THE
ENCYCLOPEDIA
OF
AMERICAN CATHOLIC HISTORY

THE
ENCYCLOPEDIA
OF
AMERICAN CATHOLIC HISTORY

Edited by

Michael Glazier and Thomas J. Shelley

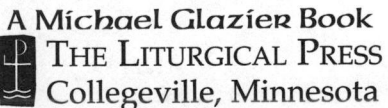

A Michael Glazier Book
THE LITURGICAL PRESS
Collegeville, Minnesota

A Michael Glazier Book published by The Liturgical Press

Cover design by David Manahan, O.S.B.

Copyediting by Aaron Raverty, O.S.B., and Annette Kmitch; typesetting by Kathy Borchert, Julie Surma, and Monica Weide; index preparation by Kelly Haeg and Lisa Twomey; photo selection by David Manahan, O.S.B., and Ann Blattner

1	2	3	4	5	6	7	8

Library of Congress Cataloging-in-Publication Data

The encyclopedia of American Catholic history / edited by Michael
    Glazier and Thomas J. Shelley.
        p.   cm.
    "A Michael Glazier book."
    Includes bibliographical references and index.
    ISBN 0-8146-5919-5 (alk. paper)
     1. Catholic Church—United States—History—Encyclopedias.
  2. United States—Church history—Encyclopedias.   I. Glazier,
Michael.   II. Shelley, Thomas J.
  BX1406.2.E53   1997
  282'.73'03—dc21
                                     97-41221
                                         CIP

To Mary, the Mother of the Lord,
who had a special place in the lives
of the immigrants and their descendants
who made American Catholicism.

Contents

Introduction

On the doorstep of a new century over sixty million Catholics look back and celebrate their history which is an integral part of the great American saga. Catholicism in the United States was built and supported by immigrants and the descendants of immigrants and *The Encyclopedia of American Catholic History* tells their story. This is the first encyclopedia of its kind; there has never been a reference work on American Catholicism comparable to this volume. Beginning with Columbus, it spans half a millennium covering the men, women, and events that shaped Catholic life in a vast and diverse nation.

The Encyclopedia of American Catholic History contains over a million words, and its entries are alphabetically arranged for convenient use by researchers and general readers. The primary aim of each entry, whether it reflects some original research or summarizes existing scholarship, is to provide basic information, while its bibliographical citations open the road to further study. The interpretations and opinions expressed in the entries are those of the authors rather than the editors. Contributors were given full freedom with one guiding reminder, that truth, not edification, was to be the sole criterion of their work. Only thus could a true evaluation of the Catholic experience in the United States be made.

Due to the limitation of space, most entries are brief. But longer treatment is given to basic topics such as the early Spanish, French, and English missions; Frontier Catholicism; the waves of immigration; and the Catholic struggles for education. Other subjects, which were often neglected in the past, are given greater consideration. These include the role of women, Native Americans, and the growth of Catholicism in the fifty States.

The encyclopedia lists essential data on all Catholic colleges and universities and on all religious institutions of men and women, but it was not feasible to have a separate entry on each. Therefore, a representative selection was made and articles were written on some of the larger and smaller colleges and universities; and the same procedure was adopted with the religious orders and congregations. Unfortunately, space did not permit the inclusion of every important person or event in American Catholic history. Selecting the final list of contents was a slow process, and winnowing down possible entries was often a disheartening task.

The American Catholic Church has been the home to a vast variety of people. The notable men and women who appear in these pages are truly the representatives of countless millions who are known to God alone. But American Catholicism today is the living monument to their lives and labors. Knowing their history gives us confidence, and *The Encyclopedia of American Catholic History* is a celebration of their faith.

Michael Glazier / Thomas J. Shelley

Acknowledgments

Dr. Christopher J. Kauffman of The Catholic University of America encouraged this project from its inception, and the editors are deeply grateful for his good counsel and constructive suggestions. A special note of thanks is tendered to Dr. Charles Nolan, Archivist of the Archdiocese of New Orleans; Dr. Jeffrey M. Burns, Archivist of the Archdiocese of San Francisco; Dr. Christine Krosel, Archivist of the Diocese of Cleveland; Rev. Wilfred P. Schoenberg, S.J., Archivist Emeritus of the Oregon Province of the Society of Jesus; Sister Mary Nona McGreal, O.P., of Project OPUS, Chicago; and Mr. Joseph G.E. Hopkins, Larchmont, New York.

Dr. Philip Gleason of the University of Notre Dame, Rev. Gerald P. Fogarty, S.J., of the University of Virginia, and Dr. Tricia T. Pyne of Wheeling Jesuit College were ever helpful, and their aid and suggestions were invaluable and appreciated. Amongst the many others to whom we are indebted are two scholars from Louisville, Kentucky: Brother Thomas J. Spalding, C.F.X., of Spalding University and Rev. Clyde Crews of Bellarmine College; Rev. John T. Monaghan of Cardinal Spellman High School, Bronx, New York; Rev. Thomas A. Lynch; Mr. Anthony D. Andreassi of Xavier High School, New York City; Sister Regina Melican, O.P., and the staff of the Archbishop Corrigan Memorial Library, St. Joseph's Seminary, Dunwoodie, New York.

The publisher and editors are thankful to Robert Lockwood of Our Sunday Visitor, publishers of *The Catholic Almanac,* and to Jeanne LoGiurato Hanline of *The Official Catholic Directory* (P. J. Kenedy & Sons / R. R. Bowker) for kind permission to reproduce their lists of: Archdioceses, Dioceses, Archbishops and Bishops; American Bishops of the Past; Religious Institutes of Men in the United States; Religious Institutes of Women in the United States; Diocesan and Interdiocesan Seminaries; Universities and Colleges in the United States.

Finally, the editors offer their gratitude to the staff of The Liturgical Press, but especially to Rev. Michael Naughton, O.S.B., director; Mr. Mark Twomey, managing editor; Brother Aaron Raverty, O.S.B., for invaluable editorial assistance; to Mrs. Joan Ricker for her computer and administrative help; and thanks to Mrs. Colleen Stiller who carefully supervised the production of this work.

M.G. / T.J.S.

A

ABBELEN, PETER M. (1843–1917)

Priest, German-American leader. Abbelen was born in Germany on August 8, 1843, and was educated in Gaesdonk and Munster. After emigrating to the U.S.A., he entered St. Francis Seminary in Milwaukee and was ordained a priest on January 2, 1868. Abbelen taught and did pastoral work in La Crosse, Chippewa Falls, and Prairie du Chien. Abbelen was a theological consultant for the Third Plenary Council of Baltimore (1884) and served as the vicar general for the Archdiocese of Milwaukee from 1906–17. Throughout his work as a priest, he championed the preservation of the German language and culture for German Catholic immigrants and fought off attempts by some American bishops to "Americanize" German immigrants. He was a strong advocate of separate parishes for Germans and for the policy of forcing the children of German immigrants to attend only schools attached to German parishes.

In 1886 he authored the famous "Memorial on the German Question," a petition addressed to Roman authorities complaining of the mistreatment of German-American Catholics by the English-speaking American hierarchy and asking for special consideration for German-American Catholics. Propaganda Fide, the Roman congregation responsible for the American Church, rejected Abbelen's proposals, a decision that was considered a victory for "Americanist" forces under the leadership of Archbishop John Ireland of St. Paul and Bishop John Keane of Richmond (later rector of The Catholic University of America). Abbelen was named a monsignor in 1907 and died on August 24, 1917.

See also GERMAN CATHOLICS IN AMERICA.

Barry, Colman, O.S.B. *The Catholic Church and the German Americans.* Milwaukee, 1953.

ANTHONY D. ANDREASSI

Peter Abbelen

ABBEY OF GETHSEMANI

The Abbey of Gethsemani, located among wooded hills at Trappist, Kentucky, is the oldest monastery of the Cistercians of the Strict Observance (popularly known as

Trappists) in the United States. It was founded in 1848 by French Cistercian monks from Melleray Abbey in Brittany. Friendship with Bishop Benedict Flaget of Bardstown/Louisville was instrumental in bringing the monks to Kentucky. The forty-five founders settled on property purchased from the Sisters of Loretto.

Dom Eutropius Proust, the founder and first abbot of Gethsemani, led the pioneer monks until his resignation in 1860, when he returned to Melleray in France. During the first years there were very few vocations and even fewer who persevered. The first American-born choir monk to persevere was Frederic Dunne, who was elected fifth abbot in 1935. He received Thomas Merton (Fr. Louis) into the novitiate in December of 1941. Merton's writings, especially *The Seven Storey Mountain,* which was published in 1948, would have a profound effect on the monastic life as well as on the Church at large. Vocations greatly increased in the years following its publication, which coincided with the end of World War II.

Trappist community celebrating Mass

Gethsemani's expansion began during the abbacy of Dom Frederic Dunne, with the foundation of the Monastery of the Holy Spirit in Conyers, Georgia, in 1945, and Holy Trinity Abbey in Huntsville, Utah, in 1947. Following the death of Dom Frederic Dunne in August of 1948, Dom James Fox, founding superior of the first foundation in Conyers, Georgia, was elected sixth abbot of Gethsemani. The expansion continued by making a third foundation at Mepkin, Moncks Corner, South Carolina, in 1949, and a fourth one at Genesee, Piffard, New York, in 1951. Gethsemani launched a fifth foundation, New Clairvaux, in the Sacramento Valley, at Vina, California, in 1955. In 1966 Gethsemani assumed the paternity of a foundation near Santiago, Chile, originally begun by St. Joseph's Abbey, Spencer, Massachusetts. Since then the monks have moved to a more isolated location at Rancagua, and have renamed the monastery Miraflores.

From its earliest days the monks of Gethsemani welcomed visitors and retreatants, and for about fifty years conducted a school for boys on the property. The latter burnt down in 1913, never to be rebuilt. By that time there were sufficient schools in that part of Kentucky, so that the monks could concentrate on their specific vocation, the contemplative life of prayer in silence and solitude. Men, and more recently women (since 1989), retreatants are welcomed at Gethsemani for some days of retreat during which they follow the prayer life of the community.

See also CISTERCIANS, MONKS AND NUNS (O.C.S.O.; O.CIST.); MERTON, THOMAS.

Flanagan, Raymond. *Burnt Out Incense.* New York: Kenedy, 1949.
Kelty, Matthew. *Aspects of the Monastic Calling.* Trappist, Ky.: Abbey of Gethsemani, ca. 1980.
Merton, Thomas. *The Waters of Siloe.* New York: Harcourt Brace, 1949.

PATRICK HART, O.C.S.O.

ACADEMIC FREEDOM AND CATHOLIC HIGHER EDUCATION

Academic freedom is a term that traditionally refers to a teacher's right to express his or her opinions without fear of recrimination from those in authority. It also pertains to the right of the student to carry out a vocation of exploring various fields of knowledge and coming to conclusions that may differ from that of the teacher. However, in the history of higher education in the United States, the main concern has been with the freedom of the teacher, rather than that of the student. Since most of the colleges were founded by religious denominations, the question of academic freedom often related to the strictures placed on faculty by church bodies rather than governments. Most of the time, civil authorities tended to avoid entanglement with private institutions.

In the twentieth century, defense of academic freedom has been made by two major professional groups: the American Association of University Professors and the regional accrediting agencies that determine standards and evaluate performance. Among the areas examined are the extent to which institutions comply with AAUP principles and the commitment they show to an environment of freedom on their campuses.

In addition to the freedom of the professor there is also the question of institutional autonomy, a distinct but related concept. Subject to an ever-increasing set of federal and state regulations regarding equal opportunity and nondiscrimination, and Church concern about orthodoxy in teaching religion or theology, the institution itself must defend freedom to teach and to learn. During both World

Wars academic freedom on all campuses, public and private, was curtailed, and in the postwar zeal of the McCarthy era it was buried in the rhetoric of anticommunist propaganda. Rebukes for criticism of McCarthy and challenges to any pro-Communist or even Socialist statements were experienced on many campuses, Catholic as well as state or other private universities. In this era, academic freedom was attacked by government more than by Church.

Until 1938 there was little general discussion of academic freedom on Catholic campuses at the annual gatherings of the National Catholic Education Association (College and University Department). Between then and 1967 most treatments of the topic on the part of Catholic leaders were limited to proclaiming the freedom of faculty to "teach what is true." In the fifties and sixties faculty handbooks of several Catholic universities stated that "Faculty are free to teach provided their statements are not contrary to the teaching of the Catholic church or the Constitution of the United States." This blending of faith and patriotism which characterized the postwar era was a distinct danger to academic freedom.

In March of 1967 Dr. Philip Gleason delivered an address at the annual NCEA meeting in which he reflected on the amazing shift that had occurred in the previous two years. A major event that had served as a catalyst for the new attention to academic freedom was the faculty strike at St. John's University, Queens, New York, in December of 1965. The role played by the American Association of University Professors and the Middle States Association of Colleges and High Schools in the St. John's dispute served as a wake-up call to the administrators of other Catholic universities. Confrontations in the name of academic freedom were also experienced at several other institutions: Dayton, Marquette, and The Catholic University of America, to name a few of the most visible.

The relationship of academic freedom to institutional autonomy was evidenced with regard to speaker policies, organized demonstrations for civil rights and/or Vietnam, the free speech movement, student rights, and general campus disorders. It was not just the freedom of individual faculty or students but the right of the university to govern itself—institutional autonomy—that was threatened by both federal and state policies. In some states, loyalty oaths were required for all faculty in both public and private institutions; in the seventies, colleges were required to submit policies for handling campus disorders or face state penalties. These problems were shared with all institutions of higher learning and for the most part were settled by the courts as questions of civil liberties rather than of academic freedom although that consideration was not totally ignored in the debate.

Today, the understanding of academic freedom among most Catholic higher education leaders is that articulated in the Land O'Lakes document of 1967: "The Catholic university today must be a university in the full modern sense of the word, with a strong commitment to and concern for academic excellence. To perform its teaching and research functions effectively the Catholic university must have a true autonomy and academic freedom in the face of authority of whatever kind, lay or clerical, external to the academic community itself. To say this is simply to assert that institutional autonomy and academic freedom are essential conditions of life and growth and indeed of survival for Catholic universities as for all universities."

This assertion has dominated all subsequent discussion of the topic. It has not always been interpreted in conjunction with the further statement in *Land O'Lakes:* "Distinctively, then, the Catholic university must be an institution, a community of learners or a community of scholars, in which Catholicism is perceptibly present and effectively operative." The reconciliation of these two commitments constitute the core of the debate that has gone on since 1967.

Regarding academic freedom as a positive value in the search for knowledge and wisdom, advocates within the Catholic community have pressed for adherence to the 1940 principles enunciated by the American Association of University Professors in this regard. Until 1970 the AAUP recognized the need for exceptions to some of these principles in Church-related universities, insisting only that such limitation be made known at the time of hiring. However, in the wake of the St. John's strike, the AAUP set up a special committee to reexamine this concept of approved limitations, and the report of that committee asserted that AAUP no longer held that such limitations were acceptable among institutions which wished to be considered "true" universities. In this, they had the concurrence of Protestant and Catholic leadership organizations.

Since that time, Catholic colleges and universities have conformed to AAUP standards and have generally fought vigorously any challenge by church authorities to limit the freedom of faculty or students within their institutions. The lengthy dialogue between the Congregation of Catholic Education in Rome, the American hierarchy and the presidents of Catholic colleges and universities from 1967 to 1990 resulted in a recognition of "institutional autonomy" and "academic freedom" as essential components of a Catholic university. John Paul II in *Ex corde ecclesiae* writes that "[every Catholic university] possesses that institutional autonomy necessary to perform its functions effectively and guarantees its members academic freedom, so long as the rights of the individual person and of the community are preserved within the confines of the truth and the common good." The concept is expanded in a footnote which defines "institutional autonomy" as meaning "that the governance of an academic institution is and remains internal to the institution," and that "academic freedom is the guarantee given to those involved in teaching and research that, within their specific specialized branch of knowledge and according to the methods proper to that specific area, they may search and publish the results of this search, keeping in mind the cited criteria, that is, safeguarding the rights of the individual and of society within the confines of the truth and the common good."

Having achieved this agreement on the meaning of the terms and the necessity of implementing such values in Catholic universities and colleges, the leadership is still faced with the task of prudential judgments as to "the confines of truth" and "the common good."

Since 1980 the specific problems on Catholic campuses have tended to deal with the teaching of theology. Most visible among these cases are that of the Rev. Charles Curran of the pontifical faculty of The Catholic University of America and Dr. Daniel Maguire of Marquette University. Although there had been earlier instances of ecclesial sanctioning of Catholic theologians, the fact that in the 1980s there was instant media presentation of their views put a new twist on the old question of academic freedom. Since both of these men are in the field of moral theology where ecclesiastical judgments involve pastoral reservations about the topics being considered, the traditional understanding of academic freedom came under new scrutiny.

Probably neither the American bishops nor the faculties on the campuses of Catholic colleges and universities would dissent from the approval given in *Ex corde ecclesiae* to the concepts of academic freedom and institutional autonomy. Nevertheless, agreement is lacking as to whose judgment prevails in determining "the confines of truth" and "the common good." The responsibility of peers in the academy, the committees charged with hiring and evaluation of faculty, the administrators who ratify such evaluation, and the trustees who hold ultimate governing authority in the institution must be exercised in the light of the mission of the university. The Church community and its bishops must recognize the legitimate internal authority of the institution to safeguard its commitment to academic integrity while, at the same time, the universities must recognize the legitimate concern of the Church to safeguard its own tradition and hand it on to the next generation. The Catholic tradition testifies to the link between the life of faith and the free exercise of the intellect. It is the tension between these various goals and constituencies that will continue to color the way in which academic freedom is understood by American Catholic higher education.

See also CATHOLIC EDUCATION, HIGHER; CURRAN (CHARLES) CONTROVERSY, THE.

Annarelli, James John. *Academic Freedom and Catholic Higher Education.* New York: Greenwood Press, 1987.
Curran, Charles E. *Catholic Higher Education, Theology, and Academic Freedom.* University of Notre Dame Press, 1990.
Gallin, Alice, O.S.U. *American Catholic Higher Education: Essential Documents, 1967–1990.* University of Notre Dame Press, 1992.
Schrecker, Ellen W. *No Ivory Tower.* New York: Oxford University Press, 1986.

ALICE GALLIN, O.S.U.

ACADIANS IN AMERICA

Seventeenth-century settlers of present-day Nova Scotia, and their descendants in the United States and Canada. A permanent French settlement was established on the shores of the Bay of Fundy in 1610. Acadia, and its three principal population centers at Port-Royal, Grand Pré, and Beaubassin, elicited considerable British animosity as it represented the potential northern limit of their own expansion. Acadia served as a pawn in the French and British contest for control of North America. The colony was attacked repeatedly within its first century of existence before definitively passing into British hands at the Treaty of Utrecht (1713).

British authorities, aware of Acadian improvements to the colony, impeded the migration of the inhabitants into remaining French territories, this despite treaty provisions guaranteeing freedom of movement to them, their goods, and their chattels. Early attempts at imposing an unqualified Oath of Allegiance failed since the Acadians feared a surrender of religious rights and possible forced military service against the French.

The impasse was broken by 1730 with a verbal "Qualified Oath" that left the Acadians in possession of their faith and allowed for their neutrality in time of war. While the vast majority of Acadians remained neutral during and after the War of the Austrian Succession, commencing in 1744 in North America, certain among them did not. The missionary LeLoutre succeeded in whipping up anti-British activity among the native Micmac and Malecite peoples, an effort in which some few Acadians came to participate.

The decision to deport the entire Acadian population of the region was taken by the acting Governor Charles Lawrence and his superiors, and was carried out beginning in the fall of 1755. Originally less than half of the estimated 18,000 Acadians were rounded up, and shipped to the British seaboard colonies. The majority of Acadians escaped into "Acadie Française" (New Brunswick) or to the Ile St-Jean (Prince Edward Island) or Ile Royale (Cape Breton). Over the succeeding decade the majority of these refugees were arrested as well, and a great many were deported. Deaths from disease and general physical wretchedness would become legion.

In order to destroy Acadian cohesiveness and identity, seaboard colonial officials parceled out nuclear families to individual towns and placed them, at least initially, on the public dole. Where Acadians were allowed to remain in groups, food and shelter were grudgingly provided. Children were frequently bound out in apprenticeship. Virginia refused its allotment of Acadians and sent them instead to England where they remained as prisoners of war until 1763. In South Carolina and Georgia, many refugees were placed in indentured servitude.

While some individuals did attempt escape by land or sea, the majority of Acadians had to await the Treaty of Paris of 1763 to regain their freedom. Those who were under arrest at Halifax or who had managed to elude capture began life anew on the rocky coasts of New Brunswick, in remote parts of Nova Scotia, or on the islands of the Gulf of St. Lawrence. Massachusetts Acadians walked to Quebec and the Maritimes. Many in Pennsylvania and Maryland sailed for Spanish Louisiana, where they were joined twenty years later by most of the survivors of the Virginia allotment. These had languished in England until 1763, been sent to France, and had survived ill-starred schemes to colonize Santo Domingo, the Falkland Islands, and less-than-desirable tracts in metropolitan France. Numerous Acadians in the seaboard colonies had likewise voyaged to Santo Domingo where they succumbed to tropical fevers.

Louisiana Acadians were settled outside Creole New Orleans by colonial authorities. Principal locations included the "Acadian Coast," a stretch of Mississippi riverbank fifty miles north of New Orleans; the Attakapas District, centered about St. Martinville on the Bayou Teche; the upper Bayou Lafourche; and the Opelousas area.

After the turn of the nineteenth century, Anglo-American capital would make possible large-scale sugar plantations, and result in the displacement of numerous Acadians from prime river frontage. The ensuing westward migration to the prairie country made Vermillionville (later renamed Lafayette) the capital of Louisiana's French Triangle.

Despite its ability to absorb individuals from other backgrounds, most notably German and Spanish arrivals who both preceded and followed the exiles to Louisiana, "Cajun" culture proved remarkably resistant to change in its essentials. It retained its rural, French-speaking, and staunchly Catholic character well into the twentieth century. Public education in English, increased urbanization, and the homogenizing effect of World War II, served inevitably to undermine traditional Cajun culture. Efforts in the 1970s to recapture ethnic pride and halt the disappearance of spoken French have met with some success.

See also FRENCH-CANADIAN CATHOLICS IN AMERICA.

Arsenault, Bona. *Histoire des Acadiens*. Carleton, Quebec: CHAU, 1988.
Brasseux, Carl A. *Scattered to the Wind*. Lafayette, La.: Center for Louisiana Studies, 1991.
Conrad, Glenn R. *The Cajuns: Essays on Their History and Culture*. Lafayette, La.: Center for Louisiana Studies, 1983.
Dormon, James H. *The People Called Cajuns*. Lafayette, La.: Center for Louisiana Studies, 1983.
LeBlanc, Dudley J. *The Acadian Miracle*. Lafayette, La.: Evangeline Publishing Co., 1966.

ALBERT H. LEDOUX

ADORERS OF THE BLOOD OF CHRIST (A.S.C.)

Religious congregation of women. The Adorers of the Blood of Christ began in Acuto, Italy, a small mountain town southeast of Rome. There Maria de Mattias, a young woman from Vallecorsa, came in 1834 "not merely to teach school, but to found a monastery as well." Inspired by Gaspar del Bufalo, a Missionary of the Precious Blood, and directed by his confrere Giovanni Merlini, Maria hoped the religious congregation would provide young women with a cultural and spiritual formation so much needed in that time and place. As Adorer-Apostles under the banner of the Precious Blood, sisters would spread the knowledge and love of God and the redeeming Blood of Christ.

A group led by Ursula Behringer began in Steinerberg, Germany, in 1845. Upon hearing of Maria de Mattias' foundation in Acuto, with her concept of adoration in action, the Steinerberg sisters moved toward affiliation. By 1860 there was formal incorporation into the Italian congregation. The difficulties experienced by religious in Germany under Bismarck and the request for sisters from German immigrant parishes in the U.S.A. led to the journey of sisters to the United States in 1870 to meet this need.

In 1875 Clementine Zerr, leader of the group which maintained ties with Maria's foundation, established a convent in Ruma, Illinois. Ruma became the vicariate of the Adorers in the U.S.A. In 1902 Mother Clementine opened

A.S.C. Memorial Sculpture, Ruma, Illinois

a central house in Wichita, Kansas, for the sisters teaching in small rural schools in Kansas. Both areas grew rapidly, and in 1929 Ruma and Wichita became provinces.

A vicariate was also established in Alton, Illinois, under Pauline Schneeberger, who had entered the community in Austria. In 1925 they moved to Columbia, Pennsylvania, and eventually became the Province of Columbia.

The chief ministry of the sisters was education, most often in small rural parishes where the sisters shared the life of the parish, nurturing and strengthening the faith of the German immigrants among whom they worked. In the Columbia province, the issue of integration in the schools was vigorously addressed. The sisters were active in civil rights and in empowering minorities, especially the Croatians and blacks whom they served.

Eventually there were institutional ministries: an orphanage in Alton, Illinois; St. Teresa's Academy in East St. Louis; St. Clement Hospital in Red Bud, Illinois (a first for the congregation); St. John's Academy in Wichita, Kansas; St. Francis Hospital in Carlsbad, New Mexico; St. Ann's Home and St. Joseph's Academy in Columbia, Pennsylvania. Later other institutions were opened, including homes for the elderly and Sacred Heart (Kansas Newman) College in Wichita in 1933.

The American sisters did not confine their ministries to the United States. In 1930, sisters from Ruma went to China; in 1960, to Puerto Rico. In 1995 they served in Bolivia, Guatemala, and Liberia, where, in 1992, five sisters from Ruma became "Martyrs of Charity." Five young Liberian women are now in Ruma, preparing to return to their country to carry on the work of the gospel. The Wichita province sent missionaries to Brazil in 1947, and in succeeding years established many clinics and schools along the Amazon, attracting women who now form the Province of Manaus.

In 1968 sisters began work in Guatemala, and in 1973 they began a foundation in Korea. Members of all three provinces have given leadership in addressing social issues, with strong interest in environmental justice, empowerment of women and the disenfranchised, and advocacy for the poor. Their connections with ten other provinces in Europe and South America, in a congregation of 2,100 members, make them part of a global mission.

Adoration leading to redemptive action is the charism motivating all works of evangelization, liberation, and education. The power of prayer is demonstrated especially by sisters who find this their living mission in later years.

See also WOMEN RELIGIOUS IN AMERICA.

HELEN STRECK, A.S.C.

AFRICAN AMERICAN CATHOLICS

Although African American Catholics have never been as noteworthy as African American Protestants, nor as nu-

merous as many Catholic ethnic groups, few have played as supportive a role in the history of American Catholicism. In almost every area of American Catholic history, African Americans have made their contribution. In almost every period black Catholics were to be found in almost every corner of this country.

The history of African American Catholics is inextricably connected with the nation's history. This history can be divided into the following periods: the period before the Civil War; the period of Reconstruction and after; the civil rights movement; and the period following the assassination of Martin Luther King, Jr.

The Colonial Period

Catholicism arrived in the United States with the settlement of St. Augustine by the Spaniards in 1565 in what is now northern Florida. The settlement was to protect the Spanish colonies in the Caribbean and Latin America. Documentary evidence on the population is supplied by the parochial registers of the Church of St. Augustine, particularly the baptismal registers. In these registers beginning with the first page the baptism of blacks, both slaves and free, are so designated in the margins of the text. In fact, the entries also indicated the origin of many of the blacks, the status of their parents, and the status of their sponsors. Beginning with 1783, the period when the Spaniards returned to Florida after a hiatus of twenty-one years following the British victory in the Seven Years War, separate baptismal registers, marriage registers, and death registers were kept for blacks. These registers portray a society that was Catholic in religion, Spanish in language, and African and Latin in culture.

By 1700 the Spanish were threatened by the English colonies to the north, particularly in the Carolinas. To weaken the economy, the Spaniards encouraged English slaves to enter the Florida territory where, upon entrance into the Catholic church, they were assured of their freedom. The baptismal registers reflect the influx of English slaves into the Floridas, some coming from as far north as Maryland. In 1738 the first all-black town was created and named Santa Teresa de Mose. It was composed of ex-British slaves, many of them members of the black militias that had existed in St. Augustine since the end of the previous century. Under their leader, Francisco Menendez, regular forays against English settlements in Georgia took place in partnership with the Yamassee natives, traditional allies of the Spaniards. In fact, the death registers for blacks indicate that black and mulatto soldiers were regularly garrisoned in St. Augustine. Other sources indicate that free black youths were educated together with white youths in the school operated by the local priest.

Spanish-speaking black colonists were also found throughout the southwestern United States. Los Angeles was founded in 1781 with eleven families from two villages in northern Mexico. The census carefully distinguished the racial mixture of each family member. Two men were Spaniards, two were blacks, seven were Native Americans, four were mestizos, and seven were mulattos.

The French settled along the Mississippi River from Canada to the Gulf where they established the city of New Orleans in 1718. In what would later become the Middle West of the United States many of the French inhabitants had Native American and African slaves. Inasmuch as French law obligated slave holders to baptize their slaves, many blacks in Cahokia, Kaskasia, St. Louis, Ste. Genevieve, and Vincennes were Catholics. Although his birthplace is uncertain, Jean Baptiste Pointe du Sable, black and Catholic, was a successful trader, woodsman, and honorary member of the Potawatomi, one of whom he married. He was also the first settler of the future city of Chicago. He was buried in the Catholic cemetery of St. Charles in Missouri in 1818.

In Louisiana and along the Gulf coasts, black Catholics made their own contribution to the French Catholic culture of that region. Black slaves were routinely baptized in New Orleans, Mobile, and in the rural areas. The extent of the evangelization seems to have varied according to time and period. Because of the increase of unions between white men and female blacks, their descendants, the "free people of color," began to have a prominent role in the Gulf coast region in Louisiana, Florida, and southern Alabama. Certain regions such as Natchitoches in northern Louisiana and Chastang and Mon Luis Island in Alabama were the centers of a flourishing Afro-French Catholic culture which thrived on its insularity and developed its own folk culture. To this day certain family names indicate the origin and French Catholic heritage of individuals now living in other regions of the country.

Recent historical studies have pointed out two particular characteristics of Creoles of color society: initiative and independence. Social conditions encouraged wealthy white men to form illicit unions with women of color. These unions were everything but marriage unions. The death of the male, however, often left the woman and her children without protection or means. Thus was created a climate of immorality and ambiguity. Creoles of color like many other blacks in other sections of the country often had one or two slaves themselves. They had to rely heavily upon their own creative instincts to survive in a hostile environment. A few became very wealthy and were generous in their turn to the black community. The Widow Bernard Couvent, originally from Africa, at her death in 1837 left property for the establishment of a free school for black orphans. The school still exists.

Maryland was the home of black Catholics in the English-speaking colonies. The area around Baltimore and Washington, D.C., the plantations and farm land of Calvert County and St. Mary's County, nurtured the growth of a traditionally African American Catholic community. At the end of the eighteenth century this community was enlarged by the influx of Haitian refugees of color. At the beginning of the nineteenth century many Catholic slaves accompanied Maryland Catholic slaveowners to the center of Kentucky, creating another traditionally black Catholic area around Nelson county.

Slaveholders

Despite the fact that the Catholic Church was never split in half over the question of slavery as were many Protestant churches, slavery was never only a Protestant problem. Catholics were as implicated in it as were Protestants. Priests and bishops, religious and laity owned slaves. The Jesuits in Maryland and Missouri were slaveholders. The Vincentians in Missouri owned slaves. Capuchins in Louisiana were slaveowners. Bishops like Louis William du Bourg of New Orleans, Michael Portier of Mobile, and John Carroll in Baltimore owned slaves. Carmelite, Visitation, and Ursuline nuns were slaveholders, and so were many others. Many would argue that slavery was not intrinsically evil. Still, few dealt seriously with the fact that Pope Gregory XVI in 1839 condemned the slave trade and by implication condemned slavery itself.

Bishop John England in a series of articles published in his diocesan newspaper, *The United States Catholic Miscellany,* would seek to prove that slavery had never been considered an evil in itself by ecclesiastical authorities and Catholic theologians. Above all he wished to protect the pope from being called an abolitionist by his fellow Southerners. Still, he never sought to answer how an institution that destroyed family life, that encouraged sexual immorality, that dehumanized men, women, and children, and that resulted in violence and cruelty could ever be considered a good. In "Letters to Forsythe," England's major concern was to show his fellow Southerners that Catholicism fitted into the American scene.

The bishop of Natchitoches, Auguste Martin, in his pastoral letter of 1861 went even further by making slavery a good fitting into God's providential design in bringing the wretched Africans to this country. His letter narrowly missed condemnation by the Holy See because the war ended. On the other hand, one Catholic bishop broke ranks with his colleagues and took a public stand for the emancipation of the slaves on the eve of the Civil War. That bishop was John Baptist Purcell (1800–83), archbishop of Cincinnati. The Catholic Church in the United States was never divided by the slavery question, but it never resolved the moral issues raised by American slavery. As a result American bishops failed to carry out the Church's historic mission to be the voice of conscience no matter what the dangers, no matter what the trials.

African American Religious Women

Despite the cruelties and the limitations of slavery, the religious life developed in the midst of the African American Catholic community in the early 1800s. As early as 1824, Charles Nerinckx (1761–1824), a Belgian priest in Bardstown, Kentucky, who was the founder of a community known as the Sisters of Loretto, began a community composed of three young black women, former students of the Sisters of Loretto. Nerinckx proposed to send these religious women into the plantations and farms of Kentucky to catechize and minister to the slaves. Unfortunately, Nerinckx was forced out of office because of his austerity. His successor disbanded the infant community.

Jacques Joubert de la Muraille (d. 1843), a French-born Sulpician in Baltimore, who had worked previously in Haiti, became the chaplain for the Haitians of color, recent refugees, who worshiped in the basement chapel of St. Mary's Seminary on Paca Street in Baltimore. He learned of the teaching carried out by four Haitian women under the leadership of Elizabeth Lange (d. 1882). From the beginning these women wished to become religious sisters. Archbishop James Whitfield (1770–1834) of Baltimore recognized them as a religious community in 1829, known as the Oblate Sisters of Providence. Two years later they received papal recognition from Pope Gregory XVI. The education of black children was their principal apostolate. At once they began an academy for black girls together with an orphanage. Black women joined them; some were freed slaves, arriving at the convent with their manumission papers in hand. They endured hardship and even public hostility. They persevered and can rightfully lay claim to being one of the first authentically American religious communities.

Therese Maxis Duchemin, one of the four original founders of the Oblate Sisters of Providence, received permission to accompany Fr. Louis Gillet, C.Ss.R., to Monroe, Michigan, where in 1845 she and Sr. Ann Constance, also from the Oblate Sisters of Providence, began a new congregation, the Sisters, Servants of the Immaculate Heart of Mary, known as the I.H.M. Sisters. A misunderstanding with the bishop of Detroit, Peter Paul Lefevere (1804–69), resulted in her leaving the community at Monroe along with Sr. Ann Constance, and finally spending long years of exile with the Grey Nuns in Ottawa, Canada. She returned to the I.H.M.s in West Chester, Pennsylvania, where she died in 1892.

The Sisters of the Holy Family was the second community of black sisters in this country. Founded in 1842 by two free women of color, Henriette Delille (1813–62) and Juliette Gaudin (1808–87), the latter originally from Haiti, the community began as a community of women of color ministering to young black girls as teachers and to invalid sick slaves as nurses. Josephine Charles (1812–85),

also a free woman of color, joined the two founders in 1843. The infant community had to face many obstacles, including hostility from the local community. At first the city did not accept these women as religious. A certain acceptance was only accorded following the yellow fever epidemic of 1853 when the sisters gave of themselves unstintingly in nursing the sick. They finally were able to wear their religious habit on the street in 1872, ten years after the death of Henriette.

Benevolent Societies

African Americans formed their own self-help organizations early in the eighteenth century. Many of these organizations were the means whereby poor blacks could pay into a central fund and later withdraw sufficient funds for financial aid for one's burial, for assistance for a member's family, or in times of illness. One of the oldest of these mutual aid societies was the Free African Society founded in Philadelphia in 1787 by Richard Allen (1760–1831), who became the founder of the African Methodist Episcopal Church.

Recent research has shown that black Catholics also had mutual aid societies. In Baltimore the Society of the Holy Family met weekly for prayer, for hymn singing, and for reflection in the basement of the cathedral hall. Thanks to the journal kept from 1843 to 1845 by the Sulpician priest who served as chaplain, we know details of the meetings, the membership roll, the financial arrangements, and the disbursement of funds, and this information provides an insider's view of black Catholic lay spirituality. There is some evidence that this particular society moved its location to the chapel of the Oblate Sisters of Providence and continued its work. The *Catholic Directory* for that period indicated the existence of other mutual aid societies, particularly the Tobias Society, about which little is known. Mutual aid societies also existed in the black Catholic community of New Orleans. Three of these were: the Christian Doctrine Society, the Société des Artisans de Bienfaisance et d'Assistance Mutuelle, and Dieu Nous Protège.

Black lay Catholics also belonged to another form of religious society. These were the confraternities or pious unions connected with some devotion. Three were established in Baltimore at the end of the eighteenth century and early in the nineteenth. The membership lists with the date of enrollment are contained in a notebook in the Sulpician Archives of Baltimore. The oldest, the Confraternity of Our Lady of Mount Carmel, which began under the direction of Bishop John Carroll in 1796, contained the names of blacks, male and female, slave and free. The very first entry on January 7, 1796, had four names, three of whom were black women; one of whom, a female mulatto, was free. More than half of the entries on fifty-five pages, between the years 1786 and 1841 show that black Catholic men and women, many of them slaves, had the kind of piety that prompted them to enroll in a confraternity honoring the Virgin and to wear the Carmelite scapular.

The lists of two other confraternities, that of Our Lady of Help and of the Holy Rosary, both for the first half of the nineteenth century, also contained the names of blacks, mostly women, both slaves and free. The presence of black Catholics in what was essentially associations of piety and devotion suggests very strongly that in Baltimore and probably elsewhere the black Catholic population was not bereft of spiritual ministration. When this is coupled with the evidence of mutual aid societies among black Catholics, it seems clear that future research will reveal a more active black Catholic community than previously thought. In Baltimore at least part of this activity can be probably traced back to the Oblate Sisters of Providence.

Black Catholics and the Civil War

The major black abolitionists and the leading black religious leaders during the period of the Civil War and its aftermath were Protestants. Hence, it is surprising to recognize the first black soldier to die in the Civil War was a Louisiana black Catholic, Captain André Cailloux, of the first regiment of the First Louisiana Native Guard Infantry, black troops raised by General Benjamin Butler, the Union commander of the forces that occupied New Orleans since 1862. Butler turned to the Free People of Color for recruits for three regiments. Cailloux became an officer in the first regiment. He was killed on May 27, 1863, as the Union troops stormed Port Hudson, a Confederate stronghold thirty miles north of Baton Rouge on the Mississippi River. This action by black Catholic soldiers under the leadership of Cailloux was the first display of courage and sacrifice by black troops in the Civil War.

At the close of the Civil War, the American bishops came together for the Second Plenary Council of Baltimore in 1866. Martin J. Spalding (1810–72), archbishop of Baltimore and apostolic delegate for the plenary council, wanted the council to discuss proposals for the evangelization of the freed slaves. Spalding had proposed to the Curia that it would be good if one man, preferably a bishop, could coordinate on the national level all the efforts made for the spiritual ministry of the blacks; for as he wrote, "four million of these unfortunates are thrown on our Charity . . . it is a golden opportunity for reaping a harvest of souls." In the end the American bishops, during a very acrimonious discussion, rejected any notion of a national ordinary who might seem to impinge on the authority of the respective bishops. As a result the bishops developed no national plan, except to turn their eyes toward Europe with the hope that religious orders would answer the call to the apostolate.

In 1871 the Mill Hill Fathers, an English missionary society, came to Baltimore with the purpose of evangelizing blacks. In 1892 the American branch severed all ties with Mill Hill in England and became known as the Society of St. Joseph of the Sacred Heart or the Josephites. Their apostolate remained missionary service to African Americans. At the beginning of this century the German missionary congregation, the Society of the Divine Word, undertook mission work among Southern blacks beginning its apostolate in 1906 in Vicksburg, Mississippi. Other religious orders such as the Spiritans, the Benedictines, and the Jesuits continued their ministry among black Catholics both in the North and in the South.

Black Vocations

Unlike the policy of the Catholic Church in many mission countries at this period which supported the development of a native clergy, there was little effort made to recruit black youths for the priesthood in the United States. Racial animosity towards blacks was endemic in American society throughout the nineteenth century. Catholics, including members of the hierarchy, found it impossible to accept any notion of social equality between whites and African Americans. Most frankly believed that black men could not live a moral life. For this reason, bishops were unwilling to support the ordination of blacks to the priesthood.

This did not deter blacks from seeking entrance into the priesthood. William A. Williams, a convert originally from Virginia, sought entrance as early as 1853 into the Urban college attached to the Congregation of the Propaganda in Rome. Although he became a student in 1855, Williams was forced to discontinue since he could find no American bishop willing to adopt him. Williams returned to the United States and eventually became a librarian at The Catholic University of America.

The first black priest in American history was James Augustine Healy (1830–1900), eldest of ten children. His father, Michael Morris Healy, was originally from Ireland and came to central Georgia where he laid out a plantation. His mother was a slave on the plantation, as a result all of the children were slaves as well. Thanks to the future bishop of Boston, John Fitzpatrick, the first four sons of Michael Healy studied at Holy Cross College in Massachusetts. Three of his sons became priests and two of his daughters nuns. James was ordained as the first black American priest in Paris in 1854 for the Diocese of Boston. James would later become the first black bishop in United States history in 1875, when he was ordained bishop of Portland, Maine. His brother, Alexander Sherwood Healy (1836–74), was ordained a priest for the Diocese of Boston in Rome in 1858. He also received a doctorate in canon law. His was the promise of a brilliant career cut short by an early death in the same year that his brother became a bishop.

The strangest experience of all was the career of the second brother, Patrick Francis Healy, S.J. (1834–1910), who was ordained a Jesuit priest in Belgium in 1864 and became president of Georgetown University in Washington, D.C., in 1874. Patrick Healy was sufficiently light skinned to pass for white; blacks were not admitted as students until almost a century later. Healy is considered the second founder of the university. By his efforts it became a modern, up-to-date institution of higher learning.

The Healy brothers never saw fit to immerse themselves into the black Catholic community of the time. Many scarcely knew about three black priests in the country at that time. When Augustus Tolton (1854–97), born a slave in Missouri, sought to enter the priesthood in the late 1870s, no American seminary would accept him. Thanks to the efforts of some Franciscans, Tolton was accepted into the Urban College in Rome in 1880. Although originally destined to become a missionary in Africa, Cardinal Giovanni Simeoni (1816–92), prefect of the Congregation of Propaganda (that was responsible for the Church in the United States at the time), insisted that America must see a black priest and that Tolton would return to the United States. Ordained in 1886, Tolton served in the diocese of Alton (later Springfield), Illinois. Because of the harassment of a neighboring priest in Quincy, Tolton received permission to move to Chicago where he was made the pastor of the first black parish in 1889.

Tolton was the first black priest who was readily recognizable as black. A man of simplicity and accessibility, he was honored and loved as their pastor by black Catholics all over the country. Tolton's life was not an easy one. He died at the age of forty-three in 1897.

In his book, *Desegregating the Altar,* Stephen Ochs has studied the careers of the early black Catholic priests. Following Tolton and the Healy brothers, only five black priests were ordained between 1891 and 1910. Between 1910 and 1930, only three priests were ordained. Little support was given the first black priests. They faced hostility, discrimination, and mistrust. It was, in fact, pressure from the Holy See that finally brought about the establishment of a seminary for the training of black priests. With clear support from Pope Pius XI, the Society of the Divine Word opened a seminary to train black men for priesthood in the society, first in Greenville, Mississippi, in 1920, later in permanent buildings in Bay St. Louis, Mississippi, in 1923. With the first ordination class of 1934, the number of black priests began to increase. Between 1934 and 1944, twenty-three black men were ordained to the priesthood.

The Role of Black Lay Catholics

African American Catholics at the end of the nineteenth century were in a much different situation than many other ethnic groups in the United States. Among many ethnic groups, the priest played a central role as leader and

African American family in the 1950s

spokesman. Among American blacks, the black preacher also played the same role. Black Catholics had almost no priests. The priests they had occupied no leadership role within the Church. As a result, the black Catholic laity began to occupy a position of leadership and initiative that was unusual in the period. It was the African American laity that helped define their position within the Church, their expectations from the Church, and their understanding of their own gifts.

Two African American laymen dominated black Catholic history at the end of the nineteenth century and after World War I. They were Daniel Rudd (1854–1903) and Thomas Wyatt Turner (1877–1978). Both were deeply loyal to the Catholic Church, and both were men of action. Both realized a program, both knew temporary success, and both had a long-term impact on the Church.

Daniel Rudd was born a slave in Bardstown, Kentucky. He attended high school after the Civil War in Springfield, Ohio. Shortly thereafter in 1887 he began publishing a black weekly newspaper which soon turned into a black Catholic weekly newspaper, *American Catholic Tribune,* eventually published in Cincinnati and then in Detroit, ceasing publication toward the end of the 1890s. Rudd was thoroughly convinced that the Catholic Church would raise up the African American people and aid them to overcome racism and racial discrimination. He predicted a massive conversion to Catholicism by American blacks.

In keeping with this conviction, he organized five black Catholic lay congresses, the first of their kind in the United States. These were meetings of black Catholic delegates (male) elected by parishes from all over the country, and they were held in Washington, D.C. (1889), Cincinnati (1890), Philadelphia (1892), Chicago (1893), and Baltimore (1894). These congresses had three effects: they provided a forum for the black Catholic laity which had never existed before; they provided a meeting place to discuss the meaning of Catholicism in relation to their racial identity; they imputed an identity and created a unity for black Catholics as a people in the face of Protestant blacks and white Catholics. These results were made evident in the public declarations and speeches made at each congress. In these statements the participants expressed a love for the Catholic faith and a sophisticated awareness of Catholic teaching on race and social issues. They did not hesitate to express their need for specific aid that the Church could give to them as a people.

Thomas Wyatt Turner was the son of sharecroppers in southern Maryland. Like Rudd he was from a traditional black Catholic milieu. While Rudd was a newspaperman and a publicist, Turner was a university professor, first at Howard University in Washington, D.C., and then at Hampton Institute in Virginia. By 1916 Turner had organized a group of black Catholic leaders known at first as the Committee for the Advancement of Colored Catholics. By 1924 the committee had become the Federated Colored Catholics. Turner wanted an organization that was under black lay leadership, that was action-oriented, and that was geared to bring about change. Turner wanted black Catholics to be on an equal footing with white Catholics in terms of education, lay organizations, and access to the priesthood. To this end, letters were written, conventions were held, and pressure was brought to bear on the American hierarchy, the Josephites, and the apostolic delegate.

In the end Turner faced opposition from William Markoe, S.J. (1892–1969), and John LaFarge, S.J. (1880–1963), both of whom were outspoken opponents of racism and supporters of the black Catholic apostolate. On the other hand, they preferred that stress be placed on integration and interracial cooperation and discussion. In the end there was a split between the Jesuits and Turner in 1932. It led to the slow demise of the Federated Colored Catholics. It resulted in LaFarge's establishment of the New York Catholic Interracial Council in 1936. In time many would see that the approach taken by Turner which stressed black lay leadership and strategy for change was the best means for black Catholics as they moved into the civil rights period.

Black Catholics and Civil Rights

The civil rights movement began in 1955 with the arrest of Rosa Parks in Montgomery, Alabama. As a movement it found its dynamism and its inspiration in the leadership provided by the black Protestant Churches. Neither the Catholic Church nor black Catholic priests or laity emerged as leaders in the movement. By the mid-twentieth century black Catholics numbered nearly four hundred thousand out of a black population of fifteen million. Thanks to the generosity of Blessed Katherine Drexel (1858–1955), founder of the Sisters of the Blessed Sacrament, who used her enormous fortune for the evangelization of Native Americans and African Americans, the only black Catholic institution of higher learning, Xavier University in New Orleans, was founded by her in 1931. Many Catholic schools and parishes for African Americans were to be found in ever increasing numbers in northern cities.

A third black Catholic sisterhood, the Franciscan Handmaids of Mary, was established in Savannah, Georgia, in 1916 and moved to Harlem, New York, in 1922. By 1958 a hundred black priests had been ordained in the United States. In the perception of blacks the Roman Catholic Church was seen as friendly but far removed from African American history and culture. Only in 1958 did the Roman Catholic bishops of the United States make a formal statement regarding the moral issues of racism.

Large-scale involvement in the civil rights movement followed upon the call of Martin Luther King, Jr., to the clergy of the United States to come to Selma, Alabama, for the voter registration drive. Following the assassination of King in April of 1968, black Catholic priests from all over the country at a meeting in Detroit formed the National Black Catholic Clergy Caucus. That same year black sisters formed the National Black Sisters Conference. Black seminarians and black lay Catholics followed later forming a national association of black seminarians and black lay Catholic caucuses in various cities. In 1971 the National Office of Black Catholics was formed as an umbrella organization for the diverse black Catholic activist groups. For the first time since the Federated Colored Catholics, African American Catholics had taken the initiative to confront racism within the Church. In the wake of the Second Vatican Council, black Catholics began to incorporate into the Catholic liturgy art, symbols, and music from African American history and culture. Black Catholics began to reexamine their own history within the American Catholic experience.

Black Catholics and Art

Black Catholics participated in the Harlem Renaissance of the 1920s through the poetry and fiction of Claude McKay (1890–1948). McKay, born in Jamaica, came to the United States just before the First World War. He lived in Russia for a while, where he became a Communist but soon was disillusioned by the activities of the Communist Party. McKay became a Catholic in 1944. He had been nursed during a serious illness by the members of a Catholic lay organization located in Harlem, Friendship House. His writings at the end of his life, both his poetry and his essays, revealed the peace he found in Catholicism.

Ellen Tarry, born in Alabama in 1906 and a convert to the Catholic Church, has been the author of numerous books for young adults. As a young member of the Harlem Renaissance, she brought to it her Catholic perspective in her autobiography, *The Third Door.*

The first African American sculptress was Edmonia Lewis, born in 1845, the daughter of an African American father and a Native American mother, from an Ojibwe tribe in upper New York. After studying at Oberlin College in Ohio, she received her first instructions in sculpturing in Boston. She went to Rome in 1866 where she acquired a studio and spent the rest of her life. Sometime after this date, Edmonia Lewis became a Catholic. Pope Pius IX personally visited her studio. Many of Lewis's works were displayed in exhibitions in the United States. A few of them are still on display in the National Museum of American Art in the nation's capital. The date of her death is uncertain, but it was sometime after 1909. She was buried in Rome.

Mary Lou Williams (1910–81), jazz pianist, composer, and arranger, was born in Atlanta but grew up in Pittsburgh. She entered the world of African American jazz music when she was sixteen, soon becoming a well-known pianist. She became famous for her jazz arrangements. At the height of her career, she gave up her music, disillusioned by the music world. About this time (1957) she converted to the Catholic faith. She returned to jazz music, but this time concentrating on composing religious music in the jazz idiom, something very new and original. She composed a cantata for St. Martin de Porres in 1962 and several Masses in the jazz idiom, one of which was performed at St. Patrick's Cathedral in New York and at the Church of the Gesù in Rome. She died in 1981.

Mary Lou Williams, jazz musician and composer

African American Catholics have made a distinctive contribution to liturgical music in the United States. Artists and composers such as Clarence Rivers, Rawn Harbor, Edward Bonnemere, Grayson Brown, and many others have changed the course of Catholic Church music in the United States.

African American Catholics in the 1990s

In 1989 George Stallings, priest of the Archdiocese of Washington and arguably one of the best African American Catholic preachers, severed his connection with the Holy See to establish the Imani Temple as headquarters of the African American Catholic Rite. Stallings had vainly sought the permission of the cardinal archbishop of Washington to establish an African American Rite parish, with a quasi-independent status and liturgy. The cardinal's refusal was met with Stallings' departure from the Church. With this action, the African American community saw its first schism. The following year, Bruce Greening, a Salvatorian priest, who had accompanied Stallings into schism, broke from him and established the Independent African American Catholic Rite in Washington, D.C.

Stalling's action was a turning point for the black Catholic community. Agreeing with many of his criticisms of American Catholicism, the black Catholic community, nevertheless, in general did not follow him or Greening into schism. On the contrary, the community has become stronger in its fidelity to Catholicism. In the United States today, black Catholics have become a recognized, vibrant part of the American Church. In 1988, Beverly Carroll was named director of the Secretariat for African American Catholics of the National Council of Catholic Bishops. In most dioceses where a substantial community of blacks is to be found, some type of Office of Black Catholic Ministry has been instituted. This has provided a means for black Catholics to let their voices be heard by the bishops of the United States.

These same bishops issued a pastoral letter in 1979, *Brothers and Sisters to Us,* which called for an end to racism and described it as a sin against the dignity of God's sons and daughters. Five years later the ten black bishops of the United States issued a pastoral letter, *What We Have Seen and Heard,* in which they called for black Catholics to take on responsibility for their own evangelization.

In the last third of the twentieth century, the black Catholic community is growing in numbers and influence. Part of this is the result of Haitian immigration; another source is the continuing conversion of black adults. Out of a population of thirty million blacks, there are some two million black Catholics. The black Catholic community is the fifth largest African American religious body; it is almost equal in membership to the Episcopal Church in the United States. There are thirteen bishops, three of whom are ordinaries, approximately three hundred priests, four hundred permanent deacons, and about five hundred sisters.

One of the contributions that the Catholic Church in America has made to African Americans has been in the area of education. A survey conducted in 1991 showed that black Catholics who attended Catholic schools were 40 percent more likely to graduate from college than other blacks. Overall indications such as jobs, income, and college education were found to be more likely of attainment by graduates from Catholic schools than by those who came through the public schools. Catholic education from all indications has made a difference for the black community.

Concomitant with this development has been the growth of academic studies among black Catholics. In the last two decades, an Institute for Black Catholic Studies at Xavier University has prepared white and black students for ministry in the black community. The institute has also fostered ongoing studies by black Catholic scholars in the area of theology, Scripture, ethics, and religious history. These studies are in response to the earlier scholarship among African American Protestant scholars and the increasing activity of African and Afro-Latin students, both Protestant and Catholic, in French-speaking, English-speaking, and Portuguese-speaking Africa and Latin America.

The five black Catholic congresses at the end of the nineteenth century gave a voice and an identity to the black Catholic community of which it had been deprived since the days of slavery. In the past decade the black Catholic community has revealed once again its gifts and its strengths in its contributions to the American Catholic Church in the world today. In 1987 in Washington, D.C., and in 1992 in New Orleans, there was celebrated the sixth and the seventh black Catholic congresses. The liturgy, the conferences, the enthusiasm, the fervor all indicate a people who have left their mark on the Roman Catholic Church of the United States, a Church that is no longer European nor immigrant, neither white nor Anglo, a Church that is truly global in its outreach and universal in membership and undertaking.

See also CIVIL RIGHTS MOVEMENT AND CATHOLICS, THE; CIVIL WAR AND CATHOLICS, THE; HEALY, JAMES AUGUSTINE; RUDD, DANIEL; SLAVERY AND AMERICAN CATHOLICS; STALLINGS SCHISM, THE; TURNER, THOMAS WYATT; WILLIAMS, MARY LOU.

Davis, Cyprian, O.S.B. *The History of Black Catholics in the United States.* New York: Crossroad, 1990.

Landers, Jane. "Gracia Real de Santa Teresa de Mose: A Free Black Town in Spanish Colonial Florida." *American Historical Review* 95 (1990) 9–30.

Nichols, Marilyn. *Black Catholic Protest and the Federated Colored Catholics, 1917–1933: Three Perspectives on Racial Justice.* The Heritage of American Catholicism. New York: Garland Publishing, 1988.

Ochs, Stephen. *Desegregating the Altar. The Josephites and the Struggle for Black Catholic Priests, 1871–1960.* Baton Rouge: Louisiana State University Press, 1990.

____. "A Patriot, A Priest and A Prelate: Black Catholic Activism in Civil-War New Orleans," *U.S. Catholic Historian* 12 (1994) 49–75.

CYPRIAN DAVIS, O.S.B.

ALABAMA, CATHOLIC CHURCH IN

For more than its first half-century, colonial history in Alabama was Catholic. A parish was formally erected by the bishop of Quebec at the French settlement of Mobile in 1704. It survived a period of English rule (1765–80) to emerge with new life under Spanish hegemony (1780–1813). A missionary bishop, Michael Portier (1795–1859) was appointed for the state and the Territory of Florida in 1826, and the Diocese of Mobile was established in 1829. Early support from the Society of the Propagation of the Faith made it viable.

Missionary efforts to Native Americans left no lasting results and the Catholic population grew from French and Spanish settlers through the addition of later and larger numbers of Irish immigrants. Germans came in the mid-nineteenth century and by the end of that period Italian families had settled especially in northern Alabama. Slavery as well as frequent outbreaks of yellow fever accounted for a relatively slight foreign-born population and the number of Catholics advanced slowly over the years. They numbered but 10,000 in 1850 and 21,700 by the turn of the century, located for the most part in Mobile, Montgomery, and, after 1872, in Birmingham.

Education and Religious Communities

Alabama's oldest college, Spring Hill, was founded at Mobile in 1830 and after 1847 was entrusted to the Jesuits. A second Catholic college, St. Bernard's, began at Cullman where Benedictine monks had undertaken care of German immigrants and organized an independent abbey by 1891. Visitation sisters from Georgetown, D.C., began a convent and girls' school at Mobile in 1832. Daughters of Charity from Emmitsburg, Maryland, arrived in 1841 to staff an orphanage made necessary by deaths from frequent epidemics of yellow fever. Later they provided hospital facilities in Mobile, Birmingham, and Montgomery. Other religious communities made possible a strong parochial school system in the cities. A Benedictine motherhouse at Cullman and an independent Convent of Mercy at Mobile sent teaching sisters throughout the state.

The peninsular part of Florida was separated from the diocese in 1850 so that Alabama's second bishop, John Quinlan (1826–83), faced less responsibility but more acute problems after 1860. Civil War and Reconstruction seriously hampered Catholic growth. Service of religious sisters as military nurses and priests as chaplains, however, did much to dispel religious prejudice. Those postwar years did see growth in the northern part of the state as a result of the discovery of iron ore and coal at Birmingham. But a need to repair war damages joined to a depressed economy statewide left the diocese encumbered with a crushing debt.

A lack of resources made it impossible to minister to the newly freed slaves. Though a "creole" school existed in Mobile as early as 1850, specifically black Catholic schools and parishes, then seen as an advance in ministry, would not develop until the time of the fifth bishop, Edward P. Allen (1853–1926), at the century's end. Despite its twenty-year history (1900–22), a college to train black catechists near Montgomery under the direction of the Josephite Fathers did not succeed. That community and later efforts of the Edmundites at Selma gave somewhat of a Catholic context to the 1965 civil rights march led by Dr. Martin Luther King, Jr., from Selma to Montgomery where participants headquartered at the City of St. Jude.

Twentieth-Century Growth

Thomas J. Toolen (1886–1976) succeeded Allen in 1927 and in his forty-two years of leadership saw phenomenal growth in the Church of Alabama. Wartime prosperity in the 1940s accompanied Catholic population increase, especially in the area of Huntsville where much of early space technology was located at Redstone Arsenal. By 1968, after ten counties of northwest Florida were detached from the diocese, the Catholic population had reached 101,000 who were served by 150 parishes. The following year Toolen resigned to make way for a new diocese at Birmingham where Joseph Gregory Vath (1918–87) became the first bishop. The Diocese of Mobile was entrusted to John L. May (1922–94). In 1980 May was transferred to St. Louis as archbishop. Later that year a new metropolitan jurisdiction was formed comprising the states of Alabama and Mississippi, and Oscar H. Lipscomb (1931–) was appointed first archbishop of Mobile.

Catholics of more than local note connected with Alabama are the Rev. Abram J. Ryan (1838–86), poet-priest of the South; Admiral Raphael Semmes (1809–77), captain of the Confederate warship *Alabama;* Admiral, later U.S. Senator, Jeremiah A. Denton (1924–); and members of the Bruno Family of Birmingham whose philanthropy has benefited religious, educational, and health efforts statewide.

The Catholic population of Alabama is 132,181 within a total statewide of 4,001,555.

See also PORTIER, MICHAEL.

Carroll, Mary Teresa Austin, R.S.M. *A Catholic History of Alabama and the Floridas.* New York, 1908.

Curley, Michael J., C.Ss.R. *Church and State in the Spanish Floridas* (1783–1822). Washington, 1940.

Kenny, Michael J., S.J. *Catholic Culture in Alabama.* New York, 1931.

Lipscomb, Oscar H. "The Administration of Michael Portier, Vicar Apostolic of Alabama and the Floridas, 1825–1829, and First Bishop of Mobile, 1829–1859." Ph.D. dissertation, The Catholic University of America, 1963.

———. "The Administration of John Quinlan, Second Bishop of Mobile, 1859–1883." *Records of the American Catholic Historical Society of Philadelphia 78* (March–December 1967) 3–163.

Lovett, Rose Gibbons. *The Catholic Church in the Deep South.* Birmingham, 1980.

✠ OSCAR H. LIPSCOMB

ALASKA, CATHOLIC CHURCH IN

Alaska, a vast landmass at the northwestern extremity of the North American continent, purchased by the U.S.A. from Russia in 1867 for $7,200,000, organized as a Territory in 1912 and officially admitted into the Union in 1959 as the forty-ninth state, comprises 591,004 square miles and is nearly one fifth the size of the rest of the continental United States.

Early Missionaries

"Discovered" by Vitus Bering in July 1741, Alaska was first touched by Catholicism in 1779, when, on Ascension Day, May 13, the Franciscan priest Juan Riobó, a member of a Spanish exploratory expedition sailing out of San Blas, Mexico, celebrated Mass near present-day Craig in southeastern Alaska. Known at the time as "Russian America," Alaska was, ecclesiastically speaking, as yet a "no-man's land." That changed in 1847 when Modeste Demers was consecrated the first bishop of Vancouver Island and given jurisdiction over the island of that name and all British and Russian possessions as far north as the "glacial sea."

The Oblates of Mary Immaculate were the first Catholic missionary priests to enter Alaska. Jean Séguin spent the winter 1862–63 at Fort Yukon—accomplishing nothing. In 1870 Émile Petitot visited Fort Yukon briefly. Two years later Bishop Isidore Clut and Auguste Lecorre arrived at Fort Yukon with a view to establishing a permanent mission there. They too met with little success. In the summer of 1873 they went down the Yukon River to St. Michael, where they were favorably received and enjoyed a modicum of evangelizing success. Clut returned to Canada that same summer. Lecorre spent the winter 1873–74 at St. Michael. In the summer of 1874, when he learned that Alaska was under the jurisdiction of the bishop of Vancouver Island, he too returned to Canada.

Archbishop Seghers

Meanwhile, Alaska's southeastern part was also being visited by Catholic missionaries. In 1867 a secular priest, Joseph Mandart, visited the panhandle briefly. In 1873

Charles J. Seghers, newly consecrated bishop of Vancouver Island, made his first of five trips to Alaska. He visited Sitka, Kodiak, and Unalaska. In 1877, accompanied by Mandart, he visited the northern interior. The two arrived at Nulato in August and spent the following twelve months there and in the surrounding area, engaged in missionary work. In May 1879 Seghers founded a mission at Wrangell and put Fr. John Althoff in charge. In 1885 Seghers—now an archbishop—established a mission at Sitka and put Fr. William Heynen in charge.

In 1886 Seghers set out for Alaska on what was to be the last journey of his life. He had with him two Jesuits, Paschal Tosi and Aloysius Robaut. The party had as its goal the establishment of missions in Alaska's northern interior, especially at Nulato, which Seghers still fondly remembered from his earlier stay there.

The archbishop, the two Jesuits, and a Catholic layman, Francis Fuller—who was already giving signs of mental instability—left Victoria on July 13, 1886. On September 7 they arrived at the confluence of the Stewart and Yukon Rivers, still in Canadian territory, where the two Jesuits were to spend the winter doing missionary work, while Seghers and Fuller pushed on toward Nulato. It was late in the season for river travel, but Seghers was most eager to get to Nulato, fearing that Protestant ministers would arrive before him and take over the area.

As Seghers and Fuller made their way down the Yukon, their boat, traveling conditions, and Fuller's mind all deteriorated rapidly. On October 4 they arrived at Nuklukayet, where they abandoned their boat and waited for the river to freeze solid enough for sled travel. On November 19 they again set out for Nulato. On November 27, with Nulato still a good distance away and travel difficult because of deep snow, the party camped. Early the next morning, the demented Fuller fired a shot into Seghers as he bent over to pick up his mittens. He died instantly.

The following spring, 1887, Tosi and Robaut came down the Yukon into Alaska, where they learned of Seghers' death. Immediately Tosi took passage for the Pacific Northwest to confer with Rocky Mountain mission superior, Joseph M. Cataldo, S.J. When Seghers was given Tosi and Robaut for the trip north in 1886, he was given them simply as traveling companions. There was no intention to commit the Jesuits to the Alaska Mission. Upon Tosi's urging, Cataldo decided then and there that the Jesuits would, for the time being, take charge of at least parts of Alaska. A long-term commitment would need Rome's approval. Armed with all the faculties the vicar general of Vancouver Island could give him, Tosi returned to Alaska in the summer of 1887 to organize the systematic development of missions in northern Alaska. In 1892, during a private visit with Pope Leo XIII in Rome, Tosi so moved him with his account of Alaska that Leo told him: "Go, and make yourself pope in those regions!"

Ecclesiastical Organization

In 1894 the Holy See separated Alaska from the Diocese of Vancouver Island and made it a prefecture apostolic, with Tosi as prefect apostolic. At the same time, the Jesuit general separated Alaska from the Rocky Mountain Mission and made it an independent mission with Tosi as general superior. Failing health led to his being replaced as prefect apostolic in 1897 by John B. René, S.J. He, in turn, was replaced in 1904 by Joseph R. Crimont, S.J. In 1916 Alaska became a vicariate apostolic, and in 1917 Crimont was consecrated a bishop to serve as Alaska's first vicar apostolic. Upon his death in 1945, he was succeeded by his coadjutor since 1939, Bishop Walter J. Fitzgerald, S.J., who died two years later. He was followed in 1948 by Francis D. Gleeson, S.J., Alaska's last vicar apostolic.

From time to time Alaska's vastness and its greatly varied geographic and ethnic makeup prompted those in authority, both in Rome and Alaska, to consider the desirability of dividing it into several ecclesiastical districts. In 1951 Rome decreed the erection of Alaska's first diocese, the Diocese of Juneau, comprising at the time Alaska's panhandle and much of south-central Alaska. Dermot O'Flanagan was its first ordinary.

When the Juneau diocese was established, Gleeson moved to Fairbanks, where he continued on as vicar apostolic of the rest of Alaska. (Up to 1951 all of Alaska's ecclesiastical leaders after Tosi had made Juneau their headquarters.) In 1962, however, the vicariate became the Diocese of Fairbanks and Gleeson its ordinary. In 1966 the 138,985 square miles Archdiocese of Anchorage was established. This left the Juneau diocese with 37,566 square miles and the Fairbanks diocese with 409,849. Joseph T. Ryan was Anchorage's first archbishop.

Gleeson retired in November 1968 and was succeeded as bishop of Fairbanks by Robert L. Whelan, S.J. O'Flanagan resigned the Juneau see in June 1968. For two years then Ryan administered the Juneau diocese. In 1970 Francis T. Hurley became auxiliary bishop to Ryan and administrator of Juneau as Ryan's vicar. In 1971 he was named ordinary of the Diocese of Juneau. In December 1975 Ryan became Coadjutor Military Vicar of the U.S. Armed Forces. The following year Hurley became archbishop of Anchorage and administrator of Juneau. From 1979 to 1995 Michael H. Kenny was Juneau's ordinary. And since Whelan's retirement in 1985, Michael J. Kaniecki has been Fairbanks' ordinary.

Missions and Parishes

In northern Alaska, the Nulato Mission, founded in 1887, rightly claims primacy. The Holy Cross Mission and boarding school was founded in 1888, and the Nelson Island Mission in 1889. The mission and boarding school at Akulurak near the mouth of the Yukon, St. Joseph's, was opened in 1894, struggled along for four years, then the school was closed. The mission at St. Michael dates from 1898, the Nome parish from 1901, the Fairbanks parish from 1904. Reopened as St. Mary's in 1905, the boarding school at Akulurak flourished until 1951, when it was moved to the new St. Mary's on the Andreafsky River. Various other missions, stations, and schools were opened in the course of the years, principal among them the Pilgrim Springs Mission and boarding school north of Nome in 1918, the King Island Mission in 1929, the Kotzebue Mission also in 1929, and the Barrow Mission in 1954.

In Alaska's panhandle, pioneer parishes were established in the following places: Wrangell (1879); Juneau and Sitka (1885); Skagway (1898); and in Ketchikan (1903). In Alaska's south-central area: Seward and Valdez (1905); Cordova (1908); Anchorage (1915); Kodiak (1944); and Dillingham (1948).

Women Religious and Clergy

Schools and hospitals, staffed primarily by sisters, have been part of the Alaskan Catholic scene for well over a century. In 1886 the Sisters of St. Ann opened a hospital and school in Juneau. They served at Holy Cross from 1888–1957, and at Akulurak, 1894–98. In 1899 they began almost a century of service at Nulato. Douglas, Fairbanks, Skagway, Sitka, Glennallen, and Anchorage, too, were scenes of their labors. The Sisters of Providence were in Nome to operate a hospital and a school from 1902–18. In 1910 they began a ministry of hospital work and teaching in Fairbanks that was to last well over half a century. They have been operating a major hospital in Anchorage since 1938. They have also taught school there.

Ursuline nuns have been in Alaska since 1905 when they went to Akulurak to staff the St. Mary's Mission boarding school there. In 1951, when that school was moved to the new St. Mary's, they moved with it and staffed it till it was closed in 1987. They were at the Pilgrim Springs Mission from 1919–41. The Sisters of St. Joseph of Peace began operating a hospital in Ketchikan in 1923, and teaching school there in 1946. Among pioneer sisters in Alaska must be numbered also the Grey Nuns of the Sacred Heart. In 1944 they took over management of the Kodiak hospital. Since 1952 the Little Sisters of Jesus have had fraternities in Nome, Fairbanks, and on Little Diomede Island. In more recent years many sisters of various orders and congregations have served in many of Alaska's communities in a variety of ministries. In recent decades numerous members of the Jesuit Volunteer Corps have served throughout Alaska. The Catholic radio station in Nome, KNOM, has been staffed mainly by volunteers.

The whole of Alaska was, for the most part, under the care of Jesuits from 1887 to 1951, when the Diocese of Juneau was erected. They were virtually the only clerics and male religious serving in Alaska during those sixty-odd years. Several Brothers of Christian Instruction were part of the Holy Cross staff from 1905–09. In 1918, in Juneau, J. Edgar Gallant became the first priest ordained in and for Alaska. Diocesan priest William F. Walsh was pastor at Kotzebue, 1929–30. Gradually other diocesan priests began to take over parishes, mainly in Alaska's southern parts. In more recent decades diocesan priests and religious priests and brothers have been serving in a great variety of ministries in all three of Alaska's dioceses and at military bases.

Catholic Alaska Today

While Catholic Alaska is not overly impressive in terms of numbers (according to the 1994 *Official Catholic Directory* the Archdiocese of Anchorage had 26,612 Catholics out of a total population of 363,835; Fairbanks 17,356 out of 133,467; Juneau 6,051 out of 75,043), it has achieved a certain degree of maturity. A glance into the current *OCD* reveals that its three dioceses resemble in the main most other U.S. dioceses. However, the geographic and ethnic makeup of Alaska gives rise to some major differences. Many communities are "bush" communities—communities widely separated from one another and unconnected by roads—that can be reached only by airplane, boat, or snowmachine. This makes ministry in Alaska time-consuming and expensive. To save time and cut costs, Archbishop Hurley and Bishop Kaniecki fly their own planes. The Anchorage and Juneau dioceses have relatively few Alaskan native Catholics. Fairbanks, on the other hand, has many—most of them Athapaskans and Central Yup'ik Inuits. Among the latter, there are around forty permanent deacons. Alaska, too, knows prejudice and racial tensions, but for the most part Alaskans have traditionally prided themselves in being governed by a tolerant, personal folk philosophy of "live and let live."

From the outset Alaskan Catholics have, in all areas, been part of mainstream Alaskan life. This is strikingly evident in the area of politics. Among the more prominent Catholics in Alaska's political life have been: Mike Stepovich, Alaska's last territorial governor; Walter J. Hickel, twice Alaska's governor, and secretary of the interior under President Nixon; Frank Murkowski, U.S. Senator; George Sullivan and Tom Fink, mayors of Anchorage; Edward Merdes, president of the International Junior Chamber of Commerce and Alaska State Senator.

Alaska, "the Last Frontier," is still in a state of becoming. This is true too of the Catholic Church in Alaska.

Cantwell, Margaret. *North to Share*. Victoria, Canada: Sisters of St. Ann, 1992.

Champagne, Joseph-Etienne. "First Attempts at the Evangelization of Alaska." *Etudes Oblates* 2 (1943) 13–22.

Llorente, Segundo, S.J. *Jesuits in Alaska*. Portland, Oreg.: Graphic Arts Center, 1969.

Mousseau, Gilles. "L 'Affaire d 'Alaska. A propos du Voyage de Mgr. Clut dans l'Amérique Russe en 1872." *Etudes Oblates* 5 (1946) 161–88.

Renner, Louis L. *Pioneer Missionary to the Bering Strait Eskimos: Bellarmine Lafortune, S.J.* Portland, Oreg.: Binford & Mort., in collaboration with Dorothy Jean Ray, 1979.

____. "Fr. Aloysius Bobaut, S.J.: Pioneer Missionary in Alaska." *Eskimo* 37 (no. 20, New Series, 1980–81) 5–16.

Savage, Alma H. *Dogsled Apostles.* New York: Sheed & Ward, 1942.

Schoenberg, Wilfred P. *Paths to the Northwest: A Jesuit History of the Oregon Province.* Chicago: Loyola University Press, 1982.

Shideler, John C., and Hal K. Rothman. *Pioneering Spirit: The Sisters of Providence in Alaska.* Anchorage, Alaska: Providence Hospital, 1987.

Steckler, Gerard G. "The Diocese of Juneau, Alaska." *Historical Records and Studies* 47 (1959) 234–54.

____. "The Foundation of the Alaskan Catholic Missions." *Studies in Mediaevalia and Americana: Essays in Honor of William Lyle Davis, S.J.* Spokane, Wash.: Gonzaga University Press, 1973, 129–50.

Yzermans, Vincent A. *St. Rose of Wrangell: The Church's Beginning in Southeast Alaska.* St. Paul, Minn.: North Central Publishing Company, 1979.

LOUIS L. RENNER, S.J.

ALEMANY, JOSEPH SADOC (1814–98)

First archbishop of San Francisco. Joseph Alemany was born July 13, 1814, at No. 9 Rambla del Paseo in the ancient town of Vich, Spain, the third youngster of Antonio Alamany and Micaela de los Santos Cunill. In 1830 Joseph Alemany (he preferred and always used the "e" rather than the "a") entered the Priory of Santo Domingo and, on September 23, 1831, took solemn vows as a member of the Order of Preachers (Dominicans) at which time he was given the name "Sadoc."

After philosophical studies at Tremp's Priory of San Jaime de Pillars and theological training at Gerona's Priory of Our Lady's Annunciation, Joseph completed his sacerdotal preparations at Viterbo's Priory of Santa Maria dei Gradi. He was ordained to the priesthood by Bishop Gaspar Bernardo Pianetti on March 11, 1837, at Viterbo's cathedral of San Lorenzo.

Following reception of a lectorate in theology and extensive courses in English at the Urban College of Propaganda Fide, Fr. Alemany was sent to the United States. Arriving on April 2, 1840, he was assigned to St. Joseph's Priory in Somerset, Ohio. Naturalized as an American citizen on April 15, 1841, Fr. Alemany served at Zanesville, Nashville, and Memphis. He was elected master of novices in 1847 and the following year he was named major superior for St. Joseph's province in which capacity he attended the Seventh Provincial Council of Baltimore.

Bishop of Monterey

Appointed Bishop of Monterey on May 31, 1850, by Pope Pius IX, Alemany was consecrated (ordained) on June 30, 1850, in Rome's Church of San Carlos al Corso by Giacomo Cardinal Franzoni, assisted by Archbishop Giovanni Stefanelli and Patriarch Guiseppe Valerga.

Disembarking at San Francisco on December 6, 1850, the newly appointed bishop of Monterey immediately journeyed to Santa Barbara, where he presented himself to the vicar capitular of the vacant jurisdiction, Fray Jose Maria Gonzalez Rubio. He was formally installed on January 28. While in Santa Barbara, Alemany issued his first pastoral letter in which he exhorted Catholics in California to a greater "purity of morals" in the practice of their faith.

By the end of the following year, Alemany had established himself at Monterey where he designated the presidio Chapel of San Carlos Borromeo as his cathedral. On December 21, 1851, at Alemany's request, the Diocese of Monterey was separated from its attachment to the Metropolitan District of Mexico City. Alemany also took steps to establish a vicariate for peninsular California. He invoked a diocesan synod which was held in San Francisco on March 19–23, 1852.

While attending the First Plenary Council of Baltimore, Bishop Alemany initiated proceedings for the recovery of the Pious Fund of the Californias, a legal action that remained prominent in American juridical annals until its ultimate solution in 1967. On July 17, 1853, Alemany laid the cornerstone of what would become St. Mary's Cathedral in San Francisco.

Archbishop of San Francisco

On July 29, 1853, Pope Pius IX created the Metropolitan District of San Francisco with Alemany as its first archbishop, a distinction bestowed on only six other districts during the longest pontifical reign in history. On November 18, 1855, Alemany was invested with the sacred pallium by his suffragan, Bishop Thaddeus Amat, C.M., of Monterey.

Alemany oversaw erection of the vicariate apostolic of Marysville on September 27, 1860, and the selection of Eugene O'Connell as its first incumbent. O'Connell subsequently became bishop of Grass Valley (later Sacramento).

Alemany attended all of the sessions of Vatican Council I, 1869–70, where he actively supported the definition of papal infallibility. He spoke several times to the assemblage, always with distinction and poise. In thirty-five years, Alemany's flock in San Francisco grew to an impressive 400,000 Catholics, served by 160 clergymen in 131 churches and twenty-five chapels and stations.

After prolonged negotiations with the Sacred Congregation of Propaganda Fide, Alemany secured the appointment of a coadjutor archbishop in the person of Patrick W. Riordan in 1883. Upon acceptance of his resignation by Pope Leo XIII, on December 28, 1884, Joseph Sadoc Alemany was given the titular see of Pelusium. He returned to Spain, where he spent the final years of his life as a humble religious in the Order of Preachers.

Death claimed the prelate on April 14, 1888, in the city of Valencia, where he was endeavoring to reestablish his order's ancient province of Aragon. He was interred on the epistle side of the main altar in the chapel of Santo Domingo. Alemany's remains were disinterred in January of 1965 and returned to San Francisco where, after services conducted in old St. Mary's Cathedral, he was placed in a vault alongside his successors at Holy Cross Mausoleum in Colma, California.

See also CALIFORNIA, CATHOLIC CHURCH IN; DOMINICANS (O.P.).

McGloin, John B., S.J. *California's First Archbishop. The Life of Joseph Sadoc Alemany, O.P.* St. Louis: Herder and Herder, 1966, 412.

Weber, Francis J. *Joseph Sadoc Alemany. Harbinger of a New Era.* Los Angeles: Dawson's Book Shop, 1973, viii, 70.

FRANCIS J. WEBER

ALEXIAN BROTHERS

Religious congregation of men. As a loose confederation of locally autonomous houses, the Alexian Brothers developed in three major areas in post-Reformation Europe: the Catholic Netherlands, Cologne, and Aachen. The Aachen community reached international status in 1866 with the original foundation in Chicago and in 1875 with the first house in Manchester, England. The ministries were diverse; in Aachen they were in charge of large asylums for the mentally ill and the severely retarded; in the United States they were primarily engaged in general hospitals in response to the desperate need to provide basic health care for the continuous stream of immigrants; in England they were at first burial brothers but soon developed nursing homes and provided home nursing.

First American Foundations

After visiting five cities, Br. Bonaventure Thelen, "the Rector of America," received Bishop James Duggan's permission to establish a house in Chicago. The first Alexian Brothers' hospital was actually a small infirmary on Dearborn and Shiller Avenues with room for only six patients. By contrast, Chicago's Mercy Hospital could accommodate 150 patients. By the fiftieth anniversary of the Chicago hospital in 1916, there were three other Alexian facilities located principally in German-American areas: St. Louis (1870), Oskosh, Wisconsin (1873), a hospital for the mentally ill and severely retarded, and Elizabeth, New Jersey (1893). Besides the location of the houses, the predominantly German character of the community was manifested in their tradition to limit their nursing to male patients.

German-American conservatism was also manifested in an anti-modern governance structure that prohibited fundraising efforts, such as fairs because they entailed excessive contact with the secular world. However, advances of pace-setting German medical science were immediately incorporated in their hospitals. Except for one provincial, Paul Pollig, a liberal who proposed election of provincials according to the republican ethos of the United States, traditional authoritarianism dominated the Alexians until the mid-twentieth century.

World War I, the rise of American vocations and the open-ended character of modernization of medical science fostered an Americanization process among the community. Simultaneously, nursing had become a middle-class profession. Though subjected to long hours and a strong dependency upon attending physicians, the three-year education program eventually broke down pervasive antimodern attitudes and rules governing the Alexian way of life. For example, a crisis of authority occurred in Chicago in the mid-1940s that resulted in a special visitation to mediate polarization. This resulted in expanding the personal responsibility of brothers and relaxing the rigid monastic routine. These adaptations to the professionalization of this nursing community prepared the brothers for the changes in the rule of life that occurred as a result of Vatican Council II.

Post-Vatican II Changes

In accord with the pattern of renewal and reform, the Alexian Brothers held extended chapter meetings in 1968–69 to compose a new constitution. In general the document authorized a team governance model, an apostolic healing ministry as the source of spirituality, both of which were based upon a retrieval of the original charism.

Br. Felix Bettendorf, who had presided over the foundation of the hospital in San Jose, was the first American superior general (1967–76). He guided the congregation through the post-Vatican Council II period, laid the groundwork for official affiliation of the Aachen congregation with the German and Belgian houses. Br. Warren Longo, a voice for new ministries in health care, has been involved in formation and administration of the provinces and general congregation. Br. Philip Kennedy, a long-time President and CEO of the Elk Grove Hospital, has a graduate degree in Public Health from Yale that represents post-Vatican II professionalism. Br. Dominic Walsh is the first nurse from the English/Irish province to serve as superior general.

With drastically reduced numbers, the American Alexians pursue the ministry of healing in diverse ways: they have nursing home and retirement facilities in Signal Mountain, Tennessee, and Milwaukee, Wisconsin, general hospitals in Elk Grove, Illinois, St. Louis, Missouri, and San Jose, California. Just as they originally gathered together in the fourteenth century to care for those struck by epidemics, the most recent Alexian ministry is at Bonaventure House in Chicago, a hospice for men and women with AIDS. This manifestation of the vitality of the original charism sustains hope and promise among the brothers during the last years of the twentieth century.

Archives of the American Province are located in Elk Grove, Illinois.

Kauffman, Christopher J. *Tamers of Death, The History of the Alexian Brothers 1300–1789.* Vol. I. New York: Seabury Press, 1976.

_____. *The Ministry of Healing, The History of the Alexian Brothers, 1789 to the Present.* Vol. II. New York: Seabury Press, 1978.

CHRISTOPHER J. KAUFFMAN

ALLEN, FRED (1894–1956)

Entertainer. Born John Florence Sullivan, in Cambridge, Massachusetts, on May 31, 1894, he began his career in entertainment by performing juggling and ventriloquism. His first performance was while he was an employee of the Boston Public Library: he performed as a juggler at an employee Christmas party. Allen performed on amateur circuits and vaudeville tours and entertained under a variety of names including Paul Huckle and Freddy St. James.

Upon return from a tour in Oceania in 1916, he adopted the name Fred Allen and ascended to stardom as evidenced by top billing in the prestigious Palace Theater in New York City. He appeared in *The Passing Show* (1922) and *The Greenwich Village Follies.* After marrying fellow performer Portland Hoffa in 1927, Allen appeared in *The Little Show* (1929) and *Three's a Crowd* (1930). He entered the medium of radio in 1932, signed with Columbia Broadcasting System and, with Hoffa, starred in *Town Hall Tonight* in 1934 through 1939. In 1939 the show was renamed *The Fred Allen Show* with Allen not only starring in it, but also writing most of the 273 episodes.

In 1940 he started the enormously popular radio show the *Texaco Star Theater* which presented a weekly cast of characters of "Allen's Alley" such as Mrs. Pansy Nussbaum, Senator Beauregard Claghorn, and Ajax Cassidy among others. Allen appeared in the movie *Love Thy Neighbor* (1940) and wrote two autobiographical books, *Treadmill to Oblivion* (1954) and *Much Ado About Me* (1956). Allen's dry wit and superb timing influenced a generation of performers. He died in New York City on March 17, 1956.

LISELLE DRAKE

ALLEN, GRACIE (1905–64)

Entertainer. Allen was born in San Francisco, California, on July 26, 1905, to Edward Allen, an entertainer, and Margaret Darragh Allen. Her father fostered Gracie's entertainment career by allowing her to make her stage debut at the age of three years. Gracie joined her father and three sisters later on the stage after leaving Star of the Sea Convent at age fourteen. She performed for several years with the Larry Reilly Company. There was a brief hiatus from the stage to secretarial school during which she met George Burns in 1922. Together they formed a new act: Burns and Allen.

Four years after they met, they were married in Cleveland, Ohio. Under contract with the Keith Theater chain, Burns and Allen became a very popular vaudeville act in the late 1920s and graduated to the medium of radio in 1930 by appearing on the Eddie Cantor show. They were later offered a contract with Columbia Broadcasting System and by the end of the decade their show was one of the most popular radio programs in the country.

The 1930s also marked their debut into the medium of motion pictures. Among the several movies featuring Burns and Allen were *The Big Broadcast* (1932) and *College Holiday* (1936). The couple also had a television show in the 1950s again with enormous success. In 1958 Gracie retired from portraying the preposterous characterizations that had made her both famous and one of America's most beloved female entertainers. She died in Los Angeles, California, on August 2, 1964.

LISELLE DRAKE

ALLOUEZ, CLAUDE JEAN (1622–89)

Jesuit, missionary, explorer. Allouez was born in Saint Didier-en-Forez, France, June 6, 1622. Allouez entered the Jesuit novitiate of Toulouse in 1639, and was ordained in 1655. He arrived in New France three years later, where

Fred Allen

he ministered to the settlers of the St. Lawrence Valley and studied the Huron and Algonquin languages. In 1660, Allouez was chosen superior of the residence at Trois-Rivières and an appointment as vicar general to the bishop of Quebec followed in 1665. Fr. Allouez was instrumental in establishing an enduring Jesuit presence in the Great Lakes region.

Between 1665 and the year of his death, he preached to around twenty Native American nations. He was especially appreciated among the Illinois and wrote an Illinois-French prayer book. His superior, Fr. Dablon, estimated that Allouez had baptized between ten and twenty thousand neophytes. His command of Algonquin languages was evidenced in 1671. When the king of France claimed possession of a large territory in the west, Fr. Allouez delivered the address for the occasion to the attending Native American headmen. The *Jesuit Relations* contain extracts from his journals (esp. 1667–76) which provide the earliest descriptions of the Illinois nation. He also laid the foundations for the St. Francis Xavier Mission in 1673. In the United States, recognition of his endeavors is most noticeable in Wisconsin. In 1899, the Wisconsin Historical Society dedicated a monument to Fr. Allouez at De Pere, one of the centers of his extensive missionary activities.

KEES-JAN WATERMAN

ALTER, KARL J. (1885–1977)

Archbishop of Cincinnati. Karl J. Alter was born on August 18, 1885, in Toledo, Ohio, the son of John and Elizabeth Kuttner Alter. Educated at St. John University in Toledo and at St. Mary Seminary in Cleveland, he was ordained by Bishop James Farrelly of Cleveland on June 4,

Karl J. Alter

1910. He was the first priest ordained for the newly established Diocese of Toledo. After serving in parishes in Lima and Leipsic, he was appointed Diocesan Director of Catholic Charities in 1914, a position which he held until 1929. From 1929 to 1931 he served as the director of the National Catholic School of Social Service. Elected to the see of Toledo on April 17, 1931, he was consecrated on June 17 by Archbishop John McNicholas of Cincinnati whom he would succeed as archbishop nineteen years later. As bishop of Toledo, Alter oversaw an extensive building program which included the completion of Blessed Virgin Mary of the Rosary Cathedral which had been planned by Bishop Joseph Schrembs and begun by Bishop Samuel Stritch, Alter's two predecessors as bishop of Toledo.

Alter was promoted to the metropolitan see of Cincinnati on June 21, 1950. As he did in Toledo, Alter engaged in an extensive building program in the archdiocese, undertaking 130 major building projects in his nineteen years as archbishop. Among the most notable of these projects was the restoration of St. Peter in Chains Cathedral which was rededicated in 1957 and the completion of St. Gregory preparatory seminary. In addition, Alter oversaw the building of seven new Catholic high schools, a new orphanage and a new home for the aged, as well as the construction of parish churches, convents, rectories, and parochial schools. In 1954 he convoked the fifth synod of the archdiocese which resulted in a thoroughly recodified body of laws governing the archdiocese. Long interested in Catholic Action, Alter took steps to reorganize structures which would give the laity the effective means of exercising the lay apostolate. Particularly important in this respect was his reorganization of the Archdiocesan Councils of Catholic Men and Women. In the area of social welfare and social justice, Alter frequently served as a spokesman for social legislation, including minimum wage laws and federal aid to education. He served as an advisor on social legislation to both the NCWC and the Ohio Department of Welfare. On the national level, he served consecutive terms as chairman of the Administrative Board of the NCWC. During the preparatory stages of the Second Vatican Council, Alter was appointed to the Central Preparatory Commission for the council and later served on the council's Commission for Bishops and the Government of Dioceses. In the post-Vatican II period he oversaw the implementation of the liturgical changes, established an Archdiocesan Pastoral Council, and ordered the establishment of parish councils in every parish. After his retirement in 1969, he continued to reside in Cincinnati where he died on August 23, 1977.

See also OHIO, CATHOLIC CHURCH IN.

The Church in Cincinnati, 1921–1971. (Sesquicentennial booklet containing articles reprinted from *The Catholic Telegraph*).

THOMAS W. TIFFT

AMAT, THADDEUS (1811–78)

Missionary, bishop. Thaddeus Amat was born on December 21, 1811, in Barcelona, Spain, the son of Pedro and Martha (Brusi) Amat. He was received into the Congregation of the Mission (Vincentians) on January 4, 1832, and was ordained a priest on December 23, 1837, by Archbishop Hyacinthe Louis de Quélen of Paris.

Amat arrived in New Orleans on October 9, 1838. He served at posts in Perryville, Cape Girardeau, and St. Louis, Missouri, until 1847 when he became rector of St. Charles Borromeo Seminary in Philadelphia. He also attended the Seventh Provincial Council of Baltimore in1849. Amat was consecrated (ordained) bishop of Monterey on

Thaddeus Amat

March 12, 1854, by Giacomo Cardinal Franzoni in the chapel of Propaganda Fide, Rome. He arrived in California with the relics of Saint Vibiana under whose patronage he erected a cathedral in 1876. He was installed at Monterey November 25, 1855.

Amat issued his first pastoral letter in 1854 and authored a catechism on matrimony (1864) which was used widely throughout the United States. He moved to Southern California and had the name of the diocese changed to Monterey-Los Angeles in 1859. He attended the sessions of Vatican Council I (1869–70) and brought to an end the first phase of the settlement for the Pious Fund of the Californias (1875). He also engaged in a protracted canonical dispute with the Franciscans at Santa Barbara.

Bishop Amat died at Los Angeles on May 12, 1878, and was interred beneath the main altar in St. Vibiana's Cathedral. In 1962, his remains were moved to the episcopal vault at Calvary Mausoleum.

See also CALIFORNIA, CATHOLIC CHURCH IN.

Weber, Francis J. *California's Reluctant Prelate. The Life and Times of Right Reverend Thaddeus Amat, C.M.* Los Angeles: Dawson's Book Shop, 1964, xv, 234.

FRANCIS J. WEBER

AMERICA

America is a weekly Catholic journal of opinion that has appeared continuously since April 17, 1909. The founder was John J. Wynne, S.J. (1859–1948), who also conceived the idea of the *Catholic Encyclopedia,* the first volume of which appeared in 1907 under his direction. From 1892 Wynne edited a devotional Catholic monthly, *The Messenger of the Sacred Heart.* Determined to publish materials less devotional and more wide-ranging, so that readers might "find God in all things," he had by 1902 divided that earlier journal in two: *The Messenger of the Sacred Heart,* which remained the organ of the Apostleship of Prayer, and *The Messenger,* a Catholic magazine of more general interest. He wanted *The Messenger* to be yet "more solid and serious," and by 1909 the improved version appeared as *America.* This title was meant to show the new magazine's scope, and the subtitle "Catholic Review of the Week" specified its point of view.

From the beginning the magazine has been the work of Jesuits from across the United States, and this breadth of origin was reflected in the first editorial board, composed of Jesuits from all the U.S. provinces of the Society of Jesus then existing. Wynne himself, a peremptory if industrious character, lasted only a few months as editor of *America,* but the editorial formula he devised lasts to this day—editorial comment, short articles, and reviews of arts and letters.

Issues and stances that have characterized the history of the publication would include the following. It promoted racial and social justice from the 1930s through the 1960s with the contributions of longtime editors like John LaFarge, S.J., and Benjamin Masse, S.J. During the Spanish Civil War (1936–38), the magazine was sympathetic to Spanish Catholics and therefore tended to support the Catholic aspects of Franco's cause, and on this issue the magazine parted company with liberal U.S. journals with which it is sometimes compared. On the other hand, *America* in the early 1950s, under the editorship of Robert Hartnett, S.J., criticized Senator Joseph McCarthy, who was often championed by Catholics of that day for his supposed anti-communism, and the magazine and its editor suffered for that principled stand. In the 1960s the magazine enthusiastically reported and supported Vatican Council II, and America Press Inc. published the first available English edition of council documents. Between 1960 and 1970, C. J. McNaspy, S.J., one of the associate editors, enlivened the magazine's appreciation of liturgy, music and the fine arts.

A review of the magazine's history or of any given issue reveals that *America* strives for balance, preferring analysis to ideology. A historical example was its editorial of August 17, 1968, carefully dissenting from that part of Pope Paul VI's encyclical *Humanae vitae* which said all forms of artificial birth control are inherently evil.

America retains a loyal readership, especially among the hierarchy and other leaders and managers of the Catholic Church in the United States, lay and religious. During the post-Vatican II period, the editors have consistently promoted conciliar reform, but they have struck a balance between the extremes of liberal and conservative opinion in the reforming Church, acting as a bridge for Church dialogue. This opens the magazine to the criticism that it is bland or uncommitted, but it adheres to an analytical rather than crusading tone, and it consistently wins prizes from the Catholic Press Association. The weekly press run in 1995 stood at 35,000.

Editors in chief of recent decades have been: Thurston Davis, S.J. (1955–68, d. 1986), who acquired the magazine's present headquarters on W. 56 St. in Manhattan and who raised the readership to a historical high in the early 1960s; Donald R. Campion, S.J., (1968–74, d. 1988), who was one of the editors of the first English edition of the documents of Vatican II; Joseph A. O'Hare, S.J. (1974–84); George W. Hunt, S.J. (1984–present).

The balance favored by these editors has given the magazine a reputation for temperateness that its founding editor did not always share. But such steadiness has enabled the magazine to fulfill throughout the twentieth century the vision of its founder, who wrote in the first issue: "The object, scope and character of this review are sufficiently indicated in its name—*America*: A Catholic Review of the Week."

See also CATHOLIC MAGAZINES AND PERIODICALS; JESUITS IN AMERICA, THE.

America, April 11, 1959 (50th Anniversary Issue).

Ciani, John L., S.J. "A Man With Too Many Ideas." *America* (December 19, 1992) 494–98.

Hunt, George W., S.J. "America: How Did It Happen?" *America* 170 (April 9, 1994) 8–11.

THOMAS H. STAHEL, S.J.

AMERICAN BISHOPS, NECROLOGY OF

Information includes: dates; place of birth if outside the U.S.; date of ordination to the priesthood; titular see in parentheses of bishops who were not ordinaries; indication, where applicable, of date of resignation.

Abbreviation code: abp., archbishop; bp., bishop; v.a., vicar apostolic; aux., auxiliary bishop; coad., coadjutor; ord., ordained priest; res., resigned.

A

Acerra, Angelo Thomas, O.S.B. (1925–90): ord. May 20, 1950; aux. Military Services archdiocese (Lete), 1983–90.

Ackerman, Richard H., C.S.Sp. (1903–92): ord. Aug. 28, 1926; aux. San Diego (Lares), 1956–60; bp. Covington 1960–78 (res.).

Adrian, William L. (1883–1972): ord. Apr. 15, 1911; bp. Nashville, 1936–69 (res.).

Ahr, George W. (1904–93): ord. July 29, 1928; bp. Trenton, 1950–79 (res.).

Albers, Joseph (1891–1965): ord. June 17, 1916; aux. Cincinnati (Lunda), 1929–37; first bp. Lansing, 1937–65.

Alemany, Joseph Sadoc, O.P. (1814–88): b. Spain; ord. Mar. 11, 1837; bp. Monterey, 1850–53; first abp. San Francisco, 1853–84 (res.).

Alencastre, Stephen P., SS.CC. (1876–1940): b. Madeira; ord. Apr. 5, 1902; coad. v.a. Sandwich Is. (Arabissus), 1924–36; v.a. Sandwich (Hawaiian) Is., 1936–40.

Alerding, Herman J. (1845–1924): b. Germany; ord. Sept. 22, 1869; bp. Fort Wayne, 1900–24.

Allen, Edward P. (1853–1926): ord. Dec. 17, 1881; bp. Mobile, 1897–1926.

Alter, Karl J. (1885–1977): ord. June 4, 1910; bp. Toledo, 1931–50; abp. Cincinnati, 1950–69 (res.).

Althoff, Henry (1873–1947): ord. July 26, 1902; bp. Belleville, 1914–47.

Amat, Thaddeus, C.M. (1811–78): b. Spain; ord. Dec. 23, 1837; bp. Monterey (title changed to Monterey-Los Angeles, 1859), 1854–78.

Anderson, Joseph (1865–1927): ord. May 20, 1892; aux. Boston (Myrina), 1909–27.

Anderson, Paul F. (1917–87): ord. Jan. 6, 1943; coad. bp. Duluth (Polignana), 1968–69; bp. Duluth, 1969–82 (res.); aux. Sioux Falls, 1983–87.

Anglim, Robert, C.Ss.R. (1922–73): ord. Jan. 6, 1948; prelate Coari, Brazil (Gaguari), 1966–73.

Annabring, Joseph (1900–59): b. Hungary; ord. May 3, 1927; bp. Superior, 1954–59.

Appelhans, Stephen A., S.V.D. (1905–51): ord. May 5, 1932; v.a. East New Guinea (Catula), 1948–51.

Armstrong, Robert J. (1884–1957): ord. Dec. 10, 1910; bp. Sacramento, 1929–57.

Arnold, William R. (1881–1965): ord. June 13, 1908; delegate of U.S. military vicar (Phocaea), 1945–65.

Atkielski, Roman R. (1898–1969): ord. May 30, 1931; aux. Milwaukee (Stobi), 1947–69.

B

Babcock, Allen J. (1898–1969): ord. Mar. 7, 1925; aux. Detroit (Irenopolis), 1947–54; bp. Grand Rapids, 1954–69.

Bacon, David W. (1815–74): ord. Dec. 13, 1838; first bp. Portland, Me. 1855–74.

Baldwin, Vincent J. (1907–79): ord. July 26, 1931; aux. Rockville Centre (Bencenna), 1962–79.

Baltes, Peter J. (1827–86): b. Germany; ord. May 31, 1852; bp. Alton (now Springfield), Ill., 1870–86.

Baraga, Frederic: See Baraga, Frederic.

Barron, Edward (1801–54): b. Ireland; ord. 1829; v.a. The Two Guineas (Constantina), 1842–44 (res.) missionary in U.S.

Barry, John (1799–1859): b. Ireland; ord. Sept. 24, 1825; bp. Savannah, 1857–59.

Barry, Patrick J. (1868–1940): b. Ireland; ord. June 9, 1895; bp. St. Augustine, 1922–40.

Bartholome, Peter W. (1893–1982): ord. June 12, 1917; coad. St. Cloud (Lete), 1942–53; bp. St. Cloud, 1953–68 (res.).

Baumgartner, Apollinarls, O.F.M. Cap. (1899–1970): ord. May 30, 1926; v.a. Guam (Joppa), 1945–65; first bp. Agana, Guam, 1965–70.

Bayley, James Roosevelt (1814–77): convert, 1842; ord. Mar. 2, 1843; first bp. Newark, 1853–72; abp. Baltimore, 1872–77.

Bazin, John S. (1796–1848): b. France; ord. July 22, 1822; bp. Vincennes (now Indianapolis), 1847–48.

Beaven, Thomas D. (1851–1920): ord. Dec. 18, 1875; bp. Springfield, Mass., 1892–1920.

Becker Thomas A. (1832–99): ord. June 18, 1859; first bp. Wilmington, 1868–86; bp. Savannah, 1886–99.

Beckman, Francis J. (1875–1948): ord. June 20, 1902; bp. Lincoln, 1924–30; abp. Dubuque, 1930–46 (res.).

Begin, Floyd L. (1902–77): ord. July 31, 1927; aux. Cleveland (Sala), 1947–62; first bp. Oakland, 1962–77.

Bell, Alden J. (1904–82): b. Canada; ord. May 14, 1932; aux. Los Angeles (Rhodopolis), 1956–62; bp. Sacramento, 1962–79 (res.).

Benincasa, Pius A. (1913–86): ord. Mar. 27, 1937; aux. Buffalo (Buruni), 1964–86.

Benjamin, Cletus J. (1909–61): ord. Dec. 8, 1935; aux. Philadelphia (Binda), 1960–61.

Bennett, John G. (1891–1957): ord. June 27, 1914; first bp. Lafayette, Ind. 1944–57.

Bergan, Gerald T. (1892–1972): ord. Oct. 28, 1915; bp. Des Moines, 1934–48; abp. Omaha, 1948–60 (res.).

Bernardin, Joseph L. (1928–96): ord. April 26, 1952; aux. Atlanta (Lugura), 1966–72; abp. Cincinnati, 1972–82; abp. Chicago, 1982–96; cardinal 1983.

Bernarding, George, S.V.D. (1912–87): ord. Aug. 13, 1939; first v.a. Mount Hagen, Papua New Guinea (Belabitene), 1960–66; first bp., 1966–82, and first abp., 1982–87 (res.), Mount Hagen.

Bidawid, Thomas M. (1910–71): b. Iraq; ord. May 15, 1935; U.S. citizen; first abp. Ahwaz, Iran (Chaldean Rite), 1968–70; Chaldean patriarchal vicar for United Arab Republic, 1970–71.

Bilock, John M. (1916–94): ord. Feb. 3, 1946; aux. Byzantine-rite Munhall, now Pittsburgh (Pergamum), 1977–95.

Binz, Leo (1900–79): ord. Mar. 15, 1924; coad. bp. Winona (Pinara) 1942–49; coad. abp. Dubuque (Silyum), 1949–54; abp. Dubuque, 1954–61; abp. St. Paul and Minneapolis, 1962–75 (res.).

Biskup, George J. (1911–79): ord. Mar. 19, 1937; aux. Dubuque (Hemeria), 1957–65; bp. Des Moines, 1965–67; coad. abp. Indianapolis (Tamalluma), 1969–70; abp. Indianapolis, 1970–79 (res.).

Blanc, Anthony (1792–1860): b. France; ord. July 22, 1816; bp. New Orleans, 1835–50; first abp. New Orleans, 1850–60.

Blanchet (brothers): **Augustin M.** (1797–1887): b. Canada; ord. June 3, 1821; bp. Walla Walla, 1846–50; first bp. Nesqually (now Seattle), 1850–79 (res.). **Francis N.** (1795–1883): b. Canada; ord. July 19, 1819; v.a. Oregon Territory (Philadelphia, Adrasus), 1843–46; first abp. Oregon City (now Portland), 1846–80 (res.).

Blanchette, Romeo R. (1913–82): ord. Apr. 3, 1937; aux. Joliet (Maxita), 1965–66; bp. Joliet, 1966–79 (res.).

Blenk, James H., S.M. (1856–1917): b. Germany; ord. Aug. 16, 1885; bp. San Juan, 1899–1906; abp. New Orleans, 1906–17.

Boardman, John J. (1894–1978): ord. May 21, 1921; aux. Brooklyn (Gunela), 1952–77 (res.).

Boccella, John H., T.O.R. (1912–92): b. Italy, came to U.S. at age of two; ord. Mar. 29, 1941; abp. Izmir, Turkey, 1968–78 (res.); tit. abp. Ephesus.

Boeynaems, Libert H., SS.CC. (1857–1926): b. Belgium; ord. Sept. 11, 1881; v.a. Sandwich (Hawaiian) Is. (Zeugma), 1903–26.

Bohachevsky, Constantine (1884–1961): b. Austrian Galicia; ord. Jan. 31, 1909; ap. ex. Ukrainian Byzantine Catholics in U.S. (Amisus), 1924–58; first metropolitan of Byzantine Rite archeparchy of Philadelphia, 1958–61.

Boileau, George, S.J. (1912–65): ord. June 13, 1948; coad. bp. Fairbanks (Ausuccura), 1964–65.

Bokenfohr, John, O.M.I. (1903–82): ord. July 11, 1927; bp. Kimberley, S. Africa, 1953–74 (res.).

Boland, Thomas A. (1896–1979): ord. Dec. 23, 1922; aux. Newark (Irina), 1940–47; bp. Paterson, 1947–52; abp. Newark, 1953–74 (res.).

Bona, Stanislaus (1888–1967): ord. Nov. 1, 1912; bp. Grand Island, 1932–44; coad. bp. Green Bay (Mela), 1944–45; bp. Green Bay, 1945–67.

Bonacum, Thomas (1847–1911): b. Ireland; ord. June 18, 1870; bp. Lincoln, 1887–1911.

Borgess, Caspar H. (1826–90): b. Germany; ord. Dec. 8, 1848; coad. bp. and ap. admin. Detroit (Calydon), 1870–71; bp. Detroit, 1871–87 (res.).

Bourgade, Peter (1845–1908): b. France; ord. Nov. 30, 1869; v.a. Arizona (Thaumacus), 1885–97; first bp. Tucson, 1897–99; abp. Santa Fe, 1899–1908.

Boylan, John J. (1889–1953): ord. July 28, 1915; bp. Rockford, 1943–53.

Boyle, Hugh C. (1873–1950): ord. July 2, 1898; bp. Pittsburgh, 1921–50.

Bradley, Denis (1846–1903): b. Ireland; ord. June 3, 1871; first bp. Manchester, 1884–1903.

Brady, John (1842–1910): b. Ireland; ord. Dec. 4, 1864; aux. Boston (Alabanda), 1891–1910.

Brady, Matthew F. (1893–1959): ord. June 10, 1916; bp. Burlington, 1938–44 bp. Manchester, 1944–59.

Brady, William O. (1899–1961): ord. Dec. 21, 1923; bp. Sioux Falls, 1939–56; coad. abp. St. Paul (Selymbria), June–Oct. 1956; abp. St. Paul, 1956–61.

Brennan, Andrew J. (1877–1956): ord. Dec. 17, 1904; aux. Scranton (Thapsus), 1923–26; bp. Richmond, 1926–45 (res.).

Brennan, Francis J. (1894–1968): ord. Apr. 3, 1920; judge (1940–59) and dean (1959–67) of Roman Rota; ord. bp. 1967; cardinal 1967.

Brennan, Thomas F. (1853–1916): b. Ireland; ord. July 14, 1880; first bp. Dallas, 1881–93; aux. St. John's, Newfoundland (Usula), 1893–1905 (res.).

Brizgys, Vincas (1903–92): b. Lithuania; U.S. citizen, 1958; ord. June 5, 1927; aux. Kaunas, Lithuania (Bosano), 1940; exiled 1944; resided in U.S. (Chicago archdiocese) from 1951.

Broderick, Bonaventure (1868–1943): ord. July 26, 1896; aux. Havana, Cuba (Juliopolis), 1903–05 (res.).

Brondel, John B. (1842–1903): b. Belgium; ord. Dec. 17, 1864; bp. Vancouver Is., 1879–84; first bp. Helena, 1884–1903.

Brossart, Ferdinand (1849–1930): b. Germany; ord. Sept. 1, 1892; bp. Covington, 1916–23 (res.).

Brust, Leo J. (1916–95): ord. May 30, 1942; aux. Milwaukee (Suelli) 1969–91 (res.).

Bruté, Simon G. (1779–1839): b. France; ord. June 11, 1808; first bp. Vincennes (now Indianapolis), 1834–39.

Buddy, Charles F. (1887–1966): ord. Sept. 19, 1914; first bp. San Diego, 1936–66.

Burke, James C., O.P. (1926–94): ord. June 8, 1956; prelate of Chimbote, Peru (Lamiggiga), 1967–78 (res.).

Burke, Joseph A. (1886–1962): ord. Aug. 3, 1912; aux. Buffalo (Vita), 1943–52; bp. Buffalo, 1952–62.

Burke, Maurice F. (1845–1923): b. Ireland; ord. May 22, 1875; first bp. Cheyenne, 1887–93; bp. St. Joseph, 1893–1923.

Burke, Thomas M. (1840–1915): b. Ireland; ord. June 30, 1864; bp. Albany, 1894–1915.

Busch, Joseph F. (1866–1953): ord. July 28, 1889; bp. Lead (now Rapid City), 1910–15; bp. St. Cloud, 1915–53.

Byrne, Andrew (1802–62): b. Ireland; ord. Nov. 11, 1827; first bp. Little Rock, 1844–62.

Byrne, Christopher E. (1867–1950): ord. Sept. 23, 1891; bp. Galveston, 1918–50.

Byrne, Edwin V. (1891–1963): ord. May 22, 1915; first bp. Ponce, 1925–29; bp. San Juan, 1929–43; abp. Santa Fe, 1943–63.

Byrne, Leo C. (1908–74): ord. June 10, 1933; aux. St. Louis (Sabadia), 1954–61; coad. bp. Wichita, 1961–67; coad. abp. (Plestra) St. Paul and Minneapolis, 1967–74.

Byrne, Patrick J., M.M. (1888–1950): ord. June 23, 1915; apostolic delegate to Korea (Gazera), 1949–50.

Byrne, Thomas S. (1841–1923): ord. May 22, 1869; bp. Nashville, 1894–1923.

C

Caesar, Raymond R., S.V.D. (1932–87): ord. June 4, 1961; coad. bp. Goroka, Papua New Guinea, 1978–80; bp. Goroka, 1980–87.

Caillouet, L. Abel (1900–84): ord. May 7, 1925; aux. New Orleans (Setea), 1947–76 (res.).

Canevin, J. F. Regis (1853–1927): ord. June 4, 1879; coad. bp. Pittsburgh (Sabrata), 1903–04; bp. Pittsburgh, 1904–21 (res.).

Cantwell, John J. (1874–1947): b. Ireland; ord. June 18, 1899; bp. Monterey-Los Angeles, 1917–22; bp. Los Angeles-San Diego, 1922–36; first abp. Los Angeles, 1936–47.

Carrell, George A., S.J. (1803–68): ord. Dec. 20, 1827; first bp. Covington, 1853–68.

Carroll (brothers): **Coleman F.** (1905–77): ord. June 15, 1930; aux. Pittsburgh (Pitanae), 1953–58; first bp. Miami, 1958–68 and first abp., 1968–77. **Howard J.** (1902–60): ord. Apr. 2, 1927; bp. Altoona-Johnstown, 1958–60.

Carroll, James J. (1862–1913): ord. June 15, 1889; bp. Nueva Segovia, P.I., 1908–12 (res.).

Carroll, John (1735–1815): ord. Feb. 14, 1761; first bishop of the American hierarchy; first bp., 1789–1808, and first abp., 1808–15, of Baltimore.

Carroll, John P. (1864–1925): ord. July 7, 1886; bp. Helena, 1904–25.

Carroll, Mark K. (1896–1985): ord. June 10, 1922; bp. Wichita, 1947–67 (res.).

Cartwright, Hubert J. (1900–58): ord. June 11, 1927; coad. bp. Wilmington (Neve), 1956–58.

Caruana, George (1882–1951): b. Malta; ord. Oct. 28, 1905; bp. Puerto Rico (name changed to San Juan, 1924), 1921–25; ap. del. Mexico (Sebastea in Armenia), 1925–27; internuncio to Haiti, 1927–35; nuncio to Cuba, 1935–47 (res.).

Casey, James V. (1914–86): ord. Dec. 8, 1939; aux. Lincoln (Citium), Apr.–June, 1957; bp. Lincoln, 1957–67; abp. Denver 1967–86.

Casey, Lawrence B. (1905–77): ord. June 7, 1930; aux. Rochester (Cea), 1953–66; bp. Paterson, 1966–77.

Cassata, John J. (1908–89): ord. Dec. 8, 1932; aux. Dallas-Ft. Worth (Bida), 1968–69; bp. Ft. Worth 1969–80 (res.).

Cassidy, James E. (1869–1951): ord. Sept. 8, 1898; aux. Fall River (Ibora), 1930–34; bp. Fall River, 1934–51.

Chabrat, Guy Ignatius, S.S. (1787–1868): b. France; ord. Dec. 21, 1811; coad. bp. Bardstown (Bolina), 1834–47 (res.).

Chanche, John J., S.S. (1795–1852): ord. June 5, 1819; bp. Natchez (now Jackson), 1841–52.

Chapelle, Placide L. (1842–1905): b. France; ord. June 28, 1865; coad. abp. Santa Fe (Arabissus), 1891–94; abp. Santa Fe, 1894–97; abp. New Orleans 1897–1905.

Chartrand, Joseph (1870–1933): ord. Sept. 24, 1892; coad. bp. Indianapolis (Flavias), 1910–18; bp. Indianapolis, 1918–33.

Chatard, Francis S. (1834–1918): ord. June 14, 1862; bp. Vincennes (now Indianapolis—title changed in 1898), 1878–1918.

Cheverus, John Lefebvre de (1768–1836): b. France; ord. Dec. 18, 1790; bp. Boston, 1810–23 (returned to France, made cardinal 1836).

Christie, Alexander (1848–1925): ord. Dec. 22, 1877; bp. Vancouver Is., 1898–99; abp. Oregon City (now Portland), 1899–1925.

Clancy, William (1802–47): b. Ireland; ord. May 24, 1823; coad. bp. Charleston (Oreus), 1834–37; v.a. British Guiana, 1837–43.

Clavel Mendez, Tomas Alberto (1921–88): b. Panama; ord. Dec. 7, 1947; bp. David, Panama, 1955–64; abp. Panama, 1964–68 (res.); vicar for Hispanics, Orange, Calif., diocese.

Cody, John P. (1907–82): ord. Dec. 8, 1931; aux. St. Louis (Apollonia), 1947–54; coad. bp. St. Joseph, Mo., 1954–55; bp. Kansas City-St. Joseph, 1956–61; coad. abp. 1961–62; ap. admin., 1962–64, and abp., 1964–65, New Orleans; abp. Chicago, 1965–82; cardinal, 1967.

Cohill, John Edward, S.V.D. (1907–94): ord. Mar. 20, 1936; first bp. Goroko, Papua New Guinea, 1967–80 (res.).

Collins, John J., S.J. (1856–1934): ord. Aug. 29, 1891; v.a. Jamaica (Antiphellus), 1907–18 (res.).

Collins, Thomas P., M.M. (1915–73): ord. June 21, 1942; v.a. Pando, Bolivia (Sufetula), 1961–68 (res.).

Colton, Charles H. (1848–1915): ord. June 10, 1876; bp. Buffalo, 1903–15.

Conaty, Thomas J. (1847–1915): b. Ireland; ord. Dec. 21, 1872; rector of Catholic University, 1896–1903; tit. bp. Samos, 1901–03; bp. Monterey-Los Angeles (now Los Angeles), 1903–15.

Concanen, Richard L., O.P. (1747–1810): b. Ireland; ord. Dec. 22, 1770; first bp. New York, 1808–10 (detained in Italy, never reached his see).

Condon, William J. (1895–1967): ord. Oct. 14, 1917; bp. Great Falls, 1939–67.

Connare, William G. (1911–95): ord. June 14, 1936; bp. Greensburg, 1960–87 (ret.).

Connolly, James L. (1894–1986): ord. Dec. 21, 1923; coad bp. Fall River (Mylasa), 1945–51, bp. Fall River, 1951–70 (res.).

Connolly, John, O.P. (1750–1825): b. Ireland; ord. Sept. 24, 1774; bp. New York, 1814–25.

Connolly, Thomas A. (1899–1991): ord. June 11, 1926; aux. San Francisco (Sila), 1939–48; coad. bp. Seattle, 1948–50; bp, 1950–51, and first abp. Seattle, 1951–75 (res.).

Conroy, John J. (1819–95): b. Ireland; ord. May 21, 1842; bp. Albany, 1865–77 (res.).

Conroy, Joseph H. (1858–1939): ord. June 11 1881; aux. Ogdensburg (Arindela), 1912–21; bp. Ogdensburg, 1921–39.

Conwell, Henry (1748–1842): b. Ireland; ord. 1776; bp. Philadelphia, 1820–42.

Cooke, Terence J. (1921–83): ord. Dec. 1, 1945; aux. New York (Summa), 1965–68; abp. New York, 1965–83; cardinal 1969.

Corbett, Timothy (1858–1939): ord. June 12, 1886; first bp. Crookston, 1910–38 (res.).

Corrigan, Joseph M. (1879–1942): ord. June 6, 1903; rector of Catholic University, 1936–42; tit. bp. Bilta, 1940–42.

Corrigan, Michael A. (1839–1902): ord. Sept. 19, 1863; bp. Newark, 1873–80; coad. abp. New York (Petra), 1880–85; abp. New York, 1885–1902.

Corrigan, Owen (1849–1929): ord. June 7, 1873; aux. Baltimore (Macri), 1908–29.

Cosgrove, Henry (1834–1906): ord. Aug. 27, 1857; bp. Davenport, 1884–1906.

Cosgrove, William M. (1916–92): ord. Dec. 18, 1943; aux. Cleveland (Trisipa), 1968–76; bp. Belleville, 1976–81 (res.).

Costello, Joseph A. (1915–78): ord. June 7, 1941; aux. Newark (Choma), 1963–78.

Cote, Philip, S.J. (1896–1970): ord. Aug. 14, 1927; v.a. Suchow, China (Polystylus), 1935–46; first bp. Suchow, 1946–70; imprisoned by Chinese Communists, 1951; expelled from China, 1953; ap. admin. Islands of Quemoy and Matsu, 1969–70.

Cotter, Joseph B. (1844–1909): b. England; ord. May 3, 1871; first bp. Winona, 1889–1909.

Cotton, Francis R. (1895–1960): ord. June 17, 1920; first bp. Owensboro, 1938–60.

Cousins, William E. (1902–88): ord. Apr. 23, 1927; aux. Chicago (Forma), 1949–52; bp. Peoria, 1952–59; abp. Milwaukee 1959–77 (res.).

Cowley, Leonard P. (1913–73): ord. June 4, 1938; aux. St. Paul and Minneapolis (Pertusa), 1958–73.

Crane, Michael J. (1863–1928): ord. June 15, 1889; aux. Philadelphia (Curium), 1921–28.

Crétin, Joseph (1799–1857): b. France; ord. Dec. 20, 1823; bp. St. Paul, 1851–57.

Crimont, Joseph R., S.J. (1858–1945): b. France; ord. Aug. 26, 1888; v.a. Alaska (Ammaedara), 1917–45.

Crowley, Timothy J., C.S.C. (1880–1945): b. Ireland; ord. Aug. 2, 1906; coad. bp. Dacca (Epiphania), 1927–29; bp. Dacca, 1929–45.

Cunningham, David F. (1900–79): ord. June 12, 1926; aux., 1950–67, and coad. bp., 1967–79, Syracuse (Lampsacus); bp. Syracuse, 1970–76 (res.).

Cunningham, John F. (1842–1919): b. Ireland; ord. Aug. 8, 1865; bp. Concordia, 1898–1919.

Curley, Daniel J. (1869–1932): ord. May 19, 1894; bp. Syracuse, 1923–32.

Curley, Michael J. (1879–1947): b. Ireland; ord. Mar. 19, 1904; bp. St. Augustine, 1914–21; abp. Baltimore, 1921–39; title changed to abp. Baltimore and Washington, 1939–47.

Curtis, Alfred A. (1831–1908): convert, 1872; ord. Dec. 19, 1874; bp. Wilmington, 1886–96 (res.).

Cusack, Thomas F. (1862–1918): ord. May 30, 1885; aux. New York (Temiscyra), 1904–15; bp. Albany, 1915–18.

Cushing, Richard J. (1895–1970): ord. May 26, 1921; aux. Boston (Mela), 1939–44; abp. Boston, 1944–70; cardinal 1958.

D

Daeger, Albert T., O.F.M. (1872–1932): ord. July 25, 1896; abp. Santa Fe, 1919–32.

Daley, Joseph T. (1915–83): ord. June 7, 1941; aux. Harrisburg (Barca), 1964–67; coad., 1967–71, and bp., 1971–83, Harrisburg.

Daly, Edward C., O.P. (1894–1964): ord. June 12, 1921; bp. Des Moines, 1948–64.

Damiano, Celestine (1911–67): ord. Dec. 21, 1935; apostolic delegate to South Africa (Nicopolis in Epiro), 1952–60; bp. Camden, 1960–67.

Danehy, Thomas J., M.M. (1914–59): ord. Sept. 17, 1939; ap. admin. v.a. Pando, Bolivia (Bita), 1953–59.

Danglmayr, Augustine (1898–1992): ord. June 10, 1922; aux. Dallas-Ft. Worth (Olba), 1942–69 (res.).

Dargin, Edward V. (1898–1981): ord. Sept. 23, 1922; aux. New York (Amphipolis), 1953–73 (res.).

David, John B., S.S. (1761–1841): b. France; ord. Sept. 24, 1785; coad. bp. Bardstown (Mauricastrum), 1819–32; bp. Bardstown (now Louisville), 1832–33 (res.).

Davis, James (1852–1926): b. Ireland; ord. June 21, 1878; coad. bp. Davenport (Milopotamus), 1904–06; bp. Davenport, 1906–26.

Davis, James P. (1904–88): ord. May 19, 1929; bp. 1943–60, and first abp., 1960–64, San Juan, P.R.; abp. Santa Fe, 1964–74 (res.).

Dearden, John F. (1907–88): ord. Dec. 8, 1932; coad. bp. Pittsburgh (Sarepta), 1948–50; bp. Pittsburgh, 1950–58; abp. Detroit, 1958–80 (res.); cardinal 1969.

De Cheverus, John L.: See Cheverus, John.

De Falco, Lawrence M. (1915–79): ord. June 11, 1942; bp. Amarillo, 1963–79 (res.).

De Goesbriand, Louis (1816–99): b. France; ord. July 13, 1840; first bp. Burlington, 1853–99.

De la Hailandière, Celestine (1798–1882): b. France; ord. May 28, 1825; bp. Vincennes (now Indianapolis), 1839–47 (res.).

Delany, John B. (1864–1906): ord. May 23, 1891; bp. Manchester, 1904–06.

Demers, Modeste (1809–71): b. Canada; ord. Feb. 7, 1836; bp. Vancouver Is., 1846–71.

Dempsey, Michael R. (1918–74): ord. May 1, 1943; aux. Chicago (Truentum), 1968–74.

De Neckere, Leo, C.M. (1799–1833): b. Belgium; ord. Oct. 13, 1822; bp. New Orleans, 1829–33.

Denning, Joseph P. (1907–90): ord. May 21, 1932; aux. Brooklyn (Mallus), 1959–82 (res.).

De Saint Palais, Maurice (1811–77): b. France; ord. May 28, 1836; bp. Vincennes (now Indianapolis), 1849–77.

Desmond, Daniel F. (1884–1945): ord. June 9, 1911; bp. Alexandria, 1933–45.

Dimmerling, Harold J. (1914–87): ord. May 2, 1940; bp. Rapid City, 1969–87.

Dinand, Joseph N., S.J. (1869–1943): ord. June 25, 1903; v.a. Jamaica (Selinus), 1927–29 (res.).

Dingman, Maurice J. (1914–92): ord. Dec. 8, 1939; bp. Des Moines, 1968–86 (res.).

Dobson, Robert (1867–1942): ord. May 23, 1891; aux. Liverpool, Eng. (Cynopolis), 1922–42.

Dolinay, Thomas (1923–93): ord. May 16, 1948; aux. Passaic Byzantine Rite (Tiatira); 1976–81; first bp. Van Nuys Byzantine Rite, 1981–90; coad. abp., 1990–91, and abp., 1991–93, Pittsburgh Byzantine Rite.

Domenec, Michael, C.M. (1816–78): b. Spain; ord. June 30, 1839; bp. Pittsburgh, 1860–76; bp. Allegheny, 1876–77 (res.).

Donaghy, Frederick A., M.M. (1903–88): ord. Jan. 29, 1929; v.a. Wuchow, China (Setea), 1939; first bp. Wuchow, 1946. expelled from China, 1955.

Donahue, Joseph P. (1870–1959): ord. June 8, 1895; aux. New York (Emmaus), 1945–59.

Donahue, Patrick J. (1849–1922): b. England; ord. Dec. 19, 1885; bp. Wheeling, 1894–1922.

Donahue, Stephen J. (1893–1982): ord. May 22, 1918; aux. New York (Medea), 1934–69 (res.).

Donnellan, Thomas A. (1914–87): ord. June 3, 1939; bp. Ogdensburg, 1964–68; abp. Atlanta, 1968–87.

Donnelly, George J. (1889–1950): ord. June 12, 1921; aux. St. Louis (Coela), 1940–46; bp. Leavenworth (now Kansas City—title changed in 1947), 1946–50.

Donnelly, Henry E. (1904–67): ord. Aug. 17, 1930; aux. Detroit (Tyrnbrias), 1954–67.

Donnelly, Joseph F. (1909–77): ord. June 29, 1934; aux. Hartford (Nabala), 1965–77.

Donohoe, Hugh A. (1905–87): ord. June 14, 1930; aux. bp. San Francisco (Taium), 1947–62; first bp. Stockton, 1962–69; bp. Fresno, 1969–80 (res.).

Donovan, John A. (1911–91): b. Canada; ord. Dec. 8, 1935; aux. Detroit (Rhasus), 1954–67; bp. Toledo, 1967–80 (res.).

Doran, Thomas F. (1856–1916): ord. July 4, 1880; aux. Providence (Halicarnassus), 1915–16.

Dougherty, Dennis (1865–1951): ord. May 31, 1890; bp. Nueva Segovia, P.I., 1903–08; bp. Jaro, P.I., 1908–15; bp. Buffalo, 1915–18; abp. Philadelphia, 1918–51; cardinal, 1921.

Dougherty, John J. (1907–86): ord. July 23, 1933; aux. Newark (Cotena), 1963–82 (res.).

Dougherty, Joseph P. (1905–70): ord. June 14, 1930; first bp. Yakima, 1951–69; aux. Los Angeles (Altino), 1969–70.

Dowling, Austin (1868–1930): ord. June 24, 1891; first bp. Des Moines, 1912–19; abp. St. Paul, 1919–30.

Dozier, Carroll T. (1911–85): ord. Mar. 19, 1937; first bp. Memphis, 1971–82 (res.).

Driscoll, Justin A. (1920–84): ord. July 28, 1945; bp. Fargo, 1970–84.

Drossaerts, Arthur J. (1862–1940): b. Holland; ord. June 15, 1889; bp. San Antonio 1918–26; first abp. San Antonio, 1926–40.

Drumm, Thomas W. (1871–1933): b. Ireland; ord. Dec. 21, 1901; bp. Des Moines, 1919–33.

Drury, Thomas J. (1908–92): ord. June 2, 1935; first bp. San Angelo, 1962–65; bp. Corpus Christi, 1965–83 (res.).

Dubois, John, S.S. (1764–1842): b. France; ord. Sept. 28, 1787; bp. New York, 1826–42.

Dubourg, Louis William, S.S. (1766–1833): b. Santo Domingo; ord. 1788; bp. Louisiana and the Two Floridas (now New Orleans), 1815–25; returned to France; bp. Montauban, 1826–33; abp. Besancon 1833.

Dubuis, Claude M. (1817–95): b. France; ord. June 1, 1844; bp. Galveston, 1862–92 (res.).

Dufal, Peter, C.S.C. (1822–98): b. France; ord. Sept. 29, 1852; v.a. Eastern Bengal (Delcon), 1860–78; coad. bp. Galveston, 1878–80 (res.).

Duffy, James A. (1873–1968): ord. May 27, 1899; bp. Kearney (see transferred to Grand Island, 1917), 1913–31 (res.).

Duffy, John A. (1884–1944): ord. June 13, 1908; bp. Syracuse, 1933–37; bp. Buffalo, 1937–44.

Duggan, James (1825–99): b. Ireland; ord. May 29, 1847; coad. bp. St. Louis (Gabala), 1857–59; bp. Chicago, 1859–80 (res.). Inactive from 1869 because of illness.

Dunn, Francis J. (1922–89): ord. Jan. 11, 1948; aux. Dubuque (Turris Tamallani), 1969–89.

Dunn, John J. (1869–1933): ord. May 30, 1896; aux. New York (Camuliana), 1921–33.

Dunne, Edmund M. (1864–1929): ord. June 24, 1887; bp. Peoria, 1909–29.

Dunne, Edward (1848–1910): b. Ireland; ord. June 29, 1871; bp. Dallas, 1893–1910.

Durick, Joseph Aloysius (1914–94): ord. May 23, 1940; aux. bp. Mobile-Birmingham (Cerbali), 1955–64; coad. bp. Nashville, 1964–69 (ap. admin. 1966–69); bp. Nashville, 1969–75 (res.).

Durier, Anthony (1832–1904): b. France; ord. Oct. 28, 1856; bp. Natchitoches (now Alexandria), La., 1885–1904.

Dwenger, Joseph, C.Pp.S. (1837–93): ord. Sept. 4, 1859; bp. Fort Wayne, 1872–93.

Dworschak, Leo F. (1900–76): ord. May 29,1926; coad. bp. Rapid City (Tium), 1946–47; aux. Fargo, 1947–60; bp. Fargo, 1960–70 (res.).

Dwyer, Robert J. (1908–76): ord. June 11, 1932; bp. Reno, 1952–66; abp. Portland, Ore., 1966–74 (res.).

E

Eccleston, Samuel, S.S. (1801–51): ord. Apr. 24, 1825; coad. bp. Baltimore (Thermae), Sept.–Oct., 1834; abp. Baltimore, 1834–51.

Egan, Michael, O.F.M. (1761–1814): b. Ireland; first bp. Philadelphia, 1810–14.

Eis, Frederick (1843–1926): b. Germany; ord. Oct. 30, 1870; bp. Sault Ste. Marie and Marquette (now Marquette), 1899–1922 (res.).

Elder, William (1819–1904): ord. Mar. 29, 1846; bp. Natchez (now Jackson), 1857–80; coad. bp. Cincinnati (Avara), 1880–83; abp. Cincinnati, 1883–1904.

Elko, Nicholas T. (1909–91): ord. Sept. 30, 1934; ap. admin. Byzantine exarchy of Pittsburgh (Apollonias), Mar.–Sept. 1955; exarch, Sept., 1955–63, and first eparch, 1963–67, of Pittsburgh; tit. abp. Dara, 1967, with assignment in Rome; aux. bp. Cincinnati, 1971–85 (res.).

Elwell, Clarence E. (1904–73): ord. Mar. 17, 1929; aux. Cleveland (Cone) 1962–68; bp. Columbus, 1968–73.

Emmet, Thomas A., S.J. (1873–1950): ord. July 30, 1909; v.a. Jamaica (Tuscamia), 1930–49 (res.).

England, John (1786–1842): b. Ireland; ord. Oct. 11, 1808; first bp. Charleston, 1820–42.

Escalante, Alonso Manuel, M.M. (1906–67): b. Mexico; ord. Feb. 1, 1931; v.a. Pando, Bolivia (Sora), 1943–60 (res.).

Espelage (brothers): **Bernard T., O.F.M.** (1892–1971): ord. May 16, 1918; bp. Gallup, 1940–69 (res.). **Sylvester J., O.F.M.** (1877–1940): ord. Jan. 18, 1900; v.a. Wuchang, China (Oreus), 1930–40.

Etteldorf, Raymond P. (1911–86): ord. Dec. 8, 1937; apostolic delegate, 1969–73, and nuncio, 1973–74, to New Zealand (Tindari); pro-nuncio to Ethiopia, 1947–82.

Eustace, Bartholomew J. (1887–1956): ord. Nov. 1, 1914; bp. Camden, 1938–56.

Evans, George R. (1922–85): ord. May 31, 1947; aux. Denver (Tubyza), 1969–85.

F

Fahey, Leo F. (1898–1950): ord. May 29, 1926; coad. bp. Baker City (Ipsus), 1948–50.

Falconio, Diomede, O.F.M. (1842–1917): b. Italy; ord. Jan. 3, 1866, Buffalo, N.Y.; missionary in U.S. and Canada; returned to Italy; bp. Lacedonia, 1892–95; abp. Acerenza e Matera, 1895–99; ap. del. Canada (Larissa), 1899–1902, U.S., 1902–11; cardinal 1911.

Farley, John (1842–1918): b. Ireland; ord. June 11, 1870; aux. New York (Zeugma), 1895–1902; abp. New York, 1902–18; cardinal 1911.

Farrelly, John P. (1856–1921): ord. Mar. 22, 1880; bp. Cleveland, 1909–21.

Fearns, John M. (1897–1977): ord. Feb. 19, 1922; aux. New York (Geras), 1957–72 (res.).

Fedders, Edward L., M.M. (1913–73): ord. June 11, 1944; prelate Juli, Peru (Antiochia ad Meadrum), 1963–73.

Feehan, Daniel F. (1855–1934): ord. Dec. 29, 1879; bp. Fall River, 1907–34.

Feehan, Patrick A. (1829–1902): b. Ireland; ord. Nov. 1, 1852; bp. Nashville, 1865–80; first abp. Chicago, 1880–1902.

Feeney, Daniel J. (1894–1969): ord. May 21, 1921; aux. Portland, Me. (Sita), 1946–52; coad. bp. Portland, 1952–55; bp. Portland, 1955–69.

Feeney, Thomas J., S.J. (1894–1955): ord. June 23, 1927; v.a. Caroline and Marshall Is. (Agnus), 1951–55.

Fenwick, Benedict J., S.J. (1782–1846): ord. June 11, 1808; bp. Boston, 1825–46.

Fenwick, Edward D., O.P. (1768–1832): ord. Feb. 23, 1793; first bp. Cincinnati, 1822–32.

Fink, Michael, O.S.B. (1834–1904): b. Germany; ord. May 28, 1857; coad. v.a., 1871–74, and v.a., 1874–77, Kansas and Indian Territory (Eucarpia); first bp. Leavenworth (now Kansas City), 1877–1904.

Finnigan, George, C.S.C. (1885–1932): ord. June 13, 1915; bp. Helena, 1927–32.

Fisher, Carl, S.S.J. (1945–93): ord. June 2, 1973; aux. Los Angeles (Tlos), 1987–93.

Fitzgerald, Edward (1833–1907): b. Ireland; ord. Aug. 22, 1857; bp. Little Rock, 1867–1907.

Fitzgerald, Edward A. (1893–1972): ord. July 25, 1916; aux. Dubuque (Cantanus), 1946–49; bp. Winona, 1949–69 (res.).

Fitzgerald, Walter J., S.J. (1883–1947): ord. May 16, 1918; coad. v.a. Alaska (Tymbrias), 1939–45; v.a. Alaska, 1945–47.

Fitzmaurice, Edmond (1881–1962): b. Ireland; ord. May 28, 1904; bp. Wilmington, 1925–60 (res.).

Fitzmaurice, John E. (1837–1920): b. Ireland; ord. Dec. 21, 1862; coad. bp. Erie (Amisus), 1898–99; bp. Erie, 1899–1920.

Fitzpatrick, John B. (1812–66): ord. June 13, 1840; aux. Boston (Callipolis), 1843–46; bp. Boston, 1846–66.

Fitzsimon, Laurence J. (1895–1958): ord. May 17, 1921; bp. Amarillo, 1941–58.

Flaget, Benedict, S.S.: *See* FLAGET, BENEDICT JOSEPH.

Flaherty, J. Louis (1910–75): ord. Dec. 8, 1936; aux. Richmond (Tabudo), 1966–75.

Flannelly Joseph F. (1894–1973): ord. Sept. 1, 1918; aux. New York (Metelis), 1948–70 (res.).

Flasch, Kilian C. (1831–91): b. Germany; ord. Dec. 16, 1859; bp. La Crosse, 1881–91.

Fletcher, Albert L. (1896–1979): ord. June 4, 1920; aux. Little Rock (Samos), 1940–46; bp. Little Rock, 1946–72 (res.).

Floersh, John (1886–1968): ord. June 10, 1911; coad. bp. Louisville (Lycopolis), 1923–24; bp. Louisville, 1924–37; first abp. Louisville, 1937–67 (res.).

Flores, Felixberto C. (1921–85): b. Gaum; ord. Apr. 30, 1949; ap. admin. Agana, Guam (Stonj), 1970–72; bp., 1977–84, and first abp. Agana, 1984–85.

Foery, Walter A. (1890–1978): ord. June 10, 1916; bp. Syracuse, 1937–70 (res.).

Foley (brothers): **John S.** (1833–1918): ord. Dec. 20, 1856; bp. Detroit, 1888–1918. **Thomas** (1822–79): ord. Aug. 16, 1846; coad. bp. and ap. admin. Chicago (Pergamum), 1870–79.

Foley, Maurice P. (1867–1919): ord. July 25, 1891; bp Tuguegarao, P.I., 1910–16; bp. Jaro, P.I., 1916–19

Ford, Francis X., M.M. (1892–1952): ord. Dec. 5, 1917; v.a. Kaying, China (Etenna), 1935–46; first bp. Kaying, 1946–52.

Forest, John A. (1838–1911): b. France; ord. Apr. 12, 1863; bp. San Antonio, 1895–1911.

Fox, Joseph J. (1855–1915): ord. June 7, 1879; bp. Green Bay, 1904–14 (res.).

Franz, John B. (1896–1992): ord. June 13, 1920; first bp. Dodge City, 1951–59; bp. Peoria, 1959–71 (res.).

Fulcher, George A. (1922–84): ord. Feb. 28, 1948; aux. Columbus (Morosbisdus), 1976–83; bp. Lafayette, 1983–84.

Furey, Francis J. (1905–79): ord. Mar. 15, 1930; aux. Philadelphia (Temnus), 1960–63; coad. bp. San Diego, 1963–66; bp. San Diego, 1966–69; abp. San Antonio, 1969–79.

Furlong, Philip J. (1892–1989): ord. May 18, 1918; aux. Military Vicar (Araxa), 1956–71 (res.).

G

Gabriels, Henry (1838–1921): b. Belgium; ord. Sept. 21, 1861; bp. Ogdensburg, 1892–1921.

Gabro, Jaroslav (1919–80): ord. Sept. 27, 1945; bp. St. Nicholas of Chicago (Byzantine Rite, Ukrainians), 1961–80.

Galberry, Thomas, O.S.A. (1833–78): b. Ireland; ord. Dec. 20, 1856; bp. Hartford, 1876–78.

Gallagher, Michael J. (1866–1937): ord. Mar. 19. 1893; coad. bp. Grand Rapids (Tiposa in Mauretania), 1915–16; bp. Grand Rapids, 1916–18; bp. Detroit, 1918–37.

Gallagher, Nicholas (1846–1918): ord. Dec. 25, 1868; coad. bp. Galveston (Canopus), 1882–92; bp. Galveston, 1892–1918.

Gallagher, Raymond J. (1912–91): ord. Mar. 25. 1939; bp. Lafayette, Ind., 1965–82 (res.).

Gallegos, Alphonse, O.A.R. (1931–91): ord. May 24, 1958; aux. Sacramento (Sassabe), 1981–91.

Gannon, John M. (1877–1968): ord. Dec. 21, 1901; aux. Erie (Nilopolis), 1918–20; bp. Erie, 1920–66 (res.).

Ganter, Bernard J. (1928–93): ord. May 22, 1952; first bp. Tulsa, 1972–77; bp. Beaumont, 1977–93.

Garcia Diego y Moreno, Francisco, O.F.M. (1785–1846): b. Mexico; ord. Nov. 14, 1808; bp. Two Californias (now Los Angeles), 1840–46.

Garriga, Mariano S. (1886–1965): ord. July 2, 1911; coad. bp. Corpus Christi (Syene), 1936–49; bp. Corpus Christi, 1949–65.

Garrigan, Philip (1840–1919): b. Ireland; ord. June 11, 1870; first bp. Sioux City, 1902–19.

Gartland, Francis X. (1808–54): b. Ireland; ord. Aug. 5, 1832; first bp. Savannah, 1850–54.

Garvey, Eugene A. (1845–1920): ord. Sept. 22, 1869; first bp. Altoona (now Altoona–Johnstown), 1901–20.

Gercke, Daniel J. (1874–1964): ord. June 1, 1901, bp. Tucson, 1923–60 (res.).

Gerken, Rudolph A. (1887–1943): ord. June 10, 1917; first bp. Amarillo, 1927–33; abp. Santa Fe, 1933–43.

Gerow, Richard O. (1885–1976): ord. June 5, 1909; bp. Natchez-Jackson (now Jackson), 1924–67 (res.).

Gerrard, James J. (1897–1991): ord. May 26, 1923; aux. Fall River (Forma), 1959–76 (res.).

Ghattas, Ignatius, B.S.O. (1920–92): b. Nazareth, Israel; ord. July 7, 1946; bp. Newton for Greek Melkites, 1990–92.

Gibbons, Edmund F. (1868–1964): ord. May 27, 1893; bp. Albany, 1919–54 (res.).

Gibbons, James (1834–1921): ord. June 30, 1861; v.a. North Carolina (Adramyttium), 1868–72; bp. Richmond, 1872–77; coad. Baltimore (Jonopolis), May–Oct., 1877; abp. Baltimore, 1877–1921; cardinal 1886.

Gilfillan, Francis (1872–1933): b. Ireland; ord. June 24, 1895; coad. bp. St. Joseph (Spiga), 1922–23; bp. St. Joseph, 1923–33.

Gill, Thomas E. (1908–73): ord. June 10, 1933; aux. Seattle (Lambesis) 1956–73.

Gilmore, Joseph M. (1893–1962): ord. July 25, 1915; bp. Helena, 1936–62.

Gilmour, Richard (1824–91): b. Scotland; ord. Aug. 30, 1852; bp. Cleveland, 1872–91.

Girouard, Paul J., M.S. (1898–1964): ord. July 26, 1927; first bp. Morondava, Madagascar, 1956–64.

Glass, Joseph S., C.M. (1874–1926): ord. Aug. 15, 1897; bp. Salt Lake City, 1915–26.

Gleeson, Francis D., S.J. (1895–1983): ord. July 29, 1926; v.a. Alaska (Cotenna), 1948–62; first bp. Fairbanks, 1962–68 (res.).

Glenn, Lawrence A. (1900–85): ord. June 11, 1927; aux. Duluth (Tuscamia), 1956–60; bp. Crookston 1960–70 (res.).

Glennon, John J. (1862–1946): b. Ireland; ord. Dec. 20, 1884; coad. bp. Kansas City, Mo. (Pinara), 1896–1903; coad. St. Louis, April–Oct., 1903; abp. St. Louis, 1903–46; cardinal 1946.

Glorieux, Alphonse J. (1844–1917): b. Belgium; ord. Aug. 17, 1867; v.a. Idaho (Apollonia), 1885–93; bp. Boise, 1893–1917.

Gorman, Daniel (1861–1927): ord. June 24, 1893; bp. Boise, 1918–27.

Gorman, Thomas K. (1892–1980): ord. June 23, 1917; first bp. Reno, 1931–52; coad. bp. Dallas–Ft. Worth (Rhasus), 1952–54; bp. Dallas–Fort Worth (now Dallas), 1954–69 (res.).

Grace, Thomas (1841–1921): b. Ireland; ord. June 24, 1876; bp. Sacramento, 1896–1921.

Grace, Thomas L., O.P. (1814–97): ord. Dec. 21, 1839; bp. St. Paul, 1859–84 (res.).

Graner, Lawrence L., C.S.C. (1901–82): ord. June 24, 1928; bp. Dacca, 1947–50, and first abp., 1950–67 (res.).

Granjon, Henry (1863–1922): b. France; ord. Dec. 17, 1887; bp. Tucson, 1900–22.

Graves, Lawrence P. (1916–94): ord. June 11, 1942; aux. Little Rock (Vina), 1969–73; bp. Alexandria (now Alexandria-Shreveport), 1973–82 (res.).

Graziano, Lawrence, O.F.M. (1921–90): ord. Jan. 26, 1947; aux. Santa Ana, El Salvador (Limata), 1961–65; coad. San Miguel, El Salvador, 1965–68; bp. San Miguel, 1968–69 (res.).

Greco, Charles P. (1894–1987): ord. July 25, 1918; bp. Alexandria, La., 1946–73 (res.).

Green, Francis J. (1906–95): ord. May 15, 1932; aux. Tucson (Serra), 1953–60, coad. May–Oct., 1960, and bp. Tucson, Oct. 26, 1960–1981 (ret.).

Green, Joseph J. (1917–82): ord. July 14, 1946; aux. Lansing (Trisipa), 1962–67; bp. Reno 1967–74 (res.).

Grellinger, John B. (1899–1984): ord. priest July 14, 1929; aux. Green Bay (Syene), 1949–74 (res.).

Greteman, Frank H. (1907–87): ord. Dec. 8, 1932; aux. Sioux City (Vissala), 1965–70; bp. Sioux City, 1970–83 (res.).

Griffin, James A. (1883–1948): ord. July 4, 1909; bp. Springfield, Ill., 1924–48.

Griffin, William A. (1885–1950): ord. Aug. 15, 1910; aux. Newark (Sanavus), 1938–40; bp. Trenton, 1940–50.

Griffin, William R. (1883–1944): ord. May 25, 1907; aux. La Crosse (Lydda), 1935–44.

Griffiths, James H. (1903–64): ord. Mar. 12, 1927; aux. New York and delegate of U.S. military vicar (Gaza), 1950–64.

Grimes, John (1852–1922): b. Ireland; ord. Feb. 19, 1882; coad. bp. Syracuse (Hemeria), 1909–12; bp. Syracuse, 1912–22.

Grimmelsman, Henry J. (1890–1972); ord. Aug. 15, 1915; first bp. Evansville, 1945–65 (res.).

Gross, William H., C.Ss.R. (1837–98): ord. Mar. 21, 1863; bp. Savannah, 1873–85; abp. Oregon City (now Portland), 1885–98.

Grovas Felix, Rafael (1905–91): b. San Juan, Puerto Rico; ord. Apr. 7, 1928; bp. Caguas, P.R., 1965–81 (res.).

Grutka, Andrew G. (1908–93): ord. Dec. 5, 1933; first bp. Gary, 1957–84 (res.).

Guertin, George A. (1869–1932): ord. Dec. 17, 1892; bp. Manchester, 1907–32.

Guilfoyle, George H. (1913–91): ord. Mar. 25, 1944; aux. New York (Marazane), 1964–68; bp. Camden 1968–89 (res.).

Guilfoyle, Richard T. (1892–1957): ord. June 2, 1917; bp. Altoona (now Altoona-Johnstown), 1936–57.

Guilfoyle, Merlin J. (1908–81): ord. June 10, 1933; aux. San Francisco (Bulla), 1950–69; bp. Stockton, 1969–79 (res.).

Gunn, John E., S.M. (1863–1924): b. Ireland; ord. Feb. 2, 1890; bp. Natchez (now Jackson), 1911–24.

H

Haas, Francis J. (1889–1953): ord. June 11, 1913; bp. Grand Rapids, 1943–53.

Hacker, Hilary B. (1913–90): ord. June 4, 1938; bp. Bismarck, 1957–82 (res.).

Hackett, John F. (1911–90): ord. June 29, 1936; aux. Hartford (Helenopolis in Palaestina), 1953–86 (res.).

Hafey, William (1888–1954): ord. June 16, 1914; first bp. Raleigh, 1925–37; coad. bp. Scranton (Appia), 1937–38; bp. Scranton, 1938–54.

Hagan, John R. (1890–1946): ord. Mar. 7, 1914; aux. Cleveland (Limata), 1946.

Hagarty, Paul L., O.S.B. (1909–84): ord. June 6, 1936; v.a. Bahamas (Arba), 1950–60; first bp. Nassau, Bahamas, 1960–81 (res.).

Haid, Leo M., O.S.B. (1849–1924): ord. Dec. 21, 1872; v.a. N. Carolina (Messene), 1888–1910; abbot Mary Help of Christians abbacy, 1910–24.

Hallinan, Paul J. (1911–68): ord. Feb. 20, 1937; bp. Charleston, 1958–62; first abp. Atlanta, 1962–68.

Hammes, George A. (1911–93): ord. May 22, 1937; bp. Superior 1960–85 (res.).

Hanna, Edward J. (1860–1944): ord. May 30, 1885; aux. San Francisco (Titiopolis). 1912–15; abp. San Francisco, 1915–35 (res.).

Hannan, Jerome D. (1896–1965): ord. May 22, 1921; bp. Scranton, 1954–65.

Harkins, Matthew (1845–1921): ord. May 22, 1869; bp. Providence, 1887–1921.

Harper, Edward, C.Ss.R. (1910–90): ord. June 18, 1939; first prelate Virgin Islands (Heraclea Pontica), 1960–77, and first bishop (prelacy made diocese of St. Thomas), 1977–85 (res.).

Harris, Vincent M. (1913–88): ord. Mar. 19, 1938; first bp. Beaumont, 1966–71; coad. bp. Austin (Rotaria), Apr. 27–Nov. 16, 1971; bp. Austin, 1971–85 (res.).

Hartley, James J. (1858–1944): ord. July 10, 1882; bp. Columbus, 1904–44.

Harty, Jeremiah J. (1853–1927): ord. Apr. 28, 1878; abp. Manila, 1903–16; abp. Omaha, 1916–27.

Hastrich, Jerome J. (1914–95): ord. Feb. 9, 1941; aux. Madison (Gurza), 1963–69; bp. Gallup, 1969–90 (ret.).

Hayes, James T., S.J. (1889–1980): ord. June 29, 1921; bp. of Cagayan, Philippines, 1933–51; first abp. Cagayan, 1951–70 (res.).

Hayes, Nevin W., O. Carm. (1922–88): ord. June 8, 1946; prelate Sicuani, Peru (Nova Sinna), 1965–70; aux. bp. Chicago, 1971–88.

Hayes, Patrick J. (1867–1938): ord. Sept. 8, 1892; aux. New York (Thagaste), 1914–19; abp. New York, 1919–38; cardinal 1924.

Hayes, Ralph L. (1884–1970): ord. Sept. 19, 1909; bp. Helena 1933–35; rector North American College (Hieropolis) 1935–44; bp. Davenport, 1944–66 (res.).

Healy, James A. (1830–1900): ord. June 10, 1854; bp. Portland 1875–1900.

Heelan, Edmond (1868–1948): b. Ireland; ord. June 24, 1890; aux. Sioux City (Gerasa), 1919–20; bp. Sioux City, 1920–48.

Heffron, Patrick (1860–1927): ord. Dec. 22, 1884; bp. Winona, 1910–27.

Heiss, Michael (1818–90): b. Germany; ord. Oct. 18, 1840; bp. La Crosse, 1868–80; coad. abp. Milwaukee (Hadrianopolis), 1880–81; abp. Milwaukee, 1881–90.

Helmsing, Charles H. (1908–93): ord. June 10, 1933; aux. bp. St. Louis (Axomis), 1949–56; first bp. Springfield-Cape Girardeau, 1956–62; bp. Kansas City-St. Joseph, 1962–77 (res.).

Hendrick, Thomas A. (1849–1909): ord. June 7, 1873; bp. Cebu, P.I., 1904–09.

Hendricken, Thomas F. (1827–86): b. Ireland; ord. Apr. 25, 1853; bp. Providence, 1872–86.

Hennessy, John (1825–1900): b. Ireland; ord. Nov. 1, 1850; bp. Dubuque, 1866–93; first abp. Dubuque, 1893–1900.

Hennessy, John J. (1847–1920): b. Ireland; ord. Nov. 28, 1869; first bp. Wichita, 1888–1920; ap. admin. Concordia (now Salina), 1891–98.

Henni, John M. (1805–81): b. Switzerland; ord. Feb. 2, 1829; first bp. Milwaukee, 1844–75; first abp. Milwaukee, 1875–81.

Henry, Harold W., S.S.C. (1909–76): ord. Dec. 21, 1932; v.a. Kwang Ju, Korea (Coridala), 1957–62; first abp.

Kwang Ju, 1962–71; ap. admin. p.a. Cheju-Do, Korea (Thubunae), 1971–76.

Herzig, Charles E. (1929–91): ord. May 31, 1955; first bp. Tyler, 1987–91.

Heslin, Thomas (1845–1911): b. Ireland; ord. Sept. 8, 1869; bp. Natchez (now Jackson), 1889–1911.

Heston, Edward L. (1907–73): ord. Dec. 22, 1934; sec. Sacred Congregation for Religious and Secular Institutes, 1969–71; pres. Pontifical Commission for Social Communications, 1971–73; tit. abp. Numidea, 1972.

Hickey, David F., S.J. (1882–1973): ord. June 27, 1917; v.a. Belize, Br. Honduras (Bonitza), 1948–56; first bp. Belize, 1956–57 (res.); tit. abp. Cabasa, 1957–73.

Hickey, Thomas F. (1861–1940): ord. Mar. 25, 1884; coad. bp. Rochester (Berenice), 1905–09; bp. Rochester, 1909–28 (res.).

Hickey, William A. (1869–1933): ord. Dec. 22, 1893; coad. bp. Providence (Claudiopolis), 1919–21; bp. Providence, 1921–33.

Hillinger, Raymond P. (1904–71): ord. Apr. 2, 1932; bp. Rockford, 1953–56; aux. Chicago (Derbe), 1956–71.

Hines, Vincent J. (1912–90): ord. May 2, 1937; bp. Norwich, 1960–75 (res.).

Hoban, Edward F. (1878–1966): ord. July 11, 1903, aux. Chicago (Colonia), 1921–28; bp. Rockford, 1928–42; coad. bp. Cleveland (Lystra), 1942–45; bp. Cleveland, 1945–66.

Hoban, Michael J. (1853–1926): ord. May 22, 1880; coad. bp. Scranton (Halius), 1896–99; bp. Scranton, 1899–1926.

Hoch, Lambert A. (1903–90): ord. May 30, 1928; bp. Bismarck, 1952–56; bp. Sioux Falls, 1956–78 (res.).

Hodapp, Robert L., S.J. (1910–89): ord. June 18, 1941; bp. Belize (now Belize-Belmopan), 1958–83 (res.).

Hodges, Joseph H. (1911–85): ord. Dec. 8, 1935; aux. Richmond (Rusadus), 1952–61; coad. Wheeling, 1961–62; bp. Wheeling (now Wheeling-Charleston), 1962–85.

Hogan, John J. (1829–1913): b. Ireland; ord. Apr. 10, 1852; first bp. St. Joseph, 1868–80; first bp. Kansas City, 1880–1913.

Horstmann, Ignatius (1840–1908): ord. June 10, 1865; bp. Cleveland, 1892–1908.

Howard, Edward D. (1877–1983): ord. June 12, 1906; aux. Davenport (Isauropolis), 1924–26; abp. Oregon City (title changed to Portland, 1928), 1926–66 (res.).

Howard, Francis W. (1867–1944): ord. June 16, 1891; bp. Covington, 1923–44.

Hughes, John J. (1797–1864): b. Ireland; ord. Oct. 15, 1826, coad. bp. New York (Basilinopolis), 1837–42, bp. New York, 1842–50, and first abp., 1850–64.

Hunkeler, Edward J. (1894–1970): ord. June 14, 1919; bp. Grand Island, 1945–51; bp. Kansas City, Kans. 1951–52; first abp. Kansas City, 1952–69 (res.).

Hunt, Duane G. (1884–1960): ord. June 27, 1920; bp. Salt Lake City, 1937–60.

Hurley, Joseph P. (1894–1967): ord. May 29, 1919; bp. St. Augustine, 1940–67.

Hyland, Francis E. (1901–68): ord. June 11, 1927; aux. Savannah-Atlanta (Gomphi), 1949–56; bp. Atlanta, 1956–61 (res.).

Hyle, Michael W. (1901–67): ord. Mar. 12, 1927; coad. bp. Wilmington, 1958–60; bp. Wilmington, 1960–67.

I

Iranyi, Ladislaus A., Sch. P. (1923–87): ord. Mar. 13, 1948; U.S. citizen, 1958; ord. bp. (Castel Mediano), July 27, 1983, for spiritual care of Hungarian Catholics living outside Hungary.

Ireland, John (1838–1918): b. Ireland; ord. Dec. 21, 1861; coad. bp. St. Paul (Marobea), 1875–84; bp. St. Paul, 1884–88, and first abp. St. Paul, 1888–1918.

Ireton, Peter L. (1882–1958): ord. June 20, 1906; coad. bp. Richmond (Cyme), 1935–45; bp. Richmond, 1945–58.

Issenmann, Clarence G. (1907–82): ord. June 29, 1932; aux. Cincinnati (Phytea), 1954–57; bp. Columbus, 1957–64; coad. bp. Cleveland (Filaca), 1964–66; bp. Cleveland, 1966–74 (res.).

Ivancho, Daniel (1908–72): b. Austria-Hungary; ord. Sept. 30, 1934; coad. bp. Pittsburgh Ruthenian Rite (Europus), 1946–48; bp. Pittsburgh Ruthenian Rite, 1948–54 (res.).

J

Janssen, John (1835–1913): b. Germany; ord. Nov. 19, 1858; first bp. Belleville, 1888–1913.

Janssens, Francis A. (1843–97): b. Holland; ord. Dec. 21, 1867; bp. Natchez (now Jackson) 1881–88; abp. New Orleans, 1888–97.

Jeanmard, Jules B. (1879–1957): ord. June 10, 1903; first bp. Lafayette, La., 1918–56 (res.)

Johannes, Francis (1874–1937): b. Germany; ord. Jan. 3, 1897; coad. bp. Leavenworth (Thasus), 1928–29; bp. Leavenworth (now Kansas City), 1929–37.

Johnson, William R. (1918–86): ord. May 28, 1944; aux. Los Angeles (Blera), 1971–76; first bp. Orange, 1976–86.

Jolson, Alfred, S.J. (1928–94): ord. June 14, 1958; bp. Reykjavik, Iceland, 1988–94.

Jones, William A., O.S.A. (1865–1921): ord. Mar. 15, 1890; bp. San Juan, 1907–21.

Joyce, Robert F. (1896–1990): ord. May 26, 1923; aux. Burlington (Citium), 1954–57; bp. Burlington 1957–71 (res.).

Juncker, Henry D. (1809–68): b. Lorraine (France); ord. Mar. 16, 1834; first bp. Alton (now Springfield), Ill., 1857–68.

Junger, Aegidius (1833–95): b. Germany; ord. June 27, 1862; bp. Nesqually (now Seattle), 1879–95.

K

Kain, John J. (1841–1903): ord. July 2, 1866; bp. Wheeling, 1875–93; coad. abp. St. Louis (Oxyrynchus), 1893–95; abp. St. Louis, 1895–1903.

Katzer, Frederick X. (1844–1903): b. Austria; ord. Dec. 21, 1866; bp. Green Bay, 1886–91; abp. Milwaukee, 1891–1903.

Keane, James J. (1856–1929): ord. Dec. 23, 1882; bp. Cheyenne, 1902–11; abp. Dubuque, 1911–29.

Keane, John J. (1839–1918): b. Ireland; ord. July 2, 1866; bp. Richmond, 1878–88; rector of Catholic University, 1888–97; consultor of Congregation for Propagation of the Faith, 1897–1900; abp. Dubuque, 1900–11 (res.).

Keane, Patrick J. (1872–1928): b. Ireland; ord. June 20, 1895; aux. Sacramento (Samaria), 1920–22; bp. Sacramento, 1922–28.

Kearney, James E. (1884–1977): ord. Sept. 19, 1908; bp. Salt Lake City, 1932–37; bp. Rochester, 1937–66 (res.).

Kearney, Raymond A. (1902–56): ord. Mar. 12, 1927; aux. Brooklyn (Lysinia), 1935–56.

Keiley, Benjamin J. (1847–1925): ord. Dec. 31, 1873; bp. Savannah, 1900–22 (res.).

Kelleher, Louis F. (1889–1946): ord. Apr. 3, 1915; aux. Boston (Thenae), 1945–46.

Kellenberg, Walter P. (1901–86): ord. June 2, 1928; aux. New York (Joannina), 1953–54; bp. Ogdensburg, 1954–57; first bp. Rockville Centre, 1957–76 (res.).

Kelley, Francis C. (1870–1948): b. Canada; ord. Aug. 23, 1893; bp. Oklahoma. 1924–48.

Kelly, Edward D. (1860–1926): ord. June 16, 1886; aux. Detroit (Cestrus), 1911–19; bp. Grand Rapids, 1919–26.

Kelly, Edward J. (1890–1956): ord. June 2, 1917; bp. Boise, 1928–56.

Kelly, Francis M. (1886–1950): ord. Nov. 1, 1912; aux. Winona (Mylasa), 1926–28; bp. Winona, 1928–49 (res.).

Kelly, Patrick (1779–1829): b. Ireland; ord. July 18, 1802; first bp. Richmond, 1820–22 (returned to Ireland; bp. Waterford and Lismore, 1822–29).

Kennally, Vincent, S.J. (1895–1977): ord. June 20, 1928; v.a. Caroline and Marshall Islands (Sassura), 1957–71 (res.).

Kennedy, Thomas F. (1858–1917): ord. July 24, 1887; rector North American College, 1901–17; tit. bp. Hadrianapolis, 1907–15; tit. abp. Seleucia, 1915–17.

Kenney, Lawrence J. (1930–90): ord. June 2, 1956; aux. Military Services archdiocese (Holar), 1983–90.

Kenny, Michael H. (1937–95): ord. Mar. 30, 1963; bp. Juneau, 1979–95.

Kenny, William J. (1853–1913): ord. Jan. 15, 1879; bp. St. Augustine, 1902–13.

Kenrick (brothers): **Francis P.** (1796–1863): b. Ireland; ord. Apr. 7, 1821; coad. bp. Philadelphia (Aratha), 1830–42; bp. Philadelphia, 1842–51; abp. Baltimore, 1851–63. **Peter** (1806–96): b. Ireland; ord. Mar. 6, 1832; coad. bp. St. Louis (Adrasus), 1841–43; bp. 1843–47, and first abp. 1847–95, St. Louis (res.).

Keough, Francis P. (1890–1961): ord. June 10, 1916; bp. Providence, 1943–47; abp. Baltimore, 1947–61.

Kevenhoerster, John B., O.S.B. (1869–1949): b. Germany; ord. June 24, 1896, Collegeville, Minn.; ord. tit. bp. Camuliana, 1933; p.a., 1933–41, and v.a., 1941–49, of Bahamas.

Keyes, Michael, S.M. (1876–1959): b. Ireland; ord. June 21, 1907; bp. Savannah, 1922–35 (res.).

Kiley, Moses E. (1876–1953): b. Nova Scotia; ord. June 10, 1911; bp. Trenton, 1934–40; abp. Milwaukee, 1940–53.

Killeen, James (1917–78): ord. May 30, 1942; aux. Military Vicariate (Valmalla), 1975–78.

Klonowski, Henry T. (1898–1977): ord. Aug. 8, 1920; aux. Scranton (Daldis), 1947–73 (res.).

Kocisko, Stephen (1915–95): ord. Mar. 30, 1941; aux. Byzantine ap. ex. Pittsburgh (Teveste), 1956–63; first eparch Passaic, 1963–68; eparch, 1968–69, and first metropolitan of Pittsburgh, 1969–91 (ret.).

Kogy, Lorenz S., O.M. (1895–1963): b. Georgia, Russia; ord. Nov. 15, 1917; U.S. citizen, 1944; patriarchal vicar for Armenian diocese of Beirut (Comana), 1951–63.

Koudelka, Joseph (1852–1921): b. Austria; ord. Oct. 8, 1875; aux. Cleveland (Germanicopolis), 1908–11; aux. Milwaukee, 1911–13; bp. Superior, 1913–21.

Kowalski, Rembert, O.F.M. (1884–1970): ord. June 22, 1911; v.a. Wuchang, China (Ipsus), 1942–46; first bp. Wuchang, 1946–70 (in exile from 1953).

Kozlowski, Edward (1860–1915): b. Poland; ord. June 29, 1887; aux. Milwaukee (Germia), 1914–15.

Krautbauer, Francix X. (1824–85): b. Germany; ord. July 16, 1850; bp. Green Bay, 1875–85.

Kucera, Louis B. (1888–1957): ord. June 8, 1915; bp. Lincoln, 1930–57.

L

Lamb, Hugh (1890–1959): ord. May 29, 1915; aux. Philadelphia (Helos), 1936–51; first bp. Greensburg, 1951–59.

Lamy, Jean B.: See Index.

Lane, Loras (1910–68): ord. Mar. 19, 1937; aux. Dubuque (Bencenna), 1951–56; bp. Rockford, 1956–68.

Lane, Raymond A., M.M. (1894–1974): ord. Feb. 8, 1920; v.a. Fushun, Manchukuo (Hypaepa), 1940–46; sup. gen. Maryknoll, 1946–56.

Lardone, Francesco (1887–1980): b. Italy; ord. June 29, 1910; U.S. citizen 1937; nuncio to various countries (tit. abp. Rhizaeum), 1949–66 (res.).

Laval, John M. (1854–1937): b. France; ord. Nov. 10, 1877; aux. New Orleans (Hierocaesarea), 1911–37.

Lavialle, Peter J. (1819–67): b. France; ord. Feb. 12, 1844; bp. Louisville, 1865–67.

Lawler, John J. (1862–1948): ord. Dec. 19, 1885; aux. St. Paul (Hermopolis), 1910–16; bp. Lead (now Rapid City), 1916–48.

Le Blond, Charles H. (1883–1958): ord. June 29, 1909; bp. St. Joseph, 1933–56 (res.).

Ledvina, Emmanuel (1868–1952): ord. Mar. 18, 1893; bp. Corpus Christi, 1921–49 (res.).

Leech, George L. (1890–1985): ord. May 29, 1920; aux. Harrisburg (Mela), Oct.–Dec., 1935; bp. Harrisburg, 1935–71 (res.).

Lefevere, Peter P. (1804–69): b. Belgium; ord. Nov. 30, 1831; coad. bp. and admin. Detroit (Zela), 1841–69.

Leibold, Paul F. (1914–72): ord. May 18, 1940; aux. Cincinnati (Trebenna), 1958–66; bp. Evansville, 1966–69; abp. Cincinnati, 1969–72.

Leipzig, Francis P. (1895–1981): ord. Apr. 17, 1920; bp. Baker, 1950–71 (res.).

Lemay, Leo, S.M. (1909–83): ord. Apr. 15, 1933; v.a. North Solomon Is. (Agbia), 1961–66; first bp. Bougainville, 1966–74 (res.).

Lenihan (brothers): **Mathias C.** (1854–1943): ord. Dec. 20, 1879; first bp. Great Falls, 1904–30 (res.). **Thomas M.** (1844–1901): b. Ireland; ord. Nov. 19, 1868; bp. Cheyenne, 1897–1901.

Leonard, Vincent M. (1908–94): ord. June 16, 1935; aux. Pittsburgh (Arsacal), 1964–69; bp. Pittsburgh, 1969–83 (ret.).

Leray, Francis X. (1825–87): b. France; ord. Mar. 19, 1852; bp. Natchitoches (now Alexandria, La.), 1877–79; coad. bp. New Orleans and admin. of Natchitoches (Jonopolis), 1879–83; abp. New Orleans, 1883–87.

Leven, Stephen A. (1905–83): ord. June 10, 1928; aux. San Antonio (Bure), 1956–69; bp. San Angelo, 1969–79 (res.).

Ley, Felix, O.F.M. Cap. (1909–72): ord. June 14, 1936; ap. admin. Ryukyu Is. (Caporilla), 1968–72.

Lillis, Thomas F. (1861–1938): ord. Aug. 15, 1885; bp. Leavenworth (now Kansas City, Kans.), 1904–10; coad. bp. Kansas City, Mo. (Cibyra), 1910–13; bp. Kansas City, Mo., 1913–38.

Lootens, Louis (1827–98): b. Belgium; ord. June 14, 1851; v.a. Idaho and Montana (Castabala), 1868–75 (res.).

Loras, Mathias (1792–1858): b. France; ord. Nov. 12, 1815; first bp. Dubuque, 1837–58.

Loughlin, John (1817–91): b. Ireland; ord. Oct. 18, 1840; first bp. Brooklyn, 1853–91.

Lowney, Denis M. (1863–1918): b. Ireland; ord. Dec. 17, 1887; aux. Providence (Hadrianopolis), 1917–18.

Lucey, Robert E. (1891–1977): ord. May 14, 1916; bp. Amarillo, 1934–41; abp. San Antonio, 1941–69 (res.).

Ludden, Patrick A. (1838–1912): b. Ireland; ord. May 21, 1865; first bp. Syracuse, 1887–1912.

Luers, John (1819–71): b. Germany; ord. Nov. 11, 1846; first bp. Fort Wayne, 1858–71.

Lyke, James P., O.F.M. (1939–92): ord. June 24, 1966; aux. Cleveland (Furnes Maior) 1979–90; ap. admin. Atlanta, 1990–91; abp. Atlanta, 1991–92.

Lynch, Joseph P. (1872–1954): ord. June 9, 1900; bp. Dallas, 1911–54.

Lynch, Patrick N. (1817–82): b. Ireland; ord. Apr. 5, 1840; bp. Charleston, 1858–82.

Lyons, Thomas W. (1923–88): ord. May 22, 1948; aux. bp. Washington, D.C. (Mortlach), 1974–88.

M

McAuliffe, Maurice F. (1875–1944): ord. July 29, 1900; aux. Hartford (Dercos), 1923–34; bp. Hartford, 1934–44.

McCafferty, John E. (1920–80): ord. Mar. 17, 1945; aux. Rochester (Tanudaia), 1968–80.

McCarthy, Joseph E. (1876–1955): ord. July 4, 1903; bp. Portland, Me., 1932–55.

McCarthy, Justin J. (1900–59): ord. Apr. 16, 1927; aux. Newark (Doberus), 1954–57; bp. Camden, 1957–59.

McCarty, William T., C.Ss.R. (1889–1972): ord. June 10, 1915; military delegate (Anea), 1943–47; coad. bp. Rapid City, 1947–48; bp. Rapid City, 1948–69 (res.).

McCauley, Vincent J., C.S.C. (1906–82): ord. June 24, 1943; first bp. Fort Portal, Uganda, 1961–72 (res.).

McCloskey, James P. (1870–1945): ord. Dec. 17, 1898; bp. Zamboanga, P.I., 1917–20; bp. Jaro, P.I., 1920–45.

McCloskey, John (1810–85): ord. Jan. 12, 1834; coad. bp. New York (Axiere), 1843–47; first bp. Albany, 1847–64; abp. New York, 1864–85; first U.S. cardinal 1875.

McCloskey, William G. (1823–1909): ord. Oct. 6, 1852; bp. Louisville, 1868–1909.

McCormick, Patrick J. (1880–1953): ord. July 6, 1904; aux. Washington (Atenia), 1950–53.

McCort, John J. (1860–1936): ord. Oct. 14, 1883; aux. Philadelphia (Azotus), 1912–20; bp. Altoona, 1920–36.

McDevitt, Gerald V. (1917–80): ord. May 30, 1942; aux. Philadelphia (Tigias), 1962–80.

McDevitt, Philip R. (1858–1935): ord. July 14, 1885; bp. Harrisburg, 1916–35.

McDonald, William J. (1904–89): b. Ireland; ord. June 10, 1928; aux. Washington (Aquae Regiae), 1964–67; aux. San Francisco, 1967–79 (res.).

McDonnell, Charles E. (1854–1921): ord. May 19, 1878; bp. Brooklyn, 1892–1921.

McDonnell, Thomas J. (1894–1961): ord. Sept. 20, 1919; aux. New York (Sela), 1947–51; coad. bp. Wheeling, 1951–61.

McEleney, John J., S.J. (1895–1986): ord. June 18, 1930; v.a. Jamaica (Zeugma), 1950–56; bp. Kingston, 1956–67; abp. Kingston 1967–70 (res.)

McEntegart, Bryan (1893–1968): ord. Sept. 8, 1917; bp. Ogdensburg, 1943–53; rector Catholic University (Aradi), 1953–57; bp. Brooklyn, 1957–68.

McFadden, James A. (1880–1952): ord. June 17, 1905; aux. Cleveland (Bida), 1932–43; first bp. Youngstown, 1943–52.

MacFarland, Francis P. (1819–74): ord. May 1, 1845; bp. Hartford, 1858–74.

McFaul, James A. (1850–1917): b. Ireland; ord. May 26, 1877; bp. Trenton, 1894–1917.

McGavick, Alexander J. (1863–1948): ord. June 11, 1887; aux. Chicago (Marcopolis), 1899–1921; bp. La Crosse, 1921–48.

McGeough, Joseph F. (1903–70): ord. Dec. 20, 1930; internuncio Ethiopia, 1957–60; apostolic delegate (Hemesa) S. Africa, 1960–67; nuncio Ireland, 1967–69.

McGill, John (1809–72): ord. June 13, 1835; bp. Richmond, 1850–72.

MacGinley, John B. (1871–1969): b. Ireland; ord. June 8, 1895; bp. Nueva Caceres, 1910–24; first bp. Monterey-Fresno, 1924–32 (res.).

McGolrick, James (1841–1918): b. Ireland; ord. June 11, 1867; first bp. Duluth, 1889–1918.

McGovern, Patrick A. (1872–1951): ord. Aug. 18, 1895; bp. Cheyenne, 1912–51.

McGovern, Thomas (1832–98): b. Ireland; ord. Dec. 27, 1861; bp. Harrisburg, 1888–98.

McGrath, Joseph F. (1871–1950): b. Ireland; ord. Dec. 21, 1895; bp. Baker City (now Baker), 1919–50.

McGucken, Joseph T. (1902–84): ord. Jan. 15, 1928; aux. Los Angeles (Sanavus), 1940–55; coad. bp. Sacramento, 1957–62; abp. San Francisco, 1962–77 (res.).

McGuinness, Eugene (1889–1957): ord. May 22, 1915; bp. Raleigh, 1937–44; coad. bp. Oklahoma City and Tulsa (Ilium), 1944–48; bp. Oklahoma City and Tulsa, 1948–57.

McGurkin, Edward A. M.M. (1905–83): ord. Sept. 14, 1930; bp. Shinyanga, Tanzania, 1956–75 (res.).

McIntyre, James F. (1886–1979): ord. May 21, 1921; aux. New York (Cirene), 1941–46; coad. abp. New York (Palto), 1946–48; abp. Los Angeles, 1948–70 (res.); cardinal, 1953.

MacKenzie, Eric F. (1893–1969): ord. Oct. 20, 1918; aux. Boston (Alba), 1950–69.

McLaughlin, Charles B. (1913–78): ord. June 6, 1941; aux. Raleigh (Risinium), 1964–68; first bp. St. Petersburg, 1968–78.

McLaughlin, Thomas H. (1881–1947): ord. July 26, 1904; aux. Newark (Nisa), 1935–37; first bp. Paterson, 1937–47.

McMahon, John J. (1875–1932): ord. May 20, 1900; bp. Trenton, 1928–32.

McMahon, Lawrence S. (1835–93): ord. Mar. 24, 1860; bp. Hartford, 1879–93.

McManaman, Edward P. (1900–64): ord. Mar. 12, 1927; aux. Erie (Floriana), 1948–64.

McManus, James E., C.Ss.R. (1900–76): ord. June 19, 1927; bp. Ponce, P.R., 1947–63; aux. New York (Banda), 1963–70 (res.).

McMullen, John (1832–83): b. Ireland; ord. June 20, 1858; first bp. Davenport, 1881–83.

McNamara, John M. (1878–1960): ord. June 21, 1902; aux. Baltimore (Eumenia), 1928–47; aux. Washington, 1947–60.

McNamara, Martin D. (1898–1966): ord. Dec. 23, 1922; first bp. Joliet, 1949–66.

McNeirny, Francis (1828–94): ord. Aug. 17, 1855; coad. bp. Albany (Rhesaina), 1872–77; bp. Albany, 1877–94.

McNicholas, John T., O.P. (1877–1950); b. Ireland; ord. Oct. 10, 1901; bp. Duluth, 1918–25, abp. Cincinnati, 1925–50.

McNicholas, Joseph A. (1923–83): ord. June 7, 1949; aux. St. Louis (Scala), 1969–75; bp. Springfield, Ill., 1975–83.

McNulty, James A. (1900–72): ord. July 12, 1925; aux. Newark (Methone), 1947–53; bp. Paterson, 1953–63; bp. Buffalo, 1963–72.

McQuaid, Bernard J. (1823–1909): ord. Jan. 16, 1848; first bp. Rochester, 1868–1909.

McShea, Joseph M. (1907–91): ord. Dec. 6, 1931; aux. Philadelphia (Mina), 1952–61; first bp. Allentown, 1961–83 (res.).

McSorley, Francis J., O.M.I. (1913–71): ord. May 30, 1939; v.a. Jolo, P.I. (Sozusa), 1958–71.

McVinney, Russell J. (1898–1971): ord. July 13 1924; bp. Providence, 1948–71.

Machebeuf, Joseph P. (1812–89): b. France; ord. Dec. 17, 1836; v.a. Colorado and Utah (Epiphania), 1868–87; first bp. Denver, 1887–89.

Maes, Camillus P. (1846–1915): b. Belgium; ord. Dec. 19, 1868; bp. Covington, 1885–1915.

Maginn, Edward J. (1897–1984): b. Scotland; ord. June 10, 1922; aux. Albany (Curium), 1957–72 (res.).

Magner, Francis (1887–1947): ord. May 17, 1913; bp. Marquette, 1941–47.

Maguire, John J. (1904–89): ord. Dec. 22, 1928; aux. New York (Antiphrae), 1959–65; coad. abp. New York (Tabalta), 1965–80 (res.).

Maher, Leo T. (1915–91): ord. Dec. 18, 1943; first bp. Santa Rosa, 1962–69; bp. San Diego, 1969–90 (res.).

Mahoney, Bernard (1875–1939): ord. Feb. 27, 1904; bp. Sioux Falls, 1922–39.

Maloney, David M. (1912–95): ord. Dec. 8,1936; aux. Denver (Ruspe), 1961–67; bp. Wichita, 1967–82 (res.).

Maloney, Thomas F. (1903–62): ord. July 13, 1930; aux. Providence (Andropolis), 1960–62.

Manning, Timothy (1909–89): b. Ireland; ord. June 16, 1934 (Los Angeles archd.); American citizen, 1944; aux. Los Angeles (Lesvi), 1946–67; first bp. Fresno, 1967–69; coad. abp. Los Angeles (Capri), 1969–70; abp. Los Angeles, 1970–85 (res.); cardinal 1973.

Manogue, Patrick: *See* MANOGUE, PATRICK.

Manucy, Dominic (1823–85): ord. Aug. 15, 1850, v.a. Brownsville (Dulma), 1874–84; bp. Mobile, Mar.–Sept., 1884 (res.); reappointed v.a. Brownsville (Maronea) (now diocese of Corpus Christi), 1884–85.

Mardaga, Thomas J. (1913–84): ord. May 14, 1940; aux. Baltimore (Mutugenna), 1967–68, bp. Wilmington, 1968–84.

Marechal, Ambrose, S.S. (1766–1828): b. France; ord. June 2, 1792; abp. Baltimore, 1817–28.

Markham, Thomas F. (1891–1952): ord. June 2, 1917; aux. Boston (Acalissus), 1950–52.

Marling, Joseph M., C.Pp.S. (1904–79): ord. Feb. 21, 1929; aux. Kansas City, Mo. (Thasus), 1947–56; first bp. Jefferson City, 1956–69 (res.).

Marshall, John A. (1928–94): ord. Dec. 19, 1953; bp. Burlington, 1972–91; bp. Springfield, Mass, 1991–94.

Martin, Augustus M. (1803–75): b. France; ord. May 31, 1828; first bp. Natchitoches (now Alexandria), 1853–75.

Marty, Martin, O.S.B. (1834–96): b. Switzerland; ord. Sept. 14, 1856; v.a. Dakota (Tiberias), 1880–89; first bp. Sioux Falls, 1889–95; bp. St. Cloud, 1895–96.

Marx, Adolph (1915–65): b. Germany; ord. May 2, 1940; aux. Corpus Christi (Citrus), 1956–65; first bp. Brownsville, 1965.

Matz, Nicholas C. (1850–1917): b. France; ord. May 31, 1874; coad. bp. Denver (Telmissus), 1887–89; bp. Denver, 1889–1917.

May, John L. (1922–94): ord. May 3, 1947; aux. bp. Chicago (Tagarbala), 1967–69; bp. Mobile, 1969–80; abp. St. Louis, 1980–92 (res.).

Mazzarella, Bernardino N., O.F.M. (1904–79): ord. June 5, 1931; prelate Olancho, Honduras (Hadrianopolis in Pisidia), 1957–63; first bp. Comayagua, Honduras, 1963–79.

Medeiros, Humberto S. (1915–83): b. Azores; U.S. citizen, 1940; ord. June 15, 1946; bp. Brownsville, 1966–70; abp. Boston, 1970–83; cardinal 1973.

Meerschaert, Theophile (1847–1924): b. Belgium; ord. Dec. 23, 1871; v.a. Oklahoma and Indian Territory (Sidyma), 1891–1905; first bp. Oklahoma, 1905–24.

Melcher, Joseph (1806–73): b. Austria; ord. Mar. 27, 1830; first bp. Green Bay, 1868–73.

Mendez, Alfred, C.S.C. (1907–95): ord. June 24, 1935; first bp. Arecibo, P.R., 1960–74 (res.).

Messmer, Sebastian (1847–1930): b. Switzerland; ord. July 23, 1871; bp. Green Bay, 1892–1903; abp. Milwaukee, 1903–30.

Metzger, Sidney M. (1902–86): ord. Apr. 3, 1926; aux. Santa Fe (Birtha), 1940–41; coad. bp. El Paso, 1941–42; bp. El Paso, 1942–78 (res.).

Meyer, Albert (1903–65): ord. July 11, 1926; bp. Superior, 1946–53; abp. Milwaukee, 1953–58; abp. Chicago, 1958–65; cardinal, 1959.

Michaud, John S. (1843–1908): ord. June 7, 1873; coad. bp. Burlington (Modra), 1892–99; bp. Burlington, 1899–1908.

Miege, John B., S.J. (1815–84): b. France; ord. Sept. 12, 1844; v.a. Kansas and Indian Territory (now Kansas City) (Messene), 1851–74 (res.).

Mihalik, Emil J. (1920–84): ord. Sept. 21, 1945; first bp. Parma (Byzantine Rite, Ruthenians), 1969–84.

Miles, Richard P., O.P. (1791–1860): ord. Sept. 21, 1816; first bp. Nashville, 1838–60.

Minihan, Jeremiah F. (1903–73): ord. Dec. 21, 1929; aux. Boston (Paphus), 1954–73.

Misner, Paul B., C.M. (1891–1938): ord. Feb. 23, 1919; v.a. Yukiang, China (Myrica), 1935–38.

Mitty, John J. (1884–1961): ord. Dec. 22, 1906, bp. Salt Lake, 1926–32; coad. abp. San Francisco (Aegina), 1932–35; abp. San Francisco, 1935–61.

Moeller, Henry (1849–1925): ord. June 10, 1876; bp. Columbus, 1900–03; coad. abp. Cincinnati (Areopolis), 1903–04; abp. Cincinnati, 1904–25.

Molloy, Thomas E. (1884–1956): ord. Sept. 19, 1908; aux. Brooklyn (Lorea), 1920–21; bp. Brooklyn, 1921–56.

Monaghan, Francis J. (1890–1942): ord. May 29, 1915; coad. bp. Ogdensburg (Mela), 1936–39; bp. Ogdensburg, 1939–42.

Monaghan, John J. (1856–1935): ord. Dec. 18, 1880; bp. Wilmington, 1897–1925 (res.).

Montgomery, George T. (1847–1907): ord. Dec. 20, 1879; coad. bp. Monterey-Los Angeles (Thmuis), 1894–96; bp. Monterey-Los Angeles (now Los Angeles), 1896–1903; coad. abp. San Francisco (Auxum), 1903–07.

Mooney, Edward (1882–1958): ord. Apr. 10, 1909; ap. del. India (Irenopolis), 1926–31; ap. del. Japan, 1931–33; bp. Rochester, 1933–37; first abp. Detroit, 1937–58; cardinal, 1946.

Moore, John (1835–1901): b. Ireland; ord. Apr. 9, 1860; bp. St. Augustine, 1877–1901.

Mora, Francis (1827–1905); b. Spain; ord. Mar. 19, 1856; coad. bp. Monterey-Los Angeles (Mosynopolis), 1873–78; bp. Monterey-Los Angeles (now Los Angeles), 1878–96 (res.).

Morkovsky, John L. (1909–90): ord. Dec. 5, 1933; aux. Amarillo (Hieron), 1956–58; bp. Amarillo, 1958–63; coad. bp. Galveston-Houston (Tigava), 1963–75; bp. Galveston, 1975–84 (res.).

Morris, John (1866–1946): ord. June 11, 1892; coad. bp. Little Rock (Acmonia), 1906–07; bp. Little Rock, 1907–46.

Morrow, Louis La Ravoire, S.D.B. (1892–1987): ord. May 21, 1921; bp. Krishnagar, India, 1939–69 (res.).

Mrak, Ignatius (1810–1901): b. Austria; ord. July 31, 1837; bp. Sault Ste. Marie and Marquette (now Marquette), 1869–78 (res.).

Mueller, Joseph M. (1894–1981): ord. June 14, 1919; coad. bp. Sioux City (Sinda), 1947–48; bp. Sioux City, 1948–70 (res.).

Muench, Aloysius (1889–1962): ord. June 8, 1913; bp. Fargo, 1935–59 (res.); apostolic visitator to Germany, 1946; nuncio to Germany 1951–59; cardinal 1959.

Mugavero, Francis J. (1914–91): ord. May 18, 1940; bp. Brooklyn, 1968–90 (res.).

Mulcahy, John J. (1922–94): ord. May 1, 1947; aux. bp. Boston (Penafiel), 1975–92 (res.).

Muldoon, Peter J. (1862–1927): ord. Dec. 18, 1886; aux. Chicago (Tamasus), 1901–08; first bp. Rockford, 1908–27.

Mullen, Tobias (1818–1900): b. Ireland; ord. Sept. 1, 1844; bp. Erie, 1868–99 (res.).

Mulloy, William T. (1892–1959): ord. June 7, 1916; bp. Covington, 1945–59.

Mulrooney, Charles R. (1906–89); ord. June 10, 1930; aux. Brooklyn (Valentiniana), 1959–81 (res.).

Mundelein, George (1872–1939): ord. June 8, 1895; aux. Brooklyn (Loryma), 1909–15; abp. Chicago, 1915–39; cardinal, 1924.

Murphy, Joseph A., S.J. (1857–1939): b. Ireland; ord. Aug. 26, 1888; v.a. Belize, Br. Honduras (Birtha), 1923–39.

Murphy, T.(Thomas) Austin (1911–91): ord. June 10, 1937; aux. Baltimore (Appiaria), 1962–84 (res.).

Murphy, William F. (1885–1950): ord. June 13, 1908; first bp. Saginaw, 1938–50.

Murray, John G. (1877–1956): ord. Apr. 14, 1900; aux. Hartford (Flavias), 1920–25; bp. Portland, 1925–31; abp. St. Paul, 1931–56.

Mussio, John K. (1902–78): ord. Aug. 15, 1935; bp. Steubenville, 1945–77 (res.).

N

Najmy, Justin, O.S.B.M. (1898–1968): b. Syria; ord. Dec. 25, 1926; ap. ex. Melkites (Augustopolis in Phrygia), 1966–68.

Navagh, James J. (1901–65): ord. Dec. 21, 1929; aux. Raleigh (Ombi), 1952–57; bp. Ogdensburg, 1957–63; bp. Paterson, 1963–65.

Neale, Leonard (1746–1817): ord. June 5, 1773; coad. bp. Baltimore (Gortyna), 1800–15; abp. Baltimore, 1815–17.

Nelson, Knute Ansgar, O.S.B. (1906–90): b. Denmark; ord. May 22, 1937; U.S. citizen, 1941; coad. bp. Stockholm, Sweden (Bilta), 1947–57; bp. Stockholm, 1957–62 (res.)

Neraz, John C. (1828–94): b. France; ord. Mar. 19, 1853; bp. San Antonio, 1881–1894.

Neumann, John, St.: *See* NEUMANN, ST. JOHN.

Newell, Hubert M. (1904–87): ord. June 15, 1930; coad. bp. Cheyenne (Zapara), 1947–51; bp. Cheyenne, 1951–78 (res.).

Newman, Thomas A., M.S. (1903–78): ord. June 29, 1929; first bp. Prome, Burma, 1961–75 (res.).

Niedhammer, Matthew A., O.F.M. Cap. (1901–70): ord. June 8, 1927; v.a. Bluefields, Nicaragua (Caloe), 1943–70.

Nilan, John J. (1855–1934): ord. Dec. 2, 1878; bp. Hartford, 1910–34.

Noa, Thomas L. (1892–1977): ord. Dec. 23, 1916; coad. bp. Sioux City (Salona), 1946–47; bp. Marquette, 1947–68 (res.).

Nold, Wendelin J. (1900–81): ord. Apr. 11, 1925; coad. bp. Galveston (Sasima), 1948–50; bp. Galveston-Houston, 1950–75 (res.).

Noll, John F. (1875–1956): ord. June 4, 1898; bp. Fort Wayne, 1925–56 (pers. tit. abp., 1953).

Northrop, Henry P. (1842–1916): ord. June 25, 1865, v.a. North Carolina (Rosalia), 1881–83; bp. Charleston, 1883–1916.

Noser, Adolph, S.V.D. (1900–81): ord. Sept. 27, 1925; v.a. Accra, British W. Africa (now Ghana) (Capitolias), 1947–50; bp. Accra, 1950–53; v.a. Alexishafen, New Guinea (Hierpiniana), 1953–66; abp. Madang, Papua New Guinea. 1966–75 (res.).

Nussbaum, Paul J., C.P. (1870–1935): ord. May 20, 1894; first bp. Corpus Christi, 1913–20 (res.); bp. Sault Ste. Marie and Marquette (now Marquette), 1922–35.

O

O'Boyle, Patrick A. (1896–1987): ord. May 21, 1921; abp. Washington, D.C., 1948–73 (res.); cardinal 1967.

O'Brien, Henry J. (1896–1976): ord. July 8, 1923; aux. Hartford (Sita), 1940–45; bp. Hartford, 1945–53, and first abp. Hartford, 1953–68 (res.).

O'Brien, William D. (1878–1962): ord. July 11, 1903; aux. Chicago (Calynda), 1934–62.

O'Connell, Denis J. (1849–1927): b. Ireland; ord. May 26, 1877; aux. San Francisco (Sebaste), 1908–12; bp. Richmond, 1912–26 (res.).

O'Connell, Eugene (1815–91): b. Ireland; ord. May 21, 1842; v.a. Marysville (Flaviopolis), 1861–68; first bp. Grass Valley, 1868–84 (res.).

O'Connell, William H. (1859–1944): ord. June 7, 1884; bp. Portland, 1901–06; coad. bp. Boston (Constantia), 1906–07; abp. Boston, 1907–44; cardinal, 1911.

O'Connor (brothers), **James** (1823–90): b. Ireland; ord. Mar. 25, 1848; v.a. Nebraska (Dibon), 1876–85; first bp. Omaha, 1885–90. **Michael, S.J.** (1810–72): b. Ireland; ord. June 1, 1833; first bp. Pittsburgh, 1843–53; first bp. Erie, 1853–54; bp. Pittsburgh, 1854–60 (resigned, joined Jesuits).

O'Connor, John J. (1855–1927): ord. Dec. 22, 1877; bp. Newark, 1901–27.

O'Connor, Martin J. (1900–86): ord. Mar. 15, 1924: aux. Scranton (Thespia), 1943–46; rector North American College, Rome, 1946–64; abp., 1959 (Laodicea); nuncio to Malta, 1965–69; pres. Pontifical Commission for Social Communications, 1964

O'Connor, William A. (1903–83): ord. Sept. 24, 1927; bp. Springfield, Ill., 1949–75 (res.).

O'Connor, William P. (1886–1973): ord. Mar. 10, 1912; bp. Superior, 1942–46; first bp. Madison, 1946–67 (res.).

O'Dea, Edward J. (1856–1932): ord. Dec. 23, 1882; bp. Nesqually (now Seattle—title changed in 1907), 1896–1932.

Odin, John M., C.M. (1800–70): b. France; ord. May 4, 1823; v.a. Texas (Claudiopolis), 1842–47; first bp. Galveston, 1847–61; abp. New Orleans, 1861–70.

O'Donaghue, Denis (1848–1925): ord. Sept. 6, 1874; aux. Indianapolis (Pomaria), 1900–10; bp. Louisville, 1910–24 (res.).

O'Donnell, Cletus F. (1917–92): ord. May 3, 1941; aux. Chicago (Abritto), 1960–67; bp. Madison, 1967–92 (res.).

O'Dowd, James T. (1907–50): ord. June 4, 1932; aux. San Francisco (Cea), 1948–50.

O'Farrell, Michael J. (1832–94): b. Ireland; ord. Aug. 18, 1855; first bp. Trenton, 1881–94.

O'Flanagan, Dermot (1901–73): b. Ireland; ord. Aug. 27, 1929; first bp. Juneau, 1951–68 (res.).

O'Gara, Cuthbert, C.P. (1886–1968): b. Canada; ord. May 26, 1915; v.a. Yuanling, China (Elis), 1934–46; first bp. Yuanling, 1946–68 (imprisoned, 1951, and then expelled, 1953, by Chinese Communists).

O'Gorman, James, O.C.S.O. (1804–74): b. Ireland; ord. Dec. 23, 1843; v.a. Nebraska (now Omaha) (Raphanea), 1859–74.

O'Gorman, Thomas (1843–1921): ord. Nov. 5, 1865; bp. Sioux Falls, 1896–1921.

O'Hara, Edwin V. (1881–1956): ord. June 9, 1905; bp Great Falls, 1930–39; bp. Kansas City, Mo., 1939–56 (title changed to Kansas City-St. Joseph, 1956).

O'Hara, Gerald P. (1895–1963): ord. Apr. 3, 1920; aux. Philadelphia (Heliopolis), 1929–35; bp. Savannah (title changed to Savannah-Atlanta in 1937), 1935–59 (res.); regent of Romania nunciature, 1946–50 (expelled); nuncio to Ireland, 1951–54; ap. del. to Great Britain, 1954–63; tit. abp. Pessinus, 1959–63.

O'Hara, John F., C.S.C. (1888–1960): ord. Sept. 9, 1916; delegate of U.S. military vicar (Mylasa), 1940–45; bp. Buffalo, 1945–51; abp. Philadelphia, 1951–60; cardinal, 1958.

O'Hara, William (1816–99): b. Ireland; ord. Dec. 21, 1842; first bp. Scranton, 1868–99.

O'Hare, William F., S.J. (1870–1926): ord. June 25, 1903; v.a. Jamaica (Maximianopolis), 1920–26.

O'Hern, John F. (1874–1933): ord. Feb. 17, 1901; bp. Rochester, 1929–33.

O'Leary, Thomas (1875–1949): ord. Dec. 18 1897; bp. Springfield, Mass., 1921–49.

Olwell, Quentin, C.P. (1898–1972): ord. Feb. 4, 1923; prelate Marbel, P.I. (Thabraca), 1961–69 (res.).

O'Meara, Edward T. (1921–92): ord. Dec. 21, 1946; aux. St. Louis (Thisiduo), 1972–80; abp. Indianapolis, 1980–92.

O'Regan, Anthony (1809–66): b. Ireland; ord. Nov. 29, 1834; bp. Chicago, 1854–58 (res.).

O'Reilly, Bernard (1803–56): b. Ireland; ord. Oct. 16, 1831; bp. Hartford, 1850–56.

O'Reilly, Charles J. (1860–1923): b. Canada; ord. June 29, 1890; first bp. Baker City (now Baker), 1903–18; bp. Lincoln, 1918–23.

O'Reilly, James (1855–1934): b. Ireland; ord. June 24, 1880; bp. Fargo, 1910–34.

O'Reilly, Patrick T. (1833–92): b. Ireland; ord. Aug. 15, 1857; first bp. Springfield, Mass., 1870–92.

O'Reilly, Peter J. (1850–1924): b. Ireland; ord. June 24, 1877; aux. Peoria (Lebedus), 1900–24.

O'Reilly, Thomas C. (1873–1938): ord. June 4, 1898; bp. Scranton, 1928–38.

Ortynsky, Stephen, O.S.B.M. (1866–1916): b. Poland; ord. July 18, 1891; first Ukrainian Byzantine Rite bishop in U.S. (Daulia), 1907–16.

O'Shea, John A., C.M. (1887–1969): ord. May 30, 1914; v.a. Kanchow, China (Midila), 1928–46; first bp. Kanchow, 1949–69 (expelled by Chinese Communists, 1953).

O'Shea, William F., M.M. (1884–1945): ord. Dec. 5, 1917; v.a. Heijon, Japan (Naissusz), 1939–45; prisoner of Japanese 1941–42.

O'Sullivan, Jeremiah (1842–96): b. Ireland; ord. June 30, 1868; bp. Mobile, 1885–96.

Ott, Stanley J. (1927–92) ord. Dec. 8, 1951; aux. New Orleans (Nicives), 1976–83; bp. Baton Rouge, 1983–92.

Oves Fernandez, Francisco Ricardo (1928–90) b Cuba; ord. Apr. 13, 1952; aux. Cienfuegas, Cuba (Montecorvino), 1969–70; abp. Havana, 1970–81 (res.); resided in El Paso, Tex., diocese from 1982.

P

Pardy, James V., M.M. (1898–1983): ord. Jan. 26, 1930; v.a. Cheong-Ju, Korea (Irenopolis), 1958–62; first bp. Cheong-Ju, 1962–69 (res.).

Paschang, Adolph J., M.M. (1895–1968): ord. May 21, 1921; v.a. Kong Moon, China (Sasima) 1937–46; first bp. Kong Moon, 1946–68 (expelled by Communists, 1951).

Pechillo, Jerome, T.O.R. (1919–91): ord. June 10, 1947; prelate Coronel Oviedo, Paraguay (Novasparsa), 1966–76; aux. Newark, 1976–91.

Pellicer, Anthony (1824–80): ord. Aug. 15, 1850; first bp. San Antonio, 1874–80.

Peñalver y Cardenas, Luis (1749–1810): b. Cuba; ord. Apr. 4, 1772; first bp. Louisiana and the Two Floridas (now New Orleans), 1793–1801; abp. Guatemala, 1801–06 (res.).

Perché, Napoleon J. (1805–83): b. France; ord. Sept. 19, 1829; abp. New Orleans, 1870–83.

Pernicone, Joseph M. (1903–85): b. Sicily; ord. Dec. 18, 1926; aux. New York (Hadrianapolis) 1954–78 (res.).

Perry, Harold R., S.V.D. (1916–91), ord. Jan. 6, 1944; aux. New Orleans (Mons in Mauretania), 1966–91.

Persico, Ignatius, O.F.M. Cap. (1823–95): b. Italy; ord. Jan. 24, 1846; bishop from 1854; bp. Savannah, 1870–72; cardinal, 1893.

Peschges, John H. (1881–1944): ord. Apr. 15, 1905; bp. Crookston, 1938–44.

Peterson, John B. (1871–1944): ord. Sept. 15, 1899; aux. Boston (Hippos), 1972–32: bp. Manchester, 1932–44.

Phelan, Richard (1828–1904): b. Ireland; ord. May 4, 1854; coad. bp. Pittsburgh (Cibyra), 1885–89; bp. Pittsburgh, 1889–1904.

Pinger, Henry A., O.F.M. (1897–1988): ord. June 27, 1927; v.a. Chowtsun, China (Capitolias), 1937–46; first bp. Chowtsun, 1946 (imprisoned, 1951 then released, 1956 and expelled by Chinese Communists).

Pinten, Joseph G. (1867–1945): ord. Nov. 1, 1890; bp. Superior, 1922–26; bp. Grand Rapids, 1926–40 (res.).

Pitaval, John B. (1858–1928): b. France; ord. Dec. 24, 1881; aux. Santa Fe (Sora), 1902–09; abp. Santa Fe, 1909–18 (res.).

Plagens, Joseph C. (1880–1943): b. Poland; ord. July 5, 1903; aux. Detroit (Rhodiapolis), 1924–35; bp. Sault Ste. Marie and Marquette (title changed to Marquette, 1937), 1935–40; bp. Grand Rapids, 1941–43.

Portier, Michael (1795–1859): b. France; ord. May 16, 1818; v.a. Two Floridas and Alabama (Olena), 1826–29; first bp. Mobile, 1829–59.

Prendergast, Edmond (1843–1918): b. Ireland; ord. Nov. 17, 1865; aux. Philadelphia (Scilium), 1897–1911; abp. Philadelphia, 1911–18.

Primeau, Ernest J. (1909–89): ord. Apr. 7, 1934; bp. Manchester, 1960–74 (res.); director Villa Stritch, Rome, 1974–79 (res.).

Proulx, Amedee W. (1932–93): ord. May 31, 1958; aux. bp. Portland, Me. (Clipia), 1975–93.

Purcell, John B. (1800–83): b. Ireland; ord. May 20, 1826; bp., 1833–50, and first abp., 1850–83, Cincinnati.

Q

Quarter, William (1806–48): b. Ireland; ord. Sept. 19, 1829; first bp. Chicago, 1844–48.

Quigley, James E. (1855–1915): b. Canada; ord. Apr. 13, 1879; bp. Buffalo, 1897–1903; abp. Chicago, 1903–15.

Quinlan, John (1826–83): b. Ireland; ord. Aug. 30, 1852; bp. Mobile, 1859–83.

Quinn, William Charles, C.M. (1905–60): ord. Oct. 11, 1931; v.a. Yukiang, China (Halicarnassus), 1940–46; first bp. Yukiang, 1946–60 (expelled by Chinese Communists, 1951).

R

Rademacher, Joseph (1840–1900): ord. Aug. 2, 1863; bp. Nashville, 1883–93; bp. Ft. Wayne, 1893–1900.

Rappe, Louis Amadeus (1801–77): b. France; ord. Mar. 14, 1829; first bp. Cleveland, 1847–70 (res.).

Rausch, James S. (1928–81): ord. June 2, 1956; aux. St. Cloud (Summa), 1973–77; bp. Phoenix, 1977–81.

Ready, Michael J. (1893–1957): ord. Sept. 14, 1918; bp. Columbus, 1944–57.

Reed, Victor J. (1905–71): ord. Dec. 21, 1929; aux. Oklahoma City and Tulsa (Limasa), 1957–58; bp. Oklahoma City and Tulsa, 1958–71.

Regan, Joseph W., M.M. (1905–94): ord. Jan. 27, 1929; prelate Tagum, Philippines (Isinda), 1962–80 (res.).

Reh, Francis F. (1911–94): ord. Dec. 8, 1935; bp. Charleston 1962–64; bp. Saginaw, 1969–80 (res.).

Rehring, George J. (1890–1976): ord. Mar. 28, 1914; aux. Cincinnati (Lunda), 1937–50; bp. Toledo, 1950–67 (res.).

Reicher, Louis J. (1890–1984): ord. Dec. 6, 1918; first bp. Austin, 1948–71 (res.).

Reilly, Edmond J. (1897–1958): ord. Apr. 1, 1922; aux. Brooklyn (Nepte), 1955–58.

Reilly, Thomas F., C.Ss.R. (1908–92): ord. June 10, 1933; prelate San Juan de la Maguana, Dominican Republic (Themisonium), 1956–69; first bp. San Juan de la Maguana, 1969–77 (res.).

Résé, Frederic (1791–1871): b. Germany; ord. Mar. 15, 1823; first bp. Detroit, 1833–71. Inactive from 1841 because of ill health.

Reverman, Theodore (1877–1941): ord. July 26, 1901; bp. Superior, 1926–41.

Reynolds, Ignatius A. (1798–1855): ord. Oct. 24, 1823; bp. Charleston, 1844–55.

Rhode, Paul P. (1871–1945): b. Poland; ord. June 17, 1894; aux. Chicago (Barca), 1908–15; bp. Green Bay, 1915–45.

Rice, Joseph J. (1871–1938): ord. Sept. 29, 1894; bp. Burlington, 1910–38.

Rice, William A., S.J. (1891–1946): ord. Aug. 27, 1925; v.a. Belize, Br. Honduras (Rusicade), 1939–46.

Richter, Henry J. (1838–1916): b. Germany; ord. June 10, 1865; first bp. Grand Rapids, 1883–1916.

Riley, Thomas J. (1900–1977): ord. May 20, 1927; aux. Boston (Regiae), 1956–76 (res.).

Riordan, Patrick W. (1841–1914): b. Canada; ord. June 10, 1865; coad. abp. San Francisco (Cabasa), 1883–84; abp. San Francisco, 1884–1914.

Ritter, Joseph E. (1892–1967): ord. May 30, 1917; aux. Indianapolis (Hippos), 1933–34; bp., 1934–44, and first abp. Indianapolis, 1944–46; abp. St. Louis, 1946–67; cardinal 1961.

Robinson, Pascal C., O.F.M. (1870–1948): b. Ireland; ord. Dec. 21, 1901; ap. visitor to Palestine, Egypt, Syria and Cyprus (Tyana), 1927–29; ap. nuncio to Ireland, 1929–48.

Rohlman, Henry P. (1876–1957): b. Germany; ord. Dec. 21, 1901; bp. Davenport, 1927–44; coad. abp. Dubuque (Macra), 1944–46; abp. Dubuque, 1946–54 (res.).

Rooker, Fraderick Z. (1861–1907): ord. July 25, 1888; bp. Jaro, P.I., 1903–07.

Ropert, Gulstan F., SS.CC. (1839–1903): b. France; ord. May 26, 1866; v.a. Sandwich (now Hawaiian) Is. (Panopolis), 1892–1903.

Rosati, Joseph, C.M.: See Index.

Rosecrans, Sylvester (1827–78): ord. June 5, 1853; aux. Cincinnati (Pompeiopolis), 1862–68; first bp. Columbus, 1868–78.

Rouxel, Gustave A. (1840–1908): b. France, ord. Nov. 4, 1863; aux. New Orleans (Curium), 1899–1908.

Rummel, Joseph (1876–1964): b. Germany; ord. May 24, 1902; bp. Omaha, 1928–35; abp. New Orleans, 1935–64.

Ruocco, Joseph J. (1922–80): ord. May 6, 1948; aux. Boston (Polignano), 1975–80.

Russell, John J. (1897–1993): ord. July 8, 1923; bp. Charleston, 1950–58; bp. Richmond, 1958–73 (res.).

Russell, William T. (1863–1927): ord. June 21, 1889; bp. Charleston, 1917–27.

Ryan, Edward F. (1879–1956): ord. Aug. 10, 1905; bp. Burlington, 1945 56.

Ryan, Gerald J. (1923–85): ord. June 3, 1950; aux. Rockville Centre (Munatiana), 1977–85.

Ryan, James (1848–1923): b. Ireland; ord. Dec. 24, 1871; bp. Alton (now Springfield), Ill., 1888–1923.

Ryan, James H. (1886–1947): ord. June 5, 1909; rector Catholic University, 1928–35; tit. bp. Modra, 1933–35; bp., 1935–45, and first abp. Omaha, 1945–47.

Ryan, Patrick J. (1831–1911): b. Ireland; ord. Sept. 8, 1853; coad. bp. St. Louis (Tricomia), 1872–84; abp. Philadelphia, 1884–1911.

Ryan, Stephen, C.M. (1826 96): b. Canada; ord. June 24, 1849; bp. Buffalo, 1868–96.

Ryan, Vincent J. (1884–1951): ord. June 7, 1912; bp. Bismarck, 1940–41.

S

Salpointe, John B. (1825–98): b. France; ord. Dec. 20, 1851; v.a. Arizona (Dorylaeum), 1869–84; coad. abp. Santa Fe (Anazarbus), 1884–85; abp. Santa Fe, 1885–94 (res.).

San Pedro, Enrique, S.J. (1926–94): b. Cuba; ord. May 18, 1957; aux. bp. Galveston-Houston (Siccesi), 1986–91; coad. bp. Brownsville, Aug.–Nov., 1991; bp. Brownsville, 1991–94.

Scanlan, Lawrence (1843–1915): b. Ireland; ord. June 28, 1868; v.a. Utah (Laranda), 1887–91; bp. Salt Lake (now Salt Lake City), 1891–1915.

Scannell, Richard (1845–1916): b. Ireland; ord. Feb. 26, 1871; first bp. Concordia (now Salina), 1887–91; bp. Omaha, 1891–1916.

Scheerer, Louis A., O.P. (1909–66): ord. June 13, 1935; bp. Multan, Pakistan, 1960–66.

Schenk, Francis J. (1901–69): ord. June 13, 1926; bp. Crookston, 1945–60; bp. Duluth, 1960–69.

Scher, Philip G. (1880–1953): ord. June 6, 1904; bp. Monterey-Fresno, 1933–53.

Schexnayder, Maurice (1895–1981): ord. Apr. 11, 1925; aux. Lafayette (Tuscamia), 1951–56; bp. Lafayette, La., 1956–72 (res.).

Schierhoff, Andrew B. (1922–87): ord. Apr. 14, 1948; aux. La Paz, Bolivia (Gerenza), 1969–82; v.a. Pando, Bolivia, 1982–87.

Schinner, Augustine (1863–1937): ord. Mar. 7, 1886; first bp. Superior, 1905–13; first bp. Spokane, 1914–25 (res.).

Schlaefer Berg, Salvator, O.F.M. Cap. (1920–93): ord. June 5, 1946, v.a. Bluefields, Nicaragua (Fiumepiscense), 1970–93.

Schlarman, Joseph H. (1879–1951): ord. June 29, 1904; bp. Peoria, 1930–51.

Schlotterback, Edward F., O.S.F.S. (1912–94): ord. Dec. 17, 1938; v.a. Keetmanshoop, Namibia (Balanea) 1956–89 (res.).

Schmidt, Matthias W., O.S.B. (1931–92): ord. May 30,1957; aux. Jatai, Brazil (Mutugenna), 1972–76; bp. Ruy Barbosa, Brazil, 1976–92.

Schmitt, Adolph G., C.M.M. (1905–76): b. Bavaria, U.S. citizen 1945: v.a. Bulawayo (Nasai), Rhodesia (now Zimbabwe), 1951–55; first bp. Bulawayo, 1955–74 (res.). Murdered by terrorists.

Schmondiuk, Joseph (1912–1978): ord. Mar. 29, 1936; aux. Philadelphia exarchate (Zeugma in Syria), 1956–61; eparch Stamford, 1961–77; abp. Philadelphia, 1977–78.

Schott, Lawrence F. (1907–63): ord. July 15, 1935; aux. Harrisburg (Eluza), 1956 63.

Schrembs, Joseph (1866–1945): b. Germany; ord. June 29, 1889; aux. Grand Rapids (Sophene), 1911; first bp. Toledo, 1911–21: bp. Cleveland, 1921–45.

Schuck, James A., O.F.M. (1913–93): ord. June 11, 1940; prelate Cristalandia, Brazil (Avissa, 1959–78), 1959–88 (res.).

Schuler, Anthony J., S.J. (1869–1944) ord. June 27, 1901; first bp. El Paso, 1915–42 (res.).

Schulte, Paul (1890–1984): ord. June 11, 1915; bp. Leavenworth, 1937–46; abp. Indianapolis, 1946–70 (res.).

Schwebach, James (1847–1921): b. Luxembourg; ord. June 16, 1870; bp. La Crosse, 1892–1921.

Schwertner, August J. (1870–1939): ord. June 12, 1897; bp. Wichita, 1921–39.

Scully, William (1894–1969): ord. Sept. 20, 1919; coad. bp. Albany (Pharsalus), 1945–54; bp. Albany, 1954–69.

Sebastian, Jerome D. (1895–1960): ord. May 25, 1922; aux. Baltimore (Baris in Hellesponto), 1954–60.

Seghers, Charles J.: *See* SEGHERS, CHARLES JOHN.

Seidenbusch, Rupert, O.S.B. (1830–95): b. Germany; ord. June 22, 1853; v.a. Northern Minnesota (Halia), 1875–88 (res.).

Senyshyn, Ambrose, O.S.B.M. (1903–76): b. Galicia; ord. Aug. 23, 1931; aux. Ukrainian Catholic Diocese of U.S. (Maina). 1942–56; first bp. Stamford (Byzantine Rite), 1958–61; abp. Philadelphia (Byzantine Rite), 1961–76.

Seton, Robert J. (1839–1927): b. Italy, ord. Apr. 15, 1865; tit. abp. Heliopolis, 1903–27. Grandson of St. Elizabeth Seton.

Shahan, Thomas J. (1857–1932): ord. June 3, 1882; rector, Catholic University of America, 1909–27; tit. bp. Germanicopolis. 1914–32.

Shanahan (brothers): **Jeremiah F.** (1834–86): ord. July 3, 1859; first bp. Harrisburg, 1868–86. **John W.** (1846–1916): ord. Jan. 2, 1869; bp. Harrisburg, 1899–1916.

Shanley, John (1852–1909): ord. May 30, 1874; first bp. Jamestown (see transferred to Fargo in 1897), 1889–1909.

Shanley, Patrick H., O.C.D. (1896–1970): b. Ireland; ord. Dec. 21, 1930; U.S. citizen; prelate Infanta, P.I. (Sophene), 1953–60 (res.).

Shaughnessy, Gerald, S.M. (1887–1950): ord. June 20, 1920; bp. Seattle, 1933–50.

Shaw, John W. (1861–1934): ord. May 26, 1888; coad. bp. San Antonio (Castabala), 1910–11; bp. San Antonio, 1911–18; abp. New Orleans, 1918–34.

Shea, Francis R. (1913–94): ord. Mar. 19, 1939; bp. Evansville, 1970–89 (res.).

Sheehan, Edward T., C.M. (1888–1933): ord. June 7, 1916, v.a. Yukiang, China (Calydon), 1929–33.

Sheen, Fulton J. (1895–1979): ord. Sept. 20, 1919; aux. New York (Caesarina), 1951–66; bp. Rochester, 1966–69 (res.); tit. abp. Newport.

Shehan, Lawrence J. (1898–1984): ord. Dec. 23, 1922; aux. Baltimore and Washington (Lidda), 1945–53; bp. Bridgeport, 1953–61; coad. abp. Baltimore (Nicopolis ad Nestum), Sept.–Dec., 1961; abp. Baltimore 1961–74 (res.), cardinal 1965.

Sheil, Bernard J. (1886–1969); ord. May 21, 1910; aux. bp. Chicago (Pegae), 1928–69; tit. abp. Selge, 1959–69.

Shubsda, Thaddeus A. (1925–91): ord. Apr. 26, 1950; aux. Los Angeles (Trau), 1977–82; bp. Monterey, 1982–91.

Smith, Alphonse (1883–1935): ord. Apr. 18, 1908; bp. Nashville, 1924–35.

Smith, Eustace, O.F.M. (1908–75): ord. June 12, 1934; v.a. Beirut, Lebanon (Apamea Cibotus). 1958–73 (res.).

Smith, Leo R. (1905–63): ord. Dec. 21, 1929; aux. Buffalo (Marida), 1952–63; bp. Ogdensburg, 1963.

Smyth, Clement, O.C.S.O. (1810–65): b. Ireland; ord. May 29, 1841; coad. bp. Dubuque (Thennesus), 1857–58; bp. Dubuque, 1858–65.

Soenneker, Henry J. (1907–87): Ord. May 26, 1934; bp. Owensboro, 1961–82 (res.).

Spalding, John L. (1840–1916): ord. Dec. 19, 1863, first bp. Peoria, 1876–1908 (res.).

Spalding, Martin J. (1810–72): ord. Aug. 13, 1834; aux. Louisville (Lengone), 1848–50; bp. Louisville, 1850–64; abp. Baltimore, 1864–72.

Spellman, Francis J. (1889–1967): ord. May 14, 1916; aux. Boston (Sila), 1932–39; abp. New York, 1939–67; cardinal 1946.

Spence, John S. (1909–73): ord. Dec. 5, 1933; aux. Washington (Aggersel). 1964–73.

Stang, William (1854–1907): b. Germany; ord. June 15, 1878; first bp. Fall River, 1904–07.

Stanton, Martin W. (1897–1977): ord. June 14, 1924; aux. Newark (Citium) 1957–72 (res.).

Stariha, John (1845–1915): b. Austria; ord. Sept. 19, 1869; first bp. Lead (now Rapid City), 1902–09 (res.).

Steck, Leo J. (1898–1950): ord. June 8, 1924; aux. Salt Lake City (Ilium), 1948–50.

Stemper, Alfred M., M.S.C. (1913–84): ord. June 26, 1940; v.a. Kavieng (Eleutheropolis), 1957–66; first bp. Kavieng, 1966–80 (res.).

Stock, John (1918–72): ord. Dec. 4, 1943; aux. Philadelphia (Ukrainian Rite) (Pergamum), 1971–72.

Stritch, Samuel (1887–1958): ord. May 21, 1909; bp. Toledo, 1921–30; abp. Milwaukee, 1930–39; abp. Chicago, 1939–58 cardinal 1946.

Sullivan, Bernard, S.J. (1889–1970): ord, June 26, 1921; bp. Patna, India, 1929–46 (res.).

Sullivan, Joseph V. (1919–82): ord. June 1, 1946; aux. Kansas City-St. Joseph (Tagamuta), 1964–74; bp. Baton Rouge, 1974–82.

Swanstrom, Edward E. (1903–85): ord. June 2, 1928; aux. New York (Arba), 1960–78 (res.).

Sweeney, James J. (1898–1968): ord. June 20, 1925; first bp. Honolulu, 1941–68.

Swint, John J. (1879–1962): ord. June 23, 1904; aux. Wheeling (Sura), 1922; bp. Wheeling, 1922–62.

T

Takach, Basil (1879–1948): b. Austria-Hungary; ord. Dec. 12, 1902; first ap. ex. Pittsburgh Byzantine Rite (Zela), 1924–48.

Tanner, Paul F. (1905–94): ord. May 30, 1931; gen. sec. NCWC (now USCC), 1958–68; tit. bp. Lamasba, 1965; bp. St. Augustine, 1968–79 (res.).

Tarasevitch, Vladimir L., O.S.B. (1921–86): b. Byelorussia (White Russia); ord. May 26, 1949; ap. visitator (with residence in Chicago) for Byelorussians outside Soviet Union (Mariamme), 1983–86.

Taylor, John E., O.M.I. (1914–76): ord. May 25, 1940; bp. Stockholm, Sweden, 1962–76.

Thill, Francis A. (1893–1957): ord. Feb. 28, 1920; bp. Concordia (title changed to Salina in 1944), 1938–57.

Tief, Francis J. (1881–1965): ord. June 11, 1908; bp. Concordia (now Salina), 1921–38 (res.).

Tierney, Michael (1839–1908): b. Ireland; ord. May 26, 1866; bp. Hartford, 1894–1908.

Tihen, J. Henry (1861–1940): ord. Apr. 26, 1886; bp. Lincoln, 1911–17; bp. Denver, 1917–31 (res.).

Timon, John, C.M. (1797–1867): ord. Sept. 23, 1826; first bp. Buffalo, 1847–67.

Toebbe, Augustus M. (1829–84): b. Germany; ord. Sept. 14, 1854; bp. Covington, 1870–84.

Toolen, Thomas J. (1886–1976): ord. Sept. 27, 1910; bp. (pers. tit. abp., 1954), Mobile, 1927–69 (res.).

Topel, Bernard J. (1903–86): ord. June 7, 1927; coad. bp. Spokane (Binda), Sept. 21–25, 1955; bp. Spokane, 1955–78 (res.).

Tracy, Robert E. (1909–80): ord. June 12, 1932; aux. Lafayette, La. (Sergentiza), 1959–61; first bp. Baton Rouge, 1961–74 (res.).

Treacy, John P. (1890–1964): ord. Dec. 8, 1918; coad. bp. La Crosse (Metelis), 1945–48; bp. La Crosse, 1948–64.

Trobec, James (1838–1921): b. Austria; ord. Sept. 8, 1865; bp. St. Cloud, 1897–1914 (res.).

Tuigg, John (1820–89): b. Ireland; ord. May 14, 1850; bp. Pittsburgh, 1876–89.

Turner, William (1871–1936): b. Ireland; ord. Aug. 13, 1893; bp. Buffalo, 1919–36.

Tyler, William (1806–49): ord. June 3, 1829; first bp. Hartford, 1844–49.

U–V

Unterkoefler, Ernest L. (1917–93): ord. May 18, 1944; aux. Richmond (Latopolis) 1962–64; bp. Charleston, 1964–90 (res.).

Van de Velde, James O., S.J. (1795–1855): b. Belgium; ord. Sept. 16, 1827; bp. Chicago, 1849–53; bp. Natchez (now Jackson), 1953–55.

Van de Ven, Cornelius (1865–1932): b. Holland; ord. May 31, 1890; bp. Natchitoches (title changed to Alexandria, 1910), 1904–32.

Van de Vyver, Augustine (1844–1911) b. Belgium; ord. July 24, 1870; bp. Richmond, 1889–1911.

Vath, Joseph G. (1918–87): ord. June 7, 1941; aux. Mobile-Birmingham (Novaliciana), 1966–69; first bp. Birmingham, 1969–87.

Vehr, Urban J. (1891–1973): ord. May 29, 1915; bp. 1931–41, and first abp. Denver, 1941–67 (res.).

Verdaguer, Peter (1835–1911): b. Spain; ord. Dec. 12, 1862; v.a. Brownsville (Aulon), 1890–1911.

Verot, Augustin, S.S. (1805–76): b. France; ord. Sept. 20, 1828; v.a. Florida (Danaba), 1856–61; bp. Savannah, 1861–70; bp. St. Augustine, 1870–76.

Vertin, John (1844–99): b. Austria; ord. Aug. 31, 1866; bp. Sault Ste. Marie and Marquette (now Marquette), 1879–99.

Vogel, Cyril J. (1905–79): ord. June 7, 1931; bp. Salina, 1965–79.

Vonesh, Raymond J. (1916–91): ord. May 3, 1941; aux. Joliet (Vanariona), 1968–1991 (res. May; d. Aug.).

W

Wade, Thomas, S.M. (1893–1969): ord. June 15, 1922; v.a. Northern Solomons (Barbalissus), 1930–69.

Wadhams, Edgar (1817–91): convert, 1846; ord. Jan. 15, 1850; first bp. Ogdensburg 1872–91.

Waldschmidt, Paul E., C.S.C. (1920–94): ord June 24, 1946; aux. Portland, Ore. (Citium) 1978–90 (res.).

Walsh, Emmet (1892–1968): ord. Jan. 15, 1916; bp. Charleston, 1927–49; coad. bp. Youngstown (Rhaedestus), 1949–52; bp. Youngstown, 1952–68.

Walsh, James A., M.M. (1867–1936): ord. May 20, 1892; cofounder (with Thomas F. Price) of Maryknoll, first U.S. established foreign mission society and first sponsor of a U.S. foreign mission seminary; superior of Maryknoll, 1911–36; tit. bp. Syene, 1933–36.

Walsh, James E., M.M. (1891–1981): ord. Dec. 7, 1915; v.a. Kongmoon, China (Sata), 1927–36; superior of Maryknoll, 1936–46; general secretary, Catholic Central Bureau, Shanghai, China, 1948; imprisoned by Chinese communists, 1958–70.

Walsh, Louis S. (1858–1924): ord. Dec. 23, 1882; bp. Portland, Me., 1906–24.

Walsh, Thomas J. (1873–1952): ord. Jan. 27, 1900; bp. Trenton, 1918–28; bp., 1928–37, and first abp. 1937–52, Newark.

Ward, John (1857–1929): ord. July 17, 1884; bp. Leavenworth (now Kansas City), 1910–29.

Waters, Vincent S. (1904–74): ord. Dec. 8, 1931; bp. Raleigh, 1945–74.

Watson, Alfred M. (1907–90): ord. May 10, 1934; aux. Erie (Nationa), 1965–69; bp. Erie 1969–82 (res.).

Watterson, John A. (1844–99): ord. Aug. 9, 1868; bp. Columbus, 1880–99.

Wehrle, Vincent, O.S.B. (1855–1941): b. Switzerland; ord. Apr. 23, 1882; first bp. Bismarck, 1910–39 (res.).

Welch, Thomas A. (1884–1959): ord. June 11, 1909; bp. Duluth, 1926–59.

Weldon, Christopher J. (1905–82): ord. Sept. 21, 1939; bp. Springfield, Mass., 1950–77 (res.).

Whealon, John F. (1921–91): ord. May 26, 1945; aux. Cleveland (Andrapa), 1961–66; bp. Erie, 1966–69; abp. Hartford, 1969–91.

Whelan, James, O.P. (1822–78): b. Ireland; ord. Aug. 2, 1846; coad. bp. Nashville (Marcopolis), 1859–60; bp. Nashville, 1860–64 (res.).

Whelan, Richard V. (1809–74): ord. May 1, 1831 ; bp. Richmond, 1841–50, bp. Wheeling, 1850–74.

White, Charles (1879–1955): ord. Sept. 24, 1910; bp. Spokane, 1927–55.

Whitfield, James (1770–1834): b. England; ord. July 24, 1809; coad. bp. Baltimore (Apollonia), 1828; abp. Baltimore, 1828–34.

Wigger, Winand (1841–1901): ord. June 10, 1865; bp. Newark, 1881–1901.

Willging, Joseph C. (1884–1959): ord. June 20, 1908; first bp. Pueblo, 1942–59.

Williams, John J. (1822–1907): ord. May 17, 1845; bp., 1866–75, and first abp., 1875–1907, Boston.

Willinger, Aloysius J., C.Ss.R. (1886–1973): ord. July 2, 1911; bp. Ponce, P.R., 1929–46; coad. bp. Monterey-Fresno, 1946–53; bp. Monterey-Fresno, 1953–67 (res.).

Winkelmann, Christian H. (1883–1946): ord. June 11, 1907; aux. St. Louis (Sita), 1933–39, bp. Wichita, 1939–46.

Wood, James F. (1813–83): convert, 1836; ord. Mar. 25, 1844; coad. bp. Philadelphia (Antigonea), 1857–60; bp., 1860–75, and first abp., 1875–83, Philadelphia.

Woznicki, Stephen (1894–1968): ord. Dec. 22, 1917; aux. Detroit (Peltae), 1938–50; bp. Saginaw, 1950–68.

Wright, John J. (1909–79): ord. Dec. 8, 1935; aux. Boston (Egee), 1947–50; bp. Worcester, 1950–59; bp. Pittsburgh, 1959–69; cardinal, 1969; prefect Congregation of the Clergy, 1969–79.

Wurm, John N. (1927–84): ord. Apr. 3, 1954; aux. St. Louis (Plestia), 1976–81; bp. Belleville, 1981–84.

Y–Z

Young, Josue (1808–66): ord. Apr. 1, 1838; bp. Erie, 1854–66.

Zaleski, Alexander, M. (1906–75): ord. July 12, 1931; aux. Detroit (Lybe), 1950–64; coad. bp. Lansing, 1964–65; bp. Lansing 1966–75.

Zardetti, Otto (1847–1902): b. Switzerland; ord. Aug. 21, 1870; first bp. St. Cloud, 1889–94; abp. Bucharest, Rumania, 1894–95 (res.).

Zuroweste, Albert R. (1901–87): ord. June 8, 1924; bp. Belleville, 1948–76 (res.).

(Source: The Catholic Almanac.)

AMERICAN CATHOLIC HISTORICAL ASSOCIATION (ACHA)

A national learned society whose purpose is to promote knowledge of the history of the Catholic Church broadly considered and to advance historical scholarship among American Catholics and other members of the association. It was founded in Cleveland, Ohio, during Christmas week of 1919 by a group of historians who wished to bring more Catholics into the main professional organization, the American Historical Association (AHA), of which it became an affiliated society. A former president of the AHA, J. Franklin Jameson, advised and encouraged the founders, and in recognition of his help the ACHA later conferred on him the only honorary membership it has ever awarded. It was incorporated under the laws of the District of Columbia and is recognized by the United States Catholic Conference.

Until 1966, by an unwritten bylaw excluding clerics, all the presidents and first vice presidents (who succeed automatically to the presidency) were laymen; in that year Philip Hughes was the first priest to be president. Priests had often been second vice presidents from the beginning, and women occasionally from 1955 on. The first woman, Annabelle M. Melville, became president in 1989. The first non-Catholic president, Albert C. Outler, held office in 1972. Three of the presidents subsequently became presidents of the AHA, namely, Carlton J. H. Hayes, David Herlihy, and Caroline Walker Bynum. The first permanent secretary was Peter Guilday, one of the founders and a priest-professor at The Catholic University of America, where the executive office has always been located. His successors were John Tracy Ellis (1941–61), who was also president in 1969, and Robert Trisco (1961–), who also became treasurer in 1983.

Since its founding the ACHA has held annual three-day meetings in large cities in conjunction with the AHA with only three exceptions (all in the first decade). It regularly sponsors sessions jointly with the AHA and the American Society of Church History and sometimes with other specialized societies. Besides those winter meetings, since 1972 the ACHA has held a two-day meeting each spring in a different place, usually at a Catholic university or college.

As its journal the ACHA adopted the *Catholic Historical Review,* a quarterly which had been published since its inception in 1915 by The Catholic University of America Press. It carries each year the address of the outgoing president and the reports of the officers and committees, as well as news about the ACHA's activities in each issue. The ACHA has published three volumes of papers presented at annual meetings and two volumes of documents edited by Leo Francis Stock *(United States Ministers to the Papal States* and *Consular Relations between the United States and the Papal States).* It also sponsored the editing, completed by Thomas O'Brien Hanley, S.J., of the *John Carroll Papers* (3 vols.).

The ACHA offers two annual book prizes. On the occasion of its twenty-fifth anniversary it established the John Gilmary Shea Prize, named after the pioneer historian of American Catholicism (1824–92); it is a cash sum given to the author of a work that in a preceding twelve-month period makes what the committee of judges considers to be the most significant contribution to the history of the Catholic Church by an American or Canadian citizen or permanent resident. The first award was conferred in 1946.

The other prize perpetuates the memory of Howard R. Marraro of Columbia University who died in 1972, bequeathing to the ACHA $10,000 to be invested as a fund, the income from which is presented to the author of the most outstanding book of the year (in English) on the history of Italy or Italo-American relations.

In 1995 the ACHA created the John Tracy Ellis Memorial Fund to aid doctoral students with their research by means of modest grants.

The membership of the ACHA reached a peak of 1,332 in 1961, and in the 1990s remained above eleven hundred. There are many members in foreign countries, especially

Canada. Membership is open to students and amateurs of history. In addition, the ACHA has appointed seven permanent corresponding fellows, who represent as many European countries. They are expected to help acquaint the members of the ACHA with professional developments in their homelands and to convey information about the ACHA's work to their countrymen who might be interested.

The ACHA is a constituent member of both the American National Committee of the International Commission for Comparative Church History and the Joint Committee of Catholic Learned Societies and Scholars, on which it is represented by a permanent delegate.

The ACHA is the recognized collective Catholic voice in the historical profession of the United States.

ROBERT TRISCO

AMERICAN CATHOLIC QUARTERLY REVIEW

A semipopular journal of opinion that was published in Philadelphia from 1876 to 1924. The first editor (1876–89) was the Rev. James A. Corcoran, a professor at St. Charles Seminary, Overbrook, and one of the country's leading Catholic theologians. The review featured articles on theology, philosophy, history, literature, and apologetics, which tended to be longer and more substantial than similar articles in the *Catholic World* and *Ave Maria*. In the early years contributors included Orestes Brownson, James Cardinal Gibbons, Bishop John Lancaster Spalding, Bishop John J. Keane, John Gilmary Shea, and other prominent American Catholics whose articles (as John Tracy Ellis pointed out) are now primary sources on these men. A frequently discussed topic in the heyday of Darwinism was the compatibility of Christianity and evolution, which was the subject of several articles in the review by the Notre Dame scientist Fr. John A. Zahm, C.S.C., and the English biologist St. George Mivart.

In the 1890s and early 1900s, the review frequently carried articles by professors at The Catholic University of America, including John A. Ryan, William Kerby, Edward A. Pace, Thomas J. Shahan, Charles Grannan, and Thomas Bouquillon. Over the years the ideological range of the contributors was especially noteworthy with conservatives like Condé Pallen, Msgr. Thomas Preston, and Salvator Brandi, S.J., rubbing shoulders with "Americanists" like Dr. Edward McGlynn and the English "Modernist" George Tyrrell, S.J. Circulation declined from 7,500 in 1910 to less than 1,500 in 1923. There is a general index for volumes 1–25 (1876–1900).

See also CORCORAN, JAMES ANDREW.

Appleby, R. Scott. *"American Catholic Quarterly Review."* *Religious Periodicals of the United States,* ed. Charles H. Lippy. Westport, Connecticut, 1986, 18–21.

THOMAS J. SHELLEY

AMERICAN CATHOLIC SEXUAL ETHICS

To date, the story of the actual sexual experience of American Catholics has not been told. The ecclesial and theological history demonstrates a constant struggle to relate Roman Catholic sexual ethics to the American context. From the eighteenth century, Catholic clergy warned that Catholics would be corrupted by their association with those outside the faith. "Keeping company" with non-Catholics—in, e.g., their dances, festivities and amusements, dating or marriage—undermines the Catholic sexual ethic. That ethic identified heterosexual marriage as the sole locus for sexual activity, and heterosexual marriage between Catholics as the norm. This ethic had developed in the European moral manuals that Americans later adapted to their country. Scholars attribute the style and substance of American Catholic sexual ethics to the immigrant Church, whose French and Irish priests were inheritors of a rigorist, Jansenist tradition (Ellis, 1971).

Nineteenth-Century Teaching

Many seminaries in the United States used American moral manuals, e.g., Archbishop Francis Patrick Kenrick's *Theologia Moralis* (1841) and the Sabetti-Barrett *Compendium Theologiae Moralis,* for instruction in sexual ethics. Sexual ethics is treated under certain key headings in the manuals: the sixth and ninth commandments, the sacrament of matrimony, and the cardinal virtue of temperance. The sixth and ninth commandments prohibit sins of impurity, in deeds and in thoughts. As manuals for confessors, the texts identify sexual sins in terms of their gravity. Fornication, adultery, incest, rape, abduction and sacrilege, as well as masturbation, sodomy, and bestiality are sins of impurity. So too are certain touches, looks, reading, and conversation; they are dangerous if they lead to venereal pleasure. There is no *parvitas materiae*—no small or slight matter—in the sixth and ninth commandments; all sexual sins contain grave matter.

The matrimony section of the manuals describes the ritual and ethics of marriage. Although spouses owe the marital debt, it is occasionally reasonable for them to refuse sexual relations (danger of venereal disease, risk to life, unreasonable frequency of demands). Also listed are the prohibitions of any interference (contraception or "onanism") with the proper end of the marital act.

Both priests and moral theologians warned that occasions of sins of impurity and dangers to the sacrament of matrimony are posed by the non-Catholic presence, especially by mixed marriages. Parallel approaches to sexual sin are found in Catholic revival movements of the nineteenth century, whose preachers taught a "rigorous moralism," with drunkenness and impurity identified as the two major sins (Dolan, 1978).

The synodal and conciliar legislation of the American Church, in addition to the national pastorals of the American bishops, demonstrates the resolution of the U.S. hierarchy to defend the indissolubility of marriage and to prevent mixed marriages. The longest decree of the first National Synod in 1791 is on the sacrament of matrimony. Councils and pastorals of 1840, 1866, and 1884 condemn mixed marriages; ringing condemnations of divorce emerge from the 1866 Second Plenary Council. The Church's fears that mixed marriages will destroy Catholics' faith are summarized in the Baltimore Catechism (1889).

Toward the end of the nineteenth century, significant changes in American theology, including moral theology, occur, but are thwarted by papal condemnations of Americanism and Modernism in 1899 and 1907. The changes do not extend to sexual ethics, where American theologians remain faithful to the manuals. Adolphe Tanquerey places sexual questions in separately bound volumes, and in the appendix, of his manual, and appears stricter than Kenrick (Gardella, 1985).

Twentieth-Century Developments

By 1911, the sterilization of criminals and of the mentally defective is a pressing question for Catholic moralists, as some states pass sterilization legislation. The disagreement among theologians is noteworthy; according to John A. Ryan, Catholics may disagree because the papal teaching is ambiguous. When Ryan addresses the new subject of "birth control" in 1916, however, there is "no possibility of a difference of opinion" (Ryan, 1916). The 1919 National Pastoral rejects contraception as "detestable." The letter states that both men and women must maintain purity before marriage, and criticizes divorce, "our national scandal."

In the 1940s and 1950s, theologians discuss a range of sexual questions. Rhythm and other means of birth control take center stage; other prominent topics include sterility tests, sterilization, courtship and marriage, artificial insemination, the problem of divorce, *amplexus reservatus* (vaginal penetration without orgasm), *copula dimidiata* (partial vaginal penetration), homosexuality, psychiatry, and the Kinsey reports. By the 1950s, American moral theologians have distinguished their ethic from the European in one way: John Connery argues that in the United States, dances are not an occasion of sin. Meanwhile, the effect of personalism begins to appear in the ethic of marriage, as ethicists emphasize the secondary (unitive) aspects of marriage while continuing to identify procreation as primary (Ford and Kelly, vol. l).

In the 1950s and 1960s, contraception predominates. Rhythm is the cynosure, as moral theologians ask what circumstances justify Catholic limitation of family size. The opposition to artificial birth control is vigorous. In anticipation of the nation's first Catholic president, theologians discuss whether a Catholic president should sign laws permitting contraceptives (Connery, 1959). By 1964,

theologians are divided about the subject of birth control. Jesuit Richard McCormick suggests that probabilism applies to contraception. Meanwhile Americans, including bishops and John Ford, John Noonan, Patrick and Patricia Crowley, serve on the papal birth control commission. Noonan's historical analysis of contraception provides powerful scholarly impetus for a change in official Church teaching, while John Ford defends traditional teaching in the name of papal authority. From this point on, sexual ethical questions are inextricably linked to ecclesiological questions of the magisterium's authority.

On July 29, 1968, Pope Paul VI issues the prohibition of artificial birth control, *Humanae vitae.* Charles Curran presents a statement by dissenting theologians in Washington, D.C. The board of trustees of The Catholic University authorizes an investigation of its professor Curran; in 1968, the Board of Inquiry clears Curran—in this round of inquiry. Meanwhile, other theologians, joined by numerous bishops, defend Paul VI. Germain Grisez, Joseph Boyle, and William E. May are consistent defenders of the magisterial teaching in the United States.

Humanae vitae is the watershed in American Catholic sexual ethics, as large numbers of American Catholics dissent from the papal teaching. Surveys suggest that American Catholic use of contraceptives parallels that of non-Catholics. Post-*Humanae vitae,* American Catholics challenge other aspects of the Church's sexual teaching. Divorce and remarriage, premarital sexual relations, reproductive technology, homosexuality, and the roles of men and women in marriage and the family become controverted questions for American Catholics and their theologians. Throughout the 1970s, Catholic hospital policies on sterilization are questioned.

In 1975 the Congregation for the Doctrine of the Faith reaffirms prohibitions on masturbation, homosexuality, and premarital sex as intrinsically evil actions, and reasserts the traditional teaching on parvity of matter, in *Persona Humana.* In 1977 a committee of the Catholic Theological Society of America writes *Human Sexuality* in an effort to relate the Christian tradition of sexual ethics to the North American context. The authors replace the traditional ends of marriage, "procreative" and "unitive," with "creative" and "integrative" goals; sexuality should foster "creative growth toward integration." The reaction to the book—loud praise *and* loud protest among American theologians—illustrates the pluralism of opinion in the American Catholic community. Anthony Kosnik is disciplined for his participation in the project.

Jesuit John McNeill's 1976 book, *The Church and the Homosexual,* asks Catholics to reconsider traditional prohibitions on all homosexual activity. McNeill is silenced after the book's publication, and is dismissed from the Jesuits in 1988 when he breaks his silence to criticize a 1986 Vatican letter on homosexuality.

A 1986 Vatican ruling finds Charles Curran "not suitable nor eligible to teach Catholic theology" because of his writings on contraception, masturbation, abortion, euthanasia, premarital sex, homosexuality, sterilization, and artificial insemination.

The late André Guindon argued that over the past twenty years American Catholic sexual ethics has undergone a "substantial paradigmatic shift" from the act-centered manualist tradition. Yet he warned that contemporary Catholic moralists still "construe 'sex' as genital acts . . . most Catholic moralists seem to buy the inventory of sexual activities wholesale from the old textbooks which they denigrate in their theoretical considerations" (Guindon 1987, 315). Guindon's alternative "sexual lifestyles" approach was investigated by the Congregation for the Doctrine of the Faith in 1992.

In the 1980s and 1990s, public attention turned to the sexual ethics of Catholic clergy who confronted serious charges of sexual misconduct and sexual abuse.

Pope John Paul II has reiterated traditional Catholic moral theology and sexual ethics in his encyclicals *Veritatis Splendor* and *Evangelium Vitae*. The encyclicals have been interpreted as in part a critical response to the permissive sexual climate of the United States. As in the eighteenth century, American Catholics at the end of the twentieth century are warned to resist any American interpretations of sexuality that violate the traditional prohibitions of the unchanging Roman Catholic sexual ethic.

See also CURRAN (CHARLES) CONTROVERSY, THE.

Connery, John, S.J. "May A Catholic President Sign . . . ?" *America* 102 (December 12, 1959) 353–54.

Dolan, Jay P. *Catholic Revivalism: The American Experience 1830–1900.* Indiana: University of Notre Dame Press, 1978.

Ellis, John Tracy. "The Formation of the American Priest: A Historical Perspective." *The Catholic Priest in the United States.* Collegeville, Minn.: St. John's University Press, 1971, 3–110.

Ford, John C., S.J., and Gerald Kelly, S.J. *Contemporary Moral Theology.* Westminster, Md.: The Newman Press, 1958, 1963.

Gardella, Peter. *Innocent Ecstasy: How Christianity Gave America an Ethic of Sexual Pleasure.* New York: Oxford, 1985.

Guindon, André. "Sexual Acts or Sexual Lifestyles: A Methodological Problem in Sexual Ethics." *Eglise et Théologie* 18 (1987) 315.

Lawler, Ronald, Joseph Boyle, Jr., and William E. May. *Catholic Sexual Ethics: A Summary, Explanation and Defense.* Huntington, Ind.: Our Sunday Visitor, Inc., 1985.

McCormick, Richard A., S.J. *Notes on Moral Theology 1965–1980.* Lanham, Md.: University Press of America, 1981.

_____. *Notes on Moral Theology 1981–1984* Lanham, Md.: University Press of America, 1984.

Noonan, John T., Jr. *Contraception: A History of Its Treatment by the Catholic Theologians and Canonists.* New York: New American Library, 1967.

Ryan, John A. "Family Limitation." *American Ecclesiastical Review* 54 (1916) 684–96.

LESLIE C. GRIFFIN

AMERICAN CATHOLIC SPIRITUALITY

Basic Concepts

"Spirituality," as used in this article, refers to the lens through which people interpret and transform their lives in view of ultimate values. To use an analogy: a kaleidoscope is composed of colored pebbles, glass planes, and mirrors which rotate in variegated patterns. The pebbles represent the various components of Catholic living: doctrine, beliefs, ascetic and devotional practices, family, parish, attitudes about the body, relationship to culture, involvement in society, etc. The planes and mirrors represent spiritualities, which arrange the components in patterns as the context changes. Spirituality focuses life, giving it direction and coherence.

"American Catholic spirituality" refers to the various spiritualities arising out of the geographic, historical, and cultural experiences of Catholic people living in the area now encompassed by the United States. The ways in which they have interpreted and transformed their lives have shifted to reflect the place, time, and culture in which they lived. Most of their spiritual traditions were received from Europe. Yet, as time went on these European traditions developed in the peculiarly American mix of ethnic pluralism, the separation of Church and state, democracy, capitalism, and individualism. The study of American Catholic spirituality is still in its early stages. Some major figures and movements have been analyzed, but significant gaps remain.

Spanish Colonies

Columbus' landing on the island of San Salvador in 1492 opened a new world to Spanish exploration, a conquest that brought wealth to the mother country but decimated the Native American population. Hernán Cortéz entered Mexico in 1519. Missionaries accompanied the conquistadors. The first mission in what is now the U.S.A. was established in 1565 in St. Augustine, Florida. Later foundations developed from the conquest of Mexico; churches and settlements were established in Arizona (1598), New Mexico (1598), Texas (1659), and California (1769).

Belden C. Lane has suggested that a key aspect of both Spanish culture and spirituality is the stoic acceptance of pain and a "passion for twisting impoverished pain into radiance" (*Landscapes,* 78; see 74–85 for full discussion). The missionaries were prepared to suffer and even face martyrdom for the spread of the faith. A profound respect for suffering can still be seen in the spirituality of the Catholics of the Southwest, especially Mexican Americans.

The spirituality of the Spanish missions developed in the clash of cultures. The missionaries saw the Native Americans as pagans who would face eternal damnation unless they were enlightened by the gospel. Some (though not all) supported the bloody and repressive practices of the conquistadors. One priest reported, "The Indians, being children of fear, are more strongly appealed to by the glistening of the sword than by the voice of five missionaries" (Dolan, *Experience,* 47). The missionaries also used moral force. In their preaching they painted vivid pictures of the fires of hell in order to frighten the Native Americans into converting. "Conversion" usually meant changing the Native Americans into Europeans.

Patrick W. Carey has suggested that various missionaries pursued two divergent strategies: separation and incorporation, on the one hand, and affirmation of Native American culture on the other (*Catholics,* 6). The most common strategy involved separating the Native Americans from their nomadic culture and incorporating them into the stable, semimonastic lifestyle of the missions. The missionaries provided a structure which included "regular hours of prayer, a cycle of annual liturgical celebrations, a cult of Mary and the saints, seasons of fasting, and daily catechetical instruction" (Carey, *Catholics,* 6). The Native Americans were also taught other skills, such as farming or crafts, to incorporate them into the settled life of the mission. Junípero Serra (1717–84), the founder of several California missions, adopted this approach. Other missionaries, such as Eusebio Kino, S.J. (1645–1711), while approving of missions, attempted to use Native American language and culture to explain Christian concepts.

French Colonies

French exploration of the New World began under Jacques Cartier in the early sixteenth century. French missionaries began evangelizing Native Americans in Acadia in the early seventeenth century. French exploration—and missionary endeavors—followed the waterways: down the St. Lawrence River, throughout the Great Lakes, and down the Mississippi to New Orleans.

The French evangelization of Native Americans was carried on principally by the Jesuits. As in the case of the Spanish, their European culture came into conflict with the culture of the Native Americans. The early Jesuits attempted to adapt to their nomadic lifestyle, but this approach "proved ineffective in establishing a stable Christian life among the tribes" (Carey, *Catholics,* 10). The missionaries then moved to a strategy of "reductions," similar to the Spanish missions. These were enclaves in which converted Native Americans would be separated from their unconverted counterparts. In the reductions the Native Americans could be introduced to the catechism and to a routine of spiritual discipline. Like the Spanish, the Jesuits

also followed a strategy of frightening people into conversion. One report from the *Jesuit Relations* says, "We have given here, within four or five months, some Instructions on Hell by means of certain Mournful Songs and some spectacular representations, which have had considerable influence on our savages" (Dolan, *Experience,* 52). The Jesuits were, however, more willing than the Spanish to learn the languages of the native peoples.

Seventeenth-century France witnessed a time of cultural, political, and spiritual grandeur. Lane notes that in France one finds a "spirituality that thrived on images of hierarchical authority, whether these were defined as heavenly, royal, or sacerdotal" (87). The grandeur of royalty, seen most clearly at the palace of Versailles, was also applied to God and to the heavenly queen, Mary. One adopted an attitude of abnegation and self-abasement in the face of such majesty (Lane, 87–89). One could expect suffering on earth in order to prepare for the glories of heaven. Kateri Tekakwitha (ca. 1656–80) embodies this spirituality. The young Mohawk woman became a model Christian after her baptism in 1676. She was revered for her devotion to prayer, fasting, and penance. She made a private vow of celibacy. Her tomb became a place of pilgrimage, and she was declared "Blessed" in 1980.

The Jesuits believed that just as the early Church was built upon the blood of martyrs, so too would be the Church in the new world. Carey notes, "the Jesuits' missionary spirit was tied to their mystical and physical identification with Jesus, even to the point of suffering and death" (*Catholics,* 248). Jesuits Isaac Jogues (1607–46) and Jean de Brébeuf (1593–1649) endured heroic sufferings and painful deaths in bearing witness to the gospel.

English Colonies

In 1633 Cecil Calvert, an English Catholic, obtained from King Charles I a charter for a propriety colony, which he named Maryland. His efforts to found a colony received support from wealthy Catholics, but from the beginning Maryland was religiously pluralistic. He persuaded some Jesuits to accompany him on his first voyage (1634), asking them to minister to colonists and Native Americans alike. English-speaking Catholics faced a set of circumstances quite different from their Spanish and French coreligionists. They were surrounded by Protestant culture and conscious of their minority status. John Carroll, first bishop of Baltimore, spoke to a congregation: "Your particular circumstances call upon you for uncommon watchfulness over yourselves, and unusual exertions in all the exercises of the Xtian [i.e., Christian] life. The impressions made by your conduct will be lasting impressions" (Curran, *Spirituality,* 132).

The spirituality of English Catholic colonists was rooted in their experience of being a religious minority. After the Glorious Revolution of 1688 Catholics in Maryland were excluded from participation in politics, though some Catholic families still enjoyed social and economic prestige. Richard Challoner (1691–1781), the English bishop who published *Garden of the Soul* in 1740, became the most influential spiritual writer among Anglo-American Catholics. He taught a down-to-earth piety which emphasized "strong moralism, the promotion . . . of mental prayer for everyone, and some knowledge of affective prayer" (Chinnici, *Living Stones*, 10). The direct, personal experience of God was open to all. These values fitted well into the colonists' lifestyle. They attended to their duties, held prayer services in their homes (since priests were often not available), and did not call public attention to their Catholicity.

John Carroll, the first bishop of Baltimore (elected by his clergy in 1789), offers a clear embodiment of English colonial spirituality. Joseph P. Chinnici has suggested that Carroll fostered "a communal spiritual life reflecting the compatibility between Catholicism and the value of religious liberty." Carroll in his preaching sought to impart an attitude of "tolerance, mutual respect, and rational argument" (6 and 7). His positive view of the human person presumed a close connection between nature and grace. Rational preparation could open one to the influence of God's grace. Such a view was well suited to the colonies' pluralistic environment, where diverse groups could appeal to a common rationality if not to a common set of beliefs.

Chinnici has suggested that Carroll's spirituality was built upon three pillars: religious exercises, moral conduct, and "fervor" (26–34). For religious exercises, Carroll fostered participation in the sacraments and the reading of Scripture. He especially recommended reception of penance and the Eucharist. He had the Douay-Reims translation of the Bible printed in the colonies in 1790. In his view upright moral conduct would deflect criticism of Catholics. Chinnici summarizes Carroll's recommendations in his lenten pastoral letter of February 1792: "temperance, self-denial, fasting, voluntary mortification, discipline, meditation, reading, and works of charity" (29). Catholics should do their duty in all things and seek conformity to God's will. Finally, Carroll, encouraged Catholics to have "fervor." Chinnici notes that *fervor* meant interiority, a piety centered in the will and its dispositions. It signified, above all . . . 'Transforming into our hearts the sentiments and affections of Jesus Christ'" (30).

Elizabeth Ann Seton (1774–1821), the first American-born person to be canonized, also lived during this time of republican Catholicism. She was born into a well-to-do Episcopalian family in New York and, at age nineteen married a merchant, William Seton. From 1794 to 1798 the Setons' business thrived but took a turn for the worse after that. In addition, William became ill with tuberculosis. Elizabeth accompanied William to Italy, where he hoped to recuperate, but he died there in 1803. Elizabeth was left a young widow with five children. She was be-friended by a local family, the Filicchi's, who introduced her to Catholicism. After much soul-searching she joined the Catholic Church in 1805. She eventually started a school for girls in Baltimore in 1808 and in 1809 moved the school to Emmitsburg, Maryland, where she also began her religious congregation, the Sisters of Charity.

Mother Seton encountered much suffering in her life. She faced poverty after becoming accustomed to a life of comfort; she attended the deaths of her husband, her oldest daughter, and other close relatives; she faced rejection from her family after she became a Catholic; she struggled to found a religious congregation. Yet her spirituality was marked by confidence in God and even joy in her lot. Her letters attest to her profound devotion to prayer, but her spirituality also has an active cast. She wrote to one of her sisters, "This is not a country, my dear one, for Solitude and Silence, but of warfare and crucifixion" (Kelly and Melville, 35). Her biographers suggest that her spirituality was especially marked by three loves: for her newfound faith, for God, and for the Eucharist. She told her spiritual director, "Now I think for every spark of desire I have ever had to love our God and to show I love, I have a towering flame" (65). Mother Seton's Sisters of Charity now serve across the nation. She was beatified in 1975.

1815–66

The years 1815–66 brought enormous changes both in the Catholic population and in the nation's reaction to the Catholic Church. During this time the Catholic population increased 1,300 percent, "from about 318,000 in 1830—3 percent of the total American white population—to 4.5 million in 1870, representing about 13 percent of that population. By 1850 Catholicism was the largest single denomination in the country" (Carey, *Catholics*, 31). This influx of immigrants sometimes led to virulent anti-Catholic attitudes. Anti-Catholic riots occurred throughout the 1830s, 1840s, and 1850s, and prejudice against Catholics culminated in the founding of the Know-Nothing Party. This changed cultural context gave rise to two distinguishable Catholic spiritualities: that of the immigrant Church, which by far influenced the greater number of Catholics, and that of the upper classes who were affected by American Romanticism. These spiritualities differed in their views of the human person, American culture, the Church, and asceticism.

Church of the Immigrants

Under the leadership of strong episcopal spokesmen such as Martin John Spalding (1818–72), archbishop of Baltimore, and John Hughes (1797–1864), archbishop of New York, the immigrant Church developed a spirituality focused upon the local parish. The newcomers often felt alienated from Anglo Protestant culture. They spoke languages other than English and held different cultural values. Spalding noted the evil of the prejudice they often encountered: "The serpent of religious bigotry soon entered into this fair paradise, marring its beauty, infecting its hitherto virgin atmosphere with its poisonous breath" (*Miscellanea* [Baltimore: John Murphy & Co., 1869] 605). The parish would thus became the spiritual home for people who had been uprooted from their native land and felt unwelcome in their adopted country.

Socially and economically, the needs of immigrants were addressed through parish confraternities, associations, and credit unions. Spiritually, their needs were addressed through parish missions, which sought to stir up more fervent reception of the sacraments, and through devotions to the Holy Spirit, the Sacred Heart, the Blessed Sacrament, and to Mary and the saints. Often such devotions were publicly celebrated. Ann Taves notes that "by the middle decades of the nineteenth century, the reception of the sacraments was overshadowed for most lay Catholics by devotional practices" (viii). Devotions helped preserve people's cultural and ethnic identity and distinguished Catholics from the Protestant culture.

John Neumann (1811–60), superior of the Redemptorists in the United States and later bishop of Philadelphia, embodied the spirituality of devotionalism. In the mid-1850s he established the Archconfraternity of the Blessed Sacrament, and he fostered the Forty Hours devotion. Chinnici notes that Neumann "emphasized the social cohesion created by orderly and devout participation in church services, frequent reception of the sacraments, pious practices, and membership in confraternities" (70).

Immigrant spirituality emphasized the corporate and hierarchic nature of the Catholic Church. The divinely instituted Church stood against Protestant mainline culture and challenged the capitalist economy. The Church offered a vision of community in contrast to the individualism and self-interest taking over the culture. "Avarice," complained Spalding, "is the besetting sin of the age. Ours is, emphatically, the enlightened age of *dollars and cents!*" (394). Jesus, on the other hand, preached "a religion which solaced and raised up the poor" (133). Jesus could identify with the immigrants' experience, and they in turn with his. The Church's discipline, Hughes also noted, could restrain passion, keep a focus upon the common good, and ennoble the human heart (Chinnici, 61).

American Catholic Romanticism

The years 1815–66 also saw the emergence of a spirituality very different from that of the immigrant Church, a spirituality eager to dialogue with American culture rather than stand against it. Carey has labeled this movement "American Catholic Romanticism." ("American Catholic Romanticism, 1830–1888," *Catholic Historical Review* 64 [October 1988] 590–606). The founders of the movement, Orestes Brownson (1803–76) and Isaac Hecker (1819–88), both converts to Catholicism, were products of the intellectual movements stirring in New England in the mid-nineteenth century.

Orestes Brownson, the older of the two, was a prolific writer whose works have never been fully collected but would run to over thirty volumes. Brownson embodied the restless spirit of his age and journeyed through a series of spiritual and intellectual conversions. In 1832 he started a study of French and German and a systematic reading of theology and philosophy, a project which would last the rest of his life. He converted to Catholicism in 1844 and remained a Catholic until his death in 1876.

Brownson's spirituality was deeply influenced by his intellectual quest. Early in his study (1832) he came under the influence of the French philosopher Victor Cousin (1792–1867). Cousin was interested in the subject-object dialectic and attempted to establish an objective foundation for knowledge outside of the subjective categories of thinkers like Kant and Hegel. Brownson wrote that "man lives not by himself alone, but by communion with an object not himself; and his actual life partakes alike of the object and the subject" (Carey, *Brownson,* 242). He agreed with Cousin that God is most deeply available through intuition: "the race lives by immediate communion with God, therefore inspired by him, and hence in its normal state aspires to him" (246). Nonetheless, this intuitive grasp of God needed to be strengthened by rational reflection.

In discussing spiritual discipline, Brownson fell within Catholic revivalism (see Dolan, *Revivalism*). Brownson believed that Christian living involved one's heart as well as one's head. "Religion must appeal to the heart, rouse the passions, strike on the senses, affect the sensibilities. It must awaken enthusiasm . . . ." (Carey, *Brownson,* 252). He supported parish retreats and missions as means for awakening people from spiritual slumber. He especially encouraged lay spirituality: "in our own country, if we mean religion shall prosper, the Church take root and flourish in the land, we must leave laymen free to do all that laymen can do . . ." (Chinnici, 101). He recommended the reading and study of Scripture as important means of spiritual growth. He also recommended personal prayer and meditation, especially the type of meditation described in St. Ignatius' *Spiritual Exercises* (Carey, *Brownson,* 44). He often warned against the excesses of sentimental devotionalism.

Isaac Hecker (1819–88) also became a leading spokesperson for American Catholic Romanticism. He was born into a German immigrant family in New York City. After a few years of elementary education he joined his brothers in the family business, a bakery. By the mid-1830s the Hecker brothers had also become deeply involved in social reform, an interest that would mark the remainder of Hecker's life.

Hecker had a mystical bent and powerful spiritual experiences. An 1844 diary entry reads, "Where shall we find

God? Within. How shall we hear the voices of angels? Listen with the inner ear" (Chinnici, 110). He met Brownson in 1841 and continued to seek the older man's advice for the next few years, finally entering the Catholic Church in 1844. The following year, he joined the Redemptorists with the intention of preaching to the Protestant majority in the United States. After his novitiate and seminary studies in Belgium and Holland he was ordained to the priesthood in 1849 and sent to the United States to preach missions to English-speaking Catholics. Problems arose within the Redemptorists, however, and eventually in 1858 Hecker received the blessing of Pope Pius IX to begin a new religious order, the Paulists, dedicated to converting the United States to Catholicism. "My vocation," he said, "was to labor for the conversion of my non-Catholic fellow countrymen" (Chinnici, 95). His approach to Protestants was warm and friendly, quite in contrast to the polemics of the day, and he was much in demand as a public speaker. His 1855 book, *Questions of the Soul,* attracted many readers. He also made use of mass media, founding the journal the *Catholic World* (1865) and the Catholic Publication Society (forerunner to Paulist Press) (1866).

Hecker's spirituality focused upon the Holy Spirit. The Holy Spirit was at work both in the individual soul and in the Church. The Church provided a structure within which the deepest longings of the soul could be met. Attending to the Spirit within required spiritual practices such as asceticism (to quiet the longings of the body), meditation, contemplative prayer, silence, and interior recollection (Chinnici, 110–12). Attending to the Spirit within the Church implied reception of the sacraments, attendance at liturgical prayer, and participation in devotions.

Hecker also believed in evolutionary progress. The Spirit was leading the world into a new age in which Catholicism would be typified by the United States rather than Europe. "Christianity," he wrote, "is promised a reception from an intelligent and free people, that will give forth a development of unprecedented glory" (Chinnici, 96). He urged Catholics to be actively involved in culture and politics.

After Hecker's death, his writings became embroiled in European discussions of the relationship between Catholicism and democracy. Eventually his critics won the ear of Pope Leo XIII, and on January 22, 1899, the pope issued a letter, *Testem benevolentiae,* which condemned a system of beliefs he labeled "Americanism." Chinnici notes that this letter "marked for the first time the entrance of the Roman magisterium into the self-definition of American Catholic spiritual life" (132). From now on, and well into the twentieth century, American spiritual writers would struggle with what Chinnici labels a "fractured inheritance": in the Leonine view state and Church, nature and grace, secular and sacred, exist side by side in separate worlds. The integration of "personal experience, Catholic identity, and American culture" was lost (133).

A third convert to Catholicism, Rose Hawthorne Lathrop (1851–1926), fits neither "immigrant" or "romantic" categories. She was the youngest daughter of the writer Nathaniel Hawthorne. At age twenty she married George Lathrop; the couple both became published authors. In 1891 she and George joined the Catholic Church; by 1896 strains in the marriage prompted her to leave her husband. In 1894 she had moved into the slums of Manhattan's Lower East Side with the intent to care for indigent women who were dying of cancer. She cared for some in her meager quarters and visited others in their homes. Her devotion to these dying outcasts anticipated some movements within contemporary spirituality. Her deep experiences of Jesus' love for her and her love for him prompted her to serve the poorest of the poor. Similar to persons with HIV/AIDS, cancer patients were often neglected because the disease was little understood, and many doctors thought it was contagious. Hospitals sometimes shunned cancer patients because they could not be healed. Rose, anticipating today's hospice movement, asserted the dignity of those who were dying. She eventually became Mother Mary Alphonsa, foundress of the Dominican Congregation of St. Rose of Lima (1900), also known as the Servants of Relief for Incurable Cancer. Her congregation published a magazine, *Christ's Poor,* in which she shared her teachings and wrote of the rights and dignity of the poor.

Twentieth-Century Popular Movements

Creativity, change, and growth have continued to mark American Catholic spirituality in the twentieth century. Before examining some of the major figures of this century one would do well to recall that most Catholics live their spirituality through involvement in their parish and in popular devotions.

Catholic spirituality is rooted in word and sacrament, especially the celebration of the Eucharist. The strong parish life which developed in the immigrant Church has carried into the twentieth century. For many Catholics the local parish remains a primary source of spiritual nourishment, a place for reflection on Scripture and for celebration of the Eucharist and of significant transitions in one's life. Parish-based organizations, such as the Saint Vincent de Paul Society, the Altar and Rosary Society, and the Knights of Columbus (to name but a few) have continued to provide many lay persons with a forum for involvement in the Church's mission.

In addition, many Catholics continue to be nurtured by devotionalism, especially by devotion to Mary. Several movements within the Church have fostered the development of lay spirituality.

The eucharistic movement flowered in the first half of the new century. The Confraternity of Perpetual Adoration was begun in 1893; it gave some structure to lay spirituality. Chinnici reports that these confraternities "promoted frequent communion, attendance at benediction, visits to the Blessed Sacrament, and eucharistic processions" (146). National Eucharistic Congresses, drawing thousands of the faithful, were held regularly throughout these decades.

The retreat movement grew out of the many lay associations, parish missions, and confraternities of the immigrant Church (for a general discussion see Chinnici, 157–71). In 1911 several lay persons in New York City considered forming a national retreat movement. Various organizations for laymen developed in the 1920s. The women's retreat movement also developed in association with the Sisters of the Cenacle. Statistics indicate widespread involvement. For example, in 1965, 176 retreat houses for men served 189,000 adults and 70,000 youths. In 1972, a new organization, Retreats International, was begun, with its headquarters at the University of Notre Dame. In 1977 the men's and women's divisions were merged. The years after Vatican II have brought a renewal of retreats based upon the *Spiritual Exercises* of St. Ignatius. During such retreats the retreatant meets individually with a director rather than attending lectures. The retreat movement remains very much alive; the 1995 *Catholic Almanac* lists nearly 350 retreat houses in the United States.

The Christophers, founded by Maryknoll priest James Keller (1900–77), provide another example of a Catholic popular movement. After joining Maryknoll in 1921, Keller gradually developed the concept of applying the principles used by Maryknoll missionaries in foreign countries to the United States. The lay missionaries which he envisioned would preach the gospel to American culture. He called them "Christophers" because they would carry Jesus to the marketplace. Response to his ideas was so positive that he began building an organization. He adapted the mass marketing procedures of modern corporations to his movement (a strategy that some Catholic leaders criticized) and spread the Christopher's message through books (such as his *You Can Change the World,* 1948), brochures, a newsletter *(Christopher News Notes),* a television program (1952), one minute radio spots (1957), and a magazine *(Catholic Missions).* By 1954 *Christopher News Notes* was reaching 800,000 readers. He made famous the motto, "It is better to light one candle than to curse the darkness."

Finally, the charismatic movement has touched the lives of hundreds of thousands of Catholics. Charismatic spirituality includes "baptism in the Spirit, reception of gifts of the Spirit, such as glossalalia [i.e., speaking in tongues], prophecy, healings, and deliverance from evil" (*New Dictionary of Catholic Spirituality,* s.v. "Charismatic Renewal"). Charismatic and Pentecostal traditions have deep roots in American religion, but the modern Catholic phenomenon began in 1967 among faculty and students at Duquesne University in Pittsburgh. It quickly spread to university communities in South Bend, Indiana, and East Lansing, Michigan, and later throughout the country. The South Bend community formed national structures such as the National Service Committee, the annual Catholic Pentecostal Conference, and the magazine *New Covenant,* begun in 1971. The U.S. bishops have noted the lay nature of this movement: "From its beginnings . . . it has been largely led, taught, discerned and participated in by lay people" (*Pastoral Statement on the Catholic Charismatic Renewal,* 6). Though the movement's leaders have sometimes been criticized for being authoritarian and sexist, they have also accomplished much good. The movement supports family life, especially the education of young people in the faith; it meets many people's longing for community; it sponsors thousands of prayer groups; and it has established several covenanted communities.

In addition to these popular movements, certain individuals have arisen to voice new understandings of American Catholic spirituality. Some of these significant voices will now be examined.

Neo-Thomistic Activists

By the early years of the twentieth century the United States was in the midst of an economic and social revolution. The country was shifting from its rural roots to an urban, industrial power. John A. Ryan (1869–1945), a diocesan priest from St. Paul, Minnesota, and William J. Kerby (1870–1936), a diocesan priest from Dubuque, Iowa, shared the conviction that the American Catholic Church had to become more centralized if it were to respond to the problems facing it and the nation. Ryan eventually became director of the Social Action Department of the newly formed National Catholic Welfare Conference (forerunner of the United States Catholic Conference). He was the leading spokesperson for Catholic social teaching and an active supporter of Roosevelt's New Deal. Kerby was the main force behind the formation of the National Conference of Catholic Charities (1910) and served as secretary of this organization until 1920.

Of the two activists Kerby had the greater influence on spirituality. In 1919, while making an annual retreat, he resolved to gradually withdraw from his many activities and devote himself to spiritual writing and preaching retreats. He became one of the most sought after directors for priestly retreats, and he also wrote many articles as editor of the *American Ecclesiastical Review* from 1927 to 1936.

Prior to his ordination in 1892 Kerby was sent to The Catholic University of America to receive his licentiate in theology. There he came under the influence of the Belgian Thomist Thomas Bouquillon (1840–1902). Kerby learned his fundamental theological principles (nature/grace, reason/revelation, nature/supernature) from Bouquillon and throughout his life retained a Thomistic understanding of spiritual growth. Nonetheless he placed traditional Catholic asceticism in dialogue with American culture in creative ways. Many of his spiritual writings have been collected in two books: *Prophets of the Better Hope* (1922) and *The Considerate Priest* (1937). Kerby emphasized an inductive approach to spirituality focused upon personal experience at a time when spiritual writers often took a deductive approach, deriving conclusions from universal principles. He urged Christians (and especially the clergy) to be active and involved in social issues, not to withdraw into a Catholic ghetto. His emphasis on rational analysis, the natural virtues, and active engagement spoke deeply to many Catholics, lay as well as clerical. Perhaps more than any other spiritual writer of his time Kerby understood that modern industrial society placed new demands upon Christian asceticism. He realized that "charity" had to now be applied to social structures and not simply to individual poor people; hence social action to address injustices became a new form of charity.

The Personalists

Neo-Thomistic activism reflected the optimism of American culture through the 1920s. Ryan and Kerby trusted in scientific research and rational bureaucratization to address the social problems of the time. The Great Depression and subsequent developments in the 1930s, however, called their optimism into question. A new generation of Catholics saw the collapse of capitalism, on the one hand, and the rise of totalitarian leaders (Hitler in Germany, Mussolini in Italy, Stalin in the Soviet Union) on the other. They sought a middle way between capitalism and totalitarianism and found a solution in "personalism," which sought to reconstruct social and political life through the spiritual rebirth of individuals. This philosophy was first articulated by the Frenchman Emmanuel Mounier. The personalists sought a synthesis between the holy and the ordinary, between faith and action.

Virgil Michel (1890–1938), a Benedictine from Collegeville, Minnesota, was one of America's prominent personalist thinkers and for several years the leader of liturgical renewal in the United States. In 1924 he was sent to Europe to study philosophy. While in Europe, he came in contact with the liturgical renewal occurring among the Benedictines. He brought a passion for liturgical renewal when he returned to the United States, founding the magazine *Orate Fratres* (later *Worship*) and The Liturgical Press in 1926. Unlike the Europeans, however, Michel linked liturgical renewal to social reform. Participation in the liturgy should be balanced by concern for one's neighbor, since both actions express the Church as the body of Christ. His writings covered a variety of topics: sociology, economics, education, art, and politics. His promising career was ended by his early death at the age of forty-eight.

A second manifestation of personalist spirituality can be seen in "Catholic Action" groups, which trace their origin to the Belgian social activist Canon Joseph Cardijn (1882–1967). Cardijn believed in the principle of "like affecting like." Workers would be the best people to evangelize workers; students to evangelize students. He fostered a lay spirituality of preaching the gospel through one's ordinary tasks. Jay P. Dolan describes Cardijn's method: "people would systematically observe and discuss their environment, judge the situation in the light of the gospel, and then act" (*Experience,* 415).

"Catholic Action" was most evident in the Archdiocese of Chicago under the administration of Samuel Cardinal Stritch, archbishop from 1939 to 1958. Cardijn's ideas were introduced there by a speaker at 1938 clergy summer school for social action. One of those in attendance was Msgr. Reynold Hillenbrand (1909–79), rector of Mundelein Seminary. Hillenbrand and other sympathetic priests began to gather interested laity to form Catholic Action groups; among these were the Christian Family movement, Young Christian Workers, Young Christian Students, the Catholic Labor Alliance, and the Catholic Interracial Council. Thousands of Catholics were involved in this movement. By 1947, for example, Young Christian Worker groups existed in thirty-five cities. By 1967, an estimated 40,000 couples in the United States and Canada belonged to the Christian Family movement. In Europe, Catholic Action was guided by the hierarchy. In the United States, however, many Catholic Action groups eventually came under the direction of lay leadership. The Christian Family movement, for example, was ably led by Chicagoans Patrick (1911–74) and Patricia (1913–) Crowley.

A third manifestation of personalist spirituality can be found in Catholic radicalism. Spokespersons for this view included two lay women, Dorothy Day (1897–1980) and Catherine de Hueck Doherty (1896–1983), and a priest of the Archdiocese of Washington, D.C., Paul Hanly Furfey (1897–1992). Thomistic activists like Ryan and Kerby had sought to form coalitions with people who agreed with their position on the basis of reason and natural law. The radicals, on the other hand, appealed to the gospel. They interpreted the New Testament literally. Rather than form coalitions to influence social legislation they established alternative communities which would witness to the gospel message: Day at the Catholic Worker (1933) and Doherty in Friendship House (1938), both in New York City, Furfey at Fides House in Washington, D.C. (1940). Here they sought to live out the corporal works of mercy by providing food, shelter, or clothing to the poor who came to them. The radicals supported Virgil Michel's liturgical renewal; they participated in the liturgy and even the Divine Office on a daily basis. Of these three, Day became the most prominent spiritual writer. She had the journalist's gift for portraying the profound spiritual significance of the everyday struggles of the workers, the poor, the homeless. She inspired many Catholics through her column, "Little by

Little," in the *Catholic Worker* newspaper, which she co-founded with Peter Maurin (1877–1949) in 1933. She also reached readers through her autobiographical works, *The Long Loneliness* (1952) and *Loaves and Fishes* (1963).

Thomas Merton

Thomas Merton (1915–68) is American Catholics' best-known spiritual writer. His parents, Owen Merton (from New Zealand) and Ruth Jenkins (from the United States), were both artists. He traveled widely as a youth, especially after the death of his mother when he was six years old. He attended schools in France and England and finally ended up, in 1935, at Columbia University in New York City. There he obtained his B.A. in 1938 and his M.A. in 1939. He joined the Catholic Church in 1938 and, after receiving his M.A., taught at St. Bonaventure's University in western New York until 1941, when he entered the Trappist Monastery of Our Lady of Gethsemani in Kentucky.

Merton's 1948 autobiography, *The Seven Storey Mountain,* became a bestseller and catapulted him to fame. A gifted and prolific writer, he published over sixty books (some of them posthumous). He was not, however, a systematic thinker; many of his books are reworkings of his journals. In his early writings Merton shows a triumphalistic attitude about both Catholicism and monasticism. His interests broadened as he matured and found his own voice. He came to understand that his life was inherently paradoxical, and one of its central paradoxes was that his monastic vocation put him at the heart of his culture rather than isolated him from it. He carried on a wide correspondence with people all over the world. He wrote about the reform of monasticism, and argued successfully for the restoration of the hermit lifestyle. During the 1960s he began to write about the threat of nuclear weapons, the need to oppose the Vietnam War, and the racism which blighted American culture. He had a lifelong interest in literary criticism and was himself a published poet. He also became interested in interreligious dialogue and argued that western monks had much to learn from the spiritual traditions of the East. He died while attending an ecumenical monastic meeting in Bangkok, Thailand, in 1968.

Merton believed that his own spiritual search embodied the dark side of life in the twentieth century: spiritual emptiness, shallow consumerism, addiction to violence. Perhaps for this reason his writings have touched many people and have been translated into several languages. His major theme, however, is the unity of contemplation and action. Chinnici has suggested that "Merton's significance can been seen in his focus on the unity of all vocations in the contemplative experience of God" (206). Merton believed that all people were called to contemplation. A classic treatment of this theme can be found in his 1962 masterpiece, *New Seeds of Contemplation.*

Vatican II and Beyond

The theological, ecclesial, and pastoral changes initiated by Vatican Council II (1962–65) have been widely documented and need not be discussed here. Vatican II's effects on American Catholic spirituality are, perhaps, less thoroughly understood. Only a few broad strokes can be painted here.

First, the council called for a return to the Scriptures. At the academic level this has led to a renaissance of Catholic biblical scholarship; at the popular level one finds a widespread hunger for Scripture. Many Catholics pray over the Scriptures, read the Bible, or participate in Bible study through classes or reflection groups. Contemporary Catholic spirituality is more likely to be biblical, whereas the spirituality of nineteenth-century Catholics was more often based on devotional prayer books.

Second, the council called for a return to the liturgy. The Church Fathers and Mothers saw participation in liturgy and sacrament as a primary source of spiritual nurture. The Church has sought, then, to encourage lay participation in the sacraments and to play down the role of paraliturgical devotions.

Third, the council emphasized the importance of the human person. This has led Catholic theology to reappropriate experience as a theological category. Much contemporary spirituality focuses upon a person's experience of the divine call in his or her life. The 1980s and 1990s have witnessed a widespread interest in spirituality throughout the American culture, not simply among Roman Catholics. Within American Catholicism one finds renewed interest in ancient practices like meditative reading, contemplative prayer, spiritual direction, and retreats. Many Catholics seek a deeper understanding of the relationship between spirituality and psychology. More recently, advances in understanding of ecology and new scientific cosmologies have prompted interest in the relationship between spirituality and cosmology.

Emphasis on experience has particularly led to the emergence of voices in the tradition which have previously been overlooked, especially the voices of women and ethnic minorities. Feminist writers are exploring spiritualities which provide a healthy balance to overly masculinized traditions. And African American, Hispanic, and Asian peoples are reclaiming their spiritual roots. There is today a deeper appreciation of plurality within the Catholic community.

Today one can find a plurality of spiritualities within the Catholic community: charismatic, Hispanic, African American, feminist, masculine, creation centered, to name but a few. As the kaleidoscope continues to turn, it reveals beautiful and dazzling variations of the ways in which Christians appropriate the mystery of Jesus.

See also AMERICANISM; BROWNSON, ORESTES AUGUSTUS; CARROLL, JOHN; CHRISTOPHERS, THE; DAY, DOROTHY; HECKER, ISAAC; LITUR-

GICAL MOVEMENT IN AMERICA, THE; MERTON, THOMAS; MICHEL, VIRGIL; SETON, ELIZABETH ANN BAYLEY.

Carey, Patrick W. *Orestes A. Brownson: Selected Writings.* New York: Paulist Press, 1991.

____. *The Roman Catholics.* Westport, Conn.: Greenwood Press, 1993.

Chinnici, Joseph P. *Living Stones: The History and Structure of Catholic Spiritual Life in the United States.* Maryknoll, N.Y.: Orbis, 1996.

Curran, Robert Emmett. *American Jesuit Spirituality: The Maryland Tradition, 1634–1900.* New York/Mahwah, N.J.: Paulist Press, 1988.

Dolan, Jay P. *The American Catholic Experience: A History from Colonial Times to the Present.* Garden City, N.Y.: Doubleday & Company, Inc., 1985.

____. *Catholic Revivalism in the United States, 1830–1900.* University of Notre Dame Press, 1977.

Kelly, Ellin, and Annabelle Melville. *Elizabeth Seton: Selected Writings.* New York/Mahwah, N.J.: Paulist Press, 1987.

Lane, Belden C. *Landscapes of the Sacred.* Mahwah, N.J.: Paulist Press, 1988.

Lozano, John M. *Grace and Brokenness in God's Country: An Exploration of American Catholic Spirituality.* Mahwah, N.J.: Paulist Press, 1991.

Taves, Ann. *The Household of Faith: Roman Catholic Devotions in Mid-Nineteenth-Century America.* University of Notre Dame Press, 1986.

BRUCE H. LESCHER

AMERICAN CATHOLIC WOMEN

The history of American Catholic women is not substantially different from that of their Protestant sisters. They both inherited the same traditions from a patriarchal Church. Conventional theology from St. Paul to St. Augustine to St. Thomas, supported by the Hebrew Scriptures and Church Fathers, confined woman's activities to home and children. She was, they claimed, naturally submissive and pious, designed by God for either virginity or motherhood. To live outside these constraints was not only unfeminine but unnatural, a threat to civilized society.

Some women unquestioningly accepted these precepts, hailing them as the guarantor of female dignity and the means of exalting their sexual identity. Often they had very little patience with critics, especially those Catholics in the last third of the twentieth century, who assailed this inheritance as an impediment to developing their full potential as humans and Christians. Other women, however, without contesting these strictures, interpreted them as a means of increasing their opportunity to obtain equality in Church and state.

But most common were practicing Catholics who in their day-to-day lives subverted these dicta by developing new interests outside the family, becoming wage-earners, influencing politics, and changing society. Their actions forced churchmen to revise their views on women's right to work, to vote, to be educated on a level with men, and to limit the number of children they bore.

Thus there are no typical Catholic women in the American past. Instead one finds foremothers to match the variety of positions found in today's Church. Even those labeled as "radicals" can assert that they are only the current participants in an enduring struggle for equality in Church and state.

Establishing the Traditions

Little is known of Catholic women in Colonial America for not only were they few in number, but their lives were shaped for the most part by conventional values. Thus their conduct seldom attracted the attention of notetakers. However, in the Catholic colony of Maryland they played a role that was so prominent in spreading and preserving the faith that it shocked clerical observers into recording their achievements. One woman, Margaret Brent, who was the executor of the estate of Governor Leonard Calvert, directly contravened the behavior expected of females. When the Maryland Assembly rejected her request for two seats in that body, she then protested against all of their proceedings.

However, with the establishment of the Anglican Church, Catholicism in Maryland, as in the other English settlements, was preserved primarily in the home. This was the God-given domain of the mother who supervised family rituals and presided over religious feasts and fasts.

An alliance with Catholic France during the War for Independence mitigated anti-Romanist prejudice, making it easier for some Catholic women to champion the Revolution. They did so by performing such feminine tasks as nursing and by stepping from their sphere to rally women to the patriot cause. They raised money for the poorly supplied Continentals and gathered intelligence information for the rebels by crossing British lines. One woman, Mary Digges Lee, was even thanked by George Washington for her achievements in support of the Revolution.

With American adherence to the separation of Church and state, the Catholic population grew rapidly after 1776. The country's first bishop, John Carroll (Baltimore), to nourish his flock in a Protestant environment, urged European orders of nuns to come to the United States and establish schools. He also encouraged the formation of American teaching communities, the first of which, the Sisters of Loretto of the Foot of the Cross, was established to serve those Catholics who had moved west into Kentucky. The most renowned of these new communities was the Sisters of Charity of Emmitsburg. This order was founded by one of the era's many converts, St. Elizabeth Ann Seton, the founder of the parochial school system in the United States.

By 1852 nuns had established over one hundred academies to prepare young ladies for their primary mission in life—motherhood. Virtues such as piety, modesty, subservience, and gentleness were emphasized along with social graces, the French language, drawing, dancing and music. Some dismissed the curriculum as merely "ornamental studies" but according to Bishop John England (Charleston, South Carolina) this was precisely the type of education that prepared young ladies for heaven.

Increasingly, however, the nuns' concept of educating for motherhood came to include training their young charges to be effective teachers of their sons who someday would be society's movers and shakers. Consequently, attention began to be placed on the so called "masculine branches of learning" such as science, Latin, and math and with the hope these future mothers would grow intellectually after graduation. An even greater challenge to the dominant educational philosophy was the lifestyle of the very nuns who supposedly were its exemplars. They resided in a self-governing community of women and were confident, independent and authority figures to many. Consequently they were compelled to protect their way of life from clerical interference. Even Seton struggled with male authorities, and then, like many strong-minded religious women, she blamed herself for being too assertive rather than blame males for being too intrusive. She concluded she was "illy qualified" for leadership as she lacked "a pliancy of character."

Other superiors suffered from the same alleged character defect. Resenting challenges to episcopal authority, especially from laywomen and women religious, bishops tried to obtain unquestioned obedience from nuns. Sometimes they established their own religious orders with special vows of obedience. They also forced communities to separate from their motherhouses, intervened in elections, diverted funds, and even drove recalcitrants from their diocese. Occasionally convents were placed under interdict, supervisors excommunicated or deposed, and sacraments denied. The hierarchy generally shared the belief of Bishop Celestine de la Hailandière (Vincennes, Indiana) that to oppose a bishop was to rebel against God and that the least priest in a diocese had more power over sisters than their superior general. Even St. Rose Philippine Duchesne was refused absolution, Communion, and public renewal of her vows because she resisted clerical interference in the community she founded, the Religious of the Sacred Heart in America.

Early Challenges to Tradition

Despite these trials the numbers of women religious continued to grow and by the end of the century they outnumbered male churchmen in every diocese. They were four times as numerous as priests, and bore the brunt of selfless service to the poor, the ill, the orphaned and the immigrant. In so doing women religious eroded clerical perceptions of what it was to be feminine for they displayed the so-called masculine virtues of courage and self-reliance as they defied anti-Catholic attacks and the ravages of cholera. Sisters courageously performed missionary work among Native American tribes, Hawaiian lepers, and isolated Inuits. They defied mores, and sometimes the law, by teaching slaves. Two communities of African American nuns, the Oblate Sisters of Providence (1829) and Sisters of the Holy Family (1843) opened schools, orphanages, and old-age homes for American blacks. Mother Mary Katherine Drexel established the Sisters of the Blessed Sacrament for Indians and Colored People (1891) and the only African American Catholic College, Xavier University of New Orleans.

Consecrated women were considered an exception to the teaching of nineteenth-century ethicists that God's plan for woman was motherhood and a home where she would reign and comfort man. Forces allegedly threatening this divine design—employment, suffrage, feminism, male-style education—were assailed by these moralists. Although they contended that woman's piety and moral superiority could ennoble and uplift man, as a daughter of Eve, she was also consciously or not, an occasion of sin. Consequently, one of her duties was to protect man against temptation as well as to preserve her own greatest treasure and source of power—her virginity.

However, there were Catholic women who defied this ideal. As early as the eighteenth century, according to confessional documents, Catholic females actively prevented conception and, failing that, sometimes induced miscarriages. However, it was the violation of sexual morality outside of marriage that Catholic churchmen found so disgraceful. Large numbers of Irish girls resorted to prostitution in cities such as Philadelphia and Chicago, and in New York it was reported in 1855 that nearly half of the two thousand harlots were Catholic. Abortions, too, increased among Catholics, so much so that one physician described them as "shockingly prevalent among Irish-Americans" and therefore urged the Archbishop of Cashel, Ireland, to discourage emigration of females to the United States.

Primarily it was women religious who dealt with these concerns: staffing working girls houses and teaching trades to unskilled females. To reduce abortions, orphanages were established and by the 1870s there was a hospital for unmarried mothers in nearly every diocese. Furthermore, although Archbishop John Hughes (New York) believed fallen women could never be redeemed, two communities of sisters adopted their rehabilitation as a special mission.

But more common than direct violations of woman's sphere was an unconscious defiance of it. Catholic women began to apply their God-given talents to the world at large, not just to the domestic area. Some found opportunity in church work. Joanna England, sister of the bishop, edited the *U.S. Catholic Miscellany,* the first Catholic newspaper in the nation. Others raised funds for churches, hospitals, orphanages, schools, missions, the aged and the poor. They aided sisters in administering schools and established and maintained institutions for society's flotsam: prisoners, fallen women, and immigrants. By midcentury it was observed that laywomen were not only esteemed and loved by the masses, but that they had done more good than the clergy. Therefore, it was alleged they did not need political rights or equality with men in order to change society.

Nevertheless, some devout females assumed both rights and equality in church disputes. Early in the century many women of St. Mary's parish, Philadelphia, advocated "trusteesism," lay ownership of the church structure. Half a century later a disproportionate number of females supported the excommunicated Fr. Edward McGlynn and continued to attend his Anti-Poverty Society meetings even though New York's Archbishop Michael A. Corrigan declared attendance a serious sin. At the same time, defying their excommunication by Bishop Richard Gilmour, women continued to join the Cleveland chapter of the Ladies Land League, an organization to support land reform in Ireland.

Religious scholars in promulgating desirable female characteristics ignored the problems of wage earners who were so far removed from their ideal woman. Catholic females were employed as live-in domestics or toiled in the unskilled, low-paying, sewing trades. Many worked because they were unmarried and alone (there were more single female Irish immigrants than any other nationality), or to send money to relatives in the old country. Others supplemented their husband's meager salary or were widows. But all found conditions deplorable. By the end of the Civil War the number of wage-earning Catholic females had increased to such numbers that moralists began to direct some of their teachings to these exploited women. These scholars, who still contended motherhood was the natural vocation and employment was only a temporary expedient until marriage, reflected dominant middle-class concepts. They urged working women to be loyal to their employers and to accept minimal wages as the will of God. Hard work, they claimed, would please both employer and Creator and be rewarded here and hereafter.

Without directly challenging the domesticity to which the Church would relegate them, Catholic women earned money, became independent, and found an outlet for their intelligence and creativity by writing. Most of their short stories and novels lacked literary merit, but served a valuable didactic function. They were designed to foster Catholicism in a Protestant society by disarming and converting non-Catholics as well as educating Catholics in doctrine and ritual. Furthermore, their stories illustrated the dangers of dissolute living and the temporal and spiritual rewards of a moral life style. As might be expected these novelists betrayed a class bias: practically all were politically conservative, opposed woman suffrage, and ignored social justice. However, like nuns, they presented a role model different from the values they extolled. By their self-sufficiency and through their female characters they exposed readers to a world of strong, assertive women. Their heroines were not characters to whom things happened, but were the shapers of events. More often than not, the superiority of these female heroines ennobled, redeemed, and reformed pliable males. Occasionally these authors were criticized for depicting such powerful women, but only two, Mary Agnes Tincker and Kate O'Flaherty Chopin, directly attacked the era's female stereotype.

The difference between ideology and reality in Catholic women's roles was further dramatized by the westward movement when 350,000 pioneers descended on the Pacific Coast from 1841 to 1869. Although most women moved west as a result of a male decision and while on the trail continued to fulfill gender roles such as cooking, washing, and tending the children, the distinction between masculine and feminine blurred. Neither Native American attacks, bitter cold, baking sun, hunger, or fatigue distinguished between sexes. Furthermore, it was frequently women who maintained the morale and drive of a dispirited caravan. In 1841 when the Donner party was entrapped in a mountain pass and finally resorted to cannibalism, Elizabeth Breen, mother of eight, despite the presence of her husband, distributed the stores, nursed the sick and kept hope alive. Thirteen year old Virginia Reed was so moved by Breen's faith that she converted to Catholicism. Once at their destination, pioneer women continued to cross gender barriers, managing farms, fighting Native Americans, directing businesses, and in lawless frontier cities teaching school and running boarding houses.

Nuns, too, displayed the same daring—traversing through hostile territory to primitive areas where they lived and worked under challenging conditions. They opened schools, hospitals, and orphanages, often erecting the actual structure themselves. They tended Native Americans, freebooters, criminals, and adventurers in their effort to bring the Church and compassion to the West. Sr. Blandina (Rose Maria Segale) nursed a wounded partisan of Billy the Kid; as a result Billy always treated Sisters of Charity with kindness and respect. More traditionally in 1876 Blandina raised funds in Santa Fe for an orphanage, hospital, and industrial school for Native American females.

The Civil War and Aftermath

The Civil War gave Catholic women an opportunity to participate in the most significant political event of their lifetime in the name of patriotism. In supporting their section of the country they skirted the restraints of domesticity by rolling bandages, sewing flags, raising money for soldier relief, and encouraging males to enlist. With their men at war they assumed new responsibilities in the home, farm, or plantation. Because of a labor shortage, made all the more critical by wartime industrial expansion, thousands of city girls found employment in manufacturing and sometimes in sales. Since many of the new workers were mothers, a Catholic day nursery, probably the first of its type, was opened in New York City.

Woman's role was directly challenged by those who followed their husbands onto the battlefield, served as scouts, enlisted disguised as men, or engaged in espionage. The most famous Civil War spy, Rose O'Neal Greenhow, insisted that her Northern captors recognize her right to attend Mass.

The best-known Catholic women's contribution to the war was that of sisters who nursed for the Union and the Confederacy. The only class of women with experience in nursing and hospital management, they provided about 20 percent of all military nurses, despite the North's special effort to recruit Protestants and the South's early reliance on African Americans. These women tended wounded on both sides including prisoners. They ignored enemy lines, advanced and retreated with their armies, and risked smallpox, typhoid, and enemy fire. Some died as a result of military service.

During the war Northern feminists rallied to the Republican cause, adopting as their credo "After the slave—then the woman." Following Appomattox feminists demanded a woman suffrage amendment to the federal constitution. Since 1848, when New Yorkers met at Seneca Falls advocating female voting rights, prominent Catholic churchmen and scholars had assailed that proposal. Their criticism now became more strident and was augmented by two prominent Catholic women. Ellen Ewing Sherman, the wife of General William T. Sherman, and Madeline Vinton Dahlgren, author and widow of Admiral John Dahlgren, assumed the leadership of female remonstrants. They used political means to advance their contention that political responsibilities were irreconcilable with woman's nature, ability, and character. By 1879 a leading suffragist, Civil War hero, and prominent minister, Thomas Wentworth Higginson, concluded that one of the major impediments to that reform was Catholics. This view remained quite common through the years, despite suffrage advocacy by a handful of clergy and a substantial number of Catholic women.

The Reform Movement

Catholic opposition to the women's vote did not necessarily mean opposition to female participation in other reform movements. As the nineteenth century drew to a close, Catholics increasingly believed that woman's moral excellence need no longer be confined to the home, but should be exercised on behalf of all of society—a sort of Catholic version of the Social Gospel movement. Among those advancing this idea were Eleanor Donnelly, author

of over fifty volumes of poetry; Emma Forbes Cary, vice regent of Trinity College; and Alice T. Toomey, president of Cliff Haven summer school. Publications such as the *Catholic World* and *American Catholic Quarterly Review* also advanced this concept as well as the more liberal members of the hierarchy including Bishop John Lancaster Spalding (Peoria) and Archbishop John Ireland (St. Paul).

One of the immediate effects of this interpretation of women's role was improved education. Convent schools, as part of a more liberal curriculum, began to emphasize the need to develop women's skills. Summer schools, evening schools, and reading circles reached an entirely new class of women with offerings designed to attract working girls and wives. It became necessary to prepare additional women for careers in teaching when the Third Plenary Council of Baltimore (1884) urged the establishment of parish schools. Since females were excluded from Catholic colleges and discouraged from attending secular ones, the establishment of institutions of higher education was essential. In 1896 Notre Dame Institute in Maryland became the first four-year American Catholic college for women, and was soon followed by other academies. Trinity College in Washington, viewed by many as the capstone of Catholic women's education, in 1900 became the first Catholic institution founded as a four-year woman's college. By 1925 there were fifty-one liberal arts Catholic colleges for women whose curriculum was concerned primarily with teacher training, but which also promoted motherhood and religion. This latter objective was sometimes emphasized at the expense of professional aims as the colleges sought to meet the criticism that higher education was a danger to faith.

In addition to teaching school, middle-class Catholic women, lay and religious, were able to exercise their special gifts by answering the challenges posed by an influx of immigrants. They established foundling homes, ministered to desolate women, taught trades, and ran employment services. One of the most successful in aiding newcomers was St. Frances Xavier Cabrini. Despite criticism from several churchmen, Catholic women followed their Protestant sisters into the settlement house movement—live-in residences for reformers in poor immigrant neighborhoods. By 1915 there was at least one Catholic settlement house in every major diocese.

An outgrowth of this movement was the social service profession, first given academic status in a Catholic institution at Loyola University of Chicago in 1914. Among the prominent reformers whose careers were shaped by this profession were Kate Barnard and Caroline Gleason. Barnard was twice elected to four-year terms as state Commissioner of Charity in Oklahoma, ten years before women were enfranchised in that state, and Gleason was head of the Oregon State Industrial Welfare Commission before entering religious life as Sr. Miriam Theresa of the Sisters of the Holy Names of Jesus and Mary. Other areas in which Catholic women reached out to the less fortunate were in running day nurseries, volunteering as nurses in the Spanish-American War, and serving in the Catholic temperance movement.

Although deeply involved in social problems Catholic activists continued to extol the domestic lifestyle. Two of the many were Margaret Buchanan Sullivan and Mary Boyle O'Reilly. Sullivan, one of the most brilliant journalists of her era, believed in subservience to men and in the primacy of family life. O'Reilly, a director of the Women's Educational and Industrial Union, wartime nurse in Belgium, and undercover newspaper reporter, repeatedly advocated female traditionalism.

Even though many women were able to reconcile public service with femininity, churchmen often worried that such action would undermine faith. Nevertheless, such perceptions did not prevent two of the more conservative members of the hierarchy, Archbishop Michael Corrigan (New York) and Bishop Bernard McQuaid (Rochester) from using a woman as their agent in Rome. Ella B. Edes, an American doing secretarial work for the Congregation of Propaganda, reported on Roman politics and leaked private information to these religious leaders. She apparently even influenced the conservative direction of some policies. Edes was the ideal representative of the foes of Americanism, the alleged heresy that the American Church was a threat to Roman authority. In her own words she had come to "hate modern ideas, progress, evolution, and especially and above all modern woman."

Trade Unions

Large numbers of Catholic women entered the work force and even when employed in "feminine" tasks such as taking in boarders, they grew in confidence and independence. The activities of these young women were no longer restricted to the family circle or the parish church. Now they were more likely to select their husband and less likely to defer to priestly and parental authority. In time they rejected the notion that marriage was an escape from long hours, low wages, and oppressive working conditions, and turned instead to trade unions. In so doing they substituted assertiveness for submissiveness, the very change that many churchmen feared.

The first prominent Catholic female labor leader, Augusta Lewis Troup, was a convert who served the International Typographical Union as corresponding secretary. She pressed for equal pay and championed suffrage as a means of improving working conditions. A mother of twelve, Elizabeth Flynn Rodgers, founder of the first female union in Chicago, was head of all Knights of Labor assemblies in that city, except for the stockyards, and established the Women's Catholic Order of Foresters, an insurance society. The career of the first full-time female labor organizer, Leonora Barry, a widowed millworker and mother of two, reflected the limitations that Catholicism sometimes enjoined on working women. Barry organized factory workers, raised strike funds, and agitated for equal pay and improved working conditions. Devoutly religious, she nevertheless was admonished by some churchmen for these "unladylike" endeavors, a criticism that was not entirely at odds with her own convictions. Barry believed that woman's divinely instituted normal role was that of homemaker. Women should work only when absolutely necessary; unions although responsible for protecting mothers-to-be, were to be run by men "as God intended."

Probably the most significant female Catholic labor leader was Mary E. Kenney, hired as the American Federation of Labor's (AFL) first woman organizer by its president, Samuel L. Gompers. Even after her marriage she established a federal labor union, spoke out on behalf of the poor and exploited, and volunteered for settlement duties. A year after her husband's death (1902) she cofounded the National Women's Trade Union League (NWTUL) in order to organize and educate working women and to press for legislation protecting them. Like Lake and other Catholic female labor leaders, she was an exponent of suffrage assailing its critics as "enemies of the people." Unlike Lake, but like the second generation of Catholic women labor leaders, she contended that women had a right to earn wages.

Other Catholic women played major roles in labor history by organizing for the AFL and the Congress of Industrial Organizations, establishing unions for waitresses, glove workers, and telephone operators and holding key posts in the NWTUL, including that of president. Eva MacDonald Valesh exemplified the newer assertiveness of working women. Hired as an organizer and writer for the AFL, she quit when Gompers refused to put her name on the masthead of the *Federationist,* the union's official publication. Convinced by this incident that there was little justice for women in trade unions, Valesh dedicated herself to the suffrage cause.

By the beginning of the twentieth century, many second-generation Catholic immigrant women had entered the professions, especially public education. Victimized by a gender-based pay scale and without the vote as a means of influencing school committees and tax structures, teachers turned to unions and suffrage for relief. Catholic educators were responsible for establishing teacher's unions in New York and Chicago and for using these organizations to obtain more professional treatment and to agitate for the ballot.

Ethnicity

Nearly as significant as wage earning in abrading Catholic conventions were the ethnic loyalties of American women. For example, Italian women established female auxiliaries to the Sons of Italy and joined the Italian Mutual Benefit Association and the Italian Girls Industrial League. In 1916, when the Irish-American pastor of the Italian church in Trenton, New Jersey, planned to reduce his debt by renting the parish school to the city, bands of females armed with clubs and sticks blocked the entrance to the school forcing the pastor to retain the Italian order of nuns who administered it.

Ethnic parishes and organizations were usually not viewed as endangering woman's assigned role. However, their activities fostered nationalism and led to political activity. Furthermore, when religion and patriotism were intertwined in subjected Catholic countries, religious rites became political acts, weakening once again female domesticity.

The Polish Women's Alliance, founded in 1898 to foster nationalism, published its own weekly, convened national assemblies, and soon began to support women's rights. Among Polish Catholic nationalists were the noted actress Helena Modjeska and Mary Olzewski Kryszak, founder and president of a local Alliance chapter and a representative in the Wisconsin legislature for sixteen years. To preserve Lithuanian heritage and lobby for a free homeland, the American Lithuanian Roman Catholic Women's Alliance was begun in 1914 under the banner, "Serve Church and County." Political activities on behalf of the Lithuanian cause were exceptions to the Alliance's policy of discouraging participation in public affairs.

Contrary to historian Hasia R. Diner's assertions, Irish-American women were not only involved in nationalistic endeavors but probably were more active than any other group in identifying with their homeland's struggle. In addition to preserving history and tradition, and raising money for patriotic groups, they became directly involved in Ireland's quest for freedom. Almost immediately after the establishment of the Fenian Brotherhood in 1859 emphasizing the necessity of force in winning independence, a Sisterhood was begun. Its members were denounced from the altar as "bad women" by Chicago's Bishop James Duggan. Irish-American women assisted males in the secret Clann-na-Gael, established Ladies Land Leagues, were arrested at rallies for Irish freedom, testified before Congress on Ireland's behalf, sold Irish nationalist newspapers at church doors, and were arrested for picketing the White House in the name of Ireland. Many of these partisans and other women seeking freedom for their European homeland, like working-women, evolved into suffragists.

Women Suffrage

With the growth of the suffrage movement, clerical opposition became even more discordant, associating that reform with anti-Catholicism, birth control, and socialism. Archbishop Sebastian J. Messmer (Milwaukee) condemned the vote as a panacea for those who refused to accept the "essential inequality of men and women." The newly published (1912) *Catholic Encyclopedia,* whose article on women asserted that the female soul was inferior to that of the male, described antisuffrage organizations as "the voice of common sense."

Clerical opposition was joined by an unusual coalition of Catholic females who used political means to deny their fitness for political responsibilities. One of the most outspoken of these remonstrants was Katherine E. Conway, novelist, essayist, editor of the Boston *Pilot,* pioneer in Catholic reading circles and member of the Board of Massachusetts Prison Commissioners. Among other prominent women who asserted that suffrage would undermine the home and lead to socialism were Caroline Corbin, social worker and long-time president of the Illinois antisuffrage association and Martha Moore Avery, a socialist convert, who before her entrance into the Church had been a suffragist.

But the forces of change could not be stilled. Enfranchisement increasingly appealed to middle-class Catholic women who, unlike its critics, saw it as a means of protecting the family and enhancing women's position. Jane Campbell, founder and president of the Philadelphia County Woman Suffrage Association, whose every meeting began with a prayer, claimed that suffrage would force political parties to nominate good men thereby insuring justice for women. Other influential Catholic suffragists, who advocated ballot extension as an opportunity to exercise womanly virtues, were the writer Mary Blake; Sara McPike, mainstay of the St. Catherine's Welfare Association of New York; Helen P. McCormick, the first female assistant district attorney in Brooklyn; and Hortense Ward, the first Texas woman admitted to the bar and the first female to practice before the United States Supreme Court.

Catholic suffragists were not content to lobby, petition, write, debate, and testify. Inspired by English militants, some adopted less ladylike tactics. Mary O'Toole, president of the District of Columbia Equal Suffrage Association, organized and conducted street corner rallies as did Teresa O'Leary Crowley, a lawyer and mother of three. Crowley, moreover, conducted a campaign that ousted eight Massachusetts antisuffrage state senators and was a major participant in a coalition that defeated an antisuffrage United States senator. Margaret Foley, a member of the WTUL who had studied militant tactics in England, trailed antisuffrage politicians throughout Massachusetts disrupting rallies and heckling candidates. She was so successful that the national woman suffrage organization sent her on a tour throughout the country. In 1918 Foley was appointed an officer in the Margaret Brent Suffrage Guild, a Catholic organization, on whose behalf she established local chapters and testified before the state legislature.

Although described by her confessor "as gentle a woman as I have ever met," the most daring of all the Catholic suffragists was Lucy Burns, who spent more days in jail in behalf of voting rights than any other woman. Burns, who had been incarcerated for suffrage demonstrations in England, was cofounder of the Woman's Party whose object was to make militancy relevant to the American struggle. She edited its journal, crisscrossed the country on its behalf, was arrested for picketing the White House and forced fed for resorting to a hunger strike when her demand to be treated as a political prisoner was rejected.

As the demand for suffrage intensified, clergy increasingly began to support it, endorsing the proposal not as a matter of justice, but usually as a means of protecting women, especially working females. More commonly, however, they considered the vote a means for morally superior women to purify politics by the injection of feminine virtues. The Los Angeles *Tidings* proclaimed, "In the hands of woman the ballot becomes a sacred trust, a power for good." As suffrage was extended by several states and then the federal government (1920), clerical critics became priestly proponents—the most significant of whom was Cardinal James Gibbons (Baltimore). Although expressing regret that "women had taken the plunge into the deep," Gibbons even urged nuns to vote. Catholic periodicals and organizations began to assert that female voting was necessary to protect the nation from feminists, socialists, and radicals. What once had been a threat to an orderly Christian society had become the means of preserving it.

World War I and Aftermath

One of the major factors in convincing the male power structure to amend constitutions on behalf of female suffrage was women's achievements in World War I. Catholic women joined their Protestant compatriots in defense production, in the navy as yeomenettes, and in the Woman's Land Army tending crops. However, what many women saw as opportunities, clerics often saw as dangerous temptations luring women out of their sphere into men's occupations. By earning wages females would become less dependent on males thereby losing their qualities as Christian ladies. These fears were reflected in the Bishops' Pastoral of 1919 where woman's responsibility in the home was emphasized and her role in the workforce ignored. The program of Social Reconstruction in the same year encouraged employers to hire men rather than women and implied that working females should be eased into lower-paying occupations.

However, the Church found ways for Catholic women to support the war effort without jeopardizing their special qualities. The National Catholic War Council, established by the hierarchy to coordinate Catholic participation in the struggle, had a special subcommittee on women. Headed by a cleric, who believed females were incapable of administering the organization, all leadership positions, including that of executive secretary, were filled by men.

Under the committee's direction, local women's organizations ran service clubs for soldiers, worked with the Red Cross, cared for military dependents, raised relief funds, and taught first aid. Moreover, the women's committee opened facilities at training camps and ports of embarkation where women, properly chaperoned, could visit soldiers. Community houses were established in major cities to provide employment services, recreation, and educational opportunities, as well as residences for young women seeking wartime employment. At the conclusion of hostilities these evolved into Catholic settlement houses.

One of the enduring achievements of the committee was the institution of the National School of Social Service at The Catholic University of America in Washington. The school, whose original purpose was to train young women for wartime social work at home and abroad, became in time a regular graduate division of the University, the National Catholic Service School. Of its World War I graduates, 127 served abroad, operating residences for nurses, Red Cross volunteers, refugees and orphans.

The War Council was so successful that at Gibbon's request Rome approved a similar hierarchical peacetime organization, the National Catholic Welfare Conference (NCWC). A division of this organization was the newly formed National Council of Catholic Women (NCCW) whose function was to guide women's organizations and reconstruct society along Catholic lines by influencing legislation. The council's chair, Bishop Joseph Schembs (Toledo), interpreted his duty as requiring the protection of home, family, and education from feminist assaults. However, in defending traditional feminine roles, the council provided a dramatic model for Catholic women who chose a career rather than a family. Agnes Regan, executive secretary for twenty years, developed special programs for working women, lobbied for social legislation, frequently testified before Congress, and was active in world peace programs. At the same time Regan defended more traditional concerns by railing against birth control and an equal rights amendment to the national constitution.

As mores changed, birth control, an unmentionable topic for nineteenth-century Catholic female authors, appeared in the works of several twentieth-century women. The many novels of Lucille Papin Borden and Katherine Thompson Norris, like their nineteenth-century counterparts, promoted Catholic values and large families and directly assailed birth control. Norris's first book *Mother* (1911) was praised by one critic as "the most smashing single blow ever delivered by the press to the creeping cult of birth control" and Borden attributed the World War II occupation of France as just deserts for the practice of contraception in a degenerate nation.

Quite different was Margaret Culkin Banning, author of over one hundred short stories and forty books, many with Catholic settings. Banning, who described herself as an "arrogant, hard-shelled, old style feminist," condemned fornication, but quite shockingly allowed her heroines to "be unchaste—but not for long." In *The Vine and the Olive* (1964), a novel praised by Dr. John Rock, one of the developers of the birth control pill and implicitly sanctioned by Cardinal Richard Cushing (Boston), Banning encouraged family planning. However, she also extolled ladylikeness, family responsibility, and surprisingly, the supremacy of a husband's interests over those of his wife.

Birth control was but one manifestation of what many churchmen, Catholic and Protestant, viewed as a moral breakdown in the 1920s. This collapse of virtue, allegedly characterized by female sexual laxness, was often attributed to the extension of suffrage to women. Churchmen responded by repeatedly reminding Catholic women of their destiny, warning of their responsibility not to tempt men, and alerting them to a series of dangers: bobbed hair, close dancing, cosmetics, sex education, divorce, indecent dress and especially birth control. Clerics began to emphasize the sinfulness of family planning because they were convinced their parishioners were ignoring earlier warnings against this practice. The first extensive exposition on the subject in 1916 was followed three years later by the Bishops' Pastoral condemning it as "a detestable thing" leading to "race suicide." In 1922 the NCWC condemned it as an "affront to all genuine Christians." Catholic publications and homilists spread these injunctions to every parish. However, the evil denounced was the limitation of families, not the means of controlling birth. As a result rhythm was usually ignored or occasionally censured. Nevertheless, despite admonitions from the press, pulpit, and papacy and to the despair of moralists, many Catholics continued the practice—in a survey of 509 Catholic women in 1940, 53 percent defied the Church ban on contraceptives.

One means of fighting this alleged degeneracy was a renewed emphasis on traditional values in women's colleges. Critics demanded these institutions pay more attention to preparing students for motherhood and family responsibilities and denounced the overemphasis on professional preparation. They also assailed coeducation as irreconcilable with the ends of female education. Despite higher academic standards, the encouragement to graduate work, and the introduction of more traditionally "male" courses and majors, Catholic colleges did not abandon their mission of readying ladies for family life. They assumed a dual objective: preparation for a career as well as marriage and motherhood.

With the ratification of the Nineteenth (Suffrage) Amendment, many Catholic women, with little criticism from the clergy, entered politics serving in a variety of local and state offices. However, the first Catholic congresswoman, Mae Hunt Nolan, a widow, was unable to reconcile political life and womanliness. After succeeding her husband for one term, she refused to run for another, declaring "Politics is entirely too masculine to have any attraction for feminine responsibilities." Mary Hopkins Norton, a New Jersey Democrat, had no such difficulty. As a matter of fact precisely because women had more moral sense than men, Norton believed they should enter politics, applying Christian values to social problems. During the 1920s Norton struggled to repeal the Eighteenth (Prohibition) Amendment and pushed for tariff reduction. Later as chair of the House Labor Committee she was responsible for significant wage and hour legislation.

Depression and War

Another way of serving society was ministering to the unemployed during the Great Depression. Many women undertook charitable and relief work. One of the most famous, Genevieve Garvan Brady, founded the National Women's Committee on Welfare and Relief Mobilization. Dorothy Day's Catholic Worker movement was designed to serve the needy and to assist workers. In addition to publishing her own paper, succoring strikers, and raising relief funds, Day established hospitality houses staffed by volunteers to provide room, board, and hope to the poor. Despite her radicalism in fighting injustice, Day was a traditional Catholic, especially on women's issues. She had some reservations about Vatican II, was apprehensive about feminism, and adamantly opposed birth control and the sexual revolution.

Like Day, Baroness Catherine de Hueck was a social revolutionary and a religious conservative, who believed that women had equality and status equal to men because of the Church. A devotee of the lay apostolate, de Hueck established interracial residences staffed by volunteers who lived and worked with the poor—especially African Americans.

Also in the interwar years two new major religious communities were established. Mary Rogers, a Smith College graduate, founded the Maryknoll Sisters (1920), a foreign mission society which by 1940 had thirty-five missions in Asia. Anna Dengel established the Medical Missionaries of Mary (1936), after Cardinal Dennis Dougherty (Philadelphia) convinced the Vatican to revise its prohibition on nuns practicing medicine.

As World War II approached, Catholic women reflected the nation's division over Franklin D. Roosevelt's foreign policies. On the one hand there was Day's Catholic Worker which opposed the President's efforts to assist the allies and denounced peacetime conscription. Unlike most critics of the administration's internationalism, Day's opposition was rooted in religious pacifism. As a result hers was the only Catholic organization to encourage and sustain the handful of World War II Catholic conscientious objectors. Day continued her campaign against militarism for which she was jailed in the 1950s and, as Patricia Neal has written, was "midwife in the formation of Catholic pacifist peace organizations . . . during the Vietnam War." Sharing Day's assessment of Roosevelt's policies was

Kathleen Norris. The novelist was president of Mothers of America, a pacifist organization, and one of the founders of America First, an isolationist body.

On the other hand, an adjunct of the NCWC, the Catholic Association for International Peace (CAIP) in which women held key positions and whose mainstay was its executive secretary Elizabeth Sweeney, accepted Catholic just war teaching. As a result the CAIP supported revision of the neutrality acts and aid to Britain. Also espousing Roosevelt's policies was the American-Irish Defense Association founded by Frances Sweeney, a one-woman crusader against anti-Semitism and isolation in Boston. Ironically its first formal meeting was held on December 7, 1941, the day Pearl Harbor was attacked. Sweeney shifted the association's objective to assisting the allies and warring on prejudice—especially anti-Semitism. This campaign embroiled her with supporters of the anti-Semitic Anglophobe, Rev. Charles E. Coughlin and with Cardinal William O'Connell, who allegedly threatened her with excommunication.

Once the United States entered the conflict, Catholic leaders, as in World War I, united behind the war effort. As early as the spring of 1941, the NCWC established the National Catholic Community Service (NCCS) with a special women's division to provide for the spiritual, material, and educational needs of men and women in the military and defense industries. The NCCS, chaired by Alice S. Hooley, former NCCW president, trained leaders at the National Catholic School of Social Service. Under the aegis of this organization 137 clubs and 490 houses were established in the United States and abroad, and clothing was collected, bonds sold, and scrap metal gathered.

There was little, if any, criticism of this type of wartime activity for women. However, defense work was different. Many of the hierarchy feared the effects of industrial employment on Catholic women, or any woman, for that matter. Modesty, family responsibility, and even faith itself would be endangered. There seemed to be general agreement with Bishop John A. Duffy's (Buffalo) assessment that, if the nation lost women's role in the home, it lost the war. For the most part the Catholic press echoed the clergy's views; those few who supported working women did so cautiously and with restrictions. Lost in the tumult were the voices of Banning and Helen White, president of the American Association of University Women; the latter even advocated drafting females.

This area, military service for women, was of greatest concern to churchmen and frequently decried by them. The most celebrated opponent, Bishop John J. O'Hara, auxiliary to the military vicar, maintained that to keep women from military service, soldiers would willingly peel their own potatoes and darn their own socks. More vociferous was Bishop James Cassidy (Fall River, Massachusetts) who urged women not to enlist because the Women's Aux-

iliary Army Corps (WAAC) contravened the teachings and principles of the Church. As a rule the Catholic Press shared his fears; the Brooklyn *Tablet* asserted service would degrade women by bringing back "the pagan, female, goddess of de-sexed lustful sterility."

The army, the first branch to accept females, campaigned assiduously to assure critics, especially Catholics, that military service was consonant with morality and femininity. Hooley, of the Women's division of the NCCS, was appointed to a committee to select officer candidates. Captain Louise E. Golden, a former English teacher, was assigned to WAAC public relations where she concentrated on resolving Catholic fears. She wrote for Catholic periodicals and lectured before Catholic groups, contending that military service increased women's religious devotion and prepared them to raise families. Furthermore, she compared enlistees and their relationship to military rules and traditions with that of nuns' relationship to their communities.

In time Catholic criticism began to abate. Msgr. Michael J. Reedy of the NCWC averred that army life strengthened "womanly character." Catholic journals began publishing sympathetic accounts of women's military experiences. Even Bishop O'Hara was moved to report that the WAC "seems to be working out." The historian, Anne E. Allen, attributed this shift of opinion to the large number of Catholic enlistees, estimated at over 25 percent.

Among these recruits were two Catholic women destined to become directors of the corps. Neither had patience with feminists and both were able to reconcile military life with ladylikeness. Elizabeth P. Hoisington, the first female brigadier general in American history, was dubbed "The Lady" by her troops for emphasizing femininity. Mary A. Hallaren believed her subordinates with "all the force of their female nature" were protecting "the Christian dignity of womanhood" from Communism.

The cold war struggle with atheistic Communism increased Catholic approbation of women in the armed forces. Hallaren relied on clergy to help recruiting, Cardinal Francis J. Spellman (New York), the military vicar, declared military women had earned the gratitude of their country, and, most revealing, Pope Pius XII blessed the work of Hallaren and Captain Joy Hancock, director of women in the navy.

Perceptions of women's proper province were changed by the war. Thus it appeared as if an equal rights amendment (ERA) first introduced in 1923, might become part of the United States Constitution. The first Catholic congresswoman to support the proposal (1943), New York's Winifred C. Stanley, was joined by other Catholic women such as Banning and Mary Merrick, founder of the Christ Child Society. However, the opposition from the institutional Church overwhelmed the voices of these supporters. A myriad of Catholic women's organizations rallied to defend the family and the special nature of women from the ERA's dangers, often asserting it would menace mothers-to-be by invalidating protective legislation. The House of Representatives' adverse report on the amendment (1943) was attributed to Catholic opposition and accordingly proponents were urged to recruit and organize Catholic women.

Dorothy Shipley Granger, a Maryland activist and longtime ERA advocate, ignored her husband's injunctions and established the St. Joan Society of Catholic Women. The organization immediately endorsed and lobbied for the proposal, vigorously objecting when Catholics implied their opposition represented the Church. St. Joan's was buffeted by some Catholic groups and the orthodoxy of its members was impugned. Granger described a meeting with NCCW officials as "beautifully refined torture . . . the boys who made the Inquisition rolled in their graves in envy." However, Bishop Edward J. Fitzmaurice (Wilmington) and Cardinal Dougherty had quietly encouraged these women and in 1945 Dougherty stunned his colleagues and shocked many American Catholics by publicly endorsing the amendment. But it was too late. The return to normalcy had begun.

Americans in the late 1940s and 1950s sought to recapture a past that never was—one where every woman found happiness in knowing her place and not moving therefrom. Catholics joined in this cacophony, blaming society's ills on emancipated women, urging men to reassert their authority and women to return to a passive home life. Once again there was renewed emphasis on the evils of family planning. However, as in earlier decades, Catholics appeared to pay little heed to this teaching. By 1945 over 80 percent of Catholic wives polled were using some means of birth control, over half of whom were using a method condemned by the Church.

One of the forms of Catholic renewal in those years was the Grail established in the United States in 1940 to reinvigorate traditional values. This was to be achieved by training young women to accept the challenges of Christianity and cultivate the feminine virtues of spirituality and compassion. By 1953 over 6,000 women had completed Grail programs and missionaries were being prepared for service abroad. In promoting orthodoxy the Grail blamed the employment of women for the increase in birth control, divorce, and juvenile delinquency. Although conventional at its inception, by emphasizing women in the Church, the Grail began to challenge customary thinking by developing a theology of women that included nonsexist worship.

Another effort to restore conventional roles were demands for schools and colleges to stress again domestic responsibilities for women. Bishop Edwin V. O'Hara (Kansas City) seemed to speak for many when he defined the purpose of Catholic education, "to make manly men and womanly women" with no attempt of "raising the woman's fallen destiny upon an equal pedestal with man." Although most Catholic professionals believed it necessary to educate women differently from men in order to develop their special gifts and even though domestic programs were added to the curriculum, there were no substantial educational changes. In women's colleges nuns continued to provide strong role models, females assumed leadership in student government and extra-curricular activities, and as Abigail McCarthy has pointed out, a disproportionate number of alumnae of the era entered politics.

Belief in the primacy of family values and the unique qualities of women did not preclude public careers; Kathryn Granahan, Clare Boothe Luce, and Jane Hoey all shared conventional attitudes. Granahan, after representing Pennsylvania in Congress, was named Treasurer of the United States. Playwright and Congresswoman Luce, who entered the Church in 1946, was instrumental in Dwight Eisenhower's nomination for the presidency and was rewarded by being named ambassador to Italy (1953). Hoey, who held a number of administrative positions in the New Deal, was for eighteen years the first director of the Bureau of Public Assistance under the Social Security Administration.

Rather than restoring traditional roles, the postwar years paved the road for additional change. Large numbers of women either rejected tradition or reconciled it with a less feminine lifestyle. Moreover, laywomen were assuming responsible positions on Catholic publications, and nuns, in keeping with Pius XII's injunction to adjust to the modern world, were moving toward the cutting edge of fundamental change. Communities began to modify their regulations and require professional training for members. Religious superiors met to exchange ideas and discuss problems and sisters began their own journal, the *Sister Formation* Bulletin.

Contemporary Developments

With federal equal pay legislation (1963), the Civil Rights Act (1964) and the establishment of the National Organization of Women (1966), the decade of the 1960s issued in an era of turmoil and change for American women. For Catholics the change was even more profound. Pope John XXIII in *Pacem in Terris* (1963) seemed to give approbation to these developments by writing that "women will not tolerate being treated as mere material objects, but demand rights befitting a human person in domestic and public life." The documents and spirit of Vatican Council II (1962–65) unleashed clerical restraints on females by condemning every type of discrimination, including sexual, and affirming woman's right to a state of life, education, and political participation equal to that of man. Furthermore, by defining the Church as the People of God, the council encouraged collegiality and theological analysis of magisterial pronouncements—first publicly manifested in the United States by the questioning of *Humanae vitae* (1968), an encyclical unexpectedly reaffirming Vatican teachings on contraception. The council also called upon nuns to adjust to the changed conditions and culture of the contemporary world and ordered all communities to consider renewal. As a result women, lay and religious, to an unprecedented extent began to question authority, demand new roles, enter politics, push for social justice and openly deliberate questions of sexual morality. On the other hand, many Catholics interpreting these actions as revolutionary, sought stability and order by stressing institutional authority and tradition.

Having already begun to reassess "antiquated customs" as enjoined by Pius XII, nuns were major participants in the women's movement. Many abandoned the habit, relocated into small communities, demanded just wages, moved into the secular world and demonstrated for civil rights and an end to the war in Vietnam—and shocked much of the laity by courting arrest for acts of civil disobedience. Such actions appeared sanctioned when, despite Vatican trepidations, the Conference of Major Superiors of Women changed its focus and title to the Leadership Conference of Women Religious (LCWR) (1971) and began to emphasize social justice and the "empowerment of women." Its spokesperson, Mary Theresa Kane, Sister of Mercy, in publicly welcoming John Paul II to the United States (1979), urged the pope to hear the appeals of women that all ministries be open to their sex. The "new" nun like her nineteenth-century counterpart frequently encountered resistance from the hierarchy. Unsuccessful struggles with their bishops over rules resulted in one half of the Sisters of Glenmary of Cincinnati and over four hundred Immaculate Heart of Mary Sisters of Los Angeles leaving their community.

Further exacerbating the tensions between the old and new visions of women was the equal rights amendment. Due in large part to the efforts of NOW, the ERA was resurrected, and in 1972 was approved by Congress and submitted to the states for ratification. Although supported by a majority of Catholics and such organizations as the LCWR, National Coalition of Nuns, and St. Joan's Alliance of Catholic Women, the amendment encountered powerful Catholic opposition, especially from the NCCW which described it as a threat "to the nature of women." The Bishops' Ad Hoc Committee on Women and Society in the Church at first seemed to share these fears. However, in 1978 it planned to issue a pro-ERA statement after obtaining approval of the National Conference of Catholic Bishops (NCCB). When this step became public, the NCCB was inundated with protests resulting in the bishops' administrative committee reaffirming its earlier position that the amendment should be "closely scrutinized" because of its "doctrinaire character and broad sweep." However, in an unprecedented action twenty-three bishops issued a joint statement calling upon legislators to rat-

ify the amendment. But to no avail. A Catholic, Phyllis Stewart Schlafly, who personified the resurgent conservatism of the late 1970s and 1980s, more than any single person was responsible for its defeat. She had organized the opposition and denounced the amendment as weakening the family and leading to abortion, lesbianism, and the drafting of women.

Probably the most divisive issue was that of ordination. As early as 1963 the newly formed United States Chapter of St. Joan's International Alliance, whose goal was equality in Church and State, raised the issue of ordination. Then in 1975, the first Women's Ordination Conference (WOC) in Detroit was attended by 1200 registrants (1100 of whom were nuns, 500 turned away). Enthusiasm for female priests was not curbed when Cincinnati's Archbishop Joseph L. Bernardin, spokesman for the NCCB, reiterated the Church's prohibition against women's ordination. Nevertheless, ordination was seen as an act of justice in the resolutions of 1340 representatives at Call to Action, a 1976 conference convened by American bishops. Hoping to end the controversy the Vatican issued *Inter Insigniores* (1976) asserting that the priesthood must be confined to males for "we can never ignore the fact that Christ is a man."

But no longer was the dictum *Roma locuta est, causa finita est* appropriate. Instead, at the Baltimore WOC meeting (1978) attended by two thousand men and women, it was decided to go beyond ordination and question the institutional framework of the Church. This approach was reflected in the conference's theme, "New Woman, New Church, New Priestly Ministry" and in the establishment of Womanchurch at a Chicago gathering of 1,400 in 1983. Womanchurch contends it is not in exile but in exodus from the patriarchy, "a new theological and practical standpoint . . . to claim authentic theological growth of being church."

Among those who found communion in this movement were two Sisters of Notre Dame. "We are Catholics . . . we pray with our Womanchurch." In 1984 Congresswoman Geraldine Ferraro, Democratic nominee for vice president, was admonished by the hierarchy for separating her political and personal views on abortion. This rebuke led to an advertisement in the *New York Times* sponsored by Catholics for a Free Choice, founded in 1972 and chaired by "I think I'm a good Catholic" Frances Kissling. Entitled "A Diversity of Opinion Regarding Abortion Exists Among Committed Catholics," the ad was signed by two priests, two brothers, twenty-six nuns, and forty-seven laity. The Vatican succeeded in forcing retraction from all the religious—albeit ambiguously worded by several—except for Barbara Ferraro and Patricia Hussey, who resigned from their community.

Other nuns also resisted Vatican directives. Agnes Mary Mansour, a Sister of Mercy for thirty years and former president of Mercy College, was director of Social Services for the State of Michigan. Conservative objections to the small portion of her departmental budget for medical abortions resulted in the pope ordering her to resign. Although personally opposed to abortion, she instead left her community. Elizabeth Morancy, a member of the Rhode Island legislature, and Arlene Violet, a candidate for attorney general in that state, also left the Sisters of Mercy rather than follow Rome's directive and abandon a commitment to public service. Cardinal Joseph Ratzinger of the Congregation for the Defense of the Faith was moved to remark that American nuns were contaminated by feminist mentality.

To resolve the issues raised by Catholic women, the American bishops decided to produce a pastoral letter on women. If they hoped by this means to reconcile differences and reclaim those who appeared to be drifting from orthodoxy, they failed. After nine years of preparation, testimony from 750,000 women and four drafts of the document, for the first time in history a pastoral letter was defeated 137–110 (two-thirds needed for approval). Each draft was more pleasing to the Vatican and less pleasing to masses of women as the emphasis shifted from areas of agreement such as equal pay and equal opportunity to areas of disagreement and even confrontation. Earlier drafts had urged the inclusion of women in ministries, condemned the sin of sexism, outlined the difficulties facing single, divorced, and lesbian women, and acknowledged the disagreement of people of faith over ordination and contraception. To some, and especially to Rome, where it was believed bishops should be teachers not listeners, these drafts not only ignored the rights of husbands and children but rejected tradition. In the final draft sexism was no longer a sin, merely a moral and social evil, ordination was no longer a question, it was theologically unacceptable and implicitly a closed subject. A handful of bishops publicly objected to that draft for pastoral reasons or because it precluded the possibility of ordination. The pastoral now had become a referendum on women's issues. Feminists pressed for its rejection, undertaking a letter writing campaign, lobbying bishops, and advertising in the *National Catholic Reporter*.

Defeat of the pastoral appeared to be a victory for Catholic feminists especially when it was followed by the pope's approval of an interpretation of canon 230 allowing for altar girls. However, opposition to what some saw as a clerical surrender to feminism became more strident. Conservatives accused feminists of trivializing sexuality and gender, of undermining the family and the dignity of women while emasculating men. Feminists were assailed as "offensive and destructive." It was asserted that female altar servers would contribute to the shortage of priests by driving boys from the altar and would encourage women's ordination. Those who had criticized feminists for scorning Church pronouncements now rapped this change as a

pastoral error. One critic even attributed the pope's approval to the condition brought about by his pain and suffering.

One of those troubled by the presence of female altar servers was Mother Angelica, of the Eternal Word Television Network. Mother Angelica, who appeared twice weekly on hourlong programs, claimed to reach an audience of thirty-eight million with her message on the evils of feminism and ordination. Also protesting altar girls were the bishops of Arlington, Virginia, and Lincoln, Nebraska, and Helen Hitchcock, founder of Women for Faith and Family. This organization's purpose was to assist orthodox Catholic women in "their efforts to provide witness to their faith, both in their families and the world." It grew rapidly and in a few years had a staff of ten, sixty thousand members, a newsletter, and convened conferences in Australia and England. Hitchcock even detected feminist penetration in the United States Catholic Conference and the NCCW, offering as some of her evidence the use of inclusive language by these agencies. Other new groups reflecting the more traditional feminine perspective were the United Catholic Women of America whose 40,000 members seek to restore Marian values, the National Institute for Womanhood a "pro-family, prowoman, pro-church" organization and a new religious order, Sisters for Life, founded by Cardinal John J. O'Connor (New York) to protect the sacredness of life, particularly that of the unborn child.

These organizations must have been pleased when the Vatican, urged on by Mother Angelica, refused to approve the English translation of the Universal Catechism because of its inclusive language. Despite the fact that American bishops in 1990 had called for every effort to make biblical translations as inclusive as a faithful translation permits, a new and more traditional translation was undertaken, delaying publication for two years. Inclusive language became an even more divisive issue when it was the basis for the Vatican's rejection of the New Revised Standard Version of the Bible three years after its approval by American bishops.

Traditional views appeared even more vindicated by John Paul II's *Ordinatio Sacerdotalis* (1994) stating that "priestly ordination is to be reserved to man alone." To preclude further debate the Pope asserted that this judgment "is to be definitively held by all the church's faithful." Nevertheless some theologians attacked the concept of "definitive" and supporters of ordination continued their campaign describing the document as "simply unacceptable." To placate these men and especially women, American bishops by a vote of 220 to 10 in November 1994 approved a Pastoral Reflection on Women in the Church and Society. In it they called for inclusive language in catechetical and religious materials, rejected sexism, advocated female participation in every possible aspect of church life and, after considerable debate, rejected as antagonistic an amendment condemning "radical feminism." Nevertheless, the pastoral described *Ordinatio Sacerdotalis* as "a clear affirmation of Catholic teaching" and resulted in WOC conducting a prayerful protest outside the bishops' hotel. Eighty to ninety others including Auxiliary Bishop Thomas Gumbleton (Detroit) held a vigil at the National Shrine for full ministry for women. The director of the LCWR simply stated that the dialogue about ordination must continue, which it has despite the Pope's Letter to Women on the eve of the United Nations World Conference on Women (1995).

The Pontiff, who gave thanks for the "mystery of women," acknowledged that historical conditioning has been an obstacle to women's progress but qualified his apology for Catholic participation by asking, "if objective blame has belonged to not just a few members of the church." Much more forthright were his calls for equal pay, protection for working mothers, legislation to protect women from domestic violence and his recognition of the positive achievements of women's liberation. To critics, however, these pronouncements paled, as he once again reaffirmed complementarity thereby limiting the potential of women and helping to justify his restatement of an exclusively male priesthood.

A new factor in the equation between churchmen and women is that many Catholics in the United States are now Latin Americans with gender attitudes emphasizing subservience to males and family responsibilities. Exceptions have always existed and will probably increase. Urbanization, working females, women-headed families, and a history of less Roman domination, most likely will result in a path similar to that taken by other Catholic women. However, no matter what the future direction, it will be impossible for the Church to assume "that women are inferior to men" as it has during much of its history.

See also CATHOLICS AND AMERICAN LITERATURE; SUFFRAGE MOVEMENT AND AMERICAN CATHOLICISM; WOMEN RELIGIOUS IN AMERICA.

Burleigh, Anne H., ed. "The Valiant Woman," a special edition of *Crisis: A Journal of Lay Catholic Opinion* 12 (June 1994).

"Disputed Questions: Authority, Priesthood, Women." *Commonweal* 123 (2) (January 20, 1996).

Ewens, Mary. *The Role of the Nun in Nineteenth Century America: Variations on the International Theme.* New York: Arno, 1978.

Kenneally, James. *The History of American Catholic Women.* New York: Crossroad, 1990.

Kennelly, Karen, ed. *American Catholic Women: A Historical Exploration.* New York: Macmillan, 1989.

Pope John Paul II. "Letter to Women." *Origins* 25 (July 27, 1995).

Weaver, Mary Jo. *New Catholic Women: A Contemporary Challenge to Traditional Religious Authority.* Bloomington: Indiana University Press, 1995.

JAMES J. KENNEALLY

AMERICAN CATHOLICS: 1492–1815

The history of Europeans and Catholics in territories presently under the United States flag is for the initial one hundred and twenty years the story of Spanish exploration and settlement, beginning with Christopher Columbus's arrival on September 19, 1492, at "a beautiful large island we called Borinquén." Spaniards had come to Puerto Rico. Vicente Yáñez Pinzón, captain of the *Niña,* would later be named *corregidor* or governor of Puerto Rico, which he thoroughly explored in 1505 during his third voyage to the new world. Juan Ponce de León became *corregidor* in 1508, Dominican and Franciscan friars began laying the foundations of Church life, opening churches and a school. The Diocese of San Juan was established in 1511, and on Christmas day, 1512, Bishop Alfonso Manso began a twenty-two year episcopate. He was the first "American" bishop.

Spanish Settlements

Permanent settlements on the mainland began with St. Augustine, Florida, on August 28, 1565, and closed with San Francisco Solano in Sonoma, California, in 1823, two years after Mexico's declaration of independence from Spain. Havana-based explorations had less lasting success than did those from New Spain, the capital of which was Mexico City. Spanish ships ranged along the Atlantic coast. In 1525 Esteban Gómez in the *Anunciada* explored from Newfoundland to Florida, sailing into the later Hudson River and Chesapeake Bay. Others traversed the Gulf Coast, and from 1539–42 Hernando De Soto led a hunt for gold through much of the present southeastern United States, as far as Arkansas.

To protect shipping in the Bahamas Channel between those islands and the mainland, Spain founded its one successful major East Coast settlement at St. Augustine. Secular priests manned the parish of Nombre de Dios; hospitals and a seminary were opened; and in the early seventeenth century there were even resident bishops from time to time. But the colony was mosquito-infested and marginal in Spain's grand colonial design. The European population remained small and poor. Efforts of the recently founded Jesuit Order at missionary work among the native tribes floundered. Their first superior, Pedro Martínez, had been killed in 1566, and eight more perished on a missionary expedition to the banks of the Rappahannock River in Virginia. They transferred their efforts to Mexico. Franciscans were more successful in evangelizing Florida, Georgia, and the Carolinas, although in 1597 five were martyred in Georgia. The Florida colony passed to England from 1763–83 and was again Spanish from 1783–1821, but Catholic life was feeble.

The Spanish arc stretching westward to California was intersected by Louisiana, a French colony from 1699–1766.

Texas, which had been explored as early as 1518–19, was always thinly populated by Europeans centered in missions and presidios like San Antonio (1718). By 1810, there were only 4,100 Europeans, a quarter of them soldiers. The Yankee immigration that would change the face of Texas was just beginning.

The Southwest, explored from "New Spain" or Mexico, seemed more promising. Coronado's expedition in the 1540s reached as far as modern Kansas, where Franciscan Juan de Padilla died, the first American martyr, in 1542. Construction of the city of Santa Fe, New Mexico, began in 1610. A people of mixed native and Spanish ancestry grew in a feudal society of wealthy rancheros and poor peons. Many of the natives were Christianized by Franciscan friars, but ties to ancestral religions remained strong. In 1680 a Pueblo revolt ousted the Spaniards and shattered the Christian community. The Europeans were back in 1692, but church organization never recovered until it was replaced by a new form of ecclesiastical government after the 1848 United States takeover. Arizona was originally also evangelized by Franciscans, but the mission was developed by Jesuits led by Eusebio Kino (d. 1711), cattle rancher, geographer, and indefatigable explorer and missioner, who founded the mission of San Xavier del Bac. After King Charles III expelled the Jesuits from his empire in 1767, Franciscans returned to care for the Church until Mexican independence led to their departure in the 1820s. The missions were only partially successful, more so among the more agricultural peoples and less among the nomadic hunter-gatherer tribes.

Modern American California was largely ignored by the Spaniards until the late-eighteenth-century threat of Russian colonization prompted a joint military-missionary effort. Juan Rodríguez Cabrillo had explored the California coast in the early 1540s, but not until 1768 did the Spanish move north. Beginning with San Diego, a chain of missions was created over a half-century, closing with San Francisco Solano (1823) in Sonoma. Blessed Junípero Serra (d. 1784) was the moving spirit of the California missions, which were secularized by the Mexicans in 1834. The Diocese of the Two Californias, established in 1840, had a population of four thousand Europeans when United States forces occupied the capital of Monterey in 1846, while the Native American population continued in steady decline. The discovery of gold and Yankee annexation were about to create a new California with a population that by 1849 reached 100,000 from all corners of the world.

French Empire in America

The most sophisticated society to develop in colonial times along the southern flank of what became the United States was the creole population of Louisiana and adjoining areas. Spaniards and French mingled with Rhinelanders and German Swiss. African slaves began to be imported in the 1720s, their lives regulated by the 1724 *code noir*. A distinct mulatto population developed, and French creoles were joined in the 1750s by Acadian ancestors of the modern Cajuns. France controlled the Great Lakes region, the Illinois country on the upper Mississippi and Louisiana and the Gulf Coast until 1766. Initial settlements in the south were at Biloxi (1699), Mobile (1702), and New Orleans (1718). The clergy were chiefly Capuchins and, until their 1763 expulsion from France's empire, Jesuits. Ursuline nuns established in 1727 the first religious women's convent in the future United States. The years of Spanish control (1766–1803) were marked by a severe priest shortage, but an auxiliary bishop of Santiago, Cuba, became in 1781 the first resident bishop in New Orleans. The Diocese of Louisiana and Florida was created in 1793 and Luis Peñalver became in 1795 its first incumbent. In the waning days of Spanish rule, the influence of the Enlightenment and of the French Revolution disturbed the colony. With the coming of more Yankee immigrants, the Spanish rulers retreated from earlier religious toleration. From 1781–1829 the most powerful single individual in the Louisiana Church was the Spanish Capuchin Antonio de Sedella, long-time pastor of the New Orleans cathedral, where he worked in close alliance with the "marguilliers," or lay church wardens. The first bishop under American rule was the Frenchman Louis William DuBourg, named in 1815. He lived up river in St. Louis and only in the final three years of his tenure (1823–26) took up residence in New Orleans.

France's American empire stretched in a great arc from Quebec and Montreal on the St. Lawrence to the Mississippi delta. Settlements between the two anchoring areas were few and far between. France did not come to the New World primarily to colonize, but to gather furs. Small trading posts and mission stations were the norm. Detroit (1701) was for many years the only substantial town in the interior. The first frontier was among the Abenaki in Maine, where Jesuits labored from 1613–1764. Raids back and forth between the Abenaki and English settlers were a regular feature of life. The Abenaki remained loyal to Catholicism, and when many of them joined in the American Revolution, one condition of their participation was that the Yankees provide Catholic priests to tend their spiritual needs.

The founder of French Canada, Samuel de Champlain, chose alliance with the Hurons over their enemies, the Iroquois confederacy. Consequences for French America and for the Church, which was an integral part of it, were momentous. Eventually the Hurons were virtually wiped out in a genocidal war in 1648–49, during which the five Canadian Jesuit martyrs died. Three others had been killed by the Mohawks at Auriesville (New York) in 1642 and 1646. Later efforts by Jesuits and Franciscans were partially successful among some of the Iroquois tribes. Blessed Kateri Tekakwitha (1656–80), of Algonquin-Mohawk ancestry was known as the "Lily of the Mohawks." But Iroquois alliance first with the Dutch and then the English was generally a factor inhibiting Catholic growth. Missionaries—Jesuits, Franciscans, priests of the Quebec seminary—pushed west into the Great Lakes region. Jesuit Jacques Marquette in 1673 accompanied Louis Jolliet on a 2,700-mile round trip down the Mississippi as far as the confluence with the Arkansas. Friar Louis Hennepin was the first European to describe Niagara Falls, and he spent six months as a Dakota (Sioux) captive in Minnesota.

Other friars were with La Salle's expedition to the mouth of the Mississippi in 1682. But institutional development was slow because of the tiny settled population. While Louisiana by 1763 had nine thousand people, the entire Illinois country numbered only a thousand whites and blacks by that year of French departure. There was no substantial population growth until the United States takeover. Sébastien Meurin, the last Jesuit, continued a lonely ministry from the 1763 expulsion of his order until he died in 1777. His successor in the vast Illinois country was a Quebec seminary priest, Pierre Gibault. In post-Revolutionary days, war with the pro-British tribes ended the French missionary era, although the first priest of the American era was a French Sulpician, Gabriel Richard, assigned by Bishop John Carroll to Detroit in 1798. Before his death in 1832, Richard helped found the University of Michigan, founded the first Catholic newspaper in the United States, and was the first priest to serve in the U.S. Congress, as delegate from the Michigan Territory from 1823–25.

The English Colonies

Roman Catholic history in English America began when the tiny ships *Ark* and *Dove* made landfall on St. Clement's Island in the Potomac River on March 25, 1634. They carried two hundred colonists sent out by Caecilius Calvert, second Lord Baltimore, to found his new colony, which he named "Maryland" after Charles I's Queen Henrietta Maria. Calvert was a Roman Catholic. So were the colony's lieutenant governor, his brother Leonard Calvert, the colonial secretary John Lewger, and the military commander, Thomas Cornwallis. Roman Catholics predominated among the "gentlemen adventurers," the political, social, and economic elite who formed the first Maryland assembly, but Protestants were from the first a majority in the overall population.

In matters of religion, Lord Baltimore, like his father, the first baron, was remarkably tolerant in an intolerant age. That had been their policy in a previous colony, Avalon in Newfoundland. It remained their policy in Maryland. The founding documents clearly distinguished political loyalty, due to the sovereign and religious loyalty to one's own conscience. No church was established or subsidized. Catholic worship was public, an anomaly in England's Protestant empire, but as long as Catholics controlled

Maryland, the rights of Protestants were meticulously protected. The Jesuit priests Andrew White and John Gravenor arrived on the *Ark* as gentlemen adventurers and soon had a prosperous and successful ministry; but when their successors claimed clerical privileges common in Europe's Catholic countries, they were refused. A Church-state relationship was established which simply prescinded from canon law. It was based on separation of the two, combined with a guarantee of free exercise of religion. This was stated in an act of assembly in 1639. Ten years later, when Protestant participation in the assembly had increased, the more restrictive toleration act of 1649 was enacted.

During the English civil war, Protestant colonists seized power in Maryland and Catholic rights were curbed. Then from 1660–89 the Calverts' proprietary rule was restored, and the Catholic community prospered. A school opened at Newtown, sons and daughters of the gentry were sent to Flanders for schooling, forty-nine men and thirty-three women entered seminaries or religious houses. Many returned in colonial and early federal days to work as Jesuit priests in Maryland and Pennsylvania. Three American women returned in 1790 as foundresses of the first American Carmel.

There were Catholics also on the 'Northern Neck' of Virginia, the peninsula between the Potomac and the Rappahannock, centering on the plantations of the Brent family. Scattered indentured Catholic servants in Virginia generally were unchurched, but itinerant priests from Maryland served the Brents. Better organized were missions in Delaware and Pennsylvania begun in 1706. Quakers tolerated Catholics, and Mass was first publicly said in Philadelphia in 1708. In 1729 the "City of Brotherly Love" had a resident priest, and in 1733 St. Joseph's, the first town church in colonial English America, opened. A second group of Pennsylvania Catholics began in 1717 when John Digges led Marylanders into rich farmlands in the colony's southeastern counties. They were soon joined by Catholics among the "Pennsylvania Dutch" recruited by William Penn's agents in the Rhineland and Palatinate. These rural Catholics, together with the polyglot population that developed in Philadelphia, foreshadowed the multinational shape of the future American Catholic Church. They were served throughout the colonial period by English and German Jesuits.

New Jersey and New York both knew colonial Catholics. Small communities were served by circuit-riding Jesuits from Pennsylvania. For twenty years Catholics were prominent in the Duke of York's government of the New York colony, where in 1674 toleration for "all persons of what Religion soever" had been decreed. Irish Catholic Governor Thomas Dongan established in 1683 a Jesuit school on the "King's Farm" and planned to replace French Jesuit missionaries among the Iroquois with their English brethren, but these plans came to naught in the wake of the 1688 "Glorious Revolution" which drove King James II from England's throne, and English-style penal laws against Catholics ended toleration of them until 1806.

Catholics were few and far between in colonial New England. There is no record of a corporate presence, and only isolated individuals stand out like Ann Glover, hanged as a witch in Boston in 1688. On the borderland with Quebec, Franciscan and Jesuit missionaries labored with the Abenaki, and Jesuit Sebastian Râle was killed in a 1724 raid by Massachusetts militia on the village of Norridgewock on the Kennebec. The Abenaki remained faithful even after the Jesuits' forced withdrawal in 1764, and made it a condition of their help for the American Revolution that a blackrobe, and not a Protestant preacher, be sent to minister to them.

Catholics and the Revolution

Outbreak of the American Revolution coincided with the worldwide suppression of the Jesuit Order by Pope Clement XIV. The priests in Maryland and Pennsylvania were left to their own devices and for a decade continued under the last Jesuit superior, John Lewis. Despite notable anti-Catholicism displayed by many of the Patriot party, Roman Catholics generally sided against the British. The wealthiest person in the colonies, Charles Carroll of Carrollton, hazarded his fortune for the cause, served in the Continental Congress, and signed the Declaration of Independence. He was part of the new nation's first diplomatic mission to Canada, on which he was accompanied by his cousin, Fr. John Carroll. The latter's brother Daniel signed the Federal Constitution, as did Catholic businessman Thomas FitzSimons of Philadelphia. Other Philadelphia Catholics were active in supplying Washington's troops, and Captain John Barry has a claim to be called "Father of the U.S. Navy." Maryland and Pennsylvania Catholics served in the Continental Army, as did Catholic officers from France and Poland.

The Church in the New Republic

Writing to Rome in 1783, a committee of Catholic clergy celebrated the birth of religious toleration: "In these United States, our Religious system has undergone a revolution, if possible, more extraordinary than our political one." Fr. John Carroll became the leader of the Catholic community. He spoke eloquently on the subject of religious liberty, organized the ex-Jesuits, and in 1784 was named superior of the mission. Four years later the priests elected him first bishop of Baltimore.

An immigrant flood soon diversified the Catholic population. Churches sprang up in seaboard cities, often for different national groups and built by laypeople who hired and fired pastors. Lay trustees' challenges to episcopal authority were a feature of early American Church life. Meanwhile, Carroll launched Catholic higher education with

Georgetown College and St. Mary's Seminary, both opened in 1791. Catholics moved to western Pennsylvania, where, after 1799, Fr. Demetrius Gallitzin was a towering figure. In 1775 Catholic settlement of the "Holy Land" of Kentucky began in Nelson and Scott Counties, where the first priest settled in 1787. The Illinois country came under the bishop of Baltimore in 1791, and the addition of the Louisiana Territory in 1803 demanded new organization. In 1808 Carroll was named archbishop of Baltimore with suffragan sees in Boston, New York, Philadelphia, and Bardstown, Kentucky.

Teaching and social-service sisters followed upon establishment in 1790 of the Port Tobacco Carmel. The "Pious Ladies" of Georgetown, who had assisted a refugee group of Poor Clares running a school there, made initial vows as Visitation nuns in 1816. Their foundress was Teresa Lalor, and Bishop Leonard Neale was their patron. Elizabeth Ann Bayley Seton (1774–1821), canonized as the first American-born saint in 1975, began life as a member of the Church of England, married businessman William Seton, with whom she had five children, but after his death (1803) became a Roman Catholic in 1805 and in 1809 made private vows. She had a school in Baltimore, that moved to Emmitsburg, site of the first free Catholic school and the first academy for girls. She was foundress of the Sisters of Charity in the United States. They soon branched out to establish an orphanage in Philadelphia (1814), and another in New York (1817). The American Daughters of Charity and several congregations of Sisters of Charity trace their origins to Emmitsburg. In New York City, one of the sisters' main supports was the saintly black Haitian Pierre Toussaint (1766–1853), whose cause for canonization has been introduced.

Three women's communities grew out of Kentucky Catholicism: the Sisters of Loretto at the Foot of the Cross (1812), whose foundress was Mary Rhodes, directed by the rigidly ascetical Belgian priest Charles Nerinckx. They spread through the Midwest and into the later Rocky Mountain states. In the same year (1812), three young Kentuckians headed by Catherine Spalding began the Sisters of Charity of Nazareth, following a rule based on the Vincentian rule of the Emmitsburg sisters, although not affiliated with them. Fr. John Baptist David, S.S., was their adviser. Thomas Wilson, O.P., was the animator of the third Kentucky foundation, the Dominican Sisters of St. Catherine (1822), whose first superior was Maria (Mother Angela) Sansbury. Farther west, St. Rose Philippine Duchesne, R.S.C.J. (1769–1852), a disciple of St. Madeleine Sophie Barat, brought the Religious of the Sacred Heart to Missouri in 1818, where they opened the first free Catholic school west of the Mississippi. Known to the Native Americans among whom she later worked as "the woman who prays always," Philippine Duchesne was canonized in 1988 by Pope John Paul II. Apart from a few refugee

Trappistines and Poor Clares fleeing the French Revolution, these communities were the only women's congregations in the United States, along with the Louisiana Ursulines whose continuous history dates from 1727. The later impressive multiplication of religious communities had to await the immigrant flood after 1815.

When the American Revolution ended, most of the Catholic clergy were ex-Jesuits. They affiliated in 1805 with the remnant of their order existing in the Russian Empire, and in 1814 the entire Society of Jesus was restored. Its American branch became prominent in education, parish missions, and in work among Native Americans. Occasional Franciscans, Capuchins, and Dominicans served parishes in eastern states, while Matthew Carr and John Rosseter founded in 1796 the Augustinian community in Philadelphia from which Villanova University had its origins. Edward Fenwick, O.P., later bishop of Cincinnati, brought the first Dominican community (1805) to the Ohio River valley. Invited by Bishop DuBourg, Vincentians led by Felix DeAndreis and Joseph Rosati began their ministry in the Midwest in 1818 in Missouri. Together with the Sulpicians, who in 1791 had founded St. Mary's Seminary, Baltimore, they became the premier seminary educators in the American Church, while many of both communities also served as frontier missionaries. Like the women's communities, men religious did not multiply beyond these initial foundations until the immigrant flood began.

When John Carroll died in 1815, he was succeeded as archbishop of Baltimore by his coadjutor, Leonard Neale. There were five other dioceses within the United States. In Boston the effective Jean Lefebvre de Cheverus presided over a New England Catholic population of some 4,600, 750 of them Native Americans in Maine, the rest Irish and French immigrants with a sprinkling of Yankee converts. He left for France in 1823 and died there a cardinal. New York was less fortunate. The first resident bishop, John Connolly, O.P., arrived only in 1815 to a diocese torn by disputes with lay trustees. The same was even more true of Philadelphia, where Franciscan Michael Egan died in 1814 after a troubled four years as bishop. The intellectual center of early Catholicism, site of publication of the "Carey Bible," beginning in 1789, Philadelphia also saw defections from the Catholic Church among its prominent families and sometimes tumultuous struggles over control of its churches. New Orleans, administered by Carroll until 1815, has been mentioned above. St. Louis became a coequal center during the residence there (1815–23) of Bishop DuBourg. Bardstown, Kentucky, with Benedict Joseph Flaget, S.S., as bishop for forty years until his death in 1850, developed a vibrant frontier Catholicism. With the end of the Napoleonic wars in Europe, a new era opened for the Catholic Church in the United States, that of massive European immigration. The initial colonial/federal phase was over.

Dolan, Jay P. *The American Catholic Experience.* Garden City, 1985.
Ellis, John Tracy. *American Catholicism.* rev. ed. Chicago, 1969.
Hennesey, James, S.J. *American Catholics.* New York, 1981.
Melville, Annabelle M. *John Carroll of Baltimore.* New York, 1955.
Metzger, Charles H., S.J. *Catholics and the American Revolution.* Chicago, 1962.

JAMES HENNESEY, S.J.

AMERICAN CATHOLICS: 1815–1865

Between 1815 and 1865 the most obvious feature of the Catholic Church in the United States was the huge increase in the size of the Catholic population. In 1785 John Carroll had reported to Rome that there were about 25,000 Catholics in the new republic, one percent of the total population. By 1820 that number had increased to almost 200,000. Thereafter, the size of the Catholic community grew rapidly due to a steady stream of immigrants from Europe, principally from Ireland and Germany. At the time of the First Plenary Council of Baltimore in 1852, there were some two million Catholics in the United States, making the Catholic Church the single largest religious denomination in the country. Fourteen years later, at the time of the Second Plenary Council in 1866, the size of the Catholic community had doubled to almost four million. The growth of the hierarchy was equally impressive. In 1815 there was only one archdiocese (Baltimore) with five suffragan sees (Boston, New York, Philadelphia, Bardstown, and New Orleans); by 1866 there were no fewer than seven archdioceses (Baltimore, Oregon City, Cincinnati, New York, New Orleans, St. Louis, and San Francisco) and thirty-six dioceses.

Immigration

Patrick Carey calculated that in 1866 approximately 78 percent of the American Catholics were of either Irish or German ancestry (*The Roman Catholics,* 32). The Irish immigrants tended to congregate in the larger cities of the eastern seaboard and the Midwest and in New Orleans, which was the second biggest port of entry for Catholic immigrants before the Civil War. Emmet Larkin estimated that only about 40 percent of the prefamine Irish were regular churchgoers, leaving the American clergy with the task of turning nominal Catholics into practicing Catholics. The Irish had advantages possessed by none of the other Catholics immigrants. Not only were they familiar with the English language, but they also were accustomed to anti-Catholic bigotry and they had a tradition of voluntaryism, i.e., voluntary financial support of the Church. Lawrence McCaffrey concluded that "the Irish were the only Catholic group that could have led an American Catholic Church with a diverse European immigrant constituency into an accommodation with the dominant, Anglo-American Protestant culture" (*The Irish Diaspora in America,* 9).

The German immigrants tended to be better off economically than the Irish and to emigrate as families rather than as individuals. Many settled in the farmlands and cities of the Midwest, giving rise to talk of the German triangle of Milwaukee, St. Louis, and Cincinnati. The German Catholics brought with them a rich liturgical tradition unknown to the Irish, and they demonstrated their penchant for organization by developing a network of national parishes, parochial schools, German-language Catholic newspapers, and fraternal societies. The first national parish in the United States, Holy Trinity Church in Philadelphia, was organized by German-speaking Catholics in that city in 1788.

Like the laity, the antebellum hierarchy and clergy were also composed largely of immigrants. In 1818 Archbishop Ambrose Maréchal of Baltimore reported to Rome that he had in his archdiocese fifty-two priests of seven different nationalities. At the opening session of the Second Plenary Council in 1866, thirty of the forty-seven prelates were foreign-born immigrants. However, the Irish domination of the American hierarchy was not as pronounced in this period as it was after the Civil War due to a substantial contingent of French and French-Canadian bishops, especially in the frontier dioceses west of the Mississippi.

Lay Trusteeism

The growth of the Catholic population created a need for new parishes and priests to staff them. Often the initiative for new parishes came from the laity, who collected funds, purchased property for the erection of a church, and then sought to enlist the services of a priest. The lay leaders or "trustees" frequently claimed the same rights in parish management as the American Protestant laity or the Catholic aristocracy in Europe. The American Catholic clergy generally resisted this assertion of lay power and often regarded it as an effort to introduce American notions of political democracy into the government of the Church. Conflict between clergy and lay trustees was frequently exacerbated by ethnic differences or by the attempt of an assertive pastor to use the lay trustees against the bishop. In New York, Philadelphia, Buffalo, Norfolk, Charleston, and elsewhere, bitter disputes led to excommunications, interdicts, and appeals to Rome. One legacy of lay trusteeism was a fear of lay power on the part of the clergy. In John Carroll's day, the Maryland Catholic gentry and the wealthy Catholic merchants of New York and Philadelphia played a prominent role in church affairs. In the early nineteenth century, however, lay influence waned, especially after the First Provincial Council of Baltimore in 1829, which outlawed the lay ownership of church property.

Religious Communities

The early nineteenth century saw the modest beginnings of the vast network of Catholic schools in the United States. In New York City in the 1820s and 1830s a few lay-operated "free schools" existed in the basements of churches and sometimes received government funding. The real expansion of the Catholic school system came only after midcentury with the rapid and extensive growth in the number of women religious, who were the backbone of the system. Between 1830 and 1870, forty-seven communities of sisters came to the United States from Europe, and several American communities had already been founded, including Mother Seton's Sisters of Charity. However, as late as 1850, according to Karen Kennelly, there were only 1,344 women religious in the whole country (*American Catholic Women,* 25).

Despite their limited numbers, women religious also started the first Catholic charitable institutions in the United States. The Sisters of Charity opened orphanages in Philadelphia in 1814 and in New York in 1817, and in 1828 they established the first Catholic hospital in the United States, the Mullanphy Hospital in St. Louis. The Sisters of Mercy opened Houses of Mercy for immigrant girls in New York, New Orleans, and other port cities. Two communities of African American sisters were founded, the Oblate Sisters of Providence in Baltimore in 1829, and the Sisters of the Holy Family in New Orleans in 1842. One year earlier, at Notre Dame, Indiana, the Brothers of the Holy Cross made the first permanent establishment of brothers in the United States.

Anti-Catholic Bigotry

One consequence of the growth of the Catholic community was the revival of anti-Catholic bigotry, a phenomenon that had been pervasive in the colonial period but had virtually disappeared during the American Revolution. It now reappeared in full force, especially in the large cities of the East, where there was widespread resentment of poor Catholic immigrants. Ray Allen Billington, in his classic *Protestant Crusade,* delineated the successive waves of this anti-Catholic bigotry.

It began in the 1830s in New York and Philadelphia with professional bigots who founded anti-Catholic newspapers such as *The Protestant* of George Bourne and the *American Protestant Vindicator* of William Craig Brownlee. Anti-Catholic agitators sponsored lectures about the horrors of the confessional and convent life, and provoked priests and Protestant ministers into public debates that produced more heat than light. A particular bugbear was the fear that the pope wished to annex the Mississippi Valley, an accusation which found expression in 1834 in Samuel F. B. Morse's *Foreign Conspiracy against the Liberties of the United States.* In that same year the first serious violence occurred when a mob burned down the Ursuline convent in Charlestown, Massachusetts. The most famous "literary" product of this scurrilous campaign was the *Awful Disclosures of the Hôtel Dieu Nunnery of Montreal,* a salacious and mendacious account of convent life supposedly written by an escaped nun with the improbable name of Maria Monk. Published in New York in 1836, it was actually the work of several Baptist ministers and became the *Uncle Tom's Cabin* of the Protestant Crusade.

In the 1840s the Protestant Crusade entered a new phase when Catholics protested against the mandatory use of the Protestant version of the Bible in the public schools and demanded a proportionate share of public funds for their own schools. Mainline Protestant churches now entered the fray with accusations that the Catholics wished to drive the Bible from the public schools and to raid the public treasury. In 1844 nativist riots in Philadelphia led to the death of thirteen protesters and the destruction of three Catholic churches. When nativist agitators threatened to take similar action in New York City, Bishop John Hughes prevented mob violence by placing armed guards around the city's Catholic churches. "By the middle of the 1840's," said Billington, "the American [Protestant] churches were able to present a virtually united front against Catholicism" (*Protestant Crusade,* 181). The Protestant Crusade reached high tide in the 1850s, assisted by the record number of poor Catholic immigrants who poured into the United States during the Great Famine in Ireland. Another factor was the ill-advised visit to the United States in 1853 of Archbishop Gaetano Bedini whose tour of the United States provoked anti-Catholic demonstrations in several cities. The main source of organized anti-Catholicism in this decade was the Order of the Star-Spangled Banner, a secret society which in 1854 evolved into the American Party or, as it was usually called, the Know-Nothing Party.

The Know-Nothings experienced meteoric success in 1854, electing forty-three congressmen and five senators, and winning control of several state governments. "Our Praise-God-Bare-Bones Parliament," was the Boston *Pilot*'s description of the Massachusetts legislature elected in the fall of 1853. One of the main objectives of the Know-Nothings in Congress was the enactment of a twenty-one year naturalization law, something which they were unable to achieve. In New York state, however, in 1855 the state legislature enacted the Putnam Bill, requiring lay ownership of church property. In that same year riots in Louisville resulted in over twenty deaths. By the middle of the decade, according to Billington, "the anti-Catholic forces were numerically stronger than at any time before in the country's history" (314). Catholics feared that in 1856 the Know-Nothings would gain control of the White House. However, their candidate, Millard Fillmore, won only 25 percent of the popular vote, and American voters soon lost interest in the Protestant Crusade as they turned their attention to the impending crisis over slavery and secession.

Conversions to Catholicism

Oddly enough, the revival of anti-Catholic bigotry coincided with the reception into the Catholic Church of a number of prominent converts. Several of them came from the clergy of the Episcopal Church, which was feeling the impact of the Oxford Movement in America. Among them were James Roosevelt Bayley, who later became archbishop of Baltimore, Thomas Preston, a future vicar general of the Archdiocese of New York, and Levi Silliman Ives, the Protestant Episcopal bishop of North Carolina.

In 1844, the year of the nativist riots in Philadelphia, both Isaac Hecker and Orestes Brownson entered the Catholic Church. Brownson was a self-educated Vermont Yankee who for the next twenty years single-handedly turned out the first serious periodical produced by American Catholics, *Brownson's Quarterly Review.* Hecker, after an unhappy interlude as a Redemptorist, founded the Society of Missionary Priests of St. Paul the Apostle (Paulists) with the intention of promoting a rapprochement between the Catholic Church and American civilization. Respected and revered in his lifetime, after his death Hecker became a controversial figure as the reputed godfather of the "Americanism" that was condemned by Pope Leo XIII in 1899.

The 1840s also witnessed the reception into the Catholic Church of Edgar Wadhams, who in 1872 became the first bishop of Ogdensburg; Richard Gilmour, who became the second bishop of Cleveland in the same year; and Augustine Hewit, who in 1889 was to succeed Isaac Hecker as the second superior of the Paulists. Other converts included James Frederick Wood, the first archbishop of Philadelphia, and Thomas Becker, the first bishop of Wilmington, as well as Jedediah Huntington and James McMaster, both of whom became prominent Catholic journalists.

The Antebellum Hierarchy

The growing influence of the immigrants, and especially the Irish immigrants, in the antebellum American Catholic Church was reflected in the changing ethnic composition of the hierarchy. John Carroll was a native of Maryland. The three most prominent American bishops in the following half century were Irish immigrants: John England, Francis Patrick Kenrick, and John Hughes.

As bishop of Charleston from 1820 to 1842, England described himself as bishop of the smallest and poorest diocese in the world. In a report to Rome in 1832, he said that he had 11,000 Catholics spread over three states among a total population of 1,800,000. England claimed that he lived off Vienna, Munich, and Lyons, meaning the Austrian, Bavarian, and French missionary aid societies. Despite the small size of his diocese and its meager resources, England became a national figure. He defused the issue of lay trusteeism by giving his diocese a written constitution with specific responsibilities entrusted to the laity. He wrote his own catechism, started his own seminary, and in 1822 established the country's first strictly Catholic newspaper, the *United States Catholic Miscellany.* He also gave his fellow American bishops a sense of their collegial identity by promoting the provincial councils of Baltimore. His biographer, Peter Guilday, said: "No bishop since has surpassed him in eloquence or in appreciation of the American mind and heart."

In contrast to England, Francis Patrick Kenrick was a shy, bookish seminary professor who in 1830 was made coadjutor to the aged and eccentric Bishop Henry Conwell of Philadelphia. He inherited a diocese of 50,000 square miles with thirty-five priests, only one of whom was American-born. For eighteen of his twenty-one years in Philadelphia, Kenrick made an annual visitation of his diocese, which usually lasted three months. In 1851 he was promoted to archbishop of Baltimore where until his death in 1864 he found himself increasingly uncomfortable as a Northerner in a strongly Southern city. Despite his administrative duties in Philadelphia and Baltimore, Kenrick wrote a four-volume manual of dogmatic theology, a three-volume manual of moral theology (both in Latin), translated the whole Bible into English, wrote several scriptural commentaries, and left a voluminous correspondence.

John Hughes had neither the erudition of Kenrick nor the sophistication of England, but he was more popular with his flock than either of them because he was the embodiment of the militant Immigrant Church in its confrontation with an unfriendly WASP America. An Irish immigrant who was ordained a priest of Philadelphia in 1826, Hughes was named coadjutor of New York in 1837, fourth bishop in 1842, and first archbishop in 1850. Early in Hughes' career in New York, two highly publicized issues placed him at center stage in the American Catholic Church. First, in 1841 he criticized the anti-Catholic bias of the New York City public schools and unsuccessfully demanded a share of public funds for the city's Catholic schools. Then in 1844 he confronted the forces of nativism and used armed guards to protect New York's Catholic churches from mob violence. Recognition of Hughes' national prominence came from the highest quarter during the Civil War when the United States government asked him to visit France on behalf of the Union cause. At his death in 1864, he was the best known, if not the best loved, Catholic prelate in the United States.

Hughes' style of leadership was unabashedly authoritarian, epitomized in his response to two protesting priests that "he would teach them County Monaghan canon law and send them back to the bogs whence they came." Jay Dolan commented that "Hughes ruled like an Irish chieftain, and the Irish respect for the hierarchy of power made his task all the easier" (*The Immigrant Church,* 165). Such unity was useful in combating the Know-Nothings, but it left the clergy and laity with little of the leadership role that John Carroll had once envisioned for them in the American Church. Hughes has also been faulted for per-

petuating a ghetto mentality among his flock, especially through his decision to create a Catholic school system. David O'Brien believed that such a decision "pointed away from the republican ideal of tolerant good will and equal responsibility and toward a subculture nourished in conflict" (*Public Catholicism,* 49).

Westward Expansion

In 1840s, as a result of the annexation of Texas, the Mexican War, and the settlement of the border dispute with Great Britain in the Pacific Northwest, the boundaries of the United States were extended to the Pacific, creating a major pastoral problem for the American bishops. Fortunately, they could draw upon the services of French missionaries, several of whom became outstanding figures in the westward expansion of American Catholicism. Jean-Marie Odin, who became vicar apostolic of Texas in 1841, was responsible for a diocese of almost 400,000 square miles with about 10,000 nominal Catholics and a handful of priests. His counterpart in Santa Fe in 1850, Jean Baptist Lamy, was only slightly better off with 25,000 Catholics and nine priests. Other French-born bishops faced similar odds in laying the foundations of the Church west of the Mississippi. Among them were Jean Mathias Loras in Dubuque, Joseph Crétin in St. Paul, Joseph Machebeuf in Denver, and John Salpointe in Arizona.

In California, where the Anglo population jumped from 4,000 to 100,000 between 1846 and 1850, the key figure was Joseph Alemany, a Spanish-born Dominican, who became bishop of Monterey in 1850 and the first archbishop of San Francisco in 1853. Perhaps the most resourceful of these pioneer bishops was François Blanchet, a French-Canadian who was appointed vicar apostolic of the Oregon Territory in 1843. In 1846, at a time when there were no more than 10,000 Catholics in the Pacific Northwest, he persuaded the Holy See to establish a whole new ecclesiastical province in the area with himself as the first archbishop of Oregon City and his brother Augustin as one of his suffragan bishops. In those same years Pierre De Smet and his fellow Jesuits established a network of Indian missions that stretched from Missouri to Washington.

Slavery and the Civil War

Although the question of slavery became the great moral issue in the United States after 1830, the abolitionist cause found few supporters among American Catholics, especially among Irish-American Catholics, to the dismay of the greatest Irishman of the day, Daniel O'Connell, who chastised his kinsmen in America for their failure to denounce what he called "the filthy aristocracy of the skin." In the Southern states, with rare exceptions, Catholics accepted the existence of the peculiar institution with the same equanimity as their Protestant neighbors. In 1841, Bishop England expressed his personal antipathy to slavery, but added: "When it can and ought to be abolished is a question for the legislature, not for me." In that same year Bishop Francis Kenrick wrote in his moral theology textbook: "Nothing should be attempted against the laws, nor anything done or said that would make [slaves] bear their yoke unwillingly."

The issue of slavery did not shatter the institutional unity of the Catholic Church (as it did in the case of the Methodists, Baptists, and Presbyterians), but the Civil War left American Catholics divided along regional lines. Several Southern prelates, notably Bishop Auguste Martin of Natchitoches and Bishop Augustin Verot of St. Augustine, were outspoken apologists for slavery, and Bishop Patrick Lynch of Charleston traveled to Rome in 1864 as an emissary of the Confederacy. In the North, a few prelates such as Archbishop John Purcell of Cincinnati and Bishop Josue Young of Erie voiced strong support for the abolition of slavery. Most shared the sentiments of Archbishop John Hughes of New York, who told the Secretary of War in 1861 that most Northern Catholics "are willing to fight to the death for the support of the Constitution, the Government and the laws of the country, but, if . . . they are to fight for the abolition of slavery, then indeed they will turn away in disgust from the discharge of what would otherwise be a patriotic duty."

Catholics served in both Union and Confederate armies since both sides were eager to raise Irish regiments and brigades. Among the most prominent Catholics were Union army general Philip Sheridan and Confederate Secretary of the Navy Stephen Mallory. Some thirty Catholic chaplains served in the Confederate army, and perhaps forty served in the Union army, one of them the newly ordained John Ireland. One of the most impressive contributions came from the sisters, over five hundred of whom served as nurses caring for the wounded on both sides of the conflict.

The war was a disaster for the Catholic Church in the South where it had already been weak in numbers before the war. Not only were many churches destroyed, but the war led to the impoverishment of the Catholic gentry and the dispersal of many of their emancipated slaves. In 1865 Archbishop Martin Spalding of Baltimore pointed out to Archbishop John McCloskey of New York that many ex-slaves were unchurched and receptive to evangelization by Catholics. "Four million of these unfortunate beings are thrown on our charity," said Spalding. "It is a golden opportunity for reaping a harvest of souls which neglected may not return." At the Second Plenary Council of Baltimore in 1866, Spalding proposed the creation of a special nonterritorial diocese for blacks, but his proposal met strong opposition from many of his fellow bishops. Instead, the bishops in 1866 decided to concentrate their limited resources on caring for the millions of Catholic immigrants who continued to pour into the country in ever-increasing numbers.

See also IRISH CATHOLICS IN AMERICA; NATIVISM; SLAVERY AND AMERICAN CATHOLICS; TRUSTEEISM; WOMEN RELIGIOUS IN AMERICA.

Billington, Ray Allen. *The Protestant Crusade*. New York, 1938.

Carey, Patrick W. *The Roman Catholics*. Westport, Connecticut, 1993.

——. *People, Priests and Prelates: Ecclesiastical Democracy and the Tensions of Trusteeism*. Notre Dame, 1987.

Crews, Clyde F. *American and Catholic: A Popular History of Catholicism in the United States*. Cincinnati, 1994.

Dolan, Jay P. *The American Catholic Experience*. Garden City, 1985.

Ellis, John Tracy. *American Catholicism*. Chicago, rev. ed., 1969.

Hennesey, James, S.J. *American Catholics*. New York, 1981.

Kennelly, Karen, ed. *American Catholic Women*. New York, 1989.

McCaffrey, Lawrence J. *The Irish Diaspora in America*. Bloomington, Indiana, 1976.

O'Brien, David. *Public Catholicism*. New York, 1989.

Rice, Madeleine Hooke. *American Catholic Opinion in the Slavery Controversy*. New York, 1944.

Vicchio, Stephen J., and Virgina Geiger, eds. *Perspectives on the American Catholic Church, 1789–1989*. Westminster, Maryland, 1989.

THOMAS J. SHELLEY

AMERICAN CATHOLICS: 1865–1908

Between the end of the Civil War and the turn of the century, the United States Church reflected the growth of the nation which was emerging on the world scene. In 1866 the American bishops assembled for the Second Plenary Council of Baltimore, under the presidency of Archbishop Martin John Spalding as delegate. They expressed the unity of the Church after a war that left some Protestant denominations divided. They also passed legislation, earlier adopted for the provinces of St. Louis and Baltimore, restricting priests' rights. But they also articulated their theology of the episcopacy in a decree that stated that "bishops, whether gathered in council or dispersed throughout the world, when teaching and judging together with the Sovereign Pontiff, the Bishop of Rome, are endowed from on high with the gift of inerrancy, so that their body or college cannot err."

In 1869 they found this collegial tradition threatened when they gathered for the First Vatican Council, the first ecumenical council with American participants. Most of them believed that papal infallibility could be defined as a doctrine, but that such definition was inopportune. Some, however, like Archbishop Peter R. Kenrick of St. Louis, judged it to be merely a theological opinion that not even an ecumenical council could elevate to a doctrine. Like most members of the minority opposed to infallibility, Kenrick absented himself from the final solemn definition on July 18, 1870. His delay in submitting to the definition until

January 2, 1871, became a *cause célèbre.* One American bishop, however, Edward Fitzgerald of Little Rock, remained at the council for the final session to cast one of two votes against the definition. His immediate submission, however, prevented the type of controversy that surrounded Kenrick.

In the postbellum years, anti-Catholicism was for the most part no longer aimed at individual Catholics, but at bishops who sought a share of public funds for parochial education. Some bishops sought a means of accommodation. In Poughkeepsie, New York, for example, the local pastor devised a system according to which the local public school board leased his school during the school day and supervised the secular education. Such an arrangement displeased some Catholics. James McMaster, editor of the *New York Freeman's Journal,* protested to the Congregation of Propaganda, the missionary department of the Roman Curia, to which the U.S. Church was subject, and was instrumental in obtaining an "instruction" on parochial schools. Written by the Holy Office in 1875 and promulgated in 1876 by Propaganda, the instruction urged the construction of more parochial schools and stated that parents were to send their children to these schools unless they provided the bishop with a sufficient reason, such as the unavailability or inadequacy of the parish school. This instruction later became part of the legislation of the Plenary Council in 1884.

In 1875 the Holy See recognized the growing strength and maturity of the U.S. Church by naming the first American cardinal, Archbishop John McCloskey of New York. He seems to have been chosen because not only was New York the largest American city, but also because he had been neutral, if not insignificant, during the Vatican Council's debates on papal infallibility.

Institutional Expansion

The nation and the church were still rapidly expanding, especially in the Midwest. At the same time McCloskey received his red hat, the Holy See established four new archdioceses. From the metropolitan province of St. Louis, it carved out the new provinces of Milwaukee under Archbishop John Martin Henni and Santa Fe under Archbishop Jean Baptist Lamy. From the province of Baltimore came the new province of Philadelphia under Archbishop Frederick Wood, and from that of New York came the new Province of Boston under Archbishop John Williams. The vastness and variety of the country fascinated, if it did not mystify, the papal legate, Mgr. Cesare Roncetti, who brought the red biretta for McCloskey and the bulls for the new archbishops. He left a vivid account of the Gregorian chant in the cathedrals of Boston and Philadelphia, the cannon salute that greeted him from the Milwaukee seminary as he passed by on the steam boat on Lake Michigan from Chicago, the ethnic diversity in Milwaukee where the bulls

were read in Latin, English, and German. But he decided not go to Santa Fe when he learned that he faced the danger of being scalped on the long journey by stage coach and horseback. In 1875 Chicago had not been named an archdiocese, because its bishop, James Duggan, was in an insane asylum. The diocese was governed by a coadjutor, Thomas Foley, whose death in 1880 paved the way for Chicago's elevation to an archdiocese with Patrick Feehan as the first archbishop.

In the meantime, new leaders were coming to the fore. In 1872 Spalding in Baltimore had died and was replaced by James Roosevelt Bayley. Even at that early date, the second choice for the nation's oldest see was James Gibbons, the vicar apostolic of North Carolina, who had been the youngest bishop at Vatican Council I. Only a few days before Spalding's death, however, Bishop John McGill of Richmond had died. Gibbons was named to succeed him, while retaining North Carolina. In 1877, he was named coadjutor to Bayley who died before Gibbons even reached Baltimore. As archbishop of Baltimore until his death in 1921, Gibbons would be the dominant figure in the hierarchy. Present for his installation was Bishop George Conroy of Ardagh, Ireland, who had come to Canada on a temporary mission and was commissioned to make a visitation of the American Church. His report to Propaganda in 1878 was a devastating critique of the American bishops, particularly for their strained relations with their priests. It provided the basis for some of the Roman proposals for the legislation of the Third Plenary Council.

In the meantime, other changes were made in the hierarchy. In 1880, at McCloskey's request, Bishop Michael Augustine Corrigan of Newark was named coadjutor of New York. Far to the west, San Francisco's first archbishop, Joseph Sadoc Alemany, asked for a coadjutor in 1883. California retained little of its earlier Spanish tradition and had become populated by English-speakers, many of them from Ireland. Alemany's choices were all Irish or Irish-American priests. The Pope selected Fr. Patrick W. Riordan from Chicago. The same year, Wood died in Philadelphia. Since his suffragans were unable to reach a clear consensus on candidates, Propaganda transferred Patrick J. Ryan, coadjutor archbishop of St. Louis since 1872, to Philadelphia.

The vastness and the diversity of the nation was both its strength and its weakness. Bishops of the Midwest, with its growing population of German immigrants, felt the need for another national council to legislate for their needs, but eastern bishops resisted the plea. In 1883, however, the Holy See summoned the American archbishops to a meeting in Rome to prepare for the Third Plenary Council. In preparing its agenda, Propaganda had before it not only Conroy's report but also the instruction on schools. This Roman meeting brought to the fore some of the issues that would soon divide the Church in the U.S.A. First, at the two earlier plenary councils, the archbishop of Baltimore had been delegated to preside, a right that would have been his *ex officio* had he been the primate. For the 1884 council, Propaganda had actually named an Italian archbishop to preside as delegate, but the Americans succeeded in having Gibbons replace him as delegate. Second, the congregation proposed some legislation that the bishops considered unsuited for the American Church, such as cathedral chapters to assist the bishop in governing his diocese.

Third Plenary Council of Baltimore

On November 8, 1884, 71 bishops and archbishops, and 38 abbots and superiors of religious orders of men processed into Baltimore's Cathedral of the Assumption for the opening of the council that would last a month. Its legislation, except as modified by the codes of canon law of 1917 and 1983, continues to govern the Church in the U.S.A. In regard to parochial schools, the bishops decreed that every parish was to have a school within two years of the council unless the bishops judged otherwise; Propaganda later granted only an extension of time. Under pressure from Roman authorities, the council provided that some parishes should have rectors who were to be irremovable and have a vote, together with the diocesan consultors, in the selection of their bishop; for the first time since the election of John Carroll, priests had a voice in the selection of their bishop. To provide for the growing number of suspect secret societies, the bishops decreed that each case was to be referred to the full body of the archbishops; if they failed to grant unanimous approval, the case was then to be referred to Rome. This decree led to annual meetings of the archbishops from 1890 to 1919. The council also legislated for the establishment of The Catholic University of America.

The council, unfortunately, did little to head off the divisions within the Church, but it did bring into prominence a number of new leaders, especially John Ireland, bishop of St. Paul. Reflecting the ethnic tension in the American Church, he chafed at being a suffragan of the German-dominated province of Milwaukee. In 1888, he became the first archbishop of St. Paul. He was to become the dominant figure in the movement to accommodate the Church to American culture. While he was in Rome late in 1886 promoting the establishment of his new province, he also took a leading role in gaining approval of the statutes for the new university. This, in turn, brought him into direct contact with Bishop John J. Keane, then bishop of Richmond, who was designated the university's first rector, and Denis J. O'Connell, a priest of Richmond and protege of Gibbons, who had just been named rector of the American College in Rome. The three initiated the formative phase of the liberal party within the U.S. hierarchy, as they responded to a series of issues that all arose during this critical period.

Controversial Issues

First, during the fall of 1886, a group of German-American Catholics sent Fr. Peter Abbelen of Milwaukee to Rome with a petition complaining of their treatment in the American Church and asking for German vicars general in dioceses with German populations, for German national parishes to be given equal status with English-speaking territorial ones, and for the adult children of German immigrants to be required to attend German national parishes. Second, Rome was then investigating whether to tolerate the Knights of Labor, an early labor union, about which the archbishops had failed to reach unanimous agreement. Related to this was the desire of some bishops, especially Archbishop Corrigan of New York, to have the Holy See condemn the works of Henry George, a social reformer, who had the support of the Knights of Labor and had run for mayor of New York. During his campaign, Fr. Edward McGlynn spoke publicly in his favor, contrary to his archbishop's command, and was first suspended from the priesthood and later excommunicated in July 1887.

As these events were unfolding, the Holy See again paid homage to the American Church. In October 1885 McCloskey had died. In June 1886 Pope Leo XIII named Gibbons the nation's second cardinal—he would in fact be the only one until 1911. In February 1887 Gibbons arrived in Rome formally to receive his red hat at the consistory in March. He joined Ireland, Keane, and O'Connell in addressing the divergent issues on which they had been working. In one memorial to Propaganda, he defended the Knights of Labor as a legitimate labor organization; in a second, he urged that, instead of a condemnation of George, there be an encyclical on the social question. In an address when he took possession of his titular church, he praised religious liberty in the United States. Finally, as a member of the Congregation of Propaganda, he attended its meeting that responded to Abbelen. Prior to Abbelen's arrival in Rome, the American bishops had already given their opinion that German-speaking parishes should have the same status as English-speaking ones. The congregation accepted this opinion, but rejected Abbelen's other demands.

Gibbons' support of the labor movement won for the U.S. Church the permanent loyalty of the laboring class. In 1888, the Holy See granted toleration to the Knights of Labor, who had already agreed to modify their constitutions to conform with Church teaching. In 1891, moreover, Leo XIII published *Rerum Novarum,* the first encyclical on the social question. While Thomistic in content, it owed its inception to Gibbons' request.

In the meantime, The Catholic University of America opened in 1889, in a ceremony coinciding with the centennial of the hierarchy and the first of two lay Catholic congresses. With Keane as rector, the university became closely identified with Ireland's Americanizing program.

But the U.S. Church continued to be composed of immigrants, increasing numbers of whom after 1880 came from Italy, Poland, and eastern Europe. The last named brought with them a different rite, including a married clergy. Ireland initially tried, unsuccessfully, to have Rome impose the Latin Rite on the U.S.A. But most of all, he became the symbol of opposition to German-Americans. In 1890 he led the archbishops, who had a consultative vote on vacant archdioceses, in an unsuccessful effort to prevent the appointment to Milwaukee of Frederick Katzer, the nominee of both the eligible priests of Milwaukee and the bishops of the province. He proposed, instead, Bishop John Lancaster Spalding of Peoria, on the grounds that he spoke German. The tension between German and English speakers, mainly of Irish extraction, flowed across the Atlantic. In December 1890 the European branches of the St. Raphael Society, originally founded in Germany by Peter Paul Cahensly, met in Lucerne, Switzerland. They drew up a memorial for Propaganda, which Cahensly took to Rome. Among other things, it called for representation in the hierarchy of each ethnic group. O'Connell then wrote a series of articles that appeared in the Associated Press, datelined Rome, Brussels, and Berlin. They accused Cahensly of acting in behalf of the German government, which, reportedly, expressed its pleasure at Katzer's appointment to Milwaukee. Cahensly only exacerbated the situation when he and his Italian colleague, Marchese Volpe-Landi, submitted a second memorial stating that sixteen million immigrants and their descendants had been lost to the Church in the U.S.A. because of lack of pastoral care. Although the Holy See rejected Cahensly's proposals and all the American archbishops, including Katzer, repudiated foreign intervention into the U.S. Church, President Benjamin Harrison expressed his concern about such intervention to Gibbons.

The School Question

But Ireland aroused yet more controversy with his plan at Faribault and Stillwater to have the public school board lease his parochial schools during the school day and supervise the secular education. Although the plan did not essentially differ from that in Poughkeepsie, Ireland had earlier praised the public schools and his new plan gave rise to a debate over the right of the state to educate. He explained his plan to the archbishops at their annual meeting in 1891, and he later claimed, erroneously, that they had given their approval. At the same time, he supported a law in Wisconsin requiring that English be the language of instruction in all schools, public or religious. This intensified ethnic tension, for German-American Catholics argued that the German language was essential for preserving their culture and religion. Moreover, Ireland's praise of public education and his granting the right to the state to supervise secular education in his schools was construed

in Europe as his surrendering what the church in Germany had fought to preserve during the *Kulturkampf,* the right of the Church to educate. Many English-speaking bishops in the United States also opposed Ireland's plan. Corrigan of New York was his most bitter adversary on the grounds that the plan surrendered too much to the state and that Ireland was too intent on Americanizing the Church and its immigrants. But, other bishops, like Spalding, who were usually his supporters, likewise dissented from his plan.

In the spring of 1892, Ireland personally presented his position in Rome. In a memorial to Propaganda, he argued that, if the Church did not accommodate itself to American culture, a *Kulturkampf* was as possible in the U.S.A. as it had been in the German Empire. Propaganda declared that his school plan could be tolerated *(tolerari potest),* but Corrigan had procured a copy of Ireland's supposedly secret memorial and assembled his suffragans to challenge Ireland's plan and to deny that a *Kulturkampf* was possible. Leo XIII personally rejected Corrigan's arguments that he had been swayed by Ireland's threat of an outbreak of anti-Catholicism.

Archbishop Francesco Satolli

Ireland had won his case, but he paid a price. He and O'Connell agreed to accept a papal legate to discuss the school question and probably to remain as a permanent delegate to the hierarchy. They then devised a complex plot to bring the delegate, Archbishop Francesco Satolli, to the U.S.A. They had Satolli named an official legate for the opening of the Columbian Exposition, the World's Fair in Chicago, commemorating the 400th anniversary of Columbus' landing. They furthermore kept Corrigan ignorant of the plans, so that, when the ship conveying Satolli and O'Connell as his secretary docked in New York, Corrigan was absent from the reception committee—an absence that was construed as a snub. Ireland and Gibbons then accompanied Satolli to Chicago for the opening of the fair. In November, Satolli addressed the annual meeting of the archbishops and delivered fourteen points on the school question, drafted by O'Connell. He supported Ireland, called for cooperation of Church and state in establishing schools, and urged religious education of children who were not in parochial schools. He then asked the archbishops for their opinion on having a permanent delegate; only Ireland voiced approval to the proposal. Satolli drove a further wedge between Ireland and Corrigan by removing McGlynn's excommunication, without notifying Corrigan.

On January 14, 1893, Satolli was named the first permanent apostolic delegate to the U.S. hierarchy, an office that would remain until January 1984 when the U.S.A. and the Holy See established diplomatic relations and Archbishop Pio Laghi, then the apostolic delegate, became the first pronuncio or ambassador to the U.S. government.

Satolli's appointment was the first step toward increased Vatican involvement in the U.S. Church. Although Satolli never lost his admiration for Ireland, he soon became critical of Gibbons, especially for his participation, together with Keane and Ireland, in the World's Parliament of Religions, an early ecumenical meeting, held in Chicago in 1893. The delegate's sharp report to Rome on the cardinal's activities brought a response from the Holy See prohibiting Catholic participation in such ecumenical gatherings that remained in force until the eve of Vatican Council II.

In the meantime, under the progressive leadership of such men as Gibbons and Ireland, lay activity increased. Between 1889 and 1894, African American Catholics held five national congresses, and there were two general Catholic congresses, the first, mentioned above, in 1889, and the second, in 1893, in conjunction with the Columbian Exposition. But such activity was linked with the fate of the episcopal leadership.

In January 1895 the American progressives received a further setback when Leo XIII issued his apostolic letter, *Longinqua Oceani*. The Pope warned against seeing the American separation of Church and state as an ideal to be exported to Europe and stated that the American Church would flourish even more if it enjoyed some privilege in law. Moreover, later that year, Leo XIII demanded Denis O'Connell's resignation as rector of the American College in Rome. He was replaced by William Henry O'Connell, the future archbishop of Boston and cardinal. In 1896, the Pope also asked for Keane's resignation as rector of The Catholic University, although the Pope stated he merely desired the rector to serve only one six-year term. Keane became a consultor to Propaganda and the Congregation of Studies, and took up residence in Rome, where Denis O'Connell continued to reside as the vicar for Gibbons' titular church. They became the Roman representatives of what now became known as Americanism.

Americanism

Americanism grew out of a series of factors. First, in 1892, Leo XIII and his secretary of state, Cardinal Mariano Rampolla del Tindaro, had called for French Catholics to support the Third Republic (the *Ralliement*). The papal policy was premised in part on the desire to gain French support against Italy, Austria-Hungary, and the German Empire to end the Roman Question, the status of the Pope after the city of Rome fell to the forces of Italy in 1870. But Ireland and his followers saw it as a move toward republican government, and in France, his speeches and sermons were translated as a blueprint for how Catholics could embrace republicanism. Second, the *Life of Father Hecker* by Walter Elliott, C.S.P., was translated into French. Isaac Hecker, a convert, had founded the Paulists in 1859. He stressed the indwelling of the Holy Spirit within each person as the motivation for activity within the world. He therefore

stipulated that members of this congregation were to respond to the Spirit and not take the religious vows of religious orders, but were to be ready to do so. He was not a trained theologian, however, and frequently used terms, such as "natural virtues," in a way that was misleading when they were put in the scholastic language of the day.

It was not so much that the translation of Hecker's biography was faulty as that it was impossible to translate the American cultural experience to France. Hecker was transformed into the priest of the marketplace rather than the cloister, one who espoused a life of individual action rather than of obedience to external authority. He became the icon of a new spirituality and the darling of those Frenchmen in the *néo-chrétienne* movement who were trying to create a Church freed from dogmatic restrictions.

As the debate over Americanism now became international, the American progressives sought to capitalize on the publicity, but, at the same time, explain their position. At the fourth Catholic International Scientific Congress at Fribourg, Denis O'Connell explained "A New Idea in the Life of Father Hecker." He began by distinguishing between political and ecclesiastical Americanism. Political Americanism was derived from the Declaration of Independence, which stated that "all men are created equal and are endowed by their creator with certain unalienable rights." This, he stated, was an expression of the British and American common law, according to which a subject had rights independent of what the state granted. In contrast, he argued that according to the Roman law the subject had only those rights that the government granted. He concluded that the common law was more in accordance with the dignity conferred on one by baptism than the Roman Law, which was, incidentally, the basis of canon law.

When O'Connell turned to ecclesiastical Americanism, he trod onto more controversial territory. By his time, the accepted theology of Church-state relations was that ideally, i.e., in theory, there should be a union of Church and state. Where such union was impossible, a hypothesis could be tolerated, i.e., a situation in which the Church had its liberty, while it strove for full union. Citing the First Amendment, he pointed out that the U.S. government was placing restrictions on itself in regard to religion. Moreover, he continued, were a Church to be established, it would be Protestant. He further declared that, though the theory of union of Church and state might be "beautiful," it led government officials, little versed in Catholic doctrine, to usurp the Church's rights. He concluded, therefore, that the American hypothesis worked at least as well as the theory.

O'Connell's speech became one of the key documents in the controversy over Americanism. In the meantime, what had been merely a war of ideas between the Old World and the New turned into a war of arms in the Spanish-American War. At the eleventh hour, Leo XIII asked

Ireland to make a fruitless intervention with President William McKinley. The U.S. victory meant not only the emergence of the nation as a world power, but the annexation of Puerto Rico, Cuba, and the Philippine Islands, which had been previously under Spanish control. Ireland and O'Connell, in expressions of chauvinism, both saw this as the way of Providence in extending Americanism. But they misread the tenor of the times.

During the summer of 1898, Leo XIII appointed a committee to investigate Americanism—other committees were looking at biblical scholarship emanating from the École Biblique in Jerusalem and the writings of John A. Zahm, C.S.C., an American, on evolution. To the conservative European theological mindset, all these issues were intertwined. On January 22, 1899, the Pope issued his apostolic letter, *Testem benevolentiae*. Acknowledging that the controversy over Americanism arose from the translation of the life of Hecker into French, he, nevertheless, addressed the letter to Gibbons. While praising the loyalty Catholics should have to their respective nations, he challenged certain aspects of what he considered to be Hecker's thought. He condemned watering down doctrine in order to gain converts and the apparent denial of the need for external authority. In a crucial section, the Pope addressed the relationship between nature and grace.

The letter condemned those who rejected "all external guidance" as "superfluous" or even "as somewhat of a disadvantage." He reproached those who implied that previous ages had "received a lesser outpouring of the Holy Spirit." On the contrary, he asserted that the "illumination of the Holy Ghost" was essential for one to accept the gospel and, as evidence, he cited the Second Council of Orange held in 529. That council had condemned semi-Pelagianism, and its citation by the Pope served as a warning that the Americanists were suspected of denying the need for grace. Leo also charged that those who spoke of the abundance of the Spirit in the present age seemed also to "extol beyond measure the natural virtues as more in accordance with the ways and requirements of the present day." This implied to the Pope that "nature . . ., with grace added to it," was "weaker than when left to its own strength."

Few American Catholics, bishops or otherwise, probably understood the theological implications of the misreading of their tradition. While the Pope had not directly addressed the questions of the separation of Church and state and of religious liberty, he clearly implied that "liberty" meant the rejection of the need for external authority—and of grace. The response of the bishops in the U.S. was predictable. Ireland, Gibbons, and their supporters denied that the heresy existed. The bishops who had been neutral in the previous controversies simply acknowledged receipt of the letter. But Corrigan and Katzer both thanked the Pope for exercising his infallible magisterium in eradicating the heresy. In northern Italy, where Catholics were debating papal temporal power, the bishops of the provinces of Vercelli and Turino likewise thanked the Pope for exercising his infallible office.

The condemnation of Americanism cast the American Church into a dogmatic slumber from which it would not awaken until the 1940s. In November 1903 Gibbons became the first American to participate in a papal conclave. But Pius X ushered in a new era of intellectual repression as he sought to stamp out Modernism, which he condemned in 1907. The Catholic University of America, the bastion of progressive thought in the 1890s, lapsed into intellectual mediocrity, as erstwhile progressive leaders, like Gibbons and Denis O'Connell, who had become rector in January 1903, worked to remove from the university any taint of Modernism, even if it meant impugning the reputation of outstanding biblical scholars such as Henry Poels from Holland. The Holy See, moreover, began to restructure the American hierarchy. In 1902, Corrigan, the only archbishop of New York since 1875 not named a cardinal, died. The aging Leo XIII appointed as his successor John Farley, who had been a moderating influence during the 1890s. But a new wind was blowing through the American Church, of which William O'Connell was the symbol. In 1901 he was appointed bishop of Portland, Maine, although he had not been nominated. In 1905 he became coadjutor archbishop of Boston, although, again, he had not been nominated. At Williams' death in 1907 he became archbishop and, in 1911, was named a cardinal together with Farley. In 1908 the U.S. Church was removed from the Congregation of Propaganda and thereafter reported to the Pope through the Consistorial Congregation. Although this resulted from a restructuring of the Roman Curia, nevertheless, the U.S. Church was no longer considered a missionary territory.

Ellis, John Tracy. *The Life of James Cardinal Gibbons, 1834–1921.* Milwaukee: Bruce Publishing Co., 1952.

Fogarty, Gerald P., S.J. *The Vatican and the American Hierarchy from 1870 to 1965.* Collegeville, Minn.: Michael Glazier, 1985.

Hennesey, James, S.J. *American Catholics: A History of the Roman Catholic Community in the United States.* New York: Oxford University Press, 1981.

McAvoy, Thomas T., C.S.C. *The Great Crisis in American Catholic History.* Chicago: Henry Regnery Co., 1957.

O'Connell, Marvin R. *John Ireland and the American Catholic Church.* St. Paul: Minnesota Historical Society Press, 1988.

GERALD P. FOGARTY, S.J.

AMERICAN CATHOLICS: 1908–1965

Catholicism in the United States during the first two-thirds of the twentieth century was characterized by many transitions: from a Church of immigrants to a Church of the establishment; from a Church of the cities to a Church of the suburbs; from seemingly limitless institutional expansion to the beginnings of contraction; from stability in its liturgical and devotional forms to dramatic change. A new era began in June 1908 when the Vatican removed the Church in America from the jurisdiction of the Sacred Congregation de Propaganda Fide. This administrative action, largely unfelt by most Catholics, ended the designation of the United States as mission territory, placing it on a par with the longer established churches of Europe. By the close of the Second Vatican Council in December 1965, enthusiasm for reform and renewal was widespread, but the prospect of unanticipated change was likewise emerging.

Social Composition

As the century opened, American Catholicism had a solid population base established by large-scale immigration in the nineteenth century. Catholics of Spanish, French, English, and Caribbean origin had been present in the territory encompassed by the United States from the beginning of the nation's history, but it was the massive immigration from Ireland, starting in the 1840s and continuing largely unabated into the twentieth century, which had the decisive effect. By 1850 Catholicism had become the largest single religious denomination in the country, a distinction it retains to this day, and continued expansion seemed inexorable. Catholic immigration also became more diverse even as it grew. Emigrants from the countries of southern and eastern Europe arrived in large numbers, adding Italians, Poles, Lithuanians, Portuguese, Slovaks, and Lebanese to the Irish, German, French-Canadian, Hispanic, and African American Catholics already in the country. With the passage of laws restricting immigration in the 1920s, the influx of newcomers was temporarily halted, only to begin again in the 1970s and 1980s, with America by then attracting Catholics largely from Latin America and Asia.

Throughout the first half of the twentieth century, these immigrants supported an impressive expansion of their Church's institutional presence. New dioceses and parishes were created to accommodate the expanding population. Schools at all levels, from the elementary grades through universities and graduate professional schools, rivaled the public educational system in many places. Social welfare institutions of all kinds—hospitals, orphanages, residential facilities serving specific populations, and eleemosynary agencies—flourished under Catholic auspices. Staffing this institutional infrastructure were impressive numbers of priests and religious women and men. A comparison of the aggregate dimensions of the Church at the beginning and end of the period is telling. In 1908 the American Church consisted of 93 dioceses, more than 1,200 parishes, and approximately 6,000 schools, serving a Catholic population of about 14 million; there were 15,000 priests and 50,000 religious sisters. In 1965, the results of sustained growth were evident everywhere. By then, there were 142 dioceses, 17,000 parishes, almost 14,000 schools, 58,000 priests, and 180,000 nuns; the population was estimated at 45 million.

Catholics proved themselves eager and able to achieve upward social mobility and its rewards. At the beginning of the century, American Catholicism was a largely urban phenomenon, and its people consisted predominantly of members of the working class. The desire for advancement was strong, however, and education offered a means for achieving that goal. While college attendance was rare among the immigrant generation, from the 1930s on a steadily increasing number of their sons and daughters, many of them aided by the G. I. Bill of Rights (1944), received higher education and were able to advance into the professional work force. By the 1950s, this phenomenon contributed to a large-scale move to the suburbs, and American Catholicism thus replicated in new communities the impressive building and organizational growth which had characterized the earlier urban Church. The fruits of material success were apparent both here and abroad. Church finances at home depended on large numbers of small contributions rather than the reverse, and by the end of the Second World War, American Catholic financial support was essential to international efforts as well. Reversing its position in the nineteenth century, the American Church became a net exporter of missionaries, and enthusiasm for such groups as the Maryknoll fathers and sisters (both founded 1911) was strong.

Institutional and Public Life

Perhaps understandably for a hierarchical Church, Catholicism was frequently characterized by its leadership, and more than one generation of strong diocesan bishops dominated church affairs. While many nineteenth-century bishops had been immigrants themselves, by the twentieth century the overwhelming majority were native born. Though identifiably American in citizenship and manners, the hierarchy of the United States in this period was also being "Romanized." Changes at the Vatican in the method of appointing bishops made solidarity with the papacy and its administrative apparatus the most important factor in the making of episcopal appointments. In contrast to more distinctive national expressions of Catholicism elsewhere, the American Church became singularly Roman and papal in its outlook.

Powerful, intensely loyal bishops came to represent the Church in America, both to its own members and to outsiders. Cardinals George Mundelein (1872–1939; archbishop of Chicago, 1915–39), William O'Connell (1859–1944; archbishop of Boston, 1907–44), and James Francis McIntyre (1886–1979; archbishop of Los Angeles, 1948–70) all used the force of their personalities to affect events locally and nationally, but no leader better symbolized the sense of American Catholicism's having "arrived" than Cardinal Francis Spellman (1889–1967; archbishop of New York, 1939–67). Exercising influence in the higher councils of the Church worldwide, playing an often decisive role in the appointment of bishops to smaller dioceses in this country, and applying the pressure of Catholic numerical strength to political issues, Spellman became a kind of "American Pope," the de facto primate of the Church in the United States. In order to increase their collective impact, the bishops had organized themselves into a National Catholic War Council in 1917, which continued after the First World War as the National Catholic Welfare Conference (NCWC). Reorganized in 1966 as the National Conference of Catholic Bishops (and a subsidiary group, the United States Catholic Conference), this body became the means for local bishops to work together on issues of concern to the Church as a whole and on matters of public policy.

At the same time, laypeople played an increasingly prominent role in Church activities and programs throughout the twentieth century. Traditionally organized into parish (e.g., Knights of Columbus), ethnic (e.g., the German Central-Verein), and other locally based groups, the laity had a more coordinated impact as the century advanced. The National Council of Catholic Men and the National Council of Catholic Women (both founded 1922), together with the Catholic Youth Organization (founded 1930), served as umbrella organizations, and groups with more specialized interests were also formed. A National Catholic Rural Life Conference was established in 1923 to advance the cause of those American Catholics living outside the cities; the Catholic Church Extension Society (founded 1905) promoted domestic missionary endeavor in areas with small Catholic populations.

In addressing problems of social welfare, Catholics proved particularly active. The NCWC Social Action Department, directed for many years by Fr. John A. Ryan (1869–1945), had issued its pioneering "Bishops' Program for Social Reconstruction" in 1919, and Catholic interest in issues of economic and social justice was sustained. Patrick Callahan (1865–1940) of Louisville, Kentucky, spearheaded a Catholic Conference on Industrial Problems in 1923, and associations of Catholic trade unionists flourished in many dioceses. By the far the most enduring of such efforts was the doctrinally conservative but socially radical Catholic Worker movement, organized in the late 1920s by Dorothy Day (1897–1980), a convert to Catholicism, and Peter Maurin (1877–1949), a French émigré philosopher; in 1933 they began publishing their influential newspaper, *The Catholic Worker*. Other publications intended for a broad audience also appeared, including the Jesuit-run *America* (1909 and thereafter) and the independent lay journal *Commonweal* (1924 and following).

Under these clerical and lay leaders, Catholicism came to exert an increasingly strong role in American public life. In the East and Midwest, Catholic politicians established an enduring hegemony in municipal, state, and congressional politics. American Catholics were frustrated when one of these, Governor Alfred E. Smith (1873–1944) of New York, rose high enough to run for the presidency in 1928, only to be defeated after a bitter campaign in which his religion was held by many voters as a disqualification for the nation's highest office. Though Catholic voters were an important component of President Franklin Roosevelt's New Deal coalition and Catholic politicians were usually found on the moderately liberal, Democratic side of the political spectrum, they were also represented elsewhere. Wisconsin's Senator Joseph McCarthy (1908–57) set much of the political agenda of the 1950s by alleging Communist infiltration of American government and institutions, and he drew enthusiastic support from his fellow Catholics, including several prominent members of the hierarchy. The equally aggressive John Birch Society (founded 1958), though religiously unaffiliated, also attracted a large Catholic following, helping to characterize American Catholics as the nation's most stalwart anticommunists during this period.

Catholic influence also extended beyond elective politics into broader areas of public culture. Concern over a perceived deterioration of public morals led many bishops, priests, and laypeople to reassert traditional standards and values. In many states, for example, attempts to relax strict laws on birth control and abortion were successfully blocked by strong Catholic opposition. Through the exercise of their local influence, bishops often had effective authority to censor books, movies, and stage productions. Following repeated denunciations by Catholic leaders, the movie industry in 1930 adopted a Motion Picture Production Code, written largely by a Catholic layman and a Jesuit priest. At the same time, the hierarchy and laity supported the Legency of Decency (founded 1934), which published ratings of movies for their moral content and organized successful boycotts of objectionable productions and theaters. If they could condemn the developing mass media, however, Catholics could also use it to advantage. In the 1950s, they enjoyed great success with the new medium of television, which made church ceremonies visible and accessible as never before. Some Catholics even became "stars": an auxiliary bishop of New York, Fulton J. Sheen (1895–1979), held audiences spellbound with his weekly inspirational broadcast, which for a time was the most popular program on television.

Worshiping Life

Twentieth-century American Catholicism was also characterized by a flourishing liturgical and devotional life. Rates of sacramental participation and weekly Mass attendance, though never reliably measured, were consistently high. Church buildings of a wide variety of styles were constructed to accommodate impressive numbers of regular churchgoers. Reinforced by the Catholic school system and by parish based organizations for men (principally the Holy Name Society, founded 1909), women (local sodalities of the Virgin), and children (the CYO), Catholic identification almost always meant Catholic practice, and "falling away" was both strongly stigmatized and rare. In the 1930s a movement to increase lay participation in the liturgy was organized by Paul Hanley Furfey (1896–1992), a priest from The Catholic University of America in Washington, and Virgil Michel (1890–1938), a Benedictine theologian from St. John's Abbey in Minnesota. The movement's impact was limited at the time, though it did provide a foundation for some of the liturgical renewal which followed the Second Vatican Council.

Apart from the formal sacramental requirements of the Church, American Catholics also developed an impressive array of other devotional practices. Novenas, parish missions, retreats for the laity, and other religious activities brought large numbers to church on occasions other than Sunday Mass, and these devotions wove themselves into the weekly and annual cycles of Catholic life. In many places, guilds, organized along occupational lines (doctors, nurses, lawyers, teachers, even telephone operators), combined social gatherings with religious ceremonies. Marian devotions such as recitation of the rosary were widely popular, with the months of May and October set aside for special observance; parish May processions, climaxed by the adorning of a statue of Mary with a floral crown, attracted large crowds. Eucharistic devotions, especially benediction of the Blessed Sacrament and nocturnal adoration of the exposed consecrated Host, were likewise popular. The display in the home and the personal use of so-called sacramentals—devotional pictures, statues, holy cards, blessed medals, scapulars, palm branches from Holy Week services, and so on—were common and served as distinguishing marks of Catholic affiliation. Even little things, such as the prohibition against eating meat on Friday (a requirement that was abolished in the United States in 1966), assumed great importance in fixing Catholic identity, both for Catholics themselves and for other Americans.

Popular devotional life often took distinctive shape along the lines of ethnicity and gender. Some groups deemphasized weekly Mass attendance in favor of other practices. Italian Catholics, for instance, organized annual *feste* in honor of the Virgin or particular patron saints, in which several days of street processions, carnivals, feasting, and public celebration became the focus of religious expression. Many Polish and Lithuanian Catholics favored the Forty Hours devotion, three days of intense prayers and sermons before the Eucharist. Hispanic Catholics often emphasized the penitential aspects of their faith, with laypeople publicly reenacting Christ's passion. Church authorities did not always view such practices benignly, fearing that they distracted Catholics from regular religious practice; in addition, interethnic rivalry was often at the root of such tensions. The all-male hierarchy and clergy may also have been uncomfortable with the prominent role played by laywomen in establishing and maintaining the popularity of these practices. Even so, popular devotions survived this hostility and added a rich texture to American Catholic practice.

Tensions

Although American Catholicism seemed self-confident and untroubled in this period, a number of tensions persisted, both within the Catholic community and between Catholics and others. Overt hostility toward the Church in America had a long history in the nineteenth century, with periodic resurgences of anti-immigrant and anti-Catholic agitation, and this pattern persisted in the twentieth century. Members of the American Protective Association (founded 1887) vowed never to vote for or hire a Catholic, for instance, and in the 1920s a reinvigorated Ku Klux Klan directed more of its energies against Catholics than against the black Americans who were its primary targets both before and after that. The Klan achieved significant political power in several Midwestern states, and it played an important role in the defeat of Al Smith in the presidential election of 1928. Voters in Oregon had attempted to outlaw the Catholic school system in 1922, approving a referendum which compelled all school age children to attend public schools, but the law was declared unconstitutional by the U.S. Supreme Court in 1925. Subsiding during the communal crises of the depression and the Second World War, anti-Catholicism revived again thereafter. President Harry Truman's proposal to appoint an American ambassador to the Vatican in 1947 was blocked by a storm of protest, and writer Paul Blanshard's best-selling *American Freedom and Catholic Power* (1949) rehearsed old assertions that Catholicism was inherently subversive of American political institutions.

Catholics responded by articulating a new understanding of the proper relation between church and state. The Jesuit theologian, John Courtney Murray (1904–67), moved away from traditional notions that Catholics had a responsibility to attempt the religious conversion of their fellow citizens. Criticized initially by many in the hierarchy itself, Murray's assertion of the fundamental right of all people to choose their own religious practice, expressed in his 1961 book, *We Hold These Truths*, was affirmed for the Church internationally in the Vatican II document on religious liberty of 1965. The "Catholic issue" emerged again in the election of 1960, when John F. Kennedy (1917–63), scion of two Irish Catholic families in Massachusetts, ran for the presidency. Several well-known Protestants, including the popular inspirational writer Norman

Vincent Peale, openly questioned whether a Catholic could serve as president, but Kennedy defused this criticism in a landmark speech to a conference of ministers in Houston, Texas, in September 1960, defending his ability to keep his religious beliefs separate from his politics; his election two months later was generally taken to have settled the question permanently.

If American society often looked on Catholics with suspicion, the hostility could also run in the opposite direction. Fr. Charles Coughlin (1891–1979), pastor of the Shrine of the Little Flower in Royal Oak, Michigan, initially gained popularity in the early 1930s for his devotional radio broadcasts. In Catholic neighborhoods, all activity seemed to stop on Sunday afternoons while Coughlin was on the air. At first a supporter of the New Deal, Coughlin turned hostile as the depression deepened, attributing all the nation's troubles to a supposed conspiracy between monied establishment interests and Jews. Unsuccessfully backing a fringe presidential candidate in 1936, Coughlin displayed increasingly profascist views as the Second World War approached, and he was finally silenced following American entry into the war at the end of 1941.

Shortly after the war, just as Catholics were moving into the mainstream of American life and improving their relations with non-Catholics, the reassertion of Catholic distinctiveness had one last gasp. Beginning in 1949, a popular Jesuit poet and essayist, Leonard Feeney (1897–1978), and a group of followers, many of them converts associated with Harvard University, gained notoriety for aggressively preaching that there was no salvation outside the Catholic Church. Feeney's attacks were initially directed mainly against other Catholics whom he judged insufficiently rigorous but, like Coughlin before him, he quickly hit on Jews as the center of all religious and social problems; his street-corner preaching took on an ugly anti-Semitic character. Both the Vatican and the American Church were embarrassed by Feeney's hateful language and rejected his theological views: he and his followers were formally excommunicated in 1954. A more tolerant attitude toward other denominations, a live-and-let-live approach to religious difference, had generally taken root among American Catholics and was reinforced by the Second Vatican Council.

Catholics also participated in the civil rights struggles of the 1950s and 1960s, and this sometimes produced tensions within the Church. American Catholicism had had a mixed record at best on matters of race: there was widespread support for slavery before the Civil War and only half-hearted work on behalf of African Americans after it. By the turn of the century some sustained efforts, such as those of the Sisters of the Blessed Sacrament, founded in 1891 by Philadelphia heiress Katherine Drexel (1858–1955), were evident. Local branches of the Catholic Interracial Council (founded 1934) appeared in many dioceses, and these councils cooperated with groups from other denominations to promote racial equality. The issue came home to Catholics over the desegregation of parochial schools. Archbishop Joseph Ritter (1892–1967) of St. Louis took the lead in this, ordering the integration of schools there in 1947, while Archbishop Patrick O'Boyle (1896–1987) of Washington pursued a similar policy. Their flocks accepted these changes dutifully if not always enthusiastically, but farther south there was trouble. When Archbishop Joseph Rummel (1876–1964) of New Orleans ordered the desegregation of Church institutions in Louisiana, he faced stiff opposition from white Catholic politicians. In 1962 he excommunicated three of these, including Leander Perez (1891–1969), the boss of Plaquemines parish, for their resistance.

Vatican II and After

American Catholics were at least as surprised as members of the Church elsewhere when Pope John XXIII called for an ecumenical council of the Church, which assembled at the Vatican for its first session in October 1962. This unpreparedness notwithstanding, many bishops, priests, religious, and laypeople from the United States came to play important roles in both the preparations for and the deliberations of Vatican II. More than sixty Americans were designated *periti* ("experts") in various subject areas, helping to draft the documents that were then debated, revised, and adopted by the council. During the three years of meetings, American bishops frequently participated in the discussions and helped shape the council's outcome. Cardinal Albert Meyer (1903–65; archbishop of Chicago, 1958–65), an experienced scholar, was influential in promoting renewed Catholic interest in the Bible, while Archbishop Paul Hallinan (1911–68; archbishop of Atlanta, 1962–68) played a prominent role in forging the most visible changes to come from the council, the revisions of the liturgy. The vernacular, whether English or the mother tongue of a parish's particular ethnic population, was now the language of the Mass and the sacraments, and more active lay participation in the form of spoken responses and congregational singing became the norm. When Pope Paul VI visited New York in October 1965, delivering a passionate speech for peace at the United Nations and celebrating an open-air Mass in Yankee Stadium, American enthusiasm for the renewal of the Church set forth by Vatican II was at its apogee.

The enthusiasm endured, and lay American Catholics took on increasingly responsible roles in the life of the Church. Less welcome changes were also ahead. A sharp decline in the numbers of religious vocations of men and women began almost immediately after 1965, and many of those already ordained or in vowed religious life left their ministries for lay careers. Enrollment in Catholic schools declined, and the rate at which baptized Catholics gave up the practice of their faith increased steadily. Many factors have been identified as contributory causes for these evidences of institutional contraction: rising levels of education and affluence leading to religious indifference; the collapse of an all-pervading Catholic culture and the loss of a sense of mystery which came with the vernacular liturgy; lay dissatisfaction with certain official Church teachings such as Paul VI's restatement in 1968 of the traditional prohibition against "artificial" birth control. These and other factors all played some role, but for those who maintained their Catholic identity, the American Church was a renewed and challenging place. Because Catholicism in the United States had become, like other American denominations, a voluntary Church, one which individuals deliberately chose to be a part of rather than merely inheriting membership from their immigrant parents, it exerted a strong and committed hold on its members.

Dolan, Jay P. *The American Catholic Experience: A History from Colonial Times to the Present.* New York, 1985.

Halsey, William M. *The Survival of American Innocence: Catholicism in an Era of Disillusionment, 1920–1940.* New York, 1980.

Hennesey, James. *American Catholics: A History of the Roman Catholic Community in the United States.* New York, 1981.

Kauffman, Christopher J., ed. *Makers of the Catholic Community: Historical Studies of the Catholic People in America, 1789–1989.* 6 vols. Notre Dame, 1989.

JAMES M. O'TOOLE

AMERICAN CATHOLICS: 1965–1995

American Catholics in 1960 were both secure and expectant. Secure in their role as the nation's largest religious group who had largely left behind them immigrant poverty and status. Secure too in a complex of traditions and experiences that set them apart as a distinctive people instantly identifiable within the American spectrum: fish on Friday; confession on Saturday; Latin Masses; lenten fasts and ashes; habited nuns; May processions and novenas. These were a generous, somewhat disciplined people who in matters religious were rarely accustomed to theological questioning or dissent. Few foresaw that by 1965 the structures of that secure world would be coming apart.

They were also an expectant people as well. In November 1960 the nation had elected John F. Kennedy as the first president of Catholic faith, thus shattering the last invisible barrier to full initiation into American political life. When Kennedy was assassinated on November 22, 1963, the televised Catholic funeral helped to unify the nation. In the next generation, over twenty-five Catholics would serve in the presidential cabinet, compared to but six in the first 150 years of national life. By 1965 Catholics had become the largest religious group represented in Congress, with over one hundred members. But by 1965 Catholics were also beginning a new era, less secure and more challenging.

The Council: Prelude to Unforeseen Change

Pope John XXIII was already a beloved figure to people of many faith traditions when he summoned the first ecumenical council of the twentieth century to Rome. At the Second Vatican Council (1962–65), especially through the writings of Maryland Jesuit John Courtney Murray, the American experience of pluralism and freedom of faith left its imprint on the church worldwide in the Declaration on Religious Liberty.

The council was to mark an epochal transformation in the life and attitudes of American Catholics. Peter Steinfels, writing a generation later, concisely summarized the scope and pervasiveness of change:

> The Second Vatican Council . . . affirmed the active participation of the laity in worship and the responsibilities of bishops along with the Pope. It avoided condemnations, took a sympathetic stance toward the modern world, endorsed freedom of religion and conscience and emphasized that holiness was found in marriage, everyday work and the struggle for justice as well as in prayer and priestly life.
>
> The revised liturgy expressed the new egalitarianism and communal participation. The church authorized celebration of the Mass in local languages rather than in Latin. . . . Most importantly the new liturgy, along with the other, less visible changes, shattered many Catholics' assumption that their church's rules and practices were immutable and beyond discussion (*New York Times*, May 29, 1994).

The generation before the council has been identified as the era of institutional (or "brick and mortar") Catholicism because of its extraordinary energy for constructing parishes, schools, hospitals, and other institutions. The generation that followed the epochal event in Rome might be called participational (or "flow-chart") Catholicism as the typical diocese found itself filled with a network of new agencies, committees, and commissions.

Often these more collaborative bodies included diocesan and parish councils as well as clerical and religious senates. There also appeared a veritable alphabet of commissions concerned with such areas as black ministries, continuing education, due process, ecumenical affairs, evangelization, family relations, finance, lay ministries, liturgy, media, social justice, spirituality, vocations, or youth ministry.

A Time of Involvement and Dissent

The deepened sense of commitment and involvement extended well beyond church structures for postconciliar

American Catholics. In considerable numbers they cast themselves into national civic concerns. The National Conference of Catholic Bishops had issued a letter in 1958 titled "The National Race Crisis," supportive of the civil rights struggle; soon many Catholics at grassroots level became involved in integration committees, marches, and picket lines.

On the tortured issue of the morality of the war in Southeast Asia, some Catholics like the clerical Berrigan brothers, Daniel and Philip, turned to radical stances of opposition. Most notably the "Catonsville Nine"—including six current or former members of religious orders—were prosecuted for breaking into a draft board office on May 17, 1968. Other Catholics in large numbers found more conventional means of dissent; by 1971, over half of Catholics polled were in opposition to the war. The bishops, in their *Resolution on Southeast Asia* of the same year, declared that "whatever good we hope to achieve through continued involvement in this war is now outweighed by the destruction of human life and of the moral values that it entails." There were, of course, American Catholics who took a counter position, supporting the war to its conclusion in 1973.

In that same year of 1973, the Supreme Court of the United States, in its *Roe v. Wade* decision, handed down on January 22, rendered abortion legal in America. Along with people of other religious traditions, Catholics became outspoken in their opposition to the ruling. The bishops addressed the abortion issue repeatedly and with special urgency in their pronouncements. They did so within a complex of a "consistent life ethic" in which they spoke out as well on a wide spectrum of social issues: positively in such areas as education, gun control, health care, housing, welfare, and women's rights; negatively on the death penalty, discrimination, and euthanasia. Their best-known documents, widely perceived as politically liberal when they were issued in the Reagan presidential years, were *The Challenge of Peace* (1983) and *Economic Justice for All* (1986). By the late 1980s, according to Gallup poll reports, 68 percent of Catholics favored cuts in military spending, while 77 percent wanted to see more government spending on social programs.

Within the Church itself in America, a tradition of dissent became manifest in 1968 over an issue that was not directly related to the Second Vatican Council: birth control. In the encyclical *Humanae vitae* of July 29, 1968, Pope Paul upheld traditional Catholic natural law teaching disallowing the use of artificial contraception. Many priests were numbered among the first public protesters, and in the Archdiocese of Washington, thirty-nine clerics were suspended for their stance. While a highly visible case, it was not a typical one. In increasing numbers, as revealed by frequent national surveys, a majority of lay Catholics reported their own variance from the papal teaching.

"Selective Catholicism"?: The Evidence of the Polls

From the middle 1960s forward, another new phenomenon entered the American Catholic scene: the papal visit. Large crowds greeted Pope Paul VI in 1965, and Pope John Paul II in his mainland United States visits of 1979, 1987, and 1993. Whenever the Holy Father came to call, pollsters went into a frenzy of surveying Catholics on controversial issues.

While many cautioned that faith and morality are not fashioned by popular voting, and although there would be numerical variations, results have remained fairly consistent. A Gallup Poll of 1993 found 72 percent of American Catholics favoring the ordination of married men as priests, with 64 percent supporting the ordination of women (*National Catholic Reporter,* October 8, 1993).

An additional poll of the same year sponsored by *USA Today,* CNN and Gallup, found that the following percentages said they could remain "A good Catholic" even if they:

Use artificial birth control 81%
Do not go to Mass regularly 67%
Do not go to confession yearly 66%
Divorce and remarry without
   a church annulment 61%
Have an abortion 51%
Have sex outside marriage 48%
Engage in homosexual acts 35%

(*USA Today,* August 17, 1993)

Not surprisingly, this growing phenomenon of "cafeteria Catholicism" set off impassioned discussions of polarity among church leaders and scholars. Such organizations as Catholics United for the Faith (1967) and the Fellowship of Catholic Scholars (1977) were founded as conservative counterforces.

The papacy of John Paul II has been termed "restorationist" for its highly publicized attempts to rein in dissent. These efforts included the appointment of highly orthodox prelates as American diocesan bishops; pronouncements reasserting traditional praxis, such as the prohibition of the clerical ordination of women; and the presentation of an oath of fidelity for new theology professors in seminaries and universities (1989). In 1986 Fr. Charles Curran was dismissed from his teaching post at The Catholic University of America over controversial stances especially in areas of sexual morality.

Spiritual and Interfaith Energies

The existence of controversies should not obscure the fact that the postconciliar years have been a time of immense social and spiritual energy. Sponsored by the National Conference of Catholic Bishops, The Call to Action Conference in Detroit in October 1976 represented an unprecedented gathering of laity, religious, and clergy to plan in collaborative deliberation for the betterment of Church and society. Catholics also maintained a high profile of interfaith collaboration and cooperation throughout the nation. Beginning with formal theological consultations with Anglicans and Eastern Orthodox in 1965, American Catholicism has increasingly entered honest and hospitable dialogues with leaders of other denominations. Relationships of mutual understanding have been nurtured as well with other faiths, especially Islam and Judaism. The Vatican diplomatic recognition of Israel in 1994 significantly enhanced the Jewish-Catholic discussions.

Such interfaith contacts have ranged far beyond the theological and institutional levels to frequent grassroots sharing of Catholics with persons of other faith commitments in prayer, religious education, and social service. Among themselves, Catholics experienced a range of both new and renewed forms of spiritual intensity. These included the Charismatic movement, Cursillo, Engaged Couple and Marriage Encounter Groups, Marian piety (especially focused around events at Medjugorje) and parish renewal programs such as RENEW. Catholics also had newly declared American saints to venerate in these years, including Mother Elizabeth Ann Seton (1975), John Nepomucene Neumann (1977), and Rose Philippine Duchesne (1988).

Expanded Roles of Women and Minorities

A significant number of articulate feminist theologians representing a spectrum of opinion emerged within American Catholicism in the generation after the Second Vatican Council. Issues have ranged from inclusive language, to women's ordination, to ways of imaging God. Several new organizations sprang into existence such as the liberal Women's Ordination Conference (1976) or Womenchurch (1983); and the more traditional Women for Faith and Family (1984).

Women had meanwhile in these years assumed many new ministerial roles and administrative tasks (e.g., as parish administrators, diocesan chancellors, or marriage tribunal directors). After the Vatican had reiterated opposition to the ordination of women, the American Bishops in 1994 issued "Toward Strengthening the Bonds of Peace," a document that called for alternative ways for women to share in decisional roles within the Church.

The complexion and leadership of American Catholicism was changing markedly in the postconciliar generation. By the 1990s, Hispanics constituted nearly 20 percent of the Catholic people, and in about a dozen western dioceses accounted for half of the population. Over twenty Hispanic bishops took their place among the nation's bishops. The number of African American Catholics had risen to about a million and a half (about 2.5 percent of the Catholic population), with ten black bishops serving in the nation's hierarchy. A national Office for Black Catholics was established in 1970. Catholic charity organizations were responsible for bringing to America a sizable number of refugees as well, notably Vietnamese and Haitians. Additionally, Catholicism revealed an increased official sensitivity to empowering Native Americans, while admitting candidly that early missionary efforts had often treated the first Americans unjustly.

Catholics in the Public Eye

As America's largest religious community, Catholicism was frequently analyzed in the nation's press and broadcast media. In addition to coverage of conflicts and dissent, the media often provided favorable profiles of Catholics in politics, social causes, and ecumenical endeavors; they also were called upon to report cases of clerical pedophilia.

It would be impossible to name the many highly placed Catholics in public service of this generation. In New York in 1994, the governor and two U. S. senators were of the Catholic faith, as well as the mayor of New York City. Controversial political figures on the national scene included Robert Kennedy (d. 1968) and Edward Kennedy, senators from New York and Massachusetts, respectively; Eugene McCarthy, presidential candidate in 1968; Geraldine Ferraro, vice-presidential candidate in 1984; and Henry Hyde, congressman from Illinois, especially visible in the Right To Life movement.

It was typical of this age that the theologians most profiled in the national press were often controversial figures; in an earlier era, if theologians were reported on at all, it would have been as remote and dusty scholars. Among those prominent in the public eye have been Raymond Brown, John Dominic Crossan, Charles Curran, Mary Daly, Avery Dulles, Elizabeth Johnson, Richard McBrien, Richard McCormick, Richard Neuhaus, Rosemary Radford Ruether, Elisabeth Schüssler-Fiorenza, and David Tracy. Other Catholics who made a notable impact on the American scene were African American liturgist Sr. Thea Bowman (d. 1990); conservative editor William F. Buckley; labor leader Cesar Chavez (d. 1993); Richard Cardinal Cushing, archbishop of Boston (d. 1970); Catholic Worker founder Dorothy Day (d. 1980); sociologist and novelist Andrew Greeley; and Francis Cardinal Spellman, archbishop of New York (d. 1967).

In a class nearly by himself was Thomas Merton (1915–68), a Trappist priest of the Kentucky Abbey of Gethsemani. Called "the American Augustine," Merton was a renaissance figure who wrote prodigiously and learnedly on a wide range of issues: Catholic history, liturgy and spirituality; ecumenical relationships; Oriental faiths; art and literature; civil rights and nuclear weapons. Poet and critic, monk and mystic, Merton's work remains highly influential and has made him a candidate for the century's most widely known Catholic spiritual writer in America. While Merton wrote little fiction, he very much revered it. Among the outstanding fiction writers who were nurtured by Catholicism, mention might be made of Edwin O'Connor (d.

1968), Flannery O'Connor (d. 1964), Andre Dubus, Mary Gordon, William Kennedy, and Walker Percy (d. 1990).

Gain and Loss: A Comparative Statistical Glance

Drawing on statistics from the *Official Catholic Directory* for 1962 and 1994, the following comparative chart can be drawn:

	1962	1994
Catholic Population	42,876,665	59,858,042
Archbishops	34	45
Bishops	195	344
Sisters	173,351	94,431
Brothers	11,502	6,510
Priests	55,581	50,320
Permanent Deacons	0	11,123
Seminarians	46,189	5,726
Parishes	17,156	19,787
Colleges & Universities	278	232
College & University Students	336,604	664,777
Hospitals	816	609
High Schools	2,435	1,360
High School Students	945,785	632,620
Elementary Schools	10,630	7,292
Elementary Students	4,451,893	2,032,853

Conclusion

Catholics today, worshiping in nearly 20,000 parishes, make up about 23 percent of the American population. While they are predominantly of Western liturgical observance, such Eastern traditions as the Antiochene, Armenian, Chaldean, and Constantinopolitan are represented as well. Catholics are a study in ethnic diversity. In such archdioceses as Chicago or Los Angeles, Sunday liturgy is conducted in well over two dozen languages.

The number of Americans identifying themselves as Catholic also presents a picture of a people divided over several controversial issues. American ideals of democracy and pluralism, higher educational levels, increasing lay assertiveness and participation, deeper historical consciousness, intensified ecumenical encounters, the distrust of practically any authority figure in America since the turmoil of the 1960s and Watergate in the 1970s—all these have had a profound impact on the experience of Catholics in America in the postconciliar generation.

These are a people who have had to experience a great deal of cultural change in a short span of time. Within two decades, they watched the departure of thousands of priests and religious from the clerical or community ranks. Many American Catholics grew in affluence, moved to suburbs, and lost something of treasured neighborhood and ethnic roots. They witnessed many old securities ebb away and new vitalities come to birth.

And yet, American Catholics remain a people who seem to find a common identity around the great verities: classic dogmas of faith; sacramental, scriptural, and spiritual experiences; celebration of life in community; and commitment to personal and social morality. They also cling—however diversely—to their rootedness to Rome. Through the papacy and bishops, they find a bonding to a worldwide community of faith as well as historical connectedness to the ancient faith of the Gospels.

Though many of their traditions have been subjected to sustained and unprecedented self-criticism in this generation, American Catholics find in their faith energies and expectations for enhancing the lives and hopes of themselves and their society. Most would probably agree with the words of Joseph Cardinal Bernardin of Chicago in a *New York Times* interview of December 11, 1994:

> We are a church polarized. . . . We have to bring it back together. . . . We need a greater sense of humility for our failings, a greater sense of reaching out for what joins us rather than looking for what can divide us.

See also CATHOLIC PEACE MOVEMENT, THE; *HUMANAE VITAE:* ITS RECEPTION IN AMERICA; MERTON, THOMAS; VATICAN II AND AMERICAN CATHOLICS.

Briggs, Kenneth A. *Holy Siege: The Year That Shook Catholic America.* San Francisco, 1992.

Carey, Patrick. *The Roman Catholics.* Westport, Connecticut, 1993, esp. 115–46.

Dolan, Jay. *The American Catholic Experience.* Garden City, New York, 1985.

Gallup, George, and Jim Castelli. *The American Catholic People: Their Beliefs, Practices and Values.* New York, 1987.

Greeley, Andrew. *The Catholic Myth: The Behavior and Beliefs of American Catholics.* New York, 1990.

Hennesey, James. *American Catholics.* New York, 1981.

Kelly, George. *The Battle for the American Catholic Church.* Garden City, New York, 1979.

Kennedy, Eugene. *Tomorrow's Catholics, Yesterday's Church.* New York, 1988.

Neuhaus, Richard. *The Catholic Moment: The Paradox of the Church in the Postmodern World.* San Francisco, 1987.

Steinfels, Peter. "Searching Its Soul: The American Catholic Church." *New York Times,* May 29–31; June 1, 1994.

Weaver, Mary Jo. *New Catholic Women: A Contemporary Challenge to Traditional Religious Authority.* San Francisco, 1985.

CLYDE F. CREWS

AMERICAN CATHOLICS, PERCENTAGE OF POPULATION

(*Source: The Official Catholic Directory, 1995;* figures are as of Jan. 1, 1995. Total general population figures at the end of the table are U.S. Census Bureau estimates for Jan. 1 of the respective years. Archdioceses are indicated by an asterisk.)

State Diocese	Catholic Pop.	Total Pop.	Cath. Pct.	State Diocese	Catholic Pop.	Total Pop.	Cath. Pct.
Alabama	**132,745**	**4,002,552**	**3.3**	**Illinois**	**3,594,618**	**11,540,432**	**31.1**
*Mobile	65,558	1,452,506	4.5	*Chicago	2,330,000	5,680,388	41.0
Birmingham	67,187	2,550,046	2.6	Belleville	116,707	861,193	13.6
Alaska	**51,764**	**578,735**	**8.9**	Joliet	496,326	1,383,027	35.9
*Anchorage	27,411	366,473	7.5	Peoria	233,558	1,430,200	16.3
Fairbanks	18,058	133,467	13.5	Rockford	250,617	1,079,500	23.2
Juneau	6,295	78,795	8.0	Springfield	167,410	1,106,124	15.1
Arizona	**710,402**	**3,782,271**	**18.8**	**Indiana**	**739,550**	**5,524,454**	**13.4**
Phoenix	356,593	2,628,300	13.6	*Indianapolis	215,349	2,201,503	9.8
Tucson	353,809	1,153,971	30.7	Evansville	88,237	468,820	18.8
Arkansas				Ft. Wayne-S. Bend	153,491	1,096,876	14.0
Little Rock	82,843	2,424,000	3.4	Gary	182,349	734,339	24.8
California	**7,857,437**	**31,601,761**	**24.9**	Lafayette	100,124	1,022,916	9.8
*Los Angeles	3,595,414	10,330,409	34.8	**Iowa**	**509,541**	**2,770,921**	**18.4**
*San Francisco	420,567	1,700,000	24.7	*Dubuque	215,021	923,000	23.3
Fresno	320,422	2,175,450	14.7	Davenport	106,504	707,123	15.1
Monterey	167,850	839,253	20.0	Des Moines	86,920	671,381	12.9
Oakland	485,183	2,192,235	22.1	Sioux City	101,096	469,417	21.5
Orange	580,535	2,484,789	23.4	**Kansas**	**376,680**	**2,399,399**	**15.7**
Sacramento	364,000	2,842,890	12.8	*Kansas City	179,200	952,000	18.8
San Bernardino	590,045	3,000,000	19.7	Dodge City	39,670	209,536	18.9
San Diego	670,787	2,730,027	24.6	Salina	56,301	328,480	17.1
San Jose	374,412	1,497,648	25.0	Wichita	101,509	909,383	11.2
Santa Rosa	113,105	771,950	14.6	**Kentucky**	**354,823**	**3,696,475**	**9.6**
Stockton	175,117	1,037,110	16.9	*Louisville	185,325	1,139,022	16.3
Colorado	**502,293**	**3,432,108**	**14.6**	Covington	79,089	403,104	19.6
*Denver	332,000	2,358,754	14.1	Lexington	40,803	1,376,114	3.0
Colorado Springs	75,264	585,739	12.8	Owensboro	49,606	778,235	6.4
Pueblo	95,029	487,615	19.5	**Louisiana**	**1,330,672**	**4,283,444**	**31.1**
Connecticut	**1,359,102**	**3,281,787**	**41.4**	*New Orleans	482,868	1,328,996	36.3
*Hartford	796,355	1,824,574	43.6	Alexandria	48,050	400,478	12.0
Bridgeport	343,388	828,713	41.4	Baton Rouge	225,390	774,287	29.1
Norwich	219,359	628,500	34.9	Houma-Thibodaux	104,538	202,000	51.8
Delaware				Lafayette	353,002	543,000	65.0
Wilmington	157,566	1,009,937	15.6	Lake Charles	79,198	259,425	30.5
District of Columbia				Shreveport	37,626	775,258	4.8
*Washington	440,000	2,296,507	19.1	**Maine**			
Florida	**1,892,527**	**13,595,245**	**13.9**	Portland	233,555	1,227,927	19.0
*Miami	729,152	3,388,511	21.5	**Maryland**			
Orlando	286,551	2,707,836	10.6	*Baltimore	467,358	2,722,904	17.2
Palm Beach	198,818	1,357,592	14.6	**Massachusetts**	**2,952,484**	**5,980,979**	**49.4**
Pensacola-				*Boston	1,962,432	3,764,200	52.1
Tallahassee	60,487	1,214,986	5.0	Fall River	350,450	700,440	50.0
St. Augustine	109,896	1,434,434	7.7	Springfield	315,650	806,634	39.1
St. Petersburg	335,637	2,206,983	15.2	Worcester	323,952	709,705	45.6
Venice	171,986	1,284,903	13.4	**Michigan**	**2,116,870**	**9,407,630**	**22.5**
Georgia	**268,383**	**6,182,033**	**4.3**	*Detroit	1,325,571	4,266,654	31.1
*Atlanta	199,973	3,848,100	5.2	Gaylord	87,189	421,449	20.7
Savannah	68,410	2,333,933	2.9	Grand Rapids	148,584	1,109,795	13.4
Hawaii				Kalamazoo	104,192	968,535	10.7
Honolulu	209,166	1,172,000	17.8	Lansing	228,542	1,641,750	13.9
Idaho				Marquette	73,783	313,915	23.5
Boise	113,375	1,134,000	10.0	Saginaw	149,009	685,532	21.7

State Diocese	Catholic Pop.	Total Pop.	Cath. Pct.
Minnesota	**1,178,701**	**4,481,442**	**26.3**
*St. Paul and Minneapolis	701,811	2,606,151	26.9
Crookston	44,114	236,100	18.7
Duluth	82,000	400,000	20.5
New Ulm	72,405	277,461	26.1
St. Cloud	149,176	433,427	34.4
Winona	129,195	528,303	24.5
Mississippi	**108,044**	**2,654,794**	**4.1**
Biloxi	63,704	674,769	9.4
Jackson	44,340	1,980,025	2.2
Missouri	**826,433**	**5,136,812**	**16.1**
*St. Louis	548,775	2,027,351	27.1
Jefferson City	80,115	750,700	10.7
Kansas City- St. Joseph	145,623	1,299,555	11.2
Springfield- Cape Girardeau	51,920	1,059,206	4.9
Montana	**128,572**	**776,230**	**16.6**
Great Falls-Billings	62,160	351,858	17.7
Helena	66,412	424,372	15.6
Nebraska	**345,747**	**1,597,250**	**21.6**
*Omaha	208,167	790,159	26.3
Grand Island	53,714	290,429	18.5
Lincoln	83,866	516,662	16.2
Nevada			
Reno-Las Vegas*	193,346	1,400,000	13.8
New Hampshire			
Manchester	319,453	1,125,000	28.4
New Jersey	**3,247,472**	**7,820,158**	**41.5**
*Newark	1,325,838	2,656,693	49.9
Camden	425,066	1,274,400	33.3
Metuchen	477,900	1,140,396	41.9
Paterson	368,914	1,019,101	36.2
Trenton	649,754	1,729,568	37.6
New Mexico	**425,598**	**1,737,275**	**24.5**
*Santa Fe	260,129	926,635	28.1
Gallup	40,169	355,640	11.3
Las Cruces	125,300	455,000	27.5
New York	**7,330,849**	**18,195,419**	**40.3**
*New York	2,307,262	5,159,500	44.7
Albany	403,403	1,315,414	30.6
Brooklyn	1,657,619	4,252,262	39.0
Buffalo	760,935	1,628,713	46.7
Ogdensburg	144,602	425,622	34.0
Rochester	348,166	1,379,052	25.2
Rockville Centre	1,336,197	2,811,265	47.5
Syracuse	372,665	1,223,591	30.5
North Carolina	**201,758**	**6,993,189**	**2.9**
Charlotte	97,232	3,519,890	2.8
Raleigh	104,526	3,473,299	3.0

State Diocese	Catholic Pop.	Total Pop.	Cath. Pct.
North Dakota	**160,009**	**651,707**	**24.6**
Bismarck	64,295	261,307	24.6
Fargo	95,714	390,400	24.5
Ohio	**2,205,339**	**11,043,720**	**20.0**
*Cincinnati	542,000	2,886,700	18.8
Cleveland	813,406	2,795,813	29.1
Columbus	207,036	2,145,693	9.6
Steubenville	46,724	511,607	9.1
Toledo	319,778	1,479,041	21.6
Youngstown	276,395	1,224,866	22.6
Oklahoma	**140,221**	**3,194,967**	**4.4**
*Oklahoma City	89,105	1,938,467	4.6
Tulsa	51,116	1,256,500	4.1
Oregon	**303,988**	**3,038,000**	**10.0**
*Portland	274,803	2,646,500	10.4
Baker	29,185	391,500	7.5
Pennsylvania	**3,613,052**	**11,979,755**	**30.2**
*Philadelphia	1,438,564	3,777,995	38.1
Allentown	257,575	1,084,189	23.8
Altoona-Johnstown	129,124	643,493	20.1
Erie	229,259	874,074	26.2
Greensburg	200,492	685,335	29.3
Harrisburg	227,242	1,867,124	12.2
Pittsburgh	768,381	2,022,057	38.0
Scranton	362,415	1,025,488	35.3
Rhode Island			
Providence	641,761	1,003,000	64.0
South Carolina			
Charleston	102,245	3,643,000	2.8
South Dakota	**157,144**	**711,591**	**22.1**
Rapid City	38,951	211,591	18.4
Sioux Falls	118,193	500,000	23.6
Tennessee	**145,470**	**4,974,270**	**2.9**
Knoxville	34,487	1,860,218	1.9
Memphis	56,898	1,373,000	4.1
Nashville	54,085	1,741,052	3.1
Texas	**4,053,437**	**17,931,981**	**22.6**
*San Antonio	639,236	1,766,574	36.2
Amarillo	38,148	386,574	9.9
Austin	240,100	1,638,245	14.6
Beaumont	86,420	541,354	16.0
Brownsville	669,605	829,359	80.7
Corpus Christi	350,500	759,800	46.1
Dallas	294,125	2,682,302	11.0
El Paso	516,725	725,242	71.2
Fort Worth	176,086	2,060,943	8.5
Galveston-Houston	777,340	4,052,706	19.2
Lubbock	39,818	448,640	8.9
San Angelo	78,850	674,500	11.7
Tyler	37,177	1,126,596	3.3
Victoria	109,307	239,146	45.7

State Diocese	Catholic Pop.	Total Pop.	Cath. Pct.
Utah			
Salt Lake City	76,425	1,860,000	4.1
Vermont			
Burlington	146,332	575,691	25.4
Virginia	**464,000**	**6,394,600**	**7.2**
Arlington	294,101	2,037,600	14.4
Richmond	169,899	4,357,000	3.9
Washington	**495,996**	**5,312,896**	**9.3**
*Seattle	353,100	4,143,900	8.5
Spokane	78,696	707,996	11.1
Yakima	64,200	461,000	13.9
West Virginia			
Wheeling- Charleston	106,779	1,793,477	6.0
Wisconsin	**1,544,560**	**4,919,688**	**31.4**
*Milwaukee	598,884	2,080,883	28.8
Green Bay	379,431	836,600	45.3
La Crosse	227,710	773,427	29.4
Madison	252,323	847,428	29.8
Superior	86,212	381,350	22.6
Wyoming			
Cheyenne	47,008	467,000	10.1
Eastern Churches	**462,714**	—	—
Military Archdiocese	**1,483,083**	—	—
Outlying Areas	**2,841,691**	—	—
Grand Totals '95	**60,190,605**	**261,653,497**	**23.0**
Grand Totals '94	**59,858,042**	**259,353,627**	**23.1**
Grand Totals '85	**52,286,043**	**237,232,946**	**22.0**

*Reno-Las Vegas diocese made two separate dioceses in 1995. Catholic and total population figures are from the *1995 Annuario Pontificio.*

AMERICAN COLLEGE OF LOUVAIN, THE

The story of The American College of Louvain cannot be told apart from the story of The Catholic University of Louvain. For nearly a century and a half, the "Louvain Method" and the Louvain spirit at The American College have inspired and shaped leaders for the Church in North America, giving the United States at least thirty-four bishops and more than two thousand priests.

The Catholic University of Louvain

The Catholic University of Louvain, *Alma Mater Omnium Universitatum Catholicarum,* was founded by Pope Martin V on December 9, 1425. It is the oldest continuous Catholic university in the world. Its faculty of theology was established in 1432.

By the sixteenth century, Louvain's faculty of theology had already begun to make significant impact on biblical and theological scholarship. Three outstanding Louvain professors come immediately to mind: Pope Adrian VI, Erasmus of Rotterdam, and Justus Lipsius. Adrian VI had studied at Louvain, later became professor and still later rector of the university. After becoming Pope, he gave his home (Adrian VI College) to the students of theology. In 1517 the great Renaissance humanist, Erasmus, laid the foundations for Louvain's "back to the sources" methodology by establishing at Louvain his Collegium Trilingue for the comparative study of Latin, Greek, and Hebrew versions of the Bible. One of his successors at Louvain, Justus Lipsius, became the creator of modern textual criticism.

Louvain's professors of theology took an active role in the reforming work of the Council of Trent (1545–63). And at the Second Vatican Council, four hundred years after Trent, the University of Louvain provided more *periti* than any other university in the world. At Vatican II, Louvain's Gerard Philips was a prominent participant in the deliberations which led to the formulation of the dogmatic constitution *Lumen gentium.*

The American College of Louvain

The American College was founded in 1857 under the leadership of Bishop Martin J. Spalding, bishop of Louisville, Kentucky, and Bishop Peter Paul Lefevere, bishop of Detroit, Michigan. In 1856, Fr. Peter Kindekens, vicar general of the Diocese of Detroit, had been sent to Rome by Francis P. Kenrick, archbishop of Baltimore, to establish an American college at Rome. Upon his arrival in Rome, Kindekens ran into difficulties everywhere he turned and was forced to abandon the project. Even Pio Nono (Pope Pius IX) had given up hope for an American college in Rome, at least for the present. On his way back to the United States, Kindekens visited his native Belgium and found the Belgian bishops and the rector of the University of Louvain very supportive of the establishment of an American College at Louvain. Shortly after Peter Kindekens' return to the United States, the American bishops approved a project, and by February 1857, Kindekens was back in Louvain to become the first rector of The American College of the Immaculate Conception which began, at the present site of the college, in a vacant butcher shop. That building had actually been part of the College of Aulne founded by the Cistercians in 1629.

By the time of its fiftieth anniversary in 1907, The American College could boast of international renown, strong support from the United States, one hundred and twenty students, a personal blessing from Pope Pius X and the successful completion of its first major building campaign!

At the outbreak of the First World War, the University of Louvain suspended classes; the rector of The American

College, Jules de Beeker, volunteered the buildings of the college for the establishment of a Red Cross station (flying the Stars and Stripes), and the program of priestly formation at The American College was reduced to six seminarians who were ordained by the papal nuncio in 1915. It was in fact only through these six students at The American College that the Catholic University of Louvain continued to function in the year 1914–15. Following the First World War, The American College—like the city of Louvain—lived through the pains of growth and postwar reconstruction, achieving stability by 1939 when the Second World War was on the horizon.

It was in fact in December 1939, when seminarians left for their Christmas vacation, that the College felt obliged to close. Despite the heavy bombardment of Louvain, the buildings of The American College continued to stand and housed the remnants of the University of Louvain Library which had been burned by the enemy for the second time.

In 1949 the American bishops debated the future of The American College. They knew that, following a second world war, the college would require tremendous human and financial resources. In the end, convinced of the value and need of Louvain-trained priests for the United States, they voted to reopen the College in 1952 under the rectorship of Fr. Thomas F. Maloney from the Diocese of Providence, Rhode Island.

Under Maloney and his successor, Msgr. Paul D. Riedl from the Diocese of Springfield, Massachusetts, The American College not only continued but began once again to flourish. By 1955 the college had one hundred and fourteen students representing twenty-six dioceses in the United States. By 1965 student enrollment represented thirty-six American dioceses.

In the years following the Second Vatican Council, The American College has greatly transformed and enhanced its seminary program of priestly formation. That transformation and development, begun under Msgr. Riedl, was continued during the rectorships of Fr. Clement Pribl (1970–72), Archdiocese of Oklahoma City; Fr. Raymond F. Collins (1972–78), Diocese of Providence; and Fr. William J. Greytak (1978–83), Diocese of Helena.

In the 1980s under the leadership of the eleventh rector, Fr. John Costanzo (1983–88) from the Diocese of Pueblo and the twelfth rector, Msgr. Thomas P. Ivory (1988–92) from the Archdiocese of Newark, The American College embarked upon its most extensive building renovation program since the early days of this century. The final touches to that phase of renovation were applied during the rectorship of Fr. Melvin T. Long (1992–93) of the Diocese of Salina. He was succeeded as rector by Vincentian Fr. David E. Windsor.

Aubert, Roger. "Le Collège Américain de Louvain. 1857–1957." *Le Centenaire du Collège Américain, Annua Nuntia Lovaniensa, Fasculus XIV.* Louvain: Editions Universitaires, 1958.

Cross, Richard E., and Eugene L. Zoeller. "The Story of The American College." *The American College Bulletin,* 1957. XXXVI:28–91.

Sauter, John A. *The American College of Louvain, 1857–1898.* Louvain: Publications Universitaires de Louvain, 1959.

Van der Heyden, Joseph. *The Louvain American College.* Louvain: Fr. & R. Ceuterick, 1909.

JOHN A. DICK

Related Document

FATHER KINDEKENS APPEALS FOR AN AMERICAN COLLEGE AT LOUVAIN, NOVEMBER 5, 1856

The first institution to be established abroad by the Catholic Church of the United States was the American College in Louvain, Belgium. When some of the American bishops were in Rome in December, 1854, for the definition of the dogma of the Immaculate Conception the idea of founding a college in the Eternal City was discussed, and among the chief promoters of the plan was Francis Patrick Kenrick, Archbishop of Baltimore. When, therefore, the Belgian-born Father Peter Kindekens (d. 1873), vicar-general of the Diocese of Detroit and pastor of Immaculate Conception Church, Adrian, was sent to Rome in the spring of 1856 on business for his ordinary, Peter P. Lefevere (1804–1869), Kenrick asked him to look for a location for a college. In the letter printed below Kindekens explained the reasons for his failure in Rome, but the brighter prospects which he had found in his native Belgium. Upon his return to the United States he sent out a circular to the American hierarchy, the substance of which is contained in his letter to Kenrick. But he met with very little success and the only two bishops who gave any practical response were Martin J. Spalding of Louisville and his own ordinary. It was due, therefore, to these two prelates that the college opened at Louvain on March 19, 1857, with Kindekens as rector, a post he held until 1860. By the time the institution celebrated its golden jubilee in 1907 it had furnished nearly 700 priests to the American Church. Most of these were European-born, but as the years went on there was an increasing number of Americans who were sent to the college by their bishops in order to avail themselves of the superior advantages of study offered by the famous Catholic University of Louvain.

(*Source*: Archives of the Archdiocese of Baltimore, Kindekens to Kenrick, Detroit, November 5, 1856.)

MY LORD: WHEN, DURING THE PAST SUMMER, AT ROME, I endeavored with the utmost diligence, by your special request to look for and secure a suitable location for the projected "American College" in that City, I found that not only is it impossible at present, but that it will probably remain impossible for some time to come, to establish such an institution in the Holy City. In point of fact, the Holy Father assured me that, under present circumstances (the occupation of Rome by the French, etc.) he could not say when it would be in his power to assign a suitable building for the purpose.

On my return, passing through Belgium, I learned that an earnest wish prevailed among persons of distinction to establish there a college for the foreign missions. I resolved at once to secure the fruits of these happy dispositions for the missions of the United States with the following success:

I obtained a promise from the Count Félix de Mérode[1] of the sum of between 50,000 and 60,000 francs towards founding a College for the Missions in the United States, in any city of Belgium of my choice.

His Eminence the Cardinal Archbishop of Malines,[2] and several other Prelates with whom I had the honor to speak on the subject, assured me of their warmest sympathies and promised their co-operation.

A subscription in aid of the foundation of the establishment will be opened in the columns of the Catholic journals of Belgium, as soon as I can assure them that the Right Rev. Bishops of the United States (or some of them) are earnestly engaged in promoting the good work.

The Rector of the University of Louvain[3] (the city selected for the College) has promised his aid, and is prepared to grant all we may reasonably require of the University, to secure the success and prosperity of the contemplated institution.

From the above, Your Lordship will easily perceive that the object of the Institution in Belgium would be, 1st, To serve as a nursery of properly educated and tried clergymen for our missions; and 2d. to provide the American Bishops with a college to which some at least of their students might be sent to acquire a superior ecclesiastical instruction and a solid clerical training, without much expense, as the College will require no other Professors than those for the English and German languages.

The basis of the government of the institution will be that of the "Propaganda" at Rome, and each Diocese of the United States will profit of its fruits in proportion to the amount it may have furnished towards the foundation, etc. For it could not be reasonably expected that the Catholics of the United States should have no share in the honor and merits of founding an institution designed exclusively for their benefit.

Will Your Lordship be kind enough to inform me, at your earliest convenience, whether you desire to take part in the work, and, if so, what amount your diocese may possibly furnish, by collection in the various congregations, or by any other way you may think proper, towards the proposed Institution.

Your Lordship is also requested to nominate the person whom you may wish to charge with the execution of the work and to become the Rector of the Institution, at least for the time being. An early reply is urged as necessary, as I must write to the Count de Mérode to inform him whether the design is entered upon by the Bishops of the United States in a manner worthy of success, or whether it may not be necessary to abandon the project and leave him free to apply his alms towards building a Church in Brussels as was his original intention. You will please also to offer any suggestions which you may judge proper on the subject.

[1]Félix de Mérode-Westerloo (1791–1857) belonged to one of the most distinguished families in Belgium. He held successively the portfolios of foreign affairs, war, and finance in the cabinets of King Leopold I. He was the father of Frédéric F.-X. de Mérode (1820–1874), Archbishop of Melitene, who figured prominently in the government of the Papal States under Pius IX. The elder de Mérode died before he learned that the project for which he had offered the money was to become a reality. This loss left Kindekens with only $2,000 to start the college, a sum which he had been given in equal shares by Bishops Spalding and Lefevere.

[2]Engelbert Sterckx (1792–1867) was made Archbishop of Malines in 1832 and a cardinal in 1838.

[3]Pierre F.-X. de Ram (1804–1865), a distinguished church historian, was the first rector of the Catholic University of Louvain when it was restored in 1834.

Source: John Tracy Ellis, ed. *Documents of American Catholic History*. Vol. 1: 1493–1865. Wilmington, Del.: Michael Glazier, 1987, 315–17.)

AMERICAN ECCLESIASTICAL REVIEW

In December 1887, somewhat disgruntled at the efforts of the editor of its journal called *The Pastor*, the management of Frederick Pustet and Company approached a priest of the Archdiocese of Philadelphia, the Rev. Herman Joseph Heuser (1851–1933), to rescue the company's investment. As a result, the first issue of the *American Ecclesiastical Review*, a journal for priests and seminarians, appeared in January 1889.

The German-born, American-trained Heuser, a faculty member at St. Charles Borromeo Seminary of Philadelphia, had been working with Msgr. James Andrew Corcoran, the founding editor of the *American Catholic Quarterly Review*. Heuser insisted that an entirely new journal be started, one which would assist priests in their pastoral duties, while helping in their continued education beyond the walls of a seminary. He hoped that the new periodical would also stimulate the growth of intellectual endeavor by American Catholic clergy and seminarians, as well as provide a resource for encouraging and guiding lay collaborators. He intended the journal to carry out this charge with fidelity to Rome, and without polemical debate. Using words of St. Paul (1 Cor 14:5), he gave the *Review* the motto "For the Upbuilding of the Church."

Heuser soon discovered that the formula he had set for the *Review*, which carried feature articles as well as "departments" devoted to the presentation of ecclesiastical documentation, responses to letters from readers, and book reviews, could not avoid the controversies rocking the Catholic Church in the United States in the 1890s and 1900s, i.e., over education, Americanism, and Modernism. While publishing the insights of more progressive minds, the journal became identified with the conservative forces of the day. Nevertheless, through his prodigious work as editor and author, publisher and business agent, Heuser managed to provide what he had promised to his readers, while making it the cornerstone of other publishing ventures and numerous charitable endeavors.

In December 1901, as a result of a short-lived proposed merger with the *Irish Ecclesiastical Review,* the journal became the *Ecclesiastical Review.* The name remained until 1943. While Heuser continued as editor until 1927, he began to look to The Catholic University of America for help. Rev. William J. Turner, a philosophy professor, was temporary editor from 1914 to 1919, and Msgr. William J. Kerby succeeded Heuser in 1927 when the founder gave the *Review* and all its assets to the university under the direction of a specially appointed board of trustees. Kerby, while bringing some of his interest in Catholic social teaching to the review, followed Heuser's original program.

Kerby's successors included Joseph LaRue (1936–44), Joseph Clifford Fenton (1944–63), Patrick Granfield (1963–71), and James P. Clifton (1971–75). Several changes took place during Fenton's editorship. While the journal, which had returned to its former title, became an organ of The Catholic University of America, it was guided to address the movement of the Church into an ecumenical age from the conservative point of view held by its editor, Fenton, and his chief associate, the Redemptorist Francis J. Connell. During this time the *Review* became involved in debates with scholars contributing to other journals, such as *Theological Studies* and the *Catholic Biblical Quarterly.* Nevertheless, it remained basically faithful to its charter until it ceased publication in 1975.

See also CATHOLIC MAGAZINES AND PERIODICALS.

Appleby, R. Scott. "American Ecclesiastical Review." *Religious Periodicals in the United States,* ed. C. Lippy. Westport, Connecticut, 1986, 21–25.
Ellis, J. T. "Sixtieth Birthday of the *American Ecclesiastical Review." American Ecclesiastical Review [AER]* 121 (October 1949) 261–80.
Granfield, P. "Seventy-five Years of the *American Ecclesiastical Review." AER* 150 (January 1964) 18–32.
Hubbert, J., C.M. "For the Upbuilding of the Church": The Reverend Herman Joseph Heuser, D.D., 1851–1933." 3 vols. Ph.D. dissertation, The Catholic University of America, 1992.

JOSEPH G. HUBBERT, C.M.

AMERICAN FEDERATION OF CATHOLIC SOCIETIES

The American Federation of Catholic Societies resulted from the desire of American Catholics to create an umbrella organization for the various Catholic fraternal and benevolent societies that flourished in the later nineteenth century. This same desire for organizational unity manifested itself in other initiatives such as the various Catholic Unions that appeared in the larger cities in the 1870s, in the Catholic Congresses that were held in 1889 and 1893, and in the federation of Catholic societies that was organized in the Diocese of Pittsburgh in March 1900. A prime mover in the Pittsburgh federation was the Knights of St. John, a German-American fraternal society.

Origins

The Knights of St. John were also instrumental in convening a meeting in New York City on Thanksgiving Day, 1900, at which delegates from some fourteen Catholic societies agreed to lay the groundwork for a national federation of the country's Catholic societies. Among the societies represented were the Ancient Order of Hibernians, the Catholic Benevolent Union, the Staats Verbund, and the Catholic Total Abstinence Union of America, but not the country's largest Catholic fraternal organization, the Knights of Columbus. At another organizational meeting in Long Branch, New Jersey, in August 1901, the delegates adopted a temporary constitution and agreed to call their organization the American Federation of Catholic Societies of the United States. In December of that year, the AFCS held its first convention which drew approximately 250 delegates from 24 states.

In order to emphasize the lay character of the new organization, the AFCS deliberately refrained from seeking the approval of the hierarchy, and an unwritten rule prohibited any cleric from serving as a member of the executive board. The AFCS hoped to act as a unified Catholic lay voice on such contentious public issues as the federal government's Native American policy, the settlement of the Church's land claims in the recently acquired Philippine Islands, and the right of priests to administer the sacraments in state institutions. However, there was also a positive thrust to the activities of the AFCS. Inspired by the encyclicals of Pope Leo XIII and the work of comparable European Catholic organizations, the AFCS sought to evangelize America through the dissemination of Catholic social and moral teachings.

From the very beginning there were differences among the members of the AFCS over the nature and purpose of the organization. Some of the constituent societies, especially the German-American organizations, resisted efforts at centralization from fear that it would encroach on their own autonomy. Two bishops, James A. McFaul of Trenton, New Jersey, and Sebastian Messmer of Green Bay, Wisconsin, gave strong support to the AFCS, but others (such as Cardinal James Gibbons and Archbishop John Ireland) were fearful that the AFCS would draw the Church into partisan politics and thus provide ammunition to anti-Catholic bigots. "Americanist" prelates like Ireland and newspaper publisher Humphrey J. Desmond feared the influence within the AFCS of German-Americans like Arthur Preuss, who said bluntly in October 1901: "If the Federation is not to be the ground work for a Catholic Centre Party . . . it will do more harm than good and deserve to die abornin'."

Development and Decline

Despite a shaky beginning, by the time that the AFCS held its fourth annual convention in 1904, it was a well-established organization with members in thirty-eight states. It could boast of eleven state federations and three hundred county federations. Ten national organizations had affiliated with the AFCS, including the Central-Verein, the Irish Catholic Benevolent Union, and the Catholic Order of Foresters (but still not the Knights of Columbus). The AFCS often shared and supported the efforts of evangelical Protestants to promote Sunday observance and temperance laws, and to combat immoral plays and posters. The social action apostolate of the AFCS expanded significantly in 1911 with the creation of a Social Service Commission with Bishop Peter Muldoon of Rockford, Illinois, as chairman and labor priest Peter Dietz as secretary. The AFCS kept in touch with its members through a *Bulletin* and *Weekly Newsletter*, and it often acted as a Catholic lobby on both the state and national levels.

After 1908 two major structural changes altered the character of the AFCS. First, the constitution was amended at the 1908 convention to provide for the admission of diocesan federations as well as Catholic societies. Henceforth recruitment efforts were concentrated on attracting more diocesan and parish organizations. Secondly, this shift from a federation of lay societies to a federation of diocesan organizations was accompanied by a shift from lay to ecclesiastical control of the AFCS. At the 1908 convention in Boston, Archbishop William Henry O'Connell told the delegates: "In a word, the faithful are to be taught, to be led, to be fed, not by whomsoever they choose, much less by themselves, but by those divinely constituted in their office of teacher, leader, guide and shepherd, by Christ's own authority."

In 1917 O'Connell reported that it was the consensus of the U.S. archbishops that "the Federation should be responsible to the hierarchy as a body." At the convention of the AFCS in the fall of that year the organization was remodeled to become mainly a federation of diocesan organizations, each of which was under the control of the local bishop. In recognition of the changed character of the organization, the name was changed in 1917 to the Catholic Federation of the United States.

While this reorganization of the AFCS was in progress, in order to meet the wartime needs of the American Catholic Church, Fr. John J. Burke, C.S.P., created a new national organization, the National Catholic War Council. The American bishops found the new organization so useful that they decided to continue it after the war as the National Catholic Welfare Council (later changed to Conference). One of the specialized agencies of the NCWC was the Department of Lay Organizations which soon established a National Council of Catholic Men whose first convention took place in Washington, D.C., in September 1920. By that time, the AFCS was largely a moribund organization and was quietly replaced by the NCCM. The historian of the AFCS, Alfred J. Ede, summarized the rise and fall of the organization in one sentence. "What had begun as a lay organization and had been gradually ecclesiasticized," he said, "now disappeared into a bureau created by the American hierarchy."

Ede, Alfred J. *The Lay Crusade for a Christian America: A Study of the American Federation of Catholic Societies, 1900–1919.* New York, 1988.

Gorman, Mary Adele Francis, O.S.F. "Federation of Catholic Societies in the United States." Ph.D. dissertation, University of Notre Dame, 1962.

THOMAS J. SHELLEY

AMERICAN PROTECTIVE ASSOCIATION

Anti-Catholic and anti-immigrant secret society, founded by Henry F. Bowers at Clinton, Iowa, March 13, 1887.

Organized nativist activity in the United States largely ceased from the mid-1850s thru the 1870s, when slavery, war, and Reconstruction dominated the national political debate. The catalyst for renewed activity lay in the immigration tallies, which, beginning with the 1880s, surpassed a half million yearly.

Further nativist alarm was experienced in 1884, when American Catholics were obligated by their bishops to send their children to Catholic schools, and to construct new schools where such did not exist. Many Americans saw this as a threat to the public schools, and they became convinced of this when subsequent demands were made by Catholics for public education monies. In addition, American institutions seemed at the mercy of hordes of naturalized voters.

Among the many patriotic organizations founded in the 1880s was the American Protective Association, organized along hierarchical lines similar to the old Know-Nothings. Its members were bound by oaths to support only Protestants for public office and to deny assistance to Catholic causes of any kind. The A.P.A. grew slowly at first but gradually assumed leadership among the various nativist societies. It held to a four-part platform: restriction of immigration; knowledge of English as a prerequisite for naturalization; a longer waiting period before naturalization; and opposition to Catholics occupying elected office.

The A.P.A. was not above using forgeries to advance its cause. Chief among these was a reputed letter from the American bishops to their flocks urging the formation of a Catholic party, and papal "Instructions to Catholics" (1892), commanding Catholics to kill all heretics on the feast of St. Ignatius Loyola, July 31, 1893.

The encyclical *Rerum Novarum* was labeled by nativists as a Catholic conspiracy to control labor, while the Catholic faith of Terence Powderly sufficed to brand his Knights of Labor a Romanist plot. The appearance at the Columbian Exposition in 1892 of the first apostolic delegate to the United States, Archbishop Francesco Satolli, and his subsequent residence in Washington, D.C., was seen by many as further proof of papal designs on the American government.

The A.P.A. reached its apogee between 1893 and 1895. Economic hard times had resulted in increased unemployment, and had branded the immigrant as an unwanted competitor for jobs. The association made its greatest impact in the upper Midwest, the West, and the Northeast. It succeeded in winning control of municipal governments in Detroit, Milwaukee, and Kansas City, but had no significant impact on the state and national level. However, on both the state and national levels politicians used the A.P.A. to their own advantage.

Internecine squabbles further pitted Republican Party partisans against association president William J. Traynor who wished the A.P.A. to constitute a party unto itself. Implication in religious riots in Butte, Montana, Kansas City, and Boston in 1894 and 1895, as well as charges of internal corruption, led to the disintegration of the association. After the 1896 presidential elections, where its influence was negligible, the A.P.A. faded from the public scene until its final demise in 1911.

See also KU KLUX KLAN; NATIVISM.

Bennett, David H. *The Party of Fear.* Chapel Hill: University of North Carolina Press, 1988.

Curran, Thomas J. *Xenophobia and Immigration 1820–1930.* Boston: Twayne, 1975.

Kinzer, Donald L. *An Episode in Anti-Catholicism: The American Protective Association.* Seattle: University of Washington Press, 1964.

Williams, Michael. *The Shadow of the Pope.* New York: McGraw-Hill, 1932.

ALBERT H. LEDOUX

Related Document

THE SECRET OATH OF THE AMERICAN PROTECTIVE ASSOCIATION, OCTOBER 31, 1893

After the breakup of the Know-Nothings with the Civil War there was no organized movement against the Catholic Church in the United States until March 1887, when Henry F. Bowers (1837–1911) and six associates founded the American Protective Association at Clinton, Iowa. The founders were drawn from no single political or religious group, there being among the original seven two Republicans, two Democrats, one Populist, and one Prohibitionist, with two of no religion and one each a Methodist, Lutheran, Baptist, Presbyterian, and Congregationalist. The A.P.A. grew slowly at first, but by 1894 they made significant gains in the elections of that year and by 1896 it was estimated that they numbered approximately a million members with the chief strength centered in the Middle West. The issue of Bryanism and free silver split their ranks in 1896, and as Arthur Meier Schlesinger remarked, "Both major parties snubbed the A.P.A., and the movement withered as suddenly as it had grown" ("A Critical Period in American Religion, 1875–1900," *Proceedings of the Massachusetts Historical Society,* LXIV [1932], 546). The A.P.A. lingered on, however, until 1911, and during the 1890s they did a great deal of harm among many Americans who were taken in by their lying propaganda, the most fantastic item of which was published in the *Patriotic American* of Detroit on April 8, 1893, and purported to be an encyclical of Pope Leo XIII instructing the American Catholics to rise on the feast of St. Ignatius Loyola, July 31, 1893, and massacre all heretics in the country. The secret oath of the A.P.A., a copy of which follows, came to light late that year through the exposé of the St. Paul *Globe* and through the efforts of Henry M. Youmans (1832–1920), defeated congressman from the eighth district of Michigan, to unseat William S. Linton (1856–1927), his opponent, who, he contended, was a member of the A.P.A.

(*Source:* Michael Williams. *The Shadow of the Pope.* New York: McGraw-Hill Book Co., Inc., 1932, 103–4.)

I DO MOST SOLEMNLY PROMISE AND SWEAR THAT I WILL ALways, to the utmost of my ability, labor, plead and wage a continuous warfare against ignorance and fanaticism; that I will use my utmost power to strike the shackles and chains of blind obedience to the Roman Catholic church from the hampered and bound consciences of a priest-ridden and church-oppressed people; that I will never allow any one, a member of the Roman Catholic church, to become a member of this order, I knowing him to be such; that I will use my influence to promote the interest of all Protestants everywhere in the world that I may be; that I will not employ a Roman Catholic in any capacity if I can procure the services of a Protestant.[1]

I furthermore promise and swear that I will not aid in building or maintaining, by my resources, any Roman Catholic church or institution of their sect or creed whatsoever, but will do all in my power to retard and break down the power of the Pope, in this country or any other; that I will not enter into any controversy with a Roman Catholic upon the subject of this order, nor will I enter into any agreement with a Roman Catholic to strike or create a disturbance whereby the Catholic employees may undermine and substitute their Protestant co-workers; that in all grievances I will seek only Protestants and counsel with them to the exclusion of all Roman Catholics, and will not make known to them anything of any nature matured at such conferences.

I furthermore promise and swear that I will not countenance the nomination, in any caucus or convention, of a Roman Catholic for any office in the gift of the American people, and that I will not vote for, or counsel others to vote for, any Roman Catholic, but will vote only for a Protestant, so far as may lie in my power. Should there be two Roman Catholics on opposite tickets, I will erase the name on the ticket I vote; that I will at all times endeavor to place the political positions of this government in the hands of Protestants, to the entire exclusion of the Roman Catholic church, of the members thereof, and the mandate of the Pope.

To all of which I do most solemnly promise and swear, so help me God. Amen.

[1]A sample of A.P.A. literature which made their intent clear was the 56-page pamphlet put out by a certain J. H. Jackson of Forth Worth, Texas, supreme vice-president of the organization, entitled *The American Protective Association. What It Is, Its Platform and Roman Intolerance* (n.p., n.d.). In the preface Jackson remarked that he had been a member for eighteen months and had read everything he could find on the Catholic Church and had become convinced that there was an urgent need to combat its power. When he learned "that the Roman pope gave his subjects no right to think for themselves," he declared "this is a false assumption of authority, which American manhood cannot, and will not, submit to" (p. 3).

(*Source:* John Tracy Ellis, ed. *Documents of American Catholic History.* Vol 2:1866–1966, Wilmington, Del.: Michael Glazier, 1987, 483–5.)

AMERICAN REVOLUTION AND CATHOLICS, THE

At the outbreak of the American War for Independence in 1775, Catholics were, for the most part, a negligible presence in the thirteen British seaboard colonies. Although precise figures do not exist, it is estimated that Catholics numbered perhaps twenty-five thousand in a colonial population of two and one half million. The largest concentrations of Catholics were in Maryland, which had been founded by the Catholic Calvert family, and in Pennsylvania, where the religious freedom clause in William Penn's colonial charter accorded Catholics more freedom than elsewhere in the colonies. In 1785, less than four years after the British surrender at Yorktown, Fr. John Carroll, first superior of the American missions, listed approximately 15,800 Catholics in Maryland and 7,000 in Pennsylvania. These were served by twenty-four former Jesuit priests. Additional Catholics were scattered in Massachusetts, New York, New Jersey, Delaware, Virginia, and in the former French settlements in the Mississippi valley. In addition to the restrictions on the public practice of their faith that pertained in all the colonies except Pennsylvania, Catholics were also legally disenfranchised in every colony, and could neither vote nor hold public office.

Anti-Catholic Sentiment

The extent of Catholic disenfranchisement, even in Maryland, was demonstrated by the 1773 exchange of letters between Charles Carroll of Carrollton and Daniel Dulany, Jr., in the *Maryland Gazette.* Under the pen name *Antilon,* Dulany, the provincial secretary, undertook to defend the action of Governor Robert Eden arbitrarily extending an unpopular Fee Bill for the support of the Anglican Church in the colony. Carroll, one of the wealthiest men in the colonies and a Catholic, responded to Dulany as *First Citizen* on behalf of the patriot cause. A series of four letters was exchanged in the *Gazette.* When it appeared that Dulany had been bested in the argument, he attacked Carroll's right to join in the debate since, "He is not a Protestant," and thus was not accorded full citizenship "on account of his principles, which are distrusted."

Anti-Catholic sentiment was exacerbated in the immediate pre-Revolutionary period by the passage in Parliament of the Quebec Act in 1774. This legislation accorded religious toleration, and even support of the clergy, to the French-speaking Catholics in Canada, a territory which had passed from France to Britain in the 1763 Treaty of Paris. The New England patriots were particularly vociferous in their opposition to the establishment of "popery" in a nearby province of British North America. The Suffolk County [Massachusetts] Resolves of September 9, 1774, considered the Quebec Act, "dangerous in an extreme degree to the Protestant religion, and to the civil rights and liberties of all Americans." Among those who spoke or wrote against the religious provisions of the Quebec Act were John Adams, Samuel Adams, Alexander Hamilton, John Jay, Philip Livingston, and Richard Henry Lee. This outpouring of anti-Catholic invective helped assure the reluctance of Canadians to make common cause with the American Revolution.

Catholics and the Patriot Cause

By 1776, however, the realities of a possibly lengthy struggle had begun to settle in among the patriots. The advantages of recognition and assistance from Catholic France and Canada made antipopery sentiment and activity less desirable among Americans. As part of this about-face, the Continental Congress dispatched the first American diplomatic mission to Canada in April 1776. Officially the mission consisted of Pennsylvania's Benjamin Franklin, and two Marylanders: Samuel Chase and Charles Carroll, the only Catholic member of Congress. Unofficially, Carroll was asked to enlist the support of his cousin, Fr. John Carroll. The mission was doomed to failure. The Canadians, led by Bishop Jean-Olivier Briand of Quebec, were content under the English and understandably suspicious of the Americans. Perhaps the one positive result of the mission was the respect and friendship that grew from the solicitude and medical care extended by Fr. Carroll to the ailing Franklin.

With the outbreak of hostilities the colonial Catholics saw little difference with regard to their religious situation between the two combatants. They had no compelling reasons to be grateful for their past treatment by the British, nor excessively hopeful for their status in an independent American state. In addition the Catholics were too separated by geography, ethnic background, and lack of religious organization and communication to be able to espouse the Revolution as a body, or to make a common contribution to the patriot cause. The example and treatment of Charles Carroll in the wake of the Carroll-Dulany debates may have swayed some of his fellow Maryland Catholics, but that was the exception. By and large the Catholics made their decision for or against independence for individual reasons, and many opted for the patriot cause.

Maryland Catholics

Southern Maryland, especially Charles and St. Mary's Counties, was the one area where Catholics were heavily concentrated. Here, Catholic disenfranchisement notwithstanding, Catholics were elected to the General Committee, the Committee of Correspondence, and as delegates to the newly independent state's constitutional convention. Catholics enlisted heavily in the local militia with such Catholic families as Abell, Boarman, Boone, Brooke, Fenwick, Mattingly, Mudd, Neale, Purcell, and Spalding contributing considerable manpower. The entire cadre of officers in the Lower Battalion of St. Mary's County was Catholic led by Colonel Ignatius Fenwick, Jr.

Maryland's southern counties were important sources of provisions for the Continental Army. Like their neighbors, the former Jesuits in southern Maryland sold supplies from their plantations to the army. As a result, the area was often the object of British raiding parties, and the clergy suffered along with their flock. Fr. George Hunter's house at Port Tobacco was burned by the British, and Fr. James Walton at St. Inigoe's Manor suffered similar depredations.

Pennsylvania Catholics

Other groups of Catholics also contributed to the war effort. The Catholics of Pennsylvania were no less patriotic than their Maryland coreligionists, contributing manpower to the famous Pennsylvania Line. In addition more than a dozen of the sons of St. Mary's parish in Philadelphia aided their country on the seas as privateers. Others served in the fledgling United States Navy. The great chain that stretched across the Hudson at West Point to prevent British traffic on the river was fabricated by the German and Irish ironworkers of northern New Jersey, many of whom were Catholic. Much of the munitions for Washington's army also came from this source.

Despite their small numbers, several Catholics rose to prominence in the patriot cause. Charles Carroll was elected to the local Committee of Correspondence, and to Maryland's Constitutional Convention, where he helped draft the new state's organic document. He also represented Maryland in the second Continental Congress. Carroll's membership on the important congressional Board of War provided Washington with crucial support during the "Conway Cabal." He was the only Catholic to sign the Declaration of Independence, and was the last surviving signer at his death in 1832. Daniel Carroll, cousin of Charles and brother of Fr. John, served in the Maryland Senate, and represented that state in the Continental Congress and the Constitutional Convention. He was a signer of both the Articles of Confederation, and the United States Constitution.

The only other Catholic to sign the federal constitution was Philadelphia's Thomas FitzSimons. During the war, FitzSimons helped to raise and outfit a regiment, and saw service at Princeton. FitzSimons and his brother-in-law and partner, George Meade, raised funds for Washington's troops at Valley Forge and outfitted privateers that preyed on British shipping.

Philadelphia's Catholic community also produced two important patriots in Stephen Moylan and John Barry. Moylan recruited a contingent of soldiers who rushed to the defense of Boston at the outbreak of the war. During 1776 he served subsequently as aide-de-camp to Washington and quartermaster general of the Continental Army. Later Moylan raised a cavalry unit, and became commander of the Fourth Continental Dragoons, eventually reaching the rank of brigadier general. Moylan's three brothers, James, John, and Jasper, were all involved in noncombatant support of the Revolutionary cause both at home and in Europe. The naval exploits of Captain John Barry, "the father of the American Navy," delighted and encouraged his contemporaries. Barry was the first American officer to take a British warship.

Two other Philadelphia Catholics contributed their medical expertise to the war effort. Doctor Joseph Cauffman, Jr., lost his life while serving as medical officer on the frigate *Randolph,* and nurse Mary Waters, according to Benjamin Rush, "served the whole war in the military hospitals." Three European Catholics, the Marquis de Lafayette, engineer Thaddeus Kosciusko, and cavalry officer Casimir Pulaski all contributed mightily to Washington's ultimate victory.

Catholic Clergy

Although not numerous, the Catholic clergy also supported the patriot cause. In Philadelphia, Fr. Ferdinand Farmer refused the chaplaincy of a regiment of Catholic loyalists raised by General Howe. Farmer wrote that the offer "embarrasseth me on account of my age and several other reasons." Later Farmer was appointed a trustee of the University of Pennsylvania and took the oath of allegiance to the commonwealth, the first priest to hold public office in the new nation. On the eastern shore of Maryland, Fr. Joseph Mosley took the oath of allegiance to the new state himself and counseled his parishioners. He reported, "Every Roman Catholic took [the oath] in good time, under my direction, none excepted." Fr. Pierre Gibault, a native of Montreal serving in the Illinois country, exercised his influence on behalf of George Rogers Clark in securing the Northwest Territory for the new nation.

The Revolutionary Era changed the lives of American Catholics in a profound way. Opportunities for public and military service opened up for Catholics and allowed them to show their mettle as well as their patriotism. Many non-Catholic leaders had their prejudices challenged as they were exposed to a lived Catholicism for the first time in the Philadelphia Catholic community and in dealings with the French and Spanish. If there was not a complete change of heart from the pervasive anti-Catholicism of the colonial period, that sentiment was at least tempered in the Revolutionary Era, and toleration began to prevail on a public level. Faced with the challenges of revolution, most American Catholics espoused the patriot cause, fought nobly for their new nation's independence, and helped to secure a liberty which would have far-reaching consequences for the life of their Church.

Ellis, John Tracy. *Catholics in Colonial America.* Baltimore: Helicon, 1965.

Hanley, Thomas O'Brien, S.J. *The American Revolution and Religion: Maryland 1770 to 1800.* Washington, D.C.: The Catholic University of America Press, 1972.

———. *Charles Carroll of Carrolton: The Making of a Revolutionary Gentleman.* Washington, D.C.: The Catholic University of America Press, 1970.

———. *Revolutionary Statesman: Charles Carroll and the War.* Chicago: Loyola University Press, 1983.

Metzger, Charles H., S.J. *Catholics and the American Revolution. A Study in Religious Climate.* Chicago: Loyola University Press, 1962.

RAYMOND J. KUPKE

Related Document

GEORGE WASHINGTON BANS GUY FAWKES DAY IN THE ARMY, NOVEMBER 5, 1775

The American Revolution served to dissipate to some extent the prejudices which had operated so strongly against Catholics all through the colonial period. Among the many indignities which they had had to suffer was to witness in most of the principal towns on November 5 of each year a commemoration of the fateful attempt of Guy Fawkes to blow up the houses of parliament at London in 1605. At these colonial celebrations one of the principal attractions was the burning of the pope in effigy. Washington's sense of decency put a stop to this practice among the troops under his command at the siege of Boston. His general orders were written while the Commander in Chief was still

seemingly confident that the effort to bring the French Catholics of Canada in on the side of the revolting colonies would succeed, and he used that as his main motive for issuing the order.

(*Source:* John C. Fitzpatrick, ed. *The Writings of George Washington.* Washington: United States Government Printing Office, 1931, 4:64–5.)

General Orders
Head Quarters, Cambridge, November 5, 1775

AS THE COMMANDER IN CHIEF HAS BEEN APPRIZED OF A DEsign form'd for the observance of that ridiculous and childish custom of burning the Effigy of the pope—He cannot help expressing his surprise that there should be Officers and Soldiers in this army so void of common sense, as not to see the impropriety of such a step at this Juncture; at a Time when we are solliciting, and have really obtain'd, the friendship and alliance of the people of Canada, whom we ought to consider as Brethren embarked in the same Cause. The defence of the general Liberty of America: At such a juncture, and in such Circumstances, to be insulting their Religion, is so monstrous, as not to be suffered or excused; indeed instead of offering the most remote insult, it is our duty to address public thanks to these our Brethren, as to them we are so much indebted for every late happy Success over the common Enemy in Canada.

(*Source:* John Tracy Ellis, ed. *Documents of American Catholic History.* Vol. 1:1493–1865. Wilmington, Del.: Michael Glazier, 1987, 136.)

AMERICANISM

Americanism is the name assigned to a controversy which divided the Catholic Church in the United States in the late nineteenth century and arose in Europe after the publication of a biography of Paulist founder Isaac Hecker. In the United States the most important issue was the proper pastoral policy for dealing with immigrant Catholics and their children, a question which eventually centered on the parochial school. In Europe the debate was about the significance for the universal Church of the Catholic experience in the United States. The episode concluded in 1899 when Pope Leo XIII, in an apostolic letter, *Testem benevolentiae,* addressed to the bishops of the United States, condemned a series of propositions which he associated with the term "Americanism."

Divisions Among U.S. Bishops

In the last two decades of the nineteenth century a series of issues divided the American Church and hierarchy. While individuals shifted sides of specific issues, two identifiable groups emerged. One group, led by Archbishop John Ireland of St. Paul, favored rapid assimilation of Catholic immigrants and special efforts to demonstrate Catholic allegiance to American institutions and ideals.

These bishops took the initiative to establish The Catholic University of America, and Ireland attempted to reopen the school question, resisting the all-out commitment to parochial school education approved at the third Plenary Council of Baltimore in 1884. New York archbishop Michael Corrigan led the opposition, which received support from German-American Catholics and from others suspicious of Ireland's enthusiastic American nationalism.

Personal animosities worsened the division, which in the 1890s came to focus on efforts to win the support of the newly appointed papal representative in the United States, Archbishop Francesco Satolli. In 1895 the Vatican signaled its concern in a papal letter which strongly endorsed The Catholic University but insisted on submission to papal authority and warned against holding the United States arrangements of Church-state separation and religious liberty as good in themselves and worthy of imitation in other countries. This was followed by the removal of key supporters of Ireland from important positions.

The controversy reached Europe in the form of a debate about the meaning of the success of the Catholic Church in the United States. Liberal Catholics argued that the American experience demonstrated the wisdom of religious liberty and an open attitude toward modern culture, while conservatives warned that liberty and accommodation would divide the Church and undermine its doctrinal and moral authority. This division had marked European Catholic life since the French revolution a century before. The Vatican consistently took the conservative side, rejecting modern liberties and working to strengthen ecclesiastical authority, a process of internal centralization and condemnation of modern culture that climaxed with the First Vatican Council of 1869–70. American Catholics were aware of these divisions, but their differences were more limited.

In 1897 an abridged translation of Walter Elliott's biography of Isaac Hecker appeared in France. Liberals pointed to Hecker as a symbol of a more effective response to freedom and democracy, conservatives found in his writings and liberal commentary on them evidence of laxness, if not heresy. While polemical literature centered on Hecker, larger issues such as the Church-state question invariably arose. Accused Americans argued that they championed a political Americanism of freedom and democracy but rejected an ecclesiastical Americanism which would introduce those ideas into the Church's internal life. Conservatives, encouraged by Ireland's enemies in the United States, insisted that even such limited accommodation of modern ideals would damage the Church.

Testem benevolentiae

In 1898, to quiet the increasingly bitter public exchanges surrounding what was coming to be called "Heckerism" and "Americanism," the Pope took the debate under advisement. After a period of intense lobbying by both sides,

Leo XIII wrote an apostolic letter, *Testem benevolentiae,* to James Cardinal Gibbons of Baltimore. The letter addressed "certain opinions . . . concerning the manner of living the Christian life." The principles on which these opinions were based, the Pope wrote, could be reduced to one: "that, in order the more easily to bring over to Catholic doctrine those who dissent from it, the Church ought to adapt herself somewhat to our advanced civilization, and relaxing her ancient rigor, show some indulgence to modern popular theories and methods." In fact, the Pope insisted, Catholicism admitted no modifications "according to the diversity of time and place." The Church's teaching office "has constantly adhered to the same doctrine, in the same sense and in the same mind."

After listing a number of ideas supposedly associated with Hecker, including undue emphasis on the interior action of the Holy Spirit, minimizing the need for spiritual direction and other forms of "external guidance," and preferring the active to the passive virtues as appropriate for modern life, Leo summed up the problem: "We cannot approve the opinions which some comprise under the head of Americanism. If indeed by that name be designated characteristic qualities which reflect honor on the people of America, conditions of your commonwealth, or the laws and customs which prevail in them, there is surely no reason why we should deem it should be discarded. But, if it is to be used not only to signify but even to commend the above doctrines, there can be no doubt that our Venerable Brethren the bishops of America would be the first to repudiate and condemn it, as being especially unjust to them and to the entire nation as well. For it raises the suspicion that there are some among you who conceive of and desire a church in America different from that which is in the rest of the world."

The conditional clauses left American bishops room to deny that such doctrines were present in the United States, but the condemnation nevertheless dealt a death blow to the liberal party. Hecker's reputation was badly damaged, Ireland and his associates became far more cautious in their public statements and alertly submissive to Vatican decisions. Debate about the wisdom of parochial schools ended, and Catholic decision-making became far more secretive.

Together with other changes, such as the appointment of the papal delegate to the American Church, the end of the periodic national councils through which the U.S. bishops had legislated for their Church in the nineteenth century, and the appointment of an increasing number of Roman-trained and -oriented bishops, the apostolic letter marked a major turning point in American Catholic history. For many years national projects remained weak, pastoral strategies designed to encourage dialogue with non-Catholics came under suspicion, and intellectual reflection on American experience was circumscribed. Not for another sixty years would there be an opportunity to reexamine the Catholic position on religious liberty.

A "Phantom Heresy"?

For many years historians regarded Americanism as a "phantom heresy," the product of bitter liberal-conservative divisions in Europe and chronic anti-Americanism in European Catholic circles. The Americanism which worried Pope Leo XIII had no basis in the realities of Catholicism in the United States. The American Catholics under suspicion in 1899 in fact did not hold the positions named in the encyclical. After Vatican II, historians began a reassessment, many concluding that Hecker and others indeed accepted many of the points condemned by Rome, but not in the sense that the Pope understood them. They also argued that many of the so-called Americanist ideas corresponded with theological ideas endorsed by Vatican II. And on several of the most contested issues, most notably religious liberty, Americans were united. This issue was resolved in the Americanists' favor at the council, but other issues, such as the balance between Catholicism's unifying doctrines and discipline and modifications according to regional cultural differences, once again became debated issues in the Church.

Americanism, in short, now appears as one episode in a long series of controversies surrounding the Church's role in the modern world. In the universal Church those usually ended with the defeat of liberal Catholicism, at least until the middle of the twentieth century. In the United States the continuing arrival of millions of Catholic immigrants limited the appeal of an Americanizing strategy based on affirmation of American ideals and institutions. In chastened form, these ideas found support among the American Church's small middle class. They would revive with the dramatic expansion of that class after World War II, and find their vindication in the endorsement of religious liberty by the Second Vatican Council.

See also GIBBONS, JAMES CARDINAL; HECKER, ISAAC; IRELAND, JOHN; PAPAL REPRESENTATION IN AMERICA.

Ellis, John Tracy. *The Life of James Cardinal Gibbons*. Milwaukee, 1952. II:1–80.

Fogarty, Gerald P., S.J. *The Vatican and the American Hierarchy from 1870 to 1965*. Wilmington, 1985, 143–94.

Klein, Félix. *Americanism: A Phantom Heresy*. Atchison, Kansas, 1951.

McAvoy, Thomas T. *The Great Crisis in American Catholic History, 1895–1900*. Chicago, 1957.

O'Brien, David J. *Isaac Hecker, American Catholic*. New York, 1992.

Reher, Margaret. "Leo XIII and Americanism" *Theological Studies* 34 (1973) 679–89.

U.S. Catholic Historian 11 (3) (Summer 1993). The entire issue is devoted to "The Americanist Controversy."

DAVID O'BRIEN

Related Document

POPE LEO XIII'S APOSTOLIC LETTER *TESTEM BENEVOLENTIAE* ON AMERICANISM, JANUARY 22, 1899

Only once in the history of the Catholic Church in the United States was its orthodoxy of doctrine called in question. The episode grew out of a series of differences within the hierarchy due to the liberal and conservative approach of the bishops to problems such as the secret societies, the teachings of Henry George, and Catholic participation in the World's Parliament of Religions at Chicago in 1893. The flourishing state of American Catholicism had meanwhile attracted the attention of European observers, especially in France where the Church was harassed by the policies of anticlerical governments. As a consequence some French Catholic leaders advocated a closer imitation of the Church in the United States, a policy which aroused violent dissent among the more conservative leaders of the French Church. A crisis ensued when a careless French translation of *The Life of Father Hecker* (New York, 1891) by Walter Elliott, C.S.P., appeared in 1897. The controversy became so heated on both sides of the Atlantic over American teaching and methods that Leo XIII finally took the matter into his own hands and after careful investigation issued a letter to Cardinal Gibbons on the subject. The pope was careful to say that the erring doctrines had been imputed to the American Catholics by a foreign source, that the issue had nothing to do with the legitimate patriotism of the Americans, and that he was not accusing the Catholics of the United States of holding these views; he was merely warning that if such doctrines were being taught, they were erroneous. Following the publication of the pope's letter the bishops of the Provinces of Milwaukee and New York thanked Leo XIII for saving the American Church from the threat of heresy. The more common reaction in the United States, however, was that embodied in the reply of Cardinal Gibbons to the pontiff on March 17, 1899, when he said: "This doctrine, which I deliberately call extravagant and absurd, this Americanism as it has been called, has nothing in common with the views, aspirations, doctrine and conduct of Americans' (John Tracy Ellis, *The Life of James Cardinal Gibbons, Archbishop of Baltimore, 1834–1921* [Milwaukee, 1952] II:71).

(*Source:* John J. Wynne, S.J., ed. *The Great Encyclical Letters of Pope Leo XIII*. New York: Benziger Bros., 1903, 441–53.)

WE SEND YOU THIS LETTER AS A TESTIMONY OF THAT DEVOTED affection in your regard, which during the long course of Our Pontificate, we have never ceased to profess for you, for your colleagues in the Episcopate, and for the whole American people, willingly availing Ourselves of every occasion to do so, whether it was the happy increase of your church, or the works which you have done so wisely and well in furthering and protecting the interests of Catholicity. The opportunity also often presented itself of regarding with admiration that exceptional disposition of your nation, so eager for what is great, and so ready to pursue whatever might be conducive to social progress and the splendor of the State. But although the object of this letter is not to repeat the praise so often accorded, but rather to point out certain things which are to be avoided and corrected, yet because it is written with that same apostolic charity which We have always shown you, and in which We have often addressed you, We trust that you will regard it likewise as a proof of Our love; and all the more so as it is conceived and intended to put an end to certain contentions which have arisen lately among you, and which disturb the minds, if not of all, at least of many, to the no slight detriment of peace.

You are aware, beloved Son, that the book entitled, "The Life of Isaac Thomas Hecker," chiefly through the action of those who have undertaken to publish and interpret it in a foreign language, has excited no small controversy on account of certain opinions which are introduced concerning the manner of leading a Christian life. We, therefore, on account of Our apostolic office, in order to provide for the integrity of the faith, and to guard the security of the faithful, desire to write to you more at length upon the whole matter.

The principles on which the new opinions We have mentioned are based may be reduced to this: that, in order the more easily to bring over to Catholic doctrine those who dissent from it, the Church ought to adapt herself somewhat to our advanced civilization, and, relaxing her ancient rigor, show some indulgence to modern popular theories and methods. Many think that this is to be understood not only with regard to the rule of life, but also to the doctrines in which the *deposit of faith* is contained. For they contend that it is opportune, in order to work in a more attractive way upon the wills of those who are not in accord with us, to pass over certain heads of doctrines, as if of lesser moment, or to so soften them that they may not have the same meaning which the Church has invariably held. Now, Beloved Son, few words are needed to show how reprehensible is the plan that is thus conceived, if we but consider the character and origin of the doctrine which the Church hands down to us. On that point the Vatican Council says: "The doctrine of faith which God has revealed is not proposed like a theory of philosophy which is to be elaborated by the human understanding, but as a divine deposit delivered to the Spouse of Christ to be faithfully guarded and infallibly declared. . . . That sense of the sacred dogmas is to be faithfully kept which Holy Mother Church has once declared, and is not to be departed from under the specious pretext of a more profound understanding" (*Const. de Fid. cath.,* c. iv).

Nor is the suppression to be considered altogether free from blame, which designedly omits certain principles of Catholic doctrine and buries them, as it were, in oblivion. For there is the one and the same Author and Master of all the truths that Christian teaching comprises: *The only-begotten Son who is in the bosom of the Father (John,* i, 18). That they are adapted to all ages and nations is plainly deduced from the words which Christ addressed to His apostles: *Going therefore teach ye all nations: teaching them to observe all things whatsoever I have commanded you: and behold I am with you all days even to the consummation of the world (Matthew,* xxviii, 19). Wherefore the same Vatican Council says: "By the divine and Catholic faith those things are to be believed which are contained in the word of God either written or handed down, and are proposed by the Church whether in solemn decision or by the ordinary universal magisterium, to be believed as having been divinely revealed" (*Const. de Fid. cath.,* c. iii). Far be it, then, for any one to diminish or for any reason whatever to pass over anything of this divinely delivered doctrine; whosoever would do so, would rather wish to alienate Catholics from the Church than to bring over to the Church those who dissent from it. Let them return; indeed, nothing is nearer to Our heart; let all those who are wandering far from the sheepfold of Christ return; but let it not be by any other road than that which Christ has pointed out.

The rule of life which is laid down for Catholics is not of such a nature as not to admit modifications, according to the diversity of time and place. The Church, indeed, possesses what her Author has bestowed on her, a kind and merciful disposition; for which reason from the very beginning she willingly showed herself to be what Paul proclaimed in his own regard: *I became all things to all men, that I might save all (Corinthians,* ix, 22). The history of all past ages is witness that the Apostolic See, to which not only the office of teaching but also the supreme government of the whole Church was committed, has constantly adhered *to the same doctrine, in the same sense and in the same mind* (Conc. Vatic., *ibid.,* c. iv): but it has always been accustomed to so modify the rule of life that, while keeping the divine right inviolate, it has never disregarded the manners and customs of the various nations which it embraces. If required for the salvation of souls, who will doubt that it is ready to do so at the present time? But this is not to be determined by the will of private individuals, who are mostly deceived by the appearance of right, but ought to be left to the judgment of the Church. In this all must acquiesce who wish to avoid the censure of Our predecessor Pius VI, who proclaimed the 18th proposition of the Synod of Pistoia "to be injurious to the Church and to the Spirit of God which governs her, inasmuch as it subjects to scrutiny the discipline established and approved by the Church, as if the Church could establish a useless discipline or one which would be too onerous for Christian liberty to bear."

But in the matter of which we are now speaking, Beloved Son, the project involves a greater danger and is more hostile to Catholic doctrine and discipline, inasmuch as the followers of these novelties judge that a certain liberty ought to be introduced into the Church, so that, limiting the exercise and vigilance of its powers, each one of the faithful may act more freely in pursuance of his own natural bent and capacity. They affirm, namely, that this is called for in order to imitate that liberty which, though quite recently introduced, is now the law and the foundation of almost every civil community. On that point We have spoken very much at length in the Letter written to all the bishops about the constitution of States; where We have also shown the difference between the Church, which is of divine right, and all other associations which subsist by the free will of men. It is of importance, therefore, to note particularly an opinion which is adduced as a sort of argument to urge the granting of such liberty to Catholics. For they say, in speaking of the infallible teaching of the Roman Pontiff, that after the solemn decision formulated in the Vatican Council, there is no more need of solicitude in that regard, and, because of its being now out of dispute, a wider field of thought and action is thrown open to individuals. A preposterous method of arguing, surely. For if anything is suggested by the infallible teaching of the Church, it is certainly that no one should wish to withdraw from it; nay, that all should strive to be thoroughly imbued with and be guided by its spirit, so as to be the more easily preserved from any private error whatsoever. To this we may add that those who argue in that wise quite set aside the wisdom and providence of God; who when He desired it especially in order the more efficaciously to guard the minds of Catholics from the dangers of the present times. The license which is commonly confounded with liberty; the passion for saying and reviling everything; the habit of thinking of and of expressing everything in print, have cast such deep shadows on men's minds, that there is now greater utility and necessity for this office of teaching than ever before, lest men should be drawn away from conscience and duty. It is far, indeed, from Our intention to repudiate all that the genius of the time begets; nay, rather, whatever the search for truth attains, or the effort after good achieves, will always be welcomed by Us, for it increases the patrimony of doctrine and enlarges the limits of public prosperity. But all this, to possess real utility, should thrive without setting aside the authority and wisdom of the Church.

We come now in due course to what are adduced as consequences from the opinions which We have touched upon; in which if the intention seem not wrong, as We believe, the things themselves assuredly will not appear by any means free from suspicion. For, in the first place, all external guidance is rejected as superfluous, nay even as somewhat of a disadvantage, for those who desire to devote themselves to the acquisition of Christian perfection; for the Holy Ghost, they say, pours greater and richer gifts into the hearts of the faithful now than in times past; and by a certain hidden instinct teaches and moves them with no one as an intermediary. It is indeed not a little rash to wish to determine the degree in which God communicates

with men; for that depends solely on His will; and He Himself is the absolutely free giver of His own gifts. *The Spirit breatheth where He will (John* iii, 8). *But to every one of us is given grace according to the measure of the giving of Christ (Ephesians,* iv, 7) . For who, when going over the history of the apostles, the faith of the rising Church, the struggles and slaughter of the valiant martyrs, and finally most of the ages past so abundantly rich in holy men, will presume to compare the past with the present times and to assert that they received a lesser outpouring of the Holy Ghost? But, aside from that, no one doubts that the Holy Ghost, by His secret incoming into the souls of the just, influences and arouses them by admonition and impulse. If it were otherwise, any external help and guidance would be useless. "If any one positively affirms that he can consent to the saving preaching of the Gospel without the illumination of the Holy Ghost, who imparts sweetness to all to consent to and accept the truth, he is misled by a heretical spirit" (*Conc. Arausic.,* II, can. vii). But as we know by experience these promptings and impulses of the Holy Ghost for the most part are not discerned without the help, and, as it were, without the preparation of an external guidance. In this matter Augustine says: "It is he who in good trees co-operates in their fruiting, who both waters and cultivates them by any servant whatever from without, and who by himself gives increase within" (*De grat. Christi,* c. xix). That is to say, the whole matter is according to the common law by which God in His infinite providence has decreed that men for the most part should be saved by men; hence He has appointed that those whom He calls to a loftier degree of holiness should be led thereto by men, "in order that," as Chrysostom says, "we should be taught by God through men" *(Hom. i. in Inscr. altar.).* We have an illustrious example of this put before us in the very beginning of the Church, for although Saul, who was *breathing threatenings and slaughter (Acts* c. ix), heard the voice of Christ Himself, and asked from Him, *Lord what wilt Thou have me to do?* He was nevertheless sent to Ananias at Damascus: *Arise and go into the city and there it shall be told thee what thou must do.* It must also be kept in mind that those who follow what is more perfect are by the very fact entering upon a way of life which for most men is untried and more exposed to error, and therefore they, more than others, stand in need of a teacher and a guide. This manner of acting has invariably obtained in the Church. All, without exception, who in the course of ages have been remarkable for science and holiness have taught this doctrine. Those who reject it, assuredly do so rashly and at their peril.

For one who examines the matter thoroughly, it is hard to see, if we do away with all external guidance as these innovators propose, what purpose the more abundant influence of the Holy Ghost, which they make so much of, is to serve. In point of fact, it is especially in the cultivation of virtue that the assistance of the Holy Spirit is indispensable; but those who affect these novelties extol beyond measure the natural virtues as more in accordance with the ways and requirements of the present day, and consider it an advantage to be richly endowed with them, because they make a man more ready and more strenuous in action. It is hard to understand how those who are imbued with Christian principles can place the natural ahead of the supernatural virtues, and attribute to them greater power and fecundity. Is nature, then, with grace added to it, weaker than when left to its own strength? and have the eminently holy men whom the Church reveres and pays homage to, shown themselves weak and incompetent in the natural order, because they have excelled in Christian virtue? Even if we admire the sometimes splendid acts of the natural virtues, how rare is the man who really possesses the habit of these natural virtues? Who is there who is not disturbed by passions, sometimes of a violent nature, for the persevering conquest of which, just as for the observance of the whole natural law, man must needs have some divine help? If we scrutinize more closely the particular acts We have above referred to, we shall discover that oftentimes they have more the appearance than the reality of virtue. But let us grant that these are real. If we do not wish *to run in vain,* if we do not wish to lose sight of the eternal blessedness to which God in His goodness has destined us, of what use are the natural virtues unless the gift and strength of divine grace be added? Aptly does St. Augustine say: "Great power, and a rapid pace, but out of the course" (*In Ps.,* xxxi, 4). For as the nature of man, because of our common misfortune, fell into vice and dishonor, yet by the assistance of grace is lifted up and borne onward with new honor and strength; so also the virtues which are exercised not by the unaided powers of nature, but by the help of the same grace, are made productive of a supernatural beatitude and become solid and enduring.

With this opinion about natural virtue, another is intimately connected, according to which all Christian virtues are divided as it were into two classes, *passive* as they say, and *active;* and they add the former were better suited for the past times, but the latter are more in keeping with the present. It is plain what is to be thought of such division of the virtues. There is not and cannot be a virtue which is really passive. "Virtue," says St. Thomas, "denotes a certain perfection of a power; but the object of a power is an act; and an act of virtue is nothing else than the good use of our free will" (I. II. a. I), the divine grace of course helping, if the act of virtue is supernatural. The one who would have Christian virtues to be adapted, some to one age and others to another, has forgotten the words of the Apostle: *Whom he foreknew he also predestinated to be made conformable to the image of His Son* (*Romans,* viii, 29). The Master and exemplar of all sanctity is Christ, to whose rule all must conform who wish to attain to the thrones of the blessed. Now, then, Christ does not at all change with the progress of the ages, but is *yesterday and to-day, and the same forever* (*Hebrews,* xiii, 8) . To the men of all ages, the phrase is to be applied: *Learn of Me because I am meek, and humble of heart* (*Matthew,* xi, 29) and at all times Christ shows Himself to us as becoming *obedient unto death* (*Philippians,* ii, 8) and in every age also the word of the Apostle holds: *And they that are Christ's have crucified their flesh with the vices and concupiscences* (*Galatians,* v, 24). Would that more would cultivate those virtues in our days, as did the holy men of bygone times! Those who by humbleness of spirit, by obedience and abstinence, were *powerful in word and work,* were of the greatest help not only to religion but to the State and society.

From this species of contempt of the evangelical virtues, which are wrongly called *passive,* it naturally follows that the mind is imbued little by little with a feeling of disdain for the religious life. And that this is common to the advocates of these new opinions we gather from certain expressions of theirs about the vows which religious orders pronounce. For, say they, such vows are altogether out of keeping with the spirit of our age, inasmuch as they narrow the limits of human liberty; are better adapted to weak minds than to strong ones; avail little for Christian perfection and the good of human society, and rather obstruct and interfere with it. But how false these assertions are, is evident from the usage and doctrine of the Church, which has always given the highest approval to religious life. And surely not undeservedly. For those who, not content with the common duties of the precepts, enter of their own accord upon the evangelical counsels, in obedience to a divine vocation, present themselves to Christ as His prompt and valiant soldiers. Are we to consider this a mark of weak minds? In the more perfect manner of life is it unprofitable or hurtful? Those who bind themselves by the vows of religion are so far from throwing away their liberty that they enjoy a nobler and fuller one—that, namely, *by which Christ has set us free* (*Galatians,* iv, 31).

What they add to this—namely, that religious life helps the Church not at all or very little—apart from being injurious to religious orders, will be admitted by no one who has read the history of the Church. Did not your own United States receive from the members of religious orders the beginning of its faith and civilization? For one of them recently, and it redounds to your credit, you have decreed that a statue should be publicly erected. And at this very time, with what alacrity and success are these religious orders doing their work wherever we find them! How many of them hasten to impart to new lands the life of the Gospel and to extend the boundaries of civilization with the greatest earnestness of soul and amid the greatest dangers! From them no less than from the rest of the clergy the

Christian people obtain preachers of the Word of God, directors of conscience, instructors of youth, and the entire Church examples of holy lives. Nor is there any distinction of praise between those who lead an active life and those who, attracted by seclusion, give themselves up to prayer and mortification of the body. How gloriously they have merited from human society, and do still merit, they should be aware who are not ignorant of how *the continual prayer of a just man* (*James,* v, 16) especially when joined to affliction of the body, avails to propitiate and conciliate the majesty of God.

If there are any, therefore, who prefer to unite together in one society without the obligation of vows, let them do as they desire. That is not a new institution in the Church, nor is it to be disapproved. But let them beware of setting such association above religious orders; nay rather, since mankind is more prone now than heretofore to the enjoyment of pleasure, much greater esteem is to be accorded to those *who have left all things and have followed Christ.*

Lastly, not to delay too long, it is also maintained that the way and the method which Catholics have followed thus far for recalling those who differ from us is to be abandoned and another resorted to. In that matter, it suffices to advert that it is not prudent, Beloved Son, to neglect what antiquity, with its long experience, guided as it is by apostolic teaching, has stamped with its approval. From the word of God we have it that it is the office of all to labor in helping the salvation of our neighbor in the order and degree in which each one is. The faithful indeed will most usefully fulfil their duty by integrity of life, by the works of Christian charity, by instant and assiduous prayer to God. But the clergy should do so by a wise preaching of the Gospel, by the decorum and splendor of the sacred ceremonies, but especially by expressing in themselves the form of doctrine which the apostles delivered to Titus and Timothy. So that if among the different methods of preaching the word of God, that sometimes seems preferable by which those who dissent from us are spoken to, not in the church but in any private and proper place, not in disputation but in amicable conference, such method is indeed not to be reprehended; provided, however, that those who are devoted to that work by the authority of the bishop be men who have first given proof of science and virtue. For We think that there are very many among you who differ from Catholics rather through ignorance than because of any disposition of the will, who, perchance, if the truth is put before them in a familiar and friendly manner, may more easily be led to the one sheepfold of Christ.

Hence, from all that We have hitherto said, it is clear, Beloved Son, that We cannot approve the opinions which some comprise under the head of Americanism. If, indeed, by that name be designated the characteristic qualities which reflect honor on the people of America, just as other nations have what is special to them; or if it implies the condition of your commonwealths, or the laws and customs which prevail in them, there is surely no reason why We should deem that it ought to be discarded. But if it is to be used not only to signify, but even to commend the above doctrines, there can be no doubt but that our Venerable Brethren the bishops of America would be the first to repudiate and condemn it, as being especially unjust to them and to the entire nation as well. For it raises the suspicion that there are some among you who conceive of and desire a church in America different from that which is in the rest of the world. One in the unity of doctrine as in the unity of government, such is the Catholic Church, and, since God has established its centre and foundation in the Chair of Peter, one which is rightly called Roman, for where Peter is there is the Church. Wherefore he who wishes to be called by the name of Catholic ought to employ in truth the words of Jerome to Pope Damasus, "I following none as the first except Christ am associated in communion with your Beatitude, that is, with the Chair of Peter; upon that Rock I know is built the Church; whoever gathereth not with thee scattereth" (*S. Ambr. in Ps.,* xi, 57).

What We write, Beloved Son, to you in particular, by reason of Our office, we shall take care to have communicated to the rest of the bishops of the United States, expressing again that love in which we include your whole nation, which as in times past has done much for religion and bids fair with God's good grace to do still more in the future.

To you and all the faithful of America We give most lovingly as an augury of divine assistance Our Apostolical Benediction.

(*Source:* John Tracy Ellis, ed. *Documents of American Catholic History.* Vol. 2:1866–1966. Wilmington, Del.: Michael Glazier, 1987, 537–47.)

ANCIENT ORDER OF HIBERNIANS

The Ancient Order of Hibernians is a Roman Catholic fraternal organization composed of individuals of Irish birth or descent. The order traces its origins to Ireland and the year 1565, a time of great religious and national conflict between Ireland and England. Following the collapse of the Catholic military alliance a secret organization was formed and under various names over the following centuries protected the persecuted Church and clergy. The members frequently acted as watchmen during the sacrifice of the Mass which had been forbidden by law.

Much of the early history of the A.O.H. is obscure as a result of its necessity to maintain secrecy. As restrictions on the Church eased somewhat in the late eighteenth and early nineteenth centuries, the organization increasingly turned to actions designed to ease the plight of the Irish tenant farmer. Under colorful local names like the

Whiteboys, the Terry Alts or the Ribbonmen, the proto-A.O.H. societies clandestinely exerted pressure on the landlords and their agents, a class of people almost entirely alien in religion and sentiment. In the first decades of the nineteenth century the tide of Irish emigration carried the order to Britain and in 1836 to America.

The A.O.H. in America was founded near St. James Church on the Lower East Side of Manhattan in 1836. The order spread to most of the Irish immigrant centers on the East Coast and slowly extended itself westward to California by the 1860s and a few decades later to Canada. The early role of the A.O.H. was again the direct defense of the Catholic Church then struggling against hostility and persecution. On several occasions armed members of the order acted to defend church buildings from attack, most notably during the attempts on the old St. Patrick's Cathedral in New York in 1844.

Responding to the often pitiful conditions of the poor immigrants, the A.O.H. built up an extensive network of benefits for its members in the event of sickness or death. An active social and athletic program provided the members and the Irish community with a variety of dances, concerts, picnics, excursions, and sports programs. Political and cultural developments in Ireland were closely followed and funds were sent to Ireland for a variety of causes, not the least of which was the promotion of an Ireland free from foreign rule.

Almost every Catholic parish in the urban areas where the Irish had settled as well as many rural communities had their branches, called divisions, of the order. The local division often worked in close alliance with the neighborhood parish and most of the charitable activities were consequently directed towards Catholic institutions and causes. Divisions of Hibernian Ladies first appeared in the 1890s and were also to be found working at the parish level.

The Ancient Order of Hibernians is organized today in approximately thirty states and Canada. The current membership, unlike that of seventy-five years ago, is overwhelmingly composed of those who are Irish by descent rather than by birth.

See also IRISH CATHOLICS IN AMERICA; IRISH CATHOLIC IMMIGRANTS, HISTORICAL BACKGROUND.

Emmons, David M. *The Butte Irish: Class and Ethnicity in an American Mining Town, 1875–1925.* Urbana: University of Illinois Press, 1989.

Funchion, Michael F., ed. *Irish American Voluntary Organizations.* Westport, Conn.: Greenwood Press, 1983.

O'Dea, John. *History of the Ancient Order of Hibernians.* Philadelphia: National Board A.O.H. 1923.

Ridge, John T. *Erin's Sons in America: The Ancient Order of Hibernians.* New York: A.O.H. 150th Anniversary Committee, 1986.

JOHN T. RIDGE

ANDERSON, MARY ANTOINETTE (1859–1940)

Actress. Mary Antoinette Anderson was born on July 28, 1859, in Sacramento, California. Her mother, Marie Antoinette Leugers, was a conservative Roman Catholic, and maintained her own family's prohibition of theatricals. Her father, Charles Henry Anderson, volunteered for the Confederate army and was killed in 1867. Anderson and her mother had since moved to Louisville to be close to her uncle, Fr. Anthony Mueller. Anderson's and Mueller's preparations for her life of service were altered when her mother remarried in 1868. Her stepfather, Dr. Hamilton Griffin, was a patron of the arts. Anderson soon became interested in music and drama and under Griffin's guidance (he would later serve as her manager), made her debut in Louisville as Juliet at age sixteen. She made her New York debut two years later in 1877 in *The Lady of Lyons* as Pauline. Despite little formal training, her beauty and intelligent choice of roles helped make her one of America's most famous actresses. The highlights of her many roles included performances in *Pygmalion* and *Galeta, Guy Mannering,* and *The Hunchback.* In 1885, she was invited to appear at the Shakespeare Memorial Theatre in Stratford-upon-Avon as Rosalind in *As You Like It.* In 1887 she returned to England to perform the dual roles of Perdita and Hermoine in *The Winter's Tale,* a theatrical first.

Anderson retired from the stage in 1889, at age thirty. In the same year, she married Antonio de Navarro, a wealthy American and they returned to England. She raised two children, Jose Maria and Elena Antonia, in addition to a son who died at birth. Anderson made a few appearances in support of the Allied effort in the First World War, but this was the extent of her professional appearances after her marriage. She died on May 29, 1940, at her home in Worcestershire, England.

Anderson, Mary Antoinette. *A Few Memories.* 1896.

———. *A Few More Memories.* 1936.

Archer, William. "Miss Mary Anderson." *The Theatre* (October 1, 1885).

Derrick, Patty D. "Rosalind and the Nineteenth-Century Woman: Four Interpretations." *Theatre Survey* 26 (2) (1985)143–62.

Dictionary of American Catholic Biography, s.v., "Mary Antoinette Anderson."

Sawyer, Raymond. "The Shakespearean Acting of Mary Anderson 1884–1889." Unpublished Ph.D. dissertation, University of Illinois, 1974.

COLLEEN J. MATAN

ANTHONY OF THE ASCENSION AND COMPANIONS

Missionaries. Carmelite friars of the Teresian Reform had reached Mexico (then New Spain) in 1588; fifteen more arrived in 1597 hoping to work as missionaries in New

Mexico. However, because that area had already been entrusted to the Franciscans, the viceroy of New Spain promised the Discalced Carmelites the next available missionary opportunity. Thus, when the king of Spain ordered a new exploration of the California coast, the viceroy chose the merchant Sebastian Vizcaino as commander, and three Discalced Carmelite friars—Andrew of the Assumption, Anthony of the Ascension, and Thomas of Aquinas—as chaplains, missionaries, chroniclers, and cartographers. Though Andrew was the superior, Anthony became better known to later historians through his detailed record of the journey.

The Vizcaino expedition set sail from Acapulco on May 5, 1602, reaching San Miguel (which they renamed San Diego) after seven months; here Andrew celebrated the first Mass on the Pacific Coast of what is now the United States on November 12, 1602. Proceeding further, mapping and naming the sites, they reached the Monterey peninsula the following month, celebrating the first Mass in upper California in mid-December. The Discalced Carmelite missionaries named the area "Carmelo," and the river "Río Carmelo." Throughout the journey, the missionaries also made promising contacts with the indigenous peoples. After returning to Mexico, Anthony of the Ascension continued to urge further missionary efforts in California until his death in 1636, but nothing came of it until the work of Franciscan missionaries such as Junipero Serra over a century later, who named his "Carmelo" mission in memory of these early friar-explorers.

Kroll, C. D. "Unknown and Uncelebrated: California's First Mass." *Carmelite Digest* 4 (Spring 1989) 3–9.

O'Brien, J. P. "California Missions, Part II: Spanish Voyages from Mexico North to California; the Carmelites." *Arms of the Cross* 4 (1985) 1–12.

Rohrbach, P.-T. *Journey to Carith: The Story of the Carmelite Order.* Garden City, N.Y.: Doubleday, 1966, 327–28.

Wagner, H. R., ed. *Spanish Voyages to the Northwest Coast of America in the Sixteenth Century.* San Francisco: California Historical Society, 1929.

STEVEN PAYNE, O.C.D.

ANTI-COMMUNISM AND AMERICAN CATHOLICS

Origins

Roman Catholics opposed Communism right from the beginning. Karl Marx, Freidrich Engels, and the other nineteenth-century European theorists of Communism regarded religion in general, and Christianity in particular, as an "opiate," a drug which clouded believers' minds. They argued that religion obscured social-class lines, that the promise of heaven encouraged a spirit of resignation rather than resistance on earth, and that it stalled the development of a revolutionary spirit among industrial workers. Early Communists, such as the leaders of the Paris Commune in 1870–71, were fiercely anti-Catholic. The gruesome murder of Archbishop Darboy of Paris during the Commune intensified Catholics' conviction that Communism and Catholicism were implacable enemies.

But influential Catholics agreed that Communism was a response to the injustices of the industrial revolution, which made tens of thousands of ill-paid working people dependent on the erratic business cycle. The Church must draw on its own resources to offer a superior alternative both to heartless capitalism and to Communism. Cardinal Henry Manning of Westminster, an energetic English convert, helped Pope Leo XIII in drafting *Rerum Novarum* (1891), an encyclical letter which condemned the injustices of industrial society, capitalist wage slavery, and neglect of the poor in the new cities. It also condemned Socialism and Communism for their opposition to private property and their atheism. *Rerum Novarum* became the foundational document of Catholic anti-Communism, first in Europe, then in America.

The American Situation

The United States, like Western Europe, was becoming an urban and industrial society in the late nineteenth century. But American Socialists, unlike their European counterparts, were not opposed to Christianity. In fact a long radical tradition among American workers took Jesus, the carpenter of Nazareth, as an inspirational figure. Socialist Party leader Eugene Debs himself wrote an admiring biography of Jesus, *The Supreme Leader,* and Socialist meetings often began and ended with prayers. Tensions developed in the early years of the twentieth century when George Herron, a Congregationalist minister and Socialist Party leader, was involved in a divorce scandal. Martha Moore Avery, a Marxist theorist who had recently converted to Catholicism, denounced Herron in her book *Socialism: The Nation of Fatherless Children* (1903). In it she argued that Socialists and Communists saw all institutions, even marriage, as no more than the product of prevailing social conditions. To her, by contrast, marriage was a sacrament, valid at all times, and not to be replaced in the future by the Socialist idea of dissoluble unions based on "sex fondness." Avery decided, soon after her conversion, to break away from the Socialist Party and to organize the Militia of Christ, an anti-Communist Catholic workers' organization which followed the teaching of *Rerum Novarum.*

Communist ideology, advocating violent revolution rather than a peaceful evolution into Socialism, continued to divide the American left before the First World War. These tensions were greatly intensified with the Russian Revolution of 1917. After their seizure of power, Lenin and the Bolsheviks launched the Third International, urging Communists throughout the world to follow policy "lines" issued from Moscow rather than local Socialist initiatives. The official atheism of the Soviet regime and its persecution of Russian Christians hardened Catholic opposition to the Revolution. The American Catholic bishops responded to the Revolution and the dislocations of the war with their "Program of Social Reconstruction" (1919), drafted by Msgr. John A. Ryan and issued in the midst of the postwar "Red Scare." In this wide-ranging declaration the bishops came out in favor of minimum wages, unemployment insurance, the rights of trade unions, a social security program to protect the elderly, public housing, cooperative ownership and management of businesses, and government control of monopolies. With this program they hoped to address the issues which tempted working men and women to join the Socialist and Communist Parties and to show that their Church was equally aware of the problems and dedicated to radical solutions. In practice, unfortunately, the bishops did not lobby very vigorously for fulfillment of their program during the 1920s, and in that decade they could even be found opposing federal legislation to restrict child labor.

The Great Depression and the Dictators

American Catholics united in opposition to President Franklin Roosevelt's decision to grant diplomatic recognition to the Soviet Union in 1933. They were also angered by his sympathetic treatment of anti-Catholic revolutionaries in Mexico in the 1930s and demanded that he remove Ambassador Josephus Daniels who had praised the revolutionary General Elias Calles. Their opposition to Communism led them to place some faith in the Italian dictator Benito Mussolini in the 1920s and early 1930s. Mussolini's Fascists had stamped out Italian Communism in the early 1920s and, in the Lateran Treaty of 1929, had made peace with Pope Pius XI, ending a sixty-year stand-off between the Vatican and the Italian civil authorities. Historian Ross Hoffman of Fordham University spoke for many American Catholics in 1936 when he wrote that Fascism was an effective barrier against "the pestilential heresy of Communism." Catholic sympathy towards Mussolini cooled only in the late 1930s when he allied Italy with Nazi Germany.

The outbreak of the Spanish Civil War in 1936 intensified the ideological conflicts of the era. Spanish Republicans, given military aid by the Soviet Union, persecuted the Catholic Church. In the first months of the war the Republicans slaughtered thousands of priests, monks, and nuns, and burned down churches and convents. In consequence, most American Catholics regarded the rebel leader, General Francisco Franco, as the savior of the Catholic Church, and often described him as a latter day crusader or even as "the George Washington of Spain." Only a handful of American Catholics had the temerity to point

out that Franco's anti-Communist soldiers, many of them African Moors, were committing equally hideous atrocities. When *Commonweal* ventured this line of criticism bishops throughout America preached against the lay journal, which found its subscriptions falling precipitously. "To the leaders of American Catholicism," writes Catholic historian David O'Brien, the Spanish Civil War seemed "a clear confrontation of Christianity and civilization with Communism and barbarism" (86).

Meanwhile at home the Great Depression of the 1930s gave American Communism greater appeal than ever before, and for a time it won the support of influential intellectuals like Edmund Wilson, Theodore Dreiser, and Malcolm Cowley. Catholic bishops denounced the Communists and, in most cases, threw their weight behind Roosevelt's New Deal, which they saw as a democratic capitalist alternative to revolution. Other Catholics recommended more drastic action, among them the Detroit priest Charles Coughlin, always a fanatical anti-Communist, and Dorothy Day, founder of the Catholic Worker movement. They both cited Pius XI's new social encyclical *Quadragesimo Anno* (1931) which amplified the message of *Rerum Novarum* and underlined the condemnation of Communism. Dorothy Day, another convert, understood perhaps better than any other American Catholic the sense of desperation among poor unskilled workers which led them to welcome the American Communist Party's bold plans for sweeping away capitalism once and for all. Her writings from the depression decade chided prosperous Catholics for their complacency and inertia beside the hard-working, hands-on Communist activists she met every day in the New York slums.

The Second World War

America's political alliance with the Soviet Union in the Second World War posed a problem to American Catholics. After Pearl Harbor in December 1941 they agreed that Japan and Germany must be defeated, but they did not welcome an alliance with Hitler's Eastern enemy, the Soviet Union. While American government propaganda sang the praises of "Uncle Joe" Stalin, Catholic bishops reminded their flocks that this could be no more than an alliance of convenience, and they cited Pius XI's uncompromisingly anti-Communist encyclical *Divini Redemptoris* (1937). Archbishop Francis Beckman of Dubuque warned in a wartime sermon that "the Christ-haters of Moscow and their international brethren . . . may well take note of the Church-Militant when she becomes aroused" and foresaw the postwar conflict between America and the Soviet Union. Historian George Sirgiovanni notes that "anyone who admired Communism had to hate religion because the Communist millennium could not be achieved so long as organized religion endured" (151).

New York's Cardinal Francis Spellman acted as President Roosevelt's unofficial messenger to the Vatican during the war, and enjoyed the confidence of Pope Pius XII. For a time in 1944 and 1945 Pius considered trying to mitigate his anti-Soviet policy, but cautious diplomatic feelers, again undertaken by Spellman, led to no substantive change. As the war ended Catholic antagonism to the Soviet Union hardened even more quickly than American antagonism, especially when Stalin made it clear that he intended to dominate Catholic Poland and the rest of Eastern Europe. Spellman's biographer John Cooney summarizes, "The Vatican became the first power to declare the Cold War on the Soviet Union, and Spellman played a key role in the struggle. He was entrusted with getting the United States to provide the cold steel needed to back up the Church's moral fervor." Cooney adds that "he welded his Church and nation to the goal of obliterating Communism wherever it appeared" (145). Throughout the tense cold war years which followed, Presidents Truman, Eisenhower, and Kennedy could rely on Spellman's leadership to maintain an almost absolutely militant anti-Communism among all American Catholics.

The Cold War and McCarthyism

Anti-Communism was a domestic issue as well as the leading foreign policy concern in postwar America. First President Harry Truman, then Senator Joseph McCarthy, launched investigations into the loyalty of federal employees, and many state and local authorities and private employers followed suit, aiming to sniff out employees who belonged to the Communist Party. These investigations, remembered collectively as McCarthyism, were particularly acute between 1950 and 1953, when for the first time American soldiers fought against Communist soldiers, in the Korean War. McCarthy, a war veteran and Wisconsin senator, was himself a Catholic, and he won eager support from most of the Catholic press and bishops. Investigating committees, such as his Senate Subcommittee on Internal Security, urged former Communists to name their old colleagues. By then, ironically, the American Communist Party had lost most of its members and would never again wield any domestic influence. But even ex-Communists who were slow to denounce old colleagues could find themselves out of work.

Among the most ardent ex-Communists was Louis Budenz, who had lapsed from the Catholic faith during his Communist years but had rejoined the Church after renouncing Communism in 1946. His autobiography, *This is My Story* (1947), exposed what he now saw as the wickedness and duplicity of Communism. It made him a hero to Catholic reviewers and a villain to American civil libertarians who saw him as a liar and a traitor to his friends. Budenz, who knew personally most of America's prominent Communists, became a regular participant in trials and hearings aimed against them.

Commonweal was one of the few Catholic journals to criticize McCarthyism for its excesses, but *Commonweal*'s editors were themselves passionate anti-Communists. They merely thought that McCarthy's reckless accusations of treason, sometimes against blameless men of the highest probity, were going to give the real and necessary cause a bad name. A new anti-Communist journal, *National Review,* was launched by William F. Buckley, Jr., a Catholic layman, in 1955. He and his brother-in-law, L. Brent Bozell, a Catholic convert and McCarthy speechwriter, had published *McCarthy and His Enemies* in 1953, defending the senator's techniques and arguing that America was, in effect, a nation at war against international Communism and was justified in taking drastic steps to secure its internal apparatus. Buckley and Bozell continued to defend the work of the House Committee on un-American Activities and other internal security investigations well into the 1960s.

Catholic anti-Communism was not confined to intellectuals and politicians. It also had a vigorous life among ordinary Catholics throughout the nation. For example, a farmer's wife, Mrs. Mary Ann Van Hoof, saw an apparition of the Blessed Virgin Mary near her home in Necedah, Wisconsin, in 1950. The Virgin warned her about the danger of Communism and the need to fight against it with intensified prayer. Thousands of pilgrims gathered at the site and joined in spontaneous prayer meetings, even though the local bishop cautiously refrained from giving the new cult any official sanction. Continuing a practice begun during the Second World War some Catholic communities arranged novenas (nine-day prayer sessions) in the hope that they could generate the spiritual energy to convert the Russian masses to Christianity and so bring Communism to an end.

The Hungarian Revolution of 1956 led to another upsurge of Catholic anti-Communism, partly because one of its symbolic figureheads was Cardinal Joszef Mindszenty of Budapest. Mindszenty was released from a Communist jail and entered Budapest in triumph. But when Russian tanks arrived to crush the uprising a week later Mindszenty, fearing for his life, sought sanctuary in the American embassy. The rebellion over, the Soviet authorities refused to grant Mindszenty a safe conduct out of the country, the embarrassed American ambassador refused to hand him over, and so he stayed in the embassy for the next eighteen years, a living symbol of uncompromising Catholic opposition to Communism. Hungarian refugees in New Brunswick, New Jersey, erected a statue of Mindszenty outside one of their churches and Catholic "Mindszenty Clubs" studied the character of International Communism and its challenge to the Church.

The Vietnam Era

Not long after the Korean truce and just before the Hungarian rising, French forces finally abandoned their long anti-Communist war in their Southeast Asian colony, Vietnam. A settlement signed in Geneva in 1954 did not endure and by 1960 a Communist insurgency, the Viet Minh, was trying to capture the southern, non-Communist zone and reunite the country under Ho Chi Minh. An American Catholic doctor, Tom Dooley, had already made a name for himself in Vietnam by caring for Catholic refugees from the north seeking resettlement after the Geneva treaty. His popular books encouraged American Catholics to see the war as one more confrontation of "Godless Communism" with Christian civilization.

As the American presence in Vietnam began to escalate, first with "advisors" under President Kennedy, then with combat soldiers under President Johnson following the Tonkin Gulf Resolution of 1964, Catholics remained firmly committed to the fight. Cardinal Spellman visited the American troops in Vietnam at Christmas, 1966, and told them that they were fighting in "a war for civilization."

By then, however, a small minority of Catholics, priests and laity alike had begun to doubt the wisdom of the American policy. Did either America or Vietnam really stand to benefit from so ruthless a war, with its far-ranging destruction? A young Catholic named Roger LaPorte set fire to himself on November 9, 1965, outside the United Nations building in New York, dying to protest against the war. Two priest-brothers, Daniel Berrigan, S.J., and his brother Philip Berrigan, S.S.J., were among the first to join antiwar protests, Daniel telling a crowd that in a war like that in Vietnam, "man stands outside the blessing of God. He stands, in fact, under His curse." Daniel Berrigan visited North Vietnam in 1967, much to the consternation of his superiors, who continued to hold conventional anti-Communist views of the war. The Berrigans then undertook a series of dramatic demonstrations against the military draft. They threw vials of their own blood over draft files in Baltimore, and, a few months later, set fire to draft files in Catonsville, Maryland, with homemade napalm.

The bishops' early indignation at antiwar protesters abated in the late 1960s. Strongly influenced by Vatican II, by Pope John XXIII's encyclical *Pacem in Terris* (1963), and by the later writings of Thomas Merton, an influential Trappist monk, they too began to see that the Vietnam War raised nettlesome questions of proportionality and justice even for uncompromising anti-Communists. The Tet Offensive of 1968 also raised the specter of American defeat and made army propaganda ring hollow. An unwinnable war in Southeast Asia was eroding public confidence in the government, fragmenting society, and doing little to help America (or Christianity) in the conflict against the Soviet Union. The bishops therefore wrote a pastoral letter in support of conscientious objection in 1968, reversing a century-long policy in which they had denied that refusing to fight in the nation's wars was an option for Catholics.

Twilight of Communism

The era of Vatican II witnessed experiments throughout the Catholic world. Among the more surprising theological developments was "liberation theology," which began among Latin American Catholic intellectuals but soon spread to American seminaries and divinity schools. Liberation theologians such as Gustavo Gutierrez and Juan Luis Segundo argued that Christ showed a "preferential option for the poor," and that his work in the modern world consisted of fighting against capitalist "structures of oppression" in the Third World. The rhetoric often sounded decidedly similar to that of Latin American Communists, and liberation theologians identified popular insurgencies in Nicaragua and El Salvador—whose leaders were avowed Marxists— as Christian liberation movements. Rosemary Ruether, an American Catholic theologian, was among the pioneers of a feminist liberation theology, adapting the Latin Americans' insights to the study of women as an oppressed group, though in a less obviously Marxist framework.

By 1980 most American Catholic bishops and intellectuals hesitated to use the blistering anti-Communist language their predecessors had favored. That year, indeed, they set about drafting a pastoral letter on the issue of nuclear weapons and deterrence theory, and concluded, in their final draft (1983), that American foreign policy ought not to be based on the threat of widespread annihilation, even if the putative enemy was Communist. At the same time, however, the emergence of a Polish pope, John Paul II, and a new generation of anti-Communist protests, which began with the Solidarity movement in his native land, invigorated Catholic anti-Communism in Europe. American Catholic neoconservatives, led by Michael Novak and Richard J. Neuhaus, a convert from Lutheranism, argued that the basic cold war situation was unchanged and that Catholics should not relax their vigilance against either the Soviet Union or Communism. They condemned liberation theology as a dangerous entering wedge for Communism.

For them, as for most Americans, the events of 1989–91, when Communist regimes collapsed throughout Eastern Europe and the Soviet Union, confirmed their faith that the democratic free societies of the West provided a superior and more durable model of social organization than totalitarian, atheistic Communism. By the early 1990s the only surviving Communist regimes were Cuba and China, both of which completely lacked the idealistic radiance which Communism had generated in the first half of the century. For a century America's Catholic leaders had declared, sometimes boldly, sometimes anxiously, that the Church would outlive Communism just as it had outlived other deadly rivals in the past. By 1991 they found that history had vindicated their faith.

See also COMMONWEAL; McCARTHY, JOSEPH RAYMOND; RYAN, JOHN AUGUSTINE; SPANISH CIVIL WAR AND AMERICAN CATHOLICS, THE; SPELLMAN, FRANCIS CARDINAL.

Allitt, Patrick. *Catholic Intellectuals and Conservative Politics in America: 1950–1985*. Ithaca, N.Y.: Cornell University Press, 1993.

Cooney, John. *The American Pope: The Life and Times of Francis Cardinal Spellman*. New York: New York Times Books, 1984.

Crosby, Donald. *God, Church, and Flag: Senator Joseph McCarthy and the Catholic Church*. Chapel Hill: University of North Carolina Press, 1978.

Meconis, Charles. *With Clumsy Grace: The American Catholic Left, 1961–1975*. New York: Seabury, 1979.

O'Brien, David. *American Catholics and Social Reform*. New York: Oxford University Press, 1968.

Sirgiovanni, George. *An Undercurrent of Suspicion: Anticommunism in America During World War II*. New Brunswick, N.J.: Transaction, 1990.

PATRICK ALLITT

ANTI-SEMITISM AND AMERICAN CATHOLICS

Catholics and Jews arrived in what were to become the thirteen original colonies and later the United States at approximately the same time. Catholics established the colony of Maryland in 1634; the first Jews arrived in New Amsterdam (later renamed New York) in 1654. Both were minorities in the dominant Protestant culture. Neither Catholics nor Jews were allowed in most of the English colonies, and if they were, they had no rights. Situations fluctuated depending on who was in power, but Rhode Island, Pennsylvania, New York, and the Carolinas permitted non-Protestants some freedom of worship at various periods.

By the time of the American Revolution, the population of the nascent United States included approximately 3,000,000 Protestants, 30,000 Catholics, and 2,000 Jews. Catholic-Jewish interaction in the colonial or early national period was minimal. Both groups struggled to maintain their identity in the newly established nation which provided religious toleration—and the promise of religious liberty. The fear of proselytizing by Protestants caused both Catholics and Jews to develop close-knit religious communities in this first wave of immigration.

Nineteenth Century

With the revolutions in Europe (1830, 1848), and the potato famine in Ireland (1840s), the Irish and German immigrations brought Catholics and Jews in substantial numbers to the United States in the pre-Civil War period. Catholics found themselves caught in a xenophobic quagmire. Protestant fear of the papacy resulted in anti-Catholic riots and the burning of convents. Jews tended to be spectators in the midst of the Protestant-Catholic turmoil. It was the American Jewish woman Rebecca Gratz who noted during that period:

> The present outbreak is an attack on the Catholic Church, and there is so much violent animosity between that sect and the Protestants that unless the strong arm of power is raised to sustain the provisions of the Constitution of the United States, securing to every citizen the privilege of worshipping God according to his conscience, America will no longer be the happy asylum of the oppressed and the secure dwelling place of religion (Rebecca Gratz, "Rebecca Gratz on Religious Bigotry," *American Jewish Archives* V [2] [June 1953] 114).

Her inherent sympathy for the plight of the Catholics and her insight into the dangers of bigotry in the United States, provide a helpful reflection on Jewish-Catholic relations in this period.

The word "anti-Semitism" was coined in 1879 by the German journalist Wilhem Marr. Prior to that, hatred of Jews was basically "anti-Judaism"—rejection of Jews for religious reasons (i.e., they had not accepted Jesus as Messiah, or had "crucified Christ"). However, the mid-nineteenth-century studies of Charles Darwin and his scientific work on the theory of evolution had implications in the social sphere vis-à-vis racism. Would-be sociologists appropriated ideas such as "the survival of the fittest" to support the superiority of the Nordic and Anglo-Saxon people. Southern and Eastern Europeans were considered inferior. These were the very people who migrated to the United States in large numbers from 1880–1924. Polish and Russian Jews (Orthodox, many of them Hasidic) arrived on the east coast along with Polish and Italian Catholics and Orthodox Christians from Greece and Russia. All of them were aliens in an Anglo-Saxon-Protestant nation and were the targets of the "100 percent Americanists."

The exclusion of both Catholics and Jews from employment opportunities was common. Protestant country clubs and elite schools discriminated against both groups, but particularly the Jews. There was some ethnic animosity between Jews and Irish, and between Jews and other predominantly Catholic groups, but these same communities found themselves with common concerns such as prohibition against intermarriage, adherence to dietary laws, a strong sense of family and tradition, and ancient liturgies to nourish their souls in an alien culture.

World War I and After

With the entry of the United States into World War I, Catholics, Protestants, and Jews joined together to provide chaplains for servicemen and aid for refugees. The National Catholic War Council (later the National Catholic Welfare Conference) found itself cooperating during the war years with the Federal Council of Churches (Protestant), and the Joint Distribution Committee representing Jewish organizations. This was the advent of national interfaith cooperation in America. It continued in the postwar period as the three groups made efforts to deal with the rising social problems revolving around a living wage, reasonable working hours, and a safe environment for workers.

The 1920s saw the revival of the Ku Klux Klan which targeted African Americans, Catholics, and Jews. The election of 1928 in which Governor Al Smith of New York became the first Catholic to be the nominee of a major party for the U.S. presidency unleashed fear and hostility toward Catholics. Efforts were made by groups such as the National Conference of Christians and Jews (founded 1928) to alleviate mounting prejudice against Jews and Catholics.

With the advent of the depression in 1929, the desire to find a scapegoat for the monetary problems and high unemployment focused upon the Jews. The radio sermons of Fr. Charles E. Coughlin exacerbated Catholic-Jewish relations using religion to inflame the anti-Semitic climate. Between the World Wars, Jews were attacked as either Bolsheviks who were responsible for the Russian revolution or as international bankers who were controlling national finances to the detriment of the ordinary person. This anti-Semitic hysteria reached a high point in 1938.

The Holocaust and Vatican Council II

After World War II, with the discovery of the death camps, the reality of the Holocaust caused Christians to consider the truly destructive power of anti-Semitism. Following the immediate horror and initial denial regarding the destruction of European Jewry, Catholic, Protestant and Jewish scholars started collaborating on projects such as the Dead Sea scrolls. New research and scholarship—biblical and historical—provided the groundwork for the documents of Vatican Council II.

Catholics, with few exceptions, had not been allowed to participate in ecumenical or interreligious dialogue for centuries. It was Pope John XXIII who specifically directed Cardinal Augustine Bea, S.J., to develop a draft document on the relationship of the Catholic Church with the Jews which was eventually incorporated into *Nostra aetate* (Declaration on the Relationship of the Church to Non-Christian Religions). Although it did not include a condemnation of the charge of deicide against the Jews as some had wished, Article no. 4 stated explicitly:

> Indeed, the Church reproves every form of persecution against whomsoever it may be directed. Remembering, then, her common heritage with the Jews and moved not by any political consideration, but solely by religious motivation of Christian charity, she deplores all hatreds, persecutions, and displays of antisemitism leveled at any time and from any source against the Jews.

The National Conference of Catholic Bishops in their "Guidelines for Catholic-Jewish Relations" promulgated in 1975 not only reiterated the condemnation of anti-Semitism but encouraged interreligious dialogue. Article 6 stated:

> Proselytism, which does not respect human freedom, is carefully to be avoided. While the Christian, through the faith life of word and deed, will always witness to Jesus as the risen Christ, the dialogue is concerned with the permanent vocation of the Jews as God's people, the enduring values that Judaism shares with Christianity and that together, the Church and the Jewish people are called upon to witness to the whole world ("Guidelines for Catholic-Jewish Relations," National Conference of Catholic Bishops [Washington, D.C., 1985], publication no. 966, p. 4).

These documents and the initiatives they generated, while not eradicating anti-Semitism in the Church in the United States, laid the groundwork for remarkable progress in the relationship between Jews and Christians in the second half of the twentieth century.

See also COUGHLIN, CHARLES EDWARD; VATICAN COUNCIL II AND AMERICAN CATHOLICS.

Athans, Mary Christine. "Anti-Semitism—or Anti-Judaism?" *Introduction to Jewish-Christian Relations,* eds. Michael Shermis and Arthur E. Zannoni. New York, 1991.

____. *The Coughlin-Fahey Connection: Father Charles E. Coughlin, Father Denis Fahey, C.S.Sp., and Religious Anti-Semitism in the United States, 1938–1954.* New York, 1991.

Dinnerstein, Leonard. *Anti-Semitism in America.* New York, 1994.

Jaher, Frederick C. *A Scapegoat in the New Wilderness: The Origins and Rise of Anti-Semitism in America.* Cambridge, Massachusetts, 1994.

Pawlikowski, John. *Catechetics and Prejudice.* New York, 1973.

MARY CHRISTINE ATHANS, B.V.M.

ARBEZ, EDWARD PHILIP (1881–1967)

Biblical scholar. He was born in Paris on May 16, 1881, and came to America in 1901 in the middle of his seminary training as he wanted to join the Sulpicians and become part of their "American mission." He attended The Catholic University of America and was ordained in 1904. He was assigned to St. Patrick's Seminary in Menlo Park, California, where for over twenty years he taught multiple subjects including Hebrew and Scripture. He then moved to The Catholic University of America where he found the opportunity to make good use of his many linguistic talents. He was recognized for his expertise in Semitic languages, and in 1943 he was chosen to head the Semitic Languages Department.

For years he was dissatisfied with the Catholic approach and meager contribution to contemporary biblical studies. To widen the scholastic horizon, he crusaded for the foundation of the Catholic Biblical Association in 1936. He was wont to point out that Rome's fettering of biblical research and its restrictive approach to scriptural studies were a damaging disservice to the Church. When in 1943 Pius XII issued *Divino Afflante Spiritu,* the emancipation proclamation for Catholic scholars, Arbez was one of the first to advocate a new American translation of the Bible by Catholic scholars, and his hope was realized when *The New American Bible* was launched. He died in Washington, D.C., on December 27, 1967.

See also CATHOLIC BIBLICAL ASSOCIATION (CBA).

Hill, W. F. "Rev. Edward P. Arbez, S.S." *Catholic Biblical Quarterly* 23 (1961) 113–24.

MICHAEL GLAZIER

ARCHAMBAULT, ALEX (ca. 1850–1911)

Missionary. When Bishop Louis Lootens, the first vicar apostolic of Idaho, arrived in Idaho City in February 1869, he brought with him a young priest from Montreal, Canada, named Alex J. A. Archambault. Not long after, the bishop gave Fr. Archambault charge of St. Joseph's Church in Idaho City.

Press reports of the day indicate that he started teaching the fall term of his first year in the Boise Basin because the Sisters of the Holy Names had pulled out of St. Mary's Academy, Idaho City, and there was no one else available to teach. Archambault continued to teach school in Idaho City for six years, but renamed the school St. Joseph's Academy. He also attended to the churches in Idaho City, Centerville, and Pioneerville on weekends, traveling to the mountain towns on horseback.

In January 1876 he contracted diphtheria and postponed reopening the school while he tried to regain his health. The school never reopened.

In 1877 two other priests left the Boise Basin to accept posts elsewhere, leaving Archambault as the only priest in South Idaho for some time. The *Owyhee Avalanche* reported after one of his visits to Owyhee County: "During the two weeks the Rev. Gentleman spent in this vicinity, he was constantly at work, either holding service or visiting families here and elsewhere. He left a most favorable impression here and all will be glad to see him return."

The hard work took a heavy toll on Archambault's health. By the time other priests arrived to assist him, he was forced to request a transfer to Oregon in hope the coastal country would help his health. He left his post as pastor of St. John's in Boise City on July 6, 1880, to serve as rector of St. Francis Church in Portland, Oregon. While there he taught in St. Michael's College where Fr. Alphonsus Glorieux was president. Glorieux later was named the first bishop of Idaho. In 1882 Archambault returned to Canada to live in retirement until his death in January 1911.

In the *History of the Diocese of Boise, 1863–1952,* authors Fr. Cyprian Bradley, O.S.B., and Bishop Edward Kelly said Fr. Archambault's labors "laid one more solid stone beneath the foundation of the Diocese of Boise."

COLETTE COWMAN

ARIZONA, CATHOLIC CHURCH IN

Christian evangelization first occurred in what is modern Arizona in 1539 when Estebanico, a Black Moor, carried a cross before him to announce the coming of a Spanish expedition. The first rudimentary ideas of the gospel were spoken by Fray Marcos de Niza on his quest for the seven cities of Cíbola that turned out to be only stone and adobe pueblos. And the colonizing expedition of Francisco Vásquez de Coronado that crossed Arizona into New Mexico fared poorly indeed as an occasion for conversion of the native peoples it encountered. For the next two centuries the presence of the Church was largely confined to organized missionary activity of the Franciscans and the Jesuits. The few, dispersed, secular clergy who were in evidence labored exclusively with tiny Spanish settlements.

Franciscan and Jesuit Missionaries

Like its geography, Arizona's ecclesiastical history is divided by the massive Mogollon Rim and the Gila River which together cut the state into north and south. The northern sector forms part of the Colorado Plateau that slopes toward the upper Río Grande valley in New Mexico. After the successful entry of Juan de Oñate into New Mexico in 1598, Franciscan missionaries made contact with the Zuñi and Hopi peoples to the west. Conversion was a difficult struggle and ended effectively after the Pueblo Revolt of 1680, but not before several Franciscans had given their lives. The southern sector below the Gila was only introduced to Christianity in the late seventeenth century by the famed Jesuit missionary, Eusebio Francisco Kino. His work among the indigenous tribes dwelling south of the Gila from its exit out of the mountains to the Colorado met with memorable success. But mission expansion stalled for a score of years after his death until the visit of the bishop of Durango (Mexico), Benito Crespo, who urged the crown for more missionaries. This resulted in staffing missions in the northern Pimería Alta (which would become southern Arizona in the mid-1800s). Expansion was interrupted by a bloody Piman revolt in 1751 that took the lives of two Jesuit missionaries, Tomás Tello and Henrique Ruhen. Although the mission frontier was slowly advancing in the south, the north held out firmly against accepting missionaries among the Hopi mesas.

Jesuit hopes for expansion to the north and west were dashed by Charles III's edict of expulsion in 1767. A handful of Franciscans tried to maintain the extant missions, but the stringent reforms of the Bourbon monarchs stifled the nascent Church in the desert. However, the expulsion of the Jesuits occasioned the arrival of Fray Francisco Tomás Hermenegildo Garcés, a Franciscan from Querétaro, Jalisco. His close alliance with the military forces placed him on several important expeditions such as the opening of the overland trail to California. Tragically, Garcés and three

Franciscan companions were martyred in the infamous Yuma massacre in 1781. The last quarter of the eighteenth century witnessed some impressive church construction in the desert communities, the most spectacular being San Xavier del Bac which was completed in 1797.

Mission San Xavier del Bac, Arizona

Diocese of Sonora

Until the establishment of the Diocese of Sonora in 1779, the Church in Arizona remained almost exclusively a missionary church under the auspices of the Spanish *patronato real* and under the administration of regular clergy. A few secular clergy served the mining towns and at least three priests surrendered their lives in service of the Church. Bishop Antonio de los Reyes, a Spaniard and the first bishop of Sonora, had been one of the Franciscan missionaries, but he differed sharply with his companions on frontier policy. After his death in 1787, José Joaquín Granados was consecrated bishop and concentrated his activities in Culiacán, Sinaloa. He was momentarily followed by Damián Martínez de Galinzoga who in a few short months was transferred to Spain. Then Pius VI named Francisco Rouset as bishop; he served the vast diocese for the next nineteen years until his death in 1814.

While Mexico staggered under the effects of its War of Independence, the next and fifth bishop of Sonora was consecrated—Bernardo Martínez Ocejo, a Carmelite friar. Traveling the diocese tirelessly until his death in 1825, Bishop Martínez was not replaced until 1837. His successor, Lázaro de la Garza, had been the rector of the cathedral of Mexico City, returning there as archbishop in 1850. He left Sonora in the hands of Pedro Loza, the last bishop of Sonora to hold sway over Arizona. With the Gadsden Purchase in effect in 1854, Loza finally ceded the church's jurisdiction and possessions in 1860 to Bishop Jean Baptist Lamy of Santa Fe through the auspices of Fr. Joseph Machbeuf.

Under American Rule

After a long, checkered history of missionaries, itinerant bishops, and political uncertainties, the Church in Arizona was beginning to show a new identity. Under terms of the Treaty of Guadalupe Hidalgo, which granted vast sections of northern Mexico to the brash, expansionist United States, and under the terms of the sale of huge portions of the desert northwest, heavy responsibilities were being placed on the heirs apparent to the Catholic population of the recently acquired territories. The Baltimore-dominated American Church grasped for its quickest solution to the problem of ministering to the new lands by sending French missionaries who were becoming well established in the Midwestern states. Little consideration was given to the immense cultural differences they would encounter in Spanish and Native American settlements that had been Catholic for centuries! And once again the geography of Arizona proved too much for the bishop of Santa Fe, so the southern portion of the diocese was made into a new bishopric to be administered by Jean Baptiste Salpointe, who had ministered in southern Arizona for some four years.

In 1868 Arizona was made a vicariate apostolic with Salpointe as bishop-elect. He was consecrated bishop in Clermont, France, in 1869, returning the following year with several volunteer priests for the new diocese. Once again in the desert, he searched the nation for volunteers to staff hospitals and schools. His ambitious service transformed Tucson and the young diocese. Then in 1884 he left Arizona to become coadjutor archbishop of Santa Fe. The vicariate apostolic was placed in charge of Peter Bourgade who had come to the desert with Salpointe's volunteers fifteen years before. In 1897 Bourgade was appointed the first bishop of Tucson. Then in 1899, Bourgade, plagued with health problems, followed Salpointe's footsteps into the archbishopric of Santa Fe where he served until his death in 1908. The Arizona Church was handed over to another French missionary, Henry Regis Granjon, from Lyons.

Twentieth-Century Developments

As the twentieth century dawned, Granjon held the reins with high hopes for educating the populace of the diocese, but he died suddenly in 1922 at the age of fifty-nine; his successor was the long-lived Daniel J. Gercke, a native of Philadelphia, Pennsylvania. Consecrated at forty-nine, Gercke survived through his retirement in 1960 at eighty-six years of age. He was succeeded by Bishop Francis J. Green, who witnessed the real growth of the Church in Arizona with the establishment of the Diocese of Phoenix in 1969, headed by Bishop Edward McCarthy.

The Church in the Southwest was experiencing growing pains in the second quarter of the twentieth century because immigrants from Europe and the eastern U.S. were settling in the formerly tiny towns. And the Church's problems continued to be divided between urban and missionary apostolates. In 1939 the Diocese of Gallup split off from Santa Fe to minister to the sprawling native reservations including most of northern Arizona. The first bishop was a Franciscan, Bernard Espelage. Twenty years later he was succeeded by Jerome Hastrich who, on his retirement in 1990, handed the miter over to Donald Pelotte, S.S.S., the first Native American bishop to work in Arizona.

Bishop McCarthy was raised to the archbishopric of Miami and James Rausch headed the fairly young diocese until his unexpected death in 1981; he was succeeded by Thomas O'Brien who saw Phoenix become the largest Catholic population center in Arizona. Bishop Green of Tucson retired in 1981 and an auxiliary bishop in Los Angeles, Manuel Moreno, became the first Hispanic bishop in Arizona since the time it was broken away from Sonora.

Hence, the history of the Church in Arizona is a tale of missionary evangelization for over four centuries, a condition that still prevails, and of a largely immigrant population—first Hispanic, then Anglo and Mexican. The mixture and the isolation from frequent ministry has led to pockets of traditionalism, folk-Catholicism, and liberal accommodation in every era.

Bolton, Herbert Eugene, ed. *Kino's Historical Memoir of Pimería Alta: A Contemporary Account of the Beginnings of California, Sonora and Arizona by Father Eusebio Francisco Kino, S.J., Pioneer Missionary, Explorer, Cartographer and Ranchman, 1683–1711.* 2 vols. Cleveland, 1919; repr. New York, 1976.

____. *Rim of Christendom: A Biography of Eusebio Francisco Kino.* New York, 1936.

Burrus, Ernest J., S.J., ed. *Kino and Manje: Explorers of Sonora and Arizona.* St. Louis and Rome, 1971.

Coues, Elliott. *On the Trail of a Spanish Pioneer: The Diary and Itinerary of Francisco Garcés in His Travels through Sonora, Arizona and California, 1775–1776.* New York, 1900.

Nordmeyer, Robert E., Kieran McCarthy, and Charles Polzer. *Shepherds in the Desert: A Sequel to Salpointe.* Tucson, 1978.

Salpointe, Jean Baptiste. *Soldiers of the Cross: Notes on the Ecclesiastical History of New Mexico, Arizona and Colorado.* Banning, California, 1898.

CHARLES POLZER, S.J.

ARKANSAS, CATHOLIC CHURCH IN

Less than fifty years after the first voyage of Christopher Columbus, and some sixty-six years before the first permanent English settlement in North America, Roman Catholics first entered what would become Arkansas. Hernando De Soto was the first European to see and then cross the Mississippi River on June 18, 1541. After crossing this mighty stream, De Soto erected a cross and knelt before it singing the *Te Deum,* a traditional Catholic hymn of praise. This was a first Catholic Christian religious service ever held in what would become Arkansas. De Soto stayed in the future state a little less than a year, and Spain, occupied by its vast holdings in Central and South America, basically abandoned this area. While both brief and rather shallow, this was Arkansas' first experience with Catholicism.

Colonial Period

More than 130 years would pass before another Catholic missionary penetrated Arkansas. Fr. Jacques Marquette, S.J., and fur trapper Louis Jolliet had come down from French Canada and journeyed southward down the Mississippi River to the mouth of the Arkansas River. They stayed for about two weeks in July 1673 before returning north. Nine years later Robert Cavalier de La Salle returned to the lower Mississippi River valley, claimed the whole region for France, and named it Louisiana after his monarch, King Louis XIV. To one of his lieutenants, Henri De Tonti, La Salle gave a land grant and Tonti returned in 1686 to found the first European settlement in Arkansas near the junction of the Arkansas and Mississippi Rivers. The Arkansas Post, as it was called, was abandoned ten years later and there would be no permanent settlement again for another quarter century. On November 1, 1700, the first recorded Mass in Arkansas was said by Fr. Jacques Gravier, S.J., a French missionary traveling down the Mississippi River from Canada.

France refounded the Arkansas Post in August 1721, but there was little effort made to colonize the area and convert the natives. Fr. Paul du Poisson, S.J., labored as a missionary among the native Arkansas peoples for two years, 1727–29, but he was martyred near Natchez, Mississippi, on November 28, 1729. (This was exactly 114 years to the day before the establishment of a Catholic Diocese of Arkansas.) Very few Catholic missionaries came to Arkansas during the eighteenth century or during the first four decades of the nineteenth century. Until the diocese was erected in 1843, the longest time a priest had stayed in Arkansas was eight years, and that was Jesuit missionary Fr. Louis Carette, S.J., 1750–58.

The Spanish assumed control of the western half of the old Louisiana Territory, which included Arkansas. The Spanish eventually put all their territory in Florida and Louisiana under a diocese centered in New Orleans in 1793. After decades of serving as a mission outpost of larger Catholic parishes in what would now be known as Missouri, the Arkansas Post was made a separate parish in 1796, with its first resident pastor in almost forty years. Fr. Pierre Janin, a French diocesan priest fleeing from the French Revolution, stayed at the Arkansas Post for three and a half years. Janin attempted and failed to build a church at the post and he departed by late December 1799. After Napoleon pressured Spain to hand him Louisiana, the French dictator then turned around and sold it to the United States in 1803. Forty years after this transfer, and upon the recommendation of the Fifth Provincial Council in Baltimore, Pope Gregory XVI erected the Diocese of Little Rock on November 28, 1843. Its boundaries, the document stated, would embrace the state of Arkansas.

Diocese of Little Rock

For the duration of the nineteenth century, Arkansas' sole diocese had two Irish-born prelates, Andrew Byrne (1802–62) and Edward M. Fitzgerald (1833–1907). After arriving in 1844, Byrne spent eighteen years in this struggling diocese on the southwestern frontier. He never had more than ten priests, yet he founded Arkansas's first Catholic College of St. Andrew in Fort Smith in 1849 and brought the Irish Sisters of Mercy to the diocese. In the year they arrived, 1851, the Mercy Sisters opened St. Mary's Academy in Little Rock, the state's oldest continuous educational institution. By the end of his tenure as bishop, the Mercy Sisters were operating convent schools in Fort Smith and Helena. In 1850 the Little Rock diocese was made a part of the New Orleans metropolitan province. If Bishop Byrne had an opinion of slavery, he never recorded it nor owned any slaves. During the Know-Nothing uproar of the 1850s, Byrne stayed out of political disputes and instead sought diligently, yet unsuccessfully, to build up his flock by supporting Catholic migration to the state. He traveled twice to his homeland in search of clergy and immigrants, yet by the end of his tenure as bishop, there was no noticeable increase of Catholic population, which numbered about one percent of the white population in 1860. Byrne died in Helena, Arkansas, and was buried in the garden of the St. Catherine's Convent of the Mercy Sisters. In 1881 his successor had his remains removed to Little Rock and placed under the newly constructed Cathedral of St. Andrew.

The disruption of the Civil War meant that Arkansas would not see another Catholic bishop for almost five years. In the interim, Bishop Byrne's last vicar general, Irish-born Fr. Patrick Reilly, would serve as apostolic administrator. In the summer of 1866 word came from Rome that Fr. Edward Fitzgerald, pastor of St. Patrick's Church in Columbus, Ohio, and priest of the Archdiocese of Cincinnati, was to be the second bishop of Little Rock. Fitzgerald initially rejected the appointment in September, and this prompted Pope Pius IX to issue to the young priest a *mandamus,* a command under holy obedience to accept the Arkansas diocese. By the time Fr. Fitzgerald received this order from Rome in early December, he had attended the Second Plenary Council in Baltimore with his archbishop, John B. Purcell. At the council Fitzgerald changed his mind about the appointment and decided to go to Little Rock where he arrived on St. Patrick's Day, 1867.

Bishop Edward Fitzgerald

Edward M. Fitzgerald would prove to be a unique Catholic bishop for his time and the most significant prelate in the history of the Arkansas Church. Only thirty-three at the time of his appointment, he was the youngest Catholic bishop in the United States, if not the world. He distinguished himself in the universal Church by being one of two bishops in the world, and the only English-speaking prelate, to cast his vote against the declaration of papal infallibility at the First Vatican Council in 1870. This action, plus his opposition to the setting up of Catholic schools in each parish at the Third Plenary Council in 1884, and his sympathy with the early labor movement, clearly mark him out as one of the more interesting and overlooked American bishops of the nineteenth century. Throughout his career, however, he defended doctrines like papal infallibility and implemented policies like Catholic schools, positions from which he had publicly dissented. He was not punished for his views, as he turned down promotions to two archdioceses (Cincinnati and New Orleans), plus offers of other dioceses.

Like his predecessor, Fitzgerald sought to bring immigrants to the state to bolster the Catholic population. Some Irish migrants continued to arrive, but they were now outnumbered by larger contingents of German, Swiss German, and Polish Catholic immigrants who came between 1870–90. These newcomers settled mainly, but not exclusively, along the Little Rock-Fort Smith Railroad in the Arkansas River valley, and in northeastern Arkansas. Italian Catholics came to Sunnyside Plantation in southeastern Arkansas in 1895, and many of these immigrants would leave that area three years later to found Tontitown in the Ozarks. Other Italians, migrating from the old country through Chicago, set up a little community about forty miles west of Little Rock in 1915. There were small pockets of Slovaks, Czechs, and Austrians scattered across the state. By 1890 Arkansas would have its highest rate of foreign-born residents, only 1.7 percent of the white population. (This was at a time when the U.S.A. as a whole had a foreign-born population of 16.8 percent.) In a similar pattern with that of Bishop Byrne, this met with only limited success; by the end of the century, only one percent of the white population were Catholics. In contrast to his predecessor, however, Fitzgerald actively sought to increase his flock by converting African Americans to Catholicism, yet this too had met with only limited success by the turn of the century.

Bishop Fitzgerald could point to a great deal of institutional growth during his years as bishop. He arrived in 1867 with only six priests for the whole state; there were by 1900 twenty-one diocesan priests and twenty-two priests belonging to either the Benedictines or the Holy Ghost Fathers, two religious orders brought to the diocese through his efforts. Only nine Catholic churches stood when he came; by the turn of the century, there were fifty-one edifices across the state. Bishop Fitzgerald's active career as bishop ended when the prelate suffered a stroke in January 1900, although he continued to live in St. Joseph's Hospital in Hot Springs until his death in February 1907. The day-to-day operations of the diocese were conducted by his last vicar general, German-born Benedictine Fr. Fintan Kraemer.

Twentieth-Century Developments

For the bulk of the twentieth century, the Arkansas church has had only three prelates; in fact the Little Rock diocese is unique in that it has had only five bishops in more than 150 years of its existence. Two of the three twentieth-century bishops, John B. Morris (1866–1946) and Andrew J. McDonald (1923–), were of Irish-American ancestry and were born outside the state. Only one, Albert L. Fletcher (1896–1979), was born in Arkansas; both of his parents were converts to Catholicism.

Bishop Morris came from Tennessee in the summer of 1906 as a coadjutor bishop for Bishop Fitzgerald. Once Fitzgerald died, Morris automatically became Arkansas's third bishop. Over the next four decades, Morris would oversee great institutional growth and development.

During the episcopacy of Bishop Morris, the nation as a whole, and Arkansas in particular, witnessed a serious outburst in anti-Catholic and antiforeign sentiments, especially during the two decades after 1910. Agrarian-populist editor Tom Watson published his anti-Catholic weekly paper which sold well throughout the South. A national anti-Catholic weekly published out of Springfield, Missouri, known as *The Menace* was started a year later, and by 1914 it had a million subscribers. In Magnolia, Arkansas, a Baptist minister published his own anti-Catholic publication called *The Liberator*. In 1915 the Arkansas General Assembly passed a convent inspection act which allowed local authorities to inspect convents and rectories at different occasions. This act remained law until it was quietly repealed in 1937. On April 23, 1917, just seven days after the U.S.A. declared war on Germany, the sheriff of Logan County entered Subiaco Benedictine monastery and destroyed the only wireless in the area, believing that it might be receiving messages from the Imperial German government.

During the 1920s the Ku Klux Klan made a major revival throughout the United States and it was quite powerful in certain areas of the state. The Klan, however, was not as strong in Arkansas as it was in other southern states. Arkansans voted for the national Democratic presidential candidate Alfred E. Smith in 1928, even though he was a Roman Catholic Governor from New York and supported repealing prohibition. (A major factor in the vote could also have been the fact that Al Smith's vice-presidential running mate was Arkansas senator Joseph T. Robinson.)

Morris made vigorous attempts to convert blacks to Catholicism and established Catholic schools for blacks. When he came to Arkansas there were only two fledgling black parishes; by 1946 there were nine black Catholic parishes and seven of them had schools. By the time Bishop Morris died in 1946, Arkansas Catholicism had exhibited strong and substantial growth. When he came in 1906, there had been sixty priests in the diocese; four decades later, there were 154 priests. While there had been 150 sisters in Arkansas in 1900, by 1946 there were 582 religious sisters working in schools, hospitals, and orphanages. Twenty Catholic high schools and sixty parish schools were operating, instructing some 7,710 students throughout the state. Between 1905–45, the number of Catholic hospitals had increased from four to nine. This was all from a Catholic population which numbered only 35,196. Catholics were now just over 2 percent of the white population and amounted to 1.7 percent of the total population.

If Bishop Morris served longer than any of his twentieth-century counterparts, Bishop Albert L. Fletcher would lead the diocese during its most turbulent era. A native of Little Rock, though raised in western Arkansas, Fletcher graduated from both Little Rock College and St. John's Seminary. He became the first Arkansan ever to be raised to the American hierarchy on April 25, 1940. That day he became auxiliary bishop to Bishop Morris and helped the aging prelate deal with diocesan affairs. After Morris died, Fletcher did not have the right of succession, but Pope Pius XII named this native son head of the Little Rock diocese. He was the only Arkansas prelate ever to be consecrated in Little Rock in a ceremony in February 1947.

Integration and Change

Bishop Fletcher's twenty-five years as bishop would not be tranquil. In 1957 eyes of the nation and the world focused upon the racial strife centering around the integration of the Little Rock public schools. Throughout the strife, the Catholic prelate called for calm and peaceful integration in his public pronouncements. In a locally published catechism, Bishop Fletcher wrote in 1960 that segregation and racial hatred were morally wrong. While integration would start to be implemented within the diocese, this would hurt the number of black parishes and schools. In 1961 there were eleven black parishes and seven schools; eleven years later there were only three black Catholic schools and churches still in operation. Bishop Fletcher attended all four session of the Second Vatican Council between 1962–65. The Arkansas bishop made thirteen suggestions at the council and nine were accepted into the documents.

In the twenty years after the end of World War II, Arkansas Catholicism continued to experience real growth. By 1960, for the first time since the census started counting in 1850,

Arkansas Catholics made up more than 2 percent of the population. Ten years later, by the end of Bishop Fletcher's era as bishop, Catholics made up 2.8 percent of the population, the highest in state history. At the close of the Second Vatican Council in 1965, there were 190 priests working in the diocese, an all-time high for the diocese. It was also an all-time high for religious sisters, with 693 working within the diocese. There were thirteen Catholic hospitals and sixty Catholic schools with over 10,980 students.

Three years prior to his resignation, Bishop Fletcher asked Rome for an auxiliary bishop. Lawrence P. Graves (1916–94), a native of Texarkana, was the second native Arkansan to become a Catholic bishop. He was consecrated as auxiliary bishop on April 25, 1969. History did not repeat itself, and Graves did not succeed Fletcher. In the summer of 1972 Pope Paul VI named a priest from Savannah, Georgia, to be the next bishop. Bishop Fletcher retired and died in Little Rock in December 1979. Bishop Graves became the bishop of Alexandria-Shreveport in 1973 and served for nine years until ill health forced his retirement. He died in Alexandria, Louisiana, in January 1994.

Andrew J. McDonald arrived in Little Rock in September 1972. He headed the diocese during a time when the American Catholic Church as a whole experienced a substantial decline in religious vocations, and Arkansas was not immune to this trend. The number of active priests in the state dropped between 1965–95 from 190 to 131; over the past three decades the number of sisters fell from 693 to 364. The number of Catholic schools dropped from sixty to thirty-six over the past thirty years and the number of students fell from 10,980 to 6,695. Catholic hospitals also decreased slightly, from thirteen to eleven. Overall the *percentage* of the Catholic population has declined slightly between 1970–90, from a high of 2.8 percent to 2.5 percent, meaning that the number of Catholics in the state now equaled what it had been in 1960.

However, most of the decline of Catholic population and in students and schools happened during the 1970s. After 1980, the Arkansas church witnessed increases in both population and Catholic schools. In 1980 there were 59,911 Catholics in the state; fifteen years later that number stood at 82,843. The diocese has opened new Catholic schools. Some 10,344 students were receiving some Catholic instruction outside of regular schools by 1995. Three black Catholic parishes and one black Catholic school were still in operation within the diocese. Catholic growth has also been augmented by a new wave of Catholic immigrants from Latin America and refugees from Southeast Asia. Bishop McDonald has created diocesan ministries for both groups of these new arrivals.

Guy, Francis S. "The Catholic Church in Arkansas, 1541–1843." M.A. thesis, The Catholic University of America, 1932.

Lucey, John M. "A History of the Catholic Church in Arkansas." *Publications of the Arkansas Historical Association* 2:424–61. Little Rock: Democrat Printing and Lithograph Co., 1908.

_____. "History of Immigrants to Arkansas." *Publication of the Arkansas Historical Association* 3. Little Rock: Democrat Printing and Lithograph Co., 1911, 201–19.

Weibel, Eugene J., O.S.B. *Forty Years Missionary in Arkansas.* Trans. Mary Agnes Voth, O.S.B. St. Meinrad Abbey Press, 1968.

Woods, James M. "To the Suburb of Hell: Catholic Missionaries in Arkansas, 1803–1843." *Arkansas Historical Quarterly* 48 (Autumn 1989) 217–42.

_____. *Mission and Memory: A History of the Catholic Church in Arkansas.* Little Rock: August House Publishing Company, 1993.

JAMES M. WOODS

AUGUSTINIANS (O.S.A.)

In the Beginning

Although the Order of Saint Augustine was not formally established in the United States until the end of the eighteenth century, several Augustinian friars had already landed on U.S. soil in the last quarter of the seventeenth century, among them Henri de la Motte, who worked among the native peoples of Maine, and John Facundus Skerret who was a missionary in Virginia about 1680.

The Augustinians as an order put down roots in the U.S.A. in 1796 when Matthew Carr and John Rosseter, both friars of the Irish province, founded St. Augustine Church in Philadelphia. Although the initial donations for the church were most encouraging, and included gifts from prominent citizens (among them George Washington), it was another five years before the church was used for worship and several more years before the edifice was fully completed. The delays were due to a lack of funds and frequent outbreaks of yellow fever, the latter phenomenon not uncommon in seaport cities of that era.

While St. Augustine's Church was being built, neither Fr. Carr nor Fr. Rosseter remained idle. In addition to continuing missionary work in southeastern Pennsylvania, Fr. Carr in 1799 became pastor of St. Mary's Church in the oldest part of Philadelphia, followed in the post by Fr. Rosseter in 1801. Carr was also appointed by Bishop John Carroll of Baltimore to be his vicar general in eastern Pennsylvania, Delaware, New Jersey, and New York. One of Carr's more onerous duties was to settle the schism that occurred at Philadelphia's Holy Trinity Church. This incident was part of the more general Trusteeism crisis that affected the U.S. Roman Catholic Church generally in the early part of the nineteenth century. St. Augustine's Church was spared this problem because Carr had had the foresight to incorporate legally the Order of Hermits of St. Augustine in the state of Pennsylvania in 1804.

The First Three Decades

Although they legally incorporated themselves in 1804, the Augustinians as a separate province had already been canonically established on August 27, 1796, under the name of Our Lady of Good Counsel. The document granted certain powers to Fr. Matthew Carr and allowed for the reception and profession of new members. However, new members were very slow in coming. As of the death of Fr. Matthew Carr in 1820, only one permanent friar had been added, Michael Hurley, born in Ireland but raised in Philadelphia, who later would not only succeed Carr but also make the survival of the order possible. Between 1824 and 1828 he was the only Augustinian in the U.S.A. Then in 1828 two recently ordained Irish friars, William and Nicholas O'Donnell, landed in Philadelphia. While engaging in parochial ministry at St. Augustine's, the latter also became editor of *The Catholic Herald*, a Philadelphia weekly. After ten years in Philadelphia, Nicholas O'Donnell and his cousin James, the first Augustinian to profess vows in the U.S.A., went to Brooklyn, New York, to serve at St. Paul's Church. While there, they also engaged in missionary work on Long Island. Due to difficulties with John Hughes, the new bishop of New York, Nicholas O'Donnell had to give up St. Paul's in 1846. Between 1832 and 1843, only one man, Thomas Kyle of Galway was received as a novice. But then in 1843 three new members were added, one of whom, William Harnett, a native Philadelphian, served as teacher and administrator at Villanova College, master of novices, and parish priest.

During the 1840s two important events occurred, at the center of which were two notable friars, Patrick Moriarty and John Possidius O'Dwyer. It was due to Moriarty's vision that the Augustinians seized the opportunity in 1841 to purchase the two-hundred-acre Belle Air farm about ten miles west of Philadelphia, that had been put up for sale by the widow of John Rudolph, a wealthy merchant. It was the future site of Villanova University, which was founded as a college in 1841–42.

At the beginning of 1844, the number of Augustinians had grown to twelve, and St. Augustine's parish was flourishing. However, there was also an increase in the anti-immigrant, and anti-Catholic, spirit, exemplified by the Native American Party, "a political organization dedicated to the vindication of Protestantism and bitterly opposed to immigrants, especially those who were Catholics" (Ennis). The tension increased in Philadelphia, until an explosion occurred on May 6, 1844, lasting for three days. Although there were no personal casualties among the Augustinians, their church of St. Augustine and the valuable theological library of more than 3,000 volumes were destroyed by the rioters. Fifty years of hard work had gone down the drain, but the friars were not defeated and began to make plans to rebuild. Moriarty left for Europe to raise funds for

a new St. Augustine's, a venture that was unsuccessful. In the meantime, however, Fr. O'Dwyer and his companions built a temporary chapel, and started their own campaign to raise funds, one that was so successful that a larger and more beautiful edifice was completed and consecrated by Bishop Francis Patrick Kenrick on November 5, 1848.

1840 to 1874

Between 1844 and 1874, the year the first provincial chapter was held, the Augustinians grew in numbers, both in friars and in houses. The period of real growth began in 1851, after Patrick Moriarty returned once again and became commissary general. In the greater Philadelphia area between 1851 and 1855, the Augustinians opened St. Denis Church in Havertown and Our Mother of Consolation Church in Chestnut Hill, and St. Nicholas of Tolentine Church in Atlantic City, New Jersey. In 1858, John McCloskey, bishop of Albany (later cardinal archbishop of New York), invited the Augustinians to take charge of two parishes, St. John's in Lansingburg (later North Troy) and St. Mary's, Waterford, New York. Between 1860 and 1870, under the pastorship of Thomas Galberry, later the bishop of Hartford, Connecticut, a new church was built at Lansingburg, dedicated to St. Augustine. During this same decade the friars established other houses in the Albany diocese, at Schaghticoke, Hoosick Falls, Cambridge, Greenwich, and Mechanicville. In 1874, in the Diocese of Ogdensburg, northwest of Albany, the friars took on St. James the Minor parish.

In contrast to the foundations in upstate New York, which could be described as rural, the Augustinian foundations in Massachusetts were urban, with the exception of St. Augustine parish in Andover. Lawrence, Massachusetts, became in the second half of the nineteenth century a haven for immigrants. Not a very large city, it was nevertheless a city of churches, the Augustinians having several of them in close proximity. During the tenure of Patrick A. Stanton as commissary general the oldest parish in Lawrence, St. Mary's, was established in 1861 along with St. Augustine's in Andover. Since James O'Donnell had been working in the area since 1848, there was already a large church, which later became a school. A new cathedral-size church was dedicated by Bishop John Williams of Boston in 1871. St. Mary's most famous pastor was Fr. James T. O'Reilly, who "exercised a dominant influence over the people and the affairs of Lawrence" (Ennis).

It was also during Fr. Stanton's time in office (1858–66) that Villanova College developed a theological faculty. That the college was able to do so was the result of Stanton's request to the prior general in Rome, John Belluomini, to send teachers to the U.S.A. Of the two teachers who did come, it was Pacifico Neno, later prior general himself, who had the greater effect on Villanova. He served as regent of studies and taught the courses in dogmatic and moral theology as well as canon law; in 1878 he was elected the second prior provincial of the U.S. province. One of Neno's colleagues at Villanova, Thomas Middleton, was first president of the American Catholic Historical Society of Philadelphia, which he helped to organize.

The First Provincial Chapter to the End of WWII

With the granting of province status under the name of St. Thomas of Villanova on August 25, 1874, by the prior general, the Augustinians in the U.S.A. had come of age. Their last commissary general became their first prior provincial. Thomas Galberry, elected in December by the first provincial chapter, had held this office less than a year when he was appointed the fourth bishop of Hartford, Connecticut, an office he tried to refuse. He was ordained that city's bishop on March 19, 1876, and served his people well until he died of tuberculosis two years later.

During the 1880s only one new foundation was made, Our Mother of Good Counsel parish, Bryn Mawr, Pennsylvania, just down the road from Villanova College. In the last decade of the nineteenth century, the most important event was the first visitation by a prior general, Sebastian Martinelli. Two years later, in 1896, he became the second apostolic delegate to the U.S.A.; in 1901 he was made cardinal by Pope Leo XIII. At the very end of the decade, during the provincial administration of John J. Fedigan, the friars established Our Lady of Good Counsel parish on Staten Island, New York. It was also Fr. Fedigan who began a major building expansion program at Villanova College, and who initiated the Villanova province's first missionary activity, in Cuba after the Spanish-American War.

In January 1899, Fr. Fedigan sent Fr. William A. Jones, later bishop of San Juan, Puerto Rico, and Br. George Woolsey to Cuba, where they took charge of the small chapel of San Agustin in Havana. In 1901, Fr. Jones set up the Colegio San Agustin, and in 1903 Augustinians moved into the parish of El Cristo. From these modest beginnings other foundations emerged later in the twentieth century under the inspired leadership of Fr. Lorenzo Spirali, including the establishment of the Universidad de Santo Tomas de Villanueva, which was declared a pontifical university in 1957, just a few years before the Augustinians were expelled by Fidel Castro.

For the Augustinians in the U.S.A., the twentieth century could be labeled one of "growth and expansion." In the first decade, under the leadership of Martin J. Geraghty, the longest serving provincial in the history of the Villanova province, the friars established houses of formation at Villanova College, and funded two parishes in Chicago, St. Rita and St. Clare of Montefalco, with a school attached to the former. In the Bronx, St. Nicholas of Tolentine parish was founded to serve a largely Irish immigrant population. Today it serves a largely Latino population. The city of Philadelphia once again became the site of a new parish, St. Rita of Cascia, to serve Italian immigrants, while in Rosemont near Villanova a school and chapel were opened. Italian immigrants were also the motivating force for the establishment of what came to be known as the Vice Province of Our Mother of Good Counsel, located in South Philadelphia and southern New Jersey. The vice province has now ceased to exist; the parish of St. Nicholas of Tolentine in Philadelphia, and St. Augustine Preparatory High School in Richland, New Jersey, have been joined to the Villanova province.

During World War I only one foundation was made, St. Nicholas of Tolentine, Jamaica, Queens, New York. Between the two wars, the minor seminary was transferred to Staten Island, a novitiate was opened in New Hamburg, New York, and a theologate was built in Washington, D.C. A preparatory high school was built in Malvern, Pennsylvania. In the Midwest three parishes were opened in Michigan, in Detroit, Grosse Point, and Flint, one in Oconomowoc, Wisconsin. The friars also established St. Thomas High School in Rockford, Illinois, and Cascia Hall, a preparatory high school in Tulsa, Oklahoma. The friars also moved to the West Coast, establishing St. Augustine's High School and St. Patrick's Church, San Diego; Villanova Preparatory High School and St. Thomas Aquinas Church, Ojai; and Our Lady of Good Counsel Church, Hollywood.

During World War II, twenty-five Augustinian friars served as chaplains in the armed forces. Villanova College celebrated its centenary, and the Chicago province of Our Mother of Good Counsel was created.

The Postwar Expansion

After World War II, the order experienced the most extensive expansion period in its history in the U.S.A. In 1947, Merrimack College was opened in North Andover, Massachusetts, as well as the university in Cuba, already mentioned. In addition to these institutions of higher learning, two diocesan high schools were established in the East, Archbishop John Carroll High School in Washington, D.C., and Msgr. Bonner High School in Drexel Hill, Pennsylvania. Three other high schools were founded in the Midwest, Mendel Catholic High School, Chicago; Austin Catholic Preparatory School, Detroit; and Augustinian Academy, St. Louis. The Chicago province also opened two houses of formation that no longer function as such.

On June 16, 1952, the Congregation for the Propagation of the Faith granted permission for the Villanova and Chicago provinces jointly to enter the Diocese of Nagasaki, Japan. There are now several other houses in Japan, including Tokyo, Fukuoka, and Nagoya, and a house of formation in Tanashi City, all with at least one Japanese friar. Japan became a vicariate in 1995.

In 1953 Augustinian friars opened their first house in the state of Florida, the parish of Our Lady of the Angels in Jacksonville. On January 1, 1957, the vice province of St. Augustine was established in California. The 1960s saw the establishment of a third college, Biscayne College (later St. Thomas University, which was relinquished in the 1980s) in Miami, Florida. New parishes were founded in Dania, Casselberry, and Golden Gate, Florida, and Austin Preparatory High School was established in Reading, Massachusetts. Both the Villanova and Chicago provinces once again jointly set up missions in Peru, in what is now the Diocese of Chulucanas. The first convent of Augustinian Sisters of Contemplative Life was established in 1968 in Holland, Michigan, and later moved to their present location in St. Louis, Missouri. There are also the Sisters of Saint Thomas of Villanova, founded by a French Augustinian, Ange Le Proust, during the nineteenth century, working in Norwalk, Connecticut, and the Sisters of the Incarnation and Most Blessed Sacrament working in Texas, both of which are aggregated to the order.

The Chicago province closed Olympia Fields as a theologate and built St. John Stone Friary in 1971 to house the students attending the Chicago Theological Union. In 1985, this province accepted a high school in New Lenox, Illinois. The vice province of California, in the meantime, not only became a province in 1969, but also expanded into the northern part of the state with a parish in Castro Valley and a retreat house in Gold Hill, Oregon. The California province of St. Augustine is distinguished more by its concern for social justice than for any other type of apostolic work. In 1969, for example, it took on the sponsorship and management of a low-income housing project in the town of San Ysidro, near the U.S.-Mexican border.

Ennis, Arthur J., O.S.A. *The Augustinians: A Brief Sketch of Their American History from 1796 to the Present.* Villanova, Pa.: Augustinian Press, 1985.

____. *No Easy Road: The Early Years of the Augustinians in the United States, 1769–1874.* New York, 1993.

____. "The Founding of the Augustinians in the United States (1796)." *Analecta Augustiniana* 41 (1978) 285–312.

Tourscher, Francis E., O.S.A. *Old St. Augustine's with Some Records of the Work of the Austin Friars in the United States.* Philadelphia, 1937.

EDWARD J. ENRIGHT, O.S.A.

AVE MARIA

On May 1, 1865, the first issue of *Ave Maria,* a religious magazine for Catholic families, rolled off a new printing press on the campus of the University of Notre Dame near South Bend, Indiana. Though advised against it by colleagues and members of the hierarchy, Fr. Edward F. Sorin launched the weekly publication amidst fanfare and bravado, as he had undertaken many ambitious projects since landing in New York City from France nearly twenty-four years before. To most everyone else's amazement, *Ave Maria* continued to be published without missing an issue until March 21, 1970, when it died a quiet death, victim of high costs and declining circulation, like the majority of its contemporary periodicals.

Sorin was quite used to skeptics and naysayers. He had founded Notre Dame itself on a wintry day in 1842, on an isolated tract of land just north of South Bend, Indiana. From the start he called his little boarding school a "university," though it would take many decades to reach that august goal and stature. His family magazine, dedicated to the same Blessed Mother whom he would honor with a huge golden statue on top of a giant dome on the main building of his university, was also destined for greatness.

To give the journal a good foundation and secure beginning, the French-born but thoroughly Americanized Holy Cross priest at the same time expanded the rudimentary printing plant at Notre Dame with a new press, and used the readily available labor of priests, brothers, and sisters of the local Holy Cross community. He had brought them here or recruited most of them in the first place; and he kept on challenging them with visionary new projects.

His closest collaborators were Sister (later Mother) Angela who did much of the editorial work and Br. Stanislaus who ran the printing press. Together with dedicated laypersons, they enthusiastically began to fulfill the dream of Sorin to publish a well-written and edifying family newspaper, "devoted to the honor of the Blessed Virgin." As Sorin's own duties and activities multiplied and spread farther across the country and the Atlantic as superior general of the Congregation of Holy Cross, in 1868 Sr. Angela's brother, Fr. Neal Gillespie, assumed editorship. Almost to the end, a group of brothers, known as "canvassers," went from door to door in many cities and towns across the U.S.A. to sell the magazine. And at home many young brothers and sisters gave their life's labor to putting out the weekly magazine.

By 1875, when Fr. Gillespie was forced to retire because of poor health, the circulation had topped 8,000 subscribers. Fr. Daniel E. Hudson became editor at that time and continued in that position until 1930. Under his leadership the magazine grew in circulation (to 35,000) and stature. By the time of its silver jubilee, practically all English-speaking Catholic writers of note had contributed to its pages, a tradition carried on until its demise in 1970.

Even a cursory survey of the 190 bound volumes of the periodical shows the care with which it was produced. It was meant to be readable and attractive to the families who received it, from its earliest issues, with small type, rough-quality paper, two columns, and sixteen pages, to its final years with larger type and artistic layout, many photographs and illustrations, and limited use of color.

Throughout its 105 years of publication, the reader of *Ave Maria* was always challenged by editorials and commentary, informed by news notes and documentary sources, entertained by features for different age groups, and assisted in prayer and reflection by articles on faith, liturgy, and Christian living.

Women authors and articles about women were common, lovers of poetry were not ignored, and children and youth were never forgotten. The magazine tried to be spiritually edifying to Catholics, rather than defending the faith against attackers or explaining it to outsiders. It was meant to be "popular" in the best sense of the word—for the people, not the scholars or theologians.

The editors, particularly Fr. Hudson who shepherded the magazine during more than half its existence, were aware of the vast reservoir of Catholic authors and thought in the U.S.A. Social, political, and religious issues in an American context, and Church and ecumenical issues on a global scale, were dealt with openly and in an informative manner.

While always situating the Church in this country within the Church universal, the editors managed to bring together the best of Catholic journalistic endeavors and present them to a receptive audience which was growing in its own appreciation of the Church's contributions to society.

In its latter years, many of the articles and series were turned into small paperback books which sold widely through parishes and Catholic bookstores. The mission of book publishing expanded rapidly after the magazine ceased publication and now Ave Maria Press, one of the major American Catholic publishing houses, carries forward the daring dream of Fr. Sorin and his associates.

See also HOLY CROSS, CONGREGATION OF (C.S.C.); SORIN, EDWARD F.; REEDY, JOHN L.

DAVID E. SCHLAVER, C.S.C.

AVERY, MARTHA (1851–1929)

Social activist, writer. Martha Gallison Moore Avery was born on April 6, 1851, in Steuben, Maine. The child of Albion and Katherine Moore, she was raised in the Unitarian faith. She was a vocal proponent of socialism in the late nineteenth century who later embraced Catholic social teaching and led various lay groups. A founder of the First Nationalist Club of Boston (est. 1888) who joined the Socialist Labor Party in 1891, she saw in socialist ideals a remedy for the conditions created by an increasingly industrialized society.

From 1892–95 she lectured and served as a member of the Massachusetts state committee of the Socialist Labor Party. She founded the Karl Marx Class, a meeting ground for socialists (later renamed the Boston School of Political Economy) with socialist colleague David Goldstein in 1896, and in 1898 she was a delegate to the national convention of Daniel De Leon's Socialist Trade and Labor Alliance.

Four years later, however, both she and Goldstein rejected socialism, seeing in its hostility toward religion and its sanctioning of violence and free love a serious threat to family and social stability. Increasingly sympathetic to Catholic social views, she converted to Catholicism in 1904 and began a quarter-century career as an antisocialist propagandist. Together with Goldstein, and with backing from various Catholic organizations, she wrote an array of articles, pamphlets, and books (notably *Socialism: The Nation of Fatherless Children*).

As chair of the legislative committee, and later president of the Boston Catholic lay group Common Cause Society, she fought for child labor laws, minimum wage legislation, reduced working hours, and employer liability. She lectured publicly and, with the support of Boston's Cardinal William O'Connell, taught and preached on street corners. The latter practice became the apostolate of the Catholic Truth Guild, which she founded with Goldstein in 1906 (the guild changed its name in 1935 to Catholic Campaigners For Christ).

A lifelong campaigner for social justice and economic equity, she upheld a conservative stance on several key issues of her day, namely women's suffrage and birth control, both of which she opposed. She died in Medford, Massachusetts, in 1929.

American Catholic Who's Who, 1911.

Avery, Martha Gallison Moore, and David Goldstein. *Socialism: The Nation of Fatherless Children.* Boston, 1903; 2nd ed., 1911.

____. *Bolshevism: Its Cure.* Boston, 1919.

____. *Campaigning for Christ.* Boston, 1924.

____. "Is Socialism the Remedy?" *Irish World* 24 (January 1903) 4–5.

____. "The Spread of Social Disorder" *America* 14 (November 6, 1915) 78–79.

Campbell, Debra. "David Goldstein and the Lay Catholic Street Apostolate, 1917–41." Ph.D. dissertation, Boston University, 1982.

Corrigan, D. Owen. "Martha Moore Avery: Crusader for Social Justice." *Catholic Historical Review* 54 (April 1968) 17–38.

____. "A Forgotten Yankee Marxist." *New England Quarterly* 42 (March 1969) 23–43.

Goldstein, David. *Autobiography of a Campaigner for Christ.* Boston, 1936.

JOSEPH QUINN

B

BADIN, STEPHEN (1768–1853)

Missionary. An exile from the French Revolution, born on July 17, 1768, seminarian Badin arrived in America in 1792. At Baltimore on May 25, 1793, in a ceremony performed by Bishop John Carroll, Badin became the first priest to be ordained in the United States. Appointed the same year to the Kentucky missions by Carroll, Badin walked as far as Pittsburgh, then went by flatboat to his assignment.

Stephen Theodore Badin

In Kentucky, Badin served for a year at Scott County in the Bluegrass, removing in 1794 to the central part of the new state. Here at St. Stephen's Farm near Pottinger's Creek (in present-day Marion County), he established the center of his missionary labors. Most of his time was spent on horseback traveling to far-flung Catholic settlements. Until the arrival of Benedict J. Flaget, the first bishop of the West, Badin was the undisputed leader of Kentucky Catholics.

A man of stern morality, Badin quarreled with many of his parishioners. He also engaged in a lengthy dispute with Flaget over deeds to property, resulting in his departure for France in 1819. He returned to the U.S.A. to work among the Potawatomis and Irish immigrants. In northern Indiana, he acquired and donated the land on which the University of Notre Dame would eventually stand. Badin died in Cincinnati on April 19, 1853, and now lies buried at Notre Dame.

See also AMERICAN CATHOLICS: 1492–1815; KENTUCKY, CATHOLIC CHURCH IN.

Schauinger, J. Herman. *Stephen T. Badin*. Milwaukee, 1956.

CLYDE F. CREWS

BAKER, JOSEPHINE (1906–75)

African American dancer and singer who introduced *le jazz hot* to France in the 1920s. Baker was born in St. Louis, Missouri, probably on June 3, 1906. She worked her way out of a life of poverty by joining a dance troupe from

Philadelphia at the age of sixteen. Later she joined the chorus of a show in Boston and in 1923 moved to New York City where she danced in the chorus of *Shuffle Along* and *Chocolate Dandies* on Broadway, as well as in the floor show of Harlem's Plantation Club.

Because career advancement for African Americans in the United States was restricted in the 1920s, Baker went to Paris in 1925 where she danced at the Théâtre des Champs-Elysées in *La Révue nègre* and also appeared in the *Folies Bergère*. Her flamboyant style, which appealed to the French, propelled her into the limelight, and in 1926 she opened her own nightclub, *Chez Josephine*. In 1937 she became a French citizen.

For the next fifty years, Baker continued her career as a dancer, began singing professionally in 1930, and made several movies before the outbreak of World War II. During the war, she worked with the Red Cross and French Resistance, entertained troops in Africa and the Middle East, and was awarded the Croix de Guerre and the Legion d'Honneur with the rosette of the Resistance.

Baker's marriage to Jean Lyon, a French industrialist, had been annulled in 1940, and in 1947 she married Jo Bouillon, a French orchestra leader. She began an "experiment in brotherhood" in 1950 by adopting babies of various nationalities and races—twelve in all—and rearing "her rainbow family," as she called it, at Les Milandes, her estate in southwestern France.

Although she retired from the stage in 1956, the burdens of maintaining her estate forced her to accept the starring role in the musical *Paris* in 1959. She traveled often to the United States during the 1960s to participate in civil rights demonstrations. Following a triumphant return to the New York stage in 1973, she returned to Paris where she died two years later, on April 12, 1975.

Papich, Steven. *Remembering Josephine Baker.* Indianapolis, 1976.

MARIANNA McLOUGHLIN

BALTIMORE CATECHISM, THE

The Baltimore Catechism is so-called because it was commissioned by the Third Plenary Council of Baltimore in 1884. It belongs to the genre of "small catechisms" intended primarily for the instruction of children in Christian doctrine. The original edition had 421 questions and answers divided into 37 chapters that explained the Apostles' Creed, the Seven Sacraments, and Ten Commandments. In commissioning the catechism, the bishops saw it as a means of promoting uniformity in catechetical instruction and introducing the children of immigrants to the prayer forms and devotional practices of the American Church. Composed in English, it was to be translated in other languages and was intended to displace other catechisms then in use. In 1941 the bishops issued a revised Baltimore Catechism that substantially reorganized and slightly enlarged the text of the 1884 edition.

The nineteenth century witnessed a proliferation of catechisms, some original works, some translations. As early as 1827 Archbishop Ambrose Maréchal of Baltimore expressed a fear of what might result from a "multiplicity of discordant catechisms." The First and Second Plenary Councils of Baltimore in 1852 and 1866 recommended that a standard catechism be used in all dioceses. The proposals were never implemented because the American bishops favored a version of the "Carroll Catechism," associated with the name John Carroll, the country's first bishop, while Rome pushed for an adaptation of St. Robert Bellarmine's Small Catechism, widely used throughout the Catholic world. Before the Third Plenary Council convened in November 1884, Archbishop James Gibbons of Baltimore appointed a committee to look into the matter. Upon receiving the committee's report the council instructed the members to "select a catechism and if necessary emend it, or to start from scratch if they would feel it the necessary and opportune thing to do."

Before the council adjourned, the bishops were given a draft of the new catechism, said to have been prepared by Msgr. Januarius de Concilio, a pastor from Jersey City who was present at the council as the theologian of Bishop James O'Connor of Nebraska. The bishops were instructed to send suggestions for changes in the text to Bishop John L. Spalding of Peoria. Spalding, working in New York, assisted by de Concilio, completed the final text of *A Catechism of Christian Doctrine, Prepared and Enjoined by the Order of the Third Plenary Council of Baltimore* by the end of February 1885. The published work carried an imprimatur by John Cardinal McCloskey of New York and the approval of Gibbons, in his role as apostolic delegate, but Spalding held the copyright in his own name. Within months Spalding issued an abridged version, about half the size of the original, that was commonly known as "Baltimore No. 1," but it never gained the popularity of the original.

Rather than a work from scratch, the Baltimore Catechism was largely a compilation of questions from existing catechisms, notably the Carroll Catechism, the Butler-Maynooth Catechism, and catechisms by Bishop David, Bishop Verot, and Msgr. McCaffrey. The Baltimore Catechism had hardly appeared before it became the target of severe criticisms, many from bishops. The critics faulted the catechism's pedagogical method which they said was repetitious and dull, and its theological shortcomings, especially its perfunctory treatment of prayer and its failure to distinguish teachings of greater and lesser importance.

Bishops acknowledged the shortcomings of the 1884 edition, but it was 1941 before a revised text was published. The episcopal committee for the Confraternity of

Christian Doctrine engaged the Rev. Francis J. Connell, C.Ss.R., professor of moral theology at The Catholic University of America, as editor and theological advisor. The 1941 edition increased the number of questions to 499, including a section on the Lord's Prayer, reordered the contents so that the Commandments were treated before the sacraments, and added an appendix titled, "Why I Am a Catholic." It was followed by a revision of "Baltimore No. 1," and in 1943 by a First Communion edition. "Baltimore No. 3," a text intended for use by adults, appeared in 1949. It had the same questions as the 1941 edition, but the answers were more lengthy and included pertinent quotations from the Scriptures.

The Baltimore Catechism continued in general use until the eve of the Second Vatican Council.

See also CATHOLIC EDUCATION, PAROCHIAL; SPALDING, JOHN LANCASTER.

Bryce, Mary Charles. *Pride of Place: The Role of the Bishops in the Development of Catechesis in the United States.* Washington, D.C.: The Catholic University of America Press, 1984.

Marthaler, Berard L. *The Catechism Yesterday and Today. The Evolution of a Genre.* Collegeville, Minn.: The Liturgical Press, 1995.

BERARD L. MARTHALER

BANNON, JOHN B. (1829–1913)

Chaplain-soldier, Confederate commissioner. Bannon was born in Roosky, County Roscommon, Ireland, in 1829. He was educated at the Royal College of St. Patrick at Maynooth, County Kildare, and was ordained in 1853. Soon after he volunteered to go to the United States to work with Irish emigrants. He went to St. Louis, Missouri, where he served in that city's parishes until the outbreak of the Civil War, when he decided to become a chaplain for the Confederacy. Leaving without his bishop's permission, he soon caught up with many of his former parishioners who had enlisted under General Sterling Price in the First Missouri Confederate Brigade, where he served as a volunteer chaplain until he received his official commission in 1863. His battlefield heroics earned him the title of the Confederacy's "fighting Chaplain."

He undertook the first of several diplomatic missions for the Confederacy when he was appointed Confederate Commissioner to Ireland in 1863. There he orchestrated an all-out propaganda campaign not only to explain the Confederate position to the Irish, but also to stop the flood of Irish immigrants who had been pouring into the Union army. In 1864 he accompanied Bishop Patrick Lynch of Charleston, South Carolina, who had been appointed Confederate Commissioner to Europe, on a trip to Rome for what was an unsuccessful attempt to secure papal recognition of the Confederacy.

Unable to return to the South because of the Union naval blockade, Bannon went to Ireland where he joined the Jesuits in 1865. He served at St. Ignatius University College Church and St. Francis Xavier Church in Dublin and became renowned for his preaching skills through the mission band he formed. He died in Dublin in 1913.

See also CIVIL WAR AND CATHOLICS, THE.

TRICIA T. PYNE

BARAGA, FREDERIC (1797–1868)

Missionary, bishop. Frederic Baraga, the "Snowshoe Priest," was born into a middle-class family in Slovenia on June 29, 1797. By age fifteen he was an orphan. At the University of Vienna he was greatly influenced by St. Clement Mary Hofbauer, C.Ss.R. After completion of a law degree in 1821, he chose a new direction for his life. He broke off his marriage engagement, renounced his substantial inheritance, and entered the seminary in Ljubljana. Ordained in 1823, he became a renowned and beloved parish priest in his native Slovenia. He encouraged devotion to the Blessed Sacrament and to the Blessed Mother, and was the first person to write a popular devotional prayer book in the Slovene vernacular language.

Frederic Baraga

Through the Leopoldine Society, the Austrian missionary-aid society which assisted the American missions, Baraga volunteered to work among the Native Americans of Michigan. His first mission was among the Ottawas at Arbre Croche (near present-day Petoskey) where he baptized 547 natives in twenty-eight months. In 1835 Baraga began to search for souls in the more remote north—first at LaPointe (Apostle Islands, Wisconsin), and then at L'Anse, Keeweenaw Bay. A letter he wrote to his sister reveals his missionary spirit: "L'Anse is an unpleasant, sad sterile place" . . . he said, "only the desire to help the poor Indians attain eternal happiness keeps me here. I have here . . . no comforts, often times barely the necessities of life; but what consolation . . . for on the Day of Judgment . . . my good children in Christ will surround me and give their testimony."

His diary indicates how this refined, well-educated man, accustomed to upper-class European amenities, spent his time in the isolated forests of Upper Michigan. Every morning no matter how cold or uncomfortable, he rose at 4 A.M. for meditation and prayers. During the summer months, when travel was easy by canoe, he cared for the spiritual needs of the native peoples through Mass, baptisms, marriages, confessions, and instructions. For years he was the only priest along the southern shoreline of Lake Superior. During the winter months he taught school, and continued his travels on snowshoes regardless of the distance or the weather. He spent long winter nights compiling the first Ojibwe dictionary, grammar, catechism, and other devotional books. When the U.S. government threatened to move the natives to western reservations, he purchased lands for them with his own funds, thus allowing them to remain. He kept constant vigil against efforts of the fur traders to sell them liquor.

By 1845 Baraga's efforts also reached out to the growing members of European immigrants who poured into the Upper Peninsula as a result of the discovery of copper and iron ore. And so Baraga spoke French, German, English, Slovenian, and Italian as well as Ottawa and Ojibwe for the salvation of souls. In 1857 he became Upper Michigan's first bishop, but this honor did not alter his lifestyle. An eyewitness described him in 1862: "The Bishop was then 64 years of age and his health had greatly failed. The winter was extraordinarily severe and we had about 6 feet of snow. But the Bishop went from one wigwam to another, visiting the Indians. . . . When it was to rescue a soul he never counted the distance. . . . The Bishop, half frozen, was sitting on a little sleigh about two inches higher than the ground dragged by a small Indian dog. . . . Our Lord in his travels used to ride an ass, but our bishop was perfectly satisfied to have a dog for riding."

In 1866 Bishop Baraga transferred his see from Sault Ste. Marie to Marquette. He suffered a stroke while attending the Second Plenary Council in Baltimore in 1866. Though critically ill, he insisted on returning to Marquette to die among his beloved native people. A few days before his death, a priest visitor recalled: "The Bishop pointed to a tin box on a library shelf . . . he asked me to take the key for the box from under his pillow. . . . With his weak, trembling hand the Bishop opened the box and told

(me) to take the money in it, $20.00. 'I don't need any more money—take it [for the Indians].'"

On January 19, 1868, the worn-out missionary commended his soul to the Lord.

See also MICHIGAN, CATHOLIC CHURCH IN.

Ceglar, Charles A. *Bishop Frederic Baraga.* 2 vols. London, Ontario, 1991–92.

Gregorich, Joseph. *The Apostle of the Chippewas: The Life Story of the Most Rev. Frederic Baraga, the First Bishop of Marquette.* Chicago, 1932.

Lambert, Bernard J. *Shepherd of the Wilderness: A Biography of Bishop Frederic Baraga.* Marquette, 1974.

Rezek, Antoine. *History of the Diocese of Sault Ste. Marie and Marquette.* Chicago, 1906.

Verwyst, Chrysotomus, O.F.M. *Life and Labors of Rt. Rev. Frederic Baraga.* Milwaukee, 1900.

Walling, Regis M., and N. Daniel Rupp, eds. *Diary of Bishop Frederic Baraga.* Detroit, 1990.

N. DANIEL RUPP

BARONI, GENO (1931–84)

Priest, social activist. Geno Baroni was born the son of an immigrant coal miner from Italy in Acosta, Pennsylvania. After studying at Mt. St. Mary's College in Emmitsburg, Maryland, he was ordained in 1956. After serving as a priest in ethnic parishes in working-class neighborhoods near his home, he worked in Johnstown and Altoona, Pennsylvania, where he served as assistant pastor and high-school teacher. He then moved to Washington, D.C., during the troubled 1960s to study at The Catholic University of America. He soon began working in the Washington inner city and helped in mediating differences between blacks and whites during the riots of the late 1960s.

During the early 1960s, Baroni worked particularly with the poor in all ethnic groups, improving inner-city life for those groups and defusing interracial tensions based solely on those of each ethnic group not knowing much about the other. Most of his work during this time was done in Washington's St. Paul and St. Augustine parishes, two of the city's foremost black parishes in the 14th Street, N.W., area.

He continually fought against the stereotype of America as a melting pot; he saw it more as "the most pluralistic society in the world." He felt the former idea should be dismissed. He believed that having everyone try to be alike was wrong, and that individuals should try to find themselves in their racial identity and then develop new ways "that respect cultural differences, different lifestyles, and different value systems."

He served as an assistant secretary of Housing and Urban Development during the Carter administration from 1977 to 1980, at the time, the highest cabinet-level position bestowed upon a priest. During this time he worked at establishing joint partnerships with the private and public sectors for revitalization of the Church and community. He worked persistently at preserving the Italian, Polish, Irish, and other ethnic neighborhoods.

When the Carter administration made changes in 1980, Baroni was one of those to lose his job; and Archbishop James A. Hickey appointed him special assistant for community affairs in the Washington archdiocese. Baroni was one of many responsible for developing the concept for the Campaign for Human Development, the bishops' multimillion-dollar antipoverty program.

Prior to his employment with HUD, Baroni was the president of the National Center for Urban Ethnic Affairs, an organization which he founded in 1971. He won a major victory during his time as its president when Congress passed a law banning the practice of "redlining," the denial of mortgages to certain neighborhoods based on ethnicity. Baroni also helped in organizing over forty neighborhood groups throughout the U.S.A. and raising millions for their causes. Baroni, widely known as a "gadfly" because of his continuous work to preserve urban ethnic neighborhoods and their identities, died on August 7, 1984, at the age of fifty-three, after an extensive battle with cancer.

L. FRANKLIN CARTER

BARRY, CATHERINE GERALD (1881–1961)

Religious, educator. Barry was born on March 11, 1881, to Michael and Catherine Dixon Barry in Inagh, County Clare, Ireland, and was given the name Catherine Bridget. As a young woman Barry emigrated to the United States, worked for some time, and in 1913 entered the novitiate of the Congregation of the Most Holy Rosary of the Dominican Sisters in Adrian, Michigan. In 1914 she took simple vows, took the name Gerald, and began a career in teaching. Recognized early for her leadership skills, she was principal in several schools beginning in 1914. In 1921 she was named mistress of novices, an important and prestigious office, and she held this post until 1933 when she was elected prioress general of the community and remained general superior for almost thirty years.

While prioress general, Barry helped organize and direct the rapid expansion of the community and its apostolates. The number of sisters increased from 930 to 2,400. The congregation opened two senior colleges, a teacher's college, four secondary schools, and sisters from her community began staffing seventy elementary schools. Barry believed strongly in the importance of the sisters' own education and sent over two hundred sisters for graduate study. In 1952 she became the first chairperson of the National Congress of Religious in the U.S.A., and in 1956 she led the Chicago meeting of this group that eventually become the Conference of Major Superiors of Women's Religious Institutes. Mother Barry died at the mother-house of the community in Adrian, Michigan, on November 20, 1961.

See also DOMINICANS (O.P.).

ANTHONY D. ANDREASSI

BARRY, COLMAN JAMES (1921–94)

Benedictine monk, historian, and educator, Barry was born on May 21, 1921, in Lake City, Minnesota. He entered St. John's University at Collegeville, Minnesota, in 1938 and received a degree in history with honors four years later. He professed vows as a member of the St. John's Benedictine community in 1943 and was ordained to the priesthood in 1947.

Barry then began graduate work at The Catholic University of America where he majored in American religious history under the guidance of Msgr. John Tracy Ellis, who by word and example inspired him at every turn. His master's thesis, completed in 1949, was published as *The Catholic University of America, 1903–1909, The Rectorship of Denis J. O'Connell,* by The Catholic University of America Press in 1950. His doctoral dissertation, *The Catholic Church and German Americans,* was published by Bruce Publishing Company, Milwaukee, in 1952.

Upon his return to St. John's in the early 1950s, Barry began a notable career as a professor of history and as an administrator until 1971. It was during this period that he found time to continue his research and to publish numerous historical volumes. Some of the titles were: *Readings in Church History,* 3 volumes (1959–65); *American Nuncio: Cardinal Aloysius Muench* (1969); *Upon These Rocks (Catholics in the Bahamas)* (1973).

Colman Barry

During Barry's tenure as St. John's seventh president from 1964 to 1971, a variety of new institutions were established, including the first affiliate of Minnesota Public Radio; the Center for Ecumenical and Cultural Research, a residential center for religious and social study; and the Hill Monastic Microfilm Library, a microfilm collection of monastic manuscripts from around the world.

Upon the completion of his presidential term Fr. Colman received an invitation to serve as a visiting professor of Church history at Yale Divinity School during the 1972–73 school year. While there he gave one of the Nathaniel W. Taylor Lectures. He spoke on the topic, "The Church Divided: A Catholic Question." While at Yale, Fr. Colman received word in March of 1973 that he had been selected as the first dean of the new School of Religious Studies at The Catholic University of America where he served until 1977.

It was during his time as dean that he was elected president of the American Catholic Historical Association, a post which he held in 1976, the bicentennial of the United States. At the annual meeting in December held in Washington, D.C., he delivered his presidential address which he entitled: "The Bicentennial Revisited."

Barry was also the recipient of five honorary degrees and was awarded the papal medal, *Pro Ecclesia et Pontifice,* at The Catholic University of America in 1977. He died at St. John's Abbey on January 7, 1994, continuing his writing and research like his Benedictine model of the eighth century, St. Bede the Venerable, until the Lord called him.

See also BENEDICTINES (O.S.B.).

VINCENT TEGEDER, O.S.B.

BARRY, JOHN (1745–1803)

Naval officer, "Father of the U.S. Navy." John Barry was born in Tacumshane, County Wexford, Ireland. The son a malt house clerk, young Barry went to sea at the age of ten, a not uncommon occurrence in that day. The boy's natural abilities helped him to rise quickly; by 1761 he had emigrated to Philadelphia and had become master of his own ship. He became wealthy as a shipowner but still ardently supported the American Revolution. In 1776 Congress appointed him captain of the brig *Lexington,* and he had the distinction of being the first American naval officer to engage the enemy at sea. He served on the Delaware River in 1777, protecting the supply lines of the American army at Valley Forge and keeping the British from the city. But when Admiral Richard Howe brought in overwhelming numbers of warships, Barry had to abandon the campaign and even scuttle his vessel.

In 1778 Barry commanded a frigate out of Boston, but he lost the ship in an engagement with two British vessels. In 1780 he commanded the *Alliance,* which captured two British ships off Sandy Hook, New Jersey, in an engagement which made Barry's reputation as a tactician and

in which he was wounded. He sailed to France in 1783 and returned home via Cuba in order to escort a merchant ship. Off the coast of Florida he successfully protected the merchantman in an engagement with a British frigate. As it happened, this was the last naval battle of the Revolution, giving Barry the distinction of having fought both the first and last naval engagements of that conflict.

He returned to his mercantile career after the war, and he sailed to Canton, China. In 1794, the federal government officially established the United States Navy and commissioned Barry "senior captain" to supervise the construction of the new fleet. He was also given command of the nation's premier warship, the *United States.* From 1798 to 1801 he directed naval operations in the West Indies during the United States' undeclared war against revolutionary France. In 1803 President Thomas Jefferson assigned him the command against the Barbary pirates, but Barry had to decline because of illness, and he died a few months later on September 13. Barry ranks as one of the great patriots of the Revolutionary period, since his initial wealth as a shipowner derived from British control of the seas, and many wealthy colonials became Tories rather than jeopardize their station; he also ranks as one of the founders of the American navy. Gilbert Stuart painted his portrait. He died in Philadelphia on September 13, 1803.

Blanco, Richard, ed. *American Revolution, 1775–1783: An Encyclopedia.* New York, 1993. I:101–102.

Clark, W. B. *Gallant John Barry.* New York, 1938.

DAB 1:654.

NCE 2:127–28.

JOSEPH F. KELLY

BARRY (LAKE), LEONORA MARIE (1849–1930)

Union organizer and temperance advocate. Leonora Barry was born on August 13, 1849, to John Barry and Granger Brown Kearney Barry in County Cork, Ireland. She was their only child. When she was still a small child (1852), her family emigrated to the United States and settled on a farm in St. Lawrence County, New York. In 1871 Leonora married William E. Barry, an Irish painter and musician. They had three children, one of whom died at the age of eight. William himself died in 1881.

In order to support herself and her two sons, Barry took a job as an unskilled garment factory worker in Amsterdam, New York, earning sixty-five cents a week. By 1884 low pay and harsh working conditions led her to join the Knights of Labor, an organization dominated by Irish Catholic men and women and interested in social reform as well as the cause of the worker. Barry quickly became very active in the organization. She became a full-time employee in 1886. During her four years at the Knights of Labor, she traveled around the country advocating reforms in working conditions and trying to organize the women members, a project whose difficulty was increased by internal struggles within the organization. Her achievements with the Knights of Labor included being credited with a crucial role in the enactment of the first Pennsylvania Factory Inspection Act of 1889, a feat she accomplished without lobbying among legislators because she deemed such behavior unladylike.

Even as Barry labored to improve working conditions for factory workers, she maintained a rather traditional view of women's place in society. She believed that women's role in relation to men, both privately and publicly, was to support men in their positions. Thus, she encouraged women to remain at home unless economic necessity dictated otherwise. Accordingly, when Leonara married Obadiah Read Lake, an employee of the *St. Louis Globe-Democrat,* in 1890, she resigned from her position at the Knights of Labor in order to work at home.

For Leonora, however, working at home did not mean abdicating from a role in public life. She became active in several reform movements, including the women's suffrage movement. In 1893 she delivered an address to the congress of women at the World's Columbian Exposition in Chicago entitled "The Dignity of Labor." She was also a member of the Women's Christian Temperance Union, an officer of the Catholic Total Abstinence Union of America, and the founder of the Catholic Women's Temperance Union. She wholeheartedly supported the Volstead Act, a piece of legislation designed to provide for strong enforcement of the eighteenth amendment, which prohibited the sale, transportation, and production of intoxicating liquors. Leonora saw the "evil of drink" as a threat to the sanctity of the family. Furthermore, she believed that the success of the temperance movement depended on women's involvement since they were the foundation of the Church, the ones who actually motivated the men to go to Mass.

Leonora continued to keep public speaking engagements until 1928. She succumbed to cancer of the mouth on July 15, 1930, at Minooka, Illinois, her home since 1916.

Bland, Joan. *Hibernian Crusade: The Story of the Catholic Total Abstinence Union of America.* Washington, D.C., 1951.
Carey, Patrick. *The Roman Catholics.* Westport, Conn.: Greenwood Press, 1993, 178.
Diner, Hasia R. *Erin's Daughters in America.* Baltimore: Johns Hopkins University Press, 1983, 100–02.
Joliet Herald-News, July 16, 1930.
Levine, Susan. "Labor's True Woman: Domesticity and Equal Rights in the Knights of Labor." *Journal of American History* 70 (2) (September 1983) 331–39.
NAW, 1:101–2, s.v. "Barry."
Who's Who in America, 194–95, s.v. "Barry."
Women's Who's Who of America, 1914–15, s.v. "Lake."

PATRICIA DeFERRARI

BARRY, TERESA (1814–1900)

Religious superior. Born in Cork, Ireland, in 1814, Teresa Barry was brought to the United States as a child by her aunts, Mary O'Gorman and Honora O'Gorman. In November 1829 they moved from Baltimore to Charleston to become the first members of the Sisters of Charity of Our Lady of Mercy, the religious congregation founded by Bishop John England on the model of the Sisters of Charity at Emmitsburg, Maryland.

During the founder's lifetime, Sr. Teresa taught school while simultaneously caring for the orphans placed with the community, and, attending the victims of the frequent cholera and yellow fever epidemics. In 1835 Bishop England appointed her to the community council. When he died, April 11, 1842, she was directing a school for free colored children. In 1844 Teresa Barry was elected mother superior, an office she held at intervals for a total of thirty-nine years.

Mother Teresa headed the community during the Civil War. Under her leadership sisters staffed a Confederate hospital at Montgomery White Sulphur Springs, Virginia, and cared for the Union soldiers who were hospitalized or imprisoned in Charleston. In gratitude, Congress appropriated twelve thousand dollars in 1871 to help rebuild the motherhouse.

In October 1882 Mother Teresa achieved a long-time goal with the opening of St. Francis Xavier Hospital in Charleston. Plans for a nursing school were in place at the time of her death on May 18, 1900. What a foundress is for other religious congregations, Mother Teresa Barry has become for the Sisters of Charity of Our Lady of Mercy.

Madden, Richard C. *Catholics in South Carolina: A Record.* Lanham, Md.: University Press of America, Inc., 1985.
"A Southern Teaching Order: The Sisters of Mercy of Charleston, S.C., 1829–1904." *Records of the American Catholic Historical Society* 15 (September 1904) 249–65.

ANNE FRANCIS CAMPBELL, O.L.M.

BARRY UNIVERSITY

The opening of Barry College, now Barry University, in September 1940 was the result of careful planning by three members of the Barry family from County Clare, Ireland: Bishop Patrick Barry, then head of the St. Augustine, Florida, diocese and the person for whom the college was named; Mother Mary Gerald Barry, superior of the Dominican Sisters in Adrian, Michigan; Msgr. William Barry, founder and pastor of St. Patrick's parish in Miami Beach, Florida; and by John Graves Thompson, a Miami lawyer.

As legal representative, Thompson purchased forty acres of scrub palm in Miami Shores for twenty-four thousand dollars in May 1939. There were five original buildings:

Cor Jesu Chapel, built and furnished by Margaret Brady Farrell from Albany, New York; Adrian Hall, a classroom-administration unit; La Voie Hall, the dining hall and home economics laboratories; and Kelley and Farrell Houses, residence halls. The Adrian Dominican Sisters financed these last four buildings.

That same year Barry was incorporated under the laws of the state of Florida as a college of liberal arts and recognized as a Catholic institution of higher education for women. The original faculty numbered fourteen, twelve of whom were Adrian Dominican sisters. The forty students who matriculated were offered a curriculum which included eleven majors.

Mother Gerald Barry was president of Barry from 1940 until her death in 1961. Because she resided in Adrian, Michigan, she appointed executive vice presidents who lived on campus. Her successor, Mother Mary Genevieve Weber, asked the general council to elect a president who would live on campus.

The council chose Sr. Dorothy Browne as the first resident president in 1963. During her administration, Barry College began the first school of social work in South Florida, and built the Monsignor William Barry Library and Weigand Center.

In 1974 the board elected Sr. Trinita Flood as president, and she made Barry coeducational in all areas. The board of trustees elected Sr. Jeanne O'Laughlin, O.P., as president in 1981. Unlike her predecessors, she had not taught. In her first year at Barry she received board approval to change the status of the college to that of a university, reorganized the administration of the university, explored and began new programs of instruction, and continued renovation of the campus.

During Sr. Jeanne's presidency, the D. Inez Andreas School of Business, the James G. Garner School of Computer Science, the St. Francis-Barry Health and Rehabilitation Center, the Health and Sports Center, the Lillian Rooney Powers and Samuel J. Powers Jr. Human Services building and four residence halls were completed.

In a short period Barry grew from a small liberal arts college to a comprehensive university of 7,000 students with doctoral programs in education, podiatric medicine, and social work. Currently, there are nine schools: Adult and Continuing Education, Arts and Sciences, Business, Education, Human Performances and Leisure Sciences, Natural and Health Sciences, Nursing, Podiatric Medicine and Social Work.

See also CATHOLIC UNIVERSITIES AND COLLEGES.

EILEEN F. RICE, O.P.

BARRYMORE, ETHEL (1879–1959)

Actress. Born in Philadelphia, Pennsylvania, into a family of famous actors, Barrymore was educated there by

Ethel Barrymore

the Sisters of Notre Dame de Namur, to whom she dedicated her 1955 autobiography *Memories*. While serving as an apprentice in New York to her uncle, comedian John Drew, she began her long association with manager Charles Frohman, and had her first leading role as Stella De Gex in his road production of *His Excellency the Governor* in 1900. One year later Barrymore became a star as Madame Trentoni in the Broadway hit *Captain Jinks of the High Horse.* Her success continued over the years in such hits as *A Doll's House* (1905); *Tante* (1913); *Our Mrs. McChesney* (1915); *The Lady of the Cameuias* (1917); and *The Constant Wife* (1926). In 1928 the Shuberts' Ethel Barrymore Theater, named in her honor, opened in New York.

In 1909 Barrymore married Russell Griswold Colt, son of Samuel Pomeroy Colt, chairman of the United States Rubber Company. The couple had three children. They were divorced in 1923; however, Barrymore, as a Catholic, considered the divorce "merely legal" and never remarried.

Barrymore's last great stage success was in *The Corn is Green* (1940–42), although she appeared in many subsequent Broadway shows. Best known for her work in the theater, she also acted in television and film. She won an Academy Award as best supporting actress in 1944 for her portrayal of Ma Mott in *None But the Lonely Heart.* Barrymore appeared in twenty films between 1946 and 1957, as well as in various drama and variety-comedy series on television. One of America's leading actresses, renowned for her talent, warmth, and beauty, she died in Hollywood, California, on June 18, 1959.

Alpert, Hollis. *The Barrymores.* New York, 1965.
Barrymore, Ethel. *Memories: An Autobiography.* New York, 1955.
Barrymore, Lionel. *We Barrymores.* New York, 1951.

Peters, Margo. *The House of Barrymore*. New York, 1990.

K. N. McCARTHY

BARZYŃSKI, VINCENT MICHAEL (1838–99)

Missionary, pastor. Wincenty Michał [Vincent Michael] Barzyński was born in Sulisławice, Poland, on September 20, 1838. After studying at the seminary in Lublin from 1856, he was ordained a secular priest on October 28, 1861. While assistant pastor in Tomaszów he took an active part in the Polish January Insurrection against the Russians in 1863. With its failure he fled to Kraków but was arrested by the Austrian authorities and spent ten months in prison. Deported to Paris in 1865, he was attracted to the Congregation of the Resurrection, an order founded in Paris in 1836 by Polish émigré priests to unite Catholicism and the cause of Polish national independence. Moving to Rome, he joined the Congregation of the Resurrection, making his vows on September 18, 1866. On the following day he left for the United States as one of three priests sent by the Resurrectionists to Texas where he served as organizer and pastor of St. Michael's parish in San Antonio.

In 1874 he became pastor of St. Stanislaus Kostka Church in Chicago, serving there until his death in 1899. Barzyński was a leading organizer of Polish immigrants in America, calling the first meeting of the Polish Roman Catholic Union in Chicago on October 10, 1874. In 1875 he and several others founded the *Towarzystwo Księży Rzymsko-Katolickich Polskich w Stanach Zjednoczonych* [Association of Polish Roman Catholic Priests in the United States] to promote clerical unity, assist bishops, and provide guidance to the laity. Among his many other accomplishments, he founded the first Polish secondary school in Chicago, an orphanage and hospital, organized nearly forty societies and associations, established a parish savings and loan association that served as a model for other such efforts, introduced the Sisters of the Holy Family of Nazareth to the United States, and assisted in the formation of twenty-five other parishes. In 1877 he established the Polish Publishing Company, an important means of maintaining the faith among Polish immigrants and their offspring, which published the first Polish American school textbooks, missals, devotional books, and pamphlets on Polish heritage. Barzyński's company published the religious newspaper *Kropidło* [*The Aspergillum*] and in 1890 he founded the influential Catholic newspaper *Dziennik Chicagoski* [*Chicago Daily News*] to oppose Masons, socialists, and anticlerical elements. By 1893 St. Stanislaus Kostka was considered the largest Catholic parish in the world, eventually numbering some 50,000 parishioners. In 1898 he became first provincial superior of the Resurrectionists in America. He died in Chicago on May 2, 1899.

JAMES S. PULA

BAUDIER, JOSEPH ROGER (1893–1960)

Writer, historian, journalist, activist. Joseph Roger Baudier was born in New Orleans on July 30, 1893, son of Jean Alexandre Baudier, II, and Louise Angela Baudier. He was orphaned at six and raised with the help of elderly aunts who filled his childhood with Creole stories and traditions. He attended St. Philip's School in the French Quarter (1898–1906) and St. Anthony College (seminary) in Santa Barbara, California (1909–13), working in the interim.

Baudier taught at St. Francis Orphanage in Watsonville, California (1913–18), and served briefly in the army (1918–19). Returning to New Orleans, he became a clerk for the Southern Pacific Railroad (1919–27), commercial artist, freelance writer, and trade journalist and editor. His early trade articles on baking and plumbing reflected his talent for storytelling and historical research. Baudier married Mary Mabel Demarest of New Orleans; the couple had three children: Mary Mabel, Jr., Joseph Roger Jr., and Ann Marie.

When Archbishop John Shaw reestablished a local Catholic newspaper, *Catholic Action of the South*, in 1932, Baudier was tapped as associate editor (1932–41) and later editor (1941–49). In 1949 he returned to the trade journals and was appointed the archdiocese's first official chronicler.

Baudier was the South's most prolific Catholic historian of the mid-twentieth century; his books, monographs, articles, special newspaper supplements, and signed columns number more than 270. His major publications include: *The Catholic Church in Louisiana* (1939); *The Eighth National Eucharistic Congress* (1941); *Anchor and Fleur-de Lis: The Knights of Columbus in Louisiana 1902–1962* (with Millard Everett: 1962); and the history of St. Louis Cathedral that sold more than 700,000 copies. He wrote, edited, or contributed to fifty-four major supplements of *Catholic Action of the South*.

Baudier wrote forty-five booklets and numerous articles on Catholic parishes, organizations, and institutions. His major trade journal series included the history of sanitation in New Orleans (*Southern Plumber*, 1930–32) and history of the bread-making customs of the native peoples of the Southwest (*Mixer*, 1932). He was an organizer and first secretary (1932–34) of Louisiana State Bakers Association.

Baudier authored a weekly column, "Historic Old New Orleans"—a major source of Creole traditions, folklore, and beliefs—in *Catholic Action of the South* (1933–60). He was active in the Knights of Columbus, the Catholic Committee of the South, the Archconfraternity of St. Ann, Associated Catholic Charities, and the Holy Name Society. He handled publicity for numerous Catholic events and organizations, especially the Eighth National Eucharistic Congress (1938).

Baudier was a long-time advisor to Archbishop Joseph Rummel. His research, columns and editorials supported workers' rights and the continuing efforts of Archbishop Rummel to foster the rights of African Americans and the desegregation of Catholic parishes, schools, and organizations. Baudier was named a Knight of St. Gregory (1943). He received France's *Palmes Académiques* (1950) and an honorary doctorate from Notre Dame Seminary (1958), the first layman to be so honored.

Baudier died in New Orleans, November 30, 1960. Louisiana pastor-educator-historian Henry C. Bezou commented that Baudier was not only a Renaissance man—writer, historian, artist, organizer, poet, editor, journalist, and publicist—but also "the most unique Catholic layman in the twentieth century."

Roger Baudier Papers in Archives of the Archdiocese of New Orleans (AANO) and Baudier Family.

Catholic Action of the South, 1932–60.

Nolan, Charles E. "A Passion for History: Roger Baudier, Sr." Presentation to the Louisiana Historical Association, March 27, 1993 (copy in AANO).

Nolan research papers for Baudier biography.

CHARLES E. NOLAN

BAUER, BENEDICTA (1803–65)

Religious superior. Maria Anna Bauer was born on July 17, 1803, in Pielenhofen, Germany. At the age of seventeen, she entered the Dominican Holy Cross Convent in Ratisbon, Germany, and took the name Benedicta. From 1845 to 1858, she served as superior of her order. In this role, she sent many missionary sisters to the United States to establish parochial schools for German-speaking immigrants and to establish an American Dominican convent in Brooklyn, New York (1853), the first of numerous Dominican convents for which she was responsible throughout the United States.

Mother Benedicta came to the United States herself in 1858 and served in convents in New York, Ohio, Tennessee, and Wisconsin. Between 1862 and 1863 she and two companions built a permanent independent Dominican motherhouse, St. Catherine of Siena Convent, and a parochial school at Racine, Wisconsin. Her continuing efforts resulted in four additional educational institutions in Wisconsin and increased membership in the Dominican community. Mother Benedicta died on October 13, 1865, at St. Catherine of Siena Convent.

See also BENEDICTINES (O.S.B.).

Carey, Patrick W. *The Roman Catholics.* Westport, Conn.: Greenwood Press, 1993, 178–79.

Kohler, Mary Hortense. *Life and Work of Mother Benedicta Bauer.* Milwaukee, 1937.

PATRICIA DeFERRARI

BAYLEY, JAMES ROOSEVELT (1814–77)

Convert, archbishop. James Roosevelt Bayley was born into a prominent New York family on August 23, 1814. St. Elizabeth Ann Bayley Seton was his father's half-sister, and Uncle Isaac Roosevelt, his mother's brother, was the great-grandfather of Franklin D. Roosevelt. He was educated at Mount Pleasant Classical Institution, Amherst College, and Trinity College, Hartford, where he graduated in 1835. Like his father and grandfather, Bayley initially pursued medical studies, but after a year he switched to the ministry. After private studies with Samuel Farmar Jarvis in Middletown, Connecticut, Bayley was ordained to the Episcopal priesthood on February 14, 1840, while serving as rector of St. Andrew's Church, Harlem, New York.

Bayley's reading of the Church Fathers and Church history, as well as conversations with Fr. (later Cardinal) John McCloskey sowed doubts in his mind about the claims of his Church. In 1841 Bayley resigned his rectorship, and, later that year his concerned grandfather sent him to Rome to see firsthand the weaknesses of Catholicism. The opposite prevailed and Bayley was received into the Catholic Church at the Gesù on April 28, 1842. After studies at Saint-Sulpice, Paris, and New York, he was ordained at New York on March 2, 1844. He served first as vice president of St. John's College, Fordham, and successfully oversaw the transfer of that school from the diocesan clergy to the Jesuits. After a brief pastorate on Staten Island, Bayley was named secretary to Archbishop John Hughes. He served Hughes for seven years during a tumultuous period marked by immigration, growth, and nativism.

First Bishop of Newark

Bayley attended the First Plenary Council of Baltimore in 1852, one result of which was the recommendation of a new diocese for New Jersey. On July 29, 1853, Bayley was named first bishop of Newark. He was consecrated at New York, together with the new bishops of Brooklyn and Burlington, on October 30, 1853, and installed in Newark's St. Patrick's Cathedral two days later. Bayley's New Jersey years were happy and energetic. He crisscrossed the state by train and carriage, preaching, confirming, and lecturing. The state's Catholic population, expanded by immigration, doubled during his episcopate to 80,000, and the new bishop set about to better provide for their needs. Eighty new churches were built in Bayley's nineteen years as bishop, and the Catholic school population grew from 1,500 to 20,000.

Bayley strove to put the new diocese on a firm footing. In 1856 he founded a men's college at Madison to provide for the training of new priests and named it after his aunt. Two years later, he prevailed upon the New York and Cincinnati Sisters of Charity to assist him in founding a New Jersey branch of his aunt's congregation. And in 1860,

James Roosevelt Bayley

tine's Church in Washington, D.C., the largest church for blacks in the nation.

Personally generous, Bayley was interested in the Native American missions and the North American College at Rome. He was a friend and backer of Isaac Hecker in his efforts to establish the Paulists. He had an interest in American ecclesiastical history, and wrote two short works, *Brief Sketch of the Early History of the Catholic Church on the Island of New York* (1853), and *Memoirs of the Rt. Rev. Simon Wm. Gabriel Bruté, D.D., First Bishop of Vincennes* (1860). He also encouraged the historical efforts of John Gilmary Shea and opened the Baltimore archives to him.

Beset by ill health, Bayley pressed for the appointment of Bishop James Gibbons of Richmond as his coadjutor. Bayley had already left for Europe to recover his health by the time of Gibbons's appointment on May 27, 1877. Returning in August, Bayley died in his old room at the cathedral rectory in Newark on October 3, 1877, and was buried beside his aunt in Emmitsburg, Maryland.

See also MARYLAND, CATHOLIC CHURCH IN; NEW JERSEY, CATHOLIC CHURCH IN.

Spalding, Thomas W. *The Premier See. A History of the Archdiocese of Baltimore, 1789–1989.* Baltimore and London: The Johns Hopkins University Press, 1989.
Sullivan, Edwin Vose. "James Roosevelt Bayley." *The Bishops of Newark 1853–1978.* South Orange, N.J.: Seton Hall University Press, 1978, 1–22.
———. "An Annotated Copy of the Diary of Bishop James Roosevelt Bayley, First Bishop of Newark, New Jersey, 1853–1872." Ph.D. dissertation, University of Ottawa, 1956.
Yeager, M. Hildegarde. *Life of James Roosevelt Bayley, First Bishop of Newark and Eighth Archbishop of Baltimore 1814–1877.* Washington, D.C.: The Catholic University of America Press, 1947.

RAYMOND J. KUPKE

he oversaw the move of Seton Hall College to South Orange, while the Sisters of Charity moved their motherhouse to Madison. In the same year, Immaculate Conception Seminary at Seton Hall commenced instruction in theology. Bayley conducted diocesan synods in 1856 and 1868 and pressed the state legislature into passing an act providing for the civil incorporation for Catholic parishes. One of his last acts as bishop was to secure the site of Newark's present cathedral.

Bayley's activities were not restricted to New Jersey. He traveled to Europe in 1862 and 1867. He participated in the Second Plenary Council of Baltimore in 1866, and in the First Vatican Council where he was part of the "inopportunist" minority. A forceful writer, Bayley became nationally known from his pastorals as an advocate of Catholic schools and the temperance movement.

Archbishop of Baltimore

On July 30, 1872, Bayley was named archbishop of Baltimore in succession to Martin J. Spalding. A reluctant primate, Bayley's brief tenure in America's oldest see was unhappy and less productive than his Newark years. Already suffering from Bright's disease, Bayley found his see city uncomfortable and unhealthy, and often traveled to New Jersey and elsewhere for his health. Bayley's principal accomplishment in Baltimore was to introduce a more businesslike approach to diocesan and parish structures in a see long accustomed to more casual arrangements. His 1876 pastoral letter appealed for greater generosity from his flock, and he managed to retire the cathedral debt and consecrated the fifty-five-year-old structure on May 25, 1876. Three weeks later Bayley dedicated St. Augus-

BECKER, THOMAS ANDREW (1832–99)

Bishop. Becker was born in Pittsburgh, Pennsylvania, on December 20, 1832, a son of John and Susannah Walker Baker. He attended the Allegheny Institute and Mission Church and Western University in Pittsburgh. Later, while completing his studies at the University of Virginia where his brother Samuel was a professor of ancient languages, he was received into the Catholic Church and baptized on May 22, 1853, at Winchester, Virginia. At the time of his conversion to Catholicism, his parents, who were strict Scotch-Irish Covenanter Presbyterians, required him and his brother Samuel to change their name from Baker to Becker. Thereafter he was often mistakenly thought to be German although his parents were northern Irish.

He was accepted as a candidate for the priesthood by John McGill, bishop of Richmond, and while teaching

Thomas A. Becker

school pursued studies under Fr. Plunkett, pastor of Martinsburg, West Virginia, until his departure for the College of the Propaganda, Rome, in June 1855. As a student in Rome, he attracted notice for his piety, scholarliness, and remarkable talent for both ancient and modern languages. After receiving his doctorate in theology, he was ordained by Cardinal Patrizi in the Basilica of St. John Lateran on June 18, 1859.

His first assignment was as assistant pastor in St. Peter's Cathedral, Richmond, Virginia, where he remained until January, 1860. He was then appointed pastor of St. Joseph's Church in Martinsburg, West Virginia, with the care of Winchester, Berkeley Springs, and the adjacent counties. An important task early in his pastorate was the completion of a new church in Martinsburg, begun by Fr. Plunkett. Early in 1863, when the town of Martinsburg was occupied by Union troops, Fr. Becker, a secessionist, was sent under arrest to Washington for refusing to pray publicly for President Lincoln and for actively aiding the Confederacy by passing information through the Southern spy, Belle Boyd, as well as for directly helping the Mosby raiders when they stormed Martinsburg to free Confederate prisoners.

First Bishop of Wilmington

Archbishop Francis P. Kenrick of Baltimore eventually obtained his release by appealing to President Lincoln, and in July 1863 placed him on the faculty of Mount Saint Mary's College, Emmitsburg, Maryland. There he was an instructor in dogma, Scripture, and Church history until July 1864 when he was summoned to Baltimore to serve as secretary to Archbishop Martin J. Spalding. While on the cathedral staff, he collaborated with Spalding in the publication of the *Catholic Miscellany*. When the Second Council of Baltimore convened in October 1866, Becker was one of the theologians appointed to assist at the assembly. At the council's close, Becker returned to the Richmond cathedral to serve as assistant rector. During this time he conducted a school for eighty boys, and published a *Vade Mecum* prayer book. He was named the first bishop of Wilmington, Delaware, upon its establishment on March 3, 1868. He was consecrated bishop in Baltimore along with James Gibbons at the Basilica of the Assumption on August 16, 1868. Archbishop Martin J. Spalding was the chief consecrator while Bishop McGill of Richmond and Bishop Whelan of Wheeling were co-consecrators. Thirty-six years of age, the scholarly and energetic new bishop plunged into the task of evangelizing the vast missionary district of the Delmarva peninsula which was his diocese.

His influence was felt on a national scale, particularly in the field of education. He was one of the first to advocate the founding of a national Catholic university, expressing his views in two articles published in the *American Catholic Quarterly Review* in 1876: "Shall We Have A University?" and "A Plan for a Proposed Catholic University." Again in the *American Catholic Quarterly Review* in 1878, he dealt with the then highly controversial subject of labor unions, upholding the right of labor to organize, and pronouncing upon the morality of certain of their practices.

In 1877 his impressive performance caused him to be considered as a successor to the ailing Archbishop James Roosevelt Bayley of Baltimore. In 1878 Bishop Becker masterfully refuted Delaware Episcopalian bishop Alfred Lee's public accusations against the Church in a published reply circulated throughout the city of Wilmington. Bishop Becker collaborated with Gibbons in preparations for the Third Plenary Council of Baltimore, held in November 1884. Gibbons appointed him to prepare the important chapter on the education of the clergy.

Bishop of Savannah

As early as September 1879 he became discouraged by what he felt was lack of progress in his diocese, and requested transfer from Wilmington, but it was not until seven years later that his request was granted. In May 1886 at the age of fifty-four, he was transferred to the see of Savannah, Georgia. He served as the sixth bishop of Savannah for thirteen years. In January 1895 his people presented him with a purse, and Bishop Becker sailed for Rome and the Holy Land. On his visit to Rome, he petitioned the Holy See to move his residence from Savannah to Atlanta. The request was not granted because the Holy See felt it inopportune to transfer the see at that time. The Savannah Cathedral of St. John the Baptist burned in

1898. Bishop Becker began its reconstruction, but did not live to see its completion. Having contracted malaria, he was failing in health generally. While substituting for one of his priests at St. Joseph's Orphanage and Church, Washington, Georgia, he received the last rites of the Church from Fr. Benjamin Keiley, his close associate of more than thirty years, and died there on July 29, 1899. Interment was in Cathedral Cemetery, Savannah, Georgia.

See also DELAWARE, CATHOLIC CHURCH IN; GEORGIA, CATHOLIC CHURCH IN.

Peterman, Thomas J. *The Cutting Edge, Life of Thomas A. Becker First Catholic Bishop of Wilmington and Sixth Bishop of Savannah (1831–1899)*. Philadelphia: Cooke Publishers, 1982.
____. *Priests of a Century, 1868–1968, Diocese of Wilmington, Delaware*. Philadelphia: Cooke Publishers, 1970, 15–17.
____. "Thomas Andrew Becker, the First Catholic Bishop of Wilmington, Delaware, and the Sixth Bishop of Savannah, Georgia, 1831–1899." Ph.D. dissertation, The Catholic University of America, 1981.

THOMAS J. PETERMAN

BECKMAN, FRANCIS (1875–1948)

Archbishop. Francis Joseph Beckman was born in Cincinnati, Ohio, on October 25, 1875. He was educated at Mt. St. Mary of the West Seminary in Cincinnati and at The Catholic University of Louvain and the Pontifical Gregorian University in Rome where he received a S.T.D. degree in 1908. Returning to the United States as a young priest (he had been ordained on June 20, 1902), he taught theology at Mt. St. Mary Seminary from 1908 to 1912 and then served as rector of the seminary from 1912 to 1924. While rector of the seminary, he founded the Catholic Students' Mission Crusade. He also energetically encouraged the Catholic Action Movement, retreats, pilgrimages, and the enthronement of the Sacred Heart in homes.

He was appointed bishop of Lincoln, Nebraska, on December 23, 1923, and also served as apostolic administrator of the Diocese of Omaha from June 1, 1926 to July 4, 1928. He was appointed archbishop of Dubuque, Iowa, on January 17, 1930. In Dubuque he organized the Midwest (later National) Antiquarian Association and an extensive art museum at Columbia (later Loras) College. Seeing the European war of 1939 mainly as an opportunity for Stalinist Communism, he became involved in the America First Movement and even in the no-third-term movement of 1940 against Franklin D. Roosevelt. The last of his national broadcasts from Dubuque peace rallies or from studios came one month before the bombing of Pearl Harbor.

To support his pious projects Beckman was induced by a mining agent, Phillip Suetter, later found guilty of criminal fraud, to sell promissory notes privately and invest heavily in placer gold mines in Oregon and California. Massive bank loans and sales of art objects were required to buy back the notes. A papal investigation begun in 1941 ended in 1944 with the appointment of a coadjutor archbishop and Beckman's resignation in 1946. After his resignation, he was appointed titular archbishop of Phulla. He died in Chicago on October 17, 1948. His years in Dubuque were remembered as a splendid experience in an otherwise bleak time.

See also IOWA, CATHOLIC CHURCH IN.

Fogarty, Gerald P., S.J. *The Vatican and the American Hierarchy from 1870 to 1965*. Wilmington, 1985.
Wilkie, William E. "Seeds Must Die." *Seed/Harvest, a History of the Archdiocese of Dubuque*, ed. M. K. Gallagher, 1987, 79–105.

WILLIAM E. WILKIE

BEDINI, GAETANO (1806–64)

Archbishop, papal envoy to the United States. Bedini was born in Sinigaglia, Italy, on May 15, 1806.

He served in the largely symbolic post of papal governor of Bologna from 1849 to 1852, at a time when Austrian armies controlled this region of the Papal States and ruled by martial law. Bedini would subsequently be denounced in America for military executions over which he had exercised no personal control.

The newly named titular archbishop of Thebes and nuncio to Brazil arrived in the U.S.A. on June 30, 1853, to investigate then-current problems: trusteeism; anti-Catholic agitation; dangers posed to Catholic children by the

Gaetano Bedini

common schools, among others. After conveying papal greetings to President Franklin Pierce, Bedini sojourned in many northern cities accompanied by New York archbishop John Hughes. He also visited Montreal and Quebec City.

Greeted courteously by civic and ecclesiastical authorities, Bedini was frequently burned in effigy by local mobs, and denounced as the "Butcher of Bologna" by anti-Catholic speakers such as Alessandro Gavazzi a renegade Italian priest, and by the nativist press. The greatest disturbance occurred in Cincinnati on Christmas 1853, when a crowd of perhaps a thousand marched on the cathedral. A tired Bedini sailed from New York February 3, 1854. Guarding against a final nativist confrontation, he was smuggled out to Staten Island and brought aboard his oceangoing ship in a rowboat. Bedini later served as Secretary of the Congregation of Propaganda Fide. On March 18, 1861, he was named bishop of Viterbo-Toscanella, and on September 27 of the same year, was created cardinal with the titular church of Santa Maria sopra Minerva. He died in Viterbo, Italy, on September 6, 1864.

See also HUGHES, JOHN; PAPAL REPRESENTATION IN AMERICA.

Guilday, Peter. "Gaeto Bedini, An Episode in the Life of Archbishop John Hughes." *Historical Records and Studies* 23 (1933) 87–170.
Shaw, Richard. *Dagger John.* New York: Paulist, 1977.

ALBERT H. LEDOUX

BEGIN, FLOYD LAWRENCE (1902–77)

Bishop. Begin, the first of seven children, was born on February 5, 1902, in Cleveland to Peter and Stella McFarland Begin. After completing his studies in Cleveland schools, Begin decided to study for the priesthood and was sent to North American College where he was ordained on July 31, 1927.

Begin completed his doctoral studies in philosophy and theology in Rome and served as an assistant to the rector of North American College. Returning to Cleveland in 1930, he was named vice chancellor and secretary to Bishop Joseph Schrembs. His duties included coordination of the Seventh National Eucharistic Congress held in Cleveland in 1935. In 1938 he became *officialis* of the tribunal and director of the diocesan chapter of the National Council of Catholic Men.

On March 27, 1947, he was named auxiliary bishop of Cleveland. His consecration took place on May 1, 1947, in St. Agnes Church in Cleveland. On January 23, 1949, Begin was appointed pastor of this same church. St. Agnes parish, once very affluent, was located in the Hough neighborhood that was undergoing rapid racial and economic change. Begin started an evangelization program that featured personalized invitations, home visits by the Legion of Mary, and instruction classes. He fought with unre-

sponsive city bureaucracy for better services. He and other clergymen organized for community betterment.

On February 21, 1962, the Vatican announced the creation of three new California dioceses: Oakland, Santa Rosa, and Stockton. Begin was selected to head the Oakland diocese.

On April 28, 1962, he was installed as the bishop of Oakland. Begin started a practice of visiting each parish and institution annually. He spoke out for criminal justice reform, fair housing, and the rights of farm workers. He became the first American bishop to condemn the American invasion of Cambodia in 1970.

Begin had attended the Second Vatican Council and served on its administrative tribunal. He supported liturgical renewal and Oakland's Cathedral of St. Francis de Sales was the first to be renovated for the new liturgy. During his administration sixteen new parishes were established; twenty churches and fifteen mission centers were constructed along with additional schools.

He died in Oakland on April 26, 1977, after a brief illness.

Blatnica, Dorothy A. "In Those Days": African-American Catholics in Cleveland, 1922–1961. Ph.D. dissertation, Case Western Reserve University, Cleveland, 1992.
Catholic Voice. Special supplement (April 20, 1972) 1–10, 12–20; (May 2, 1977) 1.
Diocese of Oakland. *News Release,* March 1, 1977; April 14, 1977.
Hynes, Michael J. *History of the Diocese of Cleveland—Origin and Growth (1847–1952).* Cleveland, 1953.

CHRISTINE KROSEL

BELLARMINE COLLEGE

On October 3, 1950, Bellarmine College was opened under the sponsorship of the Roman Catholic Archdiocese of Louisville and the assistance of the Conventual Franciscan Friars. In 1949 Archbishop John A. Floersh had appointed Msgr. Alfred F. Horrigan as first president of the liberal arts college for men. Its motto is *In Veritatis Amore* ("In the Love of Truth"). The site of the college had been the location of Bishop William George McCloskey's seminary, Preston Park, from 1871–1909; and later the location of orphanages staffed by the Sisters of Charity of Nazareth. Bellarmine was one of the first colleges in the Commonwealth of Kentucky to be open to all races because the restrictive "Day Law" was repealed in 1950.

In 1968 Bellarmine merged with Ursuline College, a Catholic women's college founded in 1938 by the Ursuline Sisters of Louisville. At the time of this merger, Archbishop Thomas J. McDonough ceded ownership and governance of the college to an independent governing board of trustees. The student body became coeducational. The archbishop of Louisville serves as chancellor of the college and a member of the board of trustees. Bellarmine's second president and the first layperson to hold the office was Dr. Eugene V. Petrik who served from 1972 until 1990. He was succeeded by the current president, Dr. Joseph J. McGowan, Jr.

In 1963 the Trappist monk and author Thomas Merton (1915–68) accepted the invitation of Msgr. Horrigan and Bellarmine's dean, Fr. John T. Loftus, O.F.M. Conv., to establish a "Merton Room" collection. In 1967 it became the official depository of his manuscripts and archival materials, now numbering over 40,000 items. After Merton's accidental death in Asia, December 10, 1968, the Merton Legacy Trust governed use and publication of materials housed in the Bellarmine Merton Center Collection. In the spring of 1995 the abbot of Gethsemani, the Merton Legacy Trust, and the president of Bellarmine established The Thomas Merton Center Foundation, Inc., to promote programs and study of Merton's spiritual, ecumenical, cultural, and social interests. In January of 1997 Bellarmine's new library opened with a new Merton Center wing housing its Merton collection, research space, and exhibits.

Bellarmine established its first graduate program in 1975 with the MBA degree. In 1981 graduate programs in Education were introduced. Masters of Science in Nursing (1984), Master of Social Administration (1986), Master of Arts in Teaching (1986), and the Master of Arts in Liberal Studies (1992) also became part of the college's curriculum.

Bellarmine began in 1955 to present the prestigious Bellarmine Medal to persons of civil and moral excellence on the national or international level. Recipients include: Henry Cabot Lodge, Mother Theresa of Calcutta, Jesse Jackson, Lech Walesa, and Arthur Ashe. Although its history has evolved into the status of independent but Church-related liberal arts college, Bellarmine intentionally identifies itself as a Catholic college.

See also CATHOLIC UNIVERSITIES AND COLLEGES.

GEORGE KILCOURSE

BENEDICTINES (O.S.B.)

It was not until midway through the nineteenth century that the Benedictine Order made its presence felt in the United States. Before that time, individual Benedictine monks made their way to North America as missionaries. Peter Joseph Didier, Charles Guny, and Louis Leopold Moni were all examples of Benedictine priest-monks who left their European monasteries in the turmoil of the aftermath of the French Revolution.

The immediate cause of European Benedictines emigrating to the United States was the increasing wave of German-speaking Catholic immigrants who arrived in America during the middle decades of the nineteenth century. This

St. Benedict of Nursia

coincided with several movements that affected European Benedictine houses. Benedictine monasticism itself experienced an unprecedented renewal in the years 1830–80. Part of that renewal was seen in a resurgence of interest in missionary activity to foreign lands. Many Benedictine communities looked back to the monastic missionary accomplishment of the Middle Ages in the evangelization of Europe as a model for what would be required of the people of the New World. A steady stream of petitions from an American episcopate desperate for religious personnel also moved the monasteries into action.

Boniface Wimmer and the Founding Vision: Eichstätt and Metten

Among the Benedictines representative of the missionary impulse in European houses was a young, outspoken, Bavarian priest from the German abbey of Metten. Convinced of the urgent need to establish a Benedictine monastery in North America, the thirty-six-year-old monk boldly petitioned his abbot and the Congregation for the Propagation of the Faith in Rome for permission to leave Europe and establish a monastery in the United States. Despite resistance from superiors and community members, Boniface Wimmer won the approval of Rome and the good will and financial backing of King Ludwig I of Bavaria. In 1846 he arrived in Cambria County, Pennsylvania, with eighteen prospective candidates. In that same year, Wimmer moved to property near Latrobe, Pennsylvania, at the invitation of the bishop of Pittsburgh, Michael O'Connor. At the outset, Wimmer was clear about his purpose in coming to the United States: to provide for the sacramental care of the German-speaking Catholics of North America, provide them with a seminary to supply a safeguard of future priestly and religious vocations, schools to insure a Catholic education for their children, and a monastery that would serve as a cultural and religious lifeline for an immigrant community whose ties with its European Catholic traditions had been severed.

In 1851 Wimmer drew up plans to bring Benedictine women to the United States. That year he visited the Benedictine convent of nuns in Eichstätt, Bavaria. In 1852 he won the approval of the Eichstätt superior and the support of the Ludwig Missionsverein. That same year three Benedictine sisters from Eichstätt arrived in St. Marys, Pennsylvania, under the leadership of Benedicta Riepp. For the next ten years, Wimmer and Riepp engaged in a struggle to determine the respective autonomy of their communities. The effort of the women to establish a Benedictine identity was hampered by the authority exercised over them by the local ordinary and Rome's decision to exclude all American Benedictine women from solemn vows, placing them in the canonical category of sisters rather than nuns.

Early Expansion

Nonetheless, the Bavarian Benedictine transplants expanded quickly. Wimmer became known as the patriarch of American monasticism. By the time of his death in 1887, he had established a formidable network of monastic foundations from the mother abbey of St. Vincent in Latrobe. As members of the American Cassinese Congregation, they ranged from Colorado and Kansas in the West, to Alabama, Georgia, Kentucky, and North Carolina in the South, Illinois in the Midwest, and New Jersey in the East. The major work of the monks was pastoral assistance and education. Educational institutions of higher education that claim a link with this period include St. Vincent College, Latrobe, Pennsylvania; Kansas Benedictine College, Atchison, Kansas; Belmont College, North Carolina; St. Anselm's College, Manchester, New Hampshire; and Benedictine University, Lisle, Illinois. The priest-monks of these houses served an increasingly diverse group of Americans, encompassing not only German-speaking immigrants, but African Americans in the South and Native Americans in the Upper Midwest, as well as Czech and Slovak ethnic groups.

The growth of the Benedictine sisters paralleled this, often accompanying the monks. The Eichstätt sisters who settled in St. Marys, Pennsylvania, started new communities in Erie (1852), Johnstown (1870) and Carrolltown (1870), Pennsylvania. They worked with the monks in St. Cloud, Minnesota (1857), Newark, New Jersey (1857), Covington, Kentucky (1859), Atchison, Kansas (1863), Ferdinand, Indiana (1867) and Richmond, Virginia (1868). Other foundations were made in Chicago, Illinois (1861), St. Joseph, Minnesota (1863), Elizabeth, New Jersey (1868),

Nauvoo, Illinois (1874), Pittsburgh, Pennsylvania (1878), Ridgley, Maryland (1887), St. Leo, Florida (1889), Duluth, Minnesota (1892), and Cullman, Alabama (1898). The work of these communities consisted primarily in elementary school teaching, though members were frequently pressed into service as private tutors, missionary catechists, and even cooks and church caretakers.

The Swiss-Americans

In addition to the properly German branch of Benedictines, there was another arm of Benedictine men and women from Switzerland who came to North America. Benedictine monks from the Swiss abbeys of Einsiedeln and Engelberg, and Benedictine sisters from the Swiss convents of Maria Rickenbach, Melchtal, and Sarnen all established foundations in the United States in the nineteenth century.

One of the precipitating factors in their decision to respond to the requests of American bishops was the precarious political situation in Switzerland in the mid-nineteenth century. The Swiss government at this time threatened to dissolve a number of Benedictine schools and monasteries. So partially as a way of creating a religious refuge, partially as a response to the promptings of a number of Swiss Benedictines whose appetites were sharpened by the promotional literature of American missionaries, the Swiss abbey of Einsiedeln sent monks to St. Meinrad, Indiana, in 1854. After some early setbacks and a number of changes in superiors, two young monks from Einsiedeln were sent to St. Meinrad in 1860, Martin Marty and Fintan Mundwiler. These two priests provided leadership for the Indiana community during the next forty years. Their work was remarkably similar to that of the American Cassinese Congregation. They established a seminary and college. They also maintained an extensive work of pastoral assistance to the immigrant. Under the direction of Martin Marty, the St. Meinrad community also committed itself to the care of the Native American Plains Indians of the Dakota Territory. St. Meinrad went on to found daughter houses in Subiaco, Arkansas, in 1878, and in Gessen, Louisiana, in 1890.

About twenty years after St. Meinrad's foundation, the Swiss abbey of Engelberg decided to put down roots on American soil. The abbot of Engelberg, Anselm Villiger, was concerned about the deteriorating security of Benedictine houses with respect to the Swiss government. So when he received a letter in 1872 from Bishop John Hogan of St. Joseph, Missouri, inviting him to start a monastic house in his diocese, the timing was right. The Engelberg chapter voted to go ahead with the American enterprise. As was the case with St. Meinrad, the first monastic foundation of Engelberg, Conception Abbey, had its future determined by two men sent from Switzerland, Frowin Conrad and Adelhelm Odermatt. Conrad was appointed superior of Conception from the day of its founding in 1873. He remained superior for the next fifty years. In that time, he guided Conception through its pioneer stages and gave it a distinctly monastic and liturgical character, even as it continued the work of education and missionary assistance. Adelhelm Odermatt left Conception in 1881, seeking to make a foundation on the West Coast. Eventually, he found a site in the Willamette Valley of Oregon, where in 1882 he started the community of Mount Angel.

In 1881 the Holy See recognized the Swiss-American Congregation of monks. Along with the American Cassinese Congregation, it was to serve as one of the two major organizational entities for American Benedictine monks.

Prior to his departure for America, Frowin Conrad was chaplain for a group of sisters in Maria Rickenbach. This community followed the Rule of St. Benedict and dedicated themselves to perpetual adoration of the Blessed Sacrament. A year after his arrival in Missouri, Conrad wrote to the superior of Maria Rickenbach, Gertrude Leüpi, asking for sisters to come to Conception. Five Benedictines from Maria Rickenbach arrived at Conception in 1874. Within a short time, the sisters divided into two missions, one at Conception, and one at nearby Maryville. The group at Maryville gave evidence of a desire for missionary work. So it was that in the early 1880s they took up work in the Dakotas (Yankton, 1887) and in Mt. Angel, Oregon (1882). The sisters at Conception moved to nearby Clyde, Missouri, and there initiated a more cloistered observance. This community became the basis for the Benedictine Congregation of the Sisters of Perpetual Adoration.

An additional group of Swiss Benedictine sisters came from the monastery at Sarnen in 1884 to Oregon, eventually settling in Cottonwood, Idaho. Another Swiss monastery, Melchtal, made a foundation in Sturgis, South Dakota, in 1889. That community relocated to Rapid City in 1964.

Benedictine Sisters: Growth and Canonical Status

American Benedictine sisters engaged in a long struggle to achieve autonomy. After more than a half century of attempts to organize, Rome recognized the Congregation of St. Scholastica in 1930. Succeeding years witnessed the establishment of the Congregation of St. Gertrude and the Congregation of St. Benedict for Benedictine women. The Congregation of Perpetual Adoration was the last of the women's congregations to be formed that represented a nineteenth-century origin. All of the above congregations, along with later American communities of the Benedictine Missionaries of Tützing, the Olivetan Benedictines of Jonesboro, the Congregation of the Sisters of Jesus Crucified, and the Subiaco Congregation, retained canonical status as *suores*, or sisters, without solemn vows. American communities in Bethlehem, Connecticut, Greensburg, Pennsylvania, and Boulder, Colorado, all were given status as *moniales*, and with their cloistered life were able to take solemn vows.

Development of American Benedictine Monks

In addition to the two major congregations of American monks already mentioned, the twentieth century saw communities founded from the English Benedictine Congregation, (Portsmouth, Rhode Island, Washington, D.C., and St. Louis, Missouri), the Congregation of St. Ottilien (Newton, New Jersey, and Norfolk, Nebraska), the Camaldolese Congregation (Big Sur and Oakland, California), the Belgian Congregation of the Annunciation (Valyermo, California), and the Sylvestrian Congregation (Oxford, Michigan). Other notable American foundations made in the middle of the twentieth century were those of Mount Saviour (New York), Weston (Vermont), and Christ in the Desert (New Mexico), all characterized by smaller numbers and a more contemplative orientation.

The presence of large numbers of immigrant Catholics in the United States dictated the nature of work that was adapted by Benedictines. Two apostolic works took on special prominence: education, and a wide variety of pastoral assistance.

Education

The rapid numerical expansion of the American Catholic Church in the latter part of the nineteenth century was matched by the growth of Benedictine communities of the major congregations of women and men. Educational institutions were in the forefront of this growth. Communities of men were distinguished for constructing a system of Benedictine seminaries. High school and college seminaries evolved throughout the first century of Benedictine presence. Some were shoestring operations that soon went out of existence. Others served for a time until the forces of changing demographics and dwindling numbers required a conversion of institutional apostolates. A proof of the maturity and broadening network of Benedictine schools was the organization after World War I of a National Benedictine Educational Association. It was unusual in its intercongregational character. It issued an association *Bulletin*, and for over twenty years spearheaded the advancement of excellence in American Benedictine education.

By the middle of the twentieth century, there were over ten monasteries with seminary schools. On the college level, both Conception Abbey in Missouri and St. Joseph Abbey in Covington (Louisiana) boasted of free-standing seminaries. Perhaps the best known of the schools of theology were those at St. Vincent, Latrobe (Pennsylvania), St. Meinrad (Indiana), St. John's, Collegeville (Minnesota), and Mount Angel (Oregon).

Both men and women Benedictines became known for the quality of their secondary education. On the college and university level, monks and sisters pooled their resources to staff colleges in Atchison (Kansas), Lisle (Illinois), Bismarck (North Dakota), and Lacey (Washington).

Women's colleges of St. Benedict and St. Scholastica (St. Joseph and Duluth, Minnesota), and Mount Marty (Yankton, South Dakota), and Mary (Bismarck, North Dakota) attested to the long-term commitment of Benedictine sisters to higher education. Comparable institutions affiliated with monasteries of men included Benedictine College, Atchison (Kansas), Belmont Abbey College, Belmont (North Carolina), St. Anselm College, Manchester (New Hampshire), St. Gregory's College, Shawnee (Oklahoma), and St. Leo's College, St. Leo (Florida). In the decade of the 1990s, an Association of Benedictine Colleges and Universities was formed to promote dialogue and the enhancement of a Benedictine spirit at these schools.

Even more diverse were the Catholic communities being served by Benedictine high schools. By the twentieth century, the majority of American Benedictine communities of men and women staffed some type of secondary school. A great number of these closed their doors in the period of change after Vatican II. However, numerous examples of schools that stood the test of time remained. Notable cases of college preparatory academies run by Benedictine sisters include St. Scholastica, Chicago, and St. Mary's Academy, Nauvoo (Illinois), and Marian Heights Academy, Ferdinand (Indiana). Monasteries at Morristown and Newark (New Jersey), Marmion and St. Procopius (Illinois), Mount Michael, Elkorn (Nebraska), Subiaco (Arkansas), and St. Andrew's, Cleveland (Ohio), all could point to long traditions of running college preparatory schools.

Noteworthy in this regard was the English Benedictine Congregation. The first English Benedictine monastery in the United States was in Portsmouth, Rhode Island. Established under the aegis of Downside Abbey in 1919. After the community's transferral to Fort Augustus Abbey, Scotland, they began a preparatory school in 1926. Another English foundation made in the 1920s from Fort Augustus was St. Anselm's, in Washington, D.C. They began a secondary day school for boys in 1942 that continues today. A third English house was founded from Ampleforth Abbey in 1955 in St. Louis. Like the other two English houses, St. Louis set up a secondary day school for boys.

Woodside Priory in California, originally a member of the Hungarian Congregation of Benedictines and later transferred to the American Cassinese Congregation, maintained a prep school from the time of their arrival in the United States during the late 1950s.

Pastoral Works

In addition to their contributions in the field of Catholic education, American Benedictines distinguished themselves in the field of pastoral ministry. The staffing of a vast number of parishes typified the growth of American monks in their years of growth. Indeed, by the beginning of the twentieth century a sizeable majority of American Benedictine monks were ordained priests. In the second half of the twentieth century, as small parishes were consolidated and priesthood vocations declined, many of these pastoral posts were relinquished.

Already in their early years of growth, a considerable number of Benedictine sisters began work in the medical field, operating hospitals and clinics to provide health care for immigrants. In this instance as well, a large portion of the medical care institutions that were once run by Benedictine communities gave way in the last decades of the twentieth century to corporate control. More typical in later years were community programs of constructing and converting residences for the elderly and infirm, one of the indices of an aging American society at the end of the twentieth century.

Missionary Enterprises

Though the original impetus of American Benedictines was to establish mission stations for German-speaking immigrants, the scope of missionary work broadened by stages.

Especially notable were the number of communities committed to working with the Native Americans. In the nineteenth century, Benedictine monks from the communities of St. Meinrad (Indiana), St. John's (Minnesota), Conception (Missouri), Sacred Heart (Oklahoma), and Mount Angel (Oregon) served missions and schools for a range of Native American tribes. Benedictine sisters from Ferdinand (Indiana), St. Joseph (Minnesota), Yankton (South Dakota), and Mount Angel (Oregon), assisted the monks in their work with the Native Americans, often laboring under primitive conditions.

Two monasteries were founded with the specific intent of ministering to the Native American. One, Sacred Heart Monastery (Oklahoma), was founded by the French Benedictine Isidore Robot in 1876. Robot was named the first prefect apostolic of the Indian Territory. The monastery eventually was transferred to the American Cassinese Congregation and opened St. Gregory College in Shawnee (Oklahoma). In 1950 Blue Cloud Abbey in South Dakota was founded. Not only was its primary pastoral service to the Native American, but it was the only monastery named after a Native American.

The American South, largely devoid of significant Catholic population, was targeted by Boniface Wimmer as a place for early expansion. Monasteries in North Carolina (Belmont), and Alabama (St. Bernard's) were founded by Wimmer, and there followed communities in Florida (St. Leo's), Georgia (Savannah), and Virginia (Richmond). Before the end of the nineteenth century, Swiss-American monks also established monasteries in Arkansas (New Subiaco) and Louisiana (St. Joseph).

The Benedictine sisters were often companions to the monks, with women's communities taking root in Cullman (Alabama), St. Leo (Florida), Covington (Kentucky), Covington (Louisiana), Shoal Creek (Arkansas), and Bristow (Virginia).

As the flow of immigrants changed, so did the complexion of American Benedictines. By the beginning of the twentieth century, Czech communities of Catholics were served by Benedictine houses of men and women around Chicago, and Slovak Catholics had a center in Cleveland with St. Andrew's monastery.

The twentieth century witnessed a widening of missionary work beyond the borders of the United States. The American Cassinese sent monks to China in the 1930s, only to have Japanese occupation and World War II cut short their efforts. Nonetheless, by 1960 there were two foundations of American monks on Taiwan, and one in Tokyo. Benedictine sisters from Minnesota followed in the footsteps of the monks from Peking, China, to Taiwan. Latin America was to have the largest influx of American Benedictines as missionaries. Although an attempt by Boniface Wimmer to found a monastery in Ecuador in the 1880s failed, it anticipated later successful efforts in the twentieth century. After World War II, St. John's Abbey made foundations in Mexico (Tepeyac) and Puerto Rico (San Antonio Abad) that eventually became independent abbeys. Benedictine sisters from Atchison, Kansas, founded a community in Mexico City at the same time. St. Benedict's Abbey (Kansas) and St. Vincent's (Pennsylvania) accepted monastic missions in Brazil shortly after the Mexican foundations. But the real surge of missionary work took place in the early 1960s. In that era, the Swiss-American monks started two communities in Mexico (Cuernavaca and Morelia), three in Guatemala (Esquipulas, Sololá, and Coban), one in Peru and one in Belize. Benedictine sisters made their own foundations in Guatemala, Colombia, and Peru. Cassinese monks also started communities and staffed schools in Colombia (Bogotá) and the Bahamas (Nassau).

Another mode of missionary presence came with the contributions of American Benedictines to AIM (the Alliance for International Monasticism). The United States section of AIM took the lead in the last quarter of the twentieth century, collecting funds and effecting solidarity with the 275 Benedictine and Cistercian monasteries found in Third World countries.

Liturgy

The norms and customs of community worship in the first American Benedictine foundations were essentially derived from the prevailing practices in European houses. Moreover, a pioneer environment for both men and women often dictated that full choral recitation of the Divine Office and musical resources were sacrificed to the expedients of pastoral work.

By the twentieth century, however, American Benedictines became the primary purveyors of what was known in Europe as the liturgical movement. Fr. Virgil Michel, a priest of St. John's Abbey in Minnesota, was the instrumental figure in carrying the principles of the liturgical movement in Europe to the United States. In doing so, it was Michel's peculiar genius to integrate these principles into the social and educational mission of the American Catholic Church. On one hand, Michel's prolific translations and articles on liturgy in the decade of the 1930s popularized the liturgical reform, something that formerly had been the preserve of academicians and ecclesiastics, for a wide segment of the laity. Michel's writings were also imbued with a vision of social justice that incorporated the best aspects of both scholarly research and modern communications. Under his efforts, St. John's became the authoritative voice for the liturgical movement in the United States. The journal *Orate Fratres* (later known as *Worship* magazine) appeared in 1926 and was later expanded by The Liturgical Press and the Popular Liturgical Library.

Michel was not alone in promoting the work of liturgical reform. Another monk, Fr. Michael Ducey, helped organize the "Liturgical Days" (in imitation of the Belgian Benedictine Dom Lambert Beauduin). This led, in turn, to the first National Liturgical Week in October, 1940, held in Chicago under the auspices of the Benedictine Liturgical Conference of the United States. In subsequent years, liturgical weeks were held in St. Paul (Minnesota), St. Meinrad (Indiana), and St. Procopius (Illinois), after which the Benedictine Conference handed on leadership for these annual meetings to the National Liturgical Conference.

Benedictines had also advanced the cause of the recovery of Gregorian chant and polyphony in the first decades of the twentieth century. By the middle of the century, American Benedictines, such as the future abbot primate, Rembert Weakland, promoted a mix of contemporary culture and musical forms to help renew a liturgical music that was rooted in more traditional forms.

Benedictine communities such as Conception Abbey and St. John's Abbey served as designated centers for liturgical experimentation during the years immediately preceding Vatican Council II. American Benedictines also took on a leadership position in the liturgical reform of the council, spearheaded by Fr. Godfrey Diekmann of St. John's Abbey.

In the postconciliar era, a wave of new Benedictine liturgists contributed to liturgical renewal. They included Fr. Aidan Kavanagh of St. Meinrad, Fr. Kilian McDonnell of Collegeville, and Sr. Mary Collins of Atchison (Kansas). In the area of musical composition, Benedictine musicians began meeting in 1966. One of the fruits of their work was the *Benedictine Hymnal*. The Monastic Liturgy Forum, an organization of American Benedictine men and women, formed in 1988, provided yet another vehicle for advancing liturgical life and spirituality within monastic communities and the Church.

Ecumenism

Throughout its early history, an atmosphere of ecumenism was not a prominent feature in American Benedictine life. This is not surprising in an American Catholic Church that saw itself in an adversarial role with the prevailing Protestant ethos. But even when American Catholics found themselves in a combative and apologetic stance toward other religious faiths, Benedictines reflected a broader ecumenical perspective. In the 1920s, the Benedictine community of St. Procopius, Lisle (Illinois), took a first step in facilitating Church unity by accepting the invitation of Pope Pius XI to further dialogue and promote reconciliation with the Eastern-rite Churches. Their work bore fruition in the establishment of Holy Trinity Monastery in Butler, Pennsylvania, in 1948. In 1946 the Anglican Benedictine monastery of Nashdom, England, founded an American house at Three Rivers, Michigan. The monastery of St. Gregory which grew from this foundation eventually became an independent abbey and took an active role in ecumenical exchange with other Catholic American monastic houses. The work of fostering wider ecumenical contacts, undertaken by many communities in an informal manner in the years leading up to Vatican II, was given a formal and institutional status with the erection of the Institute for Ecumenical and Cultural Research at St. John's Abbey, Collegeville, in 1967. Collegeville was one of many monastic sites in America that became favorite settings for ecumenical meetings. One of the other fruits of this ecumenical atmosphere was the attraction of many non-Catholics to become Benedictine lay oblates and integrate monastic spirituality into their writing. The names of Esther De Waal, Eric Dean, Patrick Eastman, Kathleen Norris, and Patrick Henry, are among the most noteworthy examples of non-Catholic lay oblates.

Collegeville's role as a center of ecumenical activity and a responsive voice to pastoral concerns was also seen in the establishment of the Interfaith Sexual Trauma Institute, a result of several meetings with representatives from various religious denominations hosted by the monastic community in the 1990s on the problem of sexual abuse.

An ecumenical development that reached beyond the United States was the North American Board for East-West Dialogue. Established by the Benedictine Confederation in 1978 to assume a leading role in the dialogue between Christianity and the great religions of the East, it fostered conversation and exchange to monastics of Eastern religions. The board changed its name to Monastic Interreligious Dialogue in 1993, continuing its work of understanding and ongoing exchange of resources and information, particularly with the Buddhist tradition.

Scholarship and Spirituality

Largely because of the missionary-oriented character of the first generations of American Benedictines, opportunities for scholarly pursuits and the development of a distinctive spirituality were limited. However, one of the results of those monastic houses involved in the work of higher education was an increasingly skilled group of teachers with advanced degrees. By the middle of the twentieth century, it was commonplace for Benedictine communities to have a number of their members with doctorates in various disciplines. Many communities of monks regularly sent monks to Europe for theological studies, but there were also considerable numbers of those who attended secular universities.

A noted advance in the theological education of Benedictine women came in the 1950s with the establishment of the Benedictine Institute of Sacred Theology at St. Joseph, Minnesota. This anticipated a full-scale involvement of Benedictine sisters in programs of theological education in the period after Vatican Council II. The conciliar mandate for a return to sources prompted houses of women to enlist their members in programs of research and study. The fruits of these efforts were seen in renewal documents such as *Climb Along the Cutting Edge* (1977). The Benedictine community of St. Scholastica in Atchison launched a semiannual periodical, *Benedictines,* that focused on Benedictine spirituality. They also conducted an annual Monastic Institute at their house during the years of renewal in the 1970s and 1980s. The project to prepare an American commentary on the *Rule* of Benedict, *RB 1980,* was ably assisted by an editorial staff that included Srs. Imogene Baker, Augusta Raabe, Raphael Joseph, Elizabeth Mason, Angelo Haspert, and Joan Taylor. Beginning in 1964, Sr. Theresa Doyle, in her position as editor of the *American Benedictine Review,* extended "A Call for Monastic Scholars" that provided a forum for what proved to be an extensive public discussion on the nature of monasticism and the Benedictine charism.

Benedictine men and women took a more active role in the disciplines of biblical studies, patristics, liturgy, Church history, and spirituality in the years of the twentieth century. The immense popularity of the monastic writings of Thomas Merton generated an awareness of American monastic life that continued in the period of religious renewal in the second half of the twentieth century. The *American Benedictine Review,* a scholarly journal sponsored by American Benedictine men and women, was started in 1950. It was intended "to serve as an agency to stimulate and promote the interests and activities of American Benedictines and to cultivate and transmit the best traditions of Benedictine life and scholarship." This journal was a byproduct of the American Benedictine Academy, an organization of American Benedictine monastics that was begun in 1945. Both the *Review* and the Academy continue their work today.

A signal reflection of the vitality of American scholarship came in the form of the publication of a critical English translation and commentary of the *Rule* of Benedict, *RB 1980,* published under the auspices of a consortium of Benedictine scholars in the United States. The more contemplative side of the Benedictine tradition also emerged as a font of scholarly work in this period, as seen in the volumes of the *Cistercian Studies* and *Cistercian Fathers* series of publications and the quarterly journal, *Cistercian Studies.* Benedictine sisters of Petersham (Massachusetts) in the 1980s began St. Bede's Publications, in addition to their yearly *Word and Spirit* magazine, as a means of furthering study of Benedictine spirituality. Typical of the climate in which contemplative monastic living attracted people in the latter part of the twentieth century was the journal *Monastic Studies,* originally a product of Mt. Savior Monastery in New York.

Interest in the study of the Benedictine charism also led to the establishment of a Monastic Studies program at St. John's School of Theology in Collegeville, and an annual summer Monastic Institute which attracted monastic men and women reflecting the entire range of American Benedictines.

With the advent of the Internet and computerized communication in the 1990s, Benedictine communities of men and women incorporated technology into their corporate apostolates and promotional materials. Benedictine communities in the United States, notably the monasteries of Christ in the Desert (New Mexico), Mount St. Benedict (Pennsylvania), and St. John's (Minnesota), were in the vanguard of this new development.

Leadership

From its earliest days, the Benedictine Order in the United States provided outstanding examples of leadership in the American Catholic Church. Boniface Wimmer was not only a charismatic authority figure in his own right, but he could claim a spiritual paternity of numerous abbots and bishops. Bishops Rupert Seidenbusch (St. John's, Minnesota), Louis Fink (St. Benedict's, Kansas), Leo Haid (Belmont, North Carolina) and Martin Marty (St. Meinrad, Indiana) were all influential Benedictine prelates in the nineteenth century. A century later, Benedictines were still prevalent in the nation's hierarchy, with Archbishops Rembert Weakland (St. Vincent's, Pennsylvania-Milwaukee), Daniel Kucera (St. Procopius, Illinois-Dubuque), and Daniel Buechlein (St. Meinrad, Indiana-Memphis and Indianapolis), and Bishops Joseph Gerry (St. Anselm's, New Hampshire-Manchester, New Hampshire and Portland, Maine) and Jerome Hanus (Conception, Missouri-St. Cloud, Minnesota, and Dubuque, Iowa).

For many years, sisters who were superiors of religious communities were some of the few women in the Catholic Church who had an opportunity to exercise leadership. It was not atypical to have some women serve as superior for twenty to thirty years. When combined with a dynamic sense of mission and a clear vision of monastic life in the Church, this could have profound effect. Srs. Lucy Dooley of Atchison (Kansas), and Jerome Hunt of Yankton (South Dakota), are just two examples of superiors whose leadership over several decades in the twentieth century shaped the character of their communities and the Church they served for years to come.

American Benedictine sisters surfaced in a variety of leadership positions in the period after Vatican Council II. Sr. Joan Chittister headed the Leadership Conference of Women Religious and articulated themes of religious renewal and monastic identity for many. The leadership for the Catholic peace organization, Pax Christi, was supplied by Benedictine Sisters of Erie, Pennsylvania, for several decades. Benedictine women also took on prominent roles as advocates of peace and justice issues in the American Catholic Church of the 1970s and 1980s.

Another sign of the maturing of American monasticism was the influence it had beyond the boundaries of the United States. The election of Abbot Rembert Weakland as abbot primate at the Congress of Abbots in 1967 represented a new stage in having an American monk direct the Benedictine Confederation at a crucial juncture in their history. The election of Abbot Jerome Theisen of St. John's Abbey as abbot primate in 1992 and Abbot Marcel Rooney of Conception Abbey in 1996 reaffirmed the capacity for leadership of American Benedictines. In a similar vein, American Benedictine sisters exercised a significant role in directing the dialogue of religious renewal in the postconciliar period, both in the United States and abroad.

Within the renewal process of the second part of the twentieth century, American Benedictines reclaimed and reaffirmed many of their monastic values. They also faced anew the same vital questions that their nineteenth century founders confronted. How to maintain an equilibrium between a life of separation from the world and active ministry in the same world? How to accept the tension of living an enclosed life in a stable monastic community while being responsive to the desire of the Church to draw upon the resources of that same community? How to strike a balance between serving as a spiritual leaven in American culture and not being transformed in turn by the secular ethos of that culture? The representatives of Benedictine life in the United States who answered these questions at the end of the second millennium were at once more diversified, more assimilated, and more grounded in Benedictine identity than their pioneer forebears. But they also were monastics who appreciated the legacy of faith and perseverance that those forebears had passed on to them, one that continues to serve as an effective force in the American Catholic Church.

See also LITURGICAL MOVEMENT IN AMERICA, THE; MONASTICISM IN AMERICA; ST. JOHN'S ABBEY.

Barry, Colman, O.S.B. *Worship and Work.* Collegeville, Minn.: The Liturgical Press, 1994.

Hollermann, Ephrem, O.S.B. *The Reshaping of a Tradition: American Benedictine Women 1852–1881.* Winona, Minn.: St. Mary's Press, 1994.

Oetgen, Jerome. *An American Abbot.* Latrobe, Pa.: Archabbey Press, 1976.

Rippinger, Joel, O.S.B. *The Benedictine Order in the United States: An Interpretive History.* Collegeville, Minn.: The Liturgical Press, 1990.

Sutera, Judith, O.S.B. *True Daughters: Monastic Identity and American Benedictine Women's History.* Atchison, Kans.: Benedictine College Press, 1987.

JOEL RIPPINGER, O.S.B.

Related Document

BONIFACE WIMMER OUTLINES THE FUTURE OF THE BENEDICTINE ORDER IN THE UNITED STATES, NOVEMBER 8, 1845

The origin of the work of the monks of St. Benedict in the United States was owed to Boniface Wimmer (1809–87), one of the first five novices to be received at the Abbey of Metten after its restoration in 1830. This Bavarian-born religious began dreaming about an American foundation for the spiritual care of German immigrants as early as 1843. In 1845 Wimmer discussed the American situation with a fellow countryman, Peter Henry Lemcke (1796–1882), then pastor of a congregation at Carrolltown in western Pennsylvania, on the latter's visit to Munich. He likewise spoke with Canon Josef Salzbacher (1790–1867) of Vienna who had been in the United States three years before, and with the Vienna-born Frederick de Held (1799–1881), provincial of the Belgian province, to which the Redemptorists' American missions were subject. It was a period when there was a great deal of criticism in German and Austrian Catholic circles about the money they gave through the Ludwig-Missionsverein and Leopoldinen Stiftung for their compatriots in the United States, being channeled off to non-German projects by Irish-American bishops. In answer to reports brought back by men like Salzbacher and de Held, Wimmer composed the document that follows and had it published anonymously. Fired by his zeal for the missions in the New World, and having secured the permission of his superiors, Wimmer set out in July 1846, with four ecclesiastical students and fourteen young laymen who desired to embrace the Benedictine life in the United States. Accepting the offer of Michael O'Connor (1810–72), first Bishop of Pittsburgh, to have his little community settle on some church lands in Westmoreland County, he invested his eighteen companions with the religious habit on October 24, 1846, and thus inaugurated his great work. Wimmer opened a college and a seminary in 1848 at St. Vincent's Priory and in August 1855 Pope Pius IX granted his petition and raised his foundation to the rank of

an abbey and at the same time made Wimmer president of the newly founded American congregation of Benedictines. During his forty years of unceasing labors he sent out missionaries from St. Vincent's who founded six future abbeys: St. John's in Minnesota (1856), St. Benedict's in Kansas (1857), Belmont in North Carolina (1876), St. Bernard's in Alabama (1876), St. Procopius in Illinois (1885), and Holy Cross in Colorado (1886), besides numerous smaller missions in parishes in twenty-five states which by 1885 were ministering to over 100,000 souls, especially among German, Irish, and Italian immigrants. By the time he died Wimmer had more than fulfilled the dream about which he had written over forty years before, in a document which is in many ways the charter of the American Benedictines since the aims and methods it embodied were consistently and successfully developed in the United States.

(*Source*: Augsburg *Postzeitung,* November 8, 1845. This document was printed as an appendix in Colman J. Barry, O.S.B., *Worship and Work. St. John's Abbey and University, 1856–1956* Collegeville, 1956, 345–51.)

EVERY CATHOLIC WHO CHERISHES HIS FAITH MUST TAKE A deep interest in missionary labors; but religion as well as patriotism demands that every German Catholic should take a special interest in the missions of America. To us it cannot be a matter of indifference how our countrymen are situated in America. I, for my part, have not been able to read the various and generally sad reports on the desolate condition of Germans beyond the ocean without deep compassion and a desire to do something to alleviate their pitiable condition. Thus, I have given much thought to the question of how they might be practically assisted. It is not difficult to understand what should be done—more German-speaking priests should be found laboring for the spiritual welfare of our countrymen in America. The only question is how to get priests and what kind of priests will do the work most successfully. The answer to the second question will also give the solution for the first. I do not wish to offend anyone, but my opinion is that secular priests are not the best adapted for missionary labors. History shows that the Church has not availed herself of their services to any great extent in missionary undertakings. I do not mean to say that a secular priest cannot labor effectually within a limited territory in America, for there are many who labor successfully even at the present day. But they cannot satisfy themselves. They are in great danger of becoming careless and worldly-minded. I cannot agree with Dr. Salzbacher when he says that the spiritual needs of our countrymen can be provided by perambulating missionaries, who go about like the Wandering Jew from forest to forest, from hut to hut; for unless such a missionary be a *Saint* not much of the spiritual man would remain in him, and even then by such transient visits not much lasting good could be accomplished. The missionary, more than any other priest, stands in need of spiritual renewal from time to time, consolation and advice in trials and difficulties. He must, therefore, have some place where he can find such assistance: this may be given by his bishop but he will find it more securely in a religious community—in the midst of his confrères.

He should also have a home to receive him in his old age or when he is otherwise incapacitated for missionary labors; he should have no worldly cares, otherwise he might neglect or even forget his own and others' spiritual welfare. All this can be had only in a religious community. For this reason, therefore, religious are better adapted to missionary work than secular priests. In a community the experiences of the individual become common property; all have a common interest, stand together and have the same object in view. A vacancy caused by death or otherwise can be filled more readily and having fewer temporal cares, they can devote themselves more exclusively to the spiritual interests of themselves and others. Thus, all other things being equal, a religious priest in a community should be able to work more effectively on the missions than the secular priest who stands alone.

The next question is: What religious Order is most adapted for the American missions, not to convert the native Indians but to provide for the spiritual necessities of German immigrants?

As far as I know the only Religious in the strict sense of the word now found in America are the Jesuits and Redemptorists. The missionaries of the Middle Ages, the Benedictines, Dominicans, and Franciscans are not yet represented in the New World, except by a few individuals who do not live in monasteries.[1] The Jesuits devote their energies principally to teaching in colleges; their students are mostly from the higher classes of society and many of them belong to Protestant families. Many Jesuits are also doing excellent work among the Indians, and others have charge of congregations in cities near their colleges. But while they accomplish so much in their sphere of labors, they can do little for Germans, because few of them speak their language. The Redemptorists are doing noble work for our countrymen in the States: in cities and thickly settled country districts they have large congregations, and also do what they can for others as traveling missionaries. Some secular priests likewise go about among the scattered Catholics doing good, but they naturally and necessarily concentrate in cities where there is a large Catholic population.

We see, therefore, that much is being done in America; very much, indeed, when we consider the small band of priests and the difficulties under which they labor. But as yet nothing has been done for the stability of the work, no provision has been made for an increase of German-speaking priests, to meet the growing demand for missionary laborers. It is not difficult to see that secular priests, whose labors extend over a district larger than a diocese, can do nothing to secure reinforcements to their own number. But why have the Redemptorists and Jesuits not accomplished more in this line? By his vows neither the Jesuit nor the Redemptorist is bound to any particular place, but he must always be prepared to leave his present position at the command of his superiors, and may also request, if not demand, his removal for weighty reasons. This has many advantages, but for America it seems to me also to have disadvantages. For the successor of the one who has been removed will require a long time to become acquainted with all the circumstances with which his predecessor was familiar, and even the uncertainty as to how long he will remain at any particular place will be an obstacle in his way. Moreover, the fact that Jesuits generally receive only the children of richer families, many of whom are Protestants, into their institutions, because they depend upon them for their sustenance, and that the Redemptorists are by their statutes required to devote themselves to missionary work, and can, therefore, not be expected to take charge of seminaries, gives us no reason to hope that the spiritual wants of Americans, particularly of German-Americans will be provided for by native German-speaking priests. And in case the mission societies of Europe should unexpectedly be rendered incapable of supplying money or reinforcements in priests, the situation would become even more serious. But even supposing that everything remains as it is, we cannot hope to have an efficient supply of priests as long as we have no means of securing a native clergy for the United States of America. For the number of those who are educated at Alt-Oetting[2] or elsewhere in Germany is not in proportion to the continually increasing emigration to America, not to speak of the natural increase of Germans in America itself. Jesuits and Redemptorists are, therefore, doing noble work in America and their number should be increased as much as possible; but they will scarcely be able to remove the chief cause of the deficiency of German-speaking priests. We need not speak of the Dominicans and Franciscans; there are very few German Dominicans, and the present social condition of America seems not to call for Mendicant Friars.

We now come to the Benedictines, who are not as yet represented in the United States. In my opinion they are the most competent to relieve the great want of priests in America. In support of my opinion I will adduce some facts: but I must again state that I have not the remotest intention of belittling the efforts and successes of other religious Orders; on the contrary, I am desirous of seeing them labor in the same field, side by side with the Benedictines.

History abundantly proves:

1. That we owe the conversion of England, Germany, Denmark, Sweden, Norway, Hungary, and Poland almost exclusively to the Benedictines, and that in the remaining parts of Europe Christendom is deeply indebted to them.

2. That the conversion of these countries was not transient but lasting and permanent.

3. That this feature must be ascribed to the fact that the Benedictines are men of stability; they are not wandering monks; they acquire lands and bring them under cultivation and become thoroughly affiliated to the country and people to which they belong, and receive their recruits from the district in which they have established themselves.

4. That the Benedictine Order by its Rule is so constituted that it can very readily adapt itself to all times and circumstances. The contemplative and practical are harmoniously blended; agriculture, manual labor, literature, missionary work, education were drawn into the circle of activity which St. Benedict placed before his disciples. Hence they soon felt at home in all parts of Europe and the same could be done in America.

When we consider North America as it is today, we can see at a glance that there is no other country in the world which offers greater opportunities for the establishment and spread of the Benedictine Order, no country that is so much like our old Europe was. There are found immense forests, large uncultivated tracts of land in the interior, most fertile lands which command but a nominal price; often for miles and miles no village is to be seen, not to speak of cities. In country districts no schools, no churches are to be found. The German colonists are scattered, uncultured, ignorant, hundreds of miles away from the nearest German-speaking priest, for, practically, they can make their homes where they please. There are no good books, no Catholic papers, no holy pictures. The destitute and unfortunate have no one to offer them a hospitable roof, the orphans naturally become the victims of vice and irreligion—in a word, the conditions in America today are like those of Europe 1000 years ago, when the Benedictine Order attained its fullest development and effectiveness by its wonderful adaptability and stability.

Of course, the Benedictine Order would be required to adapt itself again to circumstances and begin anew. To acquire a considerable tract of land in the interior of the country, upon which to found a monastery, would not be very difficult; to bring under cultivation at least a portion of the land and to erect the most necessary buildings would give employment for a few years to the first Benedictine colony, which should consist of at least two or three priests and ten to fifteen brothers skilled in the most necessary trades.

Once the colony is self-supporting, which could be expected in about two years, it should begin to expand so that the increased number of laboring hands might also increase the products and revenues to be derived from the estate. A printing and lithographing establishment would also be very desirable.

Since the Holy Rule prescribes for all, not only manual labor and the chanting of the Divine Office, but also that the monks should devote several hours a day to study, this time could be used by the Fathers to instruct the Brothers thoroughly in arithmetic, German grammar, etc., thereby fitting them to teach school, to give catechetical instruction and in general to assist in teaching children as well as grown persons.

Such a monastery would from the very start be of great advantage to German settlers, at least to those who would live near it. They would have a place where they could depend upon hearing Mass on Sundays and hear a sermon in their own language; they would also have a place where they could always be sure to find a priest at home to hear their confessions, to bless their marriages, to baptize their children, and to administer the last sacraments to the sick if called in time.

Occasionally the Superior might send out even the Brothers two by two to hunt up fallen-away Catholics, to instruct children for their first Communion, etc. All subsequent monasteries that might be established from the mother house would naturally exercise the same influence.

So far, the services rendered by the Benedictines would not be extraordinary; any other priests or religious could do the same, except that they would not likely be able to support themselves without assistance from Europe; whereas a community of Benedictines, when once firmly established, would soon become self-sustaining.

But such a monastery if judiciously located would not long remain isolated; all reports from America inform us that the German immigrants are concentrating themselves in places where churches have been erected or where a German-speaking priest has taken up his residence. This would also be found, and to a greater extent, if there were a monastery somewhere with a good school. In a short time a large German population would be found near the monastery, just as in the Middle Ages, villages, towns, and cities sprang up near Benedictine abbeys. Then the monks could expect a large number of children for their school, and in the course of time, as the number of priests increases, a college with a good Latin course could be opened. They would not be dependent upon the tuition fee of the students for their support, which they could draw from the farm and the missions (though these would not be a source of much income in the beginning). Thus they could devote their energies to the education of the poorer classes of boys who could pay little or nothing, and since these boys would daily come in contact with the priests and other monks, it could scarcely be otherwise but that many of them would develop a desire of becoming priests or even religious. I am well aware that to many readers these hopes and expectations will appear too sanguine, since all efforts at securing a native American clergy have hitherto failed so signally. But we must remember that the annals of the missions as well as the oral reports of priests who have labored in America, inform us that these efforts were more theoretical than practical, that there was a desire of making such efforts, but they were not really made, and that those which were really made were more or less restricted to the English-speaking clergy, and that in general there were neither sufficient means nor sufficient teachers to train a native German-speaking clergy. It is said that the young American is not inclined to devote himself to the sacred ministry because it is so easy for him to secure a wife and home; that the American has nothing in view but to heap up the riches of this world; that fathers need their sons on the farms or in the workshops and, therefore, do not care to see them study. But, let me ask, is it not the same here in Europe? Are the rich always pleased when their sons study for the priesthood? Are all Germans in America well-to-do or rich? Are they not as a rule the very poorest and to a certain extent the menials of the rest? Moreover, is the first thought of a boy directed to matrimony? Is it any wonder that he should show no inclination for the priesthood when he sees a priest scarcely once a year; when divine services are held in churches which resemble hovels rather than churches, without pomp and ceremony, when the priest has to divest himself of his priestly dignity, often travels on horse-back, in disguise, looking more like a drummer than a priest, when the boy sees nothing in the life of a priest but sacrifice, labor, and fatigue?

But all this would become quite different if boys could come in daily contact with priests, if they received instructions from them, if the priest could appear to advantage, better dressed and better housed than the ordinary settler, if young men could learn from observation to realize and appreciate the advantages of a community life, if they could learn to understand that while the life of a priest requires self-denial and sacrifice, his hopes of a great reward are also well grounded. Yes, I do not doubt but that hundreds, especially of the lower classes, would prefer to spend their lives in well regulated monasteries in suitable and reasonable occupations, than to gain a meager livelihood by incessant hard labor in forest regions. Let us remember that here in Bavaria from the year 740 to the year 788 not less than 40 Benedictine monasteries were founded and the communities were composed almost entirely of natives from the free classes, who had enjoyed the advantages of freedom in the world and could have chosen the married state without any difficulty or hindrance. Why should we not reasonably expect the same results in the United States where the conditions are so similar?

But such a monastery in North America would not draw its recruits exclusively from the surrounding country, but also from the great number of boys, who either during the voyage or soon after their arrival in America lose their parents and thereby become helpless and forsaken. An insti-tution, in which such unfortunate children could find a home, would undoubtedly be a great blessing for that country. And where could this be done more easily than in Benedictine monasteries as described above, in which young boys could not only attend school, but also do light work on the farm or in the workshops and according to their talents and vocation become priests or at least educated Christians and good citizens. Surely, many of these would gladly join the community as brothers or priests, and thus repay the monastery for the trouble of educating them.

In this way a numerous religious clergy could soon be secured, and then some of the Fathers might be sent out to visit those Catholics who scarcely ever see a priest; occasionally at least they might preach the word of God and bring the consolations of religion even to those who live at a great distance from the monastery; small congregations could be established, and the seminary could soon furnish a goodly number of the secular clergy.

But where could the Benedictines be found to establish such a monastery in North America, and where are the necessary means for such an undertaking? The writer is informed that there are several Fathers in the Benedictine Order here in Bavaria who would gladly go upon such a mission, and with regard to Brothers there would be no difficulty whatever; within a few years not less than 200 good men have applied for admission into one of our monasteries. It is a well known fact that of those who are studying for the priesthood many are joining the Redemptorist Order simply because it offers them the hope of becoming missionaries in America.

The necessary funds could easily be supplied by the Louis Mission Society.[3] Bavaria annually pays 100,000 florins into the treasury of this Society. Would it be unfair to devote one tenth of this sum to the establishment of monasteries in America, especially since just now hundreds of our own nationality are seeking homes in the United States, and consequently the money contributed would be used to further the interests of Germans in general and our countrymen in particular? Could a better use of such contributions be made or could anything appeal more loudly to our national patriotism? Is it right that we should continually look after the interests of strangers and forget our own countrymen? Moreover, whatever would be done for the Germans would advance the well-being of the entire Church in America. We must not stifle our feelings of patriotism. The Germans, we hear it often enough, lose their national character in the second or third generation, they also lose their language, because like a little rivulet they disappear in the mighty stream of the Anglo-American population in the States. Is this not humiliating for us Germans? Would this sad condition of affairs continue if here and there a German center were established, to which the stream of emigration from our country could be systematically directed, if German instruction and sermons were given by priests going forth from these centers, if German books, papers, and periodicals were distributed among the people, if German boys could receive a German education and training, which would make themselves felt in wider circles?

Let us, therefore, no longer build air castles for our countrymen in America. Let us provide for their religious interests, then their domestic affairs will take care of themselves. Benedictine monasteries of the old style are the best means of checking the downward tendencies of our countrymen in social, political, and religious matters. Let Jesuits and Redemptorists labor side by side with the Benedictines; there is room enough for all and plenty of work. If every Religious Order develops a healthy activity within its sphere, the result will be doubly sure and great. North America will no longer depend upon Europe for its spiritual welfare, and the day may come when America will repay us just as England, converted by the Benedictines, repaid the continent of Europe.

[1] Wimmer was unaware that Edward D. Fenwick, O.P. (1768–1832), first Bishop of Cincinnati, had opened St. Rose Priory near Springfield, Kentucky, as the first Dominican convent in the United States as early as December 1806.

[2] Wimmer was doubtless referring here to the seminary for candidates to the diocesan priesthood at Altötting, permission for which he had received from King Ludwig I of Bavaria. Altötting was the site of a popular shrine to our Lady where Wimmer had served as an assistant priest for a short time.

[3] The Ludwig-Missionsverein was founded in Munich in December, 1838, to assist German Catholic emigrants. Between 1842 and 1922 the society contributed $886,504.52 to the Catholic missions in the United States.

(*Source:* John Tracy Ellis, ed. *Documents of American Catholic History*. Vol. 1:1493–1865. Wilmington, Del.: Michael Glazier, 1987, 279–88.)

BENDIK, CRESCENTIA (1901–82)

Religious educator and superior. Sr. Crescentia was born Catherine Mary Bendik on October 28, 1901, in Plymouth, Pennsylvania, in the heart of the state's anthracite coal mining district. On January 9, 1916, while still a teenager, Catherine cast her lot with the Sisters of SS. Cyril and Methodius, a pioneer community not yet seven years old founded to educate Slovak immigrant children in American ways while preserving their rich heritage of faith. During her sixty-three years of service to the Church, Sr. Crescentia grew with the community in broadening its charism in the Church.

As general superior from 1946–58, prior to Vatican II, Sr. Crescentia already initiated spiritual reform within her community by emphasizing personal responsibility in prayer, in professional development, and in concern for the larger Church and world. She encouraged the pursuit of theological studies and was on the cutting edge of preparing sisters for geriatric ministry.

Though founded primarily to minister to Slovak peoples, under her aegis the first sisters responded to requests beyond ethnic boundaries. They were the first seven "Northern sisters" to minister to the people of South Carolina, at St. Patrick's, Charleston. In the North, they also ministered in territorial parishes. They coped with objections from Slovak-American pastors and parishioners who complained of "abandonment."

Sr. Crescentia's keen interest in ecumenical, civic, and social issues, as well as in biblical studies and the charismatic movement never waned, even in her "retirement" years where, at Villa St. Cyril, Highland Park, Illinois (the home for the aged she had founded in 1957), she implemented new models of pastoral caring. On August 8, 1982, Sr. Crescentia died unexpectedly in the midst of those who came to see in her a model of "living life to the full" in spite of declining health and limited resources.

PARACLETA AMRICH, SS.C.M.

BENSON, WILLIAM SHEPHERD (1891–1957)

Admiral. He was born on a plantation in Bibb County, Georgia, on September 25, 1891. He chose a naval career and graduated from the U.S. Naval Academy in 1877. He married Mary Augusta Wyse in 1879. Benson served on various naval missions and taught at the academy in 1890–93. He commanded the midshipmen there in 1907–08 and was promoted to captain. In 1913–15 he was appointed commandant of the Philadelphia Naval Yard, and then became the first chief of naval operations and a rear admiral; and was promoted to admiral in 1916. In 1917 he was awarded the Laetare Medal. He was naval advisor to the U.S. peace commissioner in Paris in 1919. On his retirement, Benson—a convert in early life and a devout Catholic during his career—became active in Catholic causes. He was chosen as the first president of the National Council of Catholic Men in 1921–25. He died in Washington, D.C., on May 20, 1957.

MICHAEL GLAZIER

BENTIVOGLIO, ANNA MARIA (MADDALENA) (1834–1905)

Foundress. Born in Rome on July 29, 1834, her education was at Trinità dei Monti and at a convent school in Turin. In July 1864, at age thirty, she followed two of her sisters into the Poor Clare monastery of San Lorenzo in Panisperna (Rome) and chose the name Maria Maddalena of the Sacred Heart. In 1874 the monastery was visited by Mother Ignatius Hayes, of the Third Order Regular of St. Francis, who, with the approval of the bishop of St. Paul, was intent on establishing a Poor Clare convent in Belle Prairie, Minnesota. Maddalena and her blood sister Costanza accepted the invitation. Prior to leaving Rome, the Bentivoglio sisters had an audience with Pius IX, who encouraged them to be faithful to their mission of establishing a cloister of Poor Clares of the Primitive Observance in America. M. Maddalena, at the same time, was appointed abbess of the new foundation. Together with Mother Hayes, they left on September 27, 1875, and arrived in New York City on October 12, 1875.

Difficulties

Circumstances, however, changed on their arrival, and since their Franciscan spiritual director, who had traveled with them, had advised them not to proceed to Minnesota, M. Maddalena wrote to the Franciscan minister general in Rome for new instructions. The answer came in June 1876: abandon Minnesota and try to establish a foundation in New York. The two sisters then approached John Cardinal McCloskey of New York, but were told that their way of life was against the spirit of the country. They next visited (August 1876) Archbishop James Wood of Philadelphia and received a similar response. The bishops wanted teachers and nurses and not contemplatives. Informed of their rejection in Philadelphia, Archbishop Napoleon Perché of New Orleans invited them to his diocese, where they arrived on March 11, 1877. When the Franciscan visitor to the convent judged New Orleans too humid, and complained that the sisters did not have their own Franciscan chaplain, he directed (July 1877) the community to transfer to Cleveland, where they were to merge with a group of Poor Clare Colettines. As long as M. Maddalena followed the Colletine constitutions and customs, she realized she could not fulfill her mission of establishing a cloister of the Primitive Observance in America and, hence, she and her group, after six months in Cleveland, left (February 1878) for New York.

Foundations

In response to an invitation from Bishop O'Connor in Omaha, the sisters went there and succeeded (September 1878) in founding their first stable community. With the increase of vocations, a daughter house was established in New Orleans in 1885, and another in Evansville (Indiana) in 1897. To this latter M. Maddalena went and remained until her death on August 18, 1905. In view of her reputation for holiness, the cause for her beatification was introduced in Rome in 1969.

See also WOMEN RELIGIOUS IN AMERICA.

Barth, Pius J., O.F.M. "With Light Step and Unstumbling Feet: Mother Maria Maddalena Bentivoglio, O.S.C. (1834–1905)." *Portraits in American Sanctity*, Joseph N. Tylenda. Chicago: Franciscan Herald, 1982, 222–34.

Cicognani, Amleto. "Mother Mary Magdalen Bentivoglio, Foundress of the Poor Clares in the United States." *Sanctity in America*. Paterson, N.J.: St. Anthony Guild, 1945, 151–56.

Zarrella, Mary Alice. *I Will . . . God's Will: A Biography of Mother Mary Magdalena Bentivoglio, O.S.C., Foundress of the Poor Clares in the United States*. Evansville, Ind.: Poor Clare Monastery Press, 1975.

JOSEPH TYLENDA, S.J.

BERNARDIN, JOSEPH CARDINAL (1928–96)

Cardinal archbishop of Chicago. Joseph Louis Bernardin was born on April 2, 1928, in Columbia, South Carolina, the son of Maria (Simion) and Joseph Bernardin, who had immigrated the previous year to the United States from Tonadico di Primiero in northern Italy. He and his younger sister, Elaine, attended Catholic and public schools in Columbia. When their father, a stonecutter, died when Joseph was six years old, they were raised by their mother.

After a year of premed studies at the University of South Carolina, Bernardin entered the seminary and studied at St. Mary's College in Kentucky, St. Mary's Seminary in Maryland, and at The Catholic University of America in Washington. He was ordained a priest of the Diocese of Charleston by Bishop John J. Russell on April 26, 1952. During his fourteen years as priest in South Carolina, Fr. Bernardin served under four bishops in many capacities, including chancellor and vicar general. With Bishop Ernest Unterkoefler, Bernardin attended the fourth session of the Second Vatican Council where he sat among the *periti*.

Joseph Cardinal Bernardin

In 1966 Pope Paul VI appointed Bernardin auxiliary bishop of the Archdiocese of Atlanta. Upon his episcopal ordination on April 26, 1966, with Archbishop Paul J. Hallinan, his first important mentor, as principal consecrator, Bernardin became the youngest bishop in the country. In

Atlanta he served as vicar general and rector of the Cathedral of Christ the King. In 1968 Bishop Bernardin was elected general secretary of the National Conference of Catholic Bishops and the United States Catholic Conference by the administrative bodies of those conferences. The bishops were reorganizing the episcopal conference according to the norms established by the Second Vatican Council, and Bishop Bernardin served as coordinator of the reorganization until the latter part of 1972.

In November 1972, Pope Paul VI appointed Bernardin archbishop of Cincinnati. He served the Ohio metropolitan see for nearly ten years. In November, 1974, his fellow bishops elected him president of the NCCB/USCC, a position he held until November 1977. In November 1980, he was appointed chair of an ad hoc committee of bishops that drafted the pastoral letter, "The Challenge of Peace," noteworthy both for its conclusions and the widespread consultation that led to the final draft being approved by all the bishops in May 1983. In recognition of his work on this committee, he received the 1983 Albert Einstein Peace Award.

Archbishop of Chicago

On July 10, 1982, Pope John Paul II appointed Bernardin archbishop of Chicago, a see left vacant by the death of John Cardinal Cody. The new archbishop immediately began to bring needed healing and reconciliation to that local Church. He set the tone at his first meeting with his priests, telling them "I am Joseph, your brother." He worked hard to restore unity and confidence in the archdiocese, established new consultative bodies and a collaborative style of leadership, and strengthened archdiocesan finances. He established the Big Shoulders Fund, which raised sixty-two million dollars in ten years for archdiocesan inner-city schools. He also closed or consolidated several parishes and schools.

During the consistory of February 2, 1983, the Holy Father made Bernardin a cardinal with the titular Church of Jesus the Divine Worker in Rome. In an address at Fordham University later that year, Cardinal Bernardin, then chair of the bishops' Pro-Life Activities Committee, articulated the need for a "consistent ethic of life," a concept that he continued to develop through the years. Acknowledging that each of the "life-issues"–affecting human life from conception to natural death and in all its circumstances–is distinct, Bernardin also demonstrated a linkage among such issues as abortion and assisted suicide, poverty, and health care. The U.S. episcopal conference adopted the Consistent Ethic of Life as the basis for its Respect Life Program from 1985 on.

As archbishop of Chicago, Cardinal Bernardin issued pastoral letters on the liturgy (1984), ministry (1985), the Church (1989), and health care (1995), as well as a pastoral reflection on Jesus and his meaning for Christian life (1985), and pastoral statements on religious education (1986), the AIDS crisis (1986), the Catholic Charismatic Renewal (1988), the permanent diaconate (1993), and an archdiocesan parish sharing program (1996).

Cardinal Bernardin served on several curial groups, including the Congregation for Sacraments and Divine Worship, the Congregation for the Evangelization of Peoples, and the Pontifical Council for Promoting Christian Unity. He was one of four elected NCCB delegates to the Synod of Bishops held in Rome in 1974, 1977, 1980, 1983, 1987, 1990, and 1994. Beginning in 1974, he was elected five times to serve on the fifteen-member Council of the Secretariat of the Synod, serving in that capacity for sixteen years before being reelected in 1994.

Cardinal Bernardin was widely recognized as a man of prayer and deep faith. His integrity, honesty, equanimity, and courage in the face of adversity became increasingly clear. Despite the fact that he became a leader in the Catholic Church's response to clerical sexual misconduct, in November 1993, Cardinal Bernardin himself was falsely accused of sexual misconduct by Steven Cook, a young man with AIDS who had been a seminarian in Cincinnati while Bernardin was archbishop there. The humiliating charges, immediately broadcast throughout the world, were withdrawn by Cook the next spring. In December 1984 the Cardinal and his accuser were reconciled in Philadelphia.

In June 1995 Cardinal Bernardin's doctors discovered that he had pancreatic cancer. The resulting surgery and treatment slowed down but did not bring to a halt his pastoral ministry, which he resumed as quickly and as fully as possible. Late in 1995 he began to experience severe, constant pain in his back because of two spinal conditions unrelated to the cancer. In mid-August 1996 he announced the establishment of a Catholic Common Ground Project designed to engage Catholics in a dialogue about various topics of disagreement within the Church but within the boundaries of ecclesial teaching. Two weeks later, Bernardin learned that the cancer had spread to his liver and was inoperable. On September 9, ten days after announcing that he had terminal cancer, Cardinal Bernardin received the Medal of Freedom, the highest U.S. civilian honor, at the White House. Cardinal Bernardin died on November 14, 1996.

Bernardin, Joseph Cardinal, and others. *The Consistent Ethic of Life.* Kansas City, 1988.
____. *The Gift of Peace.* Chicago: Loyola University Press, 1997 (published posthumously).
Kennedy, Eugene. *Cardinal Bernardin.* Chicago, 1989.
____. *This Man Bernardin.* Photography by John H. White. Chicago, 1996.
Wall, A.E.P. *The Spirit of Cardinal Bernardin.* Chicago, 1983.

ALPHONSE P. SPILLY, C.PP.S.

BIENVILLE, JEAN BAPTISTE LE MOYNE (1680–1767)

Explorer, colonial governor. The eighth son of a Canadian pioneer ennobled by Louis XIV for his great service to the crown, Jean himself joined the French Navy at the age of twelve. Wounded in battle at seventeen, he accompanied his older brother Pierre on an expedition to rediscover the mouth of the Mississippi and found a French colony there. The first settlement was made at Old Biloxi in 1699, and in 1701 Jean succeeded to the command of the colony, which he moved to Mobile Bay a year later. Bienville had great skill in conciliating the native tribes of the area, due partly to his skill in languages. But he needed workers for his colony and suggested that Indian War captives be exchanged in the West Indies for black slaves.

In 1712 Louis XIV granted Louisiana to a new company and Bienville was replaced as governor by Cadillac. In 1716 Cadillac sent him to fight the Natchez whom he reduced to obedience. Then in 1717 a company founded by John Law, a financier, took over the colony and restored Bienville to command of the province. In 1718 New Orleans was founded by him and became the capital in 1722. The wild speculation which had begun with John Law's takeover led to the bursting of the "Mississippi Bubble," and the flight of Law. Bienville continued as governor and promulgated the "Black Code," a series of restrictive regulations on blacks. In 1723 war with the Natchez tribe broke out again and lack of support from the company brought ruin upon him. He was summoned to France and deprived of all offices, but recalled in 1733 to quell the Natchez. Finally in 1740 an indecisive peace was reached and Bienville returned to Paris where he spent his declining years until his death in 1767.

JAMES HALEY

BISHOP, WILLIAM HOWARD (1885–1953)

Founder and superior general of the Glenmary Home Missioners. William Howard Bishop was born in Washington, D.C., on December 19, 1885. He was educated at Harvard University (1906–08) and St. Mary's Seminary, Baltimore (1908–15). He became pastor of St. Louis parish, Clarksville, Maryland (1917–37) a rural community which included ministry at St. Mary's chapel in Doughoregan Manor, the ancestral home of Charles Carroll, the Catholic signer of the Declaration of Independence. With the help of the Catholic Daughters of the Americas he founded and headed the League of St. Louis (1922) to support a parochial school; it became the League of the Little Flower (1924), an archdiocesan organization to supervise funding of catechetical programs and parochial education in rural parishes. He was founder and editor of its quarterly publication, *The Little Flower* (1927–37).

He was a founding member of the National Catholic Rural Life Conference (NCRLC) in 1923 and was its president (1928–34). He founded and edited the NCRLC journal *Landward* (1930), a quarterly dedicated to a back-to-the-land movement. His mission strategies were articulated in a program of pastoral activism. In opposition to rural anti-Catholic prejudice he urged enlightened cooperation; against capitalist exploitation of the land he urged the state to promote the widest possible distribution of productive property; in response to urban employment he advocated rural colonization, cooperative ownership of small factories, and domestic craft industry. He unsuccessfully attempted to form a colony of unemployed in Clarksville, one imbued with Catholic distributist ideals and open to people of all or no religious traditions. As a rural pastor he departed from a parish model that fostered Catholic separatism.

W. Howard Bishop

In 1935 he designed a plan for a religious community of Catholic rural missionaries. Influenced by the rural-mission experiences of Thomas F. Price, the missionary bands of diocesan priests promoted by the Paulists and by the foreign mission thrusts of Maryknoll, Bishop's plan was a direct-action evangelization to convert the unchurched in the rural areas through "camp meetings" led by a team of missioners who would articulate Catholicity and establish mission parishes in the hundreds of counties in rural America that he referred to as "no priest land." With the support of the founder-superior of Maryknoll, James A. Walsh, M.M., and Archbishop John T. McNicholas, O.P., of Cincinnati, the Home Missioners of America were founded in 1939. Later called the Glenmary Home Missioners, the society was composed of priests, brothers, and sisters, who later formed a separate community. In 1938 Bishop founded *The Challenge,* the society's publication. When Bishop died in Glendale, Ohio, on June 11, 1953, there were seven rural missions, twenty-one priests, eleven brothers, and twenty-nine sisters.

See also GLENMARY HOME MISSIONERS, THE.

Howard Bishop's personal papers, diaries, and correspondence are located at the Glenmary Archives in Cincinnati.

Kauffman, Christopher J. *Mission to Rural America: The Story of W. Howard Bishop, Founder of Glenmary.* Mahwah, New Jersey, 1991.

Stanten, Herman W. *Howard Bishop, Founder of the Glenmary Home Missions.* Cincinnati, 1961.

CHRISTOPHER J. KAUFFMAN

BLACK CATHOLIC CONGRESSES

Between 1889 and 1894 African American Catholics organized five national congresses. The chief architect of the first congress was Daniel A. Rudd of Cincinnati, an African American layman who was the owner and editor of the *American Catholic Tribune,* the country's only black Catholic newspaper. After attending the conventions of several white American Catholic societies, Rudd suggested the idea of holding a black Catholic congress in his newspaper in the spring of 1888. He received favorable responses from a number of black Catholic leaders, and he also secured the approval and support of Archbishop Henry Elder of Cincinnati, Fr. John Slattery, S.S.J., and Cardinal James Gibbons of Baltimore.

The first black Catholic Congress met in Washington, D.C., January 1–4, 1889, attended by eighty-five delegates, most of whom came from Washington, Maryland, and Pennsylvania. The opening ceremony was a Mass at St. Augustine's Church celebrated by Fr. Augustus Tolton, the first African American priest in the United States, at which the preacher was Cardinal Gibbons, who urged caution and moderation. "Remember the eye of the whole country is upon you," said the cardinal. "It is not the eye of friendship, but . . . criticism." A highlight of the congress was a White House reception given to two hundred participants by President Grover Cleveland. Before adjourning the delegates approved an "Address of the Congress to their Fellow Catholic Citizens" in which they called upon white Catholics to combat racial discrimination both in American society and in the American Catholic Church.

Over the next five years four other congresses were held: June 8–10, 1890, in Cincinnati; January 5–7, 1892, in Philadelphia; September 4–8, 1893, in Chicago; and October 8–11, 1894, in Baltimore. At each of these congresses the issue of racial discrimination was raised with particular emphasis on the exclusion of African Americans from Catholic schools and colleges. At the fourth congress in 1893 the delegates established a committee of grievances which sent a questionnaire to each bishop inquiring about racial discrimination in Catholic churches and institutions. At the same congress an attempt was made to organize a permanent black Catholic organization, St. Peter Claver's Catholic Union, but the organization met with only limited success.

After the first congress, the influence of Rudd waned, and the leadership of the congresses passed into the hands of a small group of dedicated black laymen (many of them converts) who included Charles H. Butler of Washington, D.C., Robert L. Ruffin of Boston, Dr. William Lofton of Washington, D.C., Frederick L. McGhee of St. Paul, James Alexander Spencer of Charleston, South Carolina, and Robert Wood of New York. The fifth congress in 1893 could muster only 38 delegates in contrast to the 85 who had attended the first congress six years earlier and the 125 who were present at the second congress in 1890. After 1894 no further congresses were held for almost a century, until the National Black Catholic Congress met in Washington, D.C., May 21–24, 1987.

Various reasons have been suggested for the demise of the black Catholic Congresses such as the hierarchy's suspicion of lay initiative, internal divisions between Southern and Northern blacks, and the general sense of hopelessness among African Americans after the *Plessy v. Ferguson* decision of the U.S. Supreme Court in 1896 sanctioning racial segregation under the "separate but equal" rubric. However, Cyprian Davis regards the congresses as a success, not a failure, because they revealed the existence of capable and dedicated lay leaders in the American Catholic black community at a time when black priests were virtually nonexistent, and they paved the way for future black Catholic movements in the United States.

See also AFRICAN AMERICAN CATHOLICS.

Davis, Cyprian, O.S.B. *The History of Black Catholics in the United States.* New York, 1990, 163–94.

Spalding, Thomas W., C.F.X. "The Negro Catholic Congresses, 1889–1894." *Catholic Historical Review* 55 (October 1969) 337–57.

THOMAS J. SHELLEY

BLACK ELK (1866–1950)

Holy Man of the Oglala. Black Elk entered the public forum through John Neihardt's classic *Black Elk Speaks: Being the Life-story of a Holy Man of the Oglala Sioux* (1932). Joseph Epes Brown then reported the man's reflections on Lakota (Sioux) religious tradition in *The Sacred Pipe: Black Elk's Account of the Seven Rites of the Oglala Sioux* (1953). These books became fonts of inspiration for Native American religious and cultural resurgence, and have been the most widely read works dealing with Native America.

Black Elk seemed to embody the different stereotypes related to native people of the pre-reservation era. Defeated warrior, saddened elder, wilderness ascetic, native ecologist, and religious philosopher, Black Elk appeared to be a paralyzed victim of Western subjugation. A large reading audience received the portrait of a man who seemed to be a relic of the past, and prisoner of irreconcilably foreign ways.

He was a young boy in Montana at "Custer's last stand" (the battle of Little Big Horn) in 1876, and a participant in the Ghost Dance movement which ended tragically at South Dakota's Wounded Knee massacre in 1890. Neihardt's text implied that this latter event was the "end of the trail" for Black Elk's people while Brown's work suggested the rebirth of traditional Lakota religion would be a hopeful answer to the holy man's lifelong prayer.

Black Elk's early years were happy ones, while his last years were thought to have been tearfully endured (since nothing specific was noted about his later life in either book). Presumably, he typified the experience of all native people who moved on a markerless path from nomadic to sedentary ways. By providing commentary for the transcripts upon which *Black Elk Speaks* was based, *The Sixth Grandfather* (1984) illumined much of the holy man's life that previously had not been told.

Michael F. Steltenkamp's *Black Elk: Holy Man of the Oglala* (1993) showed that the Lakota patriarch had been significantly misrepresented. This work fleshed out the many years not treated in previous literature as it captured the recollections of his only surviving child, Lucy Looks Twice. She reported that Black Elk converted to Catholicism in 1904,

Black Elk (1947)

and was ardent in this practice until death. She said that his religious ideology was not being correctly interpreted by persons only familiar with the published material on his life. Joined by people who knew the holy man personally (and who substantiate and expand her recollections), Lucy felt obliged to "set the record straight" for younger people who she felt were receiving incorrect information about the religious experience of her father's generation.

Black Elk was known (at least among his people) as the zealous "catechist" who both lived and preached the gospel. Using his baptismal name "Nicholas," or "Nick" (after the saint on whose feast he was baptized, December 6), he prepared people for baptism, led prayer meetings, organized social activities for the Catholic population, and served as a missionary to other reservations. Contributors to this latter work saw the importance of illuminating these many years of the man's life, and by doing so, produced an essential companion volume that completed a trilogy of Black Elk portraits. Their effort thus became the definitive biography of one of the world's most famous religious figures.

See also NATIVE AMERICANS AND THE CATHOLIC CHURCH.

Brown, Joseph Epes. *The Sacred Pipe*. Norman: University of Oklahoma Press, 1953.

DeMallie, Raymond J. *The Sixth Grandfather*. Lincoln: University of Nebraska Press, 1984.

Neihardt, John G. *Black Elk Speaks*. New York: Pocket Book Edition, 1972 [reprint].

Steltenkamp, Michael F. *Black Elk: Holy Man of the Oglala*. Norman: University of Oklahoma Press, 1993.

MICHAEL F. STELTENKAMP, S.J.

BLANC, ANTOINE (1792–1860)

First archbishop of New Orleans. Antoine Blanc was born in Sury-le-Comtal, Department of the Loire, France, on October 11, 1792, son of Laurent Blanc and Jeanne Pinand Blanc. He attended the Petit Séminaire in Verrières and St. Irenaeus Grand Séminaire in Lyons where his classmates included Jean Marie Vianney, Jean Claude Colin, and Marcellin Champagnat. He was ordained at Lyons on July 22, 1816, by Bishop Louis William DuBourg of Louisiana.

On September 4, 1817, Blanc arrived in Maryland and was temporarily "loaned" to the Bardstown diocese. He served at Vincennes (1817–20), Natchez, where he was the only priest in Mississippi (1820), Pointe Coupee, Louisiana (1820–26), and Baton Rouge (1826–31). J. Edgar Bruns observed that these years of Blanc's American formation "awakened in him a total awareness of the great potential of this nation, its people, and the role of the Church in it" (Bruns, 122).

In 1831 Blanc was called to New Orleans as vicar general. At the death of Bishop Léo de Neckère in 1833, Blanc

Antoine Blanc

became one of two diocesan administrators. In 1835 he was named bishop of New Orleans and was consecrated on November 22, at St. Louis Cathedral. He immediately convoked the clergy, stressing education and evangelization. On July 19, 1850, the province of New Orleans was established with Blanc as its first archbishop. He received the pallium in New Orleans on February 16, 1851. He was made an assistant at the pontifical throne in 1854.

Blanc visited his vast diocese by "river packet, pirogue, carriage, horseback and afoot" (Henry C. Bezou, *A Dictionary of Louisiana Biography,* s.v. "Blanc, Antoine"). His long tenure, including 1833–35, witnessed an unparalleled growth in Louisiana Catholicism. The number of churches and chapels grew from 22 to 64, the number of priests from 24 to 92, the number of religious communities from 3 to 12, including the Jesuits who returned to Louisiana in 1837. By 1860 the archdiocese included a seminary, first established at Assumption (1838); two colleges for boys; eight academies for girls; about ten free schools; two hospitals; seven orphanages; three homes for the aged; a home for delinquent girls; and the first diocesan paper, *Le Propagateur Catholique* (1842). In addition, the Diocese of Natchitoches in north Louisiana numbered seventeen priests, nineteen churches, and seven schools.

Blanc engaged in a lengthy (1837–44), public, and often bitter conflict with the St. Louis Cathedral churchwardens over his authority to appoint a cathedral pastor; the Louisiana Supreme Court ruled in Blanc's favor on June 8, 1844. Through his vicar general, Etienne Rousselon, he encouraged the establishment of the Sisters of the Holy Family, a community of African American sisters who labored among "God's poor." With strong Irish support, he weathered the attacks of nativists and Know-Nothings.

Blanc attended the First Plenary Council of Baltimore (1852); was present in Rome for the proclamation of the dogma of the Immaculate Conception (December 8, 1854); and presided over the First and Second Provincial Councils of New Orleans (1856, 1860).

Blanc guided the reestablishment of the Church in the newly independent (1836) Texas Republic, calling upon Frs. John Timon and Jean Marie Odin to visit, report on, and minister to the widely scattered communities. He saw the Diocese of New Orleans diminished in size with the creation of the Dioceses of Natchez, Mississippi (July 28, 1837), and Natchitoches (July 2, 1853), although he had to administer the Mississippi Church on several occasions.

Blanc's leadership manifested itself in many ways: his long pastoral visits to establish and nourish outlying communities; his courageous defense of the Church's role and rights in a pluralist, democratic society; his ability to attract personnel and other needed resources; his fatherly concern and support for priests and religious; his willingness to spend time ministering to individuals in need; his devotion to a diocesan seminary for training and enculturating needed clergy; his belief in and support for education as the key to rebuilding Louisiana Catholicism; and his ability to select and work with extraordinary collaborators.

Blanc died on June 20, 1860, and was buried in St. Louis Cathedral. Roger Baudier thus began a proposed biography: "Monsieur Blanc was a man of Providence, destined to turn the tide of indifference, anti-clericalism and irreligion . . . and to establish finally, after the collapse of the colonial religious efforts, the Church solidly and expand it most remarkably."

See also LOUISIANA, CATHOLIC CHURCH IN.

Blanc Papers in New Orleans Collection, Archives of the University of Notre Dame, and Archives of the Archdiocese of New Orleans (AANO).

Baudier, Roger. *The Catholic Church in Louisiana.* New Orleans, 1939.

Bruns, J. Edgar. "Antoine Blanc: Louisiana's Joshua in the Land of Promise He Opened." *Cross, Crozier and Crucible: A Volume Celebrating the Bicentennial of a Catholic Diocese in Louisiana.* Lafayette, Louisiana, 1993.

Manuscripts of incomplete biographies of Blanc by Roger Baudier and J. Edgar Bruns in AANO.

Nolan, Charles E. "Archbishop Antoine Blanc and the Growth of Louisiana Catholicism." Presentation to the Louisiana Historical Association, March 18, 1994 (copy in AANO).

CHARLES E. NOLAN

BLANCHET, AUGUSTIN MAGLOIRE (1797–1887)

First bishop of Walla Walla and brother of Archbishop François Blanchet. Augustin Blanchet was born in St. Pierre, Rivière-du-Sud, Quebec, on August 22, 1797. He was edu-

Augustin M. Blanchet

cated at the Quebec seminary and was ordained a priest on June 3, 1821. He served as a missionary to the Madeleine Islands and on Cape Breton Island for five years, and then served in parishes in the Montreal area from 1827 to 1846. In 1842 he became a canon of the cathedral in Montreal.

In 1846 Blanchet was appointed the first bishop of Walla Walla, Washington, serving as a suffragan to his brother, François, the first archbishop of Oregon City. Augustin received episcopal ordination in Montreal on September 27, 1846, and traveled to his diocese via the Oregon Trail. He arrived in Walla Walla on September 5, 1847. He established his residence first at St. Anne of the Cayuse, and then, in June 1848, he moved to The Dalles. In 1850 the Diocese of Walla Walla was transferred to Nesqually, and in October 1850, Blanchet moved to Fort Vancouver, Washington. He died at Fort Vancouver on February 25, 1887, and was buried there under the main altar of the church. In 1955 his remains were removed to Holyrood cemetery mausoleum.

See also WASHINGTON, CATHOLIC CHURCH IN.

Aubin, Georges. *Journal d'un Patriote.* Montreal, 1992.

Kowrach, Edward J., ed. *Journal of a Catholic Bishop on the Oregon Trail.* Fairfield, Washington, 1978.

Schoenberg, Wilfred P. *A History of the Catholic Church in the Pacific Northwest, 1743–1983.* Washington, 1987.

GEORGE BROWN

BLANCHET, FRANCIS NORBERT (1795–1883)

Archbishop. The Apostle of Oregon, Francis Norbert Blanchet, was born in St. Pierre, Rivière du Sud, Quebec, Canada, on September 30, 1795, the son of Pierre Blanchet

and Rosalie (Blanchet) Blanchet. In 1810 he enrolled in the Quebec Seminary and was ordained on July 18, 1819. His first assignment was at the Quebec Cathedral, but the next year he went to Richibucto in New Brunswick, to minister for seven years to the native Micmac, and French and English settlers. In 1827 he accepted the parish of St. Joseph de Soulanges in Cedres near Montreal.

The Columbia Mission

An opportunity to respond to requests from French-Canadian settlers in the Oregon Country presented itself in 1836, and Fr. Blanchet was appointed vicar general for the Columbia mission, but the Hudson's Bay Company, in whose brigade he traveled, delayed his departure until May 3, 1838. At Red River Fr. Modeste Demers, the second priest destined for the mission, joined the group. For almost six months more they toiled across Canada, arriving at Fort Vancouver on November 24, 1838.

The two priests immediately began their missionary work, at first only north of the Columbia River. Through the influence of Dr. John McLoughlin of the Hudson's Bay Company, missions south of the river were permitted, and on January 6, 1839, Fr. Blanchet celebrated the first Mass in what became the state of Oregon, at St. Paul Mission.

For almost four years, the two missionaries served the people of the Oregon Country without ever seeing another priest. In 1841 the Oregon missionaries received a letter from Peter De Smet, the Jesuit missionary then in the Rocky Mountains, at last responding to repeated requests for Blackrobes from the Native Americans. In June 1842 he came to Fort Vancouver, and the three priests met to decide the fate of the Church in Oregon. As a result of this conference,

Francis N. Blanchet

Fr. De Smet went to Europe to bring more personnel, Fr. Demers went to extend the mission into British Columbia and Fr. Blanchet remained alone to convince his superiors by letters that Oregon should become a vicariate apostolic.

Several months later his solitude was broken by the arrival of Frs. John B. Bolduc and Anthony Langlois who had been on their way from Canada by ship for over a year. On August 12, 1844, Fr. De Smet returned with reinforcements, including four Jesuits, three lay brothers, and six Sisters of Notre Dame de Namur.

Oregon Vicariate and Archdiocese

Pope Gregory XVI named Fr. Blanchet vicar apostolic for Oregon on December 1, 1843, but the news reached Oregon on November 4, 1844. Fr. Blanchet left in December 1844 for consecration, which took place in Montreal, Canada, on July 25, 1845. From Canada he went to Europe to find more personnel for his vast vicariate, gathering a large group of seminarians, priests and more Sisters of Notre Dame de Namur.

During his travels, Bishop Blanchet developed a plan calling for establishing an ecclesiastical province in Oregon, including an archdiocese and seven suffragan sees. He won Pope Gregory XVI's support, but the Pope died before giving formal approval. Pope Pius IX, his successor, endorsed a somewhat modified plan, and on July 24, 1846, the Archdiocese of Oregon City was created. Francis Blanchet became archbishop of Oregon City; his brother, Augustine Blanchet, became bishop of Walla Walla; and Modeste Demers became bishop of Vancouver Island. Signing of the treaty making Oregon a part of the United States at virtually the same time made the See of Oregon City the second archdiocese in the United States.

Return to Oregon

Upon his return to Oregon in August 1847, Francis Blanchet and Oregon Catholics celebrated their new status until the Whitman massacre occurred. Blaming Dr. Marcus Whitman, a Protestant missionary, for diseases devastating their tribes, Native Americans killed the Whitmans and eleven others. Catholics were involved only to the extent that Augustine Blanchet, newly arrived to set up the Diocese of Walla Walla in the area, was negotiating with the Native Americans for a residence. Many citizens accepted the claim by Rev. Henry Spalding, who had been saved from death by Fr. John B. Brouillet, one of Augustine Blanchet's priests, that Catholics plotted the massacre. Bishop Augustine Blanchet, driven out of his diocese by the unrest after the massacre, took refuge at St. Paul Mission, where the archbishop held the first provincial council of Oregon in 1848. Shortly before this, on November 30, 1847, he had consecrated Modeste Demers as bishop of Vancouver Island in the first episcopal consecration in the Pacific Northwest.

Another setback occurred with the discovery of gold in California, when much of the Oregon population, including many Catholics, hurried off to the gold rush. Already reeling under heavy debt for overzealous construction projects, the archdiocese saw its membership and support disappear. Clergy and religious left the area and schools closed.

In spite of these disturbances, the Church's work in Oregon went on. Francis Blanchet attended the First Plenary Council of Baltimore in 1852, the second in 1866, and the First Vatican Council in 1869–70.

After almost five years without nuns in Oregon, the archbishop himself brought the Sisters of the Holy Names to Portland in 1859 to establish schools. With support from the archbishop and the St. Vincent de Paul Society, the Sisters of Providence opened St. Vincent's Hospital in Portland in 1875.

Archbishop Blanchet led the fight for Catholic reservations under Grant's Peace Policy, being instrumental in the formation of the Bureau of Catholic Indian Missions.

Retirement

Archbishop Blanchet moved the seat of his see to Portland in 1862, and in 1878 began construction of a new cathedral. He was ready to retire, but the Holy See refused to accept his resignation, installing a coadjutor bishop, Charles Seghers, former bishop of Vancouver Island. Francis Blanchet retired to St. Vincent's Hospital in 1881 where he died on June 18, 1883, at the age of eighty-seven. Charles Seghers conferred on him the title "Apostle of Oregon," in his funeral oration. At his own request Francis Blanchet was buried in the cemetery at St. Paul, where the Church in Oregon originated.

See also OREGON, CATHOLIC CHURCH IN.

Bagley, Clarence B. *Early Catholic Missions in Old Oregon.* 2 vols. Seattle, 1932.

Blanchet, Francis N. *Historical Sketches of the Catholic Church in Oregon.* Fairfield, Wash.: Ye Galleon Press, 1983.

Lyons, Letitia. *Francis Norbert Blanchet and the Founding of the Oregon Missions, 1838–1848.* Washington, D.C.: The Catholic University of America Press, 1940.

Munnick, Harriet. *Priest's Progress.* Portland, Oreg.: Binford & Mort, 1989.

O'Hara, Edwin. *Pioneer Catholic History of Oregon.* Centennial ed. Paterson, N.J.: St. Anthony Guild Press, 1939.

PATRICIA BRANDT

BLIEMEL, EMMERMAN (1831–64)

Missionary and Confederate army chaplain. Emmeran Bliemel was born in Ratisbon, Bavaria, on September 29, 1831. He was educated at St. Michael's Abbey, Metten,

Bavaria, but felt called to leave his homeland to minister to German Catholics who had emigrated to America. Therefore, when he finished his studies in 1851, he left Germany and entered the Benedictine novitiate of St. Vincent Abbey at Latrobe, Pennsylvania.

After learning the English language, he taught mathematics in the abbey college. In 1852 he made solemn vows as a Benedictine monk and began his education for the priesthood. Four years later he was ordained by Bishop Michael O'Connor of Pittsburgh, Pennsylvania. For several years he traveled on horseback to minister at various parish communities throughout Pennsylvania, including Hollidaysburg, Johnstown, Elk County, Butler, and Warren.

In 1860 Fr. Bliemel was sent to St. Joseph parish, Covington, Kentucky, from where he served the surrounding area, including southern Ohio. In the fall of that year, he answered a request from the bishop of Nashville, Tennessee, for priests to serve in the diocese and was granted permission by his Benedictine superiors to serve as pastor of the small German parish of the Assumption in Nashville.

After the fall of Fort Sumter in April 1861 and the eruption of civil war, Bliemel's parish began to disintegrate, especially as Union troops began moving south and captured the city. Although he believed in the Southern cause, Bliemel was allowed more freedom than the general population of the city and carried on his priestly ministry among the sick and wounded Union soldiers. However, military authorities began to suspect that he was using his privileges to smuggle medicine to Confederate troops, and he was even arrested when caught carrying four ounces of morphine, and another time for supposedly writing treasonable articles for the *Freeman's Journal.*

In 1863 Union troops commandeered Assumption Church for use as a hospital. Having no parish and after several requests to join the Tenth Tennessee Regiment ("The Bloody Tenth") as a chaplain, Bliemel was finally given permission to join the Confederate unit in the fall of 1863. The regiment was among the Confederate troops that participated in the battle of Jonesborough, Georgia, on August 31, 1864, in which some 1,500 men were killed. Bliemel went to the aid of the wounded and dying, assisting the litter bearers.

When the order to pull back was given, Bliemel was caught in heavy Union fire that followed the retreat. He was hearing the confession of Colonel William Grace, commander of the Tenth Tennessee who went down in the attack, when he was struck in the head on August 31, 1864, at Jonesborough, Georgia.

Bliemel had the distinction of being the first U.S. Catholic chaplain to die while serving in battle and the only chaplain to die during the Civil War. In 1983 the Sons of Confederate Veterans posthumously awarded him the Confederate Medal of Honor.

See also CIVIL WAR AND CATHOLICS, THE.

Germain, Aidam Henry. *Catholic Military and Naval Chaplains.* Washington, D.C., 1929, 111–12.

Meaney, Peter J., O.S.B. "Valiant Chaplain of the Bloody Tenth." *Tennessee Historical Quarterly* 41 (1) (1982) 37–47.

Plaisance, Aloysius, O.S.B. "Heroic Confederate Chaplain." *The American Benedictine Review* (June 1966) 210.

MARIANNA McLOUGHLIN

BOEHM, CHARLES (1853–1932)

Pioneer Hungarian priest in America. Charles Boehm was born on June 13, 1853, in Selmec-banya, Hungary, to Felix and Julia Urbanszky Boehm. Boehm was a gifted student, excelling at St. Stephen Seminary in Esztergom and at the University of Vienna. On July 16, 1876, he was ordained to the priesthood for the Archdiocese of Esztergom. Boehm's first assignment was as assistant at Maria Nostra. He would later serve as administrator at Nagy-Modro and pastor at Maria Nostra.

Hungarian immigration to America increased in the 1880s. Many Hungarians were attracted to the U.S.A. by the promise of jobs in American mills, but their language and culture isolated them. The Cleveland Hungarian community desperately needed a priest and Boehm answered the call. Arriving in Cleveland in December 1892, he started the first Magyar parish in America and was instrumental in the establishment of other churches.

Boehm began the necessary organization and fundraising for his parish of St. Elizabeth located in the Buckeye-Woodland area of Cleveland. He was anxious about the fate of other Hungarians scattered throughout the United States. He feared that, without some religious contact, their faith would be endangered. In 1894, therefore, he began editing and writing *Magyarorszagi Szent Ersebet Amerikai* [St. Elizabeth of Hungary's Herald in America], now known as *The Catholic Hungarian Sunday*. Boehm used the paper and personal visits as a means of finding and organizing scattered Hungarian communities throughout the U.S.A.

In 1907, after founding a second Hungarian parish in Cleveland and one in the village of Fairport Harbor, Ohio, he left Cleveland to aid other Hungarian communities. Using Buffalo as a base, he established churches in Missouri, Pennsylvania, Ohio, Newark, and New Jersey. He stabilized the struggling Buffalo congregation of St. Elizabeth and established a school.

In 1923 Boehm returned to Cleveland where he resumed the pastorate of St. Elizabeth Church. In 1925 he became a domestic prelate. When he retired from pastoral work in 1927, he began a ministry to the mentally ill patients in Cleveland State Hospital. He died on April 9, 1932, in Cleveland.

See also HUNGARIAN CATHOLICS IN AMERICA.

Msgr. Boehm Memorial Foundation. *Memorial Booklet Commemorating the 25th Anniversary of the Death of Msgr. Charles Boehm.* Fairport Harbor, 1957.

Carr, Michael W. *A History of Catholicity in Northern Ohio and in the Diocese of Cleveland.* Vol. II. Cleveland, 1903.

Catholic Universe Bulletin, April 15, 1932, 1, 4.

Karpi, Francis A. *For God and Country, Msgr. Charles Boehm.* Youngstown, 1985.

Papp, Susan M. *Hungarian Americans and their Communities of Cleveland.* Cleveland, 1981.

CHRISTINE L. KROSEL

BOHACHEVSKY, CONSTANTINE (1884–1961)

Archbishop. Constantine Bohachevsky was born June 17, 1884, into a priestly family at Manaiw, Galicia. After studies at Lviv and Innsbruck, he was ordained a priest at Lviv on January 31, 1909. He returned to Innsbruck for the doctorate in sacred theology which was conferred in 1910, and later studied Oriental Patrology at Munich. Over the next dozen years he held several teaching, pastoral, and administrative posts at Lviv and Przemysl, culminating with his appointment as vicar general of the Przemysl diocese. He served as a chaplain in the Austrian Army on the Italian front in 1916. While rector of the Przemysl Cathedral, he was briefly imprisoned near Krakow for his vocal defense of the needs of Ukrainians in Poland.

After World War I, the Holy See decided to divide the Byzantine exarchate in the United States into separate jurisdictions for Galicians (Ukrainians) and Transcarpathians (Ruthenians). On May 20, 1924, Bohachevsky was appointed titular bishop of Amisus and Ukrainian exarch of Philadelphia. He was consecrated at Rome together with Basil Takach, the Ruthenian exarch, on June 24, and arrived in the United States on August 15, 1924.

Bohachevsky's early years as exarch were marked by considerable dissension. He strove to reestablish clerical and parochial discipline in an exarchate which had been without a bishop for more than eight years. In addition, the failure of Ukraine to achieve political independence led to dissatisfaction with Bohachevsky among more nationalistic Ukrainians in America and fueled defections to the Ukrainian Orthodox Church which was perceived by some as more patriotic.

Bohachevsky was convinced that education was the key to the growth and stability of the exarchate. He introduced a seminary system with the opening of St. Basil's Preparatory Seminary at Stamford, Connecticut (1933), St. Basil's College Seminary at Stamford (1939), and St. Josaphat's Theologate at Washington (1941). In line with his efforts to develop a parochial school system, Bohachevsky introduced a teaching order, the Sisters Servants of Mary

Immaculate into his jurisdiction (1935), and founded an American Ukrainian community, the Missionary Sisters of the Mother of God, at Stamford in 1944.

Because World War II made periodicals from Europe less available, Bohachevsky founded a diocesan journal, *The Way/Shlakh* in 1940. The clergy of the exarchate were augmented by the introduction of the Basilian monks (1932), Byzantine Franciscans (1945), and Redemptorists (1946). After the war, as a result of the perilous situation of the Church in Eastern Europe, Bohachevsky and other bishops in the West exercised more extensive leadership in the Ukrainian Catholic Church.

In the 1950s the growth of the exarchate and Bohachevsky's leadership were recognized. On May 20, 1954, he was named titular archbishop of Beroe. On July 20, 1956, New England and New York were separated from the exarchate and a new jurisdiction established at Stamford. And on August 6, 1958, Philadelphia was made a metropolitan see. Bohachevsky was installed as archbishop of Philadelphia of the Ukrainians on November 1, 1958, before twelve thousand faithful in Philadelphia's Convention Hall. Bohachevsky died at Philadelphia on January 6, 1961.

See also EASTERN CATHOLIC CHURCHES IN AMERICA.

Procko, Bohdan P. *Ukranian Catholics in America. A History.* Lanham, Md.: University Press of America, 1982.

Sochocky, Isidore. "The Ukrainian Catholic Church of the Byzantine-Slavonic Rite in the U.S.A." *Ukranian Catholic Metropolitan See, Byzantine Rite, U.S.A. November 1, 1958.* Philadelphia: Archbishop's Chancery, 1959.

RAYMOND J. KUPKE

BONAPARTE, CHARLES JOSEPH (1851–1921)

Secretary of the Navy, U.S. Attorney General. Born in Baltimore on June 9, 1851, the grandson of Napoleon's youngest brother (Jerome), and the son of Jerome and Susan May Williams Bonaparte, he was educated by tutors and in private schools near Baltimore. He graduated from Harvard University in 1872 and from Harvard Law School in 1874. Married in 1875 to Ellen Channing Day, Bonaparte entered politics as an Independent Republican who championed municipal reform, civil service reform, and suffrage rights for African Americans. By the 1890s, he had become a colleague as well as a strong supporter of Theodore Roosevelt and held numerous government appointments during the Roosevelt presidency.

In 1902 he served as legal advisor to the Indian Commissioners' Board investigating Indian Affairs. Later, he acted as an intermediary between the Church and Roosevelt while helping settle disputes over Church property in Puerto Rico. He supported Roosevelt's naval expansion program and, in 1905, was appointed Secretary of the

Charles J. Bonaparte

Navy. The following year, Bonaparte became U.S. Attorney General and actively initiated antitrust suits; more than fifty originated during his tenure. Largely responsible for the dissolution of the American Tobacco Company, he personally argued against other Cabinet members (primarily Elihu Root) who lobbied to quash this antitrust action. After 1909 he returned to private law practice in Baltimore but reentered politics briefly in 1912 to support Roosevelt's third party. He was a founder and president of the National Municipal League and received the Laetare Medal. Bonaparte died at his Maryland estate, Belle Vista, on June 28, 1921.

JOHN ALLEN

Related Document

CHARLES J. BONAPARTE ON THE AMERICAN EXPERIENCE OF SEPARATION OF CHURCH AND STATE, JULY 11, 1889

Charles E. Bonaparte (1851–1921) was one of the most distinguished Catholic laymen of his generation. Baltimore-born grandson of King Jerome of Westphalia, brother of Emperor Napoleon I, Harvard-trained, and from a family of wealth, Bonaparte enjoyed all the advantages which such a background afforded. He was especially noted for his zeal in behalf of good government and civil-service reform, having been one of the founders of the National Municipal League and later its president. Theodore Roosevelt appointed Bonaparte to a number of federal offices, naming him Secretary of the Navy in May 1905 and Attorney General of the United States in December 1906, where he continued to the end of the administration in March 1909 and earned for himself widespread fame as a trust-buster. He was always a devout Catholic and had very pronounced views about the need for keeping the Church free from politics and the State out of religious affairs. The excerpts from one of his public addresses that follow were all the more pertinent in being spoken at a time when the A.P.A. were on the rise. The speech was delivered at the centennial celebration of the Catholic societies of the Archdiocese of Baltimore at Bay Ridge, Maryland.

(*Source*: Charles J. Bonaparte. *The Catholic Church and American Institutions*. Baltimore: William K. Boyle & Son, 1889, 16–21.)

YOU HAVE ALL HEARD AND READ, MANY OF YOU, NO DOUBT, often, some, perhaps, *ad nauseam,* that there is an "incompatibility" between American institutions and the Catholic Church. . . . Even now it may be, perhaps, sincerely said by a Catholic who is not an American, or an American who is not a Catholic, but I cannot think this opinion is shared by any American Catholic, sufficiently informed to have an intelligent opinion. Nor need I disprove it *a priori;* we have met to commemorate its refutation by the one unanswerable test of experience.

The mustard seed planted on these shores a hundred years ago fell on no ungrateful soil; of this no better proof can be given or reasonably asked than Time has furnished in the stately tree with its deep roots and spreading branches, which has grown from that seed. . . . If we apply to the sum of American institutions the vague and much abused term "liberty," a century's history proves that liberty is good for the Catholic Church, and this is a conclusion of such moment that I feel justified in a further trespass on your patience to briefly weigh its import.

I claim the fact to have been established by a decisive experiment, but opinions may of course, differ as to its explanation; to understand, however, why American liberty has proved thus congenial to the Church, we must first appreciate what, in its essentials, our liberty is, and how it differs from political systems abroad, which usurp or masquerade in the same name. A competent and candid observer asked to indicate the countries whose history during the present century could be read with most pleasure by devout Catholics would unhesitatingly group with the United States, the great English colonies. In old Catholic countries, the Church has often contended with hostility and spoliation from the State; elsewhere she has been steadfast under persecution from non-catholic rulers of arbitrary power; but among all English speaking peoples she has gained ground, and in Canada and Australia and the United States her prosperity has been manifest and her progress rapid. What suits her in our country, then, is something we share with our Northern neighbors and our kinsmen in the great island of the Southern sea, and we share with them a large measure of individual freedom under a popular government.

The genius of our common institutions, is to let each citizen work out his own happiness with little hindrance and little help from the State; the government protects his person and property and enforces his contracts, then leaves him as nearly to himself as the exigencies of national defence and public order permit. To the ephemeral republics which this century has seen rise and fall in Europe, this spirit has been utterly alien; they may have committed the State's authority to many hands, but have made that authority ever more and more arbitrary and far-reaching; in such a republic,

> That worst of tyrants, a usurping crowd

intrudes upon every phase of a man's life, assumes to watch over his coming in and his going out, the management of his property, the education of his children, the care of his health, to dictate even the words he shall use and the clothes he shall wear. The legitimate outcome of the first system is complete religious liberty, to give any creed, not grossly repugnant to the accepted standard of public morals, a fair field, but no favor, for the State to ask only the things of Caesar, leaving to the conscience of each citizen to care for the more lasting interests which lie beyond its humbler sphere.

Under the second system, the State becomes itself a church, a church wanting, indeed, in almost all that makes a church a means of good, but with a potent influence for evil. To be consistent, a paternal government must provide a legal religion; it cannot, in the words of the Great Frederic, "let its subjects go to Hell by the road they like best," and under such a government, the Catholic Church stands face to face with a rival. The Bill of Rights of Maryland declares:

> That, as it is the duty of every man to worship God in such manner as he thinks most acceptable to Him, all persons are equally entitled to protection in their religious liberty. . . .

The aim of ecclesiastical legislation in many European countries is precisely to make all places of worship, public buildings, and all ministers of religion, of whatsoever creed or order, public functionaries, controlled by the State and maintained from the proceeds of taxation. Here the Church goes her way and does her work without caring, almost without thinking, whether the civil rulers for the time being are within or without her fold; there she may be hampered in every function of her ministry by the hostility of such rulers or more gravely embarrassed, more permanently discredited by their compromising friendship. For, even if I scandalize some worthy people by so thinking, I yet think the civil power less dangerous to the Church as a rival, even as an oppressor, than as a patron. The Church of Christ should be no hot-house plant:

> Moored in the rifted rock,
> Proof to the tempests' shock,
> The firmer they root her the harder they blow,

but when fenced about with laws, when sheltered behind privileges and prescriptions, her rugged fibre grows soft and her sturdy frame dainty. When the time of trial comes,—and come it will, for dynasties and their kingdoms, laws and the nations that made them, man and all man's works, must sometime change and pass away,—when all these screens and safe guards of a day fall around her, and she faces again the whirlwind of human error and human passion, many sapped boughs shall break and much dead wood claim the pruning knife. It is no trick of theologian's jargon that calls the Church "militant"; she is indeed a fighting body, and her conquests must be held as they were made by valor and discipline and well kept arms, not by a Chinese Wall of timid isolation. Moreover Caesar does not work for nothing: he must be paid for his protection; if he makes heresy treason, he asks that she make treason heresy, and this is little less than a ruinous price for a less than doubtful service.

Here the Church hires no mercenary defender, she guards her own by her own might; no prince or magistrate, no parliament or judge, wielding the clumsy weapon of unconvincing force, is called on to fill a mission for which her clergy have grown unworthy. Her soldiers cannot rust in barracks or cower behind intrenchments; they must meet their foes of today as all the countless spiritual heroes of her history met and conquered theirs, in the open field of argument and example with the armament of zeal and eloquence, learning and saintly life. The American priesthood is no refuge for cowardice and sloth either intellectual or physical. It has a work to do, a vast and hard and endless work, which no one else will do or try or pretend to do for it; and today, as we look back along these hundred years and then around us, we say with a just pride in the past, with a reasonable confidence in the future, and, above all, with perfect trust in the proven and abiding guidance of Almighty God, that work has been and is and will be well done!

(*Source:* John Tracy Ellis, ed. *Documents of American Catholic History.* Vol. 2:1866–1966. Wilmington, Del.: Michael Glazier, 1987, 470–3.)

BORRANO, FRANCIS XAVIER (1901–93)

Priest and publisher. He was born in San Damino d'Asli, a village in northern Italy in 1901. He became one of the first members of the Society of St. Paul (Paulines), a new congregation founded by Fr. James Alberione to spread the gospel by using advances in communication. Ordained in 1923, he took a degree in philosophy and began a publishing apostolate that lasted over sixty years. He arrived in New York with little money in 1931 and edited a paper for Italian immigrants, and with little help, took over two rundown parishes in Staten Island. He later established branches of his congregation in Australia and Cuba. In 1956 the Paulines established their first province in America, and Borrano was elected provincial. He devoted much of his time to developing a distinguished publishing list for Alba House in Staten Island and to fostering Alba Communications in Canfield, Ohio, where he died on April 16, 1993. Francis X. Borrano was a man of great courtesy and personal sanctity.

See also ITALIAN CATHOLICS IN AMERICA.

MICHAEL GLAZIER

BOSCHE, MARY AGNES (1885–1949)

Religious, educator. Sr. Mary Agnes (Edna Mary Bosche) a Sister of Notre Dame of Cleveland, Ohio, was born in Massillon, Ohio, on July 29, 1885. She received elementary education under the Sisters of Notre Dame at St. Peter School, Canton, Ohio, and secondary schooling at their Academy, Cleveland, Ohio. She entered their novitiate on December 8, 1904, and pronounced her vows on July 22, 1907. She completed undergraduate studies at St. John College, Toledo, Ohio (1920), and earned her master's degree from Fordham University, New York (1924).

After spending eighteen years as teacher and administrator in the order's high schools in Cleveland and Toledo, Sr. Mary Agnes launched a new venture in higher education. She was named first dean of Notre Dame College of Ohio, a teacher-training and liberal arts college founded in 1922 by her religious order as an answer to the national concern, current in the 1920s, for the education of women. With far-sighted vision, she shaped the spiritual, philosophical, educational, and social thrust of the college to prepare Catholic young women for leadership in the Church and American society. She provided opportunities for her students to make decisions, to become knowledgeable and articulate on current issues, to become leaders in the home and in their sphere of influence.

Sr. Mary Agnes left the college in 1943 to spend six years in writing. She published articles in magazines, and three meditation books on charity: *St. Paul's Hymn of Charity* (1937); *Practical Charity* (1939); *Bond of Perfection* (1941). Named provincial superior in 1947, Sr. Mary Agnes guided her sisters of the Cleveland province at a time of rapid development, branching out to a foreign mission in Jamalpur, India. Stricken by cancer, Sr. Mary Agnes died on July 21, 1949, a few days before her sixty-fourth birthday.

Arntz, Mary Luke, S.N.D. *Remembering Sister Mary Agnes.* Chardon, Ohio, 1994.

MARY LUKE ARNTZ, S.N.D.

BOSTON COLLEGE

Boston College, a Jesuit university founded in 1863, experienced in its beginnings the anti-Catholic and anti-Irish

Boston College

bias of the dominant Anglo-Protestant New England population. When the Jesuits, planning to establish a church and college, purchased a sizable piece of property in the heart of Boston, a group of 925 Protestant citizens petitioned city authorities to forbid the building of a Catholic church on the site. Although a counter-petition in support of the Jesuits was made by an enlightened group of twenty-five Protestant leaders, including Edward Everett, a former governor and Harvard president, Rufus Choate, a former U.S. senator, and William Prescott, the noes carried the day and the Jesuits were forced to locate in the South End of Boston.

Boston College's first president, Fr. John Bapst, had suffered physical abuse by Protestant extremists in Maine before coming to Boston. A native of Switzerland, Fr. Bapst served as a missionary to the Penobscot natives of Maine while also ministering to the French and Irish Catholics of the region. A radical Protestant group called Know-Nothings, who had considerable national influence in the 1840s and 1850s, warned Fr. Bapst to stay out of the town of Ellsworth. When he insisted on celebrating Mass there, he was hauled from his house, taken out of town on a rail, and tarred and feathered. Public outcry against such violence helped lessen public anti-Catholicism.

Despite these anti-Catholic antecedents, Boston College managed finally to welcome its first students in September 1864. The college's struggle for land took place in the 1850s, the decade after the great famine in Ireland that drove thousands of Irish people to Boston. Some of the sons of those Irish immigrants were teenagers when Boston College opened in the next decade and while enrollments were small, the enrollment compared favorably with many public and private colleges of the era. Indeed, before the end of the nineteenth century the Jesuits were looking for a larger site for the burgeoning institution.

Like all American Jesuit colleges of the time, Boston College offered a strictly classical, liberal arts education, and since the Archdiocese of Boston had no preparatory seminary then, substantial numbers of the priests of the archdiocese received their early training in Boston College. Often more than 50 percent of the graduating class entered the seminary. Boston's first two cardinals—William Cardinal O'Connell and Richard Cardinal Cushing—attended Boston College.

In 1913 the college moved to it present location in Chestnut Hill, just outside of Boston, with an ample campus and beautiful neo-Gothic buildings. After World War I, the College began to evolve towards university status with the establishment of graduate programs and the professional schools of law, business, nursing, social work, and education. Enrollment exploded after World War II and students began to enroll from all across America. Coeducation was introduced in all undergraduate divisions in 1970. For many years the Jesuit community has been one of the largest in the world, usually numbering about 135. Many of the Jesuits are from Third World countries, pursuing graduate study. In the 1980s the Jesuit community and the university established a multimillion-dollar foundation to support the Jesuit Institute, a research center of Catholic theology and thought. Also begun then was the Institute for Religious Education and Pastoral Ministry. In 1995 a national survey ranked Boston College's graduate program in theology seventeenth in the country.

In 1995 Boston College enrolled some 8,500 undergraduate and some 4,000 graduate students. Its endowment ranked it among the top fifty universities in America.

See also JESUITS IN AMERICA, THE.

Donovan, Charles F., S.J., David Dunegan, S.J., and Paul A. Fitzgerald. *The History of Boston College from its Beginnings to 1990.* Boston, 1990.
Donovan, Charles F., S.J. *Boston College: Glimpses of the Past.* Boston, 1994.

CHARLES F. DONOVAN, S.J.

BOULET, JOHN BAPTIST (1834–1919)

Missionary. Like many pioneer priests, John Baptist Boulet was a man of many talents. In the course of his long life, he was a school teacher, a missionary to Native Americans, a founder of the Church in the Pacific Northwest where he built from scratch, or completed, at least ten churches, and a printer and publisher of significant Catholic Americana. For the latter he has, for a priest, a unique claim to fame.

Born in Quebec province in Canada on July 20, 1834, Boulet attended school in his native town and then a semi-

nary at St. Hyacinth. Uncertain about his future, he moved to Vermont to learn English, then to Holyoke, Massachusetts, to earn a living. He worked in a cotton mill, studied and taught night classes for others. Eventually he met Napoleon St. Onge, another French-Canadian, who changed his life.

St. Onge was a seminarian who had agreed to teach boys at Bishop Augustin Blanchet's Holy Angels College in Vancouver, Washington, while he prepared for ordination for the Nesqually diocese. He persuaded Boulet to join him at Holy Angels, and after ordination, to join him at a mission for the native Yakima. Boulet remained with him for four years. The experience confirmed him in his desire to be a priest. He returned to Vancouver and studied theology with the bishop, while he served as his secretary. On July 19, 1874, he was ordained; thus his amazing life as a priest began.

Forty-five years of life remained to him. He began as a missionary "to all the Indian missions in Clark, Skamania and Lewis Counties." He was transferred later to missions along the Northwest Coast, where he built his churches. One of these was in a white settlement called Fairhaven. Today it is called Bellingham and it is a large city. Meanwhile Boulet had acquired a printing press. In Vancouver he called it St. James Press and when he moved north to Tulalip, he called it St. Ann's Press. On this, two pages at a time, he printed his booklets and later his two magazines, *The Youth's Companion* and subsequently *The Glad Tidings.* He did all of the work himself, typesetting, printing, binding and mailing copies, most of them to eastern American subscribers who paid for his churches. On February 22, 1911, Boulet was invested as a monsignor at Bellingham. Eight years later, on August 4, 1919, he died peacefully in the Lord.

The Bellingham Herald, November 17, 1906.
Catholic Sentinel, February 23, 1911.
Schoenberg, Wilfred P., S.J. *A History of the Catholic Church in the Pacific Northwest 1743–1983.* Washington, 1987.
_____. *Jesuit Mission Presses in the Pacific Northwest: A History and Bibliography of Imprints 1876–1899 Plus Other Early Catholic Presses and a Critical Study of the Lapwai Press 1839–1846.* Fairfield, Washington, 1994.

WILFRED P. SCHOENBERG, S.J.

BOUQUILLON, THOMAS (1842–1902)

Priest, moral theologian, and educator. Thomas Bouquillon was born in Warrenton, Belgium, on May 16, 1842. He studied in the seminary at Bruges, was ordained a priest in 1865, earned his doctorate in theology from the Gregorian University in Rome in 1867, and began teaching moral theology in the seminary at Bruges. In 1877 he was appointed to teach moral theology at the new Catholic University of Lille but withdrew in 1885 to the Benedictine monastery at Maredsous apparently to concentrate on his research. But in 1889 he accepted the invitation to become the first professor of moral theology at the newly founded Catholic University of America. This brilliant, committed, and tireless scholar taught, published, and greatly contributed to the intellectual life of The Catholic University of America until he died in 1902.

Bouquillon, a true scholar with a love of books, a magnificent personal library, and a deep interest in history, was recognized as the leading intellectual of the faculty and was the first to introduce the German seminar to university education in the United States. His many articles in three languages—Latin, French, and English—often appeared in the journals associated with his various institutional commitments. Although he wrote on a broad number of social, historical, and theological subjects, moral theology was his primary field. His *Theologia moralis fundamentalis* was first published in 1873 but greatly expanded in subsequent editions of 1890 and 1903. He also published *De virtutibus theologicis* (1878) and *De virtute religionis* (2 vols., 1880).

Bouquillon was a committed neoscholastic who exuberantly praised and followed the program of renewal proposed by Pope Leo XIII who made Thomas Aquinas the model and teacher for Catholic theology and philosophy. Bouquillon interpreted the history of theology in the light of its acceptance or rejection of Thomism. Thanks to the renewal of Thomism the Church in the latter part of the nineteenth century could now address the culture and problems of the times and refute naturalism especially in its two principal forms of rationalism and liberalism.

In journal articles and even in his textbooks, Bouquillon, in the light of his neoscholasticism, strongly criticized the manuals of moral theology as being separated from other theological disciplines and more interested in cataloguing the opinions of theologians of the last three centuries than in striving for truth. However, his *Theologia moralis fundamentalis* does not really follow Aquinas but accepts the purpose (training of confessors as judges) and model (a legal model with law as the objective norm and conscience as the subjective norm of morality) of the manuals together with their close association of canon law with moral theology. However, his discussion of these realities is more in-depth and scholarly than the approach of the manuals.

Bouquillon's pamphlet, *Education: To Whom Does It Belong?* (1891), employing in a very scholarly and objective way the teaching of Aquinas on the role of the state, proposed a special and proper right of the state to teach human knowledge (not religion) as supplementing the rights of individuals and families. This and subsequent articles supported the practice of Archbishop John Ireland of St. Paul of working for closer cooperation of Catholics with public schools and embroiled Bouquillon in a bitter controversy with more conservative theologians, bishops, and even the influential Italian Jesuit journal, *Civiltà Cat-*

tolica. This controversy together with his belonging to the liberal majority at The Catholic University and his role in the exoneration of Edward McGlynn, identified Bouquillon with the Americanist approach of liberal nineteenth-century Catholicism in the United States.

Bouquillon's classes and journal articles showed a great interest in and knowledge of the social sciences, the understanding of which was necessary to apply properly the principles of moral theology to contemporary realities. He strongly supported the establishment of a school of social sciences at The Catholic University of America and was the intellectual mentor of William J. Kerby, the first proponent of professional Catholic social work and an organizer of Catholic Charities, and of John A. Ryan, the leading Catholic figure in social thought in the United States in the first half of the twentieth century. Bouquillon died in Brussels, Belgium, on November 5, 1902.

Curran, Charles E. "Thomas Joseph Bouquillon: Americanist, Neo-Scholastic or Manualist?" *Proceedings of the Catholic Theological Society of America* 50 (1995) 156–73.

Nuesse, C. Joseph. "Thomas Joseph Bouquillon (1840–1902): Moral Theologian and Presursor of the Social Sciences in the Catholic University of America." *Catholic Historical Review* 72 (1986) 601–19.

Reilly, Daniel F. *The School Controversy (1891–1893)*. Washington, D.C.: The Catholic University of America Press, 1943.

CHARLES E. CURRAN

BOYLE, ELIZABETH (1788–1861)

Convert, religious superior. Elizabeth Boyle was born near Baltimore, Maryland, on October 16, 1788, to a Protestant family of English origin. She was baptized and received into the Catholic Church on April 24, 1808, by Fr. John Moranvillé, pastor of St. Patrick's Church, in the Fells' Point section of Baltimore. Two years later she joined Mother Elizabeth Seton's fledgling sisterhood at Emmitsburg, Maryland. She made her vows with seventeen other young women at Emmitsburg on July 19, 1813.

In 1820 Elizabeth became superior of St. Joseph's Orphan Asylum in Philadelphia, and, on November 24, 1822, she was appointed superior of St. Patrick's Orphan Asylum in New York City. When John Dubois came to New York as its third bishop in 1826, Elizabeth Boyle greeted him as an old friend. Again in 1838, when John Hughes arrived in New York as coadjutor to the aging Dubois, she welcomed him as someone whom she had known since his student days at Mount St. Mary's Seminary in Emmitsburg. As New York heaved under immigration turbulence, Elizabeth Boyle struggled to maintain her orphanage.

In mid-1840s, when the Sisters of Charity of Emmitsburg initiated affiliation with the Paris-based Daughters of Charity, the problem of the care of male orphans (which was forbidden by the French rule) reached crisis proportions in New York City. In late 1846, sisters in New York who were unwilling to abandon this work, separated from Emmitsburg to form the Sisters of Charity of St. Vincent de Paul under the jurisdiction of Bishop John Hughes. Of 62 Sisters of Charity in New York at that time, 29 returned to Emmitsburg; 33 remained in New York where they operated three orphan asylums, three academies, and six parochial schools. On December 31, 1846, the sisters elected Elizabeth Boyle as first Mother of the new community.

One of Elizabeth Boyle's first tasks was to establish a motherhouse for the New York Sisters of Charity. With a loan of $10,000 from the trustees of St. Patrick's Cathedral, she purchased property and an old frame house at McGowan's Pass, an area of upper Manhattan that ten years later was to be incorporated into Central Park. She called her modest motherhouse Mount St. Vincent. In 1849, during Elizabeth Boyle's term as superior, the New York Sisters of Charity also established their first mission, in Halifax, Nova Scotia.

Elizabeth Boyle's three-year term of office expired on December 8, 1849. Although she was eligible for reelection, Hughes did not want her to serve for another term. She asked him: "And what shall I do, Your Grace? Shall I return to the orphans?" In the presence of all the sisters, he replied: "You will now take the last place in the community, Mother, and apply yourself to reading the lives of the saints." At the time she had been a superior for thirty-five years, but she obediently went to St. Joseph's Half-Orphan Asylum on Sixth Avenue in Greenwich Village where she served as a simple sister for the next two years. When the new Roman Catholic Orphan Asylum was opened at Fifth Avenue and Fifty-First Street on October 1, 1851, Elizabeth Boyle was appointed the superior and remained there until her death on June 21, 1861.

From her life work she left the guidance of penniless youth as hall mark to her daughters. Revered for her devotion to duty and appreciation of the Immigrant Church, Elizabeth Boyle transmitted to the congregation as heritage the pioneer spirit of Mother Seton and a practical love of the poor.

See also WOMEN RELIGIOUS IN AMERICA.

Sister Marie de Lourdes Walsh. *Mother Elizabeth Boyle, Mother of Charity.* New York, 1955.
____. *The Sisters of Charity of New York, 1809–1959.* 3 vols. New York, 1960.

ANNE COURTNEY, S.C.

BOYS TOWN

Irish immigrant priest Fr. Edward J. Flanagan founded Father Flanagan's Boys' Home, known as the original Boys Town, in 1917, in Omaha, Nebraska. He began this mission by providing a "hotel" for homeless and down-and-out workers, not far from St. Patrick's Catholic Church in Omaha, where he was assistant pastor. He noticed a common thread in the hopelessness of these men—neglect, indifference, and ignorance had shaped their lives as adolescents. Fr. Flanagan decided to address the problem at the root. He felt that if he could catch a child before he fell into these problems, he could make a difference. He received consent from his archbishop and borrowed ninety dollars from his friend, Jewish businessman and attorney Henry Monsky. On December, 12, 1917, Fr. Flanagan opened the doors of a drafty Victorian house in downtown Omaha to a half-dozen boys.

Word spread of the friendly Omaha priest's mission to help wayward boys. As the number of needy boys increased, Flanagan had to look for larger quarters. He purchased a farm ten miles west of downtown Omaha. He moved the boys to that location October 22, 1921. It became the incorporated Village of Boys Town, Nebraska, in 1936—Fr. Flanagan's "City of Little Men." With the help of the community and donors across the country, Fr. Flanagan built facilities for the boys. He changed the way America thought of her troubled children in the 1920s and 1930s by pioneering alternative education, vocational training, and self-government instead of prison. From the early days until 1974, the boys lived in large dormitories on campus, although plans were underway during Fr. Flanagan's era to build cottages that were homes to fewer boys. In 1974 Boys Town moved from institutional care to family-based care. Today, each of the one hundred homes at Boys Town or at Boys Town sites across the country, has a group of six to eight youths. Highly trained professional married couples called Family-Teachers care for the youth. These couples form a warm, caring family with their youths, guiding and instructing them on a twenty-four-hour basis and seeing that their physical, spiritual, emotional, and treatment needs are met. Boys Town began accepting girls into its programs in 1979. Now, about 40 percent of the children in residential care are girls.

Boys Town began expanding its services to other parts of the country in 1983 as part of its mission of changing the way America cares for her troubled children. It now has residential care and other programs in sixteen cities in eleven states and the District of Columbia. The other programs are oriented toward family preservation and prevention and include emergency shelters, treatment foster care, in-home crisis counseling, and parent training.

Boys Town operates a state-of-the-art National Research Hospital specializing in communication disorders and an Omaha inner-city alternative high school for "at-risk" youth. Boys Town also shares its expertise and training with child-care providers, teachers, school administrators, and mental health-care workers as well as treatment foster care programs, family preservation services, emergency shelters, and parent-training programs. The Boys Town National Hotline handles more than 500,000 calls each year from children and parents.

See also FLANAGAN, EDWARD J.

JOHN MELINGAGIO

BRADY, NICHOLAS (1878–1930)

Financier, philanthropist. Nicholas Frederic Brady was born in Albany, New York, on October 25, 1878, the son of Anthony Nicholas Brady and Marcia Myers Brady. His father, a self-made businessman whose education ended at the age of twelve, left an estate of seventy million dollars at his death in 1913. The elder Brady was born in France of Irish parents who emigrated to the United States when he was a child. Although baptized a Catholic, Anthony Brady ceased to practice his faith for most of his life and raised his children in the faith of his devoutly Episcopalian wife.

Young Nicholas was educated at the Albany Academy and Yale University from which he graduated in 1899. He followed his father into a Wall Street career. In 1912, at the age of thirty-four, Brady was president of the New York Edison Company, one of the largest utilities in the United States. By the time of his death, he was chairman of the board of both the New York Edison Company and the Brooklyn Edison Company as well as a director of over one hundred corporations. An extremely wealthy man, he once explained that he sold his three-masted yacht to one of the Vanderbilts because, he said, "I think there are better ways of spending money than to keep forty men on her all year when I use her for only three weeks."

On August 20, 1906, Brady married Genevieve Garvan, a devout Catholic from Hartford, Connecticut. Shortly before his marriage, Brady was received into the Catholic Church and thereafter became an active Catholic layman. The Bradys maintained a private chapel in their Long Island mansion, Inisfada, where Nicholas regularly served daily Mass. On vacation trips to his winter home in Florida, he even obtained permission from the apostolic delegate to have Mass celebrated in his private railroad car.

The Bradys owned a villa in Rome, Casa del Sole, where they spent several months each year and attracted an influential clerical clientele, including Cardinal John Bonzano, former apostolic delegate to the United States, and two rising young stars in the Vatican Secretariat of State, Giuseppe Pizzardo and Francis J. Spellman. Brady's benefactions to the Church amounted to some twelve million dollars, including a donation of one million dollars to construct the Jesuit novitiate in Wernersville, Pennsylvania. Brady's generosity to the Church was rewarded with his appointment as a papal chamberlain and later as a papal duke. He appeared in his latter capacity in full regalia at the Eucharistic Congress in Chicago in 1926 where he was caught in the violent thunderstorm that drenched the participants during the final day of the proceedings. His colorful outfit was ruined, but he was heard to remark, "Thank God, I shall not have to wear that uniform again." In 1929 he became the first American to receive the Supreme Order of Christ, a papal decoration usually reserved for heads of state.

Brady was regarded as an enlightened employer who tried to implement the teachings of the papal social encyclicals, although in 1919 he told Archbishop Patrick Hayes of New York that he disapproved of the Bishops' Program of Social Reconstruction because it advocated such measures as a minimum wage and compulsory sickness insurance. Brady died in New York City on March 27, 1930, and was buried in the crypt beneath the chapel of the Jesuit novitiate of St. Isaac Jogues in Wernersville, Pennsylvania.

Daly, James J., S.J. *Nicholas Frederic Brady: A Memoir.* New York, 1935.

THOMAS J. SHELLEY

BRONDEL, JOHN BAPTIST (1842–1903)

First bishop of Helena, Montana. John Baptist Brondel was born on February 23, 1842, in Bruges, Belgium, to Charles Joseph Brondel and Isabella Becquet Brondel. He was educated by the Xaverian Brothers and attended St. Louis College in Bruges. He entered The American College of Louvain in 1861 and was ordained on December 17, 1864, at Mechlin, Belgium. After more schooling, partly to learn English, he was assigned to the Diocese of Nesqually in the Washington Territory (now the Archdiocese of Seattle), under Bishop Augustin M. A. Blanchet.

Fr. Brondel dreamed of ministering to Native Americans, but had little contact with them in thirteen years of teaching at a boys' school and as pastor at Steilacoom (also called Steilicom) on Puget Sound. After becoming bishop of Vancouver Island and Alaska in 1879, he visited many tribes in his diocese and established a mission among the Kayokuot (Kyuquot) of Alaska.

As bishop, he succeeded Bishop Charles J. Seghers, a classmate from Belgium who had become archbishop of Oregon City. Later that year, Archbishop Seghers visited Montana Territory and recommended that its two vicariates apostolic be consolidated and that a resident vicar apostolic be appointed. Bishop Brondel received the appointment in 1883 and arrived in the territory on June 19. He established his residence at Helena, the territorial capital.

Six months later, he petitioned the Vatican to raise the vicariate to a diocese. Pope Leo XIII created the Diocese of Helena and named him its first bishop on March 7, 1884. Bishop Brondel supported Native American missions and schools, and the religious priests and sisters who ministered to them. He encouraged the religious orders to establish schools, hospitals and orphanages.

He convened synods in 1884, 1887, and 1891. Discussions included a diocesan college and a new cathedral, but he was destined not to see those dreams fulfilled. He was successful in another way. In 1903 he petitioned the pope to erect three more dioceses in Montana. Only one more was established with the see at Great Falls.

With his encouragement, the Helena diocese grew steadily. Sixteen churches grew to sixty-five, four hospitals to eight, two academies to seven, two parochial schools to nine, four diocesan priests to thirty-eight, twelve religious priests to fifteen, and one seminarian to eleven. He died November 3, 1903, in Helena after several illnesses and was buried there.

See also MONTANA, CATHOLIC CHURCH IN.

Flaherty, Cornelia M. *Go with Haste into the Mountains, a History of the Diocese of Helena.* Helena: Diocese of Helena with Falcon Press Publishing Co., 1984.

Palladino, L. B., S.J. *Indian and White in the Northwest.* Baltimore: John Murphy & Company, 1894.

Schoenberg, Wilfred P., S.J. *A History of the Catholic Church in the Pacific Northwest.* Washington, D.C.: Pastoral Press, 1987.

M. CATHERINE TILZEY

BROTHERS OF THE CHRISTIAN SCHOOLS (F.S.C.)

St. John Baptist de La Salle (1651–1719), eldest son of the king's magistrate of Rheims, a canon of the cathedral, and doctor of theology, would have lived and died a holy but uneventful life had not Providence intervened. First his spiritual director, Blessed Nicholas Roland, died and in his will requested Fr. John to secure royal recognition for a group of sisters founded to educate poor girls. Then, the young canon became involved with some barely literate young men trying to teach poor boys in the rundown charity schools of the city parishes, a group with no professional status, no standards, and little motivation to stay with the job. "People who live lower than my own valet," La Salle was to say of them in later years.

Almost by accident, Fr. La Salle assumed the leadership of this nondescript band of teachers. Initially he helped pay their rent; then he moved them into a house near his own. When he saw at closehand how uncultured and uneducated they were, he invited them to his home for meals, and to the shock and chagrin of the family, invited them to live there. Finally, in 1682, he moved with them to a rented house in a poor neighborhood, from which this first community staffed its schools.

The university system, which provided a classical education from grade school to the doctorate, had existed for centuries, but was accessible only to those who, like La Salle, could afford to pay, or who were willing to endure years of penury in the "Latin Quarters" of college towns. Apart from the university schools, there were "little schools" which also charged tuition. Pastors were supposed to provide charity schools for the poor, but in most of these administration was vague, teachers were incompetent and poorly paid, students were unkempt and undisciplined, attendance was sporadic, and facilities were inadequate.

La Salle's Innovations

To meet the educational needs of the poor, La Salle not only established a unique form of the religious life, but also founded teacher-training schools for the laity. He set up weekend programs of study for working teenagers, special education programs for needy students, a boarding school with offerings in advanced technical and pre-professional courses unavailable elsewhere, and an institution to care for juvenile delinquents. When King James II fled to France after the Battle of the Boyne, La Salle formed classes for the children of Irish Catholics who followed him into exile.

Students were to be taught in French, not Latin. They were to be taught in groups, not one-on-one while the others engaged in busywork or worse. Assigned to classes according to their ability, they were promoted when deemed capable of advanced work. Teachers were to keep grade books and lesson plans, which were examined by the principal and inspector of schools at frequent intervals. To guide his Brothers he wrote *The Rule; The Management of Christian Schools; A Collection of Various Topics About the Religious Life; Meditations for Sundays, Feasts, and Time of Retreat; A Method of Interior Prayer,* and numerous letters. He wrote a catechism, and a book on politeness which was used to teach reading. La Salle, with his early brothers, revolutionized education, set standards that transformed teaching into a profession, and established a new religious congregation in the Church, but at the cost of his ambition, fortune, lifestyle, and reputation. People thought he was crazy, his family disowned him, the educational establishment bombarded him with lawsuits, and Church authorities hounded him relentlessly.

Nevertheless, from the time of La Salle's death in 1719 his congregation grew steadily, and on the eve of the French Revolution in 1789 there were over a hundred schools in France and three in Italy. The brothers were almost obliterated during the Revolution, and a number of brothers were martyred, but in 1802 Napoleon ordered the congregation restored, and it spread beyond the borders of France. In 1816 an attempt was made to establish the brothers in Ste. Genevieve, Missouri; in 1837 a permanent foundation was established in Montreal; and in 1845 the brothers opened Calvert Hall College High School in Baltimore. Bishop Hughes of New York presided at the first American habit-taking ceremony of the brothers in St. Patrick's Cathedral in 1849. The brothers opened their first American college in St. Louis in 1849, and a year later, they were welcomed to New Orleans. In 1859 St. Michael's College, now the College of Santa Fe, was founded in New Mexico. At the height of the Civil War (1863), Manhattan College in New York and La Salle University in Philadelphia were founded; and in 1868, eight brothers arrived in San Francisco. In 1878 brothers displaced by the Chicago Fire established Christian Brothers' University in Memphis. The brothers in America had grown to five provinces and a hundred schools in less than forty years.

All of the early foundations suffered financial and other hardships, but the communities in the South had more than their share. The worst disaster was yellow fever, which caused the death of some forty brothers in less than twenty years and brought the work of the brothers in the South to a temporary halt. The province of New Orleans was reestablished by intrepid French brothers who had been driven from France to Mexico by the anticlerical laws of 1904, and from Mexico to the United States by the Revolution of 1914. They remained under the jurisdiction of France until after World War II, and the brothers did not return to New Orleans itself until 1949.

The Latin Question

Some of the bishops of the nineteenth-century United States regarded the public school system, with its public reading of the King James Bible, as a danger to the faith, and made every effort to set up parochial schools which would enable immigrants to adjust to their Protestant milieu, learn skills to enhance their earning power, and nurture religious vocations so badly needed in the burgeoning American Church. Brothers were eagerly sought to staff parish schools, college preparatory academies, child-care institutions, and colleges. Elementary schools and welfare institutions were traditional to the brothers' ministry, but the other schools created a problem, because in order to prepare students for college in those days, it was necessary to teach them the classical languages, and colleges needed a Classics Department to qualify for accreditation. But Latin, as we have seen, was forbidden in the brothers' schools. At first the prohibition was informally waived, but by the end of the nineteenth century the European superiors of the Christian Brothers felt that the rule against Latin should be enforced.

This caused consternation and dismay, but the superiors remained adamant, even removing American administrators from office and exiling them to remote schools in Europe and Asia. Appeals from the American hierarchy to the brothers' superiors and to the Roman Curia were viewed as a manifestation of the so-called "Americanism" heresy, and were rejected. Most schools managed to survive by having laypersons teach the classics and by introducing modern languages, business, science, and engineering courses into the curricula; and finally through the efforts of Cardinals Gibbons, Dougherty, Mundelein, and Hayes (each had a brothers' college in his archdiocese, and the latter two were "Brothers' boys" from Manhattan College), Pope Pius XI in 1923 directed the brothers to permit the teaching of the classics. Vocations to the brotherhood, stagnant since the turn of the century, rose, and before long almost every large city in the country had at least one brothers' school, producing its share of Catholics loyal to their Church and their schools. Ironically, the first non-French superior of the order, Br. Charles Henry Buttimer, was an American who had earned his doctorate in Latin; and Br. Exuperian, the assistant superior general who so bitterly opposed the teaching of Latin in American schools, has been formally proposed for canonization.

Expansion and Diversification

The second quarter of the twentieth century saw rapid expansion of Catholic education in the United States, particularly in large high schools built and supported financially by a diocese or parish, and staffed by religious who received a subsistence salary. For the brothers this had to include support for the brothers at the school, the training of new brothers, the care of the retired, and assessments from the generalate in Europe. Meager finances were stretched to the breaking point, and sometimes beyond, especially during the Great Depression, and to this day brothers' recreations are enlivened by stories arising from the hardships and privations of the period. Nevertheless, the system not only provided education for the middle-class Catholics, but underwrote the costs of the professional training which states were beginning to insist upon. As child labor laws and the growth of trade unions generated a greater need, the brothers placed more of their men into secondary education.

World War II curtailed enrollments nationwide, but at its end the brothers' colleges expanded tremendously to accommodate veterans taking advantage of the G.I. Bill, and the movement to the suburbs created a demand for many new high schools. Fortunately, vocations were at unprecedented heights, and houses of formation were joyfully constructed to receive them. Brothers easily qualified for the workshops in science, math, and foreign languages that were developed in reaction to Sputnik's launching in 1957, and returned from these with techniques to make excellent schools even better. Stirred by Vatican Council II, the Christian Brothers became more flexible in their religious customs. They were no longer obliged to wear the habit, nor did they receive a new name when they entered the order, and they could undertake new ministries, including the teaching of girls. At the same time, the radical upheaval caused many brothers to leave the congregation and in consequence schools had to be staffed with laypersons or closed entirely. Several general chapters considered the problem of diminishing numbers, and evolved the concept of "shared mission" as it became clear that La Salle's charism was a legacy not only for the brothers, but for the entire Church. They instituted the "Lasallian Volunteers," a group of dedicated young laypersons who live in community with the brothers and share the work of their apostolate. Teachers, whatever their status or wherever they taught, shared the mandate of Christ to "teach all nations," and the genius of John Baptist de La Salle could serve as a beacon to all.

In the region of English-speaking North America, besides the province of Toronto, six American provinces serve the areas of Long Island-New England, New York, Baltimore, the Midwest, New Orleans-Santa Fe, and San Francisco. In 1993, 1,177 brothers staffed 6 elementary schools, 9 junior high schools, 51 high schools, 7 colleges and universities, 8 child-care institutions, 9 group homes, and 7 retreat centers. A number of apostolates extend beyond the classroom. For example, St. Mary's Press of Winona, Minnesota, pioneered the teaching of religion through attractive texts rather than the traditional catechism, and publishes many educational texts and other materials. Christian Brothers Services, established in Chicago, offers support and consultation expertise for all administrative details connected with contemporary school administration, from insurance and employee health benefits to computerized scheduling and grade reporting to purchase of school supplies. Dozens of clients in school systems throughout the country benefit from these services. Christian Brothers Investment Services was founded by Brs. Joel Damian Wilhelm and Louis DeThomasis to advise financial officers and directors of development on making the best use of resources in these days of ever rising expenses.

Outstanding Brothers

Brothers have always been active in their own fields of expertise. Br. Boutolph Schneider (1833–1906), founder of the College of Santa Fe, was superintendent of schools for Santa Fe County and a charter member of the School Board of the Territory of New Mexico. He is the only American Christian Brother to have a statue erected in his honor. Br. Maurelian Sheel (1842–1917), founder of Christian Brothers' University, Memphis, was delegated by the American hierarchy to direct the Catholic exhibit at the Chicago Columbian Exposition of 1893. At age fifteen, Br. Azarias Mullaney (1847–93) began a teaching, writing, and lecturing career that led to friendships with Cardinal John Henry Newman and other leading intellectuals of the time. Br. Potamian O'Riley (1846–1917), first dean of Manhattan College's School of Engineering, collaborated with Guglielmo Marconi, and, constructing most of the apparatus himself, was the first person to use an X-ray for medical purposes in Ireland. Br. Amandus Leo Call, another engineering dean at Manhattan College, helped to design the Triborough Bridge.

Br. Barnabas McDonald (1865–1929) founded the Columbian Squires and made Lincoln Hall, New York, a model for the care of juvenile offenders that was copied throughout the nation. In more recent times Br. Dennis Edward Yuergens (1870–1960) was active in the National Catholic Educational Association and many other learned societies throughout his long life. Br. Timothy Diener, "Brother Cellarmaster," developed innovative growing techniques while head of Christian Brothers' Winery in Napa, California. For many years the profits from this

Barnabas McDonald

venture supported the work of the brothers in California. Br. Alfred Brousseau (1907–88), a provincial of that district, was an authority on the Fibonacci number series in mathematics. Br. Anthony Wallace (1910–90) wrote and lectured extensively, especially on the evaluative criteria of the Middle States Accreditation Association. Br. Luke Salm, theologian and author, has served as president of the Catholic Theological Society of America. Br. Nicholas Sullivan is an internationally known speleologist and past president of the Explorers' Club, and Br. Patrick Ellis is president of The Catholic University of America.

American brothers serve in Africa, the Philippines, the Middle East, and Central America, where in 1982 Br. James Miller was killed by those who opposed his work with the poor natives of Guatemala. In addition to their founder, three brothers have been canonized: St. Miguel Febres Cordero, a catechist and Spanish scholar from Ecuador; St. Benilde Romançon, a French elementary school principal responsible for numerous religious vocations; and St. Mutien-Marie Wiaux, who led a life of simple piety in a Belgian boarding school. In addition, there are nineteen beatified brothers, the majority of whom were martyred by the Communists during the Spanish Civil War.

See also CATHOLIC EDUCATION, PAROCHIAL.

Battersby, William J. *Christian Brothers in the United States, 1900–1950.* 2 vols. Winona, Minn.: St. Mary's College Press, 1976.

Isetti, Ronald E. *The Gentle American: The Life and Times of Brother Charles Henry Buttimer, First American Superior General of the Brothers of the Christian Schools.* Landover, Md.: Christian Brothers Publications, 1994.

Salm, Luke. *A Religious Institute in Transition: The Story of Three General Chapters.* Landover, Md.: Christian Brothers Publications, 1989.

WILLIAM QUAINTANCE, F.S.C.

BROUILLET, JEAN BAPTISTE (1813–84)

Native American missionary, vicar general, founder and director of the Catholic Bureau of Indian Affairs. Brouillet was born December 11, 1813, at St. Jean Baptiste de Rouville, Province of Quebec, Canada. The son of a farmer, Brouillet entered St. Hyacinthe Seminary in 1826 and was ordained for the Diocese of Montreal on August 27, 1837. He taught philosophy at the College of Chambly, Quebec, and was assistant and pastor at various parishes in the province for the next few years.

In 1847 he was granted permission to become a missionary in the Northwest for Bishop Augustin Blanchet, Diocese of Walla Walla (Diocese of Nesqually). The party of missionaries began their overland journey from Montreal to the Oregon Territory in spring 1847. Upon their arrival at Fort Walla Walla in October 1847, Brouillet opened St. Anne's mission among Cayuse natives near the Umatilla River along what is now the southeastern border of Washington. Tension between missionaries and Native Americans had been rising, and on November 29, 1847, Protestant missionary Dr. Marcus Whitman and others were killed in an attack by the Cayuse. Brouillet's involvement in the aftermath of the Whitman Massacre led to accusations that the Catholic missionaries and the Hudson's Bay Company were ultimately responsible for the tragedy. Belief in the culpability of the Catholic Church in the massacre was so widespread that Brouillet wrote a pamphlet in 1848 in defense of his actions. It was reprinted in 1856 as Executive Document No. 38, Thirty-Fifth Congress, First Session, House of Representatives.

Brouillet was appointed vicar general of the Diocese of Nesqually and became known as a strong mediator and administrator. His pastoral work involved ministry to Native Americans and French-Canadians in the Pacific Northwest.

Jean Baptiste Brouillet

His work as vicar general often sent him to Washington, D.C., on business relating to church land claims and the care of Native American missions. Bishop Blanchet released Brouillet in 1874 to labor on behalf of Catholic native missions throughout the country. That same year, he established the Bureau of Catholic Indian Missions. He also worked with General Charles Ewing, Commissioner for Indian Affairs, in administering the complex details of President Grant's peace policy. He died on February 5, 1884, in Washington, D.C., from complications of muscle paralysis suffered during a snowstorm in the Dakotas. He is buried at Mt. Olivet Cemetery in Washington, D.C.

Brouillet, J.B.A. "True Account of the Whitman Murder." Ferndale, Washington, 1912.

Kowrach, Edward, J., ed. *Journal of a Catholic Bishop on the Oregon Trail.* Fairfield, Wash.: Ye Galleon Press, 1978.

Rahill, Peter J. *The Catholic Indian Missions and Grant's Peace Policy, 1870–1884.* Washington D.C.: The Catholic University of America Press, 1953.

Thomas, Marian Josephine, S.H.N. "Abbé Jean-Baptiste Abraham Brouillet: First Vicar General of the Diocese of Seattle." Master's thesis, Seattle University, 1950.

CHRISTINE TAYLOR

BROUN, HEYWOOD (1888–1939)

Journalist. Broun was born on December 7, 1888, in Brooklyn, New York. The son of Heywood Cox and Henriette Brose Broun, he studied at the Horace Mann School, New York City, and attended Harvard University (1906–10). He left before graduation and began a career in journalism at the New York *Morning Telegraph.* In 1912 he joined the New York *Tribune* as a sportswriter and was a war correspondent in France during World War I (1917–19).

For the next two years, Broun was literary and drama critic for the *Tribune.* He then joined the staff of the New York *World,* where he began his daily column, "It Seems to Me," which dealt with current controversial issues, such as the Ku Klux Klan, labor unions, and the Sacco and Vanzetti case. His defense of the two alleged murderers led to his dismissal from the *World* in 1928.

Broun was hired by the Scripps-Howard papers and continued his column, becoming one of the most widely syndicated columnists in the country. In 1930 he ventured into politics, running unsuccessfully on the Socialist ticket for a U.S. Congressional seat. His support for unions led to his organizing the American Newspaper Guild in 1933, and he served as its president until his death.

When the *World* merged with *The Telegram* in 1931, he wrote for the new paper until 1939 when he left because of political differences with the publisher and joined the staff of the New York *Post.* From 1935 until his death, he also wrote a column, "Shoot the Works," for *The New Republic.*

Selections from his newspaper columns were published as collections in *Seeing Things at Night* in 1921 and *Pieces of Hate* in 1922. His other publications include an autobiographical novel, *The Boy Grew Older* (1926); *The Sun Field* (1923); *Gandle Follows His Nose* (1926); *Anthony Comstock* (1927), a study of censorship; and *Christians Only* (1931), a study of anti-Semitism.

Following the death of his first wife, Ruth Hale, in 1934, Broun married Connie Madison, a dancer. On May 23, 1939, he was baptized a Catholic by Msgr. (later Archbishop) Fulton J. Sheen. He died in Stamford, Connecticut, on December 18, 1939.

Kramer, D. *Heywood Broun.* New York, 1949.
_____. *Heywood Broun As He Seemed to Us.* New York, 1940.

MARIANNA McLOUGHLIN

BROWNE, MARY DeSALES (1826–1910)

Mercy Sister. Born in Pennsylvania, Fannie Browne was one of the first postulants to enter the Mercy Community at Pittsburgh. Her pastor, Fr. O'Connor, traveled to Ireland in 1845 and accompanied Sr. Francis Xavier Ward and the first Mercy Sisters to America. Her three sisters followed her example: Sr. Regina died at twenty-four in Washington, D.C., while nursing during the Civil War; Sr. Josephine became superior of the Buffalo, New York, foundation; Sr. Vincent accompanied Sr. DeSales to Mississippi. Sr. DeSales began her ministry at the orphanage in Pittsburgh; next, she and four sisters went to Washington, D.C., to the Washington Infirmary, a teaching hospital.

In 1860 she led a group of six sisters to Vicksburg, Mississippi, where they successfully operated a school for a year before the Civil War. During the war the sisters became Confederate nurses, traversing Mississippi and Alabama under most austere circumstances, nursing the wounded from such battles as Shiloh, Corinth, and Jackson. After the siege of Vicksburg in1863, Grant's occupation forces refused to return the school to the sisters until President Lincoln intervened. Both he and Jefferson Davis paid tribute to the nursing efforts of the Mercy Sisters.

In 1875 Sr. DeSales survived the horrendous yellow fever epidemic during which all the parish priests, six sisters, and half the population of the Vicksburg area died. Twenty orphans were left to her care. Under her leadership and example over twenty Mercy schools and hospitals were eventually established throughout Mississippi, which were served by over two hundred sisters.

See also SISTERS OF MERCY OF THE AMERICAS (R.S.M.).

PAULINUS OAKES, R.S.M.

BROWNSON, HENRY FRANCIS (1835–1913)

Soldier, lawyer, author. The son of Orestes Brownson and Sarah Healy Brownson was born in Canton, Massachusetts, on April 6, 1835. As a boy he became a Catholic when his father converted in 1844. He was educated at Holy Cross College and Georgetown University and graduated in 1851. He continued his studies for two years with the Jesuits and spent two further years at Munich. On his return to America he studied law and was admitted to the New York bar. He joined the Union army and received head and debilitating hand wounds at the battle of Chancellorsville. He was captured and was briefly imprisoned by the Confederate army. He remained in the army until 1871 and retired with the rank of major. He formed a successful law partnership in Detroit with Philip Van Dyke, whose sister, Josephine, he had married in 1868. He became a versatile writer and a contributor to *Brownson's Quarterly Review.* He wrote a three-volume biography of his father, *Life of O. A. Brownson,* and also edited a twenty-volume collection of his father's writings. He initiated the first Catholic Congress in Baltimore in 1889, and was awarded the Laetare Medal the same year. He died in Detroit on December 19, 1913.

MICHAEL GLAZIER

BROWNSON, ORESTES AUGUSTUS (1803–76)

Convert, philosopher, journalist, apologist. Born on September 16, 1803, in Stockbridge, Vermont, Orestes Brownson converted to Catholicism in 1844, at the age of forty-one. He was part of the religious ferment and turmoil of his own New England culture prior to his conversion and he brought much of that excitement and challenge into the Catholic community. From the time of his youth in Stockbridge,

Vermont, Brownson experienced that part of the New England culture that was in religious fluidity, nonconformity, and dissent. Unlike his more famous contemporaries Ralph Waldo Emerson and other American nonconformists, however, Brownson lived on the edge and outskirts of the New England culture of wealth, formal education, and privilege. Born into a poor family in Vermont, he lost his father, a Presbyterian, to death when he was three, and because of the family's poverty he was separated from his siblings and his mother, a Restorationist Universalist, when he was six. From his sixth to his fourteenth years, he lived with parental guardians who were Congregationalists.

Orestes A. Brownson

Early Life

In 1817 Brownson rejoined his mother and siblings. With numerous other Vermonters, the Brownsons migrated West to Ballston Spa, New York, where they hoped to find more favorable living conditions than they had in Vermont. In Ballston Spa, Brownson identified himself first with his mother's Universalism, and then, after a revival experience, he became a Presbyterian. At the age of twenty, after only nine months as a Presbyterian, he returned to his former Universalism because of intellectual difficulties he had with a Calvinist emphasis on human depravity and predestination.

In 1824 and 1825 he taught school, first in Detroit and then in Elbridge, New York. In 1826 he went to Vermont to become a Universalist minister. Shortly after his ordination he returned to the Finger Lakes region of upstate New York where he married Sally Healy, one of his former students, and began preaching in a variety of small parishes.

In upstate New York Brownson also edited a number of journals for the Universalists. As an editor and jour-

nalist, he became, like many of the Universalists, a severe critic of the revivalism that was moving across the so-called "Burnt-Over" district of upstate New York during the late 1820s. By 1829, however, he left the Universalist ministry after he had criticized some Universalist pastors for their "narrow denominationalism" and "priestcraft." He became a *persona non grata* among Universalists, moreover, after he supported Fanny Wright and the *Free Inquirer,* a journal that espoused radical social reforms and called for the economic rights of workingmen. By 1830 he considered himself a "free thinker."

Brownson soon discovered that he could not advocate social reform without religion. In 1831, therefore, he returned to the ministry, but this time as a nondenominational preacher in Ithaca, New York. By 1832, after reading the Unitarian William Ellery Channing, he began to modify the religious rationalism of his early twenties and to emphasize the universal value of the religious sentiment. That same year he accepted a Unitarian pastorate in Walpole, New Hampshire. There he began to read some of the French and German romantics. His turn to the romantic impulse became evident in a number of articles he published in various East Coast Unitarian journals, where he came to the attention of the Bostonian literary and religious establishment.

In 1834, seeking a wider audience and a larger congregation for his ministry, he accepted a pastorate in Canton, Massachusetts. His two-year stay there brought him into closer communication with movements in Boston Unitarianism and with some of the leading lights of the Boston intelligentsia. By the summer of 1836, through the influence of George Ripley, he was invited to take up a pastorate among the workingmen of Boston.

In Boston he established a "Society for Christian Union and Progress" (1836), an attempt to reach the workingmen of the city with the message of Christianity. At the same time he became editor of the *Boston Reformer,* a journal in which he criticized Christian pastors for their failures to identify Christianity itself with needed economic and social reforms. In 1835 he also became a charter member of the Transcendentalist Club, a discussion group of romantically inclined advocates of reform in Christianity and society.

While continuing as pastor to workingmen in Boston, he established in 1838 the *Boston Quarterly Review* (1838–42), a widely distributed and distinguished journal of opinion on religion, literature, and politics. In the midst of the political campaign of 1840, he wrote his famous "Essay on the Laboring Classes," a burning Marxist-like critique of the economic structures of society. That essay called for revolutionary economic and political reforms, including the abolition of hereditary descent of property, and alienated him from those in the Boston democratic political and religious establishment.

Between 1840 and 1842 Brownson underwent another gradual intellectual transformation after he read the French St. Simonian Pierre Leroux. With the help of Leroux he moved away from the rationalism and subjective romanticism of his early days and began to develop a concept he and Leroux called "Life by Communion." This theory placed positive value on objective revelation, tradition, and the Church as media of the divine life, which alone, he argued, made social and spiritual progress and reform possible. In 1844 he established a new journal, *Brownson's Quarterly Review* (1844–64: 1872–75), for the dissemination of his new ideas and in October of that year he announced that he had entered the Catholic Church because he had decided that that Church was the only valid medium of the salvific life.

Conversion to Catholicism

His conversion further alienated him from his former Unitarian associates and reinforced their view that Brownson was intellectually and emotionally unstable. Although since 1842 prominent Unitarians had observed Brownson's gradual intellectual movement toward Catholic Christianity, they were unprepared for his postconversion attacks upon Unitarian and Transcendentalist ideals because those attacks appeared to be incompatible with his own former doctrines. In fact, his immediate postconversion arguments in favor of the necessity of the Catholic Church and his opposition to Unitarianism and Transcendentalism were based upon a post-Tridentine apologetic that he had learned from Boston's bishop John Bernard Fitzpatrick. Those views were indeed not in clear continuity with his earlier doctrine of life by communion.

From 1844 until 1855 Brownson edited his *Quarterly* under the guidance of Bishop Fitzpatrick and lectured extensively throughout the United States and Canada. His lectures as a new convert to Catholicism attracted as much popular attention in the American Catholic community as did those of apostate priests in the Protestant community.

Brownson became a celebrity in the American Catholic community, but he also experienced as many difficulties in Catholicism as he had in Protestantism. The American bishops who had endorsed his journal in 1849 withdrew that support in 1854 because a number of bishops felt that his articles on exclusive salvation, his attacks on his fellow convert John Henry Newman, and his extreme positions on the temporal authority of the pope were unnecessarily provocative if not heterodox. In the midst of nativist attacks upon Catholicism in the 1840s and 1850s, moreover, many Irish Catholic clergy, and especially Irish Catholic lay editors, were furious with Brownson's articles supporting the Americanization of the Irish. Brownson argued that Catholicism was above any specific national culture, but he did so in ways that alienated the Irish Catholics whom he criticized, among other things for identifying their own culture with Catholicism.

During the 1850s Brownson's Catholic intellectual life took another turn. In 1849 he read the Italian Catholic ontologist Vincenzo Gioberti whose views he believed had some affinities with his own pre-Catholic doctrine of life by communion. Gradually after 1850 he came more and more under the influence of ontologist principles which became the foundation for his view of the relationship of God to human beings and of the Church to culture. His ontologism was particularly evident in his most important post-Civil War book on politics, *The American Republic* (1865), and in his 1873 "Essays on the Refutation of Atheism." This approach, too, got him in trouble with the papal-favored neoscholastics who considered the ontological method heretical or at least heterodox. Although Brownson was a strong advocate of papal authority (he called himself an "ultra Ultramontane"), he did not support the rising neoscholastic tradition even after it was reinforced by the First Vatican Council (1870) and by numerous nineteenth-century papal decisions.

In 1855, in the midst of his intellectual movement toward ontologism and traditionalism, Brownson, his wife and eight children left Boston and the tutelage of Bishop Fitzatrick for what he hoped would be an open intellectual environment in New York City. From 1855 until the end of the Civil War, he edited his journal from New York City, gained the support of a number of clergy, continued lecturing throughout the nation, tried to demonstrate the necessity of the Catholic Church for the preservation of American ideals of freedom under the law, and generally favored the compatibility of Catholicism and American culture.

At the beginning of the Civil War, Brownson lost some Catholic support for his journal when he advocated emancipation as a means of ending the Civil War, a position that was extremely unpopular with many American Catholics. Loss of subscribers, depression over the length and tragedies of the Civil War, the deaths of two sons who were killed in the war, and a desire to produce a major philosophical treatise on American politics contributed to the cessation of his journal in 1864, the year of Pope Pius IX's Syllabus of Errors.

After 1864 Brownson began to criticize what he considered an emerging secularized culture. To combat secularism, he developed an intellectual defense for theism and demonstrated the vital importance of a theistic view of culture. In the early 1840s he had believed that the most pressing intellectual problem in American religious culture was a defense of the necessity of the Church as the medium of salvation. By the post-Civil War years, he asserted that the defense of theism itself had become the fundamental problem in Western culture.

In 1866 he published his major philosophical treatise on politics, *The American Republic,* to demonstrate the communion (not institutional union) of religion (theism) and politics, believing that "political atheism" (i.e., the separation of religion and politics) was the imminent threat to American culture. Although he was philosophically and theologically alienated from the developing Catholic scholastic tradition, he became a champion of Pope Pius IX's assault upon relativism, subjectivism, and accommodationism. Although he did not accept everything in Pius IX's Syllabus of Errors (he thought, for example, that the pontiff's decree on separation of Church and state was misguided and in fact too extreme), he did believe that the papal spirit of opposition to the world was the right one for a new world culture that Brownson himself believed was heading toward naturalism in philosophy, science, education, literature, and politics. Brownson's rejection of secularism, however, was based upon his own ontological principles, not upon the neoscholastic ideology that was behind the papal opposition.

In 1873, after some years of conflict with Augustine Hewit, the Paulist editor of the *Catholic World,* and other Catholics who favored the scholastic revival, Brownson resumed his own *Quarterly Review.* For two years he published his philosophical and political critiques, but age and failing health forced him to again cease publication in 1875. He then moved to Detroit to live with his favorite son Henry. He died there on April 17, 1876.

Brownson was perhaps the one American Catholic most knowledgeable about mid-nineteenth-century philosophical currents in Europe and America. The periodic shifts in his intellectual orientations revealed his intellectual curiosity, his openness to argumentation, and his creative ability to adapt his own thought to what he perceived to be the changing needs of contemporary culture. Behind the frequent changes, however, was the constant search for new ways of explaining the communion of God with human beings and human culture. He called upon the American Catholic community to engage the vital questions of nineteenth-century intellectual and religious culture, but that immigrant community was unprepared for this task. Not until the twentieth century was Brownson's work picked up again—first by Virgil Michel and then by a host of other scholars in the later half of the twentieth century.

Brownson, Henry F., ed. *The Works of Orestes A. Brownson.* 20 vols. Detroit: Thorndike Nourse, 1882–87.
____. *The Life of Orestes A. Brownson.* 3 vols. Detroit: Henry F. Brownson, 1898–1900.
Carey, Patrick W., ed. *Orestes A. Brownson: Selected Writings.* New York: Paulist Press, 1991.
Ryan, Thomas R. *Orestes A. Brownson: A Definitive Biography.* Huntington, Ind.: Our Sunday Visitor Press, 1975.
Schlesinger, Arthur, Jr. *A Pilgrim's Progress. Orestes A. Brownson.* Boston: Little, Brown, and Co., 1939.

PATRICK W. CAREY

BRUMIDI, CONSTANTINO (1805–80)

An Italian-American painter whose fame is based mainly upon frescoes, both in Italy and the United States. Born in the summer of 1805 in Rome, his early studies began at Rome's Academy of Fine Arts before his admission to the Accademia di San Lucia at the age of thirteen, where he studied under Vincenzio Camucci and Antonio Canova. Early paintings include commissions for Roman palaces and the Vatican (the latter by Popes Gregory XVI and Pius IX). The Vatican commission specified the restoration of several Raphael frescoes, for which Brumidi worked as a member of a team of four Roman painters; alone, he painted Pius IX's portrait. Brumidi's tenure at the Vatican lasted three years, before the political upheavals in 1849 prompted his emigration to New York City; in 1859 he attained U.S. citizenship. Portraiture and church adornments at St. Stephen's Church in New York City and the cathedral in Mexico City complemented Brumidi's first major U.S. work, *Cincinnatus at the Plough* (1855). This work, which decorates the U.S. Capitol's agriculture committee room, introduced fresco painting in the United States. Thereafter, the creation of other allegorical frescoes to adorn the Capitol comprised the bulk of his work, of which the most famous is *Apotheosis of Washington* (1865). This work, in the rotunda, depicts George Washington and other American heroes in the company of gods and goddesses. One digression from his work at the U.S. Capitol was the adornment of Philadelphia's cathedral with frescoes of Saints Peter and Paul. Brumidi's and other artists' work on the Capitol during the American Civil War was in response to Lincoln's mandate for the continuation of the Capitol's restoration as a symbolic demonstration of national unity. In 1879 Brumidi's fall from his scaffold while painting the frieze around the rotunda's circumference eventually proved fatal. He died on February 19, 1880.

LISELLE DRAKE

BRUNINI, JOHN (1868–1954)

Attorney. John B. Brunini was born in Vicksburg, Mississippi, on December 25, 1868, son of Alexander Brunini and Teresa Gatti, Italian immigrants who came to Yazoo City on the eve of the Civil War and moved to Vicksburg during the later war years. John attended local Catholic schools and received his law degree from the University of Virginia. He was admitted to the Mississippi bar in 1891. He served *gratis* as attorney to the Diocese of Natchez for more than forty years and was active in the Knights of Columbus and the Catholic Committee of the South.

Brunini married Blanche Mary Stein on December 9, 1895; their eight children included Joseph, the first Mississippi-born bishop of the Diocese of Jackson; John, a New York Catholic editor *(Spirit)* and author; Alex and

Edmund, attorneys; Charles, who died in infancy; and three daughters, Beatrice, Blanche, and Marjorie.

Although he never sought elected state or national office, Brunini was a friend and advisor to Mississippi senators and governors—"a power in the State Democratic party and a natural leader in civic affairs" (*CAS,* November 11, 1954). He served in many civic roles, including chairman of the Mississippi Highway Commission, and played a major role in the restoration of Vicksburg's National Military Park.

Brunini was instrumental in derailing proposed state legislation to ban white teachers from all schools for African Americans including Catholic schools (1914) and to enact a convent inspection law (1916). He successfully argued before the U.S. Supreme Court the Sisters of Mercy's right to inherit the Botto estate despite the state's attempt to confiscate it; he later played a major role in repealing the state law forbidding bequests to religious institutions.

In 1929 Brunini became the first Mississippian to be named a Knight of St. Gregory; in 1951 sons Alex and Edmund became the state's fourth and fifth Knights of St. Gregory. John received an honorary law degree from Georgetown University. Brunini died at Vicksburg on November 8, 1954, and was buried there. Bishop Richard Gerow noted that Brunini was "an example not only of family . . . , but also of his integrity in his profession and his religious life" (Gerow Diary, November 10, 1954).

John Brunini clipping file, in Archives, Diocese of Jackson.
Bishop Joseph Brunini family papers.
Catholic Action of the South (CAS), November 11, 1954.
Gerow Diary, in the Archives, Diocese of Jackson.
Gunn Correspondence, in the Archives, Diocese of Jackson.

CHARLES E. NOLAN

BUHLMEIER, EMMA (MOTHER THOMASINA) (1859–1926)

Religious foundress. Mother Mary Thomasina, O.P., was foundress of the Congregation of St. Thomas Aquinas in 1888 in Washington Territory. Born in New York City on September 29, 1859, and baptized as Emma Buhlmeier, she later attended a Dominican convent school in that city. An uncommonly devout child, she persuaded her widowed mother and the superior of Holy Rosary Convent in New York to accept her as a postulant when she was only twelve years old. She was not allowed to receive her habit until 1874 because of her age. At that time she was given her name in religion, Sr. Mary Thomasina of the Blessed Sacrament. After her profession of vows, she was sent to St. Dominic Convent in New Jersey, where, despite her tender years, she was appointed novice mistress. In 1885 the Jersey City Dominicans opened a new convent in Lima, Ohio, and Sr. Thomasina was made superior.

At this time the Jersey City Dominicans belonged to the Second Order of Dominicans, with members committed to contemplative lives that had to be modified by periodic permissions for their work of teaching. Sr. Thomasina, convinced that this Second Order was not compatible with the duties required for teaching, suggested a basic change in their status—that they change to Third Order. Most sisters strongly opposed any change. Eventually Sr. Thomasina received permission from Dominican and Church authorities to establish a Third Order Congregation in the Pacific Northwest. Thus it happened that in October 1888, with two sisters, de Chantal and Aloysia, she traveled west to Pomeroy, Washington Territory, and founded the Congregation of St. Thomas Aquinas. At the request of Bishop Aegidius Junger, bishop of Nesqually, they opened a school there on October 29.

Pomeroy did not prove to be satisfactory. After many hardships, the three sisters with their novices moved to Seattle where they remained only a short time, because a new pastor of the parish wanted a larger order for his teachers. Meanwhile, Sr. Thomasina received documents from Rome, dated April 11, 1890, according to which her new congregation was canonically established in the Third of the Dominican Orders. She was given, by these accounts, the title of "Mother."

Leaving Seattle with her sisters for nearby Tacoma, Mother Thomasina acquired land and began over. In the course of time she established the motherhouse there, acquiring the more common congregation name, "The Tacoma Dominicans," as opposed to "The Everett Dominicans" in the same state of Washington. In Tacoma, Mother Thomasina established the novitiate, an academy for girls, a school for boys, which later became the Northwest's only military academy, and a college. When she died on April 18, 1926, while visiting Everett on business, she left a vibrant congregation with twelve convents of her sisters teaching in as many schools in the state of Washington.

See also DOMINICANS (O.P.); WASHINGTON, CATHOLIC CHURCH IN.

Burton, Katherine. *All the Way to Heaven.* Tacoma, 1958.
Flanagan, Mary Rita, O.P. *The Work of the Sisters of St. Dominic of the Congregation of St. Thomas Aquinas in the Diocese of Seattle, 1888–1951.* Seattle, 1951.

WILFRED P. SCHOENBERG, S.J.

BURKE, JOHN (1859–1937)

U.S. Treasurer, judge, governor. Born in Keokuk County, Iowa, on February 25, 1859, Burke was the son of Irish immigrants John and Mary Ryan Burke. He was educated in local public schools and at the University of Iowa, where he received his law degree in 1886. Admitted to the Iowa bar, Burke practiced law in Des Moines with a brother. In 1888, he moved to the Dakota Territory where he continued his law practice and was elected state representative in 1890 and state senator in 1892. Burke married Mary Kane in 1891; they had four children.

In 1906 Burke became the first Roman Catholic elected governor of North Dakota. Holding office for an unprecedented three terms between 1907 and 1913, he was a progressive Democrat who initiated liberal legislation dealing with corrupt practices, lobbying, primary elections, and public utilities control, among other issues. A contender for the vice-presidential nomination at the Democratic National Convention in 1912, Burke was appointed United States Treasurer in 1913 by President Woodrow Wilson. He served until 1921 when he became an associate in a brokerage business in New York, and later practiced law privately in North Dakota. Known as "Honest John," Burke was elected associate justice of the North Dakota Supreme Court in 1924. He was that court's chief justice from 1929 to 1931, and again from 1935 until his death in Rochester, Minnesota, on May 14, 1937.

Glabb, Charles N. "John Burke and the North Dakota Progressive Movement, 1906–1912." Unpublished M.A. thesis, University of North Dakota, 1952.

K. N. McCARTHY

BURKE, JOHN E. (1852–1925)

Diocesan priest of New York. John E. Burke was born in Brooklyn, New York, on January 22, 1852, the son of John and Catherine Burke. He studied at St. Francis Xavier College in Manhattan and at Mt. St. Mary's Seminary in Emmitsburg, Maryland. He completed his studies for the priesthood at the North American College in Rome. Ordained on August 4, 1878, in Rome, he was first assigned to Epiphany Church in Manhattan where the pastor was Fr. Richard Burtsell. Burke was named the first pastor of St. Benedict the Moor Church in November 1883, having been involved with the activity surrounding its establishment by Burtsell, who was interested in the pastoral care of New York's African American Catholics.

The church, the first parish church established for African American Catholics north of the Mason-Dixon Line, had as its members laborers and domestic workers from the city area as well as distinguished black politicians including Dr. John E. W. Thompson, the U.S. minister and consul general to Haiti from 1885–91.

In December 1886 Burke opened an orphanage for black children in the parish house and named it St. Benedict's Home. The home was established to meet the needs of those children who apparently were prevented by their racial classification from being admitted to other Catholic institutions in the city at this time. The home was later moved to Rye, New York, in suburban Westchester County. It remained there until the site was closed in 1941 and the children were moved to the Mission of the Immaculate Conception in Staten Island, New York. With the shift of Manhattan's black population northward, St. Benedict's Church was moved to smaller quarters in midtown.

In 1907 Burke was named executive director of the Catholic Board for Mission Work Among the Colored People, an organization established by the American bishops at the prompting of Rome. Burke worked for the next eighteen years with a group of priests from various dioceses who toured the country seeking donations for the support of black Catholic churches. During his tenure as director, eighty mission churches and sixty-six schools were either wholly or partially established by the board, and 217 teaching sisters were paid a regular salary through funds raised by the board. Burke was named a domestic prelate by Pius X in October 1914 in recognition of his work "for the colored people." He died in Mount Vernon, New York, on May 7, 1925.

Arlotta, Jack M. "'Before Harlem': Black Catholics in the Archdiocese of New York and the Church of St. Benedict the Moor." *Dunwoodie Review* 16 (1992–93) 69–108.
Davis, Cyprian, O.S.B. *History of Black Catholics in the United States.* New York, 1990.

JACK M. ARLOTTA

BURKE, JOHN JOSEPH (1875–1936)

Paulist. Born June 6, 1875, in New York City to immigrant Irish parents, John J. Burke attended St. Francis Xavier High School and then the College of St. Francis Xavier, both on the Lower West Side. After graduating from college in 1896, he entered the Missionary Society of St. Paul the Apostle, commonly known as the Paulists, a community founded by Isaac Hecker. Burke studied for the priesthood at the Paulist seminary in The Catholic University of America, Washington, D.C., and was ordained on June 9, 1899. He remained at the university for two more years to earn a licentiate in theology.

Editor of the Catholic World

Following completion of his degree, Burke did a brief stint of parish work followed by another of giving parish missions. In 1903 the Paulist community appointed him assistant editor of its magazine the *Catholic World.* After an apprenticeship of only one year, he took over the editorship of the entire Paulist publishing enterprise: the *Catholic World, The Leader* (a magazine for youth), and the Catholic Publication Society (later called Paulist Press). Prior to the papal condemnation of Modernism (1907), Burke published articles by such avant garde theologians as George Tyrrell, S.J. Thereafter, the theological writings in the magazine hewed to a strict orthodoxy. In the years following the condemnation, Burke promoted social reform

John J. Burke

through articles by men like sociologist William J. Kerby and moral theologian John A. Ryan. He served as editor of the *Catholic World* until 1922. During his tenure, his theological thinking matured.

Burke's theology blended two complementary notions: the religious ideals of Hecker and the doctrine of the Mystical Body of Christ. Like Hecker, Burke believed that only "the truth of the Catholic Church would vivify, explain, redeem and sanctify every field of human activity and every faculty and power of man." The bearers of this redemptive truth were lay persons who grasped "the lesson of continued and abiding prayer: of learning to live in the presence of God: of seeking the guidance of the Holy Spirit within." Such Spirit-filled people "out in the marketplace, in shop or in office . . . would have the opportunity to explain the doctrines of the Church: to lay down the right ethical principle on a social, economic or labor problem." Timidity had no place in the life of the Catholic Christian. "The individual Catholic layman [was] not only to be prepared, but actually to speak: to be aggressive: vigilant of opportunity: with initiative and energy: carrying into every corner, to every ear that would listen, the message of the Catholic truth." Like Hecker, Burke saw a deep compatibility between the principles on which the United States was founded and those of the Catholic Church. Indeed, the two were practically interchangeable. The principles of the Constitution, "if rightly carried out to their full logical term, would lead to Catholic truth, as of Catholic truth they were born." Like Hecker, he believed that the way to convert America was to show "the true American that his very first principles were a preparatory declaration of the Catholic Faith" ("Father Hecker and Present Problems," *Catholic World* 110 [January 1920] 564–71).

While stressing the role and power of the individual to inject Catholic truth into everyday life, Burke used the doctrine of the Mystical Body of Christ to tie those individuals into a unity. "The individual must eagerly and earnestly perfect himself," he wrote; "yet this perfecting of self is not an unrelated, but a social act. The individual is not alone, he is a member of Christ and of Christ's kingdom . . . what he thinks and does affects for good or ill the entire society of his fellows. . . . [W]e are knit to one another more closely than words can describe because we are all one in Christ, and Christ is all in all, the Saviour, the One Man Who has incorporated all men and all creation into himself" (from translator's preface of Abbé Anger, *The Doctrine of the Mystical Body of Christ: According to the Principles of the Theology of St. Thomas,* trans. John J. Burke [New York: Benziger Brothers, 1931]). This doctrine gave Burke a framework within which to take a national view of Catholicism. America's entry into the First World War convinced him that the Church must act as a unit. "The individual, the parish, the society, the diocese, must emphasize and sacrifice itself unto that larger Catholic unity of which each is a reflection and from which each borrows its title," declared Burke. "That Catholic unity must in turn be employed in the solution of the national problems" (quoted in Michael Williams, *American Catholics in the War: National Catholic War Council, 1917–1921* [New York: Macmillan Company, 1921] 119).

National Catholic War Council

Acting on these beliefs, Burke participated in national organizations and efforts. In 1911 he helped establish the Catholic Press Association. When America declared war on Germany in 1917, he founded the Chaplain's Aid Association to provide priests in the military with all the accoutrements necessary for their ministry. Shortly thereafter he organized the National Catholic War Council to coordinate the Catholic war effort and to represent Catholic views to the government. After the American archbishops assumed control of the War Council, Burke served as chairman of the council's Committee on Special War Activities, which oversaw a variety of subcommittees that mobilized Catholic lay men and women, monitored legislation, maintained historical records, and handled postwar reconstruction. To advise the War Department on how best to maintain the moral tone in and around military camps, he formed and chaired an interdenominational group known as the Committee of Six, including representatives from the Catholic, Protestant, and Jewish faiths. In recognition of all his war work, the War Department awarded Burke the Distinguished Service Medal.

General Secretary of the NCWC

Perhaps Burke's greatest efforts for national Catholic action came after the war. In 1919 the American hierarchy organized itself as the National Catholic Welfare Conference (NCWC) to promote Catholic activity, social welfare work, education, and aid to immigrants. The hierarchy implemented its decisions through an Administrative Committee of bishops, which operated a multibranch secretariat in Washington, D.C. Burke was selected as general secretary of the Washington office, a position that gave him the daily, on-site supervision of all the NCWC departments, and thereby of all national Catholic activities. For the final seventeen years of his life he labored tirelessly to organize the laity, to foster and protect Catholic education, to encourage social reform along Catholic lines, and to protect the Church's legislative interests. To provide a theological foundation for such national activities, Burke translated two French treatises on the Mystical Body, *Christ in the Christian Life According to Saint Paul* by J. Duperray and *The Doctrine of the Mystical Body of Christ According to the Principles of the Theology of St. Thomas* by Abbé Anger, published in English in 1927 and 1931 respectively. He then brought forward his own meditations on the Mystical Body in a book entitled *Christ in Us* (1934). In 1927 the Vatican conferred an honorary doctorate in sacred theology on Burke for all his work with the NCWC.

The Church in Mexico

From 1926 until his death, a matter that deeply involved Burke, both as general secretary of the NCWC and as liaison of the Vatican, was a resolution of the Church-state conflict in Mexico. Beginning in 1925 the Mexican government began a persecution of the Catholic Church, countered by a church strike (the suspension of all worship services), an economic boycott, and the Cristero Rebellion. Working through the U.S. State Department and in close collaboration with Dwight Morrow, ambassador to Mexico, Burke twice met with Mexican President Plutarco Elías Calles to pave the way for a *modus vivendi,* which was finally reached in June 1929. The adjustment, however, was short-lived, lasting only until 1932 when the persecution was gradually revived. Burke insisted that President Franklin D. Roosevelt bring informal pressure to bear on the Mexican government for a resolution of the conflict. The president did so and arranged for Assistant Secretary of State Sumner Welles to act as go-between for Burke and the Mexican ambassador to the United States in the process of ending the persecution. At the time of Burke's death, many churches in Mexico had reopened, and a special papal envoy had toured that country as the first step toward the appointment of a new apostolic delegate there. The month before his death, Burke was made a domestic prelate (monsignor) in reward for all his service as general secretary of the NCWC.

He died suddenly in Washington on October 30, 1936, of an occluded coronary artery.

See also PAULISTS (C.S.P.).

Catholic Action 18 (1936), the entire December issue.

McKeown, Elizabeth. *War and Welfare: American Catholics and World War 1.* New York and London: Garland Publishing, Inc., 1988.

Piper, John F., Jr. "Father John J. Burke, C.S.P., and the Turning Point in American Catholic History." *Records of the American Catholic Historical Society of Philadelphia* 92 (March–December 1981) 101–13.

Sheerin, John B., C.S.P. *Never Look Back: The Career and Concerns of John J. Burke.* New York: Paulist Press, 1975.

Slawson, Douglas J. *The Foundation and First Decade of the National Catholic Welfare Council.* Washington, D.C.: The Catholic University of America Press, 1992.

____. "The National Catholic Welfare Conference and the Church-State Conflict in Mexico, 1925–1929." *The Americas* 47 (July 1990) 55–93.

____. "The National Catholic Welfare Conference and the Mexican Church-State Conflict of the Mid-1930s: A Case of *déjà vu.*" *Catholic Historical Review* 80 (January 1994) 58–96.

DOUGLAS J. SLAWSON

BURNETT, PETER (1807–95)

Oregon and California pioneer. Peter Hardeman Burnett was born in Nashville, Tennessee, on November 15, 1807, the eldest son of George and Dorothy Burnet. Peter grew up on a farm in Missouri. At the age of nineteen he returned to Tennessee to work in a hotel; he also added the second "t" to his name to make it "more complete and emphatic." After becoming a clerk in a store, Burnett married Harriet W. Rogers in 1828. The following year he purchased the store, but after three unsuccessful years he moved back to Missouri heavily in debt. Burnett studied law, and in 1839 he became a practicing lawyer; in 1840 he was appointed prosecuting attorney for the Liberty District.

Still in debt and with his wife's health failing, Burnett emigrated to Oregon, arriving in October 1843. After helping to found Linnton, Burnett moved to a farm on the Tualatin Plains of the Willamette Valley. The same year he was chosen as a member of Oregon's legislative committee. In 1845 he was appointed judge of the supreme court of Oregon; the following year Burnett converted to Catholicism.

In 1848 he joined the gold rush, arriving in California in November 1848. Burnett became attorney and agent for John A. Sutter, Jr., and in 1849 (after leaving Sutter's employ) he was named judge of the superior tribunal of California. A strong supporter of California statehood, Burnett was elected governor in November 1849 in an election which ratified the state constitution. Burnett resigned on January 9, 1851, and returned to private law practice. In 1857 he was appointed to the state supreme court, serving until 1858. With two partners, Burnett founded the Pacific

Bank in San Francisco in 1863. In 1880 he retired and published his memoirs; he died on May 17, 1895, in his San Francisco home.

Burnett, Peter Hardeman. *Recollections and Opinions of an Old Pioneer.* New York: D. Appleton and Company, 1880.

____. *The Path Which Led a Protestant Lawyer to the Catholic Church.* New York: D. Appleton and Company, 1860.

Clark, Malcolm, Jr. *The Eden Seekers.* Boston: Houghton Mifflin Company, 1981.

MICHAEL SOCOLOW

BURTSELL, RICHARD (1840–1912)

Priest, canon lawyer, diarist. Richard Burtsell was born in New York City on April 13, 1840, where he attended local Catholic schools. His father, John, was born in the United States and was a businessman. The Burtsell family claimed that their ancestors had emigrated to Maryland from Wales in the 1640s, but there is little evidence to substantiate this claim. His mother, Dorothea Morrogh, was born in Cork, Ireland, and came to New York shortly before the Great Famine (1845–48). At the age of eleven, Burtsell began studies for the priesthood at the Sulpician Seminary in Montreal. From there he went to Rome for studies at the Urban College of the Propaganda where he earned degrees in philosophy and theology. After ordination in Rome in 1862, Burtsell was assigned to St. Ann's Church in Manhattan where Thomas Scott Preston, a conservative Episcopalian convert, was pastor.

From 1865 until his death, Burtsell kept a detailed diary of his life and work as a priest. Although only a small part of this diary has ever been published, most of it survives

Richard Burtsell

in the Archives of the Archdiocese of New York, It contains almost five thousand pages of entries and runs almost continuously until his death in 1912. Since Burtsell was influential in ecclesiastical circles beyond New York, this diary is an excellent resource for information on the American Catholic Church and its more important, and often controversial, events and persons.

In December 1867 Archbishop John McCloskey assigned Burtsell to found Epiphany parish in Manhattan where he remained as pastor until 1890. Though he lacked a formal degree in canon law, Burtsell was well versed in the field and was often called upon by other priests to represent them in canonical cases against their bishops. Burtsell served as a consultant for Dr. Edward McGlynn in his conflict with Archbishop Michael Corrigan of New York. Because of his association with McGlynn and other liberal-minded clerics, Burtsell was held suspect by Archbishop Corrigan. Corrigan removed him in 1890 as pastor of Epiphany and banished him to an upstate parish, St. Mary's in Rondout, near Kingston. Although he appealed his case, Rome found in favor of Corrigan. After this, Burtsell poured himself into pastoral work in his new parish, and was partially vindicated when he was named a monsignor by Archbishop John M. Farley in 1904. A hardworking pastor and an accomplished self-taught canon lawyer, Burtsell fought hard to protect the rights of ordinary priests from highhanded bishops who ignored canon law. He died of pneumonia on February 4, 1912, in Kingston, New York.

Callahan, Nelson A., ed. *The Diary of Richard L. Burtsell, Priest of New York.* New York, 1978.

Cohalan, Florence D. *A Popular History of the Archdiocese of New York.* Yonkers, 1983.

Curran, Robert Emmett, S.J. "Prelude to 'Americanism': The New York Accademia and Clerical Radicalism in the Late Nineteenth Century." *Church History* 47 (March 1978) 48–65.

____. *Michael Augustine Corrigan and the Shaping of Conservative Catholicism in America, 1878–1902.* New York, 1978.

ANTHONY D. ANDREASSI

BUTIN, ROMAIN FRANÇOIS (1871–1937)

Marist priest, Scripture scholar, linguist, archeologist, professor, and founding member of the Catholic Biblical Association of America. Romain [Romanus] François Butin was born in the town of Saint Romain d'Urfé in eastern France on December 3, 1871. At the age of nineteen he came to the United States. He entered the Society of Mary, the Marists, completing his theological studies in Washington with ordination in 1897. From 1912 until his death in 1937, Butin taught Semitic languages and literature at The Catholic University of America. In 1926 he was chosen as annual professor and acting director of the American School of Oriental Research in Jerusalem, collaborating there with William F. Albright and providing the Harvard expeditions to Sinai with translations of hitherto indecipherable inscriptions.

Butin's most important contributions include his work on the origins of the alphabet, a Hebrew Grammar, and his initiative in establishing the Catholic Biblical Association of America. While working for the Episcopal Committee of the Confraternity of Christian Doctrine with other scholars in 1936 on a revised edition of the Rheims version of the New Testament, Butin proposed a permanent association of Catholic Scripture scholars. He submitted a tentative plan to the American bishops, and this led to the formation of the Catholic Biblical Association, which acknowledged at Butin's death that his energetic zeal and untiring efforts were largely responsible for its existence. Fr. Romain Butin died in an automobile accident in University Park, Maryland, December 8, 1937.

See also CATHOLIC BIBLICAL ASSOCIATION (CBA).

Butin, Romain François, S.M. *The Ten Nequdoth of the Torah.* Baltimore, 1906.
_____. *Progressive Lessons in Hebrew.* Washington, 1915.
Numerous articles and book reviews for professional journals.

PHILIP GAGE, S.M.

BUTLER, MARY JOSETTA (1904–95)

Religious, innovator in liberal education. Born (December 27, 1904) and raised in Chicago, Sr. Josetta taught in the public schools before entering the Sisters of Mercy. The first woman to earn a Ph.D. in chemistry at the University of Illinois, she then joined the faculty of St. Xavier College, Chicago. Later, as dean, Sr. Josetta led the college to distinction in liberal education for women. Grants from the Fund for the Advancement of Education and Carnegie Endowment assisted St. Xavier to develop and implement an innovative continuum of liberal education from first grade through college.

She advocated completion of college studies by sisters before they assumed professional roles. She rallied support to the Sister Formation Conference which aimed to strengthen development of the intellectual, spiritual, and professional life for women religious. She joined other Sisters of Mercy in transforming these goals into action.

Besides her engagement in associations of higher education, Sr. Josetta held leadership positions with the Conference of Major Superiors of Women, Movement for a Better World—U.S. and International, and the Sisters of Mercy.

Her vision of Mercy's worldwide mission launched the Overseas Education Program. Through her efforts, 69 Catholic institutions funded college scholarships for 270 religious sisters from 10 Third World countries as their contribution to mutual understanding and appreciation of cultural diversity. She died on February 24, 1995.

See also SISTERS OF MERCY OF THE AMERICAS (R.S.M.).

Butler, Mary Josetta, R.S.M., and Claudette Dwyer, R.S.M. *Overseas Education Program.* Chicago: Sisters of Mercy of the Americas, 1980.
The Liberal Education of the Christian Person: Saint Xavier College Self-Study. Chicago: Saint Xavier College, 1965.
Perlmutter, Oscar William. "A Program for Liberal Education." *Commonweal* LIX (17) (January 29, 1954) 423–26.

CLAUDETTE DWYER, R.S.M.

BUTLER, PIERCE (1866–1939)

Associate Justice of the U.S. Supreme Court. Born to Irish immigrants in a log farmhouse near Northfield, Minnesota, on March 17, 1866, Butler earned his B.S. degree in 1887 from Carleton College and was admitted to the Minnesota bar in 1888. Butler married Annie Cronin in 1891; they had eight children. Appointed assistant county attorney in 1891, Butler was elected county attorney in 1893 and 1895, but was defeated for state senator in 1906. Leaving politics, he began his association with the firm which became Butler, Mitchell and Doherty, and was known for his work in federal cases testing the application of the Sherman Anti-Trust Act. Butler was also renowned for his expert representation of railway corporations, particularly in rate cases, like the *Minnesota Rate Cases.*

In 1922 Butler was nominated to the U.S. Supreme Court by President Warren Harding. Confirmed as associate justice the same year, Butler served for sixteen years, writing more than 300 majority opinions and 140 dissents, becoming, in Justice Holmes' words, a "monolith" on the Court. Philosophically opposed to centralization of power in the federal government, Butler regularly voted to strike down government regulation of business. From 1933 he became the leader of the Court's conservative bloc, which tried to resist New Deal legislation. Butler was a chief target of President Roosevelt's "court packing" scheme in 1937. He died in Washington, D.C., on November 16, 1939, bringing to an end an important era in the Supreme Court.

Brown, F. J. *The Social and Economic Philosophy of Pierce Butler.* CUA Studies in Sociology 13, Washington, D.C., 1945.
Noonan, John T., Jr. "The Catholic Justices of the United States Supreme Court." *Catholic Historical Review* 67 (3) (1981) 369–85.

K. N. McCARTHY

BYRNE, ANDREW (1802–62)

First bishop of Little Rock, a diocese which both then and now encompasses the whole state of Arkansas. He was born in Navan, about forty miles northwest of Dublin, Ireland, the son of a Robert and Margery Moore Byrne. There is no record of Andrew Byrne's actual date of birth; yet, according to Irish parish records, he was baptized on December 3, 1802. Since his given name was Andrew, he may have been born on November 30, the feastday of St. Andrew. Little is known of his early life or education except that while a seminarian in Navan, Byrne heard Bishop John England of Charleston, South Carolina, recruiting priests. Answering the call, Byrne arrived in Charleston by the early 1820s. He completed his priestly formation under Bishop England who ordained him on November 11, 1827.

As the Charleston diocese then included both the Carolinas and Georgia, Byrne's first assignment was in North Carolina. He returned to Charleston in 1830 to become pastor of St. Mary's Church. In 1833 he accompanied Bishop England to the Second Provincial Council in Baltimore as vicar general. Byrne's relationship with Bishop England apparently deteriorated and he left the Charleston diocese in 1836. He transferred to the Diocese of New York where he made a name for himself as a pastor in New York City, becoming the founding pastor of St. Andrew's Church in 1842.

First Bishop of Little Rock

Byrne's proven abilities as pastor, his connection with New York bishop John Hughes, plus his prior Southern experience, all made him a natural choice for a diocese on the southwestern frontier. Pope Gregory XVI erected the Diocese of Little Rock on November 28, 1843; Byrne was consecrated as Arkansas's first Roman Catholic bishop in Old St. Patrick's Cathedral on March 11, 1844. He arrived in Little Rock three months later with just two priests to minister to all of Arkansas.

There was a Catholic church in Little Rock, known as St. Joseph's, built in the early 1840s. The priest who built this structure, however, left the state and sold the deed to a Catholic priest in New Orleans. Byrne raised funds to purchase another lot where he built his Cathedral of St. Andrew, dedicated on November 1, 1846. Throughout his eighteen years as bishop, Byrne never had more than ten priests at one time. He maintained the diocese with funds from the Austrian-based Leopoldine Society and the French-based Society for the Propagation of the Faith. Using this support, Byrne purchased land, sustained his clergy, and started schools. He founded the College of St. Andrew at Fort Smith in 1849. He journeyed to Ireland to persuade the Sisters of Mercy to locate a convent in Little Rock by 1851, the year these sisters opened what became known as Mount St. Mary's Academy, Arkansas's oldest educational institution. By the Civil War, Mercy Sisters were also operating convent schools in Fort Smith and Helena.

During the nativist, anti-Catholic, Know-Nothing uproar of the 1850s, Byrne studiously avoided political disputes, particularly those involving slavery. He owned no slaves and his correspondence yields no opinion on the subject. Like many Catholic prelates of the period, Byrne probably saw the issue as not one of moral or religious concern.

Bishop Byrne was quite dissatisfied with his position at first. At the Sixth Provincial Council in Baltimore in 1846, he persuaded his fellow bishops to petition the Vatican to abolish the Arkansas diocese so that he could be moved to the newly created Diocese of Buffalo. Rome dismissed this recommendation and refused the bishop's later request for a transfer in 1853. In 1850 the Arkansas diocese was attached to a newly created ecclesiastical province of New Orleans. With bishops from Mississippi, Alabama, Texas, and northern Louisiana, Byrne attended provincial councils in 1856 and 1860.

Byrne attempted to attract clergy and laity from his native land during the 1850s, yet Catholics numbered only one percent of Arkansas's population by 1860. His last trip to Ireland in 1858–59 yielded few recruits. The Civil War closed the College of St. Andrew in 1861, and the war disrupted some international communications, making it difficult for him to secure funds from Europe. Byrne died on June 10, 1862, in Helena, at St. Catherine's Mercy Convent. He was buried in the convent garden, but his successor, Bishop Edward M. Fitzgerald, had his remains placed in the crypt below his recently constructed Cathedral of St. Andrew on November 30, 1881. Though he had his share of disappointments and frustrations, Byrne persevered and laid the foundations of the Church so securely that the diocese survived, despite years of civil war and a five-year absence of a successor bishop.

See also ARKANSAS, CATHOLIC CHURCH IN.

Archives of the Archdiocese of New Orleans, Old Ursuline Convent in New Orleans.

Archives of the Diocese of Little Rock, St. John's Catholic Center, Little Rock, Arkansas.

Archives of the University of Notre Dame.

Clarke, Richard N. *Lives of the Deceased Bishops of the Catholic Church in the United States.* 2 vols. New York, 1872, 265–67.

Diocesan Historical Commission. *A History of Catholicity in Arkansas.* Little Rock, Arkansas, 1925, 9–11.

Little Rock *Arkansas Gazette,* obituary, June 28, 1862, 2.

Woods, James M. *Mission and Memory: A History of the Catholic Church in Arkansas.* Little Rock: August House Publishing Company, 1993, 55–72.

JAMES M. WOODS

BYRNE, THOMAS SEBASTIAN (1841–1923)

Fifth bishop of Nashville. Byrne was born in Hamilton, Ohio, in 1841, and was educated at St. Thomas Seminary,

Bardstown, Kentucky; Mount St. Mary of the West Seminary, Cincinnati, Ohio; and the North American College in Rome. He began his long episcopate in Nashville on July 25, 1894. His diocese then comprised the entire state. Until Byrne, it was a "Propagation" diocese, basically missionary in character and kept afloat by missionary funds. Byrne turned Nashville into a modern Catholic diocese, with a stable central administration and strictly observed geographical parishes. Order and discipline were his watchwords. He fostered a new spirit of pride and confidence in Tennessee Catholics, partly through his establishment of new churches, schools, and hospitals, and by his sponsorship of organizations like the Knights of Columbus, the Ladies of Charity, and orphanages. He was a pioneer in starting churches and schools for the blacks.

Byrne was himself no bleeding heart. He was starkly severe and aristocratic, devoted to Rome and the papacy, suspicious and intolerant of anything not Catholic. Born in Hamilton, Ohio, near the Cincinnati he felt his home base all his life, he was a laborer in his youth and a rather late vocation, entirely self-educated. He was a proud American. His support of the national interest in the Spanish-American War was quoted the country over, asserting the position of American Catholics as against Catholic Spain. An indefatigable author and translator, he became a well-known figure in the American hierarchy, a warm and articulate supporter of the new Catholic University of America. He was a great builder, often taking a hand himself with hod and trowel. He died on September 4, 1923, in the shadow of the new cathedral he had built in Nashville.

See also TENNESSEE, CATHOLIC CHURCH IN.

Stritch, Thomas. *The Catholic Church in Tennessee: The Sesquicentennial Story.* Nashville, 1987.

THOMAS STRITCH

C

CABOT, JOHN (ca. 1450–98)

Explorer. Cabot was born in Genoa, Italy, ca. 1450 and become a Venetian citizen in 1476. Determined to make an all-water voyage to the East, Cabot went to England around 1484 to find sponsorship for such an expedition. After Columbus's discoveries, King Henry VII of England issued Cabot and his three sons a patent for his own exploration. In May 1497 Cabot left Bristol, England, with an expedition sailing west looking for the supposed "Northwest Passage" to the Orient. After reaching either Newfoundland or Cape Breton Island, Cabot returned to England believing that he had succeeded in reaching the Orient (Asia).

In 1498 Cabot made a second voyage, now looking for Japan. His party sailed down the Eastern Coast of what is now the U.S.A. and possibly explored as far south as the Chesapeake Bay area. Shortly after his return to England, Cabot died in Bristol in late 1498. Much of England's later claims to North America were based on the early explorations by Cabot. John Cabot's second son, Sebastian, probably accompanied his father on his two expeditions. Later Sebastian led his own exploration and possibly entered Hudson Bay, although this is not entirely clear.

ANTHONY D. ANDREASSI

CABRINI, FRANCES XAVIER (1850–1917)

Missionary and saint. The first American citizen to be canonized a saint (1946). Mother Cabrini came to the United States in 1889 to help Italian immigrants. She died at

St. Frances Xavier Cabrini

Chicago in 1917. Together with her Missionary Sisters of the Sacred Heart of Jesus, a religious community she had founded in Italy in 1880, Mother Cabrini established a network of educational, health care and social service institutions and programs for Italians across the United States.

Early Life

Maria Francesca Cabrini was born in 1850 at Sant'Angelo Lodigiano in the province of Lombardy in northern

Italy. From infancy she experienced delicate health and remained frail throughout her life. Her father, a relatively prosperous farmer, was able to provide a good education for his children. Maria Francesca became a licensed elementary public school teacher in 1868. Third Order Franciscan and laywoman active in parish ministry, she held in her heart the dream of becoming a religious sister and a missionary to the Orient. She realized part of the dream in 1880 when she established a new sisterhood dedicated to the missions. Mother Cabrini relinquished her desire to evangelize in the East when urged by Bishop John Baptist Scalabrini of Piacenza to go to the aid of Italian immigrants in America, and mandated to do so by Pope Leo XIII who knew of the needs of those who had gone West to the United States to build new lives in a new land.

New York

On March 31, 1889, Mother Frances Xavier Cabrini and six Missionary Sister companions arrived in Manhattan. The first works entrusted to them included an orphanage for daughters of Italian immigrants and ministry among poor Italians in St. Joachim's Parish. Hearts aflame with love, Mother Cabrini and her sisters cared for the orphans and began religious instruction for children and adults in the parish. They also visited poor families in their homes, the sick in city hospitals and the incarcerated in city jails. Elementary education was started in the orphanage and in the parish. Additional sisters were called from Italy to help in the apostolic works. An American novitiate was soon opened in West Park, New York. New York City became the site of the first of Cabrini's Columbus Hospitals, intended primarily for the care of Italian immigrants but open to all nationalities.

It was also in New York that Mother Cabrini took on the administration of additional parochial schools and industrial schools, where embroidery and other practical arts were taught. She and her sisters assumed responsibilities for religious societies for boys and girls, retreats for women and begging expeditions among the poor to provide the wherewithal for the works on their behalf.

Missionary to America

Mother Cabrini was not one to stay put. Determined to be a bearer of the love of Christ to humankind, Frances Xavier Cabrini, despite a strong fear of water growing out of a near drowning accident as a child, would in her lifetime undertake twenty-three ocean voyages to Europe, North, Central, and South America bringing the Good News of God's love to those in need. Her main focus of attention was, however, the United States of America and her nine missionary journeys to the U.S.A. were marked by prodigious accomplishments on behalf of her beloved immigrants. After New York, outreach extended to New Orleans' demoralized Italian colony following the lynchings there of eleven Italian men. In New Orleans the Missionary Sisters gave courageous service in two yellow fever epidemics, set up an orphanage and schools and visited immigrants in rural Louisiana. In response to the pleas of Italian clergy, parish schools were opened in Newark, Chicago, Denver, Seattle, Los Angeles, and Philadelphia. With fathers victims of work-related accidents, particularly in mining areas, and mothers frequently succumbing to tuberculosis, orphanages were also set up in Denver; Arlington, New Jersey; Seattle; Los Angeles; and Philadelphia.

Additional hospitals were opened in Chicago and Seattle and included outpatient dispensaries and training schools for nurses. To generate income for the medical care of the poor, private facilities were furnished for paying patients. Sisters assigned to the hospitals, like those associated with schools and orphanages, took on catechetics in Italian parishes and visited Italian prisoners.

Mother Cabrini made frequent visits to all of her foundations in the United States and paid careful attention to the details of administration and the expansion of facilities.

"Education of the Heart"

While responsible for health care, child care and social service institutions, Mother Cabrini remained first and foremost an educator. Her philosophy of education was based on a pedagogy of love. Her profound religious faith gave vitality to her educational ideals. For Mother Cabrini, all education was to be God-centered. She adopted a holistic approach to education, advocating instruction in science, mathematics, history, language, and literature, stressing the importance of music, drama, art, physical education, and sports. She did not separate intellectual education from what she termed "education of the heart." This, she characterized, was a "feeling for God in an environment of affective relationships in which education becomes an act of love." Cabrini wanted teachers in her schools, both her own Missionary Sisters and lay teachers, not just to speak of values but to live them in an environment of love.

Mother Cabrini was also an advocate, to a degree, of bilingual education. While English was to be the basis of all instruction, some time was devoted daily to learning to read and write and speak Italian. Cabrini wanted to give the children a deeper sense of their cultural heritage and to instill in them pride in being of Italian descent.

Evangelization

The Institute of the Missionary Sisters of the Sacred Heart of Jesus was founded to spread the reign of Jesus Christ by means of evangelization which Mother Cabrini saw as inflaming all those with whom they came in contact with the love of Christ. Italian immigrants who had little formal instruction in their Catholic faith were prepared for the sacraments of penance, Holy Communion, and confirmation. Those who knew the rudiments of their faith were gently reevangelized. The Missionary Sisters in urban and rural areas encouraged baptism of children, regularization of marriages in church, and return to practice of the Catholic religion. The sisters brought groceries and clothing to the poor, helped to find work for the unemployed and interceded on behalf of prisoners wrongfully accused, always striving to lead those they assisted to the God of Love.

The institutions which Mother Cabrini founded established her role as an advocate for Italian immigrants, but her advocacy went far beyond buildings. In general each foundation became a center serving the socioreligious needs of the immigrants and from which extensive immigrant outreach programs were launched.

Later Life, Death, and Glory

During her years in the United States, Mother Cabrini extended her contacts throughout the country with members of the American hierarchy, civil leaders, Italian clergy and the Italian American communities, where she was much loved. She took great pride in the fact that graduates of her schools and orphanages were making their way in life, that the quality of patient care in her hospitals continued to improve, that new opportunities for religious instruction were willingly accepted by her sisters in their ever-widening circles of parish outreach programs, and that regular visits to the jails, prisons and mines continued.

Mother Cabrini brought hope and help to those in many countries, but her greatest achievements, and the ones for which history will remember her, are her pioneering missionary works among Italian immigrants in the United States.

Following exhaustive Vatican processes of beatification and canonization, Mother Cabrini was declared Blessed on November 13, 1938, only twenty-one years after her demise at Columbus Hospital, Chicago, and on July 7, 1946, she became the first United States citizen to become a saint. In 1950 Pope Pius XII formally proclaimed St. Frances Xavier Cabrini the "Patroness of Immigrants."

See also ITALIAN CATHOLICS IN AMERICA.

Borden, Lucille Papen. *Francesa Cabrini: Without Staff or Scrip.* New York: Macmillan, 1945.

DeLora, John P. "Corrigan, Cabrini and 'Columbus': The Foundation of Cabrini Medical Center, New York City." M.A. thesis, St. Joseph's Seminary, Dunwoodie, 1994.

DiGiovanni, Stephen M. *Archbishop Corrigan and the Italian Immigrants.* Huntington, Ind.: Our Sunday Visitor, 1994.

Green, Rose Basile, ed. and trans. *Mother Frances Xavier Cabrini.* Chicago: Missionary Sisters of the Sacred Heart, 1984.

Maynard, Theodore. *Too Small a World.* Milwaukee: Bruce Publishing Co., 1945.

Serpentelli, Giovanni, trans. *The Travels of Mother Frances Xavier Cabrini.* Exeter, England, 1925; and Chicago: Missionary Sisters of the Sacred Heart, 1944.

Sullivan, Mary Louise, M.S.C. *Mother Cabrini: "Italian Immigrant of the Century."* New York: Center for Migration Studies, 1992.

MARY LOUISE SULLIVAN, M.S.C.

CADILLAC, ANTOINE DE LA MOTHE (1658–1730)

Explorer and French colonial governor. Cadillac was born in France on March 5, 1658, of a minor nobleman and came to America in 1683 after rising to the rank of lieutenant in the army. He had a home in Port Royal (now Annapolis Royal, Nova Scotia) and lived for a short time on his grant in Maine. In 1694 the governor of Canada, Count de Frontenac, gave him command of Mackinac, the most important post in the western part of New France.

However, in 1697 the crown ordered the withdrawal from the western outposts and Cadillac returned to Canada. In 1699 he went to France to present his plan for a post on the Detroit River to protect the fur trade of the west from the English. The plan was accepted in 1701 and he set out with some colonists to found Detroit. Since for some time he had opposed the moral severity of the Jesuits, he invited the Recollet (Franciscan) missionaries to undertake the care of souls there, and he planned to invite all the western tribes to send their converts to them.

Cadillac had hoped to make Detroit his lifelong family home, but in 1711 he was appointed governor of Louisiana. During his three years as governor, he complained of poor conditions there and sought to enrich himself. In 1716 he was recalled to France and spent his last years in his native Provence. In Detroit, Cadillac's name is memorialized by buildings and monuments in his honor. Despite his tendency to complain about living conditions and to make enemies, he was an able and clever leader. His broad vision and brilliant plans for extending French power in the western parts of America contrasted with his reluctance to sacrifice personal gain for their fulfillment. In Louisiana his failure in leadership embittered his last years. He died in France on October 15, 1730.

JAMES HALEY

CAHENSLY, SIMON PETER (1838–1923)

German Catholic layman and social reformer. He was a shipping merchant from Limburg an der Lahn, in Germany. While living in Le Harve, France, in 1861, Cahensly, a devout Catholic, began working for the welfare of German emigrants to the United States under the auspices of the St. Vincent de Paul Society. Appalled by the conditions that German emigrants were compelled to endure during their sea voyage to America, and concerned that the Catholics among them were falling prey to the Protestant immigrant aid societies which greeted them on the other side of the Atlantic, Cahensly made an appeal for assistance for the emigrants at the annual gathering of German Catholic Societies, the *Katholikentag* held in Trier in 1865. Building on the support for his cause that he received at this and subsequent meetings of German-speaking Catholics, Cahensly established "Der St. Raphaelsverein zum Schutze Katholischer deutscher Auswander" in 1871.

The St. Raphaelsverein

Established to help emigrants in every possible way, before, during and after the completion of their voyages, the lay-led St. Raphaelsverein soon employed agents at ports of embarkation through out Europe. However, the success of the "St. Raphaelsverein" was hindered by a number of obstacles, including the general hostility of the Prussian government, the lack of international cooperation on emigration issues on both sides of the Atlantic, and the seeming indifference of the American Catholic hierarchy to numerous requests from Cahensly for pastoral care of the immigrants once they reached the United States.

Cahensly's frustration with the apparent neglect of German Catholic immigrants by the Church in the United States, led him to support German-American Catholic opposition to the policies of rapid "Americanization" pursued by many of the American hierarchy. Cahensly also antagonized some of the American bishops with his pessimistic assertions in the *St. Raphaelsverein Blatt,* and before *Katholikentag* gatherings in Germany, that millions of German Catholics in America were being lost to the faith because they were neglected upon their arrival and because they were being denied the right to religious services and schools conducted in their own language. Despite tensions with the American hierarchy, Cahensly finally succeeded in establishing an American branch of his organization, the "St. Raphael Society," in 1883 under the patronage of Archbishop Michael Corrigan of New York with Bishop Winand Wigger of Newark as president. In 1889 a mission house, the "Leo House," was opened in New York, financed by the contributions of the American members of the St. Raphael Society.

The "Lucerne Memorial"

Throughout the 1880s Cahensly's organization had expanded in Europe to include seven branches for other national groups. At the December 1890 Meeting of the Directors of the European Societies in Lucerne, Switzerland, a "Memorial" was drawn up and approved by the fifty-one delegates from the various national societies for presentation by Cahensly to Pope Leo XIII. The "Lucerne Memorial" stated that over ten million Catholic immigrants had been lost to the faith in America and requested that more be done to provide priests, parishes, and schools for the immigrants to minister to them in their own language. The memorial also requested that every language group be represented among the bishops chosen for service in America.

After the "Lucerne Memorial" was presented to Leo XIII in April 1891, heated public controversy ensued. Opponents of the memorial among the American clergy claimed that the supporters of the memorial were attempting to establish separate "language" churches under their own bishops within the American Church and they labeled this supposed plot "Cahenslyism." They also asserted that the memorial was the result of collaboration between German Catholic elements in the United States and the Prussian government for the purpose of "Germanizing" America. The fact that Cahensly had been a member of the German Reichstag in 1885 was thought by some to give credence to this accusation. Archbishop John Ireland of St. Paul accused Cahensly of meddling in American domestic affairs and succeeded in having him denounced from the floor of the United States Senate.

In June 1891 Leo XIII declined to accede to the memorial's request regarding the appointment of bishops, and referred the other concerns raised by the petition to the American hierarchy.

As the controversy was closely related to the ethnic tensions which plagued the Church in America at this time, it was slow to die. For years afterwards the proponents of the rapid Americanization of Catholic immigrants would regularly use the term "Cahenslysism" as an epithet for those German and conservative Catholics who opposed their policies. However, within the German Catholic community "the great Cahensly" was fondly honored as "the Father of the Immigrant."

See also CORRIGAN, MICHAEL; GERMAN CATHOLICS IN AMERICA.

Barry, Colman. *The Catholic Church and German Americans.* Milwaukee: Bruce Publishing Company, 1953.

Fogarty, Gerald P. *The Vatican and the American Hierarchy from 1870 to 1965.* Wilmington, Del.: Michael Glazier Press, 1985, 44–61.

Gleason, Philip J. *The Conservative Reformers, German-American Catholics, and the Social Order.* University of Notre Dame Press, 1968.

RORY T. CONLEY

CAHILL, T. JOE (1877–1964)

Philanthropist. Born August 7, 1877, in Camp Carlin, Wyoming Territory, a supply depot in Wyoming's pioneer days where his parents had settled after their marriage, T.

Joe knew what the frontier life was all about and how important a church community was in that life. He was serving as an altar boy in Cheyenne's first Catholic church, St. John the Baptist, in 1887, when Wyoming became the Diocese of Cheyenne; and his father was serving in the territorial legislature when Wyoming became a state three years later in 1890. T. Joe Cahill was a horse wrangler and a frontier sheriff in his early days whose law enforcement work brought him into contact with one of the West's most controversial bad men, Tom Horn.

Throughout his life, he was a prime mover and spokesperson for Cheyenne Frontier Days worldwide. The contacts he made in this arena allowed him and his wife, Susan Brady, who he married March 3, 1901, to successfully practice their greatest philanthropy, the support of St. Joseph's Orphanage in Torrington, Wyoming. Hardly a week went by from the time of the establishment of the children's home in 1930 until his death in the late summer of 1964 that he did not forward checks to the bishop made out by friends from all over the world. When he would talk to anyone about the Cheyenne community's big annual celebration, he would always include a pitch for St. Joseph's. He was honored for this service to the Church and to St. Joseph's by Pope Pius XII who appointed him a Knight of St. Gregory on January 25, 1946.

He spent the last years of his life making daily visits to cheer the patients at DePaul Hospital in Cheyenne and sending birthday congratulations to everyone he knew. The church in Wyoming marked his passing at a funeral Mass on August 18, 1964, at St. Mary's Cathedral with Bishop Hubert M. Newell officiating.

GLORIA S. CARLSON

CALDWELL SISTERS, THE

Philanthropists. Mary "Mamie" Gwendolin Byrd Caldwell was born in Cincinnati, Ohio, October 21, 1863, to multimillionaire William Shakespeare Caldwell and Kentucky Belle Mary Eliza Breckenridge. A second girl, Mary Elizabeth "Lina" Breckenridge, was born December 26, 1865, in the same city, but was baptized a month later in New York by Martin John Spalding, archbishop of Baltimore. In 1867, Mrs. Caldwell died. The girls were enrolled in 1872 at the Sacred Heart Academy in Manhattanville where they met the chaplain, Fr. John Lancaster Spalding, the archbishop's nephew. Two years later Shakespeare Caldwell passed away. At the Third Plenary Council of Baltimore in 1884, John Lancaster Spalding, then bishop of Peoria (Illinois), executed a provision in Caldwell's will which had encouraged Mamie to donate a third of her estate, reportedly $300,000, toward the establishment of The Catholic University of America in Washington, D.C. The donation was contingent upon Mamie's stipu-

lation that she be considered the foundress. The cornerstone to Caldwell Hall was laid on May 24, 1888.

Lina donated money to build the university chapel in which she was married by Spalding on June 17, 1890, to a German diplomat, Baron Kurt von Zedwitz. Later that year the pope awarded Mamie the Golden Rose. In 1893, Spalding, along with the United States Trust Company, were made cotrustees of the Caldwell estate. On May 8, 1896, Lina gave birth in Berlin to a son, Waldemar Konrad. Less than four months later, his father was killed in a boating accident in the South Sea. On October 19, 1896, Mamie was married by Spalding at St. Joseph's Church in Paris to Marquis Jean des Monstiers Merinville, a French nobleman. But the union was unhappy from the start.

Two years later while attending the Founder's Day Celebration at The Catholic University, Mamie donated $5000 to establish a scholarship for the diocese of Peoria and promised that she and Lina would give an additional $10,000 endowment. In July 1900, Mamie received the Laetare Medal, but later that year after suffering a stroke she privately expressed doubts about the Catholic faith. Lina quietly left the Church in 1901; then, the following year, assaulted Spalding's character just as he was being considered for the vacant Chicago see. Archbishop Patrick W. Riordan of San Francisco investigated her vague accusations, and, based on a report from an unnamed priest that Spalding had maintained a twenty-year-long affair with Mamie, Riordan recommended that Spalding's name be removed from the *terna*. Neither sister ever confirmed the allegations, but in 1904, Mamie publicly renounced Catholicism and in 1906, Lina published *The Double Doctrine of the Church of Rome,* a pamphlet which claimed to unveil hypocrisy within ecclesiastical ranks.

Mamie succumbed to Bright's disease on October 10, 1909, while aboard the *Konprinzessin Cecile* docked in New York. With heart trouble Lina died on December 16, 1910, at the Carlton Hotel in Frankfurt. Both women were interred at the public Cave Hill Cemetery in Louisville, Kentucky, under a monument which depicts the two sisters embracing each other.

See also CATHOLIC UNIVERSITY OF AMERICA, THE; SPALDING, JOHN LANCASTER.

Gollar, C. Walker. "The Double Doctrine of the Caldwell Sisters." *Catholic Historical Review* 81 (3) (July 1995) 372–97.

Nuesse, C. Joseph. *The Catholic University of America: A Centennial History.* Washington, D.C., 1990.

Sweeney, David Francis, O.F.M. *The Life of John Lancaster Spalding.* New York, 1965.

Zedwitz, Baroness von [nee Mary Elizabeth Caldwell]. *The Double Doctrine of the Church of Rome.* New York, 1906.

C. WALKER GOLAR

CALIFORNIA, CATHOLIC CHURCH IN

The history of the Catholic Church in California begins with the arrival of Fr. Junipero Serra, O.F.M., in 1769, and the establishment of Mission San Diego de Alcala. At the age of fifty-five, Serra volunteered to lead the bold venture of evangelizing the northernmost outpost of New Spain. Over the next fifteen years, he established eight additional missions including Mission San Carlos Borromeo in present day Carmel in 1770, which became his headquarters. Serra served as Father President of the California missions until his death in 1784. His successor, Fermin Lasuen, O.F.M., served from 1784–1803, and established another nine missions. By 1823 twenty-one missions dotted California's coastline, populated by an estimated 20,000 Native American converts, or neophytes as they were called. Under Lasuen, mission life became more complex, buildings became more substantial, and the mission economy more sophisticated as irrigation and other technologies enhanced mission production. California missions were regarded as highly successful in terms of the number of converts, and in the economic productivity of the missions. From 1810 until 1834 the survival of California depended upon the productivity of the missions.

The California Missions

The missions were an integral part of the Spanish program to colonize their northernmost territory. Theoretically, the missions were temporary institutions with a twofold purpose. First, they were to evangelize and convert the native peoples of California to Catholicism and to nurture their newfound faith. Second, they were to teach the neophytes European ways, particularly the European industrial arts and agriculture. The conversion of the native Californian was thus religious and cultural. Once the native neophyte was prepared, he or she was to be released into the general population, and become an ordinary citizen of the Spanish empire. Unfortunately, this last stage was never reached in the California missions. From 1769 until 1834 the Franciscan padres did not believe the natives were ready to take their place in Spanish (and later Mexican) society. They believed that, if the native peoples were released from the missions, they would be preyed upon by the military and other settlers. Their belief was sadly borne out by the plight of the mission natives following the secularization of the missions in 1834.

In recent historiography, the California missions have been attacked by historians and Native American activists who portray the missions as a diabolical system designed to torture, enslave, and destroy the native peoples of California. Much blame has been heaped on Fr. Serra. These criticisms, while understandable, are not well grounded in the historical record. Though the missions were not utopian societies, they did work to protect and nurture the native people. Much of the venom in recent scholarship springs from an attempt to debunk the California mission myth that is so deeply imbedded in the California psyche. The myth originated with the publication of Native American rights advocate Helen Hunt Jackson's novel *Ramona* in 1884. Jackson attempted to inspire a Native American rights movement by contrasting an idyllic mission system populated by loving padres and native peoples, who dwelt together in harmony to the greed and rapacity of the Yankee-Anglo culture which was destroying the remainder of the indigenous peoples. Unfortunately, the novel failed to rouse interest in the plight of the native; instead it initiated the California Mission Revival, which celebrated a mythic mission utopia. It is the tenacity of this myth in the California popular imagination that has led to the vicious and, at times, ahistorical attacks on the missions in current scholarship and in popular culture.

Three issues standout in the current controversy—forced labor, disease, and punishment. The missions and the missionaries are accused of enslaving the native peoples against their will, and forcing them to provide the labor to keep the missions productive. No evidence exists to support this accusation. The padres repeatedly emphasized that all neophytes converted willingly and with knowledge of what conversion entailed. Once converted, the native peoples were required to remain at the mission. If neophytes left the mission without permission, soldiers were sent to find them, and force the neophytes to return. Critics contend that natives were forced to return to provide the needed workforce. In reality, the theological understanding of salvation necessitated the capture and return of the neophytes, *once* converted. The padres believed that once they converted native persons, they were responsible for their souls. If the native was allowed to leave the mission, he or she might backslide and resort to indigenous religious practices. In addition, access to the sacraments was thought crucial in achieving salvation; if the

Santa Barbara Mission

natives were outside the mission community, they would have to live without the sacraments and thus invite damnation. As a result, the padres insisted that the neophytes remain at the mission.

Troublesome to many of the indigenous peoples were the punishments used at the mission to provide order and to discourage runaways, namely the lash and the stocks. These punishments may have been unobjectionable to Spanish culture, but to the natives these were devices reserved for one's enemies, not to be used on one by so-called friends, particularly friends who were announcing a loving God.

Most troublesome was the widespread presence of disease brought by Europeans. Childhood diseases, such as the measles, and other common illnesses, proved devastating to natives who did not have the necessary immune system to combat them. Before the first European explorers arrived, the indigenous population was estimated at about 350,000. By the end of the mission era, the number had declined to 100,000. Though the missions were not willfully culpable of inflicting the disease on the native community, such a distinction was lost on many Native Americans. Many rejected the new found faith because it lacked the power to protect them from the various diseases. The padres too suffered discouragement at their inability to prevent the spread of disease.

At the emotional heart of the current debate is the move to canonize Junipero Serra. Opponents argue that canonization would be an insult to native peoples, as Serra was part of the colonization efforts that led to the destruction of native peoples and native culture. Proponents of canonization argue that Serra was a good and holy man, who loved and defended the indigenous Californians, and should be praised for defending their interests against the military and secular interests. Canonization proceedings for Serra were begun in 1934. He was declared venerable in 1985 and beatified in 1988. The debate will continue, though it reflects less on the mission era than on current cultural conflicts within the Church and the social arena.

Secularization of the Missions

In 1833 the Mexican government decreed an end to the California missions. Since 1821, when Mexico achieved its independence from Spain, forces had worked to secularize the California missions. Secularization meant removing the temporal power of the missions and reducing them to the status of ordinary parishes. The Spanish Franciscans were to be replaced by Mexican secular priests. The great economic enterprise of the missions was to be dismantled and the neophytes "released," free to go wherever they desired. In theory, the missions' land, livestock and other possessions were to be divided among the natives to provide them with a stake in the new social order,

and to assist them in becoming regular citizens. This did not happen. The mission padres opposed secularization arguing that the indigenous peoples were unprepared to fend for themselves in Mexican society. The padres were right. The condition of the California natives worsened with the closing of the missions.

Mexican California

In conjunction with the secularization of the missions, the Mexican government tried to encourage immigration and settlement of California by offering large land grants to prospective settlers. Between 1734 and 1736, more than seven hundred land grants totaling over eight million acres were given to individuals. A wealthy, landed elite, who called themselves "Californios" emerged to fashion life in California. Ranchos became the center of California social and economic, as well as religious life. Rancheros developed a "rich, family centered devotional practice to maintain their faith life" (Engh, 7). These practices were often noninstitutional in character, and often in conflict with more formal, "American" forms of worship.

More formal Church life was established in California in 1840 with the creation of the first California diocese, the Diocese of Ambas (both) Californias, which included all of Baja and Alta California. Franciscan Francisco Garcia Diego y Moreno was named the first bishop, and set up his headquarters at Santa Barbara in Alta California, appointing a vicar forane to oversee the Church in Baja California.

Diego y Moreno confronted two problems that haunted each of the early bishops on the West Coast—a scarcity of qualified clergy and a lack of funds. Diego y Moreno should have been able to draw on money from the Pious Fund, a trust fund established to fund missionary endeavors in Alta California. Unfortunately, the Mexican government confiscated the funds, and provided little alternate support for the Church in California. Diego y Moreno tried to establish a system of tithing, but this program met with little success among California's elite Californio population, and cost him much popularity. In 1842, in an attempt to provide a source of qualified clergy for his diocese, he opened a seminary at Mission Santa Barbara that was moved in 1844 to Mission Santa Ines. On January 1, 1846, he ordained three priests for his diocese, but the seminary never provided an adequate number of new clergy.

After six years of frustration, Garcia Diego y Moreno died in 1846 of tuberculosis. The diocese was left in the hands of his able assistant Jose Gonzalez Rubio, who served as administrator from 1846 until 1850.

During Rubio's administration, events occurred over which he had no control, that fundamentally transformed California, and the Church in California. In 1846 war broke out between the United States and Mexico, culminating in 1848 with the signing of the Treaty of Guadalupe Hidalgo that ceded California to the United States. In the same year, gold was discovered by James Marshall at Sutter's Mill near Sacramento, touching off the California gold rush. Over the course of the next decade thousands of gold-hungry argonauts flooded the state in search of instant fortunes. As a result, California went from being a quiet Mexican province to a bustling mix of cultures that was admitted as a state of the United States in 1850 without ever having had territorial status. The gold rush condensed California history, giving it a population base and influence beyond its years. San Francisco was an "instant city," where, as Carey McWilliams put it, "all the lights came on at once."

The Church immediately set about trying to provide some ecclesial order. In 1849 two French Canadian priests from Oregon established St. Francis of Assisi parish in San Francisco, the first nonmission church in the City. In 1850, the first American Catholic diocese in California, the Diocese of Monterey, was established and Dominican Joseph Sadoc Alemany appointed its first bishop. Alemany quickly realized that San Francisco was a more appropriate episcopal seat and that California was too vast to be effectively administered by one bishop and one diocese. In 1853 the Archdiocese of San Francisco was established with Alemany as archbishop. The Diocese of Monterey became a suffragan diocese of San Francisco, and covered all of California from Gilroy south. In 1854 Thaddeus Amat, C.M., was appointed as bishop of Monterey, though he moved his episcopal residence to Los Angeles in 1859. In 1860 a vicariate of Marysville was created consisting of the gold regions, with Eugene O'Connell, former seminary professor from All Hallows College in Ireland, appointed vicar apostolic. From this vicariate the Diocese of Grass Valley was formed in 1868, with O'Connell as bishop. In 1886 it became the Diocese of Sacramento under the leadership of Bishop Patrick Manogue.

The New Missionary Era

Alemany, Amat, and O'Connell were truly missionary bishops, confronted with vast territories and meager resources. The main concern of these bishops was to revive the basic ecclesial institutions which had fallen into disarray since the secularization of the missions, and to provide for the basic needs of their people. Alemany's vast archdiocese included a wide diversity of peoples, from the landed Californio elite that found their social and economic status caught in a downward spiral to the distressed Native American remnant to the multitude of immigrant groups brought by the gold rush. Amat's task was no less daunting, although southern California developed much more slowly than the San Francisco area. When Amat arrived in California in 1855, he had only sixteen priests at

his disposal to serve a diocese of over 80,000 square miles. O'Connell faced similar problems trying to serve the vast and rugged gold country which contained a highly mobile and transient population. Historian Henry Walsh, S.J., noted, "The early missionary realized his ministry was to be carried out in an unbounded parish, made up of rugged hills and isolated gulches and ravines; that his parishioners were constantly on the move, on foot or mule" (Walsh, 19). Stable church life was slow in coming.

The missionary bishops faced the same basic problems that had confronted Garcia Diego y Moreno, namely, a lack of qualified clergy and a scarcity of funds. Alemany and Amat each established seminaries in their respective dioceses, but neither enterprise was long-lived, nor did they provide an adequate number of new clergy. For many years California relied on priests and seminaries outside the state. A major source of priests for the state was Ireland, especially graduates from All Hallows Missionary College who supplied the majority of Irish immigrant clergy to California. The first stable seminary in California was not established until 1898 with the opening of St. Patrick's Seminary in Menlo Park for the Archdiocese of San Francisco. The Archdiocese of Los Angeles waited until 1939 to open its major seminary, St. John's in Camarillo. The missionary bishops also arranged to have several orders of religious men establish houses in California during this era: to the Franciscans were added the Dominicans, Jesuits, and Vincentians.

All three bishops tried to put their young dioceses on a firm financial basis. Alemany found himself in the somewhat embarrassing position of looking for funds beyond the archdiocese despite the fact that his diocese was in the midst of what outsiders perceived as gold-rich California. Unfortunately for Alemany, most gold miners had a different agenda than the Church. All three bishops succeeded in obtaining funds from the Society of the Propagation of Faith in Lyons and Paris. More importantly, Alemany succeeded in validating the mission lands as property of the Church of California in accordance with the California Land Act of 1851. Sixteen of the missions fell within Amat's diocese and five in Alemany's. The outside funds and the land validation provided a needed boost to the Church in California.

Alemany also sought to recover money for the Church in California from the government of Mexico, contending that Mexico had illegally confiscated the money of the Pious Fund. Negotiations and proceedings to resolve the Pious Fund would continue until 1966. Alemany won an initial judgment in 1875, but the major decision in favor of the archdiocese's claim did not occur until 1902, under the direction of Alemany's successor, Patrick William Riordan. In the first case held at the Permanent Court of Arbitration at The Hague Tribunal, the archdiocese won a major award. Unfortunately, complete payment of the award was upset by the Mexican Revolution in the 1910s, and final restitution was not made until 1966.

The Immigrant Church in California

The defining feature of California Catholicism was and continues to be the constant influx of immigrant groups. Northern California, particularly San Francisco, was transformed into a cosmopolitan center as a result of the immigrant waves brought on by the gold rush. Alemany attempted to provide for the needs of his ethnically diverse flock in a culturally sensitive manner. First, he attempted to provide priests who spoke the language of each community. For example, in 1854, he obtained the services of Chinese priest Fr. Thomas Cian to minister to the growing Chinese population. Unfortunately, Cian spoke the wrong dialect; he did, however, speak fluent Italian, having studied in Rome, and so Alemany appointed him pastor to the Italians of San Francisco. In the 1880s, Italian-born Fr. Gregory Antonucci repaid the favor by establishing a Chinese mission in San Francisco, and later serving as a vicar apostolic in China.

In addition to appointing priests who spoke the immigrants' language, Alemany also tried to ensure that his priests were culturally sensitive and properly trained to work in a multicultural environment. Finally, he established national parishes when necessary, establishing parishes for the French (1856), Germans (1860), Spanish-speaking (1875), and Italians (1884). Though national parishes were used, they were never relied upon to the extent that they were in Eastern and Midwestern urban centers.

Amat faced a different situation in southern California, which did not experience significant growth until the 1880s. Amat's diocese retained a distinctly Hispanic cast. In Los Angeles, Catholic life centered around the Old Plaza Church, Our Lady, Queen of the Angels, popularly known as "La Placita." Amat showed less patience with the Hispanic spirituality he encountered than did Alemany in the north. Amat attempted to "Americanize" and "Romanize" the southern California faithful. He did not want Catholics to appear too foreign. Historian Michael Engh writes, "He envisioned a local Catholic community, Roman in orientation, uniform in expression, and obedient to him in its actions" (Engh, 175). His attitude brought him into conflict with his Californio flock, whose festive religious celebrations lacked the decorum Amat desired. His attempt to establish his authority also brought him into conflict with the remaining Mexican Franciscans living at Mission Santa Barbara. Present in this conflict was a dispute over Hispanic religious practices allowed by the Franciscans, but which did not fit into Amat's plan.

Alemany and Amat's successors, Patrick William Riordan, and Francisco Mora continued to face an influx of immigrants. Throughout the nineteenth century the Irish, Germans, and Italians were the primary Catholic immigrant groups. At the start of the twentieth century these groups were joined by Portuguese, Mexicans, and Filipino immigrants, the latter two groups increasing in number after 1910 and 1920 respectively.

Attempts were made to evangelize the predominantly non-Catholic Asian groups, the Chinese and the Japanese. After several halting attempts, a Chinese mission was established by the Paulists in 1902 at Old St. Mary's parish in San Francisco. Los Angeles opened a Chinese Catholic Center in 1942. In 1913 both San Francisco and Los Angeles, under the guidance of Fr. Albert Breton, opened missions for the Japanese.

The Catholic immigrant experience in California differed from that in other states in that white Catholics suffered comparatively little discrimination, although the Irish did suffer some abuse during the 1850s in San Francisco. Nativist hostility was directed primarily at people of color, especially the Chinese, Japanese, Mexican, and Filipinos. Only in the latter two groups did anti-Catholicism and anti-immigrant feeling merge. White immigrant groups enjoyed significant upward social mobility. Though the majority remained solidly working class, a significant number of Irish, Italians, and Germans moved into San Francisco's and the state's economic elite including the Tobins, Sullivans, Phelans, Donahues (Irish), Gianninis, DiGiorgios, Gallos (Italian), and Wensingers (German). The experience of these Catholic immigrant groups was generally more positive than it had been on the East Coast.

Despite the milder form of anti-Catholicism on the West Coast, California Catholics, as had Catholics elsewhere in the nation, developed a separate culture complete with Catholic institutions of all kinds—schools, hospitals, orphanages, and other charitable and educational institutions—to preserve the immigrants' Catholic faith and culture. Brick-and-mortar Catholicism was firmly rooted in California to meet immigrant needs. With massive building programs went massive debt, much of Catholic life revolved around fundraising. Bazaars, festivals, raffles, dinners, dances, and regular appeals became standard features of California Catholicism.

Great emphasis was placed on the church building itself. An impressive church building reflected not only the community's love of God, but also the fact that the immigrant community had made it in California. Three impressive cathedrals were constructed in the nineteenth century—Old St. Mary's (1854), and new St. Mary's (1891) in San Francisco, and St. Vibiana's (1876) in Los Angeles.

Women Religious

At the base of the immigrant Church were countless, devoted men and women religious, who provided the personnel to staff the separate Catholic institutional order. From the beginning of the American Church in California, sisters were present, most notably the Dominican Sisters of Mission San Rafael (1850), the Sisters of Notre Dame de Namur (1851), the Daughters of Charity (1852), the Presentation Sisters (1854), and the Sisters of Mercy (1854). These were the earliest groups established in the Archdiocese of San Francisco. San Francisco also gave birth to an indigenous religious order in 1872, the Sisters of the Holy Family, specializing in child welfare and home health care. In Los Angeles, the earliest and most significant group was the Daughters of Charity, who arrived in 1856 and established a hospital and orphanage. In 1871 the Sisters of the Immaculate Heart of Mary arrived in the diocese to establish and teach in Catholic schools. This is not an inclusive list of all the orders who worked in California; dozens of other orders arrived and worked selflessly for the building of the Church in California.

The Mexican Catholic Community

By 1900, San Francisco and Los Angeles had developed two distinctively different Catholic cultures. San Francisco was a cosmopolitan city that contained a large foreign-born population, and significant numbers of Catholics and Jews. In contrast, Los Angeles grew during the 1880s largely from transplanted Midwesterners and Easterners who took advantage of the cheap railroad rates to migrate to Southern California. Los Angeles citizens, as a result, tended to be native-born, more conservative, and more Protestant.

The most significant immigrant group to come to southern California was the Mexican. Following the gold rush, Mexican immigration to California slowed considerably until 1910 when the onset of the Mexican Revolution caused significant dislocation, propelling countless emigrants and exiles into California. Intense persecution of Catholics during 1926 to 1929, and again between 1934 and 1936, sent many Catholics to California. In the late 1920s an estimated 150,000 exiles had migrated to southern California. In addition to the push of the revolution, there was the pull of California agribusiness and industry which relied on a cheap, mobile labor force, and actively recruited immigrants from Mexico. By 1928 Los Angeles was the second largest Mexican city in the world, second only to Mexico City. Immigration from Mexico remained high through the 1990s, except for a brief period during the depression of the 1930s, when Mexicans were encouraged to return to Mexico.

The arrival of so many immigrants from Mexico presented the Church in southern California with enormous pastoral problems. Under the direction of Bishop John J. Cantwell and his department of Catholic Charities, a practical response was worked out. The four main goals of the Church in evangelizing the Mexican community were to educate Mexicans in Catholic doctrine, validate Mexican marriages, provide charitable relief where necessary, and protect the Mexican faithful from Protestant evangelization. To achieve these goals, the Church relied on settlement houses (particularly in the 1920s and earlier), charitable agencies, the Confraternity of Christian Doctrine (CCD) and the Catholic school, and Mexican parishes and missions. The latter were particularly important in Los Angeles during the 1920s, with twelve Mexican parishes established during the period 1923–28. Throughout the era, the Church sought to assist in the Americanization of the Mexican in both the civic and religious arenas.

Following World War II, the Church in California supported community organizing efforts in the Mexican community, particularly the efforts of the Community Service Organization. This commitment to community organizing intensified in the 1960s. Currently within the Mexican American Catholic community experiments with basic ecclesial communities are underway. As of 1995, the Mexican/Mexican American community represents an increasingly large segment of the Catholic population in California, and presents a "promise and challenge" to the Church in California.

The Heyday of California Catholicism 1920–60

By the 1920s, southern California superseded northern California as the most populous region in the state, and Los Angeles superseded San Francisco in population and importance. By 1936, the Diocese of Los Angeles was raised to the status of an archdiocese, and in 1953 the archbishop of Los Angeles, James Francis McIntyre, was named the first cardinal in the state's history. While the nineteenth century belonged to San Francisco, the twentieth century has belonged to Los Angeles.

San Francisco's decline began in 1906 when a powerful earthquake and the tragic fire which ensued razed a large portion of the city. The Church suffered significant damage: twelve churches were completely destroyed and many other archdiocesan properties, including the recently opened St. Patrick's Seminary, suffered significant damage. Archdiocesan property loss was estimated at more than six million dollars. Archbishop Riordan was not present in San Francisco, but upon his return he rallied the city in an emotional speech before the Citizen's Committee of San Francisco in which he asserted, in the words of St. Paul, "I am a citizen of no mean city, although it is in ashes," and he vowed, "We shall rebuild." Within two years, eleven of the twelve damaged parishes had reopened. Though the city and the church of San Francisco did rebuild, their preeminence in the state was at an end.

Los Angeles continued to grow with the emergence of Hollywood and the film industry, the expansion of California agriculture, and the growth of the oil industry. The

Church also grew and developed under the leadership of two impressive bishops—John J. Cantwell, who served from 1917 until 1947, and James Francis McIntyre, who served from 1948 until 1970. Both episcopacies covered eras of enormous growth. During Cantwell's episcopacy the Catholic population of the Archdiocese of Los Angeles grew from 178,233 in 1917 to 601,200 in 1947. The number of priests grew from 276 to 658; the number of parishes from 128 to 218; the number of Catholic grade schools from 43 to 115, with the number of students increased from 6,959 to 42,877. During McIntyre's era the growth continued with the creation of 82 new parishes, and the number of Catholic schools tripled. McIntyre placed special emphasis on the construction of new Catholic schools, diverting funds intended for the construction of a new cathedral to subsidize the construction of new Catholic schools.

The Archdiocese of San Francisco likewise witnessed large growth under the leadership of Archbishop John J. Mitty, who served from 1935 until 1961. During his episcopacy the number of Catholics in the archdiocese increased from 405,000 to 1,125,000. The number of parishes grew from 171 in 1935 to 256 in 1961. In addition, Mitty sponsored 563 major building projects, ranging from schools and churches to hospitals and high schools.

In the midst of this enormous growth Mitty imposed order. He effectively organized and centralized the administration of the archdiocese, streamlining and energizing the Church's bureaucratic agencies. He revolutionized archdiocesan finances, being one of the national pioneers in establishing the system of central archdiocesan banking. Under this system, parishes and archdiocesan agencies were required to deposit surplus funds with the archdiocesan bank. When parishes needed a loan, they were to obtain a loan through the archdiocesan bank rather than a private bank. The system gave the archbishop greater control over the financial structure of his archdiocese. Los Angeles adopted the system pioneered by Mitty.

Like San Francisco, the period 1920 to 1960 was also a time of centralization in Los Angeles. In the early 1920s, Cantwell attempted to organize his diocesan Catholic charities, culminating in the creation of the Catholic Welfare Bureau in 1926. In 1923 he established the Confraternity of Christian Doctrine (CCD) to better facilitate the religious education of public school children. Various other archdiocesan agencies were formed, reformed, and strengthened.

Mitty's greatest legacy to the Church in northern California was the creation of a highly motivated and well-trained diocesan clergy, which Mitty claimed was the equal of any religious order. Priests were sent to graduate school to obtain advanced degrees before being placed in charge of some diocesan agency. He sponsored "special work" such as his creation of an Archdiocesan Mission Band,

which took the place of religious orders in giving missions throughout the archdiocese, and his creation of a Spanish Mission Band to work among the migrant and bracero fieldworkers. This latter group was to assist in the discovery and development of Cesar Chavez, Dolores Huerta, and the United Farmworkers (UFW). Under Mitty, the clerical morale of the priests of the Archdiocese of San Francisco reached an all-time high.

Cantwell and McIntyre also successfully built up their archdiocese. Cantwell developed a number of programs to benefit the ever-increasing number of Mexican Catholics in his archdiocese. Besides creating Mexican parishes and subsidizing charities that assisted the Mexican people, Cantwell mandated that his seminarians study Spanish, and that they be instructed in the basics of Mexican culture. Cantwell's concern for his Mexican flock earned him the title of "the Irish-born champion of the Mexican people."

Cantwell also addressed the issue of ministry to African American Catholics who had begun arriving in significant numbers after World War I. He established St. Victor's Center in 1922 and St. Odilia's parish in 1927. The first African American national parish in San Francisco was not opened until 1938 with the creation of St. Benedict the Moor. During World War II and after, a large number of African Americans were drawn to California by the availability of jobs in the war and defense industries. At the very time the civil rights movement was gearing up, California was confronting its first major influx of African Americans.

The Unrest of the 1960s

California was the focal point of much of the social turmoil that racked the 1960s throughout the United States. The civil rights movement, student protests and antiwar demonstrations, the war on poverty, and the counterculture, all fundamentally challenged the foundations of American and California life that had perdured through the 1950s. Besides these traumas, Catholics experienced the equally troubling and rapid changes introduced into the Church by the Second Vatican Council. As a result, traditional authority, both secular and religious, was challenged, undermined, and ultimately eroded.

For the first time in their history, Catholics became involved in social protests in a major way. The 1950s saw the struggling beginnings of the Catholic Interracial Council in California, as Catholics became increasingly involved in the civil rights movement. Of particular note was the battle in 1964 against the repeal of the Rumford Fair Housing Act, or Proposition 14, as it came to be known. Every Catholic bishop in California except Cardinal McIntyre issued a statement against the proposition. The proposition passed and many criticized McIntyre for his silence on the issue. One of his priests, William DuBay, accused McIntyre of forbidding his priests from speaking on the racial issue. DuBay also petitioned the pope to remove McIntyre for "abuse of authority." The DuBay incident was the most sensational of the conflicts encountered by McIntyre during the 1960s. McIntyre also engaged in celebrated disputes with the Immaculate Heart of Mary Sisters, whose attempts to renew their order found little favor in the Los Angeles chancery, and the highly publicized dispute with the radical Mexican rights group, Catolicos por La Raza, protesting the dedication of St. Basil's in 1969. In 1970 McIntyre was succeeded by Archbishop Timothy Manning, whose less confrontational style did much to rebuild the Church in Los Angeles, which he served as archbishop until 1986.

The Church in San Francisco was not exempt from protest. In 1962 the San Francisco Cathedral burned to the ground. A new cathedral employing rather daring and striking modern design was built and dedicated in 1971; however, its construction engendered significant protest from those who believed the money spent on the cathedral would be better spent on the poor. Equally as troubling for Archbishop Joseph McGucken (1962–77) was agitation for priests' rights through the creation of a Priests Association, which at one point threatened a strike by the priests of the archdiocese, and supported the first due process case in the American Catholic Church.

Throughout the decade Catholics from all over California rallied to support Cesar Chavez and the UFW's grape and lettuce boycotts. Participation in these boycotts brought protest within parishes and families that previously had been little concerned with such matters.

The New Immigrant Church

Just as significant as the social protests was the change in the immigration law in 1965 that resulted in a massive influx of new immigrants: Mexicans, South and Central Americans, Filipinos, Vietnamese, Koreans, Chinese, and other Asian groups, and the Polish. Between 1970 and 1980, 1,868,000 immigrants entered California, earning for the state the title of "the new Ellis Island." The Church is once again faced with the problem of how best to assist these new immigrants in becoming established in the United States, and in becoming part of the California Church. Most dioceses in the state have inaugurated special ethnic offices with the mandate to assist priests and other church workers to be more culturally sensitive to the newly arriving immigrants. When necessary, special missions have been established to serve the immigrant community.

In 1962 California became the most populous state in the Union. As the state has grown, so has the Church, and from 1936 forward there have been attempts to provide better service to Catholics by creating smaller dioceses which could be more responsive. In 1936, when Los Angeles was made an archdiocese, the southernmost counties were broken off to form the Diocese of San Diego. In 1949 the Diocese of Monterey-Fresno was created. Separate dioceses of Fresno and Monterey were created in 1967. In 1962 the Archdiocese of San Francisco was split to create the dioceses of Santa Rosa, Stockton, and Oakland, and in 1981 the Diocese of San Jose was created. In 1976 the Diocese of Orange was created from Los Angeles, and in 1978 the Diocese of San Bernardino was separated from San Diego. The Archdiocese of Los Angeles remains the largest diocese and the most powerful in the state, and one of the most powerful in the nation. Cardinal Roger Mahoney has served the archdiocese since 1986. The archdiocese is well on its way to complete an amazing one hundred million dollars capital fundraising campaign.

One of the most innovative, interesting, and controversial developments of the 1990s was the attempt by the Archdiocese of San Francisco under the direction of Archbishop John Quinn (1977–96) to fashion a "Pastoral Plan" to bring the Church into the twenty-first century. Most controversial was the closing of ten city parishes, including the city's oldest parish, St. Francis. Overlooked in the controversy was the creation of a school for lay leaders, the creation of more lay liturgists, and innovative youth and service programs. The future will judge the wisdom of the Pastoral Plan.

See also ALEMANY, JOSEPH SADOC; AMAT, THADDEUS; CHAVEZ, CESAR; RIORDAN, PATRICK; SERRA, JUNIPERO.

Burns, Jeffrey M. "Building the Best: A History of Catholic Parish Life in the Pacific States." *The American Catholic Parish: A History from 1850 to the Present,* ed. Jay Dolan. Vol. II. Mahwah, N.J., 1987.

———. "The Mexican Catholic Community in California." *Mexican Americans and the Catholic Church, 1900–1965,* eds. Jay Dolan and Gilbert Hinojosa. Notre Dame, 1994.

Dwyer, John. *Condemned to the Mines: The Life of Eugene O'Connell.* New York, 1976.

Engh, Michael. *Frontier Faiths: Church, Temple and Synagogue in Los Angeles, 1846–1888.* Albuquerque, 1992.

Englehardt, Zephryn. *Missions and Missionaries of California.* Vols. I–IV, 1915–29.

Gaffey, James. *Citizen of No Mean City: Archbishop Patrick Riordan of San Francisco.* Wilmington, N.C., 1976.

Geiger, Maynard. *The Life and Times of Junipero Serra.* Washington, D.C., 1959.

McGloin, John. *California's First Archbishop: The Life of Joseph Sadoc Alemany.* New York, 1966.

Walsh, Henry. *Hallowed Were Those Gold Dust Trails: The Story of the Pioneer Priests of Northern California.* Santa Clara, 1946.

Weber, Francis. *Century of Fulfillment: The Roman Catholic Church in Southern California, 1840–1947.* Mission Hills, California, 1990.

JEFFREY M. BURNS

Related Document

THE CHURCH IN SAN FRANCISCO IN
THE DAYS OF THE GOLD RUSH, JUNE 15, 1853

At no time in the nineteenth century were there enough native-born priests in the United States to care for the rapidly increasing Catholic population. No foreign country was more generous in supplying priests for the American Church than Ireland, and no institution of that land sent so many to the American missions as All Hallows College, Dublin, which had been established as a missionary seminary in 1842. Among the best known of the All Hallows men in the United States was Eugene O'Connell (1815–1891). He had come out to California for the first time in 1851 to collect funds but was induced by Bishop Alemany to remain and assist him with his infant seminary. O'Connell returned to the faculty of All Hallows in 1854 and remained there until 1861 when he was appointed the first Vicar Apostolic of Marysville, California. In 1868 he was made first Bishop of Grass Valley, a see that was the predecessor to the present Diocese of Sacramento. The following letter to Father David Moriarty, president of All Hallows, contains some picturesque details on the type of surroundings in which the Church operated in San Francisco in the years immediately after the gold rush.

(*Source: All Hallows Annual, 1953–1954*. Dublin: Browne and Nolan, Ltd., 1954, 152–53.)

SAN FRANCISCO
June 15th [1853]

My dear Father Moriarty,

Your welcome letter, after an unsuccessful search about the solitude of Santa Ynez,[1] reached me a few days ago in this noisy city. How then can I express to you my gratitude for your kind invitation to All Hallows after my wanderings in the Far West? I only await the arrival of one of the six missionaries whom Dr. Alemany[2] expects from All Hallows previous to my departure. You would really pity the poor Bishop were you to see the fluctuating soldiers he has to fight his battle; like Dr. Whelan[3] of Virginia, he was obliged to make the two seminarians he has swear to remain with him. Therefore, under these circumstances, I presume on your leave to remain. . . .

You must, I'm sure, have received letters from Dr. Alemany since March 5th which shew you the urgent need he has of Irish clergymen and the provision he is making to secure a constant supply from All Hallows now, in order to keep up an unbroken succession in this diocese of All Hallows missionaries. For the present, he can do no more for the institution than he has done, in consequence of being engaged in building St. Mary's Cathedral, which it is calculated will cost $100,000—a work he is *bound (ut dicunt Americani)* to get through with, for many reasons, but principally to secure a fire-proof church in the neighborhood, that he himself and his clergymen may be without the daily and nightly apprehension of being *burnt out*. Owing to the scarcity of stone in this country and the dearness of brick-buildings, most of the houses here are constructed of wood and the six or seven fires that have already occurred haven't taught many to make an effort to build brick houses. Since the Bishop transferred me from Santa Ynez to this city about three or four months ago, there has been a fire almost every month and the value of thousands of dollars consumed. . . .

The temporal burnings of which I am speaking naturally remind me of the everlasting ones which they presage to thousands of the citizens of San Francisco, unless they stop in their career of iniquity. The rage for duelling, the passion for gambling and barefaced depravity prevail to a frightful degree. . . . Venus has numerous temples erected to herself in this city but, thank God, the Catholic church is not deserted all the while. The two Catholic churches are crowded every Sunday and, notwithstanding the enlargement of one of them by Architect O'Connor (nephew of the Bishop), it is full to overflowing. William Hamill,[4] formerly of Maynooth, is the teacher of the Bishop's English school, *vice* Doctor Barry who was translated to the Dolores seminary with a salary of $50 a month. Mr. Hamill's salary is $60 a month in consideration of his acting as Sexton to the church—in fact $50 a month is the salary even of cooks in this country.

I don't know whether you are aware of some of our California liberties which beat the Gallican ones hollow. Take, for example, that of eating meat *toties quoties* on every Friday except the Fridays in Lent—and don't infer from this that the finest salmon in the world don't abound on our shores! There is again the universal custom of smoking cigars (*secluso scandalo ullo*), so that it is rather singular to be seen without a cigar save at Mass or at meals. The only scandal to my knowledge given by a smoking clergyman was owing to his having repeatedly put the *ignited end* into his mouth instead of the opposite extreme. Hence you perceive it is neither the simple fact of smoking *per se*, nor of drinking *per se*, but the unlucky combination of both by a clergyman which makes him confound both ends of a lighted cigar. Then, and not till then, do the ladies and gentlemen receive a slight shock!

Oh, my dear Father and brothers, please all pray for me and my speedy return to Alma Mater, where I hope to find rest for my soul.

Adieu, dear Father, until then.

Eugene O'Connell

[1] The diocesan seminary, of which O'Connell was rector, was first established at Santa Inez and moved early in 1853 to Mission Dolores in San Francisco.

[2] Joseph S. Alemany, O.P. (1814–1888), born in Spain, was named first Archbishop of San Francisco six weeks after O'Connell's letter was written.

[3] Richard V. Whelan (1809–1874) was first Bishop of Wheeling.

[4] William J. Hamill, born in County Antrim, Ireland, arrived in San Francisco in 1851; he later became the first editor of the *Monitor*, San Francisco's weekly Catholic newspaper. No identification of Barry could be found.

(*Source:* John Tracy Ellis, ed. *Documents of American Catholic History.* Vol. 1:1493–1865. Wilmington, Del.: Michael Glazier, 1987, 304–6.)

CALLAN, CHARLES JEROME (1877–1962)

Biblical scholar and theologian. Callan wrote and edited over forty theological works in his lifetime, many of them in collaboration with his confrere and close friend, John Ambrose McHugh, O.P. Together they played a significant role in the liturgical and catechetical movements occurring in the United States in the earlier part of the twentieth century.

Born on December 5, 1877, in Lockport, New York, and educated by the Jesuits at Canisius College in Buffalo, Callan entered the Dominican Order in 1899. Ordained to the priesthood along with McHugh in 1905 by James Hartley, bishop of Columbus, he went on to obtain the order's degree of lector in sacred theology at the University of Fribourg, Switzerland, in 1907. Twenty-four years later, he was awarded the degree of master in sacred theology after completing the rigorous examination with distinction.

Shortly after his return from Switzerland, he was assigned in 1909 to the Dominican House of Studies in Washington where he initially taught philosophy and later sacred Scripture. Six years later, both Callan and McHugh were transferred from the faculty in Washington to the small parish of the Holy Rosary in Hawthorne, New York, where they spent the rest of their lives in a threefold apostolate of parochial work, theological writing, and teaching at the nearby Maryknoll seminary which had recently been established for the training of foreign missionaries.

The team of Callan and McHugh first achieved national prominence when, in 1916, they accepted the additional responsibility of jointly editing the *Homiletic and Pastoral Review,* a position they held for over thirty years. Through their efforts, the journal experienced phenomenal growth in readership and prestige. Upon McHugh's death in 1950, Callan continued on as sole editor for another seven years, at which point his own failing health necessitated the appointment of Aidan Carr, O.F.M. Conv., as associate editor to carry on the bulk of the work.

During the early years at Hawthorne, Callan produced several commentaries on the Gospels, the Acts of the Apostles, and the letters of Paul. However, his best-known works are those he coauthored with McHugh. These include *A Parochial Course of Doctrinal Instruction* (1920), *Moral Theology* (1930), and *Program for a Four-Year Course of Catechetical Instructions* (1937). They also produced several devotional works and prayer books, including *Dominican Sisters' Office Book* (1912), *Blessed be God* (1925), and an English translation of *The Catholic Missal* (1936).

When, in 1935, the American bishops decided that a new English translation of the Scriptures from the Latin Vulgate was needed to replace the Douay-Rheims version, Callan and McHugh were among the biblical scholars invited to sit on the editorial board. In addition to their involvement with this project, they also completed the editing of a previously unpublished translation of the New Testament from the original Greek by their fellow Dominican, Francis Aloysius Spencer. Spencer had completed the translation in 1913 but died before it could be published. Their edited version of the Spencer translation, complete with introductions to each of the books and over one thousand critical notes, appeared in 1937.

Callan's scholarship in the field of biblical studies was further recognized in 1940 when he was appointed a consultor to the Pontifical Biblical Commission by Pope Pius XII. He was the first native-born American to be so honored.

In 1954 failing health forced him to retire from his teaching at Maryknoll, though he continued to write and edit. Two years later he received permission from his superior to reside with friends in Milford, Connecticut, who had offered to care for him as his condition deteriorated. He died there on February 26, 1962, and is buried at Maryknoll next to McHugh.

See also DOMINICANS (O.P.); MARYKNOLL.

JOHN LANGLOIS, O.P.

CALVERT FAMILY, THE

A family prominent in seventeenth-century British politics that oversaw the founding of the colony of Maryland.

George Calvert

Son of Leonard Calvert and Alice Crossland, born in 1580 or 1582 at Kipling, Yorkshire, George was the first in a family of prosperous farmers to attend university. He received his bachelor of arts from Oxford University in 1597. After his graduation, he made the customary tour of the continent, during which he probably met Sir Robert Cecil, then ambassador of Elizabeth I to the Court of France. During the tenure of Cecil as Lord Treasurer, young Calvert served him as his personal secretary.

The following year, on September 3, 1606, he was appointed prothonotary and keeper of the writs, bills, files, records, and rolls within the Province of Connaught and Thomand in Ireland. In 1609 George Calvert appears among the patentees in the new charter granted to the Virginia Company. He was named clerk to the Privy Council in 1613. A favorite of James I, he was knighted by him in 1617. Two years later, Calvert was made one of the secretaries of state, and in 1620 was elected to Parliament as the representative for the University of Oxford.

George Calvert, first Lord Baltimore

By this time, Calvert had become a partisan of a proposed marriage between the Prince of Wales and the Infanta Maria of Spain, daughter of Philip III. The marriage was to cement an alliance with Spain to the detriment of France. The French party would eventually win the day, with Charles' marriage to the Bourbon princess Henrietta Maria. By then Calvert had withdrawn from active participation in politics and had embarked on his first overseas venture.

On February 8, 1621, Calvert acquired a substantial grant of land in Ireland from James I. Consisting of 2,300 acres in County Longford, the land became his on the condition that all its inhabitants take the oath of supremacy.

In 1624 Calvert made public his conversion to Roman Catholicism, and resigned his post as secretary of state. James I accepted the resignation but retained him as Privy Councillor. Such was his favor with the king that the latter allowed him to take a modified oath of allegiance and, on February 16, 1625, erected Calvert's Irish estate into the manor of Baltimore from which a baronial title would derive.

Efforts at colonizing the New World had long interested Calvert. Besides his earlier membership in the Second Virginia Company, he had also been one of the eighteen members of the New England Company in 1622. During this same year he applied for a patent for a proposed settlement on the coast of Newfoundland. "Avalon," as the colony would be called, would draw its name from the mythical location of the first Christian mission in Britain. After heavily subsidizing this colony with his own funds for a number of years, Calvert visited Avalon in the summer of 1627. He returned the following summer, accompanied by his second wife and his children by his first spouse, Anne Mynne, whom he had married in 1604 and who had died in 1622.

Much to his dismay, he found himself obliged to defend the settlement, as well as English fishing boats who plied local waters, from naval attacks by the French. Calvert was successful in his efforts, capturing a number of prisoners and sending French vessels back to England as prizes of war.

A single winter sufficed to convince the Lord Proprietary of Avalon of the impracticability of large-scale colonization. Along with his wife and family, as well as some forty other colonists, he sailed to Virginia. Local leaders there were well aware of Calvert's colonial designs and of his Catholic faith. In an attempt to cause his departure, he was offered the Oath of Supremacy. Unable to acknowledge King Charles as head of the Church, Calvert declined the oath.

Calvert did take note of the vast tracts of unexplored and uncolonized land to the north and south of Virginia. The original charter of the province had been invalidated in 1623, with title to all unsettled lands reverting to the king. Upon returning to England, Calvert sought and received an additional grant of land from Charles I consisting of all present-day Maryland and Delaware, as well as substantial portions of present-day Pennsylvania and West Virginia. Calvert proposed the name "Crescentia" for his new colony, but Charles prevailed, and the name "Maryland" was given, in honor of his queen Henrietta Maria. The first Lord Baltimore died on April 15, 1632, leaving his eldest son Cecilius to succeed to his titles and estates. It was the second Lord Baltimore who became the first Lord Proprietary of Maryland on June 20, 1632.

Cecilius Calvert

Named for his father's early patron, Cecilius (b. 1606), was accorded remarkable powers as lawgiver and landowner in his colony. Maryland was to constitute a "Palatinate." The Proprietary, and not Parliament, would levy taxes. He was the supreme legislator with full rights to impose laws upon his colonists. In practice, however, the inhabitants would be given great latitude in formulating and enforcing their own laws. In most legal matters the Proprietary would limit his role to giving or withholding assent.

Some Virginia planters launched the first formal attack on the Charter in July 1633, alleging that a settlement already existed within the boundaries of Maryland; that the Palatinate powers were too broad and a threat to individual liberties; and, paradoxically, that Marylanders would enjoy greater freedoms and tend to draw settlers from other established colonies. The challenge, while brushed aside, had the effect of convincing the Lord Proprietary to remain in England to defend his interests and those of

Maryland. It is supposed that he had otherwise intended to accompany the first colonists to the New World.

Cecilius Calvert, second Lord Baltimore

Two ships, the *Ark* and *Dove,* were outfitted at Baltimore's own expense and departed the Isle of Wight on November 22, 1633. The colonists consisted of some twenty gentlemen and two hundred to three hundred laborers and craftsmen. They arrived at Barbados on January 3, 1634, were at Point Comfort, Virginia, by the end of the following month, and celebrated their first Mass in Maryland, on St. Clement's Island, March 25, 1634. Shortly afterward, a colonial capital was established at St. Mary's.

In 1629 Cecilius Calvert was married to Anne Arundel, daughter of Thomas Arundel, Baron of Wardour and Count of the Holy Roman Empire. The Lord Proprietor never visited his colony, instead confiding its governance to his brother Leonard, accompanied by yet another brother, George. Leonard Calvert would oversee the colony's affairs until his death, June 9, 1647.

It would seem that the principal motive of the Proprietary lay in the founding of a colony where Catholics could live and worship in peace. Establishing an exclusively Catholic colony was out of the question for two reasons. The assent of a Protestant sovereign could hardly have been expected for such a scheme, no matter how valuable the elder Calvert's past services had been. In addition, Protestant immigration would sooner or later eclipse that of the Catholics, leading to further turmoil. Cecilius Calvert's status as Proprietary allowed him to establish religious toleration for all Christians as a foundation of his colony. Such was the practice from the time of the first plantation, a policy which was enshrined in law in the "Act Concerning Religion" or "Act of Toleration" of 1649. This law was the first of its kind in the English colonies.

Official policy or not, religious toleration was not universally accepted by the colonists. Profiting from the turmoil of the early Commonwealth period in England, the Puritans at Providence in Ann Arundel County convened an assembly in October 1654, from which all Catholics were excluded. A new "Act Concerning Religion" overturned that of 1649 and stripped Catholics of their civil rights. Cromwell reconfirmed the Proprietary in his rights and privileges in 1658, but religious toleration would only survive as long as the Proprietary's rights remained intact.

After the death of his brother Leonard in 1647, Cecilius Calvert continued to rule through governors, and was known for great liberality toward his colonists. Lands were sold at nominal fee. A silver and bronze coinage was provided the settlers in 1658, paid for by the Proprietary. Cecilius survived the turmoil of English politics of the Civil War period and the subsequent Commonwealth, as well as the machinations of Virginia partisans who sought to limit his power and the relative autonomy of Maryland. Cecilius spent his last years in retirement. He died on November 30, 1675, and was succeeded by his son Charles.

Charles Calvert

The third Lord Baltimore and second Lord Proprietary of Maryland, was born in 1628 and served as governor of Maryland beginning in 1661. After the death of his father, Charles visited England, but soon returned to America. In 1684, he moved to England and remained there until his death.

It was during the tenure of the second Lord Proprietary that the Calvert family fortunes in Maryland began to sour. The first of the blows was dealt by William Penn who, with the connivance of James, Duke of York, later James II, received a grant of land that substantially overlapped the lands already ceded by the Crown to the Calverts. In fact, the original northern boundary of Maryland ran in an east-west line to the north of present-day Philadelphia. The present-day state of Delaware also lay within the Calvert domain, yet Penn had designs on this territory as well. Conflicting boundary lines would lead to much confusion and not a little bloodshed until the borders were formally surveyed in the next century and Maryland ceded much of the contested land.

Religious toleration, the centerpiece of Calvert policy in Maryland, would come to an end with the accession of William III and Mary II to the English throne in 1689. Maryland Protestants, maintaining that local Catholics posed a grave danger to their security (although outnumbering these by an estimated twelve-to-one), convinced William III to suspend the Maryland charter. Maryland ceased to be a free Palatinate and in essence became a crown colony, while the Proprietary ceased being a prince and was reduced to an absentee landlord.

In 1713 Charles Calvert's eldest son and heir, Benedict Leonard, formally abjured Catholicism. The third Lord Baltimore survived another year, dying February 24, 1714.

Benedict Leonard Calvert

The fourth Lord Baltimore and third Lord Proprietary of Maryland, cut off from the family fortunes by his father, had these restored upon the death of the elder Calvert. He himself would survive his father by little more than a year, dying April 5, 1715.

Charles Calvert

The Proprietorship of Maryland which had been taken from his Catholic grandfather, was restored to the Fifth Lord Baltimore by George I. The work of a quarter century could not be undone, however, and English Common Law came to be further extended into the colony's legal structure. The old days of the Proprietary lawgiver were definitely over.

Charles Calvert, born September 29, 1699, knew great success at Court, serving the Prince of Wales in various capacities. On December 10, 1731, he was elected a Fellow of the Royal Society. He sat in Parliament in 1734, representing St. German's in Cornwall, and again in 1741 and 1747, for the County of Surrey. On March 9, 1741, he was appointed Junior Lord of the Admiralty, and in April, 1747, Cofferer to the Prince of Wales and Surveyor of the Duchy Lands of Cornwall. He died April 24, 1751, in London.

Frederick Calvert

The last of the Calverts was born in 1731 and succeeded to his father's titles upon the death of the latter. In 1753, he married Lady Diana Egerton, youngest daughter of the Duke of Bridgewater. A would-be author, the sixth Lord Baltimore published two works of dubious literary value in 1763 and 1769. His relations with his Maryland province were chiefly financial, and consisted in the collecting of the taxes necessary to his own extravagant way of life. In 1768, he was brought to trial for sexually assaulting a woman. Although acquitted, he was condemned in the court of public opinion. He died at Naples, September 14, 1771, leaving no legitimate issue. Frederick willed the Province of Maryland to his illegitimate son, Henry Harford, but the American colonies were by this time on the brink of revolt. With independence, the Proprietary rights of the Calverts came to an end.

See also MARYLAND, CATHOLIC CHURCH IN.

Browne, William Hand. *George Calvert and Cecilius Calvert.* New York: Dodd, Mead, and Co., 1890.

____. *Maryland: The History of a Palatinate.* Boston: Houghton Mifflin, 1884.

Fogarty, Gerald P., S.J. "Property and Religious Liberty in Colonial Maryland Catholic Thought." *Catholic Historical Review* 72 (October 1986) 573–600.

Krugler, John J. "Lord Baltimore, Roman Catholics, and Toleration: Religious Policy in Maryland during the Early Catholic Years." *Catholic Historical Review* 65 (January 1979) 49–75.

Morris, John G. *The Lords Baltimore.* Baltimore: Maryland Historical Society, 1874.

ALBERT H. LEDOUX

Related Document

THE CHARTER OF MARYLAND, JUNE 20, 1632

Sir George Calvert (c. 1580–1632), one of the chief secretaries and favorites of King James I of England, belonged to that rather rare breed of men who do not hesitate to forfeit a promising political career when it conflicts with their religious convictions. After his conversion to Catholicism in 1625, Calvert resigned his royal secretaryship, although he continued to employ the favor which he retained at court to secure a haven of religious peace in the English colonies for his harassed coreligionists. Attempts to establish a settlement in Newfoundland and Virginia having failed, the first Baron of Baltimore died before he could fulfill his dream. But in June, 1632, Charles I redeemed his father's promises by issuing a generous charter to Baltimore's son, Cecilius Calvert. In view of the anti-Catholic laws of the mother country, and the hostility and suspicion that permeated the government of Charles I in all that related to Catholicism, it is not surprising to find the charter encouraging the erection of churches in the colony which were to be "dedicated and consecrated according to the Ecclesiastical Laws of our Kingdom of England. . . ." In actual fact, however, religious toleration for all Christians was preserved by Calvert, and by reason of the tact and common sense of the proprietor and his Catholic representatives in the colony that policy endured until it was abolished in 1654 by the Puritans who had overthrown Baltimore's government.

(*Source*: Francis Newton Thorpe, ed. *The Federal and State Constitutions.* Washington, D.C.: Government Printing Office, 1909, III, 1677–86.)

. . . II. WHEREAS OUR WELL BELOVED AND RIGHT TRUSTY Subject Caecilius Calvert, Baron of Baltimore, in our Kingdom of Ireland . . . being animated with a laudable, and pious Zeal for extending the Christian Religion, and also the Territories of our Empire, hath humbly besought Leave of Us, that he may transport, by his own Industry, and Expense, a numerous Colony of the English Nation to a certain Region, herein after described, in a Country hitherto uncultivated, in the Parts of America, and partly occupied by Savages, having no Knowledge of the Divine Being, and that all that Region, with some certain Privileges, and Jurisdiction, appertaining unto the wholesome Government, and State of his Colony and Region aforesaid, may by our Royal Highness be given, granted, and confirmed unto him, and his Heirs.

III. Know Ye, therefore, that We . . . by this our present Charter . . . do Give, Grant, and Confirm, unto the aforesaid Caecilius, now Baron of Baltimore, his Heirs, and Assigns, all that Part of the Peninsula, or Cherosonese, lying in the Parts of America, between the Ocean on the East, and the Bay of Chesapeake on the West . . .

IV. Also We do Grant . . . unto the said Baron of Baltimore . . . all Islands and Islets within the Limits aforesaid, all and singular Islands and Islets, from the Eastern Shore of the aforesaid Region, towards the East, which have been, or shall be formed in the Sea, situate within Ten marine Leagues from the said Shore . . . And furthermore the Patronages, and Advowsons of all Churches which (with the increasing Worship and Religion of Christ) within the said region . . . hereafter shall happen to be built, together with Licence, and Faculty of erecting and founding Churches, Chapels, and Places of Worship, in convenient and suitable places, within the Premises, and of causing the same to be dedicated and consecrated according to the Ecclesiastical Laws of our Kingdom of England, with all, and singular such, and as ample Rights, Jurisdictions, Privileges, Prerogatives, Royalties, Liberties, Immunities, and royal Rights, and temporal Franchises whatsoever, as well by Sea as by Land, within the Region . . . aforesaid, to be had, exercised, used, and enjoyed, as any Bishop of Durham, within the Bishoprick or County Palatine of Durham, in our Kingdom of England, ever heretofore, hath had, held, used, or enjoyed or of Right could, or ought to have, hold, use, or enjoy.

V. And we do by these Presents . . . Make, Create, and Constitute Him, the now Baron of Baltimore, and his Heirs, the true and absolute Lords and Proprietaries of the Region aforesaid, and of all other the Premises (except the before excepted) saving always the Faith and Allegiance and Sovereign Dominion due to Us . . . To Hold of Us . . . as of our Castle of Windsor, in our County of Berks, in free and common Soccage, by Fealty only for all Services, and not in Capite, nor by Knight's Service, Yielding therefore unto Us . . . Two Indian Arrows of these Parts, to be delivered at the said Castle of Windsor, every Year, on Tuesday in Easter Week: And also the fifth Part of all Gold and Silver are, which shall happen from Time to Time, to be found within the aforesaid Limits.

VI. Now, That the aforesaid Region . . . may be eminently distinguished above all other Regions of that Territory . . . Know Ye, that . . . We do . . . Erect and Incorporate the same into a Province, and nominate the same Maryland, by which Name We will that it shall from henceforth be called.

VII. And . . . We . . . do grant unto the said now Baron . . . and to his Heirs, for the good and happy Government of the said Province, free, full, and absolute Power, by the tenor of these Presents, to Ordain, Make, and Enact Laws, of what kind soever, according to their sound Discretions, whether relating to the Public State of the said Province, or the private Utility of Individuals, of and with the Ad-

vice, Assent, and Approbation of the Free-Men of the same Province, or of the greater Part of them, or of their Delegates or Deputies, whom We will shall be called together for the framing of Laws, when and as often as Need shall require, by the aforesaid now Baron of Baltimore . . . and in the Form which shall seem best to him . . . and duly to execute the same upon all Persons, for the Time being, within the aforesaid Province, and the Limits thereof, or under his or their Government and Power . . . by the Imposition of Fines, Imprisonment, and other Punishment whatsoever; even if it be necessary, and the Quality of the Offence require it, by Privation of Member, or Life . . . So, nevertheless, that the Laws aforesaid be consonant to Reason and be not repugnant or contrary, but (so far as conveniently may be) agreeable to the Laws, Statutes, Customs and Rights of this Our Kingdom of England.

XVII. Moreover, We will, appoint, and ordain, and by these Presents, for Us, our Heirs and Successors, do grant unto the aforesaid now Baron of Baltimore, his Heirs and Assigns, from Time to Time, forever, shall have, and enjoy the Taxes and Subsidies payable, or arising within the Ports, Harbors, and other Creeks and Places aforesaid, for Wares bought and sold, and Things there to be laden, or unladen, to be reasonably assessed by them, and the People there as aforesaid, on emergent Occasion; to whom We grant Power by these Presents, for Us, our Heirs and Successors, to assess and impose the said Taxes and Subsidies there, upon just Cause and in due Proportion.

XVIII. And Furthermore . . . We . . . do give . . . unto the aforesaid now Baron of Baltimore . . . full and absolute Licence, Power, and Authority . . . that he assign, alien, grant, demise, or enfeoff so many, such, and proportionate Parts and Parcels of the Premises, to any Person or Persons willing to purchase the same, as they shall think convenient, to have and to hold . . . in Fees-imple, or Fee-tail, or for Term of Life, Lives, or Years; to of the aforesaid now Baron of Baltimore . . . by . . . such . . . Services, Customs and Rents of This Kind, as to the same now Baron of Baltimore . . . shall seem fit and agreeable, and not immediately of Us. . . .

XIX. We . . . also . . . do . . . grant Licence to the same Baron of Baltimore . . . to erect any Parcels of Land within the Province aforesaid, into Manors, and in every of those Manors, to have and to hold a Court-Baron, and all Things which to a Court-Baron do belong . . .

(*Source:* John Tracy Ellis, ed. *Documents of American Catholic History.* Vol. 1:1493–1865. Wilmington, Del.: Michael Glazier, 1987, 95–98.)

CANA CONFERENCES

This lay movement originated in a series of retreats given to married couples by the Jesuit priest John P. Delaney. After hearing of Delaney's success in this work, a group of lay Catholics in St. Louis requested Edward Dowling, S.J., to conduct a similar retreat for them. Dowling did so in October 1944, calling his reflections a "Cana Conference," and it sparked a demand for similar retreats.

These retreats were unlike earlier retreats given by priests for married laypersons. Dowling intended his talks to deal not with spirituality in a rarefied sense but instead to deal with the everyday things of life experienced by married men and women in a spiritual way. Also Dowling conducted his conferences in a more relaxed and informal fashion than the way in which Catholic retreats were usually conducted prior to the Second Vatican Council (1962–65). The popularity of Cana Conferences grew. The emphasis on the importance of family life and community was welcomed by laypeople throughout the United States, and many American bishops began setting up formal diocesan structures to deal with Christian family life and its needs.

Soon the movement expanded to working with engaged couples under the title, "Pre-Cana Conferences," as well as with the widowed, "Naim Conferences," and "Bethany Conferences" for single Catholics. Many dioceses now make Pre-Cana conferences compulsory for couples preparing for Christian marriage. The Cana Conference movement was important in the history of spirituality in the American Church in that the Church formally recognized that the spiritual needs of lay Catholics were different from those of priests and religious and developed formal structures to deal with them.

Clemens, A. H. *The Cana Movement in the U.S.* Washington, 1953.

ANTHONY D. ANDREASSI

CANISIUS COLLEGE

Canisius College owes its existence to the persistent efforts of Bishop John Timon, the first bishop of Buffalo, to provide higher education for his diocese. Bishop Timon appealed repeatedly to the Jesuits to start a college, but the shortage of manpower and money made them reluctant to undertake such a project. However after several unsuccessful attempts to establish Catholic higher education in the Buffalo area, Canisius College got underway in 1870. Patterned after the European model, which did not distinguish between high school and college, Canisius began as a Jesuit classical college in downtown Buffalo, New York.

Bismarck's *Kulturkampf* in Germany provided an unexpected benefit to the infant college. Jesuits were expelled from Germany and many of them came to the United States, providing numerous recruits for the faculty and likewise giving a decidedly German orientation to the college in those early years. In 1912 the college was separated from the high school and college classes moved to a new location, while the high school remained at the original site.

The end of the Second World War saw a massive increase in the number of students and physical facilities. Begun as a classical college on the European style, over the years Canisius has introduced a variety of programs, graduate and undergraduate, taught by an increasingly diverse faculty. From one small building located in downtown Buffalo to thirty-eight buildings presently on its urban campus and with more construction planned, Canisius has continued to grow. Canisius graduates are unusually well represented among the professional and business leaders of western New York and the college has been able to preserve a high academic reputation.

See also CATHOLIC UNIVERSITIES AND COLLEGES.

Brady, Charles. *Canisius College: The First Hundred Years.* Buffalo, N.Y.: Canisius College, 1969.
Harney, Thomas E. *AMDG A History of Canisius College.* Vol. I. New York: Vantage Press, 1971; Vol. II. Smithtown, N.Y.: Exposition Press, 1981; Vol. III. New York: Vantage Press, 1988.

JOHN GARVEY, S.J.

CANON LAW SOCIETY OF AMERICA

Foundation

The Canon Law Society of America (CLSA) is a professional association dedicated to promotion of the study and application of canon law in the Roman Catholic Church.

The first canon law society in the Western hemisphere, the CLSA was founded on November 12, 1939, in Washington, D.C., at the invitation of Most Rev. Joseph Corrigan, rector of The Catholic University of America. Sixty persons attended the first meeting, largely from alumni of the university's school of canon law. Membership levels later reached more than eighteen hundred members. The first president was the Rev. William Doheny, C.S.C., prominent canonist and later prelate auditor of the Roman Rota. The early annual meetings were convened in New York City on the occasion of the annual convocation of the Alumni and Friends of CUA. These meetings were typically one half day in length, consisting of a scholarly presentation, discussion, business meeting and elections. Eventually the meetings evolved to a period of several days and were located in various cities across the United States. Lay members were first admitted in 1949. The meeting agenda reflected typical canonical interests, chiefly related to chancery practice, marriage annulments, and religious life.

Revision of Canon Law

The announcement in 1959 by Pope John XXIII of the Second Vatican Council and the revision of canon law occasioned a new direction of CLSA activities. Extensive involvement was expended during the conciliar and postconciliar years for the revision of canon law. As early as

1960, the CLSA circulated a survey of areas of potential reform in canon law which resulted in a series of recommendations. The 1964 annual meeting in San Francisco was a significant moment in CLSA history when new leadership was elected which served to chart the future direction of the society's involvements for the revision of canon law and postconciliar renewal.

With the formal commencement of the revision of the 1917 Code of Canon Law after the conclusion of Vatican II, the CLSA provided recommendations and critiques of the various proposed revisions. Although the CLSA was not an official consulting body to the Roman commission responsible for the revision of canon law, the CLSA entered into a collaborative working relationship with the American hierarchy through the National Conference of Catholic Bishops. This was a very fruitful process. The CLSA's participation included not only the critique of proposed technical revisions, but also endeavored to incorporate into the revision process an alertness to other substantive issues from a multidisciplinary methodology.

This involvement in the revision of the law precipitated numerous CLSA symposia and studies on issues which occupied the attention of the Catholic Church in the immediate postconciliar era. A significant example of CLSA involvement was the administration of justice in the marriage annulment process. The CLSA proposed to the American bishops a streamlined system of tribunal procedures. These procedures, known as the American Procedural Norms, received approval from Rome in 1970. These norms significantly impacted upon the ability of American marriage tribunals to respond more justly and efficiently to rapidly increasing numbers of petitions for annulments. With the promulgation of the revised Code of Canon Law in 1983, these norms ceased to have effect, although their influence is detectible in some areas of the revised law.

The postconciliar spirit continued to animate many CLSA projects and activities. Various symposia were sponsored by the CLSA which investigated areas such as due process in the Church, selection of bishops, sexism and Church law, and lay ministry. A series of permanent seminars explored various canonical-theological issues such as the Church as communion, official ministry, and the Church as mission. Workshops were sponsored for bishops to assist their understanding of the revised canon law. These activities represented a new era in canon law which promoted a greater integration of theology in the science of canon law, especially the ecclesiological teachings of Vatican Council II. Since 1973 the society annually bestows the Role of Law Award to a canonist who exemplifies in ministry the furtherance of Church law as a pastoral means of serving God's people.

Publications

The CLSA published in 1983 an English language translation of the 1983 code (*Code of Canon Law, Latin-English*

Edition). The publication of an extensive canon law commentary (*The Code of Canon Law: A Text and Commentary*, Paulist Press, 1985) was a major contribution to canonical literature on the revised code. The many symposia, workshops and annual meetings of the CLSA have resulted in numerous publications. The CLSA has evolved into a major publisher of canonical studies, having published more than sixty titles.

The CLSA administrative offices are located on the campus of The Catholic University of America.

"The Canon Law Society of America." *The Jurist* 1 (1941) 92–94.

Canon Law Society of America, *Reflections on the Occasion of the 50th Anniversary*. Washington: Canon Law Society of America, 1988.

Green, T. J. "The Canon Law Society of America and the Revision of the Code: Historical Reflections and Continuing Concerns." *The Jurist* 53 (1993) 1–21.

PATRICK COGAN, S.A.

CANTWELL, JOHN J. (1874–1947)

Archbishop. A native of Limerick, Ireland, Cantwell was born on December 1, 1874, the first of fifteen children of Patrick and Ellen O'Donnell Cantwell. Upon completion of his studies in Sacred Heart College at the Crescent in Limerick, John entered St. Patrick's Seminary at Thurles in 1892 as a clerical aspirant for the Archdiocese of San Francisco. He was ordained on June 18, 1899, by Bishop Robert Browne. In San Francisco, Fr. Cantwell served as curate at St. Joseph's parish in Berkeley, where he organized the Newman Club at the University of California. In 1904 he was made secretary to Archbishop Patrick W. Riordan and, a decade later, he was appointed vicar general.

Named bishop of Monterey-Los Angeles in 1917, Cantwell was consecrated at St. Mary's Cathedral on December 5. He was installed at Los Angeles a week later in St. Vibiana's Cathedral. Cantwell served as chief shepherd for thirty years, first as bishop of Monterey-Los Angeles (1917–22), then as bishop of Los Angeles-San Diego (1922–36) and, finally, as archbishop of Los Angeles (1936–47). California became the first state in the union to have two metropolitan provinces when Los Angeles was advanced to that rank in 1936.

During the longest tenure yet served by a residential prelate in California's southland, Cantwell oversaw the erection of both a major and a minor seminary, sixteen hospitals and clinics, 205 churches, thirty-four high schools, and forty-three elementary schools. Among Cantwell's other major accomplishments was the establishment of the Catholic Motion Picture Actor's Guild of America (1923) which evolved into the Legion on Decency (1934); an outreach to Mexicans fleeing to Southern California as political and religious refugees (for which he received the

Golden Rose of Tepeyac), and the numerical expansion of his see from 178,000 to 601,000 Catholics in an area twice divided during his incumbency.

When the archbishop died at Los Angeles on October 30, 1947, a local newspaper observed that "no career in public life was better marked with works of importance and benefit towards our society as a whole than that of John J. Cantwell."

See also CALIFORNIA, CATHOLIC CHURCH IN.

Weber, Francis J. *John Joseph Cantwell, His Excellency of Los Angeles.* Hong Kong: Cathay Press Limited, 1971.

FRANCIS J. WEBER

CAPITAL PUNISHMENT AND AMERICAN CATHOLICS

American Catholic moral and intellectual reflection on the issue of capital punishment is consistent with traditional Church teaching over the centuries with the notable exception, however, of developments that have occurred in the most recent deliberations of the American Catholic bishops, particularly in the process which resulted in the 1980 statement of the National Conference of Catholic Bishops. This article will review, briefly, the history of American Catholic reflection on the question and will outline the significant events which have resulted in the most current expression of American ecclesiastical leadership.

Traditional Teaching

Fr. D. M. Campion's essay in the *New Catholic Encyclopedia* articulates the key elements in the history of Catholic theological thinking on the question of the death penalty. The most prominent figure is that of St. Augustine of Hippo who provides the theological rationale that figures in subsequent theological assessments, most notably that of Aquinas in the *Summa Theologiae II-II.* The central contention is that the state, for the sake of the defense of the public order, may undertake the execution of those whose crimes directly violate the right to life of the innocent. Since such actions directly compromise the right to life of all citizens, the state may invoke capital punishment in order to preserve the common good of the social order.

Professor James Megivern of the University of North Carolina has researched the long tradition of Church teaching and argues persuasively that, while Augustine frequently supported the sentence of capital punishment, in all instances where it was imposed, however, he argued for clemency rather than execution (*The Death Penalty*). Furthermore, Megivern argues that were it not for the issue of heresy, the death penalty would never have achieved the status that it subsequently acquired in theological assessments of Church-state relations. A reappraisal of such a long-

standing tradition in Church teaching by the American Church required the confluence of important twentieth-century theological developments in the ecclesial understanding of human rights with a political and social climate resulting in "de facto" diminution of the death penalty in the period between 1930 and 1969 in the United States. Megivern's analysis cogently outlines this process and will provide the framework for subsequent remarks. However, it is worthwhile noting that American theological thinking in the traditional manuals of moral theology indicates a uniform acceptance of the tradition. A case in point is the work of the nineteenth-century prelate, Francis Patrick Kenrick.

Kenrick, who served as archbishop of Baltimore, addresses the question in his three-volume work, *Theologia Moralis,* which appeared in 1841. Kenrick begins his appraisal by noting the opposition of the twelfth-century heretical group, the Waldensians, to the practice of capital punishment. Kenrick responds with a catalogue of theological commentary from sacred Scripture to Aquinas in favor of capital punishment. Kenrick's Latin commentary is interesting in its inclusion of references from the common law tradition, notably Blackstone, and concludes with an endorsement of the American Constitutional protection against deprivation of life without due process of law. However, Kenrick does not challenge this tradition and is content to repeat it with common law glosses.

The substance of the tradition, according to Kenrick, is that the state enjoys the right to execute a criminal, when necessary, for the defense of the common good. Kenrick's discussion of the question, however, makes no mention of the 1764 challenge of Cesare Beccaria questioning the right of the state to inflict the death penalty, nor is there reference to the dissident voices of Tertullian and Lactantius in the patristic period. The acknowledgment of "necessity" is intriguing, since it anticipates the much later argument for the rejection of the death penalty by the American hierarchy who challenge the "necessity" of the penalty in order to defend public order.

Opposition to the Death Penalty

Against the backdrop of widespread humanitarian concern for human rights, significant American voices were raised in opposition to the death penalty. Dr. Benjamin Rush is widely acknowledged as the earliest proponent for abolition in his essay in opposition to public execution in 1787. The diverse religious communities in American life were a strong force for abolition, especially the Quaker churches who were also in the forefront of the antislavery movement. Abolitionist sentiment is evident in the varying practices of the states with Michigan being the earliest, in 1864, to oppose the death penalty. For an American Catholic community preoccupied with caring for the multifaceted pastoral needs of burgeoning immigrant communities and overcoming the hostile legacy of nativism, few theological resources were available for extended sociopolitical critique of the death penalty until after the Second World War.

Nonetheless, there are significant American Catholic concerns about the practice that can be documented. For example, an editorial comment in the May 2, 1931, issue of *America* magazine suggests that while the state "may" inflict the capital penalty, there is no requirement that it "must" do so. A bibliographical review of theological commentary on the death penalty in prominent American ecclesiastical journals from the turn of the century up to the present, particularly in *Commonweal, America, Theological Studies,* and the *American Ecclesiastical Review,* generally reveals a rehearsal of the received tradition, but with significant support for alternatives to capital punishment raised in the form of reader responses to the journals. A significant article by the Catholic pacifist, Gordon Zahn, in the pages of *Commonweal* ("A Pacifist Looks at the Question of Abortion"), argues for the moral symmetry of pacifist opposition both to warfare and the violence of abortion. This linkage anticipates the "seamless" web argument to connect the broad range of issues affecting human life developed by Cardinal Joseph Bernardin in the 1980s.

Critical reflection on various forms of violence can be found in American Catholic literature. For example, discussion of the question of prize-fighting in the highly regarded "Notes on Moral Theology" in *Theological Studies* discloses near unanimity among American moralists in opposing the violence of this practice in the face of widespread societal approval. Fr. John Ford, on another front, was virtually alone in registering opposition to the saturation bombing campaign of the American military in his now famous essay in the 1943 volume of *Theological Studies*. Nonetheless, these critical responses to the question of violence are an important witness to the resources in the Catholic tradition of social justice to which the bishops return in response to the challenges of the civil rights movement and the legacy of the Vietnam War.

Several factors form an important context for the bishops' 1980 statement. From 1930 until 1969, the number of executions in the United States declined from a high of 199 to zero. The "de facto" absence of executions, as the political scientists Zimring and Hawkins have noted, anticipates the corollary development of "de jure" legislation for abolition. Furthermore, the continuing high percentage of public support for the death penalty is attributable, according to the authors, to the enduring "symbolic" value of the penalty as an expression of social resistance to high crime rates. Once abolition occurs, rates of public approbation decline. At least one factor influencing the reconsideration of the hierarchy is this factual phenomenon of dramatically decreased recourse to capital punishment. Secondly, the Supreme Court in its 1972 case, *Furman v. Georgia,*

challenged the procedures whereby the penalty was applied, in effect, rendering invalid all existing state statutes. The flurry of activity to reinstate the penalty, notwithstanding, the public policy debate was joined. Thirdly, Fr. D. M. Campion's prescient entry in the *New Catholic Encyclopedia* forecasted that subsequent Catholic reconsideration of the question would be influenced by the expansive embrace of a universal understanding of human rights as well as a "dynamic" understanding of natural law.

The appearance of Pope John XXIII's *Pacem in Terris* retrieved and expanded the natural law affirmation of human rights and gave approbation to the philosophical affirmation of personalism in the writings of leading continental thinkers in the twentieth century, notably, Emmanuel Mounier and Jacques Maritain. The distinctive theological contribution of John Courtney Murray, S.J., to the conciliar debate on religious liberty took the form of a closely reasoned historical assessment of the American democratic experience to demonstrate that democratic structures do not necessarily militate against the legitimate interests of the Church thereby yielding a more optimistic appraisal of Church-state relations.

American Bishops and Capital Punishment

This attention to concrete "praxis" as a source for theological analysis is reflected in the pastoral letters of the American hierarchy on nuclear weaponry and the economic order and is also reflected in their 1980 reappraisal of the death penalty. The precipitating events, however, for this reassessment were the Supreme Court's response to *Furman v. Georgia* in *Gregg v. Georgia* (1976) which held that the penalty of death does not "violate the Constitution" followed in short order by convicted murderer Gary Gilmore's request for execution in 1977. The 1980 statement, however, has important antecedents.

In 1974 the bishops declared their opposition to the death penalty on the basis of their commitment to the inviolable value of human life. In 1978 the bishops issued a pastoral letter, "Community and Crime," in which they argued that recourse to capital punishment leads to "further erosion of respect for life in our society." This statement continued, with numerous scholarly citations, to acknowledge the discriminatory application of the death penalty in the past (e.g., although the Supreme Court in the *McClesky* decision of 1987 rejected the argument that racial discrimination is an argument for its abolition, it is a matter of fact that of 376 people executed in Georgia from 1930 to 1987, 304 were black men), and disputed claims that the death penalty is an effective deterrent. In November 1980 the bishops by a vote of 145 to 31, with fourteen abstentions, resolved that the death penalty be abolished as a "manifestation of our belief in the unique worth and dignity of each person from the moment of conception, a creature made in the image and likeness of God."

The crucial theological argument that is made in the statement rests upon a conviction that respect for human life is an interdependent, interlocking moral principle with that of the common good of the social order. A unifying thread of coherence links church opposition to abortion, euthanasia, the death penalty, nuclear warfare, or any other threat to the integrity of human life. This thread is one of inviolable dignity and is captured by Cardinal Bernardin of Chicago as the "seamless web" argument, a metaphor drawn from the biblical account of the seamless garment of Jesus in John's narrative of the Lord's passion.

The statement does not seek to contravene the traditional argument affirming the right of the state to exercise capital punishment. Rather, the strategy adopted by the bishops to support the position for abolition is to highlight six "inherent difficulties" that reflect a "praxis," experiential-based theological analysis of the morality of capital punishment. The bishops find the justification to be wanting on several counts. There is the possibility of mistake, the problem of delays in implementation, the frank acknowledgment of discriminatory application of the penalty against the poor and racial minorities, the fact that the penalty extinguishes the possibility of reform, the anguish that the imposition of the penalty brings to the criminal, loved ones and those charged with witnessing the event, the increasingly acrimonious atmosphere engendered by the existence of the death penalty, and unfair and discriminatory sentencing practices.

Professor Megivern's trenchant analysis of church tradition identifies two important continental theologians, Canon Jacques Leclerq of Louvain and Fr. Johannes Ude, who, in the 1930s, broke ranks with the traditional defense of the state's right to kill on the basis of public "necessity." According to Leclerq, the state has the "mission" to defend life, and in modern society the death penalty lacks legitimacy. Ude, who witnessed the execution of a retarded youth under Nazi tyranny, contends that the Christian defense of the death penalty has been a betrayal of gospel nonviolence. Both theologians score the tradition for its defense of a state's "right" to kill without sufficient attention to the limits inherent in such a "right." Megivern insightfully highlights the importance of post-World War II theological developments in Scripture and ecclesiology which accentuate the importance of historical-critical scholarship which, in turn, leads to the resounding affirmations of human dignity in the conciliar decrees on the Church and the pastoral constitution on the Church (respectively, *Lumen gentium* and *Gaudium et spes*).

Fr. Robert Drinan, S.J., former congressman from Massachusetts, has been an outspoken advocate for abolition of the death penalty, concurring with Cardinal Bernardin's assessment that its continued existence contributes to the "increased brutalization of society." Drinan speculates that the high rate of support among American Catholics for the death penalty (more than 70 percent in most surveys) may be attributable to the perception that killing is permissible when American interests are at stake. There is no scientific validation for this perception, but Drinan further speculates that the pressure of international law as well as the fact that America is joined by oppressive political regimes such as China and Iran in imposing the death penalty may provide incentives for a reevaluation of public support in the future.

In summary, the American bishops have charted a new course for the American Church on the issue of capital punishment by invoking a more universalistic appeal to basic human rights and the inviolable dignity of the human person as a sacred moral value. While the American Catholic population at large continues to share widely held public attitudes in favor of the death penalty, influenced in large measure by fears of widespread crime and social disorder, official Church leadership, including Pope John Paul II's opposition to the death penalty in 1983, has committed the Church to a different discernment akin to the processes whereby slavery was also accepted and then subsequently rejected by the public.

See also BERNARDIN, JOSEPH CARDINAL; KENRICK, FRANCIS PATRICK.

Bedau, Hugo Adam, ed., *The Death Penalty in America.* 3rd ed. England: Oxford University Press, 1982.

Corrado, Dennis, and James Hinchey. *Shepherds Speak, American Bishops Confront the Social and Moral Issues that Challenge Christians Today.* New York: Crossroad, 1986.

Drinan, Robert F. *The Fractured Dream, America's Divisive Moral Choices.* New York: Crossroad, 1991.

Langan, John. "Capital Punishment." *Theological Studies* 54 (March 1993) 111–25.

Megivern, James J. *The Death Penalty: An Historical and Theological Survey.* New York: Paulist Press, 1997.

Nolan, Hugh. *Pastoral Letters of the United States Catholic Bishops, Volume III 1962–1974 and Volume IV 1975–1983.* Washington, D.C.: United States Catholic Conference.

Zimring, Franklin, and Gordon Hawkins. *Capital Punishment and the American Agenda.* Cambridge University Press, 1986.

JEREMIAH J. McCARTHY

Related Document

ENLARGING THE DIALOGUE ON A CONSISTENT ETHIC OF LIFE, MARCH 11, 1984

The so-called life issues of abortion, capital punishment, euthanasia, hunger, war—each a single aspect of human rights in general—have been the subject of intense and often bitter debate among Americans in the generation since World War II. In the course of the debate on these topics deep differences have arisen and that within the Catholic community of the United States, as well as within the broader national society. In an effort to establish a linkage between these individual issues that is based on general moral principles relating to life itself, there has evolved what has been called the "seamless garment" approach. In the William Wade Lecture at Saint Louis University in March, 1984, Joseph Cardinal Bernardin, Archbishop of Chicago, sought to advance that approach by showing how each single life issue has relation to the whole.

(*Source: Origins,* 13. April 5, 1984, 705–09.)

I FIRST WISH TO EXPRESS MY APPRECIATION TO ST. LOUIS University for the invitation to deliver the 1984 Wade Lecture. The William Wade lecture series is a fitting way to celebrate Father Wade's life as a priest, a philosopher and a teacher. His interest in the moral issues confronting today's church and society was an inspiration to all who knew him. I hope that my participation in this series will help to keep alive his memory and his ideals.

Three months ago I gave a lecture at Fordham University honoring another Jesuit educator, Father Robert Gannon, and addressed the topic of a consistent ethic of life. That lecture has generated a substantial discussion both inside and outside the church on the linkage of life issues, issues which I am convinced constitute a "seamless garment." This afternoon I would like extend the discussion by expanding upon the idea of a consistent ethic of life.

The setting of a Catholic university is one deliberately chosen for these lectures. My purpose is to foster the kind of sustained intellectual analysis and debate which the Jesuit tradition has cultivated throughout its history. The discussion must go beyond the university, but it will not occur without the involvement of Catholic universities. I seek to call attention to the resources in the Catholic tradition for shaping a viable public ethic. I hope to engage others in the church and in the wider civil society in an examination of the challenges to human life which surround us today and the potential of a consistent ethic of life. The Fordham lecture has catalyzed a vigorous debate; I seek to enlarge it, not to end it.

I will address three topics today: 1) the case for a consistent ethic of life; 2) the distinct levels of the problem; and 3) the contribution of a consistent ethic to the church and society generally.

I. The Logic of the Seamless Garment

The invitation extended to me for both the Gannon Lecture at Fordham and the Wade Lecture today asked that I address some aspect of the bishops' pastoral, "The Challenge of Peace: God's Promise and Our Response." While I would gladly have spent each lecture on the question of war and peace, I decided that it was equally necessary to show how the pastoral is rooted in a wider moral vision. Understanding that vision can enhance the way we address specific questions like the arms race.

When I set forth the argument about this wider moral vision—a consistent ethic of life—it evoked favorable comment, often from individuals and groups who had supported the peace pastoral but found themselves at odds with other positions the Catholic Church has taken on issues touching human life. At the same time, the Fordham address also generated letters from people who fear that the case for a consistent ethic will smother the Catholic opposition to abortion or will weaken our stance against the arms race.

Precisely in response to these concerns, I wish to state the essence of the case for a consistent ethic of life, specifying why it is needed and what is actually being advocated in a call for such an ethic. There are, in my view, two reasons why we need to espouse a consistent ethic of life: 1) the dimensions of the threats to life today; and 2) the value of our moral vision.

The threat to human life posed by nuclear war is so tangible that it has captured the attention of the nation. Public opinion polls rank it as one of the leading issues in the 1984 election campaign; popular movements like the nuclear freeze and professional organizations of physicians and scientists have shaped the nuclear question in terms which engage citizens and experts alike. The church is part of the process which has raised the nuclear issue to a new standing in our public life. I submit that the church should be a leader in the dialogue which shows that the nuclear question itself is part of the larger cultural, political, moral drama. Pope John Paul II regularly situates his examination of the nuclear issue in the framework of the broader problem of technology, politics and ethics.

When this broader canvas is analyzed, the concern for a specific issue does not recede, but the meaning of multiple threats to life today—the full dimension of the problems of politics and technology—becomes vividly clear. The case being made here is not a condemnation of either politics or technology, but a recognition with the pope that on a range of key issues "it is only through a conscious choice and through a deliberate policy that humanity can be saved." That quote from the Holy Father has unique relevance to nuclear war, but it can be used creatively to address other threats to life.

The range of application is all too evident. Nuclear war threatens life on a previously unimaginable scale; abortion takes life daily on a horrendous scale; public executions are fast becoming weekly events in the most advanced technological society in history; and euthanasia is now openly discussed and even advocated. Each of these assaults on life has its own meaning and morality; they cannot be collapsed into one problem, but they must be confronted as pieces of a larger pattern.

The reason I have placed such stress on the idea of a consistent ethic of life from the beginning of my term as chairman of the pro-life committee of the National Conference of Catholic Bishops is twofold; I am persuaded by the interrelatedness of these diverse problems, and I am convinced that the Catholic moral vision has the scope, the strength and the subtlety to address this wide range of issues in an effective fashion. It is precisely the potential of our moral vision that is often not recognized even within the community of the church. The case for a consistent ethic of life—one which stands for the protection of the right to life and the promotion of the rights which enhance life from womb to tomb—manifests the positive potential of the Catholic moral and social tradition. It is both a complex and a demanding tradition; it joins the humanity of the unborn infant and the humanity of the hungry; it calls for positive legal action to prevent the killing of the unborn or the aged and positive societal action to provide shelter for the homeless and education for the illiterate. The potential of the moral and social vision is appreciated in a new way when the systemic vision of Catholic ethics is seen as the background for the specific positions we take on a range of issues.

In response to those who fear otherwise, I contend that the systemic vision of a consistent ethic of life will not erode our crucial public opposition to the direction of the arms race; neither will it smother our persistent and necessary public opposition to abortion. The systemic vision is rooted in the conviction that our opposition to these distinct problems has a common foundation and that both church and society are served by making it evident.

A consistent ethic of life does not equate the problem of taking life (e.g., through abortion and in war) with the problem of promoting human dignity (through humane programs of nutrition, health care and housing). But a consistent ethic identifies both the protection of life and its promotion as moral questions. It argues for a continuum of life which must be sustained in the face diverse and distinct threats.

A consistent ethic does not say everyone in the church must do all things, but it does say that as individuals and groups pursue one issue, whether it is opposing abortion or capital punishment, the way we oppose one threat should be related to support for every systemic vision of life. It is not necessary or possible for every person to engage in each issue, but it is both possible and necessary for the church as a whole to cultivate a conscious explicit connection among the several issues. And it is very necessary for preserving a systemic vision that individuals and groups who seek to witness to life at one point of the spectrum of life not be seen as insensitive to or even opposed to other moral claims on the overall spectrum of life. Consistency does rule out contradictory moral positions about the unique value of human life. No one is called to do everything, but each of us can do something. And we can strive not to stand against each other when the protection and the promotion of life are at stake.

II. Levels of the Question

A consistent ethic of life should honor the complexity of the multiple issues it must address. It is necessary to dis-

tinguish several levels of the question. Without attempting to be comprehensive, allow me to explore four distinct dimensions of a consistent ethic.

First, at the level of general moral principles, it is possible to identify a single principle with diverse applications. In the Fordham address I used the prohibition against direct attacks on innocent life. This principle is both central to the Catholic moral vision and systematically related to a range of specific moral issues. It prohibits direct attacks on unborn life in the womb, direct attacks on civilians in warfare and the direct killing of patients in nursing homes. Each of these topics has a constituency in society concerned with the morality of abortion, war and care of the aged and dying. A consistent ethic of life encourages the specific concerns of each constituency, but also calls them to see the interrelatedness of their efforts. The need to defend the integrity of the moral principle in the full range of its application is a responsibility of each distinct constituency. If the principle is eroded in the public mind, all lose.

A second level of a consistent ethic stresses the distinction among cases rather than their similarities. We need different moral principles to apply to diverse cases. The classical distinction between ordinary and extraordinary means has applicability in the care of the dying but no relevance in the case of warfare. Not all moral principles have relevance across the whole range of life issues. Moreover, sometimes a systemic vision of the life issues requires a combination of moral insights to provide direction on one issue. At Fordham I cited the classical teaching on capital punishment which gives the state the right to take life in defense of key social values. But I also pointed out how a concern for promoting a public attitude of respect for life has led the bishops of the United States to oppose the exercise of that right.

Some of the responses I have received on the Fordham address correctly say that abortion and capital punishment are not identical issues. The principle which protects innocent life distinguishes the unborn child from the convicted murderer. Other letters stress that while nuclear war is a threat to life, abortion involves the actual taking of life, here and now. I accept both of these distinctions, of course, but I also find compelling the need to relate the cases while keeping them in distinct categories. Abortion is taking of life in ever growing numbers in our society. Those concerned about it, I believe, will find their case enhanced by taking note of the rapidly expanding use of public execution. In a similar way, those who are particularly concerned about these executions, even if the accused has taken another life, should recognize the elementary truth that a society which can be indifferent to the innocent life of an unborn child will not be easily stirred to concern for a convicted criminal. There is, I maintain, a political and psychological linkage among the life issues—from war to welfare concerns—which we ignore at our own peril: a systemic vision of life seeks to expand the moral imagination of a society, not partition it into airtight categories.

A third level of the question before us involves how we relate a commitment to principles to our public witness of life. As I have said, no one can do everything. There are limits to both competency and energy; both point to the wisdom of setting priorities and defining distinct functions. The church, however, must be credible across a wide range of issues; the very scope of our moral vision requires a commitment to a multiplicity of questions. In this way the teaching of the church will sustain a variety of individual commitments. Neither the Fordham address nor this one is intended to constrain wise and vigorous efforts to protect and promote life through specific, precise forms of action. Both addresses do seek to cultivate a dialogue within the church and in the wider society among individuals and groups which draw on common principles (e.g., the prohibition against killing the innocent), but seem convinced that they do not share common ground. The appeal here is not for anyone to do everything, but to recognize points of interdependence which should be stressed, not denied.

A fourth level, one where dialogue is sorely needed, is the relationship between moral principles and concrete political voices. The moral questions of abortion, the arms race, the fate of social programs for the poor and the role of human rights in foreign policy are public moral issues. The arena in which they are ultimately decided is not the academy or the church, but the political process. A consistent ethic of life seeks to present coherent linkage among a diverse set of issues. It can and should be used to test party platforms, public policies and political candidates. The church legitimately fulfills a public role by articulating a framework for political choices, by relating that framework to specific issues and by calling for systematic moral analysis of all areas of public policy.

This is the role our bishops' conference has sought to fulfill by publishing a statement on political responsibility during each of the presidential and congressional election years in the past decade. The purpose is surely not to tell citizens how to vote, but to help shape the public debate and form personal conscience so that every citizen will vote thoughtfully and responsibly. Our statement on political responsibility has always been, like our respect life program, a multi-issue approach to public morality. The fact that this statement sets forth a spectrum of issues of current concern to the church and society should not be understood as implying that all issues are qualitatively equal from a moral perspective. As I indicated earlier, each of the life issues—while related to all the others—is distinct and calls for its own specific moral analysis. Both the statement and the respect life program have direct relevance to the political order, but they are applied concretely by the choice of citizens. This is as it should

be. In the political order the church is primarily a teacher; it possesses a carefully cultivated tradition of moral analysis of personal and public issues. It makes that tradition available in a special manner for the community of the church, but it offers it also to all who find meaning and guidance in its moral teaching.

III. A Pastoral and Public Contribution

The moral teaching of the church has both pastoral and public significance. Pastorally, a consistent ethic of life is a contribution to the witness of the church's defense of the human person. Publicly, a consistent ethic fills a void in our public policy debate today.

Pastorally, I submit that a church standing forth on the entire range of issues which the logic of our moral vision bids us to confront will be a church in the style of both Vatican II's *Gaudium et Spes* and in the style of Pope John Paul II's consistent witness to life. The pastoral life of the church should not be guided by a simplistic criterion of relevance. But the capacity of faith to shed light on the concrete questions of personal and public life today is one way in which the value of the Gospel is assessed. Certainly the serious, sustained interest manifested throughout American society in the bishops' letter on war and peace provides a unique pastoral opportunity for the church. Demonstrating how the teaching on war and peace is supported by a wider concern for all of life may bring others to see for the first time what our tradition has affirmed for a very long time: the linkage among the life issues.

The public value of a consistent ethic of life is connected directly to its pastoral role. In the public arena we should always speak and act like a church. But the unique public possibility for a consistent ethic is provided precisely by the unstructured character of the public debate on the life questions. Each of the issues I have identified today—abortion, war, hunger and human rights, euthanasia and capital punishment—is treated as a separate, self-contained topic in our public life. Each is distinct, but an ad hoc approach to each one fails to illustrate how our choices in one area can affect our decisions in other areas. There must be a public attitude of respect for all of life if public actions are to respect it in concrete cases.

The pastoral on war and peace speaks of a "new moment" in the nuclear age. The pastoral has been widely studied and applauded because it caught the spirit of the new moment and spoke with moral substance to the issues of the new moment. I am convinced there is an open moment before us on the agenda of life issues. It is a significant opportunity for the church to demonstrate the strength of a sustained moral vision. I submit that a clear witness to a consistent ethic of life will allow us to grasp the opportunity of this open moment and serve both the sacredness of every human life and the God of life who is the origin and support of our common humanity.

(*Source:* John Tracy Ellis, ed. *Documents of American Catholic History.* Vol. 3:1966–1986. Wilmington, Del.: Michael Glazier, 1987, 888–95.)

CARDINALS IN THE AMERICAN CHURCH

With Pope John Paul II's selection of Archbishops Adam Maida of Detroit and William Keeler of Baltimore as cardinals in 1994, the total number of cardinals in the history of the American Church numbered thirty-nine. The selection of these prelates occasions some observations about the men chosen for the pope's highest honor and the sees or offices they held that led to this honor. Usually, but not always, the appointment to certain archdioceses brings with it the red hat. The first cardinal in the United States, for example, was Archbishop John McCloskey of New York in 1875. His successor, however, Michael Augustine Corrigan, did not receive the red hat, an honor given to every other archbishop of New York since 1902.

East Coast Dioceses

The supposed prestige or historical significance of an archdiocese is likewise no guarantee that its incumbent will become a cardinal. Baltimore, for example, is the nation's oldest diocese, but it is not the primatial see, a title formally refused by the Holy See in the 1850s, because of fear of the growing independence of the American hierarchy. Baltimore received the nation's second red hat in 1887, when James Gibbons was elevated. In 1903, he was the first American to attend a conclave, which elected Pius X. But his long life—he died in 1921—and the prominence he enjoyed as the nation's unofficial primate led Archbishop Giovanni Bonzano, the apostolic delegate, to warn Roman officials that never again should a man be appointed to Baltimore who would assume the role Gibbons had in the national Church. Gibbons' two successors, therefore, did not become cardinals. Despite its historical significance, moreover, Baltimore is no longer as important as other sees. In other words, while appointment to New York virtually guarantees a red hat, Baltimore's honor is more to the person than to the place. Even in those sees, usually occupied by cardinals, some incumbents had to wait an unusually long period before receiving the honor.

By the early twentieth century, other Catholic centers were developing first on the East Coast and later in the Midwest. In 1911 Pius X named the third and fourth cardinals in the U.S.A., John Farley of New York, who had been a moderating influence in the archdiocese during the episcopate of his predecessor, Corrigan, and William Henry O'Connell of Boston, an appointment which represented a combination of an honor given both to the place and the person. Boston had begun to rival New York as an important East Coast Catholic center, and O'Connell had carefully cultivated Roman contacts to gain his promotion first as bishop of Portland, Maine, and later coadjutor to Archbishop John Williams of Boston. The appointment of Farley and O'Connell brought to three the total number of American cardinals. In 1914, however, only Farley managed to get to the conclave that elected Benedict XV. In 1918, however, Farley died. In the same year, Dennis Dougherty was transferred from Buffalo to Philadelphia and, in 1921, was the first archbishop of Philadelphia to be named a cardinal, an honor given to all his successors. With the death of Gibbons later that year, the number of American cardinals was again reduced to two. In the conclave that elected Pius XI to succeed Benedict XV in 1922, neither of the Americans reached Rome in time to participate, an event that led O'Connell to have Vatican officials to extend the time within which cardinals were to assemble in Rome after the death of a pope.

The Midwest

But the population centers of the American Church were then expanding beyond the East Coast. In 1925 Pius XI increased the number of American cardinals to four by naming two more Americans, Patrick Hayes, who had succeeded Farley in New York in 1918, and George Mundelein, who had become archbishop of Chicago in 1915 after the Holy See rejected all the candidates proposed by the priests of the diocese and bishops of the province. Mundelein set about to display the importance of his Midwestern see in 1926 by sponsoring the International Eucharistic Congress, the first held in the U.S.A., in Chicago and on the grounds of his new seminary. Every archbishop of Chicago since that time has received the red hat. Other Midwestern cities were also increasing in prominence. In 1937 Detroit was elevated to an archdiocese, with the appointment of Edward Mooney, then the bishop of Rochester and former apostolic delegate to India and later Japan.

On the eve of World War II, other important changes occurred in the hierarchy that indicated there would be future cardinals. In 1938 Hayes died. Before his successor could be named, Pius XI died. O'Connell, together with Dougherty and Mundelein managed to attend the conclave to elect Cardinal Eugenio Pacelli, the secretary of state, as Pius XII. It was the third conclave that Americans attended and the only one for which O'Connell managed to arrive in time. For him, its outcome was ironic, for it was no secret among the bishops that he and his auxiliary, Francis J. Spellman, enjoyed, at best, strained relations, and Spellman and the new pope were on very close terms. Soon after Pius XII took office, he named Spellman archbishop of New York. But then, Mundelein died unexpectedly. Archbishop Samuel Stritch was then transferred from Milwaukee to Chicago. War, however, prevented the naming of any new cardinals. Moreover, in 1944 O'Connell of Boston died and was succeeded by Richard Cushing, who, unlike his predecessor, had received all his education at the Boston seminary.

After World War II

In 1946 Pius XII held the first of two consistories of his pontificate. He added four new American cardinals: Spellman of New York, Stritch of Chicago, Mooney of Detroit, and John J. Glennon of St. Louis. Together with Dougherty, American cardinals now numbered five. Glennon, who had been archbishop of St. Louis since 1902, however, died in Ireland before returning to his see. His successor, Joseph Ritter, would have to wait until 1961 to get his red hat. In other words, the honor to Glennon seems to have been as much to the person as to the see. Cushing of Boston was probably passed over at this time because he had been in office for a short time. In 1953 Pius XII held his second consistory, but named only one American, James Francis McIntyre of Los Angeles, the rapidly growing metropolis on the West Coast to which McIntyre had been named the second archbishop in 1948. That San Francisco, an archdiocese since 1853, was passed over may have been due to two factors. Los Angeles had become the larger of the two cities in the only state to have two archdioceses, and McIntyre was a protégé of Spellman, under whom he had served as auxiliary and coadjutor. Both the city and the person were being rewarded. Since McIntyre, every archbishop of Los Angeles has become a cardinal.

The fact that Cushing was passed over in 1953, however, warrants some explanation. His archdiocese had gone through the turmoil of the excommunication of Father Leonard Feeney, who taught that those not in formal communion with the Catholic Church could not be saved. Pius XII may have been dissatisfied with the archbishop's handling of the case or with his pastoral style of governance. Another possibility is that Cushing did not have the support of Spellman, who had, however, played a role in his appointment to Boston. In short, being archbishop of Boston in the 1950s did not ensure that one would become a cardinal. Whatever may have been Spellman's role in delaying the promotion of Cushing, he was directly responsible for the promotion of another leading prelate, John F. O'Hara, C.S.C., former president of the University of Notre Dame. After serving as Spellman's auxiliary in the Military Ordinariate, O'Hara had become bishop of Buffalo in 1945 and then, with Dougherty's death in 1951, archbishop of Philadelphia. That he was not made a cardinal in 1953 can be attributed to his short time in office.

1958 was a transitional year for the Church, American and universal. Stritch had been transferred from Chicago to Rome to become pro-prefect of Propaganda, but he died shortly thereafter. His successor in Chicago was Albert Meyer, like Stritch, formerly the archbishop of Milwaukee. In October, Pius XII died. The three American cardinals, Spellman, Mooney, and McIntyre, went to the conclave that elected John XXIII, but Mooney died just before it opened. At his first consistory, in 1958, John XXIII elevated both O'Hara of Philadelphia and Cushing of Boston to the cardinalate. The following year, he named as cardinals both Meyer of Chicago and Aloysius Muench, former bishop of Fargo, who had been nuncio to Germany and then served in the Curia. In 1960 O'Hara died in Philadelphia and was replaced by John Krol. In 1961 the pope elevated Ritter of St. Louis to the college of cardinals. Omitted from these three consistories was Mooney's successor in Detroit, John Dearden. Nevertheless, at six, the number of American cardinals was its highest in history up to that time. When Vatican Council II opened in October 1962, five of them were in attendance—Muench had died shortly before.

Vatican Council II and After

In June 1963 John XXIII died. The five Americans attended the conclave to elect Paul VI. In February 1965, Paul VI held his first consistory and appointed one American cardinal, Lawrence Shehan of Baltimore, the second archbishop of the nation's oldest see to attain the honor. An alumnus of the North American College and archbishop since 1961, he had been an able, if unoriginal, contributor to the first three sessions of the council. In this case, the honor seems clearly to have come to the man personally rather than to the see, especially in light of the fact that both Dearden and Krol, who had been in office at least as long, were passed over. The number of American cardinals was, however, again reduced to five with the death of Meyer, shortly before the opening of the final session of the council in 1965. He was succeeded by John Cody, former archbishop of New Orleans.

Of all the American cardinals, more have been appointed since Vatican II than in all the years previously. In 1967, Paul VI named four new American cardinals: Krol, Cody, Patrick O'Boyle, who had become the first archbishop of Washington 1947, and Francis Brennan, a member of the Curia. That same year, both Spellman and Ritter died. To New York, Paul VI named Terence Cooke, an auxiliary bishop who received all his education in New York; to St. Louis, he named John Carberry, a Roman alumnus. At his next consistory in 1969, Paul VI elevated both of them to the college of cardinals, together with Dearden and Bishop John Wright of Pittsburgh, who was assigned to the Curia. That Cooke received his red hat so soon after assuming office can be attributed to the great significance of New York. The rapid promotion of Carberry in contrast to his predecessor, who had to wait for more than a decade, might be explained in terms of the need for a strong voice in defense of papal policies then being challenged in the wake of *Humanae vitae* in 1968. The selection of Wright, a Roman-trained theologian, coincided with Paul VI's efforts to internationalize the Curia. The choice of Dearden, who had served in Detroit since 1959, was virtually mandated by his able administration of a diocese rapidly going through racial change and turmoil and the respect with which he was regarded by the other bishops who had elected him president of their national conference.

In the meantime, Paul VI required that all bishops, including cardinals, submit their resignations upon reaching the age of seventy-five. Cardinals over eighty, moreover, were no longer eligible to vote in a conclave. The first American cardinal affected by the new regulations was McIntyre, who submitted his resignation in 1970 at the age of eighty-four. He was succeeded by Timothy Manning, who had served as auxiliary bishop under John J. Cantwell, the first archbishop of Los Angeles. In 1970, moreover, Cushing died in Boston. His successor, Humberto Medeiros, had been bishop of Brownsville, Texas. In 1973 Paul VI named both Manning and Medeiros cardinals. Manning, born in Ireland, and Medeiros, born in the Azores, brought to the select group of American cardinals the further distinction that, aside from Farley and Glennon, they were the only ones not born in the U.S.A. In addition, the pope honored the oldest diocese in U.S. territory and, perhaps, the nation's growing Hispanic population by conferring the red hat on Luis Aponte Martinez of San Juan, Puerto Rico. During his pontificate, Paul VI named only one more cardinal to the American Church. In 1973 O'Boyle retired in Washington. His successor, William Baum, former bishop of Springfield-Cape Girardeau, received his red hat in 1976, the year of the nation's bicentennial. In 1980 he was transferred to the Roman Curia.

Pope John Paul II

When Paul VI died in 1978, there were twelve American cardinals, three of whom, McIntyre, O'Boyle, and Shehan, were ineligible to vote because of their age. In that tragic year, the Americans had to make two trips to Rome, the first to elect John Paul I, and, a little over a month later, to elect John Paul II. In 1980 John Paul II transferred Baum to the Curia and replaced him in Washington with James Hickey, former rector of the North American College in Rome and bishop of Cleveland. In 1982 Cody of Chicago died to be replaced by Joseph Bernardin, former secretary general of the USCC/NCCB and archbishop of Cincinnati. A year later, John Paul II named him a cardinal. Bernardin had been educated at The Catholic University of America. His short term in office before receiving the red hat was more than offset by the breadth of his previous experience and his deft handling of the situation in Chicago torn by scandals during the last days of Cody.

In 1983 both Cooke in New York and Medeiros in Boston died. To Boston, the pope appointed Bernard Law, the first graduate of Harvard College to be elevated to the episcopate, who had received his seminary education at several American seminaries. He had been bishop of Springfield-Cape Girardeau, where he had succeeded Baum. To New York, the pope named John J. O'Connor, who had been

educated at the Philadelphia seminary before entering the U.S. Navy, where he earned a Ph.D. at Georgetown University and rose to the rank of admiral as the Chief of Navy Chaplains. After serving as auxiliary for the military ordinariate in New York, he was named bishop of Scranton. In 1985, in the first consistory after their appointment, the pope named both Law and O'Connor cardinals. The appointment of both to important sees and their elevation to the cardinalate in the next consistory is illustrative of the combination of the man and the see—the pope would appoint to such dioceses only men he intended to elevate to the red hat.

Yet, there are certain anomalies. Washington is an important see, and Hickey certainly had the proper credentials. Yet he had to wait until 1988 to receive his red hat. In 1981 Dearden had retired in Detroit and was succeeded by Edmund Szoka, who likewise was named a cardinal in 1988 and was subsequently transferred to the Curia. In St. Louis, Carberry retired in 1979, but his successor, John May, never received the red hat, although he had been president of the National Conference of Catholic Bishops. Appointment to St. Louis does not automatically guarantee a red hat.

In 1985 Manning of Los Angeles retired and was succeeded by Roger Mahony. Early in 1988 Krol retired and was replaced in Philadelphia by Anthony J. Bevilacqua, former bishop of Pittsburgh. In 1991 both Bevilacqua and Mahony were elevated to the college of cardinals in the second consistory after their appointments. Completing the roster of American cardinals were William Keeler of Baltimore and Adam Maida of Detroit. In 1989 Keeler succeeded Archbishop William Donald Borders, who had retired. In 1990 Maida became archbishop of Detroit when Szoka was appointed to the Curia; he is, incidentally, the first alumnus of St. Mary's Seminary in Baltimore since Gibbons to receive the red hat, although he did graduate studies in Rome. In 1994 both were elevated to the sacred college in the second consistory after their appointments. It could well be argued that neither had been in office long enough to be elevated at the first consistory at which they were eligible in 1991. Yet, a brief tenure in office did not preclude the elevation of Bernardin, O'Connor, and Law at the first consistory at which they would have been eligible, but in each of these cases their predecessors had died—Chicago and New York have never had a retired archbishop, and Boston's Cushing lived for only one month after retirement.

Tentative Conclusions

From this overview, certain tentative conclusions can be drawn about what archdioceses and men receive red hats. First, appointment to New York, Boston, and Chicago, seems automatically to mean the incumbent will be named a cardinal at the next consistory. Granted the limits on the number of cardinals in the sacred college, these sees have a priority. Second, the archbishops of Washington, Los Angeles, Philadelphia, and Detroit can expect to receive a red hat, but not at the first consistory for which they would be eligible, especially if their predecessors are still alive and under the age of eighty. Finally, when the archbishops of Baltimore and St. Louis are named cardinals, they, rather than their sees, are being recognized.

Roman seminary education has also played an important, though not an essential role in the selection of cardinals. Of the entire group, seventeen (McCloskey, Farley, O'Connell, Dougherty, Mundelein, Stritch, Mooney, Spellman, Meyer, Shehan, Brennan, Cody, Krol, Carberry, Dearden, Wright, and Keeler) studied for the priesthood in Rome. Another six (Manning, Baum, Hickey, Szoka, Bevilacqua, and Maida) did graduate work there. Yet of the twelve cardinals in the U.S.A. appointed since 1973, five (Medeiros, Bernardin, Law, O'Connor, and Mahony) received their education entirely in this country.

Equally important as the sees whose incumbents receive red hats are the Roman congregations to which each cardinal is assigned. In 1887, for example, Gibbons was appointed to the Congregation of Propaganda, but was able to make only one meeting, the one held when he received his red hat. In 1914 and again in 1922, American cardinals were prevented by distance from even getting to the conclaves. With the advent of air travel, American cardinals can not only make it to conclaves but also attend the meetings of the congregations of which they are members and, therefore, have a direct influence on both the American and the universal Church. Membership in the Congregation of Bishops, which nominates bishops to the pope, obviously has more immediate importance than membership in, for example, the Congregation of Saints.

In addition to the cardinals who occupied residential sees in the U.S.A., other men who served in the American Church were later elevated to the sacred college. Jean Lefebvre de Cheverus, the first bishop of Boston, was later named bishop of Montauban in France and then archbishop of Bordeaux, where he became a cardinal in 1836. Ignatius Persico, former apostolic delegate in Bombay, was bishop of Savannah from 1870 to 1872. He then returned to Rome and was named a cardinal in 1893. Fr. Camillo Mazzella, S.J., the first dean of the Jesuits' Woodstock College in 1869, was summoned back to Rome to teach in 1878 and was named a cardinal in 1887, the same year as Gibbons. In addition, ten prelates have served as apostolic delegates between 1893 and 1984, when the U.S.A. and the Holy See established diplomatic relations and the office was transformed into a nunciature: Francesco Satolli, Sebastian Martinelli, Diomede Falconio, Giovanni Bonzano, Pietro Fumasoni-Biondi, Amleto Cicognani, Egidio Vagnozzi, Luigi Raimondi, Jean Jadot, and Pio Laghi, who became the first pro-nuncio in 1984. All but Jadot, the only non-Italian prelate in the group, were named cardi-

nals on occasion of their leaving their American posts. Service as delegate and, presumably, pro-nuncio in the U.S.A. virtually assures the appointee of an eventual red hat.

GERALD P. FOGARTY, S.J.

CAREY, MATHEW (1760–1839)

Author, political economist, publisher, bookseller. Carey was born in Dublin, Ireland, on January 28, 1760. The son of a baker, Carey apprenticed himself as a printer at the age of fifteen. In 1779 he was forced to flee to France for a year after publishing a pamphlet attacking the penal code against Irish Catholics.

After returning to Ireland, he founded the radical *Volunteer's Journal* in 1783. In 1784, as a result of attacks on the Irish Parliament and administration, he was arrested and held briefly in Newgate Prison. After his release he emigrated to America on September 7, 1784.

Carey arrived in Philadelphia on November 1, 1784. The Marquis de Lafayette, whom Carey had met in France, lent him $400.00 which he used to start *The Pennsylvania Evening Herald* in January 1785. The paper became popular by printing the debates of the Pennsylvania House of Assembly.

Mathew Carey

In January 1787 Carey began publishing *The American Museum,* the first literary magazine in the United States. In 1790 he published the first edition of the Douai Bible printed in the United States. During the 1790s Carey's publishing and bookselling business became one of the largest in the United States. He published and sold books on a variety of subjects. He published numerous Catholic doctrinal and devotional works as well as subsequent editions of both the Douai and King James versions of the Bible. He also took advantage of the lack of copyright laws to publish American editions of popular English authors.

In 1791 Carey married Bridget Flahavan. They had nine children, of whom six survived to adulthood, including the economist Henry Carey.

After selling his newspaper in 1788, Carey expressed his political activities through his pamphlets. Carey was a political independent and fervent nationalist. His anti-English feelings drove him towards the Democrats although he supported much of the Federalist economic program, including a national bank. In 1814 Carey published *The Olive Branch* to promote national unity between the Democrats and Federalists.

After the War of 1812, Carey became a leading advocate of a protective tariff to support American manufacturing. In 1819 he helped to found the Philadelphia Society for the Promotion of National Industry. In 1820 he published *The New Olive Branch* in which he tried to reconcile agricultural, commercial, and manufacturing interests. He also wrote pamphlets in support of canals and railroads.

Carey was involved in a number of philanthropic endeavors. In 1791 he helped to found the nonsectarian Sunday School Society of Philadelphia. The following year he helped to organize the Hibernian Society for the Relief of Emigrants from Ireland. In 1793 he was actively involved in relief work during the yellow fever epidemic in Philadelphia and published two pamphlets on the epidemic. He also wrote and worked in support of orphans, female workers, retired soldiers, and Greek and Polish independence.

During the 1820s Carey became involved in the trustee controversy at St. Mary's Church in Philadelphia. As in other areas, Carey tried to reconcile the two sides. After the resolution of the dispute, he helped organize the "Vindicators of the Catholic Religion from Calumny and Abuse" to defend the Catholic Church from criticism it had received as a result of the trustee dispute. Carey's personal stand on Catholicism was never revealed. One of his biographers views Carey as a Gallican who favored an American Catholic Church free from interference from Rome. He died in Philadelphia on September 16, 1839.

See also CATHOLIC BOOK PUBLISHING; AMERICAN REVOLUTION AND CATHOLICS, THE.

Carey, Mathew. *Autobiography.* Brooklyn, N.Y.: Research Classics, 1942. (Reprinted from *New England Magazine* [July 1833–December 1834] 1833–34.)

Green, James N. *Mathew Carey: Publisher and Patriot.* Philadelphia: The Library Company of Philadelphia, 1985.

Maier, Eugene F.J. "Mathew Carey, Publicist and Politician (1760–1839)." *Records of the American Catholic Historical Society* 39 (2) (June 1928) 71–154.

Rowe, Kenneth M. *Mathew Carey: A Study in Economic Development.* Baltimore: Johns Hopkins University Press. 1933.

"Selections from the Correspondence of the Deceased Mathew Carey." *Records of the American Catholic Historical Society.* Vol. 9 (1898) 352–84, 468–80; Vol. 10 (1899) 102–11, 345–53, 457–63; Vol. 11 (1900) 67–69, 213–14, 338–50; Vol. 12 (1901) 96–105; Vol. 13 (1902) 237–47.

SHAWN WELDON

CAREY, THOMAS (1904–72)

Priest, educator, theatrical producer. Thomas Carey was born in Chicago, Illinois, on June 14, 1904. He was a graduate of Providence College and was ordained a priest in 1932. In 1935 he was awarded a Ph.D. from The Catholic University of America. The next five years, Carey served the university as an assistant professor of psychology. In 1932, while at The Catholic University, Carey cofounded (with Urban Nagle) the Blackfriars Guild, which was dedicated to producing dramas in the Catholic tradition. The Guild grew to attain representation in twenty cities. In 1937 Carey founded the Blackfriars Institute of Dramatic Arts at The Catholic University, which later evolved into the university's Department of Speech and Drama. In 1941, Carey and Nagle founded the Blackfriars Guild Theater in New York City. After attaining complete control of the theater in 1951, Carey produced forty-three of the seventy-five plays produced by the guild. During his career, he also served as the first secretary of the National Catholic Theater Conference, and assistant national director of the Holy Name Society from 1940 to 1952. The closing of the Blackfriars Guild Theater preceded Carey's death on May 8, 1972, by six weeks: the building in which the theater was housed was razed.

See also HARTKE, GILBERT.

LISELLE DRAKE

Thomas Carey

CARMELITE FRIARS (O. CARM.)

In the latter part of the seventeenth century four Carmelites from France served French workers in present-day Louisiana and worked among the Native Americans of the area. Three other French Carmelites were chaplains to French naval vessels sent to aid the colonies in their revolution against England. Two Irish Carmelites, educated in Spain, served in West Florida and Louisiana in the late 1700s until the early years of the next century while the area was under Spanish control.

No effort was made by these Carmelites to make permanent establishments in the United States. The first attempt towards this goal was made by Cyril Knoll and Xavier Huber who came from Straubing, Germany, in 1864 to serve, after some abortive efforts, at St. Joseph's Hill, Indiana. In four months they left to serve German immigrants at Leavenworth, Kansas, and in the next year took over a parish at Pottawatomie Creek, later renamed Scipio. In September 1866 this group bought the Redemptorist convent and parish in Cumberland, Maryland, which was turned into a novitiate.

In 1867, to meet the demand for English speakers, two young Irish priests who had been trained in Rome arrived in Cumberland and were joined in the next year by two Netherlanders who had worked in England. These latter, Anastasius Smits and Brother Berthold Lenders, left in 1869 to take over a parish in Fort Lee, New Jersey. The previously mentioned Irishmen, Peter Thomas Meagher and Theodoric McDonald, took charge of a parish in Upper Marlboro, Maryland. The Carmelite general, Angelo Savini, sent from Rome a group of six Irish priests and foundations followed at Paducah and Louisville, Kentucky. All of these houses were made into a commissariate in 1874. Louisville and Upper Marlboro were abandoned the following year.

The Carmelites in the two Kansas foundations were placed under the jurisdiction of the general in 1869, and they opened a monastery in Niagara Falls, Canada, in 1875. Knoll had accepted St. Peter's Parish in Butler, Pennsylvania (1873), and when he had finished paying the Redemptorists for the Cumberland house, he sold it to the Capuchins. The superior in Kansas, Albert Heimann, and Knoll in 1878 united their jurisdictions with Knoll as superior. General Savini united these houses under Anastasius Smits in 1881. Smits gave up Paducah and confirmed the Niagara Falls house as a novitiate.

Savini made Pius Mayer, later to be general of the order, the commissary superior in 1886. He moved the novitiate to New Baltimore, Pennsylvania, where he also established a house of studies. This foundation, Scipio, Pittsburgh, Niagara Falls, Englewood (New Jersey), and Leavenworth were formed into a province on February 20, 1890, with the title of the Most Pure Heart of Mary. Membership consisted of twenty-eight priests, fourteen brothers, and two clerics.

Commissariate of the South

In 1882 four German-born Carmelites secretly left Scipio to join a local German resident who was emigrating to West Texas. They offered the first Mass in a tent in Grelton Springs that August. They erected a church and school and successfully sought funds and students in Germany. John Neraz, bishop of San Antonio, sought and obtained their regularization from Savini.

These Carmelites regularly served nine missions traveling a distance of two hundred miles on the Texas and Pacific Railway besides visiting seven communities in Southeast New Mexico and seven more remote and lawless ones south of Tazah. Drought and rainstorms in 1886 brought about the abandonment of many farms. A scandal in the community brought about a Savini-initiated visitation by Pius Mayer who recommended the erection of a commissariate with Anastasius Peters in charge. This Savini did in 1890.

What made the commissariate possible was that the Texas drought drove some Carmelites into Louisiana where they established a parish at Bayou Pierre in 1888. A novitiate was established there, and when one of the community became the postmaster, he changed the name of the town to Carmel. Their pastorate included the care of all of De Soto Parish.

Scandals in the community brought about an apostolic visitation. In its wake the community dwindled and the commissariate was dissolved in 1896. The members joined the newly established American province or remained on the missions as diocesan priests.

In 1899 five Dutch Carmelites came to Tusker, Mississippi, to staff a previously established mission among the Choctaws. The area covered six counties of eastern Mississippi and included four white communities. In 1900 the provincial chapter urged expansion of the mission to white communities as a means of support of the missions. A parish was taken in New Athens, Illinois (Diocese of Belleville), but a debt on the parish school prevented any diversion of funds from this new work.

The United States government decided to move Native Americans to a territory established for them in the area of the present state of Oklahoma. The Netherlands' chapter of 1903 decided to abandon the mission but suggested that those wanting to remain should be joined to the American province or the recently established Carmelites in New York. The 1903 chapter of the American province agreed to accept the mission. Four Carmelites left in 1903 with the Native Americans for Antler, Oklahoma, where traveling by horse they served an area of 12,000 square miles. The mission was abandoned in 1904 with most of the Carmelites returning to the Netherlands.

The Church of St. Cecilia in Englewood, New Jersey, was the center for missions throughout the then rural Bergen County. Eventually, eight Carmelite parishes came into existence and today these, along with four foundations in Canada, and the missions in Peru, constitute the Eastern Commissariate. In 1949 missions had been established in Lima, Peru, and Santiago, Chile, but the latter was abandoned in 1970. The Peruvian mission flourished and to it was added the prelature *nullius* of Sicuani consisting of an area separated from the Archdiocese of Cuzco.

St. Cyril's Priory was established in Chicago in 1900 and from there was founded Mt. Carmel High School. This apostolate expanded over the years and about a dozen high schools were established. Chicago also became the headquarters of the Little Flower Society founded by Albert Dolan in 1923. A shrine to the saint was built at St. Clara's Church, now closed, and this was the depository of relics of the saint and a center of devotion to her fostered by the many books written by Dolan. This has all been moved to Darien, Illinois. These Chicago houses along with others at Joliet, Mundelein, Kansas, and Kentucky constitute the Midwestern Commissariate.

A house of studies was opened in Washington, D.C., in 1926 and this eventually became Whitefriars Hall (1939), a theologate, which has now become a residence with the students attending Washington Theological Union.

Mt. Carmel High School in Los Angeles as well as the parish nearby of St. Raphael's were transferred from the New York Carmelites in 1957 to this Chicago-based province. Other parishes and schools in Arizona, California, and Texas became the Western Commissariate of the province.

The New York Carmelites

An Irish Carmelite, Michael Moore, was visiting the United States in 1887 and chanced to meet James McMahon, a wealthy New York priest who offered the Carmelites an endowed foundation on Manhattan's Upper West Side. Archbishop Michael Corrigan of New York would not allow them to accept this offer on the grounds there were already too many churches in the area. The Carmelites in turn reported the archbishop to the Congregation for the Propagation of the Faith for denying them this opportunity. While Corrigan was explaining his actions to the Roman authorities, John Bartley, the Irish provincial, came to New York to see McMahon and investigate for himself this remarkable offer. Corrigan, having just undergone a long and bitter conflict with Dr. Edward McGlynn, offered Bartley a new parish carved from McGlynn's former parish of St. Stephen's. Seeing he would never be allowed to accept McMahon's offer, Bartley accepted this offer to which was attached the care of Bellevue Hospital. Three Irish Carmelites, Edward Southwell, Michael Daly and Paul McDonnell, arrived in March 1889 to begin Our Lady of the Scapular parish on First Avenue and 28th Street. A church was soon erected and a school was opened in 1904.

Southwell was anxious to begin a separate jurisdiction of the order and with this as his goal later accepted Corrigan's offer of a parish in Tarrytown, New York, which was begun in October 1896. A mission was established in nearby Elmsford (1905) but was given to the care of the archdiocese as a parish in 1912 in exchange for Our Lady of Mount Carmel in Middletown to which became attached as a mission a previous foundation at Otisville (1910) which itself included a number of missions. In 1917 a seminary and novitiate, St. Albert's, was opened in Middletown. The new parish of St. Simon Stock in the Bronx was given to the Carmelites in 1920 enabling this group, previously subject to the Irish province, to became a commissariate in 1922. This became a province under the name of St. Elias in 1931 with Lawrence D. Flanagan as the first provincial. A foundation at Auburn, New York, successively a novitiate, house of studies, and a high school existed from 1947 to 1970. Other establishments are Williamstown—originally a novitiate and now a retreat house—a parish in Troy, New York, a community in Rochester, New York, a parish and high school in Boca Raton, Florida, a parish in Brooklyn and a pre-novitiate house in Tappan, New York.

The Manhattan parish of Our Lady of the Scapular was a center for devotion to St. Therese and Our Lady of Knock, but when the parish was merged with that of St. Stephen's in 1989, these activities were moved to the former preparatory seminary in Middletown, which became the provincial headquarters and a retirement home for aged Carmelites.

In 1995 there were two Carmelite provinces in the United States. The province of the Most Pure Heart of Mary, located in Darien, Illinois, consisted of 249 priests and 21 brothers who administered 36 parishes and 5 high schools in 15 dioceses. The province of St. Elias, in Middletown, New York, consisted of 68 priests and two brothers who administered 10 parishes, two retreat houses and one high school in 10 dioceses.

Isacsson, Alfred, O. Carm. *Carmel in New York.* 3 vols. Middletown, N.Y., 1978–84.

Smet, Joachim, O. Carm. *The Carmelites.* Vol. 4. Darien, Illinois, 1985.

ALFRED ISACSSON, O. CARM.

CARMELITE FRIARS, DISCALCED (O.C.D.)

Though no permanent community of Discalced Carmelite friars was successfully established in the United States until the twentieth century, the Carmelite Reform inaugurated by St. Teresa of Avila (1515–82) had contacts in the New World almost from its beginnings. Friars of the Teresian Reform had reached Mexico by 1588. In 1602, three members of the province of New Spain (Andrew of the Assumption, Anthony of the Ascension, and Thomas of Aquinas) served as chaplains, missionaries, cartographers, and chroniclers for the Vizcaino expedition along the California coast. They named many sites along the coastline, and were the first to celebrate Mass on the Pacific shore of what would later become the United States, but were unable to obtain permission to return for a more substantial missionary effort.

Carmelite Missionaries

From 1625 to 1636, Simon Stock of St. Mary, O.C.D. (Thomas Doughty), head of the Discalced Carmelite mission in England during penal times, urged the Sacred Congregation for the Propagation of the Faith to send missionaries to the English-speaking colonies on the Eastern seaboard, to counteract the inroads of Protestantism among the indigenous peoples. He showed particular interest in the Avalon colony, and later in Virginia and New England. Though the Congregation finally authorized his missionary efforts, Simon Stock saw the project pass to Capuchins and Jesuits due to personnel shortages among the Discalced friars.

In 1720, in response to a request from the Company of the West and after obtaining permission from superiors in Rome, the provincial of the Discalced Carmelites in France authorized three (later four) friars to work as missionary chaplains in the Louisiana Territory. John Matthew of St. Anne served in Old Biloxi and Mobile; nearby, Charles of St. Alexis ministered among the Apalache people. Joseph of St. Charles was stationed in New Orleans as pastor of St. Louis parish, which would later become the cathedral. However, when the Gallican bishop de St. Vallier of Quebec learned that the Carmelites had received their commission directly from Rome, without consultation of the French crown or hierarchy, he expelled them from the territory and entrusted it to the Capuchins. The Carmelites reluctantly returned to France in 1723.

Though no friars of the Teresian Reform accompanied the four Discalced Carmelite nuns who established the first community of religious women in the newly independent United States at Port Tobacco, Maryland, in 1790, individual Discalced Carmelite men ventured to this country as missionaries during the late eighteenth and early nineteenth centuries. Paul of St. Peter (1746–1826) from Germany had originally come as a military chaplain to foreign troops fighting on the side of the colonists at the Battle of Yorktown, and later returned to serve for many years as a missionary along both sides of the Mississippi until his death in 1826. The Irish friar Paul of St. Patrick (b. 1750) worked in Pennsylvania in the late 1780s. Discalced Carmelites from Bavaria built a monastery and church in Paterson, New Jersey, in 1875, as a house of refuge from Bismark's *Kulturkampf,* but sold them to the

Franciscans when they were withdrawn in 1879 to help with a new foundation at Geleen in the Netherlands.

Holy Hill

In 1905 Bavarian friars returned, seeking a suitable locale for a new foundation. The following year, Archbishop Sebastain Messmer of Milwaukee offered them Holy Hill, a site in the Kettle Moraine region (about thirty miles outside the city) originally sacred to the local Menominee tribe and already an active Marian shrine, featuring a large handcarved wooden statue of Our Lady brought from Germany for the Philadelphia World's Fair of 1875.

Four Bavarian Discalced Carmelite friars (Eliseus Mackina, Irenaeus Berndl, Adam Modlmayer, and Alphonse Merl) took formal charge of Holy Hill on July 2, 1906; a larger shrine church and monastery were built in 1931 and 1938 respectively, with the present shrine chapel (which houses the famous statue of Mary, Help of Christians, and attracts thousands of pilgrims and visitors each year) constructed in 1956.

In 1912 Bavarian friars from Holy Hill also accepted a Milwaukee parish, and built the church and monastery of St. Florian. That same year, Spanish friars from the province of Catalonia arrived in Arizona, establishing houses at Tucson, Phoenix, Sonora, and various mission stations.

Twentieth-Century Developments

In 1913 friars from the Spanish province of Valencia returned to Mexico to help rebuild the Mexican province, shattered by persecutions, but were themselves soon expelled by Pancho Villa. Seeking refuge in the United States, they first went to Holy Hill, but at the instruction of their Spanish superiors began looking southward for possible places to minister to the Spanish speaking, settling finally in the diocese of Oklahoma City in the small town of Pittsburg. Joined by others, these friars took on numerous mission parishes, and eventually established communities in Oklahoma City (1922), San Antonio (1926), Dallas (1944 and 1951), Little Rock (1952), and most recently New Orleans. In 1935 they achieved canonical recognition as the province of St. Thérèse, the first in the United States.

Meanwhile, a former missionary of the Castile province working in Cuba, José Maria Isasi, transferred to the Catalonian province and, with several Catalonian friars imported from Arizona, founded a monastery in Washington, D.C., near The Catholic University, in 1916. This foundation served for decades as a house of studies, and more recently as the home of *Spiritual Life* (a quarterly begun in 1955) and ICS Publications (specializing in contemporary translations of Carmelite classics).

After the Spanish Civil War, and at the urging of Fr. Thomas Kilduff (then prior of Washington), the generalate of the order juridically joined the Washington foundation to the two existing communities in the Milwaukee archdiocese; together they founded a new house in Boston in 1942. In 1947 this union officially became the Province of the Immaculate Heart of Mary, and additional communities were later established in Peterborough, New Hampshire (1953), Hinton, West Virginia (1968), Chicago (1995) and elsewhere. The Washington province also began a missionary effort in the Philippines in 1947, and in 1995 took charge of the order's house of studies for English-speaking Africa in Nairobi, Kenya.

Irish Discalced Carmelites arrived in California in 1924, establishing their first house in Alhambra. Other foundations followed in Redlands (1952), Oakville (1955), and San Jose (1959). These houses were later joined to the existing monasteries in Arizona in 1964, to form the nucleus of what would officially become the California-Arizona province of St. Joseph in 1983. More recently, this province has inaugurated the quarterly, *Carmelite Digest,* besides establishing a new house in Berkeley (1981) and an Institute of Spirituality at St. Cecilia Parish in Stanwood, Washington, near Seattle (1989).

In 1949 Discalced Carmelites from Poland founded a monastery in Munster, Indiana, to minister to the Polish-speaking in the Chicago area; more recently the Polish Carmelites accepted a parish in Corona, Florida, in 1988. That same year, friars of the Castile province inaugurated the Nuestro Señora del Monte Carmelo Spiritual Life Center in Miami. Just north of the U.S. border, friars from Malta have established a house for English-speaking Canada in London, Ontario, while the Avignon-Aquitaine Province of France has brought French-speaking friars back to the Quebec province with a foundation in Montreal.

In recent years especially, the Discalced Carmelite friars in the United States have focused on the promotion of prayer and spirituality, broadly understood, through spiritual direction, publications, shrine and parish ministry, retreat houses, spirituality centers, "desert" communities, collaborative efforts with the Carmelites of the Ancient Observance (e.g., through the Carmelite Institute) and work with the Carmelite nuns and laity. The first U.S. community of the Discalced Carmelite Third Order (now called Secular Order of Discalced Carmelites) was established in New York City in 1910. Though the Discalced friars themselves remain fewer than two hundred in the United States, these primarily lay affiliates of the order now number roughly seven thousand nationwide. Together with some sixty Carmels of contemplative nuns, and about a dozen affiliated institutes of consecrated life (including the Servants of the Paraclete, Carmelite Sisters of Charity, Carmelite Sisters of the Most Sacred Heart of Los Angeles, and the Carmelite Sisters of St. Therese of Oklahoma), the Discalced Carmelite friars and laity have helped add a strong element of Teresian Carmelite spirituality to the American scene.

Kearns, M. *Holy Hill: Its History.* Hubertus, Wis.: Discalced Carmelite Friars, 1987.
Leahy, E. *Vintage of Grace: The Discalced Carmelite Friars in California 1923–1982.* San Jose, Calif.: Carmelite Seminary, 1983.
Pignatiello, C. P. *The Unshod: The Men of Carmel!* Munster, Ind.: Pignatiello Enterprises, 1981.
Rohrbach, P.-T. *Journey to Carith: The Story of the Carmelite Order.* Garden City, N.Y.: Doubleday & Co., 1966, ch. 10: "Carmel in America."

STEVEN PAYNE, O.C.D.

CARMELITE NUNS AND SISTERS (O. CARM.)

Founded in 1452 during the generalate of John Soreth, the Carmelite Sisters of the Ancient Observance (O. Carm.) are cloistered and dedicated to a strictly contemplative life. The first monastery in the United States was at Allentown, Pennsylvania, founded from Holy Cross convent near Naples by Sister Teresa of Jesus in 1931. The Carmelite general, Elias Magennis, was instrumental in beginning this foundation. From here, foundations have been made in Wahpeton, North Dakota (1954), Ashville, North Carolina (1956–1978), Hudson, Wisconsin (1963). Wahpeton in turn founded the Carmel of Our Lady of Grace, San Angelo, Texas, in 1988.

The Congregation of Our Lady of Mount Carmel originated with a group of Carmelite Third Order members whom Fr. Boutelu, with the assistance of Mother St. Paul Bazire, organized as a religious community whose apostolate was social work. This was done in 1824, but the group was undone by the July Revolution of 1830 in France and Boutelu came to the United States to exercise his ministry. Settled in Louisiana, he asked two of the group's members, Teresa Chevrel and Sr. Augustine Clerc, in 1833 to come to Louisiana. Bishop Leo de Neckere welcomed them and his successor, Bishop Anthony Blanc, committed to their care a school in New Orleans for African-American girls. Eventually the Louisiana sisters became separated from the refounded French group and formed their own congregation. The sisters were affiliated to the Carmelite Order in 1930. As the sisters gained more candidates, they opened more schools. Except for brief ventures in British Honduras and among native Americans in Oklahoma, the sisters are engaged primarily in educational work in Louisiana and the Philippines. Education has expanded from the classroom to include hospitals, social services, religious education, campus ministry, pastoral and retreat work.

The Institute of the Sisters of Our Lady of Mount Carmel was founded in 1854 by Mother Maria Teresa di Gesù (Maria Scrilli, 1825–1889) at Montevarchi, but the fledgling group was dispersed by the anticlerical laws of 1860. The group continued living in secrecy and discovered a second foundress in 1862 in Mother Maria di Gesù (Clementina Mosca) who headed the group until her death in 1934. The Institute was affiliated to the Carmelites in 1929. The sisters came to the United States beginning in 1947 to do domestic work at Carmelite seminaries in Hamilton, Massachusetts; Niagara Falls, Ontario; and Washington, D.C. These ministries having ended, the sisters' ministry is now child care and education, which they carry out in Washington, D.C., and Peabody, Massachusetts.

Mother Angeline Teresa McCrory became a Little Sister of the Poor in 1914. She saw a need to care for the aged and ailing who were not impoverished. With the intention of caring for these people in a personal manner employing privacy and freedom, she and six companions left the Little Sisters in 1929 with the blessing of Patrick Cardinal Hayes of New York. The first foundation was St. Patrick's Home in Van Cortlandt Park, Bronx, New York, utilizing an old RCA building. Through friendship with and the mediacy of Dionysius L. Flanagan, the Carmelite Sisters for the Aged and Infirm became affiliated with the order in 1931. The motherhouse is in Avila-on-Hudson, Germantown, New York, and the sisters operate homes throughout the United States and one in Ireland.

Clara Perrins (1876-1949) was born in Handsworth, Birmingham, England, converted to Catholicism at the age of sixteen and changed her family name to Ellerker. Having dedicated herself to social service, she formed, under the direction of Vincent McNabb, O.P., a community which included her mother and sister. In 1908 the group were professed as Dominican tertiaries with Clara taking the name of Mary of the Blessed Sacrament. The Dominican connection prompted bishops from that order to give them places in Port of Spain, Trinidad, and Duluth, Minnesota. Mother Mary of the Blessed Sacrament was attracted to St. Thérèse of Lisieux and the growth of this devotion in her life brought her to see the Carmelite provincial, Lawrence Diether, in Chicago. This resulted in affiliation with the Carmelites in 1927.

The work of the Corpus Christi Carmelite sisters is social services and religious education. They have foundations in the United States, England, Ivory Coast, Grenada, Guyana and Trinidad and Tobago.

The Mission Family "Donum Dei" was founded with three members by Fr. Marcel Roussel at St. Denis, France, in 1950. On February 22, 1987, the group was recognized as a Carmelite Third Order Secular. The Donum Dei apostolate is the evangelization of those far from Christian life. The main group consists of women who want to follow Christ while working in a profession. There are also branches for mothers, youths, and adult laypersons trying to live a life of holiness in the world. Donum Dei has two foundations in the United States, New York City and Middletown, New York.

ALFRED ISACSSON, O.CARM.

CARMELITE NUNS, DISCALCED (O.C.D.)

Anglo-American Tradition

The first community of religious women in the thirteen original states was founded in Charles County, Maryland, in 1790. It was *contemplative* and Carmelite. Three foundresses, returning to the newly formed United States the same year John Carroll was ordained its first bishop, were Americans of the Anglo-Catholic gentry reaching back to the beginnings of the Maryland colony. All four nuns were members of English-speaking monasteries in Hoogstraten and Antwerp, important centers for the English recusant community in the seventeenth and eighteenth centuries.

British colonials from Maryland began crossing the ocean to become Carmelites in 1742 so that by the last quarter of the eighteenth century the seed for Carmel in America had taken root producing strong American leadership for the English Teresians. While Mary Margaret Brent, prioress of Antwerp, was primary in planning the foundation, it was her close collaborator from Charles County, Bernardina Matthews, prioress in Hoogstraten Carmel from 1771–90, who assumed on Brent's death the task of leading the first Carmelite foundation to their native Maryland. The other founders were Bernardina's nieces, Mary Eleanora and Mary Aloysia Matthews from Hoogstraten, their uncle, Charles Neale, chaplain at Antwerp Carmel after the suppression of the Jesuits, and Clare Joseph Dickinson, a London-born Antwerp Carmelite who became prioress of the new monastery in 1800 on the death of Bernardina.

Port Tobacco and Baltimore

The Carmelites established their monastery on a farm at Port Tobacco in southern Maryland and dedicated it on October 15, 1790, to the Sacred Hearts of Jesus, Mary, and Joseph. Bought and managed by their chaplain, Neale, and worked by slaves brought as dowry by the daughters of the Maryland gentry, the farm supported the Anglo-American community in their poor, simple life of prayer for forty years. There are significances to this foundation, the country's only Carmel for seventy-three years, that demand attention. First, it was rooted in an Anglo-American Catholic religious culture that prized the values of religious toleration, mutual respect, and freedom of conscience. Even when women from other ethnic groups joined them, beginning with the first Irish immigrant only in 1837, the community did not take on the face of the immigrant Church. Second, in their spirituality, the American-born foundresses stood within the moderate humanistic French school as it was mediated to them through both the English Jesuit inheritance in Maryland and the Lowlands and the central elements of Teresian/Carmelite spirituality brought to the Low Countries from Spain in 1607 by the successors of Teresa of Avila, Anne of Jesus (Lobera) and Anne of St. Bartholomew (Garcia). Third, a second strand of spirituality coexisted from the beginning. A leaning in Charles Neale and Clare Joseph toward the more rigoristic continental French school evidenced suspicion of the passions and stressed rational control, mortification, obedience to rule and superior and a certain approach to meditation relative to contemplation. Fourth, a level of cultural and intellectual life characteristic of the Maryland Catholic gentry and the English Teresians was cherished as is verified by the thirteen-hundred-book library brought to the foundation. Fifth, relationships were central to the nuns' contemplative prayer mission: with their families, the Jesuits with whom they often shared family ties, the French Sulpicians establishing the first U.S. seminary, the earliest bishops beginning with John Carroll, the various founders including Elizabeth Seton.

Following the deaths of Bernardina and Clare Joseph and driven by the economically depressed condition of Charles County, the aging of the slaves, the failure of the farm and the death of Neale, the community closed the monastery at Port Tobacco and moved to Baltimore in 1831. To support themselves, since begging had "become very odious to the Catholics of [the] city," they opened in 1832 "The Carmelite Sisters Academy for the Education of Young Ladies" of all religious denominations, one of the first four such academies in the original states. For twenty years, three or four of the nuns, Teresa (Juliana Sewall) chief among them, staffed the school. Although in 1792 Bishop John Carroll had obtained a rescript from Propaganda Fidei allowing the nuns to teach, they had refused Carroll's request believing teaching was contrary to their contemplative charism. When the survival of their contemplative life depended upon it, however, they accepted "the full confirmation of the dispensation for teaching" secured by Archbishop James Whitfield. The school was one manifestation of the enduring historical tension between solitary prayer and ministry that has characterized the order since the early movement from eremitical beginnings on Mount Carmel to mendicant status/ministry in European urban centers.

Baltimore Carmel relocated again in 1873 and 1961. In 1990 this first community celebrated its bicentennial and with it Carmel in the U.S.A.

Foundations: Baltimore Branches

Seven branches with forty-seven U.S. foundations grew on the Baltimore tree. The second Carmel was founded in St. Louis in 1863 at the invitation of Archbishop Peter R. Kenrick and with the support of Francis P. Kenrick, archbishop of Baltimore. A sad peculiarity of this foundation, made during the Civil War, was that a period of community conflict was resolved when the five foundresses led by Mothers Gabriel Boland and Alberta Smith departed Baltimore. Only fourteen years later St. Louis Carmel established New Orleans Carmel, the first of eleven monasteries founded on the St. Louis branch between 1877 and 1965.

In 1890 the third branch of fourteen monasteries (–1965) began to grow when the fourth Carmel was founded in Boston with the experienced leadership of Mother Beatrix Magers. Among her four companions from Baltimore were two future foundresses, Sr. Gertrude McMaster, the founding prioress of Philadelphia Carmel in 1902, and Sr. Augustine Tuckerman, a native Bostonian who led the foundation to Santa Clara in 1908.

Foundresses left Baltimore for Brooklyn in 1907 (Teresa McMaster); Seattle in 1908 (Raphael Keating and Cyril McDougal); Davenport in 1911 (Clare Nagle and Aloysius Heiker); Wheeling in 1913 (Joanna Sneeringer and Mary Magdalen Potts); New York City in 1920 (Teresa Cawley and Agnes Garvin): five branches with twenty foundations made throughout the U.S.A. between 1907–61.

Although all these foundations traced their origins to a Carmelite life rooted in Anglo-Catholic religious culture, nevertheless, these Carmels largely took on the religious culture of the immigrant Church. They were marked by the cultural/ethnic/educational backgrounds and interpretations of the women who founded them. The result was small autonomous communities with local relationships and jurisdiction, the strength of the Carmel dependent on the quality of local leadership and formation.

Foundations: Mexican Branch

Between 1915 and 1934 the government's persecution of the Church in Mexico gave birth to four refugee Carmels in the U.S.A. with their own distinctive history and identity. The first Mexican Carmels were established in Puebla and Mexico City at the same time Teresa of Avila's disciples were founding Carmel in France (1604) and the Low Countries. Like the Beguines received into the order as the first Carmelite nuns in 1452, the foundresses of Puebla were lay women, Spaniards from Huelva in Andalusia. Ana and Beatriz Nuñez, young orphaned noblewomen, made a treacherous year long trip to "New Spain." Joined later by two other women, Dona Elvira Suarez, a Spanish widow, and Dona Juana Fajardo, they eventually began leading lives of "solitude, prayer and mortification" under the direction of a Jesuit, Alonso Ruiz. They were in 1604 received into the order when the first Discalced Carmelite monastery in continental America was established in Puebla under the patronage of Jesus, Mary, and Joseph. In 1616 a similar community was founded in like circumstances in Mexico City: that is, with the encouragement of the first Discalced Carmelite friars from Spain. The foundresses, Mary Inez of the Cross and Mariana of the Incarnation, were originally Sisters of the Congregation of Jesus and Mary. Guadalajara Carmel was founded from Puebla in 1695; from Mexico City, Queretaro in 1803, Durango in 1853 with help from Queretaro, and Tulancingo in 1905 via the foundations of Contreras (1704) and Villa de Guadalupe (1896).

After more than half a century of suffering from a painful series of expulsions from their monasteries, the near demise of their communities and repeated persecution occasioned by the revolutions under Juarez and later Carranza and Calles, the nuns of these four Carmels finally fled to the U.S.A. The Guadalajara Carmel saw its members disbanded for forty-four years between 1860 and 1904. Following a brief respite for regrouping, the years from 1914–27 were ones of upheaval, eviction, hiding and arrest, until finally the nuns sought refuge in San Francisco in 1927. Having been exiled from Mexico, the Queretaro community, led by Mother Mary Elias, lived briefly in Havana Carmel before settling definitively in Grand Rapids, Michigan, in 1916. Between 1919 and 1950 they made two foundations in Mexico and five in the U.S.A. beginning with Buffalo (1920). Though the Tulancingo nuns under the leadership of Mother Teresa Massieu also fled to Havana Carmel, they returned for some years to Mexico, to enormous poverty and suffering, before finally seeking refuge in Dallas, Texas, in 1928. The odyssey of the San Antonio Carmel is the most convoluted. In 1917 the Durango Carmelites were dispersed and two sisters fled to San Antonio. All reunited in Durango in 1918. When Calles outlawed the existence of religious houses in 1926, the community sought refuge in Tucson, Arizona, but after three young sisters died, they returned to Mexico City in 1931. They fled permanently to San Antonio only in 1934 from where a foundation was made to Houston in 1958.

The Mexican branch of the U.S. Carmelite nuns accounts for seventeen foundations made between 1916 and 1992 and their brave, stark history has undoubtedly influenced the direction of their development. They paid a high price for a Carmelite indentity; the charism in them is marked by a collective experience of loss and persecution. Little prestige was associated with their status either as religious in Mexico or as immigrants in the U.S.

Foundations: French Branch and Other Shoots

In 1927 two former Third Order Carmelite Religious, Marie Joseph (Justine Solignac) and Marie Genevieve, from a community in Gignac, France, began a Discalced Carmelite monastery in Altoona (soon moved to Loretto), Pennsylvania. Educated by the Visitandines in Washington, D.C., where her father was in the French diplomatic corps, Justine was the niece of Placide Chapelle, archbishop of Santa Fe and later archbishop of New Orleans with whom she had lived and worked. How much the two women were motivated by earlier desires to be Carmelite nuns, how well they understood the irregularity of their foundation since they were *not* Discalced Carmelite nuns, or whether they

intended to deceive either the leadership in the Church or order or those received into the community whose vows were subsequently invalid, are questions difficult to answer. Three facts remain: first, the foundresses, having been released from their vows, left their community in Gignac, France, with the support of Chapelle and the specific intention of founding a Carmel in the U.S.A.; second, in view of the anomaly of the foundation, the Sacred Congregation for Religious in 1934 had to grant a sanation validating the foundation; third, the precise origins of the community were kept secret from those who later entered. Still, life was passed on to four foundations between 1947 and 1961. The third in Elysburg, Pennsylvania, not only amalgamated in 1977 with the Wheeling Carmel, a Baltimore foundation, but also began a Byzantine rite Carmel in Sugarloaf, Pennsylvania, in 1977.

Two shoots from Asian Carmels enriched Carmel in the U.S.A.: the Guam monastery from Malaysia in 1966 and the Hawaii Carmel from Hong Kong in 1973. Furthermore, shoots sprouted abroad from U.S. communities: Hsinchu, Taiwan, from Santa Clara in 1954; Naga City, Philippines, from Baltimore (and Manila) in 1949; Finland from San Rafael in 1988; and personnel assistance for Nairobi from Cleveland in 1952.

As foundations proliferated, in very human, limited situations and people, most motivated by faith and love, others possibly driven by a need for power, and still others by the experience of persecution, a life that witnessed to the experience of God and the value of contemplative prayer spread across the country. There the mystical tradition of Carmel was kept alive and available.

Federation and Associations

Following Pius XII's promulgation of the apostolic constitution *Sponsa Christi* (1950), the movement toward federation among the monasteries began, the seed of a renewal to come. Unknown to the U.S. nuns, prior general of the order, Fr. Silverio, opposed federation and sabotaged its implementation. However, the vision of collaboration, unity and mutual help did not die "in spite of the blocks set up by some of the nuns themselves, by their own leadership [in the order], by certain US Bishops and even by the Holy See itself" (Kuenstler). Four associations, not federations, were eventually formed along ideological rather than geographical or foundation lines: Carmelite Communities Associated (CCA) now with fourteen member Carmels (1970); St. Teresa's Association with twelve (1975), including a new foundation of the association erected in Port Tobacco in 1989; Mary, Queen of Carmel Association with thirteen (1976); the St. Joseph Association with four (1976). Three associations were promptly approved by the Holy See. Because some of the members of CCA had publicly criticized *Venite Seorsum* (1969), a Vatican document on enclosure for nuns, and had participated in the Association of Contemplative Sisters (ACS), CCA was denied approval until 1993. After twenty years, collaboration has begun among three of the associations.

Vatican II and Renewal

The renewal mandated by Vatican II has given rise to two major interpretations of Carmelite life. One focuses on the ministry of contemplative prayer and the retrieval of mysticism, particularly Teresa of Avila, John of the Cross, Thérèse of Lisieux, etc. This reading of the charism stresses *presence* (*Ad gentes,* no. 18) and is willing to experiment with various ways the life of contemplative prayer/liturgy can be lived and shared with the people. It values solitary prayer and shared life in a community of equals. The other highlights *separation* from the world and a literal fidelity to the life as it has been lived in the past. It values preservation, therefore, and sees enclosure as the essential *manifestation* of contemplative Carmelite life. Although these two readings seem to be a contemporary expression of the order's age-old tension between solitary prayer and community, the hermit emphasis and the mendicant effort, communities are diverse and complex, spread along a continuum between these two poles. If renewal, ongoing theological and psychological education, experimentation and self-government had been encouraged by the male generalate following Vatican II, if distrust had not been institutionalized in the order, we might have seen a different scenario among the existing sixty-five U.S. Carmels.

Constitutions

Nowhere is this more evident than in the history of the revision of the *Constitutions* authorized by Vatican II. Due to the structures of jurisdiction in the order, the autonomy of monasteries, the generalate's discouragement of federation, the consequent lack of structures of collaboration and representation among the nuns, and deep attachment to the so-called "Constitutions of St. Teresa," new legislation was not promulgated until 1990–91. Then *two* constitutions were engineered and approved by the Holy See. Thirty years of struggle ended with a division of the Discalced Carmelite Nuns into two definitive groups, one with *Constitutions* in the mind of Vatican II; a second with an adapted text of the "Constitutions of Alcala," a 1581 revision by the friars' chapter of the text written by Teresa of Avila in 1567.

See also DICKINSON, FRANCES; MATTHEWS, ANNE.

Chinnici, J. "The Politics of Mysticism: Church, State and the Carmelite Tradition." *Symposium, Carmel 200.* Baltimore, 1990.

Currier, C. W. *Carmel in America.* Darien, Ill.: Carmelite Press, 1989. Bicentennial edition of 1889 history.

Discalced Carmelite Nuns. *Carmel in the United States 1790 to 1990.* Eugene, Oreg.: The Queen's Press, 1990.

FitzGerald, C., ed. *The Carmelite Adventure, Clare Joseph Dickinson's Journal of a Trip to America.* Baltimore: Carmelite Sisters, 1990.

Stewart, G. C. *Marvels of Charity: History of American Sisters and Nuns.* Huntington, Ind.: Our Sunday Visitor, 1994, 46–51.

CONSTANCE FITZGERALD, O.C.D.

CARMELITES, TWO BRANCHES

The worldwide Carmelite Order had its eremitical beginnings at the dawn of the thirteenth century on Mount Carmel in Palestine. Within the century Carmelites migrated to Europe and joined the great mendicant surge; they moved into city and university, striking an uneasy balance between contemplation and apostolic ministry. In 1452 the long affiliation of women with the order was recognized when the Beguines of "Ten Elsen" in Guelders were received into the order.

In 1562, during the Counter-Reformation, Teresa of Avila initiated in Spain a reform of both nuns and friars setting the stage for the separation of the Carmelites into two orders by 1593: The Carmelites of the Ancient Observance and the Discalced Carmelites (the Teresian Reform). While the nuns have stressed primarily the contemplative role, the friars have always included the mendicant or ministry role.

CONSTANCE FITZGERALD, O.C.D.

CARNEY, FRANCIS W. (1915–82)

Priest, educator, and social activist. Francis W. Carney was born in Cleveland, Ohio on February 17, 1915, to Michael and Margaret Carney. Carney studied at John Carroll University before entering St. Mary Seminary in Cleveland. He was ordained on December 20, 1940, after completing his studies at the North American College in Rome and at The Catholic University of America.

After parish ministry, Carney was named a professor at Sisters College (later St. John College) in 1945 where he developed expertise in ethical and social issues, especially labor issues. In 1948 he established the Institute for Social Education at St. John College. The institute was modeled on the lines of a labor school, but Carney had expanded the curriculum to include general education, and ethical and religious courses besides those pertaining to labor and management skills.

The Diocese of Cleveland further utilized Carney's knowledge on ethical issues when he was named the first director of its Family Life Bureau in 1951. Carney developed a marriage preparation program and became a skilled defender of the Church's stance against artificial birth control. In addition to his educational responsibilities, Carney was also an advocate for labor unions. He helped oppose the open shop legislation proposed in 1958 for Ohio. In 1956 he became a member of the Department of Social Action of the Ohio Catholic Conference.

Carney believed that religious people had a responsibility to the larger society. In 1963 he joined a group determined to combat the prejudice and misinformation put forth by extremist groups. This organization, the National Committee for Civic Responsibility, received national prominence when it exposed the falsity of the book *None Dare Call It Treason,* which had alleged that a national conspiracy existed between government officials and other societal leaders. Carney also served on various civic boards and planning agencies. His last years were plagued by illness and he died on January 8, 1982, in Cleveland.

See also OHIO, CATHOLIC CHURCH IN.

Papers of Msgr. Francis W. Carney, 1948–70. Archives, Diocese of Cleveland.

Papers of Family Life Bureau, 1951–70. Archives, Diocese of Cleveland.

Papers of the Institute of Social Education, 1948–72. Archives, Diocese of Cleveland.

CHRISTINE L. KROSEL

CARROLL, AUSTIN (1835–1909)

Religious, educator. Born in Tipperary, Ireland, on February 23, 1835, Margaret Anne Carroll was one of nine children of a Clonmel merchant family. Her parents William and Margaret Strahan Carroll gave priority to both faith and learning. Their highly educated daughter Margaret joined Catherine McAuley's Sisters of Mercy in Cork, where she professed her religious vows as Mary Austin and was missioned to America in 1856. There she assisted Irish Mercies to spread their works and schools in the Northeast and Midwest for ten years before she was sent to establish convents and schools across the South. Serving alternately as superior or assistant in either New Orleans or Mobile, she welcomed several hundred sisters to these Mercy Centers which gradually staffed parish schools from Appalachicola, Florida, to Texas.

Mother Austin worked to broaden and increase educational opportunities as she opened forty-eight schools, including eleven secondary schools, and thirteen schools for black children in Gulf Coast towns without black schools. Her other outreach programs for special needs were free daycare for toddlers, vocational training for their mothers and immigrant women, and night schools for newsboys and poor working youths. She enriched every school and many parishes with libraries, and strengthened the typical finishing school curriculum with as much math and science as the boys studied. She encouraged the girls to write and produce plays and challenged them to prove their intellectual ability in college.

Besides establishing shelters in New Orleans for orphans, poor elderly women, girls between jobs, and newsboys, Mother Austin and her Mercies brought food, care, and prayer regularly to the sick poor in their homes. While their schools were closed during lethal epidemics of yellow fever, however, she and her sisters nursed untiringly to save the stricken. Austin considered the Mercy fever martyrs who died to save others as responsible for the influx of Mercy candidates after each epidemic. A mixture of courage and compassion, Austin gave prisoners weekly instructions, protested the death penalty, gave no quarter to the clergymen who tried to change the Mercy Rule or community ministries, and used the power of the press to obtain matrons for the women's jail.

An acclaimed author whose twenty books and numerous articles assisted in the financing of her black schools and other charitable works, Austin considered writing just a sideline. Between her 1866 *Life of Catherine McAuley* the Venerable Mercy founder, and the fourth volume of her *Annals of the Sisters of Mercy* in 1895, Austin wrote several school plays with strong heroines, realistic stories of lively children, lives of saints, and translations of French and Spanish spiritual works. Besides fulfilling Austin's aim, to preserve early data that otherwise could be lost, the McAuley biography and the *Annals* worked to unify the traditions of Mercies around the world.

The last decade of her forty years in the South were spent in the Diocese of Mobile, where she died on November 29, 1909, and was buried in the cathedral cemetery. Obituaries across the country noted that she was as prolific in establishing schools, libraries, and shelters as she was in generating books, compassion, and companions, including three of her blood sisters who also became Mercies. The New Orleans's *Morning Star* of December 4, 1909, announced that the "Mercy Order had lost, except for its noted foundress, its greatest and most distinguished member . . . and the Church one of its noblest daughters."

See also SISTERS OF MERCY OF THE AMERICAS (R.S.M.); HOUSES OF MERCY (MERCY HOMES).

Muldrey, Mary Hermenia. *Abounding in Mercy: Mother Austin Carroll.* New Orleans, 1988.

Papers of Austin Carroll, 1858–1909. Archives, Sisters of Mercy, New Orleans.

HERMENIA M. MULDREY, R.S.M.

CARROLL, CHARLES (OF CARROLLTON) (1737–1832)

Statesman, signer of the Declaration of Independence. Carroll, the only son of Charles Carroll II of Annapolis and Elizabeth Brooke, was born in Annapolis on September 19, 1737. His family played an important role in the colonial history of Maryland. His grandfather, Charles, known as "the Attorney General," or the "Founder," came to Maryland from England, and was appointed attorney general by Charles Calvert, the third Lord Baltimore in 1688. After the overthrow of James II of England, a rebellion broke out in Maryland aimed at overthrowing Lord Baltimore's government. This colonial counterpart to the Glorious Revolution included the removal of the "Attorney General" from office. In return for his service, Lord Baltimore endowed him with more than six Maryland manors. Charles Carroll inherited that property through his father and became very wealthy.

Charles Carroll

Education

Carroll was educated at the Bohemian Manor Academy, which was conducted secretly by the Society of Jesus in defiance of Maryland law. His cousin, John, the future archbishop of Baltimore, was also educated there, and the two of them went on to the English Jesuit college of St. Omer, France. After St. Omer, his education continued with a year at the Jesuit college at Rheims and the College of Louis le Grand in Paris. He studied law in Bourges and practiced in Paris and London. After sixteen years in Europe, he returned to Maryland in February 1765.

Upon his return, his father gave him Carrollton Manor, a ten-thousand acre estate in Frederick County. From then on he signed his name "Charles Carroll of Carrollton," to distinguish himself from his father. In 1768 he married Mary Darnell, with whom he had seven children.

Public Career

By 1770 Carroll became a spokesman for resistance to unfair colonial taxes. In 1773 he waged a war of words with jurist Daniel Delany through the pages of the *Maryland Gazette*. Carroll, under the pen name "First Citizen," protested Delany's support of taxes for officeholders' fees and stipends for the clergy of the Established Church. Carroll's viewpoint, that taxes should not be levied without the consent of the people's representatives, had many supporters and made Carroll well known.

Due to these articles in the *Maryland Gazette* Carroll's political career flourished. He supported armed resistance to England and advocated independence. In 1776 he, along with Benjamin Franklin, Samuel Chase, and his cousin John (now a priest), was part of a diplomatic mission to Canada sent to secure an alliance. Although the mission failed, it propelled Carroll into a place of importance in the fight for independence. In 1776 the Maryland delegates to the Continental Congress voted for independence due to Carroll's influence. In July he was elected to the Continental Congress, and on August 2, 1776, he signed "Charles Carroll of Carrollton" on the Declaration of Independence.

During the Revolutionary War he was on the Board of War, but resigned from the Continental Congress in 1778 to become a senator in the Maryland senate, where he served as president from 1787–89. He worked toward the ratification of the Constitution, although he refused the chance to be an emergency delegate to the Constitutional Convention in Philadelphia. He became a leader in the Federalist Party, and was elected to the United States Senate in 1789. Preferring to work in the Maryland senate, he resigned from the U.S. Senate in 1792 because of a new law that prohibited state legislators from serving in Congress.

Carroll's public service ended in 1800, the year of Thomas Jefferson's campaign for president, which he opposed. After Jefferson's victory, Carroll went into semiretirement, commenting seldom on public affairs. The only notable exception was his opposition to the War of 1812. He spent the rest of his life in studious pursuits, including a comparative study of religions. In his last public appearance he laid the cornerstone for the Baltimore and Ohio's new railroad, July 4, 1828. He died four years later, on November 14, 1832, at Doughoregan Manor, near Baltimore, at the age of ninety-five. He had the distinction of being the last surviving signer of the Declaration of Independence.

See also AMERICAN CATHOLICS: 1492–1814; AMERICAN REVOLUTION AND CATHOLICS, THE; MARYLAND, CATHOLIC CHURCH IN.

Hanley, Thomas O'Brien. *Charles Carroll of Carrollton: The Making of a Revolutionary Gentleman.* Washington, D.C.: The Catholic University of America, 1970; repr. Chicago, 1970.

———. *Revolutionary Gentleman: Charles Carroll and the War.* Chicago: Loyola University Press, 1983.

Rowland, Kate Mason. *The Life of Charles Carroll of Carrollton, 1737–1832, with His Correspondence and Public Papers.* 2 vols. New York and London, 1898.

Smith, Ellen Hart. *Charles Carroll of Carrollton*. Cambridge, 1942; repr. New York, 1971.

JOSEPH M. McLAFFERTY

Related Document

CHARLES CARROLL'S DEFENSE OF HIS RELIGIOUS BELIEFS, 1773

In the struggle for American independence the Catholics joined with their fellow countrymen without reserve. Among their number no one played a more prominent and honorable role than Charles Carroll of Carrollton (1737–1832), signer of the Declaration of Independence, who from the time he entered politics in 1773 until his retirement in 1800 filled a number of important state and federal offices. The occasion which brought him to public notice was the appearance on February 4, 1773, of the first of a series of letters when he published in the *Maryland Gazette* over the pen name of "First Citizen." Carroll had been roused by Daniel Dulany's ("Antillon") attempt to defend the arbitrary action of Governor Robert Eden in proroguing the Maryland assembly and reaffirming by proclamation officers' fees and stipends for the clergy of the established church. With the development of the debate the argument broadened and in the end Carroll's effective polemics not only vanquished Dulany but helped to swing the Maryland election of May 1773, in favor of the patriot party who had opposed the royal governor. In the course of the exchange Dulany sought to discredit Carroll by an attack on his religion. This appeal to prejudice angered the Catholic statesman and he struck back in defense of his political and religious beliefs. The excerpts from his letters of May 16 and July 1, 1773, which follow illustrate Carroll's method of meeting the insinuations against his religious faith.

(*Source*: Kate Mason Rowland. *The Life of Charles Carroll of Carrollton, 1737–1832, With His Correspondence and Public Papers*. New York: G. P. Putnam's Sons, 1898, I, 284–85, 316, 359.)

MARYLAND GAZETTE, MAY 6, 1773

In vindication of his conduct, Antillon has not endeavoured to convince the minds of his readers by the force of reason, but *"in the favourite method of illiberal calumny, virulent abuse and shameless asseveration to affect their passions"* has attempted to render his antagonist ridiculous, contemptible and odious; he has descended to the lowest jests on the person of the Citizen, has expressed the utmost contempt of his understanding, and a strong suspicion of his *political and religious principles*. What connection, Antillon, have the latter with the Proclamation? Attempts to rouse popular prejudices, and to turn the laugh against an adversary, discover the weakness of a cause, or the inabilities of the advocate, who employs ridicule, instead of argument. *"The Citizen's patriotism is entirely feigned"*; his reasons must not be considered, or listened to, because his *religious principles* are not to be trusted. Yet if we are to credit Antillon, the Citizen is so little attached to these principles, *"That he is most devoutly wishing for the event,"* which is to free him from their shackles.

What my speculative notions on religion may be, this is neither the place nor time to declare; my political principles ought only to be questioned on the present occasion; surely they are constitutional, and have met, I hope, with the approbation of my countrymen; if so Antillon's aspersions will give me no uneasiness. He asks, who is this Citizen? A man, Antillon, of an independent fortune, one deeply interested in the prosperity of his country: a friend to liberty, a settled enemy to lawless prerogative. . . .

. . . I comprehend fully, Antillon, your threats thrown out against certain religionists; to shew the *greatness of your soul,* and your utter detestation of malice, I shall give the public a translation of your Latin sentence; the sentiment is truly noble, and reflects the highest lustre on its author or adopter; *Eos tamen laedere non exoptemus, qui nos laedere non exoptant,* we would not wish to hurt those who do not wish to hurt us;—in other words, "I cannot wreak my resentment on the Citizen, without involving all of his religion in one common ruin with him; they have not offended me, it is true, but it is better that ninety-nine just should suffer, than one guilty man escape—a thorough paced politician never sticks at the means of accomplishing his ends; why should I, who have so just a claim to the character?" These, Antillon, are the sentiments and threats, couched under your Latin phrase, which *you even* were ashamed to avow in plain English. . . .

Ibid., July 1, 1773

. . . The Citizen did not deliver his sentiment only but likewise the sentiment of others. We Catholics, who think we were hardly treated on occasion, we still remember the treatment though our resentment hath entirely subsided. It is not in the least surprising that a man incapable of forming an exalted sentiment, should not readily comprehend the force and beauty of one. . . . To what purpose was the threat thrown out of enforcing the penal statutes by proclamation? Why am I told that my conduct is very inconsistent with the situation of one, who "owes even the *toleration* he enjoys to the favour of government"? If by instilling prejudices into the Governor, and by every mean and wicked artifice you can rouse the popular resentment against certain religionists, and thus bring on a persecution of them, it will then be known whether the toleration I enjoy, be due to the favour of government or not. . . .

(*Source*: John Tracy Ellis, ed. *Documents of American Catholic History*. Vol. 1:1493–1965. Wilmington, Del.: Michael Glazier, 1987, 128–30.)

CARROLL, DANIEL (1730–96)

Maryland statesman and signer of the Federal Constitution of the United States, Carroll was born in Upper Marlboro, Maryland on July 25, 1730. Three well-known Carroll families emigrated to Maryland from Ireland in 1688,

1715, and 1720. Drastic penal laws in England and the loss of family estates were some of the incentives that drove immigrants to the new world. Daniel Carroll II descended from this third line of Carrolls. His father, Daniel Carroll I (1696–1751), came in 1720 and acquired extensive lands from the Patuxent River to the present-day borders of the District of Columbia. Like many other Catholic families, Daniel Carroll I purchased slaves and "imported Protestant rather than Catholic servants on whom there was double duty." To Daniel Carroll and his wife, Eleanor Darnall (1706–96), were born seven children among them Daniel Carroll II and John Carroll, the first archbishop of Baltimore.

Private Life

The Carrolls like many Irish families came to Maryland because they believed that this colony was a haven for all believers. They soon realized that with the accession of William and Mary in England in 1688 Catholics were subject to the onus of "double taxing," deprived of the right to vote, to worship, hold office, and most importantly, deprived of an education. Daniel Carroll was, undoubtedly, taught by his mother whose excellent French education fitted her for this task. At the age of twelve he was sent to the College of St. Omer, a famous English Jesuit refugee school in French Flanders. For six years he received an excellent education in theology, philosophy, classics, political philosophy, and public speaking. He returned to the colonies the same year that his brother, John, and his cousin, Charles Carroll, began their studies at St. Omer's.

Born into a wealthy family, enhanced by the marriage of his father to Eleanor Darnall, the intellectual and wealthy granddaughter of Henry Darnall I, an heir to the prosperous merchant business of his father, Daniel Carroll II's background enabled him to enter political life with confidence. At twenty-two, Daniel Carroll married Eleanor Carroll, a "very distant cousin" of Charles Carroll of Carrollton and daughter of Daniel Carroll of Duddington and Ann Rozier, the heiress of Cerne Abbey in England. It was through this marriage that two Carroll lines became closely related.

Public Life

In 1776 at the time of the American Revolution Maryland permitted Catholics the right to vote within property qualifications and to serve in political office. For almost twenty years Carroll was a public servant not only in his native state, Maryland, but also in the Federal government. Carroll was elected to the State Council of Maryland in 1777 and reelected for five consecutive terms. He believed that the people were the broad base of government and that it could survive only through this vision—a belief not totally shared by Charles Carroll of Carrollton.

Carroll was elected senator in the Maryland legislature (1781–92), state delegate to the Continental Congress (1781–83), chairman of the Maryland-Virginia project to promote navigation on the Potomac River (1785), a member of the Constitutional Convention (1787), a member of the First House of Representatives (1789–91), and was appointed one of three commissioners to survey the District Territory for the permanent seat of government of the United States (1791–95).

While serving in the Maryland Senate, Carroll was named a delegate to the Continental Congress. The Maryland delegates refused to subscribe to the Articles of Confederation until those states that held western lands ceded them to the federal government. When this was accomplished, Daniel Carroll and John Hanson signed on March 1, 1781.

On May 26, 1787, Carroll was called to Philadelphia to serve in the Constitutional Convention to consider the emendation of the Articles of Confederation. One of the most important achievements of Carroll was furthering legislation that aimed at preserving the safeguards which he deemed necessary for the establishment of the new government. He championed a strong centralization of the federal government but, at the same time, measures aimed at preserving and guaranteeing democracy at both the state and national levels. With James Madison and James Wilson, Carroll insisted that the people be regarded as the real source of power in the new government and that individual rights be recognized and guaranteed. The strong opposition in Maryland to the ratification of the Constitution is evidenced by the frequent letters Carroll wrote in the *Maryland Journal* in favor of the Constitution under the name of "A Friend of the Constitution" and the many letters to and from James Madison. The final victory for ratification was in great part due to Carroll's competence and persistence. Maryland ratified the Constitution as the seventh state of the union.

Carroll served as a delegate to the First United States House of Representatives along with Thomas FitzSimons of Philadelphia, the other Catholic signer of the Constitution. Carroll was instrumental in influencing the passage of the First and Tenth Amendments. With Madison, he urged that "no religion should be established by law" and that "powers not delegated to the government be reserved to the states or to the people."

Carroll received an appointment January 22, 1791, from President Washington as one of three commissioners to plan the erection of the national capitol. After many difficulties and conflicts with Mayor Pierre L'Enfant whose insubordination ultimately resulted in his dismissal, Andrew Ellicott, a well-regarded surveyor, completed the plans. After serving four years Carroll resigned, the last of the commissioners to serve.

Daniel Carroll, "a gentleman of unbounded philanthropy" both to the Catholic Church and to the Irish immigrants in this country, died at the age of sixty-six in Rock Creek, Maryland, the same year as the death of his mother. Daniel Carroll's place of burial is unknown.

See also MARYLAND, CATHOLIC CHURCH IN.

Burnett, Edmund Cody. *Letters of Members of the Continental Congress.* 8 vols. Washington, D.C., 1821–36.

Geiger, Virgina. *Daniel Carroll, A Framer of the Constitution.* Washington, D.C., 1943.

———. *Daniel Carroll, One Man and His Descendants.* Baltimore, Maryland, 1979.

Ives, Joseph M. "Daniel Carroll." Unpublished manuscript in the Georgetown University Library, LaFarge Papers.

Purcell, Richard J. "Daniel Carroll, Framer of the Constitution." *Records of The American Catholic Historical Society* 52 (2) (June 1941) 67–87; 137–60.

VIRGINA GEIGER, S.S.N.D.

CARROLL, JOHN (1736–1815)

First bishop and archbishop of Baltimore and founder of the American Catholic hierarchy. John Carroll was born at Upper Marlboro, Maryland, on January 8 (or 19), 1736, the fourth of seven children of Daniel Carroll, merchant and planter, and Eleanor Darnall. Though but remotely related on his father's side to the more famous Carroll branch that produced Charles Carroll of Carrollton, he was through his mother a second cousin of the latter. Through his mother he could also claim descent from some of the leading families of England. John was probably baptized in the chapel of the newly built mansion of his uncle Henry Darnall III called "His Lordship's Kindness." The uncle would soon after take communion in the Church of England in order to hold public office and then flee the province when caught embezzling public funds. John would have more than his share of blacksheep relatives.

John Carroll

Early Years

John Carroll was probably instructed first by his mother, who had been educated in the convent school of the Sepulchrine nuns of Liège, which training, the historian John Gilmary Shea claimed, "gave him the ease, dignity, and polish which marked him through life." In 1747 he was sent to a school recently established by the Jesuits at Bohemia Manor in Cecil County and in 1748, with his cousin Charles Carroll, to the Jesuit school of St. Omer in French Flanders. At the latter his brother Daniel and many other Maryland Catholics received a solid grounding in the classics. Daniel returned to Maryland the year John arrived to pursue the life of a planter and later politician. John entered the Jesuit novitiate at Watten nearby on September 8, 1753, and took his first vows two years later. From Watten he went to the English College at Liège to pursue his studies in philosophy and theology. On February 14, 1761, he was ordained a priest by the auxiliary bishop of Liège. In 1762, having finished his studies, he began to teach philosophy at the English College. By 1767 he was teaching at the Jesuit college in Bruges. After a year's tertianship in Ghent Carroll took his final vows on February 2, 1771. Not long after he began a continental tour as chaperon for the young Charles Philip Stourton, a future baron, a broadening experience for them both.

Carroll's goal was Rome, where the pope was on the verge of suppressing the Society of Jesus. They lodged for a time at the Jesuit College of Nobles in Bologna, where Carroll first met his future friend and faithful correspondent Charles Plowden. By the fall of 1772 Carroll was in Rome incognito. "What a revolution of ideas," he wrote a friend in February, "do all these proceedings produce in a mind accustomed to regard this city as the seat of Religion" (*John Carroll Papers,* 1:29). When word of the suppression finally reached him in Bruges, he wrote his mother, "The greatest blessing which in my estimation I could receive from God, would be immediate death" (32). The suppression of June 21, 1773, made the unhappy Marylander his "own man," and the following year he returned to America and another revolution.

Creating a Church

In Maryland Carroll resided with his mother at Rock Creek, where his brother Daniel built a chapel for him to serve the Catholics of the neighborhood. In 1776 he was asked by the Continental Congress to accompany a mission to Canada consisting of Benjamin Franklin, Samuel Chase, and his cousin Charles Carroll. Though he questioned the propriety of a minister of religion's being involved in political affairs and entertained small hope of winning over the Canadians, he felt it his patriotic duty to go. Snubbed by the local clergy on the orders of the bishop of Quebec, Carroll took an early opportunity to accompany the ailing Franklin back to Philadelphia.

Carroll's sympathies were with the revolutionary cause, which he saw as favorable to the future of the Church in the new nation. With independence ratified by treaty in 1783, he wrote jubilantly to an official in Rome that "our Religious system has undergone a revolution, if possible, more extraordinary, than our political one." It was "a blessing and advantage, which is our duty to preserve & improve with the utmost prudence" (80–81). When a cousin, Charles Henry Wharton, wrote a work to justify his conversion to the Protestant Episcopal Church suggesting that Roman Catholicism was inimical to a free society, Carroll felt compelled to publish in 1785 a 115-page rebuttal, *An Address to the Roman Catholics of the United States of America,* his most ambitious literary effort. In it he argued that "America may come to exhibit a proof to the world, that general and equal toleration, by giving a free circulation to fair argument, is the most effectual method to bring all denominations of Christians to an unity of faith" (140). At this point in his career Carroll also favored a liturgy in the language of the people and a recognition of papal power as extending only to spiritual matters. In 1785 he fought a bill that would have laid a tax for the support of clergymen in Maryland. To at least two American newspapers he sent essays demanding equal rights for Roman Catholics.

With independence Carroll realized something must be done for the support of the clergy, almost all former Jesuits, and the protection of their properties. In the face of the apathy and irresolution of his former colleagues, he took the initiative in 1783 by calling several priests to White Marsh, Maryland, where a constitution was framed from a plan he had outlined. It provided for a chapter of the clergy elected from three districts. To the chapter, which would meet regularly, would be entrusted the former Jesuit properties and responsibility for the conduct of the clergy in temporal matters. Only then did the ex-Jesuits petition the Holy See to grant the necessary spiritual faculties to their former superior, Fr. John Lewis. Rome meanwhile, through the French foreign minister, approached the American representatives in Paris. When told that the Holy See was free to make any arrangement for the new nation it wished, Congress having nothing to do with religion, the pope, at Franklin's recommendation, named Carroll instead of Lewis "Superior of the Mission in the thirteen United States" on June 9, 1784.

Not wishing to be under the Congregation of the Propaganda Fide, which was charged with missionary territories, Carroll informed the cardinal prefect, Leonardo Antonelli, that it would be impolitic to create for the new nation a vicar apostolic directly under this curial congregation.

When the time was right, he insisted, the United States should have a diocesan bishop chosen by its own clergy. A compromise that was something of an anomaly would eventually be worked out: the American clergy would, for the first time only, be allowed to elect their bishop, but this diocesan bishop would be under the Congregation of the Propaganda. Troubles in New York and Philadelphia, plus the antics of wandering priests, soon convinced Carroll and the chapter that a bishop was needed. Carroll was elected almost unanimously. On November 6, 1789, by the pontifical brief *Ex hac apostolicae,* Baltimore, where Carroll had lived since 1786, was made the first diocese of the United States with Carroll its bishop. On August 15, 1790, he was raised to the episcopacy in the chapel of the Weld family, Lulworth Castle, Dorset, England, where his friend Charles Plowden was chaplain, by Bishop Charles Walmesley, vicar apostolic of the Western District.

Bishop of Baltimore

In November 1791 Carroll held the only synod of his twenty-five-year episcopacy. It concerned itself mostly with the administration of the sacraments and support of the Church. Nothing was legislated in the area of education, Carroll's principal concern. As early as 1786 he had pushed for the creation of what would come to be called Georgetown College. Its first student was finally admitted in November 1791, a little more than a month after the French Sulpicians, who had broached the possibility to Carroll in England, opened St. Mary's Seminary in Baltimore. In 1805 the Sulpicians would also establish St. Mary's College in Baltimore and in 1808 Mount St. Mary's College and Seminary in Emmitsburg. Carroll would likewise give his approval to the founding of Visitation nuns, who in 1799, under the direction of Leonard Neale, his successor, would begin the Visitation Academy in Georgetown. In 1805 Carroll would urge English Dominicans to begin a priory and college in Kentucky for the large number of Maryland Catholics migrating thither. In 1809 he would encourage Elizabeth Seton to establish the American Sisters of Charity for the education of girls. He was not successful, however, in inducing the Carmelites, who had come to Maryland in 1790, to take up the work of education.

An unfortunate rivalry in the field of education developed between the former Jesuits and the Sulpicians. Although Carroll tended to favor the Sulpicians, upon whom he had come to lean heavily for advice, he took the lead in effecting a restoration of the Society of Jesus in Maryland in 1805, without informing Rome, by an affiliation with the Russian Jesuits, who had been protected from suppression by Catherine the Great.

Carroll encouraged the building of churches by trustees in the manner of Episcopalian vestries. This he saw as the best way to secure church property and involve the laity in the governance of the Church. Trustees, however, proved unruly in the port cities of New York, Philadelphia, Charleston, and even Baltimore. Despite assertions to the contrary by such historians as John Gilmary Shea and Peter Guilday, Carroll never repudiated the system, which worked well in the rural churches of Maryland. Trustees proved indispensable in the erection of the magnificent cathedral that Carroll began in 1806, engaging the noted architect Benjamin Henry Latrobe.

More vexing than troublesome trustees were the many problem priests with whom Carroll had to contend. One of the most notorious was Simon Felix Gallagher of Charleston, an eloquent alcoholic with a large following. Carroll's policy towards such priests was one of forbearance, even kindness. One of his accomplishments ignored by historians was his ability to tame such troublemakers, even Gallagher. It was, however, the presence of irresponsible and contentious priests that probably convinced Carroll of the inadvisability of episcopal elections by the clergy.

Archbishop of Baltimore

Carroll's inability to govern a diocese coterminous with the United States was apparent from the start. As early as 1793 he was told to consult his clergy on the choice of a coadjutor. The consultation took the form of an election, and the lot fell to Lawrence Graessl, a former Jesuit. He died, however, before the briefs arrived. A second coadjutor, Leonard Neale, was chosen, probably also by election, in 1795 but a miscarriage of the briefs prevented his being raised to the episcopacy until 1800. Neale proved of little help. In 1804 Carroll was given the administration of the Danish West Indies and other nearby islands that were under no ecclesiastical jurisdiction and in 1805 the Louisiana Territory. Finally, on April 8, 1808, Baltimore was raised to an archdiocese with four suffragan sees: Philadelphia, New York, Boston, and Bardstown, Kentucky.

Carroll himself ordained the bishops he had chosen for all but New York. That choice he had left to the Holy See, but Bishop Richard Luke Concanen died in Europe soon after his consecration. Not only was Carroll obliged to continue his care of New York but also of Philadelphia, where Bishop Michael Egan, in poor health, proved incapable of dealing with a variety of troublemakers. While Boston and Bardstown were in the capable hands of John Cheverus and Benedict Flaget respectively, Carroll was unable to send out the man he had chosen as administrator of Louisiana, William DuBourg, until 1813.

Although Carroll came to appreciate the support of the Congregation of the Propaganda, he and his suffragans attempted to deal directly with the pope. This effort, as well as that of filling the empty sees of New York and Philadelphia after Egan's death in 1814, was frustrated by the imprisonment of Pius VII and the unsettled condition of the Holy See.

Carroll's last years were particularly troubled ones. War with England prevented him from holding the provincial council he had planned. He was compelled to complain of foreign interference in the choice of bishops for the orphaned sees. He had to suffer independent-minded Jesuit superiors. At the time of the restoration of the society in 1814 he refused to surrender at once the powers, properties, and parishes the superior demanded. His death after a brief illness on December 3, 1815, brought respite but occasioned a universal outpouring of regret.

The Maryland Tradition

John Carroll has sometimes been criticized by historians for having abandoned such enlightened goals as a vernacular liturgy and the election of bishops, for having relinquished the "republican blueprint" he had fashioned in the 1780s. While it is true that he evidenced a greater conservatism as bishop than he had shown as a priest, in authority he faced increasingly obdurate and complex problems. The destructive character of the French Revolution and "furious democracy," moreover, served to moderate attitudes born of the American Revolution. Carroll was a Federalist, who regarded property as a social separator. To whatever extent he may have looked to Europe for models after becoming a bishop, however, he was still the architect of the Maryland tradition in American Catholicism.

Born of an ardent patriotism, Carroll's own devotion to such American principles as freedom of conscience and separation of Church and state were readily communicated to his coreligionists in America. To friends and acquaintances abroad he continually held up his native land as a model for imitation. No minister of religion, moreover, contributed more to the ecumenical spirit that stamped the early national period than did Carroll. He developed close friendships with almost all the leaders of other denominations.

This easy association Carroll accomplished largely by the leadership he exerted in promoting civic improvement. As early as 1782 he found a place on the original board of trustees for St. John's College in Annapolis and was elected its president in 1788. He would also be elected to the board of Baltimore College but declined the office of provost because of age. He was prominent in the founding and in the management of such organizations as the Library Company of Baltimore, of which he was proudest, the Baltimore Female Humane Association, the Maryland Society for Promoting Useful Knowledge, and the Baltimore General Dispensary. Carroll's example led other Catholics to immerse themselves in the affairs of the larger community, to lend their talents to civic enterprises.

Catholic piety in the Carroll era was simple and personal. Carroll did not wish Catholic worship, or the display of Catholic piety, to be a source of dissension. On one occasion he wrote disapprovingly of a Corpus Christi procession conducted by a pastor on the streets of Baltimore. Carroll wished the Catholic populace to blend imperceptibly into the social fabric. He governed a Church with a minimum of institutions and associations and had little inclination to create strictly Catholic ones.

In its relationship with the Holy See Carroll wished a measure of autonomy for the American Church. Although he overcame his initial distrust of the Congregation of the Propaganda, he was not overly generous in the information he supplied the Roman authorities nor overly conscientious in following their directives. At the same time, he instilled in his spiritual children a deep loyalty to the pope as a symbol of unity.

This amalgam of attitudes and values that was the Maryland tradition would be the chief legacy that John Carroll bequeathed to the Church of which he was founder and father.

Guilday, Peter. *The Life and Times of John Carroll, Archbishop of Baltimore.* New York, 1922.

Hanley, Thomas O'Brien, ed. *The John Carroll Papers.* 3 vols. Notre Dame, Indiana, 1976.

Hennesey, James, S.J. "An Eighteenth-Century Bishop: John Carroll of Baltimore." *Archivum Historiae Pontificiae* 76 (1978) 171–204.

Melville, Annabelle M. *John Carroll of Baltimore: Founder of the American Catholic Hierarchy.* New York, 1955.

Spalding, Thomas W. *The Premier See: A History of the Archdiocese of Baltimore 1789–1989.* Baltimore, 1989.

———. "John Carroll: Corrigenda and Addenda." *Catholic Historical Review* 71 (1985) 505–18.

THOMAS W. SPALDING

Related Documents

JOHN CARROLL IS APPOINTED SUPERIOR OF THE AMERICAN MISSIONS, JUNE 9, 1784

The recognition of American independence by Great Britain in the provisional treaty of November 30, 1782, confronted the Holy See with a difficult and unprecedented situation. Obviously the jurisdiction of the Vicar Apostolic of the London District over American Catholics could no longer be exercised and some substitute would have to be found. But an overseas republic with a strong tradition of hostility toward the Church, wherein the priests themselves were known to oppose the appointment of a bishop, did not offer a promising prospect for direct negotiations. In his perplexity, therefore, Lorenzo Cardinal Antonelli (1730–1811), Prefect of Propaganda, turned to France, the new republic's ally, for guidance. He first raised the question with the nuncio at Paris on January 15, 1783, and for the next year and a half the correspondence continued and ultimately involved a number of officials, including Benjamin Franklin, the American Minister to France. Finally Propaganda reached a decision by naming John Carroll (1735–1815) as superior of the American missions with very limited faculties. Thus did there come about the first step toward giving a form and government to the Church in the United States. The following letter of Antonelli to Carroll informed him of his appointment, acknowledged that it was only a temporary arrangement, and asked for more information on the state of Catholicism in the new country.

(*Source*: Latin text in Donald C. Shearer, O.F.M. Cap., ed. *Pontificia Americana. A Documentary History of the Catholic Church in the United States, 1784-1884.* Washington: The Catholic University of America Press, 1933, 58–59; English translation by John Gilmary Shea, *History of the Catholic Church in the United States.* New York: John G. Shea, 1888, II, 243–45.)

ROME, JUNE 9, 1784

Very Rev. Sir:

In order to preserve and defend Catholicity in the Thirteen United States of North America, the Supreme Pontiff of the Church Pius VI, and this sacred Congregation, have thought it extremely proper to designate a pastor who should, permanently and independently of any ecclesiastical power, except the same Sacred Congregation, attend to the spiritual necessities of the Catholic flock. In the appointment of such a pastor, the Sacred Congregation would have readily have cast its eyes on the Rev. John Lewis if his advanced age and the labors he has already undergone in the vineyard of the Lord, had not deterred it from imposing on him, a new and very heavy burden; for he seems to require repose rather than arduous labor. As then, Rev. Sir, you have given conspicuous proofs of piety and zeal, and it is known that your appointment will please and gratify many members of that republic, and especially Mr. Franklin, the eminent individual who represents the same republic at the court of the Most Christian King, the Sacred Congregation, with the approbation of his Holiness, has appointed you Superior of the Mission in the thirteen United States of North America, and has communicated to you the faculties, which are necessary to the discharge of that office; faculties which are also communicated to the other priests of the same States, except the administration of confirmation, which is reserved for you alone, as the enclosed documents will show.

These arrangements are meant to be only temporary. For it is the intention of his Holiness soon to charge a Vicar-Apostolic, invested with the title and character of bishop, with the care of those states, that he may attend to ordination and other episcopal functions. But, to accomplish this design, it is of great importance that we should be made acquainted with the state of the orthodox religion in those thirteen states. Therefore we request you to forward to us, as soon as possible, a correct report, stating carefully the number of Catholics in each state; what is their condition, their piety and what abuses exist; also how many missionary priests labor now in this vineyard of the Lord; what are their qualifications, their zeal, their mode of support. For though the Sacred Congregation wish not to meddle with temporal things, it is important for the establishment of laborers, that we should know what are the ecclesiastical revenues, if any there are, and it is believed there are some. In the meantime for fear the want of missionaries should deprive the Catholics of spiritual assistance, is has been resolved to invite hither two youths from the states of Maryland and Pennsylvania, to educate them at the expense of the Sacred Congregation in the Urban College; they will afterwards, on returning to their country, be substitutes in the mission. We leave to your solicitude the care of selecting and sending them. You will make choice of those who have more promising talents and a good constitution, who are not less than twelve, nor more than fifteen years of age; who by their proficiency in the sanctuary may give great hopes of themselves. You may address them to the excellent archbishop of Seleucia, Apostolic Nuncio at Paris, who is informed of their coming. If the young men selected are unable to defray the expenses of the voyage, the Sacred Congregation will provide for them: we even wish to be informed by you frankly and accurately of the necessary traveling expenses, to serve as a rule for the future. Such are the things I had to signify to you; and whilst I am confident you will discharge the office committed to you with all zeal, solicitude and fidelity, and more than answer the high opinion we have formed of you, I pray God that he may grant you all peace and happiness.

L. Card. Antonelli, Prefect

Stephen Borgia, Secretary

(*Source:* John Tracy Ellis, ed. *Documents of American Catholic History.* Vol. 1:1493–1865. Wilmington, Del.: Michael Glazier, 1987, 142–44.)

CARROLL ANSWERS AN ATTACK UPON THE CATHOLIC FAITH, 1784

One of the most unpleasant duties which John Carroll, first superior of the American Catholics, had to perform in the year of his appointment was to answer an attack made upon the Catholic faith by an apostate priest. Charles H. Wharton (1748–1833) was a Maryland-born ex-Jesuit like Carroll himself who had served for some years as chaplain to the Catholics in Worcester, England. After his return to the United States he had published at Philadelphia in the early summer of 1784 *A Letter to the Roman Catholics of the City of Worcester.* The following excerpts from Carroll's reply indicate something of his method as well as the method used by Wharton in his efforts to justify his action. Carroll was a warm admirer of the religious toleration which was then becoming a reality in the United States and he was pained at the prospect of disrupting the present harmony between Americans of different religious beliefs by engaging in religious controversy. The priests of that day were accustomed to charges against the church, but by reason of the nature and source of Wharton's publication they felt it could not be ignored, and they were agreed that Carroll was the man to answer it.

(*Source: An Address to the Roman Catholics of the United States of America.* By a Catholic Clergyman [John Carroll]. Annapolis: Frederick Green, 1784, 59–60, 113–15.)

I WILL NOT DENY, THAT I WAS SURPRISED WHEN I READ THE first passage cited by the Chaplain; it appeared so opposite to the principles which St. Chrysostom had laid down in several parts of his works. It was a mortifying circumstance, that I could not conveniently have recourse to that holy doctor's writings, nor minutely examine the passage objected, together with its context. I procured a friend to examine the edition of Chrysostom's works, belonging to the public library at Annapolis; he has carefully and repeatedly read the 49th homily on St. Matthew; and not one syllable of the Chaplain's citation is to be found in it. After receiving this notice, I was for some time doubtful, whether it might not be owing to a difference in the editions. I could not persuade myself, that he, who so solemnly calls heaven to witness for the impartiality and integrity of his inquiry, would publicly expose himself to a well-grounded imputation of unpardonable negligence, in a matter of such serious concern. But I have now the fullest evidence, that the passage, for which Chrysostom on Matthew, hom. 49, is quoted, is not taken from that father. It is extracted from a work of no credit, supposed to be written in the 6th century, entitled, *The unfinished work on Matthew.* But had it ever been fairly quoted from him, the Chaplain would not have had so much cause for triumph as he imagines. For the passage, he adduces, carries with it equal condemnation of the protestant and catholic rule of faith. . . .

I have now gone through a task, painful in every point of view, in which I could consider it. To write for the public eye, on any occasion whatever, is neither agreeable to my feelings, my leisure, or opportunities; that it is likewise disproportioned to my abilities, my readers, I doubt [not], will soon discover. But if reduced to the necessity of publishing, I would wish that my duty led me to any species of composition, rather than that of religious controversy. Mankind have conceived such a contempt for it, that an author cannot entertain a hope of enjoying those gratifications, which in treating other subjects may support his spirits and enliven his imagination. Much less could I have a prospect of these incitements in the prosecution of my present undertaking. I could not forget, in the beginning, progress, and conclusion of it, that the habits of thinking, the prejudices, perhaps even the passions of many of my readers, would be set against all the arguments, I could offer; and that the weaknesses, the errors, the absurdities of the writer would be imputed to the errors and absurdity of his religion. But of all considerations the most painful was, that I had to combat him, with whom I had been connected in an intercourse of friendship and mutual good offices; and in connection with whom I hoped to have consummated my course of our common ministry in the service of virtue and religion. But when I found these expectations disappointed; when I found that he not only had abandoned our faith and communion, but had imputed to us doctrines foreign to our belief, and having a natural tendency to embitter against us the minds of our fellow-citizens, I felt an anguish too keen for description; and perhaps the Chaplain will experience a similar sentiment, when he comes coolly to reflect on this instance of his conduct. It did not become the friend of toleration to misinform, and to sow in minds so misinformed, the seeds of religious animosity.

Under all these distressful feelings, one consideration alone relieved me in writing; and that was, the hope of vindicating your religion to your own selves at least, and preserving the steadfastness of your faith. But even this prospect should not have induced me to engage in the controversy, if I could fear that it would disturb the harmony now subsisting amongst all christians in this country, so blessed with civil and religious liberty; which if we have the wisdom and temper to preserve, America may come to exhibit a proof to the world, that general and equal toleration, by giving a free circulation to fair argument, is the most effectual method to bring all denominations of christians to a unity of faith.

The motives, which led the Chaplain to the step he has taken, are known best to God and himself. For the vindication of his conduct, he appeals to the dictates of conscience with a seriousness and solemnity, which must add greatly to his guilt, if he be not sincere. He is anxious to impress on his readers a firm conviction, that neither views of preferment or sensuality, had any influence on his determination. He appears to be jealous, that suspicions will arise unfavourable to the purity of his intentions. He shall have no cause to impute to me the spreading of these suspicions. But I must entreat him with an earnestness suggested by the most perfect good will and zealous regard for his welfare, to consider the sanctity of the solemn and deliberate engagement, which at an age of perfect maturity he contracted with Almighty God. . . .

(*Source:* John Tracy Ellis, ed. *Documents of American Catholic History.* Vol. 1:1493–1865. Wilmington, Del.: Michael Glazier, 1987, 145–47.)

THE FIRST AMERICAN REPORT TO PROPAGANDA ON CATHOLICISM IN THE UNITED STATES, MARCH 1, 1785

Father John Carroll did not find his appointment as superior of the American Catholic missions to his liking, but from the time he received word of it in late November 1784, he set about to fulfill the duties of the office as efficiently as he possibly could. One of his most pressing tasks was to furnish Propaganda with the data they had requested concerning the condition of the Church in the United States. For that purpose Carroll turned to the twenty-four priests then in the country and asked them to supply him with the facts on their missions. From the reports submitted to him, and from his own knowledge, he composed the document which follows. It has interest as being the most

authentic account of the state of the Church at that time, as well as being the first of a lengthy series of reports on American Catholicism which found their way into Propaganda's archives from 1784 until 1908 when the American Church was removed from the jurisdiction of that congregation.

(*Source:* The original Latin was published from a photostat of the document in the archives of the Congregation de Propaganda Fide by Peter Guilday, *The Life and Times of John Carroll, Archbishop of Baltimore, 1735–1815.* New York: Encyclopedia Press, 1922, I, 223–25; the translation is taken from John Gilmary Shea, *History of the Catholic Church in the United States.* New York: John G. Shea, 1888, 11, 257–61.)

Report for the Eminent Cardinal Antonelli Concerning the State of Religion in the United States of America

1. On the Number of Catholics in the United States

THERE ARE IN MARYLAND ABOUT 15,800 CATHOLICS; OF these there are about 9,000 freemen, adults or over twelve years of age; children under that age, about 3,000; and above that number of slaves of all ages of African origin, called negroes. There are in Pennsylvania about 7,000, very few of whom are negroes, and the Catholics are less scattered and live nearer to each other. There are not more than 200 in Virginia who are visited four or five times a year by a priest. Many other Catholics are said to be scattered in that and other States, who are utterly deprived of all religious ministry. In the State of New York I hear that there are at least 1,500. (Would that some spiritual succor could be afforded them!) They have recently, at their own expense, sent for a Franciscan Father from Ireland, and he is said to have the best testimonials as to his learning and life; he had arrived a little before I received the letters in which faculties were transmitted to me, communicable to my fellow-priests. I was for a time in doubt whether I could properly approve this priest for the administration of the sacraments. I have now, however, decided, especially as the feast of Easter is so near, to consider him as one of my fellow-priests, and to grant him faculties, and I trust that my decision will meet your approbation. As to the Catholics who are in the territory bordering on the river called Mississippi and in all that region which following that river extends to the Atlantic Ocean, and from it extends to the limits of Carolina, Virginia and Pennsylvania,—this tract of country contains, I hear, many Catholics, formerly Canadians, who speak French, and I fear that they are destitute of priests. Before I received your Eminence's letters there went to them a priest, German by birth, but who came last from France; he professes to belong to the Carmelite order: he was furnished with no sufficient testimonials that he was sent by his lawful superior. What he is doing and what is the condition of the Church in those parts, I expect soon to learn. The jurisdiction of the Bishop of Quebec formerly extended to some part of that region; but I do not know whether he wishes to exercise any authority there now, that all these parts are subjects to the United States.

2. On the Condition, Piety, and Defects, etc., of Catholics

In Maryland a few of the leading more wealthy families still profess the Catholic faith introduced at the very foundation of the province by their ancestors. The greater part of them are planters and in Pennsylvania almost all are farmers, except the merchants and mechanics living in Philadelphia. As for piety, they are for the most part sufficiently assiduous in the exercises of religion and in frequenting the sacraments, but they lack that fervor, which frequent appeals to the sentiment of piety usually produce, as many congregations hear the word of God only once a month, and sometimes only once in two months. We are reduced to this by want of priests, by the distance of congregations from each other and by difficulty of travelling. This refers to Catholics born here, for the condition of the Catholics who in great numbers are flowing in here from different countries of Europe, is very different. For while there are few of our native Catholics who do not approach the sacraments of Penance and the Holy Eucharist, at least once a year, especially in Easter time, you can scarcely find any among the newcomers who discharge this duty of religion, and there is reason to fear that the example will be very pernicious especially in commercial towns. The abuses that have grown among Catholics are chiefly those, which result with unavoidable intercourse with non-Catholics, and the examples thense derived: namely more free intercourse between young people of opposite sexes than is compatible with chastity in mind and body; too great fondness for dances and similar amusements; and an incredible eagerness, especially in girls, for reading love stories which are brought over in great quantities from Europe. Then among other things, a general lack of care in instructing their children and especially the negro slaves in their religion, as these people are kept constantly at work, so that they rarely hear any instructions from the priest, unless they can spend a short time with one; and most of them are consequently very dull in faith and depraved in morals. It can scarcely be believed how much trouble and care they give the pastors of souls.

3. On the Number of Priests, Their Qualifications, Character and Means of Support

There are nineteen priests in Maryland and five in Pennsylvania. Of these two are more than seventy years old, and three others very near that age: and they are consequently almost entirely unfit to undergo the hardships, without which this Vineyard of the Lord cannot be cultivated. Of the remaining priests some are in very bad health, and there is one recently approved by me for a few months only, that in the extreme want of priests I may give him

a trial: for some things were reported of him, which made me averse to employing him. I will watch him carefully, and if anything occurs unworthy of priestly gravity I will recall the faculties granted, whatever inconvenience this may bring to many Catholics: for I am convinced that the Catholic faith will suffer less harm, if for a short time there is no priest at a place, than if living as we do among fellow-citizens of another religion, we admit to the discharge of the sacred ministry, I do not say bad priests, but incautious and imprudent priests. All the other clergymen lead a life full of labour, as each one attends congregations far apart, and has to be riding constantly and with great fatigue, especially to sick calls. Priests are maintained chiefly from the proceeds of the estates; elsewhere by the liberality of the Catholics. There is properly no ecclesiastical property here: for the property by which the priests are supported, is held in the names of individuals and transferred by will to devisees. This course was rendered necessary when the Catholic religion was cramped here by laws, and no remedy has yet been found for this difficulty, although we made an earnest effort last year.

There is a college in Philadelphia, and it is proposed to establish two in Maryland, in which Catholics can be admitted, as well as others, as presidents, professors and pupils. We hope that some educated there will embrace the ecclesiastical state. We think accordingly of establishing a Seminary, in which they can be trained to the life and learning suited to that state.

John Carroll

March 1, 1785

(*Source:* John Tracy Ellis, ed. *Documents of American Catholic History.* Vol. 1:1493–1865. Wilmington, Del.: Michael Glazier, 1987, 147–50.)

CARROLL, JOHN PATRICK (1864–1925)

Second bishop of Helena, Montana. Carroll was born on February 22, 1864, in Dubuque, Iowa, to Martin Carroll and Catherine O'Farrell Carroll. He attended the local parish school and St. Joseph College, graduating in 1883. He earned his Doctor of Divinity degree at the Grand Séminaire in Montreal and was ordained there on July 7, 1889. He taught at St. Joseph's and was president from 1894 to 1904. He was consecrated bishop of Helena on December 21, 1904, in Dubuque and installed on January 30, 1905, in Helena.

He expanded Catholic institutions in Helena, founding a boys' high school and college in 1909 to develop a native clergy. It is now Carroll College. He built a new cathedral, St. Helena Cathedral, which was started in 1908 and consecrated in 1924. Thirty parishes were established and fifty churches were built during his episcopacy. The bishop encouraged the Norbertines and the archbishop of Cashel, Ireland, to send priests and invited eight religious communities to Montana. Diocesan priests increased from twenty-four to eighty-nine, parochial schools from nine to twenty-three, and hospitals from five to nine.

He died of a stroke November 4, 1925, while traveling to Rome for an *ad limina* visit.

See also MONTANA, CATHOLIC CHURCH IN.

Flaherty, Cornelia M. *Go with Haste into the Mountains, a History of the Diocese of Helena.* Diocese of Helena with Falcon Press Publishing Co., 1984.
Palladino, L. B., S.J. *Indian and White in the Northwest.* Baltimore: John Murphy & Company, 1894.
Schoenberg, Wilfred P., S.J. *A History of the Catholic Church in the Pacific Northwest.* Washington, D.C.: Pastoral Press, 1987.

M. CATHERINE TILZEY

CARSON, CHRISTOPHER "KIT" (1809–68)

Frontiersman, trapper, guide, Indian agent, soldier. Carson was born on December 24, 1809, in Madison County, Kentucky, the fifth of ten children to Revolutionary War veteran Lindsay Carson and his second wife, Rebecca Robinson. In 1811 the family moved to Boone's Lick, Missouri, where, in 1818, Carson's father was killed in an accident. Carson's mother apprenticed him to a Franklin, Missouri, saddler, David Workman in 1825, but Carson ran away in 1826, joined an expedition to Santa Fe in New Mexico and continued on to Taos where he worked at various jobs.

Carson converted to Catholicism after being persuaded by Padre Antonio José Martinez that it was necessary if Carson wanted to court and marry Josefa Jaramillo. Josefa was born in 1830 in Río Arriba County, New Mexico, to Don Francisco Jaramillo and Apolonia Vigil, one of the most prominent Spanish Catholic families in the Southwest. Carson was baptized on January 28, 1842, and married Josefa on February 6, 1843, in Guadalupe Church, with Padre Martinez presiding and George Bent as a canonical witness.

During the conquest of California, Carson was active against Mexican forces and Native Americans until U.S. forces captured Los Angeles in August of 1846. Ordered by General Stephen Kearny to remain as a guide, Carson fought at the battle of San Pasqual, escaped through the lines with Lieutenant Edward Fitzgerald Beale to bring reinforcements from San Diego, and, in January of 1847, fought in the battles to recapture Los Angeles.

After returning to Taos, Carson fought Native Americans and took up farming until the summer of 1853 when, while driving sheep to Sacramento, Carson discovered he had been appointed an Indian agent in Taos to two tribes of Utes. For more than seven years, Carson served the Utes well. He was also called upon to serve as an army guide and to help negotiate peace with the Cheyenne, Arapaho, and Navaho. Around 1856, Carson, who was illiterate, dictated a brief autobiography to Army surgeon Lieutenant-Colonel De Witt C. Peters.

At the beginning of the Civil War, Carson resigned as an Indian agent and organized the First New Mexican Volunteer Infantry. He was commissioned a lieutenant-colonel in July 1861, and promoted to full colonel in September. He fought in the battle of Valverde on February 21, 1862, in campaigns against Mescalero Apaches and Navahos in 1862 and against the Kiowas and Comanches during the fall of 1864. In his final battle at Adobe Walls in Texas on November 25, 1864, Carson, with four hundred men, attacked between three thousand and five thousand Native Americans. For his wartime service, he was commissioned a brevet brigadier general in March, 1865. During the summer of 1866 Carson received command of Fort Garland in western Colorado but, suffering from a tracheal tumor, he resigned his commission and was mustered out in November of 1866. In the spring of 1868, he and his family moved to Boggsville, Colorado, where he was appointed Superintendent of Indian Affairs for the Colorado Territory and was immediately invited to Washington, D.C., to confer with a deputation of Utes. During the trip Carson sought medical attention in Boston and New York, but without success. He returned home in early April and, on April 23, Josefa died. Carson, his health declining, was moved to Fort Lyon on May 14, where he died on May 23, 1868.

Carter, Harvey Lewis. *'Dear Old Kit': The Historical Christopher Carson.* Norman: University of Oklahoma Press, 1968.
Estergreen, M. Morgan. *Kit Carson: A Portrait in Courage.* Norman: University of Oklahoma Press, 1962.
Guild, Thelma S., and Harvey L. Carter. *Kit Carson: A Pattern for Heroes.* Lincoln: University of Nebraska Press, 1984.
Peters, De Witt C. *The Life and Adventures of Kit Carson, the Nestor of the Rocky Mountains.* New York: W.R.C. Clark and Co., 1858.

DONALD L. STELLUTO

CARTIER, JACQUES (1491–1557)

Explorer. In April 1534, ten years after Verrazano returned from his exploration of the coast of North America for France, a Breton navigator, Jacques Cartier, sailed for the New World. He reached Newfoundland and sailed up the St. Lawrence River, believing he had found a new route to China and the East Indies.

Returning to North America the following spring, Cartier entered the Gulf of St. Lawrence and ascended the river to the later site of Quebec, a rocky promontory on its northern banks. The natives greeted his arrival with curiosity and friendship, but tried to dissuade him from going further by warning him of unseen dangers.

Cartier ignored them and took his smallest galleon up river as far as navigable, then advanced in small boats to a large settlement where a thousand natives thronged the shore in greeting. The settlement was Hochelaga, later to be the site of Montreal, after the name Cartier gave to a nearby mountain. As winter approached, Cartier retraced his course to Stadacona (Quebec), and waited out the winter. There scurvy struck his company and twenty-five men died before the disease was checked. When spring arrived, Cartier headed back to France, taking with him by force some of the native chiefs who had befriended him.

Then in May 1541 Cartier crossed the Atlantic once again and moved up the St. Lawrence. Other ships in the expedition were delayed and did not reach Newfoundland until April 1542.

At the harbor of St. John they met Cartier's ships on their way home. Cartier, discouraged by sickness among his company, a new aloofness among the natives, and the dim economic prospects for the colony, had abandoned New France. Contrary to orders, he escaped with his vessels under cover of night and returned to France for good.

Nonetheless, he had opened up the door to the interior of the American continent for later French explorers, missionaries, and settlers. They were to spread the French flag and the Catholic faith from the St. Lawrence westward to the Great Lakes and beyond, and southward down the Mississippi to New Orleans in the following centuries. He died in St.-Malo, France, on September 1, 1557.

LaRoncière, Charles. *Jacques Cartier et la découverte de la Nouvelle-France.* Paris, 1931.

JAMES HALEY

CASEY, SOLANUS (1870–1957)

Capuchin friar and healer. Casey was born on November 25, 1870, near Prescott, Wisconsin. He was one of the sixteen children of Irish immigrants Bernard and Ellen Murphy Casey. Young Bernard grew to manhood on the family's Wisconsin farm, and later worked as a sawmill laborer, prison guard, and streetcar conductor. The last of these jobs took him to Superior, Wisconsin, where he experienced his call to the priesthood.

His formal education having stopped after eighth grade, the twenty-year old Bernard was sent to the "German" seminary of St. Francis de Sales in Milwaukee to prepare for the diocesan priesthood. Five years later, his mediocre grades and an inadequate grasp of German and Latin resulted in his dismissal. The faculty still believed in his vocation, however, and urged him to seek admittance into a religious community. He took the Capuchin habit in Detroit on January 14, 1897, and was given the name "Solanus." At the end of his novitiate in July of 1898, he entered the Capuchin seminary in Milwaukee.

Venerable Solanus Casey

His difficulty with foreign languages made progress in theological studies difficult. Convinced of his religious fervor, yet concerned that Solanus' grasp of Church doctrine was less than adequate, the Capuchin superiors decided to ordain him a "priest simplex" or "Mass priest." Faculties to preach and to hear confessions were to be withheld. Fr. Solanus would be able to deliver only informal religious talks and could never speak on Catholic doctrine. He could hear confessions only in cases of dire emergency, and only when no other priest might be available. Accepting these humbling conditions, Fr. Solanus was ordained by Archbishop Sebastian Messmer on July 24, 1904, in Milwaukee's Capuchin Church of St. Francis.

After an initial assignment as sacristan and porter at Sacred Heart Friary in Yonkers, New York, he was sent in July 1918, to Our Lady of Sorrows Friary in Manhattan. Here he was once again named sacristan, as well as director of the Young Ladies' Sodality. Three years later he found himself at Our Lady of the Angels Friary in Harlem. It was here that Fr. Solanus' name began to be known outside the friary walls.

Those visitors to the monastery who sought divine favors were often urged by Fr. Solanus to enroll themselves or a loved one in the Franciscan "Seraphic Mass Association." In so doing, they would share in the spiritual benefits from the Masses offered by Capuchins worldwide. Word began to spread of favors received by those personally enrolled by Fr. Solanus. The friar always denied any personal involvement in the obtaining of favors, pointing instead to the divine power that flows from the Mass. Yet his admirers noted his evident holiness of life and his frequent ability to foretell the future. He would often name the hour that one person might recover from an illness, or the fact that another individual would succumb. Remarkable stories of healings and conversions reached the ears of the provincial, Fr. Benno Aichinger, who in turn commanded Fr. Solanus to keep a detailed record of special favors granted through the Seraphic Mass Association.

Solanus was transferred to St. Bonaventure Friary in Detroit in August of 1924. From here the priest's reputation as a miracle worker spread even further. The porter was given the additional responsibility of blessing the sick with a relic of the True Cross at special Wednesday afternoon services. During the depression years, he often led "begging" expeditions in the city, on behalf of the friary's soup kitchen. His devotion to Christ in the Eucharist and to the Blessed Mother was well known. Lengthy periods of prayer before the tabernacle lay at the heart of his spirituality.

By 1945, with his health beginning to fail, Solanus was sent into semiretirement at St. Michael's Friary in Brooklyn. A further transfer to St. Felix Friary in Huntingdon, Indiana, followed in April of 1946. His increasing feebleness necessitated medical trips to Detroit. Although he celebrated his fiftieth anniversary of ordination on a visit to Detroit, his final transfer to the city did not occur until May 10, 1956. On the following January 14, he celebrated the sixtieth anniversary of his entrance into community. Death occurred in Detroit on July 31, 1957, after a one-month hospital stay.

On June 19, 1982, the Cause for Sainthood of Fr. Solanus Casey was officially approved by Pope John Paul II. Recognition of the relics occurred on July 8, 1987, at which time Fr. Solanus' body was removed from the friary cemetery, clothed in a new habit, and reinterred in St. Bonaventure Church. Final documentation was submitted to the Congregation for the Causes of Saints on October 10, 1992.

See also FRANCISCANS (CAPUCHINS).

Derum, James Patrick. *The Porter of Saint Bonaventure's.* Detroit: Fidelity Press, 1968.

ALBERT H. LEDOUX

CASTAÑEDA, CARLOS (1896–1958)

Historian, educator. Carlos Eduardo Castañeda was born in Camargo, Mexico, on November 11, 1896. He moved to the United States in 1908, and received his Ph.D. from the University of Texas, Austin, in 1932. He became a naturalized citizen in 1936, he taught at The Catholic University of America, the University of Mexico, the College of William and Mary, and the University of Texas, where he remained from 1946 until his death in 1958. He received a Doctor of Laws, *honoris causa,* in 1941 from St. Edward's University, and in 1951 from The Catholic University of America.

Castañeda wrote over eighty articles and pamphlets as well as the seven-volume *Our Catholic Heritage in Texas, 1519–1950* (1936–58), for which he is best known. Additionally, Castañeda wrote *The Mexican Side of the Texan Revolution* (1928) and *The Finding of Texas* (1939). He served as president of the American Catholic Historical Association from 1939–40, and was regional director for the Fair Employment Practices Committee in the Southwest during World War II. He was made a Knight of the Equestrian Order of the Holy Sepulchre by Pope Pius XII in 1941, and a Knight Commander of the Order of Isabel the Catholic of Spain at the recommendation of the Spanish Academy in 1950. He was a member of Phi Beta Kappa, served on the board of editors of the *Hispanic American Historical Review,* and was an advisory editor of *The Americas,* published by the Academy of American Franciscan History. He was a delegate to the First Congress of Historians of the United States and Mexico, and to the First Congress of Philosophy held in Mendoza, Argentina, in 1948.

ANN DOWART

CATALA, MAGIN (1761–1830)

Missionary. Fray Catalá was born on January 29, 1761, at Montblanch (Tarragona province), Spain, and entered the Franciscan Order in Barcelona on April 4, 1777. After studies in Barcelona he was ordained in Gerona in February 1785. Having read about the order's missions in Mexico and California, he volunteered for that apostolate and in the autumn of 1786 sailed from Cádiz and most probably arrived in Veracruz, Mexico, at the end of that year. He spent the next six years at the Apostolic College of San Fernando in Mexico City, where he studied mission methods and Native American languages, and preached missions to the local people.

California Missionary

In 1793 he was appointed to the Native American missions in Upper California, but on his arrival in Monterey he was assigned as chaplain to a Spanish vessel making an expeditionary trip to Nootka Sound (Vancouver Island, Canada). After the ship's return he went (August 1794) to the Santa Clara mission, the eighth (founded in 1777) in the long chain of California missions, and there spent the remaining thirty-six years of his life.

Not long after his arrival, Fray Catalá was afflicted with inflammatory rheumatism that increasingly debilitated him to the extent that he had great difficulty in walking and riding. This, however, did not keep him from visiting the neighboring missions or traveling as far as the San Joaquin Valley, some hundred miles distant, to search out unconverted natives and invite them to the Christian mission or to one of the indigenous rancherias that surrounded it. In view of his health, he left the management of the material aspects of the mission to others, for the most part, and concentrated on the mission's spiritual life, namely, instructing catechumens, catechizing neophytes, and administering the sacraments. The Santa Clara mission was one of the best regulated, and no California mission recorded as many baptisms, or marriages, or deaths. Fray Catalá, from September 1, 1794, to October 27, 1827, personally performed 3,067 baptisms and 1,905 marriages.

Holy Man of Santa Clara

During the last two years of his life, when he could no longer ascend the pulpit or stand at the altar rail, he spoke to his flock from a chair placed in front of the rail. After an exemplary, industrious, and edifying life, he died on November 22, 1830, and was buried on the following day in the sanctuary of the mission church he had built. So revered was he in life that the mission native peoples referred to him as the "Holy Man of Santa Clara." Many interesting incidents are associated with his life, but the more fascinating ones are his prophecies. He was known to interrupt his instructions and sermons and ask his audience to pray for someone who was, at that moment, dying. Later news verified that the individuals for whom he had prayed, had died at the moment he had requested the prayers. He likewise predicted that a large city would rise on the site of Yerba Buena and that the houses built there would be destroyed by earthquake and fire. Yerba Buena became San Francisco in 1847, and in 1906 it suffered earthquake and fire. Because of the manifest devotion that the native peoples continued to show toward Fray Catalá, Archbishop Joseph Alemany of San Francisco initiated the cause for his beatification in 1884.

See also CALIFORNIA, CATHOLIC CHURCH IN; FRANCISCAN FRIARS.

Engelhardt, Zephyrin, O.F.M. *The Holy Man of Santa Clara or Life, Virtues, and Miracles of Fr. Magin Catala, O.F.M.* San Francisco: James Barry, 1909.

The Laurelwood Mission: A Documentary History of Santa Clara de Asís. Published by Francis J. Weber, editor. 1–2, 117–20, 136–38.

McKevitt, Gerald, S.J. *The University of Santa Clara: A History 1851–1977.* California: Stanford University, 1979.

Tylenda, Joseph N., S.J. "Beloved of God and Men: Father Magín Catalá, O.F.M. (1761–1830)." *Portraits of American Sanctity.* Chicago: Franciscan Herald, 1982, 122–33.

Weber, Francis J. *Catholic Footprints in California.* Newhall, Calif.: Hogarth, 1970, 128–30.

JOSEPH TYLENDA, S.J.

CATALDO, JOSEPH M. (1837–1928)

Missionary. Born in Terrasini, Sicily, Cataldo joined the Society of Jesus in Palermo at the age of fifteen. Turmoil associated with the unification of Italy brought about the expulsion of the Jesuits from the island, however, and Cataldo

had to complete his formation in Rome. Here he volunteered to join the Jesuit's Rocky Mountain Mission in America. Accepted, Cataldo had to first complete his theological studies in Louvain, Belgium, where he was ordained, and then learn English in Boston. During his first winter in America, Cataldo developed an illness that doctors diagnosed as tuberculosis. As a result, in 1863 his superiors sent him to Santa Clara College to recover his health. The climate in California agreed with Cataldo, so much so that by 1865 he could reinstate himself as a volunteer for the Rocky Mountain Mission. Assigned to work among the Coeur d'Alenes and Spokanes, Cataldo ultimately became most closely associated with the Nez Perces of present-day Idaho. Except for brief excursions to Alaska and Europe, Cataldo essentially lived the rest of his life in the Pacific Northwest.

Slight of build, the Native Americans called Cataldo "Dried Salmon." The appearance deceived because the priest exhibited not frailty but uncommon energy as a missionary. A tireless and fearless traveler, even into his eighties, Cataldo never allowed inclement weather, unimproved roads, or threats of warfare to halt his rounds to the native villages. It was not in Cataldo's nature to be overtly loving or sensitive, and that included his confreres in the society, yet the native peoples recognized in him an honesty and devotion they respected. When Chief Joseph made his decision in 1877 to abandon his homeland rather than accept a smaller reservation, his obvious esteem for Cataldo's counsel led some federal agents to blame the priest for the Nez Perce war that followed.

Cataldo was an extraordinarily effective missionary. To begin, he came to his assignment well prepared. While living at Santa Clara College, Cataldo learned the customs of the Rocky Mountain tribes from Fr. Gregory Mengarini, S.J., a missionary who had gone west in 1841 with Fr. Peter John De Smet, S.J. With each passing year Cataldo increased his knowledge and sensitivity to the culture of the native peoples. Second, Cataldo had a facility for learning languages and he quickly mastered ten native tongues. Cataldo's presence at a camp or a council assured there would be open communication. Finally, Cataldo earned the regard of tribal leaders when, as superior of the Rocky Mountain Mission from 1877 to 1893, he dedicated himself to bringing education to their people. Cataldo not only established boarding schools at a dozen reservations, but he also recruited priests and sisters to staff them and he founded Gonzaga College as a central boys' school to integrate native students with whites.

Carriker, Robert C. "Joseph M. Cataldo, S.J.: Courier of Catholicism to the Nez Perces." *Churchmen and the Western Indians,* eds. Clyde A. Milner and Floyd A. O'Neil. Norman: University of Oklahoma Press, 1985.

____. "Direct Successor to De Smet: Joseph M. Cataldo, S.J. and the Stabilization of the Jesuit Indian Missions of the Pacific Northwest, 1877–1893." *Idaho Yesterdays* 31 (1–2) (Spring/Summer 1987).

The Cataldo papers are in the archives of the Oregon Province of the Society of Jesus.

ROBERT C. CARRIKER

CATHOLIC BIBLICAL ASSOCIATION (CBA)

A scholarly society for the service of the faith through the promotion of biblical scholarship.

Origin

The formation of the Catholic Biblical Association (CBA) was, in a sense, a byproduct of the desire of Bishop Edwin V. O'Hara, chair of the Episcopal Committee on the Confraternity of Christian Doctrine, to have the Challoner-Rheims New Testament (NT) revised. Early in 1936 O'Hara called a meeting of American Catholic Scripture scholars who should help to plan and implement the project. On the occasion of this meeting a proposal was presented to form a permanent association of American Catholic biblical scholars and the group readily agreed to act on it. A group of about fifty scholars met on October 3, 1936, and by their vote brought the Catholic Biblical Association of America into existence. Edward P. Arbez was elected its first president and Bishop O'Hara was accorded the unofficial title of "Father and Founder" of the CBA. A committee was appointed to draw up a constitution and bylaws, and these were approved and adopted in 1937. It was incorporated in the District of Columbia in 1941 and reincorporated in 1958. Initially the CBA was under the patronage of the Confraternity of Christian Doctrine (CCD). While the translation and revision of the Bible were in the forefront of concerns in the early years (and continues to be an important work of the association), the broader purposes are to promote the scholarly study of the Bible through meetings and publications, and to disseminate the fruits of genuine biblical scholarship to other scholars and to the faithful.

Bible Translation

O'Hara's aim of revising the Challoner-Rheims NT, based on the Vulgate (Vlg), was realized by the publication, in 1941, of the CCD NT; in the meantime work had begun on revising the Old Testament (OT), again based on the Vlg. But in 1943 the publication of *Divino Afflante Spiritu,* with its emphasis on the importance of biblical scholarship and recourse to biblical languages, encouraged the switch to a totally new translation of both OT and NT from the original languages. The Book of Genesis appeared in 1948, and other sections of the OT followed at intervals. In the final stages the work took on a more ecumenical aspect, with contributions from non-Catholic Scripture scholars, and when the completed work, including the NT, appeared in 1970, it was given the title "The New American Bible" (NAB). This translation, in addition to its use for private study and devotion and for study in formal classes, was incorporated into the lectionary used for Mass throughout the United States. Further work was undertaken to revise the NAB NT, and this revision was completed in 1987. A revision of the NAB Psalter was begun in 1988; the work was completed and approved in 1991. Revision of the rest of the OT was begun in 1994.

Membership

From its early meeting of fifty scholars the CBA has grown to almost thirteen hundred active and associate members. Active members must have the Licentiate in Sacred Scripture (S.S.L.) from the Pontifical Biblical Institute in Rome or the equivalent in graduate training or publication; associate members must have done graduate studies in Scripture or have taught Scripture for a specified time on the major seminary or college level. There are no confessional restrictions for membership, and many non-Catholics and Jews are members of and active in the association. A general meeting of the association is held each year, normally in August; meeting activities include the presentation of papers, seminars, task forces (groups which concentrate on a particular area of study over a period of years), panel discussions, and reports on work in progress. There are various regional chapters. The CBA also promotes biblical study by providing some support to scholarship students in doctoral Scripture programs, to young scholars after graduation, and by providing help in funding archeological digs.

The CBA is a constuent society of the Council of Societies for the Study of Religion and a member of the Joint Committee of Catholic Learned Societies and Scholars.

Publications

The Catholic Biblical Quarterly is the official organ of the CBA; its first issue appeared in 1939. It carries scholarly articles and notes in Scripture and related fields, an extensive book review section, as well as news of the association's annual meeting and other pertinent notices; its circulation is worldwide and in excess of four thousand. The first volume of the Catholic Biblical Quarterly—Monograph Series appeared in 1971 and additional volumes have been published regularly since then. *Old Testament Abstracts* began to be published in 1978. It provides summaries and bibliographical information on articles and books in all major languages from all over the world; in 1995 almost three thousand books and articles were abstracted; its worldwide circulation is in excess of two thousand.

See also ARBEZ, EDWARD PHILIP; CATHOLIC BIBLICAL SCHOLARSHIP IN AMERICA; O'HARA, EDWIN.

Fogarty, Gerald P. *American Catholic Biblical Scholarship: A History from the Early Republic to Vatican II.* San Francisco: Harper and Row, 1989, 222–29 and passim.

Jensen, Joseph, O.S.B. "Fifty-Six and Counting." *Supplement to The Catholic American Biblical Quarterly* 54 (1992) 15–16.

Rossiter, Francis S. "Forty Years Less One: An Historical Sketch of the C.B.A. (1936–1975)." *Supplement to The Catholic Biblical Quarterly* 54 (1992) 1–14.

JOSEPH JENSEN, O.S.B.

CATHOLIC BIBLICAL SCHOLARSHIP IN AMERICA

Catholic biblical scholars seek to understand the texts of sacred Scripture in their own time and on their own terms (historical criticism), to make clear the language and literary character of these texts (literary criticism), and to help theologians, preachers, teachers, and the People of God as a whole to grasp better the possibilities and challenges posed by the texts (biblical theology). In the U.S.A. Catholic biblical scholarship has been influenced strongly by official documents of the Roman Catholic Church about biblical matters and at times has interacted creatively with persons and movements in American religious and cultural history.

Before 1943

The two papal encyclicals that gave direction to American (and other) Catholics in biblical study during the late nineteenth and early twentieth centuries were Pope Leo XIII's *Providentissimus Deus* (1893), which warned especially against Rationalism, and Pope Benedict XV's *Spiritus Paraclitus* (1920), which warned against Modernism. Both encyclicals encouraged scientific biblical study but always within the framework of the Catholic theological tradition.

The best scientific Catholic biblical scholarship of the time was done by Marie-Joseph Lagrange, O.P., and his coworkers at the Ecole Biblique de Jérusalem (founded in 1890). These French Dominicans were among the first serious archeologists and explorers of the Holy Land. They were also aware of the new literary-critical studies on the Pentateuch and the Gospels in Germany, and tried to mediate some of their perspectives to Catholics. Due in part to ecclesiastical suspicions toward Lagrange and his colleagues, the Jesuits were asked to found the Pontifical Biblical Institute in Rome (in 1909) and so strongly influenced the training of many American Catholic teachers and scholars.

The history of American Catholic biblical scholarship from the early republic (John Carroll) to Vatican II has been admirably chronicled and interpreted by Gerald P. Fogarty, S.J. The major figures in his story include Francis P. Kenrick who in the mid-1800s produced new English translations based on the Latin Vulgate; Henry Poels who contended that the Pentateuch was a compilation of several sources put together after Moses' time and was forced to leave his teaching post at The Catholic University of America in 1910; Francis Gigot, S.S., whose positions on certain biblical matters aroused opposition among conservative American Catholic theologians and ecclesiastics in the early 1900s; Charles A. Briggs, a famous and controversial Protestant scholar, who tried unsuccessfully to mediate on behalf of liberal Catholics against the charges of Modernism; and Bishop Edward V. O'Hara who in 1936 set in motion the project to prepare a new American translation of the Bible.

To avoid charges of Modernism (and perhaps reflecting the marginal social status of most immigrant Catholics), American Catholic biblical scholars in this period were cautious and conservative. Almost all were priests, trained in Europe, and serving as seminary professors. The center of the seminary curriculum was dogmatic theology—for which biblical scholars supplied prooftexts for apologetical arguments. Catholic scholars appealed especially to patristic and other Church traditions in their argumentation. The professors at the only research-oriented university—The Catholic University of America—were watched closely with respect to orthodoxy since the Poels affair. On the whole, there was little or no ecumenical outreach to biblical scholars of other denominations (who in turn looked upon Catholic scholars as saying what they were told to say).

The genius of American Catholicism (some say) has been its ability to create and sustain institutions that have had lasting impact for its people. Shortly before World War II Catholic biblical scholars began two institutions that continue to shape biblical scholarship in the U.S.A. In 1936 the Catholic Biblical Association of America was founded to promote scientific biblical study among Catholics, with the express purpose of revising the Rheims-Douay-Challoner Bible, then the only version approved for English-speaking Catholics. In 1939 the first fascicle of the *Catholic Biblical Quarterly* appeared. Although the early issues were somewhat parochial in their topics, methods, and viewpoints, this journal would eventually provide an important outlet for the best scientific scholarship that members of the Catholic Biblical Association (and others) would produce in the years to come.

From 1943 to 1965

Pope Pius XII's 1943 encyclical *Divino Afflante Spiritu* marked a new era in Catholic biblical study. It encouraged Catholic biblical scholars to return to the original Hebrew and Greek texts (rather than the Latin Vulgate) in their translations. It urged them to look first for the literal meaning of the biblical texts, to study the Bible in its ancient historical context, and to pay particular attention to the literary forms used by the sacred authors and to the cultural assumptions that they brought to their writings.

These new and now officially approved currents in Catholic biblical scholarship came to post-World War II America most immediately through seminary professors trained at the Pontifical Biblical Institute in Rome and the Ecole Biblique de Jérusalem. They were well expressed in the books and articles of John L. McKenzie, S.J.; Frederick L. Moriarty, S.J.; Bruce Vawter, C.M.; and David M. Stanley, S.J. These scholars and their contemporaries had philological and historical training, read widely in French and German scholarship, wrote in an accessible and attractive way, and influenced the next generation of scholars.

The theological training of several important scholars of the post-Vatican II generation was supplemented by exposure to the literary and archeological remains of the Ancient Near East either at The Catholic University of America under Edward P. Arbez, S.S., or at Johns Hopkins University under the Methodist layman, William Foxwell Albright. The Oriental Seminary directed by Albright was open to Protestant, Catholic, Jewish, and other students. It provided the best training in ancient languages, archeology, and culture done in a broadly humanistic perspective. Not a denominational or specifically religious program, it gave the scholars who studied under Albright a common historical methodology and framework, as well as a network of colleagues that had important implications for the ecumenical openness of American Catholic scholarship after Vatican II.

From 1965 Onward

Vatican II's Dogmatic Constitution on Divine Revelation (*Dei Verbum*) issued in 1965 made its own the major points of *Divino Afflante Spiritu* and the 1964 instruction by the Pontifical Biblical Commission on the historical truth of the Gospels, which insisted that the Gospels be read at three levels: Jesus, the early church, and the evangelists. It also emphasized the primacy of God's self-revelation in Scripture, the unity of Scripture and tradition, the importance of the Old Testament, and the central role of Scripture in Catholic theology and life.

The official endorsement of the new directions in Catholic biblical scholarship by a conciliar statement of the highest theological rank gave a burst of energy to American scholars that has continued and grown even stronger. After many years of planning and drafting, the *New American Bible* was completed in 1970 by members of the Catholic Biblical Association (including a few Protestant scholars). A revised version of the New Testament appeared in 1986, and the Old Testament is in the process of revision. The Catholic Biblical Association became increasingly attractive to non-Catholics because of its scholarly seriousness, intellectual openness, and concern with theological matters. The *Catholic Biblical Quarterly* quickly became one of the most respected scholarly journals in the world, and its pages were opened to all competent scholars. Two of the most important bibliographical tools—*New Testament Abstracts* (1956–) and *Old Testament Abstracts* (1978–)—are produced under Catholic auspices. Testimony to the sophistication and maturity of Catholic biblical scholarship in the U.S.A. as well as to its pastoral sensitivity can be found especially in *The Jerome Biblical Commentary* (1968) and in its revised version (about 70 percent new) entitled *The New Jerome Biblical Commentary* (1990), as well as in *The Collegeville Bible Commentary* (1989). These large one-volume commentaries treat the entire Bible, synthesizing modern scholarship and making it available to teachers, preachers, and all who wish to study Scripture.

Individual American Catholic biblical scholars who achieved international prominence since Vatican II include Patrick W. Skehan on the Dead Sea scrolls; Mitchell Dahood, S.J., on the Psalms and Ugaritic poetry; Roland E. Murphy, O. Carm., on the Wisdom literature; Elisabeth Schüssler Fiorenza on feminist hermeneutics and the role of women in early Christianity; and John P. Meier on the historical Jesus. But the two most prominent U.S. Catholic biblical scholars since Vatican II have been Raymond E. Brown, S.S., and Joseph A. Fitzmyer, S.J. Brown wrote massive commentaries on John's Gospel (1966, 1970), the Gospel infancy narratives (1977), the Johannine epistles (1982), and the passion narratives (1994). Fitzmyer produced classic commentaries on Luke's Gospel (1981, 1985) and Romans (1994), and established himself as one of the foremost experts on Aramaic and on the Dead Sea scrolls. Brown and Fitzmyer (both products of the Albright program at Johns Hopkins) collaborated with Catholic and Protestant exegetes on *Peter in the New Testament* (1973) and *Mary in the New Testament* (1978)—books that showed that exegetes from different denominational backgrounds could come to basic agreement on topics that had long separated the Churches.

Since Vatican II Catholic biblical scholars have been active participants and chief officers in the larger nondenominational biblical organizations: the Society of Biblical Literature, the Society for New Testament Studies, and the American Schools of Oriental Research. They have been invited to contribute to various projects sponsored by these organizations and to be part of the editorial teams for the Nag Hammadi documents and the Dead Sea scrolls. Catholic biblical scholarship in the U.S.A. retained its roots in and commitment to the Church while cooperating in the wider ventures that constitute international and interconfessional biblical scholarship.

Since Vatican II Catholic biblical scholarship in the U.S.A. has become less clerical and more representative of the Church's membership. Up to 1965 almost all Catholic biblical scholars were priests trained in a few Catholic institutions. Since then there has been a dramatic involvement of lay scholars trained at various universities (Harvard, Yale, Chicago, Notre Dame, Louvain, etc.). Perhaps in part because they were excluded from priestly ordination, many American Catholic women have pursued academic training in theology and have become especially prominent in biblical studies. The new generation of Catholic biblical scholars in the U.S.A. is engaged in all the new directions of biblical research: Jesus research, social-science interpretation, feminist hermeneutics, rhetorical criticism, etc. What they do is best explained by the Pontifical Biblical Commission's 1993 document entitled *The Interpretation of the Bible in the Church.*

See also CATHOLIC BIBLICAL ASSOCIATION (CBA).

Bergant, D., and R. J. Karris, eds. *The Collegeville Bible Commentary.* Collegeville: The Liturgical Press, 1989.

Brown, R. E., J. A. Fitzmyer, and R. E. Murphy, eds. *The Jerome Biblical Commentary.* Englewood Cliffs, N.J.: Prentice-Hall, 1968.

_____. *The New Jerome Biblical Commentary.* Englewood Cliffs, N.J.: Prentice-Hall, 1990.

Collins J. J., and J. D. Crossan, eds. *The Biblical Heritage in Modern Catholic Scholarship.* Wilmington, Del.: Glazier, 1986.

Fogarty, G. P. *American Catholic Biblical Scholarship: A History from the Early Republic to Vatican II.* San Francisco: Harper & Row, 1989.

Senior, D. P., ed. *The Catholic Study Bible.* New York: Oxford, 1990.

DANIEL J. HARRINGTON, S.J.

CATHOLIC BOOK PUBLISHING

There was practically no Catholic publishing in colonial America. The restrictive anti-Catholic laws in most of the thirteen colonies had little or nothing to do with it. There was no publishing as there weren't enough Catholics to support it. Prior to 1776 some Catholic literature was imported by individuals, but only eight titles were printed in the colonies, and these were mostly sponsored by a few missionaries. We know that in 1774 Robert Molyneux, S.J., arranged the publication of Challoner's *Garden of the Soul* and sponsored Robert Bell's printing of *A Manual of Catholic Prayers.* Works by Thomas More and Fénelon and *The Imitation of Christ* were among the other titles that comprise the totality of Catholic publishing in colonial times.

The Beginning

Christopher Talbot of Philadelphia is recorded as the first American Catholic publisher as in 1784 he published Joseph Reeve's *New History of the Old and New Testament.* However the first publisher of any significance was Matthew Carey (1760–1839). He was born in Dublin and as a young man he was sought for writing a seditious pamphlet and fled to Paris where he met Benjamin Franklin

and Lafayette from whom he borrowed some money that he used to start a printing business on his return to Dublin where again he became enmeshed in anti-English activities and was jailed in Newgate Prison. On his release he fled to Philadelphia, became a private publisher, and issued the first American edition of the *Douay Bible.* He became prominent for his political opinions and created a variegated publishing company which published both secular and religious titles.

Eugene Commiskey followed Carey's lead in Philadelphia, and published over sixty-four titles including a series of bibles, *The Catholic Family Library,* and Lingard's *History of England.* Fielding Lucas Jr., who had worked with Matthew Carey, brought Catholic publishing to some prominence in Baltimore. He subsidized his Catholic publications by successfully marketing secular titles including maps and atlases. From 1833 to 1837 he issued the *Catholic Almanac and Laity's Directory.* In the course of his working career Lucas was a Protestant and became a Catholic during his final illness.

Immigrants

The nineteenth was the century of immigrants, and their coming transformed every facet of American life and changed the course of Catholic publishing. In 1830 there were 318,000 Catholics in America; by 1840 they numbered 630,000; and by 1850 there were between 1,088,000 and 1,606,000. Successive waves of Irish, German, and Italian immigrants dramatically altered the demographic composition of the United States, and by 1900 there were 12,000,000 Catholics, comprising 15.5 percent of the population. With this ongoing growth the scope of Catholic publishing expanded.

Eugene Willging (1909–65), who pioneered the serious study of Catholic magazine, newspaper, and book publishing, estimated that 9,122 books were published between 1831 and 1900. Many of these were catechetical, scriptural, liturgical, and devotional, and some were American editions of works that originated in England and Ireland. Boston, New York, and Philadelphia were the principal publishing centers. Apart from Fielding Lucas Jr., mentioned above, the list of publishers included: Donahoe (Boston); Pustet, Kenedy, Sadlier, Benziger, Shea, Dunigan (New York); McGrath, Dunnigham (Philadelphia); Kelly, Pret, Hedien, O'Brien (Baltimore). There were many others less notable; and some of the publishing houses that survived into the twentieth century dominated the scene in the second half of one century and the first half of another.

Nineteenth and Twentieth Centuries

John Kenedy (1794–1866), an immigrant from Kilkenny, Ireland, published an abridged edition of Rodriguez's *The Practice of Christian Perfection* in Baltimore in 1832. Thus began a publishing dynasty which lasted over a century and a quarter. Moving to New York, he opened a bookstore and trained his son, Patrick John (1843–1906), in the basics of the book trade. On his father's death, Patrick John reincorporated the company as P. J. Kenedy & Sons and expanded the publishing list with a steady flow of liturgical, biographical, and devotional titles, and by the acquisition of the inventories of companies in financial trouble.

His sons Louis (1882–1956) and Arthur (1878–1951) expanded the business and their *Official Catholic Directory* (1913–) became the company's most lucrative asset. The last generation of Kenedys in the publishing business established a strong editorial policy and were adept at co-publishing books with foreign publishers particularly with Burns, Oates and Washbourne of London. After Vatican II, the business retrenched and the firm was sold to Crowell Collier Macmillan.

The Benziger imprint appeared on 937 books before 1900. The firm was founded in 1853 by Louis Benziger and his cousin A. N. Aldrich in New York. It was the offshoot of a Swiss company founded by their grandfather and it later became independent and specialized in educational, liturgical, and devotional titles. Branches were founded in Cincinnati (1860) and Chicago (1887) and these catered to German-American parishes and customers. The company expanded to San Francisco (1929) and Boston (1937). It prospered until the post-Vatican II era when liturgical publishing underwent an unprecedented upheaval. It was then acquired by Crowell Collier Macmillan.

Two Irish immigrants, James (d. 1869) and Denis (d. 1885) Sadlier, founded the most durable Catholic publishing house in the United States. In 1840 James went to Montreal and established a Canadian branch. He married Mary Anne Madden (1820–1903) who became a celebrated novelist and the guiding editorial planner in the Sadlier company. The firm had started by serializing Butler's *Lives of the Saints* and the Bible, and gradually became a leading imprint in the textbook field. Over the years, its list was practical and contained such works as *Catholic Directory and Ordo* (1864–96); series on geography and English; *Sadlier's Baltimore Catechism with Study Guides*. As the leading catechetical publisher it later pioneered such formative projects as the *On My Way* series; and Sadlier became the dominant company in the Catholic educational field.

The German-owned firm of B. Herder was a leading publisher and supplier of books and religious goods for the German-American Catholics in the Midwest. Beginning in the 1920s, it promoted more theologically rich spiritual titles and was the publisher of Columba Marmion, O.S.B., and Reginald Garrigou-Lagrange, O.P. Changes in the liturgy and the transformation of Catholic attitudes which followed the Second Vatican Council doomed some companies, including B. Herder of St. Louis and Pustet which had been founded in 1865 in New York. They did not adapt to the new situation.

John Joseph Murphy (1812–80) of Baltimore was a versatile Irish immigrant publisher. Prior to 1900, he published 684 secular and religious titles including almanacs and historical works, and he sold over two million copies of *The Faith of Our Fathers* by Cardinal Gibbons. The company survived until 1934 when it was absorbed by P. J. Kenedy.

The Paulist Fathers played a unique role in Catholic publishing since 1866 when Isaac Hecker (1819–88) launched the Catholic Publication Society in New York. It devoted itself exclusively to book publishing; and, unlike many other houses, it had no affiliated church goods business. Hecker entrusted the running of C.P.S. to Lawrence Keogh (1832–90). Under his direction, the society published almost a thousand titles. After Keogh's death the society declined, reviving after 1913 with the imprint of the Paulist Press, and published literally thousands of pamphlets. Thus the Paulist Press became identified as a pamphlet publisher for almost half a century. Under the aegis of Paulists Alvin Illig and Kevin Lynch, the press was revitalized in the 1960s and became the largest Catholic book publisher in the English-speaking world. In 1962 it acquired the Newman Press and its valuable backlist including *The Ancient Christian Writers* series. The Paulist Press differed from other religious publishers by catering to all sections of the community: theologians, ecumenists, counselors, canonists, women religious, clergy, educators, liturgists, and children.

Expansion and Diversity

The growth of Catholic publishing in the United States during the closing years of the nineteenth century and the opening decade of the twentieth was due to a number of factors: (a) The growth of the Catholic population, which had increased to 12,000,000 by 1900; (b) the increased number of clergy and parishes. From 1830 to 1900 the number of active priests had grown from 232 to almost 10,000. And the growth of religious sisters, working in various educational and charitable activities, leaped from 448 in 1830 to 46,000 in 1900; (c) the Third Plenary Council of Baltimore (1884) had a phenomenal impact on Catholic life. It mandated the establishment of an elementary school and a branch of the Confraternity of Christian Doctrine in every parish, and it also planned the writing of a series of (Baltimore) catechisms which formed the basis of religious education for decades. These events spurred the growth of all areas of book publishing. Catholics saw that education was the gateway to prosperity, and Church leaders sought to make Catholics in the twentieth century an educated community.

Quality and Maturity

The pontificate of Pius X (1903–14) had a profound influence on the Church in America. His liturgical reforms brought changes to the structure of the parish, changed its educational life, and created an upsurge of liturgical and devotional publishing. In 1908 Pope Pius removed the United States from the jurisdiction of Congregatio de Propaganda Fide and removed its mission status. But the Pope's crusade against Modernism was too often handled by officials with more zeal than charity, and this created an environment of suspicion, suppression, and censorship which hampered Catholic intellectual life for two generations. This partly explains why America produced so few notable Catholic scholars in the first half of the twentieth century.

The first important publishing event of the new century was the publication of *The Catholic Encyclopedia* (fifteen volumes and index), published between 1907 and 1914. It was an impressive achievement and proved the maturity and ability of American scholars. Its editors were Charles Herbermann, Edward Pace, Condé Pallen, Thomas Shahan, and John Wynne, S.J. They brought together a distinguished phalanx of contributors from America and elsewhere to create a great reference work which held the field until it was replaced by McGraw-Hill's *New Catholic Encyclopedia* in 1964. (In 1929 two of its editors, Edward Pace and John Wynne, produced *The New Catholic Dictionary* for general use.)

The Liturgical Press, founded in 1925 by the pioneering liturgist Virgil Michel, O.S.B., was one of the most influential Catholic publishers in the twentieth century. Its books, booklets, and magazines persistently fostered the liturgical education of clergy and laity. Its authors such as Cipriano Vaggagini, Clifford Howell, and A. G. Martimort were the pathmakers in the liturgical field; and its hymnals and missalettes became aids to renewal for millions of Americans. Under the direction of William Heidt, O.S.B., in the 1950s, it published Pius Parsch's set *Year of Grace,* which before and after Vatican II had a wide and profound liturgical influence. Its New and Old Testament *Reading Guides* did more than any other publications to restore Catholic interest in scriptural reading and study. The company kept its pioneering course by publishing basic reference works during the last decades of the twentieth century. It issued encyclopedias on theology, Eastern Christianity, early Christianity, sociology, liturgy, *The Modern Catholic Encyclopedia,* and the *Collegeville Pastoral Dictionary of Biblical Theology.*

Sheed and Ward had a significant place in American Catholicism. It was founded in London in 1926 by Frank Sheed, a scholarly Australian of Irish stock, and his wife Maisie Ward, the daughter of Wilfrid Ward. Sheed, who became more English than the English, was a talented author, lecturer, and translator. His translation of *The Confessions of St. Augustine* is a standard work; and Ward was a reputable biographer of G. K. Chesterton and others. Sheed and Ward started a branch in New York in 1928 and introduced Americans to the best of European Catholic writing. The firm published Karl Adam, Henri de Lubac, Romano Guardini, G. K. Chesterton, Hilaire Belloc, Christo-

pher Dawson, Allison Peers, Hans Küng, Edward Schillebeeckx, and scores of other distinguished authors. Its books were tastefully designed, and its list had an intellectual dignity. While the older companies, such as Kenedy, Sadlier, Benziger, Herder and others, published traditional liturgical, spiritual, and theological titles, Sheed and Ward strove to broaden horizons and eschewed duplicating the works of others. Some companies, such as Catholic Book Publishing, did better financially publishing missals and prayerbooks; but Sheed and Ward opted for quality theology, spirituality, history, philosophy, and poetry. In the upheaval after Vatican II, Sheed and Ward seemed to lose touch with the needs of the changing times, and went broke. (Its name was later purchased by the *National Catholic Reporter* for its subsidiary book company.)

William Eckenrode was a perceptive Marylander who in the late 1930s decided to sell books by mail to a growing Catholic population. His Newman Bookshop became a large operation which served North America. It sold books of all publishers, and eventually slipped into publishing under the editorial stewardship of John McHale. The Newman Press imprint appeared on thousands of titles until it was taken over by the Paulist Press in 1962.

While Newman Bookshop became the biggest distributor of Catholic titles, a number of book clubs contributed in a lesser way. In the 1920s the Catholic Book Club was founded in New York by America Press and promoted quality titles. The Bruce Publishing Company established the Catholic Literary Foundation that found its market mainly with institutions and clergy. The Catholic Digest Book Club promoted popular books for a large market. The Spiritual Book Associates was founded by James Kane in New York in the 1950s. It offered select spiritual titles, and was eventually purchased by Ave Maria Press of Notre Dame. Thomas More Book Club was founded by Dan Herr of the Thomas More Association to cater to an educated readership.

Prior to the Second Vatican Council (1962–65), American publishers became aware of growing interest in biblical literature. Fr. John L. McKenzie pioneered to bring the insights of modern research down to the grassroots level. In 1956 the Bruce Publishing Company of Milwaukee issued McKenzie's *The Two-Edged Sword* which was one of the most respected scriptural books in the century. (Bruce was a fairly traditional publisher of textbooks, theology and liturgical books since 1891.) In 1965 it successfully published McKenzie's landmark *The Dictionary of the Bible* which Crowell Collier Macmillan kept in print for decades after purchasing Bruce.

Vatican II and Publishing

The Second Vatican Council engendered great hope, fundamental changes and also called for painful adjustments.

One of the unforeseen phenomenon was the resignation and departure of thousands of women religious from their congregations and the unprecedented flood of requests by priests for laicization. Novitiates and seminaries were often almost emptied by the sharp decline in vocations during the 1970s. This upheaval adversely affected every facet of religious publishing.

Two new companies, Herder and Herder and Helicon Press, invigorated Catholic publishing prior to the Council. Herder and Herder, a subsidiary of Herder of Freiburg, introduced reputable German authors and titles, and eventually endeavored to foster American authors. The company published Karl Rahner's *Theological Investigations* (after Helicon Press published the first volume). Helicon and Herder and Herder were publishers of distinguished authors: Hans Reinhold, Godfrey Diekmann, Gerard Sloyan, Edward Schillebeeckx, Frederick McManus, Yves Congar and scores of other talented writers. Helicon faded out in the 1970s. Herder and Herder went through several transformations and changes of name. As Crossroad Publishing Company it published pioneering authors such as Elizabeth Shüssler-Fiorenza, Elizabeth Johnson, and David Tracy. In 1995 the company split into two independent corporations: Crossroad Publishing Company and Continuum Publishing Company.

Maryknoll priest Miguel D'Escoto, who later became the foreign minister in the Sandanista government in Nicaragua, founded Orbis Books in 1970. It became the forum for writers from the Third World, including the creators of liberation theology in South America. Philip Scharper, its editorial director, focused attention on social issues for over fifteen years and introduced authors such as Gustavo Gutierrez to English-speaking readers. After Scharper's death, Robert Gormley continued the tradition but widened the company's perspective when interest in liberation theology declined.

Our Sunday Visitor which had dominated the Catholic newspaper field for generations, acquired the *Catholic Almanac* and published popular titles between 1970–90. It came to life in the 1990s, under the direction of Robert Lockwood, with some very useful reference and biographical titles. Alba House, run by the Society of St. Paul, was part of the society's international publishing operations. Under the direction of Francis X. Borrano, S.S.P., it published a solid list of theological, ecumenical, and spiritual titles.

Irish-born Michael Glazier launched a new company in Delaware which published scholarly works, both secular and religious. Glazier felt that American Catholic publishing had been dependent for too long on European scholars. The company launched commentaries on the Old and New Testaments and series on theology, patristics, mysticism, and biblical spirituality. These works were mostly written by North American authors. Glazier also launched a new series of encyclopedias to service the English-speaking world, the first of which was *The New Dictionary of Theology*. One of the company's notable achievements was the translation from the Aramaic of all the extant Aramaic Targums, most of which had never been published in English. The company was eventually merged with The Liturgical Press in 1990.

Books with a conservative or traditional slant marked the quality list issued by the Franciscan Herald Press during the 1960s and 1970s. Then came Servant Books which grew out of the charismatic movement and also issued some staunch conservative titles. The Ignatius Press, founded by conservative Joseph Fessio, S.J., published some noted authors such as Hans Urs von Balthasar and Cardinal Josef Ratzinger; and reprinted the works by G. K. Chesterton, while also issuing such useful works as John A. Hardon's *Treasury of Catholic Wisdom*.

Popular and Academic

Since the American publication of Newman's *Apologia pro Vita Sua,* secular and university publishers have spasmodically and selectively published Catholic titles. Charles Scribner & Sons published Jacques Maritain's major titles, and Random House had Etienne Gilson on its list. Teilhard de Chardin's *The Phenomenon of Man* and his most important works were issued by Harper and Row (later HarperCollins). Thomas Merton's *Seven Storey Mountain* was published by Harcourt Brace, and New Directions became his principal publisher. In the 1950s Doubleday established a separate Catholic department under the able direction of publisher John J. Delaney, who initiated *Image Books,* the reputable paperback imprint series that brought the Catholic classics and contemporary works of durable quality to a wide readership. Delaney published *The Jerusalem Bible* (after Sheed and Ward turned it down), and he personally wrote several reference works including the valuable *Dictionary of American Catholic Biography.* Doubleday also published Raymond Brown's *The Birth of the Messiah* and *The Passion of Jesus.* Besides Brown, other Catholic scholars such as Joseph Fitzmyer and Mitchell Dahood contributed to Doubleday's *Anchor Bible,* the most significant commentary published to date in the English-speaking world. Prentice-Hall, through its subsidiary Hawthorn Books, published Catholic works for an educated readership; and the monumental *The Jerome Biblical Commentary* edited by Raymond Brown, Joseph Fitzmyer, and Roland Murphy, was first published in 1964 by Prentice-Hall. In 1996 Pope John Paul II's *Crossing the Threshold of Hope* was published by Random House. In the closing decades of the twentieth century HarperCollins became a leading publisher of Catholic authors such as Richard McBrien, Robert Schreiter, Luke Timothy Johnson, John Dominic Crossan.

Oxford University Press published major works of Catholic interest including James Hennesey's *American Catholics* (1981), J.N.D. Kelly's *Dictionary of the Popes* (1986), and Gerald O'Collins *Christology* (1995). Catholic university presses also made some important contributions: Notre Dame, under the direction of James Langford, published a distinguished list of philosophical and ecumenical studies and published such historians as Philip Gleason and Jay Dolan; Georgetown published some focal studies on ethics by Richard McCormick, S.J., and others; and The Catholic University's great contribution was the *Church Fathers* series which had over 155 large volumes by 1997.

See also CATHOLIC MAGAZINES AND PERIODICALS; CATHOLIC PRESS (NEWSPAPERS), THE.

Delaney John J. *Dictionary of American Catholic Biography.* New York, 1984.

Lehmann-Haupt, A. *The Book in America.* 2nd ed. New York, 1951.

Modern Catholic Encyclopedia. Collegeville, Minn.: The Liturgical Press, 1994.

New Catholic Encyclopedia. New York, 1967.

A Survey of Catholic Publishing in the U.S., 1831–1900. Eleven master's theses are on one roll of microfilm. Washington, D.C., 1960.

MICHAEL GLAZIER

CATHOLIC CHARITIES

The term "charity" carries a rich assortment of meanings. It is a theological virtue and a practical response to human need, a type of social organization and a major component of modern welfare provision. The history of charity in all of these senses reflects the changing social and political circumstances of the Christian churches. The community of goods and rudimentary local organization of the early Church evolved with the development of diocesan administration, and the burden of responsibility for the needy shifted to the "bishop's house." Monasteries assumed a large share of the work of caring for the wayfarer and the sick in medieval Christianity, and the guilds and confraternities of the new cities and towns contributed a range of services in the late Middle Ages. The Reformation and the development of the modern state brought another major shift in the organization and administration of charity by dramatically increasing the role of public officials in caring for the needy. The evolution of Christian charity in the modern period shows the dominant influence of modern secular welfare practices.

Although the Catholic Church adjusted its social programs in response to national and international developments, it insisted on the importance of the ancient ideal of charity. Personal service and almsgiving continued to hold a central place in Catholic teaching and practice, even as the Church championed a modern program of social justice aimed at removing the root causes of human need. The history of Catholic charity in the United States reveals an especially complex encounter between tradition and modernity. Catholic social provision has been characterized by both determined resistance to the secularization of charity, and by a deliberate accommodation to the emergence of the modern welfare state.

Catholic Charities in the Nineteenth Century

Catholics first encountered organized American social provision in the rapidly multiplying private charities of the nineteenth-century Protestant "benevolent empire." The empire consisted of an extensive network of local organizations, which assumed responsibility not only for welfare provision but also for public morals. Thousands of volunteers from the prosperous classes created institutions and agencies to aid and control their less fortunate neighbors.

After the Civil War, as the tide of immigration continued to bring millions of newcomers to the United States, charity leaders began to demand reforms in public welfare practices, specifically urging state and local governments to take a more active role in the work of aiding and controlling the poor. In response to this pressure, cities and states began to appoint independent boards of public charity. Public custodial institutions—almshouse and poorhouses—were gradually shut down and replaced with specialized institutions for dependent and handicapped children, and for the mentally and chronically ill. Meanwhile, new penitentiaries and reformatories marked the evolution of public concern for the welfare of delinquents and adult criminals.

Convinced that handouts pauperized their recipients, many states and cities also ceased to provide outdoor relief, relying instead on the volunteer activities of private charities organizations to address the commonplace needs of the poor. To support the work of these private providers, a growing number of cities and states provided funding for organizations that offered institutional care for the poor.

Their poverty and their immigrant status caused Catholics in the United States to become the major clients of this emerging system of social welfare. Inundated by waves of newcomers, the Church could not meet the need, and Catholics soon filled the rosters of non-Catholic social agencies and public poorhouses. They also became regular inmates of prisons and houses of detention.

Their plight stimulated coreligionists to exertions on their behalf that sometimes reached heroic proportions. Immigrant and benevolent societies provided collective assistance along national and ethnic lines, and by midcentury, volunteer organizations like the Society of St. Vincent de Paul and the Ladies of Charity began to develop institutions and services in parishes and dioceses. Following the pattern of Protestant benevolence, the work remained local, remedial and voluntary. Although funding was limited by the slender means of most Catholics, and by competing demands for money to finance churches and schools, Catholic charities had one peerless asset—the contributed services of religious orders. With some notable exceptions, congregations of religious women assumed responsibility for the work of caring for the poor. Their hospitals, asylums, foundling homes, and protectories were the backbone of nineteenth-century Catholic charities.

The cause of needy children was the centerpiece of Catholic efforts. Concerned to save children from Protestant proselytizers, Catholics worked strenuously to "provide for their own," while dedicated Protestants strove with equal energy to rescue needy children from the purportedly baneful and antidemocratic control of the Catholic Church. Methodist and Presbyterian child-placers were charged with stealing the faith of thousands of dependent Catholic children, while Protestant reformers bitterly criticized the methods of Catholic orphanages and foundling homes. The literature of child care in the nineteenth century resounded with recriminations on both sides, as the battle for Catholic children drove a permanent wedge between Catholic and non-Catholic welfare efforts.

New York City

The battle over charity and children was headquartered in New York City, home to major Protestant reform societies and a growing army of needy Catholic children. The system of public provision for private charities that evolved in New York became the leading example of the complex forces of resistance and accommodation that characterized the development of American Catholic charities in the latter half of the nineteenth century. The use of public funds to support children in private institutions was already an established practice in the state when Catholics successfully influenced a new state law governing the care of dependent children. The artful lobbying of Catholics resulted in a stipulation that the religious background of needy youngsters must be honored in any plans made for their care. Because the religion of a majority of the needy children of New York was Catholic, the revised Children's Law (1875–9) guaranteed that greatly increased public funding would be available to Catholic organizations caring for dependent children.

Religious orders of women responded immediately to the new law. The Sisters of Charity led the way, using per capita payments from the city to support their institutions and insulate themselves against the uncertainties of private giving. Soon the populations in their asylums and foundling homes began to grow at an explosive rate. The vast majority of the children sheltered by the nuns were not true orphans, but youngsters whose parent or parents could not care for them. Along with the consolations of religion, the nuns provided a basic social safety net for thousands of parents, tiding them over until they could reclaim their children, or carrying the children into adulthood.

The efforts of religious women were supported by dedicated lay volunteers, and by the political clout of Catholic politicians, who honed their skills as rough-and-tumble apprentices in the Tammany machine. Their efforts made New York Democracy the guarantor for dependent children in Catholic institutions, insuring steady public funding and benevolent oversight. Tammany's support for the children of the poor demonstrated its strength in the city, and anchored the machine's growing public welfare agenda. By the second decade of the twentieth century, Tammany representatives in the New York state legislature sponsored a "market basket" full of welfare measures that anticipated the programs of the New Deal.

The Bishop's House

As America moved into the twentieth century, the informal and voluntary patterns of Protestant benevolence gave way to the organizational reforms of Progressivism. Size, abstract rationality, and professionalization had already begun to erode time-tested methods of intuition and common sense in business and public administration. Similar pressures soon detached American social provision from its religious and humanitarian roots, and transformed it into "scientific charity" and professional "social work."

Although Catholics resisted the secularization of charity, the forces of urbanization and industrialization inevitably altered their traditions along with those of Protestants and Jews. The change in Catholic charity is most apparent in the major shift from parish-based and voluntary forms of assistance, to diocesan and professional bureaucracies of charity. The new look was first introduced by local conferences of the Society of St. Vincent de Paul. In the first two decades of the century, in cities like New York, Baltimore, Brooklyn, and Detroit, the Vincentians began to create citywide "special works," in order to address needs that transcended the boundaries of the city parishes. Local Vincentian conferences also began to hire "paid workers" to provide more regular service to the poor, and to act as their representatives in the juvenile courts.

The success of the United War Work financial campaign during World War I convinced many Catholic bishops that central financing of charities would net large returns. Archbishop Patrick Hayes of New York immediately sought the help of professional fundraisers to build an archdiocesan fundraising organization, and he hired social surveyors to report on the hundreds of independent initiatives of charity in the archdiocese. With this support, Hayes created a new central office of Catholic charities, and charged it with responsibility for funding and supervising social provision in the archdiocese.

Other bishops followed Hayes' lead and increased their control over the independent and volunteer charitable activities of their dioceses. Building on the Vincentian pattern, they created centralized bureaucracies to administer Catholic work, appointing diocesan priests as directors of the new bureaus. These clergy-executives were expected to bring the institutions and charitable organizations of their dioceses under the close control of the chancery. Fundraising activities were gradually consolidated, and annual charity campaigns replaced the more traditional initiatives of volunteer organizations. Although many midsized cities and Midwestern dioceses began to participate in local Community Chests (and therefore to submit their charities to non-Catholic boards for approval), the biggest dioceses preferred to remain independent. The public funding available to Catholic children, and the returns from the annual archdiocesan fund drive, allowed Cardinal Hayes to resist plans for community financing in New York City. New York Catholic Charities did not participate in a community financing program until after Hayes' death in 1938.

To accomplish the goal of modernizing social services, the diocesan directors began to hire professional social workers. The new profession of social work developed rapidly after World War I, and the bulk of its practitioners were women. Hundreds of Catholic women took advantage of social work lectures and classes offered at Loyola University of Chicago, Boston College, St. Louis University, and the National Catholic School of Social Service in Washington. Some of them also took advanced degrees from secular universities and from non-Catholic schools of social service. Their advent into the institutional and organizational work of Catholic charities marked a signal development in the involvement of lay women in the pastoral work of the Church.

Armed with the methods of social work leader Mary Richmond, and eager to provide both spiritual and social assistance to coreligionists, professional social workers inaugurated a new era in Catholic charities. They introduced methods of case work that reformed traditional child care practices and expanded family and protective work. Their case records also reflected their determination to involve themselves with the religious condition of their clients. Catholic social workers who remained in the diocesan charities bureaus shouldered responsibility for checking on marriage and baptismal records, and urged clients to avail themselves of the resources of the sacraments and of personal prayer. Social workers also carried the concerns of the church into non-Catholic welfare circles, where they played a growing part in shaping local, state and national policy on social provision. As members of professional boards and associations, and representatives of Catholic interests in community and state councils, their outreach guaranteed a new degree of Catholic influence in public life.

New methods of professional social work, and the growing authority of social workers, challenged many diocesan charity executives to seek comparable credentials. The non-Catholic New York School of Social Work was a prominent choice for priests from the New York archdiocese and beyond. Robert Keegan, the first director of Catholic Charities of New York, and his assistant and future cardinal-archbishop of Washington, Patrick O'Boyle, both developed their social work credentials there, as did the director of the Children's Division of the archdiocese, Bryan McEntegart, the future rector of The Catholic University of America and bishop of Brooklyn. As the New Deal began to pump millions of federal dollars into local and state economies, these executives worked strenuously to preserve and enlarge the role of Catholic diocesan charities in the emerging welfare state.

The New Deal

Their efforts made Catholic charities the chief medium through which the Church responded to New Deal social legislation. The diocesan organizations of charity and their umbrella organization, the National Conference of Catholic Charities (NCCC), actively sought to influence the legislation and administration of public funds. Their two chief concerns were the Federal Emergency Relief Act and the Social Security Act. The secretary of the NCCC, John O'Grady, monitored Catholic interests on Capitol Hill, while diocesan charity executives in New York, Chicago, Denver, Baltimore, Cincinnati, and St. Louis, worked to develop their influence in city and state welfare programs.

Catholic directors preferred work programs rather than outright relief, and they championed the ideal of subsidiarity, freshly articulated in Pius XI's *Quadragesimo anno,* to reinforce their demand for a large degree of local control in social provision. Traditional Catholic resistance to federal government programs softened considerably during the crisis, but charities leaders continued to insist that administrative control of federal funds should rest with state and city agencies. They also argued that federal and state programs should use private charities and welfare agencies to administer public funds.

Meanwhile, Catholic social workers moved into key positions in the new federal and state welfare programs. Chicago social worker, Rose McHugh, who provided extensive consultation to diocesan charities in the 1920s, left Catholic service to become assistant commissioner of welfare for New York state, and then director of social surveys for the Social Security Administration. After getting her start in Catholic charities, Mary Gibbons directed New York's first massive depression relief program, the Bureau of Home Relief, and then became deputy commissioner of welfare for the state. A number of other Catholic social workers across the country also moved out of diocesan charities to take positions in state government, and several went to the federal Children's Bureau to administer new government programs for children.

New Yorker, Jane Hoey, moved from the position of assistant director of the city's private Council of Social Agencies to become chief of the new federal Bureau of Public Assistance of the Social Security Administration in Washington. Her first task was to persuade the states to pass enabling legislation that would allow federal funds to reach dependent children. When pressed by representatives of Catholic charities to support their efforts to include private agencies in the federal relief chain, Hoey refused. Her Aid to Dependent Children program sent payments through public welfare agencies to qualified parents, without the mediation of private case work. Hoey agreed with New Dealer Harry Hopkins, her long-time colleague, that public dollars should be spent only by public agencies. Her position implicitly rejected the model offered by New York's collaboration with private providers and deeply annoyed many of the clergy who ran the diocesan charities agencies.

As a result of New Deal experiments, the United States began to develop the elements of a permanent welfare state. The beginning was manifestly inadequate. Entitlement programs began to provide insurance plans for the unemployed and for retirees, based on assumptions about male family breadwinners. The plans covered only a portion of the work force, and contained major racial and gender barriers. The major assistance program, Aid to Dependent Children, was viewed as "welfare" rather than as a rights-based "entitlement," and states stipulated eligibility rules and means tests for recipients. The crucial question of federal support for health and housing went unresolved until the 1960s.

Diocesan Catholic charities agencies continued their efforts to develop staff and standards, and to improve their institutions in order to provide better service for needy Catholics and to meet requirements for public funding. The days of the large congregate institutions for children were over, but religious communities continued to offer dedicated service to dependent and handicapped children and the elderly. The central bureaus relied on the services of professional social workers, who remained in staff positions under ecclesiastical direction. Catholic lay volunteers, who had been so much a part of Catholic charities in early stages of development, were in scarce supply in the diocesan organizations of the middle decades of the twentieth century, in spite of sporadic efforts by clergy and professional social workers to draw them back into the work. Numbers of lay Catholics were instead attracted to new, grassroots movements, where their role was inevitably larger, and where there was much less concern for the niceties of bureaucratic red tape. Notable among these efforts was the Catholic Worker, whose guiding spirit, Dorothy Day, was roundly critical of strategies and practices of the diocesan charity agencies.

As the federal role in social provision continued to expand after World War II, Catholic social and economic mobility also increased. The G.I. bill and generous student loan programs made higher education widely available, while welfare coverage for individuals increased through the extension of Social Security, and through Medicaid and Medicare programs developed during the 1960s and 1970s. In spite of these developments, however, poverty continued to deepen in what Michael Harrington called America's "economic underworld." Poverty among people of color remained intractable, as it did in rural areas and city slums. The "feminization of poverty" captured headlines, even as the Reagan administration attempted to reverse the pattern of government involvement in welfare in the 1980s; and the children of single mothers constituted a fast-growing population of the poor.

The combined resources of Catholic charities agencies, which totaled more than one and a half billion dollars a year in the 1990s, remains devoted largely to the care of women, children, and families. Catholic charities opened their doors to needy persons of all religious persuasions (and of none) in the 1960s and in spite of the cutbacks at federal, state, and local levels, which have seriously eroded the financial base of these agencies, they continue to be the leading private provider of care in the United States.

Brown, Dorothy, and Elizabeth McKeown. *The Poor Belong to Us: Catholic Charities and American Welfare.* Harvard University Press, 1997.

Gavin, Donald P. *The National Conference of Catholic Charities, 1910–1960.* Milwaukee: Bruce Press, 1962.

Oates, Mary J. *The Catholic Philanthropic Tradition in America.* Bloomington: Indiana University Press, 1995.

O'Grady, John. *Catholic Charities in the United States: History and Problems.* Washington: The National Conference of Catholic Charities, 1931.

ELIZABETH McKEOWN

CATHOLIC CONGRESSES OF 1889 AND 1893

The inspiration for a lay Catholic congress came from Henry Brownson, son of Orestes Brownson, who had been impressed with the success of such congresses in Germany and Belgium. Brownson conceived the idea of organizing an American Catholic lay congress to be held in conjunction with the celebration of the centennial of the United States Catholic hierarchy in Baltimore in 1889. He first approached Fr. Augustine Hewitt, superior general of the Paulists, whose founder, Isaac Hecker, had once urged American Catholics to imitate the example of the German and Belgian Catholics. Hewitt, however, declined to associate the Paulists with this lay venture. Brownson then turned to William J. Onahan, a prominent Chicago layman, who gave the project his enthusiastic support.

The next step was to secure the approval of the hierarchy. Cardinal James Gibbons was cool to the proposal, fearful that such a Catholic gathering would provoke a backlash of anti-Catholic bigotry, especially at a time when the American Protective Association was reaching the height of its influence. Through the intervention of Archbishop John Ireland, however, Brownson and Onahan obtained the guarded approval of Gibbons, but only after Onahan, acting on his own initiative, agreed to the appointment of an episcopal advisory committee with veto power over the papers to be read at the congress. Brownson had little choice but to agree to this condition, but he complained that Onahan had "no broad views of what the laity could do for religion, if they were encouraged to act freely and spontaneously." Peter L. Foy, a Catholic journalist in St. Louis, shared Brownson's frustration and said that the hierarchy had shown "want of confidence in the laity."

The Congress of 1889

The congress took place in Baltimore on November 11 and 12, 1889. The pope conveyed his blessing through Cardinal Mariano Rampolla, papal secretary of state, and appointed as his representative to the congress Archbishop Francesco Satolli, the papal delegate to the centennial celebration of the hierarchy. On the day before the opening of the congress, Archbishop Ireland announced in the Baltimore cathedral that "laymen have in this age a special vocation." The opening speech was given by John Gilmary Shea, who spoke—appropriately enough—on "Catholic Congresses." Henry Brownson delivered an address on "Lay Action in the Church." Charles Bonaparte discussed "The Independence of the Holy See," and Henry J. Spaunhorst, president of the Central Verein, read a paper on Catholic societies. Other participants spoke on such topics as Catholic education, Sunday observance, and the relationship of capital and labor. Both the Catholic press and secular newspapers gave favorable coverage to the congress.

After the conclusion of the congress, Cardinal Gibbons sent a glowing report to Rome telling Pope Leo XIII that the congress "was a triumph for the Catholic Church." However, when efforts were made a few years later to hold a second congress, Gibbons did his best to prevent it. "We know not what wild elements may be let loose at the Congress," he told Archbishop Ireland, "and who can control them?" Ireland himself waffled about the advisability of a second congress, but the faithful William Onahan pushed ahead with his plans, and the second Lay Congress, first scheduled for 1892, was held in Chicago in 1893 in conjunction with the Columbian Exposition of that year. The U.S. archbishops appointed an advisory committee consisting of Archbishop Ireland, Bishop Camillus Maes of Covington, Bishop John Foley of Detroit, and Bishop Matthew Harkins of Providence. Neither Henry Brownson nor Peter Foy took part in the preparations.

The Congress of 1893

The second congress took place in Chicago from September 4 to September 9, 1893. Three days were devoted to speeches on various aspects of Leo XIII's recent encyclical *Rerum Novarum*. Another major topic was the value of Catholic societies, a topic known to be of concern to the Pope. According to the historian of the Catholic Congresses, Sr. Mary Adele Francis, O.S.F., the second congress was not as successful as the first. She attributes the disappointing results to the attempt to cover too many topics in a brief time span.

She also notes that few laymen expressed interest in holding a third congress. "Apparently," she explains, "[lay] Catholics in the United States were not ready to assume the type of leadership necessary for successful congresses." Messrs. Brownson and Foy might have offered their own explanation and wondered if the American bishops were prepared to allow the laity to assume the leadership necessary for the success of such congresses. Even Americanist prelates like Gibbons and Ireland took alarm at the prospect of a lay congress that would not be under the direct control of the hierarchy. On the eve of the Chicago congress, Gibbons told Ireland that he and the other American archbishops "would try to kill it, or that failing, to determine that this should be the last congress." He succeeded beyond his expectations.

Abell, Aaron I. *American Catholicism and Social Action: A Search for Social Justice, 1865–1950.* Garden City, 1960, 99–117.

Francis, M. Adele, O.S.F. "Lay Activity and the Catholic Congresses of 1889 and 1893." *Records of the American Catholic Historical Society of Philadelphia* 74 (March 1963) 3–23.

THOMAS J. SHELLEY

CATHOLIC EDUCATION AND GOVERNMENT AID

Historian James Hennesey traces Catholic education in English North America to the colony of Maryland where, in 1653, wealthy farmer Edward Cotton bequeathed to the Society of Jesus his horse and mare, "the stock and all its increase to be preserved and the profit made use of for the use of a school." The next three and one-half centuries would recast Catholic education and English North America. A revolution, a constitution, industrialization, immigration, and war would transform the simplicity of horse and mare to the complexities of Church and state.

In 1789 the United States Congress drafted the First Amendment, which reads in part that "Congress shall make no law respecting an establishment of religion, nor prohibiting the free exercise thereof." That same year it reenacted the Northwest Ordinance, which reads in part that "religion, morality, and knowledge being necessary to good government and the happiness of mankind, schools and the means of education shall ever be encouraged." In 1839 Horace Mann, Secretary of the Massachusetts Board of Education, established the first state normal school in the United States. Mann, troubled by "a riot of almost unheard-of atrocity" between Catholics and Protestants in Boston two years earlier, advocated nonsectarian reading of the Bible in the school.

Such mixed messages have characterized the history of government aid to Catholic education in the United States. The Roman Catholic Church and the United States government have been at various times adversaries and allies. The arena of discussion of government aid has shifted from the states and the courts to the White House and Congress, then back again. As the debate enters the twenty-first century, it will yield new arguments, new milestones—and old contradictions.

Adversaries

The Catholic Church's early position on government aid reflected the anxieties of a minority Church confronting a Protestant culture. Substantial immigration to the United States from Mexico and northern and western Europe in the first half of the nineteenth century invited hostile and often violent Protestant reaction. The immigrant Church therefore adopted its own separate course in education. After Bishop John Hughes' unsuccessful effort to secure public funds for Church-controlled schools in New York City in 1841, and the religious riots provoked by Philadelphia Bishop Francis Kenrick's attempt to end exclusive use of the King James Bible in that city's public schools in 1844, the Church inaugurated an ambitious campaign to construct a network of parochial, or parish, schools. The bishops at the First Plenary Council of Baltimore in 1852 pledged to finance these schools with Church revenues.

The rise of Catholic schools helped explain the Blaine Amendment, a proposal by Republican Representative James Blaine of Maine to outlaw government aid to religious schools. The constitutional amendment passed the House and failed in the Senate in 1876, but it became the model for similar restrictions in several state constitutions.

The second major influx of immigrants to the United States at the turn of the twentieth century came primarily from Mexico, southern and eastern Europe, and east Asia, and included over a million Catholics in each of the decades between 1880 and 1920. The bishops at the Third Plenary Council of Baltimore in 1884 responded by ordering a parochial school built for every parish church.

A 1922 Oregon referendum threatened this parochial school system by approving a proposed state law prohibiting attendance at nonpublic schools during school hours. The Sisters of the Holy Names of Jesus and Mary joined a nonsectarian private school, Hill Military Academy, in challenging the result of the referendum in court. In 1925, in *Pierce v. Society of Sisters,* a decision that James Hennesey calls the "Magna Carta for Catholic education in the United States," the Supreme Court ruled unanimously that the Oregon government could regulate nonpublic schools, but it could not effectively abolish them.

The proposed Oregon statute heightened the Catholic bishops' suspicion of government. The National Catholic Welfare Conference (NCWC, the bishops' social welfare organization) expressed the fear in 1941 that federal aid to public education would lead to federal control of all education.

Allies

As the United States moved toward cultural homogenization during World War II, many Catholics reassessed their views toward the majority culture and toward their government. In 1944 Congress and President Franklin Roosevelt enacted the Servicemen's Readjustment Act, or G.I. Bill of Rights, by which the federal government financed college tuition, fees, and living expenses for up to four years of public or nonpublic higher education for veterans of World War II (and later the Korean and Vietnam Wars). The G.I. Bill would send large numbers of Catholics to college and would help reshape Catholic higher education. Later that same year, the NCWC concluded that, since public school classroom and teacher shortages had made federal aid to public elementary and secondary education virtually inevitable, Catholics should now fight for their share of the largesse.

The Arena: The States and the Courts

During the next decade, as federal aid bills weathered religious, racial, and ideological challenges, the focus of government aid toward Catholic education returned to the states and the courts. In 1947 the Supreme Court, in *Everson v. Board of Education,* upheld the constitutionality of a New Jersey statute permitting the state to reimburse nonpublic school parents for their children's transportation to and from school. The court majority thus subscribed to the "child-benefit theory" in dismissing the plaintiff's contention that such aid violated the First Amendment's separation of Church and state.

A year later, in *Illinois ex rel v. Board of Education,* the court ruled unconstitutional a Champaign, Illinois, released-time religious education program in the public schools, sponsored by a council of Catholic, Jewish, and Protestant groups. The court majority maintained that the program abridged the First Amendment by permitting use of the public schools to aid religious groups in spreading their beliefs.

The court appeared to reverse itself in 1952 by ruling a New York released-time plan constitutional. The program allowed public schools to release pupils during the school hours to receive instruction at religious centers. In its majority opinion in *Zorach v. Clauson,* the court distinguished between the on-campus Champaign and off-campus New York programs, noting that the former blended secular and sectarian education, while the latter separated them.

The Arena: The White House and the Congress

In 1958 the Cold War supplanted the Constitution as the greatest ally of proponents of government aid to Catholic schools. Spurred by the Soviet launch of Sputnik I the previous year, Congress and President Dwight Eisenhower enacted the first significant legislative concession to Catholic education, the National Defense Education Act. The act provided federal loans to college students and federal grants for mathematics, science, and foreign language instruction at nonpublic as well as public elementary, secondary, and higher education institutions.

Congressional proponents of government aid to Catholic schools pressed forward, undeterred by the Supreme Court's *Engel v. Vitale* (1962) and *Abingdon Township v. Schempp* (1963) decisions prohibiting official prayers and Bible readings in public schools. President Lyndon Johnson signed the Higher Education Facilities Act of 1963, which authorized federal grants and loans for construction of facilities at public and nonpublic colleges and universities.

The climax of three decades of congressional debate over federal aid to public and nonpublic schools came in 1965 with the passage of the Elementary and Secondary Education Act. Title I of the act allocated monies to be distributed by state education officials to assist local school district projects directed at underprivileged children. These funds could finance "shared-time" programs by which nonpublic school pupils attend classes at public schools. Title II provided for the purchase through public agencies of textbooks and other materials, as well as the expansion of school libraries, for nonpublic as well as public school children. Title III earmarked funds for "supplemental services and centers" open to public and nonpublic school children. Though technically a "categorical aid" measure like the NDEA, the scope of the ESEA was broad enough to satisfy proponents, and to offend opponents, of general federal aid (for classroom construction and teachers' salaries).

The Higher Education Act of 1965 marked a final victory for supporters of federal aid to nonpublic schools. For the first time, the federal government provided scholarships for students at public and nonpublic colleges and universities.

The Arena: The States and the Courts Again

Just as the door to Capitol Hill was opening for Catholic education, the doors to Catholic schools were closing. From 1940 to 1960, according to George La Noue, Catho-

lic elementary and secondary school enrollments increased at a rate three times that of the public schools. By the 1960s, nine of every ten nonpublic schoolchildren, and one of every nine schoolchildren, attended Catholic elementary and secondary schools. But from 1964 to 1984, according to Jay Dolan, 40 percent of Catholic high schools and 27 percent of Catholic elementary schools closed.

The Catholic school crisis invited many explanations, including the decline in religious vocations, the fall in the Catholic birth rate, the social acceptance of Catholics in public schools, and the ideological impact of the Second Vatican Council (1962–65). The rising cost of Catholic education was the refrain heard most often from the leading interest groups—the Department of Education of the United States Catholic Conference (formerly the NCWC), the National Catholic Education Association (the professional association of Catholic school teachers and administrators), and Citizens for Educational Freedom (a citizens' group).

And government aid remained the most popular solution. In 1968, in *Board of Education v. Allen,* the Supreme Court upheld the constitutionality of a New York law permitting the purchase with public funds of secular textbooks for parochial schools. By 1969 *U.S. News and World Report* counted twenty-five states with some form of aid to nonpublic schools. Twenty-three states offered free bus transportation, eight provided secular textbooks, three supplemented the salaries of teachers of secular subjects, and one issued tuition tax credits.

But the salary-supplementary laws would not survive the courts. In 1971 the Supreme Court ruled unconstitutional the Pennsylvania *(Lemon v. Kurtzman)* and Rhode Island *(Earley v. Dicenso)* salary-supplementary laws, and upheld a lower-court decision overturning the Connecticut salary supplementary statute. In each case, the court rejected the separation of "secular" and "sectarian" aspects of parochial school education to allow the teachers of the former to receive public funds. In the *Lemon* decision, the court added a third criterion to the 1963 *Schempp* formula for interpreting the First Amendment: not only whether legislation "is a mask to advance religion" or if its primary effect is to help or harm religion, but whether it embodies an "excessive government entanglement" with religion.

Three years later, tuition tax credits failed the *Lemon* test. In separate decisions, the Supreme Court ruled that New York and California laws permitting tuition reimbursements to parents of nonpublic schoolchildren constituted "an excessive governmental entanglement with religion."

No such entanglement existed at the higher education level, however. In its 1971 *Tilton v. Richardson* decision, which upheld the Higher Education Facilities Act of 1963, the court's five-member majority argued that, unlike church-related primary and secondary schools, religious colleges and universities do not practice "religious indoctrination."

The Arena: The White House and the Congress Again

Richard Nixon became the first president to strongly advocate government aid for parochial schools. In his first term he established the Commission on School Finance and the President's Panel on Nonpublic Education. Among the former group's recommendations were federal cash vouchers for parents of school-age children to choose public or nonpublic schools. The major recommendation of the latter group was a federal income tax credit for tuition for low- and middle-income parents of nonpublic schoolchildren.

Nixon endorsed first vouchers, then tuition tax credits, but over one hundred parochiaid bills failed in Congress during his presidency. The high-water mark for parochiaid came four years after the end of the Nixon Administration. In 1978 a tuition tax credit bill won in the House but lost in the Senate. Jimmy Carter had promised a presidential veto if the measure had passed.

In 1982 President Ronald Reagan proposed a tuition tax credit for low- and middle-income parents of nonpublic schoolchildren. In 1983 and 1985 Reagan prescribed vouchers for low-income parents of public and nonpublic schoolchildren. In 1989 President George Bush opposed tuition tax credits, but in 1992 he proposed vouchers for low- and middle-income parents of nonpublic schoolchildren. But the Reagan and Bush proposals suffered a similar fate: death in Congress.

The Arena: The States and the Courts Again

The legislative failures of the Reagan and Bush Administrations and the election of parochiaid opponent Bill Clinton to the presidency in 1992 returned the issue to the states and the courts, where parochiaid experienced mixed results. Victory came in 1983, in *Mueller v. Allen,* when the Supreme Court upheld a Minnesota law permitting tax deductions for parents of nonpublic as well as public schoolchildren. In 1988 the court cited the *Tilton* decision in upholding the 1981 Adolescent Family Life Act, which provided federal funds for public and nonprofit private agencies that encouraged alternatives to abortion through counseling and educational services for teenage girls.

In *Lamb's Chapel v. Center Moriches Union Free School District* in 1993, the court unanimously held that a public school district must rent school facilities to religious groups during nonschool hours as long as the facilities are open to other community groups. In the same year, in *Zobrest v. Catalina Foothills School District,* the court permitted a publicly-funded sign-language interpreter to serve a deaf Catholic student enrolled in a Catholic school.

Defeat arrived in 1985, in *Aguilar v. Felton* and *Grand Rapids v. Ball,* when the court struck down New York City and Grand Rapids, Michigan, programs under which public school teachers offered remedial education and other special services in parochial schools. In *Lee v. Weisman* in 1992, the court prohibited clergy from offering prayers at public school commencements. In *Board of Education v. Grumet* in 1994, the court overturned a New York law creating a unique public school district for special education of disabled Hassidic Jewish schoolchildren. The United States Catholic Conference had filed an *amicus curiae* brief in favor of New York's "legislative accommodation of religion."

By 1995 the prognosis for government aid to Catholic education appeared uncertain. Proponents could cite the 4 percent of American college students and 10 percent of American elementary and secondary school pupils enrolled in Catholic educational institutions; the twenty-two states that permit some form of government aid to nonpublic elementary and secondary education; the control by Republicans (recently more sympathetic to parochiaid than Democrats) of both houses of Congress for the first time in forty years; and the three dissenting and two concurring opinions in the *Grumet* decision, which presaged a reversal of the *Aguilar* and *Ball* verdicts. Opponents could note a 1994 study by John Witte of the University of Wisconsin that attacked the nation's only current voucher experiment in Milwaukee's secular nonpublic schools, and the defeat of voucher ballot initiatives in three states. The history of government aid to Catholic education in the United States thus offers an ambiguous past, which portends a contentious future.

Coughlin, John. "Religion, Education, and the First Amendment." *America* 168 (May 15, 1993) 12–15.

"Crisis Hits Catholic Schools." *U.S. News and World Report* (September 29, 1969) 33.

Dolan, Jay. *The American Catholic Experience.* New York: Doubleday, 1985.

Hennesey, James. *American Catholics: A History of the Roman Catholic Community in the United States.* New York: Oxford University Press, 1981.

Spring, Joel. *The American School 1642–1845.* New York: Longman, 1986.

LAWRENCE McANDREWS

CATHOLIC EDUCATION, HIGHER

Because Catholics in the colonial era were few in numbers and labored under severe disabilities, they were unable to found permanent schools. Hence the story of American Catholic higher education begins only after independence and falls into two periods of about a century each. The first, the age of the old-time Catholic college, extends from 1789 when Georgetown college was founded to 1889 when The Catholic University of America opened its doors. The modern era, from the 1890s to the present, has been dominated by the struggle to bring Catholic institutions into line with ongoing organizational and ideological changes in the larger academic world without sacrificing their distinctive religious identity. Both of these century-long epochs can be subdivided into shorter spans, two in the case of the first, three in that of the second. Seminary education will be dealt with in what follows only insofar as it touches on the development of institutions for lay men and women.

The Old-Time Catholic College: Beginnings

From the 1780s to the 1840s, the founding of Catholic colleges was a major concern of the bishops and was closely linked to the overall growth of the Church; both in that era and later, colleges likewise figured prominently in the development of religious communities. Academies for young women soon outnumbered the men's schools; though not called colleges, they resembled the men's schools in many respects. By performing a service highly valued by the larger society, these schools (both men's and women's) generated financial support for the religious communities operating them; they also recruited new vocations and provided a base for further expansion.

Because schools served these important functions, it is understandable that, despite the role the bishops played in founding colleges, religious communities have dominated Catholic higher education. In fact, the same reason that made bishops want colleges—the shortage of clerical personnel—made them eager to attract to their dioceses male religious orders which could, among other things, assume responsibility for running the colleges.

The bishops wanted colleges because they desperately needed priests for the rapidly growing Catholic population, and they visualized the colleges as sources of vocations and places where clerical prospects could be given part of their training. Indeed, it was possible through much of the nineteenth century for a clerical prospect to receive all the training he would get at one venue, for college and seminary were often combined in the same institution. In such a "mixed" college/seminary, the lower-level lay students provided the base of support on which the whole institution rested; a much smaller number of prospective priests served as teachers and prefects (i.e., disciplinary overseers) in the college, while at the same time receiving instruction in philosophy and theology.

These features can be noted in the history of the earliest Catholic colleges. John Carroll, the first American Catholic bishop, was quite explicit in stating that his principal motive in founding Georgetown was to recruit priests and begin their training. He regarded the establishment of this school, which was the first institutional project he undertook, as essential to the future well-being of the Church in America.

Even before Georgetown could be opened, however, Bishop Carroll acquired a real seminary when the Sulpicians in Paris, seeking refuge from the French Revolution,

offered to open what came to be known as St. Mary's Seminary in Baltimore (est. 1791). Until it began to attract substantial numbers of seminarians, Sulpician émigrés helped out at Georgetown; but in 1799, St. Mary's Seminary spun off a college for lay students (St. Mary's College) to provide a basis for support and serve as a feeder for the seminary. A few years later, another Sulpician offshoot—Mount St. Mary's in Emmitsburg, Maryland (est. 1808)—developed into an even clearer example of a mixed college/seminary. In the meantime, control of Georgetown was gradually being assumed by the Society of Jesus, which had been suppressed in 1773 but was fully reconstituted in 1814. From then on vocational recruitment and clerical training at Georgetown were focused on the society.

The Jesuits became by far the most numerous and important order engaged in higher education. By the 1840s they had taken over several other colleges originally founded by bishops, the most important being St. Louis University, which became the base for further Jesuit expansion in the vast area drained by the Mississippi, Missouri, and Ohio rivers. Aside from the Sulpicians, the only other orders to establish colleges before 1840 were the Dominicans (briefly in Kentucky) and the Vincentians (in Missouri).

The Jesuits were also particularly influential because their reputation as educators extended back to the sixteenth century. John Carroll, himself a member of the society before its suppression, patterned Georgetown after the Jesuit schools familiar to him as a student and teacher in the Low Countries, and the Jesuit system likewise served as a model for other Catholic colleges. Whether Jesuit or not, these schools were quite small; 100 to 150 students was considered a healthy enrollment. Throughout this early period, non-Catholic students were welcomed at Catholic colleges (as well as women's academies) and often accounted for a third or more of the student body.

Since students enrolled as young as ten to twelve years of age, the great majority were really doing secondary-level work; until after the Civil War, probably only about 5 percent completed the full college course and earned a bachelor's degree. One reason Catholic schools were so bottom-heavy with young students was that Catholic educators, especially the Jesuits, defined the college differently from most Americans. To them a "college" was a school like the German *Gymnasium* or the French *lycée*—one that offered in a unified program of about six years the same course content that English and American educators divided between two institutions, a four-year secondary school and the first two years of college.

This anomalous organizational structure would prove in time to be a major problem. But it was not so obvious a handicap in the early years, when nearly all American colleges were small denominational schools that depended heavily on their own "preparatory departments." More troubling to Catholic educators was the fact that they had to de-emphasize the classical languages, which they regarded as the core of the college curriculum, in order to satisfy parental demands for more practically oriented studies.

The Old-Time Catholic College: Consolidation

In the middle decades of the nineteenth century, higher education, along with other aspects of American Catholic life, passed from its rude beginnings to a stage of expansion and consolidation. The most basic element in this transition was the fantastic growth of the Church brought on by immigration. In the thirty years before the Civil War, the Catholic population shot up three-and-a-half times faster than the overall American population, reaching an estimated total of 3.1 million in 1860.

The impact of rapid growth on higher education was reflected in the founding of forty-two Catholic colleges in the 1850s, a number equal to the total founded in the previous sixty years. Many were established by religious communities new to the American scene. Thus the Congregation of Holy Cross founded Notre Dame (1842); the Benedictines, St. Vincent (1846) and St. John's (1857); the Marianists, what was to become the University of Dayton (1850); the Christian Brothers, Manhattan (1853); and the Franciscans, St. Bonaventure (1856). The Jesuits, reinforced by newcomers exiled by revolutionary upheaval in Italy and Germany, multiplied their schools (e.g., Santa Clara, est. 1851); the Vincentians added Niagara (1856); and the Augustinians, who had been around for years, opened Villanova in 1842.

As the religious communities increasingly took over the work of higher education, the bishops played a less active role (although Seton Hall opened under diocesan auspices in 1856). Bishops responsible for new dioceses were still keenly interested; but in the more settled regions, the Church's growing size and maturity made it possible for bishops to erect free-standing seminaries, after which they were no longer so concerned about the colleges. In addition, the need to provide parochial schooling for Catholic youngsters demanded more of the bishops' attention from the 1840s onward; this too distracted them from higher education for lay people. However, their efforts to attract teaching orders to staff the parochial schools paved the way for the establishment of colleges by communities of brothers and, in later years, sisters as well.

Among the colleges that survived (perhaps one out of three), the more successful broadened their course offerings and adjusted in other ways to American practice— for example, by calling the first two or three years of the course "preparatory" and the latter part "collegiate." St. Louis University and Georgetown launched medical schools before the Civil War, but the former was short-lived; a few years after the war, Notre Dame and Georgetown established law schools. However, Catholic colleges still retained the combined secondary-collegiate organizational structure described above. The inability of such institutions to meet the intellectual and religious challenges of the day became increasingly evident by the 1870s and accounted for the growing conviction that American Catholics needed a real university of their own.

The promoters of this movement, especially Bishop John Lancaster Spalding of Peoria, Illinois, were inspired by Cardinal Newman's *Idea of a University,* but they conceived of the university more along continental than English lines. It was to bear the same relation to the existing Catholic colleges as German universities did to the *Gymnasia* of that nation. Being of a higher "grade," it would not compete with the colleges for students; rather it would provide a model for emulation and thus indirectly elevate the whole system. After being talked about for several years, the project was approved at the Third Plenary Council of Baltimore in 1884; five years later the Catholic University of America (CUA) began operation.

The New Era: Organizational Modernization

For the first ten years of its existence CUA was deeply embroiled in the controversies over "Americanism," but it was less directly affected by the Modernist crisis in the first decade of the twentieth century. Both of these episodes grew out of Catholic efforts to respond to social change and new currents of thought in the natural sciences, biblical scholarship, and philosophy. The "liberal" responses championed by Americanists and Modernists were decisively rejected by Church authorities, and neoscholasticism was prescribed as the official Catholic answer to the philosophical and theological problems raised by modern thinkers.

Neoscholasticism had a tremendous influence on Catholic higher education, but it did not really make itself felt until the 1920s. By that time, far reaching organizational changes had already taken place; these too constituted a response to the challenges of modernity, this time in the social and institutional realms.

The founding of CUA was itself a major landmark. Intended from the outset to operate at the graduate level, CUA was part of the university revolution that transformed American higher education in the late nineteenth century. In addition, it served as a key diffusion point from which the methods and spirit of that revolution radiated outward to other Catholic schools. After 1900, Catholic colleges in urban centers, especially Jesuit schools, experienced their own "university movement." It consisted primarily in adding professional schools (law, medicine, etc.) and other vocationally oriented programs in engineering, journalism, pedagogy, and so on. Except at CUA, however, genuine graduate work was virtually nonexistent at Catholic institutions until the 1920s.

In the meantime, Catholic colleges modernized themselves in organizational terms, a reform basic to everything that happened later. It was forced by larger shifts that brought about a crisis affecting all collegiate educators at the turn of the century. The problem centered on "articulation" (i.e., how different levels of schooling relate to each other), which was precisely where Catholic institutions, still predominantly composed of prep students, departed most obviously from prevailing norms.

The crisis was precipitated by the rapid growth of American education at all levels, especially the burgeoning of free public high schools; by an accompanying increase in the number of "new subjects" (e.g., history and English) being taught; and by the decline of the "prescribed curriculum" in favor of the "elective" principle. This combination of changes made the already blurry dividing line between secondary and collegiate education murkier than ever. In reaction, educators from both levels came together in a series of ad hoc committees and permanent organizations (e.g., the College Entrance Examination Board) to differentiate clearly between high school and college, and to establish definite criteria whereby students' progress through each could be measured. Both the high school "unit" and college "credit hour" were introduced during this movement of "standardization," and the regional accrediting associations became its quality-control agencies.

Catholic colleges, with their combined secondary-collegiate coverage, could no longer continue on the old basis once the standardizing movement got under way. This reality was underscored by the contemporaneous "drift" of Catholic students to "secular" universities, which caused considerable alarm among Catholic educators. The Catholic Educational Association (organized, 1904; word "national" added, 1927) played a vital role in the crisis by providing a forum for the exchange of information and a vehicle for undertaking common action. Its leaders, most notably James A. Burns, C.S.C., campaigned for freestanding Catholic high schools and for "standard colleges," i.e., four-year postsecondary schools that met the standards generally agreed upon by accrediting agencies. Reform was painful, especially for the Jesuits who were strongly committed to the traditional arrangement, but by the early 1920s the battle was over. Preparatory departments were eliminated, and Catholic colleges thereafter resembled all others in terms of organizational structure, credit-hour requirements, and so on.

Another major institutional development of this era was the phenomenal growth of Catholic women's colleges. The first to develop from an already existing academy was Notre Dame of Maryland, which received its college charter in 1896; four years later, Trinity College, the first to be established de novo, opened its doors in Washington, D.C. By 1926 twenty-five colleges for women constituted more than a third of the sixty-nine institutions accredited by the Catholic Educational Association.

The general opening of opportunities for women was fundamental to this institutional explosion, but the growth of education itself was the key variable. The vast expansion of schooling at all levels required increasing numbers of teachers, and certification requirements for teachers were being continuously upgraded. As schoolteaching became both feminized and professionalized, the demand for higher education for women was bound to grow. Since religious orders of women were heavily engaged in teaching in parochial schools and academies, it made sense for them to open colleges. Here their own members could receive the training they needed, and offering collegiate work for lay women, many of whom also became school teachers, met an existing demand and was a natural next stage of evolution in what the sisters were already doing.

Higher Education in the Era of the Catholic Renaissance

From the 1920s to the early 1960s, American Catholicism flourished in terms of numerical growth, institutional vigor, and spiritual vitality. The latter quality was especially notable in the middle years of this epoch, which contemporaries called an intellectual and cultural revival, or a Catholic Renaissance. Under the influence of this outlook, Catholic colleges and universities took a countercultural line, mounting a stringent critique of secularism and claiming to offer a prescription for human culture deeper and truer than the prevailing materialism of modern American society.

Negatively, the new Catholic self-confidence rested on the widely shared perception of cultural crisis that followed upon the calamity of World War I and was reinforced by subsequent economic collapse and the rise of totalitarianism. These developments proved, as Catholics saw it, that the modern world was headed for destruction. Positively, the key element in the Catholic Renaissance was the Scholastic Revival, or return to the thought of St. Thomas Aquinas, which was officially launched by Pope Leo XIII in 1879 and imposed in more rigorous fashion after 1907 as an antidote to the errors of the Modernists.

The Scholastic Revival (also referred to as neoscholasticism or neo-Thomism) reached this country as a fullfledged movement just as Catholic colleges were completing the standardizing process described above. Heavy credit-hour requirements in neoscholastic philosophy imposed on Catholic collegians by the late 1920s served to reinforce the religious identity of institutions that had recently undergone organizational modernization. These courses also buttressed the student's religious belief by harmonizing the truths of faith with the findings of reason, thereby constituting the basis for a practical "philosophy of life." And thanks especially to the natural-law teaching that was an intrinsic feature of the system, neoscholasticism could serve as the foundation upon which to build a Catholic culture. In short, neoscholastic philosophy formed the cognitive framework around which the whole intellectual edifice of Catholic higher education was built from the 1920s through the 1950s. (The teaching of theology was confined to the seminaries until near the end of this period.)

"Catholic Action," the participation of lay people in socioreligious works sanctioned by ecclesiastical authority, added a note of apostolic fervor to the Catholic Renaissance in the thirties and forties. Only a small minority of undergraduates became Catholic Action "militants," but the ethos of the movement permeated the Catholic campus scene. It meshed with interest in papal social teaching, the labor movement, and combating Communism; it was also linked to campaigns against indecent movies, pulp fiction, and birth control, and with the promotion of sound family life through academic study and organizations like the Cana Conference and the Catholic Family Movement.

The final academic manifestation of the Renaissance was a midcentury movement to embody the Catholic worldview in a more effectively "integrated" undergraduate curriculum. By that time, however, Catholic liberals were already deploring the tendency toward separatism, or "ghettoism," that was the obverse side of the drive to create a Catholic culture. The liberals endorsed the religious premises on which the drive rested, but their dissatisfaction with its practical outcome reflected a more positive attitude toward the modern world. This assimilationist mindset soon inspired a degree of self-criticism—initiated by Msgr. John Tracy Ellis's 1955 essay, "American Catholics and the Intellectual Life"—that amounted to a de facto rejection of the Catholic Renaissance as such.

Upward social mobility and Catholic participation in World War II were basic to assimilationist tendencies, but two more strictly academic factors were also involved—the sheer growth of Catholic higher education and deeper involvement in graduate work.

Between 1920 and 1960, the number of Catholic colleges and universities increased by only 78 percent (from 130 to 231), but their total enrollment mushroomed from 34,000 to over 300,000. Already in 1920, laypersons constituted three-quarters of the faculties of the institutions classified as universities; by 1960, the lay faculty was even more dominant there and outnumbered the religious faculty everywhere except in the women's colleges. As they grew larger, diversified their curricular offerings, and became more administratively complex, the tone-setting Catholic institutions could not help being progressively assimilated to the overall academic culture, even though it was still regarded as "secular." This was especially the case after World War II, when an increasing proportion of new faculty members received their graduate training in leading non-Catholic universities.

Graduate work in Catholic universities (other than CUA) really began in the 1920s, mostly at the master's degree level, and often in summer sessions heavily patronized by sisters intent on upgrading their academic qualifications to teach in their own high schools and colleges. Graduate work was thus keyed to the massive expansion of education already mentioned, and attracted lay students too as growing undergraduate enrollments created a demand for teachers while simultaneously giving more young people an introduction to the intellectual life.

A very weak showing in the first national review of graduate programs (in 1934) made Catholic educators more sensitive to the need for stringent quality standards, causing the Jesuits in particular to redouble their efforts. During the post-World War II expansion, full-time doctoral-level work developed at eight or ten Catholic universities. Although the proportion of American doctorates they produced was minuscule—about 3 percent from the mid-1950s through the mid-1960s—commitment to graduate work hastened the academic acculturation of Catholic universities to prevailing national norms.

Vatican II and the New Configuration

In the mid-1960s what had previously been a gradual transition in Catholic higher education suddenly accelerated. Three factors combined to produce the ensuing revolution: (1) the ongoing processes of social and academic assimilation already noted; (2) changes in the Church's doctrinal and disciplinary stance stemming from the Second Vatican Council; and (3) the seismic upheaval in American society brought on by the racial crisis, the Vietnam War, the rise of the New Left, and other movements which contributed to widespread turmoil on the nation's college campuses.

The onset of radical change was dramatized by a series of spectacular eruptions over academic freedom at St. John's (New York), the University of Dayton, CUA, and elsewhere, during which a few dissident Catholic professors argued that an institutional religious commitment was irreconcilable with the true nature of higher education. While rejecting this extreme, a group of outstanding Catholic educators issued the "Land O'Lakes Statement" (1967) asserting that a Catholic university "must have a true autonomy and academic freedom in the face of authority of whatever kind, lay or clerical, external to the academic community itself." Since theology was now being taught at Catholic universities, this kind of claim caused uneasiness among bishops, the Church's official teachers of doctrine, and set off an extended dialogue between Rome and American Catholic educators which has continued to the present.

The laicization of boards of trustees, which also began in the late 1960s, constituted a practical move toward autonomy, since it transferred ultimate authority over an institution from the sponsoring religious community to an independent board numerically dominated by laypersons. But the effective influence of religious communities was more seriously weakened by a massive exodus from their ranks and a drastic falling-off of new vocations. Membership in the Jesuits, the most important teaching community, declined by more than a third between 1965 and 1990. Comparable losses among communities of religious women were especially damaging to women's colleges because the sisters bore more of the teaching load in those schools. At least two dozen have closed over the past thirty years; approximately four times that number survived, many by becoming coeducational or offering nontraditional programs. Curricular requirements, especially in philosophy and religion, were loosened up in all Catholic colleges, as were regulations governing student life.

Accompanying these changes was a collapse of intellectual confidence, even among those who did not simply reject Catholic schools as outmoded ghetto institutions. The self-criticism of the fifties had become an almost hateful repudiation of virtually everything "preconciliar," neoscholasticism most emphatically included. But since agreement on this philosophical system had served for two generations to reconcile faith and reason, its sudden abandonment left Catholic educators unable to explain what the religious commitments supposedly built into their schools had to do with the academic and scholarly activities carried on there (which have continued to improve). The resulting perplexity about how to offer a convincing answer to the question, "What *difference* does it make for a place to be Catholic?" gave rise to what was first called an identity crisis and is still being discussed as a problem.

The Catholic identity issue is basic to the ongoing dialogue with Rome as to the proper relationship between academic institutions and ecclesiastical authorities. A spiritually rooted commitment to social service has been suggested as meeting the need for a new religious rationale for Catholic higher education, but it is by no means universally accepted. Many faculty members consider the religious character of an institution far less important than its academic quality, and object to taking religion into consideration in hiring. Others, however, are increasingly concerned about the threat of secularization, and believe that it demands systematic attention if Catholic higher education is to meet the deepest challenge of modernity in its most recent form.

Curran, Robert Emmett, S.J. *The Bicentennial History of Georgetown University: Volume I, From Academy to University, 1789–1889.* Washington, D.C.: Georgetown University Press, 1993.

Gleason, Philip. *Contending with Modernity: Catholic Higher Education in the Twentieth Century.* New York: Oxford University Press, 1995.

Leahy, William P., S.J. *Adapting to America: Catholics, Jesuits, and Higher Education in the Twentieth Century.* Washington, D.C.: Georgetown University Press, 1991.

Nuesse, C. Joseph. *The Catholic University of America: A Centennial History.* Washington, D.C.: The Catholic University of America Press, 1990.

Power, Edward J. *Catholic Higher Education in America: A History.* New York: Appleton-Century-Crofts, 1972.

PHILIP GLEASON

CATHOLIC EDUCATION, PAROCHIAL

While one form or another of Catholic schooling has existed in what is now the United States since the early seventeenth century, such schooling has taken different shapes at various times. These largely have mirrored shifts within both American Catholicism and the broader culture within which it has been situated.

Colonial Education

Initially, the Church provided schooling in the colonial territories belonging to the French and Spanish. These served a constituency of colonists and Indians, utilizing both traditional literacy and classical curricula and various forms of vocational education.

Throughout most of the rest of the present-day United States, Catholicism was a minority religion, and its educational arrangements reflected this fact. Maryland, founded as a Catholic refuge in 1634, witnessed the establishment of its first Catholic school by Ralph Crouch in 1640. After Anglicanism became the colony's established religion in 1692, however, education by the Anglo-American Catholic community went underground.

Quaker religious tolerance made Pennsylvania the only place in which Catholicism could be practiced freely during much of the colonial era, and it was here that Catholic schooling flourished. In 1745 or 1746 the Jesuits founded a school at Bohemia Manor in territory claimed by both Maryland and Pennsylvania with the hope that the ambiguous border would protect them from persecution. Around 1743 two Jesuits from Germany began schools for the growing community of German immigrants near Conewago and at Goshenhoppen. About ten years later, the Jesuits Ferdinand Farmer (Steinmayer) and Robert Molyneux arrived from Germany and founded schools at two Philadelphia parishes. These activities represented almost the entire scope of Catholic education in the British colonies during this era, since anti-Catholic laws prevented the foundation of schools virtually everywhere else.

The Federal Era

The first really significant growth of Catholic schooling occurred in the early federal period. Gabriel Richard, a Sulpician priest working in the Northwest Territory, founded a seminary and girls' school in 1804 at what would later be Detroit, and published the first English language American Catholic textbook, *The Child's Spelling Book,* in 1809.

Still, however, Catholic school development was sporadic. The Catholic community during this period was quite small, fairly poor, and lacked the presence of communities of religious women. This latter especially was a critical factor retarding institutional development.

Initial attempts at school formation by small, transient communities of sisters whose origins were European met with failure. While several communities established schools, there were either not enough personnel to staff them, or the community found it impossible to survive at that particular location, and moved elsewhere.

It was only with the formation of communities of native-born religious sisters that Catholic schools became a genuine possibility. The first of these was a group of "pious ladies" who gathered together at Georgetown in 1814. These women, who eventually became a convent of the Visitation Order, founded a school that taught reading, writing, arithmetic and geography. Although the beginnings were difficult due to the small pool of available students, the sisters hung on, and by 1832 their school was enrolling a hundred students. The foundation of another American sisterhood, the Sisters of Charity, by the Anglican convert Elizabeth Bayley Seton in 1809, led to the formation of a school at Emmitsburg, Maryland, in 1810 and to eight more by 1828. In 1812 two more communities were founded in Kentucky, the Sisters of Loretto and the Sisters of Charity of Nazareth, and were followed ten years later by a community of Dominicans. These sisterhoods founded several schools on the Kentucky frontier, especially in the locale of Bardstown, an early Catholic center.

Within a few years, European communities had established themselves in the United States with sufficient members to carry on educational works until Americans joined them. The Sisters of St. Joseph arrived in 1836, and were followed by the Sisters of Providence and Sisters of Notre Dame de Namur in 1844. These sisterhoods were the first in a vanguard of European religious communities that would contribute greatly to the establishment and growth of Catholic schooling in the young nation.

While American Catholic schooling's beginnings were largely in the small towns of the Middle Border, its real growth took place in the nation's growing urban areas. The first Catholic school in New England was begun by the Ursulines in Boston in 1820. The school, which was eventually transferred to Charlestown and burned in the anti-Catholic riots of 1834, enrolled over one hundred girls in its first year, teaching a curriculum of both classical and practical subjects. In New York, which despite its cosmopolitan character had maintained anti-Catholic legislation until 1784, the first Roman Catholic free school was established in 1800 and by 1806 had become the second largest denominational school in a city where such schools were the predominant form of instruction, enrolling two hundred twenty pupils at two sites. Besides the schools founded as a result of the early efforts of Farmer and Molyneux, the German Catholics of Philadelphia's Holy Trinity parish established a school to meet their needs in 1789. In 1818 the Religious of the Sacred Heart established both an academy and parochial school at St. Charles, Missouri, near St. Louis, and a branch at Grand Coteau, Louisiana, in 1821.

During this period, Catholic education was generally a small-scale enterprise, characterized by the poverty of both institutions and constituents, severe teacher shortages (those who did teach were frequently expected to serve as church sextons or organists), and a sparse and dispersed Catholic population numbering fewer than half a million in 1830. Despite such disadvantages, there were at least two hundred Catholic schools in existence by 1840, with about half west of the Alleghenies in the territory of America's westward expansion.

Immigration and School Formation

During the period from 1830 to the turn of the century, American Catholic schooling expanded at a dramatic pace. This increase mirrored the growth of the nation's Catholic population which increased from around 500,000 in 1830 to eight million by 1884, doubling each decade. The first wave of this immigration included large numbers of Irish escaping the potato blight of 1821 and famine of 1845. Also important were large numbers of Germans fleeing difficult economic conditions or the abortive revolutions of 1848.

Key to the development of Catholic education was the appearance of immigrant religious who would provide the cheap labor necessary to staff the schools. By 1884, over forty new communities of religious women and eleven of brothers had arrived in the United States and begun their ministries here.

Besides immigration and the availability of teachers, Catholic school formation was also aided by internal forces supporting educational development as well as external ones that caused Catholics to draw together more closely. For many immigrant communities, especially non-English speakers, schooling was an important way of maintaining their unique ethnic and cultural identities in the face of the overwhelmingly dominant Protestant Anglophone mainstream. The establishment of ethnic parishes frequently included schooling as an important component of their mission of cultural preservation. Thus, Lithuanians in Chicago complained that the Catholic school was turning their children into Poles, a function of the pastor's decision to employ Polish sisters to staff it when Lithuanian religious proved impossible to obtain.

The external pressure of a hostile mainstream culture also encouraged Catholics to create unique institutions in which they would not be stigmatized for their beliefs. Nativism, especially in the urban centers of the Northeast, helped create a culture of difference that provided Catholics with a well-defined identity whether they desired it or not.

These latter forces combined to blight the bishops' expectations of accommodation with the elites who controlled the developing common school systems. Initially, Catholics were successful in many locales in obtaining shares of the state school fund, leading to the hope that Catholic schooling might become part of the publicly-subsidized educational network. Illustrative of such arrangements were the Lowell Plan (1831–52) in Massachusetts and the Poughkeepsie Plan (1873–98) in New York, which provided state support for Catholic schools, including teacher salaries. As the common school movement took a more definite shape, however, state funding began to be channeled exclusively to the schools it sponsored. Disillusioned by various attempts either to achieve state funding for Catholic schools or to merge such institutions into the common school system, the bishops turned increasingly to the development of a parallel network of institutions. While the admonitions encouraging the establishment of Catholic schools given by the First Provincial Council of Baltimore in 1829 were fairly mild, Catholic bishops insisted with increasing frequency and force from this point on that establishment of an alternative system of schooling was the only viable option remaining to them. More and more pressure was placed on pastors and parents alike to found and support such a separate network of parochial schools.

The impetus given to school formation by the convergence of all of these forces was mirrored in the rapid growth in both quantity and scope of Catholic education. In the Archdiocese of Cincinnati, for example, the number of children attending Catholic schools had increased to around 15,000 by 1866, representing over 37 percent of the city's school attendance and raising fears for the long-term viability of public education. In New York City, the "School War" of 1841–42 fought by Bishop John Hughes with the Public School Society, a Protestant philanthropic group that sought to establish free schools, had the effect of speeding the development of separate Catholic schools, while school foundations were unremarkable events in the Diocese of Philadelphia after 1830.

The Late Nineteenth and Early Twentieth Centuries

The intensification of most of the internal and external forces in the late nineteenth and early twentieth centuries drove Catholic schooling at an even more frenetic pace. The Catholic population swelled from nine million in the 1890s to twenty million in the 1920s, the result of immigration from southern and eastern Europe, especially Austria-Hungary, Italy and Poland. Even greater cultural disjuncture from the mainstream than was true of earlier immigrants tended to promote school development, as did the passage

of Progressive-era child labor legislation. The increasingly powerful hierarchy, too, was strong in its promotion of Catholic schools and condemnation of "godless" public ones. The legislative high point was reached at the Third Plenary Council of Baltimore in 1884 which mandated the establishment of a grammar school in each parish within two years. In several dioceses, synods were held in the following years that reinforced the plenary council's position to the extent of threatening the removal of pastors who failed to establish parochial schools.

While broad religious, cultural, and political forces drove Catholic school establishment, however, the pace of school formation was uneven. Factors such as regional and ethnic peculiarities helped to account for such differences. For example, in 1880, 94 percent of Chicago's parishes had schools that enrolled 22 percent of the city's school-age children, while Boston, with a proportionally higher Catholic population, had schools in only 37 percent of its parishes and attendance at these represented only 10 percent of the school-age population. Here, the difference is explained by the striking ability of Boston's Catholic leadership to co-opt the public schools, blunting the need for a separate educational network.

The rate of school formation also differed on the basis of ethnicity. Chicago's Poles outnumbered Italians by two to one in 1900, but had thirteen times as many schools. This difference probably reflected the cultural biases immigrants brought from their homelands, which for Italians included a tradition of churches and schools funded solely by gifts and endowments rather than popular contributions.

In some places, too, parents were more oriented toward public schooling as a channel of upward mobility for their children. The attitudes of local bishops were also a factor: John Williams of Boston was no more a promoter of Catholic schooling after the Third Plenary Council of Baltimore than he had been before. Archbishop John Ireland of St. Paul, while a supporter of Catholic education, was also in favor of Catholic attendance at public schools as a means toward assimilation. A speech he gave praising public education at the National Educational Association in 1890 provoked considerable controversy, and was repudiated by some of his fellow bishops. He also came under fire for the compromise that he approved in 1891 by which two Catholic schools in the small towns of Faribault and Stillwater were taken over by the local school boards, thereby receiving public funding but still retaining their Catholic teachers. His actions seemed to receive Vatican approbation with the publication of the *Fourteen Points* of Archbishop Francesco Satolli, the first apostolic delegate to the United States, in 1892 which both promoted Catholic schools and allowed for the possibility of state institutions. Conservative prelates such as Bernard McQuaid in Rochester and Michael Corrigan in New York strenuously opposed this new direction, and successfully argued their case in Rome. Finally, Vatican officials issued a decree that allowed Ireland's experiment to continue but forbade its duplication in other dioceses. These sobering results blunted much of whatever Catholic enthusiasm still existed for cooperation with public schooling.

While a few bishops supported public schooling as a viable alternative to parochial education, they were in a distinct minority. The first decades of the twentieth century were a time of growth and consolidation for Catholic education. In 1908 America officially ceased to be a missionary country, an acknowledgment of the more established character of its Catholic community. While restrictive immigration laws in the 1920s stopped the flow of European Catholics to the United States, a high birth rate and increasing prosperity fueled the development of Catholic schools. The Catholic population by 1920 had reached over 19 million, with an increase in Catholic school attendance from around 400,000 in 1880 to 1.7 million. Dioceses began to imitate the administrative structure of public schooling. The first diocesan school board was established in New York in 1886 and several other dioceses created school offices shortly thereafter. The role of these agencies, however, differed substantially from their public counterparts. Central Catholic school units served a function that was largely one of record keeping and broad policy enforcement. For most purposes, the schools continued to be governed by the local pastors and principals. The formation of the Catholic Educational Association in 1904 signaled the concern with establishing a national professional organization.

In other respects, too, the saga of Catholic school formation paralleled that of public schooling. During the last decades of the nineteenth century, the public high school became America's normative secondary institution. Catholics, too, saw an advantage in the "people's college," especially for those not going on to higher education, and began to establish comparable institutions, with the first, Catholic High School of Philadelphia, founded in 1890.

Secular teacher education had become professionalized by the late nineteenth century, with two-year teachers' colleges providing the normative training. While communities of religious women previously had viewed religious profession as the only necessary credential for teaching in a parochial school, this external pressure motivated them to obtain formal instruction as well. The first in-service training appeared in New York in 1905, and was followed here and in other places by extension classes. By the early 1920s, over a dozen colleges across the country were replicating The Catholic University of America's Sisters College by offering summer credential and degree programs for religious women educators.

The position of Catholic schools, too, was ensured by the U.S. Supreme Court case of *Pierce v. the Society of Sisters*. In 1922 Oregon had passed an initiative promoted by the Ku Klux Klan and Scottish Rite Masons requiring children aged eight to sixteen to attend public schools. The law was challenged by the Sisters of the Holy Names of Jesus and Mary who staffed a number of schools in the state. In 1925 the Supreme Court rejected Oregon's contention that the law was necessary to insure Americanization and affirmed the rights of parents to select the appropriate educational environment for their children. The decision settled once for all the right of Catholic schools to exist and fueled the development of parochial education during the era.

The Mid-Twentieth Century

The years between the end of World War I and the Second Vatican Council were times of tremendous expansion for Catholic parochial schooling. During these years, despite the temporary downturn during the Great Depression, the number of Catholic schools doubled and the number of pupils tripled. In the first half of the century, the growth is largely accounted for by the increasing prosperity of the Catholic community, allowing it to establish institutions for its perpetuation.

That proponents of parochial schooling saw it as a unique expression of Catholic culture is clear. Critiques of public education for its "godless" character are common in Catholic periodicals of the era, as is distaste for forms of education based on the implicit premise that the secular and sacred ought to be dichotomized. "Secularism," "paganism," and "indifferentism" are all epithets hurled at the competing public schools during the era. The Progressive pedagogy pioneered by John Dewey is constantly lambasted as a result of perceptions that it pandered to children's worst instincts and lacked meaningful discipline. The testing movement was also criticized as a threat to the primacy of the individual. Catholic concern about communists in the public schools began in the 1930s and continued for the next several decades. This fear was coupled with that

Sister with students

of progressivism by those who saw the latter as a communist stalking-horse.

The peak years of Catholic school growth occurred between 1950 and 1960. While this was largely an artifact of the postwar "baby boom," it also mirrored concern over the maintenance of a distinctive Catholic culture. Thus, while public elementary enrollments grew by 142 percent during this period, Catholic numbers increased by 171 percent. An indication of Catholic assimilation into the mainstream was the increased acceptance of educational psychology, though without most of the Freudian elements then in vogue, and a somewhat greater attention in the curriculum to schooling's social dimensions. In 1954 the National Catholic Educational Association established a department of special education to address the dearth of such facilities in Catholic education. Even in these growth years, however, nearly half of the Catholic school-age population did not attend parochial schools.

In the political arena, Catholic mobilization once again to obtain a share of state and especially, of federal, funding created tensions between the Church and the rest of American society. Indeed, it became axiomatic in educational politics from 1950 to 1965 that general federal aid to education was impossible since Catholics would oppose any legislation that excluded parochial schools, and many others would reject legislation that included them. In the process of these political struggles, Catholics ended up more estranged than ever from public school advocates, who saw them as "spoilers" in any attempt to obtain federal aid for primary and secondary schooling.

Race also exerted a political force in the development of Catholic school policy. Even before the 1954 U.S. Supreme Court decision *Brown v. the Board of Education* that eventually resulted in the desegregation of public education, some Catholic dioceses had begun to take steps in this direction. Because the success of such efforts depended on the local political ecology and especially, on the willingness of the ordinary to promote such activities, movement on this front was uneven. Washington, San Antonio and St. Louis were early pioneers in school desegregation, while dioceses in the deep South moved more slowly. In cities like Chicago, local bishops found themselves opposed by individual pastors and congregants, and managed the process of desegregation only by continual application of steady pressure.

The Era of Crisis ·

The mid-1960s witnessed the beginning of what was to be a dramatic change in the course of Catholic parochial education. Some dioceses experienced enrollment drops of nearly 20 percent in a single year. Between 1966 and 1968 alone, 637 Catholic elementary and secondary schools closed, principally in inner city and rural areas, while only 207 new ones were opened. The period from 1965 to 1975

witnessed a drop of 35 percent in grammar school enrollments, though the high school population continued to increase. Partially, this was the result of demographic forces and especially, the ending of the "baby boom." More far-reaching cultural forces also played a part. American Catholics had become more assimilated into the mainstream culture and, as a result, more secularized. The Second Vatican Council appeared to validate such shifts to complete participation in the wider culture, and encouraged more focused critics like Mary Perkins Ryan who in her 1968 book *Are Parochial Schools the Answer?* argued that Catholic education was generally inferior to that of public schooling, and encouraged a "ghetto mentality" that was anti-ecumenical in spirit. Fixed resources, she argued, were better spent on broadly-based parish religious education programs. Especially significant was the fact that such critiques were being made not by a public school advocate but by a noted Catholic laywoman. A more muted note was sounded by Andrew M. Greeley and Peter H. Rossi in their 1966 study, *The Education of American Catholics,* when they found no evidence that schools were absolutely necessary for the survival of the American Church, but opined that they had been worth the efforts expended to establish them.

Another major factor affecting parochial education during this era was a rapid change in the character of school staffs. Cultural shifts had helped bring about a massive exodus of clergy and especially, of religious women. The situation was compounded by a significant reduction in the number of religious vocations and a decreasing preference for teaching as their primary ministry by many religious women who remained. In 1950, fewer than 20 percent of Catholic elementary teachers were lay. By 1979, the number was over 70 percent. While many welcomed predominantly lay-staffed schools as concrete expressions of new theology of the laity emerging from the Second Vatican Council, others saw such schools as transmitting a diluted Catholic culture. More obviously, the necessity of paying significantly greater wages to lay teachers than had been given to religious transformed the economics of parochial education. Schools that had been able to function as de facto common schools, serving virtually all the children of a parish and charging nominal tuition now were forced to increase fees in order to remain solvent. This, in turn, placed significant strain on the budgets of many parishes and eliminated families unable to pay the costs and unwilling to ask for tuition assistance. Thus, in many instances, the center of gravity of parish life shifted from the parochial school to other activities.

Contemporary Developments

Developments since the mid-1970s make the future and direction of parochial schooling unclear. On the one hand, both the number of institutions and students have continued to decline. On the other, both sets of declines since the early 1980s are proportionately the lowest since the mid-1960s, suggesting that the situation may have stabilized. Moreover, there is sketchy evidence that the Catholic schools may be developing new constituencies. Since 1970–71, the Hispanic population of Catholic schools has risen from 5 to over 8 percent, and that of Asian Americans from 0.5 to 1.8 percent. Thus, parochial education may have begun to develop a constituency among newer immigrants. This is occurring, however, in a different climate than was the case during the century of mass immigration beginning around 1830. The external pressure of religious discrimination in public education that confronted earlier immigrants is notably lacking. A critical internal difference has also proved important to the dynamics of Catholic school development among the newcomers. Unlike previous immigrant groups, more recent arrivals tend not to have brought clergy and religious with them. Thus, the schools that serve them inevitably have significant numbers of lay teachers, many of whom are not from the native culture. These factors also exercise a retarding influence on the sort of school development that characterized earlier ages.

By the 1970s, Catholic schools in many urban areas had come to function as alternatives to problematic public school systems. This represented a new mission for parochial education since, for the first time in the history of such schools in the United States, many of their African American constituents were not Catholics. Such schools appear to have been most successful when they operated on the one hand as virtually independent religious schools with few ties to local parishes or on the other were intensely connected with parishes as vehicles for evangelization. The inability of most constituencies to provide long-term financial support for such schools, however, raises questions about their viability.

In the final analysis, there is not enough data to predict the future of American Catholic parochial education. The complex matrix of forces that have impacted on such schools in the past are still in enough flux to make their future uncertain. To the extent that American Catholics sense their own culture as uniquely different from that of the mainstream, and possess the resources necessary to establish institutions to propagate that culture, Catholic schooling will continue to have a place of importance in the life of the American Church.

Buetow, Harold A. *Of Singular Benefit.* New York: The Macmillan Company, 1970.

Cross, Robert. "Origins of the Catholic Parochial Schools in America." *American Benedictine Review* 16 (1965) 194–219.

Lannie, Vincent P. "Church and School Triumphant: Sources of American Catholic Educational Historiography." *History of Education Quarterly* 16 (1976) 131–45.

Lazerson, Marvin. "Understanding American Catholic Educational History." *History of Education Quarterly* 16 (1977) 297–310.

Sanders, James W. *Education of an Urban Minority.* New York: Oxford University Press, 1977.

F. MICHAEL PERKO, S.J.

CATHOLIC EDUCATION, SCHOOL STATISTICS

The status of Catholic educational institutions and programs in the United States and outlying areas at the beginning of 1995 was reflected in figures (as of January 1) reported by *The Official Catholic Directory, 1995.*

Colleges and Universities: 235 (U.S., 229; Outlying Areas, 6).

College and University Students: 656,905 (U.S., 635,648; Outlying Areas, 21,257).

High Schools: 1,350 (823 diocesan and parochial; 527 private). U.S., 1,238 (728 diocesan and parochial; 510 private). Outlying Areas, 112 (95 diocesan and parochial; 17 private).

High School Students: 652,054 (378,847 diocesan and parochial; 273,207 private). U.S., 614,798 (348,448 diocesan and parochial; 266,350 private). Outlying Areas, 37,256 (30,399 diocesan and parochial; 6,857 private).

Public High School Students Receiving Religious Instruction: 798,072 (U.S., 776,228; Outlying Areas, 21,844).

Elementary Schools: 7,210 (6,911 diocesan and parochial; 299 private). U.S., 7,050 (6,774 diocesan and parochial; 276 private). Outlying Areas, 160 (137 diocesan and parochial; 23 private).

Elementary School Students: 2,023,976 (1,949,989 diocesan and parochial; 73,987 private). U.S., 1,975,652 (1,910,305 diocesan and parochial; 65,347 private). Outlying Areas, 48,324 (39,684 diocesan and parochial; 8,640 private).

Public Elementary School Students Receiving Religious Instruction: 3,401,284 (U.S., 3,320,104; Outlying Areas, 81,180).

Non-Residential Schools for Handicapped: 93 (U.S., 92; Outlying Areas, 1). **Students: 11,241** (U.S., 11,229; Outlying Areas, 12).

Teachers—167,768. U.S., 162,799: Lay Persons, 146,264; Sisters, 12,603; Priests, 2,329; Brothers, 1,534; Scholastics, 69. **Outlying Areas, 4,969:** Lay Persons, 4,462; Sisters, 366; Priests, 111; Brothers, 30.

Seminaries—218 (72 diocesan; 146 religious). U.S.: 202 (67 diocesan; 135 religious). Outlying Areas: 16 (5 diocesan; 11 religious).

Seminarians—5,083 (3,522 diocesan; 1,561 religious). U.S.: 4,964 (3,475 diocesan; 1,489 religious). Outlying Areas: 119 (47 diocesan; 72 religious).

CATHOLIC EDUCATION, SCHOOL SUPERINTENDENCY

Beginnings

The diocesan superintendency, like its public school counterpart, evolved to fill a need. Initially, school boards/boards of inspectors were instituted to supervise schools within the diocese. These early boards were composed of pastors named by their bishop. As the number of schools increased so, too, did the work of the inspectors. Soon the demands began to infringe on the pastors' parish responsibilities. This led to their recommendation that one of their group be appointed full-time inspector who could do the day-to-day work and report regularly to the board.

One of the early diocesan school boards was instituted in 1886 in the Archdiocese of New York, a result of the archdiocese's fifth synod. Two years after its establishment (1888) the first diocesan inspector (superintendent), the Rev. William E. Degnan, was appointed. The appointment was among the clergy appointments which appeared in the April 18, 1888, issue of *The American Catholic News* (the archdiocesan newspaper) and read: "Rev. William E. Degnan, D.D., of St. Mary's Church, New York, has been made superintendent of the parochial schools of the archdiocese. He will probably reside at St. Mary's Church, New York, and his duty will be to visit the different parochial schools and attend to the advancement of education. His action will be subject to the rulings of the regular school board of the archdiocese." He served one and a half years and was replaced by the Rev. Michael J. Considine.

In 1889 the Rev. Nevin F. Fischer was appointed superintendent in the Philadelphia archdiocese. Omaha was next with the Rev. S. F. Carroll, followed by Brooklyn with Rev. John L. Belford. The list continued growing with appointments in Boston, Pittsburgh, Baltimore, Buffalo, and Springfield, Massachusetts. The first lay superintendent, Attorney Wilfrid J. Lessard, served the Diocese of Manchester, New Hampshire, from 1919–32. Today each diocese has a person in a similar position.

As new superintendents were named, they would confer with practicing superintendents regarding the role and its functions. These early superintendents occupied themselves and their time developing an organization of schools in their dioceses.

The work of the early superintendents included visiting each school, examining teachers and students, evaluating the course of studies, and meeting with the pastor. After the visit, he prepared a report incorporating the status of inspected persons and items and recommendations for improvement. Later a summary of these reports was submitted to the school board and bishop.

After the period of system organization, superintendents focused on teacher and administrator preparation and curriculum issues. In the 1940s and thereafter, they became involved in securing support from state and national governments for students and parents. This continues today with voucher and tax credit efforts. After Vatican Council II and the enrollment peak of the 1960s, they encountered new challenges, including declining enrollment, school closings, decreased religious and increased numbers of lay teachers and administrators, substantially increased budgets resulting from the religious/lay staffing changes, the questioning of the value of Catholic schools resulting in the redefinition of their role in the Church's mission, and the maintenance of the Catholic identity of the schools. Today they wrestle with the use of technology, new moral and ethical issues precipitated by societal and cultural changes, and students whose demographic characteristics are significantly different from those of an early period, e.g., increased numbers from single-parent families.

Since the early part of the century, superintendents have not had to face these issues alone but have worked together regularly redefining their roles and functions and addressing the changing school challenges. Again, like their public school colleagues, an organization was needed to gather them to share experiences and share ideas.

Superintendents' Organization

Like many organizations the diocesan superintendents' group was born out of need. Bishop Thomas J. Conaty, the rector of The Catholic University of America, aided in the founding of the Educational Conference of Seminary Faculties, the Association of Catholic Colleges, and the Parish School Conference, which in 1904 joined to form the Catholic Educational Association (CEA and later NCEA).

The Parish School Conference was an outgrowth of the Association of Catholic Colleges and served as the organization for superintendents, board members and principals. In 1908 the superintendents became a Section of the CEA Parish School Department whose object of organization was: "To form a union for the purpose of preparing and discussing papers, and the exchange of ideas on subjects pertaining to the general and special work of superintending and supervising parish schools."

The first chair of the group was the Rev. Philip R. McDevitt, Philadelphia superintendent and later fourth bishop of Harrisburg, Pennsylvania. In their formative years (1908–35) the issues commanding most attention were administration, curriculum, religious education, and teachers.

The next phase began in 1936 after the group successfully petitioned the NCEA Board to become a department. During the departmental years (1936–71) the organization's principal issues remained administration, curriculum, teachers, and religious education, but the new topics of public relations and the media were added.

Following Vatican Council II dioceses began reorganizing their offices to implement the council's documents and education offices were included in that reorganization. New positions and titles such as vicar for education, superintendent of education, and director of religious education began appearing. This change was reflected in the redefining of the superintendents' department and in 1972 it assumed a new form and title, Chief Administrators of Catholic Education (CACE). It underwent a second reformation in 1979 which resulted in three divisions: total education (vicars), schools (superintendents), and religious education (directors of religious education).

During the CACE period, the group elected its first lay president, J. Alan Davitt (New York State Catholic Superintendents Executive) 1977–79, and first woman, Sr. Anne C. Leonard, C.N.D. (superintendent, Oklahoma City), 1991–94.

In its nearly ninety-year history, CACE and its predecessors have served as the forum for superintendents and other diocesan educational leaders. The annual conferences, beginning in Cincinnati in 1908, have provided these leaders with camaraderie, new ideas, and the opportunity to speak with one voice on national issues.

CACE programs.
The *Proceedings and Addresses of the National Catholic Educational Association* 1904–66.

JOHN AUGENSTEIN

CATHOLIC ENCYCLOPEDIA, THE

The Catholic Encyclopedia is best described by its subtitle, *An International Work of Reference on the Constitution, Doctrine, Discipline, and History of the Catholic Church.* The first volume appeared in March 1907 followed by subsequent volumes at consistent and regular intervals. Volume XVI, a detailed index, was published in April 1914 bringing to completion a work that for over half a century was to be the premier source of information on the Catholic Church in the English-speaking world. Two supplementary volumes were published in 1922 and 1950–58 (the latter published by the Gilmary Society).

At the turn of the century the market was flooded with general and special encyclopedias, but all of them fell short in presenting the Catholic story with committed integrity. There was a need for a reliable, scholarly, and authoritative Catholic encyclopedia. Two years before the actual work on the encyclopedia began, a group of five scholars began a series of meetings to lay the groundwork for this ambitious project. In January 1905 these same five individuals were named to the board of editors and the following month they were elected members of the board of directors of the publishing company that was to produce *The Catholic Encyclopedia.* These original editors, Charles G. Herbermann, Edward A. Pace, Condé B. Pallen, Thomas J. Shanan, and John J. Wynne, S.J., remained with the project and guided it to completion.

In February 1906 the editors issued a pamphlet in which they pledged themselves to excellence. In general terms they mapped out the scope, aim, and special characteristics of the encyclopedia. The work was to be a comprehensive and authentic account of the entire cycle of Catholic doctrine, history, actions, and interests. It was to present all that the institutional Church had done for the welfare of humankind, her failures and triumphs, and the accomplishments of her members throughout the course of history. It would differ from general encyclopedias in that it would omit material that had no relation to the Catholic Church. However, since the Church had been such an integral part of human history for almost 2,000 years, *The Catholic Encyclopedia* would chronicle the contributions that Catholics had made in all areas of knowledge. Its audience was to be all inclusive: world-famous theologians, the Catholic clergy, the Catholic laity, and interested Protestants.

Scholars from both sides of the Atlantic representing the major religious orders, seminaries, colleges and universities, joined the editors to suggest and to prepare the articles. The result was this impressive list of contributors: Australia 14, Austria 45, Belgium 63, Canada 88, Central and South America 44, Denmark 1, France 120, Germany 105, Great Britain 186, Holland 33, Ireland 118, Italy 37, the Orient 9, Portugal 2, Scandinavia 2, Spain 8, Switzerland 11, and the United States 559.

The work was applauded by Catholic and non-Catholic critics alike for its detailed articles on medieval literature, history, philosophy, art, and other subjects on which theology had an impact. Accolades were given for the detailed index, the comprehensive and signed articles, the extensive bibliographies, the generous illustrations, and the numerous biographies. On the downside, it was considered less comprehensive than its French counterparts such as the *Dictionnaire de Théologie Catholique.* Its narrow interpretation of events and ideas as well as its somewhat biased treatment of Protestantism were shortcomings which received justifiable criticism.

Writing in *America* (11 [April 18,1914] 8–9), the editor in chief, Charles E. Herbermann, expressed his gratitude to the 28,000 subscribers whose financial generosity had brought the work to completion. He thanked the three American cardinals, the hierarchy, the priests, and the thousands of lay men and women throughout the United States who had supported the project. He especially praised the stockholders, headed by Cardinal John Farley, because of their commitment to and interest in the work. He summed it up saying, "To tell the truth, *The Catholic Encyclopedia* owes its existence to the great Catholic Church itself, to the faith and zeal of its priesthood and its laity, to their intelligence and self-sacrifice, to the Catholics of the United States, but also to the scholars of the Universal Church."

Because of the profound changes that had taken place in the world in general and the Catholic Church in particular during the twentieth century, it became clear that this work could not be updated through supplements. Although the *New Catholic Encyclopedia* (1967–79) was to supersede this somewhat outdated classic, the original *Catholic Encyclopedia* continues to be of value for coverage not found in more modern works.

The Catholic Encyclopedia and Its Makers. New York, 1917.

REGINA A. MELICAN, O.P.

CATHOLIC HEALTH CARE

To trace the history of Catholic-hospital ministry in the United States entails an exploration of several contexts: the development of medical science, particularly the modernization of hospitals and the professionalization of personnel; immigration and the formation of ethnic and religious identities manifested in hospitals within a pluralist society; regional and frontier influences; sexism and racism as reflected in the history of hospitals; varieties of episcopal leadership and the diverse historical charisms of women and men religious; and the devotionalism and spirituality related to the care of the sick. Woven throughout this essay is a thematic thread of pastoral ministry: priests were primarily engaged in sacramental ministry until the rise of pastoral care departments after Vatican Council II; sisters, brothers and lay nurses were unofficially involved in pastoral care, as they brought prayer and Christian compassion to their critically ill patients whom they viewed as *alter Christus*. As St. Vincent de Paul said to the Daughters of Charity in hospital ministry: "When you leave your prayers for the bedside of a patient, you are leaving God for God. Looking after the sick is praying."

Role of Women Religious

Though women religious nursed in hospitals owned by physicians, cities, counties, states, mining companies and railroads, though they responded to epidemics of cholera and yellow fever and though they represented 20 percent of the nursing "corps" in the Civil War and nursed during the Spanish-American War, this essay will focus on ministry in Catholic hospitals. With an emphasis upon the intersection of religion and culture within the principal periods in Catholic and hospital history, this brief comprehensive study will highlight Catholic identities in health care.

Elizabeth Seton's Sisters of Charity, the first community of women religious founded in the United States, was also the first to staff a hospital. The Baltimore Infirmary owned by a group of physicians successfully sought the sisters as nurses in 1823. This soon became the hospital of the University of Maryland. Another group of Sisters of Charity had staffed the state mental hospital near Baltimore, but soon opened their own mental hospital, Mt.

St. Vincent's, near Baltimore, the first Catholic mental hospital in the United States. Though the Ursuline Sisters had charge of a hospital in New Orleans in the early eighteenth century before it was incorporated in the United States, the first extant Catholic hospital was founded in St. Louis, Missouri, in 1828. In response to a request from Joseph Rosati, C.M., bishop of St. Louis, who had received land and funds from John Mullanphy, an Irish-American millionaire, four Sisters of Charity arrived from Emmitsburg on November 5, 1828. Some three weeks later they took charge of the hospital. Officially entitled St. Louis Hospital, it was frequently referred to as Mullanphy Hospital. Of course, Rosati, a Vincentian of the religious family of Vincent de Paul and Louise de Marillac's Daughters of Charity, was very pleased to welcome the American sisters modeled after the Daughters.

The hospital was a three-room log cabin, with the sisters living in the kitchen area so that the two remaining rooms would be for patients. After an inauspicious beginning, the hospital soon became too small for the needs of the city. In 1830 Bishop Rosati wrote to the Leopoldine Foundation in Austria, a strong source of funds for American missionary endeavors. He described the hospital ministry of the sisters: "This is the means Divine Providence makes use of in order to preserve the lives of a number of laborers, sailors, negroes and others, who are received gratis, and treated with kindness and solicitude." With the help of John Mullanphy and other benefactors, the sisters and patients moved into a brick building that could accommodate sixty patients. The new facility opened in 1832, the year of a cholera epidemic in St. Louis and many other cities throughout the nation.

Of the sixteen communities of women religious in the United States in 1849, five nursed in hospitals. The Sisters of Charity, who would soon merge with the French Daughters of Charity, were in charge of five hospitals; Bishop John Hughes of New York assumed direct control of the Sisters of Charity in his diocese; during the cholera epidemic the New York community founded St. Vincent's Hospital. The Sisters of Charity of Nazareth, founded in 1812 by Catherine Spalding and John B. David, S.S., had nursed cholera patients in Kentucky and Tennessee during the epidemics. Each of two European communities, the Sisters of Mercy and the Sisters of St. Joseph, had charge of one hospital in Pittsburgh and Philadelphia respectively. The size of these hospitals ranged from the old charity hospital in New Orleans, which was a state institution with five hundred patients that the Sisters of Charity staffed since 1834, to the hospital in Pittsburgh where the Sisters of Mercy could accommodate eight patients. Hence, during the 1849 cholera epidemic there was a small but effective Catholic presence in contrast to 1832 when only the Sisters of Charity and the Oblate Sisters of Providence, the first African American community of women religious founded in 1829, nursed in Baltimore city almshouses and special cholera hospitals.

The Sisters of Charity and other communities founded in America easily absorbed the ethos of the young republic. For example, in the description of St. John's Infirmary of Milwaukee for the 1850 *Metropolitan Catholic Almanac,* it was noted that "Any patient may call for any clergyman he may prefer. But no minister whether Protestant, or Catholic, will be permitted to preach to, to pray aloud before, or interfere religiously with, such patients as do not ask for the exercise of his office. The rights of conscience must be held paramount to all others." This recognition of conscience stands in stark contrast to several other private and public hospitals, dominated by a strongly evangelistic Protestant ethos, where priests were discouraged from ministering to Catholic patients. This was particularly evident in the Northeast during the first wave of immigration, 1840–60, which fostered nativism and anti-Catholicism.

There were also German-Irish tensions in Philadelphia and New York; for example, Bishop John Neumann enthusiastically supported the 1855 foundation of the Sisters of the Third Order of St. Francis who opened a twenty-bed hospital in 1860. As a strong preservationist of tradition, Neumann reflected the general trend that presumed the preservation of the faith within the context of German language and culture.

Bishop John Hughes, who strongly asserted Catholic identity amidst a hostile climate, struggled to have Catholic chaplains officially recognized as salaried staff of public hospitals. He sponsored the opening of St. Vincent's Hospital in New York under the supervision of his own sister, Angela Hughes, S.C. From the bishop's point of view the hospital provided Catholics with a refuge from the snares of religious prejudice and Protestant proselytism. As one of the sisters at the Catholic hospital in Lowell remarked, "A Protestant hospital existed, but a priest could not enter its precincts and a Catholic conveyed to its wards was exposed to dying without the sacraments."

Sisters on The Western Frontier

In contrast to the strong institutional development within the immigrant Church during the second half of the nineteenth century, the Church in Seattle, Salt Lake City, and San Antonio was missionary, self-reliant, activist, pragmatic and open to the plasticity of culture on the expanding rim of the westward expansion of the nation. Though the frontier was peopled by Catholics of every ethnic group and though there were parishes that reflected ethnic rivalries, there was a distinctive regional flavor to Catholicism that developed in pioneer conditions.

In response to the demands of the health-care mission, women religious stressed the active apostolate rather than contemplative prayer and tended to be more self-determined than their sisters in the structured and institutionalized Northeast. In many towns the sisters' hospital was the only facility available. Without sufficient numbers of priests, these sisters acted as "priest-chaplains" invoking the presence of God in prayer and ministry. The sisters' pastoral care blended with nineteenth-century women's sphere of domestic life to impose a touch of refinement on the rough edges of frontier existence.

In response to a 1852 request from Bishop Augustine Blanchet of Nesqually, Washington, whose see city was in Fort Vancouver, five Sisters of Charity of Providence arrived there in 1856 to establish a school and a hospital. Founded in Quebec in 1843, the sisters were influenced by the Daughters of Charity. As superior of the Fort Vancouver mission, Mother Joseph Pariseau worked with an ad hoc group of Catholic, Protestant, and Jewish women who, in interfaith cooperation so characteristic of the frontier, raised money for furnishings and a pharmacy for the one-room hospital, "a small wooden building of 16' x 24' with four windows."

Known as "the builder," Mother Pariseau had learned carpentry and supervision of construction work from her father. She personally rode horseback through the mining communities to raise money for the sisters' mission projects. When the sisters moved to Portland, Oregon, she designed a seventy-five-bed hospital. With only twenty-three priests to serve a sprawling Catholic population of about twenty thousand, the St. Vincent's Hospital (1875) represented a singular Catholic presence on the frontier. When Mother Pariseau died in 1902, there were two provinces of 250 professed Sisters of Providence, many of whom were nursing in the eleven hospitals located in Washington and Oregon. Considered the first architect of the Northwest by the American Institute of Architects, Mother Pariseau's missionary endeavors were memorialized when she was chosen to represent the state in Statuary Hall in Washington, D.C. She was the fifth woman and first woman religious to be so honored. However, a bas-relief monument to "Nuns of the Battlefield" had been erected in the nation's capital in 1924 to honor the Civil War Nurses. The sister-nurses in the Civil War and those of the frontier, such as the Sisters of Providence in Washington, the Sisters of Charity of Leavenworth, the Sisters of St. Joseph of Carondolet, the Holy Cross Sisters, the Sisters of Mercy, and the Sisters of Charity of the Incarnate Word not only responded to the health-care needs of the West but in the process undermined the anti-Catholicism and nativism so frequently manifested in American history.

Expansion of Catholic Hospitals

In 1875, a decade after the Civil War, the number of Catholic hospitals numbered about 175. During the next twenty-five years medical science had experienced significant progress—germ theory, aseptic surgery, the pathology laboratory, later the x-ray, expansion of residency programs such as gynecology, orthopedics, and opthalmology. By the turn of the century anesthesiology and clinical pathology were entering the residency specialties in medicine. All of this changed the hospital from a working-class setting for the severely ill and injured—those too poor to be attended at home—to a middle-class institution for diagnosis, treatment, and curing illnesses.

The precipitous increase in the number of hospitals reflects these modern developments of medical science and nursing education: from 178 in 1872 to 4,000 in 1910; Catholic hospitals from 75 in 1872 to nearly 400 in 1910. Schools and hospitals were established by sisters representing the new immigrant groups from Germany, the Austro-Hungarian Empire, and Italy; of the forty-nine new foundations of women religious begun between 1870 and 1890, thirty-nine originated in Europe, eight in Canada, and twelve in the United States. Refugees from Bismarck's *Kurturkampf* dominated the twenty-six foundations in the 1870s. The Franciscan Sisters of the Sacred Hearts of Jesus and Mary founded Pius Hospital (later St. Anthony's) in St. Louis, St. Joseph's in Milwaukee, and St. Mary's in Racine, Wisconsin. Other German communities, such as the Poor Sisters of St. Francis Seraph of the Perpetual Adoration, founded St. Joseph's Hospital in Omaha, Nebraska, and six other hospitals in Colorado, Wisconsin, and Indiana, as well as facilities in Columbus and Lincoln, Nebraska. Mother Frances Xavier Cabrini, founder of the Italian Missionary Sisters of the Sacred Heart, established New York's Columbus Hospital in 1892, followed by hospitals in Chicago and as far west as Seattle.

The modernization of the Catholic hospital represents the convergence of subcultures; while they provided for progressively modern care of their patients, religious communities were anchored in a subculture fearful of the secular drift of the modern world. Protective canopies of an ethnic and religious cloth were symbols of the Catholic separatism with its traditional piety, those devotional practices and prayers to particular saints known for miraculous cures and a myriad of associations such as the Apostolate of Suffering, which gave religious meaning to physical and emotional pain and anguish. The centralization of authority structures and the revised code of canon law added thick layers to the boundaries of religious separatism, particularly as the rules governing the enclosure were imposed upon communities of women religious committed to an activist apostolate of nursing. Though these structures fragmented the prayer life and nursing ministry, the sense of pastoral ministry prevailed, but it was more restrictive than the proactive character of frontier health-care ministry.

The Mayo Clinic, in Rochester, Minnesota, perhaps the most prominent of the modern medical centers, is attached to St. Mary's Hospital, with its origin in 1889 associated with Dr. William Mayo, the physician-father of two sons who also became physicians and Sister Alfred Moes, founder of the Rochester Franciscans, a woman characterized by intelligence, energy, and determination. Built with room for only thirty patients, St. Mary's was on the threshold of modernity. Soon a nursing school was founded which was later integrated into the College of St. Teresa in Winona.

The 1893 World's Columbian Exposition was a tribute to Chicago as a railroad, shipping, and manufacturing center of the nation. Over twenty-seven million visitors witnessed a "veritable encyclopedia of civilization." By 1900 Chicago's population exceeded one million, thus becoming the nation's "second city." Chicago became an archdiocese in 1880; by 1900 it numbered about 660,000 Catholics in an area of 10,379 square miles, 168 of which comprised the city. Of all the states reporting to a survey in 1903, Illinois had the largest number of Catholic hospitals; of the 118 hospitals, 43 were Catholic. The majority of the Catholic hospitals, many of which were staffed by German-American sisters, were in small towns. For example, in the Diocese of Peoria there were nine hospitals located in Bloomington, Danville, Kewanee, LaSalle, Lincoln, Macomb, Peoria, Rock Island, and Streator. Patient capacity ranged from 15 to 175. The Catholic population of the diocese was about 123,000, which implies that these institutions, like most private hospitals, served the general population of one million with only seven hospitals. Mercy Hospital, the oldest Catholic facility, grew with the city. By 1910 it had three hundred beds and was affiliated with the School of Medicine of Northwestern University.

Professionalization of Health Care

Modernization engendered increasing professionalization of nursing. The American schools of nursing were inspired by Florence Nightingale, who had visited the Daughters of Charity Hospital in Paris and who had worked with the Sisters of Mercy in the Crimean War and who had opened St. Thomas School of Nursing in London in 1860. Like St. Thomas, both Catholic and non-Catholic schools stressed a religious and moral commitment within a context increasingly influenced by medical science; the doctors composed the faculties of the early schools. The Catholic schools represented a Catholic domesticity and even conveyed a convent atmosphere with its devotional subculture; they placed the caping ceremony within the religious context, a special liturgy in the hospital or school's chapel. St. John's Hospital in Springfield, Illinois, sponsored by the Hospital Sisters of St. Francis founded in Germany (1844) opened the first Catholic nursing school in the United States in 1886, thirteen years after the first schools were opened in New York, New Haven, and Boston. In

1915, the year the Catholic Hospital Association held its first annual convention, there were 220 Catholic nursing schools, most of which were three-year programs with twelve-hour shifts of hospital-based nursing service.

The Catholic Hospital Association's (CHA) mission was to mediate modernity, particularly through the standardization movement, to sponsor professional education for religious and lay nurses, and to promote a strong Catholic identity in what was perceived as an increasingly threatening secular society. The CHA has been a prism refracting the trends and patterns in Catholic health care, such as the conflicts between religious and secular values.

Characteristic of the clericalization of most Catholic societies in the twentieth century, priests dominated the CHA; and, in accord with the tendencies of patriarchal governance, the men elaborated on the ascribed roles of women religious in a modern Catholic hospital. During this period from 1890 to 1950, the emphasis was on Catholic idealism or romanticism infused into the separate spheres of health care—e.g., the guilds of Catholic physicians and Catholic nurses—that anchored modernity in traditional religious understanding. However, in the practical quotidian life of the hospital, modernization and professionalization were inexorably affecting the religious ethos. For example, during this period many sisters attained graduate degrees in hospital administration, a countervailing force to the male dominance of the profession. Professionalization entailed social mobility into the middle class and tended to affect self-perceptions and social expectations. The CHA, though founded as a separate religious organization, drove a wedge into the religious boundaries as it promoted widespread participation in professional societies and developed a positive consciousness of the relationship between Catholicism and modern health care. The CHA leadership during the 1930s and 1940s tended to fragment this relationship into separate religious and medical spheres, but CHA's mission was emblematic of the advance of modernity in the religious climate of Catholic hospitals.

The Catholic hospital's response to African Americans reflected the generally deplorable racist attitudes in society. In his 1928 book, *The Catholic Church and the Negro,* John T. Gillard, S.S.J., reported that of the 612 Catholic hospitals the overwhelming majority segregated blacks into their own wards, and he could find only two private rooms designated for blacks. He was appalled that black sisters "were forced to accept hospitalization in wards," a situation that reflected the general discrimination against African Americans entering white communities of women religious. However, several communities of women religious were responding to the need for health care among blacks in the South during the 1940s and 1950s. The first hospital established as an integrated facility with black physicians on the staff was St. Vincent's in Kansas City

(1953) that was spearheaded by Bishop Edwin O'Hara. In 1948, Archbishop Joseph E. Ritter of St. Louis integrated Catholic education that included nursing schools. By the 1950s some communities of women religious became integrated.

The Second Vatican Council represents a shift to a new religious consciousness rooted in historical understanding of Scripture, theology, ecclesiology, and the distinctive character of the religious life. Religious involved in health care experienced renewal chapters or general assemblies which were extended constitutional conventions that composed fundamental documents delineating new understandings of community, governance, spirituality, and ministry, and entailed a commitment to respond to the poor, oppressed, alienated, and marginalized. Gradually many sisters and laywomen involved in health care absorbed a feminist perspective into the new religious consciousness that profoundly affected the critique of society, Church, and educational and health care institutions. Concurrently, during the years 1965–75, there was a precipitous decline in vocations to the religious life and a rising awareness of the value of the laity in leadership positions. The significant trends in hospital ministry have been represented particularly as an agenda of John E. Curley, Jr., president of the CHA since 1979: to strengthen ecclesial affiliation, to initiate a transformationist model for leadership, and to clearly articulate Catholic identity within the contexts of health-care reform.

In the public place of the hospital, with its paucity of traditional religious symbols, a missionary consciousness, rooted in new understandings of ecclesiology, Scripture, pastoral care, and the roles of the laity, is infused into the ethos of Catholic health care. The recent formation of new missionary identities of Catholic health care is characterized not by the mix of European tradition and republican ethos but rather with a blend of religious renewal and health-care reform mediated in a climate of American pluralism.

See also WOMEN RELIGIOUS IN AMERICA.

Kauffman, Christopher J. *Ministry and Meaning, A Religious History of Catholic Health Care.* New York, 1995.

Liptak, Dolores, R.S.M., and Ursula Stepsis, S.C.A., eds. *Pioneer Healers, Women Religious in American Healthcare.* New York, 1989.

CHRISTOPHER J. KAUFFMAN

CATHOLIC IMMIGRATION TO AMERICA

Introduction

When Catholics first came to the Western Hemisphere, "America" had to be further identified as Spanish or Portuguese or French or British America. In this essay, "America" means the territory that eventually fell within the geographic borders of the United States. "Catholic migration" is also a vague concept. The United States has never asked immigrants to state their religion. Instead, scholars commonly identify certain places of origin as "Catholic countries," and assume religious identity from national identity. Nor is the definition of an immigrant clear, since many migrants can be more precisely defined as transient labor, refugees, etc. Finally, since all American Catholics have some migrant roots, the story of Catholic immigration to America is the story of American Catholicism, and intertwines with other elements of Catholic history. In order to impose some coherence, this essay will describe the waves of U.S. migration, the strategies of pastoral care used, and the development of a national-level approach to migrant pastoral care.

Chronology of Migration

The first Catholic migrant to reach the Western Hemisphere, Christopher Columbus, was himself a Genoese, but he sailed under Spanish patronage and therefore opened the way for Spanish migration, with other European countries soon following. At its height Spanish America extended from Florida west to California, and south to Cape Horn. The French, another Catholic nation, claimed territory from the St. Lawrence River to the Great Lakes and south to the Gulf of Mexico. Portuguese Catholics colonized Brazil. England was not a Catholic country, but an English Catholic family, the Calverts, received a land grant which they named Maryland and which they opened to all professed English Christians who believed in the Trinity. The English colony of Pennsylvania was even more tolerant, and attracted non-English immigrants, including German Catholics. By the eighteenth century internal problems led Spain to neglect its colonies. After 1756 European warfare limited migration to the Americas. In 1763 France lost its North American mainland colonies to England and Spain. In 1815, when the Napoleonic Wars ended and migration could resume, one element of modern migration was in place: European emigrants left lands controlled by their native governments and entered lands controlled by other governments, including the United States.

Migration increased after 1815, reached its first peak in the early 1850s, and subsided in the 1860s. The factors shaping this wave were: (1) the end of the War of 1812, which reopened safe transatlantic travel; (2) the industrialization of England and parts of northern Germany, which led some farmers and artisans to choose to continue their trades in America rather than switch trades and remain at home; (3) the Irish potato famine of the 1840s, and, to a lesser extent, the German revolutions of 1848, which disrupted those areas' societies and economies. Special mention should be made of the Mexican-American War. This did not increase migration, but, when the United States took the northern third of Mexico after the war, a number of Mexicans automatically became citizens of the United States.

During the 1850s peak, the proportion of Catholic migrants was especially high, because the potato famine hit southern and western Ireland especially hard. Socioeconomic and cultural forces increased the Catholics' visibility. The impoverished famine Irish clustered in the northeastern cities near the new mass-circulation newspapers and the large concentrations of native Protestants who had just passed through a religious revival. As a result the anti-immigrant backlash of the 1850s had strong anti-Catholic overtones. Political parties such as the Know-Nothings equated foreignness with Catholicism. Such parties scored election victories in seacoast states with heavy immigration, such as Massachusetts and Maryland. The newly elected legislatures in turn passed laws designed to minimize the perceived threat of Catholic migration. The most noted were the convent inspection laws which required communities of women religious to open their doors to state-appointed committees checking to insure that no woman was held there against her will.

Another wave of migration took place between 1880 and 1920. This wave included Scandinavians and eastern European Jews, and also noticeable groups of Catholics, Poles, Italians, German Catholics (whose position at home had been rendered uncomfortable by the *Kulturkampf*), and Oriental-rite Catholics from Eastern Europe. The Catholic migrants included some highly transient groups. Italians, especially, came to the United States to earn money to use in the home country. Socioeconomic factors again made the Catholics visible as poor Italians and Poles congregated near sources of wage labor. In the 1890s the equivalent of the Know-Nothings was the American Protective Association. In the 1920s, the revived Ku Klux Klan widened its scope to include anti-immigrant sentiment, anti-Semitism, and especially anti-Catholicism. In some ways, non-Catholic opposition to these migrants was ironic. Within the faith, Catholics whose roots lay in earlier migrations doubted whether the newcomers were good Catholics.

Beginning in 1921, the U.S. government enacted a series of laws limiting immigration on a racial or national basis. "Desirable" countries such as the northwestern Protestant European nations, were granted large numbers of visas, and "undesirable" countries such as Russia and the nations in southern and eastern Europe, received few visas. (Chinese immigration had been restricted since 1882 and Japanese immigration had been restricted since 1907; in 1924 Congress created the Asian Barred Zone, forbidding migration from much of Asia.) Between the 1920s and the 1960s Americans thought of themselves as having closed the door to international migration. Migration within the United States was supposed to have replaced migration from outside it. African Americans moved from the rural South to meet wartime urban labor needs during

World War I and II, and continued to leave the South when cotton-harvesting was mechanized after World War II, thus throwing many farmworkers off the land.

Catholic ethnic groups continued to migrate between the 1920s and 1960s. Farmers in need of harvesters turned to Mexicans, organized by the U.S. government in various *braceros* programs. Some individuals, such as Archbishop Robert Emmet Lucey of San Antonio, Texas, provided pastoral care and advocacy for these migrants. Nations that suffered during World War II or during the early stages of the cold war were able to send some refugees to the United States.

In 1965 Congress passed legislation ending the national quota system. The new laws set total migration from the Eastern Hemisphere at 170,000 and that from the Western Hemisphere at 120,000, with each country in both hemispheres getting a maximum of 20,000 visas per calendar year. Rather than emphasize racial desirability, the United States emphasized family unification, welcoming individuals with skills and training that the U.S. economy needed, and sheltering refugees. At that point, the law aroused little controversy; the great age of migration had been over for forty years, and the refugees from World War II had largely been resettled.

New wars, however, produced new refugees, for example, refugees from Vietnam after 1975. Other conflicts created refugees from Cambodia, Laos, Guatemala, El Salvador, Nicaragua, and Haiti. The Refugee Act of 1980 reflected these changed conditions. It increased the maximum permissible number of migrants per year to 320,000, the maximum number of refugees to 50,000, defined refugees more broadly than previous laws (which had emphasized protecting those fleeing Communism), and created an office to handle refugee affairs.

During the 1980s, two other issues regarding immigration became of great public interest. The first was the impact of migrants on the U.S. economy. While some complained that immigrants took jobs from those already in the United States, employers of migrant farmworkers pointed out that the immigrants took jobs that Americans themselves were unwilling to take. Debate raged about whether immigrants used more public services that they paid for through taxes. This question could not be answered without knowing how many immigrants there were; there was a widespread sense that uncounted people had entered the United States without going through the Immigration and Naturalization Service. The federal government tried to satisfy these concerns via the 1986 Immigration Reform and Control Act, which facilitated legalization of those illegally in the country, prohibited employers from knowingly hiring illegal aliens, and made special provisions for international migrant farmworkers.

Such laws did not address continuing cultural concerns. No one resurrected the antebellum arguments against Catholic immigrants, but they used similar-sounding arguments against nonwhite migration, claiming that the migrants were too culturally different to assimilate. The major legislative expression of this concern has been a campaign to make English the official language of the United States.

In this situation, the Church has assumed two responsibilities. First, it maintains its traditional concern for the material and spiritual care of Catholic migrants. Second, it has taken on the duty of proclaiming Church teaching regarding the ethics of migration, the moral imperative to recognize and preserve the dignity of human beings in the sometimes difficult position of being strangers in a strange land.

Strategies of Pastoral Care

The antebellum migration overwhelmed the small number of old-stock Catholics living on the East Coast near the new migrants, so that the first pastoral care strategy American Catholics practiced came from the migrants themselves and was intended to protect the Catholic faith from anti-Catholic nativists. Historian Jay P. Dolan has shown how the urban Irish and Germans, led by individuals such as Archbishop John J. Hughes of New York, subsidized by donations from groups such as the Society for the Propagation of the Faith in Lyons, and aided by the inexpensive labor of religious vowed to poverty, built a network of Catholic institutions. Catholics provided schools from elementary through university levels, so that younger students did not have to read non-Catholic Bible translations and older ones did not have to attend another denomination's compulsory chapel. The sick went to Catholic hospitals where their chaplains were free to visit. Dependent children went to Catholic orphanages rather than being placed in foster care away from the Catholic community. The St. Vincent de Paul Society paralleled the work of such groups as the New York Association for Improving the Condition of the Poor and provided food, fuel, clothing, and money to allow the poor to remain in their homes. Institutions provided specialized care for the aged, handicapped or delinquent under Catholic auspices. The alternative Catholic world became a source of controversy as the descendants of the antebellum immigrants who had built and used them become sufficiently well-off as to have little need of them. Did they still protect Catholics from the evils of Protestantism and secularism, or did they provide reasons for non-Catholics to suspect Catholics were not fully part of modern society?

This Catholic world was challenged by the migration that began gathering momentum in the 1880s. English-speaking Irish dominated the established institutions, and could not effectively help non-English-speakers. The new immigrants also complained of incidents of intra-Catholic prejudice. American Catholics feared the Italian laity preferred festas and devotions to the sacraments, and they had such trouble with Oriental-rite Catholicism that parts of the Oriental (i.e., Byzantine) tradition, especially the married clergy, were severely compromised by migration. The result was that within the Catholic world there developed smaller worlds providing care in particular languages, such as German immigrant aid societies, Polish seminaries, French-Canadian national parishes, Italian orphanages, dioceses for Oriental-rite Catholics.

In the 1890s, those who supported the strategy of caring for immigrant Catholics by helping them to preserve their homeland languages and customs made an effort to have this strategy become a Church-wide policy. The leaders in this movement were the directors of the European-based immigrant-aid societies. The earliest of these societies was the St. Raphael Society for the Protection of German Catholic Emigrants, founded in 1871 and directed by Peter Paul Cahensly, a German entrepreneur and philanthropist. His society became a model for other national societies with the same name, the most notable being the St. Raphael Society for Italian Emigrants, founded by Bishop Giovanni Battista Scalabrini and directed by a layman, Giovanni Battista Volpe-Landi. On December 9–10, 1890, representatives of the national St. Raphael Societies met in Lucerne, Switzerland, and drafted a document, the Lucerne Memorial, addressed to Pope Leo XIII. The document alluded to tremendous losses to the Catholic faith caused by migration, and explained that the remedy lay in enabling migrants to carry with them not just their faith, but the entire culture of their Catholic homeland. Cahensly presented the Lucerne Memorial to Pope Leo XIII on April 16, 1891. In the past Leo had shown some interest in providing migrants with pastoral care in their native languages. He had written a letter of introduction, *Quam Aerumnosa,* for Bishop Scalabrini's Society of Saint Charles, a community of priests dedicated to the Italian migrant apostolate. However, in 1891 Leo did not accept the Lucerne Memorial's suggestions. The basic Roman policy was that the national parishes in use in the U.S.A. were sufficient.

American Catholic ordinaries' opinions as to proper migrant care varied. Historian Dolores Liptak has shown how a succession of archbishops of Hartford fostered pastoral care along linguistic lines, recruiting priests who spoke the necessary languages, sending local clergy abroad to learn newcomers' languages and customs, and authorizing national parishes which, unlike territorial parishes, did not draw their congregations from specific geographical boundaries but ministered to all who spoke a particular language. Biographers such as Edward Kantowicz have shown how other individuals, such as George Cardinal Mundelein of Chicago, minimized ethnic pastoral care. The bishops shared common opinions regarding the Lucerne Memorial. The American hierarchy's real objection to the Lucerne Memorial was the call for ethnic representation within the episcopacy. However, the American ordinaries also objected to the Lucerne Memorial's preservation of various languages and customs. The hierarchy's long-term goal was to present the United States with immigrants who, while holding on to their Catholic faith, adopted the English language and American ways and so proved, contrary to anti-immigrant, anti-Catholic nativists, the compatibility of Catholicism and American patriotism.

American entry into World War I promoted two trends relevant to American Catholic migrant care. It prompted the nationalizing of many institutions, including American Catholicism, and it intensified American patriotism. This combination led the American Catholic hierarchy to develop a new strategy of immigrant pastoral care, at least insofar as Catholic migrants in transit were concerned. After World War I, the hierarchy established a permanent national organization, then called the National Catholic Welfare Council, and erected within it a Bureau of Immigration. That bureau replaced the multitude of St. Raphael Societies doing welfare work among immigrants in port cities. During the 1920s, it was NCWC Bureau of Immigration agents who met ships, helped Catholic immigrants through reception procedures, protected them from fraud at the money exchanges and railroad stations, and provided guidance as to how to get settled in the United States.

The NCWC Bureau of Immigration recognized the anti-Catholic implications of the 1920s quota legislation, but it also agreed with those who argued that limiting new immigration allowed the United States to concentrate on absorbing and Americanizing the migrants it already had. In the 1930s the impetus for migration changed from that of seeking economic betterment in a new country to that of fleeing fascism or war in the old country. The NCWC became more interested in refugee work and thus in immigrant advocacy, specifically the altering of U.S. immigration legislation. After World War II, the NCWC expanded and institutionalized its role as an advocate for immigration legislation based not on nationalism but on human need. Historian Frank Cavaioli has explained how the NCWC called for Italian Americans to organize themselves to press for legislation that would overturn the quota system which treated Italians as undesirable immigrants. Accordingly, Italian American Catholics created the American Committee on Italian Migration (ACIM) in 1951. ACIM became one of the lobbyists, first for emergency legislation allowing Italian refugees to enter the U.S.A. above quota limitations, and then for a general revision of immigration law. By the time that revision came—the law passed in 1965 was not fully implemented until 1968—the need to admit Italian refugees was largely over.

When Catholic migration increased again, the Church followed its tradition of providing at least temporary care in the migrants' home languages. New socioeconomic conditions, however, shaped the new ethnic care in a different way. Some Catholic immigrants still congregated in large cities, but those cities already had as many parishes as they could afford to maintain. Rather than build new parishes, therefore, local bishops often established new outreach programs from old parishes. Francis Cardinal Spellman, for example, took St. Benedict the Moor, New York's first parish for African Americans, and made it a center of Puerto Rican ministry.

The Development of Modern Pastoral Care

Leo XIII's *Quam Aerumnosa* was written for Italian migrants, but utilized ideas with universal application. World War I slowed papal progress in developing Italian migrant pastoral care, and also alerted the papacy to the more general problem of migration. On August 1, 1952, Pius XII issued *Exsul Familia*, an apostolic constitution which established fundamental teaching regarding migration and also laid down a basic policy of providing spiritual care. He also created what is now the Pontifical Council on Migrants and Itinerant Peoples to provide ongoing attention to these issues. The Holy See has cast its net broadly and considers as migrants those who move for personal reasons, refugees, and also tourists, nomads, pilgrims and those whose occupations require constant travel (e.g., airline personnel, sailors, circus performers, etc.).

On the national level, the U.S. Conference of Catholic Bishops has several venues for proclaiming Catholic moral teaching regarding migration. It has made migration the theme of one major pastoral letter, *Together a New People* (1986). It issues shorter statements on some specific situations such as pending legislation or the care of particular groups of migrants. The USCCB has a committee devoted to migration, and several of its other committees—e.g., Hispanic Affairs—also touch on the issue. The U.S. Catholic Conference on Migration and Refugee Services in Washington, D.C., carries out Church teaching. It makes educational resources available to American dioceses for National Migration Week, works with local communities to resettle refugees, and promotes the care of itinerant workers. A number of other national Catholic agencies cooperate in specific aspects of migrant care. The National Catholic Rural Life Conferences does pastoral and advocacy work on behalf of migrant farmworkers, the Catholic Committee for Refugees and Children coordinates international adoptions and the care of refugee minors, and the Catholic Legal Immigration Network provides counsel to those who need legal aid in immigration matters.

Each American diocese has its own structure for ministry to migrants. Again, the definition is very broad. Sees with international airports must tend to migrants in transit; those in agribusiness areas care for migrant farmworkers; others have welcomed refugees; and nearly every place has communities of recently arrived immigrants. Although few individuals remain permanently in the condition of migrants, migration itself is a feature of modern life. The Catholic Church is developing strategies and structures to provide proper spiritual and material care for these members of the human family.

See also CATHOLIC POPULATION, HISTORICAL GROWTH; GERMAN CATHOLICS IN AMERICA; HISPANIC CATHOLICS IN AMERICA; HUNGARIAN CATHOLICS IN AMERICA; IRISH CATHOLICS IN AMERICA; ITALIAN CATHOLICS IN AMERICA.

Barry, Colman J., O.S.B. *The Catholic Church and German Americans*. Milwaukee: Bruce, 1953.

Bronder, Saul E. *Social Justice and Church Authority: The Public Life of Archbishop Robert E. Lucy*. Philadelphia: Temple University Press, 1982.

Cavaioli, Frank J. "Chicago's Italian Americans Rally for Immigration Reform." *The Family and Community Life of Italian Americans: Proceedings of the Thirteenth Annual Conference of the American Italian Historical Association . . . 1980*, ed. Richard N. Juliani. New York: American Italian Historical Association, 1983.

Diaz-Stevens, Ana Maria. *Oxcart Catholicism of Fifth Avenue: The Impact of the Puerto Rican Migration upon the Archdiocese of New York*. University of Notre Dame Press, 1993.

Dolan, Jay P. *The Immigrant Church: New York's Irish and German Catholics, 1815–1865*. Baltimore: The Johns Hopkins University Press, 1975.

Ellis, John Tracy. *Catholics in Colonial America*. Baltimore, 1965.

Fogarty, Gerald P., S.J. "The American Hierarchy and Oriental Rite Catholics, 1890–1907." *Records of the American Catholic Historical Society of Philadelphia* 85 (1974) 17–28.

Kantowicz, Edward R. *Corporate Sole: Cardinal Mundelein and Chicago Catholicism*. University of Notre Dame Press, 1983.

Linkh, Richard M. *American Catholicism and European Immigration, 1900–1924*. New York: Center for Migration Studies, 1987.

Liptak, Dolores, R.S.M. *European Immigrants and the Catholic Church in Connecticut, 1870–1920*. New York: Center for Migration Studies, 1987.

Marchetto, Ezio, C.S. *The Catholic Church and the Phenomenon of Migration: An Overview*. New York: Center for Migration Studies, 1989.

Tomasi, Silvano M., C.S. "Immigrants and the Catholic Church in the United States." *Immigration Experience in the United States: Policy Implications*, eds. Mary G. Powers and John J. Macisco, Jr. New York: Center for Migration Studies, 1994, 73–87.

MARY ELIZABETH BROWN

CATHOLIC-JEWISH RELATIONS IN AMERICA

Catholics and Jews share many common experiences in the United States as immigrant communities. Both stood on the fringes of American society—economically, politically, culturally. Both suffered various forms of social and political discrimination for many years. Signs in New York, Chicago and other metropolitan areas often excluded both from housing and job opportunities. "Catholics and

Jews Need Not Apply" was not unknown in advertisements and public signs.

It was this joint social experience that gave rise to the initial contact and cooperation between Jews and Catholics in the United States. Labor unions in particular were an area where the two groups formed important coalitions to press for improved wages and working conditions. These coalitions began as early as the 1920s. They reached a crescendo during the period of the New Deal when Catholic, Jewish, and some Protestant labor and religious leaders mobilized effectively to support a major overhaul of the U.S. social system.

This period of intense social collaboration was not accompanied by an equally bold examination of specifically religious understandings of the other inherited from their respective traditions. Nonetheless, it can be argued that indirectly it contributed to major efforts in religious reinterpretation that began in earnest with the Second Vatican Council.

The U.S. Catholic hierarchy at Vatican II played a decisive role in the development and passage of the historic statement on the Church's Relationship to the Jewish People which became chapter four of the Council's Declaration on Non-Christian Religions known as *Nostra aetate*. Without the active and strong support of the American bishops, this statement may never have secured conciliar approval. Certainly there were individual Catholic scholars and leaders, including the U.S.-based Msgr. John Oesterreicher (originally from Austria), founder of the Institute of Judaeo-Christian Studies at Seton Hall University and its important publication *The Bridge,* who deserve great credit for passage of the document on the Jews. These experts played a significant role in convincing the bishops to vote for the change. And the contributions of Jewish leaders present at the council, such as Rabbi Marc Tanenbaum and Zach Schuster of the American Jewish Committee, and Rabbi Arthur Gilbert and Joseph Lichten of the Anti-Defamation League, proved significant. But certainly the very positive experience of working with the Jewish community for several decades in the common effort for social justice made the U.S. hierarchy far more receptive to supporting a major theological restatement of the Catholic understanding of the relationship with Jews than they might otherwise have been.

Groundwork for Religious Dialogue

The major effort to develop a specifically religious dialogue with Jews in the United States is basically the result of Vatican II's *Nostra aetate,* though some important groundwork was laid for it by the significant investigations of Catholic textual materials covering literature, social studies, and religion which took place at St. Louis University in the late fifties and early sixties under the overall direction of Fr. Trafford P. Maher, S.J., of its Sociol-

ogy Department. The research itself was undertaken by three women religious, Sr. M. Linus Gleason, C.S.J. (literature materials), Sr. M. Rita Mudd, F.S.C.P. (social studies texts), and Sr. Rose Thering, O.P. (religion texts). It is interesting to note that Sr. Thering's study was the last in the Catholic series. This was deliberate. The project directors were concerned at the time that criticism of religion texts which had achieved a kind of "sanctity by association" might disturb many Catholics. Hence the decision was made to begin with the literature and social studies materials.

It was the study of the religion texts by Sr. Thering that brought to light particular problems with respect to the Jews and their religious tradition. While Jews were virtually unrepresented in the literature materials and they were the least visible of the nine religious/racial/ethnic outgroups examined in the study, when it came to the social studies materials, they appeared as the most visible group in the religion materials for all publishers without exception. In one way, this was hardly an unexpected finding. It is in fact almost impossible to present Christianity—particularly such aspects as revelation, the life of Jesus and the origins of the early Church—without significant reference to Jews and Judaism.

The overwhelming majority of negative references concerning Jews were concentrated around the themes of: (1) the Jewish rejection of Christianity and the consequent divine curse inflicted on this people; (2) the Jewish role in the crucifixion; and (3) the role of the Pharisees at the time of Jesus. These negative portrayals of Jews and Judaism were not confined to a few marginal textbook series, but were present in the then most widely used materials in Catholic schools and religious education programs.

The religion study in particular proved decisive in terms of Catholic-Jewish relations in the United States. Completed as a doctoral dissertation in 1961, its results were used effectively to convince American bishops at the Second Vatican Council of the need for a positive conciliar declaration on the Jews. It also served as the basis for a series of meetings with major Catholic textbook publishers which, especially after Vatican II, resulted in a wholesale reorientation in descriptions of the Catholic-Jewish relationship, responsibility for the crucifixion and Jesus' links with specific Jewish movements of his own time. A fundamentally negative picture was transformed in a relatively short period to an essentially positive one. The effect of the studies became even more widespread with the eventual publication by Fr. John T. Pawlikowski, O.S.M., of Chicago's Catholic Theological Union of their basic findings with further analysis in the volume *Catechetics and Prejudice* (Paulist, 1973).

There was also a parallel study of Jewish educational materials undertaken at this time by Dr. Bernard D. Weinryb at Dropsie College in Philadelphia as part of a tri-faith project sponsored by the American Jewish Committee. On the whole, Dr. Weinryb's study (which never received the same national circulation as its Catholic equivalent) showed Jewish educational materials far less concerned with outside groups (including Catholics) than their Christian counterpart texts.

Follow-up studies on Catholic teaching materials relative to their portrayal of Jews and Judaism were undertaken by Dr. Eugene Fisher at New York University in the seventies (published as *Faith Without Prejudice,* Paulist, 1977) and by Dr. Philip A. Cunningham at Boston College in the nineties (published as *Education for Shalom,* The Liturgical Press, 1994). Both studies revealed widespread incorporation of the vision of Vatican II's *Nostra aetate* and recent scholarship in nearly all Catholic textbook series. The classical stereotypes have all but disappeared and the sense of a positive Jewish-Christian bonding being presented by Pope John Paul II and other Church leaders is appearing with increasing frequency.

The Role of the NCCB

Another important stimulus for implementation of Vatican II's historic declaration on the Church and the Jewish People has come from the statements of the U.S. Catholic Bishops' Conference as a whole as well as individual leaders such as Cardinals John O'Connor of New York, Bernard Law of Boston, Joseph Bernardin of Chicago and William Keeler of Baltimore and bishops such as Francis Mugavero of Brooklyn who served as episcopal advisor to the NCCB's Secretariat for Catholic-Jewish Relations. The National Conference of Catholic Bishops launched the implementation of *Nostra aetate* in the United States soon after its passage in 1965. They established an office for promoting knowledge and understanding of the Vatican document with Fr. Edward Flannery as its first director. He was eventually succeeded by Dr. Eugene J. Fisher who continues to hold that position within the restructured Secretariat for Ecumenical and Inter-religious Affairs directed by Fr. John Hotchkin. Another influential voice within the Bishops' Conference has been Msgr. George Higgins who has chaired the National Advisory Committee on Catholic-Jewish Relations whose members include diocesan officials responsible for Catholic-Jewish relations from various parts of the country as well as Catholic scholars such as Celia Deutsch (Sisters of Sion), Eva Fleishner, Daniel Harrington, S.J., Michael McGarry, C.S.P., and John T. Pawlikowski, O.S.M.

The work of the Bishops' Office for Catholic-Jewish Relations has been strengthened over the years by a series of important statements in the spirit of Vatican II. The first of these appeared in March 1967. It sought to translate the vision of the council into a set of concrete recommendations to Catholic dioceses across the country, focusing on the development of local dialogue groups,

improved preaching on Jesus' Jewishness and the Church's continuing links to the Jewish People, revamping of textbooks and prayerbooks in keeping with *Nostra aetate* and cooperation in the field of social action.

On the tenth anniversary of the Conciliar Declaration on the Jews in 1975, the U.S. Bishops reaffirmed their continuing commitment to the process they encouraged in their 1967 document. They especially encouraged all dioceses to establish appropriate mechanisms for implementation of *Nostra aetate,* urged homilists and liturgists to pay particular attention to the presentation and interpretation of biblical texts in order "to promote among the Catholic people a genuine appreciation of the special place of the Jewish people as God's first-chosen in the history of salvation and in no way slight the honor and dignity that is theirs," and encouraged Catholic scholars to address the theological and biblical issues raised by the Church's new understanding of its relationship with the Jewish People.

Additional documents on special issues such as preaching, passion plays, etc., as well as practical guidelines for the dialogue, have been issued by the Bishops' Office on Catholic-Jewish Relations, sometimes in collaboration with other offices. One of those with the greatest potential impact was prepared in collaboration with the Bishops' Committee on the Liturgy in whose name it appeared in September 1988. Entitled *God's Mercy Endures Forever: Guidelines on the Presentation of Jews and Judaism in Catholic Teaching,* it makes specific recommendations for preaching during each of the major liturgical seasons in light of the Christian-Jewish bonding that emerged from Vatican II.

Jewish-Catholic Dialogue

National Jewish leaders and their organizations have cooperated over the years with the Bishops' Conference in developing programming based on these documents for teachers, seminarians, clergy and scholars. Rabbis Arthur Gilbert and Marc Tanenbaum, both of whom were present at Vatican II, were among the early Jewish partners. Subsequently others at the Anti-Defamation League and the American Jewish Committee which Rabbis Gilbert and Tanenbaum respectively represented, including Rabbis Leon Klenicki and A. James Rudin and Mrs. Judith Banki, joined the effort. The conference collaborated on occasion with other Jewish organizations such as the Union of American Hebrew Congregations (e.g., a joint study guide on the U.S. Bishops' Pastoral Letter on Peace) and the Synagogue Council of America (e.g., a series of conferences at Notre Dame University on religious values and social issues).

Throughout the country from Los Angeles to Houston to Detroit to Brooklyn local statements and guidelines were developed by Catholic and Jewish leaders, often working in close collaboration. These often served as a stimulus for the growth of local dialogue groups with noteworthy efforts along this line in Los Angeles, Tulsa, Milwaukee, Chicago, Detroit, Brooklyn, Dayton, Mobile, and Albuquerque. The Dayton dialogue in particular is significant because it gave birth in 1973 to the first National Workshop on Catholic-Jewish Relations which brought together diocesan leaders and scholars for several days of intense discussion on theological and practical issues. This National Workshop which, beginning with its second meeting in Memphis was opened to all Christians, has become an important gathering point for the leaders in the Christian-Jewish dialogue as well an opportunity to introduce people in various sectors of the country to the basics of the ongoing discussion. The National Workshop has met (now every two years) in such cities as Boston, Detroit, Milwaukee, Pittsburgh, Los Angeles, Tulsa, Chicago, Baltimore, and Minneapolis.

Higher educational institutions have also provided important leadership in the implementation of *Nostra aetate*. The Institute for Judaeo-Christian Studies at Seton Hall University has pioneered graduate programs in Christian-Jewish studies and its Education Department has provided extensive opportunities for study trips to Israel under the leadership of Dr. Rose Thering of its faculty. Seton Hill College near Pittsburgh has developed a program in Holocaust education for Catholic teachers. The Catholic Theological Union in Chicago has incorporated the services of Rabbi Hayim Perelmuter as a full member of its faculty since the school's inception in 1968. Together with fellow faculty member Fr. John T. Pawlikowski, O.S.M., Rabbi Perelmuter has developed a unique "Sabbath experience" seminar which all students for the basic degree are required to take. Sacred Heart University in Connecticut, under the leadership of Rabbi Jack Bemporad, is developing a comprehensive program in Christian-Jewish studies. Hebrew Union College in Los Angeles has worked collaboratively with the Archdiocese of Los Angeles in developing programs for clergy education. And the Spertus Institute of Jewish Studies (Chicago), through its Cardinal Bernardin Center for Eastern European Jewry, has pioneered programs in Jewish-Polish Catholic relations under the direction of Rabbi Byron Sherwin. The University of St. Thomas in St. Paul has also developed considerable programming, including academic conferences whose results are made available nationally.

Catholics and Jews have cooperated, often as part of broader coalitions, to address particular national and international issues. One important one was the cause of Soviet Jewry. Sr. Ann Gillen played a prominent leadership role in this effort. Another was support for the formal recognition of Israel by the Holy See, an effort in which Cardinals John O'Connor of New York, William Keeler of Baltimore, and Bernard Law of Boston exercised a leading role.

Cooperation to resolve occasional public tensions between Catholics and Jews also has been in evidence in recent years, particularly at the leadership level. In part, this is a result of the deep bonds established through the dialogue. When a major controversy occurred, for example, over the establishment of a cloistered convent at the Auschwitz concentration camp near Krakow, Poland, U.S. Catholic and Jewish leaders were instrumental in the eventual resolution of this crisis which began in 1986 and continued through 1989. The interventions of the U.S. cardinals, as well as the meetings Cardinal Joseph Glemp held with Jewish leaders in Washington (coordinated by the U.S. Catholic Conference) and Chicago (hosted by the Cardinal Bernardin Center at Spertus Institute of Jewish Studies), proved decisive in helping diffuse the tension.

Contemporary Issues

Controversies still remain between U.S. Jews and Catholics, and are likely to continue for the foreseeable future. Issues continuing to generate disagreements include abortion, sexuality, governmental aid for private schools, the record of Pope Pius XII during the Holocaust, among others. Questions have been raised by Jewish leaders in the dialogue such as Rabbis A. James Rudin and Leon Kelnicki regarding the continued presentation of Jews and Judaism in certain sections of the new Catholic catechism despite their recognition of the catechism's basic incorporation of the perspective of *Nosta aetate*.

On occasion, however, certain groups of Jews have joined Catholics in coalitions on specific issues such as abortion. This is especially the case for some members of the Orthodox Jewish community which by and large has opposed theological dialogue with Catholics (or any other religious group) on specifically religious questions. In some traditional areas of disagreement between Catholics and Jews in America such as state aid to private schools, there has been a measure of reevaluation recently which has brought segments of the non-Orthodox Jewish community closer to the Catholic view than in previous years.

There is no question that the more than quarter century since the appearance of Vatican II's *Nostra aetate* has produced a profound and permanent transformation of Catholic-Jewish relations in the United States. Just as the U.S. hierarchy played a pivotal role in the passage of the conciliar declaration on the Jews, so the American Church is continuing to set the pace in terms of implementation of the document. Countries in Europe and Latin America often look to the U.S.A. for assistance as they launch their own efforts in Jewish-Catholic reconciliation. Tensions and disagreements will no doubt continue to challenge the new bonding created by the dialogue. But in key areas such as education there is simply no question of going back to the preconciliar theology of the Jewish-Catholic relationship. What was fundamentally negative has now been solidly placed on a positive course. Grass roots dialogues and academic study of the Jewish-Catholic relationship will continue without interruption even if the relations between the two communities at the institutional level experience an occasional impasse.

See also ANTI-SEMITISM AND AMERICAN CATHOLICS; ECUMENISM IN AMERICA.

Athans, Mary Christine. *The Coughlin-Fahey Connection: Father Charles E. Coughlin, Father Denis Fahey, C.S.Sp., and Religious Anti-Semitism in the United States, 1938–1954.* New York: Peter Lang, 1991.

Cunningham, Philip A. *Education for Shalom: Religion Textbooks and the Enhancement of the Catholic and Jewish Relationship.* Collegeville, Minn.: The Liturgical Press, 1995.

Fisher, Eugene J. *Faith Without Prejudice: Rebuilding Christian Attitudes Toward Judaism.* New York: Crossroad, 1995.

Herberg, Will. *Protestant, Catholic, Jew: An Essay in American Religious Sociology.* Garden City: Doubleday, 1955.

Pawlikowski, John T., O.S.M. *Catechetics and Prejudice: How Catholic Teaching Materials View Jews, Protestants and Racial Minorities.* New York: Paulist Press, 1973.

Sharper, Philip, ed. *American Catholics: A Protestant-Jewish View.* New York: Sheed & Ward, 1959.

JOHN T. PAWLIKOWSKI, O.S.M.

CATHOLIC LAYMEN'S ASSOCIATION OF GEORGIA, THE

Thomas E. Watson, former Congressman and Populist Party candidate for the presidency of the United States, began a campaign against the Roman Catholic Church in his publications in 1908. "Swatting the Pope" proved a successful political ploy, and Watson controlled Georgia politics for most of the following decade. He influenced the Georgia legislature to enact the Convent Inspection Act in 1916. The law required grand juries to inspect convents for evidence of wrongdoing and to question the "inmates" as to whether they were being held against their will.

The National Council of the Knights of Columbus, represented by Patrick H. Callahan of Louisville, Kentucky, and Benedict Elder of Cincinnati, Ohio, offered financial support to Georgia Catholics for the purpose of countering anti-Catholic allegations. Georgia Catholics, who numbered only 15,000 in 1916, had enjoyed friendly relations with their neighbors until Tom Watson began to target them.

Bishop Benjamin Keiley called upon each parish in the state to send delegates to a meeting in Macon on September 24, 1916. He told the laymen that after the passage of the Convent Bill he could no longer advise them to remain silent. The convention adopted the resolution proposed by Patrick H. Rice of Augusta to form the Catholic Laymen's Association of Georgia. Augustine Long of Macon was elected president. Rice headed the finance committee and James J. Farrell, an Augusta journalist, chaired the publicity bureau.

The patriotism of Georgia Catholics during the World War contrasted sharply with Watson's diatribes against the war as a popish plot. In 1919 Farrell's publicity bureau culled 3,576 clippings dealing with Catholic matters from Georgia newspapers and found only one hundred antagonistic. Within two years the bureau had compiled a file of 27,000 correspondents. Local branches of the association had been organized in each city and $85,000 collected to finance the work of the publicity bureau. The association's successful campaign against bigotry attracted the attention of Catholics in other states.

The elections of 1920 which swept Warren Harding into the presidency made Tom Watson a United States Senator. Watson used his newspaper, the *Columbia Sentinel,* to rally his Georgia followers. He attacked *The Bulletin,* the association's paper, and defended the practice of lynching. When he went to Washington he continued to circulate his newspaper in Georgia. In one of his first editorials from the Senate Office Building, he wrote that some of the 65,000 girls reported missing in the United States might be found in Bishop Keiley's "slave pens" in Savannah.

Dick Reid, editor of *The Bulletin* and the leading spokesman for the association, collected enough copies of the *Columbia Sentinel* to mail one to each senator. In his next editorial, Watson accused Reid of attacking him, and warned that his Augusta friends would retaliate. Reid circulated that editorial around also with the comment that it must be the first time that an editor threatened someone for circulating his editorials. Watson's reputation was further damaged by his unsubstantiated allegations about the brutality of army officers. He fell into a depression marked by heavy drinking and died on September 25, 1922.

With their chief antagonist silenced, Georgia Catholics experienced an improved climate of opinion. Georgia's overwhelming vote for Catholic Al Smith in 1928 demonstrated that swatting the pope had lost its clout in Georgia.

In 1940 Dick Reid left Georgia to edit *The Catholic News* of New York. Coincidentally, both he and Benedict Elder died in January 1961. By that time the Catholic Laymen's Association had ceased operating. It had served its purpose. In 1966 the Georgia Legislature quietly repealed the Convent Inspection Act.

See also KU KLUX KLAN; NATIVISM; SMITH, ALFRED EMANUEL.

The Bulletin of the Catholic Laymen's Association, with other records of the association, may be found in the Archives of the Diocese of Savannah, Georgia.

Cashin, Edward J. "Thomas E. Watson and the Catholic Laymen's Association of Georgia." Ph.D. dissertation, Fordham University, New York, 1962.

Mulherin, Mary Jeanne, I.H.M. "The First Five Years of the Catholic Laymen's Association of Georgia." Master's thesis, The Catholic University, Washington, D.C., 1954.

EDWARD J. CASHIN

CATHOLIC LIBRARY ASSOCIATION, THE

Through the impetus of the Rev. Paul J. Foik, C.S.C., librarian of the University of Notre Dame, librarians banded together in 1921 to form a library section in the Catholic Education Association, later renamed the National Catholic Education Association. The section was approved the following year. Fr. Foik remained the chair of the section until 1929 when a constitution was drawn up and a petition for withdrawal from NCEA was granted in order to relieve that organization of the financial responsibilities of the bibliographic work in hand. Thus began the Catholic Library Association. Also, in 1929 the *Catholic Periodical Index* published by H. W. Wilson Company, began under the editorship of Francis E. Fitzgerald, who assumed also the chair of CLA and the editorship of the *Catholic Library World,* the official journal of the association.

In 1931, CLA, with no more than two hundred members, elected the Rev. William N. Stenson its first president. The young, struggling association saw two presidents die in office, but Laurence Leavey managed to keep the CPI alive.

In 1946 he was hired as the first full-time executive secretary and remained in the position until 1951. In 1949 Sr. Mary Reparata Murray became the first woman president. The Regina Medal was created in 1959 to reward high standards for the writing of good literature for children. In 1960 Matthew R. (Dick) Wilt became the executive director and in 1962 was able to create a permanent headquarters for the association in Haverford, Pennsylvania. He retired in 1987, being recognized for years as the pillar of CLA.

With the whole nation cooperating with the federal government's policies for library development in 1964, membership in the national organization rose to 4,085. Membership fluctuated thereafter. By 1970 it had declined to 2,800, but in 1975 when the convention was again held with the NCEA, there were 3,357 members. However, by 1980, membership had again dropped to 2,240 and in the 1990s there were fewer than a thousand members. In 1992 its headquarters were closed.

In 1968 the *Catholic Periodical Index* and the *Guide to Catholic Literature* were combined into the *Catholic Periodical and Literature Index.*

See also CATHOLIC BOOK PUBLISHING.

PAUL J. OSTENDORF, F.S.C.

CATHOLIC MAGAZINES AND PERIODICALS

Catholic periodicals of the nineteenth and twentieth centuries ran the gamut of interest from foreign and domestic missionary work and religious education to youth-oriented activities and matters of general religious interest. They also included academic journals on biblical and theological studies, as well as those that served to support the faith of professionals in a particular field. Most periodicals had a specific apostolic mission that was tied to serving the interests of the Catholic Church.

Since a periodical's life depended to a great extent on the financial "bottom line," those that could not maintain a circulation sufficient to meet the journal's costs, or were not subsidized by a religious organization, were quickly abandoned. As a result, many magazines had a relatively short life span.

Nineteenth-Century Periodicals

The *Metropolitan (Catholic Monthly Magazine),* published in Baltimore, was the first U.S. Catholic periodical; however, it lasted only a year, from January to December 1830. In March 1830, the first Catholic periodical for youth, the *Expostulator,* was founded and edited by Bishop Benedict Joseph Fenwick of Boston with the purpose of explaining the tenets of the Catholic faith. It also folded within a year.

Attempts to publish periodicals, such as *Protestant's Abridger and Expositor* and *Catholic Expositor,* for Catholic readers in the years before the Civil War, met similar fates.

Although writers and editors were competent, financial resources were scarce. Also, it was an era when Catholic doctrines were being attacked by anti-Catholic forces, and Church authorities realized that weekly news journals were more important than periodicals.

Some periodicals, however, had a longer life span, such as the *St. Joseph's College Minerva* published by St. Joseph's College, Bardstown, Kentucky, from 1834–36. It focused on national and foreign literature before succumbing to the weekly trend.

In 1842 the Baltimore-based monthly *Religious Cabinet* provided its readers with domestic and foreign news and commentaries, as well as with literary features. A year later it was renamed *United States Catholic Magazine,* but in 1849 it became the official weekly newspaper of the Baltimore archdiocese. The monthly *Metropolitan,* which featured general information on religion, education, and literature, was introduced in 1853, but it folded within six years.

The first Catholic literary magazine west of the Mississippi River was the *Catholic Cabinet* (1843–45), founded and edited by Bishop Peter R. Kenrick of St. Louis. Besides items of a religious and historical nature, it offered reprinted and abridged articles from contemporary European magazines.

Perhaps the best-known and most important periodical of the time was the *Brownson Quarterly Review* begun by Orestes Brownson in 1844 shortly before his conversion to Catholicism. Each issue featured articles on religion, philosophy, and general literature, usually written by Brownson. The *Review* continued publication through the Civil War, publishing its last issue in 1865.

In the 1860s religious congregations began publishing for the general Catholic population rather than solely for their own members. Some of those periodicals found a successful formula and lasted into the twentieth century. The *Catholic World* (1865), founded by Paulist Fr. Isaac Hecker for the purpose of converting America, focused on issues relating to the Catholic Church; *Ave Maria* (1865), published by the Congregation of the Holy Cross at the University of Notre Dame, promoted Catholic devotions and family life; *Messenger of the Sacred Heart* (1866–the 1970s), the major nineteenth-century publication of the U.S. Jesuits, featured devotional literature, fiction, poetry, and academic articles on faith. A spinoff in 1907 named *Messenger* was abandoned two years later shortly before *America* was inaugurated.

Attempts also were made in the 1860s to revive magazines for Catholic youth. Those considered the best of this genre were a Paulist publication, *Young Catholic* (later the *Leader,* 1870–1923), and *Guardian Angel,* published in Philadelphia 1867–1909. *Catholic Young People's Friend,* published in Chicago, began publication in 1877 and lasted well into the latter half of the twentieth century.

The last three decades of the nineteenth century saw the emergence of several important publications: the *Woodstock Letters* (1872), which recorded activities of the U.S. Jesuits and became a valuable source of American Catholic Church history; the revival of *Brownson's Quarterly Review* (1873–75); the *American Catholic Quarterly Review* (1876–1924); and *Donohoe's Magazine* (1879–1908), which featured light fiction, biographies, and book reviews, and became the most popular monthly of its period, reaching a circulation of 42,775 in 1897 (in 1908 it was bought by the *Catholic World*).

Reviews for clergy, Church history magazines, and parish journals, including *American Ecclesiastical Review* (1889–1914; 1919–27), *American Catholic Historical Researches* (1884–1912) in Philadelphia, and *Sacred Heart Review* (1888–1918) in Cambridge, Massachusetts, were among some fifty magazines that began publication in the 1880s.

In the 1890s emphasis was placed on quality journalism, which resulted in new family magazines, as well as several journals that focused on education, devotion, doctrine, and social work. Among the most successful of these were the Dominicans' *Rosary Magazine* (1891); *St. Anthony Messenger* (1893), published by the Franciscan friars of St. John the Baptist province; *Emmanuel* (1895), a publication of the Congregation of the Blessed Sacrament; and the Benedictines' *St. Joseph's Magazine.*

American Catholic journalism received a boost at the end of the century with the work of William Henry Thorne and Arthur Preuss. In the *Globe* (1889–1904) and the *Fortnightly Review* (1894–1935), respectively, they offered forthright comments and candid opinions on issues that affected the Church. Their work served to measurably improve the standard of nineteenth-century Catholic magazines.

Twentieth-Century Periodicals

The nineteenth century had seen an influx of Catholic immigrants to the United States. As a result, the purpose of many publications was to strengthen the faith of Catholics and to defend the Church against doctrinal attacks. The efforts of some publishers during that time to broaden the intellectual horizons of their readers were largely unsuccessful. The *New York Review,* a scholarly journal published at St. Joseph's Seminary, Dunwoodie, New York, from 1905 to 1908 was a victim of the Modernist crisis.

During the first half of the twentieth century, the Catholic hierarchy exerted more control over the Catholic press; however, those magazines published by religious congregations continued their mission to inform Catholics of contemporary issues that would affect daily Christian life. Among those periodicals was the weekly *America* (1909) founded by Jesuit Fr. John J. Wynne (editor of the *Messenger of the Sacred Heart*) to provide commentary from a Catholic perspective on issues and events in politics, religion, and the arts. In 1965 it was the largest weekly journal in the United States with a circulation of 100,000. At the end of the twentieth century, it continues to command international ecumenical respect.

Many early twentieth-century periodicals focused on foreign and domestic missions. Among those were: *Extension* (1906), published by the Catholic Church Extension Society to report on activities and issues of the American home missions; and *The Field Afar* (1907), published by the Maryknoll priests and brothers and renamed *Maryknoll,* the first American Catholic magazine to promote the foreign missions. (A Spanish-language edition, *Revista Maryknoll* began publication in 1980.) Eventually, many other religious congregations published magazines depicting their mission work, including *Far East* (1918), published by the Columban Fathers, and *Mission,* a publication of the Society for the Propagation of the Faith.

The list of general interest magazines that began in the nineteenth century and continued publication into the twentieth century expanded with the addition of *The Lamp* (1903), published by the Franciscans of Peekskill, New York; *Liguorian* (1913), published monthly by the Redemptorists with articles on spirituality and Catholic teaching for readers of all ages; and the *Sign* (1921), published by the Passionists, containing articles, reports, and comments on world affairs, as well as entertaining features.

In 1924 a lay-edited weekly, *Commonweal,* was established in New York with the purpose of applying Christian tradition, experience, and culture to the daily problems that Christians face. In the 1990s *Commonweal* continues to provide articles from notable authors on public affairs, religion, literature, and the arts. The *U.S. Catholic,* founded in 1935 by the Claretians in Chicago, provides the opportunity for informed Catholics to discuss the issues they face in their daily lives.

Periodicals that focused on reprints became popular during the twentieth century. Such publications included *The Catholic Mind* (1902), which offered articles and speeches by leading Catholic figures, as well as papal speeches and statements of the hierarchy; *Catholic Digest* (1936), which features articles of general interest; *Theology Digest* (1953), which provides condensations of theological articles appearing in the United States and abroad; *The Family Digest* (1945), which contained articles promoting and supporting Catholic family life; *Cross Currents* (1950), which offers its readers essays and studies that explore the implications of Christianity for modern life; and *The Pope Speaks* (1954), which consists of selected papal speeches, letters, and other documents.

Although journals for juveniles were published in the nineteenth century, none of them survived except the *Young Catholic Messenger* (1885), which was published in Dayton, Ohio. George Pflaum, Sr., continued its publication and added companion publications, *Junior Catholic Messenger, Our Little Messenger,* and *Treasure Chest,* all of which were used in parochial schools and religious education classes throughout the United States well into the 1960s. *Catholic Youth* (1914), was published by the Salvatorian Center in Wisconsin, and *Catholic Boy* (1932) and *Catholic Miss* (1942), at the University of Notre Dame. *Visions* and *Venture* were inaugurated in 1975 by *Our Sunday Visitor,* Huntington, Indiana, to spread the gospel message through Sunday Scriptures (bought in 1980 by Peter Li Inc.). In 1979 the Daughters of St. Paul began publication of *My Friend* for children aged six through twelve. *You! Magazine* was introduced in 1987 by Veritas Communications (California), attracting young readers to learn truths of the faith by using a contemporary and visually appealing format.

Scholarly journals (many of which are still being published in the 1990s) began to proliferate in the last half of the century. Such periodicals, which focused on Scripture, canon law, theology, and/or religious education, included the *Homiletic and Pastoral Review* (1900), *Thought* (1926), *The Thomist* (1939), *Theological Studies* (1940) *Lumen Vitae* (1946), *Chicago Studies* (1962), *Continuum* (1963), *The Living Light* (1964), and *The New Theology Review* (1987), which was founded by the Catholic Theological Union, published by Michael Glazier, and had the largest circulation among theological journals in the English-speaking world (now published by The Liturgical Press).

Orate Fratres (1926) led the way among liturgical publications. The monks of St. John's Abbey, Collegeville, Minnesota, published the journal to promote greater understanding of the liturgy. In 1951 its name was changed to *Worship,* and it quickly was regarded as one of the principal pioneering forums for liturgical renewal and reform prior to the Second Vatican Council.

The Catholic Biblical Association founded two periodicals that were widely respected for the quality of their scholarship—*Catholic Biblical Quarterly* (1939) and *Old Testament Abstracts* (1978). Both the latter and *New Testament Abstracts* (1956), founded by the Weston School of Theology, are considered essential for Scripture scholars and reference libraries. In the aftermath of the Second Vatican Council and a resurgence of interest in Scripture by the average Catholic, *The Bible Today* (1962), published by The Liturgical Press, became the chief organ for promotion of popular scriptural studies.

Following the Second Vatican Council (1962–65), the religious press realized the need among Catholics for instruction and encouragement with respect to the changes and "openness" wrought by the council fathers. As a result, many publications sprang up to deal with concerns in liturgy and religious education and with the promotion of social justice.

Among the periodicals that served the professional development of religion teachers and catechists were *Religion Teacher's Journal* (1966), *The Catechist,* and *Today's Catholic Teacher* (1967). Offering assistance for parish staff and personnel was *Today's Parish* (1969). Several periodicals offered resources for liturgical ministers and musicians: *Liturgy 90* (1970), *Celebration* (1972), *AIM: Liturgy Resources* (1973), and *Modern Liturgy* (1973).

Salt of the Earth (1981), published by the Claretians, promoted ideas for putting faith into action. *Crisis* (1982), a journal of lay Catholic opinion on contemporary and Church issues, was published by the Brownson Institute at Notre Dame (Indiana) University. *The Critic* (1985), a publication of the Thomas More Association, focused on American Catholic culture.

Special needs among Catholics also prompted publication of periodicals such as *New Covenant* (1971) and *The Bread of Life* (1978) for the Catholic Charismatic Renewal movement; *Catholic Singles World* (1982); *CGA World* (1981) for Catholic senior citizens; and *Catholic Parent* (1993). Those who were interested in how the beliefs and traditions of the Church have influenced culture and faith found such information in *Catholic Heritage* (1991).

The American Catholic press, and particularly Catholic periodicals, have "come a long way" in the twentieth century. By emerging from the orbit of Church authority, the Catholic press was transformed from an entity solely concerned with "saving the saved" into a vehicle that provided average Catholics not only with inspiration and education, but also gave them the means to become knowledgeable and concerned about the Church's evangelical and social mission. As John G. Deedy, Jr., noted in *The Religious Press in America,* "The Catholic press should be concerned in a maximum degree with the wide world and the broad common good, as distinct from the precincts of the church and the good circumscribed by Catholic interests and partisanship."

See also CATHOLIC BOOK PUBLISHING; CATHOLIC PRESS (NEWSPAPERS), THE.

Lippy, Charles H., ed. *Religious Periodicals of the United States.* Westport, Connecticut, 1986.

MARIANNA McLOUGHLIN

CATHOLIC MEDICAL ETHICS IN AMERICA

The last several decades have seen a remarkable growth in biomedical ethics in the United States. Indeed, many contemporary scholars forget that medical ethics has been an important field of study within Roman Catholic theology for all of this century in the United States and for centuries before in Europe. Recent claims that "bioethics" was born in the 1970s often forget that this "new" field owes much to American Catholic medical ethics.

European Catholic Roots

Early Works. Medicine and religion have long been related to one another. Many societies combined the work of health provider and spiritual leader. This changed for the West when Hippocrates introduced the method of investigation, diagnosis, and prescription. From then until the fifth and sixth centuries C.E., physicians were not usually priests or monks. When Roman structures collapsed in the early Middle Ages, however, Christian monks took over the practice of medicine, seeing it as a part of their religious duties rather than as their primary vocation. This lasted through the twelfth century.

Thomas Aquinas and other major theologians introduced into Western Christianity a theological matrix which again made medical advances possible. For them the study of nature was a way of giving glory to God. This theological change served as a basis for the advancement of "scientific" medicine within a theocentric Christian environment. A true secularization of medicine occurred in the eighteenth century with the Enlightenment. Now physical and spiritual healing were separated and religion was privatized and often seen as the enemy of science.

The development of medical ethics as a distinguishable area within Catholic moral theology is related to these changes in the relationship of Christianity and medicine. The more medicine became separate from religion, the more theologians and pastors attended to it and tried to establish a dialogue with physicians. Thus the *Summae* for confessors in the High Middle Ages add for the first time a special section concerned with the moral obligations of physicians. The post-Tridentine manuals of moral theology did the same.

Pastoral Medicine. With the eighteenth century and the Enlightenment a new rubric came into common use to describe what was becoming a recognized field of study. "Pastoral Medicine" investigated the relationship of religion and medicine. Pastors and theologians wrote to physicians about the spiritual and ethical implications of medicine; doctors taught pastors how to provide first aid and hygiene to their parishioners. The topics included in these disparate works were varied indeed; anything which had to do with soul and body could be part of the literature. But as the field of study changed from the eighteenth to the late nineteenth century, many of these topics disappeared and ethical issues were emphasized. The principle of selection by the beginning of the twentieth century was primarily the actual professional practice of health care personnel.

The first work in pastoral medicine available in English for American readers was Carl Cappellmann's *Pastoral Medicine,* translated in 1878 from the Latin original. This work was the first to emphasize the moral topics which previously had been often only one minor subdivision of pastoral medicine.

The Early Period (1900–40)

For reasons which will become apparent, Catholic medical ethics in the United States can be divided into three periods. The first preceded the Second World War and the papacy of Pius XII. It was a time when American Catholics were able to deal with medical issues more or less on their own terms, and the approach they took showed this relative isolation. After the war, during the papacy of Pius XII, some questions arose which required a defense of the Catholic position. This brought some change in emphasis into the discipline from 1940 up to the Second Vatican Council. The third period is the postconciliar one and it has been a time of rapid and even radical change, when Catholics are now no longer alone, and when health care ethics has become an ecumenical and rapidly growing field.

Name and Definition. Beginning just before the turn of the century, Catholic moral theologians, especially in the United States, developed a specific subdivision of moral theology which would later be known as "medical ethics." At least thirteen books written before 1940 by American Catholic scholars were works in medical ethics. Several of these saw multiple editions and revisions.

The first American book in the field, written in 1897 by the Belgian-born Jesuit theologian Charles Coppens, was directed explicitly to medical students at the John A. Creighton Medical College in Omaha. The title, *Moral Principles and Medical Practice,* shows the emphasis on the immediately practical concerns which characterizes the discipline in the United States. Coppens' work is also interesting from the perspective of the rubric with which to designate the discipline. As his subtitle, *The Basis of Medical Jurisprudence,* shows, Coppens calls it "medical jurisprudence." In professional medicine at that time two rubrics were available which might have been used: "medical ethics" and "medical jurisprudence." The first of these would ultimately be accepted, but not without resistance. This was due to the fact that the "medical ethics" of the professional medical associations was not in any real sense the moral (ethical) investigation of health care. Rather it dealt largely with questions of medical etiquette and its approach was often self-serving. Its goal was to defend the prestige of the medical profession. Moral theologians recognized this, and were reluctant to adopt the term as rubric for their discipline. Some explicitly rejected it. Coppens' suggestion was never widely accepted, but it is an example of the hesitation moralists of the period had in using the seemingly more obvious "medical ethics."

After Coppens' book, a series of works were written by Catholic scholars. Some of these followed his lead in emphasizing moral questions; others stressed the issues typical of works in pastoral medicine. The first American work to use the rubric "pastoral medicine," physician Alexander E. Sanford's 1904 *Pastoral Medicine: A Handbook for the Catholic Clergy,* is a good example of the older approach. It teaches medicine to clergy.

There were other similar books, but soon the American discipline came to emphasize primarily the moral dimensions of medical practice. Thus the topics included were those procedures that nurses and physicians encountered in their professional practice. Since these tended to be mostly physical interventions to cure physical ailments, Catholic medical ethics naturally began to analyze these more than the wider spiritual, psychological, and structural questions connected with health care. It came to be "physicalist" and "individualist."

One example of this emphasis was the trend in some of the literature to underline the problem of abortion. Coppens' book stressed this topic, as did Andrew Klarmann's 1904 *The Crux of Pastoral Medicine: The Perils of Embryonic Man,* which argues that abortion ought to be the only issue central to pastoral medicine.

Associations and Journals. The founding of two major Catholic associations with their respective journals was of considerable significance. The Catholic Hospital Association of the United States and Canada was begun in 1915. Its journal, *Hospital Progress,* now *Health Progress,* began publishing in 1920. The Association was affiliated in 1933 with the American Catholic hierarchy. When the CHA was founded in 1915, there were 541 Catholic hospitals in the United States. The number grew rapidly through the 1950s (by 1963 there were 857), and the influence of the CHA in establishing moral policy within the hospital system increased. The National Federation of

Catholic Physicians' Guilds was formed in 1932 and began that year its publication of the *Linacre Quarterly,* which has consistently emphasized medical moral issues.

Methodology. The area of methodology is complex and problematic. American Catholic Medical Ethics, in dialogue with European Pastoral Medicine, developed a methodology which enabled it to arrive at universally applicable solutions to medical ethical questions. The method was based on a cause-and-effect analysis applied largely through the principle of double effect. Contemporary critics of this method have called it "physicalism." Physicalism is an emphasis in moral analysis on the physical and biological properties and goals of the action under consideration. In the Catholic medical ethics of this period, this emphasis was dominant to the relative neglect of other aspects of human behavior, such as social, psychological, relational, and spiritual aspects.

Catholic moralists did not intend, of course, to eliminate these other realities when doing ethics. Indeed, it was their stated purpose to investigate the practice of medicine precisely from the spiritual and moral perspective. And they include important theological principles such as God's role in ruling human life and the meaning of human suffering in the context of Jesus' redemptive love. Nonetheless, the actual analysis of medical procedures subordinates these themes from Christian anthropology to a method which reaches its final conclusions on the basis of act analysis. A particularly clear example of this approach is found in Patrick Finney's 1922 manual, *Moral Problems in Hospital Practice: A Practical Handbook.* Similar is the important analysis of ectopic pregnancies by T. Lincoln Bouscaren in his doctoral dissertation of 1933, permitting as "indirect" some abortions which until then had been forbidden. His solution made physicalism a more precise instrument for use in Catholic medical ethics.

The Middle Period (1940–60)

It is during the next two decades that Catholic medical ethics established itself, especially in the United States, as a self-conscious field of study with its own sense of definition and method. Whereas the early period had no truly comprehensive works, the 1940s and 1950s produced a significant number of more or less complete manuals.

Name and Definition. The first, and arguably the most important of the manuals was that of Charles McFadden, an Augustinian priest who taught at Villanova University. His *Medical Ethics* was the most widely used manual of the time and saw six editions between 1946 and 1967. McFadden's use of the phrase "medical ethics" as title of his manual was influential in leading the discipline to accept the rubric as its name. But McFadden takes care to disassociate his meaning of the term from that used in the medical profession. While they are interested in etiquette, he will deal with morality. McFadden's book includes the entire range of issues that came to constitute the material definition of Roman Catholic medical ethics of the time. The emphasis is practical. Most emphasized are questions of direct physical medical intervention (abortion, mutilation, sterilization, euthanasia, artificial insemination).

The most important American Catholic medical ethicist of the period was the Jesuit moralist Gerald Kelly. Educated in Rome, Kelly taught for twenty-six years at St. Mary's College in Kansas. From 1947 to 1953 he wrote "Notes on Moral Theology" for *Theological Studies*. His articles were consistently cited by Catholic authorities and by other authors.

In the late 1940s the CHA appointed a committee, with Kelly as its chairman, to develop an ethical code. The result was the "Ethical and Religious Directives for Catholic Hospitals." First formulated in 1949, revised in 1954 and again in 1971 (and most recently, with significant change, in 1995), the directives were not intended to be binding on individual dioceses unless the bishop so directed. They quickly became the accepted code, however, which was seen as binding in American Catholic hospitals.

Gerald Kelly wrote a number of articles concerning the issues addressed in the Directives. First published from 1949 to 1954 as five booklets, *Medico-Moral Problems* was revised and published as a one-volume book in 1958.

The 1950s saw the publication of a number of new manuals in Catholic medical ethics, among them those of John Kenny, Edwin Healy, Thomas O'Donnell, and Patrick O'Brien. Kenny and Healy use the rubric "medical ethics" in their titles; by now this is an accepted designation. All show the emphasis on physical interventions for physical illnesses which has become typical. Catholic medical ethics has now become a self-conscious field of study. Its goal is to analyze and make ethical judgments concerning those procedures which physicians and nurses do in their professional practice. In this analysis it is still, in 1960, virtually alone.

Methodology. The middle period of American Catholic medical ethics (1940–60) continues the pervasive use of the same physicalist criteria we have already noted. The major manuals of these two decades found the principle of the double effect, with its cause and effect precision, especially apt at supporting ethical judgments on the procedures stressed in modern medicine. But in addition to this there was an often subtle yet significant increase in the role that Church authority, particularly the authority of Pope Pius XII, played in medical ethical analysis. Thus, in addition to physicalism, American Catholic medical ethics came increasingly under the influence of what I have called "ecclesiastical positivism."

Whereas in the earlier period the emphasis was on working out the fundamental methodology and in developing the specifications needed to apply it to difficult cases, now there is a shift toward a defense of these principles and conclusions. Whereas earlier literature is directed mainly to Catholic readers, and presumes their agreement, now both Catholics and non-Catholics may need convincing. Catholics are thus urged to respect the inerrant authority of the Church. Non-Catholics, too, are asked to respect the decisions of the Catholic magisterium, which is said to be the only authority capable of correctly interpreting the natural law. Since the natural law binds all people, the interpretations of the Catholic magisterium are said to bind everyone as well. The obvious question of how the natural law, which is supposed to be available to "unaided human reason," can be known in fact only by the Catholic hierarchy, was seldom raised at the time, and has never received a satisfactory answer.

One of the causes for this shift toward ecclesiastical positivism was the increasing integration of Catholics into the mainstream of American life. Second and third generation Catholics refused to stay in Catholic ghettos and spread out into the American culture. As they did, Catholic hospitals became an important part of the American health care system, offering medical services to non-Catholics, who in turn became more active in the Catholic institutions. The Second World War also increased the interaction of Catholics and others in medicine. Thus what had needed (or had seemed to need) little defense in a literature directed mainly to Catholics now came to demand a more explicit apologetic.

The degree of interest shown by Pope Pius XII in medical ethics also contributed to the emphasis on Church authority. Until then, there had been relatively few papal interventions in the area. But during the forties and fifties Pope Pius XII and his curial officials issued large numbers of statements of various kinds on medical ethics. These were listed in a number of the manuals and gathered into anthologies. Thus, although Catholic medical ethics still proclaimed that its teachings were based on natural law and not on magisterial decree, in practice it was often the decisions of the Pope which caused American Catholic moralists to change their ideas and how they expressed them.

The combination of physicalism and ecclesiastical positivism is apparent in McFadden's *Medical Ethics*. He clearly insists that his is a work in ethics, based on the natural law and not on specifically Catholic or Christian sources of revelation. Yet his manual stresses the pronouncements of the magisterium and often cites them as part of his analysis. In one instance he explicitly changes his mind from an earlier edition, based not on reasoning but on a statement of Pius XII. Gerald Kelly also demonstrates the growing importance during these decades of magisterial decisions. The manuals of Kenny, Healy, O'Donnell, and Finney and O'Brien differ in some emphases, but are essentially similar.

A number of important issues were analyzed and conclusions reached during these decades. In some cases American Catholic medical ethics made substantial contributions to what must be seen as humane and theologically valid judgments. Possibly the most significant of these is the development and application of the traditional concepts of "ordinary" and "extraordinary" means of preserving and prolonging life. Pope Pius XII revived this centuries-old distinction, insisting that it was not morally obligatory to make use of unreasonably burdensome or humanly useless treatment to prolong life. In this way Catholic medical ethics developed a tradition which remains of value today in supporting a national consensus opposed to the technological vitalism of some approaches to modern medicine.

The Later Period (1960 to the Present)

Perhaps the most obvious characteristic of recent American Catholic medical ethics is that it is no longer the single most important source of medical ethical scholarship. There has been an unprecedented growth in American medical ethics in the last three decades. Indeed, except for certain methodological discussions it is no longer possible to locate Catholic medical ethics as truly distinct. Catholics now join theologians from other traditions and philosophers who represent no particular religious tradition.

Name and Definition. Whereas American Catholics medical ethics before the 1960s stressed individual medical procedures, today it has extended its topical array to include both individual and structural issues connected directly or indirectly to medicine and biology. This is due partly to the ecumenical growth in the field and partly to the changing emphasis since Vatican II within Catholic moral theology toward including structural issues.

The name given to the discipline reflects this definitional change in emphasis. Though "medical ethics" remains one of the accepted rubrics, it has been joined by "bioethics," "biomedical ethics," and "health care ethics." Each suggests the centrality of "life" and "health" rather than that of professional medicine.

Methodology. The physicalist and positivist frameworks of the forties and fifties are now being challenged from both within and without the Catholic community. Emphasis on the physical analysis of individual acts has been replaced by an emphasis on the human person considered as individual and as social being, the human person adequately considered. The principle of double effect, once of central importance, has been challenged by a less precise but arguably more adequate methodological approach.

Similarly, much of contemporary American Catholic medical ethics has been critical of ecclesiastical positivism. Perhaps now themes of central symbolic significance in Christian anthropology such as the meaning of God's sovereignty over creation and the meaning of human suffering may be freed to engage us in the vital task of discerning, in Catholic theological context, the meaning of human life, thus enabling American Catholic medical ethics to continue its distinctive contribution.

Kelly, David F. *The Emergence of Roman Catholic Medical Ethics in North America: A Historical, Methodological, Biographical Study.* New York: Edwin Mellen, 1979.
____. "The History of American Catholic Medical Ethics." *Perspectives on American Catholicism, 1789–1989,* eds. Virgina Geiger and Steven Vicchio. Westminster, Md.: Christian Classics, 1989, 253–74.
McCormick, Richard A. *Health and Medicine in the Catholic Tradition.* New York: Crossroad, 1987.
O'Rourke, Kevin D., and Philip Boyle, eds. *Medical Ethics: Sources of Catholic Teaching.* 2nd ed. Washington, D.C.: Georgetown University Press, 1993.

DAVID F. KELLY

CATHOLIC NEAR EAST WELFARE ASSOCIATION

Catholic Near East Welfare Association (CNEWA) is a special agency of the Holy See established to support the pastoral mission and institutions of the Catholic Churches of the East and to provide humanitarian assistance to the needy and afflicted without regard to nationality, race, or religion. It also has been entrusted by the Holy Father with responsibility for promoting the union of the Catholic and Orthodox Churches.

CNEWA works on behalf of the Christian East—that is, those lands in which, from ancient times, the majority of Christians have been members of the various Eastern Churches. Its mandate extends to the Churches and peoples of the Middle East, Northeast Africa, India, and Eastern Europe, and to Eastern Catholics everywhere. It raises and distributes funds to help meet the material and spiritual needs of the people it serves.

Establishment

During the years immediately following the First World War, Pope Benedict XV and Pope Pius XI made it their mission to do all that they could to bring material and spiritual aid and relief to the countries and peoples in need. They were supported in this great work of charity by the generosity of the faithful of the whole world and in particular by the Catholics of the United States of America. The Holy See's appeals for aid, especially in the years 1921–23 for the relief of famine victims in Russia, were wholeheartedly and generously responded to by the American people, and various American associations were organized to assist the needy in Russia and other regions of the Near East.

On March 11, 1926, Pope Pius XI decided to unite permanently into one organization and under one administration all the American associations working for assistance to Russia and other areas of the Near East and in general working for the same goals as the Sacred Congregation for the Oriental Church and the Pontifical Commission for Russia. This new pontifical organization was to be called the Catholic Near East Welfare Association. It was placed under the immediate direction of the archbishop of New York, and he was invited to form a governing body for it selected from the American hierarchy. The funds raised by the new association were to be placed directly at the disposition of the Pope, who would disburse them in response to the requests for assistance coming to him from all over the world or recommended to him by CNEWA itself.

The first president of CNEWA, Fr. Edmund A. Walsh, S.J., stated that the Pope wished it to function as a central Catholic welfare agency to "materially assist the Holy See to meet the daily increasing demands made on the Holy Father for assistance in humanitarian works, in the field of education, and in social welfare work all over the world, as well as in distinctly religious and missionary activities."

On July 30, 1927, Pius XI wrote to Fr. Walsh to express his gratitude to American Catholics for their generosity and his satisfaction that CNEWA was now constituted on a permanent basis as a pontifical organization. The next year, on October 23, 1928, the Pope sent an autographed letter to the bishops of the United States praising the work of both the Society for the Propagation of the Faith and of CNEWA, expressing his appreciation for the funds raised and transmitted to him by both of the organizations, and distinguishing their respective roles.

The Pontifical Mission for Palestine

On June 18, 1949, the work of humanitarian and charitable assistance of the Holy See for Palestine and all those afflicted by war there was consolidated and formalized with the establishment of the Pontifical Mission for Palestine. Its direction was entrusted to the secretary of CNEWA, and it was mandated to conduct its activities in Palestine and in the neighboring countries of the Middle East so as to make available to every exiled or needy Palestinian the charity of the Pope and of all Catholics of the world.

CNEWA was asked by the Holy See to assist the Pontifical Mission for Palestine in accomplishing its work. Because the Mission lacked civil status in the United States, CNEWA made appeals for its work and collected funds for it. CNEWA also provided the administrative and financial support necessary for the Pontifical Mission's operations in addition to most of the means of assistance for the persons it served.

Pope Paul VI later broadened the scope of the Pontifical Mission, charging it to assist, without regard to nationality or religion, all who suffer as a result of the repeated conflicts which have devastated Palestine and neighboring regions of the Middle East. The Pontifical Mission serves both as the Holy See's relief and development agency for the Middle East and as the operating agency of CNEWA for that part of the world.

In the following years, innovative programs of person-to-person sponsorship of the education and formation of individual seminarians and novices and of the care of individual orphaned or needy children were developed by CNEWA with great success. Also the membership of CNEWA gradually expanded to include Catholics in Canada and, to a lesser extent, Mexico and other countries, to the point that CNEWA became the principal animator and collector in North America of assistance for the Near East.

The governing body of CNEWA is a board of trustees. The number of trustees is nine, one of whom is the archbishop of New York *ex officio;* the remaining eight trustees are elected for terms of four years by the board itself from among the cardinals, archbishops, and bishops of the United States and Canada. The trustees meet at least once every year on a date fixed by the archbishop of New York.

The principal office of CNEWA is located in New York City. In addition to an administrative office in Vatican City, it has regional offices and staff in Addis Ababa, Amman, Beirut, and Jerusalem.

ROBERT L. STERN

CATHOLIC PEACE MOVEMENT, THE

Introduction

In the 1960s American society experienced a tremendous upheaval which resulted in the questioning of most of the cultural and religious principles and ideals which had previously undergirded it. In this same period the Catholic Church experienced some of the greatest challenges to its relevance on the issues of war and social justice.

The issues raised by the nuclear arms race and the national divisions over the Vietnam War caused many Catholics to respond to what they saw as the challenge of Vatican Council II to look at war "with an entirely new attitude." Subsequent years witnessed an unprecedented growth of the pacifist position within the American Catholic community.

In these years of anti-Vietnam War and anti-arms race fervor there emerged within the American Catholic community its most radical antiwar movement. This loosely organized movement of thought and political action represented the most developed Catholic critique of American society and the most radical expression of American Catholic antiwar sentiment. Rooted in the thought and ideals of the Catholic Worker movement of the 1930s, the

Catholic peace movement which emerged in the 1960s represented a uniquely American evolution of Catholic social thought which called upon the Catholic community to embrace a revolutionary agenda for transforming American society and establishing world peace.

The Catholic Worker Movement

Founded in 1933 by Dorothy Day to implement the social philosophy of Peter Maurin, The Catholic Worker was the first American Catholic pacifist group, and has been the most long-lived radical movement in American Catholicism. While decidedly a minority within Catholicism, the Catholic Worker has exercised a tremendous influence on the thinking of many Catholics concerned with social reconstruction.

It is paradoxical of the ideology of Peter Maurin and the Catholic Worker that, while it is associated with the radical elements of American Catholicism, it is actually a product neither of the American left nor of liberal Catholicism, but rather of the European right. The Catholic Worker ideology rests upon the repudiation of most of the ideas developed during the Enlightenment which became the fundamental tenets of the philosophical liberalism underlying the structure of American economics, politics and society. In that lay the radicalism of the Catholic Worker.

The Catholic social ideal to which Maurin looked blended a literal interpretation of the Christian Gospels with medieval ecclesiastical institutions and modern papal social teaching. Maurin believed that the gospel provided a blueprint for the social order, and that under the guidance of the Church medieval society had succeeded in creating a social order based on personal responsibility and cooperation in seeking the common material and spiritual good. The modern bourgeois culture which supplanted that of the medieval world was judged by Maurin and the Catholic Worker to be fundamentally opposed to human fulfillment, because it inculcated a spirit of competitive exploitation, and demanded that there always be a class of exploited at the mercy of the powerful. Thus the Catholic Worker, unlike most American Catholic liberal reformers, viewed capitalism as a wholly evil force, inimical to Christian love, for it organized life around the profit motive.

The Catholic Worker rejection of capitalism also extended to the other current social ideologies which presented themselves as revolutionary alternatives to capitalism, especially socialism and communism. Both capitalism and its ideological rivals were seen as focusing on peoples' acquisitive desires and being premised on class conflict rather than cooperation.

As its alternative, the Catholic Worker did not seek to provide a strategy for dealing with particular social problems, but rather a "total idea" or way of life aimed at the regeneration of society. The core of the Catholic Worker social ideal was its philosophy of Christian personalism, which amounted to the attempt to live a literalist interpretation of the Sermon on the Mount, and the integration of the spiritual and material aspects of life through one's participation in the political, economic, and social concerns of the world. Thus, cultural change was seen as essentially a religious commitment to a countercultural community whose witness invites individuals to change their lives.

The concrete forms which the Catholic Worker took to create Christian community were the establishment of farm communes and houses of hospitality for the service of the poor. These communities sought to bring together scholars and workers to clarify thought in the light of the gospel and to unite theory and praxis in living voluntary poverty and practicing the corporal works of mercy. Through these base communities Dorothy Day and the Catholic Worker, since the 1930s, provided one of the most consistent Catholic presences in the support of labor strikes, the civil rights movement, and the wider American peace movement.

During the forties and fifties the Catholic Worker movement became associated with two characteristics which it would bequeath to the subsequent development of radical American Catholicism: anarchism and pacifism.

Anarchism reflected the Catholic Worker conviction that freedom is the gift of God in Christ which must be prophetically affirmed in the face of all determinist philosophy and state coercion. Freedom demands resisting all the implicit and explicit ways in which society controls individuals and forces them to conform to standards which demean them as persons and destroy their sense of conscience and personal responsibility. Pacifism, Dorothy Day insisted from the inception of the Catholic Worker, is the only philosophy in accord with the Christian life demanded by Christ in the Sermon on the Mount. Thus nonviolence became the Catholic Worker norm for all political action aimed at social change.

This anarchistic pacifism created a tension within the philosophical approach of the Catholic Worker to social change, which would continue to mark radical Catholicism and set the Catholic Worker and its philosophical offspring apart from the world view of mainstream Catholicism.

The Catholic Worker did not address the question of how to combine its personalist approach, which preserves the values of person and community, with the necessity of the state and the creation of intermediate social structures. Similarly, the pacifism of the Catholic Worker did not allow it to develop a theory of force and its use, and simply presupposed all coercion to be destructive. It regarded the state's use of force in law enforcement and punishment as self-evidently unjust, but did not deal with the state's role in restraining evil or how this was to be done. The failure of the Catholic Worker to develop its ideas into a theory of society and social change which admitted a place to the state, left it in a position of being a source of personalist protest rather than an organizing focus for a wider movement for social change. Yet as the nurturing womb of radical American Catholicism, the Catholic Worker would make possible the emergence in the 1960s of a new and more visible generation of Catholic activists and writers who would articulate the radical Catholic critique of American society as part of the national response to the nuclear arms race and the war in Vietnam.

Catholic Pacifism and Resistance—the 1960s

As the decade of the 1960s dawned, secular and religious peace movements had already begun to experience a revival in the United States and Western Europe. The immediate impetus to this revival in the United States was the atmospheric testing of the hydrogen bomb. Yet the issue quickly grew to focus on the continued development of the nuclear arms race. From the mid-sixties to its termination in 1975, the escalating American intervention in Vietnam provided the strongest and most divisive stimulus to the growth of national debate not only on the nuclear arms race, but also on the morality of modern war and the moral character of the values and aims underlying American national policy.

This period also spurred the revival of a more radical pacifist movement in American society. In 1957 radical American pacifists joined to form the Committee for Non-Violent Action (CNVA), in the effort to go beyond traditional individual pacifist objection to war, and to create an organized pacifist movement capable of disrupting U.S. military policy and working to transform American cultural values. As these efforts developed during the sixties, their goals expanded beyond the protesting of bomb tests and the construction of nuclear weapons, to visionary demands for unilateral disarmament and efforts to link the peace and civil rights movements into a common effort to transform society.

Within the American Catholic community, the Catholic Worker played a significant role in the revival of the American radical pacifist movement with its campaign of organized civil disobedience in protest against the civil defense drills in New York City during the closing years of the fifties. In the early sixties American Catholic pacifists received great encouragement from the encyclical *Pacem in Terris* of John XXIII, but they found their most significant breakthrough in the acceptance of pacifism as a legitimate moral option by Vatican Council II. Particularly because of growing reaction to the war in Vietnam, pacifists experienced in the 1960s and 1970s an unprecedented rise in acceptance and prominence within the American Catholic community, without ever losing their minority status.

While not all of those associated with the development and articulation of radical Catholic pacifism during these years were part of the Catholic Worker movement, it was still the Catholic Worker tradition which provided the basic intellectual heritage for these developments, as well as their organizational womb. In 1962 members of the Catholic Worker, under the leadership of Eileen Eagan, reactivated the American branch of PAX in affiliation with the English Catholic peace movement of the same name. PAX concentrated on working for change within the institutional Church, and actively lobbied for the pacifist position at the Second Vatican Council. In 1964 Catholic Workers, James Forrest, Thomas Cornell, and Martin Corbin joined with Rev. Philip Berrigan, S.S.J., to form the Catholic Peace Fellowship (CPF), in affiliation with the Protestant organization, the Fellowship of Reconciliation. The CPF sought to integrate Catholic peace activities into the wider American peace movement, as well as to continue the Catholic Worker tradition of civil disobedience and nonviolent resistance to war. Thus, by 1964 the Catholic Worker, PAX, and the CPF constituted the organizational backbone of the first viable American Catholic peace movement. As this movement developed, those who articulated the social perspectives of Catholic pacifism and organized radical Catholic political activism did not constitute a cohesive monolithic group. Yet they shared critical judgments on American society, and the place of the Church within it, that would give rise to the most radical social critique and antiwar activism in American Catholic history.

American Catholic Pacifists

Three men emerged in these years as the most prominent and systematic expositors of American Catholic pacifist thought: Gordon Zahn, who was one of the few Catholic conscientious objectors during World War II; the Trappist monk and prominent spiritual writer, Thomas Merton; and James Douglass, author of the *Non-Violent Cross,* which was regarded as one of the most systematic and influential expositions of a theology of nonviolence produced in the 1960s and 1970s. The writings of these three men greatly facilitated the rise in status and respectability which pacifism acquired in the American Catholic community during the 1960s.

In the similarity of themes, in the thought of these men can be found the parameters of the social vision which guided radical American Catholic pacifism from 1960 into the 1980s. There are several clear themes which they continue from the earlier Catholic Worker heritage.

First, they rejected the conventional definition of the conflict between the capitalist West and the communist

East. For these more radical Catholics the conflict between the Western and communist powers was not the fundamental conflict with which the Christian was to be concerned, for both power blocs were seen as competing giants spawned by the same antihuman, technological culture. The obligation of the Christian was not the defense of Western democracy, but the defense of humanity against a technocratic civilization that was rapidly subjecting human life and freedom to its own need for control.

Perhaps one of the most significant features in this radical Catholic social vision was the emergence of a more anti-American theme. Particularly with the experience of the Vietnam War, the traditional Catholic pacifist critique of modern culture became a critique of American society and power as the dominant expression of the destructive power of technological civilization.

Secondly, these radical Catholics rejected as inadequate, or as a compromise of Christian faith, the tradition of just-war teaching. Yet all would argue that by the terms of that very tradition, no modern war could be justified.

Thirdly, all insisted on the primary necessity of reestablishing a cultural sense of the responsibility and competency of the individual conscience to judge and resist actions of the state.

Fourthly, they all sought to redefine the Christian's relationship to the state in a way that transcends the either-or dichotomy of sectarian withdrawal or the establishment of a Christian state. In this regard, there remained, particularly in the work of Zahn and Douglass, the same tension found in the Catholic Worker vision between the call to transform society and the inability to provide an adequate theory for the Christian assumption of responsibility for the operation of the state.

At the heart of this effort to redefine the relationship of the Christian community to the state was the effort to articulate a pacifism of resistance. That is, a pacifism that went beyond individualistic nonparticipation in war to an active, nonviolent, communally based resistance to injustice, and which offered an alternative means to armed force for national self-defense.

Antiwar Activists

This search for a pacifism of resistance would give rise to the most radical expression of Catholic antiwar activity in what became known as the Catholic resistance movement. The chief architects of this movement were two priest brothers, Daniel Berrigan, S.J., and Philip Berrigan, S.S.J., who on May 7, 1968, led seven associates into the Catonsville, Maryland, draft board, took Selective Service records outside, and burned them with homemade napalm. The group became known as the "Catonsville Nine." Philip Berrigan had earlier led the "Baltimore Four" in a similar action, in which he and three companions poured blood on the draft files in the Baltimore Customs House. The term "Catholic Left" or "Catholic resistance movement" was the label applied to the activities of the Berrigan brothers and a growing number of peace activists who engaged in similar acts of disruptive civil disobedience from the Catonsville action in 1968 to the trial of the "Harrisburg Seven" in 1972. In this trial Philip Berrigan and six others were charged with conspiracy to kidnap Secretary of State Henry Kissinger and destroy heating tunnels for government buildings in Washington, D.C.

In the 1960s the draft had become the chief target for concretizing antiwar sentiment. Members of the Catholic Worker had already been committed to helping people resist the draft when in October 1965, Catholic Worker David Miller became the first man to publicly burn his draft card after such actions had become illegal. This act marked the high point of Catholic Worker protest against the draft. By 1968 a deep sense of frustration had grown within the American peace movement over failure to stop the Vietnam War, and within Catholic antiwar groups over failure even to obtain a condemnation of the war from the institutional Church.

The emergence of the Catholic resistance movement marked a new and culminating phase in radical Catholic efforts to resist war and commit themselves to nonviolent revolution for American society. The Catholic resistance movement also embodied the most extreme anti-American expression of the radical Catholic pacifist critique of society. As Philip and Daniel Berrigan stated, their decision for the Catonsville action reflected a complete disillusionment with American and Western society, and a deep sense of the systemic character of injustice in America as well as a negative view of American influence in the world. Thus, with the Catholic resistance movement, the Catholic pacifist critique of power became most pointedly the critique and rejection of American power.

With the ending of the U.S. involvement in Vietnam, the mainstream American Catholic debate on war and peace would turn to the issue of the nuclear arms race as the focus of its ongoing development. Public attention to the war and peace debate within the American Catholic community would turn to the debate within the American hierarchy over the morality of U.S. nuclear policy. Radical Catholic pacifists, such as the Berrigans, would continue to use civil disobedience as a method to protest the continued possession and development of nuclear weapons. Yet radical Catholic pacifists would cease to have the prominence that the national division over Vietnam had given them. Not surprisingly, the most visible focal point of the radical pacifist presence in the Catholic community continued to be the Catholic Worker movement, whose theoretical perspectives and communal activity had such a formative influence on the Catholic antiwar activities of the 1960s and 1970s. The Catholic Worker continues to be the oldest radical pacifist movement in American Catholicism.

See also CATHOLIC WORKER MOVEMENT, THE; CONSCIENTIOUS OBJECTION (AND OBJECTORS) IN AMERICA; DAY, DOROTHY; MAURIN, PETER; MERTON, THOMAS.

Au, William A. *The Cross, the Flag and the Bomb: American Catholics Debate War and Peace.* Westport, 1985.

Cornell, Thomas C., and James H. Forrest, eds. *A Penny A Copy.* New York, 1968.

Day, Dorothy. *The Long Loneliness.* New York, 1952.

Douglass, James. *The Non-Violent Cross: A Theology of Revolution and Peace.* New York, 1968.

———. *Resistance and Contemplation: The Way of Liberation.* Garden City, 1972.

McNeal, Patricia F. *The American Catholic Peace Movement.* New York, 1968.

Meconis, Charles. *With Clumsy Grace: The American Catholic Left, 1961–1975.* New York, 1979.

Merton, Thomas. *Faith and Violence: Christian Teaching and Christian Practice.* Notre Dame, 1968.

Zahn, Gordon. *War, Conscience and Dissent.* New York, 1967.

WILLIAM A. AU

CATHOLIC PHILANTHROPY IN AMERICA

When in 1789 John Carroll of Baltimore was appointed the first American bishop, his congregation numbered approximately 30,000. At that time, there were no organized Catholic charities, although Ursuline nuns had cared for orphans in the Louisiana Territory since 1734. In 1791, however, the First Synod of Baltimore urged the Catholic community to give generously to benefit their neighbors in need. Institutional charity commenced in 1805 when Visitation sisters in Georgetown, D.C., opened a boarding school and applied its tuitions to finance a day school for poor girls and to support a number of boarding orphans. Several years later, aided by Bishop Carroll and a few laypersons, Elizabeth Bayley Seton, founder of the Sisters of Charity, established a similar school in Baltimore. This funding arrangement continued to mark Catholic charities for many years. Since working-class congregants could not endow charitable institutions adequately, boarding school tuitions were indispensable for the maintenance of the sisters and the poor they served.

Early Nineteenth Century

Soon benevolent laity were calling on sisterhoods for help in meeting the needs of growing numbers of immigrants. The challenges they faced in the 1820s and 1830s were vastly eclipsed by those of succeeding decades. A flood of impoverished immigrants in the 1840s, including 1.5 million from Ireland alone, caused church membership to soar from about 663,000 in 1840 to three million in 1860. Their poverty stimulated the development of new religious communities dedicated to parochial school teaching, nursing, and every variety of social work. These groups were to remain an essential component of Catholic philanthropy until the late twentieth century. Their religious approbation and the lifetime commitment of their members assured the stability of the charitable institutions and schools they conducted. At the same time, they were free to mobilize quickly to meet new social needs as they emerged across the nation.

Young women from every social class, far more than their brothers, were attracted to these religious communities. As a result, while there were few sisters in America before 1840, their ranks swelled consistently thereafter. They soon became the most notable feature of the Church's charity organization, and, indeed, they were unique in American religious philanthropy. Given nineteenth-century restrictions on women's public activities, their unusual lifestyle and remarkable benevolent enterprise captured the attention, and, in time, the admiration of citizens of all faiths.

Until the 1860s, Catholic charitable institutions remained, for the most part, small and parish-based. Clerical and lay leaders struggled to involve laity of every social class in their support on a continuing basis. The subscription society, founded to finance a specific institution, was an early stratagem. In the 1830s a membership subscription was approximately $1.50 per year. The charity fair, with its promise of entertainment, proved more popular than the subscription society among poor and working-class parishioners. Managers of charitable institutions also appreciated the fair since its returns were cash in hand, whereas subscription pledges were not always honored. By the 1850s, the charity sermon had become another important fundraising technique. Directors of orphanages, in particular, competed with one another for the most eloquent preachers, since they attracted huge audiences and generated immediate, badly needed funds for the institutions. The exemplary oration of the era stressed the spiritual rewards that accompanied giving to the poor, especially to helpless orphans.

Wealthy Catholics gave generously, but their numbers were sparse for much of the nineteenth century. They, like their working-class coreligionists insisted that the needs of the poor, the elderly, the sick, and children should always take priority over other church projects such as church and seminary construction. Ironically, the fact that, unlike other charitable institutions, Catholic hospitals accepted some payment for service led many parishioners to conclude erroneously that they were less in need of assistance than other institutions that served the poor. Early hospitals, for the most part, were small, informal, and open to all, regardless of religious affiliation or type of illness. In 1860 eighteen cities had Catholic hospitals; by 1885 there were 154. They were usually owned as well as managed by sisterhoods, and financed by the sisters' contributed labor and by a weekly charge for those who could afford to pay. But, in fact, patient fees were minimal, and a majority of those cared for paid nothing. As a result, nineteenth-century hospitals were invariably in serious financial difficulty.

Later Nineteenth Century

After the Civil War, the organization of Catholic charities slowly began to change. The pre-war convent school that accommodated a few orphans was now giving way to the large orphanage in which some education was provided. A large institution was thought to be more cost-effective than a number of small parish establishments operating independently of each other. The huge diocesan orphanage with an industrial school attached quickly became the most visible Catholic philanthropic response to the social crises facing major American cities. By 1897 the New York Catholic Protectory, with 3,296 children enrolled, had become the nation's largest child-caring institution. A movement to organize benevolent laity on a national basis commenced in the mid-1850s when the German Roman Catholic Verein in St. Louis united numerous groups engaged in various good works. The St. Vincent de Paul Society and the Irish Catholic Benevolent Union followed suit in the next decade.

The 1880s saw the beginning of the second great wave of Catholic immigrants from Europe, this time from Canada, Italy, Hungary, Poland, and Lithuania. Over the next thirty years, these newcomers were to account for a 4.8 million increase in church membership. Like their predecessors, they settled heavily in the nation's larger cities. The harsh urban environment of the era and the enormity of the social problems accompanying unregulated economic activity impelled charity leaders to rethink the Church's traditional approach to philanthropy. They urged less focus on institution-building and more attention to collaboration with Protestant benevolent organizations and with government social agencies. They insisted that, if the Church was to play an influential role in mainstream philanthropic forums, its charitable institutions could no longer continue to operate autonomously. All would have to observe policies and procedures established by diocesan charitable bureaus.

Twentieth-Century Developments

The St. Vincent de Paul Society spearheaded the charity centralization movement in 1901 by opening a cross-parish agency for child placement in Baltimore. This step paved the way for the establishment of the National Conference of Catholic Charities in 1910. Although rank-and-file laity and sisterhoods resisted the reform initiative, the rapid professionalization of social work and the formation of the National Catholic Welfare Conference in 1919 ensured its implementation in dioceses across the nation. Whereas before World War I only five dioceses had established charitable bureaus, by 1931 the total had reached thirty. Local bishops presided over these diocesan bureaus, appointing clergy and wealthy laymen to sit on their advisory boards. Under episcopal direction, these boards formulated policies for all diocesan charities and supervised their operations.

At the same time, seemingly endless appeals by charitable institutions and religious communities for financial contributions persuaded bishops to push more vigorously for consolidation of charity fundraising. To this end, they launched annual diocesan-wide charity drives to benefit all charities of their dioceses. They anticipated several benefits from the new approach: it would allow all to give; it would raise more money; it would cost little to administer; and it would enable bishops to control the allocation of financial contributions.

By the 1960s, professional fundraisers were being paid to conduct these annual drives. Their secular values, however, were often at odds with the philosophy of religious charity. Efficiency, class differences, and civic consciousness rather than the gospel message permeated charity campaign literature and solicitation strategies. "Painless giving" replaced sacrificial giving, and gifts of money received more attention than voluntary service. Nonetheless, because professional fundraising promised improved financial returns, its potentially harmful long-term consequences were overlooked. These changes in charity financing, like the concurrent centralization of the charities themselves, gradually undermined the traditional understanding among grassroots Catholics that everyone, regardless of economic circumstances, has a role to play in the charitable activities of the Church.

An unexpected and sustained decline in the number of women joining and remaining in sisterhoods, commencing in the late 1960s, brought the crisis in Catholic philanthropy to public attention. As the cost of labor in thousands of parochial schools and charitable institutions escalated dramatically, it was obvious that financial contributions were lagging far behind requirements. The Catholic community, now solidly middle class, was simply not supporting church charities in proportion to its means. By 1980 the Catholic Church ranked behind other major religious denominations in the annual amount contributed by practicing households to the Church. Nor has this disturbing situation ameliorated in the 1990s. The critical challenge facing American Catholics today is to reclaim the radical values and genuine popular participation that for so long distinguished their collective benevolence.

Gavin, Donald P. *The National Conference of Catholic Charities, 1910–1960.* Milwaukee: Bruce Press, 1962.
Greeley, Andrew, and William McManus. *Catholic Contributions: Sociology and Policy.* Chicago: Thomas More Press, 1987.

McManus, William. "Stewardship and Almsgiving in the Roman Catholic Tradition." *Faith and Philanthropy in America: Exploring the Role of Religion in America's Voluntary Sector,* eds. Robert Wuthnow and Virginia A. Hodgkinson. San Francisco: Jossey-Bass Publishers, 1990.

National Conference of Catholic Bishops. *Stewardship: A Disciple's Response.* Washington, D.C.: U.S. Catholic Conference, 1992.

Oates, Mary J. *The Catholic Philanthropic Tradition in America.* Bloomington: Indiana University Press, 1995.

____. "Economic Change and the Character of Catholic Philanthropy." *Religion, the Independent Sector, and American Culture,* eds. Conrad Cherry and Rowland Sherill. Atlanta: Scholars Press, 1992.

MARY J. OATES

CATHOLIC POPULATION, HISTORICAL GROWTH

Estimating the number of Catholics—or of any religious denomination—living in the United States at various historical periods is more difficult than it appears. The U.S. census has never included a question on this subject. Throughout the nineteenth century, figures for the Catholic population were "incredibly inflated" (Finke and Stark, 110). Nineteenth-century estimators had vested interests in assuming the largest number of Catholics possible—as many as twenty-four million in 1870, according to some publications. For Protestants, such overwhelming Catholic population growth mobilized their own members to donate funds for proselytization, increased the influence of nativist demagogues, and "explained" the declining percentage of Americans who belonged to mainline Protestant denominations (Finke and Stark, 112). For Catholics, who knew that nowhere near 24,000,000 congregants were attending their services, high estimates served to reinforce Church claims of the immigrants' vulnerability to losing their faith, and the necessity of increased donations and personnel to remedy the situation.

The inflated estimates had been obtained by simply counting all the immigrants arriving in each decade from "Catholic" countries and assuming a high subsequent birth rate. But many Irish immigrants were Protestants from Northern Ireland, and many French immigrants were Huguenots. Other countries posed similar problems. To obtain a more accurate estimate, Gerald Shaughnessy multiplied the number of immigrants from various countries by the percentage in that country who were Catholic (Shaughnessy, 1925). Shaughnessy's more conservative figures became the standard ones cited in later histories (e.g., Hennesey, 1981). More recent researchers claim, however, that even this technique may overestimate the Catholic population, since the Catholics and Protestants in a country may have had different migration rates (Finke and Stark, 111). This seems to have been especially true

of France, whose Protestants were much more likely to emigrate than its Catholics were.

Other methods have also been used to measure the Catholic population. Finke and Stark use the decennial Census of Religious Denominations, which was compiled by the U.S. Census Bureau between 1890 and 1936. Other researchers have tended to discount this source, since it was based on figures collected from local churches rather than on individual responses. Finke and Stark, however, maintain that asking the pastor or elders of a church to provide membership figures was *more* likely to be accurate than asking individual Americans to give their denominational affiliation. Individuals are notoriously prone to exaggerate their religious involvement and to claim that they are members of a denomination whose doors they have not darkened in thirty years. Local churches had less to gain by over-reporting their membership and were, in any event, rigorously checked by Census officials (Finke and Stark, 8). The Census Bureau ceased its efforts to enumerate religious bodies after 1936. More recently, however, the Glenmary compilations of "Churches and Church Membership in the United States" have used a similar method to estimate denominational membership (Quinn and others, 1982; Bradley and others, 1992).

A third way to estimate the numbers of denominational adherents is by a nationwide sample survey. The technology for drawing a sufficiently accurate sample has only been available since the 1950s. Even so, the technique remains expensive, and few researchers used it to estimate denominational membership. The most recent such attempt, the National Survey of Religious Identification, was conducted in 1990 (Kosmin and Lachman, 1993).

A further complication arises when one wishes to estimate the *percentage* of Americans who were Catholic, as compared to the percentage belonging to other denominations. Catholics counted children in their membership figures; Methodists and Baptists, among many other Protestant denominations, did not. When comparing percentage figures, therefore, denominational figures have to be adjusted to include (or exclude) children.

Table I lists the U.S. Catholic population, as determined by each of the above methods. Throughout the nineteenth century, it can be seen that the Finke and Stark figures are lower than Shaughnesey's estimates. In the twentieth century, the Glenmary estimates tend to be lower than Hennesey's, while Kosmin's and Lachman's 1990 estimate is lower than Glenmary's. The estimates given by the Official Catholic Directory tend to be higher than both.

Geographic Distribution

The Catholic population has never been evenly distributed across the country. In 1860 Rhode Island was the most Catholic state, with 21.4 percent of its people Catholic.

California was next (19%), followed by Louisiana (16%) and Minnesota (14.8%). These Catholics were, however, from different ethnic groups: Irish and Italian in the case of Rhode Island, Latino in California, French Cajun in Louisiana, and German in Minnesota (Finke and Stark, 114). By 1890 New Mexico was the most Catholic area (77%), followed by Arizona (37.5%), Rhode Island (33%), Massachusetts (32.3%) and Minnesota (24.5%) (Finke and Stark, 114). In 1990, according to the Glenmary studies, the most Catholic states were all in the Northeast: Rhode Island (63.1%), Massachusetts (49.2%), Connecticut (41.8%), New Jersey (41.3%), and New York (40.5%). Other Catholic states in 1990 included Louisiana, Wisconsin, Illinois, New Mexico, and Pennsylvania. Between 30 and 32 percent of the population of each of these states were Catholic (Bradley and others, 12–36).

Ethnic Distribution

If estimating the size of the Catholic population in a given historical period is difficult, estimating its ethnic composition is even more so. Prior to 1840, most Catholics were of English descent, with substantial percentages of French in Louisiana and the Mississippi valley. Irish, Germans, and (in the West) Hispanics comprised the majority of Catholics between 1840 and 1880; substantial numbers of Poles, Italians, Slovenes, Slovaks, and French-Canadians were added to the mix between 1880 and 1920. The exact percentages, however, cannot be computed. However, several current surveys estimate the ethnic composition of U.S. Catholics today; the most recent figures are given in Table II.

Table I
Estimates of the Catholic Population of the United States, 1790–1990

	Total Catholic Population	Percent of U.S. Population
1790	24,000–40,000[a]	0.6–1.0%
1820	195,000[b]	2.0%
1830	318,000[b]	2.5%
1840	663,000[b]	3.9%
1850	1,088,000[c]–1,606,000[b]	4.7–6.9%
1860	2,439,000[c]–3,103,000[b]	7.8–9.9%
1870	3,555,000[c]–4,504,000[b]	8.9–11.3%
1880	6,259,000[b]	12.5%
1890	7,343,000[c]–8,909,000[b]	11.7–14.2%
1900	12,041,000[b]	15.8%
1906	14,211,000[c]	16%[c]
1910	16,363,000[d]	17.8%
1916	15,722,000[c]	16%[c]
1920	18,000,000[d]	17.0%
1926	18,605,000[c]	16%[c]
1930	20,000,000[d]	16.3%

	Total Catholic Population	Percent of U.S. Population
1940	21,000,000[d]	15.9%
1960	42,000,000[d]	23.4%
1980	47,502,000[e]–49,812,000[d]	21.0–22.0%
1990	46,004,000[f]–53,385,000[g]	18.5–21.5%
1995	60,190,605[h]	23.2%

[a]Cogley and Van Allen, 1, 25.
[b]Shaughnessy, 71, 262.
[c]Finke and Stark, 113, 248.
[d]Hennesey, 173, 207, 237, 283–284, 329.
[e]Quinn and others, 1.
[f]Kosmin, 15.
[g]Bradley and others, 1.
[h]Official Catholic Directory, 1995, 2020.

Table II
Ethnic Composition* of U.S. Catholics, 1995

Irish	25%
German	23%
Italian	20%
Spanish/Mexican/Hispanic	11%
Polish	11%
French	10%
English	7%
Native American	3%
Czechoslovakian	2%
Scottish/Scotch	2%
Indian	2%
Puerto Rican	2%
African American	2%
Other groups (Portuguese, Filipino, Norwegian, Asian)	1% each
Other	13%
Don't Know	3%

*"What ethnic group or groups are most important in your ancestry?" (Some respondents mentioned more than one group.)

(*Source:* Davidson and others, forthcoming.)

See also AFRICAN AMERICAN CATHOLICS; FRENCH-CANADIAN CATHOLICS IN AMERICA; GERMAN CATHOLICS IN AMERICA; HISPANIC CATHOLICS IN AMERICA; IRISH CATHOLICS IN AMERICA; ITALIAN CATHOLICS IN AMERICA; POLISH CATHOLICS IN AMERICA; SLOVAK CATHOLICS IN AMERICA.

Bradley, Martin B., and others. *Churches and Church Membership in the United States, 1990.* Atlanta: Glenmary Research Center, 1992.

Cogley, John, and Rodger Van Allen. *Catholic America.* Expanded and updated edition. Kansas City, Mo.: Sheed and Ward, 1986.

Davidson, James, and others. *Catholic Faith and Morals: Unity and Diversity in Today's Church.* Our Sunday Visitor Press, forthcoming.

Finke, Roger, and Rodney Stark. *The Churching of America 1776–1900.* New Brunswick, N.J.: Rutgers University Press, 1992.

Hennesey, James, S.J. *American Catholicism: A History of the Roman Catholic Community in the U.S.* New York: Oxford University Press, 1981.

Kosmin, Barry A., and Seymour P. Lachman. *One Nation Under God: Religion in Contemporary American Society.* New York: Harmony Books, 1993.

Quinn, Bernard, and others. *Churches and Church Membership in the U.S., 1980.* Atlanta: Glenmary Research Center, 1982.

Shaughnessy, Gerald. *Has the Immigrant Kept the Faith?* New York: Macmillan, 1925.

PATRICIA WITTBERG, S.C.

CATHOLIC PRESS (NEWSPAPERS), THE

Although the purpose of Catholic newspapers has been viewed from various perspectives during the past two centuries, the Roman Catholic Church in the United States has consistently taken the attitude that the Catholic press is not only a public relations tool, but also a means to counteract attacks from its adversaries—both within and without the Church. Catholic newspapers have evolved from the use of a primitive printing press by a nineteenth-century missionary priest in the Northwest Territory to electronic technology in the twentieth century.

With the United States' ever-expanding development, the bishops soon realized the need for a quick and effective means of communication with the faithful. Bishops, therefore, looked to the Catholic press as an avenue through which the faith could be interpreted for life in American society. That role of the Catholic media has continued, with modifications, over the past two centuries.

Nineteenth-Century Newspapers

No history of Catholic newspapers would be complete without the mention of the Irish national press in America. Although those nineteenth-century journals focused primarily on news from Ireland, they also provided support in the faith for Irish Catholic immigrants and essentially became forerunners of the Catholic press in the United States.

Irish-American newspapers were published mostly in New York, Boston, and Philadelphia, where large Irish populations had settled. Prominent among those journals in the early 1800s were the *Shamrock* or *Hibernian Chronicle* (1810), *Globe and Emerald* (1824–27), *Irish Shield* (1828), *Irish Advocate* (1831), *Green Banner* (1835), and in the south the *Irishmen and Charleston Weekly Register* (1829).

Although the *Michigan Essay* is considered the pioneer of all Catholic journals (founded in 1809 by the Rev. Gabriel Richard, a missionary in the Northwest Territory), the first strictly religious newspaper established in the United States in defense of Catholic doctrine was the *United States Catholic Miscellany.* Bishop John England of Charleston, S.C., saw a need to counteract the attacks

upon Catholic doctrines and practices that were being made in the secular press.

In 1822, therefore, he began publication of the weekly newspaper, which reached six hundred Catholics residing in North and South Carolina and Georgia, to provide simple explanations and defense of the Catholic faith. Even though his venture had little support from the rest of the U.S. Church, it continued uninterrupted until the Civil War (1861).

In New York, Catholics looked to the *Truth Teller* (1822–55) for news about the Church until the publication of the *Catholic Register* in 1839. However, in 1841 the *Register* merged with the *Freeman's Journal* and became the *Freeman's Journal and Catholic Register,* which was sold by the diocese to James Alphonsus McMaster, who made it one of the most respected journals of the time.

Early religious-oriented weekly newspapers were owned mainly by lay publishers or had some affiliation with a religious order. The Boston *Pilot* (1829) originated with the *Literary and Catholic Sentinel,* a Jesuit journal. However, the early *Pilot,* owned by Patrick Donahoe, was more a national newspaper read by Irish immigrants throughout New England. The *Pilot* was bought by Boston's archbishop in 1876 but did not become the official newspaper of the diocese until 1908.

The Rev. Edward D. Fenwick was a true pioneer in establishing newspapers that had episcopal approbation. Before being appointed bishop of Cincinnati, he founded *The Catholic Press* (1829–33) in Hartford, Connecticut. Following his arrival in Cincinnati, he began publication of the *Catholic Telegraph* (1831) "to aid the diffusing of a correct knowledge of the Roman Catholic faith." The *Telegraph* has been continuously published for more than 165 years with only a short suspension in 1832 due to a cholera epidemic in the city. The journal was so successful that it became the official organ of the Dioceses of Louisville, Cleveland, Vincennes, and Detroit in 1850.

In 1832 New York Catholics had access to the *Weekly Register and Catholic Diary,* and *Shepherd of the Valley* became a source of information and inspiration for Catholics in the Mississippi River basin.

An attempt was made in Washington, D.C., in 1833 to publish a newspaper for Catholics living in the area of the nation's capital. However, the *Catholic Journal* survived only one year. In 1836 the *Catholic Advocate,* which had evolved from the *St. Joseph's College Minerva,* was founded by Benjamin J. Webb and moved from Bardstown, Kentucky, to Louisville. The Louisville newspaper became *The Record* following a twenty-nine-year merger with Cincinnati's *Catholic Telegraph* in 1850.

Also in 1833, the Rev. John Hughes (later archbishop of New York) began the *Catholic Herald* in Philadelphia to refute charges made against the Church in the *Christian Advocate.* The *Herald* was intended originally as a forum for a series of discussions between Catholics and Presbyterians. In 1856 the *Herald* consolidated with the *Visitor,* and ten years later its name was changed to *Catholic Standard.* In 1895 it merged with the *Catholic Times* to become the present-day *Catholic Standard and Times.*

Diocesan newspapers that began publication in the 1840s were the *Pittsburgh Catholic* (1844) and the Baltimore *Catholic Mirror* (1849), which evolved from early attempts at publishing a monthly magazine for Catholics. In 1913 it became the archdiocese's present-day *Catholic Review.*

Following the Civil War and the pioneer westward migration, Catholic newspapers began to emerge as a more important means for bishops to communicate with the faithful. Several diocesan newspapers as well as *The Wanderer,* a national newspaper founded by Joseph Matt at Assumption Church in St. Paul, Minnesota, trace their beginnings to the latter half of the nineteenth century. *The Wanderer* has remained in the Matt family for three generations and has continued through the twentieth century to maintain its reputation as the organ of conservatism on Catholic issues.

Among those diocesan newspapers established at that time were the *Catholic News* of New York, founded by Herman Ridder in 1886 and privately owned until purchased by the archdiocese in 1981; the *Monitor* (1858), which served the faithful of the San Francisco archdiocese for 126 years until a monthly periodical, the *San Francisco Catholic* (1985–95), was inaugurated; the *Catholic Sentinel* (1870) of Portland, Oregon, which was privately owned until 1928 when it became a diocesan organ.

Among the chain of newspapers owned by Humphrey J. Desmond of Milwaukee were the *Catholic Citizen,* predecessor of the diocese's *Catholic Herald* (1869); the St. Paul *Northwestern Chronicle;* the *Catholic Journal* of Memphis, Tennessee; *New Century* of Washington, D.C.; and the Sioux City *Iowa Catholic Citizen.*

Other weekly diocesan newspapers that trace their origins to this time were: in the 1870s, the *Michigan Catholic* (1872), *Western New York Catholic* of the Buffalo diocese (1873), *Catholic Universe Bulletin* (1874) of Cleveland, *Catholic Times* (1875) of Columbus, Ohio, and the *Providence Visitor* (Rhode Island) (1875); in the 1880s, the Davenport, Iowa, *Catholic Messenger* (1882), and the *Catholic Courier* (1889) of Rochester, New York; in the 1890s, the Chicago *New World* (1892), *Catholic Sun* (1892) of Syracuse, New York, *Today's Catholic* (1892) of San Antonio, Texas, Los Angeles *Tidings* (1895); *Catholic Spirit* (1895) of Wheeling-Charleston, West Virginia, *Catholic Times* (1896) of Springfield, Illinois, *Catholic Northwest Progress* (1897) of Seattle, Washington, *Catholic Transcript* (1898) of Hartford, Connecticut, and *Intermountain Catholic* (1899) of Salt Lake City, Utah.

Several attempts were made during the 1800s at publishing a daily newspaper for Catholics in English, including the New York-based *American Citizen* (1835–41) and the *Catholic Telegraph* (1875). In 1902 the Chicago *New World* also made a foray into the arena but its efforts were short-lived. However, thirty-five foreign-language newspapers did fairly well in the nineteenth century, including *Narod Polski* (1886) and *Jednota* (1891), published in Polish and Slovak as well as English, respectively. Others that survived well into the twentieth century included *Draugas* (Lithuanian) and *Dziennik Chicagoski* (Polish).

Essentially, historians view early Catholic journalism as a struggle to maintain the civil and religious liberty of a people who were often seen by their non-Catholic neighbors as subversive of the U.S. government.

Twentieth-Century Newspapers

Many Catholic newspapers were still privately owned during the early 1900s. At that time there were 63 weekly newspapers and 145 foreign-language publications in 16 languages (including periodicals). One of the more interesting phenomena during the twentieth century has been the rise and fall of diocesan newspaper circulation. In 1908 the Brooklyn (New York) *Tablet* had a circulation of 13,000; in 1964 it reached 138,871; and by 1996 had dropped to 84,796. Likewise, the Cincinnati *Catholic Telegraph* dropped from about 70,000 in the 1960s to 27,000 in the 1990s. However, some newspapers increased circulation during the latter half of the century, such as the Baltimore *Catholic Review* from 44,496 to 67,724 and the *Pittsburgh Catholic* from around 90,000 to 109,589.

Economics had an influence on the prosperity of many diocesan newspapers. Two models emerged as dioceses began to assume control, using the newspapers as "partisan house organs" for communication with the faithful. Some were purely nonprofit institutional journals while others were expected to rely heavily on profits from advertising revenue. In many dioceses, publication costs were covered by subsidies from parishes. In such cases, parishes were expected to pay an annual rate according to the number of declared parishioners. Over the years, however, as diocesan costs increased in other areas of operation, a combination of subsidy, subscription, and advertising revenue emerged as the means for a newspaper's survival. Those factors also affected subscription costs as evidenced from the rise in rates of many papers at one dollar or two dollars a year in the early 1900s to twenty dollars and twenty-five dollars by the end of the century.

Pre-World War II diocesan newspapers continued to be public relations tools, concentrating on disseminating the Church's viewpoints on controversies that arose. Following World War II, however, editors realized the need for more thorough coverage of national and international Church news as college education became a norm for the average Catholic and professional journalists began to enter the field. Consequently, diocesan newspapers took on a sharper image and broadened their horizons to become not just the platform whereby a bishop could express an opinion, but also an independent voice for the people.

In his encyclical *Humani generis,* Pope Pius XII encouraged this trend by stating that the press should strike a balance between "mute servility" and "uncontrolled criticism." He also noted in a radio address to the 1957 Catholic Press Association convention that free discussion would be legitimate and that apart from issues of faith and morals each person could hold and defend individual opinions.

With its liberating spirit, the Second Vatican Council pushed those boundaries even further. Many bishops eased the once-strict control they exerted over their diocesan newspapers and encouraged editors to tackle substantive issues that affected American society. As a result, critical social topics, such as racism and birth control as well as liturgical matters, Church authority, and diocesan fiscal responsibility, made their way onto the pages of diocesan newspapers.

Although diocesan editors ventured slowly into such uncharted waters and were influenced by a bishop's expectations, national newspapers under lay control set the standard for the 1960s and 1970s by being more committed to serving public interest. Foremost among those journals was the *National Catholic Reporter* (1964), which began as a diocesan newspaper in Kansas City-St. Joseph, Missouri, with Robert Hoyt as editor. When the newspaper's daring approach to news became too controversial for diocesan tastes, it became independent and continued to prosper under lay leadership with a circulation of 48,000 by the mid-1990s.

Another national newspaper that made an impact on the U.S. Church scene was the *National Catholic Register* (1924), considered moderately conservative in outlook. It evolved from a chain of papers begun in 1900 in Denver by Thomas Jefferson Casey. The chain grew to include papers for 33 dioceses with a combined circulation of 778,196 by the 1960s. However, the chain dissolved during the latter half of the twentieth century, and along with *Catholic Twin Circle,* the *Register* was purchased by Circle Media, Inc., in 1995.

A similar history is recorded by *Our Sunday Visitor* (OSV), which was founded in 1912 by Rev. John Francis Noll (later bishop of Fort Wayne, Indiana) as a means to instruct the faithful against anti-Catholic attacks. In 1937 the newspaper expanded to another diocese and by 1964 OSV published 11 diocesan editions, a national edition for Canada, and a national news edition with a combined circulation of 892,148. As dioceses withdrew from the chain during the 1970s and 1980s, only the national edition (a weekly news magazine) remained by the end of the century with a circulation of 91,000.

Chains on a smaller scale included the collaboration of dioceses, such as the Catholic Quality Newspapers of Northern Ohio, which published editions for Cleveland, Toledo, and Youngstown until the 1980s when the chain was discontinued. The *Catholic Herald* with editions for Milwaukee, Madison and Superior, Wisconsin, has survived into the 1990s with a combined circulation of 77,697, although it had reached 172,313 in the 1960s. A collaboration that took shape in the 1980s was *The Florida Catholic,* whereby the Diocese of Orlando published editions for six dioceses in Florida, reaching a combined readership of 137,100.

Such cooperation often meant survival for a diocesan newspaper. As circulation and financial resources decreased, many dioceses cut publication to biweekly or monthly, and even changed to a newsletter format or a weekly page in a community newspaper. Most papers also began using desktop publishing with state-of-the-art graphics and color to enhance their products and entice readers, in an effort to compete with secular publications and electronic media.

Those newspapers experiencing difficulty were able to draw on expertise from the Catholic Press Association (CPA), which was formed in 1911 in Columbus, Ohio, from an earlier organization, American Catholic Press Association (1908). The CPA was founded to "assist members in publishing effective periodicals according to the demands of technical standards, and the truths of human reason and the Catholic faith."

CPA statistics note that in 1964 there were 121 weekly Catholic newspapers in the United States with a circulation of 4,569,230, and 13 foreign-language newspapers with a readership of 195,434. By the end of the century, the CPA listed among its member publications five national newspapers, 167 diocesan newspapers, and 13 Eastern-Rite publications, with a total circulation of 5,859,310, as well as 19 foreign-language newspapers with a circulation of 306,1288. However, foreign-language publications had fared better in the nineteenth century with a total of 524 newspapers at one time or another, serving immigrant Catholics from both eastern and western European countries. By 1900 that number had decreased to 145, which included both newspapers and magazines.

Editors of Catholic newspapers often found themselves in a quandary during the 1980s and 1990s when some bishops began once again to reassert more control over diocesan news content. Although Pope John Paul II urged the Catholic press to be a means for continuing dialogue between Church leadership and membership, editors had to determine "how to provide a forum for dissent and accurate news while [their papers were] officially sponsored by the diocese" (William J. Thorn, "The History and Role of the Catholic Press").

See also CATHOLIC BOOK PUBLISHING; CATHOLIC MAGAZINES AND PERIODICALS.

Deedy, J. G. "The Catholic Press." *The Religious Press in America,* ed. Martin E. Marty. New York, 1963.

Foik, Paul J. *Pioneer Catholic Journalism.* New York: U.S. Catholic Historical Society, 1930.

New Catholic Encyclopedia 3:314–26.

Thorn, William J. "The History and Role of the Catholic Press." *Reporting Religion Facts and Faith,* ed. Benjamin J. Hubbard. Sonoma, California, 1990.

Willging, E. P., and H. Hatzfeld. *Catholic Serials of the 19th Century in the U.S.: A Descriptive Bibliography and Union List.* 2nd ser. Washington, 1959– .

MARIANNA McLOUGHLIN

CATHOLIC RELIEF SERVICES

Prologue

The story of Catholic Relief Services is a story about the U.S. Catholic Church, its leaders and members. CRS, first known as WRS, War Relief Services, was founded in 1943 by the American bishops to assist victims of war. The bishops called upon American Catholics to give from their substance as well as from their abundance. Hundreds of thousands of Catholics and others responded with financial donations, clothing, volunteer service, and supportive prayers. It is also a story about human relationships, for CRS is an organization in which very talented, highly motivated women and men dedicate their best efforts to feeding hungry people, clothing victims of natural disasters, and sheltering families made homeless by war, famine, and disease.

For fifty-one years, CRS staff persons in countries all over the world have continued to respond to emergencies, like earthquakes—in India, Italy, Mexico, Colombia, and the Philippines—volcanic eruptions and cyclones in Bangladesh, drought and famine in Ethiopia, Sudan, Mozam-

Catholic Relief Services

bique, Somalia, displacement of people through wars—in Cambodia and Vietnam, the former Yugoslavia, Angola, Iraq, Sudan, and El Salvador. They oversee the distribution of food and collaborate with local groups—especially Church agencies—to dig wells and canals, implement agricultural schemes for improved yield, set up credit unions and village banking operations, sponsor health clinics for mothers and children, provide training for demobilized military personnel, and support education for community leaders. The successes and struggles of CRS "field" personnel are mirrored in the work of (currently) 150 men and women at CRS World Headquarters in Baltimore who clearly understand that theirs also is a response to the gospel imperative of the Beatitudes.

The Middle East and Europe

In the year 1943, thousands of Polish women and children, along with elderly men, were caught in a diaspora stretching from Asiatic Russia through the Middle East and Africa all the way to Mexico. War Relief Services assigned Fr. Aloysius J. Wycislo of Chicago to oversee relief activities on behalf of these refugees. By 1943 more than 250,000 Polish refugees, evacuees and deportees had found haven in Iran, Palestine, Egypt, Kenya, Uganda, Tanganyika, the Rhodesias, South Africa, India, England, Scotland and Mexico.

Wycislo recalls celebrating Christmas Mass that year in Bethlehem, sharing the night watch in the Shepherds Field with thousands of Polish refugees, and notes that he and they would travel a long and hard road together before the peace they prayed for that night would become a reality. "By the middle of 1944," said Wycislo, "WRS-NCWC had relief projects for Polish refugees in 22 cities and towns in the Holy Land. Before the end of that year, 61 recreation and welfare centers dotted the Italian peninsula, serving Polish troops. . . . [WRS distributed] almost $800,000 worth of precious medicines, food, clothing and other welfare and recreational supplies for Polish refugees whose exile forced them to await the end of the war in this cradle of civilization."

Meanwhile, in Europe in 1944, Fr. Andrew P. Landi of New York arrived in Rome to begin what was to become the largest food program in CRS history. As the Allied troops moved up the Italian peninsula, the agency followed right behind, setting up centers for distribution of clothing, food and medicines. Fr., later Msgr., Landi received numerous decorations from the Italian government and other governments for his work on behalf of the poor. He served as assistant executive director for fifteen years after returning from Italy in 1967.

In other countries of Europe, War Relief Services bent its efforts to the monumental task of rehabilitating and resettling Iron Curtain refugees. Germany especially was in shambles. It was impossible for the country to take care of its own population, let alone care for the millions of DPs in the UNRRA and, later IRO, refugee camps. The inspiring work of WRS in the camps is memorialized in the writings of Eileen Egan and Alfred A. Schneider, both of whom long served the mission of the agency, in Germany and elsewhere. James Norris joined WRS in 1946 and lent his prodigious intellect to organizing and supervising the agency's rehabilitation efforts in Europe and, later, to running the International Catholic Migration Commission. It was because of the scope and size of the refugee program, which War Relief Services was still addressing far into the 1950s throughout Europe and Asia, that the "War" agency, set up for the duration, was converted to a permanent relief and development agency under the present title Catholic Relief Services.

U.S. Catholic Support

During these postwar years and since, American Catholics have regularly "plugged in" to the work of CRS through the annual Thanksgiving Clothing Collection and the Laetare Sunday, or ABOA [American Bishops Overseas Appeal] collection. The National Council of Catholic Women and other religious groups have taken on special projects in collaboration with CRS, so that the effort has been truly representative of the entire U.S. Catholic community.

Korea, 1952. CRS staff, working with Maryknoll missioners and others, provided emergency relief for the refugees streaming over the border from North Korea, and collaborated in several development projects that steadily improved the lot of the uprooted Koreans. In Hong Kong and Macao, CRS cared for thousands of refugees from mainland China. From 1953 to the end of the war, literally hundreds of CRS staff went to Vietnam to deliver basic relief services and establish longer-term development projects among the displaced thousands of North Vietnamese who were trying to find a peaceful existence in the south. Many readers will recall the heroic work of Patricia Smith, a medical doctor and member of the Grail, who labored among the Montagnards in the central highlands of Vietnam from 1959 to 1975. Beginning with community health care, Dr. Smith soon took on surgery and hospital administration. She built a hospital in Kontum and provided basic health and surgical services for a people literally caught in the middle of the war.

Africa. Across the world, a new order was dawning in Africa. By 1960 independence was being secured by many of the former colonies but not without tremendous hardship and dislocation of peoples. CRS was sponsoring mother/child health and nutrition programs as well as distributing food in many parts of Africa as revolution was in the making. Agency folklore describes Monsignor Wilson Kaiser, the founder of CRS's Africa mission, traversing the continent in a jeep, setting up centers for food and medicine distribution and making friends with the villagers.

One of the most dramatic stories in CRS history describes the hair-raising night flights of planes bringing needed supplies to the starving Biafran people who were at war with the federal government of Nigeria during the period 1968–70. Edward Kinney, assistant to the executive director of CRS, arranged for the purchase of four cargo planes from the U.S. government, adding them to a small fleet already chartered by CRS and its partners in Joint Church Aid. Through this humanitarian effort, over one hundred tons of relief goods were daily flown in and distributed to the needy. A classic illustration of CRS's traditional stance of nonpartisanship was the fact that CRS continued its programs in Federal Nigeria while running this ad hoc airline with its partners in Joint Church Aid to bring emergency humanitarian supplies to the rebelling province of Biafra.

1970–present. In 1976 Catholic Relief Services had in-country resident staff and programs in forty-one countries in all parts of the world. During that year alone, it shipped 705,312,960 gross pounds (3,205,968 MT) of food that fed more than 8,000,000 people. Later in the decade, CRS mounted a gigantic medical relief effort in the refugee camps set up along the Thai border with Cambodia. This program involved the services of hundreds of medical interns from Fordham, Georgetown, and Tufts Universities. Heroic service was offered in the mercy convoys that traversed the border areas of that region.

The 1980s witnessed unprecedented famine in Ethiopia, where CRS joined with other Church groups to form the Joint Relief Partnership, which operated the largest food distribution network in the country. In the Middle East, the situation was volatile. On January 8, 1985, in Lebanon, CRS's program director, Fr. L. Martin Jenco, was kidnapped and held captive for nineteen months. His harrowing story is well known. In Central America, CRS worked with the nearly 2,000,000 refugees displaced by the war in El Salvador, providing them with basic necessities for survival. But more than that, the CRS staff fostered creative, self-determined community activities that offered training for the people to produce their own food and other material needs. Through the years, hundreds of U.S. staff, many of whom grew up in the Peace Corps, and thousands of national staff, have lived the gospel message of love, expressing that love in solidarity with their brothers and sisters in 131 different countries throughout the world.

In the 1990s the agency is, ironically, reliving some of its earliest relief efforts as CRS staff in Bosnia-Herzegovina, Croatia and Macedonia, work with CARITAS and other counterpart organizations to provide relief supplies to that tragic, war-torn area. In Somalia, Catholic Relief Services personnel brought their humanitarian service of food, medical, and agricultural assistance. Across the globe, Cambodia and Vietnam once again engage the energy and resources of CRS staff, who are there to help the people in rebuilding their lives.

Epilogue

This, then, is the history of CRS in review. CRS has been called "the best-kept secret" of the U.S. Catholic Church. The secret of its success, in a nutshell, is the effective leadership of CRS and the staff's fidelity to the social teaching of the Church. In its fifty years, Catholic Relief Services has drawn on the talents and faith commitments of exceptional clerical, religious, and laypersons. The first four executive directors, Bryan J. McEntegart, Patrick A. O'Boyle, Edward E. Swanstrom, and Edwin B. Broderick, became bishops. O'Boyle was named a cardinal.

Lawrence A. Pezzullo, who succeeded Bishop Broderick as executive director, came to the agency from the U.S. diplomatic corps, and the current executive director, Kenneth F. Hackett, continues his long, distinguished career with CRS. James Norris, assistant director of CRS, addressed Vatican Council II in flawless Latin. "There will be no meaning to [Western nations'] Christian profession or humane traditions" he said, "if they forget that wealth is a trust and that property carries social obligations and that riches on the scale of the West's modern riches must be redeemed by generosity."

CRS has, in effect, actualized the social teaching of the Church. It has put theory into action with its counterparts all across the world. In a draft document prepared for CRS in 1986, Rev. Philip Land, S.J., described this wonderfully productive combination of action based on theological reflection in these words: "Christian [or as Paul VI would say, 'forward-looking'] imagination working on already gained experience" to formulate guiding principles. CRS's mission statement begins: "The fundamental motivating force in all activities of CRS is the Gospel of Jesus Christ as it pertains to the alleviation of human suffering, the development of people and the fostering of charity and justice in the world." This is the work of CRS, the work of the U.S. Catholic community.

Egan, Eileen. *Catholic Relief Services: The Beginning Years.* New York, 1988.
____. *The Works of Peace.* New York, 1965.
Kupke, Raymond J. "James J. Norris: An American Catholic Life." Ph.D. dissertation, The Catholic University of America, 1995.
McCloskey, Robert J. *A CRS Chronicle.* Baltimore, 1993.
Schneider, Alfred. *My Brother's Keeper.* Green Bay, 1981.
Solberg, Richard. *Miracle in Ethiopia.* New York, 1991.
Swanstrom, Edward. *Pilgrims in the Night.* New York, 1950.

ROSALIE McQUAIDE, C.S.J.P.

CATHOLIC RURAL LIFE MOVEMENT

The Catholic rural life movement in the United States took its origins from the weakness of the Church in rural areas. During the great migrations of the nineteenth century, Catholic immigrants crowded into the large cities of the East and Midwest where they could be most easily cared for by clergy and Church facilities. By 1900 over four-fifths of American Catholics lived in urban areas. The first phase of the Catholic rural movement consisted of efforts in the late nineteenth and early twentieth centuries by Church leaders to colonize Catholics on the land in order to strengthen the rural Church and prevent "leakage" of underserved rural Catholics to Protestantism.

The National Catholic Rural Life Conference

Around 1920 Fr. Edwin V. O'Hara of Eugene, Oregon, popularized the idea that because birthrates were much higher in rural areas than in urban districts, the Catholic Church was in danger of dying out if it continued to be centered in the unproductive cities. In November 1923 O'Hara's agitation resulted in the founding of the National Catholic Rural Life Conference, consisting of rural pastors and others interested in the well-being of the rural Church. During the 1920s, O'Hara and the NCRLC concentrated on strengthening the rural Church by such means as religious vacation schools and correspondence courses.

In the 1930s the focus of the Catholic rural life movement changed to economics in response to the nationwide depression. NCRLC leaders, blaming the depression on urbanism and industrialism, joined in the call for a back-to-the-land movement, and helped organize a number of subsistence farming communities. Catholic ruralists also supported the formation of cooperatives and government aid for poor farmers. Membership in the NCRLC boomed as the annual conventions began to attract thousands of dirt farmers as well as clerical leaders.

Monsignor Ligutti and International Affairs

In 1940 the charismatic Msgr. Luigi G. Ligutti became executive secretary of the NCRLC and redirected the Catholic rural life movement again, this time toward international affairs. As the United States became a world power during World War II and after, Ligutti expanded the role of the NCRLC to include food shipments to war-torn nations, resettlement of war refugees, representation in the United Nations' Food and Agriculture Organization, lobbying in Washington for foreign aid to developing countries, and sponsorship of seven international Catholic rural life congresses in Rome and Latin America.

From the 1960s to the 1990s, the Catholic rural life movement carried on an increasingly desperate fight to save the family farm in an age of ever-expanding agribusiness. Attempts to form a coalition of the major farm organizations, lobby for government measures to inhibit the growth of corporate farms, and support family farmers—especially during the indebtedness crisis of the 1980s—were largely unavailing, as family farmers shrank to a minuscule percentage of the population.

Finally, starting in the 1970s, the Catholic rural life movement underwent yet another metamorphosis, as it turned its attention to environmental issues. Based on the Catholic principle of stewardship, the still-active NCRLC supported soil conservation, opposed strip-mining and heavy use of insecticides, favored use of nonpolluting energy sources such as solar and wind, and even spoke out against the nuclear arms race. The Catholic rural life movement had broadened its concern for the land and its dwellers to embrace the survival of the entire planet.

See also LIGUTTI, LUIGI G.; O'HARA, EDWIN.

Dolan, Timothy M. *"Some Seed Fell on Good Ground": The Life of Edwin V. O'Hara.* Washington, D.C.: The Catholic University of America Press, 1992.

Witte, Raymond P. *Twenty-Five Years of Crusading: A History of the National Catholic Rural Life Conference.* Des Moines, Iowa: National Catholic Rural Life Conference, 1948.

Yzermans, Vincent A. *The People I Love: A Biography of Luigi G. Ligutti.* Collegeville, Minn.: The Liturgical Press, 1976.

DAVID BOVEE

CATHOLIC SOCIAL TEACHING IN AMERICA

Introduction

The social teaching of the American Catholic Church is an interesting and varied mixture, reflective of who we are as Americans and as Church and how we got that way. This teaching can be approached from several perspectives: various Church and lay organizations which engaged in social activity; the ministry of various religious orders and congregations and their many works of the apostolate; key figures in American Catholic history. Or, as in this presentation, the subject may be approached through a consideration of the documents of the American bishops either in provincial council or through the National Catholic Welfare Conference or its successor, the United States Catholic Conference.

Part of the documentary history of the social teaching of American Catholicism reflects the missionary and immigrant dimension of our history. Another part responds to specific problems the Church encountered: labor issues, racism, war, etc. And another part seeks to set an agenda for social action. Focusing on the documentary dimension provides a rich and interesting source of the history of Catholic social teaching, for a recent collection of these letters issued by the USCC contains over two hundred entries. Rather than try to categorize all of the topics presented in this collection, this article will highlight

different teachings from three major periods: first an overview of the teaching until 1919 (the year of the bishops' critical statement on social reconstruction) then material from 1919 to 1962 (the date of Vatican Council II); and finally material from 1962 to the present. All references, except those to *Economic Justice for All,* are from this collection.

Early Social Teaching: 1792–1919

Many of the early letters from the bishops or the Councils of Baltimore focused on the internal problems of a minority Church within an emerging and expanding nation. The critical issues were organizational, catechetical, and disciplinary. The key issue was establishing and building up the structure of the Church, not only in terms of hierarchy and clergy, but also of buildings.

Yet, early on the thematic problem of Church and state raised its head. In 1837 the Third Provincial Council of Baltimore, addressed this issue together with the other thematic issue of patriotism and allegiance to the state. The context was a sharp rise in anti-Catholicism and the bishops affirmed strongly Catholics' citizenship and fidelity to the Church. "When, therefore, using our undoubted right, we acknowledge the spiritual and ecclesiastical supremacy of the chief bishop of our universal church, the pope or bishop of Rome, we do not thereby forfeit our claim to the civil and political protection of the commonwealth; for, we do not detract from the allegiance to which the temporal governments are plainly entitled and which we cheerfully give" (I, 91).

An issue not addressed during these times is that of slavery. Nothing was mentioned about this in the 1852 letter and no pastoral letters were issued until 1866, a year after the end of the Civil War. While individual bishops spoke out—on both sides—on the issue of slavery, no official position was taken. Even in the pastoral letter of 1866, the topic of emancipated slaves occupies only one small paragraph which regrets that the emancipation was not accomplished more gradually, as was done with serfs after the decline of feudalism. The bishops appeal to Christian charity and zeal to respond to "the evils which must necessarily attend the sudden liberation of so large a multitude, with their peculiar dispositions and habits" (I, 204). Not until 1958 was there official recognition that racism was a moral issue.

Two of the most critical documents of this first period were the 1919 *Program of Social Reconstruction* (written by John A. Ryan of The Catholic University of America) and the 1933 letter *Present Crisis. The Program of Social Reconstruction* was written in the aftermath of World War I and spoke to the many different social and political dislocations that followed it. Part of what is interesting in this letter is its review of British political, social, and religious proposals for social renewal. While recognizing that the

American and British situations were not comparable, nonetheless the bishops found the proposals instructive.

Employment was a critical issue, particularly the reintegration of members of the armed services into the work force and resolving the role of women in the workplace. While arguing that women should not suffer any greater loss or inconvenience than necessary, the bishops noted two controlling principles: "No female worker should remain in any occupation that is harmful to health or morals"; second, "the proportion of women in industry ought to be kept within the smallest practical limits" (I, 261). Yet, even though the bishops argued that women should be returned to more domestic positions, they also argued that "those women who are engaged at the same tasks as men should receive equal pay for equal amounts and qualities of work" (I, 262).

This orientation to wage justice continued in the argument that wages not be reduced because "the average rate of pay has not increased faster than the cost of living" and because most wage earners "were not receiving living wages when prices began to rise in 1915" (I, 262). Additionally the bishops argued that the legal minimum wage should be "ultimately high enough to make possible that amount of saving which is necessary to protect the worker and his family against sickness, accidents, invalidity, and old age" (I, 262). Interesting here, the bishops argue that since the worker is in need of insurance, until the minimum wage reaches this level, the state is obligated to provide insurance to cover these contingencies. The bishops argue that the ideal is a situation in which "workers would themselves have the income and the responsibility of providing for all the needs and contingencies of life, both present and future" (I, 266).

The Middle Years: 1920–62

Several critical events occurred during these middle years of the Church's life in America. Religiously the National Catholic Welfare Conference was organized in 1919; the number of Catholic institutions such as churches, schools, and hospitals swelled enormously to respond to the growing needs of the Church; and the hierarchy, meeting annually now, continued to speak to a number of both ecclesial and national situations. Socially these were the years of the Great Depression, World War II, and the Korean War, the first efforts at integration, and the shift of the population from the farm to the city and then to the suburbs.

Generally speaking, the pastoral letters of this period become more focused and specific in their content. There were two thematic directions in these teachings. The first can be characterized as speaking to the broader social issues of the day and the second as speaking to the inner life of the Church. Frequently these two issues are joined as in frequent appeals for personal transformation as the basis for social reform. But, generally speaking, the pastorals tend to focus on one theme or the other.

Thus the program of social reconstruction begun in 1919 opened the door to a rich development of social teaching in response to some of the major issues of the day and set a general tone for this period as is evident, for example, in the letter "Present Crisis," written in 1933 during the depression. What is important to note in this letter is that, while there is still mention of individual vices such as greed and selfishness as being major factors in the depression, there is also reference to structural dimensions of the economy that needed reform. This analysis parallels the discussion by Pius XI in *Quadragesimo Anno* and applies many of his insights to the American situation.

The bishops acknowledge that the concentration of economic power in the hands of a few is in no small part a cause of the depression. This concentration leads to a threefold struggle: dictatorship in the economic sphere, the battle to acquire control of the state, and clashes between states themselves. But the bishops also make the strong and continual case that we brought such a situation on by ourselves by "divorcing education, industry, politics, business, and economics from morality and religion, and by ignoring for long decades the innate dignity of man and trampling on his human rights" (I, 378). The bishops also condemn two dominant philosophies of the day. First is "unrestrained individual economic freedom and the economic dictatorship that has succeeded it" (I, 279). This philosophy denies the solidarity of humanity and makes wealth and power ends in themselves. Second, the bishops condemn Communism because of its atheistic vision and encouragement of class warfare.

Part of the resolution of the problems of the depression, of industrialization, and urbanization is an emphasis on home ownership in rural communities. This is because cities cannot support their populations; cities crushed people's spirits, made them a ripe prey for the radicals of the day, and because the new order espoused by radicals "could be attained only through the adoption of a materialistic philosophy in which there was no place for God or religion" (I, 400). In rural communities the Church can become the center of life, the pastor can guide the people, and people will be immune from harmful teachings. But such a "reconstruction of rural civilization" (400) is not simply an escape from the evils of the city, it is an "imperative duty to see that our people shall have homes if the moral and spiritual values of life are to be conserved and if the race is to be saved from extinction" (I, 400).

From this basis, the bishops continued to speak to the critical issues of the day. Four particular social problems that they highlighted during this period were: the war, peace and its aftermath; Communism; secularism; and discrimination.

World War II was recognized by the bishops as a justifiable war, and they gave their full support to the country. However, they continued to note that such support did not mean a relaxation of moral standards, neither for those in the military nor for women now entering the work force in large numbers.

At the war's end, the bishops note in their 1945 statement *Between War and Peace:* "The war is over but there is no peace" (II, 62). The bishops took note of the clash of ideologies involved in negotiating the ending of the war. They made clear their understanding for the need to establish a social order which would produce a just and lasting peace. "A first principle for a sane reconstruction of society," the bishops said in the 1943 letter *The Essentials of a Good Peace* is "the social recognition of God's sovereignty and of the moral law" (II, 45). Additionally there is need for the establishment of international institutions to preserve peace. These too need to be grounded on this moral order. Also the bishops continued to express concern for the just treatment of victims of war, displaced persons, and prisoners of war.

The persecution of Catholics and others by Communist nations was singled out for condemnation in several letters. The issues were both attempts to destroy the Church as an institution and also the active persecution and imprisonment of Catholics. Given the 1959 judgment of the bishops in *A Statement of Freedom and Peace* that "Communism is godless, it is aggressive and belligerent, it is unbelievably cruel" (II, 217), it is no wonder that the bishops thought it to be the "overriding danger to peace and freedom" (II, 217). While negotiations must occur with the Communists, the bishops urge that the basic and irreconcilable differences between Christianity and Communism must not be forgotten. The solution to Communism that the bishops purpose is Christians exemplifying "the principles that we proclaim as Christian members of a nation dedicated to God's law" (II, 218).

The Church also looked to the inner lives of its members. One major threat to the development of a full religious life was secularism. This topic shows up as the major topic or continually recurring theme in several of the pastoral letters of this period. Secularism was defined as the "practical exclusion of God from human thinking and living" (II, 74). Secularism takes into account only human law, making its code "[e]x-pediency, decency, propriety . . ." (II, 75). This philosophy also "takes God out of economic thinking and thereby minimizes the dignity of the human person . . ." (II, 78). Secularism is also related to atheistic materialism which fosters an "excessive preoccupation with creatures. This form of materialism reveals itself as secularism in politics and government, as avarice in business and in the professions, and as paganism in the personal lives of all too many men and women" (II, 173).

A response to this is a call to personal responsibility in the world. This presupposes an acknowledgment of one's dignity as a child of God, "the free and deliberate acceptance of one's obligations in the position he occupies"; "it demands the rule of conscience"; it "recognizes that every deliberate action of the human person has a relationship with his Creator and makes him a cooperator with his Creator in forwarding the Kingdom of God" (II, 236).

This era ends with a call to personal conversion and a turning from the many temptations, social and personal, that threaten the life of the Church, the country, and the individual.

The Modern Period: 1963 to the Present

Three major issues were the focus of attention during this modern period: racism, war and peace in a nuclear age, and economic justice.

The bishops had referred to the evils of racism in many previous statements. In 1958 they explicitly spoke to this issue and strongly condemned segregation for two reasons: it imposes a stigma of inferiority and leads to "oppressive conditions and the denial of basic human rights" (II, 204). This teaching was expanded in 1963 by reiterating their teaching that the race question is "moral and religious" (III, 17). Also respect for persons and their rights is both an individual moral duty but also "a matter of civic action" (III, 17). Again in 1963 the bishops spoke of the harm to individuals and to the common good done by assigning some to second-class citizenship whether on the basis of religion or race. And in 1968 the bishops returned to the continuing problems caused by racism and argued for both the eradication of discrimination and the duty to help the poor and oppressed. Also identified in this letter are continued efforts to be made in the areas of education, job opportunities, housing, and welfare (III, 159–60). In 1979 the bishops noted that, while some changes had been made, in large part "only the external appearances have changed" (IV, 324). In this letter, the bishops call attention to the "unresolved racism that permeates our society's structures" (IV, 343) and note that, while this form of racism is less blatant, it is more subtle and more dangerous. In this letter, too, the bishops explicitly say: "Racism is a sin" (IV, 344), acknowledge that Catholics have been involved "in the mistakes and sins of the past" (IV, 348), say that Catholics have "allowed conformity to social pressures to replace compliance with social justice" (IV, 349), and regret that the Church has been for many a "racist institution" (IV, 349). This confession formed the basis for a call to repentance and for greater action to remedy these serious evils.

As the Church was addressing the issues of civil rights during this turbulent time in America, it also needed to respond to the challenges of the morality of modern warfare. This issue was first brought into focus by the Vietnam War. While acknowledging the morality of some wars and the obligation of Christians to serve in such just wars, the bishops nevertheless affirm clearly that "a Catholic can be a conscientious objector to war in general or to a particular war 'because of religious training and belief'" (III, 285). While recognizing the difficulties of the selective conscientious position, the bishops nonetheless support a modification of the law to allow for this position. Also after a period of evaluation in which the bishops were either supportive or neutral on the Vietnam War, they finally came to the conclusion in 1971 that "whatever good we hope to achieve through continued involvement in this war is now outweighed by the destruction of human life and of moral values" (III, 289). Therefore the "speedy ending of this war is a moral imperative of the highest priority" (III, 289).

In 1983 the bishops issued their most thorough statement on the morality of modern war, *The Challenge of Peace*. Drafted by a subcommittee and reviewed by experts from various fields, and refined through three drafts over several years, the letter makes three critical teachings. First, "Under no circumstances may nuclear weapons or other instruments of mass slaughter be used for the purpose of destroying population centers or other predominantly civilian targets" (IV, 532). Second, "We do not perceive any situation in which the deliberate initiation of nuclear warfare, on however restricted a scale, can be morally justified" (IV, 533). Third, in light of all the difficulties—policy, strategic, and moral—surrounding deterrence theory, the bishops propose a "strictly conditioned moral acceptance of deterrence" (IV, 543). The method of his letter has given contemporary Catholics an appropriate framework with which to evaluate the moral problems of modern warfare.

The third major theme is that of economic justice addressed in 1986 in *Economic Justice for All*. Like the peace pastoral, this letter was drafted by a subcommittee, was reviewed by a variety of experts, and went through three major drafting periods. Of critical importance is the requirement of justice. *"Basic justice demands the establishment of minimum levels of participation in the life of the human community for all persons"* (O'Brien and Shannon, 596; italics in original). From this flows a recognition that everyone has an obligation to participate in society and that society has the obligation to enable this to happen. Additionally the bishops argue that *"the obligation to provide justice for all means that the poor have the single most urgent economic claim on the conscience of the nation"* (O'Brien and Shannon, 599; italics in original). Finally, the bishops propose a simple, yet elegant, test for economic justice: *"The dignity of the human person, realized in community with others, is the criterion against which all aspects of economic life must be measured"* (O'Brien and Shannon, 584; italics in original). The full argument of the letter also spells out several practical applications of these three core moral principles.

This article highlights several key themes of the social teaching of the bishops over a more than two-hundred-

year history. The riches of these resources on social justice within the Catholic Church are the basis for both the analysis of current problems and future developments of an already rich heritage of social teachings.

See also ANTI-COMMUNISM AND AMERICAN CATHOLICS; CIVIL RIGHTS MOVEMENT AND CATHOLICS, THE; RYAN, JOHN AUGUSTINE.

Himes, Michael J., and Kenneth R. Himes, O.F.M. *Fullness of Faith: The Public Significance of Theology*. New York: Paulist Press, 1993.

Hollenbach, David, S.J. *Claims in Conflict: Retrieving and Renewing the Catholic Human Rights Tradition*. New York: Paulist Press, 1979.

____. *Justice, Peace, and Human Rights*. New York: Crossroad, 1988.

O'Brien, David J., and Thomas A. Shannon. *Catholic Social Thought: The Documentary Heritage*. Maryknoll, N.Y.: Orbis Books, 1992.

Pastoral Letters of the United States Catholic Bishops. Vols. I–IV. Washington, D.C.: National Conference of Catholic Bishops/United States Catholic Conference, 1983.

THOMAS A. SHANNON

CATHOLIC SUMMER SCHOOL OF AMERICA (CLIFF HAVEN)

The Catholic Summer School of America originated in 1892 as the Catholic equivalent of the highly successful Chautauqua Summer School established by the Methodists in the 1870s at Lake Chautauqua in upstate New York. Like the Chautauqua movement among the Methodists, the Catholic Summer School was designed to meet a growing interest in popular education among Catholics, an interest that was already evident in the popularity of Catholic Reading Circles and the lectures sponsored by various Catholic societies or "unions" in some of the larger cities of the East and Midwest.

The Catholic Summer School of America was founded by some two dozen priests and laymen at a meeting at the Catholic Club of New York City in May 1892. Many of the participants were already active in promoting Catholic popular education. Warren E. Mosher, of Youngstown, Ohio, was editor of *The Catholic Reading Circle Review;* Fr. James F. Loughlin of Philadelphia was president of the Catholic Young Men's National Union and Fr. Joseph H. McMahon had founded the Cathedral Library Reading Circle of New York. The organizers enjoyed support from the conservative and liberal wings of the hierarchy, winning the endorsement of both Archbishop Michael Corrigan of New York and Bishop John J. Keane, the rector of The Catholic University of America. The first session of the summer school took place in August of 1892 at a hotel in New London, Connecticut. It was a three-week affair during which ten priests, Br. Azarias, F.S.C., and fifteen laypeople (including three women) delivered fifty-one lectures. Estimates of the attendance varied widely from 300 to 1,000.

Cliff Haven

The following year—thanks to the largesse of a wealthy benefactor and the self-interest of the Delaware and Hudson Railroad—the school moved to a permanent site, Cliff Haven, a 450-acre farm near Plattsburg, New York, on the shores of Lake Champlain. On February 9, 1893, the state of New York granted the school a charter to conduct extension courses and to confer degrees ("pedagogical certificates"). In 1894, despite the worst economic depression of the century, the summer school attracted 1,500 students from twenty-four states for the four-week session. Over the next few years the site was transformed with the erection of an administration building, chapel, auditorium, dining hall and some thirty "cottages," which were really three-story residence halls. Before long, Cliff Haven had its own post office, laundry, barber shop, tennis courts, golf course, a steamboat pier on Lake Champlain and a trolley line to Plattsburg. From 1903 onward more than 5,000 people attended the summer school each year.

The lectures were devoted principally to philosophy, history, literature, and the humanities. Many of the speakers were nonacademics such as Fr. John Talbot Smith, Maurice Francis Egan, and Condé Pallen, but they also included Fr. William J. Kerby of The Catholic University of America, who introduced his listeners to the new science of sociology, and Fr. John A. Zahm, C.S.C., of the University of Notre Dame, who lectured on the relationship between religion and science.

Cliff Haven reached the peak of its popularity in the decade before the First World War. By that time, in addition to the Teachers' Institute, it included a full recreation program, a college camp, and the toney Champlain Club whose membership was limited to two hundred "Catholic gentlemen." Cardinal Gibbons and several of the apostolic delegates to the United States visited Cliff Haven as did three presidents of the United States, William McKinley, Theodore Roosevelt (while governor of New York), and William Howard Taft. Cliff Haven also gave rise to several similar ventures: the Western Catholic Summer School, founded in 1895; the Catholic Winter School in New Orleans, founded in 1896; and the Maryland Catholic Summer School, founded in 1900.

Inevitably, Cliff Haven also had its critics, like Arthur Preuss, the conservative editor of the St. Louis *Review,* who quoted the comment of a "learned priest" (probably Edward A. Pace) that "the only kind of lectures appropriate, timely and useful for a Catholic Summer School would be a course of plain, everyday, catechetical instruction." Other critics noted that women students out-numbered men and claimed that Cliff Haven was becoming "a marriage bureau" for single Catholics.

Enrollment seems to have declined after World War I, but in the 1930s Fordham University used Cliff Haven for summer extension courses. In the summer of 1941, it celebrated its fiftieth anniversary (one of the lecturers that year was John Courtney Murray, S.J.), but it never recovered from World War II and competition from the vast new opportunities for higher education that were available to Catholics after the war. By 1948 the Catholic Summer School of America had quietly faded from the scene.

DeLuca, Lorraine Susanna. "Adult Education and the Ambivalence of the Catholic Church towards Modern American Society in the Archdiocese of New York." Ed.D. dissertation, Teachers College of Columbia University, 1994, 143–56.

McMillan, Thomas, C.S.P. "The Catholic Summer School, Silver Jubilee, 1892–1916." *Catholic World* 102 (1916) 597–607.

Mooney, John A. "The Catholic Summer School." *Catholic World* 55 (1892) 532–38.

O'Neil, Alfred J. *Catholic Action* 23 (July 1941) 9–10.

Shuster, George N. "Beside Lake Champlain." *Commonweal* 14 (June 24, 1931) 211–12.

White, James Addison. *The Founding of Cliff Haven: Early Years of the Catholic Summer School of America.* New York, 1950.

THOMAS J. SHELLEY

CATHOLIC THEOLOGICAL UNION

Catholic Theological Union at Chicago was founded in 1967 as a creative response to the call for seminary *aggiornamento* issued by Vatican Council II. American Catholic seminaries, by and large, were too many and too small, were isolated from the mainstream of American education, were academic rather than professional (praxis-based) in focus, and had few, if any, ecumenical contacts. Very few were accredited.

Three religious orders in Chicago, the Franciscans, the Passionists, and the Servites, decided that a collaborative school would best serve the needs of the future. This would provide a larger faculty, library, and student body. C.T.U. was not a coalition of independent seminaries, but an autonomous school of theology, with one administration and faculty, governed by a board of trustees. Preparation for ministry was the responsibility of the school; spiritual formation of the students was remanded to the participating communities. Membership in C.T.U. was open to all religious orders of men.

Located in the Hyde Park area of Chicago, C.T.U. was adjacent to several Protestant seminaries and the University of Chicago, with its prestigious divinity school. The city and church of Chicago afforded exceptional opportunities for ministerial placements to undergird the professional program. A two-hundred-room hotel building was remodeled to serve as headquarters for C.T.U. Classes began in 1968 with a faculty of twenty-three and a student body of one hundred twenty.

Other religious orders quickly joined the new venture, closing their small seminaries. In its first year C.T.U. began educational and ecumenical collaboration with the neighboring Protestant seminaries. The University of Chicago gave special registration privileges to C.T.U. and to other Hyde Park schools of theology.

C.T.U. was fully accredited in 1972. In 1972 the Divine Word Missionaries established the Mission Program which quickly attracted a number of mission-sending societies. Eventually the program became the largest among American Catholic schools of theology. C.T.U. was opened to women in 1974, resulting in a significant presence of women at the school as students and faculty. Special programs for Hispanics and African Americans were to come a decade later.

In 1992, at the end of its first twenty-five years, C.T.U. was the official theologate for twenty-five religious communities of men. The faculty consisted of twenty-eight full-time and twelve part-time teachers. Many professors were nationally recognized in their fields of study and had published over two hundred books. The 112,000 volume library specialized in the sacred sciences, especially Catholic materials. Student enrollment was 320. Of these, 11 percent were women religious, and 38 percent were laypersons. Twenty percent of the student body was from outside the United States, including Latin America, Africa, and Asia.

Degrees offered were the Master of Arts in Pastoral Studies, the Master of Arts in Theology, the Master of Divinity, and the Doctor of Ministry. There were also certificate programs in Liturgical Studies, Biblical Spirituality, and Pastoral Studies. C.T.U.'s more than one thousand graduates were at work throughout the United States and in fifty countries worldwide.

C.T.U. serves the following communities of men (1996): Franciscans, Servites, Passionists, Augustinians, Norbertines, Society of the Divine Word, Missionaries of the Precious Blood, Claretians, Crosier Fathers, Holy Ghost Fathers, Sacred Heart Missionaries, Viatorians, Comboni Missionaries, Franciscan Capuchins, Sacred Heart Fathers and Brothers, Ukrainian Catholic Diocese, Congregation of the Blessed Sacrament, Columban Missionaries, Redemptorist Fathers, Oblates of Mary Immaculate, Xaverian Missionaries, Maryknoll Missionaries, Conventual Franciscans, Oratorians, Scalabrinians, Discalced Carmelites, Vincentians.

See also STUHLMUELLER, CARROLL.

Bechtold, Paul, C.P. *Catholic Theological Union at Chicago, the Founding Years.* Chicago: Catholic Theological Union, 1993.

PAUL BECHTOLD, C.P.

CATHOLIC TRADE UNIONISTS, ASSOCIATION OF

Any American born in the second half of the twentieth century must find it difficult to imagine what life in the United States was like in 1937, the year the Association of Catholic Trade Unionists (ACTU) was founded at Catholic Worker headquarters in New York City. This was the middle of the Great Depression. Unemployment had risen to 25 percent and in 1938 it still stood at 19 percent. Poverty, hunger, homelessness were everywhere.

However, for the first time labor had won the right to organize, thanks to President Franklin D. Roosevelt and the New Deal. From a mere 6 percent of the work force union membership was to rise to 25 percent over the next few years, on its way to 35 percent in 1955. All the passion and excitement that was later to characterize the civil rights movement or the anti-Vietnam War movement in the 1960s, then centered around the labor movement, on strike picket lines, in union halls, across bargaining tables. In 1935 the American Federation of Labor, dominated by craft unionists, had split wide open, with the more militant leaders, behind the beetle-browed, Shakespeare-quoting John L. Lewis, breaking away to form the Congress of Industrial Organizations.

The Founding of ACTU

The eleven men who gathered around the kitchen table at the Catholic Worker on February 27, 1937, were not prominent labor leaders. They were mostly obscure rank-and-file members who wanted to express their Catholic faith and to involve the Church in support of this new drive to organize the unorganized and to do something practical about poverty and social injustice. They were members of both AFL and CIO unions. They welcomed the Lewis initiative to organize the major industries into industry-wide unions. Some of them were members of corrupt old AFL unions, dominated by gunmen and racketeers. They came looking for help to free their unions from that domination. Those who were members of CIO unions were also concerned about the foothold that Communist elements had gained in some of these unions, a foothold that they were sometimes able to expand into full control.

Stalinist sympathizers in the academic community have published a number of books that maintain that this anti-communist activity was the primary, if not the sole, activity of the ACTU. This is a total fabrication. Much more typical of the ACTU's concerns was its involvement in two strikes in the late 1930s: the strike of Woolworth store clerks in New York and the strike of Chrysler auto workers in Detroit.

ACTU Activities

The saleswomen at Woolworth's had gone on strike shortly after that founding meeting of ACTU in 1937. Heywood

Broun, later a Catholic convert and then president of a new CIO union, the Newspaper Guild, had written a column for the *New York World* highlighting the miserable wages at Woolworth's—for many less than ten dollars a week for six days—and, in contrast, the great riches of Barbara ("Babs") Hutton, the much-photographed and much-married Woolworth heiress.

A society columnist defended Hutton on the ground that she had given eleven million dollars to charity. An ACTU membership meeting voted to support the strike and join the CIO picket line on 14th Street in Manhattan. One crudely lettered picket sign carried by an ACTU member read: BABS GAVE $11 MILLION TO CHARITY, *BUT* 'THE WORKERS ARE NOT TO RECEIVE AS ALMS WHAT IS THEIR DUE IN JUSTICE'—POPE PIUS XI.

Earlier, to develop its program, the ACTU had used the encyclicals of Pius XI and Leo XIII, as well as the teachings of Msgr. John A. Ryan, *The Rights and Duties of the Worker.* Among the more controversial duties that this included was the duty to join a bona fide, independent trade union—that is, independent of the employer, as contrasted with the company unions that were then being outlawed by the Democratic Congress.

In Detroit, in November 1939, Fr. Charles Coughlin, the famous radio priest, devoted his Sunday talk to an attack on the strike of Chrysler auto workers, claiming that the CIO union there was Communist-led. The ACTU already had an active chapter in Detroit, one of the fourteen chapters it was eventually to organize. It also had the support of Archbishop Edward Mooney and a network of forty labor schools that were turning out trained Catholic and non-Catholic unionists.

At a United Auto Workers (UAW) rally in Cadillac Square in downtown Detroit, attended by 40,000 auto workers, Msgr. John Mies, an ACTU chaplain, defended the UAW and the strike from the Coughlin attack and urged the crowd to stand by the strike and their union. That same night the Detroit ACTU sponsored a radio talk by another ACTU chaplain, Fr. Raymond Clancy, who refuted Fr. Coughlin point by point. Coughlin's back-to-work movement fell flat and the strike went on to a victorious conclusion.

It was this kind of pro-union, pro-CIO activity that made it possible for the ACTU to be effective in backing Walter Reuther in his fight to save the UAW from an attempted Communist takeover later in the 1940s.

By the early 1940s ACTU labor schools around the country numbered about 150, turning out about 5,000 graduates every year. Also in the field was another network, the Jesuit Labor Schools. Prominent among these was the Xavier Labor School in New York, run by Frs. Philip Carey and John Corridan. The latter, active in the fight to clean up the longshoremen's union, was the model for the priest in the popular movie, *On the Waterfront.*

ACTU members were also active in this fight, among them George Donahue, who at one point played a role similar to that of Marlon Brando in the movie.

ACTU campaigns were sometimes controversial, as against employers, racketeers, and Communists. Several chapters disaffiliated and did good work under other names, such as the Catholic Labor Alliance of Chicago led by Ed Marciniak and Bob Senser, and the Catholic Labor Guild of Boston, later simply the Labor Guild, under outstanding directors like Frs. Frank McDonnell, Mort Gavin, and Ed Boyle. A secular organization, the Association for Union Democracy, now continues the work of ACTU against corrupt and undemocratic elements in the labor movement. One of its attorneys, John Harold, along with John Sheehan and Edward Scully, provided free legal assistance through an ACTU subsidiary, the Catholic Labor Defense League.

ACTU Program

The ACTU program, somewhat unique among labor organizations in its emphasis on duties as well as rights, argued that the workers have the following rights: (1) job security; (2) income sufficient to support a family in reasonable comfort; (3) collective bargaining through union representatives freely chosen; (4) a share in the profits after a just wage and return to capital have been made; (5) the right to strike and picket peacefully for just cause; (6) a just price for the goods they buy; (7) decent working hours; (8) decent working conditions. And they had a duty to (1) perform an honest day's work for an honest day's pay; (2) join a bona fide union; (3) strike only for just cause; (4) refrain from violence; (5) respect property rights; (6) abide by just agreements freely made; (7) enforce strict honesty and democracy inside the union; and (8) cooperate with employers who respect their rights to bring about a peaceful solution to industrial warfare by establishing industry councils for the self-regulation of industry and producer cooperatives in which workers share as partners in the ownership, management, and profits of the business in which they work.

Although it gets more credit than it deserves for the elimination of significant Communist influence in the CIO in the late 1940s, several chapters of ACTU played active roles in this development. The Pittsburgh ACTU, behind the charismatic leadership of Fr. Charles Owen Rice, was important in the struggle within the United Electrical, Radio and Machine Workers Union (UE). The New York ACTU was a factor in this fight as well as in the Transport Workers Union and the Newspaper Guild. As noted, the Detroit ACTU was one of Walter Reuther's strongest supporters in the United Auto Workers.

The ACTU faded away about 1970. Changing times, postwar prosperity (of sorts), government action against labor racketeering, the disappearance of the Communist threat, the establishment of a significant labor movement, all these factors contributed to a lessening of Catholic interest. Boston's Labor Guild and its effective labor school remain almost alone in the field. From 35 percent of the labor force union membership has declined to about 16 percent, even though it is still a formidable movement of fifteen million men and women. Poverty, hunger, homelessness, and unemployment are again to be seen everywhere in the land. Perhaps it is time for a renewal of Catholic interest in the labor movement and social justice.

See also ANTI-COMMUNISM AND AMERICAN CATHOLICS; LABOR MOVEMENT AND AMERICAN CATHOLICS, THE; MONAGHAN, JOHN P.

The Labor Leader (National ACTU newspaper) and *The Wage Earner* (Detroit ACTU newspaper). Microfilm files available in New York and Boston (possibly Detroit) public libraries. So much false information has been published about ACTU that it is best to limit oneself to these reliable sources. Piehl's book is almost the only accurate commentary, especially on the subject of ACTU's relation to the Catholic Worker movement.

Piehl, Mel. *Breaking Bread: The Catholic Worker and the Origin of Catholic Radicalism in America.* Philadelphia: Temple University, 1982.

JOHN C. CORT

CATHOLIC UNIVERSITIES AND COLLEGES

(*Sources:* Catholic Almanac survey; *The Official Catholic Directory.*)

Listed below are institutions of higher learning established under Catholic auspices. Some of them are now independent.

Information includes: name of each institution; indication of male (m), female (w), coeducational (c) student body; name of founding group or group with which the institution is affiliated; year of foundation; total number of students, in parentheses.

Albertus Magnus College (c): 700 Prospect St., New Haven, CT 06511. Dominican Sisters; 1925; independent.

Allentown College of St. Francis de Sales (c): 2755 Station Ave., Center Valley, PA 18034. Oblates of St. Francis de Sales; 1965 (1,717).

Alvernia College (c): Reading, PA 19607. Bernardine Sisters; 1958 (1,292).

Alverno College (w): 3401 S. 39th St., Milwaukee, WI 53215. School Sisters of St. Francis; 1887; independent (2,450).

Anna Maria College (c): Sunset Lane, Paxton, MA 01612. Sisters of St. Anne; 1946; independent (1,797).

Aquinas College (c): 1607 Robinson Rd. S.E., Grand Rapids, MI 49506. Sisters of St. Dominic; 1922; independent (2,330).

Assumption College (c): 500 Salisbury St., Worcester, MA 01615. Assumptionist Fathers; 1904 (2,588).

Avila College (c): 11901 Wornall Rd., Kansas City, MO 64145. Sisters of St. Joseph of Carondelet; 1916 (1,413).

Barat College (c): 700 Westleigh Rd., Lake Forest, IL 60045. Society of the Sacred Heart; 1919; independent (710).

Barry University (c): 11300 N.E. 2nd Ave., Miami Shores, FL 33161. Dominican Sisters (Adrian, Mich.); 1940 (6,896).

Bellarmine College (c): 2001 Newburg Rd., Louisville, KY 40205; Louisville archdiocese; independent (2,326).

Belmont Abbey College (c): Belmont, NC 28012. Benedictine Fathers; 1876 (918).

Benedictine College (c): 1020 N. Second St., Atchison, KS 66002. Benedictines; 1859; independent (905).

Boston College (University Status) (c): Chestnut Hill, MA 02167. Jesuit Fathers; 1863 (14,455).

Brescia College (c): 717 Frederica St., Owensboro, KY 42301. Ursuline Sisters; 1950 (750).

Briar Cliff College (c): 3303 Rebecca St., P.O. Box 2100, Sioux City, IA 51104. Sisters of St. Francis of the Holy Family; 1930 (1,157).

Cabrini College (c): 610 King of Prussia Rd., Radnor, PA 19087. Missionary Srs. of Sacred Heart; 1957; private (1,473).

Caldwell College (c): 9 Ryerson Ave., Caldwell, NJ 07006. Dominican Sisters; 1939 (1,600).

Calumet College of St. Joseph (c): 2400 New York Ave., Whiting, IN 46394. Society of the Precious Blood; 1951 (1,200).

Canisius College (c): 2001 Main St., Buffalo, NY 14208. Jesuit Fathers; 1870; independent (4,789).

Cardinal Stritch College (c): 6801 N. Yates Rd., Milwaukee, WI 53217. Sisters of St. Francis of Assisi; 1937 (5,654).

Carlow College (w): 3333 5th Ave., Pittsburgh, PA 15213. Sisters of Mercy; 1929 (2,084).

Carroll College (c): Helena, MT 59625. Diocesan; 1909 (1,425).

Catholic University of America, The (c): 620 Michigan Ave. N.E., Washington, DC 20064. Hierarchy of the United States; 1887. Pontifical University (6,147).

Chaminade University of Honolulu (c): 3140 Waialae Ave., Honolulu, Hawaii 96816. Marianists; 1955 (2,300).

Chestnut Hill College (w): Philadelphia, PA 19118. Sisters of St. Joseph; 1924 (1,143).

Christendom College (c): 134 Christendom Dr., Front Royal, VA 22630. Founded 1977 (164).

Christian Brothers University (c): 650 E. Parkway S., Memphis, TN 38104. Brothers of the Christian Schools; 1871 (1,609).

Clarke College (c): 1550 Clarke Dr., Dubuque, Iowa 52001. Sisters of Charity, BVM; 1843 (1,002).

Creighton University (c): 2500 California Plazaha, NE 68178. Jesuit Fathers; 1878; independent (6,424).

Dallas, University of (c): 1845 E. Northgate, Irving, TX 75062. Dallas diocese; 1956; independent (2,995).

Dayton, University of (c): 300 College Park Ave., Dayton, Ohio 45469. Marianists; 1850 (10,750).

DePaul University (c): 1E. Jackson Blvd., Chicago, IL 60604. Vincentians; 1898 (16,747).

Detroit Mercy, University of (c): 4001 W. McNichols Rd., Detroit, MI 48221; 8200 W. Outer Dr., Detroit MI 48219. Society of Jesus and Sisters of Mercy; 1877; independent (7,774).

Dominican College of Blauvelt (c): Orangeburg, NY 10962. Dominican Sisters; 1952; independent (1,800).

Dominican College (c): 50 Acacia Ave., San Rafael, CA 94901. Dominican Sisters; 1890; independent (1,250).

Duquesne University (c): 600 Forbes Ave., Pittsburgh, PA 15282. Congregation of the Holy Ghost; 1878 (more than 9,000).

D'Youville College (c): 320 Porter Ave., Buffalo, NY 14201. Grey Nuns of the Sacred Heart; 1908; independent (1,700).

Edgewood College (c): 855 Woodrow St., Madison, WI 53711. Dominican Sisters; 1927 (1,900).

Emmanuel College (w): 400 The Fenway, Boston, MA 02115. Sisters of Notre Dame de Namur; independent (1,200).

Fairfield University (c): North Benson Rd., Fairfield, CT 06430. Jesuits; 1942 (5,300).

Felician College (c): 262 S. Main St., Lodi, NJ 07644. Felician Sisters; 1942; independent (1,041).

Fontbonne College (c): 6800 Wydown Blvd., St. Louis, MO 63105. Sisters of St. Joseph of Carondelet; 1917; independent (1,681).

Fordham University (c): Fordham Rd. and Third Ave., New York, NY 10458. Society of Jesus (Jesuits); 1841; independent (14,500).

Franciscan University of Steubenville (c): Steubenville, Ohio 43952. Franciscan Fathers; 1946 (1,800).

Gannon University (c): 109 University Square, Erie, PA 16541 (main campus); 2551 W. 8th St., Erie, PA 16505 (Villa Maria branch campus). Diocese of Erie; 1933 (3,669).

Georgetown University (c): 37th and O Sts. N.W., Washington, DC 20057. Jesuit Fathers; 1789 (11,985).

Georgian Court College (w/c): 900 Lakewood Ave., Lakewood, NJ 08701. Sisters of Mercy; 1908 (2,539).

Gonzaga University (c): Spokane, WA 99258. Jesuit Fathers; 1887 (4,495).

Great Falls, College of (c): 1301 20th St. S., Great Falls, MT 59405. Sisters of Providence; 1932; independent (1,361).

Gwynedd-Mercy College (c): Gwynedd Valley, PA 19437. Sisters of Mercy; 1948; independent (1,979).

Hilbert College (c): 5200 S. Park Ave., Hamburg, NY 14075. Franciscan Sisters of St. Joseph; 1957; independent (950).

Holy Cross, College of the (c): Worcester, MA 01610. Jesuit Fathers; 1843 (2,720).

Holy Family College (c): Grant and Frankford Aves., Philadelphia, PA 19114. Sisters of Holy Family of Nazareth; 1954; independent (2,569).

Holy Names College (c): 3500 Mountain Blvd., Oakland, CA 94619. Sisters of the Holy Names of Jesus and Mary; 1868; independent (966).

Illinois Benedictine College (c): 5700 College Rd., Lisle, IL 60532. Benedictine Monks of St. Procopius Abbey; 1887 (2,694).

Immaculata College (w): Immaculata, PA 19345. Sisters, Servants of the Immaculate Heart of Mary; 1920 (2,088).

Incarnate Word College (c): 4301 Broadway, San Antonio, TX 78209. Sisters of Charity of the Incarnate Word; 1881 (2,861).

Iona College (c): 715 North Ave., New Rochelle, NY 10801. Congregation of Christian Brothers; 1940; independent (6,247).

John Carroll University (c): 20700 North Park Blvd., Cleveland, OH 44118. Jesuits; 1886 (4,300).

Kansas Newman College (formerly Sacred Heart College) (c): 3100 McCormick Ave., Wichita, KS 67213. Sisters Adorers of the Blood of Christ; 1933 (1,954).

King's College (c): Wilkes-Barre, PA 18711. Holy Cross Fathers; 1946 (2,330).

La Roche College (c): 9000 Babcock Blvd., Pittsburgh, PA 15237. Sisters of Divine Providence; 1963 (1,813).

La Salle University (c): 1900 W. Olney Ave., Philadelphia, PA 19141. Christian Brothers; 1863 (6,000).

Le Moyne College (c): Syracuse, NY 13214. Jesuit Fathers; 1946; independent (2,757, full-time, part-time, graduate).

Lewis University (c): Romeoville, IL 60441. Christian Brothers; 1932 (4,399).

Loras College (c): 1450 Alta Vista St., Dubuque, IA 52004. Archdiocese of Dubuque; 1839 (1,993).

Lourdes College (c): 6832 Convent Blvd., Sylvania, OH 43560. Sisters of St. Francis; 1958 (1,670).

Loyola College (c): 4501 N. Charles St., Baltimore, MD 21210. Jesuits; 1852; combined with Mt. St. Agnes College, 1971 (6,261).

Loyola Marymount University (c): 7101 W. 80th St., Los Angeles, CA 90045. Society of Jesus; Religious of Sacred Heart of Mary, Sisters of St. Joseph of Orange; 1911 (5,957).

Loyola University (c): 6363 St. Charles Ave., New Orleans, LA 70118. Jesuit Fathers; 1912 (5,000).

Loyola University Chicago (c): 820 N. Michigan Ave., Chicago, IL 60611. Society of Jesus; 1870 (15,000). Mallinckrodt College (Wilmette) and Mundelein College (Chicago) became part of Loyola University Chicago, in January and June, 1991, respectively.

Madonna University (c): 36600 Schoolcraft Rd., Livonia, MI 48150. Felician Sisters; 1947 (4,200).

Magdalen College (c): RFD #2, Box 375, Warner, NH 03278; Magdalen College Corporation; 1973 (60).

Manhattan College (c): 4513 Manhattan College Pkwy., Riverdale, NY 10471. De La Salle Christian Brothers; 1835; independent (3,600). Cooperative program with College of Mt. St. Vincent.

Marian College (c): 45 S. National Ave., Fond du Lac, WI 54935. Sisters of St. Agnes; 1936 (2,510).

Marian College (c): 3200 Cold Spring Rd., Indianapolis, IN 46222. Sisters of St. Francis (Oldenburg, Ind.); 1851; independent (1,352).

Marist College (c): Poughkeepsie, NY 12601. Marist Brothers of the Schools; 1946; independent (4,300).

Marquette University (c): P.O. Box 1881, Milwaukee, WI 53201. Jesuit Fathers; 1881; independent (10,700).

Mary, University of (c): 7500 University Dr., Bismarck, ND 58504. Benedictine Sisters; 1959 (1,855).

Marygrove College (c): 8425 W. McNichols Rd., Detroit, MI 48221. Sisters, Servants of the Immaculate Heart of Mary; 1910; independent (1,238).

Marylhurst College (c): Marylhurst, OR 97036. Srs. of Holy Names of Jesus and Mary; 1893; independent (1,339).

Marymount College (w): Tarrytown, NY 10591. Religious of the Sacred Heart of Mary; 1907; independent (1,138). Coed in weekend degree programs.

Marymount Manhattan College (w): 221 E. 71st St., New York, NY 10021. Religious of the Sacred Heart of Mary; 1936; independent (1,330).

Marymount University (c): 2807 N. Glebe Rd., Arlington, VA 22007. Religious of the Sacred Heart of Mary; 1950; independent (4,167).

Marywood College (c): Scranton, PA 18509. Sisters, Servants of the Immaculate Heart of Mary; 1915; independent (3,068).

Mater Dei College (c): 5428 State Highway 37, Ogdensburg, NY 13669. Sisters of St. Joseph; 1960; independent (506).

Mercyhurst College (c): 501 E. 38th St., Erie, PA 16546. Sisters of Mercy; 1926 (2,466).

Merrimack College (c): North Andover, MA 01845. Augustinians; 1947 (2,105).

Misericordia (College Misericordia) (c): Dallas, PA 18612. Religious Sisters of Mercy of the Union; 1924 (1,822).

Molloy College (c): 1000 Hempstead Ave., Rockville Centre, NY 11570. Dominican Sisters; 1955; independent (2,149).

Mt. Aloysius College (c): Cresson, PA 16630. Sisters of Mercy; 1939.

Mount Marty College (c): Yankton, SD 57078. Benedictine Sisters; 1936 (1,100).

Mount Mary College (w): 2900 N. Menomonee River Pkwy., Milwaukee, WI 53222. School Sisters of Notre Dame; 1913 (1,524).

Mount Mercy College (c): 1330 Elmhurst Dr. N.E., Cedar Rapids, IA 52402. Sisters of Mercy; 1928; independent (1,200).

Mount St. Clare College (c): 400 N. Bluff Blvd., Clinton, IA 52732. Sisters of St. Francis of Clinton, Iowa; 1918 (513).

Mount St. Joseph, College of (c): 5701 Delhi Rd., Cincinnati, OH 45233. Sisters of Charity; 1920 (2,648).

Mt. St. Mary College (c): Newburgh, NY 12550. Dominican Sisters, 1959; independent (1,823).

Mount St. Mary's College (c): Emmitsburg, MD 21727. Founded by Fr. John Dubois, S.S., 1808; independent (1,286).

Mount St. Mary's College (w/c): 12001 Chalon Rd., Los Angeles, CA 90049 and 10 Chester Pl., Los Angeles, CA 90007 (Doheny Campus). Sisters of St. Joseph of Carondelet; 1925. Coed in music, nursing and graduate programs.

Mt. St. Vincent, College of (c): 6301 Riverdale Ave., Bronx, NY 10471. Sisters of Charity; 1847; independent (1,300). Cooperative program with Manhattan College.

Neumann College (c): Concord Rd., Aston, PA 19014. Sisters of St. Francis; 1965; independent (1,335).

New Rochelle, College of (w/c): 29 Castle Pl., New Rochelle, NY 10805 (main campus). Ursuline Order; 1904; independent (6,000). Coed in nursing, graduate, new resources divisions.

Niagara University (c): Niagara Univ., NY 14109. Vincentian Fathers and Brothers; 1856 (2,862).

Notre Dame, College of (c): 1500 Ralston Ave., Belmont, CA 94002. Sisters of Notre Dame de Namur; 1868; independent (1,730).

Notre Dame du Lac, University of (c): Notre Dame, IN 46556. Congregation of Holy Cross; 1842 (10,000).

Notre Dame College (w): 4545 College Rd., Cleveland, OH 44121. Sisters of Notre Dame; 1922 (688).

Notre Dame College (c): 2321 Elm St., Manchester, NH 03104. Sisters of Holy Cross; 1950; independent (1,291).

Notre Dame of Maryland, College of (w): 4701 N. Charles St., Baltimore, MD 21210. School Sisters of Notre Dame; 1873 (3,215).

Ohio Dominican College (c): Columbus, OH 43219. Dominican Sisters of St. Mary of the Springs; 1911 (1,713).

Our Lady of Holy Cross College (c): 4123 Woodland Dr., New Orleans, LA 70131. Congregation of Sisters Marianites of Holy Cross; 1916 (1,360).

Our Lady of the Elms, College of (w): Chicopee, MA 01013. Sisters of St. Joseph; 1928 (1,174).

Our Lady of the Lake University of San Antonio (c): 411 S.W. 24th St., San Antonio, TX 78207. Sisters of Divine Providence; 1895 (3,338).

Parks College of Saint Louis University (c): Cahokia, IL 62206. Jesuits; 1927; independent (600).

Pontifical Catholic University of Puerto Rico (c): Ponce, PR 00731. Hierarchy of Puerto Rico; 1948; Pontifical University (12,100).

Portland, University of (c): 5000 N. Willamette Blvd., Portland, OR 97203. Holy Cross Fathers; 1901; independent (2,800).

Presentation College (c): Aberdeen, SD 57401. Sisters of the Presentation; 1951 (451).

Providence College (c): River Ave. and Eaton St., Providence, RI 02918. Dominican Friars; 1917 (6,100).

Quincy University (c): 1800 College Ave., Quincy, IL 62301. Franciscan Friars; 1860 (1,250).

Regis College (w): Weston, MA 02193. Sisters of St. Joseph; 1927; independent (1,200).

Regis University (c): 3333 Regis Blvd., Denver, CO 80221. Jesuits; 1887 (9,091).

Rivier College (c): Nashua, NH 03060. Sisters of the Presentation of Mary; 1933; independent (2,759).

Rockhurst College (c): 1100 Rockhurst Rd., Kansas City, MO 64110. Jesuit Fathers; 1910 (2,625).

Rosary College (c): 7900 W. Division St., River Forest, IL 60305. Dominican Sisters; 1901 (1,855).

Rosemont College (w): Rosemont, PA 19010. Society of the Holy Child Jesus; 1921 (749).

Sacred Heart University (c): 5151 Park Ave., Fairfield, CT 06432. Diocese of Bridgeport; 1963; independent (5,600).

St. Ambrose University (c): Davenport, IA 52803. Diocese of Davenport; 1882 (2,585).

Saint Anselm College (c): Manchester NH 03102. Benedictines; 1889 (1,937).

Saint Benedict, College of (w): 37 S. College Ave., St. Joseph, MN 56374. Benedictine Sisters; 1913 (1,736). Sister college of St. John's University, Collegeville (see below).

St. Bonaventure University (c): St. Bonaventure, NY 14778. Franciscan Friars; 1858; independent (2,500).

St. Catherine, College of (w): 2004 Randolph Ave., St. Paul, MN 55105. Sisters of St. Joseph of Carondelet; 1905 (2,763).

St. Edward's University (c): 3001 S. Congress Ave., Austin, TX 78704. Holy Cross Brothers; 1885; independent (3,107).

St. Elizabeth, College of (w): 2 Convent Rd., Morristown, NJ 07960. Sisters of Charity; 1899; independent (1,599). Coed in graduate and weekend college programs.

St. Francis, College of (c): 500 N. Wilcox St., Joliet, IL 60435. Sisters of St. Francis of Mary Immaculate; 1920; independent (1,100).

St. Francis College (c): 180 Remsen St., Brooklyn Heights, NY 11201. Franciscan Brothers; 1884; private, independent in the Franciscan tradition (2,166).

St. Francis College (c): 2701 Spring St., Fort Wayne, IN 46808. Sisters of St. Francis; 1890 (993).

St. Francis College (c): Loretto, PA 15940. Franciscan Friars; 1847; independent (2,020).

St. John's University (c): 8000 Utopia Pkwy., Jamaica, NY 11439 (Queens Campus); 300 Howard Ave., Grymes Hill, Staten Island, NY 10301 (Staten Island Campus). Vincentians; 1870 (19,105).

St. John's University (m): Collegeville, MN 56321. Benedictines; 1857 (1,643). All classes and programs are coeducational with College of St. Benedict (see above).

St. Joseph, College of (c): Clement Rd., Rutland, VT 05701. Sisters of St. Joseph; 1954; independent (500).

Saint Joseph College (w/c): 1678 Asylum Ave., West Hartford, CT 06117. Sisters of Mercy; 1932 (1,859). Women's college in undergraduate liberal arts. Coed in graduate school and Weekend College.

Saint Joseph's College (c): Standish, ME 04084. Sisters of Mercy; 1912 (716, campus; also has external degree program with more than 5,000 students nationwide).

Saint Joseph's College (c): Rensselaer, IN 47978. Society of the Precious Blood; 1891 (1,030).

St. Joseph's College (c): 245 Clinton Ave., Brooklyn, NY 11205 (1,114) and 155 Roe Blvd., Patchogue, N.Y. 11772 (2,303). Sisters of St. Joseph; 1916; independent.

St. Joseph's University (c): 5600 City Ave., Philadelphia, PA 19131. Jesuit Fathers; 1851 (6,000).

Saint Leo College (c): Saint Leo, FL 33574. Order of St. Benedict; 1889; independent (7,148).

St. Louis University (c): 221 N. Grand Blvd., St. Louis, MO 63103. Society of Jesus; 1818; independent (12,000).

Saint Martin's College (c): Lacey, WA 98503. Benedictine Monks; 1895 (891 main campus; 494 extension campuses).

Saint Mary, College of (w): 1901 S. 72nd St., Omaha, NE 68124. Sisters of Mercy; 1923; independent.

Saint Mary College (c): Leavenworth, KS 66048. Sisters of Charity of Leavenworth; 1923 (905).

Saint Mary-of-the-Woods College (w): St. Mary-of-the-Woods, IN 47876. Sisters of Providence; 1840 (1,215).

Saint Mary's College (w): Notre Dame, IN 46556. Sisters of the Holy Cross; 1844 (1,500).

St. Mary's College (c): Orchard Lake, MI 48324. Secular Clergy; 1885 (375).

St. Mary's College (c): Moraga, CA 94575. Brothers of the Christian Schools; 1863 (4,000).

Saint Mary's University of Minnesota (c): Winona, MN 55987. Brothers of the Christian Schools; 1912 (1,300 undergraduate, 6,300 graduate).

St. Mary's University of San Antonio (c): One Camino Santa Maria, San Antonio, TX 78228. Society of Mary (Marianists); 1852 (4,200).

Saint Meinrad College (m): St. Meinrad, IN 47577. Benedictines. Liberal Arts.

St. Michael's College (c): Colchester, VT 05439. Society of St. Edmund; 1904 (2,092).

St. Norbert College (c): De Pere, WI 54115. Norbertine Fathers; 1898; independent (2,092).

Saint Peter's College (c): 2641 Kennedy Blvd., Jersey City, NJ 07306. Society of Jesus; 1872; independent (3,025).

Saint Rose, College of (c): 432 Western Ave., Albany, NY 12203. Sisters of St. Joseph of Carondelet; 1920; independent (4,001).

St. Scholastica, College of (c): 1200 Kenwood Ave., Duluth, MN 55811. Benedictine Sisters; 1912; independent (1,849).

St. Thomas, University of (c): 2115 Summit Ave., St. Paul, MN 55105. Archdiocese of St. Paul and Minneapolis; 1885 (10,161).

St. Thomas, University of (c): 3800 Montrose Blvd., Houston, TX 77006. Basilian Fathers; 1947 (2,298).

St. Thomas Aquinas College (c): Sparkill, NY 10976. Dominican Sisters of Sparkill; 1952; independent, corporate board of trustees (2,100).

St. Thomas University (c): 16400 N.W. 32nd Ave., Miami, FL 33054. Archdiocese of Miami; 1962 (2,488).

Saint Vincent College (c): Fraser Purchase Rd., Latrobe, PA 15650. Benedictine Fathers; 1846 (1,237).

St. Xavier University (c): 3700 W. 103rd St., Chicago, IL 60655. Sisters of Mercy; chartered 1847 (4,400).

Salve Regina University (c): Ochre Point Ave., Newport, RI 02840. Sisters of Mercy; 1934 (2,195).

San Diego, University of (c): Alcala Park, San Diego, CA 92110. San Diego diocese and Religious of the Sacred Heart; 1949; independent (6,381).

San Francisco, University of (c): Ignatian Heights, San Francisco, CA 94117. Jesuit Fathers; 1855 (6,564).

Santa Clara University (c): Santa Clara, CA 95053. Jesuit Fathers; 1851; independent (7,514).

Santa Fe, College of (c): Santa Fe, NM 87501. Brothers of the Christian Schools; 1947 (1,600).

Scranton, University of (c): Scranton, PA 18510. Society of Jesus; 1888; independent (5,100).

Seattle University (c): Broadway and East Madison, Seattle, WA 98122. Jesuit Fathers; 1891 (5,025).

Seton Hall University (c): South Orange Ave., South Orange, NJ 07079. Diocesan Clergy; 1856 (9,688).

Seton Hill College (w): Greensburg, PA 15601. Sisters of Charity of Seton Hill; 1883 (921).

Siena College (c): Loudonville, NY 12211. Franciscan Friars; 1937 (3,350).

Siena Heights College (c): 1247 E. Siena Heights Dr., Adrian, MI 49221. Dominican Sisters; 1919 (1,850).

Silver Lake College of Holy Family (c): 2406 S. Alverno Rd., Manitowoc, WI 54220. Franciscan Sisters of Christian Charity; 1935 (1,000).

Spalding University (c): 851 S. 4th Ave., Louisville, KY 40203. Sisters of Charity of Nazareth; 1814; independent (1,218).

Spring Hill College (c): 4000 Dauphin St., Mobile, AL 36608. Jesuit Fathers; 1830 (1,117).

Stonehill College (c): 320 Washington St., North Easton, MA 02357. Holy Cross Fathers; 1948; independent (2,949).

Thomas Aquinas College (c): 10000 N. Ojai Rd., Santa Paula, CA 93060. Founded 1971 (225).

Thomas More College (c): Crestview Hills, Covington, KY 41017. Diocese of Covington; 1921 (1,335).

Trinity College (w): Colchester Ave., Burlington, VT 05401. Sisters of Mercy; 1925 (973).

Trinity College (w): 125 Michigan Ave. N.E., Washington, DC 20017. Sisters of Notre Dame de Namur; 1897 (1,100). Coed in graduate school.

Ursuline College (w): 2550 Lander Rd., Cleveland, OH 44124. Ursuline Nuns; 1871 (1,446).

Villanova University (c): 800 Lancaster Ave., Villanova, PA 19085. Order of St. Augustine; 1842 (11,100).

Viterbo College (c): 815 S. 9th, La Crosse, WI 54601. Franciscan Sisters of Perpetual Adoration; 1890 (1,160).

Walsh University (c): 2020 Easton St. N.W., North Canton, Ohio 44720. Brothers of Christian Instruction; 1958 (1,480).

Wheeling Jesuit College (c): 316 Washington Ave., Wheeling, WV 26003. Jesuit Fathers; 1954 (1,430).

Xavier University (c): 3800 Victory Pkwy., Cincinnati, OH 45207. Jesuit Fathers; 1831 (6,180).

Xavier University of Louisiana (c): 7325 Palmetto St., New Orleans, LA 70125. Sisters of Blessed Sacrament; 1925; lay-Religious administrative board (3,490).

Catholic Two-Year Colleges

Ancilla College (c): Donaldson, IN 46513. Ancilla Domini Sisters, 1937.

Aquinas College (c): 4210 Harding Rd., Nashville, TN 37205. Dominican Sisters; 1961 (380). Offers B.A. in Elementary Teacher Education.

Assumption College for Sisters: 350 Bernardsville Rd., Mendham, NJ 07945. Sisters of Christian Charity; 1953 (25).

Castle College: 21 Searles Rd., Windham, NH 03087. Sisters of Mercy; 1963; independent (313).

Chatfield College (c): St. Martin, OH 45118. Ursulines; 1971 (300).

The College of St. Catherine-Minneapolis (c): 601 25th Ave. S., Minneapolis, MN 55454. Sisters of St. Joseph of Carondelet (1,232).

Donnelly College (c): 608 N. 18th St., Kansas City, KS 66102. Archdiocesan College; 1949 (752).

Don Bosco Technical Institute (m): 1151 San Gabriel Blvd., Rosemead, CA 91770. Salesians; 1969 (105).

Holy Cross College (c): Notre Dame, IN 46556. Brothers of Holy Cross; 1966 (455).

Manor Junior College (c): 700 Fox Chase Road, Jenkintown, PA 19046. Sisters of St. Basil the Great; 1947 (640).

Maria College (c): 700 New Scotland Ave., Albany, NY 12208. Sisters of Mercy; 1963 (950).

Marymount Palos Verdes College (c): Rancho Palos Verdes, CA 90274. Religious of the Sacred Heart of Mary; independent (1,068).

St. Catharine College (c): St. Catharine, KY 40061. Dominican Sisters; 1931 (375).

St. Gregory's College (c): Shawnee, OK 74801. Benedictine Monks; 1876 (300).

Springfield College in Illinois (c): 1500 N. Fifth St., Springfield, IL 62702. Ursuline Sisters; 1929 (455).

Trocaire College (c): 110 Red Jacket Pkwy., Buffalo, NY 14220. Sisters of Mercy; 1958; independent (1,105).

Villa Maria College of Buffalo (c): 240 Pine Ridge Rd., Buffalo, NY 14225. Felician Sisters 1960; independent (400).

CATHOLIC UNIVERSITY OF AMERICA, THE

A decision to establish a "principal seminary" for advanced study around which a university could develop was made by the Roman Catholic bishops of the United States on December 2, 1884, during their Third Plenary Council of Baltimore. The desirability of a university had been suggested on earlier occasions. At Baltimore, the foremost proponent, John Lancaster Spalding, first bishop of Peoria, himself of old-line American stock, persuaded a majority of his brother bishops of "the immigrant Church" that so long as they would "look rather to the multiplying of schools and seminaries than to the creation of a real university" the progress of American Catholics was sure to be "slow and uncertain." At hand was a prospective gift of $300,000 from his protégée, Mary Gwendoline Cald-

Caldwell Hall

well of Newport, Rhode Island. It made possible the beginning. There were, however, continuing objections to the project from Bishop Bernard McQuaid of Rochester and his metropolitan, Archbishop Michael A. Corrigan of New York, from some Jesuits, and later, in the institution's early years, from German-American Catholics.

A university committee of bishops, priests, and laymen soon named the institution, determined upon its location in Washington, D.C., and in 1886 appointed its first rector, John Joseph Keane, bishop of Richmond. Pope Leo XIII, who encouraged the project from its beginning, formally approved it on April 10, 1887. Incorporation in the District of Columbia followed on April 21. After the recruitment of professors in Europe and the drafting of constitutions that were approved by the Pope on March 7, 1889, and after the completion of the first building, later named Caldwell Hall, the university opened officially on November 13, 1889.

Governance had been delegated by the bishops to a board of trustees. Originally it consisted of the seventeen incorporators and their successors. It was enlarged considerably after amendment of the corporate charter by an act of Congress in 1928. Lay membership was minimal until 1968 when new bylaws provided for equal numbers of clerical and lay members. In 1995 there were fifty trustees. They govern a complex institution with a campus of 154 acres.

Academic Organization

Expansion from theology into the arts and sciences began in 1895 with the opening of what Keane called "the faculties for the laity" in a new building named for the donor, Msgr. James McMahon of New York. Instruction in law and in technology were included. Although initially the institution had been dedicated to graduate instruction exclusively, students without baccalaureate degrees could then study law. Undergraduate instruction in other fields was authorized in 1904. Academic reorganization or dissolution of faculties and departments, which had already begun, continued at frequent intervals as in other institutions.

The most comprehensive academic reorganization occurred in 1930, during the administration of James Hugh Ryan, later archbishop of Omaha, when, following prevalent American patterns, a College and Graduate School of Arts and Sciences and a School of Engineering and Architecture were established. The undergraduate program of liberal education that was developed was particularly distinctive and had a widespread enduring influence. In 1947 the National Catholic School of Social Service and in 1954 the Columbus School of Law, both of which had been founded in Washington after World War I, were incorporated into the university. In 1973 organization of the School of Religious Studies consolidated the former Schools of Theology and Canon Law and the Department of Religion and Religious Education, and in 1975 the College and Graduate School were consolidated into a single School of Arts and Sciences. In 1995 the university included Schools of Architecture and Planning, Arts and Sciences, Engineering, Law, Library and Information Science, Music, Nursing, Philosophy, Religious Studies, and Social Service. Its Theological College, directed by the Sulpicians, was serving diocesan seminarians from the entire country.

Distinctive Contributions

In the context of American higher education generally, the most significant contribution of the university was in its role as the principal channel through which the modern American university movement, begun with the opening of the Johns Hopkins University in 1876 and now worldwide in its influence, entered the American Catholic community. The Catholic University of America was one of the first three American institutions to dedicate itself to graduate study in recognition of research as well as instruction as a basic university purpose. It developed library collections to serve this aim. In 1900 it became a charter member of the Association of American Universities. In 1995 it still awarded more academic doctoral degrees than any other Catholic institution in the United States.

From its beginning, the university made a particularly visible contribution to the Church through its preparation of teachers, many of them diocesan priests or members of religious communities of men and women, for Catholic schools, seminaries, colleges, and universities. The Catholic Sisters College, its adjunct from 1911 until 1964, served this purpose before women were admitted to graduate study, in 1928, and before their admission to all departments in the College of Arts and Sciences, which was a process not completed until the 1950s. A summer session was held in the Catholic Sisters College until summer sessions were offered by the university itself, beginning in 1929. Other particularly visible contributions to the Church have been made through the preparation of diocesan officials in canon law and in social work. The university is the only institution in the United States authorized to confer higher ecclesiastical degrees.

Programs of affiliation have also provided distinctive services to Catholic institutions. A program for secondary schools and colleges, begun in 1912 and strengthened after 1947, placed emphasis upon assisting institutions to prepare for accreditation by the appropriate state, regional, and national agencies. Its termination in 1968 was a mark of its success.

Conspicuous service was extended to Catholic elementary and—with less impact—secondary schools by a Commission on American Citizenship established in 1939. It provided a curriculum guide and a series of eight elementary school readers that were used for more than two decades, as well as sponsorship of related activities. At another level, continuing education begun in 1949 as an outreach to the local community, is now an offering of a Metropolitan College that includes baccalaureate programs for adults.

Current Instructional Role

Inevitably, the size and composition of the university's student body has changed from time to time. Enrollment reached its peak to date in 1979 when 8,595 individuals were registered for instruction.

Three recent changes in the composition of the student body are notable. The most conspicuous is the change in the proportion of clerics and religious. As recently as the early 1960s, their proportion was about 30 percent of all students enrolled. During the first semester of the academic year 1993–94, they were only a little more than 3 percent of the total. Almost all were post-baccalaureate students and about 70 percent were enrolled in the School of Religious Studies.

In view of the historic aim and actual role of the university in the past, a decline in the proportion of its graduate students is a more significant mark of academic change. Increases in the proportions of undergraduates and of post-baccalaureate students in professional fields are its counterparts. Undergraduates—90 percent of whom are enrolled full-time—now comprise about 40 percent of the total number of students. Students in fields other than arts and sciences, philosophy, and religious studies now comprise almost two-thirds of the total post-baccalaureate enrollment.

The effects of these changes become clearer when another, the increase in the number of part-time, post-baccalaureate students, is related to them. Currently (1996), about 58 percent of all post-baccalaureate students are enrolled part-time, and about 64 percent of those in graduate studies are so enrolled. In its impact upon the character of the institution, there appears to be a shift to professional education that is more significant than the growth of undergraduate numbers in the student population.

Although it was expected initially that instructional costs would be funded by income from endowment, sufficient funds have never been received from this source. In 1903 Pope Pius X authorized the bishops of the United States to establish an annual collection for the university. It was the introduction of this collection that enabled the university to survive the loss of 60 percent of its early endowment in the following year. Currently about $5,000,000 is realized from the collection each year.

Ellis, J. T. *The Formative Years of the Catholic University of America.* Washington, D.C.: American Catholic Historical Association, 1946.

Nuesse, C. Joseph. *The Catholic University of America, A Centennial History.* Washington, D.C.: The Catholic University of America Press, 1990.

C. JOSEPH NUESSE

Related Document

THE LAYING OF THE CORNERSTONE OF THE CATHOLIC UNIVERSITY OF AMERICA, MAY 24, 1888

At the Second Plenary Council of Baltimore in October, 1866, the idea of a university for American Catholics was seriously discussed for the first time by the hierarchy, although nothing came of it at that time. In the interval between the plenary councils of 1866 and 1884 the subject continued to be urged by a number of leaders such as Thomas A. Becker (1832–1899), first Bishop of Wilmington, Isaac T. Hecker (1819–1888), founder of the Paulists, and by none more insistently than Bishop Spalding of Peoria. It was Spalding's notable sermon of November 16, 1884, during the Third Plenary Council, and the fact that he was able to secure the first substantial grant of funds, that helped to make the project a reality. It was fitting, therefore, that when the cornerstone of Caldwell Hall, the original building, was laid in the presence of President Grover Cleveland and a large assembly of distinguished guests, Spalding should have been chosen to deliver the principal address. The university opened on November 13, 1889, with forty-six students; the enrollment in February, 1956, was 3,350 students divided among the ten schools of the university.

(*Source*: John Lancaster Spalding, "University Education," *Education and the Higher Life*. Chicago: A. C. McClurg and Co., 1891, 178–79, 193, 195–98.)

THE SPECIAL SIGNIFICANCE OF OUR AMERICAN CATHOLIC history is not found in the phases of our life which attract attention, and are a common theme for declamation; but it lies in the fact that our example proves that the Church can thrive where it is neither protected nor persecuted, but is simply left to itself to manage its own affairs and to do its work. Such an experiment had never been made when we became an independent people, and its success is of worldwide import, because this is the modern tendency and the position toward the Church which all the nations will sooner or later assume; just as they all will be forced finally to accept popular rule. The great underlying principle of democracy,—that men are brothers and have equal rights, and that God clothes the soul with freedom,—is a truth taught by Christ, is a truth proclaimed by the Church; and the faith of Christians in this principle, in spite of hesitations and misgivings, of oppositions and obstacles and inconceivable difficulties, has finally given to it its modern vigor and beneficent power. . . .

The aim the best now propose to themselves is to provide not wealth or pleasure, or better machinery or more leisure, but a higher and more effective kind of education; and hence whatever one's preoccupation, whether social, political, religious, or industrial, the question of education forces itself upon his attention. Pedagogy has grown to be a science, and chairs are founded in universities to expound the theory and art of teaching. The learning of former times has become the ignorance of our own; and

the classical writings have ceased to be the treasure-house of knowledge, and in consequence their educational value has diminished. . . . The ancients, indeed, excel us in the sense for form and symmetry. There is also a freshness in their words, a joyousness in their life, a certain heroic temper in their thinking and acting, which give them power to engage the emotions; and hence to deny them exceptional educational value is to take a partial view. But even though we grant that the study of their literatures is in certain respects the best intellectual discipline, education, it must be admitted, means knowledge as well as training; and thorough training is something more than refined taste. It is strength as well, and ability to think in many directions and on many subjects. Nothing known to men should escape the attention of the wise; for the knowledge of the age determines what is demanded of the scholar. And since it is our privilege to live at a time when knowledge is increasing more rapidly even than population and wealth, we must, if we hope to stand in the front ranks of those who know, keep pace with the onward movement of mind. To turn away from this outburst of splendor and power; to look back to pagan civilization or Christian barbarism,— is to love darkness more than light. Aristotle is a great mind, but his learning is crude and his ideas of Nature are frequently grotesque. Saint Thomas is a powerful intellect; but his point of view in all that concerns natural knowledge has long since vanished from sight. What poverty of learning does not the early mediaeval scheme of education reveal; and when in the twelfth century the idea of a university rises in the best minds, how incomplete and vague it is! Amid the ruins of castles and cathedrals we grow humble, and think ourselves inferior to men who thus could build. But they were not as strong as we, and they led a more ignorant and blinder life; and so when we read of great names of the past, the mists of illusion fill the skies, and our eyes are dimmed by the glory of clouds tinged with the splendors of a sun that has set.

Certainly a true university will be the home both of ancient wisdom and of new learning; it will teach the best that is known, and encourage research; it will stimulate thought, refine taste, and awaken the love of excellence; it will be at once a scientific institute, a school of culture, and a training ground for the business of life; it will educate the minds that give direction to the age; it will be a nursery of ideas, a centre of influence. The good we do men is quickly lost, the truth we leave them remains forever; and therefore the aim of the best education is to enable students to see what is true, and to inspire them with the love of all truth. Professional knowledge brings most profit to the individual; but philosophy and literature, science and art, elevate and refine the spirit of a whole people, and hence the university will make culture its first aim, and its scope will widen as the thoughts and attainments of men are enlarged and multiplied. Here if anywhere shall be found teachers whose one passion is the love of truth, which is the love of God and of man; who look on all things with a serene eye; who bring to every question a calm, unbiassed mind; who, where the light of the intellect fails, walk by faith and accept the omen of hope; who understand that to be distrustful of science is to lack culture, to doubt the good of progress is to lack knowledge, and to question the necessity of religion is to want wisdom; who know that in a God-made and God-governed world it must lie in the nature of things that reason and virtue should tend to prevail, in spite of the fact that in every age the majority of men think foolishly and act unwisely. . . .

(*Source:* John Tracy Ellis, ed. *Documents of American Catholic History.* Vol. 2:1866–1966. Wilmington, Del.: Michael Glazier, 1987, 464–66.)

CATHOLIC WORKER MOVEMENT, THE

The Catholic Worker movement was founded in 1933 during the Great Depression by Dorothy Day at the urging of Peter Maurin. It is best known for houses of hospitality located in rundown sections of many cities, although a number of Catholic Worker centers exist in rural areas. Food, clothing, shelter and welcome are extended by unpaid volunteers to those in need according to the ability of each household. In 1995 there were 134 Catholic Worker communities, all but three of them in the United States. "Our rule is the works of mercy," said Dorothy Day. "It is the way of sacrifice, worship, a sense of reverence."

The Catholic Worker is also the name of a newspaper published by the Catholic Worker community in New York City. From 1933 until her death in 1980, the editor was Dorothy Day, a journalist who was received into the Catholic Church in 1927. Writers for the paper have ranged from young volunteers to such notable figures as Thomas Merton, Daniel Berrigan, and Jacques Maritain. (Many Catholic Worker communities also publish newsletters or journals chiefly for local distribution.)

Beyond hospitality, Catholic Worker communities are known for their activity in support of labor unions, human rights, cooperatives, and the development of a nonviolent culture. Those active in the Catholic Worker movement are often pacifists—people seeking to live an unarmed, nonviolent life. During periods of military conscription, Catholic Workers have been conscientious objectors to military service. Many of those active in the Catholic Worker movement have been jailed for acts of protest against racism, unfair labor practices, social injustice, and war.

Catholic Worker communities have refused to apply for federal tax exempt status, seeing such official recognition as binding the community to the state and limiting the movement's freedom. With its stress on voluntary poverty, the Catholic Worker has much in common with the early

Franciscans, while its accent on community, prayer and hospitality has Benedictine overtones. "We try to shelter the homeless and give them clothes," Dorothy Day explained, "but there is strong faith at work. We pray. If an outsider who comes to visit us doesn't pay attention to our prayings and what that means, then he'll miss the whole point."

It is unlikely that any religious community was ever less structured than the Catholic Worker. Each community is autonomous. There is no board of directors, no sponsor, no system of governance, no endowment, no paychecks, no pension plans. Since Dorothy Day's death, there has been no central leader.

See also CATHOLIC PEACE MOVEMENT, THE; DAY, DOROTHY; MAURIN, PETER.

Cornell, Tom, Robert Ellsberg, and Jim Forest, eds. *A Penny a Copy: Writings from The Catholic Worker.* Maryknoll, N.Y.: Orbis, 1995.

Coy, Patrick, ed. *A Revolution of the Heart.* Philadelphia: Temple, 1988.

Miller, William. *A Harsh and Dreadful Love.* New York: Liveright, 1973.

Piehl, Mel. *Breaking Bread: The Catholic Worker and the Origin of Catholic Radicalism in America.* Philadelphia: Temple, 1982.

Troester, Rosalie Riegle. *Voices from the Catholic Worker.* Philadelphia: Temple, 1993.

JIM FOREST

Related Document

DOROTHY DAY DESCRIBES THE LAUNCHING OF *THE CATHOLIC WORKER* AND THE MOVEMENT BEHIND IT, MAY, 1933

The great depression of the 1930's set on foot numerous projects throughout the United States for the relief of the immense army of unemployed. During this period of severe distress the charitable agencies of the Church were taxed as never before, but there was no more distinctive and inspiring example of Catholic charity than that of the Catholic Worker Movement. Through its houses of hospitality, its organization of farming communes, and its program of discussion groups, study clubs, and publications disseminating the social doctrines of the Church, the Catholic Worker Movement not only gave a new start in life to many of the victims of the depression, but it likewise inspired and trained young Catholic workers and intellectuals who in the years that followed found their way into other enterprises like the Association of Catholic Trade Unionists and the Catholic youth movement. The undertaking was due in the main to Dorothy Day (1898–1980) who had been a member of the Socialist Party, the I.W.W., and communist affiliates and who knew, therefore, at first hand what the social philosophy was from the angle of the left. In December, 1927, she became a convert to Catholicism, and when the depression struck she channeled her zeal and love for the poor in a way that proved eminently practical for countless men and women who had been cut adrift from their normal walks of life. In the excerpts from her memoirs that follow she tells of the beginnings of the movement's best known publication, as well as something about how the original house of hospitality was operated in its early days.

(*Source: The Long Loneliness. The Autobiography of Dorothy Day*. New York: Harper & Bros., 1952, 182–86.)

WE STARTED PUBLISHING *THE CATHOLIC WORKER* AT 436 East Fifteenth Street in May, 1933, with a first issue of 2,500 copies. Within three or four months the circulation bounded to 25,000, and it was cheaper to bring it out as an eight-page tabloid on newsprint rather than the smaller-sized edition on better paper we had started with. By the end of the year we had a circulation of 100,000 and by 1936 it was 150,000. It was certainly a mushroom growth. It was not only that some parishes subscribed for the paper all over the country in bundles of 500 or more. Zealous young people took the paper out in the streets and sold it, and when they could not sell it even at one cent a copy, they gave free copies and left them in streetcar, bus, barber shop and dentist's and doctor's office. We got letters from all parts of the country from people who said they had picked up the paper on trains, in rooming houses. One letter came from the state of Sonora in Mexico and we read with amazement that the reader had tossed in an uncomfortable bed on a hot night until he got up to turn over the mattress and under it found a copy of *The Catholic Worker*. A miner found a copy five miles underground in an old mine that stretched out under the Atlantic Ocean off Nova Scotia. A seminarian said that he had sent out his shoes to be half-soled in Rome and they came back to him wrapped in a copy of *The Catholic Worker*. These letters thrilled and inspired the young people who came to help, sent by Brothers or Sisters who taught in the high schools. We were invited to speak in schools and parishes, and often as a result of our speaking others came in to help us. On May Day, those first few years, the streets were literally lined with papers. Looking back on it, it seemed like a gigantic advertising campaign, entirely unpremeditated. It grew organically, Peter used to say happily, and not through organization. "We are not an organization, we are an organism," he said.

First there was Peter, my brother and I. When John took a job at Dobb's Ferry, a young girl, Dorothy Weston, who had been studying journalism and was a graduate of a Catholic college, came to help. She lived at home and spent her days with us, eating with us and taking only her carfare from the common fund. Peter brought in three young men from Columbus Circle, whom he had met when discussing the affairs of the world there, and of these one became bookkeeper (that was his occupation when he was employed), another circulation manager, and the third married Dorothy Weston. Another girl came to take dictation and help with mailing the paper, and she married the circulation manager. There were quite a number

of romances that first year—the paper appealed to youth. Then there were the young intellectuals who formed what they called Campion Committees in other cities as well as New York, who helped to picket the Mexican and German consulates and who distributed literature all over the city. Workers came in to get help on picket lines, to help move dispossessed families and to make demonstrations in front of relief offices. Three men came to sell the paper on the street, and to eat their meals with us. Big Dan had been a truck driver and a policeman. The day he came in to see us he wanted nothing more than to bathe his tired feet. That night at supper Peter indoctrinated him on the dignity of poverty and read some of Father Vincent McNabb's *Nazareth or Social Chaos*. This did not go over so well, all of us being city people, and Father McNabb advocating a return to the fields, but he made Dan Orr go out with a sense of a mission, not worrying about shabby clothes or the lack of a job. Dan began to sell the paper on the streets and earned enough money to live on. He met others who had found subsistence jobs, carrying sandwich signs or advertising children's furniture by pushing a baby carriage, a woman who told fortunes in a tea shop, a man who sold pretzels, which were threaded on four poles one on each corner of an old baby carriage. He found out their needs, and those of their families, and never left the house in the morning without bundles of clothes as well as his papers.

Dan rented a horse and wagon in which to deliver bundles of the paper each month. (We had tried this before he came but someone had to push the horse while the other led it. We knew nothing about driving a wagon.) Dan loved his horse. He called it Catholic Action, and used to take the blanket off my bed to cover the horse in winter. We rented it from a German Nazi on East Sixteenth Street, and sometimes when we had no money he let us have the use of it free for a few hours. It rejoiced our hearts to move a Jewish family into their new quarters with his equipment.

Dan said it was a pious horse and that when he passed St. Patrick's Cathedral, the horse genuflected. He liked to drive up Fifth Avenue, preferably with students who had volunteered their help, and shout, "Read *The Catholic Worker*" at the top of his lungs. He was anything but dignified and loved to affront the dignity of others.

One time he saw me coming down the street when he was selling the paper in front of Gimbel's and began to yell, "Read *The Catholic Worker!* Romance on every page." A seminarian from St. Louis, now Father Dreisoner [*sic*], took a leaf from Dan's book and began selling the paper on the corner of Times Square and at union meetings. He liked to stand next to a comrade selling *The Daily Worker*, and as the one shouted "Read *The Daily Worker*," he in turn shouted, "Read *The Catholic Worker* daily." Between sales they conversed. . . .

Peter, the "green" revolutionist, had a long-term program which called for hospices, or houses of hospitality, where the works of mercy could be practiced to combat the taking over by the state of all those services which could be built up by mutual aid; and farming communes to provide land and homes for the unemployed, whom increasing technology was piling up into the millions. In 1933, the unemployed numbered 13,000,000.

The idea of the houses of hospitality caught on quickly enough. The very people that Peter brought in, who made up our staff at first, needed a place to live. Peter was familiar with the old I.W.W. technique of a common flophouse and a pot of mulligan on the stove. To my cost, I too had become well acquainted with this idea. Besides, we never had any money, and the cheapest, most practical way to take care of people was to rent some apartments and have someone do the cooking for the lot of us. Many a time I was cook and cleaner as well as editor and street seller. When Margaret, a Lithuanian girl from the mining regions of Pennsylvania, came to us and took over the cooking, we were happy indeed. She knew how to make a big pot of mashed potatoes with mushroom sauce which filled everyone up nicely. She was a great soft creature with a little baby, Barbara, who was born a few months after she came to us. Margaret went out on May Day with the baby and sold papers on the street. She loved being propagandist as well as cook. When Big Dan teased her, she threatened to tell the "pasture" of the church around the corner.

To house the women we had an apartment near First Avenue which could hold about ten. When there were arguments among them, Margaret would report them with gusto, giving us a blow-by-blow account. Once when she was telling how one of the women abused her so that she "felt as though the crown of thorns was pressing right down on her head" (she was full of these mystical experiences), Peter paused in his pacing of the office to tell her she needed to scrub the kitchen floor. Not that he was ever harsh, but he was making a point that manual labor was the cure of all such quarreling. Margaret once told Bishop O'Hara of Kansas City that when she kissed his ring, it was just like a blood transfusion—she got faint all over.

Jacques Maritain came to us during these early days and spoke to the group who were reading *Freedom and the Modern World [sic]* at that time. He gave special attention to the chapter on the purification of means. Margaret was delighted with our distinguished guest, who so evidently loved us all, and made him a box of fudge to take home with him when he sailed for France a few weeks later.

Ah, those early days that everyone likes to think of now since we have grown so much bigger; that early zeal, that early romance, that early companionableness! And how delightful it is to think that the young ones who came into the work now find the same joy in community. It is a permanent revolution, this Catholic Worker Movement. . . .

(*Source:* John Tracy Ellis, ed. *Documents of American Catholic History.* Vol. 2:1866–1966. Wilmington, Del.: Michael Glazier, 1987, 625–29.)

CATHOLIC WORLD, THE

After the end of the American Civil War, the founder of the Paulists, Isaac Thomas Hecker, was able to act on his dream of launching a national Catholic magazine. It was a daring step, for several Catholic periodicals had appeared and quickly failed. Yet, issue after issue, Hecker filled the 140 pages of the *Catholic World* with first-rate writers and promising beginners. He culled articles from the best British and continental periodicals. The second issue published John Henry Newman's *Dream of Gerontius*. Later issues featured Orestes Brownson and poems by Aubrey de Vere.

Editors of the Catholic World

When Hecker died in 1888, a cofounder of the Paulists, Fr. Augustine Hewit, became its second editor. Hewit had studied for the ministry of the Episcopal Church. Then, influenced by John Henry Newman's conversion to Catholicism, he became a Catholic in 1846 and was ordained a Catholic priest in 1847. Hewit was editor of the *Catholic World* from 1888 to 1897.

An important subeditor from 1889–93 was Paulist author and missionary, Fr. Walter Elliott. It was Elliott who built a Catholic press building called the Columbus Press which in 1913 became the Paulist Press. A French translation of Elliott's *Life of Father Hecker* would trigger the Americanism controversy.

In 1897 the *Catholic World*'s third editor was Fr. Alexander P. Doyle. Doyle recast the magazine to a more popular level in format and content. He preferred the short stories of Irish novelist Canon F. S. Sheehan and the poetry of Francis Thompson to more scholarly articles. In 1897 Hilaire Belloc appeared in the *Catholic World*. In 1904 Fr. (later Msgr.) John J. Burke became its fourth editor. Burke restored the *Catholic World* to its old excellence. In 1911 with other Catholic journalists he cofounded the Catholic Press Association.

In 1922 the Paulists appointed Fr. James Martin Gillis its fifth editor. Gillis was considered the finest Paulist orator of the twentieth century. The *Catholic World* saw its highest circulation ever in his twenty-six years as editor. For twenty-seven years, Gillis also wrote a column, "Sursum Corda," nationally syndicated by the NC News Service. From 1948 to 1971 Fr. John Basil Sheerin served as its sixth editor. Sheerin won journalism honors for his editorial courage in such issues as ecumenism, race relations, civil rights, and peace, and he was himself a specialist in the Jewish-Catholic dialogue.

In 1972 Fr. Kevin A. Lynch, C.S.P., president of the Paulist Press, established an editorial board consisting of the senior editors of the Paulist Press. The magazine also went from monthly to bimonthly publication, with each issue focusing on one major theme. Over the years, the *Catholic World* received many national awards from the Catholic Press Association for *general excellence.* In 1996, after 131 years of continuous publications, the *Catholic World* was discontinued.

See also HECKER, ISAAC; PAULISTS (C.S.P.); SHEERIN, JOHN BASIL.

THOMAS E. COMBER, C.S.P.

CATHOLIC YOUTH ORGANIZATION (CYO)

See SHEIL, BERNARD JAMES.

CATHOLICS AND AMERICAN LITERATURE

See BROWNSON, ORESTES AUGUSTUS; COLUM, PADRAIC; CONWAY, KATHERINE E.; DORSEY, ANNA; HORGAN, PAUL; McGINLEY, PHYLLIS; MERTON, THOMAS; O'CONNOR, EDWIN; O'CONNOR, FLANNERY MARY; O'REILLY, JOHN BOYLE; PERCY, WALKER; POWERS, JESSICA; REPPLIER, AGNES; SADLIER, MARY; SHUSTER, GEORGE NAUMAN; WOLFF, MADELEVA.

CENSORSHIP

Historical Background

History records the use of censorship by rulers, popes, and societies. The office of censor, from which the term is derived, was established in Rome in 443 B.C.E. The censor conducted the census and regulated the morals of the citizens. While in the past, censorship dealt primarily with offensive written materials, the modern world views censorship more restrictively because of the search for knowledge and freedom of speech and expression. Nevertheless, censorship is still employed when certain teachings and views are questionable and condemned by a majority or a governing body.

Censorship is a type of prohibition that restricts the propagation of certain ideas through various types of media: theater, written materials, books, art, film, and audio-visual technologies. The content of these various media can be objectionable for religious, moral, political, or social reasons. Frequently the content is of a sexual nature, but it can also deal with dissident teachings and prejudice of a religious, racist, ethnic, sexist, political, nationalist, and ageist nature. When common observance or a majority opinion, theory, or political view hold sway, dissident views are often repressed through censorship. The purpose can be to eliminate competition, attain unity and strength, to arrive at purity of doctrine, or to impart morals that promote the common good of a society.

Methods of restriction can include forbidding the publication and use of texts, cessation of funding, removal of materials such as art pieces from public viewing, and public notification of condemned matter through lists. Censorship can be proscriptive or restrictive. Proscriptive censorship forbids the reading of certain kinds of books, while restrictive censorship aims to control the circulation of books to certain classes of people such as minors. This also pertains to films, science research, and works of art.

Historical Precedent

Censorship has been used widely throughout history by governments that determined what was beneficial for the character and development of its citizens. The early Greeks and Romans practiced censorship to promote the welfare of the regime and the character development of its citizens. In Greece, people were censored if they did not observe religious holidays and respect the gods of the city, although Athens celebrated a more liberal view. However, their openness was limited as seen in the 399 B.C.E. conviction of Socrates for subverting the minds of the youth. In the *Republic,* Plato writes that law shapes the opinions of the community and dissenters undermine common morality or destroy the institutions of the society. Authority defines what is acceptable material to be written and taught.

Religious Censorship

Ancient Israel also used censorship to achieve its goals. The Israelites and their leaders were corrected by prophets who held the believers to a firm religious vision. A noted example is the daring challenge of the prophet, Nathan, to King David who had seriously breached religious norms by taking Bathsheba for his wife. The purpose of the law was to set people free to worship God. The Israelites had restrictions regarding religious observance even in the voicing of God's name. The unobservant Jew could be severely punished, possibly with stoning.

Christianity developed its own forms of censorship. Early Christianity defined Church doctrine and condemned opposing teachings as heretical; heretics were usually expelled from the community. The most noted form of early censorship is the *Index Librorum Prohibitorum* whose origins can be traced back to the fifth century C.E. The *Index* maintained orthodox thought of the Roman Catholic Church as summarized in the creeds. If certain books challenged the teachings of the canonical texts or established credal statements, they were condemned. The leadership of the Church determined what was orthodox doctrine but at times secular leaders also defined acceptable doctrine for members of an empire or society.

Censorship reached an unprecedented level during the Middle Ages when the Church founded the Inquisition because it feared the spread of heresies. Cruel punishments of torture, imprisonment, exile, and death were imposed on heretics from the twelfth century until the Inquisition was abolished during the French Revolution. "The names of hostile witnesses were withheld, anonymous informers were used, the accusations of personal enemies were allowed, the accused were denied the right of defense, or of defending counsel; and there was no appeal" (Johnson,

253). Moreover, from the fourteenth to the eighteenth centuries, many people were persecuted as witches for superstitious, religious, political, or social reasons, or because of various psychic disturbances. Religion and politics were so intermingled that condemnation was effected often by both as in the cases of Joan of Arc in France (1431) and Thomas More in England (1535). Followers of Luther, such as Matthaeus Judex (1528–64), confronted civil courts that were attempting to censor the writings of theologians during the sixteenth century. Similar attempts at censorship were made in England. During the sixteenth and seventeenth centuries, English authors avoided censorship by employing certain hermeneutic principles that created double meanings of a text. An author, like Ben Jonson in *King Lear* or Teresa of Avila in *Interior Castle,* could comment on contemporary issues and so avoid censorship by the authorities. The Inquisition was particularly strong in Spain and spread to the Spanish colonies in the New World. England, Germany, Russia, and Italy also employed various types of censorship. The United States recalls its own practice of burning witches at the stake in colonial days.

Contemporary Practices

With the Enlightenment in the seventeenth century came new perspectives on religious freedom and political liberty. Efforts were made to remove government censorship of written texts seeing restraints as associated with Roman Catholic practices. Freedom of speech and freedom of the press were bolstered in England with John Milton's "Areopagitica" that advocated the abolishment of censorship. American judges often turned to English legal opinion which led American courts to follow English developments in law rather closely. For example, the Cockburn judgment in England after 1868 helped American judges define terms as "lewd," "lascivious," "indecent," and "obscene" (Craig, 127). Based on England's laws, the United States followed suit. The First Amendment to the Constitution in the United States, ratified in 1791, states that

> Congress shall make no law respecting an establishment of religion, or prohibiting the free exercise thereof; or abridging the freedom of speech, or of the press, or the right of the people peaceably to assemble, and to petition the Government for a redress of grievances.

This amendment protects not only written texts but also art, moral and scientific inquiry, advertising, and public discourse. While there have been numerous challenges to this amendment and varied interpretations, the force of freedom of speech and freedom of the press stands as an important American right.

With time there was a need to regulate published materials. The United States courts took a tough legal view on obscenity which even led to an attack on Walt Whitman for having a censored book in his desk. American Puritanism reached a high peak under Anthony Comstock who judged as obscene anything that favored sex. As a vice crusader, he was instrumental in passing the Comstock Act of 1873 which tightly regulated obscene publications, including contraceptive literature. For forty years Mr. Comstock conducted a "reign of terror" in the publishing world until his death in 1915, the year he represented the United States at the International Purity Congress. Comstock's work continued under John S. Sumner who effected the prosecution of those offending the Obscenity Act.

A more lenient shift in opinion occurred in the 1930s which began the reform of legal procedures involving obscenity and seizures of materials. Nevertheless, in 1933, American Customs agents seized reproductions of frescoes in the Sistine Chapel, painted at the command of Pope Paul III, and painted loincloths on Michaelangelo's figures. "Comstockery" gradually subsided and was defeated when the courts cleared James Joyce's *Ulysses* of obscenity in 1933. The efforts of the American Civil Liberties Union helped to clear many printed works and works of art from condemnation. Under Judge Bok a more modern and lenient rule replaced that of Chief Justice Cockburn. However, the ruling of Judge Bok was swept away in 1957 when the United States Supreme Court decided that obscenity was not within the area of protected speech and press under the First Amendment. The states could enact their own obscenity laws which were to exclude serious literature but act against commercial pornography.

The movie industry used restraint in its beginning stages. However, with competition for viewers from television, with rising costs, and changes in the movie-going audience, self-imposed restraints grew lax. In 1930 the first Motion Picture Code of the Motion Picture Association of America (MPAA) was published. It laid down three general principles that bound all members. The MPAA strictly enforced its code due to the pressure from the Legion of Decency founded in 1934.

Roman Catholic Church and Regulation of Media

While the film industry began some form of self-regulation, it did so only under public pressure. As early as 1927, a list of general moral principles for guidance of movie producers was written by Mr. Martin Quigley and Fr. Daniel Lord, S.J. The "Don'ts and Be Careful's" was accepted by the industry in 1930 as its "Production Code." Conscientious Catholics were concerned about the moral fiber of the motion picture industry not only because of the scandals of prominent actors and actresses but also because of the moral dangers of the motion pictures themselves (Kelly and Ford). Despite the 1930 code of the MPAA, the moral tone of movies continued to degenerate because the code lacked the force of organized public opinion. The Legion of Decency had the organizational power to pressure the movie industry by classifying its films. The group that wrote the Legion's document sought the endorsement of the American Catholic bishops and obtained from the apostolic delegate a statement of approval. At their annual meeting in 1933, the American bishops decried the immorality of films and set up an Episcopal Committee on Motion Pictures to organize a campaign. The Legion of Decency asked that Americans take a pledge to oppose the "dangers of salacious and immoral pictures and to take action against them." Objectionable movies were to be boycotted. About one hundred sixty reviewers were guided by Martin Quigley's book, *Decency in Motion Pictures,* and two publications of the National Catholic Welfare Conference in classifying films as A-I, A-II, B, C. Lists of endorsed and "condemned" films were published.

In 1936 Pope Pius XI published his encyclical, *Vigilanti cura,* which praised the Legion of Decency and its supporters. This encyclical is considered the magna carta of the Church's position on morality in motion pictures. About twenty years later in 1955, Pius XII delivered two allocutions that used the themes of the encyclical and further strengthened the campaign for morality in motion pictures. On this same subject, members of the hierarchy have issued innumerable documents. Catholic Action groups were charged with educating the public on good films. The effectiveness of the campaign caused the movie picture industry to elevate its moral standards and to revise its Production Code in 1956. At the urging of the U.S. Senate, more liberalization of the code was effected and the film industry began to explore themes such as race relations, homosexuality, adultery, narcotics, and sexuality. About the same time, England passed the Obscene Publications Act in 1959. The preamble states the act is "to provide for the protection of literature and to strengthen the law concerning pornography." This law defines as an offense punishable by fine or imprisonment, the publication of an obscene article, reading material, sound records and films, showing of pictures, sculpture, and other objects intended for viewing.

Catholic Church, Civil Legislation and Regulation of Printed Material

Two types of censorship are in effect today. One governs prepublication materials and is employed by the Roman Catholic Church in its use of the imprimatur. With the close of Vatican Council II, the Roman Catholic Church in 1966 abolished the *Index.* In 1975 the Church established a new discipline on censorship of books with the decree, *Ecclesiae pastorum,* that placed the rules for the imprimatur into Book Three of the 1983 Code of Canon Law (cc. 822–32). In the revised code a structure is provided for censorship of matter contrary to Church teaching on faith and morals. Responsibility for censorship now lies principally with the bishop of a diocese, who is to compile a list of censors who aid both him and the diocesan curia in judging the content of a proposed text. The bishop can entrust the judgment of books to his appointed censor who considers only the teachings of the Church concerning faith and morals as proposed by the ecclesiastical magisterium. The censor is to submit an opinion in writing: if favorable, permission will be granted to publish the text; if unfavorable, no permission will be granted, and reasons are communicated by the bishop to the author. The imprimatur, a stamp of approval indicating orthodox teaching, is necessary only for those books considered most official and whose need for accuracy calls for special screening, such as biblical and liturgical texts, prayer books, catechisms, school textbooks, and religious literature sold or distributed in churches.

A second type of censorship is broader and governs postpublication materials. Here Church officials publicly voice disapproval of materials considered to be morally offensive. This type of censorship can involve sanctions on the publisher who can seek protection under the law. While the government of the United States has made attempts to repress prepublication of written materials such as the *Pentagon Papers,* it does so only with great difficulty. This form of censorship is problematic, since it may concern legitimate defense of the country or individuals, diplomatic and administrative efficiency, or confidential matters. Movies, texts of music, and textbooks deemed offensive, have been the subject of censorial efforts. A more recent dilemma involved the government's financial support of certain projects in the arts, science, and education. Some charge the government is legislating taste, while others believe the removal of financial support belies the First Amendment guarantee of freedoms. Education of the public to understand the work of individuals in postpublication may help solve the problem to some extent.

Censorship exists to maintain moral and civic standards of thought, belief, and decorum. As with all law, censorship is to serve the common good. Contrary to those who believe the purpose of law is to enlarge personal freedom, the goal of law is justice which, depending upon the circumstances, may at times demand more freedom and at other times reasonable restrictions. The shifting philosophical, religious, and political systems of the age use various standards to judge which works are acceptable. While established to maintain laudable values such as freedom, extreme forms of censorship have had devastating results that have led to a contemporary aversion for censorship of any type.

Alec, Craig. *Suppressed Books: A History of the Conception of Literary Obscenity.* New York: The World Publishing Company, 1963.

Connell, Francis J., C.Ss.R. "Pope Pius XII and the Legion of Decency." *American Ecclesiastical Review* 137 (1957) 392–99.

Gardiner, H. C. "Censorship." *NCE* (1967) 3:391–92.

Johnson, Paul. *A History of Christianity.* New York: Atheneum, 1977.

Kelly, Gerald, S.J., and John C. Ford, S.J. "The Legion of Decency." *Theological Studies* 1 (1957) 387–433.

Skinner, James M. *The Cross and the Cinema: The Legion of Decency and the National Catholic Office for Motion Pictures.* Westport, Conn.: Praeger, 1993.

Walsh, Frank. *Sin and Censorship: The Catholic Church and the Motion Picture Industry.* New Haven: Yale University Press, 1996.

ELIZABETH WILLEMS, S.S.N.D.

CENTRAL-VEREIN/CATHOLIC CENTRAL UNION OF AMERICA, THE

The Catholic Central Union of America was founded in 1855 when delegates from several German Catholic benevolent societies gathered in Baltimore and established "Der Deutsche Romisch-Katolische Central Verein von Nord Amerika." The "Central-Verein," as it was known, was a national federation of parish mutual aid societies whose primary purpose was to provide support for their members in cases of poverty. Gradually, through its annual conventions, the Central-Verein became the organizational voice of German-American Catholics on a broad range of issues with a particular interest in the welfare of German Catholic immigrants. During the 1880s and 1890s, when questions regarding the establishment of German national parishes and schools divided the Church in America, the Central-Verein promoted the cohesiveness of German Catholics, although the organization itself shied away from an active role in the disputes.

With the inevitable Americanization of German-speaking immigrants and the unfortunate collapse of the Verein's "Widows and Orphans Fund" at the turn of the century, the Central Union appeared to have lost its reason for existence. However, under the leadership of Nicholas Gonner, Joseph Matt, and Frederick Kenkel, and inspired by Pope Leo XIII's encyclical, *Rerum Novarum* (1891), the Central-Verein found new purpose as a proponent of social reform. Reorganized in 1905 with a "Central Bureau" in St. Louis under the directorship of Kenkel, the Central-Verein enjoyed a decade of renewed vitality and its membership peaked in 1916 at 125,000. The new focus of the organization centered on educating American Catholics about the Church's social teaching, especially as it related to the competing evils of capitalism and socialism. In addition to sponsoring classes and providing pamphlets on social questions of the day, in 1909 the Central Bureau of the Central-Verein began publishing its own journal, the *Central Blatt and Social Justice Review.* The new strength of the Verein enabled it to establish in 1916 an affiliated organization for women, the National Catholic Women's Union.

However, American entry into the war with Germany in 1917 and the traumatic effect that World War I had on the ethnic identity of the German-American community led to a loss of interest in the Central-Verein. By 1930 its membership had fallen to 86,000 and the combined effects of the end of German immigration, the depression, and a second war with Germany guaranteed that the Central-Verein could no longer survive as a distinctively German ethnic organization. Thanks to the foresight of Kenkel and others, the Central Bureau and its journal, *The Social Justice Review,* continue to promote Catholic social reform. The offices of the Central Bureau in St. Louis also maintain an important library and archive of sources on German Catholic history in America.

See also CAHENSLY, SIMON PETER; GERMAN CATHOLICS IN AMERICA; KENKEL, FREDERICK P.

Barry, Colman J., O.S.B. *The Catholic Church and German Americans.* Milwaukee: Bruce Publishing Company, 1953.

Gleason, Philip. *The Conservative Reformers: German-American Catholics and the Social Order.* University of Notre Dame Press, 1968.

RORY T. CONLEY

CHAMPLAIN, SAMUEL DE (ca. 1567–1635)

French explorer and colonial governor. Having first sailed the Americas in the Spanish service and seen the Pacific, Champlain brought a report of what he had seen back to his native France. King Henry IV was pleased and sent him on a voyage to Canada in 1603. By means of the St. Lawrence River, explored by Jacques Cartier sixty years before, Champlain hoped to find a direct route to China. At the same time he worked indefatigably to colonize New France, evangelize the native tribes, and establish a strong government. For this last purpose he undertook the construction of a fort at Quebec in 1608.

In 1609 he ventured down the Richelieu River with his Huron allies to the lake later named for him in New York State. There near Ticonderoga they met an Iroquois war party of the Mohawk tribe. Champlain fired his arquebus and killed an Iroquois chief, earning for the French the undying enmity of the Iroquois. After the battle he sought to alleviate the torture of the Iroquois captives by the Hurons but without much success.

In the following years Champlain traveled westward, exploring Lakes Huron and Ontario, opening the way for future French exploration of the Mississippi valley. Champlain hoped to develop New France as an agricultural colony, but the quick profits to be made in the fur trade were more appealing in the short run. This prevented the rapid growth of population in New France and helped lead to its defeat in 1756 in the colonial struggle with England. In spite of this, the culture of French Catholic Quebec remains Champlain's enduring monument today. He died on December 25, 1635, in Quebec and was buried there.

Morison, Samuel Eliot. *Samuel de Champlain, Father of New France*. Boston, 1972.

JAMES HALEY

CHANATH, NICEPHOR (1855–98)

Ruthenian Catholic priest. Born in Uzhorod, in present-day Ukraine, in 1855, Nicephor Chanath was orphaned at an early age and was raised by a grandmother. After studies at Uzhorod and Presov, he received his theological degree from the Imperial Theological School in Budapest. Following the custom of the Ruthenian (Greek Catholic) Church, Chanath returned to Uzhorod and was married shortly before his priestly ordination in 1881. Unfortunately his wife died after only one year of marriage.

Chanath's early priestly assignments were at Uzhorod in the chancery of the Munkacevo Eparchy and as a teacher in the Imperial Greek Catholic Preparatory School. Because of his ability, Chanath was sent by his bishop to serve the needs of the growing Ruthenian community in the United States. He came to America in May 1891, and became the first resident pastor of St. Michael's parish in Passaic, New Jersey.

Chanath arrived during troublesome times for the Ruthenian Church in America. The few clergy were disorganized and many of the immigrant Ruthenian faithful were without spiritual assistance in their own rite. The American Catholic bishops were also at odds over the proper approach to the new immigrant groups in general. Hence the Ruthenian clergy were not always well received by the local Latin bishops, many of whom were particularly suspicious of a married clergy. Just two months before Chanath's arrival, Fr. Alexis Toth had led his Minneapolis congregation into Russian Orthodoxy and was encouraging other clergy and faithful to defect from Catholic union.

In this volatile situation, Chanath emerged as an early leader of the Ruthenian clergy who remained faithful to Rome. He was selected as one of three members of the "Priests' Committee" which sought to regularize spiritual assistance to Ruthenian congregations, stem the tide of defections to Orthodoxy, and represent the Ruthenian clergy to the Latin bishops. In February 1892 he helped organize the Greek Catholic Union, a fraternal organization for the Ruthenian faithful. At a September 1893 meeting in Olyphant, Pennsylvania, Chanath was selected as the clergy's chief spokesman and advisor, a role which appears to have been confirmed by the apostolic delegate. Under the patronage of Bishop John Lancaster Spalding of Peoria, Chanath addressed the American archbishops at their annual meeting in November 1892, pleading unsuccessfully for faculties for married and widowed clergy, and for a Ruthenian vicar general. He reiterated this plea in October 1894. At the end of that year, Chanath assumed the pastorate of St. Mary's, Scranton, Pennsylvania, replacing a young priest who had defected to Orthodoxy.

By 1897 Chanath's call for a Ruthenian superior or vicar general had won acceptance by many of the archbishops and with Rome, but Chanath was not to live to see this development. In ill health and worn out by labors and controversies, Chanath died on December 31, 1898, and was buried at Scranton.

Fogarty, Gerald P., S.J. "The American Hierarchy and Oriental Rite Catholics, 1890–1907." *Records of the American Catholic Historical Society of Philadelphia* 85 (March–June 1974) 17–28.

Procko, Bohdan P. "The Establishment of the Ruthenian Church in the United States, 1884–1907." *Pennsylvania History* XLII (April 1975) 137–75.

Simon, Constantin, S.J. "The First Years of Ruthenian Church Life in America." *Orientalia Christiana Periodica* 60 (1994) 187–232.

RAYMOND J. KUPKE

CHANCHE, JOHN MARY JOSEPH (1795–1852)

First bishop of Natchez. John Mary Joseph Chanche was born in Baltimore on October 4, 1795, the son of John Chanche and Catherine Provost. He was educated at St. Mary's College and St. Mary's Seminary in Baltimore. He was ordained to the priesthood there on June 5, 1819, and he joined the Sulpicians on July 5, 1819. He taught at St. Mary's College and St. Mary's Seminary in Baltimore (1818–35) and served as college president (1834–40). On December 15, 1840, he was appointed the first bishop of the Diocese of Natchez, Mississippi, after previously declining

John J. Chanche

nominations to the coadjutorships of Baltimore, Boston, and New York. He was consecrated in Baltimore on March 14, 1841.

Chanche arrived in Natchez on April 18, 1841. His new diocese comprised 46,000 square miles and had more than 375,000 inhabitants; in addition to Catholic communities at Natchez, Vicksburg, and the Gulf Coast, an unknown number of Catholics were scattered throughout Mississippi. The state had no Catholic church or institution and was served by two priests at Natchez and Vicksburg. Chanche immediately spelled out a pastoral vision that included Catholics, Protestants, blacks, and Native Americans, although the latter were neglected during his tenure.

The new bishop recruited personnel and solicited funds in Europe and the United States; established churches and mission stations throughout the state (eleven churches and thirty-two stations at his death); began educational and orphanage programs; and built a large, Gothic cathedral in Natchez that became a symbol of the Catholic Church's presence in Mississippi. The cathedral debt drained much of Chanche's time and energy during his later years.

Chanche died on July 22, 1852, in Frederick City, Maryland, and was buried in Baltimore. Chanche was an eloquent preacher, capable theologian, and good administrator. He imposed great privations on himself to help with the cathedral debt. He was a bishop of "extraordinary courage, zeal and foresight" (Pillar, 50).

See also MISSISSIPPI, CATHOLIC CHURCH IN.

Gerow, Richard O. *Catholicity in Mississippi*. Natchez, 1939.
Nolan, Charles E. *St. Mary's of Natchez: the History of a Southern Catholic Congregation, 1716–1988*. Natchez, 1992.
Pillar, James J. *The Catholic Church in Mississippi, 1837–1865*. New Orleans, 1964.

CHARLES E. NOLAN

CHARISMATIC RENEWAL

The Catholic Charismatic Renewal is the name given to a movement in the Catholic Church of those who have undergone the experience called Baptism of the Holy Spirit. It has been referred to as the "third stream" of the worldwide Pentecostal movement, and was, in fact, called Catholic Pentecostalism in the first years of its existence. It originated among some faculty and students of Midwestern universities in early 1967, and from this beginning has become an international movement. Within seven years there was a meeting of charismatics from thirty-four countries in Grottaferrata, Italy, and in 1975 an International Congress was held in Rome on Pentecost. And since 1972, formal dialogue sessions between Roman Catholics and Classical Pentecostals have been conducted, with the admittedly limited goal of increasing understanding between the two confessions.

The "first stream" of this movement is that of Classical Pentecostalism; nourished in the Wesleyan and Holiness strains of nineteenth-century American Protestantism, it began at the turn of the century with the appearance of glossolalia in the congregations of storefront churches in Kansas and California. Because this so-called neo-Pentecostalism aroused fear and was rejected by established denominations, participants often formed new churches.

The "second stream" developed in 1953 when the Full Gospel Businessmen's Fellowship was organized to encourage openness to the Spirit in members of mainstream Protestant churches. The experience of Catholics at Duquesne, Notre Dame, and Michigan State Universities, and the rapid spread of what were called "Catholic Pentecostal" prayer groups, is thus the "third stream" of a Christian experience which is marked by a powerful sense of the presence of God and by the frequent appearance of the extraordinary charisms of tongue-speaking, prophecy, and healing.

That the movement was so quickly accepted by the official Church is attributed to certain decisions of the Second Vatican Council: its (contested) recognition in *Lumen gentium* of the existence of charisms, its embracing of the necessity of ecumenism, and its insistence that the call to holiness is central to Church life.

Growth in the number of participants and prayer groups was rapid between 1967 and the later 1970s, when a loss of momentum and splits in some of the communities founded during the first decade weighed heavily on the movement and occasioned some reorientation. In the mid-nineties, prayer groups, covenant communities, popular and scholarly publications, a revitalized National Service Committee, and the ongoing Roman Catholic-Pentecostal Dialogue give evidence of the Renewal's impact.

Origins

The university faculty and students who first experienced the intense form of prayer called Baptism in the Spirit were already linked by friendship, educational experience, and a desire to become more active laypersons. Many had participated in the Cursillo movement and were members of Bible study and prayer groups; others were Notre Dame graduate students who had been undergraduates at Duquesne. Ralph Kiefer, a professor of theology at Duquesne, had done his graduate work at Notre Dame, and maintained contacts there; through the Cursillo he had become acquainted with Steve Clark and Ralph Martin, staff members of the Michigan State student parish, and also of the National Cursillo.

Kiefer and William Storey often met with Duquesne faculty members for prayer and discussion, and took part in liturgical, ecumenical, and civil rights activities. In August 1966, at the National Cursillo Convention, Clark and

Martin introduced them to David Wilkerson and John Sherrill's *The Cross and the Switchblade*. Kiefer and Storey had been investigating Baptism in the Spirit, and with their fellow faculty members were praying the *Veni, Creator Spiritus* for one another; the further reading of John Sherrill's *They Speak with Other Tongues* convinced them that they should meet someone who had experienced glossolalia.

In late 1966 they sought and found this in a prayer group led by a Presbyterian woman; invited to attend, they were favorably impressed with the quality of the Scripture sharing and the solid theology of Christian life. Kiefer asked to have hands laid on himself, and reported the experience of Baptism in the Holy Spirit. In mid-February, thirty people gathered for a weekend of prayer, preparing for it by reading *The Cross and the Switchblade* and meditating on the first four chapters of Acts. On Saturday night, shunning a party planned for relaxation, many found their way to the chapel; there they experienced a powerful sense of the presence and power of Christ and the Spirit. The news was quickly relayed to the friends at Notre Dame and East Lansing.

Kiefer visited Notre Dame in early March; he was heavily questioned, but subsequently, several persons prayed for and received Baptism in the Spirit. A few weeks later, a weekend of prayer attracted an overflow crowd from Notre Dame, St. Mary's, and Michigan State. Some of the publicity which resulted was bizarre, and the Friday night meetings thereafter were crowded with the sincere and the curious. In the smaller, more personal meetings which were then arranged, a notable transformation and deepening of faith was clearly evident among many who attended.

Because of the widespread publicity, some of the earliest participants prepared informational panels for Notre Dame's several thousand summer school students, and organized small prayer sessions for them. From members of these groups they learned that there were others who had had a private experience of extraordinary prayer, but there was no other case of a group experience. In 1969 early leaders Kevin and Dorothy Ranaghan could write that "the Holy Spirit is being poured out on hundreds of people with little or no human connection or organized effort."

In November 1968 the NCCB recommended that its Committee on Doctrine make a formal study of what was then called the "Pentecostal Movement." Its November 1969 report gave cautious approval to the movement, declaring it to be theologically sound, noting that it had fostered the spiritual life, attracted its members to the reading of Scripture, and left them with a deeper understanding of their faith. The report was cautious, however, and contained references to an "emotional, demonstrative style of prayer," and unfortunate remarks about the "mistakes" of Classical Pentecostalism. A 1975 report by the Committee on Pastoral Research and Practices noted the strengths and fruits of the movement, but added the need for discernment to determine the authenticity of the gifts that accompanied it and expressed hesitations about its ecumenical dimensions. A 1984 statement of the Bishops' Liaison Committee confirmed the earlier reports.

Leadership and Organization

Most of those who first experienced the extraordinary gifts of the Spirit had already worked toward renewal in the Church; Steve Clark, converted at Yale in 1960, was distressed at his fellow Catholics' individualistic approach to their faith. As graduate students in philosophy, he and Ralph Martin discovered the Cursillo movement, and brought it to Notre Dame in 1963. Later, as National Cursillo Staff members, they proposed to implement its ideal of community at Michigan State through a network of small and large groupings which were aimed at creating an environment where Christians could flourish. In 1969, after the initial surge of charismatic experience, they began what would become the Word of God covenant community at Ann Arbor. A similar community, the People of Praise, was founded in South Bend by Kevin Ranaghan and Paul DeCelles; an earlier effort there, True House, was disbanded in 1974.

Peter Hocken divides the history of the Charismatic Renewal into three periods, according to the character of the leadership. From 1967–76, it was formed by the communities in Ann Arbor and South Bend. 1976–81 was a period during which there were severe criticisms of this original leadership and the community model which had developed; rival publications were begun. The period from 1981 to the present has been marked by a search for a vision to replace that of the beginnings; in 1986 evangelization became a central focus, and most recently, an effort to bring the renewal to the heart of the Church.

The leadership structures that developed were influenced by two diverging forces: (1) the covenant communities that grew up in South Bend and Ann Arbor, (where Martin and Clark joined the Catholic chaplaincy in 1969); and (2) the gradual aligning of the movement more deeply with ecclesial structures through parish-based prayer groups, the appointment of diocesan liaisons, and the establishment of diocesan renewal offices. The "diocesanization" of the renewal movement was in part a reaction to the heavy ecumenical membership in some covenant communities; there is some evidence that central Catholic beliefs and sacramental life were downplayed in the effort to be inclusive. In addition, the communities at South Bend and Ann Arbor, which were especially ecumenical, developed a discipline of headship which lacked the wisdom available in sacramental confession and the tradition of spiritual direction; some of the groups' later strains seem related to these facts.

Covenant communities, which have grown out of prayer group members' desire for a more committed community life, are distinctive of United States charismatic renewal; elsewhere, communities are modeled on religious life. While ostensibly stemming from early prophecies about the Spirit's call for a community, the influence of Clark and Martin, who were already convinced of the force of communities as a radical strategy for transforming environments, cannot be discounted. Community members aim to live an authentic Christian life in the world in a shared lifestyle, seeing themselves as a sign to Church and world. Some hold goods in common, but most retain private ownership and tithe. The status granted to such associations of the faithful by the new Code of Canon Law provides a basis for their belonging to the mainstream of life in the Church.

A 1993 survey of existing covenant communities by Theophane Rush received responses from twenty-three of the possibly forty known groups; of these, four were formed in the 1960s, most between 1970 and 1979, and none after 1984. In 1975 the Ann Arbor and South Bend communities formed an association of communities, which disbanded in 1981. In 1991 debate over "headship"—the exercise of authority and the freedom of members—as well as a rethinking of the concept of community vis-à-vis the meaning of covenant, caused splits in the two communities, and their numbers are somewhat diminished. Similar criticisms of the activities of the Servants of Christ the King on the campus of Steubenville University were made by the local bishop. Rush concluded, however, that despite serious difficulties in some groups, the overall picture is one of "stability and fidelity to the grace and call of Baptism in the Spirit."

From the earliest years, the Word of God and People of Praise communities provided significant organization and resources for the movement. A communications center, begun in a garage by volunteers in 1969 to prepare teaching materials, had an annual business of one million dollars in 1975, when it became the Charismatic Renewal Service. Ann Arbor's *Pastoral Newsletter,* begun in 1972 as an aid to prayer groups, grew to a circulation of 70,000 as *New Covenant* by the late 1970s. A National Service Committee, composed largely of members of these two communities, developed educational material and sponsored conferences at Notre Dame which grew to an attendance of 30,000 by 1974, after which regional conferences became the norm. Reorganized in 1985, it moved to offices outside Washington, D.C.

Theology

When the term "charismatic" arose at Vatican Council II in the preparation of *Lumen gentium,* it had so lapsed from theological currency, that the *Dictionnaire de Théologie Catholique* did not have an entry for it; only the persua-

sive arguments of Cardinal Suenens allowed it to remain in the text. While the earliest reports from Duquesne and Notre Dame include instances of the extraordinary charisms of glossolalia, healing and prophecy, there are equally frequent descriptions of an overpowering sense of the presence of God which left in its wake a lively faith. Ralph Kiefer once commented that "the world of the supernatural suddenly became as real as the natural." An exact characterization of the experience which participants undergo cannot be made: not all persons receive the gift of tongues; not all have an immediately powerful experience, but rather undergo a slow transformation. Francis Sullivan, S.J., notes that what people experience are the changes that take place in their lives; naming this as Baptism in the Spirit is a theological interpretation of the experience.

Ecumenical Impact

Although the "Catholic Pentecostals" of the early days of the renewal received great assistance and empathy from local Pentecostals and members of the Full Gospel Businessmen's Fellowship, the eventual choice of "charismatic renewal" to designate the movement reflects the fact that there are clear differences in the interpretation given by the Catholic Church to these experiences, and that deep conflicts exist between Catholicism and Classical Pentecostals. Progress in understanding, however slow, is being made. Following a preliminary dialogue in 1970–71, arising from the activities of Jan Cardinal Willebrands and the Classical Pentecostal leader David DuPlessis, there has been a formal Roman Catholic-Classical Pentecostal Dialogue. The goal of the meetings is simply that of removing misunderstanding; long-standing suspicion on the part of Pentecostals, who have suffered often violent persecution in Catholic countries, makes such a limitation necessary. Such memories mean, for some Pentecostal participants, that even being associated with the dialogue can cause loss of appointments in their own communion. The sessions have twice been held in the United States; Kilian McDonnell, O.S.B., of St. John's Abbey, Collegeville, Minnesota, who was early invited to participate in a sociological research project on Pentecostal phenomena, and who facilitated the introduction of David DuPlessis into Catholic circles, has produced many writings and documents of the movement and was cochair of the meetings.

Evaluation

Before Vatican II, it was not conceivable that a renewal movement which originated outside the Catholic Church would have been so readily accorded approval; the fact that the original participants were able to recognize the importance of the role of theology in their interpretation of events contributed substantially to its acceptance. A tension persists as to whether the movement is that of one spirituality competing among many, or whether it should be considered as the core of ecclesial renewal. Hocken notes that all churches face the question of how it is related to other currents of renewal; only Catholics, however, continue to describe themselves as "charismatics."

The late 1980s saw a consolidation and development of the activities in the National Service Committee which was incorporated separately from community structures in 1975. It moved to the Washington, D.C., area in 1990, and its activities have expanded to include education, leadership training, a focus on youth, ethnic outreach, conferences and a "Heart of the Church" project which has sponsored two major consultations on the theological foundations of the charismatic renewal movement. In addition, it maintains contact with the leadership of other movements, including Cursillo, Focolare, and Marriage Encounter, as well as Evangelization 2,000, U.S. Bishops' offices and the Pontifical Council for the Laity in Rome.

Among the reevaluations following upon declining numbers and difficulties within covenant communities is the suggestion that the "postcharismatic" person may be one of the Renewal's greatest gifts to the Church, and that the movement itself might be considered a formation program which highlights the operation of the charisms and gives to those who participate a transforming experience of the presence of God and opens them to further charisms, especially those of service.

See also AMERICAN CATHOLIC SPIRITUALITY.

Hocken, Peter. "The Charismatic Movement in the U.S." *Pneuma* 16 (2) (1994) 191–214.

McDonnell, Kilian, O.S.B., ed. *Presence, Power, Praise.* 3 vols. Collegeville, Minn.: The Liturgical Press, 1980.

O'Connor, E. D. *The Pentecostal Movement in the Catholic Church.* Notre Dame, 1971.

Ranaghan, K., and D. *Catholic Pentecostals.* New York, 1969.

Rush, Theophane. "Covenant Communities in the U.S." *Pneuma* 16 (2) (1994) 233–46.

Sullivan, F. A. "Catholic Charismatic Renewal." *The Dictionary of Charismatic and Pentecostal Movements,* eds. S. M. Burgess and G. B. McGee. Grand Rapids, 1988.

MARY BARABARA AGNEW, C.PP.S.

CHARLOT, CHIEF (ca. 1831–1910)

Native American Kalispel chief (also known as Stem-hak-kah, Little-Claw-of-the-Grizzly-Bear). Charlot was born in the Bitterroot country of northern Idaho. His father, Chief Victor, named him after a French trader.

Charlot became chief in 1870. Two years later he confronted United States' President Ulysses S. Grant's order, prompted by settlers' pressures, to move his tribe to the Jocko or Flathead Reservation in western Montana. When Charlot refused, citing the provisions of the 1855 Hell Gate Treaty, Special Commissioner James A. Garfield obtained other tribal agreements and replaced Charlot with subchief Arlee (Ale). Subsequently Arlee and about 80 followers moved to the Flathead Reservation while some 350 remained with Charlot.

Known for his staunch friendship with the whites, Charlot grew disillusioned and angry. In sympathy, Peter Ronan, Flathead Indian Agent, took Charlot and five headmen to a conference in Washington, D.C., to effect a compromise but Charlot remained intractable.

During the late 1880s settlers' continuing influx into the Bitterroot made the tribal hunting livelihood almost impossible, and Charlot's band became increasingly more destitute. Finally in 1889 the government sent General (Ret.) Henry B. Carrington to Stevensville to confer with Charlot and ultimately make final arrangements for the relocation of Charlot's group.

In 1891 Charlot and his remaining two hundred followers moved to the Flathead Reservation. He lived the next nineteen years on the reservation, but he continued to be bitter toward a government which had taken his country and imposed an alien life upon his people.

See also NATIVE AMERICANS AND THE CATHOLIC CHURCH.

Fahey, John. *The Flathead Indians.* Norman: University of Oklahoma Press, 1974.

Harrison, Michael. "Chief Charlot's Battle with Bureaucracy." *Montana, the Magazine of Western History* 10 (October 1960) 27–33.

Ronan, Peter. *Historical Sketch of the Flathead Indian Nation from the Year 1813 to 1890.* Helena, Mont.: Journal Publishing Company, 1890; repr. 1965.

JOAN BISHOP

CHAVEZ, CESAR (1927–93)

Founder of the United Farmworkers (UFW), labor organizer, human rights leader; the charismatic leader who successfully organized the nation's migrant farmworkers, a group previously considered unorganizable by organized labor.

Chavez was born on March 31, 1927, near Yuma, Arizona, to Juana Estrada and Librado Chavez, the second of five children. The Chavez family worked their small farm until 1939, when unpaid taxes forced them off their land and into the migrant labor force that traveled through Arizona and California harvesting crops. In 1944, Cesar temporarily escaped the migrant life by joining the U.S. Navy. In 1946 he returned to Delano, California, where he married a Delano native, Helen Fabela, in 1948; together they raised a family of eight children. In 1952 they settled in San Jose in the Mexican barrio Sal Si Puedes (Get Out if You Can), where Cesar had obtained a job in a lumberyard.

Cesar Chavez

Early Union Activities

In 1952 Cesar met two men who fundamentally altered the course of his life—the Rev. Donald McDonnell and Fred Ross. McDonnell, a Roman Catholic priest, was working among migrant farmworkers in the San Jose area when he encountered the young Chavez. McDonnell introduced and immersed Chavez in the social teachings of the Catholic Church, particularly the great papal encyclicals that referred to the right of labor to organize. Fred Ross was a community organizer working for Saul Alinsky's Chicago based Industrial Areas Foundation, who was attempting to establish the Community Service Organization (CSO) among the Spanish-speaking in California. Ross provided the practical methodology for applying McDonnell's social philosophy. The CSO sought to identify and promote the community's natural leaders. The first night Ross met Chavez at an informal house meeting, he wrote in his diary, "I think I've found the guy I'm looking for" (Levy, 102). The house meeting was a key organizing technique used by the CSO and one that Chavez effectively used in the early days of organizing the UFW.

Chavez joined Ross and the CSO, working on voter registration and citizenship drives. In 1958 he became executive director of the CSO in California. That same year he had a taste of labor organizing as the CSO became involved in the strike of the largely Mexican United Packinghouse Workers in Oxnard, California. In 1962, at the annual CSO state convention, Chavez attempted to move the CSO into organizing California's migrant farmworkers into a union. When the CSO declined, asserting that it was a civil rights organization, not a labor union, Chavez broke from the CSO, and with the assistance of Dolores Huerta, set about establishing the National Farmworkers Association (NFWA).

Between 1962 and 1965, Chavez utilized the techniques he had learned from the CSO to enroll members into his union, but his greatest asset was his intense dedication, untiring work ethic, and his personal charisma. The union grew slowly, claiming 1,200 members by 1965. In that year, the Agricultural Workers Organizing Committee (AWOC), an AFL-CIO affiliate made up largely of Filipino workers and led by Larry Itliong, called a strike against the table grape growers in Delano. Chavez was not certain his union was strong enough to endure a major strike; nonetheless, on September 16 (a major Mexican holiday), 1965, the NFWA voted to join the AWOC-initiated strike. The strike was to last five years, and became the biggest agricultural strike in California history.

United Farmworkers Association

Following the vote to strike, the NFWA enjoyed a burst of popularity enrolling an additional 2,700 members. Within a year the NFWA and AWOC had merged to form the United Farmworkers Organizing Committee (UFWOC), officially chartered by the AFL-CIO. The name was later changed to the UFWA.

During the five-year strike, Chavez became a major national figure, and his central philosophy and strategy were defined, tested, and refined. At the heart of Chavez's movement, popularly known as "La Causa" (The Cause), was a firm commitment to nonviolence. Chavez drew on the teachings of Jesus, St. Francis of Assisi, Gandhi, the example of Martin Luther King, Jr., and the counsels of his mother to define his philosophy of nonviolence. He believed that the greatest strength the farmworkers had was the inherent justice of their cause. Violence only undermined the validity of the farmworkers' claim; nonviolence would most effectively bring the public on to the side of the farmworkers and result in victory. Also central to Chavez's philosophy was his belief in the essential human dignity of each farmworker; thus, his movement sought not only improved working conditions but a fundamental affirmation of the worker's dignity. The method of protest had to be in accord with that dignity.

Methods and Techniques

Chavez's and the UFW's commitment to nonviolence was repeatedly put to the test. In 1967 several growers invited the Teamsters in to organize their workers, thereby undermining Chavez's efforts. This tactic was repeated in 1970, and again in 1973. The Teamsters were not averse to employing violence. By 1968 many in the UFW, frustrated by the length of the strike, and beset by the aggressive harassment from California agribusiness and the Teamsters, began to question the union's nonviolence. In response, Chavez employed another Gandhian technique to restore discipline and morale within the movement—the fast. The fast was carried out in an overtly religious manner with Chavez attending Mass daily. His fast succeeded in recommitting the movement to nonviolence. The fast became a standard discipline Chavez used over the next three decades.

Chavez also learned from the black civil rights movement. He made use of the protest march to publicize the plight of the farmworker, but as in many things he gave the march a religious twist referring to it as a "peregrina" (pilgrimage), a term which spoke to his largely Catholic following, and to the condition of their lives. The first major march occurred in the first year of the strike; beginning in March 1966 the farmworkers marched more than three hundred miles from Delano to Sacramento, the state capital, carrying UFW banners, the U.S. flag, and a banner with the image of Our Lady of Guadalupe on it. (Chavez made use of explicitly Mexican symbols—the Aztec eagle and Our Lady of Guadalupe—to bolster the movement, a practice that caused occasional protest from the Filipino workers.) During the march to Sacramento, one of the major growers, Schenley Industries, signed a contract with the UFW in April 1966.

The most effective weapon used by Chavez and the UFW was the economic boycott. In 1968, as the strike dragged on, Chavez called for a boycott of table grapes to pressure the growers into negotiating. The response of Church and community groups in support of the Union was impressive, and succeeded in placing significant pressure on the growers. In 1969 supermarkets that carried nonunion grapes were boycotted and picketed. The pressure exerted by the boycott resulted in a series of contracts being signed with the UFW, giving the UFW contracts for 85 percent of the table grapes market.

Further Battles

Chavez had no time to revel in his success. The same year, new contracts with lettuce growers were being negotiated in the Salinas Valley. Again the Teamsters were invited in. As one grower acknowledged, "The Teamsters are a trade union; Chavez's union is a civil rights movement;" as such the growers preferred the Teamsters. Chavez responded by initiating a lettuce boycott.

In 1972 valuable time and energy, which should have been used in organizing the basic structures of the UFW, were diverted into a bruising political campaign. The California Farm Bureau successfully placed an initiative on the California ballot, Proposition 22, that threatened to outlaw the use of the economic boycott, limit union voting to nonseasonal workers, and included several other stipulations designed to shackle the UFW's efforts. Again, showing extraordinary political skill, Chavez mobilized the electorate to defeat the proposition by a whopping 58 percent to 42 percent margin.

The following year, 1973, the table grapes' contracts came up for renewal in the San Joaquin Valley, and again the Teamsters were invited in. Despite what came to be

known as the Teamster "reign of terror," in which two workers were killed, Chavez and the UFW remained true to the principles of nonviolence. Again, effectively using the economic boycott, Chavez emerged victorious.

In 1975, with the assistance of California governor, Edmund G. "Jerry" Brown, Jr., Chavez and the UFW scored a significant legislative victory with the passage of the Agricultural Labor Relations Act, bringing to an end a decade of strife in California agriculture. The act made significant guarantees to the UFW—the right to collective bargaining for farmworkers, the right to chose a union by secret ballots, the right to boycott, and the right of seasonal migrant laborers to vote in union elections. The act also set up the Agricultural Labor Relations Board to oversee union elections, and to oversee the implementation of the ALRA. The first chair of the board was Bishop Roger Mahoney, future cardinal archbishop of Los Angeles. In 1977 the UFW and the Teamsters signed a jurisdictional agreement, bringing to an end their competition.

Later Years

By 1978 the UFW's membership rolls peaked at 100,000. After achieving its major goals, the UFW set about establishing themselves as a working trade union. For a variety of reasons, membership dropped to 12,000 by 1984. Some blamed the union's emphasis on the charismatic leadership of Chavez; without a cause, interest in the movement waned. Others blamed an increasingly hostile ALRB appointed by Governor George Deukmejian. In 1984 Chavez launched a new boycott of grapes to protest the dangerous pesticides to which farmworkers were being exposed. Health issues had always been a major focus of Chavez. The new boycott failed to catch the public's imagination and so had little effect. The union continued to plod on until Cesar's untimely death in Yuma, Arizona, on April 23, 1993.

The greatest achievement of Chavez's life was his successful organization of the nation's migrant labor force, a group previously thought to be unorganizable. But his importance transcends that of a mere labor organizer, no matter how successful. Cesar Chavez was a deeply spiritual man, whose profound conviction of the absolute worth and dignity of each individual, his firm commitment to the philosophy and discipline of nonviolence, and his untiring work on behalf of the dispossessed made him a hero and inspiration to a generation of Americans, and a symbol of what America should be.

See also LABOR MOVEMENT AND AMERICAN CATHOLICS, THE.

Daniel, Cletus. "Cesar Chavez and the Unionization of California's Farmworkers." *Labor Leaders in America,* eds. M. Dubrofsky and W. Van Tine. Urbana: University of Illinois Press, 1987.

Griswold del Castillo, Richard, and Richard Garcia. *Cesar Chavez: A Life of Struggle and Sacrifice.* Norman: University of Oklahoma Press, 1995.

Levy, Jacques. *Cesar Chavez: Autobiography of La Causa.* New York: Norton, 1975.

London, Joan, and Henry Anderson. *So Shall Ye Reap: The Story of Cesar Chavez and the Farmworker Movement.* New York: Thomas Crowell, 1970.

Taylor, Ronald. *Chavez and the Farm Workers.* Boston: Beacon Press, 1975.

JEFFREY M. BURNS

CHAVEZ, DENNIS (DIONISIO) (1888–1962)

U.S. Senator. Dennis Chavez was born on April 8, 1888, in Los Chavez, New Mexico, to Paz Sanchez and David Chavez. Although he had only an eighth-grade education, he was an assistant engineer in the Albuquerque engineering department (where his family had moved when he was still a child) from 1905–15. He married Imelda Espinosa in 1911. Chavez became involved in the 1916 reelection campaign of Senator Andribus A. Jones as an interpreter. Following Jones's victory, Chavez served as an U.S. Senate clerk. While in Washington, he petitioned to take a special examination and was admitted to Georgetown University Law School, from which he received his L.L.B. in 1920. Chavez returned to Albuquerque after his graduation and began a long career in New Mexico politics, first as a state senator from 1923–24, then as a U.S. Representative from 1930–36. Although Chavez was defeated for the U.S. Senate by Bronson Cutting in 1934, he was appointed to serve out the remainder of Cutting's term following Cutting's death in 1935. Chavez then served as U.S. Senator from New Mexico from 1936–62. His career interests included New Deal legislation, Latin American affairs, and Native American and Puerto Rican issues. He died in Washington, D.C., on November 18, 1962. In 1976 the new federal building in Albuquerque was designated the Senator Dennis Chavez Federal Center. The centennial of his birth was celebrated on April 8, 1988, and was designated as "Dennis Chavez Day" by a joint resolution of Congress.

Lujan, Joe Roy. "Dennis Chavez and the Roosevelt Era, 1933–1945." Ph.D. dissertation, University of New Mexico, 1987.

Vigil, Maruillo, and Roy Lujan. "Parallels in the Career of Two Hispanic U.S. Senators." *Journal of Ethnic Studies* 13 (4) (1986) 1–20.

Welsh, Michael. "The United States Corps of Engineers in the Middle Rio Grande Valley, 1935–1955." *New Mexico Historical Review* 60 (3) (1985) 295–316.

COLLEEN J. MATAN

CHEVERUS, JEAN-LOUIS (1768–1836)

Missionary, archbishop, cardinal. Jean-Louis-Anne-Madeleine Lefebvre de Cheverus was born January 28,

Jean Cheverus

1768, in the parish of Notre Dame de Mayenne, the eldest of six children born to Jean-Vincent-Marie Lefebvre de Cheverus and Anne-Charlotte Lemarchand de Noyers. After graduating from the College of Louis-le-Grand in Paris, Jean went on to the seminary conducted by the Fathers of the Oratory, Saint Magloire, and on December 18, 1790, was ordained to the priesthood. Refusing to take an oath to uphold the Civil Constitution of the Clergy, Cheverus was forced to leave his native land in 1792. After four years in England, he accepted an invitation to go to America.

On October 3, 1796, Fr. Jean Cheverus arrived in Boston and set to work helping Fr. François Matignon minister to a small community of French and Irish immigrants, as well as to Native Americans in northern Maine. The cooperative spirit of the two priests did much to reduce the strong anti-Catholic prejudices of the Puritan town. Although Cheverus was asked to return to France in 1801, he chose to continue his work in Boston.

Seeking larger quarters for their expanding congregation, the priests were aided by the generosity of many non-Catholics and on September 29, 1803, they dedicated the new Church of the Holy Cross on Franklin Street. Five years later, on April 8, 1808, when Pope Pius VII created four new dioceses in the United States, Jean Cheverus was named first bishop of Boston. Although he was saddened by the death of Fr. Matignon in 1818, Cheverus tended to his parishioners and often traveled to Maine to serve his Native American converts. Perhaps his greatest accomplishment was to earn the respect of prominent Bostonians and establish a strong Church in a region where Catholics once suffered persecution.

Early in 1823, Cheverus agreed to return to France to become bishop of Montauban. In 1826 King Charles X named him to succeed the archbishop of Bordeaux, and in April 1836 Pope Gregory XVI named Cheverus to the College of Cardinals. On July 19, 1836, at the age of sixty-eight, Jean Lefebvre de Cheverus died and was mourned throughout France. He was buried with great ceremony in Bordeaux, in the nave of Saint-André.

Cauwenbergh, E. van. "Jean-Louis Lefebvre de Cheverus." *Dictionnaire d'Histoire et de Géographie ecclésiastiques*. Paris, 1953, 12:650.

Hamon, Andre J. M. *The Life of Cardinal Cheverus*. Trans. Robert M. Walsh. Philadelphia, 1839.

Lord, Robert H. "Jean Lefebvre de Cheverus, First Catholic Bishop of Boston." *Proceedings of the Massachusetts Historical Society* 65 (1933) 64–78.

Melville, Annabelle M. *Jean Lefebvre de Cheverus 1768–1836*. Milwaukee, 1958.

THOMAS H. O'CONNOR

CHINIQUY, CHARLES (1809–99)

Ex-priest and anti-Catholic speaker. Chiniquy was born on July 30, 1809, at Kamouraska, Lower Canada (Quebec), and ordained on September 21, 1839, in Quebec City.

A powerful orator, widely hailed as the Canadian "Apostle of Temperance," Chiniquy's personal behavior forced his departure from the Quebec archdiocese in 1846, from the Oblate novitiate at Longueuil in 1847, and from the Diocese of Montreal in 1851, the last for improper behavior toward women. Repeating his indiscretions in the Diocese of Chicago, Chiniquy was suspended and later excommunicated by Bishop Anthony O'Regan for continuing to administer the sacraments.

Chiniquy and about one thousand of his followers at St. Anne, Illinois, affiliated in 1859 with the Presbyterian Synod of Chicago. This relationship ended in 1862 with Chiniquy's being defrocked for conduct unbecoming a minister. A year later Chiniquy and his congregation affiliated with the Presbyterian Synod of Canada.

Chiniquy would become known as an anti-Catholic polemicist, as well as the first systematic proponent of Jesuit and papal complicity in the Lincoln assassination. Lincoln had in fact defended Chiniquy in an 1856 libel trial and was alleged to have spoken to him of a papist plot in Washington in August of 1861. This coincided with his reputed offer to make Chiniquy secretary to the U.S. legation to France, and his own antipapal spy. Further meetings between Chiniquy and Lincoln were alleged to have taken place in Washington in early June of 1862, and on June 8, 1864.

Lincoln's presidential papers mention no such meetings. Furthermore, his personal secretary, John Hay, never noted Chiniquy's presence in Washington. While Chiniquy's allegations received a wide circulation in their day, these

were subsequently discredited. He died on January 16, 1899, in Montreal, Quebec.

Chiniquy, Charles. *Fifty Years in the Church of Rome*. Toronto: Toronto Willard Tract Depository, 1888.

Hanchett, William. *The Lincoln Murder Conspiracies*. Urbana: University of Illinois Press, 1986.

Trudel, Marcel. *Chiniquy*. Montreal: Editions du Bien Public. 2nd ed. Trois Rivières, 1955.

ALBERT H. LEDOUX

CHIROUSE, EUGENE CASIMIR (1821–92)

The Apostle of Puget Sound. Chirouse was born in France, May 8, 1821, and joined the Order of the Oblates of Mary Immaculate. He left Le Havre harbor in February of 1847, bound for America. Wild storms swept the *Zuric*, tossing and beating the ship. The captain said: "For thirty years I have sailed the Atlantic and never have I seen the like!" After two months at sea, they finally reached New York. He went on to St. Louis and prepared for the long journey over the Oregon Trail, reaching Fort Walla Walla on October 4, 1847. He was ordained January 2, 1848.

His first assignment was at St. Rose Mission among the Yakima natives. In March 1852 he reopened St. Anne Mission near Umatilla, caring for the Cayuse people. Due to war conditions, on December 8, 1856, he went to Priest Point (Olympia) on Puget Sound. In Tulalip he built a log building to serve as residence, church, and school. He ministered at Swinomish, Lummi, Mukleshoot, Fort Madison, and to numerous indigenous peoples near the reservations. With help of the government, he built a school where he housed, clothed, and fed the students. Along with his teaching and his active ministry, he served as the agent of the Indian Bureau, preserving peace. He spent thirty-one fruitful years on Puget Sound. He then went to New Westminister, British Columbia, in 1878, where he spent fourteen years in active ministry working among the indigenous peoples of Fraser River valley.

In January 1892 he suffered a stroke and passed away May 28, 1892. He was small in physical stature but a giant of spirituality and he was loved by both the natives and the whites.

Schoenberg, Wilfred P., S.J. *A History of the Catholic Church in the Pacific Northwest, 1743–1983*. Washington, D.C.: The Pastoral Press, 1987.

EDWARD J. KOWRACH

CHRISTIAN BROTHERS, CONGREGATION OF (C.F.C.)

The Congregation of Christian Brothers (C.F.C.) is a teaching congregation founded in 1802 by Edmund Rice, a wealthy merchant of Waterford, Ireland. Recognizing the need to educate the young of his native Ireland, where the British penal laws and other restrictions had reduced the Catholic majority to destitution and ignorance, Rice disposed of his successful business and devoted his life to raising the living standard of his fellow Irish Catholics. He was soon joined in this mission by others, the work prospered, and schools were opened in other Irish towns. In 1808, with six companions, Rice pronounced religious vows and took the name of Br. Ignatius. In 1822 Br. Rice and his companions received a papal brief placing the congregation under the papacy. The brothers then held their first general chapter and elected Br. Rice the first superior general. In 1844, at the age of eighty-two, Br. Ignatius Rice died at the congregation's first school, Mt. Sion, in Waterford City, where his remains rest in a special chapel.

In 1993, after studying the sanctity and greatness of Br. Rice's life and work, the Congregation of Saints formally recommended to Pope John Paul II that he be declared Venerable. On April 6, 1995, at a special ceremony in the Vatican, the Holy Father gave his official approval to a miracle attributed to the intercession of Venerable Brother Edmund Ignatius Rice. This decision marked the final stage to the declaration of beatification which was held in St. Peter's Basilica, Rome, in 1996. The feastday of Blessed Edmund Ignatius Rice is May 5.

The congregation spread to distant areas as needs arose to educate the young of various dioceses. In 1995 there were four provinces in Australia, two in the United States, two in Ireland, one each in Canada, England, India, South Africa and New Zealand, and regional districts in Papua New Guinea, Zambia, and West Africa. In addition, there were many mission schools throughout the globe, all attesting to the worldwide missionary vision presented and cultivated by Br. Edmund Ignatius Rice in the early nineteenth century.

Christian Brothers in America

The Christian Brothers came to North America in 1876 with the opening of a school in St. John's, Newfoundland. In 1906, at the invitation of Msgr. James W. Power, pastor of All Saints Church, New York City, the congregation opened a primary school in that parish in the Harlem section of the borough of Manhattan. In 1909, with the establishment of All Hallows Institute in New York City, the brothers began a widespread system of secondary schools. With these establishments as the cornerstone, the schools in Newfoundland and the United States were combined in 1916 to become the North American province. The first provincial superior of the American province was Br. Patrick J. Ryan, who was also one of the four brothers who initially came to the United States in 1906 to establish All Saints Parish School.

In 1940 the opening of Iona College in the city of New Rochelle, a community only a short distance north of New York City, marked the congregation's entrance into the area of American Catholic higher education. During World War II the Christian Brothers at Iona College struggled with a dangerously declining student body population. With the end of the war, however, Iona burgeoned and at the close of the twentieth century Iona College was nationally known and respected with a student population of approximately 7,500 men and women in both undergraduate and graduate degree programs.

The Christian Brothers in North America have also been most willing to commit their resources of manpower and finances to help the poor of other continents. Over the years, North American Brothers have been sent to Africa, Latin America, and the West Indies. In 1966, under the leadership of Br. Arthur A. Loftus, the first American-born superior general of the congregation, the American province opened its first school in Peru in the city of Arequipa. This first mission school has resulted in the establishment of a number of schools in that nation with an increasing number of Peruvian vocations. This decision to staff missionary schools in distant lands among peoples of different cultures reflects the continuation of the compassionate concern of Br. Ignatius Rice for the poor of all lands.

Eventually, the American province in the United States and Canada extended from the Atlantic to the Pacific Oceans, including an establishment in the state of Hawaii. In order to administer such a large area two provinces, East and West, were established in 1966 and in 1967 a separate province was created for Canada.

In 1995 the two provinces had 343 brothers who were stationed in 16 dioceses throughout the U.S. as well as in Peru and West Africa. In the U.S. in 1995 the brothers operated Iona College, 14 high schools, and 4 grade schools.

See also MEN, RELIGIOUS ORDERS AND CONGREGATIONS.

HARRY DUNKAK, C.F.C.

CHRISTIAN BROTHERS UNIVERSITY

Christian Brothers University, Memphis, Tennessee, first opened its doors to twenty-six students in November 1871 as Christian Brothers College. Throughout its history, the college, now the university, and the secondary school bearing the same name but located on a separate property since 1965, have been under the sponsorship of the De La Salle Christian Brothers. From its foundation until 1915, Christian Brothers College operated as both a high school and a college. World War I forced the suspension of college work, which was not resumed until 1940 with the opening of a junior college division. World War II forced the temporary closing of the junior college division from 1943 until 1946. The present four-year college program was inaugurated in 1953; university status was granted in 1991.

Christian Brothers University offers professionally oriented undergraduate degree programs in four schools:

Arts, Sciences, Engineering, and Business. In addition, the university offers two graduate degrees: a Master's in Business Administration (MBA) in a regular and executive or accelerated format and a Master's in Engineering Management (MEM). It enrolls about 1,700 students annually.

See also CATHOLIC UNIVERSITIES AND COLLEGES.

Battersby, W. J., F.S.C. *The Christian Brothers in Memphis, A Chronicle of One Hundred Years 1871–1971.* Memphis, Tenn: Christian Brothers College, 1971.
____. *Brother Maurelian.* Winona, Minn.: St. Mary's College Press, 1968.

MICHAEL J. McGINNISS, F.S.C.

CHRISTIAN FAMILY MOVEMENT (CFM)

A lay, married couples' social action movement which uses Canon Joseph Cardijn's "observe-judge-act" formula for Catholic Action. CFM attempts to transform the environment in which families find themselves and to make family life easier. It is not enough to focus on internal family relationships; families are affected and dependent upon societal institutions. Thus, if better family life is to be created, these institutions must be changed. The basic unit of CFM is the section, which consists of six couples, and when possible, a chaplain. Section members meet regularly to "observe" their environment, "judge" whether or not what they observed is in accordance with the gospel message of Jesus, and then "act" to lessen the distance between reality and the gospel ideal. Each meeting is divided into a Gospel inquiry (fifteen minutes), in which the word of God is studied; a Liturgy inquiry (fifteen minutes), in which the Mass is studied; and finally a Social inquiry (forty-five minutes), in which the Cardijn formula is employed. Special emphasis is placed on action; groups are not to be mere study clubs. Like other Cardijn-inspired groups, CFM is a "like-to-like" apostolate, which in CFM's case means family ministers to family.

Origins

CFM grew out of a number of Catholic Action groups operating in the mid-1940s in Chicago, South Bend, New York, and Wisconsin. Particularly important in the formation of CFM were, in Chicago, Pat and Patty Crowley, and their mentor and major CFM theorist, Msgr. Reynold Hillenbrand, and in South Bend, Indiana, Bernie and Helene Bauer and their guide, Fr. Louis Putz, C.S.C. A key year in CFM's emergence as a national organization was 1949. In June, fifty-nine lay delegates and twelve chaplains from eleven cities met at Childerly Retreat House in Wheeling, Illinois, just outside of Chicago, to forge a national organization. A national coordinating committee was created, with the Crowleys selected as the committee's chair; the following year, at the second national gathering at St. Procopius Abbey in Lisle, Illinois, the Crowleys were selected as the executive secretary couple, a position they held until 1970. Indeed, from 1949–70, the charismatic leadership of the Crowleys so dominated the movement that they were often referred to as Mr. and Mrs. CFM. The Childerly meeting also named *Act,* the newsletter of Adult Catholic Action in Chicago and begun in 1946, as the official publication of CFM. It also designated Chicago as the headquarters for the movement. Later that year, the basic manual for the creation of a CFM section was published entitled, *For Happier Families: How to Start a Catholic Family Action Section,* though it came to be known as the "little yellow book." The following year, the St. Procopius meeting adopted "The Christian Family Movement" as the official name of the movement.

Expansion and Development

During the 1950s, the national coordinating committee enunciated CFM's primary goals as "serving," "educating," and "representing" families. The committee, while attempting to respect the local genius of each CFM section, also sought to provide some coherence, direction, and unity to the movement to make it a national force. In 1950 and every year following, the national committee published an inquiry booklet that focused on one or two major themes that sections throughout the country were to use in the coming year. In 1950 the theme was "Economics and Family Life," and the following year, it was the "Family and World Crisis." In addition to the annual booklet, a yearly convention was held to gather CFMers from across the United States. Beginning in 1951, the convention was held at the University of Notre Dame in South Bend, Indiana. The conventions exposed members to leading theologians, sociologists, liturgists, and other scholars, who explored the latest thinking in their various fields. The conventions also gave members a chance to meet other CFMers from across the United States and Canada and to form personal relationships with them. The conventions grew in popularity, attracting more than 5,000 participants by 1959. The coordinating committee, the annual inquiries, the annual conventions, and the Crowleys succeeded in giving CFM a national presence.

Even with the national thrust, the success of CFM depended on its effectiveness at the local level. Some complained that the national programs were too remote or complex to be relevant to the local scene. Nonetheless, thousands of actions were carried out at the local section level ranging from simple acts of neighborliness to becoming involved in local politics to setting up a babysitting service or credit union to assisting handicapped children. The list of actions as reported in *Act* is virtually endless. One of the most significant and popular early actions was to sponsor and promote Cana and Pre-Cana Conferences. Cana focused more on internal family relationships and complemented CFM's social action approach to the family apostolate. Another popular early action was to invite foreign students who were attending college in the United States to dinner during holidays. This simple action blossomed into a more ambitious foreign student exchange program, with an International Student Committee established by CFM in 1955. Students exposed to CFM carried it home to their native lands and CFM expanded worldwide. CFM enjoyed wide popularity in Spanish-speaking nations with the creation of the *Movimiento Familiar Cristiano* (MFC), which hosted its first convention in Montevideo, Uruguay, in 1957. The international thrust of CFM became an integral part of the movement resulting in the creation of the Foundation for International Cooperation (FIC) in 1960, and the International Confederation of the Christian Family Movement (ICCFM) in 1966.

CFM membership continued to grow throughout the 1950s, peaking in the early 1960s with a membership of more than 40,000 couples. While CFM remained a significant force through most of the 1960s, by the late 1960s its membership and influence had begun to decline significantly. In many ways, CFM was a victim of the social and theological traumas that rocked the nation and the Church during that era. These traumas exacerbated an internal tension which had existed within CFM since its inception—a split between those who saw the movement primarily as a social action movement designed to transform the social order, and those who belonged to CFM primarily to enhance the quality of their own family life. The split, one CFMer noted, was between "social apostles" and "family apostles." In 1964–65, the annual inquiry booklet confronted the topic of race relations, a particularly controversial issue as it coincided with a crucial moment in the civil rights movement. The following year the annual inquiry focused on the international scene just as protests against the Vietnam War were beginning to escalate. As social strife increased, as protests and urban rioting became common events, many CFMers retreated from the broad social vision encouraged by the CFM national coordinating committee to more limited family concerns. Unwittingly, CFM contributed to its own decline by introducing the Marriage Encounter movement (the English-speaking version) to the United States at its annual Notre Dame convention in 1967. Marriage Encounter, begun in Spain in the early 1960s, focused on internal family relationships and intrafamily communication; it spent little time worrying about the environment in which the family found itself. Marriage Encounter grew and prospered during the 1970s, superseding CFM as the primary family movement in the American Church.

Vatican II and After

The Second Vatican Council and the spirit it unleashed also affected the movement. Pat and Patty Crowley served on the Papal Birth Control Commission, and solicited the personal testimonies of CFMers from around the world as to their experience with birth control, or the lack of it. Impressed by thousands of personal testimonies of struggle, the Crowleys sided with the Commission's majority report which called for a revision of the Church's traditional teaching on birth control. When Pope Paul VI rejected the majority report, and reasserted the Church's traditional teaching in *Humanae vitae,* the Crowleys publicly dissented. The Crowleys' dissent cost them the support of many bishops, and several long-time supporters, including Monsignor Hillenbrand. CFM also lost episcopal support as the Movement became increasingly ecumenical. In 1965 an Episcopal version of *For Happier Families* was published and sections formed. At the 1967 convention, several non-Catholics addressed the convention, and at the 1971 convention, an Episcopal priest allegedly concelebrated at the convention Mass. CFM's ecumenical thrust was going too fast for many and cost it many supporters, particularly among the American hierarchy.

In 1970 the Crowleys resigned as the executive secretary couple, and were replaced by Ray and Dorothy Muldoon. CFM continued to function, but it was no longer the significant force it had once been, though the MFC remained popular in Spanish-speaking parishes. In 1981, CFM headquarters moved from Chicago to Ames, Iowa. Though the CFM continues to struggle in the 1990s, its tremendous impact on the American Catholic Church of the 1950s and 1960s must not be forgotten. CFM successfully prepared a generation of lay leaders for action inside and outside the Catholic Church in the United States and throughout the world.

See also CROWLEY, PATRICIA; CROWLEY, PATRICK.

Burns, Jeffrey M. *American Catholics and the Family Crisis, 1920–1962.* New York: Garland Press, 1988.

Kotre, John. *Simple Gifts: The Lives of Patrick and Patty Crowley.* New York: Andrews and McMeel, 1979.

Lucey, Rose. *Roots and Wings: Dramas and Doers in the Christian Family Movement.* San Jose: Resource Publications, 1987.

JEFFREY M. BURNS

CHRISTOPHERS, THE

Founded as a movement in 1945 by Fr. James Keller, a Maryknoll Missioner, the purpose of The Christophers is to encourage all people to appreciate their uniqueness and to take personal responsibility in seeking constructive solutions to today's problems. The philosophy which continues to guide the nonprofit organization was summed up by Fr. Keller (1900–77): "Each one of us has, by the grace of God, the power to change the world for the better. Every act of care and concern for others has a ripple effect, touching many lives. Where there is hate, bring in love; where there is darkness, carry light."

This message is spread through various media activities. *Christopher News Notes,* a free newsletter published ten times a year, reaches hundreds of thousands in 125 countries. *Ecos Cristóforos,* the Spanish edition, is produced six times a year. Each issue covers one topic ranging from prayer and spirituality to personal and family life. *Light One Candle,* a syndicated newspaper column, and *Encienda Una Vela,* the Spanish-language translation, along with *Three Minutes a Day,* a series of books offering daily reflections, are other Christopher publications.

Since 1952 The Christophers have also produced a weekly television program, *Christopher Closeup,* which appears on commercial and cable outlets across the United States. Christopher Awards are presented annually for books, motion pictures and television specials that aspire to the highest values of the human spirit. Since the 1980s, the James Keller Youth Award has singled out those who serve the interests of today's young people. The Christopher Leadership Course, conducted by the Gabriel Richard Institute (U.S.A.) and the Lumen Institute (Canada), develops communications and public speaking skills.

STEPHANIE RAHA

CISTERCIANS (MONKS AND NUNS) (O.C.S.O.; O. CIST.)

The Cistercians are named after the abbey of Citeaux, located outside Dijon, in southeastern France. This monastery was founded in 1098 by St. Robert of Molesme and twenty of his monks as a renewal of the Benedictine life. The reform quickly caught on and within a century there were hundreds of Cistercian monasteries established in all parts of Christendom. Historical situations led to the order developing congregations along national and ideological lines. In 1892, under the auspices of Pope Leo XIII, the order was divided into the Cistercian Order of the Stricter Observance (commonly called Trappists) which retains the aim of the founders of the order and seeks to live a contemplative monastic life, and the Order of Cistercians (usually referred to as the Common Observance) which is open to various apostolic activities, especially schools. There are, however, some strictly contemplative communities among the Common Observance.

Cistercian life was sadly in decline in France when North America was being colonized. For their part the Spanish and Portuguese colonizers wanted only mendicants like the Franciscans and Jesuits who could be active evangelizers, not monks. The rest of the colonial powers had long since cleared their countries of monks. Communities of nuns spontaneously arose in some of the colonies and one in Lima even adopted the Cistercian usages. There is also the curious fact that a number of Cistercians were sent to the New World as bishops. But it was over three centuries after Columbus claimed the lands of this hemisphere for the Lord before the Cistercian monks established their first permanent community.

Beginnings in the United States

It was the turmoil following the French Revolution that finally sent the first Cistercians to the shores of North America. The Trappists, under the leadership of Fr. Urban Guillet, arrived in America first. They landed in Baltimore on September 4, 1803, and after exploring sites in Pennsylvania, Missouri, Illinois, and Kentucky, they finally joined a group of monks who had landed in New York under the guidance of Dom Augustine de l'Estrange. They occupied an abandoned Jesuit college and established a monastery and an orphanage on the site where St. Patrick's Cathedral stands today. When peace came to France in 1815, the Trappists returned to France to reestablish their monasteries there.

However, one saintly monk was convinced that God wanted the Trappists in America. Fr. Vincent de Paul Merle "missed" the boat at Halifax and stayed on in Nova Scotia to prepare for a permanent foundation which was established in Tracadie by monks from Bellefontaine (Maine-et-Loire, France), La Trappe (Soligny-la-Trappe, France) and Aiguebelle (Montjoyer, France) in 1825 under the title of Notre Dame de Petit Clairvaux. After many struggles the community flourished and sent monks to establish a second house in Quebec, Notre Dame de l'Esprit Saint, which in turn sent monks to Old Monroe, Missouri, in 1872. However, pastoral cares soon engulfed the monks at Old Monroe, and the Monastery of the Immaculate Conception evolved into the parish of the Immaculate Conception and was taken over by the Archdiocese of Saint Louis. The early parish records bear the names of the Trappists who baptized and presided at weddings and funerals.

In the meantime, in 1848 the abbey of Notre Dame de Melleray in France sent a group of monks to establish the abbey of Our Lady of Gethsemani near Bardstown, Kentucky, and in 1849 the abbey of Our Lady of Mount Melleray in Ireland sent monks to begin Our Lady of New Melleray Abbey near Dubuque, Iowa.

The abbey of Petit Clairvaux suffered several devastating fires in the 1890s and recruitment continued to be very slow, so the monks accepted an invitation from the bishop of Providence and transferred their community in 1900 to Valley Falls, Rhode Island, and adopted the name Our Lady of the Valley. Shortly after that the troubles in France, which carried fear of religious persecution and the expulsion of religious, brought more Trappists to America to prepare a possible refuge. These French monks settled in Oregon at a site called Jordan. However, the foundation was short-lived as the religious climate improved in France and the monks were called home.

When the monks of Petit Clairvaux at Our Lady of the Valley celebrated their centenary, there were three well-established communities in the United States.

The Rapid Expansion of the Mid-Twentieth Century

Our Lady of the Valley began to truly flourish under Dom Edmund Futterer (abbot from 1945 to 1961). In 1948 he sent monks to establish a monastery near Pecos, New Mexico. The site, however, proved unsuitable for the monks' usual agrarian occupations so the community moved to Lafayette, Oregon, not far from the site of the Jordan foundation. There they retained their original title of Our Lady of Guadalupe. Our Lady of the Valley itself was destroyed by fire on the feast of St. Benedict in the Holy Year of 1950. As the area had become quite developed, Dom Edmund used the opportunity to relocate the rapidly growing community to Spencer, Massachusetts. The site of the new monastery was atop a high hill so the name of the community was again changed to the abbey of Our Lady of Saint Joseph.

Dom Edmund sent out two more colonies of monks to other parts of the United States: Holy Cross Abbey, Berryville, Virginia, and Saint Benedict's Abbey, Snowmass, Colorado, as well as two colonies to begin the order in South America, in Argentina and Chile. Gethsemani Abbey established new monasteries in some rather challenging places: in Georgia (Our Lady of the Holy Spirit Abbey, Conyers—where the monks were greeted with a burning cross in front of their barn monastery); in Utah (Our Lady of the Holy Trinity Abbey, Huntsville—in the heart of Morman country); in South Carolina (Our Lady of Mepkin Abbey, Moncks Corner, which looks to Clare Booth Luce as their foundress. She and her family, including Henry Luce, are buried at the abbey.). Other foundations were made in upper New York State (Our Lady of the Genesee Abbey, Piffard) and in California on the old Stanford Estate at Vina (Our Lady of New Clairvaux). And New Melleray Abbey sent a group of monks to establish Assumption Abbey near Ava in the Missouri Ozarks. In twelve years (1944–56) the American Trappists grew from three monasteries to twelve, from about three hundred monks to over a thousand.

The extraordinary growth of the Cistercians in the United States after the Second World War has been too exclusively attributed to the influence and writings of Thomas Merton. His contribution was and continues to be considerable. But the large influx began some years before his famous autobiography, *The Seven Storey Mountain,* was published. More credit than is usually given needs to be assigned to Fr. Raymond Flanagan, also a monk of Gethsemani and author of many volumes. His trilogy, *Three Religious Rebels, The Family Who Overtook Christ* and *Burnt-out Incense,* along with his very popular *The Man Who Got Even With God,* were used by God to draw many to the Cistercian life. More at source, credit should be

given to Raymond and Merton's abbot, Dom Frederic Dunne. Dom Frederic came from a literary background and appreciated the power and ministry of the printed word and its compatibility with the Cistercian life. He generally encouraged literary output at Gethsemani. The many pamphlets: *A Trappist speaks. . . .,* found on the racks in the back of most Catholic churches in the United States in the 1940s, made the Cistercian life and its meaning known to a vast number of the Catholic faithful.

This early literary activity of the American Cistercians (Our Lady of the Valley's Father Raphael produced his own best-selling conversion story, *The Glory of Thy People,* and there were others) was largely of a rather popular vein and reflected only very partially the rich and deep scholarly work that was being produced by their European confreres, little of which was known on this side of the Atlantic. A number of the scholarly journals, such as *Collectanea, Citeaux, Analecta Cisterciensia* and *Cistercium,* were beginning to circulate in America, but few of the American monks were fluent in the European languages and very few copies reached libraries outside the monasteries. It was only in 1965 that the American Cistercians collaborated with the other English-speaking Cistercians to inaugurate *Cistercian Studies Quarterly.*

The Twentieth-Century Renewal of Cistercian Life

The life of the many new members who entered the order in the 1940s and early 1950s at Gethsemani, Our Lady of the Valley/Spencer, and New Melleray was very much what was found in the usages that had been in force for some decades. Some adaptations were made to respond to the crowded conditions and some indulgences were allowed the many very young. Those under twenty-one were not allowed to observe the full Trappist fast and slept till 4:00 A.M. The intense heat of Georgia summers made a visiting abbot general realize that the local cotton was a better fabric for the monks' robes than the wool of the French sheep. Automation of the farms and heavy construction work on the new monasteries postulated more practical clothing for work time.

Dom Edmund Futterer was elected abbot of Our Lady of the Valley in 1945, though he had actually been superior or virtually superior for many years. Dom James Fox was elected abbot of Gethsemani in 1948; he had been superior at Conyers since its founding. Both had come to the Cistercians from the Passionists where they were confreres. Yet they offered very different approaches to the Cistercian life. Dom James had some U.S. Navy experience in his background and discipline was very important to him. The Trappist asceticism appealed to him, and he presented it with a down-home piety.

Dom Edmund was a keen musician with a very highly cultivated sense for the beautiful. The destruction of Our

Lady of the Valley by fire on the feast of St. Benedict (March 21) in the Holy Year of 1950 gave him the opportunity to create a wholly new and traditionally beautiful monastery at Spencer. He was deeply influenced by the writings of Dom Columba Marmion and had a great love for contemplative prayer. For a few years Dom James was the Father Immediate or canonical visitor of Dom Edmund's community, but the election in 1951 of the abbot of Bellefontaine, Dom Gabriel Sortais, as abbot general led to the recognition of Bellefontaine as the more authentic motherhouse for the Spencer community. New Melleray, reflecting the Irish tradition of the order, had a flavor uniquely different from the other two monasteries.

The election of Dom Gabriel, a man with all the command and leadership qualities of a French general, as abbot general of the order, heralded new times for the Cistercians. The renewal began with the general chapter of 1953, which introduced what seemed like very radical changes in those times. In the heavily bureaucratic Church of the preconciliar days, practically every decision of the general chapter had to be approved by the Sacred Congregation for Religious in Rome. After waiting ten months for a response, Dom Gabriel pressed the congregation, noting the approach of another chapter. (In those days the order still had annual chapters as postulated by the original constitutions of the order, the Charter of Charity. They now take place every three or four years.) The congregation replied: The changes proposed are too sweeping and demanded a plenary chapter. (Every five years there was a plenary chapter to which all the abbots were expected to come, even those in far off lands.) All that was granted was fifteen more minutes of sleep on working days. (Some of the monks laughed for fifteen minutes.)

The move to return to the simplicity of primitive Citeaux had begun. Step by step the duplications and accretions in the liturgical life were removed, reducing the hours in choir from six or seven to three or less, allowing more time for *lectio* and contemplation. Only after the Second Vatican Council would the vernacular be allowed and greater freedom be given to the local community to create its own liturgical worship.

Another initiative forwarded by Dom Gabriel and sanctioned subsequently by the council, has not received equally widespread acclaim and has left problems still to be solved. That was the "unification" of the communities. Because of the work already initiated by the abbot general, when the council's Decree on the Appropriate Renewal of the Religious Life called for only one class of members in monasteries, the Cistercians were ready for this change. Within weeks of the close of the council, the Decree of Unification was approved by Rome. This decree provided that, while respecting the acquired rights of the lay brothers to retain their professed status, henceforth there would be only one class of monks in the Cistercian community.

Those who were lay brothers could change over to the new monastic status.

For a time, until the approval of the new constitutions, lay brothers had the option of choosing a simplified monastic status—monks without all the obligations traditionally laid upon Cistercian monks—or they could enter fully into the way of the Cistercian "choir" monk, whose choir obligations were actually to be rapidly simplified. The Decree of Unification virtually demanded this simplification, for if there were to be no more lay brothers, the monks would have to take on longer hours of work. The decree, in accord with a more primitive monastic tradition, emphasized the discretion and discernment of the abbot in determining each monk's participation in community prayer and work. But this change has not adequately responded to the problem that the Cistercian founders sought to solve by the inauguration of lay brothers: how to celebrate a full choral office, fully support the monastery from the labor of the community's hands, and still have adequate holy leisure to live a truly contemplative life. With a reduction of numbers, the problem has become more and more acute in some communities.

In 1969 the first official renewal chapter of the order produced a sweeping Statute on Unity and Pluralism which reduced all the previous usages to little more than suggestions, replacing them with eleven principles that were to guide each community in the creation of its own usages or guidelines or customs. Gone were the days when a monk could visit any house in the order and know exactly when each event was going to take place, how it was going to be done, and could fully enter into the Latin prayers and minutely prescribed ceremonies. At the same time it has been surprising how a relatively few statutes, along with the dynamic force of age-old custom and spirit, have been able to maintain such a commonness in the way Cistercian life is lived in the communities not only in the United States but around the world.

Like all the other religious and monastic orders, as soon as the Second Vatican Council was over, plans were made to begin work on new constitutions. As the first renewal chapter was assembled at Citeaux in 1967 (significantly it proved to be the last general chapter to meet at Citeaux), many thought it would be a relatively easy task that could be completed in two renewal chapters. The wide-ranging suggestions, not to say confusion, that appeared at the chapter should have quickly warned every one that they were venturing upon a much more revolutionary task. A necessary eye had to be kept on the development of the new Code of Canon Law, and that too went through a long and difficult evolution. It was only shortly after the promulgation of the new code that the long arduous task was brought to a conclusion in 1984 in Holyoke, Massachusetts, at the first general chapter held outside of Europe, and a text was submitted to the Holy See for approval.

The years under the Statute of Unity and Pluralism, struggling with the Decree of Unification, had been good in that the new constitutions came much more out of a lived experience. The Holy See demanded some compromises of the order—the monks and nuns not only wanted to remain one order but wanted complete equality. On the whole, however, the new constitutions are a fine document which leaves room for evolution and the development of even better solutions to the challenges of living a stable contemplative life in a rapidly changing world. The United States participants brought a great deal to the development of the new constitutions; their contribution was blended with the contributions of other nations to the great enrichment of all.

In the early 1960s the American abbots began to meet informally. They were soon joined by the abbesses, who still had to obtain numerous permissions to come out to such meetings. Then at times they were joined by other groups such as the novice masters and mistresses or delegates from the communities. This evolved into a structure which was fully incorporated into the new constitutions: the Regional Meeting. Though continuously looked upon with suspicion by some because of the history of the order breaking into national or regional congregations, these meetings have played a significant role in the evolution of the Cistercian life and proved to be real support groups for the superiors.

The American Communities in
the Latter Part of the Twentieth Century

Of the original three American abbeys, Gethsemani and Spencer have remained the large ones. One of the foundations, the first, Conyers, approaches them in size and has given birth to a foundation in South America. The other foundations have generally remained smaller. The communities offer a broad spectrum in size from the largest abbey in the order, Saint Joseph's, Spencer, to an annex of only two or three monks, Oxford, North Carolina. This, along with regional culture which is quite marked in the monasteries, has produced a rich variety in the way Cistercian life is lived in the United States today.

As the decade of the fifties drew to a close, Pope John XXIII encouraged two friends, Cardinal Richard Cushing of Boston and Dom Edmund Futterer (whose abbey of Spencer was actually in the Boston archdiocese when it was first conceived), to look to South America. The cardinal started the Saint James Society which sent many diocesan priests on a tour of mission duty. Dom Edmund sent the group that had built Spencer and Snowmass to build Nuestra Señora de los Angeles near Azul, Argentina. In the last years of his abbatial service he went on to inaugurate the community in Chile and to lay plans for other communities of nuns and monks. In the succeeding decades monasteries from other countries joined the Americans in building up the Cistercian presence in South America. Many monks in the United States communities had an opportunity to spend some time in Latin America. The expansion still goes on and United States communities continue also to provide chaplains for the nuns south of the border.

Another outreach of the United States communities was the corporate sponsorship of a foundation in the Philippines. This kind of collaboration in launching a new house was exceptional and harkened back to the founding of Petit Clairvaux by monks from several abbeys. Assumption Abbey, Ava, now serves as the motherhouse though the founders came from Mepkin, Conyers, Gethsemani, and Holy Trinity, and the first abbot, Dom Joseph Chu-Cong, came from Spencer.

The growth has not stopped there. Saint Joseph's adopted a Benedictine foundation in North Carolina—Holy Mother of God Monastery, Oxford. In 1978 Our Lady of the Genesee Abbey (Piffard, New York) adopted a diocesan monastery in Nigeria, Our Lady of Mount Calvary, Awhum. New Clairvaux turned its interest to the Orient, first adopting the refugee monks from communist China who had gathered on Lantao Island near Hong Kong, the monastery of Our Lady of Joy. They then went on to start a new community in Taiwan above Shuili.

In the American Cistercian communities today, the office is celebrated with simplicity and sobriety and with a solemnity proportionate to the resources of each community. There is a clear commitment to self-support, as each community finds several means to attain this and at the same time devotes a good bit of communal labor to maintaining a beautiful contemplative environment. The standard of living reflects the area within which the community is located. It is generally middle class with certain significant expressions of poverty and, if the truth be told, elements of affluence. Care is taken to ensure contemplative time and space for each monk and nun, not without some struggle. *Lectio divina,* that truly monastic kind of reading that opens out into prayer, is generally better understood and practiced. Continued effort is being made, especially by pooling resources, to upgrade the educational programs available to the young monks and nuns. There is certainly much more mutual collaboration and sharing among the monks and nuns to the enrichment of all. According to the decision of each community, the abbot may now be elected for six years or for an indeterminate term of office with retirement at seventy-five.

The Order of Cistercians (Common Observance)

With the encouragement of Abbot General Janssens, the first group of Cistercians of the Common Observance came to the United States from Austria in 1928 and established Our Lady of Spring Bank near Oconomowoc,

Wisconsin. Their ideal was to establish a more contemplative observance. The community has always remained quite small even though they received an influx of Hungarian monks after the Second World War and then a number of monks from the Trappists. The former went on in 1956 to establish Our Lady of Dallas Abbey, which not only operates a preparatory school but also provides the theology faculty for the University of Dallas. Some of the latter group then proceeded to establish Saint Mary's Priory, New Ringgold, Pennsylvania. The Spring Bank community also sponsors a parochial monastery, Our Lady of Gerowval, Rose Hill, Mississippi. Spring Bank Abbey itself moved to Sparta, Wisconsin.

The great Italian abbey of Casamari in 1967 founded a small monastery near Mont Laurel, New Jersey: Our Lady of Fatima.

The Cistercian Nuns

The Cistercians of the Strict Observance are the one order in the Church where the men and women form strictly one religious order, sharing in the chapter and together electing their general. This is the fruit of a long evolution that began in the time of the Cistercian founders.

Some Trappistines actually accompanied the exiled monks who came to the United States in the early nineteenth century. These, however, were not strictly Cistercian nuns, but a sort of third order created by Dom Augustine de l'Estrange. Arriving first in Boston, they eventually transferred to New York. They enjoyed a good American recruitment. When it came time for the Trappists to return to France, the American nuns were given the option of remaining in their own country or accompanying the monks to France. Only four opted to remain in the United States. They joined the Daughters of Charity at Emmitsburg where they lie buried today.

It was Dom Edmund Futterer who prepared the way for the first permanent Trappistine convent in the United States by sending American candidates to Canadian and Irish convents. In 1949, with the help of some Irish nuns, these returned to the United States to establish Mount Saint Mary's Abbey, Wrentham, Massachusetts. Mother Angela Norton, the first American abbess, led this community through more than thirty years of growth and transition and established convents in Iowa (Our Lady of the Mississippi, Dubuque), Arizona (Santa Rita Abbey, Senoita), and Virginia (Our Lady of the Angels, Crozet). In 1962 a charismatic abbess from Belgium, Mother Miriam Dardeen, brought a small group of nuns to northern California and established Our Lady of the Redwoods near Whitethorn.

The Common Observance also brought their nuns to establish a small nunnery at Prairie du Sac, Wisconsin, not far from the Spring Bank community. The Valley of Our Lady Monastery has continued to live a quiet contemplative life there.

Contributions

The Cistercians of the Strict Observance have always seen their primary contribution to the Church and to the world to lie in their quiet, prayerful lives. At the heart of the Church and at the heart of the particular diocese in which they are established, they devote the largest part of their waking hours to prayer, in choir and in private, and to *lectio*. They are also committed to offering an open hospitality, providing a place of quiet and apartness and spiritual guidance for any who come seeking it. In recent years many of the communities have significantly upgraded their guest facilities and have begun to welcome members of the opposite sex. Retreat programs are simple, offering mainly silence and solitude, with spiritual fathers or mothers available for consultation and instruction in prayer. In the 1970s there came forth from Spencer a practical, simple teaching on contemplative prayer that has popularly become known as Centering Prayer.

Apart from this prayerful presence at the heart of the Church, probably the most significant and well-known contribution made by the Cistercians to the Church in the United States and indeed to the nation and the world has been that made by Fr. Louis, better known as Thomas Merton. This Trappist monk shared the fruit of his contemplation, animated a social conscience, and led the way in interreligious dialogue through a steady flow of books and articles as well as a very extensive correspondence and a generous hospitality and finally a fatal journey to Asia. His lively existential approach has spoken powerfully to the American Catholic community.

With the support and encouragement of Fr. Louis, Fr. M. Basil Pennington, in 1968, established Cistercian Publications, an ambitious project which has sought to publish all the significant writings of the early Cistercian Fathers and Mothers in English translation as well as a series of Cistercian Studies. In 1969 he inaugurated the annual Cistercian Studies Conference which has grown in size and international character and has been integrated with the annual Medieval Conference sponsored by Western Michigan University, Kalamazoo. Three years later he transferred the publications to the university campus and united with it in the sponsoring of the Institute of Cistercian Studies. Fr. Basil himself has published over forty books reflecting Cistercian spirituality and ecumenical concerns.

Another significant contribution has been made by Abbot Thomas Keating. After serving the Spencer community for twenty years as their abbot, he went on to father the Contemplative Outreach, an international lay movement bringing contemplative prayer into the lives of ordinary people, priest and lay alike, at the parish level. For this he has developed a presentation of the ancient monastic way of prayer which has become popular under the name of

Centering Prayer. He has also shared the fruit of his contemplation through a number of published volumes.

There have been other contributions from Cistercian writers: Fr. Louis Lekai was the foremost monastic historian of this century. Sr. Lillian Thomas Shank brought her expertise to the study of nuns. Fr. Chrysogonus Waddell published an important series of liturgical texts and has done much to develop Cistercian chant. Sr. Miriam Pollard, Fr. William Menniger, Fr. Charles Cunningham and others have added to the wealth of spiritual literature available to American Catholics.

The Common Observance have made their particular contribution to the American Church in the establishment of a fine preparatory school at their abbey in Dallas as well as serving on the faculties of the University of Dallas and other universities.

See also ABBEY OF GETHSEMANI; AMERICAN CATHOLIC SPIRITUALITY; MERTON, THOMAS.

Breit, Marquita, and Robert Daggy, *Thomas Merton. A Comprehensive Bibliography.* New York: Garland, 1986.

Lekai, Louis J., O. Cist. *The Cistercians. Ideals and Reality.* Ohio: Kent State University Press, 1977.

Pennington, Basil M., O.C.S.O., *The Cistercians.* Collegeville, Minn.: The Liturgical Press, 1992.

_____. *Monastic Life. A Short History of Monasticism and Its Spirit.* Petersham, Mass.: Saint Bede's Publications, 1989.

Sullivan, Mary Christina. "Some Non-Permanent Foundations of Religious Orders and Congregations of Women in the United States (1793–1850)." *Historical Records and Studies* 31 (1940) 7–118.

M. BASIL PENNINGTON, O.C.S.O.

CISZEK, WALTER (1904–84)

Jesuit missionary. He was born of Polish immigrant parents in Shenandoah, Pennsylvania, on November 4, 1904. When he expressed a desire to become a priest, he was sent for his high school studies to Saints Cyril and Methodius Seminary in Orchard Lake, Michigan, and there he remained for college as well. During his final year he decided to become a Jesuit and on September 7, 1928, entered the novitiate in Poughkeepsie, New York.

Russian Mission

In early 1929 the novices were told of a letter of Pius XI calling upon Jesuits to prepare for missionary work in Russia. Shortly after taking vows (September 1930), Ciszek wrote to the Jesuit general volunteering for the mission. He was accepted but was told to continue studies until further notification. He studied philosophy (1931–34) at Woodstock College (Maryland), and sailed for Europe during the summer of 1934. That fall he began to study theology at Rome's Gregorian University and pursued Russian studies at the Russicum. He was ordained in Rome on June 24, 1937.

Since conditions in Russia were such that it would have been imprudent to send missionaries there, Ciszek was assigned to work among the Russian Catholics in Albertyn, Poland. He arrived in November, 1938. On September 1, 1939, Germany invaded Poland, and on October 17, Russia occupied Albertyn. Ciszek decided to penetrate further into Russia, the better to minister to the spiritual needs of its Catholics. As Vladimir Lypinski, a widower, without family, he signed on with a lumber company to work in the Urals and left Lvov on March 19, 1940. After a two-week trip in boxcars, he and his fellow workers arrived at the Chusovoy lumber camps.

Prisoner

On June 22, 1941, Germany invaded Russia, and early the following morning Ciszek was arrested as a German spy and sent to prison in Perm. During his first interrogation he learned that the Russians had known his true identity and that he was a priest. He was subsequently transferred to Moscow's Lubyanka Prison. Interrogations were frequent but he always responded in the same way: his reason for being in Russia was spiritual and not political. On July 26, 1942, he was convicted as "a Vatican spy" and sentenced to fifteen years of hard labor. He remained in confinement in Lubyanka and, though the war had ended in May 1945, he was detained there until June 1946 when he was taken to Siberia to begin his sentence of hard labor.

After six months at Krasnoyarsk, Ciszek was moved (December 1946) to the Norilsk area, where he remained until 1953. During those years he was assigned to various camps and performed a variety of jobs: e.g., coal miner and construction worker. In October 1953 he was sent to the nearby Kayerkhan mines and in April 1955 was released after serving fourteen years and nine months of his sentence. He left camp as a free man on April 22 and made his way to Norilsk, where he found a job and resumed priestly activity. Because his apostolic work attracted attention, the police asked him to leave the city in 1958. He then made his way to Abakan, found a job as an auto mechanic and worked there until 1963, when he was told to go to Moscow, where an official of the American consulate met him.

Freedom

Ciszek arrived in New York City on October 12, 1963, and joined the John XXIII Center for Eastern Christian Studies at Fordham University. He spent the remaining years of his life giving conferences and retreats. His *With God in Russia* relates his life under the Soviets and his *He Leadeth Me* tells of the faith that had sustained him during those years. He died on December 8, 1984; his cause for beatification is under consideration.

Ciszek, Walter J. *With God in Russia*. New York: McGraw-Hill, 1964.

_____. *He Leadeth Me*. Garden City, N.Y.: Doubleday, 1973.

Crane, W. O. "A Man of Courage." *Homiletic and Pastoral Review* 80 (June 1980) 44–46.

Roccasalvo, Joan L. "Allow God to Lead." *Homiletic and Pastoral Review* 86 (August–September 1986) 55–56.

JOSEPH N. TYLENDA, S.J.

CIVIL RIGHTS MOVEMENT AND CATHOLICS, THE

Introduction

When the civil rights movement began, the Catholic community—for many historical reasons—found itself by and large standing on the sidelines. As the movement unfolded, Catholics joined often as followers and in a few instances made a pivotal difference. This movement came almost exclusively through an informal network of individual lay people and key "activist" priests and nuns. While the institutional Church made little overall contribution, a handful of individual bishops took significant risks, particularly in the desegregation of Catholic schools.

By the time Dr. Martin Luther King, Jr., was killed, many people felt that the problem of race in American society had been solved and that only time was needed for racial justice to work its way throughout American institutions, including the Catholic Church. During the ensuing years, the Catholic Church began changing and offered tremendous potential for any future progress on civil rights simply by being responsive to its own newly expanding constituency, since more than 40 percent of its members were from ethnic minorities, mostly Hispanic, by the mid-1990s.

The special perfidious slavery that took on the form of racism was invented in the Americas as a justification for economic development. ("Historically, racial prejudice, in the strict sense of the word, that is, awareness of the biologically determined superiority of one's own race or ethnic group with respect to others, developed above all from the practice of colonization and slavery at the dawn of the modern era" [*The Church and Racism. Towards a More Fraternal Society,* Pontifical Commission Justitia et Pax, Vatican City, 1988]).

Very few Catholics settled in the Southern United States in the area where slavery became established. They were not among the colonists who gained control of large tracts of land and then sought out cheap labor to farm this land. Some of the worst rioting by the "underclass" in this country, for instance, was not by blacks, but by the Irish, particularly in New York and Chicago (the first in response to President Lincoln's draft as many a Catholic young man was fodder for the North's war machine to free the slaves).

The White Ethnic Church

As Catholic migration increased, the Catholic white ethnic parishes played a significant role in creating a secure environment for its members, serving as job placement centers, establishing local savings and loan institutions, teaching the young, representing its people to the large community and in endless ways working for the civil rights of its own particular group.

Priests such as Msgr. Peter Adamski, pastor of St. Stanislaus parish in Buffalo, or Fr. Roberto Balducelli, O.S.F.S., of St. Anthony's in Wilmington, Delaware, had as much power in the ethnic portions of their respective cities as did the mayors of these communities. But this focus was myopic and the ultimate goal was to protect white ethnic enclaves while integrating these white ethnics into the employment and service opportunities of the general community.

Even before the advent of the civil rights movement, a few prominent Catholic leaders took the initiative in promoting racial justice. In the late 1940s both Archbishop Patrick O'Boyle of Washington and Archbishop Joseph Ritter of St. Louis integrated the Catholic schools in their archdioceses. In that same decade most Catholic colleges dropped the racial barriers to admission. In New Orleans, Archbishop Joseph Rummel took a strong position on integration of Catholic organizations and churches and eventually Catholic schools, although he then kept delaying the implementation of school integration because of the threat of losing public services and opposition from some of his clergy. At a later date, Bishop Joseph Brunini of Natchez Jackson, in a bold attempt to have a black priest made the ordinary of a diocese, appealed to Rome to split his diocese, and to have the new diocese headed by his one black priest, Joseph Lawson Howze.

But, despite common perception, it was not usual for leadership in other churches, especially those in the African American community, to struggle for civil rights. They, possibly even more than white ethnic parish leadership, kept their agenda to more narrowly defined "spiritual" interests and also served as brokers and conduits from the larger American institutions into the African American communities. Rev. Martin Luther King, Jr., was breaking ground when he built his efforts on the back of a bus boycott organized by E. D. Nixon, said by some to be the real founder of the civil rights movement.

The National Catholic Conference for Interracial Justice

It was the National Catholic Conference for Interracial Justice (NCCIJ), under the skilled and unassuming leadership of a layman, Mathew Ahmann—one of the few Catholic organizations with no formal ties to the institutional Church—that spearheaded and coordinated Catholic involvement in the civil rights cause. It was this organization that focused for Dr. King—as he himself has noted—the civil rights movement as principally a religious or moral cause.

This Catholic civil rights effort had been founded in 1934 by Jesuit Fr. John LaFarge. Fr. LaFarge drew together an interracial group of Catholics who hired as their director a white layman, George Hunton, and called their effort the Catholic Interracial Council of New York. Other councils eventually formed throughout the country and by the 1960s there were some 150 of them.

In 1958 the Catholic Interracial Council of Chicago, chaired by R. Sargent Shriver (then head of the Chicago Board of Education and later, a Kennedy official and the first Peace Corps director) and directed by Lloyd Davis (later to become vice president of the Martin Luther King, Jr. Center for Non-Violent Social Change and director of the Martin Luther King, Jr., Holiday Commission) with Msgr. Daniel Cantwell as chaplain, called for a meeting of these councils as well as other activist Catholic groups.

The NCCIJ was officially chartered in 1960 and began its role as support to the burgeoning civil rights movement. Among various activities, it was one of the ten cochairs of the 1963 March on Washington, selected by the civil rights leaders as a way of addressing a threatened boycott of the march by Washington Archbishop Patrick O'Boyle. Sr. Margaret Traxler, NCCIJ Education Director, and a team of sisters, all with doctorates, conducted 110 workshops and summer schools, some for public schools and corporations, on all aspects of civil rights and racism. (The exposure these nuns received and the networking that took place as they traveled throughout the country had a tremendous impact on the renewal of religious orders.)

NCCIJ promoted the establishment of human relations offices under diocesan auspices, starting in Detroit, St. Louis and New Orleans. It organized and served as secretary for the Black Clergy Caucus. Under NCCIJ's Thomas Gibbons, Project Equality programs were established in various dioceses to promote affirmative action in local dioceses.

Catholic Conference on Religion and Race

In 1963 a three-day meeting, organized by the NCCIJ, entitled the Conference on Religion and Race and cochaired by Rev. King, Rabbi Abraham Heschel of New York and Cardinal Albert Meyer of Chicago, brought together leaders from seventy-eight denominations and major church organizations. This meeting was covered extensively by the media throughout the United States and made a significant contribution to highlighting the civil rights movement as a moral cause. This conference was the first significant participation of the Catholic Church in an American interdenominational endeavor and led to the development of numerous local interdenominational efforts and organizations.

Selma

One Sunday in May 1965, a shocking movie, *The Rise and Fall of the Third Reich,* was broadcast throughout the nation. As the movie ended, program broadcasts were interrupted with scenes of black marchers being clubbed and charged by police on horses as the marchers were crossing the Edmund Pettus bridge in Selma, Alabama, in support of voting rights legislation.

The next morning, when a call came in to Mr. Ahmann at NCCIJ from Rev. King asking for a mobilization of the Catholic community in support of the Selma marchers, he found the organization already in action. Mathew Ahmann had discovered that the local Catholic bishop in Alabama was sending word to his fellow bishops asking them to forbid their church members to come to Selma. Ahmann knew he had to act fast if he was to gain Catholic Church involvement.

One of his first contacts was Msgr. Geno Baroni, a well-known Washington, D.C., inner-city priest. Floyd Agostinelli, diocesan social action director, informed Msgr. Baroni that a call would be coming to him from the auxiliary bishop forbidding him to go to Selma. Msgr. Baroni rushed out the door for the airport. As soon as Ahmann heard that Msgr. Baroni had taken off from National Airport (after futile attempts by the bishop to intercept him at Dulles Airport), Ahmann put out the word that Cardinal Patrick O'Boyle's key social activist priest was going to Selma, implying the archbishop's approval.

Catholic Interracial Council members and a few key activist nuns and priests from many dioceses ran for airplanes, two of them chartered by St. Louis developer Charles Vatterott. Many of these participants were tended to as they arrived in Selma by the Edmundite Fathers under the leadership of Fr. Maurice Ouellet, who, forbidden to participate in the marches, instead played a key role in supplying "hotel" and meeting space for the movement.

While this Catholic Church participation made a significant visible statement and gained credibility for the cause, it had as great an impact on those who had come to Selma and were moved by what they experienced. Selma was the first mass movement of whites into the civil rights marches of the 1960s; it was also a "coming out" of the Catholic Church in a major way into the social arena. White Selma marchers were disproportionately Catholic with high media attention given particularly to nuns in habit.

Local Activists

Throughout the civil rights era, there were often some priests or religious women—many of them motivated by the Selma experience—who at times spearheaded activity, but more often organized or articulated support in the local dioceses and religious orders.

Jesuit Louis Twomey appealed to Jesuit General Pedro Arrupe in Rome to issue a decree ordering all Jesuits to get involved in civil rights. Sociologist Joseph Fichter, S.J., lectured and wrote on the need for a multicultural church. Inner-city pastor, Fr. James Groppi of Milwaukee, led highly dramatic and tense marches into the Polish Southside Catholic community backed by the skilled strategizing and organizing of Fr. Patrick Flood.

Sr. Marilyn Morehauser, a Marquette student, played a strong role in establishing Freedom Schools in Milwaukee. Walter Hooke, an Urban League and Catholic Interracial Council activist in California, was brought into United Parcel Services to refocus UPS on affirmative action and multicultural concerns. Fr. James Sheehan, Fr. Norman Thomas and Hope Brophy in Detroit, inspired by the leadership of Msgr. Clement Kerns, carefully guided Cardinal John Dearden to progressive leadership. Fr. Sheehan, along with League Life Insurance executive Joseph Hansknecht and John Yorke, developed comprehensive, archdiocesan-wide training in race relations through Project Commitment, which became Project Understanding in Pittsburgh under the hand of Sr. Mary Dennis and spread to other dioceses.

Of special note was the migrant farm laborer, Cesar Chavez, who, inspired by the social encyclicals, moved the civil rights agenda beyond that of the black community as he organized a nationwide grape boycott and a farm laborer movement impacting heavily on the Spanish-speaking community.

Then there was Msgr. John Shocklee in St. Louis; Dr. Claude Organ in Omaha and his brother, Henry Organ, in California; Fr. George Clements in Chicago; Fr. Eugene O'Boyle in San Francisco; Fr. Joseph Connolly and Fr. Henry Offer, S.S.J., in Baltimore; Fr. Donald McIlvane in Pittsburgh; Fr. David Finks in Rochester, New York; Fr. Bernard Law, later cardinal, in Jackson, Mississippi; Fr. John McCarthy, later bishop, in Houston; Fr. Edward Flahavan in the Twin Cities; Henry Cabirac, John Nelson, and John Sisson in New Orleans; Msgr. Daniel Cantwell, CIC chaplain in Chicago.

The Aftermath

In 1967 Msgr. John Egan utilized the network of activists involved in NCCIJ, broadened the agenda and constituency and established the Catholic Committee for Urban Ministry, at a time when Catholic activists were shifting their interest away from civil rights towards Vietnam and eventually other peace and justice issues.

As the civil rights movement itself ground down with the death of Dr. King, Msgr. Geno Baroni—under the umbrella of the National Center for Urban Ethnic Affairs—began organizing in the white ethnic communities in order to give a positive thrust to what was being manipulated as a backlash to civil rights by national and local political figures.

By the time Dr. King had been killed, the "simple," more visible goals of the civil rights movement, e.g., access to water fountains and bathrooms, integrated buses and lunch counters, major civil rights legislation, were in place. Beginning to come into focus was the fact that racism was closely intertwined with economic conditions and systemic and institutional forces. Civil rights leaders, including Dr. King, finding themselves with little access to these economic and institutional forces, became frustrated and, like Don Quixote, began riding off in all directions. Some, having benefited from the civil rights movement, lost their interest as did the general populace who thought the legislation in place would in time force changes throughout the system. Middle-class blacks took advantage of progress made and moved out of the inner-city communities. Also, beginning about 1973, major economic shifts in society began taking shape, further alienating the inner cities.

Meanwhile, the Catholic Church, long the bastion of white ethnic neighborhoods surrounding the black inner-city communities, found itself viewed not just a white ethnic church, but also an immigrant church and a minority church. Middle-class blacks became converts, having been educated in the Catholic school system. The schools had opened their doors to minorities after losing a large percent of their Catholic students. This was possibly the greatest contribution the Church has made to minority advancement.

Haitians and Cubans headed to U.S. shores in every way possible. North Vietnamese Catholics, who had fled from the North to the South because of Communism, were among the most likely once again to flee to the United States as the Vietnam War ended. Catholic Hispanics by the millions fled turmoil and poverty in Mexico, El Salvador, and Nicaragua. The Catholic white ethnic populations of the late 1800s and early 1900s were followed by the mass influx of nonwhite Catholics in the last half of the twentieth century.

The Church today finds itself to be still an immigrant and ethnic church, presently heavily middle- and upper-class white, but with a vibrant nonwhite minority, now 40 percent and growing. It is also a major institution in American society and its people control or have significant leverage in many of the economic and political institutions.

Because of its basic turf orientation or local neighborhood organizational focus, its interrelated structures, its moral mission, its white ethnic composition surrounding many inner-city minority neighborhoods, the Catholic Church has possibly more potential than any other institution in American society for building bridges among ethnic communities and for impacting on the economic and social forces that can help to bring about social change consistent with the goals and hopes of the civil rights movement.

Unfortunately, this opportunity also comes at a time when the Church institutional leadership has turned inward and is buffeted and threatened by internal Church considerations. For very different reasons and despite its present potential, it is largely in the same position it found itself in during the height of the civil rights era—disengaged. The last significant effort by the national Church was an outstanding pastoral letter *(Brothers and Sisters to Us)* issued in 1969 calling for institutional change for Church and society. A committee headed by African American auxiliary bishop Joseph Francis of Newark was able to overcome opposition from other bishops to issue this pastoral inspired by the insights of Josephite activist Fr. Joseph McManus, S.S.J., but the decree has often since been referred to as the best kept secret of the Catholic Church in America.

"The Black Catholic Community, 1880–1987." *U.S. Catholic Historian* 7 (2, 3) (1988).

"The Black Catholic Experience." *U.S. Catholic Historian* 5 (1) (1986).

Davis, Cyprian, O.S.B. *The History of Black Catholics in the United States.* New York, 1990.

LaFarge, John, S.J. *Interracial Justice.* New York, 1937.

———. *The Race Question and the Negro.* New York, 1943.

Ochs, Stephen J. *Desegregating the Altar: The Josephites and the Struggle for Black Priests.* Baton Rouge, 1990.

JEROME B. ERNST

Related Document

THE AMERICAN CATHOLIC BISHOPS AND RACISM, NOVEMBER 14, 1958

It would be difficult to think of any problem that has done more to disturb the internal peace of the United States than discrimination against various groups on the score of race or nationality. Friction between whites and native Indians and Negroes has been a fairly constant phenomenon in American history, but it has been especially acute in regard to the latter since World War II. That some American Catholics have been influenced by racist doctrines is, unfortunately, true, and had they accepted the Church's teaching on this subject there would probably be more than 675,000 colored people and 125,000 Indians among the American Catholics at the present time (1961). Yet strenuous efforts have not been lacking in recent years on the part of members of the hierarchy to emphasize in a practical way the Church's mission to men of all races and nationalities. And these efforts have produced effective results, even if in certain localities race prejudice has not permitted more progress to be made. For example, Joseph E. Ritter, Archbishop of St. Louis, ordered the integration of the schools of his archdiocese in September, 1947, seven years in advance of the Supreme Court's ruling of May,

1954. Likewise in the autumn of 1948 integration of the Catholic schools of the national capital was begun at the instance of Patrick A. O'Boyle, Archbishop of Washington, and in June, 1951, Vincent S. Waters, Bishop of Raleigh, instituted the same policy in all the churches and diocesan institutions of his southern see. Nationally speaking, however, the situation has yielded—if at all—only after great resistance. It was with that background that the Catholic bishops determined to set forth in detail the Church's doctrine on this controversial question.

(*Source:* "Discrimination and the Christian Conscience." New York *Times,* November 14, 1958.)

FIFTEEN YEARS AGO, WHEN THIS NATION WAS DEVOTING ITS energies to a World War designed to maintain human freedom, the Catholic Bishops of the United States issued a prayerful warning to their fellow citizens. We called for the extension of full freedom within the confines of our beloved country. Specifically, we noted the problems faced by Negroes in obtaining the rights that are theirs as Americans. The statement of 1943 said in part:

"In the Providence of God there are among us millions of fellow citizens of the Negro race. We owe to these fellow citizens, who have contributed so largely to the development of our country, and for whose welfare history imposes on us a special obligation of justice, to see that they have in fact the rights which are given them in our Constitution. This means not only political equality, but also fair economic and educational opportunities, a just share in public welfare projects, good housing without exploitation, and a full chance for the social advancement of their race."

In the intervening years, considerable progress was made in achieving these goals. The Negro race, brought to this country in slavery, continued its quiet but determined march toward the goal of equal rights and equal opportunity. During and after the Second World War, great and even spectacular advances were made in the obtaining of voting rights, good education, better-paying jobs, and adequate housing. Through the efforts of men of good will, of every race and creed and from all parts of the nation, the barriers of prejudice and discrimination were slowly but inevitably eroded.

Because this method of quiet conciliation produced such excellent results, we have preferred the path of action to that of exhortation. Unfortunately, however, it appears that in recent years the issues have become confused and the march toward justice and equality has been slowed if not halted in some areas. The transcendent moral issues involved have become obscured, and possibly forgotten.

Our nation now stands divided by the problem of compulsory segregation of the races and the opposing demand for racial justice. No region of our land is immune from strife and division resulting from this problem. In one area, the key issue may concern the schools. In another it may be conflicts over housing. Job discrimination may be the focal point in still other sectors. But all these issues have one main point in common. They reflect the determination of our Negro people, and we hope the overwhelming majority of our white citizens, to see that our colored citizens obtain their full rights as given to them by God, the Creator of all, and guaranteed by the democratic traditions of our nation.

There are many facets to the problems raised by the quest for racial justice. There are issues of law, of history, of economics, and of sociology. There are questions of procedure and technique. There are conflicts in cultures. Volumes have been written on each of these phases. Their importance we do not deny. But the time has come, in our considered and prayerful judgment, to cut through the maze of secondary or less essential issues and to come to the heart of the problem.

The heart of the race question is moral and religious. It concerns the rights of man and our attitude toward our fellow man. If our attitude is governed by the great Christian law of love of neighbor and respect for his rights, then we can work out harmoniously the techniques for making legal, educational, economic, and social adjustments. But if our hearts are poisoned by hatred, or even by indifference toward the welfare and rights of our fellow men, then our nation faces a grave internal crisis.

No one who bears the name of Christian can deny the universal love of God for all mankind. When Our Lord and Savior, Jesus Christ, "took on the form of man" (Phil. 2, 7) and walked among men, He taught as the first two Laws of life the love of God and the love of fellow man. "By this shall all men know that you are my disciples, that you have love, one for the other." (John 13, 35) He offered His life in sacrifice for all mankind. His parting mandate to His followers was to "teach all nations." (Mat. 28, 19)

Our Christian faith is of its nature universal. It knows not the distinctions of race, color, or nationhood. The missionaries of the Church have spread throughout the world, visiting with equal impartiality nations such as China and India, whose ancient cultures antedate the coming of the Savior, and the primitive tribes of the Americas. The love of Christ, and the love of the Christian, knows no bounds. In the words of Pope Pius XII, addressed to American Negro publishers twelve years ago, "All men are brothered in Jesus Christ; for He, though God, became also man, became a member of the human family, a brother of all." (May 27, 1946)

Even those who do not accept our Christian tradition should at least acknowledge that God has implanted in the souls of all men some knowledge of the natural moral law and a respect for its teachings. Reason alone taught philosophers through the ages respect for the sacred dignity of each human being and the fundamental rights of man. Every man has an equal right to life, to justice before the law, to marry and rear a family under human con-

ditions, and to an equitable opportunity to use the goods of this earth for his needs and those of his family.

From these solemn truths, there follow certain conclusions vital for a proper approach to the problems that trouble us today. First, we must repeat the principle—embodied in our Declaration of Independence—that all men are equal in the sight of God. By equal we mean that they are created by God and redeemed by His Divine Son, that they are bound by His Law, and that God desires them as His friends in the eternity of Heaven. This fact confers upon all men human dignity and human rights.

Men are unequal in talent and achievement. They differ in culture and personal characteristics. Some are saintly, some seem to be evil, most are men of good will, though beset with human frailty. On the basis of personal differences we may distinguish among our fellow men, remembering always the admonition: "Let him who is without sin . . . cast the first stone . . ." (Jn. 8, 7) But discrimination based on the accidental fact of race or color, and as such injurious to human rights regardless of personal qualities or achievements, cannot be reconciled with the truth that God has created all men with equal rights and equal dignity.

Secondly, we are bound to love our fellow man. The Christian love we bespeak is not a matter of emotional likes or dislikes. It is a firm purpose to do good to all men, to the extent that ability and opportunity permit.

Among all races and national groups, class distinctions are inevitably made on the basis of like-mindedness or a community of interests. Such distinctions are normal and constitute a universal social phenomenon. They are accidental, however, and are subject to change as conditions change. It is unreasonable and injurious to the rights of others that a factor such as race, by and of itself, should be made a cause of discrimination and a basis for unequal treatment in our mutual relations.

The question then arises: Can enforced segregation be reconciled with the Christian view of our fellow man? In our judgment it cannot, and this for two fundamental reasons.

1) Legal segregation, or any form of compulsory segregation, in itself and by its very nature imposes a stigma of inferiority upon the segregated people. Even if the now obsolete Court doctrine of "separate but equal" had been carried out to the fullest extent, so that all public and semi-public facilities were in fact equal, there is nonetheless the judgment that an entire race, by the sole fact of race and regardless of individual qualities, is not fit to associate on equal terms with members of another race. We cannot reconcile such a judgment with the Christian view of man's nature and rights. Here again it is appropriate to cite the language of Pope Pius XII. "God did not create a human family made up of segregated, dissociated, mutually independent members. No; He would have them all

united by the bond of total love of Him and consequent self-dedication to assisting each other to maintain that bond intact." (September 7, 1956)

2) It is a matter of historical fact that segregation in our country has led to oppressive conditions and the denial of basic human rights for the Negro. This is evident in the fundamental fields of education, job opportunity, and housing. Flowing from these areas of neglect and discrimination are problems of health and the sordid train of evils so often associated with the consequent slum conditions. Surely Pope Pius XII must have had these conditions in mind when he said just two months ago: "It is only too well known, alas, to what excesses pride of race and racial hate can lead. The Church has always been energetically opposed to attempts of genocide or practices arising from what is called the 'color bar.'" (September 5, 1958)

One of the tragedies of racial oppression is that the evils we have cited are being used as excuses to continue the very conditions that so strongly fostered such evils. Today we are told that Negroes, Indians, and also some Spanish-speaking Americans differ too much in culture and achievements to be assimilated in our schools, factories, and neighborhoods. Some decades back the same charge was made against the immigrant, Irish, Jewish, Italian, Polish, Hungarian, German, Russian. In both instances differences were used by some as a basis for discrimination and even for bigoted ill-treatment. The immigrant, fortunately, has achieved his rightful status in the American community. Economic opportunity was wide open and educational equality was not denied to him.

Negro citizens seek these same opportunities. They wish an education that does not carry with it any stigma of inferiority. They wish economic advancement based on merit and skill. They wish their civil rights as American citizens. They wish acceptance based upon proved ability and achievement. No one who truly loves God's children will deny them this opportunity.

To work for this principle amid passions and misunderstandings will not be easy. It will take courage. But quiet and persevering courage has always been the mark of a true follower of Christ. We urge that concrete plans in this field be based on prudence. Prudence may be called a virtue that inclines us to view problems in their proper perspective. It aids us to use the proper means to secure our aim.

The problems we inherit today are rooted in decades, even centuries, of custom and cultural patterns. Changes in deep-rooted attitudes are not made overnight. When we are confronted with complex and far-reaching evils, it is not a sign of weakness or timidity to distinguish among remedies and reforms. Some changes are more necessary than others. Some are relatively easy to achieve. Others seem impossible at this time. What may succeed in one area may fail in another.

It is a sign of wisdom, rather than weakness, to study carefully the problems we face, to prepare for advances, and to by-pass the non-essential if it interferes with essential progress. We may well deplore a gradualism that is merely a cloak for inaction. But we equally deplore rash impetuosity that would sacrifice the achievements of decades in ill-timed and ill-considered ventures. In concrete matters we distinguish between prudence and inaction by asking the question: Are we sincerely and earnestly acting to solve these problems? We distinguish between prudence and rashness by seeking the prayerful and considered judgment of experienced counselors who have achieved success in meeting similar problems.

For this reason we hope and earnestly pray that responsible and sober-minded Americans of all religious faiths, in all areas of our land, will seize the mantle of leadership from the agitator and the racist. It is vital that we act now and act decisively. All must act quietly, courageously, and prayerfully before it is too late.

For the welfare of our nation we call upon all to root out from their hearts bitterness and hatred. The tasks we face are indeed difficult. But hearts inspired by Christian love will surmount these difficulties.

Clearly then, these problems are vital and urgent. May God give this nation the grace to meet the challenge it faces. For the sake of generations of future Americans, and indeed of all humanity, we cannot fail.

Signed by members of the Administrative Board, National Catholic Welfare Conference, in the name of the Bishops of the United States:

Francis Cardinal Spellman, Archbishop of New York
James Francis Cardinal McIntyre,
Archbishop of Los Angeles
Francis P. Keough, Archbishop of Baltimore
Karl J. Alter, Archbishop of Cincinnati
Joseph E. Ritter, Archbishop of St. Louis
William O. Brady, Archbishop of St. Paul
Albert G. Meyer, Archbishop of Chicago
Patrick A. O'Boyle, Archbishop of Washington
Leo Binz, Archbishop of Dubuque
Emmet M. Walsh, Bishop of Youngstown
Joseph M. Gilmore, Bishop of Helena
Albert R. Zuroweste, Bishop of Belleville

(*Source:* John Tracy Ellis, ed. *Documents of American Catholic History.* Vol. 2:1866–1966. Wilmington, Del.: Michael Glazier, 1987, 646–52.)

CIVIL WAR AND CATHOLICS, THE

Roman Catholics, North and South, lay and clergy, participated in the American Civil War out of loyalty to their respective sections, to enhance their place in American society, and with hopes to overcome nativist prejudice against them. During the war era, the United States was in the midst of industrial growth pains and agricultural decline which heavily impacted upon the system of labor. Caught in the middle, immigrant Catholics, North and South, clashed with natives over jobs. As society attempted to adjust to economic change, the political parties and the government system felt the chaos of those times. Recently formed nativist political parties attacked Catholic Democrats. Attitudes toward the place of government in that great upheaval launched a debate over the role of institutional life in the private sector, and inevitably brought the Catholic Church into that vortex of change. Even foreign relations at times become embroiled in battles over religious institutions as accusations were made that Catholics were more loyal to Europe and Rome than to their adopted country. Religious beliefs of Catholic people and the Church were caught up in the economic, social, and political turmoil of the age. In addition, the absence of an official Church position on slavery or the desperate sectional conflict left American Catholics adrift to act largely in the interests of their regions. All of these issues were exacerbated further when Catholics joined the war effort.

Northern Catholics During the Civil War

Northern Catholics participated in the war effort as ordinary soldiers and as officers, behind the lines in war-related jobs, as authors of partisan wartime propaganda, and through many charitable efforts. A number of Catholic generals had major roles in crafting the Northern victory, including William R. Rosecrans in Tennessee and Philip Sheridan in the Valley of Virginia. General William Tecumseh Sherman had been baptized Catholic, and General George L. Meade descended from a prominent Philadelphia Catholic family. Lesser but important Catholic general officers included Fenian Society leaders Thomas Meagher and Michael Corcoran, and General James Shields. Catholic Admiral Benjamin F. Sands ably served the United States Navy on the high seas.

Ordinary soldiers early flocked to the banner. They did so in part because of enlistment bonuses and the promise of future business opportunities which they hoped would allow them to leave the squalid conditions of the cities. Others joined out of devotion to their new nation. Ethnic differences and prejudices soon separated Northern troops, as enrolling officers learned to organize them along ethnic lines. The Hibernian Benevolent Society assisted to raise and equip such Irish regiments as the Ninth Massachusetts Volunteers, the New York Sixty-ninth Irish Volunteers, and the celebrated Twentieth Maine of Gettysburg fame. Irish troops were gaily decked out in uniforms with shamrock emblems and carried green banners into combat. Carl Schurz's famous Missouri Germans also fought valiantly at Gettysburg. In all approximately 150,000 Irish

and 175,000 Germans participated in the Union military cause. Some were recently recruited from the old country, but most had lived in the United States for a time. Those Catholic troops were used in the most hazardous of wartime conditions, as they often were selected to lead the charge in hopeless situations. General Meagher's Irish Brigade began the war some 5,000 strong, and after Chancellorsville dwindled to a mere 520 troops ready for duty. Those who saw Meagher's men try to carry Marye's Heights at Fredericksburg described it as abject slaughter. Accused of being aliens and disloyal Democrats, Catholic troops often felt the sting of Yankee prejudice. But generals like Sherman praised Catholic troops for their valor.

Due to prejudice, poor working conditions, and competition for jobs, Catholics at home became wary about military service and at times rioted over their plight. In the coal fields of eastern Pennsylvania ethnic Catholics fought among themselves for unskilled job opportunities. They often felt discriminated against in industrial jobs in the Midwest. In New York City Irish Catholic laborers clashed with black workers over menial jobs. When renewed draft efforts after Gettysburg seemed to single out the Irish in early July 1863, they went on a rampage that left at least 120 people dead. Irish thugs burned the Colored Children's Orphanage and the offices of the nativist New York *Tribune*. Ironically, it was an Irish-led police force which ultimately put down that riot, and probably forestalled riots in other Northern cities.

Jobs lured Irish and other Catholics to the United States, and at least 800,000 came over to work in war plants and take the places of native farmers who went off to fight. The passage of the Homestead Act in 1862 also served as a means to bring immigrants to these shores during the War. In the factories which produced war material the Catholic work force held the least enviable jobs, but they gained skills which could help them after the war. Work and living conditions were horrible for the Catholic people. At times German workers in Wisconsin towns rebelled against their unsafe working conditions. Chicago's infamous Third Ward became a symbol of wartime privation for Irish Catholics. Squalid housing, poor diets, and rampant crime made the Third Ward a place to avoid. Despite those horrid living conditions, the Catholic workers behind the lines ably served the Union cause.

Behind the Northern lines the Catholic press and church leaders kept up a steady and at times divisive propaganda war in support of and in opposition to the war. New York City Catholic Democrat James McMaster edited the *Freeman's Journal*, a scurrilous racist and pro-Confederate periodical. Antagonisms over politics, treatment of Catholic soldiers, and horrible family conditions behind the lines no doubt led to Catholic journalists' associations with the antiwar Copperheads. But other church writers such as Fr. Edward Purcell of Cincinnati and the editor of the New

York *Katholiche Kirchenzeitung* took strong positions in favor of the Union, and early supported the emancipation of the slaves. Midwestern bishops especially supported the war as they regarded it as a means to prove nativists wrong in their accusations that Catholics were un-American. Archbishop John Hughes of New York took a special interest in the Union cause. He flew the United States flag from the roof of his cathedral, actively recruited troops, preached on loyalty of the Constitution, supported the laws of the land, and opposed riots. The archbishop was sent to France to keep that country from recognizing the Confederacy. In all, the war of words and deeds revealed the Northern Catholic Church divided over what was good for its flock. But Northern Church leaders mainly supported the Union, even if their efforts caused some to worry about the question of separation of Church and state.

A field Mass during the Civil War

In charitable work the Church perhaps made its greatest contribution to the Union war effort and to the lives of ordinary Catholics. Some forty chaplains served in the front lines to minister to the needs of Catholic soldiers. They heard confessions, gave absolution, preached on temperance, and proselytized for conversion, and they took heroic risks as battles raged around them. Catholics remained aloof from the Protestant-controlled United States Sanitary Commission, and instead formed their own charitable organizations for the wounded troops and their families left behind in the war. They set up relief food kitchens and expanded orphanages for Catholic children, often beyond their capacity. The religious Sisters of Charity held hospital jobs and even went into the front lines to tend to wounded soldiers. When public charitable groups were overwhelmed with the task of feeding and clothing women and children, the Church hierarchy stepped in to help. But the Church was unable to provide enough aid, as even orphanages were forced to shut down for lack of staff. Since

even teaching sisters and priests served in the war effort, Catholic schools at times had to close. The clergy who remained taught the children about patriotic Catholic soldiers in the front lines, and in that manner assisted Catholic youth to become patriotic Americans.

Southern Catholics During the Civil War

During the war Southern Catholics also ably served their own people and contributed mightily to the Confederate war effort. The Church did not break formally with Northern Catholics, but its minority status and the issue of slavery divided Southern Catholics. Southern Catholics lived mostly in Louisiana and Maryland, although border and coastal cities, and towns along the Mississippi River had large numbers of Catholics, some of whom had recently arrived in the South. Those from the urban border areas and those most recently settled in the South had conflicted loyalties, and mainly remained neutral or joined the Union cause. Recent German Catholic immigrants to Nashville and San Antonio, trapped within the Confederacy, received rough treatment. Some were murdered, and others were forced to flee from their homes. Most Southern Catholics, however, fought for and aided the cause of the Confederacy.

Soldiers usually were organized according to their ethnicity, as separate New Orleans Creoles and Richmond Irish regiments fought and died together. The Eighth Alabama Regiment was also an Irish regiment. Those ordinary soldiers often fought far from their homes, participated in many campaigns, and served the cause valiantly. But Southern Catholic troops also came in for nativist prejudice, and many claimed that despite their valor they were passed over for promotion.

Catholic elites had long lived in certain areas of the lower South and the border slave states, and they held leadership positions beyond their numbers, and certainly in better posts than their Northern opponents. General Pierre G. T. Beauregard of Louisiana stands out as one of the greatest Confederate commanders, as he was a major strategist of the Confederate war effort. The cousins Louis and Paul Hébert, both brilliant engineers, ably served the cause as leaders in Louisiana. William J. Hardee whose well-known book of *Tactics* was a primer for soldier training was a Catholic. The leading Maryland Catholic to serve in the Confederate army was Major General William Whiting, who had been number one in his class at West Point, but did not live up to his promise. The great Admiral Raphael Semmes, commander of the cruiser *Alabama* and a legendary Confederate naval commander, originally came from a Maryland Catholic family before he settled in Mobile.

Catholic leaders also held major civilian commands in the Confederacy. Notable was Stephen Mallory, Confederate Secretary of the Navy. Commissary General of the

Confederacy and close friend of President Jefferson Davis, Lucius B. Northrup had converted to the Church before the war. Creole Catholics from Louisiana served in the Confederate Congress, as did Arkansas Catholic David Carroll, descended from a prominent Maryland family. Henry Watterson of Louisville, Kentucky, edited a pro-Confederate newspaper. The infamous Confederate spy, Belle Boyd, the "Rebel Rose," was also a Maryland Catholic.

Behind the lines ordinary Catholics worked in railroad construction, in factories, as longshoremen on the docks, and in the dangerous jobs on the river levees. They often clashed with black laborers in the urban South, and some of them went over to the Union side. They faced job competition, dangerous tasks, poor pay, and ethnic prejudice. But a number of them learned the skills necessary for postwar occupational opportunities. Alas, many would have to leave the South because those jobs disappeared in the ruined economy. Wealthy Catholic bankers, lawyers, and businessmen from the cities no doubt turned their talents to the Confederate cause. A number, however, seemed to owe no loyalty to any cause, and they absconded back to the old world with their wealth and talent.

Priests and religious also served the Confederacy as chaplains and in the hospitals. The famous poet-priest Fr. Abram Ryan was a chaplain. The New Orleans Redemptorist James B. Sheeran became famous for his conversion practices. Some thirty other priests served in the front lines as poorly paid, untrained, and courageous men of the cloth. Those in religious orders, like the Emmitsburg Daughters of Charity, worked in hospitals and aided the wounded on both sides. In all, some eight hundred nuns served in the war. The Church also attempted to feed and clothe wives, widows, and children of the Catholic soldiers, after the task proved overwhelming for civilian authorities. At times urban Catholic women rioted for food and shelter, despite Church efforts.

The Church hierarchy and its various publications also sought to keep up the morale of soldiers and civilians with a constant stream of attacks on Yankee perfidy and defense of slave society. *Charleston Catholic Miscellany* set the standard of support for the Confederacy. Fr. Ryan's bishop also encouraged him to publish war poetry, and he became the poet laureate of the Confederate cause with his patriotic efforts. Some border state bishops were unable to support the Confederate war effort. The resignation of Bishop James Whelan of Tennessee and subsequent removal to the North was a blow to Catholic loyalty in the Middle South. Bishop Martin J. Spalding of Louisville, who hoped to remain neutral during the war, nevertheless supported slavery and wrote an important pamphlet in 1863 entitled *A Dissertation on the American Civil War.* That major defense of slavery, which also supported Catholic education for ex-slaves, was said to have influenced Vatican policy on the Civil War.

Also interested in Rome's position on the Confederacy was Bishop Patrick Lynch of Charleston who traveled to Rome in behalf of the Confederate government. Bishop Augustin Verot of St. Augustine and Savannah had previously written a pamphlet based on a fastday sermon which circulated widely in the Confederacy during the war. This major document by a Catholic bishop supported secession, urged Catholics to fight for the South, but also warned Catholic planters about ill-treatment of their slaves. Verot's pamphlet became a major statement about the morality of slavery and the duties of Catholic masters to their slaves. Bishop Verot was also one of the first Southern Catholics to advocate training for ex-slaves once the war had ended. Bishop John McGill of Richmond was an ardent supporter of the Confederacy, and he personally raised and armed a regiment of Irish troops.

The Northern military invasion of the South and its generals reacted to the ardent Catholic support of the Confederate cause. Northern troops confiscated Church property. Churches were used as barns, and burned when the troops left. Bishop William Elder of Natchez was for a time forced to flee his home because he refused to honor Yankee requests that he pray for the Union cause. Union troops occupied a Savannah Catholic graveyard during Sherman's March to the sea and they violated the premises. Southern Catholics thus were left with horrible memories of Yankee behavior which would influence their postwar devotion to the Southern cause and their enmity toward the North.

Aftermath

In so many ways, the Civil War had caused hardships for the nation's Roman Catholics. From privation and starvation, to loss of jobs, to many deaths in combat, lay persons in the North and the South suffered mightily. The war also proved costly to the Church in forcing schools and orphanages to close, and in the destruction of Church property. But Catholics had also a taste of public service and took pride in their contributions to the war effort. Heroic generals took their places in the lexicon of American Catholic lore. Chaplains and nuns and their unselfish wartime activities on behalf of the people no doubt helped to overcome nativist charges of their disloyalty. Catholic workers, although their wages were depressed, gained job and factory skills, and a number were able to become farmers. Through these opportunities they were prepared to enter the mainstream of American labor, at least until the next economic crisis placed them again at the bottom of the job market. Alas, even before the war had officially ended, Catholics were implicated in President Lincoln's assassination, as members of the Surrat family were charged with having aided the assassin. The issue of disloyalty again surfaced. Church leaders also attempted to confront the serious immediate postwar labor crisis and the plight of the ex-slaves and Northern free black people. The Church opened schools and offered training to black people. It also made an effort to convert them, but black people did not join the Catholic Church in large numbers, either in the North or the South.

Blied, Benjamin. *Catholics and the Civil War.* Milwaukee, 1945.

Charleston Catholic Miscellany [formerly *United States Catholic Miscellany*].

Germain, Aidan H., O.S.B. *Catholic Military and Naval Chaplains, 1776–1917.* Washington: The Catholic University of America Press, 1929.

Hennesey, James, S.J. *American Catholics.* New York: Oxford University Press, 1981.

Lipscomb, Oscar H. "The Administration of John Quinlan: Second Bishop of Mobile, 1859–1883." *Records of the American Catholic Historical Society of Philadelphia* 78 (1967) 1–163.

New York *Freeman's Journal.*

Osborne, William A. *The Segregated Covenant: Race Relations and American Catholics.* New York: Harper and Row, 1967.

JON L. WAKELYN

Related Documents

BISHOP LYNCH PRESENTS THE SOUTH'S CASE FOR SECESSION, AUGUST 4, 1861

Unlike some of the Protestant churches, the organizational unity of the Catholic Church in the United States remained intact during the slavery controversy and the Civil War. But that did not mean that there were not deep sectional differences of opinion among the Catholics of the North and the South on the issues at stake. These differences were high-lighted for the general public when the New York *Metropolitan Record* of September 7, 1861, published an exchange of correspondence between Patrick N. Lynch (1817–1882), Bishop of Charleston, and Archbishop John Hughes of New York on responsibility for the war. Lynch had outlined his views for Hughes in a letter on August 4, and the latter took the somewhat unusual step of replying through his own newspaper on the grounds that, by reason of the disruption of the mails, it was his only chance of acknowledging Lynch's communication. He decided, therefore, to print his reply of August 23 and, as he told the Bishop of Charleston, "without special permission publish your letter at the same time. In this way it may happen that during the war, or afterwards, my answer will come under your inspection" (Lawrence Kehoe, ed., *Complete Works of the Most Rev. John Hughes, Archbishop of New York* [New York, 1865] II, 513). Lynch may have learned of Hughes' action because shortly thereafter he published the full text of his letter to the archbishop in his own diocesan paper. The exchange between the prelates attracted widespread attention and complete texts of the letters, together with accompanying editorials, were carried by the New York *Herald, Times,* and *Tribune.* In its issue of September 4, 1861, James Gordon Bennett's *Herald* stated that the "statesmanlike views and admirable temper" of the correspondence "will obtain for it a widespread and attentive consideration both here and abroad." The *Herald*'s editorial took occasion to read a lecture to some of the

Protestant clergy whose extreme statements were in striking contrast to the calm and tempered opinions of Lynch and Hughes, recommending the bishops' letters to "all the abolitionist and secessionist parsons throughout the country."

(*Source:* Charleston *Catholic Miscellany,* September 14, 1861.)

MOST REVEREND DEAR SIR:

The mails are so completely paralyzed that it is hard to get a letter from outside the Confederacy. Papers are scarcely ever seen. That, however, Jefferson would think a blessing, on the ground that "he who is simply ignorant is wiser than the one that believes error." A paragraph which has gone the rounds of the Southern papers, states that your Grace has spoken strongly against the war policy of the Government of the United States, fraught with much present suffering, and not calculated to attain any real advantage. What a change has come over these States since I wrote you a long letter last November, and even since I have had the pleasure of seeing you last March. All that I anticipated in that letter has come to pass, and more than I looked for. All the hopes cherished last spring of a peaceful solution have vanished before the dreadful realities of war. What is before us, who can say? Missouri, Maryland and Kentucky are nearer secession now than Virginia, North Carolina and Tennessee were four months ago. Missouri is a battle field. I think that President Davis, after the victory of Stone Bridge, will probably throw a column into Maryland. Kentucky will, ere long, be drawn into the struggle, and the United States will, in less than ten months, be divided in two not unequal parts, marshalling hundreds of thousands of men against each other.

This war is generally dated from the bombardment of Fort Sumter. There we fired the first gun, and the responsibility is charged on us. But, in reality that responsibility falls on those who rendered the conflict unavoidable—The South, years ago, and a hundred times, declared that the triumph of the abolition or anti-slavery policy, would break up the Union. They were in earnest. When that party, appealing to the people on the Chicago platform, elected their candidate by every free State vote (excepting New Jersey, which was divided,) South Carolina seceded, and other States were preparing to do so. They were in earnest. Yet, as the people disbelieved it, or heeded it not at the ballot, so Congress heeded it not at Washington, and stood doggedly on the Chicago platform endorsed by the people.— This consummated success. The Confederate Government was formed. The dogged obstinacy of the Black Republicans at Washington last winter made all the South secessionists. Still there was peace. The new Administration professed an intention to preserve it. Peace gave time, and time can work wonders. The Confederate Government did not put much faith in those professions. The same hallucination as to their power, which rendered the Black Republicans arrogant and impracticable in Congress, would, it was apprehended, lead them to attempt to crush out secession by force.—And nothing was left undone to be prepared for this event should it occur.

Meanwhile Commissioners were at Washington to arrange a peaceful separation. Favorable intimations were privately given them, and they had hopes of success.

Nine Governors, however, it is said, put the screws on the Cabinet, which resolved on a war policy, and, as silently as they could, made warlike naval preparations. Then, after a month, the Commissioners were refused admission or dismissed, and it was plainly announced that here would be no negotiation. At this time other facts were coming to light here, in Charleston, where our batteries had, for a month or more silently looked on Fort Sumter. During the time of peaceful professions two special messengers (Fox[1] and Lamon[2]) from President Lincoln visited Fort Sumter. Before being allowed to go thither they gave their word of honor to our Governor that their object was really peaceful. The hotel conversation of the latter was very frank, it is said. Gentlemen here supposed that President Lincoln before ordering the evacuation wished, by these personal friends, to see, as it were, personally, and not simply to learn through official channels, how matters stood at Fort Sumter. When time rolled by without such an order, and it was rumored that the Cabinet had succumbed to the pressure of the Governors, the mails were stopped to and from Fort Sumter. Among the letters seized was one from Major Anderson[3] to President Lincoln, discussing the details of the plan of reinforcement, forwarded to him from Washington by these messengers. Our authorities were thus made aware of the breach of faith towards them, and of the details of the plan itself.

Then came the special messenger of the President, announcing that he intended revictualing the fort, quietly, if permitted, forcibly, if resisted; then the account of the sailing of the fleet from New York. The fort was at once attacked and taken without waiting their arrival. The attack was not made until the offer of negotiation and peaceful arrangement had been rejected, and until the United States Government was in the act of sending an armed force. But it is of little use now to inquire on whom the responsibility rests; we have the war on us, with all its loss of life and long train of evils of every kind. It is the latest, perhaps the strangest instance history gives us, *quam parva sapientia regitur mundus*. Here was a country, vast, populous, prosperous and blessed in all material interest, if any country was. The south producing Cotton, tobacco, sugar, rice and naval stores for the supply, as far as needed, of the North and Northwest, to the value of, perhaps, $50,000,000 a year, and exporting to foreign countries over $220,000,000; the Northwest producing chiefly grain, and supplying the North and the South, and when the European crops failed, having, as last winter, a large European market; the North manufacturing and supplying the South and the Northwest, and struggling to compete with foreign goods abroad, and doing the trading and commerce of the South and the Northwest.

Could the material interests of all the sections be more harmoniously and advantageously combined than in this Union, where each was free to develop to the fullest extent those branches of industry in which it could excel, and could draw from the others those products which it needed, but could not produce as well or as cheaply as they could? Even a child could see the vast benefits to all from this mutual co-operation. No wonder that in all material interests the country was prospering to an extent that intoxicated us and astonished the world. We claimed to be pre-eminently sagacious in money matters. The Yankees, I believe, ranked next after the Chinese, in their keenness in business; yet they especially, with an inconceivable blindness, have originated, fostered and propagated a fanatical party spirit which has brought about a result foretold from the beginning, both North and South, as the inevitable consequence of its success.

Taking up anti-slavery, making it a religious dogma, and carrying it into politics, they have broken up the Union. While it was merely all intellectual opinion they might discuss it as they pleased; they might embrace it as they did any other ism. Even their virulent use and misrepresentation we scarcely heeded, provided they did not obtrude them upon us at home. We, as Catholics, might everywhere smile at this additional attempt to "reform" the teachings of our Savior. And the Protestants, South, could have churches and associations of their own. But when they carried it into politics, gaining one State Government after another, and defining their especial policy by unconstitutional laws and every mode of annoying and hostile action, and finally, with increased enthusiasm and increased bitterness, carrying the Presidential election in triumph, and grasping the power of the Federal Government, what could the South do but consult its own safety by withdrawing from the Union? What other protection had they? The Senate, which had still a Democratic majority? They had seen the House of Representatives pass into the hands of their enemies, and each session saw an increasing majority there. The Executive had gone for four years. Their own majority in the Senate was dwindling fast, while on the Territorial question not a few of the Northern Democrats were unsound. To the Supreme Court? That had spoken in the Dred Scott decision. The North would not sustain it, and the Black Republicans scouted it; and moreover, in a few years President Lincoln would have the privilege of placing on the bench new judges from the ranks of his party. To the sober second thought of the people? But this was no new issue on which they were taken by surprise. For years and years it had been discussed; North and South it had been denounced as fraught with disunion and ruin; and yet the Northern people had gradually come to accept it. But the South had spoken so often and so strongly of disunion, without doing anything, that the Northern people had no real belief that any evil consequences would ensue; they did not understand the full bearing of their action. At least, let them understand something of this before all hope of appeal to them is abandoned. Well, South Carolina seceded—other States were preparing to follow her. The matter was taken up in Congress. Many Southerners hoped that then, when the seriousness of the questions could no longer be doubted, something might be done. How vainly they hoped, the Committees of Congress showed. The alternative was thus forced on the South either of tame submission or of resistance. They did not hesitate. They desired to withdraw in peace. This war has been forced upon them.

It was necessary in the beginning. It brings ruin to thousands in its prosecution. It will be fruitless of any good. At its conclusion the parties will stand apart exhausted and embittered by it; for every battle, however, won or lost, will have served but to widen the chasm between the North and South, and to render more difficult, if not impossible, any future reconstruction. Will it be a long war, or a short and mighty one? The Cabinet and the Northern press has pronounced for the last. Yet this is little more than an idle dream. What could 400,000 men do?

I do not think there is a General on either side able to fight 50,000 men. And the North would need eight or ten such Generals. Certainly the 40,000 under McDowell,[4] after five hours' fighting, fought on mechanically without any generalship. The higher officers had completely lost the guiding reins. On our side the Southern troops ought to have been in Washington within forty-eight hours. But the 40,000 on the Confederate side was, I apprehend too unwieldy a body for our Generals. Did not Bonaparte say that not one of his Marshals could general fifty thousand men in battle?

Soult[5] could bring them to the field, and place them properly, but could go no further.

But without Generals, what could 400,000 men do against the South? By force of numbers, and a great loss, they might take city after city. But unless they left large permanent garrisons, their authority would die out with the sound of their drums. Such an army marching through a country covered with forests and thickets and occupied by a population hostile to a man, and where even schoolboys can "bark a squirrel," would be decimated every hundred miles of its progress by a guerrilla warfare, against which it could find no protection. This mode of attacking the South can effect nothing beyond the loss of life it will entail, and the temporary devastation that will mark the track of the armies.

But it is probable that circumstances would again, as they have done, overrule the designs of the Washington Cabinet, and make the war slow, long and expensive—

one to be decided, less by battles than by the resources and endurance of the combatants.

That portion of the former United States will suffer most in such a contest and must finally succumb, which is least able to dispense with the support it received from the other two sections. How the North can do without our Southern trade, I presume it can judge after three or four months' trial. But it would seem that the failure to sell to the South one hundred and twenty millions of their manufactures each year the stoppage of so much of their shipping interest as was engaged in the two hundred and twenty millions of our foreign exports and the return importations, and in our internal coasting trade, together with the loss of the profits and commissions on so vast a business, must have a very serious effect, too, that I see no way of escaping. Truly the North has to pay dearly for its whistle of Black Republicanism. The Northwest depended partially on the South for a market for its productions, and so far will suffer from the loss of it. It must also be incidentally affected by commercial embarrassments at the North. They will assuredly have enough to eat and to wear, but the "fancy" prices of real estate and stocks, by which they computed their rapidly increasing wealth, must fall in a way to astonish Wall-street. Should their own crops fail, as they sometimes do, or should the European crops be abundant, their commerce will fall. Yet, as the mass of the poor will have all that they ever get anywhere—food and raiment, and that without stint—the Northwest will suffer comparatively little.

How long will it fare with the South should the war be long and so powerfully waged as to require the Southern Confederation to keep say 100,000 men-in-arms, and if the ports are strictly blockaded? This is an important question, and one that can be answered only from a practical knowledge of the habits, resources and disposition of the Southern people. Our needs will be provisions, clothing, money for the government and war expenses, and for the purchase from abroad of what we absolutely require, and are not already supplied with.

As for provisions, I am satisfied that this season we are gathering enough for two years' abundant supply. Every one is raising corn, wheat and stock. On this point the South need not envy the Northwest. Again, manufactures are springing up on all sides, In this State we are providing for our wants—from lucifer matches and steam engines to powder and rifled cannon. Clothing, too, though of a ruder texture and sometimes inferior quality, is abundantly made and easily procured. The supply of tea and coffee will, I presume, in time run out. This will put us to some trouble, but otherwise, neither for provisions nor for clothes, will the South be seriously inconvenienced.

The blacks (by-the-bye more quiet and orderly now, if possible, than before) will remain devoted to agriculture, while the rapidly increasing demand for home productions of every kind gives ready employment to the poorer classes of the whites.

What amount of gold and silver there is within the Confederate States I can only guess at—I suppose about $25,000,000. But as the greater part of our expenses are at home, any currency we are satisfied to use will do, whether Bank bills, Confederate bonds or Treasury notes. When we go abroad, it must be with gold or with Cotton. This last is the spinal column of our financial system. The following is the proposed mode of operating with it: Two millions, or two and a half of bales will be conveyed to the Confederate Government, to be paid for in bonds or Treasury notes. This Cotton will be worth, at ordinary prices, one hundred millions of dollars. If it can be exported at once, it is so much gold. If it is retained, it will form the security for any loan that may be required abroad. The other third of the Cotton will be sold by the planters as best they can on their own account.

The chief difficulty is the blockade, which may prevent the export and sale abroad of the Cotton. A loan on it as security, while it is still unshipped, and scattered in numberless small warehouses, could not easily be affected.

Up to the present time, and for six months more, the blockade, so far from doing any serious injury, has, on the contrary, benefitted, and will continue to benefit the South, forcing us to be active, and to do for ourselves much that we preferred formerly to pay others to do for us. I presume that next January, with a crop of three and a half or four millions of bales on hand, the South would become very restive under a strict blockade. *Should it continue twelve months longer property at the South would go down as they say it has in New York.*

But, before that time comes, another very serious complication arises—how England and France will stand the cutting off their supply of an article on which depend two-thirds of the manufacturing interests of the one and one-third of those of the other? They cannot, try they ever so much, supply the deficiency. As far as the feelings of England are concerned, and, I presume, those of France, too, both nations are decidedly and bitterly anti-slavery; but neither will be guilty of the mistake of the North, and utterly sacrifice vast interests for the sake of a speculative idea. If they find that they cannot do without Southern Cotton, they will interfere, first probably to make peace, and if that effort fails, then in such other manner as will secure for them what will be a necessity. Mr. Seward's[6] letter to Dayton,[7] and its reception in Europe, the transportation of troops to Canada, and Admiral Milne's declaration as to the inefficiency of the blockade, are straws already showing the possible course of future events. Is the Federal Government strong enough for a war with England and France in addition to that with the South?

One other warlike course remains—to capture and hold all the Southern ports, and thus seek to control commerce, independent of secession, leaving the interior of the South to fret and fume as it pleases. This is the problem of belling the cat. The Northern forces would have to capture Norfolk, Charleston, Savannah, Wilmington, N.C., Pensacola, Mobile, New Orleans and Galveston, besides some fifteen other smaller points. At each of them they would find a Stone Bridge; and even if they succeeded, they could only hold military possession and be forever in arms against the attacks of the State authorities. Peace would never be established by any such course. It would not be successful, and even if successful, it would only hamper the South, it would never subjugate it.

The separation of the Southern States is *un fait accompli.* The Federal Government has no power to reverse it. Sooner or later it must be recognized. Why preface the recognition by a war equally needless and bloody? Men at the North may regret the rupture; as men at the South may do. The Black Republicans overcame the first at the polls, and would not listen to the second in Congress, when the evil might have been repaired. They are responsible. If there is to be fighting, let those who voted the Black Republican ticket shoulder their musket and bear the responsibility. Let them not send Irishmen to fight in their stead, and then stand looking on at the conflict, when, in their heart of hearts, they care little which of the combatants destroy the other.

Most Reverend dear Sir, I am surprised and somewhat ashamed of the length to which my pen has run. But the night is hot—too hot for sleep. I arose from my couch, and have spent a couple of hours speaking to you as frankly and unreservedly as you have ever kindly allowed me to do. A trip to New York would be agreeable for more reasons than one. But that is impossible. Next to that I would like to see a file of the Record.[8] That, too, is impossible. Nothing seems now to span the chasm but that bridge of Catholic union and charity, of which your grace spoke so eloquently last St. Patrick's Day.

I must thank you, too, for your article in my defence against Tracy. He was a poor man with a growing family whom, at Rev. Mr. O'Connell's[9] instance, Bishop Reynolds[10] allowed to live on a place in Newberry District, belonging to him, rent free, and as an act of charity I did not trouble him. He says I saw him there once, years ago. Perhaps so, I do not remember. The first time I remember seeing him, was here in Charleston, after his expulsion. He was driven off, because he was suspected for years, and charged by the neighbors with stealing, and buying stolen goods habitually—was once tried and convicted—and afterwards, they were satisfied, continued the practice.

Commending myself to your holy sacrifices, I have the honor to remain, most Reverend dear Sir, your Grace's sincere and respectful son in Christ.

✝ P. N. LYNCH, D.D., S.C.[11]

[1]Gustavus V. Fox (1821–1883) was named Assistant Secretary of the Navy by Lincoln's government in August, 1861.

[2]Ward H. Lamon (1828–1893), a former Law partner of Lincoln in Illinois, had been sent to Charleston as the president's personal agent in March, 1861.

[3]Robert Anderson (1805–1871) was the Union Commander at Fort Sumter.

[4]General Irvin McDowell (1818–1885) and his Union army were routed by the Confederate forces at Manasses Junction, Virginia, on July 21, 1861.

[5]Marshal Nicolas-Jean-de-Dieu Soult (1769–1851) was one of the most prominent of Napoleon's generals.

[6]William H. Seward (1801–1872) was Lincoln's Secretary of State.

[7]William L. Dayton (1807–1864) had been appointed American Minister to France in 1861.

[8]Hughes had started the *Metropolitan Record* in July, 1859, after falling out with McMaster of the *Freeman's Journal*.

[9]There were two priests of that name in the Diocese of Charleston at that time, Jeremiah J. and Lawrence P. O'Connell.

[10]Ignatius Reynolds (1798–1855) ruled the See of Charleston as its second bishop from 1844 to 1855.

[11]Patrick N. Lynch was consecrated as third Bishop of Charleston on March 14, 1858. In the spring of 1864 he received an official commission from President Jefferson Davis to go to Rome with the hope that he could win recognition for the Confederacy from the government of Pope Pius IX. The mission ended in failure, however, and it was not until late in 1865 that Lynch was able to return to his diocese after a presidential pardon had been won for him through the efforts of Archbishop Martin J. Spalding of Baltimore.

Hughes concluded his lengthy letter to Lynch by stating that there remained nothing for him to add except "that the Catholic faith and Catholic charity which unites us in the spiritual order, shall remain unbroken by the booming of cannon along the lines that unfortunately separate a Feat and once prosperous community into two hostile portions, each arrayed in military strife against the other" (Kehoe, *op. cit.*, II, 520).

(*Source:* John Tracy Ellis, ed. *Documents of American Catholic History.* Vol. 1:1493–1865. Wilmington, Del.: Michael Glazier, 1987, 347–56.)

A CATHOLIC CHAPLAIN WITH THE UNION ARMIES, OCTOBER 2, 1862

Ever since Canadian-born Father Louis E. Lotbinière (1715–1786) was commissioned by the Continental Congress in January, 1776, to serve as chaplain to Colonel James Livingston's regiment of Canadian volunteers, Catholic priests in one capacity or another have been rendering spiritual aid to the American armed forces. Early in the Civil War President Lincoln informed Archbishop Hughes of New York that he had appointed three Protestant ministers as hospital chaplains, and he added, "If you perceive no objection, I will thank you to give me the name, or names, of one or more suitable persons of the Catholic Church, to whom I may, with propriety, tender the same service" (Archives of the Archdiocese of New York, Lincoln to Hughes, Washington, October 21, 1861). Eventually sixty-seven priests were enrolled as chaplains in the field with the Union and Confederate armies, together with a number of hospital and volunteer chaplains and nearly 500 sisters from over twenty congregations who cared for the wounded in hospitals. Among the Union chaplains Father Peter P. Cooney, C.S.C. (1822–1905), was one of the most prominent. He was attached to the 35th Regiment, Indiana Volunteers, from October, 1861, to June, 1865, and saw service in

Kentucky, Tennessee, and Georgia during which time he conceived a deep admiration for the piety of General William S. Rosecrans (1819–1898), a convert to Catholicism from his days at West Point, and it was Cooney who received General David S. Stanley (1828–1902) into the Church early in 1864. The following letter depicted for his brother experiences which have been met by all chaplains who have seen active fighting with the American armies.

(*Source:* Thomas T. McAvoy, C.S.C., ed. "The War Letters of Father Peter Paul Cooney of the Congregation of Holy Cross." *Records of the American Catholic Historical Society of Philadelphia,* XLIV. March 1933, 67–69.)

LOUISVILLE, KENTUCKY
October 2, 1862

My dear Brother:

After a long silence I am happy to have an opportunity to write you a few lines. Since I last wrote my health has never been better. It seems as if my health grows better as my hardships and fatigues increase; for all that I had to undergo since I entered on this new field of duty could not equal what I had to endure last month.

We started from McMinnville, Tennessee on the last day of August and we have been marching nearly ever since. We arrived here a few days ago, having traveled, without stopping but [for] the necessary rests, over three hundred miles and nearly the whole time in a dense cloud of dust, so that we looked like so many millers. There [were] between sixty and eighty thousand soldiers with us, making a fearful army. When we arrived here Munfordsville, Kentucky, we prepared for a battle, as the Southern troops were nearly as many as we were at this place and they have the benefit of a strong fortification. We stopped a day and a night to prepare for the battle between two large armies. I heard confessions all that night—no sleep. I sat eight hours without getting off my seat. It was a very cool night; for the nights, as a general thing, are colder in the South than in Michigan or Indiana but the days are warmer. About twelve o'clock, my legs were perfectly benumbed, until one of the poor soldiers brought me a blanket to roll around my thighs; for they think more of an inconvenience to me than I do myself. You might hear them whispering to one another words of sympathy for me. They little knew the joy that was in my breast, midst all these trials, when I considered how much God was doing with the hands of his unworthy son.

If [you] were to see my confessional that night you would laugh. In the evening one of the soldiers came to me and said: "Father, will you be hearing tonight?" "Indeed I will, my dear, with God's help," I answered and I jocosely asked him in presence of the others, "Did you not know I was hearing all day?" "No Father," said he, very innocently, and he noticed the joke only when the next commenced to laugh. I find it an advantage sometimes in camp to crack a joke with them; it cheers them up and enlivens the monotony of camp life. "What will you do Father," said one, "for a place to hear confessions in?" (For we were in the open field). "Never mind," I answered, "come this way four or five of you." They came and we made three stacks of guns, four guns in each, in this shape V, [and] the bayonets were locked into each other. Then we got three blankets, two covering two sides hanging on the bayonets; the other covered the top, leaving the front open. And in this I sat all night. This is a piece of architecture that you will not find in Monroe. Here the poor fellows came, impressed with the idea that perhaps this would be the last confession of their lives. Some of the officers gave me their wills and then went to confession. But it would take volumes to tell all.

Here, dear Brother, in such places life is valued as it ought—as worth nothing. That night I baptized a non-commissioned officer who was to that time an Episcopalian. But we came to Munfordsville the next day and the rebels had run away. We caught only the hind ones who could not keep up. All the march we were up at two o'clock in the morning; and generally it was ten or eleven o'clock before we could get to bed, without tents, but the broad canopy of heaven. I alone had a tent along but some nights it would be five miles behind in the wagon train. So you see we have "high living" when you come to add to this, that the men had to march some times eight hours without anything to eat.

The whole army started yesterday from here towards Bardstown forty miles from here to meet the enemy. I follow them tomorrow morning. I shall take a trip home to rest about the end of the month. I think the drafting system is given up, so you need not be troubled about it. Pray, pray, dear Brother, for me and for yourselves and heaven shall be our reward.

Your Brother,
P. P. Cooney, *Chaplain*
35th Reg. Ind. Vol.

Write immediately and let me know how my mother and all the folks are. Give my love to all. Direct your letter to me Chaplain 35th Reg. Ind. Vol., Louisville, Kentucky.

(*Source:* John Tracy Ellis, ed. *Documents of American Catholic History.* Vol. 1:1493–1865. Wilmington, Del.: Michael Glazier, 1987, 376–8.)

THE NURSING SISTERS IN THE MILITARY HOSPITALS OF VIRGINIA, JANUARY, 1862–APRIL, 1865

One of the most inspiring—and little known—chapters of the Civil War was written by the nearly 500 members of twenty or more congregations of religious women who nursed the wounded in the military hospitals of both the North and South. Among the most prominent of these congregations were the Daughters of Charity of St. Vincent de Paul whose mother house at Emmitsburg, Maryland, was only a few miles distant from the battlefield at Gettysburg. Speaking of that memorable encounter in July, 1863, Sister Camilla O'Keefe (1815–1887), a contemporary, stated, "They fought until the evening of the 3rd, advancing by their movements more and more towards our peaceful Vale, so that our buildings and the very earth trembled from their cannons" (Archives of St. Joseph's Central House, Emmitsburg, "Notes, 1863," p. 22). There is record of at least 232 of the Daughters of Charity who engaged in nursing the troops during the war. On September 20, 1924, a monument to the "Nuns of the Battlefield" was unveiled in Washington across the street from St. Matthew's Cathedral to commemorate the deeds of these heroic women of the many congregations who gave their services to the wounded soldiers. The following document of Sister Angela Heath (1830–1912), who saw service from January, 1862, to April 13, 1865, four days after the surrender of Lee at Appomattox, gives a good idea of the difficulties encountered by the sisters as they moved from one hospital to another during the campaigns of the Old Dominion.

(*Source:* Archives of St. Joseph's Central House, Emmitsburg, Maryland. "Annals of the Civil War, 1861–1865." Pp. 95–98.)

LEFT RICHMOND FOR MANASSES ON THE 9TH. OF JANUARY 1862, at the solicitation of Dr. Williams[1] Medical Director of the Army of the Potomac. We were five in number, & found, on taking possession, 500 patients, sick & wounded of both armies. Mortality was very great, as the sick poor had been very much neglected. The wards were in a most deplorable condition, & strongly resisted all efforts of the broom to which they had long been strangers, & the aid of a shovel was found necessary. At best, they were but poor protection against the inclemency of the season & being scattered, we were often obliged to go through snow over a foot deep, to wait on the sick. For our own accommodation we had one small room, which served for dormitory, chapel, &c, &c. & when we were fortunate enough to get a chaplain, the holy sacrifice was daily offered in a little corner of our humble domicile. The kitchen, to which what we called our refectory, was attached, was, I do not think I exaggerate when I say a quarter of a mile from our room, & often it was found more prudent to be satisfied with two meals than to trudge through the snow for a third, which at best, was not very inviting, for the culinary department was not under our control, but under that of negroes, who had a decided aversion for cleanliness. On an average, ten died every day, & of this number, I think I may safely say, four were baptized, either by Fathers Smoulders [sic][2] & Feeling [sic][3] or by our Sisters. It happened several times that men, who had been until then totally ignorant of our faith, & I may say even of God, sent to us in the middle of the night, when they found that they were dying, & begged for baptism which astonished as well as consoled & edified us. On the 13th of March we received orders from Gen. Johnson [sic],[4] to pack up quietly & be ready to leave on six hours' notice, as it was found necessary to retreat from that quarter.

Oh the horrors of war! We had scarcely left our post than the whole camp was one mass of flame, & the bodies of those who died that day, were consumed. Our next field of labor was the military hospital at Gordonsville. We were but three in number & found 200 patients very sick—pneumonia and typhoid fever prevailing. Here again privations were not wanting. The sick were very poorly provided for, although the mortality was not as great as at Manasses. . . . Father S. who was our chaplain at that time received about twenty-five into the communion of the Church some of whom died shortly after. One morning as Sister Ann Estelle[5] was visiting her patients before Mass, one called from the lower end of the ward, "Oh! Sister, Sister, do come & save me, let me die in the church that you Sisters belong to. I believe all that you believe." Father S. who was vesting for mass, was at first unwilling to wait on him until after, but as Sister insisted that no time was to be lost, he went and baptized him, & as we knelt at the "Et verbum caro factum est," he expired. The approach of the Federals compelled us to leave Gordonsville on Easter Sunday, & we retreated "in good order" to Danville. . . . Here we found 400 sick much better provided for than in M. or . . . . Most of our patients were Catholic, at least in name, for many had almost forgotten their duties as such, but it was our consolation to see them entering upon them again with the simplicity of children. The zeal of good Father S. led many to a knowledge of our holy religion & about 50 were baptized. In Nov. the Medical Director removed our hospital to Lynchburg as there was no means of heating that in Danville. Our number had increased to five as the hospital was larger & contained 1000 patients, whom we found in a most pitiful condition. The persons who were in charge, had a very good will, but not the means of carrying it out, & although the fund was ample, the poor patients were half starved owing entirely to mismanagement. As we passed through the ward the first time, accompanied by the Dr., a man from the lower end called out, "Lady, oh lady—for God's sake gave me a piece of bread." To give you an idea of the care the sick had received, it will be sufficient to say that though the whole establishment had been cleaned for our reception, some of the Sisters swept up the vermin in the dust pan. The doctors soon placed everything under our control, & with a little economy the patients were well provided for, & order began to prevail. Father Gache,[6] a zealous & holy Jesuit, effected much good & removed many prejudices from the minds of those whom a faulty education had made enemies—bitter enemies of our holy faith. During the three years that we remained in L. he baptized 100. . . . The approach of the Federals placed our hospital in imminent danger & it was decided to move the sick & hospital stores to Richmond. The Surgeon General of the Confederate Army[7] begged that we would take charge of the Stuart hospital in that city which we did on the 13th. of Feb. 1865. We were then 10 in number, & as usual, we found plenty to do to place the sick in a comfortable situation, which we had just accomplished when the city was evacuated, & on the 13th. of April, the hospital being dispensed with, we left R. for our sweet valley home.

[1]An effort to identify Williams further was unsuccessful.

[2]Egidius (Giles) Smulders, C.Ss.R. (1815–1900), was a Dutch-born priest, chaplain of the Eighth Louisiana Infantry, who served throughout the entire war.

[3]Henry Fehlings (1822–1888), a German-born priest, who was dispensed from his vows as a Redemptorist in May, 1861, and died as pastor of St. Mary's Church, Utica, New York.

[4]Joseph E. Johnston (1807–1891) was in command of the Confederate troops in northern Virginia at this time.

[5]An effort to identify this religious was not successful.

[6]Hippolite Gache, S.J. (1817–1907), was a chaplain who entered the service from Louisiana.

[7]Samuel Preston Moore (1813–1889) was Surgeon General of the Confederate Army.

(*Source:* John Tracy Ellis, ed. *Documents of American Catholic History.* Vol. 1:1493–1865. Wilmington, Del.: Michael Glazier, 1987, 368–70.)

CLARETIANS

The Claretians are a religious community of Catholic priests, brothers, and laypeople who are engaged in spiritual, social, and educational works in fifty-four countries around the world. They number more than 3,000 professed members. They take their name from St. Anthony Claret, a nineteenth-century Spanish missionary preacher, writer, and promoter of religious and social renewal.

Claret formed the order (Sons of the Immaculate Heart of Mary) in Vich, Spain, in 1849. Soon afterward, he was appointed the archbishop of Santiago, Cuba, where he served for seven years and fought for the freedom of slaves and other social reforms. He later became the personal chaplain to Queen Isabella II of Spain and established a major publishing house there. He was declared a saint by Pope Pius XII in 1950.

The Claretians first came to the U.S.A. from their province in Mexico in 1902 and began a ministry to Spanish-speaking people in San Antonio, Texas. They steadily extended their ministry into Arizona, California, the Midwest, and East Coast. The Claretian Eastern province is based in Chicago and the Western province in Los Angeles.

Mission work has been a part of the Claretian tradition from the beginning. The United States Eastern province developed a mission in Guatemala in 1965. Currently, Claretian priests and lay missionaries from the United States and the UK/Irish province work in three mission centers that serve between twenty and sixty small agricultural and fishing villages. The missions are dedicated to parish work, health and education programs, and land reform.

The Claretians in the Western province staff San Gabriel Mission, one of the original California missions founded by the Franciscans. They also staff Our Lady, Queen of Angels Church (Plaza), the largest Hispanic parish in the country. They have a retreat center and offer special outreach to troubled youths in Los Angeles. They serve in other parish ministries in California, Arizona, and Texas.

The Claretians maintain the National Shrine of St. Jude which they founded in Chicago in 1929. Over the years, the shrine has attracted thousands of St. Jude patrons to its novena services, and the St. Jude League receives annually hundreds of thousands of letters of thanks and petition.

Following the example of their founder, Claretians in the United States and around the world are active in publishing. Claretian Publications in Chicago publishes two highly regarded national magazines, *U.S. Catholic,* which serves as a forum for lay Catholics, and *Salt of the Earth,* a resource for parish-based social justice. Other Claretian Publications include Martin Marty's *Context, U.S. Parish, Bringing Religion Home, Generation, Nuestra Parroquia,* and *El Momento Católico.*

The Claretians throughout the country are dedicated to social justice and urban development. In South Chicago, they have helped fund the building of Villa Guadalupe, a low-income seniors' retirement complex, and Guadalupe Homes, houses for low-income families. They also manage medical centers for poor and indigent families, provide counseling services, and sponsor youth-formation and summer ministry programs. Since the late 1970s, they have directed campus ministry at Southwest Missouri State University in Springfield, Missouri.

JENNIFER TOMSHACK

CLARKE, MARY FRANCES (ca. 1803–87)

Religious leader. Mary Frances Clarke, founder of the Sisters of Charity of the Blessed Virgin Mary, was the daughter of Cornelius Clarke and Catherine Quartermas. The exact date of Mary Frances' birth in Dublin, Ireland, cannot be documented. It was either March 2, 1803 or 1806. Clarke and four of her friends opened Miss Clarke's Seminary in 1832, a school for young girls too poor to attend the convent schools.

A missionary from the United States convinced the five young women to move to Philadelphia in 1833 to teach the children of the Irish immigrants. There the women met Fr. Terence Donaghoe who encouraged them to organize as a religious congregation, the Sisters of Charity of the Blessed Virgin Mary (B.V.M.s). Clarke became the mother superior and they opened a school for poor girls.

When, in 1843, Mathias Loras, bishop of Dubuque, invited the congregation to educate children of Native Americans and of pioneer farmers, Clarke responded by sending five sisters to open a school in Dubuque in the Iowa Ter-

Mary F. Clarke

ritory. Later that year Loras convinced the other fourteen sisters and Fr. Donaghoe also to settle in Dubuque.

These women religious led by Clarke attracted other young pioneer women. During her lifetime 440 joined the congregation. She sent them to teach in schools opened for children of the pioneers moving westward. Clarke maintained close contact with her sisters through letter writing, encouraging the women who experienced great hardship living in primitive conditions. The congregation began as a circle of friends and Clarke's letters continued that relationship.

Her letters also revealed a collaborative and compassionate leadership style. During Clarke's fifty-four years as mother superior, she established forty parochial schools and nine boarding academies. The last school she opened before her death on December 4, 1887, was in San Francisco. On August 27, 1984, Mary Frances Clarke was inducted into the Iowa Women's Hall of Fame for her role in the education and religious formation of the American frontier.

See also WOMEN RELIGIOUS IN AMERICA.

Coogan, Jane, B.V.M. *The Price of Our Heritage.* 2 vols. Dubuque, Iowa: Mt. Carmel Press, 1975.

Doran, Lambertina, B.V.M. *In the Early Days.* St. Louis: Herder, 1911.

McGuire, Pulcheria, B.V.M. *Annals* (1905). Unpublished. B.V.M. Archives, B.V.M. Center, Dubuque, Iowa.

Smith-Noggle, Laura, ed. *My Dear Sister.* Correspondence and Notes of Mary Frances Clarke. Dubuque, Iowa: Mt. Carmel Press, 1987.

KATHRYN LAWLOR, B.V.M.

CLORIVIÈRE, JOSEPH PIERRE PICOT DE (1768–1826)

Soldier, priest. Clorivière was born in Nantes, France, on November 4, 1768. The son of Michel Alain Picot and Renée Jeanne Roche Picot, he was educated at the College of Rennes and at the Royal Military School of Paris. He served as an officer in the King's Guards, but resigned his commission in 1791. He soon became associated with the Chouans, the counterrevolutionary movement founded in the west of France. In 1800 he was implicated in a plot to assassinate Napoleon, but eluded arrest and went into hiding until 1803 when he emigrated to Savannah, Georgia, and changed his name to Picot de Clorivière. In 1806 he entered St. Mary's Seminary in Baltimore, Maryland, to study for the priesthood. Upon his ordination in 1812, he was sent to St. Mary's Church in Charleston, South Carolina.

He made a trip to France in 1814 and on his return to Charleston one year later was informed by the pastor and the church's trustees that he had been replaced with another priest during his absence. The events that followed would place Clorivière at the center of one of the Church's most contentious episodes in the early nineteenth century, often referred to as "the Charleston schism." The conflict was finally resolved in 1818 when Archbishop Ambrose Maréchal sent Fr. Benedict Fenwick, S.J., to mediate the dispute. In the end, Clorivière was reassigned, becoming chaplain to the Visitation Convent in Washington, D.C., the city in which he died. Because of his generous support of the sisters, he is often referred to as the convent's second founder and is buried in the crypt there.

Carey, Patrick W. *People, Priests and Prelates: Ecclesiastical Democracy and the Tensions of Trusteeism.* Notre Dame, 1987.

TRICIA T. PYNE

COADY, CLARE (1875–1935)

Educator and religious. Margaret Ann Coady was born in New Orleans on October 3, 1875, daughter of Joseph Coady and Mary Jane Farley. Raised in the Irish Channel and Mount Carmel Orphan Asylum in New Orleans, she entered the Sisters of Mount Carmel, New Orleans, on September 2, 1891; she professed first vows on July 27, 1894, and final vows on July 24, 1902. She taught at Abbeville, Lafayette, and Thibodaux in Louisiana as well as at Vinita in Indian Territory from 1894 to 1913. She was principal and superior at Mount Carmel Academy in Lafayette, 1909–15 and 1931–35.

She served two terms as her community's superior general, 1915–31. During her tenure, the community took charge of three parochial schools in New Orleans as well a school in Westwego; opened Mount Carmel Academy in the Lakeview section of New Orleans, 1926; established a state-approved normal school in New Orleans, 1923; won state approval for community high schools; and fostered state certification for teaching sisters. She encouraged spiritual renewal among the sisters through personal example, legislative changes, and motherly supervision. Under her leadership, the Louisiana community was affiliated to the main branch of the Carmelite Order in 1931.

She died at Lafayette, Louisiana, on March 22, 1935, and was interred there. Her leadership as superior general reflected an emphasis on a solid personal spirituality and the growing educational professionalism among Louisiana's religious communities.

See also LOUISIANA, CATHOLIC CHURCH IN.

Mother Clare Coady Papers in Archives of the Sisters of Mount Carmel, New Orleans, Louisiana.
Nolan, Charles E. *Mother Clare Coady: Her Life, Her Times and Her Sisters.* New Orleans: 1983.

CHARLES E. NOLAN

COCKRAN, WILLIAM BOURKE (1854–1923)

Lawyer, U.S. Congressman. Cockran was born on February 28, 1854, in Sligo, Ireland, to Martin and Harriet Knight Cockran. Following his early education in Ireland and France, Cockran emigrated to New York in 1871, avoiding his parents' plan that he pursue a clerical vocation. He was able to study part-time at night while teaching at a Catholic girls' academy and serving as principal of a public school in Tuckahoe, New York. He was admitted to the New York bar in 1876.

William Bourke Cockran

Cockran practiced law in Mt. Vernon, New York, for two years before moving to New York City where he began a career in politics. While Cockran's entire career was consistently distinguished by oratorical abilities that he often used on behalf of the rights of immigrants, his party loyalties were less consistent. He began his political career in New York as the delegate for the Irving Hall Democracy, a faction opposed to Tammany, at the Democratic State Convention at Albany in 1881. In 1884, however, he gained national attention at the Democratic National Convention when, this time as a Tammany delegate, he delivered a speech attacking the nomination of Grover Cleveland.

Cockran was elected to the House of Representatives in 1886, 1890, and 1892. Because of his opposition to the free coinage of silver, he broke with the Democratic Party and opposed William Jennings Bryan, siding with William McKinley in the 1896 presidential campaign. His "Sound Money" speech at Madison Square Garden in New York City is considered the high point of his oratorical efforts. His commitment to the Republican Party was short-lived, however, and in 1900 he returned to the Democratic Party largely because of "the brutal imperialism of McKinley." He was subsequently elected to Congress in 1904 and served until 1909. The campaign of 1912 saw another shift of loyalties as Cockran embraced the cause of Theodore Roosevelt, an embrace which did not preclude frequent vocal criticism of Roosevelt. His membership in the Republican Party was longer lived this time, but ultimately he returned to the Democrats. He came back into national attention in 1920 when he delivered a rousing speech supporting the presidential nomination of New York State Governor Alfred E. Smith. He returned to the House that year, serving until his sudden death on March 1, 1923.

McGurrin, James. *Bourke Cockran: A Free Lance in American Politics.* New York, 1948.

United States Sixty-Eighth Congress, First Session, May 4, 1924, House. *W. Bourke Cockran: Memorial Addresses Delivered in the House of Representatives in Memory of W. Bourke Cockran, Late Representative from New York.* Washington, 1925.

RICHARD G. SMITH

CODY, JOHN CARDINAL (1907–82)

Cardinal archbishop of Chicago. John Patrick Cody was born in St. Louis, Missouri, on December 24, 1907, and was ordained for the Archdiocese of St. Louis on December 8, 1931. Named auxiliary bishop of St. Louis (titular bishop of Appollonia) in May 1947, he served there until being named coadjutor bishop of St. Joseph, Missouri, in January 1954. In 1956 he was appointed bishop of Kansas City-St. Joseph, where he remained until 1961. In that year, he was named coadjutor archbishop of New Orleans; a year later he was appointed administrator, and

John P. Cardinal Cody

by November 1964 he became archbishop of New Orleans. (It was the third successive diocese in which he had been named coadjutor with the right of succession to an aging bishop.) In New Orleans, he took a strong stand in favor of integration, including the public excommunication of several prominent Catholic politicians when they refused integration within their civil parishes.

In June 1965 he was named eleventh bishop, sixth archbishop of Chicago, succeeding Cardinal Albert Meyer. On June 26, 1967, Paul VI named him a cardinal priest, the fourth cardinal in Chicago history. He served for seventeen years.

Early Career

Cardinal Cody was a classic careerist. He spent ten years in Rome, first as a seminarian (1927–31) and then as vice rector of the North American College and a staff member of Cardinal Eugenio Pacelli's (later Pius XII) Secretariat of State from 1932 to 1938. Another staff member at the time was a diplomat named Giovanni Battista Montini, who would become Paul VI and would appoint Cody to Chicago. (Cody used to boast that he had been named a bishop a full seven years before Montini. It was a classic non sequitur, but it may explain why Paul VI was so reluctant to remove him from office years later.)

Recalled to St. Louis in 1938, Cody was made personal secretary to Archbishop (later Cardinal) John Glennon. He established his *Romanità* even before he was consecrated bishop. In February 1946 he accompanied Archbishop Glennon to Rome where the ailing prelate was to receive the cardinal's red hat. En route home, already near death, Glennon stopped in his native Ireland. Meanwhile, Cody's mother was dying in St. Louis. He chose to remain with Glennon, who died on the same day that Cody's mother was buried.

The see of Chicago was vacant sixteen months before Cody was named to Chicago. According to Peter Hebblethwaite, biographer of Paul VI, the long delay was evidence of a titanic battle for the vacant throne. Cody enjoyed the support of Cardinals Francis Spellman of New York and James McIntyre of Los Angeles, together with the support of the apostolic delegate, Egidio Vagnozzi, who was Cody's old Roman classmate.

Archbishop of Chicago

Cody arrived in Chicago in a special railroad car that underscored his imperial style. He immediately dismissed a group of aging pastors and began to centralize all authority which his predecessors Albert Meyer (1958–65) and Samuel Stritch (1939–58) had preferred to delegate to others. Chicago had thrived under the permissive style of Stritch and Meyer for over twenty-five years. It was a center of liturgical reform, civil rights, labor movements, and family apostolates such as the Cana Conference and the Christian Family Movement. Known for its massive parishes, many of its pastors were de facto bishops who came to resent Cody's high-handed style. It was viewed as a reversion to an earlier era under the autocratic Cardinal George Mundelein (1915–39).

Nonetheless, Cody introduced many benefits for both clergy and lay employees. He instituted a health insurance plan for priests, initiated a pension plan for both clerical and lay employees, and established a personnel board. However, his autocratic style was not in step with the changing times. It was a period when large numbers of priests were resigning from the active ministry. (Chicago lost over three hundred.) The subsequent shortage of priests and funds caused Cody to close parishes. By 1966 his high-handed style had so incensed his priests that they formed a de facto union, the Association of Chicago Priests (ACP). Initially, Cody tried to cooperate with them, but within a few years, tensions had grown so strong that they soon came to view appeals to his authority as challenges. When the ACP publicly censured both Cody and his auxiliaries, all contact was broken.

Although often viewed as a restorationist, Cody had sensitive political radar. He sensed the mind of Rome on certain key issues, particularly those coming out of Vatican Council II. Thus, he revamped the seminary curriculum, replacing the rectors. He established a permanent diaconate program which rapidly became the largest in the U.S.A. He promoted desegregation in the parishes and the schools, even meeting privately with Dr. Martin Luther King, Jr., and giving generous subsidies to the black and Hispanic inner city parishes that survived the budget cuts. Yet he drew sharp criticism for his lavish spending on his

pet projects, the Catholic Television Network of Chicago (CTN/C), which proved a failure, and his renovation of Holy Name Cathedral on which he lavished over three million dollars. The first project displayed his vision but was severely hobbled by his style; the second project was vitally necessary but was carried out with such secrecy that his clergy rebelled even more.

Cody's obsession with detail caused him to ignore the growing disaffection of his priests and people. He insisted on signing all checks and reading all chancery correspondence. Despite incredibly long workdays, the backlog continued to accumulate. His compliant staff tended to echo his style. As a result, the gap between the chancery and the parish continued to widen.

Later Years

By the early 1980s, Cody's style began to unravel. He had become more suspicious and reclusive. Having succeeded to three dioceses after being named coadjutor, he began to fear that he would suffer the same fate. His problems were compounded when rumors began to surface that he had diverted much of the archdiocesan insurance business to a David Dolan Wilson, the son of Cody's stepcousin in St. Louis. There is no evidence that young Wilson cheated the archdiocese, but the coincidence could not be ignored. Rumors were rampant that the beleaguered cardinal was having an affair with Helen Dolan Wilson, who had relocated to Chicago and had a luxury apartment not far from Cody's mansion.

The rumors grew so strong that by 1981, the United States Attorney's office opened an investigation of Cody's finances. The suspicion was that he had diverted diocesan funds for personal use, including the purchase of a home in Florida for his stepcousin. There is evidence that she was on the payroll of the archdiocese, although there was no evidence of her work product and, after brief employment in some poorly defined position, she received a generous pension. It remains entirely possible that whatever support Mrs. Wilson received came from the cardinal's personal funds. Further, no one was able to substantiate any evidence of an affair.

Cody's final days were spent fending off charges that, by this time, had become front-page news, especially in the *Chicago Sun-Times*, which published a long investigative piece. Following his death, stories surfaced that his old friend, Paul VI, had hesitated about removing him from office. Allegedly, the necessary papers were on John Paul I's desk, but he died after a thirty-one-day reign. According to former *New York Times* correspondent Tad Szulc's biography of John Paul II, Cardinal Karol Wojtyla, enjoyed Cody's support before the conclave which would elect him pope in 1978. Further, when John Paul II visited Chicago, Cody arranged a lavish welcome. The Pope's support insured that Cody would not be removed from office.

Now nearing his seventy-fifth year, Cody's health began to fail, even as he fended off his attackers. The once vast and vigorous archdiocese drifted considerably while he spent much of his final days with lawyers. He died in his mansion on April 25, 1982. Within three months, with uncharacteristic haste, John Paul II appointed Joseph L. Bernardin of Cincinnati to succeed him.

See also ILLINOIS, CATHOLIC CHURCH IN; LOUISIANA, CATHOLIC CHURCH IN; MISSOURI, CATHOLIC CHURCH IN.

Code, Joseph B. *Dictionary of the American Hierarchy.* New York, Joseph F. Wagner, 1964.

Dahm, Charles. *Power and Authority in the Catholic Church: Cardinal Cody in Chicago.* University of Notre Dame Press, 1981.

Skerrett, Ellen, Edward B. Kantowicz, Steven M. Avella. *Catholicism Chicago Style.* Chicago: Loyola University Press, 1993.

R. TIMOTHY UNSWORTH

COGLEY, JOHN (1916–76)

Writer and journalist. Cogley was born in Chicago on March 16, 1916, to John F. Cogley and Ann Geenty. His mother died giving birth to him. Maternal relatives were never a factor in his life, and his father who married again and had another family was somewhat detached from him. The only relative who was unequivocally devoted to his interests was his paternal grandmother. After receiving a parochial school elementary education, he won a scholarship to St. Philip High School, run by the Servites. For his second year of studies, he switched to the Servite's preparatory seminary for those who intended to enter the

John Cogley

order and continued through graduation. He then decided, however, that he would not continue on and begin collegiate seminary studies for the priesthood.

Early Years

Then, his grandmother died and he was mostly on his own in difficult economic times. He found occasional jobs and earned enough to enroll in two courses at Loyola University and also took free evening courses in philosophy at nearby Rosary College. In 1937 he found a copy of the *Catholic Worker,* was impressed by it, and attended a meeting of a new Catholic Worker group that had been organized on the west side of Chicago by a black physician, Arthur G. Falls. This led to a period of full-time involvement with the Catholic Worker that eventually included the direction of a soup kitchen and a house that provided shelter to as many as three hundred men. It also led to Cogley's first journalistic work as the editor of the *Chicago Catholic Worker,* an eight-page monthly. Through the *Catholic Worker,* Cogley met and worked with Al Raser, James O'Gara, Ed Marciniak, Tom Sullivan, and Theodora Schmidt, a recent graduate of the University of Chicago who worked as secretary to Saul Alinsky, the social activist. While the *Catholic Worker* was officially pacifist, Cogley and his colleagues felt Hitler had to be stopped by force and they entered military service. This happened a few weeks after Cogley married Theodora Schmidt on April 6, 1942.

Editor of Commonweal

By the war's end, they were the parents of two children, and, thanks to the education benefits of the G.I. Bill of Rights, Cogley finished his undergraduate degree at Loyola University and continued on for graduate studies in Thomistic philosophy at the University of Fribourg in Switzerland. While finishing his degree at Loyola, he had with James O'Gara founded and edited *Today,* a national Catholic student publication. He continued freelance writing during his graduate studies and upon returning to the United States in 1949, was offered the position of executive editor of *Commonweal* by Edward Skillin, the editor in chief. There, to gain some extra income for the family that expanded ultimately to six children, Cogley added the writing of a column to his regular editorial duties. He left *Commonweal* in 1955 to work for Robert Hutchins and the Center for the Study of Democratic Institutions, but continued his widely admired *Commonweal* column which established him as the most prominent American Catholic journalist and lay leader of his generation.

Other Activities

His first project for the Center was to direct a study of blacklisting in the radio, television and motion picture industry and the resulting two-volume report showed how the lives and careers of hundreds had been damaged. Summoned by the House Committee on Un-American Activities, he courageously resisted the committee's pressure to reveal his sources, while testifying without an attorney at his side because he explained: "I didn't see why I had to have anybody on hand to protect my rights before a group of Congressmen." He had himself accepted a draft in 1954 to run for Congress on the Democratic ticket losing in a heavily Republican district.

In 1960 he served as an aide in the presidential campaign of John F. Kennedy, contributing crucially as the "principal architect" of Kennedy's famous televised speech and discussion with a group of Protestant clergymen in Houston. The presentation is credited with defusing Kennedy's Catholicism as a campaign issue, and with being a key element in his eventual victory over Richard M. Nixon. In 1968 Cogley joined the campaign staff of Senator Eugene J. McCarthy, an old friend whose moral courage he admired.

In 1965 he had left the Center to join the *New York Times* as Religion News Editor. He covered the final session of Vatican Council II, winning a prize from the Catholic Press Association for his coverage. In 1967 he returned to the Center in Santa Barbara where he became a senior fellow and founding editor of *Center Magazine*. He also wrote two books, *Religion in a Secular Age* (1968) and *Catholic America* (1973).

Like many Catholics, Cogley found the 1968 encyclical on birth control, *Humanae vitae*, to be disappointing. Syndicated as a columnist in some twenty diocesan Catholic papers, he wrote a final piece giving fundamental dissent from the encyclical as his reason for discontinuing the column. Later, he resumed writing for the independent Catholic press.

In 1973, however, he was formally accepted into the Episcopal Church. His wife and six children did not join him in the move. He said he felt no hostility toward the Catholic Church or its leadership, and that he was not at all confident that he would be a better Christian as an Anglican, but that he thought he could be "a more honest one." In 1974 he suffered a serious cerebral stroke. During an extended recovery he wrote the autobiographical *A Canterbury Tale* (1976). He also applied to the Episcopal diocese of California for ordination to the priesthood and was accepted. Ordained a deacon in January 1976, he was developing a special ministry among the aging and looking forward to ordination later in the year when he died of a heart attack on March 29.

See also COMMONWEAL; CATHOLIC WORKER MOVEMENT, THE; *HUMANAE VITAE:* ITS RECEPTION IN AMERICA.

Cogley, John. *Catholic America.* Expanded and updated by Rodger Van Allen. Kansas City, Mo.: Sheed & Ward, 1986, esp. 217–24.

Van Allen, Rodger. *The Commonweal and American Catholicism.* Philadelphia: Fortress Press, 1974.

RODGER VAN ALLEN

COLLEGE OF ST. SCHOLASTICA

The College of St. Scholastica in Duluth, Minnesota, was founded in 1912 by a group of Benedictine sisters who saw higher education as an extension of their mission in the Duluth area, where they had already been establishing schools, hospitals, and orphanages.

Their first college courses were offered to six young women. The first baccalaureate class was graduated in 1926. In 1996 St. Scholastica, the only independent college in northeastern Minnesota, educated nearly 2,000 men and women, and had more than 9,000 alumni.

The College of St. Scholastica's story began in the 1880s when sisters from St. Benedict's Convent at St. Joseph, Minnesota, were sent to the booming frontier harbor city of Duluth. With the establishment of the Duluth diocese in 1889 a plan was developed to have the sisters break ties with their motherhouse in the St. Cloud, Minnesota, diocese and establish an independent Benedictine community in Duluth. The head of this effort was Mother Scholastica Kerst, the former prioress of St. Benedict's.

See also CATHOLIC UNIVERSITIES AND COLLEGES.

ROBERT ASHENORACHER

COLORADO, CATHOLIC CHURCH IN

Historians are agreed that the first Catholics to enter the present bounds of Colorado were Spanish pioneers and missionaries. Just when, however, the first of these Spanish parties penetrated the confines of the Centennial State has not been definitely determined. A possible opinion is that Coronado and his entourage cut across the plains in what is now southeastern Colorado in the year 1541. Every Spanish cavalcade of exploration was always accompanied by several chaplains and with Coronado's expedition there were Franciscan priests. Following this opinion, the Catholic history of the state could have begun with Coronado in 1541. Within the first ten years of the eighteenth century there were at least two Spanish missions within the territory of Colorado.

Diocese of Denver

In 1849 the territory of Colorado was placed officially by the Holy See under the vicariate apostolic of New Mexico. This continued until 1868 when the Holy Father established the vicariate of Colorado and appointed Fr. Joseph Machebeuf as first bishop. This first bishop visited every part of a state which contained miles and miles of prairies as well as mountains over 14,000 feet. The tremendous zeal and leadership of Bishop Machebeuf were formally recognized by the Holy Father, who, on August 16, 1887, made the vicariate of Colorado the Diocese of Denver with Bishop Machebeuf as its first bishop and the Rev. Nicholas C. Matz coadjutor bishop with the right of succession. Bishop Machebeuf began his work as bishop of Colorado in 1868 with three priests, two schools, ten sisters and about 18,500 Catholics.

One of the great highlights of his episcopate occurred in 1884 when the Jesuits agreed to come to Morrison, Colorado, to open a college for men. Bishop Machebeuf gave them a forty-two-room, two-story, stone resort hotel which had been owned by the territorial governor of Colorado, John Evans. The college opened on September 15, 1884, as the College of the Sacred Heart, with a faculty of nine Jesuits and twenty-four students. Three years later the Jesuits moved the college to Denver on a forty-acre site at West 52nd Avenue and Lowell Boulevard. In 1919 the college was renamed Regis College, in honor of St. John Francis Regis, a seventeenth-century French Jesuit. The Jesuits have been a mainstay of the Church in Colorado throughout the years, operating Regis College, now Regis University, Regis High School, and staffing many parishes.

When Bishop Machebeuf died on July 10, 1889, the Catholic population of the State was forty thousand, served by 64 priests and 168 sisters. The majority of the priests who served the church in Colorado during this period were from France and Ireland. The first religious orders of women to make a major commitment to Colorado were the Sisters of Loretto from Nerinckx, Kentucky. They staffed many elementary and secondary schools as well as founding, in 1864, St. Mary's Academy for girls and Loretto Heights College. Bishop Machebeuf had a great love for Catholic schools and established sixteen parish schools, nine academies for young ladies, one orphanage, one protective home, and one college for men. At his death, throughout the state there were 49 churches, 53 chapels, 85 mission stations and 11 Catholic hospitals.

Bishop Matz succeeded Bishop Machebeuf as the second bishop of the diocese. During his tenure, thousands of people from all parts of Europe emigrated to the United States. The advent of the railroads brought many of these emigrants to Colorado. Bishop Matz was very conscious of making the church available to every nationality and he established special parish churches for the Italians, the Germans, the Polish, the Irish, and the Spanish. He was especially happy to welcome Mother Frances Xavier Cabrini when she came to Denver and established a parish school at the Italian parish of Mount Carmel and an orphanage for all children. Mother Cabrini also established a Shrine to our Blessed Mother in the mountains adjacent to Denver which is visited each year by thousands of people and is still served by the Sisters of Mother Cabrini.

One of the great events in his years as bishop was the building of St. Thomas Seminary as a training institution for prospective priests for Colorado and the surrounding states. The Vincentian Fathers in 1907 agreed to staff the seminary and continued to do so until 1995. It was under the leadership of Bishop Matz that ground was broken for the erection of a cathedral which has aptly been called: "The Pinnacled Glory of the West." Ground was procured on Colfax Avenue, two blocks from the state capitol, and upon it was erected one of the most impressive Gothic cathedrals in the United States. The administration of Bishop Matz was characterized by educational expansion and reaching out to people of every race. His administration was greatly blessed by the generosity of laypeople like J. K. Mullen, a poor Irishman who became a multimillionaire flour miller and emerged as a financial angel of the Denver diocese. It is estimated that he contributed over two million dollars to the Church during his lifetime. Two of his special projects which still bear his name are Mullen High School and the J. K. Mullen Home for the Aged. At the death of Bishop Matz, the Catholic population was over 110,000, with 88 churches with resident priests and 133 mission churches. Bishop Matz died on August 6, 1917.

A little over a month later, on September 18, 1917, Bishop J. Henry Tihen of Lincoln, Nebraska, was appointed third bishop of Denver. Bishop Tihen headed the Diocese of Denver for thirteen years. It was a period which witnessed extraordinary expansion following the ending of the First World War. The Catholic population increased during these thirteen years from 110,000 to 136,000, served by 123 diocesan priests and 106 religious order priests,

John H. Tihen

an increase of 55 priests in 13 years. There were 111 churches with resident pastors and 144 mission chapels. The diocese had two colleges with 423 students, one seminary with 95 seminarians, four academies for young ladies, 49 parish elementary schools, four orphanages, one industrial school, and 12 hospitals. Bishop Tihen founded the Catholic Charities of Denver under the capable leadership of Fr. John R. Mulroy in February 1927. His first office was two rooms in the Railroad Building at 1515 Larimer Street. Catholic Charities has grown to serve many needs of the Church and is found in every aspect of community life. Bishop Tihen retired on September 2, 1931, and he lived in Wichita, Kansas, where he had served as a young priest, until he died on January 14, 1940.

The Right Reverend Urban J. Vehr, rector of Mt. St. Mary of the West Seminary, Norwood, Ohio, was appointed by the Holy Father to succeed Bishop Tihen. For the third time, a bishop of Colorado had earlier roots in the state of Ohio. Both Bishop Machebeuf and Bishop Matz had served the Church in Ohio. Bishop Vehr was a bishop who measured up to every challenge and tried to reach the heart of every person. He strengthened all phases of the Catholic Charities programs, especially during the depression years, and he provided visible and compassionate leadership during the Second World War. He made it his personal challenge to administer the sacrament of confirmation in every parish and to use that occasion to visit personally with the priests and people.

Archdiocese of Denver

On January 6, 1942, the Holy See recognized the status and growth of the Diocese of Denver by naming the diocese an archdiocese with Bishop Vehr as the first archbishop. The Diocese of Pueblo was also established at this time. The Diocese of Pueblo comprised basically the southern half of the State of Colorado and the Archdiocese of Denver the northern half of the state. To assist Archbishop Vehr in the administration of the archdiocese, Fr. David Maloney was consecrated auxiliary bishop on January 4, 1961. During the thirty-six years of Archbishop Vehr's episcopate, Catholicism flourished. Church membership tripled and he ordained 162 priests for the archdiocese. He served with a chancery staff of three priests and was always available. On February 22, 1967, Archbishop Vehr retired. He was seventy-five years of age. He died on September 19, 1973. Upon his death, the *Rocky Mountain News* placed this headline over his obituary: "One of the brightest and loving stars ever to shine in Colorado."

Under God's providence, a very gentle shepherd was sent to succeed Archbishop Vehr. On February 22, 1967, Pope Paul VI appointed Bishop James V. Casey of Lincoln, Nebraska, as the successor of Archbishop Vehr. On his shoulders fell the task of implementing the directives of Vatican Council II and accomplishing this during the difficult decades of the 1960s and 1970s. The tenor of his years as archbishop were reflected in his opening remarks on the day of his installation at the cathedral: "I do not come to you as one thinking he has all the answers. I do not even know all the questions. I come to walk with you as a gentle and loving shepherd." His life as archbishop fulfilled this comment among the priests and people. He showed special concerns for the poor, the homeless, and the forgotten. He sought to achieve the goals of Vatican II in every parish and he provided outstanding leadership in involving laymen and laywomen in the life and programs of the Church. Often using laypersons, the archbishop created many new offices: Aging, Campus Ministry, Catholic Youth Services, Chicano Concerns, Data Processing, Family Life Services, Handicapped Services, Low-income Housing, Justice and Peace, Major Giving, Parish Councils, Priestly Personnel, Prison Ministry, Pro-Life, Single Adults, and the Parish Renew Program. Under his direction, a seven-story building was purchased to house the personnel for these programs and it was named The Catholic Pastoral Center.

On April 23, 1969, Msgr. George Evans was installed as the auxiliary bishop of Denver. He served in this post until his death on September 13, 1985. The continued growth of the archdiocese was noted by the Holy See when it appointed Fr. Richard Hanifen as auxiliary bishop in 1974. A year later, Archbishop Casey created the vicariate of Colorado Springs and appointed Bishop Hanifen as episcopal vicar. On January 30, 1984, Colorado Springs was made a diocese and Bishop Hanifen was selected as its first bishop. Archbishop Casey made many plans for the celebration of the centennial of the archdiocese during the year 1987. He asked each parish to write a history of the parish and to present it to the archives of the archdiocese so that the history of the diocese would always be remembered. He asked Professor Tom Noel to write a history which Professor Noel completed for the centennial year under the title, *Colorado Catholicism*. But Archbishop Casey did not live to see the centennial year. The gentle shepherd died on March 14, 1986. His last public letter was to the state legislature urging passage of a bill to provide potable water and portable toilets for migrant workers. At his funeral, Governor Richard Lamm of Colorado said: "There aren't many people I would call inspired, but I truly believe Archbishop Casey's gentleness has inspired all of us."

Denver's sixth bishop and third archbishop came from Baltimore, the hometown of Catholicism in the United States. On July 30, 1986, J. Francis Stafford was canonically installed as the archbishop of Denver. He formally accepted the spiritual care of 310,000 Catholics. One of the most dramatic events in the history of the Church in Colorado occurred in August, 1993, when His Holiness

Pope John Paul II visited Denver for World Youth Day. Over 300,000 people attended the papal Mass in Cherry Creek Park. The community was captivated by the love and prayerfulness of the Pope and the thousands of young people who came to Denver to celebrate their faith. His visit will never be forgotten. Since 1986 the Denver Metropolitan area has seen an increase of 14 percent in population. Within the Archdiocese of Denver are Regis University, five high schools, 36 elementary schools, 148 parishes and missions, Samaritan Shelter for the Homeless, Seton House for those suffering from AIDS, as well as extensive programs to reach out to meet the spiritual, physical, and social needs of the Catholic community. A special emphasis continues to be placed on the Hispanic community comprising a significant percentage of the Catholic population.

In the summer of 1996 Archbishop Stafford relinquished his post as archbishop of Denver to accept an appointment in Rome as president of the Pontifical Council on the Laity. He was replaced by Bishop Charles J. Chaput, O.F.M. Cap., bishop of Rapid City, South Dakota. Chaput was appointed archbishop of Denver on February 8, 1997, and installed on April 7, 1997. At the age of fifty-two, Chaput was the youngest archbishop in the country and the first Native American to be made an archbishop.

In 1995 there were 527,408 Catholics in Colorado in a total population of 3,594,784. There were 196 parishes in the three Colorado dioceses, 272 diocesan priests, 180 religious order priests, 149 permanent deacons, 44 brothers, and 729 sisters (of whom 53 were engaged in teaching). There were 16 Catholic hospitals in the state, one Catholic college (Regis University, Denver), seven high schools, and 47 elementary schools.

Feely, Thomas Francis. "Leadership in the Early Colorado Catholic Church." Ph.D. dissertation, University of Denver, 1973.
Howlett, William J. *Life of Bishop Machebeuf.* Pueblo, Colo.: Franklin, 1908; repr. Regis College, Denver, 1973.
Jones, William. *History of Catholic Education in the State of Colorado.* Washington: Catholic University of America Press, 1955; repr. Denver *Catholic Register,* 1961.
Noel, Thomas J. *Colorado Catholicism.* Denver: University Press of Colorado, 1989.
____. *History of Catholic Education in the State of Colorado.* Washington, D.C.: The Catholic University of America Press, 1955.
O'Ryan, William, and Thomas H. Malone. *History of the Catholic Church in Colorado.* Denver: C. J. Kelly Press, 1961.
WILLIAM JONES

COLUM, MARY (MOLLY) (1887–1957)

Critic, editor, teacher. Mary (Molly) Colum was born Mary Catherine Gunning Maguire in Ireland on June 13, 1887. After the death of her parents, Colum was raised by her maternal grandmother, Catherine Gunning, and after her death by relatives until she was sent to the St. Louis Convent Boarding School in Monaghan and later abroad to a German convent school. She described her convent education as one that "was regarded as a means of fitting our souls for good rather than as a preparation for life." However, the French emphasis at St. Louis not only prepared her to read modern languages at the Royal University, which became the National University by the time she took her B.A., but it also provided the foundation in classics and in modern literature that established her as a comparativist in her literary sensibility.

Colum's university years coincided with the early years of the Irish literary revival in Dublin. She later recalled, "Between Abbey Street and College Green, a five minute's walk, one would meet every person of importance in the life of the city at a certain time in the afternoon." She organized a student society called the Twilight [Celtic Twilight] Literary Society and, as its president, she became active in Dublin's literary and artistic circles. W. B. Yeats, whom she called the most remarkable person she ever knew, encouraged her to abandon her interest in writing fiction for criticism.

Colum remained in Dublin after taking her degree teaching for Patrick Pearse at his bilingual girls' school, St. Ita's. With fellow teachers Thomas MacDonagh and Padraic Colum and David Houston of the College of Science, she founded *The Irish Review* in 1911. It ran until 1915. English journals praised her first review essay of John Millington Synge's *Collected Works* that appeared in the first number of the *Review.*

Colum married poet and playwright Padraic Colum in 1912. She described his rather odd proposal and her acceptance in her autobiography, *Life and the Dream* (1947). After a tearful scene with a rejected suitor, Padraic said, "I think that to save yourself trouble, you should marry me. Then these fellows will leave you alone and you don't have to go through anymore of these scenes." She responded, "All right, Colum; maybe that would be best."

They accepted the offer of passage to America from Padraic's aunt in 1914. They planned to stay only a few months while Padraic gave some lectures; however, except for visits abroad and three years in France, the Colums spent the rest of their lives in the United States. When they settled in New York, Colum went to work at *Women's Wear* translating articles about French fashion, interviewing designers, and writing occasional theater features. Later her excellent critical mind found outlets in the major literary journals of the day: *Scribner's, The Dial, The New Republic, The Saturday Review of Literature, The New York Times Book Review,* and the *Tribune.* Colum also wrote for *The Forum* and served as its literary editor from 1933–40.

Colum received the first of her two Guggenheim Fellowships in 1930. The fellowship financed a three-year stay in France. Colum's project was a comparative study of the continental and English origins of literary modernism called *From These Roots* (1937). Her work received an award for criticism from the American Academy. Her second fellowship in 1938 brought the Colums back to an uneasy Europe on the brink of war. They visited Germany to see life in the Third Reich for themselves. They left Paris just after the Munich appeasement.

The Colums settled on Central Park West in New York; they both taught, sometimes the same class, at Columbia University until 1956. They were a contrast: Padraic small, modest, and gentle, and Molly, formidable and highly opinionated. She won most of the arguments. During this time Colum produced her second book, her autobiography, *Life and the Dream* (1947), an account of her life from boarding school to her return from Europe in 1938. The book's strength is its re-creation of literary Dublin before World War I from the viewpoint of a lively undergraduate woman. The memoir reveals Colum's critical personality, her demanding intellect and her penchant for lionizing literary and social celebrities. Her opinions were respected in literary and publishing circles, and she influenced William Savage of Charles Scribner's Sons to publish Jacques Maritain and Etienne Gilson, who played leading roles in the intellectual life of France.

Colum's last work was *Our Friend James Joyce* (1958), a book written jointly with Padraic. Colum's chapters expanded on anecdotes from *Life and the Dream* and concentrated on Joyce's Paris years. She included affecting accounts of their efforts to help Joyce's schizophrenic daughter Lucia. The book was unfinished when Colum died in New York on October 22, 1957.

Bowen, Zack. *Padraic Colum. A Biographical-Critical Introduction.* Carbondale: Southern Illinois University Press, 1970.

Colum, Mary. *Life and the Dream.* Garden City, N.Y.: Doubleday, 1947.

MAUREEN MURPHY

COLUM, PADRAIC (1881–1972)

Poet, dramatist, novelist, folklorist, biographer, writer of travel and children's literature. He was born in Longford, Ireland, at the Longford Workhouse on December 8, 1881. There, where his father Patrick Collumb was Master, Colum's early years were spent among "strays and tramps [who] congregated, and [he] was entertained by the gossip and history of old men and old women who were survivals from an Ireland that had disappeared." He used his Workhouse experience in his play *Thomas Muskerry* (1910).

Colum lived in Longford until 1896 when his father accepted the position of Station Master of the Sandy Cove Railway Station. After leaving the Glasthule National School, Colum joined the Irish Railway as a clerk in the

Padraic Colum

Irish Railway Clearing House and became active in the Irish nationalist and cultural organizations of his day: the Gaelic League, the Irish Volunteers and literary society, Cumann na nGaedheal. His early lyrics published in *The United Irishman* brought him to the attention of W. B. Yeats and of AE (George Russell) who wrote to the artist Sarah Purser in 1902, "I have discovered a new Irish genius and announce his name—Columb." AE published some of Colum's best lyrics in *New Songs* (1904).

While Colum was gaining notice as a poet, he was developing a reputation as a dramatist. In 1903 his anticonscription play *The Saxon Shillin'* was produced by the Irish National Theatre Society, but it was his play *Broken Soil,* later revised as *The Fiddlier's House,* also produced in 1903, that prompted Lady Gregory to name Colum along with Synge as new Abbey playwrights. Colum's play *The Land* (1905), a play based on the Land Act of 1903, was a popular as well as a critical success and established the historically based, realistic peasant play in the Abbey Theatre repertoire. The third of his trilogy of early plays *Thomas Muskerry* was published in 1910. The earliest plays were Colum's finest. He returned to drama late in life when he wrote, among other works, five oneact plays in the style of the Japanese Noh drama based on Irish historical themes.

Following the success of his first book of poetry, *Wild Earth* (1907), an American patron, Thomas Hughes Kelly, financed Colum to five years of full-time writing. During that time, Colum helped to found *The Irish Review* (1911–15). In 1912 Colum married Mary Catherine (Molly) Maguire who taught for Patrick Pearse and was active in Dublin literary circles where she had made a reputation for herself as a critic. In 1914 the Colums emigrated to an aunt in Pittsburgh. Colum helped produce plays at the Carnegie Institute while Molly taught. From 1914 to his death on January 11, 1972, Padraic Colum was "the Catholic presence" in American literary circles.

After a few months, the Colums moved to New York where Colum accepted an offer to supply children's stories to the *New York Sunday Tribune* for eight dollars a week. A collection of these stories, *The King of Ireland's Son* (1916), with illustrations by Willy Pogany was the first of twenty books of children's stories and adaptations from the classics, folklore, and mythology. The Hawaiian government commissioned two collections of Polynesian lore for school children: *At the Gateway of the Day* (1924) and *The Bright Island* (1925); they were published in a single volume, *Legends of Hawaii* (1937).

The Colums went to Paris in 1930 where they renewed their friendship with James Joyce, a period they later described in their jointly authored *Our Friend James Joyce* (1958). The depression drove the Colums back to America in 1933 where they settled on Central Park West for the rest of their married life. Both started teaching at Columbia University in 1956. After Molly's death in 1958, Colum began to lecture widely about literary Dublin, for by then he was the sole link with the Irish Renaissance. He continued to write poetry and to experiment with drama until his death in Enfield, Connecticut, on January 11, 1972. He is buried with Molly on the Hill of Howth.

Colum's best work is his earliest: his lyric poetry with its direct language, regular meter and rhyme, and its evocation of rural Ireland and his realistic peasant plays. Whatever his genre, Colum reminded his reader of the orality of the Irish literary tradition. In his introduction to Colum's *Collected Poems* (1953), praising his craftsmanship and his humanity, John L. Sweeney called Colum "a new singer in an old tradition."

Colum received a number of honors during his lifetime. He was elected president of the Poetry Society of America (1938–39) and was their Medalist in 1940. He was awarded honorary degrees from the National University of Ireland (1951) and Columbia University (1958). Other awards included a fellowship from the Academy of American Poets (1952), the Lady Gregory Award from the Academy of Irish Letters (1953), and the Regina Medal from the Catholic Library Association (1961), and election to the American Academy of Arts and Letters (1963).

Colum's published work includes: *Castle Conquer* (1923), *The Collected Poems of Padraic Colum* (1953), *Cross Roads in Ireland* (1930), *The Fiddler's House* (1907), *The Flying Swans* (1957), *The King of Ireland's Son* (1916), *The Land* (1905), *Legends of Hawaii* (1937), *My Irish Year* (1912), *Ourselves Alone: The Story of Arthur Griffith and the Origin of the Irish Free State* (1959), *The Poet's Circuits, Collected Poems of Ireland* (1960), *The Road Round Ireland* (1926), *Thomas Muskerry* (1910), and *Wild Earth* (1907).

Bowen, Zack. *Padraic Colum. A Biographical-Critical Introduction.* Carbondale: Southern Illinois University Press, 1970.
Sternlicht, Sanford. *Padraic Colum.* Boston: Twayne, 1985.

MAUREEN MURPHY

COLUMBUS, CHRISTOPHER (ca. 1451–1506)

Explorer. In spite of several imaginative attempts to prove otherwise, Christopher Columbus (Cristoforo Colombo) was born in or near Genoa, Italy. Columbus himself was a major contributor to the myth of his origins by never discussing his background except in the most general terms. He appears to have been ashamed of his lowly roots, a major reason for insisting that Ferdinand of Aragon and Isabella of Castile grant him and his descendants noble titles as part of his reward for discovering a new route to the markets of Asia.

Early Life

Although as a youth Columbus worked with his father, a weaver, like other ambitious Genoese youths he subsequently took to the sea, eventually going west where Genoese seamen, merchants, and financiers were actively involved in Portuguese and Castilian expansion into the Atlantic. His marriage (ca. 1478–79) to Dona Felipa Perestrello e Moniz, the daughter of a Portuguese nobleman who ruled Porto Santo, one of the Madeira islands, brought Columbus into contact with those engaged in the exploration of the Atlantic and of the west coast of Africa with the support of Prince Henry the Navigator (1394–1460).

Christopher Columbus

Although Columbus's life before 1492 is obscure, it is clear that by the time he sailed on his first voyage he had acquired a great deal of experience at sea, a wide knowledge of the available geographical information, and a broad acquaintance with contemporary travel literature about Asia. He had sailed as far to the west as Iceland and as far south as the Gulf of Guinea. In addition, he was acquainted with Ptolemy's *Geography* (2nd cent. C.E.), *The Book of Marco Polo* (1254–1324), the Bible, and a wide range of late medieval spiritual writings, especially Franciscan, that predicted the imminent end of the world.

The central event of Columbus's life was the series of four voyages (1492, 1493, 1498, 1502) that revealed the existence of the Americas to the European world. In asserting that he could reach Asia by sailing westward, Columbus was not making a radical break with existing geographical knowledge but rather was building on it. Like his contemporaries, he knew the earth was round and he was aware of the range of estimates concerning its circumference. Also, like them, he assumed that the earth's surface consisted of large land masses divided by comparatively narrow bands of water.

On the basis of this set of assumptions Columbus sought financial support for a voyage that would enable Europeans to reach Asia and deal directly with merchants in the spice trade. This would not only be advantageous to European merchants and consumers, but it would also strike an economic blow at the Muslim merchants who had blocked European access to Asia and its markets since the fifteenth century.

Unable to convince the Portuguese to support his plan, perhaps because they were convinced that having discovered the Cape of Good Hope (1485), they had found the key to the direct sea route to Asia, Columbus sought help elsewhere, eventually winning the support of Ferdinand and Isabella. With the financial support of the Spanish monarchs, the collective knowledge of Portuguese seamen about the Atlantic, the written record of geographical and travel literature, and his own extensive experience, Columbus set sail in 1492.

Goals and Results of His Voyages

The quincentennial celebration of Columbus's first voyage generated a great debate about his motives for sailing and the long-term consequences of the voyages. Columbus's initial agreement with Ferdinand and Isabella stressed finding a route to Asia, but throughout his career Columbus always had several motives and he emphasized different ones at different times. After the first voyage failed to locate a route to Asia, Columbus tended to emphasize the importance of converting the peoples whom he had met to Christianity along with economic reasons for occupying the Caribbean islands. Furthermore, in addition to using the wealth of the Americas to enrich himself and

his family as well as the monarchs who supported his voyages, Columbus also stressed the importance of using the gold of the Americas to finance a last great crusade that would free the Holy Land from the Turks. While these motives might appear contradictory to a twentieth-century observer, they were quite compatible with the fifteenth-century outlook.

As for the consequences of Columbus's voyages, most of the consequences that modern critics condemn were unintended. Neither Columbus nor his successors intended the destruction of the indigenous peoples and societies that they encountered because they needed them to provide a labor supply to exploit the resources of the lands the Spanish occupied.

In terms of the goals that Columbus articulated throughout his career, his life was a mixture of successes and failures. On the one hand, contrary to popular myth, he died a rich man, although the noble status and high offices he sought for his family were slow in coming. On the other hand, he had not found the route to the riches of Asia that he had sought, although he always believed that he had reached Asia and never realized that he had reached lands completely unknown to the ancient and medieval geographers and travelers whose works he had read. Furthermore, his career as a colonial governor had ended in disgrace when he was removed from office and returned to Spain in chains (1500) after his third voyage. Finally, his dream of a last great crusade fueled by the riches he found was not to be. He died on May 20, 1506.

In the final analysis, Columbus was neither the radical innovator who recognized that the earth was round when everyone else believed it was flat, the image of Columbus that Washington Irving created in the early nineteenth century, nor was he some wild-eyed, greedy fanatic who plotted the destruction of the peoples of the Americas. Rooted in centuries of European expansion, especially against the Muslims who were driven out of Spain only months before he sailed in 1492, Columbus's life and career bridged the medieval and the early modern periods of European, Christian expansion. The same medieval religious, dynastic, and economic motives that drove Columbus, continued to drive early modern European missionaries, merchants, and adventurers overseas in succeeding centuries.

Fernández-Armesto, Felipe. *Columbus.* Oxford: Oxford University Press, 1992.

Flint, Valerie. *The Imaginative Landscape of Christopher Columbus.* New Jersey: Princeton University Press, 1992.

Morison, Samuel Eliot, ed. and trans. *Journal and Other Documents on the Life and Voyages of Christopher Columbus.* New York: The Heritage Press, 1963.

____. *Admiral of the Ocean Sea.* 2 vols. Boston: Little, Brown, 1942.

Phillips, William D., Jr., and Carla Rahn Phillips. *The Worlds of Christopher Columbus.* Cambridge University Press, 1992.

JAMES MULDOON

Related Document

THE BULL *INTER CÆTERA* OF POPE ALEXANDER VI, MAY 4, 1493

When the news of the success of Columbus' first voyage reached Europe it was rumored that the energetic King John II of Portugal was preparing to dispute the Spanish claims to the new territories. Ferdinand and Isabella, therefore, sent a hurried appeal to Pope Alexander VI (1492–1503), asking that he confirm their possession of the lands discovered by Columbus. As a consequence, the pontiff issued several documents in the year 1493, the best known being that which drew the imaginary "line of demarcation" which assigned to Spain all lands west of a meridian 100 leagues west of the Azores and Cape Verde Islands. Although the line was later changed to Portugal's advantage, the bull *Inter caetera*—known from the first words of the original Latin text—is included here to illustrate, among other things, the prestige which the Holy See enjoyed at the time for settling disputes between nations.

(*Source:* Frances Gardiner Davenport, ed. *European Treaties bearing on the History of the United States and Its Dependencies to 1648.* Washington: Carnegie Institution of Washington, 1917, I, 75–78.)

ALEXANDER, BISHOP, SERVANT OF THE SERVANTS OF GOD, to the illustrious sovereigns, our very dear son in Christ, Ferdinand, king, and our very dear daughter in Christ, Isabella, queen of Castile, health and benediction. We have indeed learned that you, who for a long time had intended to seek out and discover certain islands and mainlands remote and unknown and not hitherto discovered by others, to the end that you might bring to the worship of our Redeemer and the profession of the Catholic faith their residents and inhabitants, having been up to the present time greatly engaged in the siege and recovery of the kingdom itself of Granada were unable to accomplish this holy and praiseworthy purpose; but the said kingdom having at length been regained, as was pleasing to the Lord, with a wish to fulfill your desire, chose our beloved son, Christopher Columbus, a man assuredly worthy and of the highest recommendations and fitted for so great an undertaking, whom you furnished with ships and men equipped for like designs, not without the greatest hardships, dangers, and expenses, to make diligent quest for these remote and unknown mainlands and islands through the sea, where hitherto no one had sailed; and they at length with divine aid and with the utmost diligence sailing in the ocean sea, discovered certain very remote islands and even mainlands that hitherto had not been discovered by others; wherein dwell very many peoples living in peace, and, as reported, going unclothed, and not eating flesh. . . . wherefore, as becomes Catholic kings and princes . . . you have purposed . . .

to bring under your sway the said mainlands and islands. . . . And, in order that you may enter upon so great an undertaking with greater readiness and heartiness endowed with the benefit of our apostolic favor, we, of our own accord, not at your instance nor the request of anyone else in your regard, but out of our own sole largess and certain knowledge and out of the fullness of our apostolic power, by the authority of Almighty God conferred upon us in blessed Peter and of the vicarship of Jesus Christ, which we hold on earth, do by tenor of these presents, should any of said islands have been found by your envoys and captains, give, grant, and assign to you and your heirs and successors, kings of Castile and León, forever, together with all their dominions, cities, camps, places, and villages, and all rights, jurisdictions, and appurtenances, all islands and mainlands found and to be found, discovered and to be discovered towards the west and the south, by drawing and establishing a line from the Arctic pole, namely the north, to the Antarctic pole, namely the south, no matter whether the said mainlands and islands are found and to be found in the direction of India or towards any other quarter, the said line to be distant one hundred leagues[1] towards the west and south from any of the islands commonly known as the Azores and Cape Verde. With this proviso, however, that none of the islands and mainlands, found and to be found, discovered and to be discovered, beyond that said line towards the west and south, be in the actual possession of any Christian king or prince up to the birthday of our Lord Jesus Christ just past from which the present year 1493 begins. . . . Furthermore, under penalty of excommunication *latae sententiae* to be incurred *ipso facto*, should anyone thus contravene, we strictly forbid all persons of whatsoever rank, even imperial and royal, or of whatsoever estate, degree, order, or condition, to dare without your special permit or that of your aforesaid heirs and successors, to go for the purpose of trade or any other reason to the islands or mainlands . . . apostolic constitutions and ordinances and other decrees whatsoever to the contrary notwithstanding. . . . Let no one therefore, infringe, or with rash boldness contravene, this our recommendation, exhortation, requisition, gift, grant, assignment, constitution, deputation, decree, mandate, prohibition, and will. Should anyone presume to attempt this, be it known to him that he will incur the wrath of Almighty God and of the blessed apostles Peter and Paul. Given at Rome, at St. Peter's, in the year of the incarnation of our Lord one thousand four hundred and ninety-three, the fourth of May, and the first year of our pontificate.

[1]The old Spanish *legua* was the equivalent of about 2.63 miles, although the Spaniards used another standard in California the exact equivalent of which was never determined.

(*Source:* John Tracy Ellis, ed. *Documents of American Catholic History.* Vol. 1:1493–1865. Wilmington, Del.: Michael Glazier, 1987, 1–3.)

COMMONWEAL

The oldest Catholic independent journal of opinion in the United States was founded by Catholic laity in 1924. Spearheading the movement of a group called the Calvert Association (named after George Calvert, the first Lord Baltimore, the Roman Catholic founder of Maryland) was Michael Williams, a journalist who had worked for Fr. John J. Burke, C.S.P., as assistant director of the Press Department of the National Catholic Welfare Council. In 1922, Williams left that post with the idea of founding an intellectual Catholic weekly of comparable literary excellence to *The Nation* and *The New Republic*.

The first gathering of what was later known as the Calvert Associates met at the Hotel Belmont in New York on the evening of October 19, 1922. The group consisted of four priests and nine laymen. It included one non-Catholic, the distinguished architect Ralph Adams Cram of Boston. Among the clerics were Francis Clement Kelly of Chicago who later became the bishop of Oklahoma, and Lawrason Riggs of the Washington banking family who would serve as Catholic chaplain at Yale until 1943. Carlton J. H. Hayes of Columbia University and Summerfield Baldwin of Harvard University were perhaps the most notable of the laymen. The group quickly reached agreement that they wanted a review that would be "expressive of the Catholic note" in literature, the arts, and in the discussion of economics and social topics. A special committee was set up to launch a financial campaign, and when the group met a month later, six thousand dollars had been subscribed to a preliminary fund.

It was decided that the magazine should be lay edited and that it should not be an instrument of the Church. It was logical, therefore, to look to the laity for financial support. The group elected Thomas F. Woodlock, an editor of the *Wall Street Journal* as their first president, and Michael Williams as secretary. Williams, however, was the chief promoter and fundraiser. During the next two years he toured the country addressing meetings in many of the larger cities, eventually achieving pledges of more than $250,000. Williams also supplied the name *The Commonweal* as being most indicative of the purpose of the new journal. He also became the journal's founding editor. His selection for this position by the mostly Ivy League and affluent Catholics associated with the journal's establishment was quite an achievement for an impoverished lad whose formal education had ceased at the age of thirteen.

Also crucial to *Commonweal's* early years, was George N. Shuster, a 1912 graduate of the University of Notre Dame who returned there to teach English after his service in a bilingual intelligence unit in World War I. He became the chairman of the English Department and in 1922 published *The Catholic Spirit in Modern English Litera-ture*. In 1924, however, he came to New York to work for his doctorate at Columbia University, and soon after became *Commonweal's* managing editor. Some highlights of the Williams and Shuster years at *Commonweal* from 1924 to 1938 included the self-critique of Catholic intellectual life, the Al Smith presidential candidacy in 1928, liturgical renewal, and early warnings regarding Nazi Germany.

In 1938, in the context of editorial disagreements regarding the Spanish Civil War and a financial crisis for the magazine, Edward S. Skillin and Philip Burnham, two junior staffers on the journal, bought *Commonweal* for a nine-thousand-dollar settlement with its creditors. Burnham left after several years, but Skillin who had started with the magazine in 1933 continued on as editor until 1967 and as publisher after that, serving even at this writing in his ninety-first year. Skillin, who gradually acquired full ownership of *Commonweal,* established the Commonweal foundation in 1982 to ensure the continuation of its work after his death.

Commonweal has faced continuing financial challenges throughout its years, and is sustained today by its subscribers and the Commonweal Associates, contributors of relatively small amounts that collectively keep the operation going. Its subscribers number only about twenty thousand, but its influence is significant both inside and outside of the Catholic community. It has a well-established tradition of civility on its pages where both intellectual vigor and courtesy prevail.

A significant part of *Commonweal's* success throughout the long Skillin era has been the distinction of his own work and that of his successors as editors in chief: James O'Gara (1967–84), Peter Steinfels (1984–88) and Margaret O'Brien Steinfels (1988 to the present). In addition, there have been many remarkable staff editors including John Cogley, Daniel Callahan, William Pfaff and John Leo.

Some highlights of these years included the McCarthy period, during which *Commonweal's* critical evaluation of Senator McCarthy led to an attempt by McCarthy to smear the magazine itself. Other highlights included Vatican Council II (which was a great vindication for *Commonweal* and the commitment to Catholic renewal associated with its pages), the Vietnam War, economic justice, serious and sustained attention to abortion, and the Restoration Catholicism of Pope John Paul II.

Commonweal has been an independent intellectual voice in American Catholicism and American life in general. History has shown it to have been correct in its analysis of most of the big issues it has faced, which is the highest praise for a journal of opinion. Most importantly, *Commonweal* has sustained in its pages a conversation that has frequently been at the cutting edge of the creative inculturation of Catholicism in the United States. It is not surprising that it has been called "perhaps the most important symbol and achievement of the American Catholic laity."

See also COGLEY, JOHN; SHUSTER, GEORGE NAUMAN; SPANISH CIVIL WAR AND AMERICAN CATHOLICS, THE; WILLIAMS, MICHAEL.

Bredeck, Martin J. *Imperfect Apostles: The Commonweal and the American Catholic Laity 1924–1976.* New York: Garland Publishing, 1988.

Clements, Robert Brooke. *"The Commonweal, 1924–1938: The Williams-Shuster Years."* Ph.D. dissertation, University of Notre Dame, 1972.

Van Allen, Rodger. *The Commonweal and American Catholicism.* Philadelphia: Fortress Press, 1974.

____. *Being Catholic: Commonweal from the Seventies to the Nineties.* Chicago: Loyola University Press, 1993.

RODGER VAN ALLEN

CONCANEN, RICHARD LUKE (1747–1810)

Dominican friar, first bishop of New York. Concanen was born in Kilbegnet, County Roscommon, Ireland, on December 27, 1747. At the age of seventeen he left Ireland forever, traveling to Louvain where, on September 14, 1764, he entered the Irish province of the Order of Preachers. The following year he was sent to Rome where he was to spend virtually all of the rest of his life. He was ordained a priest in Rome on December 22, 1770. From 1769 until 1792, Concanen lived at San Clemente, the Roman headquarters of the Irish Dominicans. From 1792 until 1808 he resided at the Minerva, the Dominican generalate, and served as an assistant to the Dominican master general. During these latter years Concanen also acted as the Roman agent for several Irish bishops, for Bishop John Carroll of Baltimore, and for Bishop John Milner (vicar apostolic of the Midland District in England).

Twice Concanen declined nomination to Irish dioceses. In 1798 he turned down Kilmacduagh, and in 1802 he turned down Raphoe. During the controversy over the "Veto Question"—the proposal to give the British government the right to veto episcopal appointments in return for Catholic Emancipation—Concanen shared Milner's opposition to the proposal. He also opposed the suggestion that the British government should pay the salaries of the Catholic clergy on the grounds that it would lessen their dependence on the bishops and the people.

In 1808, when the Diocese of Baltimore was made a metropolitan see with four new suffragan dioceses, Archbishop Carroll failed to recommend a candidate for the Diocese of New York. The Holy See selected Concanen for the post. He received episcopal ordination on April 24, 1808, in the Dominican church of St. Catherine in Rome. Due to the state of war between England and France, Concanen was unable to reach his new diocese. In June 1810 he went to Naples, hoping to secure passage on a ship leaving for the United States. He died suddenly in Naples on June 19, 1810, and was buried on the next day in the local Dominican church. On July 9, 1978, Terence Cardinal Cooke dedicated a memorial tablet identifying his tomb as that of the first bishop of New York.

See also NEW YORK, CATHOLIC CHURCH IN; DOMINICANS (O.P.).

Cohalan, Florence D. *A Popular History of the Archdiocese of New York.* Yonkers, 1983, 21–24.

Hughes, Vincent R., O.P. *The Rt. Rev. Richard Luke Concanen, First Bishop of New York (1747–1810).* Freiburg, 1926.

O'Daniel, Victor F., O.P. *"Concanen's Election to the See of New York (1808–1810)."* *Catholic Historical Review* 2 (1917) 19–46.

THOMAS J. SHELLEY

CONFERENCE OF MAJOR SUPERIORS OF MEN (CMSM)

The Conference of Major Superiors of Men in the United States, Inc. (CMSM) was founded on September 27, 1956. It was canonically established by decree of the Sacred Congregation for Religious and Secular Institutes on December 15, 1959.

With a membership of 265 abbots, superiors general, and provincials, the conference represents 22,000 religious priests and brothers in the United States. It has three purposes: to support major superiors and serve as a resource for them in their leadership role; to promote dialogue and collaboration with other major groups in the Church and society, and to provide a corporate influence and voice for male religious in the United States through national and regional structures.

CMSM is divided into six regions which meet three times a year. Regional meetings serve as the means for networking leadership, providing peer support, providing educational programs, and conducting conference business. In addition, the entire membership meets annually at a national assembly. The assembly serves as a forum for discernment on religious life and ministry and for decision-making by all the members on issues pertinent to the conference. Every three years the national assembly is held in conjunction with the Leadership Conference of Women Religious.

The conference is governed by a national board composed of the president, vice president, secretary/treasurer, the six regional chairpersons, and the six at-large representatives. The president is elected for a term of two years with other board members serving three-year terms. CMSM publishes a monthly newsletter, an action alert devoted to issues of justice and peace, and, seasonally, a journal of original articles of interest to leadership. Leadership workshops are held annually with other in-service programs scheduled as needed. The conference has a number of standing committees, e.g., finance, priestly formation, justice and peace, and special projects, as well as ad hoc committees dealing with specific issues. Special projects are also undertaken that benefit leadership as well as the members of the religious congregations.

The conference maintains contact with other religious conferences throughout the world as well as with Roman congregations and councils. Every five years in conjunction with the Canadian Religious Conference and the Confederation of Latin American Religious an inter-American meeting is held bringing together between one to two hundred leaders of men's and women's religious congregations. In this country, the conference maintains close working relationships with the National Conference of Catholic Bishops and the Leadership Conference of Women Religious. CMSM is also one of the sponsoring organizations for the CMSM-LCWR-NATRI Legal Office and the National Religious Retirement Office, as well as the Commission on Religious Life and Ministry, composed of members of the National Conference of Catholic Bishops, the Conference of Major Superiors of Men, the Leadership Conference of Women Religious, and the Council of Major Superiors of Women Religious. The national office, located in Silver Spring, Maryland, is headed by a full-time executive director.

See also MEN, RELIGIOUS ORDERS AND CONGREGATIONS OF.

STEVEN HENRICH, O.S.C.

CONFRATERNITY OF CHRISTIAN DOCTRINE, THE

Origins

The Confraternity of Christian Doctrine has a long history as the Church's official association of persons devoted to the catechetical mission of the Church. It had its origins in Milan, Italy, in 1536, when a young priest, Castello de Castellano, formed the Company of Christian Doctrine for the purpose of conducting schools of Christian doctrine. In 1560, the Confraternity of Christian Doctrine, with the approval of Pope Pius IV, became the official association of persons devoted to teaching religion to children and adults in Rome. In 1571 Pope Pius V formally approved the established organization and recommended that it be established in all parishes. Thirty-nine years later the Sacred Congregation of Indulgences decreed that it be established in every parish.

Pope Pius X

In the United States, while many women and men, both lay and religious, devoted themselves to teaching religion, it took the encyclical *Acerbo Nimis,* issued by Pope Pius X in 1905 to provide the impetus to stimulate interest in the Confraternity of Christian Doctrine. The document stated:

> In each and every parish the society known as the CCD is to be canonically established. Through this Confraternity, the

pastors, especially in places where there is a scarcity of priests, will have lay helpers in the teaching of the Catechism, who will take up the work of imparting knowledge both from a goal for the glory of God and in order to gain the numerous indulgences granted by the Sovereign Pontiffs.

This emphasis on the CCD prompted Fr. Joseph B. Collins (director of the National CCD Center for forty years) to call *Acerbo Nimis* the Magna Carta of the CCD (*New Catholic Encyclopedia* 4:155).

In 1918, the Code of Canon Law, promulgated by Pope Benedict XV, incorporated the decree that the Confraternity of Christian Doctrine be established in every parish. In 1923 Pope Pius XI called for the establishment of a Catechetical Office in the Sacred Congregation of the Council to regulate and promote catechetical activity in the Church.

The National Center

In the early 1900s the CCD was established in large dioceses such as New York and Los Angeles, but it was not until the 1930s that it became a national movement in the United States. Through the vision and zeal of Bishop Edwin V. O'Hara of Great Falls, Montana, a headquarters was established in Washington, D.C., at The Catholic University of America in 1933. He was appointed chairman of an episcopal committee named in 1934. That same year, at the invitation of Bishop O'Hara, fifteen diocesan directors of CCD met for the first time. In 1935 a National CCD Center was set up as part of the National Catholic Welfare Conference. That same year, the first National Catechetical Congress was held in Rochester, New York, and the diocesan directors of the confraternity continued to meet annually.

The National CCD Center sponsored annual congresses until 1941, after which these large meetings were held every five years until 1971. In that year the last International Catechetical Congress was held in Miami, Florida, in October 1971.

The National Center functioned as a source of information and published literature on all facets of Confraternity promotion and programs. It sponsored the Confraternity translation of the Scriptures which was later revised and published as the *New American Bible.* It also published *Our Parish Confraternity,* a monthly bulletin of leadership and programming from 1942 until 1966.

As more and more dioceses appointed diocesan directors responsible for the establishment of the CCD in the parishes, the National Center saw the need for developing materials which would help them in their work. For schools of religion and religious vacation schools, manuals were published and periodically revised. Programs for parents of preschool children, discussion club materials for adults, and literature for the Apostles of Good Will, who reached beyond the Church, were also developed.

Diocesan CCD Directors and the National Center

While the diocesan directors had met annually for thirty-one years, it was not until 1966 that a more formal structure for their organization was proposed. By this time virtually every diocese had a Diocesan Office of Religious Education and a structured religious education program for the parishes. Teacher training became a parish or diocesan responsibility, but the National Center sponsored CCD leadership courses at Catholic colleges and universities during the summer. The diocesan directors felt the need for a more effective means of communication with the Episcopal Committee and the National CCD Center. With the approval of the Episcopal Committee, the diocesan directors formed a national committee with each province electing a representative. The National Committee met in 1967. An interim constitution was drawn up and the organization was named the National Conference of Diocesan Directors of Religious Education (NCDD).

Recognizing that the work of the NCDD and the National Center were so closely allied, in 1969 both groups agreed that it would be beneficial to have the executive secretary of the NCDD also in a staff position at the National Center. This alliance continued until 1975 when a major reorganization of the United States Catholic Conference occurred and the National CCD Center was dissolved.

U.S.C.C. Department of Education

In the 1975 reorganization the functions of the National CCD Center were partially assumed by the Representative for Religious Education. That person also continued to function as the executive secretary of the NCDD. The Episcopal Committee of the Confraternity of Christian Doctrine had ceased to exist in 1969, when its responsibilities were given to the U.S.C.C. Committee on Education. The COE formulates and recommends policy to the Administrative Board of the U.S.C.C., the governing board for conference activities.

In 1982 a decision was made by the bishops to discontinue structural linkage with all national organizations. The NCDD elected to become an independent national organization. It has since extended its membership and been renamed the National Conference of Catechetical Leadership (NCCL).

Official Organizational Structure

In 1973 an office was established under the National Conference of Catholic Bishops to develop a national catechetical directory to provide policies, norms and guidelines for catechetical ministry in the United States. *Sharing the Light of Faith, the National Catechetical Directory for Catholics of the United States* gives a brief reference to the CCD in the preface, but does not allude to it in the chapter on organizational structures. It states: "The *General Catechetical Directory* states that a conference of bishops should have a permanent structure to promote catechetics on the national level. The Department of Education of the United States Catholic Conference, through its religious education component, has the mission of carrying out the catechetical policies of the bishops of the United States."

For forty years the National CCD Center promoted the Confraternity of Christian Doctrine. It prepared for and contributed to the catechetical revival in the post-World War II era. Although the National CCD Center was dismantled in 1975, the work and spirit of the CCD continue. The professional parish religious education directors, the Representatives for Catechetical Ministry and Adult Education in the U.S.C.C. Department of Education, the National Conference of Catechetical Leadership, the Religious Education department of the National Catholic Educational Association, as well as colleges and universities which offer religious education degrees, all provide leadership in catechetical ministry. The publishers of catechetical textbooks and supplementary materials provide professional teaching tools. In addition, the thousands of volunteer catechists whose dedicated commitment enables them to proclaim the Christian message to children and adults in parish and diocesan religious education programs throughout the United States continue what began in Milan 459 years ago.

See also CATHOLIC EDUCATION, PAROCHIAL; O'HARA, EDWIN.

Collins, Joseph B. "Edwin V. O'Hara." *The Confraternity Comes of Age.* Paterson, N.J.: Confraternity Publications, 1956, 1–27.
_____. "The Episcopal Committee of the CCD." *The American Ecclesiastical Review* 169 (November 1975) 610–20.
_____. "The National Center for the CCD." *The American Ecclesiastical Review* 169 (December 1975) 690–702.
Middleton, John S., ed. *A Handbook of the CCD.* New York: Benziger Brothers, 1937.
Spellacy, Marie Elizabeth. "The Evolution of the Catechetical Ministry Among the Mission Helpers of the Sacred Heart: A Case Study." Ph.D. dissertation, School of Religious Studies, The Catholic University of America, 1984, 71–82; 110–17.

MARIELLA FRYE, M.H.S.H.

CONNECTICUT, CATHOLIC CHURCH IN

Beginnings

The Catholic Church was unwelcomed in the English colonies of Connecticut and Qunnipiack, which territories later became the state of Connecticut. Proscribed by law, as were all religious groups and churches dissenting from the established Congregational Church, the normative sacramental and administrative life of the Church could not be established. Bound by expressly anti-Catholic oath, no man within the colonies could own land, exercise any influence in local government affairs, or inherit land or property, unless first publicly denouncing the Roman Catholic Church, the pope, and various Catholic doctrines. Few Catholics, consequently, settled within the boundaries of these colonies, other than a few Irish indentured servants and about 400 French-speaking Acadians, political exiles from Nova Scotia who were forcibly settled in the Connecticut area in 1756 by the British government (DiGiovanni, xviii).

The first real Catholic missionary was Fr. John Thayer, a priest from Boston, who made his way throughout the state in search of Catholics, and celebrated Mass in the home of Noah Webster in West Hartford, on April 10, 1791. Not until the Revolutionary War did the Connecticut population encounter large numbers of Catholics, primarily French troops with their chaplains, bivouacking and traversing the colony in order to engage the British in battle.

This remained the case until 1818, when a new constitution was ratified for the state, allowing freedom of religion. With freedom to establish and exercise their faith, and a growing number of jobs in the state whose economy was slowly changing from agriculture to industry, large numbers of immigrants began to arrive, primarily French and Irish, the majority of whom were Roman Catholic. By 1823 the Catholics of Hartford petitioned Bishop Jean Cheverus of Boston, under whose jurisdiction they were since 1808, for a resident priest. He visited the city in May, celebrating Mass and baptizing the children of the community, among whom were Francis Clerc, Mary Mulligan, and Robert Webb (O'Donnell, 183). Since Hartford had the largest Catholic community in the state, boasting 120 communicants by 1830, the first Catholic church in Connecticut was founded there. Holy Trinity Church, established in an abandoned Protestant church, was placed under the care of Fr. Bernard O'Cavanagh, Connecticut's first resident priest, on August 26, 1829. The church was moved to a new location, dedicated and opened on June 17, 1830. Later in the year, Connecticut's first Catholic school opened in the basement of Holy Trinity Church, organized and operated by the lay members of the community. This marks the true beginning of the Church's organization in Connecticut. Hartford was the center from which all subsequent missionary activity in the state proceeded.

New Haven followed suit, opening its own Catholic church in 1832, under the guidance of Fr. James McDermott. In 1842 the small Catholic community of Bridgeport opened its own St. James Church, led by Fr. Michael Lynch.

Diocese of Hartford

As the number of Catholics slowly grew within Connecticut, 720 Catholics within the 220,955 total estimated population of the state, a need for more organization and priests within the southern portion of New England was seen if the future of the Church was to be secured. Dur-ing the Fifth Provincial Council of Baltimore in 1843, Bishop Benedict Fenwick of Boston asked the council fathers to petition the pope to establish such a new diocese. Despite objections by some bishops that the proliferation of dioceses in New England was superfluous, Pope Gregory XVI erected the Diocese of Hartford on November 28, 1843, with jurisdiction over Catholics in the states of Connecticut and Rhode Island, and led by its first bishop, William Tyler (DiGiovanni, xxviii, 241).

At the time of his appointment, Tyler could count only 2 percent of the state population—4,817 Catholics—as members of his Church, with three priests, and four churches in Connecticut. Since Hartford had only 600 Catholics, compared with the Catholic community of Providence, Rhode Island, with more than 2,000 members, Bishop Tyler petitioned Rome to transfer his residence there, which was granted in 1844. The bishops of Hartford remained in Providence until the establishment of that see in 1872.

The diocese's acute lack of funds and clergy hindered Tyler's work to establish normative Catholic life for the ever-increasing number of immigrant Catholics arriving in the state as industry and railroad construction began in earnest in New England (O'Donnell, 128).

Following Bishop Tyler's death in 1849, the vicar general of the Diocese of Buffalo was appointed to Hartford. Fr. Bernard O'Reilly was consecrated bishop of Hartford on November 10, 1850. In a letter to the Propagation of the Faith in Lyons, France, O'Reilly outlined the program for his administration and that of his successors through the 1860s. He wrote, "We can do little without sufficient number of priests, and we cannot save the children without a Catholic education. All the influences which are here are against our religion's [influence], and . . . it is only by great zeal, purely Catholic education and sufficient number of priests, that we can save our own and make progress against heresy" (DiGiovanni, 2).

To realize his plan, to some degree, O'Reilly petitioned the Propagation of the Faith in Lyons, as well as the various Irish seminaries, especially All Hallows, searching for priests and funds.

The first Sisters of Mercy arrived in Providence in 1851. Mother Mary Xavier Warde, and Srs. Mary Camillus O'Neil, Mary Joana Fogarty, Mary Josephine, and Mary Paula Lombard immediately became the objects of scorn, and received rough treatment in Providence by those unfriendly toward the Church (Carroll, *Leaves from the Annals of the Sisters of Mercy,* 389). Despite this, they flourished. In 1852 the sisters came to Hartford, opening a school in the basement of St. Patrick Church, while others went to New Haven to begin teaching at St. Mary Church. Both groups later opened girls' academies and an orphan asylum.

As the number of Catholics increased, primarily because of Irish immigration, the resources of the diocese were stretched. During the decade of 1850–60, the largest settlements within Connecticut were to be found in Hartford, New Haven, and Fairfield counties. During this decade, the majority of Irish immigrants to the United States were Roman Catholic, and practiced a faith freshly enlivened by Catholic Emancipation in Great Britain, the temperance preaching of the Capuchin priest, Theobald Mathew, and the political preaching of Daniel O'Connell, which united Catholicism with Irish nationalism.

The secondary result of such a rapid increase in Catholic numbers was a rise in anti-Catholic sentiment within the state. With the advent of the Know-Nothing party, with its platform against immigrants and Catholics, and with the election of its gubernatorial candidate, William T. Minor in May 1855, the Church found itself in some difficulty. Preachers, press and politicians worked, and succeeded, in effecting anti-Catholic legislation within the state concerning Church incorporation, ownership of land, and the rights of bishops and clergy. They also worked to "convert" Catholics to Protestantism, and began a campaign falsely claiming the loss to the Catholic faith of millions of immigrants, once arrived in America.

Bishop O'Reilly was lost at sea in early 1856. With the discrediting of everything foreign by the nativist forces, three priests of Hartford wrote to urge Rome to permit an election by the priests themselves of an American-born priest as bishop (DiGiovanni, 129). Rome acknowledged the truth of the priests' statements, but independently appointed Francis Patrick McFarland as the third bishop of Hartford. He was the first bishop consecrated in New England, on March 14, 1858. He quietly worked to overcome the threats from the Know-Nothing and anti-Catholic forces within the state, which were ultimately undermined by the coming of the Civil War, which also speeded up the industrialization of the state and, consequently, the arrival of more and more immigrants, primarily Irish and German. To assist the German Catholics, McFarland organized Connecticut's first national parish, St. Boniface, in New Haven in 1868.

McFarland introduced the Sisters of Charity into Connecticut in 1864, assigning them the care of the New Haven orphan asylum. He later welcomed the first religious order of men into Connecticut, assigning the Order of Friars Minor to St. Joseph Church, Winsted, in 1865.

Late Nineteenth Century

In 1872 the Diocese of Providence was erected. McFarland returned the episcopal residence to Hartford, establishing St. Joseph parish as his new cathedral. Connecticut's Catholic population had exploded to nearly 140,000, served by seventy-seven priests in seventy-six churches and sixty chapels and mission stations.

McFarland died in 1873 and was succeeded by Thomas Galberry, the first provincial of the Augustinians in the United States, who was consecrated fourth bishop of Hartford in March 1876. Ordinary of the diocese for only twenty months, Galberry won the respect of all for his holiness and unflagging zeal, compared often to the late Bishop McFarland. He established the newspaper *Connecticut Catholic* in 1876, which later became the *Catholic Transcript,* laid the cornerstone for St. Joseph Cathedral, and succeeded in making one pastoral visitation of the entire diocese (O'Donnell, 165).

Immigration rapidly increased during the administrations of the two subsequent bishops. Lawrence Stephen McMahon, vicar general of Providence, who served as bishop of Hartford from 1879–93, was faced with increasing numbers of Catholic immigrants from southern and eastern Europe. McMahon followed the policy of his predecessors, training American and Irish-born students in European and Canadian seminaries as a means of supplying priests to the growing immigrant Catholic population. He also introduced the La Salette Fathers and the Missionaries of the Congregation of Saint Charles Borromeo, who ministered respectively to the French-Canadian and Italian communities in Connecticut (Liptak, 96).

Connecticut received more individual immigrant groups during these years than any other state, necessitating McMahon to create forty-eight new parishes, of which thirteen were national parishes for these groups. This further enhanced rumors that Hartford would be elevated to the archiepiscopal dignity and Connecticut formed into a new ecclesiastical province (*Connecticut Catholic,* February 4, 1888).

In 1882 the Rev. Michael McGivney, assistant priest at St. Mary Church, New Haven, began a lay organization for mutual protection and the spiritual growth of its members. At first composed primarily of Irish immigrants, the Knights of Columbus became the most influential and largest lay Catholic organization in the country. With a desire to protect the Catholic faith of its immigrant members, while instilling in them a love for their adopted country, the Knights performed and continue to perform great work for its members and the Church.

The sixth bishop of Hartford was Michael Tierney, who was raised in Norwalk, Connecticut, and served as the rector of various churches throughout the diocese. His nomination was preceded by another petition for "home rule" by the Hartford priests who had submitted Tierney's name as their first choice. His appointment by Pope Leo XIII, while independent of those wishes, was welcomed by all (DiGiovanni, 150).

The Catholic population of Connecticut had grown to nearly 150,000, served by 122 priests in ninety-eight churches. Tierney worked to improve priestly life by instituting mandatory priestly retreats, yearly theological examinations of the clergy, and founded St. Thomas Seminary in 1897. He opened Catholic hospitals in Hartford, Waterbury, Bridgeport, Willimantic, and New Haven, and orphanages in New Haven and Hartford. He also labored to assist workers by supporting labor unions and supporting the Catholic Temperance Union. Tierney also introduced into the diocese the Sisters of the Holy Ghost, or "White Sisters," The Little Sisters of the Poor, and the Sisters of the Good Shepherd.

Twentieth Century

Catholic education was seen as important for Catholic life, and it grew within Connecticut during Tierney's years, with the number of parish schools increasing from forty-eight to eighty by 1908. Improvements in the quality of Catholic education were also made. Guided by Rev. Patrick J. McCormick, assistant priest at Saint Augustine Church in Bridgeport, who served as the Diocesan Supervisor of Schools in 1906, a standardized curriculum and improved training for teaching sisters were pursued throughout the state.

The Rev. John J. Nilan served as the seventh bishop, being installed nearly two years after his predecessor's death, on April 28, 1910. Nilan's primary work was to bolster and support the numerous institutions and works begun by his predecessor, whether in education, health care, seminary preparation or immigrant ministry (Liptak, 55).

In 1934, following Nilan's death, Maurice F. McAuliffe was named bishop of Hartford. With a background in seminary work and teaching, McAuliffe worked to strengthen his clergy, as well as bolster family life within the diocese. Fostering the Legion of Decency, and establishing a diocesan-wide Catholic Youth Organization, parish clubs, and Parent-Educator groups, he sought to protect Catholic youth and families from the effects of the more destructive aspects of American culture (DiGiovanni, 180).

Desirous that the Jesuits work within the diocese in the field of education, McAuliffe approved their plan to open Fairfield College Preparatory School in 1942 and Fairfield University of Saint Robert Bellarmine in 1945. He established the Diocesan Labor Institute to promote papal social teaching and assist the working Catholics, and influenced work among blacks and other minority Catholics. One of his primary works was the support he gave to the American war effort during the Second World War, urging clergy and laity alike to join to defend the country as Catholics and Americans.

Henry J. O'Brien succeeded McAuliffe in 1945, and immediately dedicated diocesan funds and staff to find homes for orphans and to assist persons displaced by the war, and to secure employment, counseling, and other assistance to those returning from wartime service (DiGiovanni, 185).

Archdiocese of Hartford

By 1953 the Diocese of Hartford had the largest Catholic population of any American diocese after Brooklyn. It was decided to divide the diocese, raise it to the dignity of an archdiocese, and establish two new dioceses, Bridgeport and Norwich, adding Providence to complete the newly created province. O'Brien's subsequent years were dedicated to the reorganization of his archdiocese and the overseeing of the stabilization of the new Hartford province. He attended the Second Vatican Council and worked to implement the decrees of the council in Hartford.

John Francis Whealon succeeded as archbishop of Hartford in March 1969. A biblical scholar, Whealon devoted much of his ministry to preaching and to furthering the study of Holy Writ in the light of the teachings of Vatican II.

He implemented the decrees of the council within the archdiocese, and steered his Church through the turbulent years of the 1970s and 1980s, working against racism, and instituting a number of social programs for the underprivileged and marginalized. Whealon died in August, 1991, and was succeeded by Archbishop Daniel A. Cronin, translated from the see of Fall River.

The histories of the newly established dioceses of Bridgeport and Norwich began with the work of Bishops Lawrence J. Shehan in Bridgeport, and Bernard J. Flanagan in Norwich. Urban crime, youth problems, threats to family life, the growing fear of Communism and the cold war, crumbling industry and the beginning of the flight to the suburbs all called for new answers and solutions.

Under Bishop Shehan, the Diocese of Bridgeport, composed of only Fairfield County in southwestern Connecticut, was to begin its existence devoted to improving Catholic education. The first Catholic high school of the diocese, Notre Dame in Bridgeport, was completed in September, 1957, followed by two others in Norwalk and Stamford. Shehan supported and encouraged efforts to strengthen CYO programs and to foster vocations to the priesthood and religious life. Fifteen new parishes were established to meet the needs of the growing numbers of Catholics settling in the suburbs throughout Fairfield County. The needs of immigrant groups, especially the Hungarians, Portuguese, and Hispanics were also recognized and specialized ministries were initiated to meet their needs. In 1960 the Carmelite Sisters of the Aged and Infirm were brought to the diocese to begin St. Joseph Manor in Trumbull.

In 1961 Bishop Shehan was transferred to his home diocese of Baltimore, as the coadjutor archbishop. Bishop Walter W. Curtis succeeded Shehan in Bridgeport, beginning a pastoral plan that would, in his words, "provide a seat in Catholic schools for every Catholic child in the Diocese of Bridgeport." His plan created parish schools in nearly every parish throughout the diocese, and completed Shehan's vision of five diocesan high schools.

By 1963 there were thirteen Catholic high schools and academies, and fifty-eight elementary schools and two Catholic universities, one, Sacred Heart University in Bridgeport, founded by Bishop Curtis.

As a Father of the Second Vatican Council, most of Bishop Curtis' administration was concerned with the implementation of the decrees of the council and the subsequent legislation and pastoral programs initiated by the NCCB, following the council. This included social concerns, work among the growing number of Catholic immigrants, especially the Hispanics and Asians, improved health care, and ministries to divorced and remarried Catholics and to various other groups.

In 1988 Bishop Edward M. Egan was named the third bishop of Bridgeport, arriving from New York where he had served as an auxiliary bishop for three years.

The Diocese of Norwich comprises the counties of Middlesex, New London, Tolland, and Windham in eastern Connecticut, as well as Fishers Island, in Suffolk County, New York.

Bishop Bernard J. Flanagan, the first bishop of the diocese, spent his nearly six years organizing and improving Catholic life within his primarily rural diocese. With industrial centers such as New London, with the naval bases and shipyards, as well as the smaller mill towns, the diocese labored to organize more strongly Catholic life, especially through the encouragement of vocations to the priesthood and religious life. In 1959 Bishop Vincent J. Hines succeeded Bishop Flanagan, and piloted the diocese through the years of change brought on by the Second Vatican Council. By 1963 there were approximately 174,325 Catholics in a total population of 412,000 inhabitants, served in sixty-six parishes and seventeen missions, by 119 diocesan and eighty-eight religious priests. Such religious communities as the Society of St. Edmund, the La Salette and Capuchin Fathers, and the Jesuits, Oblates of Mary Immaculate, Marian Fathers, Brothers of St. Francis Xavier and the Basilian Fathers all worked within the diocese. There were seven Catholic high schools and twenty-six Catholic elementary schools for the nearly 12,000 Catholic students. Religious women within the diocese at this time were the Franciscan Missionary Sisters, Daughters of the Holy Ghost, Felicians, Religious of the Cenacle, Filippini Sisters, Sisters of the Holy Family, Sisters of Mercy, Sisters of the Immaculate Conception, Sisters of the Precious Blood, Sisters of St. Joseph, and Sisters of Charity.

In 1975 Bishop Daniel P. Reilly was named to the Diocese of Norwich, and continued until his appointment as bishop of Worcester, Massachusetts. His years of ministry have continued the implementation of the decrees of Vatican II, in the areas of Catholic education, lay participation in the mission of the Church, social programs and civil rights, and ecumenism. Bishop Daniel A. Hare was appointed to Norwich on September 12, 1995.

In 1995 there were 1,353,693 Catholics in Connecticut in a total population of 3,269,846. Catholics constituted 41 percent of the total population, one of the highest in the nation. Connecticut's Catholics were served by 389 parishes, 836 diocesan priests, 298 religious priests, 412 deacons, 108 brothers, and 1,926 sisters. There were 5 Catholic hospitals in the state, 6 Catholic universities and colleges, 24 high schools, and 127 elementary schools.

Carroll, Teresa Austin. *Leaves from the Annals of the Sisters of Mercy.* New York, 1889.

DiGiovanni, Stephen M. *The Catholic Church in Fairfield County 1666–1961.* New Canaan, 1987.

Duggan, Thomas S. *The Catholic Church in Connecticut.* New York, 1930.

Liptak, Dolores A. *European Immigrants and the Catholic Church in Connecticut, 1870–1920.* New York, 1987.

O'Donnell, James H. *The Diocese of Hartford.* New York, 1900.

Shehan, Lawrence. *A Blessing of Years; The Memoirs of Lawrence Cardinal Shehan.* Notre Dame, 1982.

STEPHEN M. DiGIOVANNI

CONNELL, FRANCIS (1888–1967)

Redemptorist priest, moral theologian. Francis J. Connell was born in Boston, Massachusetts, on January 31, 1888. Connell graduated from Boston College before entering the Congregation of the Most Holy Redeemer (Redemptorists). Professed in 1908 and ordained in 1913, Connell was chosen for graduate studies in Rome which were postponed until 1921 because of wartime conditions in Europe. He worked briefly in pastoral ministry in Brooklyn and taught dogma at Mount St. Alphonsus, the Redemptorist theologate in Esopus, New York. Connell obtained the doctorate in sacred theology from the Angelicum in Rome in 1923 and returned to Mount St. Alphonsus to teach. In 1940 Connell accepted the chair of moral theology at The Catholic University of America in Washington,

Francis J. Connell

D.C., and served as chair of the Department of Theology from 1949–57. He retired from the university in 1958 and then served as special dean of the religious on campus until his death on May 12, 1967. Connell was a prolific writer and his clear and popular style made him one of the most authoritative voices in moral theology in the United States. In 1920 Connell began an association with the *American Ecclesiastical Review* that continued throughout his career. His column "Answers to Questions in Moral Theology," was widely read. Connell published a number of books including *Outlines of Moral Theology* (Milwaukee, 1953), *Morals in Politics and the Professions* (Westminster, Maryland, 1946), and a revised edition of the Baltimore Catechism. In his attempts to bring the Roman Catholic moral tradition to bear on cultural and political problems unique to the United States, Connell represented a distinctively American voice in moral theology.

Granfield, Patrick, O.S.B. "An Interview with Father Connell." *American Ecclesiastical Review* 157 (August 1967) 74–82.

TERRENCE J. MORAN

CONNELLY, CORNELIA (1809–79)

Foundress of the Society of the Holy Child Jesus. She was born in Philadelphia, Pennsylvania, on January 15, 1809. She established the congregation at Derby, England, in 1846 and remained superior general until she died. During her lifetime, the community made foundations in the United States and France, ultimately spreading to Ireland, Switzerland, Wales, and Italy. It also fostered the foundation of autonomous congregations in Nigeria (the Handmaids of the Holy Child Jesus), and in Ghana (the Sisters of the Infant Jesus). Today, the motherhouse of this international congregation is located in Rome.

Despite the raging Civil War, Mother Connelly sent missionary sisters to Towanda, Pennsylvania, in 1862. Conditions there were miserable, not as advertised by the dishonest agent of the community's benefactor, the Duchess of Leeds. After struggling for almost two years, the sisters relocated to Sharon Hill in the Philadelphia area and operated successfully thereafter. Mother Connelly visited Sharon Hill in 1867. Specializing in education, the sisters opened and operated numerous schools and established Rosemont College in 1921. In 1995 the 311 American members were active in 29 dioceses and archdioceses in a variety of apostolates. A series of extraordinary events in the foundress's life led to the establishment of the society and a long series of painful trials attended struggles to preserve her creation.

Early Years

Born into a well-to-do Philadelphia family, Cornelia Augusta Peacock received an excellent education from private tutors. At age twenty-three she married Pierce Connelly, a newly ordained Episcopalian minister. The newlyweds moved to Natchez, Mississippi, where Pierce assumed the rectorship of Trinity Church. His preaching, charm, and wit made him popular while Cornelia's grace and beauty gained the couple many friends. Two children blessed the union. During their third and fourth years in Natchez, Pierce gradually became a convinced Roman Catholic. On September 6, 1835, he announced from the pulpit of Trinity Church his resignation and belief in Catholicism. This sermon and the letter of resignation to his bishop were printed and broadcast, becoming national and international topics of interest. Cornelia also found herself drawn to Catholicism. After the couple consulted with Bishop Joseph Rosati (1789–1843) in St. Louis, Cornelia joined the Church. Pierce, however, determined to visit Rome for final conversion.

Conversion and Difficulties

Intrigued with Pierce and fascinated by the beautiful Cornelia, Roman society and high-ranking ecclesiastics made them welcome. Over the next two years, Pierce made important contacts in Rome and England, notably with the Earl of Shrewsbury and with Nicholas P. Wiseman, the rector of the English College. Pierce openly broached the subject of his possible ordination as a Catholic priest, greatly disturbing Cornelia. Financial setbacks forced the family to return to the United States in 1838 where Pierce obtained a teaching post at St. Charles College, the newly established Jesuit college in Grand Coteau, Louisiana. Cornelia taught music at the nearby convent of the Society of the Sacred Heart. Two more children blessed the marriage. During their five years at Grand Coteau deep pain afflicted Cornelia twice: the tragic death by scalding of their third child and Pierce's final decision to seek ordination, something that would require Cornelia's agreement to enter religious life. In 1845 the family went to England and subsequently to Rome.

Pierce's ordination involved Pope Gregory XVI (1765–1846) and various Vatican officials. Saddened, Cornelia acquiesced in Pierce's decision and agreed to a Bill of Separation and to entering the Roman convent of the Society of the Sacred Heart as a semipermanent novice taking the younger children with her. Pierce was ordained on July 6, 1845.

After some months in the convent, Cornelia determined against permanent membership, gradually evolving a plan for founding a new congregation to be devoted to teaching. Pierce departed for England and, encouraged by Pope Gregory XVI, Cornelia accepted Bishop Wiseman's invitation to found her new congregation in England. He directed her to property in Derby where she and three companions established a convent and school. Women seeking admission to the new community appeared almost immediately.

Cornelia and Pierce Connelly

Despite signed promises made concerning the children and the Deed of Separation, Pierce continued seeking control over Cornelia. He visited her unannounced in March 1848, supposedly to discuss the society's proposed rule. Bishop Wiseman had advised Cornelia not to see Pierce and the visit greatly upset her. Nonetheless, Pierce returned to Derby once more. This time Cornelia refused to receive him despite the fact that Pierce had removed the children to the continent and cut off her communications with them. Humiliated, Pierce instituted a suit for restoration of conjugal rights in the Anglican Court of Arches, ultimately gaining a favorable verdict. Anti-Catholicism was running high in England and the case became a *cause célèbre* on both sides of the Atlantic. Bishop Wiseman provided Cornelia both legal and moral support while the English press pilloried her, making Cornelia seem an unnatural mother and faithless wife. Mortified and hurt, she maintained her silence. The Privy Council ultimately upheld her position.

Pierce renounced the Catholic Church and became an anti-Catholic activist. He eventually settled in Florence, Italy, as rector of the American Episcopal Church where he published anti-Catholic tracts and attacks on Cornelia. He alienated the children from their mother. Pierce died in 1883, still not reconciled to the Church.

Following the trial, Cornelia moved her growing community to St. Leonard's due to property title problems at Derby. Here physical conditions were much improved, but years of new trials awaited her. Relations between her and Cardinal Wiseman (elevated in 1850) became strained, due to his lack of understanding of her problems. Constant financial demands and incidents of disloyalty by some sisters pressured her and the community the rest of her life. Her final battle was in defending the rule that she had written for the community and had submitted to Rome. Cardinal Wiseman and several English bishops, desiring diocesan control rather than pontifical status and annoyed by her independence, delayed approval until after her death. Her rule was finally approved in 1893. Investigations into her private devotional life have established that her love for God was intense. Mother Cornelia Connelly was declared Venerable in 1992.

See also WOMEN RELIGIOUS IN AMERICA.

Dehey, Elinor Tong. *Religious Orders of Women in the United States.* Hammond, Ind.: W. B. Conkey Company, 1930.

Flaxman, Radeagunde. *A Woman Styled Bold: The Life of Cornelia Connelly 1809–1879.* London, England: Dartman, Longman and Todd, 1991.

Wadham, Juliana. *The Case of Cornelia Connelly.* New York: Pantheon, 1957.

GEORGE STEWART, JR.

CONNOLLY, JOHN (1747/48 or 1751–1825)

Dominican friar, bishop. John Connolly was born in the parish of Monknewtown, County Meath, Ireland.

Many historians have either overlooked or minimized John Connolly's role and contributions to the Catholic Church in the United States. To correct this, Dominican historian Victor O'Daniel (1868–1960) researched primary sources in an unpublished manuscript appended to another study he called "Carbry Case Appendices: Appendix F.," 235–303, completed in 1939 (Dominican Archives, Providence College, Rhode Island). O'Daniel verified the year of Connolly's birth, corrected negative interpretations, and illuminated the man as a true pastor who, at age sixty-four, was consecrated bishop and removed from his life of teaching, administration, and Church diplomacy to serve in the New World.

John Connolly

Educated at Holy Cross College (Louvain, Belgium), Connolly was ordained September 24, 1774, in Malines, and sent to teach at the Irish Dominican College of the twin convents of San Sisto and San Clemente in Rome. Over a period of thirty-seven years there he held offices of regent of studies, prior, procurator, theologian-librarian of the famous Casanate Library (Minerva), and served as Roman agent to Irish bishops. In 1798 Napoleon's troops invaded Rome, imprisoning Pope Pius VI, and confiscating Church property. Connolly maintained a lone Dominican presence at San Clemente during the French occupation, and helped to preserve that historic site from damage, having refused allegiance to Bonaparte three times (Leonard E. Boyle, *San Clemente Miscellany I: the Community of SS. Sisto e Clemente in Rome* [Rome: S. Clementem, 1977]).

Second Bishop of New York

Connolly succeeded to a number of offices vacated by his former teacher, Luke Concanen, O.P., who was consecrated first bishop of New York in 1808, but who died in 1810 in Naples awaiting a ship to America. John Connolly was consecrated second bishop of New York in Rome on November 6, 1814, by Cardinal Brancadoro. As the War of 1812 closed, Connolly left for his new diocese in January 1815, stopping first in Belgium where no bishop had exercised faculties in fourteen years, and then in Ireland to recruit for the New World. A week before the death of John Carroll on November 24, 1815, he arrived in New York after so long a crossing that he was thought to have been lost at sea. His diocese, administered by Jesuits Anthony Kohlmann and Benedict Fenwick in the intervening years, comprised the whole state of New York and northern New Jersey and about 15,000 Catholics, most of whom were Irish and poor, served by only four priests.

The next ten years held many tensions, particularly between Irish and French clergy, but in 1817 alone Connolly brought the Sisters of Charity from Emmitsburg, Maryland, to New York, opened a free school in the basement of the small cathedral, founded an orphan asylum, and was co-consecrator of Archbishop Ambrose Maréchal in Baltimore. Problems of the trustee system developed in several dioceses—New York was no exception, and 1818–20 were very difficult years. But the people loved their bishop who drudged night and day for his flock, even during the yellow fever epidemic of 1822–23, and despite lack of personnel and funds. During his tenure (the era of building the Erie Canal) he ordained five priests, and churches were established in Brooklyn, Paterson, Utica, Auburn, Carthage, Rochester, and elsewhere. In ill health from 1823, he continued to act as pastor. He died in New York City on February 6, 1825. Thirty thousand persons are reported to have turned out for his funeral. He was buried at Old St. Patrick's Cathedral and later his remains were moved to an unmarked vault, where they were not rediscovered until February 1976, and reinterred in the crypt of Old St. Patrick's Cathedral.

See also DOMINICANS (O.P.); NEW YORK, CATHOLIC CHURCH IN.

Cohalan, Florence D. *A Popular History of the Archdiocese of New York.* Yonkers, 1983, 29–38.

ANNA M. DONNELLY

CONRARDY, LOUIS LAMBERT (1841–1914)

Missionary. Born in Liège, Belgium, July 12, 1841, Louis Lambert Conrardy was ordained June 15, 1866. After almost four years as parish priest at Stavelot, where he was known for his charitable works, he left for India, becoming a missionary, from 1871 to 1874, in the Pondicherry area.

After study at the American College at Louvain, he came to the Archdiocese of Oregon City in November 1874. By January 1875 he was resident missionary at the Umatilla Indian Reservation, but in his zeal, he ministered to Catholics over a wide area as well. Controversy over treatment of the native peoples, as well as growing interest in leper missions, convinced him to go to Molokai in 1888 to work with Fr. Damian. Conrardy attended Fr. Damian on his deathbed, administering the last sacraments to him. He remained at Molokai eight more years, then visited Chinese leper colonies. Realizing that he needed more medical education, Conrardy entered the University of Oregon Medical School in Portland, from which he graduated in April 1900. He continued his education at the University of Liège, later collecting money in Europe to start a leper colony in China.

Robbed of part of his collection in San Francisco, Conrardy continued on to China where be bought land on Shek Lung Island near Canton and established his leper colony. Government officials eventually recognized his efforts and provided some assistance.

In 1914 he contracted pneumonia and died on August 24, 1914, in a Hong Kong hospital. At his request, he was buried, wrapped in a mat, in that city's Catholic cemetery.

Dease, A. "First Class Leper Man." *Ave Maria* 38 (December 9, 1933) 746–50.

O'Connor, Dominic. *A Brief History of the Diocese of Baker.* St. Benedict., Oreg.: Benedictine Press, 1966.

Van der Heyden, J. "Father L. Conrardy, Leper Missionary in Hawaii and China." *Records of the American Catholic Historical Society of Philadelphia* 30 (December 1919) 303–08.

Walsh, J. E. "Father Conrardy, the Chinese Damien." *Field Afar* 27 (October 1931) 270–73.

PATRICIA BRANDT

CONSCIENTIOUS OBJECTION (AND OBJECTORS) IN AMERICA

Before 1965 and the Second Vatican Council's recommendation "that laws make humane provisions for the case of those who for reasons of conscience refuse to bear arms . . ." (Second Vatican Council, Pastoral Constitution on the Church in the Modern World, no. 79) the issue of conscientious objection was generally ignored by Catholics. From its earliest days, of course, the Church has honored as saints individuals who refused or evaded orders for military service they believed contrary to the demands of conscience. For some—St. Martin of Tours, for example—the objection was comprehensive, rejecting participation in any war as "unlawful" for those who had chosen to be "soldiers of Christ." Others suffered martyrdom for rejecting specific wars or commands they considered immoral in purpose or in the means employed. The beloved Curé d'Ars, St. John

Vianney, was a "conscientious deserter," going into hiding rather than accept orders to serve in Napoleon's forces.

Legal Status in the U.S.A.

Today conscientious objection is a legal classification conferring exemption from conscript military service. In the United States, although earlier wars may have involved enforceable calls for "volunteer" combat duty, formal conscription was introduced during the Civil War (though allowance was made for paid substitutes for those who objected to serving). In World War I and subsequent wars, conscription has been universal for males except for designated categories of deferments.

No formal provision was made for religion-related exemption until World War I when President Wilson approved noncombatant alternatives for members of the historic "peace churches" (Society of Friends, Mennonites, Church of the Brethren, etc.) whose tenets forbade participation in war. Approximately 4,000 such exemptions were granted.

However, neither the government nor Church authorities recognized conscientious objection as a legitimate option for Roman Catholics. Following the conversion of Constantine and the theological concessions introduced by Augustine, traditional Catholic moral teachings distinguished between "just" and "unjust" wars. Coupled with the "presumption of justice" routinely granted to the established secular authority, this effectively excluded Catholics from such recognition. The few Catholics known to have refused service were subjected to severe treatment in military prison and/or mental hospitals.

World War II and After

In World War II the situation improved, but slightly. Here, too, exemption from conscript service was keyed to "peace church" definitions; but the "radical" Catholic Worker movement through its Association of Catholic Conscientious Objectors helped gain recognition for the few Catholics (135 of approximately 12,000) assigned to the alternative Civilian Public Service program. Given the procedural difficulties encountered by Catholics, the men in CPS were almost certainly outnumbered by Catholic men sentenced to prison for violations of the conscription law. Most of these violations involved refusal to comply despite the prevailing belief that Catholics could not be conscientious objectors.

Few though they were, the men assigned to ACCO-sponsored CPS camps and units provided the precedent establishing legitimacy of their position under the law and (to a lesser extent) within the Catholic religious community as well. In the Vietnam War Catholic conscientious objectors—and more activist "resisters"—became a major element in the antiwar movement.

The Second Vatican Council's declaration already cited gives evidence of further progress as does the increasing number of pastoral letters and directives issued by the U.S. Catholic hierarchy and, perhaps most surprising of all, the opinion expressed by Pope John Paul II in a 1984 talk to an audience of young parishioners in Rome describing conscientious objection as "a sign of maturity when people manage to accept another form of public service that is not military service."

The destructive nature of modern war with its indiscriminate weapons and strategies provides further justification for Catholic conscientious objection. Vatican II's condemnation of the bombing of entire areas and their populations as "a crime against God and man himself" has inspired a thoroughgoing reassessment of the traditional "just war" theory by professional theologians and responsible Church leaders.

This brings us back to those men in prison (and St. John Vianney). During the Vietnam War years the public was scandalized by the number of young men who went into "exile" as draft-evaders in Canada or even chose desertion from the armed forces in protest against a war they could no longer justify and duties they believed immoral. Legalism notwithstanding, these deserve to be counted and respected as conscientious objectors—even though the law still discriminates by limiting legal recognition to claimants who reject "war *in any form*," in effect excluding Catholics and members of other "mainstream" Churches which still accept the possibility of a theoretically "just" war.

Prospects for broadened recognition of conscientious objection are promising. Over the past twenty-five years the U.S. Catholic bishops have repeatedly proposed revising the law to allow for "selective" conscientious objection. Nations which formerly made no provision for such exemption from military service now have policies often more generous than ours. Most significant of all, in 1987 the UN Human Rights Commission endorsed conscientious objection as "a legitimate exercise of the right of freedom of thought, conscience, and religion."

See also CATHOLIC PEACE MOVEMENT, THE; DAY, DOROTHY; PAX CHRISTI U.S.A.

Finny, Torin R.T. *Unsung Hero of the Great War.* New York: Paulist Press, 1989.
Vatican Council II. Pastoral Constitution on the Church in the Modern World, nos. 79–80.
Zahn, Gordon C. *Another Part of the War: The Camp Simon Story.* Boston: University of Massachusetts Press, 1979.

GORDON C. ZAHN

CONSIDINE, JOHN J. (1897–1982)

Missionary. John J. Considine, Maryknoll missioner, mission theorist and educator, was born in New Bedford, Massachusetts, October 9, 1897. He completed his seminary studies at Maryknoll Seminary and was ordained to the priesthood on May 26, 1923. The following year he earned a licentiate in theology at The Catholic University of America where he wrote a study on the missionary thought of Ramón Lull. He was then assigned to Rome where he was to serve Maryknoll and the Congregation for the Propagation of the Faith during the next ten years (1924–34).

He directed the assembling of Maryknoll's exhibit for the Vatican Missionary Exhibition of 1925. This experience brought him into contact with mission representatives from all parts of the world and inspired his first book *A Window on the World*. In 1926 he assisted the Congregation for the Propagation of the Faith in reorganizing its department of statistics, and the following year he established for the congregation the multilanguage Fides International News Service and served as its first director.

In 1934 Considine returned to the U.S.A. to serve on the general council of the society. He was reelected in 1936 and served in this position until 1946. During 1943–46 he was vicar general. His office enabled him to continue to visit missionaries overseas and to lecture widely in the U.S.A.; as a director of Maryknoll's publications, he further developed and systematized the mission education efforts initiated by the society's cofounders. In his brief *World Christianity* (1945) he highlighted the societal dimensions of Christian doctrines. After 1946 Considine continued to coordinate Maryknoll's mission publications. With the collaboration of Maryknoll sisters he promoted the preparation of new high-school textbooks for social studies emphasizing the oneness of the human family. He also worked with J. Franklin Ewing, S.J., in developing programs of mission studies at Fordham University. His missiology lectures there and at Maryknoll Seminary provided stimulating working background for young missioners.

In 1945 Considine made his first trip to Latin America. Local bishops and other observers informed him that the fundamental problem in the Latin American Church was an insufficiency of priests. He published his survey as a *Call for Forty Thousand* [priests] (1946). In 1954 he organized a conference in Lima, Peru, at which he aided Maryknollers to examine critically the approaches they had been using during their first decade in Latin America.

In 1960 he readily accepted the request of the U.S. bishops to organize for them a Latin America Bureau; a year later he was named director and served until 1968. In 1961, when Pope John XXIII urged that more North American apostolic personnel be sent to Latin America, the bureau sponsored a program of formation and language study in Cuernavaca, Mexico, and later in San Juan, Puerto Rico. Through the Papal Volunteer program (PAVLA), Considine encouraged the participation of U.S. laity.

Considine retired in 1968 and spent his final years doing mission research at Maryknoll. He died May 4, 1982.

See also MARYKNOLL.

Considine, John J. *World Christianity*. Milwaukee: Bruce, 1945.

Costello, Gerald M. *Mission to Latin America*. Maryknoll, N.Y.: Orbis, 1979.

McGurkin, Edward A. "Fr. John J. Considine." *Profiles of Maryknollers*. Privately printed. Maryknoll, N.Y., 1983, 13–24.

WILLIAM D. McCARTHY, M.M.

CONWAY, KATHERINE E. (1853–1927)

Journalist, novelist, poet, professor, clubwoman, and first woman editor of Boston's Catholic newspaper, the *Pilot*. Born in Rochester, New York, Conway attended a Sacred Heart Convent School in New York City. Her father, an English emigrant, had been forced to flee Great Britain because of his Chartist affiliations, while her mother came from a family of educated women. Conway's journalism career began in 1875 under a pen name with some articles for a Catholic monthly. Three years later, after her father suffered significant financial losses, she obtained work at the Buffalo *Catholic Union and Times*. Moving to Boston in 1883, she joined the *Pilot* as assistant editor to John Boyle O'Reilly. Her first major assignment was the Catholic Centenary Congress in Baltimore, 1889.

The next Catholic Congress, held in 1893 in Chicago simultaneously with the World Columbian Congress of Women, led Conway to defend equal representation for women. Still, she campaigned against a separate woman's day for Catholics, and further undermined her position by delivering a paper advocating traditional notions of female domesticity and motherhood. Conway's subsequent career was marked by its opposition between demands for female educational, occupational, and wage equality, and loyalty to the conservatism of the Catholic Church on gender roles. For example, although Conway had opposed woman suffrage, when women received the vote in 1920 she acknowledged their duty to register. Moreover, she objected to the registration requirement that women reveal their ages on the grounds that employers might arbitrarily discriminate against aging women. Nonetheless, like certain middle-class professional women of that era, she viewed her own career as a deviation from the "normal" path of Christian marriage and motherhood.

From the 1890s until her death Conway was active in the abundant organizations formed by Catholic laity in this era to promote reading and intellectual life. Notably, Conway became the second woman elected to the Boston Union, succeeded O'Reilly as president of a prominent Catholic reading group, and became the first woman to edit the *Pilot* after the departure of James J. Roche in 1905. To sustain the paper Conway worked without salary and spent her own savings. In 1907 she received the prestigious Laetare Medal of the University of Notre Dame for her writing. In 1912 she was awarded the *Pro Ecclesia et Pontifice* medal by Pope Pius X. In 1908, however, as

Archbishop William O'Connell took over the *Pilot*, Conway was dismissed. She traveled for a year in Europe before returning to teach English at Saint Mary's College for Women in South Bend, Indiana (1911–16). Poor health, however, forced her to stop in 1916. Returning to Boston she found employment with John Fitzgerald's Democratic weekly, *The Republic*, until it folded in 1926. In the years before her death Conway contributed occasional, unsigned editorials to the *Pilot*.

As an Irish-American writer, Conway helped fashion a bourgeois Catholicism whose impact extended well beyond New England. Her series of self-improvement and etiquette books in the 1890s showed Catholics how to become well liked and well read. As such, Conway's work served the assimilationist phase of early twentieth-century American Catholics, in whose subculture women were assigned antiworldly, domestic goals. Other nonfiction publications include a biography of a Boston politician, Charles Donnelly, and histories of the Good Shepherd Sisters in New York, Newark, and Boston. Her novels manifested the uneasy amalgam of realism and sentimentalism that typified her Irish-American literary cohort (Fanning, 153). Her poetry, largely religious, emphasized the theme of meaningful death (McDannell, *AWW* 1:394). The Conway papers at Boston College contain diaries, speeches, and correspondence. Archives of the Archdiocese of Boston house the *Pilot*'s records; University of Notre Dame Archives has correspondence with editor Rev. Daniel Hudson.

See also CATHOLIC PRESS (NEWSPAPERS), THE; O'CONNELL, WILLIAM CARDINAL; *PILOT*, THE; O'REILLY, JOHN BOYLE.

Conway, Katherine. *Bettering Ourselves*. Boston, 1899.

——. *Lalor's Maples*. 4th ed. Boston, 1909.

Fanning, Charles, ed. *The Irish Voice in America*. Lexington, Kentucky, 1990.

Kane, Paula M. *Separatism & Subculture: Boston Catholicism, 1900–1920*. Chapel Hill, North Carolina, 1994.

Kenneally, James K. *The History of American Catholic Women*. New York, 1990.

McDannell, Colleen. "Catholic Women Fiction Writers, 1840–1920." *Women's Studies* 19 (3/4) (1991) 385–405.

——. "Katherine Conway." *American Women Writers: A Critical Reference Guide from Colonial Times to the Present*, ed. Lina Mainiero. 4 vols. New York, 1979–82, 1:393–94.

PAULA M. KANE

CONWAY, RACHEL (1827–1911)

Religious superior and foundress. In 1848 twenty-one-year-old Ellen Conway was received as Sr. Rachel into the Dominican community that Fr. Samuel Mazzuchelli was organizing in Wisconsin. A year later, when the tiny, poverty-stricken community was on the verge of disbanding, the decision regarding its future was given to the youngest, novice Rachel Conway, who declared, "In the name of God, let us remain together." Thus she became one of the "Four Cornerstones" of the Sinsinawa Dominican Congregation. In 1866 Sr. Rachel transferred to the Kentucky Dominicans, and in 1873 she was one of the six sisters sent from Kentucky to establish a new foundation in Illinois. Thus she became one of the foundresses of the Springfield Dominicans.

On October 15, 1874, in obedience to a telegram from Bishop Baltes, at the request of President U.S. Grant, Sr. Rachel, together with Sr. Josephine Meagher, unveiled the statue of Abraham Lincoln at the dedication of Lincoln's monument at Oak Ridge Cemetery in Springfield. The President had insisted upon this honor as a token of public gratitude to all the "Nuns of the Battlefield" who had served during the Civil War.

After twenty years as a gifted though self-effacing musician and teacher, Sr. Rachel was confined by a crippling illness to a wheelchair. Until her death, her room was her refuge from public attention and a mecca for young and old, who delighted in her gracious company. Strangely, Sr. Rachel's death on Lincoln's birthday in 1911 coincided with a three-day celebration in Springfield of the anniversary of Lincoln's death. There had to be a divine irony in the final scene: As her funeral procession passed Lincoln's Monument, the bells of Oak Ridge Cemetery tolled, and a military guard of honor stood at the entrance of Calvary Cemetery where she was buried.

See also DOMINICANS (O.P.).

LINDA TONELLATO, O.P.

CONWELL, HENRY (ca. 1745–1842)

Second bishop of Philadelphia. Henry Conwell was born ca. 1745, at Moneymore, Derry, Ireland, served twenty-five years as vicar general of the Archdiocese of Armagh before being named bishop of Philadelphia at the age of seventy-five. Offered the see of Madras, India, or Philadelphia, he chose the latter which had remained vacant since the death in July 1814 of Michael Egan, the first bishop of Philadelphia. Conwell was ordained a bishop in London on September 24, 1820, and arrived in Philadelphia in November of that year.

Trusteeism, in particular the Hogan schism, dominated Henry Conwell's episcopacy. It was further troubled by the return from Ireland of the Dominican William V. Harold, a major figure in the Egan episcopacy. Harold had been the choice of many Philadelphians as Egan's successor but Rome judged him unqualified. Conwell believed that lay usurpation and the unprincipled conduct of some of the clergy threatened the American Church with extinction. He felt that the trustees were intent on a national referendum on lay rights in the Church.

The Hogan Schism

William Hogan, an Irish priest of questionable background and reputation, initiated a breech with the bishop in December 1820, by refusing to live in the clerical residence and announced his own preaching schedule. Conwell, who saw in Hogan another Luther or John Knox, suspended him, subsequently excommunicating him in May 1821. Episcopal rights were pitted against a claim of the trustees to select and present pastors in increasingly bitter public confrontations which endured beyond the departure of Hogan from Philadelphia. The board of trustees of St. Mary's Cathedral elected in 1821 supported Hogan, excluded Conwell from its membership and refused to recognize him as pastor of St. Mary's. The 1822 trustee election produced a riot serious enough to be reported in the New York, Baltimore, and Washington press.

The trustees sought a change in the charter to exclude clerical membership. In both instances they were successful in the state legislature, but in the first case (1821) the state supreme court nullified the change and in the second (1823) the governor vetoed the bill. The legislature refused to consider a third effort.

Rome's response to events, particularly to trustee appeals, ended Hogan's role but not the trustee issue itself. Pius VII in August 1822 denounced Hogan by name and the trustees for subverting Church order and discipline in claiming a new right to appoint and remove pastors. Hogan accepted this, obtained Conwell's absolution on condition of leaving the diocese, but he failed to do so until a year later.

The trustees presented another Irish priest, Thaddeus O'Mealy, as pastor of St. Mary's. O'Mealy was subsequently excommunicated by the bishop in November 1823 for ignoring Conwell's prohibition against performing any ecclesiastical functions. Sent to Rome by the trustees in April 1825 to "negotiate a concordat" recognizing the rights of the trustees, O'Mealy submitted to Rome instead.

Conwell's Pact with the Trustees

The bishop and trustees agreed in October 1826 to a compromise pact of uncertain initiative. It recognized Conwell as bishop and senior pastor of St. Mary's; each party dropped any pending suits against the other; the setting of clerical salaries was left to the board; Conwell accepted review by the trustees of episcopal appointments at St. Mary's parish.

The pact did not bring peace. Most of the American hierarchy protested the settlement. The diocesan vicar general, William Harold, O.P., wrote Rome in November 1826 denouncing the pact. Propaganda Fide, in a decision confirmed by Pope Leo XII, condemned the pact in April 1827 for overthrowing episcopal authority and discipline. William Harold became an issue. Bishop Conwell removed him as vicar general in December 1826 for insulting language and behavior toward him, and in April 1827 suspended Harold's faculties. The trustees now supported Harold, petitioning Rome for his restoration and for the removal of the bishop. Yet in October 1827, Conwell, about to undertake a diocesan visitation, appointed Harold one of two pastors of St. Mary's. Harold was subsequently ordered by Rome to move to Cincinnati. He delayed a year and went to Ireland instead.

In August 1827 Propaganda Fide requested Conwell's presence at Rome. The bishop delayed and in March 1828 was ordered to Rome. He left for Rome in July. Expected to provide a thorough report of affairs in Philadelphia, he failed to do so and was prohibited from leaving Rome until he agreed he would not return to America; he was to be allowed to reside anywhere he wished in Europe. Conwell instead fled Rome in April 1829 and consequently was suspended in September 1829. Arriving in the United States in October, he was not permitted to participate in the First Provincial Council of Baltimore, although the bishops requested Rome to absolve him and lift the censure. Conwell was allowed to remain in Philadelphia, but with the diocese governed by a coadjutor, Francis Patrick Kenrick, named bishop of Arath *in partibus*. Conwell died on April 22, 1842.

Conwell's episcopal visitations were not extensive; the furthest reached Carlisle in south-central Pennsylvania. He ordained ten priests. He made two trips to Quebec, 1822 and 1823, seeking funds to build a new cathedral church and to obtain nuns to establish an Ursuline house in Philadelphia; he had some success with the former but not with the latter.

See also PENNSYLVANIA, CATHOLIC CHURCH IN.

Carey, Patrick W. *People, Priests, and Prelates: Ecclesiastical Democracy and the Tensions of Trusteeism.* University of Notre Dame Press, 1987, passim.

Ennis, Arthur J., O.S.A. "The New Diocese of Philadelphia." *History of the Archdiocese of Philadelphia,* ed. James Connelly. Philadelphia, 1976, 79–112.

Griffin, Martin I. J. "The Life of Bishop Conwell." *Records of the American Catholic Historical Society of Philadelphia* 24 (1913) 16–24, 162–78, 217–50, 348–61; 25 (1914) 52–67, 146–78, 217–48, 296–341; 26 (1915) 64–77, 131–65, 227–49; 27 (1916) 74–87, 145–60, 275–83, 359–78; 28 (1917) 64–84, 150–83, 244–65, 310–47; 29 (1918) 170–82, 250–61, 360–84.

Tourscher, Francis E., O.S.A. *The Hogan Schism and Trustee Troubles in St. Mary's Church Philadelphia, 1820–1829.* Philadelphia: Peter Reilly Co., 1930.

THOMAS R. GREENE

COOKE, TERENCE CARDINAL (1921–83)

Cardinal archbishop. Terence J. Cooke was born in New York City on March 1, 1921, the youngest of three chil-

Terence Cardinal Cooke

dren of Michael Cooke and Margaret Gannon Cooke, who were both natives of County Galway, Ireland. They named him after Terence MacSwiney, the nationalist Lord Mayor of Cork who had died six months earlier from his celebrated hunger strike protesting British occupation policies in Ireland. When Terence was five years old, his family moved from the Morningside Heights section of Manhattan to the northeast Bronx where he attended St. Benedict's parochial school. After the death of his mother in 1930, her sister, Mary Gannon, joined the family to help rear Terence and his older brother and sister. Terence decided to study for the priesthood upon graduation from elementary school in 1934 and enrolled in Cathedral College, the minor seminary of the Archdiocese of New York. In 1940 he entered St. Joseph's Seminary, Dunwoodie, and was ordained a priest on December 1, 1945, by Francis Cardinal Spellman in St. Patrick's Cathedral.

Immediately after ordination, Fr. Cooke was assigned to graduate studies in social work, first at the University of Chicago, then in the National Catholic School of Social Service at The Catholic University of America, where he obtained a master's degree in 1949. From 1949 to 1954 he was assigned to the Youth Division of Catholic Charities; in 1954 he became procurator of St. Joseph's Seminary where his administrative efficiency brought him to the attention of Cardinal Spellman, who selected him as his secretary in 1957.

Thereafter, Cooke's star ascended rapidly as he advanced from vice chancellor (1958) to chancellor (1961) to vicar general and auxiliary bishop (1965). At Spellman's death in December 1967, Cooke was the youngest of ten auxiliary bishops. His appointment as the seventh archbishop of New York on March 8, 1968, was unexpected (especially to Archbishop John J. Maguire, the coadjutor *without* right of succession) and was widely attributed to Spellman's influence *d'outre tombe*. On April 4, 1968, Cooke also succeeded Spellman as military vicar for the United States Armed Forces. He was appointed a cardinal on April 28, 1969.

Archbishop of New York

Cooke became archbishop of New York during a tumultuous period of civil rights demonstrations and student protests provoked by the Vietnam War. On the day of his installation, April 4, 1968, Dr. Martin Luther King Jr. was assassinated, leading to riots in many American cities. That evening Cooke left a reception to travel to Harlem and plead for racial peace. Cooke also had to face the unsettling aftermath of Vatican Council II. Between 1967 and 1983 the number of diocesan priests in New York declined from 1,108 to 777. There was an even more abrupt decline among women religious, from 8,955 to 5,178. The total Catholic population of the archdiocese remained approximately the same (1,800,000), but only because large numbers of Hispanic immigrants replaced several hundred thousand middle-class Catholics who moved to the suburbs outside the archdiocese. Sacramental statistics indicated a sharp drop in religious practice. Between 1967 and 1983, the number of infant baptisms fell from 50,000 to 31,000 per year, and church weddings declined from 15,000 to 8,200 per year.

The age of expansion in the archdiocese had ended by the time that Cooke took over the reins. Between 1939 and 1967 Cardinal Spellman had established forty-five new parishes. Under Cooke there was a net gain of four new parishes. The archdiocese needed a leader with the financial expertise to husband carefully the available resources, and Cooke excelled in this particular role. No check stub or requisition slip was too insignificant for his attention, and, at board meetings of Catholic institutions, he regularly demonstrated an encyclopedic knowledge of budgets and balance sheets. One of his most effective stratagems was the creation of the Inter-Parish Finance Commission, which levied an assessment on all parishes and used the income to subsidize poorer parishes. Largely as a result of this system, only thirty-one of the 305 Catholic elementary schools were forced to close despite a massive decline in enrollment (from 167,000 to 88,000) and the departure of three-quarters of the teaching sisters. Cooke also appointed the first black and Hispanic auxiliary bishops in the history of the archdiocese, and, in his capacity as military vicar, he continued Spellman's custom of visiting American troops overseas.

Critics complained that Cooke's financial wizardry was not matched by comparable leadership qualities or long-term vision. In such areas as the Hispanic apostolate and the academic quality of the diocesan seminary, Cooke was faulted for failing to continue the innovative policies of his predecessor. He was sensitive to criticism from the secular press and tended to avoid open confrontation on controversial issues. In public he displayed a cheery smile and exuded an aura of unquenchable optimism. With the clergy he was affable but a stickler for ecclesiastical propriety. He had a native ability to deflect a discussion of substantive issues into inoffensive pleasantries. His penchant for conciliation spared New York the polarization that occurred among the clergy of some other dioceses in the wake of Vatican Council II.

In August 1983 Cooke announced that he was terminally ill with cancer, a lymphoma condition for which he had been secretly receiving medical treatment for the previous eight years. During the following six weeks, his faith and courage made a deep impression on many New Yorkers. After his death on October 6, 1983, huge crowds filed past his bier in St. Patrick's Cathedral and over 900 priests attended his funeral. The tabloid New York *Daily News* commented: "On Cardinal Cooke's final day a line from Shakespeare seems uniquely appropriate: 'Nothing in his life became him like the leaving of it.' This was a man who showed us all how to pass from time to eternity with courage and grace." He was buried under the main altar of St. Patrick's Cathedral.

See also NEW YORK, CATHOLIC CHURCH IN .

Diaz-Stevens, Ana Maria. *Oxcart Catholicism on Fifth Avenue: The Impact of the Puerto Rican Migration upon the Archdiocese of New York.* University of Notre Dame Press, 1993.

Groeschel, Benedict J., C.F.R., and Terrence L. Weber. *Thy Will Be Done: A Spiritual Portrait of Terence Cardinal Cooke.* New York: Alba House, 1990.

Shelley, Thomas J. *Dunwoodie: The History of St. Joseph's Seminary.* Westminster, Md.: Christian Classics, 1993.

THOMAS J. SHELLEY

COPE, MARIANNE (1838–1918)

Missionary, religious superior. Barbara Cope was born in Germany on January 23, 1838. She was foundress of the Franciscan Mission to Hawaii and is primarily remembered as the leader of the first contingent of sister-nurses to the sick of Hawaii especially to those suffering from Hansen's disease (leprosy).

During her lifetime she was decorated with the royal medal of Kapiolani by Hawaiian royalty for her leadership on behalf of the sick poor; she was celebrated in musical compositions dedicated to her by the famed leader of the Royal Hawaiian band, Captain Henry Berger; and she was commemorated both in poetry and prose by Robert Louis Stevenson. Honors and tributes to her heroic charity continue after her death.

Marianne Cope

When her family emigrated to Utica, New York, from Hesse-Darmstadt, Germany, in 1840, Barbara Cope was its youngest member, a child of less than two years. At the age of twenty-four she felt free enough of family responsibilities to be able to follow her religious vocation, and she chose the name Marianne as a Sister of St. Francis.

She spent nearly a decade as a teacher and then as principal in newly established Catholic schools for German immigrants. She also was a founding member of two of the first Catholic hospitals in the United States, both of which were initiated by her religious community in the 1860s. She herself directed one of these hospitals, St. Joseph's, the first in Syracuse, New York, from 1870–77. All these experiences helped to prepare her for a special ministry in Hawaii.

Mission to Hawaii

In 1883, at the urgent request of the leaders of the Hawaiian kingdom, she did what no other secular or religious leader in the United States, Canada or Europe saw fit to do. Her community accepted the challenge to go to the aid of two hundred leprosy patients who had been isolated in a hospital near Honolulu, Oahu, bereft of nursing care. The call for sacrifice also included the challenge of extending hospital service elsewhere in the Hawaiian Islands when called upon to do so.

An arduous journey and exposure to a dangerous disease would face all who joined her at the quarantined Kakaako hospital, near Honolulu. The conditions were almost unspeakable. The sisters started their efforts by cleaning up the filth in the series of wooden buildings filled with rats and by bathing the patients who were covered with sores and vermin. The patients who had been left to die unattended were fed and cared for. Wards were set up in a manner that the strong and violent could no longer take undue advantage of the weak.

The small force of seven sisters was soon divided as, in 1884, Mother Marianne set up the first hospital for non-leprous patients on Maui. She returned soon to Kakaako to rid the place of the corrupt superintendent who was abusive to the patients. In 1885 she saw the need to give up her own position of authority as head of her community in Syracuse, New York. That same year a home was opened on the Kakaako hospital grounds for the female children of leprosy patients who lived endangered lives at the Molokai settlement. The situation had become more pressing because the leprosy of Fr. Damien DeVeuster had been confirmed earlier that year.

In November 1888 the Franciscan mission was extended to Kalaupapa, Molokai, a desolate place where hundreds of leprosy patients were exiled. Mother Marianne had accepted charge of a home for leprous girls and women. When Fr. Damien died five months later, she also took charge of the home he had initiated for men and boys.

Upon the death of Mother Marianne thirty years later on August 9, 1918, the Honolulu *Advertiser* praised her in these words. "Mother Marianne, without the blare of trumpets, came to Hawaii to do whatever was required of her. Living apart from the world and its comforts, she labored in the cause of a stricken people. She faced each task with unflinching courage and smiled sweetly through it all. Her life of sacrifice came to an end."

The legacy of Mother Marianne of Molokai continues with medical centers and schools both in New York state and Hawaii under the auspices of the Sisters of Saint Francis of Syracuse. Her cause for sainthood is in the discussional stage in Rome.

See also DAMIEN, FATHER/JOSEPH DE VEUSTER.

Hanley, Sr. Mary Laurence, O.S.F., and O. A. Bushnell. *Pilgrimage and Exile.* Honolulu: The University of Hawaii Press, 1990.

SR. MARY LAURENCE HANLEY, O.S.F.

CORCORAN, JAMES ANDREW (1820–89)

Theologian and editor. He was born in Charleston, South Carolina, on March 30, 1820, the son of John Corcoran and Jane O'Farrell Corcoran of County Longford, Ireland. His parents came to Charleston in 1816. James's father and sister died three years later. By 1832 James's mother had died also, leaving him and his brother to the care of a family friend.

James attended school at the Philosophical and Classical Seminary of Charleston, established in 1822 by Bishop John England. James was noted for his brightness and piety. Bishop England was aware of his desire to be a priest

James A. Corcoran

and he selected him to be educated at the Urban College of the Propaganda in Rome. On May 16, 1834, James Corcoran enrolled in the Urban College. He received several awards for his scholarly accomplishments in Latin oratory and poetry, Greek language and philosophy. It was at the Urban College James met several other American students, including Benedict J. Spalding, George A. Hamilton, James O'Connor, William O'Hara, and James F. Wood. James was ordained on December 21, 1842, by Cardinal Fransoni, Prefect of the Propaganda.

In May of 1843 he received his doctorate in sacred theology and returned to Charleston around November of 1843. Around 1846, James Corcoran, Patrick N. Lynch, and Augustine F. Hewit began preparing the writings of Bishop John England for publication. This important project was completed in 1848. In 1850 James Corcoran took over the editorship of the *United States Catholic Miscellany,* the local Catholic newspaper that had been established by Bishop John England in 1822 to defend the Roman Catholic Church against her attackers.

At this time in the United States, the political situation was critical for the Church, as large numbers of Catholic immigrants continued to pour into the country, thus arousing fear among the Protestants. The Know-Nothing Party was becoming strong and their anti-Catholic stand was widely publicized. Corcoran fought this anti-Catholic group with much vigor and intellectual quality. His writings did much to shape the Catholic thinking of the time.

The 1860s produced many political changes in the U.S.A., including the decline of the Know-Nothing Party and the rise of the Republican Party. Corcoran believed that the anti-Catholic forces had succeeded in gaining control of the government. This event, along with his Southern heritage, caused him to take a strong pro-Confederacy stance, for he believed that the Confederacy offered the American Catholic Church its best hope for survival. When South Carolina seceded from the Union in 1860, Corcoran gave his strong approval. In January of 1861 he changed the name from *United States Catholic Miscellany* to *Charleston Catholic Miscellany*. Because of the change of name, Corcoran came under much criticism especially from Archbishop John Hughes of New York. On December 11, 1861, a large fire broke out in Charleston, burning much of the city, including the Catholic cathedral and the *Miscellany* office. Corcoran left Charleston in 1862 to aid victims of a yellow fever epidemic in Wilmington, North Carolina.

Corcoran served in several important positions. Because of his command of Latin he was elected secretary of the Eighth and Ninth Provincial Councils of Baltimore, 1855 and 1858. In July 1868 the United States archbishops appointed Corcoran as the American theologian to Vatican Council I. He arrived in Rome a year before the opening of the council, where he and others began preparation for the *schemata* of the council. The question of papal infallibility dominated the council, but Corcoran, along with several American bishops, was opposed to any formal definition of papal infallibility.

At the close of the council in 1870, Corcoran returned to Charleston and then to Philadelphia, where in 1871 he accepted a chair of Dogmatic Theology at the newly built St. Charles Seminary in Overbrook. In 1872 he served as rector for a period of one year resigning because of poor administrative skills. Late in 1875, Brownson's *Quarterly Review* had been discontinued. To fill the demand for a learned Catholic quarterly, the *American Catholic Quarterly Review* was established with Corcoran as the editor. The first issue appeared in January 1876, and contained Corcoran's introductory article, "Salutatory."

Corcoran continued to serve the Church in many capacities. At the First Provincial Council of Philadelphia, he acted as secretary. When Pope Leo XIII proposed the Third Plenary Council of Baltimore, Corcoran accompanied the United States archbishops to Rome as their theologian for the preliminary meetings in 1883. Made a monsignor in Rome, Corcoran returned to the United States to serve as secretary to the Third Plenary Council in Baltimore in 1884. He died in Philadelphia on July 16, 1889.

Archbishop John J. Keane ranked Corcoran with Orestes Brownson and Isaac Hecker in terms of his influence on American Catholic intellectual life. "Our great philosopher, our great missionary, and our living encyclopedia of sacred learning," he called them.

See also CATHOLIC MAGAZINES AND PERIODICALS.

Keane, John J. "Monsignor Corcoran." *American Catholic Quarterly Review* 14 (October 1889) 738–48.

Lofton, Edward. "Reverend Doctor James Andrew Corcoran and the 'United States Catholic Miscellany.'" *Records of the American Catholic Historical Society of Philadelphia* 93 (March, December 1982) 77–101.

Lowman M. "James Andrew Corcoran: Editor, Theologian, Scholar, 1820–1889." Ph.D. dissertation, St. Louis University, 1958.

EDWARD LOFTON

CORDERO, PAULA (1908–91)

Religious publisher. Born Adele Cordero in 1908, she grew up in Priocca, Italy. Adele entered the new congregation of the Daughters of St. Paul and received the name "Paula." When Sr. Paula and Sr. Anita, her younger companion, left for the U.S.A. in 1932, they had little money, few friends, and did not know the language. They faced an America gripped by the Great Depression.

An apartment in Bronx, New York, became the sisters' home and they began the Pauline mission of producing and distributing religious books and pamphlets. Gradually, more sisters were sent from Italy. Young women began to join and the first American Daughter of St. Paul, Sr. Mary Celeste Carini, received the religious habit. In other countries it was common to see Daughters of St. Paul bringing religious literature to people. It soon became familiar on New York's busy streets too. Time and again the sisters explained their new and unique mission. In 1938, the sisters moved to Staten Island, New York, because their community had grown so much.

Their founder, Fr. James Alberione, and first superior general, Mother Thecla Merlo, kept in close contact with the sisters and visited them until World War II began. Lack of communication with the motherhouse in Rome and their families during the war was painful. After the war, communication lines were reopened. Mother Paula obtained permission to move to larger property. In 1949 an estate in Derby, New York, became the first novitiate house of the Daughters of St. Paul in America. There the sisters made significant strides in printing and binding religious material. They filled the convent with typesetting machines, printing presses, and binding equipment. The buildings were piled high with paper for the press. Before the sisters knew it, they were even storing books in their bedrooms. Mother Paula knew it was time to move again.

During these years, Mother Paula sent sisters to open new convents and bookcenters throughout the country. She asked Cardinal Cushing of Boston for permission to open a novitiate there. Cushing welcomed the sisters to his archdiocese and in 1956 the community moved to their new home: a hilltop in suburban Boston.

In 1995 the sisters staffed twenty-one Pauline Book and Media centers from coast to coast and in Toronto, Canada. From these centers they reach out to people everywhere. Internationally they are in over fifty countries.

Mother Paula died in 1991.

See also WOMEN RELIGIOUS IN AMERICA.

Daughters of St. Paul. *Communicators for Christ.* Daughters of St. Paul: Boston, 1972.
____. *Daughters of St. Paul, 50 Years of Service in the USA—1932–1982.* Boston: St. Paul Editions, 1982.

KATHLEEN MARIA MITCHELL, F.S.P.

CORRIGAN, MICHAEL (1839–1902)

Early Life

Third archbishop of New York. Michael Augustine Corrigan was born in Newark, New Jersey, on August 13, 1839. He was the fifth of nine children of a wealthy immigrant Irish couple, Thomas, a cabinet-maker turned merchant, and Mary (English) Corrigan. Of frail health, his earliest schooling was at home and then at a small academy conducted by his godfather. At fourteen he began collegiate studies at St. Mary's College in Wilmington, Delaware, and two years later entered Mt. St. Mary's College in Emmitsburg, Maryland. In 1859, having graduated first in his class, he sailed for Rome under the auspices of his bishop, James Roosevelt Bayley, to begin studies for the priesthood as a member of the first class of the North American College. Continuing academic success in Rome led to graduate studies in theology after his ordination in 1863. With a doctorate in hand a year later, he returned to Newark to become director of the seminary at Seton Hall College as well as professor of sacred Scripture and dogmatic theology. Named president of the school in 1869, Corrigan used his family wealth to overcome the financial crisis which was threatening to close the institution. When Bayley was appointed archbishop of Baltimore in 1873, the thirty-four-year-old Corrigan succeeded him as bishop of Newark.

Bishop of Newark

Despite the depressed times, the diocese under Corrigan added sixty-nine churches and missions within seven years, an expansion of its parishes by more than a third to meet the pressing needs of its rapidly growing immigrant population. The increase in priests was even greater. The centralization of ownership and administration of diocesan property under Corrigan as corporation sole meant stable finances and uniform practices. A comprehensive schedule of recurring episcopal visitations of parishes and regular conferences for priests were innovations of the new bishop which also promoted uniformity and accountability. By 1880 the impressive achievements of Corrigan made him the choice of the ailing cardinal archbishop of New York, John McCloskey, for coadjutor with the right of succession. With the death of Cardinal McCloskey in October 1885, Corrigan became the ordinary of the more than 600,000 Catholics in New York City and the seven adjoining counties to the north.

Archbishop of New York

As coadjutor, Corrigan immediately became the chief administrator of the archdiocese. To New York he applied the reforms he had instituted in Newark, visiting all parishes, reorganizing the bureaucracy, and consolidating the school system. And, given the needs of the largest and most rapidly growing Catholic community in the nation, Corrigan was responsible for the greatest period of expansion in the archdiocese's history. During his tenure as coadjutor and then ordinary, he established ninety-nine parishes, opened seventy-five schools, and brought in twenty-four communities of religious men and women to staff them and other ministries. Charitable institutions proliferated, culminating with the establishment of the Association of Catholic Charities in 1902. For the education of his clergy, which more than doubled in the two decades of his episcopacy, the archbishop built at the cost of nearly a million dollars St. Joseph's Seminary in Dunwoodie, a massive complex which opened in 1896 under the Sulpicians.

As the representative of Cardinal McCloskey, Corrigan played a key role, together with James Gibbons of Baltimore, in the planning and the conduct of the Third Plenary Council of Baltimore in 1883–84, affecting everything from priests' rights to the establishment of a university. When, in the aftermath of the council, activists for the German-American Catholic community, by then representing the largest Catholic immigrant body, began to pressure Rome for equal rights for German-American parishes and

Michael A. Corrigan

special vicars general for Germans in dioceses with large German-speaking populations, Corrigan, while supporting the establishment of separate parishes for large ethnic groups, including the Germans, led a successful effort of the four East Coast archbishops (Baltimore, Boston, New York, and Philadelphia) to persuade Rome to forestall any action in behalf of the German-Americans. In his own diocese he was persistently concerned about meeting the particular needs of the various ethnic groups. For the largest group of recent Catholic immigrants in the city, the Italians, Corrigan turned to Italy for missionaries. In 1883 John Bosco sent members of his community, the Salesians, to New York at the archbishop's request. Five years later Corrigan secured a group of Scalabrinians, and a year after that Mother Frances Xavier Cabrini came with her Missionary Sisters of the Sacred Heart, all to work with the surging Italian population in New York in establishing, with Corrigan's support, independent parishes, an orphanage, and a hospital.

The McGlynn Controversy

For more than a decade the archbishop was involved in a dispute with one of his priests, Edward McGlynn, that had national and international repercussions and served as a catalyst for Corrigan's emergence as a leader of anti-progressive forces within the Church. McGlynn, the pastor of the largest parish in the city, St. Stephen's, had long been an advocate and implementer of social reform. In 1886 he became a prominent supporter of Henry George's bid to become mayor of New York, despite a previous warning from Rome to desist from his advocacy of George's radical proposals for economic reform. Corrigan suspended McGlynn for his obstinacy, and after the election (in which George finished a surprisingly close second), the archbishop, in a rare exercise of Catholic episcopal authority on a matter touching the socioeconomic order, issued a pastoral letter condemning, without naming, George's land theories. At the prodding of other prelates who were convinced that McGlynn was a heterodoxical menace who needed to be silenced, Corrigan appealed to Rome to take action; in the meantime he removed McGlynn from St. Stephen's, despite the violent opposition of his parishioners. Two papal summons having failed to bring McGlynn to Rome, in July 1887 he was excommunicated, which touched off a firestorm of protest in New York City and many other Catholic urban areas where McGlynn had become a popular social reformer and promoter of democracy both within society and the Church. As the *New York Times* depicted the controversy, "It is a question whether the Catholic Church in America is to be Americanized and brought into harmony with the spirit of our institutions or whether it is to Romanize those institutions."

In fact the core of McGlynn's substantial support in New York came not from workers but middle-class clerical and lay Catholics who embraced the priest's promotion of their rights within the Church. Pastoral letters, clerical loyalty oaths, the transfer of priests, and the prohibition under sin of attending meetings of McGlynn's Anti-Poverty Society all failed to break the opposition. A request by the archbishop for a Roman condemnation of Henry George brought only a decision to put George's major work, *Progress and Poverty* on the Index of forbidden books, but to disallow the promulgation of this ruling out of fear of a hostile reaction in the United States. Corrigan then lobbied for an explicit papal declaration of the right of private property. Leo XIII's *Rerum Novarum* in 1891 with its condemnation of "certain obsolete opinions" denying any individual ownership of land was taken by the archbishop as vindication of his stand against McGlynn. And yet McGlynn remained a rallying point for dissidents.

Opponent of "Ultra-Americanism"

The McGlynn case helped shape the ideological divisions that formed among the American hierarchy in the late 1880s and 1890s. The attempt of certain prelates, including John Ireland of St. Paul, to intercede on McGlynn's behalf with Roman authorities, gave Archbishop Corrigan and his colleagues grounds for their initial suspicion of the liberal tendencies later to be called "Americanism." As early as 1890 Corrigan was warning Roman officials of "the ultra-Americanism" of an episcopal cabal bent on imposing their liberal program on the Church in the United States. A covert struggle arose among the American hierarchy for episcopal appointments to key sees, such as Milwaukee and Cleveland, in most of which contests the conservatives prevailed. The conflict became public over the issue of public versus private education, when a pamphlet war broke out between surrogates of Ireland and Corrigan over whether the state or the parent (through the Church) had the primary right to educate. The controversy then centered on an experimental program that Ireland had secured in two Minnesota towns in which parochial schools received public funding along with state regulation. Archbishop Corrigan and other champions of parochial education, fearing Ireland's program would undermine Catholic commitment to an autonomous system, took their protests to Rome. A special Vatican commission concluded that Ireland's experiment could be tolerated, but disagreement persisted over the significance of the toleration, whether it meant an exception or an alternative to the prevailing model of parochial education.

When Archbishop Francisco Satolli was appointed apostolic delegate in 1892 to deal with the school issue and the status of McGlynn among others, Corrigan soon found himself in open opposition to the delegate's endorsement of Ireland's educational plan and his exoneration of McGlynn's orthodoxy. Corrigan refused to receive back the now reinstated priest and surreptitiously led a campaign to discredit the delegate. Ironically his opposition to Satolli, a delegate of the Secretariate of State, strengthened his standing in certain Vatican quarters, which opposed the Secretariate of State's *Ralliement* policies, particularly Propaganda Fide under whose jurisdiction the United States still fell. The delegate subsequently made a pressured peace with Archbishop Corrigan and took increasingly conservative positions on education, dissident priests, and other divisive issues.

Americanism

When "Americanism" became an international issue in 1897 with the publication of Abbé Felix Klein's translation of Walter Elliott's *Life of Father Hecker*. Corrigan could afford to rely on his powerful allies in Rome to ensure a disfavorable Roman reaction. *Testem benevolentiae* did not disappoint. Corrigan quickly congratulated the pontiff on his condemnation of "the multiplicity of fallacies and errors" disguised "as good and Catholic doctrines under the specious title of 'Americanism.'" Despite the attempts of Ireland, Gibbons, and others to depict "Americanism" as a phantom heresy, Corrigan's reading of the encyclical was the one that stuck and the conservatives capped a pyrrhic victory that left the Church in the United States more dependent on Rome and less collegial than it had ever been.

In February 1902, while preparing to lead a pilgrimage of prominent lay Catholics to Rome, the archbishop suffered a fall, contracted pneumonia, and died of heart failure on May 2, 1902.

See also GIBBONS, JAMES CARDINAL; McGLYNN, EDWARD; NEW YORK, CATHOLIC CHURCH IN.

Cohalan, Florence D. *A Popular History of the Archdiocese of New York*. New York: United States Catholic Historical Society, 1983.

Curran, Robert Emmett, S.J. *Michael Augustine Corrigan and the Shaping of Conservative Catholicism in America, 1878–1902*. New York: Arno Press, 1978.

DeLora, John P. "Corrigan, Cabrini and 'Columbus': The Foundation of Cabrini Medical Center, New York City." M.A. thesis, St. Joseph's Seminary, Dunwoodie, 1994.

DiGiovanni, Stephen M. *Archbishop Corrigan and the Italian Immigrants*. Huntington, Ind.: Our Sunday Visitor, 1994.

Mahoney, Joseph F., and Peter J. Wosh, eds. *The Diocesan Journal of Michael Augustine Corrigan, Bishop of Newark, 1872–1880*. Newark and South Orange: New Jersey Historical Society and the New Jersey Catholic Historical Records Commission, 1987.

McAvoy, Thomas T., C.S.C. *The Great Crisis in American Catholic History, 1895–1900*. Chicago: Regnery, 1957.

Shelley, Thomas J. *Dunwoodie: The History of St. Joseph's Seminary Yonkers, New York*. Westminster, Md.: Christian Classics, 1993.

ROBERT EMMETT CURRAN, S.J.

COUDERT, FRÉDÉRIC RENÉ (1832–1903)

Lawyer. Frédéric René Coudert was born on March 1, 1832, in New York City to Charles Coudert, a native of France, and Jeanne Clarisse du Champ. Coudert entered Columbia College at the age of fourteen and graduated with honors in 1850. He was admitted to the New York State bar in 1853 and with his brother subsequently established an international law practice which handled a large volume of patent, trademark and extradition cases. His expertise in international law and clarity of thought and communication led to his appointment as counsel to the French, Italian, and Spanish governments.

Coudert had a strong interest in politics as an independent Democrat and deep convictions about the importance of the newly established civil service. However, he consistently turned down prestigious political positions, including appointments to both the New York State Court of Appeals and the United States Supreme Court and to the post of minister to Russia. He was a delegate to the Antwerp Conference (1877), which revised the rules of general average for losses at sea and the International Conference at Berne (1880), which codified the law of nations. He also argued at the Bering Sea seal fisheries dispute in Paris (1893–95) and at the Venezuela and British Columbia boundary dispute (1896). Coudert took an active role in serving local needs as commissioner of the New York City public schools (1883–84), president of the Columbia University Alumni Association and a trustee of the University (1890–1901), and as seventh president of the Association of the Bar of New York City.

A committed Roman Catholic, Coudert delivered a series of addresses under the auspices of the Catholic Union (1873), was president of the United States Catholic Historical Society, and aided in the administration of the St. Vincent de Paul Orphan Asylum. His published work includes *International Law, the Rights of Ships* (1895) and *Addresses: Historical, Political, Sociological* (1905). Coudert died in Washington, D.C., on December 20, 1903.

Fuller, Paul. "Frédéric Coudert." *Historical Records and Studies* 3 (2) (1904) 343–50.

RICHARD G. SMITH

COUGHLIN, CHARLES EDWARD (1891–1979)

Priest, radio commentator. Fr. Charles E. Coughlin, known as "the radio priest," was popular as a radio preacher and political activist in the United States in the period between the world wars. He was an only child born to parents of Irish ancestry (Thomas and Amelia Mahoney Coughlin) in Hamilton, Ontario, Canada, in 1891. At the age of thirteen he entered the preparatory seminary at St. Michael's College, Toronto, to begin studies for the priesthood. In

Charles E. Coughlin

1911 he was the president of the first graduating class to receive a degree from the University of Toronto and the newly federated St. Michael's College. He joined the Congregation of St. Basil, attended St. Basil's Seminary in Toronto, and was ordained to the priesthood in 1916.

From 1916–18 Coughlin taught psychology, English, and logic at the Basilian's Assumption College in Windsor, Ontario. Because it was adjacent to the Michigan border, he frequently served in parishes in Detroit on weekends. Due to changes in the Basilian Order in Canada in 1918, Coughlin decided to join the diocesan clergy, and on February 6, 1923, he was incardinated into the Diocese of Detroit.

The Radio Priest

In 1926, after three brief and successful assignments, Coughlin's bishop, Michael J. Gallagher, asked him to build a new parish in Royal Oak, a suburb of Detroit. The new congregation was to be named for the recently canonized saint, Thérèse of Lisieux, affectionately known as "The Little Flower of Jesus." Coughlin's first radio program, a broadcast of one of his sermons, was a fundraising effort for the new parish and was aired on October 17, 1926, over WJR in Detroit.

Coughlin's style of sermonizing changed, however, with the advent of the depression. He spoke more of sociopolitical issues and the frustration of the people. He attacked Bolshevism and became an "authority" on Communism and monetary issues. By 1930, CBS picked up his program nationally, and he had an estimated forty million listeners. Short-wave from Philadelphia carried his voice all over the world on "The Golden Hour of the Little Flower."

Coughlin's speeches were often framed in the language of the scholastic philosophy and theology of the Neo-Thomistic revival popular among Catholics in that period. He was strongly influenced by the social encyclicals *Rerum Novarum* (1891) of Leo XIII and *Quadragesimo Anno* (1931) of Pius XI. Coughlin is credited with popularizing these documents and their support for the rights of the working classes through his radio addresses. He was a beacon of hope to many people suffering during the depression.

Coughlin was a devotee and supporter of Franklin D. Roosevelt prior to the election of 1932. He was led to believe that he would have a place of influence in F.D.R.'s administration if Roosevelt should be elected. He used his influence on the airwaves to support F.D.R. and coined the expressions "Roosevelt or Ruin," and "The New Deal is Christ's Deal." However, President Roosevelt did not look to Coughlin for advice after his election. As a result, the "radio priest" felt rejected and angry, and became a rabid anti-New Dealer.

Coughlin's own popularity, however, was still on the rise. He was second only to Roosevelt as a radio orator in the 1930s. It has been said that on Sunday afternoons in the summers one could walk down many a city street and never miss a word of his sermons because every household was tuned to his program. He conveyed warmth, compassion, and hope. Speaking to large audiences in venues such as Madison Square Garden, he could stir up the crowd by playing on fears of godless Communism.

National Union for Social Justice

In 1934 Coughlin founded the National Union for Social Justice, and in 1936 he began publication of his weekly newspaper, *Social Justice*. At that time he decided it was imperative to oppose Roosevelt in the upcoming election. He joined with the Rev. Gerald L. K. Smith (Protestant minister and heir apparent of the recently assassinated Huey P. Long), and Dr. Francis P. Townsend (physician and founder of a program for the elderly in California), to form the Union Party. They chose Congressman William Lemke of North Dakota as their presidential candidate, and Thomas O'Brien, District Attorney of Boston, for their vice-presidential nominee. Both were colorless figures and the campaign was dominated by Coughlin and Smith. At one point "the radio priest" overextended his theatrical techniques, ripped off his Roman collar, and called Roosevelt a liar and betrayer. Many Catholics were shocked by his behavior, and the Vatican was disturbed. Coughlin's superior, Bishop Gallagher, however, was supportive of him to the end. Coughlin promised that, if Lemke did not receive nine million votes, he would go off the air.

Roosevelt won the election by a landslide, and Coughlin temporarily retired from the radio and public life. With Bishop Gallagher's death in January 1937, however, Coughlin returned to the airwaves, stating that it was the bishop's dying wish. With the appointment of Edward Mooney as archbishop of the newly reorganized Archdiocese of Detroit, Coughlin found that he had a superior who wanted to supervise his activities. Rather than submit to what he considered censorship, Coughlin cancelled his 1937–38 radio season. Through the efforts of his fans, however, the Vatican was deluged with mail, begging that "the radio priest" be reinstated. In 1937 Coughlin met with the apostolic delegate, Amleto Cicognani, and in January 1938 he resumed his broadcasting.

Coughlin and Anti-Semitism

In his earlier years Coughlin was not overtly anti-Semitic. In 1934 he invited Jews to join the National Union for Social Justice. As the years progressed, however, his disenchantment with Roosevelt focused on what he perceived to be undue Jewish influence in F.D.R.'s administration. He sought scapegoats, and they were usually Jews. He pronounced Jewish names in exaggerated fashion and challenged people to deal with the international bankers by "turning the money changers out of the temple." His radio speeches became more angry and vitriolic. He was labeled one of the "demagogues of the depression."

With the rise of fascism in Europe, Coughlin became radically anti-Semitic. More and more he relied on the document *The Protocols of the Elders of Zion*, now known to be (and long suspected of being) a forgery. It purports to describe a Jewish conspiracy to take over the world. He presented extended commentaries in *Social Justice* condemning Jews as both Bolsheviks and bankers, Communists and greedy capitalists. In November–December 1938 his radio speeches became violent. He began to rely on the writings of an Irish theologian, Fr. Denis Fahey, C.S.Sp., which provided him with a theological rationale for his anti-Semitism and allowed him to portray the alleged Jewish conspiracy in a theological framework.

More than once Hitler appeared on the cover of *Social Justice*. Coughlin exhibited sympathy toward the German leader and described Nazism as "a defense mechanism against Communism." He continued with this approach even after the entrance of the U.S.A. into the war. In 1942 *Social Justice* had its mailing privileges revoked by the U.S. Government, and President Roosevelt sent word to Archbishop Mooney that, if Coughlin was not curtailed, he would be indicted under the Espionage Act of 1917.

Coughlin received the directive of his archbishop in a spirit of obedience, although he confided to his friend Fahey that he thought it was related to "the almost universal ecclesiastical subservience to Franklin D. Roosevelt who is surrounded by high Masons and dominated by crafty Jews" (Athans, 182).

The "radio priest" was silent on political issues after 1942. He continued as pastor of the Shrine of the Little Flower until his retirement in 1966. Although he wrote a few small volumes, often with apocalyptic emphases, denouncing Communism and Vatican Council II, his later years were largely spent in seclusion. He died on October 27, 1979, at his home in Birmingham, Michigan.

See also ANTI-SEMITISM AND AMERICAN CATHOLICS; NEW DEAL AND AMERICAN CATHOLICS, THE.

Athans, Mary Christine. *The Coughlin-Fahey Connection: Father Charles E. Coughlin, Father Denis Fahey, C.S.Sp., and Religious Anti-Semitism in the United States, 1936–1942*. New York: Peter Lang, 1991.

Bennett, David H. *Demagogues in the Depression: American Radicals and the Union Party*. New Brunswick, N. J.: Rutgers University Press, 1969.

Brinkley, Alan. *Voices of Protest: Huey Long, Father Coughlin, and the Great Depression*. New York: Vintage Books, 1983.

Marcus, Sheldon. *Father Charles E. Coughlin: The Tumultuous Life of the Priest of the Little Flower*. Boston: Little, Brown and Company, 1973.

Tull, Charles J. *Father Coughlin and the New Deal*. New York: Syracuse University Press, 1965.

Warren, Donald. *Charles Coughlin, the Father of Hate Radio*. New York: Free Press, 1996.

MARY CHRISTINE ATHANS, B.V.M.

COUNCIL OF MAJOR SUPERIORS OF WOMEN RELIGIOUS

The Council of Major Superiors of Women Religious is a canonically erected conference of major superiors, established under canons 708 and 709 of the Code of Canon Law, to promote mutual support among major superiors of women's religious congregations and to foster coordination and cooperation with the bishops' conference and with individual bishops, under the governance of the Holy See.

In late 1989 and in 1990, a significant number of women major superiors in the United States saw the need for organizational unity among themselves through a new, canonically erected conference. They held consultations and meetings throughout 1991. A Steering Committee was formed to draft the statutes of the proposed new Council of Major Superiors of Women Religious in the United States of America. In February 1992 major superiors met in New York and signed a petition requesting the canonical erection of the new council. The Decree of Erection was given in Rome on June 13, 1992. The first National Assembly was convened at Techny, Illinois, in October of the same year, at which time the twelve-member board of directors and four officers were elected. The council began with 99 individual members representing 62 congregations. Its membership grew to 152 major superiors representing 104 congregations by the close of 1994.

In November 1994 the Council of Major Superiors of Women Religious was invited by the National Conference of Catholic Bishops, the Leadership Conference of Women Religious, and the Conference of Major Superiors of Men into full participation in the Commission on Religious Life and Ministry.

See also WOMEN RELIGIOUS IN AMERICA.

MOTHER VINCENT MARIE, O.C.D.

COURTNEY, MAUREEN (1944–90)

Missionary. Killed in Zelaya, Nicaragua, January 1, 1990. Born in Milwaukee, Wisconsin, May 12, 1944, Maureen enjoyed a happy childhood and adolescence. Graduated from Divine Savior High School, and, after experiencing "a hundred million miracles of grace," Maureen entered the Congregation of St. Agnes. She completed her education at Marian College in Fond du Lac, then successfully taught in elementary schools in Wisconsin and East Harlem. Ardently desiring missionary work, in 1978, she left for Waspam, Nicaragua to work among the native Miskito people. In her journal, she wrote: "I count each day among the Indian people a blessing. They have received me as a daughter and taught me many things." A woman of strong convictions, Maureen could still write when the country was torn by war: "It does not matter to the poor what party we belong to. What matters most is our desire to walk with them and struggle with them to bring about a better tomorrow."

When the Sandinistas evacuated the people from their home in Waspam, Maureen accompanied them to resettlement camps, forming sewing cooperatives, teaching, doing pastoral ministry, cooperating with Church and government in health and agricultural programs to benefit the people. On New Year's Day 1990, Maureen with two other sisters and Bishop Paul Schmitz were enroute to a meeting with Miskito leaders when they were ambushed. Maureen and Sr. Teresa de Jesus Rosales were killed.

Weidman, Patricia, C.S.A. "Witness of a Life: Maureen Courtney, CSA, (1994–1990)." *Sisters Today* 63 (2) (March 1991) 124–28.

LEANNE SITTER, C.S.A.

COUVENT, JUSTINE FERVIN (1750–1837)

Ex-slave and philanthropist. She is usually known as "Madame Couvent" or "La Veuve Couvent" (The Widow Couvent), for she had married Gabriel Bernard Couvent, a carpenter, who died in 1829. There being no children of the marriage, he left his entire estate to her.

She was born in an unknown locality during the 1750s, probably in Africa. Brought to Louisiana probably as a slave, presumably she obtained emancipation. In any case, as a "free woman of color" she amassed wealth in money and real estate. Unfortunately, little is known of her life and work, but it is recognized that she had a solid sense of business and a dedication to education, the opportunity for which she had herself been deprived. By her will, drawn up about five years before her death, she left an endowment for a school, initially for orphans of "free persons of color"; her will placed the institution under the protection of the Catholic clergy. Madame Couvent's school, originally bilingual and coeducational, was launched in the 1840s; it evolved and faced difficulties, but it survived until a merger in 1994. Rodolphe-Lucien Desdunes praised her generosity in life and death. Her name was also given to a public school in New Orleans in 1939 but was removed in 1994 because, it was reported, she had been a slaveowner.

Madame Couvent died in New Orleans June 28, 1837.

Desdunes, Rodolph-Lucien. *Nos Hommes et Notre Histoire.* Montreal, 1911; English translation, Baton Rouge, 1973.

CHARLES EDWARDS O'NEILL

COVENANT HOUSE

Covenant House began in 1969 when Fr. Bruce Ritter, a conventual Franciscan priest, provided a night of shelter in a snow storm for six young runaways. From his small apartment on the lower east side of Manhattan where those first youngsters slept on the floor, Covenant House grew into the largest shelter program for homeless young people in the United States.

In addition to food, shelter, clothing and crisis care, Covenant House offers a variety of services to homeless youth including health care, education, vocational preparation, drug abuse treatment and prevention programs, legal services, recreation, mother/child programs, transitional living programs, street outreach, a national crisis telephone hotline, assistance in finding long-term living accommodations, and aftercare.

In 1996 Covenant House provided residential and non-residential services to over 44,000 youths in five countries. Approximately 13,000 young people came into Covenant House Crisis Shelters and Rights of Passage Programs. Another 13,000 received help in Community Service centers or in aftercare and prevention services. Outreach workers served another 18,000 youths on the street. The Covenant House Nineline (1-800-999-9999) received over 88,000 crisis calls from youngsters all over the country who needed immediate help and had nowhere else to turn.

Incorporated in 1972, Covenant House grew from its quarters in the Greenwich Village tenements to a group home program to its first Crisis Center in Times Square in 1977. In December 1979 the Crisis Center moved to its present location on 41st Street and 10th Avenue on Manhattan's west side.

In 1977 Fr. Ritter began a Faith Community, a group of full-time volunteers who give a year of service to young people, pray together every day and live a simple community life based on the example of St. Francis. In 1996 the Faith Community numbered approximately forty members.

Expansion Outside New York

Covenant House's first ten years were characterized by steady growth in the New York City program. The second decade was marked by expansion to fourteen other cities in six countries:

Location	Year
Antigua, Guatemala	1981
Toronto, Canada	1982
Houston, Texas	1983
Ft. Lauderdale, Florida	1985
New Orleans, Louisiana	1987
Tegucigalpa, Honduras	1987
Guatemala City, Guatemala	1988
Anchorage, Alaska	1988
Los Angeles, California	1988
Mexico City, Mexico	1988
Newark & Atlantic City, New Jersey	1990

In the eighties the complexity and diversity of the program grew with the needs of the young people. In 1986 a transitional program known as Rights of Passage began. In addition to shelter for up to eighteen months, the "Rights" program provides education, employment and counseling services, and a volunteer mentor works one-on-one with each of the young men and women in the program.

Outreach programs were begun at many of the agency's locations to work with the kids on the street and to encourage them to come into the Crisis Centers. Covenant House's blue vans are familiar sights in places where kids congregate on the street. In the 1980s special programs for young mothers and their children were also started at several locations to help these young women face the difficult challenge of caring for their children as single parents.

In February 1990 Fr. Ritter resigned from the agency as the result of allegations of personal and financial impropriety. No legal findings regarding the allegations against Fr. Ritter were made. In the year following Fr. Ritter's resignation, the agency was forced to downsize as a result of a reduction in financial support. Fortunately, the agency was able to keep all its major residential services in place.

Following an investigation of the allegations by Covenant House's board of directors, Sr. Mary Rose McGeady, D.C., was appointed president of the agency in August 1990. Sr. Mary Rose came to the agency from her position as associate executive director of Catholic Charities of the Diocese of Brooklyn. Her professional career in human services and caring for homeless and disturbed children and their families spans some forty years.

In 1994 the agency renovated a large facility in Toronto to serve homeless children and completed construction of a new building in Los Angeles. Covenant House began offering services to young people at risk in Washington, D.C., in the spring of 1995. A new facility in Detroit began functioning in the summer of 1997.

The hallmark of Covenant House is the agency's policy of "Open Intake" whereby no child or teenager is turned away on the first visit, but rather is accepted on a "no questions asked" basis. Only serious misconduct or refusal to make use of proffered services limits repeat visits. By almost any standard the growth of Covenant House has been dramatic. The agency's budget of seventy-three million dollars in fiscal year 1996 was supported almost entirely (95 percent) by private contributions from hundreds of thousands of generous donors who make this work possible.

RICHARD HIRSCH

COVEYOU, WALTER (1894–1929)

American missionary to China. William Coveyou was born at Petoskey, Michigan, on October 17, 1894. He entered the Passionists on February 13, 1912, taking the religious name of Walter. He was ordained a priest in Chicago by George Cardinal Mundelein, on May 29, 1920.

In 1921 when the first American Passionists were leaving for the new mission in China, Fr. Walter volunteered to go with them, but instead he was assigned to the Passionist monastery in Cincinnati. During his years in Cincinnati he organized various activities to raise money among the Catholics of the city. He spoke at the meetings of various Catholic organizations. He also participated in the work of Catholic Student Mission Crusade, conducting mission rallies throughout Ohio. He wrote articles for the newly founded Passionist magazine, called *The Sign*, becoming in time its promoter in the Midwest. In every way possible he publicized the missions in Cincinnati.

In June 1928 the provincial announced that Fr. Walter, with two newly ordained Passionists, would be going to China. That summer the three Western missionaries were in Cincinnati on August 26 for the formal departure ceremony. His farewell to the Queen City was a huge demonstration of the people's esteem for Walter.

Once in China, Walter devoted some months to studying Chinese—a language, he said "the devil must have invented." In April he joined some of the other missionaries in making the annual retreat at the end of which he, Godfrey Holbein, and Clement Seybold left for their new assignments. Their journey took them through bandit country, stopping at night at a village inn. The next morning, as they continued their journey, they were halted by a gang of sixteen armed bandits who led them up the mountain and there each one met instant death with a shot in the head. It was April 26, 1929. The first American Catholic missionaries had shed their blood in China.

The news of their deaths was published throughout the country and in Europe. The federal government in Washington investigated their deaths. Among Catholics they were hailed as "martyrs."

See also PASSIONISTS (C.P.).

Carbonneau, Robert E., C.P. "Life, Death and Memory: Three Passionists in Hunan China and the Shaping of an American Mission Perspective in the 1920s." Ph.D. dissertation, The Catholic University of America, Washington, D.C., 1992.

Caufield, Caspar, C.P. *Only a Beginning.* Union City, N.J.: Passionist Press, 1990.

Mercurio, Roger, C.P. *The Passionists.* Collegeville, Minn.: The Liturgical Press, 1991.

ROGER MERCURIO, C.P.

CREIGHTON, EDWARD (1820–74)

American entrepreneur and philanthropist. Creighton was born August 31, 1820, near what would become Barnesville, Belmont County, Ohio, the fifth of nine children of Irish immigrants, James Creighton and Bridget Hughes Creighton. With a farm background and minimal rural schooling, at the age of nineteen he began driving freight wagons between Cincinnati and Cumberland, Maryland. The next year he received a contract to organize repair work on the National Road between Cumberland and Springfield, Ohio. Recognizing the changes in communication that would parallel the development of the American West, he conceived a scheme for unifying the nation's telegraph system, which in the middle of the nineteenth century consisted of small private companies linking pairs of nearby cities. From 1847 to 1859 he built more than a thousand miles of telegraph wire connecting the Midwest with the East and the South.

The Western Union Company

At this time Eastern business leaders Jeptha Wade, Ezra Cornell, and Hiram Sibley, with the last as president, dedicated themselves to the same plan for their company, Western Union. After moving to the three-year-old city of Omaha in 1857 to engage in the freighting business, Creighton joined the Western Union group with the plan of constructing a telegraph line from the Missouri River to the Pacific Ocean. The discovery of a desirable route was his responsibility, and depending on the maps of John C. Frémont, who had explored the west in the 1830s, and on the reports of Mormon leader Brigham Young, Creighton set out

for the Pacific on November 18, 1860, by stagecoach. Traveling alone from Julesburg, Colorado, he encountered the fiercest of winter conditions for twelve days between Salt Lake City and Carson City, arriving in the Nevada town exhausted and nearly snow-blind. Nevertheless, he continued overland to San Francisco, returning to New York by way of the Isthmus of Panama with Jeptha Wade to recommend a specific route for the telegraph.

In the spring of 1861 construction began, with W. H. Stebbins in charge of work eastward from Salt Lake to Julesburg and Creighton responsible for the line westward from Julesburg. Creighton had previously shown unusual skill at managing large numbers of laborers; now he displayed equal ability in dealing with the Native Americans along the route. His primary challenge was obtaining supplies; besides provisions, insulators and tools, cedar poles had to be procured from as far away as 240 miles for construction sites on the treeless plains. Nevertheless, the project was completed on October 24, and the first message sent on the line was to his wife back in Omaha.

Other Business Ventures

Creighton's reward for this work was being made Superintendent of the Omaha-to-Salt Lake division of the Western Union Company, as well as a large amount of the corporation's stock, which almost immediately appreciated more than twentyfold. He turned next to real estate development in his adopted city, and erected office blocks and a hotel. In 1863, with the Kountze brothers, prominent Omaha investors, he organized the city's First National Bank, of which he became president, and also operated banks in Denver and Central City, Colorado. He served as president of the Omaha and Northwestern Railroad Company, and influenced the choice of Omaha/Council Bluffs as the starting point for the Union Pacific Railroad.

Creighton is credited with leadership in the development of the extensive Great Plains cattle industry, as well. In 1867 he drove three thousand head of cattle from Schuyler, Nebraska, to Cheyenne County in the western part of the state. Some of the herd were separated and given up for lost in a blizzard in the state's central Sand Hills, but were found thriving in the rich and well-watered grassland there in the spring. It was judged that cattle could indeed thrive in land previously considered economically useless, and the area thus was developed as one of the chief cattle-raising regions of the West.

By the end of the 1860s, his was the largest fortune in the state of Nebraska. Philanthropy, especially towards his Church, had occupied Creighton's thoughts from the beginning of his association with the western plains. He gave the majority of the money required for the erection of Omaha's first permanent Catholic church, supported a Catholic church in Laramie, Wyoming, and aided the Sisters of Charity of Leavenworth, Kansas, in establishing convents in Denver and in Helena, Montana. Always conscious that his immigrant family's poverty had prevented him from getting even a second-rate education, he expressed to his wife, the former Mary Lucretia Wareham, a desire to endow a free college for the children of the poor or the recently immigrated. Creighton died, intestate, in Omaha of apoplexy on November 5, 1874, but his widow, who survived him by little more than a year, indicated in her will that $100,000 be spent to endow an institution to be known as "Creighton College." Opening in 1878, the college was placed by Omaha bishop James O'Connor in the hands of the Jesuits, and has developed into the present Creighton University.

Casper, Henry, S.J. *The Catholic Church in Nebraska.* Vols. I–III. Milwaukee: The Bruce Publishing Company, 1960–66.

McDermott, Clare. *The Creighton University: Its Story 1878–1937.* Omaha, Nebr.: Creighton University Archives, 1937.

Mullens, P. A., S.J. *Creighton Biographical Sketches of Edward, John A., Mary Lucretia and Sarah Emily.* Omaha, Nebr.: Creighton University, 1901.

Olson, James C. *History of Nebraska.* Lincoln: University of Nebraska Press, 1955.

Sorenson, Barbara. "A King and a Prince among Pioneers: Edward and John A. Creighton." M.A. thesis, Creighton University, Omaha, 1961.

THOMAS A. KUHLMAN

CREIGHTON, JOHN ANDREW (1831–1907)

Pioneer business leader and philanthropist. John Andrew Creighton was born on October 15, 1831, in Licking County, Ohio, the youngest child of James Creighton of County Monaghan, Ireland, and Bridget Hughes Creighton of County Armagh. For the first four decades of his long life, he lived and worked in the shadow of his older brother Edward, whose leadership in developing the transcontinental telegraph made him one of the best-known entrepreneurs in the American West, as well as one of the wealthiest citizens on the frontier. After Edward's sudden death at the age of fifty-one, however, John took advantage of opportunities not only to increase the extended Creighton family's financial assets but to embark on a broad program of religious and financial philanthropy, eventually receiving national and papal honors. One result was that in the last years of his life and for decades thereafter, John was every bit as well known as his brother, and somewhat surprisingly in a republic and in the still rather rough West, he would be universally referred to as "Count Creighton."

Business Activities

While Edward, like John's other siblings, had known poverty as a child in a poor, rural part of Ohio still itself a frontier area, and had had no opportunities for more than a few months of formal education, John spent the years 1852–54 at St. Joseph's College in Somerset, Ohio, newly organized by the Dominicans. Nevertheless, in 1859 he joined Edward in the construction of telegraph lines, and then settled in Omaha, employed first as a clerk in a store, and then as the store's owner and as a freighter delivering supplies to gold miners in Colorado and other western states or territories.

The development and the physical dangers of the Rocky Mountain area would absorb Creighton's energies throughout the middle part of his life. He assisted his brother in the travels required for the establishment of the Western Union telegraph lines, and also provided livestock and supplies for Brigham Young as the Mormon leader pioneered the Great Basin. He ran stores in Virginia City, Nevada, and Alder Gulch, Montana, cattle operations in Wyoming, and, again in Montana, gold and copper mines and a bank.

In 1868 he married Sarah Emily Wareham, the Dayton-born younger sister of Edward's wife Mary Lucretia, and after that based his activities in Omaha. He was president of the Omaha Nail Works, an incorporator in 1883 and director of the Omaha Union Stockyards and its associated bank and railroad, and at the time of his death was the president of the city's First National Bank. In 1884 he was a delegate to the Democratic National Convention in Chicago, at which Grover Cleveland was nominated for president.

Philanthropic Work

Mary Lucretia's death, fifteen months after her husband Edward's, placed John in the position of directing the spending of one of the largest fortunes in the West. Working closely with Omaha's first bishop, James O'Connor, he gave the money for the establishment of the Franciscan sisters in Columbus, Nebraska, in 1877, and the next year for the establishment of the Poor Clares in Omaha. He paid for the erection of Eden Hill, the Poor Clare monastery in 1880. The primary object of his support, however, was the Jesuit university bearing the family name, founded with a bequest by Mary Lucretia Creighton. In 1887 he donated the money for the construction of the campus church, St. John's, and was the principal benefactor of the university's teaching hospital, St. Joseph's, and the John A. Creighton Medical College.

John Creighton, like many of the Catholic business leaders in Omaha, also took an active interest in the economic and political situation in late nineteenth-century Ireland, and in 1879 he attended the national convention in Chicago of the Irish Catholic Colonization Association, promoted by Bishop John Ireland of St. Paul. Along with John Boyle O'Reilly, editor of the *Boston Pilot,* and John Fitzgerald of Lincoln, president of the Irish National League in America, Creighton was one of the seven laypersons and seven bishops constituting the executive board of the colonization society. Subsequently, he worked with Bishop John Lancaster Spalding of Peoria on the development of an Irish-American colony in Greeley in central Nebraska.

For these and other activities, Creighton was made first a Knight of St. Gregory and then in 1895 a Count of the Papal Court by Pope Leo XIII. He was awarded the Laetare Medal by the University of Notre Dame in 1900. He died in Omaha on February 7, 1907.

See also CREIGHTON, EDWARD.

Casper, Henry, S.J. *The Catholic Church in Nebraska.* Vols. I–III. Milwaukee: The Bruce Publishing Co., 1960–66.

McDermott, Clare. *The Creighton University: Its Story 1878–1937.* Omaha, Nebr.: Creighton University Archives, 1937.

Mullens, P. A., S.J. *Creighton Biographical Sketches of Edward, John A., Mary Lucretia and Sarah Emily.* Omaha, Nebr.: Creighton University, 1901.

Savage, James W,. and John T. Bell. *History of the City of Omaha.* New York: Munsell and Co., 1894.

Sorenson, Alfred. *The Story of Omaha from the Pioneer Days to the Present Time.* Omaha: National Printing Company, 1923.

Sorenson, Barbara. "A King and a Prince among Pioneers: Edward and John A. Creighton." M.A. thesis, Creighton University, Omaha, 1961.

THOMAS A. KUHLMAN

CREIGHTON UNIVERSITY

Creighton University is operated by the Society of Jesus in Omaha, Nebraska. It currently enrolls more than 6,400 students in nine undergraduate, graduate, and professional schools and colleges.

Creighton University was founded in 1878 with a bequest from Mary Lucretia Creighton, widow of pioneer Omaha businessman Edward Creighton. Creighton, who made his fortune as a developer of the first transcontinental telegraph line and as a pioneer cattle rancher, often told his wife that he wished to endow a school for boys in Omaha. Edward Creighton died in 1874 and Mary Lucretia Creighton passed away just fourteen months later in early 1876. Her will included a $100,000 trust for the establishment of a university to bear her husband's name. Omaha bishop James O'Connor was given the task of launching the school, and he called upon the Jesuits for help. Creighton College opened on September 7, 1878, under the leadership of its first president, the Rev. Romanus A. Shaffel, S.J. Because of the poor state of education on the American frontier, the university would not award its first bachelor's degrees until 1891.

Edward Creighton's brother, John Creighton, was an early benefactor of Creighton University. He and his wife,

Sarah Emily, donated more than one million dollars to the young frontier university and in 1892 founded what would become the Creighton University School of Medicine. Creighton University grew rapidly in the twentieth century. It has awarded more than 50,000 degrees since 1891. Other notable dates in the university's history include the establishment of the Creighton University School of Law in 1904; the establishment of the Creighton University School of Dentistry and the beginning of pharmacy programs at Creighton in 1905; the 1920 formation of the Creighton College of Commerce, Accounts and Finance, which in 1956 became the College of Business Administration; the 1926 appointment of a Dean of Graduate Studies, marking the official beginnings of a graduate school; and the 1928 addition of nursing to the university's curriculum.

True to Mary Lucretia Creighton's wishes, Creighton was established as a free school for boys and was the only free Catholic university in the nation until 1924, when it began charging tuition in the College of Arts and Sciences. Women were not admitted to undergraduate education until 1913, when they were enrolled as part-time students in summer sessions. In 1931 women were enrolled as full-time students. However, all Creighton graduate programs admitted women from their establishment. Creighton's first woman student was enrolled in the School of Medicine in 1892.

Today (1996) the university offers forty-six undergraduate majors, fourteen preprofessional programs, six professional degrees, and twenty-one master's or doctor of philosophy degree programs.

See also CATHOLIC UNIVERSITIES AND COLLEGES.

MICHAEL MORRISON, S.J.

CRÉTIN, JOSEPH (1799–1857)

Missionary, bishop. Joseph Crétin was born on December 10, 1799, to Joseph and Mary Jane (Mery) Crétin. He studied classics in the seminary of Meximieux, philosophy at L'Argentière and Alix, and theology at St. Sulpice in Paris. Ordained on December 20, 1823, for the Diocese of Belley, he ministered between 1823–38 in Ferney, a Calvinist stronghold, where he founded a college for boys.

Wanting missionary work, Crétin accepted Bishop Mathias Loras' invitation to work in the Dubuque diocese. Starting in 1839, he preached among the Winnebago, built St. Gabriel's Church in Prairie du Chien, and served as rector of St. Raphael's Cathedral and as vicar general. On July 23, 1850, Crétin was appointed first bishop of St. Paul. He was consecrated in Belley on January 26, 1851, and on July 2 took possession of his see.

It included some 30,000 Native Americans, 6,000 settlers, and 1,000 Catholics served by three priests in three small churches. He brought in Sisters of St. Joseph of Carondolet, Sisters of the Propagation of the Faith, Brothers of the Holy Family, and monks of St. Benedict. These coworkers collaborated with diocesan priests to establish twenty-six new churches, thirty-five stations, a theologate with four students, a hospital, and over two dozen schools. When Crétin died on February 22, 1857, St. Paul numbered about 50,000 Catholics served by twenty-seven priests.

Ireland, John. "Life of the Rt. Rev. Joseph Crétin." *Acta et Dicta* 5.1 (July 1917) 3–66; 5.2 (July 1918) 170–205.

Reardon, J. M. *The Catholic Church in the Diocese of St. Paul.* St. Paul, Minn.: North Central Publishing Company, 1952, 61–121.

JOHN WHITNEY EVANS

CRIMMINS, JOHN DANIEL (1844–1917)

Contractor, philanthropist. John Daniel Crimmins was born on May 18, 1844, in New York City of Irish immigrant parents Thomas and Johanna O'Keefe Crimmins. Educated at St. Francis Xavier College in New York City, he became a member of his father's contracting firm by the age of twenty-one, and later succeeded his father as its head. Crimmins' firm, employing at times as many as 12,000 workers, built more than four hundred buildings and many public works, including most of the elevated railways in New York City. Throughout all of his business endeavors, he was considered a model employer. Crimmins was an influential figure in local politics, serving as New York City Parks Commissioner, and he was appointed to the Greater New York Charter Revision Commission by Governor Theodore Roosevelt.

Crimmins was one of the few Catholic millionaires of his time and became an indispensable aide to New York

John D. Crimmins

Archbishop Michael Corrigan, especially in connection with Corrigan's extensive building projects, including St. Joseph's Seminary, Dunwoodie. For his work, Crimmins was made a Knight Commander of the Order of Saint Gregory by Pope Leo XIII and a Papal Count by Pope Pius X. A member of many Irish-American organizations such as the American-Irish Historical Society and the Friendly Sons of St. Patrick, Crimmins also maintained an interest in Irish-American history, writing two extensive books on the subject.

In 1925 his son, Thomas Crimmins, compiled and published *The Diary of John D. Crimmins* in order "to keep fresh in the memories of all those who knew him, his love and pride in his Church, his family, his friends and his work" (Preface). This compilation of over 240 separate diary entries, letters, etc., includes valuable information for those interested in the building and development of New York City during Crimmins' lifetime, as well as the growth of the Archdiocese of New York during this period from the viewpoint of one of Archbishop Corrigan's closest advisers. The archives of the American-Irish Historical Society in New York City contain an extensive collection of Crimmins' papers, books, etc. He died in New York on November 9, 1917.

Crimmins, John D. *St. Patrick's Day: Its Celebration in New York and Other Places.* New York, 1902.

The Diary of John D. Crimmins. New Rochelle, 1925.

KEVIN J. O'REILLY

CROATIAN CATHOLICS IN AMERICA

Introduction

The history of the Croatian Catholic people in the United States has not been formally documented. The primary sources of this information are the individual histories of the several Croatian Catholic parishes in the Eastern, Midwestern and Western states, along with the historical accounts provided by various Croatian organizations, principally the local lodges of the Croatian Catholic Union, a fraternal benevolent insurance society, founded in 1921. The following documentation provides a brief summary or overview of the Croatian Catholic communities in America.

Croatian Immigration to America

It is very difficult to establish when the first Croatian Catholic came to the American continent. Some written documents indicate that individuals or small groups of Croatian Catholics (notably seafarers from the Dalmatian coastal regions) landed on this continent two or three hundred years ago. But in the late 1890s and early 1900s, many Croatians, the majority of them Roman Catholics, began emigrating to the United States. Many were economic immigrants, while others considered themselves political refugees. Like other immigrants of that period, they looked for employment wherever jobs could be found. Many of them, mostly single young men but often married men with or without their families, settled in small towns as coal miners or in larger cities as steelworkers. Within a comparatively short period of time Croatians could be found all over the United States from New York to California, from New Orleans to Minneapolis-St. Paul.

A new wave of Croatian Catholic immigrants began to arrive after World War II. These were mostly political refugees, including orphans whose parents had been killed during the war, individuals and families fleeing Yugoslavia's Communist regime. Most of these Croatians settled in established Croatian colonies, often among relatives and friends.

Croatian priests and other professionals working among the Croatian immigrants assumed that this would be the end of Croatian immigration. But, beginning in 1965, America saw a new influx of Croatians, some of them political refugees, most of them younger families seeking economic security and a prosperity impossible to find in Yugoslavia. Those arriving in the 1960s and the decades that followed settled mostly in larger cities. These immigrants were better educated and more liberal than their forebears in America, but they were also influenced by the new European standard of life and opposed to the Communist ideology forcefully imposed upon them in the totalitarian state of Yugoslavia. They sought "the good life"—a decent job, a balanced education for their children, good housing and utilities, the ability to be vocal in their political views in democratic America, and the freedom to live out their deeply rooted religious convictions. Gradually this new wave of immigrants joined Croatian Catholic parishes and organizations, and soon became the contemporary bearers of Croatian Catholic culture and tradition in the United States. Currently only a small number of Croatian Catholics continue to emigrate, mostly those who have relatives already well established in America.

Croatian Priests and Parishes

Croatian priests, mostly diocesan clergy, came in precious few numbers with the earliest immigrants towards the end of the nineteenth century. They were true missionaries. They traveled from place to place wherever their people settled, preaching parish missions and organizing religious, cultural, and benevolent societies. Often the priest was the only educated member of the Croatian colony, and thus they had to assume leadership roles; moreover, they were among the first to learn English well and often served as translators and interpreters. Their primary responsibility, however, was the organization of Croatian Catholic parishes in the urban centers with substantial Croatian

populations. Thus, at the beginning of this century there were Croatian churches in Pittsburgh and Steelton, Pennsylvania, New York, Chicago, and other cities. The oldest parish is St. Nicholas Church in Pittsburgh, founded in 1894; several others were erected in the early 1900s.

During the period 1910–40 more Croatian priests came to the United States to work among their people, mostly younger men and mostly religious order priests, beginning in 1912 through 1940. Many of these were Franciscans from various Croatian provinces, mostly friars from the Hercogovinian province in Mostar.

A good number of Croatian priests, religious and diocesan, came to the United States following World War II. As the Croatian immigrant community grew and spread, new parishes needed to be organized. Thus the life of the immigrant priest, like the lives of his people, became more parish centered, more stable.

After the 1960s, a new wave of younger Croatian priests, influenced by Vatican Council II and the continental pastoral theology that followed in its wake, arrived in the United States. They organized new and visionary programs, including Croatian-language radio programs, and often bridged the gap between Croatians and other Catholics in their dioceses through various religious and ethnic activities.

Much has been accomplished for the Croatian immigrants in the United States during the past hundred years, as evidenced by the number of Croatian Catholic parishes and social, cultural, athletic, and religious organizations that have been established coast to coast. One of the largest organizations, founded in 1921, the Croatian Catholic Union of the U.S.A. and Canada, with headquarters in Hobart (Gary), Indiana (a fraternal benefit society), was spearheaded by immigrant Croatian priests; today CCU has lodges in many states and throughout Canada as well. Based on the religious principles and fraternal system, the Croatian Catholic Union through its benevolent, charitable, educational, religious, sports, and patriotic programs and activities, serves multiple needs of its members and the Croatian people in the United States and Canada.

Present Status of Croatian Catholic in the United States

While precise figures are unavailable, Croatian Catholics in the United States, both those born in Croatia and those born in the United States of Croatian-born parents and/or grandparents, who have direct contact with the Church, number approximately 250,000 to 300,000. According to the United States Census Bureau of Statistics (1990) there were over 544,270 Croatian Americans who identify themselves as being of Croatian descent or being born in Croatia. In addition to that, many Croatian Americans identify themselves as Yugoslavs, Slavs, Dalmatians, Bosnians, Austrians, or Austro-Hungarians. Based on other historical sources there are approximately three million Croatian-Americans in the United States.

It is equally difficult to present in this context an in-depth study of the pastoral work that has been and continues to be accomplished among Croatian Catholics in America. The following is a brief summation with a few general remarks.

Currently in the United States, the following religious communities work among Croatian Catholics, with the majority of these religious themselves being Croatian-born. The Croatian Franciscan Custody of the Holy Family, with headquarters in Chicago, was established by the Order of Friars Minor (O.F.M.) in 1926, and currently numbers thirty-seven friars. In the early 1940s the friars established a printery at their Chicago friary, Croatian Franciscan Press, and began publishing and editing the Croatian *Danica* [*The Morning Star*], a weekly newspaper, and the monthly *Glasnik* or *Croatian Catholic Messenger*. The annual *Kalendar* or Almanac edited by the friars provided American Croatians with well-written articles by Croatian priests and lay intellectuals in the United States and elsewhere, as well as other useful information.

Even before being officially established in 1926, the Croatian Franciscan friars traveled throughout the United States, establishing and assisting in Croatian parishes and keeping alive the religious and national sentiments of their people. Today the Croatian Custody is ministering at parishes in Milwaukee and West Allis, Wisconsin, St. Louis, New York City, Detroit, Chicago (two congregations), and in Bethlehem and Sharon, Pennsylvania, as well as in seven Canadian parishes serving the thousands of Croatian immigrants in Canada. This community has done much for the spiritual and material welfare of many Croatian immigrants during the past seventy-five years.

Other Croatian religious communities of men ministering among the Croatian immigrants in America include the Dominicans, who staff two Chicago Croatian parishes; the Conventual Franciscans serving congregations in Gary, Indiana, and Lackawanna, New York; the TOR Franciscan friars service parishes in the Pittsburgh area as well as Washington, D.C. In addition, Franciscans (O.F.M.) from the Dalmatian province of Split, Croatia, serve parishes in California and Canada.

Many secular priests from various dioceses in Croatia are serving the spiritual and cultural needs of American Croatians and have founded several parishes. Currently, they serve in New York, New Jersey, Cleveland, and elsewhere in Ohio, Florida, and Los Angeles, and San Pedro in California. Several men of Croatian descent have been ordained for dioceses throughout the United States.

Along with the male religious, various Croatian religious sisters from the early years of this century to the present day have ministered among Croatian immigrants, most visibly in several parish schools (many now closed) established by the Croatians. These religious orders include the Adorers of the Precious Blood of Jesus, based for most of this century in Columbia, Pennsylvania; the Daughters of Divine Charity in Akron, Ohio; the School Sisters of St. Francis of Christ the King based in Lemont, Illinois; the Dominican Sisters in Chicago and the Franciscan Sisters in San Jose, California. Many Croatian-born sisters, as well as those born in the United States of Croatian ancestry, have served as principals and teachers at various Croatian parochial schools, and in more recent years, they have worked with young parishioners, instructing them in religious education classes and Croatian language and culture classes. As with other ethnic groups in the United States, the role of the teaching sister among the Croatians cannot be overestimated.

Conclusion

Croatian Roman Catholics in America form a vital part of the American Catholic Church. This is due in large measure to the pioneering and ongoing efforts of their priests and sisters, whose witness has enabled the Croatian immigrant community and their children and grandchildren born in the United States to remain faithful to their Catholicism and their Croatian roots. With the liberation of Croatia in 1990 and its establishment once again as a sovereign and democratic nation, it is expected that Croatian emigration to the United States will continue to decline.

Croatian Catholic Union of the U.S.A. and Canada 70th Anniversary Celebration. Gary, Indiana, 1991.

Golden Jubilee of the Croatian Franciscan Custody of the Holy Family. Chicago: Croatian Franciscan Press, 1976.

"Katolicka Crvka i Hrvati izvan Domovine." *Hrvatsko Dusobriznistvo u Sjevernoj Americi/Croatian Pastoral Health Care in North America* 1 (Zagreb 1980) 174–91.

Prpic, George J. *The Croatian Immigrants in America.* 4th printing. New York: Philosophical Library, 1980.

PAUL MASLACH

CROOKS, JULIA (1838–1924)

Foundress. Born in New York City on September 22, 1838, Julia Crooks was the youngest of the nine children of Ramsay and Emily Pratte Crooks. Her father was representative, manager, and later president of the American Fur Company, founded by John Jacob Astor, and her mother was descended from several of the old French families in the St. Louis area, all involved in the fur trade. Julia was tutored at home and also at the New York Academy of the Sacred Heart. Fluent in English and French, she was a frequent traveler across country and overseas.

Julia Crooks entered the Dominican Order at the monastery at Oullins, France, on Pentecost Monday, June 2, 1873.

The name she received upon her admission was Marie de Jésus. She made her profession on August 16, 1874, as a Dominican dedicated to a life of perpetual adoration. From the beginning, her prioress, Mère Marie Dominique de Jésus, prepared her for a possible American foundation with special direction and training.

Soeur Marie de Jésus was acquainted with the bishop of Newark, Michael Augustine Corrigan, through her niece, Marie Gourd, who was subsequently married to his brother, Dr. Joseph Corrigan. Favorably disposed, Bishop Corrigan expressed a desire and willingness to receive a foundation of Dominican nuns of perpetual adoration into his Newark diocese. He confirmed this on a visit to Oullins in 1876, following an *ad limina* visit to Rome.

The transferal of the Dominican nuns from France was accomplished on a small scale: the tiny missionary band which left Oullins on June 24, 1880, was composed of Mother Mary of Jesus with three companions: Mother Domenica, Sr. Emmanuel and Sr. Mary of Mercy, a novice. Embarking from Le Harve, they reached New York on July 6, 1880.

The community lived in a house on Sussex Ave. in Newark until April 1884 when the Monastery of St. Dominic was formally opened with fifteen sisters. It was there that Sr. Mary of Mercy made her religious profession in February 1881, the first of its kind in this country.

When Bishop Corrigan was called to become the archbishop of New York, he promised Mother Mary of Jesus, "You shall follow me." Prior to his construction of the archdiocesan seminary, he asked for a foundation of nuns of perpetual adoration who would pray especially for the seminarians and priests. This foundation was made by Mother Mary of Jesus with seven companions in May 1889. By its completion the following year, twenty sisters were able to move into Corpus Christi Monastery in the Bronx.

Her final act of service was the foundation at Menlo Park, California, in 1921. Blind during the last few years of her life, she gave up all but the little spiritual direction and charities she could perform from the infirmary. She died on May 4, 1924.

See also DOMINICANS (O.P.).

MARY OF JESUS, O.P.

CROQUET, ADRIEN-JOSEPH (1818–1902)

Missionary. Croquet was born in Braine-l'Alleud, Belgium, in 1818, three years after the battle of Waterloo. An elder sister was to marry a Mercier and mother the famous cardinal. Croquet was educated at the seminary of Malines and was ordained in 1844. After ordination he spent an additional two years of study at The Catholic University of Louvain and then served for twelve years as a curate in his native parish in Braine-l'Alleud. Fourteen years after ordination he volunteered for America. After some

months of studying English at the new American College in Louvain and a year's pastoral apprenticeship in Oregon, he was assigned in 1860 to an Indian reservation recently created at Grand Ronde.

He also served coastal tribes and, when officially tolerated, the Siletz Reservation. Until 1876 he served settlers in the nearby Willamette Valley. Grand Ronde included some Canadian tribesfolk who had come west as trappers and who now influenced the rest to choose Catholics as missionaries.

Croquet was not an original evangelist but routinely used Blanchet's Chinook *Catechism* and Demers' *Prayers and Hymns*. He never tried to baptize the nearby sacred mountain or to Christianize the ritual dancing. He struggled for a sisters' school, to raise a Christian generation, but even this proved a minor success. His real success lay in his total gift of himself and of all he had and in his refusal to think ill of these potential children of God.

After almost forty years of service in Oregon, in 1898 Croquet retired to his native Belgium. He died on August 15, 1902, in Braine-l'Alleud.

Cawley, Martinus, O.C.S.O. *Father Crockett of Grand Ronde.* Lafayette, Oregon, 1985.

Schoenberg, Wilfred P., S.J. *A History of the Catholic Church in the Pacific Northwest.* Washington, D.C., 1987.

Van der Heyden, J. "Monsignor Adrien J. Croquet, Indian Missionary." *Records of the American Catholic Historical Society of Philadelphia* 16 (1905) 121–61, 268–95, 456–62; 17 (1906) 86–96, 220–42, 267–88.

MARTINUS CAWLEY, O.C.S.O.

CROSBY, HARRY LILLIS "BING" (1903–77)

Entertainer and singer. Harry Lillis Crosby was born on May 2, 1903, in Tacoma, Washington. He earned the nickname "Bing" due to his affection for a comic strip called "The Bingville Bungle." After the Crosby family moved to Spokane, Washington, Crosby attended Gonzaga High School and, in 1921, Gonzaga University. While at law school at Gonzaga University, Crosby sang and played drums as a member of a local ensemble called the Musicaladers. In 1925 Crosby left the university and went to Los Angeles with a friend, Al Rinker. Crosby and Rinker performed in vaudeville and in 1927 joined the Paul Whiteman band. The team was unsuccessful in New York City and Whiteman dropped the two from the band. Success came shortly thereafter, however, when the twosome joined Harris Barris to form a group called the Rhythm Boys. It was Crosby's recording of *I Surrender Dear* (1932) that thrust him into the national limelight. Stage, motion picture, and radio show offers followed.

Throughout his career, Crosby appeared in approximately seventy motion pictures beginning with the *King*

Harry "Bing" Crosby

of Jazz in 1930. In 1940 Crosby, Bob Hope and Dorothy Lamour made the movie *The Road to Singapore.* The success of this movie spawned a whole series of "The Road to . . . " movies between 1940 and 1952, which included *The Road to Zanzibar* (1941), *The Road to Morocco* (1942), and *The Road to Bali* (1952). His performance as Father O'Malley in *Going My Way* (1944) won him an Academy Award. His last movie was *Stagecoach,* made in 1966. In 1952 Crosby made his television debut in a telethon with Bob Hope. Although Crosby did not star in a regular television series, he made several television specials that were very popular.

Despite the variety of media in which he performed, Crosby was known primarily as a singer. He became known as a "crooner" of sentimental songs in motion pictures. His recordings of "White Christmas" and "Silent Night" became two of the most popular songs of the century. Crosby died in Madrid, Spain, on October 14, 1977, of a heart attack.

LISELLE DRAKE

CROWLEY, PATRICK (1911–74)

Business lawyer and cofounder of the Christian Family Movement. Patrick Francis Crowley was born on September 23, 1911 in Chicago, Illinois, to Jerome Crowley, lawyer, and Henrietta O'Brien. He graduated from the University of Notre Dame in South Bend, Indiana, in 1933, and received his law degree from Loyola University of Chicago in 1937. On October 16, 1937, he married Patricia "Patty" Caron in Chicago. They moved to suburban Wilmette, where they raised five children (one adopted),

and cared for almost fifty foster children. Together they were instrumental in the creation of the Christian Family Movement during the 1940s.

From 1949 until 1970 they served as CFM's executive couple, and were responsible for the expansion of CFM throughout the world. In 1966, they assisted with the creation of the International Confederation of the Christian Family Movement (ICCFM) and served as its second president couple. They also served on the Papal Birth Control Commission from 1964 until 1967, publicly siding with the majority report, which called for a revision of the Church's traditional teaching on birth control. Their view was rejected by Pope Paul VI in his encyclical *Humanae vitae.* They received numerous awards including the Laetare Medal from the University of Notre Dame in 1966. In 1971 Pat was diagnosed with cancer. He died on November 20, 1974.

See also HUMANAE VITAE: ITS RECEPTION IN AMERICA.

JEFFREY M. BURNS

CURLEY, JAMES MICHAEL (1874–1958)

Politician. James Michael Curley was born in Boston, on November 20, 1874, and died on November 12, 1958, in Jamaica Plain, a section of his native city. The son of Michael and Sarah (Clancy) Curley, he received a primary and secondary education in Boston's public schools before he began a political career which dominated the politics of Boston for at least a half century. At the same time, he lived a family life of bereavement since his first wife and most of his nine children predeceased him. A local rather than a national politician, he was the inspiration for Edwin O'Connor's novel, *The Last Hurrah,* and left his mark on

James M. Curley

Boston with the support of the city's Irish population, especially in South Boston where he is still revered as a hero.

Curley began his rise by concentrating on local politics. After winning a seat on the Boston Common Council in 1899, he was elected to the Massachusetts General Court in 1902. Subsequently, he served as an alderman (1904–09) in Boston and as a member of the Boston City Council (1910–11) before going on to higher office.

Elected to the United States Congress in 1910, Curley represented the Twelfth District of Massachusetts for two terms at a time when William Howard Taft and Woodrow Wilson occupied the White House. During this period, he successfully defeated an effort to unseat him because he had spent time in jail for taking a civil service exam for a friend in 1904. Like many Democrats in Congress, he was unsuccessful in attempting to eliminate the literacy test for immigrants. Then, having enough of the politics of Washington after four years, in 1913 Curley decided to run for mayor of Boston, the first of ten attempts in his long career.

Mayor of Boston

Successful in his first bid for that office, Curley resigned his congressional seat on February 2, 1914, and began to make a deep impression on his native city. Concentrating patronage in his own hands, he dispensed favors in such a way as to strengthen his political power with his constituency, not even hesitating at times to wink at the law. Understandably, this approach to politics did not always benefit him as his defeat by Andrew J. Peters in 1917 made clear. However, Curley was able to make a comeback in the election of 1921 and continue to care for his supporters by funding municipal projects such as hospitals, parks, and schools. Ambitious for more power, he ran for the office of governor of Massachusetts but was defeated by Alvan T. Fuller in 1924. Prevented from succeeding himself as mayor in 1926, he continued as president of the Hibernia Savings Bank from 1919 to 1938, during which time he was elected mayor of Boston in 1929.

With Franklin Delano Roosevelt coming upon the national scene, Curley turned his attention to presidential politics. When he was sidetracked by the elite in the state party, Mayor Curley circumvented them and became a delegate from Puerto Rico at the party's national convention. Having campaigned vigorously for the New York Governor in 1932, Roosevelt offered the Bostonian the ambassadorship to Poland, but Curley rejected it.

Governor of Massachusetts

Disappointed with Roosevelt, Curley ran successfully for governor of Massachusetts in 1934 and took advantage of the programs of the New Deal to improve the state's roads, bridges, and other facilities. However, when he ran for the

United States Senate against Henry Cabot Lodge, Jr. in 1936, Curley failed, especially since many of Boston's voters believed that the governor was doing so to get back at Roosevelt. Subsequently, Curley tried to win back his seat at City Hall in 1937 and in 1941, but Maurice J. Tobin, a former protégé, defeated him on both occasions. And, between those setbacks, Leverett S. Saltonstall, a popular and prominent Brahmin politician, beat Curley for governor of Massachusetts in 1938.

Nevertheless, despite those four losses, Curley did have a few more victories before his career came to an end. Elected to the United States Congress from the Eleventh District of Massachusetts in 1942, he served there until he was elected mayor of Boston for the fourth time in 1945. Found guilty of defrauding the mails, Curley had to govern from a federal penitentiary until President Harry S. Truman, at the instigation of United States Congressman John W. McCormack, a Democrat from Boston, had him released and pardoned. Thereafter, having embarrassed his supporters, Curley never won an election, losing his bids for mayor of Boston in 1949 and 1955, an indication that he was a relic of another generation.

See also IRISH CATHOLICS IN AMERICA; NEW DEAL AND AMERICAN CATHOLICS, THE.

Beatty, Jack. *The Rascal King*. Reading, Massachusetts, 1992.
Curley, James Michael. *I'd Do It Again*. Englewood Cliffs, 1957.
The Curley Papers, mainly scrapbooks of clippings, are at the College of the Holy Cross.
Dinneen, Joseph F. *The Purple Shamrock*. New York, 1949.

VINCENT A. LAPOMARDA, S.J.

CURLEY, MICHAEL JOSEPH (1879–1947)

Archbishop of Baltimore. Michael Joseph Curley was born in Athlone, County Westmeath, Ireland, on October 12, 1879, the son of Michael Curley, a fairly prosperous farmer, and Maria Ward. He attended the Marist Brothers' school in Athlone until age sixteen, then went to Mungret College, Limerick, conducted by the Jesuits, to study for the priesthood. Though he originally dreamed of being a missionary to the Fiji Islands, the visit of a bishop of Florida to Mungret led him to volunteer his services for that underdeveloped part of the Catholic world. After receiving a bachelor's degree from the Royal University in Dublin, he entered the Urban College of the Propaganda in Rome in 1900 to prepare himself for the life of a missionary in the United States. He was ordained by Cardinal Pietro Respighi, vicar general of the pope, on March 19, 1904.

In Florida Curley was sent by the bishop of St. Augustine to a parish at DeLand that encompassed 7,200 square miles, greater by a thousand than the archdiocese he would later govern. He lived in a rented room above a store and took his meals in a diner where a five-dollar ticket bought

Michael J. Curley

him twenty-one meals. In 1914 he served nine months as chancellor and secretary to the bishop, then was himself named bishop of St. Augustine on April 3, 1914, and raised to the episcopacy on June 30 by the bishop of Savannah. In 1917 he attracted national attention by battling a convent inspection bill and later an act forbidding sisters to teach "colored" children. On August 10, 1921, he was named to succeed the venerable Cardinal James Gibbons as archbishop of Baltimore. He took possession of the premier see on November 21.

Archbishop of Baltimore

In his first years in Baltimore Curley devoted himself to the work of consolidation, centralization, and the implementation of Vatican directives, goals already achieved by the larger archdioceses. In 1922 he organized the Office of Education, in 1923 the Bureau of Catholic Charities, and in 1925 the Society for the Propagation of the Faith. The achievements of which he was proudest were in education; by 1926 he felt that he could boast, "I defy any system of grammar school education in the United States to prove itself superior to the system that is being maintained in the Archdiocese of Baltimore." He energized such societies as the Holy Name, Knights of Columbus, Catholic Daughters of America, and International Federation of Catholic Alumnae, charging them with such tasks as the support of Catholic schools, poor relief, and defense of the Church.

In time Curley won a reputation as a battler as well as that of a builder. He was the most outspoken and militant prelate in America in the interwar years. Among the crusades he launched were those against the anticlerical governments of Mexico and Spain, the salacious movies coming out of Hollywood, and the Catholic Foundation movement for the establishment of Catholic centers at secular universities, which Curley felt undermined Catholic schools. He was the first American bishop to speak out forcefully against Communism, persuading the bishops in 1936 to conduct a study of its influence in America. In Baltimore and Washington he established labor schools to disseminate papal teachings on social justice and to counter the activities of the Communist party in local unions. Curley was quick to demand apologies for what he considered slurs against the Catholic Church, waging a bitter campaign against the Baltimore *Sun* when one of its reporters compared Hitler to Ignatius Loyola.

A Warrior Bishop

Though he avoided involvement in local politics, Curley was outspoken in his criticism of the foreign policy of the Roosevelt administration. On this and other matters his public statements proved often a source of embarrassment to the administrative committee of the National Catholic Welfare Conference, with whom he was often at odds. In 1936 Curley submitted his resignation to the conference when ordered to dissolve a corporation he had created for Mexican relief. Curley was also frustrated in his efforts to make a true university of The Catholic University in Washington, of which he was, as archbishop of Baltimore, the chancellor. The dismissal of the rector whom he supported Curley also took as a rebuke.

Curley had, in fact, no close friends among the American bishops and was the first archbishop of Baltimore not to be recognized as leader of the Catholic Church in the United States. On July 22, 1939, however, he was named also archbishop of the newly created Archdiocese of Washington, but he continued to govern the two archdioceses as a unit. Unaware of the bombing of Pearl Harbor, Curley responded to a reporter in a flippant manner concerning the catastrophe. The interview was used by those who wished to silence him to have the apostolic delegate deliver an admonition. Pained by the reproof, Curley made no pronouncements on political affairs for the rest of his life.

Perhaps the majority of his spiritual children in the two archdioceses he governed came to admire this bluff and blunt Irishman so unlike his irenic predecessor, in whose shadow Curley lived throughout his years in Baltimore. In his disdain for the values of mainstream America, Michael Curley, in fact, put himself at odds with the Maryland tradition begun by Carroll and revived by Gibbons. His contribution to the Catholic militancy of the interwar years was, perhaps, unequalled. As a builder he also had few equals, doubling the institutions and personnel in his twenty-five years in Baltimore.

Much of this was accomplished from a hospital bed. Curley suffered from a number of ailments, among them sinusitis, shingles, and high blood pressure. He suffered a number of strokes that induced partial paralysis, blindness, and on May 16, 1947, death. Archbishop John Mc-Nicholas of Cincinnati, a former antagonist, summed up the many assessments of his episcopacy. In Curley's death, he declared, "the Church loses a warrior prelate for its unchangeable teachings . . . , a champion of Christian education of our youth, a friend of the missions, and almoner of the poor." Curley was, perhaps, the most honest and forthright of American bishops. Even his critics admired his directness and candor as they deplored his lack of tact. Even more did those who really knew him admire his simplicity of life and love of the poor. He tried, in fact, to live as poorly as the poor he never patronized.

See also FLORIDA, CATHOLIC CHURCH IN; MARYLAND, CATHOLIC CHURCH IN.

Fitzpatrick, Vincent de Paul. *Life of Archbishop Curley: Champion of Catholic Education.* Baltimore, 1929.

Spalding, Thomas W. *The Premier See: A History of the Archdiocese of Baltimore, 1789–1989.* Baltimore, 1989.

THOMAS W. SPALDING

CURRAN (CHARLES) CONTROVERSY, THE

The "Charles Curran Controversy" for more than two decades attracted the interest of a wide spectrum of the American public as well as that of many outside the United States. The duration of the conflict and the intensity of the discussion it engendered involved an increasingly complex web of issues and personalities.

Charles Curran, born in 1934, was ordained a priest of the Diocese of Rochester, New York, in Rome in 1958. Three years later he received doctorates in sacred theology from the Pontifical Gregorian University and in moral theology from the Accademia Alfonsiana, and began teaching at St. Bernard's Seminary in Rochester, New York. In 1965 he was named an assistant professor in the Department of Theology of The Catholic University of America in Washington, D.C. In his writings and lectures around the country he supported the opinion that the Catholic Church could change its position on artificial contraception, an issue then in the hands of a papal commission. On April 17, 1967, he was informed that the board of trustees would not renew his contract. Students and faculty rallied in protest against this decision. The theological faculty unanimously declared that they "cannot and will not function unless and until Father Curran is reinstated" and invited other professors to join them. The faculty of the university, four hundred to eighteen, supported the strike which effectively closed the university. On April 21, the board rescinded its action and offered Curran a new contract with tenure and promotion to associate professor. As a result of the strike Curran came to be identi-

Charles Curran

fied as a leading proponent for the Church to change its teaching on birth control.

Curran and Humanae vitae

On July 29, 1968, Pope Paul VI issued the encyclical *Humanae vitae* which affirmed the Church's prohibition of artificial contraception. In response Curran composed a statement recognizing the possibility of dissent from such noninfallible teaching. This statement was eventually signed by six hundred individuals qualified in theology. Although other such statements were issued, this was the first and, originating at The Catholic University, it drew the most attention from the public and the press.

In September 1968 The Catholic University Board of Trustees called for a university inquiry to determine if The Catholic University signers had thereby violated their responsibility as professors of theology. In April 1969 the faculty inquiry committee vindicated the declaration and the actions of the professors. The board of trustees received the report but did not accept its spirit and tenor.

In the following years, Curran continued to lecture and write on such topics as homosexuality, divorce, sterilization, and abortion. He also directed his attention to questions of medical ethics and, in the mid-1970s moved into the field of social ethics. In 1971 he was promoted to the rank of ordinary professor.

Eight years later, in August 1979, Cardinal Franjo Seper, prefect of the Congregation for the Doctrine of the Faith, informed Curran that he was under investigation and, in fact, had been for several years. Seper's letter included "Observations" on Curran's teachings, to which Curran responded two months later. In February 1981 the congregation requested that Curran further address additional aspects of the original observations. To this letter he responded in June 1982.

Ratzinger and Curran

A year later, in June 1983, the new prefect, Cardinal Josef Ratzinger, asked Curran if he wished to revise his positions which were "in clear public dissent from the magisterium." In August 1984 Curran sent his response, which Ratzinger acknowledged in October.

Meanwhile, it was becoming clear that the Holy See was taking an active interest in developments in American Catholic theology, in particular in the area of ethics. The imprimatur was withdrawn from Philip Keane's *Sexual Morality* and the Congregation for the Doctrine of the Faith pointed out errors in Anthony Kosnick's *Human Sexuality*. In July 1984 Pope John Paul II began a series of talks on *Humanae vitae* and a Vatican spokesman, commenting to the press, noted that Curran was among those theologians whose opinions contesting *Humanae vitae* were causing confusion and doubt among the faithful.

Curran then offered to move from The Catholic University's Department of Theology, an ecclesiastical faculty subject to special Vatican regulations, to the Department of Religion and Religious Education, a department which was not part of the ecclesiastical faculty.

In September 1985 Curran received a letter from Ratzinger asking him to retract and reconsider his positions on contraception, direct sterilization, abortion, euthanasia, masturbation, premarital intercourse, homosexual acts, and the indissolubility of sacramental marriage. Curran was warned that, if he did not retract, he would not be considered a Catholic theologian and could not teach in the name of the Church. Curran then offered to cease teaching his course in sexual ethics and to accept a document pointing out "errors" in his theology as long as it still acknowledged him as a Catholic theologian.

Archbishop James Hickey of Washington, chancellor of The Catholic University, brought the proposed compromise to Rome in January 1986 and met with Pope John Paul II and Cardinal Ratzinger. Upon his return, Hickey informed Curran that Rome would not allow him to teach in the name of the Church while holding the positions under discussion.

In a final attempt at resolution, Curran, accompanied by Msgr. George Higgins and Rev. William Cenkner, O.P., dean of the School of Religious Studies of The Catholic University, traveled to Rome in March 1986. There, accompanied by Rev. Bernard Häring, C.Ss.R., he met in March 1986 with Ratzinger and officials of the congregation. No compromise was reached.

On August 18, 1986, the congregation informed Curran that he could "no longer be considered suitable nor eligible to exercise the function of a professor of Catholic theology." Archbishop Hickey told Curran that he was initiating the "withdrawal of the canonical mission which permits (him) to teach theology at this University." Curran responded that he would fight the dismissal using both academic and legal avenues of due process.

Curran and The Catholic University

The following January Curran was suspended from teaching in an ecclesiastical faculty pending the outcome of the proceedings to withdraw his canonical mission to teach in the name of the Church. He considered the suspension unjustified on the grounds that many of his courses did not fall into the areas to which the congregation took exception. Curran accused Hickey of prejudging the case and declared the suspension to be a "punishment unprecedented in the American university environment." This Hickey denied. The university then canceled Curran's classes. Barred from teaching at The Catholic University, Curran received an academic leave and accepted a visiting professorship in Catholic Studies at Cornell University.

The Catholic University Board of Trustees twice postponed decision on the matter and finally on April 12, 1988, withdrew Curran's license to teach Catholic theology while declaring that he still possessed tenure and could teach outside the ecclesiastical faculty of the Department of Theology. Curran had previously offered to teach outside this department and accepted the board decision while disagreeing with it. The board further required that Curran sign a statement that he would not teach Catholic theology and that he would not teach theological students. Upon receipt of these restrictions, Curran rejected the offer and sued the university for breach of contract.

The lawsuit was complex, involving the intertwining of canon and civil law. In February 1989 the court ruled against Curran stating that "(t)he withdrawal of the canonical mission was not a breach of Professor Curran's contract." Recognizing that this "dispute is merely a piece of a larger struggle that has been raging in Catholic higher education," the court determined that the general principles of contract interpretation must govern its decision. The court also stated that it "must avoid impermissible entanglement of the 'state' in the affairs of the church."

The "Charles Curran Controversy" occurred during a time of momentous change in the American theological enterprise and in the life of the Catholic Church in the United States. Pastoral concern was stimulated by the public nature of the controversy. Ease of communication, a contentious Catholic press, a secular press which, since Vatican Council II had taken a serious interest in the Catholic Church, a more sophisticated Catholic laity, an academy of Catholic theologians independent of direct hierarchical control and protected by tenure, the interest of other

Christians and of non-Christians in Catholic issues, all combined to keep each move in this intricate case before the eyes of the public.

The controversy, born in the area of sexual ethics, expanded to include issues such as the right to dissent from non-infallible teachings, the role of the hierarchical magisterium in relation to the academy of theologians, the role of the theologian in the Church, the definition of theology itself, and academic freedom in Catholic institutions of higher education. It involved theologians in the United States and throughout the world, academic administrators, the press, the American judicial system, the Roman Curia, and the Pope himself. The resultant discussion highlighted divisions within the Catholic Church in the United States and, in the opinion of some, deepened those divisions. Many of the questions which it stimulated have not yet been resolved.

Since 1991 Charles Curran has been Elizabeth Scurlock University Professor of Human Values at Southern Methodist University. In the course of his career, he has served as president of the Catholic Theological Society of America, the Society of Christian Ethics, and the American Theological Society.

Curran, Charles E. *Faithful Dissent.* Kansas City, Mo.: Sheed & Ward, 1986.

Curran, Charles E., and Richard A. McCormick, eds. *Dissent in the Church.* New York: Paulist Press, 1988.

May, William W., ed. *Vatican Authority and American Catholic Dissent: The Curran Case and its Consequences.* New York: Crossroad, 1987.

Origins, vols. 15–18.

ROBERT J. WISTER

CURRAN, JOHN (1859–1936)

Labor priest. In the early twentieth century, Fr. John Curran of Wilkes-Barre, Pennsylvania, earned a national reputation as an outspoken supporter of the country's miners as they struggled to improve wages and working conditions. The priest was a friend to John Mitchell, 1870–1919, the head of the United Mine Workers; he was a long-time confidant of Theodore Roosevelt, 1858–1919, who wrote about the help he received from Fr. Curran during the great anthracite strike of 1902 in his *Autobiography:* "The man in Wilkes-Barre who helped me most was Father Curran; I grew to know and trust and believe in him, and throughout my term in office, and afterward, he was not only my staunch friend, but one of the men by whose advice and counsel I profited most in matters affecting the welfare of the miners and their families."

John Curran was born in Hawley, Pennsylvania, on June 20, 1859. His family moved to Avoca, a small mining community not far from Wilkes-Barre. As a boy, Curran spent

John Curran

eight years working in the mines where he gained firsthand knowledge of the miners' plight. The experience shaped his loyalties and helped him to form lifelong commitments to the workingman and to the temperance movement.

By day Curran worked in the mines; during the evenings he attended public school. As a teen, he attended Wyoming Seminary, a private school under the jurisdiction of the Wyoming (Pennsylvania) Conference of the Methodist Episcopal Church. He graduated with honors and matriculated at St. Vincent's College, Latrobe, where he received his degree in 1882. That same year he entered the Grand Séminaire at Montreal. He was ordained a priest for the Diocese of Scranton on August 22, 1887.

While serving as an assistant pastor in Carbondale, a mining town near Scranton, Curran gained national attention by championing the cause of the United Mine Workers who started a crippling anthracite coal strike on May 12, 1902. During the 163 days the men stayed out, Curran worked closely with John Mitchell to present the miners' case to the American public. Eventually, President Theodore Roosevelt, upon the advice of Fr. Curran, intervened as the coal shortages were affecting the nation's economy. Roosevelt formed a valued friendship with the priest, even traveling to Wilkes-Barre in 1912 to participate in a celebration of the priest's silver jubilee of ordination. The friendship continued until Roosevelt's death in 1919.

Over the years, Curran involved himself in a number of labor disputes; and always he gained the respect of the unionized workers as well as that of the owners. His interest in labor matters never waned. In 1933, just three years before his death, Curran traveled to Washington to mediate a labor dispute that had shut down mining operations in northeastern Pennsylvania. Curran was also a tireless advocate of total abstinence from alcoholic beverages. The priest served as a vice president of the Anti-Saloon League of America and held many positions in the Catholic Total Abstinence Union.

Named a domestic prelate by Pope Pius XI in 1930, Curran continued to lead an active life as pastor, labor mediator, public speaker, and advisor to the White House. In a February 2, 1932, telegram, he advised President Herbert Hoover to move against Japan. Until his death on November 7, 1936, Fr. Curran remained one of the most prominent Catholic priests of the early twentieth century. His ecumenical friendships, his mediation skills, and his access to powerful political leaders, including the President of the United States, made John Joseph Curran a singularly unique American Catholic clergyman.

See also LABOR MOVEMENT AND AMERICAN CATHOLICS, THE.

Earley, James B. *Envisioning Faith: The Pictorial History of the Diocese of Scranton.* Devon, 1994.
Gallagher, John P. *A Century of History: The Diocese of Scranton, 1868–1968.* Scranton, 1968.
Roosevelt, Theodore. *An Autobiography.* New York, 1929.

JAMES B. EARLEY

CURTO, GREGORIO (ca. 1804–87)

Singer, composer, organist, music educator. He was born ca. 1804 in Tortosa, Spain. Curto was educated in Paris, later serving as organist at the Cathedral of Soissons, and *maître de chapelle* at the Sorbonne. John Davis, impresario of the *Théâtre d'Orleans* of New Orleans, aware of his work at the *Théâtre des Italiens* in Paris, arranged for Curto's appearance in New Orleans in 1830. On May 2, 1832, A. Curto, was appointed organist of the St. Louis Cathedral of the same city. He held that post through December 4, 1841. However, he directed music for the dedication of the extensively renovated cathedral on December 7, 1851. City directories reflect his development as a musician in New Orleans. He first appears in the 1832 city directory as A. Curto (an actor) residing at 93 St. Ann St. The 1834 city directory lists a Mr. Curteaud as "parish organist" (the cathedral was the city's only parish church at the time). Subsequent city directories list him as a "professor of music."

He composed the operas *Le Nouvel Hérmite* (1834), *Amour et Folie* (1834), *Sardanapale* (1838), and *Le Lépreux* (1845). However, the bulk of his compositions are sacred. From 1855 to 1883 he set religious texts in Latin, French, and English. As organist-choirmaster of St. Theresa in New Orleans, he composed nine Masses, published in the mid-1850s as a series entitled *Musique Religieuse de L'Eglise de Ste. Thérèse.* The Masses were followed by

25 Motets à Une, Deux, Trois, et Quatre Voix avec Accompagnement d'Orgue. Curto's sacred music received acceptance in New Orleans, New York (J. Fischer & Bros. published many of his works) and Paris, where his *Grand Mass* was performed at St. Eustache. As a composer of secular music, he aligned himself with leading literary figures, as well as cultural and charitable institutions. He died in New Orleans on November 19, 1887.

Lemmon, Alfred E. "Music in St. Louis Cathedral from 1725 to 1844." *Cross, Crozier, and Crucible.* Lafayette: Archdiocese of New Orleans and the Center for Louisiana Studies, 1993, 489–504.
New Orleans Times-Democrat, November 20, 1887.

ALFRED E. LEMMON

CUSHING, RICHARD CARDINAL (1895–1970)

Archbishop of Boston (1944–70) and cardinal. Cushing was born on August 23, 1895, in South Boston, Massachusetts, of working-class parents. He studied briefly at Boston College and then at Saint John's Seminary, Brighton, Massachusetts. He was ordained to the priesthood in 1921. Instead of receiving parochial assignments, Cushing was appointed to the staff of the diocesan office of the Society for the Propagation of the Faith. There he distinguished himself for his fundraising ability and his support for American involvement in foreign missions. He was made director of the office in 1928 and, even after becoming archbishop, maintained his strong support for its work. In 1958, for example, he was largely responsible for forming the Society of Saint James the Apostle, an organization which sent priests from the United States to Latin America.

Richard Cardinal Cushing

As a churchman, Cushing was noted for a vivid, outgoing personality. Most previous American Catholic leaders, including his own predecessor in Boston, Cardinal William O'Connell, had been remote and imposing figures, but Cushing cultivated a more approachable public persona. He always enjoyed mugging for news cameras, especially with children and the elderly. He delighted in taking groups of nuns to professional baseball games and amusement parks. His unusual speaking voice, a singsong nasal twang, became increasingly familiar to the general public through his pioneering radio and television broadcasts of Catholic ceremonies in the 1940s and 1950s. This apparently democratic style made him a popular favorite among local Catholics as he became successively auxiliary bishop of Boston (1939), administrator of the archdiocese (April 1944), and finally archbishop (November 1944). He was elevated to the cardinalate in 1958 by Pope John XXIII.

During Cushing's tenure as archbishop, the Boston church experienced an impressive institutional expansion. By the end of World War II, three of every five people in Massachusetts were Catholics, and this population was shifting out of the larger cities and into the suburbs. Cushing increased the number of parishes in the archdiocese by one-third to 410, and he opened many schools, hospitals, and social welfare institutions. He gave special support to work on behalf of mentally retarded children and adults. He also encouraged lay involvement in church activities, supporting formation of associations for the laity, often organized around occupational categories. Never a leader in liturgical reform, he nonetheless supported the changes instituted by the Second Vatican Council. His own participation in the council was limited, though he did take a part in shaping the decree on Catholic relations with non-Catholics (*Nostra aetate*, October 1965), which reversed the earlier church tradition of blaming Jews for the death of Jesus.

Cushing was also known for an eagerness to involve himself in secular politics. He was a staunch Cold Warrior during the 1950s, speaking and writing widely on the dangers of the Communism and, like many of his fellow American bishops, supporting Senator Joseph McCarthy. He also backed Robert Welch and the John Birch Society, which had its headquarters just outside Boston. He took an active part in state and local politics, helping defeat a referendum liberalizing the Massachusetts birth control laws in 1948, and his strong support for urban renewal in Boston in the 1950s and 1960s was essential to its success. His most visible political connection was with the family of President John F. Kennedy. Behind the scenes, he helped defuse the so-called Catholic issue of the 1960 campaign, and he later assisted Attorney General Robert Kennedy in raising money for the ransom of prisoners captured during the Bay of Pigs invasion. He remained close to the family in good times and bad, delivering an invocation at Kennedy's inauguration, presiding over the President's funeral in 1963, and publicly endorsing the controversial marriage of Jacqueline Kennedy to Aristotle Onassis in 1968.

Steadily declining health cast a shadow over Cushing's final years. Poor administrative controls brought on massive archdiocesan debt, and declining religious vocations seemed to suggest that the institutional Church had expanded beyond its ability to sustain itself. Even so, Cushing's tenure came to be remembered as an age of confidence for Catholicism in Boston and elsewhere. He died on November 2, 1970.

See also MASSACHUSETTS, CATHOLIC CHURCH IN; VATICAN COUNCIL II AND AMERICAN CATHOLICS.

Cutler, John Henry. *Cardinal Cushing of Boston.* New York, 1970.

Dever, Joseph. *Cushing of Boston: A Candid Portrait.* Boston, 1965.

Devine, M. C. *The World's Cardinal.* Boston, 1964.

Fenton, John H. *Salt of the Earth: An Informal Portrait of Richard Cardinal Cushing.* New York, 1965.

JAMES M. O'TOOLE

CZECH CATHOLICS IN AMERICA

Although some Czech (Bohemian, Moravian, and Silesian) immigrants arrived in America in the seventeenth and eighteenth centuries, the "golden age" of the Czech immigrants began in 1860s and the era culminated in the joint efforts of the Czechs and Slovaks for the independence of Czechoslovakia during World War I. Like other Czechs, the Czech Catholics settled in all parts of the country, though their main settlements were in Illinois, Iowa, Kansas, Maryland, Michigan, Minnesota, Missouri, Nebraska, North Dakota, New York, Ohio, Oklahoma, Oregon, Texas, Virginia, Wisconsin, and Canada. They built and rallied around hundreds of churches, parishes, schools, and monasteries, such as the Benedictine monastery of St. Procopius, Lisle, Illinois, and the parishes of the Redemptorists in New York and Baltimore.

Parishes and Organizations

The first Czech parish was founded in St. Louis in 1854, followed by the establishment of the Czech mother parish in Chicago, located in "Praha," where some families through self-initiative and effort built and dedicated a church to St. Wenceslaus in 1863. A few years later, St. John's parish was established. By 1925 eight Czech Catholic churches were organized in various sections of the city and its suburbs. Each parish had an ethnic school, different in manner from the Czech secularist counterparts by its manner of pupil attendance. Each was a day school rather than a weekend institution.

One of the characteristics of the Czechs is their love of organization. The Czech Catholics in Chicago (as in other places) had their fraternal benevolent societies such as the Czech-Roman First Catholic Central Union, the Czech-Roman Catholic Central Union of American Women, and an organization of the Catholic Foresters and Forestresses. Like their secularist counterparts, the Catholic societies became sponsors, builders and supporters of an orphanage and home for old people; they supported the manifold needs of the Church.

The St. Wenceslaus and St. Ludmila Association established the first Czech Catholic church in New York in 1874; a church of St. Cyril and Methodius was built a year later. After 1887, the Redemptorists took over the pastoral care of the New York Czech Catholics and built a church to Our Lady of Perpetual Help, which is also the shrine of the Infant of Prague in the United States.

In Iowa the largest Czech community was in Cedar Rapids where the Czech Catholics in 1882 built a church dedicated to St. Wenceslaus, the patron saint of the Czech nation. A schoolhouse was added, and later the St. Wenceslaus High School was erected where Sisters of Mercy worked as teachers. In 1905 a large church of St. Ludmila was dedicated, and in 1914 the St. Ludmila Catholic School was established where Sisters of Notre Dame taught Czech children in the vicinity.

Catholic Czechs in Texas built their first church at Ross Prairie in 1859; later the church was moved to Hostýn, named after a well-known pilgrimage place in Moravia. The lack of Czech priests hampered progress and the first congregations were served by Polish and German priests. Josef Chromčík was the first Czech Catholic priest who came to Texas in 1872; he took over the congregation at Fayetville and served surrounding communities. Fr. Chromčík was joined later by several other Czech priests.

As in other settlements, the Czech Catholics in Texas established schools in connection with their churches. One of the main subjects taught was the Czech language that they tried to preserve, since Czech was the language used in the churches for more than a century. In the first quarter of this century the Czech language was taught in the Catholic seminaries, academies, and at several universities. In Texas it was still taught at some of them in 1995.

As in Chicago, New York, Iowa, and other places, in Texas several organizations or clubs arose. The first organization, called the First Texas Czech-Moravian Benevolent Society, was established by the Czech Catholics at Bluff in 1879. It became a unit of the Second Roman-Catholic Central Union in 1883. In 1889 the Czech Catholic organization in Texas formed the Czech Catholic Union of Texas that still exists today. Another still-existing organization is the Catholic Family Fraternal of Texas, originally named the Czech Roman Catholic Benevolent Union of Texas Women, founded in 1897.

One of the more prominent Czech Catholics was John Nepomucene Neumann, fourth bishop of Philadelphia, who is considered a founder of the American parochial school system. He was canonized in 1977. Among outstanding Czech scholars in the United States were world-renowned Byzantinologist, Msgr. Francis Dvorník of Harvard University; Msgr. Ludvík Němec, author of several books and many articles on the subject of religion and Church-state relations; Dr. Joseph Čada, authority on immigration history who was chairman of the History Department at Chicago Teachers College. Among the bishops and archbishops of Czech background were or are John L. Morkovsky, bishop of Galveston-Houston; Daniel W. Kucera, archbishop of Dubuque, Iowa; Jerome Hanus, archbishop of Dubuque, Iowa; John G. Vlazny, bishop of Winona, Minnesota; Emil A. Wcela, auxiliary bishop of Rockville Centre, New York.

In addition to elementary and secondary schools, the Czech Catholics established institutions such as St. Procopius College, Lisle, Illinois. The college carries the name of one of Bohemia's saints. The college has recently witnessed an unprecedented development in its history by becoming a coeducational institution and earning recognition for its scientific research. The college was founded by the Czech Benedictines. In the Czech community in the U.S.A. several Benedictine abbots have been very influential, e.g., Leo Ondrak and Valentine Skluzacek.

Newspaper and Periodicals

The Czech Catholics established many periodicals, most of which have folded over the years. The first was *Katolické noviny* published in Chicago in 1867. Its life was short. Since there was a substantial Czech community in St. Louis in January 1872, Msgr. Joseph Hessoun founded the Catholic semiweekly *Hlas* which was published until 1950. *Hlas* was the most influential organ of Czech Catholics in the United States until the end of the nineteenth century when the Czech (Bohemian) Benedictine Press was established in Chicago. The Benedictines founded a weekly *Katolík* in 1893 and a daily *Národ* in 1894. (*Národ* became a weekly in 1960.) They also established *Katolický dělník/Catholic Workman,* official organ of the Catholic Workman, a Czech Catholic fraternal union, published in Czech and English. In 1975 the periodicals *Katolík* and *Národ* were succeeded by a weekly *Hlas Národa/Voice of the Nation;* it became a biweekly in the 1990s.

In Halletsville, Texas, a Czech Catholic weekly *Nový Domov* first appeared in 1895; in 1925 another Czech Catholic weekly, *Našinec,* was founded in Granger, Texas. The Czech Catholic missions and parishes published monthly bulletins. *Organ of Czech Catholic Foresters* was published in Chicago, 1910–50; it was the official publication of the Czech Catholic Foresters Organization that had

113 affiliated branches. Several other short-lived periodicals were published in Chicago, Cleveland, and other cities. In the 1950s the Czech Catholic anti-communist exiles published *Orel* (Nebraska) and *Křesťanská demokracie* (New York).

Organization and Assimilation

For decades some of the "old Czech Catholic settlers" belonged to gymnastic organizations called Catholic Sokols or Sokol-Orels. After the complete Communist takeover of Czechoslovakia, some of the post-1948 exiles founded the Czechoslovak Orel in Exile that carried the torch of Orel, a Catholic gymnastic organization in Czechoslovakia, proscribed by the Communist regime. It engaged in religious, educational, gymnastic, and cultural work as dictated by the postulate—their nation's liberation. Among the many events that ought to be mentioned are the erection of a marble statue of the Virgin Mary in Exile, Lisle, Illinois (the statue was transferred to Prague, Czech Republic, in 1993), and the organizing of three world unionistic congresses in Lisle. The *Orel* was one of the leading members of the Alliance of Slav Orels, Catholic Sokols, and a member of the International Federation of Gymnasts in Paris, etc. The Orels took part in the building of the Czech National Chapel of Our Lady of Hostýn in honor of St. John Neumann in the National Shrine, Washington, D.C.

In the spring of 1917 in Cleveland, Ohio, *Národní svaz českých katolíků,* the National Alliance of Czech Catholics, was founded and the organization joined other secular organizations that advocated and worked for independence of the Czechs and Slovaks. During World War I branches of the alliance were established in cities with Czech populations and most of them continue to be the spokesmen of Czech Catholics in their localities. Unfortunately, the number of those who identify themselves as Czech-Americans declines year after year. The Czechs have assimilated themselves into the American society faster than any other ethnic group. There are very few "Czech parishes" now, although the names of the churches show that they were built by the Czech immigrants. While many Czech Catholics belong to clubs and organizations which are not exclusively Catholic, some are organized in the National Alliance of Czech Catholics whose headquarters are in "Velehrad," Cicero, Illinois. Affiliated with the alliance are fraternal organizations such as the Catholic Workman, Czech Catholic Union, Czech Catholic Union of Texas, K.J.T., Czech Family Fraternal of Texas K.J.Z.T., Czech Associated Courts, C.O.F., Velehrad, North American Pastoral Center (California), Czech Mission (Los Angeles, California), and Czechoslovak Orel Abroad.

Čapek, Thomas. *The Czechs (Bohemians) in America.* New York, 1920.

———. *Slavs in the United States 1850–1940.* Chicago, 1943.

———. *Padesát let českého tisku v Americe.* New York, 1911.

Czechoslovak National Council of America, *Panorama. A Historical Review of Czechs and Slovaks in the United States of America.* Cicero, Illinois, 1970.

Habenicht, Jan. *Dějiny Čechů amerických.* St. Louis, Missouri, 1910.

Jerabek, Esther. *Czechs and Slovaks in North America. A Bibliography.* New York and Chicago, 1976.

JOSEF KALVODA

D

DABLON, CLAUDE (ca. 1618–97)

Jesuit, missionary and explorer. Dablon was born in Dieppe, France, ca. 1618. Not much is known concerning his education and background. After entering the Society of Jesus, he was sent to Canada as a missionary. When Dablon arrived in Quebec in 1655, his superior immediately sent him south of Lake Ontario. The Onondaga nation of the Iroquois Confederacy, who dwelled in that area, had for a number of years requested missionaries to live and work in their villages.

In 1661 he accompanied Fr. Gabriel Druillettes and five other Frenchmen on an expedition to Hudson Bay. The objective of this mission was to establish whether this "northern sea" was connected to the elusive Northwest Passage. Another goal was to commence missionary work among the Cree inhabitants of the area. Seven years later, Frs. Dablon, Claude Jean Allouez, and Jacques Marquette explored the area around Lake Superior. Dablon established Sault Ste. Marie, Michigan, in 1668 and was appointed superior of the western missions in 1669. In that capacity he dispatched Fr. Marquette down the Mississippi River.

His appointment as superior general of the Jesuit missionaries in New France brought him back to Quebec in 1671. He served two terms in this position (1671–80 and 1686–93). His contributions to the *Jesuit Relations* (esp. 1655–72) contain quite adequate descriptions of some interior regions of America and its native inhabitants. In 1678, Dablon also arranged and edited for publication the letters and charts of Marquette's expedition down the Mississippi River.

KEES-JAN WATERMAN

DABROWSKI, JOSEPH (1842–1903)

Priest and educator. Dabrowski was born in Zoltance, Poland, on January 27, educated at Lublin Gymnasium and the University of Warsaw, fought in the unsuccessful Polish uprising of 1863 against Czarist Russia, fled to Germany, then continued his studies at Lucerne and Berne, Switzerland. He then went to Rome to study for the priesthood and was ordained in 1869. After ordination Dabrowski emigrated to the United States, bringing the Felician Sisters to the United States in 1874 to assist him in his work with Polish Catholics in Wisconsin. In eleven years as a parish priest he built two churches, a mission chapel, parochial school, convent, and rectory. He assisted the Felician Sisters in establishing a novitiate and in setting up a printing shop, which published Polish textbooks for elementary grades.

In 1882 Dabrowski transferred his activities from Polonia, Wisconsin, to Detroit, Michigan, where he was to spend the last two decades of his life guiding the expansion of the Felician Sisters, their schools, and their publications. Dabrowski was also a central figure in the founding of SS. Cyril and Methodius Seminary and St. Mary's High School in 1885 for training bilingual Polish-American priests.

Dabrowski became even more significant to the development of Midwestern Polish-American Catholicism when he became entangled in the 1885–98 "Kolasinski Affair." Around Dabrowski would crystallize a group of ethnic Poles who were opposed to the colorful Fr. Dominik Kolasinski, a Detroit parish priest whom Dabrowski replaced after Kolasinski was accused of financial misconduct by

407

Detroit bishop Caspar Borgess and the parish trustees. Despite attempts to remain focused on the construction and development of the seminary and the education of Polish Catholic youth, Dabrowski was compelled to witness the fracture of the fledgling Polish community over what had begun as a conflict between Kolasinski and his bishop. Dabrowski died at his Detroit seminary on February 15, 1903.

See also POLISH CATHOLICS IN AMERICA.

Boyea, Earl. "Father Kolasinski and the Church of Detroit." *Catholic Historical Review* 74 (July 1988) 420–39.

Paré, George. *The Catholic Church in Detroit, 1701–1888.* Detroit: Wayne State University Press, 1983.

Tentler, Leslie. *Seasons of Grace: A History of the Catholic Archdiocese of Detroit.* Detroit: Wayne State University Press, 1990.

MARIA MAZZENGA

DAHOOD, MITCHELL (1922–82)

Biblical scholar. He was born on March 8, 1922, in Anaconda, Montana. In 1941 he joined the English province of the Society of Jesus and was ordained at Weston College, Massachusetts, on June 19, 1954. Dahood combined a flair for languages and an abiding love of the Scriptures. He studied Semitic languages under William Foxwell Albright at Johns Hopkins University and received his doctorate in 1951. For over a quarter of a century (1956–82) he was a respected and good-humored professor on the faculty of the Pontifical Biblical Institute in Rome where he enthusiastically advocated the importance of Urgaritic and Eblaite for a better understanding of the Bible. He wrote profusely and lectured widely in Europe and America, and his views were often original and sometimes controversial. He wrote the three-volume commentary on the Psalms for the Anchor Bible, and was president of the Catholic Biblical Association in 1981. He died on March 8, 1982, while praying in the Church of Santa Maria in Via in Rome.

Obituary notice. *Catholic Biblical Quarterly* 44 (1982) 470–71.

MICHAEL GLAZIER

DALEY, RICHARD JOSEPH (1902–76)

Mayor of Chicago. Daley was born in Chicago on May 15, 1902, educated in parochial schools and at DePaul University's Law School. He was admitted to the Illinois bar in 1933, but within a few years, he was devoting his primary energies to politics. He served in the State Assembly from 1936–38 and in the State Senate from 1939–46. For one year, 1949–50, he was Director of Revenue for the State of Illinois. In 1955 he was elected mayor of Chicago, a position he held without significant opposition

Richard J. Daley

for twenty-one years. He was chairman of the Cook County Democratic Party for twenty-three years.

Daley was mayor of "the city that works," as one national news magazine dubbed Chicago. Although not known as a reflective man, he loved that definition and bristled at the suggestion that he presided over "a political machine." Machine or not, it was the most effective and smooth-running administration that most cities have ever known. Long after civil service had decimated the ward and patronage system in other cities, Daley's fifty wards, virtually all of them presided over by Democratic committeemen, flourished.

Widely held to be, personally, a dollar-honest mayor, Daley was worldly in his judgment of people in politics using their clout to make money. He was tolerant of politicians who became rich on what was called "honest graft," e.g., city-connected law business, real estate deals, etc. Daley's rationale has been described as: "It takes money to be in politics; so as long as it's not immoral or illegal, what was wrong with making some money if you had a chance?"

It is clear, however, that many politicians crossed the line. The system permitted the mayor to pay modest salaries because many of his strategically placed aldermen and appointees could compensate with generous contributions to their campaign chests. Daley himself appears to have been free from the temptation to steal; he was more concerned with power. Even before federal reporting legislation was introduced in 1976, as chairman of the Cook County Democratic Party, he collected an estimated $15 million in contributions which he controlled completely. There is no evidence that he took any for his personal use.

During the Daley years, Chicago ran smoothly for most of its citizens. Potholes were fixed; garbage was collected; there was clean water and sewers. Minority neighborhoods did not fare as well, however, and the civil rights movement caused considerable tensions.

Daley had little interest in national politics, but he campaigned vigorously for the election of John F. Kennedy in 1960, delivering Cook County and thus Illinois to the nation's first Catholic president. The electoral votes were enough to give Kennedy a narrow victory over Richard M. Nixon.

In 1968, during the Democratic National Convention held in Chicago, the Chicago police were accused of using brutal tactics to subdue demonstrators. Daley supported his police while other politicians termed the demonstrations "a police riot." The experience angered Daley, then in his sixty-sixth year. It marked the beginning of the end of his influence within the state and in Washington, although at his final election in 1976 he garnered an impressive 58 percent of the votes. The aging mayor felt that control of his world was being snatched away from him bit by bit. He tried desperately to elbow his way to the side of Jimmy Carter in the 1976 presidential election. But changing times and mores had severely hobbled the last big city boss. (His son, Richard M. Daley, can still reasonably claim this title. In April 1995 he was elected to his fourth term as mayor.)

Daley, a devout Catholic, enjoyed an easy relationship with the Church. Again, his immense clout insured that churches and schools received preferential service. Daley's rationale was simple: the Catholic Church was one of the most effective social agencies in the city, all at little or no cost. He died in Chicago on December 20, 1976.

O'Connor, Len. *Requiem: The Decline and Demise of Mayor Daley and His Era.* Chicago: Contemporary Books, 1977.

R. TIMOTHY UNSWORTH

DALY, JOHN AUGUSTIN (1838–99)

Dramatist and theatrical manager. Born in Plymouth, North Carolina, on July 20, 1838, Daly's interest in theater was sparked when he moved with his family to New York City in 1849. A member of several amateur dramatic societies, Daly became drama critic of the New York *Sunday Courier* in 1859, and was writing for five New York newspapers by 1867. In addition to criticism, essays, and short stories, Daly wrote plays, many of which were successfully produced, including *Leah the Forsaken* (1863) and *Under the Gaslight* (1867). Daly is credited with writing more than ninety plays, many adapted from English, French, and German originals, although it is said that he collaborated closely with his brother Joseph, a judge.

In 1869 Daly married Mary Duff; they had two sons. The same year he stopped writing for newspapers and began

John A. Daly

managing New York's Fifth Avenue Theater. Over the next thirty years, Daly became America's most famous and influential theater manager: the most prominent actors and actresses appeared in his plays on his stages in New York; and later, in London. Daly was known for the methods he introduced to theater management. He demanded intensive rehearsals and careful attention to script, scenery, lighting, costumes, and makeup. He directed all actors, even those with star status, with the ensemble in mind. Although Daly was reproved by some employees for his autocratic style, his productions were popular and critical successes. He received Notre Dame University's Laetare Medal in 1894, and died on June 7, 1899, while visiting Paris.

Daly, J. F. *The Life of Augustin Daly.* New York, 1917.
Felheim, M. *The Theater of Augustin Daly.* Boston, 1956.
Wilmeth, Don B., and Rosemary Cullen, eds. *Plays by Augustin Daly.* Cambridge, England, 1984.

K. N. McCARTHY

DALY, MARCUS (1841–1900)

Businessman. A Montana mining entrepreneur, Daly was born in Ireland and emigrated to the United States at the age of fifteen. After mining stints in California, Nevada, and Utah, Daly moved to Butte, Montana, in 1879 and worked at the Walker brothers' Alice mine. He then acquired the Anaconda Silver Mine. Daly was one of the first to capitalize on the value of copper ore in the region. He built the town of Anaconda with its huge smelter and established the *Anaconda Standard* newspaper, one of the best in the state. His company contributed to Catholic institutions including St. Ann's Hospital in Anaconda.

Daly's initial friendship with Butte mining magnate, William A. Clark, turned into a bitter personal and business rivalry that dominated Montana politics between 1888 and 1900. Frederick Augustus Heinze became the third of the battling copper kings.

In 1895 Daly consolidated his vast mining operations, including railroads and lumber companies, into the Anaconda Copper Company. Five years later to avoid outside investment, he created the Amalgamated Copper Company, a holding company that enlarged the Anaconda Company.

Daly was married to Margaret Evans in 1872 and built a mansion, orchards, and racing horse stables in Hamilton in Montana's Bitterroot valley.

Glasscock, C. B. *The War of the Copper Kings.* New York: Bobbs Merrill, 1935.

Malone, Michael P. *The Battle for Butte: Mining and Politics on the Northern Frontier, 1864–1906.* Seattle: University of Washington Press, 1981.

Toole, K. Ross. "Marcus Daly, A Study in Business Politics." Master's thesis, Montana State University, 1947.

JOAN BISHOP

DAMIEN, FATHER/JOSEPH DE VEUSTER (1840–89)

Fr. Damien, "The Leper Priest of Molokai," was born Joseph De Veuster at Tremeloo, Belgium, January 3, 1840.

He entered the Congregation of the Sacred Hearts of Jesus and Mary on February 2, 1859, and professed his vows at the order's motherhouse in Paris on October 7, 1860. In 1863 Damien volunteered to replace his priest-

Father Damien

brother Pamphile, then sick with typhus, as missionary to Hawaii. He arrived at Honolulu, March 19, 1864, and, on May 21, was ordained in the Honolulu cathedral by Bishop Louis Maigret, SS.CC. Damien's labors on the "Big Island" of Hawaii lasted until May 10, 1873, when he sailed for Molokai.

Since 1865 Hawaii's rigid segregation laws had forced the removal of all lepers to an isolated promontory on the island of Molokai. Between 1866 and 1873 an estimated 40 percent of the exiles died uncared-for. The settlements were dominated by the strongest of the residents, to the detriment of the weak.

Some 816 residents witnessed Damien's arrival. Faced with appalling social conditions and a general lack of medical care, the priest set about constructing dwelling houses for the inhabitants, personally providing medical attention to the sick in their huts, and seeing that the dead were properly buried. He founded an orphanage for the younger patients, and pleaded for improved supplies and treatment from the Royal Board of Health.

Newspaper stories of his work led to widening public recognition. Liliuokalani, regent for her brother King Kalakaua, named Damien "Knight Commander of the Royal Order of Kalakaua" on September 12, 1881. An American, Joseph Dutton (d. 1931), would volunteer in 1886 to become Damien's assistant. Mother Marianne Cope (d. 1918) would arrive with her Third Order Sisters of St. Francis in 1889.

Damien's diagnosis of leprosy in 1884 led to even greater renown. Certain English patrons, chief among them Edward Clifford and the Anglican clergyman Hugh B. Chapman, contributed large sums of money and supplies to further Damien's work.

The priest's waning years were marked by political troubles with the Royal Board of Health and with his own religious superiors. The former, composed of Americans, had no desire to see English influence expanded in the islands via English alms. The latter, Bishop Herman Koeckemann and Fr. Leonor Fouesnel, both Sacred Hearts Fathers, thought that Damien's reputation overshadowed the work of other island missionaries. They also feared for Church freedom in the face of growing hostility from the Board of Health. As a final insult, Damien had to endure the prevalent misconception that leprosy was a byproduct of syphilis.

Damien succumbed to his illness on April 15, 1889, and was buried on Molokai. In death, his fame continued to spread. On January 27, 1936, in response to a formal request by the Belgian government, Damien's remains were disinterred and shipped back to his homeland. Damien's cause for sainthood, initiated two years later, has thus far resulted in his beatification. Pope John Paul II declared him blessed on June 4, 1995, at ceremonies in Belgium.

A secular tribute to Damien occurred on April 15, 1969, when his bronze likeness was unveiled in Washington,

D.C. He and Kamehameha I, unifier of the Hawaiian islands, would henceforth represent the fiftieth state in the Statuary Hall of the Capitol.

See also COPE, MARIANNE.

Bunson, Margaret. *Father Damien.* Huntington, Ind.: Sunday Visitor, 1989.

Daws, Gavan. *Holy Man.* New York: Harper and Row, 1973.

Jourdain, Vital. *The Heart of Father Damien.* Milwaukee: Bruce, 1955.

ALBERT H. LEDOUX

DAMMANN, GRACE COWARDIN (1872–1945)

Religious of the Sacred Heart. Dammann was born in Baltimore, Maryland, on July 9, 1872, the eldest of six children of Francis Dammann and Eileen Cowardin. She was educated at Visitation Convent, Georgetown, and was instrumental with Mary Merrick, a girlhood friend, in the beginnings of the Holy Childhood Association. In 1898 she entered the Society of the Sacred Heart in Albany, New York, where she also made her final profession in 1906.

A teacher and administrator in the schools of the Religious of the Sacred Heart in Albany, New York City, Philadelphia, and London, England, she was named superior and finally president of Manhattanville College in New York in 1930. Mother Dammann was a recognized leader in educational circles and a fearless champion of racial equality.

In 1933 the Manhattanville student body adopted the Manhattanville Resolutions, eight resolutions embodying the principles of Catholic social justice toward blacks. In 1938 Dammann accepted the first black student at Man-

Grace Cowardin Dammann

hattanville. She explained this decision in the address "Principles vs. Prejudice," given to the Manhattanville Alumnae Association. Using the social teachings of the Church, Mother Dammann responded to the objections raised against the decision. She kept in touch with the non-Catholic leaders of the black press and did much to counter the bitterness resulting from the lack of vision among Catholics on the race question.

As a leader in the field of Catholic higher education, Mother Dammann promoted the importance of a full-time faculty for Catholic colleges as early as 1935. The benefit plans for faculty that she developed at Manhattanville were far in advance of the norm for even secular colleges at the time. An active member of the National Catholic Education Association, Dammann chaired the Eastern Regional Unit of the College Department in 1941 and served on the committees on Policies and Plans as well as Finance. She also contributed a chapter, "The Catholic College for Women" in *Essays on Catholic Education in the United States,* ed. Roy Deferrari, C.U.A., Washington, 1942.

Mother Dammann held memberships in the NCEA, National Rural Life Conference, NAACP, Catholic Association for International Peace, American Catholic Philosophical Association, National Conference of Christians and Jews, and the Catholic Art Association. She died at Manhattanville College in New York City on February 13, 1945.

MARGARET PHELAN, R.S.C.J.

DAUGHTERS OF CHARITY OF ST. VINCENT DE PAUL (D.C.)

The Daughters of Charity in the United States trace their origin to Elizabeth Bayley Seton: wife, mother, widow, convert, and recognized foundress and patroness of the Catholic education system in the United States. Ironically, Elizabeth Seton's Episcopalian background had included her outstanding service to the poor in New York City, earning her the title "the Protestant Sister of Charity." After the death of her husband in 1803, she opened a little school in Manhattan to support herself and her children. Now a Catholic, Mrs. Seton moved to Baltimore at the suggestion of the French Sulpicians and opened a school there. Bishop John Carroll of Baltimore had met Elizabeth Seton when he administered the sacrament of confirmation at New York on May 25, 1806. He was immediately charmed by the small gentlewoman's radiance and wit. Carroll soon learned that his confidence in this convert's sincerity was well founded. It began to appear that she had a vocation for the life of a religious.

Foundation of the Early Community

On July 31, 1809, Elizabeth, now called Mother Seton, her children and four companions moved into the Fleming farmhouse on a piece of property in western Maryland, near Emmitsburg, which was offered to her by Samuel Cooper, a wealthy seminarian. This date, July 31, 1809, is generally considered the foundation of the Sisters of Charity of St. Joseph. The French Sulpicians became the guardians of the fledgling community. These Sulpicians were well acquainted with the Daughters of Charity founded by St. Vincent de Paul and St. Louise de Marillac, and knew that St. Louise had opened a school for poor girls in 1641 in the Faubourg St. Denis in Paris. They realized the importance of Catholic education if the Church were to prosper in the United States, and saw in Elizabeth Seton a possible instrument of God for the establishment of this work. In 1810 Mother Seton obtained a copy of the rules of the French Daughters of Charity through Fr. Benedict Flaget, a Sulpician. The first chapter of their rule explains the purpose of the Daughters of Charity: "The principal end for which God has called and assembled the Daughters of Charity is to honor Our Lord Jesus Christ as the source and model of all charity, serving him corporally and spiritually in the person of the poor" (Daughters of Charity, *Constitutions and Statutes,* 1983, 5). The sisters adopted these rules and followed them as closely as the conditions of the developing country permitted. This done, the American foundation was now able to grow rapidly in membership and in works of service.

Union with the International Community of the Daughters of Charity

Many events led to the permanent union of the Emmitsburg group with the French community. Since 1810 they had been observing the rules and living under the guidance of the Sulpician Fathers in the United States. In 1845, "the Very Reverend Louis de Courson, the new Superior General of the Sulpicians, ordered his American provinces to withdraw from all works save their primary objective, the seminary" (Crumlish, *1809–1959,* 59). Fr. de Courson asked the Very Reverend Jean-Baptiste Etienne, C. M., the superior general of both the Vincentians and the Daughters of Charity, to grant full incorporation of the Emmitsburg community into the international Community of the Daughters of Charity. Archbishop Samuel Eccleston of Baltimore asked Fr. John Timon, a Vincentian, to urge the superiors of the Daughters of Charity to finalize the affiliation of the Emmitsburg community which officially occurred in 1850. By that time the sisters were laboring in nineteen cities from the East Coast to the west bank of the Mississippi.

The Apostolates of the Daughters of Charity

Education was not the sole interest of Mother Seton and her followers. They also had very much at heart the needs of the sick and the orphans after the manner of their prototypes, the Daughters of Charity in France. Even from the

early days, the challenges presented by the huge waves of immigration and subsequent health and social problems called for the generous response of the Emmitsburg community. From the humble beginnings in a small, one-room school the community's works expanded to include orphan asylums, each with an internal school, which also accepted the neighborhood children. Small hospitals or clinics were opened and the sisters visited the homes of immigrants to tend to social needs. Over the years requests came for the sisters to provide services in many cities and dioceses.

Expansion of the Daughters of Charity

Young women continued to respond to the call of Christ, permitting further spread of the community across the continent to the Pacific Coast. The sisters arrived in San Francisco in 1852 and, "despite the discouraging and primitive conditions, the sisters bravely set to work and public generosity seconded their endeavors" (Crumlish, *1809–1959,* 75).

The American Civil War, fought in so great a degree close to Emmitsburg, had a prolonged effect on the entry of the sisters into the provision of health care. Soldiers of both sides of the conflict benefited from the selfless work of the sisters. The nursing skills developed by the sisters during the periods of epidemics were well tested. They established field hospitals and transports carrying the wounded to safe areas. The Daughters of Charity, already organized and available, provided over fifty percent of the nurses working with the military. They performed these same services in 1898 during the Spanish-American War in field and ship hospitals. These sisters were the early models for the Army Corps of Nurses.

The Daughters of Charity Today

Like many American communities, the Daughters of Charity are to be found in multiple apostolates. A history of the Daughters of Charity in the United States, written in 1990, offers a rationale for this diversity of works: "Changes in the apostolic services reflect two priorities: concern for and ministry to the poor and a thrust toward services in areas where the unchurched are numerous or where Catholic presence is minimal" (Hannifin, *Daughters of the Church,* 260).

The Daughters of Charity are recognized leaders in the delivery of health care in the United States. In 1986, they established the Daughters of Charity National Health System (DCNHS), a network of over fifty-one hospitals, psychiatric facilities, nursing homes, and free-standing clinics. In an effort to bring health care closer to the consumer, sisters visit the homebound and elderly and serve as midwives in poor and rural areas. The desire to meet the needs of the poor has led the sisters into many facets of social welfare.

Crumlish, Sr. John Mary. *1809–1959.* Emmitsburg, 1959.

Hannifin, Sr. Daniel. *Daughters of the Church: A Popular History of the Daughters of Charity in the United States, 1809–1987.* Brooklyn: New City Press, 1990.

ELAINE WHEELER, D.C.

DAVID, JOHN BAPTIST (1761–1841)

Missionary, bishop, and a member of the Society of St. Sulpice. David was ordained a priest in 1785, and began his clerical career as a seminary professor at Angers. Because of the terrors of the French Revolution, David removed to America as a missionary in 1792. He served as parish priest in southern Maryland and then as professor at Georgetown College. When his friend and colleague Benedict Flaget was appointed bishop in Kentucky, David volunteered his services to the new frontier diocese.

In 1811 David was named director of the newly established St. Thomas Seminary in Nelson County. When an attempt was made to have David transferred to the post of bishop of Philadelphia, Flaget appealed to Rome to have his colleague appointed coadjutor bishop in Kentucky. Rome agreed, and David was accordingly the first bishop to be consecrated in the West, the ceremony taking place at the Bardstown cathedral, August 15, 1819.

In 1812 David had been instrumental, along with Catherine Spalding, in the founding of the Sisters of Charity of Nazareth. A prayer book by David, *True Piety,* was published in 1824; and his *Catechism of the Catholic Religion* in 1825. In a confusing scenario, Flaget resigned in 1832, hoping that Guy Chabrat would be named bishop. Rome appointed David instead, much to Flaget's and David's consternation. David tendered his resignation at once, remaining bishop of Bardstown only until the Holy See restored Flaget to that office in 1833. David fell ill in April 1841 and asked to end his days among the Sisters of Charity. He died on July 12, 1841, and is buried at the motherhouse cemetery at Nazareth.

See also KENTUCKY, CATHOLIC CHURCH IN.

Fox, Columba. *The Life of the Right Reverend John Baptist Mary David.* New York, 1925.

CLYDE F. CREWS

DAY, DOROTHY (1879–1980)

Social activist. Dorothy Day, founder of the Catholic Worker movement, was born in Brooklyn, New York, November 8, 1897. The family later moved to San Francisco.

Early Years

After surviving the San Francisco earthquake in 1906, the Day family moved into a tenement flat in Chicago's South

Dorothy Day

Side. It was a big step down in the world made necessary because John Day was out of work. Day's understanding of the shame people feel when they fail in their efforts dated from this time.

It was in Chicago that Day began to form positive impressions of Catholicism. Later in life she would recall her discovery of a friend's mother, a devout Catholic, praying at the side of her bed. Without embarrassment, she looked up at Day, told her where to find her daughter, and returned to her prayers. "I felt a burst of love toward [her] that I have never forgotten," Day recalled.

When John Day was appointed sports editor of a Chicago newspaper, the Day family moved into a comfortable house on the North Side. Here Dorothy began to read books that stirred her conscience. Upton Sinclair's novel, *The Jungle,* inspired Day to take long walks in poor neighborhoods in Chicago's South Side. It was the start of a lifelong attraction to areas many people avoid.

Day had a gift for finding beauty in the midst of urban desolation. Drab streets were transformed by pungent odors: geranium and tomato plants, garlic, olive oil, roasting coffee, bread and rolls in bakery ovens. "Here," she said, "was enough beauty to satisfy me."

Day won a scholarship that brought her to the University of Illinois campus at Urbana in the fall of 1914. But she was a reluctant scholar. Her reading was chiefly in a radical social direction. She avoided campus social life and insisted on supporting herself rather than live on money from her father. Dropping out of college two years later, she moved to New York where she found a job as a reporter for *The Call,* the city's only socialist daily. She covered rallies and demonstrations and interviewed people ranging from butlers to labor organizers and revolutionaries.

She next worked for *The Masses,* a magazine that opposed American involvement in the European war. In September, the post office rescinded the magazine's mailing permit. Federal officers seized back issues, manuscripts, subscriber lists and correspondence. Five editors were charged with sedition.

In November 1917 Day went to prison for being one of forty women in front of the White House protesting women's exclusion from the electorate. Arriving at a rural workhouse, the women were roughly handled. The women responded with a hunger strike. Finally they were freed by presidential order.

Returning to New York, Day felt that journalism was a meager response to a world at war. In the spring of 1918, she signed up for a nurse's training program in Brooklyn.

Her conviction that the social order was unjust changed in no substantial way from her adolescence until her death, though she never identified herself with any political party.

Her religious development was a slower process. As a child she had attended services at an Episcopal Church. As a young journalist in New York, she would sometimes make late-at-night visits to St. Joseph's Catholic Church on Sixth Avenue. The Catholic climate of worship appealed to her. While she knew little about Catholic belief, Catholic spiritual discipline fascinated her. She saw the Catholic Church as "the church of the immigrants, the church of the poor." In 1922, in Chicago working as a reporter, she roomed with three young women who went to Mass every Sunday and holy day and set aside time each day for prayer. It was clear to her that "worship, adoration, thanksgiving, supplication . . . were the noblest acts of which we are capable in this life."

Her next job was with a newspaper in New Orleans. Living near St. Louis Cathedral, Day often attended evening Benediction services. Back in New York in 1924, Day bought a beach cottage on Staten Island using money from the sale of movie rights for a novel. She also began a four-year common-law marriage with Forster Batterham, an English botanist she had met through friends in Manhattan. Batterham was an anarchist opposed to marriage and religion. In a world of such cruelty, he found it impossible to believe in a God. By this time Day's belief in God was unshakable. It grieved her that Batterham didn't sense God's presence within the natural world. "How can there be no God," she asked, "when there are all these beautiful things?" His irritation with her "absorption in the supernatural" would lead them to quarrel.

Conversion to Catholicism

What moved everything to a different plane for her was pregnancy. She had been pregnant once before, years earlier, as the result of a love affair with a journalist. This resulted in the great tragedy of her life, an abortion. The affair and its awful aftermath had been the subject of her novel, *The Eleventh Virgin.* The abortion, Day concluded in the years following, had left her barren. "For a long time I had thought I could not bear a child, and the longing in my heart for a baby had been growing," she confided in her autobiography, *The Long Loneliness.* "My home, I felt, was not a home without one."

Her pregnancy with Batterham seemed to Day nothing less than a miracle. But Batterham didn't believe in bringing children into such a violent world. On March 3, 1927, Tamar Theresa Day was born. Day could think of nothing better to do with the gratitude that overwhelmed her than arrange Tamar's baptism in the Catholic Church. "I did not want my child to flounder as I had often floundered. I wanted to believe, and I wanted my child to believe, and if belonging to a Church would give her so inestimable a grace as faith in God, and the companionable love of the Saints, then the thing to do was to have her baptized a Catholic."

After Tamar's baptism, there was a permanent break with Batterham. On December 28, 1927, Day was received into the Catholic Church. A new period commenced in her life as she tried to find a way to bring together her religious faith and her radical social values.

In the winter of 1932 Day traveled to Washington, D.C., to report for *Commonweal* and *America* magazines on the Hunger March. She watched the protesters parade down the streets of Washington carrying signs calling for jobs, unemployment insurance, old age pensions, relief for mothers and children, health care and housing. What kept Day on the sidelines was that she was a Catholic and the march had been organized by Communists, a party at war not only with capitalism but also with religion.

It was December 8, the feast of the Immaculate Conception. After witnessing the march, Day went to the Shrine of the Immaculate Conception where she expressed her torment in prayer: "I offered up a special prayer, a prayer which came with tears and anguish, that some way would open up for me to use what talents I possessed for my fellow workers, for the poor."

Peter Maurin

Back in her apartment in New York the next day, Day met Peter Maurin, a French immigrant twenty years her senior. Maurin, a former Christian Brother, had left France for Canada in 1908 and later made his way to the United States. When he met Day, he was a handyman at a Catholic boys' camp in upstate New York, receiving meals, use of the chaplain's library, living space in the barn, and occasional pocket money.

During his years of wandering, Maurin had come to a Franciscan attitude, embracing poverty as a vocation. His celibate, unencumbered life offered time for study and prayer, out of which a vision had taken form of a social order instilled with basic values of the gospel "in which it would be easier for men to be good." A born teacher, he found willing listeners, among them George Shuster, editor of *Commonweal* magazine, who gave him Day's address.

As remarkable as the providence of their meeting was Day's willingness to listen. It seemed to her Maurin was an answer to her prayers, someone who could help her discover what she was supposed to do. What Day should do, Maurin said, was start a paper to publicize Catholic social teaching and promote steps to bring about the peaceful transformation of society. Day readily embraced the idea. If family past, work experience and religious faith had prepared her for anything, it was this.

Day found that the Paulist Press was willing to print 2,500 copies of an eight-page tabloid paper for fifty-seven dollars. Her kitchen was the new paper's editorial office. She decided to sell the paper for a penny a copy, "so cheap that anyone could afford to buy it."

On May 1, the first copies of *The Catholic Worker* were handed out on Union Square.

Few publishing ventures meet with such immediate success. By December, 100,000 copies were being printed each month. Readers found a unique voice in *The Catholic Worker*. It expressed dissatisfaction with the social order and took the side of labor unions, but its vision of the ideal future challenged both urbanization and industrialism. It wasn't only radical but religious. The paper didn't merely complain but called on its readers to make personal responses.

The Catholic Worker Movement

For the first half year *The Catholic Worker* was only a newspaper, but as winter approached, homeless people began to knock on the door. Maurin's essays in the paper were calling for renewal of the ancient Christian practice of hospitality to those who were homeless. In this way followers of Christ could respond to Jesus' words: "I was a stranger and you took me in." Maurin opposed the idea that Christians should take care only of their friends and leave care of strangers to impersonal charitable agencies. Every home should have its "Christ Room" and every parish a house of hospitality ready to receive the "ambassadors of God."

Surrounded by people in need and attracting volunteers excited about ideas they discovered in *The Catholic Worker*, it was inevitable that the editors would soon be given the chance to put their principles into practice. Day's apartment was the seed of many houses of hospitality to come. By the wintertime, an apartment was rented with space for ten women, soon after a place for men. Next came a house in Greenwich Village. In 1936 the community moved into two buildings in Chinatown, but no enlargement could possibly find room for all those in need. Mainly they were men, Day wrote, "grey men, the color of lifeless trees and bushes and winter soil, who had in them as yet none of the green of hope, the rising sap of faith."

Many were surprised that, in contrast with most charitable centers, no one at the Catholic Worker set about reforming them. A crucifix on the wall was the only unmistakable evidence of the faith of those welcoming them. The staff received only food, board and occasional pocket money. The Catholic Worker became a national movement. By 1936 there were thirty-three Catholic Worker houses spread across the country. Due to the depression, there were plenty of people needing them.

The Catholic Worker attitude toward those who were welcomed wasn't always appreciated. These weren't the "deserving poor," it was sometimes objected, but drunkards and good-for-nothings. A visiting social worker asked Day how long the "clients" were permitted to stay. "We let them stay forever," Day answered with a fierce look in her eye. "They live with us, they die with us, and we give them a Christian burial. We pray for them after they are dead. Once they are taken in, they become members of the family. Or rather they always were members of the family. They are our brothers and sisters in Christ."

Some critics justified their objections with biblical quotations. Didn't Jesus say that the poor would be with us always? "Yes," Day once replied, "but we are not content that there should be so many of them. The class structure is our making and by our consent, not God's, and we must do what we can to change it. We are urging revolutionary change."

The Catholic Worker also experimented with farming communes. In 1935 a house with a garden was rented on Staten Island. Soon after came Mary Farm in Easton, Pennsylvania, a property finally given up because of strife within the community. Another farm was purchased in upstate New York near Newburgh. Called the Maryfarm Retreat House, it was destined for a longer life. Later came the Peter Maurin Farm on Staten Island, which later moved to Tivoli and then to Marlboro, both in the Hudson Valley. Day came to see the vocation of the Catholic Worker was not so much to found model agricultural communities as rural houses of hospitality.

Pacifism and Nonviolence

What got Day into the most trouble was pacifism. A nonviolent way of life, as she saw it, was at the heart of the gospel. She took as seriously as the early Church the command of Jesus to Peter: "Put away your sword, for whoever lives by the sword shall perish by the sword." For many centuries the Catholic Church had accommodated itself to war. Popes had blessed armies and preached Crusades.

In the thirteenth century St. Francis of Assisi had revived the pacifist way, but by the twentieth century, it was unknown for Catholics to take such a position.

The Catholic Worker's first expression of pacifism, published in 1935, was a dialogue between a patriot and Christ, the patriot dismissing Christ's teaching as a noble but impractical doctrine. Few readers were troubled by such articles until the Spanish Civil War in 1936. The fascist side, led by Franco, presented itself as defender of the Catholic faith. Nearly every American Catholic bishop and publication rallied behind Franco. *The Catholic Worker,* refusing to support either side in the war, lost two-thirds of its readers. Those backing Franco, Day warned early in the war, ought to "take another look at recent events in [Nazi] Germany." She expressed anxiety for the Jews and later was among the founders of the Committee of Catholics to Fight Anti-Semitism.

Following Japan's attack on Pearl Harbor and America's declaration of war, Dorothy announced that the paper would maintain its pacifist stand. "We will print the words of Christ who is with us always," Day wrote. "Our manifesto is the Sermon on the Mount." Opposition to the war, she added, had nothing to do with sympathy for America's enemies. "We love our country. . . . We have been the only country in the world where men and women of all nations have taken refuge from oppression." But the means of action the Catholic Worker movement supported were the works of mercy rather than the works of war. She urged "our friends and associates to care for the sick and the wounded, to the growing of food for the hungry, to the continuance of all our works of mercy in our houses and on our farms."

Not all members of Catholic Worker communities agreed. Fifteen houses of hospitality closed in the months following the U.S. entry into the war. But Day's view prevailed. Every issue of *The Catholic Worker* reaffirmed her understanding of the Christian life. The young men who identified with the Catholic Worker movement during the war generally spent much of the war years either in prison, or in rural work camps. Some did unarmed military service as medics.

The world war ended in 1945, but out of it emerged the cold war, the nuclear-armed "warfare state," and a series of smaller wars in which America was often involved. One of the rituals of life for the New York Catholic Worker community beginning in the late 1950s was the refusal to participate in the state's annual civil defense drill. Such preparation for attack seemed to Day part of an attempt to promote nuclear war as survivable and winnable and to justify spending billions on the military. When the sirens sounded on June 15, 1955, Day was among a small group of people sitting in front of City Hall. "In the name of Jesus, who is God, who is Love, we will not obey this order to pretend, to evacuate, to hide. We will not be drilled into fear. We do not have faith in God if we depend upon the Atom Bomb," a Catholic Worker leaflet explained. Day described her civil disobedience as an act of penance for America's use of nuclear weapons on Japanese cities.

The first year the dissidents were reprimanded. The next year Day and others were sent to jail for five days. Arrested again the next year, the judge jailed her for thirty days. In 1958 a different judge suspended sentence. In 1959 Day was back in prison, but only for five days. Then came 1960, when instead of a handful of people coming to City Hall Park, five hundred turned up. The police arrested only a few, Day conspicuously not among those singled out. In 1961 the crowd swelled to two thousand. This time forty were arrested, but again Day was exempted. It proved to be the last year of dress rehearsals for nuclear war in New York.

Another Catholic Worker emphasis was the civil rights movement. As usual Day wanted to visit people who were setting an example and therefore went to Koinonia, a Christian agricultural community in rural Georgia where blacks and whites lived peacefully together. The community was under attack when Day visited in 1957. One of the community houses had been hit by machine-gun fire and Ku Klux Klan members had burned crosses on community land. Day insisted on taking a turn at the sentry post. Noticing an approaching car had reduced its speed, she ducked just as a bullet struck the steering column in front of her face.

Vatican Council II and Vietnam

Concern with the Church's response to war led Day to Rome during the Second Vatican Council, an event Pope John XXIII hoped would restore "the simple and pure lines that the face of the Church of Jesus had at its birth." In 1963 Day was one of fifty "Mothers for Peace" who went to Rome to thank Pope John for his encyclical *Pacem in Terris.* Close to death, the Pope couldn't meet them privately, but at one of his last public audiences blessed the pilgrims, asking them to continue their labors.

In 1965 Day returned to Rome to take part in a fast expressing "our prayer and our hope" that the council would issue "a clear statement, 'Put away thy sword.'" Day saw the unpublicized fast as a "widow's mite" in support of the bishops' effort to speak with a pure voice to the modern world.

The fasters had reason to rejoice in December when the Constitution on the Church in the Modern World was approved by the bishops. The council described as "a crime against God and humanity" any act of war "directed to the indiscriminate destruction of whole cities or vast areas with their inhabitants." The council called on states to make legal provision for conscientious objectors while describing as "criminal" those who obey commands which condemn the innocent and defenseless.

Acts of war causing "the indiscriminate destruction of . . . vast areas with their inhabitants" were the order of the day in regions of Vietnam under intense U.S. bombardment in 1965 and the years following. Many young Catholic Workers went to prison for refusing to cooperate with conscription, while others did alternative service. Nearly everyone in Catholic Worker communities took part in protests. Many went to prison for acts of civil disobedience.

Probably there has never been a newspaper so many of whose editors have been jailed for acts of conscience. Day herself was last jailed in 1973 for taking part in a banned picket line in support of farmworkers. She was seventy-five years old.

Day lived long enough to see her achievements honored. In 1967, when she made her last visit to Rome to take part in the International Congress of the Laity, she found she was one of two Americans—the other an astronaut—invited to receive Communion from the hands of Pope Paul VI. On her seventy-fifth birthday the Jesuit magazine *America* devoted a special issue to her, finding in her the individual who best exemplified "the aspiration and action of the American Catholic community during the past forty years." Notre Dame University presented her with its Laetare Medal, thanking her for "comforting the afflicted and afflicting the comfortable." Among those who came to visit her when she was no longer able to travel was Mother Theresa of Calcutta, who had once pinned on Day's dress the cross worn only by fully professed members of the Missionary Sisters of Charity.

Long before her death November 29, 1980, Day found herself regarded by many as a saint. No words of hers are better known than her brusque response, "Don't call me a saint. I don't want to be dismissed so easily." Nonetheless, having herself treasured the memory and witness of many saints, she is a candidate for inclusion in the calendar of saints. The Claretians have launched an effort to have her canonized.

"If I have achieved anything in my life," she once remarked, "it is because I have not been embarrassed to talk about God."

See also CATHOLIC PEACE MOVEMENT, THE; CATHOLIC WORKER MOVEMENT, THE; MAURIN, PETER.

Coles, Robert. *Dorothy Day: A Radical Devotion.* Reading, Mass.: Addison-Wesley, 1987.
Cornell, Tom, Robert Ellsberg, and Jim Forest, eds. *A Penny a Copy: Writings from The Catholic Worker.* Maryknoll, N.Y.: Orbis, 1995.
Day, Dorothy. *The Long Loneliness.* Chicago: Saint Thomas More Press, 1993.
Ellsberg, Robert, ed. *Dorothy Day: Selected Writings.* Maryknoll, N.Y.: Orbis, 1992.
Forest, Jim. *Love is the Measure: A Biography of Dorothy Day.* Maryknoll, N.Y.: Orbis, 1994.
Miller, William. *Dorothy Day: A Biography.* New York: Harper & Row, 1982.

JIM FOREST

DAY, VICTOR (1866–1946)

Priest. Msgr. Victor Day was administrator of the Helena, Montana, diocese four times, and vicar general for forty-five years under five bishops. He was born on March 29, 1866, in Desselghem, Belgium, to Henri De Brabandere and Febronie Van der Zyppe. He was educated at the College of Saint-Amand, Courtrai, the minor seminary of Roulers and the major seminary in Bruges. He was ordained on May 23, 1891, and traveled to western Montana in 1893.

Bishop John Baptist Brondel appointed him rector of the Cathedral of the Sacred Hearts and vicar general of the diocese in 1894. He was incardinated into the diocese in 1900 and became administrator when Bishop Brondel died in 1903.

Under Bishop John P. Carroll, Day helped to plan and build the Cathedral of St. Helena and wrote a book on its construction. He wrote extensively, including translations of Gottfried Kurth's *The Church at the Turning Points of History* (1918) and *What Are the Middle Ages?* (1921).

He was made a domestic prelate (monsignor) June 19, 1911. Msgr. Day also served Bishops George F. Finnigan (1927–32), Ralph L. Hayes (1933–35), and Joseph M. Gilmore (1936–62). He retired in 1939 and died on November 7, 1946.

See also MONTANA, CATHOLIC CHURCH IN.

Flaherty, Cornelia M. *Go with Haste into the Mountains, a History of the Diocese of Helena* Helena: Diocese of Helena with Falcon Press Publishing Co., 1984.
Palladino, L. B., S.J. *Indian and White in the Northwest.* Baltimore, Md.: John Murphy & Company, 1894.
Schoenberg, Wilfrid P., S.J. *A History of the Catholic Church in the Pacific Northwest.* Washington, D.C.: Pastoral Press, 1987.

M. CATHERINE TILZEY

DeANDREIS, FELIX (1778–1820)

Missionary. DeAndreis was born on December 12, 1778, in Demonte, in Italy's Piedmonte region, and after a classical education entered (November 1797) the Congregation of the Mission (Vincentians) in Mondovì. As a result of Napoleon's prescriptions imposed on Italy, studies in seminaries were disrupted and when the Vincentian seminary was suppressed, DeAndreis transferred for a time to Turin and then to the Collegio Alberoni in Piacenza. After ordination (August 1802), he gave missions and retreats in the towns and villages surrounding Piacenza and likewise taught at the Collegio Alberoni. When north Italy's weather began to wreak havoc with his health, he moved (1806) to Rome, where he was in charge of the formation of his congregation's seminarians and gave conferences and retreats to priests and bishops as well as missions in the Roman countryside.

In 1815 Louis William DuBourg, the newly consecrated bishop of New Orleans, after hearing DeAndreis preach, asked him to come to Louisiana and establish a seminary. DeAndreis and others who accepted the bishop's invitation, sailed from France on June 12, 1816, and arrived at Baltimore on July 25. Because of disturbances in New Orleans, the missionaries were now to go to St. Louis. On their way they visited Bishop Benedict Joseph Flaget in Bardstown (Kentucky), where the group remained for a year and where DeAndreis taught at St. Thomas Seminary.

After DeAndreis' arrival in St. Louis in January 1818, Bishop DuBourg appointed him vicar general of Upper Louisiana and pastor of the procathedral. He likewise established a seminary for the training of the local clergy and was one of its professors. He also opened a novitiate for the Vincentians. Less than three years after his arrival he died in St. Louis on October 15, 1820, with a reputation for holiness. During his brief period on the missions, he translated prayers into the local Native American tongue and began work on a Native American catechism. He is acknowledged as the founder of the Vincentians in America. The cause for his beatification was introduced in Rome in 1918.

See also VINCENTIANS (C.M.).

Cicognani, Amleto. "The Venerable Felix de Andreis, C.M. Vicar General of Upper Louisiana." *Sanctity in America.* Paterson: St. Anthony Guild, 1945, 77–82.

Easterly, Frederick J., C.M. *The Foundation of the Vincentians in the United States, 1816–1835.* Washington, D.C.: The Catholic University of America, 1938.

_____. "Many Things in a Short Time: Venerable Felix DeAndreis, C.M. (1778–1820)." *Portraits in American Sanctity,* ed. Joseph N. Tylenda. Chicago: Franciscan Herald, 1982, 44–56.

JOSEPH N. TYLENDA, S.J.

DEARDEN, JOHN FRANCIS (1907–88)

Cardinal archbishop. Born on October 15, 1907, in Valley Falls, Rhode Island, John Dearden went on to become one of several Cleveland priests promoted to the office of bishop during the episcopate of Archbishop-Bishop Edward F. Hoban. He came to great public prominence during and after the Second Vatican Council. As bishop of Pittsburgh, he was involved, like most American bishops of the 1950s, with numerous building projects to meet the ever-expanding educational, religious, and social need of

John Francis Cardinal Dearden

a rapidly increasing Catholic population. He was the first American bishop promoted to a vacant diocese by Pope John XXIII and, after going to Detroit in 1958, he was one of three American bishops appointed to the Doctrinal Commission on Faith and Practice (known as the Theological Commission) that Pope John XXIII had established to prepare for the Second Vatican Council. From 1959 to 1962 Dearden was involved in the preparation of conciliar documents. During the council he served on a number of conciliar commissions. He attended all four sessions of the council and during the last three sessions spoke to the council frequently from the floor.

After the council, Dearden was elected a member of the United States Bishops Commission on the Liturgical Apostolate and became the national episcopal leader in the implementation of English in the liturgy. Pope Paul VI also appointed him a member of the Secretariat for Non-Christian Religions, where he demonstrated the ecumenical concerns of the council. In 1966, when the American bishops established the National Conference of Catholic Bishops, Dearden was elected presiding bishop, an office he held for five years. During his years in this tremendously significant position (1966–71), the American Church experienced a host of inner conflicts that challenged both authority and tradition. His warm and gentle understanding of the concerns of others, his naturally conservative theological orientation and his progressive openness to reforming conciliar directions combined to make him a remarkably effective leader in times of turmoil and upheaval. Unlike many of his brother bishops, whose study had been in the area of canon law, Dearden was always the theologian reflecting his own education and his bent of mind. On occasion, when asked how radically he had changed from a rather formal and unbending young priest and bishop to the open-hearted and patient archbishop of Detroit, he would say, smiling, "I simply was obedient to the Church."

Dearden was instrumental in his archdiocese and in the American Church at large in extending to the laity and the clergy a participation in the life of the Church. In 1969, he finalized and promulgated an archdiocean synod (called Synod '69) which was the result of participation of all segments of the archdiocese for more than two years.

In 1976, to celebrate the bicentennial of the United States, the U.S. bishops planned two major events. One was a eucharistic congress, led by John Cardinal Krol of Philadelphia. The other was a National Justice Conference, entitled "Call to Action," led by Cardinal Dearden in Detroit. Preparations for "Call to Action" included hearings in designated regions and small group discussions in parishes around the country. From this process, there emerged consensus and recommendations from the grassroots on issues such as racism, the laity, women, sexuality, divorced Catholics, youth, and the quality of preaching. In October 1976 over two thousand delegates and observers met in Detroit to discuss and vote on the recommendations. Toward the end of the four-day conference, Cardinal Dearden was called upon to address the participants. As he came forward, all present rose to their feet and gave him a thunderous ovation lasting nearly twenty minutes.

In 1977 John Dearden suffered a major heart attack. After a period of convalescence, he resumed his office as archbishop of Detroit. He participated in the conclaves choosing Pope John Paul I and Pope John Paul II in 1978. In 1980, feeling a decline in health, Cardinal Dearden submitted his resignation as archbishop of Detroit to Pope John Paul II. The resignation was accepted and from 1980 until his death on August 1, 1988, John Dearden resided in Detroit.

His funeral took place in Blessed Sacrament Cathedral, Detroit. After the ceremony, as the procession began to take him to his grave, a tremendous ovation came forth from the packed church. It swelled and was sustained as a thunderous applause for fully ten minutes. As in 1976, so in 1988 and countless other times, the ovation spoke of the way people felt about John Cardinal Dearden.

Major events in Dearden's life may be summarized as follows: Education: St. Mary Seminary, Cleveland, 1924–28; North American College, Rome 1928–32; Pontifical Gregorian University, Rome 1932–34. Ordained 1932; pastoral work St. Mary's parish, Painesville, Ohio (Diocese of Cleveland) 1934–37; faculty St. Mary Seminary, Cleveland 1937–44; rector St. Mary Seminary, Cleveland 1944–48; coadjutor bishop of Pittsburgh 1948–50; bishop of Pittsburgh 1950–58; archbishop of Detroit, 1958–80; president, National Conference of Catholic Bishops 1966–71; Cardinal 1969–88; named to Worldwide Synod of Bishops, 1969, 1971, 1973 and 1975; Retired 1980–88.

See also VATICAN COUNCIL II AND AMERICAN CATHOLICS.

Hughes, Jane Wolford, ed. *In the Midst of His Flock, John Cardinal Dearden.* Detroit: Publications Office, Archdiocese of Detroit, 1980.

Tentler, Leslie Woodcock. *Seasons of Grace, a History of the Catholic Archdiocese of Detroit.* Detroit: Wayne State University Press, Great Lakes Books Edition, 1990.

NELSON J. CALLAHAN

DE ARVIDE, MARTÍN (?–1632)

Missionary, martyr. Martin de Arvide was born in Puerto de San Sebastian, Spain, at an unknown date. Arvide professed his vows as a Franciscan at the Convento de San Francisco, Spain, in 1612 and was sent with twenty-five other Franciscans to work in the New Mexico mission. There he labored among the Native American tribes, establishing the mission of San Lorenzo at Picurís, where he remained until 1628. Upon learning that the Jémez tribe had deserted their pueblos and were living in the mountains because of famine conditions and attacks by the Navajo tribe, he obtained permission from his superior, Fray Alonso de Benavides, and the territory's governor, Felipe Zotylo, to go and work among them. For the next four years he remained with the Jémez, helping to reestablish their community and restore peace to the area. In 1632 he was asked to establish a new mission among the Zipias tribe of Sonora. He was killed en route to Sonora by members of the Zuñi tribe. Known as the Apostle of Picurís, there is a monument dedicated to him at the Church of San Lorenzo.

TRICIA T. PYNE

DE BRÉBEUF, JEAN (1593–1649)

Saint, martyr, and French Jesuit missionary to French Canada. He was born on March 25, 1593, in Conde-sur-Vire, France, and studied at the University of Caen, 1609–10. At the age of twenty-four he entered the Jesuit novitiate at Rouen and was ordained in February 1622. He served as procurator of the Jesuit college at Rouen for the next two years.

In 1625 Jean de Brébeuf landed in Quebec with hopes of sailing up the St. Lawrence in order to work among the Huron Nation. After an earlier abortive attempt, Jean de Brébeuf, with help from Samuel de Champlain, left Quebec for the Huron territory, Huronia, in July 1626. The eight-hundred-mile trip to Huronia, a land south of present-day Georgian Bay, took three to four weeks.

He and other missionaries were forced to return to Quebec and then eventually to France in 1629 due to the capitulation of Quebec to the Kirke brothers fighting on behalf of English interests. However, with the signing of the treaty of Saint-Germain-en-Laye in 1632, France regained

Martyrdom of Jean de Brébeuf

control of New France and the Jesuit missionaries were able to return to Quebec and Huronia. Brébeuf and others made the arduous journey to Huronia in the summer of 1634. Shortly after arriving, the Jesuit missionaries established a small residence in one of the Huron villages. From this residence and its successors, Jean de Brébeuf and companions traveled throughout this area which was about forty miles long and twenty miles wide and at its height had thirty thousand people.

Brébeuf was head of this missionary territory for the next few years, and his writings, especially his *Relations,* illustrate his vast knowledge of the Hurons' language, customs, and suspicions. Despite the work of Jean de Brébeuf and others, evangelization was slow, and they often came under the suspicion of Huron chiefs who blamed them for smallpox epidemics and Iroquois attacks, which by 1639 had reduced the population to twelve thousand people.

From 1641 to 1644 Jean de Brébeuf served the Huron mission from Quebec as procurator. After acting as procurator he returned to Huronia and the next few years saw improvement in relations among the missionaries and Hurons. In March 1649, while working in the Huron village of St. Louis, Jean de Brébeuf and a companion, Gabriel Lalement, were captured by the Iroquois. After an extensive torture, he died on March 16, 1649. On June 29, 1930, Pius XI bestowed the title of saint and martyr upon Jean de Brébeuf and seven of his companions (Isaac Jogues, Gabriel Lalement, Charles Garnier, Antoine Daniel, Noel Chabanel, René Goupil, Jean de la Lande).

Brébeuf, Jean de. *Travels and Sufferings of Father Jean de Brébeuf among the Hurons of Canada as Described by Himself.* Trans. Theodore Besterman. London, 1938.

Macdougall, Angus. "Jean de Brébeuf/1593–1649." *Martyrs of New France,* ed. Angus Macdougall. Midland, Ontario: Martyrs Shrine, 1972.

Talbot, Francis X. *Saint Among the Hurons: The Life of Jean de Brébeuf.* Garden City, N.Y.: Doubleday and Company/Image Books, 1956.

JOSEPH M. McLAFFERTY

Related Document

"INSTRUCTIONS FOR THE FATHERS OF OUR SOCIETY WHO SHALL BE SENT TO THE HURONS," BY JEAN DE BRÉBEUF, S.J., 1637

One of the most resplendent periods in the history of French Catholicism occurred in the seventeenth century, and no finer pages in that history have been written than those which describe the heroic sacrifices made by the French Récollets, Jesuits, and other missionary priests in their efforts to win the Indians of France's North American colonies to the Catholic faith. That effort began in what is today Canada, but as time went on it was extended to areas south and west that embraced large sections of the present United States. Among the leaders of the Jesuits was an intrepid Norman, Jean de Brébeuf (1593–1649), who entered upon his extraordinary missionary career in 1625 at the age of thirty-two, and who persisted amid almost incredible suffering and privation until he was captured, tortured, and put to death in 1649 by a roving band of Iroquois in a raid on St. Ignatius and St. Louis Missions near Georgian Bay. Brébeuf had worked with the Huron Indians for several years and he could thus enlighten his confreres as to how they should conduct themselves among the savages. The following account was written in 1637 and foreshadowed the life of self-denial that awaited the missionaries. It was incorporated into the relation for 1637 by Paul le Jeune, S.J. St. Jean de Brébeuf was canonized by Pope Pius XI in 1930, along with seven of his fellow Jesuit martyrs of North America, of whom three met their deaths within the area of the present Diocese of Albany, New York.

(*Source:* Reuben Gold Thwaites, ed. *The Jesuit Relations and Allied Documents.* Cleveland: Burrows Brothers Co., 1898, XII, 117–23.)

THE FATHERS AND BRETHREN WHOM GOD SHALL CALL TO THE Holy Mission of the Hurons ought to exercise careful foresight in regard to all the hardships, annoyances, and perils that must be encountered in making this journey, in order to be prepared betimes for all emergencies that may arise.

You must have sincere affection for the Savages,—looking upon them as ransomed by the blood of the son of God, and as our brethren with whom we are to pass the rest of our lives.

To conciliate the Savages, you must be careful never to make them wait for you in embarking.

You must provide yourself with a tinder box or with a burning mirror, or with both, to furnish them fire in the daytime to light their pipes, and in the evening when they have to encamp; these little services win their hearts.

You should try to eat their sagamité or salmagundi in the way they prepare it, although it may be dirty, half-cooked, and very tasteless. As to the other numerous things which may be unpleasant, they must be endured for the love of God, without saying anything or appearing to notice them.

It is well at first to take everything they offer, although you may not be able to eat it all; for, when one becomes somewhat accustomed to it, there is not too much.

You must try and eat at daybreak unless you can take your meal with you in the canoe; for the day is very long, if you have to pass it without eating. The Barbarians eat only at Sunrise and Sunset, when they are on their journeys.

You must be prompt in embarking and disembarking; and tuck up your gowns so that they will not get wet, and so that you will not carry either water or sand into the canoe. To be properly dressed, you must have your feet and legs bare; while crossing the rapids, you can wear your shoes, and, in the long portages, even your leggings.

You must so conduct yourself as not to be at all troublesome to even one of these Barbarians.

It is not well to ask many questions, nor should you yield to your desire to learn the language and to make observations on the way; this may be carried too far. You must relieve those in your canoe of this annoyance, especially as you cannot profit much by it during the work. Silence is a good equipment at such a time.

You must bear with their imperfections without saying a word, yes, even without seeming to notice them. Even if it be necessary to criticise anything, it must be done modestly, and with words and signs which evince love and not aversion. In short, you must try to be, and to appear, always cheerful.

Each one should be provided with half a gross of awls, two or three dozen little knives, called jambettes (pocket-knives), a hundred fishhooks, with some beads of plain and colored glass, with which to buy fish or other articles when the tribes meet each other, so as to feast the Savages; and it would be well to say to them in the beginning, "Here is something with which to buy fish." Each one will try, at the portages, to carry some little thing, according to his strength; however little one carries, it greatly pleases the Savages, if it be only a kettle.

You must not be ceremonious with the Savages, but accept the comforts they offer you, such as a good place in the cabin. The greatest conveniences are attended with very great inconvenience, and these ceremonies offend them.

Be careful not to annoy anyone in the canoe with your hat; it would be better to take your nightcap. There is no impropriety among the Savages.

Do not undertake anything unless you desire to continue it; for example, do not begin to paddle unless you are inclined to continue paddling. Take from the start the place in the canoe that you wish to keep; do not lend them your garments, unless you are willing to surrender them during the whole journey. It is easier to refuse at first than to ask them back, to change, or to desist afterwards.

Finally, understand that the Savages will retain the same opinion of you in their own country that they will have formed on the way; and one who has passed for an irritable and troublesome person will have considerable difficulty afterwards in removing this opinion. You have to do not only with those of your own canoe, but also (if it must be so stated) with all those of the country; you meet some to-day and others to-morrow, who do not fail to inquire, from those who brought you, what sort of man you are. It is almost incredible, how they observe and remember even the slightest fault. When you meet the Savages on the way, as you cannot yet greet them with kind words, at least show them a cheerful face, and thus prove that you endure gayly the fatigues of the voyage. You will thus have put to good use the hardships of the way, and already advanced considerably in gaining the affection of the Savages.

This is a lesson which is easy enough to learn, but very difficult to put into practice; for, leaving a highly civilized community, you fall into the hands of barbarous people who care little for your Philosophy or your Theology. All the fine qualities which might make you loved and respected in France are like pearls trampled under the feet of swine, or rather of mules, which utterly despise you when they see that you are not as good pack animals as they are. If you go naked, and carry the load of a horse upon your back, as they do, then you would be wise according to their doctrine, and would be recognized as a great man, otherwise not. Jesus Christ is our true greatness; it is He alone and His cross that should be sought in running after these people, for, if you strive for anything else, you will find naught but bodily and spiritual affliction. But having found Jesus Christ in His Cross, you have found the roses in the thorns, sweetness in bitterness, all in nothing.

(*Source:* John Tracy Ellis, ed. *Documents of American Catholic History.* Vol. 1:1493–1865. Wilmington, Del.: Michael Glazier, 1987, 49–51.)

DE CORPA, PEDRO, AND FOUR COMPANIONS (d. 1597)

In the vicinity of San Agustín, the embryonic capital of Spain's settlement on the East Coast of North America, Spanish Franciscans were engaged in missionary activity by 1577. From that base they expanded their apostolic work to the territory along the coast, from Cumberland Island to Parris Island, and inland to the mid-peninsula. In the heart of that extensive stretch was the area known as Guale.

In 1584 eight more Franciscan friars arrived from Spain. With this increase of laborers, it became possible to initiate intensified apostolic work among the Guale natives.

One of the principal problems the missionaries encountered was that the chiefs *(caciques)* commonly had several wives. Their example contradicted the missionaries' teaching of monogamic Christian marriage. In September 1597 five friars working among the Guales were slain. The occasion of this violence was the missionaries' strong condemnation of the bad example of Juanillo, the young Catholic chief, commonly regarded as in line to become head of the tribe. He resented the correction of his bigamy and the admonition on the part of the missionaries. Five missionaries were slain within one week.

The first victim was Fray Pedro de Corpa, the superior of the mission. Fray Pedro was born in Villabilla, near Madrid, about the year 1560. Ordained to the priesthood probably about 1584, he came to the New World in 1587. On the morning of September 14, 1597, as he prepared to celebrate Mass, a group of natives, led by Juanillo, burst into his house and clubbed him to death.

The second friar to die was Fray Blas Rodríguez. Born in the Province of Caceres, as a young man he became a friar in the Franciscan Province of San Gabriel. Assigned to Mission Santa Clara in Tupiquí, where Juanillo, heir presumptive to the headship of the Guale tribe, resided, Fray Blas had to warn the young brave that his scandalous example in taking a second wife made him unworthy of becoming *cacique* of the tribe. In retaliation Juanillo launched the rebellion against the friars in general. Fray Blas was martyred on September 16 of that year.

Fray Miguel de Anon was the third friar to be slain. A native of Badajóz, he was a genuine son of St. Francis. Coming to Florida in the year 1595, he won the admiration of all who knew him. He was slain on the Island of Santa Catalina on September 17, the feast of the Stigmata of St. Francis. A lay brother, Fray Antonio de Badajóz was a member of the Franciscan Province of San Gabriel. He had come to Florida in 1587, and excelled in his command of the native language. He readily put his services at the disposition of his priestly fellow-friars and of the converts among the people. With Fray Miguel he was slain on the feast of the Stigmata of St. Francis.

The fifth friar killed in the uprising was Fray Francisco de Veráscola. He was the youngest of the five martyred missionaries, when he was slain being slightly over thirty-one years of age. His notable vitality made him especially popular among the young people of his mission, where he was accustomed to take part in their vigorous games. He had been put in charge of the mission to be founded on the island of Asao; to obtain materials needed for its construction he had gone to San Agustín before the revolt broke out. On his return to his post, he was treacherously attacked and brutally slain on the shore as he was about to land.

See also FRANCISCAN FRIARS.

Gannon, Michael V. *The Cross in the Sand.* 3rd ed. Gainesville, Florida, 1985.
Geiger, Maynard, O.F.M. *The Franciscan Conquest of Florida.* Washington, D.C., 1937.
Lanning, John Tate. *The Spanish Missions of Georgia.* Chapel Hill, 1935.

ALEXANDER WYSE, O.F.M.

DEFERRARI, ROY JOSEPH (1890–1969)

Classical scholar and educator. Roy Joseph was born on June 1, 1890, in Stoneham, Massachusetts, to Agostino Gianbattista Deferrari and Maria Crovo Deferrari, Italian immigrants. Roy was the fourth of six children who lived to adulthood. He studied in Stoneham's elementary school but traveled to Melrose for his high school education because his parents had learned that Melrose gave its students a better preparation for college than did Stoneham at that time, and they felt that quality education merited the extra effort and expense. During these years Roy also worked in his family's grocery store. He attended college at Dartmouth and received his bachelor of arts degree in 1912. He then studied for his doctorate at Princeton University. Upon receiving his Ph.D. in 1915, he was appointed to the faculty at Princeton and taught there for three years. After serving in the Army Air Service in World War I, Roy Deferrari joined the faculty of The Catholic University of America as Head of the Department of Greek and Latin on December 9, 1918.

The Catholic University of America

As head of the Greek and Latin Department, Deferrari helped build the department's reputation in patristics through his scholarly publications, his teaching and his administration. Early in his long career at The Catholic University, Deferrari became involved in the administration of the university. His administrative positions included director of the Summer Session, dean of the Graduate School of Arts and Science, chairman of Catholic University's Committee on Affiliation, and Secretary General of the University (1937–60). He took part in planning the reorganization of the university in 1930. He also encouraged the university's move toward enrolling women in its undergraduate programs and racially integrating the student population. Deferrari became well known for his administrative abilities early in his career. He was frequently recruited as a consultant on academic administration to colleges and universities, to members of the American hierarchy, and to major superiors of religious congregations in North and South America and in the Far East. He served on the Managing Committee of the American School of Classical Studies in Rome, The Dean's Conference of the Association of American Universities, and the Executive

Committee of the Middle States Association of Colleges and Secondary Schools. In 1945 President Truman named him to a mission of college educators sent to Japan to advise General MacArthur on education problems. Deferrari was awarded thirteen honorary degrees and was named a Knight of St. Sylvester by Pope John XXIII.

Publications

Deferrari was a part of many publications during his years at The Catholic University. In collaboration with colleagues and students, he developed several indexes and concordances, including a complete index of the *Summa Theologiae* of St. Thomas Aquinas (1956), *A Concordance of Lucan* (1940), *A Concordance of Ovid* (1939), *A Concordance of Prudentius* (1932), and *A Concordance of Statius* (1943). In addition, he edited the proceedings of workshops on college curricula, college administration, and the particular challenges of Catholic higher education. He also produced four books in a widely used series of Latin textbooks. He served as editor of the series *The Fathers of the Church, A New Translation*, which came to The Catholic University of America Press in 1947 largely through his own efforts. He was the sole translator of several volumes in the series, including *St. Basil, Letters; St. Ambrose, Theological and Dogmatic Works;* and *Orosius, Against the Pagans*.

Roy Deferrari's personal pride was his family—his parents, brothers and sisters, wife, children and grandchildren. His professional commitment of nearly fifty years was, in his own words, "to the importance of effective integrated Catholic education," whereby he meant primary, secondary and higher education appropriately rooted in religious instruction. He believed that Catholic teachers must strive to integrate their particular subject not only with other academic subjects and with the daily life of students but also with the spiritual life, "since the two are integrally related and are essentially one." After more than forty years of service to The Catholic University of America, Deferrari retired from its faculty in 1960. He died in Washington, D.C. on August 24, 1969.

See also CATHOLIC UNIVERSITY OF AMERICA, THE.

Deferrari, Roy J. *A Complete System of Catholic Education Is Necessary*. A Reply to *Are Parochial Schools the Answer?* by Mary Perkins Ryan. Boston: The Daughters of St. Paul, 1964.

———. *A Layman in Catholic Education: His Life and Times*. Boston: The Daughters of St. Paul, 1966.

———. *Memoirs of the Catholic University of America 1918–1960*. Boston: St. Paul Editions, 1962.

PATRICIA DeFERRARI

DEGGS, MARY BERNARD (CLEMENTINE) (1846–96)

Free woman of color, religious sister, and late nineteenth-century community journalist. Born Clementine Deggs (also Diggs) at Stony Point near Baton Rouge, Louisiana, on November 9, 1846, she was baptized into the Catholic Church in June, 1854. On May 7, 1873, she entered in New Orleans the Holy Family Sisters, a community of free women of color, founded by Henriette Delille in 1842. She made her first profession on August 14, 1875, taking the name Mary Bernard.

On March 19, 1894, Deggs began to record the history of her community in journal form. She wrote brief sections at each sitting, often leaving a thought or story half-finished and returning to the same story in later pages. Deggs recounts the community's history from its "umble [humble]" origins and depicts its spirit in candid, detailed portraits of five community leaders whom she knew personally. These personal portraits capture the community's spirituality, rooted in the call to work for "God's glory and his poor." The community is particularly called to minister to and uplift "our people" against a background of growing racism and oppression that coincided with the enactment of Jim Crow laws.

Deggs' journal is one of the remarkable women's journals of the late nineteenth century, centering on a community of women rather than an individual. The journal captures the way race, class, and gender, shaped the sisters' lives and work/ministry. Its unique linguistic style reflects Deggs' French and African background, teaching ministry, and often self-taught writing skills.

Deggs continued her journal until a few days before her death in New Orleans on March 26, 1896. She was buried in St. Louis Cemetery Number 2 in New Orleans.

Davis, Cyprian, O.S.B., Virginia Meacham Gould, Charles Nolan, and Sylvia Thibodeaux, S.S.F. "In That 'Umble House': The 1894–96 Holy Family Sisters Journal of Sister Bernard Deggs." Presentation to the American Catholic Historical Association, January 3, 1997.

Journal of Sister Mary Bernard Deggs and related records in Holy Family Sisters Archives, New Orleans.

Hart, Mary Francis Borgia. *Violets in the King's Garden: A History of the Sisters of the Holy Family of New Orleans*. New Orleans, 1976.

VIRGINIA MEACHAM GOULD AND CHARLES E. NOLAN

DELANEY, JOHN (1910–85)

Author, editor. A native New Yorker and a graduate of the College of the City of New York, he spent sixty years in the book business, close to fifty of which were devoted to Catholic publishing and writing. Beginning as a clerk, he later managed a retail book store, became a publisher's representative, handled advertising and promotion for several publishers, and was involved in mail order and book club activity as well.

Widely regarded as the dean of American Catholic publishing, Delaney conceived and developed Image Books, the premier line of Catholic paperbacks in this country, which began publishing in 1954 as a special imprint of Doubleday & Company. (The imprint remains alive as of this writing, more than four decades later.) From 1955 to 1967 he was also editor of the Catholic Family Book Club, the Catholic Youth Book Club, and Echo Books. He was president of the Religion Publishing Group from 1966 to 1968. He retired as director of the Catholic Book Department at Doubleday in 1976. Additionally, under his influence, effort, and tutelage, the English translation of the monumental *Jerusalem Bible* became a reality in the United States in 1966.

A four-time winner of the Thomas More Medal for his contributions to Catholic literature, Delaney was also recipient of the Catholic Press Association-Catholic Digest Award, as well as a Christopher Award for "his achievements in bringing high quality religious books to readers for 20 years." A frequent speaker before such groups as the Catholic Library Association, Delaney also published numerous magazine and newspaper articles. He was author of *Dictionary of Saints* (1980) and *Dictionary of American Catholic Biography* (1984), coauthor of *Dictionary of Catholic Biography* (1961) and *A Guide to Catholic Reading* (1966), translator of *The Practice of the Presence of God* (1977), and editor of fourteen works that include the six-volume Catholic Viewpoint Series (1956–61), *A Woman Clothed with the Sun* (1959), the four-volume Catholic Perspective Series (1966–68), and *Why Catholic?* (1979).

A man of vision, tenacity, and steadfast loyalty to his "mission" in the Church, Delaney worked with some of the greatest theologians and literary figures of this century. Throughout, he maintained the balance required of any good editor, recognizing the editor's crucial role in bringing ideas to printed fruition. And for him, as he remarked in a 1979 speech, "it has been a rich and rewarding experience." Undergirding that personal satisfaction, however, was "the hope that the books published under my aegis have played some role in advancing the message Christ has for all of us and that the Church for nineteen centuries, in good times and in bad, has tried to proclaim."

See also CATHOLIC BOOK PUBLISHING.

PATRICIA A. KOSSMAN

DELAWARE, CATHOLIC CHURCH IN

The earliest documented visit of a priest to what is now Delaware occurred in 1674 when the bishop of Quebec sent Jean Pierron to Maryland to investigate the need for a confirmation tour. The first-known Catholic to have settled in the area was Jacobus Seth, a Dutch sea captain, who received a grant of land near Lewes. In 1701 Joseph Weldon, a Catholic farmer from Maryland, settled in the southwestern corner of what is now New Castle County and began what developed by the 1730s into Delaware's largest community of Catholics during the colonial period.

By 1745 a second community evolved south of Dover around the Cain, Lober, and other families in present-day Willow Grove. The Jesuits founded a two-hundred-acre mission station there and attended it from Cecil County, Maryland, from 1747 to 1785. A third mission developed somewhat later in upper New Castle County at Cuba Rock where Mass was celebrated at the home of Con Hollahan. In 1772 the Jesuits established a two-hundred-acre mission nearby on which a chapel was built.

A host of French refugees who fled a 1795 revolution in Saint Domingue (now Haiti), took up residence in Wilmington. They settled amidst the existing Irish community, the members of which worked mainly at powder mills along the Brandywine River. During that time, Mass was celebrated for the French at the home of John Keating by Frs. Etienne Faure and Adrian Cibot. The Irish were cared for by priests from St. Mary's Church in Philadelphia. From 1794 to 1804 two Augustinians, John Rosseter and Matthew Carr, ministered to their needs, and from 1799 to 1804, a Capuchin, Charles Whelan.

Early Nineteenth Century

Fr. Patrick Kenny arrived from Ireland that year to begin a thirty-six-year ministry for Catholics at five stations and one church in Pennsylvania and Delaware. He lived at Coffee Run, where a log cabin had been built. Until 1808 when Delaware became part of the Diocese of Philadelphia, the territory was served by priests from both Maryland and Pennsylvania. In 1808 Fr. Kenny laid the cornerstone for St. Peter Church in New Castle and, in 1816, for Wilmington's St. Peter Church that eventually became the cathedral for the Wilmington diocese.

During the 1800s several waves of European immigrants added large numbers of Catholics to Wilmington parish rosters. Parishes were soon established to minister to their needs: St. Joseph on the Brandywine and St. Patrick for the Irish; Sacred Heart served the Germans; St. Hedwig and St. Stanislaus Kostka, the Poles; and St. Peter's Cathedral, St. Thomas and St. Anthony of Padua, the Italians.

During those years parochial and private schools were built and staffed by several religious communities. The Daughters of Charity of Emmitsburg, Maryland, Sisters of St. Joseph of Chestnut Hill, Pennsylvania, Benedictines from Newark, New Jersey, Felician Sisters of Lodi, New Jersey, Franciscan Sisters of Glen Riddle, Pennsylvania, Dominicans and Oblates of St. Francis de Sales all established foundations in the diocese. Also, the Daughters of Charity opened St. Peter Orphanage in 1830 for the many children whose parents had been killed by explosions at the powder mills.

Diocese of Wilmington

Wilmington was part of the Diocese of Philadelphia until 1868 when Pope Pius IX established a new diocese, encompassing Delaware and the Eastern Shore counties of Maryland and Virginia. The two Virginia counties were returned to Richmond in 1972. Thomas A. Becker was named the diocese's first bishop and headed the see until 1886. During his Wilmington tenure, Bishop Becker established eighteen churches, including the first Catholic church in Dover, and brought the Visitandines to the diocese to open an academy that was later staffed by the Ursulines when the Visitandines became a cloistered community.

The second ordinary of the diocese, Bishop Alfred A. Curtis, in his eleven-year tenure built twelve new churches, saw that individual parishes were legally incorporated, and enabled the Visitandines to establish a monastery. The Catholic population continued to grow over the next eighty-eight years. Four bishops—John J. Monaghan, Edmond J. FitzMaurice, Michael W. Hyle, and Thomas J. Mardaga—provided parishes, churches, schools, a hospital, and a Newman Center, as well as religious education resources. Robert E. Mulvee, who has placed strong emphasis on collegiality in diocesan administration, was installed as seventh bishop of the Wilmington diocese in 1985.

In 1994 the population of Delaware was 709,000, of which 17 percent (119,037) was Catholic.

Esling, Charles A. H. "Catholicity in the Three Lower Counties, or Planting of the Church in Delaware." *Records of the American Catholic Historical Society of Philadelphia* 1 (March 1886) 117–60.
Peterman, Thomas J. *Priests of the Century, 1868–1968.* Wilmington, Delaware, 1971.
____. "Thomas Andrew Becker, the First Catholic Bishop of Wilmington, Delaware, and Sixth Bishop of Savannah, Georgia, 1831–1899." Ph.D. dissertation, The Catholic University of America, 1981.
Quigley, Robert Edward. "Catholic Beginnings of the Delaware Valley." *History of the Archdiocese of Philadelphia,* ed. James F. Connelly. Philadelphia, 1976.

THOMAS J. PETERMAN

DE LEON, PONCE (ca. 1460–1521)

Explorer. Ponce de Leon was born to a noble family in San Servos in the province of Campos, Spain. As a young man he was a page in the court of Pedro Nuñez de Guzman and helped defend Spain against the Moors of Granada. In 1493 he accompanied Columbus on his second voyage to the New World and settled on the island of Hispaniola. He soon become an aide to the Spanish governor, Nicholas de Ovanda, excelled in this, and in 1502 was given command of the region around Higuey in the present-day Dominican Republic. Tantalized by stories from the native peoples about great treasure on the nearby island of Borinquen (Puerto Rico), in 1508 he set out on an expedition to find these treasures. He discovered gold, was named governor of the entire island, grew very rich and established the first European settlement there. However his stay there was short-lived, and in 1512 he was replaced as governor by Diego Columbus.

Still desirous of fortune, he set out for the island of Bimini in search of a fabled "fountain of youth." Instead of landing in Bimini, he wound up exploring the Atlantic coastline of present-day Florida although Ponce thought this region was an island. The area received its appellation from its Spanish explorers either for its lush flora or because it was discovered during Eastertide ("Pascua Florida"). His explorations took him up the Gulf coast of Florida as far as Cape Romano. Unsuccessful in finding a fountain of youth, in 1514 he was given jurisdiction by the Spanish crown of both Bimini and this new-found "island" of Florida. After an unsuccessful campaign against the Carib Indians south of Borinquen and a brief visit back to Europe, Ponce de Leon returned to Florida in 1521 to found a colony. His nascent settlement was destroyed by a local people, and he was wounded in this attack. He died of his injuries while traveling to Cuba.

ANTHONY D. ANDREASSI

DELILLE, HENRIETTE (1813–62)

Religious foundress. The youngest of three children, Henriette Delille was born in 1813 in New Orleans, Louisiana, in 1813, to Jean Baptiste Delille-Sarpy, a white Creole, and his mistress, Marie Joseph "Pouponne" Dias, a free woman of color. Delille's free black relatives were French-speaking, Roman Catholic Creoles.

Her early education consisted in learning how to be a mistress for a wealthy man—cultivating the charms needed for such a position, as well as studying music, dance, and French literature. However, Delille's mother taught her how to nurse and to prepare folk remedies from roots and herbs.

When she was eleven years old, Delille met a French nun of the Dames Hospitaliers who had opened a school in New Orleans in 1823 for young free girls of color. That meeting changed the course of her life, teaching her the value of prayer, how to teach religion to slaves, and how to minister to the needy.

Within a few years, Delille refused to attend social functions and condemned her older relatives' lifestyle of extramarital affairs. Even though her mother encouraged

Delille to enter a convent in France, she preferred to remain in New Orleans to continue her work there among the indigent.

In 1836 she joined a group of white and Creole women of color to establish a religious community, the Sisters of the Presentation. However, because of the community's interracial membership, the local Catholic Church hierarchy and the civil government reacted unfavorably, and the community disbanded.

The prospect of reestablishing a community increased when Fr. Etienne Jean François Rousselon, a French priest, arrived in New Orleans in 1837. When he became pastor of St. Augustine Parish in a Creole suburb, Delille was among a group of free women of color who was given permission by the bishop to form a religious community known as Sisters of the Holy Family.

In 1847, when the state legislature passed an act requiring incorporation of nonprofit societies, a lay Association of the Holy Family was formed to support the sisters. The association built a hospice in 1849 so the order could more easily conduct their ministry to the sick, aged, and poor. During epidemics of yellow fever, cholera, and malaria, the sisters had to open an annex to the hospice in 1860.

When Delille died in 1862, the order numbered only twelve sisters. The order had been permitted to accept only Creole free women of color, but following the Civil War the sisters gained permission to admit former black bondswomen into the community. Gradually, the sisters began to receive wider acceptance and acclaim from Church authorities for their work; however, it was not until 1872 that the Sisters of the Holy Family were permitted to wear religious habits.

An ironic footnote to Delille's life occurred in 1881 when the order purchased for their headquarters the former Orleans Ballroom in the French Quarter. The old dance floor, on which interracial alliances were inaugurated, became the convent chapel. Delille died November 16, 1862, in New Orleans.

Detiege, Audrey Marie, S.S.F. *Henriette Delille, Free Woman of Color: Foundress of the Sisters of the Holy Family.* New Orleans: Sisters of the Holy Family, 1976.

Hart, Mary Francis Borgia, S.S.F. *Violets in the King's Garden: A History of the Sisters of the Holy Family of New Orleans.* New Orleans: Sisters of the Holy Family, 1976.

Smith, Jessie Carney, ed. *Notable Black American Women.* Detroit: Gale Research Inc., 1992, 270–72.

MARIANNA McLOUGHLIN

DEMERS, MODESTE (1809–71)

Missionary. Honored as cofounder of the Church in Oregon and founder of the Church in British Columbia, Modeste Demers was born October 11, 1809, at St. Nicholas,

Quebec, Canada, son of Michel and Rosalie (Foucher) Demers. After education at the Quebec Seminary, he was ordained by Bishop Joseph Signay on February 7, 1836. His first mission at Trois-Pistoles, Quebec, lasted a year, and in 1837 Bishop Joseph Provencher persuaded the young priest to minister to the Native Americans at his Red River Mission, while awaiting orders to go to the Columbia mission in the Oregon Country. On July 10, 1838, Fr. Demers left for Oregon with his superior, Vicar General Fr. Francis Blanchet, and a Hudson's Bay Company brigade. During the long trip he celebrated the first Mass in the British Columbia interior at Big Bend on October 14, 1838.

The Oregon Mission

Within weeks of his arrival at Fort Vancouver on November 24, 1838, Demers' linguistic facility enabled him to preach, translate prayers, and teach hymns to the natives. From 1839 to 1844 he worked mainly in Native American missions north of the Columbia River, but in 1842 he began missionary work with tribes in the interior of British Columbia. While Francis Blanchet was in Europe from 1844–47, during which time the Oregon vicariate became the Archdiocese of Oregon City, Demers was pastor of Oregon City parish, building St. John's Church, which became the first cathedral, as well as serving as Oregon's vicar general, supervising church and school construction throughout the Oregon mission.

Bishop of Vancouver Island

Modeste Demers reluctantly accepted the post of bishop of Vancouver Island when Archbishop Francis Blanchet officiated at the first episcopal consecration in the Pacific Northwest at St. Paul on November 30, 1847. After attending the first provincial council of Oregon City in 1848, Demers departed at once for Europe to find support for his priestless and penniless diocese. On his return to North America he celebrated the first Mass in Seattle in August, 1852, before entering his see city of Victoria for the first time.

Bishop Demers brought Sisters of St. Anne from Quebec in 1858 to establish the Catholic school system on Vancouver Island. That same year the Oblates of Mary Immaculate entered the diocese, opening St. Louis College in Victoria in 1863, as well as beginning intensive work with the native tribes.

Diocese Reduced

At Bishop Demers' suggestion, the size of his vast diocese diminished when the mainland became the vicariate of British Columbia in 1863. The Oblates left Victoria for the new vicariate in 1866.

Constantly short of funds, Demers experienced great difficulty in attracting priests and building facilities, although he managed to erect St. Andrew's Cathedral, which he consecrated on December 5, 1858.

Demers participated in the First Vatican Council in 1869–70. On the way to the council, he suffered a compound leg fracture in a train accident in France. Shortly after his return to Victoria, he suffered a stroke from which he never recovered. He died July 28, 1871, and is buried in St. Andrew's Cathedral in Victoria.

See also OREGON, CATHOLIC CHURCH IN.

Hill, J. M. "The Most Reverend Modeste Demers, D.D. First Bishop of Vancouver Island." *Report of the Canadian Catholic Historical Association,* 1953, 29–35.

Lamirande, Emillien. "L'Implantation de l'Eglise Catholique en Colombie-Britannique 1838–1948." *Revue de L'Université d'Ottawa* 28 (June–December 1958) 213–15, 323–63, 453–87.

Morice, Adrian G. *History of the Catholic Church in Western Canada.* 2 vols. Toronto: Musson Book Co., 1910.

Steckler, Gerard G., S.J. "Charles John Seghers: Missionary Bishop in the American Northwest, 1839–1886." Ph.D. dissertation, Seattle, University of Washington Press, 1963.

PATRICIA BRANDT

DEMJANOVICH, MIRIAM TERESA (1901–27)

Spiritual writer. Teresa was born on March 26, 1901, in Bayonne, New Jersey, of parents who had immigrated to the United States in 1884 from Bardejov, Slovakia. The family belonged to the Byzantine Ruthenian Rite. She studied in Bayonne's local schools and on completing her high school education she felt called to the convent, but in view of her mother's illness and eventual death (1918), she considered it her duty to remain home and keep house for her father. In 1919 she began her studies at the College of St. Elizabeth, operated by the Sisters of Charity, in Convent Station (New Jersey), and after graduation (1923) taught English at St. Aloysius school in Jersey City. In February 1926, shortly after her father's death, she entered the Sisters of Charity and in the following May received the religious habit and the name Miriam Teresa.

While following her novitiate schedule, at the same time, beginning in June 1926, she taught at the academy affiliated with the convent. Because of her remarkable progress in the spiritual life, even before her entrance into religion, her spiritual director, with the knowledge of her superior, asked her to write conferences and instructions for her sister novices, which he then read to the community, without the community knowing the true author. In November of that year she became ill and when there was no sign or hope of her getting better, she was permitted to make her profession on April 2, 1927. She died on the following May 8. The conferences that she wrote were published in 1928 under the title *Greater Perfection.* Because of her reputation for holiness, the informative process investigating her cause for beatification was begun in December 1945.

Cicognani, Amleto. "Sister Miriam Teresa Demjanovich (1901–1927)." *Sanctity in America.* Paterson: St. Anthony Guild, 1945, 223–28.

Demjanovich, Charles C., ed. *Greater Perfection: Conferences of Sister Miriam Teresa.* New York: Kenedy, 1928.

Geis, M. Zita, S.C. "Unto Greater Perfection: Sister Miriam Teresa Demjanovich, S.C. (1901–1927)." *Profiles in American Sanctity,* ed. Joseph N. Tylenda. Chicago: Franciscan Herald, 1982, 298–311.

Maynard, Theodore. *The Better Part.* New York: Macmillan, 1952.

Sister of Charity. *Sister Miriam Teresa (1902–1927).* New York: Benziger, 1936.

JOSEPH TYLENDA, S.J.

DENECHAUD, CHARLES ISIDORE, SR. (1879–1956)

Attorney, civic and lay religious leader. Charles Isidore Denechaud was born in New Orleans on January 3, 1879, the son of Edward Francis Denechaud and Juanita Del Trigo. He attended the College of the Immaculate Conception, Tulane University (LL.B., 1901) and Loyola University (LL.D, 1924), all in New Orleans. He was admitted to the Louisiana bar and federal courts in 1901. He married Rose Stafford of Ontario, Canada, on October 30, 1907; the couple had four children: Rosemary, Kathleen, Charles I. Jr., and Margaret.

Denechaud was a member of New Orleans, Louisiana, and American Bar Associations and a professor of Civil Law at Loyola University where he received an honorary Doctor of Law Degree (1932). He served as attorney for Catholic Archdiocese of New Orleans; Loyola University; WWL Radio and later Television; and the New Orleans Chapter of American Red Cross among others.

Denechaud served in Paris as Overseas Commissioner for the National Catholic Welfare Council (1918–20). He was a special assistant to U.S. Attorney General and was appointed chairman of the local Disaster Relief Committee of the American Red Cross by Secretary of Commerce Herbert Hoover (1936). He served on numerous civic boards including the Louisiana State Welfare Board; the Commission on American Citizenship; the Louisiana State Hospital Board; the Board of Administrators of Charity Hospital; the Board of Commissioners of New Orleans City Park; the Board of Managers of the Hospital Association of New Orleans which he helped to organize; and the Board of Trustees of Catholic University of America. He also served on the Board of Directors of the National American Bank of New Orleans; the International Trade Mart; the United Service Corporation; the Louisiana League for the Hard of Hearing; the New Orleans Chapter of the

Red Cross; the Marquette Association for Higher Education; St. Mary's Boys' Orphan Asylum; Lakeshore Hospital; the Catholic School Board of the Archdiocese of New Orleans; and the Delgado Museum of Art. He served as chairman of the Board of Advisors of the Hôtel Dieu and Xavier University.

He served as district deputy of the Knights of Columbus (1904–17); president of the Federation of Catholic Societies of Louisiana (1908–12); national president of the American Federation of Catholic Societies (1912–14); chairman of the Executive Committee for the Diocesan Seminary Fund (1919); chairman of the Laymen's Committee for the Eighth National Eucharistic Congress (1938); member of the Executive Committee of the National Catholic Educational Association; and treasurer and member of the Executive Committee of National Council of Catholic Men.

Denechaud contributed "The Catholics of the South," to *Catholic Builders of the Nation* (1923). He was made a Knight of St. Gregory (1924) and Papal Chamberlain of the Cape and Sword to Pope Pius XI (1938); he received numerous other awards.

Denechaud died in New Orleans on October 21, 1956, and was interred in Metairie Cemetery. He was called "one of the most eminent attorneys of his time" (Davis, II:36). Archbishop Joseph F. Rummel eulogized him as "a Christian gentleman who dedicated his life to the service of God, the Church, civic interests and society."

Davis, Edwin Adams. *Catholic Action of the South*, October 28, 1956, and passim.
———. *The Story of Louisiana*. New Orleans, 1960.

CHARLES E. NOLAN

DENVER CATHOLIC REGISTER

He may have been a diminutive man at five feet, four inches, but from 1913 until his death in 1960, Msgr. Matthew Smith, editor in chief of the *Denver Catholic Register* and the *Register System of Newspapers* cast a long shadow on the face of Catholic journalism in the United States. Under his innovative leadership, the *Register* courageously confronted the Ku Klux Klan, and in its peak years, had a circulation of 800,000, and published 38 diocesan weeklies nationwide.

The Early Years

The later success of the *Register* could not have been foreseen during the efforts to produce a Catholic newspaper in the early days of Colorado Catholicism.

Established as a diocese in 1887, Colorado was a vast, untamed territory. In 1884 the *Colorado Catholic* became the first Catholic newspaper in the state. Taking over sole control of the journal in 1890 was Fr. Thomas Malone,

pastor of Denver's St. Joseph Redemptorist parish. When Fr. Malone combined the finances of his parish with the newspaper, a series of confrontations ensued with Bishop Nicholas Matz.

Succeeding Colorado's pioneer bishop Joseph Machebeuf in 1889 Bishop Matz faced not only daunting pastoral and financial responsibilities, but also the rebellious Fr. Malone, who used the pages of the *Colorado Catholic* to regularly attack the French-born prelate, most notably over Bishop Matz' handling of Bishop Machebeuf's estate and the establishment of Mt. Olivet Cemetery, still the official cemetery of the Archdiocese of Denver.

The Birth of Denver Catholic Register

In 1905, frustrated by Fr. Malone's continued use of the *Colorado Catholic* to challenge his authority, Bishop Matz decided that the diocese should have its own official newspaper. On August 11, 1905, the *Denver Catholic Register* was born. But it was not until eight years later when Matz hired Matthew J. Smith, a young telegraph editor from a southern Colorado newspaper, *The Pueblo Chieftan*, that the fortunes of this struggling diocesan weekly began to turn around.

One of six children of an Irish immigrant family, Matthew John Willfred Smith was born in Altoona, Pennsylvania, on June 9, 1892. After the death of his wife from tuberculosis, Matthew's father began to send his children one by one to semiarid Colorado, where the dry climate was healthier. At the age of twenty-one, Matthew Smith arrived in Pueblo. Having four years' newspaper experience with the *Altoona Tribune*, the young Smith quickly landed a job with the *Chieftan* as a telegraph editor. After a few months, Smith ventured to Denver where he met with another transplanted Pennsylvanian, Fr. Hugh McMenamin, the owner of the *Denver Catholic Register*. He offered the cub reporter a job, and in October 1913 appointed Smith editor.

The new editor immediately began to change the face of the *Register* by employing the use of photographs, bold headlines and establishing a system of parish stringers so that the vast diocese could have a more local feel. He also convinced Bishop Matz to make the *Register*, though still privately owned, the official diocesan newspaper. Bishop Matz agreed, under the condition that Fr. McMenamin put his imprimatur on the content. Matthew Smith also began studying for the priesthood at St. Thomas Seminary, in between his editorial duties.

In 1921 Bishop J. Henry Tihen, who succeeded Bishop Matz in 1917, decided to purchase the *Register* for five thousand dollars from Fr. McMenamin's Catholic Publishing Company. Within a year, the *Register* had moved out of the offices it had shared with a livestock journal. In 1923 Matthew Smith was ordained a priest, with the primary duty of overseeing the growing diocesan weekly.

Two years later, the *Register* again moved into larger quarters, while at this same time taking on the Ku Klux Klan, which made the *Register* and its feisty Irish editor well known outside Catholic Church circles.

Confronting the Klan

The Ku Klux Klan in Colorado, seizing upon the antiforeign sentiment that sprang from World War I, began to dominate Colorado politics in the 1920s. At its peak, the KKK controlled the Colorado General Assembly, and had among its members the governor of Colorado and the mayor of Denver.

Along with other crusaders, Fr. Smith—in the face of recurring threats—challenged the Klan routinely in his editorials, listed the names of Klansmen in the *Register,* and in the 1925 city elections, named the candidates for public office who were Klan sympathizers. Despite their large numbers in the political infrastructure of Colorado, the KKK was never able to translate their bigoted ideology into any sustaining type of legislation. In his 1948 memoirs, the then Msgr. Smith gave some insight into the reasons why: "I was never long in the dark . . . about what the organization was doing," he wrote. "John Galen Locke, grand dragon of the Klan . . . told me, after the movement was virtually dead, that I had accurate inside information. He thought that I must have had five or six spies in the organization. I did not have one. There were a number of political leaders in Colorado who had agents in the Klan. They kept me well informed."

The Register *System of Newspapers*

By 1927 the KKK influence was waning, and Fr. Smith began implementing other changes in the *Register.* Now in its own publishing plant in Denver, the first national edition of the *Register* was launched. In a unique arrangement, diocesan news was printed on the front page of the local edition, with national and international news inside.

In 1929 the *Register* published its first paper for a diocese outside Colorado when it began printing issues for the dioceses of Fresno and Monterey, California. Expanding and enlarging its plant in 1934, 1938, and 1940, by the time Denver was established as an archdiocese in 1941, the *Register* had become one of the most widely circulated religious newspapers in the world.

The End of an Era

By the mid-1950s, however, many dioceses began breaking away from the *Register* system, seeking more editorial autonomy. By the time of Msgr. Smith's death in 1960, the end was in sight for the network he had founded, as rival publications began to emerge.

When he assumed control of the archdiocese in 1967, Archbishop James V. Casey found the circulation of the *Register* system dwindling and deeply in debt. To ease the financial crunch, he sold the system to Twin Circle Publishing of Culver City, California, thus ending what had been a chain of Catholic newspapers unlikely ever to be rivaled again.

Now a thirty-page tabloid, in 1995 the *Denver Catholic Register* has a circulation of 87,000, making it one of Colorado's most widely distributed weekly newspapers.

But the enduring legacy of Msgr. Matthew Smith's vision can still be seen by the number of Catholic newspapers across the United States that still bear *Register* name on their flags and mastheads.

See also CATHOLIC PRESS (NEWSPAPERS) IN AMERICA.

Johnson, Richard S. "Inspiring the Faith." *Empire* magazine. Supplement to the *Denver Post,* March 4, 1979.

McNeill, Charles J. "The Catholic Church in Colorado." *Colorado,* eds. Leroy R. and Ann Hafen. Denver, 1953, 519–22.

Noel, Thomas J. *Colorado Catholicism.* Denver, 1989.

Noel, Thomas J., and Stephen J. Leonard. *Denver: Mining Camp to Metropolis.* Denver, 1990.

Smith, Matthew J. "Memoirs." Serialized in the *Denver Catholic Register,* 1948–49.

KEITH COFFMAN

DE OÑATE, JUAN (ca. 1549–ca. 1626)

Spanish explorer. Born ca. 1549 into a family that was both politically and financially influential in New Spain (Mexico), Oñate became active in the king's service at an early age. His father, Cristóbal de Oñate, was one of the richest men in the Americas and was named governor of Nueva Galicia in 1538. His mother, Dona Cathalina de Salazar, was a daughter of Gonzalo de Salazar who held the post of royal factor.

Although his maternal grandfather was an enemy of Hernán Cortés, Oñate married Isabel Tolosa, a descendant of Cortés and Montezuma; the couple had two children. In 1595 Oñate received a royal contract to explore and colonize the territory north of Mexico. Political maneuverings delayed the expedition of four hundred settlers, natives, and cattle until 1598.

After claiming the land for the Spanish crown and naming it New Mexico, Oñate established San Juan de los Caballeros, about thirty miles north of present-day Santa Fe, New Mexico. He governed the territory from there and organized districts for political and religious purposes. However, in 1599 the Pueblos at Acoma revolted, and he reportedly used cruel measures to suppress the revolt.

From his base in New Mexico, Oñate led expeditions to Kansas in 1601 and to the Gulf of California in 1605—all in search of reputed riches that he could claim for the Spanish crown. During his absences, discontent had grown in the colony, and Oñate petitioned the crown to appoint a new governor, which did not occur until 1609.

In 1614 he was tried on charges of misconduct in office, mistreatment of soldiers and native peoples, and disobedience to viceregal orders. He was convicted and sentenced not only to perpetual banishment from New Mexico, but also from Mexico for four years and fined six thousand ducats. Oñate was unsuccessful in 1622 in obtaining an appeal of his sentence; however, he may have obtained a pardon from the king in 1624 when he requested a position in Mexico or the Philippines—a request that was denied.

Even though Oñate's exploration opened up vast territory in the New World to Spanish control, he had found no treasures on his expeditions. Therefore, his accomplishments were neither appreciated nor acknowledged by Spanish authorities at the time. Only through the writings of Gaspar de Villagrá, one of Oñate's lieutenants who recorded the explorer's exploits in *Historia de la Nueva Mexico,* has Oñate's role in history been remembered and celebrated.

Who Was Who in American History. History Volume 1607–1896. Chicago: Marquis Who's Who Inc., 1967, 215.

MARIANNA McLOUGHLIN

DE PADILLA, JUAN (ca. 1500–42)

Missionary and martyr. Little is known about the first priest martyred in territory which later became part of the United States. He joined the Friars Minor in Spain, and in 1528 sailed as a missionary to Mexico. He was actively connected with several expeditions and was zealously engaged in missionary activities. He founded Franciscan friaries at Tzapoltán and Tamasula, and was chosen as superior at Tulantzingo. He was a seasoned missionary and traveler when he joined Francisco de Coronado's expedition to New Mexico in 1540. He visited the Hopi Pueblos, and stayed for about two months with the Rio Grande Pueblos. When in early 1542 Coronado decided to return to Mexico, Juan de Padilla decided to stay and work among the natives. With Andres de Campo, his Portuguese companion and some assistants including some native Wichita men, he decided to trek to Quivera where he was well received. While traveling, an unidentified native killed him near what is now Herington, Kansas.

MICHAEL GLAZIER

Related Document

JUAN DE PADILLA, THE PROTOMARTYR
OF THE UNITED STATES, IS MURDERED
BY THE PLAINS INDIANS, c. 1542

In the three centuries between the entrance of the first priests into Florida in the early 1520's and the founding of the last of the California missions at San Francisco Solano in July, 1823,

hundreds of Catholic missionaries labored in every section of what was to become the United States in an effort to convert the native Indians to Christianity. In the attempt many of these men met death at the hands of the savages. On the epochal exploring expedition of Coronado which started north from old Mexico in February, 1540, and during the next two years traversed so large a part of the American Southwest, there were three Franciscan friars, Fathers Juan de Padilla and Juan de la Cruz, and Brother Luis de Ubeda (DeEscalona). When Coronado turned back in disappointment in the spring of 1542 the friars remained behind in the hope of evangelizing the Indians. Soon thereafter Padilla was murdered by the red men and thus became the protomartyr of the future United States; the other two were never heard from again. In the account which follows, written by one of Coronado's soldiers, Pedro de Castañeda, he described the little that is known about the fate of the friar. The exact date and location of Padilla's death are uncertain, although most authorities think it took place shortly after Coronado's departure southward and probably occurred somewhere in southern Kansas.

(*Source:* "The Narrative of the Expedition of Coronado by Castañeda," Frederick W. Hodge and Theodore H. Lewis, eds. *Spanish Explorers in the Southern United States, 1528-1543.* New York: Charles Scribner's Sons, 1907, 372–74; now included in *Original Narratives of Early American History,* copyright Barnes & Noble, Inc., New York.)

WHEN THE GENERAL, FRANCISCO VÁSQUEZ,[1] SAW THAT everything was now quiet, and that his schemes had gone as he wished, he ordered that everything should be ready to start on the return to New Spain by the beginning of the month of April, in the year 1543 [1542].

Seeing this, Friar Juan de Padilla, a regular brother of the lesser order, and another, Friar Luis [De Escalona], a lay brother, told the general that they wanted to remain in that country—Friar Juan de Padilla in Quivira, because his teachings seemed to promise fruit there, and Friar Luis at Cicuye.[2] On this account, as it was Lent at the time, the father made this the subject of his sermon to the companies one Sunday, establishing his proposition on the authority of the Holy Scriptures. He declared his zeal for the conversion of these peoples and his desire to draw them to the faith, and stated that he had received permission to do it, although this was not necessary. The general sent a company to escort them as far as Cicuye, where Friar Luis stopped, while Friar Juan went on back to Quivira with the guides who had conducted the general, taking with him the Portuguese, as we related, and the half-blood, and the Indians from New Spain. He was martyred a short time after he arrived there, as we related in the second part, Chapter 8.[3] Thus we may be sure that he died a martyr, because his zeal was holy and earnest.

Friar Luis remained at Cicuye. Nothing more has been heard about him since, but before the army left Tiguex[4] some men who went to take him a number of sheep that were left for him to keep, met him as he was on his way to visit some other villages, which were fifteen or twenty leagues from Cicuye, accompanied by some followers. He felt very hopeful that he was liked at the village and that his teaching would bear fruit, although he complained that the old men were falling away from him. I, for my part, believe that they finally killed him. He was a man of good and holy life, and may Our Lord protect him and grant that he may convert many of those peoples, and end his days in guiding them in the faith. We do not need to believe otherwise, for the people in those parts are pious and not at all cruel. They are friends, or rather, enemies of cruelty, and they remained faithful and loyal friends.

After the friars had gone, the general, fearing that they might be injured if people were carried away from that country to New Spain, ordered the soldiers to let any of the natives who were held as servants go free to their villages whenever they might wish. In my opinion, though I am not sure, it would have been better if they had been kept and taught among Christians. . . .

[1]Francisco Vásquez Coronado (1510–1554) was Governor of Nueva Galicia and leader of the expedition.

[2]Cicuye was synonymous with Pecos in New Mexico.

[3]At the point referred to Castañeda stated: "A friar named Juan de Padilla remained in this province, together with a Spanish-Portuguese and a negro and a half-blood and some Indians from the province of Capothan in New Spain. They killed the friar because he wanted to go to the province of the Guas [possibly the Kaw or Kansa Indians], who were their enemies. . . . The Indians from New Spain who accompanied the friar were allowed by the murderers to bury him . . ." (364–65).

[4]Tiguex was situated at the site of Bernalillo on the Rio Grande River in what is today New Mexico.

(*Source:* John Tracy Ellis, ed. *Documents of American Catholic History.* Vol. 1:1493–1865. Wilmington, Del.: Michael Glazier, 1987, 9–10.)

DePAUL UNIVERSITY

DePaul University has been a significant force in the Chicago area for almost one hundred years. In 1995 it included 16,700 students in eight colleges and schools on five campuses, and international programs and partnerships with governments and institutions around the globe. It was the largest Catholic university in the Midwest and the second largest in the country. It is an urban university which has influenced the development of two of the Chicago's neighborhoods: Lincoln Park where it has its original campus, and the south Loop, its downtown campus.

In 1898, at the request of the first archbishop of Chicago, the Vincentian Fathers (Congregation of the Mission) opened St. Vincent's College as a small liberal arts school in a three-story building on the near north side of Chicago. The first students were young men from immigrant, working-class families who desired a classical and professional education. The growing college was rechartered in 1907 as DePaul University, named for its patron, St. Vincent de Paul, the founder of the Congregation of the Mission whose vision and values were reflected in the academic curriculum and student programs. This new charter was an attempt to establish a Catholic university with the highest standards of scholarship and excellence. The charter excluded any test of religious persuasion for admission or faculty hiring, and students of all religions and races found a welcome home at DePaul. In 1911 DePaul was one of the first Catholic universities in the country to offer degrees to women students.

The university expanded rapidly by affiliating with the Illinois College of Law (1912), opening the School of Music (1912) and the College of Commerce (1913). In 1915, to accommodate the working students, the commerce and law classes were moved to the Loop (downtown).

The School of Education was established in 1962 to unify and enhance teacher education which was being done in several colleges. A nontraditional, competency-based undergraduate and graduate school for adults which combined life experience with academic study was opened in 1972 as the School for New Learning. DePaul acquired the prestigious Goodman School of Drama in 1978 and renamed it the Theatre School ten years later. The School of Computer Science, Telecommunications and Information Systems was established in 1995. Expansion into the suburbs started in 1975 with the opening of the O'Hare campus, followed by the Oak Brook campus in 1986 and the South campus (Oak Forest) in 1993. Making higher education accessible to the qualified poor and disadvantaged has always been a priority for DePaul. In the early years the focus was on the sons and daughters of immigrants. In 1996, 25 percent of the student body were people of color.

See also CATHOLIC UNIVERSITIES AND COLLEGES.

JOHN MINOGUE, C.M.

de RÉMUR, SIMON BRUTÉ (1779–1839)

Missionary, educator, bishop. He was born on March 20, 1779, in Rennes, France, of Simon Bruté de Rémur and Jeanne Renée Le Saulnier de Vauhelle Vatar. During the Terror, he witnessed the execution of priests and nobles and brought some prisoners the Eucharist. He graduated first in his medical class in Paris in 1803, but chose to become a Sulpician, being ordained on June 11, 1808. He knew Félicité de Lamennais at this time and kept in correspondence with him all his life, trying to reconcile him to the Church in the early 1830s. While teaching theology at Rennes, he responded to Benedict Flaget's 1810 visit and left with him for the United States as a missionary, taking his five thousand books as well. He served at St. Mary's Seminary, Baltimore (1810–12, as professor; 1815–18, as president), and at Mount St. Mary's College, Emmitsburg (1812–15, as professor; 1818–34, as president), and left the Sulpicians in 1826 when the college ceased to be in their care. While in Emmitsburg he served as spiritual director to Mother Elizabeth Seton, each holding the other in affection.

Despite a reputation for restlessness, moodiness, a poor pronunciation of English, and weak management skills, he was consecrated the first bishop of Vincennes (now Indianapolis) on October 28, 1834. He had five difficult years on this frontier as he increased the clergy and churches, recruited in Europe, and began educational institutions (a seminary, a girls' academy, and a college) for his 25,000 Catholics. This intellectual died at Vincennes on June 26, 1839, after two years of poor health.

Bayley, J. *Frontier Bishop: The Life of Bishop Simon Bruté.* Huntingdon, Ind., 1971.

Kauffman, C. *Tradition and Transformation in Catholic Culture: The Priests of Saint Sulpice in the United States from 1791 to the Present.* New York, 1988.

McAvoy, Thomas T. *The Catholic Church in Indiana, 1789–1834.* New York, 1940.

Trisco, Robert. *The Holy See and the Nascent Church in the Middle Western United States, 1826–1850.* Rome, 1962.

EARL BOYEA

DE SMET, PETER JOHN (1801–73)

Jesuit missionary. De Smet was born on January 30, 1801, in Dendermonde, Belgium. He made his initial landing on the St. Louis levee at the close of May 1823. Still in religious training as a novice, De Smet was then preparing for membership in the Society of Jesus. As a young immigrant of Belgium background, De Smet was also working to gain a mastery of the English language.

Peter J. De Smet

Fifty years later—almost to the day—the newspapers of St. Louis reported on the termination of De Smet's career. Noting details of the funeral service, the press also provided an obituary tribute to this priest who had gained an exceptional public reputation: "The St. Louis University Church was thronged last evening with people anxious to take a last look at the familiar face. . . . The funeral today will be one of the largest ever witnessed in the city."

Within that half century, De Smet had indeed become widely known. He had gained an outstanding reputation in both the city and the country he had gratefully adopted, and in the Old World as well. It was a reputation based upon a unique relationship between De Smet and the Native Americans of the West.

De Smet and the Native Americans

This Native American–De Smet relationship was spiritual: De Smet was "Blackrobe," a revered leader whose services were requested by the religious-minded Indians. It was a lasting relationship: two successive generations of tribal leaders sought De Smet's guidance. Also, in extent it was a quasi-universal relationship: Blackrobe served the diverse tribes of the Buffalo culture—a people spread across the central and northern plains—and he was also similarly related to the tribes of the Pacific Northwest. According to various knowledgeable people of the period, De Smet was reported to have been "the most influential white man on the Great Plains."

Yet, how did such a relationship, one exercised beyond the frontier, contribute to the elevation of De Smet into prominence in the non-native world? It was a special combination of factors—some, unique to the period—that fashioned De Smet's standing as "the most widely known American Jesuit of the nineteenth century."

Within the central half of that century, the status of these indigenous peoples was abruptly altered. The golden age of their Buffalo culture was so quickly terminated by the destruction of their native economy— the tremendous herds had answered all their material needs—that the tribes were plunged into utter impoverishment. In the 1840s De Smet had been so impressed by their achievements that he dreamed of the possibility of fashioning an independent Native American Empire. Already by 1851, at the First Fort Laramie Treaty Council, conditions had been so altered that De Smet endorsed the government's proposal pointing to "peaceful coexistence." By 1868—the Second Fort Laramie Treaty—the total extinction of the herds was being finalized; and De Smet and native leaders realized that major cultural adjustments were required in order to avoid tribal extinction.

Within that half century, De Smet's thinking, as based upon his firsthand experiences in the native world, became widely known. His writings, mostly in the form of

Pauline epistolary reports, were popularized by translations into the various European languages. "In journeys, often," this Peter was also like the renowned Paul. De Smet spent only about one-third of his days at his St. Louis University headquarters. He established this travel record for his time: in addition to nine business trips to Europe, some twenty departures were made from the St. Louis levee on westward voyages up "my beloved Missouri." More than any other St. Louisan, De Smet lived the twofold activity symbolized by the Arch at the Gateway City: De Smet experienced and reported the national Westward Expansion—as an invasion.

De Smet and the Jesuits

Through the third quarter of that century, the official assignments of Jesuit De Smet were Jesuit-oriented. He served the Missouri province Jesuits as their "procurator," and this, through a tense period of "procuring" the needed funding, as well as of supervising the financial operations. In addition, he was their main "procurer" of necessary manpower: consequent to his European trips, De Smet as an early "vocation director" led almost one hundred candidates to join his Missouri brethren. Further—and prior to the formal recognition of such a term and office—De Smet labored effectively as "public relations director" for the Jesuits. Directly, then, as a field missionary, De Smet served the tribes for only ten years; yet, throughout his lifetime, he managed to combine his personal Native American apostolate with his assigned Jesuit services.

This combination of his talents and interests, both personal and religious, as well as his labors on official assignments—all led De Smet into marketplace activities that were regarded as unique for the priest of his day. Consequent to a factual appreciation of his intercessory influence with tribal leaders, De Smet was courted by the generals of the army of the West; by the merchant princes working out of the frontier; and by the political leaders engaged in directing the Westward Expansion effected in this half century. In a special and highly demanding role, Blackrobe De Smet served in a praiseworthy manner. He died on May 23, 1873.

See also JESUITS IN AMERICA, THE.

Carriker, Robert C. *Father Peter John de Smet: Jesuit in the West.* Norman: University of Oklahoma Press, 1995.

Chittenden, Hiram M., and Albert T. Richardson. *Life, Letters and Travels of Father Pierre-Jean De Smet, S.J., 1801–1873* 4 vols. New York, 1905; repr. New York, 1969.

Killoren, John J., S.J. *"Come, Blackrobe": De Smet and the Indian Tragedy.* Norman, Oklahoma, 1994.

Laveille, E., S.J. *The Life of Father De Smet, S.J., 1801–1873.* New York, 1915.

JOHN J. KILLOREN, S.J.

DE SOTO, HERNANDO (ca. 1500–42)

Explorer. De Soto was born in Barcarrota, Spain, to a poor noble family. He was educated at the University of Salamanca under the patronage of Pedrarias Davila. In 1519 he accompanied Davila to Central America and served in his army there. He served in the forces that conquered the native peoples in both Honduras and Nicaragua and in

Hernando De Soto

1532 went to Peru. After discovering the capital of the Incas, he was made ambassador to Atahualpa, leader of the Incas. De Soto become rich from the booty taken from the Incas, returned to Spain, and in 1537 married Ines de Bobadilla, daughter of Davila. Soon his wanderlust returned; he sold his property in Spain, and he was made governor of Cuba by the Emperor Charles V. In 1539 he and an army left Cuba for Florida in search of great treasure. Fed by rumors of great wealth, De Soto wound up traveling as far as Oklahoma crazed with the hope of finding enormous treasures. Throughout these travels De Soto treated his Native Americans with extreme cruelty and contempt in order to control them. He was not successful in finding treasure and died of a fever on the Mississippi River around May 21, 1542. His companions unceremoniously dumped his corpse in the Mississippi River for fear that Native Americans might discover that the great conqueror was dead and revolt.

ANTHONY D. ANDREASSI

DICKINSON, FRANCES (1755–1830)

Carmelite prioress. Frances Dickinson was born in London, England, on July 12, 1755. Her father was George

Dickinson and her mother's family name was Halford. She had brothers, at least one sister and was educated by the Ursulines in Paris. In 1772 she joined the Carmelites in Antwerp, bringing a dowry of one hundred pounds sterling, was professed as Clare Joseph of the Sacred Heart in 1773, and at thirty-five left as a missionary for Maryland, never again to see family or friends.

Her legacy includes a diary of the three-month ocean voyage from the Netherlands made by the four founding Carmelites and two ex-Jesuits in 1790. Impressive for its honesty, sense of humor, and lack of drama in the face of extreme conditions, the diary does not hide the disdain which she and her cultured companions felt for the captain's mean, revolting behavior. It reveals an overwhelming sense of God's intervention in ordinary events and deep desires for frequent Communion familiar to Teresian and Ignatian spirituality but frowned upon by Jansenists and the more rigorous French spirituality.

Like her predecessor, Bernardina Matthews, Clare Joseph transmitted to the first American Carmelites the positive value of freedom of conscience, reinforcing it in her last illness. She helped to compile the *Pious Guide to Prayer and Devotion,* published in 1792 by the Georgetown Jesuits and designed in part to refute the Jansenist criticism of the Sacred Heart devotion. However, she also left numerous spiritual writings indicative of a tendency toward a more rigoristic tradition, one she shared with Jesuit Charles Neale, her chief collaborator in the guidance of the community. He lived at Port Tobacco until his death. One cannot overestimate the influence of this partnership on the development of Carmelite life. Clare Joseph's relationships with the first U.S. bishops, John Carroll, Leonard Neale, Simon Bruté, Benedict Flaget, Ambrose Maréchal, and all the early Jesuits, including Benedict Fenwick, underline the value she placed on friendship in contemplative prayer ministry. This is a notable part of her legacy. When Clare Joseph died after thirty years as prioress at the Port Tobacco Carmel on May 27, 1830, twenty-nine Carmelites had been professed in the first U.S. Carmel, ten of these during Bernardina's lifetime.

See also CARMELITE NUNS, DISCALCED (O.C.D.).

Curran, R. E., ed. *American Jesuit Spirituality: The Maryland Tradition, 1634–1900.* New York: Paulist Press, 1988.
FitzGerald, C. *The Carmelite Adventure.* Baltimore: Carmelite Sisters, 1990.
Hardman, A. *English Carmelites in Penal Times.* London: Burns Oates and Washbourne, 1936.
Spalding, T. *The Premier See: A History of the Archdiocese of Baltimore, 1789–1889.* Baltimore: Johns Hopkins University Press, 1989, 1–5.

CONSTANCE FITZGERALD, O.C.D.

DIEGO Y MORENO, FRANCISCO GARCIA (1785–1846)

Bishop. Francisco Garcia Diego y Moreno was born on September 17, 1785, at Lagos de Moreno, Mexico, the son of Francisco and Ana Maria (Moreno) Gracia Diego. Invested with the religious habit of the Order of Friars Minor at the College of Nuestra Señora de Guadalupe on November 26, 1801, Francisco was ordained priest on November 14, 1808, by Bishop Primo Feliciano Marin de Porras of Linares.

Upon completion of his service as novice master for the Franciscan community at Zacatecas, Fray Francisco Garica Diego was elected Comisario-Prefecto of the missions attached to the apostolic college. In 1832 he led a contingent of friars to peninsular California and then north to Alta California, arriving at Santa Clara Mission where he labored for several years.

On April 27, 1840, Pope Gregory XVI erected the Diocese of Both Californias naming Fray Francisco Garcia Diego as the proto-bishop of the new jurisdiction. The friar was consecrated by Bishop Antonio Maria de Jesus Campos on October 4, 1840 at the National Shrine of Our Lady of Guadalupe.

Upon his return to Alta California, Bishop Garcia Diego took up residence at Santa Barbara Mission where he lived for the relatively few years of his episcopal tenure. Beyond opening a seminary at Santa Inés Mission, he was frustrated in bringing his other objectives to completion because of the economic, political, and religious challenges in the region.

He succumbed on April 30, 1846, probably from tuberculosis. He is buried in a vault on the epistle side of the sanctuary at Santa Barbara Mission.

Weber, Francis J., trans. and ed. *The Writings of Francisco Garcia Diego y Moreno.* Los Angeles, 1976.

FRANCIS J. WEBER

DIETZ, PETER E. (1878–1947)

Labor priest, social activist. Peter Ernest Dietz was born on the Lower East Side of Manhattan on July 10, 1878, the son of German immigrant parents. Peter acquired an interest in the plight of labor at an early age when he accompanied his father to meetings of the fledgling labor movement. These formative experiences gave direction to his adult commitments as a priest.

At age sixteen, Dietz entered the seminary. Over the next ten years, the seminarian formed a particular vision of his vocation that combined ordained ministry with activism in economic reform. Bouts with severe depression and uncertainty about his unique priestly role made this decade of his life particularly difficult. Two years of study

(1900–02) in Moedling, Germany, provided the distance needed for him to understand the unique opportunities offered in the United States. Dietz came to the conviction that his nation's democratic traditions made possible economic reform based upon Catholic social teaching. He returned to America in 1902 invigorated by a commitment to dedicate his priesthood to establishing a Catholic-grounded economic reform. He completed his studies at The Catholic University of America in 1903. Cardinal Gibbons ordained him for the Cleveland diocese the following year.

Soon after his arrival in his new diocese, Dietz joined in the local and national activities of the Central-Verein. His practical plan for social reform appeared in the *Central Blatt and Social Justice,* the Verein's principal publication. From 1909 to 1910, Dietz edited the paper's English section, an initiative begun by the young priest. The brevity of his term reflects a disagreement between the priest and Frederick P. Kenkel, the Verein's Central Bureau social education director. Dietz constantly sought programs that included practical directives for implementing theory. Kenkel did not agree with the educational approach.

The Militia of Christ

Dietz next turned his attention to establishing direct Catholic influence among labor union leaders. His scheme involved the founding of the Militia of Christ for Social Service that would draw its membership from Catholics active in the American Federation of Labor (AFL) and other trade unions. By founding this organization, Dietz hoped to confirm the Catholic Church's defense of labor through a specific plan of social reform. He also hoped the Catholic presence might counter the anti-Catholic attitudes promoted by Protestant and more especially Socialists in the unions. Dietz sought an official alliance with the AFL but failed to garner labor leaders' support for a formal link. The militia did attract several hundred labor leaders but most active members served in cities like Chicago, Milwaukee, and St. Louis. Dietz's desire to establish a national network of Catholic labor leaders remained unfulfilled.

American Federation of Catholic Societies

While working to establish the militia, Dietz also participated in the American Federation of Catholic Societies (AFCS). In 1910 he served as AFCS representative at the 1910 AFL convention, the same meeting that gave birth to the Militia of Christ. Two years later, the AFCS established a Social Service Commission, for which Dietz served as executive secretary. Dietz also edited *Social Service,* the militia's official organ, which appeared in the AFCS Bulletin under "Newsletter."

As in other endeavors, Fr. Dietz hoped to establish a national Catholic voice for social reform, in this case by integrating the militia's purposes into the AFCS's Social Service Commission. He recognized the potential benefits for the militia which needed national connections and financial support. The integration never occurred.

Also consistent with his earlier commitments, Dietz challenged the Commission to devise an action plan for implementing social and economic reform. Lack of episcopal enthusiasm for such a plan ensured inaction. Despite frustrating setbacks, Dietz remained editor of the AFCS's newsletter until 1918, when AFCS disbanded the Social Service Commission. The AFCS itself had become part of the National Catholic Welfare Conference which contained a Social Action Department under the leadership of Dietz's longtime friend, John A. Ryan.

Beginning in 1915, Dietz committed himself to yet another project: the American Academy of Christian Democracy. The school was to train laity, both men and women, in Catholic social teaching as well as in the democratic principles undergirding the United States political and economic system. The academy, initially located in Hot Springs, North Carolina, attracted several women students. In 1917 the school relocated to a Cincinnati hospital where a greater Catholic population made student recruitment easier. Later that same year, the school moved to Ault Park, Ohio, to take advantage of nearby Catholic faculty. Fifty women graduated from Dietz's academy and became known as "White Cross Nurses."

American School of Labor

Receiving the financial backing from the AFL in 1922, Peter Dietz transformed the women's academy into the American School of Labor. It was to educate Catholics in Leo XIII's teachings pertaining to labor organizing. Unfortunately, Dietz was unable to implement his plans due to a conflict with Cincinnati's Archbishop Henry Moeller who forced the priest to leave the diocese. The priest's association with labor, perceived by business leaders as a social and economic threat, may have been the primary reason for his dismissal.

Peter Dietz spent the remainder of his life as a parish priest in the Archdiocese of Milwaukee, Wisconsin. He founded St. Monica's parish in Whitefish Bay, a Milwaukee suburb. He remained in this parish until his death in 1947. Evidence of his former days as labor priest appeared at St. Monica's when the parish formed it own credit union, a first in Wisconsin. His procedure provided general guidelines for other parishes who established these community-based financial institutions.

Peter Dietz's various attempts to fulfill his chosen mission as a labor priest anticipate much of the effective Catholic involvement in the U.S. economic realm. The specific plan of action which he wanted from the Central-Verein came in the 1919 Bishops' Program of Social Reconstruction. His commitment to the AFCS as a means of coordinating Catholic social activism became subsumed under the NCWC's Social Action Department. His lay schools for educating the laity in Catholic social teaching anticipate the Catholic labor schools by nearly twenty years. With very few resources and little support, Dietz led the way in organizing Catholics for the tasks of social and economic reform. He died in Milwaukee on October 11, 1947. Dietz's gravestone rightly proclaims his humble life of service: "Champion of Labor—Founder of St. Monica's congregation."

See also RYAN, JOHN AUGUSTINE.

Abell, Aaron I. "The Reception of Leo XIII's Labor Encyclical in America. 1891–1919." *The Review of Politics* 7 (October 1945) 464–95.

Fox, Mary Harrita. *Peter E. Dietz, Labor Priest.* University of Notre Dame Press, 1953.

Mitchell, John J. *Critical Voices in American Economic Thought.* New York: Paulist Press, 1989.

SANDRA YOCUM MIZE

DIVINE WORD MISSIONARIES

The Society of the Divine Word in North America, *Societas Verbi Divini* in Latin or S.V.D., is part of the worldwide society founded by Blessed Arnold Janssen in Steyl, Netherlands, in 1875. Br. Wendelin Meyer, the first S.V.D. to enter the United States in 1895, came to sell German Catholic magazines to German-speaking Americans. He was soon joined by other priests and brothers from Ger-

Arnold Janssen, founder

many and Holland, and in 1909 they opened the first seminary in the United States to train young men exclusively for the foreign missions. This was at Techny on the north side of Chicago, where the priests and brothers, in imitation of their founder, quickly set up a flourishing press apostolate and pioneered the Lay Retreat Movement. Vocations soon began to pour in, and in 1912 another seminary was established in Girard, Pennsylvania, followed over the next years by nine more, stretching from Massachusetts to California.

Shortly after their arrival, Divine Word Missionaries began to work in the African American apostolate. In 1919 a boarding school for black youth was established in Greenville, Mississippi, as a first step towards a minor seminary. This effort was formally continued with the opening in 1923 of St. Augustine's Seminary in Bay St. Louis, Mississippi, to train African Americans for the priesthood and brotherhood, the first concerted effort of its kind in the South. The first four black Divine Word Missionaries were ordained in 1934. Since then African American members of the Society of the Divine Word have been sent not only to minister to blacks in America, but to Africa and New Guinea, to the West Indies and to other missions entrusted to the society as well.

When the Divine Word Missionaries came to the United States, it was itself a mission country, and so one of the first things they had to do was develop mission awareness. Fr. Clifford King, while still a seminarian, founded the Catholic Students' Mission Crusade in 1918 for just this purpose. In its day it proved to be one of the most successful ventures of its kind, enlisting, literally, millions of students in its ranks over the years. Many people of an earlier generation also still remember the pagan babies they ransomed with their small donations, thus stimulating their awareness of the missions. The Mission League and the Mission Mass League were also effective reminders that every American had a mission obligation, while *The Little Missionary,* a magazine for the youth, found its way into Catholic schools all over the country.

The S.V.D. Today

From the beginning, the American branch of the Society of the Divine Word has been part of an *international* mission-sending society whose members now come from sixty-two countries. They all receive their appointments from their superior general in Rome to any one of the sixty lands where they are active. Thus nationalities from sixty-two countries are mixed in the missions to which they are sent, as well as in the United States itself. Because mission funds are also distributed centrally by the superior general, the financial contributions of more wealthy countries are thereby more equitably shared with less wealthy countries. Since the beginning this international approach to mission has proved to be very useful for the society, most especially perhaps in the numbers of members it now has in Asia, India, and Africa, where the Society of the Divine Word continues to flourish and grow.

Shortly after Vatican II, a watershed event in the Catholic Church of the twentieth century, vocations to high school seminaries dropped precipitously; soon all of these institutions were closed. Notions of "mission" broadened. Methods of intellectual and spiritual formation changed from the structured, group-oriented, isolated style to the flexible, more individualistic and engaged-with-the-world manner so familiar now. Today the Society of the Divine Word operates a college seminary in Epworth, Iowa, which prepares future missionaries, both brothers and priests, together. True to tradition, this college is also international in scope and cross-cultural in character. From here graduates enter novitiate, after which, as Divine Word missionaries, they proceed to the Chicago Theological Union (CTU) for their theology. This has become a very important educational center for ministry in the Church, whose Mission Studies Program was identified by several accrediting agencies in 1971 as "strong and giving every indication of becoming a center of missiology in the United States" (Bechtold, 213). This prophecy, according to Paul Bechtold, the founding president of CTU, has happily been fulfilled. Elsewhere he says: "The Program in World Mission is largely the history of the Divine Word Missionaries at the school. While all of the communities who were at CTU at its beginnings had a mission-sending apostolate, no group had world mission as its primary work. A vibrant program in mission studies awaited a missionary society to sponsor and staff it" (Bechtold, 194).

In its own way, in changing times but in continuity with the aims of its founder, the Society of the Divine Word continues to foster mission awareness, to be a model of community in diversity, and to prepare missionaries for the twenty-first century.

See also MEN, RELIGIOUS ORDERS AND CONGREGATIONS OF.

Alt, Josef. *Arnold Janssen SVD, Briefe in die Vereinigten Staaten von Amerika, herausgegeben und kommentiert von Josef Alt SVD.* Nettetal: Steyler Verlag, 1994.

Bechtold, Paul, C.P. *Catholic Theological Union at Chicago: The Founding Years, 1965–1975, History and Memoir.* Chicago: Catholic Theological Union, 1993.

Ochs, Stephen J. *Desegregating the Altar: The Josephites and the Struggle for Black Priests, 1871–1960.* Baton Rouge: Louisiana State University Press, 1990.

ERNEST BRANDEWIE

DOHEN, DOROTHY M. (1924–84)

Sociologist. A professor of sociology at Fordham University and an authority on spiritual and ascetic literature, Dohen was also a writer and editor. As a young adult, she had been in the forefront of the Catholic lay apostolate movement as it developed in the United States after World War II. She sought to construct and practice throughout her life a lay spirituality that included prayer, work for social justice, and ecumenism. Any efforts toward social reform not rooted in compassion and a vision beyond the merely secular, Dohen deemed inadequate. Of the Christian vocation she wrote, "The secular hero dies once; the saint dies daily."

After graduating from the College of Mount St. Vincent in 1945, Dohen spent time with the Grail and Young Christian Workers before beginning to publish articles in Catholic magazines, such as *The Torch, Integrity, Commonweal,* and *Blackfriars.* Her first book on spirituality, *Vocation to Love* (1950) was followed by *Journey to Bethlehem* (1958). For four of the intervening years she served as editor of *Integrity,* a journal that went defunct in 1956, her last year at the helm. Published by lay Catholics, *Integrity* described itself as "dedicated to the task of discovering the new synthesis of Religion and Life for our times." Its goal anticipated by several years what would become one of the major themes articulated at the Second Vatican Council, that the Church, in order to play its proper role in the modern world, needs to look closely at the signs of the times. Dohen adopted the same focus for her professional career and personal life, regarding the relation of faith to society as the central problem of faith in the modern world.

In an effort to better analyze social and cultural conditions, Dohen embarked on the study of sociology at Fordham University, receiving her M.A. in 1959 and Ph.D. in 1966. Her first major sociological work, *Woman in Wonderland* (1960), looks at the changing role of women in modern society.

Nationalism and American Catholicism (1967), however, was her most significant and best-known work. In it Dohen analyzes the efforts of six U.S. Catholic bishops representing the full sweep of U.S. history—John Carroll of Baltimore, John England of Charleston, John Hughes of New York, John Ireland of St. Paul, James Gibbons of Baltimore, and Francis Spellman of New York; plus, as a control, Bishop John Lancaster Spalding of Peoria. Each tried to work out a relationship between the Church and the dominant culture. Dohen begins the book (published while the U.S.A. was enmeshed in the Vietnam War) in a journalistically timely fashion with Cardinal Spellman quoting Stephen Decatur, "My country . . . right or wrong." Her historical account then moves backward through the controversies over the founding of The Catholic University of America, Americanism, problems that attended the huge influx of Irish immigrants, early American anti-Catholicism, and the role of Catholics in the revolutionary period.

Succinctly put, Dohen's thesis was that the American experience of religious pluralism tends to identify sacred symbols with secular ones and national goals with religious goals. It does so, and has done so since the beginning of the nation, because our particular brand of pluralism itself precludes the establishment of a common religion. Consequently, the state's goals and ideals serve as the common ground around which all religions can rally, whether Protestant, Catholic, or any other. By using the bishops' own words from public statements and speeches, Dohen illustrates the ways in which these prelates attempted to show how Catholic America is, and how American the Church is. Each bishop in his own way tried to persuade his constituency and their critics of the compatibility of democracy and faith. Dohen's caveat is that such pluralism dilutes the distinctive character and contribution of each particular religion, perhaps even religion in general.

An outstanding teacher and scholar in the field of sociology, Dohen edited (1970–72) *Sociological Analysis,* the Journal of the Association of the Sociology of Religion. After 1967, however, she produced no major sociological research of her own.

In an article published in *Commonweal* after her death, Rev. Joseph P. Fitzpatrick, S.J., a close colleague and mentor, wrote of Dohen, "Her private life with the Lord was a life of profound spiritual experience, a life kept hidden from even her closest friends. It was a life completely of faith, but also a hidden darkness in which she faced alone the terrible mystery of unbelief."

She died of cancer on January 3, 1984, at her home in Manhattan.

Dohen, Dorothy M. *Nationalism and American Catholicism.* New York: Sheed & Ward, 1967.

Fitzpatrick, Joseph P., S.J. "A Lay Apostle." *Commonweal* (June 1, 1984) 325–27.

Obituary in *New York Times,* January 1, 1984.

KAREN SUE SMITH

DOHERTY, CATHERINE DE HUECK (1896–1985)

Russia

Spiritual writer and social activist. Catherine de Hueck Doherty (nee Kolyschkine) was born in Nijni-Novgorod, Russia, on August 15, 1896. Her mother, Emma Thompson Kolyschkine, was of French and English descent, and her father, Theodore Kolyschkine, came from the Russian landed gentry. Her mother was Lutheran but deeply influenced by the Orthodox faith; her father was Orthodox with possible Polish Roman Catholic influence from his mother's family. Catherine was baptized and raised in the Russian Orthodox Church. Part of her early education was

Catherine de Hueck Doherty

with the Catholic Sisters of Sion in Alexandria, Egypt. Her exposure to the "two lungs of East and West" in her deeply Christian home with its influences of Eastern and Western Christianity shaped her later vision and mission. Married at the age of fifteen to her first cousin, Baron Boris de Hueck, Catherine served as a Red Cross nurse during World War I. Forced to flee Russia during the Bolshevik revolution, the young couple almost starved before they were liberated and escaped to England. Catherine was received into the Catholic Church in November 1919 in England. In 1921 they arrived in Toronto, Canada, and their son, George, was born in July of the same year.

The search for work eventually took Catherine to New York where she obtained a number of menial jobs to support herself and her family. A respite from this period of frequent physical hunger with its attendant depression and desperation came when she was launched as a lecturer with the Chautauqua Lecture Bureau. This was followed by a period as a lecturer with the Catholic Near East Welfare Association. During this period she came in contact with Fr. Paul Wattson, founder of the Friars of the Atonement at Graymoor, Garrison, New York, and spent some time there with the community.

Friendship House

She experienced the words of the gospel: "Go, sell what you possess and give to the poor, and come, follow me." This inspired her to a course of action that led to the establishment of Friendship House in Toronto—the first of the two communities that she founded. Following the ideas of Catholic Action, Friendship House offered assistance to those who needed food, clothing, and Christian literature, and it represented an attempt by laypeople to live out the social encyclicals such as *Rerum Novarum* and *Quadragesimo Anno*. During this period she met Dorothy Day, cofounder of the Catholic Worker movement, who was engaged in a similar type of work in New York. This led to a friendship and a correspondence between the two women that spanned some forty years.

In 1938 Catherine established a house in Harlem, New York, and here as elsewhere she showed herself as a pioneer in promoting interracial justice in the Catholic Church in America. Although her work was sometimes misunderstood, it attracted a great deal of interest, and influenced, for example, the young Thomas Merton who served as a volunteer at the Harlem Friendship House. It was here, too, that Catherine met her second husband, Eddie Doherty, after her first marriage had been annulled in 1937. But the success of Friendship House was marred by internal strife. Catherine wanted to establish a rural apostolate, assisting the poor, but a number of the Friendship House community felt that the scope of their activity should be confined to the interracial apostolate. This division, coupled with the problem, as some saw it, of Catherine's authoritarian leadership style, eventually led to the departure of Catherine and her husband Eddie to Combermere, Ontario, in 1947, and the establishment of her second community, Madonna House. Located in a small village some two hundred miles north of Toronto and about one hundred and twenty miles west of Ottawa, this was to be the site of her most enduring legacy to the Church.

Madonna House

Over time Catherine severed her connections with the Friendship House movement and concentrated her energies on building a community that eventually allowed her to give fuller expression to her Russian background in a Western environment. The community which developed is comprised of priests and laypersons who promise to observe the evangelical counsels of poverty, chastity, and obedience. Its spirituality is a blend of Eastern and Western Christianity, with the aim of building a community of love in the spirit of Nazareth.

Here Catherine introduced to the Western world her idea of *Poustinia*, which means "desert" in Russian. This experience of solitary prayer and fasting before the Lord in a single room set apart for this purpose is an integral part of the spiritual life at Madonna House. This development of interior silence is done within an active community which values physical labor. In 1995 the Madonna House facilities at Combermere served as a training center for the over two hundred members (called staff workers) and applicants, and for the twenty-three mission houses located in Canada, the U.S.A., West Indies, England, France, Brazil, Africa, and, most recently, in Russia. In addition, there were more than one hundred associate priests spread throughout the world.

The community numbers are augmented by the invitation extended to visitors, by the ministry to families at the Summer Cana Colony and the preseminary program offered for eight months of the year within the Madonna House community life.

Catherine died at Combermere on December 14, 1985, surrounded by members of her community. She was buried in the local cemetery at Combermere beside her late husband, Eddie, who died in 1984. Apart from her pioneering roles in the lay apostolate, interracial justice, and the introduction of her Eastern spirituality to the Western world, her reputation as a spiritual writer continues to grow with the publication of her writings by Madonna House. Her life story is told in *Tumbleweed* and *Cricket in My Heart* by Eddie Doherty; in her own autobiographical reflections, *Fragments of My Life,* and in *Katia* by Fr. Emile Brière. Her spirituality may be further explored in *Poustinia* and *The Gospel without Compromise*. The bishop of Pembroke—the diocese in which Madonna House is located—appointed Fr. Robert Wild, a priest of Madonna House, as vice postulator, to gather materials for the possible opening of a cause for the canonization of Catherine Doherty.

Doherty, Catherine de Hueck. *Fragments of My Life*. Notre Dame, Ind.: Ave Maria Press, 1979.

_____. *The Gospel without Compromise*. New Canadian ed. Combermere: Madonna House Publications, 1989.

_____. *Poustinia. Christian Spirituality of the East for Western Man*. Notre Dame, Ind.: Ave Maria Press, 1974.

Doherty, Eddie. *A Cricket in my Heart*. San Antonio: Blue House Press, 1990.

_____. *Tumbleweed*. New Canadian ed. Combermere: Madonna House Publications, 1989.

Duquin, Lorene Hanley. *They Called Her the Baroness: The Life of Catherine de Hueck Doherty*. New York: Alba House, 1995.

JARLATH QUINN

DOMENEC, MICHAEL (1816–78)

Bishop, seminary professor. Domenec was born on December 27, 1816, in Ruez, Tarragona, Spain. He began his schooling in Madrid but was forced to flee to Paris with his father for political reasons. In 1832 he joined the Congregation of the Mission (the Vincentians) and began studies for the priesthood in Paris, but in 1838 he emigrated to the United States and finished his studies at St. Mary's Seminary in The Barrens, Missouri. He was ordained on June 29, 1839, and began teaching at St. Mary's Seminary and in 1845 went to teach in St. Charles Seminary in Philadelphia. After doing pastoral work, Domenec was named second bishop of Pittsburgh in 1860. His time there was difficult, since he had to deal with the problems associated with Civil War (1861–65) and the subsequent economic depressions. He was a strong defender of the Union and went on a mission to his native Spain on behalf of the federal government. After the Diocese of Pittsburgh was divided in 1876, he took the less important see, Allegheny City. (The two dioceses were reunited in 1889.) Domenec was considered an inopportunist at the First Vatican Council but later accepted the definition of papal infallibility. He retired as bishop of Allegheny City on July 27, 1877, because of poor health and died on January 7, 1878, in Spain.

Fogarty, Gerald P., S.J., *The Vatican and the American Hierarchy from 1870 to 1965*. Collegeville, Minn.: The Liturgical Press, 1982.

ANTHONY D. ANDREASSI

DOMINICANS (O.P.)

Members of the Dominican Order (Order of Preachers) have been on mission in the United States for more than two centuries. The mission given them by Dominic de Guzman (1170–1221) from the founding of the order is to proclaim the word of God by preaching, teaching and example, while they are sustained by life in common.

The single mission of the Order of Preachers embraces many ministries, developed as needed to bring the word of God to persons in varying societies and circumstances. St. Dominic had this in mind when he urged the first members to identify with each culture through the use of the vernacular languages. For the same purpose he asked the preachers to meet all people as mendicants, ready to exchange gifts and necessities with others in the spirit of Jesus and the apostles.

The Order of Preachers is composed of men and women of four branches: friars, who may be priests or brothers; cloistered nuns; sisters; and laity. Dominic de Guzman was called to ministry in the universal Church. His followers have proclaimed the gospel around the world to peoples never known to the founder, including those of the Americas.

Early Missionaries to the United States

Three centuries after the death of St. Dominic in 1221 the first Dominicans landed on the Atlantic coast with Spanish colonists, arriving in 1526 near the current site of Georgetown, South Carolina. Among them was the friar Antonio de Montesinos, whose vehement protests against the conquerors' oppression of the native peoples have been acclaimed as the first voice for liberty raised in the New World. When the intended colony failed, Montesinos returned to his prophetic preaching in the Caribbean. However, other Dominicans followed him into the southern region of the present United States. These included Fray Luis Cancer who was martyred in Florida, and the men who accompanied De Soto and other explorers into regions along the Gulf Coast. Friars of Mexico, which then extended north beyond the Rio Grande, evangelized the natives of the present Texas, some losing their lives in that endeavor. After them, nearly two centuries intervened before the Preachers came to stay.

The continuing presence of Dominicans in the United States began in 1786. A friar of the Irish province, John O'Connell, was assigned to New York, the nation's temporary capital, to serve primarily as chaplain at the Spanish legation. Following O'Connell more than twenty friars, the majority from Ireland, were sent as missionaries to the new nation. Of these the first twelve served with Bishop John Carroll in the vast Diocese of Baltimore, then the only one in the United States.

One of the Preachers on mission with John Carroll was Francis Antoninus Fleming, the bishop's vicar general for the Northern District, which extended from New York to Maine. Fleming, like several of his confreres, met death while caring for victims of yellow fever. Among the other friars were William O'Brien, pastor of New York's first parish, St. Peter's on Barclay Street; Anthony Caffrey, founder of St. Patrick's, the first parish in the rising 'Federal City' of Washington, D.C.; and John Ceslas Fenwick, an American of the English province, who lived and labored with the Jesuits in southern Maryland.

When the single see of Baltimore was divided in 1808 to form five dioceses one of these, New York, was given as its first bishop the Irish Dominican, Luke Concanen. After his episcopal ordination in Rome his passage to the

Saint Dominic

United States was delayed so long by Napoleon's embargo on ships leaving Italy that death overtook him before he could leave. A second Irish friar, John Connolly, was then appointed bishop of New York (1815–25).

Foundations in the First Half-Century

The initial move toward founding a Dominican province in the United States was made by Edward Dominic Fenwick, O.P., an American descendant of early Maryland colonists. Fenwick entered the Order of Preachers of the English province in 1788, after completing his studies at the Dominican college of Holy Cross in Belgium. While serving for ten years in the English province he dreamed of establishing an American province of the order in his native Maryland. The dream was realized finally by Fenwick and three English friars, with the support of Dominican superiors in Rome and the encouragement of Bishop John Carroll. However, Carroll requested that the province be founded far from Maryland, out in frontier Kentucky, where the first westward-moving Catholics were begging for priests.

The Dominican Province of St. Joseph was established in 1806 at St. Rose, Kentucky, near Bardstown. In 1811 the Dominicans welcomed to the ecclesiastical outpost of Kentucky the first bishop on the western frontier, Benedict Joseph Flaget. In his Bardstown diocese the friars served as itinerant preachers, instructors in their college of St. Thomas Aquinas, and pastors of the earliest parishes formed in the wilderness. The people responded favorably to their pastoral ministry, finding their practices more acceptable than the rigorous ones of the veteran French missionary Stephen Theodore Badin and his Belgian coworker Charles Nerinckx.

As itinerant missionaries the friars traveled widely among the settlers in Kentucky; then Edward Fenwick ventured north across the Ohio River into the forests of Ohio. There in 1818 he and his Dominican nephew, Nicholas Dominic Young, built the first Catholic church in the state, a log cabin at Somerset in Perry County dedicated to St. Joseph. Three years later Fenwick was named the first bishop of Cincinnati (1821–32) and given the spiritual care of Catholics in the whole region of present-day Ohio, Michigan, and Wisconsin. In the beginning the only priests in the diocese were his Dominican brothers, who with the zealous people formed the earliest parishes in Ohio and built the first Catholic churches.

While planning the foundation of the friars in the United States Edward Fenwick hoped to have American sisters to share in their mission. This hope was realized in 1822 when nine young women, answering the call of the provincial, Samuel Thomas Wilson, became the first American Dominican Sisters, known today as the Congregation of St. Catherine of Siena. The founding members began their common life in a crowded log cabin near Cartwright Creek and began their teaching in a school opened in a still house. Angela Sansbury, of one of the pioneer families from Maryland, was the first to make her religious profession and the first to be elected by her community as prioress. She merits the title of foundress of Dominican Sisters in the United States.

At the call of Bishop Fenwick, four of the Kentucky sisters were sent to Ohio in 1830 to establish the community and academy of St. Mary's in the settlement at Somerset. There, as in Kentucky, they shared in the Dominican mission as teachers. As Fenwick noted, they undertook "the role of missionary among us." Following a disastrous fire the community and academy moved in 1868 to Columbus, Ohio, where they assumed the title, "St. Mary of the Springs."

Dominican preachers were called south to Tennessee, which had few Catholics and no priest, with the appointment in 1837 of the first Catholic bishop of Nashville. He was Richard Pius Miles, O.P., a native of Kentucky, who welcomed to the diocese several friars from Kentucky and Ohio with whom he had served as missionary and provincial. Among them were Joseph Alemany, who would later become the first archbishop of San Francisco; and Thomas Langdon Grace, who was subsequently named the bishop of St. Paul. In 1846 Dominican sisters were sent from both Kentucky and Ohio to Memphis, to form a new community and academy of St. Agnes in collaboration with the friars of St. Peter's parish. Less than three decades later, Memphis sisters and friars alike gave their lives in caring for victims of the yellow fever epidemic.

In 1860 the Ohio sisters of St. Mary's sent four members to the cathedral city of Nashville, Tennessee, at the request of the second bishop of Nashville, James Whelan, O.P. These sisters founded the Congregation and Academy of St. Cecilia. During the Civil War they found themselves on the Tennessee battlefront. Later sisters went from Nashville to Memphis as volunteers to nurse the victims of the yellow fever, for whom some gave their lives.

The ministry of the Order of Preachers to Native Americans, fur traders, and pioneer Americans of Michigan and Wisconsin was initiated by their bishop, Edward Fenwick, in the territory once evangelized by the French Jesuits. In 1830 he assigned the newly ordained Samuel Mazzuchelli to the missions of the old Northwest, then in the territory of Michigan. Subsequently the Italian-American missionary became the first Dominican to serve the Church in the new dioceses of St. Louis, Detroit, Dubuque, Milwaukee, and Chicago. In 1844 he initiated at Sinsinawa Mound, Wisconsin, the third collaborative foundation of Dominican friars and sisters: a province of the friars which was short-lived, and in 1847 the Sinsinawa Dominican Sisters. The cause of Samuel Mazzuchelli, the first American Dominican missionary proposed for canonization, was advanced in 1993 when he was named Venerable by the Holy See.

The fourth collaborative mission of Dominican men and women in the United States was initiated in California in 1850 by Dominican friars and sisters who accompanied Joseph Alemany to his bishopric in Monterey. There Alemany and Sadoc Vilarrasa, a fellow Spanish missionary who had been serving with him in Ohio, founded the friars' province of the Holy Name. At the same time Alemany's hope for sisters was fulfilled by Mary Goemaere, a Dominican from Paris, with Aloysia O'Neill and Frances Stafford from St. Mary's, Somerset. These founded the community that became the Congregation of Holy Name of San Rafael.

Early Members of the Dominican Laity

The foundations laid by Edward Fenwick included not only those of friars and sisters, but also of members of the Dominican laity, then known as the Third Order. In 1807, while the Kentucky venture was only started, Fenwick wrote to Luke Concanen in Rome to ask about receiving men and women as lay Dominicans. He said he thought that the Third Order, if he understood it well, could be established "with benefit to the pious people and much honour to our Lord."

Little is known about the first lay Dominicans in the United States. Among their sparse records preserved from the early nineteenth century is that of the reception of one Betsy Wells by the Dominican friars at St. Rose in 1826. Another, in 1829, records the reception of two men, George Shock and John Roi, into the Third Order. In 1833 Bishop Flaget of Bardstown praised the "virtuous lay women," presumably tertiaries, among the Dominicans at St. Rose who nursed the cholera victims there. The lay Dominicans at Somerset, Ohio, included two named Fanny and Theresa Naughton who served St. Joseph Convent all their adult lives. The early records pertained only to individuals. No references to early chapters or meetings of tertiaries have been discovered.

Mission to the Immigrants

In 1853, after the foundation of the order in Kentucky, Ohio, Tennessee, Wisconsin, and California by friars and sisters on mission together, the first Dominican women came from Europe to serve in the American Church. These were four cloistered nuns from the Monastery of Holy Cross in Regensburg, Bavaria, led by Josepha Witzlhofer. Called to America to provide education for German Catholic immigrants, they settled in Williamsburg, New York, later an area of Brooklyn. They tried valiantly to combine their monastic way of life with the strenuous work of conducting a school. In 1868 the nuns met another urgent need of the people by opening the first hospital conducted

by American Dominican sisters. By 1900 the Brooklyn community and the many foundations across the United States which branched ultimately from Holy Cross Monastery in Bavaria had become congregations of active Third Order sisters. Many years later, in 1947, the Brooklyn sisters moved their motherhouse to Amityville, New York.

Another Dominican community formed for the education of German immigrants began in Racine, Wisconsin, in 1862. The foundress was Maria Benedicta Bauer, who, when prioress of Holy Cross Monastery in Bavaria, had sent the four nuns from Regensburg to Brooklyn in 1853. The Racine sisters, like their predecessors in Brooklyn, evolved from a contemplative monastic community to become an active congregation.

Only six years after the coming of the nuns from Bavaria to the Brooklyn convent of Holy Cross, German Catholics in lower Manhattan requested sisters from Brooklyn to open a monastery and school at St. Nicholas parish. The reply was favorable. The sisters soon welcomed young women to their novitiate on Second Street, and in 1869 became an autonomous monastery, with Mary Augustine Neuhierl as prioress. By 1883 this community had developed into a congregation with branch houses and moved their motherhouse up the Hudson to Newburgh, New York.

Dominican nuns from Ireland also came to help immigrants to the United States at midcentury. In response to a call from a pastor in New Orleans, Mary John Flanagan and five other nuns from Dublin opened a parish school in that city of French and Spanish culture in 1860. Coming from a contemplative monastery, as did the nuns from Germany, they struggled in this new environment with the ambiguities of a cloistered life in active ministry until they became the Congregation of St. Mary's of New Orleans.

Beginnings in the Second Half-Century

In 1873 seven sisters from the original Dominican community in Kentucky traveled to mid-Illinois to open a school and convent at Jacksonville. A year later, two of these sisters were requested to participate with President Ulysses Grant in an unusual event: the unveiling of a statue of Abraham Lincoln at his tomb in Springfield, the state capital. Grant asked them to represent all the religious women who had served during the Civil War in prisons and hospitals and on the battlefields; women whom President Lincoln had warmly praised, as Grant recalled. The sisters fulfilled the President's request and returned to their less public ministry in Jacksonville. Later their motherhouse was moved to Springfield.

As immigration increased and the move from farm to city accelerated, new needs of the people challenged Dominicans to undertake ministries new and old. The urban ministry of the friars was expanded with their move to New York City in 1867, which was followed by the transfer of the eastern provincial center from St. Rose, Kentucky, to St. Vincent Ferrer parish, New York City. The western province of Holy Name moved in turn to San Francisco and opened parishes as far north as Portland, Oregon. Added to the founding of new parishes was another form of urban ministry: the weeklong missions which the friars undertook as preaching teams called "mission bands" in far-flung towns and cities.

Attention to evolving human needs led to new foundations and ministries among the Dominican sisters. Catherine Antoninus Thorpe was led by such a need in 1876 to found a new community in New York, with the guidance of the Dominican provincial John Rochford. These Dominican sisters who later moved to Sparkill, New York, were established to provide for indigent women and dependent children. The numbers of orphans had multiplied rapidly after the Civil War, owing not only to battle fatalities and recurring epidemics, but also to the many deaths of immigrants enroute to the United States. Women who left family farms for work in city factories were equally in need of assistance.

Lucy Eaton Smith, a convert, was inspired by the example of Catherine Antoninus Thorpe and also challenged by the needs of women. In 1880 she founded in Albany, New York, a Dominican congregation which would offer women the opportunity for spiritual retreats related to the contemplative aspects of the sisters' lives; and also would provide residences for working women in the cities. Under the patronage of St. Catherine de Ricci the sisters of the community she established continue this dual ministry, centered at the motherhouse now located at Elkins Park, Pennsylvania.

Four congregations of American Dominican sisters, all dedicated primarily to education, formed new branches in the 1880s. Sisters from Newburgh, New York, established a community in Jersey City in 1881. These became a congregation which moved their motherhouse later to Caldwell, New Jersey. From Columbus, Ohio, a group of sisters led by Mary Agnes Magevny traveled to distant Galveston, Texas, in 1882 to make a foundation which later moved to Houston. The record for long-distance travel to new beginnings was made when sisters from Brooklyn, urged by Joseph Alemany, the Dominican archbishop of San Francisco, responded to the educational needs of German immigrants in California. By 1888 these sisters became the Dominican congregation of Mission San Jose, under the leadership of Maria Pia Backes. In the same year, sisters from the Jersey City community, led by Thomasina Buhlmeier, made a new foundation on the West Coast at Tacoma, Washington.

During the final decade of the nineteenth century two more American branches of the fast-growing "tree" whose seedling was sent from Bavaria became new congregations. From Newburgh came the sisters who formed the congregation of Blauvelt, New York, in 1891. Their ministry for orphans had begun years earlier when Mary Ann Sammon, foundress of the new branch, brought homeless children into the Manhattan cloister to be cared for by the nuns. The second new branch, the Grand Rapids Sisters, originated as a Michigan province of the Newburgh congregation, from which the members were separated in 1894 by the arbitrary action of the bishop of Grand Rapids. They became an independent congregation under the leadership of Aquinata Fiegler.

The initial ministry of Dominican sisters among Franco-Americans began with a call from Canadian friars at work in New England. Mary Bertrand Sheridan and several Dominican sisters from Washington, D.C., responded to that call in 1892 by founding a community and school in Fall River, Massachusetts.

In 1896 a Dominican congregation unique in its single ministry was founded by Rose Hawthorne Lathrop, the daughter of Nathaniel Hawthorne. The members' compassionate ministry for the poor is found in their title: the Servants of Relief for Incurable Cancer. Their motherhouse is at Hawthorne, New York.

Monasteries of Contemplative Nuns

The earliest foundation of women in the Order of Preachers was that of the contemplative nuns established by St. Dominic as a part of the Preaching of Jesus Christ at Prouille, France. Theirs was the fourth branch of the order to be established permanently in the United States. The nuns who had come at mid-century from monasteries in Germany and Ireland were cloistered contemplatives. Their active apostolate had compelled them to live in increasing dependence upon dispensations from their constitutions until each foundation, encouraged by successive masters of the order, made the decision to become an active congregation of Dominican sisters.

The first permanent American foundation of cloistered nuns was made in 1880. Four nuns from Ouillins in France, a monastery whose origins went back to Prouille, came to Newark, New Jersey, to found the Monastery of St. Dominic, dedicated to perpetual adoration. The founding prioress, Mary of Jesus, was an American. By 1889 members of the Newark foundation opened a second monastery in the Bronx, New York; and in 1906 one in Detroit, now at Farmington Hills.

New Jersey was the site in 1891 of a second monastic foundation from Europe. Four nuns of the Perpetual Rosary, founded in Belgium, opened a monastery in Union City. By 1910 they had established five more monasteries in as many states: Milwaukee, Wisconsin, in 1897; Catonsville, Maryland, in 1899; Camden, New Jersey, in 1900; Buffalo, New York, in 1905; and in 1909, La Crosse, Wisconsin. The La Crosse nuns moved in 1984 to Washington, D.C.

Emerging Chapters of Dominican Laity

Records of Dominican laity in the early nineteenth century were not only sparse but limited to the reception or profession of individuals. From the second half of the century there exist records of chapters of lay Dominicans who met regularly, studied and prayed together, and introduced others to the spirituality and apostolic charity of the Order of Preachers. Chapters were encouraged by the Dominican friars in their parishes, as at San Francisco in 1863, by sisters in schools and by nuns in their monasteries. Chapter news was given in the friars' *Rosary Magazine* from its inception in the last quarter of the nineteenth century. Large, active chapters of men and women were found during that period in parishes in San Francisco, St. Paul, Louisville, New York City, Boston, and Lewiston, Maine. The articles showed the zeal of the tertiaries in those chapters.

Early Twentieth Century

The first founding of a Dominican community of sisters in the twentieth century took place in Kansas, far from the concentration of Dominicans on the East and West Coasts. It was from Holy Cross in Brooklyn, however, that the former prioress, Antonina Fischer, set out to found eventually in 1902 the Great Bend congregation of Dominican Sisters.

In 1910 Mary Walsh obtained official recognition by the Church for a community of women she had gathered earlier in New York to offer health care to the poor in their homes. These Dominican Sisters of the Sick Poor later moved their central house to Ossining on the Hudson.

The California friars who began their foundation in 1850 at Monterey had been obliged for lack of frontier resources and personnel to set aside their status as a full province in 1864 and assume that of a congregation. But by 1912 the province of the Holy Name was fully restored, with their central house in San Francisco and parishes in cities located chiefly along the Pacific Coast.

Monasteries of nuns of the order multiplied in the decade between 1915 and 1925, with eight new foundations established at great distances from one another. Nuns from Newark opened a monastery in Cincinnati in 1915 and another in Los Angeles in 1924. From Farmington Hills, Michigan, a new community was formed in Albany, New York, in 1915; and in New Jersey a group from Union City opened a house in Summit in 1919. From the Bronx monastery a foundation was made in Menlo Park, California, in 1921. Nuns from Catonsville, Maryland, established a monastery in West Springfield, Massachusetts, in 1922 and another in Lancaster, Pennsylvania, in 1925. In the same year, the monastery at Camden opened a daughter-house at Syracuse, New York.

Two widely separated provinces of the Newburgh congregation became autonomous congregations in 1923. The first province founded at Aberdeen, Washington, in 1890, now became the Dominican congregation of Everett, later Edmonds, Washington. The second group had become a province of the Newburgh congregation in 1892, centered at Adrian, Michigan. In 1923 that province became autonomous and their provincial, Camilla Madden, became the first prioress of the new Adrian congregation.

At the end of the 1920s individual sisters of the Caldwell congregation, by arrangement between the bishops of Cleveland and Newark, were given the choice of remaining in the New Jersey congregation or joining a new branch of the order at Akron, Ohio. This second Ohio Dominican congregation, founded a century after the pioneer community at Somerset, was established in 1929.

New Developments

On the eve of World War II the friars of St. Joseph province had grown in membership and outreach, from the Atlantic to the Rocky Mountains and from the Canadian border to the Gulf of Mexico. The master of the order, Martin Gillet, proposed the formation of a new province of friars to serve the central United States. The province of St. Albert the Great was established in 1939, with headquarters in Chicago.

Friars of the three American provinces served as chaplains for the armed forces in World War II. During and after the war they ministered to increasing numbers of Catholics who moved to the cities and required new or expanded parishes.

American friars then took part, thanks especially to the initiative of Walter Farrell, in promoting the study of theology among the laity. For women and men throughout the country they initiated Thomist Associations, regional study groups, the publication of books and periodicals, and theology courses in numerous colleges and universities.

In the decade of the 1940s four monasteries of nuns were formed from existing foundations: Elmira, New York, from Buffalo; Lufkin, Texas, from Farmington Hills, Michigan; and North Guilford, Connecticut, from Summit, New Jersey. The fourth foundation, from Catonsville, Maryland, brought an interracial, intercultural monastery to Marbury, Alabama.

After 1950 two communities of Dominican sisters became independent of their European motherhouses. One whose members came originally from Czechoslovakia to Pennsylvania in 1923 became the congregation of Oxford, Michigan, in 1950, under the leadership of Mary Joseph Gazda. The second group had come from an Irish Dominican community in Lisbon, Portugal, to serve in the state of Oregon. They formed in 1952 the autonomous Dominican congregation of Kenosha, Wisconsin, with Mary Vincent Mullins as their major superior.

In the same decade two new communities were established for catechetical ministry among adults and children. The Marian Dominican Catechists of Boyce, Louisiana, were founded in 1954 by Bishop Charles Greco to serve in the diocese of Alexandria, Louisiana. Another Louisiana foundation, the Eucharistic Missionaries, had been established for catechetics and related ministries in 1927 by Catherine Bostick and Margaret Grouchy. Thirty years later they were affiliated to the Order of Preachers.

In 1979 the friars of the eastern and central provinces initiated the collaborative founding of a new province, using a process unique in the history of the order. They combined personnel and resources to establish together the new Southern province of St. Martin de Porres, centered at New Orleans. The friars of this province launched their mission in the South with a verbal motif given them by the master of the order: "A New Birth in Hope."

Dominican sisters who had come from Speyer, Germany, in 1925 to serve in the northwestern states became the autonomous American congregation of Spokane, Washington, in 1986.

Laity in the Twentieth Century

Members of the Dominican laity in the United States have developed their contemplative-apostolic role in the Order of Preachers within each province of the friars. Chapters now exist in thirty-three states, and their members collaborate with Canadians in the CANAM organization. In 1985 they welcomed to Montreal lay Dominicans from all continents to celebrate the seven hundredth anniversary of the founding of the Third Order in 1285. Looking toward the future they emphasized the need to recognize and make known the elements of Dominican spirituality which many lay Catholics seek to live. The new *Rule* of 1987 supports and encourages these elements.

A broad vision of the laity was proposed at the first International Conference of the Dominican Family in Bologna in 1983. Led by the master of the order, Vincent de Couesnongle, the delegates from every continent, representing all four branches of the order, broadened the concept of "lay Dominican" to include all men and women who "look to Dominic and the Order for inspiration" *(Bologna Document)*. In the United States these include women and men invited by many congregations of Dominican Sisters to be their associates.

Dominican Teachers and Learners

The first Dominican school in the United States was opened by the friars in a Kentucky farmhouse in 1806. It became the College of St. Thomas Aquinas with both men and boys in attendance, as was customary in the earliest institutions; and one of the boys was Jefferson Davis, who remembered with pleasure the year he spent with the friars. The college was closed by 1830, as were other schools and colleges established later by the friars at Somerset, Ohio, and Sinsinawa, Wisconsin. In the meanwhile the Dominican sisters in 1822 had opened St. Mary Magdalen's

school, which in turn, over a century later, became a college that survived. The two Kentucky institutions initiated the educational ministry offered subsequently by American Dominicans for almost two centuries.

The early sisters founded academies as well as primary schools to encourage the continuing education of pioneers and immigrants, especially of women. Some taught in the first public schools of the north central states. Before mid-century, and increasingly after the Plenary Council of 1884, they staffed parish schools. These multiplied rapidly as bishops and pastors requested, pleaded or demanded that sisters be sent to teach in their parishes. In this way Dominican sisters as well as friars committed themselves to the development of the local Church throughout the nation.

Secondary education offered by Dominican sisters, like that of other religious women, usually originated in their own academies for girls, of which many became collegiate institutions. The needs of urban families led to the opening of numerous Dominican high schools, some of them conducted by the friars. In later years Dominicans have administered or taught in secondary schools sponsored by parishes, dioceses, or other religious orders. Many alumni of these high schools, and also of colleges, have entered religious life because of their association with women and men of the order.

Among the early friars one of the deterrents to full Dominican life was the lack of traditional emphasis on study, that basic element given to the order by St. Dominic. Advanced study of theology and philosophy was often sacrificed to build up the Church as settlers moved into Kentucky, Ohio, Tennessee, and California. A few friars were sent to Europe to study; and men from Europe were sometimes appointed to the post of Regent of Studies for brief periods. But not until 1905 was the first proper Studium set up in Washington, D.C., adjoining the new and struggling Catholic University of America. In 1936 the Holy Name province opened the College of St. Albert in Oakland, which later became the Dominican School of Theology and Philosophy and joined the Graduate Theological Union at Berkeley. By 1941 the province of St. Albert the Great established a house of studies, which became in 1964 the Aquinas Institute of Theology at St. Louis, offering graduate degrees to religious and lay men and women. Subsequently, the new Southern province of St. Martin de Porres and that of St. Albert the Great formed one house of studies at Aquinas Institute.

In the early 1900s Dominican sisters attended colleges and universities in increasing numbers at home and abroad, although few Catholic institutions would admit women. The congregations who had personnel qualified for faculty posts in higher education began to establish colleges for women. In 1904 bachelor's degrees were first granted by the Dominican Sisters of St. Clara College at Sinsinawa, which under the name Rosary College later moved to River Forest, Illinois. The San Rafael Sisters were the second congregation to open a college for women, the Dominican College of San Rafael, which first conferred degrees in 1917. Well into the century, all Dominican colleges for women became coeducational institutions.

In succeeding years Dominicans founded the institutions listed here which grant bachelor's or higher degrees:

Institution	Founding Sponsor	Degrees Granted
Rosary College	Sinsinawa Dominicans	1904
Dominican House of Studies	St. Joseph Province	1906
Dominican College of San Rafael	San Rafael Dominicans	1917
Providence College	St. Joseph Province	1918
Siena Heights College	Adrian Dominicans	1924
Ohio Dominican College	Columbus Dominicans	1927
Albertus Magnus College	Columbus Dominicans	1928
Dominican School of Theology and Philosophy	Holy Name Province	1936
Aquinas College	Grand Rapids Dominicans	1942
Barry College	Adrian Dominicans	1942
Edgewood College	Sinsinawa Dominicans	1942
Caldwell College	Caldwell Dominicans	1943
Mt. St. Mary College	Newburgh Dominicans	1958
Dominican College of Blauvelt	Blauvelt Dominicans	1959
Molloy College	Amityville Dominicans	1959
St. Thomas Aquinas College	Sparkill Dominicans	1963
Aquinas Institute of Theology	St. Albert Province	1964

Among collegiate institutions which have granted associate degrees are St. Catherine Junior College of St. Catherine, Kentucky (1931); Aquinas Junior College of Nashville, Tennessee (1961); and Queen of the Holy Rosary College, Fremont, California (1979).

Many friars and sisters have engaged in campus ministry at a variety of institutions, including those sponsored by Catholic and Protestant churches, independent colleges, and universities. Paralleling this ministry are Dominican projects in adult education among the disadvantaged and immigrants, prisoners, and handicapped persons.

American society and the Church have benefited from Dominican scholars in a variety of national and international institutions, whether as professors of theology in various graduate schools, individual instructors, or scholars doing advanced research.

Health Care

St. Dominic preached human dignity and the worth of the human body to oppose the Cathar belief that whatever was physical and material was evil. Catherine of Siena put Dominic's preaching to work not only in her teaching but in her loving care of the sick. American Dominicans have also put teaching into practice in caring for the health needs of the people. Friars and sisters in Kentucky were commended by their bishop for the care of cholera victims in the 1830s. During the Civil War members of the order served as chaplains and nurses on the battlefield. In the 1870s sisters and friars gave their lives caring for victims of yellow fever in Tennessee.

The first Dominican hospital was founded in New York by the Brooklyn sisters (later Amityville) in 1869. Home health care for the destitute was introduced in New York by Mary Walsh and the Dominican Sisters of the Sick Poor. Today, Dominican men and women participate in a broad range of burgeoning health services and related areas of pastoral and social ministry. They conduct and staff hospitals, medical centers, and nursing homes; also urban and rural clinics for the poor, in which Dominican sisters are physicians and nursing staff. Hospitals are conducted currently by the following congregations:

Adrian:
   Dominican Santa Cruz Hospital, Santa Cruz, California
   St. Rose Dominican Hospital, Henderson, Nevada
Great Bend:
   Central Kansas Medical Center, Great Bend, Kansas
   St. Catherine Hospital, Garden City, Kansas
   St. Joseph Memorial Hospital, Larned, Kansas
Kenosha:
   Holy Rosary Medical Center, Ontario, Oregon
   St. Catherine's Hospital, Kenosha, Wisconsin
   Mercy Hospital, Merced, California
San Rafael:
   St. Joseph's Medical Center, Stockton, California
   St. Mary's Regional Medical Center, Reno, Nevada

Springfield:

St. Dominic-Jackson Memorial Hospital, Jackson, Mississippi

St. Mary-Rogers Memorial Hospital, Rogers, Arkansas

Significant study, research, and publication have been done in the field of medical ethics by friars of the provinces of St. Albert the Great and St. Martin de Porres.

Missions Abroad

Only in 1908 did the Church in the United States emerge from its former mission status. Soon afterward American Dominicans began to send members on mission to other countries. The first were the sisters from Mission San Jose, who in 1910 opened a school and then a novitiate in Mexico. In 1912 the Maryknoll Sisters of St. Dominic were founded by Mary Joseph Rogers at Hawthorne, New York, to be the first American Dominican congregation of sisters founded specifically to serve in the foreign missions. They were given official approval of the Church in 1920.

The first American friars to staff a foreign mission were those of St. Joseph province, who in 1924 sent men to Kienning-Fu in south China and later invited the Sisters of St. Mary of the Springs, Ohio, to join them.

The Dominican nuns of Los Angeles opened in 1959 the first monastery of Americans at Karachi in Pakistan, following the earlier initiative of the friars of St. Joseph province.

As members of the order began to hear the call of peoples outside their own nation, a special summons to the lands of Latin America was sounded by Pope Pius XII in the 1950s. Many sisters and friars responded, leading to their continued ministry, with emphasis on human rights and justice, in Latin America and elsewhere. At the close of the twentieth century Dominican men and women of the United States offer a variety of ministries in the following mission fields:

Bahamas:	Caldwell
Belize:	Kentucky
Bolivia:	St. Albert, Columbus, Maryknoll, Sinsinawa, San Rafael
Brazil:	San Rafael, Maryknoll
China:	Columbus, Maryknoll
Colombia:	Amityville
Dominican Republic:	Adrian
El Salvador:	Maryknoll, Sinsinawa
Guatemala:	Akron, Houston, Maryknoll, San Rafael
Honduras:	St. Albert, St. Martin de Porres
Jamaica:	Blauvelt
Kenya:	St. Joseph, N. Guilford, Racine, St. Albert, Maryknoll, Adrian
Mexico:	Holy Name, Mission San Jose, Racine, San Rafael
Nigeria:	St. Albert, Great Bend
Pakistan:	St. Joseph, Sparkill, Los Angeles Monastery
Panama:	Maryknoll, Adrian
Peru:	St. Joseph, St. Martin de Porres, Columbus, Springfield, Sparkill, Grand Rapids, Kentucky, Maryknoll
Philippines:	Maryknoll: Los Angeles, Summit, Corpus Christi
Puerto Rico:	Adrian, Amityville, Columbus, Newburgh
Romania:	Kentucky
S. Africa:	Adrian
Trinidad:	Sinsinawa
Virgin Islands:	Adrian

Additionally, Maryknoll serves in these locations: Chile, Ecuador, Hong Kong, Indonesia, Japan, Korea, Nepal, New Guinea, Nicaragua, Samoa, Sudan, Taiwan, and Tanzania.

On Mission to the United States

Dominicans have come on mission to the United States from other lands since the first Spanish friars arrived in the Southeast and Southwest. In the nineteenth century, members of the order from England, Ireland, Germany, France, and Spain served among and with Americans. At the close of the twentieth century Dominican women and men have continued to come on mission from other nations. The following list shows the nation and Dominican group from which they come, and the location of their provincial or regional headquarters in the United States:

Canada:	Dominican Friars of Canadian Province; Lewiston, Maine
France:	Dominican Rural Missionaries; Abbeville, Louisiana
	Presentation Sisters of St. Dominic; Dighton, Massachusetts
	Roman Congregation; Iowa City, Iowa
Ireland:	Dominican Sisters of Cabra; New Orleans, Louisiana
Italy:	Religious Missionaries of St. Dominic; Corpus Christi, Texas
Philippines:	Dominican Sisters of Manila; Pen Argyle, Pennsylvania
Poland:	Dominican Sisters of Poland; Justice, Illinois

S. Africa:	Oakford Dominican Sisters; Mountain View, Texas
Spain:	Dominican Friars, Province of Spain; San Diego, Texas
Vietnam:	Dominican Sisters of Ho Nai; Houston, Texas Dominican Friars of Vietnam: Houston, Texas

Collaboration within the Order

From the time that friars invited women to participate in their Dominican mission in Kentucky, collaboration among branches of the order has remained an important factor, although sometimes disregarded in American Dominican history.

The original organization for collaboration in the United States, the Dominican Leadership Conference, was initiated in 1935 as a conference of Dominican mothers general. Today it sponsors intercommunication among major superiors of American congregations and provinces, holds an annual meeting, and encourages various forms of collaboration by means of the following groups:

PARABLE Conference for Dominican Life and Mission. Staff members provide "Encounter with the Word" retreats; study tours to the Lands of Dominic and Central American missions; and preaching teams for parish missions.

Project OPUS: A History of the Order of Preachers in the United States. Researchers from the four branches of the order are engaged together in this undertaking, the first integrated history of the American Dominicans.

Las Casas Ministry. Conference members support this ministry among native peoples, especially the Cheyenne and Arapaho, by volunteer service and support.

Dominican Charism and Emerging World Order. A committee formed to assess the needs of the global community and prepare for a new world order.

U.S. Dominican Collaboration. A committee to promote regional conferences and action in the Dominican Family.

Because preaching the word of God takes priority in the mission of the order, Dominican men and women are appointed as *Promoters of Preaching* in their respective branches to collaborate in proclamation of the word. For many years friars and sisters have formed preaching teams to serve parishes throughout the nation. One example of a specialized ministry is the Dominican Missionary Preaching Team which moves with migrant workers to help them form vital base communities, *comunidades eclesiales de base,* among them.

Representatives of the four provinces of men and several congregations of women form the official Liturgical Commission of the Order of Preachers in the United States, whose studies and conferences have produced significant publications for the order and the Church.

Collaboration in programs of initial formation of members began in 1976 with nationwide conferences for novices. These have led to the launching of a common novitiate for congregations of Dominican women. Joint sponsorship by leaders of St. Albert and St. Martin de Porres provinces has provided a novitiate and house of studies for men of the two provinces. The California Dominicans sponsor conferences for novices of the women's congregations and Holy Name province.

In 1975 American monasteries of Dominican contemplative women initiated the Conference of the Nuns of the Order of Preachers of the United States, which organizes intermonastic study weeks and communication and publishes *Dominican Monastic Search* to support contemplative life.

Going beyond collaboration to convergence, some Dominican congregations by choice of the members have united to become a single entity in the final decade of the twentieth century. After many years of study and deliberation, members of the three congregations of Fall River, Ossining, and Newburgh in 1995 merged into one that their members named the Dominican Congregation of Hope. Using a similar process, the Spokane Sisters in the same year joined the Sinsinawa congregation. These actions resulted from the traditional Dominican practice of communal decision-making. They were influenced chiefly by two realities. One was the current diminishment of numbers in each congregation. The other, resulting from years of prayer and study together, was the recognition of the way the charism of the order was profoundly present in each of the congregations. This reality would only be intensified by their union of life and mission.

See also FARRELL, WALTER; FENWICK, EDWARD; FLEMING, FRANCIS ANTONIUS; HARTKE, GILBERT; HOLY NAME SOCIETY IN AMERICA; LANTHROP, MARY ALPHONSA/ROSE HAWTHORNE; MAZZUCHELLI, SAMUEL; MILES, RICHARD PIUS; O'BRIEN, WILLIAM VINCENT.

Ashley, Benedict M., O.P. *The Dominicans.* Collegeville, Minn.: The Liturgical Press, 1990.

Culburtson, Diana, O.P., ed. *Rose Hawthorne Lathrop: Selected Writings.* New York: Paulist Press, 1993.

Murray, Mary Cecilia, O.P. *Other Waters: A History of the Dominican Sisters of Newburgh, N.Y.* Old Brookville, N.Y.: Brookville Books, 1993.

Parmisano, Fabian Stan, O.P. *Mission West: The Western Dominican Province, 1850–1966.* Oakland, Calif.: Western Dominican Province, 1995.

Petit, Loretta, O.P. *Friar in the Wilderness: Edward Dominic Fenwick O.P.* Chicago: Project OPUS, 1994.

Schwind, Mona, O.P. *Period Pieces: An Account of the Grand Rapids Dominicans, 1853–1966.* Grand Rapids, Michigan, 1991.

MARY NONA McGREAL, O.P.

DONGAN, THOMAS (1634–1715)

Soldier and colonial governor of New York. Dongan was born in County Kildare, Ireland, a younger son of Sir John Dongan, Baronet. He became a soldier, spending several years in France in the service of Louis XIV before receiving an appointment from Charles II in 1677 as lieutenant-governor of Tangier, which was under British rule. In 1682 he was appointed governor of New York by James, the Roman Catholic Duke of York. The province at that time contained all of New York itself and the dependencies of Pemaquid, Martha's Vineyard, and Nantucket; it became a royal province upon the ascension of James to the British throne.

Dongan himself was a Catholic, but his term as governor was marked with great religious tolerance. In 1683 the colonial legislature passed a Charter of Liberties and Privileges giving religious toleration to all Christians. He attempted to develop the province by establishing geographically clearer boundaries. He recognized the growing power of the French in the north and the growing influence of French Jesuits over the Iroquois in that region. He protested strongly to De la Barre and the Marquis de Denonville, successive governors of Canada, but, by the winter of 1687–88, Dongan found it necessary to raise an armed force for the defense of Albany. In 1688 Sir Edmond Andros succeeded Dongan as governor. Dongan remained in New York and fell victim to the anti-Catholic sentiment accompanying the Revolution of 1689 in the colonies. He returned to England in 1691, and upon the death of his older brother in 1698 became the second Earl of Limerick. He lived to see the French government recognize the English protectorate over the Iroquois by the Treaty of Utrecht in 1713. Dongan died on December 14, 1715.

Christoph, Peter R., ed. *The Dongan Papers, 1683–1688.* 2 vols. Syracuse University Press, 1993–96.

Driscoll, John T. "The Charter of Liberties and the New York Assembly in 1683." *Historical Records and Studies* 4 (1906) 5–53.

Kennedy, John H. *Thomas Dongan, Governor of New York (1682–1688).* Washington, 1930.

Phelan, Thomas P. *Thomas Dongan, Colonial Governor of New York.* New York, ca. 1933.

RICHARD G. SMITH

Related Document

NEW YORK'S GRANT OF RELIGIOUS TOLERATION, OCTOBER 31, 1683

On two occasions in American colonial history Catholics held the office of governor of a colony. In both instances religious toleration was granted to all Christians. We have already seen how the early Calverts made provision for such toleration in Maryland. The second case was in New York under Colonel Thomas Dongan (1634–1715), appointed governor in 1682 by the Duke of York, the future James II, himself a Catholic. The new governor summoned the first representative assembly in the history of the colony in October, 1683, and sponsored the passage by that body of the Charter of Liberties and Privileges. Dongan's broad grant of religious freedom endured in New York until 1688 when James II lost his throne, the governor was recalled, and Jacob Leisler's usurping government disfranchised the Catholics.

(*Source:* Hugh Hastings, Supervisor, *Ecclesiastical Records of the State of New York.* Albany: James B. Lyon, 1901, II, 864–65.)

. . . THAT NO PERSON OR PERSONS, WHICH PROFESS FAITH IN God by Jesus Christ, shall at any time, be any ways molested, punished, disquieted, or called in question for any difference in opinion or matter of religious concernment, who do not actually disturb the civill peace of the Province, but that all and every such person or persons may, from time to time, and at all times freely have and fully enjoy his or their judgements or consciences in matters of religion throughout all the Province, they behaving themselves peaceably and quietly and not using this liberty to Licentiousnesse nor to the civill injury or outward disturbance of others.

Provided always, that this liberty, or anything conteyned therein to the contrary, shall never be construed or improved to make void the settlement of any public Minister on Long Island, whether such settlement be by two thirds of the voices in any Towne thereon, which shall always include the minor part; or by subscriptions of perticuler inhabitants in said townes; Provided, they are the two thirds thereof: Butt thatt all such agreements, covenants and subscriptions thatt are there already made and had, or thatt hereafter shall bee in this manner consented to, agreed and subscribed shall att all time and times hereafter, bee firm and stable:

And in confirmation hereof, it is enacted by the Governor Councell, and Representatives: That all such sums of money so agreed on, consented to, or subscribed as aforesaid, for maintenance of said public ministers, by the two thirds of any towne on Long Island, shall always include the minor part, who shall bee regulated thereby: and also such subscriptions and agreements as are beforemenconed, are and shall be always ratifyed, performed and payed, and if any towne of said Island, in their public capacity of agreement with any such minister or any perticuler persons, by their private subscriptions aforesaid, shall make default, deny, or withdraw from such payments so covenanted to, agreed upon, and subscribed thatt in such case, upon complaint of any Collector appointed and chosen by two thirds of such towne upon Long Island, unto any Justice of that County, upon his hearing the same, he is hereby authorized, empowered, and required to issue out his warrant unto the constable or his deputy or any other person appointed for the collection of said rates or agreement, to levy upon the goods and chattells of the said delinquent or defaulter, all such sums of money so covenanted and agreed to be paid, by distresse, with costs and charges, without any further suit in law, any lawe, custom or usage to the contrary in any wise notwithstanding; provided always, the said sum or sumes be under forty shillings, otherwise to be recovered as the law directs.

And whereas all the respective Christian Churches now in practice within the City of New York, and the other places of this Province, do appear to be privileged *[sic]* Churches, and have been soe established and confirmed by the former authority of this Government; Bee it hereby enacted by this present Generall Assembly, and by the Authority thereof, That all the said respective Christian Churches be hereby confirmed therein, and thatt they and every of them shall from henceforth, forever, be held and reputed as privileged Churches, and enjoy all their former freedoms of their religion in Divine Worship and Church Discipline; and thatt all former contracts made and agreed on for the maintenances of the several ministers of the said Churches, shall stand and continue in full force and vertue, and thatt all Contracts for the future to be made, shall be of the same power; and all persons that are unwilling to perform their part of the said contract shall be constrained thereunto by a warrant from any Justice of the Peace; Provided it be under forty shillings, or otherwise, as the law directs; Provided also That all other Christian Churches that shall hereafter come and settle within this Province, shall have the same privileges.

(*Source:* John Tracy Ellis, ed. *Documents of American Catholic History.* Vol. 1:1493–1865. Wilmington, Del.: Michael Glazier, 1987, 116–18.)

DOOLEY, THOMAS A. (1927–61)

Physician, social activist. Dr. Thomas A. Dooley was an American Catholic folk hero of the cold war era. Born in St. Louis to a prominent family (his paternal grandfather, Thomas A. Dooley, Sr., was a well-known, self-made Irish-American industrialist), Thomas A. Dooley, III, attended the Jesuits' St. Louis University High School, the University of Notre Dame, and St. Louis University Medical School.

Dooley was an aspiring socialite who took five years to graduate from medical school. With few prospects in St. Louis, he enlisted in the United States Navy Medical Corps in the summer of 1954 and was soon assigned to temporary duty in Vietnam, where the Navy was about to embark on a massive refugee operation involving nearly one million North Vietnamese Catholics. Following the triumph of the Viet Minh over the French at Dienbienphu, the Geneva Accords mandated free passage for those Vietnamese wishing to settle either in the pro-Communist North or in the fledgling, pro-Western Republic of South Vietnam, under the leadership of the Catholic mandarin,

Thomas Dooley

Ngo Dinh Diem. Lt. Thomas A. Dooley worked tirelessly on behalf of the Catholic refugees from his base in Haiphong Harbor. In May 1955 he was awarded South Vietnam's highest honor; more importantly, he was urged by American intelligence operatives to write an account of his contribution to the "Passage to Freedom."

Dr. Tom Dooley's first book, *Deliver Us From Evil* (1956), was a best-seller and was condensed by the *Reader's Digest* in fourteen foreign-language editions. Dooley became an international celebrity and leading spokesman for the Diem regime in the U.S.A., but while on a lecture tour he was suddenly forced to resign from the Navy following a lengthy investigation into his homosexual behavior. The same members of the intelligence community who had closely monitored Dooley's career—including the CIA's legendary psychological warfare specialist, Lt. Col. Edward G. Lansdale—now arranged for Dooley's "rehabilitation," beginning with his voluntary service in a private medical mission known as "Operation Laos." Although Dooley was essentially blackmailed into returning to Southeast Asia, he quickly came to love his work there and, as his "handlers" had hoped, he became an enormous public relations "asset" to U.S. interests in the region.

Dooley was especially admired by American Catholics for his anticommunism and his selfless devotion to the suffering peoples of Southeast Asia. Although this relationship was exploited by American policymakers, it was totally authentic. Following the publication of *The Edge of Tomorrow* (1958), his account of "operation Laos," Dooley became perhaps the most popular Catholic in the U.S.A., garnering numerous honorary degrees from Catholic colleges as well as a host of awards from such groups as the Christophers. He also became an honorary member of a missionary order, the Oblates of Mary Immaculate. When he contracted malignant melanoma in 1959, millions participated in prayer vigils (his September 1959 surgery in New York City was filmed for an award-winning CBS documentary, "Biography of a Cancer"). A postoperative lecture tour netted well over one-million dollars for MEDICO, a medical aid program he had helped to launch in 1958. Dooley published a third best-selling book, *The Night They Burned the Mountain* (1960), and returned to Southeast Asia to supervise MEDICO's expanding clinic programs. He died of cancer on January 18, 1961, one day after his thirty-fourth birthday.

A Gallup Poll of American adults in December 1959 found that Dooley was the seventh most-admired man in the world. Senator John F. Kennedy was the only other Catholic on the list. Dooley helped pave the way for the election of Kennedy as president of the United States by demonstrating that a devout Catholic could serve effectively as the head of a nonsectarian, international program designed to bring medical aid *and* Americanism to the Third World. President Kennedy would cite Dooley's example in launching the Peace Corps. A formal campaign for Dooley's canonization was launched in the 1970s, but it was later suspended due to the complexities of his character.

See also VIETNAM WAR AND AMERICAN CATHOLICS, THE.

Dooley, Agnes W. *Promises to Keep: The Life of Dr. Thomas A. Dooley.* New York, 1962.

Dooley, Thomas A. *Dr. Tom Dooley's Three Great Books.* New York, 1960.

Fisher, James Terence. *Dr. America: The Lives of Thomas A. Dooley, 1927–1961.* Amherst, Massachusetts, 1996.

Monahan, James. *Before I Sleep: The Last Days of Dr. Tom Dooley.* New York, 1962.

JAMES TERENCE FISHER

DORCY, MARY JEAN (1914–88)

Religious and artist, Frances Emma Dorcy was born in Anacortes, Washington, in 1914 to William and Emma Dorcy. The youngest of eight children, she learned sharing even before shearing. It was perfectly in keeping with her background that she become a religious and spent her life using her unique talent of silhouette cutting to the inspiration of so many.

Frances entered the Dominican Sisters, Congregation of Holy Cross, Everett, Washington, in 1932, making profession on January 18, 1934, as Sr. Mary Jean Dorcy. Having entered a community with firm roots in education, she went to Gonzaga University for her first degree, then to Fordham University, and finally to Oakland College of Arts and Crafts for her degree of Master of Fine Arts.

No part of literature or art went unexplored by Sr. Jean. In children's literature she produced a series of self-illus-

Silhouette by M. Jean Dorcy

trated lives of the saints; in adult literature, *Shepherd's Tartan* and *St. Dominic's Family;* in silhouette cutting, *My Shady Hobby* and *Spring Comes to the Hill Country,* the contents of which brought her both national and international acclaim because of their delicacy, intricacy, and outstanding originality. Her output in this form was prodigious. She cut literally thousands of pieces, her favorite subjects being flowers, children, and her lifelong inspiration—Our Lady.

Coming as she did from the rugged northwest country, Sr. Jean had a deep sense of her historical background which she pursued in conjunction with missionary and Native American lore. This knowledge welled over into years of catechetical work among Washington Native American tribes and eventually caused her to volunteer for work at the orphanage run by Fr. William Wasson just outside Mexico City. There she taught English composition and religion, as well as sewing to the girls and tailoring to the boys as their career training. The latter included the creation of fabulous Mexican dancing costumes. She died on May 5, 1988, and is remembered for her art.

See also DOMINICANS (O.P.).

EDWINA SWEENEY, O.P.

DORION, MARIE (?–1850)

Madame Marie Dorion, as she is remembered in history, was an Iowa Native American woman who was married to a fur trapper by the name of Pierre Dorion. Her claim to fame rests on her heroic conduct in saving her children. Her ordeal was first made known by Washington Irving in his classic book, *Astoria.*

Dorion, a French Canadian, was a member of the Astor overland expedition to Oregon in 1810. His wife and two small sons accompanied him. Near what is now North Powder in eastern Oregon, Marie gave birth to another child in 1811. This child later died in her arms.

Subsequently, one section of the expedition, including the Dorions, established a winter camp for gathering furs in a remote region of the upper Snake River. Here all the men were killed by hostile natives. Warned by one of them before he died, Marie realized that the only chance for life was instant flight. "With great difficulty, she caught two of the horses belonging to the party, then collecting her clothes and a small quantity of beaver meat and dried salmon, she packed them upon one of the horses . . . on the other she mounted with her two children and hurried away from the dangerous neighborhood." Traveling west in the deep snow, she reached, at length, "a range of the Rocky Mountains, near the upper part of the Wallah-Walla River. Here she chose a wild, lonely ravine, as her place of winter refuge."

She had a buffalo robe and three deerskins and with these and branches of cedar and bark, she made a crude dwelling. She killed the horses and smoked their flesh for food. Here she and the children spent the winter.

In mid-March, when their food was nearly gone, Marie packed what was left, slung it upon her back, and with her children, she walked west, seeking help. Eventually she arrived at Fort Walla Walla, more dead than alive.

Marie settled in the Willamette Valley in Oregon, where she married a man named Louis Vernier about whom little is known. Later she married John Toupin who survived her. She died, respected by all, in 1850, and was buried beneath the original Church of St. Louis.

See also NATIVE AMERICANS AND THE CATHOLIC CHURCH.

Carey, Charles H. *General History of Oregon.* Portland, 1971.
Irving, Washington, *Astoria.* Portland, 1967.
Munnick, Harriet Duncan. *Catholic Church Records of the Pacific Northwest: St. Louis Register, Volume I (1845–1868) St. Louis Register, Volume II (1869–1900).* Portland, 1982.

WILFRED P. SCHOENBERG, S.J.

DORSEY, ANNA (1815–96)

Novelist. Ann Hanson McKenney Dorsey was born on December 12, 1815, in Georgetown, D.C., into a well-established family of Quaker ancestry, the daughter of William McKenney, a Methodist minister and navy chaplain, and Cloe Ann Lanigan McKenney. Receiving a good education at home, Anna won recognition for her youthful literary talents with the publication of her verse. In 1837 she married Lorenzo Dorsey, whose job with the U.S. Post Office took them to Washington, D.C. They had five children. Their only son died as a Union soldier in the Civil War. A daughter, Ella Loraine Dorsey, emulated her mother's career as an author of Catholic fiction.

Anna Dorsey's own literary career in light Catholic fiction began after she and her husband, inspired by the Oxford Movement, converted to Catholicism. One of her first novels, *The Student of Blenheim Forest* (1847), narrates a Virginia gentleman's gradual conversion to the Roman Catholic Church. Approximately thirty other publications followed, all providing edifying accounts of Catholic convictions within the twists and turns of the nineteenth-century novel. Her *Coaina, Rose of the Algonquins* (1867) appeared in two dramatized versions and was translated into German and Hindustani. She also examined the deleterious impact of slavery and its incompatibility with Catholic convictions in novels like *The Old Gray Rosary*. Her writings were enormously popular among her contemporaries appearing not only as books but also as serials in Catholic magazines like *Ave Maria*. Anna Dorsey received the Laetare Medal from the University of Notre Dame and two apostolic blessings from Pope Leo XIII. She died on December 25, 1896, in Washington, D.C.

See also CATHOLICS AND AMERICAN LITERATURE.

Allen, Suzanne. "Dorsey, Anna Hanson McKenney." *American Women Writers.* New York, 1979.
Donnelly, E. C. *Round Table of American Catholic Novelists* (1897).
Dorsey, Anna Hanson McKenney. *A Tale of the White and Red Roses* (1846).
_____. *The Student of Blenheim Forest* (1847).
_____. *Oriental Pearl* (1848).
_____. *Flowers of Love and Memory* (1849).
_____. *Guy, The Leper* (1850).
_____. *"They're Coming, Grandad!" A Tale of East Tennessee* (1865).
_____. *The Flemings or Truth Triumphs* (1869).
_____. *The Old Gray Rosary* (1870).
_____. *Tangled Paths* (1879).
_____. *Adrift* (1887).
_____. *Warp and Woof* (1887).
_____. *Palms* (1887).
_____. *Zoe's Daughter* (1888).
"Dorsey, Anna Hanson (McKenney)." *The Feminist Companion to Literature in English.* New Haven, 1990.
Seraphine, M., O.S.U. *Immortelles of Catholic Columbian Literature* (1896).

SANDRA YOCUM MIZE

DORSEY, JOHN H. (1874–1926)

Teacher, pastor, and missionary to African Americans in the South. John Henry Dorsey was the first African American Josephite priest to be ordained in the U.S.A. Born in Baltimore in 1874, he studied at St. Joseph's Seminary there and received his B.A. and M.A. degrees at St. Mary's

John H. Dorsey

Seminary (Maryland). He was ordained as a Josephite in 1902.

The Josephite priests, then led by John R. Slattery, were directing their efforts at evangelizing African Americans, and Slattery saw the cultivation of an African American priesthood as the most effective means to accomplish this. Subsequently, Fr. Dorsey spent the great majority of his years in the priesthood ministering to African Americans in the South.

He taught at St. Joseph's College for Negro Catechists in Montgomery, Alabama, in 1903–04, and returned there in 1907 to serve as the chief prefect for boys. From 1903–07, he was an assistant pastor, then pastor, of St. Peter's Church in Pine Bluff, Arkansas. He served as a missionary in Montgomery in 1908–09, and in various Southern states from 1913–17.

He founded the Knights of Peter Claver—a fraternal and mutual aid society—in 1909, and was its national chaplain from then until 1923. He served as pastor of St. Monica's Church, Baltimore, from 1918–24.

Fr. Dorsey's ministry was marked by frequent uprooting due to poor health and to the resistance he encountered within the Josephite community, as well as from the African American Catholics he was sent to serve. He was erroneously charged with sexual misconduct, and, in an argument with a parent in 1924 over a disciplinary measure, he was beaten with a piece of wood. The assault caused him to become paralyzed, and he died two years later.

See also AFRICAN AMERICAN CATHOLICS.

"Death of Father Dorsey, Colored Priest, After Lingering Illness." *Colored Harvest* 14 (September–October 1926) 10.

Foley, Albert S. *God's Men of Color: The Colored Catholic Priests of the United States, 1854–1954.* New York, 1955; repr. New York, 1969.
New York Times, July 2, 1926, 19.
Ochs, Stephen J. *Desegregating the Altar: The Josephites and the Struggle for Black Priests, 1871–1960.* Baton Rouge, Louisiana, 1990.
____. "The Ordeal of the Black Priest." *U.S. Catholic History* 5 (1986) 45–66.
"Our Father Harry Dorsey." Baltimore *Afro-American,* July 10, 1926, 1–2.

JOSEPH QUINN

DOUGHERTY, DENNIS CARDINAL (1865–1951)

Cardinal archbishop. Dougherty was born in Ashland, Pennsylvania, August 16, 1865, to Bridget Henry Dougherty and Patrick Dougherty, the sixth of their ten children. His Irish immigrant parents had located in Schuylkill County, an anthracite mining region, where Dennis picked coal as a lad. He attended the local public schools, for want of an accessible Catholic alternative. Though an excellent student, at age fourteen he was denied entrance to St. Charles Borromeo Seminary, Overbrook, because of his youth. Accepted by Sainte-Marie College, Montreal, Canada, he studied there for two years; then he transferred to Saint Charles. In 1885 Archbishop Patrick J. Ryan sent Dougherty to the North American College in Rome where his proficiency in scholastic theology was noticed by Pope Leo XIII. On May 31, 1890, Cardinal Lucido Parocchi ordained Dougherty in the Basilica of St. John Lateran.

Dennis Cardinal Dougherty

Bishop in the Philippines

His first clerical assignment returned the young priest to St. Charles Seminary, where he taught a wide range of subjects and served as comptroller. In the aftermath of the Spanish-American War, Leo XIII appointed Dougherty the first United States bishop to the recently acquired Philippine Islands. On June 14, 1903, in the Church of SS. John and Paul, Rome, Cardinal Francesco Satolli consecrated Dougherty for the war-weary see of Nueva Segovia. In serious need of episcopal encouragement and attention, 171 parish priests were responsible for almost 1,000,000 souls. With generous contributions he personally solicited from American Catholics, Dougherty was able to rebuild and restore churches, the cathedral, and the diocesan seminary, where American troops had been billeted.

Dougherty also resolved the "Aglipay schism" precipitated by the Holy See's refusal to appoint a native bishop, as had been requested by the largely Filipino diocesan clergy. Consequently, under the leadership of Padre Gregorio Aglipay, church properties were seized. The American civil authorities stood by, fearful lest they further aggravate the situation. Despite advice to the contrary, Dougherty refused to initiate legal action against the recalcitrant priest. Rather, he shifted the proof of ownership onto Aglipay. After prolonged litigation of seven years, the courts determined that Père Gregorio was unable to substantiate his claim. This important decision set a legal precedent which would prevent future dissidents from wresting property from the original congregation.

In 1907 Dougherty played a significant role in the provincial council of Manila. Shortly after, he was given the larger see of Jaro, where he was installed on June 21, 1908. An able equestrian, Dougherty was able to reach the most remote areas of his far-flung diocese. He personally ministered to long-neglected lepers; he reorganized and virtually rebuilt the diocese. His heroic labors were recognized by Rome; he was brought home in 1915, profoundly affected by his missionary experience.

Buffalo and Philadelphia

On June 7, 1916, Cardinal John Farley of New York installed Dougherty as bishop of Buffalo. Two years later when he left the diocese to become archbishop of Philadelphia, he had liquidated a debt of almost one million dollars, established over a dozen new parishes, revitalized and expanded the parochial school system.

Dougherty was consecrated by Cardinal James Gibbons on July 10, 1918, the first native son to occupy the see of Philadelphia; three years later he became the fifth American to be named a cardinal. His episcopal style was authoritarian; his thirty-three year tenure, lengthy; his accomplishments, many. Gifted with a keen sense of real estate, "God's bricklayer," as he called himself, he opened

one hundred-twelve new parishes, twelve hospitals, and eleven homes for the elderly. He dedicated one hundred forty-five new elementary schools. His most significant contribution to Catholic education was the unique system he inaugurated of free Catholic high schools. Open to every archdiocesan Catholic youth, the tuition was paid by their pastors. The Cardinal increased the number of these schools to fifty-three. They were staffed primarily by diocesan priests and women religious to whose number Dougherty added twenty-five new communities of sisters.

A National Figure

In 1921 the veteran missionary became president of the National Commission for Catholic Missions among the Colored People and Indians; Dougherty served in that capacity for almost two decades. This position brought him in frequent contact with Mother [now Saint] Katharine Drexel, whose work he considered "the crowning glory of the Diocese." In 1934 Dougherty invited another foundress, Anna M. Dengel, to establish the motherhouse for her fledgling Medical Mission Sisters in his archdiocese. It was especially to facilitate these sisters' work with poor women in India that Dougherty persuaded Pope Pius XI to change canon law to allow women religious to practice obstetrics.

Dougherty acted swiftly when he learned that children of the Catholic elite in Peru were attending Protestant Anglo-American schools. As the local ordinary of the sisters, Servants of the Immaculate Heart of Mary, he ordered the sisters to Lima. There they opened an English-speaking academy in 1922, the first North American sisters to establish a foundation in South America.

His ardent promotion of Thérèse of Lisieux's canonization, prompted the French to call him "the Cardinal of the Little Flower." When, in 1926, St. Charles Borromeo's new four-million-dollar preparatory seminary opened, it had, at Dougherty's instigation, a cloister garden built to replicate the one at Lisieux. It was the seminary which most profited from his financial acumen. Under his watchful eye, the annual diocesan seminary collection became the largest of its kind in the world—the new seminary was debt-free upon completion.

In his later years, Dougherty became dean of the American hierarchy. He used this position judiciously. One of his rare public interventions was in support of the Legion of Decency, monitor of the motion picture industry. Another was against universal military training. On the eve of the cold war, he convoked several anti-Communist demonstrations, each attended by tens of thousands. A man of conservative temper, his 1945 public support for the Equal Rights Amendment, opposed by many of his coreligionists, was newsworthy.

On May 31, 1951, the sixty-first anniversary of his ordination to the priesthood, Dougherty died suddenly as he was preparing for his daily routine of administrative duties. He was entombed in Philadelphia's Cathedral of Saints Peter and Paul.

See also PENNSYLVANIA, CATHOLIC CHURCH IN.

Gallagher, John J., ed. *Official Jubilee Volume: Life and Works of His Eminence, D. Cardinal Dougherty and History of St. Charles Seminary* (1928).

Nolan, Hugh J. "Cardinal Dougherty: An Appreciation." *Records of the American Catholic Society of Philadelphia* 62 (1951) 135–41.

____. "Cardinal Dougherty's Services." *Ave Maria* (September 8, 1951) 295–96.

____. "The Native Son" *The History of the Archdiocese of Philadelphia,* ed. James F. Connelly. Wynnewood, Pennsylvania, 1976, 339–418.

Reher, Margaret Mary. "Den[n]is J. Dougherty and Anna M. Dengel: The Missionary Alliance," *Records of the American Catholic Historical Society of Philadelphia* 101 (1990) 21–33.

____. "Get Thee to a [Peruvian] Nunnery: Cardinal Dougherty and the Philadelphia IHM's." *Records of the American Catholic Historical Society of Philadelphia* 103 (1992) 43–51.

Rowan, John, ed. *Official Jubilee Volume: Fifty Years of Notable Achievement in the Life of His Eminence, Dennis Cardinal Dougherty, 1890–1940* (1940).

MARGARET MARY REHER

DOUGHERTY, JOHN J. (1907–86)

Biblical scholar and educator. John Joseph Dougherty was born at Jersey City, New Jersey, on September 16, 1907. He attended St. Peter's Preparatory School, Jersey City, Seton Hall College, South Orange, New Jersey, and Immaculate Conception Seminary, Darlington, New Jersey.

John J. Dougherty

After graduation from Seton Hall in 1930 he was sent to the North American College, Rome, and received the licentiate in sacred theology from the Gregorian University in 1934. He was ordained a priest at Rome on July 23, 1933.

Scholar and Educator

Dougherty returned to Rome for two periods, 1934–37 and 1947–48, for studies at the Pontifical Biblical Institute and study and travel in Jerusalem and the Middle East. He received the licentiate in sacred Scripture in 1937 from the institute, and was awarded the doctorate in 1948, one of only five persons to possess the degree in the United States. In 1937 he was appointed professor of sacred Scripture at Immaculate Conception Seminary, Darlington, where he would remain for twenty-two years. Dougherty was very much a part of the renaissance in biblical studies after *Divino Afflante Spiritu,* wrote many articles on biblical topics, and translated the book of Deuteronomy for the *New American Bible.* His 1959 popular introduction to the Bible, *Searching the Scriptures,* was named one of the ten best religious books of the 1950s by *America* magazine.

Dougherty's scholarship, combined with a ready wit and resonant speaking voice, made him a popular lecturer beyond New Jersey. He became a regular speaker on "The Catholic Hour" radio program sponsored by the National Council of Catholic Men. When the program moved to television in 1951, Dougherty moved to the new medium. He collaborated with Pulitzer Prize author Paul Horgan in a popular 1957 broadcast, "Rome Eternal," for "The Catholic Hour." This program won the Sylvania Award for Exceptional Merit in 1958, and the following year Dougherty was presented with the first Catholic Television Arts Award from the National Council of Catholic Men. In 1956 he was named to the Pontifical Commission for Motion Pictures, Radio and Television.

In November 1959 Dougherty was named thirteenth president of Seton Hall University, and presided over the school during the turbulent 1960s. He expanded the university's programs and oversaw the building of thirteen million dollars in new facilities. Both coeducation and computers made their debut at Seton Hall during the Dougherty years.

Auxiliary Bishop of Newark

On November 17, 1962, Dougherty was named titular bishop of Cotenna, and auxiliary bishop of Newark. He was consecrated in Newark's Sacred Heart Cathedral together with Bishop Joseph A. Costello on January 24, 1963. As bishop, he participated in the last two sessions of the Second Vatican Council. In addition to his university and pastoral duties, Dougherty's talents were regularly tapped by his fellow American bishops. He chaired the USCC Committee on Social Development and World Peace, and the NCCB Committee on International Affairs; and was a member of the NCCB Committees on the Liturgy and on Priestly Formation. He also served on the Vatican Committee on Peace Studies, and the Governor's Commission on Civil Disorder which looked into the causes of the 1967 Newark Riots. He represented the American Bishops on the International Commission on English in the Liturgy, where he served as vice chairman, and at the United Nations, 1964–72. In the latter role Dougherty hosted Pope Paul VI during the pontiff's visit to Holy Family Church, "the UN parish," during his historic visit to New York in October 1965. Feeling that "the Church in the U.S. should become more articulate in the matter of peace," Dougherty became an early critic of the Vietnam War and encouraged bringing that conflict to the negotiation table.

Dougherty resigned the Seton Hall presidency in 1969 and was named pastor of St. Rose of Lima, Short Hills. Here he brought his peace and justice work to the local scene, promoting ecumenism and "twinning" St. Rose with a needy parish in inner-city Newark.

In 1977 Dougherty resigned his pastorate and returned to Seton Hall as scholar-in-residence. Here, as chairman of the New Jersey Catholic Historical Records Commission, he hoped to complete a book on the history of New Jersey Catholicism. The bishop suffered a stroke while cheering at a Seton Hall basketball game in January 1980, and never recovered full mobility. He resigned from pastoral office in September 1982. Dougherty died at Teaneck, New Jersey, March 26, 1986.

See also NEW JERSEY, CATHOLIC CHURCH IN.

"Bishop John J. Dougherty . . . 50 Years Ministry to the Archdiocese of Newark. A Commemorative Issue." *The Advocate,* December 29, 1982.

"Bishop Dougherty Remembered." *The Advocate,* March 26, 1986.

RAYMOND J. KUPKE

DOWLING, AUSTIN (1868–1930)

Archbishop. Austin Dowling was born in New York City on April 6, 1868, to Irish immigrants Daniel and Mary Teresa (Santry) Dowling. Having graduated with honors from Manhattan College in 1887, he enrolled in St. John's Seminary, Brighton, Massachusetts. Between 1890–92 he earned a licentiate in sacred theology at The Catholic University of America.

Ordained for the Diocese of Providence on June 24, 1891, Dowling served as parish priest, professor of church history, and editor of the *Providence Visitor* before becoming rector of Sts. Peter and Paul Cathedral in 1905. On April 25, 1912, he was consecrated first bishop of the Diocese of Des Moines, where he served until taking possession of St. Paul on March 25, 1919.

Here Dowling presided over a see that grew from about 265,000 to 280,000 members. He concentrated more on promoting schools than in opening new parishes. He established a Catholic Teachers' College and a diocesan Bureau of Education, opened two new high schools and a preparatory seminary, and initiated religious vacation schools in rural areas. He also incorporated the Bureau of Catholic Charities, and promoted the Council of Catholic Men and the Holy Name Societies. Dowling also helped to organize the National Catholic Welfare Conference. He served on its administrative board, and as treasurer and secretary of its Department of Education, when the conference successfully defended the freedom of religion and parental choice in education that the Oregon law of 1922 threatened to undermine.

Dowling died in St. Paul on November 29, 1930. Archbishop McNicholas described his years as "twelve glorious pages in the history of Church of the Northwest."

O'Connell, M. R. "The Dowling Decade in St. Paul." Master's thesis, St. Paul Seminary, 1955.

Reardon, J. M. *The Catholic Church in the Diocese of St. Paul.* St. Paul, Minn.: The North Central Publishing Company, 1952, 436–505.

JOHN WHITNEY EVANS

DOWLING, EDWARD (1898–1960)

Jesuit priest. He was born in St. Louis, Missouri, September 1, 1898. After service as a private in the U.S. Army, a summer as a semiprofessional baseball catcher, and a year as a reporter for the *St. Louis Globe Democrat,* Dowling entered the Jesuits in 1919 at Florissant, Missouri. In the Jesuit novitiate, both his struggle to accept incurable spinal arthritis and his own dark night of the soul—a year without God's comfort—grounded him in a sensitivity both to those suffering and the right group for help.

At the end of Dowling's Jesuit training, Fr. Daniel Lord, S.J., chose him to be on the staff of the *Queens Work* and the Summer School of Catholic Action. A reporter quipped the job was a cover for his real mission: "God's ambassador to humanity." Some students he taught discovered Alcoholics Anonymous in the late 1930s and invited Dowling to his first AA meetings in Chicago. Dowling—impressed by the movement—took the train to New York in November of 1940 and met Bill Wilson, the cofounder of AA.

That meeting began a friendship that would last until Dowling's death in 1960. Dowling used the twelve steps of AA to start the CANA Conference for couples which spread across America in the 1940s. The St. Louis AA group challenged Dowling to stop his compulsive smoking with the twelve steps. He did, and would be the first to suggest the twelve steps could be used for other compulsions in a 1960 article in the AA publication, *The Grapevine.* Both Bill W. and Dowling knew their other compulsions: Dowling from overeating and Bill from smoking and dependency relationships.

When Bill W. came in the 1950s to write his commentary, *Twelve Steps and Twelve Traditions,* he asked Dowling to send him a copy of *The Spiritual Exercises of St. Ignatius.* Bill read the "Two Standards" meditation in the *Exercises.* For Dowling this meditation is the heart of AA: God blesses the depths of humiliation and suffering. Bill asked that Dowling's quote, "God resists the proud, assists the humble. . . . The shortest cut to humility is humiliations, which M has in abundance," be on the dust jacket for the third edition of the Big Book. In the 195 letters between them, Dowling calls Bill W. to humility and discernment as Bill faced decisions about taking part in psychic or LSD experiments.

Dowling called for AA leadership "to be on tap not on top." Bill would turn down honors (an honorary doctorate from Yale) and call for AA anonymity with the imagery of the "Two Standards" meditation. Dowling was a firm believer all his life in democracy and proportional representation. Dowling rejoiced that AA democratized therapy, taking it from the expensive couch to kitchen coffee klatches.

Dowling spent the last night of his life (April 2, 1960) talking with AA couples as he prepared to give a CANA conference the next morning in Memphis. At his death Bill W. would write, "He was the greatest and most gentle soul that I may ever know."

See also GAVIN, IGNATIA.

AA Comes of Age. New York, 1957.

Fitzgerald, Robert, S.J. *The Soul of Sponsorship. The Friendship of Father Ed Dowling, S.J., and Bill Wilson in Letters.* Center City, 1995.

Mel B. *New Wine. The Spiritual Roots of the Twelve Step Miracle.* Center City, 1991.

ROBERT FITZGERALD, S.J.

DOYLE, MICHAEL FRANCIS (1877–1960)

International lawyer and diplomat. A Philadelphia native born on July 12, 1877, Doyle was educated at the University of Pennsylvania, admitted to the Pennsylvania bar in 1897, and completed postgraduate work from 1897–99. During World War I, he served as a designee of the U.S. State Department to assist Americans stranded in Europe. He provided special counsel to the American legation in Switzerland and the American embassy in Austria and participated as an organizer of U.S. relief efforts to Belgium and to Ireland.

Doyle provided counsel to several Irish revolutionaries including Sir Roger Casement (who was found guilty of high treason and hanged by the British) and Eamon de Valera, a New York City native and Sinn Fein activist in the 1916 Irish uprising. Thereafter, he assisted with the drafting of the constitution of the Irish Free State. In 1910 he assisted in the establishment of the National Conference of Catholic Charities as well as the Catholic Near East Welfare Association. In 1922 the State Department appointed Doyle as counsel for Haiti and Santo Domingo. From 1929–39, Doyle served as chair of the American Committee of the League of Nations in America; during this fruitful decade of this career, Doyle enjoyed several special appointments: in 1932, to the Inter-American Conference for Peace (Buenos Aires); in 1938, to the International Court of Arbitration at the Hague (an appointment renewed by President Truman); in 1945, as special counsel to the president of the Philippine Republic. In 1937 Doyle won from the USSR government the privilege on behalf of Americans in Moscow to receive aid from American missionaries. In the twelve year span from 1937 to 1945, Doyle held the position of president of the American Electoral College for four consecutive terms. In the last year of his life, he was made a papal chamberlain, an honor which followed numerous other ones bestowed by the Vatican. He died on March 20, 1960, in his native city.

LISELLE DRAKE

DREXEL, KATHARINE (1858–1955)

Blessed Katharine Drexel, dubbed by journalists in discussing details of her life at the time of her demise as the "millionaire nun," died on March 3, 1955, but left behind a profound legacy of a true Christ-filled life. On November

Mother Katharine Drexel

26, 1858, Catherine Mary was born to Francis Martin Drexel, a noted Philadelphia banker, and Hannah Langstreth Drexel. Shortly after Catherine's birth Hannah Drexel died and Francis then married Emma Bouvier, who became a very devoted mother to Catherine and her sister, Elizabeth. Catherine had no formal education in schools, having been instructed by governesses at her home in Philadelphia, though her intellectual faculties were extensively developed by her numerous travels in the United States and abroad, as well as by her intimate participation in many social activities.

At the death of her stepmother (1883) and her father (1885), she inherited a sizable fortune which she ultimately used for her missionary endeavors in the community of sisters which she established. During a personal visit with Pope Leo XIII in 1883 Catherine asked His Holiness what could be done for the "Indians and Colored People" (as they were then called) in the United States. The Pope answered, "Daughter, why don't you become a missionary?" She left in tears. Upon return to Philadelphia, her home, she consulted with her spiritual director, Bishop James O'Connor of Omaha, Nebraska, about entering a cloistered Carmelite community because of her contemplative nature and because she was attracted to their way of life and their daily reception of Holy Communion. At that time religious communities, other than contemplatives, could approach the Communion rail only three times weekly. The bishop insisted on Catherine establishing her own community to respond to the specific request of the Pope and assured her permission would be given for daily reception of Holy Communion by the sisters. To prepare for this task she entered the novitiate of the Sisters of Mercy in Pittsburgh, Pennsylvania. At that time it was customary for sisters to adopt a name other than their baptismal name, but she assumed the name of Sr. Katharine. As head of the community she often signed correspondence to those who knew her well as "M.K.D.," Mother Katharine Drexel.

New Foundation

Her own foundation, known as Sisters of the Blessed Sacrament for Indians and Colored People, but now officially called Sisters of the Blessed Sacrament, was canonically founded on February 12, 1891. Because of her substantial financial holdings a reconciliation with the vow of poverty was necessary. Archbishop Patrick J. Ryan of Philadelphia settled the issue and informed Katharine, "You retain the possession and the administration, but you have to promise *in case of my requiring* it, that you would renounce your possessions."

In her lifetime she expended nearly twenty million dollars yielded from the income of her parents' estate by establishing and maintaining some sixty missions to care for the education of Native and African Americans to whom she and her sisters dedicated their lives. She focused her work and love on the nation's poorest and most oppressed. She met with fierce opposition in her work, never, however, fleeing a battle, but conducted her efforts with such refinement and style that she impressed her enemies and won their respect. One of her greatest triumphs was in establishing Xavier University in New Orleans, the only Catholic university for blacks in America.

When she died in 1955, at the age of ninety-seven, she left a great legacy of solid accomplishments. As mother general, she founded forty-nine convents for her sisters, set up training courses for catechists and teachers, and built sixty-two schools and Xavier University.

At the time of her death her reputation for holiness was so all-pervasive that people in great numbers began visiting her burial place at the motherhouse in Cornwell Heights (now Bensalem), Pennsylvania, and insisted that her cause for beatification and canonization be undertaken. The cause was opened in 1964 by John Cardinal Krol, archbishop of Philadelphia, and her writings were approved by the Congregation of the Causes of the Saints on November 9, 1973. The results of that preliminary searching inquiry were sent to Rome, and Pope John Paul II officially introduced the cause of this holy woman (the official beginning of the apostolic process) on November 17, 1979. She was beatified by Pope John Paul II on November 20, 1988, and her feast day is March 3.

Duffy, Consoela Marie, S.B.S. *Katharine Drexel: A Biography* Philadelphia, 1965.

JAMES McGRATH

Related Document

MOTHER KATHARINE DREXEL DRAFTS THE CONSTITUTIONS OF HER CONGREGATION, MAY 25, 1907

When the history of twentieth-century Catholicism in the United States is finally written there will be no more honored name than that of Mother Katharine Drexel (1858–1955). Granddaughter of Francis M. Drexel (1792–1863), the Austrian-born immigrant who came to Philadelphia in 1817 and in 1838 opened a brokerage office that led in time to the world famous banking house of Drexel & Company, Katharine and her two sisters became the heiresses of an immense fortune upon the death of their father in 1885. Having been the recipient of the finest type of religious training from her pious father and step-mother, Katharine Drexel was deeply impressed by the appeal of the bishops of the Third Plenary Council in 1884 for help to the Indian and Negro missions. In a private audience of Leo XIII in January, 1887, she spoke of this interest, whereupon the pontiff was prompted to ask, "Why not become a missionary yourself, my child?" That settled Miss Drexel's vocation for life. Guided by James O'Connor (1832-1890), first Bishop of Omaha, who as the pastor of Homesburg, Pennsylvania, had known the Drexel family very well, she made her novitiate with the Sisters of Mercy in Pittsburgh and in February, 1891, she took the veil and with thirteen other women launched the Sisters of the Blessed Sacrament for Indians and Colored People. Even before her entry into the religious life Miss Drexel had given a million dollars to the missions for these two races, and all during the next sixty-four years she continued to pour her vast wealth into the cause by building dozens of churches, chapels, schools, and other missionary buildings. At Mother Katharine's death the community numbered 511 professed religious stationed in fifty-one houses located in twenty-one states and the District of Columbia. The sisters staff sixty-two schools, including forty-nine elementary, twelve high schools, and the only Catholic Negro university in the country, Xavier University of New Orleans, founded in 1925, and having a faculty of 115 with over 1100 men and women students. Not only did Mother Katharine use all of her tremendous income for the advancement of the Catholic faith among the American Indians and Negroes, but she and her congregation have likewise given generously to missions for these races in Alaska, Canada, Africa, and the British possessions. Mother Katharine herself drew up the first draft of the constitutions of her community after it had been in existence for sixteen years, and the following document—the original written in her own hand—embodied a rough outline of her aims and objectives. The decree of final approbation for the sisters' rule was granted by the Holy See in May, 1913.

(*Source:* Archives of St. Elizabeth's Convent, Cornwells Heights, Pennsylvania, *Constitutions of the Sisters of the Blessed Sacrament for Indians and Colored People* [photostat].)

Concerning the Nature of the Congregation & the Manner of Living in the same

CHAPTER I
Nature & Object of the Congregation.

1. The primary object which the Sisters of this religious Congregation purpose to themselves is their own personal sanctification.

2. The secondary & special object of the members of the Congregation is to apply themselves zealously to the service of Our Lord in the Blessed Sacrament by endeavoring to lead the Indian & Colored Races to the knowledge & love of God, & so make of them living temples of Our Lord's Divinity.

CHAPTER II
The Means of Carrying out the Object.

3. The principal means by which the Sisters of the Blessed Sacrament for Indians & Colored People are to procure their own perfection & the education, sanctification & salvation of the Indian & Colored Races are the following:—

(1 The faithful observance of the three simple vows of Poverty, Chastity & Obedience according to the approved Constitutions of the Congregation, & the faithful observance of these same Constitutions.

(2 A complete consecration of themselves, body & soul, to the service of their Eucharistic Lord, by a special devotion to the Blessed Sacrament, so that through Him they may sanctify in an especial manner their two-fold apostolate of prayer & work as set forth in these Constitutions.

(3 Frequent prayer, especially at the Holy Sacrifice of the Mass & at Holy Communion, to draw down upon themselves & upon the souls of the Indian & Colored the graces that will save them.

(4 As a further means of accomplishing this work, the members of this Congregation are according to circumstances, [to] undertake

1) To instruct the Indian & Colored Races in religious & other useful knowledge according to their needs & capacities;

2) To care for their orphans & spiritually or corporally destitute children;

3) To attend to their sick by visiting them in their homes, or by the conducting of hospitals;

4) To visit their homes in order to look after their spiritual & temporal welfare;

5) To visit & instruct Indian & Colored inmates of prisons;

6) To shelter distressed & deserving women of these Races;

7) To aid in as far as they are able needy priests, religious communities & other reliable persons engaged in missionary work among the Indian & Colored Races.

(*Source:* John Tracy Ellis, ed, *Documents of American Catholic History.* Vol. 2:1866–1966. Wilmington, Del.: Michael Glazier, 1987, 574–76.)

DRISCOLL, CHARLES MARY (1859–1934)

Augustinian. Charles Mary Driscoll was born on June 18, 1859, in Lawrence, Massachusetts. Having spent some time as a lay student at Villanova College, he was received as an Augustinian novice December 8, 1879, and was ordained in Rome on December 23, 1883. Over the next seven years he served at Villanova in formation, and as a parish priest, including his first stint as a pastor. After fours years in Italy he returned to the U.S.A. in 1894 only to be elected as prior provincial in the chapter that year. Almost immediately he had to mediate a dispute between an Augustinian pastor in Atlantic City and the bishop of Trenton.

Highly respected by Archbishop Patrick Ryan of Philadelphia, Driscoll was appointed to serve as a judge for John Neumann's beatification process. After completing his term of office in 1898, he returned to Massachusetts where he served as pastor of several parishes. He also served in the curia of the Boston archdiocese, as well as acting as chaplain of the Knights of Columbus.

For the next ten years beginning in 1910, he served as pastor at parishes in New York City, upstate New York, and Philadelphia. In 1917, on the death of the prior provincial, he was appointed to fill out the term. When he went to Rome in 1920 for the general chapter, he was appointed to the office of assistant general. Completing this assignment in 1925, he returned to Villanova where for all but his last two remaining years he was in ill health, dying at St. Rita's parish in South Philadelphia on December 19, 1934.

See also AUGUSTINIANS (O.S.A.).

EDWARD ENRIGHT, O.S.A.

DRUMGOOLE, JOHN CHRISTOPHER (1816–88)

Priest, social reformer, and founder of the Mission of the Immaculate Virgin and St. Joseph's Union. John Drumgoole was born on August 15, 1816, in Granard, County Longford, Ireland. He emigrated to New York City as a young boy of eight years to greet his widowed mother, Bridget, who had taken the journey to America ahead of him to find work as a housemaid. Young John Drumgoole was educated in old St. Patrick's Cathedral Parish School located at Mott and Prince Streets in lower Manhattan. After reaching his fourteenth birthday, he abandoned school to support his mother and quickly acquired employment as a cobbler's assistant. Since he was in the habit of attending daily Mass, John was asked to be the sexton of St. Mary's Church which had been founded in 1826.

While at St. Mary's Church, John inquired about the possibility of becoming a priest. However, his lack of a formal education, his responsibilities to his mother, and his advanced age appeared to be insurmountable obstacles. Nonetheless, Drumgoole studied at both St. John's College at Rose Hill (now Fordham University) and the newly founded St. Francis Xavier College in New York City. In September 1865, he entered Our Lady of Angels Seminary in Niagara, New York, for theological studies. At fifty-two years of age, he was ordained to the priesthood by Bishop Stephen Ryan of Buffalo on May 22, 1869, and was appointed to the staff of his former parish, St. Mary's Church.

New York city was already infamous for the thousands of immigrants who had crowded into its grimy tenements. Even as late as 1868, over forty thousand children were unaccounted for and homeless. Catholics were particularly concerned about the fate of Catholic orphans and homeless young people. Many of them were eventually sent to Protestant institutions or were boarded with Protestant families who subjected them to intensive proselytism.

In 1871 Drumgoole offered his services to St. Vincent's Home, a boarding house for boys which had been recently opened by the St. Vincent de Paul Society and located at 53 Warren Street in lower Manhattan. With Archbishop John McCloskey's approval, Drumgoole left his parish work to create a nonterritorial "parish" of thousands of homeless youngsters. He quickly gathered many boys from the streets and brought order to their lives with a daily schedule of work and prayer. When he obtained a bigger facility next door to St. Vincent's, he added a program of classroom instruction and recreation in this new institution, which he called Newsboys' Home.

In 1881, with the help of the Franciscans Sisters of Buffalo, Drumgoole opened the Mission of the Immaculate Virgin for the Protection of Homeless and Destitute Children on the corner of Lafayette and Great Jones Street. The financial backing for his programs came from members of his St. Joseph's Union (who donated dues on an annual basis) and from the sale of his publication, *The Homeless Child Magazine*. In 1882 Drumgoole was able to purchase three farms located on Staten Island, which he designated Mount Loretto. In that location, which offered a refuge from the city streets, both boys and girls received a thorough vocational education and the institution became one of the largest orphanages in the United States, staffed by eighty Franciscan sisters.

Drumgoole became internationally known and even won the commendation of Pope Leo XIII and St. John Bosco. The seventy-two-year-old Drumgoole died at Mount Loretto on March 28, 1888. A victim of the Great Blizzard of 1888, his death certificate noted that he died of pneumonia and exhaustion.

Burton, K. *Children's Shepherd: The Story of John Christopher Drumgoole.* New York, 1954.

Jacoby, George Paul. *Catholic Child Care in Nineteenth-Century New York.* Washington: The Catholic University of America Press, 1941, 158–75.

THOMAS A. LYNCH

DUBOIS, JOHN (1764–1842)

Bishop, missionary, educator. John Dubois was born in Paris, France, on August 24, 1764. He was educated in Paris at the College of Louis le Grand, the Seminary of St. Magloire and the Sorbonne, and was ordained a priest in that city by the archbishop on September 22, 1787. His first assignment was to the large parish of St. Sulpice where he had additional responsibilities as chaplain to a mental institution.

In 1791, as the French Revolution entered a more radical and anticlerical phase, Dubois fled to the United States, settling in Virginia where he ministered to small Catholic communities in Richmond and Norfolk. In 1794 Bishop John Carroll assigned him to Frederick, Maryland, where he remained until 1808 when he shifted the site of the parish to Emmitsburg. From both locations, Dubois cared for the pastoral needs of Catholics scattered over a wide area of Maryland and northern Virginia.

John Dubois

Founder of Mt. St. Mary's Seminary

In 1808 Dubois embarked on a new career when he founded a preparatory seminary in Emmitsburg. Following a common practice of financing such institutions, Dubois also opened the seminary to lay students. In 1808 the total enrollment consisted of only seven students but grew to sixty by 1812. As Mt. St. Mary's College and Seminary, Dubois' school continues to exist today as a flourishing seminary and as the third-oldest Catholic college in the United States. In 1807 Dubois himself joined the Society of Saint Sulpice, the French religious community which in 1791 had founded the first Catholic seminary in the United States, St. Mary's Seminary in Baltimore. In the early nineteenth century, relations between St. Mary's Seminary and Mt. St. Mary's Seminary were often strained.

In addition to his pastoral and academic duties in Emmitsburg, Dubois took on additional responsibilities in June 1809 when Elizabeth Ann Seton and her companions took up residence in the village. Dubois acted as spiritual director to her and her companions and then served as their superior when they received ecclesiastical approval for their rule and were formally recognized as American Sisters of Charity.

Third Bishop of New York

Dubois began still another career when he was appointed the third bishop of New York on May 23, 1826. His episcopal ordination took place in Baltimore on October 29, 1826, and he was installed in New York on November 4, 1826. It proved to be an extremely difficult assignment. The Diocese of New York comprised all of New York state and the northern half of New Jersey, 51,334 square miles. When Dubois made a tour of the diocese in 1828, he covered some 3,000 miles. In addition to the size of the diocese, Dubois had to contend with the scarcity of churches and priests, and the poverty of the rapidly increasing Catholic immigrant population. Moreover, many of the Irish immigrants resented the appointment of a French-born bishop instead of Fr. John Power, the popular Irish-born pastor of St. Peter's Church, who had administered the diocese for twenty-one months prior to Dubois' appointment.

In an appeal for funds to the archbishop of Vienna in 1836, Dubois reported that there were 200,000 Catholics in his diocese with only thirty-three completed churches and thirty-eight priests to serve them. "The poverty of the Catholics," he said, "of which Europeans have no conception . . . is responsible for our having so few churches and priests."

Lay trusteeism was a major problem for Dubois in several of his churches, including his own cathedral, where the trustees threatened to refuse to pay his salary. Dubois' administration in New York also coincided with the outbreak of a wave of serious and sustained anti-Catholic bigotry. In 1836 New York City was the place of publication of one of the most notorious of all the anti-Catholic books of the era, Maria Monk's *Awful Disclosures of the Hôtel Dieu Nunnery in Montreal,* a fabricated "exposé" of convent life.

One of Dubois' great ambitions was to provide the diocese with its own seminary. Between 1833 and 1837, he laboriously constructed a seminary building in Nyack, New York, but it burned to the ground in 1837 just as it neared completion. That same year the aging and ailing Dubois requested and received a coadjutor, John Hughes, a Philadelphia priest who had been a student under him at Mt. St. Mary's Seminary. Dubois ordained him a bishop in Old St. Patrick's Cathedral on January 7, 1838. After Dubois suffered several strokes, in August 1839 Hughes was made the administrator of the diocese. Dubois died in New York on December 20, 1842, and was buried at his direction beneath the sidewalk in front of old St. Patrick's Cathedral. He is supposed to have said: "Bury me where the people will walk over me in death as they wished to do in life." His exact burial site was soon forgotten and was only rediscovered in 1976.

See also MOUNT ST. MARY'S COLLEGE AND SEMINARY; NEW YORK, CATHOLIC CHURCH IN; SETON, ELIZABETH ANN BAYLEY.

"Bishop Dubois on New York in 1836." *Historical Records and Studies* 10 (1917) 124–29.

Cohalan, Florence D. *A Popular History of the Archdiocese of New York.* Yonkers, 1983, 39–52.

Shaw, Richard. *John Dubois: Founding Father.* Yonkers and Emmitsburg, 1983.

THOMAS J. SHELLEY

DuBOURG, LOUIS WILLIAM (1766–1833)

Educator and bishop. Born in Saint-Domingue, the two-year-old William was sent by a prosperous but recently widowed father to his grandparents in France. Educated in Bordeaux and Paris, he was always a Frenchman at heart. Ordained a priest in Paris in 1790, the 1792 Jacobin stage of the Revolution turned him into a nonjuring émigré in Spain where a gift for languages became apparent.

Two years later the Abbé DuBourg was in Baltimore where he joined the Society of St. Sulpice and began his American career as a schoolman. Bishop John Carroll appointed him president of Georgetown College in 1796. After a misadventure in a Sulpician college in Cuba he returned to Baltimore and founded St. Mary's College and Seminary in 1799. In that capacity he invited Elizabeth Ann Seton to Baltimore to begin her seminal work of parochial education in the young Republic of the United States and supported her foundation of the Sisters of Charity in Emmitsburg.

His career as prelate in the Mississippi Valley began when Archbishop John Carroll appointed him apostolic administrator of the Diocese of Louisiana and the Floridas, a notoriously difficult post. DuBourg arrived in New Orleans in 1812. Confrontations with the pastor of the Cathedral, Padre Antonio de Sedella (Père Antoine), dogged him. Acknowledged by Orleanians to be intelligent, gracious, zealous, and, indeed, French-born and French-speaking, he was still an outsider. A moment of prestige was the January 1815 public ceremony of Thanksgiving at the cathedral honoring the victorious General Andrew Jackson. With the apparent end of the Napoleonic Wars, DuBourg left for Rome, arriving there only after delays in the chaotic France of the summer of 1815.

Louis William DuBourg

Bishop of Louisiana

On September 24 in the Church of Saint-Louis des Français, DuBourg was consecrated bishop for the Diocese of Louisiana. He spent the next two years using a gift for recruiting talented personnel and a flair for collecting funds for his frontier American diocese. Fearful of a hostile reception in New Orleans, where his friendship with the restored Bourbons was denounced, the new bishop decided to reside in Upper Louisiana, building a cathedral in St. Louis. Thus Vincentians founded the Seminary of St. Mary of the Barrens in Upper Louisiana and the Ladies of the Sacred Heart, led by Philippine Duchesne, began their American educational apostolate there. Bishop DuBourg also invited Flemish Jesuits, stranded in Maryland, to come west to evangelize the Native American nations. His recruits who had gone to Lower Louisiana founded parishes in Grand Coteau, Thibodaux, and Vermilionville (Lafayette). In 1823 Joseph Rosati, C.M., was appointed coadjutor bishop and DuBourg took up residence in New Orleans where, although hostility remained, he received strong support from the Ursuline nuns. On their move to a new site, their French Quarter convent became his episcopal residence. DuBourg, whose enthusiasm led to overreaching and consequent disappointments, nonetheless demonstrated a remarkable resilience throughout his whole career. In 1826, however, he resigned his see when his effort to establish a seminary in Lower Louisiana failed. He returned to France and was appointed bishop of Montauban at the request of King Charles X; shortly before his death on December 12, 1833, he was promoted to the Archdiocese of Besançon.

See also LOUISIANA, CATHOLIC CHURCH IN; SULPICIANS (S.S.).

Melville, Annabelle M. *Louis William Dubourg.* 2 vols. Chicago, 1986.

EARL NIEHAUS, S.M.

DUCHEMIN, THERESA MAXIS (1810–92)

Religious. The first American-born African American woman to become a religious, and pioneer in the founding of two religious congregations: the Oblates of Providence and the Sisters, Servants of the Immaculate Heart of Mary, Theresa Maxis was born in Baltimore in 1810. She was the daughter of a Haitian refugee and a British military officer and was raised within the African American community by her mother's guardians, the Duchemins.

In 1829 Theresa became one of the founding members of the Oblates of Providence. The young community soon faced serious problems due to lack of support for an African American religious congregation. Ultimately, the congregation was ordered not to receive any new candidates. During this time, Theresa met Louis Florent Gillet, C.Ss.R., a Belgian missionary who was looking for sisters to educate young women in Michigan.

In 1845 Theresa left the Oblates and traveled to Monroe, Michigan, in order to found the Sisters, Servants of the Immaculate Heart of Mary. She become the first general superior. In 1855 the Redemptorists withdrew from the diocese, and Bishop Peter Paul Lefevre, angered by this action, appointed a diocesan priest—Edward Joos—as superior and director of the I.H.M. Congregation. Mother Theresa was thus replaced.

Three years later (1858), the I.H.M.s were invited to open a mission in Pennsylvania. Mother Theresa was anxious to do so. In 1859, when seeking permission to open another mission in Pennsylvania, Theresa was refused. She protested vigorously and was deposed by Bishop Lefevre and ordered to the leave the diocese.

Theresa went to Pennsylvania and was rejected by the bishop of Scranton. She took shelter with the Grey Nuns in Ottawa. She remained there for seventeen years, and claimed her I.H.M. title throughout her time of exile. She continuously sought to be allowed to return to the I.H.M.s. Finally, in 1885, a new bishop of Philadelphia allowed her to return to West Chester, Pennsylvania. She was never allowed back to Scranton or to Monroe. She died in West Chester, Pennsylvania, in 1892.

Theresa Maxis was a woman of color who knew discrimination, oppression, and rejection. Even as her life reminds us of the injustices that can be perpetuated in the name of religion and order, her courage reminds us that faith and steadfast love are gifts of the women who have gone before us.

See also AFRICAN AMERICAN CATHOLICS; SISTERS OF THE IMMACULATE HEART OF MARY (I.H.M.).

JULIANA CASEY, I.H.M.

DUCHESNE, ROSE PHILIPPINE (1769–1852)

Religious, missionary, and saint. Philippine was born on August 29, 1769, in Grenoble, France, the second of eight children born to Pierre-François Duchesne and Rose-Euphrosine Périer. Both the Duchesne and Périer families were well-to-do bourgeois clans active in mercantile and political affairs in the French province of Dauphiné. Pierre-François would serve as a representative in local politics, while Philippine's first cousin, Casimir-Périer, would achieve his greatest fame several decades later as prime minister in the early years of the July monarchy.

The family was composed of fervent Catholics. Five of the six sisters of Philippine's father would become Sisters of the Visitation. In spite of his early ties to the Church, Pierre-François Duchesne would gradually become a free thinker and devotee of the Enlightenment. Mme. Duchesne, for her part, remained devoted to the Catholic faith

Rose Philippine Duchesne

of her ancestors and sought to preserve it in the hearts of her children.

Religious in France

It was during the two-year period, starting in 1781, that she spent with the Visitandines of Grenoble in preparation for her First Communion that Philippine felt the first stirrings of a religious vocation. Encountering the opposition of her family, she returned home and awaited the year 1788 before entering religious life. It was during this period that the desire was awakened in her to one day become a missionary in America.

The Grenoble Visitation convent, Ste-Marie-d'en-Haut, was largely unaffected by the revolutionary decree of February 13, 1790, banning all monastic orders in France. Religious women were specifically exempted from the order, especially if they engaged in education or works of charity. This exemption was revoked on August 18, 1792, with the abolition by the revolutionary government of all religious orders for women.

With the closing of her convent, Philippine returned to her family. At their country home outside Grenoble, she attempted to maintain the essence of the Visitation Rule with a cousin, Julie Tranchand, a Visitation nun from the monastery at Romans. Philippine returned to Grenoble during the height of the terror to organize works of charity for the poor, as well as to offer material and spiritual support to priests in prison or in hiding. She and her helpers would be called the "Ladies of Mercy."

Still sensing the call to religious life, Philippine would, over the course of the next few years, attempt to join a group of Visitandines in exile. The group at nearby St-Marcellin was headed by her own aunt, Mother Claire-Euphrosine Duchesne, but Philippine's attachment to them proved short-lived.

After a pilgrimage to the tomb of St. Francis Regis at LaLouvesc in 1800, Philippine resolved to dedicate her life to teaching the poor. She arranged, on December 10, 1801, to rent her former monastery at Ste-Marie-d'en-Haut, and therein to reintroduce the Visitation Rule. This unfortunate venture lasted little more than two years, and was ended by dissension within the community.

The four remaining nuns adopted a new name, "Daughters of the Propagation of the Faith," on March 3, 1803, and the following year sought admission into the Society of the Sacred Heart, founded in 1800 by Madeleine-Sophie Barat. With Mother Barat herself acting as mistress of novices, the Ste-Marie convent became the second foundation of the new community and was transformed into a novitiate. In January of 1805, the first of Mother Duchesne's many requests to serve in the American missions would be denied by Mother Barat.

Between 1805 and 1815, Mother Duchesne bore the responsibility for the convent school at Grenoble, and for the first part of this period, the role of mistress general as well. After the adoption in Rome of a constitution and rules for the Society of the Sacred Heart in November of 1815, and the convoking of the society's second general council, Mother Duchesne was named secretary general, with residence in Paris.

Missionary in America

The year 1817 saw the visit to France of Louis DuBourg, bishop of Louisiana and the Two Floridas. Because of his urgent plea for missionaries, and a personal meeting between the bishop and Mother Barat, permission was obtained for Mother Duchesne and a first contingent of nuns to travel to America. The necessary preparations took many months to accomplish, and the missionaries only set foot in the New World on May 25 of the following year, after spending ten weeks at sea.

Mother Duchesne and her companions enjoyed the hospitality of the Ursulines at New Orleans for several weeks before receiving permission to head up-river by packet boat to St. Louis. Bishop DuBourg resolved that the sisters should take up residence at St. Charles, Missouri, and not at St. Louis. According to the bishop's wishes, the sisters were to set up a school for local white children. After traveling this great distance, Mother Duchesne was frustrated in her immediate desire to work among the native peoples of the Mississippi Valley.

Because of an abundant correspondence between Mother Duchesne, on the one hand, and her family and Mother Barat on the other, we can trace the progress of her work and that of her sisters in America. During her first decade in the New World, Mother Duchesne suffered all the extremes of physical deprivation that the frontier had to offer. Precarious finances, and the difficulty encountered by her family and Mother Barat in efficiently transferring funds from Europe to America, only served to compound her worries.

After a year-long stay at St. Charles, the convent school was removed to Florissant, Missouri. The fall of 1820 witnessed the entry into the society of its first American vocation, Mary Layton. At the instigation of Bishop DuBourg, the community sent a delegation of sisters to Louisiana in 1821 to establish a foundation near Opelousas.

Mother Duchesne served as superior to her sisters in the Mississippi Valley, and possessed authority from Mother Barat to buy or sell property in the name of the society. The authority to establish definitively new foundations, appoint religious personnel anywhere in the world, and make important executive decisions remained vested in Mother Barat in far-off France. Significant decisions had to be referred to her, or at the very least submitted to her for ratification. This would remain the case until 1839, when various visitatrixes would be appointed for the society. Given the chain of authority that existed in the earliest days, the inevitable delays in sending and receiving mail constituted a further impediment to the smooth functioning of the society.

In spite of these handicaps, the society made impressive strides, and by the close of the 1820s, it could count six institutions in the United States, staffed by 64 religious, educating more than 350 students. While fourteen of the religious had come from France, the remaining fifty were American-born.

On November 30, 1831, Mother Barat acceded to Mother Duchesne's oft-stated request, and relieved her of her weighty duties as superior in America. The relief was short-lived as Bishop Joseph Rosati of St. Louis disagreed with the decision and caused Mother Duchesne to remain in office. The year 1834 brought a change of residence to Mother Duchesne, back to Florissant from St. Charles.

With the arrival of the visitatrix, Mother Elizabeth Galitzin, in the fall of 1840, Mother Duchesne would be finally relieved of her duties as superior. She would assume residence in the society's "city house" in St. Louis with the only seniority being that of her years of profession. Here she would have spent her declining years except for a happy convergence of opinions.

Missionary to the Native Americans

After Gregory XVII urged the society to engage in mission work among Native Americans, three sisters were appointed to this task. Due to her advanced years, Mother Duchesne was not among those named. The quick intercession of her Jesuit friend, the local missionary Fr. Peter Verhaegen, caused Mother Duchesne to be included in the mission band.

Their destination was a Potawatomi village at Sugar Creek, Kansas, inhabited by a people who had formerly lived in Michigan, but who had been displaced by the federal government. While a significant number of the tribespeople had already embraced Catholicism, much work remained for the sisters and the Jesuit Fathers to accomplish.

Mother Duchesne arrived at Sugar Creek in July of 1841. Her age, her generally frail health, and her inability to master the Potawatomi tongue all combined to limit the material assistance that she could offer to the missionary effort. She would spend long hours nursing sick tribe members, however, and quickly gained a reputation for sanctity among her new neighbors. The Potawatomi would christen her "Quah-Kah-Ka-num-ad," or "woman who prays always," in honor of the extensive periods of time she spent kneeling before the Blessed Sacrament.

Devotion to the Sacred Heart of Jesus and to the Blessed Sacrament had indeed always constituted the essence of her spirituality. Her habit of keeping lengthy night vigils before the tabernacle had long ago been noticed by her sisters, who furthermore marveled that these extended sessions of prayer and their attendant lost hours of sleep, in no way impeded Mother Duchesne's daytime energy.

Her evangelical poverty was also legendary. Her repeatedly patched habit and veil served as a poignant sign of her renunciation of the riches of this world. No false sense of dignity prevented her from embracing the most arduous of manual labor.

The arrival of the visitatrix, Mother Galitzin, to the Sugar Creek Mission on Palm Sunday 1842 marked the beginning of the end of Mother Duchesne's work among the Potawatomi. The visitatrix deemed the elderly nun too frail to continue living at the village, and decreed Mother Duchesne's return to St. Louis. The missionary life among the native people which she had so ardently desired for decades was about to come to an end, less than a year after it started. Under obedience, Mother Duchesne returned to St. Louis and spent her remaining years at the society's house at St. Charles. She died November 18, 1852, having attained her eighty-third year.

Mother Duchesne's remains were interred in the community cemetery at St. Charles. After lying in the ground for three years, encased in a plain wooden coffin, her body was exhumed in preparation for reburial in a recently constructed oratory. The corpse was found to be incorrupt at this time, although it later succumbed to the laws of nature. Mother Rose Philippine Duchesne was beatified May 12, 1940, and on July 3, 1988, was pronounced a saint of the Church by Pope John Paul II. Her feastday occurs on the anniversary of her death on November 18.

See also SACRED HEART, SOCIETY OF THE (C.S.C.J.); WOMEN RELIGIOUS IN AMERICA.

Callan, Louise, R.S.C.J. *Philippine Duchesne, Frontier Missionary of the Sacred Heart.* Westminster, Md.: Newman Press, 1965.
Cruz, Joan Carroll. *The Incorruptibles.* Rockford, Ill.: Tan, 1977.

ALBERT H. LEDOUX

DUDZIK, MARY THERESA (1860–1918)

Foundress. She was born on August 30, 1860, in the hamlet of Plocicz in western Poland and was given the name Josephine at baptism (Mary Theresa was her name in religion). After her early education she trained to be a seamstress. The family migrated to Chicago in May 1881 and there she resumed her sewing to help support the family. She was active in her local parish and when the Third Order of St. Francis was organized, she was named mistress of novices.

Chicago began to see hard times in the late 1880s; unemployment increased and the soup-kitchen lines grew longer. Josephine felt she had to extend her hand to Chicago's poor and homeless, so after her father's death in May 1889, she brought several destitute women into her home and cared for them. After four years of crowded living, she thought of buying a house for her ladies and of asking friends among the members of the Franciscan tertiaries to dedicate themselves to the poor and homeless. Under the guidance of the pastor of St. Stanislaus' parish, Josephine's plan went into effect on December 8, 1894, and on the following December 23, she was elected the group's first superior. Thus was founded the Franciscan Sisters of Bl. Kunegunda, known since 1970 as the Franciscan Sisters of Chicago.

To support themselves and the women under their care, the first members took in sewing, did laundry and housework. Since Josephine's home was much too small to house a convent and a hospice for homeless women, she purchased property in Avondale. Construction began in September 1897, and on March 25, 1898, the sisters and the women moved to their new St. Joseph's Home.

On October 4, 1898, the pastor of St. Stanislaus parish, who remained the sisters' spiritual guide, unexpectedly removed Josephine (he gave no cause) as superior and appointed another. Josephine was subsequently placed in charge of the laundry and when vocations increased she was likewise placed in charge of formation. On January 1, 1909, the sisters' spiritual guide reappointed Josephine as superior—the incumbent had proved to be a failure because of inexperience. At the congregation's first general chapter (August 1910), which Josephine prepared, Josephine, because of animosity among the delegates who thought her view of religious life too strict, was not elected to any position of authority. She spent her remaining years taking care of the community's garden and died on September 20, 1918.

Though she had never been the congregation's mother general, nevertheless, she is rightfully acknowledged as the community's foundress. The canonical process for her beatification opened in Chicago in 1979 and on March 26, 1994, Pope John Paul II published the decree proclaiming her a person of extraordinary virtue.

See also POLISH CATHOLICS IN AMERICA.

Malak, Henry M. *Theresa of Chicago.* Lemont, Ill.: League of the Servant of God Mother Mary Theresa, 1975.

Tylenda, Joseph N. "With Charity towards All: Mother Mary Theresa Dudzik, O.S.F. (1860–1918)." *Portraits in American Sanctity.* Chicago: Franciscan Herald, 1982, 250–64.

JOSEPH TYLENDA, S.J.

DUFFY, FRANCIS PATRICK (1871–1932)

Educator, military chaplain. Duffy was born in Cobourg, Ontario, Canada, on May 2, 1871, and died in New York City on June 26, 1932. He was the third of eleven children born to Patrick and Mary Ready Duffy, working-class Irish-Canadians whose families had fled the famine in their native land. He received a scholarship to St. Michael's College, Toronto, Canada, where he earned his baccalaureate degree in 1893. Through a Jesuit friend he obtained a position in the preparatory department of St. Francis Xavier College, New York City, where he earned a master's degree and decided to begin studies for the priesthood. He entered St. Joseph's Provincial Seminary at Troy, New York, in 1894. Duffy was ordained for the Archdiocese of New York at his home parish in Canada on September 6, 1896, by Bishop Richard A. O'Connor of Peterborough.

Francis P. Duffy

Seminary Professor

He attended The Catholic University of America, Washington, D.C., where he obtained the S.T.B. degree in 1898. These studies were cut short when Duffy contracted typhoid fever and was sent to St. Joseph's Hospital in Yonkers, New York, to recover. Following his illness he began a fourteen-year assignment (1898–1912) teaching philosophy and theology at the newly established St. Joseph's Seminary at Dunwoodie, New York. Dunwoodie's first rector, Sulpician Edward R. Dyer, called Duffy "one of the most efficient men I have ever seen work in a seminary." Duffy once described his own attitude to scholarship by saying: "Lack of faith is not our difficulty unless it be that worst form of infidelity which fears to look at the truth. Our main drawback is a certain intellectual sloth which masquerades as faith."

Along with Dunwoodie colleagues John Brady and James Driscoll, Duffy founded and served as associate editor of the *New York Review* (1905–08), a scholarly journal with a constructive emphasis on contemporary apologetics, especially in the area of biblical exegesis. As an editor, Duffy's influence marked every issue of the *New York Review;* however, his major scholarly contribution to the *New York Review* was the "Notes" which appeared at the end of each issue. These "Notes" summarized and commented upon developments in contemporary European and American Catholic intellectual life. This section, considered one of the finest aspects of the *New York Review,* was one of the first to be dropped when the journal came under suspicion during the "Modernist" crisis. The *New York Review* was forced to cease publication in the spring of 1908.

Pastor and Military Chaplain

In 1912 Duffy founded Our Savior parish in the Bronx, where he quickly built a church, school, and convent. While remaining pastor of Our Savior, Duffy was appointed, on John Cardinal Farley's nomination, a military chaplain from 1916–17 with the "Fighting Sixty-Ninth" Regiment of the New York National Guard. He accompanied the regiment to France late in 1917 and remained a chaplain until 1920. Duffy said that he never regretted being a military chaplain.

Duffy's tolerance made him popular with the chaplains and soldiers of various creeds. He also received official recognition for his work, and was decorated with the Distinguished Service Cross and Medal, the Croix de Guerre, and the Legion of Honor, and became the best-known American military chaplain of World War I. Duffy published his chronicles of the war in *Father Duffy's Story* (1919), which includes a historical appendix by Joyce Kilmer, a personal friend of Duffy killed in the war.

Duffy as a Public Figure

Following the war, Duffy was made pastor of Holy Cross parish on West Forty-Second Street, Manhattan (1920–32).

He also served as president of the Catholic Summer School of America, Cliff Haven, New York. Throughout his life, Duffy was a man ahead of his time who took great interest in ecumenism and education, both as a pastor and a military chaplain. It was because of his theological expertise and ecumenical sensitivities that Duffy became involved in the "Catholic Issue" of the 1928 presidential election campaign. In March 1927 the *Atlantic Monthly* published a letter from a distinguished Episcopalian lawyer, Charles Marshall, who stated the Protestant difficulties with the traditional Catholic understanding of Church-state relations. Marshall not only expressed the concerns of many American Protestants, but also publicized the opinions of some right-wing Catholics who insisted that the Catholic Church could not tolerate "erroneous" religions.

Alfred E. Smith, fearing a growing concern among the American people about his own Catholicism, employed Duffy's help in drafting a reply which appeared in the April 1927 issue of the *Atlantic Monthly*. Duffy prepared a clear statement enabling Smith to show the harmony between Church teaching and American political principles. Unfortunately, such explanations seemed irrelevant to millions of voters who continued to harbor fears of a Catholic in the White House, as Smith discovered on Election Day. However, Duffy's arguments in this regard remain significant in that they anticipate the critically important scholarship in the 1950s and 1960s of Jesuit John Courtney Murray which helped to shape the Second Vatican Council's explanation of religious freedom.

Duffy devoted much time in his final years to writing and public speaking. Duffy never was made a monsignor, a common honor for priests who had achieved far less than he had done. He was, however, the best-known priest in New York. At his death in 1932, a newspaper ran a cartoon of a wealthy lady trying to get into St. Patrick's Cathedral for Duffy's funeral, which attracted 25,000 people. A burly cop was barring her way. She said to the cop: "But I was a friend of Father Duffy." The cop replied: "Lady, everybody in New York was a friend of Father Duffy." Five years following his death, his statue was placed in Times Square making him the first priest to be so honored in the State of New York.

See also MODERNISM IN AMERICA; *NEW YORK REVIEW;* WORLD WAR I AND AMERICAN CATHOLICS.

DeVito, Michael J. *The New York Review (1905–1908)*. New York: United States Catholic Historical Society, 1977, 25–30.
Duffy, Francis P. "Does Theology Preserve Religion?" *American Ecclesiastical Review* 25 (1901) 372–90.
____. *Father Duffy's Story*. New York: George H. Doran Company, 1919.
Flick, Ella M. E. *Chaplain of the Sixty-Ninth Regiment*. Philadelphia: Dolphin Press, 1935.

Purcell, Richard J. "Francis Patrick Duffy." *Dictionary of American Biography*. Supplement I, 267–69.
Shelley, Thomas J. *Dunwoodie, The History of St. Joseph's Seminary, Yonkers, New York*. Westminster: Christian Classics, 1993.
____. "'What the Hell is an Encyclical': Governor Alfred E. Smith, Charles Marshall, Esq., and Father Francis P. Duffy." *U.S. Catholic Historian* 15 (2) (Spring 1997) 87–107.
RICHARD G. SMITH

DUFFY, FRANK J. (1867–1950)

Lay Catholic activist and banker. Frank J. Duffy was born in St. Louis, Missouri, in 1867. He came to Natchez, Mississippi, around the turn of the century where he worked as a manager for the Southern Railway and Light Company. He later entered the banking and hotel businesses. He was also a successful planter in nearby Concordia Civil Parish in Louisiana.

Duffy was an active civic leader and parish advisor at St. Mary's Cathedral in Natchez. He served for many years on the Cathedral School financial advisory board that was established in 1915, was active in the St. Vincent de Paul Society, contributed generously to charitable causes, and was "a leading figure in all community work." Duffy served as president of the local Association of Commerce (1915–17).

Duffy's most noteworthy contribution followed the 1929 failure of the local Bank of Commerce. Duffy, as bank president, felt a personal responsibility to all customers and, over the years "dug into the personal fortune he had earned and saved to pay each depositor, dollar for dollar." Duffy left in his adopted Mississippi home an enduring memory of social justice and community responsibility that is unique, or at least rare, in American banking history.

Frank Duffy died in Natchez on January 5, 1950, and was buried in Calvary Cemetery in St. Louis, Missouri. His generous bequest to St. Mary's parish was an important factor in building a new parish school.

Natchez *Democrat,* January 6, 1950; *Catholic Action of the South,* January 12, 1950.
Nolan, Charles E. *St. Mary's of Natchez: The History of a Southern Catholic Congregation, 1716–1988*. Natchez, 1992.
St. Mary's Parish, Natchez, Pulpit Announcements and Organizational Minutes in parish archives, passim.
CHARLES E. NOLAN

DUNN, MARY FLAVIA (1856–1945)

Religious. An outstanding educator whose influence played a part, not only in the development of Catholic education, but also in the evolution of secular education in Oregon.

Mary Flavia was born of Irish immigrant parents in Sacramento, California. After the family moved to Oregon, she was educated by the Sisters of the Holy Names of Jesus and Mary, first in St. Paul, Oregon, and later in Salem, Oregon. Graduated from Sacred Heart Academy, Salem, in 1875, she entered the Sisters of the Holy Names in 1876. After eleven years in the missions, she returned to St. Mary's in Portland to assume the duties of senior class teacher and of Provincial Directress of Studies for the Sisters of the Holy Names in Oregon and Washington. It was at this time that her great work in the field of education began.

In 1893 she established a college at St. Mary's academy, Portland, with full accreditation from the state of Oregon, in spite of many bigots who opposed any growth of Catholicism in the area. She founded three normal schools for women in Oregon and Washington and obtained competent educators to conduct them. Certification for her teachers was a high priority for her. She established summer schools and teacher institutes which offered college courses geared towards the subjects needed to meet state requirements for teacher certification. She recognized the need for higher degrees and sent her sisters to far-off Catholic universities to obtain them, a practice unheard of in those days. She also supervised curricula, wrote courses of study, visited classes, admonished and encouraged teachers, and continually strove for the advancement of excellence in the schools run by the Sisters of the Holy Names. Because of the guidance and farsightedness of this valiant educator, the Catholic schools in Oregon and Washington offered excellent education for those who elected to attend them.

Sr. Flavia's zeal did not stop at the school doors. She did all she could to combat bigotry that threatened every phase of Catholic education in the state. After many months of effort, prayer, and collaboration with others working to save the schools, the notorious Oregon School Bill of 1922 was declared unconstitutional by the United States Supreme Court in 1925. Catholic schools were no longer in jeopardy from the Ku Klux Klan and other enemies. To honor the fiftieth anniversary of her religious community's presence in Oregon and Washington, Sr. Mary Flavia wrote the history of these first fifty years. The book, entitled *Gleanings of Fifty Years,* has been a valuable source of information for succeeding generations. Her death in 1945 brought to a close a long and fruitful career.

Dunn, Mary Flavia. *Gleanings of Fifty Years.* Portland, 1909.

ROSEMARIE KASPER, S.N.J.M.

DUQUESNE UNIVERSITY

Duquesne University, run by the Society of the Holy Ghost (Spiritans), first opened its doors as the Pittsburgh Catholic College of the Holy Ghost in October 1878 with an enrollment of forty students and a faculty of seven. From a humble original location on Wylie Avenue in the city's

uptown section to its present beautifully self-contained campus, Duquesne provides a hilltop vista overlooking one of the nation's most attractive cities.

In 1911 Duquesne was granted university status by the Commonwealth of Pennsylvania. The Schools of Law, Business, and Theater Arts admitted women students in 1915. By 1927 all remaining schools at the university admitted women students.

Duquesne's recent growth has been significant with more than 9,000 students in nine schools of study, including the College and Graduate School of Liberal Arts (1878); and the Schools of Law (1911); Business Administration (1913); Pharmacy (1925); Music (1926); Education (1929); Nursing (1937); Health Sciences (1990); Natural and Environmental Sciences (1994). Duquesne's nine schools offer degree programs on the baccalaureate, professional, master's, and doctoral levels.

See also CATHOLIC UNIVERSITIES AND COLLEGES.

JOHN MURRAY

DUTTON, IRA BARNES (1843–1931)

Lay missionary. Better known as "Brother Joseph of Molokai," Ira Dutton was born to a Congregationalist family in Stowe, Vermont, on April 27, 1843. He later moved to Wisconsin, from which state he enlisted in the Union army at the age of eighteen. Serving in the Civil War for four years, he rose to the rank of captain. At the end of the conflict, he obtained a position in the War Department, where he served in the Claims Department for ten years. During this period, Dutton entered into a short-lived and unhappy marriage that lasted one year. For a time, he engaged in loose living and heavy drinking.

He made a spiritual rediscovery, converting to Catholicism in 1883. Shortly thereafter he joined the Trappists, entering the monastery of Our Lady of Gethsemani in Kentucky where he spent two years.

Having learned of the work of Fr. Damien De Veuster among the lepers of Molokai in the Hawaiian islands, Dutton made his way on foot to San Francisco in 1886. It was his intention to work among the lepers and to atone for his past life. He arrived on Kalaupapa, Molokai Island, in June 1886, where he was met by Fr. Damien. Dutton remained on the island until his death forty-five years later. He served as a lay brother, assuming the name of Joseph. When Fr. Damien died in 1889, Br. Joseph took on the duties of administrative assistant of the colony. He worked among the lepers, nursing them and continuously striving to improve their living conditions. Among other accomplishments, he founded the Baldwin Home, a residence for leper men and boys.

In his later years, Dutton was honored for his work on Molokai by the Hawaiian government. As illness and old age took their toll, Br. Joseph found it necessary to go to a hospital in Honolulu where he died, at the age of eighty-eight, on March 26, 1931. At the time of his death, he was praised as "an incentive to virtue . . . a man who for many years had preached the loving charity of Our Lord Jesus Christ."

See also DAMIEN, FATHER/JOSEPH DE VEUSTER.

"Brother Joseph of Molokai." *America* 45 (April 11, 1931) 5–6.

PATRICK J. McNAMARA

E

EASTERN CATHOLIC CHURCHES IN AMERICA

The Vatican Council II called the members of the Catholic Church to esteem the institutions, liturgical rites, ecclesiastical traditions, and the order of Christian life of the Eastern Catholics. In its Decree on the Catholic Eastern Churches it declared:

> History, tradition and very many ecclesiastical institutions give clear evidence of the great debt owed to the Eastern Churches by the Church Universal. Therefore the holy council not merely praises and appreciates as is due this ecclesiastical and spiritual heritage, but also insists on viewing it as the heritage of the whole Church of Christ. For that reason this Council solemnly declares that the churches of the East like those of the West have the right and duty to govern themselves according to their own special disciplines. For they are guaranteed by ancient tradition, and seem to be better suited to the customs of their faithful and to the good of their souls (no. 5).

This article will focus primarily on the Eastern Catholics and their various rites in the U.S.A. To do so properly it is necessary first to see the early Churches of the Christian East from which the present Eastern Catholics living in America have evolved.

History of the Eastern Churches

When the term *Eastern Churches* is used, it refers to those Churches which evolved in the eastern half of the Roman Empire in the first five centuries of Christianity and others that were dependent upon the beginning Churches, even though the daughter Churches were and still are found outside of the original boundaries of the Roman Empire. The chief centers of civil administration became the ecclesiastical centers since Christianity flourished mostly in populated urban centers.

The Emperor Theodosius in the fourth century divided the prefecture of Illyricum into an eastern and western part with the boundary line separating the eastern and western halves of the empire which ran along the Sava, Drina, and Zeta Rivers to the Adriatic Sea. All lands west of the line belonged ecclesiastically to the Latin or Roman Church, while all lands eastward belonged to the respective Eastern Churches in that territory.

All Eastern Christian Churches evolved out of the ancient patriarchates of Constantinople, Alexandria, and Antioch, while the Churches of Armenia and Persia developed outside of the Roman Empire. Thus we find the roots for the five leading Eastern Christian rites which followed along the territories of the five ecclesiastical jurisdictions, namely, the Alexandrian, Antiochene (or Western Syrian), Byzantine, East Syrian, and Armenian.

The Persian or East Syrian Church was formed through the fifth-century heresy called Nestorianism, which taught that Jesus Christ had two natures, divine and human, but it was the human Jesus, born of Mary as a human person, who died for us. This heresy was condemned in the Council of Ephesus in C.E. 431.

In the Council of Chalcedon in C.E. 451, the heresy of Monophysitism, which taught that the human nature of Jesus was absorbed into his divinity, was condemned. This resulted in the formation of the Armenian, Coptic, and Syrian Churches, called *Orientals*. These Churches no longer belonged to the "one, holy, catholic and apostolic Church," as did the remaining Eastern Orthodox, Byzantine, and the Roman Churches.

Through a gradual estrangement, climaxed by the Latin Crusaders who sacked Constantinople in 1204 and the disputes about the primacy in jurisdiction of the pope of Rome over the other Eastern patriarchs, there resulted the *schism* that divided the Roman and the Byzantine Orthodox Churches from each other. Two ecumenical councils at Lyons in 1274 and at Florence in 1439, were called to reunite the Western and Eastern Churches, but to no lasting success.

The Rise of the Uniate Churches. With the Counter-Reformation Council of Trent in the sixteenth century, the Roman Church evolved a strong, monarchical ecclesiology, unknown in the ancient Eastern Churches that had stressed jurisdiction in terms of collegiality. The Roman attitude with regard to the Orthodox and Oriental Churches became one of uniformity and obedience to the authority of the pope of Rome. A great missionary effort led by the Jesuits, Dominicans, and Franciscans working in those Eastern countries from the sixteenth century into modern times strove to "reunite" the Eastern Churches with Rome, while Rome would promise to allow the Eastern Churches to retain their liturgical rituals and elements of their canonical disciplines. This policy has given rise to the term *uniatism,* used chiefly by the Eastern Christian Church leaders. It was primarily meant to vilify any Eastern Christians who sought reunion with Rome.

Yet this faulty, unecumenical approach to reunion imposed many unwanted effects upon the "reunited" Orthodox and Oriental Christians, as will be pointed out in regard to the Eastern Catholics in America.

Reunions with Rome. The first reunion of Orthodox with Rome was brought about in the *Union of Brest* in 1595–96, and brought into union with Rome the largest group of Slav Orthodox living in the Orthodox Metropolitan Province of Kiev from which modern-day Catholic Ukrainians claim their origin.

Other Slav unions among the Podcarpathian Rusins with Rome were the *Union of Uzhorod* in 1646 and the *Union of Mukachevo* in 1771. The union among the Assyrian Nestorians was brought about in 1681 in the city of Diarbekir in modern Iraq.

Various Eastern Catholic patriarchates were established, as that of the Syrian Catholics in 1663 and in 1729 of the Catholic Melkites. The Catholic Armenian Patriarchate was set up as a result of the union in Sis, Cilicia, in 1742 and the Coptic Catholic Patriarchate was erected in Cairo in 1895. Other smaller groups among the Romanian Orthodox and those Orthodox Slavs living in Yugoslavia and

Bulgaria entered into union with Rome. The most recent reunion took place in Kerala, India, in 1930, when Mar Ivanios led a large group of Indian Jacobites to form the Catholic Malankar Church.

The Maronites, originally centered in Lebanon, today have no counterpart among the Orthodox and Oriental Christian Churches and claim they have never broken their union with the Roman Church.

Eastern Catholic Churches in the U.S.A.

According to the 1994 statistics (see *The Official Catholic Directory* [New Providence, N.J.: P. J. Kenedy & Sons, 1994] 1144–68), the population of Eastern Catholics in America numbers approximately 550,000.

Eastern Catholics in U.S.A.

Rite	Membership	Parishes	Dioceses
1. Ruthenian	192,537	341	4
2. Ukrainian	138,250	201	4
3. Chaldean	55,800	11	1
4. Maronite	55,740	51	1
5. Armenian	38,000	6	1
6. Melkite	27,000	44	1
7. Romanian	5,200	15	1
8. Syro-Malankara	N.A.	6	0
9. Syro-Malabar	N.A.	6	0
10. Russian	N.A.	3	0
11. Belarusian	N.A.	1	0

As indicated above, the majority of Eastern Catholics in the U.S.A. belong to the Slavic ethnic groups, all using the Byzantine Rite. Keeping in mind the above distributions, let us look more closely at the historical roots and present situation of the Eastern Catholics in U.S.A.

Eastern Catholics first arrived in America with the mass immigration of Eastern Catholic Slavs, mostly Ukrainians and Ruthenians, who came out of the regions that in the nineteenth century belonged to the Austro-Hungarian Empire. To develop the coal and steel industries of Pennsylvania and Ohio chiefly, agents were sent to the poverty-stricken, unindustrialized Slavic regions of the Austro-Hungarian Empire to arrange that whole villages would come en masse to America.

At this time the Vatican called these groups *Ruthenians* (*Rutheni* in Latin) and included all the Slav immigrants among the Ukrainians, Belarusians, Slovaks, and Ruthenians. This group of Eastern Catholics preferred and even today prefer to call themselves *Rusyns*.

The Ruthenian Catholic Church

The majority of the first Eastern Catholics were those who today constitute the Ruthenian Church in America, often called simply *Byzantine Catholic Church,* since it "americanized" more rapidly than the strictly so-called Ukrainian Church, by using English in all their services. This was due to the fact that it embraced Slavs coming from Slovakia and Hungary, as well as from Yugoslavia.

These Catholics petitioned their European bishops to send them Byzantine Catholic priests to minister to them. What followed was a tragic drama of these Slavic Catholics in America seeking to hold on to the traditions of their Byzantine heritage, while the Vatican sought to control them by placing them under the local Latin-Rite bishop. A circular letter of the Congregation for the Propagation of the Faith (that handled such matters of missionary concern in 1890) to the Ukrainian and Carpathian hierarchies in Europe, insisted that only celibate priests or widowers without their children would be allowed to work in America (see Archimandrite Victor J. Pospishil, *Ex Occidente Lex—From the West—The Law* [Carteret, N.J., 1979] 25).

Over 200,000 Eastern Catholics, without any bishop of their own, but finding themselves under Latin local bishops (who had little understanding of their Eastern traditions) turned to the Russian Orthodox in America to accept them as Orthodox. Finally in 1907 they received their first Slavic Byzantine bishop when Rome appointed the Basilian monk, Soter Stephen Ortynsky, the first Byzantine Catholic bishop in America. What sent so many of these Catholics into the Russian Orthodox Church was the Vatican's decree, *Ea Semper,* in 1907, which would not allow Ortynsky to have any jurisdiction over his people, since he would be a representative of the apostolic delegate in Washington, D.C. Compulsory celibacy was imposed and many other "latinizations" were demanded.

In 1913 Ortynsky received full episcopal jurisdiction, independent of the Latin-Rite bishops but still under the supervision of the apostolic delegate. Because Ortynsky was of Ukrainian descent, the Ruthenians demanded to have their own Ruthenian bishop and this was granted in 1924 with Bishop Constantine Bohachevsky as the Ukrainian bishop and Basil Takach as the ordinary for the Ruthenians in America.

The final reason why so many thousands of Byzantine Catholics in the United States turned to the Russian or Ukrainian Orthodox Churches was the issuance of the papal decree *Cum Data Fuerit* on March 1, 1929 (*A.A.S.* 21 [1929] 152–59). It stated: "In the meantime, as has already several times been decreed, priests of the Greek-Ruthenian Rite who wish to go to the United States of North America and stay there, must be celibate" (Art. 12). This led to the formation in 1936 of the *American Carpatho-Russian Orthodox Greek Catholic Diocese* under the jurisdiction of the patriarch of Constantinople which now numbers 110,000 members.

Pospishil states that about 1,347,000 today are Slav Orthodox in America and that "more than 90 percent are former Catholics of Byzantine Rite and their offspring, according to private judgments expressed by Orthodox churchmen" (Pospishil, 59). He estimates that only 22 percent of the Eastern Slav Catholic immigrants to America have remained as Catholics united to Rome.

Today, the Ruthenian Catholic Church has the largest number of Eastern Catholics in the U.S.A. As indicated in the distributions listed earlier, they number 192,537 with 341 parishes in four dioceses. The metropolitan archdiocese was established in February 21, 1969, with headquarters in Pittsburgh. It numbers 101,122 members. The other dioceses are: the Byzantine Catholic Diocese of Passaic, established July 31, 1963, with headquarters in West Paterson, New Jersey, with 72,500 members; the Byzantine Diocese of Parma, Ohio, established on February 21, 1969, with 15,650 members; and the Byzantine Diocese of Van Nuys, California, established December 3, 1981, with 3,265 members.

Metropolitan Archdiocese of Philadelphia Ukrainian

This was first established as a diocese on May 28, 1913, under the first Eastern Rite Catholic bishop in America, Bishop Ortynsky, and on August 6, 1958, it was elevated to a metropolitan archdiocese. It has its headquarters in Philadelphia, Pennsylvania, and numbers 73,500 members. Besides this metropolitan archdiocese there are three other Ukrainian dioceses: (1) the Ukrainian Catholic Diocese of Stamford, Connecticut, established on August 8, 1956, with 34,822 members, embracing the territories of New York and the New England states; (2) the Ukrainian Catholic Church of Chicago of the St. Nicholas diocese, comprising all of the states west of the western borders of Ohio, Kentucky, Tennessee, and Mississippi, which was established on July 12, 1961, and has 18,201 members; (3) the Ukrainian Catholic Diocese of St. Josaphat in Parma, Ohio, which was established on December 3, 1963, and has 11,727 members.

Eparchy of St. Thomas, the Chaldean Catholic Diocese

This was established as a diocese on September 14, 1986. Its members originally immigrated to America from the Middle East, especially from Iraq and Iran. It is headquartered in Southfield, Michigan, outside of Detroit, and numbers 55,800, with eleven parishes.

Diocese of St. Maron of Brooklyn, New York

This Maronite diocese extends its jurisdiction throughout all of the U.S.A. and has a bishop and an auxiliary bishop. It was created as a diocese on November 11, 1971. The ancestors of the members of this diocese came to America mainly from Lebanon, Syria, and Iraq. It is made up of fifty-one parishes with 55,740 members.

Armenian Catholic Exarchate of the U.S.A. and Canada

In the U.S.A., the Catholic Armenians are found in six parishes spread out in the states of New York, California, Massachusetts, Michigan, New Jersey, and Pennsylvania. They form an apostolic exarchate with a bishop having jurisdiction over all Armenian Catholics in Canada and the U.S.A. Their ancestors came to America mainly from Lebanon, Syria, and Turkey. This Church was established as an exarchate (not yet an official diocese) on July 3, 1981. The members number 38, 000, with six parishes.

Eparchy of Newton of the Melkite Catholics in the U.S.A.

The word *Melkite* comes from the Syriac *malka* or the Arabic *malek* or *melek* meaning king or emperor. The name was first used by the Monophysites to deride those Byzantine Christians who remained faithful to the Christian Byzantine emperors who held the Christology taught by the Council of Chalcedon (451). Today, the term is used in its most limited sense to refer to the Orthodox of the Byzantine Rite who became reconciled with Rome in 1744. The present Catholic patriarch of the Melkite Catholics bears the title of Greek Catholic Patriarch of Antioch and All the East, of Jerusalem and of Alexandria.

The Catholic Melkite Church is governed by the bishop of Newton, Massachusetts, and an auxiliary bishop. It was established as a diocese on July 15, 1976, with the entire U.S.A. as its territory. It is made up of fifty-one parishes and 55,740 members.

Romanian Catholic Diocese of Canton, Ohio

The roots of this Romanian diocese extend back to Transylvania, now a part of modern-day Romania. In order to have equal religious and political rights under Leopold I, emperor of the Holy Roman Empire, who had annexed Transylvania in 1687 by defeating the Turks, a union with Rome was brought about in 1700. This union was abolished under the Communists in 1948 and most of the five Catholic dioceses were given to the Romanian Orthodox Church. Many of those Byzantine Catholics who were able to escape from the Communist rule formed the diocese of St. George in Canton, Ohio.

This diocese was established on December 4, 1982. It comprises fifteen parishes with 5,200 members, centered primarily in the states of Ohio and Michigan.

Missions under the Local Roman-Rite Hierarchy

Russian Catholics in America have never numbered more than a few hundred and therefore are considered a mission under the supervision of the Latin hierarchy in the territory where such parishes are found. There are three such parishes, one in New York City, another in San Francisco, and a third in El Segundo, California.

Belarusian Catholics have their roots, like the Catholic Ukrainians, in the Union of Brest (1595–96). The Belarusian Byzantine Catholic Church was suppressed by the Russian tsarist government in the nineteenth century. A community emerged of some 30,000 Byzantine Catholics after World War I in the area of modern Belarus, then a part of Poland. In America there is only one parish of Christ the Savior in Chicago.

The Syro-Malankara Catholics in America stem from the Syro-Malankar Jacobites who united with Rome under Mar Ivanios in 1930. Although in America they have not developed sufficiently in numbers to constitute a diocese, they are under the jurisdiction of the local Roman-Rite bishop. They have thriving parishes in Chicago, Dallas, Houston, New York, Philadelphia, Washington, D.C., and Toronto.

The Syro-Malabar Catholics are rapidly growing in America with about ten priests in ten parishes. In India, primarily in Kerala, they number about three million Catholics with many vocations to the priesthood and religious orders. In the U.S.A. these Catholics are under the supervision of the local Latin bishop.

Coptic Catholics have parishes in Brooklyn and Los Angeles and are made up of Coptic Catholics from the Coptic Catholic Patriarchate of Cairo.

The Future of Eastern Catholics in America

Through intermarriages, especially between Eastern and Roman Catholics, plus the diminishing number of immigrants coming from the original areas of these Catholic Rites in Europe, Africa, the Middle and Near East, and India, with some exceptions, we see a continued decrease in the numbers of Eastern Catholics in America. Often the mobility of modern living brings about an uprooting of such Eastern Catholics from their Eastern parishes to a locality where there is no Eastern parish and such Catholics are usually assimilated into the Roman Catholic Rite.

Latinization. Latinization is defined by Donald Attwater as "the modification of Eastern liturgies, customs, and modes of thought by undiscriminating adoption of foreign practices and submission to foreign influences that mostly come from the West" (*The Christian Churches of the East*, I, 27). A glaring example of such turning away from the ancient traditions of their Eastern Christian patrimony has been the enforced celibacy for the Eastern Catholic dioceses in U.S.A. from 1929 with the papal decree *Cum Data Fuerit* that forbade the ordination of any married man to the diaconate and priesthood for service in Eastern Catholic parishes in the U.S.A.

The removal of icons and the replacing of them with statues, the use of Latin-Rite devotions, and the removal of the icon screen, have all removed Eastern Catholics away from their traditions and their unique piety of many centuries. Some Eastern Churches have developed a "low Mass" that is recited and abbreviated from the traditional Eastern Liturgy. A lack of monasticism in America among the Eastern Catholic Churches has been replaced by apostolic religious orders modeled on Roman-Rite communities, much to the neglect of the deep roots of Eastern Christian mysticism.

The Challenge. There is a great need as Vatican II Council told Eastern Catholics for their religious leaders and the faithful to remain true to their Eastern Christian traditions and to return to them if for any reason they have been lost:

> All members of the Eastern Churches should be firmly convinced that they can and ought always preserve their own legitimate liturgical rites and ways of life, and that changes are to be introduced only to forward their own organic development. They themselves are to carry out all these prescriptions with the greatest fidelity. They are to aim always at a more perfect knowledge and practice of their rites, and if they have fallen away due to circumstances of times or persons, they are to strive to return to their ancestral traditions (Decree on the Catholic Eastern Churches, no. 5).

Another needed endeavor for the growth of Eastern Catholics in America is a better formation of the members of the Eastern Catholic hierarchy, priests, and also the laity in their Eastern Christian patrimony in Scripture, theology, and canon law; their unique and ancient forms of piety, music, art and architecture. They also need to develop a greater understanding and use of the mystical symbols that in Eastern Christianity play a great role in emphasizing the doctrine and practice of discovering the trinitarian theophanies in our human existence through the power of the resurrected, cosmic Christ working in our present world to bring to completion all of God's creation.

No matter how few are the numbers of Eastern Catholics in the U.S.A. compared to the number of Roman-Rite Catholics, there must be a sincere and effective appreciation for all Eastern Catholics as full members of the Church. They preserve the ancient elements of Christian living that will redound to the building up of the entire Church. Pope John Paul II often quotes from Yves Congar's statement: "The Church must breathe fully with its two lungs: the Eastern Churches and the Western."

Maloney, G. "Eastern Churches." *New Catholic Encyclopedia* 5:13–21.

Pospishil, V. *Ex Occidente Lex: The Eastern Catholic Churches under the Tutelage of the Holy See of Rome.* Carteret, New Jersey, 1979.

Robertson, R. *The Eastern Christian Churches.* 3rd ed. Rome, 1993.

Roccasalvo, J. *The Eastern Catholic Churches: An Introduction to Their Worship and Spirituality.* Collegeville, Minn.: The Liturgical Press, 1993.

Taft, R. *Eastern-Rite Catholicism: Its Heritage and Vocation.* Mahwah, New Jersey, 1963.

GEORGE A. MALONEY, S.J.

ECKERT, JOHN (STEPHEN) (1869–1923)

Capuchin friar and pastor. Eckert was born of German immigrant parents in Ontario (Canada) on April 28, 1869. His elementary education was in Berlin (now Kitchner) Ontario, and he later attended a school operated by the Resurrectionists for young men thinking about the priesthood. He subsequently entered the Capuchin Order at St. Bonaventure Monastery in Detroit, and on receiving the habit in 1891 he also received the name Stephen. Since the German tongue was used in seminary classes, and in view of the fact that English was his first language, he found studies difficult. Nevertheless, he persevered. In 1892 he was assigned to Milwaukee, where he began his theological studies and was ordained to the priesthood on July 2, 1896.

The years following ordination were spent in New York City and environs. In 1897 he was assigned to Sacred Heart parish in Yonkers and in 1906, though hoping to be assigned to a mission in the South among blacks, he was transferred to Our Lady of the Angels in Harlem, which was, at that time, predominantly Slavic and Italian. When superiors needed someone who spoke English to minister in a parish quickly losing its German character, he was assigned in 1907 to St. John's Church on West 30th Street in mid-Manhattan. His first experience with blacks came when several families moved into the parish. Since these families did not feel at home in an Irish parish, he thought of buying an old Protestant church for his new black converts, but before he could do anything, he was reassigned (1909) to Our Lady of the Angels. Now, in addition to his parish work, he began preaching parish missions in various parts of the United States.

In July 1913 Eckert was transferred to St. Benedict the Moor "Mission for the Colored" in Milwaukee and was its first resident pastor. Out of the 2,000 black residents in that area, only 84 were Catholics. He began a house-to-house visitation, and held instructions for converts. Enrollment in his school soon increased. He also opened a club room, an employment agency for girls and women and a day nursery. The money to operate his mission he received from the whites in the area and used the honoraria from his missions and retreats. In 1921 he was appointed the mission's fundraiser, while another Capuchin took over daily administration. In January 1923 he preached a Forty Hours devotion in Britt (Iowa), but after preaching and hearing confessions, he began to feel ill. He returned to Milwaukee, where pneumonia set in. He died on February 16, 1923. In 1958 a statue in his memory was erected next to St. Benedict the Moor parish in Milwaukee, with the inscription

"Apostle and Champion of the Colored Race." The cause for his beatification was begun in 1959.

See also FRANCISCANS (CAPUCHINS).

Bittle, Berchmans, O.F.M. Cap. *A Herald of the Great King: Stephen Eckert, O.F.M. Cap.* Milwaukee: St. Benedict the Moor Mission, 1933.

Crosby, Michael, O.F.M. Cap. "Minister to Urban Blacks: Father Stephen Eckert, O.F.M. Cap. (1869–1923)." *Profiles in American Sanctity,* ed. Joseph N. Tylenda. Chicago: Franciscan Herald, 1982, 266–82.

JOSEPH TYLENDA, S.J.

ECUMENISM IN AMERICA

Circumstances in the nineteenth century did not favor a friendly attitude toward other Churches on the part of the Catholic immigrants. Yet a global interest in religion was manifest in the writings of Orestes Brownson after his conversion in 1844, and in the pastoral initiatives of Isaac Hecker, both of whom had been influenced by the literary and religious movement of the Transcendentalists. As Hecker founded the first American Catholic religious community of men—the Paulists—he formed an institution that would share his concerns about the basic spirituality of other Churches and religions in America. At the official level the American hierarchy was in general remarkably open. Not only did the bishops accept the pluralism of their society, but following Bishop John England of Charleston and Archbishop John Ireland of St. Paul, they even regarded it as the logical consequence of the freedom of the act of faith. It was in part the desire to equip the Church with the qualities of mind needed to prosper in a religiously plural society that lay behind the creation of The Catholic University of America in 1887. And the conviction that the American Catholic Church could meet other churches and religions at the highest level of intellectuality inspired the decision of Cardinal James Gibbons, archbishop of Baltimore, and John Ireland, to organize a Catholic participation in the World's Parliament of Religions in Chicago (1893). But Leo XIII's critique of what he called "Americanism" (*Testem benevolentiae,* 1899) resulted in a later retrenchment of the hierarchy behind a strict adherence to the spirit of the Counter-Reformation.

The "Unionist" Ideal

It was also Leo XIII's conception of Christian reunion by conversion to Rome ("unionism") that dominated the thought of the few who were concerned about disunity among Christians in the first decades of the twentieth century. On the one hand there was so little concern for the rites and rights of Byzantine Catholic immigrants, that, despite immemorial tradition, the Congregation for the Oriental Church imposed the Latin discipline of clerical celibacy on the Oriental clergy in the U.S.A. (decree *Cum Data Fuerit,* March 1, 1929). On the other hand the reunion of Christendom was envisioned as the "return" of all "dissidents" to Latin Catholicism. The effective conversion of Lewis Wattson (Fr. Paul) and the Friars of the Atonement from the Episcopal Church to the Catholic Church (1908), and the rejection by Benedict XV in 1917 and Pius XI in 1928 *(Mortalium animos)* of Catholic participation in the Faith and Order and the Life and Work movements confirmed this basic orientation, with the result that the emergence of the ecumenical movement in 1910 and its subsequent development were not echoed in American Catholicism until the 1950s.

Seeds of an Ecumenical Opening

In 1949 the rejection by Archbishop Richard Cushing of Boston, of Leonard Feeney's narrow interpretation of the axiom *Extra ecclesiam nulla salus,* implicitly opened a door to better relations with Protestants, all the more so when it was supported by a letter from the Holy Office (*Suprema haec,* August 8, 1949). Meanwhile, the growing pressures of a free society upon American Catholics made unavoidable a degree of pluralism that was alien to the spirit of the Counter-Reformation and that opened the possibility of an ecumenical attitude. During World War II the chaplains' corps of the Armed Forces was a school of practical ecumenism. So were the chaplaincies and "Newman Centers" in secular universities. Various degrees of fraternity with other Christians came naturally to lay movements like Dorothy Day's Catholic Worker or Catherine de Hueck's Friendship House, and to publications like *America* (Society of Jesus), the *Catholic World* (Paulist Fathers), or *Commonweal* (run by a team of laypersons). Occasional exchanges of friendly letters between Catholics and other Christians were promising: in 1954 between James Cardinal McIntyre of Los Angeles and Russian Orthodox bishop Athenagoras Kokkinakis, on the occasion of the ninth century of the separations of 1054; from 1955 to 1957 between Gerald O'Hara, bishop of Savannah, and a Southern Baptist minister, Dick Hall. The Catholic Theological Society of America heard papers on Protestant theology in 1953 and 1955, and on the ecumenical movement in 1954.

Discovery of Ecumenism

The discovery of ecumenism was slowly taking place, in theological and historical courses offered by a growing number of Catholic colleges and universities, in the development of a theology of democracy by John Courtney Murray, S.J., in the writings of Gustave Weigel, S.J., on the ecumenical movement and on Protestant theology, notably on the thought of Paul Tillich. Ecumenical gestures were also made. In 1945, Helen Iswolsky, a Byzantine Catholic born in Russia and recently arrived from France, started *The Third Hour,* an ecumenical journal of irregular periodicity, and, under the same title, a gathering of Orthodox, Catholics, Anglicans, and Protestants who met in New York City for lectures and conversation. The Russian Center of Fordham University hosted solid theological conversations between several Orthodox (notably Georges Florovsky and Alexander Schmemann) and Catholic theologians. In the 1950s Barbara Simonds, an Anglican in New York City, initiated ecumenical pilgrimages to Canterbury and Rome. In 1955 my volume, *The Catholic Approach to Protestantism,* with a preface by George Shuster, marked the first clear departure from the conversion conception of Christian reunion.

The way, however, was not entirely smooth. John Courtnay Murray had adversaries in several seminaries. In 1954 Samuel Cardinal Stritch, archbishop of Chicago, sent no observers to the second assembly of the World Council of Churches in Evanston, and forbade Catholics to attend. Yet in 1958 Edward Hoban, bishop of Cleveland, delegated Gustave Weigel, S.J., and John Sheerin, C.S.P., as official observers to a meeting of the American section of the Faith and Order Commission at Oberlin College. On the whole, however, the Catholic Church in the U.S.A. was, on the eve of Vatican Council II, generally unprepared for the ecumenical opening of John XXIII. A few Jesuits were pioneers. Conversations with other Christians or with Jews were occasionally organized in some monasteries. But the few religious communities that had inherited from their foundation or their subsequent history an interest in the reunion of Christians were not directly involved in the ecumenical movement. Through university chaplaincies and their publication, the *Catholic World,* the Paulists were moving in an ecumenical direction. The Friars of the Atonement were engaged in the spiritual ecumenism of the Octave of Prayer for the Unity of Christians, but in the unionist direction of their founder. Before 1955, the Assumptionists were not active on the lines of their founder's intention to work for the unity of the Church.

Vatican Council II

It was the experience of Vatican II by bishops and *periti* that effectively brought ecumenism to the fore. No American bishop was among the members of the Pontifical Secretariat for Christian Unity at its creation by John XXIII in 1960, though a Paulist priest (James Cunningham) was a member, and three consultants (Edward Hanahoe, S.A., John Oesterreicher, George Tavard, A.A.), and two officials of the Secretariat (John Long, S.J., and Thomas Stransky, C.S.P.) were also from the U.S.A. Three bishops were added during the second session of the council: Charles Helmsing (Kansas City-St. Joseph), who presented to the council the *relatio* on chapter two of the decree on Ecu-

menism on October 6, 1964; Ernest Primeau (Manchester, New Hampshire); and Lawrence Cardinal Shehan (Baltimore). Before the end of the council, the Bishops' Committee for Ecumenical and Interreligious Affairs (BCEIA) was created in the U.S. Catholic Conference, and contacts were soon made with several Churches with a view to the initiation of dialogues along the lines of *Unitatis redintegratio* and the postconciliar Ecumenical Directory (1967 and 1970).

Bilateral Dialogues

Since 1965 official dialogues have taken place between representatives of the BCEIA and the following Churches: Lutheran (with participation of the Missouri Synod), Episcopal, Presbyterian and Reformed, Methodist, Disciples (soon becoming an international dialogue), Southern Baptist, Orthodox, Ancient Oriental. A number of joint theological statements have been issued, among which the nine documents of *Lutherans and Catholics in Dialogue,* published from 1965 to 1994, have achieved international recognition.

Popular Ecumenism

Ecumenism in America in the years that followed Vatican II was also characterized by its popular aspect. Many dioceses established Commissions for Ecumenism. Booklets published by the Paulist Press inspired "living-room dialogues" in many parts of the country, with the participation of local laity and clergy. The officers in charge of the Commissions for Ecumenism formed a National Association of Diocesan Ecumenical Officers (NADEO). This is primarily concerned with grassroots ecumenism; it works in close association with a similar organism in the Episcopal Church (EDEO); and it has inspired an annual convention, the National Workshop on Christian Unity. Ecumenical "covenants," which include a commitment to mutual prayer and to a degree of common action, have been signed between Catholic parishes and congregations of other Churches, and even between dioceses and the corresponding judicatories of several Protestant Churches.

Conclusion

Undoubtedly the popular dimension of American ecumenism has receded since the death of Paul VI. Yet the official dialogues continue. These are increasingly turning to the future and considering the requirements of full communion and the conditions for the restoration of organic unity among all Christians.

The Ecumenist (1962–).
The Journal of Ecumenical Studies (1964–).
Tavard, George H. *The Catholic Approach to Protestantism.* New York: Harper, 1955.

_____. *Two Centuries of Ecumenism.* Notre Dame, Ind.: Fides Publishers, 1960.

Weigel, Gustave. *A Catholic Primer on the Ecumenical Movement.* Westminster, Md.: Newman Bookshop, 1957.

GEORGE H. TAVARD

EDES, ELLA B. (1832–1916)

Journalist. Born in Charlestown, Massachusetts, on December 7, 1832, she was the only surviving child of the merchant Captain Robert F. Edes of Charlestown, Massachusetts, and Henrietta Birkhead Phelps Edes of New Haven, Connecticut. Three other siblings all died within one year of their birth. Her father drowned at sea aboard his cargo ship, *Groton,* on passage from New Orleans to Marseilles, on September 18, 1836. She claimed blood relationship with Peter and Benjamin Edes who were active as printers, publishers, and revolutionaries in the late 1700s in Boston. It was within the confines of Peter Edes's domicile in the North End one placid midnight that the plans for the Boston Tea Party were methodically engineered. She was also the maternal niece of Jonathan Mayhew Wainwright, Episcopal bishop of New York.

Of her early years and education few details are known, but after her father's death, she lived with her mother (until her early death in 1856) and her aunts Jennette Phelps Beers and Elizabeth Phelps Chetwood and assorted cousins in Elizabethtown, New Jersey. It is surmised that on February 25, 1852, she was converted to Catholicism by James Roosevelt Bayley, secretary to Archbishop John Hughes. As sole heiress to her mother's considerable estate and beneficiary of that fortune, she was able to cast off her provincial background and to move permanently to Rome.

Edes in Rome

In 1860 she emigrated with her lifelong companion Eliza McBride (another convert from her New Jersey neighborhood and daughter of Scottish shipping magnates) to the Eternal City. There she found fortuitous employment as secretary to Cardinal Alessandro Barnabò, prefect of the Sacred Congregation for the Propagation of the Faith in the Piazza di Spagna. Gradually over the course of the years she became untitled daring lobbyist for the Ultramontane cause. Her presence inside Propaganda proved invaluable to conservative American bishops in their disputes with their more liberal confreres in the American hierarchy.

For the American conservatives, Edes at the palazzo of Propaganda was a match made in heaven. In that place she ripened into that most vital but dangerous personage, an agent with an agenda, who was at the beck and call of her political cronies and powerful allies. She interfered as much as was humanly possible. She pursued and ultimately won access to the decisions and judgments of that busy bureaucracy before they were published and disseminated them by cable and telegram to her friends in America. She also tried to convince and influence the decision-makers at Propaganda. More often than not, she succeeded handsomely in swaying them to her point of view.

At first she translated apostolic declarations from Italian to English and afterward the depositions of advocates who pleaded and negotiated their cases in Rome. She also compiled newspaper notices and clippings regarding the worldwide state of the clergy from the international press, gathering them into dossiers. Later she accumulated authority by her familiarity with officials and functionaries within their intimate hierarchical networks. Among her acquaintances she numbered popes Pius IX and his successor, Leo XIII, whose encyclical, *Testem benevolentiae,* concluded the Americanist "crisis" in January 1899.

Edes's convocations and dinners were legendary, and she once noted: "They are always offering to do me any favor I wish." Staunch loyalty was her credo, and her mission to demonstrate her fidelity was paramount. There was nothing she would not attempt to do to advance the interests of her protectors or to promote their clerical standing. Edes was the ultimate faithful servant. She was outspoken but diplomatic, her convictions were solid and unshakable, her fealty as devout as the creed she professed. It is well known that she leaked confidential information containing private minutes of secret meetings to Archbishop Michael Corrigan of New York and Bishop Bernard McQuaid of Rochester. She planted false stories and erroneous details in stories she transmitted in her news columns. Rumors of her prowess and the lengths to which she tergiversated became the stuff of myth and lore.

Her adversaries among the progressives complained bitterly about her behavior and blamed her for every defeat they suffered, imagined or real. It was said by her enemies, who vilified her as "La Signora," that she was not above committing crimes of stealing and forging documents, bribing Propaganda personnel to filch files and printers to stop the presses in mid-type for the purpose of obtaining advance copy. Those whom she antagonized fought back, sullying her reputation with insults. They called her "a sanctimonious spinster become scandalmonger," "an unsucculent . . . sour and wintry virgin," "a gossip-monger . . . among the plague of garrulous old women" who haunted Holy Cities. This personal warfare did not deter Edes from her sacred duty, and she retaliated in print. She relished deflating the petty, pompous, arrogant, and the ambitious.

Edes's Roman "Letters"

Edes's greatest contribution was in the prolific and vigorous "letters" she wrote for various secular and religious newspapers and journals as "special Roman correspondent" over a career that spanned thirty years. An editorial announcement in 1899 stated: "The letter . . . will furnish not only the most readable news from Rome but the most reliable, for unquestionably of all Roman correspondents the well known lady . . . is the best and trustiest." This was no self-serving hyperbole, for she wrote her mother tongue with idiomatic conciseness and had a lively mocking style which combined venom and vitriol. Among those literary media in which her famous byline "E" appeared were (in chronological order): the New York *Herald,* New York *World,* Brooklyn *Daily Eagle, Osservatore Romano,* London *Tablet, Freeman's Journal and Catholic Register, Catholic News, Catholic Review,* Brooklyn *Citizen, Dublin Review,* and *Ave Maria.*

Unlike other correspondents of the day who roved the continent, she never traveled outside her adopted country, preferring always to slake her curiosity at home. Her book-strewn apartment at 21 Via delle Mercede, crowded with statues and images, was a famous stopover for clerical dignitaries and managing editors and writers, among whom were James Edwards, Daniel Hudson, John Talbot Smith, William Hickey, and James McMaster. Unable to care for herself after 1900, she moved to Piscina in northern Italy, the village of her erstwhile domestic Rosita Orsi, and died there on February 27, 1916.

Much of her later life after Rome is shrouded in mystery. It is verified that she destroyed her voluminous papers. Only her furniture survived. Other witnesses' diaries which have come to light in recent years suggest that recipients of her copious correspondence were encouraged to burn the material. Ironically hundreds of letters still remain and can be consulted in the archives of the Archdioceses of Baltimore, New York, St. Paul, and Cincinnati, and the Dioceses of Cleveland and Rochester, the University of Notre Dame, and the Abbey of St. Paul's Outside the Walls in Rome, and the American Catholic Historical Society of Philadelphia.

See also AMERICANISM; CORRIGAN, MICHAEL.

Curran, R. E. *Michael Augustine Corrigan and the Shaping of Conservative American Catholicism, 1878–1902.* New York: Arno, 1978.

Fogarty, G. P. *The Vatican and the Americanist Crisis: Dennis J. O'Connell, American Agent in Rome.* Rome: Universita Gregoriana, 1974.

McNamara, R. F. "Ella Edes." *New Catholic Encyclopedia,* 5:102.

O'Connell, M. R. *John Ireland and the American Catholic Church.* St. Paul: Minnesota Historical Society, 1988.

BRUCE KUPELNICK

EGAN, MAURICE (1852–1924)

Author, journalist, diplomat. Maurice Francis Egan was born in Philadelphia, Pennsylvania, on May 24, 1852, the

Maurice Egan

son of Maurice Florent Egan, an Irish immigrant from Tipperary, and Margaret MacMullen Egan, a native of Philadelphia. He was educated at Dr. Martin's Latin School, St. Philip's parochial school, and LaSalle College, Philadelphia, where he received the B.A. degree in 1873, and the M.A. degree in 1875. For the following three years, 1875–78, Egan taught and studied philosophy at Georgetown University. In 1878 he moved to New York City where he spent the next ten years as a journalist and assistant editor of *Magee's Weekly, Illustrated Catholic American, Catholic Review,* and the *Freeman's Journal.*

In 1888 Egan accepted an invitation to become professor of English literature at the University of Notre Dame where he remained until 1896 when he accepted a similar offer from The Catholic University of America. In 1907 President Theodore Roosevelt appointed Egan minister to Denmark. In the following years he twice refused an offer to become ambassador in Vienna and remained in Copenhagen throughout World War I, only resigning in 1918 when ill health forced him to relinquish the post. As minister to Denmark, Egan played a key role in the purchase of the Danish West Indies (the American Virgin Islands) by the United States in 1917.

Egan wrote thirty-five books and received the Laetare Medal from the University of Notre Dame in 1911. In 1880 he married Katherine Mullin; they had three children.

Egan, Maurice Francis. *Recollections of a Happy Life.* New York, 1924.

THOMAS J. SHELLEY

EGAN, MICHAEL (1761–1814)

First bishop of Philadelphia. Michael Egan was born in Ireland in 1761, was educated at Louvain and Prague, and was guardian of the Franciscan house at Rome from 1787 until he returned to the Irish Mission in 1790. He arrived in the United States possibly before 1798, certainly by January 1802, when he appears as assistant to the pastor of the Lancaster, Pennsylvania, congregation. He was reputed a good preacher, an important talent in a Protestant milieu, and able to preach in German. In April 1803 Egan became one of the pastors at St. Mary's parish, Philadelphia, and was elected a trustee in April 1804.

Michael Egan, supported by Bishop John Carroll, petitioned Rome in December 1803 to establish a Franciscan province in the United States. Members of the order would be subject to call by the bishop similar to the Augustinians. Rome assented but with the stipulation that the property be vested in Bishop Carroll or someone not of the order. A benefactor donated three hundred acres in Indiana County in western Pennsylvania in August 1806, but the disturbed conditions of the Philadelphia Church prevented the establishment of the province during Bishop Egan's tenure. The property passed to Bishop Conwell.

Bishop of Philadelphia

In April 1808 the Diocese of Baltimore, which covered the entire United States, was divided, and the suffragan sees of Philadelphia, New York, Boston and Bardstown, Kentucky, were established. Archbishop Carroll had recommended Michael Egan as bishop of Philadelphia, although he felt Egan lacked robust health, experience and "a greater degree of firmness in his disposition" (Griffin, 24). The new bishops were consecrated only in October 1810 followed by a meeting of the hierarchy and the issuing of Regulations of Ecclesiastical Discipline for the Governance of the Church. A provincial council was scheduled for 1812, but this first provincial council did not meet until 1829. The new diocese included the entire states of Pennsylvania, Delaware, and southwestern New Jersey. St. Mary's parish, the cathedral parish, and the wealthiest and most populous of American congregations, was one of four in Philadelphia.

Finding German-speaking priests for Holy Trinity in Philadelphia and in Lancaster, staffing parishes, and diocesan visitations were normal difficulties for the ordinary. Bishop Egan, in four years as ordinary, made but one western visitation—a three-month trip in 1811. There was one priest in the Pittsburgh region at the time.

Contention with trustees over clerical salaries and difficulties with two Irish Dominican priests, William V. Harold and William's uncle James Harold, marked Bishop Egan's episcopacy. The trustees refused to increase the annual salary in October 1810, but did so for the bishop and two assistants in December when informed that the salary was inadequate. Then, following renovations to St. Mary's, the board in April 1812 proposed a reduction of salaries and dismissal of one of the pastors. When offered a reduced payment in August, Egan initiated a pamphlet war with a circular, *Appeal to the Congregation;* the trustees responded, offering to allow Archbishop Carroll to settle the dispute. Egan, concerned that the trustees might attempt the removal of clerical membership from the board by seeking a charter amendment in the state legislature, compromised in December 1812. No legislative petition would be forwarded and Egan disavowed primary responsibility for the *Appeal* but admitted that clergy had sometimes interfered with trustee elections. A last clash occurred in July 1813 when a new board offered the first installment of a two-third reduction in salary it had mandated. The bishop refused to accept this and threatened to withhold absolution. The matter was still unsettled when Egan died in July 1814.

Fr. William V. Harold, strongly recommended by Archbishop Troy of Dublin, had arrived in November 1810. Fr. James Harold arrived March 1811. William became vicar general of the diocese. They supported the bishop in his dispute with the trustees. Both signed the above *Appeal.* Yet, when health reasons forced Egan to preach less, William Harold insisted he was obligated to preach only every third Sunday; James Harold refused a transfer to Pittsburgh. In February 1813 they publicly resigned, William possibly because Egan did not want him as coadjutor with right of succession, possibly over concern the bishop was sacrificing them to the trustees. William subsequently returned to Ireland, followed some months later by his uncle.

The effect was a further dispute with the trustees who appealed to Archbishop Carroll in an effort to restore William Harold. Carroll urged Egan to consider it but Egan refused. It continued beyond the bishop's death. In the six-year interregnum before the appointment of Bishop Conwell, efforts were made by some trustees to restore Fr. William Harold as pastor and even to name him bishop. The last such appeal reached Rome in 1818. Rome felt William Harold was not suitable.

See also PENNSYLVANIA, CATHOLIC CHURCH IN.

Ennis, Arthur J., O.S.A. "The New Diocese of Philadelphia." *The History of the Archdiocese of Philadelphia,* James F. Connelly. Philadelphia, Pennsylvania, 1976, 63–79.

Griffin, Martin, I. J. *History of Rt. Rev. Michael Egan, DD: First Bishop of Philadelphia.* Philadelphia, 1893.

THOMAS R. GREENE

EL SALVADOR, FOUR MARTYRS OF (1980)

Nineteen-eighty was a bloody year in El Salvador. Thousands of people—catechists, trade unionists, students, members of peasant organizations—were murdered by the military and death squads as the country fell headlong into civil war. The Church was not spared. On March 24, 1980, Archbishop Oscar Arnulfo Romero was assassinated while celebrating Mass. He joined a growing list of church leaders and pastoral workers who had taken up the cause of the poor and suffered persecution and martyrdom because of it.

In the last months of 1980 during the Salvadoran civil war, the four North American churchwomen, Maura Clarke, M.M., Jean Donovan, Ita Ford, M.M., and Dorothy Kazel, O.S.U., often collaborated to transport refugees and supplies. On the evening of December 2, 1980, Jean and Dorothy met Ita and Maura at the San Salvador airport, as they returned from the Maryknoll Sisters' Regional Assembly in Nicaragua. Shortly afterwards, their van was stopped by national guardsmen in civilian clothes. The four women were taken into the countryside where they were raped, shot, and buried in a shallow common grave and found the next day. In May 1984 the five national guardsmen who abducted the women were convicted of murder, the first time that members of the Salvadoran security forces had ever been brought to justice.

Maura Clarke, M.M.

Mary Elizabeth Clarke, always known as Maura, was born on January 13, 1931, in Manhattan, New York, the eldest of three children of Irish-born John and Mary McCloskey Clarke. Growing up in Rockaway Beach, Queens, she attended Saint Francis de Sales Grade School, Stella Maris High School, and Saint Joseph College for Women for one year. In 1950 she entered the Maryknoll Sisters Congregation and made final vows in 1953. Graduating from Maryknoll Teachers College in 1954, Maura taught at St. Anthony's School in the Bronx, until she was assigned to the desolate mining town of Siuna, Nicaragua, in 1959.

From 1970 to 1976 she worked with basic Christian communities in Managua. After the devastating earthquake of 1972, she helped people to rebuild their lives during the tumultuous and repressive Somoza regime. In 1977 Maura returned to Maryknoll, New York, as a member of the Maryknoll Sisters World Awareness Team which, in her words, served as "a channel for awakening real concern for the victims of injustice in today's world."

In August 1979 Maura went to El Salvador in response to the plea for more Maryknoll sisters. After the death of Sr. Carla Piette in a flash flood on August 23, Maura decided to join Ita Ford, Carla's companion, in emergency relief work with refugees in Chalatenango: "The courage and suffering of these people never ceases to call me," she wrote.

During the Maryknoll Regional Assembly in Managua, Nicaragua, in November 1980, the sisters' mission presence in El Salvador was evaluated and strongly affirmed. Maura spoke of her own fear of the violence but said she felt strong "not in myself, but in the sense that the Lord will be faithful to me and his great love will take care of it."

Jean Marie Donovan

Jean Donovan was born to Patricia and Raymond Donovan on April 10, 1953, in Stamford, Connecticut. She studied in the Westport, Connecticut, school system, graduating from Staples High School in 1971. She matriculated at Mary Washington College in Fredericksburg, Virginia, and spent her junior year at University College in Cork, Ireland. She received her MBA degree from Case Western Reserve in Cleveland in 1977 and joined the accounting firm of Arthur Anderson. She left to do volunteer work in El Salvador with the Cleveland Mission Team in 1978, receiving training in missionary work at Maryknoll, New York, and Huehuetenango, Guatemala. In August 1979 she joined the team in El Salvador working with the poor, especially pregnant women and young children. Jean kept the team books, being the only accountant and, as the war escalated, was occasionally called upon to help to transport refugees and supplies. This was her ministry from August 1979 until December 2, 1980, when she and Dorothy Kazel, O.S.U., Maura Clarke, M.M., and Ita Ford were murdered by the Salvadoran military. Jean's change from an account executive to a missionary probably can be traced back to her junior year abroad in Ireland where she met an Irish missionary priest. She then began thinking in terms of repaying God for all that she had been given. Jean was perfect for her work, having a great sense of humor which, along with faith, is all that is necessary to keep one sane in circumstances such as those she encountered in El Salvador. As she said, "I am not up for suicide, but I can't leave the children." She had promised them she would always come back.

Ita Ford, M.M.

Ita Ford, the second of three children, was born in Brooklyn, New York, on April 23, 1940, to Mildred and William Ford. Ita attended Visitation Academy Grade School, Fontbonne Hall High School and Marymount Manhattan College. In 1961 she joined Maryknoll, but before final vows was dismissed for health reasons. For the next seven years Ita was editor of high-school English and religion texts with Sadlier Publishing Company in New York.

In 1971 Ita reentered Maryknoll, was professed the following year and missioned to Chile in March 1973. She lived and worked in the Población La Bandera on the outskirts of Santiago until late 1977, where she ministered with basic Christian communities, helping to organize soup kitchens during the repressive Pinochet regime. She returned to Maryknoll for a reflection year before final vows in 1978.

Ita had grown increasingly aware of the violent situation in El Salvador and was drawn to respond to the call for help from the Salvadoran Church led by the prophetic

Monseñor Oscar Arnulfo Romero. During this time, she was in an automobile accident and her injuries prevented her from traveling until late 1979. Just as she was to depart for her assignment to El Salvador, Monseñor Romero was murdered. "We believe that his death will bear fruit," Ita wrote, "and it's part of the Christian mystery we celebrate this Holy Week; and in that same Christian tradition, we'll go to El Salvador."

In 1980 Ita, joined by Sr. Carla Piette, M.M., also from the Chile Region, began to aid refugees through the Emergency Committee of the Vicariate of Chalatenango. On August 23, 1980, Piette was killed in the flash flood. Ita almost miraculously survived this tragedy, and though grief-stricken, was determined to continue their ministry for refugees.

While at the Maryknoll Regional Assembly in November 1980 in Nicaragua, Ita read this quotation of Monseñor Romero's the night before she and Sr. Maura Clarke, M.M., returned to El Salvador: "Christ invites us not to fear persecution because . . . one who is committed to the poor must risk the same fate as the poor . . . : to disappear, to be tortured, to be captured and to be found dead."

Dorothy Kazel, O.S.U.

The second and youngest child of Lithuanian-American parents, Joseph and Malvina Kazel, "Dorothea Lu" was born on June 30, 1939, in Cleveland, Ohio. After graduating from high school in 1957, Dorothy completed a teacher certification program at St. John's College, Cleveland, and taught for a year. In 1960 she joined the Congregation of the Ursuline Sisters of Cleveland. After first profession in 1963, Dorothy earned her B.A. degree and teaching certificate in stenography-typing and social studies. For nine years she ministered to adolescent young women as teacher and guidance counselor at two of the Ursuline schools: Sacred Heart Academy (1965–72), and Beaumont School (1972–74). She also volunteered at a multiservice agency for the inner-city poor, a hospital for the chronically ill, a women's correctional facility, and at a parish where she taught catechism to deaf children. Her first experience of cross-cultural mission was in the summer of 1969 when she taught religion to Native Americans of the Papago tribe in Topawa, Arizona.

In 1974 Dorothy became a member of the Cleveland Diocesan Latin American Team in El Salvador. For the next six years she did pastoral work in the three parishes staffed by the Cleveland team in Chirilagua, La Union, and La Libertad. In the final months of 1980 Dorothy's ministry expanded to include the transportation of refugees and supplies to refugee centers.

Just days before Dorothy was murdered, she wrote to the Cleveland diocese:

If we look at this little country of El Salvador as a whole, we find that it is . . . a country that is writhing in pain—a coun-try that daily faces the loss of so many of its people—yet a country that is waiting, hoping, and yearning for peace. The steadfast faith and courage which our leaders have to continue preaching the Work of the Lord even though it may mean "laying down your life" . . . is a most vivid realization that JESUS is HERE with us.

JUDITH NOONE, M.M.

ELDER, WILLIAM HENRY (1819–1904)

Archbishop. William Henry Elder was born on March 22, 1819, in Baltimore, Maryland, to Basil Spalding Elder and Elizabeth Snowden. He was one of thirteen children. At the age of twelve he was enrolled at Mt. St. Mary's College in Emmitsburg. At this time the president of the college was Fr. John B. Purcell whom Elder would later succeed as archbishop of Cincinnati. In June 1837, Elder graduated from the classical course at the college.

The next five years were spent studying theology at Mt. St. Mary's. In 1842 his superiors sent him to study at the Urban College in Rome. He was ordained a priest on March 29, 1846, in the chapel of the Urban College. Upon his return to Maryland he was appointed professor of dogmatic theology at his alma mater. He held this position for the next ten and a half years.

He was consecrated as bishop of Natchez (Mississippi) on May 3, 1857, in the cathedral at Baltimore by Archbishop Francis Kenrick, Bishop John McGill of Richmond, and Bishop James F. Wood of Philadelphia. The Diocese of Natchez at that time embraced the entire state of Mississippi.

In 1864, during the Union occupation of Natchez, Brigadier General Y. M. Tuttle issued a decree that in all churches prayers should be said for the President of the United States and for the success of the Union army. In keeping with his policy of neutrality, Bishop Elder refused to have the prayers said in his parishes. On July 23, Bishop Elder was imprisoned under military guard in Vidalia, Louisiana. He wrote letters of appeal to both Abraham Lincoln and secretary of war Edwin Stanton. His letters of appeal were successful. The decree was rescinded, and he was released from military imprisonment on August 12, 1864.

He traveled to Rome in 1867 to attend the centennial celebration of the death of SS. Peter and Paul, and again in 1869 to attend the First Vatican Council. In 1878 a yellow fever epidemic raged through the Diocese of Natchez. He, personally, ministered to the sick and dying in the diocese, and sent many of his priests to minister at Vicksburg where they were badly needed. During Bishop Elder's ministrations to his people he himself contracted the disease, but eventually recovered.

On January 30, 1880, he was appointed coadjutor with right of succession to Archbishop John Purcell of Cincinnati and he became archbishop on July 4, 1883. Elder had been appointed to Cincinnati to straighten out the financial failure of Archbishop Purcell. This task was to prove to be beyond his capabilities, and the legal battles surrounding the financial failure were not to be settled until nearly half a year after his death in 1904.

His greatest contribution to the Archdiocese of Cincinnati was reforming and organizing the diocesan administration. He instituted the office of the chancellor, insisted on annual reports from all the parishes, and established ecclesiastical courts and other canonical bodies necessary for the new administration. In 1887 he reopened Mt. St. Mary's Seminary of the West, which had closed it doors during the early years of Purcell's financial difficulties.

In 1902 Archbishop Elder petitioned Rome for a coadjutor. On April 27, 1903, Henry Moeller, the bishop of Columbus, was appointed to the coadjutorship with the right of succession. Almost immediately Archbishop Elder relinquished the administration of the archdiocese to Bishop Moeller. Elder died in Cincinnati on October 31, 1904.

See also MISSISSIPPI, CATHOLIC CHURCH IN; OHIO, CATHOLIC CHURCH IN; SLAVERY AND AMERICAN CATHOLICS.

Campbell, James Harold. "New Parochialism: Change and Conflict in the Archdiocese of Cincinnati, 1878–1925." Ph.D. dissertation, University of Cincinnati, 1982.

Character Glimpses of Most Reverend William Henry Elder, D.D.: Second Archbishop of Cincinnati. Cincinnati: Frederick Pustet & Co., 1911.

Gerow, R. O., ed. *Civil War Diary (1862–1865) of Bishop William Henry Elder, Bishop Of Natchez.* Diocese of Natchez-Jackson Mississippi: Most Reverend R. O. Gerow, 1960.

Husscy, M. Edmund. *The 1878 Financial Failure of Archbishop Purcell.* Cincinnati: Cincinnati Historical Society, 1978.

Lamott, John H. *History of the Archdiocese of Cincinnati, 1821–1921.* Cincinnati: Frederick Pustet Company, Inc., 1921.

DON H. BUSKE

ELLARD, GERALD (1894–1963)

Liturgical scholar. Gerald Ellard stood as one of the principal spokesmen of the American Roman Catholic liturgical movement from its origins in the mid-1920s up to the time of the Second Vatican Council forty years later. He influenced American Catholicism through his lectures, his teaching and his extensive publication. While his speaking and writing were, for the most part, at the level of high-popularization, his background in liturgical history and research gave his work the credibility it needed as background for liturgical reform and renewal.

Education for Liturgical Reform

Ellard was born on October 8, 1894. He spent his childhood and youth in Wisconsin, Michigan, New Mexico, and

Gerald Ellard

finally, in Denver, Colorado, finishing his high-school years at the local Jesuit college. In 1912 he entered the Society of Jesus at the age of seventeen. His first spark of interest in liturgy came during his novitiate years when he was given a hand-sized copy of the Roman Missal, but serious attention to this dimension of Catholic life developed only some years later.

After the usual Jesuit course of studies including philosophy and theology with a period of high-school and college teaching in between the two, Ellard was ordained a priest in St. Louis in 1926. A year later he left for Austria where he completed his final year of Jesuit formation before beginning his doctoral studies in Germany. During his years of theological study in preparation for the priesthood he met two other American liturgical pioneers, Dom Virgil Michel, O.S.B. (of St. John's Abbey in Collegeville, Minnesota), and Msgr. Martin Hellriegel (of O'-Fallon, Missouri, just outside St. Louis). Hellriegel and Ellard became friends sometime after 1923 once they came in contact through their mutual interest in liturgical renewal. Ellard was invited to O'Fallon to celebrate Christmas in 1925 and there met Michel, himself a guest of Hellriegel. Late on Christmas Eve the three discussed an American liturgical journal, already in the planning stages at Collegeville. During their conversation that evening they hit on the idea for the journal's title, *Orate Fratres,* words taken from the Latin text of the Mass, which highlighted the social dimension of Christian worship. (*Orate Fratres* eventually changed its name to *Worship* and remains in publication to the present day.)

By the time Ellard left for his studies in Europe in 1927, he had already contributed about twenty articles on the value of liturgical renewal, published, for the most part, in *America, Catholic World,* and *Queen's Work,* all journals aimed at the wider American Catholic public. This style of productivity was to set the pattern of Ellard's professional life and contribution to the American liturgical movement.

During his years in Europe Ellard finished his doctorate in liturgy and medieval history at the University of Munich. His dissertation, "Ordination Anointings in the Western Church before 1000 A.D.," won him the highest possible acclaim by the faculty and was later published in 1933. The lengthy holiday periods scattered through the academic year at Munich enabled Ellard to observe the liturgical movement in Europe, and to meet many of the leaders of that movement.

He traveled to what had become centers of focus for liturgical research and renewal: Maria Laach, Klosterneuberg, Mont César, and Solesmes among others. His reports and reflections from these visits found expression in articles published in *America, American Ecclesiastical Review* and, of course, *Orate Fratres.* He met Josef Jungmann, Pius Parsch, and Ildefons Herwegen, all pillars of the liturgical movement in Europe and of what was to grow into the American movement.

1930s: Christian Life and Worship

Once he had returned to the United States in 1931, Ellard began teaching at St. Louis University. This assignment, however, lasted only a year. In 1932 the Jesuit seminary moved from St. Louis to St. Mary's College in Kansas. Ellard joined the faculty there and this was to remain his home until his death just over thirty years later. Each of those three decades could be named by a major volume of Ellard's, calculated at its time to meet the ongoing needs of American Catholics in their journey of liturgical awareness, and, eventually, of liturgical change.

Not long after his return to teaching, Ellard wrote the book which remains one of the most significant of his contributions to the American liturgical movement: *Christian Life and Worship.* Published in the fall of 1933, the book went through several editions and sold over 63,000 copies over the next thirty years, maintaining a fairly consistent volume of sales over those same years. Originally intended as a college textbook, *Christian Life and Worship* grounded the liturgy as the worship of the entire body of Christ, head and members. Ellard confronted what he saw as three fundamental problems in American Catholic piety: a generally limited understanding of the Mass along with a strong strain of spiritual individualism and a failure to relate Holy Communion to the action of the Mass. All three problem areas reflected a general lack of appreciation of the communal dimension of life in the Church. A better understanding of Christian worship had to be based on a better understanding of Christian life itself.

The doctrine of the Mystical Body of Christ, while an ancient theme in Christianity, had only begun to resurface in the scholarly world in the nineteenth century and to color seminary teaching and popular consciousness by the 1930s. In an article published in 1932 in *Thought,* Ellard names the Mystical Body doctrine as that "on which the whole (liturgical) movement rests."

During this same decade of the 1930s Ellard joined the teaching staff of the annual "Summer School of Catholic Action," a group organized by Daniel Lord, S.J., which traveled from city to city over the summer months, offering a weeklong program of lecture, prayer, and social life for those involved in the sodality movement. Ellard taught classes and organized dialogue Mass participation for all present. One survey indicated that in the course of Ellard's twenty summers with the S.S.C.A. more than 100,000 laypeople, religious, and priests heard of the liturgical awakening for the first time and most of them had their first experience of the dialog Mass.

1940s: The Dialog Mass

By the early 1940s, the foundations for liturgical reform had been laid by the pioneers of the movement in the United States. The first National Liturgical Week was held in Chicago in the summer of 1940, bringing together the enthusiasts of the liturgical movement, most of whom were solo voices in their own local liturgical wastelands. These conventions would encourage the pioneers in their prophetic work until the promulgation of *Sacrosanctum Concilium,* the Second Vatican Council's Constitution on the Sacred Liturgy, still twenty-three years away. The 1940s saw, as well, two encyclical letters of Pope Pius XII which gave official grounding and recognition to the liturgical movement, *Mystici Corporis* in 1943 and *Mediator Dei* in 1947.

Once again, Ellard sensed the more immediate need of American Catholics to know more about liturgical reform. In 1940 he published *Men at Work at Worship: America Joins the Liturgical Movement;* in 1942, *The Dialog Mass: A Book for Priests and Teachers of Religion;* and, in 1948, an annotated edition of *Mediator Dei.* As Ellard saw the directions the movement was taking, he hastened to supply the rationale for those directions at a popular level.

In 1948 Ellard published another volume, *The Mass of the Future,* which signaled coming decades of liturgical change, but the book came at a time when many American Catholics were not ready for that signal! Backed by his thorough knowledge of liturgical history, Ellard sketched out a form of the Mass which more accurately reflected the early Christian understanding of the liturgy before it became overlaid with later medieval accretions. Actually the Mass of the future which Ellard suggested in 1948 was only slightly different from the reformed Mass liturgy which emerged from the reforms of Vatican Council II twenty years later. But in 1948 many Catholics, including bishops, priests, and laity were not even ready to hear that the Mass had a past let alone a future!

1950s: The Mass in Transition

Soon, however, fear of history gave way to a number of officially sanctioned liturgical changes, albeit minor ones, which were based on the best historical research. One of the more significant of those changes was the reordering of the Holy Week liturgy in 1955. Once the "scandal" of *any* liturgical change had been worked through, American Catholics became more and more interested in the history which explained the changes. *The Mass of the Future* was revised and published in 1956 under a new title, *The Mass in Transition*. Liturgical change had become, by that time, a fact of life. Ellard's work in the 1950s and 1960s was no longer groundbreaking; the ground of liturgical change had been broken! Ellard and his colleagues were now pressed to encourage and explain the liturgical evolution whose momentum would build during the twenty years ahead.

Conclusion

From the early 1950s on, poor health had, to some extent, slowed Ellard's pace but it did not put an end to his active career of teaching, lecturing, and writing. In late March of 1963 he took an active part in a Roman Catholic-Protestant Colloquium held at Harvard Divinity School. But, just after the end of that colloquium, Ellard's heart began to fail and he died on April 1 that year, eight short months before the promulgation of the Second Vatican Council's liturgical constitution, the consummation of the work of Ellard and so many of his contemporaries.

However, the groundwork had been laid. A small but well-informed and well-formed band of American Catholics did understand the rationale of liturgical renewal and were able to use their preparation to help others to understand. Thomas J. Carroll, a past president of the National Liturgical Conference, preached the eulogy at a special memorial Mass for Ellard a few days after his death. His words sum up Ellard's contribution: "To many he was a symbol—a symbol of liturgical life and growth. . . . He traveled with us to the threshold of a new day. He led us toward that day."

See also LITURGICAL MOVEMENT IN AMERICA, THE.

Diederich, Everett, S.J. "Rev. Gerald Ellard, S.J." *Yearbook of Liturgical Studies*. Notre Dame, Indiana, 1963, 4:3–10.
Klein, J. Leo, S.J. "The Role of Gerald Ellard (1894–1963) in the Development of the Contemporary American Catholic Liturgical Movement." Ph.D. dissertation, Fordham University, 1971.
Leonard, William J., S.J., "The Liturgical Movement in the United States." *The Liturgy of Vatican II: A Symposium in Two Volumes,* ed. William Barauna. English ed. Jovian Lang, O.F.M. Chicago, Illinois, 1966, 2:293–312.
____, ed. *Liturgy for the People: Essays in Honor of Gerald Ellard, S.J. (1894–1963)*. Milwaukee, Wisconsin, 1963.
J. LEO KLEIN, S.J.

ELLIOTT, WALTER (1842–1928)

Priest, author, missionary. Elliott was born on January 6, 1842, in Detroit to immigrant Irish parents, Robert T. Elliott and Frances O'Shea. He entered the University of Notre Dame but left before graduation. He then went to Cincinnati to study law at a U.S. Attorney's office. In 1861 he volunteered for the Union army and served with the Fifth Ohio Volunteers for four years. After the war, Elliott returned to Detroit, was admitted to the bar and began practicing as an attorney. After hearing Isaac Hecker preach in 1867, he decided to enter Hecker's fledgling religious community, the Missionary Society of St. Paul the Apostle (Paulists), and was ordained on May 5, 1872. He spent most of his priestly ministry conducting missions for non-Catholics in the East and Midwest and put great emphasis on breaking down Protestant stereotypes of Catholics. He was also a leader in the temperance movement.

Together with fellow Paulist Alexander Doyle, Elliott founded in 1902 the Apostolic Mission House on the campus of The Catholic University of America in Washington, D.C. This was a center for the education and training of diocesan priests for evangelization work in the U.S.A. When Hecker's health began to fail in 1886, Elliott interrupted his work to care for him until his death in 1888.

Walter Elliott

During their time together, Elliott wrote his famous biography, *The Life of Father Hecker.* First appearing serially in the *Catholic World,* this work was published in book form in 1891 with an introduction by Archbishop John Ireland of St. Paul and an imprimatur from Archbishop Michael Corrigan of New York. Elliott's difficulties began when the book was later translated into French with a preface by the Abbé Felix Klein. This modified French edition—especially Klein's preface—caused an uproar with conservative French Catholics. It led in 1899 to *Testem benevolentiae,* Pope Leo XIII's condemnation of "Americanism," a heresy of a nebulous origin and nature. Unaware of many of the theological and political implications in his book, Elliott was disturbed and hurt by the controversy that it caused. He spent much of the remainder of his life at the Mission House as rector, professor, and rector emeritus. He died in Washington, D.C., on April 18, 1928, and was buried in the crypt beneath the Church of St. Paul the Apostle in Manhattan. Joseph McSorley, the Paulist historian, praised him by saying, "His loyal attachment to Father Hecker, of whom he always declared himself the humble disciple, became the medium by which the personality of the Founder, in a certain measure, was stamped upon the second and third generation of Paulists."

See also AMERICANISM; PAULISTS (C.S.P.).

McSorley, Joseph, C.S.P. "Father Elliott." *Catholic World* 128 (June 1928) 296–305.

ANTHONY D. ANDREASSI

ELLIS, JOHN TRACY (1905–92)

Historian and educator. John Tracy Ellis was in his lifetime the dean of Catholic Church historians in the United States, continuing the pioneer efforts of John Gilmary Shea and succeeding his own mentor in the field, Peter J. Guilday. Ellis surpassed his predecessors in recognition from the wider academic community and in the impact of his work challenging Catholic educational and intellectual endeavors.

Early Years

Born on July 30, 1905, at Seneca, Illinois, Ellis was the elder of two sons of Elmer Lucien and Cecilia Murphy Ellis. The family was not wealthy and John Tracy undertook part-time employment to complete his undergraduate years at St. Viator College, Bourbonnais, Illinois. His father was not of the Catholic faith, a circumstance that left Ellis with a lifelong respect for religious differences.

Pursuing an early and consistent interest in history, young Ellis enrolled for graduate study at The Catholic University of America, Washington, with help provided by a Knights of Columbus scholarship. He also worked

John Tracy Ellis

as a speech teacher at the Sulpician Seminary and for Father Fulton J. Sheen as part-time secretary. Later the historian would say of this experience, "I found these jobs both financially rewarding and congenial as well." He finished the Ph.D. program in 1930 and thereafter taught at St. Viator College (1930–32) and at Winona, Minnesota, in the College of St. Teresa (1932–34).

At Winona, Ellis made the decision to study for the priesthood with the concurrence of the local bishop who understood the priest's primary work would be in an academic setting. He returned to Catholic University as a student in the Sulpician Seminary (now Theological College) and also taught history. John Tracy Ellis was ordained a priest by Bishop Francis M. Kelly of Winona in the chapel at the College of St. Teresa on June 5, 1938. Later in life he was incardinated as a priest of the Archdiocese of Baltimore (1947). In 1955 he was named a domestic prelate by Pope Pius XII.

The Catholic University of America

Appointed an instructor in history immediately after ordination, Ellis was promoted to assistant professor in 1941 and in that year took a sabbatical to prepare for the role of directing graduate studies in American Catholic history. The time was spent at Harvard University in study and research, and practical exercise of the principles of serious scholarship which had early emerged in the life of John Tracy Ellis and remained as his "signature." Correspondence from early years indicates his exposure to academic mediocrity and his impatience to correct it. The Catholic University offered such an opportunity; Ellis returned there as an associate professor in 1943 and moved to the rank of full professor in Church history in 1947. Earlier, in 1941, he became the managing editor of the *Catholic Historical Review* and would remain in that post for twenty-one years.

Equally adept in scholarly research and writing and in the graduate formation of historians, Ellis provided a record of outstanding achievement in both tasks. He is remembered for lectures as appealing as they were instructive. He required his own exacting standards of accuracy and honesty of those who studied under him. Earlier publication of his doctoral dissertation, *Anti-Papal Legislation in Medieval England, 1066–1377* (1930), was followed in this period by *Cardinal Consalvi and Anglo-Papal Relations, 1814–1824* (1942); *The Formative Years of The Catholic University of America* (1946); and *The Life of James Cardinal Gibbons, Archbishop of Baltimore, 1834–1921* (1952). This last work brought John Tracy Ellis attention and applause from a nonacademic public and safely secured his name among American Catholic historiographers. A text as remarkable for its exhaustive treatment as for its style captured the full fabric of Catholic life for the period in which Cardinal Gibbons often took center stage. The honest treatment of sensitive material set a new standard for ecclesiastical history as welcome to readers as it was reassuring to historians.

American Catholics and the Intellectual Life

The issue, and publication, for which John Tracy Ellis is best known was an outcome of a lecture given in the spring of 1955 at the annual meeting of the Catholic Commission on Intellectual and Cultural Affairs. "American Catholics and the Intellectual Life" was published that autumn in *Thought* and later issued under the same title in book form (Chicago, 1956). Grounded in statistical analyses of achievement, data assembled from the late 1920s to the present indicated that Catholics as individuals and Catholic institutions as nurturers of intellectual life both failed to measure up to the national norms. As an historian Ellis was in a strong position to discount such negative causes as immigrant origins and religious prejudice. The principal cause, he concluded, lay with Catholics themselves "in their frequently self-imposed ghetto mentality which prevents them from mingling as they should with their non-Catholic colleagues, and in their lack of industry and habits of work."

James Hitchcock aptly described the aftermath: "The thesis was essentially correct, and rarely has a speaker had the gratification of seeing so much talk and action follow on his words, so much effort expended to overcome the problems he had identified." In the extended debate which followed Ellis was afforded a forum for two long-held convictions: the proliferation of Catholic educational facilities diluted their effectiveness, and faculty were too often inadequately prepared and improperly utilized. His was an early voice that recognized an emerging level of maturity and independence on the part of lay Catholics and noted current deficiencies in programs of priestly formation. Openly critical of triumphal attitudes in the Church that led to unreality and self-deception, Ellis welcomed changes embodying openness and honesty in the wake of Vatican Council II. His expertise in history coupled with an instinctive grasp of current issues made John Tracy Ellis much in demand as speaker and writer.

Teacher and Writer

Ellis continued as professor of church history at The Catholic University until 1964. For the remainder of this period he authored, or edited, volumes that are standard in his field: *American Catholicism* (1956); *Documents of American Catholic History* (1956); and *Guide to American Catholic History* (1959), successor to *A Select Bibliography. John Lancaster Spalding, First Bishop of Peoria, American Educator* was published in 1963 as was a collection of speeches and essays, *Perspectives in American Catholicism*.

John Tracy Ellis moved to the University of San Francisco as professor of Church history in 1964 and remained there for twelve years. He continued to publish: *Catholics in Colonial America* (1965), *A Commitment to Truth* (1966), and *Essays in Seminary Education* (1967).

Much consulted as a commentator and critic in the post-Vatican II years, the historian responded with characteristic blend of scholarly insight, honesty, and deep faith in the Church. His work at times reflected the Church's shortcomings, but never demeaned her successes and optimistically accepted her role and mission. An editorial collaborator and contributor to the *New Catholic Encyclopedia* (1967), Ellis undertook a similar task for *The Catholic Priest in the United States: Historical Investigations* (1971).

Taking leave from the University of San Francisco, John Tracy Ellis accepted invitations as visiting professor at Brown University (1967) and the University of Notre Dame (1970). The years 1974–76 found him in Rome as scholar in residence at the North American College and with an opportunity to teach at the Gregorian and Angelicum Universities. Returning to The Catholic University of America as professorial lecturer in Church history in 1977, Ellis remained active in teaching until several years before his death. Work in this last period included: *Catholic Bishops: A Memoir* (1983) and *Faith and Learning: A Church Historian's Story* (1988). His eightieth birthday marked the occasion for a festschrift published by Michael Glazier, *Studies in Catholic History* (1985).

Ellis's major publications exist amid a corpus of some four hundred titles. Peer recognition included twenty honorary doctorates and other accolades such as the Laetare Medal from the University of Notre Dame. As was true of Guilday, John Tracy Ellis's graduate students formed a legacy that would continue his work aptly described in mid-career by Paul J. Hallinan: "No present Catholic writer has plied the historian's trade so patiently—the search of archives, the reading of dry newspaper columns and reels of dim microfilms; the personal interviews, and day-by-day perusal of collateral history. His results have been in the best tradition of objective history, masterfully told." The dedicated priest-historian closed his life near The Catholic University at the Jeanne Jugan Residence where one of the staff said, "He greeted the cleaning women everyday the same way he did visiting cardinals." Ellis died on October 16, 1992, and is buried in Seneca, Illinois.

Bowden, Henry Warner. *Church History in an Age of Uncertainty*. Carbondale and Edwardsville: Southern Illinois University Press, 1991, 196–206.

"A Church Historian's Personal Story: An Interview with Monsignor John Tracy Ellis Conducted by Eugene C. Bianchi." *Records of the American Catholic Historical Society of Philadelphia* 92 (March–December 1981) 3–42.

Ellis, John Tracy. *Faith and Learning: A Church Historian's Story*. Lanham, Md.: University Press of America, 1989.

———. "Fragments from My Autobiography, 1905–1942." *The Review of Politics* 6 (October 1974) 565–91.

Higgins, George G. "A Historian Who Made History." *Commonweal* 119 (November 6, 1992) 5–7.

Minnich, Nelson H. and others, eds. *Studies in Catholic History in Honor of John Tracy Ellis*. Wilmington, Del.: Michael Glazier, 1985. Contains a bibliography of Ellis's publications compiled by Mark A. Miller, 674–738.

Shelley, Thomas J. "The Young John Tracy Ellis and American Catholic Intellectual Life." *U.S. Catholic Historian* 13 (Winter 1995) 1–18.

Symposia on John Tracy Ellis. *Records of the American Catholic Historical Society of Philadelphia* 104 (Spring–Winter 1993) 1–30.

✠ OSCAR H. LIPSCOMB

ELSENSOHN, ALFREDA (1897–1989)

Educator. Sr. Alfreda Elsensohn, a member of the Benedictine Order at the Monastery of St. Gertrude in Cottonwood, Idaho, was born in Grangeville, Idaho, in 1897 and later moved with her family to Mount Idaho. Here she had her earliest contact with the Chinese who inspired a later book. She wrote the botany teachers' manual, *The Flora of the Camas Prairie Region*, from her experience with the abundant wildflowers in the area.

After joining the Benedictines in Cottonwood in 1915, she taught at the elementary level, continued her summer studies, and earned her bachelor of science and master of science degrees. Beginning in 1931, Sr. Alfreda taught botany, biology, and taxidermy at St. Gertrude's Academy, motivating her students to collect various specimens. Today the collection has grown into a varied display of natural science and historical artifacts, such as the Polly Bemis collection and the Rhoades-Emmanuel oriental collection, which are housed in the museum building on the grounds of the monastery. This museum, built in 1980, is dedicated to Sr. Alfreda.

As a budding researcher and historian, Sr. Alfreda published many articles in *The Echo of St. Gertrude's*, a periodical published by the Benedictine Sisters. She later wrote several historical books: *Pioneer Days in Idaho County*, Volumes I and II; *Idaho Chinese Lore;* and *Idaho County's Most Romantic Character: Polly Bemis*.

In 1969 Sr. Alfreda was honored as Idaho Writer of the Year. In 1970 she received the Governor's Award of Arts and Humanities from Governor Don Samuelson. She died in 1989.

See also BENEDICTINES (O.S.B.).

CARM TERNES, O.S.B.

EMMET, THOMAS ADDIS (1828–1919)

Surgeon. Born near Charlottesville, Virginia, on May 29, 1828, to John Patten Emmet, professor of science at the University of Virginia, and Mary Tucker Emmet, he was also the grandnephew of Irish patriot Robert Emmet. A student at the University of Virginia for one year, Emmet transferred to Jefferson Medical College in Philadelphia, Pennsylvania, and graduated in 1850. He became a physician at Emigrants' Refuge Hospital, Ward's Island, New York City in 1851. He married Catherine R. Duncan in 1854; they had six children. In 1855 Emmet joined the Woman's Hospital, New York City, as assistant gynecologist; serving the hospital for forty-five years. He became its chief surgeon in 1861. Renowned for his surgical skills, he developed new methods of treating childbirth injuries, including the Emmet operation to repair tears in the womb. His 1879 medical text, *Principles and Practices of Gynecology*, became a standard in the field.

Emmet was also an amateur historian who compiled an extensive collection of early American letters, prints, and manuscripts, now housed in the New York Public Library. An advocate of political home rule for Ireland, Emmet criticized English governance of the country in his two-volume *Ireland Under English Rule*. He converted to Catholicism in 1897; received the Laetare Medal from the University of Notre Dame in 1898; and in 1906 was named by Pius X a Knight Commander of the Order of Saint Gregory. Emmet died in New York City on March 1, 1919.

See also IRISH CATHOLICS IN AMERICA.

Emmet, T. A. *Incidents of My Life*. New York, 1911.

Marr, James Pratt. *Pioneer Surgeons of the Woman's Hospital: The Lives of Sims, Emmet, Peaslee and Thomas.* Philadelphia, 1957.

K. N. McCARTHY

ENGELHARDT, ZEPHYRIN (1851–1934)

Missionary, historian, archivist. Engelhardt was born in Bilshausen, Hanover, Germany, on November 13, 1851, and baptized Charles Anthony. Shortly thereafter his parents emigrated to Covington, Kentucky. Engelhardt joined the Order of Friars Minor at Teutopolis, Illinois, in 1873, taking the name Zephyrin, and was ordained in 1878. He was sent to work with the Menominee Native American Mission at Kenosha, Wisconsin, in 1880. He labored as a missionary for the next twenty years among the Menominees in Kenosha and Superior and among the Ottawas at Harbor Springs, Michigan. A student of Native American dialects, he published *Kachkenohamatwon Kesekoch (Guide to Heaven),* translated from Ojibwe to Menominee in 1882, and a catechism, *Kateshim,* also in Menominee, in 1884. After working among the Ottawas in Harbor Springs, he founded the Indian monthly *Anishina Enamiad (Praying Indian)* in the Ottawa language in 1896. He wrote his first studies of the Franciscan Mission while at Harbor Springs, *The Franciscans in California* (1897) and *The Franciscans in Arizona* (1899).

After 1900 he devoted the rest of his career to writing California mission histories in his capacity as historian and archivist of the Franciscan province of Santa Barbara. A prolific writer, he published over thirty historical works related to the California mission during his career, including his four-volume *Missions and Missionaries of California* (1908–15) and *The Holy Man of Santa Clara* (1909), and close to two hundred articles. His papers and correspondence are housed at the Santa Barbara Mission Archives.

See also FRANCISCANS (CAPUCHINS); NATIVE AMERICANS AND THE CATHOLIC CHURCH.

TRICIA T. PYNE

ENGLAND, JOHN (1786–1842)

First bishop of Charleston, South Carolina. John England was born in Cork, Ireland, September 23, 1786, the son of Thomas and Honora (Lordan) England. He studied law for two years. In 1802, England entered St. Patrick College, Carlow, to prepare for the priesthood. In the seminary, he made a private vow consecrating himself to God for a foreign mission under the patronage of the Mother of God. He was ordained on October 11, 1808, at the age of twenty-two by special dispensation, in St. Mary Cathedral, Cork, by Bishop Francis Moylan, a younger brother of General Stephen Moylan, an aide to General George Washington.

John England

England was assigned to the Cork cathedral until 1817. He served as chaplain to the North Presentation Convent, the Magdalen Asylum, and the city jail, and as president and teacher at St. Mary's College, a seminary for the education of priests. He founded and edited a magazine, *The Religious Repertory,* and managed a secular paper, *The Cork Mercantile Chronicle.* In 1817 England was appointed parish priest in Bandon, sixteen miles from Cork City. He was consecrated the first bishop of Charleston in St. Finbar's Church, Cork, on September 21, 1820, and arrived in Charleston on December 30, 1820. England died in Charleston on April 11, 1842. During his years as bishop, England journeyed to many parts of the U.S.A. and made four trips to Europe. He was also appointed apostolic delegate to negotiate a concordat with Haiti.

Irish Background

England was one of the first priests ordained in Ireland after the penal times. Seminaries had been open less than ten years when England began his studies at Carlow. But with the opening of seminaries and financial support from the British government came the desire of the government to have the veto over the appointment of Irish bishops. The Holy See and the Irish bishops were willing to allow this veto in exchange for the opening of the seminaries and other privileges. John England was one of the leaders in opposing the veto and organizing lay Catholics in opposition to the veto. The Irish bishops finally opposed the veto as well.

At Cork jail, England would see prisoners sentenced to the penal colony in Australia. No priests were allowed in Australia to serve these Catholic prisoners. Using the pages of the *Chronicle,* he pleaded the cause of Catholics in Australia. Within days the matter was taken up in the House of Commons and the British government allowed Catholic priests to go to Australia. England is considered one of the founders of the Catholic Church in Australia.

Twice, England had asked to go to America as a missioner. Twice he had been refused. In 1820 England came to his American mission, the Diocese of Charleston, comprising North Carolina, South Carolina, and Georgia. England found three priests and about 5,000 Catholics when he arrived. He issued a pastoral letter to the people telling them of his appointment and of his love for the United States and its Constitution, the first pastoral letter to the American people. Within six weeks he began his first journey through the diocese. England's *Diary* tells of the journeys of the first three years throughout his three-state diocese. He asked the archbishop of Baltimore if a Baltimore priest who served as his vicar general might be allowed to stay. The archbishop told him that, if he would stay in Charleston, he would not need another priest. England had different ideas. As he traveled he sought to unify the scattered Catholics. He commissioned them to meet on Sundays for worship. He commissioned some to teach. In one town, he found only one Catholic but on leaving he found another, a young lad. He noted in his diary that he must write these men and commission them to meet on Sundays for worship. He formed book societies, open to all, as a way of reaching those who were not Catholic.

Diocesan Initiatives

England's most important contribution may be that he saw the government of the United States and its democratic institutions as a desirable place for the Catholic Church. England believed that separation of Church and state was a good for the Church as well as for the state. He valued freedom of religion. In 1826 he addressed the U.S. Congress and spoke of the compatibility of the United States Constitution and the Catholic Church. John England was the first theoretician of separation of Church and state and freedom of religion. He greatly influenced the young American Church in its acceptance and involvement in American constitutional democracy and contributed to a trend that would lead the universal Church to replace the older ideal of union of Church and state with John England's ideal of a free Church in a free society.

In the diocese, England saw the need to unite the scattered Catholics into congregations and to communicate to them a sense of belonging to the Catholic Church. He founded the first regularly published Catholic newspaper, the *United States Catholic Miscellany.* He engaged agents in the diocese, around the country, and in Europe to obtain subscriptions. He published news of the Church in the United States and Europe and articles of teaching and poetry. The *Miscellany* would connect scattered Catholics with the diocese and the world Church. England was the first to publish an English-language *Missal for the Laity* in the United States. England used a missal that had been published earlier and had been in use in England and Ireland but he added a one-hundred-page introduction about the Mass. To accompany the *Missal,* England issued the *1822 Directory For the Laity* that indicated the Masses and feasts for each day of the year. England included articles about the U.S. dioceses and Catholic institutions, and the *Directory* could be called the first history of the U.S. Catholic Church. The bishop published two catechisms for teaching the faith. One was a simple *Catechism for Children.* The *Miscellany,* the *Missal,* and the *Catechism* assisted the local congregations in their worship and in their instruction in the faith.

Diocesan Constitution

St. Mary's Catholic Church in Charleston had a troubled history. When England arrived he would not accept the church as his cathedral. He purchased land and built another church to be the cathedral. He was dissatisfied with the way St. Mary's was governed. England faced the difficulty of too much control by trustees. He sought to empower the laity to cooperate but not to dominate. England wrote a *Constitution for the Diocese of Charleston.* It contained the creed, protected the Church's teaching and its discipline. The bishop's freedom to appoint and transfer priests and the priest's rights were protected.

The *Constitution* spoke of the government of the Catholic Church and how each portion of the Church must live in accordance with the laws of the wider portion but that within those laws there was great room for self-government and initiative. An elected vestry was set up for each parish. The vestry would choose the lay workers of the parish and take care of the needs of the Church. Each parish would choose lay delegates to an annual diocesan convention. The convention consisted of the House of Clergy and the House of Lay Delegates. The bishop reported on the condition of the diocese and its projects and needs. The houses deliberated separately and reported their resolutions to the bishop for his approval.

The *Constitution* listed the powers of the convention, which included disposing of the general fund of the diocese, examining all but the spiritual matters of institutions of its own creation, and appointing officers of such institutions. The House of Clergy was to examine the spiritual matters of these institutions. After listing the powers of the convention, the *Constitution* invited the convention to consider any other matter of interest and to present its advice and requests to the bishop.

Twenty-eight conventions were held in the diocese between November 1823 and November 1840. There were twenty-six state conventions and two diocesan conventions. Another convention was planned for November 1841 but England was delayed in returning to the diocese and it was canceled. His successor neglected the *Constitution* and its conventions. England came to a diocese that had been troubled with clerical and lay difficulties for may years. Under England's *Constitution* the diocese was at peace. England faced the question of lay trustees and devised a method empowering the laity to collaborate in the mission of the Church.

The conventions gave England the opportunity to ask the clergy and lay people in his diocese to offer suggestions for matters to be discussed at the provincial councils. After these councils England would also report to the conventions and ask for the help of the gathered delegates to implement the decrees of the provincial councils. The conventions connected the scattered congregations to the diocese and through the convention these congregations could speak to the province. It is no wonder that England saw the need and the importance of the provincial councils and insisted that they be held regularly. Because of his insistence on the holding of the councils, he is called the Father of the Baltimore Councils. England's *Constitution* continues to provide a collaborative model for the American Church.

Clergy and Religious

Within the diocese, England founded and encouraged a number of institutions. In 1829 he organized the Sisters of Charity of Our Lady of Mercy, a congregation that continues its work of education and of serving the needy. He invited the Ursuline sisters from Blackrock, Cork, to the diocese. He founded the Society of St. John the Baptist to support the mission work in the diocese. Two mutual benefit societies were formed to help with burial expenses and to assist workers who were sick and their survivors. These were the Brotherhood of San Marino and the St. Joseph's Mutual Benefit Society. England founded a Classical and Philosophical School in 1822, and the St. John the Baptist Seminary for the training of priests in 1825. The Charleston Seminary educated some sixty priests including four who were named bishops: Andrew Byrne of Little Rock, John Barry of Savannah, Patrick Lynch of Charleston, and John Moore of St. Augustine. James Corcoran, theologian and *peritus* at the First Vatican Council, and Augustine Hewitt, an editor of England's *Works* and a founding member of the Paulist Fathers, were also graduates of the Charleston Seminary.

The need for clergy in his diocese led England to propose that a seminary be established in Ireland for the needs of the American Church. Neither the American nor the Irish bishops were in favor of this new proposal. The idea for a mission seminary in Ireland bore fruit in the establishment of All Hallows Seminary by John Hand some years later. England made arrangements for the education of priests for his diocese with the presidents of Carlow College and St. Patrick's College, Maynooth. England preached about the needs of his own diocese and published in Ireland a booklet about the Church in North Carolina, South Carolina, and Georgia. England also reported on the Charleston mission and the other U.S. missions to the Leopoldine Society in Vienna and the Society for the Propagation of Faith in Lyons which had given support to the American Church.

Native Americans and Blacks

England raised two other mission concerns with the American bishops. Native Americans were being placed on reservations and freed blacks were going to Liberia, a country established for African Americans returning to Africa. England proposed that missions be established to serve the Catholics among these peoples. The U.S. bishops did not accept responsibility for this work. So England, while in Rome in May 1833, submitted two reports to the Holy Father about the need for these missions. Rome invited the Society of Jesus to accept these two new missions. The Jesuits accepted the work among the Native Americans in the U.S.A. but not the mission in Africa. In 1841 Rome requested the bishops of New York, Philadelphia, and Charleston to establish a mission for the Catholics in Liberia. Edward Barron, vicar general of the Philadelphia diocese, John Kelly, pastor in Albany, New York, and Dennis Pindar, lay catechist from Baltimore undertook this first foreign mission effort of the U.S. Catholic Church, arriving in Cape Palmos on January 31, 1842. John England preached in the cathedral at Baltimore on December 5, 1841, about the mission to Liberia. In the 1843 pastoral letter of the Fifth Provincial Council, the U.S. bishops told American Catholics that their prayers or alms could not be better applied than toward the new missionary establishments among the Native Americans and the Africans.

The concordat that England worked out between Haiti and the Catholic Church was not accepted by the Holy See but was similar to one accepted by Haiti and the Holy See some years later. In Haiti, Bishop England ordained a black seminarian, George Paddington, to the priesthood. England was the first U.S. bishop to ordain a black man to the priesthood.

England recognized slavery as the greatest moral evil that could come to a society. However, he thought abolition of slavery was impossible and was the duty of civil government and not of the Church. In a final letter on "Domestic Slavery" published in the *Miscellany* in 1842, England said that he was opposed to the continuation of slavery but that the abolition of slavery was up to the legislature and not him. In his *Letters on Domestic Slavery,*

England narrowly interpreted the Holy See's teachings as against the slave trade but not as condemning the ownership of slaves. Here was a flaw in his vision of a free Church in a free society.

England's life and work are a witness to the energy, vision, and accomplishment that can accompany a person animated by an awareness that one is on mission from Christ.

See also NATIVE AMERICANS AND THE CATHOLIC CHURCH; SLAVERY AND AMERICAN CATHOLICS; SOUTH CAROLINA, CATHOLIC CHURCH IN.

Carey, Patrick. *An Immigrant Bishop: John England's Adaptation of Irish Catholicism to American Republicanism.* Yonkers, New York, 1982.

Clarke, Peter. *A Free Church in a Free Society: The Ecclesiology of John England, Bishop of Charleston, 1820–1842: A Nineteenth-Century Bishop in the Southern United States.* Hartsville, South Carolina, 1982.

Grant, Dorothy F. *John England, American Christopher.* Milwaukee, 1949.

Guilday, Peter. *Life and Times of John England, 1786–1842.* 2 vols. New York, 1927.

Messmer, Sebastian G., ed. *The Works of the Right Reverend John England, First Bishop of Charleston.* 7 vols. Cleveland, 1908.

O'Brien, Joseph L. *John England, Bishop of Charleston: Apostle to Democracy.* New York, 1944.

Reynolds, Ignatius A. *The Works of the Right Reverend John England, First Bishop of Charleston.* 5 vols. Baltimore, 1849.

Rousseau, Richard W., S.J. "Bishop John England and American Church-State Theory." Ph.D. dissertation, St. Paul University, 1969.

____. "The Greatness of John England." *American Ecclesiastical Review* 168 (1974) 196–206.

PETER CLARKE

Related Document

LETTER OF RIGHT REV. JOHN ENGLAND, D.D., FIRST BISHOP OF CHARLESTON, TO M—.

CHARLESTON, SOUTH CAROLINA, MAY 27, 1829

My Dear Sir:

When I was appointed Bishop of the diocese of Charleston, towards the close of the year 1820, I found myself burdened with the spiritual care of three large States, together containing about a million and a half of people, in fact about one-seventh of the whole population of the United States.

The white people were mainly of English and Irish extraction, with some Protestant and Huguenot families that had come hither from France at the time of the revocation of the Edict of Nantes. Virginia and the Northern New England States had contributed many fortune-hunters. There were Catholic refugees from the island of St. Domingo; also a few Frenchmen who had succeeded in escaping the horrors of the (French) Revolution; lastly, a number of emigrants from Ireland and from the State of Maryland.

In general the Catholics were poor and the objects of immense prejudice, and they had no clergy.

Many of the slaves, especially such as had accompanied the French refugees, were Catholics, and nearly all were located at Charleston, Savannah and Augusta.

Several Indian tribes, also, were found within the diocese; but they were sadly neglected through lack of priests.

My jurisdiction extends from 30° 60' to 36° 50' North Lat., and from the Atlantic to 85° 20' west of the Greenwich meridian. It covers the Chattahouchee River and over the Yellow Mountains to 80°—making in all a territory of 133 thousand square miles.

I found upon my arrival one small brick church in South Carolina; in Georgia, one log and two frame edifices—in all four churches. In South Carolina there were probably two hundred communicants; in Georgia, one hundred and fifty; in North Carolina, twenty-five—a total of three hundred and seventy-five.

In Georgia and South Carolina there were only three priests. In coming over from Ireland I had brought along, at my own expense, three more whom I had ordained. Those who were already here did not long remain with me. Still I managed to obtain three others, so that I was enabled to assign two to Georgia, three to South Carolina, and I personally attended to the pastoral wants of North Carolina as soon as I had completed my visits to the chief religious centres of the other two States.

In 1821 I tried to establish a college, hoping thereby to make enough as a teacher to maintain a few theological students; but the Protestant ministers, discovering my purpose, induced those co-religionists of theirs who had entrusted their children to me to withdraw them again.

Debts hung over all the churches; and yet to-day I have my seminary, and, despite the pecuniary difficulties that beset me, I have raised many young candidates for Holy Orders. The only help I received was a sum of five hundred dollars, forwarded to me by Pope Leo XII.

Death deprived me of two of my Irish priests. The two whom they had replaced had left on account of the exhausting labors of their charge and the lack of the necessaries of life. I then procured three others, but had eventually to dismiss them. I have educated twenty subjects. Eight of them, who received Holy Orders at my hands, are now on the mission working zealously and accomplishing much good. Four are still at the seminary; four others died—a priest, a subdeacon and two not yet in minor orders. Two others who had become priests and two students left the diocese.

Eighteen to twenty priests would be needed to meet the present requirements of the diocese, as well as a professor of theology to take my place at the seminary, leaving me free to attend my special duties.

Apart from actual expenses, I still owe at least a thousand dollars, to cover the outlay incurred by the establishment of the seminary and the maintenance of the students. Furthermore, I need a library.

There are at the present time eight churches in this diocese—three frame edifices in Virginia,* one being at Savannah, another at Augusta, the other at Locust Grove, and the foundations are laid for three others.

In South Carolina there are three, one frame and one brick. Charleston has one brick and one frame church, and the foundations are laid for two more.

In North Carolina there are two frame churches—one of which is situated at Washington and the other at Fayetteville. Three others are being planned.

The number of communicants this year is as follows:

At Charleston	850
In other parts of South Carolina	100
In Georgia, about	350
In North Carolina, about	150
Total in 1829	1150
Total in 1820	375
Increase	775

Finally I have a seminary, about two hundred converts, and my diocese is in running order. Yet I am deeply in debt and need much help.

Kindly then, my good friend, beseech the Society of the Propagation of the Faith to give my work their earnest attention.

Other bishops have received much. I have received nothing, while my diocese is the most extensive and the most needy in the United States.

Praying God to bless you, I am,

Yours sincerely,
✝ John, Bishop of Charleston

*This should be *Georgia*.

(*Source: Historical Records and Studies*, Vol. 11, Part 1, October 1900, 141–44. Published by the United States Catholic Historical Society.)

ETLIN, AUGUSTINE ALFRED (LUKAS) (1864–1927)

Artist, editor. He was born on February 28, 1864, in Sarnen, Switzerland, and had his early schooling with the Benedictines in his hometown. He then attended (1880–86) the college attached to the Benedictine abbey at Engelberg. After graduation, and in view of his decision to become a Benedictine, he left for the United States on September 9, 1886, and entered Conception Abbey in Missouri, a daughter house of Engelberg. At the time of his profession the following year (November 1887), he received the name Lukas.

As a student in Switzerland, Etlin demonstrated his artistic ability and during his early years as a monk painted the large mural of the Immaculate Conception in the apse of the monastery church as well as several murals on the side walls. Later, when the church suffered damage because of a tornado, he supervised (1893) their restoration.

In 1892, the year after his ordination, Etlin was appointed chaplain to the Benedictine Sisters of Perpetual Adoration in nearby Clyde, and remained such for thirty-five years, until his death. His own intense devotion to the Eucharist led him to publish (1905) the magazine *Tabernacle and Purgatory,* through which he hoped to increase in its readers a greater esteem for the Mass and to encourage frequent Communion. After World War I, when poverty was widespread in Europe, he used the pages of the magazine to initiate an appeal for funds to benefit hungry children and homeless religious. When this appeal met with great success, he again used the magazine to seek funds for scholarships for seminarians in Europe's poor dioceses. These monies, collected in the United States, were sent abroad to bishops and religious superiors and were used to support seminarians in their studies. Etlin was in charge of the program, which later became known as *Caritas,* for seven years (1920–27) and during this period he assisted some 2,800 seminarians.

In addition to his work as chaplain and as editor, he also taught religion at St. Joseph's Academy for girls. On December 16, 1927, he and a friend had to drive to nearby St. Joseph (Missouri), and on their return their car was hit by another vehicle, and Etlin was severely injured and died on the way to the hospital. Inasmuch as he had a reputation for holiness during life, the informative process, a preliminary step in the cause for beatification, was formally opened in 1960.

Malone, Edward, O.S.B. *Fr. Lukas Etlin, O.S.B.: Apostle of the Eucharist.* Clyde, Miss.: Benedictine Convent of Perpetual Adoration, 1961.
Meyer, Louis, O.S.B. "Apostle of the Eucharist: Father Lukas Etlin, O.S.B. (1864–1927)." *Portraits of American Sanctity,* ed. Joseph N. Tylenda. Chicago: Franciscan Herald, 1982, 264–96.

JOSEPH TYLENDA, S.J.

EXTENSION SOCIETY, CATHOLIC CHURCH

The Catholic Church Extension Society of the United States of America was established in 1905 to aid in spreading the faith in rural and isolated areas of the country. Its founder was Fr. Francis Clement Kelley, a priest from Lapeer, Michigan, who recognized that many rural parishes like his own were underserved in terms of priests and facilities. Fr. Kelly secured the sponsorship of Archbishop James Quigley of Chicago, and the first meeting of the

Extension Society was held at the archbishop's residence on October 18, 1905. Nineteen prelates, priests, and laymen were present at the founding meeting. Archbishop Quigley became chancellor and chairman of the board of governors of the organization, and Kelley was elected the first president.

Kelley's Leadership

The Extension Society quickly outgrew its first headquarters in Kelley's rectory in Lapeer, and in 1906, moved to Chicago, which has remained its home ever since. As mail and contributions flooded in, Kelley hired more clerical help. He obtained increased prestige for the society in 1907 when Pope Pius X granted his approval along with special indulgences for members. In 1910 the same pontiff elevated Extension to the status of a pontifical institute, giving it immunity from a possible lapse in archdiocesan support.

At first, the Extension Society concentrated on building chapels, rectories, and schools in isolated areas where Catholics had no parish facilities. The society adopted the practice of offering a grant for construction if the local bishop and parish would double the amount. Another way of financing construction was the memorial chapel, in which a contributor would have a chapel named after a deceased relative. Kelley devised many innovative ways of raising money, including charitable gift annuities, the Child Apostles club, the Dollar Club, and the sale of colorful calendars. Extension brought religious services into isolated areas by means of "chapel cars" (railroad cars converted into chapels), "motor chapels" (automobiles similarly modified), and "chapel boats" (for use in Louisiana bayous). In 1909 a Women's Auxiliary, later renamed the Order of Martha, was formed to sew vestments and altar linens to be given to the missions.

Extension Magazine

In 1906 Kelley published the first issue of *Extension Magazine*. Although the primary purpose of *Extension* was to promote the missions, under Kelley's guidance it added articles on Church and family issues, fiction, and lavish illustrations, and soon became one of the most popular general Catholic publications. In the 1950s *Extension* reached its greatest circulation, over 500,000.

In 1924 the first phase of the Extension Society's history came to an end when Kelley was appointed bishop of Oklahoma City, bringing to a close his tenure as the society's president. By this time, Extension had a firm foundation: It was collecting close to one million dollars a year, and was estimated to have constructed half of all the Catholic churches built in the United States since its founding. Kelley handed over leadership of the society to his long-time collaborator Msgr. William D. O'Brien. As president for the next thirty-eight years, O'Brien continued Kelley's policies by increasing the amount of money raised and keeping *Extension* a general mass-circulation magazine. In 1961 he founded the Extension Lay Volunteer Program, which sent two thousand teachers, nurses, and parish workers to the rural missions over the next ten years.

Later Developments

Later presidents of the Extension Society included Msgr. Joseph Lux (1962–68), Archbishop John May (1968–70), Fr. Joseph Cusack (1970–79), Fr. Edward Slattery (1979–94), and Fr. Kenneth Velo (1995–). These leaders presided over a contraction and modernization in the activities of the society. After years of declining circulation, May transformed *Extension* from a general family magazine to one more narrowly focused on promoting the missions. His successors gave increased emphasis to financial accountability and the development of planned giving. In 1978 Extension began granting the annual Lumen Christi Award that honored "persons making outstanding contributions to the American home missions." From its founding to 1995, the Extension Society distributed over $230 million in every American state and dependency, and constructed over 10,500 church buildings.

The Extension Society was an early manifestation of an awakening of American Catholics to the underserved nature of the rural and isolated areas of the United States. At a time when over four-fifths of American Catholics lived in urban areas, Kelley's organization directed the Church's attention to the neglected countryside. Extension pioneered Catholic efforts in rural areas which later included the American Board of Catholic Missions, the Glenmary Missioners, and the National Catholic Rural Life Conference.

See also KELLEY, FRANCIS CLEMENT.

Gaffey, James P. "The Catholic Church Extension Society." *Catholics in America, 1776–1976,* ed. Robert Trisco. Washington, D.C., 1976, 193–96.

_____. *Francis Clement Kelley and the American Catholic Dream.* 2 vols. Bensenville, Illinois, 1980.

Kelley, Francis C. *The Story of Extension.* Chicago, 1922.

Leopold, Claudia. "Making a Difference in Mission America." *Extension* (October 1995) 9–15.

DAVID BOVEE

F

FAGAN, HARRY A. (1939–92)

Social activist. Fagan, the son of Harry and Jane Fagan, was born on December 15, 1939, and educated in Cleveland. After studies at John Carroll University, Fagan joined the advertising staff of the *Plain Dealer*, a Cleveland daily newspaper. In 1969 Fagan's concern about social justice led him to volunteer for service with the Cleveland diocese's recently established social justice agency, the Commission for Catholic Community Action. Fagan became a facilitator for the agency's Action for a Change project, a program designed to educate people to review and respond to societal issues in the light of the Church's social justice teachings.

His volunteer activities led him to the directorship of the Heights Community Congress. Under Fagan's leadership this grassroots neighborhood group successfully resisted real estate agents who were racially steering clients in the integrated suburb of Cleveland Heights. Switching from advertising to advocacy, Fagan became a full-time member of the Commission for Catholic Community Action in 1970. In 1976 he was named director of the organization.

Fagan built up a network of neighborhood organizations in the urban areas of the diocese. With the commission providing technical assistance, these local groups questioned authorities regarding various inequities. Fagan clashed with politicians including Cleveland's mayor Dennis Kucinich, who alleged that Fagan controlled these neighborhood groups. In 1983 Fagan came to New York City to cofound the National Pastoral Life Center, a group designated to facilitate pastoral and social ministry throughout the American Church. He died in New York City on December 9, 1992.

National Pastoral Life Center News Release, December 10, 1992.
Papers of the Commission for Catholic Community Action, 1969–83. Archives, Diocese of Cleveland.

CHRISTINE L. KROSEL

FAIRFIELD UNIVERSITY

Fairfield University was founded in 1942 in Fairfield, Connecticut, by the New England Province of the Society of Jesus as the twenty-sixth Jesuit institution of higher education in the United States and was originally incorporated as Fairfield College of St. Robert Bellarmine.

A state charter was granted in 1945, and the first class of 303 male students, including 140 veterans of World War II, arrived in 1947 for classes in the College of Arts and Sciences, held in two buildings. The first rector-president was John A. McEleney, S.J.

The first classes in graduate education followed in 1950 and were coeducational. Women were admitted to the undergraduate program in 1970 and Fairfield University expanded to become a comprehensive university with the Graduate School of Education and Allied Professions (1963), School of Nursing (1970), the School of Business (1978), the School of Continuing Education (1979) and the BEI School of Engineering, a part-time evening program acquired through a merger (1994).

In 1995 the university had grown to include more than 30 buildings and had an enrollment of almost 3,000 full-time undergraduates, 1,200 part-time undergraduates, 800 graduate students in business, education, and nursing, and 3,000 adults pursuing noncredit programs for career advancement or personal enrichment.

See also CATHOLIC UNIVERSITIES AND COLLEGES.

ALOYSIUS KELLY, S.J.

FARIBAULT-STILLWATER SCHOOL PLAN

A chief concern of the American hierarchy during the nineteenth century was the need to provide religious education for Catholic youth. The public or "common school" with its historical roots in sectarian Protestantism was deemed by many to threaten the faith of Catholic children.

Responding to a request on the part of the bishops of the Cincinnati province, the Sacred Congregation of Propaganda Fide issued an instruction on November 24, 1875, admonishing prelates to keep Catholic children away from schools that endangered their faith. Parents were to be permitted, for grave reasons, to send their children to public school, but with due precaution lest the faith of their children be compromised.

Nine years later, the assembled bishops at the Third Plenary Council of Baltimore decreed the erection of a parochial school in every parish where such a school did not yet exist. The local bishop was to decide of possible exceptions. Obstructionist clergy would be liable to removal. Unconvinced parishioners were to be helped by the local bishop to find the means to build and operate a school. The parental exception of the 1875 instruction was repeated.

Archbishop Ireland and the Public Schools

Against this backdrop, Archbishop John Ireland of St. Paul spoke before the National Education Association in July 1890. He lauded the public schools' attempt at educating all children irrespective of race or creed. He maintained that religion deserved a place in the curriculum, since its banishment from education would be disastrous. He proposed that denominational schools be funded from the public purse, as was already the custom in many parts of Europe. Lacking this, he advocated the so-called "Poughkeepsie Plan" already in existence since 1873 in one parish in New York, whereby the public school district rented the parochial school building during business hours, parochial school personnel was maintained, and religious instruction was given after the official close of the school day.

Angry reaction soon broke out, reaching even to Rome. Cardinal Rampolla, the Papal Secretary of State, requested an evaluation of Ireland's theories from Cardinal Gibbons of Baltimore. The latter responded by voicing complete confidence in the Minnesota prelate.

The theories of Archbishop Ireland were put into effect the following summer when, after obtaining the ordinary's approval, the pastor of Immaculate Conception parish in Faribault, Minnesota, placed his school building at the disposition of the public school authorities. The pastor of St. Michael's in Stillwater was authorized to do likewise.

In essence the "Poughkeepsie Plan" was repeated. The sisters were to receive forty dollars monthly (a fifteen dollar increase), and the school district was to make itself responsible for educational materials, equipment, and upkeep of the buildings. The solution seemed a fair one to many. "Double taxation" of parents was alleviated; the financial burden of the parish school was removed from the shoulders of the parishioners; the faith of the children was safeguarded.

Divisions Among American Catholics

Archbishop Ireland, no stranger to controversy, was assailed on several fronts: by Protestants who decried the destruction of the public school; by Catholics who feared state control of education; by German-American groups, both lay and clerical, who suspected that the plan would ultimately be used to undermine the German language and customs that they sought to preserve. While Ireland could count on the support of Cardinal Gibbons of Baltimore, his opponents were seconded by Archbishops Frederick Katzer of Milwaukee and Michael Corrigan of New York.

A war of pamphlets was soon underway. The Rev. Thomas Bouquillon of The Catholic University of America espoused the pro-Faribault position in a work entitled *Education: To Whom Does It Belong?* and conceded certain state powers over education. In turn, the Rev. René I. Holaind, S.J., in *The Parent First* denied any automatic state prerogatives. Other pamphlets were to follow.

Archbishop Ireland explained his plan to the assembled archbishops at their St. Louis meeting, November 28, 1891, doing so to the apparent satisfaction of all. Charges were being mounted in Rome, however, against the archbishop's orthodoxy. The Jesuit journal *la Civiltà Cattolica*, reputed to enjoy the confidence of the Vatican, published seven articles between December 1891 and April 1892, denouncing the Faribault-Stillwater plan and its champion.

The embattled archbishop traveled to Rome to defend himself personally. In a February 21, 1892, "memorial" to the Sacred Congregation of Propaganda, he emphasized that the Faribault-Stillwater plan was in no way original. Variants of the plan were in effect in some ten dioceses. Faced with the choice of closing parish schools for lack of funds, or negotiating a shared-use agreement with the public school board, the latter was certainly to be preferred. Chief among his Catholic antagonists were the Germans whose arguments had less to do with Church-state relations than with cultural concerns. Also, evidence of organized Jesuit resistance was not lacking.

Tolerari Potest

Rome ruled favorably in April 1892, using the term *tolerari potest* with respect to the Faribault-Stillwater plan. Archbishop Ireland immediately claimed vindication, while his opponents maintained just as loudly that he had been condemned. In their view, *tolerari potest* merely indicated that, in this specific instance, an evil could be tolerated. They denied that any permission had been granted to extend the plan elsewhere.

In November of 1892, at the yearly archbishops' meeting in New York, apostolic delegate Francesco Satolli reaffirmed the binding force of the decrees of the Third Plenary Council of Baltimore and further stipulated that in the absence of outright state aid Catholic schools might adopt the Faribault-Stillwater plan.

Many bishops remained unconvinced. After demanding and receiving personal statements from all American bishops, Pope Leo XIII wrote to Cardinal Gibbons on May 31, 1893. In a text that he requested be communicated to every American prelate, the Pope reaffirmed Archbishop Satolli's pronouncements of the previous fall. In a bid to stem further rancor, the Pope also pleaded for an end to bickering among bishops. Under obedience, the prelates complied.

In Stillwater, the "plan" would die after just a year in operation, a victim of local Protestant opposition. One year later the Faribault experiment would likewise come to an end because of differences between the parish and the school district.

See also BOUQUILLON, THOMAS; CATHOLIC EDUCATION, PAROCHIAL; IRELAND, JOHN; POUGHKEEPSIE SCHOOL PLAN.

Burns, J. A., and Bernard J. Kohlbrenner. *A History of Catholic Education in the United States.* New York: Benziger, 1937.
Fogarty, Gerald P., S.J. *The Vatican and the American Hierarchy from 1870 to 1965.* Wilmington, Del.: Michael Glazier, 1985.
Moynihan, James H. *The Life of Archbishop Ireland.* New York: Harper & Bros., 1953.
Reardon, James Michael. *The Catholic Church in the Diocese of St. Paul.* St. Paul, Minn.: North Central Publishing Company, 1952.
Roemer, Theodore. *The Catholic Church in the United States.* St. Louis: B. Herder, 1950.

ALBERT H. LEDOUX

FARLEY, JAMES (1888–1976)

Politician and Postmaster General. James Aloysius Farley was born in Grassy Point, New York, on May 30, 1888. He began his career as a bookkeeper at Universal Gypsum Company in 1906 after graduating from Packard Commercial School in New York City.

After serving three terms (1912–19) as town clerk in Stony Point, New York, he moved back to New York City where he served successively as port warden of the Port of New York, member and chairman of the New York State Athletic Commission, and legislator in the New York State Assembly. In 1926 Farley established a building materials firm that merged with five other companies in 1929, and he became president of the newly formed General Builders Supply Corporation until 1933.

He became prominent in politics when he was named secretary of the New York State Democratic Committee in 1928 and organized Franklin Delano Roosevelt's campaign for New York governor. In 1930 he was named chairman of the state committee and two years later organized Roosevelt's presidential campaign while serving as chairman of the Democratic National Committee.

During the campaign, he successfully orchestrated a deal in which the Texas and California delegations promised to support Roosevelt in return for the vice-presidential nomination of John Nance Garner. In recognition of Farley's successful efforts, Roosevelt appointed him to the cabinet post of Postmaster General.

Farley organized Roosevelt's second reelection campaign in 1936, but resigned his cabinet post in 1940 when he disagreed with Roosevelt over seeking a third term. Farley allowed his name to be placed in nomination at the convention. Although his bid was unsuccessful, he continued in politics, serving as chairman of the New York State Democratic Committee, once again opposing Roosevelt's reelection bid in 1944.

Following that election, Farley dropped out of politics, spending the remainder of his working years in the private sector. He served as chairman of the board of the Coca Cola Export Corporation and president of the General Builders Supply Corporation until retiring in 1973. Farley received many awards and honorary degrees and wrote two books, *Behind the Ballots* (1938) and *Jim Farley's Story* (1948). He died in New York City on June 9, 1976.

See also NEW DEAL AND AMERICAN CATHOLICS, THE.

MARIANNA McLOUGHLIN

FARLEY, JOHN CARDINAL (1842–1918)

Cardinal archbishop. John Murphy Farley was born on April 20, 1842, in Newtown Hamilton, County Armagh, Ireland, the fourth and youngest child of Philip Farrelly and Catherine Murphy Farrelly. He was educated at local schools and at St. Macartan's College in County Monaghan. After the death of his parents, in 1864 he emigrated with his surviving brother and sister to the United States and lived with his uncle, Patrick Murphy. That same year he attended St. John's College, Fordham, and in 1865 he entered St. Joseph's Provincial Seminary in Troy, New York, the major seminary of the Archdiocese of New York. In 1866 he was sent to the North American College in Rome where he was ordained a priest on June 11, 1870.

John Cardinal Farley

Upon his return to New York, Farley spent two years as a curate in St. Peter's Church in Staten Island, then served as secretary to Cardinal John McCloskey from 1872 until 1884, when he became pastor of St. Gabriel's Church, a large midtown Manhattan parish. In 1872 he changed the spelling of his name from Farrelly to Farley. Throughout the administration of McCloskey's successor, Archbishop Michael Augustine Corrigan (1885–1902), Farley remained pastor of St. Gabriel's Church. In 1891 he was also appointed vicar general, and in 1895 he became New York's first auxiliary bishop. He succeeded Corrigan as the fourth archbishop of New York on September 15, 1902, and was made a cardinal on November 27, 1911.

Archbishop of New York

A cautious and peace-loving man, Farley made it a high priority to heal the divisions in the diocesan clergy caused by the dispute between Archbishop Corrigan and Dr. Edward McGlynn. As a gesture of reconciliation, Farley conferred the still relatively rare title of monsignor on both Richard Burtsell and Patrick McSweeny, two of Corrigan's sharpest critics. Six other priests were made monsignors at the same time, an unprecedentedly lavish bestowal of Roman honors, leading John Talbot Smith to comment that "he had made half the clergy purple and the other half blue."

In contrast to the dramatic growth of the archdiocese in the nineteenth century, the Catholic population registered only a modest increase under Farley, from about 1,200,000 in 1902 to about 1,300,000 in 1918, an indication that middle-class Catholics were already beginning to move from Manhattan to the suburbs outside the archdiocese.

Much of the increase in population was due to the huge influx of Italian immigrants. Farley continued Corrigan's policy of providing pastoral care for these immigrants, who numbered about 500,000 by 1918. Unlike Corrigan, Farley made a deliberate effort to employ diocesan priests rather than religious orders in this apostolate. During his administration, the number of Italian parishes more than doubled, from eighteen in 1903 to forty-four in 1918.

Education was another area of impressive growth during Farley's years. Fifty new parochial schools were opened, doubling the enrollment on the elementary level. Catholic higher education also made notable progress. In 1904 St. John's College became Fordham University, and three women's colleges were founded in the early years of the century, the College of New Rochelle (1904), the College of Mt. St. Vincent (1910), and Manhattanville College of the Sacred Heart (1917). Unlike Archbishop Corrigan, Farley was a staunch supporter of The Catholic University of America, earning for him the gratitude of James Cardinal Gibbons. He also was a patron of the *Catholic Encyclopedia.*

In September 1903 Farley opened the archdiocese's first preparatory seminary, Cathedral College, a six-year day school, which represented a daring American innovation in seminary education. The preliminary work had been done by Archbishop Corrigan, but Farley brought it to fruition.

Farley and Dunwoodie

Farley's relationship with the major seminary, St. Joseph's Seminary, Dunwoodie, was more ambivalent. During the planning stages of Dunwoodie in the 1890s, Farley had strongly opposed Corrigan's plan to entrust the seminary to the Society of St. Sulpice. In 1906 Farley indicated to the six Sulpician members of the faculty that he would be willing to incardinate them into the diocese and to retain them on the Dunwoodie faculty. When five of the six Sulpician professors accepted his offer, he unilaterally terminated the relationship with the Sulpicians.

In 1905 Farley had given his support to the publication of the *New York Review,* a scholarly theological journal founded by three Dunwoodie professors, James F. Driscoll, Francis P. Duffy, and John F. Brady. Farley's support of the journal was a major factor in persuading the five Sulpicians to become New York diocesan priests. After the publication of the encyclical *Pascendi Dominici Gregis* in 1907, however, both the seminary and the journal came under suspicion of Modernism. The following year the journal ceased publication and the rector, James Driscoll, was forced to resign in 1909.

A major cause of concern for Farley between 1910 and 1916 was a series of state and city investigations of Catholic charitable institutions in the archdiocese which generated a considerable amount of unfavorable publicity. Farley's successor, Patrick Cardinal Hayes, remedied the situation in 1920 by creating the Catholic Charities of the Archdiocese of New York. Farley published two books, *History of St. Patrick's Cathedral* (1908) and *The Life of John Cardinal McCloskey* (1918), the second actually ghostwritten by Peter Guilday.

Like his first patron, John Cardinal McCloskey, Farley kept a low profile and avoided public confrontations. "He loved peace, especially in ecclesiastical circles," said Msgr. Michael J. Lavelle, his vicar general, who lauded Farley for the fact that he was never the object of criticism in the secular press. Lavelle also credited Farley with unifying a divided presbyterate. "There is not a clique or a faction in the diocese," he claimed at the time of Farley's death. Farley died of pneumonia on September 17, 1918, and was buried beneath the high altar of St. Patrick's Cathedral.

Brown, Mary Elizabeth. *Churches, Communities and Children: Italian Immigrants in the Archdiocese of New York, 1880–1945.* New York: Center for Migration Studies, 1995.

Cohalan, Florence D. *A Popular History of the Archdiocese of New York.* Yonkers, 1983, 177–214.

Ellis, John Tracy. "Cardinal Gibbons and New York." *Historical Records and Studies* 39–40 (1952) 5–32.

Farley's papers are in the archives of the Archdiocese of New York.

Hayes, Patrick J. "John Cardinal Farley, Archbishop of New York." *Historical Records and Studies* 6 (2) (1913) 5–68.

Kelly, Neil J. "'Orphans and Pigs Fed from the Same Bowl': Catholics and the New York Charities Controversy of 1916." M.A. thesis, St. Joseph's Seminary, Dunwoodie, 1991.

Lavelle, Michael M. "John Cardinal Farley, Archbishop of New York." *The Ecclesiastical Review* 10 (February 1919) 113–25.

Shelley, Thomas J. "John Cardinal Farley and Modernism in New York." *Church History* 61 (1992) 350–61.

See also MODERNISM IN AMERICA; NEW YORK, CATHOLIC CHURCH IN; *NEW YORK REVIEW.*

THOMAS J. SHELLEY

FARRELL, WALTER (1902–51)

Dominican theologian and writer. Walter Raphael Farrell was born in Chicago, Illinois, on July 21, 1902. His early education was in parochial schools and at Archbishop Quigley Preparatory Seminary in Chicago. In September 1920 he entered the Dominican novitiate at St. Joseph's Priory, Somerset, Ohio, where he professed his vows on September 15, 1921. His study of philosophy and theology took him first to St. Rose of Lima Priory, Springfield, Kentucky (1921–22), and then to the Dominican House of Studies, Washington, D.C. (1922–28), where he was ordained on June 9, 1927, and earned the S.T.L. degree in 1928. He then pursued graduate studies at the University of Fribourg, Switzerland (1928–30), and was awarded the S.T.D. degree in 1930.

Upon returning to the United States he taught theology at St. Joseph's Priory, Somerset, Ohio (1930–33), and then at the Dominican House of Studies, Washington, D.C. (1933–48). In 1939 he was named regent of studies for the Dominican province of St. Joseph (New York) and president of the Pontifical Faculty of Theology, positions that he continued to hold until 1948. He was awarded the degree of Master of Sacred Theology by the Dominican Order in 1940. For two years during World War II (1943–45) he left the classroom to minister as a naval chaplain, serving on the U.S.S. *Yorktown* for a year. Farrell had elected to join the new province of St. Albert the Great (Chicago) in 1940, although he continued to serve as regent for the province of St. Joseph. In 1948 he returned to his new province and taught theology at the Dominican House of Studies, River Forest, Illinois, until his death in 1951.

Farrell is best known for his four-volume work, *A Companion to the Summa* (1938–42). Originating in a series of lectures given in New York under the auspices of The Catholic Thought Association, these volumes sought "to furnish a rational defense of the faith for the ordinary Catholic and to open St. Thomas to the layman who has no professional philosophical or theological knowledge" (Foreword). He was instrumental in April 1939 in launching *The Thomist,* a speculative quarterly to promote scientific and creative investigation of Thomistic thought. Making the thought of St. Thomas Aquinas accessible to the laity also inspired his participation as a lecturer in the Thomist Association during his last years in Chicago. In addition to frequent articles in Catholic journals, Farrell was a well-known retreat master and preacher. He died in River Forest, Illinois, on November 23, 1951.

See also DOMINICANS (O.P.); THOMISM IN AMERICA.

Brennan, Robert Edward, O.P. "Walter Farrell, O.P., Apud Posteros Sacer." *The Thomist* 15 (2) (April 1952) 199–208.

Coffey, Reginald M., O.P. "The Very Reverend Walter Farrell, O.P., S.T.M." *American Ecclesiastical Review* 126 (April 1952) 271–78.

DAVID F. WRIGHT, O.P.

FAUST, MATHIAS (1878–1956)

Franciscan friar, religious superior. One of the most distinguished members of the Order of Friars Minor in the United States, Mathias (Constantine) Faust was born in Oberbimbach, Germany, on March 30, 1878. As a youth he emigrated to the United States, and at the age of nineteen he was received into the Franciscan Order in Paterson, New Jersey. Ordained to the priesthood in 1906, two years later he was named novice master, an office he was to hold for eleven years. Elected minister provincial of Holy Name province in 1919, he served in that office during four mandates of three years each (1919–22 and 1931–37).

In the regulatory interval between his second and third term of that triennial office he served as guardian and pastor of the well-known St. Francis Friary and Church in midtown New York's shopping area. During the time he was guardian-pastor he supervised the renovation of the well-known Franciscan Shrine on 31st Street.

At the outbreak of World War II, he was named the delegate of the Franciscan Minister General for North and Central America, having jurisdiction over ten provinces and eight commissariats of that vast territory. During that period he was responsible for the establishment of the world-renowned Franciscan Institute at St. Bonaventure University; likewise at that time he promoted the establishment of the Academy of American Franciscan History with its seat in suburban Washington.

At the end of World War II he was elected procurator general of the Order of Friars Minor, with responsibility for the order's dealings with the Holy See, an office that he held for six years (1946–51), with residence at the generalate of the order in Rome. Having discharged that delicate office for six years, he returned to the United States. During the next four years, residing in New York, he was delegate general for the commissariats of the order in the United States and Central America.

He died in New York City on July 27, 1956. At his funeral he was eulogized and praised for his contributions to the Church and the order, in a panegyric given by his lifelong friend and associate, Fr. Thomas Plassmann, before the final absolution given by Cardinal Spellman. He is buried in the friars' plot in Holy Sepulcher Cemetery, Paterson, New Jersey.

See also FRANCISCAN FRIARS.

ALEXANDER WYSE, O.F.M.

FEEHAN, PATRICK (1829–1902)

First archbishop of Chicago. Feehan was a native of County Tipperary, Ireland. He began his seminary training at Maynooth, but completed it in St. Louis where he was ordained on November 1, 1852. During his thirteen years in St. Louis, Feehan taught in the seminary at Carondelet, served as its president (1854–57), and served as a pastor. Feehan's dedication to the sick and wounded was demonstrated during the periodic cholera epidemics and his attention to wounded Civil War soldiers. This educated, pious, and respected priest became the bishop of Nashville in November 1865. His fifteen years in Nashville were filled with the successes of establishing new parishes, building an orphanage, and bringing new religious orders to the diocese. Offsetting these accomplishments was the toll which the various cholera and yellow fever epidemics took on the religious and clergy of the diocese. Over seventy priests and sisters died in service to victims of yellow fever during the 1870s.

First Archbishop of Chicago

When Feehan was installed as the first archbishop of Chicago on November 28, 1880, he inherited a church that had experienced tremendous growth since the 1871 Chicago fire. During his twenty-two years as archbishop, the Catholic population almost quadrupled from approximately 230,000 to 800,000. The new archbishop was known for his administrative abilities, remained conservative in fiscal matters, prudential in his judgments, and respected the opinions of his clergy (Shanabruch, 36–37). Feehan's lifelong interest in education made him a natural choice as the head for the committee on schools at the Third Plenary Council of Baltimore (1884). Although by nature a person who avoided controversy, Feehan gave a dramatic speech in defense of the Ancient Order of Hibernians at a meeting of the American archbishops on secret societies. One of the best-known episcopal orators of the day, John Ireland, later said that Feehan's speech was "one of the most eloquent" he had heard (Kirkfleet, 239–40). When Chicago hosted the 1893 World's Columbian Exposition, Feehan participated in a number of Catholic and ecumenical activities. He was the president for the organizing committee of the second lay Catholic congress. He spoke at the Catholic Education Day held in conjunction with the exposition. Feehan also gave a welcome address to the members of the World's Parliament of Religions. Such public visibility was unusual for Feehan, who is remembered for "rare excursions" into the public view (Sanders, 133).

Ethnic Conflicts

The final years of Feehan's life were marred by two controversies which disrupted the unity of the Catholic Church in Chicago. Although Polish Catholics in Chicago were served by priests from the Congregation of the Resurrection, a number of parish disputes had erupted between their supporters and opponents. In 1894, many parishioners at St. Hedwig's parish wanted their Resurrectionist pastor removed and his young associate, Anthony Kozlowski, appointed in his place. The conflict escalated to the point that Feehan dismissed the associate. Appeals to the apostolic delegate, continuing demonstrations at the parish, and contacts with Old Catholics brought the affair to a crisis point in September 1895. Although the apostolic delegate urged various steps for reconciliation, Feehan was unwilling to surrender his right to appoint the pastor of his choice. Anthony Kozlowski's excommunication on September 27, 1895, was Feehan's final word on the matter. The schismatic Kozlowski, who had consecrated his own church when Feehan refused, later was ordained a bishop by an Old Catholic bishop. At least one thousand families from St. Hedwig joined Kozlowski's independent Catholic Church.

Ethnic conflict between Irish-born priests and American-born priests of Irish descent surfaced in the selection of an auxiliary bishop for Chicago. When Peter Muldoon, Feehan's chancellor, was selected as the second auxiliary for Chicago in 1901, some twenty Irish-born priests from the archdiocese sent a letter to the apostolic delegate, Sebastiano Martinelli, accusing Muldoon of immorality and drunkenness. Although these charges were dismissed by Martinelli, Fr. Jeremiah Crowley, who presented the defamatory letter to Martinelli, resigned his parish in protest. Muldoon's consecration took place without any violence. Crowley later wanted to rescind his resignation, but he refused Feehan's condition that he apologize for the defamation. When Crowley asked for an ecclesiastical trial, he was told to submit to Feehan. He refused and was excommunicated. The Muldoon-Crowley affair resulted in a Roman investigation, requested by Bishop John Spalding (Peoria), into Feehan's management of the archdiocese. Feehan was cleared of the charges by Martinelli. Three attacks of pneumonia in two years had physically weakened Feehan. He died on July 12, 1902.

See also ILLINOIS, CATHOLIC CHURCH IN.

Kirkfleet, Cornelius J. *The Life of Patrick Augustine Feehan.* Chicago: Matre & Co., 1922.

Parot, Joseph John. *Polish Catholics in Chicago, 1850–1920.* DeKalb: Northern Illinois University Press, 1981.

Sanders, James W. *The Education of An Urban Minority: Catholics in Chicago, 1833–1965.* New York: Oxford University Press, 1977.

Shanabruch, Charles. *Chicago's Catholics: The Evolution of An American Identity.* University of Notre Dame Press, 1981.

Stritch, Thomas. *The Catholic Church in Tennessee.* Nashville: Catholic Center, 1987.

Sweeney, David Francis. *The Life of John Lancaster Spalding.* New York: Herder & Herder, 1965.

Trisco, Robert F. "The Holy See and the First 'Independent Catholic Church' in the United States." *Studies in Catholic History,* eds. Nelson H. Minnich, Robert B. Eno, S.S., and Robert F. Trisco. Wilmington, Del.: Michael Glazier, 1985, 175–238.

MARTIN ZIELINSKI

FEENEY, LEONARD (1897–1928)

Jesuit priest, writer, and controversialist. Leonard Feeney was born in Lynn, Massachusetts, on February 15, 1897, and ordained a Jesuit priest, June 20, 1928. He was considered one of the most gifted, celebrated, scorned, colorful and controversial clergymen of his time. An internationally published author, teacher, preacher, poet, and humorist, he fell from grace in the late 1940s when he was censured by Archbishop (later Cardinal) Richard Cushing of Boston in what came to be known as the "Boston

Leonard Feeney

Heresy Case" and dismissed from the Jesuit Order. He was publicly excommunicated by decree of the Holy Office on February 4, 1953, an action approved and confirmed by Pope Pius XII.

Early Years

After finishing courses at Weston College in Massachusetts and publishing a volume of poetry, *In Towns and Little Towns* (America Press, New York, 1927), Fr. Feeney was sent by his Jesuit superiors to study ascetical theology at St. Beuno's College in Wales, and English literature at Oxford. On his return in 1931, he taught at Boston College and published another book of verse, *Riddle and Reverie* (Macmillan, New York, 1933), *Fish on Friday*, an imaginative collection of essays (Sheed & Ward, London, 1934), and children's poems in *Boundaries* (Macmillan, New York, 1935).

While serving as literary editor of *America* magazine from 1936 to 1940, he was named one of the nation's top fifteen living Catholic authors by Webster College in Missouri, along with Agnes Repplier, Theodore Maynard, and Fulton Sheen. In 1936 more of his poems appeared in *Song for a Listener* (Macmillan, New York), and his series of Advent sermons at St. Patrick's Cathedral that year received much attention in the press, including an article in *Time* magazine reporting on one of these talks. During his years at *America* he also wrote a biography of Elizabeth Bayley Seton, *An American Woman* (America Press, New York, 1938), and collaborated with Nathalia Crane on *The Ark and the Alphabet* (Macmillan, New York, 1939).

In New York, Feeney befriended a number of Jews, some of whom he received into the Catholic Church. For years he would boast about these Jewish "converts" and said they had a greater claim on Christianity than he did. He spoke with respect of the importance of the "Jewishness" of Jesus and Mary. In the 1930s he mocked Hitler in print. He also suggested during this same period that it was time for the Church to appoint a black American as cardinal, and he was one of the few churchmen of his generation to condemn the dropping of atomic bombs on Japan at the end of World War II as a racist act. In later years, when he was accused by his critics of being a bigot and a racist, all this seemed so much out of character to those who knew him.

St. Benedict Center

In 1940 Leonard Feeney was reassigned to teach at Boston College and was introduced to a group of young Catholic students at Harvard University organized by Catherine Clarke, Avery Dulles, and Christopher Huntington. Clarke soon took leadership of the group which became known as St. Benedict Center. Dulles and Huntington both left to study for the priesthood and were never associated with the later controversy that came to focus on Father Feeney, Catherine Clarke, and St. Benedict Center.

Feeney was invited to speak at the student center and soon became a fixture there, offering courses and also working with young men and women who wished to become Catholics. Fr. John J. Wright, a young priest who had recently returned from studies in Rome to become secretary to Archbishop Cushing, was a frequent visitor and recommended to Cushing that Feeney be assigned full time to the center. Cushing, who also accepted an invitation to visit with the students there, petitioned the Jesuit provincial for Feeney to be appointed the Center chaplain.

Before long, St. Benedict Center became a very popular meeting place for Catholic students in the greater Boston area. John F. Kennedy, while campaigning for Congress, visited Feeney at the center and asked to try on the brown derby that Al Smith, the first Catholic candidate for the U.S. presidency, had given the priest in gratitude for an essay he had written about the famous hat during Smith's 1928 campaign against Herbert Hoover. Kennedy's brother and sister, Robert and Eunice, attended some of Feeney's lectures. Robert F. Kennedy later confronted Feeney at the center when the priest began to profess a strict interpretation of the theological dictum, "There is no salvation outside the Church—*Extra ecclesiam nulla salus*"—and walked out, never to return.

But, before the controversy over salvation became the focus of St. Benedict Center, it was a lively and intellectually stimulating magnet for hundreds of young people. Great numbers appeared at Fr. Feeney's overcrowded lectures, sometimes spilling out into the street where they listened through the open doorway. One of these students was Humberto Medeiros, a seminarian at the time, and later archbishop of Boston. Many of the nation's leading Catholic intellectuals befriended Feeney and came to hear him speak. Clare Booth Luce, a convert to Catholicism

who would later become a member of the U.S. Congress and ambassador to Italy, was often Feeney's guest at St. Benedict Center and wrote occasional pieces for the center publication, *From the Housetops*. He also made friends in Hollywood among the growing number of Catholics in the film industry, and this enhanced his national standing. Frank Sheed and Masie Ward visited Feeney at St. Benedict Center, as well, and in 1943 Sheed & Ward published *The Leonard Feeney Omnibus,* a collection of his prose and verse.

Events leading to the end of World War II seemed to be a turning point for Fr. Feeney. There were Jesuits living in Hiroshima when the atom bomb devastated the city. Horrified at the wholesale destruction of innocent human life in this new phase of warfare, Feeney worried what the consequences of this act might be for human civilization. He bitterly opposed the enrollment of Jesuit priests as students at Harvard, because he felt they took courses taught by professors who were either atheists or proponents of views opposed to Catholic teaching. He accused these fellow Jesuits of not speaking out in defense of the Church. And he encouraged many of the Catholic students he worked with to drop out of Harvard and to go to Catholic colleges instead.

The Boston Heresy Case

By 1947 Fr. Feeney had come to the conclusion, encouraged by Clarke and a number of his young followers, that the world was in such a sorry state because Catholics no longer held a strict interpretation of the doctrinal teaching that there is no salvation outside the Church, i.e., only Roman Catholics can be saved. Feeney, Catherine Clarke, and several St. Benedict Center students launched a public campaign in defense of their rigid view, and in 1949 four of his disciples were fired from their teaching positions at Boston College and Boston College High School after they wrote a letter accusing the Jesuit college of heresy, because its faculty was teaching students that "there is salvation outside the Church and that any man can be saved without submission to the authority of Our Holy Father, the Pope." The *New York Times* carried the story of the firings on its front page and the controversy became widely known in the national press as "The Boston Heresy Case." Soon after, Feeney also accused Archbishop Cushing, his secretary—by then auxiliary bishop John Wright—and Jesuit superiors of heresy for holding the same views on salvation.

That same year, Pope Pius XII personally reviewed and revised a document later issued by the Holy Office, and now known by the title *Suprema Haec Sacra,* in which it was forcefully stated that, although the Catholic Church will never cease to preach "that infallible statement by which we are taught that there is no salvation outside the

Church," the dogma must be understood "in that sense in which the Church herself understands it." In order for someone to be saved, it explained, "it is not always required that he be incorporated into the Church as an actual member, but it is necessary at least to be united to her by desire and longing."

Archbishop Cushing removed Fr. Feeney's faculties to perform priestly functions, preach, or teach religion. He decreed that any Catholics who frequented St. Benedict Center or assisted its activities would forfeit the right to receive the sacraments of penance or Eucharist. After an investigation of the matter, Fr. Feeney was dismissed from the Jesuit Order in 1949 and was summoned to appear before the Vatican's Holy Office for a hearing. He packed his bags and prepared to go to Rome, but was then convinced by Catherine Clarke that, if he went, he would be locked up or sent by Vatican officials to a monastery and never return to the St. Benedict Center. Bowing to her pressure, he did not go and, because of this "grave disobedience to Church authority," the Holy Office declared him excommunicated. Pope Pius XII approved the decree and made the excommunication a matter of law.

The Slaves of Mary

Those who remained loyal to St. Benedict Center formed their own order of religious brothers and sisters, The Slaves of the Immaculate Heart of Mary, under the leadership of Fr. Feeney as its spiritual director and Catherine Clarke as superior of the whole group of men and women. Husbands were separated from wives, and their children were raised apart from their parents by sisters appointed by Feeney and Clarke. For years the community gathered each Sunday on Boston Common, where Feeney preached to anyone who would listen that all must become Catholics to be saved. His verbal attacks against Jews and Protestants for what he felt was their refusal to convert to the Catholic faith grew more bitter. In these sessions he also continued to attack Archbishop Cushing and other local Church authorities for their "heresy." Confrontations with the crowds who came to the Common to hear him and jeer were sometimes violent and police were assigned regularly to keep order. It was during this period that he became known as a hater of Jews and, indeed, much of his bitter rhetoric was openly anti-Semitic.

Ironically, one of the few who later privately defended Fr. Feeney from the charge that he was a racist anti-Semite was one of Boston's leading Jews, Abram Sachar, founder and long-time president of Brandeis University, an institution often the target of Feeney's sharp criticism. Sachar said, near the end of his life, that though he had never met Feeney, he was convinced that the priest's widely publicized protest of a Catholic chapel being built on the Brandeis campus was rooted in a "doctrinal problem" and not

an expression of anti-Semitism. Still, even a number of Fr. Feeney's closest followers who stayed with the priest to the end were embarrassed about that period of intemperate rhetoric that was so hurtful to Jews and Catholics alike.

In 1957 St. Benedict Center moved from the Archdiocese of Boston into the Diocese of Worcester, to a sprawling farm in the quiet village of the town of Harvard, Massachusetts, called Still River. It was there that they now shunned publicity and settled down to monastic community life, continued to publish literature on their beliefs and dispatched members around the country selling their pamphlets and books, including Catherine Clarke's 1950 record of the "Boston Heresy Case," *The Loyolas and the Cabots,* a detailed account of what she interpreted as the unholy conspiracy of both Jesuits and Protestant Boston Brahmins in silencing Fr. Feeney and burying the Catholic doctrine of salvation.

Vatican II and Reconciliation

Vatican Council II confirmed what Pope Pius XII had taught in *Suprema Haec Sacra,* going further, in its Dogmatic Constitution on the Church, to say: "Those also can attain to everlasting salvation who through no fault of their own do not know the gospel of Christ or his Church, yet sincerely seek God and, moved by grace, strive by their deeds to do his will as it is known to them through the dictates of conscience" (LG 2:16). In his later years, through the efforts of Humberto Cardinal Medeiros of Boston, Bishop Bernard Flanagan of Worcester, and Cardinal John Wright, who had become the Vatican's Prefect of the Sacred Congregation for the Clergy, Fr. Feeney was reconciled with the Church he had so vehemently insisted was the only means of salvation. Because of his age and the onset of senility, only recitation of a creed as an act of faith was required.

On November 22, 1972, the excommunication was lifted quietly and without publicity in Cambridge, Massachusetts, where Fr. Feeney's troubles had begun a quarter century before. He died at the age of eighty on January 30, 1978, still believing his strict interpretation of the salvation doctrine, and was buried on the grounds of the institution he had founded. Most of his followers are also now reconciled with the Church. One of them, Rt. Rev. Gabriel Gibbs, is the first abbot of the newly established Benedictine Monastery of St. Benedict at the same place in Still River where the community had lived together as members of St. Benedict Center.

Pepper, George B. *The Boston Heresy Case in View of the Secularization of Religion.* Lewiston/Queenston: Edwin Mellen Press, 1988.

Potter, Gary. *After the Boston Heresy Case.* Monrovia, Calif.: Catholic Treasures Books, 1995.

Sennot, Thomas Mary. *They Fought the Good Fight.* Monrovia, Calif.: Catholic Treasures Books, 1987.

Silk, Mark. *Spiritual Politics: Religion and America Since World War II.* New York: Simon and Schuster, 1988.

Sullivan, Francis A., S.J. *Salvation Outside the Church?* New York: Paulist Press, 1992.

RICHARD J. SHMARUK

FELBER, MARY ANSELMA (1843–83)

Foundress. Mother M. Anselma Felber came to America determined to begin a monastic foundation devoted to adoration of Christ in the Blessed Sacrament. Sent to the U.S.A. from Switzerland with four other sisters to help the Conception Abbey monks teach the children of German immigrants, she felt that "adoration is our main task, the school is secondary."

Elizabeth Felber was born January 21, 1843, in Canton Lucerne, Switzerland. At the age of sixteen she entered the newly founded convent of Benedictine Sisters of Perpetual Adoration high in the Swiss Alps near the shrine of Our Lady of Rickenbach. When sent to America, Mother Anselma was thirty years old and had been assistant to the prioress of Rickenbach.

Through all the difficulties of language barriers, new customs, hard work, and long hours, Mother Anselma and her little group persevered. By May 1882 they were in their new monastery at Clyde, Missouri. In the daily chronicle Mother Anselma prayed: "Make us always understand better and live the spirit of our Order, the spirit of perpetual adoration." In August 1883, after nine years in America, Mother Anselma died worn out by ill health and hard labor.

See also BENEDICTINES (O.S.B.).

MARY JANE ROMERO, O.S.B.

FELICIAN SISTERS

The Felician Sisters, officially known as the Congregation of Sisters of St. Felix of Cantalice (C.S.S.F.), (more informally as the Felician Sisters), Third Order Regular of Saint Francis, an international pontifical community that traces its American beginning to the late nineteenth century. Founded in Warsaw, Poland, in 1855 by Blessed Mary Angela Truszkowska, the community was only nineteen years old when five sisters arrived in rural Wisconsin in 1874 to establish the American foundation whose membership was to outnumber that of its European counterpart.

Felician Sisters in the U.S.A.

The Felician Congregation was the first of the religious communities founded in Poland that sent sisters to serve Polish immigrants whose entry to the United States was at its highest from the 1880s to the end of World War I.

Asked by the Rev. Joseph Dabrowski, missionary priest to the Polish immigrants, and future founder of SS. Cyril and Methodius Seminary, Detroit (later Orchard Lake), Michigan, to teach in his parish school in Polonia, Wisconsin, and to open a novitiate, the original band of five sisters was never supplemented by European reinforcements, but experienced a rapid growth that resulted in the formation of seven provinces throughout the United States. These include the first or founding province in Livonia, Michigan, which was originally established in Polonia, Wisconsin (1874); and provinces in Buffalo, New York (1900); Chicago, Illinois (1910); Lodi, New Jersey (1913); Coraopolis, Pennsylvania (1920); Enfield, Connecticut (1932), and Rio Rancho, New Mexico (1953). Later evangelization efforts of the American Felicians extended ministry boundaries to Mexico (1943–46; 1992); Puerto Rico (1941 46); France (1956–71); Germany (1956–77); Canada (1937–52); and Kenya (1989), and were directly responsible for the establishment of provinces in Curitiba, Brazil (1950), and Ontario, Canada (1953).

Ties with the Felician Congregation in Europe were never severed, and the American provinces maintained their status as juridical entities under a general administration that was headquartered in Poland until 1950 when a provisional generalate was set up in Ponca City, Oklahoma, followed by relocation of the congregation's generalate in Rome, Italy, in 1953. Six of the congregation's nine superior generals have been American Felicians elected to the community's highest executive office.

The Felician Apostolates

Originally invited to teach the children of Polish immigrants, the Felician Sisters soon after their arrival in Wisconsin began additional apostolates to serve the needs of the American Church. Among these were the housing and care of orphans and pastoral service to adults and to the Ojibwe, Winnebago, and Menomini native peoples of the region.

Education, however, remained the Felician Sisters' principal ministry as they continued to accept schools and to even print textbooks as needed. By 1900 the American foundation—which included 320 professed members, 40 novices, and 98 postulants—was conducting 41 parish elementary schools in 11 states from Wisconsin to Massachusetts. At that time also, the sisters were on the staff of a small hospital in Wisconsin and were running four homes for orphaned children, two homes for the elderly, and a home for Polish and Lithuanian immigrants in New York City. Nearly one hundred years later, on the threshold of the twenty-first century, the Felician Sisters recorded sixteen hundred professed members, five novices, and two postulants serving the American Church in twenty-one states reaching from Maine to California.

Earliest efforts to prepare and train teaching sisters led to the establishment of teacher training programs and normal schools as early as 1882 followed by the later incorporation of junior and senior colleges in six of the seven U.S. provinces. Of these, three continue as institutions of higher learning, educating men and women in the liberal arts and career-oriented programs: Madonna University, Livonia, Michigan; Felician College, Lodi, New Jersey; and Villa Marie College of Buffalo.

Involved in all the usual areas of education at parochial, diocesan, and community-sponsored institutions, the Felician Sisters also conduct special education programs for exceptional children and those with learning disabilities and direct academic programs, vocational training, and workshop employment for mentally disabled adults. They continue to sponsor learning centers, a school of music, and remedial programs.

With parish school closings and school consolidations of the 1970s, the Felician Sisters broadened the scope of their teaching apostolate to encompass full-time ministry in catechetical centers and religious education programs. In the aftermath of changing child welfare policies at the state level that ended the sisters' residential care of orphans during the 1960s, provinces developed and expanded child day care programs and undertook new residential type programs for the care of children with multiphysical disabilities and administered group homes for mentally challenged adults.

The Felician Sisters' earliest missionary efforts in service to the Polish immigrant population were paralleled by ministry to blacks and Native Americans and to later groups of Asian and Latin American immigrants. Following World War II, provinces worked with displaced Polish refugees in the United States, Mexico, Germany, and France.

In the decades between 1939 and 1962 six provinces administered a total of twenty hospitals in twelve states, Canada, and Puerto Rico, that included more than a dozen small community hospitals, of which nearly half closed before 1950. Three provinces continue sponsorship of four hospitals in Illinois, Maine, Michigan, and Wisconsin while sisters of three other provinces are on the staffs of hospitals in Florida, New Jersey, New Mexico, and Pennsylvania.

Additional areas of service in health care and related social ministry which the Felician Sisters have assumed include nursing homes, hospice and AIDS ministry, adult day care, senior residence complexes, and a senior clergy village. Still other apostolic services in which they are involved are pastoral ministry and Christian services in parishes; chaplaincies in schools, hospitals, and prisons; management of soup kitchens and food pantries; ministry to the homeless and disadvantaged; retreat work; youth ministry; spiritual direction and counseling; house of prayer ministry; and administrative and office responsibilities in diocesan and Vatican departments.

In each of their provincial house chapels, the Felician Sisters enjoy the privilege of daily exposition of the Blessed Sacrament, which gives tangible expression to the centrality of the Eucharist in their lives and underscores their vision as an apostolic congregation seeking to fulfill its mission in the Church through contemplation and action.

See also POLISH CATHOLICS IN AMERICA; WOMEN RELIGIOUS IN AMERICA.

Grabowski, Mary Bonaventure. *Felician Sisters: History of the Sisters of St. Felix of Cantalice.* Newark, N.J.: Johnston Letter Co., Inc., 1993.
Ziolkowski, Mary Janice. *The Felician Sisters of Livonia, Michigan: First Province in America.* Detroit: Harlo Press, 1984.

MARY JANICE ZIOLKOWSKI, C.S.S.F.

FENTON, JOSEPH (1906–69)

Priest, theologian. Joseph Clifford Fenton was born January 16, 1906, in Springfield, Massachusetts, the son of Michael Francis and Elizabeth (Clifford) Fenton. He received the A.B. degree in 1926 from Holy Cross College; the S.T.L. and J.C.B. degrees in 1930 from the University of Montreal; the S.T.D. degree from the Angelicum in Rome in 1931. Ordained a priest on June 14, 1930, he served as a curate at Immaculate Conception Church, Easthampton, Massachusetts, 1931–32, and at St. Joseph's Church, Leicester, Massachusetts, 1933–34. He taught philosophy at St. Ambrose College, Davenport, Iowa, 1934–35, and special dogmatic theology at St. Bernard's Seminary, Rochester, New York, 1936–38. From 1938 to 1963 he taught fundamental and dogmatic theology in the School of Sacred Theology at The Catholic University of America. He was editor of the *American Ecclesiastical Review* from 1944 to 1963.

He was named a papal chamberlain in 1951 and a domestic prelate in 1954, when he also received the papal medal *Pro Ecclesia et Pontifice.* An adviser to the Sacred Congregation for Seminaries and Universities from 1950 to 1967, he was appointed a member of the preparatory Theological Commission and then of the Doctrinal Commission of the Second Vatican Council. He left The Catholic University in December 1963 to become pastor of St. Patrick's Church, Chicopee Falls, Massachusetts, where he died July 7, 1969.

Fenton was the author of numerous articles, almost all of them published in the *AER,* and of six books: *The Theology of Prayer* (1939), *The Concept of Sacred Theology* (1941), *We Stand with Christ* (1943), *The Calling of a Diocesan Priest* (1944), *The Concept of the Diocesan Priesthood* (1951), *The Catholic Church and Salvation* (1958).

As a theologian, Fenton was trained and thought within the classic neoscholastic framework. Not an original scholar, he was a passionate advocate of traditional methods and positions and promoter of the papal magisterium, defending them with vigor and little nuance not only against outsiders but, especially in the years between the Second World War and the Second Vatican Council, against the slightest tinge of liberalism and the threat of a revival of Modernism in the Church. In temperament and style he was an intransigent who sympathized with the integrists of the anti-Modernist reaction and their successors. As editor of the *AER* he used the journal as a forum in which to defend Catholic suspicion of modernity, which he saw as only the latest moment in the ancient and perennial warfare between the kingdom of Satan and the kingdom of God. He took part in a number of controversies: on membership in the Church, salvation outside the Church, biblical scholarship, Church and state, and religious freedom. On the last two of these issues, he opposed and actively sought a Roman rejection of the views of John Courtney Murray; in 1954, when procedures against Murray were initiated in the Holy Office, Fenton wrote two reports quite critical of the Jesuit. Officially informed of the quiet measures taken against Murray later that year, he was frustrated by the refusal of Rome to make them known.

On Vatican II's preparatory Theological Commission Fenton worked on the subcommission that wrote the schema on the Church, but, despite his close association with Cardinal Ottaviani, his personality and intransigence soon marginalized him even within that group. Nor did he have much influence in the Commission on Faith and Morals during the council, when he was also hampered by a series of heart attacks. He was not happy with the direction taken by the council, whose texts adopted a quite different orientation and method and vindicated many of the positions Fenton had devoted himself to opposing.

See also AMERICAN ECCLESIASTICAL REVIEW; MURRAY, JOHN COURTNEY; THEOLOGY IN AMERICA.

JOSEPH A. KOMONCHAK

FENWICK, BENEDICT JOSEPH (1782–1846)

Educator, bishop. Benedict Joseph Fenwick was born on September 3, 1782, in St. Mary's County, Maryland, the son of George Fenwick II and Margaret Medley. A graduate of the Georgetown Academy, Benedict attended St. Mary's Seminary at Baltimore, and on June 11, 1808, was ordained as a Jesuit. After nine years in New York as vicar general and as rector of St. Peter's Church, in April 1817 Fenwick was named president of Georgetown College. The following year he was sent to Charleston, South Carolina, where he settled a trustee controversy with such dispatch that he was appointed vicar general to the two Carolinas and Georgia.

In 1825, after serving as a chaplain to various religious orders, Fenwick again served briefly as president of Georgetown College before being named to succeed Jean Cheverus

Benedict J. Fenwick

as bishop of Boston. Despite limited resources and only a handful of priests, Fenwick expanded the small cathedral in Boston, constructed numerous churches in all parts of New England, and ministered to the Penobscot and Passamaquoddy natives in Maine.

Concerned with the needs of the poor, he founded the Ladies Charitable Society for Clothing Poor Children, established the St. Vincent's Orphan Asylum, and constantly urged individual parishes to organize similar relief societies. To help immigrants move out of the city slums, he founded the short-lived utopian community of Benedicta in northern Maine.

Because of the growing numbers of Irish Catholics in Boston, Bishop Fenwick found it necessary to protect his people against those who attacked their homes, and who burned the Ursuline convent to the ground. In September 1829, in order to defend the faith, he founded *The Jesuit, or Catholic Sentinel,* a weekly newspaper he later renamed the *Pilot.* In August 1842 he convened the first clergy retreat, and later convened the first diocesan synod in order to help clarify priestly duties and sacramental procedures.

An educator himself, Fenwick attempted to establish Catholic "pay schools" for the boys and girls of the diocese. His great dream of establishing a Jesuit college in Massachusetts was realized in November 1843 with the opening of the College of the Holy Cross in Worcester. Although he detached Rhode Island and Connecticut as separate dioceses, he was still responsible for his own diocese that included Massachusetts, Maine, New Hampshire, and Vermont.

Burdened with increasing responsibilities and failing health, Fenwick chose young Fr. John B. Fitzpatrick as his coadjutor. On August 11, 1846, Benedict Joseph Fenwick, the second bishop of Boston, died at the age of sixty-three and was buried on the grounds of Holy Cross College.

See also MASSACHUSETTS, CATHOLIC CHURCH IN.

Angela, Mary, S.M. *Sown in Granite: Glimpses of Events and People Associated with the Life of Benedict Joseph Fenwick, S.J.* Worcester, Mass., 1963.

Lord, Robert H., John E. Sexton, and Edward Harrington. *History of the Archdiocese of Boston.* 3 vols. Boston, 1945; II:3–385.

THOMAS H. O'CONNOR

FENWICK, EDWARD (1768-1832)

First bishop of Cincinnati. Edward Dominic Fenwick was born on August 19, 1768, in St. Mary's County, Maryland. He received his early education on Fenwick Manor before entering Holy Cross College in Bornheim, Belgium, in 1784. The English Dominicans who conducted the college so impressed young Fenwick that he himself joined the order in 1788 and made his profession as a Dominican two years later. After theological studies he was ordained on February 23, 1793. For slightly more than ten years he taught and held various administrative positions both at Holy Cross College and later at the college at Carshalton, near London, where the English Dominicans had taken refuge from the French Revolutionary forces.

In 1804 Fenwick received permission to found a Dominican house in his native country and returned to the United States in November of that year. Bishop John Carroll directed him to Kentucky as a possible location for the new foundation. Upon investigation and after sending a favorable report to both Bishop Carroll and to his Dominican superior in Rome, Fenwick was appointed the superior of the new province in the United States on June 22, 1805. Purchasing five hundred acres of land near Springfield, Kentucky, he launched a building program which, when completed in 1812, included a priory, a college, and a church known as St. Rose's. In October 1807 at his own request, he was released from his position as Dominican superior and began missionary work in Kentucky. He later expanded his work to include Ohio where after 1816 he concentrated his efforts. Because of his work in Ohio he is called the "Apostle of Ohio." When the Diocese of Cincinnati was established on June 19, 1821, it was only natural that Fenwick should be named the first bishop. The territory of the diocese was contiguous with the civil boundaries of Ohio, with Michigan and the eastern part of the old Northwest Territory being temporarily attached to the new diocese for administration. There were approximately six thousand Catholics in Ohio.

First Bishop of Cincinnati

After episcopal consecration at St. Rose's Church on January 13, 1822, by Bishop Benedict Flaget of Bardstown, Fenwick arrived in Cincinnati in March 1822. Because the only church in the area was located on the outskirts of the city and was inaccessible in the spring due to muddy roads, Fenwick purchased a lot on Sycamore Street between Sixth and Seventh Streets and had the church moved to this location. This would serve as his first cathedral. In May 1823 he journeyed to Europe partly to recruit priests and religious and raise money, but also to resolve a dispute which had arisen between himself and Bishop Flaget over the use of Dominican personnel in Ohio. This trip proved to be successful in every respect. He received substantial contributions from Pope Leo XII, the Lyons Association of the Propagation of the Faith, and from collections taken up in Belgium, England, and Holland. He recruited four priests and one Sister of Mercy for work in the new diocese. He was also successful in his negotiations over the use of Dominican personnel with a second Dominican province being established in Ohio. When this arrangement was later annulled, the Dominicans were united under Fenwick as superior, a step which allowed the bishop to use Dominicans in Ohio.

The years after Fenwick's return from Europe in March 1825 were busy ones. A new cathedral was built on the site of the old one and dedicated to St. Peter on December 17, 1826. While his first attempt to open a seminary in 1825 failed, Fenwick persevered and in 1829 opened St. Francis Xavier Seminary in the same frame building which had served as his first cathedral. A new seminary building was completed in 1831. In order to combat anti-Catholic

Edward Fenwick

propaganda, a newspaper, the *Catholic Telegraph,* was founded in 1831. Ever mindful of the need to bring priests and religious into the diocese, the bishop recruited the Sisters of Charity of Emmitsburg and the Dominican sisters from Kentucky. By 1831 the diocese had grown to the point that there were twenty-two churches and twenty-four priests active.

Plagued with poor health during his later years, Fenwick continued to make annual visitations of his diocese. It was in the course of such a visitation to northern Ohio and Michigan that he contracted cholera, dying at Wooster, Ohio, on September 26, 1832. Originally buried there, his remains were later transferred to Cincinnati with final burial at St. Joseph Cemetery in Cincinnati.

See also DOMINICANS (O.P.); KENTUCKY, CATHOLIC CHURCH IN; OHIO, CATHOLIC CHURCH IN.

Hynes, Michael J. *History of the Diocese of Cleveland, 1947-1952.* Cleveland, 1953.

Jurgens, W. A. *A History of the Diocese of Cleveland, Vol. I: The Prehistory of the Diocese to its Establishment in 1947.* Cleveland, 1980.

Lamott. *History of the Archdiocese of Cincinnati, 1821-1921.* New York, 1921.

O'Daniel, V. F., O.P. *The Right Rev. Edward Dominic Fenwick, O.P.* 2nd ed. Washington, 1921.

THOMAS W. TIFFT

FERMI, ENRICO (1901–54)

Nuclear physicist. Fermi was born in Rome, Italy, on September 29, 1901. He was the youngest of three children born to Albert and Ida de Gattis Fermi. Having decided at an early age to become a physicist, he earned a doctorate from the University of Pisa at the age of twenty-one, writing a thesis on research that he had done with X-rays. Following appointments at the University of Florence and the University of Rome (where he developed a statistical model of the atom), he began research in nuclear chemistry in 1933.

When Fermi traveled to Sweden in 1938 to receive the Nobel Prize for physics, he and his family emigrated to the United States. They had secretly planned such a move because scientific research had become too confining under the Italian Fascist government. Upon his arrival in the United States, Fermi was appointed professor of physics at Columbia University, where he began research on nuclear fission.

In 1942 he transferred to the University of Chicago and led the team of scientists who built the first atomic pile. He then joined the team of scientists who worked on the Manhattan Project at Los Alamos, New Mexico, ultimately producing the first controlled, self-sustaining nuclear chain reaction—forerunner of the modern nuclear reactor, which produced a controlled flow of energy from a source other than the sun.

The Fermis became American citizens in 1944. In 1946 he was named Distinguished-Service Professor for Nuclear Studies at the University of Chicago and received the Congressional Medal of Merit. At the University of Chicago, he continued his studies on nuclear particles and served as a consultant in construction of the synchrocyclotron, a large particle accelerator.

His experimental work led to the first successful demonstration of atomic fission, the basic principle of both nuclear power and the atomic bomb. He was elected a foreign member of the Royal Society of London in 1950, was honored by the president of the United States in 1954 with the Award of Merit, had element number 100 named for him, and an award—the Enrico Fermi Award—established in his honor, which he was the first to receive. Fermi died in Chicago, Illinois, on November 28, 1954.

Fermi, Laura. *Atoms in the Family.* 1954; repr. 1987.
Latil, Pierre de. *Enrico Fermi: The Man and His Theories.* 1966.
Segrè, Emilio. *Enrico Fermi: Physicist.* 1970.

MARIANNA McLOUGHLIN

FERREE, WILLIAM J. (1905–85)

Marianist priest and educator. William J. Ferree was born in Dayton, Ohio, on November 15, 1905, joined the Society of Mary (Marianists) in Dayton, Ohio, and completed studies for the priesthood at the University of Fribourg, Switzerland, where he was ordained in 1937. In 1942 he received a Ph.D. from The Catholic University of America. The subject of his dissertation was the act of social justice. Recognized as a significant contribution on the topic, it also was a focus of his life's activities. While in Switzerland he became associated with *Pax Romana,* and for many years served as its international chaplain. It was also this association that led him to found the U.S. Office of the Catholic Bureau of Inter-American Collaboration, acting as its secretary until it became affiliated with the National Catholic Welfare Conference

From 1953 to 1956 he was rector of The Catholic University of Puerto Rico, which was entrusted to the Marianists. Allied to his association with Pax Romana was his interest in and work with the Catholic Action movement among university students in the United States. John XXIII designated him as a consultor of the Pontifical Commission on the Apostolate of the Laity in preparation for the Second Vatican Council. His work in Catholic Action complemented his concerted effort to promote sodalities as a central Marianist apostolate. He saw commitment to this work as an essential mark of faithfulness to the founding vision of the Society of Mary because it was from the Sodality of Bordeaux, an organization of apostolic Christians begun by William Joseph Chaminade in the beginning of the nineteenth century in France, that the Marianists had emerged. From the time of his seminary training, Ferree was devoted to recapturing that original spirit and communicating it to his fellow religious.

To that end he developed a synthesis of Chaminade's thought that continues today to serve as a fundamental work in the religious formation of Marianists. He established an archives for his home province, with the intent that it would become a Marianist research center and he edited various Marianist publications. He was elected a member of the Council of the General Administration (1956–66), named president of Chaminade College, Honolulu (1967–68), and then appointed provincial of the province of Cincinnati (1968–73). He died in Dayton, Ohio, on August 30, 1985.

See also MARIANISTS (S.M.).

Brisbane, Colin Stuart, and William J. Ferree, S.M. *An Introduction to Economic and Social Development.* Rome, 1966.

Ferree, William J., S.M. *The Act of Social Justice.* Washington, D.C.: The Catholic University of America Press, 1942.

_____. *Administration and Social Justice.* 2nd ed. Fribourg: Regina Mundi, 1962.

_____. *Introduction to Catholic Action.* Rev. ed. Washington, D.C.: The Youth Department, National Catholic Welfare Conference, 1940.

_____. *Introduction to Social Justice.* New York: Paulist Press, 1948.

JOSEPH H. LACKNER, S.M.

FICHTER, JOSEPH H. (1908–94)

Jesuit sociologist. Joseph Fichter was born on June 10, 1908, in Union City, New Jersey. He was a high-school dropout and a construction worker when at the age of twenty he conceived the desire to be a priest. He entered the Jesuits at Grand Coteau, Louisiana, in 1930. After his ordination in 1942 he studied sociology at Harvard University. His first research project was a sociological survey of a New Orleans parish, but, due to objections of the clergy of the diocese and his Jesuit superiors, only the first volume, *Southern Parish* (1951), of a projected four-volume study appeared. He went on to write forty scholarly volumes not counting his textbook which was popular in four languages. From 1965 to 1970 he held the Chauncey Stillman Chair of Catholic Studies at Harvard University. He also lectured at major universities all over the world, including many in the United States. His home base was Loyola University of New Orleans and it was in New Orleans that he died on February 23, 1994.

See also CIVIL RIGHTS MOVEMENT AND CATHOLICS, THE; JESUITS IN AMERICA, THE.

THOMAS A. CLANCY, S.J.

FIRST CATHOLIC SLOVAK LADIES ASSOCIATION

The First Catholic Slovak Ladies Union was established on January 1, 1892, in Cleveland, Ohio. Mrs. Anna Hurban, a Slovak immigrant, recognized that the death or disability of wife or mother could be just as devastating to a family as the loss of a wage earner. With the support of her pastor, Rev. Stephen Furdek, Hurban and eight other women went door to door recruiting women for this new fraternal insurance society. The society not only provided fraternal life insurance, but its purposes were to assist and comfort the widowed and orphaned; to encourage members to remain true to their Catholic faith and to maintain their ties to Slovakia by preserving the Slovak language and culture.

In 1899, when the society incorporated as a fraternal benefit society, it had grown to 1,859 members in eighty-three branches in seventeen states. The monthly dues of ten cents which provided two hundred dollars in benefits made membership attractive.

The First Catholic Slovak Ladies Union realized that children needed insurance and by 1905 it became the first fraternal to extend coverage to young girls. The Junior Order of the First Catholic Slovak Ladies Union came into being and sponsored scholarships, drill teams, and socials to recruit members. This effort was so successful that in 1921 coverage was extended to young boys.

Claims resulting from the influenza epidemic of 1918 nearly destroyed the financial solvency of the association. The fraternal made the difficult decision to realign their rates to insure financial solvency. This decision sustained them during the depression. During the Second World War the fraternal was able to contribute to the cost of chaplain supplies and three fighter planes (with other Slovak societies), and it mounted successful war bond drives among its membership.

At its fiftieth anniversary in 1942, the fraternal had 65,000 members and twelve million dollars in assets. By 1950 the assets had nearly doubled. In 1955 a scholarship fund was established for college and high-school students. The First Catholic Slovak Ladies Union began planning its long-cherished goal of a home for elderly members which was financed by a popular cookbook of Slovak and American recipes. Property was purchased in Beachwood, Ohio, and the $1.3 million Villa Sancta Anna Home was dedicated in 1960. Originally planned as a home for the elderly, it evolved into a fully equipped nursing home.

Like the First Catholic Slovak Union, the First Catholic Slovak Ladies Union supported the SS. Cyril and Methodius Institute in Rome.

Since 1945 five other fraternals have merged with the First Catholic Slovak Ladies Union. In 1967 the fraternal changed its name to First Catholic Slovak Ladies Association. It currently has 87,000 members in 600 local groups located in nine regions. Since 1914 it has been publishing *Zenska Jednota,* formerly a newspaper, now a magazine entitled *Fraternally Yours, Zenska Jednota.*

See also SLOVAK CATHOLICS IN AMERICA.

Barton, Josef J. *Peasants and Strangers: Italians, Rumanians, and Slovaks in an American City.* Cambridge, 1975.
First Catholic Slovak Ladies Association. *Reflections of the Past: Centennial Anniversary of Fraternal Progress.* Middletown, 1992.
Fischer, Carolyn A., and Carol A. Schwartz, eds. *Encyclopedia of Associations.* Volume 2. Gale Research, Inc., 1995.
Pap, Michael S. *Ethnic Communities of Cleveland.* University Heights, 1973.

CHRISTINE L. KROSEL

FIRST CATHOLIC SLOVAK UNION

The First Catholic Slovak Union, born of a merger of several Slovak fraternal societies, was first organized in Cleveland, Ohio, in 1890, mainly through the vision and dedication of a Slovak priest, Rev. Stephen Furdek.

Like his countrymen, Furdek was from the impoverished rural lands of eastern Slovakia. He realized that only communal effort could preserve the faith and culture of the Slovak immigrants and help these rural people find their way in industrial America. These immigrants and their families were particularly vulnerable to destitution if the wage earner died or became disabled. Dying without funds for a proper burial was a particular disgrace.

Fraternal insurance societies had already found acceptance in America. Furdek realized that such a society could provide both protection for families and provide a means of unifying the Slovak community and involving it in the work of the Church. By the early 1890s there were approximately 277 Slovak societies in America.

Furdek established the St. Joseph Society in Cleveland in 1889 and a few months later called for a convention of societies. Eight societies responded and ten delegates met in Cleveland in September of 1890. These eight societies from Ohio, Pennsylvania, Minnesota, and Illinois merged to form the First Catholic Slovak Union *(Prva Katolicka Slovenska Jednota).* The purpose of this new society, to promote the spiritual and temporal welfare of its members, was summed up in its motto "For God and Nation."

Furdek encouraged lay leadership, but he still provided the inspiration. In 1891 he became the publisher of the fraternal's newspaper, *Jednota (Union),* which provided religious, social, and economic instruction and information. Determined to keep the First Catholic Slovak Union financially stable, Furdek convinced the leadership to set up a reserve system so that they would be in compliance with the state insurance laws. Furdek envisioned a complex educational and charitable system maintained by the

First Catholic Slovak Union. Acreage was purchased in 1909 north of Middletown, Pennsylvania. The land became the site of a printing complex, an orphanage in 1914, and a motherhouse for the Slovak Sisters of SS. Cyril and Methodius who cared for the children.

Besides these works, the First Catholic Slovak Union offered generous support in the founding of three hundred Slovak churches in America and Canada, one hundred fifty parochial schools, and assistance to religious communities serving the Slovaks. It provided scholarships for the children of members. In 1965, the year of its seventy-fifth anniversary, the First Catholic Slovak Union donated the acclaimed Jednota Chapel of Our Mother of Sorrows in the National Shrine of the Immaculate Conception in Washington, D.C. In the same year the First Catholic Slovak Union contributed $100,000 to the SS. Cyril and Methodius Institute in Rome, a Slovak Catholic seminary dedicated to providing priests for Slovakia once the Communists were ousted.

The society now numbers 80,000 members in eighteen state groups and sixty local chapters. Besides its fraternal and charitable works, the society operates the Slovak Museum and Archives, which is the largest private collection of Slovak material in the world. Its newspaper is circulated in thirty-one countries.

See also SLOVAK CATHOLICS IN AMERICA.

Barton, Josef J. *Peasants and Strangers: Italians, Rumanians, and Slovaks in an American City, 1890–1950.* Cambridge, 1975.
Fischer, Carolyn A., and Carol A. Schwartz, eds. *Encyclopedia of Associations.* Volume 2. Gale Research, Inc. 1995.
"Ninety-Fifth Anniversary of the First Catholic Slovak Union." *Jednota.* September 4, 1985.
Pap, Michael S. *Ethnic Communities of Cleveland.* University Heights, 1973.

CHRISTINE L. KROSEL

FITZGERALD, EDWARD (1833–1907)

Second bishop of Little Rock. Edward Mary Fitzgerald was born in the city of Limerick on the west coast of Ireland. His baptismal certificate, dated October 26, 1833, does not reveal his exact birth date, but an early account of his life claims October 13, then the feast day of St. Edward the Confessor. While his father was Irish, his mother was of German descent. He migrated to the United States with his family in 1849. The following year he entered St. Mary of the Barrens Seminary in Perryville, Missouri; two years later he enrolled at St. Mary's Seminary in Cincinnati, Ohio. On August 22, 1857, Archbishop John Purcell of Cincinnati ordained the twenty-three-year-old cleric.

Fr. Fitzgerald's first assignment was St. Patrick's Church in Columbus, Ohio. The young priest brought unity to this

Edward Fitzgerald

divided parish and so Archbishop Purcell allowed him to stay there for nine years. Fitzgerald became an American citizen on October 11, 1859.

On June 22, 1866, Fitzgerald received a note from Pope Pius IX informing him that he was to be the bishop of Little Rock. The young priest rejected the appointment. He soon reconsidered this decision while attending the Second Plenary Council in Baltimore in October 1866. His reconsideration must not have reached Rome for he received from the Pope in early December a *mandamus,* an order to accept the Arkansas diocese under holy obedience. On February 3, 1867, at his parish church, Archbishop Purcell consecrated him Arkansas's second Catholic prelate. At thirty-three, he was now America's youngest bishop.

Bishop of Little Rock

Fitzgerald arrived in Little Rock on St. Patrick's Day, where he quickly discovered what five years without a bishop and a Civil War could do to a diocese. (The Diocese of Little Rock had been without a bishop since the death of Andrew Byrne on June 10, 1862.) Financially the diocese was almost destitute, with only six priests to serve the whole state. In 1869 he was summoned to Rome to attend the First Vatican Council. Fitzgerald distinguished himself the following year by being one of only two Catholic prelates in the world to vote against the declaration of papal infallibility. His one negative vote was the first after 491 consecutive votes in favor of the declaration. When the tally ended, this large-framed Irishman knelt before the pontiff and submitted to the council's decision. In a public address later, the Arkansas bishop stated that while he always believed in the doctrine, he felt its declaration

would hamper Catholic evangelization efforts. Fitzgerald's vote did *not* damage his career. Pope Leo XIII, successor to Pius IX, considered him for the Archdioceses of Cincinnati and New Orleans, and three or four other dioceses as well. Compelled under a *mandamus* to go Arkansas, Fitzgerald stubbornly spurned all offers of promotion or transfer out of his adopted state.

Returning to Arkansas in 1870, Fitzgerald would enjoy an active episcopal career that spanned three decades, with the Diocese of Little Rock experiencing great institutional growth. In 1867 he had only a half-dozen priests; by 1900 there were twenty-one diocesan and twenty-two priests belonging to either the Order of St. Benedict (Benedictines) or the Congregation of the Holy Ghost (Holy Ghost Fathers). When he came in 1867, he had two seminarians; by 1900 he had twenty-five young men studying for the priesthood at Subiaco Abbey in Logan County. When he arrived there were only nine churches; at century's end there were fifty-one edifices with forty chapels and mission stations attached to parishes. Where once there had been roughly twenty sisters and one religious order in Arkansas, there were four religious orders of women and 150 sisters ministering in schools and hospitals thirty-three years later.

It was under his administration that four main Catholic medical facilities were established. Fitzgerald opened Arkansas's first Catholic hospital, St. Vincent's Infirmary, in Little Rock in 1888, staffed by the Sisters of Charity of Nazareth. It is still the oldest such institution in the state. By 1900 St. Vincent's would be joined by two other Catholic hospitals which are still operating: St. Joseph's in Hot Springs, conducted by the Sisters of Mercy, and St. Bernard's in Jonesboro, served by the Olivetian Benedictine Sisters. In 1905, in the twilight of his episcopacy, the Mercy Sisters in Fort Smith opened St. Edward's Hospital, named for his patron saint.

Bishop Fitzgerald attempted to attract Catholic foreign migration into the state, while also trying to convert blacks to Catholicism. These efforts yielded few results as the percentage of Catholics in the state by 1900 amounted to just less than one percent of the total population, an incremental increase from the time he became prelate. Fitzgerald established Arkansas's oldest black Catholic parish in Pine Bluff in 1895, and a year later he had six black Catholic schools opened, but only two were left a decade later.

Bishop Fitzgerald continued to play a major role within the American Church. He delivered the opening sermon for the Third Plenary Council in Baltimore in 1884, and dissented from the decision of his colleagues at this meeting to set up a Catholic school in each parish. This disagreement did not stop him from founding Catholic schools; thirty-two were in existence by 1900 with 1,837 students enrolled. Throughout much of 1893, Bishop Fitzgerald administered the newly created Diocese of Dallas until a new bishop was appointed. He also represented Archbishop Francis Janssens of New Orleans at a conference of archbishops held in Philadelphia in 1895.

On January 17, 1900, Bishop Fitzgerald's active years of ministry came to an abrupt end; he suffered a stroke in Jonesboro, and spent the rest of his life confined to St. Joseph's Hospital in Hot Springs. Vicar General Fr. Fintan Kraemer, O.S.B., ran the affairs of the diocese for the next six years until John Baptist Morris was named as coadjutor bishop. Fitzgerald celebrated his fortieth anniversary as bishop on February 3, 1907, but eighteen days later he died. His remains were brought to Little Rock where a funeral Mass was celebrated on February 27. He is buried under the present-day Cathedral of St. Andrew, the edifice he had constructed in 1881.

See also VATICAN COUNCIL I, AMERICAN PARTICIPATION IN.

Archives of the Diocese of Little Rock, St. John's Catholic Center, Little Rock, Arkansas.
Hennesey, James J., S.J. *The First Council of the Vatican: American Experience.* New York: Herder & Herder, 1963, 100–282.
Woods, James M. *Mission and Memory: A History of the Catholic Church in Arkansas.* Little Rock: August House Publishing Company, 1993, 85–162; 185–88.

JAMES M. WOODS

FITZGIBBON, MARY IRENE (1823–96)

Sister of Charity. Mary Irene was born in London, England, on May 11, 1823. Her Irish parents had emigrated first to England, then to the United States, settling in Brooklyn in 1831. Stricken during the summer cholera plague of 1849, mentally alert but reduced to immobility, she had a vision of children calling to her; and she vowed, if spared, to give her life to the service of God.

Fully recovered, she entered the newly organized New York Sisters of Charity in 1850. For almost twenty years she worked at St. Peter's School, Barclay Street. The social chaos of post-Civil War years, evident in infanticide and child abandonment, challenged Sr. Irene to respond to the "calling children" of her dream. With civic and religious advice, congregational blessing and a gift of five dollars from the sisters, she organized a social agency for foundlings in 1869 which became the New York Foundling Hospital. An abandoned girl left on the doorsteps the night she opened her haven led the way for thousands of children, forcing moves to larger quarters and appeals to private and public charities.

The New York Foundling Hospital acquired such a favorable reputation that physicians interested in public health and child betterment voluntarily guided the medical department, business men lent their financial expertise, and women organized a powerful auxiliary. Her third Foundling Asylum, an entire city block at 68th Street and Lexington Avenue, was the agency's home for eighty-eight years. In addition to organizing and overseeing all departments, Sr. Irene supervised the adoption of children. At least twice a year, special orphan trains carried groups of children to homes across the United States, the Foundling maintaining final supervision to the child's majority. For twenty-seven years she infused her work with Christian love and respect for human suffering: this legacy of hope still flourishes at the New York Foundling Hospital. She died in New York City on August 14, 1896.

Damroth, William J. "The New York Foundling Hospital and Its Foundress, Sister Mary Irene Fitzgibbon." M.A. thesis, St. Joseph's Seminary, Dunwoodie, 1993.
Jacoby, George P. *Catholic Child Care in Nineteenth-Century New York.* Washington, 1941.
Sisters of Charity. *The New York Foundling Hospital: Its Founders and Its Place in the Community.* New York, 1944, 176–190.
Walsh, Marie de Lourdes. *The Sisters of Charity of New York, 1809–1959.* 3 vols. New York, 1960.

ANNE COURTNEY, S.C.

FITZPATRICK, JOHN BERNARD (1812–66)

Bishop. John Bernard Fitzpatrick was born in Boston on November 15, 1812, one of five children. His father, Bernard, had emigrated from Ireland and operated a tailor shop; his mother, Eleanor, had been born in Boston, and her father, James Flinn, had fought in a Massachusetts regiment during the Revolutionary War. An honors graduate of the Boston Latin School, John was sent by Bishop Benedict Fenwick to the minor seminary of Saint-Sulpice in Montreal, and then to the order's major seminary in Paris. On

John B. Fitzpatrick

June 13, 1840, Fitzpatrick was ordained to the priesthood, and returned to Boston where only three years later he was appointed coadjutor bishop of Boston with the right of succession. When Bishop Fenwick died in 1846, the thirty-four-year-old Fitzpatrick became the third bishop of Boston, much to the approval of native Bostonians who regarded him as a man of learning and culture.

Fitzpatrick had hardly settled into his new post when the great potato famine sent thousands of impoverished Irish Catholic immigrants flooding into Boston. Throughout his twenty years as bishop of Boston, Fitzpatrick worked to contain the outbreaks of violence between hostile nativist groups and resentful Catholic immigrants. Even with the formation in 1854 of the anti-Catholic American Party—called the Know-Nothing Party—Fitzpatrick cautioned the members of his flock to obey the laws and to avoid violent confrontation as he resorted to the courts to guarantee the constitutional rights of Catholics as American citizens.

Despite limited funds, Fitzpatrick was eventually responsible for the construction of at least seventy new churches throughout the diocese. He also enlarged the facilities of St. Vincent's Orphan Asylum, and created the House of the Angel Guardian for homeless boys. He helped restore the College of the Holy Cross after a disastrous fire in 1852, and saw his own dream of a college in the city for the sons of immigrant families realized with the opening of Boston College in 1863.

In 1862, after the outbreak of the Civil War, in spite of deteriorating health, Fitzpatrick traveled to Belgium where he served in an unofficial capacity as a spokesman for the Union cause. Returning to Boston in August 1864, he had his friend, Fr. John J. Williams, appointed as his successor, and on February 13, 1866, Bishop John Fitzpatrick quietly passed away. He was buried in the small cemetery chapel Bishop Cheverus had built in South Boston. A decade later, his remains were moved to the new Cathedral of the Holy Cross in Boston's South End.

See also CIVIL WAR AND CATHOLICS, THE; MASSACHUSETTS, CATHOLIC CHURCH IN.

Grozier, Richard. "The Life and Times of John Bernard Fitzpatrick, Third Roman Catholic Bishop of Boston." Ph.D. dissertation, Boston College, 1966.
Lord, Robert H., John E. Sexton and Edward Harrington. *History of the Archdiocese of Boston*. Boston, 1945, II:389–776.
O'Connor, Thomas H. *Fitzpatrick's Boston, 1846–1866: John Bernard Fitzpatrick, Third Bishop of Boston*. Boston, 1984.

THOMAS H. O'CONNOR

FITZPATRICK, JOSEPH (1913–95)

Jesuit priest, sociologist, social reformer. Joseph Fitzpatrick was born in Bayonne, New Jersey, on February 22, 1913. He entered the Society of Jesus on August 14, 1930, at Wernersville, Pennsylvania, and was ordained a priest on June 24, 1943, at Woodstock, Maryland. He joined the Fordham faculty in 1949, after earning his doctorate in sociology at Harvard University, where his dissertation on labor-management practices on Wall Street reflected his earlier experience with the Xavier Institute of Industrial Relations in New York City. He retired from the Fordham faculty in 1983 when he was named professor emeritus of sociology, but he remained active, both in scholarly publication and in community organizations, until his death on March 15, 1995.

Fr. Fitzpatrick was known internationally for his work in migration studies, particularly Latin American immigration, with special attention to the experience of Puerto Rican immigrants in New York City. Recalling his own roots, Fitzpatrick drew parallels between the treatment of Irish immigrants to New York City in the mid-nineteenth century and the experience of immigrants from Puerto Rico to New York City a century later. His work *Puerto Rican Americans: The Meaning of Migration to the Mainland* (Prentice-Hall), provided the scholarly foundation for his continued advocacy for a more generous acceptance of the new immigrants by the old and for a national policy on immigration that would, in his words, support "the quintessentially American experience of allowing access to opportunity."

From 1961 until 1971 Fitzpatrick lectured each summer at the Center of Intercultural Formation in Cuernavaca, Mexico, founded by his good friend and close colleague, Ivan Illich. During this same period, he also lectured each summer at the Catholic University of Puerto Rico. In 1959 he founded at Fordham an independent Department of Sociology and Anthropology and served as its chairman from 1959 until 1964 and again from 1970 to 1972. Fr. Fitzpatrick's influence can be measured by the fact that at the International Migration Conference held at Fordham in 1991 all of the participants in the conference, with the exception of Fitzpatrick and two other Fordham colleagues, were scholars from other institutions who had studied under Fitzpatrick and earned their doctoral degrees at Fordham.

Fr. Fitzpatrick was also active in a variety of community organizations, serving on the board of the Puerto Rican Legal Defense and Education Fund from 1972 until his death and as president of the Puerto Rican Family Foundation. He took particular delight in being named Puerto Rican Man of the Year in 1978, the only Irishman to be so designated. His was one of the earliest and most eloquent voices to call the attention of the Catholic Church in the United States to the pastoral challenge of an expanding Hispanic Catholic population in this country. His belief that the Church must respond to the need for greater inculturation was the theme of his study, *One Church,*

Many Cultures: The Challenge of Diversity (Sheed and Ward). Fitzpatrick also published scores of articles in such publications as *Commonweal, America,* and *The Catholic Sociological Review.* He was the recipient of honorary degrees from several universities, including Loyola University of Chicago and the Catholic University of Puerto Rico. He died in New York City on March 15, 1995.

Fitzpatrick, Joseph P., S.J. "The Latin American Church in the United States." *Thought* 59 (23) (June 1984) 244–54.
____. *One Church, Many Cultures: The Challenge of Diversity.* Kansas City, Mo.: Sheed and Ward, 1987.
____. *Paul: Saint of the Inner City.* Mahwah, N.J.: Paulist Press, 1990.
____. *Puerto Rican Americans: The Meaning of Migration to the Mainland.* 2nd ed. Englewood Cliffs, N.J.: Prentice-Hall, 1987.
____. "The Puerto Ricans." *The Harvard Encyclopedia of American Ethnic Groups.* Cambridge, Mass.: Harvard University Press, 1980.

JOSEPH O'HARE, S.J.

FITZSIMONS, THOMAS (1741–1811)

Merchant and signer of the Federal Constitution. Thomas FitzSimons was born in Ireland, probably in County Wicklow. From records in St. Mary's Church in Pennsylvania, we know he was registered in that colony as early as 1760. His family, background, early life, and education are almost unknown.

Private Life

Soon after his arrival in America, FitzSimons married Catherine Meade, daughter of Richard Meade, a prosperous and successful brokerage and shipping owner who had made a fortune trading in the West Indies. Because of his interest in this enterprise, FitzSimons became a partner in his father-in-law's company. George Meade's son, Richard, an officer in the United States Navy, and his grandson, General George Gordon Meade, the famous hero of the battle of Gettysburg, brought prominence to the family name.

True to the Irish tradition, FitzSimons was interested in the affairs of his native land and in 1777 founded with other Irish immigrants, Catholic and Protestant, the Friendly Sons of St. Patrick in America. Pennsylvania at that time enjoyed a greater degree of religious toleration than any other colony, but it still insisted that suffrage be limited to property holders who subscribed to the 1720 test oath, which no believing Catholic could accept. Consequently, FitzSimons could not hold any civil office but, with the American Revolution, requirements prohibiting religious observance and holding of office by Catholics were abolished.

Public Life

Filled with an ardent zeal for patriotic reform, FitzSimons engaged in a number of public activities. He served on the Committees of Correspondence, the Pennsylvania Navy Board and, through his mercantile firm, contributed to the support of the Continental Army. He was commander of the Militia and, during this time, supervised the procuring of military equipment. His interests were varied. He was an overseer of the poor, was instrumental in preventing mobs from obtaining paper money in the face of worthless continental money, and served in various volunteer groups for the city. After the adoption of the Articles of Confederation, FitzSimons was elected representative from Philadelphia to the New Congress in 1782 and served for one year. His views on financial matters won the support of Alexander Hamilton. FitzSimons urged that a tariff be placed on imported goods and he labored earnestly but without success to induce the government to pay arrears after demobilization for the veterans of the Revolutionary War. After his retirement from Congress, he urged the people to remove the restrictions on religious and political qualifications in the Pennsylvania constitution. This revised constitution stayed in effect until 1838 when it was again modified. Convinced of the weakness of the Articles of Confederation, FitzSimons urged that a Constitutional convention be called either to revise or to draft a new constitution for the federal government.

In 1787 a Constitutional convention met in Philadelphia. FitzSimons and Daniel Carroll of Maryland were the only two Catholic delegates elected to serve, and later both signed the final document. Because of his financial expertise, FitzSimons was appointed to important committees of commerce concerned with trade and exports. He also urged that the new constitution be ratified by each state as "it would be an honor not only to this legislature but of the states also." FitzSimons was not elected to the ratification committee, but he did work independently to achieve its goal.

In 1788 FitzSimons was chosen a member of the first House of Representatives and again supported Hamilton's financial policies. However, he did not agree with Hamilton that a permanent national debt should be allowed. FitzSimons was opposed by Jefferson and Madison because of his support of the National Bank and his opposition to the Whiskey Rebellion. The inability of President John Adams to be a strong leader worried FitzSimons, and he feared that, if Adams controlled the government, it would result in "the destruction of our government." FitzSimons was known as a believer in a strong federal government, in limited suffrage to freeholders because of the growing fear of mob reactions, and of the necessity for the ratification of treaties by both the House and the Senate. He served in the House of Representatives from 1789–95.

FitzSimons actively involved himself as a founder and trustee of the First National Bank of America, president of the Insurance Company of North America from 1790–1811, and president of the Philadelphia Chamber of Commerce. He was a member of the board of the Pennsylvania Hospital, and served on the board of trustees of the University of Pennsylvania. He contributed financially to the Catholic churches in Philadelphia, Georgetown College, and to the historic synagogue, Mikvah Israel. He was likewise an ardent promoter of public education.

For a long period FitzSimons had a successful career in the mercantile business and often invested money in land speculation with Robert Morris. Unfortunately, he met with serious financial reversals and never regained his former financial security. Because he was a politician of integrity and a shrewd and competent business executive, FitzSimons earned the reputation of one who "died rich in the esteem, affection and gratitude of all classes of fellow citizens." Disappointment, failure, and sorrow dogged him to the end, and he died August 26, 1811, childless, nearly ruined financially, and alone, cared for only by his housekeeper. However, his work as a state and national leader gave him a special place in history recognized and cherished by his followers.

See also AMERICAN REVOLUTION AND CATHOLICS, THE.

Garvan, Anthony B. "Thomas FitzSimons." *New Catholic Encyclopedia* 5:953.

Martin, Asa Earl. "Thomas Fitzsimons." *Dictionary of American Biography* 6:444–55.

Purcell, Richard J. "Thomas Fitzsimons, Framer of the American Constitution." *Studies* 27 (June 1938) 273–90.

VIRGINA GEIGER, S.S.N.D.

FLAGET, BENEDICT JOSEPH (1763–1850)

Missionary and bishop. Flaget was born in the Auvergne region of France, and was ordained a priest of the Society of St. Sulpice in 1788. As a result of the anti-Catholic climate of revolutionary France, the young cleric emigrated to the United States as a missionary, arriving at Baltimore in 1792. After a brief period on the Indiana frontier at Vincennes, he returned to the East in 1795 to teach at Georgetown College in Washington. From 1798 to 1801 Flaget was part of a failed attempt to found a college in Havana, Cuba. He became subsequently a professor at St. Mary's Seminary in Baltimore.

In 1808 Pope Pius VII erected the Diocese of Bardstown, Kentucky, naming Flaget as its first bishop. After a two-year attempt at avoiding the post, Flaget was consecrated the first bishop of the West by Bishop John Carroll at St. Patrick's Church, Fells Point, Baltimore, in November 1810.

Flaget arrived at Bardstown in the summer of 1811 and quickly turned his energies to planning the West's first

Benedict J. Flaget

seminary (St. Thomas) and first cathedral (St. Joseph). He would also encourage his clerical and lay coworkers to establish an array of academies, colleges, parishes, and religious communities of women. In less than a generation, Flaget's frontier diocese would be exporting men and women to positions of Catholic leadership across the young nation.

Very much a missionary bishop, Flaget traveled on horseback throughout his vast diocese to preach, administer the sacraments, and adjudicate disputes, the latter at times involving issues of trusteeism. He would also be deeply involved in making recommendations for the creation of new frontier dioceses as well as of their first episcopal leaders.

In 1832 Flaget attempted to resign his post, citing age and infirmity. A storm of protest arose among the laity because the bishop had not consulted anyone on his action; and he had sought to have the unpopular French-born priest Guy Chabrat named as his successor. After adroit maneuvering in both Bardstown and Rome, Flaget resumed his episcopal responsibilities in 1833.

The aging prelate returned to Europe in 1836, reporting to Pope Gregory XVI on his twenty-five-year tenure. The number of Catholics in Kentucky had doubled; priests had increased sixfold; a wide range of institutions had been founded; new dioceses had been formed. The Pope sent the prelate on a preaching tour of France where several of his listeners claimed miraculous healing of ailments through his intercession.

Returned to Kentucky, Flaget supervised the transfer of the seat of the diocese from Bardstown to the rapidly growing city of Louisville in 1841. As his last public act, in 1849, the dying bishop blessed the placing of the cornerstone of Louisville's Cathedral of the Assumption, where he now lies buried.

Flaget was a man of great personal affability, who held special affection for his Protestant fellow-citizens. His piety, as revealed in letters and diary entries, was deep but often troubled. As early as 1811 he had written to Simon Bruté: "The details of administration dry up my heart. I try to inspire all who come to me with love of [God], but I speak coldly because I love only feebly." And in 1849 he wrote to Archbishop Samuel Eccleston of Baltimore: "My heart is in desolation and my head is absolutely empty."

Flaget was a man of complexity: a slave owner who made the pastoral care of blacks a special concern; a decisive administrative leader who suffered profoundly because of his own delicate feelings and sensibilities; a disciplined spiritual master who knew much of the soul's dark night. According to his letters, he drew strength from sacrament, Scripture, silences, nature, and deep friendships. The prelate is still deeply revered as the "saintly Flaget" in Kentucky where several institutions—and even a Boy Scout Trail—have borne his name.

See also KENTUCKY, CATHOLIC CHURCH IN.

Crews, Clyde F. "Benedict Joseph Flaget." *Patterns of Episcopal Leadership,* ed. Gerald P. Fogarty. New York, 1989.

Lemarié, Charles. *A Biography of Msgr. Benedict Joseph Flaget.* 3 vols. Bardstown, 1992.

Spalding, Martin John. *Sketches of the Life, Times and Character of Benedict Joseph Flaget.* Louisville, 1852.

CLYDE F. CREWS

FLANAGAN, EDWARD J. (1886–1948)

Founder of Father Flanagan's Boys' Home at Boys Town, Nebraska. Flanagan was born on July 13, 1886, in Leabeg, County Roscommon, Ireland. He attended elementary school in Drimatample, Ireland, and entered Summerhill College, Sligo, Ireland, in the fall of 1900. In 1904, Flanagan graduated from Summerhill with honors and sailed for the United States where he hoped to enter the seminary and begin his life as a priest. In 1906 Flanagan graduated with an undergraduate degree from Mt. St. Mary's College in Emmitsburg, Maryland. He then enrolled in St. Joseph's Seminary, Dunwoodie, New York, but was forced to leave within the year due to poor health which eventually led to a lifelong problem with respiratory difficulties.

Flanagan's parents, who had immigrated to the United States, were also living in New York. Together, they moved to Omaha, Nebraska, where Flanagan's older brother, Patrick, was a parish priest. Seeing promise in Flanagan, the bishop of Omaha sent him to study at Gregorian University in Rome in the fall of 1907. Illness again struck, and in 1908 Fr. Flanagan was forced to return to Omaha to recuperate.

Edward J. Flanagan

In 1909 the bishop of Omaha sent Flanagan to the mountain air in Innsbruck, Austria, where he enrolled in the Royal and Imperial Leopold Francis University. On July 26, 1912, Flanagan was ordained a priest in Innsbruck, Austria. Following a brief assignment at St. Patrick's Church in O'Neill, Nebraska, Flanagan was appointed assistant pastor to St. Patrick's parish in Omaha in March 1913.

In the summer of 1916, a catastrophic drought resulted in widespread unemployment among farm laborers. They filled the streets of Omaha. Responding to this crisis, Flanagan opened a Workingmen's Hotel in January of 1916. At the time he wrote: "I knew . . . that my life's work . . . lay in the rehabilitation of these men. And yet, my methods were so basically wrong. . . . In talking with the men, I learned that they had been orphaned at childhood. . . . Or they were members of large families where income was not sufficient to care for them. . . . I knew that my work was not with these shells of men, but with the embryo men—the homeless waifs who had nowhere to turn, no one to guide them." Flanagan formed a new approach: By helping boys at an early age, he could prevent them from becoming homeless men.

Boys Town

On December 12, 1917, Fr. Flanagan opened Father Flanagan's Boys' Home in a rented boarding house in Omaha. By April of 1918, the population of the Home reached the point where Flanagan was forced to rent a larger home located on 13th Street in Omaha. In 1921, two years after Flanagan became a citizen of the United States, the Boys' Home moved west of Omaha, to a 160-acre property called Overlook Farm.

Flanagan then began a remarkable personal effort to change the way the nation thought about its homeless children. In an effort to raise public consciousness about the plight of homeless children and to raise funds, he began a nationally syndicated radio program in the 1920s. He successfully encouraged numerous national press stories about his program and his boys. He briefly tried raising money by sending a group of Boys Town entertainers out on the road. In 1938 the Academy Award-winning motion picture, *Boys Town,* pushed Fr. Flanagan and the Home further into the national spotlight. Boys Town became a household name. Flanagan made best use of this by touring the United States discussing his views on child care and juvenile delinquency, fighting for the "boy nobody wants."

In 1941 Flanagan established a Foundation Fund which he hoped one day would grow large enough so that the proceeds from it would help pay for the annual costs of operating the Home. This was a realization of an idea which Flanagan first introduced in a published article in 1930. He realized how difficult it was every year to raise enough money to care for severely troubled or indigent children. Today, annual proceeds from the fund pay for approximately one-third of Boys Town's annual operating costs. In 1994 Boys Town's programs (including its National Hospital) provided care and treatment to more than 20,000 boys and girls.

In 1946 Flanagan was named to a national panel for the study of problem children and delinquency by U.S. Attorney General Tom Clark, and Boys Town became internationally known. He was appointed a member of the Naval Civilian Committee by Secretary of the Navy James Forestall, on April 7, 1947. During that year, he made a trip to Japan and Korea to study child welfare problems at the invitation of General Douglas MacArthur and the U.S. War Department. Flanagan presented his completed report to President Harry S. Truman in 1947.

Impressed by Flanagan's work, President Truman requested that he conduct a similar tour of Austria and Germany. Flanagan left for Europe in the spring of 1948. During this tour he fell ill and died in Berlin on May 15, 1948. Funeral services were held in the Dowd Memorial Catholic Chapel, located at the heart of his beloved Boys Town, which is also the site of his final resting place.

See also BOYS TOWN.

Oursler, Fulton, and Will Oursler. *Father Flanagan of Boys Town.* Garden City, N.Y.: Doubleday and Company, Inc., 1949.

VAL J. PETER

FLEMING, FRANCIS ANTONINUS (1749–93)

Missionary. He was born in Ireland around 1749, entered the Order of Preachers at Holy Cross College, Louvain,

in 1765, and completed his studies there. Later he was assigned to another Dominican house on the continent: the College of Corpo Santo in Lisbon, Portugal, whose students remembered him with "deepest veneration and warm affection." The Portuguese knew him as an eloquent preacher, who in 1789 was recommended by the queen for a bishopric in Ireland. At that point a call from America intervened.

In 1789, when George Washington and the Congress assumed national leadership, American Catholics had no resident bishop. In that year John Carroll, superior of the American missions, welcomed Francis Fleming to Philadelphia in response to a petition from St. Mary's parish. Carroll assigned him to minister there with two other priests: Lawrence Graessl of the suppressed Society of Jesus and Christopher Keating, O.P.

Soon Carroll was praising Fleming as "a Gentleman of amiable manners & temper, & a very excellent scholar" (Carroll to Charles Plowden, October 23, 1789. *Carroll Papers,* I). He became known among Catholics and Protestants for his eloquent preaching. Along with his pastoral ministry Fleming was preceptor to the young William Joseph Gaston, the first student of Georgetown College, who became later, as chief justice of North Carolina, a defender of slaves and other minorities.

In 1790 John Carroll was made the first Catholic bishop in the United States. He appointed Francis Fleming his vicar general for the vast northern district of his diocese, which embraced the scattered Catholics of Pennsylvania, Delaware, the Jerseys, New York, and all of New England. In 1791 Fleming vigorously and publicly defended Bishop Carroll against two false accusations: his presumed favoritism on behalf of former members of the Society of Jesus, and alleged discrimination against German Catholics.

As vicar general, Francis Fleming took part in the first synod of the new Diocese of Baltimore, convoked by Bishop Carroll in November 1791. Twenty-two priests participated. They reviewed the essentials of faith and worship and drew up legislation which became the cornerstone of Catholic practice in the United States. Francis Fleming contributed to the synod out of his American experience, along with his European theological studies and teaching.

In 1793 the deadly yellow fever was brought to Philadelphia with a shipload of ailing West Indian refugees. The disease speedily ravaged the city and hundreds fled, while the priests of St. Mary's remained with the dying. Fleming and his coworker Leonard Graessl were stricken, and both died at the beginning of October.

See also DOMINICANS (O.P.).

MARY NONA McGREAL, O.P.

FLORIDA, CATHOLIC CHURCH IN (1513–1865)

The Catholic faith made its first appearance in what is now the United States on the east coast of Florida. The Spanish layman Juan Ponce de Leon planted a stone cross inside Jupiter Inlet during his voyage of discovery in 1513, and priests, both secular and regular, accompanied the discoverer on a second expedition to San Carlos Bay in 1521. The latter party was driven off by natives and no church or mission resulted. Priests formed part of subsequent expeditions to the Florida peninsula and Panhandle: those led by Pánfilo de Narváez (1528), Hernando De Soto (1539–40), Cáncer de Barbastro, O.P. (1549), and Tristan de Luna (1559–62). No missionary successes were recorded on any of those ventures.

St. Augustine

The first permanent establishment of the Church in Florida occurred at St. Augustine, founded by Pedro Menéndez de Avilés on September 8, 1565. Four secular priests with Menéndez ministered to the Spanish settlers and began a mission to the Timucuan natives of the site. Their efforts led to the founding of the country's first parish *(San Agustín)*

First Mass at St. Augustine, Florida, September 8, 1565

and first mission *(Nombre de Dios).* Jesuit missionaries were recruited by Menéndez in 1566. One was killed by natives near the mouth of the St. Johns River. A second began a mission at Charlotte Harbor, and a third took up station near present-day Miami. Neither was successful and both missions were abandoned by 1570.

The first large-scale evangelization of the Florida nations and tribes began with the arrival of Franciscan friars in 1573. In the beginning their ministry was confined to villages near and north of St. Augustine, including the Guale chiefdoms on the coastal islands of Georgia. By 1595, 1,500 converts could be counted, though two years

later a number of Guale revolted against the friars' restrictions on polygamy and killed five of them.

The garrison and civil list at St. Augustine were served by secular priests, among whom, after 1597, was Ricardo Artur (Richard Arthur), the first Irish priest to serve in this country. He presided over a parish church and a hospital. The Franciscans operated a seminary in the city. For the entire first Spanish period (1565–1763), the Florida Church was under the jurisdiction of the bishop of Santiago de Cuba, whose see was situated at Havana. In 1606 that prelate, Juan de las Cabezas de Altamirano, made an episcopal visitation to St. Augustine and traveled the mission trail northward where he confirmed both Timucuan and Guale converts, the latter now at peace again with their friars.

Expansion of the Missions

In 1607 the Franciscans began to push westward into the forested interior of the peninsula, first to present-day Palatka and Gainesville, thence to the juncture of the Santa Fe and Suwannee Rivers, finally to the rolling farmlands around Tallahassee where they were to have their greatest successes in the seventeenth century. In 1612 the Franciscan missionary system in Florida and Cuba was raised to the dignity of a province under the title Santa Elena de la Florida. Forty-three additional friars arrived in Florida during the next three years. The period after 1632, the year of the first sizable Franciscan settlements in northwest Apalachee, as far as 1675 was a time of great numerical increase in the number of baptized natives. A census of 1655 counted 26,000 Christianized natives living in or around 38 *doctrinas,* as the mission compounds were called. There they were learning not only the catechism of Christianity but also European arts and crafts, including, in many instances, reading and writing. The mission program was not without its setbacks, including several armed rebellions against Spanish civil and military authorities, strained relations between the friars and government officials, severe poverty and hardships experienced by the friars in the field, and a constant worry among the missionaries that they were placing a mere Christian veneer over persistent aboriginal beliefs and practices.

The years 1574–75 may be said to have marked the zenith of the mission century. In those years visiting Bishop Gabriel Díaz Vara Calderón counted 30,000 converts in 36 missions. During a ten-month inspection of the mission chains north and west he confirmed 13,152 Spaniards and Native Americans and ordained seven young men from St. Augustine to the priesthood. In a lengthy report on his visitation he enumerated the *doctrinas* as well as the distances that lay between them, and wrote favorably about the converts he met: "As to their religion, they are not idolaters, and they embrace with devotion the mysteries of our holy Faith."

Decline of the Missions

During the last quarter of the century the number of Franciscans decreased and the fervor and charity of the missionaries appear to have decreased in something like the same proportion. By the 1690s soldiers in the field made frequent complaints about mistreatment of the natives by the friars. The missionaries were accused of conscripting native labor for their own service and of whipping parishioners for such offenses as being late for Mass. One thirty-seven-year veteran, Fray Blas Martínez de Robles, lamented that, except for the robes, the Franciscan Order had ceased to exist in Florida.

After the turn of the century, the Florida missions were destroyed by English governor James Moore of Carolina. In 1702 he laid siege unsuccessfully to St. Augustine, having raided the Guale mission islands on his way south. Two years later, he assaulted the missions in Apalachee, killing hundreds of Christian natives, taking about 1,000 as slaves to Carolina—it was the largest slave raid ever in the South—and sending 2,000 into exile. In additional forays into Florida during the following two years native allies of the English cleaned out the remaining mission villages in Timucua, killing some Christians and sending the rest in flight to St. Augustine. The mission era had come to an end, and the hinterland chapels would not be rebuilt.

Beginning in 1709 Florida claimed a resident bishop, an auxiliary of Santiago de Cuba. In 1746 the Crown, which in virtue of the *patronato real* governed in all substantive church matters, gave ecclesiastical jurisdiction over all Christians, including the former mission converts, to the pastor at St. Augustine. These two arrangements, with brief interruptions, lasted until 1763 when, in the Treaty of Paris, Florida was ceded to Great Britain, and the entire Catholic populations of St. Augustine and Pensacola (founded in 1698) departed for Cuba and Mexico carrying all their church furnishings and objects with them.

From Missions to Diocese

During the first five years of what would be a twenty-one-year British interregnum, Florida lacked both priests and communicants. In 1768 a Scottish physician founded an indigo plantation at New Smyrna, to which he brought 1,255 men and women, most of them Catholics, from Minorca, Italy, and Greece. A Minorcan priest, Pedro Camps, with one Augustinian assistant, was recruited to serve the colony, which experienced hardships and injustices throughout its brief nine-year existence. Finally, with permission of the British governor of East Florida, the colonists took refuge from their miseries in St. Augustine, where Camps reestablished a semblance of Catholic parish life. In Pensacola, the capital of West Florida, there was no such resuscitation until the retrocession of the Floridas to Spain in 1783.

In the treaty ending the American Revolution, Spain inherited two colonies, East Florida, which ranged as far west as the Chattahoochee River, and West Florida, which extended to the Mississippi. Over that vast jurisdiction and Louisiana a new Diocese of San Cristobal, with a see at Havana, governed from 1787 to 1795, utilizing vicariates in the two distant regions. Pensacola rarely had more than one priest in the period, but the eastern Florida parish at St. Augustine had as many as five Irish clergy for a brief period in the 1790s. One of them, Michael O'Reilly, dedicated a new stone church, which, in enlarged and renovated form, serves today as a basilica-cathedral. In 1795 the two Floridas passed to the jurisdiction of a newly erected Diocese of Louisiana.

Owing both to Spanish and French ecclesiastical squabbles over canonical authority and to disintegrating provincial governments in the Gulf region, East and West Florida languished without firm episcopal control. Even after 1821, when a single Florida, bordered on the west by the Perdido River, became a possession—later a territory—of the United States, questions remained about Florida's anomalous condition. The nearest U.S. bishop, John England, of Charleston, stepped into the breach and "looked after" Florida until 1825, when the territory and Alabama together were erected a vicariate apostolic under Bishop Michael Portier. Only two years later, Portier, unable to manage his vast jurisdiction, asked England again to look after Florida.

The absence of a strong episcopal hand in St. Augustine was one factor that led to excesses in governance of the parish by a lay Board of Wardens. Typical of lay trustee bodies elsewhere in the U.S.A., the St. Augustine board claimed authority in spiritual as well as material matters. In 1829 that arrogation resulted in the dismissal of the pastor, Edward Francis Mayne, for capricious reasons, and defiance of England's attempt to reinstate him. The matter was finally resolved by Portier's intervention. In 1829 Rome elevated Florida and Alabama to the dignity of a diocese, with a see at Mobile. At Pensacola, too, the wardens controlled the finances of the one Panhandle parish, St. Michael's, but because of the general impoverishment of the church their power was limited. In 1833 the parishioners erected their first permanent church building.

Florida was admitted to the Union as twenty-seventh state in 1845, and five years later, to the great relief of Portier, the state east of the Apalachicola River was transferred from Mobile to the newly erected Diocese of Savannah. In 1857 the same region became a vicariate apostolic, with a resident bishop, Augustin Verot, exercising powers roughly the same as those possessed by bishops in dioceses. The French-born Verot, who had worked as a Sulpician college teacher and pastor in Maryland since 1830, assumed his new duties on the eve of the Civil War. This became all the more inauspicious when, in 1861, he was named third bishop of Savannah while retaining the vicariate of Florida. On January 4, 1861, in St. Augustine, he delivered a sermon in support of slavery that was later distributed throughout the South as a Confederate tract. In the same sermon, however, he called attention to certain immoral practices within the institution and proposed a servile code for their correction. During the armed conflict, Verot, his priests, and sisters ministered to soldiers of both North and South, including the federal prisoners at Andersonville, Georgia. When the Confederate flag was lowered, finally, in 1865, Verot looked out on what he called "a heap of smoking ruins."

Gannon, Michael V. *The Cross in the Sand: The Early Catholic Church in Florida, 1513–1870.* Gainesville, 1965.

Geiger, Maynard, O.F.M. *The Franciscan Conquest of Florida, 1573–1618.* Washington, 1937.

MICHAEL GANNON

FLORIDA, CATHOLIC CHURCH IN (1865–1995)

Reconstruction on the Frontier, 1865–1920

After the Civil War, Florida's Catholics faced massive economic, social, and spiritual devastation. Five out of the state's nine churches were destroyed during the war. Undaunted, Bishop Augustin Verot, the vicar apostolic of Florida since 1858, channeled the proceeds of his begging tours in the North and Europe into a Spiritual Reconstruction. He sponsored parish missions given by Redemptorists and began the successful Southern Catholic experiment to educate newly freed slaves by recruiting eight Sisters of St. Joseph from Le Puy, France, who in 1867 opened a Catholic school for blacks in St. Augustine. By 1876 over 360 students were enrolled in seven such schools. In 1868 Verot invited the Sisters of the Holy Names of Jesus and Mary from Montreal to Key West to educate blacks and Cubans there. The sisters established an academy for whites in 1868, a school for Cuban girls in 1873, and a school for blacks in 1876; later, in 1882, they founded an academy in Tampa. By 1885 the Catholic population Key West consisted of 7,000 Cubans, 648 American whites, and 70 African Americans.

The Diocese of St. Augustine was created in 1870 with Verot as its first bishop, from territory east of the Apalachicola River (the area west of the river remained part of the Diocese of Mobile until 1968). In 1876 Verot died; Irish-born John Moore succeeded him. American William Kenny was bishop from 1902 to 1913, and Irish-born Michael Curley governed from 1914 to 1921.

In 1876 Florida was mostly a rural frontier, with Catholics numbering less than 3 percent of the population. Bishop Moore had twenty parishes and missions, seventy stations, eight diocesan and two religious priests. Moore's episco-

pacy took several directions: he began extensive recruitment of Irish-born priests; he ordained the first native diocesan priest (Edward A. Pace) in 1885; he changed the focus of the diocesan congregation, the Sisters of St. Joseph, from solely teaching blacks to establishing academies for whites and from being a French community to becoming an Irish and American one. Since Moore lacked priests, he invited the Benedictine Fathers of St. Vincent's Abbey to have the sole pastoral care of three West Coast counties in 1887. By 1889 they had established St. Leo Monastery and St. Leo College. He also asked the New Orleans Jesuits to undertake the exclusive pastoral care of the lower half of his diocese in 1888. They opened a boys' high school at Tampa in 1899. While the Benedictines worked with the German-speaking settlers in Pasco County, the Jesuits ministered to Tampa's Italians, Cubans, and Spaniards who labored in the cigar industry there. Both religious orders were needed to establish missions among new settlers. In 1919 twenty-one Jesuits served six parishes, twelve missions, and forty-six stations in South Florida.

During this frontier period, when "priestless Sundays" were commonplace, lay initiative and the domestic church were essential. Wealthy benefactors, such as Edward Bradley, Kate Jackson, and James McNichol, played a key role in building churches and schools, as did the Extension Society.

In the late 1880s and 1890s the railroad brought commerce and tourism to Florida's east and west coasts. The Spanish-American War (1898) started a trend of federal expenditures for Florida military bases, bringing new capital and new residents. In response to the national initiatives during World War I by the NCWC, Curley was first to centralize diocesan administration.

Boom and Bust, 1920–40

Bishop Curley successfully recruited priests from Ireland, so much so that by 1920 most Florida diocesan priests were Irish-born. In 1921 he completed renegotiations with the Jesuits so that diocesan priests could open badly needed parishes in South Florida. When Curley left Florida in 1921 to become the archbishop of Baltimore, Irish-born Patrick Barry succeeded him.

Barry, bishop from 1922 to 1940, continued Curley's polices of Irish recruitment. In 1923 Barry invited the Adrian Dominicans to teach in parochial schools. They opened Barry College in Miami in 1940. In 1927 the Allegany Franciscans opened St. Francis Hospital in Miami Beach, while in St. Petersburg in 1930 they began teaching parochial school and operating St. Anthony Hospital.

During the early 1920s, people from the Midwest and Northeast poured into South Florida. New parishes were founded, while older wood-frame churches were replaced by larger masonry ones. For the first time, church buildings were mortgaged, so that by 1928 the diocese had a debt of $1.6 million (over $30 million in 1990 dollars). Real estate speculators built paper fortunes, but between 1925 and 1929 the boom went bust.

The biggest problem for pastors and people during the depression was debt. Although personally inclined toward an informal leadership style, Bishop Barry collectivized and centralized his diocese through refinancing parish debts. Despite the depression, Catholic life expanded. Parish sodalities initiated annual diocesan meetings, more black parishes and schools were founded, more mission chapels were built with Extension Society help. From 1922 to 1940 the number of parishes doubled, the average size of parishes doubled (from 250 families to 500), while the number of diocesan priests increased by 160 percent. Catholics grew from being 5.3 percent to 8.4 percent of the state's population. Until 1940 pastors still had significant independence and considerable discretionary power, but that was soon to change.

The Postwar Consolidation, 1940–68

American-born Bishop Joseph Hurley directed the diocese from 1940 through 1967. A combination of a population explosion and Hurley's strong leadership brought about tremendous changes in Florida Catholicism. In 1940 Florida was the twenty-seventh largest state with a population of 1.9 million; by 1960 Florida was tenth in population with 4.9 million persons. By 1965 the state's Catholic population was 11.9 percent.

Hurley consolidated power around his office and person. Under him pastors had far less discretionary power than before. He taxed parishes excessively in order to fund real estate purchases and building construction needed for parochial and institutional expansion. Although he continued to attract priests from Ireland, Hurley put new emphasis on recruiting native Florida priests. From 1940 to 1967 he doubled the number of diocesan priests and the number of parishes, while the Catholic population tripled. In the early 1950s he created a diocesan hospital, diocesan high schools, and missions for Hispanic farm workers.

In 1958 the Diocese of Miami was created out of the lower one-third of the Diocese of St. Augustine. Miami's new bishop, Coleman Carroll, instituted a diocesan newspaper, two diocesan seminaries, and new parishes, while responding to the heavy influx of Cuban exiles, all in his first five years. By 1968 Carroll had erected forty-five new parishes, seventeen new parish schools, fifty-eight new churches, eleven new high schools, and introduced thirty-five new religious communities into the diocese.

Post-1968 Expansion

In 1968 Miami was made an archdiocese, with St. Augustine (under Hurley's successor Bishop Paul Tanner) and the new dioceses of Orlando (under Bishop William Borders) and St. Petersburg (under Bishop Charles McLaughlin) as suffragan sees. At the same time Pensacola and the Panhandle were added to the Diocese of St. Augustine. In 1975 the Diocese of Pensacola-Tallahassee was created with René Gracida as its first bishop. In 1977 Archbishop Carroll died and was succeeded by his coadjutor, Edward McCarthy. In 1984 two more dioceses were founded, Palm Beach and Venice, led by Bishops Thomas Daily and John Nevins, respectively.

This expansion to seven Florida dioceses reflected population and institutional growth. By 1990 Florida had a population of 13.2 million, making it the fourth largest state, with Catholics representing 13 percent of the population.

The post-1968 era brought new challenges to Florida Catholicism. The cultural upheavals of the 1960s, the continued influx of Hispanics (and to a lesser extent Vietnamese and Haitians), and the implementation of Vatican Council II compounded the pressures of rapid population growth. Some of the ongoing challenges to Florida Catholicism include: multiculturalism, increased bureaucratization on a diocesan and parochial level, the identity and role of Catholic education, ongoing parochial and personal renewal according to Vatican II, the secularization of society and the affluence of congregations, larger parishes (average parish size in South Florida in 1990 was two thousand families) and fewer priests per parishioner, and the continued integration of lay initiative and deliberation. With increasing bureaucratization and institutionalization, Florida Catholicism struggles to maintain its traditional adaptability, flexibility, and willingness to welcome the stranger.

As of 1995, Florida's Catholics numbered approximately 1,850,000, 14 percent of the state's population. The Archdiocese of Miami had the highest proportion of Catholics, with 21 percent, while the Diocese of Pensacola-Tallahassee had the lowest with 6 percent.

Gannon, Michael V. *Rebel Bishop: The Life and Era of Augustin Verot.* Milwaukee, Wisconsin, 1964.

Horgan, James J. *Pioneer College: The Centennial History of Saint Leo College, Saint Leo Abbey, and Holy Name Priory.* St. Leo College Press, 1989.

McNally, Michael J. *Catholic Parish Life on Florida's West Coast, 1860–1968.* St. Petersburg, Fl.: Catholic Media Ministries, 1996.

____. *Catholicism in South Florida, 1868–1968.* Gainesville: University Presses of Florida, 1984.

____. "Hurley, Joseph Patrick." *Dictionary of American Biography: Supplement Eight, 1966–70,* 294–96.

____. "A Peculiar Institution: A History of Catholic Parish Life in the Southeast, 1850–1980." *The American Catholic Parish from 1850 to the Present,* ed. Jay P. Dolan. New York: Paulist Press, 1987, 1:117–234.

Mormino, Gary R., and George E. Pozzetta. *The Immigrant World of Ybor City: Italians and Their Latin Neighbors in Tampa, 1885–1985.* Urbana: University of Illinois Press, 1987.

MICHAEL J. McNALLY

FLYNN, HELEN (1893–1979)

Educator. Helen Flynn, also known as Sr. St. Egbert, was born in Hartford, Connecticut, and studied with the Congrégation de Notre Dame in Waterbury, Connecticut. Upon completing her studies she entered the novitiate of the Congrégation de Notre Dame in Montreal. After several other assignments, she was missioned to Notre Dame Academy, Staten Island.

The congregation had come to Staten Island in 1901 at the request of Catholic laypeople who desired a quality education for their daughters. The need was a real one and, in spite of many financial struggles, Notre Dame Academy was flourishing when Sr. Helen joined the staff as Latin instructor and senior teacher.

This was a seminal period in the history of Catholic higher education. Fordham University, like so many of its sister institutions, had opened the doors of its School of Education and its Graduate School to women during World War I. The sisters at Notre Dame Academy, desirous of opening further opportunities to young women, were among the female pioneers at Fordham in the early twenties. Sr. Helen entered the graduate school as a doctoral candidate in philosophy. The sisters dreamed of opening a college for women on Staten Island, but situated it in the distant future. When Fordham established an extension center on Staten Island, Sr. Helen was asked to direct it at Notre Dame Academy. Two years later, Cardinal Patrick Hayes and his vicar general, Msgr. Michael J. Lavelle, insisted that the sisters open their college with the least possible delay.

Open it they did in 1931 in a borrowed classroom, with a student body of twelve and a faculty borrowed from Fordham University. By 1934, Sr. Helen, now its dean, had an eighteen-acre campus, a Georgian mansion, and a student body of one hundred—all of this on borrowed money, approximately $100,000. Staten Island's only college for women flourished under Sr. Helen's direction for thirty-four years until 1965 when she retired from her post as its first and founding president.

In 1970 Notre Dame College merged with St. John's University and is now a flourishing part of the area's largest Catholic university. The college had conferred over 2,000 degrees on laywomen and trained large numbers of religious of the congregation. For forty years Notre Dame College exerted an important influence on Staten Island, New York City, and neighboring New Jersey. Sr. Helen died in 1979.

MARY VIRGINIA COTTER, C.N.D.

FONTBONNE, DELPHINE (1813–56)

Sister of St. Joseph, American pioneer, and foundress of Sisters of St. Joseph of Toronto. Marie-Antoinette Fontbonne was born on December 24, 1813, at Bas-en-Basset, France, entered the Sisters of St. Joseph in Lyons in 1832, where her aunt, Mother Saint-Jean Fontbonne, was superior. In 1836 Sr. Delphine and five other volunteers were missioned to the Diocese of St. Louis; her sister Antoinette (Sr. Fébronie) was superior, and her brother Jacques, spiritual director. She became superior of the tiny and impoverished community at Carondelet, six miles south of St. Louis, where three sisters taught villagers, cared for orphans, were sacristans and formed the choir of the parish church. The pastor, Edmund Saulnier, criticized her government, apparently marked by rigidity, and she resigned office in 1839.

In 1850 Sr. Delphine went to Philadelphia as novice mistress. Urged by Bishop de Charbonnel of Toronto, she with three others made the first Canadian foundation of Sisters of St. Joseph at the orphan asylum on Nelson Street in Toronto on October 7, 1851. By 1852, a second foundation followed in Hamilton, Ontario. Sisters worked among a largely immigrant population, taking on schools, another orphanage, and nursing cholera victims in 1854. In 1855 Mother Delphine started the House of Providence for the poor, bombed in a nativist attack. When she died on February 7, 1856, victim of her service during the typhus epidemic in Toronto, she had laid foundations for seminal congregations of St. Joseph (Carondelet and Toronto), source for nearly all the Sisters of St. Joseph in the U.S.A. and Canada.

Young, Mary Bernita. *The Dawn of a New Day: A Sketch of the Life and Times of Sister Delphine Fontbonne 1813–1836.* Toronto, 1983.

——. *Dictionary of Canadian Biography* 8 (1851–60), s.v. "Fontbonne, Marie-Antoinette."

PATRICIA BYRNE, C.S.J.

FORD, FRANCIS XAVIER (1892–1952)

Maryknoll missionary, bishop, martyr. Francis Xavier Ford was born in Brooklyn, New York, on January 11, 1892, the son of Austin and Elizabeth Rellihan Ford. His father was the publisher of the *Irish World,* the New York *Freeman's Journal,* and the *Monitor.* His mother was a teacher and journalist. Young Ford attended St. Francis Preparatory School in Brooklyn and Cathedral College in Manhattan. In 1912, he was the first student to apply to the seminary of the recently established Catholic Foreign Mission Society of America (Maryknoll). Ordained in 1918, he was among the first four priests assigned to Yeungkong, China. In 1925, he was appointed superior of a newly created mission territory at Jiaying (Kaying) or Meixian (Meihsien) in northeastern Guangdong (Kwangtung) province. Ten years later, when this area became a vicariate apostolic, Ford was appointed bishop. As his episcopal motto, he chose the word *condolere,* meaning "to have compassion" (see Heb 5:2). Bishop Ford made the encyclical letter *Maximum Illud* (1919) the cornerstone of his efforts to establish an indigenous Chinese Church. His goal was a self-governing local Church, unburdened by Western institutions, and financially self-reliant. His plans envisioned not only well-trained local clergy and sisterhoods, but also well-educated laity able to give leadership and assume responsibility for building modern China. Ford was one of the first Roman Catholic bishops to emphasize participation of women religious in the task of direct evangelization. A small experiment begun with a few Maryknoll sisters in 1934 became an important contribution to enhancing the role of women in mission and in the Church.

Having served as a faithful shepherd of his people all through the years of civil strife, Civil War between the Nationalists and the Communists in China in the late 1940s, Ford was publicly humiliated and arrested by the Communists in December 1950. Four months later, he was pronounced guilty of alleged spying activities and incarcerated in the Canton provincial prison, where he died of exhaustion and illness in February 1952. F. X. Ford lived his motto of "compassion" for the Chinese people, to the ultimate sacrifice of his life.

See also MARYKNOLL.

Donovan, John F. *The Pagoda and the Cross, The Life of Bishop Ford of Maryknoll.* Maryknoll, 1967.

Lane, Raymond A. *Stone in the King's Highway, the Life and Writings of Bishop Francis Xavier Ford, M.M.* New York, 1953.

Sheridan, Robert E. *Compassion, the Spirit of Francis X. Ford, M.M.* Maryknoll, 1982.

Tsai, Mark. "Bishop Ford, Apostle of South China." *American Ecclesiastical Review* 127 (October 1952).

Wiest, Jean-Paul. "The Legacy of Bishop Francis X. Ford." *IBMR* 12 (1988) 130–35.

JEAN-PAUL WIEST

FORD, JEREMIAH (1873–1958)

University professor and scholar. Ford was born of Irish parents on July 2, 1873, in Cambridge, Massachusetts. In 1894, Ford entered Harvard after having received earlier academic training in Cork, Ireland. In 1897, he received a doctorate in Romance philology. Ford's pedagogical affiliation with Harvard began in 1895 and lasted until 1940. In 1909, he was appointed Smith professor of French and Spanish. He became chair of the Romance Languages and Literature Department from 1911 and served the university in that capacity until 1943.

During his tenure at Harvard, Ford became an internationally renowned scholar and expert on Spanish and Por-

tuguese literature. His expertise resulted in publications on Spanish language and literature including *Old Spanish Sibilants* (1900), *Old Spanish Reading* (1911), and *Main Currents of Spanish Literature* (1919). His published works also include several translations and bibliographies. He served as editor of *Speculum* from 1927–36. Ford's scholarship resulted in his election to many offices of scholarly societies including the presidency of the Dante Society (1922–40), the American Academy of Arts and Sciences (1932–33), and the American Catholic Historical Association (1935). Ford received many honors from academic institutions in the U.S. and Europe and was awarded the Laetare Medal in 1937. He retired from Harvard in 1943, was elected to the French Academy in 1945, and died on November 14, 1958.

LISELLE DRAKE

FORD, JOHN (1895–1973)

Motion-picture director. Ford was born Sean Aloysius O'Feeney on February 1, 1895, at Cape Elizabeth, Maine. He studied briefly at the University of Maine after an unsuccessful attempt to obtain an appointment to the U.S. Naval Academy. In 1914 he joined his brother, Francis, in Hollywood, working as a property man at Universal Studios and changed his name to Ford.

His diligence led to a position as assistant director and assignments on several short films and westerns. In 1919, the same year that he married Mary McBryde Smith, he signed a contract with Fox and, in 1924, directed his first successful film, *The Iron Horse,* the story of the first continental railroad.

The film introduced the genre of "big westerns," on which Ford earned his reputation and for which he won several Academy Awards for best director— *The Informer* (1935), *Stagecoach* (1939), *The Grapes of Wrath* (1940), *How Green Was My Valley* (1941), and *The Quiet Man* (1952).

His stint in the U.S. Navy was finally realized in 1941 when he headed a photographic unit for the navy and filmed the documentary *The Battle of Midway.* He left the navy with the rank of admiral in the Naval Reserve.

Ford received the American Film Institute's first Life Achievement Award in 1973, as well as the Presidential Medal of Freedom. Among the 130 films he directed were: *Young Mr. Lincoln* and *Drums Along the Mohawk* (1939), *They Were Expendable* (1945), *The Fugitive* (1947; based on Graham Greene's *The Power and the Glory*), *My Darling Clementine* (1946), *She Wore a Yellow Ribbon* (1949), *The Wagonmaster* and *Rio Grande* (1950), *The Searchers* (1956), *The Man Who Shot Liberty Valance, How the West Was Won* (1962), and *Cheyenne Autumn* (1964). He died in Palm Desert, California, on August 31, 1973.

Sinclair, Andrew. *John Ford*. New York, 1978.

MARIANNA McLOUGHLIN

FORDHAM UNIVERSITY

Comprised of four undergraduate schools (Fordham College at Rose Hill, Fordham College at Lincoln Center, The College of Business Administration, and Ignatius College) and six graduate and professional schools (The Graduate School of Arts and Sciences, The School of Law, The Graduate School of Social Service, The Graduate School of Business, The Graduate School of Religion and Religious Education, and The Graduate School of Education), Fordham offers programs on three campuses in Manhattan, the Bronx, and Tarrytown, New York. The oldest Catholic institution of higher learning in the Northeast, Fordham was founded in 1841 by John Hughes, the coadjutor bishop of New York who later became the fourth bishop and the first archbishop of New York.

Early Years

Originally called Saint John's College, Fordham opened its doors on June 24, 1841, with a student body of six. In its early years, it was presided over by a succession of short-termed presidents (among them John McCloskey, who later became the first bishop of Albany, the second archbishop of New York, and the first American cardinal), and it shared both its campus and its faculty of Vincentians and diocesan clergy with Saint Joseph's Seminary, which had preceded the college to Rose Hill in 1840. Since this arrangement proved to be unsatisfactory, in 1845 Hughes signed an agreement with Clément Boulanger, S.J., the Visitor of the Mission of the Jesuits' French province, under the terms of which the French Jesuits were to assume ownership of most of the land at Rose Hill and control of both the seminary and the college. Thereafter the fortunes of the college changed rather quickly. On April 10, 1846, the college received a charter from the state of New York granting it the power to confer degrees. On July 15 of the same year, the Jesuits arrived at Rose Hill, and Augustus Thébaud, S.J., became the president of both Saint John's College and Saint Joseph's Seminary. Under his leadership, the life of the college became more regular. Hughes, however, quickly became disillusioned with their management of the seminary. Therefore, in 1855, he removed the seminary from their care and staffed it with his own clergy. Finally, in 1860 he closed the seminary and sold the remaining property that he held at Rose Hill to the Jesuits.

Soon after their arrival, the Jesuits made Saint John's the center of their apostolic activity in New York. Thus, the community grew rapidly, and the society established both a novitiate and a scholasticate on the grounds of the college. The college's enrollment, however, remained relatively small (it awarded fewer than a hundred degrees before 1861), and its physical plant remained modest throughout most of the nineteenth century. At the turn of the century, however, under a succession of energetic presidents (John J. Collins, S.J., 1904–06; Daniel J. Quinn, S.J., 1906–11; Thomas J. McCluskey, S.J., 1911–15; Joseph A. Mulry, S.J., 1915–19; Edward P. Tivnan, S.J., 1919–24; and William J. Duane, S.J., 1924–30), the complexion of the institution changed dramatically as the college expanded its efforts to include both graduate and professional education.

Graduate Schools

In 1905 a short-lived medical school (which closed in 1921) was opened. That same year, the law school opened its doors on the Rose Hill campus. (The following year, the law school moved its operations to lower Manhattan where it remained until the establishment of the Lincoln Center campus in 1960.) In recognition of the expansion of the institution's educational mission, in 1907 the original college charter was amended and Saint John's College became Fordham University. Other schools and divisions were added in rapid succession: in 1911 the College of Pharmacy was opened; in 1916 the Graduate School of Arts and Sciences, the School of Sociology and Social Services, and Fordham Teachers' College were established; in 1917 the university inaugurated its Summer Session; in 1920 the School of Business was established, although it did not receive the power to grant degrees until 1927; and in 1923 a Manhattan division of Fordham College (later the undergraduate school of education) was erected.

With the proliferation of schools, the enrollment of the university expanded, rising from 900 in 1900 to over 6,000 by the middle of the 1920s, and the physical plant was upgraded with the construction of additional science facilities, a gymnasium, an expanded library, a seismic station, and a new residence for Jesuit faculty members on the Rose Hill campus. As a result of the upgrading it had undergone in the period of growth following the turn of the century, in 1921 the university received full accreditation from the Middle States Association of Colleges and Universities.

The presidencies of Robert I. Gannon, S.J. (1936–49), and Laurence J. McGinley, S.J. (1949–63), were marked by further expansion and some consolidation. In an attempt to streamline the university's operations in Manhattan, Gannon purchased a building on lower Broadway and moved most of the university's professional schools into it. In 1940, he built additional dormitories on the Rose Hill campus to expand the university's ability to enroll boarding students. In 1944, he founded the School of General Studies (later Ignatius College) to cater to the needs of adult and part-time students. In 1947, he founded the university's radio station, and in 1948 he renovated the university church.

McGinley's tenure was marked by the most ambitious endeavor that the university had taken since the early part of the century. In 1958 he initiated the construction of the Lincoln Center campus, a move which enabled the university both to expand its professional schools and to establish a more visible presence in Manhattan. In 1961 the Law School moved into new quarters on the campus. Following the completion of the Lowenstein Center in 1969, it was joined at Lincoln Center by the graduate schools of education, social service, and business. In addition, the undergraduate School of Education was closed and replaced at Lincoln Center by the College at Lincoln Center (later Fordham College at Lincoln Center). Not all of McGinley's energies were directed to the Manhattan campus. Following the lead of his predecessor, he built a series of new dormitories, a student center and a new residence for the Jesuit faculty at Rose Hill.

Recent Developments

As was the case with many institutions of higher learning during the 1960s, Fordham went through a period of creativity, ferment, and experimentation. In 1962 the university became the first Jesuit institution to receive a charter establishing a chapter of Phi Beta Kappa on campus. In 1964, McGinley's successor, Vincent T. O'Keefe, S.J. (1963–65), opened Thomas More College, the university's first undergraduate college for women. His successor, Leo McLaughlin, S.J. (1965–69), established the Graduate School of Business (1969), the Graduate School of Religion and Religious Education (1969), and the short-lived but lively and experimental Bensalem College. Most significantly, in 1969 the university and the Jesuit community were separately incorporated and the ownership of the university was placed in the hands of an independent, self-perpetuating board of trustees, the majority of whose members were not Jesuits.

During the presidencies of Michael Walsh, S.J. (1969–72), and James C. Finlay, S.J. (1972–84), the university went through a cautious period marked by retrenchment on the Bronx campus and expansion elsewhere. Thus, in 1971, the School of Pharmacy was closed; in 1972 the preparatory school was separated from the university and moved to a site at the edge of the campus; and in 1974 Thomas More College was merged with Fordham College. These losses at Rose Hill were offset by the opening in 1970 of the Calder Center for Ecological Study in Armonk, New York, and in 1976 of the Fordham Graduate Center on the grounds of Marymount College in Tarrytown, New York. In its sesquicentennial year (1991), the university had an enrollment of 14,500 students and a faculty of 500.

See also CATHOLIC COLLEGES AND UNIVERSITIES; JESUITS IN AMERICA, THE.

Curran, Francis S., S.J. *The Return of the Jesuits: Chapters in the History of the Society of Jesus in Nineteenth Century America.* Chicago: Loyola University Press, 1966.

Fitzgerald, Paul, S.J. *The Governance of Jesuit Colleges in the United States 1920–1970.* University of Notre Dame Press, 1984.

Gannon, Robert I. *Up to the Present: The Story of Fordham.* Garden City, N.Y.: Doubleday, 1967.

McDonough, Peter. *Men Astutely Trained: A History of the Jesuits in the American Century.* New York: The Free Press, 1992.

Shelley, Thomas J. *Dunwoodie: The History of Saint Joseph's Seminary, Yonkers, New York.* Westminster, Md.: Christian Classics, 1993.

JOSEPH M. McSHANE, S.J.

FOURNIER, ST. JOHN (1814–75)

Pioneer Sister of St. Joseph and foundress of the Congregation of Chestnut Hill, Philadelphia. Julie Alexise Fournier was born on November 12, 1814, in Arbois, France. At fourteen she entered a contemplative community in Lyons, but in 1836, joined the Sisters of St. Joseph who had recently started a mission in Missouri. After studying methods for teaching deaf-mute persons at St. Etienne, she left Lyons with Sr. Celestine Pommerel, arriving at St. Louis on September 4, 1837, and professed vows at Carondelet on December 27, 1838. Sr. St. John became superior in 1845 of St. Joseph's School for the Colored in St. Louis, closed within a year by Bishop Peter Kenrick, due to racist harassment.

Mother St. John Fournier made the first foundation of the Sisters of St. Joseph outside the St. Louis diocese in 1847 at St. John's Asylum for boys, Philadelphia. In 1851, she assisted the foundation at St. Paul, in Minnesota Territory. Recalled to Philadelphia in 1853, she opened approximately twenty-five houses in Pennsylvania, Delaware, New Jersey, and Maryland. Under the influence of St. John Neumann, Mother St. John strongly supported parish schools. Sisters of St. Joseph from Chestnut Hill served as nurses in the Civil War, and from 1865 cared for orphans of veterans. In 1870 Mother St. John sent sisters to do domestic work at St. Charles Seminary, "much against my will, but we could not refuse the bishop."

The Philadelphia congregation declined formal centralization with Carondelet in 1860. As superior general, Mother St. John taught French in the Academy and translated twelve works of piety and advice to girls (P. F. Cunningham, 1871–75). During her lifetime, Philadelphia founded the congregations of Toronto (1851) and Brooklyn (1856), and aided the beginnings of Buffalo (1854) and Baden (1869). She died on October 15, 1875.

Logue, Maria Kostka. *Sisters of St. Joseph of Philadelphia: A Century of Growth and Development 1847–1947.* Westminster, Md.: Newman, 1950.

PATRICIA BYRNE, C.S.J.

FOY, FLORVILLE (1819–1903)

Sculptor. Florville Foy, born on June 29, 1819, was a mulatto sculptor, tomb builder, and marble cutter who owned one of the most important nineteenth-century marble yards in New Orleans. His parents were Prosper Foy, a French emigrant marble cutter and planter, and Heloise Azelie Aubry, a free woman of color and native New Orleanian. Foy reportedly studied in France, but learned his trade from his father. In 1836 he opened his own tomb-building business. Among his early clients were the wardens of St. Louis Cathedral, for whom he built wall vaults in St. Louis Cemetery I; in the early years of his career, he executed the tomb designs of the city's leading architect, J.N.B. DePouilly.

Foy became one of the most successful tomb builders in New Orleans, employing a large staff of marble cutters. He lived above his studio in a three-story building on Rampart Street with an adjoining marble yard. He designed tombs, sculpture, and ornamentation; many of the elegant tombs in St. Louis Cemeteries I and II were executed and signed by Foy. His business expanded along the Gulf Coast, as he shipped impressive signed tombs to St. Michael Cemetery, Pensacola, and the Old Biloxi Cemetery. One of his early sculptures, *Child with Drum*, is in the Louisiana State Museum. With a career stretching over nearly seventy years, Foy died, a widower, in his home on March 16, 1903. Buried in a tomb in St. Louis Cemetery III far simpler than those he sculpted at the height of his powers, he helped to shape the look of New Orleans cemeteries.

PATRICIA BRADY

FRANCISCAN FRIARS

The common designation in North America for the Order of Friars Minor (O.F.M.), the largest of the three independent branches of the mendicant order founded in 1209 by St. Francis of Assisi. The Friars Minor have played a leading role in the history of the Catholic Church in America, both during the colonial period and since their reestablishment in the middle of the nineteenth century. They are presently the second largest religious order of men in the United States. The stories of the two other branches of the Franciscan Order, the Conventual Franciscans (O.F.M. Conv.) and the Capuchins (O.F.M. Cap.) are treated in other articles.

European Background

The history of the Franciscan Order is a complex maze of seemingly endless reforms and divisions—what has been described as "a fine example of triumphant anarchy." Over the course of the Middle Ages, serious disagreement arose among the friars over the interpretation of the Rule of St. Francis in light of the ministries that they had taken on in the Church. During the late fourteenth and early fifteenth centuries various movements, known collectively as the Observant Reform, began in reaction to what was perceived as a relaxed spirit in the order at large. The reformers sought a greater simplicity of lifestyle, more emphasis on contemplative prayer, and more equality between clerical and lay members of the brotherhood. Tensions between this reform party and those friars who resisted it, known as the Conventuals, grew so acrimonious that Leo X divided the order in 1517 into two independent congregations. The Observant friars, by this point the majority of the order, kept the simple name of Friars Minor (Franciscans); the other branch were styled Conventual Franciscans (O.F.M. Conv.). Because the various Observant groups had never really had a unifying focus, however, the centrifugal forces of reform soon reasserted themselves in the newly independent order. New movements arose among the Friars Minor in the sixteenth century. One of these, the Capuchins, quickly gained autonomy in 1528 and by 1619 had become a totally independent congregation (O.F.M. Cap.). But a number of other groups of "stricter observance"—Discalced, Reformed, and Recollect Franciscans—also began to distinguish themselves from the friars of the more moderate "regular observance," eventually creating their own separate provinces. By 1620 they had attained almost total autonomy while remaining within the structure of the order. Until a century ago, when Leo XIII amalgamated these various groups (1897), the Franciscans were more like a federation of provinces than a united order; the many friars who came to the Americas reflected these various divisions.

Franciscans in the Spanish Colonies

As members of an order with a long missionary tradition, Franciscans plunged into the work of evangelization among the native peoples in Spain's newly conquered territories with great enthusiasm. Between 1493 and 1820 almost 8,500 Spanish Franciscans—the vast majority from the Regular Observance—set out for the Americas, totaling over half of all the missionaries sent by that nation to the New World. The Franciscans held a virtual mission monopoly in those territories which comprised the northern frontier of the Spanish Empire, a fact evident in many place names of the U.S. Southwest. The work of these friars must be understood in light of the *patronato* which the Spanish crown exercised over all mission activities in its domains: the Council of the Indies recruited, supervised, and financially supported the friars, viewing them as agents of Christianization and "Hispanization." The friars did not ordinarily minister to the Spanish colonists; their mission was to evangelize the indigenous population, gathering them into stable communities where they could be formed into good Catholics and subjects. When in the view of the state this task was completed, it was the policy of the crown to request that the Franciscans move on, turning their flocks over to the care of the secular clergy. The friars often had a very different perception of their role than did the civil authorities, a fact that gave rise to numerous conflicts.

Two Franciscans accompanied Columbus on his second voyage to Hispaniola in 1493 and immediately began carrying out their instructions to "bring the inhabitants of the said islands and 'Tierra firme' to our Catholic faith." Larger contingents of friars arrived in the next few years, so that by 1505 they were organized into an independent province of the Holy Cross, with its motherhouse at Santo Domingo. From this base, expansion to the rest of the Antilles soon followed. Franciscans came to the mainland in 1523, beginning the evangelization of Mexico almost immediately following the conquests of Cortes. Franciscans also were part of explorations to the yet unknown territories to the north. Five friars accompanied the ill-fated Florida expeditions of Pánfilo de Narváez in 1528 and De Soto in 1539–43. Then, in 1539, Fray Marcos de Niza penetrated into the territory that is now New Mexico and Arizona. The next year Francisco Vázquez de Coronado led a major expedition of over three hundred Spaniards, including six friars, into the interior of North America. When Coronado returned to Mexico, several friars, led by Juan de Padilla, remained to evangelize the Quivira people in what is now Kansas. There they were killed by hostile tribes in the fall of 1542. They are considered the protomartyrs of the present-day United States.

However, it was only towards the end of the sixteenth century that permanent missions were finally established among Native Americans in what is now the United States. Franciscans arrived in Florida in 1573, eight years after the first permanent Spanish settlement, but a sustained mission effort did not begin until larger contingents of friars arrived in 1587 and 1595. Since the tribes in Northern Florida were town-dwellers, they generally established themselves in existing Native American villages. One chain of missions extended north among the Guale peoples from Saint Augustine along the Georgia coast; another, larger chain worked its way westward, eventually extending 250 miles to the Apalachicola River. Despite periodic uprisings, most significantly the Guale revolt of 1597 in which five friars were killed, the missions prospered. At their height in 1675, forty friars were maintaining thirty-six missions, and the bishop of Havana that year confirmed over 13,000 natives. Soon, however, these missions fell victim to the struggle between Spain and England over the lands between Charleston, South Carolina, and Saint Augustine. A series of slave-taking raids by English soldiers and their Native American allies, combined with desertion of the missions by the native peoples, quickly wiped out the Florida missions. By 1706 they had virtually disappeared.

More lasting results would come from the contemporary mission efforts in New Mexico. There friars of the Holy Gospel province in Mexico accompanied the Spanish colonizing expedition of 1598, and quickly began evangelizing efforts among the town-dwelling Pueblo nation. By the 1630s the Franciscans had established missions in some twenty-five pueblos, baptizing most of the 50,000 natives they contained. This work was interrupted by the great Pueblo Revolt of 1680, when a combination of famine, cultural dislocation, and oppression encouraged the native people to rebel, putting a temporary end to the New Mexico colony: the Spanish settlers were expelled and thirty-two friars were killed. The missions were reestablished only after the Spanish reoccupied the territory in 1692. The work of these friars over the years deeply stamped the character of New Mexico Catholicism; confraternities of lay penitents would keep alive the affective piety characteristic of Franciscan spirituality even after the friars were removed from the area.

New mission fields opened for Spanish Franciscans in the eighteenth century. The friars who would serve in them belonged to the new apostolic colleges "for the propagation of the faith" of Querétaro, Zacatecas, and San Fernando which had recently been established in Mexico. These institutions recruited friars from Spain and trained them as professional missionaries; the friars had to make a ten-year commitment to serve on the frontier. The first of these new mission fields was Texas. Threatened by French expansion in the Mississippi valley, Spanish authorities determined to take possession of this vast territory through the traditional method of military bases and Christianization of the native inhabitants. A small expedition of friars temporarily established a foothold among the Caddo peoples in east Texas in the early 1690s, but enduring missions were not established until 1716, when a larger number of friars again began work in east Texas among the Nagadoches and Adaes tribes. More significant efforts were soon begun further southwest, led by one the greatest of the borderland missionaries, Antonio Margil. Mission San Antonio, the center of this region, was established in 1718. Despite the zealous efforts of the friars, the Texas missions were never very successful in numerical terms; their highly structured life did not prove attractive to the nomadic native tribes.

The last major areas of evangelization by the Spanish Franciscans were opened up by the expulsion of the Jesuits from Mexico in 1767. The friars inherited their missions in the Pimería Alta—today the Mexican state of Sonora and Arizona south of the Gila River. Two of the missions were in what is now the United States: Tubac and San Xavier del Bac among the Papago tribe. At the time the Franciscans took them over, they had been in a state of decline for some years. The friars, led by Francisco Garcés, rebuilt these missions, eventually constructing the magnificent church which still survives at San Xavier del Bac, and embarked on an expansion program. A mission was founded at Tucson and, more adventurously, the friars began to establish a presence among the Yumas on the Colorado. There Garcés met his death in 1781, and the missionaries quickly gave up these more distant mission efforts, remaining only among the Papagos.

In what would be a more significant move, the Franciscans also took over the Jesuit missions in Baja California, and thus were called upon by the Spanish government to initiate similar efforts just two years later in Alta California in what would become the most celebrated of the colonial mission chains in the United States. This expedition was led by Junipero Serra (1713–84), who founded a mission at San Diego in 1769. Within a year another mission, San Carlos, was founded on Monterey Bay. Soon after a land party discovered a vast bay to the north, where in 1776 Serra established the mission of San Francisco. Ultimately eighteen missions were established in California by Serra and his successor, Fermin Lasuén (d. 1803); three more missions followed in the early nineteenth century. The California missions were large, prosperous complexes, the economic center of colonial life. Some of the missions housed well over a thousand natives; at their height they contained 38,000 people. There is no doubt they were effective, but the effect of the paternalistic mission system was questioned by some at the time, and continues to be a subject of scholarly debate. In all 98,000 native people were baptized by the Franciscans over the six decades of the California mission era.

All of these Spanish Franciscan mission efforts began to unravel in the early nineteenth century. The number of native peoples in the older missions in New Mexico and Texas had gradually declined over the years, as they succumbed to European diseases to which they as yet had no immunity. The California missions soon followed the same pattern. And the number of missionaries themselves also decreased sharply. The upheavals of the long Mexican Wars of Independence forced most of the Spanish friars to leave, since they would not renounce their allegiance to their mother country, and the Mexican provinces were unable to furnish adequate replacements in the frontier missions. In addition, the order in Mexico was soon subjected to various secularizing measures by the new, independent government. The number of friars in Mexico decreased precipitously, and the missions themselves were confiscated by the state. Most of the Texas missions had already been secularized in the 1790s under the Spanish government; the rest of them, plus those in Arizona and New Mexico, were turned over in 1828. Finally, in 1834, the Mexican government ordered the secularization of the California

missions—valued in the millions of dollars. The Franciscan presence gradually vanished: the last remaining friar in Texas died in 1834, and the last in New Mexico in 1848. In the latter year, when the United States took possession of California, there were only four Mexican friars remaining in the whole territory, gathered at Mission Santa Barbara. The refoundation of the Franciscan presence in the Southwest would only come later in the century with an influx of personnel from the new foundations which were established by German immigrants to the United States.

Franciscans in the French and English Colonies

The French had established a settlement at Quebec in 1608 but the small colony was without clergy until its founder, Samuel de Champlain, invited Franciscans to come to Canada in 1615. These friars, who belonged to the Recollect reform movement, were known to Champlain in France as zealous religious, and were therefore his choice to be the first missionaries in his New France. There were never more than four Recollects in Canada at any one time during these early years and they had to continually battle the hostility of the Huguenot-dominated trading company which owned the colony. Nevertheless, in addition to serving as chaplains to the Quebec outpost, they undertook missions to the Montagnais and Huron peoples, even establishing a school at Quebec for native children. Due to their limited numbers, they sought the assistance of other missionaries, and the Jesuits arrived in Canada in 1625. These early efforts came to an end in 1629 with the English conquest of Quebec; when the French repossessed the colony in 1632, the French government decided that only the Jesuits should be assigned there as missionaries.

The Recollects finally managed to return to New France in 1670. They reestablished their friary in Quebec and eventually founded two others, in Trois-Rivières and Montreal. In addition they resumed their activities as missionaries to the native peoples and served as chaplains to exploring expeditions and in military posts in the Great Lakes region. Notable among these friars was Louis Hennepin, the first European to visit Niagara Falls and the rapids of St. Anthony on the Mississippi, who later penned colorful accounts of his journeys. By 1760 there were twenty-four Recollect priests and forty-six lay brothers in Canada, 70 percent of whom were native vocations. However, this community was condemned to extinction after the English conquest of Quebec in 1763, as the new government forbade male religious communities to receive any novices. The bishop of Quebec secularized the friars in 1796 and the last priest died in 1813.

Franciscans were also active in the English colonies for almost fifty years, a fact that has often escaped notice. Although Jesuits had labored in Maryland since its founding in 1634, the position of the society in the new colony was quite tenuous at various intervals. Over the years the proprietor, Lord Baltimore, petitioned Rome for more clergy; these requests became more urgent in 1669–70 when the number of the Jesuits active in the mission fell to two. The English Franciscan province responded in 1672 by sending two friars to Maryland, followed shortly by others. These friars labored throughout southern Maryland among the sizable but scattered Catholic population. Unfortunately, the lack of English Franciscans available, combined with the worsening situation for Catholics in the colony after 1704, led the mother province to discontinue sending new men to the mission. The last Franciscan in Maryland, James Haddock, died in 1718.

Franciscans in the Early National Period, 1780–1840

The Franciscans did not again establish an organized presence in the United States until the 1840s. There were a number of "freelance" friars who came to the new nation, many due to the European political upheavals of the late eighteenth and early nineteenth centuries, but all of them labored as isolated individuals. They included both zealous missionaries and unscrupulous rogues whose superiors in Europe were gladly rid of. One colorful friar was John Baptist Caussé, a German Recollect who appeared in Philadelphia in 1784; he went further west among the German immigrant farming population, where he labored with success in the Lancaster and Conewago (Harrisburg) areas. A second friar, Theodore Brouwers, a cultivated Dutchman who had been ministering on the island of Curacao, also came to Pennsylvania in 1789, and was immediately made pastor of all of western Pennsylvania by Bishop Carroll; unfortunately his strenuous activities led to his death the following year. Caussé's subsequent scandalous behavior, including his dissipation of the substantial assets built up by Brouwers and his formation of a traveling theater troupe, caused him to be excommunicated by Carroll in 1792.

Another renegade German friar, Francis Fromm, arrived penniless in Baltimore in 1789; after several disastrous pastorates, Fromm petitioned Rome to have himself appointed bishop of German-American Catholics in the new nation. He was suspended from the priesthood by Carroll in 1795, although he continued to trouble the diocese in civil court until his death in 1799. A more constructive contribution to the new American Church was made by Michael Egan, a member of the Irish province, who also came to Pennsylvania, but with a papal rescript empowering him to make a Franciscan foundation in the new nation. The pressing pastoral duties assigned him diverted him from these plans, however. Egan was named first bishop of Philadelphia in 1808, and the genial friar died in 1814 after a brief but stormy episcopate. Another Irish friar, Charles Bonaventure Maguire, arrived after the War of 1812 in the Pittsburgh area with hopes of making a Franciscan foundation, but again, this did not materialize. Among other isolated Franciscan missionaries were the Austrian Ivo Levits, the Sicilian Francesco Caro, and the Hungarian Zachary Kunz, all of whom labored in the New York diocese. In the Midwest, Otto Skolla was a missionary to the Native Americans in Wisconsin for sixteen years during the 1840s and 1850s; the Slovenian Leo Osredkar served as a pastor in Missouri and Indiana between 1852 and 1882. All of these friars ministered alone.

Franciscan Immigrant Foundations, 1840–80

The permanent establishment of the Franciscan Order in the United States only came with the flood tide of European immigrants who arrived in the United States between 1840 and 1920. These foundations, largely uncoordinated, were all from continental Europe, a fact that would give American Franciscans a heavily "ethnic" flavor throughout the period.

The first foundation of the order was in Cincinnati. In 1838 Bishop John B. Purcell had made an extensive tour of Europe, seeking priests for the already burgeoning German-speaking population of his diocese. A Bavarian friar, Francis Huber, responded and began working in Cincinnati; despite his urgent requests for assistance, the Bavarian province was unable to supply additional friars, and so at his suggestion Bishop Purcell appealed to the Tyrolese province of Reformed Franciscans. A volunteer, William Unterthiner, arrived in 1844; he was soon made pastor of the new St. John the Baptist parish in 1845. This time, more friars followed from the Tyrol; they soon moved out to care for other German parishes in the Cincinnati area and in Louisville, Kentucky (1849). A permanent mission was established in 1850, and soon afterwards a classical *gymnasium* which could serve as a minor seminary. Although the Tyrolese mother province decided to recall these shorthanded and overworked missionaries in 1857, most of the friars serving in America decided to remain. At Purcell's request, in 1859 the Franciscan general minister constituted these eleven friars, headed by Otto Jair, as an independent custody or vice province, dedicated to St. John the Baptist. The independence of the Cincinnati friars contained with it the authority to receive novices into the order. With a number of native German American vocations beginning to enter from its seminary, the new custody slowly began to prosper. In 1866 the friars expanded into southern Indiana. The 1870s saw new foundations in Chatham, Ontario; Emporia, Kansas; and in the Diocese of Peoria, Illinois.

Meanwhile, another new foundation was beginning in the East. Through the initiative of a wealthy merchant, Nicholas Devereux of Utica, New York, in 1854 Bishop John Timon of Buffalo approached the Irish Franciscans of St. Isidore's College in Rome for missionaries for his rapidly expanding diocese. The Irish friars were unable to respond to Timon's request, but several Italians did volunteer for this new effort. Headed by Panfilo da Magliano of the Reformed province of the Abruzzi, the friars settled in 1855 into temporary quarters in Ellicottville, New York, while construction began on their permanent residence on an extensive tract of land in Allegany, New York, donated by Devereux. There St. Bonaventure's College and Seminary opened in 1858. Besides attending numerous small mission churches through a wide swath of New York's southern tier, the friars soon accepted parishes in Buffalo itself, New York City, Winsted, Connecticut, and, temporarily (1859–66), in Houston, Texas. These friars were also erected into an independent custody by Rome, dedicated to the Immaculate Conception, in 1861. One of these early missionaries was Diomede Falconio, the second president of St. Bonaventure's College, who at a later stage of his career, would return to the United States as apostolic delegate. The Immaculate Conception custody was from the outset a more diverse group than its Cincinnati counterpart. Although the majority of the early volunteers were Italians, they had come from various provinces throughout Italy, and so lacked a sense of cohesion and common traditions. Furthermore, since these friars were largely ministering among the general Catholic population rather than their own countrymen, once native vocations began entering the order at the college in Allegany, the custody became increasingly Irish in complexion.

A second German Franciscan foundation was established in the Midwest, when Bishop Henry Juncker of Alton, Illinois, appealed to the Recollect Saxon province for priests. The young provincial, Gregory Janknecht, assigned eight friars to this new mission, and in 1858 they established themselves at the village of Teutopolis, Illinois. From this base they began ministering to the farming communities of the central area of the state and started a seminary for the education of the diocesan clergy. In 1859 they assumed care of the parish in Quincy, Illinois, where a year later they opened a college for laymen. The mission continued to receive steady support from its mother province, and the friars quickly expanded their ministry, accepting German parishes in St. Louis (1862), Cleveland (1867), and Memphis (1870). In 1875 the Saxon friars were forced to leave their province due to the *Kulturkampf;* the developing American mission now became a refuge for many of the exiles. Janknecht ordered Maurice Klostermann, superior of the mission, to "make five more foundations; a large number of friars will arrive." Over a hundred of them, including all the young men in formation, came later that year. The reinforced Saxon friars quickly accepted parishes in Chicago and Indianapolis, additional places in Missouri, new rural missions in Minnesota and Nebraska, and opened missions among the Ojibwe and Menominee natives in northern Wisconsin and Michigan. In 1878 Janknecht requested that the American houses become an autonomous province, and gave the German fri-

ars the option of joining the new province or of returning to Europe when conditions permitted. In 1879 the province of the Sacred Heart, with its headquarters in St. Louis, was erected. Only thirty-seven friars eventually returned to their homeland.

The *Kulturkampf* was also the occasion for yet another foundation of German friars in the United States. The small Thuringian Custody of St. Elizabeth, with its motherhouse in Fulda, had only just begun to recover from the Napoleonic suppression, when its members were evicted from their monasteries. In 1875 a little group, led by Francis Koch, came to America to find a refuge for the dispersed friars. Landing in New York, the Fulda exiles searched unsuccessfully for a home for some months. Finally, they were received by Bishop Wadhams of Ogdensburg, who offered them a backwoods parish in Croghan, New York. Still, the superior of the Thuringian Custody, Aloysius Lauer, saw in this new foundation the Godsend he had been awaiting, and decided to send more of the friars to America. Luckily, they obtained another, more felicitous residence in 1876 when Bishop Corrigan of Newark gave them a small monastery which had been constructed by Bavarian Carmelites in Paterson, New Jersey, but who had decided not to come to America after all. The next year the friars were assigned part of the city of Paterson as a parish; Lauer transferred the headquarters of his province-in-exile there in 1878.

For all of these European Franciscans, their early foundations in the United States involved a marked break from their accustomed ministries. Their chief activities in America, determined by the needs of the immigrant populations and the urgings of bishops, were staffing diocesan parishes and conducting schools. The friars in Europe certainly had long experience with numerous pastoral ministries, especially preaching, but they very rarely had been assigned the full "care of souls"—with all its administrative responsibilities—in a parochial structure. Again, the order could boast of a long educational tradition, but its schools in Europe were largely "internal," devoted to the formation of young friars. Except for those friars from the Austrian Empire, the education of laity and diocesan seminarians was a new venture. These very different ministerial activities also brought about far-reaching changes in Franciscan life. To meet the challenges of their American missions the friars had to obtain dispensations from their rule and the constitutions of the order: to wear secular clothes, to commute the Divine Office to the recitation of the rosary, to use money, and to own property in common. It was very difficult for them to establish the customary daily structures of religious life, especially in the scattered rural parishes staffed by the friars in the Midwest. These facts often led to misunderstandings—at times real conflicts—between the American friars and their European superiors.

Franciscan Immigrant Ministry and
Western Expansion, 1880–1920

In the three decades before World War I, Catholic immigration to the United States was becoming increasingly diverse, as large numbers of Eastern Europeans and Italians also landed in America. New ethnic Franciscan foundations were soon established to minister among them. When the religious houses in Poland were suppressed by the Russian government in 1872, Augustine Zetyz, a Franciscan lay brother, decided to be a missionary among the Polish people in the United States. He went first to Cincinnati, but worked his way to the Pennsylvania mining towns; there he gradually conceived the idea of establishing a community of Polish friars in America to minister to the immigrants. In 1881 he went home to muster support for his project. Finally, with the support of his superiors, he returned to America in 1886, accepting a tract of land in Pulaski, Wisconsin, west of Green Bay. Some friar volunteers from several Polish provinces joined Zetyz over the next few years; priests were put in command of the foundation, but it remained small and destitute. In 1895 the general minister placed it under the jurisdiction of Sacred Heart province. Additional priests arrived from Poland and the friars slowly began to accept the care of additional parishes, including one in Green Bay. In 1899 a novitiate was opened, and in 1901 a minor seminary. With a solid foundation thus laid for future growth, the Pulaski friars were constituted an autonomous commissariat, dedicated to the Assumption of the Blessed Virgin, in 1910.

Other Eastern European immigrant communities coming from the Austro-Hungarian Empire were also served by Franciscans. In 1906 Casimir Zakrajsek of the Slovene province came to the United States to work among his countrymen, organizing a parish in New York. On one of his return trips to Europe to plead assistance, Fr. Casimir alerted the general minister of the order to the need for more missionaries to serve the various Slavic peoples of the Austrian Empire in America. Other friar volunteers from various Eastern European provinces soon began arriving. In 1912 the commissariat of the Holy Cross, with its headquarters in Brooklyn, New York, was erected for the Slovene, Croatian, and Slovak friars working in the United States.

In the East, an ever-increasing tide of Italian immigrants began arriving after 1880. Even before this date, the Italian friars of the Immaculate Conception custody, although mainly intent on establishing a new American foundation of the order, had begun ministering to the small numbers of their fellow Italians then in the country. As early as 1866, Leo Pacilio of the Allegany custody had been requested by Archbishop McCloskey to organize an Italian parish in Lower Manhattan. Fr. Leo purchased a former Methodist church, calling it St. Anthony of Padua; this was one of the first Italian national parishes in the United States. The friars next opened a similar parish in Boston's North End in 1873. Although the number of friar volunteers from Italy serving in the custody declined after 1880 as the number of native vocations grew, pressures from the bishops for the friars to assume more ministries became more urgent as the tide of immigrants increased. The aging Italian friars opened three more parishes in the Archdiocese of New York in the 1890s, and also extended their Italian ministry to Pittsburgh in 1895. The Italian friars of the custody began agitating for a separate entity—or at least their own formation program—in order to attract more vocations from the mother country.

Meanwhile, Leo XIII had amalgamated all the various branches of the Observant Franciscans into one Order of Friars Minor in 1897; he selected Aloysius Lauer, former provincial of Thuringia, as the first general minister of the united order. Fr. Aloysius viewed this "Leonine Union" as paving the way for a merger of the relatively small Franciscan jurisdictions on the East Coast (the friars of the Immaculate Conception Custody had been Reformed, his own Thuringian friars in the Paterson, New Jersey, foundation were Recollects). The latter group had been slowly expanding its ministerial outreach in America. With the repeal of anticlerical legislation in Germany, the headquarters of the Thuringian custody were moved back to Fulda in 1887, but the friars remained in the ministries they had established during their decade of exile. That same year the dynamic pioneer Francis Koch was asked to go West and take charge of a largely German parish in Denver, Colorado; from this base, the friars attended a far-flung chain of mission stations. Additional mission parishes were taken in New Jersey and in Sullivan County, New York. Few of these ministries of the custody in America were focused on German immigrants, and the friars working in the United States began to attract some native vocations. Anselm Mueller of Sacred Heart province was asked by the general minister to conduct a visitation of the two East Coast jurisdictions in 1898.

The final decision of the general administration of the order, announced in 1901, created a new Eastern province of the Holy Name of Jesus by amalgamating the friaries of the Paterson foundation with the non-Italian friars and ministries of the Allegany custody. Both Mueller and Rome envisioned that the new province, which numbered 113 friars, would quickly become an English-speaking, "assimilated" American community. Its first provincial was Edward Blecke of the Thuringian province. The twenty-six Italian friars, who had asked to remain independent, retained the title of the custody of the Immaculate Conception, with Athanasius Butelli as their superior. Both groups, who quickly moved to establish their headquarters in New York, moved to stabilize their new situations.

As new volunteers soon began arriving from various Italian provinces, the friars of the Immaculate Conception custody embarked on an expansion program among the burgeoning immigrant population; three additional parishes were accepted in the New York area between 1903 and 1908, and two in the Archdiocese of Boston in the following decade. In addition, the custody took steps to attract vocations from among the immigrants themselves: in 1908 land was purchased in Catskill, New York, for a minor seminary, and fifteen students arrived that fall to begin studies for the priesthood. With its future growth assured, the custody was raised to the rank of a province in 1911.

Meanwhile, the friars of the new Holy Name province worked at forging an identity. As the product of a merger of friars of two different spiritual traditions and ethnic backgrounds—German and Irish—the province experienced some inner tensions for the first two decades of its existence. The foundation of a minor seminary in Callicoon, New York, in 1901, although a major financial risk for the new province, proved to be a wise investment, as large classes began to enter in the following decade. The major ministerial expansion of Holy Name province in these first years was in northern New Jersey, where the old pioneer, Francis Koch, embarked on a program of church extension. Prior to his death in 1920, he organized over twenty congregations in the industrial towns and rural villages of the region, most of which were served by the friars. Meanwhile, the area around St. Francis Church in Midtown Manhattan was undergoing a total transformation, as commercial establishments replaced residential brownstones. The friars there began adjusting their ministry to the more transient population; in 1907 they were granted permission to offer a 12:15 lunch-hour Mass, the first church in the United States to enjoy such a privilege.

The older, established Franciscan entities in the Midwest enjoyed solid growth during these decades. By 1880, Sacred Heart province, based in St. Louis, had over two hundred members, and the friars continued to accept new parishes throughout the Midwest, mainly in German immigrant communities. One of the largest of these was St. Augustine's parish in Chicago, "Back of the Yards." The friars also deepened their involvement in their ministry to Native Americans, accepting new missions among the Ojibwe in northern Wisconsin and eastern Minnesota, and the Ottawa in northern Michigan. The friars of St. John the Baptist custody, Cincinnati, also expanded their parish ministry into Illinois, Michigan, and Kansas; their steady growth led to the custody's elevation to the rank of a province in 1886. A permanent novitiate was established in a wooded section of Cincinnati, Mt. Airy, in 1889.

It was during these years that both of these German American provinces also extended their outreach to the Western United States, thus reviving the Franciscan presence in that part of the country. Following the suppression of the California missions, a small community of Mexican friars had managed to survive at Mission Santa

Barbara; in 1845 they were reconstituted as an independent apostolic college for the training of missionaries. However, only a handful of volunteers, mainly Irish, arrived over the following decades; faced with the likely prospect of the extinction of this entity, the general minister of the order requested in 1885 that Sacred Heart province incorporate Mission Santa Barbara. With the subsequent infusion of personnel from the Midwest, not only was the future of the mission assured, but additional ministries were quickly accepted. As these new friars were almost entirely of German stock, they were soon requested to take over the existing German parishes in San Francisco (1887) and Los Angeles (1893); new ones were also founded in Oakland, San Francisco, and Sacramento. In addition, these friars were asked to accept the care of the Catholic population in Phoenix, Arizona, and its environs in 1896. Meanwhile, the original work of the Franciscans in California had been revived, when the friars accepted the care of the Pomo tribe in Lake and Mendocino Counties in 1887. Because of the great distance from their motherhouse in St. Louis, these Western friaries of Sacred Heart province were organized into a semiautonomous commissariat with a regional superior in 1896. The foundations for an eventually independent entity were laid when a new minor seminary was opened at Santa Barbara in 1901. The friars also expanded their ministry into the Pacific Northwest, accepting parishes in Oregon (1908) and Washington (1909). When the friars arrived in Arizona they had immediately resumed the former labors of the Spanish missionaries among the Papago and Pima peoples there; a central friary was established at San Xavier del Bac in 1913. Bonaventure Oblasser, one of these early missionaries, became a great self-taught scholar of the culture of the Arizona natives. The rapid growth of this Western commissariat led to the organization of an independent province, dedicated to St. Barbara, in 1915.

The friars of St. John the Baptist province, Cincinnati, also initiated an extensive ministry among both the Native American and Hispanic populations in the Southwest during these years. Encouraged by Mother Katherine Drexel and the Bureau of Catholic Indian Missions, the Cincinnati friars accepted the pastoral and educational care of the Navaho missions in 1897; the first friars arrived at St. Michaels, Arizona, in 1898. One of the early missionaries, Bernard Haile, became a noted expert in the language and culture of the Navahos. Within several years, the Franciscans were also requested to take over a large number of churches in New Mexico, both "missions" among the Pueblos and parishes in towns such as Carlsbad and Roswell, serving largely Hispanic congregations. The growing prominence of the Franciscans in New Mexico was recognized by the appointment of Albert Daeger, one of the first friar missionaries, as archbishop of Santa Fe in 1919. The friars of St. John the Baptist province also pioneered

Franciscan ministry to the African American community during these years. Once again through the initiative of Mother Drexel, the Franciscans were asked in 1907 by Bishop William McCloskey of Louisville to establish a parish for the "colored" Catholics in that city, and three years later a similar ministry was begun in Kansas City, Missouri.

Thus by 1920 the Friars Minor had established a solid presence in the United States; in that year there were almost 1,200 American friars, 700 of whom belonged to the two large Midwest provinces. The focus of the order's ministry throughout this period continued to be largely parochial and educational, almost entirely directed to working-class immigrant "ethnics." Since it was only around the turn of the century that the friars were beginning to reach out to the more assimilated Catholic population, there were few, if any Franciscans among the progressive Americanists of the time. Several friars of this era did gain public acclaim for their scholarly work: Innocent Wappelhorst's *Caeremoniale* (1887) became the standard liturgical textbook in most U.S. seminaries; Zephyrin Engelhardt began producing his monumental historical research on the history of the California missions in 1897; and Paschal Robinson, one of the few "Anglo-American" friars, became one of the most noted medieval scholars in the nation. Most Franciscan authors, however, reached out to a more popular audience. In the Midwest provinces, friars such as Bernard Hammer were among the leading writers for German immigrant Catholics. The Cincinnati friars had begun publishing the devotional *Sendbote des Gottlichen Herzes Jesu* in 1875; two other periodicals promoting the Franciscan movement among the laity appeared in the 1890s: *St. Franziskus Bote* and *St. Anthony Messenger.* The friars of the Sacred Heart province also entered this field with *The Franciscan Herald* in 1913. Franciscans also were very active in the ministry of parish missions throughout the United States, numbering such prominent preachers as Titus Hugger, Jerome Kilgenstein, and Matthew Fox.

American Franciscans also made their first ventures into the field of foreign mission work during these decades. The first priest to go to China as a missionary from the United States was one of the German friars who had come to America as an exile from the *Kulturkampf.* Remy Goette, ordained in St. Louis in 1880, volunteered the following year for the Chinese missions then staffed by several European provinces. Later in the decade he was joined by two of his brothers, also Franciscans. All in all, about a dozen American friars served in the order's Chinese missions before 1920. American friars also began volunteering for the international Franciscan custody of the Holy Land, caring for the various sanctuaries there and ministering among the Christian Arabs. A commissariat for the Holy Land was established in New York in 1882 for the purpose of procuring funds and personnel for this work. In 1897 Commissary Godfrey Schilling decided to transfer this operation to Washington, D.C. There he built the "Franciscan Monastery," Mount St. Sepulchre, which quickly became one of the leading pilgrimage destinations for American Catholics.

Assimilated American Franciscans, 1920–60

For American Franciscans, this period was one of unprecedented numerical and ministerial expansion. Earlier patterns continued with a number of new ethnic foundations: in the late 1920s, the Croatian, Hungarian, and Slovak friars laboring in the United States were able to establish their own national commissariats attached to mother provinces in Europe. And when the Soviet Union occupied Lithuania in 1940, some of the Franciscan refugees sought a haven in America, where they managed to reestablish the Lithuanian province-in-exile in 1946, with its headquarters in Kennebunkport, Maine. Yet another Franciscan custody was founded for Catholics of the Byzantine-Slavonic Rites in 1947. The commissariat of the Assumption, raised to the rank of a province in 1939, and the Immaculate Conception province also expanded their ministries among the Polish and Italian immigrant populations respectively. For the other Franciscan entities, however, this period was one of assimilation into mainstream American Catholic life. Large numbers of vocations entered the order: by 1960 there were some 4,000 American Franciscans, 750 of whom were young clerics studying for the priesthood.

This influx of vocations led all the Franciscan provinces to greatly expand and professionalize their system of "internal schools": minor seminaries, novitiates, and houses of philosophy and theology. Under the inspiration of Thomas Plassmann, the Franciscan Educational Conference was founded in 1919 to encourage cooperation in these efforts among the various jurisdictions. Also joined by Capuchin and Conventual friars, the conference did much to promote a revival of a distinctive Franciscan intellectual tradition in the English-speaking world. Fruits of this new interest were the foundation of the Franciscan Institute at St. Bonaventure University in 1941 and the Academy of American Franciscan History in Potomac, Maryland, in 1946. American scholars such as Allan Wolter and Ignatius Brady became world-renowned experts in Franciscan thought.

During these decades parochial work continued to remain the major ministerial commitment of American Franciscans, who staffed some 350 parishes by 1960. However, there were marked breaks from earlier patterns. The new parishes that were accepted increasingly tended to be those in suburbs or smaller towns where the congregations were largely assimilated Americans. Also, the complexion of many older inner-city parishes was changing dramatically, as the children of the original immigrant populations dispersed. Churches such as St. Peter's in Chicago and St. Francis in New York were transformed into devotional shrine churches, offering an array of spiritual services to transient downtown congregations. Others, like St. Boniface in San Francisco and St. Francis in Cincinnati, developed breadlines and other social services to minister to the poor populations which now surrounded them.

However, these decades also witnessed a significant diversification of Franciscan ministry. The education of lay students gained increasing emphasis, as the friars responded to the demands of the upwardly mobile Catholic population. The two small Franciscan colleges at St. Bonaventure's and Quincy, Illinois, grew dramatically after World War II; in 1937 they were joined by Sienna College, outside Albany, New York. Franciscans also committed themselves to the field of secondary education, beginning with Roger Bacon High School in Cincinnati in 1928; by 1960 the American friars staffed eight diocesan and parochial high schools.

The work of evangelization also expanded greatly. All the provinces maintained large parish mission bands during these decades, and Franciscans also became significantly involved in the lay retreat movement which blossomed after World War I; by 1960 some fifteen retreat houses were maintained by American friars. The work of "home missions" to unevangelized regions of the Southern United States also became a major priority. However, the most dramatic growth in this area was the enthusiastic commitment of American Franciscans to foreign mission work. In 1922 steps were taken by the order and the Holy See to entrust a special mission field in China to the friars of the United States; in 1923 the prefecture apostolic of Wuchang was entrusted jointly to the four largest American provinces. Subsequently, this mission became the responsibility of the Cincinnati province alone, as Sacred Heart, Holy Name, and St. Barbara provinces gradually received their own territories. The Chinese missions had to be suspended in the wake of World War II, but a number of the exiled friars quickly opened new fields in Japan and the Philippines. Meanwhile, American friars had accepted two Brazilian mission territories in 1943 and one in Honduras in 1944. Further Western Hemisphere initiatives followed in the next decade with missions in Bolivia, Jamaica, Puerto Rico, and Peru. By 1960, 250 American Franciscans were serving overseas as missionaries.

Recent Developments, 1960–95

Like almost all other American religious orders, the last three decades have been a time of euphoria, disorientation, and solid new directions for the Franciscans. The only new jurisdiction created during this period has been the province of Our Lady of Guadalupe in 1985, based in Albuquerque, New Mexico, which was formed out of the houses of St. John the Baptist province in the Southwest U.S.A. Otherwise it has been a time of dramatic change for American Franciscans. In some ways, they found themselves well-poised to move into the new directions called for by the Second Vatican Council, since over the years many of the anachronistic monastic structures which had characterized the life of European friars had already fallen into desuetude as Franciscans had adjusted to American society. On the other hand, the call for religious orders to return to the charism of their founder has forced American friars to reevaluate the high priority which they have historically placed on priestly ministry in parish settings in light of the order's renewed perception of itself as a religious brotherhood whose primary mission is simply living the gospel.

This revisioning of Franciscan life, coupled with a significant fall in the number of new recruits, has forced almost all the American provinces to withdraw their friars from a good number of the ministries which had been built up over the preceding century. In addition, the various mission fields staffed by American friars have largely achieved mature independence. At the same time, U.S. Franciscans have embarked on a number of new ministerial initiatives. Many of these, in response to the order's call for " a preferential option for the poor," serve among the new ethnic minorities, especially the Hispanic population, and address issues of social justice, especially as these affect marginalized elements of American Church and society. The 2,300 Franciscan friars in the United States in 1995 continue to make a significant contribution to the life of the Church, and the prominence of American friars in the Franciscan world was recognized by the election of John Vaughn of St. Barbara province as general minister of the order (1979–91).

Bacigalupo, Leonard. *The History of the Province of the Immaculate Conception, U.S.A.* New York, 1986.

Callahan, Adalbert. *Medieval Francis in Modern America.* New York, 1936.

"Franciscan History of North America." *Report of the Franciscan Educational Conference* 18 (1936).

Habig, Marion, ed. *The Friars Minor in the United States with a Brief History of the Order of St. Francis in General.* Chicago, 1926.

———. *Heralds of the King.* Chicago, 1958.

McCloskey, Pat. *God Gives His Grace.* Cincinnati, 1994.

Morales, Francisco. *Franciscan Presence in the Americas.* Potomac, Md., 1983.

DOMINIC V. MONTI, O.F.M.

FRANCISCANS (CAPUCHINS)

As a reform of the Franciscan Order, the Capuchins received approval in 1528 with the papal declaration, *Religionis zelus.* They quickly became known for their desire to remain faithful to the original ideals of the primitive Franciscan fraternity and for their intense blending of its contemplative and missionary energies. Capuchins were working in Africa as early as 1549 and within a hundred years fraternities were formed in Asia and the Americas.

The Seventeenth Century

The first Capuchins arrived on the North American continent in 1632 as a result of the initiatives of the newly founded Congregation for the Propagation of the Faith and the Capuchin Joseph Tremblay, principal adviser to Cardinal Richelieu, "to prevent the progress of Puritanism and to minister to the Catholic settlers." While the congregation had established the prefecture apostolic of New England on November 22, 1630, the political situation prevented its realization until 1632 when France successfully negotiated with England the restoration of her colonies in Canada. As a result of the settlement, the French Jesuits and Franciscan Recollects were assigned the missions of "New France," that is, the Province of Quebec, while the Capuchins were entrusted with the prefectures of Acadia and New England which included jurisdiction over Massachusetts Bay. In 1639 this responsibility was extended to include the provinces of Virginia and Florida, that is, all English colonies of North America.

Shortly after their arrival in present-day Nova Scotia, the Capuchins established seven mission centers. A few friars settled in New Brunswick. Others made their way to the mouth of the Penobscot River in present-day Maine where they continued the mission of the Jesuits among the Penobscot natives. In order to instill the faith more effectively, the Capuchins established a number of religious schools which provided a catechetical as well as an elementary education. While many traveled with the native peoples from their summer dwellings close to the ocean to their inland winter retreats, Leonard de Chartres built what was to become the first Capuchin church in the United States, Our Lady of Hope, near Castine in Hancock County, Maine.

During the next twenty-two years, the Capuchins ministered to the Penobscots, sharing the indigenous life of privation and austerity, and, all the while, bringing them to know the gospel. In 1654, however, the British fleet captured the French settlements of Acadia and Maine. The English Puritans of Massachusetts, eager to have these Acadian and Maine missions for themselves, persecuted the remaining French Capuchins and sent thirty-two of them to France or, in the case of Bernardin de Crépy, to an English prison. Had this persecution not occurred, the Capuchin presence in Maine would have flourished. A report sent to the Roman Congregation for the Propagation for the Faith in 1656 names twenty-six Capuchins, clerical and lay, who were working in Acadia and Maine. Effectively, however, the Capuchins were driven from what had become a thriving mission of Catholicism because of the Puritan persecution.

The Eighteenth Century

French Capuchins maintained a mission in the Diocese of Quebec, an ecclesiastical jurisdiction that embraced all the vast North American territory possessed by the French. In February 1713 the second bishop of the Diocese of Quebec, Jean Baptiste de la Croix de St. Vallier, received word that a Capuchin, Louis François Duplessis de Mornay, had been appointed his coadjutor. Four years later, de Mornay became vicar general of that part of the diocese called Louisiana. He immediately asked his French Capuchin confreres for help and, in 1720, Capuchins of the province of Champagne arrived to assist in the evangelization of Louisiana. The first Capuchins were Bruno de Langres, who arrived in New Orleans toward the end of 1722, and Philibert de Vianden, who took charge of the district from Chapitoulas, a few miles above the original boundaries of the city, to Pointe Coupée, including Les Allemands, the German Coast, and the intervening concessions. In April 1723 Bruno was replaced as superior of the Capuchin missions in Louisiana by Raphael de Luxembourg who was also vicar general of the bishop of Quebec. Raphael established, in 1725, the first school for boys in New Orleans, but it lasted only for five or six years.

On May 16, 1722, by order of the French government and with the consent of Bishop St. Vallier, the entire jurisdiction was divided among the Capuchins, Jesuits and Carmelites who were working there. The country west of the Mississippi up to the mouth of the Ohio River was entrusted to the Capuchins, the country opposite to the Carmelites, and that to the north, on both sides of the Mississippi, to the Jesuits. That same year, however, the Carmelites withdrew their men, leaving their territory to the Capuchins. Thus the care of the Church on both sides of the Mississippi became their responsibility, working continuously among the French settlers in fifteen different mission stations. A Capuchin, known simply as Jean François, was the Curé of Mobile from 1736 to 1755; three others worked among the Chapitoulas, the Natchitoches, and the Natchez, three Native American tribes situated in the Mississippi River basin, while others worked in New Orleans and the surrounding area. In 1750 a new bishop of Quebec, De Pontbriand, entrusted the jurisdiction of the area to the Jesuits. When the Society of Jesus was suppressed in 1759, however, the Capuchins once again assumed responsibility for the Church, although only nine or ten Capuchins, together with a few priests, cared for this vast territory. A Jesuit, Philiberet Francis Watrin, writing in 1765 described the Capuchin mission in Louisiana as the principal one. At New Orleans, he writes, "which then had about four thousand inhabitants, since the departure of the Jesuits, the two Capuchins are kept very busy."

Due to political developments in America, the success of the Capuchin missions changed. The Treaty of Paris in 1763 was concluded between France and England giving all the territory east of the Mississippi, except for the Isle of Orleans, to the English. Thus the area bounded by the Ohio and Mississippi Rivers and the Great Lakes was added to Britain's domain. A year earlier, on November 3, 1762, King Louis XV had, by the secret treaty of St. Ildefonso, given the Isle of Orleans and all of Louisiana west of the Mississippi to his cousin, Charles III of Spain. Thus New Orleans fell under the jurisdiction of the Spanish and all French inhabitants, including the Capuchins, were urged to depart. With the arrival of three Spanish Capuchins in 1766, the French either returned to France or concentrated their efforts in the north. In 1772, for example, Valentin de Neufchateau was ministering in St. Louis, Missouri, and Hilaire de Genevaux, the first prothonotary apostolic in what is now the United States, became responsible for the Church in Ste. Genevieve. The Capuchin Bernard de Limpach became the first resident pastor of St. Louis in 1776 and remained until 1789. A month before his arrival a palisaded church replaced the log cabin which had been the first church of Saint Louis and the following year a stone rectory was completed. After the transfer of Bernard, settlements on both sides of the Mississippi in upper Louisiana were dependent upon itinerant members of religious orders.

By 1784, however, there were eight Spanish Capuchins caring for the Church of New Orleans. In addition to those in New Orleans, the Capuchins were working in Iberville and Manchac, the present site of Galveston, Texas. The following year Anthony Ildefonsus Moreno y Arze became the pastor of St. Louis Church in New Orleans, a position he held until his death in 1829, with the exception of two years when he was forced to return to Spain because of the opposition of a clique of Spanish civil officials. In 1788 and again in 1793 fires destroyed large portions of the city. Pius VI established the Diocese of Louisiana and the Floridas on April 25, 1793. The vast territory of the original diocese, except for the area under the jurisdiction of the Diocese of Baltimore, stretched from the Rocky Mountains to the Atlantic and from Canada to the Gulf of Mexico. The territory, detached from the see of Havana, was previously part of the older Diocese of Santiago de Cuba, whose jurisdiction of the Louisiana colony had ended in 1762. Before that date, Quebec had spiritual jurisdiction over French colonial Louisiana.

While the French and Spanish Capuchins were laying the foundations of the Church in the Midwest and South, the Eastern seaboard was in the midst of throwing off the yoke of the British government. In 1775 the struggle for American independence began. It was closely monitored by the French who, understandably, favored the Americans. Three years after the revolution's beginning, four French fleets came to the aid of the Americans and with them ninety Catholic chaplains of whom twenty were Capuchins. The fleet of Count DeGrasse had nine Capuchin chaplains, that of DeGuichen seven, those of d'Estaing and de Ternay two each. While many of these friars never served on American soil, four lost their lives during the war, Nicholas, Remy, Onésime, and Barnabé. One of those arriving with the French fleet was an Irish Capuchin Charles Whelan who, after suffering as a prisoner of war, witnessed the surrender of Cornwallis.

In 1784 the law of 1700 forbidding the activity of priests was repealed. The first known priest in the New York area to have taken advantage of this change was Whelan who ministered, somewhat questionably, to the unorganized Irish, Dutch, and French Catholics of the area. In April 1785 John Carroll granted Whelan faculties to administer the sacraments and, in effect, made him the first regularly settled priest in New York City. In that same year, Whelan leased from Trinity Church property on Barclay Street where St. Peter's Church now stands. In June 1785 a group of laymen had themselves incorporated as the "Trustees of the Roman Catholic Church in the City of New York," purchased the Barclay Street property, and in October supervised the laying of the cornerstone of the new church.

Shortly afterwards, another Irish Capuchin arrived, Andrew Nugent. Leaving Dublin under the cloud of an ecclesiastical censure, Nugent was appointed assistant to Whelan, quickly established himself as a flambuoyant orator and developed a large following among the trustees. When in 1786 the trustees, won over by Nugent, demanded that he be appointed pastor, Whelan resigned and went to Pottinger's Creek, Kentucky, from 1787 to 1790. We find the restless friar again in 1790 working in Johnstown, Pennsylvania, and, ten years later, at St. Mary's Church, Wilmington, Delaware, where he died in 1806. Nugent, meanwhile, became pastor of St. Peter's for only one year when the trustees insisted on his removal. Rather than comply with his removal, Nugent established a schismatic congregation and eventually returned to Ireland.

While these events were unfolding in New York, in 1788 two German Capuchins, John Charles and Peter, either brothers whose surname was Helbron or natives of the same town, Helbron, arrived in Philadelphia, Pennsylvania. John Charles became the first "curate" of the newly built church of Holy Trinity, while Peter ministered to the Catholics of Goshenhoppen in Berks County. Two years after his arrival, John Charles returned to Europe on what may have been a fundraising tour for his heavily indebted church. He never returned for he was one of those Capuchins martyred during the French Revolution. His companion, Peter, succeeded him at Holy Trinity, was replaced in 1796 when the church's trustees demanded his removal, and then worked among the German Catholics of Sportsman's Hall (which he changed to Clear Spring) in Westmoreland County, Pennsylvania, and throughout western Pennsylvania until his death in Carlisle in 1816.

Another Capuchin, Lawrence or Sylvester Phelan, ministered to the victims of Philadelphia's yellow fever plague in 1790. Shortly thereafter, he joined Peter Helbron with whom he worked until 1795 when he established a parish in Greensburg, Pennsylvania.

The Nineteenth Century

In the nineteenth century, Capuchins were present in various parts of the eastern states. Sebastian du Rosey, a chaplain in the fleet of De Guichen, remained in or returned to minister in Maryland. His name appears as pastor of St. Mary's in Maryland; he died as pastor of St. Nicholas, Maryland, on December 27, 1813. In 1844 Ambrose Buchmeyer, a Hungarian Capuchin, became pastor of St. Nicholas Church in New York, a ministry he maintained until his death in 1861. Another Capuchin Felician Krebecz, Buchmeyer's assistant, succeeded him until his death in 1876. An Austrian Capuchin, Augustine Dantner, became pastor of New York's St. John the Baptist parish in 1853. Another Austrian Capuchin, Restitutus Tamchina, was rector of St. Augustine's Church in Pittsburgh, Pennsylvania, from 1863–68 and from 1871–74. Fabian Bermadinger of Austria was the first Capuchin to work in Wisconsin as a missionary from 1849 until his death in 1867. Beginning with 1857 and into the 1860s and beyond, nine Capuchins from Holland and Belgium, notably Augustine Spierings and Hippolyt Hoffen, came to work in the Diocese of Green Bay, and, in 1870 a Polish Capuchin, Xaverius Kralczynski, came from Poland and, two years later, ministered in Manitowoc, Wisconsin, and then in Milwaukee. Theobald Matthew, the Irish Apostle of Temperance, preached against the evil of alcohol from 1845 until 1851.

Ignazio Persico, a Capuchin bishop working in India, became the bishop of Savannah, Georgia, in 1890. Two years later, however, he resigned for reasons of health, returned to Italy where he became a member of the Roman Curia and was created a cardinal.

For the most part, the Capuchins who came to the United States during the seventeenth and eighteenth centuries were missionaries, military chaplains, or friars fleeing persecution. The first attempt at establishing a recognized jurisdiction came in 1856 not through a Capuchin initiative but through one of three Swiss diocesan priests who approached the provincial of the Swiss province, Lucius, with their dream of implanting the order in the United States. Shortly after their arrival, John Anthony Frey and Gregory Haas met with Bishop John Martin Henni, the Swiss-born bishop of Milwaukee, who permitted them to establish a foundation at Mt. Calvary, Wisconsin. In 1857, under the direction of two Swiss friars, Frey and Haas entered the order. Within twenty-five years, more fraternities were established in Milwaukee, Appleton, Fond du Lac, and Wauwatosa, Wisconsin, New York City, Fort Lee, New Jersey, and Detroit, Michigan. On August 7, 1882, the Capuchin general minister Aegidius Baldesi established the province of Saint Joseph.

Whereas the establishment of the first American province came from an inspiration born in a peaceful setting, that of the second came from a reaction to Bismark's *Kulturkampf* which banished many religious communities from German territory. Francis Xavier of Ilmuenster, provincial of the Capuchin Bavarian province, assured that Bishop Michael Domenec, bishop of Pittsburgh, would accept some of his friars, sent Hyacinth Epp, Matthew Hau, and Eleutherius Guggenbichler to begin a foundation. In 1873 they began assisting Restitutus Tamchina at St. Augustine's in Pittsburgh. When he retired to a hermitage in Glenfield, Pennsylvania, in the following year, the three assumed responsibility for the church and built a large friary. When the Carmelites decided to withdraw from their ministry in Cumberland, Maryland, in 1875, the Capuchins of the Rhine-Westphalian province, who were also seeking refuge in the United States, accepted it. Throughout these first years, however, the Bavarian friars were concerned with fostering vocations; they opened a "Seraphic School" (minor seminary) at St. Augustine's, and later purchased property in Herman, Pennsylvania, in order to establish a more suitable environment for religious formation.

In 1877 the Rhine-Westphalian Capuchins accepted responsibility for St. Mary's parish in Metamora, Illinois. The following year they founded Sacred Heart parish in Peoria, Illinois, but, since this initiative was rejected by the provincial of the Rhine-Westphalian province, it was entrusted to the friars of the Bavarian province in Pennsylvania. At this same time, Bishop Louis M. Fink of Leavenworth, Kansas, approached the Capuchins in Pittsburgh to minister to the German-Russian Catholics of Ellis County, Kansas. They accepted the invitation and, in 1878, Matthew Hau and Anastasius Joseph Mueller arrived in Herzog, where the young Hau died. His successor, Joseph Calasance Mayershofer, built a church and friary in Victoria. On August 7, 1882, on the same day as the establishment of the St. Joseph's province, the Capuchin general minister Aegidius (Giles) Baldesi founded the province of Saint Augustine.

The Twentieth Century

Since the two provinces were expanding, the general minister, Bernard of Andermatt, came in 1891 for an official visit. His secretary was an English friar, Marianus Fiege, who returned to Europe with a substantial amount of Mass stipends and donations for the support of the English province. The following year, Bernard gave permission for two English friars to travel to the United States to beg for financial aid. In 1893 Rudolph McCarthy and John Mary

Finnigan took advantage of that permission but returned within two years. Marianus Fiege and John Mary Finnigan and, later, Lawrence Blanderfield, and Sebastian Brennan set out for the same reason in 1897. There is evidence of the presence of these friars in Indiana, Wisconsin, Nebraska, Kansas, and, finally, in Mendocino, California. At the invitation of Patrick W. Riordan, archbishop of San Francisco, Marianus accepted responsibility in 1903 for establishing the Church in Mendocino County. He was joined by other English Capuchins who built churches in Fort Bragg, Ukiah, and Elk, known at that time as Greenwood. By 1914 there were six English Capuchins working in California.

As the California mission of the English province was growing, Charles J. O'Reilly, the bishop of the newly established Diocese of Baker City, Oregon, approached the Irish Capuchins for help. In 1910 Thomas Dowling and Luke Sheehan arrived in Oregon and accepted responsibility for "the missions of Bend, Crook County, Oregon . . . Umatilla, Hermiston, Stanfield, Echo, Pilot Rock, and the territory embraced in the blue line marked on Rand-McNally's present map of Oregon." A year later, Alexander Christie, archbishop of Oregon City, invited the friars to accept a mission in Roseburg. Within five years six other Irish Capuchins joined the original pioneers. In 1918, however, Bishop O'Reilly left Baker City to become bishop of Lincoln, Nebraska; he immediately asked the Capuchins to join him, and, in 1919, entrusted Sacred Heart parish in northern Lincoln to them. The following year, the English Capuchins responded to the request of the order to leave California to build up their presence in India. Archbishop Edward Hanna of San Francisco turned to the Irish Capuchins to accept responsibility for Mendocino County, which they did. In 1922 John J. Cantwell, bishop of Monterey and Los Angeles, asked the Irish friars to come to a largely Mexican parish in Watts and, then, to the Old Mission Santa Inés, in Solvang, the nineteenth of the twenty-one missions established by Junipero Serra and the Spanish friars.

As these events were taking place in the West, the Eastern United States was being inundated with immigrants, many of whom were Italians. According to the 1910 census, New York State and, more specifically, New York City became home for most of them. The Capuchins of Our Lady of Sorrows in Lower Manhattan attempted to cope with many of these immigrants and, in 1913, joined John Cardinal Farley in asking the Tuscan province for help. Raymond Tonini and Michael Gori soon came to Our Lady of Sorrows where they ministered to their compatriots until John O'Connor, the bishop of Newark, entrusted Our Lady of Pompei in Paterson to their care. The following year, two more Tuscan Capuchins arrived, enabling the two pioneers to return to their original commitment to the Archdiocese of New York. That same year, its new arch-

bishop, Patrick Hayes, gave them the parish of the Immaculate Conception in the Bronx. As more and more Tuscan friars arrived, the number of their commitments increased so that by 1926 they cared for parishes in Hoboken, Passaic, Hackensack and Orange, all in the Diocese of Newark. In 1922 the Tuscan province voted to raise their American confreres to the status of a commissariate thus encouraging them to sink their roots deep in American soil.

The next thirty years saw the two provinces of St. Augustine and St. Joseph, the Commissariate of the Stigmata, and the missions of the Irish and English friars consolidating and expanding. Capuchins began ministering in Massachusetts, Rhode Island, New York, New Jersey, Pennsylvania, Delaware, Maryland, the District of Columbia, Virginia, West Virginia, Michigan, Indiana, Wisconsin, Missouri, Nebraska, Montana, Oregon, and California. In 1948 a group of Polish friars, former prisoners of the Nazi concentration camps, unable to return to their country because of its Communist regime, sought refuge in the United States and, at the invitation of Bishop Eugene J. McGuinness in 1948, began ministering to their compatriots in Oklahoma. Twenty-two years later, they began a second friary in Oak Ridge, New Jersey. As early as 1930 the province of St. Augustine sent friars to Puerto Rico and in 1937 assumed responsibility of the mission that had originally been established by Castilian friars expelled from Venezuela in 1904. The following year the friars of the St. Joseph province established missions in Bluefields, Nicaragua, and in Guam and the Mariana Islands. In response to a request to provide pastoral care to Italian immigrants, four friars of the New Jersey commissariate established a mission in Australia in 1945.

The daily life of the friars revolved around the Eucharist, the daily celebration of the Liturgy of the Hours, and two periods of mental prayer. Their ministries, however, were diverse. The preaching apostolate was strongly emphasized in conducting retreats, parish missions, and the observance of Forty Hours. A large number of friars were involved in formation programs which embraced high school seminaries, novitiates, and programs in philosophical and theological formation. Still others were involved in parochial ministries, especially to immigrants such as Italians, Hispanics, Asians, and Russians, and to the poor. As early as 1924 the Negro Mission of St. Benedict in Milwaukee, Wisconsin, was established by Stephen Eckert. Two years later the Cheyenne Indian Mission of Montana was inaugurated.

The success of these endeavors became evident in 1950 when the provincial administration of the St. Joseph's province discussed expanding its seminary facilities in Marathon, Wisconsin, and Garrison, New York. The occasion prompted more serious discussion of the advantages of dividing what had become a large geographical jurisdiction. On February 2, 1952, the province of St.

Mary was established embracing the states of New York and New England and the mission territories of the Mariana and Ryukyu Islands. The establishment of this new province affected the English Capuchin friars in Massachusetts and Rhode Island, who now fell under the jurisdiction of the new American provincial. Within five years new foundations were established in Interlaken and Fultonville, New York, Middletown, Connecticut, Springfield, Massachusetts, and Hudson, New Hampshire.

As early as 1925 the friars of the Basque province of Navarre-Cantabria-Aragon planned on sending friars to the Southwest to minister to the ever-growing needs of the Hispanic population. The plan did not materialize until 1954 when Bienvenido de Arbeiza became pastor of Our Lady of Lourdes Church in Dallas, Texas. In 1961 the friars expanded their ministries in Texas by moving to Fort Worth and, later, to Premont and to San Antonio. Due to the situation of the Church in Cuba, the Spanish province of Castile, to which the Cuban mission was entrusted, established a friary in 1962 in New Orleans, Louisiana.

During the 1960s all the Capuchin jurisdictions grew in number, foundations, and missions. The St. Augustine province opened new houses in Ohio, Missouri, and Colorado and expanded the mission in Papua, New Guinea, which they had established in 1955. The Stigmata custody, meanwhile, expanded in Delaware and Virginia, sent friars to Australia, and, in 1964, accepted responsibility for a mission in Zambia.

More attention was given in the 1970s to the growth of all of these jurisdictions. As a result the mission of Puerto Rico entrusted to the St. Augustine province became a vice province in 1970. The custody established by the Tuscan friars became a province in 1973, that of the Irish in 1979. In 1977 the province of St. Augustine was dissolved and two new provinces were established: the one keeping the name of the Pennsylvania province of St. Augustine, the other given the new name of the Mid-American province of St. Conrad. The mission of the Mariana Islands and Guam was expanded to include the Hawaiian Islands and, in 1982, established as a vice province. Seven years later the friars in Dallas, Texas, established the vice province of Texas. The mission of Papua, New Guinea, the responsibility of the Pennsylvania and Mid-American provinces, became a vice province in 1992.

Bittle, Celestine. *A Romance of Lady Poverty*. Milwaukee: Bruce, 1933.

Lenhart, John. "The Capuchin Prefecture of New England (1630–1656)." *Franciscan Studies* 24 (1943) 21–46.

Miller, Norbert. "Capuchins in New York, Pennsylvania, Kentucky, St. Louis, and Parts of Baltimore: Pioneer Capuchin Missions in the U.S." *Franciscan Studies* 10 (1932) 170–234.

Roemer, Theodore. "Pioneer Capuchin Letters." *Franciscan Studies* 16 (1938) 4–156.

Vogel, Clause. "Capuchins in French Louisiana (1722–1766)." *Franciscan Studies* 8 (1928) 1–95.

REGIS J. ARMSTRONG, O.F.M. CAP.

FRANCISCANS (CONVENTUAL)

Beginnings

Individual Conventuals were in the West Indies since the days of Columbus. They did not, however, influence the first organized group, which came from Bavaria in 1852, and ultimately became the province of the Immaculate Conception in 1872. The founding fathers were invited by Bishop Jean Marie Odin of Galveston, Texas. The friars were Bonaventure Keller (superior), Leopold Moczygemba, Dominic Mesens (a Belgian), Anton Mueller, and Br. Giles Austin. Their special ministry at this time was the care of German and Polish immigrants. The friars were given four parishes: Castroville, Fredericksburg, New Braunfels, and D'Hanis. Connected with these parishes were twelve missions, extending westward to California and south to Mexico. Finances were at a low ebb. The annual income at New Braunfels amounted to $250, Castroville $300, and often $250, depending on the agricultural yield. Financial aid was given by Ludwigsmission Verein. In 1854 three more missionaries arrived and three additional missions were placed in their care.

Keller left Texas in 1854. He went east to Brooklyn, New York, then to Philadelphia, Pennsylvania, where he exercised his ministry at the parish of St. Alphonsus, assigned to the friars by Bishop John Nepomucene Neumann. Fr. Moczygemba took charge of Castroville and later extended his ministry to Panna Maria where there was a new Polish settlement.

In 1858 the American mission was made a commissariate and dedicated to the Immaculate Conception. Fr. Moczygemba was appointed first commissary general. Bishop John McCloskey, first bishop of Albany, invited Moczygemba to send friars to Syracuse to care for German Catholics. Since the Conventual Friars in the U.S.A. did not have sufficient personnel for both the Texas and the eastern missions, it was decided to transfer activity to the East. The provincial house was established in Syracuse, New York, in 1859 at the parish of the Assumption. From 1859 to 1872 missions were opened at Manlius (now Minoa), Oswego, Rome, Gloversville, Colosse, Little France, Johnstown, Bleecker, and Troy, New York. In 1867 Our Lady of Angels parish in Albany was entrusted to the Conventuals.

Organization

At the 1866 general chapter in Rome, Fr. Fidelis Dehm was appointed successor to Fr. Moczygemba. The Conventuals, meanwhile, acquired parishes in the Middle West:

St. Peter's (1860) and St. Anthony's (1868) in Louisville, Kentucky; St. Anthony's (1874) in Jeffersonville, Indiana; and St. Joseph's and St. Benedict's (1872) in Terra Haute, Indiana. During these years, friars were given charge of two parishes in Hoboken, New Jersey: St. Joseph and St. Francis. The Conventuals had welcomed Polish immigrants as early as 1852 at Panna Maria in Texas. They continued in this mission, first at St. Stanislaus Church in Trenton, New Jersey, and later throughout New England and the Middle West. This mission flourished. In 1906 the Polish foundations were united into the province of St. Anthony of Padua. In 1964 this province had more than two hundred priests and twenty-one lay brothers in thirty-six parishes. The province also had three seminaries: one at Granby, Massachusetts, for college and theological students; a preparatory seminary at Athol Springs, New York; and a novitiate at Ellicott City, Maryland. The friars had charge of foreign missions in the Ryukyu Islands in the Pacific and helped toward the support of the order's missions in Japan. They had three high schools in the dioceses of Buffalo, New York, as well as a Negro mission in Bessemer, Alabama.

In 1926 a new province was formed from the Immaculate Conception province and dedicated to Our Lady of Consolation. It embraced the territory west of the state of Ohio. The province opened a minor seminary at Mt. St. Francis, Indiana; a novitiate at Auburn, Indiana; a college seminary at Carey, Ohio; and a theological seminary at Clarke, Minnesota. Its priests partially staffed Bellarmine College in Louisville, Kentucky, and Central Catholic High School in Toledo, Ohio. The friars maintained, too, Our Lady of Consolation shrine at Carey, Ohio, and assisted at foreign missions in the Diocese of Ndola in Northern Rhodesia. Rupert Hillerich, a member of this province, was appointed the first prefect apostolic. In 1964 the province numbered approximately 140 priests and 30 brothers.

On July 29, 1939, the province of St. Bonaventure was formed from the province of St. Anthony. The new province took charge of all Polish parishes of the order in the Middle and Far West and opened a preparatory seminary at Crystal Lake, Illinois, and a novitiate at Lake Forest, Illinois. Its friars staffed a diocesan high school at Torrance, California, and the Minor Basilica of St. Josaphat in Milwaukee, Wisconsin. A special training school for lay brothers was founded at Kenosha, Wisconsin. The province counted about 90 priests and more than forty brothers in 1964.

Statistics

The following paragraphs represent the statistics of the Conventuals in the U.S.A. in 1994.

In 1994 the province of the Immaculate Conception had 230 solemnly professed friars, 200 priests, and 30 brothers, exercising the ministry in 40 parishes, Bl. Kateri Tekakwitha Shrine, Fonda, New York, and other min-

isterial endeavors such as theological professors, social services, college and high school teachers, retreats, preaching, missionaries, chaplaincies, and other specialized ministries. Included in this figure are friars serving in Rome and the custodies of Brazil, Costa Rica, and Canada. From the friars in Brazil, the Holy See has chosen a Conventual to serve as the bishop of the Diocese of Valenca, Bishop Elias Manning, O.F.M. Conv. Since 1991 the provincialate has been located at St. Anthony on the Hudson in Rensselaer, New York.

In 1994 St. Anthony of Padua province had friaries and parishes in the Archdioceses of Baltimore, Boston, Atlanta, Hartford, Los Angeles, and New York. The province also serves the Dioceses of Buffalo, Rochester, Birmingham, (Alabama), Bridgeport, Brooklyn, Springfield (Massachusetts), Cleveland, Paterson, Ogdensburg, Harrisburg, Johnstown, Fall River, Palm Beach, Trenton, Norwich, Portland (Maine), and Erie. The province also had friaries in Japan, Peru, and the Philippines. There were 197 priests and 27 brothers in the province.

The province of Our Lady of Consolation had friaries and parishes in Bloomington, Minnesota; Carey, Ohio; Carlsbad, New Mexico; Clarkesville, Indiana; El Paso, Texas; Grand Rapids, Michigan; Indianapolis, Indiana; Jessup, Georgia; Lansing, Michigan; Lorain, Ohio; Louisville, Kentucky; Misilla Park, New Mexico; Mt. St. Francis, Indiana; Pleasure Ridge Park, Kentucky; Prior Lake, New Mexico; San Antonio, Texas; St. Louis, Missouri; Terre Haute, Indiana; Washington, D.C.; and Waupun, Wisconsin. The province also had custodies in Kitwe, Zambia, Comayaguola, Honduras, as well as the San Antonio de Padua Formation Friary in Santa, El Salvador, and the Nuestra Señora de Guadalupe Formation Friary in Heredia, Costa Rica.

In 1994 the province of St. Bonaventure had 65 priests and 22 brothers. It had friaries in the Archdioceses of Detroit and Milwaukee, the dioceses of Peoria and Rockford, the Archdiocese of Acapulco, Mexico, and the Archdiocese of San Jose, Costa Rica.

September 18, 1981, the custody of St. Joseph Cupertino of St. Bonaventure province was recognized as a province at the Extraordinary Chapter of the Order in Assisi. One of the reasons given was that the distance between California and the Midwest warranted such a change. The new province presently has thirty-six priests and eleven brothers. The friars are involved in parish ministry, foreign missions, and education.

Hess, Roger, O.F.M. Conv. *History of the Province of St. Anthony of the Order of Friars Minor Conventual.* Massachusetts, 1984.

Smith, Jeremiah, O.F.M. Conv. *History of the Conventual Franciscans in the United States.* Union City, N.J., 1988.

JEREMIAH SMITH, O.F.M. CONV.

FRANCISCANS (THIRD ORDER REGULAR— T.O.R.)

Beginnings: The Irish Brothers

The Third Order Regular Franciscans in the United States originated with a group of Irish Brothers of St. Francis who arrived in Loretto, Pennsylvania, in 1846. These brothers took charge of a primary school founded in 1832 by Fr. Demetrius Gallitzin, the first Catholic priest to receive all his orders in this country. Gallitzin had hoped that Loretto would become a center of Catholic activity in Pennsylvania, but he died in 1840 and the brothers resumed the work of the school in 1847. This school eventually became St. Francis Academy, and was chartered as St. Francis College in 1858, functioning as an elementary school, high school, and after 1863, a college offering bachelor's degrees. The brothers were also active in schools, farms, and orphanages in what was then the Diocese of Pittsburgh at various times, and for a time staffed a school at Germantown, now part of Philadelphia.

Another group of Irish brothers came to Brooklyn, New York, in 1858. Some of these went westward in 1879 to staff a government school for Native Americans at Clontarf, Minnesota. Federal support for the school was withdrawn in 1894, and the brothers moved on to Spalding, Nebraska, a settlement established to bring Irish immigrants out of urban tenements and establish them in a farming community. The brothers began a high school and college at Spalding. Although originally from the same Irish community of Franciscan brothers, the Loretto and Spalding groups were separate in the United States. Eventually, however, they would come together to from the nucleus of the Third Order Regular in the United States.

The Third Order Regular

Beginning around 1900, efforts were being made in both Europe and America to unite various communities of Third Order brothers to the clerical community of the Third Order Regular, which had nearly become extinct in the nineteenth century. The Brooklyn brothers, led by their minister general, Br. Linus Lynch, approved a union in 1906, but were opposed by the bishop of Brooklyn, and later in 1906 they elected new leaders who opposed the union. Spalding, however, approved the union, and one-third of the Brooklyn community, led by Lynch, went to Spalding to be part of the union in 1907. Loretto joined in 1908, and in 1910 the first American province, the province of the Most Sacred Heart of Jesus, was erected. A seminary was started in Loretto in 1912 under the guidance of Fr. John P. M. Doyle, a former Brooklyn diocesan priest who had known the Brooklyn brothers well and had joined the new province in 1911.

Division of the Province

Although the primary work of the friars continued to be in the schools at Loretto and Spalding, parishes in the newly formed diocese of Altoona-Johnstown were served also, mainly by priests from the Italian province who had come to help establish the new American province. The provincial chapter of 1918 had disputed results, mainly because of questions about the role in the chapter of the Italian friars who were still attached to their province in Italy. On the calling of a new chapter in 1919, it was agreed to divide the province. The new province of the Immaculate Conception was formed as a commissariate in 1920 and raised to a province in 1925.

The Two American Provinces

The friars of Sacred Heart province remained largely based in western Pennsylvania until the 1930s, when they began to expand into parishes in the Dakotas and North Carolina, and later into missionary activity in Bihar state in India. In 1942 a fire in Loretto destroyed most of St. Francis College, including the seminary and high school. The college was rebuilt, mainly in the 1950s; the seminary moved to new property and the high school moved to Spring Grove, Pennsylvania. In 1946 the College of Steubenville, later Franciscan University of Steubenville, began. In the 1950s there were once again friars in Philadelphia as the friars taught in high schools in the archdiocese. Parishes in Florida were staffed in the 1970s, and in Texas in the 1980s. Missionary work in the Amazon Basin of Brazil began in 1962. By 1995 the 160 friars of Sacred Heart province were represented in Pennsylvania, Virginia, Florida, Texas, South Dakota, Ohio, West Virginia, and the District of Columbia.

The friars of Immaculate Conception province remained in parishes, at first in Pennsylvania but after 1950 also in West Virginia, Minnesota, and Oregon. Also in the 1950s, mission work began in Paraguay. By 1995 the seventy friars of Immaculate Conception province were represented in Pennsylvania, Florida, Ohio, West Virginia, Minnesota, and the District of Columbia.

European Provinces Active in the United States

Other European provinces of the order sent friars to serve the needs of immigrant groups in the United States. The province of St. Jerome in Croatia has served in ethnic Croatian parishes in the Diocese of Pittsburgh since 1925. The province of the Immaculate Conception in Spain has served in Spanish-speaking parishes in Texas since the 1920s. In the 1940s, these Spanish friars were the first to introduce the Cursillo movement to the United States.

Conley, Seraphin, T.O.R. *Third Order Regular of Saint Francis of Penance Resource Manual.* Rome: Convento dei Ss. Cosma e Damiano, 1994.

Doyle, John P. M., T.O.R. "History of the Third Order Regular of Saint Francis of Penance." Loretto, Pa.: Unpublished typescript, 1947.

MICHAEL TRIPKA, T.O.R.

FRANCISCAN SISTERS IN AMERICA

Sisters of the Third Order Regular of St. Francis began their participation in the Church's mission in the United States in the mid-nineteenth century. It was during this century that more and more active communities of Third Order Regular Franciscan women in Europe began to emerge from cloistered foundations or were newly founded to serve the poor, the ill, and the uneducated. These beginnings paralleled the political, religious, and social movements in Europe which caused widespread emigration to the United States. Franciscan women's religious communities developed a form of religious life in the United States adapted to frontier life in burgeoning cities and rural areas where they had been called by bishops and pastors to serve emigrants from their homeland.

These Franciscan women carried into the new world the mission given St. Francis by Christ, "to observe the Holy Gospel of our Lord Jesus Christ living in obedience, in poverty and in chastity" *(Rule).* For Francis this "evangelical" life flowed not from a common place or service to the Church and the world, but rather from a common heart, "a prophetic witness to Christ and the whole of his gospel" *(Response to the Lineamenta).* The spirituality of the Franciscan, therefore, is generated not from the needs of the world or canonical definition, but from a primary experience of the Spirit.

Third Order women religious find their basic spirituality expressed in *The Rule and Life of the Brothers and Sisters of the Third Order Regular of St. Francis,* approved by Pope John Paul II in 1982. International collaboration in study, dialogue, and a search for unity brought about this new formulation of the way of life for the Third Order. It states their charism: "The brothers and sisters of this Order are to persevere in true faith and penance. They wish to live this evangelical conversion of life in a spirit of prayer, of poverty, and of humility" (no. 2).

The Franciscan way of life expresses the values of *poverty* —detachment from earthly goods, reverence for all of God's creation, and reliance on God's loving providence; *penance*—biblical *metanoia,* that is, continuous conversion manifested in works of mercy and charity; *minority*— *minores,* servants of the Word witnessing love and compassion for others; and *contemplation*—"Within themselves, let them always make a dwelling place and home for the Lord God Almighty, Father, Son and Holy Spirit so that, with undivided hearts, they may increase in universal love by continually turning to God and to neighbor . . . and celebrate the Father's love for the world" *(Rule and Life,* nos. 8 and 9). Third Order women religious find in St. Clare of Assisi a model who not only epitomized these values in her own life, but also elaborated them in her *Rule* for Second Order Franciscans (Poor Clares), which she cofounded with St. Francis, as well as in her *Letters* to St. Agnes of Prague.

At the time Third Order sisters came to the United States, however, the Counter-Reformation Church and the demands of the frontier, as well as the constitutional and jurisdictional interpretations of the time, profoundly affected their spirituality. Recent research into the increasingly accessible Franciscan sources has brought about a deeper understanding and enlightened interpretation of the Franciscan vocation in a society experiencing throes of change similar to the days of Francis.

Of the seventy-seven women's Third Order Regular Franciscan communities listed in *The Official Catholic Directory* (1994), thirty-nine originated in the United States, although their founders may have emigrated from a European country. Of these, one is a recent reunification of two communities and one, the amalgamation of two unrelated Franciscan communities. The other thirty-eight were founded by religious congregations from fifteen countries. Most of these are provinces or some kind of subdivision of a motherhouse located outside the United States. The origins of these communities are:

Germany	11	Colombia	1
Italy	5	India	1
Austria	4	France	1
Poland	3	Brazil	1
Switzerland	3	Hungary	1
Mexico	2	Portugal	1
England	2	Spain	1
Holland	1		

The larger numbers from Germany, Italy, and Austria reflect the fact that historically, both the Regular and Secular Third Orders of St. Francis spread rapidly throughout Europe, especially in these three countries, not only during the middle and later decades of the nineteenth century, but as early as the thirteenth century with the Beguines. Eight of the communities founded by congregations with motherhouses outside the United States have become independent of their founding communities. Several with motherhouses abroad have two or more provinces.

Beginnings—Original Foundations in the United States

Of the first fourteen Third Order Regular communities of women in the United States, nine originated in this country. The first, a group of secular Franciscan Tertiaries— six women and an equal number of men, led by their pastor and his assistant—emigrated from the village of Ettenbeuren, Bavaria, to the Diocese of Milwaukee, Wisconsin, where they were received by Bishop Martin Henni, May 28, 1849. The women, led by Ottilie Dirr Zahler (Mother Aemiliana), succeeded in founding the Sisters of the Third Order of St. Francis the Seraphic. The sisters taught in the parishes of the two priests, cared for orphans, and in 1856 accepted the domestic duties at the new St. Francis de Sales Seminary in Milwaukee.

After severe trials, including the departure of the six founders, the sisters relocated the motherhouse to Jefferson, Wisconsin, in 1864. At the invitation of Michael Heiss, bishop of the newly formed Diocese of La Crosse, Wisconsin, and former spiritual director of the community, the sisters moved the motherhouse to that city in 1871. In 1873 the sisters at the seminary, with the assurance of Bishop Henni that their vows would remain intact, formed themselves into an independent community. Thirty of the 120 sisters chose this alternative and became the Sisters of St. Francis of Penance and Christian Charity; more recently entitled the Sisters of St. Francis of Assisi, Milwaukee. Having established perpetual adoration of the Blessed Sacrament in 1878, the La Crosse sisters assumed the title of Congregation of the Sisters of the Third Order of St. Francis of Perpetual Adoration. In 1973 a group of sisters separated from the La Crosse congregation to become the Institute of the Franciscan Sisters of the Eucharist with their motherhouse in Meriden, Connecticut.

The second foundation of Franciscan Third Order women occurred in 1851 when a pastor in Oldenburg, Indiana, requested the assistance of sisters from a Franciscan community in Vienna. Sr. Teresa Hackelmeier responded and with three young women from the area founded the Franciscan Sisters of Oldenburg.

In 1855, encouraged by their bishop, St. John Neumann, three women under the leadership of Anna Maria (Mother Mary Francis) Bachmann, who had come from Bavaria in 1840, founded the Sisters of St. Francis of Philadelphia. This community became the source for three more foundations: Sisters of the Third Franciscan Order, Syracuse, New York, 1860, the Sisters of St. Francis of the Third Order Regular of Buffalo, Williamsville, New York, 1863; and the Sisters of St. Francis of Millvale, Pittsburgh, Pennsylvania, 1871. Subsequently, sisters from Buffalo who were ministering in the metropolitan area of New York formed the Sisters of St. Francis of the Mission of the Immaculate Virgin (Hastings-on-Hudson), 1893. Extending the family tree once more, the Millvale Franciscans assisted in the founding of the Sisters of St. Francis of the Providence of God in 1922 for the purpose of evangelizing Lithuanian immigrants.

In 1855, at the invitation of Bishop John Timon of the newly formed Diocese of Buffalo, New York, the Rev. Panfilo Magliano, O.F.M., brought a small band of friars and brothers from Rome. After founding St. Bonaventure University and Seminary, Magliano invited three women to form the Franciscan Sisters of Allegany, New York, in 1859, for the purpose of educating children in that area.

This same Franciscan encouraged Mother Mary Alfred Moes to found the Congregation of the Third Order of St. Francis of Mary Immaculate in Joliet, Illinois, in 1865. Later, in 1877, Mother Alfred became the founder of the Sisters of the Third Order Regular of St. Francis of the Con-

gregation of Our Lady of Lourdes in Rochester, Minnesota. And in 1916, sisters from this congregation missioned in Sylvania, Ohio, became independent of the Rochester group at the request of Joseph Schrembs, bishop of Toledo.

The Franciscans of Clinton, Iowa, trace their origins to a need in Gethsemani, Kentucky, for women religious to staff a school. In 1866 the bishop sent five candidates to the novitiate of the Franciscan Sisters in Oldenburg. They returned to Kentucky and in 1869, at the invitation of John Hennessy, bishop of Dubuque, established their motherhouse in Clinton, Iowa.

Nine more original foundations occurred between 1869 and 1910. These include the Sisters of St. Francis of Penance and of Charity, Tiffin, Ohio, and the Franciscan Sisters of Christian Charity in Manitowoc, Wisconsin, 1869; in 1874 the Sisters of St. Francis of the Holy Cross, Bay Settlement, Wisconsin; and in 1890 the Sisters of St. Francis of the Immaculate Conception, Peoria, Illinois.

Elizabeth Hayes (Sr. Mary Ignatius), a convert from Anglicanism in England, came to the United States in 1873 as a missionary and founded the Franciscan Missionary Sisters of the Immaculate Conception in Belle Prairie, Minnesota. Having opened houses in various states, she established a motherhouse in Rome in 1881 and located the United States provincial house in Newton, Massachusetts. The Franciscan Sisters of Little Falls, Minnesota, became independent of the Franciscan Missionary Sisters in 1891. Sisters from Little Falls missioned in Rock Island, Illinois, in 1893, became independent in 1901, forming the Franciscan Sisters of Rock Island, Illinois. In 1988 this community amalgamated with the Sisters of the Third Order of St. Francis of East Peoria.

Eleven Franco-American women founded the Little Franciscans of Mary in Worcester, Massachusetts, in 1889. Unable to survive there, they went to the Archdiocese of Quebec, Canada, where they received canonical approval in 1892, maintaining regional headquarters, however, in Worcester.

The Franciscan Sisters of the Atonement were founded as an Episcopalian community at Garrison, New York, by Mary Francis White (Mother Lurana) with the Rev. Paul James Francis Wattson, who also founded the Friars of the Atonement. The two communities were corporately received into the Catholic Church in 1909 and affiliated with the Franciscan Order in 1921.

Foundations by European Congregations, 1858–1961

Ten congregations with motherhouses in Europe established foundations to extend their apostolates of health care and education among the immigrants. The Franciscan Sisters of the Poor, Aachen, Germany, the first of these, through the efforts of Sarah Peter, convert and laywoman, arrived in Cincinnati, Ohio, in 1858. There they served the poor especially in health care, becoming recognized for their services during the Civil War. The congregation in 1959 divided into two branches, German and American. The congregational office of the latter is located in Brooklyn, New York.

The second congregation to establish a province in the United States was the Franciscan Missionary Sisters of the Sacred Heart, F.M.S.C. At the request of the First Order Franciscans in New York City, these sisters came from Italy in 1867 and established their province in Peekskill, New York. In 1986 a group of sisters separated from this province and became the Franciscan Sisters of Peace in Haverstraw, New York.

Holland was the country of origin of the Franciscan Sisters of Penance and Christian Charity who began their work in Buffalo, New York, in 1874. This foundation grew into three provinces: Stella Niagara, New York, in 1928; Denver, Colorado, and Redwood City, California, in 1939.

The Sisters of the Sorrowful Mother of the Third Order of St. Francis of Assisi, founded in Rome by Mother Frances Streitel, a native of Germany, came to Wichita, Kansas, in 1889. Milwaukee, Wisconsin, however, became their provincial site in the United States until recent reorganization changed it to Broken Arrow, Oklahoma.

The Sisters of St. Francis of the Holy Eucharist, Independence, Missouri (originally, Franciscan Sisters of Perpetual Adoration), trace their roots to a Franciscan convent of Grimmenstein, Switzerland (1378). In 1892 five sisters emigrated to the United States to settle in Nevada, Missouri. In 1900 they became an independent community and relinquished perpetual adoration to engage in active ministries. Also founded in Switzerland, the Sisters of Mercy of the Holy Cross established a province in Merrill, Wisconsin, in 1912.

The Franciscan Missionaries of Our Lady emigrated from Calais, France, to Monroe, Lousiana, in 1913. Primarily ministering in health care they later established their provincial house in Baton Rouge.

From Naples, Italy, the Franciscan Sisters of St. Elizabeth arrived in Newark, New Jersey, in 1919 to carry out their ministry primarily in Montessori, early childhood, and elementary education. Their Delegate House is in Parsippany, New Jersey. In 1961 two more congregations from Italy made foundations: the Franciscan Missionary Sisters of Assisi in Holyoke, Massachusetts, and the Franciscan Missionary Sisters of the Infant Jesus, Cherry Hill, New Jersey.

Influence of Bismarck's Kulturkampf

The Catholic Church in the United States benefited when Bismarck's *Kulturkampf* in Germany threatened the very existence of a number of women's Third Order congregations. One of the first such foundations was the Fran-

ciscan Sisters, Daughters of the Sacred Hearts of Jesus and Mary, who at the request of the Rev. E. A. Schindel of St. Louis, Missouri, sent three sisters in 1872. The province grew and in 1947 relocated to Wheaton, Illinois.

Also in 1872, Mother Mary Odelia Berger emigrated to St. Louis. Welcomed by the pastor and people of St. Mary's parish, Mother Odelia named her newly founded community the Sisters of St. Mary of the Third Order of St. Francis. In 1894 seven members of the Sisters of St. Mary founded the Franciscan Sisters of Maryville, Missouri. These two communities reunited in 1986 under the title of Franciscan Sisters of Mary.

In 1874 Mothers Alexia Hoell and Alfons Schmid with Sr. Clara Seiter emigrated to the United States and founded the School Sisters of St. Francis in Campbellsport, Wisconsin. Milwaukee became the site of the motherhouse after a two-year period in Winona, Minnesota. This congregation also has a province in the United States, one in Germany, one in Central America, and a region in India.

The Sisters of St. Francis of the Holy Family migrated as an entire community in 1875 and the Franciscan Sisters of the Sacred Heart in 1876. The former was a young community from Herford. Facing the threat of suppression, the twenty-nine sisters having been invited by a pastor in Iowa City, Iowa, migrated to that city. In 1878 they established their motherhouse in Dubuque at the invitation of Bishop John Hennessy. Also in 1878 at the urging of John Lancaster Spalding, bishop of Peoria, Illinois, some of these sisters who had started a hospital in Peoria separated themselves from the Dubuque motherhouse to form the Sisters of the Third Order of St. Francis. It is with this community that the Sisters of Rock Island amalgamated in 1988.

The mother general of the Franciscan Sisters of the Sacred Heart with three sisters came from Baden at the invitation of a German priest and settled in Avilla, Indiana. Later that same year twenty-three more sisters joined them and they became independent of their ties to Germany. They later moved their motherhouse to Joliet and in 1964 to Mokena (Frankfort), Illinois.

From Westphalia, twenty Hospital Sisters of the Third Order of St. Francis traveled to Alton, Illinois, in 1875, dedicating themselves to health care. In 1926 they established a provincialate in Springfield, Illinois.

Also from Westphalia, the Sisters of St. Francis of Perpetual Adoration accepted the invitation of Joseph Dwenger, bishop of Fort Wayne, Indiana, to establish a foundation in his diocese. In 1875 six sisters arrived in Lafayette, Indiana. There are now two provinces located in Mishawaka, Indiana, and Colorado Springs, Colorado.

In 1875 seventeen sisters of the Congregation of the Poor Sisters of St. Francis arrived in Milwaukee, and after being received by Bishop Henni, proceeded to the motherhouse of the Manitowoc Franciscans. The remaining ten sisters of the community arrived from Germany in 1876, and the two communities merged under the title of the United States foundation, The Franciscan Sisters of Christian Charity (1869).

Foundations to Serve the Polish

A growing population of Polish immigrants into the United States attracted the ministrations of the Congregation of St. Felix of Cantalice of the Third Order of St. Francis (Felicians) as early as 1874. Five Felician Sisters arrived in Polonia, Wisconsin, in response to the persistent requests of Joseph Dabrowski, the pastor. In 1876 the foundation became a province. It was moved to Detroit (Livonia, Michigan) in 1882, and from 1900 to 1953 six more provinces were formed—in Buffalo, New York; Chicago, Illinois; Lodi, New Jersey; Coraopolis, Pennsylvania; Enfield, Connecticut; and Rio Rancho, New Mexico.

Another congregation in Poland, the Bernardine Sisters of the Third Order of St. Francis, a contemplative congregation, sent four sisters to Mt. Carmel, Pennsylvania, in 1894 to staff the parish school at the request of the pastor. They were dispensed from the cloister and during the first year transferred to Reading where they established their motherhouse. The community grew and divided into four provinces: Reading, Stamford, Connecticut; Farmington, Michigan; and Porto Alegre, Brazil.

Two congregations indigenous to the United States were founded in the late 1890s to serve Polish immigrants. The first of these originated in 1894 in Chicago and is now known as the Franciscan Sisters of Chicago. The second was founded in 1897 after a German-speaking community from Upper Silesia withdrew their sisters from the Polish parish of St. Stanislaus Kostka in Pittsburgh, Pennsylvania, except one, Sr. Colette Hilbert, a Pole. She, with four American-born Polish novices, moved to Trenton, New Jersey. There, with the help of the provincial of the Friars Minor Conventual of Syracuse, New York, the Very Rev. Hyacinth Fudzinski, they founded the Franciscan Sisters of St. Joseph who established their motherhouse in Buffalo, relocating it in 1928 to Hamburg, New York.

At the turn of the century a group of sisters of Polish extraction separated from the School Sisters of St. Francis (Milwaukee) and founded the Sisters of St. Joseph of the Third Order of St. Francis, Stevens Point, Wisconsin. As their work expanded in schools and hospitals in other states, they transferred their motherhouse in 1936 to South Bend, Indiana, and formed three provinces—Stevens Point, Bartlett, Illinois, and Garfield, Ohio.

Also in 1901 a community stemmed from the Joliet Franciscans when three of their members founded the Franciscan Sisters of Our Lady of Perpetual Help in St. Louis, Missouri, to work among the Polish immigrants in the Mississippi-Missouri valley.

The last group to come from Poland were the Servants of the Most Sacred Heart of Jesus from Cracow, who in 1959 founded a province in Cresson, Pennsylvania.

Foundations to Work among the African Americans

Although many of the Third Order Regular Franciscan women worked among the blacks, both in the South and inner cities of the United States, two congregations were founded specifically for this purpose. The Franciscan Sisters of Baltimore came to the United States from England, where their founder with other members of their Anglican community had entered the Roman Catholic Church in 1868. At the request of Cardinal Gibbons, archbishop of Baltimore, four sisters came from the motherhouse at Mill Hill, London, to Baltimore in 1881 and opened an orphanage for blacks. With the Mill Hill priests they continued ministering among the blacks. In 1958 the congregation transferred the motherhouse from Mill Hill to Baltimore, and the sisters now carry out an integrated ministry. Missionary outreach to Africa resulted in the formation of the Franciscan Missionary Sisters for Africa in 1927. They established their motherhouse in County Louth, Ireland, and have a foundation in Brighton, Massachusetts.

Approximately thirty-five years after the founding of the Franciscan Sisters of Baltimore, Mother Mary Theodore and Rev. Ignatius Lissner, S.M.A., founded the Franciscan Handmaids of the Most Pure Heart of Mary in Savannah, Georgia, to provide a "Community of Colored Sisters for Colored people." The invitation of Cardinal Patrick Hayes to staff a nursery prompted the community to send sisters to New York City in 1923 and eventually establish a motherhouse there. Societal changes have also affected this community of sisters who, without abandoning their original purpose, have opened their membership and services to all people.

School Sisters from Austria

A number of Franciscan congregations with the title of School Sisters of St. Francis trace their beginnings to a congregation founded in 1843 by a group of Secular Third Order Franciscans in Graz, Austria. The first of these to come to the United States are the Sisters of St. Francis of Christ the King. Having become an independent congregation in 1869, they established their motherhouse in Rome, and in 1909 sent sisters to the United States to work among the Slovenian and Croatian immigrants in Kansas City, Kansas. In 1926 they established their Province House in Lemont, Illinois.

A second community of School Sisters of the Third Order Regular of St. Francis also became independent of the Graz congregation when they established themselves in Czechoslovakia. In 1913 six sisters emigrated to Pittsburgh, Pennsylvania, where they established their provincialate. In 1957 another province was founded in Bethlehem, Pennsylvania.

The Sisters of St. Francis of Savannah, Missouri, also stem from an Austrian foundation of Franciscan School Sisters whose founder and first members derived their Franciscan spirituality from the Sisters at Graz. The first sisters came in 1922, opened a novitiate in Conception, Missouri, and in 1957 established their provincialate in Savannah, Missouri.

Also from Austria, but located in Vienna, the School Sisters of the Third Order of St. Francis of Panhandle, Texas, came to the United States in 1931. They located first in Bordentown, New Jersey, then in Youngstown, Ohio, before settling in Panhandle.

Sisters from Germany, 1910–30

The Sisters of St. Francis of the Immaculate Heart of Mary, whose motherhouse is now in Rome, originated in the Bavarian village of Dillingen in 1241 stemming from a group of Beguines, medieval penitents. These sisters first came to the United States in 1913 and opened a house at Collegeville, Minnesota. In 1928 they established a provincial motherhouse in Hankinson, North Dakota.

During the 1920s four Franciscan communities from Germany established foundations in the United States, the last from that country to do so in the twentieth century. Each of these engaged in some kind of health care and/or social services. In 1923 the Sisters of St. Francis of the Martyr St. George established a province in Alton, Illinois, and the Franciscan Sisters of the Blessed Virgin Mary of the Holy Angels in St. Paul, Minnesota. The Franciscan Sisters of the Immaculate Conception came to Buffalo, New York, in 1928, and the Servants of the Holy Child Jesus of the Third Order Regular of St. Francis to Staten Island in 1929, later establishing their Region House in Plainfield, New Jersey.

International Missionary Congregations

Several Third Order Regular missionary congregations have foundations and/or provinces in the United States. The Franciscan Missionary Sisters of Mary were founded in Madras, India, in 1877, specifically for work in the foreign missions. In 1904 they established a provincialate located in New York City. The motherhouse has been in Rome since 1882.

Founded in Santarem, Para, Brazil in 1910, the Franciscan Missionary Sisters of the Immaculate Conception came to the United States in 1922. Mother Maria Immaculata, the first superior general, was forced for reasons of health to remain in the United States. The motherhouse and U.S. provincialate are located in the Paterson diocese. The sisters in the United States are engaged primarily in health and educational services to the blacks and Mexicans of Texas.

The Franciscan Sisters of Mary Immaculate of the Third Order of St. Francis, founded in Switzerland, sent sisters to Ecuador in 1888. Encountering unfavorable political conditions they moved to Bogota, Colombia. In 1932 Rudolph A. Gerken, bishop of Amarillo, Texas, invited them to his diocese where they have established a provincialate. In 1981 a group of these sisters founded the St. Francis Mission Community in Amarillo as an autonomous province.

The Franciscan Missionary Sisters of St. Joseph, also called the Mill Hill Sisters, founded in England in 1883, established a regional house in Albany, New York, in 1952. These sisters engage in missionary work in Kenya, Borneo, and Malaysia.

Foundations from Mexico, Portugal, Spain, and Hungary, 1925–50

During these years Mexico was the source of two foundations in California. The Franciscan Sisters of the Immaculate Conception established a province in San Fernando, California, in 1927, during the religious persecution in Mexico. The Eucharistic Franciscan Missionary Sisters came to Los Angeles in 1943 and relocated their motherhouse there.

The Franciscan Hospitaller Sisters of the Immaculate Conception, Lisbon, Portugal, made a foundation in San Jose, California, in 1960, and the Franciscan Sisters, Daughters of Mercy, from Spain, established a Regional Delegation in Waco, Texas, in 1962. The Daughters of St. Francis of Assisi from Austro, Hungary, established a province in Lacon, Illinois, in the Diocese of Peoria in 1946.

Original U.S. Foundations, 1919–72

A variety of foundations originated in the United States as a response to perceived needs in the Church in the twentieth century. The Franciscan Sisters of the Immaculate Conception and St. Joseph for the Dying were founded in 1919 at San Carlos Parish in Monterey, California. Although teaching superseded their ministry to the ill and dying, the latter is now their primary ministry.

The Franciscan Missionary Sisters of the Divine Child were founded in 1927 in Williamsville, New York, under the auspices of William Turner, bishop of Buffalo, for the specific purpose of providing catechetical instruction and to help parish priests in their apostolate of home visitation.

A small group of women who had formed a Franciscan community to serve the poor in Pueblo, Colorado, traveled to Newark, New Jersey, in 1921, where they succeeded in founding the Capuchin Sisters of the Infant Jesus. In 1931 they established themselves in Ringwood, New Jersey, and have assumed the title, Franciscan Sisters of Ringwood.

The Sisters of St. Elizabeth, originating in 1931 in Milwaukee, have relocated to Brookfield, Wisconsin. Their primary apostolate is health care.

The Franciscan Sisters of Our Lady of Sorrows stem from the Sisters of St. Francis of the Holy Family, Dubuque. As missionaries in Hunan, China, these sisters assisted a native community, the Franciscan Missionary Sisters of Our Lady of Sorrows, founded in 1939. In 1947, when the Dubuque Franciscans recalled their sisters from China, four of them at the bishop's request transferred to the native community. Subsequently, the motherhouse was transferred to Beaverton, Oregon. Besides various ministries in the United States, these sisters retain missionary activities in Hong Kong and Taiwan.

In 1972 the Disciples of the Lord Jesus Christ, charismatics, established their community in Channing, Texas. With emphasis on contemplative living, they minister to youth and adults.

At least twelve, probably more, recently formed communities are still in the founding process. Some of these are Private Associations of the Faithful; some have advanced to the status of Public Associations of the Faithful having diocesan approval; and a few are still in the experimental stage.

Franciscan Women as Educators

At the First Plenary Council of Baltimore in 1852, the bishops of the United States reiterated the statement of the various provincial councils regarding the goal of a parochial school in every parish. This goal, combined with the belief that the Catholic faith was best preserved if learned in one's native language, motivated ethnic parishes to build schools and seek women religious to staff them. As a result, elementary and secondary education in parochial and diocesan settings became the primary ministry of most of the Franciscan women's congregations. Some also established schools and academies of their own, especially with the intent of providing secondary education to young women.

Catechetics and religious education for children and adults also became a ministry for many of the sisters, as well as Montessori, preschool, and daycare programs. These and ministries in social service, retreat, and pastoral work in parishes and health care institutions developed as communities expanded and societal needs changed.

Especially in the nineteenth century and earlier days of the twentieth, dioceses established orphanages for the care and education of children who had lost parents because of disease, war, and hazards concomitant with pioneer living. Third Order women also responded to this need by staffing diocesan institutions and sometimes establishing their own.

Many congregations have worked and continue to work among Native Americans on reservations, in parishes for the blacks in the South, among Hispanics and migrant workers. Originally missionaries in the United States, Franciscan congregations as they grew in membership sent missionaries abroad, especially to China in the 1920s until 1949. They are now found in many countries, too numerous to mention here.

A number of communities also developed schools and homes for the mentally retarded, both children and adults. The Sisters of St. Francis of Assisi (Milwaukee) sponsor four such institutions, providing care and education through the lifetime of the residents.

For the sisters, education of others meant becoming educated themselves. To this end Franciscan women began to attend institutions of higher learning and to establish normal schools and/or colleges for the education of their own members and other women religious. Presently, Franciscan Third Order women sponsor fifteen colleges which offer four-year baccalaureate degree programs and some, master's degrees. Most of these are now coeducational.

Health Care

More than half of the Third Order women's congregations are involved in some form of healing ministry which often began as home care and developed from sponsorship of a single hospital to numerous hospitals, schools of nursing, nursing homes, hospice and home care, and related social services. At least thirty congregations sponsor health-care systems, some of which constitute more than thirty entities.

Collaboration

With the friars of St. Bonaventure University, Thomas B. Plassman, O.F.M., initiated the Franciscan Educational Conference in 1919. The conference sponsored annual meetings for members of the various male branches of the order, and in 1951 began to sponsor annual meetings for the "Franciscan Teaching Sisterhoods." As equal partners today, the various Franciscan higher educational institutions are seeking greater collaboration.

The major superiors of the Franciscan communities, led by Mother Viola Leininger, O.S.F., a Millvale Franciscan, became convinced that the time had come for collaboration among themselves. They founded the Federation of Franciscan Sisters in 1965 for the purpose of working together to renew religious life as followers of St. Francis. Sixteen years later (1981), the federation widened its membership to include the Third Order Regular men and is now officially the Franciscan Federation Third Order Regular of the Sisters and Brothers of the United States. The organization shifted in 1991 to a leadership/grassroots model with six regions. The national officers and regional chairpersons constitute the national board.

In August 1993 a group of nine Franciscan women's congregations in the Midwest sponsored and organized *Clarefest* to celebrate the 800th Anniversary of Clare of Assisi's birth. More than 1,000 Franciscans of all three orders gathered at Viterbo College and St. Rose of Viterbo Convent in La Crosse to honor St. Clare through scholarly presentations of historical research, music, the arts, and liturgy.

Also, the Franciscan Orders, men and women, collaborate in support of Franciscans International, a nongovernmental organization at the United Nations. It serves its members, United Nations personnel, and other nongovernmental organizations "through collaboration, education, and action regarding care of creation, peacemaking, and concern for the poor." And so Franciscans today continue to enflesh the mission of Francis as he expressed it in the thirteenth century: "The world is our cloister."

See also WOMEN RELIGIOUS IN AMERICa.

Pazzelli, Raffalele, T.O.R. *The Franciscan Sisters.* Translated from the Italian by Aidan Mullaney, T.O.R. Steubenville, Ohio: Franciscan University Press, 1993.
"Response to the *Lineamenta* in Light of the 1994 Bishops' Statement on Consecrated Life in the Church." *Newsletter 1994.* Washington, D.C.: Franciscan Federation Third Order Regular, Washington, D.C., 1994.
The Rule and Life of the Brothers and Sisters of the Third Order Regular of St. Francis and Commentary. Washington, D.C.: Franciscan Federation, 1982.
Short, William J., O.F.M. *The Franciscans.* Wilmington, Del.: Michael Glazier, 1989.

GRACE McDONALD, F.S.P.A.

FREEMAN'S JOURNAL AND CATHOLIC REGISTER

John E. and James W. White, lawyers and nephews of the Irish poet and novelist Gerald Griffin, founded the *New York Freeman's Journal* around 1841 (giving it the name of an Irish periodical) as an independent Irish American weekly newspaper. With William E. Fitzgibbon, publisher, they requested and received approval from the Diocese of New York to merge it with the *New York Catholic Register,* thus becoming the *Freeman's Journal and Catholic Register.*

The newspaper's mission was to be "independent . . . interesting to Irishmen . . . [containing] news from every portion of the Green Isle, and information useful to the immigrants [including] accounts of the Catholic Church throughout the globe . . . [with expectation] that the columns will be enriched by contributions of . . . learned clergymen."

In 1842 James White sold the paper to Thomas Walsh and Louis Ende. Eugene A. Casserly was named editor and endeavored to carry on the newspaper's commission despite unwarranted assaults on his character from rival newspapers. In 1846 Bishop John Hughes of New York, who had founded the *Catholic Herald* in Philadelphia in 1833, bought the paper and appointed the Rev. James Roosevelt

Bayley editor. (Bayley later became bishop of Newark and then archbishop of Baltimore.) In 1854 the newspaper was formally recognized as the official organ of the New York archdiocese, and Bishop Hughes contributed articles and used it as a platform from which to defend his positions in controversies with the New York *Observer.*

James Alphonsus McMaster, who was associate editor under Bayley, bought the paper in 1848 and became editor. Through the newspaper, he expressed his interpretation of Irish problems, politics, and religion, often drawing the wrath of both civil and religious authorities. In 1857 the paper lost the archdiocese's support, but McMaster continued to consider Catholic journalism his apostolate.

The paper was suspended by the War Department from August 1861 to April 1862 because of McMaster's support of the South and states' rights, as well as his opposition to President Abraham Lincoln's military preparedness before the outbreak of war.

Although holding the distinction of being the most outstanding Catholic newspaper of its time, the *Freeman's Journal* began losing influence in the 1870s. Consequently, in order "to put new blood into the old *Freeman*" and because of serious health problems, McMaster hired Maurice F. Egan in 1881 as associate editor. Also, McMaster's son, John Alphonsus, took over as business manager and travel agent east of the Mississippi around 1884–86.

After the death of the elder McMaster in December 1886, his son inherited the paper and Egan became editor in chief and co-owner. Egan remained with the paper until accepting a position as professor of English at the University of Notre Dame in 1888. The paper was then purchased by Austin E. and Robert L. Ford, owners of *The Irish World.* In 1894 they invited the Rev. Louis A. Lambert, founder of the *Catholic Union and Times* of Buffalo, New York, and the *Catholic Times* of Philadelphia, to be editor in chief. Following Lambert's death in 1910, A. Brendan Ford assumed editorship of the paper until its demise.

During World War I, the paper adopted an antiwar policy, as well as an anti-English and pro-German stance. When the United States entered the war, many of its issues were withheld by government authorities, and the July 4, 1918, issue announced to its readers: "As we can neither . . . retract nor compromise the truth . . . we will not issue the *Freeman's Journal* until we can speak as Americans, as Christians."

Such was the end of a newspaper that had influenced many generations of U.S. Catholics and offered its readers not only a link to their national roots, but also cultural and literary features of the day as well as local and foreign Church news.

See also CATHOLIC MAGAZINES AND PERIODICALS; McMASTER, JAMES ALPHONSUS.

Willging, Eugene P., and Herta Hatzfeld. *Catholic Serials of the Nineteenth Century in the United States.* Washington, D.C.: The Catholic University of America Press, 1967. Second series. 1:111–20.

MARIANNA McLOUGHLIN

FRENCH-CANADIAN CATHOLICS IN THE UNITED STATES

From their origins on this continent, the French and French-Canadians have made their mark upon American political, social, cultural, and religious traditions. Their history on this continent stretches back to the nation's precolonial past. Three major ethnic groups, comprising a total of more than eight million persons in the U.S.A., claim French heritage: the French, French-Canadians, and Acadians (Cajuns). The 1990 Census reports over six million people claiming to be descendants of the French, and ranks them as the fifth largest group of European ancestry. Another one-and-a-half million report French-Canadian as the primary ancestry, and a half-million people descend from Acadians. While there are French descendants distributed evenly in all four regions of the U.S.A., the French-Canadians are to be found primarily in the Northeast and the Acadians in the South. French-Canadian Americans, then, are one part of that larger group sometimes called Franco-Americans.

Origins, Development, and Migrations

Any analysis of the French-Canadian contribution to Catholic life in this country is related to their struggles to preserve the ancestral language, traditions, and faith which they brought from New France (Quebec) and have long regarded as the root of their culture and identity. In the seventeenth century, the French were among the vanguard of New World explorers in North America. In 1608 Samuel de Champlain (1567?–1635) established the Quebec colony along the St. Lawrence River narrows. Sponsored by a fur-trading company, the earliest French-Canadians set up trading posts and homesteads that eventually extended from Maine and Vermont to Louisiana, the Great Lakes, and beyond the Rockies. The migratory patterns of these first settlers were formed by a search for wealth, but they also revealed a hard-working people, touched by chronic wanderlust and discontent, unwilling to be reined in by societal constraints. By 1760, 70,000 Frenchmen were scattered over the continent as explorers, missionaries, fur traders *(coureurs de bois),* and farmers *(habitants).*

An intensely religious spirit marked the French-Canadians from the earliest times of the colony, when waves of missionaries—Recollects, Franciscans, Jesuits, Capuchins, Ursulines, Sulpicians—arrived to help preserve the faith of the colonists and to convert the continent's indigenous peoples. Under the influence of François-Xavier de Laval (1623–1708), the first bishop of Quebec, a powerful Church structure was set in place, a stronghold of clericalism and zeal. Farmers and the *menu peuple* were not permitted to hold positions of authority in civic affairs or the Church, which resulted in a two-tiered society: power was concentrated in the leaders at the top, and it was exercised over a large group below who had little civic awareness but maintained a strong attachment to the Church.

Following the British conquest of New France and the Treaty of Paris (1763), the temporal and religious spheres in Quebec were intertwined and symbiotic, each depending on the other for survival, much as was the case in Old Regime France. The Church, with the parish as its hearth, was as significant to French-Canadians as their families. In these parish-centered communities, the pastor was a central and powerful figure who exercised many roles, from confidant and teacher to banker and labor mediator. Moreover, each Quebec parish was managed by a lay corporation known as the *fabrique,* or *syndique.* Its trustees, known as *marguilliers,* functioned as a council. They had oversight for all parish activities and financial affairs. If the pastor had spiritual authority in the French-Canadian community, the lay *marguilliers* exercised a strong hold over its economic life. These structures of Church life became both a source of strength and a factor of division as French-Canadians would begin their trek south and west to join the thousands "going to America."

Acadian Migrations

Since there was little contact between the communities of the St. Lawrence Valley and those of Acadia, a cultural divide grew between them despite their common antecedents. As a minority French population in English territory, when England and France were struggling for supremacy in the New World, the Acadians found themselves at a loss. By 1739 the French population of Acadia had grown from 2,000 to 8,000. At the time of the British conquest in mid-century, about 7,000 Acadians were exiled throughout the British colonies from New Brunswick to South Carolina, while 1,500 went to Quebec. When the last of the French-Acadian outposts fell to the British, 3,500 Acadians were transported back to France, but 700 of that number drowned when two ships sank in the Atlantic. Acadians were not welcome in the British colonies, where they were feared and distrusted by the local folk. They were not wanted in France, where their destitution would be a drain on already straitened finances. Many were forced to returned to Acadia and to Quebec. Many others found their way to New Orleans and Louisiana.

Québecois Migrations to New England

Unlike the Acadian migrations that resulted from enforced exile, the Québecois migrations can be traced to economic reasons. The shortage of land in Quebec became serious in the nineteenth century, and agricultural work was insufficient for the growing population. Because of its geographic proximity, its economic opportunities, and its growing textile industry, New England was the choice for two-thirds of those who moved to the United States. They came not because of religious oppression or persecution, but to improve their lot and their lives. The vast majority of French-Canadians became employed as factory workers in mill towns of New England, some of which were called "little Canadas," and included major centers of French-Canadian culture such as Woonsocket, Rhode Island; Lewiston, Maine; Worcester, Massachusetts; and Manchester, New Hampshire.

In 1850 French-Canadian immigrants to New England probably totaled less than 20,000 persons, 62 percent of whom had settled in Vermont. During the second half of the century, however, that figure rose to more than 106,000 French-Canadians settled in the six-state area. They were concentrated in northern Maine, western Vermont, and upstate New York, as well as in central and southeastern New England.

An interesting aspect of the French-Canadian migration was its fluidity. During the last quarter of the nineteenth century, economic and natural crises often kept French-Canadians moving back and forth between the U.S.A. and Canada, and sometimes from one state to another, despite their hopes for a more permanent future in the United States. Nevertheless, by 1912, 72 percent of all permanent settlers among French-Canadians in U.S. territory were in New England.

Québecois Migrations to the American Midwest

The first French-Canadian settlements in the Midwest were fur-trading posts established in the seventeenth and eighteenth centuries. Resident agricultural populations grew up around Kaskaskia, Cahokia, and Vincennes. While it was yet under Spanish rule, the new settlement of St. Louis at the mouth of the Missouri remained distinctly French in many respects. French-Canadians accounted for only 15 percent of Michigan's total population in the mid-1850s, but within a century the Midwest saw a resurgence in French-Canadian immigration. The first two waves of French-Canadian immigrants were attracted by lumbering prospects along Lake Huron and Lake Michigan, while others preferred the copper mines of the upper peninsula. Over 1,000 families settled in Kankakee County, fifty miles south of Chicago. Census records show that the California gold rush attracted 5,000 Canadian-born immigrants, which nearly depopulated some of the depressed towns along the St. Lawrence River.

In Lower Louisiana, the French population had originally been drawn from France and the Antilles. The arrival of Acadian refugees swelled their ranks and their resistance to Spanish rule, which lasted over thirty years (1766–1800) and ended with the sale of the territory to the U.S.A. by France in 1803. As any visitor to New Orleans realizes, southwestern Louisiana retained more French culture than any other part of the States, and became a living memorial to the French Empire in North America.

Elements of Survivance: Faith, Family, and Language

Historically, French-Canadians were accustomed to being a Catholic minority in a Protestant land. In New England, they perceived themselves as undesirable to both Yankees and to the Irish-American immigrants who were their competitors for work and jobs. French-Canadians were often referred to as "the Jews of New England," and "the Chinese of the eastern States." With time, the Québecois began to develop a strong sense of their culture: it was "defined by language, determined by faith and dedicated to the family" (Barkan, 392). Their vocal leaders called for a unified fight for survival, *"la survivance catholique et française."* The three means to attain *la survivance* were the safeguarding of the faith, of the language, and of their traditional family customs.

In one sense, the experience of the French-Canadians in New England was similar to that of other immigrant groups. A period of early hardship and discrimination was followed by gradual acculturation and rise to a higher social and economic position. Drawn to New England for economic gain, primarily in the burgeoning textile industry, the *habitant* relied on certain character traits in order to endure and prevail: a sense of independence, a willingness to work hard, tenacity, frugality, and patience. Rather than become assimilated and acculturated, however, French-Canadians tended to isolate themselves in tight-knit communities, remaining socially distant and defensive vis-à-vis American society. For example, when the labor union movement was initiated and factory workers began to organize for higher wages and better working conditions, French-Canadians did not join the unions. They were often hired to replace their migrant predecessors, mostly Irish, creating tensions in the workplace as well as in their civic communities.

To safeguard their faith, French-Canadians relied on strong parochial cohesion, and aggressively sought French-speaking priests to be their pastors. At the outset, Canadian bishops had resisted sending any help to their émigrés, whom they regarded as abandoning the homeland for wealth. By the turn of the century, however, with pressure from the American bishops and the people, priests from Quebec began to migrate to the United States. Their presence and leadership assured the organization of French-Canadian *survivance* for the "bewildered cultural strangers" whom they served. This dynamic corps of clergy helped them to recreate the unified socioreligious world they had once known in a new and sometimes hostile environment.

A major common goal of French-Canadians in New England was to build their own churches and schools where their language and customs would be preserved. Members of several dozen apostolic congregations sent priests, brothers, and sisters from Quebec to establish schools, orphanages, hospitals, and charitable works of every kind. The most important of these included the Dominicans, Oblates of Mary Immaculate, Assumptionists, Marists, and La Salette priests, Brothers of the Sacred Heart, the Congregation of Notre Dame, Sisters of Saint Anne, Sisters of the Holy Names of Jesus and Mary, Sisters of the Presentation of Mary, Religious of the Holy Union, Religious of Jesus and Mary, and Marianite Sisters of the Holy Cross. At the turn of the century, over 400 clergy and 2,000 women religious were engaged in apostolic work for the French-Canadian community.

The first French-Canadian parish in New England was St. Joseph's in Burlington, Vermont (1851). Within two years of its foundation, French-born Louis de Goesbriand (1816–99) became Vermont's first bishop, and did much to recruit priests for the Québecois. The number of French-language national parishes in the New England area rose from fewer than twenty in the 1870s to 138 in 1911, and to 178 in 1945.

When the demand for French-Canadian priests exceeded the supply, some bishops looked to Europe for French or Belgian recruits, while others concentrated their efforts on attracting priests, brothers, and sisters from Quebec. One historian has stated that "as with no other group, a rapidly increasing corps of clergy and religious was available to help recreate the French-Canadian kind of faith within the American environment" (Liptak, 165). But not until 1907 was the first French-Canadian, Georges-Albert Guertin (1869–1931), appointed as bishop of Manchester, New Hampshire. Schools were considered a major factor in *survivance,* and were at the heart of the parish educational endeavor to maintain the language and the faith of its children. By 1910 there were 133 French-language parochial schools in New England, which accounted for over 40 percent of all parochial schools. Because of the stress on French instruction rather than English by the clergy, these schools often became the source of conflict between French-Canadians and the hierarchy. In addition to their extensive network of primary, secondary, and vocational schools, French-Canadians founded Assumption College in Worcester, Massachusetts, for men (1904), the first to offer classroom instruction in French. In 1933 Rivier College (Hudson, New Hampshire) opened its doors as the first college for Franco-American women, directed by French-Canadian Sisters of the Presentation of Mary.

French-Canadians of the East and West established religious and social organizations in virtually every place where they settled in the nineteenth century. These associations were a way of maintaining community solidarity, establishing ties, offering assistance to newcomers in a familiar setting. Mutual-aid societies sprang up to offer charitable services and insurance benefits to recent immigrants. Parish organizations for women and men—the *Ligue du Sacré-Coeur* and the *Dames de Ste-Anne*—resembled one another, gave uniformity to parish life throughout New England, and encouraged institutional values. Some of these associations were local, autonomous, and short-lived, but many grew into regional and/or national associations, of which the best known were the *Société La Fayette* in Detroit, *Société Jacques Cartier* in St. Albans, Vermont (1848), and the *Société St-Jean-Baptiste* in New York City (1850). Women's secular societies were also founded, such as *Le Cercle de Dames Françaises,* and the *Fédération Féminine Franco-Américaine,* founded at Lewiston, Maine, in 1951 to counter the threat of assimilation by rallying women to "preserve our patrimony." One historian has estimated that over 400 of these societies were established with membership restricted to French-speaking Catholics (Wade, 148).

Conflicts and Confrontations

The French-Canadians encountered some friction with the New England Yankee population, especially during the anti-Catholic crusade of the "Know-Nothings" (1854–56). They were not helped by their isolation from other immigrant groups, nor by the hostility of Irish-American Catholics. In fact, French-Canadians in the U.S.A. of the nineteenth century experienced their bitterest controversies with the Irish-American hierarchy. Though their faith was the same, major differences in temperament, religious customs, and parish life made it appear to some that God might have to separate them even in heaven!

The recruitment of French-Canadian clergy, as we have seen, was dependent upon the local bishop, who was not always sympathetic to the cause of *survivance* or to the foundation of national parishes. One theory of Catholic inculturation supported by the American episcopate was that assimilation of immigrants should be achieved as quickly as possible in order to reduce the possibility of discrimination. Thus, many bishops opposed the desire of French-Canadians to have national parishes and French-language schools, because this would make them appear less "American" and separate them from the rest of mainstream America, as well as from their coreligionists. Other bishops thought it wiser to encourage the preservation of ethnic traditions and would have supported French-Canadians in their belief that "to lose your language is to lose your faith." This conflict of views formed the basis of a larger complex of tensions between the French-Canadians and the Irish, created by cultural differences, the language barrier, and rivalry among workers.

Several rifts occurred between the French-Canadian communities and their Irish-American hierarchy. One such eruption, known as the "Flint Affair," took place in the French-Canadian "Flint" neighborhood of Fall River, Massachusetts. In 1884 Bishop Thomas F. Hendricken (1827–86) became involved in a struggle over the naming of a pastor to replace the deceased French-Canadian pastor at Our Lady of Lourdes parish. The former pastor, Jean-Baptiste Bédard, had inaugurated the French *syndique* concept of a lay corporation for his parish, attempting to bypass the bishop's control of parish finances. When Hendricken tried to name an Irish pastor, the congregation rose up in protest, refusing to attend church services or make contributions. They eventually appealed to Rome and demanded the installation of a French or French-Canadian priest. After putting the parish under a two-year interdict, Hendricken bowed to Vatican pressures and compromised, by appointing an Irish pastor and a French-speaking curate.

A few years later, from 1894 through 1896, Danielson, Connecticut, became the scene of angry outbursts from French-Canadians who were the majority ethnic group at St. James' parish. They refused to contribute to the construction of the parish school because they claimed the Irish pastor had reneged on a promise to provide French instruction for the children. Even though peace was ultimately restored, "the memory of the adamant refusal of the French-Canadians to come to an amicable solution remained to haunt the New England Catholic leadership" (Liptak, 167). Similar clashes occurred in Brookfield, Massachusetts (1899), and Brunswick, Maine (1906).

The last significant challenge to ecclesiastical authority and the climax of all these tensions came with the "Sentinellist Affair" of the 1920s in Woonsocket, Rhode Island. The bishop of Providence, William A. Hickey, took up his responsibilities in 1921, during a period of xenophobic assaults on parochial and foreign-language schools across the nation. He hoped to centralize the control of parish funds and to emphasize the teaching of English in the schools of his diocese. To support the schools and other programs he had foreseen, he called for fundraising in the parishes. Clergy, religious and laity were sharply divided over Hickey's fundraising campaign. Opposition forces were led by one Elphège Daignault, president of the *Association Franco-Américaine.* In 1924 they began publishing their opinions in a journal, *La Sentinelle,* which supported the idea that parish property was inviolable and that Hickey's campaign was illegitimate. It called for more national parishes, in direct opposition to the Americanization policies of Bishop Hickey and the National Catholic Welfare Conference. Futile appeals were made to Rome and to Rhode Island's Superior Court, which upheld the bishop's levies as legitimate. *La Sentinelle* was banned in April 1928 and over sixty members of the faction were excommunicated.

In other areas where French-Canadians settled, the Church was able to play a positive role in the survival of national identity when the attitudes of the local episcopacy were favorable. Similar to the problems experienced in New England, French-Canadians had a great deal of difficulty securing parishes in Detroit, Michigan. Unlike New England, negotiating parish business became so troublesome that various Protestant groups were able to take advantage of the discontent to make converts. The Baptists established a Canadian congregation that came to number upward of one hundred families. Defections such as this spurred the hierarchy into action in Michigan, creating stable parish resources for the various timber towns throughout the state.

St. Mary's in Chicago, the first parish founded in the 1830s, was largely French-Canadian. Indeed, Chicago boasted a thriving French-Canadian community which enjoyed a great deal of support from the local bishop. Its parishes were administered by priests from Quebec, and its schools were staffed by Québecois religious congregations. By the late 1880s, there were second-generation French-Canadian priests and nuns to assist in their institutions. The churches maintained ties with rural communities not only in Illinois but also in Kansas.

The issue of French-Canadian defiance raised many questions in the Catholic community. Why had this happened to a group with such deep roots on this very continent, who were in many ways at an advantage over other immigrant peoples to the U.S.A.? Rather than utilize their strengths, French-Canadians opted to develop their faith and culture within a protected, closed environment of the national parish, and chose to cultivate their uniqueness within the American Church. Slow to assimilate, French-Canadians have remained on the periphery of Catholic leadership throughout this century.

Contributions of French-Canadians

The experiences of French-Canadians in the U.S.A. made them a people with strong ethnic loyalties, a deep attachment to cultural expressions of faith, and a sense of themselves as "a pluralistic community that respected the distinctiveness of its special membership" (Liptak, 170). The central place they gave to the parish and to lay leadership would become a post-Vatican II ideal for the whole Church. Their solidarity with one another and their deep attachment to family life and values offered them a tradition that transcended national borders.

Spiritually, the legacy of French-Canadians is a rich one. From their roots in France, they developed strong devotional practices toward the Eucharist, Our Lady, St. Anne, St. Joseph, St. John the Baptist. Every spring, they constructed May altars and attended the *"mois de Marie"* (Months of Mary in May and October), when the rosary was said as a parish community. The feasts of Corpus Christi and New Year's Day were celebrated with special solemnity in families as well as churches. The celebration of Mardi Gras prior to Lent reflected their *joie de vivre* in a culture that eschewed separation of the sacred and secular. Thus has the collective memory of their origins in New France found expression in this land, which has been enriched by their fierce pride and attachment to their language, culture, history, and faith.

See also ACADIANS IN AMERICA.

Barkan, Elliot Robert. "French Canadians." *Harvard Encyclopedia of American Ethnic Groups.* Cambridge, Mass.: Harvard University Press, 1981, 388–401.

Brault, Gerard J. *The French-Canadian Heritage in New England.* Hanover, N.H.: University Press of New England, 1986.

Liptak, Dolores, R.S.M. "French-Canadians Plead for *Survivance.*" *Immigrants and Their Church.* New York: Macmillan, 1989, 160–70.

Quintal, Claire, ed. *La femme franco-américaine. The Franco-American Woman.* Worcester, Mass.: Editions de l'Institut Français, 1994.

Roby, Yves. *Les franco-américains de la Nouvelle-Angleterre, 1776–1930.* Québec: Septentrion, 1990.

Sylvia, Philip T. "The 'Flint Affair': French-Canadian Struggle for *Survivance.*" *Catholic Historical Review* LXV (3) (July 1979) 414–35.

Wade, Mason. "French and French Canadians in the U.S." *New Catholic Encyclopedia* VI (1967) 143–48.

——. "The French Parish and *Survivance* in Nineteenth-Century New England." *Catholic Historical Review* XXXVI (July 1950) 163–89.

JANICE FARNHAM, R.J.M., AND BRUCE BRADLEY

FRIESS, MARY CAROLINE (1824–92)

Religious superior. For forty-two years, from 1850 to 1892, the Congregation of the School Sisters of Notre Dame in North America was led by Mother Mary Caroline Friess. Born just outside Paris, France, on August 21, 1824, Josefa Friess entered the young Congregation of the School Sisters in Neunburg vorm Wald on October 1, 1840. Sr. Mary Caroline was only twenty-two years old when she arrived in the United States on July 31, 1847, with the first band of S.S.N.D. missionaries. At the age of twenty-six she was appointed the North American major superior and, in December 1850, established the main North American motherhouse in Milwaukee, Wisconsin.

Mother Mary Theresa of Jesus Gerhardinger, founder of the congregation, believed early on that young Sr. Caroline possessed the qualities of leadership. Mother Caroline did not prove her wrong. During the years she led the congregation in North America, Mother Caroline staffed nearly three hundred parochial schools with her sisters, established sixteen orphanages, and opened almost a dozen

Mother M. Caroline Friess

congregation-sponsored academies in sixteen states and twenty-nine dioceses, serving some seventy thousand students. These schools served the children of all national backgrounds, and included schools for African American children, Native American children, and children who were deaf.

Mother Caroline accepted more than two thousand women into the congregation's North American novitiates and divided North America into the two provinces of Baltimore and Milwaukee to accommodate the rapid growth of the congregation. She sought and received a *Supplement* to the *Rule* of 1865 to accommodate the cultural differences of North America. In the words of *You Are Sent*, the congregation's constitution, Mother Caroline, "through courageous leadership, adapted the congregation to life on another continent, perceptively reading the signs of the times, risking innovative response to the needs of the new world."

Friess, Mother Mary Caroline, S.S.N.D. *The Letters of Mother Caroline Friess, School Sisters of Notre Dame,* ed. Barbara Brumleve, S.S.N.D. Winona, Minn.: St. Mary's Press, 1991.

Gerhardinger, Mother Mary Theresa, S.S.N.D. *The North American Foundations: Letters of Mother M. Theresa, S.S.N.D,* ed. M. Hester Valentine, S.S.N.D. Winona, Minn.: St. Mary's Press, 1977.

You Are Sent: Constitution and Directory of the School Sisters of Notre Dame. Milwaukee, 1986.

STEPHANIE MARY PILACHOWSKI, S.S.N.D.

FRONTIER CATHOLICISM

In their delineation of the "immigrant Church," historians of American Catholicism have largely ignored the life of the Church on the frontier and the many contributions the frontier itself has made to its development. It is a story in which the laity has played a decisive role in determining the perimeters and in many ways the parameters of their Church.

The westward extension of American Catholicism, following largely the imperatives of Manifest Destiny, has counted four significant frontiers: (1) the backwoods frontier, to a great extent the story of the Maryland Catholic diaspora; (2) the fur trappers' frontier, determined mostly by French-Canadians; (3) the mining frontier, on which the Irish played a dominant role; and (4) the Great Plains, the sod-house frontier, on which the Germans outnumbered other Catholic nationalities. In their westward advance these four frontiers breathed new life into the remnants of the earlier French and Spanish efforts at empire-building.

The Backwoods Frontier

The backwoods frontier, which transformed forest into farmland in hardly more than two generations, swept from the Appalachians to the Mississippi and beyond. It would, in its Catholic extension, include even Texas. In 1785 the first organized colony of Maryland Catholics began their annual treks to Kentucky that lasted until the War of 1812. The creek settlements of central Kentucky that they peopled would constitute the core of the first Catholic diocese of the West, that of Bardstown, Kentucky, created in 1808 with Benedict Flaget, one of the many French émigrés who would be chosen to build a hierarchy, the first bishop. By 1811, when he arrived in Kentucky, there were some thirty congregations counting some 10,000 Marylanders.

From Kentucky many of these Maryland Catholics pushed on to Missouri in the late 1790s and early 1800s and after the War of 1812 into Indiana and Illinois, often settling near the earlier French villages where they could hope to obtain the ministrations of a priest. As early as the 1790s smaller groups of Maryland Catholics migrated to Georgia and Louisiana. These families prospered to a greater degree, a number of the Georgia Catholics establishing sizable plantations in Mississippi. From Conewago in Pennsylvania and from western Maryland Catholics, including Pennsylvania Germans, began the settlement of Ohio. Many of these families pushed on to Indiana and Illinois. Beginning in the 1830s Catholics of Maryland extraction moved from Kentucky and Missouri into Texas.

There were few immigrants among the Catholic pioneers of the backwoods. An exception were the French, German, and Irish lured to the Black River area of upper New York state by the colonizing ventures begun in 1793 by James Le Ray de Chaumont and carried on in earnest by his son Vincent after 1818. By 1818 a church had been built in Whitefield, Maine, by Irish drawn to the lumber industry. Although the Irish ranged up and down the frontier, they created few Catholic settlements and many shed their traditional faith. Catholic Germans were better organized. Funneled largely through Cincinnati, they played an important role in closing the frontier in Indiana and Illinois in the 1830s and Michigan, Missouri, and Wisconsin in the 1840s.

It was, nevertheless, the Maryland Catholics more than any other who determined the viable perimeters and who funded the many institutions that made the Catholic Church of the backwoods strong and active. They created, for example, colleges and academies in Kentucky, Missouri, Indiana, Georgia, and Louisiana. To a great extent they determined the character of the trans-Appalachian Church in its rural simplicity and genuine piety. More at ease with their Protestant neighbors than the Germans and Irish who followed them, they maintained, nevertheless, a strong Catholic presence that is still evidenced in the rural areas they settled.

The Fur Trappers' Frontier

The fur trappers' frontier, with its creole entrepreneurs and Canadian *voyageurs,* is the *terra incognita* not only of Catholic historiography but also of American history in general. While the exploits of the American Mountain Men are legend, those of the Canadian trappers who taught them most everything they knew are ignored. Not only has the role of the Franco-American as explorers and town founders been largely overlooked, but also their contributions to the growth of their Church. Missionary and trapper worked often in tandem, the latter acting as guide, interpreter, and protector. The provisioners of the missionaries and their missions were often the dozen or so interrelated Catholic families of St. Louis, at the center of which was the powerful Chouteau clan, who dominated a fur trade that stretched from the headwaters of the Missouri River to Taos, New Mexico. The network they created with the indispensable labor of their *Canadiens engagés,* was as extensive as that of the Maryland Catholic diaspora. The fur-trading frontier in the Oregon Territory controlled by Canadian companies was also destined to be a part of the trapping community the *Canadiens* created.

The French-Canadian trappers worked well with Anglo-Americans, Mexican-Americans, and the Native Americans, serving as a socioeconomic bridge between the three cultures, a contribution seldom acknowledged. A legacy of the frontier they created was an almost total absence of religious bias on the part of Protestant and Catholic alike (except for a certain disdain of the Anglos for Mexicans).

The peak years of the fur trappers' frontier lasted little more than twenty years, from about 1820 to 1840, with the trade in buffalo robes till about 1860 a lingering reminder. It laid, however, the basis for the Catholic Church that took root in the localities the trappers traversed. When the *Canadiens* settled down with their half-breed families near trading posts, they created in effect the first parishes of the Great Plains and the Rockies. When they asked for priests, they usually came. One of the latter, Francis Blanchet, was able in 1846 to create an ecclesiastical province for a few hundred trappers and Native American converts with his see, Oregon City, its archiepiscopal center. Ill-schooled in American demographics, the Roman authorities readily responded to the requests of American bishops, eager to rid themselves of distant charges, to multiply dioceses and vicariates for the scattered Catholics of the fur-trapping and later mining frontiers.

The Mining Frontier

Catholics on the mining frontier counted more Irish than any other ethnic group. The Irish, moreover, played a significant part in the mining economy, 28 percent of mine owners, by one count, being of Irish background, and an even larger percentage of the mine operators. Best known of the bonanza kings was the partnership of John Mackay, James Fair, William O'Brien, and James Flood, who developed the richest mines in America, the Comstock Lode of Nevada. Another was Marcus Daly, who opened the Anaconda mines of Montana. Though these Irishmen became millionaires many times over, they began as simple prospectors, thus encouraging their compatriots to follow their example. To every strike, rush, and boom from 1848 to the end of the century the Irish were drawn. They constituted a "vagabond proletariat," who, after the Cornish miners, would provide the most desirable work force for the mining frontier.

Irishmen were not, of course, the only Catholics to work the mines. The California gold rush attracted Catholics of almost every national stripe. Even more did Colorado, where Catholic Germans, Italians, and a variety of eastern Europeans outnumbered the Irish workers. San Francisco, Denver, and Butte, Montana, however, were Irish strongholds, and a Catholic church could be found in almost every mining town. In the mining West the Irish played in politics and in the labor movement a role out of all proportion to their numbers. Mining wealth enabled them to build an impressive number of schools, orphanages, and hospitals even in the pioneering period. The mining Irish of the West moved with greater ease and confidence into the middle class than did the industrial Irish of the East.

The Prairies and the Plains

The Catholic Church of the prairies as well as the Great Plains was made possible by the railroad, particularly the transcontinentals laid after the Civil War. Many of the Irish who helped build them settled down to farming. Though they preceded the Germans in most localities, it was the latter who came to dominate the sod-house frontier. The majority perhaps came from other parts of the United States. Well-organized chains of migration stretched from the Old Northwest to Iowa, Wisconsin, and Minnesota, and to Kansas, Nebraska, and the Dakotas. Many well-provisioned colonies, however, came directly from Germany, or from Russia. The Germans whom Catherine the Great had invited to settle the Volga and Dnieper rivers of Russia, unhappy with new government demands, began their migrations in 1876, the Catholic Volga Germans settling mostly in Kansas and the Dnieper or Black Sea Germans in North Dakota. From these centers they spread throughout the West. They proved among the best farmers in the United States.

The Germans counted more rural Catholics than did any other national group. Those of the Great Plains displayed a greater stolidity, stability, and conservatism than did other Catholics there. They built larger churches and enjoyed a richer devotional life. Although as determined as the Germans of the East to have their own schools, they had not the same need for the variety of fraternal and pious associations the former created. Though hardly as political as the mining Irish, they had, it can be argued, a greater influence on the Catholic Church in that vast expanse between the Mississippi and the Rockies than did other national groups despite the preponderance of Irish bishops (except in Wisconsin).

Even less, however, than on the other Catholic frontiers did the Germans prevail numerically. In sizable numbers could be found the Irish, French-Canadians, Bohemians, and Poles, all consigned by most Catholic historians to the eastern proletariat. The prairies and plains, in fact, displayed a variegated pattern of Catholic life. In Faribault, Minnesota, for example, made famous by the school plan of Archbishop John Ireland, could be found an active German, Irish, and French-Canadian church, almost within the shadow of one another.

Frontier Clergy and Religious

The impression is often given by historians of American Catholicism that in the advance of the Church it was the clergy who raised the standards for the laity to follow, who blazed the trails and staked the claims. Quite the opposite was true. It was the laity who pushed the boundaries of American Catholicism outward and dared the institutional Church to follow. Many priests and religious did so with alacrity, but it was more often religious from Europe who responded. Many orders had their beginnings on the frontier, among the male orders the Dominicans, Vincentians, Trappists, Congregation of the Holy Cross, Swiss Benedictines, Redemptorists, Norbertines, Carmelites, Oblates of Mary Immaculate, and Conventual Franciscans, not to mention the Franciscans who had been in

California almost eighty years before Manifest Destiny claimed them for the United States. Among the many women religious orders drawn originally to the frontier from Europe or Canada were the Religious of the Sacred Heart, Sisters of St. Joseph, Sisters of Providence, Sisters of the Holy Cross, Sisters of Charity of Providence, Sisters of the Incarnate Word, Sisters of the Presentation, and Sisters of the Holy Names.

The backwoods frontier produced three native sisterhoods: the Sisters of Loretto, the Sisters of Charity of Nazareth, and the Dominican Sisters. The Sisters of Loretto and an offshoot of the Sisters of Charity of Nazareth, the Sisters of Charity of Leavenworth, proved also among the most active on the later three frontiers. Older orders came from the East to meet the needs of the pioneering settlements. Benedictine monks and nuns were conspicuous in their work among the Germans. Sisters of Mercy and various Sisters of Charity multiplied hospitals in the West. Because their numbers were fewer, the exploits of such as Sr. Blandina Segale in taming the West were more noteworthy.

The majority of frontier bishops were members of religious orders, beginning with the Sulpician Benedict Flaget in Kentucky and ending with the Dominican Joseph Alemany and the Vincentian Thaddeus Amat in California, and all were foreign-born. Among the remarkable prelates drawn from the secular clergy were Mathias Loras of Dubuque, John Baptist Lamy of Santa Fe, and Joseph Machebeuf of Denver. The outstanding missionary priests were also foreign born, among the most famous Gabriel Richard, Stephen Badin, Samuel Mazzuchelli, Francis Pierz, and Peter De Smet. Many were drawn initially to Native American work but ended up serving the American pioneers. A remarkable aspect of the foreign-born clergy and religious in general was the ease with which they adjusted to American culture.

The Frontier Legacy

There can be said to have existed in the history of American Catholicism the immigrant Church of the East and the frontier Church of the West, both quite different in their contours, activities, and values. It can be argued that the Church of the West promoted those legacies of the frontier catalogued by Frederick Jackson Turner: egalitarianism, individualism, optimism, tolerance, plasticity, a compulsion toward geographic mobility, a confidence in social mobility, and a high regard for material prosperity. It was more than a coincidence, the historian Thomas T. McAvoy, C.S.C., insisted, that the Turner thesis was being aired at a time the so-called heresy of Americanism was being propounded in theological circles in Europe. Condemned by Rome in 1899, the "heresy" was actually an amalgam of tendencies in American Catholicism that could be as-

sociated, as McAvoy observed, with the frontier: a disinclination to argue doctrinal differences; a self-directed individualism that saw little need for external guidance; a greater appreciation of the active over the passive virtues; an inclination of vowed religious to a more active involvement in the larger community; and a modification of devotional and liturgical practices.

From another perspective it can be argued that the characteristics of the Carroll Church, intensely patriotic, self-assured, optimistic, simple in its piety, involved in civic affairs, at ease with fellow Americans of whatever religious persuasion, and moderately prosperous, were perpetuated on the frontier as the "ghetto" attitudes and institutions of the immigrant Church took shape. It might also be argued that Vatican Council II represented for Americans an invitation to return to the roots that were the product of the Maryland tradition sustained by the frontier experience.

McAvoy, Thomas T., C.S.C., "Americanism and Frontier Catholicism." *Review of Politics* 5 (1943) 275–301.

Spalding, Thomas W., C.F.X. "The Catholic Frontiers." *U.S. Catholic Historian* 12 (1994) 1–15.

_____. "Frontier Catholicism." *Catholic Historical Review* 77 (1991) 470–84.

THOMAS W. SPALDING

FURDEK, STEPHEN (1855–1915)

Pioneer Slovak priest in America. Stephen Furdek was born to Stephen and Mary Stopek Furdek on September 2, 1855, in Trsztena, Slovakia, then part of the Hapsburg Empire. He began his studies for the priesthood at Nitra and Prague. Volunteering for service to the Slovak and Czech communities in Cleveland, he completed his education at Cleveland's St. Mary's Seminary and was ordained to the priesthood on July 1, 1882, by Bishop Richard Gilmour.

Though Furdek's first three assignments were at Czech parishes, he was concerned about the Slovak immigrants clustered in Cleveland's industrial zones. These immigrant millworkers had no Slovak parish, and so Furdek began celebrating Masses for them in St. Joseph Franciscan Church. At this time he established the St. Stephen Society which served both a social and mutual benefit (insurance) purpose. This Slovak community became the nucleus for St. Ladislas Church, Cleveland's first Slovak parish.

In February 1884 he was named pastor of the Czech parish of Our Lady of Lourdes in Cleveland. Despite the demands of his rapidly growing Czech parish, Furdek never abandoned his Slovak community. He believed that cooperative action rooted in both Catholicism and education could help the Slovak immigrants rise above their impoverished status.

On September 4, 1890, Furdek convened the leaders of eight Slovak Catholic fraternal organizations from various locations for a meeting in Cleveland. He convinced them that, if they merged their organizations into one national Slovak Catholic association, they could accomplish much for both the Church and their people. The resulting organization was the First Catholic Slovak Union. It was a fraternal organization, but its goals included not only protection from disability and the payment of death benefits, but also the support of Slovak parishes, institutions, and charities across the nation along with the promotion of education for Slovak youth. Furdek's genius was that, although he provided strong leadership, he empowered lay leaders who were just as committed to the organization's goals as he was.

Furdek was also a writer and educator; he established the journal *Jednota* and wrote and edited it for many years. He died on January 18, 1915, in Cleveland.

See also FIRST CATHOLIC SLOVAK UNION; SLOVAK CATHOLICS IN AMERICA.

Barton, Josef. *Peasants and Strangers: Italians, Rumanians, and Slovaks in an American City, (1890–1950).* Cambridge, 1975.

Carr, Michael W. *A History of Catholicity in Northern Ohio and in the Diocese of Cleveland.* Vol. II. Cleveland, 1903.

First Catholic Slovak Union. *Slovak Catholic Parishes and Institutions in the United States and Canada.* Cleveland, 1955.

Pap, Michael S. *Ethnic Communities of Cleveland: A Reference Work.* Cleveland, 1973.

CHRISTINE L. KROSEL

FURFEY, PAUL HANLY (1896–1992)

Priest, sociologist, educator. Paul Hanly Furfey was born in Cambridge, Massachusetts, on June 30, 1896, to James Arthur and Margaret Connell Hanly Furfey. He received his A.B. from Boston College in 1917; from there he entered St. Mary's Seminary, Baltimore, from which he received his master's degree and was ordained in Baltimore on May 25, 1922. Furfey earned a doctorate in sociology in 1926 at The Catholic University of America, Washington, D.C., and did postdoctoral work at the Universities of Berlin and Frankfurt in 1931–32. He began teaching at The Catholic University of America in 1925, and held the chair of the Sociology Department from 1940 until 1963, retiring in 1966. From 1973–75 he taught as a visiting professor of theology at The Catholic University of America.

His first book, *The Gang Age,* was published in 1926 and was soon followed by similar works, *You and Your Children* (1929), *Social Problems of Childhood* (1929), and *The Growing Boy* (1930). These early works were research- and technique-oriented, dealing with adolescent problems. *Fire on Earth* (1936) signaled a shift in his work to value-oriented analysis stressing the importance of Christian involvement in social reform. This was followed by five other books of a theological and ethical nature, whose titles indicated the challenge posed to those who were all too willing to maintain the status quo: *The Mystery of Iniquity* (1944), *The Respectable Murderers* (1966), and *The Morality Gap* (1969). He also published *The History of Social Thought* (1942), and *The Scope and Method of Sociology* (1953).

Furfey's theories and methodology raised criticism from varied quarters. Some conservative-minded Christians found "sociology" suspect, believing it fostered a "Christian radicalism" and "Christian revolutionism." Sociologists in the 1940s and 1950s, still concerned with establishing the credibility of their science, attempted to keep human behavior research strictly empirical in the positivist sense, and value-free in interpretation. Furfey's Christian interpretation and use of the term "supernatural sociology" put him at odds with many of his colleagues, Catholic and otherwise.

Furfey's social commitment was not limited to scholarship. In 1949 he led a study of the role of Catholic agencies in the social reconstruction of war-torn European nations. In Washington, he helped found and took part in the interracial living experience of the "Il Poverello" and "Fides House" communities at the center of the city's black ghettos, work which gave rise to *The Subculture of the Washington Ghetto* (1972). In the mid-1950s he spent time studying the poor of New York. Never were these studies merely academic; Furfey always went beyond empirical observation of human behavior which he believed necessarily included values and meaning. He was active in the peace movement during the Vietnam era, and in 1973 was a founding member of the International Committee of Conscience on Vietnam. His final book, *Love and the Urban Ghetto* (1978), served as a powerful summary of his dedication to the poor and underprivileged of society. In 1982 The Catholic University of America inaugurated the Paul Hanly Furfey Lecture, a series dedicated to the importance of sociology's role in serving the needs of people. He died on June 8, 1992, in Washington, D.C.

See also CATHOLIC UNIVERSITY OF AMERICA, THE.

Furfey, Paul Hanly. *Love and the Urban Ghetto.* New York: Orbis Books, 1978.

Morris, Loretta. "Paul Hanly Furfey." *Sociology of Religion* 54 (Summer 1993) 219–20.

O'Brien, David J. *American Catholics and Social Reform, The New Deal Years.* New York: Oxford University Press, 1968.

Zahn, Gordon C. "Tribute to a Mentor." *New Oxford Review* 59 (Summer 1992) 8–10.

RICHARD G. SMITH

G

GABLE, MARIELLA (1898–1985)

Religious, literary critic. A discriminating anthologist, critic, and prime mover in the Catholic literary revival, Sr. Mariella Gable, O.S.B., was both prophet and pioneer in shaping the standards of Catholic fiction in the United States, Great Britain, and Ireland from the 1940s to the 1960s. Chair of the English Department at the College of St. Benedict in St. Joseph, Minnesota (1934–58), she edited three anthologies of short stories: *Great Modern Catholic Short Stories* (1942; reissued and retitled *They Are People,* 1944), *Our Father's House* (1945), and *Many-Colored Fleece* (1950), all published by Sheed & Ward. Gable's major essays on Catholic fiction are reprinted in *The Literature of Spiritual Values* (1996). Her poetry is published in *Blind Man's Stick* (1938; 1966). She published thirty-two essays and more than forty book reviews in Catholic periodicals such as *Catholic World, Commonweal, Catholic Library World, Today,* and *The Critic.*

Gable unflaggingly challenged, defined, and redefined Catholic fiction, insisting that literature about moral and religious values must be good art and not sentimental propaganda. John Cogley says that Gable probably did more than anyone else "to show people what decent Catholic fiction looks like and to hint at what it might be." Historian Arnold Sparr praises Gable's leadership in the "search for the American Catholic novel" and for bringing J. F. Powers to the attention of the American Catholic reading public. John Harriott also pays tribute "forty years overdue" to Gable's contribution, especially "her shrewd observation that bad art makes for bad religion and that the non-believing artist may often strike a note of truth beyond the incompetent religious artist."

Gable developed a "bull's eye" literary theory: (1) fiction at the center is about the saints, the "little people" struggling to make choices between one value and another; (2) fiction next to the center deals with ethical issues such as race relations or abortion; (3) peripheral fiction is Catholic local color. She broadens this theory, however, to become inclusive and ecumenical in her seminal essay on "The Novel" (1962). Reiterating that Catholic local color alone does not make a Catholic novel, nor does Catholic subject matter or symbolism, she concludes: "Essential is the communication of spiritual and moral insights." Therefore, she reflects, perhaps one ought to talk about Christian or religious fiction rather than Catholic fiction. Her annotated list of 71 recommended authors and 306 novels range from Willa Cather's *Death Comes for the Archbishop* and Muriel Spark's *Memento Mori* to Alan Paton's *Cry, the Beloved Country* and Jose Gironella's *The Cypresses Believe in God.*

Gable passionately believed that "edification at the expense of truth is always a doubtful good." She paid a high cost for this stance. In 1958 she was ousted from the College of St. Benedict by the local bishop because of objections to the "obscene language" in J. D. Salinger's *Catcher in the Rye,* one of the books on the contemporary American literature reading list at the college. She spent four years in what she calls "assassination and exile" before being allowed to return to the College of St. Benedict in 1962, where she taught for another ten years.

Gable's essays on Georges Bernanos, Graham Greene, J. F. Powers, Flannery O'Connor, Pierre Teilhard de Chardin, and Dante Alighieri are noteworthy. Flannery O'Connor wrote to Gable in response to Gable's essay on O'Connor's fiction: "I do very much appreciate what you put into the essay and I shall learn from it myself. And save my breath by referring other people to it." Both Gable and O'Connor shared an incarnational view of the world in which human beings need to be "re-educated in love" of self, others, and God.

Cogley, John. Review of *Many-Colored Fleece. Commonweal* (December 22, 1950).

Gable, Mariella. Letters. St. Benedict's Monastery Archives, St. Joseph, Minnesota, 1916–85.

_____. *The Literature of Spiritual Values and Catholic Fiction,* ed. Nancy Hynes. Lanham, Md.: University Press of America, 1996.

Harriott, John X. "The Nun's Tales." *The Tablet* (August 12, 1989) 1.

Sparr, Arnold. *To Promote, Defend, and Redeem: The Catholic Literary Revival and the Cultural Transformation of American Catholicism, 1920–1960.* New York: Greenwood Press, 1990.

NANCY HYNES, O.S.B.

GALLITZIN, DEMETRIUS AUGUSTINE (1770–1840)

Missionary. Gallitzin was born on December 22, 1770, at the Hague, Netherlands, to Prince Dimitri Alexeivitch Gallitzin, ambassador of Catherine the Great at the Hague, and his German-born wife, Amalia von Schmettau. He

Demetrius A. Gallitzin

and his sister Marianne were baptized into the Russian Orthodox Church of their paternal ancestors, but were shaped by the dominant Enlightenment thought of the day.

Amalia, the Princess Gallitzin, returned in 1786 to the Catholic Church of her youth. Her two children were admitted to the Church on Trinity Sunday of the following year. At his subsequent confirmation, Dimitri took the name Augustine.

Young Gallitzin came of age in unstable times. He was sent to the United States rather than western Europe for his "grand tour," arriving in Baltimore on October 28, 1792. Having previously nurtured the desire to become a priest, he soon began the study of theology. To his father's dismay and his mother's delight, he was ordained a priest March 18, 1795, the first cleric to receive all minor and major orders in the United States.

He was assigned as a missionary on the Maryland-Pennsylvania border, with residence at Conewago, Pennsylvania, but in 1799 relocated 150 miles to the west at a settlement he would rechristen "Loretto."

Gallitzin spent much of his own money in providing for his colony. He was financially unprepared for the deaths of his father in 1803 and mother in 1806. In 1808 he was deprived of any income from the family estates by a decree of the Russian government aimed at nobles who abandoned the established religion. His sister maintained the allowance from her own purse, but stopped doing so shortly after her marriage in 1819.

Gallitzin gained considerable renown between 1815 and 1820 as a Catholic apologist and pamphleteer. The priest was actively mentioned as an episcopal candidate for Detroit and Bardstown, and refused an appointment to the Diocese of Cincinnati in 1821. He was appointed vicar general of Philadelphia in 1823. In his forty-one-year ministry, the "Apostle of the Alleghenies" laid the foundations for a uniquely Catholic culture that survives in the region to the present day.

He died at Loretto on May 6, 1840.

See also PENNSYLVANIA, CATHOLIC CHURCH IN.

Brownson, Sarah M. *Life of Demetrius Augustine Gallitzin, Prince and Priest.* New York: Pustet, 1873.

Lemcke, Peter Henry. *Life and Work of Prince Demetrius Augustine Gallitzin.* New York: Longmans, Green, 1941.

Sargent, Daniel. *Mitri.* New York: Longmans, Green, 1945.

ALBERT H. LEDOUX

GANNON, ROBERT I. (1893–1978)

Author, educator, university president. Robert Ignatius Gannon was born in St. George, Staten Island, New York, on April 20, 1893. Before joining the Jesuits, he received a bachelor's degree at Georgetown University, Washington, D.C. (1913), and studied at Woodstock (Maryland)

College. From 1919 to 1923, he taught at Fordham University, New York, Following his ordination to the priesthood in 1926, Gannon studied at the Pontifical Gregorian University, Rome, for his doctorate in theology and, in 1930, matriculated at Christ's College, Cambridge, England, where he received a master's degree.

Between 1930 and 1936, he served as dean at St. Peter's College, Jersey City, New Jersey, and organized the Hudson College of Commerce and Finance. During his tenure as president of Fordham (1936–49), enrollment fluctuated between 3,000 and 13,000 due to a loss of some 5,000 men to the armed services during World War II. He also served as president of the Association of Universities and Colleges of the State of New York (1946–49).

In 1949 he was assigned director of Manresa Retreat House, located on Staten Island, a post he held for three years. For six years (1952–58) he was pastor of St. Ignatius parish and rector of Loyola School and Regis High School in New York City. He was then named superior of the Jesuit Mission House, where he remained until 1967, when he became retreat master at St. Ignatius Retreat House, Manhasset, Long Island, New York.

Gannon received numerous honorary awards from colleges and universities. In addition to teaching and preaching, he also traveled as a speaker on the dinner circuit and wrote a number of books, among them a biography of Cardinal Francis J. Spellman, *The Cardinal Spellman Story* (1962). His other literary works included *Techniques of the One-Act Play* (1925), *After Black Coffee* (1947), *The Poor Old Liberal Arts* (1962), and *Up to Now: The Story of Fordham* (1967). He died in New York City on March 12, 1978.

See also FORDHAM UNIVERSITY.

MARIANNA McLOUGHLIN

GASTON, WILLIAM JOSEPH (1778–1884)

Jurist. In the first 250 years of North Carolina history only one Catholic layperson stands out as important to North Carolina history: Judge William Gaston of New Bern. Judge Gaston was born to a Catholic mother in 1778, at a time when his mother and siblings were the only Catholics in this small community. His father, Dr. Alexander Gaston, a surgeon retired from the British navy, was killed by a band of Tories in 1781.

Margaret Gaston wanted the best of Catholic educations for her son William. She had just heard of a new college opened by the Jesuit Fathers in Georgetown, Maryland, and decided to send William there. He arrived several months before Georgetown College opened and stayed with priests, first in Philadelphia and then in Georgetown, awaiting the opening of school. He was thus the first student to enroll at Georgetown, but left after two years for health reasons. Gaston completed his education at the College of New Jersey (the future Princeton University).

William Gaston

William Gaston studied law and began a practice in his native New Bern, where he soon entered into local politics. He was a southern Federalist and an outstanding southern Catholic, both oddities in his time. Gaston was elected to the North Carolina legislature and then to the U.S. Congress. There was question about his taking his seat in the legislature because of his Catholic religion, which at that time was forbidden by the state constitution. Because he could swear to the "truths" of the Protestant religion he was permitted to be seated. Later it would be Gaston who would lead the fight for the inclusion of an article of religious liberty in the new state constitution.

Gaston was interested in everything that concerned his native state, which he loved with all his being. We can see this in the state song, "The Old North State," which he wrote.

William Gaston was often thought of for the Supreme Court of North Carolina and had refused this appointment until 1833 when he was elected to the court by the state legislature. He served with distinction as a justice until his death on January 23, 1884. Cardinal Gibbons said of Gaston, "There is no man whose name is more tenderly enshrined in the hearts of the people of North Carolina. . . . His name is a household word in every town and hamlet." William Gaston served God and country without faltering.

Schauinger, Herman J. *William Gaston: Carolinian.* Milwaukee, 1949.

GERALD LEWIS

GAVIN, IGNATIA (1889–1966)

Religious. Though initially trained as a music teacher, ill health forced Sr. Ignatia Gavin of the Sisters of Charity of St. Augustine to work in the admissions office of St. Thomas Hospital, Akron, Ohio.

There she met Dr. Robert Smith and Bill Wilson, co-founders of Alcoholics Anonymous. Aware that there was "little enthusiasm about admitting people who were imbibing too freely," as she later explained, Sr. Ignatia helped Dr. Bob, as he was known in AA, to admit his first alcoholic patient, with a diagnosis of acute gastritis, to St. Thomas Hospital in 1939. Working closely with Dr. Bob and Wilson, Sr. Ignatia began the first hospital treatment center for alcoholics, which was a model for many chemical treatment programs in the United States.

"Bear in mind that the alcoholic is a person who is sick spiritually as well as physically," she wrote, anticipating a holistic health-care approach. "The ready access he is given to the Source of spiritual healing is a powerful factor in his recovery," she added.

Ten years later, Wilson noted, "One day, when the history of our fellowship is written, the great work done at St. Thomas Hospital will surely be its brightest page. Its alcoholic ward, where our infant movement was cradled, will become a place of intense interest and an object of thankful remembrance."

AA members and their sponsors helped in the special unit, counseling, doing chores, and raising money. In 1952 Sr. Ignatia left St. Thomas to open Rosary Hill Solarium at St. Vincent Charity Hospital, Cleveland, Ohio.

Often called the "angel of Alcoholics Anonymous," Sr. Ignatia died April 1, 1966, having personally helped over 15,000 alcoholics and their families, fulfilling the motto of the Sisters of Charity: "In all things, Charity."

Darrah, Mary C. *Sister Ignatia: Angel of Alcoholics Anonymous.* Chicago: Loyola University Press, 1992.

MARY DENIS MAHER, C.S.A.

GEHRINGER, SISTER MARY OF THE SEVEN DOLOURS (1895–1988)

Servite Sister. Mary Anne Gehringer was born in Detroit, Michigan, on March 23, 1895, to Anna Ottenbacher and George Gehringer. She graduated from St. Boniface High School and later attended Creighton University and the University of Iowa, where she received her degree. It is difficult to trace the course of her earthly life because she left so little information about herself.

On February 26, 1913, Mary Anne entered the Order of Servants of Mary, then located in Cherokee, Iowa. She received the habit on August 23 of the same year, at which time she was given the religious name Sister Mary of the Seven Dolours. Her first vows were professed on September 20, 1914, renewed September 16, 1917, and final or perpetual vows were professed September 19, 1920.

In the course of her long life, Sr. Dolours served in schools in Anthon, Sioux City, and Salix, Iowa. She lived much of her life in Cherokee, Iowa, where the motherhouse was located, and where Mount St. Mary's Academy and later Cherokee Junior College were also situated. It was in Cherokee that she began her life of spiritual direction in her charge of the Junior Professed.

In 1939 Sr. Dolours was named novice mistress and moved to the motherhouse in Omaha, Nebraska. She filled this important post for fifteen years. To be novice mistress may be a privilege, but it is also a heavy responsibility. To bend, shape, and mold young women in the spiritual life requires a person of integrity and deep, deep love of Jesus. This she could do, for "she was passionately in love with Jesus. He truly was for her a 'Tremendous Lover,'" according to one of her former novices.

Every sister who experienced her depth of love for God, for God-in-Christ, for Mary, Mother of Sorrows, can attest to the inspiration she was for all who, like her, wanted to give life and love as a Servant of Mary. In her notes she wrote, "Everything in my work is nothing but God to me." No sacrifice was too great or too small. She truly believed that prayer could change the world. She taught that the plain facts and natural happenings of everyday life both concealed God and revealed God to us.

Her physical presence made a difference. There was no darkness to cloud the day when Sr. Dolours came into the room for recreation. She was a tall woman, about five feet eight inches in height, and so graceful when she walked she seemed to be in rhythm. Her laughter was contagious, her singing voice beautiful. She radiated the love of Christ and taught that Jesus dwells in each person.

The particular devotions of the Servants of Mary honor the crucified Christ and the sorrowful Mother of Jesus. In their congregation the devotion to the Blessed Sacrament is also stressed. Sr. Dolours—or Mother Dolours as she was called when she was novice mistress—inculcated the love for Jesus and Mary deep in the hearts and minds of those in her charge. The wonder of her influence, the power, the permanence, was seen in the women who emerged from her guidance and were sent, missioned, to continue the spiritual message that was her gift to her congregation and to the Church.

After her fifteen years as novice mistress, Sr. Dolours was assigned as principal and superior first in Salix, Iowa, then at St. Juliana's in Detroit. By this time her strength was flagging, and she moved to St. John Berchman's in Detroit, where she stayed from 1973 until 1981. At that time she returned to the motherhouse in Omaha, but no longer as one who could work untold hours. She had come home to be cared for. As usual, she was no trouble but was unassuming and cooperative. Sr. Mary of the Seven Dolours died September 19, 1988.

MARY ADORATA WATSON, O.S.M.

GEORGETOWN UNIVERSITY

Origins

The oldest Catholic institution of higher education in the United States, Georgetown was the creation of John Carroll, who, as the first head of the Catholic community in the new republic, wanted to establish a school to nurture candidates for the ministry and citizens for the country. With the authorization of the Catholic clergy in 1786, Carroll secured a site for his academy in 1789 in the port village of Georgetown. A few months before the academy opened in a modest three-story building in January 1792, the bishop learned that the capital would be established in the neighborhood. It "gives a weight to our establishment," he noted, "which I little thought of when I recommended that situation."

Original college building, 1789

The institution struggled from its beginning for faculty, students, and resources. Emigré Sulpicians, brought to Baltimore by Bishop Carroll in 1791 to begin a seminary, supplied most of the faculty during the first decade and a half. One of them, William Louis DuBourg, president from 1796 until 1798, was primarily responsible for Georgetown becoming a college as well as an academy. The partial restoration of the Society of Jesus by the papacy in 1805 allowed Carroll to give the order the direction of the institution. For the next half-century European Jesuits constituted a substantial portion of the faculty and were responsible for the significant contributions that Georgetown made in the sciences in the nineteenth century, particularly in astronomy.

In accordance with Carroll's determination that his academy be no Catholic ghetto but "open to Students of every religious Profession," from the beginning until late in the nineteenth century religious pluralism characterized the student population at the college, with a strong minority of Protestants, Jews, and the unchurched. Likewise its location in Washington, D.C., made it an international school for students coming not only from virtually all of the states but also from the Caribbean, Canada, Europe, and Latin America.

From Academy to College

In 1815 the college secured a federal charter. Two years later it awarded its first baccalaureate degrees. During the three decades preceding the Civil War three alumni presidents of the college—Thomas Mulledy, William McSherry, and James Ryder—were responsible for an ambitious expansion of facilities and students. By the eve of the war more than three hundred students, the majority from the South, made the school technically one of the largest colleges in the country, although most of the students were still enrolled in the academy or "lower school." In 1849 a medical department in downtown Washington began under the auspices of the college.

The Civil War nearly closed the college. Federal troops briefly occupied the campus in 1861 and the government appropriated several buildings as a hospital for four months in the fall of 1862. College enrollment plummeted to seventeen. For the medical department, however, the war brought flush times as it became a major training center for surgeons for the Union armies.

From College to University

In the postwar decades Georgetown slowly grew from college to university as professional schools in law (1870) and dentistry (1901) were added, as well as a nursing school (1904) to staff the hospital, which had opened on the main campus in 1895. In this passage two presidents, Patrick Healy (1873–82) and Joseph Havens Richards (1888–98), led the way. Healy reformed the college's curriculum and made the formerly proprietary professional schools integral parts of the institution. To provide adequate library, classroom, laboratory, and residential facilities he constructed the magnificent Flemish Renaissance structure that now bears his name. Richards continued Healy's efforts to make Georgetown a true university, seeking a faculty of specialists, beginning graduate courses in the arts and sciences, revitalizing the observatory as a research facility, and building new facilities for the law and medical schools, including the hospital.

By 1914 the law school had become one of the largest in the country with more than nine hundred students. The medical school under the able leadership of George Kober successfully negotiated the reforms revolutionizing American medical education in the early part of the century. World War I transformed the main campus into a training center for the U.S. Army as the entire student body was mobilized by law into the Students' Army Training Corps.

At the close of the war the preparatory school completed its separation from the university with its relocation in suburban Maryland. That same year, 1919, President John Creeden, S.J., at the urging of government officials and alumni, established the School of Foreign Service to prepare students for careers in diplomacy and international business, the first such school in the nation. Edmund Walsh, S.J., the school's head for its first forty years, quickly made it a success; within its first five years enrollment reached five hundred.

In the 1920s the university experienced a period of overall growth, with enrollment nearly doubling and new residential and academic facilities, including a medical-dental complex, added to the main campus. Georgetown athletics, which had first gained national recognition in baseball and football in the 1890s, gained new renown in the latter under Coach Lou Little, whose teams lost but six games between 1925 and 1929.

Depression, War, and Modernization

The 1930s was a period of consolidation for Georgetown. University enrollment fell below two thousand; the college lost nearly half its students in four years. The Graduate School was formally reorganized and faculty recruited for selective programs in mathematics, the natural sciences, economics, history, and government. The second "Great War" converted the main campus from a college to a testing center for the Army. The medical school alone kept its prewar enrollment. In 1944 the Graduate School admitted women for the first time.

As in the 1920s enrollment in the next decade virtually doubled, as the G.I. Bill opened the university's doors to many who earlier could not have considered such an education. Substantial numbers of lay faculty were hired, not only on the main campus but at the medical center where Dr. Harold Jaeghers reorganized the departments and curriculum. The new hospital was opened in 1947.

Under Fr. Edward Bunn (1952–64) the university entered the modern world of higher education. Schools were restructured, and professional standards and benefits were introduced. Two new schools were divided from the School of Foreign Service: the School of Languages and Linguistics (1949) and the School of Business Administration (1955). The School for Summer and Continuing Education was organized in the 1950s. An array of academic, residential, and recreational buildings reflected the university's attempts to meet the needs of its multiversity character. Bunn also organized a structure for financial development, including a program of annual alumni contributions, the first major fundraising campaign, and the establishment of the Office of Federal Relations. His successor, Gerard Campbell, completed the modernization of the university, including the creation of an autonomous board of directors, the democratization of the undergraduate student body through the admission of blacks and women, the reform of curriculum, and the involvement of the faculty in university governance.

Becoming a National University

The 1970s and 1980s constituted the most dynamic decades in Georgetown's two centuries. The building boom was but the most visible evidence. Between 1970 and 1990 the main campus alone added a major library, five student villages, a massive academic complex (Bunn Intercultural Center), a field house, and a university center. The quality of the undergraduates continued to improve, as year after year more students applied to Georgetown, defying the national demographic trends. By the 1980s the steady number of Rhodes, Marshall, and Mellon scholarships won by Georgetown students and alumni/ae was one major indication that the undergraduates ranked with the finest in the nation. As the university began to attract outstanding candidates for positions, the faculty in the several schools increasingly gained recognition among their peers in their respective professional fields. The Graduate School in the past decade began concentrating on attaining distinction in certain fields appropriate to our tradition, location, and resources. The medical center continued to build upon its strengths in cardiology, renal medicine, and other traditional fields, while making major commitments to newer fields, most notably cancer research with the establishment of the Lombardi Center. The Law Center not only became again one of the largest schools in the country, but by the end of the 1980s ranked as one of the top ten in the country.

A large part of the attraction for both students and faculty was no doubt "the Washington connection," that "weight to our establishment" that John Carroll first realized nearly two centuries ago. The development of Washington as an intellectual and cultural center had an obvious impact on the university. Significantly during this period Georgetown began or housed three new centers connected with research in the field of social ethics and social policy: the Kennedy Institute of Ethics, the Woodstock Theological Center, and the Center for Immigration Policy and Refugee Assistance.

Strong administrative leadership in the 1970s and 1980s developed the institution's natural strengths in liberal education. Fr. Timothy Healy gave the university an unprecedentedly national voice as he became one of the most influential leaders in the realm of higher education by eloquently articulating its ideals and challenges, as well as defining the unique Catholic and Jesuit traditions that inform Georgetown. He also was instrumental in the quintupling of the institution's endowment, from forty million to more than two hundred million. Another national presence for Georgetown, beginning in 1972 and increasingly prominent after 1980, was John Thompson, whose basketball teams have had the longest period of success of any Georgetown sport in 130 years of competition.

Curran, Robert Emmett. *The Bicentennial History of Georgetown University.* Vol. 1, *From Academy to University 1789–1889.* Washington, D.C.: Georgetown University Press, 1993. Vol. 2, *The Second Century 1889–1989.* Washington, D.C.: Georgetown University Press, 1997.

Daley, John M. *Georgetown University: Origin and Early Years.* Washington, D.C.: Georgetown University Press, 1957.

Durkin, Joseph T. *Georgetown University: The Middle Years (1840–1900).* Washington, D.C.: Georgetown University Press, 1963.

Tillman, Seth P. *Georgetown's School of Foreign Service: The First 75 Years.* Washington, D.C.: Edmund A. Walsh School of Foreign Service, 1994.

ROBERT EMMETT CURRAN, S.J.

GEORGIA, CATHOLIC CHURCH IN

Spanish Missions

Catholic roots run deep in the history of Georgia, the last of the thirteen original colonies and the fourth state to be admitted to the Union (in 1788). History tells us that the first Europeans to set foot in Georgia were Spanish explorers. Juan Ponce de Leon in 1513, Alonzo de Pineda in 1519, and Francis de Gordillo in 1521 apparently led exploratory expeditions into the area that was to become Georgia. Lucas Vázquez de Ayllon established a colony in 1526 that lasted only a short time. Hernando De Soto crossed Georgia, and tradition says that one of the priests in the expedition performed a baptism in 1540 near the present city of Macon.

The actual beginnings of a colonization and missionary effort occurred in 1565 when Pedro Menéndez de Aviles recaptured the St. Johns River settlement from the French and founded the town of St. Augustine. In April 1566 he met on Santa Catalina (St. Catherines Island) the Indian Chief Guale, after whom the Georgia coast was named. Guale swore his loyalty to Spain and to Christianity, which encouraged the Spanish colonization and missionary efforts. By 1567 Jesuit missionaries were in Georgia and Friar Pedro Martinez became the first Christian martyr.

The Franciscans succeeded the Jesuits in 1573 at St. Catherines. By 1587 this was the major northern outpost for Spain; the mission flourished until 1680. A full mission consisting of church, cemetery, and friary complex was discovered by archeologists in the 1980s. The remains of 432 Guale Christian converts buried with an extraordinary number of religious objects were discovered under the church.

St. Catherines was the major mission in Georgia; however, other smaller missions were on the barrier islands and at inland sites. In the mid-seventeenth century there were thirty-eight missions in southeast Georgia and Florida with seventy Franciscans serving 25,000 Native Americans.

A small group of Guales staged an uprising in 1597 that is referred to as the Juanillo Revolt. Don Juanillo, a Christian convert and heir to the chiefdom, took a second wife according to tribal custom but contrary to Christian practice. When he was reprimanded by the missionaries, he and a group of rebels raided the missions on St. Catherines and Cumberland, causing destruction and killing five Franciscans. Called the Georgia martyrs, their cause for canonization was forwarded in 1993 to the Vatican by Bishop Raymond W. Lessard of Savannah.

St. Catherines remained Spain's most important northern outpost until British-led troops attacked it in 1680; shortly thereafter it was abandoned. This, coupled with the English colonization of Georgia, effectively removed the Spanish and their missions from the area. The final encounter between the English and Spanish was the Battle of Bloody Marsh on St. Simons Island in 1742, with the British emerging victorious.

Colonial and Revolutionary Georgia

On February 12, 1733, General James Edward Oglethorpe and his English colonists arrived at Yamacraw Bluff on the Savannah River to establish the town of Savannah in the colony of Georgia. The colony would provide a buffer between Carolina and the Spanish, settle lands desired by Spain and France, produce commodities needed in England, and serve to benefit the balance of trade. The colony was unique in that it would operate as a trusteeship for twenty-one years under a royal charter. Although the charter expressed a liberal view of religious tolerance, it specifically exempted "Papists from the free exercise of religion." There was a fear that Catholics might align themselves with the French and Spanish contenders for Georgia lands. The few Catholics in the colony were tolerated, but there was no open practice of their religion. In 1754 a ship with four hundred Acadians was sent from Nova Scotia to Savannah when the British took possession of the island. It was an attempt to break up the large French Catholic colony. Governor John Reynolds allowed them to remain because of foul weather and their low rations. Measures regulating them were passed by the assembly, and they were, in general, made to feel unwelcome. All left Georgia by 1764. Georgia, along with the other colonies, felt the injustice of British rule. Because the colony was younger and poorer than the others, it had not been at the forefront with the rebellious colonies; however, by July 1775, the citizens of Georgia informed the Continental Congress of their willingness to share in the defense of American rights. December 29, 1778, saw the fall of Savannah to the British. On October 9, 1779, American forces assisted by French naval forces commanded by Count Charles Henri d'Estaing tried to take Savannah from the British. Count Casimir Pulaski, a Polish nobleman and Roman Catholic, who had attained the rank of brigadier general with General George Washington's forces, was mortally wounded and died on October 11. Savannah remained in British hands; however, Pulaski's heroism is remembered. Savannah's historic district has both a square and a statue in his honor. Near Savannah, Fort Pulaski was built and a Georgia county bears his name.

Early Catholic Settlers

Following the Revolutionary War, settlers from other states began moving to Georgia and established farms and towns in the piedmont area. Among these were a group of Catholic families from Maryland who settled in the Locust Grove area of what was then Wilkes County. By 1792 a small log building was constructed for a church, the first Catholic Church in Georgia since those of the Spanish missions. French refugees from the Saint Domingoe slave uprisings and from the French Revolution, and the Irish seeking a better life, soon joined the Locust Grove community. Occasionally priests visited them, providing the sacraments and instruction in the faith. The Locust Grove Academy, which opened in 1818, was the first chartered school operated by Roman Catholics in the state. A new frame church named the Church of the Purification of the Blessed Virgin Mary was built in 1821 and, soon after, a full-time pastor was appointed to serve the parish. With the coming of the railroad, families moved away from Locust Grove to Sharon, which was on the railroad line. In 1877 the parish moved to Sharon, leaving only the old cemetery at Locust Grove. Today it is a mission with only a handful of Catholics, primarily descendants of the original families.

Savannah's first parish register dates from 1796, and the first church was dedicated in 1801 and is called St. John the Baptist. The parish was incorporated by the state legislature later the same year. Augusta's first parish dates from 1811 and was incorporated the same year, although Mass has been celebrated there since around 1800. Other antebellum churches were located in St. Marys, Columbus, Macon, Dalton, Washington, and Albany. Atlanta's first parish, Immaculate Conception, was started in 1846 and the first church was erected in 1848.

Georgia was a part of the Archdiocese of Baltimore until 1820 when the Diocese of Charleston was created. John England was named the first bishop. There were only three parishes in Georgia. England's visit to the state in 1821 marked the first episcopal visit since 1606 when the bishop of Santiago de Cuba, visited the missions. Bishop England was to visit on numerous occasions during which he held nine conventions of the laity and made numerous addresses before such groups as the Hibernian Society in Savannah in 1824 and the University of Georgia in 1840.

Diocese of Savannah

Bishop Ignatius Reynolds succeeded England as bishop and continued the missionary work in his large diocese. Some of the Sisters of Mercy were sent from Charleston to Savannah and started St. Vincent's Academy in 1845, which continues to educate girls 150 years later. Reynolds felt the people could be better served if the diocese were divided; therefore, the Diocese of Savannah was created on July 5, 1850, and its territory was the entire state of Georgia and east Florida.

The new diocese comprised 60,000 square miles but had only eight priests, seven parishes, and four thousand Catholics. Francis Xavier Gartland, vicar general of the Diocese of Philadelphia, was appointed first bishop. During his brief four years, he erected three new parishes, enlarged the Cathedral of St. John the Baptist, purchased acreage outside Savannah for a cemetery, and set up the administration of the new diocese. A yellow fever epidemic raged through Savannah during 1854; Gartland and his friend, Bishop Edward Barron, labored tirelessly to assist the victims. Barron had resigned as vicar apostolic of the Two Guineas and was serving as a missionary priest. Sick with the disease themselves, they continued to minister to the dying until Barron died on September 12, 1854, and Gartland died eight days later. Both were buried in Savannah's Catholic Cemetery.

The second bishop was John Barry, an Irish priest who had served in Augusta since 1827. He was appointed vicar general for the Diocese of Charleston in 1839 and continued as vicar general for the Diocese of Savannah. Noted for his missionary work and charity, he started an orphanage and school for boys in Augusta, which he moved to Savannah when he became bishop. This evolved into St. Joseph's Home for Boys. Barry went to Europe seeking aid for his poor diocese and hoping to restore his own health, broken by hard work and yellow fever. He died in Paris in 1859 and was buried there. His body was later brought first to Savannah and then to Augusta, where he was buried.

Civil War

Augustin Verot, S.S., vicar apostolic of Florida, was appointed bishop of Savannah in July 1861 while remaining vicar apostolic of Florida. His episcopate covered the tragic years of the Civil War. In correspondence with Bishop Patrick N. Lynch of Charleston, he detailed many of the war-caused problems. The Church played an active role in providing priests as chaplains and nuns as hospital nurses who comforted those suffering from the widespread devastation, ruin, and deprivation caused by the war. On two occasions Verot visited the Andersonville Prison and assigned priests to serve at the prison. Peter Whelan, vicar general, actually lived within the prison and endured many of the hardships of the prisoners. Thomas O'Reilly, pastor of Atlanta's Immaculate Conception parish, ministered to the prisoners and consoled those suffering the hardships in Atlanta. He is responsible for Sherman's army sparing Atlanta's churches.

Another priest, Emmeran Bliemel, O.S.B., a native of Bavaria but serving in the Diocese of Nashville, was released by his bishop to be a military chaplain in Georgia. He was killed at the Battle of Jonesboro on August 31, 1864, while assisting the wounded and dying on the battlefield. The Confederate Medal of Honor was awarded him posthumously. Catholic laity were in the various military companies and had special companies such as the Irish Montgomery Guards. The Catholic Church supported the war effort, aided both the Union and Confederate sick and dying, and offered praise and thanksgiving following decisive Confederate victories, according to T. Conn Bryan in his *Churches in Georgia During the Civil War.*

Reconstruction and Late Nineteenth Century

At the end of the war, Bishop Verot went to Europe to secure aid for his devastated diocese. While there he persuaded the Sisters of St. Joseph, whose foundation was in his home town of Le Puy, France, to go to Florida. In 1867 three of the eight sisters moved to Savannah and operated the Barry Male Orphan Asylum. While in Rome, he attended the First Vatican Council. He was very interested in the welfare and education of the newly freed blacks and proposed that each bishop of the Baltimore province establish churches and schools for them. Georgia was recognized as having organized the best Catholic schools for blacks in the South. The bishop entered into an unusual agreement with the public school systems of Savannah, Macon, and Augusta. Public funds would be provided for buildings and for salaries of Catholic lay teachers. This agreement existed until 1916 in Savannah but ended earlier in the other cities.

In 1870 the Florida vicariate was constituted the Diocese of St. Augustine and Verot became its first bishop. He was succeeded in Savannah by Bishop Ignatius Persico, O.F.M. Cap., who served from 1870–72. Persico had resigned as bishop of Bombay because of poor health and since 1866 had been a missionary priest in the Diocese of Charleston. Among his accomplishments were the establishment of several missions, including Brunswick and Darien, and the continuation of missionary work among blacks. He began planning for a new cathedral, but again his health forced his resignation and he returned to Italy. He later was named a cardinal.

Bishop William H. Gross, C.Ss.R., served the diocese from 1873 until his elevation to archbishop of Oregon City (now Portland) in 1885. This was a period of growth and development with parishes and schools opening throughout the state and the dedication of the new cathedral in 1876. Several Benedictine missionaries started a church and school for blacks on Skidaway Island near Savannah. Jesuits were assigned to Augusta and to Macon, where Pio Nono College had opened. The Sisters of St. Joseph's orphanage was moved to Washington, Georgia, in 1876 and became the St. Joseph's Home for Boys. The Sisters of Mercy opened Atlanta's first hospital, which continues today as a major health care provider and is known as St. Joseph's Hospital.

Bishop Thomas A. Becker transferred from the Diocese of Wilmington to Savannah in 1886. He secured the Marists to serve at Brunswick and Atlanta because of a shortage of priests. Aware of the need of additional priests for the black community, he tried unsuccessfully to secure the Josephite Fathers and sisters from Mother Katherine Drexel. Mother Drexel did not send sisters but did provide financial support for building an orphanage. A small group of Poor Clares came to the diocese to lead a cloistered life; however, the bishop asked them to conduct a school and orphanage on Skidaway for black girls. A remarkable Savannah woman who became known as Mother Mathilda Beasley was associated with them and continued operating the orphanage and school after the departure of the Poor Clares. In 1896 some of the Franciscan sisters who had withdrawn from Augusta came to the orphanage. The Sisters of St. Joseph opened their first school in Atlanta and the Little Sisters of the Poor started their work in Savannah. New churches were built and new parishes and missions were established, including St. Benedict the Moor, the first church for blacks in Savannah, and a church in Haralson County for Hungarian Catholics who had come from Pennsylvania to work in the newly planted vineyards. The cathedral was badly damaged by fire in 1898, and before it could be rebuilt Bishop Becker died.

Twentieth Century

Bishop Benjamin J. Keiley served the diocese from 1900 until 1922. Bishop Becker brought Keiley to the diocese as his vicar general, so Keiley was no stranger to the diocese or its needs. He invited the Society of African Missioners to work with the blacks, and the Rev. Ignatius Lissner, S.M.A., responded to the invitation in 1907. They took over the care of St. Benedict the Moor parish and founded Most Pure Heart of Mary and St. Mary parishes and schools in Savannah. They next established the parishes of Immaculate Conception in Augusta, Our Lady of Lourdes in Atlanta, and St. Peter Claver in Macon. The schools in Savannah and Augusta were taught by the Sisters of St.

Francis, while the Sisters of the Most Blessed Sacrament were in Atlanta. Lissner founded a community of black nuns in Savannah called the Franciscan Handmaids of the Most Pure Heart of Mary. Higher education was on the bishop's agenda, which led to the establishment of Marist College by the Marists in Atlanta in 1901. It continues today as a coeducational high school. Benedictine College in Savannah, established by the Benedictines in 1902, continues as a high school for young men.

In 1916 the Catholic Laymen's Association of Georgia was organized to combat the wave of anti-Catholicism and the revival of the Ku Klux Klan. The group wrote letters in response to attacks on Catholicism, published and distributed pamphlets about the Church, and finally, in 1920, published a newspaper, *The Bulletin of the Catholic Layman's Association of Georgia*. This was the predecessor of the diocesan newspapers, *The Southern Cross* (Savannah) and *The Georgia Bulletin* (Atlanta).

Bishop Michael J. Keyes, S.M., president of Marist College in Washington, D.C., was named ordinary in 1922 and served until 1935. Although the Great Depression occurred during his episcopate, it was a time of progress and expansion in the diocese. New churches, schools, and convents were constructed. The new St. Joseph's Home for Boys was dedicated and Atlanta's St. Joseph's Hospital was renovated.

Diocese of Savannah-Atlanta

Bishop Gerald P. O'Hara, auxiliary bishop of Philadelphia, became the ninth bishop of Savannah and was installed in January 1936. Realizing the importance of Atlanta, he requested the Holy See to designate the diocese as the Diocese of Savannah-Atlanta, which was officially done on January 5, 1937. The new Atlanta parish of Christ the King was designated as co-cathedral. Ironically, the house used as the rectory had been the Ku Klux Klan headquarters. At the dedication of the Cathedral of Christ the King on January 18, 1939, the former Imperial Wizard of the Klan was seated in the front pew with other dignitaries.

O'Hara asked the Grey Nuns of the Sacred Heart to teach at Christ the King School. He also asked the Missionary Sisters of the Sacred Heart to operate St. Mary's Hospital in Athens, and the Sisters of St. Dominic to open a free, integrated, and nonsectarian hospital for terminally ill cancer patients. Three contemplative religious orders established foundations: the Cistercian Order of the Stricter Observance (Trappists) at Conyers; the Order of the Visitation at Atlanta, now Snellville; and the Discalced Carmelite Nuns at Savannah. The Confraternity for the Laity was started. A diocesan school system with a superintendent of schools evolved to coordinate schools. Vacation schools to instruct students in religion were started in parishes without schools. Camp Villa Marie near Savannah opened

for the youth. A trailer with a chapel was acquired to broaden the missionary work in rural Georgia. Later, the Redemptorists, the Verona Fathers, and Glenmary missionaries would undertake this work.

With the United States' entry into World War II, Bishop O'Hara called on Catholics for all-out aid to the defense effort. Catholic service clubs opened near military installations, civilians volunteered for Red Cross and civil defense work, and Catholics hosted servicemen at church and in their homes. Many Catholic young men and women served in the military services and received honors, though many unfortunately died. Following the war Bishop O'Hara was given several diplomatic assignments by the Holy See and in 1950 received the personal title of archbishop. Because these assignments required that O'Hara spend extended periods of time away from the diocese, Francis E. Hyland was named auxiliary bishop in 1949.

Diocese of Atlanta

A momentous event took place July 2, 1956, when Georgia was divided into two dioceses with the establishment of the Diocese of Atlanta. It was canonically erected on November 8 and Francis E. Hyland was installed as first bishop. The new diocese comprised seventy-one counties in the north; the Diocese of Savannah retained the eighty-eight southern counties. In 1979 Atlanta ceded two counties to Savannah. Bishop Hyland directed an ambitious program for his new diocese, which involved the construction and renovation of more than fifty facilities for church use. Three diocesan high schools, including one for blacks, were constructed.

In 1957 a bill to legalize sterilization came before the state legislature and Bishop Hyland appeared before the committee sponsoring the bill; it never left the committee. Responding to an Associated Press questionnaire in 1956, the bishop felt that segregation could not endure much longer and stated, "The Catholic Church has always, and will always, condemn racism in all its various shapes and forms." In 1961 he, along with the bishops of Savannah and Charleston, issued a pastoral letter announcing their intention to integrate the Catholic schools within a year. Hyland was forced to resign because of ill health in October 1961.

Archdiocese of Atlanta

The Holy See announced the elevation of Atlanta to an archdiocese on February 21, 1962. Charleston's Bishop Paul J. Hallinan was appointed the first archbishop. The new province included the Carolinas, Georgia, and Florida. In 1968 Florida became a part of the Miami province. Archbishop O'Hara resigned the see of Savannah in 1959 and was succeeded by his auxiliary bishop, Thomas J. McDonough. Therefore, at the time of tremendous changes in Church and society both Georgia dioceses had new leaders. Bishop McDonough served until his promotion to archbishop of Louisville in 1967 and Archbishop Hallinan died in 1968.

The Second Vatican Council met in four sessions between 1962 and 1965 and formulated sixteen documents that reflected its basic emphasis of renewal and reform. This set the stage for liturgical reform, lay participation in the Church, and an active role in social justice. Archbishop Hallinan was at the forefront in all of these activities. Another interest of Archbishop Hallinan's was the campus ministry, as he had been involved with Newman Club work in Cleveland and with its national organization. To assist with this work in the archdiocese, he asked the Franciscans to take over the campus ministry at the University of Georgia, Georgia Institute of Technology, and Atlanta University. The Franciscans had staffed the Shrine of the Immaculate Conception since 1957.

Hallinan called a synod in 1966, the first bishop to hold one after Vatican II. Before the synod met there were congresses of the laity, sisters, and young adults to enable these groups to share their thoughts on the Church's role and direction following Vatican II. A full year of reflecting and planning resulted in the establishment of various archdiocesan councils and boards of priests, religious, and laity that were to act as consultative bodies to the archbishop. The synod identified areas of Church concern relevant in the 1990s: parochial, educational, social services, communications, formation of priests, and administration. Because Hallinan had contracted a severe form of hepatitis during the Vatican II sessions, an auxiliary bishop was appointed to Atlanta in 1966. This appointee was the late Joseph Cardinal Bernardin.

In the early 1960s when Cubans began fleeing communist Cuba, the Church assisted them in settling in their new homes. In 1960 a Spanish-speaking priest was appointed and an Office of the Hispanic Apostolate was established in 1980. Similar services were offered to the Asian communities who settled in Georgia. As a part of the continuing commitment to black Catholics, an Office of Black Catholic Ministry was established in 1981.

Contemporary Developments

The Catholic Church in Georgia continues its growth. In 1994 there were 293 priests, 356 religious, 167 parishes and missions, 35 schools, and a Catholic population of 263,681. Catholics make up 4 percent of the state's total population of more than 6.5 million. With the revival of the permanent diaconate there were 154 permanent deacons. More than sixty young men were in seminaries for the Georgia dioceses.

During this period the archbishops of Atlanta were Thomas A. Donnellan (1968–87), Eugene A. Marino, S.S.J. (1988–90), and James P. Lyke, O.F.M. (1990–92). In Savannah the bishops were Gerald L. Frey (1967–72) and Raymond W. Lessard (1973–95). As Georgia approaches the twenty-first century its episcopal leaders are John F. Donoghue, archbishop of Atlanta since 1993, and J. Kevin Boland, bishop of Savannah since 1995. The Catholic laity has long served the state in many leadership roles. Some of the better known representatives are U.S. Senator Patrick Walsh; Confederate generals James Longstreet and William J. Hardee; and authors Richard Malcolm Johnston, Joel Chandler Harris, Richard Reid, and Flannery O'Connor.

Davis, Cyprian. *The History of Black Catholics in the United States.* New York: Crossroad, 1990.

Gannon, Michael V. *Rebel Bishop: The Life and Era of Augustine Verot.* Milwaukee: Bruce, 1964.

McDonogh, Gary Wray. *Black and Catholic in Savannah, Georgia.* Knoxville: University of Tennessee Press, 1993.

Miller, Randall M., and Jon L. Wakelyn, eds. *Catholics in the Old South.* Macon, Ga.: Mercer University Press, 1983.

Peterman, Thomas J. *The Cutting Edge: The Life of Thomas A Becker, First Catholic Bishop of Wilmington and Sixth Bishop of Savannah.* Devon, Pa.: William T. Cook, 1982.

Shelley, Thomas J. *Paul J. Hallinan: First Archbishop of Atlanta.* Wilmington, Del.: Michael Glazier, 1989.

Thomas, David Hurst. *St. Catherines: An Island in Time.* Atlanta: Georgia Humanities Council, 1988.

ANTHONY R. DEES

GERMAN CATHOLIC IMMIGRANTS: HISTORICAL BACKGROUND

The period starting with the Napoleonic wars at the beginning of the nineteenth century and stretching down to the last decade of that century was characterized by demographic, political, and social changes such as Germany had never known before or since. It was a century of upheaval.

Most important among the factors contributing to rapid change was the population growth and mobility, including, of course, emigration. But other forces—religious, economic, and political—contributed to changes in life such as Germans had never before experienced. Thus, change itself became a great contributor to peoples' willingness to emigrate.

Demographic Changes

The population grew faster in Germany during the 1800s than ever before or ever since. In spite of the fact that hundreds of thousands of Germans emigrated, mostly to the United States, Germany's population more than doubled. Contributing to this growth was a new sexual ethic, especially prevalent among Catholics, that encouraged young people to marry at a young age with or without civil consent. The illegitimacy rate in Catholic areas of Germany skyrocketed between 1800 and 1850.

Prior to this development, marriages in Germany had been held together more by real estate transactions than by sacramental grace. During the so-called "Romantic Era" this changed. Young people married because they had fallen in love. This type of marriage was most typical of people who had little or no property. Propertied people looked down on these wild, romantic marriages. Naturally, people were attracted to a country where land was free and local authorities did not impose marriage license restrictions.

However, a declining death rate was just as important as the increasing birth rate. The last "killer famine," such as the potato famine in Ireland in the 1840s, occurred in Germany in 1770. There was a cholera epidemic in 1830 and widespread hunger in the 1840s (which hit Catholic Silesia especially hard), but these crises were minor in comparison with famines of previous centuries. They were nevertheless important in peoples' consideration to "seek their fortune" in far away lands. Starving people lack the energy to be adventuresome. Marginally nourished people have just enough energy to gamble on a better way of life.

Mobility characterized Germany's growing population. As the country gradually industrialized in the course of the entire century, the work force migrated back and forth between rural and urban environments. Most jobs were still to be found in the country, especially at seed time and harvest time. But, by the last quarter of the century, the pendulum swung the other way. Germany's major coal, steel, and chemical industries became dominant. At the same time the introduction of small electric and gasoline motors led to the industrialization of many crafts hitherto untouched by mass production. These factors led to a massive shift in the population. In 1850 Germany was a rural country, but by 1900 it was predominantly urban. Emigration was a part of the immense migration of the nineteenth century.

Motives for Emigration

Steadily improving transportation made emigration less and less of an ordeal as the century progressed. At the end of the eighteenth century an overseas voyage to a colony was a chancy proposition. Pirates, disease, ocean storms, and hunger all dashed peoples' hopes for finding paradise beyond Europe. All this changed in a hundred years' time. Shipping was safer and faster, and railroads transported people to and from harbors.

Between 1800 to 1850 material want and social unrest often motivated Germans to emigrate. Cyclical poor harvests caused bread prices to fluctuate wildly during these decades, doubling and even quadrupling prices of ordinary foodstuffs. Whereas fifty years earlier this would

have resulted in a sharp rise in the death rate, it now meant longer lines at soup kitchens until prices fell again. Under these circumstances saving money would only lead to its quick expenditure during the next inflation. The possibility of emigrating before the next poor harvest, in spite of the cost, was inviting. Many Germans left their homelands after the particularly hard times between 1817–20 and 1846–49.

Social unrest also fed emigration. German lands underwent major reforms during the era of the Napoleonic wars, one of which was a shift to a capitalist economy in place of a feudal economy. This led to enormous changes in both agricultural and handmade production, changes that were accompanied by social unrest.

For farmers capitalism meant learning how to switch from subsistence farming to market farming. Many farmers prospered, but many others went bankrupt, more in fact between 1800 and 1850 than ever since. Part of the reason for this was the lack of banks to extend credit until good harvests returned. But another important factor had to do with the secularization of Church property that took place as part of the reforms of the Napoleonic era. In heavily Catholic Bavaria and Baden (southeastern and southwestern Germany), reformers like Montgelas and Reitzenstein flooded the real estate market with lands taken from monasteries, convents, or other ecclesiastical corporations. This resulted in a large increase in the number of small farmers who found that, after the high prices sustained by the Napoleonic wars, their plots were now too small for them to make a living. Many sold out and emigrated before going bankrupt.

Capitalism and the fast-growing population also revolutionized production of durable goods. A free economy meant that guilds could not regulate production or marketing as they had in past centuries. Besides, their small-shop, low-productivity mode of operation could not produce enough goods for an increasing number of consumers. This led to sweat-shop type of production either in place of guild production or as a modification of it. In either instance the apprentice or skilled craftsman was transformed into an ordinary worker with no chance of one day becoming a master craftsman running his own shop.

Social unrest resulted. No group of people were more likely to engage in revolutionary activity than journeymen. They led the unrest in cities in 1848, causing Germany's greatest political upheaval and resulting in a national parliament that convened in the city of Frankfurt. Most of those elected to the parliament, however, believed in capitalism. This meant that the grievances of the journeymen would not be accommodated in what turned out to be Germany's first constitution. After the revolutionary fever ran its course in 1849, German governments provided some protection for old-fashioned guild production, but capitalism doomed it in the long run.

The Catholic Church and Emigration

After this the German Catholic Church developed a highly successful social program. The priest Adolf Kolping established houses in large cities for itinerant workers, and Wilhelm Ketteler, bishop of Mainz, provided new ideas about Catholic social norms, many of which eventually became official Church pronouncements. Thus, the German Church was vibrant in the nineteenth century, proving itself quite capable of defending its working-class members from socialism. Those who decided to emigrate could seek assistance from the St. Raphael's Society, established in 1870 for that specific purpose.

The unification of Germany provided an additional incentive for German Catholics to leave their homeland. In 1866 Prussia and Austria fought a war to determine which country would unite Germany. Since Prussia was Protestant and Austria was Catholic, many Germans interpreted the war as a religious conflict. When Otto von Bismarck succeeded in uniting Germany in 1871 on a "Little Germany" basis (excluding Austria), Catholics were reduced to minority status (about 36 percent of the population).

Fear of Protestant Prussia appeared to be justified when Bismarck launched an attack on Catholics in the middle years of the 1870s. Known as the *Kulturkampf*, the attack was actually inspired more by liberal secularists than by Protestant-Catholic discord or rivalry. Liberals, who were in the majority in Germany's new national parliament, wanted to limit the influence of religion on society. This led to so-called "May Laws," which embraced education, appointment of priests, civil marriage, and other sensitive issues. The legislation was blatantly prejudicial to Catholics. When the Church fought back, the *Kulturkampf* evolved into a nasty struggle that left hundreds of parishes in Prussia without priests to serve them.

The persecution of the Church in Prussia did not itself cause Catholics to leave their country. It was nevertheless important for the American Church because many priests and members of religious orders, barred from or severely restricted in their work, emigrated to the United States.

During the 1890s emigration from Germany dropped off sharply (70 to 75 percent). The wounds of the *Kulturkampf* were largely healed and Catholics showed that they were as susceptible to German nationalistic feelings as Protestants. Germans questioned the loyalty of socialists rather than Catholics. The decade of the 1890s was also a boom time economically. Cities caught up with the influx of rural workers. Housing became more adequate. The heyday of German emigration was over.

See also GERMAN CATHOLICS IN AMERICA.

Phayer, Michael. *Sexual Liberation and Religion in Nineteenth Century Europe.* London: Croom Helm, 1977.

Ross, Ronald. *Beleaguered Tower: The Catholic Dilemma in Wilhelmine Germany.* University of Notre Dame Press, 1976.
Sperber, Jonathan. *Popular Catholicism in Nineteenth Century Germany.* Princeton University Press, 1984.
Windell, George. *The Catholics and German Unity.* Minneapolis: University of Minnesota Press, 1954.

MICHAEL PHAYER

GERMAN CATHOLICS IN AMERICA

It is impossible to estimate with any precision either the total number of Catholics who emigrated to America from German-speaking Europe over the past three centuries, or the total number of German-speaking immigrants who chose to affiliate with American Catholic congregations during that same time period. What is clear, however, is the central role played by Germans within the evolution of American Catholicism. Only the Irish and the Italians contributed larger numbers of Catholics to the American population. By 1870 almost one-sixth of all American Catholics belonged to German-speaking parishes. A century later, roughly the same proportion of American Catholics still acknowledged German descent.

German significance within American Catholicism extended well beyond simple numbers, however. Three factors combined to shape a distinctive German Catholic milieu in nineteenth-century America: the embattled Catholic culture Germans brought from Europe, their minority status within the Irish-dominated American Church, and the ethnicity they shared with non-Catholic Germans. Within the national network of German-language parishes and other Church-linked institutions that they created, they nurtured distinctive patterns of piety, worship, parish life, lay-clerical relations, and schooling. Their parish-centered communities helped them adapt to American life, but it was their accustomed path to eternal salvation that they were most consciously reconstructing. Their cultural distinctiveness ensured frequent tensions with Church authorities, but they also enriched and diversified the American Catholic tradition, facilitated its broad geographical dispersion, expanded its ranks of religious, provided models for the incorporation of subsequent cultural minorities, and helped define Catholicism's place in American public life. Their distinctive milieu failed to outlive the end of mass immigration and consolidating trends within Church and society after World War I, but its enduring heritage remains significant both for American Catholicism and for the families raised within it.

The Size of the German Catholic Community

German-speaking Europe emerged from the upheavals of the Protestant Reformation united neither in religion nor in nationhood. The Peace of Westphalia of 1648 essentially froze in place existing religious loyalties and left

Germany covered by a patchwork of more than three hundred sovereign territories of widely varying sizes and character. Napoleon destroyed this system, and the thirty-eight states of the German Confederation that emerged from the 1815 peace settlement ultimately united in Bismarck's new German Empire in 1871. But the religious patchwork proved more enduring. Broad arcs of Catholic territory bracketed the new empire's Protestant core. On its eastern margins were Catholic areas originally acquired from Poland. On the west, Catholic settlement marched southward almost from the North Sea through former Hanoverian and Oldenburg territory, then bulged eastward to include much of Prussian Westphalia and westward to Prussia's broad Rhinelands before plunging south to Alsace, Lorraine, and Baden along the upper Rhine and then again eastward through Bavaria. Areas of mixed or heavily Protestant settlement penetrated this Catholic arc in the southwest; Catholic outliers found lodging to the northeast.

These complex confessional patterns make it difficult to determine the numbers, timing, or character of Catholic emigration from Germany to the United States. Something like 120,000 Germans arrived between the late seventeenth century and 1820, when the federal government began collecting immigration statistics. Roughly 5.5 million documented German immigrants followed in the century of mass immigration that ended in the 1920s. But how many were Catholic? Neither German nor American authorities compiled systematic data on religion. Nor can religion be assumed from birthplace data, since religious and political boundaries within Germany so seldom coincided. Protestant Prussia, for example, was almost 35 percent Catholic at midcentury, and three of its four districts of heaviest immigration between 1844 and 1871 had greater than average Catholic proportions. Indeed, Trier and Koblenz districts in the Rhineland were respectively 83 and 64 percent Catholic. On the other hand Bavaria, Germany's most Catholic state, was only 71 percent Catholic at midcentury, and two of its three districts with the highest emigration rates, the Bavarian Palatinate and Upper Franconia, were, at 43 percent Catholic each, also two of its three most Protestant districts. Even within districts, emigration could vary with religion. Thus at midcentury Catholics emigrated at disproportionate rates from Oldenburg (24 percent Catholic) in the north and from Baden (66 percent Catholic) in the south, while Protestants comprised a disproportionate share of emigrants from Upper Bavaria (98 percent Catholic).

Consequently, Gerald Shaughnessy's widely cited estimate (from his 1925 study, *Has the Immigrant Kept the Faith?*) that roughly one-third of the Germans who arrived in the century after 1820 were Catholic must be taken with a grain of salt. His overall estimate of an "effective" German Catholic immigration (controlling for deaths and return migrations) of about 1.3 million, or 13

percent of the period's total European Catholic immigration, may be roughly correct. But his decade by decade German figures probably understate the Catholic proportion before the Civil War, and overstate it after. Estimates based on district-level religion and emigration data suggest that Catholics may have comprised more than 38 percent of the Prussian emigration during the 1844–71 period, but only 27 percent from 1871 to 1890. Applying similar estimates to the German-born in the 1870 U.S. Census, one of the peak years of German presence in America, suggests a potential Catholic proportion among the German-Americans of 37 percent, of whom an estimated 26 percent were from the southwest states of Baden and Württemberg, 21 percent from Bavaria, 42 percent from Prussia (mainly Rhinelanders and Westphalians), and another 10 percent or so from the more northerly states of Hesse, Hanover, and Oldenburg.

Catholicism and the German Emigration

These proportions conform well to the changing logic of emigration from Catholic Germany, which ensured that Catholic overseas emigration began later and peaked earlier than the general German emigration. Europeans were never the deeply rooted, place-bound people of tradition; they could not afford to be. Local imbalances between population and available livelihoods, the labor needs of growing cities and long-distance trade, and depopulations resulting from war, famine, and disease all provoked recurring and significant mobility in traditional Europe among people seeking opportunity, employment, or land. Thus, when William Penn recruited German Pietists to help settle his new Pennsylvania colony in 1683, setting in motion German emigration to America, the main novelty in the colonizing migration was its distance.

During the following century, North America became an increasingly common goal for emigrants from overcrowded and war-ravaged southwest Germany and Switzerland, but few were Catholic. German-speaking Catholics were recruited as colonists for French Catholic Louisiana in 1718–21, where they established farms along the "German Coast" of the Mississippi above New Orleans and gradually assimilated into the French-speaking population. But Protestant Britain discouraged Catholic settlement in its colonies, and southwest German Catholics found an outlet of their own in the southeastern European territory reconquered from the Turks in the same year that Penn recruited his first German settlers. Nevertheless, the religious mix within southwest Germany meant that scattered Catholics were swept along in the transatlantic emigration of Protestant relatives and friends, and by 1740 they were sufficiently numerous that Maryland Jesuits appealed to German confreres for assistance. The first two German Jesuits arrived in Pennsylvania the following year, and by 1757 there were 949 German-speaking adults forming roughly 70 percent of Pennsylvania's Catholic population. American independence removed colonial disincentives to Catholic immigration, but Catholics were still only a tiny minority among the estimated 281,000 persons of German birth or parentage who made up some 7 percent of the U.S. population in 1790.

Only with the intensifying scale of transatlantic migration in the decades after peace was restored to Europe in 1815 was there significant increase in the Catholic share of the German emigration, and a significant expansion of the areas of Germany from which they were drawn. Catholics responded to the same forces that moved most nineteenth-century emigrants: dislocation and poverty attendant upon economic development and population growth, the lure of American opportunity, improved communication and transportation that increased its accessibility, the simple accumulation of letter-writing Germans in America. The ever-widening diffusion of the idea of emigration northward and eastward through German-speaking Europe engulfed Catholic and Protestant areas alike. But there were also specifically Catholic factors at work.

One of the most important was the intersection of European Catholic romanticism with the young American Church's need for both money and priests. American bishops and clergy on European recruiting missions found a ready response among Catholics eager to support Indian conversion and preservation of immigrant faith and nationality. This impulse was institutionalized with the 1822 establishment in Lyons, France, of the Society for the Propagation of the Faith, whose members pledged prayers and financial contributions to the foreign missions, receiving regular reports from the mission fields in return. When Friedrich Résé, a Hanoverian priest recruited in Rome by Cincinnati's first bishop in 1824, returned to Europe three years later seeking aid for the diocese, he published an informative pamphlet on Germans in the Midwest, and convinced the Austrian Emperor to found a similar society among Austrian Catholics for support of the American missions, the *Leopoldinen-Stiftung*. One of Résé's recruits, a young Swiss named Johann Martin Henni, in turn published *View of the Valley of the Ohio, or Letters about the Struggle and Resurrection of the Catholic Church in the Far West of the United States* while on another recruiting mission in 1835–36. Henni's groundwork helped Résé, when he made another European trip in 1838 as bishop of Detroit and the first German member of the American hierarchy, to convince King Ludwig I of Bavaria, who was deeply interested in preserving both the Catholicism and the Germanism of immigrants in America, to found a third such society, the Ludwig Missionsverein.

The three societies together (the SPF also had significant German membership) contributed some 8.7 million dollars to help build American dioceses, parishes, and religious congregations by World War I. But equally important was the information about American opportunities, and the reassurance about the American availability of spiritual consolation, that was carried into every corner of Catholic Germany by their detailed annual reports; by Catholic publications like those of Résé, Henni, and Joseph Salzbacher, whose 1845 book on his trip to America for the *Leopoldinen-Stiftung* described virtually every German Catholic settlement in the country; by frequent articles about American settlements that appeared in German-speaking Europe's growing Catholic press; by the sermons preached by visiting American clerics; and by reports sent back to Europe by the priests whom they recruited. By the time that Gottfried Duden's 1829 *Report on a Journey to the Western States of North America* aroused widespread interest among educated Germans in American colonization projects, Catholic Germany was well on its way to developing an efficient emigration system of its own.

But as the lack of significant emigration from France despite the popularity of the SPF suggests, knowledge of American opportunity was seldom enough to stimulate emigration in the absence of other motives. Thus the relatively disadvantaged position of Catholics within the German economy was a second factor in their maturing emigration system. Scholars still debate the extent to which Catholic culture itself played a role in their economic disadvantage. What is clear, however, is that nineteenth-century German Catholics were disproportionately rural and small-town dwellers with higher birthrates and infant death rates, and lower average incomes and educational levels, than their Protestant neighbors. They were underrepresented in the modernizing sectors of commerce, business, public service, and the professions, and overrepresented in traditional agriculture and handicrafts. Vast rural areas of overwhelmingly Catholic settlement in Bavaria, Baden, the Rhineland, and Westphalia remained what have been called "reservations of precapitalist and preindustrial economy," and even where industrialization took early root, Catholics were far more likely to be found among the factory workers than among the entrepreneurs and managers. By the late nineteenth century, these social "deficits" generated powerful Catholic demands for "parity" within German society; earlier in the century, they undergirded high levels of emigration among Catholics seeking to maintain in America traditional ways of living that were becoming unsustainable at home.

The third Catholic factor that influenced German emigration was the embattled state of German Catholicism itself. First came eighteenth-century reforms within the Church, which, under the influence of Enlightenment rationalism, attempted to curb excesses of religious practice, restrict the number of feast days, introduce vernacular singing of the Mass, and generally replace the Counter-Reformation's Baroque emphasis on worship and rite with pastoral concern for teaching and morals. This fit well with absolutist efforts to bring the Church under state control, and when Napoleon's conquests forced the reorganization of the German state system, even the Catholic states accepted the 1803 secularization of Church property and the elimination of Church territorial sovereignties as compensation for territory west of the Rhine lost to France. Throughout Germany, monasteries, convents, and seminaries were dissolved, schools and charitable institutions lost their endowments, and dioceses and parishes were left completely dependent upon state funding. Added to these dislocations were the direct consequences of a generation of warfare and French occupation. For years sees were left without bishops, parishes without priests, and when the Church took up the task of reorganization after 1815, it did so in a new political order that found Catholics a minority in every major state of the Confederation except Baden and Bavaria. Baden's Catholic majority, however, were subordinate to a Protestant state apparatus, and even Catholic Bavaria was as concerned as other German states to limit the Church's social authority. Thus Catholic renewal almost inevitably took the form of antimodern, Ultramontane loyalty to the pope as an alternative source of authority. Recurring conflicts with the state over the Church's role in issues like marriage and education punctuated the century. Catholics constructed a dense, defensive social and cultural milieu of their own within German society, whose gradual politicization began in the late 1830s and culminated in both the 1871 formation of the Catholic Center Party and Bismarck's *Kulturkampf*, essentially an effort to complete the secularization of the state that found its echo throughout much of Europe at the time.

Few Catholics shared the explicit chiliasm that in 1854 led Ambros Oschwald and his 113 followers from Baden to St. Nazianz, Wisconsin, seeking a frontier refuge for true Catholicism from the ills of modern times. Indeed, especially in southwest Germany where both rationalism within the Church and external chaos were particularly acute, the severing of traditional religious ties often eased the decision to emigrate, and not all reaffiliated with Catholicism once in America. But for others, the religious upheavals were further evidence of an old world gone awry, and in the context of Henni's 1836 insistence that America's great central valley was destined to become the "arena of most effective working and flourishing of our holy religion," reports of villagers leaving for America with banners flying and cross-bearing priests in their van begin to make sense. Religion in no sense "caused" most German Catholic emigration. But its structuring role was as evident when Franz Joseph Stallo, a rebellious Oldenburg printer whose 1831 letters from Cincinnati helped initiate emigration from northwestern Germany, turned to Résé for advice and religious guidance for his new Ohio

colony, as it was when Résé's fellow Hanoverian, Fr. William J. Horstmann, led his German flock to the Ohio wilderness two years later.

Economic difficulties exacerbated by political crisis ensured willing readers for letters like Stallo's, so that Catholic emigration began to flow strongly from northwestern Germany and northern Bavaria by the mid-1830s, and from Luxembourg and the Prussian Rhineland in the 1840s. German emigration reached its first peak in the early 1850s after the abortive liberal revolution of 1848, picked up again after the American Civil War, and peaked one last time in Germany's economic crisis of the early 1880s, before German economic growth finally absorbed the surplus population. Catholic newspapers continued to provide regular information on emigration. The *Katholische Verein Deutschlands* (the national association of Catholic societies in Germany, founded in 1848) published regular information on German Catholics in America in its annual proceedings, and in 1871 it established the *St. Raphaels-Verein* to provide advice, assistance, and spiritual care to emigrating Catholics. The association's *Leo-Haus* hostel for German Catholic immigrants opened in New York in 1889. The *Kulturkampf* of 1871–78, with its attempt to control education, the training and appointment of priests, and the exercise of ecclesiastical office, and its expulsion of non-nursing religious orders from some or all of Germany, had a greater demonstrable effect on religious than on lay emigration. Luxembourg, Switzerland, Austria, and Bohemia also sent German-speaking Catholics to America, while German-speaking Catholic descendants of eighteenth-century Black Sea colonists began emigrating in increasing numbers after Russia subjected them to military service in 1874, settling especially in Kansas and North Dakota.

The German Catholic Settlement System in the United States

By 1892, as German immigration neared its end, there were over 2,250 Catholic parishes and mission stations with German-speaking priests scattered across the United States. Not all immigrants remained Catholic, not all joined parishes with German-speaking priests, not all members of such parishes were German. Those parishes were, however, the public face of German Catholicism in America, and the 1892 *Schematismus der katholischen Geistlichkeit deutscher Zunge in den Vereinigten Staaten Amerikas* (Schematic of German-Speaking Catholic Priests in the United States of America) offers a useful overview of the settlement patterns of those who chose this German Catholic affiliation.

German Catholics concentrated in the Midwest, where Catholicism wore its most German face. Three-quarters of the parishes with German-speaking priests were located in the five Midwestern archdioceses: 21 percent in Cincinnati, 20 percent in St. Louis, 15 percent in Milwaukee, about 9.5 percent each in St. Paul and Chicago. New York (7 percent), Philadelphia (6 percent), and New Orleans (just under 6 percent) accounted for much of the remainder. The most German archdiocese was Milwaukee (40 percent); roughly 30 percent of the parishes in each of the other four Midwestern archdioceses were German, 22 percent in New Orleans, 19 percent in Oregon (still mainly pioneer territory), 18 percent in Philadelphia, and 12 percent in New York.

If Germans played a major role in establishing Catholicism in the Midwest, they also brought it to rural America. Less than 10 percent of the German parishes were in the sixteen large urban areas that had six or more German parishes each. The greatest urban concentration was in the New York area (thirty-seven German parishes). Cincinnati-Covington followed with thirty four parishes; Chicago twenty-four; St. Louis twenty-one; Pittsburgh sixteen; Milwaukee thirteen; Philadelphia eleven; Buffalo, St. Paul-Minneapolis, and Louisville, ten each; Kansas City and Cleveland, eight each; Baltimore, Rochester, and New Orleans, seven each; and Detroit six. More than 90 percent of Midwestern German parishes—many of them quite small—were outside the large cities normally associated with American Catholicism.

Like the emigration from Germany itself, this settlement pattern had a significant religious dimension. Most Catholics, like German emigrants in general, were not the poorest of the poor, but rather small landholders, agricultural laborers, and artisans who faced loss of status and livelihood if they remained at home, and who frequently emigrated in family groups. Many found opportunity as laborers, craftsmen, and entrepreneurs in America's expanding cities, but for those emigrating not just to retain but to improve a traditional way of life, the American countryside exerted a powerful pull. Federal land was available at relatively low cost even before the 1862 Homestead Act. Many immigrants came with cash from the sale of German property, and the rigors of subsistence farming in Germany prepared them for the American frontier. Devout Catholics had particular reasons to favor the countryside. Often alienated by American nativism and the secular German workers' culture that flourished in American cities after the 1830s, they found it easier to practice their religion in its traditional rural setting. They might spend a few years earning money through urban, canal, or railroad labor, but their goal often remained owning an American farm in a community shared by enough German Catholics to support its own church. The result was a settlement pattern shaped by urbanization and public works construction, land availability, and anticipated religious services, and by changing information sources, including those provided by the Church.

Until about 1830, most Catholics came from southwest Germany and arrived at the rapidly growing ports of New York, Philadelphia, Baltimore, or New Orleans, where many stayed. German services were more or less continuously available in Philadelphia after 1741, but not until 1787 was the first German congregation established there. Baltimore Germans formed their own congregation in 1799 while New Yorkers shared parish life with Irish Catholics until 1833. But the majority of Catholic Germans scattered through the Pennsylvania and Maryland countryside and moved south and west with their fellow countrymen through the Alleghenies in the late colonial and early national period, joined by new arrivals from Germany. Itinerant German Jesuits provided occasional services for this frontier diaspora, while around their mission churches at Conewago and Goshenhoppen in southeastern Pennsylvania coalesced America's first rural German Catholic parishes. Soon, in a process repeated time and again wherever a strong rural nucleus formed, these mother parishes spawned networks of daughter parishes as newcomers and the second generation ranged ever more widely to find land.

New generations of priests, like Résé and Henni in Ohio in the 1820s, repeated the process of itinerancy and parish coalescence on each new frontier. But the success of Dimitri Gallitzin (the Russian-German aristocrat who became the first American-trained priest ordained in the United States) in gathering a German colony at Loretto in Pennsylvania's Allegheny wilderness in the early nineteenth century encouraged further group settlements. By the 1830s small, formal German Catholic colonies began to scatter throughout the Midwest and Texas. Within a decade, the maturing of Catholic channels of communication and the active recruiting of bishops like Henni, Mathias Loras of Dubuque, and Joseph Crétin of St. Paul created broad expanses of German Catholic settlement in new areas of Wisconsin, Iowa, Minnesota, and later North Dakota. Buffalo, Cincinnati, St. Louis, and Milwaukee emerged as inland focal points for concentration and rural dispersion, while manufacturing centers like Pittsburgh and the Erie Canal towns also acquired significant German Catholic populations.

After the Civil War, new German Catholic communities were increasingly pioneered by the offspring of earlier settlers, and business became as important as the Church in sponsoring new colonization. A local alliance of business and Church leaders within Minnesota's expansive Stearns County settlement (1854) established a major colony for its children in Saskatchewan in 1904. But the successive ventures of the Flusche brothers in Iowa, Kansas, Texas, and Oklahoma were more typical of the period in their combination of land speculation and Catholic settlement promotion, and railroads, ranchers, lumber companies—anyone with surplus land to sell— advertised widely in the German Catholic press. The result was a renewed scatter of isolated clusters of German

Catholic settlement everywhere from southern Tennessee and northern Alabama to western Texas to southeastern Washington's Palouse. Established German parishes in the large cities continued to grow during this final settlement phase, but their growth came not only from what was now increasingly an immigration of young and single working people from Germany, but also from the cityward migration of young people raised in the rural German Catholic communities of the Midwest. German national parishes never took deep root in the new cities of the Far West.

German Catholic Clergy and Religious Orders

Equally significant for American Catholicism was the nineteenth-century immigration of religious from the German-speaking areas of Europe. With the papal suppression of the Jesuits in 1773, America's German-speaking Catholics could no longer depend on that order to supply their priests (ten German-speaking Jesuits worked in the colonies before the Revolution). They had to rely on individually immigrating priests, some recruited by priests already in America, others leaving Europe for motives ranging from missionary fervor to dislocation caused by war and the dissolution of the monasteries. Their numbers were never sufficient, their qualifications often questionable. Thus American bishops and their deputies soon began making regular recruiting trips to Europe, where the mission societies helped them find priests as well as funds.

Establishing seminaries to train candidates for the American missions seemed a way to ensure a more regular supply of German-speaking priests, and Ludwig I briefly supported such a scheme in Bavaria in 1845. Seminaries for this purpose actually operated after the Civil War in Westphalia and Belgium. Henni finally realized a similar ambition with the bilingual diocesan seminary that he established in Milwaukee in 1856. But the renewed growth of religious orders in Europe's atmosphere of Catholic revival offered a more immediate solution, if they could be induced to establish American foundations and attract their own recruits from both Europe and America. Bishops turned first to the mission-giving and preaching orders that were doing so much to revitalize Catholicism in Europe. Austrian Redemptorists were recruited for Cincinnati in 1832, soon moving to Pittsburgh and points east where they focused on urban parishes in particular. Swiss members of the Society of the Precious Blood located in northern Ohio in 1843, and Austrian Franciscans in Cincinnati the following year. Though monastic Norbertines from Austria failed to sustain their 1843 frontier Wisconsin foundation, Swiss Capuchins proved more successful there after 1856.

Most successful of all were Bavarian Benedictines from the newly restored abbey of Metten. Ambitious to help educate an American clergy and repeat on the American frontier their Christianizing role in the forests of Europe a thousand years earlier, their American-Cassinese Congregation expanded from its 1846 motherhouse of St. Vincent Abbey in western Pennsylvania to the Minnesota frontier in 1856 (founding St. John's Abbey, eventually the largest Benedictine monastery in the world), in an ever widening circle of urban priories and frontier monasteries. Their example was followed by Swiss Benedictines, anxious about possible monastic suppression in Switzerland, who established similar chains from initial foundations at St. Meinrad's Abbey in southern Indiana (1853) and Conception Abbey in western Missouri (1873). The monastic towers of both congregations were soon surrounded by the country parishes of the German Catholic farmers who settled in their shadow. The Jesuits, fully restored in 1815, always included some German-speakers in their ranks; their most important service was as mission preachers. Particularly legendary was Franz Xavier Weninger, the Austrian who crisscrossed America for more than three decades after 1848, conducting some eight hundred missions in German, English, French, and Spanish and stimulating the organization of dozens of parishes and the construction of countless churches. Only in 1868 did the German Jesuit province establish an American foundation of its own, headquartered in Buffalo and well-situated to serve as a refuge after 1871 when the *Kulturkampf* sent numerous religious in flight to America and elsewhere. The Illinois Franciscans, for example, welcomed more than eighty refugees from Westphalia in 1875, while refuge-seeking Holy Ghost Fathers brought their order to Pittsburgh.

As the various orders extended their fields of labor to new parishes and dioceses, and achieved independent status from their European superiors, they and their diocesan counterparts were soon joined by increasing numbers of recruits from the German Catholic community. In 1843 barely fifty German-speaking priests served the nation's estimated 300,000 German Catholics. By 1869, 1,169 German-speaking priests constituted some 35 percent of all American priests; only 39 of these were known to be American-born. Within a dozen years, an estimated 18 percent of the 2,067 German-speaking priests were American-born. But as late as 1910, the Chicago diocese was still recruiting directly in Germany to meet its need for German-speaking priests.

The largest single group among the immigrant priests in 1881 came from the Westphalian and Hanoverian dioceses of Münster, Paderborn, Osnabrück, and Hildesheim (30 percent of the total), followed by southwestern German dioceses (17 percent), the Prussian Rhineland (11 percent), and Bavaria (11 percent); almost 7 percent were Austrian, 6 percent Swiss. Less than one-quarter had been recruited as mature and experienced priests. More than one-third received most or all of their training in American seminaries (some 7 percent, in fact, having arrived as children), while the remainder arrived shortly before or after ordination. America was not just a mission field or place of refuge, but also a source of career opportunity for aspiring priests unable to afford a seminary education in Germany or to find an appointment there after ordination. Precisely two-thirds of the German-speaking priests by 1881 were diocesan clergy. Benedictines were most numerous among those belonging to religious orders (28 percent of the regular clergy), followed by Franciscans (23 percent), Redemptorists (20 percent), Jesuits (16 percent), and Capuchins (10 percent).

German-Americans also benefited from the great wave of women's vocations that Germany's Catholic reawakening fostered. Perhaps one-sixth of the flourishing American sisterhoods of the mid-twentieth century derived from German origins. Almost all were teaching and nursing orders. Some of the largest were recruited during the first wave of mass immigration before the Civil War, while later transplantations occurred during the *Kulturkampf,* and again in the years of American urban growth before and after World War I. By the 1840s, pastors and bishops began recruiting German-speaking nuns to staff their schools. Sisters of the Precious Blood arrived in northern Ohio from Switzerland in 1844. School Sisters of Notre Dame from Bavaria followed in 1847, soon locating their motherhouse in Milwaukee, while Bavarian Benedictine nuns joined their male counterparts in 1852. Both became among the nation's largest teaching and nursing orders. Austrian Ursulines arrived in St. Louis in 1848, Bavarian Ursulines in Louisville ten years later, Bavarian Dominicans in New York in 1853. One rural pastor brought Viennese Sisters of the Third Order of St. Francis to southeast Indiana in 1851, while another founded a new order for immigrant German women in 1858, the Sisters of St. Agnes, to ensure teachers for his rural Wisconsin parish. They later staffed the *Leo-Haus* immigrant hostel in New York. German discomfort with women as teachers for boys also fueled efforts to recruit teaching brotherhoods, like the Society of Mary, which arrived in Cincinnati from Alsace in 1849.

If schools seemed the first necessity, frequent epidemics and the fetid atmosphere of America's cities made hospitals and orphanages, staffed by nuns who spoke the immigrants' native language, a close second. In 1849 Henni solved this problem by encouraging six Bavarians who had emigrated seeking a cooperative religious life to form the Sisters of the Third Order of St. Francis Assisi. John Neumann, the Bohemian Redemptorist who became bishop of Philadelphia in 1852, similarly founded a Franciscan sisterhood for German immigrant women to care for the sick, the poor, and the orphans of his diocese, while Cincinnati's bishop recruited Franciscan Sisters of the Poor from Prussia in 1858 for the same purpose. They arrived in time to nurse the Civil War wounded in their own hospitals, in Cincinnati's Marine Hospital, and on the hospital boats of the western rivers.

Despite tensions over adapting European rules to immigrant needs and American Church governance, these and later immigrant sisterhoods quickly attracted recruits from the German communities of America. Many German parishes produced exceptionally high numbers of vocations among the second and third generations, and in these parishes women outpaced men in their choice of the religious life often two, three, or even four to one. As early as 1879, 53 percent of America's 452 Benedictine nuns were born in America. By 1903, 58 percent of the 1,814 Benedictines were native-born. Such growth meant that the expanding Church could increasingly depend on American rather than European orders. By 1892, for example, the School Sisters of Notre Dame had founded nearly three hundred schools and orphanages in sixteen states, the District of Columbia, and Ontario, numbered over two thousand members, and in 1873 with the College of Notre Dame of Maryland in Baltimore laid the basis for the first degree-granting Catholic institution of higher learning for women in America. These orders soon extended their services beyond the German community, and many German American women found their way into non-German religious orders as well. But the piety that drew them to the religious life in such numbers, and the commitment and organizational ability they demonstrated, were essential factors in the formation and sustenance of America's German Catholic milieu.

Parishes and Piety

The parish stood at the core of German Catholic life. In rural America, the prevalence of group colonization testified to the importance these immigrants placed on parishes of their own. But the pattern was no less pronounced in America's cities. When Philadelphia's German Catholics withdrew from the city's single parish in 1788 and launched a national parish of their own, they helped create American Catholicism's main nineteenth-century solution to caring for its immigrant members. It was not simply a question of national pride, though that was surely present. "Remain German, German, don't become English," pleaded King Ludwig I to the departing School Sisters of Notre Dame in 1847. This became the password for numerous Germans, Catholic and non-Catholic alike, as they adapted to an America that they often saw as culturally inferior.

Nor was it just language difference, though this too was critical. Henni's insistence that "language saves the faith" became a slogan among nineteenth-century German Catholics, reflecting not only the dependence of pastoral care upon effective communication in sermons, the confessional, and schools, but also the alternative available to disgruntled German Catholics in the German-language services of their Protestant compatriots. Bilingual parishes might have resolved this issue, but there was a further factor involved: the existence of significant national differences in traditions of worship, piety, education, and parish governance. On the one hand, Germans remained far more wedded than did their English-speaking counterparts to a Baroque culture of communal rather than individual devotionalism embodied in processions and pilgrimages, confraternities, rich orchestral music, and richly embellished churches. On the other hand, they had also absorbed greater doses of Enlightenment Catholicism's support for the vernacular (e.g., Masses sung in German), parish schools, and lay control of parish property. Thus it was no accident that conflicts over appropriate Church music were an important precipitant of the Philadelphia split in 1787. And since German language and culture seemed inseparable from the grace-filled Catholic life they sought, German support for the parochial schools that would pass both on to their children became proverbial. An estimated two-thirds of Midwestern German parishes established schools within two years of their founding, compared with just over one-quarter of their Irish counterparts.

To realize in America the immigrant vision of a traditional community permeated by religion demanded a homogeneity of values that extended beyond the Church to encompass every area of daily life. Thus German national parishes became de facto Church policy wherever German Catholics settled in significant numbers, and Germans clustered together to ensure the numbers to maintain their own parishes. Missions like Weninger's helped revitalize their faith and stimulate parish formation, but it was the immigrants themselves, often in the face of extreme poverty, who learned to meet together, form committees to raise money and build a church, and approach their bishop for parish recognition and a priest. From such lay activity emerged characteristic German parish patterns that replicated themselves across the expanding nation. In the countryside, with growing prosperity, simple log and frame churches yielded to steepled brick Gothic structures set within expansive precincts embracing rectory, school, convent, graveyard, picnic lawn, grotto, and parish hall, and flanked by the general stores, blacksmiths, and saloons of the hamlets that grew up around them. Here Germans reproduced the Baroque piety of the homeland. Village brass bands joined choir and congregation in making sacred music, and outdoor processions punctuated every major feast of the Church year, whether to the cemetery on All Souls' Day, into the fields on Rogation Days, or around the village from altar to flower-bedecked altar on Corpus Christi—the annual highpoint of every parish calendar. As early as 1755, Goshenhoppen's processions aroused the curiosity of non-Catholic neighbors. The annual parish fundraising fair became the functional equivalent of the old-country *Kirmes,* votive chapels sprouted along country lanes, and miraculous images or deliver-

ances from plague soon provided motives for reintroducing familiar habits of multiparish pilgrimage to local shrines. Parishioners pressed pastors to introduce traditional confraternities and sodalities, and no rural parish was complete without its complement of societies for adult men, Christian mothers, young men, young women, and children, as well as more specialized devotional and social organizations. The adult societies generally combined spiritual enrichment with practical support for parish needs and mutual benefit provisions.

During the formative decades of life in such parishes, the perennial shortage of priests meant fairly brief tenures and significant levels of lay initiative, but by the latter decades of the century the reign of long-serving patriarchal pastors often set in. Where German Catholic farms covered entire townships, local government often became little more than an extension of parish governance. German Catholic farmers realized early that the American system of local school control permitted them, where they dominated an area, to hire Catholic teachers for the public schools and avoid supporting a separate parochial system. Though bishops were never comfortable with this approach, it was already common in Ohio in the 1830s. Henni stressed its advantages in inviting German Catholics to settle in Wisconsin a decade later, and its prevalence throughout the rural Midwest is one reason why late nineteenth-century Germans were able to claim virtually universal compliance with the Church mandate for parochial schools. It resembled Germany's system of publicly supported parochial schools, and permitted many parishes to import also the familiar figure of the *Kirchenvater,* the lay "church father," who combined the roles (and salaries) of public school teacher, church organist, choir director, sacristan, and often—as the best educated layman in the parish—town clerk. In 1871 Henni opened the country's first Catholic normal school to train such lay teachers, bringing from Switzerland as professor of music John Singenberger, one of Europe's leading proponents of the Caecilian movement for Church music reform. Men trained at St. Francis Seminary (an estimated five hundred organists in the school's half-century of existence), and at other colleges established by German orders, played a central role in rural parishes well into the twentieth century.

After the Third Plenary Council of Baltimore in 1884 mandated that every parish have its own school, this rural system came under increasing pressure. Teaching sisters, now available in sufficient numbers, were both cheaper and more amenable to the authority of pastors and bishops than were lay teachers appointed by a lay school board. The system also received court challenges for its blurring of the boundaries between Church and state. Some parishes, of course, had relied on parochial schools taught by nuns from the outset; others hired nuns to teach in their public schools. Parishioners, fearful alike of loss of control and female teachers, often resisted Church pressure to introduce formal parochial schools. Several rural German parishes in Minnesota's St. Cloud diocese, for example, were placed under interdict for their resistance, but managed to retain variants of the older system in the face of pressure from both Church and state, far into the twentieth century.

Urban Germans lacked the settlement concentration and political control that reinforced rural efforts to shape a fully Catholic way of life, relying on institutional completeness instead. Like their counterparts in the growing cities of the homeland, and for much the same defensive reasons, German parishes in American cities developed a well-deserved reputation for the cradle-to-grave organization of life. Thus Milwaukee's pioneer German parishes quickly introduced both parish schools and what was by midcentury already a familiar spectrum of associations: devotional confraternities, mutual benefit associations, men's building societies, women's altar and rosary societies, young men's and young women's sodalities, debating, drama, singing, and purely social organizations. Designed to "rescue wandering sheep and protect the remainder from the rapacious wolves of worldliness and modernity" while promoting personal piety, they also provided immigrants with valuable schooling in the voluntarism of American public life. Urban parishes developed the same elaborate physical plants as their rural counterparts, and if the constraints of coexistence with sometimes hostile non-Catholic neighbors curtailed their processional habits, their musical traditions thrived. Cincinnatians established their first Cecilian Society in the early 1840s. Germans also united across parish boundaries to support cemeteries, orphanages, hospitals, cultural societies, and newspapers that paralleled English-speaking diocesan counterparts. The Germans enjoyed a stronger tradition of lay parish participation than did the Irish, but they also joined fewer non-Church-based ethnic societies, owing to the anticlericalism that flourished within so much of the German-American *Vereinswesen*.

The Broader German Catholic Milieu

The contours of a national German Catholic milieu began to emerge from this parish base during the decade after 1848. The impulse for self-enclosure, implicit in the structure of the emigration itself, was strengthened by American circumstances. Anticlericalism meant that practicing Catholics often felt distinctly unwelcome in secular German-American circles. At the same time, nativist prejudice was rife among native-born Americans worried about constructing a unified modern state in the face of growing cultural difference. Thus, Cincinnati's German Catholics in the 1850s had to face not only anti-immigrant nativist rioters, but anti-Catholic German rioters as well. The pressures they had fled in Germany followed them to America, and like their coreligionists back home they supplemented their parish organizations with a widening array of institutions and associations to enrich and defend their self-enclosed communities.

Among the most important was the German Catholic press. As early as 1837, Henni founded in Cincinnati America's first German-language Catholic weekly, *Der Wahrheitsfreund* (The Friend of Truth), in conscious imitation of Germany's emergent Catholic press. It gained significant national circulation, bringing German Catholic communities in America in closer touch with one another and with events in Catholic Europe. Similar publications followed elsewhere (Baltimore 1841, St. Louis 1849, New York and Buffalo 1851, Milwaukee 1852, etc.). Sixty-one German Catholic newspapers, nine of them dailies, were published during the nineteenth century; thirty-five were still in existence at century's end. A variety of other journals also provided religiously suitable reading for German Catholic households. They ranged from collections of edifying and entertaining family reading, to journals for German-speaking priests, choir directors, teachers, and farmers, associational newsletters, and popular annual calendars that combined light reading with practical and religious information. Catholic literature from Germany also circulated widely, thanks to German Catholic bookstores that began appearing by the mid-1830s, and to Catholic publishing houses like Benziger, Pustet, and Herder that established American branches beginning in the 1850s. The first German Catholic devotional books and catechisms to be published in America emerged from Pennsylvania presses as early as 1788 and 1797, respectively; the first German Catholic Bible (under Redemptorist auspices) in America was published in 1843. A profusion of American-published, German-language prayer books, saints' lives, catechisms, school texts, hymnals, apologetics, histories, and lighter literature followed, much of it now lost to both libraries and bibliographers, but all of it meant to ensure that the inner lives of German Catholics could remain as hermetically encapsulated as their outer ones.

The first, longest-lived, and most significant national German Catholic organization emerged in 1855, at a time when secular German-Americans were also organizing nationally, and seven years after the first national convention of Catholic associations in Germany. The *Deutsche Römisch-Katholische Central-Verein von Nord-America* (German Roman Catholic Central Association of North America) was an umbrella organization supporting the practical insurance interests of parish mutual benefit societies, but its annual meetings provided a platform for airing broader German Catholic concerns. In 1863 it accepted sponsorship of the Catholic normal school in Milwaukee; in 1868 it appointed two agents to aid immigrants arriving in New York and Baltimore; and in 1876 Weninger urged delegates to consider the needs of Catholic schools and press, ministry to Native Americans and freed slaves, and even political activity "to protect the Church when her rights are endangered." Local and state federations of benevolent and other types of parish societies, such as the young men's associations (to integrate mobile young workers into local Catholic communities), also became common, coordinating action on more local issues. The American Cecilian Society, founded by Singenberger in 1873, brought the European movement for the reform of sacred music to America, promoting classical polyphony, Gregorian chant, and appropriate vernacular hymns. Within twenty years it enrolled almost five thousand members and played an important role in the maturing of American Catholic music while giving Catholics a distinctive niche within the spectrum of German American musical activity.

Only in the 1880s, however, did America's German Catholics begin to approach European levels of national organization. It began with the 1883 founding of an American branch of Germany's St. Raphael Society for the protection of immigrants. Then in 1887 came the *Priester-Verein,* a national association for German American priests that soon numbered nine hundred members, as well as the first *Katholikentag,* an annual assembly of delegates from lay Catholic societies which the priests' society organized in direct imitation of the German model. The *Katholikentag* in turn prompted short-lived national associations for the German Catholic press, for young men, and for the support of poor American missions. State-level federations followed, pursuing interests of their own, as did national federations among German Catholic sub-groups like the Luxembourgers.

But because they found a political home in the Democratic Party along with most other nineteenth-century Catholics, German Catholics never formed a party of their own on the model of Germany's Center Party (founded in 1871). They remained among the Democrats' staunchest supporters, not only because the Democrats had defended them against antebellum nativists, but because they shared—and helped shape—the party's resolute opposition to modernizing governmental centralization and temperance, Sabbatarian, and school language legislation. As impoverished recent immigrants, many took little interest in the Union cause during the Civil War, serving more frequently as draftees than as volunteers, and Republican accusations of copperheadism and draft evasion—even when true—left deep scars. They were active citizens within their own communities, and rallied effectively at higher levels when the occasion demanded, as in 1889 campaigns against Illinois and Wisconsin legislation mandating English as the language of instruction in the schools. They likewise entered the labor movement as allies of the Irish rather than forming organizations of their own like those of Catholic Germany. Fear of socialist influences turned them away from many German American labor unions as

well. Only in the World War I-era struggles to preserve American neutrality and resist prohibition did much Catholic cooperation with other German American organizations occur.

Controversies Surrounding German Catholicism

Renewed American nativism, stimulated by mass immigration and advancing industrialization, provided a defensive motive for the burst of German Catholic national organizing in the 1880s. But it also owed much to consciousness of identity raised by the *Kulturkampf.* Newspapers and letters from Europe kept immigrants abreast of the struggle in the homeland. Emigrés occupied many pulpits and classrooms, and the last great wave of German immigration in the early 1880s brought into numerous American parishes a mentality shaped by the struggle and by the Catholic victory that resistance and organization achieved. But pride in the new German state also strengthened ethnic feeling, while laboriously acquired security assured many older German-American Catholic communities the resources for organization. Most immediately important, however, and ultimately problematic, was concern for the position of Germans within American Catholicism itself.

The nineteenth-century American Church tolerated rather than accepted ethnic difference. Bishops viewed national parishes as temporary solutions until assimilation permitted a single administrative system and a single Catholic culture, preferably one consonant with that of the Church's Irish majority. Germans posed problems from the beginning. For one thing, there was their association with "trusteeism," a term that came to embody not only their preference for lay management of parish temporalities, but also their reputation for quarrelsomeness. Anticlericalism and Febronianism (subordination of all but the purely spiritual to state or secular control) ran strong among the early southwest German immigrants, practically guaranteeing conflicts with an American episcopacy struggling to assert its authority. Add to that the chaos of Catholicism in Germany after secularization, the scarcity and uncertain quality of early immigrant priests, the extreme poverty of many immigrants, their lack of experience with voluntary financial support for religion, and real differences in language and religious culture separating northern (low) and southern (high) Germans not only from other American Catholics but from one another, and the recipe for conflict was complete. Parishioners quarreled with one another over which hymns to sing and where to build their churches; they quarreled with their pastors over finances and hiring teachers; they quarreled with their bishops over the appointment of pastors and control of parish property, particularly during the parish's formative years, or when a new pastor or a major decision threw accustomed ways of dealing into disarray.

Trusteeism in this broad sense was never an exclusively German problem, but because cultural differences made German parishes, from a non-German bishop's perspective, more difficult to tame, it came to be seen as a characteristically German failing. American law assumed congregations were self-governing, property-holding corporations managed by trustees, assumptions that accorded well with widespread experience in Germany with the *Kirchenrat,* or lay council, to manage parish temporalities. The first problems arose in the 1780s and 1790s, when Philadelphia and Baltimore Germans used their legal control of parish property to claim, as republican heirs to the authorities who exercised such patronage in Europe, the right to appoint their pastors. The first Baltimore Provincial Council in 1829 resolved to avoid such problems by accepting no new parishes unless property was vested in the bishop himself, and American law came to accept this practice. But the great majority of German parishes continued to enjoy real trustee governance in practical affairs well into the twentieth century, and the system functioned smoothly in dioceses like Cincinnati where it was accepted and regulated. Here six male trustees were elected annually from the active members of the parish, and met regularly with the pastor as *ex officio* chair to manage parish temporalities in the bishop's name.

Other issues also created tension. During the 1840s and 1850s there were persistent complaints that American bishops were channeling resources, including European missionary funds, to Irish rather than German parishes. Bishops initially were often content to leave German affairs to a vicar general or to the superiors of German religious orders in their dioceses, but subsequent efforts to reverse such benign neglect and regain diocesan control of now prosperous parishes often generated tussles with both parishes and religious orders. To German Catholics, bishops of their own ethnicity seemed one obvious remedy for such problems, and as early as 1799 they petitioned Rome to create a separate national diocese with its own bishop for Germans in America.

But when German Catholics finally gained a foothold in the hierarchy with the appointment of Résé to the new see of Detroit in 1833, the results were disastrous. His inability to manage his frontier diocese combined with the ethnic prejudice of other American bishops to force his removal in 1840. Thus four years later, when Henni's nomination to frontier Milwaukee made him the second German to join the hierarchy, rather than rejoicing his fellow ethnics complained of the discrimination that sent him to this "American Siberia." John Neumann's appointment to the important Philadelphia see in 1852 was cut short by his early death eight years later, and by 1870 only 11 percent of the bishops were of German heritage, only 14 percent at century's end. This disparity emerged in careful national surveys published by German priests in 1869,

1882, and 1892 to document German Catholic parishes, priests, communicants, school children, and diocesan administrators. The 1882 survey, on the eve of the push toward national German Catholic organization, found just one German archbishop, Michael Heiss (Henni's successor in Milwaukee), twelve bishops (in Green Bay, La Crosse, Detroit, Marquette, Alton, Fort Wayne, and Covington in the so-called "German Triangle" of the Midwest, as well as Leavenworth, Nesqually in Washington Territory, Savannah, Natchez, and Newark), and two apostolic vicars of nascent dioceses in northern Minnesota and Dakota.

These bishops and their German priests found themselves increasingly crossing swords with English-speaking confreres over issues like German tolerance for alcoholic beverages, intolerance for secret societies, and Ultramontanist suspicion of the rapprochement with modern America advocated during this era of mounting American nationalism by liberal prelates like John Ireland of St. Paul, who were anxious to rid the Church of its "foreign" stigma. Moreover, the maturing of the German immigration guaranteed heightened career competition among German- and English-speaking priests. Whose responsibility were the mixed-ethnicity parishes that social mobility was creating? And when national parishes for German immigrants existed within territorial parish boundaries, whose responsibility were the American-born children? Henni's 1878 proposal of Heiss as coadjutor with right of succession triggered a barrage of protest from English-speaking priests in his diocese who felt blocked from advancement, while similar protest erupted among German priests in St. Louis in 1884 over the subordinate status of national to territorial parishes. When the Third Plenary Council failed to resolve this issue, Peter Abbelen, a Milwaukee priest, delivered in 1886 a memorial to Rome from Milwaukee, Cincinnati, and St. Louis-area German priests requesting clarification, and the fat was in the fire.

Abbelen sought (and received) affirmation of the co-equal status of national parishes and the right of parents to keep their children in national parishes. But what he saw as equal rights, Ireland and his allies regarded as a demand for special privileges. The ensuing newspaper and pamphlet war converted the arcana of canon law into an issue of national pride uniting German clergy and laity, and led directly to both the *Priester-Verein* and the *Katholikentag,* which then were interpreted by Americanizing opponents as further evidence for German divisiveness and resistance to assimilation. The overt stimulus for the first *Katholikentag* was the need to raise money for the St. Raphael Society's planned immigrant hostel in New York, and the next major stage in the mounting crisis came from that society also. In 1891 its founder, Peter Paul Cahensly, a Rhineland merchant, carried to Rome a memorial from a recent Lucerne meeting requesting Church support for national parishes and foreign-language ministries in immigrant-receiving nations and immigrant representation in their hierarchies. The Lucerne Memorial was stimulated by concern for Italian immigrants in North and South America, and was signed by fifty-one delegates from seven nations. Nevertheless, grossly distorted cables to American newspapers converted "Cahenslyism" into a plot "to found a religious and political Prussia in the United States," and the resulting scandal ensured papal tabling of the Cahensly proposals. Further blows from the Americanizers followed, including Ireland's proposals to concede significant educational authority to the state, and a successful campaign to remove a conservative German theologian from the faculty of the new Catholic University of America, stimulating heightened German Catholic organization and greater demands for safeguarding their language within the Church than they might otherwise have thought to make.

The Heritage of German Catholicism

Their Ultramontanist conservatism and "make haste slowly" stance on assimilation found vindication of a kind in the 1899 papal condemnation of "Americanism." But the years of demonization and marginalization took a heavy toll. To be sure, the German Catholic milieu did not collapse overnight. The *Katholikentag* and the *Priester-Verein* disappeared, but the Central-Verein gained a new lease on life after 1905 by turning outward in a campaign to reform America in German Catholicism's own image of organic Christian corporatism. Inspired by fear of socialism and the example of Catholics in Germany, the Verein's vigorous advocacy of a range of reforms from settlement houses, labor unions, and workmen's compensation, to farm credit and agricultural cooperatives, helped inject a Catholic voice into American Progressivism while moving its members into the central currents of public debate. Under its auspices women finally emerged from the home to which German Catholic ideology traditionally relegated them, forming the National Catholic Women's Union in 1916 with a program that extended from traditional charity and mission work to encompass various women's and children's causes, opposition to birth control and abortion, and support in their own exercise of citizenship. Indeed, by the 1920s they had become the most active group within the Verein. For similar reasons, the turn of the century saw a proliferation of parish and citywide Catholic workingmen's societies, and a revitalization of the Kolping Society, a YMCA-type association that established a hesitant foothold in the United States as early as 1856. In the years after World War I, Kolping Houses in eleven American cities helped integrate the young single workers who formed a significant portion of that late Catholic immigration.

But even Abbelen had acknowledged that "gradual amalgamation . . . will come of itself, especially when and where immigration ceases," and this proved to be increasingly the case. Anti-German sentiment during World War I only hastened a process already well underway. Children raised in the rural communities moved to urban parishes, while their urban counterparts moved from the old national parishes to better neighborhoods and territorial parishes on the city fringe, where intermarriage with other Catholics—particularly the Irish—increased. One of Chicago's old German parishes had 258 baptisms in 1886, but only 75 twenty years later; attendance at the parochial school of another declined from 1,200 to 200 in the fifteen years after 1901. The city's last German national parish was founded in 1915. Nationally there were only half the number of German-only parishes in 1916 than ten years earlier—the urban second generation was more comfortable using English. As early as 1886 Heiss stipulated that Milwaukee children be taught the catechism in English as well as German to ensure that they understood their faith. Soon the city's parochial schools taught half-days in each language, and by the 1920s the language transition was virtually complete. German survived longer in the countryside, but by the 1930s most rural parishes were also well into the language transition. The German-language Catholic press declined from twenty-seven dailies and weeklies in 1913 to twenty-one in 1918 and only nine by 1937. The *Wahrheitsfreund* folded for lack of subscribers as early as 1907. Arthur Preuss founded *The Review* in 1894 to provide English readers with a German Catholic perspective; St. Paul's conservative *Der Wanderer* inaugurated its English edition in 1930.

But marginalization, war, and natural assimilative processes alone did not fully account for the dismantling of the German Catholic milieu. Bishops—German and non-German alike—aided the process. Their efforts to convert communal folk religiosity into more interiorized devotionalism undermined the logic of ethnic separatism in worship. Rationalization and bureaucratization of diocesan management weakened parish and pastoral autonomy. Bishops' loyalties to Rome took precedence over ethnicity, and they consciously pursued policies to create a unified Catholic fold. Thus, when George Mundelein, of German heritage, became archbishop of Chicago in 1915, he reined in the expansion of national parishes, mandated English in parochial schools, and drew Catholics out of ethnic parish societies to unite in broader associations like the Holy Name Society, the Knights of Columbus, and the Catholic Youth Organization. Milwaukee's Swiss-born Sebastian Messmer deliberately erased the German character of his diocesan seminary and closed its normal school in 1924. St. Cloud's Joseph Busch, of German parentage, founded a diocesan institute in 1917 to educate his deeply conservative rural flock to the needs of modern social reform, and established a Women's Guild and Mission Circles to draw women into the public life of the diocese.

But if the enclosed milieu of the German Catholic parishes faded, its heritage lived on in the self-confident Catholic ghetto of the twentieth century. In the 1960s Catholics of German descent were among the staunchest supporters of parochial schools, church attendance, marriage and family doctrine, and anticommunism. The organic conception of society so deeply embedded in the German Catholic tradition helped Europe's liturgical movement put down some of its earliest American roots in the Benedictine abbeys of rural Minnesota, Missouri, and Ohio, just as it ensured support for New Deal and subsequent reform measures promising to enhance the security of family and community. Among rural Germans it undergirded high birth rates and an exceptional commitment to farming, giving much of today's Midwestern countryside a decidedly Catholic character and preserving, in numerous rural parishes, significant elements of an older Catholic culture. In the cities, only the great parish churches bear witness to the vibrant German Catholic milieu they once harbored. Now they too are starting to disappear.

Barry, Coleman J. *The Catholic Church and German Americans.* Washington, D.C.: The Catholic University Press of America, 1953.

Carey, Patrick W. *People, Priests and Prelates: Ecclesiastical Democracy and the Tensions of Trusteeism.* University of Notre Dame Press, 1987.

Dolan, Jay P. *The Immigrant Church: New York's Irish and German Catholics, 1815–1865.* Baltimore: Johns Hopkins University Press, 1975.

Gerber, David A. *The Making of an American Pluralism: Buffalo, New York 1825–1860.* Urbana: University of Illinois Press, 1989.

Gleason, Philip. *The Conservative Reformers: German-American Catholics and the Social Order.* University of Notre Dame Press, 1968.

Rippinger, Joel. *The Benedictines in the United States: An Interpretive History.* Collegeville, Minn.: The Liturgical Press, 1990.

Rippley, La Vern J. *The German-Americans.* Boston: Twayne Publishers, 1976.

Rothan, Emmet H. *The German Catholic Immigrant in the United States 1830–1860.* Washington, D.C.: The Catholic University of America Press, 1946.

Yzermans, Vincent A. *The Spirit in Central Minnesota: A Centennial Narrative of the Church of St. Cloud 1889–1989.* St. Cloud, Minn.: Diocese of St. Cloud, 1989.

KATHLEEN NEILS CONZEN

GEROW, RICHARD OLIVER (1885–1976)

Bishop. Richard Oliver Gerow was born May 3, 1885, in Mobile, Alabama, son of Warren Gerow and Annie Skehan Gerow. He was educated at Mobile's McGill Institute, where he was a member of the first graduating class; Mount St. Mary's College, Emmitsburg, Maryland; and the North American College in Rome. He was ordained in Rome on June 5, 1909. Upon his return to the United States, Gerow served as chancellor (1910–20) and as cathedral rector (1920–24) at Mobile. He was appointed bishop of Natchez, Mississippi, on June 25, 1924, and was consecrated in Mobile on October 15, 1924.

Gerow continued to foster parish and mission expansion in both emerging cities and rural areas, blessing more than eighty churches and chapels between 1925 and 1959, many of which were built with generous assistance from the Catholic Church Extension Society. He encouraged Mississippi branches of national organizations such as the National Council of Catholic Women and the Knights of Columbus; fostered the local lay retreat movement; encouraged the establishment of strong parish youth programs including CYO, CCD, and scouting; fostered local community programs of every sort; and helped organize the Natchez Community Chest in 1925.

Gerow personally organized and indexed the diocesan archives, creating one of the richest and most accessible repositories of Southern Catholic history. He also authored or edited three books and numerous articles and presentations on Mississippi Catholicism and Natchez history.

In 1948 he moved the chancery to the rapidly expanding state capital in Jackson. He briefly participated in the Second Vatican Council. In 1964, with the prodding of Auxiliary Bishop Joseph Brunini and Fr. Bernard Law, he ordered the initial integration of Mississippi Catholic schools. In 1967 he resigned as bishop and continued to reside in Jackson where he died at St. Dominic Hospital on December 20, 1976. He is buried in Jackson.

Gerow nudged Mississippians toward greater mutual tolerance and compassion for the needy. He exercised his episcopal ministry with a "gentle influence . . . , apostolic zeal and the spirit of sacrifice" (Archbishop Joseph Rummel, 1959). "He is indeed a gentle teacher whose ways are the ways of peace," wrote the local Catholic newspaper editor in 1964.

See also MISSISSIPPI, CATHOLIC CHURCH IN.

Gerow Papers and Diaries, Archives, Diocese of Jackson.

Gerow, Richard O. *Catholicity in Mississippi.* Natchez, 1939.

———. *Cradle Days of St. Mary's at Natchez.* Natchez, 1941.

Local diocesan newspapers: October 14, 1937; October 13, 1949; November 6, 1959; October 16, 1964; passim.

Nolan, Charles E. *St. Mary's of Natchez: The History of a Southern Catholic Congregation, 1716–1988.* Natchez, 1992.

CHARLES E. NOLAN

GIBAULT, PIERRE (1735–1802)

Missionary. Pierre Gibault was born in Montreal, Canada, on April 7, 1735, the son of Pierre Gibault and Marie Joseph

St. Jean Gibault. He entered the seminary at Quebec in 1765 and was ordained three years later. He was immediately assigned to the Illinois country mission with the title of vicar general, where he joined Sébastien Meurin, S.J., the only Jesuit to remain in this region after the French suppression of his order in 1764. There he settled at Kaskaskia and labored among the French settlers and neighboring Native American tribes between Michilimakinac and the Arkansas River. After Meurin's death in 1777, he was left as the sole missionary in this region.

At the outbreak of the American Revolution, Quebec's bishop, Jean-Olivier Briand, forbade any member of his diocese, lay or clerical, to cooperate in any way with the Americans under the threat of severe sanctions. In late spring 1778, General George Rogers Clark led an expedition of 175 men into the Illinois territory with the objective of claiming this region for Virginia. In a surprise attack on the morning of July 4, he captured the unprotected town of Kaskaskia. After the town's surrender, Gibault led a citizens' delegation to meet with Clark. Believing Clark's exaggerated claims as to the extent of his military strength, together with his offer of full citizenship, U.S. protection of the region, and the right to freely practice their religion, they accepted Clark's terms and pledged their support to the American government and the state of Virginia.

After Clark revealed his intention to attack the town of Vincennes next, Gibault volunteered to travel there ahead of him to meet with the town's leaders and win their support. Clark sent an address to the people of Vincennes that was carried by Dr. Jean B. Laffont, while Gibault went along to provide spiritual counsel. As he had done in Kaskaskia, Gibault performed the critical act of absolving French settlers from their allegiance to the English Crown, and is credited with playing an influential role in persuading both the French settlers and the surrounding Native American tribes in the Illinois country to accept American rule.

For unstated reasons, Gibault was censured by his bishop in 1780 and his faculties were left unrenewed, but he remained in the Kaskaskia region for the next twelve years where he continued to perform his pastoral duties. When he sought a transfer from the mission in 1790, citing advanced age and declining health, he was rebuffed by Quebec's bishop, as he was by the American bishop, John Carroll, when he applied to join that bishop's newly created diocese. After approaching the Spanish government, he was offered a position at a parish in New Madrid in 1792, where he labored until his death on August 15, 1802.

Donnelly, Joseph P. *Pierre Gibault, Missionary, 1737–1802.* Chicago: Loyola University Press, 1971.

TRICIA Y. PYNE

GIBBONS, JAMES (1834–1921)

Archbishop of Baltimore and cardinal. James Gibbons was born in Baltimore on July 23, 1834, the son of Thomas Gibbons, a clerk, and Bridget Walsh Gibbons. He was baptized in the cathedral from which he would be buried.

James Cardinal Gibbons

Early Years

Gibbons' parents had come to the United States about 1829 but returned to Ireland in 1837. There his father ran a grocery in Ballinrobe, County Mayo, until his death in 1847. The widow and children returned to the United States in 1853, establishing their residence in New Orleans. There James worked in a grocery store until inspired by a Redemptorist retreat to become a priest. In 1855 he entered St. Charles College, the minor seminary of Baltimore, and in 1857 St. Mary's, the major seminary. On June 30, 1861, he was ordained by Archbishop Francis Patrick Kenrick of Baltimore, who had accepted him for his archdiocese. For six weeks Gibbons was assistant at St. Patrick's parish, then appointed first pastor of St. Bridget's, originally a mission of St. Patrick's. There he served as a chaplain for Fort McHenry during the Civil War.

In 1865 Archbishop Martin John Spalding summoned Gibbons to be his secretary and help prepare for the Second Plenary Council of Baltimore. At the council the assembled fathers, at Spalding's prompting, recommended Gibbons for the vicariate apostolic of North Carolina, whose creation they also recommended. Named titular bishop of Adramyttium on March 3, 1868, Gibbons was raised to the episcopacy by Spalding on August 16, 1868, the youngest of more than a thousand bishops in the Catholic world.

The vicariate, the entire state of North Carolina, had fewer than seven hundred Catholics. Gibbons made a number of converts, but finding the apologetical works available inadequate for their needs, he determined to write his own; *Faith of Our Fathers* would prove the most popular apologetical work written by an American Catholic. At Vatican Council I, where he was also the youngest bishop, he voted in favor of papal infallibility. In January 1872 Gibbons was named administrator of the Diocese of Richmond, one of Archbishop Spalding's last requests, and on July 30, bishop of Richmond, retaining his charge of North Carolina. In Richmond his principal task was providing teachers for his schools. At the wish of Archbishop James Roosevelt Bayley of Baltimore, he was named his coadjutor with right of succession on May 25, 1877. Upon Bayley's death on October 3, 1877, Gibbons became archbishop of the premier see.

Archbishop of Baltimore

In his first ten years as archbishop, Gibbons had neither large plans nor great ambitions. He believed his archdiocese well endowed in personnel and institutions, which, in fact, it was. Though he did not instigate, he put no brakes on the proliferation of parish societies that occurred throughout his administration, the knighthoods and young men's literary societies, especially in his first decade. The greatest problems with which he had to contend were those that arose from the influx of new immigrants: the Bohemians, Poles, Lithuanians, and Italians. Though his approach to most difficulties was a "masterly inactivity," he had on more than one occasion to intervene in the affairs of their troublesome parishes but was unable at one to prevent a Polish schism.

In 1884 the archbishop of Baltimore was chosen by the pope to preside over the Third Plenary Council of Baltimore, a gathering for which Gibbons initially showed little enthusiasm. The council, however, produced the most comprehensive body of legislation for the Catholic Church in America. On June 7, 1886, Gibbons was made a cardinal, the second American so honored. On March 17, 1887, he received the red hat in Rome, and a week later at his titular church, Santa Maria in Trastevere, delivered a stirring sermon in praise of his native land and its political principles.

Church Leader: 1

In Rome Gibbons formed a close bond with three other Americans in their efforts to resolve a number of problems: Bishop (soon Archbishop) John Ireland of St. Paul; John Keane, rector designate for The Catholic University to be established in Washington, D.C.; and Denis O'Connell, rector of the North American College in Rome. Together they won Roman approval for The Catholic University despite the opposition of Archbishop Michael Corrigan of New York and the Jesuits. The four prevented a Roman condemnation of the Knights of Labor and the public condemnation of the works of Henry George demanded by Archbishop Corrigan. One of Corrigan's priests, Edward McGlynn, had, despite Corrigan's prohibition, espoused the cause of George, whom Corrigan considered socialistic. The four also successfully countered a petition of German Catholics in the United States for a greater degree of autonomy that was highly critical of Irish bishops. The defense of the Knights of Labor was signed by Gibbons alone and won for him a reputation as champion of the working class.

Gibbons, Ireland, Keane, and O'Connell came to be recognized as the leaders of the "liberals" in the Catholic hierarchy; Corrigan and Bishop Bernard McQuaid of Rochester as spokesmen for the conservatives, who also included most of the German bishops. When German discontent surfaced again in what was called the "Cahensly affair," Gibbons delivered in 1891 a forceful sermon in the cathedral of Milwaukee denouncing those who would "sow tares of discord in the fair fields of the Church in America."

Though hitherto supportive of parochial schools, Gibbons rose to the defense of Archbishop Ireland in 1891 and his Faribault plan that would incorporate parish schools into the public school system, a measure strenuously opposed by Corrigan, McQuaid, the Germans, and the Jesuits. Rome declared that the plan could be tolerated, but in 1893 sent a permanent apostolic delegate to the United States, Francesco Satolli, to resolve this and other points of conflict. Satolli's initial sympathy for the liberals was indicated not only by his support of the Faribault plan but also by his lifting of the excommunication of Edward McGlynn imposed by Archbishop Corrigan. Uneasy, however, with the participation of Gibbons and Keane in the World's Parliament of Religions in 1893 and Gibbons' failure to enforce the Roman condemnation of certain secret societies in the United States in 1894, Satolli in 1895 shifted his support to the conservatives, especially in his approval of parish schools and the work of the Germans. The triumph of the conservatives was made obvious by the dismissal of O'Connell as rector of the North American College in 1895 and of Keane as rector of The Catholic University in 1896.

Despite this setback, Ireland, Keane, and O'Connell, with Gibbons' backing, promoted an agenda for the Americanization of the Catholic Church at home and abroad, especially the acceptance of such principles as the separation of Church and state and the adoption of democratic procedures. Alarmed, European conservatives, particularly in France, seized upon a biography of the founder of the American Paulists, Isaac Hecker, for which Ireland had written a glowing introduction, to have such American aberrations condemned by the Holy See. In the papal letter, *Testem benevolentiae* (January 22, 1899), addressed to Gibbons, the heresy of "Americanism" was condemned, actually a medley of beliefs such as a reliance on the Holy Spirit rather than on external guidance, a promotion of the active over the passive or supernatural virtues, and a depreciation of religious vows.

Church Leader: 2

Despite this fatal blow to the Americanizers as a whole, Gibbons continued to play the role of spokesman of the Catholic Church in America splendidly. His public utterances commanded increasing attention. His presence at important national events, usually to deliver the invocation, was given even greater coverage in the press. Gibbons developed a warm friendship with several presidents, especially Theodore Roosevelt. For the celebration of the fiftieth anniversary of his ordination to the priesthood in 1911, business in the national capital came practically to a halt so that almost every politician of note could go to Baltimore to pay their respects.

A part of Gibbons' popularity derived from the works he authored. *Faith of Our Fathers* (1876) was published many times over. Also widely read were *Our Christian Heritage* (1889), *Ambassador of Christ* (1896), *Discourses and Sermons* (1908), and *A Retrospect of Fifty Years* (1916). He contributed a number of essays to such much-read journals as the *North American Review* and *Putnams' Monthly.* His style was simple but compelling. Protestant Americans looked most often to Gibbons for an explanation of the Catholic position on contentious issues.

Gibbons' views were not always consistent. At the time of the Spanish-American War he was a pacifist, denouncing militarism and the arms race as unchristian. At the outset of World War I he was a strong proponent of preparedness, and during its course urged Catholic men to go forth and be proud of their wounds. Initially an opponent of American imperialism, under the influence of Presidents Roosevelt and Taft he urged the American bishops to oppose the Jones Act designed to dismantle the American Empire. At the local level Gibbons supported such progressive measures as city planning, public health, consumer protection, and the regulation of sweatshops. At the national level he opposed the Seventeenth, Eighteenth, and Nineteenth Amendments. The list of his denunciations of the movement for women's suffrage was embarrassingly long.

Until the day he died Gibbons exercised considerable power in the American Church. As ranking prelate he presided over the annual meetings of the archbishops that began in 1890. He also presided over the transformation of the National Catholic War Council into the National Catholic Welfare Council in 1919. After his reception of the red hat, he came to enjoy the power he seemed to win effortlessly. In 1914 he raised strong objections to the ru-

mors that the national capital would be detached from his archdiocese. He refused to have a coadjutor. He also enjoyed remarkable health until a few days before his death on March 24, 1921, at the age of eighty-seven years and eight months.

Assessment

More than any other Catholic, not excepting John Carroll, James Gibbons was embraced by his country. He was personable, outgoing, and seldom without a smile. Concern for his reputation, according to some, made him conciliatory but overly cautious. To a querulous few he was vain, devious, and timid. To most, however, he was assured, prudent, and gentle. With soothing words and disarming rhetoric he was able to retain the affection and esteem of those whose expectations he disappointed most. Quietly he worked to defuse the lay Catholic Congress movement while praising the layman's efforts. Though in print he continued to champion the cause of the working class, in practice his dealings with labor unions left much to be desired. While he fought a bill to disfranchise Maryland blacks, at a Catholic African American Congress he counseled "wisdom, forbearance, prudence, and discretion." While he complimented women for their virtue, industry, and piety, he made no effort to hide his disdain for feminists.

As the archdiocese he governed grew in prestige, it declined in proportion to the numerical and institutional indices that marked the growth of other archdioceses. Gibbons was not an institution builder because he was not a wall builder. He desired his immigrant charges to move into the mainstream as rapidly as possible. In this and in other ways he resembled the first archbishop of Baltimore. Like John Carroll, Gibbons evidenced a broad ecumenism in his association with the leaders of other denominations. In his involvement in civic affairs he also resembled Carroll. Like Carroll he was tireless in his praise of American virtues, institutions, and principles. And like Carroll he could interpret Roman directives broadly or ignore them altogether.

The Archdiocese of Baltimore, the apostolic delegate Giovanni Bonzano would report two months after Gibbons' death, was not in a flourishing condition. Gibbons had shunned acts of administration that involved responsibility or odium and had paid little attention to the decrees of the council over which he had presided. No future American bishop, Bonzano advised, must be allowed to wield the power Gibbons had.

Yet the apostolic delegate was prepared to admit that Gibbons had served the Church well in assuaging intolerance and bigotry. With consummate tact he had become the friend of people of every condition, race, and faith, so that at his death he was exalted as a patriot, a citizen, and a statesman, a man of great vision whose words on national questions were always peaceful and just. Five years before his death the Baltimore *Sun* had said the same. "The Catholic Church has given many distinguished prelates and priests to its work in this country, but none who has inspired the same general confidence and the same earnest esteem." Its explanation: "To all he seems to speak in their own tongues by some Pentecostal power, or by some subtle affinity that makes nothing human foreign to him."

See also AMERICANISM; KNIGHTS OF LABOR; MARYLAND, CATHOLIC CHURCH IN; PAPAL REPRESENTATION IN AMERICA.

Ellis, John Tracy. *The Life of James Cardinal Gibbons, Archbishop of Baltimore, 1834–1921.* 2 vols. Milwaukee: Bruce Publishing Co., 1952.

Fogarty, Gerald P., S.J., ed. *Patterns of Episcopal Leadership.* New York: Macmillan, 1989.

Spalding, Thomas W. *The Premier See: A History of the Archdiocese of Baltimore, 1789–1989.* Baltimore: Johns Hopkins University Press, 1989.

Will, Allen Sinclair. *Life of Cardinal Gibbons, Archbishop of Baltimore.* 2 vols. New York: E. P. Dutton, 1922.

THOMAS W. SPALDING

Related Document

THE ROMAN SERMON OF THE AMERICAN CARDINAL ON CHURCH AND STATE IN THE UNITED STATES, MARCH 25, 1887

Few subjects in American religious history have held more interest, or caused more controversy, than that of the relations of Church and State. From the time of Archbishop Carroll to our own day the Catholic hierarchy of the United States has repeatedly expressed its approval of the separation of Church and State as it has existed in this country since the beginning of the Republic (cf. John Tracy Ellis, "Church and State: An American Catholic Tradition," *Harper's Magazine,* CCVII [November, 1953], 63–67). The first time these views were publicly voiced in Rome was on the occasion when Cardinal Gibbons took possession of his titular Church of Santa Maria in Trastevere. The sermon was of more than ordinary significance in view of the severely strained relations at that time between the Church and the anticlerical governments of Germany, Italy, and France, countries where there had been a long tradition of union of Church and State. American Catholics were pleased with their new cardinal's pronouncement, and Father Isaac Hecker was doubtless expressing the reaction of the great majority when he remarked how well fitted Gibbons was by his "thorough-going American spirit to interpret us to the peoples and powers of the Old World" ("Cardinal Gibbons and American Institutions," *Catholic World,* XLV [June 1887], 331).

(*Source: Catholic Mirror,* Baltimore, April 2, 1887.)

IT IS TO ME EXCEEDINGLY GRATIFYING THAT THE HOLY FATHER has assigned as my titular church this beautiful and historic basilica, the first church ever erected in honor of the Virgin Mother of God; and I regard it as an auspicious circumstance that my own Cathedral Church of Baltimore, the oldest cathedral in the United States, is dedicated to our Blessed Lady. The venerable temple in which we are assembled leads us back to the days of the catacombs. It was founded by Pope St. Callixtus in the year 224. It was reconstructed by Pope Julius in the fourth century, and renovated by another Supreme Pontiff in the twelfth.

That ceaseless solicitude which the Roman Pontiffs have exhibited erecting the material temples which adorn this city, they have also manifested on a larger scale in building up the spiritual walls of Sion in every age.

Every student of history must be deeply impressed with the overruling action of the Papacy in the evangelization and civilization of the Christian world. I place these words together, for a nation is civilized in proportion as it receives the light of the Gospel. It was the vigilant zeal of the Holy See that sent Augustine to England, and Patrick to Ireland, and Pelagius to Scotland, and that sent Francis Xavier to evangelize the Indies; and all those other heroes of Christ's Church who bore, amid the sufferings and trials, the bright light of truth into the regions of pagan darkness. And coming down to a later period, scarcely were the United States formed into an independent government when Pius VI, of happy memory, established there the Catholic hierarchy and appointed the illustrious John Carroll first Bishop of Baltimore. This event, so important to us, occurred less than a hundred years ago—a long period, indeed, in our history, but how brief in that of Rome eternal! Our Catholic community in those days numbered only a few thousand souls, scattered chiefly through the States of New York, Pennsylvania, and Maryland, and were served by the merest handful of priests. Thanks to the fructifying grace of God, the grain of mustard seed then planted has grown to be a large tree, spreading its branches over the length and the width of our fair land. Where only one bishop was found in the beginning of this century, there are now seventy-five serving as many dioceses and vicariates. For their great progress under God and the fostering care of the Holy See we are indebted in no small degree to the civil liberty we enjoy in our enlightened republic.

Our Holy Father, Leo XIII, in his luminous encyclical on the constitution of Christian States, declares that the Church is not committed to any particular form of civil government. She adapts herself to all; she leavens all with the sacred leaven of the Gospel. She has lived under absolute empires; she thrives under constitutional monarchies; she grows and expands under the free republic. She has often, indeed, been hampered in her divine mission and has had to struggle for a footing wherever despotism has cast its dark shadow like the plant excluded from the sunlight of heaven, but in the genial air of liberty she blossoms like the rose!

For myself, as a citizen of the United States, without closing my eyes to our defects as a nation, I proclaim, with a deep sense of pride and gratitude, and in this great capital of Christendom, that I belong to a country where the civil government holds over us the aegis of its protection without interfering in the legitimate exercise of our sublime mission as ministers of the Gospel of Jesus Christ.

Our country has liberty without license, authority without despotism. Hers is no spirit of exclusiveness. She has no frowning fortifications to repel the invader, for we are at peace with all the world. In the consciousness of her strength and of her good will to all nations she rests secure. Her harbors are open in the Atlantic and Pacific to welcome the honest immigrant who comes to advance his temporal interest and to find a peaceful home.

But, while we are acknowledged to have a free government, we do not, perhaps, receive due credit for possessing also a strong government. Yes, our nation is strong, and her strength lies, under Providence, in the majesty and supremacy of the law, in the loyalty of her citizens to that law, and in the affection of our people for their free institutions.

There are, indeed, grave social problems which are now engaging the earnest attention of the citizens of the United States. But I have no doubt that, with God's blessings, these problems will be solved by the calm judgment and sound sense of the American people without violence, or revolution, or injury to individual right.

As an evidence of his benevolence and good will to the great republic of the West, as evidence of his appreciation of the venerable hierarchy of the United States, and as an expression of his kind condescension for the ancient See of Baltimore, our Holy Father, Leo XIII, has been graciously pleased to exalt its present incumbent in my humble person to the dignity of the purple.

For this mark of exalted favor I offer the Holy Father my profound thanks in my own name and in the name of the clergy and people under my charge. I venture also to thank him in the name of my venerable colleagues the bishops, the clergy, as well as the Catholic laity of the United States. I presume to thank him also in the name of our separated brethren of America who, though not sharing our faith, have shown that they are not insensible to the honor conferred on our common country, and have again and again expressed their warm admiration of the enlightened statesmanship, the apostolic virtues, and benevolent charities of the illustrious Pontiff who now sits in the Chair of Peter.

(*Source:* John Tracy Ellis, ed. *Documents of American Catholic History.* Vol. 2:1866–1966. Wilmington, Del.: Michael Glazier, 1987, 461–63.)

GILLESPIE, MARY OF ST. ANGELA (1824–87)

Religious superior. Born February 21, 1824, in Washington County, Pennsylvania, the third generation of her family in the United States, Eliza Gillespie was educated at

M. Angela Gillespie

the Visitation convent in Georgetown, Washington, D.C. When she joined the Congregation of Holy Cross in 1853, she was the educated, American-born woman whom the congregation's American superior, the Rev. Edward Sorin, was looking for to organize and lead his community of immigrant women. On her return from her novitiate in France in 1855, she became the directress of the newly opened St. Mary's Academy for women at Notre Dame, Indiana. From 1857 to 1860 and again from 1862 to 1865, she served as the superior of the sisters at Notre Dame.

During the Civil War, Mother Angela supervised the work of the more than eighty sisters assigned by Sorin as nurses in Union military hospitals. After the war she was the de facto editor of the *Ave Maria,* a weekly Catholic magazine started by Sorin in 1865. She also edited *The Metropolitan Readers,* a graded literature textbook series published by Sadlier.

In 1860 the sisters had been organized as an autonomous congregation, the Marianites of Holy Cross, separate from the Priests and Brothers of Holy Cross. By 1869 tension between the Marianites in the midwestern United States and the motherhouse in France was such that the Vatican approved a temporary separation that soon became permanent. The new congregation, known as the Sisters of the Holy Cross, was centered at Notre Dame, Indiana. Sorin was the ecclesiastical superior and Mother Angela was provincial superior from 1867 to 1882. Under her leadership her community expanded its work in the education of women and children and drew on the sisters' wartime experience to enter the field of health care. She died at Notre Dame, Indiana, on March 4, 1887.

See also AVE MARIA; SISTERS OF THE HOLY CROSS (C.S.C.).

Costin, M. Georgia. *Priceless Spirit.* University of Notre Dame Press, 1994.

McAllister, Anna Shannon. *Flame in the Wilderness.* Paterson, N.J.: St. Anthony Guild Press, 1944.

Notable American Women: 1607–1950. 1971, s.v. "Gillespie, Mother Angela," M. Madeleva Wolff, C.S.C.

JAMES CONNELLY, C.S.C.

GILLET, LOUIS FLORENT (1813–93)

Missionary. Louis Florent Gillet was born on January 12, 1813, in Antwerp, Belgium. In 1831, Gillet entered the Congregation of the Most Holy Redeemer (Redemptorists), which had only recently been established in Belgium. Gillet was professed in 1834 and, after completing his studies in the new Redemptorist major seminary in Wittem, Holland, was ordained in Liège on March 10, 1838. After some years of pastoral work in Europe, Gillet was sent to the new Redemptorist mission in the United States, arriving in New York in May 1843. Bishop Peter Paul Lefevre, coadjutor administrator of the Diocese of Detroit, requested the services of the Redemptorists for the French-speaking population around Detroit. Gillet and Francis Poilvache were sent to Detroit in August 1843. Gillet distinguished himself as a preacher of parish missions and was especially successful in establishing temperance societies.

In 1884 Gillet was made pastor and superior of the Redemptorist parish of St. Mary's in Monroe, Michigan. Recognizing the need for Catholic education of the young, Gillet, together with Mother Theresa Maxis Duchemin, founded the Sisters of Providence (the community was later renamed Sisters, Servants of the Immaculate Heart of Mary) on November 10, 1845. Gillet gave the community a rule based on that of the Redemptorists and the sisters dedicated themselves to education and preparation for the reception of the sacraments.

In 1847 Gillet was falsely accused of soliciting a woman. While he was totally exonerated in court, Gillet felt that he had lost the trust of his Redemptorist superiors because of the experience and impulsively asked for a dispensation from his vows, an act he later regretted. Between 1848 and 1858 Gillet ministered in a number of places in the United States and Canada. In 1853 he returned to Europe and unsuccessfully petitioned to be readmitted to the Redemptorists.

After ministering in Europe he traveled to South America with the intention of working there, but returned almost immediately to Europe. Tired after his years of wandering, Gillet answered a contemplative vocation and entered the Cistercian monastery in Senanque, France, taking the religious name of Marie Celestin. He pioneered foundations in Fontfroide, France, and spent the last years of his life in the Royal Abbey of Hautecombe-Savoy, France, where he served as novice master and prior. The last year of Gillet's life was gladdened by receiving the news that the community of sisters he had founded in Monroe and with whom he had no contact for over forty years had flourished. Gillet died on November 14, 1892. In 1929 his body was returned to Monroe and buried in the motherhouse cemetery of the Immaculate Heart of Mary Sisters.

See also REDEMPTORISTS (C.Ss.R.).

Kelly, Rosalita. *No Greater Service: The History of the Congregation of the Sisters, Servants of the Immaculate Heart of Mary, Monroe, Michigan: 1845–1945.* Privately published in Detroit, Michigan, 1948.

TERRENCE J. MORAN, C.Ss.R.

GILLIS, JAMES MARTIN (1876–1957)

Priest, editor, and author. Gillis was born on November 12, 1876, in Boston, Massachusetts. The son of James and Catherine Roche Gillis, he received his early education at Boston Latin School. He attended St. Charles College, Ellicott City, Maryland, and St. John's Seminary, Brighton, Massachusetts, before joining the Paulist Fathers in 1900. He was ordained the following year and studied theology at The Catholic University of America, Washington, D.C., until 1910, when he was assigned to the mission field.

In 1922 he was named editor of the *Catholic World.* Through his editorials and preaching, a syndicated newspaper column ("Sursum Corda"), and radio programs on "The Catholic Hour" from 1930–41, Gillis became one of the most influential American Catholic priests of his time.

James M. Gillis

A prolific author, his books included *False Prophets* (1925), *The Catholic Church and the Home* (1928), *The Ten Commandments* (1931), *Christianity and Civilization* and *The Paulists* (1932), *This One Day* (two volumes, 1939 and 1949), *So Near Is God* (1935), *On Almost Everything*

(1955), *This Mysterious Human Nature* (1956), and *My Last Book* (1957).

Gillis resigned as editor of the *Catholic World* in 1948 because of illness, but he continued to serve as a contributing editor. Many honorary degrees were bestowed on him by American Catholic colleges, and he also received an honorary doctorate in theology from the Angelicum (Pontifical University of St. Thomas Aquinas), Rome. He died in New York City on March 14, 1957, and was buried in the Crypt Church at St. Paul the Apostle, New York City.

See also CATHOLIC WORLD, THE; PAULISTS (C.S.P.).

Finley, J. F. *James Gillis: Paulist.* Garden City, N.Y.: Hanover House, 1958.

MARIANNA McLOUGHLIN

GILMOUR, RICHARD (1824–91)

Bishop. Richard Gilmour was born on September 28, 1824, in Glasgow, Scotland, son of John and Marian Callender Gilmour. He was received into the Catholic Church on August 15, 1842, in Philadelphia. He attended St. Michael Seminary, Pittsburgh, and Mount St. Mary College, Emmitsburg, Maryland. He was ordained in Cincinnati by Archbishop John Baptist Purcell on August 30, 1852. Gilmour was engaged in pastoral work in Cincinnati from 1852 to 1868, and again from 1869 to 1872, and was on the faculty of the Seminary of Mount St. Mary of the West in Cincinnati from 1868 to 1869. He was elevated to the see of Cleveland on February 15, 1872, and consecrated on April 14, 1872, in Cincinnati by Archbishop John Purcell, Bishop August Bernard Toebbe (Covington), and Bishop Casper Henry Borgess (Detroit).

Gilmour founded the *Catholic Universe,* the newspaper of the Diocese of Cleveland, in 1874. He won religious freedom for inmates of penal institutions in 1875 and secured exemption of Catholic school properties from local taxation in 1883. He also founded St. Ignatius College, was a champion of education and charity, and wrote several readers and a spelling book for use in schools, including *Bible History* in 1869. Gilmour was prominent in the Third Plenary Council of Baltimore in 1884. After the completion of that council, Gilmour, along with Bishop John Moore of St. Augustine and Bishop Joseph Dwenger of Ft. Wayne, was designated by Archbishop James Gibbons to personally bring the Acts of the Council to Rome for the acceptance of the Holy See. That process lasted until late October 1885 and involved the approval of the Baltimore Catechism, the ownership of property by religious orders in the United States, the question of irremovable rectors of parishes, the establishment of consultors to the bishop, and guidelines on the nomination of bish-

ops. Bishop Gilmour died April 13, 1891, in St. Augustine, Florida, and was buried in Cleveland.

Hallinan, Paul J. "Richard Gilmour, Second Bishop of Cleveland, 1872–1891." Ph.D. dissertation, Western Reserve University, 1963.

NELSON J. CALLAHAN

GIORDA, JOSEPH (1821–82)

Jesuit missionary. Joseph Giorda was born of a noble family near Turin, Italy, on March 19, 1821. He entered the Society of Jesus at the age of twenty-two, and later served as a seminary professor. He was regarded as a brilliant intellectual. After volunteering, he was assigned to the Rocky Mountain Mission for the Indians and arrived at Sacred Heart Mission for the Coeur d'Alenes in 1861. The Native Americans called him *Mil'Kokan,* which means "Round Head," because his face was the shape of a pie. Assigned to a dangerous mission, St. Peter's on the plains of what is now eastern Montana, he threw his enormous energies into the service of Native Americans and whites. He soon gained the respect of the former and the love of the latter, who elected him to be the first chaplain of the Montana Territorial Legislature at Virginia City.

One year after arriving at St. Peter's, Giorda was appointed as superior general of the Rocky Mountain Mission. This had fallen on evil days. Early missions had been closed. Native American indifference and wars had discouraged support, and Jesuits who had been assigned to the Rocky Mountain Mission were being reassigned to colleges in California. Giorda took firm control. He traveled to California and claimed his subjects. He brought to Montana Sisters of Providence, the pioneers of the sisterhoods. He rebuilt or founded new missions, including old St. Mary's, which had been closed in 1850. When relieved of his superiorship in 1866, he left eight mission residences where he had found but two. Thus he was given another title: The Second Founder of the Rocky Mountain Mission.

He served a second time as superior general from 1869 to 1877. Relieved of his charge because of poor health, he lingered on and died at Sacred Heart Mission on August 4, 1882.

Bischoff, William N. *The Jesuits in Old Oregon.* Caldwell, Idaho: Caxton Publishers, 1945.
Schoenberg, Wilfred P., S.J. *A History of the Catholic Church in the Pacific Northwest 1743–1983.* Washington, D.C.: Pastoral Press, 1987.
____. *Paths to the Northwest: A Jesuit History of the Oregon Province.* Chicago: Loyola University Press, 1982.
Schrems, Suzanne. "God's Women: Sisters of Charity of Providence and Ursuline Nuns in Montana, 1864–1900." Ph.D. dissertation, University of Oklahoma, 1993.

WILFRED P. SCHOENBERG, S.J.

GIRODEAU, FELICITÉ POMET (1791–1862)

Free woman of color and lay Catholic leader. Felicité Pomet was born in New Orleans on September 22, 1791, daughter of Leonard Pomet and Françoise Coco Pomet. She married Gabriel Girodeau in New Orleans on July 3, 1817. The couple settled in Natchez where Gabriel was a jeweler and businessman before his premature death in 1827. Felicité's father, husband, and brother-in-law, Antonio Girodeau, served as early trustees of the Natchez Catholic congregation.

Madame Girodeau's home welcomed numerous visiting clergy when Mississippi had no resident priest. Her closet served as a confessional; her parlor, a mission chapel. Bishop John Chanche initially stayed there upon his arrival in the newly created diocese in 1841. Her recollections, recorded by Bishop William Henry Elder in 1859, form the basis of much of the often-told early antebellum history of the Natchez Catholic community.

Widow Girodeau was to many the mother of the modern Natchez Catholic community, assisting with varied parish needs and serving as godmother to more than thirty adults and children of every race and social status. Her slaves, Betty, Alexandrine, and Anne, assisted at the cathedral for many years and served as godmothers to many black children.

Felicité Girodeau died on January 11, 1862. Cathedral pastor Mathurin Grignon characterized her as "the benefactress of the church, of the orphans, and of all in need, according to her means." She and her husband were free persons of color who crossed the color line in Mississippi and became early pillars of Mississippi's largest Catholic congregation.

Natchez and New Orleans sacramental records; Charles Nolan/ Robert Shumway research notes in Archives, Archdiocese of New Orleans.
Nolan, Charles E. *St. Mary's of Natchez: The History of a Southern Catholic Congregation, 1716–1988.* Natchez, 1992.

CHARLES E. NOLAN

GLEASON, MIRIAM THERESA (1886–1962)

Social activist. Before entering the Congregation of the Sisters of the Holy Names of Jesus and Mary, Sr. Miriam Theresa, then known as Caroline Gleason, secured passage of the first successful minimum wage and maximum hour law in the United States in 1913 in the state of Oregon.

In 1912 Fr. Edwin V. O'Hara of the Oregon Consumers' League asked Gleason, a social worker, to survey women's working conditions. To collect data, she organized a team who took jobs in factories. In a Portland paper box factory Gleason earned a total of $1.52 laboring three ten-hour days amid appalling surroundings. The team conducted thousands of interviews with women statewide on housing and living conditions. Gleason presented an uncompromising report revealing intolerable circumstances. While the league prepared legislation, she traveled the state publicizing the findings.

Sentiment was so strong for the wage-and-hour bill that it was introduced on the opening day of the 1913 legislature. Despite vigorous opposition from employers who attacked the credibility of the survey, the Oregon Supreme Court and the U.S. Supreme Court upheld the law's constitutionality, citing Gleason's report.

In 1916 Caroline Gleason entered the Sisters of the Holy Names at Marylhurst, Oregon. She chose a teaching community because of her conviction that Christian education was a prime means of achieving improved social conditions. She earned a doctoral degree in economics from The Catholic University of America, the first woman to receive a doctoral degree there. The U.S. Department of Labor published her dissertation, "Legislation for Women in Oregon."

From 1924 until her retirement in 1960, she chaired the Sociology Department of Marylhurst College. A recognized authority on women's industrial issues, she contributed at state and national levels on social and labor questions.

Sr. Miriam Theresa Gleason, aged seventy-six, died May 12, 1962, at Marylhurst.

Gleason, Miriam Theresa. "Legislation for Women in Oregon." Ph.D. dissertation, The Catholic University of America. New York: C. P. Young Co., 1924.
Lorenz, Helen Miriam. "Caroline Gleason: A Pioneer in Social Reforms." Unpublished paper, University of Oregon, 1966.
State of Oregon Bureau of Labor. *50 Years of Progress.* Salem: State Printing Department, 1953.
United States Department of Labor, Bulletin of the Women's Bureau. *Oregon Legislation for Women in Industry.* Report no. 90. Washington, D.C.: Government Printing Office, 1931.

CAROLE STRAWN, S.N.J.M.

GLENMARY HOME MISSIONERS, THE

Founded by W. Howard Bishop, a priest of the Archdiocese of Baltimore, the Glenmary Home Missioners originated in the Archdiocese of Cincinnati when Archbishop John T. McNicholas approved the tiny community of two priests and four seminarians as a diocesan society. Though the document of approval was composed in 1944, when the society began the process of applying for canonical status, it was predated 1939. The founder designed "The No Priestland Map" to highlight the need for rural evangelization by depicting the many hundreds of counties in the United States without a resident priest actively engaged in town and country mission work.

Howard Bishop was a pastor of St. Louis parish in Clarksville, Maryland, from 1917 to 1937; founder of the

League of the Little Flower to promote rural parish schools; a charter member of the National Catholic Rural Life Conference (1922), president of the conference (1928–34); and founding editor of one of its journals, *Landward*. Disillusioned with the apparent failure of the back-to-the land movement as a Christian communalist alternative to the severe economic distress in the cities, Bishop conceived a direct-action missionary order that would convert the unchurched and plant vital parishes in rural America. After receiving the endorsement of James A. Walsh, cofounder of Maryknoll, he sought an episcopal sponsor. His own ordinary, Archbishop Michael J. Curley of Baltimore, did not support Bishop's proposal for an independent missionary movement beyond diocesan strategies, but he did not obstruct his pursuit of an episcopal sponsor. Eventually Archbishop McNicholas, a close friend of James A. Walsh, welcomed Bishop into his diocese. In 1937 he became pastor of a small rural parish that included responsibility for a mission church. He soon founded a monthly, *The Challenge,* which featured illustrated articles on the desperate need to respond to the rural poor, black and white, by establishing a community of priests, brothers, and sisters.

Bishop's plan included three spheres of missionary activity: establishing a mission church as a base parish to directly evangelize the area; sending out teams to engage in street, trailer, or public-hall preaching to non-Catholics; and elevating the moral climate through social activism. The working brothers would construct and maintain buildings and property and assist in missionary works; the priests would engage in direct action evangelization; and the sisters would be trained in nursing, social work, and catechesis. In accord with the prevailing patriarchal attitudes, the men engaged in public witness while the women served the needy in the homes.

The nascent Glenmary Women Missioners, such as Dorothy Hendershoot, Opal Simon, Gertrude Kimmick, Joan Wade, and Eloise Woodward, attended conferences led by Howard Bishop and as early as 1944 three were assigned to catechetical classes, Bible school, and general home visitations. Though they considered Bishop their founder, the Glenmary Sisters became a canonically approved self-governing diocesan community in 1952. They adopted the Rule of St. Dominic, as did the Maryknoll Sisters, and were formed by Dominican Sisters.

The men's community did not experience their first official novitiate until 1951, the year Archbishop Karl Alter, who succeeded McNicholas in 1950, approved their constitution. A general chapter elected Howard Bishop first superior general. Like the Maryknoll community, the Glenmary order founded its own seminary infused with a missionary spirit, and *The Challenge* was both a mission journal and a source of fundraising. When Howard Bishop died in 1953, the society had seven rural missions; there were eleven brothers, twenty-one priests, and twenty-nine sisters.

The last two years of his life the founder had been working on a paraliturgical service for what he referred to as the "faraways," those ad hoc congregations who had no Sunday Mass in their area. The core of the service was a simple English translation of the Mass; a lay leader would read aloud and the congregation would respond as in the contemporary liturgy in the vernacular. In 1988 the Vatican approved a "Directory for Sunday Celebration in the Absence of a Priest" that has its historical analogue in Howard Bishop's "Service for Faraways." The founder's personality shifted from easy informality to rigidly closed-minded authoritarianism, while his temperament was equally mercurial. Though he occasionally generated conflict, there was a consensus on the viability of his mission vision and strategy.

Fr. Clement Bouchers, superior general from 1953 to 1964, was a warm, outgoing man who presided over the community during a period of phenomenal growth in vocations. Because the society reached its twenty-fifth birthday (1939–64) during the Second Vatican Council, Home Missioners did not need to "retrieve the charism" of their community, but rather to reflect upon their own lived experience as first-generation Glenmary Home Missioners, many of whom knew the founder.

Vatican II and After

In accord with the general experience of religious communities, Glenmary held an extended general chapter under superior general Robert Berson. It composed a new constitution reflecting the principles of adaptation to modernity, collegial governance, subsidiarity, personal responsibility, and new notions of spirituality grounded in liturgy,

Glenmary Missioners

Scripture, and apostolic witness. With the demise of the traditional authoritative system came the rise of an egalitarianism; brothers were free to pursue academic and pre-professional training as well as to choose the building trades and administrative positions. According to Vatican directives the superior of the community, entitled president, must be a priest, but brothers have served as vice presidents. During the administrations of Presidents Robert Berson, Charles Hughes, Frank Ruff, and Robert Dalton, collegiality and subsidiarity have been manifested in task forces and regional meetings dealing with the development of the pastoral role of the laity and other innovations in missionary life. There has been tension between peace and justice missionary activity and the demands of nurturing Catholics in parishes.

The Glenmary Sisters experienced a severe crisis during the period of experimentation based upon new understandings of the religious life. Under the leadership of Sr. Catherine Rumschlag, mother general (1953–67), the sisters were allowed to pursue academic and professional degree programs. New ministries included merging rural missionary urban projects to emigrants from the countryside. Continuous experimentation in modes of life, spirituality, and ministry led Archbishop Karl J. Alter to impose a moratorium on new membership and on further experimentation; he also revived customs that had been associated with a pre–Vatican Council II mentality. The conflict simmered to the boiling point when it appeared to Alter that the sisters, particularly the superior, were determined to pursue changes. Alter's response fractured the community. In 1967 nearly seventy sisters left the community to form the Federation of Communities in Service. The nineteen sisters who remained recommitted themselves to rural ministry (without the urban component), and to reform and renewal according to the Second Vatican Council. Srs. Mary Joseph Wade, Rosemary Esterkamp (both of whom knew Howard Bishop), and Christine Beckett have led the community from 1967 into the 1990s.

See also BISHOP, WILLIAM HOWARD.

Howard Bishop's personal papers, diaries, and correspondence are located at the Glenmary Archives in Cincinnati.

Kauffman, Christopher J. *Mission to Rural America: The Story of W. Howard Bishop, Founder of Glenmary.* Mahwah, N.J.: Paulist Press, 1991.

Stanten, Herman W. *Howard Bishop, Founder of the Glenmary Home Missions.* Cincinnati, 1961.

CHRISTOPHER J. KAUFFMAN

GLENNON, JOHN JOSEPH (1862–1946)

Cardinal archbishop of St. Louis. John J. Glennon was born in Kinnegad, County Westmeath, Ireland, on June 14, 1862, the son of Matthew and Catherine Glennon. He

John Joseph Cardinal Glennon

came from a family of poor farmers. After preliminary schooling, he studied for the priesthood at St. Finian College in Mullingar, Ireland. He then entered the missionary seminary of All Hallows, Dublin. On completion of his studies there in 1883, he came to the United States. Glennon was already a citizen of the United States since his father had lived for a time in this country, acquiring citizenship before returning to Ireland.

Glennon was adopted by the Diocese of Kansas City, Missouri, where he was ordained to the priesthood on December 20, 1884. A dispensation was required since he was below the legal age for ordination. His first appointment was as assistant pastor of St. Patrick's parish in Kansas City. Three years later, he was granted a sabbatical to continue his studies in Europe. Upon his return, he was appointed rector of the cathedral. He was named vicar general of the diocese and on March 14, 1896, at the age of thirty-four, he was named titular bishop of Pinara and coadjutor of the Diocese of Kansas City. His consecration took place on June 29, 1896.

On April 27, 1903, he was named coadjutor archbishop of St. Louis with right of succession to Archbishop John Joseph Kain. Upon Kain's death, Glennon became the third archbishop of St. Louis on October 13, 1903. On December 23, 1945, Pope Pius XII elevated him to the College of Cardinals. He died in his native Ireland on March 9, 1946, on his return trip from Rome.

Cardinal Glennon was best known as a builder, educator, and orator. During his forty-two years in St. Louis he directed the building of the present cathedral, major and minor seminary buildings, seven high schools, and numerous parishes. He was a trustee of The Catholic University of America and was selected to deliver the funeral sermon for Cardinal Gibbons in 1922. He was loved and revered by many people in St. Louis, but he played little role on the national scene. His biographer also pointed out that he was a person of narrow views on such issues as women's suffrage, the liturgical movement, and race relations.

See also MISSOURI, CATHOLIC CHURCH IN.

Schneider, Nicholas. *The Life of John Cardinal Glennon, Archbishop of St. Louis*. Ligouri, Missouri, 1971.

MARTIN G. TOWEY

GLORIEUX, ALPHONSUS JOSEPH (1844–1917)

Bishop. Glorieux was born in Dottignies, West Flanders, Belgium, February 1, 1844. After completing his early education, he began six years of study in the preparatory seminary in Courtrai. Having decided to offer himself to the North American missions of the West, he entered the American College in Louvain. Ordained August 17, 1867, he departed for Oregon where he took up his missionary work with headquarters in Roseburg. Four years later he was named first president of the new St. Michael's College, Portland. He was appointed vicar apostolic of Idaho on October 7, 1884, and consecrated bishop on April 19, 1884. In the vicariate he found two diocesan priests and three Jesuits. Choosing Boise as his headquarters, he became the first bishop to live in that city. For the next twenty years his name would appear in the baptismal records of nineteen parishes and missions that he faithfully served as active pastor.

When the Diocese of Boise was created on August 26, 1893, and he was named its first bishop, the records showed that the number of priests had increased from seven to sixteen, parish churches and schools from one to five, academies from two to three. Two hospitals had been built. By the time of his death on August 25, 1917, Bishop Glorieux had seen the dedication of ninety-three parish and mission churches and the building or remodeling of twenty-five grade schools, one high school, five hospitals, an orphanage, a home for the aged, a monastery, and a cathedral. Four additional communities of women religious had come to Idaho. The number of priests had increased to fifty-three. An educator, teacher, retreat master, builder, and missionary: this is how Bishop Glorieux is remembered by the Catholics of Idaho.

See also IDAHO, CATHOLIC CHURCH IN.

Bradley, Cyprian A., and Edward J. Kelly. *History of the Diocese of Boise 1863–1953*. Boise, Idaho: The Chancery Office, 1953.
Schoenberg, Wilfred P., S.J. *History of the Catholic Church in the Pacific Northwest 1740–1983*. Washington, D.C.: Pastoral Press, 1987.

Walsh, Nicholas E. *The Catholic Church in Idaho: An Overview*. Boise, Idaho: Capitol Publishers and Printers, 1990.

✝ NICHOLAS E. WALSH

GOESBRIAND, LOUIS DE (1816–99)

Bishop. Louis Joseph Marie Theodore de Goesbriand, first bishop of Burlington (Vermont), was born August 4, 1816, in the parish of St. Urbain, Finisterre, Brittany, France. He was the son of the Marquis Pierre Désiré and Emélie (Pastour de Kerjean) de Goesbriand. Educated in the local seminary and the Séminaire de St. Sulpice in Paris, he was ordained there on July 13, 1840, by Bishop Joseph Rosati, C.M., of St. Louis, Missouri.

Louis de Goesbriand

Attracted to the American missions, young Fr. de Goesbriand emigrated to Ohio, where he was engaged in missionary work for several years. When the Diocese of Cleveland was established in 1847, he was appointed vicar general, rector of the cathedral, and director of the regional seminary.

In 1853 three new dioceses were created, including the statewide Diocese of Burlington. Fr. de Goesbriand was named first bishop of the new diocese. He was consecrated in Old St. Patrick's Cathedral, New York City, on October 30 of that year by Archbishop Gaetano Bedini, papal nuncio to Brazil, assisted by Bishops John B. Fitzpatrick of Boston and Louis A. Rappe of Cleveland. De Goesbriand took for his motto a Latin phrase that would give him confidence throughout his forty-six year episcopate: *"Deus Providebit"*—God Will Provide.

On his arrival in Vermont the new bishop found five priests and ten churches serving a Catholic population of roughly twenty thousand. He at once set about organizing his new charge. Within months of his arrival he obtained from the bishop of Montreal an order of nuns to administer the new Providence Orphan Asylum and Hospital. Before two years had passed the bishop had traveled to Ireland and France to recruit priests for the diocese, and had promulgated the statutes of the first diocesan synod. Parishes were established on a timely basis, and the concept of a school in every parish was strongly encouraged. Additional orders of religious women opened houses around the state.

Undaunted by the lack of manpower due to the Civil War, Bishop de Goesbriand commenced construction of a cathedral in 1862. Work progressed slowly, but on December 8, 1867, the Cathedral of the Immaculate Conception was solemnly dedicated, the first cathedral church in New England erected as a cathedral. De Goesbriand was one of the first bishops in New England to realize that the immigration of French-Canadians from Canada into the United States, which greatly increased in the 1860s, was not just a temporary situation. He advocated the creation of "national parishes" to serve non-English speaking Catholics. He also lobbied the bishops of French Canada to send "missionary priests" to labor among their compatriots in New England.

From 1869 to 1870 the bishop attended the First Vatican Council, where he was a staunch promoter of the declaration of papal infallibility. At the Third Plenary Council of Baltimore in 1884, de Goesbriand, a prolific writer on Church matters, served on the episcopal committee on the catechism.

In 1890 the bishop observed the fiftieth anniversary of his ordination, and sought some relief from his many duties by requesting Rome to grant him an assistant. In 1892 a Burlington native, Fr. John S. Michaud, was appointed coadjutor Bishop of Burlington, with right of succession. As Bishop Michaud took over more of the episcopal functions, the old bishop gradually slowed his pace, retiring by 1895 to be "one of the orphans" at the orphanage he had established more than forty years earlier.

At the time of the appointment of Bishop Michaud, the number of priests active in the diocese had increased from the five de Goesbriand had found on his arrival in 1853 to fifty-two, and the number of churches had grown from ten to seventy-eight. The Catholic population had more than doubled, from twenty thousand to forty-six thousand.

At the orphanage Bishop Louis de Goesbriand lived quietly until his death on November 3, 1899. Born to a wealthy family, he had donated his inheritance to the needs of his diocese. Following his death the sum of $2.12 was found in his desk. This was his material legacy—his spiritual legacy is priceless.

See also VERMONT, CATHOLIC CHURCH IN.

WILLIAM GOSS

GOLDSTEIN, DAVID (1870–1958)

Lay evangelist. A socialist propagandist in the 1890s who became a pioneering lay evangelist, David Goldstein was born in London on July 27, 1870, to Jewish parents of Dutch heritage. He emigrated with his family to New York City in 1871. There he attended both public and Jewish schools and, at the age of eleven, he began working as a cigar maker, the trade of his father.

In 1888 his family moved to Boston, where he joined the Socialist Labor Party. Over the next decade, he became a leader of the party; he was chosen as its mayoral candidate in one election and he served on its seven-member national board of appeals. He also became acquainted with Martha Moore Avery, a prominent figure in the Boston party, who would become his ideological mentor over the next thirty years. Though strong advocates of the socialist cause, Goldstein and Moore became disturbed about certain practices of its adherents—i.e., their hostility toward religion and their advocacy of violence and free love—and both had left it by 1903.

Impressed with Catholic social teaching, Avery joined the Catholic Church in 1904. Partly under her guidance, Goldstein began studying the Catholic faith, and found there what he believed to be a secure foundation for both family and social vitality. In 1905, after considerable study and preparation, he was baptized in Boston's Immaculate Conception Church.

He subsequently applied his rhetorical skills to discrediting socialism and promoting and defending Catholic social positions. Together with Avery, and supported by Boston Cardinal William O'Connell, he started the Catholic Truth Guild, an evangelical-style association that sought to further the Catholic cause through street preaching and lecturing (renamed Catholic Campaigners for Christ in 1935). Goldstein spent the next twenty-five years engaged in this ministry, traveling the country as one of the foremost lay American Catholic evangelists. After World War II, he toured less frequently due to his age and changing attitudes in the Church regarding this style of ministry. He remained active, however, writing columns for the *Boston Pilot* between 1945 and 1958.

He received a number of awards over the years, including a degree of doctor of literature from Niagara University, Niagara, New York (1939); the Catholic Action Medal from St. Bonaventure's College, St. Bonaventure, New York (1946); the Distinguished Service Medal of the Franciscan Order (1947); and Knight of the Order of St. Gregory (1955). He died in Boston on June 30, 1958.

Among his published works are *Socialism: The Nation of Fatherless Children* (with Avery, 1903); *Bolshevism: Its Cure* (with Avery, 1919); *Campaigning for Christ* (with Avery, 1924); *Campaigners for Christ Handbook* (1934); and *Letters of a Hebrew Catholic to Mr. Isaacs* (1943).

His *Autobiography of a Campaigner for Christ* was published in 1936.

Campbell, Debra. "A Catholic Salvation Army: David Goldstein, Pioneer Lay Evangelist." *Church History* 52 (September 1983) 322–32.

――――. "David Goldstein and the Lay Catholic Street Apostolate, 1917–1941." Ph.D. dissertation, Boston University, 1982.

――――. "David Goldstein and the Rise of the Catholic Campaigners for Christ." *Catholic Historical Review* 72 (January 1986) 33–50.

JOSEPH QUINN

GORMAN, DANIEL MARY (1861–1927)

Bishop. Born in a log cabin in Wyoming, Iowa, April 12, 1861, Daniel Gorman was to become the first U.S. citizen to be named bishop of Boise. His two predecessors were natives of Belgium. After attending local public schools he became a rural schoolmaster. Wishing to serve the same area as a priest, he entered St. Joseph's College, Dubuque, Iowa. From there he went to St. Francis Seminary, Milwaukee. Ordained June 24, 1893, he was assigned to pastoral work at State Center, thus being launched into a twofold and lifelong career of parish priest and educator. In 1904 he was named president of his alma mater in Dubuque, where he set out to provide a larger campus and three additional buildings. In February 1917 he was created a protonotary apostolic with the title of monsignor; the following February he was appointed bishop of Boise.

On the day of his installation he promised to stress Catholic education, lay participation in the life of the Church, meeting the needs of the young, vocations to the priesthood and religious life, and provisions for health care. The records show that he kept his promises in each of these, and in several other fields. In his nine years as bishop of Boise he provided leadership in the planning and building of parishes, schools, and hospitals, and in the organization of parochial and diocesan societies throughout Idaho. The number of parochial schools doubled, parish churches and mission chapels increased 30 percent, and the care of students at the University of Moscow became one of the diocesan priorities. The number of seminarians went from four to twenty-three during his time in office. He died on June 9, 1927.

See also IDAHO, CATHOLIC CHURCH IN.

Bradley, Cyprian A., and Edward J. Kelly. *History of the Diocese of Boise 1863–1953.* Boise, Idaho: The Chancery Office, 1953.

Schoenberg, Wilfred P., S.J. *History of the Catholic Church in the Pacific Northwest 1740–1983.* Washington, D.C.: Pastoral Press, 1987.

Walsh, Nicholas E. *The Catholic Church in Idaho: An Overview.* Boise, Idaho: Capitol Publishers and Printers, 1990.

✠ NICHOLAS E. WALSH

GORRIS, HENRIETTA (1902–83)

Religious, social activist. Sr. Henrietta Gorris (born Marie Gorris) was the daughter of Henry and Anna Sulzmann Gorris, born on July 19, 1902, in Cleveland, Ohio. After completing her education in Cleveland, she entered the Mercy Hospital School of Nursing run by the Sisters of Charity of St. Augustine in Canton, Ohio. After graduation Gorris entered the Sisters of Charity of St. Augustine on December 28, 1925.

After completing her religious formation, Gorris began her nursing and administrative career as a supervisor at Mercy Hospital. In 1951 she became administrator of both Mercy Hospital and the new Timken-Mercy Hospital in Canton, whose construction she supervised. In 1962 she was transferred to Cleveland where she was named director of nursing services at Charity Hospital.

Despite her ministry to the sick, Gorris discerned a call to work as a missionary in Africa. Her superiors dissuaded her, but Gorris was still restless. At Charity she found the opportunity to volunteer and build up a network in Hough, a Cleveland neighborhood populated by impoverished African Americans. Gorris began home visits, trying to alleviate the hunger, illness, and desperation she encountered. She confided her frustrated missionary dreams to one of the priests at Hough's parish of Our Lady of Fatima. He suggested that she take Hough as her mission.

The pastor of the parish, Albert Koklowsky, S.T., lobbied the diocese and the Sisters of Charity to allow Gorris to open a mission center at his parish in April 1965. The Hough riots of 1966 made Gorris only more determined.

She recruited neighborhood and suburban volunteers to assist her. She established the Caridad (Charity and Responsibility in Deed and Duty) and Famicos (Family Cooperators) for the volunteers. Education, health care, and nutrition became the duties of Caridad, and Famicos evolved into a community-based housing rehabilitation program for low-income families. Gorris saw her volunteers as prayerful people who could work cooperatively. She recognized that the poor people must be involved as active participants.

Gorris took over the weekly column begun by Fr. Koklowsky in the diocesan paper, the *Catholic Universe Bulletin,* and used it to advocate and educate readers about poverty from 1970 until 1983. She died on October 17, 1983, in Cleveland.

Catholic Universe Bulletin. November 28, 1969; December 19, 1969; September 2, 1983.

Papers of Fatima Center, Archives, Diocese of Cleveland.

Wolff, Robert C. *Sister Henrietta of Hough—She Reclaimed a Cleveland Slum.* Chicago: Loyola University Press, 1990.

CHRISTINE L. KROSEL

Thomas L. Grace

GRACE, THOMAS L. (1814–97)

Second bishop of St. Paul. Thomas Grace was born in Charleston, South Carolina, on November 16, 1814, to Thomas and Margaret Grace. Feeling called to religious life, he attended St. Rose Priory in Springfield, Kentucky, making his profession as a Dominican on June 10, 1830. Grace completed his theological studies at the Minerva University, Rome, where he was ordained on December 21, 1839. For the next five years he pursued graduate studies, returning to St. Rose as "Lecturer in Sacred Theology."

Between 1846–59, Grace served St. Peter's parish in Memphis, Tennessee. He resisted appointment as bishop until ordered to St. Paul on January 21, 1859. Archbishop Peter Kenrick consecrated him in St. Louis on July 24, and he arrived in St. Paul five days later.

Here Grace expanded and consolidated his diocese during years of copious immigration. He convened seven synods, set up a preparatory seminary, and helped start several Catholic newspapers. He increased the total of religious orders of women to fourteen, of men to six. The number of schools rose to sixty-three, of protective homes to five, of hospitals to three. In 1884, when retiring due to ill health, Grace left 153 diocesan and regular priests ministering among some 200,000 parishioners in 195 churches and 51 missions.

Remembered for hard work and innate modesty, Grace died in St. Paul on February 22, 1897, as titular archbishop of Siunia. The *National Cyclopedia of American Biography* hailed him as fulfilling "the ideal of citizen, priest, and Christian."

See also DOMINICANS (O.P.); MINNESOTA, CATHOLIC CHURCH IN.

Reardon, J. M. *The Catholic Church in the Diocese of St. Paul.* St. Paul, Minn.: North Central Publishing Company, 1952.

JOHN WHITNEY EVANS

GRACE, WILLIAM RUSSELL (1832–1904)

Businessman, politician, philanthropist. William Russell Grace was born on May 10, 1832, in Queenstown, Ireland, the son of James and Ellen Mary Russell Grace. Young William wanted to become an officer in the British navy, but, when his father prevented it, he went off to sea, settling down two years later in Liverpool in a job his father had obtained for him. His father next brought him to Peru (1850) where he was to make his fortune. Grace earned his way to a partnership in Bryce and Company, ship chandlers, and with his brother Michael turned it into Grace Brothers and Company. He married Lillius Gilchrist in 1859, and in 1860 ill health forced him to leave Peru. By 1865 he had settled in New York City and began to organize his company, which was expanding into exports and had purchased its own ships.

But Peru continued to be the goose laying the golden eggs. Grace became an advisor to the Peruvian government, and his company imported and transported virtually all the supplies for the builders of the national railroad. He saw to the equipping of the Peruvian army, and when war broke out with Chile in 1879, he imported munitions for Peru and even supplied the navy with some ships. In spite of this help, Peru did not win the war and was left with a substantial debt. The enterprising Grace saw a once-in-a-lifetime chance, and he seized it.

Working with nervous British bondholders, he offered Peru the Grace-Donoughmore Contract, by which he agreed

William R. Grace

to assume the national debt in return for vast concessions. Although a consortium of Britons, led by Lord Donoughmore, theoretically supervised the arrangement, Grace, "the Pirate of Peru," was the real power, dominating Peruvian exports of silver and guano, owning land with mineral wealth, and getting leases for railroads. He made a fortune and also helped to develop Peru's economy. In 1895 he established W. R. Grace and Company to manage these vast holdings, which by then included the first steamship company sailing directly from New York to the west coast of South America.

Grace became involved in New York politics early on, and in 1880, running on the Democrat ticket, he became the city's first Roman Catholic mayor. He served two terms (until 1887), after which the party offered him its nomination for governor, but by then his business interests demanded his full attention. Grace was also a philanthropist, sending money to Irish relief and setting up the Grace Institute to aid the education of impoverished young women. He was a director of several banks and president of two drilling companies. His wife and he had eleven children. He died in New York City on March 21, 1904.

DAB 4:463.

Grace, Joseph Peter. *W. R. Grace, 1832–1904, and the Enterprises He Created.* New York: Newcomen Society in North America, 1953.

Hevner, Peter. *A One-sided History of Wm. R. Grace, the Pirate of Peru.* New York, 1888.

NCE 6:657.

JOSEPH F. KELLY

GRAIL IN THE UNITED STATES, THE (1940–95)

Origins

Lydwine van Kersbergen and Joan Overboss brought the Grail to the United States in April of 1940 at the invitation of Cardinal George Mundelein of Chicago. The movement was begun in Holland in 1921 by a Dutch priest, Jacques van Ginneken, S.J., and some of his students at the Catholic University of Nijmegen who were among the first Dutch Catholic women to earn a university doctorate. They were inspired by van Ginneken's vision of women's vast potential to change the world, a potential that had never been fully realized either in Church or in society, and were ready to give themselves totally as laywomen "at the disposal of the Church to help with the spreading of the Kingdom of God over the whole world." In the 1930s the Grail spread to Great Britain, Germany, and Australia, always with America in view.

Serious disagreements with the Archdiocese of Chicago led to relocation in Cincinnati, where Archbishop John McNicholas, O.P., was willing to take the risk of sponsoring a group of laywomen who wanted the autonomy to de-

(l. to r.) Joan Overboss, Lydwine van Kersbergen, and Mary Louise Tully

fine their own work. In March 1944 the group purchased a 180-acre farm on the eastern edge of Loveland, Ohio, and on July 17, Grailville opened as a "School of Apostolate" with an official blessing by Archbishop McNicholas.

Pioneering: Pre-Vatican II

Grailville quickly became the hub of a national movement with eleven other centers, ranging from New York to San Jose, California, and from Toronto to Lafayette, Louisiana, offering programs varying in length and intensity from a series of evening meetings to the full-year residential training at Grailville's Year's School. At the same time, Grailville became a crossroads, a meeting place for clergy and lay leaders interested in the new movements in the Church. The Grail pioneered in many fields, breaking new ground for the laity, for Catholic women, for women in general. As part of the liturgical movement, the Grail focused on living the liturgy, demonstrating full participation in the Mass and public prayer, devising paraliturgies to meet new needs, publishing more than twenty books and booklets on liturgical themes, together with practical suggestions for integrating the spirit of the feasts and seasons into daily life. Insisting on the importance of a Christian culture for a spiritual renewal, the Grail pioneered in producing vigorous contemporary expressions of a Christian spirit in the visual arts, in liturgical dramas, in music and dance, and disseminated these works through art and bookstores, exhibits, recordings, and publications.

In the 1950s the Grail was both pre-Peace Corps and pre-Vista. It took the lead among Catholic groups in preparing and sending teams of young American women to serve in developing countries and at the same time insisted on the importance of working with international students in this country. Grail teams from the city centers joined in the struggle for racial and economic justice, organizing buying cooperatives and credit unions in the inner cities of Detroit, Brooklyn, Cincinnati, and in rural Louisiana.

In the 1960s the Grail was in the forefront of ecumenical dialogue and opened its membership to women of other Christian traditions. It also played a part in developing modern catechetical approaches in the United States, emphasizing personalism and the relation of psychological to spiritual health.

Underlying all these pioneering efforts was the boundless faith in the potential of women and the development of a form of education—experiential, communal, holistic, participative—that was empowering for women and prepared them for leadership.

Post-Vatican II: Change and Continuity

The 1960s brought vast changes—religious, social, cultural—that the Grail met with creative adaptations while maintaining an underlying continuity of values and direction. Structurally, through an *aggiornamento* process carried on internationally from 1964 to 1967, the Grail changed from a highly centralized and hierarchical structure to a decentralized and participative form. The new structure, stressing shared responsibility, enabled all members—married, single, as well as celibate—to share as peers in policy and decision-making and to be eligible for any functional roles.

In response to social and cultural changes, the Grail focused its work in the 1970s and 1980s around three central themes: liberation, women, and religious search. The earlier concerns with racial and economic justice were broadened and deepened by a feminist liberation theology that emphasized the interconnections between the various oppressions: racism, sexism, classism, imperialism, heterosexism, militarism, destruction of the environment. The original concern for organic gardening was broadened to a vision on a planetary scale of sustainable and just lifestyles for humans on planet earth. Grailville and the Grail Center at Cornwall-on-Hudson, New York, carry on programs in ecological education that combine an earth spirituality with hands-on experience in permaculture practices.

The very themes—living faith and women's special mission—that were the source of the energy and unity of the movement in its first quarter century became sources of deep tensions in the late 1960s, as Grail members explored the implications of personalism, collegiality, and feminism. A long process of study, discussion, and experiment led to the development of a strong feminist consciousness among Grail members, including a critique of sexism in Church and society, a rejection of a psychology of complementarity, an affirmation of women as adult human beings, moral and religious agents, fully capable of doing theology and making ethical decisions. Grail programs and the publications issuing from them have been influ-

ential in the development of feminist theology and spirituality in the United States. According to Mary Jo Weaver, "their commitment to women has resulted in some stunning and influential programs. . . . The Seminary Quarter broke new ground for women and supported an emerging feminist theology that begins, not with God, but with a theological reflection on women's experience" (*New Catholic Women,* 127). Ann Patrick Ware described the Grail as "a small group with a great influence. Grailville and the Grail are known throughout the United States as a place and a group that have fostered the growth of feminism among religious women and indeed among all women."

The process of study, discussion, and experiment has led Grail members to seek spiritual nourishment on diverse paths: psychosynthesis, the intensive journal, yoga, Zen, Native American traditions, Jewish traditions, an earth-centered spirituality, and to create new symbols and rituals for community worship. In 1988 the International General Assembly formulated the Grail experience as a unity in diversity, noting that "as a faith community of women, we are learning that we are nourished and challenged by different well-springs. [We] strengthen and support one another in our search for God; urge each other to be open to the Spirit; and work toward transforming our world into a place of justice, peace and love" (*U.S. Catholic Historian,* 91–93).

Brien, Dolores E. "The Catholic Revival Revisited." *Commonweal* (December 21, 1979).

Buckley, Mary, and Janet Kalven, eds. *Women's Spirit Bonding.* New York: Pilgrim Press, 1984.

Clark, Linda, Marian Ronan, and Eleanor Walker. *Image-Breaking, Image-Building: A Handbook for Creative Worship with Women of Christian Tradition.* New York: Pilgrim Press, 1981.

Cornwall Collective. *Your Daughters Shall Prophesy, Feminist Alternatives in Theological Education.* New York: Pilgrim Press, 1981.

Davis, Florence H. "Lay Movements in New York City During the 30s and 40s." *U.S. Catholic Historian* 9 (4) (Fall 1993).

Kalven, Janet. "Women Breaking Boundaries: The Grail and Feminism." *Journal of Feminist Studies in Religion* 5 (1989).

Weaver, Mary Jo. *New Catholic Women.* San Francisco: Harper and Row, 1985.

Weaver, Mary Jo, and Debra Campbell, eds. *U.S. Catholic Historian, Grailville, Women in Community, 1944–1994.* 11 (4) (Fall 1993).

JANET KALVEN

GRANAHAN, KATHRYN ELIZABETH O'HAY (1896–1979)

U.S. Treasurer. Born in Easton, Pennsylvania, Granahan was educated in local public schools and graduated from Mt. St. Joseph College in Philadelphia, Pennsylvania. Before her marriage in 1943 to William T. Granahan, she worked in social service in the State Auditor General's Department, first as a supervisor of public assistance and later as a liaison officer. After her marriage, she worked closely with her husband, who became a five-term congressman from Pennsylvania's Second Congressional District. When her husband died in 1956, Granahan succeeded him in office, becoming the first woman elected to Congress from Philadelphia. In office for six years, Granahan served on several congressional committees and was known for her campaign against the sale and distribution of pornography through the postal service. In 1963 President John F. Kennedy named her United States Treasurer. Granahan retired from the position in 1966, and died in Norristown, Pennsylvania, on July 10, 1979.

K. N. McCARTHY

GRASSO, ELLA T. (1919–81)

Governor. The daughter of Italian immigrants, Grasso was born in Windsor Locks, Connecticut, on May 10, 1919. She was educated at Chaffee School and at Mount Holyoke College, where she earned a bachelor of arts degree in 1940 and a master of arts degree in 1942. She married Thomas A. Grasso in 1942; they had two children.

During World War II, Grasso worked in Connecticut as assistant state director of research for the Federal War Manpower Commission. Associated with the League of Women Voters, Grasso became active in Democratic Party politics, and was elected to the House of Representatives of the Connecticut General Assembly in 1952, and again in 1954. Grasso was elected Connecticut's secretary of state in 1958, and, twice reelected, served until 1970. A delegate and committee co-chair at the Democratic National Convention in 1968, she supported a minority resolution opposing continued American involvement in the Vietnam War. Grasso was elected to the United States House of Representatives in 1972. Particularly interested in health and human welfare issues, she helped pass the Emergency Employment Act of 1971 and the Higher Education Act of 1972.

In 1974 Grasso was elected governor of Connecticut, becoming the first woman ever to become an American governor in her own right. An "old style" Democrat, Grasso was criticized by some feminists for her opposition to abortion, which she refused to finance with state funds. Her administrations were marked by efforts to economize state spending in the midst of a recession. Reelected in 1978, Grasso resigned in 1980 because of illness, and died of cancer in Hartford, Connecticut, on February 5, 1981.

K. N. McCARTHY

GRAYMOOR

Graymoor is the motherhouse of the Franciscan Friars and Sisters of the Atonement located on the Hudson River in the foothills of the Catskills, about fifty miles from New York City. Founded in the Anglican Church in 1898, the purpose of this community was to work for the reunion of the Anglican and Roman Catholic communions. The name Graymoor originated with the little mission church around which the young religious community was established. The church was named St. John's-in-the-Wilderness and was erected as a mission of St. Philip's Episcopal Church in Garrison, New York, by its rector, Dr. Albert Zabriskie Gray. When some devout Episcopal women decided to renovate the dilapidated church in 1893, they named it after Dr. Gray and William Moore, a chief benefactor. It was to this church that Sr. Lurana Mary White and the Rev. Lewis Wattson had come to begin their new religious foundation. Its renovation reminded them of an earlier time when St. Francis of Assisi had restored the Church of San Damiano. St. Paul's epistle to the Romans in the King James Version gave Fr. Wattson and Sr. Lurana the name of the new community, the atonement. The words which Fr. Wattson read were: "And not only so, but we also joy in God, through our Lord Jesus Christ, by whom we have now received the Atonement" (5:11). The passage contained not only the name of the community but also pointed to its reconciling mission. Sr. Lurana was committed to follow the way of St. Francis and sought a community that would be dedicated to corporate poverty. The two founders shared a common vision for their new foundation and believed that God would bless their efforts if they continued to be faithful to that vision.

Graymoor and Christian Unity

From its very inception the community at Graymoor was dedicated to the cause of Christian unity. What was unusual was its stand from an ecclesiological perspective. While remaining Anglican and holding to the validity of Anglican orders, they confessed belief in the "full dogmatic faith of the Holy, Roman Church" and saw the pope as the successor of Peter and the center of a reunited Christendom. It was from Graymoor that Fr. Paul (the religious name Fr. Wattson assumed) promoted the cause of reunion through preaching and the publication of *The Lamp*. In the pages of *The Lamp,* Fr. Paul promoted his High-Church views which got him into difficulty in his own Church, even to the point of being accused of heresy by fellow clergy. It was from Graymoor that Fr. Paul started the Octave of Prayer for Christian Unity in 1908, which was later renamed the Chair of Unity Octave and eventually gained papal approval for its universal observance in the Roman Catholic Church. However, an inherent difficulty with this period of prayer for the unity of Christians was the fact that it was based on the notion that separated Christians should "return" to allegiance to Rome. Obviously, only Roman Catholics and some pro-Roman Anglicans could honestly observe it. It would be some years later that the Abbé Paul Couturier would refocus the Octave of prayer so that Protestants could pray together with Roman Catholics in what was to become the Week of Prayer for Christian Unity.

By 1909 Fr. Paul and Sr. Lurana's Anglican days were coming to an end. On the advice of their Anglican episcopal visitor, Bishop Kinsman of Delaware, who later entered the Roman Catholic Church, the founders, given the views they held, were encouraged to make a choice between the two Churches. Bishop Kinsman had no doubt that Fr. Paul should "give up Anglican Orders" and become Roman Catholic. Fr. Paul and Sr. Lurana determined that this was sound advice and the will of God for them. They sought corporate reception of the little religious community into the Catholic Church and it thus became the first example of corporate reception since the Reformation. But this new direction caused great difficulties for Graymoor, for they were considered traitors to their Church. Litigation was brought against the community by the trustees of the property upon which the church and convent were built. The legal battle over property lasted for a number of years until a bill was introduced in the New York legislature that authorized the transfer of the property to the sisters.

Contemporary Apostolate

As early as its Anglican days, Graymoor welcomed people of all walks of life, especially the poor and homeless. The commitment of the two founders the poor was seen in the establishment of St. Christopher's Inn for homeless men from a converted chicken house. The community was extremely poor, but they shared what they had with those who were less fortunate than themselves. The present-day St. Christopher's Inn stands as a monument to the charity of Fr. Paul and Sr. Lurana and their extraordinary commitment to the poor and needy. St. Joseph's Rehabilitation Center for alcoholism at Saranac Lake, New York, owes its existence to their spirit of outreach to broken humanity.

Through the years Graymoor has played host to hundreds of thousands of people who came "on pilgrimage" to visit the grounds, chapels, and shrines. There they found a few hours of peace in a prayerful atmosphere from sometimes very turbulent lives. The friars and sisters meet the spiritual needs of their visitors at the Graymoor Christian Unity Center, a retreat and conference facility. While *The Lamp* is no longer published, the friars now publish *Ecumenical Trends,* which keeps Christians informed on ecumenical progress today. Through the Graymoor Ecumenical and Interreligious Institute, located in New York City, the Friars of the Atonement continue to promote the Week of Prayer for Christian Unity and are involved in study and dialogue with representatives of other Christian traditions

and other faiths. In Rome the friars promote the cause of Christian unity through the Centro Pro Unione, an ecumenical center, which maintains a library, holds conferences, and publishes an ecumenical bulletin on current theological themes.

Through the years the Friars and Sisters of the Atonement have gone forth from Graymoor to proclaim the gospel of reconciliation throughout the United States and Canada, Japan, England, Brazil, and Jamaica. In each place, the friars and sisters seek to manifest the ecumenical dimension of their ministry, which had its beginning at Graymoor.

Twenty years ago, J. Stewart Wetmore, suffragan bishop of the Episcopal Diocese of New York, wrote that Graymoor stands as a great center of Christian hospitality for groups and individuals. He wrote:

> There moves in the midst of the community a fascinating joy of life. It is this freedom and acceptance that makes me feel at home among them, and on each of my visits I cast myself verbally in the role of a building inspector, there to check up on what care they are taking of "our real estate!" I report it amazingly improved since Father Paul took it with him when he and the struggling little community "went to Rome."

Today the Friars and Sisters of the Atonement at Graymoor and in every ministry where they serve continue in their efforts to create, in the spirit of Fr. Paul and Sr. Lurana, a welcoming atmosphere for people of every Church, every faith, and no faith to promote the cause of Christian unity, interfaith cooperation, and healing.

See also ECUMENISM IN AMERICA; FRANCISCAN FRIARS; WATTSON, PAUL.

Angell, Charles, and Charles Lafontaine. *Prophet of Reunion.* New York: Seabury Press, 1975.

Archives of the Friars of the Atonement, Graymoor, Garrison, New York.

Celine, Mary. *A Woman of Unity.* Garrison, N.Y.: Franciscan Sisters of the Atonement, 1956.

Cranny, Titus. *Father Paul: Apostle of Unity.* Peekskill, N.Y.: Graymoor Press, 1955.

Gannon, David. *Father Paul of Graymoor.* New York: Macmillan, 1951.

Lafontaine, Charles. *Essays in S. A. History.* Peekskill, N.Y.: Graymoor Press, 1984.

TIMOTHY MacDONALD, S.A.

GREY NUNS/SISTERS OF CHARITY OF MONTREAL (S.G.M.)

The Sisters of Charity of Montreal, Grey Nuns, were first called to the United States from their motherhouse in Montreal in 1855 to serve victims of a cholera epidemic in the Toledo, Ohio, area. In 1868 the Protectory of Mary

Immaculate was founded as an orphanage to care for the Civil War orphans in Lawrence, Massachusetts. In 1895 the Grey Nuns were invited to Cambridge, Massachusetts, to establish a hospital for the chronically ill. In 1901 St. Joseph Orphanage was opened in Nashua, New Hampshire, followed by St. Joseph Hospital in 1908. Numerous requests came from other areas of the United States for the foundation of hospitals, child-care institutions, educational facilities, and social services.

Current Ministries

Covenant Health Systems was established in 1983 to strengthen Grey Nun sponsorship of incorporated apostolates. United by the mission and philosophy of the Grey Nuns, current membership includes St. Vincent Medical Center in Toledo; St. Joseph Hospital and Trauma Center in Nashua, acute care providers; the Sisters of Charity Health System in Lewiston, Maine, which includes an acute care hospital, congregate subsidized housing for the elderly and disabled, and a long-term care facility. In Massachusetts member organizations are Youville Hospital and Rehabilitation Center in Cambridge, a chronic care and rehabilitation provider; and Mary Immaculate Health/Care Services in Lawrence, a skilled nursing facility and apartment complex for elderly and disabled people. Fletcher Allen Health Care in Colchester, Vermont, sponsored by the Religious Hospitallers of St. Joseph, is a member of Covenant Health Systems. The Grey Nuns also administer an adult day health center in Lexington, Massachusetts. In Nashua they sponsor a thrift shop and cosponsor Marguerite's Place, providing transitional housing for women and children in crisis situations. Current plans include an assisted living facility to respond to a need for affordable housing for the elderly in the Lexington area.

Missionary Activity

In 1963 four Grey Nuns traveled by cargo ship to Kabba, Nigeria, to establish a hospital, a boarding school for girls, and bush clinics. Later they staffed a school in Egbe, Nigeria. After fourteen years the Grey Nuns left the work in the hands of native sisters. Rural ministry in Dyersburg, Tennessee, engaged the Grey Nuns from 1977 to 1985. A mission for Native Americans in North Dakota involved Grey Nuns from 1971 to 1979. In Bogota, Colombia, the Foundation for the Adoption of Abandoned Children welcomed the Grey Nuns in 1978 to provide quality medical and nursing care until the children are placed for adoption all over the world.

History of the Foundress

Marie Marguerite Dufrost de Lajemmerais, the widow d'Youville, founded the Institute of the Sisters of Charity of Montreal, known as the Grey Nuns, in 1737. Born in Varennes, Quebec, October 15, 1701, Marie Marguerite lost her father when she was seven years old and from then on her life was marked by suffering—an unhappy marriage to François d'Youville, widowed at age twenty-eight, the loss of four of her six children in infancy. Unmindful of her own personal tragedies, she devoted herself to works of charity. "Her home was open to everyone who suffered from poverty, illness or other affliction, without distinction of age, nationality, sex or religion," commented Pope John XXIII at her beatification on May 3, 1959. In 1771, after a life of struggles, triumphs, and defeats, Marguerite died at the age of seventy. Over two and a half centuries later, six branches of the Grey Nuns serve Canada, the United States, Brazil, Colombia, Africa, Haiti, New Guinea, and Japan. On December 9, 1990, Pope John Paul II canonized Marguerite d'Youville, the first Canadian woman to become a saint of the Roman Catholic Church. In 1981 establishment of the Grey Nun Associate Program gave laypersons an opportunity to share in the charism and mission of the Grey Nuns.

See also WOMEN RELIGIOUS IN AMERICA.

MARIE LEFEVRE, S.G.M.

GRIFFIN, JOHN HOWARD (1920–80)

Writer and photographer. Griffin was born in Dallas, Texas, in 1920. Although he was educated in both America and Europe (mainly France), he spent most of his adult life in the Fort Worth/Dallas area. Besides his music studies with Nadia Boulanger in Paris, he became a younger member of the circle of friends surrounding Jacques and Raïssa Maritain. His interest in music led him to explore the or-

John H. Griffin

namentation of Gregorian chant, the subject of a graduate work project. But his inquiring mind brought him into the philosophical and theological world of the Maritains as well as psychology, medicine, and anthropology. When he entered the Church in 1951, he turned to Jacques Maritain to be his godfather.

His first novel, *The Devil Rides Outside,* was based on an experience while living in a Benedictine monastery as a pilgrim guest. While studying and traveling as a student in Europe, he worked in a mental hospital that was experimenting with music as a cure for mental illness. Later he became a member of the French underground during World War II, assisting Jews to escape from the Nazis, until he himself was forced to leave Europe or risk being captured by the Nazis.

After his return to the States, Griffin served in the American Army Air Force. Because of his proficiency in languages, he was assigned to Pacific islands inhabited by aborigines. This experience led him to write another novel, *Nuni.* Wounded by an exploding bomb in the war, Griffin lost his eyesight. When it was restored ten years later, he saw his wife and two oldest children for the first time.

His writings reflect the wide-ranging interests in his mature years: civil rights, anthropology, philosophy, theology, music, and photography. During the last decade of his life he devoted his energies to researching and writing the official biography of Thomas Merton. Due to failing health he was never able to complete the work, but he did publish a number of significant books on Merton, including *Follow the Ecstasy,* edited by Robert Bonazzi. Although Griffin was unable to finish the entire biography, his journals and notes help to fill out the picture of Merton's monastic journey.

Griffin is best known for *Black Like Me,* which was based on his experiences while traveling through the South in 1959 in the guise of an African American, having taken chemical injections and ultraviolet treatments to darken his skin. A Russian movie was made of Griffin's best-selling account, as well as an American film starring James Whitmore, which displeased Griffin. Fictional elements were added to enliven the story, which Griffin found revolting, not to mention the erroneous suggestion that Griffin began to have religious doubts.

In 1968 *The John Howard Griffin Reader,* edited by Bradford Daniel, was published by Houghton Mifflin, which revealed the extraordinary breadth of the author's prophetic vision. Included in this substantial volume was a condensed version of *The Devil Rides Outside* and *Nuni,* as well as several short stories like "Sauce for the Gander," a condensed version of *Black Like Me,* and a representative section of his writings on racism. There followed a fascinating section on Griffin's serious photography, portraits of Jacques Maritain, Sarah Patton Boyle, Godfrey Diekmann, Thomas Merton, Saul Alinsky, Pierre Reverdy,

John Beecher, and Bede Griffiths, among others. The final section of "Works in Progress" included two excerpts from his unfinished autobiography, *Scattered Shadows,* which his current biographer, Robert Bonazzi, is preparing for publication. Griffin died in 1980.

It is estimated that there are as many as thirty volumes of John Howard Griffin awaiting publication. When these writings are made available, including his novels, journals, and letters, we will have an even more complete picture of this great man of peace and compassion, whose social action was rooted in a nonviolent contemplative witness to the gospel.

See also CIVIL RIGHTS MOVEMENT AND CATHOLICS, THE; MERTON, THOMAS.

The John Howard Griffin Reader. Selected and edited by Bradford Daniel, with an introduction by Maxwell Geismar. Boston: Houghton Mifflin, 1968.

Griffin, John Howard. *Black Like Me.* 2nd ed., with a new epilogue by the author. Boston: Houghton Mifflin, 1977.

———. *Follow the Ecstasy: The Hermitage Years of Thomas Merton,* ed. Robert Bonazzi. Maryknoll, N.Y.: Orbis Books, 1993.

———. *The Hermitage Journals: A Diary Kept While Working on the Biography of Thomas Merton,* ed. Congar Beasley, Jr. Kansas City, Mo.: Andrews and McMeel, 1981.

Merton, Thomas, and John Howard Griffin. *A Hidden Wholeness: The Visual World of Thomas Merton.* Boston: Houghton Mifflin, 1970.

PATRICK HART, O.S.C.O.

GROSS, WILLIAM (1837–98)

Redemptorist and archbishop. William Hickley Gross, the son of James White and Rachel Hazlett Gross, was born June 12, 1837, in Baltimore, Maryland. Discouraged from becoming a priest while at St. Charles College, he nevertheless entered the Redemptorist seminary at Annapolis in 1857, made his profession on April 4, 1858, and was ordained on March 21, 1863, in Annapolis. After serving as a chaplain from 1866 to 1873, he conducted missions throughout the southern and eastern United States.

In 1873 Gross became bishop of Savannah, Georgia, his consecration taking place on April 17, 1873, in Baltimore. Finishing the cathedral in Savannah started by his predecessor, Gross energetically began rebuilding the war-ravaged Georgia church.

After his return from the Third Plenary Council of Baltimore in 1884, Gross learned of his appointment as archbishop of Oregon City. He arrived in Portland on May 23, 1885, to find another partially completed cathedral, which he dedicated on August 20, 1885. Expansion of parishes, churches, and institutions marked his administration. Besides attracting a number of established religious communities to the state, Archbishop Gross founded a congregation that became the Sisters of St. Mary of Oregon.

William H. Gross

In presiding at Archbishop Gross' investiture with the pallium in Portland on October 9, 1887, Cardinal James Gibbons of Baltimore became the first American cardinal to visit the West Coast.

In 1894 Gross built a temporary pro-cathedral in Portland, intending to build a permanent building later. On a visit to the East he died on November 14, 1898, in Baltimore, where he was buried in Holy Redeemer Cemetery.

See also GEORGIA, CATHOLIC CHURCH IN; OREGON, CATHOLIC CHURCH IN; REDEMPORISTS (C.SS.R.).

Brady, Michael. "Most Reverend William Hickley Gross, C.Ss.R., Third Archbishop of Oregon City, 1885–1898." Unpublished paper. Esopus, N.Y.: Mount St. Alphonsus Seminary, 1981.

McKenna, Stephen G. "Our Lady's Bishop." *Central Blatt and Social Justice* 24 (1931–32) 53–55, 88–89, 129–32, 176–78, 249–51, 286–87.

Ryan, Chloe M. "William H. Gross, Missionary Archbishop, Archbishop of Oregon City, 1885–1898." Unpublished paper. Marylhurst, Oreg: Marylhurst College, 1952.

Skeabeck, Andrew. "Most Rev. William Gross: Missionary Bishop of the North." *Records of the American Catholic Historical Society of Philadelphia* 65 (1954) 11–23, 102–15, 142–57, 216–29; 66 (1955) 35–52, 78–94, 131–55.

PATRICIA BRANDT

GRUENTHER, ALFRED MAXIMILIAN (1899–1983)

General. Born in Platte Center, Nebraska, on May 23, 1899, the son of Mary Shea Gruenther and Christian M. Gruenther, a newspaper editor. A precocious student, Gruenther entered West Point at fifteen and graduated fourth in the class of 1917 (because of a surplus of second lieutenants, he was not commissioned until 1918). Married to Grace E. Crum in 1922, he served at Fort Knox and later taught mathematics at West Point. He completed the Command and General Staff School in 1937 and the Army War College in 1939. Gruenther came to the attention of Army Chief of Staff George C. Marshall during the famous Louisiana Maneuvers of September 1941, which also uncovered Gruenther's friend and bridge partner, Ike Eisenhower. When Eisenhower was ordered to Europe in 1942, Gruenther went along as deputy chief of Eisenhower's staff.

Gruenther headed the combined (British and American) planning for the invasion of North Africa (TORCH). He served as chief planner for the invasion of Sicily, the invasion of Italy (Salerno), and the subsequent landing at Anzio. He remained in Italy as Mark Clark's Chief of Staff (Fifth Army) when Eisenhower returned to Britain. In 1943 Gruenther received a promotion to major-general, then the youngest officer of that rank in the U.S. Army. He moved up to Fifteenth Army Group Chief of Staff with Mark Clark in 1944. After the war, Gruenther headed the occupation forces in Austria and returned to the United States to serve as deputy commander of the National War College. In 1951 he again accompanied Eisenhower to Europe as Chief of Staff for the newly organized NATO command and, at age fifty-three, became the youngest four-star general in Army history. From 1953 to 1956 he served as Supreme Commander of this NATO force. After retirement, he held the presidency of the American Red Cross as well as numerous corporate directorships. His honors included the Laetare Medal and the

Alfred M. Gruenther

Distinguished Service Medal with two oak leaf clusters. From the 1920s onward, Gruenther directed and refereed numerous international bridge events. He died at Walter Reed Hospital in Washington, D.C., on May 30, 1983.

See also WORLD WAR II AND AMERICAN CATHOLICS.

JOHN ALLEN

GUÉRIN, MOTHER THEODORE (1798–1856)

Religious superior. Anne Thérèse Guérin was born to Laurent and Isabelle Guérin on October 2, 1798, in Etaples, France. In 1823 she entered the newly founded Congregation of the Sisters of Providence at Ruillé-sur-Loire, France, and took the name Theodore. After making her vows in September 1825, Sr. Theodore was appointed superior of a school in an industrial town in France, where she became known for her excellence in teaching mathematics.

At the request of the Bishop Celestine de la Hailandière of Vincennes, Indiana (1798–1882), Mother Theodore Guérin and several other French sisters came to the United States in 1840 to establish the Sisters of Providence. Together these women cleared a plot of land outside of Vincennes and built a convent there, which they named St. Mary-of-the-Woods. They soon established an institute for young girls in the area.

As superior of her community, Mother Theodore had several conflicts with her bishop over the community's rule. These disagreements were so deep and frequent that in 1847 Bishop de la Hailandière excommunicated her for what he considered obstinacy and disobedience. Later that same year, the bishop himself resigned his see, and his successor quickly restored Mother Theodore to her community. Under her leadership, the Sisters of Providence thrived and continued to grow. By the end of the century, the Sisters of Providence had over one thousand members and had established many educational institutions, including the College of St. Mary-of-the-Woods, Indiana, and eighty elementary schools around the country. Mother Guérin died on May 17, 1856, at her convent in St. Mary-of-the-Woods, Indiana.

Borromeo, M. *The History of the Sisters of Providence of Saint-Mary-of-the-Woods, 1806–1856.* Vol. 1. New York: Benziger Books, 1949.

Code, Joseph B. *Great American Foundresses.* New York: Macmillan, 1929.

Mug, Mary Theodosia, ed. *Journals and Letters of Mother Theodore Guérin, Foundress of the Sisters of Providence of Saint Mary-of-the-Woods, Indiana.* Saint Mary-of-the-Woods, Ind.: Providence Press, 1937.

_____. *Life and Work of Mother Theodore Guérin: Foundress of the Sisters of Providence of Saint-Mary-of-the-Woods, Indiana.* New York: Benziger Books, 1937.

PATRICIA DeFERRARI

GUILDAY, PETER (1884–1947)

Educator and Church historian. Peter Guilday, a priest of the Archdiocese of Philadelphia and professor of Church history at The Catholic University of America, was the first professional historian of American Catholicism. He was the author of scholarly biographies of Archbishop John Carroll and Bishop John England, as well as a history of the Councils of Baltimore. He was instrumental in founding the American Catholic Historical Association and the *Catholic Historical Review.*

Peter Guilday

Peter Guilday was born and raised in Chester, Pennsylvania. He attended the nation's first free Catholic high school in Philadelphia, then entered the archdiocesan seminary at Overbrook. He studied at the American College at the University of Louvain, Belgium, then returned to that university after ordination to pursue a doctorate in history. In 1914 he joined the faculty of The Catholic University of America in Washington, where he shifted his research and teaching interests to the undeveloped field of the history of Catholicism in the United States. To organize historical work among Catholics, he helped launch the *Catholic Historical Review* in 1915. At the same time he began meeting with other Catholic historians at the annual meetings of the American Historical Association and, in 1919, they formed their own organization, the American Catholic Historical Association.

For years Guilday's seminar at Catholic University provided almost the only professional training available for historians of the Catholic Church. His scholarly books and articles pioneered in offering a scholarly account of the early experience of the institutional Church. Guilday was an active supporter of projects to oppose anti-Catholic prejudice and improve the intellectual quality of the American Church. Always loyal to the hierarchy, he struggled for forty years to persuade Church leaders of the value of honest historical scholarship. He died in Washington, D.C., on July 31, 1947.

See also AMERICAN CATHOLIC HISTORICAL ASSOCIATION (ACHA); CATHOLIC UNIVERSITY OF AMERICA, THE.

Bowden, Henry Warner. *Church History in an Age of Uncertainty: Historiographical Patterns in the United States, 1906–1990*. Carbondale: Southern Illinois University Press, 1991, 9–14.

Guilday, Peter. *A History of the Councils of Baltimore, 1791–1884*. New York: Macmillan, 1932.

____. *The Life and Times of John Carroll, Archbishop of Baltimore, 1735–1815*. 2 vols. New York: Encyclopedia Press, 1922.

____. *The Life and Times of John England, First Bishop of Charleston, 1786–1842*. 2 vols. New York: The America Press, 1927.

____. *National Pastorals of the American Hierarchy, 1792–1919*. Washington, D.C.: National Catholic Welfare Council, 1923.

O'Brien, David. "Peter Guilday: The Catholic Intellectual in the Post-Modernist Church." *Studies in Catholic History: In Honor of John Tracy Ellis*, eds. Nelson H. Minnich, Robert B. Eno, and Robert Trisco. Wilmington, Del.: Michael Glazier, 1985, 260–306.

Thomas, J. Douglas. "A Century of American Catholic History." *U.S. Catholic Historian* 6 (1) (Winter 1987) 30–34.

DAVID O'BRIEN

GUINEY, LOUISE IMOGEN (1861–1920)

Essayist and poet. Guiney was born in Roxbury, Massachusetts, on January 7, 1861, and died in Chipping Campden, Gloucestershire, England, on November 2, 1920. She was the only child of Patrick Robert and Janet Margaret Doyle Guiney. Guiney's father, a Civil War officer who died when she was sixteen, left a lasting impression on her character and writing.

Her first book of verse, *Songs at the Start* (1884), was soon followed by a volume of essays, *Goose Quill Papers* (1885), and *The White Sail* (1887). These initial works established her as a poet and essayist and brought her into the Boston literary circle. After living in London from 1889 until 1891, Guiney published what she regarded as her best work, *A Roadside Harp* (1894).

During the final years of the decade she published a volume almost every year: *A Little English Gallery* (1894), *Nine Sonnets Written at Oxford* (1895), *Patrins* (1897), and *England and Yesterday* (1898). These were written and published in the midst of personal trials resulting from anti-Irish Catholic sentiment over her appointment as postmistress of Auburn, Massachusetts. Although she was eventually vindicated, Guiney resigned and took a position with the Boston Public Library.

Louise I. Guiney

In 1901 Guiney returned to England permanently, taking up residence at Oxford. There she began research on neglected authors, a task that became her subsequent life work. Her two most ambitious projects in this regard were a biography of Henry Vaughan and *Recusant Poets, 1535–1735: A Catholic Anthology from Thomas More to Pope*, both of which were incomplete at her death. She published editions of the poetry of Katherine Philips, Thomas Stanley, Lionel Johnson, and James Clarence Mangan, and smaller editions of the work of Matthew Arnold and Henry Vaughan. She also wrote three biographies: *Robert Emmet* (1904), *Hurrell Froude* (1904), and *Blessed Edmund Campion* (1908). In 1909 the "less faulty half" of her published verse was collected in *Happy Ending*.

See also CATHOLICS AND AMERICAN LITERATURE.

Brown, Alice. *Louise Imogen Guiney*. New York: Macmillan, 1921.

Fairbanks, Henry George. *Louise Imogen Guiney: Laureate of the Lost*. Albany, N.Y.: Magi Books, 1973.

Guiney, Grace, ed. *Letters to Louise Imogen Guiney*. New York: Harper and Brothers, 1926.

____. "Louise Imogen Guiney: A Comment and Some Letters." *Catholic World* 121 (August 1925) 596–603.

Tenison, Eva M. *Louise Imogen Guiney: Her Life and Works, 1861–1920*. London: Macmillan, 1923.

RICHARD G. SMITH

GURNEY, MARIAN LANE (MARIANNE OF JESUS) (1868–1957)

Foundress of the Sisters of Our Lady of Christian Doctrine. Marian Lane Gurney was born on June 6, 1868, in

New Orleans, Louisiana. She was raised as a genteel but unchurched girl in New York City and San Francisco. In her teens she attended Friends Seminary in New York City in order to prepare for college. At Wellesley, the college of her choice, she joined and remained an ardent communicant of the High Episcopal Church until she became a Roman Catholic in 1897. In 1910 she founded the Sisters of Our Lady of Christian Doctrine and was the much loved and highly respected mother general until her death on February 9, 1957, at Marydell Motherhouse and Novitiate in Nyack, New York.

Gurney's position as the organizer of St. Rose's Settlement House in New York City, the first Catholic settlement house in that city, and her influence in bringing the Confraternity of Christian Doctrine to the Archdiocese of New York had lasting effects on her approach to the immigrants she felt destined to serve. It was her merger of social service techniques and the teaching of Christian doctrine that made hers such an outstanding contribution to the plight of the people and also led to the foundation of the Sisters of Our Lady of Christian Doctrine.

In response to an appeal from a pastor on the Lower East Side of Manhattan, Gurney and four companions were brought into Cherry Hill, one of the most abandoned districts in the city. In spite of their honest, hard-working habits, the Italian immigrants were poverty stricken and drifting away from the faith. Helping these people was the challenge, and Gurney set to work to meet it. She and her companions used every device to make catechism classes as interesting as possible. Home visitation was undertaken in an attempt to interest the parents, but they had little success with this.

Distressed by this turn of events, they searched for the reason their efforts were not well received. The answer came when they realized that they were not really part of the neighborhood life; they were not in touch with its joys and sorrows. Cherry Hill, Gurney reasoned, had little desire to be taught, but would it respond to practical sympathy? Was this not the method chosen by the incarnate Lord to win the hearts of his people?

In the latter part of 1909 Gurney submitted to Archbishop John Farley a memorandum concerning the conditions in the area and her desire to live there with the hope of becoming more effective in her work. The archbishop, who was sympathetic to her suggestion, brought it to a meeting with the vicar general and several other priests who were keenly interested in the proposal.

One of the results of the meeting was a request from the archbishop that Gurney establish a house in the neighborhood, which would also be run as a day nursery. The nursery was an absolute necessity for the working mothers as well as for the success of any spiritual work undertaken there. Simultaneously, religion classes were to begin for the older children.

On June 29, 1910, the house was ready to receive those for whom these devoted and zealous women had left their home in Washington Heights. The settlement house founded by Marian Gurney and her four companions, Amelie Merceret, Margaret Coleman, Julia Foley, and Elizabeth Lammers, was on its way to becoming the center of spiritual development. By means of their unique method of teaching the catechism in the warm and friendly surroundings of a neighborhood house they succeeded in bringing the Good News to many of New York's tired, lonely, and poor. In 1961, for many reasons, Madonna House was closed. Nevertheless, the spirit of Mother Marianne and the type of work inaugurated there continues in New York as well as in New Hampshire, New Jersey, Illinois, Florida, and the Dominican Republic.

DOROTHEA McCARTHY, R.C.D.

H

HAAS, FRANCIS JOSEPH (1889–1953)

Bishop, scholar, labor expert. Francis Joseph Haas was born in Racine, Wisconsin, on March 18, 1889, the second of seven children of Peter and Mary (O'Day) Haas. He attended St. Patrick's parish school for six years and public school for five years before entering St. Francis Seminary in Milwaukee in the fall of 1904. His father owned a small grocery store, eventually invested in other real estate, and thus the Haas family lived in modest comfort.

Francis J. Haas

Haas was ordained a priest for the Archdiocese of Milwaukee in 1913, served as a parish assistant for two years, and was then assigned to teach in the college department of St. Francis Seminary. In 1919 he enrolled in The Catholic University of America in Washington for advanced studies in sociology and economics and, influenced by John A. Ryan, became a lifelong champion of labor's rights to unhindered unionization and a family wage. He received his Ph.D. degree in 1922, published his doctoral dissertation, *Shop Collective Bargaining: A Study of Wage Determination in the Men's Garment Industry,* that same year, and rejoined the faculty of St. Francis Seminary to teach the social sciences.

In 1931 Haas returned to Washington to serve as director of the National Catholic School of Social Service, an institution established in 1918 to train young women in the field of social work. With the inauguration of President Franklin Roosevelt in the spring of 1933, he was recruited to serve on various New Deal labor boards: the Labor Advisory Board of the National Recovery Administration (1933–35), the National Labor Board (1933–34), and the Works Progress Administration's Labor Policies Board (1935–39). He was recalled to Milwaukee in 1935 and served as rector of St. Francis Seminary for two years, and in 1937 he was also appointed by Governor Philip LaFollette to the Wisconsin Labor Relations Board. That same year he was named a monsignor and returned to Washington as dean of The Catholic University's newly established School of Social Science. He continued his work in labor mediation as a Special Commissioner of Conciliation for the Department of Labor, and in 1943 was named chairman of the reconstituted Fair Employment Practices Committee.

In October 1943, after only four months with the FEPC, Haas was named bishop of the Diocese of Grand Rapids, Michigan. In his ten years as bishop, he erected more than twenty new parishes, inaugurated a diocesan newspaper, expanded high school facilities, undertook major fundraising campaigns, built a home for the aged, and organized an annual Diocesan Congress to popularize the social teachings of the Church. In 1946–47 he served on President Harry Truman's Committee on Civil Rights.

Haas stood six feet tall, weighed close to two hundred pounds, and had a head of sandy hair that earned him the name "Red" Haas long before industrial leaders adopted it to suggest what they considered his leftist labor views. He read history and literature for relaxation, and had played the violin in his youth. In addition to his doctoral dissertation, he published numerous articles, pamphlets, and a major sociology textbook, *Man and Society*. He died of a heart attack in Grand Rapids on August 29, 1953, at the age of sixty-four.

See also NEW DEAL AND AMERICAN CATHOLICS, THE.

Blantz, Thomas E., C.S.C. "Francis J. Haas: Priest and Government Servant." *Catholic Historical Review* 59 (January 1972) 571–92.
_____. *A Priest in Public Service: Francis J. Haas and the New Deal.* University of Notre Dame Press, 1982.
Kennedy, Franklyn. "Bishop Haas." *The Salesianum* 57 (January 1944) 1–14.
Randall, Constance. "A Bio-Bibliography of Bishop Francis J. Haas." M.A. thesis, The Catholic University of America, 1955.

THOMAS E. BLANTZ, C.S.C.

HACHARD, MADELEINE (1704–60)

Religious. Madeleine Hachard was one of thirteen women, members of the Order of St. Ursula, who sailed from Hennebont, France, to the French colony of New Orleans in 1727. They were the first Roman Catholic religious women to come to what is now the United States. Madeleine, who was an Ursuline postulant at the time, began a series of letters to her parents prior to the journey, chronicling the preparations for the trip.

Once their vessel was seaward, she described in great detail the terrible journey which the brave women endured. Becalmed seas, storms. pirates, and treacherous sand bars tormented the pioneers at sea, while mosquito-infested swamps and a makeshift convent awaited them in Louisiana. "Everyone on our vessel, which was called *La Gironde,* said that out of any ten ships meeting the same difficulties as ours, not another would have escaped," she wrote.

In later letters to her father, Madeleine Hachard describes the fledgling colony. "The streets are very wide and are laid out in straight lines," she said. "The main street is nearly a league in length. The houses are very well built of 'collambage et mortier.'" And again, "While the women ignore facts pertaining to their salvation, they ignore nothing when it comes to vanity . . . they are dressed in velvets and damasks covered with ribbons."

After her final profession of vows on March 15, 1729, which was the first religious profession in America, the author was called Sr. St. Stanislaus. She taught the students and orphans whom the Ursulines cared for, and she managed the affairs of the order as secretary for the congregation. She died in her sleep on August 9, 1760, at the age of 56.

Hachard, Madeleine. *The Letters of Marie Madeleine Hachard 1727–28.* Trans. Myldred Masson Costa, 1974. (Source of the quotations.)

JOAN MARIE AYCOCK, O.S.U.

HAGAN, JOHN RAPHAEL (1890–1946)

Educator and bishop. John Raphael Hagan was born February 26, 1890, in Pittsburgh, Pennsylvania, the son of John and Katherine Foley Hagan. He was educated at St. Ignatius High School and College before discerning a vocation to the priesthood. He completed his studies at the North American College in Rome and was ordained on March 7, 1914, for the Diocese of Cleveland.

After serving in three Cleveland parishes, he became pastor of St. Mary's parish in Bedford, Ohio. Hagan was then appointed superintendent of diocesan schools on January 1, 1923. In that office he developed an ambitious plan for improving the elementary schools which incorporated child developmental theories and educational advances that he had observed in German and Dutch schools that he had visited. Hagan recognized that a changing American society demanded better educated citizens, and if parochial schools were to survive, they would have to meet and exceed the standards set by the state.

Hagan also recognized the plight of the religious communities of women teaching in the schools. Many communities were attempting to maintain normal schools to train their candidates for teaching careers while at the same time trying to continue the religious formation of these women. Hagan knew that the demand for teachers was so great that many young religious received inadequate educational training and suffered great stress as they tried to cope with often overcrowded classes. Hagan was concerned that these circumstances would be harmful both to the health and vocations of these teachers. He envisioned a diocesan teachers college staffed by master teachers that would provide the needed skills for these novice teachers. His dream became real when Sisters College was opened in 1928 in Cleveland.

By 1931 Sisters College was chartered as a full four-year college by the Ohio State Department of Education. In 1936 the college began granting masters' degrees in educational administration. Hagan was recognized as a pioneer in teacher education.

The depression created a financial crisis for the diocese's parochial schools. Hagan organized an ecumenical effort to get state aid for religious schools. His argument that the parochial schools saved the state funds found support with the governor and the Ohio Senate, but the Ohio House of Representatives defeated the bill in 1933.

Hagan was consecrated an auxiliary bishop of Cleveland on May 28, 1946. He died suddenly on September 28 of that year.

Hynes, Michael J. *History of the Diocese of Cleveland: Origin and Growth (1847–1952)*. Cleveland, 1953.
Papers of John R. Hagan, Archives, Diocese of Cleveland.
School Aid Issue (1933–35), Papers of Archbishop Joseph Schrembs, Archives, Diocese of Cleveland.

CHRISTINE L. KROSEL

HAID, LEO MICHAEL (1849–1924)

Abbot, bishop. Haid was born on July 15, 1849, near Latrobe, Pennsylvania, to German immigrant parents. He began his education at the Benedictine Abbey of St. Vincent in Latrobe where he entered the novitiate in 1868. He made his first profession as a monk on September 17, 1869. After theological studies, he was ordained a priest on December 21, 1872, and began working at the monastery

Leo M. Haid

college as a professor and chaplain. In 1885 he became the first abbot of Maryhelp Abbey in Garibaldi (later Belmont), North Carolina. The next year he opened a seminary there and made plans for a college for lay students. In 1887 Haid was appointed vicar apostolic of North Carolina, and on July 1, 1888, Cardinal James Gibbons of Baltimore ordained him a bishop—the first American abbot-bishop. Haid was a leader in monasticism in the United States and was responsible for establishing and overseeing Benedictine foundations in Virginia, Georgia, and Florida. He was president of the American Cassinese Congregation from 1890 to 1902. In 1910 Pope Pius X named Haid an abbot *nullius* and gave him canonical jurisdiction over eight counties in North Carolina. He died at Belmont Abbey on July 24, 1924.

See also BENEDICTINES (O.S.B.).

Baumstein, Paschal, O.S.B. "A Conflict of Mitres: The Diverse Policies and Cathedral Abbey of Bishop Leo Haid." *Word and Spirit* 14 (1992) 76–95.
———. *My Lord of Belmont: A Biography of Leo Haid*. Belmont, North Carolina, 1985.

ANTHONY D. ANDREASSI

HALLINAN, PAUL J. (1911–68)

Archbishop. Hallinan was born on April 8, 1911, in Painesville, Ohio, a small city some thirty miles east of Cleveland. He was educated in St. Mary's parochial school in Painesville, Cathedral Latin School in Cleveland, and the University of Notre Dame. Upon graduation from college, he entered St. Mary's Seminary in Cleveland and was ordained a priest of that diocese on February 20, 1937. His first assignment was to St. Aloysius Church in the Glenville section of Cleveland, a large lower-middle-class parish typical of urban American Catholicism of that era. As the youngest of the four parish priests, Hallinan devoted himself to youth work, at which he excelled. In 1942 he volunteered as an army chaplain and spent the next two and a half years in the South Pacific, island hopping from Australia to the Philippines.

Newman Apostolate

Upon return to Cleveland after the war, Hallinan began a long association with the Newman Apostolate, which was already well established in the diocese. From 1946 to 1947, Hallinan was part-time chaplain at Cleveland College, and then, from 1947 to 1958, he was full-time director of Newman Hall at Western Reserve University. The success of his work in Cleveland brought him recognition on the national level. From 1952 to 1954 he was national chaplain of the National Newman Club Federation and president

Paul J. Hallinan

of the chaplains' association. Both on the local and national levels, Hallinan emphasized the necessity for the Newman Apostolate to address the intellectual concerns of Catholic college students as well as their social and pastoral needs.

The Newman Apostolate had a broadening effect on Hallinan's own intellectual life. It brought him into contact with like-minded young priests who were interested in the latest developments in theology, liturgy and social justice. Taking advantage of the G.I. Bill of Rights, Hallinan earned a M.A. degree in history at John Carroll University and then began work on a doctorate at Western Reserve University. This in turn brought him into contact with Msgr. John Tracy Ellis with whom he struck up a warm friendship. Another source of intellectual growth was Hallinan's discovery of John Henry Newman, whom he began to read in earnest in those years.

In 1958 Hallinan was hoping for an opportunity to study history at The Catholic University of America, and then perhaps to teach history in the diocesan seminary. Instead, on September 16, 1958, he was selected to be the bishop of Charleston, South Carolina. His episcopal ordination took place in St. John's Cathedral in Cleveland on the same day that Angelo Roncalli was elected pope.

Bishop of Charleston

One could hardly imagine a greater contrast than that between the heavily industrialized Diocese of Cleveland with its large ethnic Catholic population and the Diocese of Charleston, where Catholics numbered a mere 30,000 in a population of 2,370,000, or 1.5 percent of the total population. Anti-Catholic bigotry was still a powerful force

in the state as Hallinan was to discover during the presidential election of 1960.

A more immediate problem for Hallinan, however, was the question of school desegregation, which was the cutting edge of the civil rights movement at that time. Four years earlier, the U.S. Supreme Court had outlawed segregated schools, but the Court's decision had yet to be implemented in South Carolina. In January 1961, Hallinan met with the bishops of Atlanta and Savannah, and the three of them agreed to issue a pastoral letter promising to desegregate the Catholic schools in their dioceses "as soon as this can be done with safety [and] not later than the public schools." The bishops' position did not please everyone, but it won approval from many Southern moderates in the civil rights movement. Ralph McGill, publisher of the Atlanta *Constitution*, wrote that the three Catholic bishops "say what many a silent Protestant minister would like to tell his congregation, if he had apostolic authority behind him." Hallinan did not remain in Charleston long enough to desegregate the Catholic schools, but it was done without incident by his successor, Bishop Francis F. Reh, in 1963 and 1964. However, Hallinan was able to desegregate all five Catholic hospitals in the diocese by Christmas 1959. When one of the hospital administrators expressed opposition to Hallinan's decision, he told him: "I do not believe that any thinking person would try to justify a Catholic hospital turning away sick people merely because they have black skin."

First Archbishop of Atlanta

Less than four years after coming to Charleston, on February 21, 1962, Hallinan was promoted to Atlanta, which at the same time was made a metropolitan see. Even more than Charleston, Atlanta was a statistical nightmare for its new archbishop. After conducting a census in 1963, Hallinan discovered that 83 percent of the 43,000 Catholics lived in metropolitan Atlanta. Atlanta and its suburbs contained 15 parishes; the other 69 counties in the archdiocese had only 14 parishes. Ten weeks after his installation, Hallinan announced that he would desegregate all Catholic schools by the following September. Next spring he ordered the desegregation of the two Catholic hospitals in the archdiocese. He also welcomed contacts with Protestants and Jews, and issued detailed ecumenical guidelines for his priests.

The year that Hallinan went to Atlanta also saw the opening of the Second Vatican Council, which proved to be a great learning experience for Hallinan, as it was for many bishops. Quite unexpectedly, Hallinan found himself the only American on the Liturgical Commission. He relied heavily on Msgr. Frederick R. McManus for advice and supported the reform-minded members of the commission. Hallinan was also instrumental in winning the support of many American bishops for liturgical reform. In 1963 they elected him to their Commission on the Liturgical Apostolate, and he used this position to urge his fellow bishops to implement the liturgical changes in the United States as quickly and as generously as the law allowed.

Shortly after Hallinan's return from the second session of the council, he suffered a severe attack of hepatitis which left him hospitalized for nine months in 1964 and prevented his attendance at the third session of the council. However, Hallinan recovered sufficiently to attend the fourth session where he spoke on behalf of the Declaration on Religious Liberty and submitted two written interventions, one calling for an explicit condemnation of racial discrimination, the other asking for a declaration of the status of women in the church. "In our society," he said, "women in many places and in many respects still bear the marks of inequality."

In Atlanta Hallinan remained active in the civil rights movement. When Dr. Martin Luther King Jr. received the Nobel Peace Prize in 1964, Hallinan was one of four civic leaders who took the initiative in honoring him by organizing the first biracial dinner in the city's history. Hallinan also found the time to complete his doctoral dissertation, which was a study of Richard Gilmour, the second bishop of Cleveland. He received his Ph.D. degree in history from Western Reserve University in June 1963. The Vietnam War was another public issue which engaged his attention. As with the civil rights movement and liturgical reform, Hallinan tried to formulate a balanced centrist position. In October 1966, he and his new auxiliary bishop, Joseph Bernardin, issued a pastoral letter on the war which endorsed American intervention but also stated: "We must keep insisting that our leaders fully inform us of the facts and issues."

Hallinan never really recovered from the hepatitis attack of 1964. In the beginning of 1968, his health suddenly deteriorated, and he died on March 27, 1968, from a combination of hepatitis and diabetes. He was only fifty-seven years old. Although he was a bishop for only ten years (in two of the smallest sees in the United States), he had become a national figure in the American Church.

See also GEORGIA, CATHOLIC CHURCH IN; LITURGICAL MOVEMENT IN AMERICA, THE; VATICAN COUNCIL II AND AMERICAN CATHOLICS.

Ellis, John Tracy. "Archbishop Hallinan: In Memoriam." *Thought* 43 (1968) 539–72.
____. *Catholic Bishops: A Memoir.* Wilmington, Del.: Michael Glazier, 1983, 162–78.
Hallinan, Paul J. "Richard Gilmour: Second Bishop of Cleveland, 1872–1891." Ph.D. dissertation, Western Reserve University, 1963.
Marszal, Theodore. "Pastor in the Age of Renewal: The Life and Spirituality of Paul J. Hallinan, Archbishop of Atlanta, Georgia." Ph.D. dissertation, Pontifical Gregorian University, 1980.
Shelley, Thomas J. *Paul J. Hallinan, First Archbishop of Atlanta.* Wilmington, Del.: Michael Glazier, 1989.
____. "Paul J. Hallinan." *Patterns of Episcopal Leadership,* ed. Gerald P. Fogarty. New York: Macmillan, 1989, 235–49.
Yzermans, Vincent A., ed. *Days of Hope and Promise.* Collegeville, Minn.: The Liturgical Press, 1973.

THOMAS J. SHELLEY

HARDEY, ALOYSIA (1809–66)

Religious of the Sacred Heart. Mary Ann Hardey, the daughter of Frederick William and Sarah Spalding Hardey, was born in Piscataway, Maryland, on December 8, 1809. The family migrated to Louisiana in 1821 and Aloysia attended the new convent of the Sacred Heart at Grand Coteau. There she entered in 1825, one of the first Americans to enter the society since it had come to America with St. Philippine Duchesne in 1818.

She taught at Grand Coteau and St. Michael's until 1841 when she was sent to found a house in New York. She worked in very close relationship with the foundress of the society, St. Madeleine Sophie Barat who trusted her judgment and recognized her ability. As provincial she opened twenty-five houses in the eastern United States, Canada, and Cuba. Her administrative initiative was complemented by sensitivity, balanced judgment, and heart.

She worked toward democratizing the social classes in the schools and founded a free school next to each of the academies, as well as an orphanage when necessary. She assisted the missionaries of the society to make foundations in South America and New Zealand. During the Civil War she succeeded in winning from several Union generals some protection for her Southern houses.

In 1872 the second superior general, Mother Josephine Goetz, called Mother Hardey to Paris to take up her role as assistant general. Her former labors of continuous travel and visitation were expanded in Europe where she founded several houses, developed a program of higher professional training for the religious teachers, and oversaw the formation of the religious preparing for final profession.

Laborious and active as her life had been, Mother Hardey was regarded by her associates for her deep affection, phenomenal memory for persons, and loyal support. After her death at the motherhouse in Paris on June 17, 1886, she was buried in Paris. When all religious were expelled from France (1902–09) her remains were transferred to the convent in Albany, New York.

Cunningham, Ruth. *First American Daughter.* Kenwood, Albany, N.Y.: Society of the Sacred Heart, 1981.
Garvey, Mary. *Mary Aloysia Hardey, Religious of the Sacred Heart.* New York: Longmans, Green, 1925.
Williams, Margaret, *Second Sowing.* New York: Sheed & Ward, 1942.

MARGARET PHELAN, R.S.C.J.

HARKINS, MATTHEW (1845–1921)

The second bishop of the Diocese of Providence. Harkins was called by a fellow bishop, William Stang of Fall River, "the ideal of a Catholic bishop." Born in Boston on November 17, 1845, of Irish immigrant parents, Harkins attended the public schools of Boston and later graduated from Holy Cross College, Worcester. After studies with the Benedictines in the English College at Douai, Belgium, and with the Sulpicians at Issy and St. Sulpice in Paris, he was ordained for the Diocese of Boston. As a priest and pastor in Boston, Harkins developed a lifelong friendship with Archbishop John Williams, who appointed him diocesan consultor and synodal examiner. When he was consecrated bishop on April 14, 1887, Harkins came to Providence as a priest known and respected as a pastor, an expert theologian and canonist, and as a prudent and successful administrator, all of which qualities he continued to cultivate as bishop of Providence.

Matthew Harkins

During Bishop Harkins' years, the Diocese of Providence grew to be among the largest in the country and to have one of the highest percentages of Catholics. Besides the Irish and French Canadians who had already settled in Rhode Island and in southeastern Massachusetts (which, until 1904, was part of the Diocese of Providence), large numbers of Italian, Polish, and Portuguese immigrants also came to the state along with smaller numbers of Germans, Austrians, Lithuanians, Carpatho-Russians, and Syrians. Although he looked forward to the day when the various peoples of the diocese would all use the same language in their worship, Harkins recognized the need to provide parishes where the immigrants could worship in familiar surroundings. Whenever an ethnic group was able to demonstrate its ability to support a pastor, he readily granted permission for a new ethnic parish. Because Harkins refused to give parochial assignments to priests who lacked the proper credentials, he frequently experienced difficulty in finding a suitable priest to serve new ethnic parishes. While his policy helped to preserve the unity of the Church in the diocese, the delay involved in securing a suitable priest prompted many complaints to the apostolic delegates of neglect on his part. In a highly unusual move, one group arranged to have their complaint carried to the pope by Portugal's ambassador to the Vatican. In each instance, the delegates, who knew Harkins well and whom Harkins kept well informed of the circumstances of the petition, supported the bishop and advised patience. Harkins' contemporaries would praise him for having done as much pastorally for the immigrants as had any other bishop in the country.

Bishop Harkins set an example for the rest of the American bishops in his solicitude for the physical care and spiritual protection of children and of the sick. To run the diocese's orphanages and homes for the aged, Harkins established corporations whose membership was made up primarily of the laity, thus ensuring that they might secure public as well as private financial support.

A strong advocate of Catholic education, Harkins invited the Dominicans of the province of St. Joseph to staff Providence College which they opened in 1919. Harkins was also an early supporter of The Catholic University of America and, in 1902, he was elected a member of the university's board of trustees. Through his service to the university and in the course of his travels, Harkins formed close friendships with a wide cross section of the American hierarchy. Often invited to speak on special occasions, he consistently declined such offers because he never considered himself a good orator. Instead, his influence in the American Church was confined to personal contacts with his fellow bishops, particularly in New England.

Harkins came to national attention in 1903 when his name was rumored to be among of those the Holy See was considering for appointment as coadjutor of Boston. Harkins refused to personally do anything to advance his candidacy for the post although many of his friends among the hierarchy and particularly his fellow New England bishops did. When Rome chose Bishop William O'Connell of Portland, Maine, as coadjutor to Archbishop Williams, Harkins welcomed the choice. Bishop Harkins died on May 26, 1921, two years after giving control over the administration of the diocese to his newly ordained coadjutor, Bishop William A. Hickey.

See also RHODE ISLAND, CATHOLIC CHURCH IN.

Hayman, Robert W. *Catholicism in Rhode Island and the Diocese of Providence, 1887–1921.* Providence, 1995.

ROBERT W. HAYMAN

HARLEM APOSTOLATE

Between 1905 and 1930 Harlem became the center of the African American community in New York City with over 200,00 black residents. During the same period there was a corresponding decrease in the white population of the area with the result that the Catholic parishes experienced a steep decline in the size of their congregations. In 1933 Fr. William R. McCann, the newly appointed pastor of St. Charles Borromeo Church on West 142 Street, estimated that only two percent of the black population of Harlem was Catholic. With the approval and encouragement of Cardinal Patrick Hayes, McCann inaugurated a program of evangelization that came to be known as the Harlem Apostolate.

The heart of the program was an intensive four-month course of catechetical instructions that met twice a week and used such innovative pedagogical techniques as slide presentations. The courses were advertised through street processions, letter-writing campaigns, and visits by the parish priests to the homes of potential converts. The four-month courses were offered continuously throughout the year, with each course culminating in a solemn baptismal ceremony at which a bishop often presided. In January 1934 Cardinal Hayes officiated at the baptism of seventy-two adult converts. Between 1934 and 1962, 6,538 adults were baptized at St. Charles Borromeo, with the peak year occurring in 1940 when 431 were received into the Catholic Church.

The Harlem Apostolate was expanded in 1935 to include St. Aloysius Church on West 132 Street, and further expanded in 1936 to include St. Benedict the Moor Church on West 53 Street, which had been the original black parish in New York City but was then in decline as the African American community moved to Harlem. Despite the impressive number of converts produced by the Harlem Apostolate, not all Catholics agreed with McCann's exclusive focus on evangelization. Both Fr. John LaFarge, S.J., leader of the Catholic Interracial Council of New York, and Baroness Catherine de Hueck, the founder of Friendship House, criticized the Harlem Apostolate for its lack of interest in the economic and social needs of black Americans, especially during the Great Depression.

McCann died on August 9, 1949. The Harlem Apostolate continued at St. Charles Borromeo for another decade, but gradually petered out in the turmoil of the 1960s.

"Harlem Apostolate." *Interracial Review* (August 1949) 115–16.
Howard, Clarence, S.V.D. "The Harlem Apostolate." *St. Augustine's Messenger* 18 (1940) 169–71.

Mahoney, Martin J. "Catholic Evangelization in Black Harlem: The Harlem Apostolate, 1933–1949." M.A. thesis, St. Joseph's Seminary, Dunwoodie, 1994.

THOMAS J. SHELLEY

HARRINGTON, EDWARD MICHAEL (1928–89)

Writer, social activist. Cochairman (with Barbara Ehrenreich) of the Democratic Socialists of America, the nation's largest socialist organization, and, with the exception of presidential candidates Eugene Debbs and Norman Thomas, this country's most influential Socialist spokesman, Harrington rose to fame and prominence while in his thirties, with the publication of *The Other America: Poverty in the United States* (1962). He would go on to write sixteen books and numerous articles, working as a political leader, lecturer, and a professor of political science at Queens College in Flushing, New York.

Born to an Irish Catholic family in St. Louis, Missouri, and educated by the Jesuits at the College of Holy Cross in Worcester, Massachusetts, Harrington graduated with a master's degree from the University of Chicago in the hope of becoming a poet. He even spent a year at Yale Law School before he was pulled to New York in 1949 by the prospects of leading the poet's intellectual and bohemian life.

In his early years in New York, Harrington joined Dorothy Day and the Catholic Workers, serving soup, bread, and hospitality to impoverished men on the Bowery in Manhattan's Lower East Side. This close encounter with life among the poor made a lasting impression on Harrington. Though he left the Catholic Church and the Catholic Worker in the mid-1950s, he would continue to be moved by such sights in subsequent years through his work as a union organizer and civil rights organizer. It fed the sense of moral outrage he passed on to readers in his first and most influential book.

The Other America

Harrington's descriptions of poverty in America fell like thunder on the ears of a conservative public enjoying enormous postwar prosperity, a public that had been assured in such books as Galbraith's *The Affluent Society* that widespread poverty in the nation had virtually disappeared. By contrast, Harrington estimated that a quarter of the population—many of whom worked full-time—were living in poverty. Poverty itself was like an undertow, pulling them into a subculture of misery, overpowering their efforts to rise above it. The poor, Harrington wrote, were immune to progress. Since their poverty was largely hidden, it would take an act of will for most Americans to see and address it.

Although Harrington thought it would take a Charles Dickens to rouse the nation to the side of the poor, his own book did much to change the lives of millions, particularly the elderly, for it fell into the hands of a president and vice president ready to enact progressive social policies.

The popularity of Harrington's book was due in part to Dwight MacDonald's long and favorable review of it in *The New Yorker*. Its appearance there made poverty a fashionable conversation topic among the Eastern elite cocktail set, which included policy makers in Washington, D.C. When President John F. Kennedy caught wind of the discussion and asked whether there was anything to it, an aide handed him a copy of Harrington's book. There the president read about slave-wage laborers in urban sweatshops, restaurants, and hospitals who were not protected by the minimum wage laws; laid-off miners and industrial workers in localized pockets of economic depression; isolated rural families eking out a living from the rocky soil of Appalachia; low-income field hands and migrant workers who could not partake of the bountiful harvests they helped reap; blacks whose poverty was structurally imposed through racism; and elderly men and women who lived lives of isolation and economic desperation. After reading the book, Kennedy made the abolition of poverty one of his chief domestic goals. It was one of his last directives before meeting death in Dallas the following November.

A few months later, Harrington, who had married Stephanie Gervis in Paris and with whom he had just returned to New York, was shocked at the reception awaiting him. He found himself invited to the White House as a consultant on the poverty section of President Lyndon Johnson's State of the Union address. Later his ideas found their way into the Johnson administration's War on Poverty.

Harrington's sudden success, spate of speaking engagements, and financial windfall brought on a nervous breakdown, which he worked through in four years of psychoanalysis. Although his public speaking temporarily ground to a halt, his writing and thinking about what socialism could contribute to the national common good continued. In 1965 he published *The Accidental Century* (Macmillan) and in 1968, *Toward a Democratic Left: A Radical Program for a New Majority* (Macmillan), followed by other books on political theory and several autobiographical accounts of the development of his personal and social philosophy. His 1977 book, *The Vast Majority: A Journey to the World's Poor* (Simon & Schuster), was nominated for a National Book Award.

The former chairman of the socialist party founded the Democratic Socialist Organizing Committee (DSOC) in 1973, appealing to various splinter groups within the socialist movement and the Democratic Party: feminists, minorities, environmentalists, peace activists, and trade union members. By 1981 the DSOC joined with the New American Movement, becoming the Democratic Socialists of America (DSA). DSA formed links with international socialist groups where Harrington became particularly well known. Within six years Harrington reported that the U.S. network itself represented between 30,000 and 40,000 activists.

Harrington won his first bout with cancer, but in 1987 learned that he had developed a deadlier type, cancer of the esophagus. Still he had time to finish his autobiographical account, *The Long-Distance Runner* (1988), as well as a major work outlining what international socialism could do to improve life in *Socialism: Past and Future* (1989).

Weeks before his death six hundred friends and colleagues, including United Farm Workers president Cesar Chavez and Senator Edward Kennedy, honored Harrington at a celebration in New York. Harrington won the George Polk Award and the Sidney Hillman Award, and was named a Distinguished Professor in 1988 at Queens College.

Moore, Authur J. "Remembering Mike." *Christianity and Crisis* 49 (September 11, 1989) 253–54.

Steinfels, Peter. "A Man Who Made a Difference: Michael Harrington in Our History." *Commonweal* 116 (September 8, 1989) 466–69.

KAREN SUE SMITH

HARTDEGEN, STEPHEN J. (1907–89)

Biblical scholar. Born in Philadelphia to a devout working class immigrant family, Joseph Hartdegen enrolled in St. Joseph's Seminary in Callicoon, New York, upon completing the eighth grade. He entered the Friars Minor in 1925, receiving the name Stephen, and was ordained to the priesthood in 1932. He was educated at The Catholic University of America, the Pontifical Biblical Institute, and the Franciscan Biblical Institute, Jerusalem. Upon completing his studies in 1939, he returned to Washington where he taught Scripture at his province's theologate, Holy Name College, until 1968.

Hartdegen was not a deeply original thinker or brilliant teacher, but a great organizer and a man of unflagging determination in promoting scholarly and popular study of the Bible. He was a member of the original editorial board of *The New American Bible*, serving as its executive secretary for more than a quarter of a century, from its inception in 1944 until 1970, when the completed translation was published in one volume. He later served in the same capacity for the *NAB* Revised New Testament, from 1978 until its completion in 1987. Meanwhile, from 1970 until his retirement in 1988, he was director of the United States Center for the Catholic Biblical Apostolate at the United States Catholic Conference.

Hartdegen was also active in numerous liturgical projects. He edited the American interim breviary, *The Prayer of Christians* (1971), and at the time of his death was working on the inclusive-language revision of the lectionary. On a pastoral level, he was a zealous apostle of Franciscan lay movements; in 1950 he introduced to the United States the Missionaries of the Kingship of Christ, the Franciscan secular institute.

See also CATHOLIC BIBLICAL ASSOCIATION (CBA); FRANCISCAN FRIARS.

---

di Lella, Alexander. "Stephen J. Hartdegen, O.F.M.: A Tribute." *The Catholic Biblical Quarterly* 52 (1990) 1–4.

DOMINIC V. MONTI, O.F.M.

HARTKE, GILBERT (1907–86)

Teacher. The story of Fr. Hartke and the nationally prominent Drama Department which he founded at The Catholic University of America is one and the same. Hartke was born in Chicago on January 16, 1907. His interest in theater began when he was discovered, before age seven, by the Chicago Film Colony, an early movie studio that featured him in several films, including *The Mischief Makers.*

Gilbert Hartke

In 1925, when he entered the Dominican Order, his desire to be an actor was sacrificed to the call to the priesthood. To utilize his speaking and dramatic skills, he was placed in charge of six dramatic productions during his first year in seminary. In 1935 he entered The Catholic University of America to pursue an M.A. in English. Shortly after his ordination, he and two other young friars were asked to begin The Blackfriar's Institute of Dramatic Arts. In 1937, as a result of this successful workshop,

the young Dominican was assigned the task of founding a Department of Drama—with no faculty, no money, and no building.

Fr. Hartke began by assembling a prodigious team that included Dr. Josephine McGarry Callan, the department's prestigious vocal coach; Walter Kerr, a successful playwright who became a distinguished drama critic for *The New York Times;* Alan Schneider, who became an internationally known director; and Leo Brady, who with Walter Kerr coauthored the musical biography of George M. Cohan, *Yankee Doodle Boy* (1939), that catapulted the young department into national prominence.

During the early days, Hartke managed the department on a shoestring budget. According to the Rev. Robert P. Mohan, Fr. Hartke's "unorthodox talent for keeping things together . . . was a blend of the wisdom of Aquinas and the resourcefulness of Machiavelli. To the sympathetic and affluent . . . he gave new meaning to the term mendicant friar." Indeed, those who knew him joke that when Fr. Hartke joined the Dominicans, he took the vows of "poverty, chastity and publicity."

For the first twelve years, the Drama Department lacked a permanent building. Finally, in 1948, Hartke purchased a surplus World War II movie theater for one dollar. Adapted for live performance, the "soldier's theater" served the department for twenty years until its roof caved in under a heavy Ash Wednesday snow. In the face of disaster, Hartke put his legendary charm to work and began raising the funds for a new building. Completed in 1970, the two million dollar, three-theater complex, is a testimony to his faith and visionary leadership.

Gilbert Hartke died in February 1986, but his legacy and influence on the American theater lives on in the Department he founded and the many lives he touched.

Graham, William H. "Father Hartke: The Legend and the Legacy." Introductory comments at the premiere of the docudrama, "Father Hartke: The Legend and the Legacy." (Department Archives)

McCarthy, Norman. "Give My Regards to CUA." *Catholic Standard* (May 31, 1990) 2.

Mohan, The Reverend Robert P. "Father Hartke: A Personal Memoir." *Celebrating Father Hartke: 50 Years at CUA.* 1985. (Department Archives)

BRIDGET COREY

HASSARD, JOHN (1836–88)

Journalist, literary and music critic. John Rose Greene Hassard was born in New York City on September 4 (or September 24), 1836, the son of Thomas Hassard, a civil engineer, and Augusta Greene Hassard. The family was probably of Huguenot origin, and his mother was a granddaughter of Commodore Samuel Nicholson, who had

John R. Hassard

served under John Paul Jones in the Revolutionary War. Young Hassard was reared as an Episcopalian and was a member of St. Luke's parish in Manhattan where he came under the influence of the High-Church curate, Thomas Scott Preston. In 1849 Preston was received into the Catholic Church and later became vicar general of the Archdiocese of New York. On May 27, 1851, at the age of fifteen, Hassard followed Preston into the Catholic Church and remained his lifelong friend.

Hassard graduated at the head of his class from St. John's College, Fordham in 1855 and entered St. Joseph's Seminary, Fordham, intending to study for the diocesan priesthood. However, poor health forced him to withdraw from the seminary after one year. Thereupon he served as secretary to Archbishop John Hughes of New York until Hughes' death in January 1864. Two years later Hassard published a biography of Hughes, *Life of the Most Reverend John Hughes, D.D., First Archbishop of New York* (New York, 1866), which won wide acclaim for its candid and objective assessment of the controversial prelate.

For the rest of his life Hassard devoted himself to journalism and literary criticism. He spent a few months in 1865 as the first editor of the *Catholic World*, and then served as assistant editor of Charles A. Dana's short-lived Chicago *Republican*. When that venture failed the following year, Hassard returned to New York where he was associated for the rest of his life with the New York *Tribune* as literary and music critic, editorial writer and (briefly) managing editor. He was one of the first American music critics to appreciate the work of Richard Wagner. He visited Bayreuth in 1876 and wrote a series of letters to the *Tribune* which were later published as *Richard Wag-*

ner at Bayreuth: The Ring of the Niebelungs: A Description of its First Performance in August 1876 (New York, 1877).

Hassard also wrote *The Wreath of Beauty* (New York, 1864); *A Life of Pope Pius IX* (New York, 1875), a short, popular biography of the pontiff; *History of the United States of America* (New York, 1878), an abridged version of which was used as a textbook in Catholic schools; *A Pickwickian Pilgrimage* (New York, 1881); and *New York Tribune's History of the United States* (New York, 1887).

A cultivated man who was fluent in both French and German, he was also one of the few prominent Catholic Republicans in a city where the Democratic Party still claimed the allegiance of virtually all Catholics. During his twenty years in journalism, Hassard established a solid professional reputation despite the anti-Catholic prejudices of many of his colleagues.

In 1872 Hassard married Isabella Hargous; they had no children. He died in New York City on April 18, 1888, after a long and debilitating struggle with tuberculosis.

Hecker, Isaac, C.S.P. "John R. G. Hassard." *Catholic World* 47 (June 1888) 397–400.

Kelly, Blanche Mary. "John Rose Green Hassard." *Historical Records and Studies* 15 (March 1921) 19–34.

Walsh, James J. "John R. G. Hassard" *Catholic World* 97 (June 1913) 349–59.

THOMAS J. SHELLEY

HAUGHERY, MARGARET GAFFNEY (1813–88)

Philanthropist. Margaret Gaffney was born in 1813, County Cavan, Ireland. She emigrated with her parents to Baltimore, Maryland, in 1818. Both of her parents died of yellow fever four years later, and Margaret was reared by a Welsh family who had made the ocean voyage with the Gaffneys.

In 1835 Margaret Gaffney married Charles Haughery, and they moved to New Orleans, Louisiana. Once again Margaret found herself alone when her husband and infant daughter died the following year. To support herself, she went into the dairy business, which became a flourishing enterprise, despite her handicap of not being able to read or write. She donated most of the proceeds from her business to the Daughters of Charity for their orphanage and assisted in founding the Female Orphan Society of the Sisters of Charity.

Haughery broadened her business empire by purchasing a small bakery and developed it into one of the largest such establishments in the South. Through her business enterprises, she amassed a fortune of more than half a million dollars, most of which she contributed to charitable causes.

In the aftermath of the 1853 yellow fever epidemic, which left an unprecedented number of orphans, she financially supported St. Vincent's Infant Asylum. However, her generosity knew no boundaries. During the occupation of New Orleans by Union troops in the Civil War, she carried provisions to the Confederate prisoners. In her will she bequeathed her estate not only to Catholic institutions, but also to Protestant and Jewish orphanages.

Haughery's benevolence has been commemorated by a statue in Margaret Place in New Orleans and a woman's club, named in her honor, that gives Christmas gifts to children. She died February 9, 1882, in New Orleans.

Baudier, R. *The Catholic Church in Louisiana.* New Orleans, 1939.

MARIANNA McLOUGHLIN

HAWAII, CATHOLIC CHURCH IN

Catholic missionaries first came to Hawaii, then known as the Sandwich Islands, in July 1827. Led by Fr. Alexis Bachelot, SS.CC., they were members of the Congregation of the Sacred Hearts (popularly called Picpus Fathers) from France. They were immediately opposed by the Hawaiian authorities through the influence of American Protestant missionaries who had arrived in 1820. Forced to leave, Bachelot sailed for California in December 1831 where he assisted the Franciscans at their San Gabriel Mission and was assigned as the first resident pastor of the settlement of Los Angeles.

In 1837, hoping to reestablish the Hawaii mission, Bachelot returned to the islands only to be opposed and expelled again. Seriously ill, he died at sea on December 5, 1837, and was buried in Ponape in Micronesia.

Aggravated by the ill-treatment of French subjects in the Pacific, France ordered Captain Cyril Laplace of the frigate *L'Artemise* to make certain demands on Tahiti and Hawaii. Under the threat of war, the Hawaiian kingdom submitted to Laplace's "manifesto" in July 1839 which, by and large, granted religious freedom in Hawaii.

Vicariate Apostolic

In 1833 Bishop Stephen Rouchouze, SS.CC., was appointed vicar apostolic and given jurisdiction over the vast mission of "Eastern Oceania" which included Hawaii. He arrived in Hawaii on May 15, 1840, to resume the ill-fated Bachelot mission of 1827 and sent his men to the several major islands to evangelize the native Hawaiians. Notable among them was Fr. Robert Arsensius Walsh, SS.CC., Hawaii's outstanding Catholic missionary. Establishing his mission center in Honolulu, Rouchouze initiated the building of Our Lady of Peace Cathedral. In continuous use as a Catholic cathedral, this Honolulu church is one of the oldest in the United States. In January 1841 Rouchouze departed for France to obtain more missionaries and supplies for his Oceania mission. Tragically, on his return, near the Strait of Magellan in March 1843, the ship and all aboard were lost at sea.

Fr. Louis Maigret, SS.CC., in charge of the mission at Rouchouze's departure, was chosen in 1847 to be Hawaii's second vicar apostolic with jurisdiction limited only to the Sandwich Islands. He completed the building of the cathedral in 1843; founded the first Catholic school, Ahuimanu College, in 1846; brought in the first nuns, the Sacred Hearts Sisters, in 1859. He ordained Fr. Damien De Veuster, SS.CC. to the priesthood in 1864 and later assigned him to the Island of Molokai to minister to the victims of Hansen's disease until his death there in 1889. Maigret's administration witnessed Catholic conversions of the Hawaiian people that rivaled the strong Protestant efforts. He died in 1882, after forty-two years of service in Hawaii, thirty-five years as a bishop, the longest of all the bishops who have served in Hawaii. Maigret is buried in a crypt beneath the cathedral sanctuary.

During the mission period (1827–1940), the Church in Hawaii was headed by a total of six vicars apostolic, all Sacred Heart men. After the turbulent beginning years, the mission, starting with Bishop Maigret's administration, experienced steady growth. Facing the radical changes taking place in the Hawaiian kingdom throughout the nineteenth century, the Church had to adjust to the changing situation such as a diminishing population of native Hawaiians and the growing number of foreign laborers in the thriving sugar industry. The mission fathers welcomed the new apostolate of ministering to the large colony of Catholic Portuguese immigrants.

Catholic education received a new impetus in the mission with the arrival of the Marianist Brothers (Society of Mary) to conduct schools for boys in the towns of Honolulu, Wailuku, and Hilo. That same year Mother Marianne Kopp, O.S.F., and the Franciscan Sisters of Syracuse arrived to work with Hansen's disease patients in Honolulu and on the Island of Molokai. Today the sisters continue their hospital work at Kalaupapa, Molokai.

The last vicar apostolic of the Hawaii mission was Bishop Stephen Alencastre, SS.CC., a Portuguese raised in the islands. In 1927 Alencastre brought in Maryknoll missionaries to assist with parish work in the islands. Maryknoll Sisters also came that year to staff a number of schools. The bishop started St. Stephen's Minor Seminary in Kalihi Valley, Oahu, and in March 1940, enjoyed the fruit of his labor with the ordination of three island priests. Bishop Alencastre died from illness on board the liner *Matsonia* on November 9, 1940. Like the first bishop, both were named Stephen and both had died at sea. One had begun the mission in Hawaii and the other had ended it.

Diocese of Honolulu

The new Diocese of Honolulu, comprising all the islands of Hawaii, was created on September 10, 1941. The diocese has had four bishops.

Bishop James J. Sweeney (1941–67) was a native of San Francisco. During the World War II years, he assisted with the spiritual care of the military in the islands. In 1946 he founded a new St. Stephen's Seminary in Kaneohe, Oahu, headed by the Sulpician Fathers. In 1957 he convened the first and only synod in the history of the diocese. At the ending of his administration the diocese had two minor seminaries, ten Catholic high schools, and thirty elementary schools, with an enrollment of 17,150 students and a Confraternity of Christian Doctrine (CCD) program with 22,613 public school children under religious instructions. Sweeney retired due to illness in 1966 and passed away in San Francisco in 1968.

Bishop John J. Scanlan (1967–82) was Irish-born. A priest in San Francisco since 1930, he was made auxiliary bishop for Honolulu in 1954. He attended all the sessions of Vatican Council II. He brought in nine religious communities (mostly Filipino nuns) to serve schools, hospitals, and various ministries in the diocese. Scanlan was outspoken against abortion, a vocal proponent for respect for life, and opened the Mary Jane Pearson Center for unwed mothers in 1976. In 1981 he ordained the diocese's first class of permanent deacons. He retired in 1981 at age seventy-five in a priests' retirement home in San Rafael, California, and passed away on January 31, 1997. He was laid to rest beside Bishop Maigret in the crypt of the Honolulu cathedral.

Bishop Joseph A. Ferrario (1982–93) was originally from Scranton, Pennsylvania. He came to Hawaii as a Sulpician priest to teach in the seminary and later joined the diocese as a parish priest. In 1978 he was made auxiliary bishop to Scanlan and appointed third bishop of Honolulu in 1982. Under the goals of *"Outreach, Unity, and Renewal,"* his constant exhortation was *"OUR Church!"* He reorganized the Catholic Charities program and established the Office for Social Ministry and involved the Church in various outreach programs in the local community. A strong supporter of liturgical renewal, Ferrario emphasized, through the Office of Worship, the liturgical updating of many of the parish churches. Bishop Ferrario retired in 1993 because of poor health and, with his fondness for the islands, continues to maintain his residence in Hawaii.

Bishop Francis X. DiLorenzo (1994–), a priest of the Archdiocese of Philadelphia, was made auxiliary bishop of Scranton in January 1988. DiLorenzo was appointed fourth bishop of Honolulu on October 4, 1994. He is spiritual leader of a diocese with sixty-six parishes, forty-five schools, one Catholic university, two Catholic hospitals, and an estimated 213,000 Catholics.

Gallagher, Charles. *Hawaii and Its Gods.* New York: John Weatherhill, Inc., 1975.

Schoofs, Robert. *Pioneers of the Faith.* Honolulu, Hawaii: Sturgis Printing Company, Inc., 1978.

Whelan, Harold. *The Picpus Story.* Pomona, Calif.: Christ the King Center, 1980.

Wiltgen, Ralph. *The Founding of the Roman Catholic Church in Oceania, 1825 to 1850.* Camberra: Australian National University Press, 1979.

Yzendoorn, Reginald. *History of the Catholic Mission in the Hawaiian Islands.* Honolulu, Hawaii: Honolulu Star-Bulletin, 1927.

LOUIS H. YIM

HAYES, CARLTON J. H. (1882–1964)

Historian, diplomat. Carlton Joseph Huntley Hayes was born in Afton, New York, on May 16, 1882, the son of Philetus Arthur Hayes and Permilia Mary Huntley. His ancestors had lived in this picturesque area of the southern tier of New York state for five generations. In 1900 Hayes entered Columbia University as a college freshman, beginning an association with that institution which was to last for fifty years. After receiving his Ph.D. degree in history from Columbia in 1909, he joined the history faculty of the university the following year and ended his career at Columbia as the Seth Low Professor of History (1935–50). In 1945 he was elected president of the American Historical Association.

Carlton J. H. Hayes

Hayes also achieved recognition as the author of several highly successful college textbooks in European history, *Political and Social History of Modern Europe* (1916), and *Modern and Contemporary European History* (1919), the latter written in collaboration with his colleague Jacob Salwin Schapiro. Together with Parker T. Moon, Hayes also wrote a two-volume high school text, *Ancient and Medieval History* and *Modern History*

(1923). In 1926 *Modern History* was banned from the New York City public schools on the grounds that it was "anti-Protestant" and "internationalistic." As recently as 1983, the two volumes were still in print in a revised three-volume edition.

As a historian, Hayes is best remembered for his studies of modern nationalism. In four books on the subject and in a highly regarded graduate seminar at Columbia University, he traced the evolution of European nationalism from what he regarded as a generally positive influence in the early nineteenth century to a destructive force in the twentieth century.

In 1920 Hayes married Mary Evelyn Carroll; they had two children. In 1924 Hayes was received into the Catholic Church and thereafter played an active role in American Catholic intellectual life. He was a cofounder of the National Association of Christians and Jews, served on the original editorial council of *Commonweal,* was elected president of the American Catholic Historical Association in 1930, and was awarded the Laetare Medal by the University of Notre Dame in 1946. The year after he entered the Catholic Church, Hayes said, "Those persons who have lost or obscured their faith in Christianity are likely to be the very persons who extol the national state as an end in itself and who demand that what is God's shall be rendered unto Caesar."

In 1942 Hayes began a new career when President Franklin D. Roosevelt appointed him ambassador to Spain where he remained until 1945. Critics claimed that Hayes' religion inclined him to adopt an excessively friendly attitude to the Franco regime. He defended himself from such charges in a book published after his return to the United States in 1945, *Wartime Mission in Spain*, in which he asserted that he had used his influence to prevent Spain from entering World War II on the side of Germany and Italy.

In 1950 Hayes retired to his farm in Afton, New York, where he died on September 3, 1964.

Earle, E. M., ed. *Nationalism and Internationalism: Essays Inscribed to Carlton J. H. Hayes.* New York, 1950.

Hayes, Carlton J. H. "Obligation to America." *Commonweal* 1 (December 31, 1924) 200–01; (January 7, 1925) 227–28; (January 14, 1925) 255–56.

Hughes, Arthur J. "Carlton J. H. Hayes: Teacher and Historian." Ph.D. dissertation, Columbia University, 1970.

THOMAS J. SHELLEY

HAYES, HELEN (1900–93)

Actress. Helen Hayes was the only child of Francis van Arnum Brown, a meat salesman and Catherine Estelle Hayes, the great-niece of the Irish singer Catherine Hayes. As a child her mother encouraged her interest in acting, and took in washing to get her a good education. She graduated from Sacred Heart Academy in Washington, D.C., and took her mother's surname when she embarked on a theatrical career. In 1920 she made her Broadway debut playing a part in a mediocre play, *Bab.* For the next sixty years Helen Hayes became a popular and versatile artist with memorable performances in such plays as *Mary of Scotland* (1933), *Victor Regina* (1935), *Harriet* (1943),

Helen Hayes

The Glass Menagerie (1948, 1956, 1961), *A Touch of the Poet* (1958), and *Harvey* (1970).

The winner of Tony and Emmy Awards, she disliked Hollywood but won two Oscar Awards for her performances in *The Sin of Madelene Claudet* and *Airport.* She also curtailed her work on television but gave distinguished performances in *The Snoop Sisters* (1972), *Murder Made Easy* (1983), and *Murder with Mirrors* (1985).

She was a popular figure in New York theatrical and literary circles and was closely connected with the talented group associated with *The New Yorker* including Dorothy Parker, Harold Ross, Alexander Wolcott, and Charles MacArthur, whom she married. Their only daughter Mary was born in 1930 and died of polio in 1950. The tragedy devastated Charles MacArthur and he died of alcoholism seven years later. Throughout her busy career Helen Hayes devoted much time to charitable and religious causes, and in 1972 the University of Notre Dame awarded her the Laetare Medal for her contributions to Catholic culture. Her autobiography, *My Life in Three Acts* (1990), is the story of an extraordinary lady who deservedly is an American legend.

MICHAEL GLAZIER

HAYES, PATRICK CARDINAL (1867–1938)

Cardinal archbishop. Patrick Joseph Hayes was born in New York City on November 20, 1867, to Daniel and Mary Gleason Hayes, both of whom were immigrants from Killarney, Ireland. After the death of his mother in 1872, his father, who was a longshoreman, remarried, and young Patrick lived with his father and stepmother. About ten years later, apparently for financial reasons, he moved to the home of his mother's sister and brother-in-law, Ellen and James Egan.

Patrick J. Cardinal Hayes

His education from elementary school to college took place entirely in Catholic schools in New York City directed by the Christian Brothers: Transfiguration parochial school, De La Salle Institute, and Manhattan College. Upon graduation from college with the A.B. degree in 1888, Hayes entered St. Joseph's Provincial Seminary in Troy, New York, the major seminary of the Archdiocese of New York. He was ordained a priest of the Archdiocese of New York on September 8, 1892, by Archbishop Michael A. Corrigan. He then spent two additional years of study at The Catholic University of America where he received the S.T.L. degree in 1894.

Early Career

Hayes first parochial assignment was an appointment in 1894 as curate in the Manhattan parish of St. Gabriel whose pastor was Msgr. John Murphy Farley, former secretary to Cardinal John McCloskey. Thereafter Hayes' career was closely linked to that of Farley. The following year Farley became New York's first auxiliary bishop and appointed Hayes his secretary. Farley became archbishop

of New York in 1902, and in 1903 he appointed Hayes chancellor of the archdiocese and president of Cathedral College, the newly established minor seminary. On July 3, 1914, Hayes followed in Farley's footsteps when he was named auxiliary bishop of New York and was ordained titular bishop of Tagaste on October 28, 1914. From 1915 to 1917 he also served as pastor of the large Manhattan parish of St. Stephen.

During World War I Hayes achieved national prominence. With the entry of the United States into the war in 1917, the number of Catholic army chaplains suddenly increased from twenty-five to almost nine hundred. On November 24, 1917, the Holy See appointed Hayes Military Ordinary with responsibility for the chaplains and for all Catholics in the armed forces. In 1917 the bishops of the United States also established the National Catholic War Council as a national planning and coordinating agency for the American hierarchy. Hayes was one of four bishops who served as a member of the administrative committee. He supported the continuation of the council after the war under the name of the National Catholic Welfare Council (later changed to Conference). In 1919 Hayes was one of four episcopal signatories of the progressive *Program of Social Reconstruction,* written by The Catholic University of America professor John A. Ryan, but issued in the name of the American hierarchy.

Archbishop of New York

Hayes succeeded Farley as the fifth archbishop of New York on March 10, 1919. He was appointed a cardinal on March 24, 1924. Until 1936 the archdiocese was still the largest in population of any American see, but, for the first time in history, the number of Catholics declined, from about 1,300,000 in 1919 to about 1,000,000 in 1938, due to the movement of middle-class Catholics to the suburbs and the legal restrictions on immigration from southern and eastern Europe. Despite the decline in the Catholic population, Hayes established sixty-five new parishes in the archdiocese, sixty of them in his first ten years before the onset of the Great Depression.

Hayes was a distinguished-looking man of less than medium height whose paternal visage, snow-white hair, and mellifluous voice (which was rarely heard from the pulpit of St. Patrick's Cathedral) fulfilled American expectations of a Catholic prelate. He was a shy and kindly person who avoided the limelight and turned down most invitations to participate in civic functions. However, one New York priest-historian (Henry J. Browne) noted: "Observers sometimes missed the angle of his jutting jaw which betrayed another facet of his personality." Despite his low public profile, Hayes wielded considerable political influence indirectly. Local Democratic politicians were thought to be so deferential to his wishes that the archbishop's residence at 452 Madison Avenue was popularly known as "The Powerhouse."

In the administration of the archdiocese, Hayes left great autonomy to the pastors, who enjoyed lifetime tenure and operated their parishes as petty fiefdoms. Like James Cardinal Gibbons, Hayes could have (but did not) ascribe his success to "masterly inactivity," since New York Catholicism needed little supervision from the chancery office in an era of crowded churches, obedient curates, uncomplaining sisters, and deferential laity.

One area in which Hayes excelled and made a major contribution to the American Catholic Church was in the field of social welfare work. Between 1910 and 1916 Catholic charitable institutions in New York had received considerable unfavorable publicity from a series of city and state investigative commissions. As soon as he became archbishop in 1919, Hayes instituted a professional evaluation of these institutions, which led in 1920 to the creation of the Catholic Charities of the Archdiocese of New York, a supervisory organization that set high standards of professionalism in the field of social service and was widely imitated by other dioceses throughout the United States.

In 1932 Hayes suffered a serious heart attack, which forced him to restrict his activities thereafter. He died in his sleep at St. Joseph's Camp in Monticello, New York, on September 4, 1938, and was buried beneath the main altar of St. Patrick's Cathedral. He was generally remembered with affection by both the clergy and laity as the "Cardinal of Charities."

See also NEW YORK, CATHOLIC CHURCH IN.

Browne, Henry J. "Patrick Joseph Hayes." *Dictionary of American Biography.* Supplement II, 293–95.

Cohalan, Florence D. *A Popular History of the Archdiocese of New York.* Yonkers, 1983, 215–64.

Hayes' Papers are in the Archives of the Archdiocese of New York.

Kelly, J. B. *Cardinal Hayes.* New York, 1940.

Parish Visitors of Mary Immaculate, eds. *The Cardinal of Charities.* New York, 1927.

Shea, Mary Margretta. "Patrick Cardinal Hayes and the Catholic Charities in New York City." Ph.D. dissertation, New York University, 1966.

THOMAS J. SHELLEY

HAZOTTE, MARY AGNES (1847–1905)

Cofoundress of the Congregation of St. Agnes. Born on May 7, 1847, in Buffalo, New York, Hazotte was the youngest of seven children of a French immigrant family. The Hazottes soon moved to Detroit, Michigan, where Mary received a rudimentary education at St. Mary's School, under the care of the Sisters of Notre Dame. From the time she was five, the family was shattered by a series of devastating losses. During the next years, two older sisters, a brother, and her father died. When Mary was thirteen, she lost her mother, leaving the two older brothers to support their sisters.

In 1863, when Mary was fifteen, she visited a friend who had joined a struggling religious community in Barton, Wisconsin. Named after St. Agnes of Rome, the group was established by a zealous Austrian missionary, Fr. Caspar Rehrl. After vainly trying to recruit sisters from Europe to aid him in the work of educating the children of the immigrants, he was in the process of establishing his own sisterhood.

When Mary arrived, the sisters were attempting to farm eleven acres of land with few implements and teaching with little preparation. Mary, talented and comparatively well educated, was welcomed as a great gift to the poverty-stricken community. On July 2, 1864, Mary, now Sr. Mary Agnes, and two other young women became the first professed Sisters of St. Agnes. That same day she became the society's first elected superior.

The differences of vision between the overworked priest and the seventeen-year-old superior were soon evident. Fr. Rehrl's goal of having sisters work immediately in the schools conflicted with Agnes's desire for more education and formation for the sisters. After a series of crises which almost eventuated in the dissolution of the congregation, the community split and Agnes and the majority of sisters left for Fond du Lac. There, the community was under the direction of Fr. Francis Haas, O.F.M. Cap., whose rule and direction strengthened the community and gave it a strong Franciscan orientation. Fr. Francis became the guiding personality in Agnes' life.

Critical years followed. Mother Agnes sent sisters on begging expeditions so that work could continue. In Fond du Lac, she opened a boarding school and the sisters continued to accept schools, public and parochial. Death overtook thirteen sisters in the decade after 1872, but the congregation grew. Sisters staffed schools in Wisconsin, Indiana, Illinois, Kansas, Michigan, New York, Ohio, Pennsylvania, and Texas. At the request of local doctors, she undertook to staff a fifty-bed hospital. She established a home for the aged and a sanitarium. She sent sisters to administer and manage the Leo House in New York where newly arrived immigrants would be safe from the victimization of the period.

In 1905 Mother Agnes was responsible for 206 sisters and 79 missions. Tired and ill and after months of suffering, this woman of remarkable courage and strong faith died at the age of fifty-eight in 1905.

See also ST. AGNES, CONGREGATION OF (C.S.A.).

Palen, Imogene, C.S.A. *Fieldstones '76: The Story of the Founders of the Sisters of Saint Agnes.* Oshkosh: Oshkosh Printers, 1976.

MARGARET LORIMER, C.S.A.

HEALY, GEORGE (1813–94)

Painter. George Peter Alexander Healy was born on July 15, 1813, in Boston, Massachusetts. Although he had no formal training as an artist, he went to Paris, France, in 1834 to study under Baron Antoine Jean Gros and copied in the Louvre. After setting up studios in Paris and London, his reputation as a portrait painter quickly spread. He amassed a large clientele and produced as many as fifty portraits a year.

From 1855 to 1867 and from 1892 until his death, Healy and his family lived in Chicago, but he retained an international practice. Throughout his career, he painted more than seven hundred portraits, including Pope Pius IX, Bismarck, King Louis Philippe of France, Henry Clay, Henry Wadsworth Longfellow, eleven U.S. presidents from John Quincy Adams to Ulysses S. Grant, Nathaniel Hawthorne, and Ralph Waldo Emerson.

His historical scenes, such as "Daniel Webster Replying to Hayne" and "The Peacemakers," represented in accurate detail not only the events, but also prominent persons of the era.

He was an honorary member of the National Academy of Design. His works hang in the National Gallery of Art, Corcoran Art Gallery, Smithsonian Institution, and the Capitol, Washington, D.C.; the Metropolitan Museum of Art and New York Historical Society, New York; Newberry Library, Chicago; and Virginia Museum of Fine Arts, Richmond, Virginia. He died in Chicago on June 24, 1894.

Healy, G.P.A. *Reminiscences of a Portrait Painter.* Chicago, 1894.

Mare, M. de. *G.P.A. Healy, American Artist.* New York, 1954.

MARIANNA McLOUGHLIN

HEALY, JAMES AUGUSTINE (1830–1900)

First U.S. bishop of African American heritage, Healy was born near Macon, Georgia, on April 6, 1830, of a white Irish immigrant planter and his mulatto slave wife. Healy graduated from Holy Cross College, Worcester, Massachusetts, and studied for the priesthood at Montreal and Paris. Ordained in 1854, he served as the first chancellor of the Diocese of Boston, rector of its cathedral, and pastor of a large inner-city parish.

In 1875 Healy was appointed second bishop of Portland, Maine, where he oversaw a modest expansion of the institutional Church amid increasing tensions between Irish and French-Canadian parishioners. Aligning himself with the conservatives in the American hierarchy, he viewed labor unions with suspicion and remained pessimistic about the possibilities for reconciling Catholicism and American culture. Somewhat light skinned and not always recognized as partly black, Healy seldom identified with

James A. Healy

efforts to promote the interests of African Americans, inside or outside the Church. Four of his siblings, similarly disinclined toward racial identification, also pursued religious careers: Patrick Healy (1834–1910), a Jesuit, served as president of Georgetown University; Sherwood Healy (1836–75) was a diocesan priest in Boston; Josephine Healy (1845–79) was a Sister of the Religious Hospitallers of St. Joseph, Montreal; and Eliza Healy (1846–1919) was a sister and convent superior of the Congregation de Notre Dame, Montreal. James Healy died on August 5, 1900, in Portland.

See also AFRICAN AMERICAN CATHOLICS; MAINE, CATHOLIC CHURCH IN.

JAMES M. O'TOOLE

HECKER, ISAAC (1819–88)

Priest, evangelist, theologian, founder of the Paulists. Isaac Thomas Hecker was the founder of the first religious order of men originating in the United States, the Missionary Society of St. Paul the Apostle, better known as the Paulist Fathers. Hecker was widely admired as a writer, lecturer, and organizer, but after his death his ideas became the center of a controversy which led to the condemnation of Americanism by Pope Leo XIII in 1899. Hecker's spiritual ideas received increasing attention in the years following the second Vatican Council.

Early Life

Isaac Hecker was born in New York on December 18, 1819, the third son of a solid working-class German family. He received only a limited education before joining his brothers in the family baking business. In 1842 he was stunned by a powerful religious experience which encouraged him to seek a deeper, more committed spiritual life. Guided by the famous lecturer Orestes Brownson, Hecker visited for a time at Brook Farm and Fruitlands in New England, where he became acquainted with many of the religious movements of the day. In 1844 he decided to enter the Catholic Church. A short time after his baptism, he left for Europe in the company of several other converts, to study for the priesthood with the Redemptorist Order, a missionary community which served German immigrants in the United Stares.

In 1851 Hecker, now a Redemptorist priest, returned to the United States with the other American converts to form an English-speaking mission band, offering spiritual revivals in Catholic parishes across the country. By this time Hecker was convinced he had a providential mission to convert non-Catholic Americans. In addition to the Catholic parish missions, he wrote two books, *Questions of the Soul* (1855), and *Aspirations of Nature* (1857), to persuade young Americans of the truths of the Catholic faith. In a thoroughly American apologetic, Hecker drew on his own experience as an unchurched American to argue that Catholicism alone could answer the spiritual hungers and intellectual questions arising from the American experience of religious freedom, pluralism, and social and economic progress.

The Paulists

Anxious to organize such evangelizing work, Hecker traveled to Rome in 1857 to seek permission to establish with his colleagues a new Redemptorist foundation for English-speaking mission work. As a result of taking the trip without proper permission, he was dismissed from the Redemptorists. Nevertheless, after months of negotiation, the Pope granted him permission to form a new missionary society under the authority of the American bishops. This was the beginning of the Paulists.

Under the authority of the archbishop of New York, John Hughes, the Paulists constructed a new and innovative New York parish, St. Paul the Apostle, while they continued their parish missions and began the work of organizing their religious community. In 1865 Hecker and his community launched the *Catholic World,* a monthly commentary on literature, religion, and the arts, and the Catholic Publication Society, which produced a variety of pamphlets and books. He also offered public lectures in civic halls in a number of cities, explaining Catholicism to skeptical Americans. In 1866 the convert evangelist addressed the entire U.S. hierarchy, urging them to take up the work of making America Catholic. His energetic presence and creative projects led an admiring journalist to name him "the steam priest."

In 1870 Hecker attended the meetings of the First Vatican Council in Rome. He was disappointed by that body's defensive emphasis on authority and papal infallibility, far removed from his soaring hopes for evangelization. Shortly after returning to the United States, he became seriously ill. For several years he traveled in Europe, visiting Egypt and the Holy Land. He brought his ideas together in a manifesto which predicted the advent of an age of evangelism and conversions, but no new opportunities for service presented themselves.

In 1875 Hecker returned to New York where he took up again the direction of the Paulists and the *Catholic World.* While his health deteriorated and he was plagued by tiredness, he still wrote many strong essays on controversial issues, later collected as *The Church and the Age* (1888), as well as a study of the work of the Holy Spirit. But he was worried by the continuing defensiveness of Church leaders, and he was disappointed by his Paulists' preoccupation with parishes and missions to Catholics. He died in New York City on December 22, 1888.

Hecker and Americanism

After Hecker's death, his Paulist disciple, Walter Elliott, wrote his biography, which was well received. When the book appeared in abridged translation in France, it excited sharp debate between factions of the European Church. Pope Leo XIII eventually took the issues under advisement and then, in 1899, he issued *Testem benevolentiae,* an encyclical letter addressed to the American bishops condemning many ideas which had come to be associated with Hecker. These included the claim that Catholic doctrine should be minimized in order to attract converts, that the Holy Spirit was at work in a unique way in the modern age, that there was now less need for spiritual direction for laypersons and more need for the active virtues than the passive, and that there might be a Church in the United States different from the church in the rest of the world.

The condemnation dealt a death blow to a liberal party in the American Church whose members had taken at least some of their inspiration from Isaac Hecker. His defenders could argue that the ideas condemned in the encyclical were distortions of Hecker's actual views, but his memory was placed under a shadow until years later, when new openings in the Church seemed to affirm many of Hecker's hopes.

Hecker's Legacy

Three elements of Hecker's life and work seem of particular interest. One was Hecker's emphasis on freedom. In America, with its religious diversity and competitive evangelism, faith would have to be a matter of personal conviction. Hecker thought this a good thing. He rejected

Isaac Hecker

all forms of coercion, and disliked pastoral work based on traditional loyalties, insisting that eventually these would give way to invitations addressed to the "earnest seekers" whose allegiance could only be won through persuasion. Similarly, those in the Church had to deepen their own interior spiritual life, supported, confirmed, and enriched by the sacramental life of the Church.

Second, Hecker's original religious experience led him to explore many dimensions of the interior life of the Spirit as it developed in the culture of the United States. Eventually he came to believe that God's Holy Spirit worked in three ways: in the voice of conscience within, through the Church, established as the very presence of Christ in the midst of history, and in Divine Providence, God's active guidance to historical events great and small. This threefold work of the Spirit was mutually supportive: the Church confirmed and tested the intuitions of conscience, conscience brought the doctrines of the Church to life in personal commitment and ministry, while Providence helped keep persons and institutions from self-preoccupation and illusion by calling the Church to account for the whole of humanity.

Finally, Hecker was indeed a certain kind of Americanist, one who believed that God was at work in the experience of the nation and its people. As a result, he wanted to encourage the Church and its people to set aside old world loyalties and enter fully into American life. During his lifetime the vast influx of immigrants and the lack of a broad Americanized middle class limited the appeal of Hecker's vision. But decades later his hopes for an American Church in mission to build the kingdom of God resonated with at least some American Catholics no longer anchored in the ethnic enclaves which long shaped the Church in the United States.

See also AMERICANISM; PAULISTS (C.S.P.).

Elliott, Walter, C.S.P. *The Life of Father Hecker.* New York, 1891; repr. New York, 1972.
Farina, John. *An American Experience of God: The Spirituality of Isaac Hecker.* New York, 1981.
____, ed. *Hecker Studies: Essays on the Thought of Isaac Hecker.* New York, 1983.
Holden, Vincent, C.S.P. *The Yankee Paul: Isaac Thomas Hecker.* Milwaukee, 1958.
McSorley, Joseph, C.S.P. *Father Hecker and His Friends.* New York, 1952.
O'Brien, David J. *Isaac Hecker, An American Catholic.* New York and Mahwah, 1992.

DAVID O'BRIEN

HEENEY, CORNELIUS (1754–1848)

Merchant and philanthropist. Cornelius Heeney was born in King's County, Ireland, in 1754. He emigrated to New York in 1784 and became a partner of John Jacob Astor as a fur dealer. After this short-lived partnership, Heeney established his own business, becoming a shrewd and prosperous merchant in his own right. He donated much time and money to the Catholic Church and charities. In 1785, he helped organize St. Peter's Church in New York City and served as a trustee and treasurer. He helped to obtain the property for St. Patrick's Old Cathedral and encouraged Elizabeth Ann Seton to found a Sisters of Charity academy for girls at St. Patrick's Old Cathedral in 1817, an institution he continued to support throughout his life. In 1820 Heeney became the guardian of John McCloskey, future cardinal archbishop of New York. Heeney served as state assemblyman from 1818 to 1822, and as such was one of the first New York Catholics to hold public office.

In 1835 he retired and moved to an estate in Columbia Heights, Brooklyn. This estate soon proved to be a refuge for those most in need. In 1845 he established the Brooklyn Benevolent Society to administer his estate, which has distributed an estimated two million dollars to the poor. Heeney died in Brooklyn, New York, on May 3, 1848.

Meehan, Thomas F. "A Self-Effaced Philanthropist: Cornelius Heeney, 1754–1848." *Catholic Historical Review* 4 (April 1918) 3–17.
____. "Some Pioneer Laymen in New York: Dominic Lynch and Cornelius Heeney." *Historical Records and Studies* 4 (1906) 285–301.
Sharp, John K. *History of the Diocese of Brooklyn, 1853–1953.* 2 vols. New York, 1954.

RICHARD G. SMITH

HEISS, MICHAEL (1818–90)

First bishop of La Crosse and second archbishop of Milwaukee. Heiss was born in Pfahldorf, Germany, on April 12, 1818. He attended the University of Munich and completed his studies for the priesthood at Eichstätt. He was ordained to the priesthood in 1840 at Nymphenburg.

In 1842 Heiss volunteered for service in Covington, Kentucky. A year later he affiliated himself with the newly appointed bishop of Milwaukee, John Martin Henni and accompanied him to the new diocese in 1844. Deeply devoted to the care of German-speaking Catholics, he became pastor of St. Mary's Church, Milwaukee's first German Catholic church. Ill health compelled a lengthy convalescence in Germany in 1850, but he returned to Milwaukee in 1852 where he resumed pastoral work and was secretary to the bishop. In 1856 Henni appointed him the first rector of his newly opened seminary where he taught dogma, canon law, and Scripture. Heiss was an able scholar, publishing books on matrimony (1861) and the Scriptures (1863). His writing also appeared on the pages of the German language journals *Pastoral-Blatt* and *Der Warheitsfreund*. He was active in the planning for the Second Plenary Council of Baltimore (1866). In 1868 he was nominated the first bishop of La Crosse, Wisconsin.

As bishop of this far western part of the state, Heiss spent considerable time on the road, confirming, visiting missions, and raising the organizational infrastructure of Church life. He attended the First Vatican Council in Rome (1869–71), where he was a supporter of the definition of papal infallibility.

In 1878 Archbishop John Martin Henni clearly wanted Heiss as his coadjutor in Milwaukee. However, Heiss's nomination was caught in the crossfire of a dispute between English-speaking and German-speaking clergy and bishops. Rome delayed making a decision until Henni suffered a near-fatal stroke and the matter was expedited. In April 1880, Heiss was nominated as coadjutor with right of succession. Upon Henni's demise in September 1881, he became archbishop of Milwaukee.

In diocesan affairs Heiss attempted to regularize diocesan finances and impose a tighter administration than his predecessor. He appointed a school board, imposed diocesan collections, and began paying off debts left by Henni. Heiss was an unabashed partisan for the rights of German-speaking Catholics. He warmly approved of the Abbelen Memorial of 1886 (Abbelen worked in the Milwaukee see). Moreover, he took a dim view of the establishment of The Catholic University of America, a program he believed too close to the heart of the Americanizers of the hierarchy. Toward the end of his life Heiss led opposition to the Bennett Law of 1889, which mandated English-only instruction in Wisconsin schools. He died in La Crosse on March 26, 1890.

See also GERMAN CATHOLICS IN AMERICA; WISCONSIN, CATHOLIC CHURCH IN.

Blied, Benjamin. *Three Archbishops of Milwaukee*. Milwaukee, 1955.

Johnson, Peter Leo. *Crosier on the Frontier: A Life of John Martin Henni*. Madison, 1959.

———. *Halcyon Days: The Story of St. Francis Seminary, Milwaukee*. Milwaukee, 1956.

———. *Stuffed Saddle Bags: The Life of Martin Kundig, Priest*. Milwaukee, 1942.

Ludwig, M. Mileta. *Right Hand Glove Uplifted*. New York, 1968.

O'Connell, Marvin R. *John Ireland and the American Catholic Church*. St. Paul, 1988.

STEVEN M. AVELLA

HELLRIEGEL, MARTIN BALTHASAR (1890–1981)

Liturgist. Born on November 9, 1890, in Heppenheim, Germany, Martin B. Hellriegel came to Starkenburg, Missouri, in 1906. He entered the seminary in St. Meinrad, Indiana, in 1909 for one year, and then completed his studies at Kenrick Seminary, St. Louis, Missouri. He was ordained a priest on December 20, 1914. Hellriegel served as assistant pastor for three and a half years in St. Peter's parish in St. Charles, Missouri; as chaplain to the Sisters of the Most Precious Blood, O'Fallon, Missouri, 1918–40; and as pastor and pastor emeritus 1940–81 at Holy Cross parish in St. Louis. He was raised to the rank of monsignor in 1940, domestic prelate in 1949, and to protonotary apostolic in 1964.

Having been caught up into the spirit of the 1903 *motu proprio* of St. Pius X, his motto became *"Instaurare omnia in Christo."* He never failed to insist that active participation in the holy mysteries and in the public and solemn prayer of the Church is the primary and indispensable source of the true Christian spirit. Hellriegel was also profoundly influenced by the spirit and theology of the monks of Maria Laach, Germany, particularly that of Odo Casel, O.S.B., and by Dr. Pius Parsch of Klosterneuberg, Austria, in the area of pastoral liturgy.

Achievements

Along with Virgil Michel, O.S.B., Gerald Ellard, S.J., Godfrey Diekmann, O.S.B., and others, Hellriegel became a leader in the early liturgical movement in the U.S.A. The Sisters of the Most Precious Blood in O'Fallon, Missouri, became early beneficiaries of his efforts as well as a garden where the full liturgical life grew: dialogue Mass, offertory processions, praying the Day Hours of the Roman Breviary, preparation for the proper celebration of the Liturgical Year, even the restoration of the Easter Vigil to its proper time. On Christmas Eve, 1925, in O'Fallon, Missouri, Michel, Ellard, and Hellriegel agreed on the name for the new liturgical journal, *Orate Fratres* (later *Worship*).

Hellriegel's work at Holy Cross parish (1940–81) grew out of three perceptions: the parish is the concretization of the Mystical Body of Christ, the eucharistic celebration is its central activity, and the families are its living cells.

Foremost among Hellriegel's contributions to the liturgical apostolate was his ability to convey to others (a) his own boundless enthusiasm for and response to God's benevolent design to unite all things under the headship of Christ, and (b) his clear vision of how this design becomes a present reality in the sacred mysteries or liturgy celebrated in the course of the Liturgical Year.

Vehicles Carrying His Influence

His own reverent and dynamic celebrations of the sacred liturgy were the chief carriers of his influence. In addition there were lectures, retreats, pamphlets, numerous articles (particularly in *Orate Fratres/Worship*). Even his books, *The Holy Sacrifice of the Mass* (Pio Decimo Press, 1948), and *Vine and Branches* (Pio Decimo Press, 1948), are largely compilations of lectures and articles.

Hellriegel was influential in the foundation of The Liturgical Conference, of which he served as member of the board of directors, member of the advisory council, vice president and president. He was a frequent contributor to the National Liturgical Weeks Proceedings. Another valuable vehicle for the promotion of the liturgical apostolate was the monthly magazine, *The Living Parish,* which Hellriegel edited from 1940–56.

His final days were spent in O'Fallon, Missouri, where he died on April 10, 1981. He is buried in the convent cemetery of the Sisters of the Most Precious Blood. His tombstone bears the appropriate inscription: "He loved the Church."

See also LITURGICAL MOVEMENT IN AMERICA, THE; MICHEL, VIRGIL; *WORSHIP (ORATE FRATRES).*

Barrett, Noel Hackmann. *Martin B. Hellriegel: Pastoral Liturgist.* St. Louis, 1990.
Casel, Odo, O.S.B. *La Fête de Paques dans l'Eglise des Pères.* Paris, 1963.
Seasoltz, Kevin R., ed. *The New Liturgy: A Documentation 1903–1965.* New York: Herder and Herder, 1966.

MARY PIERRE ELLEBRACHT, C.PP.S.

HENNEPIN, LOUIS (1626–1701?)

Priest, explorer. Hennepin was born on May 12, 1626, in Ath, Hainault, in present-day Belgium. Though little is known about his early life, he joined the Franciscan Recollects as a youth, was ordained a priest, and spent time preaching and begging for alms in Italy and Germany. After working in Holland, he was sent in 1675 to Quebec. After working as a hospital chaplain, in 1678 he acted as a chaplain for an expedition led by Robert de La Salle to explore lands around the upper Mississippi River. He was aboard the first European vessel, the *Griffon,* to explore the Great Lakes, and was part of a band that was the first to explore areas of the upper Mississippi. He traveled as far north as modern-day Minneapolis and was responsible for naming the Falls of St. Anthony there.

While in Minnesota, Hennepin and his fellow explorers were captured by the Dakota (Sioux) on April 12, 1681. After being rescued with the help of the French explorer Daniel Du Lhut, Hennepin returned to Quebec with Du Lhut and in 1682 went back to Europe. Here in a Franciscan friary in St. Germain-en-Laye he wrote *Description de la Louisiane* (1683), an account of explorations and dealings with the Native Americans. Although this and later works by Hennepin contain exaggerations and use materials written by others, some of his writings have value for their descriptions of early explorations of the upper Mississippi and the Native Americans living there. Hennepin fell into disfavor with the French crown under King Louis XIV and was banned from Canada. He was known to have gone to Rome where he died, probably around 1701.

Lovant, A. "Le Père Louis Hennepin: Nouveaux Jalons pour la biographie." *Revue d'Histoire Ecclésiastique* 45 (1950) 186–211.

ANTHONY D. ANDREASSI

HENNI, JOHN MARTIN (1805–81)

First bishop and archbishop of Milwaukee, Wisconsin. Born in Misanenga, Switzerland, Henni was educated in St. Gall and Lucerne, Switzerland, and the Urban College of the Propaganda in Rome. While a student in Rome, he met Fr. Frederick Résé, who invited him to the American

John M. Henni

missions in Ohio and Kentucky. In 1828, with his companion Martin Kundig, he emigrated to the United States and completed his theological studies in Bardstown, Kentucky. He was ordained to the priesthood on February 2, 1829, by Bishop Edward Fenwick, O.P. In Ohio, he worked as an itinerant missionary, briefly settling for a time in Canton and then in Cincinnati. He became pastor of Cincinnati's first German-speaking parish, Holy Trinity parish and founded *Der Warheitsfreund* in 1837, the first German Catholic newspaper in the United States. His devotion to German-speaking Catholics won him the title "the German Las Casas."

First Bishop of Milwaukee

When the Holy See erected the Diocese of Milwaukee in 1843, Henni was selected as the first bishop. This jurisdiction included all of the Territory of Wisconsin and a small portion of eastern Minnesota. When Henni arrived in Milwaukee in May 1844, in company with Fr. Michael Heiss, he found a thriving city with a small Catholic church run by his friend, Kundig. In subsequent travels around the state he discovered a total Catholic population of around 9,000, mostly located in the fertile farmlands south of the Wisconsin and Fox Rivers and along the shore of Lake Michigan.

Henni began immediately to build on the firm foundation of earlier Catholic missionaries. His first priorities were the construction of a suitable cathedral and a seminary. With help of generous benefactions from German-speaking Catholics in Bavaria and Austria he was able to build St. John's Cathedral in 1853, and St. Francis de Sales Seminary opened its doors in 1856. Henni made Milwaukee a congenial location for the large numbers of German immigrants who flooded Wisconsin in the 1840s and 1850s. To serve them he invited a number of German-speaking religious orders of men and women to establish Catholic schools. He also replicated his efforts in Cincinnati by creating a German Catholic press. *Die Seebote* first rolled off the presses in 1852 and a successor, *Die Columbia,* appeared in 1872.

Henni aggressively defended his flock against public attacks by nativists and German rationalists in the city. He was present at Vatican Council I (1869–71) and, although he opposed adding the infallibility question to the council's agenda, he ultimately voted in favor of the definition. In 1868 his jurisdiction was subdivided into two new dioceses: Green Bay and La Crosse. In 1875 Milwaukee was raised to metropolitan status and Henni became its first archbishop.

Henni's health deteriorated in the late 1870s and he petitioned Rome for a coadjutor bishop with right of succession. Henni's choice for the post, Bavarian-born Michael Heiss, the bishop of La Crosse, encountered stiff opposition from the English-speaking priests of his diocese and from "Americanist" bishops such as John Ireland. Their opposition temporarily delayed Heiss's nomination. But when Henni's health took a turn for the worse in 1880, Heiss's promotion was expedited largely with the help of the mother general of the School Sisters of Notre Dame and their chaplain, Fr. Peter Abbelen, who appealed to Joseph Hergenröther, the cardinal protector of the sisters.

Henni died in Milwaukee on September 7, 1881. His long tenure provided Milwaukee with the stability necessary for a firm foundation.

See also KENTUCKY, CATHOLIC CHURCH IN; WISCONSIN, CATHOLIC CHURCH IN.

Johnson, Peter Leo. *Crosier on the Frontier.* Madison, 1959.
____. *Halcyon Days: The Story of St. Francis Seminary.* Milwaukee, 1956.
Ludwig, M. Mileta. *Right Hand Glove Uplifted: A Biography of Archbishop Michael Heiss.* New York, 1968.
Walch, Timothy. *Catholic Education in Chicago and Milwaukee, 1840–1890.* New York, 1988.

STEVEN M. AVELLA

HERBERMANN, CHARLES GEORGE (1840–1916)

Editor, author, educator. Charles George Herbermann was born in Saerbeck, Westphalia, Germany, on December 8, 1840, the child of George and Elizabeth Stipp Herbermann. The family emigrated to New York City in 1851. Herbermann attended St. Alphonsus parochial school for two years before attending St. Francis Xavier College,

Charles G. Herbermann

earning a B.A. degree in 1858. He taught at St. Francis Xavier for eleven years while he continued his studies and earned an M.A. (1860) and Ph.D. (1865). In 1869 he began a forty-six-year career at the College of the City of New York as professor of Latin and college librarian (1873). He published editions of Sallust's *Jugurthine War* (1886) and *Bellum Catilinae* (1900), and a translation of Torfason's *History of Ancient Vinland* (1888).

The United States Catholic Historical Society, which Herbermann helped to found in 1884 with John Gilmary Shea, named him president in 1898, a position he held until his death. Under his supervision, the society published nine volumes of *Historical Records and Studies, Unpublished Letters of Charles Carroll of Carrollton* (1902), and a facsimile edition of the 1507 *Cosmographiae Introductio of Martin Waldseemüller* (1907). He himself contributed nineteen articles and numerous book reviews to *Historical Records and Studies.* He was appointed editor in chief of *The Catholic Encyclopedia* in 1905, a task he saw to its completion in 1913 despite his growing visual imparity. For his work in this fifteen-volume work of Catholic scholarship he received widespread recognition, including knighthood in the Order of Saint Gregory (1909), the *Pro Ecclesia et Pontifice* Medal (1913) awarded by Pius X, and honors from Notre Dame University, Fordham University, and The Catholic University of America. In 1916 he published *The Sulpicians in the United States.* He died in New York City on August 24, 1916.

Condon, Peter. "Charles George Herbermann." *Historical Records and Studies* 10 (1917) 8–25.

RICHARD G. SMITH

HESS, BEDE (1885–1953)

Franciscan Conventual friar. He was born on November 16, 1885, in Trenton, New Jersey, Frederick John Hess. He was thirteen years old when he entered St. Francis College (high school) in Trenton, New Jersey. At the time the regular course lasted three years. Frederick Hess completed it in two. He entered the novitiate of the Friars Minor Conventual in November 1900 and was given the name Frater Bede. Simple vows were pronounced in the following year, November 17, 1901.

As a professed cleric, he returned to Trenton to pursue his philosophical studies for two years. He was then sent to the University of Innsbruck for his theological studies.

In 1905 Frater Bede made his solemn profession in the Innsbruck Seminary chapel in the hands of Father General Dominic Reuter. He was ordained to the priesthood July 26, 1908. On December 19 of that same year, he was awarded the degree of Doctor of Theology. His first Solemn Mass was celebrated in St. Mary's Church, Rome, New York, in 1909. The following year he was assigned as lec-

tor in the college in Trenton, New Jersey, and as prefect of discipline in 1912. In that same year he was appointed a member of the original faculty in the major seminary in Rensselaer, New York.

Fr. Bede began his eighteen-year career as a member of the mission band in 1918. Then followed other contributions: editor of the *Minorite,* the first provincial periodical; national chairman of the Third Order Congress, 1925; minister general of the order, 1936. In 1948 he was elected to a third term as minister general.

His fluency in the German language served the order well during the occupation of Assisi by the Nazi Army. At the time, the general in charge of the German troops was a Catholic. The general had orders to destroy the city and, specifically, its basilica. Fr. Bede was able to dissuade him from implementing these orders.

Their parting was a sad one. The general knew well his destiny. He had disobeyed orders. Assisi and its basilica were saved. Fr. Bede Hess died August 8, 1953, in his beloved Assisi.

See also FRANCISCANS (CONVENTUAL).

JEREMIAH SMITH, O.F.M. CONV.

HEUSER, HERMAN JOSEPH (1851–1933)

Priest, scholar, educator, and founding editor of the *American Ecclesiastical Review (AER).* Herman Joseph Heuser was born in the Prussian capital of Potsdam, October 23, 1851. His early training in Europe, including enrollment in a minor seminary in Breslau, continued in Philadelphia to which he emigrated in 1868. He became a student-teacher, first in the preparatory seminary at Glen Riddle,

Herman J. Heuser

Pennsylvania, and later at St. Charles Borromeo Seminary, Overbrook, Pennsylvania, following its opening in 1871. Ordained on February 2, 1876, Heuser became a member of the seminary faculty, teaching courses in liturgy, mathematics, and languages. At the death of his mentor, Msgr. James Andrew Corcoran, he taught sacred Scripture, eventually becoming "Professor of Scriptural Introduction and Exegesis" (1912).

Heuser and the AER

Having been an editorial assistant to Corcoran, the first editor of the *American Catholic Quarterly Review,* Heuser founded the *AER* in January 1889. He remained as editor, with a brief hiatus (1914–19) until 1927. Three years after inaugurating the *Review,* Heuser also became its publisher and business agent. In time, with the assistance of Edward J. Galbally, he made the *AER* the cornerstone of a publishing company which in 1902 became known as the Dolphin Press.

The motto of the *Review,* "For the Upbuilding of the Church" (1 Cor 14:5), not only indicated Heuser's goal for the journal, but it was a guide that he followed throughout his life. As a result of his experience in seminary education, Heuser wanted the *AER* to be a resource in pastoral theology, one aimed at formation and ongoing education in ideas and matters that classroom presentations could not cover. In connection with this latter concern, he introduced the writings of the Irish priest Patrick Sheehan whose *My New Curate* was serialized beginning in 1897.

Heuser also hoped that he might encourage the intellectual ability of American clergy who could address—from their own experience and in their own idiom—the challenges facing the Catholic Church in the United States, including Americanism and Modernism. Turning, early on, to European authors, he increasingly made available the talents of American authors. His dedication to the magisterium of the Church provided Heuser and the *AER* with a conservative reputation; however, his writing reflected an openness to new ideas, and he continually sought to bring the talents of a broad spectrum of thinkers, including scholars like Loisy and Tyrrell, to the *Review.*

Although the *AER* was intended for a clerical audience, Heuser sought contributions from lay experts in certain fields of expertise and hoped the laity would benefit as a result of a better trained clergy. With his awareness of the needs of the laity heightened by his involvement in the Catholic Summer School at Cliff Haven, he moved to address those needs more directly by transforming a literary supplement to the *Review* (begun 1900) into a separate journal called *The Dolphin* in 1902. Ceasing publication of this magazine—for various reasons including his health—in 1908, Heuser continued to provide Catholic literature for the laity through the Dolphin Press.

Other Scholarly Activities

Other publishing endeavors included the short-lived journal *Church Music* (1906–09), pamphlets based on *AER* articles, and books written by Heuser himself. A number of these first appeared as serializations in his magazines, for example, *The Harmony of the Religious Life* (1902), and *The Autobiography of an Old Breviary* (1925). Heuser wrote or edited over fifteen books, in addition to numerous feature articles—published in other periodicals as well as in his own—and some two thousand book reviews.

Self-taught in a variety of fields as editor and writer, Heuser's personal interest in music, art, Church architecture, epigraphy, and Church history brought him frequent requests for advice in those areas; in connection with the latter he was an early member of the American Catholic Historical Society of Philadelphia. His knowledge of Church law drew him into working with several Philadelphia-based religious communities of women in writing, and seeking approval for, their rules. Foundations he assisted included the Sisters of Mercy (of which his sister Julia, as Mother Mary Hildegarde, was the second general superior), the Sisters of Saint Francis, and the Sisters of the Blessed Sacrament, a connection which led to a deep friendship with that order's foundress, Blessed Katherine Drexel.

Serving as a Synodal Examiner since 1886, Heuser also became an advisor to the Pontifical Commission on Anglican Orders in 1896, and, in 1907, a general censor for Catholic literature. Humbly declining any personal ecclesiastical honor, he did accept—with a view toward bringing distinction to the *AER*—the degree "Doctor of Divinity, *honoris causa,*" bestowed by Pope (St.) Pius X in 1905.

Retiring as a teacher in 1927, Heuser gave the *AER* and all of its assets to The Catholic University of America under the direction of a specially appointed board of trustees and the editorship of Msgr. William J. Kerby. While he continued to write, Heuser lived as a recluse at the seminary in his final years, and died in Philadelphia on August 22, 1933.

See also AMERICAN ECCLESIASTICAL REVIEW.

Galbally, E. "Rev. Herman J. Heuser, D.D., Founder of the *Ecclesiastical Review.*" *Ecclesiastical Review* 89 (October 1933) 337–60.
Hubbert, J., C.M. "'For the Upbuilding of the Church': The Reverend Herman Joseph Heuser, D.D., 1851–1933." 3 vols. Ph.D. dissertation, The Catholic University of America, 1992.
                                      JOSEPH G. HUBBERT, C.M.

HEWIT, AUGUSTINE FRANCIS (1820–97)

Cofounder of the Paulists, teacher, apologist. Hewit was born on November 27, 1820, in Fairfield, Connecticut, to Nathaniel Hewitt, a Congregationalist minister, and

Augustine F. Hewit

Rebecca Hillhouse. (Augustine Hewit dropped the final "t" from his family name.) He attended Phillips Academy in Andover and graduated from Amherst College in 1839. Hewit decided to prepare for the ministry and went to the Congregationalist seminary in East Windsor, Connecticut. Influenced by the Oxford Movement, Hewit became an Episcopalian and was ordained a deacon in September 1843.

Profoundly influenced by John Henry Newman's entrance into the Catholic Church, Hewit was received into full communion in 1846. After studying Catholic theology, he was ordained a priest by Bishop Ignatius Reynolds of Charleston, South Carolina. After teaching for a while in a seminary, he entered the Redemptorists in 1850 and began working with Isaac Hecker, also a Redemptorist. In 1858 he and Hecker founded the Missionary Society of St. Paul the Apostle (the Paulists) in New York City. He wrote the first constitutions of the fledgling community and was the driving force behind the *Catholic World,* which Hecker had founded in 1865. After Hecker's death, Hewit became the superior general of the Paulists in 1889 and remained in this post until his death on July 3, 1897, in New York City.

See also HECKER, ISAAC; PAULISTS (C.S.P.).

McSorley, Joseph, C.S.P. *Father Hecker and His Friends.* St. Louis, 1953.

ANTHONY D. ANDREASSI

HIGGINS, M. CORNELIA (1881–1967)

Missionary. M. Cornelia Higgins, a member of the Sisters Servants of the Immaculate Heart of Mary, was born in Phoenixville, Pennsylvania, on January 8, 1881. She has become known as the *fundadora* of the I.H.M. missions outside the continental United States.

After World War I, the United States became the world's leading creditor nation, which gave new impetus to learning English. In Lima, Peru, Anglo-American schools were opened. To the chagrin of the local archbishop Emilio Lissón, the schools were engaged in proselytizing. He communicated his concern to Cardinal Dougherty of Philadelphia, who had experienced similar fears as bishop in the Philippines when Protestant groups arrived after the Spanish American War.

In 1922 Dougherty agreed to send Philadelphia I.H.M.s to open a bilingual school for girls to teach the faith. Archbishop Lissón agreed to provide a school and convent for the sisters who arrived on December 12, 1922. Neither building was available; the sisters walked the street of Lima for three weeks to find a place. In the spring of 1923, Villa Maria, Lima, opened and in June, Mother Cornelia arrived to administer the Peruvian mission from 1923 to 1934, and again from 1939 to 1940.

In 1928 the pastor of San Antonio Church in the polyglot port city of Callao asked the sisters to open a parish school for poor children. The sisters responded immediately—parish schools were their chief work in the United States. The graduates of the bilingual secretarial program merited good jobs. In 1995 the school thrives, but the pupils are no longer desperately poor.

Msgr. Aldo Laghi, assistant to the nuncio in Peru when Mother Cornelia opened Villa Maria, became the papal nuncio in Santiago, Chile. Shortly thereafter, he requested the opening of Villa Maria, Santiago. Mother Cornelia administered it from 1941–47.

After her return to the United States, the pioneer work of Mother Cornelia continued. Today, the I.H.M. teach thousands in Peru and Chile in excellent academies and outstanding parish schools. They also direct schools in the most desolate areas of Peru and the mountains of Chile. Mother Cornelia died on June 4, 1967.

MARY CONSUELA CALLAGHAN, I.H.M.

HILDEBRAND, DIETRICH VON (1889–1977)

Philosopher. Dietrich Adolph von Hildebrand was born in Florence, Italy, on October 12, 1889. The son of Adolf von Hildebrand, a well-known sculptor, he grew up in the midst of Florentine painters and sculptors. However, he turned to the study of philosophy at an early age and went to Germany to study at the University of Munich and the University of Göttingen, where he received a doctoral degree in 1912. He converted to Catholicism in 1914.

During World War I (1914–18), he was a surgeon's assistant at the Poliklinik of Munich and went on to become

Dietrich von Hildebrand

a *Privatdozent* at the University of Munich and an assistant professor in 1924.

During the 1930s, Hildebrand managed to stay one step ahead of the Nazis, fleeing to Florence in 1933 and then to Vienna, Austria. While in Vienna, he taught at the university and founded the Catholic review *Der Christliche Standestaat,* which he also edited and in which he continued to attack Nazism. In 1938 he fled to Switzerland when the Nazis invaded Austria, and in 1939 he became a professor at the Catholic University of Toulouse and also lectured at the Grand Séminaire. A year later when France fell to the Germans, he fled to the United States via Portugal and Brazil.

In 1942 he joined the faculty of Fordham University, New York City, as a professor of philosophy. During the following years, he concentrated his teachings and writings on the methods and insights of German phenomenologists.

After the Second Vatican Council, Hildebrand felt uncomfortable with some Church teachings that resulted from the council. As a consequence, he separated himself from the mainstream of Catholic intellectual life for the remainder of his career.

He wrote more than one hundred articles on philosophy and morality, but his major work was the book *Christian Ethics* (1953). Among the more than thirty other books he wrote were: *In Defense of Purity* (1933); *Liturgy and Personality* (1943); *Transformation in Christ* (1948); *Fundamental Moral Attitudes* (1950); *The Trojan Horse in the House of God* (1967); and *Celibacy and the Crisis of Faith* (1971). He died in New Rochelle, New York, on January 26, 1977.

MARIANNA McLOUGHLIN

HILGER, INEZ (1891–1977)

Anthropologist and sociologist. Sr. Inez Hilger, O.S.B., was born in Roscoe, Minnesota, on October 16, 1891. She enjoyed telling others that because of her persistence she was the first woman to be admitted by The Catholic University of America into its regular graduate program. She received an M.A. degree in sociology from the university in 1925 and a Ph.D. degree in anthropology and sociology in 1939.

Persistence was a lifelong trait of this teacher, researcher, lecturer, and author who, after completing her doctoral studies on Ojibwe families in Minnesota, began in earnest her anthropological field expeditions to nineteen North American Native American tribes and to the Araucanians of Chile and Argentina. She studied the role of the child as part of a whole cultural and social system, and in particular, she studied the customs, beliefs, and traditions in the development and training of the child. This interest in the child was sparked by Margaret Mead, Hilger's lifelong friend whom she came to know while at The Catholic University of America. The tenacity with which Hilger approached her field work is reflected in Mead's remarks on the study completed on the Araucanians of Chile: "[It] will stand when the last Indian who knew the old ways is gone and our children's children wonder how the ethnologist of the twentieth century ever found out so much."

Hilger's final field expedition was undertaken in 1965. At the instigation of the Smithsonian Institute and supported by the National Geographic Society, Hilger, at age seventy-four, led a team to Japan and for thirteen months studied the vanishing culture of the Ainu people. This research resulted in an article in the February 1967 *National Geographic,* a research report for the National Geographic Society (1969), an educational film on the Ainu (1970), and her last book, *Together With the Ainu, A Vanishing People,* published by the University of Oklahoma Press in 1971.

In all, Hilger's publications include eight books and over seventy articles and essays. Three of her books were published by the Smithsonian Institute as part of its research series in ethnology. In addition to her American works, Hilger published articles in Argentina, Chile, and Germany. Throughout her professional career, Hilger taught and lectured in this country and abroad to colleges and universities, learned societies, and ordinary people wanting to know more about native cultures. She died in St. Joseph, Minnesota, on May 18, 1977.

Hilger's research materials are held by the Smithsonian Institute in Washington, D.C.

Hilger, Inez, O.S.B. Personal Files. St. Benedict's Convent Archives, St. Joseph, Minnesota.

DOLORES SUPER, O.S.B.

HILLENBRAND, REYNOLD HENRY (1904–79)

Seminary Rector. Hillenbrand was born in Chicago on July 19, 1904, the second of nine children of George and Eleanor Schmitt Hillenbrand. The Hillenbrands were members of Saint Michael's parish in Chicago, a parish known for active participation in the liturgy and for a commitment to social justice.

Reynold H. Hillenbrand

Hillenbrand was educated at St. Michael's parochial school, Quigley Preparatory Seminary, and St. Mary of the Lake Seminary. He was ordained a priest of the Archdiocese of Chicago in September of 1929.

In 1931 Hillenbrand was sent to Rome to study for a year at the Gregorian University. This same year Pope Pius XI issued the encyclical *Quadragesimo Anno*, which proved to have a lasting influence on Hillenbrand. In addition to the encyclical, Hillenbrand was influenced by his visits to the German Abbey of Maria Laach, Mont César in Belgium, and Klosterneuberg in Austria, all well-known liturgical centers. It was also during this year that he became aware of Canon Joseph Cardijn, the Belgian priest who in 1912 had established the Young Christian Workers movement.

Young Fr. Hillenbrand returned to Chicago in 1932 eager to implement all that he had learned in Rome and Europe. He was assigned to teach Latin and English literature at Quigley Preparatory Seminary. While teaching there he was also in residence at Holy Name Cathedral, where he was able to further his ministry in the direction of liturgical renewal and social action.

In 1936, at the age of thirty-one, Hillenbrand was appointed rector of St. Mary of the Lake Seminary. At his introduction to the students, George Cardinal Mundelein, Archbishop of Chicago, reportedly told them, "I know the seminary can be a dull place, so I've given you a man with imagination." Hillenbrand remained at the seminary for eight years during which time he effectively reshaped the liturgical life and challenged the social awareness of the students.

In 1938 the first Chicago Summer School of Social Action for priests was held at the seminary. These continued annually and were focused on liturgy as well as social action. In 1940, Hillenbrand was asked by the Benedictine Liturgical Conference to co-chair the first National Liturgical Week, to be held at Holy Name Cathedral in Chicago. This event proved very successful with the participation of some 1,260 people from across the country. This led Hillenbrand to organize the first National Summer School of Liturgy, which was held at the Chicago seminary in July 1941.

Hillenbrand was a founding member of the Liturgical Conference and held various leadership posts over the years. He was a guest speaker at numerous gatherings across the nation and worked diligently to implement and support the various Catholic Action groups.

In 1944 (amid some controversy), Hillenbrand was appointed pastor of Sacred Heart parish in Hubbards Woods, Illinois. As seminary rector, Hillenbrand had produced many priests who were socially orientated and liturgically minded and were well prepared for leadership positions both locally and nationally. As pastor he implemented many liturgical and social reforms in his own parish. In 1945 he introduced the dialogue Mass and formed a boys' choir, affirming his commitment to a music program and active participation. He established study groups and sponsored the first Cana Conference for married couples and a Pre-Cana Conference for engaged couples.

Also in 1945, Hillenbrand was appointed Coordinator of Catholic Action cells in the archdiocese. In 1947 he became National Chaplain of the Young Christian Workers, and in 1949 National Chaplain of the Young Christian Students and the Christian Family Movement. During his later years, Hillenbrand suffered greatly from medical difficulties which hampered his participation in so many of the groups to which he was dedicated.

He retired from his pastorate at Sacred Heart in 1974. His retirement years were medically difficult and he succumbed to his illnesses on May 22, 1979.

See also ILLINOIS, CATHOLIC CHURCH IN.

Avella, Steven M. "Reynold Hillenbrand and Chicago Catholicism." *U.S. Catholic Historian* 9 (4) (Fall 1990) 353–70; repr. Ellen Skerrett, Edward R. Kantowicz, and Steven M. Avella, eds. *Catholicism, Chicago Style.* Chicago, 1993, 79–94.

STEPHEN M. RYAN

HIRSCHBOECK, MARY MERCY (1903–86)

Missionary. Elizabeth Josephine Hirschboeck was born in Milwaukee, Wisconsin, on March 10, 1903, the only daughter of three children born to Stephen and Catherine Heiser Hirschboeck. Educated in Catholic schools, she was among the first women to graduate from Marquette University School of Medicine in 1928.

On December 2, 1922, while a student at Marquette, Elizabeth survived a serious automobile accident. She was convinced that her life was spared so she could consecrate it more fully to God as a religious. Although she expressed her desire to join the Maryknoll Sisters at that time, the foundress, Mary Joseph Rogers, encouraged her to complete her medical studies first. After interning at St. Francis Hospital, La Crosse, Wisconsin, Elizabeth became the first medical doctor to enter the Maryknoll Congregation in October 1928. She was given the name Sr. Mary Mercy, and was missioned to Korea after profession in 1931.

Mercy's medical skills and love for the people were quickly recognized and appreciated in the Northern Korean missions. However, in 1940 she was advised to return to the U.S.A. for treatment of a worsening asthma condition. The sentiments of the people were expressed in a letter of a commissioner which read in part: "She will be sadly missed by the Koreans here, for they loved her in a very special way. The women especially will feel her loss . . . for she was to them not only a doctor but a saint." For the next three years, always yearning to return to Korea, Hirschboeck served as infirmarian at Maryknoll, New York.

In 1943, along with three other Maryknoll sisters, Mercy was sent to pioneer a new mission in the isolated Beni jungle region of Riberalta, Bolivia. Mercy worked out of a one-room clinic until the increasing numbers of patients led the Bolivian government to construct a hospital which opened on January 1, 1946. Mercy served as administrator of this facility, later described by the country's president as "the best run hospital in Bolivia." In 1951 news of her reassignment to Korea caused much sorrow among the people of Riberalta, who petitioned the president to intercede with Maryknoll to allow her to stay. Urgent need in Korea, already engulfed in war, made the plea unavailing.

Although no civilians were being allowed into Korea, Hirschboeck wrote to General Douglas MacArthur and received permission for herself and two other Maryknoll sisters to go to Pusan to care for the tens of thousands of North Korean refugees flooding south. Together with many other religious and lay volunteers, they treated what the media began to call "the longest charity line in the world."

In 1952 Marquette University honored Hirschboeck with the degree of doctor of science, *honoris causa,* "for the example of courage and charity she affords for this troubled world. . . ." When she left Pusan in 1955, she was cited by the mayor of Pusan for her selfless service to the Korean people, and for "the great example she has given of the practical workings of the faith she represents." Back in the U.S.A., Hirschboeck was appointed administrator of Queen of the World Hospital in Kansas City, Missouri, the first intentionally racially integrated general hospital in the country.

In 1958 Mercy was elected vicaress general of the Maryknoll Sisters Congregation and served in this capacity for twelve years. Characterized by many radical changes in Church and society, those years posed challenges to all religious leaders, confronted by difficult choices and decisions.

In 1970, while serving as unit coordinator of the Senior Sisters at Maryknoll, New York, Mercy initiated the custom of "prayer ministry" whereby each sister was assigned to pray daily for a particular region or ministry of the congregation. At the age of seventy, Mercy began a new ministry of a prayer presence among the poor on the Lower East Side of New York City. She deeply cherished this experience and considered it the fulfillment of her life as a missioner. She lived there in community for thirteen more years, until health required her to retire to the Maryknoll Nursing Home, where she died a month later on September 21, 1986.

See also MARYKNOLL.

Danforth, Maria Del Rey. *Her Name is Mercy.* New York: Scribner, 1957.

CAMILLA KENNEDY, M.M.

HISPANIC CATHOLICS IN AMERICA

The Hispanic presence in what is now the United States began on Easter Day of the year 1513, when Juan Ponce de León, who had just ended his term as first governor of Puerto Rico, landed on the southeasternmost peninsula and named it after the feast, *Pascua Florida.* After a number of failed attempts at colonization, the city of San Agustín de la Florida was founded in 1565, and a stable, though slow-growing colony was begun. However, after the colony was sold to the United States in 1821, the Hispanic population dwindled and their descendants became totally assimilated. Only with the Cuban exiles of the nineteen sixties would the Hispanic presence become once again important in the peninsula.

The earliest Hispanic community which is still vigorously present in the United States dates from 1598, when an expedition of Spaniards and Tlaxcaltec Indians established the *"Nuevo Reino de México"* and founded the city of Santa Fe. Franciscan friars began a flourishing chain of missions in the native *pueblos,* and eventually a stable population, mixed in blood but Spanish in language and culture, established itself in the area, spilling over into what is now southern Colorado. Towards the end of the seventeenth century the Jesuits began their missions in the *Pimería,* a region which straddled the present states of Sonora and Arizona, under the leadership of Fr. Eusebio Kino. In the early eighteenth century the inroads of the French in Louisiana led the Viceroys of New Spain to foster Franciscan missions in the territory of Texas; a number of these missions eventually consolidated with the town of San Fernando to form the city of San Antonio. Finally, in the last decades of the eighteenth century, the danger of Russian expansion southwards from Alaska led the government to sponsor the settlement of Upper California, where Fray Junípero Serra founded a chain of Franciscan missions.

When Mexico became independent from Spain in 1821, there was a significant and deeply rooted Spanish-speaking population in New Mexico, and smaller groupings in Texas, southern Arizona, southern Colorado, and California. All of these territories, together with the barely settled areas of Utah and Nevada, became part of the new nation.

By the 1830s and 1840s the sparsely populated territories of Mexico's northern frontier had undergone a certain amount of penetration by settlers from the United States. Tensions arose between these often unruly immigrants and the Mexican government, which resulted in the revolt and de facto independence of Texas in 1836 and its admission as a state of the American Union in 1845. As a consequence of the war between Mexico and the United States which this admission provoked, the Mexican population of all these territories suddenly found itself an alien and often oppressed and despised minority in its own native lands.

Mexican-Americans

The population of these conquered territories became the original nucleus of the Mexican-American community. The Mexican population the Southwest is, therefore, the oldest continuous Hispanic presence in the United States; in fact, its original members arrived in the region as conquerors or settlers two centuries before the existence of either the United States or Mexico as nations. Unlike other ethnic groups in the United States, these nineteenth-century *Hispanos, Tejanos,* and *Californios* were not immigrants who had chosen to come to their new country; their experience was that of a conquered people who at once had long-standing roots in the land and yet had suddenly become aliens and victims of discrimination in the land of their birth and upbringing, where a new American society and a new American Church—in which there was no place for their ethos and traditions—were being planted.

Timothy Matovina has convincingly argued (Matovina, 1995) that the application to such a population of paradigms based on the immigrant experience (such as patterns of generational assimilation) can lead scholars to serious errors of interpretation and to unfulfilled projections. During the nineteenth century immigration from Mexico slowly increased the numbers of this native Hispanic population. But, while these newer arrivals were immigrants, they integrated into the already existing native community, and thus shared in its discrimination, but also in the strength of its identity. Thus the experience of the original Hispanic population of the Southwest became seminal for the later Mexican-American community.

It was only with the Mexican Revolution of 1910 that massive numbers of Mexicans began to cross the border into the United States. Not only did many supporters of the ousted dictator Porfirio Díaz (mostly from the upper and professional classes) take refuge across the border, but the Revolution also produced a period of political, social, and economic insecurity which drove many peasants and workers to seek a more stable environment in the United States. Especially after 1914 scarcity of labor and a war economy made the American job market extremely attractive to Mexicans, and Mexican labor extremely desirable to American industrial and agricultural employers. In the nineteen twenties the *Cristero* revolt against the anticlerical central government produced another great wave of immigration. By this time Mexican immigrants had begun to spread beyond the Southwest, and followed the railroad lines to the Midwestern industrial cities, founding Mexican *colonias* as far north as Chicago and Detroit. Small groups of migrant farm workers also began to settle down along the routes of their seasonal labor, sowing the seeds of *colonias* in the states of Washington and Oregon.

During the depression of the 1930s this growth was reversed. As jobs became scarce, moving to the United States became less attractive, while anti-Mexican sentiment flared up among Americans who saw immigrants as competitors for the few available employment opportunities. This led to a massive repatriation program which all too often was characterized by arbitrariness and injustice. Many families were forcibly broken up, and American citizens of Mexican descent were often deported along with their noncitizen neighbors.

With the coming of World War II, the U.S. job market and Mexican immigration again entered into a relationship of mutual attraction, and the number of immigrants swelled. A great number of Mexican-Americans participated in the war; indeed, the Mexican-American community produced an unusually high proportion of officially decorated war heroes. When these soldiers returned, they were able to take advantage of the educational and economic opportunities offered to veterans by the G.I. Bill; for many this became a gateway out of poverty into the middle class. Returning soldiers were also unwilling to accept the long-standing discrimination under which they had grown up, and began to found civil rights organizations, which claimed for Mexican-Americans the same rights enjoyed by their fellow citizens.

The civil rights efforts of the 1950s, like those of the black community in the same decade, were directed towards integration into American society. All too often this entailed de facto efforts at assimilation, with the consequent loss of language and culture. In the 1960s and 1970s, however, a more militant spirit came to the fore, which came to be characterized by the up-front use of the term *Chicano* (a word which the previous generation had considered undesirable and somewhat pejorative) as a self-identifier in place of the more sedate "Mexican-American." While the movement took a number of different forms and directions, all were characterized by a newfound pride in the *mestizo* race and heritage and an insistence on being accepted on one's own cultural terms, rather than on terms of cultural assimilation. While the generation of the 1980s and 1990s has been less militant, and many of its members prefer not to use the term *Chicano,* the gains in pride, identity, and civil rights that were achieved by the *"Chicano* generation" have been lasting, as has been the flowering in literature and the plastic and performing arts which the movement occasioned.

In terms of the Catholic Church's relation to Mexican-Americans, the 1960s and 1970s were also a watershed. Shortly after the American conquest, the American Church had begun a policy of appointing European-born missionary bishops (the Frenchmen Jean Baptist Lamy in New Mexico and Jean-Marie Odin in Texas, the Catalans Thaddeus Amat and Joseph Alemany in California) to the sees of the Southwest. These prelates were products of the nineteenth-century European Catholic ethos of "Ultramontanism," which stressed discipline and uniformity, and utilized new, nonlocal devotions to replace local variations within the Church. As immigrants to the United States, they had also become ardent admirers of American Catholicism. Their goal was to build an American Church in the newly acquired territories, a Church which could hold the loyalty of the Catholic settlers who were arriving from the East, and gain the respect of the culturally dominant Protestants. On the whole they were contemptuous of the traditional Catholicism they found among the Hispanic population, and deplored many of their devotional practices as superstitious. It was their avowed intention to break the power of native priests (such as Padre José Martínez of Taos) who defended the people's traditional Catholicism, and to replace them with European and American missionaries in tune with the attitudes and priorities of the new order.

The establishment of this American Church in place of the institutions and traditions brought by the original set-

tlers and missionaries signaled the beginning of a period of neglect and "second-class churchmanship" for the Hispanic population of the Southwest. The institutional Church's priority was the building of an American Catholic community, and while the original Catholic inhabitants were allowed to continue worshiping in their *barrio* parishes, and to a certain degree according to their ancestral traditions, not much was done to encourage them or to defend them from oppression. As the old elite families became impoverished and lost access to leadership and education, the number of Hispanic priests declined, and those who managed to get ordained had to be trained in American seminaries, where the formation process aimed to mold them in the ideal image of the American priest. Throughout the nineteenth and the early twentieth century, therefore, the institutional Church offered sacraments and charity to the Mexican-American community, but it did not stand up for its rights or provide it with leadership. Hardly a Catholic voice was raised in protest over the abuses of the Repatriation Program in the 1930s, and it was only in the 1940s that Archbishop Robert Lucey of San Antonio prodded the reluctant bishops of the Southwest into setting up a committee for the Spanish-speaking.

Often it was the lay confraternities which kept alive the religious traditions of the community. Communally powerful groups such as the *Penitentes* of New Mexico were sometimes perceived as a threat to hierarchical power, and their traditional practices as a scandal to Anglo observers, and so they were often actively opposed by the American clergy. But less threatening groups such as the *Guadalupanas* were tolerated, and even encouraged, and they quietly ensured the survival of a Hispanic Catholicism in the *barrios* and *colonias.*

In the Church, as in the secular sphere, the *Chicano* generation of the 1960s marked a turning point. The United Farm Workers' Union was led by the *cursillista* César Chávez, who inspired it with a commitment to *Chicano* identity and to a *Chicano* Catholicism which combined traditional devotions with the social action encouraged by the spirit of the Second Vatican Council. The image of Our Lady of Guadalupe became a symbol of liberation from an unjust economic and social structure, and progressive clergy and laity all over the United States rallied to *la causa.* Organizations such as PADRES (1969) and *Las Hermanas* (1971) helped Hispanic priests and religious to rediscover their roots and to provide leadership for their people. Fr. Virgilio Elizondo of San Antonio, a pioneer *Chicano* theologian, was instrumental in the foundation of the Mexican American Cultural Center (MACC), which since 1971 has trained clergy and lay leaders in the in-depth understanding of the Mexican religious and cultural ethos.

In 1970 Fr. Patricio Flores—the son of a migrant worker family—was consecrated auxiliary bishop of San Antonio;

after a period as bishop of El Paso, he returned to San Antonio as its first Hispanic archbishop. By the early 1990s there were some twenty Hispanic bishops in the American hierarchy, of whom two were natives of Mexico and ten were Americans of Mexican descent. This represents a significant achievement, and a significant change in the attitudes of the American Church, even though their percentage of the U.S. episcopate hardly represents the percentage of Hispanics in the U.S. Catholic population. From the 1960s to the present, the numbers and the strong organizational skills of the Mexican-Americans have made them the most powerful subgroup in the U.S. Hispanic Church.

Puerto Ricans

The island of Puerto Rico, visited by Columbus in 1493, was conquered by the Spaniards under Juan Ponce de León in 1508. It was one of the three original dioceses erected for the New World by Pope Julius II in 1511, and the first of them to have a resident bishop. After two centuries as a backwater of the Spanish Empire, it entered a period of progress in the nineteenth century, when together with Cuba it became the last remnant of this empire in the Western Hemisphere. With this material and cultural progress came a sense of identity as a people, which led some to a struggle for independence, and others to a struggle for home rule under the aegis of Spain.

Home Rule was in fact granted in 1898, but within a few months the island was taken over by the United States as a result of the Spanish-American War. In the wake of this conquest a strong campaign of cultural Americanization was launched, which culminated in the unilateral granting of U.S. citizenship to all Puerto Ricans in 1917, over the protests of the island's elected legislature. However, the efforts at cultural Americanization were ultimately a failure. In spite of decades in which all subjects in the island's schools had by law to be taught in English, the people of Puerto Rico passively resisted this policy, and remain primarily Spanish-speaking both in familiar situations and in literary production, using English only as a second language. And, while Puerto Ricans have come to appreciate the practical advantages of holding a U.S. passport, the people's self-identity has come to be primarily expressed over against the American identity: to be Puerto Rican means to not be *un Americano*. Even those born in the United States avoid the term "Puerto Rican American," preferring to coin terms such as "New Yorican." For the same reasons, it is important to realize that Puerto Ricans center their identity on their language and culture, which are shared by the whole community, rather than on race or color. A Puerto Rican of whatever race will identify primarily with other Puerto Ricans of any color, rather than with Americans of the same race.

While there were Puerto Rican merchants, students, and political exiles in the United States even before 1898, a significant Puerto Rican presence did not make itself felt before the 1940s. In that decade a number of factors such as overpopulation and lack of economic opportunities in the island and the setting up of affordable airfares between San Juan and New York combined to produce a massive migration to the mainland, whose impact was felt primarily by that city. In 1930 there were only 45,000 Puerto Ricans in New York, and hardly any in other mainland cities; by 1950 the number of Puerto Ricans in the mainland had risen to 301,375, of whom 81.6 percent were in New York City. While the proportion of Puerto Ricans in New York has steadily diminished in subsequent decades, and the Puerto Rican population has spread across all fifty states, about half the 2,700,000 Puerto Ricans in the U.S.A. are still found in New York City, and the number of Puerto Ricans in Chicago—the second largest Puerto Rican community on the mainland—lags far behind that of New York (Dolan and Vidal, 1994, 56, 235). This means that the policies taken by New York authorities, whether civil or religious, to deal with the sudden presence of large numbers of Puerto Ricans in the city are especially significant, since they were often imitated by other cities as Puerto Ricans spread beyond New York.

On the religious level, the most significant decision was that taken by Francis Cardinal Spellman (shortly after his arrival as archbishop) not to erect national parishes for the Puerto Ricans, but to integrate them immediately into territorial parishes. Spanish-speaking American priests would be assigned to parishes with a large Puerto Rican population, but special services in Spanish were expected to cease as the population became more comfortable with English. This policy arose from a number of concerns, among which were the Cardinal's fear that national parishes would eventually become "white elephants" in the hands of the archdiocese, and his confusion of national parishes (intended to preserve a group's language and culture, and thus usually desired by immigrants) with segregated parishes for African Americans (intended to exclude its parishioners from the territorial churches, and thus oppressive and discriminatory). Another factor, probably the most important, was the Cardinal's impatient desire to assimilate the Puerto Ricans into American Catholic mores and structures as soon as possible—ideally in one generation. This policy was at cross purposes with the instinctive aspiration of the Puerto Ricans to build communities of their own, where their language and culture would be preserved.

As a result, the Church has not had the central place in the U.S. Puerto Rican community which the national parishes gave it in earlier immigrant communities. Secular institutions such as hometown clubs, neighborhood associations, and community improvement groups such as *Aspira* have taken over the community-building role that the ethnic parishes had filled for earlier Catholic immigrants. The lack of a Puerto Rican-oriented Catholic community has also presented a great opportunity to the evangelical and pentecostal churches, whose practically autonomous storefront congregations are normally led by Puerto Rican pastors and whose worship is in a completely Puerto Rican style.

The policy of instant integration was particularly ill suited to the Puerto Rican migration because the fact that Puerto Ricans were citizens (and thus not subject to immigration controls), when combined with cheap and relatively short air travel, produced what has been called a "commuter" or "revolving door" immigration in which persons and families continually moved back and forth between New York and the island, without making an emotional commitment to the new environment. (Indeed, to this day a strikingly large number of U.S. Puerto Ricans return permanently to the island.) Not only did this mean that the people whom the archdiocese was trying to integrate had no settled intention of living and dying there; it also meant that the constant returns to the island kept reinforcing the very culture and language from which the archdiocese's policies were trying to wean them.

Further, the archdiocese did not in fact have enough Spanish-speaking priests to assign one to every parish affected by the massive migration, and (unlike earlier immigrant groups) the Puerto Ricans were not in a position to bring their own clergy with them, since the island's dioceses were already grievously understaffed. This problem was brought home to Spellman in the early 1950s by two young and talented priests, Joseph Fitzpatrick, S.J., and Ivan Illich.

In response to their suggestions the Cardinal set up an office for the Spanish-speaking apostolate, and sponsored a yearly *fiesta* in honor of Puerto Rico's patron, St. John the Baptist, which was intended to do for Puerto Ricans' visibility and self-esteem what St. Patrick's Day celebrations had done for the Irish. Most importantly, in 1956 he commissioned Illich to organize an institute at the Catholic University of Puerto Rico where American priests and seminarians could undergo intensive training in the Spanish language and Puerto Rican culture. This institute was designed to produce a generation of priests who would not only be fluent in Spanish (and thus able to staff the integrated parishes) but also able to get out of their own culture and serve the Puerto Ricans on their own cultural terms.

In the following decade the priests and religious trained by Illich became the vanguard of New York's clergy in the effort to adapt to the new visions ushered in by the Second Vatican Council and the spirit of the 1960s. However, they differed from Illich in that their vision tended to be directed towards leading the Puerto Ricans to give up their traditions and join with them, and with all other oppressed peoples in the city, in the building of a brave new world. Like Spellman's vision of assimilation, this vision, too, was at cross-purposes with the Puerto Ricans' instinctive desire to preserve their own traditions, and to self-identify by language and culture, rather than by color or class.

As the Spanish-speaking apostolate turned more and more to creative experimentation, and became more and more geared towards the disadvantaged and the "nonwhite" rather than to the Spanish-speaking, many Puerto Ricans turned to Spanish and Latin American priests who were willing to serve them in the traditional ways of Spanish culture. The *Cursillo* movement, run by the laity and advised by Spanish priests, also served as a vehicle for the preservation of a Hispanic style of religiosity, and for the creation of Puerto Rican lay leaders, which had not been fostered by the conditions of the integrated parish. In many ways the *Cursillo* and the charismatic renewal have come to serve the purposes which were formerly served by the ethnic parishes, by providing the Puerto Rican Catholic community with a space where their style of religiosity comes first, and where their potential leaders do not have to be subordinated to American leaders with a different vision and different agendas.

Because of this division of aims, the 1960s were not as productive for the Puerto Rican community as they were for the Mexican-Americans, whose leaders tended to come from their own community. Puerto Ricans have historically tended to passive resistance, and while this has assured the survival of their values in spite of major institutional efforts at assimilating them, it has not forced the institutions in question to change their aims and methods in response to their desires or priorities. The fact that the areas of greatest Puerto Rican strength happen to be major dioceses such as New York and Chicago has been an obstacle to the emergence of Puerto Rican bishops in the United States. As of this writing, there are only two Puerto Rican bishops in the mainland, and neither of them is an ordinary; neither New York nor Chicago has a Puerto Rican even as auxiliary bishop. This is particularly significant in light of the fact that by the end of the nineteen seventies the New York Puerto Rican community was already represented at the secular level by one congressman, two state senators, four state assemblymen, and two city councilmen.

Cubans

Like Puerto Rico, the island of Cuba was settled in the sixteenth century, but neglected until Spain lost its mainland colonies in the early nineteenth century. It then entered a period of intensive sugar cultivation which entailed the massive importation of African slaves. During this period the Church had lost the allegiance of the colonial government and the planter elite, which meant that the latter were not willing to allow time for the catechizing of their slaves, and the government was not willing to back the Church's efforts in that respect. As a result the slaves managed to preserve their ancestral religion, syncretized with the outward trappings of sanctocentric popular Catholicism, in a combination known as *Santería,* which has also spread to many non-African sectors of Cuban society. A grievous scarcity of priests, together with the fact that the institutional Church was controlled by the colonial government and therefore opposed to Cuban aspirations for independence, contributed to creating an unusually secularized society, in which the Church had very little influence on public or private life.

While many Cubans came to the United States as political exiles throughout the nineteenth century, most of these exiles returned to their homeland after the Spanish-American War of 1898, and the resulting independence of the island in 1902. Throughout the first half of the twentieth century Cuban immigration to the United States was insignificant. The present large Cuban community is a result of the triumph of Fidel Castro's revolution, which unseated the increasingly unpopular dictator Fulgencio Batista in 1959. At first the majority of Cubans supported the revolution, but by 1960 large segments of the population began to feel betrayed by its unmistakable turn towards Marxism. The disaffected included landowners and industrialists, professionals and shop owners, but also persons committed to private enterprise or to individualist lifestyles. The small number of committed Catholics, mostly products of the elite Catholic schools or of the Catholic associations for university students, had in many cases backed Castro out of religious principles, but they turned against his regime when its policies began to threaten the interests of the Church, especially in education.

Between 1959 and 1962 more than 155,000 Cubans came to the United States; after that it was only possible to leave Cuba clandestinely, so that the flow of exiles was reduced to a trickle. Since then the rate of migration has ebbed and flowed according to the varying relations between the American and Cuban governments, with occasional spurts of massive emigration when both governments have been willing to permit it (e.g., during the airlifts of 1966–72 and the boatlift from the port of Mariel in 1980). These later waves of emigration have included a more representative cross section of Cuban society, as many members of the lower-middle and poor classes became disillusioned with life under Marxism.

Given the American government's hostility to the Cuban revolution, Cubans who came to the United States were regarded as refugees from Communism, which meant that great efforts were made to welcome them and help them establish themselves. Given the connection between color and class in the Spanish Caribbean, white persons were disproportionately represented, especially among the first waves of exiles; this created the perception of Cubans as a white people, so that they have not been subjected to racial prejudice to the extent that other Hispanic groups have suffered. (Cubans unfortunately but understandably reacted by creating distance between themselves and those Hispanic groups which were victims of discrimination, which has created a certain amount of resentment among other Hispanics.) The presence of a large contingent of educated professionals has provided the Cuban community with leaders, and has made possible the creation of a vibrant cultural center in the Miami area, with Cuban theaters, publishing houses, and professional services. Other centers of Cuban settlement, such as Union City and West New York, in New Jersey, do not have such a flourishing cultural life, but the Cuban community still is commercially and politically strong, and socially self-sufficient. The older generation of Cubans consider themselves exiles rather than immigrants, and, while they are not objects of discrimination by American society, they have mostly chosen to resist assimilation into it, preferring to live in a "Cuba in exile" until they can return home.

Like the U.S. government, the American Catholic Church responded very positively to the Cuban exiles, which it tended to perceive as refugees from religious persecution. The Diocese of Miami in particular went out of its way to help them settle in their new environment, spending close to half a million dollars on assistance to them in just the year 1962. However, the diocese made it very clear that Cubans were expected to integrate into the American Church, to the point that priest refugees were assigned to American parishes in the suburbs, rather than to the urban areas where their compatriots were settling. Not only were national parishes written off as a possible way to minister to Cubans, but the setting up or regrouping of Catholic Cuban organizations was strongly discouraged. The fact that so many Cuban professionals formed part of the exile community, however, meant that the community was soon in a position to press for its interests, and at the ecclesiastical level this capacity was enhanced by the great number of clergy—especially exempt religious—who had fled or been expelled by the Castro regime. As a result a number of Cuban Catholic institutions, most noticeably the Jesuit *Colegio de Belén* (where Castro himself had been educated), have been refounded in Miami, and Cuban pastors are not uncommon in neighborhoods with a high proportion of Cubans. In reaction to Castro's antireligious stance, the exile community gives more importance to religion than was the case in pre-revolutionary Cuba.

Other Hispanic Groups

Dominicans, Central Americans, and South Americans have arrived in large numbers in recent years, but have not yet achieved the demographic significance of the Mexicans, Puerto Ricans, or Cubans.

Like the Puerto Ricans, Dominicans are very attached to their homeland, and fly back for frequent visits, which reinforce their culture and retard assimilation. They usually send a significant percentage of their earnings to their relatives back home, and many plan to return there eventually. The extended family serves as a network to facilitate and encourage migration. Dominican culture is much less secular than Cuban or Puerto Rican culture, and has traditionally allowed for much more co-operation between Church and state. Most bishops and priests in the republic have been natives since the nineteenth century, and they have remained close to the people; as a result, Dominican immigrants tend to be somewhat more attracted to the institutional Church than other groups.

Central American migration to the United States became significant as a result of the revolutions and counterrevolutions that have racked the region since the late 1970s. While the Reagan administration welcomed those Nicaraguans who opposed the Sandinista regime, it refused to admit refugees from nations such as El Salvador and Guatemala, whose military regimes it supported. In desperation many of them crossed the border as illegal aliens, to live in constant fear of deportation. Central Americans have become the most important Hispanic group in Washington, D.C., and have large neighborhoods in Los Angeles and other California cities, as well as a significant presence in Miami and New York.

South American immigrants range from highly skilled professionals to domestic servants, with a high proportion of middle-class persons. The nations most strongly represented are Colombia and Ecuador.

Hispanic Catholics

Conclusion

The history of Hispanic Catholicism in what is now the United States antedates the founding of the nation itself. But the encounter between the American Church and Hispanic Catholics, whether in the conquered territories of the Southwest or in the immigrant *barrios* of the Northeast, has been characterized by the effort to turn them into American Catholics, on the assumption that American Catholicism is basically superior to their traditional religiosity. It is only in recent years that scholars have begun to appreciate the Hispanics' *religiosidad popular,* and this appreciation has not yet filtered to the decision makers at either the diocesan or the local levels. A vision of unity as uniformity has led the American Church to foster an integration which barely differs from assimilation. The Hispanic community, on the other hand, has been less motivated to assimilate than other ethnic groups, who came to this country of their own free will rather than by conquest; it has also been in a much better position to resist assimilation because of its proximity to its lands of origin. Therefore, the efforts to Americanize the Hispanics have on the whole been fruitless, and all too often counterproductive.

In recent decades an increased militancy on the part of Hispanics, as well as an increased awareness of the values of other cultures on the part of American society, have led to an improvement in this situation both in secular affairs and in the Church. Hispanics are now represented in the American hierarchy, although not in proportion to their numbers in the American Catholic Church.

A series of national *Encuentros* (1972, 1977, and 1985) have raised the consciousness of the Hispanic Catholic community, and led it to begin to see itself in national rather than local terms. These have led to two collective pastoral letters (one by the Hispanic bishops in 1982 and one by the U.S. hierarchy in 1983) which present the Hispanic presence in the American Catholic community as a gift and a challenge rather than as a problem. The recommendations of the *Encuentros* have also led to a National Pastoral Plan for Hispanic Ministry that was approved by the U.S. bishops in 1987. Unfortunately, this plan does not always reflect the different and sometimes even contradictory needs of the various Hispanic groups in this country, but it is a step in the right direction.

The implementation of the Second Vatican Council's Constitution on the Liturgy has resulted in a Spanish-language liturgy which serves as a focus for the Hispanic community within the parishes, and which makes Cardinal Spellman's dream of integration more unlikely than ever. And while Hispanic vocations to the priesthood remain scarce, the restoration of the permanent diaconate, which does not require celibacy or higher education, has provided an opportunity of ordained service to thousands of Hispanic leaders, who usually spring from lay movements such as the *Cursillos* and the charismatic renewal. These permanent deacons have become a "native clergy" for the U.S. Hispanic community.

On the dark side, the financial difficulties under which many dioceses are laboring has led to the closing of many urban parishes, a national trend which diminishes the services offered to Hispanics. This situation has also led to cutbacks in the budgets allocated to Hispanic ministry at both diocesan and national levels. A number of dioceses have gone so far as to close their offices for the Hispanic apostolate, or to merge them into multicultural ministries, as if all "nonwhite" or "non-Western" groups had similar needs. Others have abolished their Hispanic diaconate training programs and merged them with the English-speaking ones, with little provision for the divergent needs of candidates and of the communities they will be serving. These are alarming trends, since they suggest that financial retrenchment may serve as an excuse for a return to a policy of Americanization. It is therefore with both hope and misgivings that the Hispanic Catholic community in the United States faces the challenges of the third millennium, and the sixth century of Hispanic Catholic presence in the Western Hemisphere.

Deck, Allan Figueroa, S.J. *The Second Wave: Hispanic Ministry and the Evangelization of Cultures.* New York: Paulist Press, 1989.

Díaz-Stevens, Ana María. *Oxcart Catholicism on Fifth Avenue: The Impact of the Puerto Rican Migration upon the Archdiocese of New York.* University of Notre Dame Press, 1993.

Dolan, Jay P., and Allan F. Deck, eds. *Hispanic Catholic Culture in the US: Issues and Concerns.* University of Notre Dame Press, 1994.

Dolan, Jay P., and Gilberto M. Hinojosa, eds. *Mexican Americans and the Catholic Church, 1900–1965.* University of Notre Dame Press, 1994.

Dolan, Jay P., and Jaime R. Vidal, eds. *Puerto Rican and Cuban Catholics in the US, 1900–1965.* University of Notre Dame Press, 1994.

Fitzpatrick, Joseph P., S.J. *Puerto Rican Americans: The Meaning of Migration to the Mainland.* Englewood Cliffs, N.J.: Prentice-Hall, 1971.

Matovina, Timothy. *Tejano Religion and Ethnicity: San Antonio, 1821–1860.* Austin: University of Texas Press, 1995.

Sandoval, Moisés. *On the Move: A History of the Hispanic Church in the United States.* Maryknoll, N.Y.: Orbis, 1990.

Stevens Arroyo, Antonio M. *Prophets Denied Honor: An Anthology on the Hispanic Church in the United States.* Maryknoll, N.Y.: Orbis, 1980.

JAIME R. VIDAL

Related Document

PASTORAL MESSAGE OF THE UNITED STATES HISPANIC BISHOPS, SUMMER, 1982.

No segment of the American Catholic community better illustrates its multiethnic composition than those of Hispanic culture and background; nor is any single ethnic group in that religious community increasing more rapidly in the United States. Taking as their point of departure the 450th anniversary of the tradition of the Blessed Virgin's apparition to the Indian, Juan Diego, in December, 1531, the bishops of Hispanic descent issued a pastoral letter in which they linked those of Hispanic ancestry in this country to the traditions that had arisen in Mexico centuries before. The beginning of that link was forged in a tentative way in 1540, only 9 years after the apparition, when Coronado launched his historic expedition into what is today the American Southwest. True, there was no uninterrupted and steady relationship; yet the intermingling of those of Spanish and Mexican birth, first with the native Indian population and later with American settlers in Arizona, California, New Mexico, and Texas became an increasingly important factor, and today the Hispanic presence has appeared in virtually every section of the United States. The implications of this development for the Church are obviously immense. The bishops here survey their problems as pastors of the Hispanics, touching upon the hardships and discrimination suffered by the latter, the need for renewed efforts in evangelization, increased vocations, as well as the Church's obligation to voice their peoples' temporal needs in such matters as employment, just wages, etc.

(*Source: Origins*, 12 [August 12, 1982] 145–52.)

FOUR HUNDRED FIFTY YEARS AFTER YOUR APPARITION IN OUR lands, we, your sons, come as the shepherds of our Hispanic people in the United States of North America. We come full of joy and hope, but we also come saddened and preoccupied with the suffering of our people

We are the shepherds of a people on the march. Walking with our people, we come to you, Mother of God and our mother, so that we may receive a renewed spirit. We want to be filled with enthusiasm to go out and proclaim the wonders of God that have taken place in our history, that are taking place at this time in our lives and that will take place in the future.

Although the world has often misunderstood us, you do understand and hold us in esteem. You too were always a pilgrim. You were always on the march. You visited your cousin Elizabeth in the mountains (Lk. 1:39-56); your Son was born at the end of your long trek from Nazareth to Bethlehem (Lk. 2:1-7); you went on pilgrimage to the temple to present Jesus (Lk. 2:21-44); you lived in exile as a threatened and pursued stranger (Mt. 2:13-15); you returned to your land after the tyrant King Herod died (Mt. 2:19-23); and you again went on the march toward Jerusalem for the feast of the Passover (Lk. 2:41-52). You were present at the beginning and at the end of the ministry of the Lord: at Cana in Galilee, when the signs of the kingdom were first manifest (Jn. 2:1-12) and at the foot of the cross (Jn. 19:25-27). And here, at the birth of the Americas, you have appeared as a sign from heaven (Rv. 12:1), new life and new light.

You went on all of your journeys, pilgrimages and marches as a poor woman at the service of Jesus, of the kingdom of God, of the poor and those in need. The Spirit covered you. You put the word of God into practice and you shared the life of Jesus with a believing people. After the death of Jesus you hoped against all hope and you were called to the heavens as the "favored one of God" (Lk. 1:28).

> You were the faithful one . . .
> You formed the body of Jesus
> and gave him to the world . . .
> You are the Mother of God and our mother . . .
> You are the mother of all the inhabitants of these lands . . .
> You are the mother of the Americas!

I. Our Pilgrimage Throughout History

> *Mientras recorres la vida*
> *Tu nunca solo estas*
> *contigo por el camino*
> *Santa Maria va*

A. The Birth of a New People

At a unique moment in the history of this world, three radically different and totally unknown worlds met: indigenous America, Africa and Europe.

The clash carried many of the indigenous people to slavery and death, and made them strangers in their own land. The Africans were violently wrenched from their lands and transplanted to far-off countries as slaves. This initiated a shock whose reverberations are experienced even today. There also began at that time a *mestizaje,* an intertwining of blood and culture that in effect brought about the birth of a new people.

The roots of our Latin American reality are grounded in their threefold inheritance. It is our identity, our suffering, our greatness and our future.

Four hundred fifty years ago, at the birth of our Latin American *mestizo* race, during the deep and sharp labor pains of our people, our mother came to be with us.

A great sign came from the sky (Rv. 12:1), a beautiful woman who visited our lands and spoke to us in our native tongue with gentle love, tenderness and compassion. You are that woman.

Just as she had been chosen for her littleness and humility, so Mary chose Juan Diego, a humble Indian. From the many she could have chosen, she singled out a poor man.

The faithful child Juan Diego listened to his mother, trusted in her and accepted her command. The bishop asked her for a sign, and she gave it to him *con gusto*—not only beautiful roses but she also gave him the first flower of all flowers: her image miraculously imprinted on Juan Diego's *tilma.*

At a painful time in our history, God gave us a great gift—the portrait of his mother, who is also our mother. Her image is the visible sign of her loving presence among us. A woman with a compassionate face and heart, but whose eyes are sad because she is conscious of the suffering of her people and hears their mourning.

Ever since then you have shared our sufferings and joys, our struggles and fiestas, and all of our attempts to bring about the reign of God. You inspire us, you stir us and you continue to walk beside us. You are the source of our identity and of the unity of our people in the Americas.

Today we come to you, our mother, filled with gratitude and admiration, to bring to you the portrait of your family, to tell you of our life and to share with you the enduring dreams of the Hispanic people of the United States of North America.

B. Our Faith

Our ancestors had a strong sense of religiosity. Their lives were centered in their God. They were a people of spiritual values, of wisdom and humanizing customs.

The missionaries brought us the knowledge of a personal God who, through his Son, invites us to a new life. The Gospel purified and enriched the beliefs of our lands.

Because of this our faith is personal and cultural, because the word was made flesh on our land when his mother arrived on the hill of Tepeyac. Little by little the Gospel has penetrated every aspect of our life and culture. It is the alpha and omega, the center of our very being. Faith penetrates our music, art, poetry, language, customs, fiestas—every expression of our life.

Faithful to our tradition we hope that the Gospel continues to transform our life and our culture.

C. Our Mestizaje

The Hispanic people of the United States of North America is a people of *mestizaje,* an interlacing of the blood and culture of the indigenous, African and European peoples. In the present reality of our people we find a new intertwining: that of the Latin American people and those of the United States. From this second *mestizaje,* the Hispanic American people begin to emerge.

We are thus a new people and within our very being we combine the cultural riches of our parents. The Virgin of Guadalupe, our *madrecita mestiza,* comes to fill with joy and blessings the painful and difficult process of our *mestizaje.*

D. Our Cultures

In the shaping of this people, many beautiful values from different cultures have been incorporated, all of which have enriched us today. Our culture is rich in imagery, art, music, dances, food, poetry, even to the point of embodying a certain sense of mischievousness.

Our language is rich in expressions that come from the Gospel. This facilitates the transmission of the word.

Our personal faith is expressed very beautifully: *Mi Padre Dios* (God my Father), *Nuestra Madrecita Maria*

(Our dear mother Mary), *Nuestro Senor y Hermano Jesucristo* (Our Lord and Brother Jesus Christ), *Mis santitos* (My little saints). A true spiritual environment is fostered in our homes and many houses even become household churches. The little altar with the crucifix, your statue, *Madrecita,* and our "little saints" hold a special place in the home. The vigil lights and blessed palms speak to us of your most holy Son. Our culture is the expression of the Gospel incarnated in our people and it is a rich form of passing on the divine teachings to new generations.

E. Our Families

It is almost impossible to explain this great gift from God. Words do not tell the whole story. For us the meaning of family is extended and includes parents, children, grandparents, aunts and uncles, "distant" relatives, neighbors, godparents and *compadres,* or intimate friends. The family is the first school of love, tenderness, acceptance, discipline and respect. In our homes we have come to experience the bonds of friendship, mutual support, concern for one another and the presence of God.

We have received from our families the thoughts and values that are the foundation and primary orientation of our lives.

The new Juan Diego who carried the message from heaven to the church of the United States was also a humble messenger: our mothers and grandmothers. They taught their sons and grandsons to pray while their fathers struggled to earn their daily bread.

Their voice has echoed insistently: "Don't miss Mass," "Marry in the church," "May God go with you." They have marked our souls with the love of God and have caused your image of Guadalupe, full of tenderness, to blossom throughout the nation.

Madrecita, you know the miseries and faults of our families. They have not been perfect. But even with their defects they have been a great source of security, community and happiness. In the most difficult moments of our march through history, our people have never lost their joy of living. Throughout all of the burdens of life we sing—even in the midst of pain.

Faith has made us a joyful people. In our fiestas we celebrate the mystery of life that, in its successes and failures, joys and sadness, birth and even death, is a gift from God.

F. People Who Fill Us with Admiration

Madrecita, our history is filled with men and women who have been a great inspiration for us. They have struggled and have given their lives that we might have a better life.

We give you thanks:

—for the Indians who suffered the pain of the conquest and who fought for the good of their people.

—for the Africans, victims of slavery and humiliation;

—for the missionaries you brought from Spain, men of apostolic vision filled with courage, love and compassion;

—for our forgotten heroes, who have remained hidden in obscurity;

—for the saints who blossomed in our lands like the roses of Tepeyac.

What joy we feel, *Madrecita,* seeing so many who have brought beauty to our people with the gifts your Son has given to them:

—the artists, writers, singers and poets who dream;

—the educators, the learned and the technicians;

—the businessmen, farmers, professionals and shop owners;

—domestic and farm workers;

—migrant workers and labor unions who give strength to the voice of the worker;

—politicians who truly represent the people;

—soldiers who have fought to defend freedom.

Madrecita, a very special thanks for the priests and religious, our co-workers in the vineyard of the Lord, who have given themselves to our people and who have truly loved them.

Without the wealth of their talents and the totality of their commitment, the Gospel of your Son would not be proclaimed in all its fullness.

We give thanks to God, *Madrecita*, for having called us to be the apostles of your Son in our day. We ask you to walk with us still.

II. Our Reality

Aunque te digan algunos
que nada puede cambiar
lucha por un mundo nuevo
lucha por la verdad

Much has been gained but the suffering continues. We are conscious of the oppression and exploitation of our people. We have seen bodies disfigured by hunger and saddened by the fear of the law; we have heard the cries of abandoned children mistreated by their own parents. We sense the loneliness of the elderly ignored by their relatives and the depression of prisoners whose greatest crime has been the lack of money to pay someone to defend them in court. We have shared the pain and the heat of farm workers and domestic laborers, the invisible slaves of modern society. In the jails and the detention camps there are some who have come to our country in search of work and freedom, yet who have been considered criminals. We have seen our youth with empty eyes because they have nothing to look forward to in life. We have been with the countless victims of the violence that grows daily in our neighborhoods and even in our families. We will not rest until all injustice is eliminated from our life.

We have shared with our people the fear that comes from racism and discrimination. The knowledge that we might be rejected, ridiculed or insulted paralyzes us.

Just as Juan Diego accepted his challenge, we now accept ours: that of being artisans of a new people.

A. Our Identity

We are people twice *mestizado*. We are in the beginning stages of our life as Hispanic Americans.

Every birth is at one and the same time joy and sadness. Our birth as a people has been the same. Constant rejection has been a part of our daily life.

Nevertheless, our parents taught us to love the United States, although the struggle has been difficult. Our people have always struggled to improve themselves. We love the peace founded on truth, justice, love and freedom (*Pacem in Terris*). We have not taken up arms against our country but instead have defended it. We have fought to eliminate the injustices that rule our lives. The road has been long and difficult, littered with many obstacles, but we have made progress and will continue ahead with firmness and determination.

B. Our Accomplishments

Morenita, we give you thanks for the many beautiful things that have been happening to us lately.

Our people are beginning to count in society. Their voice is now being heard. Each day they are becoming more responsible for the religious and social structures that shape their lives.

Your children have already celebrated pastoral conventions on a national level.

The efforts of the farm workers have brought forth their fruits. Many of our people today enjoy a better life, thanks to the heroic efforts of our leaders.

Fourteen sons of our people have been called to be successors of the apostles.

Vocations to religious life and to the priesthood are on the rise.

Catholic movements and associations have arisen, dedicated to the social and apostolic progress of our people.

We have pastoral centers dedicated to research, theological reflection, the production of materials and the formation of pastoral leaders.

The bishops have established national and regional offices to serve your people.

We give thanks to your Son for all that is being achieved. But we ask him to give us the strength and courage to continue facing the gigantic problems of our day. As John Paul II said in Mexico, "We want to be the voice of those who have no voice." The poor have the right to our love and special care.

C. Challenges

There are certain challenges in our society which we must meet.

Our betterment in social life does not mean that we forget our roots—our Latin American *mestiza* tradition. The more we value our past, the more strength will we have to launch ourselves toward the building of our future.

Development of a more human life does not mean that we allow ourselves to be enslaved and destroyed by materialism, consumerism, social climbing, the desire for continuous pleasure and immediate gratification. All of this come from the idolatry of gold. These values are the cancer of society.

The modernization of the family does not mean that we abandon the greatest treasure of our Hispanic culture. The family is in great danger today. Divorce is on the rise, the elderly are forgotten and even cheated, children are abandoned and young people make the street their home. The spirit of individualism is killing the spirit of community that is the core of the family.

Christian unity does not mean religious indifference. Ecumenism must not lead us to lose our identity as Catholics. Affirming ecumenism, we reject every type of active proselytizing which is anti-ecumenical and destructive to our people. The great diversity of fundamentalist groups and their anti-Catholic spirit divide our families and our peoples. Our response is not one of fighting against these groups nor one of speaking ill of them or their intentions, but rather we will take their activities as a challenge to us Catholics to live more authentically and apostolically the life of the Gospel.

III. Artisans of a New Humanity

Ahora que estamos unidos
juntos en la verdad
danos fuerza te pedimos
fuerza para triunfar

A. A Rediscovery of the Gospel

The greatest strength of our people comes from the rediscovery of the Gospel that is our truth, our way and our life. The power of God in us is this:

—His light illuminating the meaning of our life and the goal of our mission;

—His love transforming our hearts of stone into human hearts;

—His compassion moving us to action;

—His hope encouraging us to continue struggling even when humanly speaking there is no hope;

—His strength transforming our weaknesses and converting them into strengths for the good.

B. A Rebirth of the Church

The word of the Gospel takes human form the more it penetrates, encompasses and ennobles our culture. It is expressed by means of images, symbols, music, art and wisdom. The church is born out of our response to the word of Jesus. Today we are living a true rebirth of the Hispanic American *mestizo* church.

C. The Life of the Church

Faith comes to us from the church and calls us to be church. In time and space this life of the church takes various forms depending on concrete needs and conditions. With great joy we see:

—The birth of new parish life where each member places his or her talents at the service of the community. The wide participation of parishioners in the mission of the church is the beginning of a new day and the source of great hope for the church of the future;

—In the renewed parishes the church is the natural center of the life of the community. The parish forms leaders and moves the people to work together for the good of all;

—The base communities *(comunidades eclesiales de base)* cause the individual to experience faith and to feel like church;

—New family movements and Bible study groups have brought new life to our communities;

—The resurgence of ministries has engendered a new ecclesial life that has incorporated many into the mission of the church. We are all called to actively take part in the apostolate;

—Permanent deacons, men prepared and ordained for service to the people of God, have renewed the presence of the church in many places with their dedication and apostolic zeal.

D. Popular Expressions of Faith

The missionaries knew how to understand the Indians, discovering their desires and inclinations in order to make these the basis for evangelization. They made dances expressions of faith.

Pilgrimages and processions offered occasions for teaching Christian doctrine. They created forms such as the *pastorela,* the *posadas* and the *siete palabras* to pass on the biblical message by means of dance, drama, music and art.

These expressions of a Christian people are true gifts of the Spirit and a beautiful treasure of our people. We invite pastoral leaders and catechists to rediscover these values.

E. Catechesis

Religious education continues to be a most important task in the church. Through it we grow and mature in Christian commitment.

—Catechesis must take into account our Hispanic American tradition.

—Proper methods must be utilized, especially radio and television.

—The preparation and motivation of catechists merit special attention.

Catechesis today, as in the time of the missionaries, must be based on the Bible and church tradition, taking into account the concrete signs of the times, using the methods of our tradition: dramatic interpretations of the Gospel, artistic expression of the mysteries of faith and songs with catechetical content.

F. Liturgy

The community celebration of faith is the manifestation of the Christian life of the people. So that these celebrations might be authentically those of the people, they ought to incorporate:

—the local language of the people in the prayers, readings and preaching;

—the art of our people in the representations of sacred images.

Some forms of celebration are beginning to emerge today that incorporate these fundamental principles of the Second Vatican Council. We applaud these efforts and we hope that this liturgical dawning may continue glowing and that soon it may come to shine in all its fullness.

G. Theological Reflection

Theology helps to discover how to live and proclaim our faith. Every ecclesial community has the privilege and obligation of discovering the theological meaning of its life.

—We are grateful for the theological contributions of other local ecclesial communities and, in a very special way, we value the inspiration of the theological thought of Latin America.

—Our Hispanic American people are beginning to point out the theological significance of our identity in the United States.

—We invite our people to continue this process.

Each people and every generation has the privilege and the obligation to respond to Jesus' question to Peter. "And who do you say that I am?" (Mt. 6:15). The particular response of other local churches enriches us, but at the same time inspires and encourages us to search for our own response. Who is this Jesus who lives and speaks in our Christian people? Together we must search, formulate and proclaim our answer to this question.

H. Vocations

The blossoming of new vocations for our people fills us with joy. However, the number is minimal in relation to the need. This apostolate must grow. Many men and women can respond to the Lord's call.

Our Hispanic American *mestizaje* church will reach maturity when our people have enough vocations not only for our own needs but also for the universal mission of the church.

I. A More Authentic Following of Jesus

Christ is our only model and like him we ought to be ready to commit ourselves and to be steadfast in the proclamation of truth, always filled with compassion and mercy.

Our following of him demands us to raise our voice when life is threatened, defending and respecting everyone as persons created by God. We are obligated to fight for peace and justice.

Just as he opened up new horizons for us, so too must we raise up the farm worker, the migrant and the laborer. We must aid in the self-improvement of all in search of a better place in society.

IV. A Pilgrimage with Joy, Courage and Hope

The imitation of Christ allows us to see others in their dignity as children of God.

> *Ahora que estamos unidos*
> *juntos en la verdad*
> *danos fuerza te pedimos*
> *fuerza para triunfar*
> *¡Ven con nosotros a caminar*
> *Santa Maria, ven!*

We are heading into the 21st century!

Conscious of all that God has achieved through us, we call on our people to assume an attitude of leadership to create a more human society. We are all the church, and together we can triumph.

We invite our people to be strong co-workers with us in ministry. Jesus told every one of us: "Go out and proclaim the good news." Christians, by nature, are evangelizers. The lay person, if Christian, evangelizes.

We invite young men and women especially to place their enthusiasm, their sense of commitment and their sincerity at the service of the Gospel. May they be young apostolic bearers of the Gospel to the youth of today.

We invite our brother priests to continue living their commitment. Do not be discouraged. We always walk with Jesus. We never go alone. He gives us the strength to be enduring guardians of the faith. May we also care for our traditions and language that are the means of spreading the Gospel. May we form the lay and religious ministers that God gives us, that they may be effective co-workers with us.

We congratulate them on all the good that has been done and we invite them to be the Good Shepherd with us. May they be men of prayer, devoted sons of the *Guadalupana*.

We invite our brother and sister religious to continue giving witness to the value of the life of poverty, chastity and obedience in a world that values riches, pleasure and power. We commend them because they have been a prophetic voice for justice and peace. We invite them, according to the particular charism of their community, to be united with the efforts of the local church in which they work so that in conjunction with the bishops and the people of God of that diocese they may build up the kingdom of God.

We invite the contemplative religious to continue offering to the church the strength of their prayers and good example.

We invite our brother deacons to join our efforts and those of all the clergy in the apostolate. Faithful to their vocation as deacons, may they be men of service to the people. Let them not forget that the primary field of their apostolate is their home, their community and their place of work.

We challenge seminarians to commit themselves seriously to their studies and spiritual formation. Our people need compassionate priests with thorough knowledge of the sacred mysteries and a profound sense of the urgency of the social teachings of the church.

Nuestro Adios

O Mother of the Americas, just as you trusted Juan Diego, we beg you to trust in us, the Hispanic bishops. May you send us to places we are unaccustomed to visit; may you send us to proclaim your mandate: that a temple be built wherein we may feel the love and tenderness of our mother. We want to be the artisans and the builders of this new temple—a society in which all will be able to live as brothers and sisters. We want to build up the kingdom of God, where peace is found because hate, jealousy, lies, dissension and every kind of injustice will have disappeared.

> *Madre de Dios*
> *Madre de la Iglesia*
> *Madre de los Americas*
> *Madre de todos nosotros*
> *Ruega por nosotros.*

(Source: John Tracy Ellis, ed. *Documents of American Catholic History*. Vol. 3:1966–1986. Wilmington, Del.: Michael Glazier, 1987, 764–76.)

HOBAN, EDWARD FRANCIS (1878–1966)

Archbishop. The sixth bishop of Cleveland, Ohio, Hoban was born in Chicago, Illinois, one of eight children of William and Bridget O'Malley Hoban. Educated at St. Ignatius Preparatory College in Chicago and St. Mary Seminary in Baltimore, Hoban was ordained in Holy Name Cathedral, Chicago, July 11, 1903. He was sent to Rome for further studies and received a doctorate from the Pontifical Gregorian University in 1905.

Upon his return to Chicago, Hoban was appointed professor and treasurer of the minor seminary, Quigley Preparatory College. He was also appointed to the Chicago diocesan chancery staff and later became chancellor of the archdiocese. He was named auxiliary bishop of Chicago on November, 21, 1921. He coordinated and organized the 28th International Eucharistic Congress in Chicago in 1926.

Hoban was appointed bishop of Rockford on February 10, 1928, where he opened many elementary and high schools, modernized facilities of charitable institutions, and established a diocesan newspaper. He was named coadjutor bishop of Cleveland on November 4, 1942, serving as administrator with right of succession to ailing Archbishop Joseph Schrembs. He became bishop of Cleveland upon Schrembs' death on November 2, 1945.

The Catholic diocesan population of Cleveland grew during the Hoban years, from 546,000 in 1942 to 870,000 in 1966, even though six counties were lost to the new Diocese of Youngstown, which was formed in 1943. Hoban established sixty-one new parishes, forty-seven new elementary schools, and a dozen new high schools. In 1946 he launched a project to rebuild and remodel St. John Cathedral, and he also enlarged and expanded St. John College. He centralized child care facilities at Parmadale, opened Holy Family Cancer Home for terminally ill patients, and started an undergraduate seminary, St. Charles Borromeo, in 1953. Hoban actively promoted the lay retreat movement and the Newman Apostolate for Catholic students attending public universities and colleges. He was given the personal title of archbishop in 1951.

Bishop Hoban's personal life was enriched by his close friendship with Archbishop Amleto Cicognani, the apostolic delegate to the United States, and also resulted in unusual numbers of younger priests from the Diocese of Cleveland being nominated to episcopal sees, such as John Krol, John Dearden, and Paul Hallinan.

Van Tassel, David D., and John J. Grabowski, eds. *The Encyclopedia of Cleveland History.* Cleveland: Case Western Reserve University, 1987.

NELSON J. CALLAHAN

HOBAN, JAMES (ca. 1762–1831)

Architect. Hoban was born in Callon, County Kilkenny, Ireland, around 1762. He began his studies in Dublin schools and continued in Paris, returning to Ireland to work as an architect on several Dublin buildings. He specialized in the English Georgian style, a design he used throughout his career.

Hoban emigrated to the United States after the Revolutionary War and settled first in Philadelphia before moving to South Carolina, where he designed the state capitol, which was completed in 1791 (burned in 1865). In 1792 he moved to Washington, D.C., and submitted a plan, based on Leinster House in Dublin, for the presidential mansion. He won the competition and supervised construction of the White House and the rebuilding after its destruction by the British in 1814.

His commission included five hundred dollars and a lot in the District of Columbia, where he settled and continued his work, designing several federal office buildings, including the State and War offices (1818), as well as the Grand Hotel and the Little Hotel. He also was an assis-

tant supervisor in the construction of the U.S. Capitol, which was designed by William Thornton.

Hoban was a member of St. Patrick parish, Washington, D.C., and served on the city council. He and his wife, Susannah Sewall, had ten children. He died in Washington on December 8, 1831.

"James Hoban, The Architect and Builder of the White House and the Superintendent of the Capitol at Washington." *American Catholic Historical Researches* 24 (1907) 35–52.

Kimball, F. "The Genesis of the White House." *Century* 95 (1918) 523–28.

Maryland Historical Society, Baltimore.

Massachusetts Historical Society (Boston) Coolidge Collection.

Office of Public Grounds and Buildings, Washington, D.C.

Warner, William W. *At Peace With All Their Neighbors: Catholics and Catholicism in the National Capitol, 1787–1860.* Washington, D.C., 1994.

MARIANNA McLOUGHLIN

HOBAN, MICHAEL JOHN (1853–1926)

Bishop. The ecclesiastical career of Michael John Hoban, the second bishop of the Diocese of Scranton, Pennsylvania, is similar to that of many of the bishops who led the American Catholic Church in the late nineteenth and early twentieth centuries when many Catholic immigrants arrived in the United States. Hoban saw that this flood of Catholic immigrants required not only churches and schools, but that they also needed hospitals, orphanages, homes for the aged and infirm. Hoban met these spiritual, educational, and health-care needs as his aggressive brick-and-mortar efforts helped to change the institutional life of the Church in the Scranton Diocese. His tenure was marked by new beginnings for the Church in northeastern Pennsylvania. Yet, Hoban's career differed dramatically from his contemporaries as he was forced to confront the first major schism in the United States, the Polish National revolt in 1897.

The son of Irish immigrants, Michael Hoban was born in Waterloo, New Jersey, on June 6, 1853. His father, a railroad contractor, later relocated the family to Hawley, a small farming community in northeastern Pennsylvania. At fourteen, Hoban enrolled in St. Francis Xavier School, New York City. He remained there only one year, before transferring to Holy Cross College, Worcester, Massachusetts, where he studied from 1868 to 1871. He returned to Hawley for the next two and a half years to help with the family business. Hoban's formal education resumed in 1873 when he entered St. John's College, Fordham, New York. His stay at Fordham was brief, as the young man determined he had a vocation to the priesthood. Entering St. Charles Seminary, Overbrook, Pennsylvania, in September 1874, Hoban remained there only one year; he was then sent by Bishop William O'Hara, 1816–99, first bishop of Scranton, to the North American College in Rome. On May 22, 1880, Michael Hoban was ordained in St. John Lateran.

Returning to the Diocese of Scranton, Hoban was appointed to various pastoral assignments. On December 8, 1887, he was named pastor of St. Leo's Church, Ashley, a center of coal mining activity not far from Wilkes-Barre. There he was responsible for organizing the parish and erecting a church. His administrative and pastoral abilities became widely known. Bishop O'Hara, because of increasing responsibilities and advancing age, applied to Rome for help. Pope Leo XIII named Hoban coadjutor bishop with the right of succession. Hoban was consecrated bishop in St. Peter's Cathedral, Scranton, on March 22, 1896, by Cardinal Francis Satolli, the apostolic delegate to the United States.

With O'Hara's health in decline, Bishop Hoban took on more of the responsibilities for the operation of the diocese. His greatest challenge came in 1897 when Fr. Francis Hodur, a priest of the diocese, abandoned his pastorate to found the Polish National Catholic Church. In 1898 Bishop Hoban was compelled to excommunicate Hodur, an action that set off a long, and often bitter struggle involving the Roman Catholic Church and Hodur's followers. In an effort to heal wounds, formal dialogue between the Polish National Catholic Church and the Roman Catholic Church commenced in 1984.

Bishop Hoban succeeded to the see upon O'Hara's death on February 3, 1899. The second bishop of Scranton's episcopal career was highlighted by his personal involvement in local and national events. He was a friend and advisor to John Mitchell, 1870–1919, head of the United Mine Workers, who organized the great anthracite coal strike of 1902. In later years, Hoban entertained Mitchell and President Theodore Roosevelt at his episcopal residence. So respected were his negotiating skills that Hoban was frequently asked to arbitrate labor disputes throughout northeastern Pennsylvania.

Ever seeking to advance the institutional Church, Hoban aided in the establishment of three orders for women religious: the Sisters of SS. Cyril and Methodius; the Sisters of St. Casimir; and the Poor Sisters of Jesus Crucified and the Sorrowful Mother. During his episcopacy, two colleges for women were founded: Marywood College, Scranton, and College Misericordia, Dallas. Three hospitals were erected as well as two orphanages and a home for the aged. Under his expert leadership, the Church flourished in northeastern Pennsylvania. His death on November 13, 1926, ended a career marked by achievements that are still shaping the Church today.

A well-read, well-traveled man, Michael Hoban exemplifies the strong leadership that was exhibited by native-born American bishops who were at once sympathetic to the needs of the immigrant peoples they served at the same time they advanced policies and practices which demonstrated their unquestioning loyalty to Rome and their firm adherence to all of the teachings of the Roman Catholic Church.

See also PENNSYLVANIA, CATHOLIC CHURCH IN.

Earley, James B. *Envisioning Faith: The Pictorial History of the Diocese of Scranton.* Devon, 1994.
Gallagher, John P. *A Century of History: The Diocese of Scranton, 1868–1968.* Scranton, 1968.

JAMES B. EARLEY

HODUR, FRANCIS (1866–1953)

Leader of the Polish National Catholic Church. Francis Hodur [Franciszek Hodur] was born on April 1, 1866, in Żarki, Poland. After completing his secondary education and part of his seminary studies in Kraków, Poland, he emigrated to the United States where he completed his theological studies at St. Vincent's Seminary in Beatty, Pennsylvania, and was ordained in Scranton, Pennsylvania, August 19, 1893. He served as pastor of Holy Trinity parish in Nanicoke, Pennsylvania, from 1895 to 1897, during which time he came into conflict with his bishop over issues relating to lay control of parish property and finances, as well as the appointment of priests to parishes. Hodur, a devout Polish nationalist with socialistic inclinations, became an advocate of parishioner control over churches built and maintained by them, the use of the Polish vernacular in the Mass, and, through the use of parish committees, parishioner control over the selection of local pastors. These principles, along with the appointment of Polish bishops, became the cornerstones of Hodur's leadership of dissident parishes in northeastern Pennsylvania and elsewhere. In 1897 he accepted an invitation to become pastor of St. Stanislaus, Bishop and Martyr, parish by its laity, without episcopal sanction, and established the newspaper *Straż* [*The Guard*] through which he disseminated his ideas. Because of his defiance of ecclesiastical authority, he was excommunicated on September 29, 1898.

Gradually, however, he rose to such prominence in the independent movement that he rivaled Antoni Kozłowski in Chicago and Stefan Kamiński in Buffalo for leadership of the dissident movement nationally. When his older rivals died, he became the acknowledged leader of independentism and was elected bishop of the Polish National Catholic Church (PNCC) at its first synod in 1904. After the death of the Old Catholic Bishop Antoni Kozłowski in 1907, Hodur was consecrated bishop of the schismatic church by the Dutch Old Catholic Archbishop Gerard Van Gul in Utrecht, Holland. At its peak, Hodur's church attracted about 5 percent of those of Polish heritage in America, and eventually established several parishes in Poland. In 1946 the PNCC entered into intercommunion with the Protestant Episcopal Church, but it was terminated in the 1970s over the issue of Episcopal ordination of women. In the 1990s efforts were renewed to develop intercommunion with Rome and a general reconciliation has since occurred which many PNCC leaders feel will eventually lead to a complete *rapprochement* between their movement and Roman Catholicism. Hodur died in Scranton, Pennsylvania, on February 16, 1953.

See also POLISH CATHOLICS IN AMERICA.

Galush, William. "The Polish National Church: A Survey of Its Origins, Development and Missions." *Records of the American Catholic Historical Society of Philadelphia* 83 (1972) 131–49.

JAMES A. PULA

HOEHN, MATTHEW (1898–1959)

Teacher, librarian, author. Hoehn was born in Newark, New Jersey, on February 4, 1898, the son of Joseph Hoehn and Elizabeth Magin. He was educated at St. Benedict's Preparatory School, earned a B.A. degree from St. Anselm's College, Manchester, New Hampshire, in 1921, and entered the Benedictine Order in 1918. He was trained at St. Anselm's Seminary in Newark, professed in 1919, and ordained in 1925. He taught chemistry at St. Benedict's Preparatory School and St. Anselm's College and later studied at Fordham University. After studying library science at Columbia University, he earned a B.L.S. degree in 1936 and became the librarian at St. Benedict's Preparatory School. He also served as prior of St. Mary's Abbey in Newark from 1946 to 1956, and as an associate editor of the *American Benedictine Review.*

In 1948 he published *Catholic Authors: Contemporary Biographical Sketches, 1930–47,* containing biographical information for 620 contemporary authors of books in English who were practicing Catholics. In 1952 a second volume was published containing 374 additional biographies. Both works were acclaimed for addressing the deficiency of biographical reference works on Catholic authors of books in English. He also published an account of the rebuilding of the abbey at Monte Cassino in the first volume of the *American Benedictine Review.* Following his death in Newark on May 12, 1959, St. Benedict's Preparatory School named the Matthew Hoehn Memorial Library after him.

See also BENEDICTINES (O.S.B.).

Hoehn, Matthew, ed. *Catholic Authors: Contemporary Biographical Sketches, 1930–47.* Newark, N.J.: St. Mary's Abbey, 1948.
____, ed. *Catholic Authors: Contemporary Biographical Sketches, 1930–52.* Newark, N.J.: St. Mary's Abbey, 1952.
____. "Monte Cassino—1950." *American Benedictine Review* 1(3) (September 1950) 312–14.

DONALD L. STELLUTO

HOFSTEE, ANTHONY LEO (1903–86)

Dominican friar. Anthony Leo Hofstee was born in Utrecht, Holland, July 30, 1903, and while still a child he and his family emigrated to Everett, Washington. In 1925 he entered the novitiate of the western Dominican province in Benicia, California. He completed his clerical studies at the Dominican House of Studies in Washington, D.C., and was ordained there in 1932. He immediately returned to the West Coast and served as assistant pastor in Dominican parishes in Portland, Seattle, and in Berkeley and Vallejo, California.

At the commencement of the war with Japan, Fr. Hofstee volunteered as chaplain and in 1944 was with the U.S. Marines when they recaptured the Philippines. It was while in the Philippines that he encountered the lepers of Tala near Manila. Because of the terrible wartime conditions, the leprosaria throughout the Philippines were sorely neglected, and that of Tala was among the most abandoned. Fr. Hofstee offered his services to the Most Rev. J. O. Doherty, archbishop of Manila, who then wrote to the provincial of the western Dominicans:

> I am imploring you to allow Fr. Hofstee to offer his life for the care of these poor suffering people in the Leprosarium of Tala. These poor people have no resident priest, no mass, no altar, no Sisters to take care of them, and the only time they see a priest is when some of their number are on the point of death. . . .

Permission was granted, and in May of 1947 Fr. Hofstee took up residence in the colony's morgue, since there was no other dwelling for him at the time. He immediately set to work in his parish of six hundred lepers. Through benefactions which he was tireless in securing, he built a nursery for babies born of resident lepers, a grade school, a high school, a college, a church, a decent hospital, and through the years added to and improved these structures to satisfy the growing population, which by 1955 had reached 1,900 and eventually soared to 2,500. One of his first efforts was the securing of a group of Franciscan sisters for the nursery, which at times numbered 200 babies. He also established a chapter of the Third Order of St. Dominic composed of lepers alone who would help him in his daily ministry. Except for the doctors, sisters, and other priests and religious who would periodically visit the colony, Hofstee would allow only lepers to staff the colony's various projects, including the schools, and would himself pay their salaries from moneys received from his benefactors.

Among his chief concerns was to instill hope among the hopeless and joy in the hearts of those who, humanly speaking, could know only sorrow and pain. Thus, his establishment of schools—the lepers were to look forward with hope to their future; and his clownish activities—singing, dancing, joking till his downcast patient could only smile and laugh at the good but crazy priest.

In 1953 the apostolic nuncio of the Philippines, the Most Rev. Egidio Vagnozzi, asked Fr. Hofstee to organize the many leprosaria scattered throughout the islands into a national organization. This undertaking also bore fruit. In 1983 he received the Mother Teresa Award from the hands of Mother Teresa herself. Fr. Hofstee died at Tala, April 26, 1986. His body is entombed there in the shadow of the church he had built.

See also DOMINICANS (O.P.).

STANLEY PARMISANO, O.P.

HOGAN, JOHN B. (1829–1901)

Seminary rector, educational reformer. This Irish-born (County Clare), French trained Sulpician priest taught at Saint-Sulpice, Paris, from the year of his ordination, 1851, until 1884 when he became the first rector of St. John's Seminary in Boston. Of decidedly liberal persuasion, Hogan gravitated toward the thought of John Henry Newman, as well as toward the leading lights of the French Church, such as Charles de Montalembert and Bishop Félix Dupanloup. A master teacher, he inspired several students to cherish independent, critical thought: Maurice d'Hulst, rector of the Institut Catholique de Paris; Euxode Irenée Mignot, archbishop of Albi and an advocate of certain aspects of Modernism; Félix Klein, the noted exponent of the thought and ecclesiology of Isaac Hecker and John Ireland.

Hogan was rector of St. John's Seminary, 1884–89, and was president of Divinity College, later Caldwell Hall, the residence of the priests who were graduate students at The Catholic University of America, from its opening in 1889 to 1894. Though he was sympathetic to the Americanist views of Bishop John J. Keane, rector of the university, he was not an Americanizer but rather ran Divinity College according to a modified regimen of the French Sulpician seminaries. This so alienated the faculty residents of the college that the university senate rejected his appointment to the chair of apologetics. Hence he resigned and returned to St. John's Seminary.

Analysis of his correspondence and his book, *Clerical Studies,* clearly substantiates the case for John B. Hogan as a strong advocate of Americanist ecclesiology and a nascent Modernist understanding of Scripture. In his letters to the Paulist scholar, Augustin Hewit, Hogan criti-

cally nuances the meaning of several scriptural passages on the imminence of the Second Coming. In letters to Alfred Loisy he expressed his concurrence with the French exegete's views on historical criticism, but stated that the Church was not prepared to accept this methodology. Hogan's radical openness was utterly unfettered by the *a priori* reasoning of the neoscholastic synthesis. He criticized this prevailing theology for citing Scripture passages merely as proof texts for their ahistorical argumentation. Loisy perceived himself in harmony with much of Hogan's thought; he wrote to Baron Von Hügel, "Rome condemns in me what she approves in Hogan."

John Hogan represents that point on the intellectual spectrum where Americanism and Modernism intersect. Both were infused with a heightened historical consciousness, a critical attitude toward traditional apologetics, and a determined spirit to articulate the faith in modern terms. John B. Hogan is now recognized as a distinctive participant in the progressive intellectual movements of his times.

See also MODERNISM; *NEW YORK REVIEW.*

Hogan, John B. *Clerical Studies.* Boston, 1898.

Kauffman, Christopher J. *Tradition and Transformation in Catholic Culture: The Priests of Saint Sulpice in the United States from 1791 to the Present.* New York: Macmillan, 1988.

CHRISTOPHER J. KAUFFMAN

HOGAN, WILLIAM (1788–1848)

Priest and schismatic. Hogan was born in Ireland in 1788, and after studying at St. Patrick's Seminary, Maynooth, functioned as a priest in the Diocese of Limerick. In 1819 Hogan left Ireland and emigrated to Albany, New York, without his bishop's permission. He served in the Diocese of New York for a short time, but in 1820 he left Albany for St. Mary's Cathedral in Philadelphia. There, he was at the center of a battle between the newly arrived bishop, Henry Conwell, and the lay trustees of the cathedral. Hogan sided with the trustees and was critical of the bishop, who disliked Hogan's personality and lifestyle; Hogan lived on his own, apart from the rectory. When Hogan refused Conwell's order to live with the other priests, he was suspended. The animosity between Hogan and Conwell was played out in the press and courts.

Hogan's views, known as "Hoganism," found support among the trustees. It called for lay rights to select pastors and bishops and to hold and control ecclesiastical properties. Hogan's attempt to reform the structure of the church caused a stir in April 1822 with the trustees' election. There were two planks, one favorable to Hogan and the other favorable to Conwell and his supporter, the Irish Dominican, William Harold. Passions ran high during the campaigning and a fight broke out in front of the church. Punches and bricks were thrown before the police came to break it up. The civil courts upheld the validity of the election of Hogan's ticket. Pope Pius VII intervened in the "Hogan" schism. He sent a rebuke, *Non Sine Magno,* along with a letter to the archbishop of Baltimore, instructing him to see to it that the power of the trustees was limited. Hogan submitted, then withdrew the submission, left the country, but when he returned in 1824 he had lost favor with the trustees. Subsequently, he left the Catholic Church, married twice, managed a circus, and was admitted to the New Hampshire bar. Always a popular preacher, he lectured on the anti-Catholic circuit in North Carolina, Georgia, Massachusetts, and New Hampshire. His most famous pamphlets, published after his death, are *Nunneries and Auricular Confession* (1855), and *Popery As It Was and Is* (1856). In 1843 he was appointed U.S. Consul to Nuevitas, Cuba. He died in 1848 in Nashua, New Hampshire, unreconciled to the Church.

See also TRUSTEEISM.

Tourscher, Francis E. *The Hogan Schism and Trustee Troubles in St. Mary's Church, Philadelphia, 1820–1829.* Philadelphia: The Peter Reilly Company, 1930.

JOSEPH M. McLAFFERTY

HOLY CROSS, COLLEGE OF

The oldest Catholic college in New England, Holy Cross was opened in 1843 by the Society of Jesus on the outskirts of Worcester, at the site of an academy established in 1836 by Fr. James Fitton. The founder was Benedict Fenwick, a Jesuit and the second bishop of Boston, who named the school after his cathedral to stress its significance as a diocesan enterprise. Determined to establish Catholic education in a state whose nativists had burned the Ursuline school in Charlestown in 1834, Fenwick was also anxious to attract young men to the priesthood. Accordingly, he insisted that Holy Cross operate exclusively as a boarding school and admit only Catholic students. That made the college an anomaly within the Jesuit system, but produced the desired result: during the first fifty years, nearly half of the graduates opted for the priesthood. Denied a state charter in 1849 for a variety of reasons that included anti-Catholicism, Holy Cross awarded Georgetown University degrees until the charter was granted in 1865.

Throughout the nineteenth century, Holy Cross offered a seven-year curriculum that encompassed the principles of the *Ratio Studiorum* and resembled a European *lycée*. Students as young as eight were admitted, but the average age at admission rose to about eighteen by the end of the century. A limited number of day-students were accepted, beginning in the 1870s. After 1900 the program was altered to bring the college into conformity with American educational norms: a year of more advanced studies was added to the top of the program, the preparatory and collegiate divisions were separated; the prep school was phased out; the traditional emphasis on classical languages and philosophy was gradually reduced. Admission was no longer restricted to Roman Catholics, but a controlled and disciplined atmosphere was maintained. The mid-1960s brought an era of rapid transformation that included increasing reliance on lay faculty members and administrators, greater emphasis on individual responsibility for personal conduct and religious observance, the admission of women (1972), and shifts to an open curriculum (1970), distribution requirements (1984), and a language requirement (1990). In 1984 Holy Cross became a charter member of the Patriot League, which incorporates twenty-two intercollegiate sports and is committed to maintaining the ideal of the scholar/athlete. And in 1992 the mission statement pledged Holy Cross "to exemplify the longstanding dedication of the Society of Jesus to the intellectual life and its commitment to the service of faith and promotion of justice."

Enrollment has risen steadily since the founding—to 1,000 in 1924; 2,000 in 1964, and 2,600 in the 1990s—but the increases have been deliberately controlled to preserve the quality and atmosphere of the educational process in an exclusively undergraduate liberal arts college. By the sesquicentennial in 1993, a low faculty-student ratio, an average of fewer than twenty students per class, and a highly selective admissions policy, ranked Holy Cross among the top national liberal arts colleges. By then, the physical plant included two dozen major buildings on a campus of 174 acres; and the General Alumni Association of over 25,000 members, plus an annual giving rate above 55 percent, indicated an unusual level of loyalty to the institutional mission.

See also CATHOLIC UNIVERSITIES AND COLLEGES; JESUITS IN AMERICA, THE.

Devitt, Edward I. "College of the Holy Cross, 1843–1914." *Woodstock Letters* 64:204–37.

Kuzniewski, Anthony J., S.J. *College of the Holy Cross: One Hundred Fifty Years.* Worcester, Mass.: Holy Cross General Alumni Association, 1993.

Meagher, Walter J., and William J. Grattan. *The Spires of Fenwick.* New York: Vantage Press, 1966.

Tachikawa, Akira. "'Public' vs. 'Private' Colleges in 19th Century Massachusetts: The Ordeal of the College of the Holy Cross in 1849." *Educational Studies* 28:1–24.

ANTHONY J. KUZNIEWSKI, S.J.

HOLY CROSS, CONGREGATION OF (C.S.C.)

The Congregation of Holy Cross (men and women religious) takes its name from Sainte-Croix, a suburb of Le Mans, France, where it was founded in 1837 by Rev. Basile

Moreau (1799–1873), a priest of the Diocese of Le Mans. As superior since 1835 of both the Brothers of St. Joseph and the Auxiliary Priests of Le Mans, Moreau united the two institutes and added a women's branch, the Marianites of Holy Cross, in 1841. Papal approval of the brothers and priests was given in 1857 on condition that the women be organized as a separate congregation, which Moreau did in 1860.

At the invitation of Bishop Celestin Hailandière of Vincennes, Indiana, the congregation's first foundation in the United States was made in Daviess County, Indiana, in 1841 by six brothers under the leadership of Rev. Edward Sorin (1814–93). Within three months new members had been recruited in America. In 1842 the congregation moved to St. Joseph County, Indiana, and founded the school chartered in 1844 as the University of Notre Dame du Lac. Notre Dame became the center for most of the American Holy Cross community until 1948. The first sisters from France arrived at Notre Dame in 1843 and within a year they too began to receive local women.

By 1865 there were more sisters in the United States than in either France or Canada. A growing tension among the sisters over such issues as adaptation of their rule to life in America, whether the motherhouse should be located in France or in the United States and who should govern the sisters' congregation resulted in an indult of separation for a majority of the American sisters. In 1869 those who separated were organized as the Congregation of the Sisters of the Holy Cross. Their center was at St. Mary's, Notre Dame, Indiana. The sisters in Louisiana and in New York City remained united to the motherhouse in France. In 1883 the sisters in Canada separated from France over issues of adaptation of their rule to circumstances in Canada. They were organized as a separate congregation, The Sisters of Holy Cross and the Seven Dolors (later shortened to Sisters of Holy Cross).

Schools

In addition to conducting a college at Notre Dame, the congregation also took in orphans and maintained a trade school. The congregation also took over the direction of St. Mary's Asylum, a boys' orphanage in New Orleans, in 1849, and in 1859 started an agricultural school near that city. In 1872 the brothers and priests opened St. Joseph's College in Cincinnati and Sacred Heart College in Watertown, Wisconsin. In 1876 a school was opened in Austin, Texas, that was chartered in 1885 as St. Edward's College. Attempts of short duration were made to conduct colleges in Chicago, Galveston, and Brownsville (Texas), Lebanon (Kentucky), and New Iberia (Louisiana).

Throughout the nineteenth century the brothers and sisters started or took over the direction of more than 140 parish schools, mostly in Indiana, Illinois, Ohio, Louisiana, Mary-

land, the District of Columbia, Texas, and Utah. In 1881 the Canadian sisters began to staff parish schools in the New England states that served French-Canadian immigrants. By 1895 they were conducting thirteen such institutions.

Under the dynamic leadership of Sr. Angela Gillespie (1824–87), the Sisters of the Holy Cross rapidly expanded their commitment to the education of women in the years after the Civil War. By 1900 they had opened nineteen academies in Indiana, Illinois, Virginia, Maryland, Washington, D.C., Idaho, Utah, Texas, and California. They opened two more in the twentieth century in California and Massachusetts. The Marianites of Holy Cross opened five academies in Louisiana in the same period and five in the twentieth century (four in Louisiana and one on Staten Island, New York). Between 1918 and 1970 the Sisters of Holy Cross (Canadian) conducted six high schools in Connecticut, Massachusetts, and New Hampshire. As of 1993, only one of all these many institutions, Holy Cross Academy in Kensington, Maryland, remained under the sisters' direction.

Saint Mary's College for women at Notre Dame, Indiana, begun as an academy in 1844, bestowed its first bachelor's degree in 1898, and thereafter expanded its college program until all the high school students were moved off the campus in 1945. The Sisters of the Holy Cross also founded and conducted St. Mary-of-the-Wasatch College in Salt Lake City (1926–58), Dunbarton College of the Holy Cross in Washington, D.C. (1935–73), and Cardinal Cushing College in Brookline, Massachusetts (1952–72). A teacher-training institute for sisters founded in 1916 and conducted by the Marianites, Our Lady of Holy Cross College in New Orleans, opened its doors to the general public in the 1960s as did Notre Dame College in Manchester, New Hampshire, founded in 1950 by the Sisters of Holy Cross (Canadian).

Parishes

In 1853 Holy Cross priests began to serve St. Joseph's and St. Patrick's parishes in South Bend, Indiana. Commitments to other territorial parishes were undertaken in the 1870s: St. Bernard's in Watertown, Wisconsin, in 1872; St. Mary's in Austin, Texas, in 1874; Sacred Heart in New Orleans in 1879. In the years 1877–1901, the priests of the congregation founded or took responsibility for three Polish national parishes in South Bend and Chicago, and a German, a Hungarian, and a Belgian parish in South Bend.

The ministry of Holy Cross priests to minority ethnic groups expanded in the 1930s and 1940s when they committed themselves to eleven Mexican-American and African American parishes in South Bend and in the vicinity of Austin. Between 1950 and 1994, the priests of Holy Cross undertook to serve forty-nine additional parishes in the United States, most of them Hispanic, inner city, or rural.

Despite a decline in the number of priests available, they were still maintaining thirty of these commitments at the end of 1994.

Twentieth-Century Developments

The apostolate of higher education continued to be a priority for the men of Holy Cross in the twentieth century. Although their colleges in Watertown, Wisconsin, and Cincinnati were closed in 1912 and 1921 respectively, they took over the direction of the University of Portland in Oregon in 1902 and opened King's College in Wilkes-Barre, Pennsylvania, in 1946 and Stonehill College in North Easton, Massachusetts, in 1948. St. Edward's College in Austin was chartered as a university in 1925. When *Ave Maria,* a weekly magazine founded by Sorin in 1865 to provide Catholic literature for Americans, was forced to suspend publication in 1970, the Ave Maria Press was developed as a publisher of religious books and religious education materials.

Forced out of the parish schools by their declining numbers and the fact that pastors could hire nuns to teach for less, the Holy Cross Brothers upgraded the education of their members beginning in 1905 and concentrated on secondary schools. Between 1909 and 1968 they founded or took over the direction of thirty-three high schools in all parts of the country except the Plains, Rocky Mountain, and Pacific Northwest states. Br. Ephrem O'Dwyer (1888–1978), a provincial superior from 1946 to 1962, was the brothers' leader in focusing their efforts on secondary education. By 1984 declining numbers of brothers and school closures had occasioned the brothers' withdrawal from all but eleven of their high schools.

Hospitals

During the Civil War, approximately eighty sisters from St. Mary's and Notre Dame had served as nurses in Union military hospitals, primarily in the Midwest. By virtue of providing the nursing staff on *The Red Rover,* a navy hospital ship on the Mississippi River, the Sisters of the Holy Cross have been recognized as forerunners of the Navy Nurse Corps. In 1867 the Indiana sisters opened their first hospital in Cairo, Illinois. By 1900 the Sisters of the Holy Cross had established hospitals elsewhere in Illinois as well as in Utah, Idaho, South Dakota, Ohio, Indiana, and Missouri. In the twentieth century, others were added in California, New Mexico, and Maryland. In 1979 the Sisters of the Holy Cross combined their hospitals in a corporation, Holy Cross Health System, which has further expanded this ministry.

The Marianites took charge of the nursing duties at the French Hospital in New York City in 1885 where they remained until 1963. In 1957 the Marianites opened a hospital and a nursing home in Opelousas, Louisiana, from which they subsequently withdrew.

Structure and Missions

A North American province for the priests and brothers was erected in 1865 with Rev. Edward Sorin as provincial superior. In 1866 its scope was limited to the houses in the United States except for those in Louisiana, which depended directly on the general administration in France. In 1868 Sorin was elected the third superior general of the men of Holy Cross, an office he held until his death in 1893. He also served as ecclesiastical superior of the Sisters of the Holy Cross until 1889. When their congregation was restructured in 1946, the priests and brothers were organized as distinct societies, each with its own province but under a common superior general. By 1995 they had six provinces in the United States. The three congregations of Holy Cross Sisters, however, had dissolved separate provinces by 1994 in favor of having all their members under their general administrations or, in the case of the Marianites, under one provincial superior for all of North America.

While still in a mission territory themselves, the American Holy Cross communities had contributed personnel to their congregations' foreign missions in Bangladesh in the nineteenth century. In the twentieth century they have undertaken increasing responsibility for this mission while starting others: Chile in 1943, Brazil in 1947, Ghana and Uganda in 1958, Liberia in 1962, Peru in 1968, and Kenya in 1978. By 1995 there were more than 2,400 American Holy Cross religious in the four congregations of men and women, more than 1,100 men and almost 1,300 women.

See also SISTERS OF THE HOLY CROSS (C.S.C.); NOTRE DAME, UNIVERSITY OF.

Annales de la Congregation des Soeurs de Sainte-Croix et des Sept-Douleurs. 5 vols. St-Laurent, Quebec: Soeurs de Sainte-Croix et des Sept-Douleurs, 1930–92.

Annals of the Congregation of the Marianite Sisters of Holy Cross. New Orleans: Marianite Sisters of Holy Cross, 1951.

Costin, Georgia. *Priceless Spirit: A History of the Sisters of the Holy Cross, 1841–1893.* University of Notre Dame Press, 1994.

Hope, Arthur J. *Notre Dame, One Hundred Years.* University of Notre Dame Press, 1943.

Sorin, Edward F. *Chronicles of Notre Dame du Lac.* Ed. James T. Connelly and trans. John M. Toohey. University of Notre Dame Press, 1992.

JAMES CONNELLY, C.S.C.

HOLY GHOST (SPIRIT) FATHERS/SPIRITANS (C.S.SP.)

The first Spiritans (Holy Ghost Fathers) to set foot in what is now the U.S.A. arrived via Canada, where they had been working since 1732. A few of them who served as chaplains to the Micmacs and other tribes were recorded in Boston in 1745, and near Fort Duquesne (Pittsburgh) in the 1750s during the French and Indian Wars.

In 1793 Spiritans began to live more permanently in what is now U.S. territory. They came as refugees from Guiana's French Revolution and established themselves at St. Croix and St. Thomas, Virgin Islands. One of them became its official ecclesiastical superior and subsequently the local vicar general of the archbishop of Baltimore. In later years they served also on the mainland. Most outstanding among them was Fr. John Moranvillé.

Spiritan Province in America

Corporate involvement began only in 1872 when the Spiritans were about to be expelled from Germany by Bismarck as "Jesuit affiliated." After two desultory attempts to establish houses in Kentucky and Ohio, Fr. Joseph Strub, the exiled provincial of Germany, arrived in 1874. He chose Pittsburgh as the center of his endeavor to implant the Spiritans in the U.S.A. Here he founded a college in 1878, which developed into what is now Duquesne University, as well as a number of parishes for immigrants in Pennsylvania and Michigan. In Arkansas he took over a large sector of a railroad concession, where he settled all comers, regardless of their ethnic origins, in colonies. In two years, half a dozen churches went up in these colonies.

When Strub died in 1890, the Spiritans had spread over five states. In addition to those parishes, they took over the St. Joseph's Home for bereaved boys in Philadelphia when, one year after its founding, it had been on the verge of collapse. They also reestablished the American branch of the Holy Childhood Association; it was destined to become the largest of its branches.

Thereafter, the development continued. From 1895 on, the province opened its own junior and senior seminaries, as well as novitiates in Pennsylvania, Connecticut, and Michigan. Leaving aside the congregation's ministry to the blacks, some forty parishes on the mainland, nearly all for ethnic congregations, were staffed by Spiritans. When they spread to the West Coast in the 1940s, most parishes were among Mexican-Americans. In the 1960s the congregation also staffed a number of high schools.

Overseas missions always drew the congregation's attention. In 1875 the first American-born Spiritan sailed for Africa, and sporadically others followed until in 1931 four of them went to Puerto Rico to open a mission in Arecibo. Fr. Christopher Plunkett was the man who pioneered this venture. It became the starting point of a large string of churches and chapels with a personnel of about thirty priests. Their work was blessed with such success that in 1960 Arecibo became a diocese. Once a parish was flourishing, the priests would hand it over to the diocesan clergy to concentrate their own efforts on less developed areas.

In 1932 the province also took charge of the Kilimanjaro vicariate in present-day Tanzania. Up to about fifty priests and brothers at the same time evangelized the people there. Forty years later the original mission had given rise to five dioceses and contributed territory to three others, nearly all headed by native bishops with a native clergy.

Ministry with the Blacks in the U.S.A.

From the very start of their work in the U.S.A., the Spiritans had also paid attention to the blacks, notably in the Virgin Islands and Baltimore, serving whites and blacks indiscriminately in their parishes. From the 1870s on, however, it proved to be very difficult to start separate parishes for blacks, neglected in white parishes, because of prejudices against them. It was only in 1888 that they could open a small parish for them in Pittsburgh. Then in 1889, thanks to the interest shown by Archbishop Patrick Ryan and the Blessed Mother Katherine Drexel, the first large black parish was opened in Philadelphia. A second one there followed in 1909. The Holy Ghost Fathers had also begun to serve in the Drexel-Morrell venture called the St. Emma Agricultural and Industrial School for Blacks at Powhatan, Virginia, in 1895. Later called St. Emma Military Academy, this school produced many converts and served the blacks as such until 1971. At least three of them reached the priesthood.

Overcoming the widespread opposition to black parishes took time, but from 1911 on the Spiritans began a string of parishes for blacks in New York, Michigan, and in the Deep South in Louisiana, Arkansas, South Carolina, Alabama, etc. Their register of predominantly black congregations would reach the total of nearly seventy, to which over fifty mission chapels were attached. The personnel register shows that some five hundred Spiritans served some time in works among the blacks.

Slum clearance in the cities played havoc with black parishes in the 1960s and in addition most blacks favored integration. The Spiritans then gave up most of their parishes, except in areas without other parishes and elsewhere because some blacks felt that, if integrated, they had to lose their identity. Moreover, short of manpower from the 1970s on, the Spiritans decided to withdraw from works where they could be replaced by others and to retain only the most neglected areas.

Regarding black vocations to the priesthood and religious life, the Spiritans began to admit them to the congregation as brothers in the 1880s in Arkansas, but none of these persevered. (Outside the U.S.A., they had begun to ordain blacks in 1843, and continued to do so as a matter of course.) Although they successfully fostered candidates to the priesthood and ordained one in 1907, the difficulty of finding a suitable position for him even in black parishes in the U.S.A. made them postpone new admission to their seminaries until World War II. Early in the 1950s they could ordain three of them.

Present Membership

In 1994 there were a total of over 270 Spiritans belonging to its East and West provinces or working as members of the three Irish Spiritan groups in the U.S.A. that began to be formed in the 1970s.

Koren, Henry J. *The Serpent and the Dove. A History of the Congregation of the Holy Ghost, in the United States, 1745–1984.* Pittsburgh, 1985.

____. *A Spiritan Who Was Who in North America and Trinidad, 1732–1981.* Pittsburgh, 1983.

Ochs, Stephen J. *Desegregating the Altar: the Josephites and the Struggle for Black Priests, 1871–1960.* Baton Rouge, 1990.

HENRY J. KOREN, C.S.SP.

HOLY NAME SOCIETY IN AMERICA

The general purpose of the Holy Name Society is the honor of the name of God. The specific purpose is the public veneration of that name. The satisfactory realization of these two ideals presupposes that many intermediary objectives must be obtained. First among these is the spiritual betterment of the individual members and the reflection of their better spirituality in their personal and social lives.

Origins

In the year 1274 C.E. Pope Gregory X commissioned the Order of Preachers to preach devotion to the Holy Name of Jesus. The Dominican master general at the time, John Garabella or John of Vercelli, accepted the charge from the Holy Father which had been issued in the bull *Nuper in Concilio.* In 1564 Diego of Victoria, a Dominican friar, wrote the first *Constitution* of the Holy Name Society. It was raised to the canonical status of a confraternity with privileges and indulgences which have been expanded in the course of its history.

Beginnings in America

In the United States preaching of reverence to the Holy Name began in 1526 with Fra Antonio de Montesinos, O.P., who came to Florida with a band of three priests and a cooperator brother. The first Holy Name Society was established in 1808 at St. Charles Church, Marion County, Kentucky, by the Rev. Charles Nerinckx, a non-Dominican priest. In his own hand he listed 259 members. In 1868 or 1869 a Holy Name Society was chartered at St. Vincent Ferrer's Church, New York City, a parish staffed by the Dominicans who have responsibility and jurisdic-

tion over the Confraternity of the Holy Name. On May 20, 1877, a charter was issued to St. Patrick's Church in Lowell, Massachusetts.

Charles H. McKenna, founder

The priest generally credited with the major expansion of the society in the early twentieth century was the Dominican preacher, Charles Hyacinth McKenna, O.P. He was stationed at St. Vincent Ferrer's, New York City, in the late nineteenth century. In 1900 he was named spiritual director of the Holy Name Society for the eastern part of the United States. From 1900 until 1915 he traveled extensively establishing parish societies to the Holy Name for men and the Confraternity of the Rosary for women. To facilitate its establishment and spread, Fr. McKenna obtained from Pope Leo XIII a rescript dated May 20, 1896, granting all bishops the power to dispense from the Clementine decree forbidding more than one confraternity of the same kind in the same town or city. Prior to that, the Holy Name Society could only be established at one Dominican parish in a city. As a result of this papal decision the Holy Name Society multiplied by leaps and bounds. At the time of Fr. McKenna's death on May 21, 1917, there were no fewer than 1,734 parish societies in the U.S.A. A large number of these had been founded directly through his own efforts and sermons.

Recent Developments

In view of the great expansion of the Holy Name Society in the early twentieth century and the changes resulting from Vatican Council II with its emphasis upon the role of the laity in the Church, the idea of a national association began to be discussed. After a number of conventions and a series of deliberations, on July 25, 1975, the National Association of the Holy Name Society was incorporated under the laws of the state of Pennsylvania. It was understood by the documents of the foundation that the role of granting charters remained with the Dominicans, but the management of annual conventions and the administration of the details of organization were turned over to laymen. Louis Fink, a major contributor to the formation of the national association, special lay consultant to national headquarters, close associate of Fr. Brendan Larnen, O.P. (the last Dominican national spiritual director), and a writer in the *Holy Name Journal,* was elected the first national president. The *Constitution* was the brainchild of Louis Fink.

The *Constitution* prescribed a five-year term for the episcopal moderator and for the national spiritual director. In 1972 Bishop John L. May of Mobile, Alabama, accepted "with great pleasure" the post of episcopal moderator. In 1978 he was succeeded by Bishop James C. Timlin of Scranton, Pennsylvania. In 1983 he was followed by Bishop Joseph Maguire of Springfield, Massachusetts; then Bishop John Reiss of Trenton, New Jersey, and presently Auxiliary Bishop Michael Saltarelli of Newark, New Jersey.

See also DOMINICANS (O.P.); McKENNA, CHARLES HYACINTH.

Biasiotto, Peter R., O.F.M. *History and Development of Devotion to the Holy Name.* St. Bonaventure, N.Y., 1943.

O'Daniel, V. F., O.P. *Very Rev. Charles Hyacinth McKenna, O.P.* Holy Name Bureau, New York, 1917.

Ripple, Michael J., O.P. *Holy Name Society and Its Great National Convention.* National Holy Name Headquarters, New York, 1925.

GEORGE L. CONCORDIA, O.P.

HOMILETIC AND PASTORAL REVIEW

It all began in 1900. Joseph F. Wagner, founder of the publishing house carrying his name, decided to start a magazine for the Catholic clergy in the U.S.A. He called it the *Homiletic Monthly and Catechist,* the name it carried until it was changed to the present name in 1919.

The first editor until 1916 was Fr. John F. Brady of St. Joseph's Seminary in Dunwoodie, New York. Under his editorship the magazine offered mainly sermons and catechetical materials. He was succeeded by two Dominicans, Frs. John A. McHugh and Charles J. Callan. They changed the name to the *Homiletic and Pastoral Review* because they wanted to do more than just offer sermons. They expanded the scope of *HPR,* adding articles, Church documents, "Questions Answered," and book reviews.

Their tenure was exceptional in the annals of Catholic journalism in the United States. Fr. McHugh had been coeditor for thirty-four years when he died in 1950. Fr. Callan carried on as sole editor until 1957 when he got some help from a regular contributor, Fr. Aidan M. Carr, O.F.M. Conv., who became associate editor in October 1957. Beginning with that issue, Fr. Carr wrote the first editorial to appear and it was placed where it still resides, on the last page before the cover.

Because of declining health, Fr. Callan was able to do less and less, and so in May 1961 Fr. Carr was appointed the new editor and Fr. Callan was listed as "editor emeritus," a position that he held until his death in February 1962. So he was editor for forty-five years.

In 1970 Fr. Carr received permission to leave the Franciscans and join the Trappists in Moncks Corner, South Carolina. The last issue he edited was April 1970. For three months there was no editor until John F. Wagner, president of the company, appointed Msgr. Vincent A. Yzermans of Freeport, Minnesota, to be the editor. He served as editor until March 1971.

Fr. Kenneth Baker, S.J., assumed the editorship in April 1971, a position which he has filled until the present. In format and content, *HPR* has remained substantially the same since 1919. It is the most widely read journal of its type in the English-speaking world.

KENNETH BAKER, S.J.

HORGAN, PAUL (1903–95)

Author, historian, and biographer. Paul George Vincent O'Shaughnessy Horgan, one of the most admired and honored American writers of the twentieth century, was born in Buffalo, New York, the second of three children, of a cultured Catholic family. His father, Edward, was the vice president and treasurer of the family-operated Volksfreund Printing Co. whose managing editor was his father-in-law,

Paul Horgan

Matthias Rohr. The Horgans relocated to New Mexico in 1915 after Paul's father became ill from tuberculosis. Paul was only twelve at the time. The move occasioned his lifelong interest in, and love for, the great Southwest, and his two Pulitzer Prize-winning histories: *Great River: The Rio Grande in North American History* (1955), a veritable epic in two volumes; and *Lamy of Santa Fe: His Life and Times* (1975), which was two decades in the writing and included documentation from rarely consulted Vatican archives.

Growing up in New Mexico, Horgan went to high school in Albuquerque, after which he joined the staff of the *Albuquerque Journal,* where he wrote drama and music reviews. In 1923 he entered the Eastman School of Music in Rochester, New York, to study voice. His lifelong interest in music was epitomized in 1972 with the publications of *Encounters with Stravinsky* about which a music critic of *The New York Times,* Simon Karlensky, wrote: "Combining features of autobiography, memoir, cultural history of the American Southwest, personal confession and musical criticism, the book is an exquisitely literate record of one man's obsession with the music and person of Igor Stravinsky."

Books and Short Stories

Horgan's literary output was as far-ranging as it was prolific. In 1923 he published his first poem, "Exotics." His first short story, "The Head of the House of Wittleman," appeared in *Yale Review* in December 1929. His first book, *Men of Arms,* dates from 1931. The famed short story, *Devil in the Desert,* was issued in 1952. In 1955 he received a Bancroft Prize for *The Saintmakers' Christmas Eve.* His first two novels belong to the 1930s: *The Fault of Angels* (1933) and *No Quarter Given* (1935). The former won the Harper Prize Novel Contest. The latter was apparently one of his two favorite works. The other was *Far from Cibola,* written in twelve consecutive days and issued in 1938. *Great River* was chosen in 1957 as one of 350 books meant to be international "ambassadors" of American culture.

Following the publication of his first novel, Horgan published a book almost every year and a half. His other novels include *The Habit of Empire, The Common Heart, Main Line West, Give Me Possession, A Lamp on the Plains, Memories of the Future, A Distant Trumpet, Everything to Live For,* and *Whitewater.* Additional fiction, including unforgettable short stories, include *The Return of the Weed, Figures in a Landscape, Humble Rivers, One Red Rose for Christmas,* and *Things as They Are.* There was also a piece for children: *Toby and the Nighttime.*

The two Pulitzers were awarded for his historical contributions. But there were other histories and biographies and otherwise nonfictional works: *New Mexico's Own Chronicle, The Centuries of Santa Fe, Rome Eternal, Citizen of New Salem, Conquistadors in North American History, Peter Hurd: A Portrait Sketch from Life, Songs after Lincoln, The Heroic Triad: Essays in the Social Energies of Three Southwestern Cultures, Maurice Baring Restored,* and *Approaches to Writing.*

In 1960 Horgan was enrolled as a Fellow of the Center for Advanced Studies at Wesleyan University, Middletown, Connecticut. Two years later he was designated director. In 1967 he resigned as director to become professor of English and Permanent Author in Residency. It was at Wesleyan that Horgan spent the last decades of his busy life. He died at nearby Middlesex County Hospital on March 8, 1995, and was buried in Buffalo.

At Horgan's funeral Mass, which was celebrated at St. Peter's Church, Higganum, Connecticut, by the pastor and a longtime friend, Fr. Edward M. Konopka, an aged chalice which the author had brought back from the Southwest was used. Horgan had reclaimed a number of old, tarnished silver chalices from antique shops in and around Santa Fe. Fr. Konopka in his homily explained that the author was concerned "that these sacred vessels which had once contained the Blood of Christ would end up collecting dust in commercial shops. He would buy them and save them. . . ." Fr. Konopka made reference to Horgan's beloved short story, *The Devil in the Desert.* He said that he could almost hear Paul Horgan uttering the words of the aged missionary in the short story, namely, "But he brought a lifetime of prayer with him to death's door; and in a little while it entered there with him."

Horgan and Archbishop Lamy

Among the best known of all Horgan's works is *Lamy of Santa Fe.* The central figure is the same person immortalized by the novelist Willa Cather in *Death Comes for the Archbishop.* Willa Cather's classic defies categorization; it is history, but the history is seen through the eyes of a heroic bishop. Through him the reader witnesses the great Southwest take form, a form that has a soul. Paul Horgan's intent was clearly to write a biography of Archbishop Jean Baptist Lamy. His work is clearly history, scholarly history. One of his biographers, Robert Gish, refers to books like *Lamy of Santa Fe* as "history as biography." Yet here, too, one is graced with a vision of faith, the strong faith that inspired the antislavery bishop who defended the rights of the Native Americans and the strong faith of his people in New Mexico, then only recently acquired from Mexico.

Paul Horgan wrote reverently of priests, and of faith, and of those who embraced the faith. And he saw the world he wrote about in terms of redemption and grace. "Horgan's is a powerful moral imagination," wrote philosopher and writer Ralph McInerny in the January 22, 1995, issue of the *National Catholic Register,* "and his characters disturb by their simple verisimilitude and what they tell us about ourselves. But it would be wrong to convey the notion that Horgan's is a world of black pessimism. . . . It is human weakness, our capacity for evil, that makes goodness stand out in all its wonder. . . ."

In his classic, Horgan wrote that, following Archbishop Lamy's death, these words were recorded of him in his native France: "His death was the end of a fine day." Of Paul Horgan, the same could be recorded.

See also CATHOLICS AND AMERICAN LITERATURE.

Gish, Robert. *Paul Horgan.* Boston, 1983.

Homily for the Funeral Mass of Paul Horgan. Reverend Edward M. Konopka, St. Peter's Church, Higganum, Connecticut, March 11, 1995 (unpublished).

Liptak, David Q. "The End of a Fine Day." *The Catholic Transcript.* March 31, 1995.

____. "More Thoughts from Paul Horgan." *The Catholic Transcript.* May 2, 1995.

McInerny, Ralph. "Paul Horgan, Literary Master of the Southwest." *National Catholic Register.* January 22, 1995.

DAVID Q. LIPTAK

HORSTMANN, IGNATIUS FREDERICK (1840–1908)

Third bishop of Cleveland. Ignatius Frederick Horstmann was born on December 16, 1840, in Philadelphia, Pennsylvania. He was the third of ten children born to wealthy merchant John Horstmann and his wife Catherine Weber Horstmann. One of the first seminarians sent from Philadelphia to study at North American College in Rome, Horstmann was ordained there on June 10, 1865.

Ignatius F. Horstmann

Upon his return to Philadelphia he served as both a seminary professor and pastor. Ever interested in scholarship, he edited a book on Catholic doctrine and became president of the American Catholic Historical Society of Philadelphia. In 1855 he became chancellor of the archdiocese.

On December 14, 1891, his appointment as third bishop of Cleveland was announced. He was consecrated bishop on February 25, 1892. Horstmann took over a diocese that was growing rapidly due to immigration from southern and eastern Europe. Providing for the spiritual and in some cases the material needs of the immigrants became a major concern. Recruiting worthy priests, seminarians, and religious from Europe was his constant challenge. The strain of assimilating immigrants coupled with the economic crisis of 1893 caused dissension in several ethnic congregations. A major schism disrupted the large Cleveland Polish congregation of St. Stanislaus.

Aware that Catholics were still victims of anti-immigrant and anti-Catholic prejudice, Horstmann created the Cleveland Apostolate to Non-Catholics modeled on the Paulist method. Horstmann endorsed parochial schools in all parishes. He encouraged the use of English in ethnic parishes, but he did not demand that native languages be dropped. Like many other American bishops, Horstmann was surprised by the controversy generated in France and Rome over the so-called Americanist heresy. He was one of the first American bishops to acknowledge the concern of the Holy See and he composed the official letter accepting the papal criticism on behalf of the bishops of the Cincinnati province.

A heart condition claimed Horstmann's life on May 13, 1908, while he was on a confirmation tour in Canton, Ohio.

See also OHIO, CATHOLIC CHURCH IN; POLISH CATHOLICS IN AMERICA.

Hynes, Michael J. *History of the Diocese of Cleveland: Origins and Growth (1847–1952).* Cleveland, 1953.

Papers of Bishop Ignatius Horstmann, 1892–1908, Archives, Diocese of Cleveland.

CHRISTINE L. KROSEL

HOUSES OF MERCY (MERCY HOMES)

Established in Dublin in 1827, a Mercy Home was envisioned by Venerable Catherine McAuley, founder of the Sisters of Mercy, as a temporary lodging for poor women out of work. In the House of Mercy young women and girls could get religious and vocational instruction. The latter, dependent upon the capabilities of the needy applicant, ranged from the finest of needlework to such basic services as washing and ironing. The Mercy founder considered it better for a woman to assist with her expenses by contributing her work, rather than feel helpless as a mere recipient of charity. Length of stay depended upon one's ability to ready oneself for a position.

This type of shelter proved to be an effective method, especially in port cities in the United States, of assisting large numbers of Irish immigrants in and after the famine years. For instance, upon the arrival of Mother Agnes O'-Connor and her Dublin Mercies in New York in 1846, the sisters immediately opened a job placement office in their convent, where women applied daily for assistance in finding jobs and decent lodgings. In 1848 the Sisters of Mercy moved into a much larger convent and appropriated part of it as their first House of Mercy in New York City. Dormitories were established as well as classes in religion and instruction was given in the practical skills needed to procure a suitable job. News of the assistance available spread so rapidly to new arrivals that over a hundred young women received aid each month. Americans donated to the House of Mercy in New York and elsewhere because they liked the way the individual's talents were polished until she could better her life with her own skills, "pulling herself up by her own bootstraps," as the popular expression went.

Houses of Mercy crossed America just as the Irish Sisters of Mercy did, some going from Pittsburgh to Chicago or New England, others traveling from New York to St. Louis to New Orleans. Before the sisters were a month in the Irish Channel section of New Orleans, they rented a building for a Mercy Home. When their parish convent was completed, the Mercies followed the example of Dublin and New York by sharing a part of the convent as their House of Mercy. Mother Austin Carroll, Mercy leader in the South, soon purchased an adjacent sturdy building, established the job center and industrial training on the first floor, and created the dormitories on the other floors. Basic skills like cooking, washing, and ironing were taught on a limited scale, while most applicants perfected their sewing skills to qualify as seamstresses, couturiers, or milliners. Considerable emphasis was also placed on teaching needlework. While the young women awaited their new positions, they stitched banners for parades and vestments as well as skirts, shirts, and shrouds. This last item was first made for poor fever victims, but a "Mercy shroud" became so popular that producing them in quantity gave the Mercy Home a financial boost.

Nearly all Houses of Mercy or Mercy Homes, North or South, made religious instructions available, encouraged sodalists in spiritual growth, held evening or weekend classes to further education, and repeatedly adapted the curriculum of vocational skills taught to meet the ever-changing job openings. Mercies established social meetings and circulating libraries often to maintain contact with their Mercy Home alumnae long enough to see them settled into the Catholic life of their new parishes. When the needs of the original Houses of Mercy diminished, the buildings served other charitable needs.

See also CARROLL, AUSTIN; SISTERS OF MERCY OF THE AMERICAS (R.S.M.).

Carroll, Mary Austin. *Leaves from the Annals of the Sisters of Mercy.* Vols. 1, 3, 4. New York, 1881-95.

Muldrey, Mary Hermenia, R.S.M. *Abounding in Mercy: Mother Austin Carroll.* New Orleans, 1988.

HERMENIA M. MULDREY, R.S.M.

HOWARD, EDWARD (1877–1983)

Archbishop. Probably the most durable prelate in American Catholic history, Edward Daniel Howard was born on November 5, 1877, in Cresco, Iowa. He attended St. Joseph's College in Dubuque, Iowa, then St. Paul's Seminary in St. Paul, Minnesota, and was ordained by Archbishop John Ireland in 1906. Ireland sent him to teach in the high-school section of St. Joseph's (later Loras) College where he became principal, then dean and president of the college. In 1924 he was named auxiliary bishop of Davenport, and two years later installed as archbishop of Oregon City (now Portland in Oregon).

Howard was a pleasant, outgoing man who made friends easily, enjoyed life, seldom worried (some say he passed problems on to subordinates who did the worrying), and never was ill. He came to Oregon with an extensive educational background (although little pastoral experience) to lead a Church whose basic growth as a pioneering Church had been completed and which was ready to become a modern institution. Howard's administrative ability became a major asset as he began to change his predecessor's basically one-man operation into a complex organization. He put the Church on a firm financial footing by taking control of all borrowing throughout his archdiocese, revived the St. Vincent de Paul Society, and in 1933, during the Great Depression, started Catholic Charities in Oregon.

As archbishop his policy was to permit innovation, cautiously encouraging it as a schoolmaster might with promising students. During the 1930s he encouraged involvement in lay-led Study Clubs and supported efforts to provide for the small Catholic African American community in Portland. He permitted his close associate, Msgr. Thomas Tobin, to encourage lay participation in the Mass, while the Catholic Truth Society in 1934 published the first Mass leaflets for that purpose. As early as 1944 demonstration Masses with the priest facing the people were held in the cathedral, and after the National Liturgical Conference met in Portland, Oregon, in 1947, Howard espoused its recommendation that English be permitted in some parts of the Mass.

After World War II Howard dealt with an upwardly mobile Catholic laity, its dispersal to the suburbs, and the decline of traditional pietistic practices. He also presided over the start of providing services for Catholic refugees who, dislocated by post-World War II events, began to come to western Oregon. In 1966 at the age of eighty-nine he submitted his resignation after Pope Paul VI recommended this action for all bishops over seventy. While he considered his efforts in the field of education to have been his greatest contribution, especially his establishing of an archdiocesan high school for boys, his legacy is much broader than that. He served his archdiocese well for forty years of profound change, from the Great Depression through Vatican Council II.

During most of his nineties he continued to attend functions throughout the archdiocese, remained a popular community figure, and witnessed the installation of two successors. At a televised Mass celebrating his one-hundredth birthday, he gave the sermon in a firm voice, standing erectly and eschewing notes. He died at the age of 105 on January 6, 1983.

Brandt, Patricia, and Lillian A. Pereyra. "History of the Archdiocese of Portland in Oregon." Unpublished manuscript.

LILLIAN A. PEREYRA

HUGHES, ANGELA (1806–66)

Religious superior; younger sister of Archbishop John Hughes. Born Ellen Hughes in County Tyrone, Ireland, in 1806, the daughter of Patrick and Margaret McKenna Hughes, she emigrated to America with her family as a young girl in 1819 and attended St. Joseph's Academy, Emmitsburg, Maryland, from 1823 to 1825. In 1825 she entered the Sisters of Charity in Emmitsburg, taking the name of Sr. Mary Angela, and was professed in 1828. Thereafter she received assignments to Frederick, Maryland; Cincinnati; St. Louis; Utica, New York; and New York City. In St. Louis, from 1833 to 1837, she served at the Mullanphy Hospital, the first Catholic hospital in the United States, which had been established by the Sisters of Charity in 1828.

In 1846, as a result of a dispute with Bishop John Hughes, the Sisters of Charity in New York split into two groups. Of the sixty-two sisters in the diocese, twenty-nine returned to Emmitsburg; the remaining thirty-three sisters (including Angela Hughes) formed a new diocesan community. At the election of the first mother general on December 31, 1846, Bishop Hughes specifically forbade the selection of his sister for the post. Three years later, however, during the cholera epidemic of 1849, she was given the responsibility of establishing St. Vincent's Hospital, the first Catholic hospital in New York City and the eastern seaboard. The original facility was a rented three-story building without running water.

Sr. Angela remained superior of the hospital until December 8, 1855, when she was elected the third mother general of the Sisters of Charity of New York. Among her accomplishments was the purchase in 1857 of the site of the present motherhouse and College of Mt. St. Vincent, a fifty-five-acre tract overlooking the Hudson River in the Riverdale section of the Bronx. After completing two terms as mother general in 1861, Sr. Angela returned to her previous post as superior of St. Vincent's Hospital and served in that capacity until her death in New York City on September 5, 1866.

See also CATHOLIC HEALTH CARE.

Walsh, Marie de Lourdes, S.C. *The Sisters of Charity of New York, 1809–1959.* 3 vols. New York, 1960.
____. *With a Great Heart: The Story of St. Vincent's Hospital and Medical Center.* New York, 1965.

THOMAS J. SHELLEY

HUGHES, JOHN (1797–1864)

First archbishop of New York. John Joseph Hughes was born on April 24, 1797, in Annaloghan, County Tyrone, Ireland. He emigrated to the United States at the age of twenty, arriving in his adopted land in 1817. For three years he lived as a day laborer, constructing bridges, roads, and hiring onto the farms and plantations of Pennsylvania and Maryland. Working at the seminary of French émigré Fr. John Dubois at Emmitsburg, Maryland, he appealed for entry to study for the priesthood. Reluctant to accept the strong-willed young man, Dubois repeatedly put him off. Hughes sought and won help from Mother Elizabeth Seton, whose fledgling religious community was a part of Dubois' establishment. Bowing to her recommendation,

John Hughes

and having tested the laborer's ability to study, Dubois accepted Hughes into Mt. St. Mary's College.

He was a man studying among boys and was used as a farm overseer, a study hall disciplinarian, and, during holidays, as an itinerant fundraiser for the school. Ridiculed by anti-Catholic jibes when he solicited donations in one tavern, he debated with his ridiculers, finally winning from them rounds of applause and a hefty hatful of money. The incident marked for him the surprising self-discovery that he had a natural-born talent for swaying crowds with oratory. It was the beginning of a long career of public battles against nativists who would deny to immigrants an equal share in the civil and religious freedoms promised by the United States Constitution.

Philadelphia Priest

Ordained to the priesthood on October 15, 1826, the same year that John Dubois was called to become bishop of New York, John Hughes was sent to Philadelphia. The city was the scene of strife between the Catholic hierarchy and the lay trustees who had built and maintained their parish churches in a colonial era when anti-Catholic laws forbade ownership and governing rights to the Church's clergy. The squabbles over the borders between lay and clerical authority had become a public scandal. The newly ordained priest, who quickly became celebrated for his gifts as a speaker, avoided the lure of trustees who would have rewarded his giftedness with a comfortable sinecure. Instead, he preached the necessity of absolute hierarchical rule over all aspects of Catholic administration, winning enemies among prominent Catholic laity. He bested them in every confrontation, always preaching over their heads in a demagogic appeal to the common people to side with their clergy.

The 1830s brought a wave of anti-Catholic, anti-immigrant literature before the American public. The best-selling *Awful Disclosures* of the bogus "escaped nun" Maria Monk lent credibility to the bigoted diatribes of Samuel F. B. Morse, Rev. Lyman Beecher, and the collectivity of nativist clergymen who produced *The Protestant Vindicator Against Popery*. While other Catholic clergy remained on the polite defensive, Hughes aggressively counterattacked in numerous letters published in newspapers along the eastern seaboard.

The Rev. John Breckinridge of Princeton Theological Seminary, scion of a patrician family, decided to take the raw immigrant priest to task. He debated with Hughes in a series of newspaper exchanges and then challenged him to an oral debate. Hughes almost declined fearing that he could not reason fine points of theology well enough on his feet. He finally accepted and the series of confrontations began with the aristocratic Breckinridge assuring the packed audience that his priest opponent was "really ig-

norant of what gentlemen owe to one another." Indeed Hughes' oratorical style lacked all the customary flourishes of the day. He spoke intensely and directly and in doing so blasted away at every foolish bigotry Breckinridge introduced. At the end of the debates Breckinridge looked a good deal less aristocratic, and John Hughes was suddenly nationally famous as a spokesman for the Catholic Church and for the immigrant. His name began to appear on lists of prospective bishops sent to Rome by the American hierarchy. Two years after the debates he was named coadjutor bishop of New York.

Bishop in New York

John Dubois, the ordinary of the see, was felled by a stroke two weeks after the arrival of Hughes. He would live on as an invalid until his death on December 20, 1842. Nevertheless, the young and newly consecrated coadjutor (January 7, 1838) immediately assumed command of the diocese, becoming for all practical purposes the bishop of New York from the beginning of 1838. Dubois' dream of recreating another Mt. St. Mary's at Nyack had run aground when the nearly completed main building had burned down. Hughes rejected this site, tried another and finally settled his new college at Fordham. Throughout New York, as he had in Philadelphia, he successfully battled all attempts by lay trustees to control any aspects of the administration of their parishes. While still a coadjutor bishop, he embarked on a whirlwind tour of Europe to solicit money for the mission diocese of New York and, more importantly, to recruit religious personnel for his fast-expanding diocesan institutions.

In 1840 he waded into political waters, joining Governor William Seward in an attempt to gain public moneys to establish schools which would not be offensive to the culture and religion of New York City's immigrants. The city had no public school system. A private system was run by a board of prominent nativist clergymen and politicians. The King James Bible was read daily in classes and Protestant hymns were sung. Textbooks were filled with slurs aimed at Catholicism and the Irish.

Several conflicting bills were introduced in the state legislature to correct or to reinforce this situation. Hughes joined in the fray, attracting huge audiences as he publicly battled any and all opponents from various denominations who dared to take him on. When politicians gave evidence of playing to both sides of the issue, Hughes organized Catholics into a unified political force, urging them on at a large and well-publicized rally at Carroll Hall. In the next election only those candidates who had specifically backed the immigrant Catholic position were returned to office, forcing New York politicians, for the first time, to recognize the clout of the immigrant vote. The Maclay Bill was then passed, providing for a truly public New York City school system run by commissioners of education elected by each district. Hughes then turned the victory into a pyrrhic one. Instead of working with his defeated foes for a viable option of the moment—a pluralistic school system reflecting the cultures and beliefs of all participants—he turned his back on the situation, allowing the public system to become a completely secular institution while he then pushed to build a separate, private Catholic system.

Over the next several years the Bible gradually disappeared from classrooms as each school district voted that public schools should please no one group. Native Americans reacted violently. In 1844, when this movement extended to Philadelphia, riots erupted. While the mild-mannered Bishop Francis Kenrick pleaded for passivity and peace, several of the city's Catholic churches and buildings were burned by mobs. When the fever of riot spread northward to New York, Hughes, in sharp contrast to Kenrick, stationed armed parishioners around his churches, then called upon the mayor and warned him: "If a single Catholic Church is burned in New York, the city will become a second Moscow." No church was burned.

National public leaders began to turn to Hughes as if he were the country's Catholic leader even though this role belonged, *ex officio,* to the archbishop of Baltimore. At the beginning of the Mexican War, the ever-growing numbers of Catholic soldiers serving in the army were still mandated to attend Protestant services; this while they were called upon to invade a Catholic country. Realizing the danger of this situation, President James K. Polk sent a message to Baltimore where the bishops were then at council. He asked to see not Archbishop Samuel Eccleston, but Hughes. At the White House Hughes agreed to supply the government's request for priests who would be, not quite chaplains, but priests present to serve Catholic soldiers. Polk then asked Hughes, again unofficially, to travel to Mexico to assure Catholic leaders that the invasion of their country would not mean a destruction of their churches. Hughes seriously considered, then rejected the offer because of its shadowy, unofficial character. His careful and well-reasoned refusal further enhanced his prestige in official Washington. In 1847 he was invited to address Congress.

First Archbishop of New York

The potato blight in Ireland and the wave of revolutions which swept Europe in the late 1840s brought a tidal wave of immigrants to New York. In 1850 Hughes was made an archbishop with four new sees being created under his metropolitan jurisdiction. He continued in his staunch refusal to accommodate to any kind of lay trustee authority. When the New York State legislature, siding with the stubborn German parishioners of St. Louis Church in Buf-

falo, passed the Putnam Bill which forbade hierarchical ownership of church property, Hughes simply ignored the law, declaring it "more annoying than injurious." Trustees might technically oppose him with civil law, but they would do so in a church building with no priest assigned to them. The law was repealed.

He brooked opposition from no one. He split the Sisters of Charity in his diocese from their motherhouse in Emmitsburg, creating a new community totally under his rule; he bent the Jesuits at Fordham into submission over property disputes, and he acted with guarded suspicion toward Oxford Movement converts to Catholicism such as Isaac Hecker and Orestes Brownson. When nativist mobs threatened the life of a visiting Vatican emissary, Archbishop Gaetano Bedini, Hughes, though gravely ill with a bronchial infection, acted as his shield and took the man on a whirlwind 3,000 mile tour sometimes facing life-threatening riots in stops which included Chicago, Detroit, and Quebec. Determined to make a physical declaration to nativist America that Catholicism had arrived, he broke ground in 1858 at a sight so far north of central Manhattan as to evoke derision, there to build a new St. Patrick's Cathedral on a scale which would rival the great cathedrals of Europe.

As the nation was swept up in the issues which led to Civil War, Hughes opposed abolitionists. He opined that "slavery is the sick man of the United States," and that it should be allowed to die out gradually. Considering the social chaos which might follow immediate emancipation, he wondered: "There are in the Southern states four millions of slaves. Abolish slavery all at once and what is to become of them?"

When the war did come, Secretary of State William Seward prevailed upon his longtime friendship with Hughes to convince him to travel as an unofficial emissary to Catholic France in hope of convincing Napoleon III of the rightness of the Union cause. His trip won him laurels from the general public at home, but cool disapproval within the hierarchy of the Church, especially from Pope Pius IX who, owing to this civil endeavor of Hughes, may well have denied him the long desired red hat as the first American cardinal.

He was already ill in 1863 when, shortly after the battle of Gettysburg, the government initiated a draft for the army. New York City erupted in four days of the worst riots the United States had yet experienced. Hughes dragged himself from his sick bed to plead from his window that the rioters desist. It was his last public appearance; within six months (January 3, 1864) he was dead. He had suffered from Bright's disease for several years. Nonetheless, the riots certainly hastened his end. He had spent his adult life defending the immigrants as the victims of nativists. In this instance they had acted as the aggressors, and the fact that they did so was crushing to his spirit.

Whatever else he may have accomplished in life he had stood for a quarter of a century as the great champion of the immigrant, and it is in this role that he takes his place in American history. Owing to his lifelong flogging of "trusteeism," he can largely be credited, above any other individual in the Church, with having molded American Catholicism into a centralized clerical power structure which was to remain rigidly intact until the time of the Second Vatican Council.

See also NEW YORK, CATHOLIC CHURCH IN.

Cohalan, Florence D. *A Popular History of the Archdiocese of New York.* Yonkers, N.Y.: United States Catholic Historical Society, 1983.

Hassard, John R. G. *Life of John Hughes, First Archbishop of New York.* New York, 1866; repr. New York: Arno Press and the New York Times, 1969.

Kehoe, Lawrence, ed. *Complete Works of the Most Reverend John Hughes: First Archbishop of New York.* 2 vols. New York, 1865.

Shaw, Richard. *Dagger John: The Unquiet Life and Times of Archbishop John Hughes of New York.* New York: Paulist Press, 1977.

RICHARD SHAW

HUMANAE VITAE: ITS RECEPTION IN AMERICA

Before Vatican Council II

The debate over the moral legitimacy of contraceptive intercourse in marriage may be said to have begun in earnest within the American Catholic Church with the publication of Pope Pius XI's encyclical letter, *Casti Connubii* (On Christian Marriage). Issued on the last day of 1930, as a response to the Anglican Church's acceptance of artificial means of birth control at the Lambeth Conference in 1929, Pius XI's letter had acknowledged that there could be good reasons for married couples to defer for a time or even avoid altogether the procreation of children. And he had approved the so-called rhythm method of birth control as a means acceptable in Catholic teaching to that end. To be sure, he had also clearly and vigorously repeated the traditional condemnation of all artificial means of contraception. But the moral difference between the so-named artificial and natural means, both of which had the same intention and sought to realize the same end, was not so clear to everyone. Hence the door was opened for theological questioning and debate.

As technological advances after the Second World War produced new and more effective means of contraception, and the rhythm method proved less than effective, the debate, at least in theological journals like *Theological Studies* and the *American Ecclesiastical Review,* increased in frequency and vigor. The question of moral acceptability had to be put to every newly developed means of controlling births. The emergence of the birth control pill in the early 1960s greatly intensified the debate, for it could now be argued that the pill did not impede the natural function of sexual intercourse by imposing an artificial barrier between egg and sperm, but rather served to regulate and control the female ovulatory cycle.

As Catholic theological opinion began to incline toward the moral acceptability of the pill, hope became more widespread in the American Catholic community that the official teaching of the Church on birth control would change. The ongoing work of the Second Vatican Council, the appointment by Pope John XXIII of a special commission to consider the whole question of birth control, and the reconfirmation and enlargement of the commission by Pope Paul VI, intensified these hopes.

After Vatican II

Before *Humanae vitae* ever saw the light of day, both the Second Vatican Council and the papal birth control commission had finished their work. The council, at the explicit request of Pope Paul VI, had deliberately not taken up the birth control question. But the council's teaching on marriage and family in the landmark document *Gaudium et spes* (The Church in the Modern World), which emphasized the interpersonal love of the couple and the integrity of their sexual relationship even in the absence of children, was to have a major impact on Catholic thought in regard to sexuality. The views of the commission, though its work and report were intended to be private, found their way into the public press. Not only did 80 percent of the commission members argue for a change in Church teaching; but their arguments for the change seemed highly persuasive to many people, professional and lay alike, who read the report. Hence, even before the publication of *Humanae vitae*, American Catholic public opinion was predisposed to a quite different judgment than the one the encyclical would make.

Dissent from the encyclical's insistence "that each and every marriage act must remain open to the transmission of life" (HV 11) was almost instantaneous. The day after the publication of the encyclical (July 29, 1968), eighty-seven American theologians released a signed statement at a press conference held in the Mayflower Hotel in Washington, D.C., objecting to the encyclical on a variety of grounds. This statement quickly gained over six hundred signatures and won the support of well-known European and Canadian theologians such as Bernard Häring and Bernard Lonergan. Catholic lay opinion was reflected in severe criticisms of the encyclical which appeared in publications such as *Commonweal* and the *National Catholic Reporter. The New York Times* (September 1, 1968) reported on a Gallup poll showing 54 percent of American Catholics opposed to the papal view and only 28 percent in agreement. In the years to come polls repeatedly would show between 70 and 80 percent of American Catholics to be in practical disagreement with the teaching of their Church.

The encyclical, of course, had its strong supporters. The United States Catholic Bishops issued a pastoral letter, *Human Life in Our Day*, upholding the teaching of the encyclical in a way that allowed for less equivocation than did similar letters from other national hierarchies. But they made it clear that the teaching was not infallible and that peoples' difficulties with the teaching should be met with compassionate understanding.

Perhaps the most fascinating aspect of the whole controversy was how quickly the debate focused on issues of Church authority over against the authority of personal judgment and conscience. Few arguments worried about the morality of sexual conduct. Almost all took up the question of authority in one form or another, so that for the first time in the American Church papal authority was publicly and vigorously examined and rejected. For most Catholics in the United States *Humanae vitae* was a dead letter and artificial contraception a non-issue. And the American Catholic Bishops as a group did little to enliven the issue.

Pope John Paul II

With the election of Pope John Paul II to the Chair of Peter in 1979, the teaching of *Humanae vitae* was given fresh impetus. Long a vigorous and articulate defender of official Church teaching on sexual conduct, John Paul II frequently included a defense of *Humanae vitae* in his evangelization. In the United States this met with strong approval among self-styled orthodox Catholics who seemed to take one's position in regard to *Humanae vitae* as a litmus test of Catholic orthodoxy. But it made no difference to the actual practice of most American Catholics. It did, in some places, give an impetus to natural family planning, which was essential if the teaching of the Church had any hope of practical implementation.

What *Humanae vitae* represented in the United States was the end of an era in American Catholicism. For good or ill, the authority of the Chair of Peter was no longer received without question, and the whole matter of Catholic identity and loyalty was once again opened up to possible new understandings. As Patricia Byrne, C.S.J., has expressed it, "The question of being a 'good' Catholic is alive again, and progressive and conservative forces in the U.S. have deeply divided answers, and deeply divided ideas about the proper use of papal authority" (325).

See also AMERICAN CATHOLIC SEXUAL ETHICS; CURRAN (CHARLES) CONTROVERSY, THE.

Byrne, Patricia, C.S.J. "American Ultramontanism." *Theological Studies* 56 (2) (June 1995) 301–26.

Curran, Charles E., Robert E. Hunt, and others. *Dissent in and for the Church: Theologians and Humanae Vitae.* New York: Sheed & Ward, 1969.
Pope John Paul II. *Reflections on Humanae Vitae: Conjugal Morality and Spirituality.* Boston: St. Paul Books and Media, 1984.
Shannon, William H. *The Lively Debate: Response to Humanae Vitae.* New York: Sheed & Ward, 1970.
Smith, Janet E. *Humanae Vitae: A Generation Later.* Washington, D.C.: The Catholic University of America Press, 1991.

JAMES P. HANIGAN

HUMMEL, FREDERICK (1884–1978)

Architect. Frederick C. "Fritz" Hummel arrived in the United States from Germany at age five. His devout Catholic family settled in Anacortes, Washington, where his father, Charles F. Hummel, was employed as an architect and house builder. The depressions of 1892 forced the family to look elsewhere for work. They moved to Boise, Idaho, in 1894.

In 1896 Charles Hummel began an architectural practice with John E. Tourtellotte. His son, Fritz, joined the firm in 1909. When he joined, the firm had already established its reputation with the design of the Idaho State Capitol Building and Boise's Cathedral of St. John the Evangelist.

Fritz's career as an architect continued for sixty-seven years. He participated in the design of over one hundred projects for the Diocese of Boise, Idaho, and twelve in the adjacent Diocese of Baker, Oregon. His work with his father and brother, Frank K. Hummel, included the original design or remodeling and additions to virtually all of the churches, rectories, schools, hospitals, and other buildings of the far-flung Diocese of Boise. Fritz worked under the direction of five bishops of Boise from 1909 to 1978. He maintained close friendships with them and rendered considerable uncompensated service to them in studies and evaluations of buildings for insurance purposes, repairs, and alterations.

During his adult life, Fritz Hummel was also active in public service in Idaho and was the recognized leader of the Idaho architectural profession for which he was named a Fellow of the American Institute of Architects in 1961. Fritz died in Boise in 1978. His son, Charles, has carried on Fritz's architectural service to the Catholic Church in Idaho as a member of that same firm that Fritz's father helped to start in 1896.

COLETTE COWMAN

HUNGARIAN CATHOLICS IN AMERICA

Beginning of Hungarian Christianity

Originally, the Magyars or Hungarians came from central Asia. Under the leadership of Árpád, they conquered the whole Carpathian Basin in 896. For the next century their raids and expeditions terrified western Europe.

Due to the resistance of the western European countries and the influence of the surrounding Christianity, the Magyars began to undergo a transformation in mentality and lifestyle. When Árpád's great-grandson, Géza, assumed the reign, he showed more openness toward Christianity.

Géza's son, Vajk, was baptized in 977 and received the name "Stephen." Stephen married Gizella, sister of St. Henry, king of Bavaria, and cousin of Otto III, Holy Roman Emperor. Stephen became the ruler in 997. The grace of God inspired him to organize the Catholic Church in Hungary. Stephen received the royal crown from Pope Sylvester II. He was crowned on Christmas Day in the year 1,000. By this act he established the Hungarian Christian Kingdom. St. Stephen organized, with the blessing of the Pope, three archdioceses: Esztergom, Kalocsa, and Eger; and seven dioceses: Veszprém, Pécs, Győr, Vác, Várad, Gyulafehérvár, and Csanád.

The Benedictine Order brought Christian culture to Hungary. St. Stephen was very thankful for the Benedictines. He established ten monasteries, beginning with Pannonhalma in 996 and followed by Bakonybél, Pécsvárad, Zalavár, Zobor, Marosvar, etc. When Pope Sylvester II heard about the faithful dedication of Stephen's church organization, he said: "I am apostolic, but Stephen is a real apostle." Before his death, St. Stephen offered the Magyars and the Holy Crown into the special patronage of the Blessed Virgin/Our Lady of Hungary. He died on August 15, 1038. He was raised to the sainthood with his son, Emeric, and Gellért, the martyr bishop, in 1083.

Hungarian Emigration to the U.S.A.

After the Hungarian revolt against the Hapsburgs in 1848–49, the first migration of Hungarians to the United States began. Hungarians started to emigrate in greater numbers after the year 1880. In the second part of the nineteenth century, Hungary achieved quite successful economic growth, but it was unable to provide enough jobs for all the people.

The following statistics show how many Hungarians emigrated between 1899–1915 to the U.S.A. They were collected by Julianna Puskás (*Kivándorló Magyrok az Egyesült Államokba 1880–1940,* 460). According to these statistics, 460,498 Hungarians emigrated to the United States between 1899–1915.

Many of these immigrants came with the intention that after four or five years they would have earned enough money and would return to Hungary in order to establish a better existence. The expected money accumulated much more slowly than was expected. The First World War eventually thwarted these plans for return entirely, and many Hungarian immigrants finally decided to remain in the United States.

After World War II many more Hungarians came to the United States because they did not want to live under the Communist regime. Another large emigration of Hungarians came after the revolt of 1956. The total number of Hungarian emigrants was over 1,600,000 from 1848 to 1958.

Hungarians emigrated into different states between 1898–1915: New York, 77,336 (18.8 percent); New Jersey, 61,656 (15 percent); Pennsylvania, 123,216 (29.9 percent); Ohio, 70,302 (17.1 percent); Indiana, 10,054 (2.4 percent); Illinois, 18,446 (4.5 percent); Michigan, 9,368 (2.3 percent); Wisconsin, 4,645 (1.1 percent); Minnesota, 1,050 (0.3 percent); Missouri, 3.199 (0.8 percent); California, 438 (0.1 percent); other states, 31,846 (7.7 percent).

Hungarian Catholic Churches in the U.S.A.

Latin Rite. Hungarian Christianity was already nine hundred years old at the beginning of 1900s. The population of Hungary at that time was about 60 percent Catholic. When Hungarians came to the New World their strong faith and dedication caused them to establish their own churches and schools.

The first Hungarian Catholic priest who came to the United States, Fr. Károly Böhm, wished to organize the Hungarian Catholics into parish communities. Ordained in 1876 in Esztergom by János Cardinal Csrnoch, Fr. Böhm arrived on December 1, 1892, in Cleveland, Ohio.

Bishop Ignatius Horstmann of Cleveland had sent a letter to Cardinal Simor, archbishop primate of Esztergom, with this urgent request: *"Miserere animarum istarum ex tua regione, peribunt omnes sine tuo numine"* ("Have mercy on those souls who are from your region. They will all perish without your help.").

Fr. Böhm organized a meeting of the Hungarian people of Cleveland on December 11, 1892. As a result of this meeting, the people decided to build their own Hungarian Catholic church with St. Elizabeth of Hungary as its patron. Fr. Böhm asked for more priests from the Hungarian bishops. About one hundred priests came between 1893–1914.

Hungarian Catholics built more than sixty churches between 1892–1924. Among the earliest were in: Cleveland, Ohio, 1892, St. Elizabeth of Hungary; Hazelton, Pennsylvania, 1893, St. Ladislaus King; Toledo, Ohio, 1898, St. Stephen King; Bridgeport, Connecticut, 1899, St. Stephen King; McKeesport, Pennsylvania, 1899, St. Stephen King; South Bend, Indiana, 1900, Our Lady of Hungary; New York, New York, 1902, St. Stephen King; Fairport, Ohio, 1902, St. Anthony; Passaic, New Jersey, 1902, St. Stephen King. There were about two hundred Hungarian priests, including those in the religious orders in the 1950s, and about one hundred churches throughout the United States.

The immigrant Hungarians lived together in ethnic neighborhoods. Their spiritual, cultural, and business lives revolved around the church. They built Catholic, Byzantine, Protestant, and Baptist churches quite close to one another. They had their own businesses—grocery stores, bakeries, restaurants, butchers, barbers, tailors, etc. The Hungarian and other ethnic communities started to break up after World War II, when the younger generation moved to the suburbs. The Hungarian community now often travels from the suburbs to attend services at their Hungarian church. Many Hungarian churches now have only English-speaking priests.

Hungarian Byzantine-Rite Churches. Hungarian Greek Catholics lived in the eastern part of Hungary where they comprised about 50 percent of the population. About 50 percent of the Hungarian emigrants were Catholics. Greek Catholics numbered 14 percent. They came in great numbers because the eastern part of Hungary was very poor. The Orthodox comprised 15 percent; Reformed Christians, 17 percent; and other denominations, 4 percent.

Hungarian Greek Catholics made an extra effort to establish their own churches. Due to small numbers, they were under Byzantine-rite Bishops: Byzantine Eparchy of Parma, Ohio; Byzantine Eparchy of Passaic, New Jersey, and Archeparchy of Pittsburgh, Pennsylvania. They established thirteen Hungarian Greek Catholic churches between 1885–1916 in the United States. Among the earliest were in: Bridgeport, Connecticut, 1895, Blessed Trinity; Cleveland, Ohio, 1894, St. John the Baptist; Homestead, Pennsylvania, 1904, St. Elias; Lorain, Ohio, 1903, St. Michael. In later years, more than ten Hungarian Greek Catholic churches were built in different cities.

Hungarian Religious Institutes of Men

The Hungarian Communist Government suppressed the religious orders in 1950. The Benedictine, Piarist, and Franciscan Orders received back two high schools. The rest of the religious were dismissed from the religious community. Many of them tried to find a place in foreign countries, where they could continue their spiritual life and professional career.

Benedictine Monks. The first Hungarian Benedictine priest in the United States, Fr. Egon Jávor, O.S.B., arrived in the 1950s. Several other Benedictine priests came after him and established a house in 1956 at Portola Valley, California. They also organized Woodside Priory School in 1957. Some of them are now teaching at various colleges and universities.

Cistercian Monks. Cistercian priests (O. Cist.) had many high schools before 1950 in Hungary. The first five Cistercian priests came to the United States in the 1950s. In later years more priests joined them. They founded an abbey in Irving, Texas, in 1963. Many of the Cistercian priests teach now at the University of Dallas.

Franciscan Friars. There were two Hungarian Franciscan custodies in the United States: the custody of St. Stephen King and the custody of St. John Capistran.

CUSTODY OF ST. STEPHEN KING. This custody had its roots in the province of St. Stephen King, Transylvania, Romania. Fr. Lőrinc Biró, O.F.M., came from the province in 1920s to the United States. The following years five other friars joined him. Their motherhouse was in Youngstown, Ohio. They ministered to the following Hungarian parishes: Youngstown, Ohio; Fairfield, Connecticut; Barberton, Ohio; Farrel, Ohio; and Portage, Ohio. The friars took over the publication of the weekly newspaper, *Catholic Hungarian's Sunday,* in 1947. Fr. Károly Böhm established this newspaper in 1893 in Cleveland, Ohio. Due to declining numbers, this custody was suppressed by the General Definitorium on December 31, 1992.

The newspaper is still published by laypersons under the name *Hungarian Sunday.*

CUSTODY OF ST. JOHN CAPISTRAN. The members of this custody originally belonged to the province of St. John Capistran, Budapest, Hungary. The first friar of this custody, Fr. Bonaventure Peeri, O.F.M., came to the United States in 1922. He became the pastor of the Church of St. Stephen of Hungary (New York City) in 1922. Several other friars came and took over the care of St. Ladislaus parish, New Brunswick, New Jersey, in 1923, and Holy Assumption parish, Roebling, New Jersey, in 1925. The friars also served at St. Elizabeth Church, Carteret, New Jersey, as well as parishes in Woodbridge and Newark, New Jersey, Milwaukee, Wisconsin, and Flint, Michigan. They established a beautiful retreat house at DeWitt, Michigan, in 1954. Friars established a new Hungarian parish at Winnipeg, Canada, in 1950. They also provided care for Holy Cross Hungarian parish in Detroit, Michigan. St. John Capistran Friary was established in New York City. Again the declining numbers of the custody caused the General Definitorium to suppress it on June 30, 1993.

Jesuits. Jesuit priests emigrated to the New World in the 1950s. Most of the Jesuits went to Canada. Several Jesuit priests came to the United States in order to teach in universities. Five of them taught at Fordham University, Bronx, New York. In recent years many of the Jesuit priests returned to Hungary in order to reestablish the former Jesuit province which was suppressed by the Communist government in 1950.

Hungarian Religious Institutes of Women

Daughters of Divine Redeemer. Fr. Kálmán Kováts (pastor) invited these sisters to McKeesport, Pennsylvania, in

1912. These sisters' professions were teaching in elementary schools, caring for the sick, and serving the poor people. They worked at different Hungarian parishes. They became a province in 1924 and had about one hundred members. The motherhouse is currently in Elizabeth, Pennsylvania.

Daughters of Divine Charity. The sisters were invited to the United States by John Cardinal Farley of New York in 1913. The sisters' professions were teaching in elementary and high schools, providing a shelter for teenage girls, and caring for the poor. The first foundation was in New York City, and the sisters founded St. Joseph province in 1919. The motherhouse is in Staten Island, New York. These sisters have taught at many schools in the Hungarian parishes. They have been very successful in attracting vocations and had about four hundred members in the 1940s. Sisters of the province who worked in the Midwest founded a new province of Holy Trinity in the 1970s in Detroit, Michigan.

Social Mission Sisters. Three Sisters of the Mission Society came in 1922 to St. Margaret parish, Cleveland, Ohio. These sisters were very active in teaching catechism to boys and girls. In the first three years they instructed 1,264 children in the Catholic faith and visited 1,848 families. Their motherhouse in Saginaw, Michigan, was established in 1948. In later years they established a home for aged people in Burton, Pennsylvania.

Sisters of Mercy. The original name of these sisters is Szatmárian Sisters of Mercy (Hungary). They went to China in the 1930s. After the Communist Revolution they were expelled in 1951. When they arrived to the United States, they worked in a hospital in Trenton, New Jersey. They established their own house in 1963 in Hewitt, New Jersey. Two years later they founded the St. Joseph's Home for aged people.

Harkay, Róbert. *St. Stephen of Hungary Church, New York City in 1901–1978.* New York, 1979.

Török, Istvan. *Katolikus Magyarok Észak-Amerikában/Catholic Hungarians in North America.* Youngstown, Ohio, 1978.

DOMINIC L. CSORBA, O.F.M.

HUNTON, GEORGE (1888–1967)

Lawyer and reformer. The executive director of the Catholic Interracial Council of New York (CICNY) was born in New Hampshire on March 24, 1888. After attending Holy Cross College and Fordham Law School, Hunton began his professional career working for the Harlem Legal Aid Society in 1910. After his military service during World War I, Hunton returned to New York City and private legal practice. Hunton's work for the Harlem Legal Aid Soci-

George Hunton

ety made him conscious of the state of race relations in the United States in the early decades of the twentieth century.

In 1931 Hunton accepted a position as the executive director of the Cardinal Gibbons Institute. This educational institution for African Americans in southern Maryland had opened its doors in 1924 through the efforts of Dr. Thomas Wyatt Turner, head of the Federated Colored Catholics (FCC), and Fr. John LaFarge, S.J., a priest working in southern Maryland. Financial difficulties for the school and philosophical differences between Turner and LaFarge in the FCC brought a new direction to Hunton's life. The FCC split into factions, supporting either Turner's approach for African American rights through primarily African American leadership or LaFarge's approach through interracial cooperation. Fr. LaFarge promoted the idea of interracial justice through the work of the Catholic Interracial Council of New York which was founded on May 20, 1934. George Hunton was asked to become the executive director of the new organization and the editor of its magazine, *Interracial Justice.* The object of the CICNY was to promote practical race relations based on Christian principles. For over thirty years, George Hunton dedicated his efforts to these goals.

In the first decade of the council, Hunton worked with LaFarge, an associate editor of *America,* to educate American Catholics about the accomplishments and needs of the African American community. Through contacts with the Catholic Press Association, speaking engagements, discussions with bishops, college courses, and articles in the *Interracial Review,* Hunton promoted the message of interracial justice. He worked with the American Scottsboro

Committee to aid the nine African American men sentenced to death for rape in Alabama. He worked for the passage of federal anti-lynching legislation. When the United States began to produce war materials for Britain, he succeeded in getting African American workers hired in various defense plants. During the war years, Hunton was active in promoting the aims of the Fair Employment Practices Committee in supporting efforts for the passage of fair employment practices legislation. The 1943 Detroit race riot made many leaders aware of the critical state of race relations. On the local level, Hunton developed a plan for the New York City School Board to promote better race relations through school-community councils.

Prior to the war and in the following years, the CICNY cooperated in the efforts of the NAACP to gain civil rights for African Americans. Through his writing and in meetings with cooperative groups, Hunton advocated the legislative strategy being taken by the NAACP under the direction of Thurgood Marshall. The CICNY also supported the labor-organizing efforts of A. Philip Randolph and the Brotherhood of Sleeping Car Porters. In recognition of his efforts and contributions, Hunton was elected to the board of directors of the NAACP in 1955. The concentration on national issues affecting race relations was only part of Hunton's work. He and LaFarge helped to spread the Catholic Interracial Council movement to over twenty cities by 1960.

In 1962 Hunton retired from his position at the council. Over the years, he was recognized for his work in the field of interracial justice. In 1950 he received the *Pro Pontifice et Ecclesia* Medal with three other members of the CICNY. In 1961 the Third Order of St. Francis made him the recipient of their St. Francis Peace Medal. Hunton maintained contact with the CICNY as a consultant until his death on November 11, 1967. Although the whole field of race relations changed dramatically in the 1960s, George Hunton was one of the Catholic pioneers in the area of interracial justice in the twentieth century.

See also CIVIL RIGHTS MOVEMENT AND CATHOLICS, THE; LaFARGE, JOHN.

Hunton, George K. [as told to Gary MacEoin]. *All of Which I Saw, Part of Which I Was.* New York: Doubleday & Company, 1967.
Zielinski, Martin. "'Doing the Truth': The Catholic Interracial Council of New York, 1945–1965." Ph.D. dissertation, The Catholic University of America, 1988.
MARTIN ZIELINSKI

HURBAN, ANNA (1855–1928)

Founder of the First Catholic Slovak Ladies Union. Anna (nee Juriga) Hurban was born around 1855 in Egbell, in the Nitra district in Slovakia, then part of the Hapsburg Empire. Hurban, together with her husband Wendelin and their children, emigrated to Cleveland in the mid-1880s. Like many Slovaks, they settled in the Kinsman-Woodland area of Cleveland, a neighborhood adjacent to a number of mills. There they met Fr. Stephen Furdek, who had begun organizing the Slovaks living near St. Ladislas parish.

Hurban agreed to help Fr. Furdek organize a fraternal society for Slovak immigrant women, who were very vulnerable to impoverishment if the main breadwinner was incapacitated. On January 1, 1892, Hurban and eight other women organized the First Catholic Slovak Ladies Union. They shared the goals of the First Catholic Slovak Union, the men's group, namely, the strengthening of religion in the Slovak community, the establishment of a mutual benefit insurance company, the preservation of Slovak language and culture, and the education of Slovak youth. However, the women emphasized the care of widows and orphans.

Hurban's enthusiasm and organizational skills were evident in the fact that by 1893 the society had grown to 226 members in 16 lodges. When Hurban had the organization incorporated in Ohio on October 18, 1899, it had already grown to eighty-four units in five states. In 1905 the First Catholic Slovak Ladies Union created a junior branch for young people. In 1914 it launched its own newspaper, the *Zenska Jednota*.

Through the years Hurban held various posts as director, vice president, councilor, etc. She was present when 10,000 members gathered in Cleveland to celebrate the thirty-fifth anniversary of the organization. Total membership at that time numbered 65,000 members.

Hurban lived to see her organization endow churches and schools and provide needed support for Slovak religious communities. She died in Cleveland on July 6, 1928, after a brief illness.

See also FIRST CATHOLIC SLOVAK LADIES ASSOCIATION; SLOVAK CATHOLICS IN AMERICA.

Pap, Michael S. *Ethnic Communities of Cleveland.* University Heights, 1973.
Peluse, Martin F. "Archbishop Joseph Schrembs and the Twentieth Century Catholic Church in Cleveland, 1921–1945." Ph.D. dissertation, Kent State University, 1991.
CHRISTINE L. KROSEL

HURLEY, JOSEPH (1894–1967)

Papal diplomat and bishop of St. Augustine. Joseph Patrick Hurley was one of the most publicly outspoken American prelates during the mid-twentieth century, urging U.S. entry into the war against Nazi Germany in mid-1941, scolding "priest-rich" northern dioceses for their failure to send priests to minister to Catholic servicemen in southern

Joseph P. Hurley

training camps during World War II, and voicing relentless attacks against Communist ideology in the years following his service as the Vatican's representative in Yugoslavia in 1945–49. After the war, Bishop Hurley presided over an enormous increase in the number of Catholic communicants and institutions in Florida, where he is remembered with gratitude by the bishops of today's seven Florida dioceses for his provident investments in land for the state's future parishes.

Born in Cleveland, Ohio, on January 21, 1894, Hurley was ordained for the Diocese of Cleveland on May 29, 1919. After eight years in parish work and one year of graduate study at the University of Toulouse, France, in 1927, he was selected by Archbishop Edward A. Mooney, apostolic delegate to India, to be his secretary. In 1931 he moved with Mooney to the apostolic delegation in Japan, and served there as *chargé d'affaires* in 1933–34. In the latter year he was promoted to *addetto* (attaché) in the Papal Secretariat of State, Vatican City, where he oversaw matters relating to the U.S.A. and twice conducted special missions to Germany. In August 1940 he was appointed bishop of the Diocese of St. Augustine, which included all of Florida east of the Apalachicola River in the Panhandle.

Bishop of St. Augustine

Quickly, Hurley became identified as an uncompromising foe of Nazism, which, he argued, was the first enemy of the Church, the killer of its priests, and the despoiler of its temples. Nazism, he held, not Communism, was the country's principal enemy. Expressing these views in a national CBS radio address on July 6, 1941, he called on the country to follow President Franklin D. Roosevelt's lead

in confronting the Nazis militarily. *Time* magazine called him "the most outstanding interventionist in the U.S. hierarchy," but many northern bishops of German and Irish extraction either rebuked him or ignored him.

With victory over the Nazis assured in 1945, Hurley elevated Communism to the position of principal enemy. This conviction was deepened after October 1945, when Pius XII appointed him Regent ad interim at the Apostolic Nunciature in Belgrade, Yugoslavia, the first non-Italian prelate to be raised to the equivalent rank of nuncio. By Vatican count, the communist government of Marshal Josip Broz Tito had already killed 243 priests and imprisoned 169 others. The most noted prisoner in 1946 was Archbishop (later Cardinal) Alojzije Stepinac, of Zagreb, whom the government placed on trial. Hurley attended each day of the mock proceedings as a symbol of protest, and a wire service photograph of him bowing respectfully toward the archbishop was printed around the world. Throughout his term as regent Hurley used his own funds as well as those from the National Catholic Welfare Conference to funnel foodstuffs, clothing, and other supplies through Trieste to persecuted bishops, priests, and nuns in Yugoslavia. He departed Belgrade under awkward circumstances in 1949. Pius XII rewarded him for his service with the title of archbishop *ad personam*.

After his return to St. Augustine, Hurley continued in his energetic, sometimes strident, crusade against communism. He was the only bishop to attend the funeral of Senator Joseph McCarthy of Wisconsin, in 1957. Increasingly, his time was devoted to the burgeoning Catholic population in Florida. From 65,000 Catholics in 1940, the diocese grew to 192,000 Catholics in 1958. During that period the bishop had opened forty-eight new parishes and seventy new schools. In 1958 the southern half of the peninsula was divided off to form the Archdiocese of Miami. The division led to a famous contest over money and land between Hurley and the new ordinary, Coleman F. Carroll, which was resolved in the latter's favor. Though deprived of income from prosperous south Florida, Hurley pressed forward until his death on October 30, 1967, building an additional twenty-four parishes and thirty-three schools.

Typically thought of during his lifetime as conservative, even reactionary, Archbishop Hurley took a number of progressive positions. In 1943 he anticipated the ecumenical movement in an address at the University of Florida when he stated that the time had come "when Christians can lay aside the divisions which rose among them" and pursue "the grave obligation of exemplifying in unity that universal brotherhood of man under God which is the very core of the doctrine of Jesus Christ, the Man-God." In the same year his was one of the few hierarchical voices raised against the Nazis' "pogrom against the Jews." And he surprised many with the speed and thoroughness with which he implemented the Constitution on the Liturgy of Vatican Council II.

McNally, Michael J. *Catholicism in South Florida, 1868–1968.* Gainesville, 1982.
_____. *Catholic Parish Life on Florida's West Coast, 1860–1968.* Privately published by the author, 1996.

MICHAEL GANNON

HURLEY, MICHAEL (ca. 1780–1837)

Augustinian priest. Without Michael Hurley, "the Augustinian dream [in the U.S.A.] would have vanished" (Ennis, *No Easy Road*). Although raised in Philadelphia, he was probably born in Ireland in 1780 or 1781 to an upholsterer. Hurley entered the order in 1797, becoming its first U.S. candidate. Having been ordained to the priesthood in Rome on August 24, 1802, he returned to Philadelphia in September of 1803.

While at St. Peter's in New York from 1805 to 1807, Hurley labored "indefatigably among the victims [of a malignant fever]," petitioned successfully for both state aid to the parish schools and the abolition of the offensive and anti-Catholic oath of allegiance in the New York State Constitution. While there, he met and became a spiritual advisor to Mother Elizabeth Ann Seton.

Returning to St. Augustine's, Philadelphia, in addition to renovating the church, he enhanced the musical life of the city with both sacred and profane concerts, established a short-lived academy, formed a number of church societies, and may have been the author of a spiritual book centered on Augustine and Monica. After Fr. Matthew Carr died, for eight years Fr. Michael Hurley was the sole member of the Augustinian province in the U.S.A. During this time, he found himself embroiled in the Hogan schism at St. Mary's Church as Bishop Henry Conwell's chief representative. Perhaps Hurley's untiring involvement with the victims of an epidemic of Asiatic cholera in 1832 contributed to the onslaught of poor health which began that year and plagued him until his death in 1837.

See also AUGUSTINIANS (O.S.A.).

Ennis, Arthur J., O.S.A. *No Easy Road: The Early Years of the Augustinians in the United States 1796–1874.* New York, 1993.
Gavigan, John J., O.S.A. "Michael Hurley, c. 1780–1837." *Men of Heart.* Vol. 1.

EDWARD J. ENRIGHT, O.S.A.

I

IDAHO, CATHOLIC CHURCH IN

The Diocese of Boise, comprising the entire state of Idaho, is a suffragan see of the Archdiocese of Portland in Oregon.

Early Missionaries

The first Christian contact in the area came from French-Canadian fur trappers and *voyageurs* during the mid-eighteenth and early nineteenth centuries. There is strong evidence that the aboriginal inhabitants of Idaho heard about the Catholic faith from these mostly Catholic "mountain men."

Sometime between 1812 and 1820, a band of nineteen Iroquois migrated from the Mission of Caughnawaga near Sault St. Louis on the St. Lawrence River to Idaho. Their leader was Ignace La Mousse ("Old Ignace"). He and his fellow Iroquois intermarried and became members of the Salish (Flathead) tribe of northern Idaho. Ignace brought with him the rudiments of the Catholic religion and often spoke of the necessity of having "Black Robes" (members of the Society of Jesus) in their midst to show them the way to heaven. Ignace is called the first apostle to Idaho.

The first recorded meeting of Idaho natives with a priest occurred in September of 1831 in St. Louis, Missouri. Members of the Flathead and Nez Perce tribes had journeyed there to procure a priest for Idaho. They were initially unsuccessful, but after three more expeditions over the next decade, they achieved their long-awaited goal. In February of 1840, Fr. Pierre Jean De Smet, S.J., was ap-

pointed by Bishop Joseph Rosati of St. Louis to evangelize the Native Americans of the Rocky Mountains. He arrived in what is now Idaho on July 11, 1840, and celebrated the first recorded Mass in Idaho on July 22 at Henry Lake, near the west end of Yellowstone National Park.

On March 4, 1841, Fr. De Smet was appointed by his Jesuit superior, Fr. Peter Verhaegen of the Missouri vice province, as "Superior of the New Mission in the Rocky Mountains." In 1846, he received another assignment, but by then he had established the foundations of the Catholic Church in what is now Idaho and would later be known as the "Apostle of the Rockies."

The first Catholic Church in Idaho was built in 1843 by Fr. Nicolas Point, S.J., on the St. Joe River, near the present town of St. Maries. Later, because of heavy spring floods, the mission was moved to a new site on the banks of the Coeur d'Alene River. The new church, officially titled Sacred Heart, is popularly known as the Cataldo Mission, named after a much-loved Jesuit missionary. The new building was opened for services in 1853 and is the oldest building still standing in Idaho. It is now part of a state park and is occasionally still used for religious services.

For most of the next twenty years (1840–60), almost the only members of the Catholic Church in Idaho were members of the northern tribes of Native Americans. Numbering about four thousand, they all belonged to the Salishan family and spoke the same language. In 1862 a gold rush began in southern Idaho, especially around Idaho City in an area known as the Boise Basin. Many mining settlements sprang up in this wide basin. The population of the district soon reached the tens of thousands, many of whom had come from the exhausted gold mines of California. Thousands of these miners were Catholics, mostly Irish. Also, at this same period, refugees from the Civil War in the eastern states fled to Idaho, among other places in the West, to escape conscription and the ravages of war.

Vicariate Apostolic

At that time, there were only two Catholic secular priests in southern Idaho: Fr. Toussaint Mesplie, born in France; and Fr. André Poulin, a French-Canadian. Together they built several small frame churches in mining and farming communities across southern Idaho. On March 5, 1863, the territory of Idaho was established. Five years later, on March 3, 1868, Idaho was made a vicariate apostolic. The vicariate consisted of what is now Idaho and the western portions of what are now the states of Montana and Wyoming. The Rev. Louis Aloysius Lootens, born in Belgium, a priest of the Archdiocese of San Francisco, was named first vicar apostolic of Idaho. He was consecrated bishop in St. Mary's Cathedral in San Francisco on August 9, 1868. Archbishop Joseph Sadoc Alemany, O.P., archbishop of San Francisco and former bishop of Monterey in California, was the principal consecrator.

When Lootens arrived in the Idaho Territory, there were five churches in the south and two in the north. Boise City had no church at that time. Mass had first been celebrated there in the cabin of Mr. John O'Farrell in 1863 and continued to be used as such for several years thereafter. The cabin still stands and is the oldest existing building in Boise. The entire population of Idaho was somewhat over twenty thousand persons, half of whom were of European descent, with about six thousand Native Americans and four thousand Chinese. The total Catholic population was about 1,500.

Within a year of his arrival in Idaho, Bishop Lootens was called to Rome to participate in the First Vatican Council of 1870. When he returned from the council, the gold rush that had begun in the 1860s had vanished, leaving ghost towns throughout the territory. With only three secular priests left, a few missions supplied by Jesuits, and a debt he could not pay, Bishop Lootens submitted his resignation to Rome and left Idaho on October 20, 1875. He returned to Victoria in the Diocese of Vancouver Island, where he had been a missionary in his early priesthood. His resignation was accepted on July 16, 1876. He died on January 12, 1898, and was buried on Vancouver Island. On May 30, 1968, on the occasion of the centennial of the vicariate of Boise, his remains were transferred to Boise.

Archbishop Francis Norbert Blanchet of Oregon City (now Portland) was appointed administrator of Idaho on August 22, 1876. He was succeeded in that position on June 18, 1883, by his successor as archbishop, the Most Rev. Charles J. Seghers. A new vicar apostolic of Idaho was appointed on October 7, 1884. He was Fr. Alphonse J. Glorieux, born in Belgium, and then president of St. Michael's College in Portland. All the bishops of the Northwest were at that time in Baltimore, Maryland, attending the Third Plenary Council of Baltimore. Bishop-Elect Glorieux participated in the proceedings of the council and was consecrated bishop on April 19, 1885, by Archbishop (later Cardinal) James J. Gibbons of Baltimore in the Cathedral of the Assumption in that city.

Bishop Glorieux arrived in Idaho on June 12, 1885. By that time, both the vicariate and the territory of Idaho had been restructured to its present boundaries. Bishop Glorieux decided to make Boise City his see city and established the parish church of St. John the Evangelist as his cathedral. On his arrival, the vicariate consisted of one bishop, two secular priests, four Jesuits, and eight nuns. Of the territory's sixty thousand inhabitants, only 3,500 were Catholics. Bishop Glorieux was so short-handed that he petitioned the Holy See for a dispensation to ordain Cyril Van der Donckt nineteen months before he reached the canonically required age of twenty-four. Van der Donckt, ordained on June 24, 1887, was the first priest specifically ordained for Idaho.

Diocese of Boise

Two events greatly increased the population of Idaho during this era: the opening of vast tracts of public lands to settlement and the coming of the railroad. The territory of Idaho became the forty-third state of the Union on July 3, 1890. On August 25, 1893, the silver jubilee year of the vicariate, Boise City was established as a diocese by Pope Leo XIII and Bishop Glorieux was appointed as its first bishop. By this time, there were seven thousand Catholics in the diocese.

Beginning in 1909 and continuing for over a decade, railroad chapel cars of the Catholic Church Extension Society of the United States, crisscrossed the state. These chapel cars brought the sacraments to remote outposts where no permanent parishes had yet been established. They were enormously successful and popular. By the end of World War I, they were no longer required, but the Extension Society continues to provide support in the construction of mission churches and diocesan ministries to the present day.

Bishop Glorieux died in Portland, Oregon, on the anniversary of the establishment of the diocese, August 25, 1917.

On February 6, 1918, Msgr. Daniel Mary Gorman, a priest of the Diocese of Dubuque, Iowa, was appointed second bishop of Boise. He was born in Wyoming, Iowa, and at the time of his appointment was president of Dubuque

College. During his nine years as bishop, he added thirty-two diocesan priests, completed the cathedral in 1921, and doubled the enrollment in parish schools. He died in Lewiston, Iowa, on June 9, 1927.

The third bishop of Boise, Edward J. Kelly, was the first native of the Pacific Northwest to be appointed a bishop. His maternal grandparents had crossed the plains over the Oregon Trail in covered wagons. At the time of his appointment, he was a priest of the Diocese of Baker City, Oregon. He was consecrated in the cathedral of Baker City on March 6, 1928. During his twenty-eight years as bishop, the diocese grew tremendously. He died in Boise on April 21, 1956.

His successor was Bishop James J. Byrne, auxiliary bishop of St. Paul, Minnesota. He was installed in St. John's Cathedral in Boise on August 29, 1956. On March 7, 1962, he was appointed archbishop of Dubuque, Iowa. During his short administration in Boise, the Catholic population of Idaho had risen to over forty-four thousand and he established the diocesan newspaper, now known as the *Idaho Catholic Register*.

The fifth bishop of Boise, Sylvester W. Treinen, a priest of the Diocese of Bismarck, North Dakota, was consecrated in the cathedral of the Holy Spirit in Bismarck on July 25, 1962. He was installed in Boise on August 3 of that year.

Bishop Treinen, like his predecessor, Bishop Lootens, would soon be summoned to Rome to attend an ecumenical council. He was present at three sessions of Vatican Council II and spent the rest of his administration implementing the reforms of the council. Under his leadership, new forms of ministry were begun in Idaho, including the Catholic Education Office, the Idaho Catholic Liturgical Commission, the Search Program, Nazareth Retreat Center, the Catholic Communication Center, and the Student Centers at Idaho's three state universities. Bishop Treinen retired on August 17, 1988, and continues to serve the diocese, especially in retreat work and writing. On April 3, 1989, the sixth bishop of Boise, Msgr. Tod David Brown, a priest of the Diocese of Monterey in California, was ordained and installed as bishop in Boise.

Religious Communities

Seventeen different communities of women religious have served in the diocese. The first to arrive were three Sisters of the Holy Names who opened the first Catholic school in Idaho in December of 1868 in Idaho City. By far the most numerous have been the Benedictine Sisters of St. Gertrude's Monastery in Cottonwood, Idaho, who have been in Idaho since 1908. Among other orders represented have been the Sisters of the Holy Cross, the Sisters of Mercy, the Sisters of St. Joseph of Carondelet, and the Ursuline Sisters.

Fourteen different communities of religious men have served in the diocese. They include the Jesuits, the Salvatorians, the Redemptorists, the Oblates of Mary Immaculate, the Marists, and others. In 1968 the Benedictines established a priory which is now in Jerome, Idaho. Except for the Jesuits and the Benedictines, most of the religious communities have been represented by only a very few numbers.

Since 1966 the Diocese of Boise has staffed a parish in the city of Cali, Colombia, South America. The founder of this mission was Fr. Nicolas E. Walsh, now bishop emeritus of Yakima, Washington. To date, thirteen diocesan priests from Boise have served in the South American Mission. There are now five Colombian priests incardinated and working in Idaho.

Early in this century, many Basque people began immigrating to Idaho, primarily to work in the sheep industry of southern Idaho. There are approximately fifteen thousand persons of Basque heritage now living in Idaho, most of whom are Catholic.

Large numbers of immigrants from Mexico began arriving in Idaho shortly after the Second World War to work in the agricultural industry of southern Idaho. Thousands have settled permanently in Idaho. It is estimated that in the south of Idaho, Hispanics now constitute over half of the Catholic population. The commitment of the Church in Idaho to minister to Hispanics has a high priority in the diocese.

The present population of Idaho is somewhat over one million, of whom approximately ten percent, or 100,000, are Catholic. The Church of Jesus Christ of Latter-Day Saints (Mormons) constitute about one-fourth of the population, centered mostly in the southeastern portion of the state.

Bradley, Cyprian, and Edward J. Kelly. *History of the Diocese of Boise 1863–1952*. Boise, Idaho: Caxton Press, 1953.

Schoenberg, Wilfred P., S.J. *A History of the Catholic Church in the Pacific Northwest 1743–1983*. Washington, D.C.: The Pastoral Press, 1987.

_____. *Paths to the Northwest: A Jesuit History of the Oregon Province*. Chicago: Loyola University Press, 1982.

DONALD D. FRASER

ILLIG, ALVIN ANTHONY (1926–91)

Publisher, Paulist evangelizer. Alvin Anthony Illig was born in Los Angeles, California, on August 17, 1926—one of four sons of Katherina and Joseph Illig. His parents had emigrated to the United States from Germany. His father and brothers became successful contractors whose firm would later sponsor many of Fr. Illig's missionary efforts. Fr. Illig graduated from the Junior Seminary of the Archdiocese of Los Angeles in 1945. He then joined the Paulists and pursued graduate studies at Saint Paul's College, Washington, D.C.

Alvin Illig

In 1953 Alvin Anthony Illig was ordained a priest in New York City by Bishop Fulton J. Sheen. He was assigned to serve St. Paul the Apostle parish and the Paulist Press in New York. He also began part-time studies at New York University and Columbia University in publishing practices, advertising, and graphic arts. This began twenty years of commitment to Catholic publishing. Fr. Illig became managing editor of *Information* magazine in 1955, established a new division of Paulist Press called National Catholic Reading Distributors (NCRD), and launched the Unified Magazine Program. It was the NCRD that convinced thousands of Catholic parishes to offer more than pamphlets in their vestibules. In 1958 Illig played a key role in the merger of the Newman Press of Westminster, Maryland, and its Catholic bookstores in Baltimore, Maryland, and Washington, D.C., with Paulist Press in New York.

In 1959 Illig developed an adult education program for vocations. More than twenty-seven million booklets were distributed in the parishes of forty-seven archdioceses and dioceses, and in the three branches of the armed services. At the end of the Second Vatican Council in 1965, Illig helped launch the American edition of *Concilium,* an international publishing venture involving eight major publishing houses from seven countries.

Illig was recruited by the Catholic Library Association to found a service that would provide parochial schools with professionally selected titles for all ten of the Dewey library classifications. This project was so effective that the American Library Association asked Illig to make it

available to public schools, which Paulist Press did through a separate division called ALESCO (American Library and Education Service Company). At its height, ALESCO's processed library book service captured over ten percent of federal funds for school library work. In 1973 the Paulist Fathers sold this division to DEMCO, a Midwest library company.

In 1970 Illig was elected to a four-year term as a national consultor to the Paulist Fathers. He was reelected in 1974 and 1978.

A New Missionary Assignment

In 1973 Illig embarked on a new priestly career as a Catholic evangelizer among unchurched and inactive Catholics. He started in Pascagoula, Mississippi, with a program called Operation Share, which spread throughout the state. In 1975 Cardinal William Baum of Washington invited Illig to the nation's capital to design and develop new methods of Catholic evangelization. In 1977 Illig founded the Paulist National Catholic Evangelization Association (PNCEA), which continues today to develop evangelization programs and services for dioceses and parishes across the nation. In 1977 Illig was also appointed to the board of directors of the Princeton Religion Research Center, a division of Gallup Poll, Inc., and in that same year he became the first executive director of the National Conference of Catholic Bishop's new Committee on Evangelization.

In 1980 Illig launched his most popular magazine, *Share The Word,* a Catholic Bible study. Across the nation, groups used it and formed welcome settings where unchurched friends and neighbors or inactive Catholics could be invited for prayer and sharing. In 1983 Illig was given the *Pro Ecclesia et Pontifice* Medal by Pope John Paul II. In 1990, a year before he died, Illig used his waning energies to serve on the bishops' committee to develop a national pastoral plan for evangelization. He died on August 2, 1991. To honor him, in 1992 the United States bishops dedicated their statement of national priority, *Go and Make Disciples: A National Plan and Strategy for Catholic Evangelization in the United States,* to the memory of Fr. Alvin A. Illig.

See also CATHOLIC BOOK PUBLISHING IN AMERICA; PAULISTS (C.S.P.).

THOMAS E. COMBER, C.S.P.

ILLINOIS, CATHOLIC CHURCH IN

French Colonial and Early National Period

The story of Catholicism in Illinois begins in 1673 with the French Jesuits. In that year, Jacques Marquette, S.J., left Quebec with the explorer Louis Jolliet on a voyage of discovery down the Mississippi. In 1674 Marquette set up a mission dedicated to the Immaculate Conception among the Kaskaskia, members of the Illinois nation, near present-day Utica. Marquette left after a few days, but two other Jesuits who moved throughout the Great Lakes region continued his work. The first, Claude Jean Allouez, revived the mission in 1677. Pressure from neighboring tribes, notably the Iroquois, forced Allouez and the Kaskaskia to abandon the mission in 1680 and move south. Converts among the Native Americans were few until Jacques Gravier succeeded Allouez in 1689. Marie Rouensa-8cate8a (8 represents the phoneme *ou*), the daughter of the Kaskaskia chief, accepted the faith, setting in motion a number of other conversions, including her father's.

The Kaskaskia settlement, on the east bank of the Mississippi across from St. Louis, became the base of subsequent French economic, military, and religious efforts in the Illinois country. In 1689 Seminary Priests of the Foreign Missions of Quebec established their Mississippi valley headquarters at nearby Cahokia. Quebec's government built a chain of forts in the region to safeguard the fur trade, and soon after, French-Canadians migrated to the area. These *habitants,* who made a living by farming rather than trading fur, transformed the missions. By 1718, *le pays des Illinois,* as the French called the string of settlements, produced such an excess of grain and livestock that it became a breadbasket to the province of Louisiana. Within thirty years, the area boasted three thousand *habitants,* a third of whom were black or Native American slaves. The growing community led an autonomous existence. Distance diminished the power of the bishop of Quebec and left the Jesuits to direct the community's religious and civil affairs.

Le pays des Illinois thrived until the French and Indian War. In 1763 the French ceded their North American holdings to Britain in the Treaty of Paris. In the same year, the suppression of the Jesuits in France halted organized mission work. And the transportation of goods to Louisiana ended when the mouth of the Mississippi fell into hostile Spanish hands. As settlers left, the villages stagnated. A few priests such as Jesuit Sebastian Meurin and Pierre Gibault from the Quebec seminary worked in the area over the next few decades, but they ministered to a dwindling flock.

With the installation of John Carroll as bishop for all United States territory in 1789, administration of Illinois shifted from Quebec to Baltimore. In 1808 Pope Pius VII erected four new dioceses in the United States, including one in Bardstown, Kentucky, which was to direct affairs in Illinois. The size of the territory hampered, however, effective administration. Soon, two dioceses shared responsibility for the Church in Illinois. The western half of the state became part of the St. Louis diocese under Bishop Joseph Rosati in 1826. Eight years later, the Holy See established the Diocese of Vincennes in Indiana, and its bishop, Simon Bruté, assumed control of the eastern half. The few scattered Catholics in Illinois, who still lived in the southwestern corner of the state, had to rely on itinerant missionaries to receive the sacraments.

Nineteenth Century: 1833–1903

Immigration from Europe revived Catholicism in Illinois. Chicago became the focal point of this rebirth. Before the great waves of Europeans arrived, Chicago contained only a handful of Catholics. In 1833, the year Chicago was incorporated as a village, a group of Catholics petitioned Bishop Rosati of St. Louis for a priest. Rosati sent John Mary Irenaeus St. Cyr, a Frenchman. St. Cyr encountered 150 Catholics, most of whom were French, out of a population of 350. In October of that year, he built Chicago's first Catholic church, St. Mary's, a crude box-like structure. Poverty presented the greatest problem for the small flock; indeed, St. Cyr could not say daily Mass for lack of wine and candles. The construction of the Illinois and Michigan Canal in the 1830s and 1840s lured large numbers of Catholics to northern Illinois and changed the complexion of Catholicism there. To minister to the growing number of Irish working on the project, Bishop Bruté dispatched Fr. Timothy O'Meara. O'Meara, well liked by the Irish but not by his bishop, refused to relinquish control of St. Mary's when he was relieved of his charge in 1839. The Irish population rallied to O'Meara's side to challenge episcopal authority. Only the threat of excommunication quashed the incipient rebellion. By this time, the number of inhabitants in Chicago had grown to five thousand. Railroads had begun to converge at the growing town, and lake traffic had increased as Chicago was becoming the locus of the nation's grain, lumber, and livestock trade.

Growth of the state, coupled with the O'Meara affair, convinced the American hierarchy of the need to establish local authority in Illinois. Pope Gregory XVI responded by creating the Diocese of Chicago in 1843 to manage the entire state. William J. Quarter, Chicago's first bishop, faced the near-impossible task of bringing order to the burgeoning Catholic population. Irish men and women, fleeing famine, arrived in droves. Germans also made their way to Chicago and downstate in unprecedented numbers. To complicate matters further, Quarter did not have enough priests to minister to his new charges. To remedy the situation, he established the University of St. Mary's of the Lake as a diocesan seminary and college for young men. As a means of preempting trusteeism, or lay control of parishes, he introduced a bill in the Illinois legislature to incorporate the bishop of Chicago as a "corporation sole." Quarter and his successors would henceforth hold religious property in trust. Quarter negotiated the state's ethnic minefield by setting up parishes on a national basis. In 1846, he built St. Patrick's Church near the Irish settlement on the west side of the Chicago

River. For Germans, who made up a third of Illinois's Catholics, he imported Austrian priests to attend to the downstate population and raised money for the establishment of St. Peter's on Chicago's South Side and St. Joseph's for North Siders.

For the next twenty years, a leadership crisis forestalled stability in the state. Upon Quarter's death in 1848, Chicago's Irish lobbied for the appointment of an Irish successor; downstate German's petitioned for one of their countrymen; and French Catholics sought someone who could at least speak French. Pius IX split the difference by selecting James Oliver van de Velde, a Belgian Jesuit fluent in English, French, and German. But van de Velde ran into problems with his Irish charges when he made impertinent remarks about their drinking habits on St. Patrick's Day. Moreover, he feuded with the Irish priests running the seminary. The pope allowed a disillusioned van de Velde to leave Illinois in 1854. His replacement, Irishman Anthony O'Regan, fared even worse. O'Regan, who had no pastoral experience, angered the French community by appointing an Irishman pastor to the French parish of St. Louis. Administrative shortcomings forced O'Regan's resignation in 1857. Two years later, James Duggan was installed. Unlike his two immediate predecessors, Duggan brought a capacity for administration to his office. He immediately set about institutionalizing his sprawling see by delegating authority and imposing standards for the diocese. Between 1859 and 1869, Duggan founded fourteen additional parishes, including the diocese's first Bohemian and Polish parishes, St. Wenceslaus and St. Stanislaus Kostka. He also turned to religious orders, such as German Redemptorists and Benedictines, to staff national parishes. But the stresses of administering such a large, rancorous diocese proved too much for Duggan. In 1869 he was confined to a sanitarium where he died thirty years later.

Throughout the second half of the nineteenth century, growth in Illinois necessitated the creation of new dioceses. In 1853 the Holy See erected the Diocese of Quincy for southern Illinois. The see remained vacant until 1857 when it was moved to Alton with Henry D. Junker as its ordinary. Eventually, it was relocated to Springfield, the state's capital. Thirty years later, the Diocese of Belleville grew out of Alton to serve Catholics in the southernmost tip of the state. A new diocese was also established for central Illinois in Peoria in 1875. John Lancaster Spalding of Louisville, a chief organizer of The Catholic University of America, was appointed the first shepherd of a flock of 45,000.

The growth of Catholicism in the state—and the nation—also occasioned nativist resentment. In the 1880s with anti-Catholic sentiment on the rise nationally, Illinois nativists targeted the Catholic school system. Between 1880 and 1890, Catholic school enrollment in the state doubled. In 1889, the Republican-controlled Illinois legislature, supported by the Native American Patriotic Union and the Chicago-based American Protection Association, passed the Edwards Law, making English the mandatory language of instruction in Illinois' schools. The legislation caused an uproar in immigrant Catholic communities. To counter nativist propaganda, Catholics founded the *New World,* a weekly newspaper. In addition, they allied themselves with uneasy German Lutherans, and put their weight behind the state's Democratic Party. These efforts led to the repeal of the Edwards Law in 1893.

In 1880 the Holy See designated Chicago as the metropolitan see for the state. Illinois's first archbishop, Patrick Augustine Feehan, faced the difficult test of continuing the institutionalization of the Church while responding to mounting ethnic demands. Although an ardent Irish nationalist, Feehan's first problem arose with the Irish. As he began to rely on American-born clergy to administer the archdiocese, some Irish-born priests rebelled. Most vocal among these dissidents was Fr. Jeremiah Crowley, who paid the price of excommunication for his stubborn resistance to Feehan's plans. Feehan did not, however, attach his name to the Americanization crusade of his colleague in Minnesota, Archbishop John Ireland. His staunch opposition to the Edwards Law won him friends in the German community, but it did not allow him to overcome fears within Chicago's Polonia. In 1895 Fr. Anthony Kozlowski broke from the Church and formed the Independent Polish Catholic Church of America as a bulwark against the pressures of Americanization. Despite ethnic bickering, Feehan managed to accommodate many groups. African Americans had their first church, St. Monica's, staffed by the first black priest in the country, Augustine Tolton. Feehan also established the first Italian parish in the city. The ethnic landscape included Lithuanian, Slovak, Croat, Slovene, and Hungarian churches and schools. At the end of his tenure, the number of both national and territorial, or Irish-dominated, parishes grew to 132.

Twentieth Century: 1903–Present

By 1903 Chicago had developed into the fourth largest archdiocese in the Roman Catholic Church. Under the tutelage of James Quigley, the second archbishop of Chicago, consolidation continued and peace ensued. Quigley turned his attention to more visible institutions. He founded a number of Catholic hospitals, a preparatory seminary, and encouraged the Jesuits to open Loyola University and the Vincentians, DePaul University. Like Feehan, Quigley practiced ethnic accommodation. As the Irish vacated their cold water flats for steam heat apartments, they built new parishes in outlying areas. The Germans, on the other hand, only constructed two new national churches during Quigley's tenure—a testament to their rising socioeconomic status and ability to acculturate. Poles, however, remained as nationalist as ever. As more Poles continued to flood into Chicago, the number of Polish parishes increased from eighteen to thirty-three; and the number of students in Polish parish schools grew to over 21,000. The number of Italians in the archdiocese also swelled. Out of the archdiocese's coffers, Quigley created five Italian parishes in just a few years.

During this time, Illinois's Catholics also responded to the economic and social needs of their communities. Fr. Maurice Dorney of St. Gabriel's parish in Chicago, for example, earned a law degree to help his back-of-the-yards parishioners in their disputes with stock yard bosses. In addition, lay men and women set in motion a Catholic settlement scheme to counter the inroads of Jane Addams' nonsectarian Hull House among the Catholic poor. In 1893 the Chicago Catholic Women's League opened three settlement houses to provide material and spiritual nourishment to the city's poorest. In fact, Illinois provided some of the era's most prominent Catholic reformers. Peter Muldoon became a leading advocate of the rights of workers, first as an auxiliary bishop in Chicago, and then as the first ordinary of the Diocese of Rockford—Chicago's fourth suffragan see created in 1907. Moreover, Bishop Spalding of Peoria in 1902 was selected by President Theodore Roosevelt to arbitrate the nation's first industry-wide strike of coal miners.

By the early twentieth century, Catholics had "come of age" in Illinois. Chicago's Irish Democrats controlled a political patronage machine that would dominate local and state affairs—and at times, national politics—for more than half a century. The organization produced a steady stream of mayors that would reach its apogee with the reign of Richard J. Daley. It is fitting that at this time the archdiocese came under the rule of its first Prince of the Church, and Illinois's version of the "consolidating bishop," George Cardinal Mundelein. Mundelein, a trusted friend of Franklin Delano Roosevelt and Pope Pius XI, put Midwest Catholicism on the map. He transformed the Archdiocese of Chicago from a conglomeration of loosely organized ethnic enclaves into an efficient machine, replete with baronial splendor and national power.

Mundelein arrived in Chicago in 1916 at the age of forty-three with a clear vision of how he would run the archdiocese. The "Dutch Master" systematized and centralized the offices of the archdiocese. He consolidated all of the Church's charitable endeavors under the umbrella of Associated Catholic Charities, standardized the largest Catholic school system in the country, and created the first central bank in any diocese by funneling funds from affluent to poor parishes. Unlike his predecessors, he stressed cultural homogeneity. National parishes felt the effects. Mundelein cut aid from Italian parishes, insisting they pay their own way. As more ethnics left their inner-city na-

tional churches and schools, he converted them into territorial parishes. When Mundelein came to Chicago the archdiocese had more seminarians than any other American see but lacked its own seminary system. He therefore commissioned the erection of Quigley Preparatory Seminary, a grandiose Gothic structure a few blocks from Holy Name Cathedral. For a major seminary, he chose a site fifty miles northwest of downtown Chicago. St. Mary of the Lake, a complex of fourteen buildings in an American Colonial style, rose between 1920 and 1934. Despite a building explosion that included the construction of 250 churches, the archdiocese remained financially sound.

During this time, Chicago became a center for "Catholic Action." Two clergymen epitomize the social and political liberal Catholicism of Mundelein's day. To head his new seminary, Mundelein chose Fr. Reynold Hillenbrand who would go on to found the Young Christian Workers and Young Christian Students. A whole generation of priests, dubbed "Hilly's Men," would make their influence felt in race relations, social welfare, and liturgical reform. Bernard Sheil, the "People's Bishop," launched the Catholic Youth Organization. He also championed workers' rights, spoke out against discrimination in the Church, and countered anti-Semitism in Chicago.

By 1940 the Archdiocese of Chicago boasted 422 parishes ministering to almost 1,500,000, making it the largest diocese in the United States and nearly the world. Catholics represented one third of the population of Cook, Lake, Will, Kankakee, DuPage, and Grundy Counties. With 130,000 elementary school pupils and almost 28,000 high school students, Illinois's metropolitan see directed the largest Catholic school system in the world. In 1943, the Diocese of Joliet was carved out of the Chicago and Peoria sees. The metropolitan see retained jurisdiction over Cook and Lake Counties, the present contours of the archdiocese.

Changing demographics presented the greatest challenge the Church in Illinois faced during the next twenty-five years. Between 1940 and 1965, as growing numbers of whites moved to the suburbs and as African Americans from the South peopled inner-city parishes, Catholics had to reconsider the nature of the urban ministry. Mundelein's successor in Chicago, Samuel Cardinal Stritch, approached the issue with ambivalence. Early in his term, Stritch kept schools segregated despite growing appeals by blacks for admission. He turned a blind eye when some pastors attempted to keep blacks out of their churches and neighborhoods. To his credit, however, Stritch opposed racial exclusion in Catholic hospitals in the archdiocese. He also later reversed field in his school policy. Although he dragged his heels on integration, he promoted proselytization schemes for blacks. Frs. Joseph Richards and Martin "Doc" Farrell won many converts in Chicago's changing neighborhoods by, among other things, proposing church membership for school admission.

Others dealt with discrimination in a more forceful manner. The Diocese of Peoria initiated Project Equality, mandating that the diocese would only do business with companies that practiced equal employment opportunity for minorities. In Chicago, Albert Cardinal Meyer, archbishop from 1958 to 1964 and intellectual leader of the American hierarchy at the Second Vatican Council, pushed for the integration of Chicago's Catholic high schools and would not tolerate the exclusion of black Catholics from parish life. Two of "Hilly's Men," Frs. Daniel Cantwell and John Egan, flourished under these conditions. Cantwell, who formed the National Catholic Conference for Interracial Justice at Loyola University in 1958, coordinated Catholic participation in the civil rights struggle. Egan worked throughout the city to halt housing discrimination against Spanish-speaking Catholics and blacks. In his most memorable bout, he fought the University of Chicago and its plans to displace poor blacks from the areas surrounding the school.

At the end of the Second Vatican Council, the strength and visibility of the Catholic Church in Illinois reached their zenith. Vocations throughout the state had soared during the 1950s and early 1960s. In Chicago, for example, the number of priests had jumped to 3,000, occasioning Meyer to erect another preparatory seminary, Quigley South. Chicago remained the nation's largest diocese with 2,500,000 Catholics and 450 parishes. It also had a parochial school system surpassed only by the public school systems of New York, Los Angeles, and Chicago.

New sets of problems arose in the years after Vatican II. The issue of authority proved the most explosive in Illinois. In 1966 Bishop John Franz of Peoria gave his blessing to the first Priests' Senate in the state and one of the first in the country. Franz and his successor, Edward O'Rourke, advanced a number of the organization's proposals. These included the creation of a Due Process Commission to arbitrate disputes between the bishop and the priests of the diocese. While peace reigned in Peoria, conflict broke out in Chicago. John Cardinal Cody, archbishop from 1965 to 1982, sought to rule the archdiocese much in the way Mundelein had, by centralizing power. But times had changed. In 1966 four hundred clerics formed the Association of Chicago Priests. At first, the loosely structured organization sought to ensure the rights of younger curates and to provide a pension program for priests. Soon it grew into what *Time* magazine called "the closest thing to a priests' union." As it became clear that Cody would not delegate decision-making authority nor consult the clergy—particularly when the issue involved the closing of inner-city parishes—the association radicalized. In 1971 militancy reached a high-water mark when the organization censured Cody for not airing the clergy's views on the issue of celibacy at a conference of American bishops.

In 1994 the Catholic population in Illinois stood at more than 3,500,000, almost a third of the state's total population. By that time, Los Angeles had eclipsed Chicago as the largest archdiocese in the nation. Catholics who numbered 2,300,000 in the archdiocese accounted for 41 percent of all living within its boundaries. Illinois had just over one thousand parishes in 1994, staffed by 3,200 priests. But statewide, only twenty-seven men were ordained in 1995, down from the more than two hundred a year in the 1950s and early 1960s. The number of women religious also dropped. In the Archdiocese of Chicago, for example, almost 10,000 sisters worked in the archdiocese's schools and hospitals in 1965. Thirty years later, that figure had fallen to 3,678.

Avella, Steven. *This Confident Church: Catholic Leadership and Life in Chicago, 1940–1965.* University of Notre Dame Press, 1992.

Briggs, Winstanley. "Le Pays des Illinois." *William and Mary Quarterly* 47 (1990) 30–56.

Dahm, Charles. *Power and Authority in the Catholic Church: Cardinal Cody in Chicago.* University of Notre Dame Press, 1981.

Ekberg, Carl. "Marie Rouensa-8cate8a and the Foundations of French Illinois." *Illinois Historical Journal* 84 (1991) 146–60.

Kantowicz, Edward. *Corporation Sole: Cardinal Mundelein and Chicago Catholicism.* University of Notre Dame Press, 1983.

O'Rourke, Alice. *The Good Work Begun: Centennial History of Peoria Diocese.* Chicago: The Lakeside Press, 1977.

Shanabruch, Charles. *Chicago's Catholics: The Evolution of an American Identity.* University of Notre Dame Press, 1981.

Skerett, Ellen, Edward Kantowicz, and Steven Avella. *Catholicism, Chicago Style.* Chicago: Loyola University Press, 1993.

PATRICK GRIFFIN

Related Document

CONDITIONS IN THE DIOCESE OF CHICAGO, DECEMBER 13, 1849

During the 1840's approximately 700,000 Catholic immigrants entered the United States. Although many of them settled in the eastern states, other thousands made the trek across the mountains into the rapidly developing states of the Middle West where they found work on the canals and railroads, in the rising towns, and on the rich farm lands. It proved practically impossible for the bishops to provide priests, churches, and schools fast enough to accommodate the increase, and since most of the immigrants were very poor the financial aid of the European missionary societies was all the more welcome. The See of Chicago had been erected on November 28, 1843, and embraced the entire state of Illinois (55,947 square miles). James O. Van de Velde, S.J. (1795–1855), the second Bishop of Chicago, was consecrated on February 11, 1849, and ten months later he wrote the following letter to the Society for the Propagation of the Faith after he had completed his first visitation tour. At the time there were 80,000 Catholics in the diocese served by fifty-seven priests.

It is difficult to imagine now that the Archdiocese of Chicago with its nearly two million Catholics was so impoverished as it was a little over a century ago. Yet the condition described was typical of most of the dioceses of the Middle West at the mid-century.

(*Source: Annales de la Propagation de la Foi*, XXII [1850] 313–14.)

SINCE MY CONSECRATION, I HAVE VISITED ALMOST A THIRD of my new diocese. This episcopal journey, which corresponds to twelve hundred French leagues, has revealed to me all the misery of the flock entrusted to my care. You will judge it, Sirs, by this simple picture, whose distressing exactness I have verified with my eyes.

In general, the emigrants who arrive in this country, and who form almost all the Catholic population, are beyond the state of taking care of their particular needs. Poverty is so extensive that there is not one parish, even among the oldest, which has provided the most necessary things for the celebration of the holy liturgy. One priest sometimes has eight churches to take care of, and since for these different stations he possesses only one chalice, one missal, one chasuble, one alb, one altar-stone, he must carry all these things with him wherever he goes, no matter how tiring or how long the journey may be. As for ostensoria and ciboria, these types of articles are almost unknown in this diocese. Until the present time I have seen only three ostensoria and five ciboria in all the parishes which I have visited, over a space of 3,700 English miles. In lieu of these sacred vessels, the Most Holy Sacrament is kept either in a corporal, or in a tin box, or in a porcelein [sic] cup, etc., etc.

After these details, I believe it superfluous to give you a description of my episcopal residence. It is in harmony with the rest. I do not know if it is the most humble in the world, but at least it is certainly not the poorest in America.

(*Source*: John Tracy Ellis, ed. *Documents of American Catholic History*. Vol. 1:1493–1865. Wilmington, Del.: Michael Glazier, 1987, 300–01.)

IMMIGRATION LEGISLATION IN THE UNITED STATES

Since the adoption of the Constitution in 1787, the federal government has enacted numerous laws regarding entrance to the United States. The laws' exact provisions have varied depending on the issues facing the country and the political pressures generated by those issues. Although it has never passed legislation based directly on controlling the immigration of religious groups, such as Catholics, the federal government has responded to wartime emergencies, fears of economic competition, and economic drain, concerns about political radicalism, and racism.

Alien and Sedition Acts

The first important immigration legislation took place in 1797, when the Franco-British naval war threatened to engulf the United States. The Alien and Sedition Acts were designed to tighten security in the event of war. They included: (1) the Alien Enemies Act that permits the deportation of any migrant from a country with which the United States is at war; (2) the Naturalization Act, no longer in force, which set at fourteen years the length of time one had to reside in the United States before becoming a naturalized citizen; and (3) the Alien Act, no longer in force, which permitted the president to deport any foreign-born resident deemed dangerous to the federal government. The Alien Act came with an expiration date, the day after the president's term ended. Thus it gave the president a weapon not only against immigrants but against opposition domestic politicians whom those immigrants might support. The law's transparency and unpopularity contributed to its not being renewed or replaced. Immigrants resident in the United States and even their children, who are citizens by right of birth, have encountered hostility during wartime, but the Alien Enemies Act has remained sufficient for security needs and there has been no successor to the Aliens Act.

Nineteenth Century

Between the Napoleonic Wars' end in 1815 and the Civil War's advent in 1861, the federal government passed few laws regarding immigrants. An 1819 law required the annual enumeration of incoming migrants. An 1854 law prescribed the cubic footage allotted each immigrant aboard an incoming ship. In 1848 the Irish potato famine sent a flood of migrants toward the United States. The lack of federal laws and assistance put the burden of immigrant care on the states to which the migrants first came. Both Boston, Massachusetts, and New York created state boards of commissioners for immigrants. New York set aside Castle Garden, which was located at the tip of Manhattan and which had just finished its usefulness as a concert hall. Immigrants coming into New York via steerage (in which they had no berths in the ship but traveled in the hold, near the ship's steering mechanism, where the freight usually went) passed through Castle Garden, where authorities took statistical data on them. As anti-immigrant nativist political parties gained control in some seaboard states, they endeavored to limit immigrant influence on their states. Massachusetts, for example, had convent inspection laws to insure Catholic women religious did not hold Protestant girls who came to them as students against the girls' wills. As slavery became a more important issue, the anti-immigrant parties and their laws faded.

During the Civil War, Congress passed a contract-labor law which permitted American employers to recruit workers abroad. This law fit several needs at the time. The United States did not have within its labor force the skills, especially in steelmaking, to compete with English, Scotch, and German industries. In fact, all labor was in short supply because the war took so many potential workers to the battlefield. And the employers who wanted the labor were a class that the Republicans, in power in both legislative and executive branches, wanted to attract to their party.

In 1875 the Supreme Court ruled that immigration, as a kind of interstate commerce, was subject to federal legislation only; this put the seaboard states' commissioners of immigration out of business. The same year, the federal government began passing laws about who could and could not enter the United States; its first laws forbade the immigration of prostitutes and convict aliens. It took the federal government some time to take over from the seaboard states the work of processing immigrants. Not until 1891 did the Immigration Service open its reception station on Ellis Island. (It is worth noting that the original building burned, destroying the records gathered at Ellis Island up to that point, and all the records gathered at Castle Garden from its 1851 opening.)

The 1880s saw an increase in migration to the United States, and a shift in the origin of that migration. In the long run, the new immigrants from southern and eastern Europe integrated into the U.S. economy and enriched its culture; there is no denying there were short-term dislocations, which in turn led to legislation to placate affected constituents. In 1882 Congress began to tax incoming immigrants to pay for their processing, and barred certain classes of persons who seemed as though they might require more in services than they might give in capital or labor. It issued a renewed prohibition against convicts and new laws against "lunatics" and "idiots" (both of which had specific meanings in the Gilded Age's understanding of psychology) and also against those likely to become public charges, i.e., to go on welfare. In 1885 Congress reversed its 1864 position and forbade the importation of contract labor: at this point, the employers had a sufficient supply of labor, and Congress now worried about keeping the votes of the working classes, who complained that immigrants depressed wages and took their jobs. The most far-reaching law was the Chinese Exclusion Act of 1882. This was passed in response to the agitation of California's working classes, who argued that the Chinese depressed their wages and opportunities. Although the anti-Chinese legislation seemed to have been promulgated mainly on economic grounds, it marked Congress's first venture into limiting immigration on an ethnic, national, or racial basis.

Twentieth Century

Between the opening of Ellis Island and World War I, Congress continued to pass laws in the established vein, i.e., to exclude particular groups of persons in answer to objections from specific groups of constituents. In 1903 Congress forbade the immigration of anarchists and polygamists. In 1907 it forbade the immigration of tuberculosis patients, unaccompanied minors, a list of persons with physical or mental health conditions, and women being imported for immoral purposes. There was no further racial legislation, although in 1907 President Theodore Roosevelt negotiated with the Japanese government a "Gentleman's Agreement" whereby he pressured California to stop segregating Japanese children in San Francisco public schools, and the Empire of Japan agreed not to send immigrants to the United States.

However, the momentum for legislation that would exclude large groups of persons on the basis of their genetic makeup was growing. Charles Darwin had first alerted people to the importance of animals' inherited traits as predictors for their survival in the wild. Herbert Spencer translated Darwin to the human world by positing a list of supposedly inherited skills which allowed individuals to succeed economically. By the early twentieth century, a body of thought identified inherited skills with racial and national backgrounds. During the early twentieth century, individuals such as Madison Grant, in *The Passing of a Great Race,* claimed that old-stock Americans, with their superior economic-survival skills, would limit their birth rate so as to assure the success of each child, only to find their children outnumbered by immigrants with inferior survival skills, who had a tendency to have more children than they could support.

Since immigrants were also voters, anti-immigrant politicians took roundabout approaches to limiting immigration. Their first attempt came in 1917, when, over President Woodrow Wilson's veto, Congress passed comprehensive immigration legislation. The law (1) codified previous legislation regarding specific groups to be excluded; (2) prohibited Asian migration; and (3) imposed a literacy test. The literacy test required every individual entering the United States who was not fleeing religious persecution (or one member of the family if a whole family was coming), to read a fifty-word essay in the language of the immigrant's choice. Behind the test was the theory that inferior peoples had low literacy rates. By the 1920s, anti-immigrant politicians thought they had enough support to openly bar immigrants on the basis of supposedly natural inferiority. Arguing that in order to maintain the legacy of democratic republicanism inherited from its largely Anglo-Saxon founders the United States needed to maintain an ethnic mix approximating that of the Revolutionary era, anti-immigrant politicians proposed to freeze immigration so that newcomers never exceeded the ratios they represented in the nineteenth-century population. In 1921 Congress enacted legislation that froze America's ethnic mix at the ratios counted in the 1890 census. In

1924 the Johnson-Reed Act froze the ethnic mix at the ratios counted in the 1880 census, before the massive wave of southern and eastern European migration had really begun. Altogether European immigration was not to exceed 153,714 persons per annum, and each nation was to receive a quota, or share of that 153,714 total, based on the percentage of its nationals counted in the 1880 census. A separate piece of legislation reinforced the ban on Asian migration.

Historians have long noted that these laws worked hardships on potential immigrants. For example, as Adolph Hitler began his persecution of the Jews, his victims had one less place of safety to which to flee. The laws also sometimes worked against the best interests of the United States. In 1942, when World War II created a labor shortage, the United States and Mexico worked out the first of many *bracero* programs to encourage transient labor to assist in planting and harvesting U.S. crops; versions of this program continued until 1964. Banning Chinese immigration seemed undiplomatic when China became an ally against the Japanese, and in 1943 Congress repealed that ban. After the war, the racism of the national quota system was not only an unnecessary affront to emerging nations in Asia, Africa, and the Middle East, but it was no longer as important to bar people of particular national groups as it was to bar people of particular political ideologies. In 1946 Congress passed the War Brides Act to permit members of the Armed Forces to bring spouses and children from overseas into the United States, including those from groups excluded on racial grounds. In 1948 it passed a Displaced Persons Act to allow the admission of war refugees above the quota limits. In 1952 the McCarran-Walter Immigration and Naturalization Act recodified the country's immigration law. The major provisions were: (1) keeping the national quota system but repudiating race as a barrier to immigration or naturalization; (2) giving new nations their quotas; (3) prohibiting the immigration of fascists or communists; (4) establishing that for those nations with more potential immigrants than allowed under the quota system, preference would be given to the reunification of families and to the admission of individuals with skills in short supply in the United States.

Less than ten years later, American politicians called for an even more thorough reformation of immigration legislation. The Hart-Celler bill, better known as the Immigration Act of 1965, addressed many of these issues. This law contained the following provisions: (1) abolition of the national quotas; (2) replacement with new quotas of 290,000 migrants per annum, 120,000 from the Western Hemisphere, 170,000 from outside the Western Hemisphere, and no more than 20,000 from any one country outside the Western Hemisphere; (3) reaffirmed the preferences for the reunification of families and the importation of skilled labor.

The Hart-Celler Act paved the way for other changes in world politics and economics which in turn affected U.S. immigration. The 1973 U.S. retreat from Vietnam led to the 1975 reunification of that country under Communist auspices and an outpouring of refugees. Military action in the early 1980s in El Salvador, Guatemala, and Nicaragua generated refugees from those nations, and in the 1990s the refugees began coming from Haiti. In response to the increasing number of refugees, Congress passed a Refugee Act in 1980. The law (1) broadened the previous definition of refugee, which had been limited to those fleeing communism or persons uprooted from newly established Middle Eastern countries; (2) permitted the United States to accept 320,000 immigrants annually; and (3) permitted it to accept an additional 50,000 persons annually if those individuals were refugees.

A changing world economy has led to other changes in American immigration. The 1986 Immigration Reform and Control Act and its 1990 amendment reflected the changing economy. Its major provisions were: (1) in 1986, the law proclaimed amnesty to those who were in the United States illegally; (2) prohibited employers from hiring illegal aliens in the future; and (3) made arrangements for temporary importation of agricultural workers.

By the 1990s new issues had appeared, most of which can be summarized in terms of balancing one concern against another. For example, in the U.S. system of government, the federal government is responsible for immigrants, but providing public services for people is a local responsibility. Therefore, should the federal government subsidize services for immigrants clustered in a particular state or city? Governments which carefully police their residents and patrol their borders still suffer from international terrorist attacks. How then is one to balance U.S. legal traditions against the modern technology of terrorism? These are new questions, but the basic and largest question is an old one: how to respect the rights of human beings *qua* human beings in a world in which most countries protect their own citizens' rights, a situation which tends to marginalize the migrant and refugee?

Dinnerstein, Leonard, and David M. Reimers. *Ethnic Americans: A History of Immigration.* 3rd ed. New York: Harper and Row, 1988.

Higham, John. *Send These to Me: Jews and Other Immigrants in Urban America.* New York: Atheneum, 1975.

____. *Strangers in the Land: Patterns of American Nativism, 1960–1925.* New Brunswick: Trustees of Rutgers College, 1955

Reimers, David M. *Still the Golden Door: The Third World Comes to America.* 2nd ed. New York: Columbia University Press, 1992.

MARY ELIZABETH BROWN

INDIANA, CATHOLIC CHURCH IN

Indiana received its name in 1800 when organized as a territory and its present boundaries with statehood in 1816. But Indiana's Catholic heritage dates from the seventeenth century when explorers, missionaries, and traders criss-crossed the Great Lakes region, then part of France's New World empire. Jesuit explorer Jacques Marquette was probably the first European Catholic to visit the area when he traveled along Lake Michigan's shore in 1675. Robert de la Salle explored the present South Bend area in 1679. His party included three Franciscan Recollects led by Louis Hennepin who said Mass for the first time in the area. Around 1687 Jesuit Claude Allouez established St. Joseph Mission at today's Niles, Michigan, near the Indiana border. Allouez ministered to French soldiers and traders and the area's native inhabitants. In southwestern Indiana, around 1732, François Bissot, Sieur de Vincennes, established a fort on the Wabash River bearing its founder's name that is the state's first permanent European settlement. Vincennes is home to St. Francis Xavier parish, the state's oldest Christian congregation. Jesuits ministered there until their order was suppressed in France in 1763, the year that French North America came under British rule. The bishop of Quebec entrusted the region to diocesan priest Pierre Gibault, who visited Vincennes periodically in the 1770s. During the American Revolution, Gibault defied his distant pro-British bishop by assisting General George Rogers Clark to win over local Catholics to the American cause.

Nineteenth Century

A bishop's care for Indiana Catholics was remote under the Diocese of Baltimore, founded in 1789, but came closer when the area became part of the Diocese of Bardstown, Kentucky, formed in 1808. Catholic activity then advanced as English-stock Catholics from central Kentucky settled southern Indiana's Daviess County in the 1820s. In 1832, Stephen Badin, first priest ordained in the United States, reopened St. Joseph Mission near Niles, Michigan, dormant since 1773, and established a mission near South Bend to minister to northern Indiana's scattered Catholics.

Establishment of the Diocese of Vincennes in 1834 for Indiana, and, until 1843, eastern Illinois, brought to the state the first resident bishop, French-born Simon Bruté de Rémur. After his death in 1839, Bruté's successors, Celestine de la Hailandière (1839–47), John Bazin (1847–48), and Maurice de St. Palais (1849–77), all French natives, and Francis Silas Chatard (1878–1918), a Franco-American, developed Catholic institutional life. Their flock grew as Irish arrived to build railroads and canals, and Germans came to rural areas and urban communities. Bishops recruited religious communities from France, including the Sisters of Providence under Mother Theodore Guérin, who located at St. Mary of the Woods near Terre Haute in 1840 to begin education ministry, and the Congregation of Holy Cross under the Rev. Edward F. Sorin, who established the University of Notre Dame on Badin's property near South Bend in 1842. Nearby, Sisters of the Holy Cross began an academy in 1853 and staffed parish schools. At Indianapolis, Little Sisters of the Poor from France began care to the aged in 1873; and Daughters of Charity from Maryland in 1881 started their first hospital in the state.

For ministry to Germans, the state's largest non-English-speaking immigrant group, bishops recruited German-speaking diocesan priests especially from Alsace. Benedictine monks came from Switzerland in 1854 to establish what is now St. Meinrad Archabbey, Spencer County, to minister to rural Germans, and to conduct a seminary. German women's communities, the Sisters of St. Francis at Oldenburg (1851) and Sisters of St. Benedict at Ferdinand (1867), staffed parish schools.

The Diocese of Fort Wayne, created in 1857 for northern Indiana, attracted German immigrants. Its first bishop, John H. Luers (1858–71), began the diocese's tradition of German ethnic bishops including Joseph Dwenger (1872–93), Joseph Rademacher (1893–1900), and Herman Alerding (1900–24). German ethnic religious communities came to serve the diocese, including the men's Society of the Precious Blood that staffed parishes and St. Joseph's College (1891) at Rensselaer, the Sisters of St. Francis of Perpetual Adoration, first established at Lafayette in 1875 to staff hospitals and schools, and the Ancilla Domini Sisters, arriving at Fort Wayne in 1868 to staff schools.

Twentieth Century

Catholic immigrants were drawn to Indiana in substantial though not massive numbers. By 1890, the state had 140,118 Catholics or 6 percent of the general population of 2,192,404. Catholic growth in the state capital led to changing the name of Indiana's southern diocese from Vincennes to Indianapolis in 1898. By the early twentieth century, cities drew eastern and southern European immigrants to enrich the state's ethnic composition. Northwest Indiana's Lake County, the location of East Chicago, Gary, Hammond, and Whiting, developed Polish, Slovak, Italian, Lithuanian, and Byzantine parishes. South Bend had Polish and Hungarian parishes, while Indianapolis had substantial Italian and Slovene congregations. Later, parishes for African Americans were started in Indianapolis, South Bend, Evansville, and Gary.

Lay activity advanced with formation of the state's first council of Knights of Columbus at Indianapolis (1898). Indiana Knights founded Gibault Home for boys at Terre Haute in 1921. Daughters of Isabella and Catholic Daughters of America began in the early twentieth century their social and charitable work. Lay spirituality developed as

Indianapolis Bishop Joseph Chartrand (1918–33) encouraged frequent reception of Holy Communion.

Indiana Catholic leaders were not influential outside their local communities. An exception is the Rev. John Zahm, C.S.C., of Notre Dame, who wrote *Evolution and Dogma* (1896) to reconcile the theory of evolution with Catholic belief, but ecclesiastical authorities banned his work. Also at Notre Dame, Belgian-born, South Bend-bred Rev. James Nieuwland, C.S.C., developed synthetic rubber during the 1920s at a university becoming nationally known for football prowess and thereby a symbol to American Catholics.

As a religious minority, Indiana Catholics had long endured hostility to their faith. In the 1840s the sensational case of the Rev. Roman Weinzapfel, falsely convicted of rape, then pardoned, attracted national attention. By the early twentieth century, circulation of anti-Catholic publications stirred the Rev. John F. Noll of Huntington to found in 1912 a weekly journal, *Our Sunday Visitor*, to raise Catholics' understanding of their faith. Through his publishing company, Noll gained national influence and was appointed bishop of Fort Wayne in 1925. In the 1920s, the Ku Klux Klan rose to prominence in state politics and local community affairs based on a strong anti-Catholic and antiforeign appeal. Lay editor Joseph P. O'Mahony crusaded against the Klan through his *Indiana Catholic and Record*.

Indiana dioceses were suffragan sees of the Cincinnati ecclesiastical province until 1944, when Indianapolis became an archdiocese with Bishop Joseph E. Ritter promoted to archbishop and metropolitan of the new Indianapolis province. In 1946 Ritter was appointed archbishop of St. Louis and in 1961 a cardinal, becoming the first Indiana native to achieve the latter dignity. His successors at Indianapolis include Archbishops Paul C. Schulte (1946–70), George Biskup (1970–79), Edward T. O'Meara (1980–92), and Daniel M. Buechlein, appointed in 1992.

In 1944 the Indianapolis archdiocese was partitioned to create the Diocese of Evansville in the state's southwestern corner, and the Fort Wayne diocese was reduced in size with the creation of the Diocese of Lafayette-in-Indiana across the state's north central region. The Fort Wayne diocese, divided again in 1957 to form the Diocese of Gary in northwestern Indiana, was renamed the Diocese of Fort Wayne-South Bend in 1960.

Indiana Catholic life has long been marked by strong support of parish schools. In the twentieth century, bishops' policies were directed to founding Catholic high schools. Higher education likewise advanced as several academies and normal schools with nineteenth-century origins became degree-granting liberal arts institutions such as St. Mary of the Woods College, near Terre Haute; St. Mary's College, Notre Dame; St. Joseph's College, Rensselaer; Marian College, Indianapolis; Ancilla Domini College, Donaldson; and St. Francis College, Fort Wayne. Recent Catholic college foundings include Calumet College of St. Joseph, Whiting (1960); and Holy Cross College, South Bend (1966).

After World War II, higher learning advanced especially at the University of Notre Dame as the Rev. Theodore M. Hesburgh, C.S.C., president 1952–87, led the university to greater emphasis on scholarship. The university's influential community of scholars drawn from around the country and world included Indiana native, Rev. Thomas T. McAvoy, C.S.C., historian of American Catholicism. At the Jesuit theologate at West Baden, Indiana-born Rev. John L. McKenzie, S.J., gained national influence as author and leader in the renewal of Catholic biblical scholarship by the 1950s. Since the 1970s, St. Meinrad Seminary, Spencer County, has gained influence as a national school for ministry.

Lay Catholics have been active in the state's political life as mayors, state legislators, and members of the U S. House of Representatives, especially since World War II. It may reflect a minority status that no Catholic has been elected governor or U.S. Senator. In 1990 Indiana Catholics numbered 699,188 or 12 percent of the state's population of 5,544,159.

Alerding, Herman Joseph. *A History of the Catholic Church in the Diocese of Vincennes.* Indianapolis, 1883.

Blanchard, Charles. *History of the Catholic Church in Indiana.* Logansport, Ind., 1898.

Donnelly, Joseph P. *Pierre Gibault, Missionary, 1737–1802.* Chicago: Loyola University Press, 1971.

McAvoy, Thomas Timothy. *The Catholic Church in Indiana.* New York: Columbia University Press, 1940.

McNamara, William. *The Catholic Church on the Northern Indiana Frontier, 1789–1844.* Washington, D.C.: The Catholic University of America Press, 1931.

Schroeder, Mary Carol. *The Catholic Church in the Diocese of Vincennes, 1847–1877.* Washington, D.C.: The Catholic University of America Press, 1946.

JOSEPH M. WHITE

IOWA, CATHOLIC CHURCH IN

Before eastern Iowa was opened for settlement in 1833, few Europeans had visited the area. Among the exceptions were Fr. Jacques Marquette, S.J., and Louis Jolliet, who passed by on their journey down the Mississippi River in 1673. The first permanent European settler was Julien Dubuque, a French-Canadian Catholic, who in the late 1700s started lead mines after concluding treaties with the Native American Fox tribe. In 1832 Jesuit missionary Charles van Quickenborne is known to have baptized children in Keokuk, Iowa. A year later, Dominican missionary Samuel Mazzuchelli began his ministry in the Dubuque area and was responsible for the erection of a stone church dedicated to St. Raphael. At the time Iowa was part of the Diocese of St. Louis, which had been established in 1826.

Diocese of Dubuque

At the Third Provincial Council of Baltimore in 1837, the American bishops petitioned Rome for the erection of a new diocese for the upper Mississippi. Rome responded by establishing on July 28, 1837, the Diocese of Dubuque whose boundaries included all of Iowa, most of Minnesota, and the Dakotas east of the Missouri River. The first bishop was Mathias Loras, a French-born missionary who had been recommended for the post by Bishop Joseph Rosati of St. Louis.

Loras was born in Lyons, France, on August 30, 1792, and was ordained a priest of that diocese on November 12, 1815. In 1829 he left France to work in the Alabama missions of Bishop Michael Portier who appointed him vicar general of the diocese and president of Spring Hill College. In 1832 he resigned both of these offices in order to become an itinerant missionary throughout the state. Five years later Loras became the first bishop of Dubuque and was ordained a bishop in Mobile, Alabama, December 10, 1837, by his friend Portier.

Loras quickly discovered that his large diocese contained one priest (Mazzuchelli), three churches, one parish school, and 2,000 Catholics. Loras immediately departed for France to seek both money and clergy. He returned with two priests, Anthony Pelamourges and Joseph Crétin (who was to become the first bishop of St. Paul), and four subdeacons. At his installation in Dubuque in April 1839, Loras found approximately two hundred Catholics in the city. He traveled extensively throughout his large diocese, purchased land for future parishes, and invited to the diocese priests from the eastern states and from Europe. With the four subdeacons he established a makeshift seminary in his own residence, which evolved into the present-day Loras College and St. Pius X Seminary.

In 1843 the Sisters of Charity of the Blessed Virgin Mary moved from Philadelphia to Iowa where they opened a school for girls. The community was to prosper in Iowa and eventually numbered over 2,000 members. Another religious community was established in the state in 1849, when Trappist monks from Mount Melleray Abbey in County Waterford, Ireland, founded New Melleray Abbey near Dubuque.

In 1850 a new diocese was created in St. Paul with Joseph Crétin as the first bishop. As a result the Diocese of Dubuque was much reduced in size, with the diocesan boundaries now coterminous with those of Iowa (which had been admitted to statehood four years earlier). Although the diocesan boundaries shrank, the size of the Catholic population continued to grow due to the influx of Catholic immigrants from Ireland, Germany, Bohemia,

and Luxembourg. In 1857 Loras asked for a coadjutor, Clement Smyth, the prior of New Melleray. Loras died less than a year later, on February 19, 1858, leaving behind a growing diocese that now contained 48 priests, 60 churches, 40 mission stations, and 54,000 Catholics.

Later Nineteenth and Early Twentieth Centuries

Loras' four immediate successors were either Irish-born or of Irish ancestry: Clement Smyth, O.C.S.O. (1858–65), John Hennessey (1866–1900), John J. Keane (1900–11), and James J. Keane (1911–29). The growth of the Church was especially impressive during the long episcopate of John Hennessey as Iowa was crisscrossed with new railroad lines and large numbers of European Catholic immigrants settled in the state. Hennessey established over one hundred new parishes, encouraged the creation of parochial schools, and brought to Iowa several religious communities of women, including the Sisters of the Visitation, the Sisters of Mercy, the Sisters of the Presentation of the Blessed Virgin Mary, the Sisters of St. Francis of the Holy Family, and the Congregation of the Humility of Mary.

To meet the needs of the growing Catholic population, new dioceses were established in Davenport (1881), Sioux City (1902), and Des Moines (1911). In 1893 Dubuque was made a metropolitan see; since 1945 the province has consisted of the three suffragan Iowa sees.

For many years the Church in Iowa relied on European priests. A score of them came from France, over four hundred from Ireland, over one hundred from Germany, a score from Luxembourg, and some two dozen from the Czech-speaking areas of Europe. At first immigrant priests resided at the cathedral rectory and served outlying areas. Later many had pastoral responsibilities for one or more whole counties, traveling long distances to celebrate Mass and administer the sacraments. John Vahey ranged from Fort Dodge to Sioux City, and John Sheils covered a dozen counties from his home base in Waverly, Iowa.

Later Twentieth Century

One of the most controversial bishops in Iowa history was Francis J. L. Beckman, archbishop of Dubuque from 1930 until 1946. He was an outspoken foe of Russian communism and openly opposed American intervention on the side of the Soviet Union in World War II. A prominent member of the America First movement, Beckman publicly opposed the reelection of President Franklin D. Roosevelt in 1940 to the chagrin of both the Vatican and many American bishops.

Iowa Catholics were better prepared than many other American Catholics for the liturgical changes of Vatican Council II. Since pioneer days both priests and people have been concerned to provide good liturgy, to welcome church musicians, and to encourage lay participation. The liturgical movement came early to Iowa, aided by such groups as the Iowa Catholic Music Educators Association, the Loras Institute of Liturgical Music, the National Liturgical Weeks, and the music departments of various religious communities and Catholic colleges.

The high point of Catholic history in the state of Iowa was the visit in July 1979 of Pope John Paul II, who celebrated an outdoor Mass which attracted 350,000 people, the largest gathering in the history of the state.

In 1995 there were 525 parishes in the four Iowa dioceses, served by 800 priests (756 of them diocesan priests), 210 permanent deacons, 33 brothers, and 1,589 sisters. There were also 15 Catholic hospitals, 6 Catholic universities and colleges, 25 Catholic high schools, 138 Catholic elementary schools, and two diocesan seminaries with a combined total of 25 students. The Catholic population was 509,541 in a total population of 2,770,921. Catholics constituted 18 percent of the state's population, ranging from a high of 23 percent in the Archdiocese of Dubuque to a low of 13 percent in the Diocese of Des Moines.

Ahern, Patrick H. *The Life of John J. Keane, Educator and Archbishop, 1839–1918* Milwaukee, 1954.

Gallagher, Mary K., ed. *Seed/Harvest: A History of the Archdiocese of Dubuque.* Dubuque, 1987.

Hoffman, Mathias M. *Church Founders of the Northwest.* Milwaukee, 1939.

____, ed. *Centennial History of the Archdiocese of Dubuque.* Dubuque, 1938.

The Life of the Most Reverend Clement Smyth, D.D., O.C.S.O., Second Bishop of Dubuque, 1858–1865, Compiled by a Sister of the Visitation, H.M. Peosta, Iowa, 1937.

EDGAR KURT

IRELAND, JOHN (1838–1918)

First archbishop of St. Paul. John Ireland was born in Burnchurch, County Kilkenny, Ireland, on September 11, 1838. Early in 1849 he emigrated with his family first to Montreal and then to Burlington, Vermont, and finally to Minnesota. After elementary education in St. Paul, he was sent to the minor seminary at Meximieux in the Diocese of Belley, France, and studied theology at the Marist seminary at Montbel, near Toulon. He was ordained in St. Paul on December 22, 1861. From June 1862 to March 1863, he served as chaplain to the Fifth Minnesota Volunteers, although in later memory he would recall a period of longer service. Back in St. Paul, he helped organize the Father Matthew Total Abstinence Society, adding temperance to the many causes he would support. In 1869 Bishop Thomas Grace, O.P., named him his procurator for the First Vatican Council.

John Ireland

In 1875 he was named the first vicar apostolic of Nebraska, but, at Grace's request, was immediately appointed coadjutor bishop of St. Paul, where he was consecrated on December 21. He devised a plan with James J. Hill, the railroad magnate, to develop Catholic colonies in the Midwest along the railroad lines. In each of the colonies, he banned saloons. Though the project was not a great success because most immigrants could not afford the initial down payment, it marked Ireland as an innovative leader. In 1884, with Grace's retirement, Ireland became bishop of St. Paul, just in time to attend the Third Plenary Council of Baltimore in the fall, when he emerged as one of the greatest orators and leaders among the hierarchy.

Americanizing the Church

Ireland had a vision for Americanizing the Church. In the process, he alienated most German-Americans and some English-speaking prelates, notably Archbishop Michael A. Corrigan of New York. In 1888 he was named the first archbishop of St. Paul, which freed him from the German-American-dominated province of Milwaukee of which he had been a suffragan and thrust him into national leadership. While in Rome to present his case for the new archdiocese in 1886, he worked with Bishop John J. Keane, rector designate of the new Catholic University of America, and Denis J. O'Connell, the rector of the North American College, in gaining approval of the statutes for the university. The three formed a lifelong friendship, melded by their having to deal simultaneously with the first expressions of a series of issues that would divide the American hierarchy.

First, Fr. Peter Abbelen of Milwaukee traveled to Rome with a petition detailing the grievances of German-Americans. He demanded that national parishes be placed on an equal basis as English-speaking ones, that separate German vicars general be appointed in dioceses with German-speaking populations, and that children of German parents be required to attend national parishes even after reaching their majority. The second issue arose from the failure of the American archbishops unanimously to approve the Knights of Labor, an early labor union, whose case was now referred to Rome. Finally, some bishops, led by Corrigan, had requested the condemnation of the works of Henry George, a social reformer, who had run for mayor of New York. George had the support of Fr. Edward McGlynn, a popular New York priest, who was first suspended from the priesthood and subsequently excommunicated.

With Keane, Ireland drafted a circular letter to the American bishops protesting Abbelen's petition. With O'Connell, he won over Msgr. Eugene Boeglin, editor of the *Moniteur de Rome*, who had written against the Knights of Labor, and whose appointment as agent for the Associated Press they gained. In February 1887 the trio was joined in Rome by James Gibbons, archbishop of Baltimore, who was there to receive his red hat. Gibbons led the successful battle to gain approval of the Knights of Labor and to ward off a condemnation of George. As a member of the Congregation of Propaganda, he attended its meeting that rejected Abbelen's petition, except for the provision that national parishes could be placed on an equal status with territorial ones, an issue on which the American bishops had agreed before Abbelen's trip. But Ireland was emerging as the acknowledged leader of what became known as the liberal party in the American hierarchy.

To promote his Americanizing of the Church, Ireland sought in 1890 to prevent the appointment of Frederick Katzer as archbishop of Milwaukee, the choice of the eligible priests of Milwaukee and the bishops of the province. Shortly thereafter, the ethnic tension in the American Church was intensified by Cahenslyism, named after Peter Paul Cahensly, founder of the St. Raphaelsverein for care of German immigrants to the U.S.A. Branches of the society were founded in other European countries, in Canada, and the U.S.A. In December 1890 the European branches of the society drew up a memorial calling for, among other things, representation of each nationality in the American hierarchy. Cahensly personally took the memorial to Rome. A series of articles then appeared in the Associated Press, datelined Rome, Brussels, and Berlin, claiming that Cahensly was acting as an agent for the German government, which expressed its gratification at Katzer's appointment. O'Connell had written the articles, and Ireland publicly protested this foreign intrusion into the American Church. Cahensly then exacerbated the situation by drafting a further memorial claiming that sixteen million immigrants

or their descendants had been lost to the Church in the U.S.A.

The School Question

But one of the issues for which Ireland is best remembered is his controversial school plan. In 1890 he gave a speech to the National Education Association in which he praised public schools. A year later, he worked out an arrangement with the school boards of Faribault and Stillwater to lease his parochial schools during the school day and supervise the secular education. At the same time, he alienated German-Americans by supporting the Bennett Law in Wisconsin that would require English as the language of instruction in all schools, public and religious. His school plan, however, though not dissimilar to plans in existence elsewhere, notably in Poughkeepsie, New York, now provoked a pamphlet war on the state's right to educate. Late in 1891 Ireland explained his plan at the annual meeting of the archbishops, who did not, as he later claimed, give their consent. To some, it seemed that he was voluntarily surrendering to the state the right of the Church to educate, an issue for which the Church in Europe was then struggling.

As other bishops protested his plan to Rome, Ireland undertook a second journey to Rome in the spring of 1892. He won toleration for his plan *(tolerari potest),* though the controversy continued. Moreover, he and O'Connell agreed that Archbishop Francesco Satolli would come to the U.S.A. to discuss the school situation and especially the education of Catholic children not in parochial schools. Both knew that Satolli would probably remain as a permanent delegate to the American hierarchy. In the meantime, while Ireland was in Rome, Leo XIII called for French Catholics to rally to the Third Republic. In doing so, the pope alluded to the good relations between American Catholics and their republican government. Ireland then traveled to France to speak in behalf of Catholic support for the Third Republic and sent back to Rome glowing reports of his reception. But Ireland failed to understand that the pope was trying to get French support in ending the Roman Question and interpreted the papal action as support for republican government in general.

Apostolic Delegation

Back in the U.S.A., Ireland worked with O'Connell to devise a scheme to introduce Satolli to the U.S.A. without allowing him to fall into the hands of their enemies, especially Corrigan. They arranged for Satolli to be appointed as the papal representative at the opening of the Columbian Exposition in Chicago commemorating the 400th anniversary of Columbus's landing. Since the archbishop came officially as a representative to the government, Ireland had a government cutter meet the ship conveying

Satolli, accompanied by O'Connell as his secretary, to take him to shore. While Ireland kept Corrigan ignorant of these arrangements, on board the cutter were representatives of himself and Gibbons. Corrigan's absence was thus construed as a snub to the papal representative. At the meeting of the archbishops in November, Satolli issued fourteen points on the school questions, drafted for him by O'Connell and basically supporting Ireland. He then asked the prelates for their opinion on the pope appointing a permanent delegate. Ireland alone agreed to the proposal. He then helped arrange for Satolli to reconcile Fr. McGlynn to the Church, without any consultation of Corrigan. In January 1893 Satolli was officially named the first delegate.

With Ireland's encouragement, Keane organized Catholic participation in the World's Parliament of Religions, an early ecumenical gathering held in 1893 in conjunction with the Columbian Exposition. Satolli attended in Ireland's company, but was becoming increasingly wary of Catholics intermingling with Protestants and even non-Christians. Ideologically, he was growing closer to Corrigan and his followers. With Satolli's change in orientation, the papal attitude toward Ireland also changed. Yet, Satolli never lost his admiration for Ireland.

Americanism

Lying behind Ireland's vision of the American Church was the benefit he saw to the Church of the separation of Church and state. In 1895, Pope Leo XIII had challenged this vision in *Longinqua Oceani* in which he stated that the American proposition should not be held as the ideal and be exported to Europe. The apostolic letter signaled a new papal attitude toward Ireland and his friends. Later in 1895 O'Connell was forced to resign from the American College. A year later, Keane submitted his resignation as rector of The Catholic University. In the meantime, Ireland's sermons on republican government had been translated into French by Abbé Félix Klein, professor of literature at the Institut Catholique de Paris. Walter Elliott's *Life of Father Hecker* was then translated into French with Klein writing an introduction and polishing the text. The original biography had a preface by Ireland and the imprimatur of Corrigan and attracted little attention. In France, however, it was transformed into a program for reform, with Hecker seen as the new priest of the marketplace who shunned the cloisters of the past and as the representative of the new republican age of the Church. What had begun as Ireland's program for Americanizing the Church now became known as Americanism and it exploded on the European scene.

Abetted by O'Connell, who continued to reside in Rome, Ireland consciously made overtures to various European intellectuals. In a speech designed to win over German

leaders, he stated that his battle with German-Americans was not against any nationality but only against those who were reactionary. As controversy raged on both sides of the Atlantic, however, war broke out between Spain and the U.S.A. At the last moment, Pope Leo XIII had asked Ireland to intervene with President William McKinley, but to no avail. The American victory over Spain now provided the backdrop for the Pope to appoint a commission to study Americanism. In January 1899, Ireland again traveled to Rome, but this time he arrived too late to prevent the publication of Leo's apostolic letter, *Testem benevolentiae,* condemning Americanism. Ireland, Gibbons, and their supporters denied that the heresy ever existed, but Corrigan and Katzer thanked the pope for extirpating the heresy. Despite Ireland's efforts, Gibbons refused to allow the archbishops at their annual meeting to consider any protest against those who acknowledged the heresy existed.

Although Ireland's Americanizing program has been identified most closely with his opposition to German-Americans, he also opposed Eastern-rite Catholics who brought with them not only a different liturgy, but a married clergy. Ireland tried, unsuccessfully, to have the Holy See make the Latin Rite uniform in the U.S.A. He personally alienated one priest who subsequently entered the Orthodox Church and was responsible for converting many Catholics. In the aftermath of Americanism, however, Ireland agreed to an overture from the Austro-Hungarian emperor to send an official visitor to the American Church to investigate the welfare of Eastern-rite Catholics.

Despite numerous setbacks, Ireland continued to be a national figure. On several occasions his supporters tried, unsuccessfully, to have him made a cardinal. While he acquired a national and international reputation, he also left a lasting mark on his diocese. He founded the St. Paul Seminary, with a donation contributed by James J. Hill, who took total charge of the actual construction, but Ireland still made it a model for clerical education. He also built both the Cathedral of St. Paul, and what he called the procathedral, the Basilica of St. Mary in Minneapolis. The power of his rhetoric and oratory is preserved in *The Church and Modern Society,* a two-volume collection of his sermons and speeches. He died on September 25, 1918.

See also AMERICANISM; CATHOLIC UNIVERSITY OF AMERICA, THE; KNIGHTS OF LABOR.

Ireland, John. *The Church and Modern Society.* 2 vols. St. Paul: Pioneer Press, 1904.

Moynihan, James. *The Life of Archbishop John Ireland.* New York, 1953.

O'Connell, Marvin R. *John Ireland and the American Catholic Church.* St. Paul: Minnesota Historical Society, 1988.

GERALD P. FOGARTY, S.J.

Related Documents

ARCHBISHOP JOHN IRELAND: NO BARRIER AGAINST COLOR

Oration delivered Jan. 1, 1891

"We hold today an anniversary, most glorious in its memories, which it behoves the whole people of America to commemorate and to honor. On the first day of January, in the year of grace, 1863, by proclamation of President Abraham Lincoln, the chains of slavery, in the eye of the law of the land, fell from the limbs of three million or more men, brothers of citizens of America, and citizens of America as their brothers, and their legal emancipation logically and swiftly led to the total and practical blotting out of slavery on American soil.

"Slavery was horrid. We cannot recall it without sorrow and shame. Well may the head of the Catholic Church, Leo XIII, say in a recent letter than 'slavery is opposed to religion and to the dignity of man. . .'

"In the concrete, as practised and defended, slavery was the ownership of the human being, whose manhood was ignored, who was made to be the chattel. And how came it, I could ask in the name of justice, that the unborn child, whose father ever was a freeman, was shorn without his own fault or act, of the right to the free use of the powers of soul and body? Certain stages of civilization, it has been said, rendered slavery a social necessity. Certain stages of barbarism they should be called, and Americans should not have lowered themselves to barbarism.

"Slavery is inhuman. It is unchristian. 'There was scarcely anything,' writes Leo XIII, 'dearer to the Church from the beginning than to see slavery which oppressed so many human beings by its miserable yoke, removed and entirely destroyed.'

"The Christian religion emphasized the brotherhood of man, the value of the soul, charity to the weak and the oppressed. Slavery was the denial of Christian principles and Christian virtues. It was the denial of the freedom of the Gospel, which found access to the soul of the slave, only as the master permitted or ordained. Let us on this emancipation day thank God for the blessings of Christianity. The spirit of Christian freedom is today poured out upon the nations of the earth. The mighty social wave which is now lifting upward upon its crest the masses of the people of all lands is but another manifestation of the same heavenly spirit.

"Let us do our full duty. There is work for us. I have said that slavery has been abolished in America; the trail of the serpent, however, still marks the ground. We do not accord to our black brothers all the rights and privileges of freedom and of a common humanity. They are the victims of an unreasoning and unjustifiable ostracism. They may live, provided they live away from us, as a separate and inferior race, with whom close contact is pollution. It looks as if we had grudgingly granted them emancipation, as if we fain still would be the masters, and hold them in servitude.

"What do I claim for the black man? That which I claim for the white man, neither more nor less. I would blot out the color line. White men have their estrangements. They separate on lines of wealth, or intelligence, of culture, of ancestry . . . But let there be no barrier against mere color.

"Why a barrier of this kind? Where can we find a reason for it? Not in color. Color is the merest accident in man, the result of climatic changes. The colors of the human skin are of many different kinds, the shadings of the so-called white race are not easily numbered. Why visit with the ire of our exclusive pride the black, even into its lightest shadings, scarcely discernible to the eye from the olive dark, a shading most admired in the white family of nations?

"Not in race. Men are all of the same race, sprung from the one father and the one mother. Ethnology and Holy Writ give the same testimony. The subdivisions of race are but the accidental deviations from the parent stock, which revert to the same model as easily with the length of years as they diverted from it. The notion that God by special interposition marked off the subdivisions of the human family, and set upon each one an indelible seal of permanence is the dream of ignorance or bigotry.

"The objection is made that Negroes are of inferior intellectual part to the whites. I reply, that there are white men inferior on those lines to other white men, and still no wall of separation is built up by the latter against the former. Treat Negroes who are intellectually inferior to us, as we treat inferior whites, and I shall not complain. And as to a radical inferiority in the Negro as compared to his white brother, we can afford to deny it, in the presence of his achievements in the short years which have elapsed since restitution was made to him of his freedom, and any inferiority which exists, we may attribute to his unfortunate condition of long centuries whether in America, or his native Africa.

"We are the victims of foolish prejudice, and the sooner we free ourselves from it, the sooner shall we grow to true manhood. Is it to our honor that we persecute men because of the social conditions of their fathers? It is not so long ago since the proudest peoples of Europe were immersed in barbarism. It is not to our honor that we punish men for the satisfaction of our own pride. Why, the fact that the Negro was once our slave should compel us to treat him with liberality extraordinary, to compensate him if possible for wrong done, and obliterate in mutual forebearance and favor the sad memories of years gone by.

"The Negro problem is upon us, and there is no solution for it, peaceful and permanent, than to grant to our fellow citizens practical and effective equality with white citizens. It is not possible to keep up a wall of separation between whites and blacks, and the attempt to do this is a declaration of continuous war. Simple common sense dictates the solution. The Negroes are among us to the number of eight millions; they will here remain: we must accept the situation and abide by the consequences, whatever pride or taste may dictate.

"I would break down all barriers. Let the Negro be our equal before the law. There are States where the violation in the Negro of the most sacred personal right secured impunity before the law. In many states the law forbids marriage between white and black—in this manner fomenting immorality and putting injury no less upon the white whom it pretends to elevate as upon the black for whose degredation it has no care.

"Let the Negro be our equal in the enjoyment of all the political rights of the citizen. The Constitution grants him those rights: let us be loyal to the Constitution. If the education of the Negro does not fit him to be a voter, and an office holder, let us for his sake and our own, hurry to enlighten him.

"I would open to the Negro all industrial and professional avenues—the test for his advance being his ability, but never his color. I would in all public gatherings, and in all public resorts, in halls and hotels, treat the black man as I treat the white. I might shun the vulgar man, whatever his color, but the gentleman, whatever his color, I would not dare push away from me.

"Shall the homes of the whites be opened to the blacks, shall all meet in the parlor in perfect social equality? My answer is, that one's home is one's castle, the privileged place where each one follows his own likes and his own tastes, and no one, white or black, rich or poor, can pass the door without an invitation from the owner, and no one can pass censure upon the owner's act.

"I claim the right I grant to others—and my door is open to men of all colors, and no one should blame me. Social equality is a matter of taste; the granting of it largely depends on our elevation above the prejudice, and the identification of minds and hearts with the precepts and the counsels of the Gospel."

(*Source*: Joseph N. Moody, ed. *Church and Society: Catholic Social and Political Thought and Movements, 1789–1950*. New York: Arts, Inc., 1953, 887–89.)

ARCHBISHOP IRELAND'S VIEWS ON SOCIALISM, OCTOBER 14, 1894

By the 1890's the advance of socialism had become the cause of serious concern to many men in both Europe and the United States. This concern was heightened by the bloody Homestead Strike of 1892 and the turbulent year 1894 which saw the huge strikes of the Pullman Company and the western railroads and the march of Coxey's Army of unemployed on Washington. No American bishop was more alive to the necessity of finding cor-

rect solutions to social problems than John Ireland, first Archbishop of St. Paul (1838–1918). In the summer of 1892 Ireland had attracted national attention in France by a series of addresses, and it was not surprising, therefore, that Jules Huret, dean of the Paris correspondents, should seek an interview with him which was published in *Le Figaro* on August 29, 1894. The following reprint of the interview embodied a number of ideas which Ireland later expanded and published from his lectures in the two-volume work, *The Church and Modern Society* (St. Paul, 1905). The archbishop was a friend of the laboring man, as his strong support to Cardinal Gibbons in 1887 in the case of the Knights of Labor made evident. But he was not an uncritical admirer as he made clear in the interview he gave to the press in July of this same year when violence broke out among the strikers in Chicago.

(*Source*: *New York Times*, October 14, 1894.)

THE INTERVIEWER LAUREATE OF THE PARIS PRESS, JULES Huret[1] reports in *Le Figaro*[2] the following conversation with Archbishop Ireland:

Q.—What do you think of the Socialist predictions? Do you believe that transformations in social organizations are imminent?

A.—The transformations predicted by the Socialists seem to me to be neither imminent nor probable. What is probable, what I desire to realize as soon as possible is improvement in the condition of the mass of working men, their elevation from an intellectual and moral point of view, as much as from a material point of view. This improvement and this elevation shall have as consequences the advent of democracy and the disappearance of what is called, in Europe, the reign of the bourgeoisie. This will be accomplished without much resistance. As was said to me by a Belgian statesman, Minister Northamb:[3] "In our days, more than ever, nobody remains immovable. Some turn to reaction, others to democracy."

Observe that true democracy does not exclude, but, on the contrary, presupposes social influences. There shall always be in society men of genius, men of talent, and men of elevated character, and these men will always exert influence. A society where social influences are weak, where natural legitimate influences are replaced by others, is a society in an abnormal state. It was a great mistake of writers in France to write of directing classes. The expression is unfortunate; there are no directing classes, but there are, and there always will be, directing men.

I do not believe that there will be an extreme condensation of capital in the future. I think, on the contrary, that money shall be more generally distributed, that the workingmen shall be better paid, and, consequently, shall have more instruction. Notice what Leo XIII[4] says of diffusion of property, while talking of capital. Doubtless there shall always be great fortunes, but great fortunes are an evil only when they have been acquired by fraud and injustice, and, moreover, they are not incompatible with small fortunes;

on the contrary, often small fortunes are formed in the shadow of great ones. No other country possesses as many millionaires as the United States, and no other country possesses as small a number of poor people, whereas, no country possesses a smaller number of millionaires than Russia, and no other country contains more poor people. There shall always be great capitalists, great capitalists shall always have influence, and this influence will be increased naturally by association, but association in its turn will protect small capitalists and workingmen. Between the interests of the two classes, independently of moral and religious influences, there is and will remain the civil power, the mission of which is to enact wise laws which insure liberty, rights, the activity of all, especially of the weakest. In transitory times these laws are not easily made. But this is a fault inherent in human nature.

Q.—You are called here "the Socialist Bishop." Do you accept the adjective? Would your ideas be accepted by the Scholastic schools?

A.—The word "Socialist" has an evil ring, and before applying it to my ideas it should be defined. If by Socialists you understand those who are preoccupied by social necessities and miseries, who desire to improve the state of society, and who ask, in view of this improvement, not only action of individuals and influence of voluntary associations, but also a reasonable intervention of the civil power, yes, I am a Socialist. But if by "Socialist" you understand those who share the theories of Marx, of Benoit Malon,[5] of Greef, and others—theories which consist in denying the rightfulness of private property in land and in instruments of labor—no, I am not a Socialist.

I do not doubt that my ideas would be rejected by the Socialistic sects. Everywhere the Socialist sects are opposed to the Christian social movement. In laboring for the disappearance of the just grievances of the working class, the Christian movement takes from sectarian socialism the reason for its existence.

This is not because the promoters of the Christian social movement preach only charity and resignation. Far from this, they preach, above all, right and justice; natural right of the workingman; complete justice, social as well as individual. It is said that justice is a foundation of societies; it is also the foundation of economic order. Therefore, in the first place, justice; after justice, charity; charity may not be substituted for justice; one completes the other; in places where justice has ceased to command, charity intervenes.

Doubtless our conception of life differs essentially from that of the materialists; our reason and our faith teach us that present life is a preparation for a better life. But we are not led by this to neglect material welfare. Material welfare is not our end; it is our means. Its profession to a reasonable degree is of the highest importance for the moral and religious life of men.

Q.—Do you admit as legitimate the actual aspirations of the masses toward absolute social equality? Do you think that the natural inequalities might be reconciled with social equality?

A.—Aspirations of the masses toward social equality— I mean reasonable equality—are perfectly legitimate. Social equality is, after all, only the expression of equality from the point of view of human dignity and of Christian dignity. We must take care, however, that social equality should not be opposed to social hierarchy; parentage, service, and authority engender rights and social duties which are not the same for all; genius, talent, virtue, and riches entail consideration and give a certain moral pre-eminence which shall always be admitted. This observation is sufficient to show that social equality may be reconciled with natural inequality. Natural inequality is that of intelligence, of strength, and of health. This inequality is more or less corrected by society, which protects the weak. Social hierarchy is natural and indestructible. Something not as natural, and which may be abolished, is the great distance between the two ends of this hierarchy. It is not necessary that some should be so elevated and that others should be so degraded.

Q.—Since you admit that societies may pass through transformations, think you that the trilogy—family, religion, and property—should necessarily escape these transformations?

A.—The action of Providence, which brings everything to its end, does not prevent the natural course of things and does not suppress the liberty of man. Modifications in the form of societies are therefore possible, but family, religion, and property are essential elements of all human society. Family is the principle of human society; religion is its crown; property—considered in itself, independently of variable forms—is a condition of life, of liberty, and of progress.

The form of the family is determined by the nature of man, his physical forces, his intellectual faculties, his sentiments, and his instincts, and this form was sanctioned by Christ. It will not change, but what may be desired, what may be hoped, is more perfect realization of this form, and this realization may not be obtained except by progress in manners, customs, and laws.

The form of religion is also determined in a general manner by nature as regards its object and its principal acts. It was also determined in a special and positive manner by Christ. There shall not therefore be a new form of religion, but one may hope for a more complete intelligence and a more general and more perfect realization of the Christian idea, and consequently a more powerful influence of the Gospel on the life of individuals and of nations. Outside of Christianity there may be new religious forms, as was Mohammedanism, but these forms shall not be progressive. As for Neo-Christianity,[6] it will never be anything but amateurish religion.

Property is essential, but there is nothing absolute in its forms. These depend on the social, industrial, political, and moral situation of peoples. The history of property has occupied in France and elsewhere many learned men. Their studies cannot but throw light on questions of social philosophy.

Q.—Among the possible modifications of property, which ones would you regard favorably? What do you think of the communist theory?

A.—The form of property was not always the same at all epochs, and even to-day it is not absolutely the same in an countries. What modifications are possible, useful, and necessary depends on the conditions under which each people finds itself. Modifications may not be made by legislation. This can only give sanction. They are accomplished slowly, by progress in manners and under the sway of circumstances. An example of such modifications is the introduction and disappearance of feudal property.

The system of property which appears to me to be the most desirable should reunite the following qualities: Stimulate human activity and individual labor by assurance of just retribution; maintain the stability of the family, and favor an equitable distribution of the good things of this world.

The Communist theory takes no account of the nature of things or of the nature of man. It does not seem possible to me that it may be realized, and if it were realized the result would be fatal to civilization. Herbert Spencer[7] recently demonstrated this in the introduction which he wrote for "The Man Versus the State." Community of goods may exist among a certain number of men devoted to celibacy and to the cult of God. It might have existed in the age of gold and in a state of innocence; but it does not answer to the real state of present humanity.

Yet the present movement contains very complex elements, which may not be judged in their entirety from the point of view of morality and of civilization. There are few theories, however false they may be in their entirety, which do not contain elements of truth and of justice. The errors which they contain are often an occasion determining a more complete intelligence of the truth. Thus, it may not be denied that the Communist agitation has provoked a more adequate understanding of certain social principles and a more profound sentiment of social justice.

Q.—What is the state of the social question in America? Where, think you, do the Socialist theories have a better chance to succeed, in Europe or in the United States?

A.—The social question exists in America. Read on this subject Prof. Ely's[8] book, "The Labor Movement in America." In my opinion, the difference between our situation and that of Europe is as follows:

The social movement is expressed in the United States by numerous and powerful workingmen's associations. These associations have for their principal object to maintain good wages; they are preoccupied by the morality of their members and by professional education. You know that there are some associations which labor to maintain harmony between bosses and workmen, and to prevent strikes. I think that among the American people there are few Anarchists, few Communists, and that the number of collectivists cannot be large. They come from other countries. European immigration supplies their principal contingent. The details which Mr. Ely gives on these subjects are very interesting. As for Henry George's[9] agrarian movement, it is far from powerful.

Socialist theories have far less chance in America than in Europe. In the first place, the sentiment of personal dignity and responsibility and the spirit of enterprise are much developed in the American people. It likes and appreciates individual liberty and respects the law. These dispositions do not lead to social revolution. Furthermore, there is room in the United States for all kinds of energy. Labor there insures honorable life; then, the greater number of Americans have conquered their situation by personal valor, at the price of efforts, perils, and heroic sacrifices. They are not disposed to share with others what they have gained by so much work. Then there are philosophical, moral, and political causes which elsewhere favor the development of Socialism, and have no force in the United States. I allude to administrative centralization, intervention of the Government in the affairs of citizens, to the military regime, and to authoritative traditions.

[1] Jules Huret (1864–1915) was a famous French journalist who won early notice by his series of articles on controverted questions for *l'Echo de Paris,* and later for a series on European social questions for *Le Figaro.*

[2] *Le Figaro* began in 1825 and went through a number of changes, becoming in 1866 a daily paper which was monarchical in sympathies after the Franco-Prussian War and which continued to be an organ of conservative opinion.

[3] An effort to identify Northamb was not successful.

[4] Leo XIII's encyclical *Rerum novarum* on the condition of the working classes had been issued on May 15, 1891.

[5] Benôit Malon (1841–1893) was a French socialist who participated in the Paris Commune of 1870–1871 and later fled to Geneva where he founded *La Revanche;* Guillaume-Joseph de Greef (1842–1924) was a professor of sociology in the University of Brussels.

[6] Ireland may have been referring here to the followers of Claude-Henri de Rouvroy. Comte de Saint-Simon (1760–1825), who fostered in his last years a sort of mystical fraternalism.

[7] *Man versus the State,* to which Herbert Spencer (1820–1903) wrote an introduction, was first published in 1884 and was reprinted in 1940 by the Caxton Printers, Caldwell, Idaho.

[8] Richard T. Ely (1854–1943), at this time professor of political economy in the University of Wisconsin, was a prolific writer on social and economic questions. The latest edition of his volume, *The Labor Movement in America,* appeared in 1905.

[9] Henry George (1839–1897) was chiefly notable for his theory of the single tax on land.

(*Source*: John Tracy Ellis, ed. *Documents of American Catholic History.* Vol. 2:1866–1966. Wilmington, Del.: Michael Glazier, 1987, 489–94.)

IRELAND, SERAPHINE (1842–1930)

Religious and educator. Helen Ireland was born in Burn-church, Kilkenny, Ireland, on July 1, 1842, the daughter of Richard Ireland and Judith Naughton Ireland. When she was ten years old, her family emigrated to St. Paul, Minnesota. In 1858 Helen entered the novitiate of the Sisters of St. Joseph of Carondelet and took the name Seraphine. Her first assignments gave her teaching and administrative experience in elementary and secondary schools.

As did her brother, Archbishop John Ireland, Mother Seraphine advocated the active engagement of Catholic men and women in American social and economic life, an engagement that required a professionally competent education. Mother Seraphine believed that a program of academic excellence required sister teachers who were themselves thoroughly educated. Consequently, under her direction, many of the Sisters of St. Joseph attended college summer schools and received degrees at the University of Chicago, the University of Minnesota, and universities in Germany. She made sure that teachers and schools received state certification. After founding the College of St. Catherine (1911), the second Catholic college for women in the U.S.A., Mother Seraphine secured its accreditation by the North Central Association of Colleges and Secondary Schools.

Under Mother Seraphine's direction, the Sisters of St. Joseph of Carondelet flourished in Minnesota and the Upper Midwest. When she took office as superior in 1882, there were 162 sisters. When she retired in 1921, there were 913 sisters. During this period, she opened thirty-seven new institutions, including thirty parochial schools, five hospitals, St. Agatha's Conservatory of Music and Art (1884), and the College of St. Catherine (1911). She died in St. Paul on June 20, 1930.

Carey, Patrick W. *The Roman Catholics.* Westport, Conn.: Greenwood Press, 1993, 244–45.

Hurley, Helen Angela. *On Good Ground: The Story of the Sisters of St. Joseph in St. Paul.* Minneapolis, 1951.

PATRICIA DeFERRARI

IRISH CATHOLIC IMMIGRANTS, HISTORICAL BACKGROUND

Colonial and Pre-Revolutionary Period

In Ireland, these years saw the failure of the Stuart and Catholic Cause, the consolidation of the Protestant Succession, and the implementation of a Penal Code to ensure the Williamite Land Settlement.

Before American Independence, some 300,000 to 500,000 Irish emigrants went to the North American colonies, including established families with their servants and younger sons lacking inheritance. The majority, however, were probably indentured servants. In the 1600s, Catholics were three-quarters of the total, with settlements in Virginia and Maryland. Presbyterians (Dissenters) and Quakers increased at the end of the century.

In the early 1700s the mainland colonies replaced the West Indies as the focus of immigration, with Ulster Presbyterians in the majority. In 1754 Ireland had a population of 2.3 million. Crop failures in the 1720s and 1760s with a general famine from 1740 to 1741 affected all levels of society. The artisan class began to leave after the destruction of the woolen and linen trades in the early and late 1700s respectively. By 1779 Irish Catholics farmed here and a small but significant Catholic middle class was taking shape in the seaports with an ill-defined and varied working class beneath them.

The Penal Code

Ireland was the only European country that did not follow the religion of its ruler during the great religious upheaval of the sixteenth and seventeenth centuries. The majority of the people remained Catholic. The Penal Code, enacted between 1695 and 1714, outlawed Catholicism and its practice. It concentrated on making Catholics a landless people at a time when land ownership equaled political power. In 1661 Catholics owned 59 percent of the land; this fell to 18 percent in the 1700s. The Penal Code placed property, power, and privilege in the hands of a small colonial establishment. No real attempt was made to convert the Irish to Anglicanism, but if they did convert, then they were entitled to share power. Allowed to exist but not to prosper, Catholics became a humiliated people. Their Church functioned by stealth but managed to maintain its diocesan and parish structure, despite occasional periods of persecution, especially of its clergy.

From the towns where it was sustained by an affluent merchant class with strong ties to France and Spain, Counter-Reformation Catholicism moved out into Gaelic Ireland. A network of colleges on the continent provided education. After a rudimentary training, priests were ordained in Ireland and sent abroad for postordination training. The mendicant orders, especially the Franciscans, were a significant influence in nurturing the faith of the people. An underground Church made the home the usual place for baptisms, Mass, marriages, and funerals. The priest emerged from the penal days as the acknowledged leader of his people.

Catholic Relief

In the last decades of the 1700s, a Catholic Committee, drawn from the remnant of the old Catholic aristocracy—few but pliant towards the Crown—and a more forceful merchant middle class, sought relief from the Penal Code. The Dublin Parliament was reluctant, but the American

War of Independence and the outbreak of war between Britain and France in 1778 strongly suggested that a disaffected Ireland might be used by France against Britain. A series of Catholic Relief bills was introduced when Dublin's intransigence was overruled by London's political expediency. Catholics could now lease land, pass it on by will, and vote if they met certain freehold requirements. Furthermore, the Church could now sponsor schools. In 1795 the Royal College of St. Patrick at Maynooth was founded with government aid; it would later become the national seminary.

Despite the improvement in the Catholic position, a significant number joined the United Irishmen in the Rising of 1798. Its brutal suppression sparked a new wave of emigration among better-off Presbyterians and Catholics.

Catholic Emancipation

On the first of January 1801, a parliamentary union between Great Britain and Ireland became effective. Catholics welcomed it since they had been promised emancipation after the union. Most of the penal laws had been repealed in the 1780s and 1790s, but Catholics could not be judges, hold senior positions in the armed forces or the civil service, be members of Parliament, or be ministers of the Crown. These prohibitions affected a small percentage of Catholics.

Daniel O'Connell (1775–1847) led a mass democratic movement of Catholics to achieve emancipation. Forming the Catholic Association in 1823, he called on the Catholic clergy to collect the weekly "Catholic Rent" of one penny per adult. The movement was remarkable for its adherence to constitutional means, its political use of the Catholic clergy, and its engendering of a greater morale and self-esteem in the ordinary Catholic, springing from the perception of a common cause. Emancipation was granted in 1829. Public office was now open to Catholics. Henceforth, Catholic members of Parliament at Westminster would have a significant balancing role between the Liberals and the Tories.

While the position of Catholics generally improved, emigration continued with an estimate of 800,000 to 1,000,000 to North America in the thirty years before the Great Famine. These immigrants were more obviously Catholic and had a greater sense of Irish identity. On arrival, they became aware of a distrust of their religion and country in the prevailing Anglo-Saxon culture.

The Great Famine 1845–1850

Ireland had a population of 8.5 million in 1845; 1 million died and 1.8 million emigrated during the Great Famine. The small holders, cottiers, and laborers were the main victims. The 1841 census shows that only 7 percent of holdings were over thirty acres; 45 percent were under five acres. Over two-thirds of the population depended on agriculture. The famine caused a total restructuring of Irish society. Farms were no longer divided among the sons; now only one son inherited. The cost of keeping a farm intact among the parents and one son frequently presented the remaining siblings with a choice of the single life in rural Ireland or emigration.

After the famine, the most important social group became the small to medium-sized tenant farmer with holdings of at least thirty acres. His interests would dominate politics for the next fifty years and the Catholic Church would marry its own future to that of the tenant farmer.

Land Reform and Nationalism

Land reform and nationalism were the main issues in postfamine Ireland. The tenant farmer sought a fair rent, a fixed tenure, and the right to sell his interest in his tenancy. Despite the animosity between landlord and tenant, sometimes expressed violently, the movement remained constitutional.

The revolutionary and physical force tradition was more obvious in the struggle for national independence. The prefamine movement for the repeal of the union between Great Britain and Ireland failed despite O'Connell's leadership and his earlier success with Catholic emancipation. The secret societies, the Young Irelanders, and the Fenians believed in revolution and physical force. Remarkably, both the agrarian and national causes were successfully harnessed to the constitutional tradition led by the Irish Parliamentary Party at Westminster. The revolutionary tradition would continue underground only to resurface in 1916 after Home Rule was postponed until the conclusion of the Great War.

Postfamine Emigrants

Ireland's population fell from 5.8 million in 1861 to 4.3 million in 1926. Of the 4.5 million who left between 1851 and 1921, 3.75 million migrated to America. For the most part, they were single men and women who were better educated because of the national school system. By 1880, single women outnumbered the men. Many of them had experienced the power of peaceful organization in movements for emancipation, land reform, and national independence.

The Great Famine left a profound distrust of the land as a reliable provider; the city seemed more promising. In the passage from rural to city life, they needed protection and the skills to assimilate. They found these in the Catholic Church and the Democratic Party.

The Postfamine Church

Cardinal Paul Cullen (1803–78), archbishop of Armagh (1849–52) and of Dublin (1852–78), brought the Irish

Church in line with the Rome of Pope Pius IX. As papal legate in 1850, he called the first national synod since penal times. While opposed by his fellow bishops, Cullen led the Church through decades of growth and prosperity.

In the century after emancipation, 24 cathedrals and over 3,000 churches were built. Religious orders, founded in Ireland or from Europe, expanded into the areas of education and medicine. Church personnel grew from one priest per 2,000 Catholics in 1850 to one per 1,250 in 1870. Nuns increased from 200 in 1800 to 8,000 in 1900. Since Catholic pupils were in the majority, the national school system became a denominational one in practice, state-supported, but managed and controlled by the Church. The Presentation Sisters, Mercy Sisters, and Sisters of Charity provided education for girls while the Presentation Sisters and Christian Brothers did the same for boys. Their apostolic work was funded by the Catholic merchant families, who provided many of the first members.

At the pastoral level, the parish church became the center of Catholic life. Sacraments long celebrated in the home were now moved to the church. New devotions, including Benediction, novenas, and confraternities, were introduced. Parish missions renewed sacramental and devotional life.

The Irish Church was conscious of its responsibility to those who had gone abroad. All Hallows College (1842) was one of six Irish seminaries that provided for the English-speaking world. There was a consciousness among the clergy "that upon this country the obligation devolved in a most special manner of preaching the gospel to the many millions who acknowledged the rule or speak the language of Great Britain" (All Hallows Report, 1849). This commitment continued until the 1960s. After Irish independence, a new movement to Asia and Africa began with the establishment of five missionary societies.

From the 1850s, the Catholic Church took on many of the characteristics of an established Church. This was possible because Catholics were in the majority in a unified Ireland. With Irish independence, they formed 90 percent of the population. Political and social developments from the 1960s together with the impact of Vatican Council II brought great changes to a well-educated, more prosperous and more hopeful people, now partners in the European Economic Community, but who still know that emigration is a necessity for many.

See also IRISH CATHOLICS IN AMERICA.

Coogan, Timothy Patrick. *Ireland Since the Rising.* New York, 1966.

Corish, Patrick. *The Irish Catholic Experience: A Historical Survey.* Wilmington, Del.: Michael Glazier, 1985.

Larkin, Emmet. "The Devotional Revolution in Ireland, 1850–1875." *American Historical Review* 77 (3) (June 1972) 625–52.

Miller, Kerby A. *Emigrants and Exiles: Ireland and the Irish Exodus to North America.* New York, 1985.

Mooney, T. W., and F. X. Martin, eds. *The Course of Irish History.* New York, 1967.

Shier, Arnold. *Ireland and American Emigration from 1815 to the Famine.* Minneapolis, 1958.

COLMAN M. COOKE

IRISH CATHOLICS IN AMERICA

Immigration and Urbanization

From 1820 to 1920 approximately four and a half million Irish immigrants entered the United States. The overwhelming majority were young, single Catholics, almost evenly balanced in numbers between men and women. Until the 1970s they and their descendants shaped the personality and structure of American Catholicism, urban politics, and the labor movement.

Before the Irish arrived, the American Catholic Church was small in size. In 1789 the Church only had about thirty thousand adherents, most of them living in either Maryland or Pennsylvania. Ten percent were black slaves. One bishop and thirty priests ministered to the spiritual needs of the faithful. Because of the anti-Catholic core of American nativism, a British inheritance, the United States was not hospitable to Catholics or their religion. The American Enlightenment, with its distrust of all organized religion, especially the authoritarianism and the "superstitions" of Rome, shared the Protestant antagonism to Catholicism. Both agreed that it was a subversive threat to American culture and institutions.

With the exception of Pennsylvania, Protestant legislatures in the American colonies followed the Irish and British Parliaments in passing anti-Catholic penal laws. Despite the liberal spirit of the Declaration of Independence, the Bill of Rights, and the Constitution, many American states retained them into the nineteenth century.

American Catholics deferentially responded to American nativism, practicing their religion quietly without display. Their chapels were plain, resembling the classic simplicity of Protestant churches rather than the Romanesque, Gothic, and Baroque styles of European Catholic places of worship. Catholic priests wore ordinary clothing, and parishioners addressed them as "mister," not "reverend" or "father."

Catholics were unpretentious in their religious practices to avoid stirring nativist prejudices, and to show that they intended to blend into the American cultural landscape. Their most prominent clerical leader, John Carroll, cousin of Charles, a signer of the Declaration of Independence, attempted to create a distinctive, native-to-the-soil American Catholicism. In his early years he minimized the Roman connection, favored lay trustee control of parishes, promoted an English-language liturgy, and emphasized a theology more in tune with the rational spirit of the American Enlightenment than the devotionalism, emotionalism, and mysticism of European Catholicism.

In time, Carroll moved to the right. Once an admirer of the Enlightenment, he came to believe it responsible for the violence, Deism, and anticlericalism of the French Revolution. And when he became the first bishop and unofficial primate of the American Church, Carroll became more sympathetic to Rome's view of authority.

Although Carroll became more Ultramontane and less Gallican, he and the Anglo-American and French Sulpician clergy who served the Church in the United States did not wish her to be isolated from general American culture. They wanted American Catholics to be accepted and respected by non-Catholics. Therefore, they did not joyfully open their arms to the first wave of Irish Catholic immigrants. They believed the rude and crude newcomers would offend the sensibilities of Anglo-Americans, and increase their hostility to Catholicism. The Irish decision to settle in cities also made them undesirable aliens. Most Americans were antipathetic to urban life as conducive to corruption and vice. They thought of themselves as an essentially rural people. Jeffersonian democracy glorified the sturdy yeoman as the ideal citizen.

In his *The Personality of Ireland: Habitat, Heritage, & History* (1973), anthropogeographer E. Estyn Evans of Queen's University, Belfast, described the Irish as rural folk who viewed cities and towns as symbols of Viking, Norman, and Anglo-Saxon invaders. Therefore, it is paradoxical that tenant farmers and agricultural laborers from Ireland urbanized American Catholicism. Peasants who tilled the minuscule farms of Ireland with hoe, spade, and scythe did not possess the skills to properly farm the vast fields of America, and their Catholic communal personalities reacted against the social isolation of the rural United States. Only 15 percent of Irish-American Catholics were involved in the agrarian economy while the rest took employment in transportation, industry, construction, and domestic service. They became the proletarian pioneers of the American urban ghetto.

Focusing on the wretched social and moral environments of American cities, Catholic bishops and journalists in Ireland deplored the urban concentration of the Irish in the United States. They advised prospective emigrants to settle in rural areas. Such members of the American hierarchy as Buffalo's Bishop John Timon in the 1850s and St. Paul's Archbishop John Ireland in the 1880s and 1890s attempted to establish new and reestablish old Irish immigrants on farms where they would encounter fewer challenges to their peasant Catholic culture and values. Other prelates opposed efforts to steer the Irish away from cities. They argued that despite dangerous moral environments, they were better sanctuaries for the faith than rural areas. They said that it was easier for the Church to tend to the

spiritual needs of Catholics concentrated in metropolitan centers than those scattered throughout unfriendly Protestant nativist territory. But it was their technological limitations, their extrovert personalities, and the availability of unskilled labor, and not the advice of the Church, that determined the urbanization of Irish America.

Irish Catholics created America's first massive social problem. The transition from rural Ireland to the disease, vice, and crime-infested slums of urban America was psychologically as well as physically traumatic. City-living and a competitive economic environment eroded agrarian mores. Consequently, the Irish filled jails, mental asylums, hospitals, and orphanages. Irish ghettoes featured massive social disorder, confirming nativist views that there was a connection between Catholicism, ignorance, and barbarism, and fears that popery threatened American institutions and values.

Irish-American Catholicism

American bishops and priests not only frowned on Irish social behavior as a goad to Protestant bigotry, but they also were appalled by the quality of Catholicism that the immigrants brought with them. During his 1835 tour of Ireland, Alexis de Tocqueville observed that Catholics in Ireland were more devout than those on the Continent. As described by S. J. Connolly (*Priests and People in Pre-Famine Ireland, 1780–1845*, 1982), the ignorance and superstition of a significant proportion of the laity, a poorly educated and undisciplined clergy, and a divided and publicly quarreling hierarchy troubled early nineteenth-century Irish Catholicism. According to Patrick Corish (*The Irish Catholic Experience*, 1985), the condition of Irish Catholicism varied geographically. In relatively prosperous, modernized, partially Anglicized areas, Catholics were familiar with the teaching of the Church and consistently practiced their faith. In more primitive, impoverished, densely populated, still-Gaelicized parts of the country, the religious situation was quite different. There, people were still addicted to ancient superstitions and had a meager understanding of Catholic beliefs. Shortages of priests and chapels perpetuated their ignorance.

Many Irish immigrants who came to the United States before, during, and shortly after the Great Famine were only slightly aware of what it meant to be a Catholic, and did not think it of vital importance to attend Mass or receive the sacraments. And the social chaos and economic hardships of American cities tended to further weaken fragile religious commitments. Often Irish immigrants reacted negatively to French priests trying to minister to them. They demanded clergy of their own, putting a tremendous strain on the meager resources of the early American Church.

Unfortunately, when Irish bishops complied with the request of American colleagues to send missionaries to the American diaspora, they frequently took the opportunity to rid themselves of rebellious, licentious, and alcoholic troublemakers. In the United States they were as difficult to control as they had been in Ireland. Appeals from members of the American hierarchy, particularly Charleston's Irish-born John England, persuaded Irish prelates to send a higher caliber of priests to the United States. England and others also addressed the need for Irish-American priests by establishing their own seminaries.

In the second half of the nineteenth century the religious quality of Irish immigrants steadily improved as a result of what Emmet Larkin has described as a "Devotional Revolution" (*The Historical Dimensions of Irish Catholicism,* 1974). The famine set the stage for the transformation of Irish Catholicism. Hunger and disease took the lives of at least a million, and forced about a million and a half to emigrate, usually to the United States. Most famine victims came from the most impoverished, least-educated levels of society. The Irish exodus placed a great strain on Catholicism in the United States, Britain, and Canada, but it and hunger and fever fatalities eased the burdens of the Irish Church. The Great Hunger reduced ignorance and superstition, and the shortages of priests and places of worship.

During the last year of the famine, 1849, Pope Pius IX appointed the rector of the Irish College in Rome, Paul Cullen, archbishop of Armagh, primate, and papal envoy in Ireland. Retaining the latter two titles, in 1852 Cullen succeeded Daniel Murray as Dublin's archbishop. Fourteen years later, the pope named him Ireland's first cardinal. It was appropriate that Cullen, one of the Church's leading advocates of Ultramontanism, should draft the statement on papal infallibility at the 1870 Vatican Council. By that time he had made Ireland the devotional jewel of Roman Catholicism.

With the exceptions of Connacht and sections of Ulster, Cullen was able to secure the appointment of bishops who were loyal to Rome and to him. Under his guidance, the hierarchy discussed differences in private and presented a unified and harmonious public front. He improved clerical education and imposed clerical discipline; recruited a plentiful supply of intelligent priests, nuns, and brothers to serve the Church at home, among the diaspora, and throughout the British Empire; and built churches and schools and filled them with the most obedient, devout, and financially generous laity in the Roman fold.

Nationalism as well as the consequences of the famine and Cullen's leadership contributed to the "Devotional Revolution." Because Protestantism was a feature of British cultural colonialism, since the late sixteenth-century Irish Catholics were loyal to their religion as a mark of who they were. In the 1820s' campaign for Catholic Emanci-

pation, Daniel O'Connell expanded religion into nationality. Throughout the nineteenth century, as nationalism became firmly rooted in the hearts and minds of the people, and Anglo-Irish Protestants and Ulster Presbyterians, encouraged by British conservative politicians and no-popery British public opinion, exploited anti-Catholicism to frustrate Irish political independence, the bonds between religion and nationality became tighter. The increasing devotionalism of Irish Catholics reflected the intensity of their nationalism. Practicing the faith was a visible expression of Irishness.

Thanks to the "Devotional Revolution," postfamine emigrants were increasingly well schooled in their religion and scrupulous in its practice. Catholic influences as well as a higher standard of living due to an improving economy, the national school system, and aspects of Anglicization (Victorian morality) disciplined and polished the Irish character. Immigrants began to perceive the United States as a conduit to respectability and success rather than just a refuge from hunger and poverty. As their conduct improved, social reasons for despising them diminished. But the Irish role as religious, political, and labor leaders of an expanding, vigorous, urban Catholicism continued to fan the flames of American nativism.

By 1900 two-thirds of the American hierarchy were Irish, and their numbers as priests, nuns, and brothers far exceeded their proportion of the Catholic population. They Romanized and urbanized the American Catholic Church and made it part of an Irish spiritual empire that stretched across the English-speaking world into the outposts of the British Empire.

For two important reasons, minority status and nativist antagonism, connections between religion and nationality became even closer in the United States than in Ireland. Catholicism served as a psychological and spiritual comfort station in an alien, hostile environment, a bridge of familiarity between agrarian Ireland and American cities. The Catholic parish functioned as a rural village in an urban setting, molding and serving a cohesive social and religious community.

In addition to devotionalism and intense loyalty to Rome, the Irish transferred other dimensions of their religion to the New World. More than Continental Catholics, they had a deep admiration and respect for the clergy. Much of this affection evolved from religion and nationality relationships. Priests symbolized both. In Ireland, unlike other European Catholic countries, the hierarchy as well as the clergy came from the people, the sons of strong farmers and shopkeepers. Therefore, they had emotional as well as religious links to the laity. For a considerable time priests were the only educated Catholics in rural Ireland, the rivals of landlords. Peasants turned to them for secular as well as religious advice. Starting with the Catholic Emancipation agitation, bishops and priests played important roles in populist-nationalist and tenant-right movements.

In the United States, the Irish retained their high regard for priests, nuns, and brothers, and this affection and respect spread to other American Catholics. Irish parents contributed talented sons and daughters to the Church for worldly as well as spiritual motives. Having a son in the priesthood was a badge of honor and distinction for an entire family. Since nativist discrimination barred the doors of business and limited professional opportunities for Catholics, religion, politics, and the labor movement offered access to power and influence.

While less prestigious than the rectory, for many young Irish-American women the convent was a pleasant alternative to the hardships and frequent brutality of ethnic working-class marriages. They often witnessed mothers burdened with too many children, and verbally and physically abused by drunken, violent husbands. Intelligent, sensitive, young women from poor, sometimes dysfunctional families had to be impressed by the community of cultured women who taught them in parochial elementary and secondary schools. They admired nuns as educators and health-care providers and administrators of schools and hospitals, women who enjoyed the respect and deference of men. For example, nuns recruited some of the daughters of domestic servants and textile workers for the religious life; they encouraged others to become public schoolteachers and nurses. As the first group of professional women in the United States, sisters from a number of religious orders, some originating in Ireland, most staffed by Irish and Irish-American women, and the students they taught, led the Irish march toward middle-class respectability (Hasia R. Diner, *Erin's Daughters in America,* 1983).

Like their Irish counterparts, Irish-American priests played secular as well as religious roles. They were spiritual directors, psychologists, and social workers. Priests said Mass, heard confessions, baptized infants, visited parochial school classrooms, married young couples, anointed the sick, and buried the dead. They also attended meetings of parish organizations, listened sympathetically to the personal and family problems of the laity, and did their best to counsel solutions.

The greening of American Catholicism has provoked considerable criticism. Justifiably, other ethnic groups have complained of Irish arrogance and insensitivity to their cultural needs and expressions. Although Irish priests, nuns, and brothers often gave the impression that they represented a superior form of Catholicism, they did provide for the religious, social, and educational needs of all Catholic European nationalities. But when African Americans and Hispanics entered the cities, sometimes Irish religious leaders have been guilty of prejudice and neglect.

Catholic intellectuals, many of them Irish, have described Hibernian Catholicism as authoritarian, anti-intellectual, and puritanical. They suggest that it was unfortunate that a more sophisticated group of European Catholics had not preceded the Irish to the United States and taken the helm of the American Church. It is true that Irish clerics, serving peasants in Ireland and immigrants in the United States, emphasized a pastoral, devotional, nonintellectual brand of Catholicism. And fawning Irish subordination to the status and opinions of the clergy promoted clericalism. But criticizing the Irish for the failures and inadequacies of American Catholic intellectualism falsely assumes that there were other alternatives. From Pius IX to John XXIII, Roman Catholicism stressed devotionalism, obedience to authority, apologetics rather than rational examination of the faith, and a Thomistic philosophy more relevant to the medieval than the modern world. French, German, and Italian Catholicisms might have been more sophisticated than the Irish, but they were not more intellectual or less authoritarian. Englishman John Henry Newman, a convert from Anglicanism, was one of the very few nineteenth-century Catholic intellectuals of any originality.

Instead of a "Celtic heresy," Irish puritanism is as Roman as its devotionalism and clericalism. But it is a product of economic and social factors and Anglicization as well as Catholic obsessions with sins of the flesh. Prefamine Irish peasants displayed a healthy sexual exuberance. But after the misery of the late 1840s, attitudes toward marriage and sex turned conservative to avoid another overpopulation disaster. Catholic sexual morality sustained and sanctified long periods of and sometimes permanent celibacy. A sexual code that began as a response to necessity became a way of life, a prominent feature of the Irish Catholic personality. British Victorian definitions of respectable conduct also contributed to Irish prudery.

Although Irish Catholic puritanism involves taking Rome more seriously than other Catholics rather than Jansenism revisited, its overemphasis on sex has led to neuroses on the subject and unhealthy gender segregation in Ireland and America. It also has encouraged excessive consumption of alcohol as an alternative to sex. Too many Irish men have preferred the pub or the saloon to the home, and the comfort and escape of the bottle to the love of women. And many churchmen have tolerated this conduct as a manly fault or the lesser of two evils.

The Irish input has not been an unmixed blessing for American Catholicism, but the positives have outweighed the negatives for an immigrant Church attempting to survive and flourish in an industrial capitalist, essentially Protestant country. Having to endow Catholicism in separation-of-Church-and-state America was not an original or shocking experience for the Irish. Most other European Catholics who followed them to the New World came from authoritarian, unified Church-and-state political and religious traditions. While Catholics were 75 percent of Ireland's population, until 1868 they suffered a state-established Protestantism. Catholics, mostly poor, had to support the existence of their own Church, and did so in a most generous manner, building churches and schools, financing foreign missions as well as their own parishes, and sending vast sums to Rome.

In the United States, Irish-American pennies, nickels, dimes, quarters, and dollars paid for Catholic religious, educational, health, and social services. Irish magnanimity set a precedent and example for other Catholics. Despite the fact that the American Church was immigrant and working class, due to the loyalty and sacrifice of the laity it was able to take care of the poor, the sick, and the unwanted at a time when the state felt little or no obligation to solve the country's social problems.

Irish-American Politics

Politics was the only skill that the Irish brought from Ireland. Starting in the 1820s, nationalism mobilized the Irish masses for political action. In many ways, Daniel O'Connell's Catholic and Repeal Associations were previews of Irish-American political machines. In the 1880s, Charles Stuart Parnell's Irish Parliamentary Party was the most efficient and disciplined force in the British House of Commons.

An admirer of British radicals such as William Godwin, Thomas Paine, and Jeremy Bentham, O'Connell injected the principles of liberal democracy into the bloodstream of Irish nationalism which then politically civilized its ally, Irish Catholicism, making it unique in a Europe where Rome was a friend of aristocracy and the Old Regime, and an enemy of democracy and liberalism. De Tocqueville was surprised when he dined with Irish bishops and priests and listened to their enthusiastic endorsements of popular sovereignty. As the nineteenth century progressed, under Cullen's direction the Irish hierarchy and clergy became more authoritarian in religious matters, and more conservative on political, economic, and social issues, but they never abandoned their endorsement of the liberal democratic platform of Irish nationalism.

Probably the most valuable Irish contribution to American Catholicism was their successful effort in leading other Catholic ethnics into conformity with the American political consensus. Therefore, it was fortunate that the Irish were the first large group of Catholics to enter the United States. Their religious and political leadership was instrumental in Catholicism's adjustment to American political values.

For ideological and pragmatic reasons the vast majority of Irish-American Catholics joined the Democratic Party. Jeffersonian and Jacksonian egalitarianism appealed to victims of aristocratic privilege in Ireland and nativist elitism in the United States. But practical considerations outweighed idealism in the Irish choice of parties. Federalists, Whigs, and Republicans were anti-Catholic and anti-immigrant. Democratic politicians speeded the naturalization of Irish newcomers, found them jobs, and provided them with services in exchange for votes. The Irish began as foot soldiers in the Democratic political army, but quickly took command of their neighborhoods, and by the close of the nineteenth century dominated most large city councils north of the Mason-Dixon Line and New Orleans south of it.

Like their Catholic leadership, Irish-American political power has attracted considerable favorable and unfavorable comment. A number of historians and social scientists have praised Irish political machines for providing services to and including other ethnics in the American political process (John B. Buenker, *Urban Liberalism and Progressive Reform,* 1973; and Robert Dahl, *Who Governs? Democracy and Power in an American City,* 1961). Nativists argued that Irish politics manifested evidence of subversive Catholic influences. They also blamed it for the graft and corruption of urban governments. Irish-American scholar-politician Senator Daniel Patrick Moynihan (*Beyond the Melting Pot,* 1964), has complained that while the Irish were geniuses at acquiring power, they did not know what to do with it when they got it. He said that their peasant Catholic attitudes prevented city government's from adapting and responding to new challenges. Contradicting the inclusion thesis, in *Rainbow's End: Irish-Americans and the Dilemmas of Urban Machine Politics, 1840–1985* (1988), Stephen P. Erie maintains that Irish politics took care of the Irish and only gave minimal benefits to other ethnics. He also insists that their focus on politics as an opening to economic opportunity actually froze the Irish into blue-collar and lower white-collar jobs, blinding them to other American opportunities.

Evidence indicates that while the Irish might have perfected the graft and corruption of American politics, it existed long before their arrival, and continued in rural and urban areas that were Protestant preserves. Moynihan and Erie underestimate the Irish influences on urban progress. Anglo-Protestant reformers tended to emphasize moral rather than social improvement, and had a nativist contempt for "lesser breeds." Irish politicians did take care of their own as a first priority, but in their search for votes they did provide services to other ethnics, and were effective in building coalitions, and serving as middlemen between rival nationalities. Catholic common good values as well as practical politics motivated Irish politicians. Not only did they lead all Catholics into an American adjustment, they moved liberalism in the United States away from individualism in the direction of communalism. Irish political machines blazed the trail of the American welfare state. In Albany, New York, in the 1920s, Governor

Alfred E. Smith, a product of Tammany Hall, introduced legislative and policy precedents followed by the New Deal.

In condemning the Irish obsession with politics as economic opportunity, Erie exaggerated Irish Catholic economic potential in pre-World War II America. Nativist prejudice forced them into the Church, politics, and the labor movement as paths to power and influence. And the security of police force, fire department, government bureaucracy, and urban transport positions built a base for further occupational mobility when the American environment became friendlier to the Irish Catholic presence. Government building projects created a large number of Irish contractors who in turn hired such skilled workers as plumbers, electricians, carpenters, painters, plasterers, bricklayers, and unskilled diggers and hod carriers.

In addition to urban machines and the Church, Irish political skills were evident in the labor movement. Their leadership numbers far exceeded their proportion of the work force. Terence Powderly was the first grand master of the Knights of Labor, an attempt to organize labor on a national level. During the first decade of the twentieth century, 50 of the 110 American Federation of Labor presidencies were in Irish hands. Later, Philip Murray became the second president of the Congress of Industrial Organizations.

Despite the multitudes of Catholics entering the United States from southern and eastern Europe in the late nineteenth and early twentieth centuries, the Irish continued to lead and speak for Catholic America. In the 1930s the cardinal archbishops of the leading metropolitan sees, New York, Boston, Philadelphia, and St. Louis (a strongly German city), were Irish. German-American George Cardinal Mundelein was Chicago's first non-Irish archbishop, but his two auxiliaries, Bernard Sheil and William O'Brien, were Irish. The cardinal also built a close relationship with Mayor Edward J. Kelly, leader of one of the most effective Irish political machines in the country.

In addition to peasants from Ireland occupying American cities, there was another paradox in the Irish experience. At the same time, they were loyal to both a politically liberal and a religiously authoritarian system. They refused to see the disparity between these allegiances, insisting that the separation of Church and state divided political and religious spheres. Other Americans who distrusted Catholics in their midst could not understand how anyone conforming to the dictates of Rome could adhere to his or her country's freedom of conscience and individual liberty principles. They could not appreciate the psychological need for this duality. To the Irish, Catholicism was more than religion; it also was a culture and an ethnic identity that enabled them to survive British colonialism and American nativism. And they loved the United States because it had rescued them from poverty and oppression, and gave them freedom, dignity, and hope for the future.

Irish-American Nationalism

Although less vital than Catholicism or Democratic politics, nationalism was an important expression of Irish America. Without the passion and the dollars from the diaspora in the United States, it would have been difficult if not impossible for nationalism to have survived and triumphed in Ireland. In the 1840s Irish Americans from cities and small towns sent money to O'Connell's Repeal Association. During the 1850s and 1860s the American-based Fenian Brotherhood provided the popular name of and much of the political idealism for Irish revolutionary republicanism. In the 1870s the Clann-na-Gael developed the strategy for the New Departure, and Irish Americans provided most of the funds for its agrarian expression, the National Land League. They also contributed a considerable sum of dollars to the Home Rule Movement, 1880–1914, and its voice at Westminster, the Irish Parliamentary Party. John Devoy and other members of the Clann-na-Gael participated in planning the 1916 Easter Week rebellion, and during the Anglo-Irish War, Irish-American resources helped equip the Irish Republican Army, and Irish-American opinion was a factor in the pressure that forced Britain to concede the Irish Free State.

In *Emigrants and Exiles: Ireland and the Irish Exodus to North America* (1985), Kerby Miller defines Irish-American nationalism as an expression of alienation, the bitterness of culturally dysfunctional, impoverished Catholic Gaels lost in urban, industrial America. There is considerable truth in this thesis. Britain was the scapegoat for people forced to leave Ireland only to find misery rather than joy in the United States. But nationalism persisted after the Irish moved beyond the unskilled to the skilled working class and the lower levels of the middle class. In *Irish-American Nationalism* (1966), Thomas N. Brown explains late nineteenth-century Irish-American nationalism as a search for respectability. He points out that, despite their occupational mobility, the Irish remained socially *déclassé*. Many of them believed that other Americans did not respect them because their homeland was in bondage. They wanted to liberate Ireland to emancipate themselves from prejudice in the United States.

Instead of leading to Irish-American acceptance, anti-British nationalism offended Anglo-Protestant America, particularly before the United States entered World War I, and during the Anglo-Irish War. And often romantic commitments to Ireland delayed Irish-American adjustments to the reality of their urban industrial situation in the United States. But nationalism had many positive aspects. In addition to its role in freeing Ireland from British colonialism, it brought pride and idealism to Irish America, countering defeatist, fatalistic, and passivity elements in the Gaelic and Catholic traditions. Irish nationalism's liberal, democratic, economic, and social radicalism, compensated for the pragmatism and frequent cynicism of Irish-American politics, and for the conservatism that existed in large portions of Irish-American Catholicism.

Regional Diversity

The New as well as the Old Country molded Irish America, and since the United States is vast in size and complex in its economy and social structure, the Irish in various parts of the country had dissimilar experiences and perspectives. In Eastern cities, where the economy was more fixed, and the class system more rigid, Irish occupational and social mobility was slow. Because of poverty, nativist prejudice, and their own paranoia, they settled into defensive ghettoes of mind as well as of place. On the urban frontier of the Midwest and West, economies and social structures were fluid. Economic opportunities and necessities challenged nativism. In Midwestern and Western cities the Irish quickly moved into the skilled working class and crossed the frontiers of the lower middle class. While they remained somewhat defensive and insecure, they were more confident and optimistic than those in the East. As a result, they also were more cosmopolitan and liberal in their Catholicism and politics. These differences were revealed and fought out over the Americanization issue in the Catholic Church.

Although the Irish hierarchy and clergy accepted and adjusted to the American political situation, they split in their attitudes toward American culture. Generally, but not exclusively, the division was geographic, the East versus the Midwest and West. Archbishop Michael Corrigan of New York, and his advisor and confidant, Bishop Bernard McQuaid of Rochester, in conjunction with German prelates from the Midwest, urged their people to remain aloof from the American mainstream. In resisting cultural integration, they employed ethnicity as a shield against American Protestant and secular values. Opposition to Americanization led Corrigan and his allies into conservative stances on social issues. Preaching the redemptive powers of Christian poverty, they told their flocks to wait for justice in the next world, and attributed working-class discontent and unrest to socialist ideas represented by the Knights of Labor and other unions. Corrigan, McQuaid, and their friends shared Rome's antagonism to liberalism and Modernism, and its advocacy of the union of Church and state as an ideal. They discouraged lay leadership in education, insisting that Catholic schools existed to preserve the faith, not to produce intellectuals.

Led by Archbishop John Ireland of St. Paul, Midwestern Irish bishops and their priests believed in the American promise, and that separation of Church and state and the atmosphere of liberty would energize and expand Catholicism. They encouraged their people to socialize with non-Catholics. They experimented with parochial and public school cooperation. And they promoted a Catholic approach to education that emphasized secular as well as religious subjects. John Ireland and his associates championed organized labor, arguing that, if the Church in the United States ignored the material needs of the poor, she would lose their loyalty as she had in Europe. James Cardinal Gibbons of Baltimore, the unofficial primate of the American Church, identified with the Ireland faction. He went to Rome in 1887 and persuaded Pope Leo XIII to ignore the recommendations of Corrigan and French-Canadian bishops to issue a papal condemnation of the Knights of Labor.

Religious orders joined the struggle between Irish-American prelates. Jesuits, operating secondary schools and colleges for an upper-middle-class clientele, were rabid champions of Roman authority and religious conservatism. The Holy Cross Fathers, who had a small Catholic college, Notre Dame, in northern Indiana, and the Paulists, founded in 1858 by Isaac Hecker, a convert from New England Transcendentalism, agreed with Gibbons and Ireland that Catholicism in the United States should make adjustments to the American ethos.

In 1899 Corrigan and conservative French bishops persuaded Leo XIII to condemn such propositions as action being more significant than contemplation, natural superseding supernatural virtues, and private conscience taking precedence over Church authority as an Americanist heresy. Although Ireland and his friends protested that the Pope was censuring ideas that they had never advocated, Leo's condemnation, followed by Pius X's war on Modernism, resulted in a reign of terror against liberal ideas and values in American and European Catholic theology.

Despite an atmosphere of intellectual oppression that imprisoned Catholic thought in a neo-Thomist straitjacket, Midwestern Irish influence directed American Catholicism in a liberal social policy direction. John Ireland's St. Paul protégé, Msgr. John A. Ryan, adapting papal encyclicals to fit American situations, authored the progressive social justice agenda of the National Catholic Welfare Conference, previewing much of the New Deal, and Bernard Sheil, Chicago's auxiliary bishop, militantly defended working-class and interracial justice causes.

Unfortunately, not all Irish-American bishops, priests, and lay political and labor leaders applied their Church's social justice program to nonwhites. With few exceptions, they were slow in extending the virtue of Christian charity to African and Hispanic Americans. In many heavily Catholic cities in the 1950s, 1960s, and 1970s, Irish and other Catholics resisted educational and housing integration without much clerical censure. However, there were important exceptions to this indifference and negligence. Irish-American politicians in the Democratic Party urged and voted for civil rights legislation, and many priests, nuns, and brothers, often Irish, were active in agitating for racial equality in the North and South. In general, Catholic education has had a good record in promoting equality of opportunity and status. Inner-city parochial schools, established by the Irish and other white Catholic ethnics and still financed through their generosity, now educate African American and Hispanic-American children, filling a quality vacuum caused by the deficiencies of public education.

Acceptability and Respectability

John Fitzgerald Kennedy's 1960 election as president of the United States marked the end of the long Irish journey from unskilled, working-class pioneers of the urban ghetto to college-educated, middle-class inhabitants of prosperous city and suburban neighborhoods, from the despised targets of nativism to America's favorite ethnics. During the Kennedy presidency, John McCormack, Speaker of the House of Representatives; Mike Mansfield, Senate majority leader; John Bailey, chairman of the Democratic National Committee; George Meaney, president of the combined AFL–CIO, the most powerful labor leader in the country; and the majority of Catholic bishops were Irish. When Irish America reached this apogee, seminaries and convents were brimful of idealistic young men and women offering considerable talents to the Church; Catholic elementary and secondary schools, colleges, and universities had increasing enrollments and had modernized and improved their curricula; the laity crowded parish churches for daily as well as Sunday Masses, and frequently received the sacraments; priests, nuns, brothers, and laypeople were active in promoting social justice causes; and Irish names were prominent in the American delegation to Vatican Council II. Theologically their input was minimal, but they did succeed in persuading the council to accept American values concerning religious toleration, freedom of conscience, political democracy, and ecumenism. Irish-Americans were triumphal over their political and religious success story, but, as the old saying goes, the candle burns brightest just before it goes out.

Fading Identity

Kennedy's presidency not only symbolized the political power of Irish Catholics, it also represented their integration into American cultural and political mainstreams. Pre-1960 Irish-American Catholics, largely through the educational benefits of the G. I. Bill of Rights, had achieved middle-class respectability, and political influence in Congress as well as city government, but they still retained an ambivalence concerning their place in the United States. Psychologically they had not yet completely recovered

from nativist accusations that they were alien to the spirit of the country. Al Smith's failed presidential bid in 1928 fertilized Irish paranoia. Many attributed his defeat to anti-Catholic prejudices. Despite their economic mobility, late 1950s Irish and other Catholics were a separate cultural and social community, segregated by their own as well as by the choice of other Americans.

Kennedy's occupancy of the White House and his national and international popularity emancipated Catholic America from its inferiority complex. After the November 1960 election, John Ford, the outstanding Irish-American film director, wrote to a friend to say that for the first time he felt like a first-class citizen. Liberated from their defensive neuroses and suspicions of other Americans, Irish Catholics began to socialize with Protestant and Jewish neighbors and professional colleagues. Quite a few sent their children to prestigious public schools and state and private non-Catholic colleges and universities. Some married outside the faith. No longer was the parish an almost complete community or the focal point of Irish life.

An Irish sense of belonging and cultural assimilation led them to reconsider their complex and paradoxical allegiances to American liberal democracy and Roman Catholic authoritarianism. Pope Pius IV's 1968 encyclical, *Humanae vitae,* initiated a long and continuing conflict with the latter. Even before the Pope restated the Church's traditional opposition to artificial means of birth control, a number of American Catholics, determined on limiting the size of their families so that they could provide their children the best in health and education, and opposed to the physically and psychologically unnatural and ineffective Church-approved rhythm system, used contraceptive devices. Since a papal commission in 1967 had recommended that the Church leave family-planning decisions to private consciences, Paul IV's rejection of its advice triggered objections throughout the Western World.

Since they were the best-educated and most prosperous group of American Catholics, the Irish led the rebellion against what they considered abuses of religious authority. Once they objected to the decision on contraception, they began to question such other Roman dictates as a celibate clergy, an all-male priesthood, and the exclusion of divorced Catholics from the sacraments. While most Catholics oppose abortion on demand, a majority also tolerate if not approve it in such emergency situations as the mental and physical health of the mother, rape, and incest.

Post-Vatican II liturgical changes have offended a number of Irish Catholics on both the liberal and conservative spectrums. They miss the loss of the history and mystery of the Latin Mass and Gregorian chant. They find the vernacular liturgy, pop style music, and the emphasis on homilies uninspiring if not ugly. Conservatives believe that nothing should have changed; many liberals would have preferred the Church to remain liturgically traditional while modernizing and rationalizing her rules and theology.

Irish America's resistance to Church authority on sexual matters probably contains some of what Pope John Paul II has depicted as selfish materialism. But it is more indicative of political Americanization. Most Irish-American Catholics no longer suffer from a split personality. They refuse to accept the notion that a person can be free in one aspect of his or her life and enslaved in another. They insist that in order to command obedience and respect, authority must be reasonable. They expect the same concern and sensitivity from the Church for the needs and rights of the individual as they do from the state. In their opinion, Rome has not met this standard.

Cultural Americanization has worked against the Catholicism of Irish America beyond the question of freedom and authority. Since associations between religion and ethnicity have been such an integral ingredient in Irish identity, as Irish-Americans become more American and less Irish, their Catholic enthusiasms and loyalty diminish. The identity problem works both ways; a dwindling Catholicity has decreased Irishness. As in other areas of the American Catholic experience, the declining dual nationality and religious identities of the Irish probably preview what is happening or is about to happen with other ethnics.

Because some Irish-American Catholics object to what they consider abuses of authority, an intellectually irrelevant theology, and a boring liturgy, there has been a severe drop in Mass attendance and the reception of the sacraments, donations in Sunday envelopes, and the number of students in parochial schools. With the assimilation of Irish America into the American cultural and social mainstreams, and the wide variety of opportunities now open to them, they no longer contribute their best and brightest to the Church. Since the Irish have been the leading source of religious vocations, this has meant a quantitative and qualitative shortage of priests, nuns, and brothers to serve Catholic schools, parishes, and health-care facilities. Since Rome refuses to change its view on the ordination of married men or women, the American Church faces a bleak future of parishes either closing or functioning without a resident priest, a dismal prospect for a creed that emphasizes the Mass and sacraments.

At roughly 18 percent of the total Catholic population, the Irish are still the largest ethnic group in the Church. And they continue to be overrepresented in the hierarchy and clergy. About 50 percent of American bishops are Irish. But it would be more than a slight exaggeration to say that the American Church remains a part of an Irish spiritual empire. Embracing the best and the worst features of American life and culture, the Irish have assimilated. Catholicism no longer is the essence of their lives. And the Church, no longer an immigrant institution, has moved away from its European roots in an effort to accommodate African, Hispanic, and Asian Americans and blend them and white ethnics into an inclusive Catholicism.

Vanishing Irish-American identity is apparent in politics and nationalism as well as in religion. In the late 1960s and early 1970s, during the early stages of the civil rights conflict in Northern Ireland, and then again in the early 1980s in response to the Irish Republican Army and Irish National Liberation Army hunger strikes in Belfast's Long Kesh (Maze) prison, there was considerable Irish-American financial and emotional support for the Catholic nationalist cause in the six counties. But when it became clear that the IRA and INLA were vicious terrorist organizations that frequently killed women and children as well as British soldiers, and that they were not even representative of the Catholic minority in Northern Ireland, Irish-American sympathies for the armed struggle in the North cooled. In general, the Irish are so successful in the United States, and so preoccupied with American concerns, that the vast majority know little of nor care much for Ireland.

Quite a few of the overabundant Irish lawyers are still attracted to politics on the local, state, and national stages. But it does not have the allure of former days. No longer does anti-Catholic nativism obstruct Irish business and professional opportunities. Now Irish political skills are on display in the boardrooms of America's most powerful and prestigious corporations.

A number of prominent Irish politicians such as Thomas Foley, George Mitchell, and the Kennedys still wear the Democratic label, but Hibernian names can be found on Republican city, suburban, county, and state tickets. More than Protestants or German Catholics, Irish voters cast Democratic ballots in presidential and congressional elections, but not in the high percentages of the past. In recent elections, their choices of Democrats or Republicans are close to evenly balanced. Those voting for the latter have abandoned communal liberal values for middle-class economic interests and/or have rejected the social liberalism of Democratic Party platforms and legislation.

Since their ethnicity has become less religious and political and more cultural, Irish history and literature courses have become immensely popular on college and university campuses, and there is considerable interest in traditional Irish music. Other signs of cultural searches for identity are the successes of the mostly academic interdisciplinary American Conference for Irish Studies and the more populist Irish-American Cultural Institute.

Cultural and intellectual emphases in Irish ethnicity have not enlisted the massive support of Irish-American Catholics. Without the strong commitment to Catholicism as cultural and psychological ethnicity, and the loyalty to the Democratic Party that expressed their communal political values, they now seem almost indistinguishable from Anglo-American Protestants. Perhaps the Irish segment of the rich and colorful American ethnic mosaic was only painted glass that has faded in the bright sunshine of American opportunity and success.

_____

Adams, W. F. *Ireland and Irish Emigration to the New World from 1815 to the Famine.* New Haven, 1952.

Curran, Joseph M. *Hibernian Green on the Silver Screen: The Irish and American Movies.* Westport, Conn.: Greenwood Press, 1989.

Dolan, Jay P. *The American Catholic Experience.* New York: Doubleday, 1985.

Fanning, Charles. *The Irish Voice in America: Irish-American Fiction from the 1780s to the 1980s.* Lexington: The University of Kentucky Press, 1990.

McCaffrey, Lawrence J. *The Irish Diaspora in America.* Washington, D.C.: The Catholic University of America Press, 1984.

_____. *Textures of Irish America.* New York: Syracuse University Press, 1992.

Wittke, Carl. *The Irish in America.* Baton Rouge, 1956.

LAWRENCE J. McCAFFREY

ITALIAN CATHOLIC IMMIGRANTS, HISTORICAL BACKGROUND

The nationalism ignited by the French Revolution and the Napoleonic occupation in the early years of the nineteenth century resulted in the formation of the kingdom of Italy between 1859 and 1861. On March 17, 1861, Victor Emmanuel II, king of Sardinia-Piedmont, was proclaimed king of Italy. The leadership of the unification movement had been primarily Piedmontese, and the Italy that emerged, then a country of twenty-two million inhabitants, was to be dominated by the north. The constitution granted to Sardinia-Piedmont by King Charles Albert in 1848 became the fundamental law of united Italy. It provided for a two-house legislature, a senate entirely appointed by the king, and a Chamber of Deputies elected by a very restricted franchise. The government was essentially a parliamentary dictatorship and remained so until Mussolini came to power in 1922 and evolved his own personal dictatorship.

At the time of unification, the entire peninsula was economically and socially behind most of Western Europe. The country was predominantly agricultural, and the peasants who tended tiny plots or worked as day laborers or sharecroppers were never far from starvation. The south (the so-called Mezzogiorno), comprising all of Italy south of Rome, with two-fifths of the total population, was in general more backward and impoverished than the north. The condition of the south was the product of many factors, such as inefficient methods of agriculture, soil erosion, scarcity of water, malaria, earthquakes, banditry, and the paternalistic and unprogressive character of Bourbon rule.

The prevailing form of land tenure in the south was the large farm, the *latifondo,* which had originated in Roman times. The owners of these estates were few in number and were seldom directly involved in the management of their lands. Most peasant plots were extremely small, and the majority of the peasants were casual laborers or sharecroppers. Almost all peasants were illiterate and malnourished.

Prior to unification life in the Mezzogiorno was tolerable because the Bourbon Kingdom of the Two Sicilies (as the south was known until Garibaldi's conquest) had a small national debt, imposed light taxes, and ensured low food prices. Conditions in the south changed for the worse after unification and produced profound disillusionment, expressed in frequent insurrections against the national government and massive emigration.

Sources of Southern Discontent

The sources of discontent were both economic and political. The imposition of a grist tax on wheat and corn was a heavy burden for the peasants, while such industries as the south possessed, such as textiles, faced competition from the north. Naples under the Bourbons had been fairly prosperous, but after unification public services declined, building contracts that previously had been granted to southerners were now awarded to northerners, and thousands of southerners lost employment in the bureaucracy.

Political discontent was engendered by the national policy of centralization. The fear of Turin (Italy's first capital) was that regional autonomy would lead to national disintegration and corrupt local politics. Centralization involved the extension of the Piedmontese administrative and judicial system to the whole of Italy, regardless of local traditions. The effect of "Piedmontization" was to promote provincialism and even separatism, especially in Sicily.

The sense of southern exclusion from the government was intensified by the fact that until 1876 all prime ministers were northerners, and no political group took up the cause of the south. Political parties in the twentieth century sense of the term did not exist. Governments were ministries of the Right *(la Destra),* which were conservative, or the Left *(la Sinistra),* which were somewhat less conservative than the Right. Whether Right or Left, they were a coalition of diverse groups. For decades most politicians were inclined to deny the existence of a "southern problem."

The imposition of conscription in the early 1860s was another southern grievance since men were needed to farm the land. To avoid the draft many men joined bands of brigands. Brigandage did not originate with unification, but the new brigands received encouragement and money from Francis II, the last king of the Kingdom of the Two Sicilies, who was living in Rome. Though the brigands included criminals and fugitives from justice as well as draft evaders and impoverished peasants, the masses regarded them as heroes bent on avenging the cruelties foisted on them by a heartless national government.

Between 1862 and 1865 civil war prevailed in the southern countryside and the national government was forced to send 120,000 troops to quell the disturbances. Thousands of southerners were killed, wounded, or imprisoned. The end of Italy's war with Austria in 1866 (resulting in the acquisition of Venice) saw a revival of southern warfare against the national government. A special expeditionary force was dispatched from Genoa to put down the revolt. Among those arrested for having supported the rebels was the archbishop of Monreale.

By the late 1860s Italy faced huge deficits resulting from the wars of unification, the war against Austria, the suppression of southern insurgency, and excessive expenditures on public works and the armed services. The government's solution to the debt problem was in part the reimposition of the grist tax, which had been repealed. The enforcement of the grist tax provoked a revival of rioting, followed by a draconian military crackdown. Parish priests and monks who showed sympathy for the peasants were arrested and imprisoned.

Another method of raising money for the national treasury was the confiscation of ecclesiastical estates. The general atmosphere was conducive to such confiscation because of prevailing anticlericalism. The papacy had opposed unification, and when it was accomplished, it was at the expense of the Papal States. Rome, the last vestige of the Papal States, fell to the troops of Victor Emmanuel II in 1870. The pope retaliated by forbidding Catholic participation in national politics and in denying recognition to the kingdom of Italy.

Although the parliamentary law providing for the confiscation of Church lands had specified that the land be sold in small lots to the peasants, only the large landowners and the wealthy bourgeoisie could afford to buy the land. Peasants who bought land with borrowed money soon discovered that they could not repay the loans and were forced into bankruptcy. Tenant farmers were worse off than before because instead of paying relatively low rents to the Church, they now had to pay high rents to rapacious lay landlords. To compound the existing misery, phylloxera ruined southern vineyards in the 1870s.

An electoral law passed in 1882 while the Left governed Italy gave the franchise to about 7 percent of the Italians (up from the previous 2 percent). The south did not benefit from the franchise as much as the north because poverty, illiteracy, or hostility added few new southern voters to the electoral rolls. Through the decade of the 1880s, conditions in the south continued to deteriorate. The area lagged in education, health, and market facilities. Most peasants were casual laborers, fortunate if they could work half a year. The Church, having been deprived of its revenues, could provide little assistance.

Both north and south were severely hurt by a tariff war with France between 1887 and 1892. In addition to causing a national recession, it revived the revolutionary spirit of the Sicilians. Bank failures caused by overinvestment in the construction industry exacerbated the socioeconomic crisis. By the turn of the century two new ideologies contested the policies of the governing elite: Socialism, of Marxist inspiration, and Christian democracy, inspired by Pope Leo XIII's *Rerum Novarum*. Both were embodied in movements designed to improve the lot of the masses, but their antithetical ideologies precluded cooperation.

Emigration

The deplorable political, social, and economic conditions prevailing in Italy during the last three decades of the nineteenth century and the first two decades of the twentieth forced millions of Italians to forsake their homeland. Emigration was nothing new; in the preunification era Italians had moved around the peninsula or had gone to foreign countries in search of work. Most of the emigrants prior to the 1880s were from the north, and they went abroad to such countries as France, Germany, and Austria-Hungary. Their emigration was generally seasonal.

What was different about the emigration that occurred between 1880 and 1920 was that it was mostly southern in origin and permanent. Furthermore, these emigrants were more likely to go to the Americas, North and South, rather than to Europe. The overwhelming majority settled in the larger cities of the Eastern United States, where they often encountered discrimination and conditions as bad as those they had left behind.

In the late 1870s, 100,000 Italians were leaving each year; by 1913 this number had climbed to almost 900,000. When World War I broke out, Italy had a population of thirty-five million, but expatriated Italians numbered about six million. The government of Rome was more or less indifferent to this exodus and the Italian parliament intervened only to try to prevent speculators and steamship companies from exploiting the emigrants. The emigration to the United States would have continued indefinitely (at least until Mussolini's time) if the U.S. Congress had not enacted legislation in the early 1920s that clearly discriminated against those coming from southern and eastern Europe.

See also ITALIAN CATHOLICS IN AMERICA.

Absalom, Roger. *Italy Since 1800.* New York: Longman, 1995.

Clark, Mark. *Modern Italy 1871–1982.* New York: Longman, 1984.

Di Scala, Spencer. *Italy from Revolution to Republic.* Boulder, Colo.: Westview, 1995.

Gambino, Richard. *Blood of My Blood.* Garden City, N.Y.: Anchor Books, 1975.

Smith, Denis Mack. *Italy: A Modern History.* Ann Arbor: University of Michigan Press, 1969.

ELISA A. CARRILLO

ITALIAN CATHOLICS IN AMERICA

Missionaries to the Americas, 1492–1850

Questions of Italian spirituality shape the very beginnings of European expansion to the Americas. To earlier authors such as Samuel Eliot Morison, Christopher Columbus was the quintessential Renaissance figure who cast aside tradition and received wisdom in favor of exploration. Recent histories have depicted Columbus as the heir of the Middle Ages, a mystic driven by the sense that a Providential Creator had drawn up a destiny for each person, and that his destiny included bringing Christianity to places where it was not yet known.

Many Italian-born explorers followed in Columbus's wake. John Cabot (1450–98) sailed to Cape Breton Island for England. Enrico Tonti (1650–1704) accompanied René Robert de La Salle's French expeditions and ended his life as governor of French territory in the lower Mississippi valley. Alessandro Malaspine (1754–1810) circumnavigated the globe for Spain. None sailed under an Italian flag. The Italian peninsula was at that time divided into various principalities whose rulers either lacked resources to mount expeditions, used their resources to open Eastern trade routes, or spent their wealth trying to maintain their positions in Europe.

Similarly, Italian Catholic missionaries came to the Americas in the service of others. Rather than identify with Italy, they identified with the evangelization efforts of the religious orders of which they were members. One example is Eusebio Kino, S.J. (1654–1711), who in 1681 sailed from Cadiz to Vera Cruz. Kino founded missions in present-day southern Arizona in the San Miguel, Magdalena, Altar, Santa Cruz, and San Pedro Valleys. Calls for his beatification have sparked a debate as to the mixture of evangelization and exploitation in his and other missionaries' treatment of Southwestern tribes.

Farther northwest, Juan Maria Salvatierra, S.J. (1644–1717), pioneered the California missions, not by founding institutions but by developing financing. Spanish authorities granted the Jesuits permission to evangelize California, but declined to subsidize their efforts. Salvatierra and colleague Juan de Ugarte begged from wealthy laity, a campaign later systematized as the Pious Fund. The Jesuits administered missions in California until 1767, when the Spanish replaced that order with the Franciscans.

Similarly, Italian Catholic missionaries in New France identified not with their birthplace but with their religious community's evangelization efforts. Francesco Giuseppe Bressani, S.J. (1612–72), worked among Algonquins in Canada from 1642 to 1644, and among other tribes in Canada and northern New York from 1645 to 1650. (During the interval he was a prisoner of the Iroquois.)

Protestant England did not promote Catholic interests in its colonies. Notable Italian Catholic names appear only after 1776, when the English colonies became the United States. Some states maintained legal discriminations against Catholics, but more did not, and the constitution prohibited religious discrimination at the federal level. Neither ethnicity nor religion prevented Charles Constantine Pise (1801–66), the son of an Italian resident of Annapolis, Maryland, from serving as the first Italian Roman Catholic chaplain of the United States Senate (1832–33).

As the United States expanded westward, it continued to utilize Italians from religious orders as missionaries on its frontiers and in areas with Catholic populations too small to generate native clergy. Joseph B. Rosati, C.M. (1789–1843), came to the United States in 1815 to assist Louis William DuBourg, apostolic administrator of the upper and lower Mississippi. Rosati performed so well that DuBourg requested that Rosati be named coadjutor for New Orleans and placed in charge of the northern Louisiana Territory. At the time of Rosati's consecration in 1824 his jurisdiction stretched to the Canadian border. Rosati ended his missionary career as bishop of St. Louis (1826–43). Rosati's fellow Neapolitan, Ignatius Persico, O.F.M. Cap. (1823–95), came to South Carolina in 1867 and served as bishop of Savannah, Georgia (1870–72). Both of these were among the original states, but were mission territory insofar as the number of Catholics were concerned.

The most prominent Italian Catholic missionary in the Old Northwest was Samuel Charles Mazzuchelli, O.P. (1806–64). Mazzuchelli came to the United States in 1828 and was ordained in Cincinnati in 1830. Among his accomplishments were founding parishes in Galena, Illinois, and Dubuque, Iowa; designing church buildings and Iowa City's Old State Capitol; organizing the Sinsinawa Mound College for men and the Sinsinawa Dominican institute for women religious; service as vicar general of the Diocese of Dubuque; publication of a prayer book and memoirs; and a heroic death—he contracted his fatal illness ministering to the victims of an epidemic.

Although federal policy was to use Christian missionaries to assimilate the members of native tribes to white Anglo-Saxon culture, Italian Catholics continued to do much evangelical work. Antonio Ravalli, S.J. (1812–84), worked among the Flatheads from 1844 to 1850, and then from 1860 to his death. (The hiatus was caused by hostilities with the Blackfeet.) He became so significant in Montana history that a country was named for him. Blandina Segale, S.C. (1850–1941), worked according to the title of her memoirs, "at the end of the Santa Fe Trail." Giuseppe Maria Cataldo, S.J. (1837–1928), came to the United States in 1862. Until 1877 he worked among the Nez Perce; he wrote a prayer book and a life of Christ in the Nez Perce language. After sixteen years as superior of the Jesuits' Rocky Mountain Mission (1877–93), he returned to the field as a missionary, and continued to labor into the twentieth century.

United States higher education also benefited from Italian Catholic missionaries. Gregorio Mengarini, S.J. (1811–86), and John Nobili, S.J. (1818–56), helped found what is now the University of Santa Clara (chartered 1855). The aforementioned Giuseppe Cataldo founded Gonzaga University in Spokane, Washington. Mengarini and Nobili died at Santa Clara; other Italian missionary scholars moved in international circles of learning. Camillo Cardinal Mazzella, S.J. (1833–1900), lectured on dogmatic and moral theology at the Jesuits' Woodstock Seminary (1867–78); he later became known as a prominent neo-Thomist. Still other Italian missionary scholars took up a different field. Nicholas Russo, S.J. (1845–1902), served as president of Boston College, but died as pastor of Our Lady of Loreto Church, a converted tenement in the congested Sicilian neighborhood of Elizabeth Street, New York. Not all Italian educators were Jesuits. Italian Franciscans led by Panfilio Pierbattista da Magliano founded St. Bonaventure's College in the Diocese of Buffalo.

By the 1850s, Italian migrants had formed noticeable communities in major port cities. The first permanent Italian national parish in the United States, St. Mary Magdalen da Pazzi, was dedicated in Philadelphia in 1857. In some dioceses, clergy followed laity. Gennaro Vincenzo De Concilio (1836–98) was ordained in Genoa in 1860 and migrated to Newark. His ministry in the United States included service as assistant pastor at Our Lady of Grace, Hoboken, and St. Mary's, Jersey City, teaching theology and serving as chaplain at Seton Hall, South Orange, New Jersey, membership on the committee which compiled the Baltimore Catechism for the Third Plenary Council, and writing pamphlets opposing theistic evolution and advocating better pastoral care of Italians.

Italian Immigrants in the United States, 1880–1914

A brief introduction to Italian migratory demography will put in context Italian spiritual life and American pastoral care of the emigrants. Two factors operated to drive Italians from their homeland. Politics played a minor role. Many of the rulers of the various Italian principalities resisted the development of an Italian nation-state and attacked those who advocated it. Individuals such as Giuseppe Garibaldi (1807–82) found it expedient to leave Italy for a while. Garibaldi himself lived with fellow Italian Antonio Meucci (1808–89) at the latter's home on Staten Island, New York. Because the papacy was the secular ruler of territory in the center of Italy, and because various members of the hierarchy and several religious orders opposed the unification of the peninsula, revolutionaries such as Garibaldi saw Catholicism as part of an oppressive political and economic system. They neither practiced Catholicism themselves nor encouraged the pastoral care of migrants.

Economics was the major force pushing migrants out of Italy, and economic forces acted differently on different classes. Entrepreneurs, especially from Genoa and the surrounding territory of Liguria, gambled on the chance that they might establish successful businesses in the United States. Sometimes these gambles paid off handsomely. Historian Victor Greene describes how Luigi Fugazy (1839–1930) settled in New York as a banker for his compatriots. Such middle-class entrepreneurs became community leaders. Organizing churches was one element in their community leadership. As part of his work as community leader, Fugazy signed the incorporation papers of Our Lady of Pompeii, an Italian Catholic parish in Greenwich Village, New York.

Economic forces operated differently on those who had only their labor to sell. Historian John Zucchi described how poverty led parents to indenture their children to entrepreneurs who then took the youths to the large cities of Italy, the rest of Europe, and the United States to work as street musicians and beggars. Adolescent boys and adult men traveled far within Italy and overseas to get work as day laborers in agriculture, construction, mining, and manufacturing. Adolescent girls and women found work locally and tended the family's fields. After 1870, when Italy became a nation-state and embarked on an ambitious drive to become a European Great Power, taxes and compulsory military service were increased and extended to the impoverished southern part of Italy and to the island of Sicily. Italians responded by going farther afield in search of work and cash.

In 1880 Italian migration to the United States surpassed 10,000 per year for the first time. In 1900 it reached 100,000 per year, and remained high until World War I. Three-quarters of the migrants who came to the United States were males of working age; their goal was to find jobs that allowed them to save money and then return to Italy to use their savings to meet family needs. Four-fifths of the migrants to the United States came from southern Italy or from Sicily. Of those, half could not read or write in Italian, and in all parts of Italy it was common for people to speak dialects rather than standard Italian.

Among American Catholics there was much debate over the "Italian problem." Those charged with the pastoral care of Italians determined policy not by studying the Italians but by identifying their own goals. Ordinaries such as John Ireland and Michael Augustine Corrigan, who differed over other issues, agreed that the desirable outcome of Italian pastoral care would be church-going, law-abiding Catholics who would prove to non-Catholic Americans the compatibility of Catholicism and American patriotism. In theory, Ireland might have fostered assimilation more actively than Corrigan, but the actual situation drove all ordinaries toward the same methods of pastoral care. The Italians spoke little English and had their well-established religious customs. Other American bishops were prejudiced against them and worried that they could not support parishes or clergy. All over the United States, ordinaries began by appending Italian congregations to existing parishes and, as the number of Italians and the number of those able to minister to them increased, they moved to separate Italian national parishes staffed by secular clergy or by Italian religious orders.

The earliest religious orders in Italian migrant care had to be multilingual and multicultural. The Franciscans who came in 1866 to staff St. Anthony of Padua Church in the SoHo area of Manhattan were charged with the care of both the Italians and the English-speaking Catholics who lived within the parish's territorial boundaries. The Franciscans who came to Boston's North End in 1873 ministered to a Portuguese-Italian congregation that eventually grew into two separate ethnic communities. The members of the Society of the Catholic Apostolate who in 1884 came to New York to organize Our Lady of Mount Carmel Church in East Harlem had to minister to a congregation whose members spoke English, German, and Italian.

Besides secular clergy who migrated to the U.S.A., dioceses also utilized the services of various religious orders. The Servites came to Chicago, where they staffed many parishes and produced an able advocate of Italian pastoral care in Luigi Giambastiani, O.S.M. The Augustinians already had Italian-speaking clergy at Villanova University in the Archdiocese of Philadelphia at the time of the Italian mass migration, and so Augustinians staffed parishes in the archdiocese. They, too, produced an advocate of Italian pastoral care, Aurelio Palmieri, O.S.A.

Special mention should be made of the Pious Society of Saint Charles—the Scalabrinians. Their founder, Giovanni Battista Scalabrini (1839–1905), a native of Como, was consecrated bishop of Piacenza in 1875. On his first pastoral visit around his diocese, he discovered the extent to which the people of his area depended on migration for their livelihood. He published several pamphlets on the need for better pastoral care of Italian migrants: *L'Emigrazione Italiana in America* (1887), *Il Desegno di Legge Sulla Emigrazione Italiana* (1888), *Prima Conferenza sull' Emigrazione* (1891), and *Dell'Assistenza alla Emigrazione Nazionale e degli istituti che vi provvedono* (1891). In 1887 he founded a community of male religious to minister to Italian migrants in their new homes. The first missionaries departed for New York in 1888. The community spread rapidly, and provided clergy to widely scattered Italian settlements.

Some ordinaries assigned to the Italian apostolate secular clergy who had received part of their training in Rome and who spoke Italian. In Chicago, Edmund Dunne (d. 1929) took over the work of Paul Ponziglione, S.J., who had been teaching catechism to Italian children on Chicago's South Side. Dunne used the community as the basis for

Holy Guardian Angel parish, which was opened in 1898. He left the parish in 1905 when he was appointed bishop of Peoria. In New York, Daniel M. Burke (1858–1931) founded St. Philip Neri parish in the Bedford Park section of the Bronx, also in 1898. Burke acted as a liaison between Italian parishes and the archdiocesan bureaucracy until a fatal traffic accident cut short his career.

Few Italian secular priests migrated to the United States, and few found acceptance from American ordinaries, who regarded them as incompetent and avaricious. Numerous individual careers belied these stereotypes. Gennaro De Concilio has already been mentioned. Archbishop Michael Augustine Corrigan recruited Gherardo Ferrante (1853–1921) for New York. Ferrante served as "Italian Secretary" to Corrigan and his successors, John Cardinal Farley and Patrick Cardinal Hayes. In this capacity, Ferrante translated correspondence, acted as liaison with Italian parishes, and administered the temporal affairs of Italian communities of sisters. After World War II, clergy of Italian ancestry became more numerous and more prominent. In May 1954, the Archdiocese of New York consecrated its first Sicilian-born auxiliary bishop, Joseph Maria Pernicone. Francis Mugavero served as bishop of Brooklyn from 1968 to 1990. Joseph Cardinal Bernardin was installed as archbishop of Chicago in 1982, elevated to cardinal in 1983, and died in 1996. Other Italian-American priests moved up the ranks. Luigi Ligutti (b. 1895) was director of the National Catholic Rural Life Conference and later a member of the United Nations' Food and Agricultural Organization. Geno Baroni (1930–84) served as Assistant Secretary of Housing and Urban Development in the Carter administration.

Besides parishes, Italian clergy also worked in nonparochial institutions. The earliest was the St. Raphael Society for the Protection of Italian Emigrants, which Bishop Giovanni Battista Scalabrini and Marquis Giovanni Battista Volpe-Landi organized in 1890, using as a model the St. Raphael Society for the Protection of German Catholic Emigrants. (St. Raphael is the patron saint of travelers.) Genoa, the major northern port of Italian embarkation, and New York and Boston, the major points of Italian debarkation, had St. Raphael branches. At each branch, a chaplain attended to the migrants' spiritual and material needs. (The first chaplain of the New York branch, Pietro Bandini, was a Scalabrinian who had a previous career as a Jesuit in the Rocky Mountain Mission to Native Americans.) In Boston, Miss Eleanor Colleton managed the society's temporal affairs. Several religious orders had traditions of preaching missions and expanded to include missions in Italian. Roberto Biasotti came to the United States as a Scalabrinian but separated from the community and developed an "Italian Apostolate" associated with the Archdiocese of New York from 1912 to ca. 1917.

Women religious contributed greatly to Italian migrant pastoral care. The aforementioned Sr. Blandina Segale returned to Cincinnati from the end of the Santa Fe Trail in 1893. She and her blood sister, Justina Segale, S.C., founded the Santa Maria Institute in that city. The institute functioned as a settlement house, offering catechism instructions, English and citizenship lessons, home economics demonstrations, youth programs, and employment and welfare assistance. Sr. Blandina continued to work with Cincinnati Italians until her death at the age of ninety-one.

As Mary Louise Sullivan, M.S.C., explained in her biography, Frances Xavier Cabrini's activities earned her the title "Italian Immigrant of the Century." Cabrini (1850–1917) brought her first group of Missionaries of the Sacred Heart to New York in 1889, in conjunction with the Scalabrinians. From New York the community spread across the United States and into Latin America and South America. The missionaries founded orphanages, hospitals, and girls' schools, and engaged in home visiting, prison ministry, after-school catechism classes, and parochial school teaching.

Many other institutes of women religious entered the mission field. The Religious Teachers Filippini specialized in parochial school teaching and in the education of young women. The community's first foundation in the United States was in the Diocese of Trenton in 1910. They developed a system of bilingual education for Italian parochial school children in the diocese. The Pallottine Sisters of Charity staffed daycare centers, orphanages, parochial schools, and a hospice of the New York branch of the St. Raphael Society. The Apostoles of the Sacred Heart (also known as the Missionary Zelatrices of the Sacred Heart) first came to Boston in 1902 in conjunction with the Scalabrinians, and went into parochial school teaching in several dioceses.

The laity played several roles in the development of Italian-American Catholicism. They financed the efforts of the Italian clergy and sisters. Sometimes one wealthy layperson provided a subsidy; one reason Mother Cabrini came to New York when she did was that Mary Reid de Cesnola, wife of the Italian-born director of the New York Metropolitan Museum of Art, expressed an interest in financing an orphanage for Italian girls and wanted Italian sisters to staff it. In other cases, committees of laypeople worked together. In Boston, a group of Genoese laity dissatisfied with the management of the Italian parish organized the Società San Marco and successfully negotiated the establishment of Sacred Heart Church in Boston's North End. Luigi Bolzan, in his *Memories of an Italian Parish,* recorded how the lay trustees of Sacred Heart Church, Cincinnati, cooperated with the Scalabrinians in founding the parish, provided it with stability during its early years, and continued to look after its temporal affairs.

With great difficulty, several Italian communities preserved a distinct custom, the annual *festa. Feste,* to use the Italian plural, originated in Italy as annual communal celebrations of an area's patron saint. In southern Italy these were elaborate rituals which included processions carrying the saint's statue and evening fireworks displays. Although other Catholic ethnic groups had their own outdoor affairs (St. Patrick's Day parades, for example), American Catholics found the Italian *feste* distasteful. And, although northern Italians had similar devotions to the Madonna and the saints, they worried that southern Italian *feste* gave all Italians reputations for rowdiness. The southern Italians persisted, and succeeded in making *feste* part of the fabric of American Catholicism. Our Lady of Mount Carmel, East Harlem, was founded for Salernitani gathered to honor the patroness of their home valley. On Mulberry Street, New York, a lay society perpetuated the celebration of San Gennaro, the patron of Naples. St. Anthony of Padua in SoHo, New York, celebrated no *feste* during the period of mass migration. Since then, it has inaugurated an annual *festa* as a community builder and fundraiser.

*Maintaining an Italian, American,
and Catholic Identity since 1914*

Several factors reduced Italian migration after 1914. World War I (1914–18) brought a temporary end to migration. In 1921 the United States inaugurated a series of immigration reforms aimed at discouraging migration from southern and eastern Europe. The final form of this legislation, enacted in 1927, permitted fewer than 5,000 natives of Italy to enter the United States annually. In 1922 the Fascists assumed control of the Italian government and introduced their own emigration reforms aimed at curbing the migration of men eligible for military service. The Great Depression (1929–41), with its high unemployment rates, further discouraged migration to the United States. World War II (in the United States, 1941–45) again halted migration for several years. The 1952 McCarran-Walter Act added more restrictions to United States immigration, this time to prevent communists or fascists from entering the country. A short burst of Italian migration followed the major revision of Untied States immigration legislation in 1965. However, Italy had recovered from World War II and achieved a relatively stable economic system so that individuals no longer needed to migrate to earn a living. In the United States, this meant the reduction of pressures to care for incoming migrants, and the development of a long-running debate as to whether the Italians had been fully accepted into American society.

Another series of events resolved an issue which had influenced American Catholic stereotypes of their Italian coreligionists. In 1929, the Italian government and the Holy See signed the Lateran Treaties. These treaties still provide the basis for relations between the Vatican and the Italian nation that completely surrounds it. No longer could the Italians be stereotyped as anticlerical enemies of the papacy unlikely to make good Catholic Americans. In fact, during the cold war, Francis Cardinal Spellman mobilized Italian Americans for a campaign in which they wrote their Italian relatives in support of Italy's Christian Democrats in that party's battle with the Communists for political control.

The new acceptance of Italian Catholics made it easier for the Italian Catholics themselves to have influence on public policy. During the 1950s, the National Catholic Welfare Conference (now the U.S. Catholic Conference) called for popular lobbying to repeal laws which discriminated against potential migrants on the basis of their national origins. The American Italians, sympathizing with the Italians who were especially disadvantaged by the quota laws, organized the American Italian Committee on Migration. ACIM assisted in placing refugee Italian families, and lobbied for a general revision of the laws. The 1965 immigration legislation replaced national quotas with a system of preferences based on family reunification and job skills.

The end of mass migration by no means meant the end of Italian-American Catholic pastoral care. Elderly immigrants still required various forms of assistance, and preferred to receive aid in their native tongue and in a traditional manner, that is, through Christian charity rather than through private or public social programs. Italian parishes developed programs for senior citizens still living on their own, spiritual programs such as day-trips to religious sites, traditional devotions, and public celebrations of the Anointing of the Sick. The Scalabrinians have entered the ministry to the elderly by building and operating nursing homes.

Subsequent generations of Americans of Italian descent also call for particularized pastoral care. Those who were raised with certain religious customs wish to continue them, and to pass them on to their children. While making themselves fully a part of their local parishes, Italian immigrants and their descendants, by introducing their own religious practices, have made American Catholicism more fully a part of the universal Church.

In her work on the pastoral care of migrants in the Diocese of Hartford, Connecticut, historian Dolores Liptak noted that the Italian migration taught American Catholics how to minister to migrants. Since then, American Catholics have applied these lessons to more recent migrant groups. Parishes founded for Italians have discovered a new field for work among new migrants. Religious orders such as the Scalabrinians have also internationalized their apostolates.

Browne, Henry J. "The 'Italian Problem' in the Catholic Church in the United States, 1880–1900." *Historical Records and Studies* 35 (1946) 46–72.

Brown, Mary Elizabeth. *Churches, Communities, and Children: Italian Immigrants in the Archdiocese of New York, 1880–1945.* New York: Center for Migration Studies, 1995.
DeGiovanni, Stephen Michael. *Archbishop Corrigan and the Italian Immigrants.* Huntington, Ind.: Our Sunday Visitor, 1994.
Orsi, Robert A. *The Madonna of 115th Street: Faith Community in Italian Harlem, 1880–1950.* New Haven, Conn.: Yale University Press, 1985.
Schiavo, Giovanni E. *Italian-American History.* Vol. 2, *The Italian Contribution to the Catholic Church in America.* New York: The Vigo Press, 1949; repr. New York: Arno Press, 1975.
Tomasi, Silvano M. *Piety and Power: The Role of the Italian Parishes in the New York Metropolitan Area, 1880–1930.* New York: Center for Migration Studies, 1975.
U.S. Catholic Historian 6 (4) (Fall 1987). Special issue on Italian-American Catholicism.
Vecoli, Rudolph J. "Prelates and Peasants: Italian Immigrants and the Catholic Church." *Journal of Social History* 2 (Spring 1969) 217–68.

MARY ELIZABETH BROWN

Related Document

POPE LEO XIII'S PLEA FOR THE ITALIAN IMMIGRANTS IN AMERICA, DECEMBER 10, 1888

The first great wave of immigration to the United States before the Civil War had stamped the Catholic Church as the Church of the immigrant. That character became even more indelibly impressed during the so-called New Immigration of the years after 1880. Among the new arrivals the Italians occupied a prominent place, and since they were practically all at least nominal Catholics, it put a severe strain on the Church to provide adequate ministration for them. In 1880 there were only 44,230 Italian-born persons in the country, but by 1900 the number had risen to 484,027, and in the first decade of the twentieth century 2,104,309 arrived from Italy. Not all of these remained, however, for of all the late immigrants the Italians showed a greater tendency to return home after a time, and by 1910 it was estimated that about 800,000 had gone back to Italy. The plight of the Italians was aggravated by the abuses practiced against them through tricky labor contracts. Their condition became well known abroad and it was with a view to helping these unfortunate people, both spiritually and materially, that Pope Leo XIII addressed a special plea to the American hierarchy in December, 1888, in which he asked for their assistance in alleviating the lot of the Italian immigrants in this country.

(*Source*: Latin text, *American Ecclesiastical Review*, I [February 1889] 43–48; English translation adapted from the New York *Freeman's Journal*, January 5, 1889.)

HOW TOILSOME AND DISASTROUS IS THE CONDITION OF THOSE who for some years have been migrating out of Italy to the regions of America in search of a livelihood is so well known to you that nothing is to be gained by dwelling on it. Indeed, you see these evils at first hand and several of you have sorrowfully called our attention to them in repeated letters. It is to be deplored that so many unfortunate Italians, forced by poverty to change their residence, should rush into evils which are often worse than the ones they have desired to flee from. For very often to labors of various kinds that take away the life of the body, there is added the ruin of souls. At the outset the emigrants' crossing itself is full of dangers and injuries; for many of them fall into the hands of avaricious men whose slaves, as it were, they become, and then herded in ships and inhumanly treated, they are gradually depraved in their nature. And when they have reached the desired land, being ignorant of both the language and the locale, and engrossed in their daily toil, they become the victims of the trickery of the dishonest or the powerful by whom they are employed.[1] Those who by their own industry succeed sufficiently to assure for themselves a livelihood, associating constantly with people who regard everything from the point of view of business or profit, little by little lose the nobler feelings of human nature and learn to live like those who have set all their hopes and thoughts on this earth. To all this are added the ever present excitement of the passions, and the deceits practiced by the sects which flourish widely there to the injury of religion and which draw many into the path leading to destruction.

What is more lamentable among these evils is that because of the great multitude of these emigrants, the extent of the territory, and the local difficulties, it is by no means easy to provide these people with the saving care of ministers of God familiar with the Italian language, who would teach them the word of life, administer to them the sacraments, and provide for them timely help by which their souls might be lifted up in the hope of heavenly goods and their spiritual life be sustained and invigorated. In many places, therefore, there are very few who have a priest when they are dying, and there are many of the newly-born for whom there is none to administer the sacrament of regeneration. There are many who enter into marriage without regard to the Church's laws, and thereby give rise to an offspring similar to their parents. Thus there is everywhere with this people a decay of Christian morality and a growth of wickedness.[2]

Reflecting on all these things, and grieving at the wretched lot of so many whom we perceive to be wandering like sheep without a shepherd through steep paths and dangerous places, and at the same time mindful of the eternal Shepherd's love and warning, we have thought it our duty to render every possible help to them, to prepare wholesome nourishment, and to consult in every practical way for their good and salvation. We have been all the more inclined to enter upon this undertaking because of our love for men sprung from the same soil as ourselves, and because a sure hope inspires us that we shall not lack your own interest in the matter and your helpful assistance. Wherefore, we have taken care to have this matter con-

sidered by the Sacred Congregation of the Propaganda, and we have commanded it diligently to seek out and to examine the remedies by which so many evils and inconveniences can be removed, or at least be alleviated, and to propose to us what especially can be done both for the salvation of souls and for softening, as far as may be, the emigrants' hardships. But since the most potent cause of the growing evils is the lack of a priestly ministry through which heavenly grace is imparted and increased, we have determined to send to your country a number of priests from Italy accustomed to the language of their countrymen, to teach them the doctrine of faith and the unknown or neglected precepts of Christian life, to provide among them a salutary administration of the sacraments, to form the growing offspring to religion and good conduct, to help them in every way by advice and assistance, and to foster them by priestly care. To effect this the more conveniently we established by our letter of the 16th of November of last year, under the Fisherman's ring, an apostolic college of priests in the episcopal see of Piacenza, under the charge of our Venerable Brother John Baptist, Bishop of Piacenza,[3] so that ecclesiastics who are moved by a love of Christ may there cultivate those studies and be exercised in those employments and that sort of training by means of which they may earnestly and successfully perform the ministry of Christ for the scattered Italians and become fit dispensers of God's mysteries.

Among the students of this college, which we wish to be regarded as a sort of seminary of ministers of God for the salvation of Italians dwelling in America, we desire also that young men from your own country, children of Italian parents, be received and instructed; providing they are called to the vineyard of the Lord and have a wish to be initiated into Holy Orders, so that, having been ordained and returning to you, as many of them as there shall be need of will fulfill under your pastoral authority the work of the apostolic ministry. Nor do we doubt that on their return they will be received by you with fatherly love, and that also they will receive the necessary faculties for exercising the sacred ministry among their countrymen, subject to the admonition of the parish priest. For they will come to you to labor under the authority of those of you in whose dioceses they dwell. Especially at the outset of the work there will not, by any means, be so many of these helpers as the circumstances and times demand, nor will the labors of those who are sent be on a par with the number and needs of the faithful in such a way that the priests assigned to the care of souls can be appointed to separate and remote places. Wherefore, we deem it best that in dioceses where Italians are numerous there be common residences for these priests, so that they may go forth separately into the neighboring areas and perform their sacred functions on these expeditions. But in what manner or in what places these can best be established will be for your foresight to decide. All these things which we have thought to belong to our apostolic providence we have taken pains to signify to you in this letter. If any of you should discover, either by his own sense and judgment, or by consultation with his brethren, anything further that can be done by us for the welfare or comfort of those in whose behalf we are writing, let him know that he will do us a favor if he will carefully relate his proposal to the Sacred Congregation of the Propaganda.

From this work which we have undertaken for the care and defence of many souls that lack every comfort of the Catholic religion, we promise ourselves much fruit, especially if, as we hope, there be added for its support and protection, the interest and assistance of the faithful whose means are equal to their piety. As for the rest, praying the most benign God, Who wishes that all men shall be saved and come to the knowledge of the truth, that He will propitiously inspire this undertaking and give prosperous increase to it, we lovingly in the Lord, impart the apostolic benediction of our inmost affection to you, Venerable Brethren, and to the entire clergy and faithful over whom you are set.

Given at Rome, in St. Peter's, the 10th of December, 1888, in the eleventh year of our pontificate.

Leo XIII., Pope

[1] Leo XIII was referring here to the notorious treatment of the Italian immigrants under the *padrone* system which made them virtual slaves to their greedy fellow countrymen and others who exploited them through labor contracts in the United States and other countries. For these abuses cf. Robert F. Foerster, *The Italian Emigration of Our Times* (Cambridge, 1919), p. 390 ff.

[2] That the spiritual plight of the Italian immigrants was real may be gleaned from the statement made by Archbishop Corrigan of New York to Cardinal Manning on February 10, 1888, when he said, "There are 80,000 Italians in this city, of whom only two per cent have been in the habit of hearing Mass" (quoted in Shane Leslie, *Henry Edward Manning. His Life and Labours* [London, 1921]. p. 358). For the question of the Church and the Italian immigrants cf. Henry J. Browne, "The 'Italian Problem' in the Catholic Church of the United States, 1880–1900," *Historical Records and Studies*, XXXV (1946), 46–72.

[3] Giovanni B. Scalabrini (1839–1905), Bishop of Piacenza, founded the Congregation of Missionaries of St. Charles Borromeo of which two priests and a lay brother arrived in New York in July, 1888, to begin work among the Italian immigrants. In the following year the Missionary Sisters of the Sacred Heart of St. Francesca Cabrini (1850–1917) opened the first of their numerous American houses for the spiritual care of their fellow countrymen when Archbishop Corrigan blessed the ophanage on 59th Street, New York, on May 3, 1889.

(*Source*: John Tracy Ellis, ed. *Documents of American Catholic History*. Vol. 2:1866–1966. Wilmington, Del.: Michael Glazier, 1987, 466–70.)

IVES, LEVI SILLIMAN (1797–1867)

Episcopal bishop, Catholic convert. Levi Silliman Ives was born in Meriden, Connecticut, on September 16, 1797, and was reared in Turin, New York. He studied at Lowville Academy until his service in the War of 1812. Upon his return, he continued studies for the Presbyterian ministry at Hamilton College in Clinton, New York, but was unable to complete them because of illness. In 1819 he entered the Episcopal Church and studied theology under Bishop John H. Hobart of New York, who had been pastor and friend to Elizabeth Bayley Seton. In 1822 Ives married Rebecca Hobart, the bishop's daughter, and the following year he was ordained an Episcopal priest and was assigned to pastoral work.

Levi S. Ives

In 1831 he became the first Episcopal bishop of North Carolina. While in North Carolina, Ives supported slavery but saw the need for the evangelization of blacks and wrote a catechism for them. Influenced by the Oxford Movement and the writings of its adherents, Ives founded a community for men which greatly resembled Catholic monasticism. Challenged by his Church authorities, he dissolved this order. In 1852 he went to Rome and met with Pope Pius IX. He and his wife entered the Catholic Church soon after. His presence proved challenging to the American bishops. Ives lectured and taught widely and was the first director of the New York Catholic Protectory, a home for destitute children founded by Archbishop John Hughes. He died in New York City on October 13, 1867.

Ives, Levi Silliman. *The Trials of a Mind in Its Progress to Catholicism: A Letter to His Old Friends.* Boston, 1854.

Malone, Michael Taylor. "Levi Silliman Ives: Priest, Bishop, Tractarian and Roman Catholic Convert." Ph.D. dissertation, Duke University, 1970.

O'Grady, John. *Levi Silliman Ives: Pioneer Leader in Catholic Charities.* New York, 1933.

STEPHEN M. RYAN

J

JANKIEWICZ, MARY CAJETAN (1839–1907)

Pioneer in the educational ministry of the Felician Sisters. She was born in 1839 in Warsaw, Poland, and baptized Alexandra. She entered the Felician Congregation in 1867. An experienced teacher, she was one of the original five sisters from Poland who began the Felician Sisters' American foundation in 1874 in response to the Rev. Joseph Dabrowski's request for sisters to teach the children of Polish immigrants in his rural parish in Polonia, Wisconsin.

Sr. Cajetan, who served in various positions as teacher, principal, director of education, and provincial superior, directed teacher training programs for the rapidly growing number of candidates to the community. She was instrumental in establishing and directing the Seminary of the Felician Sisters, Detroit, which was incorporated by the state of Michigan in 1882 as a normal school to prepare candidates for teaching. She also designed a course of studies for the elementary school curriculum, and in the earliest years when textbooks were scarce, she was involved in the writing, compiling, and printing of books for classroom use. She directed sisters in complying with diocesan certification requirements and was encouraged in her efforts when fifty-four sisters successfully passed Detroit's first diocesan examination in 1887.

From 1900 to 1907 Sr. Cajetan served as the Detroit province's third provincial superior, after which she participated in the Felician Congregation's general chapter in Poland, where she was elected to the general council. Before beginning her service as a general councilor, she suffered a heart attack in Nowe Miasto where she was making a retreat and died on December 9, 1907.

See also FELICIAN SISTERS; POLISH CATHOLICS IN AMERICA.

Mother Mary Cajetan Jankiewicz

Ziolkowski, Mary Janice. *The Felician Sisters of Livonia, Michigan: First Province in America.* Detroit: Harlo Press, 1984.

MARY JANICE ZIOLKOWSKI, C.S.S.F.

JANSSENS, FRANCIS (1843–97)

Missionary priest and archbishop. Janssens was born on October 17, 1843, in Tilburg, North Brabant, the Netherlands. He was baptized Franciscus Antonius Josephus Augustinus. The Janssens family was prominent in the small town and devoutly attached to the Catholic Church. Francis was educated at the diocesan seminaries. An excellent student, he developed a special talent for music.

Francis Janssens

After hearing a sermon by Bishop John McGill of Richmond about the postbellum South and the shortage of priests there, Janssens volunteered for service in Virginia. He prepared for his overseas task at the American College at Louvain, Belgium. Once ordained, he departed in 1868 for the United States after a trip to Rome.

Janssens remained in Richmond for thirteen years. Stationed at the cathedral parish, he regularly traveled to "missions" in other parts of Virginia. Bishop McGill died in 1872 and was succeeded by James Gibbons, who remained until he was appointed coadjutor archbishop of Baltimore in 1877. After Gibbons' departure Janssens administered the Richmond diocese until the arrival of Bishop John Joseph Keane in 1878.

As a priest, Janssens was zealous and devout as well as friendly and accessible. He was also a good administrator with a fondness for keeping records—including all his sermons—and statistics. His name appeared on various *ternae* before he was appointed bishop of Natchez in 1881.

Bishop of Natchez

The Diocese of Mississippi (now Jackson) was one of the poorest and unhealthiest in the United States and most of its priests were foreign-born. Janssens managed to extinguish the debt on St. Mary's Cathedral, which could then be consecrated. He attended the Third Plenary Council of Baltimore as a junior promoter and was a member of the committee on the catechism.

In Mississippi, Janssens built churches and schools for white and black Catholics and began a short-lived minor seminary. His salary went into the diocesan treasury, which also received gifts from the Society for the Propagation of the Faith in Paris and from Dutch benefactors. After discovering a forgotten tribe of Choctaw natives in the piney woods, Janssens established Holy Rosary Mission for them.

Archbishop of New Orleans

In 1888 Janssens was appointed archbishop of New Orleans. Most of his predecessors had been French-born (as was the majority of the diocesan priests), and the appointment of a Dutchman caused quite a commotion. Janssens traveled extensively in the archdiocese, then the largest in area in the United States. Confirmation tours served to encourage the faithful as well as priests and religious, many of whom led poverty-stricken lives threatened by disease and, if they catered to the blacks, by enmity of racist whites. A great believer in education, Janssens built and staffed churches, chapels, and schools. In a diocese with a huge debt, the necessary funds were usually obtained from outside. Financial support in his work for the blacks often came from (now Blessed) Mother Katharine Drexel, who was impressed with his ideas of establishing rural schools throughout Louisiana.

During the 1890s, Janssens became embroiled in a controversy over the establishment of separate churches for the black population of New Orleans. He was in favor of this as a way of training the blacks to stand on their own feet and he advocated ordination of black priests long before his contemporaries did. Criticized as a boon to segregation, the black parishes in the archdiocese served as a cradle for the majority of black Catholics in the present United States.

Among several dozen religious orders in the diocese, Janssens was especially close to the Ursulines, who had been in Louisiana since the early days of the colony. He organized and officiated at the coronation of their statue of Our Lady of Prompt Succor as patroness of the state. He also collaborated closely with the black Sisters of the Holy Family who ran homes for orphans and the elderly. He received Mother Frances Cabrini, whose sisters are still active in the diocese. At his request, Bishop Giovanni Battista Scalabrini sent priests to work with Italian immigrants. Janssens founded an institution for deaf-mute children at Chinchuba as well as a lepers' home at Carville.

Janssens established charters for the parishes and attempted to tighten ecclesiastical discipline by organizing the Fifth Diocesan Synod. With the help of Benedictines, he founded a seminary that survives as St. Joseph's. He restored St. Louis Cathedral and the "archévêché," the oldest building in the Mississippi Valley and then the archbishops' residence. He strongly supported an anti-lottery campaign, which resulted in the defeat of pro-lottery candidates for political office. Janssens died June 10, 1897, at sea on his way to Europe and was buried in St. Louis Cathedral in New Orleans.

See also LOUISIANA, CATHOLIC CHURCH IN; MISSISSIPPI, CATHOLIC CHURCH IN.

Kasteel, Annemarie. "Archbishop Francis Janssens and the Americanization of the Church in Louisiana." *Cross, Crozier and Crucible.* Archdiocese of Louisiana in cooperation with the Center for Louisiana Studies of the University of Southwestern Louisiana, 1993, 156–69.

____. *Francis Janssens: A Dutch-American Prelate, 1843–1897.* Lafayette: The Center for Louisiana Studies, University of Southwestern Louisiana, 1992.

ANNEMARIE KASTEEL

JEANMARD, JULES BENJAMIN (1879–1957)

First bishop of Lafayette. Jeanmard was born on September 26, 1879, in Breaux Bridge, Louisiana, the seventh of nine children. He studied at St. Joseph's Seminary, Gessen, Louisiana; Holy Cross College, Worcester, Massachusetts; Kenrick Seminary in St. Louis, Missouri; and St. Louis Seminary in New Orleans, where he was ordained on June 10, 1903.

First appointed assistant at St. Louis Cathedral, he was chosen, in 1906, as secretary by Archbishop James Blenk, who made him chancellor in 1914 and nominated him as administrator in the event of his own death, which occurred in April 1917. In September the apostolic delegate requested that he study the feasibility of a new diocese in Lafayette, which was created on February 12, 1918.

Meanwhile the selection of a new archbishop was probably more difficult because of the war. The opposition to Francis Janssens, a Dutchman, had not been forgotten; after a Frenchman (Placide Chapelle) and a New Orleans-raised German (Blenk), it was time to give the city of New Orleans an American leader. On February 4 the bishop of San Antonio, John W. Shaw, was selected, but Jeanmard was to retain jurisdiction over the affairs of the archdiocese until June.

On July 4 Jeanmard was chosen as bishop of Lafayette, but his consecration was postponed until December 8, feast of the Immaculate Conception. On December 12, feast of Our Lady of Guadalupe, patroness of the Americas, he was installed as bishop of the diocese that he had helped to carve from New Orleans and that had been officially erected on May 23, 1918.

In his first sermon, he concluded in French: "I am sure that I shall enjoy your sympathy, confidence, support, and if need be, your indulgence because you are my very own." When he retired in 1956 the fruits of his labor were noteworthy with large increases in the number of priests, parishes, and schools.

Archbishop Joseph Rummel said that "Bishop Jeanmard's zeal was responsible for one of the most extensive developments of the Negro apostolate in our country." Four bishops today, natives of the diocese, would agree. Jeanmard died at Lake Charles, Louisiana, on February 23, 1957.

See also LOUISIANA, CATHOLIC CHURCH IN.

JEAN-MARIE JAMMES

JESUIT LABOR SCHOOLS, THE

A loose confederation of adult education institutes sponsored by the Society of Jesus and staffed largely by lay volunteers drawn from the ranks of labor, government, and the legal profession, the labor schools represented the American Jesuits' most important undertaking in the field of social action between the depression and the 1960s.

Role of John LaFarge

Inspired by the work that Jesuits had done with organized labor in England, France, and Belgium, the labor schools trace their origins to the work of John LaFarge, S.J., an editor of *America* and a pioneer in the field of race relations. Concerned that the inroads that Communism and organized crime were making in labor unions would weaken the Church's hold on the affections of the working class and undermine its position in American society, in the 1930s LaFarge sought to develop ways of reaching out more effectively to industrial workers. Drawing on the models presented by the Labor College at Oxford, the Young Christian Workers' Movement in Belgium, and Action Populaire in France, in 1935 LaFarge presented his superiors in New York with a comprehensive plan to establish both a network of Jesuit "labor colleges" and a national institute for social analysis.

The American provincials quickly approved his proposal and moved to put it into action. In 1936 the first of the labor colleges he proposed opened at Saint Francis Xavier parish in New York City, and an institute for social analysis (the Institute of Social Order) opened at the same site in 1939. Although the Xavier Labor School initially experienced some difficulty attracting a working-class clientele, the provincials were convinced that the new undertaking had great promise. Therefore, in the years that followed, they encouraged the foundation of a number of similar schools in industrial centers throughout the country where the Jesuits already ran colleges or universities. Eventually numbering over forty, the schools differed markedly from one another in both the number of students they enrolled and the impact they had on local labor politics. Not surprisingly, those in the metropolitan

New York area (most notably the Xavier Labor School, the Saint Peter's [Jersey City] Institute of Labor Relations, and the Crown Heights [Brooklyn] Labor School), Philadelphia (Saint Joseph's College Institute of Industrial Relations), New Orleans (Loyola University Institute of Industrial Relations), and Chicago (Loyola University School of Social and Industrial Relations), all of which benefited both from the presence of large numbers of Catholic unionists in their host cities and the services of resourceful directors, enjoyed healthy enrollments for most of their existences.

Adaptation to American Conditions

Almost immediately after their founding, the schools developed both a distinctly American style of ministry and a devoted following among the laboring classes. Hardnosed pragmatists who were more often than not the products of working class families themselves, the directors of the schools were more sensitive to local conditions and the peculiar politics and sensitivities of American labor than they were to the dreams of intellectuals or the abstract plans of Church authorities. Therefore, because they knew that the American labor movement was leery of both confessional unions and outside influence, the directors quietly discarded the European models that had so captivated LaFarge and developed an apostolic approach that was more suited to the American labor scene. Thus, they developed curricula that were more secular than religious, and that sought to teach their students those practical skills (e.g., debating, public speaking, parliamentary procedure, and mediation techniques) that would enable them to rise to positions of leadership in their respective unions. Once in power, it was hoped that the Jesuit-trained unionists would rid the unions of both radicalism and corruption, and become a nonthreatening and quietly effective apostolic force in the American labor movement.

The low-key approach followed by the labor schools and their directors proved to be remarkably effective in the short run. Throughout the 1940s and the early 1950s the schools enjoyed robust enrollments, garnered positive publicity for the Church, and quietly strengthened the relationship between the Church and organized labor. Nowhere was the work of the schools and their directors more publicized than in New York, where in the decade between 1945 and 1955 Philip Carey, S.J., and John Corridan, S.J., the directors of the Xavier Labor School, became minor celebrities whose battles against radicalism in the Transport Workers Union and gangsterism in the International Longshoremen's Association were chronicled regularly in the city's newspapers.

By the mid-1950s, however, the Jesuit labor schools (and all Church-sponsored labor schools) throughout the country experienced a dramatic falling off of interest and attendance due to a number of factors, among which were the emergence of college-based and/or union-sponsored programs in industrial relations, the postwar movements of Catholics to the suburbs and to white-collar jobs, and the passing of the Communist threat in the unions. As a result, most of the labor schools quietly went out of existence before the end of the 1950s. The few that remained either scrambled to recruit students from newly arriving immigrant groups or were absorbed into college-based programs.

Although the roots of the labor school movement can be traced to European models, and ultimately to the thought of Leo XIII, over time foreign influences became so muted (or so consciously downplayed) that it would be a serious mistake to try to understand this distinctly American form of social ministry by comparing it to any European model.

Contribution to American Catholicism

To appreciate their real achievement, one must try to understand the schools and their directors in their American context. The "labor priests" who ran them were markedly different from the "worker priests" of France. Unlike the worker priests, the directors neither lived with nor worked side by side with the men and women to whom they ministered. Unlike the worker priests, they did not have a theologically sophisticated rationale for the work they did. Normally loners who were either temperamentally or intellectually unsuited for traditional Jesuit apostolates, they created schools and developed ministerial styles that were as eccentric and individual as themselves. In fact, they staunchly resisted any and all attempts at homogenization or standardization.

Ultimately, their ministry was one of presence and quiet advocacy, both of which were aimed at reassuring ethnic immigrant workers that the Church had not abandoned them. Their goals were then quite modest, and with the exception of those few students who became members of their faculties, they did not succeed in creating a lasting following. For all that, they were a significant part of the American Church's social ministry in the middle third of the twentieth century, for their work enabled them to achieve the seemingly modest goal that they had set for themselves: the enhancement of the workers' sense of identification with the Church.

Betten, Neil. *Catholic Activism and the Industrial Worker.* Gainesville: University Presses of Florida, 1976.

McEntee, Georgina P. *The Social Catholic Movement in Great Britain.* New York: Macmillan, 1927.

McShane, Joseph M. "'To Create an Elite Body of Laymen': Terence J. Shealy, S.J., and the Laymen's League 1911–1922." *Catholic Historical Review* 78 (October 1992) 557–80.

____. "A Survey of the History of the Jesuit Labor Schools in New York: An American Social Gospel in Action." *Records of the American Catholic Historical Society of Philadelphia* 102 (Winter 1991) 37–64.

Seaton, Douglas P. *Catholics and Radicals: The Association of Catholic Trade Unionists and the American Labor Movement from Depression to Cold War.* East Brunswick, N.J.: Associated University Presses, 1981.

JOSEPH M. McSHANE, S.J.

JESUIT RELATIONS

A collection of annual reports written by Jesuit missionaries working in New France and sent to their provincial superior in Paris. When subsequently printed, these reports came to be known as *Relations des Jésuites.* The original series contains forty-one small volumes (one for each year) and covers the period from 1632 to 1672. These accounts were written by eyewitnesses living in the principal colonies of Quebec, Three Rivers, Montreal, and the Huronia Mission, or were based on reports received from these places. The accounts likewise describe, in some detail, the religion, morals, and customs practiced by the native population, their form of government and manner of warfare, as well as the labors and sufferings endured by the missionaries.

These annual reports were reprinted (3 vols., 1858) in Quebec, under the auspices of the Canadian government, as *Relations des Jésuites contenant ce qui s'est passé de plus remarquable dans les missions des Pères de la Compagnie de Jésus dans la Nouvelle-France.* This edition differs from the original in that it contains the 1673 report, an account (1616) of the Acadian Mission, and a 1626 letter from Quebec of Fr. Charles Lalemant. Toward the end of the nineteenth century Reuben Gold Thwaites began republishing the collection with an English translation facing the original Latin or French text. This seventy-three volume work is entitled *The Jesuit Relations and Allied Documents: Travels and Explorations of the Jesuit Missionaries in New France 1610–1791* (Cleveland, 1896–1901). The Thwaites edition (reprinted in 1959) surpasses that of Quebec: it adds the annual reports for the years 1673 to 1679, as well as allied documents covering the years 1610 to 1791, scholarly and bibliographical notes, and a detailed index.

Though not a continuous history of New France nor of the Jesuits' missionary endeavors among the native population, the *Jesuit Relations* do demonstrate the growth and development of the Church and delineate colonial life as well as that among native peoples.

Donnelly, Joseph P. *Thwaites' Jesuit Relations: Errata and Addenda.* Chicago: Loyola University Press, 1967.

McCoy, James C. *Jesuit Relations of Canada, 1632–1673: A Bibliography.* Paris: Rau, 1937.

New Catholic Encyclopedia 7:897–98.

Pouliot, Leon. *Étude sur les Relations des Jésuites de la Nouvelle France (1632–1672).* Montreal, 1940.

JOSEPH TYLENDA, S.J.

JESUITS IN AMERICA, THE

The first Jesuit to come to the present territory of the United States was Pedro Martínez, who was admitted to the Society in 1553 during the lifetime of St. Ignatius Loyola. He volunteered for the mission of New Spain in 1566. That same year he set out for Florida with a Spanish expedition. He was killed by hostile natives near the present site of Jacksonville, Florida, on October 6, 1566, shortly before his thirty-third birthday.

St. Ignatius Loyola

A little over four years later another expedition of Spanish Jesuits set out from the Antilles to begin a mission among Native Americans farther north. They entered Chesapeake Bay and landed in northern Virginia. But in February 1571 seven Jesuits, including brothers, scholastics, and priests, led by Fr. Juan de Segura, were slain. Thereafter the Florida Mission was abandoned, and the Jesuits were directed to Mexico where they had better success.

The only Spanish-sponsored Jesuit who had any success north of present-day Mexico was Eusebio Kino (1645–1711), who was an Italian Tyrolese by birth. He worked among the people of Pimería Alta in northern Mexico and southern Arizona with great success during the last years of a fruitful life, a great deal of which was spent in the saddle.

If the Spanish Jesuits approached from the south, the French came in from the north. In 1632 the French Jesuits definitively began their mission along the St. Lawrence

River. They reached out to the native peoples there and in so doing moved into present-day Maine and New York. The Jesuit way of helping the Native Americans was to try to turn them from nomadic hunters and warriors to sedentary farmers. This was the strategy that worked among the Guaranì in Paraguay, and that was the model that Jesuit missionaries had before their eyes well into the nineteenth century. But it never really caught on among the North American tribes. Tribal warfare also hindered the efforts of the missionaries, especially in view of the fact that the French colonial authorities allied themselves with the enemies of the five nations of the Iroquois who were the fiercest fighters of their time. Nevertheless, the Jesuits tried to evangelize the Iroquois, and some missionaries, such as Brs. René Goupil and Jean de la Lande and Fr. Isaac Jogues, three of the North American martyrs canonized by Pope Pius XI, were killed by the Iroquois, two of them near the present site of Auriesville, New York, in 1646.

The French Jesuits also ministered to tribes who lived in Maine, then a territory disputed between the English and the French. Many of the Puritan inhabitants of New England suspected the Jesuits of inciting their charges to warfare against the white Protestant settlers. Sébastien Râle, S.J. (1657–1724), who worked among the Abenaki tribe with great success from 1693, was the target of many such accusations. Of course, from his point of view he was simply defending the rights of the tribe to their own land. He was a proponent of peace negotiations, but the colonists were not in the mood to bargain. In 1724 a military expedition from Massachusetts killed Fr. Râle and brought his scalp back to Boston.

Long before this, the Canadian Jesuits had gone up the St. Lawrence River and the waterways of the Great Lakes to minister to native tribes living there. In present-day Michigan and Wisconsin they learned about the existence of a great river in the west. In 1673 Fr. Jacques Marquette teamed with the bold explorer Louis Jolliet to explore the Mississippi, which Marquette named "the river of the Immaculate Conception." Traveling by canoe they penetrated as far south as the mouth of the Arkansas River near the present site of Rosedale, Mississippi. But they were convinced at that time that the Mississippi flowed not into the Atlantic or Pacific Ocean, as had been previously thought, but into a southern sea, now known as the Gulf of Mexico.

The Mississippi thus became a new gateway into the trans-Appalachian American plains. Early in the eighteenth century there were French settlements and Jesuits along the Gulf Coast. The Jesuits were recruited because of their reputation as linguists. It was thought they would be more effective since they would learn the language of the various tribes. The Louisiana headquarters of the Jesuits was in New Orleans, but they were forbidden to minister to the settlers there. They were to occupy themselves exclusively with the Native American tribes in the hinterlands. The Jesuits purchased a plantation outside New Orleans to finance their work among the tribes.

This mission lasted until 1763 when the Jesuits, who had made many enemies in France, were banned from the territories of Louis XV. By that time twenty-five Jesuits, including three brothers, had served in Louisiana, that is, the lower Mississippi Valley. Three of them died violent deaths at the hands of the Native Americans.

The Maryland Mission

Along with France and Spain, the English were anxious to carve out colonies in North America. The first permanent English settlement was at Jamestown, Virginia, in 1607. Among those who applied to King Charles I for a charter to set up a proprietary colony was George Calvert, Lord Baltimore, an English Catholic convert from about 1624. His first attempt at colonization was in Newfoundland. After his death in 1632 his son, Cecil, received a royal charter for a colony north of Virginia which he called Maryland in honor of Charles' queen, Henrietta Maria.

One of the motives for founding the colony was religious freedom. The Puritans had already gone to the New World for the same purpose. Maryland was the first colony to pass a law granting toleration to all denominations of Christians. In November 1633 the *Ark* and the *Dove* sailed for Maryland with two hundred colonists. Among them were Frs. Andrew White (1579–1656) and John Gravenor [alias Altham], and Br. Thomas Gervase, all Jesuits. The ships arrived at St. Clement's Island on March 25, 1634, and there Mass was celebrated. In Maryland the Jesuits had religious freedom, but unlike the French and Spanish Jesuits they had no state subsidy. They were to support themselves by farming just like the other colonists. Besides the pastoral care of the Catholic colonists, who were in the minority, they also were to evangelize the native peoples.

Fr. White, who had been a seminary professor in Europe, mastered the Piscataway language and wrote a dictionary and a catechism in that language. Some other Jesuits learned the language, but in general their work among Native Americans was short-lived for several reasons. In the first place the colonists feared the natives and did not like having them around. Second, the hard life in Maryland cut down many Jesuits shortly after they arrived. Third, the toleration rule was periodically abrogated. In 1645, for example, White and Thomas Copley were arrested and sent back to England. By the time Copley returned in 1648 most of the native tribes had been driven off.

When the call went out for volunteers to go to Maryland in 1640 there were numerous enthusiastic responses from the scholastics, i.e., seminarians, as well as from priests and brothers. But the needs of England, which itself was a dangerous mission, meant that only a few were selected. There were never more than five priests and four brothers on the Maryland Mission at any one time in the seventeenth century. They lived a lonely life usually separated from other Jesuits. They were often on horseback for long journeys to widely separated families and congregations.

They established a school at Newton in 1677, which operated until the end of the century when a law was passed forbidding Catholics to conduct schools. Higher education had to be pursued abroad. Many young men went to the English Jesuit College at St. Omer in France. The Maryland Mission produced forty-three Jesuits, three Benedictines, and three secular priests. In all, twenty-one Jesuits born in America, including two future archbishops of Baltimore, John Carroll and Leonard Neale, worked in the English American colonies. In addition, there were thirty-three American women who entered convents in Europe, most of them contemplative.

In the thirteen colonies during the eighteenth century there were sporadic laws against the public profession of the Catholic faith. The Jesuits, however, with increased manpower, extended their apostolate to Maryland's eastern shore and into southeastern Pennsylvania. In 1732 Joseph Greaton (1679–1753) obtained a plot of land in Philadelphia for St. Joseph's Church. By 1773 there were thirteen mission stations in Maryland and five in Pennsylvania. They were served by twenty-three priests, all Jesuits. In all, 144 Jesuits, 30 of them brothers, had served in the mission before 1773. Though they were all members of the English province, not all of them were British. There were quite a few Belgian, French, and German missionaries, many of them brothers. One of the most prominent missionaries was Fr. Francis Farmer (born Stegmeyer, 1720–86). He worked in Philadelphia and New York City and was even named a trustee of the University of Pennsylvania.

In 1773 the Society of Jesus was suppressed worldwide by a brief, *Dominus ac Redemptor,* signed by Pope Clement XIV. Each bishop was to apply the brief in his own diocese. For a century and a half the Maryland Jesuits had operated with faculties granted by the vicar apostolic of the London district. In October 1773 Bishop Challoner wrote them a letter from London asking them to sign their names to a letter of submission which he could send on to Rome.

The suppression of the Society of Jesus could not have come at a worse time for the American Church. In the second half of the eighteenth century most of the religious orders that did missionary work declined sharply in numbers. In fact only three male religious orders grew worldwide in the eighteenth century: the Jesuits, the observant Franciscans, and the Capuchins. In the aftermath of the French Revolution many religious orders in Europe lost much of their property and many of their members. The number of diocesan priests also dropped sharply. Some of those expelled from Europe came to America, but just as the new nation was expanding there was an acute shortage of clergy worldwide.

The Interlude

For the Jesuits there was one glimmer of hope. They survived in White Russia, that is, the part of Poland and Lithuania annexed by Czarina Catherine in 1772. She was convinced that education was the first need of her empire, and she was delighted to find herself the temporal sovereign of over two hundred Jesuits whom she valued as educators. She refused to allow the papal brief of suppression to be promulgated in her territories. The Jesuits thus clung to a tender thread of life.

In the course of the next twenty years there was the upheaval of the French Revolution. Those kings who had insisted on the suppression of the Jesuits were no more. The papacy was in dire straits and disinclined to discourage those who wanted to revive the Society of Jesus. By 1804 Pope Pius VII had granted verbal permission for the Russian Jesuits to affiliate other ex-Jesuits in various countries, including the young American republic. There were ten ex-Jesuits still alive in Maryland. Five of them affiliated once more with the Society. In 1806 they accepted their first novices.

In the interval between 1773 and 1804 the ex-Jesuits in Maryland had, as diocesan priests, maintained their corporate existence as well as their property. They were practically the only Catholic clergy in the new republic. They governed themselves democratically as a select body. In 1788 they petitioned Rome for a bishop. Propaganda granted their request to select someone for the post and to advise where the episcopal see was to be located. Baltimore was chosen as the city and John Carroll as the bishop. In 1789 Carroll started a college at Georgetown outside of Washington. At the end of the eighteenth century Bishop Carroll judged that there were thirty thousand Catholics in the thirteen former colonies, two-thirds of them in Maryland.

The New Jesuits, 1814–1914

In 1814 Pope Pius VII restored the Society of Jesus worldwide. The restoration was not welcomed in largely Protestant America. After all, the British concession of religious toleration to the Catholics of Canada was one of the chief grievances that inspired the American Revolution. In 1816 John Adams wrote to Thomas Jefferson, "I do not like the Resurrection of the Jesuits. . . . Shall we not have swarms of them here?" Jefferson agreed. "This Society," he wrote, "has been a greater calamity for mankind than the French Revolution."

For the moment, however, Jesuits were very thin on the ground in America. Many of the new novices were from Europe. Thence also came a succession of superiors such as Giovanni Grassi (1775–1849), Francis Dziernozykski (1779–1850), and Anthony Kohlmann (1771–1836). Kohlmann is best known for his role in the successful legal defense of the sacramental seal of confession in a famous New York case of 1813. Charles Nerinckx (1761–1824) was not a Jesuit, but a secular priest, yet knowing the needs of the American Church he recruited various of his Belgian countrymen to come to America and join the Jesuits.

In 1821 he brought seven novices to Whitemarsh in Maryland to begin their novitiate. Unfortunately their arrival coincided with a financial crisis in the Maryland Mission. The Jesuit farms were unproductive and there was thought of dismissing the novices because the mission could not support them. At this point appeared Bishop Louis William DuBourg, a Sulpician who had been appointed bishop of Louisiana and the Floridas, a vast territory with few priests. The seat of the diocese was New Orleans, but DuBourg proposed to reside in Missouri. He invited the novices to St. Louis where they could evangelize the Native Americans. When asked their opinion about the move the novices are reported to have said, "The Indians are in the West. To the West let us go."

Thus it was that seven novices, one of whom was Pierre Jean De Smet, with their superior, Fr. Charles Van Quickenborne (1788–1837), another priest, three Jesuit brothers, and three young married slave couples set off on flat boats to go down the Ohio River. They crossed southern Illinois on foot and arrived at St. Louis, then a frontier town of less than four thousand inhabitants, on May 31, 1823. They moved to Florissant, Missouri, outside of St. Louis where the novices continued their Jesuit formation while conducting a school for Native American boys, tilling the fields, and building the log cabin in which they lived. This was the beginning of the Missouri Mission.

As time went by some of them moved up the Missouri River to evangelize the natives. Others worked in parishes in the surrounding territories. In 1829 they took over St. Louis College, which had been founded in 1818. By 1830 they were a mission independent of Maryland. By 1835 there were twenty novices at Florissant.

All the while the Jesuits were spreading out through the eastern states as well as the Midwest, where the French were active in missionary work and education along the Ohio River. In 1831 Leo De Neckere, bishop of New Orleans, was visited by four French Jesuits on their way up the Mississippi River and then the Ohio to Bardstown in Kentucky, where they were to help Bishop Benedict Flaget start a school. Bishop De Neckere had less than thirty priests in a diocese then coterminous with the state of Louisiana where there were many Catholics, especially in the southern part of the state. He managed to detain the Jesuits in Louisiana for almost a year. His successor, Bishop Antoine Blanc, went to Europe to get some Jesuits who would open a college in his diocese.

In 1837 four French priests, a novice, and two brothers arrived in New Orleans. The following year they opened St. Charles College in Grand Coteau with Fr. Nicholas Point (1799–1868) as rector. In the first twenty-five years of the New Orleans Mission a school in New Orleans was opened, and Spring Hill College, which had been founded by Bishop Michael Portier in 1830, became a Jesuit responsibility in 1847. During that quarter-century about 140 Jesuits worked along the Gulf Coast. We know the national origins of 114 of them. The French led the way with fifty-five. Other nations represented were Switzerland (fifteen), Ireland (thirteen), Germany (thirteen), Belgium (eleven), Holland (three), and America (four). There were also smatterings of Czechs, Austrians, Spanish, Italians, English, and one Slovene.

Like the Missouri Mission, the New Orleans Mission had recruiters who traveled to Europe to seek potential Jesuit missionaries. Fr. Pierre De Smet (1801–73) crossed the Atlantic sixteen times seeking men and money for the missions among the Native Americans. That was the big attraction. In the nineteenth century the Native Americans were the most celebrated aborigine people in the world. Their virtues as well as their warlike character were celebrated not only in travel books and news accounts, but in the literary productions of François de Chateaubriand, James Fenimore Cooper, and Henry Wadsworth Longfellow. The Second Provincial Council of Baltimore in 1833 had asked the Holy See to make the Native American missions the responsibility of the Society of Jesus. The following year the request was granted.

Meanwhile with every passing year the native tribes were forced farther west. In 1840 Fr. De Smet started up the Missouri River with Fr. Point, who by this time had moved from Louisiana. Their goal was the headwaters of the Missouri and the western slope of the Rocky Mountains. In subsequent years De Smet made this and similar voyages many times. Though he never mastered any Native American language, he had a certain charisma with the western tribes. His great service was the publicity and financial support he gave to his chosen apostolate. In 1844, after a recruiting trip to Europe, he sailed directly from Europe to Oregon and approached the Native Americans in the hinterlands by going up the Columbia and other rivers. He brought with him five Jesuits. This was the start of the Rocky Mountain Mission, which was the responsibility of the Turin province.

Only four years later gold was discovered in California, and two Italian Jesuits joined the rush to minister to the new crowds coming to California, as well as to beg for their mission. Once there, at the urgent request of the bishop, they took over the Santa Clara Mission with a commitment to start a college there.

Besides the attraction the Europeans felt for the Native Americans, there was also the fact that conditions were unsettled for the Church in Europe. Periodically the French or German Jesuits were banned from their homelands. Many German laypersons fled to America, and the Jesuits followed them. In 1849 over one-third of the German Jesuits were in the United States. In 1869 the German Mission was erected with headquarters in Buffalo. Their charge was to minister to German immigrants around the Great Lakes, though a number also served on the Native American missions in the West. They soon spread to Detroit, Cleveland, Toledo, and into Wisconsin, establishing schools along the way.

Another mission of the European Jesuits in the United States was headquartered in Denver. It ministered to Catholics, mostly Spanish-speaking, in Colorado, New Mexico, and the western part of Texas. Archbishop Jean Baptist Lamy, later celebrated in the Willa Cather novel *Death Comes for the Archbishop*, had appealed to the Jesuits for help when he was appointed to Santa Fe. A contingent from the Naples province arrived in 1867 and labored in the Southwest for forty-three years, mostly working in parishes but also starting a college and, in 1873, a Spanish-language review, *Revista Católica*, which circulated throughout the Southwest and Latin America for almost a century.

In the course of the nineteenth century, although the various missions still welcomed novices from Europe, they were more and more composed of native-born Americans and evolving into provinces. The superior of a province, the provincial, had a good deal more autonomy in implementing apostolic plans of action than a mere "mission superior." Maryland was the first to achieve province status in 1831; Missouri followed in 1863, New Orleans in 1907, and California in 1909. These four evolved into that natural larger administrative unit of Jesuits which is termed an assistancy. The American (now United States) assistancy was created in 1915. Thereafter New York and New England broke off from Maryland; Chicago, Detroit, and Wisconsin from Missouri; and Oregon from California to form the ten provinces of today.

In 1916 there were 2,626 Jesuits affiliated to the four original American provinces; 40 percent of them were scholastics in training for the priesthood. It should be remembered that as part of their training scholastics taught in the schools, usually for four to six years, but because of the manpower shortage some taught for much longer. Another 17 percent were lay brothers. They were true Jesuits but not destined for the priesthood. They served as cooks, farmers, builders, sacristans, doorkeepers, catechists, and teachers, sometimes at the college level. One of them, Br. Cornelius Otten (1835–1916), built five churches in the South at Galveston, Grand Coteau, Augusta, Macon, and Tampa. He was also something of an architect.

The number one apostolate of the Jesuits was education. By 1889 the Jesuits were conducting twenty-eight schools, both secondary and higher, with a total of 6,439 students. Of course, education was not as popular then as it later became. Nor was "dropout" a dirty word. One went to school as long as the inclination and money held out. In that same year, there were only 149 graduates from Jesuit schools.

But Jesuit schools faced three great problems. In the first place, they were under continual pressure from the superior general to teach a strictly classical curriculum, mostly Latin and Greek. But as the harried heads of American Jesuit schools pointed out repeatedly in their letters to Rome, American parents wanted their sons to be trained for the practical world. Slowly but surely other mundane subjects such as bookkeeping crept into the curriculum. Of the twenty-eight Jesuit schools in 1889, ten offered the classical course only; the other eighteen offered both the classical and commercial curriculum.

In the second place, the Jesuit constitutions forbade the collection of tuition from students. Elsewhere the Jesuit schools were fully endowed, which meant that the municipality or the government or a generous benefactor provided a source of income that sustained the Jesuit teaching corps and the upkeep of the building. But in nineteenth-century America there was a scarcity of wealthy patrons, at least among Catholics. For most of the Jesuit schools government financial subsidies were illegal. It was in St. Louis that this logjam was broken. To prevent the early death of his Jesuit school, Bishop Joseph Rosati of St. Louis wrote to Rome about loosening the no-tuition rule. Pope Gregory XVI granted the Jesuits a dispensation in the matter and told the Jesuit general to work out the details.

The third problem was personnel. As we have seen, the attraction of most of the European recruits to America was its missionary character and the chance to minister to souls in a land desperately short of priests. But the Jesuits found that even the most hard-pressed bishops wanted them to open schools. It was thought that schools would promote vocations to the priesthood and religious life, as well as form solid Christian laymen. It was especially hard to find rectors or presidents of schools who could pilot the ship of learning and pay all the bills. However, the Jesuits were fortunate in leadership placement because John Roothaan (their superior general from 1829 to 1853) and most of his successors were firmly convinced that the Jesuit prohibition against accepting ecclesiastical dignities should be maintained, and they usually had the clout to prevent Jesuits from being drafted as bishops. There were only four exceptions in the nineteenth century. Other religious orders in America were not so privileged.

Of course, opening a school was not as complicated then as it is now. All one needed was eight to ten Jesuits (half of them priests and the other half brothers and scholastics), a building with six classrooms, and simple living quarters for the Jesuits, plus a church or chapel.

Another factor favoring the Jesuit schools was that most of them were in urban areas. The American fashion until fifty years ago was to put colleges in remote rural areas because cities were looked upon as sinks of iniquity and breeding grounds for contagious disease. We also have to remember that state governments were not heavily committed to higher education in the nineteenth century. Of the 182 colleges founded in the United States before the Civil War that remained in operation in 1960, 161 (88 percent) were religious or Church-related. Only twenty-one were state colleges.

Besides the college churches, the Jesuits also served in many parishes and mission stations not attached to a school, although the number of these declined as the number of diocesan clergy grew. Jesuits also conducted parish missions. This was a traditional apostolate of the Jesuits from their beginnings, and it was in tune with the times in nineteenth-century America in which revivalism was an important element of all Christian religions. To be on the mission band, which was made up of those Jesuits whose principal work was giving parish missions, was the top prestige post for Jesuits. Fr. F. X. Weninger (1805–88) came from Austria to Cincinnati in 1848. After a short tour as a professor of theology he hit the road to give parish missions. By the end of his life he had given over eight hundred parish missions, most of them in the United States. The fact that he could preach in English and French as well as in his native German gave him more flexibility. He was also the author of a number of popular Catholic books of devotion and instruction, which he sold during his missions.

Two other mighty preachers from the Midwest were Frs. Arnold Damen (1815–90) and Cornelius Smarius (1823–70), both born in the Netherlands. Fr. Damen was pastor of Holy Family parish in Chicago and the founder of St. Ignatius High School. Still, he found time to preach the revival of religion all over the Midwest, the South, and the eastern seaboard. One particular feature of these missions was the pacification of family feuds. Another was celebrity conversions. During a mission in New Orleans in 1877 former Confederate General Joseph Longstreet became a Catholic partly due to Damen's preaching. Usually the local newspaper ran lengthy accounts of the sermons he delivered. In the days before television and the cinema the missions attracted people in search of entertainment as well as edification. Fr. Emmanuel de La Morinière (1856–1930), who preached throughout the South, was not primarily a preacher of missions, but he was an eloquent special-occasions preacher. Professional actors came to his sermons to study his technique.

Among Jesuit orators in the West, one of the most interesting was James Bouchard (1823–89), whose mother was a white woman raised by the Delaware tribe. She married a Delaware brave and James was the fruit of the union. He grew up a Protestant but was converted by Fr. Damen. Bouchard entered the Jesuits at Florissant in 1848 and was ordained in 1855. After various ministries in the Midwest he was sent to California in 1861. There Bouchard was an immediate success as a preacher at St. Ignatius Church. Anti-Catholic feeling was running high in northern California, and Bouchard's forte was the defense of the Church and the Jesuits. People paid to go to his lectures. He also gave missions all over the West in cities and mining towns. When he died a New York newspaper called him "the Father Damen of California."

In addition to Fr. Weninger mentioned above, there were other Jesuit authors in the nineteenth century. Fr. Peter Arnoudt (1811–65) wrote *The Imitation of the Sacred Heart,* but it remained in manuscript until it was translated into English and published in 1863. It was also translated into five foreign languages. Fr. Florentine Boudreaux (1821–24) was a Louisiana-born Acadian. He was orphaned at an early age. Friends sent him and his three brothers to St. Louis College, but Florentine dropped out and became a tinsmith. He eventually entered the Jesuits in 1841. Most of his active years were spent as a professor of chemistry. His two devotional books, *The Happiness of Heaven* (1871) and *God Our Father* (1878), emphasized the goodness and mercy of God. Both enjoyed great success in English and in foreign translations. The first was translated into seven languages.

Juvenile books were a staple of Catholic publishing in the late nineteenth and early twentieth centuries. In an 1897 catalog of Benziger Brothers, 136 books for adolescents are advertised, about 10 percent of them by Jesuits. The dominant author in this field was Francis Finn (1859–1928), who wrote twenty-seven highly successful juvenile books, many of which had great success in foreign translations.

The Age of Ledochowski, 1914–63

John Roothaan, the superior general who governed the Society from 1829 to 1853, had a special interest in the American missions. Many of the missionaries corresponded with him personally. He saw his role as making the restored Jesuits just like the old Society only more so, and during his lifetime there was a certain rigidity in the Jesuits that was not wholly consistent with the original Ignatian charism. That was also the thrust of his successors, especially Wlodomir Ledochowski, who was elected superior general at the Twenty-Sixth General Congregation in 1915, the same one that created the American assistancy.

At that time there were about seventeen thousand Jesuits worldwide. The American Jesuits numbered twenty-five hundred, 40 percent of them scholastics and 18 percent brothers. Besides missions to the Native Americans they had missions in Alaska, Jamaica, and British Honduras. They also conducted thirty-eight schools and thirty-nine parishes independent of churches attached to schools and mission stations served by the Jesuits in Alabama, Florida, southern Maryland, the Northwest, and other regions.

Gradually, as the century wore on, the regular stages of Jesuit training were put into place: two years of novitiate, two years of humanistic studies with and emphasis on English, Latin, and Greek (juniorate), three years of teaching (regency), four years of theology with ordination at the end of the third year, and a year of ascetical and spiritual training (tertianship). Even those who had attended university before their entrance usually had to run the complete course. Gradually, the old custom of keeping scholastics teaching for six years or longer disappeared under Roman pressure. Few would challenge the record of James Lonergan (1827–1918), who taught as a scholastic at Spring Hill College for seventeen years. The fifteen-year course of study was a way the Jesuits identified themselves, and it is described in Jesuit vocation literature all through the middle third of the twentieth century.

In each stage the day was divided into modules and punctuated by bells. Silence was the rule outside of the two recreation periods following the noon and evening meals. There was an opportunity for physical exercise on the weekdays with no classes usually on Thursday and Sunday. Films, radio, and newspapers were unknown or rare. The young Jesuit led his life in an endless round of classes and study periods, and only rarely left the grounds. The old-style Jesuit formation is sensitively re created by Peter McDonough in his fifth chapter, "Men Astutely Trained in Letters and Fortitude."

The houses of study were usually far removed from urban centers. The Jesuits built imposing piles of masonry in Mt. St. Michael near Spokane, Woodstock in Maryland, Weston in Massachusetts, and Poughkeepsie in New York. Other houses at St. Mary's in Kansas and Grand Coteau in Louisiana were former colleges of the Society.

Education was still the principal work of the Jesuits. In the early part of the twentieth century many Jesuit colleges were reorganized in the American fashion into high schools for boys in their early teens and colleges/universities for those eighteen and over. By 1925 there were 46,600 students in Jesuit schools, all but a few of them males.

This was only a small part of the tremendous investment American Catholics made in an elaborate educational system that by 1954 included 9,000 elementary schools, 2,300 high schools, 224 institutions of higher education, and 200 seminaries. The whole enterprise was largely staffed by brothers, priests, and sisters. For example, 86 percent of the almost seventy-seven thousand elementary Catholic school teachers were nuns.

A good number of these nuns got their college degrees from Jesuit institutions. After World War II the policy of admitting women students to Jesuit colleges and universities and the universalization of higher education, which was a result of the G.I. Bill, resulted in a further expansion of this apostolate. By 1963 the 28 institutions enrolled over 130,000 students; the 36 high schools had almost 34,000 students.

By the 1950s the Jesuits began to prepare their men seriously for work in higher education. More and more Jesuits were sent for graduate studies not only to Catholic institutions, as had been the practice in the years before, but also to other universities in America and abroad. The American Jesuits had a network of schools no other nation could match and that not even the combined Jesuit forces of all the other countries could equal.

Another high priority in the first half of the twentieth century was the *Spiritual Exercises*. Once the annual retreat was legislated for all religious, Jesuits were called upon in great numbers to "preach" retreats to nuns. In the 1950s it was a rare Jesuit priest who did not give at least one eight-day retreat to nuns during the summer months.

The movement for weekend lay retreats also gathered momentum in the twentieth century. The three decades from 1930 to 1960 were the great years for the establishment of retreat houses. By 1963 there were thirty-three houses devoted to retreats, usually of the three-day weekend variety, conducted by Jesuits. The chief flaw in this work was the rudimentary knowledge of the *Spiritual Exercises* by the men engaged in this work. There were very few serious commentaries on the text and theology of the exercises published in America, and not much demand for those that were published.

In the twentieth century Jesuits were also identified with social reform. In 1938 the Twenty-Ninth General Congregation of the Society of Jesus called on Jesuits throughout the world to respond to Pope Pius XI's call to work for a more just social order. That and the Wagner Act of 1935 inspired American Jesuits to open labor schools. By the 1940s there were about thirty labor schools in the United States, half of them under Jesuit auspices. They usually taught courses on the papal social encyclicals and ethics as well as how-to-do-it courses in grievance procedures, public speaking, bargaining, and economics. Courses usually ran for nine to eleven weeks and were conducted in the evenings. Among the most successful Jesuit "labor priests" were Denis Comey (Philadelphia), Louis Twomey (New Orleans), and Phil Carey and John Corridan (New York).

John LaFarge (1880–1963) spent most of his life as a writer and editor at *America*. He was identified with many reform movements in the American Church: the Liturgical Arts Society, the National Catholic Rural Life Conference, and the Catholic Association of International Peace. But his chief contribution was in the area of interracial justice. George Dunne's 1945 article in *Commonweal*,

"The Sin of Segregation," had an enormous impact on American Catholic thinking. It was said of Dunne that he enjoyed a distinction possessed by few moralists in all history, that of discovering a new sin.

Another important Jesuit social thinker was Joseph Husslein (1873–1952), a Midwestern Jesuit who wrote on the papal social teaching from Pope Leo XIII on. He also edited the science and culture series for Bruce Publishing Company, in which many American Jesuits were published for the first time. Thomas Hughes (1849–1939), born in England, joined the Missouri Jesuits and spent his life writing the massive *History of the Society of Jesus in North America,* which took the story down to 1773. John Wynne (1859–1948) was an energetic writer who was influential in the foundation of the Jesuit weekly *America* in 1909 and was a longtime editor of the *Messenger of the Sacred Heart.* Wynne was also one of the moving forces in the making of *The Catholic Encyclopedia* (1905–14), a monumental work, though only a minority of the contributors were Americans. Wynne also took a lively interest in the history of the seventeenth-century Jesuit martyrs who died in New York.

But the most popular twentieth-century Jesuit writer by far was Daniel Lord (1888–1956). During most of his life he was engaged in working in the Sodality of the Blessed Virgin Mary. This organization, founded in the sixteenth century and known in Europe as the Marian Congregations, was a traditional work of the Jesuits. From 1925 to 1948 he served as editor of the *Queen's Work,* the sodality periodical. In 1931 he began the Summer School of Catholic Action in various American cities, and these sessions catechized generations of young people in the social doctrine of the Church as well as in other aspects of Catholic life. All the while an endless stream of books and pamphlets flowed from his pen, almost three hundred altogether, and some of them circulated in the millions. He also wrote plays, musicals, pageants, and radio scripts that exercised an enormous influence on a generation of Catholic youth.

Around midcentury Jesuits also started a number of periodicals such as *Review for Religious* (1941) and *Theology Digest* (1952). More learned were quarterlies such as *Theological Studies* (1939) and *New Testament Abstracts* (1956).

In 1935 Calvert Alexander (1900–77) published *The Catholic Literary Revival.* Like many of his Jesuit contemporaries, he saw a real renaissance of Catholic literature. Some thirteen years later a book of biographical sketches of 620 contemporary Catholic authors who wrote in English or had works translated into that language was published (Matthew Hoehn, O.S.B., ed. *Catholic Authors,* Vol. 1, 1948). About half the authors were not Americans. They included G. K. Chesterton, Hillaire Belloc, James Brodrick, S.J., Paul Claudel, Graham Greene, Evelyn

Waugh, Etienne Gilson, Gabriel Marcel, and Romano Guardini. But there were forty-two American Jesuits profiled.

Nevertheless, in his famous 1955 lecture, *American Catholics and the Intellectual Life,* Msgr. John Tracy Ellis found that both secular and religious priests in America had been singularly lacking in intellectual achievement. "The general record of American religious has not been outstanding, nor would it profit by comparison with their European confreres."

The Crash, 1963–83

In 1963 there were 35,788 Jesuits in the world. That number was to climb to 36,038 in 1965. Of these 8,377, almost one in four worldwide, was an American. Then began a rapid decline until 1994, when the worldwide figure reached 23,179, a decline of more than one-third. The drop among American Jesuits was worse. They went from 8,377 to 4,621, a decline of 45 percent. Of course, this was a part of a worldwide phenomenon occurring among Catholic priests and religious. There have been only four periods in the history of the Church since the year 1000 when the number of priests and religious has steadily declined for more than three decades. The first was the period of the Black Death. The second was the time of the Protestant Reformation. The third was the second half of the eighteenth century. We are still experiencing the fourth.

The second half of the twentieth century opened brightly for the Jesuits. John Courtney Murray was easily the most famous American theologian in the 1950s. Both he and Gustave Weigel, his colleague on the faculty of Woodstock College, had great influence in the deliberations of the Second Vatican Council that began in 1962. The first session was rather disappointing, but in the next three years the pace picked up. The Catholic bishops of the world and a good number of observers from other faiths gathered in Rome every fall. The Church was slowly turning in a new direction. It was the end of one Christendom and the beginning of another.

In 1965 the Thirty-First General Congregation of the Jesuits convened in Rome to elect a new general. The man they chose was Pedro Arrupe, a Spanish Basque, who had made his tertianship in Cleveland before going on the Japanese mission in 1938, where he survived the atom bomb and served as master of novices and provincial. Arrupe was plainly a man not afraid of the future. He became the first Jesuit general to hold press conferences and appear on television. He did not seem disturbed by the decline in numbers nor was he frightened by change. On the occasion of his golden jubilee as a Jesuit in 1977 he said, "The figure of Abraham has always been for me an inexhaustible source of inspiration. 'Where is the Society heading?' men have asked me. My reply has always been: 'Where God is leading it.' In other words, I do not know."

Not all American Jesuits were as comfortable with ambiguity as Fr. Arrupe. One by one many of the certainties they relied on were disappearing. The first to go was the fifteen-year formation plan. As fewer and older men began to enter the novitiate, their formation was tailored more to their individual needs. As more Jesuits left and fewer entered, the plans made for growth were revealed as grandiose in the extreme. Almost every province had built massive new houses of study. The most elaborate was Shrub Oak on a beautiful estate north of New York City. It opened in 1956 and closed in 1969. St. Bonifatius, the new novitiate of the Wisconsin province, opened in 1970 and closed in 1975. Colombière College in Clarkston, Michigan, opened in 1959 and closed in 1971. Mt. St. Michael near Spokane was abandoned in 1966. When the smoke cleared in the 1980s, there were only three houses of formation that survived: the novitiates in Wernersville, Pennsylvania, and Grand Coteau, Louisiana, and the collegiate program at St. Louis University.

Some of those massive houses were sold. Others were converted to be used for retired Jesuits and spirituality centers. Most of the novitiates moved to private residences in urban centers. The collegiate programs were relocated to Jesuit universities also in cities. Finally there were two houses of theology left, one at Berkeley in California and the other at Cambridge in Massachusetts.

In the whole process the lockstep of Jesuit formation was broken forever. Most of the new houses rarely heard the sound of a bell, and life in them was far less monastic. Life in the colleges was more relaxed too. The number of telephones, television sets, and automobiles in Jesuit houses increased. Family visits and annual vacations were now formally permitted.

It is hard to exaggerate the effect that the drop in numbers had on Jesuit morale and thinking. Normally, Jesuits had an expansionist mentality. They thought of bigger schools, more schools, more houses, more retreatants, more cities, more countries. It took a long time for them to think small, or at least to think in terms of smaller numbers of Jesuits. It was no consolation to many of them that most dioceses and religious orders were having the same difficulties, or to remind themselves that, for all the Society's losses, it was still the largest religious order of men in the Church and could count among its members both gifted and generous religious.

One of the ways the Jesuits learned to confront this problem was in meetings devoted to planning. The Thirty-First General Congregation in 1965–66 had decreed that every province should have a commission of ministries to plan the future of various Jesuit works. A massive sociological survey of Jesuits and their works was commissioned and carried out. The late 1960s and 1970s were a time of meetings. Thirty or forty or more Jesuits, usu-

ally elected by age groups, gathered annually in almost every American province to consider numerous committee reports generated by their fellows. It was a move toward wide consultation of ordinary Jesuits, many of whom had never been asked their opinion before. These were the first Jesuits in the history of the society to be called upon annually or even oftener to elect other Jesuits who would have a large part in deciding their future. By the end of the 1980s this process had wound down, but there was still broader consultation than ever before in Jesuit history.

Another good thing that came out of the upheaval was a renewed appreciation of the *Spiritual Exercises* of St. Ignatius. In the 1960s the efficacy of the *Spiritual Exercises* was doubted by many Jesuits. Weekend retreats had a tendency to turn into discussion groups and several retreat houses closed. Some said that the *Spiritual Exercises* did not suit the mentality of the twentieth-century Jesuit or anyone else for that matter. The turning point came from a movement to dig deeper into the sources of Jesuit spirituality. George Ganss translated the Jesuit *Constitutions* into English. *Woodstock Letters,* the in-house Jesuit quarterly started in 1872, ceased publication in 1969. But in its last decade it published translations of some of the scholarly work going on in Europe on Ignatian spirituality. This rediscovery of the Ignatian spirit was carried on by the Institute of Jesuit Sources founded by Ganss in St. Louis. In 1969 he started the quarterly publication *Studies in the Spirituality of Jesuits.* His publication board was composed of ten Jesuits appointed by the various American provincials.

Even before that, Fr. Tom Burke, a New York Jesuit (1906–93), had begun to reprint scholarly material on the *Spiritual Exercises.* Especially interesting was the spread of personally directed retreats. The chief impetus for the spread of this movement occurred in the 1960s as a result of the meetings of the American Jesuit novice masters. They decided that instead of the usual preached conferences they gave to the novices making the full month-long exercises, they would simply see each novice daily and guide him personally through the retreat experience using the method laid down in the *Spiritual Exercises.* This was, in fact, the way St. Ignatius and the early Jesuits gave the *Spiritual Exercises.*

The fact that the number of novices in the ten American provinces had declined from a high of 408 in 1959 to 85 in 1970 made this procedure possible. Jesuits such as Dominic Marucca, Tom Walsh, and John English of Canada became apostles of this new kind of retreat. Soon personally directed retreats became popular with other Jesuits, and with nuns, diocesan priests, and laypersons. As noted above, some of the centers for these retreats were located in old houses of studies such as Milford, Colombière, Wernersville, and Grand Coteau.

The Schools

The massive changes that shook the Church and the Jesuits had an important impact on Catholic education in general and on the Jesuits in particular. Already in 1964 Fr. John Baptist Janssens, the Jesuit superior general, had approved changes in the Jesuit Educational Association, which up to that time was the organization by which the American provincials governed the high schools, colleges, and universities conducted by the Society. Soon both secondary and higher education each had its own organization.

The Thirty-First General Congregation, in concordance with the emphasis that the Second Vatican Council had placed on close collaboration with the laity, had asked "whether it would not be helpful to establish in some of our institutions of higher education a board of trustees . . . composed partly of Jesuits and partly of lay people; the responsibility of ownership and of direction shall pertain to this board" (Padberg, 238). The Jesuit institutions had already been considering the McGrath thesis, which stated that, since most Catholic institutions such as schools and hospitals were built and sustained with fundraising drives directed to the whole community they served, they were not really church property but public trusts. Applying this thesis to "their" schools, Jesuits reasoned that they did not really *own* the schools. The solution was to install a board of trustees, some of whom were non-Jesuits, as the governing body of the institution. St. Louis University was the first to take the plunge in 1967. In the next fifteen years all the Jesuit colleges and most of the Jesuit high schools followed suit. On their part the American provincials copyrighted the name "Jesuit" and reserved the right to withdraw from institutions the right to use the name if they deviated too far from Jesuit ideals.

That was the last thing the new trustees wanted. The name of Jesuit still evoked an image of excellence. Despite the rapid expansion of publicly funded higher education and the increased funding by state and local governments for public secondary education, there was still a big demand for Jesuit schools on the part of parents and their children.

The lay and clerical trustees had the power and responsibility to determine the curriculum, to select the president, to set the tuition, and to make sure the bills were paid. With fewer Jesuit teachers and ever higher goals of excellence the budgets rose rapidly. So did tuition. Inevitably the new trustees had to help raise money. They also wanted to increase the student body. One result of these factors was that by the 1990s all Jesuit institutions of higher education admitted women on equal terms with men. Even ten Jesuit high schools admitted young women.

The Jesuit institutions also saw their mission change. In general, up to World War II, their mission was to educate the children of parents who had not themselves gone to college. Now, although these institutions set aside scholarship funds for needy students, they generally became more selective in their admission policies. Even so, they felt an obligation to teach their students social justice. In general, the high schools had more success with this than the colleges, because of the introduction of a public service module in the senior year.

All of the twenty-eight Jesuit colleges and universities survived the turmoil of the 1960s and 1970s. But some of the high schools were closed or turned over to other sponsors; there were eight in all. On the other hand, since 1963 new Jesuit high schools have been started in Toledo, Sacramento, Cuyahoga Falls, Fall River, Detroit, and St. Louis. There are now forty-five Jesuit high schools in the continental United States, with a total enrollment of about thirty-six thousand students. The twenty-eight Jesuit colleges and universities in 1992–93 enrolled almost 190,000 students; in that same year they conferred 26,000 bachelor's degrees and over 17,000 professional, master's, and doctoral degrees. Fifty-three percent of those who received degrees were women.

As for the intellectual impact of Jesuits on the American scene in the post-Vatican II world, it is still too early to point to the most influential figures, but three names immediately come to mind, all of them born before 1920. Joseph Fichter (1908–94) was an outstanding sociologist especially noted for his studies of the Catholic parish and schools. Based at Loyola University of New Orleans, he was the first holder of the Stillman Chair of Roman Catholic Studies at Harvard to serve the maximum five-year term. Walter Ong has been an ornament of the humanities faculty of St. Louis University since 1953. His penetrating studies on literature and communications have won him wide renown. In 1978 he served as president of the Modern Language Association of America. Avery Dulles is one of America's best-known theologians specializing in the fields of ecclesiology and ecumenism. He was the mainstay of the theological faculty of Woodstock College until its closure in 1974. Since then he has taught at The Catholic University of America and many other outstanding American universities.

Decree Four

The Thirty-First General Congregation of the Society of Jesus, after electing Fr. Arrupe superior general, continued in two sessions in 1965 and 1966 in order to bring the law of the Jesuits into accord with decisions reached in the Second Vatican Council. It legislated changes in almost every segment of Jesuit life. The Thirty-Second General Congregation met in Rome for three months starting in December 1974 to tie up some loose ends. There were more African and Asian faces than in any previous general congregation. The body was not inclined to halt or reverse the changes legislated in the previous congregation. There was for the first time an explicit note of repentance in the decrees. The second decree (the first was introductory) opened with these words:

> What is it to be a Jesuit? It is to know that one is a sinner, yet called to be a companion of Jesus as Ignatius was. . . . What is it to be the companion of Jesus today? It is to engage under the standard of the Cross in the crucial struggle of our time: the struggle for faith and the struggle for justice which it includes (Padberg, 401).

The first sentence was developed in the rest of the second decree. The second sentence was developed in Decree Four, "Our Mission Today: The Service of Faith and the Promotion of Justice." It spoke of the poverty, hunger, and oppression in the world. It also warned that the promotion of justice is not one apostolate among others, "the social apostolate," but should be a dimension of all the apostolic endeavors of Jesuits (Padberg, 427).

Many critics of the Jesuits have seen in this decree the turning point for the Society. Whereas before the Jesuits insisted on learning, now they wanted to become social activists. But racism, absolutism, social injustice, male chauvinism, and other social ills are opposed by most persons of good will in the world today. The Jesuits have always served the poor and tried to empower the underclass. Decree Four was inspired by the 1971 Synod of Bishops who, in their final statement, *Justice in the World*, declared, "the promotion of justice . . . fully appear[s] to us as a constitutive dimension of the preaching of the Gospel."

Jesuits still run schools, give retreats, write books, and minister to parishioners. Now perhaps there is a new note in their sermons and actions. Of course, the temptation to be a "limousine liberal" content with politically correct thinking is a temptation to Jesuits just as it is for all Christians and persons of good will.

One indication that the Jesuits are interested in the promotion of justice is their increased interest in the missions. In the pre–Vatican II world each Jesuit province had its own mission. New York had the Philippines, New England had Jamaica and Baghdad, Wisconsin had Korea, and so forth. It should be noted that about 3 percent of the decline in the number of American Jesuits noted above is due to the fact that almost all the missions have been raised to the status of provinces and the American Jesuits therein are now counted as part of the new province. In a postcolonial world, the local Jesuits have to assume responsibility and the great majority of mission superiors are Jesuits of native stock.

And it has been in the Third World that Jesuit vocations have grown most rapidly or declined less steeply. Still, these "missions" need personnel and financial help. There are still offices in every American Jesuit province that beg for the missions. American friends of the Jesuits have made huge financial investments in Catholic works in Sri Lanka, India, Japan, Korea, Micronesia, and many other countries in Asia, Africa, and South America.

And there is still a stream of American Jesuits going to the missions. The "foreign missions" are an apostolate encouraged by their superiors, and there are still a number of Jesuits who want to serve there. The international apostolate, as the missions are now termed, is regarded as just another Jesuit field of labor. Jesuits are free to apply to any mission, subject to the acceptance of the mission superior.

Despite the decline in numbers there is still as high a proportion of American Jesuits serving in the missions as there ever has been. As of 1993 there were 467 American-born Jesuits serving abroad in most parts of the world. This is the largest number sent by any American male religious order.

Closure

In August 1981 Fr. Arrupe, the Jesuit superior general, had a stroke on arriving in Rome. He was the first general to fly all over the world visiting Jesuits and their friends. Two months later Pope John Paul II appointed Fr. Paul Dezza, S.J., as his delegate to govern the Society. He did not think that Jesuits were ready for a general congregation. This had a bracing effect on all Jesuits, including the Americans. In December 1982 the Holy Father allowed Fr. Dezza to summon a general congregation in September of the following year. Of the 220 delegates who gathered in Rome there were again many Africans and Asians, this time amounting to more than 15 percent of the delegates. They formally accepted Fr. Arrupe's resignation, elected Peter Hans Kolvenbach superior general on the first ballot, tidied up a few legal questions, generally affirmed the direction of the two previous congregations, finished their work in eight weeks, and went home.

The Jesuits met again in January of 1995 for a longer time in order to adapt the law of the Society to the new norms of canon law. Apart from legal matters the decrees that received the most attention were those on cooperation with the laity and the plea for social justice for women. But by this time the Jesuits seem to have experienced closure on what some of them called "the era of glorious nonsense." But it should be remembered that the Jesuits had to change along with the Church. And the changes that were delayed so long were bound to cause upheavals as well as some silliness in both bodies. It would appear, however, contrary to what some of their critics say, that the Jesuits face an uncertain future with an unsteady calm and a real desire to serve the Church and indeed all humanity. In America most of them realize that they must hand over to laypersons many of the roles they played in their schools, parishes, and other apostolates.

The novices they are attracting now tend to be older. Most of them have college degrees, a good number more than one. During the last twelve years the number of those entering in the ten American provinces has hovered around sixty each year. The retention rate is still causing concern. Whereas in the pre-World War II period and before, about 60 percent of novices who entered died as Jesuits, the figure now is projected to be less than half of that.

On the up side there are some good things to note. Jesuits by and large seem to be less infected with corporate pride than before. They cooperate more with bishops. Finally, as noted above, their missionary zeal seems to burn a little brighter.

Each of the fifty states is entitled to put two of its pioneers and/or great citizens in the National Statuary Hall in the Capitol in Washington, D.C. Among the ninety-five statues that now stand, there are thirteen Catholics. Five of them are religious: Fr. Damien de Veuster, M.SS.CC. (Hawaii); Fr. Junipero Serra, O.F.M. (California); Fr. Eusebio Kino, S.J. (Arizona); Fr. Jacques Marquette, S.J. (Wisconsin); and Mother Mary Joseph Pariseau, F.C.S.P. (Oregon). All of the remaining Catholics are laypersons, and three of them are Jesuit alumni: Charles Carroll of Carrollton (Maryland); Edward Douglass White (Louisiana); and Dennis Chavez (New Mexico). Only time will tell whether the Jesuits will play as important a part in the future of the United States as they have played in its past.

Jesuit Institutions of Higher Education in the U.S.A. in order of foundation year

Name	Location	Year founded	
Georgetown U.	Washington, D.C.	1789[1]	12
St. Louis U.	St. Louis, Mo.	1818[2]	12
Spring Hill College	Mobile, Ala.	1830[3]	1
Xavier University	Cincinnati, Ohio	1831[4]	6
Fordham University	New York, N.Y.	1841[5]	14
Holy Cross College	Worcester, Mass.	1843	3
St. Joseph's U.	Philadelphia, Pa.	1851	7
Santa Clara U.	Santa Clara, Calif.	1851	8
Loyola College	Baltimore, Md.	1852	6
U. of San Francisco	San Francisco, Calif.	1855	7
Boston College	Boston, Mass.	1863	14
Canisius College	Buffalo, N.Y.	1870	5
Loyola U. Chicago	Chicago, Ill.	1870	15
St. Peter's College	Jersey City, N.J.	1872	4
Regis U.	Denver, Colo.	1877	6
U. of Detroit-Mercy	Detroit, Mich.	1877	8
Creighton U.	Omaha, Nebr.	1879	6
Marquette U.	Milwaukee, Wis.	1881	11
John Carroll U.	Cleveland, Ohio	1886	4
Gonzaga U.	Spokane, Wash.	1887	5
Seattle U.	Seattle, Wash.	1891	5
Rockhurst College	Kansas City, Mo.	1910	3
Loyola Marymount U.	Los Angeles, Calif.	1911	6
Loyola U.	New Orleans, La.	1912	5
U. of Scranton	Scranton, Pa.	1923[6]	5
Fairfield U.	Fairfield, Conn.	1942	5
Le Moyne College	Syracuse, N.Y.	1946	2
Wheeling College	Wheeling, W.Va.	1954	1

[1] Jesuits came in 1805
[2] Jesuits came in 1828
[3] Jesuits came in 1847
[4] Jesuits came in 1840
[5] Jesuits came in 1846
[6] Jesuits came in 1942

The fourth column contains the number of students rounded off to the nearest thousand in the 1993–4 academic year.

See also CATHOLIC UNIVERSITIES AND COLLEGES; GEORGETOWN UNIVERSITY; MARQUETTE, JACQUES; MISSIONS IN COLONIAL AMERICA; MURRAY, JOHN COURTNEY; *THEOLOGICAL STUDIES.*

Becker, Joseph. *The Re-formed Jesuits.* San Francisco: Ignatius Press, 1992.

Garraghan, Gilbert. *The Jesuits of the Middle United States.* 3 volumes. Chicago: Loyola University Press, 1938.

Hennesey, James. *American Catholics.* New York: Oxford University Press, 1981.

McDonough, Peter. *Men Astutely Trained: A History of the Jesuits in the American Century.* New York: Free Press, 1992.

Padberg, John. *Documents of the Thirty-first and Thirty-second General Congregations of the Society of Jesus.* St. Louis, Mo.: Institute of Jesuit Resources, 1977.

THOMAS H. CLANCY, S.J.

JOLLIET, LOUIS (1645–1700)

Explorer. Born in Quebec in 1645 and educated by the Jesuits, Jolliet spent several years studying to be a priest. He renounced his vocation in his early twenties and became a fur trader. Shortly thereafter he was appointed by Governor Frontenac of Canada to explore the copper mines of Lake Superior accompanied by the Jesuit Fr. Jacques Marquette.

On May 17, 1673, the two with a party of five men set off westward along the northern shores of Lake Michigan. At Green Bay they entered the Fox River and crossed Lake Winnebago, where friendly natives guided them to the Wisconsin River. They glided down the placid tributary until they reached the Mississippi River on June 17, 1673.

Paddling their canoes southward, they passed grazing herds of buffalo, and on June 25 they stopped at a village of the Illinois tribe. After smoking the peace pipe with the chiefs and elders, Marquette announced that he was a messenger from God the Creator, whom they should obey. After eating and resting, they resumed their journey down the great river to its confluence with the onrushing Missouri.

A few days later they passed the mouth of the Ohio River on the left and soon afterward met another tribe of friendly natives. Three hundred miles and many days went by before they reached the Arkansas River. They had gone far enough to realize that the Mississippi emptied into the Gulf of Mexico. They headed homeward on July 17 and reached Green Bay at the end of September. After a round trip of more than twenty-five hundred miles, Jolliet went on to Quebec in August 1674 to bring the report of his discovery to the governor.

See also MARQUETTE, JACQUES.

JAMES HALEY

JONES, MARY HARRIS ("MOTHER") (1830–1930)

Labor leader, social activist. "Mother" Mary Harris Jones was born on May 1, 1830, in Cork, Ireland, and emigrated with her family to the United States as a child. Her father's work as a railroad construction laborer took them to Toronto, Canada, where Mary attended high school and teacher preparatory (or "normal") school. She taught briefly in a convent in Monroe, Michigan, opened a dress-making store in Chicago, and then returned to teaching in Memphis, Tennessee. There she met and married George Jones, an iron molder, and with him had four children. A yellow fever epidemic swept through Memphis in 1867, however, and George and the children perished.

"Mother" Mary Harris Jones

Mary suffered a further setback in 1871 when the Chicago fire took all of her belongings. Soon after this, she found renewed purpose in the incipient labor movement, attending meetings of the newly formed Knights of Labor and speaking out for improved working conditions for railroad employees and miners. She immersed herself fully in these and similar causes, thus beginning a half-century crusade on behalf of the industrial laborer.

Her petite stature, affectionate gray eyes, and wry wit belied her determination and passionate engagement. She participated in many of the labor movement's crucial battles: the American Railway Union Strike of 1894 in Birmingham, Alabama; the coal miners' strikes of 1900 and 1902 in Pennsylvania, and in 1912–13 in West Virginia; and the garment and streetcar worker strikes in New York City in 1915–16.

She often sought the help of politicians in her efforts to find just solutions to labor difficulties. She led a group of child mill laborers from Pennsylvania to Oyster Bay, New York, in order to confront President Theodore Roosevelt with the harshness of child labor; she interviewed President Taft on behalf of Mexican revolutionaries imprisoned in the United States; and she expressed her objections to the conditions of the Colorado mines in an interview with President Wilson. Despite her age, she remained active in her later years, testifying before the House Committee on Mines and Mining in 1914, and working with striking coal miners in West Virginia in 1923, at the age of 93.

Though not expressive of her religious beliefs, Mother Jones carried with her the prophet-like air of one consumed with seeking justice at every turn, and though she was confrontational by nature, she maintained both tolerance and respect for her foes. These attributes gained her the admiration of thousands of hardened working men and women. Baptized a Catholic in Ireland, she continued to practice her faith throughout her youth and early middle age. She left the Church in her activist years, when she leaned toward socialist ideals, but returned to it in the final years of her life. She died on November 30, 1930—six months after her one-hundredth birthday.

See also IRISH CATHOLICS IN AMERICA; KNIGHTS OF LABOR.

Fetherling, Dale. *Mother Jones, The Miner's Angel.* Carbondale: Southern Illinois University Press, 1974.

Kenneally, James J. *Women and American Trade Unions.* St. Alban's, Vt.: Eden Press, 1981.

Parton, Mary F., ed. *The Autobiography of Mother Jones.* Chicago: C. H. Kerr and Co., 1925.

Steel, Edward M., ed. *The Correspondence of Mother Jones.* Pittsburgh: University of Pittsburgh Press, 1985.

Tonn, Mari Boor. "The Rhetorical Personae of Mary Harris 'Mother' Jones: Industrial Labor's Maternal Prophet." Ph.D. dissertation, University of Kansas, 1987.

JOSEPH QUINN

JOSEPHITES, THE (S.S.J.)

The Josephites (St. Joseph's Society of the Sacred Heart) are a pontifical clerical society of apostolic life. The members, priests and brothers, bind themselves by perpetual promise as an apostolic community to work for the evangelization of black Americans by the preaching of the gospel and a ministry of the spiritual and corporal works of mercy.

The Josephites take their origin from the Foreign Missionary Society of England, founded by Herbert Vaughan in 1866 at Mill Hill, London. Through the agency of Fr. Michael O'Connor, S.J. (former bishop of Pittsburgh), acting for Archbishop Martin John Spalding, the first Mill Hill priests answered the plea for help to evangelize the recently released slaves. Spalding had emphasized this in the Second Plenary Council and again in the Tenth Provincial Council of Baltimore. The first four priests took over St. Francis Xavier Church on December 5, 1871. Thus began a consistent commitment to the black community by a male Catholic religious group, although they had been preceded, decades earlier, by two female groups, the Oblate Sisters of Providence and the Sisters of the Holy Family.

Mill Hill continued to grow. Men were added in America, allowing expansion to Louisville, Kentucky, Charleston, South Carolina, Marlboro, Maryland, Washington, D.C., Richmond and Norfolk, Virginia, and Wilmington, Delaware. After 1875 other mission fields were added, such as the Madras and Punjab areas in India, along with the chaplaincy to the English troops in Afghanistan, followed by Borneo and New Zealand mission fields, all of which seemed to some American interests as a weakening of commitment to the African American community. John R. Slattery, American-born and dedicated to black work, ordained at Mill Hill in 1877, American provincial from 1878 to 1883, was a leader in this point of view. After establishing the Richmond missions in 1884, he received sup-

port for an American Mill Hill Seminary, as well as approval from Vaughan and the American hierarchy. St. Joseph's Seminary was dedicated in 1888, an integrated seminary with the presence of Charles Randolph Uncles, who, on December 19, 1891, became the first African American trained and ordained in the United States. A minor seminary was established in Baltimore in 1889. By the middle of 1892, sixteen Mill Hill men were in America taking care of eight churches and two institutions.

Slattery received permission from Gibbons and Vaughan in 1892 to form a separate American society. Two in America chose to return to Mill Hill, nine joined dioceses in America, and four, together with Slattery and one from India, formed the American community. It was a diocesan institute, under Cardinal Gibbons, headquartered in Baltimore. It followed Mill Hill rules and customs until 1932, when it became a pontifical institute and received a new constitution. A new constitution and directory were approved by the society in 1981 and approved by Rome in 1984.

From 1893 to 1994 Josephites have worked in forty-two American and two Caribbean dioceses. They performed over 336,500 baptisms, 89,700 of converts. A high point in parish numbers was reached in 1954, when there were 123 parishes listed. The high point for parishioners was 1963, with over 159,000 claimed. In the same year there were fourteen high schools and sixty-seven elementary schools, caring for over thirty-eight thousand students. From the 1960s onward, with the improvements in civil rights and much greater diocesan involvement, the parish numbers have been reduced to slightly over sixty-five and the schools to twenty. The estimated number of all black Catholics in America is now well over the two million mark.

The 1984 rule stressed that the basic aims and goals of the society remained the same: it reaffirmed the commitment to work within the black community, seeking to refine the concept of integration as a pluralism of true equals and promoting clerical and lay black leadership within both the Church and the secular community. In 1994 there were over 135 priests and brothers involved in the work, aided by six priests of the Missionaries of St. Paul from Nigeria.

See also AFRICAN AMERICAN CATHOLICS IN AMERICA; DORSEY, JOHN H.

The Colored Harvest. Baltimore: St. Joseph's Society of the Sacred Heart, 1888–1960.

Davis, Cyprian, O.S.B. *The History of Black Catholics in the United States.* New York: Crossroad, 1990.

The Josephite Harvest. Baltimore: St. Joseph's Society of the Sacred Heart, 1960–95.

Ochs, Stephen J. *Desegregating the Altar: The Josephites and the Struggle for Black Priests, 1871–1960.* Baton Rouge: Louisiana State University Press, 1990.

PETER E. HOGAN, S.S.J.

Josephites: John H. Dorsey, Charles Uncles

JOSET, PETER JOSEPH (1810–1900)

Jesuit missionary. Peter Joseph Joset was born in 1810 in the French-speaking Canton of Berne, Switzerland, the youngest of five children, all boys, four of whom became priests. First educated by the local pastor, then by the clergy in the neighboring town of Delemont, he later attended the Jesuit college in Fribourg from 1826 to 1830. He entered the novitiate of the Society of Jesus on October 1, 1830. Ordained in Fribourg by Bishop Peter Tobias Yenni on September 19, 1840, he completed his Jesuit studies, then volunteered for the Rocky Mountain Mission in Northwest America. Accompanied by three other Jesuits, Peter Zerbinatti, Tiburnius Soderini, and lay brother Vincent Magri, he left Le Havre on March 20, 1843, for New Orleans, and arrived on May 18, too late to cross the plains that year.

The following year, on April 23, the four Jesuits departed for the West. When they arrived at the Green River Rendezvous in present-day Wyoming, Fr. Peter De Smet was not there to meet them as planned. Unable to secure a guide, the Jesuits, with their teamsters, seven in all, headed farther west, seeking in the vast wilderness St. Mary's Mission in present-day Montana. By an extraordinary act of Divine Providence, nearly a thousand miles from their destination they met Young Ignace, a Catholic Iroquois, who had just come from St. Mary's and guided them to the mission. Assigned to Sacred Heart Mission for the Coeur d'Alenes, Joset moved this mission from the St. Joe River to its present site at Cataldo in Idaho. He was superior general for the Rocky Mountain Missions for a brief time. Subsequently, he was at St. Paul's Mission on the Columbia River and at St. Michael's Mission near present-day Spokane. Most of his priestly life, however, was spent with the Coeur d'Alenes and, before his death on June 19, 1900, in his ninety-first year, he earned great fame among these native people as "the Apostle of the Coeur d'Alenes."

Bischoff, William N. *The Jesuits in Old Oregon.* Caldwell, Idaho: Caxton Printers, Ltd., 1945.

Schoenberg, Wilfred P., S.J. *A History of the Catholic Church in the Pacific Northwest, 1743–1983.* Washington, D.C.: Pastoral Press, 1987.

____. *Paths to the Northwest: A Jesuit History of the Oregon Province.* Chicago: Loyola University Press, 1982.

WILFRED P. SCHOENBERG, S.J.

JUDGE, THOMAS AUGUSTINE (1868–1933)

Home missionary, founder. Judge was born of Irish immigrant parents in Boston on August 23, 1868, and studied at the John A. Andrew Public School. He thought of becoming a priest, but after his father died in May 1887, he went to work at the local post office to help support the family. He completed his high school courses at night. As a result of a mission given by priests of the Congregation of the Mission (Vincentians) in his home parish in 1889, he enrolled the following year in their apostolic school at St. Vincent's Seminary in Germantown, Pennsylvania. He subsequently entered (1893) the novitiate, made his philosophical and theological studies there as well, and was ordained at St. Charles Seminary, Overbrook, on May 27, 1899.

Thomas A. Judge

After ordination Judge was appointed to do parish work in Germantown and in Emmitsburg, Maryland. In 1903 he was assigned to the Vincentian Mission Band, a task that took him through Maryland, Pennsylvania, New Jersey, and New York. His contacts with Catholic laity convinced him that many desired and endeavored to live holier lives. After his transfer in 1909 to St. John the Baptist Church in Brooklyn, he formed a group of dedicated Catholic lay women to assist him in his house visitations and to instruct children and adults. These women became the nucleus of a lay organization that came to be known as the Missionary Cenacle. In 1910 Judge was assigned to St. Vincent's Mission House in Springfield, Massachusetts, and since his preaching assignments took him to various cities in Vermont, Rhode Island, and Connecticut, he also started similar lay groups in those states.

In July 1915 he was made superior of St. Mary's Mission House in Opelika, Alabama. His area embraced 5,300 square miles and had a population of some 210,000, but of these only 120 were Catholics. Opelika had eight. Aware that he himself could not do all that had to be done, he sent an appeal to his lay missionaries up north, asking if some would come and work with him in Alabama. In 1916 the first missionaries arrived—men and women. The prejudice they had first met eventually disappeared when the people witnessed the selfless sacrifice of the Catholics in caring for the sick and dying during the 1918 influenza epidemic.

In time the members of the Missionary Cenacle expressed their desire to become religious congregations. The Missionary Servants of the Most Blessed Trinity (sisters) was founded in 1919, and the Missionary Servants of the Most Holy Trinity (priests and brothers) in 1921. From 1920 until his death, Judge served as the spiritual guide of both congregations. Though founder of both, he nevertheless always remained a member of the Congregation of the Mission. He became ill in August 1933, was hospitalized in Washington, D.C., for three months, and died on November 23 of that year.

Benson, Joachim V. *Father Judge, Man on Fire.* Holy Trinity, Ala: Cenacle Press, 1973.

Kraut, Alan M. "Thomas Judge and the Catholic Laity in the Rural South." *U.S. Catholic Historian* 8 (1989) 187–98.

O'Connor, David F. "America's Pioneer in the Lay Apostolate: Father Thomas Augustine Judge, C.M. (1869–1933)." *Profiles in American Sanctity,* ed. Joseph N. Tylenda. Chicago: Franciscan Herald, 1982.

JOSEPH TYLENDA, S.J.

K

KAMIŃSKI, STEPHEN (1858–1911)

Bishop of the Polish Independent Church of America. Stephen Kamiński [Stefan Kamiński, actually born Frydryk Raeder] was born on December 26, 1858, in the duchy of Poznań, Poland. Apparently a one-time parish organist, Kamiński joined the Order of the Franciscan Fathers (O.M.C) in Pulaski, Wisconsin. In 1896 he was ordained in Cleveland, Ohio, by the independent Archbishop Joseph René Vilatte. From then until May 3, 1907, he served as pastor of Holy Rosary parish, Buffalo, New York, where he was consecrated bishop March 20, 1898. An early leader in the Polish independent religious movement in the United States, from 1898 until his death in 1911 he edited and published *Warta* [*The Watch*], a weekly Polish paper and organ of the independent Church. By 1907 he claimed leadership of between 75,000 and 100,000 people in twenty-three parishes, but the number of parishioners is probably inflated. Consecrated bishop of the Polish Independent Church of America by the Old Catholic faction, he was never successful in institutionalizing dissent into a permanent church. Upon his death on September 19, 1911, in Buffalo, New York, the mantel of dissident leadership fell to Franciszek Hodur, who succeeded in establishing the schismatic Polish National Catholic Church by uniting many of the parishes hitherto loyal to Kamiński and Antoni Kozłowski in Chicago.

See also POLISH CATHOLICS IN AMERICA; SCHISMS (OR INDEPENDENCE MOVEMENTS) IN AMERICA.

Galush, William. "The Polish National Catholic Church: A Survey of Its Origins, Development and Missions." *Records of the American Catholic Historical Society of Philadelphia* 83 (1972) 131–49.

JAMES S. PULA

KANSAS, CATHOLIC CHURCH IN

In 1540 the Spanish conquistador Francisco Vásquez de Coronado left Mexico for the Gran Quivira in search of the fabled Seven Golden Cities of Cibola. On June 29, 1541, the Spanish crossed the Arkansas River near present-day Dodge City where Fr. Juan de Padilla, the Franciscan accompanying the expedition, offered the first Mass in the continental United States. Upon reaching the Great Plains and realizing that the search for gold was futile, Coronado returned to Mexico leaving Fr. Padilla in Kansas to evangelize the Quivira (Wichita natives). Although the exact place and date of death are uncertain, Fr. Padilla was martyred by a rival Native American tribe, thereby, becoming the protomartyr of the United States.

There are reports of missionary activity to the indigenous peoples in Kansas following Padilla's death, but no permanent effects of Catholic evangelization endured until 1822 when the Rev. Charles de la Croix journeyed as far into Kansas as the Neosho River and converted many of the Osage. It was the Jesuits from St. Louis, however, who established the first missions in the state. The one for the Kickapoo built by Fr. Charles Van Quickenborne in 1836 near Leavenworth had to be abandoned in 1847. A similar fate awaited Fr. Christian Hoecken's Pottawatomie Mission erected at Sugar Creek in 1839. The Religious of the Sacred Heart led by Mother Rose Philippine Duchesne founded a mission school for Pottawatomie girls at Sugar Creek. Although she was recalled to St. Louis in 1842, she left a legacy among the Pottawatomie as the "Woman-who-prays-always." In 1847 two Jesuits, John Schoenmakers and John Bax, together with three lay brothers, established the Osage Mission at St. Paul that served as the headquarters for the legendary journeys of Paul Ponziglione, S.J., throughout southeast Kansas. Part of Osage Mission was St. Ann's Academy for girls staffed by the Sisters of Loretto from Kentucky. Prominent among these sisters was Mother Bridget Hayden who served the mission from 1847 until her death in 1890.

Diocesan Organization

At the request of the Seventh Provincial Council of Baltimore, Pius IX established the "Vicariate Apostolic East of the Rocky Mountains to Missouri," and in 1851 Jean-Baptiste Miège, S.J., was appointed vicar apostolic of the territory. In 1855 when Bishop Miège established Leavenworth as the episcopal city, the diocese consisted of seven hundred Catholics, six completed churches, three under construction, eleven stations, and eight priests. The passage of the Kansas-Nebraska Act in 1854 and the acceptance of Kansas into the Union as the thirty-fourth state in 1861, redefined the territorial boundaries of Kansas and the Diocese of Leavenworth.

Following the Civil War, the demographic and economic development and expansion of the state prompted Miège's successor, Louis Mary Fink, O.S.B., to petition Rome for a division of the diocese which occurred in 1887 with the erection of the dioceses of Concordia under Richard Scannell and of Wichita under James O'Reilly who died before he could be installed and was succeeded in 1888 by John J. Hennessy. In 1897 diocesan boundaries were again reconfigured and remained in effect until 1951 when the western half of the Wichita diocese became the Diocese of Dodge City under John B. Franz. Salina later became the see city for the Concordia diocese and Kansas City, Kansas, replaced Leavenworth and eventually was raised to the status of an archdiocese.

Growth and Expansion

With the passage of the Homestead Act of 1863, pioneers, both migratory Americans and foreign immigrants, came to Kansas seeking 160 acres of free land for a ten-dollar filing fee. The Irish, German, French, Scandinavian, and the German Russians were among the most prominent of the settlers. These sturdy pioneers suffered and endured the hardships of frontier lawlessness, famine, blizzards, drought, economic depression, dust bowls, tornadoes, and grasshopper plagues in an effort to build their farms, businesses, and churches. Of particular importance to the economy of the state were the German Russians, many of whom were the Catholics of Russell and Ellis counties in northwest Kansas. Along with the Mennonites who settled in Marion, Harvey, and Reno counties in Central Kansas, they brought with them their prize possession, the seeds of the "turkey-red" wheat, later called winter wheat. This hardy strain, planted in autumn, could survive the brutal winters and reap an abundant harvest in summer. Along with cattle-raising, winter wheat became the agricultural life-line of the state.

These groups tended to establish small, rural, ethnic settlements where their first concern, apart from survival, was the establishment of churches and schools. In these small and distant settlements, magnificent churches were built and the parish became the focal point of religious, educational, and social life. Some churches, like St. Fidelis Church at Victoria in northwest Kansas, often called the Cathedral of the Plains, were built of native limestone for which each parish family was assessed a specific tonnage. In most cases the farmers quarried the stone, hauled it in their wagons to the church site, and were their own masons.

The rural parish schools were usually small, consisting of two classrooms staffed by the religious congregations who came with the pioneers. Given the economic conditions of the time, salaries were very low or nonexistent. During the dust-bowl years of the 1930s many congregations received no salary and were dependent upon the generosity of the people to supply both food and fuel for the convent.

Religious Communities

Along with the settlers of every ethnic and religious background were the religious orders of both men and women. Included among those early congregations which established abbeys, provincial houses, or motherhouses in the state were the Benedictine priests (1857) and sisters (1863) in Atchison, the Sisters of Charity of Leavenworth (1858), the Sisters of St. Joseph in Concordia (1883) and Wichita (1888), the Adorers of the Blood of Christ in Wichita (1902), the Dominican Sisters in Great Bend (1902), and the Sisters of Mercy in Fort Scott (1886) who later amalgamated with the St. Louis province. Other religious congregations—the Jesuits, the Passionists, the Capuchins, the Sisters of Loretto, and Sisters of St. Agnes—contributed significantly to the development of the early history of the church in Kansas but did not establish a central administration. In more recent years other congregations have founded houses in the state and many different religious congregations have been instrumental in the development of the Church.

Although education was a primary concern for most of these religious congregations, health care and the whole gamut of social services were provided. In nearly every instance, the institutions were built literally on faith. A case in point was the construction of Mt. Carmel Hospital in southeast Kansas when its supporting congregation, the Sisters of St. Joseph of Wichita, possessed the enormous asset of five dollars safely deposited in the pocket of the general superior. A primary reason for the building of the hospital was the care of the miners of the area, and the sisters personally went into the mines to collect twenty-five cents a week in family health-care insurance. This specific example is typical of these institutions as each could repeat a similar history.

Today, Kansas consists of the four above-mentioned dioceses in an eighty-two-thousand-square-mile area with a total population of 2,399,399, of which the Catholic population numbers 376,680. There are 364 parishes, twenty-one health-care and senior citizen residences, ninety-four elementary schools, sixteen secondary schools, and four institutions of higher learning in addition to a full array of other diocesan services and offices.

Beckman, Peter, O.S.B. *Kansas Monks: A History of St. Benedict's Abbey.* Atchison, 1957.

Gilmore, Julia, S.C.L. *Come North! The Life Story of Mother Xavier Ross, Foundress of the Sisters of Charity of Leavenworth.* New York, 1951.

Graves, W. W. *Life and Letters of Father Ponziglione, Shoenmakers and Other Early Jesuits at Osage Mission.* St. Paul, Kans., 1916.

Moeder, John. *History of the Diocese of Wichita.* Wichita, 1963.

Quinlan, Eileen, C.S.J. *Planted on the Plains: A History of the Sisters of St. Joseph of Wichita, Kansas.* Wichita, 1984.

Thomas, Evangeline, C.S.J. *Footprints on the Frontier: A History of the Sisters of St. Joseph of Concordia, Kansas.* Westminster, Md., 1948.

BARBARA BAER, C.S.J.

KATZER, FREDERICK XAVIER (1844–1903)

Educator, third bishop of Green Bay, Wisconsin, and third archbishop of Milwaukee, Wisconsin. Katzer was born in Ebensee, Austria, on February 7, 1844, and in 1857 began seminary studies at Freinberg in a school operated by the Jesuits. During his student years Fr. Francis Pierz, a representative of the Leopoldine Society, encouraged Katzer to serve as a priest in Minnesota. However, when he arrived in the United States in May 1864, Katzer was informed that his services were not needed. An offer from a fellow Austrian, Fr. Joseph Salzmann, to come to St. Francis Seminary in Milwaukee brought him to Wisconsin. He was ordained to the priesthood in December 1866 by Bishop John Martin Henni and taught mathematics, philosophy, and dogma at the seminary. He founded a literary and dramatic society for the German seminarians and wrote a play, *Der Kampf der Gegenwart,* in 1873 which lamented Europe's social ills and lauded his Jesuit mentors.

Frederick X. Katzer

In 1875 he moved to the Diocese of Green Bay, Wisconsin, where he served as secretary and later vicar general to Bishop Francis X. Krautbauer. He was appointed bishop of Green Bay in 1886 and consecrated on September 21, 1886, by Archbishop Michael Heiss of Milwaukee. Katzer spent four years in Green Bay, distinguishing himself by his strenuous opposition to the Bennett Law of 1889, which made the teaching of English compulsory in all Wisconsin schools. The law was repealed in 1890.

In January 1891 he succeeded Heiss and became the third archbishop of Milwaukee despite opposition from Cardinal James Gibbons of Baltimore and Archbishop John Ireland of St. Paul. The latter characterized him as "thoroughly German and thoroughly unfit to be an archbishop." Katzer was indeed closely associated with the "Germanizing" faction of the American hierarchy and believed with them that the survival of German Catholicism in America was inextricably linked to the preservation of their distinctive ethnic traits, especially language. When Pope Leo XIII rebuked the Americanists in the 1899 encyclical *Testem benevolentiae,* Katzer publicly thanked the pontiff.

Katzer encouraged the ethnic diversity of the archdiocese, which by this time was welcoming large numbers of southern and eastern European immigrants. National parishes flourished especially among the Poles whose immigration to Milwaukee was especially heavy. Katzer's benevolence toward the Poles raised their hopes that one day an auxiliary bishop of their nationality would be appointed to

Milwaukee. Katzer condemned popular fraternal organizations, which he considered forbidden secret societies. He distrusted the Populist movement and spoke against the candidacy of William Jennings Bryan in the 1896 presidential election.

Katzer died in Fond du Lac, Wisconsin, on July 20, 1903, the same day as Pope Leo XIII. He is buried with his parents in the cemetery of St. Francis Seminary, Milwaukee.

See also GERMAN CATHOLICS IN AMERICA; WISCONSIN, CATHOLIC CHURCH IN.

Blied, Benjamin. *Three Archbishops of Milwaukee.* Milwaukee, 1955.

Kuzniewski, Anthony, S.J. *Faith and Fatherland: The Polish Church War in Milwaukee.* Notre Dame, 1982.

Marsden, K. Gerald. "Father Marquette and the A.P.A.: An Incident in American Nativism." *Catholic Historical Review* 46 (April 1960) 1–21.

STEVEN M. AVELLA

KAVANAUGH, JOHN P. (1871–1940)

Attorney. John P. Kavanaugh was born on July 11, 1871, in St. Louis, Oregon. He graduated from Mount Angel College, Mount Angel, Oregon, in 1891, and received a law degree from the University of Oregon three years later. In 1902 he was appointed Chief Deputy City Attorney for the city of Portland, and in 1907 he was elected to the position of city attorney, running as a Republican. However, he showed such capability that in 1909 when he ran as an incumbent, he received the nominations of both parties and was easily reelected.

He was elected to the Multnomah County Circuit Court in 1910, serving until his retirement in 1922. That same year Oregon voters passed a Ku Klux Klan-inspired initiative amendment that would have forced all Oregon children to attend only public schools. He was one of four attorneys appointed by Archbishop Alexander Christie to challenge the constitutionality of that law. The state appealed lower-court decisions upholding the challenge up to the U.S. Supreme Court, where Kavanaugh and William Guthrie personally appeared to argue the case successfully. Gonzaga University in 1931 gave him the De Smet Medal, awarded to outstanding Catholic Northwesterners, based on his legal work establishing the unconstitutionality of the Oregon School Bill. In his public life he had a reputation as an ardent student of constitutional law and as an orator of unusual ability.

A member of the Cathedral of the Immaculate Conception parish in Portland, he was also active in the Catholic Order of Foresters and the Knights of Columbus, serving as Grand Knight of the Portland Council. He died on November 12, 1940.

Saalfeld, Lawrence J. *Forces of Prejudice: The Ku Klux Klan in Oregon, 1920–1925.* Portland, 1984.

Schoenberg, Wilfred P., S.J., *A History of the Catholic Church in the Pacific Northwest, 1743–1983.* Washington, D.C.: The Pastoral Press, 1987.

Shelley, Thomas J. "The Oregon School Case and the National Catholic Welfare Conference." *Catholic Historical Review* 75 (1989) 439–57.

JOSEPH A. SCHIWEK, JR.

KEANE, JAMES M. (1901–75)

A priest of the Order of Servants of Mary, or Servites. Keane was born in Chicago in 1901. He was best known as the founder of the Sorrowful Mother Novena which attracted crowds of more than 70,000 each Friday to Our Lady of Sorrows Church on the West Side. In 1939 other parishes began to offer the novena each week, and it spread to 2,300 churches worldwide in the 1940s and 1950s.

Devotion to the Mother of God has been an element of the Servite charism since its founding by the Seven Holy Founders in the thirteenth century. Since the sixteenth century, the order has especially been noted for its promotion of devotion to Mary under the title of Our Lady of Sorrows.

Among his Marian activities, Fr. Keane was founding editor of three magazines, *Novena Notes, Queen of the Missions,* and *The Age of Mary.* He also founded the Catholic lay organization, the Ambassadors of Mary, produced a nationwide radio program, "An Hour With the Queen of Heaven," and appeared weekly in a Chicago area television program on Mary.

From 1947 to 1953 Keane served as general councilor for the order and during that time he made new foundations for the American province of Servites in Northern Ireland (1948) and Australia (1951). He was the founding prior of Our Lady of Benburb Priory in the Archdiocese of Armagh, and in this position he recruited numerous vocations for the American province and its missions in Zululand, South Africa.

Other assignments included seminary rector, local prior, and parish and shrine ministry. From 1942–44 he was editor of *The Southern Cross,* the newspaper of the Diocese of San Diego, and he was assistant rector of the cathedral there. He died at Ladysmith, Wisconsin, in 1975.

Huels, John. *The Friday Night Novena.* Berwyn, Ill., 1977.

____. *Father Keane: Servant of Mary.* Berwyn, Ill., 1979.

JOHN HUELS

KEANE, JOHN JOSEPH (1839–1918)

Archbishop, educator. John Joseph Keane was born in Ballyshannon, Donegal, Ireland, on September 12, 1839, to Hugh Keane and Fannie Connolly Keane. He had two brothers and two sisters who died at an early age. In 1846, during the Great Famine, his family emigrated to St. John, New Brunswick, and then, in 1848, to Baltimore. He received his early education from the Christian Brothers at Calvert Hall, and, at the age of seventeen, left school to work for three years as a clerk in a dry goods store. An avid reader, he spent much of his spare time reading history and studying Latin and Greek. At the age of twenty, he decided to study for the priesthood and entered St. Charles College, Ellicott City, and then St. Mary's Seminary, Baltimore. He was ordained a priest of the Archdiocese of Baltimore by Archbishop Martin J. Spalding on July 2, 1866.

John J. Keane

Early Years

From 1866 until 1878, Keane was assigned to St. Patrick's Church in Washington, D.C., where he was an ardent supporter of the temperance movement and was instrumental in 1872 in the establishment of the Catholic Total Abstinence Union of America. A frequent visitor at St. Patrick's Church was Fr. Isaac Hecker, who invited Keane to join his Missionary Society of St. Paul the Apostle and to assume the editorship of the *Catholic World*. In 1872 Keane asked Archbishop James Roosevelt Bayley for permission to accept Hecker's invitation, but Bayley turned down his request. Nonetheless, Hecker had an enduring influence on Keane, especially in developing his devotion to the Holy Spirit. Denis O'Connell described Keane in 1897 as "Father Hecker's spiritual child in everything." One young parishioner on whom Keane had comparable influence

was Edward Dyer, the future American provincial of the Sulpicians.

In 1878 Keane was appointed the fifth bishop of Richmond. He was ordained a bishop in St. Peter's Cathedral in Richmond on August 25, 1878, by his predecessor, Archbishop James Gibbons. During his ten years in Richmond, Keane was active in combating Protestant prejudice against Catholics, fostering devotion to the Holy Spirit, and promoting the evangelization of blacks. In the city of Richmond he discovered that there were twenty-two Catholics in a black population of approximately 18,000. He never had more than about twenty-seven priests to care for a diocese that included the whole state of Virginia. From 1878 to 1882, Keane was also administrator of the vicariate apostolic of North Carolina, which had been vacant since 1872. In 1880 he offered to resign Richmond for North Carolina when the Holy See had difficulty in finding anyone to accept the unpromising missionary diocese.

The Catholic University of America

At the Third Plenary Council of Baltimore in 1884, Keane was appointed to a committee to establish a Catholic university in the United States. He was active in raising funds for the new institution, and in April 1887 (together with Bishop John Ireland of St. Paul) obtained papal approval for the university's statutes. He was formally appointed rector by the board of trustees on September 7, 1887. He was conscious of his own lack of university training, but accepted the position when the obvious candidate, Bishop John Lancaster Spalding of Peoria, refused to do so. On August 14, 1888, Keane resigned the see of Richmond and was appointed titular bishop of Jassus so that he could devote himself completely to the university, which opened on November 13, 1889. An accomplished public speaker, Keane gained a national reputation for himself and for The Catholic University of America. Some of his colleagues grew weary of what one called Keane's "fatal fluency," but Joseph Nuesse credits him with establishing The Catholic University of America "at the very outset as what is now termed a research-oriented institution."

He also became one of the leaders of the so-called Americanist wing of the hierarchy, associating himself with his friends John Ireland and Denis O'Connell on such issues as the defense of the Knights of Labor and the rapid assimilation of Catholic immigrants. On the question of compulsory education laws, he sided with Thomas Bouquillon, professor of moral theology at the university, who defended such legislation as a legitimate exercise of state authority. Together with James Cardinal Gibbons, Keane took part in the World's Parliament of Religions in Chicago in 1893. Such activities earned him the suspicion of the conservative wing of the hierarchy, most notably Archbishop

Michael Corrigan of New York, Bishop Bernard McQuaid of Rochester, and Archbishop Francesco Satolli, the first apostolic delegate to the United States. On September 15, 1896, he was removed as rector by Pope Leo XIII. Satolli later told Archbishop Patrick Riordan that the reason was that Keane's speeches contradicted Pius IX's Syllabus of Errors.

Later Years

John Lancaster Spalding criticized Keane (privately) for not protesting against his dismissal. "If the Pope had him down on all fours, kicking him each time he raised his foot," said Spalding, "the enthusiastic bishop would shout: 'See how the Holy Father honors me.'" In dismissing Keane from the university, the Pope gave him the choice of an American archdiocese or residence in Rome. Unfortunately for himself, he chose the latter, and from 1897 to 1899 he lived in virtual exile in Rome where he was made the titular archbishop of Damascus, a canon of the Basilica of St. John Lateran and consultor to the Congregation for the Propagation of the Faith and the Congregation of Studies, which he called the "Congregazione dei Sepolti Vivi [Congregation of the Buried Alive]." He resided in two rooms at the Canadian College until forced out by his nemesis Satolli—now a curial cardinal—who apparently feared Keane's influence on the students. Keane spent much of his time defending his reputation from right-wing critics. On a visit to the United States in 1897, he said: "I have never forgotten that the power of the truth consists in its presentation in all its symmetry and beauty and fulness; I have never sacrificed one tittle or iota of it; and they who assert that I have assert what is false."

In 1899 he returned to the United States to help raise funds for The Catholic University of America. On July 24, 1900, he achieved a degree of rehabilitation when he was appointed Archbishop of Dubuque. Even this papal *amende honorable* contained a sting, however, for the Pope's letter of August 18, 1900, also urged Keane to combat the errors of Americanism that he had mentioned the previous year in *Testem benevolentiae*. Said Keane to Archbishop John Ireland: "[The Pope] simply reiterates the assertion made in the encyclical—and this at the very time when he was virtually apologizing to you for saying it, and saying it was needed only in France. . . . It made me sick." In Dubuque Keane took a particular interest in Catholic education, urging pastors to build a parochial school whenever they could gather thirty or forty pupils. He also threw himself wholeheartedly into the local temperance movement, founding the Sacred Thirst Society for young men and publicly denouncing corrupt politicians as "dirty dogs." One of his proudest moments occurred on Sunday, June 16, 1907, when the saloons of Dubuque were closed for the first time in fifty years.

When Keane's health began to fail after 1909, the Holy See refused his request for either a coadjutor or an auxiliary bishop. His biographer, Patrick Ahern, commented: "It is not easy to explain the attitude of the Roman officials in their treatment of him as an old and broken man." Keane submitted his resignation as archbishop of Dubuque on January 10, 1911. He was then appointed titular archbishop of Ciana—his fifth episcopal title—and lived in the cathedral rectory until his death in Dubuque on June 22, 1918.

See also AMERICANISM; CATHOLIC UNIVERSITY OF AMERICA, THE; VIRGINIA, CATHOLIC CHURCH IN.

Ahern, Patrick H. *The Catholic University of America, 1887–1896: The Rectorship of John J. Keane.* Washington, D.C., 1949.
_____. *The Life of John J. Keane, Educator and Archbishop, 1839–1918.* Milwaukee, 1955.
Nuesse, C. Joseph. *The Catholic University of America: A Centennial History.* Washington, D.C., 1990.

THOMAS J. SHELLEY

Related Document

BISHOP KEANE'S ADMONITIONS TO CARDINAL GIBBONS, DECEMBER 29, 1886

John J. Keane (1839–1918) was one of the most colorful and forthright prelates in the group of remarkable bishops who governed the American Church in the late nineteenth and early twentieth centuries. Irish-born, he came to the United States at the age of seven, and twelve years after his ordination he was named fifth Bishop of Richmond in 1878. In August, 1888, he was formally appointed first rector of the Catholic University of America, a post for which he had no training but which brought out his talents for imaginative leadership, arresting public address, and enthusiastic promotion of a cause to which he had committed himself. Keane learned his job by serious reading and by visits to various institutions where he counseled with leading university executives. Thoroughly American in his sentiments, forthright in his view, and convinced of the necessity for a closer relationship between American Catholics and their fellow countrymen, at times his enthusiasm outran his discretion. The result was that he incurred enmity and suspicion as a liberal whose orthodoxy was not entirely sound. In September, 1896, he was summarily dismissed from the university, spent several years of exile in Rome, and was vindicated only in September, 1900, when he was named second Archbishop of Dubuque, a position he held until his resignation was accepted by the Holy See in April, 1911. Few bishops served the American Church more unselfishly and few experienced more reverses and humiliations than Keane. Yet he bore it all in a spirit of deep religious faith and at no time was known to have succumbed to embitterment. The following letter, written from Rome to Cardinal Gibbons at a time when the latter showed signs of wavering on several important questions before the Roman Curia, offers a good example of Keane's candor, courage, and steadfast devotion to what his biographer characterizes as "the best interests of the Catholic Church in the United

States even though it could have meant the loss of a powerful friend" (Patrick H. Ahern, *The Life of John J. Keane, Educator and Archbishop, 1839–1918* [Milwaukee, 1955], p. 37). It was a measure of the cardinal's magnanimity that this letter did nothing to impair their friendship and, in fact, he may even be said to have shown thereafter more resolution in his policies.

(*Source*: Archives of the Archdiocese of Baltimore, 82–J–4, Keane to Gibbons, Rome, December 29, 1886.)

Your Eminence:

We were delighted to receive yesterday your letter of the 17th. Its references to the three important points of the German question,[1] the coadjutorship of N. Orleans,[2] & the Knights of Labor,[3] were most valuable & welcome. I at once put them into three Latin documents, and handed them in to the Propaganda this morning. They will be sure to have great weight. I was very glad to be thus enabled to put your Eminence in a proper light in the Propaganda on the N. Orleans question. You were there identified with the advocacy of Dr. Chapelle's[4] nomination; and as he is sure to be the losing man, you were going down with him on the losing side. Your present advocacy of Bishop Janssens[5] puts you once more on the winning side, where you ought to be.

But I beg that you will permit me, dear and venerated friend, to go on and mention things which it is exceedingly painful for me to pen, and which only my high regard for yourself personally and for the exalted office which you hold, could induce me to write, for it is a hard task and often a risky one, to write painful truths to a friend, especially when he is a superior. Only *real* friendship can nerve one to the duty.

I find, to my intense regret, that an impression has taken shape in Rome to the effect that your Eminence is changeable in views, weak and vacillating in purpose, anxious to conciliate both parties on nearly every question; that it is hard to know, therefore upon which side you stand concerning any important question, or what weight to attach to your utterances. Hence I find a growing inclination to look elsewhere than to your Eminence for reliable information & judgments,—a tendency, not only here but among the Bishops of the United States, to look to New York rather than to Baltimore for the representative & leader of our Hierarchy.

Against this I protest with all earnestness; but they allege fact after fact in defence of their position. They say that, just as in the change of front in regard to New Orleans there is evidence that the former letter was written to please the Archbishop, and did not represent your real views as to the best & safest man, which was what they expected of you, so there was a somewhat similar change of front in regard to poor Dr. Foley,[6] whose friends, notwithstanding all explanations, feel quite sore over his having been finally abandonment [*sic*]. They offset your sentiments on the German question by the fact that the emissary of this attack secretly directed against our Hierarchy by a few German prelates, comes to Rome with a letter of introduction from your Eminence.[7] And they further allege the case of Bishop Dwenger,[8] who may be considered an arch-mover in this bad cause, who, in order to make much of himself & of his cause, had himself sent on here by your Eminence as the representative of our Hierarchy in regard to the Plenary Council,—and they overwhelm me by adding that whereas your Eminence at first asserted that you did not intend to send him, and denied that you had sent him, you later acknowledged that you had done so. We have lately been pouring out our[9] honest indignation at the charge that the signatures of the Prelates to the University petition could not be implicitly trusted as giving the real sentiment of the signers;[10] but I cannot help recognizing with what crushing force they can say to us: "Why look, even your Cardinal puts his name to statements & recommendations which he will afterwards take back or modify; if even he can send us important documents, not because he believes them best for the interests of the Church, but in order to please this one or that one, what confidence can we repose in any of these signatures?" They do not always say this in honest words; but they say it quite gallantly in meaning shrugs, and smiles, and insinuations. Even the Holy Father himself has thus intimated his apprehension that your Eminence was uncertain & vacillating in your views as to the University's location, etc.

I know well, dear & venerated friend, that whatever truth there may be in all this has its real source in your kindness of heart, your anxiety to be gracious and yielding to every one as far as you possibly can. But, as happened to the old man in the fable, by endeavoring to be over prudent and to please all, there is great danger that you eventually will please no one,—that both here and at home they will come to mistrust your consistency & strength of character, and to look elsewhere than to our beloved Cardinal for our exponent & our leader. It galls me to the heart to think that such injustice should be done to our Cardinal; to the leader whom Providence has given to us,—and it is this thought that has given me courage to write so plainly on so painful a subject. Let me hope that you will not be offended, that you will appreciate the affectionate devotedness which, next to my desire for the Church's best welfare, has been my only motive in thus writing; and let me hope that henceforth your Eminence will more than regain the lost ground, by showing such singleness, such consistency, such firmness, such nobleness, in every word and act, as to fully realize the grand ideal of your position in the fore-front of the foremost Hierarchy of the world.

From the depths of my heart I wish you a blessed & happy new year, and am ever

Your devoted servant & friend in Christ,
John J. Keane, Bp. of Rd.[11]

[1] At the time Keane wrote there was serious dissension within the Church of the United States between the Irish and German elements over the petition which Father Peter M. Abbelen of Milwaukee had presented to the Holy See in November, 1886, charging the hierarchy with neglect of the German Catholic immigrants.

[2] The question of a coadjutor with the right of succession to Francis X. Leray (1825–1887), Archbishop of New Orleans, was also in dispute.

[3] In August, 1884, the Knights of Labor in Canada had been condemned by Rome as a forbidden secret society. An effort to secure a unanimous judgment of the archbishops of the United States in favor of the knights in this country was not successful and, therefore, the question had to be referred to the Holy See for a final decision.

[4] Placide L. Chapelle (1842–1905) was named Coadjutor Archbishop of Santa Fe in 1891 and in December, 1897, was promoted to the See of New Orleans.

[5] Francis Janssens (1843–1897) had been Bishop of Natchez since 1881. In August, 1888, he was named Archbishop of New Orleans.

[6] John S. Foley (1833–1918). Foley had been on the *terne* for both the See of Savannah in 1885 and the vacancy in the Diocese of Wilmington in 1886, but in each case opposition to his candidacy arose and he was not appointed. In November, 1888, however, he was consecrated as Bishop of Detroit, a post which he filled until his death.

[7] Before he sailed for Rome on October 13, 1886, Abbelen had received a letter of recommendation from Gibbons to Giovanni Cardinal Simeoni, Prefect of the Congregation of Propaganda de Fide. The Cardinal of Baltimore had known Abbelen's good work in the Third Plenary Council of 1884, but he was not aware of the real nature of the petition which Abbelen was taking to the Holy See.

[8] Joseph Dwenger, C.PP.S. (1837–1893), was Bishop of Fort Wayne from 1872 to his death. Keane was referring here to Gibbons' appointment of Dwenger as one of the two American bishops who were charged with getting the legislation of the Third Plenary Council approved in Rome. Dwenger's conduct of that mission aroused a considerable amount of opposition among his fellow bishops.

[9] Keane's use of the plural throughout his letter referred to John Ireland (1838–1918), then Bishop of St. Paul, who was with him in Rome and who co-operated closely with Keane on all the problems of the American Church which were before the Roman Curia.

[10] At a meeting of the committee for the university held at Baltimore on October 27, 1886, they had drawn up documents for Pope Leo XIII and Cardinal Simeoni approving the plans so far made for the university. Since five other archbishops were in Baltimore at the time they were asked to sign the documents and did so. The opposition party, however, later made it known at the Holy See that some of those who signed were not really in favor of the project.

[11] There was no answer to this letter among the Keane Papers, nor a copy of such found in the archives at Baltimore. In Gibbons' diary under date of January 14, 1887, there was the unrevealing entry: "Wrote to Bp. Keane in reply to his letter from Rome of Dec. 29" (Archives of the Archdiocese of Baltimore, Diary of Cardinal Gibbons, p. 213).

(*Source*: John Tracy Ellis, ed. *Documents of American Catholic History*. Vol. 2:1866–1966. Wilmington, Del.: Michael Glazier, 1987, 437–41.)

KEATING, STANISLAUS (1843–1932)

Religious brother and educator. Thomas Keating was born in Tipperary, Ireland, on October 2, 1843. He moved to Mobile, Alabama, as a young boy and entered the Sacred Heart Brothers there on March 15, 1859, taking the name of Stanislaus. He first taught at St. Thomas, Kentucky

(1860–65), Mobile (1865–66), and Natchez, Mississippi (1866–69).

He became the founding director of St. Aloysius College in New Orleans (1869), St. Patrick's Commercial Institute in Augusta, Georgia, a free Catholic school that initially formed part of the state-operated public school system (1875), and St. Joseph's Normal School in Metuchen, New Jersey (1901). He administered schools in Bay St. Louis, Vicksburg, and Meridian, Mississippi, as well as in Indianapolis, Indiana. He also served on the community's provincial council (1886–1912).

In 1918 he asked to spend his final years working with the orphans at D'Evereux Hall in Natchez. He died there on May 22, 1932, and was buried in the brothers' cemetery at Bay St. Louis, Mississippi.

Br. Stanislaus was a man of "ceaseless energy," an enthusiastic and effective teacher, innovative administrator, and persuasive fundraiser. Many of his former students later recalled that their faith "was so deeply engrafted by him that they have always remained staunch Catholics." The Sacred Heart provincial eulogized him as a model of self-sacrificing zeal, faithful observance of the community's rule of life, continual prayer, and strong faith.

Annuaire de l'Institute des Frères du Sacré-Coeur, 1931–1932, n. 26.

Lives of the Brothers of the Sacred Heart, 1847–1986. Bay St. Louis, Miss., 1987.

Nolan, Charles E. *St. Mary's of Natchez: The History of a Southern Catholic Congregation, 1716–1988.* Natchez, 1992.

[Pierce, Macarius]. *A Century of Service for the Sacred Heart in the United States, 1847–1947.* Bay St. Louis, Miss., 1947.

CHARLES E. NOLAN

KEELY, PATRICK (1816/1820–96)

Architect. Patrick Charles Keely was born in Ireland, but little else is known about the early life of this architect of "preaching churches." The date and place of his birth is given as August 9, 1816, in Kilkenny or August 9, 1820, in Thurles. The spelling of his name is also a matter of some mystery, being spelled variously as Keely, Kiely, and Keily. Nor does Keely's architectural training appear to have occurred under established pedagogical circumstances: it is thought that he trained under his father who was also an architect. In 1841 Keely came to the United States. Keely's architectural style of church design has been called "preaching churches" because they are broad vis-à-vis their length and offer large, open interiors. The interior designs are described as stark and monumental and characteristic of the neo-Gothic or "Victorian" Gothic design which proliferated during the nineteenth century. Keely received the second Laetare Medal, conferred by the University of Notre Dame in 1884. During the course of forty-five years, from 1847 through 1892, he designed sixteen cathedrals and an estimated 500 to 700 churches. Cathedrals in Boston, Chicago, Erie (Pennsylvania), Providence (Rhode Island), and Rochester (New York), are among those designed by Keely.

Daly, W. A. "Patrick Charles Keely: Architect and Builder." Master's thesis, The Catholic University of America, 1934.

Kervick, F. W. *Architects in America of Catholic Tradition.* Rutland, Vt., 1962.

Wilson, H. L. "The Cathedrals of Patrick Charles Keely." Master's thesis, The Catholic University of America, 1952.

Withey, H. F. and E. R. *Biographical Dictionary of American Architects.* Los Angeles, 1956.

LISELLE DRAKE

KELLEY, FRANCIS CLEMENT (1870–1948)

Founder of the Catholic Church Extension Society of the United States and second bishop of Oklahoma. Born and educated in Prince Edward Island, Canada, Kelley was educated in Canada and ordained for the Diocese of Detroit in 1893. After serving as a military chaplain in the Spanish-American War and as a rural pastor, he conceived the idea of Extension. While agencies already assisted African American and Native American missions like the Commission for Catholic Missions Among the Colored People and Indians (established in 1886), large portions of white America, Kelley had observed, were as spiritually deprived as the developing pagan countries overseas. This discovery led to his unprecedented effort to galvanize the affluent dioceses of the North and East in assisting remote and deprived areas where priests were scarce and attrition

Francis C. Kelley

was high. To accomplish this goal, he established the Extension Society in Chicago in 1905 with the help of Archbishop James E. Quigley. Under his leadership, Extension rallied support for rural white Catholicism by organizing two missionary congresses, raising funds through an attractive annuity program, publishing a popular monthly called *Extension Magazine* (which featured articles on the rural missions and promoted the early fiction of promising Catholic writers), building chapels in the countryside, and providing several chapel-cars that traveled the railroad tracks of rural America.

After his appointment to Oklahoma in 1924, Kelley's interest in the home missions shifted noticeably. The godfather of the American Board of Catholic Missions (ABCM), he was the leading force in securing the approval of dividing a national collection between the foreign missions (60 percent) and the home missions (40 percent). This arrangement guaranteed an annual income for mission projects unable to support themselves. Eventually, Kelley grew disillusioned with the ABCM and Extension. Both agencies, he felt, had in time lost their overall vision to evangelize America and served as mere clearing-houses of funds which were in his view dispensed in a haphazard and careless fashion.

Though Kelley's priorities lay in the home missions, he was an extremely versatile man with interests in many fields. While shepherding a vast diocese in the Southwest for twenty years, he offered asylum to refugee bishops who had escaped persecution in Mexico. He also was the leading sponsor of a national seminary in New Mexico (1937–72) that trained Mexican seminarians and was supported by the U.S. hierarchy. He likewise was the principal publicist in this country for the oppressed Mexican Church, publishing a lurid history of that country in *Blood-Drenched Altars* (1935) that drew mixed reviews.

In addition to projects that came and went, Kelley's abiding passion was in the field of communication. In his day he was a sought-after speaker, his popular lectures and retreats across the country contributing to his support. As a writer, he edited *Extension Magazine* and developed a light and clear touch with words that was labeled "Kelleyesque." Of the dozen or so books he published, the most renowned was his autobiography, *The Bishop Jots It Down* (1939). Written with the encouragement of H. L. Mencken who regarded Kelley as a literary master, the book sought to reach beyond the Catholic community and to introduce indifferent non-Catholic readers to the beauties and glories of Catholicism. This was his most successful effort to craft the "perfect book of apologetics." Though it was able to dent the mass market, with its press run approaching 15,000 copies, it never achieved the extensive circulation Kelley had dreamed of.

Kelley's health failed after two decades as bishop of Oklahoma. In 1944 he accepted Eugene J. McGuinness as coadjutor with the right of succession. Four years later he fell into a coma and, as his friend Mencken predicted, slipped away "without regaining full consciousness" in Oklahoma City on February 1, 1948.

See also EXTENSION SOCIETY, CATHOLIC CHURCH.

Gaffey, James P. *Francis Clement Kelley and the American Catholic Dream.* 2 vols. Bensenville, Ill., 1980.
Kelley, Francis C. *The Bishop Jots It Down.* New York, 1939.
Oberkoetter, Mary Joachim, O.S.B. "A Bio-Bibliography of Bishop Francis Clement Kelley, 1870–1948." M.A. thesis, Rosary College, River Forest, Ill., 1955.

JAMES P. GAFFEY

KELLY, EDWARD JOSEPH (1890–1956)

Bishop. Born in The Dalles, Oregon, February 26, 1890, where his father was a farmer-banker, Kelly studied at St. Mary's Academy, and later entered Columbia (now Portland) University. In 1907 he entered St. Patrick Seminary, Menlo Park; in 1911 he was enrolled at the Propaganda University, Rome, where he earned doctorates in both philosophy and theology. Ordained on June 2, 1917, he returned to the Diocese of Baker, Oregon, where he served as chancellor with parish duties in the Mission of St. Joachim in Huntington. He was appointed bishop of Boise on December 16, 1927.

He quickly became known as a "take-charge" bishop. There was no parish, mission, school, convent, or hospital that did not soon feel the results of his new policy of making the bishop part of all major decisions at every level of diocesan and parochial life. He was a business man and a builder, but he did not consider these to be his principal contribution to the life of the Church in Idaho. Before all else he had committed himself to bringing the teaching of the Church to everyone in the diocese through Catholic Schools, the Confraternity of Christian Doctrine, his *Father John's Correspondence Course* for families living in the rural areas of Idaho, the *Summer Institutes for School Sisters,* the High School De Sales Clubs, and programs for Catholic students on state university and college campuses. A diocesan vocation program, the writing of catechetical texts and teachers' manuals, the writing of the *History of the Diocese of Boise, Volume I,* and the gathering of historical data for future historians were among the bishop's goals. All were achieved.

He suffered a heart attack and died while preparing for Mass, April 21, 1956.

See also IDAHO, CATHOLIC CHURCH IN.

Bradley, Cyprian A., O.S.B., and Edward J. Kelly. *History of the Diocese of Boise, 1863–1953.* Boise, Idaho, 1953.

Schoenberg, Wilfred, S.J. *History of the Catholic Church in the Pacific Northwest 1740–1983.* Washington, D.C.: The Pastoral Press, 1987.
Walsh, Nicolas E. *The Catholic Church in Idaho: An Overview.* Boise, Idaho: Capitol Publishers and Printers, 1990.

✝ NICOLAS E. WALSH

KELLY, GRACE PATRICIA (1929–82)

Princess Consort of Monaco, actress. She was born on November 12, 1929, to John B. Kelly and Margaret Majer in Philadelphia. She attended the Stevens School in Philadelphia and later went to New York to enroll in the American Academy of Dramatic Arts to prepare for a career in acting. She began by modeling and taking minor roles in early television shows, and in 1949 she landed a leading part in the play, *The Father,* with Raymond Massey. In 1951 she appeared in the Hollywood film, *High Noon,* with Gary Cooper, and this role launched a stellar career. Kelly had leading roles in the hit films *Dial M for Murder, Rear Window,* and *High Society.* In 1954 she received an Academy Award for *The Country Girl* with Bing Crosby. Kelly met Prince Rainier III of Monaco at the Cannes Film Festival in 1954. They were married in 1956 and had three children, Albert, Stephanie, and Caroline. A devout Catholic, Kelly was devoted to her family and was involved in many charitable works. In 1982, while driving in Monaco with her daughter Stephanie, she was in a serious car accident. She died the next day, September 14, 1982, of a stroke.

ANTHONY D. ANDREASSI

KENKEL, FREDERICK P. (1863–1952)

Editor and social reformer. Frederick Kenkel was born in Chicago on October 16, 1863, to sophisticated, well-to-do German immigrant parents, who had him educated by tutors and at private schools. At eighteen, he began his higher education in Germany, but after a brief period he abandoned his mining engineering studies and spent the next two years reading widely and in leisurely cultural travels.

After a short romance, he married, and in 1885 he returned to Chicago and entered the bookselling business. Three years later his wife died, and he underwent a spiritual crisis. The hitherto nominal Catholic turned to the Church and began a lifelong study of Catholic social teaching and tradition. In 1892 he remarried and returned to the uncongenial world of business, which bored him and eventually led to debilitating bouts of depression which persisted until 1901 when he found congenial work in editing a German-American Catholic newspaper in Chicago. This led to his appointment as editor of *Amerika,* a distinguished German Catholic daily in St. Louis. He held

Frederick P. Kenkel

this assignment until 1920 and became known for his keen analysis of the social and moral problems that beset America. His erudite and versatile editorials earned him the respect of the German-Americans, and he found himself deeply involved in the Central-Verein (now known as the Catholic Central-Verein) which has been the most influential German-American organization since its foundation in 1855. He skillfully recharged its energies and refocused its aims, and became director of its newly established Central Bureau.

He founded and became editor of *Social Justice Review*, the first Catholic magazine to make social reform its primary policy. The Verein's influence and membership grew, and Kenkel became a prophetic voice and spokesman for many of his coreligionists. When, in 1917, America entered the Great War against Germany, Kenkel was devastated and condemned the action as a colossal mistake. He, in his own way, became a casualty. Bitter and hurt, he found postwar America a changed world; many viewed German-Americans with resentful suspicion and this caused the rapid decline in membership in German-American organizations. A proud people became less enthusiastic about a distinctive cultural identity which Kenkel had fostered among his readers and followers. The mood of the time was inimical to his plan for social justice and reform. Kenkel became disillusioned and querulous and spoke, more in monologue than dialogue, to a sparser audience. With distorted historical selectivity, he viewed the Middle Ages as a model for Utopia and the paradigm for a just Christian society.

Yet this complex and cultured traditionalist continued to steer his own lonely course and staunchly promoted many good causes such as the liturgical movement, credit unions, and the care of refugees. Over the years he had assiduously created a magnificent library for the Central Bureau, one of the many achievements of Frederick P. Kenkel who died in 1952.

See also CENTRAL-VEREIN/CATHOLIC CENTRAL UNION OF AMERICA, THE; GERMAN CATHOLICS IN AMERICA.

Brophy, M. L. *The Social Thought of the German Roman Catholic Central Verein.* Washington, D.C.: The Catholic University of American Press, 1941.

Gleason, Philip. *The Conservative Reformers: German-American Catholics and the Social Order.* Notre Dame, 1968.

Liptak, Dolores, R.S.M. *Immigrants and Their Church.* New York, 1989.

MICHAEL GLAZIER

KENNA, JOHN EDWARD (1848–93)

U.S. Congressman and Senator. John Edward Kenna was born on April 10, 1848, in Kanawha County, Virginia (now West Virginia), the son of Edward Kenna, an Irish immigrant and self-educated lawyer, and Margery Lewis, a member of a prominent Virginia family. Edward Kenna's death in 1856 forced his widow and three children to move to her brother's farm in Missouri. Young Kenna worked on his uncle's farm and did not attend school. In 1864 Kenna joined the Confederate army and was severely wounded in the shoulder. He surrendered with his regiment in June 1865 and returned to West Virginia where he began three years of study at St. Vincent's College in Wheeling. Following two years of reading law Kenna was admitted to the bar in 1870.

Kenna became an important figure in the local Democratic Party and in 1872 he was elected prosecuting attorney of Kanawha County. In 1875 he was designated as justice *pro tempore* of the circuit court. Kenna was the youngest member of the forty-fifth Congress when elected to represent West Virginia's Third District in 1876. A seat on the Commerce Committee allowed Kenna to pursue federal aid for slack-water navigation on the Kanawha River. The Kanawha project opened up West Virginia's coal and timber resources for development. Reelected three times, Kenna was elected to the Senate before beginning his fourth term in 1883. In the Senate he became a leading advocate of railroad regulation and tariff reform. He defended President Cleveland's right to dismiss appointees approved by the Senate. Reelected in 1889, Kenna died before completing his second term. He enjoyed hunting and fishing, and as an amateur draftsman he designed both St. Joseph's Roman Catholic Church in Charleston, and his Washington home. In 1870 he married Rosa Quigg; she died four years later and he married Anna Benninghaus in 1876. He died in Washington, D.C., on January 11, 1893.

Memorial Addresses on the Life and Character of John Edward Kenna Delivered in the Senate and House of Representatives. Washington, D.C.: Government Printing Office, 1893.

MICHAEL SOCOLOW

KENNEDY, JOHN FITZGERALD (1917–63)

Background

President of the United States. John Fitzgerald Kennedy was born, on May 29, 1917, in Brookline, Massachusetts, and assassinated, on November 22, 1963, in Dallas, Texas. The second son of Joseph P. and Rose (Fitzgerald) Kennedy, he came from a family that was rooted in the politics of Boston. John went to primary schools, both public and private, in Boston and New York. Before he finished high school at Choate in 1935, he had spent his first year at Canterbury, a preparatory school run by the Catholic laity in New Milford, Connecticut. Moving on to Harvard, where he was a member of St. Paul's Catholic Club, he had been able to work for a few months in his junior year at the American Embassy in London due to his father's connections. Though he graduated *cum laude* from Harvard in 1940, his senior thesis, which dealt with England's lack of military preparation and was published later that year as *Why England Slept,* had been graded *magna cum laude.* Then, although handicapped by poor health, his father's influence helped him get into the United States Navy in World War II. Later, given a command of PT109, John became a genuine hero, receiving the Marine and Navy medals for rescuing his men after their boat had been hit by a Japanese destroyer in the Solomon Islands on August 3, 1943.

John F. Kennedy

Returning home, John Kennedy explored ways to carry on the family standard following the death of his older brother Joseph, Jr., who had been killed in a bombing flight over Europe in August of 1944. For him, public service was a civic responsibility, a lesson that he had learned early in life from his parents. Consequently, after covering the United Nations and the Potsdam Conference as a correspondent for the International News Service in 1945, he entered into national politics in the following year.

United States Congressman

Initially, Governor Maurice J. Tobin of Massachusetts wanted John to run with him as lieutenant governor in 1946, but Kennedy's father, who served the Tobin Administration in an advisory role, saw a greater opportunity in the seat left open in the Eleventh Congressional District by James Michael Curley, who was about to run for mayor of Boston again. Climbing up and down the three deckers of Charlestown's Irish neighborhood, where David F. Powers lived, Kennedy meticulously combed this and other working class areas of the district. With the help of his family and close friends like Paul B. "Red" Fay, Jr., Torbert H. Macdonald, and Kenneth P. O'Donnell, he won the primary and the election easily, as the family wealth of the Kennedys more than the party structure of the Democrats became a key element in his victory. Thus, he had a seat in Congress during the early Truman years while Tobin went down to defeat in the Republican tidal wave that swept across the nation in that postwar year of conservative triumphs.

During that aftermath of World War II, Kennedy, not unlike other Catholics in politics, was more of a parochial politician concerned about bread-and-butter issues in his working-class district rather than a national leader. Hardly a doctrinaire liberal, he was particularly interested in federal aid to education, a major issue in those days, and the new foreign policy being forged by Harry S. Truman to save the world from Communism. Even though Kennedy was frequently absent during his three terms in the United States House of Representatives, he was successful in his bid for the United States Senate in 1952 when, with the help of his family's tea parties, he defeated Henry Cabot Lodge, Jr., the incumbent, by 70,000 votes.

United States Senator

As a Senator, Kennedy's chances for national prominence improved. At St. Mary's Church in Newport, Rhode Island, with Archbishop Richard J. Cushing of Boston officiating, he forged social ties, on September 12, 1953, by marrying Jacqueline Bouvier (1929–94), who bore him Caroline (b. 1957) and John Jr. (b. 1960). Subsequently, Kennedy involved himself more in international issues, gaining attention by speaking out against American policy in Indochina and advocating an independent Vietnam as early as 1954. His book, *Profiles in Courage* (1956), which was later turned into a television series, won him a Pulitzer Prize in 1957 and kept him in the national limelight. Later, in one of the more prominent evaluations of foreign policy at the time, the young Senator spoke against the French policy in Algeria in 1957 and called for an independent Algeria. This and other statements were published in his third book, *The Strategy of Peace* (1960).

Kennedy lost his bid for the vice-presidential nomination in 1956 but was spared the blame for Adlai E. Stevenson's defeat in that year. Kennedy easily won a second term in the United States Senate by a majority of 875,000 votes in 1958 over Vincent J. Celeste. This stunning victory enabled Kennedy, a member of the Senate Committee on Foreign Relations, to turn his attention to the presidency. Then, he demonstrated that a Catholic was a viable candidate in 1960 by capturing eight of the presidential primaries, including those in Wisconsin and West Virginia, both supposedly heavily Protestant states. Here he proved that his religion was not a disadvantage and that he, at least, could win against Protestants like Hubert H. Humphrey and Lyndon B. Johnson, his major rivals. Kennedy's success was convincing to the power brokers of the Democratic Party like Edmund G. Brown in California, Richard J. Daley in Illinois, Robert F. Wagner, Jr., in New York, Michael V. DiSalle in Ohio, and David L. Lawrence in Pennsylvania, who were themselves Catholics. With such support, it was almost impossible to deprive Kennedy of his party's nomination in 1960.

Winning it at Los Angeles on the first ballot, Kennedy, to the surprise of his brother Robert, chose Lyndon B. Johnson, his bitter rival, as his running mate. Kennedy projected a younger, more vigorous, and more imaginative image than Vice President Richard M. Nixon who was nominated by the Republicans. In the ensuing debates, particularly those on television, Kennedy gained points on Nixon. As for the religious issue, which he skillfully presented in his special address to the Protestant ministers at Houston early in the campaign, Kennedy was helped in the cities of the East but hurt in the farm districts of the West. In the end, with the assistance of his running mate, Johnson, Kennedy won by a narrow margin of 34,227,000 popular votes compared to 34,109,000 for Nixon, though the electoral vote was more decisive with 303 for the senator and 219 for the vice president. Thus, John F. Kennedy became the youngest American and first Roman Catholic ever elected to the presidency.

President of the United States

Taking office on January 21, 1961, Kennedy inspired the nation with his challenge to Americans when he declared: "And so, my fellow Americans, ask not what your country can do for you; ask what you can do for your country." With this call to public service and his vision of a new frontier for the nation, the new President evoked confidence in his ability to govern, especially since he had brought into his administration distinguished Republicans such as C. Douglas Dillon as secretary of the treasury, John A. McCone to head the Central Intelligence Agency, and Robert S. McNamara as secretary of defense. At the same time, he selected prominent Democrats like Adlai E. Stevenson as United States Ambassador to the United Nations, Arthur F. Goldberg as secretary of labor, and Robert F. Kennedy, his own brother, as attorney general. The President's penchant for the exceptional in politics and culture was evident in the quality of his appointments to public office as well as in the talent of those artists, musicians, scientists and writers whom he chose to invite to the White House.

Domestic Policy

Having studied Richard E. Neustadt's book, *Presidential Power* (1960), Kennedy sought to be a strong President. In dealing with Congress, he sent it many messages on various topics such as civil rights, federal aid to education, a higher minimum wage, increased social security benefits, and Medicare for the aged. However, the President encountered strong opposition from a coalition of conservatives on each of those issues. "When I was a Congressman," he bitterly remarked in 1962, "I never realized how important Congress was. But now I do." This was particularly evident in January of 1963 when his proposal to reduce taxes as a way to stimulate economic growth was opposed by conservatives in both parties.

Consequently, despite his own willingness to compromise, Kennedy came to realize that his ability to act was somewhat restricted by that legislative body. Though he could have appealed over their heads to their constituents, he preferred to be reasonable and conciliatory. Unfortunately, this approach did not break the stalemate for the short time he was President. Though many of his proposals did influence the social programs signed into law by his successor, the promises of Kennedy's campaign remained largely unfulfilled during his own tenure of office. Thus, it became evident that the federal structure left something to be desired if the President could not more successfully lead Congress.

Yet, despite the unfulfilled promises under Kennedy, the strength of presidential power was evident in at least two ways. One was the President's decision to square off against Roger Blough of United States Steel and others to force them to back down from a price rise in April of 1962. Clearly, he was effective because he threatened the owners with an antitrust suit and used the Federal Bureau of Investigation to get back at the steel corporations. Likewise, when the South refused to cooperate in implementing changes in civil rights for blacks who, more than any group, had voted overwhelmingly for Kennedy in 1960, he used the power of the federal government to coerce submission to the federal laws, especially against Governor Ross Barnett at the University of Mississippi in 1962.

Foreign Policy

However, it was particularly in the area of foreign policy that Kennedy demonstrated the scope of his power as president when the United States faced some of its most dangerous crises. In confronting the Communist threat in Berlin, Cuba, and Southeast Asia, some revisionists conclude that the President showed himself a Cold Warrior rather than a New Frontiersman. Early in his administration, he had become so preoccupied with Cuba and tied to a plan prepared during the Eisenhower administration that the policy resulted in the fiasco of the landing at the Bay of Pigs on April 17, 1961. Without sufficient air support, the invasion of 1,400 Cuban refugees became a disaster for the administration. Some historians note that his bungling there and his poor showing at Vienna in his meeting with Nikita S. Khrushchev in June of that same year, emboldened the latter, who had overwhelmed Kennedy in the summit meeting, to test the young President over Cuba.

By that time, in October of 1962, Kennedy had learned from his past mistakes to place more confidence in the advice of generalists rather than specialists. Consequently, when he sought to outfox the American President, the Soviet leader found himself, much to his surprise, in a situation of having to fire the first shot. Kennedy had turned what Khrushchev had done upside down with his naval quarantine against the shipment of offensive weapons to Cuba. This was not unlike what he had done to Kennedy more than a year earlier in Berlin. With Khrushchev checkmated in this way, a compromise was reached, whereby Kennedy allowed the Russian to save face since appearances of superiority became more important than the realities (the threats were still there). Thus, with the crisis defused and the world saved from catastrophe, the naval quarantine was lifted on November 21, 1962.

Rather than pull the American missiles out of Turkey in exchange for removing the Soviet missiles from Cuba, as Khrushchev had demanded in his second letter (October 27), Kennedy responded to the first letter (October 26). In this way, the Soviets promised to withdraw the missiles from Cuba without any link to the missiles in Turkey provided the United States would not invade Cuba. However, the exchange of missiles was an option that the President could have used, as his secretary of state, Dean Rusk, revealed many years after the event (the removal of the *Jupiter* from Italy and Turkey had already been decided on before the crisis because they were obsolete).

In any case, Walt W. Rostow, in his work, *Diffusion of Power* (1972), one of his advisors in the State Department at the time, thought that Kennedy proved himself a masterful statesman in handling the crisis. While this is the view of the Kennedy historians such as Arthur M. Schlesinger, Jr., there are those like Richard J. Walton and Garry Wills who believe that Kennedy almost brought about a nuclear holocaust by his lack of responsibility in his preoccupation with toughness. Of course, some critics still wonder whether the Cuban Missile Crisis was really necessary, especially since the Soviets, with their submarines snaking surreptitiously through American waters for a number of years, had already targeted American cities for destruction during the cold war. Nevertheless, when it was all over, the Communists remained in Cuba, the Soviets maintained a foothold in the hemisphere, and the regime of General Ydigoras Fuentes in Guatemala, which had allowed the Central Intelligence Agency to train the troops to invade Cuba back in April of 1961, was overthrown by the United States in March of 1963.

Thereafter, there followed a lessening of tensions between the United States and the Soviet Union. In an effort to establish better communications between the two nations, a special telephone ("hot line") was installed between them on June 20, 1963. Then, following Kennedy's speech at American University in June, which impressed Khrushchev, the two nations signed the nuclear test-ban treaty that summer, on August 5, 1963, an achievement which General Maxwell D. Taylor, chairman of the Joint Chiefs of Staff, supported, and which many considered to be the President's greatest. Of course, one cannot forget how Kennedy intensified the space program by promising to put a man on the moon by 1970.

While Kennedy saved face in Latin America, he lost out in both Asia and in Europe. In Eastern Europe, early after the Vienna Summit, Khrushchev was able to put up the Berlin Wall (August 13, 1961) thereby dictating the agenda over the divided city, a situation that remained until the wall came down in 1989. Though Kennedy had shown his commitment to the city by his visit there on June 26, 1963 ("I am a Berliner"), it is questionable whether or not he lost an opportunity in the failure to resist the construction of the wall when, according to an NBC White Paper shortly after the crisis, the Soviets had been instructed to back off if the Americans were to offer resistance. Certainly, the objective fact is that the President could do nothing about Berlin short of war with the Soviet Union once the wall was in place. At the same time, Kennedy had to cope with the national ambitions of France's Charles DeGaulle who, distrustful of the Anglo-American agreement at Nassau (December 21, 1962) to establish a nuclear force for NATO, objected (January 29, 1963) to England's entrance into the Common Market.

In Asia, Kennedy had a number of hard choices. When China invaded Kashmir, on October 20, 1962, he sent aid to India until the invader withdrew after gaining favorable boundaries along the Himalayas. In Indochina, Kennedy had to agree to a neutral government in Laos, on May 16, 1961, but he had to intervene in Thailand on May 15, 1962, when the Pathet Lao broke that truce. The President tried to compensate for this loss by taking a stronger stand in Vietnam where he raised the American forces from 350 at the start of his administration to 16,000 at its end. His rationale was his firm belief in the domino theory. Unfortunately, Kennedy was falling into the trap of deepening America's involvement in a land war in Asia against the advice of military advisor General Douglas MacArthur and political advisor George W. Ball, his undersecretary of state. Michael V. Forrestal, an official in the administration, revealed that Kennedy, who had in the Senate supported the Roman Catholic leader of South Vietnam, turned white when he, as President, learned that Ngo Dinh Diem and the latter's brother were assassinated on November 2, 1963, a direct consequence of a decision Kennedy had taken in August of that year to reduce Vietnam to a colony of the United States. Evidently, the President's moral and religious beliefs had an impact on him in dealing with a situation where South Vietnam was badly divided between Catholics and Buddhists. Though Kennedy had plans to get out of Vietnam after the next presidential election, his tragic death prevented him from realizing that.

One should not overlook the extent to which Kennedy was engaged with Khrushchev in a rivalry for the nations of the Third World. While the President might have been on the defensive with respect to the Communists in Asia, Berlin, and Cuba, it can be said that he was on the offensive with them through the Alliance for Progress in Latin America and his deployment of the Peace Corps there, as well as in Asia and Africa. With the Alliance for Progress (March 13, 1961), Kennedy wanted to support democratic governments by expending twenty billion dollars over a period of ten years to advance economic development. And, by an executive order, on March 1, 1961, Kennedy had set up the Peace Corps, which sent American volunteers to help the people in the underdeveloped areas of Asia, Latin America, and Africa.

With respect to the latter, Kennedy appointed G. Mennen Williams as his assistant secretary of state for Africa. As his book, *Africa for the Africans* (1969), makes clear, Williams pursued this policy for a continent where its nations tended to pursue a policy of neutrality in the rivalry between East and West. Unfortunately, for the administration, African leaders were aware of the distinction in the United States between whites and blacks and the lack of blacks involved in shaping the State Department's policy for Africa. Understandably, the Soviet Union attacked American policy in Africa as another form of economic imperialism designed to help American business. Yet, Kennedy did appoint the first black plenipotentiary, Clifton

P. Wharton, ambassador to Norway, and he did attempt to ameliorate the racial situation at home to project a better image of the United States abroad.

Assassination

The extent of Americans' love for conspiracy theories is evident from the death of President Kennedy. The number of theories, beginning with the belief in a widespread conspiracy and coverup, which have been nourished in part by the blunders in the Warren Commission Report, is just too extensive to review. Given Oliver Stone's 1991 movie, *JFK,* it is doubtful that the conspiracy theories will ever be put to rest. That so interested an individual as Robert F. Kennedy did not pursue the matter is sufficient for some that the judgment about Lee Harvey Oswald acting alone was about all there was to it. Even if one allows for the circumstantial evidence such as Oswald's association with the Soviet Union, there is not sufficient evidence for an expert of this view like Gerald Posner, author of *Case Closed* (1993). However, even Harris Wofford, author of *Of Kennedys and Kings* (1980), is inclined toward another interpretation of Robert's failure to pursue the matter.

Speaking of the President, Robert Kennedy declared in 1964: "At least one-half of the days that he spent on this earth were days of intense physical pain." Perhaps this is why Dr. Max Jacobson gave him those injections before he met Khrushchev in Vienna in June of 1961. Since his whole life had been plagued with maladies, the urgency with which Kennedy lived was not unrelated to his poor health. While he concealed from the public his pain and his back brace, in addition to his affliction from Addison's disease, it is a measure of the man that he achieved so much. According to Robert E. Gilbert's *Mortal Presidency* (1992), "His illnesses, then, contributed to an intellectual life that left a clear imprint on his presidency" (160).

Catholic and Irish

Writers like Nancy Gager Clinch, Nigel Hamilton, Thomas C. Reeves and others have written much about Kennedy's character, especially as it related to his parents, to associates, like Sam Giancana and Frank Sinatra, and to the women, other than Jacqueline, in his life. However, one cannot discount the possibility that the revelations about his private life insofar as they relate to Inga Arvad, Judith Campbell Exner, and Marilyn Monroe, might very well have come about due to different motives than the service of the truth. That Kennedy evoked such responses was evident when a rumor, widespread in news circles in 1962 (and which responsible newspapers refused to print), alleged that the President had already been married prior to his marriage to Jacqueline Bouvier.

As for Kennedy's own Catholicism, perhaps Lawrence H. Fuchs' *John F. Kennedy and American Catholicism* (1967) said it best (229–30): "He was the antithesis of the stereo-typed separatist, parochial, anti-intellectual, superstitious, tribalistic, and fatalistic Catholic of Protestant literature and conversation. But the stereotype, while based on a core of reality, never suited hundreds of thousands of Catholics from Carroll to Spalding to Kennedy." While Fuchs' opinion can be regarded as historically accurate, it does not really reveal the force of Catholicism in Kennedy's private and public life, especially in relation to his character and leadership.

Given what has been revealed about Kennedy's private life, it is easy to forget that, despite his behavior, his life was not completely unaffected by his religious beliefs. Plagued by various ailments since his youth, he aggravated his condition with his heroism in the Solomon Islands resulting in serious crises over the years. Consequently, at least three of these life-threatening situations (in 1947, 1954, and 1955) resulted in Kennedy receiving the last rites, as they were then known, before he was given them for the last time following that tragic shooting in Dallas.

Though Kennedy did not make much of his own religion in his public life once he was elected president, it would be misleading to conclude that it did not mean much to him. That he was able to call upon the best of American Catholic intellectuals to help him with his address, on September 12, 1960, before the Greater Houston Ministerial Association during the campaign indicates that he was not at all ignorant of the teachings of his Church. Though critics focus on his lack of Catholicism, it was in the major confrontation of his presidency that his religion became a key factor.

At the time of the Cuban Missile Crisis, Pope John XXIII appealed to both Kennedy and Khrushchev. That the Pope's plea for moderation did not fall on deaf ears is clear from the subsequent address that Kennedy gave at Boston College in the spring of the following year and from Khrushchev's support of the 1962 Balzan Peace Prize for the Pope. Many of the details of this story have been related by Norman Cousins and should not be forgotten.

Moreover, President Kennedy was close to Richard Cardinal Cushing of Boston, who officiated at his marriage; he also had such contact with the Rev. Edward C. Duffy, who often offered Mass at the Kennedy Compound in Hyannis Port; and to his cousin, Rev. John F. Fitzgerald, who, like the Cardinal, assisted at his presidential inauguration. Inducted in the Knights of Columbus, on March 17, 1946, Kennedy remained a member of this largest Catholic lay organization throughout the remainder of his life. Perhaps later historians can give more attention to religion in the life of John F. Kennedy, a public servant who was both Irish and Catholic.

Yet, while there was no doubt about Kennedy's Irish background, Garry Wills, writing in *The Kennedy Imprisonment* (1981), declared (64): "To paraphrase Jacque-line Kennedy, it was unfair for the Kennedys to be treated as Irish, they were such poor Irishmen; they tried so hard to be anything but." Wills makes sense if one recalls that President Kennedy publicly declared on Columbus Day in 1962: "My grandfather John Fitzgerald, Mayor of Boston, claimed that the Fitzgeralds descended from the Geraldini family of Venice." Earlier, in his first term as congressman, Kennedy had refused to join his Massachussetts colleagues in asking the President to release and pardon James Michael Curley, a favorite of the Boston Irish.

Kennedy's Legacy

Perhaps one reason for the division among historians over the character and leadership of the President a generation after his death is that at forty-three, Kennedy was the youngest American elected president and, at forty-six, the youngest American president to die. Since his charisma, intelligence, and vigor overshadowed his mistakes while he was alive and immediately after his death, it became a challenge to historians to separate the legendary Kennedy of Camelot from the historical Kennedy of Washington. The national monument on his grave (where two of his children, one a girl stillborn in 1956, the other a boy, Patrick, who died shortly after birth in 1963, and his wife are also buried) in Washington, D.C., the statue at the State House in Massachusetts, the cenotaph at Dealey Plaza in Dallas, and the acre of ground given in his memory at Runnymede near Windsor, England, are impressive memorials which articulate what he has meant and continues to mean to many people in the United States and around the world.

Lastly, that John F. Kennedy proved how a Catholic could be president of the United States was itself an exceptional achievement. That he exemplified courage, dedication, integrity, and judgment, qualities that he had proposed as the hallmarks for his own administration in his address (January 9, 1961) to the Massachusetts Legislature, can serve as the yardsticks by which later generations can evaluate his place in history.

The John F. Kennedy Presidential Library in Boston houses his papers.

Bernstein, Irving. *Promises Kept*. New York, 1991.

Cousins, Norman. "Outstretched Hand." *Saturday Review* (February 13, 1965) 20–21.

———. "Improbable Triumvirate." *Saturday Review* (October 30, 1971) 24–35.

Goodwin, Doris Kearns. *The Fitzgeralds and the Kennedys*. New York, 1987.

Hilsman, Roger. *To Move a Nation*. Garden City, N.Y., 1967.

Manchester, William R. *The Death of a President*. New York, 1967.

Paper, Lewis J. *John F. Kennedy*. New York, 1979.

Reeves, Richard. *President Kennedy*. New York, 1993.

Schlesinger, Arthur M., Jr. *A Thousand Days.* Boston, 1965.

Sorensen, Theodore C. *Kennedy.* New York, 1965.

VINCENT A. LAPOMARDA, S.J.

Related Document

THE ISSUE OF RELIGIOUS FREEDOM IN A PRESIDENTIAL CAMPAIGN, OCTOBER 5, 1960

The presidential candidacy of Senator John F. Kennedy of Massachusetts which ended successfully in the election of November 8, 1960, was preceded by a campaign in which the Democratic candidate's Catholic faith became one of the major issues. The candidates of both major parties sought to bar the question of religion; but as one writer has stated, "the lens of national reporting was soon to focus attention on this religious imponderable as the central political question of the campaign. . . . Both candidates were to denounce the prejudice; but neither could erase the intrusion of religious feeling" (Theodore H. White, *The Making of the President 1960* [New York, 1961], p. 92). The question of the Catholic doctrine on religious freedom occupied a foremost position in the debate and gave rise to statements of the widest variety—and validity—from non-Catholic sources. In an effort to make clear their uncompromising acceptance of the American tradition of separation of Church and State, and what that implied by way of freedom for citizens of all religious faiths and none, on October 5, a month in advance of the election, a group of 166 Catholic laymen issued a statement embodying their views on this subject.

(*Source: Catholic Mind,* LIX [March–April, 1961] 179–180.)

THE PRESENT CONTROVERSY ABOUT THE CATHOLIC CHURCH and the Presidency proves once again that large numbers of our fellow-citizens seriously doubt the commitment of Catholics to the principles of a free society. This fact creates problems which extend far beyond this year's elections and threaten to make permanent, bitter divisions in our national life. Such a result would obviously be tragic from the standpoints both of religious tolerance and of civic peace.

In order to avert this, we ask all Americans to examine (more carefully, perhaps, than they have in the past) the relationship between religious conscience and civil society. We think that, in the present situation, Catholics especially are obliged to make their position clear.

There is much bigotry abroad in the land, some of it masquerading under the name of "freedom." There is also genuine concern. To the extent that many Catholics have failed to make known their devotion to religious liberty for all, to the extent that they at times have appeared to seek sectarian advantage, we must admit that we have contributed to doubts about our intentions. It is our hope that this statement may help to dispel such doubts.

To this end we make the following declarations of our convictions about religion and the free society. We do this with an uncompromised and uncompromising loyalty both to the Catholic Church and to the American Republic.

1. We believe in the freedom of the religious conscience and in the Catholic's obligation to guarantee full freedom of belief and worship as a civil right. This obligation follows from basic Christian convictions about the dignity of the human person and the inviolability of the individual conscience. And we believe that Catholics have a special duty to work for the realization of the principle of freedom of religion in every nation whether they are a minority or a majority of the citizens.

2. We deplore the denial of religious freedom in any land. We especially deplore this denial in countries where Catholics constitute a majority—even an overwhelming majority. In the words of Giacomo Cardinal Lercaro, the present Archbishop of Bologna: "Christian teaching concerning the presence of God in the human soul and belief in the transcendent value in history of the human person lays the foundation for the use of persuasive methods in matters of religious faith and forbids coercion and violence." The Catholic's commitment to religious liberty, therefore, he says, "is not a concession suggested by prudence and grudgingly made to the spirit of the times." Rather, it is rooted "in the permanent principles of Catholicism."

3. We believe constitutional separation of Church and State offers the best guarantee both of religious freedom and of civic peace. The principle of separation is part of our American heritage, and as citizens who are Catholics we value it as an integral part of our national life. Efforts which tend to undermine the principle of separation, whether they come from Catholics, Protestants or Jews, believers or unbelievers, should be resisted no matter how well-intentioned such efforts might be.

4. We believe that among the fundamentals of religious liberty are the freedom of a church to teach its members and the freedom of its members to accept the teachings of their church. These freedoms should be invulnerable to the pressures of conformity. For civil society to dictate how a citizen forms his conscience would be a gross violation of freedom. Civil society's legitimate interest is limited to the public acts of the believer as they affect the whole community.

5. In his public acts as they affect the whole community the Catholic is bound in conscience to promote the common good and to avoid any seeking of a merely sectarian advantage. He is bound also to recognize the proper scope or independence of the political order. As Jacques Maritain has pointed out, the Church provides Catholics with certain general principles to guide us in our life as citizens. It directs us to the pursuit of justice and the promotion of the common good in our attitudes toward both domestic and international problems. But it is as individual citizens and office holders, not as a religious bloc, that we make the specific application of these principles in political life. Here we function not as "Catholic citizens"

but as citizens who are Catholics. It is in this spirit that we submit this statement to our fellow Americans.

(*Source*: John Tracy Ellis, ed. *Documents of American Catholic History*. Vol. 2:1866–1966. Wilmington, Del.: Michael Glazier, 1987, 652–54.)

KENNEDY, JOSEPH P. (1888–1969)

Businessman, diplomat. Joseph Patrick Kennedy was born in Boston, Massachusetts, on September 6, 1888, and died in Hyannis Port, Massachusetts, on November 18, 1969. The son of Patrick J. Kennedy, a ward boss from East Boston, he was graduated from Harvard in 1912 and was determined to become a millionaire. Meanwhile, in 1914, with William Cardinal O'Connell officiating, he married Rose Fitzgerald (1890–1995), the daughter of John F. ("Honey Fitz") Fitzgerald, who had been mayor of Boston. Rose bore him nine children (Joseph, John, Rosemary, Kathleen, Eunice, Patricia, Robert, Jean, and Edward). Fiercely competitive, Joseph P. Kennedy became the president of a bank by age twenty-five and earned a million dollars by age thirty.

Engaging in various enterprises (banking in East Boston, shipbuilding in Quincy, managing investments in Boston, and producing motion pictures in Hollywood), Kennedy acquired vast wealth that enabled him to contribute substantially to the Democratic Party. His reputation for ruthlessness and shrewdness in dealings foreshadowed Kennedy's future actions. While many of his contemporaries were losing their fortunes during the Great Depression, his experience in making business deals and in managing stocks gave him the skills that paid off in manipulating the stock market and in trying to manipulate Franklin D. Roosevelt with whom he had become allied.

Then, following the victory of the Democrats in 1932, Franklin D. Roosevelt appointed Kennedy the chairman of the Securities and Exchange Commission (1934–35). In this position, Kennedy helped to curb some of those questionable practices that had helped him accumulate his own wealth in the previous decade. He wrote a book whose title, *I'm for Roosevelt* (1936), made clear where the Bostonian stood on economics and politics. Then, after Roosevelt had appointed Kennedy chairman of the United States Maritime Commission (1937), the President elevated him to the prestigious post of United States Ambassador to Great Britain (1937–40). But Kennedy clashed with the President over a third term and American foreign policy. Though he eventually accepted Roosevelt for a third term, Kennedy alienated the British by a blunt interview in *The Boston Globe* (November 10, 1940), thereby rendering himself ineffective as a diplomat. Therefore, he resigned as American Ambassador to Great Britain effective the following February.

While opposition to Roosevelt over a third term was not uncommon among Catholics, Kennedy's views later proved embarrassing when his son ran for the presidency. Specifically, the traditional prejudice of the ambassador's Irish heritage emerged in his opposition to helping England in its battle against the Nazis. Such a stand emanating from his roots was not unusual for the elder Kennedy who later supported Senator Joseph R. McCarthy, a Catholic, in his drive against Communists early in the 1950s.

Plagued by tragedy in his own family, Joseph P. Kennedy devoted the rest of his life in helping his children attain that scope of power in public life which he did not enjoy. Having already established them comfortably with individual trust funds and imposed upon them a competitive style of life, the elder Kennedy lived to see the triumphs and tragedies of his sons, John as the thirty-fifth President of the United States, Robert as United States Attorney General and United States Senator, and Edward as United States Senator. Suffering a stroke in December of 1961, Kennedy became an invalid until he died at the age of eighty-one.

After Nigel Hamilton came out with his unflattering portrait of their parents in his biography of John F. Kennedy, surviving members of the family publicly defended their father and mother with an op-ed in *The New York Times* (December 3, 1992). Joseph P. Kennedy is buried, with his wife, in Holyhood Cemetery, Brookline, Massachusetts.

The papers of Joseph P. Kennedy, Sr., can be found in the John F. Kennedy Presidential Library in Boston.

Beschloss, Michael R. *Kennedy and Roosevelt*. New York, 1980.

Goodwin, Doris Kearns. *The Fitzgeralds and the Kennedys*. New York, 1987.

Kennedy, Rose. *Times to Remember*. Garden City, N.Y., 1974.

Kessler, Ronald. *The Sins of the Father*. New York, 1996.

Koskoff, David E. *Joseph P. Kennedy*. Englewood Cliffs, N.J., 1974.

Whalen, Richard J. *The Founding Father*. New York, 1965.

VINCENT A. LAPOMARDA, S.J.

KENNEDY, ROBERT (1925–68)

U.S. Senator, Attorney General of the United States. Robert Francis Kennedy was born in Brookline, Massachusetts, on November 20, 1925, and died in Los Angeles, California, on June 6, 1968. The third son of Joseph P. and Rose Fitzgerald Kennedy, he was a younger brother of President John F. Kennedy to whom he was faithfully dedicated. Educated at schools such as Portsmouth Priory and Milton Academy, he was graduated from Harvard in 1948 and the University of Virginia Law School in 1951. Married in 1950 to Ethel Skakel (b. 1928), who was educated at Manhattanville College, they became the parents of eleven children (one of whom, Joseph P. Kennedy III, is a United States Congressman), making their home at Hickory Hill in McLean, Virginia. Tough and competitive like his father, Robert projected an abrasive personality compared to that of his brother John as they worked together in public life.

Robert F. Kennedy

Early Career

Kennedy's career as a lawyer began in the United States Department of Justice where he was employed in the Criminal Division during the last year of the Truman administration. That same year, he helped his older brother defeat Henry Cabot Lodge, Jr., for the United States Senate in 1952 by managing his campaign. Thereafter, he was never far from John F. Kennedy in public life while he worked as an investigator for the Permanent Subcommittee on Investigations chaired first by Senator Joseph R. McCarthy, a Republican from Wisconsin, and then by Senator John L. McClellan, a Democrat from Arkansas. Under McCarthy, Robert Kennedy had broken with the Wisconsin senator and joined with the senators of his own party when they protested the chairman's tactics in 1953. Returning to the committee, he served as its chief counsel under McClellan who kept Kennedy in that same position on a select committee investigating improper labor and management activities in 1957. In this capacity, Robert Kennedy exhibited a toughness that exposed the corruption of the labor unions, as is clear from his autobiographical account of these investigations, *The Enemy Within* (1960). These included his clashes with James R. Hoffa, the powerful boss of the International Brotherhood of Teamsters, whom Edward Bennett Williams, the prominent Washington lawyer and Catholic layman, defended. However, even though Kennedy lost that 1957 confrontation, he had helped to open the way to reforms that resulted in the Landrum-Griffin Act of 1959.

Attorney General

Meanwhile, during the 1956 presidential campaign, Robert Kennedy studied carefully what went wrong with Adlai E. Stevenson and was determined to avoid those mistakes in 1960 when he managed his brother's campaign for the presidency. Leaving the McClellan Committee, Kennedy devoted his efforts totally to the election of his brother, an experience that projected Robert himself even more clearly into the national limelight as an exceptional political figure. Chosen attorney general, he became his brother's most trusted advisor in presidential decisions, especially during the Cuban Missile Crisis in 1962 about which his own testimony, *Thirteen Days* (1969), exists. By suggesting that the President respond to Nikita S. Khrushchev's letter of October 26 and ignore the tougher one sent by the latter on October 27, Robert provided the key that helped to defuse the international crisis and save the world from a nuclear holocaust.

At the same time, Attorney General Kennedy gradually forged a record of distinction as an advocate of civil rights. Using the federal laws already on the books, the Justice Department forced interstate transportation facilities to desegregate, compelled Southern officials to obey the law on voter registration, and undermined resistance to school desegregation. All this became clear when the administration used the National Guard to admit James H. Meredith to the University of Mississippi in 1962. Thus, Robert Kennedy helped to open the way for the Civil Rights Act of 1964 which was signed into law under his brother's successor, President Lyndon B. Johnson.

Understandably, with the death of his brother, Robert went through an agonizing and traumatic experience. What influence national secrets about plots and counterplots and his own desire to protect his brother's reputation had in his refusal to pursue the investigation of the assassination beyond the decision of the Warren Commission has provoked much speculation. But it was clear that Kennedy had matured from a tough political figure who emphasized the law while he was United States Attorney General dealing with Governor Ross Barnett in Mississippi and Governor George C. Wallace in Alabama to a humane statesman more concerned about moral issues.

Coming to grips with the reality of his own situation and the crucial problems confronting the nation at home and abroad, Robert F. Kennedy made his way back to the center of politics by running for the United States Senate from New York, once he was edged out of presidential politics by President Johnson. Easily successful in this bid in 1964, he had found himself with a national platform from which to advocate reforms for the nation's most disadvantaged minorities. Subsequently, he separated himself from the foreign policies of the Johnson Administration, particularly in the United States military intervention in the Dominican Republic in 1965 and in the simultaneous escalation of the war in Vietnam. Concerned about the nation's foreign policy following the Tet Offensive by which the Vietcong opened their Lunar New Year in 1968, it was no surprise when Kennedy announced, on March 16, 1968, before Johnson bowed out of the competition (March 31), that he would challenge the President for his party's nomination.

Presidential Candidate

Perhaps, the most dramatic phase of Robert Kennedy's career came with the battles for the six presidential primaries against Senator Eugene J. McCarthy of Minnesota. The latter appealed to college students and the more prosperous middle-class liberals, particularly among Catholics, while Kennedy linked up with working class Catholics like Cesar Chavez, leader of the farm workers. In the midst of those contests when Martin Luther King, Jr., was assassinated, Kennedy, almost single-handedly, defused the wrath among the blacks, by his speech that night (April 4, 1968) in Indianapolis, Indiana, when he told the crowd that he could appreciate how they felt, having lost his own brother at the hands of a white man.

"Some men see things as they are," Kennedy used to emphasize during the campaign, "and say 'Why?' I dream of things that never were and say 'Why not?'" Such a confident outlook gave hope not only to blue-collar workers in the factories but to the disadvantaged who were marginalized like the whites in Appalachia and the blacks in Bedford-Stuyvesant, in addition to Hispanics in California. Though he lost Oregon to Senator McCarthy, the first defeat for a Kennedy, victory came to Robert in most of the presidential primaries that year. Certainly, it was his triumph in the June 5 California Primary that raised the hopes of all those Americans who had supported him in his quest for his party's nomination.

But, tragically, shortly after his victory, in the early morning of the following day, Kennedy was killed by Sirhan Bishara Sirhan, an Arab immigrant, in the Ambassador Hotel in Los Angeles. "His public legacy," Senator Edward M. Kennedy said of his brother, "is written in the achievements of those whom he inspired and who have carried on his work." A political and moral force in politics, Robert was a leader whose courage certainly made a difference for many because he held out the hope of eliminating the poverty, racism, and violence in this country. An eternal flame, burning at the site of his brother's grave in Arlington National Cemetery, where Robert is also buried, keeps that hope alive as does the presence in the United States Congress of a brother, a son, and a nephew.

On the surface, at least, Robert F. Kennedy appeared more religious than his brothers and that impression is not inaccurate. When he was at Milton Academy, he set an example for other Catholics to fulfill their Sunday obligation and, while at Harvard, he had rightly disagreed with Leonard J. Feeney, the Jesuit chaplain at the St. Benedict Center, concerning non-Catholics. Throughout his life, Robert attempted to conduct himself in accord with the teachings of his faith. That is why those who were not Catholic and worked closely with him in his brother's administration find it impossible to hold that Robert would have even countenanced, as some have alleged, a policy of assassination against people like Fidel Castro.

Though he valued very much his own religious beliefs and practices, Kennedy had sought to find purpose in his life after the tragic assassination of his brother by reading the ancient dramatists, especially Aeschylus. "Let us dedicate ourselves to what the Greeks wrote so many years ago: to tame the savageness of man and to make gentle the life of this world," he had concluded in that talk following the death of Martin Luther King, Jr., that same night in Indianapolis. Combining ancient wisdom with the religious truths of his faith, Robert F. Kennedy was able to make a difference for his generation, leaving, like his brother John, a legacy of civic responsibility for many who come after him to imitate.

Robert F. Kennedy's papers are housed in the John F. Kennedy Presidential Library in Boston.

Robert Kennedy, *In His Own Words* (New York, 1988), is an edition of his own recollections by Edwin O. Guthman and Jeffrey Shulman.

Lasky, Victor. *Robert F. Kennedy.* New York, 1968.

Navasky, Victor. *Kennedy Justice.* New York, 1971.

Newfield, Jack. *Robert Kennedy.* New York, 1969.

Schlesinger, Arthur M., Jr. *Robert Kennedy and His Times.* Boston, 1978.

Sorenson, Theodore C. *The Kennedy Legacy.* New York, 1993.

Wofford, Harris. *Of Kennedys and Kings.* Pittsburgh, 1980.

VINCENT A. LAPOMARDA, S.J.

KENNEDY, THOMAS J. (1887–1963)

Labor leader. Kennedy was born on November 2, 1887, in Lansford, Pennsylvania. At the age of twelve, he followed his father into the coal mines, and in 1900 he joined the local affiliate of the United Mine Workers of America. For the next sixty-three years, Kennedy remained dedicated to the interests of miners and all laborers, rising eventually to the office of International President of the UMW. In 1910 he was elected president of UMW District 7, which incorporated much of the anthracite region of western Pennsylvania, and in 1918 he challenged the young John L. Lewis for the vice presidency of the national union. Although Lewis defeated him by nearly a two-to-one margin in the election, the two men shared many similar ideas and goals, and Kennedy was to become one of Lewis's most valuable and trustworthy supporters during the turbulent 1930s and 1940s.

In 1925, after Lewis assumed the presidency of the UMW, he made Kennedy the union's secretary-treasurer, an office which he held for the next twenty-three years. He was the first representative from an anthracite mining area to hold a national office in the UMW, and his presence helped to ease organizational tension between the anthracite and bituminous sectors of the union. Kennedy was also a pioneer in the field of modern labor politics. In the depression years of 1930–32, Kennedy organized pressure on the state and federal governments to institute systems of unemployment insurance. In 1939 and 1940 he frequently appeared before congressional committees to urge the passage and enforcement of safety regulations in the mining industry.

In 1934 he was elected Lieutenant Governor of the State of Pennsylvania, and he used this office to the great benefit of labor. He secured state funds to study the decline of the anthracite industry and to promote research into the lung diseases that plagued miners. Most memorably, during the organizational campaign of the CIO's Steel Workers' Organizing Committee in 1936, Kennedy promised state police protection for striking steel workers. He also guaranteed that strikers would not be denied government relief if they should need it. He thus eliminated the two greatest barriers to the organization of workers. In 1938 he ran unsuccessfully for the Democratic Party's gubernatorial nomination against a Roosevelt-supported candidate in one of several Lewis-Roosevelt confrontations. Although he remained active in politics, he never again sought elective office.

During World War II, Kennedy represented labor on the National Defense Mediation Board and the National Labor Board. In 1948 he was elected vice president of the UMW, and in 1960, although Kennedy was ill himself, he succeeded the ailing John L. Lewis as president.

Kennedy was married in 1912 to Helen Melley. He was involved in a number of social and charitable organizations, including the Knights of Columbus, and he served as president of the board of directors for Hazleton (Pennsylvania) Catholic Charities. He died in Hazleton on January 19, 1963.

See also LABOR MOVEMENT AND AMERICAN CATHOLICS, THE.

Alinsky, Saul D. *John L. Lewis: An Unauthorized Biography.* New York, 1949.

Dubofsky, Melvyn, and Warren Van Tine. *John L. Lewis: A Biography.* New York, 1977.

Finley, Joseph E. *The Corrupt Kingdom: The Rise and Fall of the UMW.* New York, 1972.

Fox, Maier B. *United We Stand: The United Mine Workers of America, 1890–1990.* New York, 1990.

Levy, Elizabeth, and Tad Richards. *Struggle and Win, Struggle and Lose: The United Mine Workers.* New York, 1977.

Morgan, Alfred L. "Pennsylvania's 1938 Election." *Pennsylvania Magazine of History and Biography* 102:184–205.

Zieger, Robert H. *John L. Lewis: Labor Leader.* New York, 1988.

MATTHEW LaFLAMME

KENRICK, FRANCIS PATRICK (1797–1863)

Archbishop and theologian. Francis Patrick Kendrick was born in Dublin, Ireland, on December 3, 1797, and was educated at the College of Propaganda Fide in Rome. He was ordained a priest on April 7, 1821. Kenrick volunteered to serve in the Diocese of Bardstown, Kentucky, in response to an appeal from Bishop Benedict Flaget for a qualified theologian for his seminary. Kenrick taught all the theology courses in the major seminary. His first publications appeared while he was in Kentucky.

Francis P. Kenrick

Coadjutor in Philadelphia

Trusteeism in Philadelphia and Bishop Henry Conwell's erratic behavior led to the naming of Kenrick as coadjutor with right of succession and titular bishop of Arath, March 1830. Kenrick was familiar with the issues; he had condemned Conwell's 1826 pact with the trustees and in 1827 had suggested that Conwell be transferred to an Irish see.

Diocesan jurisdiction was in Kenrick's hands; Conwell was allowed episcopal but not jurisdictional functions. Personal relations were difficult and the arrangement lent itself to ambiguity regarding episcopal jurisdiction. Rome consequently reaffirmed in August 1831 that all episcopal jurisdiction belonged to Kenrick alone, and in September 1831 authorized Kenrick to publish this throughout the diocese.

Bishop Kenrick confronted the trustees directly in January 1831, informing them he intended to act as first pastor of St. Mary's, the cathedral church. Since the trustees maintained their claim to accept or reject pastors, the bishop placed an interdict on St. Mary's in April. In May the trustees conceded they had no right to interfere in appointing or removing pastors but claimed the right to fix clerical salaries. Kenrick accepted this but threatened an interdict should the temporal support of priests be withheld. It brought the trustee issue in Philadelphia under control, although there was a flare-up in 1850 at Holy Trinity Church. In a dispute between the pastor and the trustees over amending the charter, Kenrick suggested he be allowed to appoint the board. The congregation threatened to withhold the pastor's salary. Kenrick excommunicated the leaders and placed an interdict upon the church. It was settled by allowing the Jesuits to administer the parish. Kenrick also insisted that title to churches be in the hands of the ordinary.

While still at Bardstown, Kenrick was present as theologian to Bishop Flaget at the First Provincial Council of Baltimore in 1829. The bishops present wanted a "proven exemplar" of the Douay Vulgate, with annotation, since a number of versions existed. Kenrick undertook the revision a decade later. He published a complete New Testament in 1862, but never an edition of the entire Bible. The Ninth Provincial Council of Baltimore of 1858 had proposed that Kenrick's version, when completed, be adopted for common usage in the United States, but after his death, the Second Plenary Council of Baltimore, 1866, reversed this position.

Kenrick was a recognized theological scholar and an apologetical writer. His writings include a defense of the Real Presence in *Letters of Omega and Omicron* (1828); *The Primacy of the Apostolic See and the Authority of General Councils Vindicated* (1837); a four-volume *Theologia Dogmatica* (1840); three-volume *Theologia Moralis* (1843; 2nd ed., 1858/9) to meet specific American conditions such as the slavery issue; and a small treatise on *Baptism and Confirmation* (1842). As archbishop of Baltimore, he published *A Vindication of the Catholic Church, in a Series of Letters to the Rt. Rev. J. H. Hopkins*. Kenrick was conversant with the Oxford Movement and had high expectations of it.

Growing anti-Catholicism, evident in the anti-Catholic pamphlet literature in the 1830s and 1840s, led to the Philadelphia Know-Nothing Riots of May and July 1844. The May riot resulted from a protest by Kenrick and others over the anti-Catholic school atmosphere and textbooks. The school board ignored the complaints. Kenrick's efforts were taken as an effort to remove the Bible from the schools. The resulting riots were directed primarily against Irish Catholic churches and residences. St. Michael's and St. Augustine's Churches were burned. Kenrick was forced to order a cessation of public services; the clergy avoided the wearing of clerical dress. Kenrick himself left Philadelphia. A charge that Catholics had desecrated an American flag caused the July riot, exacerbated by the discovery of arms in the basement of St. Philip Neri's Church. The arms had been placed there for self-defense with the authorization of civil authorities. Five thousand military personnel were required to restore peace.

Diocesan Administration

Kenrick was known as a disciplinarian and builder. He held the first Philadelphia diocesan synod in 1832 which reissued the decrees of the First Provincial Council of Baltimore; it prohibited the building of new ecclesiastical structures without episcopal authorization—part of the policy of placing title of all church properties in the ordinary's name to counter trusteeism; it withdrew canonical faculties from any priest abetting lay interference in spiritual concerns of the Church and mandated the maintenance of accurate baptismal and marriage records; it decreed the use of Archbishop Carroll's catechism until one approved by Rome appeared, and dealt with clerical discipline and took steps to protect the sacraments against simony.

A second synod was held in 1842. It reaffirmed the common law of the Church and repromulgated the decrees of the Baltimore Provincial Council of 1840. It also ordered all priests of the diocese to attend quarterly clergy conferences. The third synod in 1847 repromulgated the decrees of the Fifth and Sixth Provincial Councils of Baltimore, regulated financial matters, matrimonial banns, and clerical attire, and reaffirmed the parochial rights of the Augustinians and Jesuits.

The Diocese of Philadelphia included the entire states of Pennsylvania and Delaware and southwest New Jersey (the original West Jersey colonial grant). Kenrick made nineteen diocesan visitations in his twenty-three years as ordinary, almost all in Pennsylvania, occasionally in New Jersey. His *Visitation Record* supports the picture of a disciplinarian and builder. He insisted that proper liturgy be used, that hymns not be sung in German; nor would he bless sites of new churches until he obtained the title. He recorded in detail his administration of sacraments on these diocesan visitations.

Based on his visitation experiences, Kenrick proposed to Propaganda Fide in 1835 separating western Pennsylvania into a new diocese at Pittsburgh. He was willing to become the ordinary there himself. Rome did not accept the proposal until made by the Fifth Provincial Council of Baltimore of 1843. Kenrick's candidate, Michael O'Connor, was then named first bishop.

Kenrick intended to build a seminary even before his arrival in Philadelphia. A committee report to the first diocesan synod supported him. He began by accepting students into his home; he acted as rector and theology professor until the arrival of his brother, Peter, in the school year 1833–34. He was helped by a substantial grant from the Leopoldine Society, Vienna, although this was later significantly reduced due to charges that Kenrick was unsympathetic to Germans. The seminary, which then occupied a separate house next to St. Mary's parish, was legally incorporated by the state legislature in April 1838. A larger site was purchased in 1838, and Michael O'Connor, future bishop of Pittsburgh, became rector. Vincentians (Congregation of the Mission) were brought in in July 1841 and remained in charge of the seminary for the remainder of Kenrick's episcopacy. He contemplated establishing a minor seminary, but it did not materialize.

The diocese grew dramatically during Kenrick's episcopacy. From 1830 to 1850 the number of churches grew from 22 to 92; priests from 35 to 101; charitable institutions from two to six; the Catholic population from 35,000 to 170,000. The cornerstone of the present Cathedral of St. Peter and Paul was laid September 6, 1846. His greatest educational accomplishment was the establishment of a free parochial school system attached to almost every parish. He encouraged the growing emphasis on devotional life, in particular Forty Hours Devotions, and supported, with reservation, Father Matthew's Total Abstinence Society. He felt Matthew relied more on the pledge than on religion.

Archbishop of Baltimore

Francis Kenrick became archbishop of Baltimore in 1851. He presided over the First Plenary Council of Baltimore in 1852. The council made binding on the American Church the decrees of all the provincial councils of Baltimore, urged the establishment of parish free schools, and the use of the Roman Ritual. It proposed the establishment of several new sees, including Washington, which Rome rejected. Rome did acknowledge in 1858 that Baltimore had "preeminence of place" rather than primacy in the American Church; it was suspicious of independence tendencies of a primacy. Kenrick supported the establishment of the North American College in Rome which opened December 1859, although there was not complete support for it among the American hierarchy.

Triennial provincial councils were held in 1855 and 1858, and diocesan synods in 1853, 1857 and 1863; the synod especially addressed administrative, disciplinary, and devotional matters relating to Baltimore, parish financial reports, restricting Catholic access to sacraments to parishes in which they resided.

Archbishop Kenrick, who stressed the citizen's duty of loyalty, died during the Civil War on July 8, 1863.

See also PENNSYLVANIA, CATHOLIC CHURCH IN.

Diary and Visitation Record of the Rt. Rev. Francis Patrick Kenrick, 1830–1851. Lancaster, Pa., 1916.

F. E. T. *The Kenrick-Frenaye Correspondence.* Philadelphia, 1920.

Light, Dale. "The Reformation of Philadelphia Catholicism, 1830–1860." *Pennsylvania Magazine of History and Biography* 112 (3) (1988) 375–405.

Moran, Michael. "The Writings of Francis Patrick Kenrick, Archbishop of Baltimore (1797–1863)." *Records of the American Catholic Historical Society of Philadelphia* (1930) 230–61.

Nolan, Hugh J. Francis Patrick Kenrick, First Coadjutorbishop." *The History of the Archdiocese of Philadelphia,* ed. James F. Connelly. Philadelphia, 1976, 113–208.

____. *The Most Reverend Francis Patrick Kenrick Third Bishop of Philadelphia 1830–1851.* Philadelphia, 1948.

Spalding, Thomas W. *The Premier See: A History of the Archdiocese of Baltimore, 1789–1989.* Baltimore, Md.: Johns Hopkins University Press, 1989, 154–78.

THOMAS R. GREENE

KENRICK, PETER RICHARD (1806–96)

First archbishop of St. Louis. *Noli Irritare Leonem* ("Do Not Disturb the Lion") was the fitting motto of the first archbishop of St. Louis, Peter Richard Kenrick, and well describes his character. Kenrick was born in Dublin, Ireland, on August 18, 1806, the son of Thomas Kenrick and

P. Richard Kenrick

Jane Foy. His early education was under a private tutor and later by an uncle, Fr. Richard Kenrick, pastor of the parish church. His older brother, Francis Patrick, was already a student for the priesthood at the Urban College in Rome when Peter Richard entered St. Patrick's College, Maynooth. He was ordained a priest on March 6, 1832, and was assigned to the cathedral in Dublin.

At the request of his brother, Francis Patrick (who had become the episcopal administrator of Philadelphia), he came to that city to assume the position of rector of the diocesan seminary, arriving in October 1833. Shortly thereafter he was also appointed rector of the cathedral and vicar general of the diocese and was subsequently stationed at Pittsburgh. During his time he authored three works, *Validity of Anglican Ordinations Examined, New Month of Mary,* and *The Holy House of Loretto.*

On November 30, 1841, he was named coadjutor bishop of St. Louis with right of succession and was consecrated in Philadelphia by Bishop Joseph Rosati of St. Louis. Rosati then left to take up his duties as apostolic delegate to Haiti, and Kenrick was left to administer the St. Louis diocese. Upon Rosati's death on September 25, 1843, Kenrick became bishop of St. Louis. On January 30, 1847, Pope Pius IX elevated St. Louis to the status of an archdiocese and appointed Kenrick its first archbishop. He took over a see plagued with debt and tremendous needs, both human and material. In 1843 the Diocese of St. Louis embraced Missouri, Arkansas, and the western half of Illinois. He had seventy-five priests to minister to this vast area.

During his long tenure as archbishop, Kenrick was involved in a number of controversies with fellow bishops, priests, politicians, and even the Holy See. He adopted a policy of silence during the Civil War. His diocese was bitterly divided and, although known to be pro-Southern, he felt his best policy was to remain silent and maintain a strict separation of Church and state. When the Union-controlled state legislature adopted a new constitution requiring all clergymen to take an oath of loyalty to the state before preaching or presiding at marriages, Kenrick issued a pastoral letter forbidding his priests from doing so. When one of his priests was arrested and imprisoned, Kenrick took the case to the U.S. Supreme Court and was vindicated.

Kenrick played an important role at Vatican Council I. He was one of the leaders of the opposition to the definition of the doctrine of papal infallibility. He believed that the definition was inopportune because it was contrary to American culture, and he also believed that papal pronouncements could be infallible only if supported by the world college of bishops. Rather than vote "no" on the issue, he left Rome prior to the vote and in Naples published his *Concio,* a pamphlet representing the views of the opposition. This publication was subsequently condemned by the Congregation of the Index.

His problems with Rome caused Kenrick to go into virtual retirement for the next decade. During this time the actual administration of the archdiocese was conducted by his coadjutor, Archbishop Patrick J. Ryan. Not until Ryan was appointed archbishop of Philadelphia in 1884, did Kenrick resume control of the daily affairs of the archdiocese. In the early 1890s there was a rebellion among many of his priests who sent a petition to Cardinal Gibbons, requesting a new coadjutor. Shortly thereafter, Bishop John J. Kain of Wheeling was appointed. Still, it took a suit in civil court by the Board of Consultors to force Kenrick to relinquish control of the archdiocese to Kain.

Peter Richard Kenrick died in St. Louis on March 4, 1896.

See also MISSOURI, CATHOLIC CHURCH IN; VATICAN COUNCIL I AND AMERICAN PARTICIPATION.

Miller, S.J. "Peter Richard Kenrick, Bishop and Archbishop of St. Louis, 1806–1896." *Records of the American Catholic Historical Society of Philadelphia* 84 (1973) 1–163.
O'Shea, John J. *The Two Kenricks.* Philadelphia, 1904.

MARTIN G. TOWEY

KENT, CORITA (1918–86)

Artist. Corita Kent was born Frances Elizabeth in Fort Dodge, Iowa, on November 20, 1918, the daughter of Robert Vincent Kent, businessman, and Edith Genevieve Sanders, the fifth of six children. Before Corita was five years old, the family had moved to Vancouver, Canada, then again to Hollywood, California, where the family settled. There Corita attended elementary school and high

Corita Kent

school. In 1936 she entered the Sisters of the Immaculate Heart of Mary, taking the name Sr. Mary Corita. In 1941 she received her B.A. from Immaculate Heart College. She was stationed in British Columbia, where she taught grade school, including more than one year at a school on a Native American reservation. She returned to teach art at Immaculate Heart College (IHC), receiving her master's degree in art history from the University of Southern California (USC) in 1951. She taught art at Immaculate Heart College from 1951 until 1968, serving as head of the Art Department from 1964 until 1968.

In 1951 Corita learned the art of printmaking from a course at USC and from Mrs. Alfredo Martinez, widow of the famed Mexican muralist. Printmaking and the creation of serigraphs became Corita's primary means of artistic expression. In 1952 she added colors to a black and white print that she had made as part of her master's project at USC, creating a new print which she entitled, *The Lord Is With Thee.* The print won first prize at the Los Angeles County Museum Show, and at the California State Fair. Her early art treated traditional religious themes in a nontraditional expressionistic manner. She noted, "In the early days, I was trying to make 'religious art' that would be not quite as repulsive as what was around." In another early print, *Benedictio,* she used words in her print, an innovation that was well received, and which became a standard part of her serigraphs. During this early period, Corita was significantly influenced by two professors at Immaculate Heart College: Dr. Alois Schardt and Charles Eames.

Corita spent each school year teaching, where she earned the reputation as a brilliant and demanding teacher. During the summer months, she would produce a new set of prints. During the 1950s Corita produced shows that exhibited not only her own work, but the work of her students as well, often in the form of a group project. As a result, her fame as well as that of the Art Department at IHC began to grow. By the end of the 1950s Corita was much in demand to produce shows and give lectures, which she did, traveling extensively throughout the United States. In 1958 she and her students produced a banner exhibit for the National Gallery in Washington, D.C.

By the early 1960s Corita was at the forefront of the Pop Art movement, using bright colors, simple forms, simple sayings, and openly embracing modern popular culture. She made frequent use of advertising slogans and billboard motifs in her serigraphs, attempting to illustrate the often hidden beauty of modern culture. In 1963 she created IBM's Christmas exhibit in New York City entitled, *Peace on Earth, Good Will Towards Men,* using large decorated boxes. The following year she produced a forty-foot mural entitled the *Beatitude Wall* for the Vatican Pavilion at the New York World's Fair. By 1966 her fame was clearly established. In addition, Westinghouse began commissioning one of her prints each year, which they published in such mass circulation magazines as *Time* and *Newsweek.* These publications gave Corita's work wide circulation reflecting Corita's belief that art is for everyone, not just the elites.

Corita was also in the forefront of changes occurring within the Catholic Church in the United States. In 1964 she transformed IHC's traditional Mary's Day, which honored the Mother of God, from a traditional, staid affair to a vibrant celebration, which included colorful banners carried in procession, with balloons, flowers, dancing, and concluding with a simple meal. These innovations brought her (or at least IHC) into conflict with the archbishop of Los Angeles, as did some of her "religious art," most notably her print which referred to Mary as "the juiciest tomato of them all." One observer noted that Corita was either "adored or abhorred" in Catholic circles. Corita's promotion of spontaneous celebrations culminated in her instigation of "happenings" in the late 1960s in which instant celebrations were created at traditionally mordant gatherings such as business meetings or conventions.

Two priests greatly influenced Corita in the mid-1960s: Fr. Daniel Berrigan, S.J., and Fr. Robert Giguere, S.S. Berrigan introduced Corita to the struggle for social justice, and her prints took on an increasingly political edge with prints protesting the Vietnam War such as *Stop the Bombing.* She did others in support of the civil rights movement, Cesar Chavez and the UFW, and other causes, most notably Physicians for Social Responsibility for which she created a famous billboard in 1984, which read, "We can create life without war." Though she never engaged in protest marches herself, Harvey Cox called her a "guerilla with a paint brush," as her art served as her form of protest. Fr. Giguere served as Corita's spiritual guide and most intimate confidante, assisting her in dealing with her inner anguish as an artist during a traumatic era for the Church and nation.

In 1968 Corita's intense work schedule—printmaking, teaching, lecturing, producing shows nationwide—combined with the struggles her order was facing with local Church authorities, prompted Corita to leave the sisterhood and the Catholic Church. In 1968, while taking a sabbatical in Cape Cod, Massachusetts, she decided not to return. She resettled in Boston, retired from teaching, and devoted herself completely to her art. She retained her religious name "Corita." She continued making prints, and supported herself by accepting commissions, most notably her creation of a 150-foot rainbow mural which adorned a natural gas tank in Boston for the Boston Gas Company. Equally as famous was the production of her "Love" stamp, for the U.S. Postal Service, which became the bestselling stamp of all time. The stamp was classic Corita with six lined splashes of color and the word "Love" drawn at the bottom of the stamp.

In the 1970s she was diagnosed with cancer, and underwent two operations. She waged a noble fight against the disease until succumbing to it on September 18, 1986.

Corita was a major influence in the Catholic Church during the 1960s, striking out boldly into new areas in the spirit of Vatican II. She also made major contributions to the American art scene, blurring the distinction between commercial and fine art. Her art is currently housed in more than thirty-five major museums, including the Museum of Modern Art in New York, and the Art Institute of Chicago.

No biography exists for Corita, but the UCLA Oral History Project has made transcripts of interviews with Corita available in Bernard Galm, *Los Angeles Art Community: Group Portrait: Corita Kent* (UCLA, 1977). There is also a film biography produced by Jeffrey Hayden, *Primary Colors: The Story of Corita* (South Carolina Educational Television Network and the Saint/Hayden Co., 1990).

JEFFREY M. BURNS

KENTUCKY, CATHOLIC CHURCH IN

The first Catholics came into Kentucky among the earliest settlers from the coastal colonies in 1775. They included Jane Coomes, believed to be the first teacher in Kentucky, and George Hart, the first physician. Not until 1785 did larger groups or "leagues" of Catholic families from Maryland begin to enter the region.

Catholics on the American Frontier

These settlers were almost exclusively of British lineage, although many brought with them enslaved African Americans who practiced the Catholic faith. While a few families settled in the Bluegrass, the majority chose an area of promising farmland near Bardstown in central Kentucky. Within a decade, three hundred Catholics were known to live in the area. Even two centuries later, the three rural counties of Marion, Nelson, and Washington have significant Catholic populations, and are regionally known as "The Kentucky Holy Land."

These frontier Catholics, called by their early historian Martin John Spalding "an iron race of pioneers," chose to come west in large groupings in order to sustain their ancestral faith through solidarity, and also to strengthen their appeals for a priest to come eventually to the region. Thus the earliest congregations of Kentucky were lay-gathered, in contrast to the clergy-led initial Catholic settlements on the East and West Coasts. Early lay leaders included Robert Abell, the only Catholic to serve in the 1799 state constitutional convention, and Grace Newton Simpson, widely known for her intellect and counsel.

The earliest resident priests to arrive in Kentucky were Maurice Whelan and William de Rohan, but neither remained long in pastoral service. With the arrival of the twenty-six-year-old Stephen Badin, the first priest to have been ordained in America, clerical stability came to Kentucky. With Badin as leader, other priests came to the region, most notably Charles Nerinckx and the Dominican friars who made their first American foundation in Washington County in 1805.

The First Inland Diocese of the United States

On April 8, 1808, Pope Pius VII subdivided the primal see of Baltimore by constituting the Dioceses of Boston, New York, Philadelphia, and Bardstown. To head the latter see, the first in inland America, the Holy See named Benedict Joseph Flaget, like Badin, an exile from the turmoil of the French Revolution.

This "First Bishop of the West" arrived in Kentucky in 1811, accompanied by his fellow Sulpician John Baptist David, who would himself be consecrated bishop at Bardstown in 1819. Flaget's far-flung area of responsibility covered all the land from the Great Lakes to the Deep South, and from the Allegheny Mountains to the Mississippi River. From this "mega-diocese" there would eventually be carved over thirty new dioceses, including Cincinnati, Indianapolis, Chicago, and Detroit.

With the arrival of Flaget there began an amazing burst of fervor and institutional energies. Within a dozen years, Flaget would initiate or encourage the following establishments, including many first of their kind in the American West: St. Thomas Seminary (1811); the Sisters of Loretto (1812); the Sisters of Charity of Nazareth (1812); St. Joseph Cathedral at Bardstown (1819); St. Joseph College (1820); St. Mary College (1821); and the Dominican Sisters at Springfield (1822). From such institutions and communities would emerge many of the leaders of American Catholicism in the nineteenth century.

Within the forty years of his tenure, Flaget would welcome to Kentucky the Good Shepherd Sisters, Jesuit Fathers, and the Trappist monks of Gethsemani Abbey. In addition to such eighteenth-century Holy Land parishes as Holy Cross (1785), St. Charles (1786), and Holy Mary's (1798), Flaget would be responsible for a growing network of congregations such as St. Louis at Louisville (1805), St. Peter at Lexington (1818), Holy Name at Henderson (1824), and Mutter Gottes (Mother of God) at Covington (1842).

Catholic Urban Life in the Nineteenth Century

Late in 1841, Flaget would move the seat of the diocese from Bardstown to the city of Louisville, whose population was swelling from the inflow of Germans and Irish. An anti-immigrant riot called "Bloody Monday" in that city on August 6, 1855, resulted in over twenty deaths.

Louisville's Civil War bishop was the Kentucky-born scholar and writer Martin John Spalding. He oversaw construction of the city's Cathedral of the Assumption (1852) and welcomed the Belgian Xaverian Brothers to their first American foundation (1854) as well as the German Ursuline Sisters (1858). One of Spalding's successors as bishop of Louisville was the authoritarian William George McCloskey. In his forty-year reign, McCloskey attended to institutional growth, but was frequently at the center of disputes—some glaringly public—with clergy, laity, and religious.

Covington was constituted a separate diocese in 1853. Here several religious communities took root, including the Sisters of St. Benedict (1859), the Sisters of Notre Dame (1874), and the Sisters of Divine Providence (1889). Bishop Camillus Maes officially dedicated the massive Gothic Cathedral of the Assumption at Covington in 1901.

The Twentieth-Century Experience

In 1937 Louisville was constituted a metropolitan see with both Covington and the newly established Diocese of Owensboro as suffragans. The Owensboro see contains within it many of the historic parishes and academies that had been founded in the nineteenth century as second-generation Holy Land Catholics had migrated to western Kentucky colonies. Also within its boundaries is the motherhouse of Ursuline sisters at Maple Mount (1912). The Diocese of Lexington was erected by the Holy See in 1988. Its territory covers not only the Bluegrass but also the mountainous eastern counties of Kentucky where innovative Catholic missions serving the entire community are to be found.

Several Kentuckians were in official attendance at the Second Vatican Council (1962–65) including J. L. Garrett of the Southern Baptist Theological Seminary, and Sister of Loretto Mary Luke Tobin, the only American woman auditor at the council. In these same years, Trappist monk Thomas Merton from his Kentucky abbey of Gethsemani wrote an array of highly influential books in the areas of Christian spirituality, Oriental religions, interfaith understanding, and social justice.

While Catholics are heavily represented in the Kentucky legislature, none has ever served as full-time governor of the commonwealth. In 1994 Third District (Louisville-area) Congressman Catholic Romano Mazzoli retired after twelve consecutive terms in Washington.

The Louisville area in the last generation has been noted throughout the country for its ecumenical and interfaith initiatives. The city's Cathedral Heritage Foundation (1985) and cathedral parishioners turned their old church into a nationally recognized urban emblem of faith. A center of worship, art, spirituality, and social service, it has been celebrated as a model civic symbol that is Catholic in its roots, inner-city and interfaith in its outreach.

The 385,000 Kentucky Catholics constitute 10 percent of the state's population. They are to be found in higher proportions in urban areas, along the Ohio River and in the three "Holy Land" counties. In other areas of the state, especially along the southern border and in the eastern mountains, Catholics tend to be a rarity. There are four Catholic jurisdictions in Kentucky: the Archdiocese of Louisville and the Dioceses of Covington, Owensboro, and Lexington. Some 48,000 students attend Catholic schools. Kentucky hosts the following Catholic institutions: five colleges, twenty-six high schools, and fourteen hospitals.

Crews, Clyde F. *An American Holy Land: A History of the Archdiocese of Louisville*. Wilmington, 1987.

Hayden, Judy. *This Far by Faith: The Story of Catholicity in Western Kentucky*. Owensboro, 1987.

Ryan, Paul E. *History of the Diocese of Covington, Kentucky*. Covington, 1954.

Webb, Benedict. *The Centenary of Catholicity in Kentucky*. Louisville, 1884.

CLYDE F. CREWS

KERBY, WILLIAM (1870–1936)

Priest, sociologist, editor. William Joseph Kerby is generally considered the founder of "scientific charity" for American Catholics. He was born on February 20, 1870, in Lawler, Iowa, to Daniel Kerby, merchant and banker, and Ellen Rochford. He attended St. Joseph's (now Loras) College before entering St. Francis Seminary in Milwaukee in 1889 to study for the priesthood for the Archdiocese of Dubuque. He was ordained a priest on December 21, 1892, in Dubuque by Archbishop John Hennessy of Dubuque. Kerby was sent to pursue graduate studies at The Catholic University of America (CUA) in Washington,

William Kerby

D.C., where he received his bachelor's degree in sacred theology in 1893, followed by his licentiate in 1894. At CUA he studied with and became a disciple of Fr. Thomas Bouquillon, who insisted that moral theology was not simply a matter of abstract reasoning. For Bouquillon, moral theology had to be grounded in social reality as discovered through the social sciences.

When CUA decided to begin a Department of Sociology, Kerby was chosen to head the department. He was sent to study in Europe in 1895, attending the universities of Bonn and Berlin before receiving his doctorate in social and political science from the Catholic University of Louvain in Belgium in 1897. He returned to head CUA's Department of Sociology, a position he held from 1897 until 1932. He also taught sociology at neighboring Trinity College from 1902 until 1932. Kerby was one of the pioneers of academic sociology in the United States and was *the* pioneer of academic American Catholic sociology. As opposed to his secular colleagues, Kerby never endorsed the notion of a "value-free" sociology. Instead, he was an advocate of what would later be called "supernatural sociology," which asserted that the lessons of theology and philosophy had to be incorporated into sociology. While it was incumbent upon the social scientist to study the observable, tangible world, that study presupposed the proper understanding of the nature and end of men and women. Humans were material *and* spiritual beings.

In this early era sociology and social work remained closely connected. Kerby became a strong advocate of social reform as a means of discouraging the development of socialism. He believed that, given the economic situation of the United States in 1900, socialism would naturally triumph unless the Church developed a positive program of social reform. Denunciations of socialism were no longer enough. Catholics had to develop a practical program of social reform grounded in social reality.

Kerby became involved in a number of local Catholic charitable groups but became distraught by what he perceived as the provincialism, defensiveness, and isolation of Catholic charitable efforts. In 1910 he was among the founders of the National Conference of Catholic Charities (NCCC) and served as secretary from 1910 until 1920. His intent was to create a national consciousness and sense of solidarity among Catholic charitable workers, who were spread out across the country. Every two years he organized a national NCCC conference that allowed for an exchange of ideas, techniques, and experiences. In 1921 he assisted in the creation of the National Catholic School of Social Service, for which he served as Acting Director from 1924 until 1929. He also taught sociology at the school until 1931.

Besides organizing Catholic charities, Kerby also believed Catholics should unite with non-Catholic groups who were working for similar objectives. Kerby sat on the Board of Charities for the District of Columbia from 1920 until 1926. Kerby also believed in the power of Catholic journals to educate the faithful. He edited the *St. Vincent de Paul Quarterly* from 1910 until 1916. He founded, but did not edit, the *Catholic Charities Review* in 1917, and he edited the *American Ecclesiastical Review* from 1927 until 1936.

Kerby was the primary advocate of scientific Catholic charity in the United States, sending out numerous disciples from CUA. He most clearly articulated this notion of scientific charity in his study, *The Social Mission of Charity,* published in 1921, in which he defined charity as "science ending in love." Kerby argued that while service to the poor was integral to the mission of the Church, such service could no longer be limited to simple and direct relief of the poor. In the modern age the causes of poverty had to be discovered and addressed rationally. Three things were required to make charity more efficient—study, organization, and training. Social workers, priests, and all those who worked with the poor needed to be trained in the social sciences. "Charity must be scientific," Kerby asserted (7). The social worker had to be able to identify the causes of poverty and seek to correct them. Second, "relief work is done most effectively through organization" (17). By organizing workers and agencies, resources could be pooled, knowledge shared, and mutual support provided. In addition, organized charities could serve as better advocates of the poor in the social arena. Finally, Kerby called for trained social workers and the creation of schools in which to train them. In sum, Catholic charity had to be organized on a scientific basis if it was to be effective and efficient in twentieth-century America. Through the efforts of Kerby, American Catholic charities were better organized and their personnel better trained, though there were frequent reactions against Kerby's clinical approach.

Kerby represented the Catholic wing of the Progressive reform movement that was prospering in the United States in the first decade of the twentieth century. Like his Progressive counterparts, Kerby stressed efficiency, rational planning, the use of scientific experts, central organization, professionalization, and the need for institutional as well as individual reform. All these concepts he adapted to American Catholic charities.

Kerby was made a monsignor in 1934. He died in Washington, D.C., on July 27, 1936.

See also CATHOLIC CHARITIES.

Gavin, D. *The National Council of Catholic Charities*. Milwaukee: Bruce, 1962.

Kerby, William. *The Social Mission of Charity.* Washington, D.C.: The Catholic University of America Press, 1921; repr. 1944.

Lescher, Bruce. "The Spiritual Life And Social Action in American Catholic Spirituality: William J. Kerby and Paul H. Furfey." Ph.D. dissertation, Graduate Theological Union, Berkeley, 1991.

Nuesse, C. Joseph. *The Catholic University of America: A Centennial History.* Washington, D.C., 1990.

JEFFREY M. BURNS

KILDUFF, THOMAS (1907–86)

Carmelite friar, spiritual writer. Thomas M. Kilduff was born of Irish Catholic immigrant parents in Boston. After a year as a candidate for the diocesan priesthood at St. Thomas Seminary, Denver, where he became interested in prayer, he joined in 1927 the monastery of Spanish Discalced Carmelite friars founded in Washington, D.C., in 1914 by the province of Catalonia.

One of the first Americans to enter the community, Kilduff studied philosophy in Tarragona, Spain, theology at The Catholic University of America, was solemnly professed in 1930 in spite of his reservations about the viability of the Spanish community, and was ordained a priest in 1934. He received an M.A. in philosophy from The Catholic University. In 1936, just before the Spanish Civil War interrupted the provincial chapter in Barcelona and cut off all communications, Thomas, at twenty-nine, was elected "in absentia" first American prior of the Washington house. For three years he led the fledgling foundation without any contact with superiors of the province in Barcelona since many of the friars had been imprisoned or executed by the communists. His former prior, Edward Farre, was never heard from again.

Following the war, Kilduff began negotiations in Barcelona and Rome to separate the Washington house from Catalonia and unite it with two foundations of the Bavarian province in Wisconsin. He was appointed delegate of the Carmelite general for these amalgamated houses until a new American province of Washington was finally formed in 1947. Kilduff was successively founder/prior of a monastery in Boston, novice master, provincial, initiator of a Carmelite Mission in the Philippines, and finally the first American counselor (1955–61) at the Carmelite generalate in Rome. Only the political intrigue and maneuvering of the incumbent general, Anastasio Ballestrero (later cardinal archbishop of Turin), prevented Kilduff from being elected general in the 1961 chapter. Had this happened the renewal history of the Discalced Carmelites would have developed differently and plans would have been considered with the general of the Carmelites of the Ancient Observance, Kilian Healy, to unite the two branches of the order separated since the sixteenth century.

Association with Carmelite Nuns

From 1934 onwards Kilduff fulfilled Teresa of Avila's desire that the Discalced friars should provide spiritual assistance for the Carmelite nuns. As the first Carmelite friar to gain acceptance among the U.S. nuns, he not only traveled the length and breadth of the country giving retreats, spiritual direction, sermons, conferences, and advice, but in 1965, in collaboration with the nuns, organized and moderated the first national meeting of delegates from the majority of the Carmels in the country to promote good governance and cooperation in initial formation. No one person in the order was more instrumental in guiding and encouraging among the nuns in the U.S.A. the renewal of prayer and life advocated by Vatican Council II. In spite of the obstacles put in the way by the order's conservative leadership, the (then) Sacred Congregation for Religious and even some of the nuns and friars themselves, and the lifelong consequences to his own reputation and influence, he spoke boldly at the general chapters of the friars on behalf of the nuns, emphasizing the need for "experimentation" and the participation of the nuns in the renewal of their own life and laws.

Spirituality and Retrieval of Mysticism

His contribution to the current retrieval of mysticism is significant: he played a singular role in raising up Carmelite spirituality in this country. Ernest Larkin, O. Carm., another well-known Carmelite, remarked, "For me, prior to Vatican II, the Discalced Carmelites were synonymous with Thomas Kilduff." For this reason, Thomas was a member of the Institute for Ecumenical and Cultural Research founded at Collegeville in 1965 by some of the *periti* and "non-Catholic observers" of Vatican II, among them Jean Leclerq, Bernard Häring, Godfrey Diekmann, and Quaker Douglas Steere. As he himself grew older, Kilduff shifted his ministry to the elderly and their experience of God and prayer, opening to them the *Spirituality and Contemplative Dimension of Aging.* He died in 1986.

See also AMERICAN CATHOLIC SPIRITUALITY; CARMELITE FRIARS, DISCALCED (O.C.D.); CARMELITE NUNS, DISCALCED (O.C.D.).

Emmanuel, M., S.C. "Reflections On Old Age By One Who Has Reached It." [About T. Kilduff] *Sisters Today* (January 1981).

Kilduff, Thomas, O.C.D. "Solitude Not Isolation." *Spiritual Life* 5 (June 1960).

_____. "A New Form of Austerity for the Contemporary World." *Spiritual Life* 13 (Spring 1967).

_____. "Faith Experience, Prayer and Discernment." *Spiritual Life* 23 (Spring 1977).

_____. "Prayer and Involvement." *Spiritual Life.*

_____. "Aging." *Spiritual Life* 26 (Spring 1980).

_____. "Spiritual Direction and Personality Types." *Spiritual Life* 26 (Fall 1980).

_____. "Old Age and Retirement." *The Way* 24 (October 1984).

CONSTANCE FITZGERALD, O.C.D.

KILMER, JOYCE (1886–1918)

Poet. Born Alfred Joyce Kilmer in New Brunswick, New Jersey, on December 6, 1886, he was educated there at the Rutgers Preparatory School. He attended Rutgers College for two years, then transferred to Columbia University, from which he graduated in 1908. The same year, he married Aline Murray, also a poet; they had five children. Kilmer taught high school Latin for one year in New Jersey before returning to New York where he worked for three years on the staff of the *Standard Dictionary*. Under the name Joyce Kilmer, he began contributing poems and essays to various magazines, and served as literary editor of the Episcopalian magazine, *Churchman*. In 1913 he and his wife converted to Catholicism.

Joyce Kilmer

Kilmer joined the staff of the *New York Times Sunday Magazine and Book Review* in 1913. His poems and essays were collected and published as *Summer of Love* (1911), *Trees* (1914), *The Circus* (1916), and *Main Street* (1917), among others. Kilmer enjoyed wide appeal for his charisma, youth, and talent; his poems, "Trees" and "Prayer of a Soldier in France," were popular worldwide. In World War I, Kilmer enlisted in the Seventh Regiment, New York National Guard, but transferred to the 165th Infantry, New York's famous "Fighting 69th" regiment. He was killed near the village of Seringes in France during the Battle of the Marne around July 30, 1918. A poet and an idealist, he became a symbol of the soldierly bravery of American youth in World War I.

Holliday, Roberto Cortes, ed. *Joyce Kilmer: Poems, Essays and Letters*. New York, 1940.

Jamison, Theodore R. "Joyce Kilmer, Soldier Poet: A Centenary Perspective." *New Jersey History* 1987 105 (1–2) 18–39.

Kilmer, Annie Kilburn. *Memories of My Son, Sergeant Joyce Kilmer*. New York, 1920.

K. N. McCARTHY

KINO, EUSEBIO FRANCISCO (1645–1711)

Missionary and explorer. This seventeenth-century Jesuit missionary in New Spain rises from the annals of history as an indefatigable explorer, rancher, teacher, mapmaker, and devoted apostle to thousands of native peoples in the northwest of Mexico. Born in 1645 in the tiny Tyrolese town of Segno on the edge of the Dolomite Alps, Kino pursued his education in Jesuit schools in Trent and Hall. He was the only son of Francis and Margarita Chino, persons of lesser nobility. Taken seriously ill in 1663, he vowed to enter the Society of Jesus if cured, and fully recovered he entered the upper German province in 1665. He followed the normal course of training: two years of novitiate at Landsberg, three years of philosophy at Ingolstadt, three years of teaching at Hall (Innsbruck), four years of theology at Ingolstadt, and tertianship at Oettingen. His full calendar of studies was punctuated by periods of teaching mathematics and science at Innsbruck for which he was offered a professorial chair by the Duke of Bavaria.

Kino received notice of his acceptance to the Spanish missions in 1678 and set out immediately with highest hopes of reaching China via the "Spanish door" of the Philippines. It was not to happen because he suffered shipwreck near Cadiz which delayed his transatlantic crossing until early 1681. During the nearly two years he spent

Eusebio F. Kino

in Spain, he fashioned a strong friendship by correspondence with the Duchess of Aveiro, a Portuguese patroness of the China missions. However, once arrived in New Spain, the viceroy determined to send Kino on a newly formed expedition to the Californias under Admiral Don Isidro Atondo y Antillón. While preparations were being made on the Pacific Coast, Kino engaged in an astronomical polemic with Don Carlos Sigüenza y Góngara which resulted in Kino's first book on the comet of 1680, earning the respect of Sor Juana de la Cruz.

The Californias

Leaving Mexico City in October 1681, the newly appointed rector of the California missions conferred with the bishop of Guadalajara before riding north to Sinaloa where the expedition was being outfitted. Inadvertently, Kino triggered a jurisdictional controversy between the bishop of Guadalajara and the bishop of Durango precisely over who controlled the Californias. Atondo's expedition set sail in January 1683 and landed at the Bay of La Paz, April 1. For the next three months Spain held a tenuous foothold in California which soon slipped because of imprudent decisions by Atondo to punish the natives for stealing. A second attempt to colonize the Californias was begun at San Bruno one-third the way up the eastern coast. From this vantage point Kino explored routes across the Giantess Mountains to the Pacific shores. With Matías Goñi, his Jesuit companion, Kino tried to maintain the nascent missions but to no avail because Admiral Atondo decided to abandon the venture in May 1685. The effort had failed, but the desire to return to the peoples of California deepened in Kino's heart.

The Pimería Alta

Admiral Atondo convinced the viceroy, the Conde de Paredes, that California was untenable and plans for colonization were scrapped, but Kino continued efforts to resume the abandoned missions. All efforts failed and he was reassigned to the missions of an old frontier where evangelization had been stalled for more than a half century—the Pimería Alta, made famous by Professor Herbert E. Bolton in his biography of Kino, *The Rim of Christendom*. Kino arrivéd in the Pimería in March 1687, establishing his first and headquarters mission at Cosari, later known as Dolores which was so named because of a painting Kino had been given for his first mission by Juan Correa, the renowned seventeenth-century Mexican artist. In a matter of days Kino had visited nearby native rancherias which were designated as future mission sites—San Ignacio, Magdalena, and San José de Imuris. He spent the first months with Jesuit companions along the Río San Miguel learning the intricacies of the Piman language which he always spoke with German overtones. And typi-

cal of his enthusiastic personality, he viewed the basin and range country of the upper Sonora desert as being "much like Europe." One of the legal instruments he brought with him was a recent cédula of Carlos II dispensing recent converts from labor in the mines for twenty years. The decree endeared Kino to the native peoples but brought scorn from the colonists who were intent on extracting wealth from the earth. His nearly instant success with ranching and agriculture, coupled with his firm ambitions for the betterment of his Native American charges, engendered strong reactions among the settlers and miners who wished to see him removed from the region. Within three years local residents prevailed on the Jesuit provincial to send a special *visitador* to see if the complaints had merit. The man chosen for the inspection was Padre Juan María Salvatierra, an Italian Jesuit missionary in the high mountain region of Chinipas. Salvatierra's visit only found an accomplished missionary, flourishing new mission settlements, and a native population most anxious for more missionary assistance. Fortuitously, Salvatierra was convinced by Kino that these missions were prosperous enough and close enough to the Californias to risk the reopening of that "abandoned island." The immediate result of the inspection, completed in 1691, was the assignment of several new missionaries to the Pimería Alta to assist in the expansion and development of the new rectorate.

One of the new missionaries, Francisco Javier Saeta, was stationed at Nuestra Señora de la Purissima Concepción de Caborca. A young and altruistic Sicilian, Saeta was martyred on April 1, 1695, almost before he could begin work at his westernmost post, where Kino was attempting to build a boat to sail to the Californias. The death of this first martyr of the Pimería shook the confidence of the Spaniards in the peacefulness of the Pimas Altas; then, at a council of peace the native perpetrators of Saeta's murder were cut down in a barrage of crossfire by mounted cavalry. A war of attrition broke out on both sides, but it ended with an urgent appeal to Kino to intercede for peace. The incident had been painfully similar to the punishment Atondo meted out at La Paz in 1683, which bitter experience Kino never forgot. After the frontier was again settled down in the late fall of 1695, Kino rode nonstop to Mexico City to file his own report on events and to appeal for more help. Arriving in the capital in January, Kino found messages from the Jesuit General Thyrso Gonzalez approving the division of his missionary work between the Pimería and the Californias. The general was so impressed with Kino's record that he compared him to St. Francis Xavier, the Apostle to the Indies.

The Pimería Alta and the Californias

Returning to the Pimería Alta, a new purpose overshadowed the scattered desert missions—to supply the planned missions of California. Because of the distasteful experiences with military discipline, the Jesuits determined to reopen the Californias under their own control, which was granted by the viceroy, as long as the Jesuits paid expenses. This arrangement led to the famous Pious Fund of the Californias whereby generous benefactions were invested in Mexican haciendas whose profits were spent in paying for the needs of the peninsular missions. Kino worked vigorously to increase the productivity of the Sonoran missions, especially after Salvatierra's reentry to California in 1697. A chance gift of blue abalone shells from the natives along the Gila alerted Kino to the possibility of an overland route to California. Hence, in 1699 Kino focused his attention on exploring the western deserts which he traversed with large retinues of livestock. In 1702 he crossed the Colorado River and reached the head of the Sea of Cortez, proving once again that California was not an island. Explorations continued on for the next five years, but Kino was ordered to cease explorations in 1707 and concentrate on building up the mission frontier of the Pimería Alta. For the next four years he dedicated himself to a flurry of activity that only ended with his death in Magdalena, March 15, 1711.

Discovery of Kino's Grave

Since his burial in the chapel of St. Francis Xavier in Magdalena, the indigenous peoples of northern Sonora have conducted pilgrimages to Magdalena, ostensibly to honor St. Francis Xavier despite efforts to replace that patron with St. Francis of Assisi. In 1966 a team of historians and anthropologists cooperated in the discovery and identification of Kino's grave which at the time rested just in front of the mayor's office. In 1970 an elaborate memorial plaza keyed to his grave was completed and the town's official name was changed to Magdalena de Kino. Bronze equestrian statues in his honor depict Kino as the "Padre on Horseback" in Hermosillo and Magdalena, Sonora; Phoenix and Tucson, Arizona; and in Segno, Trent, Italy. Arizona chose Kino as its second "pioneer" and honored him in the Hall of Statuary in the south wing of the U.S. Capitol. His cause for beatification was introduced in Rome in 1995.

Bolton, Herbert Eugene. *The Rim of Christendom.* New York: Macmillan, 1936; repr. New York: Russell and Russell, 1960; Tucson: University of Arizona Press, 1984.

Kino, Eusebio Francisco. *Historical Memoir of the Pimería Alta.* Trans. Herbert E. Bolton. Cleveland, 1919; repr. University of California Press, 1948.

Polzer, Charles W. *Kino Guide II: His Missions—His Monuments.* Tucson: Southwestern Mission Research Center, 1982.

CHARLES POLZER, S.J.

Related Document

REPORT OF EUSEBIO FRANCISCO KINO ON THE MISSIONS OF PIMERIA ALTA (ARIZONA) IN 1710

Father Eusebio Kino, S.J. (1644–1711), and his companions entered Pimería Alta in 1687. Pimería Alta, the home of the Upper Pimas, extended from the valley of the Alta River to that of the Gila and thus included that part of southern Arizona which was later contained in the Gadsden Purchase. In 1687 Kino established the mission of Nuestra Señora de los Dolores more than 100 miles south of Tucson. This mission became his headquarters for twenty-four years of exploration, missionary activity, and writing. Operating from this base, Kino crossed the line into Arizona and founded the Missions of San Xavier del Bac, Guévavi, and Tumacácori. The "Favores celestiales," a manuscript history by Kino of the work of himself and his associates in Pimería Alta, was discovered in 1915 by Bolton and edited by him. In the following selection from an account written in 1710, Kino summarized his efforts with a statement of possibilities for future development.

(*Source*: Herbert Eugene Bolton, ed., *Kino's Historical Memoir of Pimería Alta. A Contemporary Account of the Beginnings of California, Sonora, and Arizona by Father Eusebio Francisco Kino, S.J. . . . 1683–1711* [Cleveland: Arthur H. Clark Co., 1919] II, 234–253.)

Beginnings and Progress of the New Conquests and New Conversions of the Heathendoms of This Extensive Pimería and the Other Neighboring New Nations

IT IS WELL KNOWN THAT DURING ALMOST TWO WHOLE CENturies the royal Catholic crown of Spain has spent more than two millions and a half for new conquests and new conversions and for the extension of the Holy Evangel [Gospel], and for the eternal salvation of the souls of the Californias; but it appears that, thanks be to His Divine Majesty, the blessed time is now coming when not only the conquest and conversion of the Californias is being accomplished, but also at the same time that of these other neighboring extensive lands and nations of this North America, most of which has hitherto been unknown, and when the Lord is adding to the rather poor lands of the Californias the necessary succor of these very extensive and rich lands, abundant champaigns, and fertile rivers and valleys. . . .

As soon as I knew that the conversion of coveted California was suspended, I asked and obtained from my superiors and his Excellency permission to come meanwhile to these heathen coasts nearest to and most in sight of California, to the Guaimas and Seris; and I having arrived at the end of February, 1687, in this province of Sonora, and gone to Opossura to see the Father Visitor, Manuel Gonzales, his Reverence came with me to this post of heathen Pimas, as the father of Cucurpe, near by, Joseph de Aguilar, was asking of him a father for them. We named the place Nuestra Señora de los Dolores. It is in thirty-two degrees and a half of latitude. We entered March 12, 1687, accompanied by Father Joseph de Aguilar and his servants; and the father visitor returning the following day to observe Holy Week in his pueblos, I went inland two hours after his departure and with said Father Joseph de Aguilar and some guides, going ten leagues beyond Nuestra Señora de los Dolores, toward the west, to the good post and valley which we named de San Ygnacio, where we found even more people, although they were somewhat scattered. We returned by the north through the ranchería of Himeres, which we named San Joseph, and through that of Doagibubig, which we named Nuestra Señora de los Remedios, which rancherías immediately, thanks be to the Lord, we began reducing to new good pueblos, making a beginning of teaching them the Christian Doctrine and prayers, by means of a good interpreter and a good native helper, whom I procured from the old Pima mission of Los Ures, and of the building of the churches and houses, of crops, etc.

Afterward I made other missions, or expeditions, to the north and farther to the west, and despatched friendly messages inviting all the heathen of these environs to receive our holy Catholic faith for their eternal salvation, in imitation of these Pimas, their relatives and countrymen. Soon many came from various parts to see me for this purpose, and we arranged for the beginning of other new missions and pueblos. There came to see and to visit us, with great comfort on our part and his Father Manuel Gonzáles. He asked and obtained, through the Señor alcalde mayor, four additional alms from the royal chest, for four other new missions for this extensive Pimería; and four other missionary fathers came to it at the time when I dedicated this my first and capacious church of Nuestra Señora de los Dolores. . . .

In general, in these twenty-one years, up to the present time, I have made from the first pueblo of Nuestra Señora de los Dolores more than forty expeditions to the north, west, northwest, and southwest, of fifty, eighty, one hundred, two hundred, and more leagues, sometimes accompanied by other fathers, but most of the time with only my servants and with the governors, captains, and caciques of different rancherías or incipient pueblos from here and from the interior. . . .

With all these expeditions or missions which have been made to a distance of two hundred leagues in these new heathendoms in these twenty-one years, there have been brought to our friendship and to the desire of receiving our holy Catholic faith, between Pimas, Cocomaricopas, Yumas, Quiquimas, etc., more than thirty thousand souls, there being sixteen thousand of Pimas alone. I have solemnized more than four thousand baptisms, and I could have baptized ten or twelve thousand Indians more if the lack of father laborers had not rendered it impossible for

us to catechise them and instruct them in advance. But if our Lord sends, by means of his royal Majesty and of the superiors, the necessary fathers for so great and so ripe a harvest of souls, it will not be difficult, God willing, to achieve the holy baptism of all these souls and of very many others, on the very populous Colorado River, as well as in California Alta, and at thirty-five degrees latitude and thereabouts, for this very great Colorado River has its origin at fifty-two degrees latitude.

And here I answer the question asked of me in the letter of the Father Rector Juan Hurtasum, as to whether some rivers run into the North Sea or all empty into the Sea of California, by saying that as this Colorado River, which is the Rio del Norte of the ancients, carries so much water, it must be that it comes from a high and remote land, as is the case with the other large volumed rivers of all the world and terraqueous globe; therefore the other rivers of the land of fifty-two degrees latitude probably have their slope toward the Sea of the North, where Husson wintered. Some more information can be drawn from the maps which I add to this report; and in order not to violate the brevity which I promised herein, I will add only that in regard to the fourteen journeys for two hundred leagues to the northwest, I have written a little treatise of about twenty-five sheets which is entitled "Cosmographical Proof that California is not an Island but a Peninsula," etc.; and that of these new discoveries and new conversions in general, by order of our Father General, Thirso Gonzales, I am writing another and more extensive treatise, with maps, of which more than one hundred sheets are already written. By suggestion of his Reverence it is entitled "Celestial Favors of Jesus Our Lord, and of Mary Most Holy, and of the Most Glorious Apostle of the Indies, San Francisco Xavier, experienced in the New Conversions of these New Nations of these New Heathendoms of this North America."

(*Source*: John Tracy Ellis, ed. *Documents of American Catholic History*. Vol. 1:1493–1865. Wilmington, Del.: Michael Glazier, 1987, 24–27.)

KNAPP, JUSTINA (1863–1954)

Liturgist, artist. Sr. Justina Knapp, O.S.B., was born in Minneapolis, Minnesota, on September 17, 1863. A self-taught woman, she became an authority on Christian symbols and their meaning for liturgical worship. Her text, *Christian Symbols and How to Use Them* (Milwaukee, 1935), was one of the earliest English works on symbols at the time when the liturgical movement was beginning to take root in Catholic churches in the United States. In addition to her text, Knapp produced instruction books on the use of symbols during the Church Year. As part of these books, Knapp included page-length illustrations of the symbols, encouraging readers to duplicate them and use them for instructional purposes. The common use of these symbols in parochial school classrooms in central Minnesota (many of them staffed by members of her religious community, Sisters of the Order of St. Benedict, St. Joseph, Minnesota) and beyond was a significant visual aid in solidifying new understandings of worship stemming from the liturgical movement. Having symbols as part of the classroom environment provided easy access to them and their meaning for parish liturgy in ways that preaching could not effect.

Although Knapp had no formal education in theology or art, she headed the Ecclesiastical Art Department of her religious community from 1895 until 1940, directing as many as twenty sisters at a time in completing Church vestments that she designed, and using symbols of her own creation as a way to assist worshipers in understanding the cycles of the Liturgical Year. Knapp's understanding of the power of symbols came from her own study, and over the years she collected a library of over five hundred texts on symbols, some dating back to the sixteenth and seventeenth centuries. In addition to vestments, other needlework pieces were produced by the sisters. One, a tapestry of *St. George and the Dragon,* designed by Knapp, took 1,800 hours of work using 185 shades of color in the thread employed.

Knapp's own passionate belief in the symbol as a medium for "searching out the meaning of worship" was the impetus for her lifework of artistry and scholarship. Her artistry provided parishes with beautifully designed and executed vestments; her scholarship resulted in texts and illustrations explaining symbols and their value for worship. She died in St. Cloud, Minnesota, on June 16, 1954.

See also BENEDICTINES (O.S.B.).

Knapp, Justina, O.S.B. Personal files. St. Benedict's Convent Archives, St. Joseph, Minnesota.

DOLORES SUPER, O.S.B.

KNIGHTS OF COLUMBUS

A unique blend of faith and fraternalism, the Knights of Columbus is the largest organization of Catholic laity in the world. Over a 115-year history it has responded to the myriad needs of the local churches in the United States, Canada, Mexico, Puerto Rico, and the Philippines. This article traces the origins of Columbianism as a force in the Church and society with particular focus on its character as a Catholic antidefamation society.

History

Michael J. McGivney, the New Haven priest who founded the Knights of Columbus in 1882, implicitly fostered an American Catholic apologetic, one which extolled the harmony between religious liberty and Catholicism. McGivney's gifts were many and various. He was an unassuming pious priest who easily elicited the trust of the laity. Concerned with the strong appeal of the prohibited secret societies among Catholic youth and with the plight of the widows and children who suffered the loss of the breadwinner, he was eager to form a fraternal insurance society imbued with deep loyalties to Catholicism and to the American experience.

After many meetings McGivney and a small group of laymen decided to establish an independent society rather than become a branch of one of two existing Catholic benefit societies. In early February 1882 they placed their fledgling fraternal order under the patronage of Christopher Columbus. According to the few surviving documents, the Columbian motif represented several facets of the group's Catholic consciousness. Columbus was the symbol par excellence of the Catholic contribution to American culture. By portraying the navigator's landing at San Salvador as the Catholic baptism of the nation, the Knights were asserting religious legitimacy. Just as the heirs of the Pilgrims invoked the Mayflower as the Protestant symbol of their identity as early Americans, so the Knights invoked the Santa Maria as the symbol of their self-understanding as Catholic citizens.

One of the charter members of the order underscored the cause of Catholic civil liberty when he asserted that the order's patron signified that, as Catholic descendants of Columbus "[we] were entitled to all rights and privileges due to such a discovery by one of our faith."

For the first ten years insurance was a mandatory feature of membership in the order. In 1892 non-insurance or associate membership was established, which meant that candidates for knighthood could be drawn to the order unfettered by economic ties. After the order expanded into Massachusetts in 1892, Columbianism became more explicit. The quadricentennial of Columbus's landfall, the rise of another wave of anti-Catholicism in the form of the American Protective Association and the expansionist policies of the leadership fostered the development of Columbianism. The general spirit of patriotism, culminating in the Spanish American War, also animated the order's character. Shortly after the institution of Boston's Bunker Hill Council (1892), Thomas H. Cummings of Boston became the order's first national organizer hired to promote new council development. From New England the order expanded throughout the nation. By 1905 the Knights were in every state in the Union, five provinces of Canada, Mexico, the Philippines, and were poised to enter Cuba and Puerto Rico. The causation for this enormously successful period of expansion is primarily due to the way in which the Knights conveyed through their ceremonials their strong sense of American Catholic identity.

Appeal and Organization

Besides establishing a united front in defense of the Church, the Knights cultivated deep patriotic sentiments based upon the Catholic component in the American heritage. The initiation ceremonies were dramatic renditions of the heroic faith of Columbus, of the Catholic baptism of the American continent, and of the nobility of religious liberty and American democracy. In a sense, the ceremonials provided the candidates for knighthood with a rite of passage from old world ties to loyalty to the new republic. Basic to their ethos was the prevailing notion of manliness, that gender construction manifested in fraternal sentiments and muscular Christianity.

The Knights of Columbus consciously disentangled Catholicism from the European cultural context and, through the medium of their ceremonials, they developed a universalized notion of Catholic citizenship, one with which members of all ethnic groups could identify. The Knights extolled Catholic unity and struggled against the divisive character of ethnic particularism. Though the leaders were all second-generation Irish-Americans, they were realists on the ethnic issue. Hence, they allowed the establishment of the Teutonia Council for German-American Knights and of the Italian-American Ansonia Council, both of which were instituted in Boston during the 1890s.

Columbianism was a robust fraternal manifestation of that Americanist spirit fostered by such prelates as Cardinal James Gibbons of Baltimore, Archbishop John Ireland of St. Paul, and Bishop John J. Keane, rector of The Catholic University of America.

The Catholic fraternalists and the Americanists shared a transformationist perspective on the relationship between religion and culture. They seem to have shared the belief that as a result of the encounter between Catholicity and American culture both experienced positive change, as if Catholicism would be renewed within the freedom of the young republic and American culture would be refined by its contact with the ancient faith of Western Civilization.

Columbianism was expressed in persistently optimistic and idealistic terms but, given the K. of C. consciousness of the ever-present threat from the forces of anti-Catholicism, Columbianism was also, of necessity, a rallying ground for the defense of the faith. The optimism of the Progressive era was countered by those groups which feared that the increased immigration from southern and eastern Europe (which totaled nearly seven million between 1897 and 1914) would ultimately result in the breakdown of "American" folkways. Anglo-Saxon nativism included anti-Semitism, widespread antagonism to Italian and Slavic peoples, a resurgence of racism in the South and North, and the growth of anti-Oriental sentiment in the West and Northwest, symbolized by the canard of the "Yellow Peril." This type of nativism was on the ascendant by 1907, when the new immigration reached its peak, and was expressed in secular, even scientific, terms. Primarily aimed at immigration restriction, it was popular among urban middle and upper classes. It did not spill out as overt anti-Catholicism, because by this time these classes had developed a secular perspective through which to filter their antiforeigner animus.

Activities

In accord with the order's antidefamation character, it instituted in 1914 the Knights of Columbus Commission on Religious Prejudices. The latter was mandated "to study the causes, investigate conditions and suggest remedies for the religious prejudice that has been manifest through the press and rostrum." Under the chairmanship of Patrick Henry Callahan, then K. of C. state deputy of Kentucky and a wealthy industrialist known for his capital-labor profit-sharing plan, the commission followed its mandate to the letter. As an antidote to prejudices Callahan especially promoted the papal encyclical of 1891, *Rerum Novarum.*

Columbian lay activism manifested itself in a new field of work in 1916 when U.S. troops were stationed along the Mexican border. After learning of the needs for recreational and religious centers, the order established sixteen buildings from the Gulf of Mexico to the Gulf of California for the needs of all soldiers and for the religious needs of Catholics.

As a result of this experience, the Knights offered such services to the U.S. government when it entered World War I in April 1917. American and Canadian K. of C. "Huts" with signs saying, "Everyone Welcome, Everything Free," were established in the training camps and eventually in Europe and Asia, even to the remote area of Siberia. The order raised one million dollars during the first year. As a result of a joint drive with the Y.M.C.A., the Jewish Welfare Board, the Salvation Army, and others, the order received over thirty million dollars for its War Camp Fund.

After the war, the Knights established employment bureaus throughout the country to find jobs for veterans. They also provided college scholarships for returning servicemen and set up evening schools for veterans and all others interested in academic and vocational advancement. In January 1924 there were sixty-nine evening schools with an enrollment of more than 30,000 students. The Knights received numerous commendations for war and reconstruction work, but the greatest tribute was demonstrated by the more than 400,000 men who joined the order between 1917 and 1923.

During the 1920s Columbianism expressed itself in a variety of new programs. In response to those historians who stressed an economic interpretation of American history, who disregarded the idealism of the revolutionary period, and who ignored the contributions of the various non-Anglo-Saxon immigrant groups, the order established the K. of C. Historical Commission. The commission was charged with the responsibility "to investigate the facts of history, to correct historical errors and omissions, to amplify and preserve our national history to exalt and perpetuate American ideals and to combat anti-American propaganda by means of pamphlets . . . and by other proper means and methods as shall be approved by the supreme Assembly." Under the direction of Edward McSweeney, a former trade unionist and immigration officer on Ellis Island, the commission awarded prizes for the best historical monographs. Works of such scholars who later earned national reputations as Samuel Flagg Bemis and Allan Nevins were published by Macmillan in the Knights of Columbus Historical Series.

In the autumn of 1922, McSweeney designed a unique set of historical studies entitled, "The Knights of Columbus Racial Contribution Series." Three monographs were published in this ambitious series: *The Gift of Black Folk* by W.E.B. DuBois; *The Jews in the Making of America* by George Cohen; and *The Germans in the Making of America* by Frederick Franklin Schrader. In his introduction to each of these books, McSweeney summarized the history of immigration to America, the waves of nativism, anti-Catholicism, anti-Semitism, and the persistence of racial prejudice in the life of the nation.

In 1921 Pope Benedict XV called upon Columbianism's Catholic antidefamation character to respond to religious prejudice in Rome. The occasion was a Knights' pilgrimage to Europe, which included the unveiling of an equestrian statue of Lafayette, a K. of C. gift to the city of Metz, and which culminated in a private audience with the Pope. In his address to the two hundred Knights, Pope Benedict elaborated on how anti-Catholic propaganda was a strong factor in the Protestant evangelization of Rome and the degree to which it threatened to break down Roman youth's loyalties to the Church.

Within a year after this historic audience, the order had appointed a commission for the order's Roman project, had established a one-million-dollar Italian Welfare Fund through a per capita tax on the membership, had received permission to construct recreation centers from Benedict's successor, Pope Pius XI, and had contracted the services of a Roman engineer and architect, Enrico Galeazzi. Between 1924 and 1927 the order opened five recreation centers, the most significant of which was St. Peter's Oratory. In the 1930s this program was absorbed into the Catholic Action movement.

During the Great Depression the Knights revived their antisocialism, a crusade that included a social justice component. At the Supreme Council meeting in August 1937, held in San Antonio, the crusade was unanimously endorsed by the delegates. Supreme Knight Martin Carmody reported that the *Daily Worker,* the official voice of the American Communist Party, had frequently vented "its wrath against the Knights of Columbus." Shortly after the convention, the Supreme Board of Directors approved Carmody's proposal to hire an anti-Communist lecturer, George Hermann Derry, who had been a member of the K. of C.'s Historical Commission and who had recently resigned as president of Marygrove College in Detroit. Derry's lecture program, which was subject to the prior approval of the hierarchy, included a general public address sponsored by local Knights and an address to the clergy of the diocese on anti-Communist leadership. Though he was a fervent anti-Communist, he was also anti-Fascist.

Modernization

The administration of Luke E. Hart (1953–64), John K. McDevitt (1964–77), and Virgil C. Dechant, are identified with the modernization of the order within the context of its traditional loyalty to Church and country. Hart laid the basis for the modern insurance program that was later greatly refined by Virgil Dechant. Hart's conservatism on racial and labor issues alienated many members of the order and the hierarchy. McDevitt led a movement to reform the policy governing admissions to local councils, thereby engendering racial integration. By this policy and by cosponsoring a Human Rights Congress at Yale and fostering other programs related to social justice, McDevitt restored the confidence of the hierarchy in the order's direction. In general, John McDevitt's administration represents a synthesis of modern fraternalism and traditional faith.

Virgil C. Dechant's administration reflects his command of the insurance programs, his policy to modernize the structures of the international headquarters in New Haven, his commitment to infuse a strong social service component into the order's fraternalism, his positive response to the needs of the American Church mediated by the bishop, and his deep loyalty to the Vatican represented by the order's contributions to the pope's charities, and the Vatican's needs for architectural restoration and artistic beautification.

Under Dechant's leadership the order has experienced considerable growth. In 1995 there were 1.6 million Knights located in more than 10,000 councils. With seventeen billion dollars of insurance in force and with the widespread programs of the order, entailing contributions of nearly $92.2 million by Supreme, state, and local councils in 1989, and almost twenty-three million man-hours given to community service during that year, the Knights of Columbus still experience the vitality of their original mission to respond to the needs of the Church and to witness to the unique character of the Catholic experience in America.

See also McGIVNEY, MICHAEL J.

The papers of the order are located in the Archives of the Knights of Columbus in New Haven, Connecticut.

Kauffman, Christopher J. *Faith and Fraternalism, The History of the Knights of Columbus.* Rev. ed. New York: Simon & Shuster, 1992.

_____. *Columbianism and The Knights of Columbus.* New York: Simon & Shuster, 1992.

CHRISTOPHER J. KAUFFMAN

KNIGHTS OF LABOR

The Knights of Labor were founded in 1869 by Uriah Stephens in Philadelphia and were officially called the Noble and Holy Order of the Knights of Labor. They grew out of the garment cutters association in Philadelphia, and during the 1870s spread to the coal regions of Pennsylvania. The Knights were one of the first national labor unions and became the foremost national labor organization in the United States during the period 1879 to 1886. In 1879 Terence V. Powderly became Grand Master Workman and ushered the Knights into their period of greatest prosperity. Unlike the later American Federation of Labor (AFL), which organized only skilled craftsmen, the Knights attempted to form "one big union" with their motto, "an injury to one is the concern of all." Membership in the Knights was open to all productive workers, skilled and unskilled, male and female, black and white. Even small businessmen were considered producers. Only nonproducers such as bankers and lawyers were excluded. Unlike the AFL, which focused on short-term, bread-and-butter issues, the Knights sought to reform the entire industrial order by ushering in a cooperative society in which the evil of "wage slavery" was abolished. A society of small producers organized cooperatively would resolve most of the problems brought on by the Industrial Revolution.

The main tool the Knights intended to employ in the creation of the new cooperative order was education. Prior to real change, the workers and other members of society had to be instructed in sound economic principles. The Knights sponsored lectures and study clubs to promote this end. The Knights initially opposed the use of strikes as counterproductive; while strikes might be momentarily successful, they hindered the long-range goal of a cooperative society. To obtain short-range goals such as the eight-hour day and improved working conditions, the Knights advocated the use of primary and secondary boycotts (and even this form of protest was endorsed reluctantly). In 1885 alone, the Knights supported 196 boycotts. They came to support strikes even more reluctantly, though they found themselves repeatedly in the midst of strikes between 1883 and 1887, initiated by their rank and file. In 1885 the Knights won a major strike against railroad magnate Jay Gould, causing their membership to peak at over 700,000. The following year, the loss of a second strike against Gould, the Haymarket Tragedy, and the creation of the AFL, signaled the decline of the Knights. By 1889 membership had slipped to 120,000. In 1893 Powderly resigned, and new leadership was unable to resurrect the Knights. Though they were not officially disbanded until 1917, their period of greatest influence and prosperity was over.

The Knights and the Catholic Church

Since the Catholic Church in the United States was primarily a working-class Church in the nineteenth century, a large number of Catholics had joined the Knights. The Knights' leader, Terence V. Powderly, was also a Catholic. This presented the Church with a problem, since the Church's obsessive fear of socialism made it hesitant to endorse the workers' right to organize or to strike. In addition, the Church feared the violence associated with labor agitation, a fear exacerbated by its recent experience with the Molly Maguires in the coal fields in Pennsylvania. Compounding these fears was the Knights' oath of secrecy (though Powderly was working to remove the secretive elements of the Knights). Many early labor unions invoked secrecy oaths to protect their members from antiunion employers. The Church had been preoccupied with secret societies for more than a century following the condemnation of the Freemasons in 1734. Invoking the ban against secret societies, in 1884 Archbishop Eleazar Taschereau of Quebec had the Knights condemned in Canada. Bishop James Healy of neighboring Portland, Maine, published the ban and forbade any Knight from receiving the sacraments in his diocese.

The liberal wing of the American Catholic Church, led by Archbishop James Gibbons of Baltimore, sought to prevent the condemnation of the Knights in the United States. Powderly assured Gibbons that he would make any changes necessary in the Knights' constitution to prevent papal condemnation of the Knights. As several American archbishops agreed with the condemnation of the Knights, the matter was referred to Rome for a final decision. In February 1887 Gibbons delivered his famous "memorial" in defense of the Knights in which he acknowledged the reality of the grievances of American workers, who were oppressed by the "greed" and "avarice" of unprincipled monopolies and grasping owners. At the heart of Gibbons' argument was the claim that, if the Knights were condemned, the American working class might abandon the Church. Rome grudgingly allowed the Knights to be "tolerated." Gibbons emerged triumphant, placing the Church squarely on the side of the worker in the United States.

The controversy surrounding the Knights of Labor, in conjunction with several other events, contributed to the promulgation of Pope Leo XIII's major social encyclical, *Rerum Novarum,* in which the rights of workers were clearly and positively stated. The Knights and Powderly were not as fortunate. After 1887 the Knights declined, and in 1901 Powderly, his faith shaken by the controversy, and by his persistent struggle for Church approval despite *Rerum Novarum,* openly abandoned the Catholic Church by joining the Masons.

See also GIBBONS, JAMES CARDINAL; LABOR MOVEMENT AND AMERICAN CATHOLICS, THE; POWDERLY, TERENCE V.

Browne, Henry. *The Catholic Church and the Knights of Labor.* Washington, D.C.: The Catholic University of America Press, 1949.

Oestreicher, Richard. "Terence V. Powderly, the Knights of Labor, and Artisanal Republicanism." *Labor Leaders in America,* M. Dubofsky and W. Van Tine. Urbana: University of Illinois Press, 1987.

Roohan, James E. "American Catholics and the Social Question, 1865–1900." Ph.D. dissertation, Yale University, 1952; repr. New York: Arno Press, 1976.

Weir, Robert. *Beyond Labor's Veil: The Culture of the Knights of Labor.* State College: Pennsylvania State University Press, 1996.

JEFFREY M. BURNS

Related Document

CARDINAL GIBBONS' DEFENSE OF THE KNIGHTS OF LABOR, FEBRUARY 20, 1887

Throughout the nineteenth century which witnessed the most rapid growth of the Church in this country, the great majority of American Catholics belonged to the working classes. In a period marked by the rise of grave evils in the system of industrial capitalism it was not surprising that the workers should have resorted to secret organizations to defend their rights. In so doing there were at times real abuses, which became the source of deep anxiety to the American bishops lest these secret societies should alienate Catholics from their religious obligations. Fortunately, the hierarchy had at the time a man who possessed the wisdom to weigh the issues judiciously and the foresight to see that a severe condemnation by the Church of the Knights of Labor, the greatest labor organization of the day, would endanger the faith of thousands of Catholic workers. That man was James Cardinal Gibbons, Archbishop of Baltimore (1834–1921). In September, 1884, the Holy See had condemned the K. of L. in Canada at the request of the Archbishop of Quebec. But Gibbons was intent that this action should not be extended to his own country. Upon a visit to Rome in 1887 he prepared—with the assistance of Bishops John Ireland and John Keane—a forceful protest against such a possibility which he submitted to the Congregation de Propaganda Fide. The result was that the condemnation which some of the American bishops had sought was not issued, and Gibbons' memorial became the deciding factor in averting what would have proved a major calamity. As a consequence the tradition of friendliness between the Church and labor in the United States was established and has endured, and the alienation of the Catholic workers—which constituted so heavy a loss to the Church in the countries of western Europe—has never had a counterpart in the United States.

(*Source*: Henry J. Browne, *The Catholic Church and the Knights of Labor,* Washington: The Catholic University of America Press, 1949, 365–378.)

Your Eminence:

In submitting to the Holy See the conclusions which after several months of attentive observation and reflection,[1] seem to me to sum up the truth concerning the association of the Knights of Labor, I feel profoundly convinced of the vast importance of the consequences attaching to this question, which forms but a link in the great chain of the social problems of our day, and especially of our country.

In weighing [treating—jugeant] this question I have been very careful to follow as my constant guide the spirit of the Encyclicals, in which our Holy Father, Leo XIII, has so admirably set forth the dangers of our time and their remedies, as well as the principles by which we are to recognize associations condemned by the Holy See. Such was also the guide of the Third Plenary Council of Baltimore in its teaching concerning the principles to be followed and the dangers to be shunned by the faithful either in the choice or in the establishment of those associations toward which the spirit of our popular institutions so strongly impels them. And considering the dire [evil—funestes] consequences that might result from a mistake in the treatment of organizations which often count their members by the thousands and hundred of thousands, the council wisely ordained (n. 255) [n. 225] that when an association is spread over several dioceses, not even the bishop of one of these dioceses shall condemn it, but shall refer the case to a standing committee of all the archbishops of the United States; and even these are not authorized to condemn unless their sentence be unanimous; and in case they fail to agree unanimously, then only the supreme tribunal of the Holy See can impose a condemnation; all this in order to avoid error and confusion of discipline.

This committee of archbishops held a meeting, in fact, toward the end of last October, especially to consider the association of the Knights of Labor [at which the Knights of Labor was specially considered—spécialement pour consider]. We were not persuaded to hold this meeting because of any request on the part of our bishops, for none of them had asked for it; and it should also be said that, among all the bishops we know, only two or three desire the condemnation. But the importance of the question in itself, and in the estimation of the Holy See led us to examine it with greatest attention. After our discussion, the results of which have already been communicated to the Sacred Congregation of the Propaganda, only two out of the twelve archbishops voted for condemnation, and their reasons were powerless to convince the others of either the justice or the prudence of such a condemnation.

In the following considerations I wish to state in detail the reasons which determined the vote of the great majority of the committee—reasons whose truth and force seem to me all the more evident today; I shall try at the same time to do justice to the arguments advanced by the opposition.

1. In the first place, in the constitution, laws and official declarations of the Knights of Labor, there can clearly be found assertions and rules [though there may be found . . . things—peuvent bien se trouver des assertions ou des règles] which we would not approve; but we have not found in them those elements so clearly pointed out by the Holy See, which places them among condemned associations.

(a) In their form of initiation there is no oath.

(b) The obligation to secrecy by which they keep the knowledge of their business from strangers or enemies, in no wise prevents Catholics from manifesting everything to competent ecclesiastical authority, even outside of confession. This has been positively declared to us by their president [their chief officers—leur président].

(c) They make no promise of blind obedience. The object and laws of the association are distinctly declared, and the obligation of obedience does not go beyond these limits.

(d) They not only profess no hostility against religion or the Church, but their declarations are quite to the contrary. The Third Plenary Council commands that we should not condemn an association without giving a hearing to its officers or representatives: "auditis ducibus, corypheis vel sociis praecipuis" (n. 254).[2] Now, their president in sending me a copy of their constitution, says that he is a Catholic from the bottom of his heart [devoted Catholic—Catholique du fond de son coeur]; that he practices his religion faithfully and receives the sacraments regularly; that he belongs to no Masonic or other society condemned by the Church; that he knows of nothing in the association of the Knights of Labor contrary to the laws of the Church; that, with filial submission he begs the Pastors of the Church to examine all the details of their organization [their constitution and laws—tous les détails de leur organisation], and, if they find anything worthy of condemnation, they should indicate it, and he promises its correction. Assuredly one does not perceive in all this any hostility to the authority of the Church, but on the contrary a spirit in every way praiseworthy. After their convention last year at Richmond, he and several of the officers and members, devout Catholics [principal members—officiers et members], made similar declarations concerning their feelings[3] and the action of that convention, the documents of which we are expecting to receive.

(e) Nor do we find in this organization any hostility to the authority and laws of our country. Not only does nothing of the kind appear in their constitution and laws, but the heads of our civil government treat with the greatest respect [with respect—avec le plus grand respect] the cause which they represent. The President of the United States told me personally, a month ago [a few weeks ago—il y a un mois] that he was then examining a law for the amelioration of certain social grievances and that he had just had a long conference on the subject with Mr. Powderly,[4] president of the Knights of Labor. The Congress of the United States, following the advice of President Cleveland is busying itself at the present time with the amelioration of the working classes, in whose complaints they acknowledge openly[5] there is a great deal of truth. And our political parties, far from regarding them as enemies of the country, vie with each other in championing the evident rights of the poor workmen [workmen—pauvres travailleurs], who seek not to resist[6] the laws, but only to obtain just legislation by constitutional and legitimate means.

These considerations, which show that in this association [these associations—cette association] those elements are not to be found which the Holy See condemns, lead us to study, in the second place, the evils which the associations contend against, and the nature of the conflict.

2. That there exist among us, as in the other countries of the world, grave and threatening social evils, public injustices, which call for strong resistance and legal remedy, is a fact which no one dares to deny, and the truth of which has been already acknowledged by the Congress and the President of the United States. Without entering into the sad details of these wrongs,—which does not seem necessary here,—it may suffice to mention only that monopolies on the part of both individuals and of corporations, have already called forth not only the complaints of our working classes, but also the opposition of our public men and legislators; that the efforts of these monopolists, not always without success, to control legislation to their own profit, cause serious apprehension among the disinterested friends of liberty; that the heartless avarice which, through greed of gain, pitilessly grinds not only the men, but particularly the women and children in various employments, makes it clear to all who love humanity and justice that it is not only the right of the laboring classes to protect themselves, but the duty of the whole people to aid them in finding a remedy against the dangers with which both civilization and the social order are menaced by avarice, oppression and corruption.

It would be vain to deny either the existence of the evils, the right of legitimate resistance, or the necessity of a remedy. At most doubt might be raised about the legitimacy of the form of resistance and the remedy employed by the Knights of Labor. This then ought to be the next point of our examination.

3. It can hardly be doubted that for the attainment of any public end, association—the organization of all interested

persons—is the most efficacious means, a means altogether natural and just. This is so evident, and besides so conformable to the genius of our country, of our essentially popular social conditions, that it is unnecessary to insist upon it. It is almost the only means to invite public attention, to give force to the most legitimate resistance, to add weight to the most just demands.

Now there already exists an organization which presents a thousand attractions and advantages, but which our Catholic workingmen, with filial obedience to the Holy See, refuse to join; this is the *Masonic* organization, which exists everywhere in our country, and which, as Mr. Powderly has expressly pointed out to us, unites employer and worker in a brotherhood very advantageous for the latter, but which numbers in its ranks hardly a single Catholic. Freely [nobly—de grand coeur] renouncing the advantages which the Church and their consciences forbid, workingmen form associations [join—se forment], having nothing in common with the deadly designs of the enemies of religion and seeking only mutual protection and help, and the legitimate assertion of their rights. But here they also find themselves threatened with condemnation, and so deprived of [hindered from—privés] their only means of defense. Is it surprising that they should be astonished at this and that they ask *Why?*[7]

4. Let us now consider the objections made against this sort of organization.

(a) It is objected that in these organizations Catholics are mixed with Protestants, to the peril of their faith. Naturally, yes, they are mixed with Protestants in the workers' associations,[8] precisely as they are at their work; for in a mixed people like ours, the separation of religious in social affairs is not possible. But to suppose that the faith of our Catholics suffers thereby is not to know the Catholic workers of America who are not like the workingmen of so many European countries—misguided and perverted children, looking on their Mother the Church as a hostile stepmother—but they are intelligent, well instructed and devoted children ready to give their blood, as they continually give their means (although small and hard-earned) [hard-earned—chétifs et péniblement gagnés] for her support and protection. And in fact it is not in the present case that Catholics are mixed with Protestants, but rather that Protestants are admitted to the advantages of an association, two-thirds of whose members and the principal officers [many of whose members and officers—des deux tiers des membres et les officiers principaux] are Catholics; and in a country like ours their exclusion would be simply impossible.

(b) But it is said, could there not be substituted for such an organization confraternities which would unite the workingmen under the direction of the priests and the direct influence of religion? I answer frankly that I do not believe that either possible or necessary in our country. I sincerely admire the efforts of this sort which are made in countries where the workers are led astray by the enemies of religion; but thanks be to God, that is not our condition. We find that in our country the presence and explicit influence of the clergy would not be advisable where our citizens, without distinction of religious belief, come together in regard to their industrial interests alone. Without going so far, we have abundant means for making our working people faithful Catholics, and simple good sense advises us not to go to extremes.

(c) Again, it is objected that the liberty of such an organization exposes Catholics to the evil influences of the most dangerous associates, even of atheists, communists, and anarchists. That is true; but it is one of the trials of faith which our brave American Catholics are accustomed to meet almost daily, and which they know how to disregard with good sense and firmness. The press of our country tells us and the president of the Knights of Labor has related to us, how these violent and aggressive elements have endeavored to seize authority in their councils, or to inject their poison into the principles of the association; but they also verify with what determination these evil spirits [machinators—mauvais esprits] have been repulsed and defeated. The presence among our citizens of this destructive element, which has come for the most part from certain nations of Europe, is assuredly for us an occasion of lively regrets and careful precautions; it is an inevitable fact, however, but one which the union between the Church and her children in our country renders comparatively free from danger. In truth, the only grave danger would come from an alienation between the Church and her children, which nothing would more certainly occasion than imprudent condemnations.

(d) An especially weighty charge is drawn from the outbursts of violence, even to bloodshed, which have characterized [accompanied—charactérizé] several of the strikes inaugurated by labor organizations. Concerning this, three things are to be remarked: first, strikes are not an invention of the Knights of Labor, but a means almost everywhere and always resorted to by employees in our land and elsewhere to protest against what they consider unjust and to demand their rights; secondly in such a struggle of the poor and indignant multitudes against hard and obstinate monopoly, anger and violence [outbursts of anger—colère et le violence] are often as inevitable as they are regrettable; thirdly, the laws and chief authorities of the Knights of Labor, far from encouraging violence or the occasions of it, exercise a powerful influence to hinder it, and to keep strikes within the limits of good order and legitimate action. A careful examination of the acts of violence which have marked the struggle between capital and labor during the past year, leaves us convinced that it would be unjust to attribute them to the association of the Knights of Labor. This was but one of several associations of workers that took part in the strikes, and their chief officers, according to disinterested witnesses, used every possible effort to appease the anger of the crowds and to prevent the excesses which, in my judgment, could not justly be attributed to them. Doubtless among the Knights of Labor as among thousands of other workingmen, there are violent, or even wicked and criminal men, who have committed inexcusable deeds of violence, and have urged their associates to do the same; but to attribute this to the organization, it seems to me, would be as unreasonable as to attribute to the Church the follies and crimes of her children against which she protests.[9] I repeat that in such a struggle of the great masses of the people against the mail-clad power, which, as it is acknowledged, often refuses them the simple rights of humanity and justice, it is vain to expect that every error and every act of violence can be avoided; and to dream that this struggle can be prevented, or that we can deter the multitudes from organizing, which is their only practical means [hope—moyen pratique] of success, would be to ignore the nature and forces of human society in times like ours. The part of Christian prudence evidently is to try to hold the hearts of the multitude by the bonds of love, in order to control their actions by the principles of faith, justice and charity, to acknowledge frankly the truth and justice in their cause, in order to deter them from what would be false and criminal, and thus to turn into a legitimate, peaceable and beneficent contest what could easily become for the masses of our people a volcanic abyss, like that which society fears and the Church deplores in Europe.

Upon this point I insist strongly, because, from an intimate acquaintance with the social conditions of our country I am profoundly convinced that here we are touching upon a subject which not only concerns the rights of the working classes, who ought to be especially dear to the Church which our Divine Lord sent to evangelize the poor, but with which are bound up the fundamental interests of the Church and of human society for the future. This is a point which I desire, in a few additional words to develop more clearly.

5. Whoever meditates upon the ways in which divine Providence is guiding contemporary history cannot fail to remark how important is the part which the power of the people takes therein at present and must take in the future. We behold, with profound sadness, the efforts of the prince of darkness to make this power dangerous to the social weal by withdrawing the masses of the people from the influence of religion, and impelling them towards the ruinous paths of license and anarchy. Until now our country presents a picture of altogether different [most consolingly different—tout différent] character—that of a popular power regulated by love of good order, by respect for religion, by obedience to the authority of the laws, not a democracy of license and violence, but that true democracy which aims at the general prosperity through the means of sound principles and good social order.

In order to preserve so desirable a state of things it is absolutely necessary that religion should continue to hold the affections, and thus rule the conduct of the multitudes. As Cardinal Manning has so well written,[10] "In the future era the Church has no longer to deal with princes and parliaments, but with the masses, with the people. Whether we will or no this is our work; we need a new spirit, a new direction of our life and activity." To lose influence over the people would be to lose the future altogether; and it is by the heart, far more than by the understanding, that we must hold and guide this immense power, so mighty either for good or for evil. Among all the glorious titles of the Church which her history has merited for her, there is not one which at present gives her so great influence as that of *Friend of the People*. Assuredly, in our democratic country, it is this title which wins for the Catholic Church not only the enthusiastic devotedness of the millions of her children, but also the respect and admiration of all our citizens, whatever be their religious belief. It is the power of precisely this title which renders persecution almost an impossibility, and which draws toward our holy Church the great heart of the American people.

And since it is acknowledged by all that the great questions of the future are not those of war, of commerce or finance, but the social questions, the questions which concern the improvement of the condition of the great masses of the people, and especially of the working people, it is evidently of supreme importance that the Church should always be found on the side of humanity, of justice toward the multitudes who compose the body of the human family. As the same Cardinal Manning very wisely wrote, "We must admit and accept calmly and with good will that industries and profits must be considered in second place; the moral state and domestic condition of the whole working population must be considered first. I will not venture to formulate the acts of parliament, but here is precisely their fundamental principle for the future. The conditions of the lower classes as are found at present among our people, can not and must not continue. On such a basis no social edifice can stand."[11] In our country, especially, this is the inevitable program of the future, and the position which the Church must hold toward the solution is sufficiently obvious. She must certainly not favor the extremes to which the poor multitudes are naturally inclined, but, I repeat, she must withhold them from these extremes by the bonds of affection, by the maternal desire which she will manifest for the concession of all that is just and reasonable in their demands, and by the maternal blessing which she will bestow upon every legitimate means for improving the condition of the people.

6. Now let us consider for a moment the consequences which would inevitably follow from a contrary course,

from a lack of sympathy for the working class, from a suspicion of their aims, from a hasty condemnation of their methods.

(a) First, there is the evident danger of the Church's losing in popular estimation her right to be considered the friend of the people. The logic of men's hearts goes swiftly to its conclusions, and this conclusion would be a pernicious one for the people and for the Church. To lose the heart of the people would be a misfortune for which the friendship of the few rich and powerful would be no compensation.

(b) There is a great danger of rendering hostile to the Church the political power of our country, which openly takes sides with the millions who are demanding justice and the improvement of their condition. The accusation of being, *"un-American,"* that is to say, alien to our national spirit, is the most powerful weapon which the enemies of the Church know how to employ against her. It was this cry which aroused the Know-Nothing persecution thirty years ago, and the same would be quickly used again if the opportunity offered itself. To appreciate the gravity of this danger it is well to remark that not only are the rights of the working classes loudly proclaimed by each of our two great political parties, but it is very probably [not improbable—très probable] that, in our approaching national elections, there will be a candidate for the office of President of the United States as the special representative of these complaints and demands of the masses. Now, to seek to crush by an ecclesiastical condemnation an organization which represents nearly [more than—presque] 500,000 votes, and which has already so respectable and so universally recognized a place in the political arena, would to speak frankly, be considered by the American people as not less ridiculous as it is rash. To alienate from ourselves the friendship of the people would be to run great risk of losing the respect which the Church has won in the estimation of the American nation, and of destroying the state of peace and prosperity which form so admirable a contrast with her condition in some so-called Catholic countries. Already in these months past, a murmur of popular anger and of threats against the Church has made itself heard, and it is necessary that we should move with much precaution.[12]

(c) A third danger, and the one which touches our hearts the most, is the risk of losing the love of the children of the Church, and of pushing them into an attitude of resistance against their Mother. The whole world presents no more beautiful spectacle than that of their filial devotion and obedience. But it is necessary to recognize that, in our age and in our country, obedience cannot be blind. We would greatly deceive ourselves if we expected it. Our Catholic working men sincerely believe that they are only seeking justice, and seeking it by legitimate means. A condemnation would be considered both false and unjust, and

would not be accepted [and therefore, not binding—et ne serait pas acceptée]. We might indeed preach to them submission and confidence in the Church, but these good dispositions could hardly go so far. They love the Church, and they wish to save their souls, but they must also earn their living, and labor is now so organized that without belonging to the organization there is little chance to earn one's living.

Behold, then, the consequences to be feared. Thousands of the most devoted children of the Church would believe themselves repulsed by their Mother and would live without practicing their religion. The revenues of the Church, which with us come entirely from the free offerings of the people, would suffer immensely, and it would be the same with Peter's pence. The ranks of the secret societies would be filled with Catholics, who had been up to now faithful.[13] The Holy See, which has constantly received from the Catholics of America proofs of almost unparalleled devotedness, would be considered not as a paternal authority, but as a harsh and unjust power. Here are assuredly effects, the occasion of which wisdom and prudence must avoid.

In a word, we have seen quite recently the sad and threatening confusion caused by the condemnation inflicted by an Archbishop upon a single priest in vindication of discipline—a condemnation which the Archbishop believed to be just and necessary, but which fell upon a priest who was regarded as the friend of the people. Now, if the consequences have been so deplorable for the peace of the Church from the condemnation of only one priest, because he was considered to be the friend of the people, what will not be the consequences to be feared from a condemnation which would fall directly upon the people themselves in the exercise of what they consider their legitimate right?[14]

7. But besides the danger which would result from such a condemnation and the impossibility of having it respected and observed [putting it into effect—de la faire respecter et observer] one should note that the form of this organization is so little permanent, as the press indicates nearly every day, that in the estimation of practical men in our country, it cannot last very many years.[15] Whence it follows that it is not necessary, even if it were just and prudent, to level the solemn condemnations of the Church against something which will vanish of itself. The social agitation will, indeed, last as long as there are social evils to be remedied; but the forms of organization and procedure meant for the attainment of this end are necessarily provisional and transient. They are also very numerous, for I have already remarked that the Knights of Labor is only one among several forms of labor organizations. To strike, then, at one of these forms would be to commence a war without system and without end; it would be to exhaust the forces of the Church in chasing a crowd of chang-

ing and uncertain phantasms. The American people behold with perfect composure and confidence the progress of our social contest, and have not the least fear of not being able to protect themselves against any excesses or dangers that may occasionally arise. And, to speak with the most profound respect, but also with the frankness which duty requires of me, it seems to me that prudence suggests, and that even the dignity of the Church demands that we should not offer to America an ecclesiastical protection for which she does not ask, and of which she believes she has no need.

8. In all this discussion I have not at all spoken of Canada, nor of the condemnation concerning the Knights of Labor in Canada. For we would consider it an impertinence to involve ourselves in the ecclesiastical affairs of another country which has a hierarchy of its own, and with whose needs and social conditions we do not pretend to be acquainted.[16] We believe, however, that the circumstances of a people almost entirely Catholic, as in lower Canada, must be very different from those of a mixed population like ours; moreover, that the documents submitted to the Holy Office are not the present constitution of the organization in our country, and that we, therefore, ask nothing involving an inconsistency on the part of the Holy See, which passed sentence *juxta exposita.*[17] It is of the condition of things in the United States that we speak, and we trust that in these matters we are not presumptuous in believing that we are competent to judge. Now, as I have already indicated, out of the seventy-five archbishops and bishops of the United States, there are about five who would desire a condemnation of the Knights of Labor, such as we know them in our country; so that our hierarchy are almost unanimous in protesting against such a condemnation. Surely, such a fact ought to have great weight in deciding the question. If there are difficulties in the case, it seems to me that the prudence and experience of our bishops and the wise rules of the Third Plenary Council ought to suffice for their solution.

9. Finally, to sum it all up, it seems clear to me that the Holy See should not entertain the idea of condemning an association:

1. When the condemnation does not seem to be *justified* either by the letter or the spirit of its constitution, its law and the declaration of its leaders.

2. When the condemnation does not seem *necessary,* in view of the transient form of the organization and the social condition of the United States.

3. When it does not seem to be *prudent,* because of the reality of the grievances of the workers, and the admission of them made by the American people.

4. When it would be *dangerous* for the reputation of the Church in our democratic country, and possibly even arouse persecution.

5. When it would be *ineffectual* in compelling the obedience of our Catholic workers, who would regard it as false and unjust.[18]

6. When it would be *destructive* instead of beneficial in its effects, impelling the children of the Church to disobey their Mother, and even to join condemned societies, which they have thus far shunned.

7. When it would be almost *ruinous* for the financial maintenance of the Church in our country, and for the Peter's pence.[19]

8. When it would turn into suspicion and hostility the outstanding devotedness of our Catholic people toward the Holy See.

9. When it would be regarded as a cruel blow to the authority of the bishops of the United States, who, it is well known, protest against such a condemnation.

Now, I hope the considerations here presented have shown with sufficient clearness that such would be the condemnation[20] of the Knights of Labor in the United States.

Therefore, with complete confidence, I leave the case[21] to the wisdom and prudence of your Eminence and the Holy See.

Rome, February 20, 1887.

J. Cardinal Gibbons,
Archbishop of Baltimore.

[1] Archives of the Archdiocese of Baltimore, 82-N-3. The "official" English version, first published in the *Moniteur de Rome* on March 28, 1887, was reproduced in a number of works, among them Allen Sinclair Will, *Life of Cardinal Gibbons, Archbishop of Baltimore* (New York, 1922), I, 337–352. The lesser differences in the readings which usually show the toning down of the original French for American readers, are indicated in brackets within the text. The other variations are cited in the notes.

[2] The Latin phrase was omitted in the English version.

[3] "Leurs sentiments" was not translated.

[4] Terence V. Powderly (1849–1924), a Catholic at the time, was elected Grand Master Workman of the K. of L. in September, 1879, and held that office until November, 1893. After mentioning that Congress followed the advice of Cleveland, the English version inserted "in his annual message."

[5] "Ouvertement" was not translated.

[6] "Or overthrow" was inserted.

[7] The last sentence of the paragraph was entirely omitted in the English version.

[8] The first part of the parallel was omitted in English: "avec les Protestants dans les associations des travailleurs, précisément comme ils sont dans le travaux mêmes."

[9] "Proteste" was translated "strives and protests."

[10] In the English version this quotation is introduced with the words, "A new task is before us."

[11] The *Moniteur* version of Manning's text was cited as from, "Miscellanies, Vol. 2, p. 81," and read as follows: "I know I am treading on a very difficult subject, but I feel confident of this, that we must face it, and that we must face it calmly, justly, and with a willingness to put labor and the profits of labor second—the moral state and domestic life of the whole working population first. I will not venture to draw up such an act of Parliament further than to lay down this principle. These things (the present condition of the poor in England) cannot go on; these things ought not to go on. The accumulation of wealth in the land, the piling

up of wealth like mountains, in the possession of classes or individuals, cannot go on. No commonwealth can rest on such foundations."

[12] The English read, "Angry utterances have not been wanting of late, and it is well that we should act prudently."

[13] The variant reading in English was, "Thousands of the Church's most devoted children, whose affection is her greatest comfort, and whose free offerings are her chief support, would consider themselves repulsed by their Mother, and would live without practising their religion. Catholics who have hitherto shunned the secret societies, would be sorely tempted to join their ranks."

[14] This whole paragraph referring to the case of Dr. Edward McGlynn was elided in the English version.

[15] The English read: "It is also very important that we should carefully consider another reason against condemnation, arising from the unstable and transient character of the organization in question. It is frequently remarked by the press and by attentive observers that this special form of association has in it so little permanence that, in its present shape, it is not likely to last many years."

[16] "Les besoins" was not translated.

[17] In the *Moniteur*, it read *"localiter et juxta exposita."*

[18] The fifth reason in the official English version was. "When it would probably be inefficacious, owing to the general conviction that it would be unjust."

[19] This point was completely omitted in the *Moniteur* translation.

[20] The official English read "the effect of condemnation."

[21] The English inserted "the decision of the case."

(*Source*: John Tracy Ellis, ed. *Documents of American Catholic History*. Vol. 2:1866–1966. Wilmington, Del.: Michael Glazier, 1987, 444–57.)

KOHLMANN, ANTHONY (1771–1836)

Jesuit priest, educator, missionary, and defender of religious liberty. Anthony Kohlmann was born in Kaiserberg, Alsace, on July 13, 1771. In 1796, shortly after completing his theological studies and ordination at Fribourg, Switzerland, he entered the Fathers of the Sacred Heart, a religious institute founded two years earlier that followed the rule of the suppressed Society of Jesus. In 1800 Kohlmann joined the Society of Jesus, which still existed in Russia, and was among the Society's first missionaries to the United States. He was first stationed at Georgetown, Washington, D.C., and made frequent missionary journeys to German communities throughout Pennsylvania.

In 1808 Archbishop John Carroll appointed him administrator of the newly established Diocese of New York, which, at that time consisted of some 14,000 Catholics, two church buildings, one school, and a cemetery. He served in this post until 1815, during which time St. Patrick's Old Cathedral was constructed, a school for boys was started, and an Ursuline academy for girls was founded (1812). Unfortunately, neither of these educational institutions survived by 1815. In 1813, while rector of St. Peter's Church, Kohlmann was able to restore stolen goods to their rightful owner through his office of confessor. Kohlmann refused the owner's demand to reveal the thief's name and the case was brought to the Court of General Sessions. When Kohlmann refused to reveal the man's

identity, the judges found in favor of Kohlmann and upheld the seal of the confessional, a decision which was incorporated into the revised statutes of New York in 1828. The case provided the opportunity for Kohlmann to write a brief treatise on the nature of the sacrament of penance, which received considerable attention at the time.

Kohlmann returned to Georgetown College in 1815 as Jesuit master of novices and, from 1818 to 1820, he served as president of Georgetown College. He accepted the chair of theology at the restored Jesuit Gregoriana at Rome in 1824 and counted Joachim Pecci, later Pope Leo XIII, among his students. He died in Rome on April 11, 1836. Among his published work is *Unitarianism Philosophically and Theologically Examined* (1821).

Cohalan, Florence D. *A Popular History of the Archdiocese of New York*. Yonkers, 1983, 25–27.

Hopkins, Vincent C. "Kohlmann's Case: Religious Liberty in Question." *Historical Records and Studies* 50 (1964) 53–82.

Parsons, Wilfred, S.J. "Rev. Anthony Kohlmann, S.J." *Catholic Historical Review* 4 (April 1918) 38–51.

RICHARD G. SMITH

KOKLOWSKY, ALBERT (1916–83)

Pastor and social activist. Albert Koklowsky, the son of Lithuanian immigrants, was born on February 23, 1916, in Clifton, New Jersey. He entered the Missionary Servants of the Most Holy Trinity in 1929 and was ordained on May 18, 1944.

After assignments in Newark, New Jersey, and in Maysville, North Carolina, and a mission center for Choctaws in Philadelphia, Mississippi, and in Puerto Rico, he was named pastor of Our Lady of Fatima parish in Cleveland in 1963. The formerly Hispanic parish was in the Hough area of Cleveland, a once affluent neighborhood that had become a slum populated by African Americans.

Fr. Koklowsky set about the task of making life better for his people and educating the larger society about its responsibility. His work led to volunteers clearing debris-strewn streets and setting up playgrounds. He recruited the Sisters of Charity of St. Augustine, including Sr. Henrietta Gorris, C.S.A., to staff an outreach center at this parish. He badgered indifferent city officials for such necessary services as trash pick-up.

In 1965 he began writing a column, "A Voice from the Slums," for the Cleveland diocesan newspaper, the *Catholic Universe Bulletin*. His fiery advocacy both inspired and irritated people. He used the column as a means to educate and recruit volunteers. He helped establish community housing programs such as HOPE, Inc. (Housing Our People Economically). In 1967 he went on a fast to support the nonprofessional workers at St. Luke's Hospital, Cleveland, who were striking for union recognition.

In 1969 he was transferred to Lorain, Ohio, where he served as pastor of Sacred Heart parish, a Hispanic congregation. In 1972 he was transferred to a parish in Puerto Rico which included the poverty-stricken island of Piones. Combining faith and fundraising, Koklowsky succeeded in building a chapel for this community.

His next assignment took him to the Los Angeles archdiocese where he worked with migrants. Stricken with cancer, he died on April 1, 1983, in Orange, California. He is buried in the Trinitarian Cemetery in Holy Trinity, Alabama.

Papers of Our Lady of Fatima Parish, 1949–70, Archives, Diocese of Cleveland.

Catholic Universe Bulletin. Cleveland, Ohio. April 2, 1965; April 16, 1965; April 30, 1965; September 10, 1965; July 22, 1966; November 10, 1972; April 15, 1983.

Wolff, Robert C. *Sr. Henrietta of Hough—She Reclaimed a Cleveland Slum.* Chicago, 1990.

CHRISTINE L. KROSEL

KONINGS, ANTHONY (1821–84)

Redemptorist priest, moral theologian. Anthony Konings was born in Helmond, Holland, on August 24, 1821. He was professed as a Redemptorist in 1843 and ordained in 1844. Konings taught moral theology in the Redemptorist major seminary in Wittem, Holland, and served as provincial of the Dutch province from 1865 to 1868. In 1870 he was sent to the Baltimore province in the United States and taught moral theology at the province's major seminary, then in Ilchester, Maryland, until his death on June 30, 1884. His *Theologia moralis Sancti Alphonsi, in compendium redacta, et usui Venerabilis Cleri Americani accomodata* was published in New York in 1874 and went through five editions in his lifetime and two after his death. Konings's work was significant in its influence in propagating the moderate moral theology of St. Alphonsus among the American clergy and in its attempt to reflect on moral issues which were unique to the democratic and pluralistic American society.

See also REDEMPTORISTS (C.SS.R.).

TERRENCE J. MORAN, C.SS.R.

KOŚCIUSZKO, TADEUSZ (1746–1817)

Polish patriot and soldier. Tadeusz Kościuszko was born in Mereczowszczyzńa, Lithuania, on February 12, 1746. Born into an impoverished Polish minor gentry family, he pursued a military career and was educated at the Royal Military School in Warsaw. He arrived in Philadelphia, Pennsylvania, in 1776 to volunteer his services to the American cause. He was commissioned as colonel of engineers and during his service implemented a number of innovative improvements to American fortifications, his greatest accomplishment being the design and building of West Point. He served under General Horatio Gates at Ticonderoga (1777) and contributed to the American victory over General John Burgoyne at Saratoga. He completed his service under General Nathaniel Greene in the southern campaign.

After the war, Congress recognized his military service by promoting him to brigadier general by brevet and giving him the usual land grant that was awarded to all officers of the Continental Army. He returned to Poland in 1784 where he accepted a commission as major general in the Polish army and emerged as a national hero in the wars against Russia. He returned to Philadelphia in 1797 where he was feted by the American people. His final years were spent in France and Switzerland tirelessly working to achieve a free and independent Poland. He died in Soleure, Switzerland, on October 15, 1817.

TRICIA T. PYNE

KOUDELKA, JOSEPH MARIA (1852–1921)

Bishop. Koudelka was born on December 8, 1852, in Chilstova, Bohemia, then part of the Hapsburg Empire. At the age of sixteen, he emigrated with his parents, Markus and Anna, and his siblings to Wisconsin, where he continued his studies for the priesthood. He volunteered to serve in the Diocese of Cleveland and was ordained there on October 8, 1875.

As a deacon, Koudelka had become pastor of St. Procop Bohemian parish in Cleveland where he started a parochial school and authored a series of Bohemian-language

Joseph M. Koudelka

readers. In May 1882 he went to St. Louis to edit the Bohemian journal *Hlas,* but returned to Cleveland within a year where he established the German parish of St. Michael and built its landmark Gothic church and school. Koudelka wrote a short history of the church and composed prayer books for children and adults. He was a linguist, fluent in German, Polish, Bohemian, and English. He recruited European seminarians, priests, and religious for work in the Diocese of Cleveland. Cleveland's Bishop Ignatius F. Horstmann employed Koudelka in mediating various disputes that arose in the Slavic parishes of the diocese. Horstmann petitioned Rome for an auxiliary bishop to minister to the Slavic immigrants of his diocese and Koudelka's appointment was announced on November 29, 1907. His consecration on February 25, 1908, made him the first auxiliary bishop of special jurisdiction in America.

Horstmann's successor, Bishop John P. Farrelly, argued that he no longer needed an auxiliary, and so Koudelka was transferred to the Archdiocese of Milwaukee on September 4, 1911. On August 1, 1913, he became the second bishop of the largely rural diocese of Superior, Wisconsin. Koudelka learned Native American dialects in order to minister to those residing in his diocese. He continued to preach retreats and missions to Slavic congregations nationwide.

Koudelka requested that his funeral take place from St. Michael's parish, Cleveland, where he had spent twenty-eight years as pastor. He is buried in St. Mary Cemetery in Cleveland.

Papers of Bishop Richard Gilmour, 1873–91. Archives, Diocese of Cleveland.

Papers of Bishop Ignatius Horstmann, 1892–1908. Archives, Diocese of Cleveland.

Hynes, Michael J. *History of the Diocese of Cleveland, Origin and Growth, 1847–1952.* Cleveland, 1953.

Sheehan, Thomas W. *The Story of Saint Michael Church.* Cleveland, 1975.

CHRISTINE L. KROSEL

KOZŁOWSKI, ANTHONY (1857–1907)

Organizer of the Independent Polish Catholic Church of America. Anthony Kozłowski [Antoni Kozłowski] was born in Russian Poland in 1857. He was ordained a priest in Taranto, Italy, on August 15, 1885, came to the United States in 1894, and served as assistant pastor of St. Hedwig's parish in Chicago until 1895. In June of that year he organized the independent All Saints parish, the first parish in the "Independent Polish Catholic Church of America," which was dedicated June 16, 1895. Kozłowski and the members of the parish were excommunicated on September 29, 1895. Regardless, Kozłowski continued organizing independent parishes, and on November 21, 1897,

Bishop Edouard Herzog, the Swiss Old Catholic bishop of Berne, Switzerland, consecrated him bishop of the "Polish Catholic Diocese of Chicago." Kozłowski's organizational constitution generally mirrored the principles of the Old Catholics, but contained a clause stipulating that "the Independent Polish Church considers the Roman Pontiff as Primate of the Occident." On April 26, 1898, Pope Leo XIII personally excommunicated Kozłowski and those loyal to him. Kozłowski was a rival of Stefan Kamiński and later Franciszek Hodur for leadership of the independent movement among Polish Catholics in America, but his willingness to reach out to Episcopalians and others for allies and his reluctance to adopt Polish as the language of the Mass led to charges from his rivals that he had betrayed the independent movement's goals of promoting Polish ethnicity and Catholicism. Nevertheless, given the preeminent importance of Chicago within Polonia, he remained arguably the most influential independent leader until his death at the relatively young age of fifty in Chicago on January 15, 1907.

See also POLISH CATHOLICS IN AMERICA.

Galush, William. "The Polish National Catholic Church: A Survey of Its Origins, Development and Missions." *Records of the American Catholic Historical Society of Philadelphia* 83 (1972) 131–49.

JAMES S. PULA

KREISLER, FRITZ (1875–1962)

Composer and violin virtuoso. Kreisler was born in Vienna, Austria, on February 2, 1875. He began studying violin under his father, a prominent Vienna physician, and continued at the Vienna Conservatory where, at the age of ten, he won the conservatory's gold medal. From 1885 to 1887 he studied composition and violin at the Paris Conservatoire, earning the school's gold medal and grand prize.

At the age of thirteen, he made his New York debut, and, after several tours of the United States (1888–89), he returned to Vienna to study medicine at the university. During the intervening years until his return in 1898 to the stage as a concert violinist with the Vienna Philharmonic, he pursued the study of art in Paris and Rome and served as an officer in the Austrian army.

Kreisler's debut in Berlin in 1899 marked the beginning of a sixty-year career on the concert stage, touring both in Europe and the United States, interrupted briefly for service as a captain in the Austrian army during World War I. After Hitler came to power in Germany in 1933 and the sale and broadcast of Kreisler's music was banned, he moved to France in 1938 and became a French citizen. A year later he moved to the United States and became an American citizen in 1943.

He had married Harriet Lies Woerz, an American divorcee, in 1902. They were received back into the Catholic Church by then-Msgr. Fulton J. Sheen in 1944 and renewed their marriage vows during the ceremony.

Besides being a skilled violinist, Kreisler also composed numerous concertos, chamber music, operettas, and violin and piano solos, as well as cadenzas for Mozart, Beethoven, and Brahms concertos. In 1935 Kreisler admitted that his *Classical Manuscripts,* supposedly arrangements of works by several well-known composers, were his own compositions. Among his other original works were "Viennese Caprice" and "Pretty Rosemary Plant." He died in New York City on January 29, 1962.

Janick, H. *MusGG* 7:1742–43. Baker 869.
Lochner, L. P. *Fritz Kreisler.* New York, 1951.
New York Times (January 30, 1962) 1:4.
Pincherle, M. *The World of the Virtuoso.* Trans. L. H. Brockway. New York, 1963.

MARIANNA McLOUGHLIN

KROL, JOHN CARDINAL (1910–96)

Cardinal archbishop. John Krol was the fourth of eight children born to John Krol, Sr., a machinist, and Anne Pietruszka Krol on October 26, 1910. After graduating from a Catholic high school, he became a meat cutter, and later, a manager of a Kroger food market. He began a personal study of Catholicism after he was stumped by questions asked by a Lutheran coworker. He later decided to study for the priesthood and was ordained in 1937. After a brief assignment as an assistant pastor, he was chosen to study canon law in Rome and at The Catholic University of America. He was ordained auxiliary bishop in 1953.

Krol, a tall impressive figure, was a skilled manager and administrator, and served as a permanent undersecretary and coordinator at the Second Vatican Council (1962–65). Pope John XXIII appointed him as archbishop of Philadelphia in 1961, and Pope Paul VI elevated him to the College of Cardinals in 1967.

In Philadelphia, Cardinal Krol was a conservative prelate who regarded himself as the appointed guardian of the past. A close friend of Pope John Paul II, he approved of Vatican Council II and cautiously implemented the changes that flowed from it. For instance, he disagreed with the reception of Communion in the hand; he resisted and delayed the introduction of Saturday evening Mass in lieu of Sunday; and disapproved the revision of regulations covering marriages between Catholics and those of other faiths. He earned respect as a conservative pragmatist who spoke his mind clearly and eschewed innovation. Politically, he placed his hopes in the Republican Party and publicly endorsed Presidents Nixon and Reagan. While some of the laity and clergy viewed him as rigid and aloof, all agreed that his only concern was the spiritual welfare of the citizens of Philadelphia. The Cardinal retired in 1988, and he died at the age of eighty-five, on March 3, 1996.

See also PENNSYLVANIA, CATHOLIC CHURCH IN.

MICHAEL GLAZIER

KRUSZKA, WENCESLAUS (1868–1937)

Priest, author, spokesman for Polish-American Catholics. Wenceslaus Kruszka [Wacław Kruszka] was born in Slabomierz, Poland, on March 2, 1868. Although he studied for entry into the Society of Jesus, medical problems prevented completion of his studies, and he was sent to teach at the Jesuit high school in Chyrów from 1890 to 1891. Moving to Rome, in 1893 he graduated from the Gregorianum and decided to come to the United States. Ordained at St. Francis Seminary, St. Francis, Wisconsin, on June 16, 1895, he served from that date until February 25, 1896, as assistant pastor at St. Josaphat's parish, Milwaukee, Wisconsin. In 1896 he organized St. Wenceslaus parish in Ripon, Wisconsin, where he remained as pastor until September 18, 1909, when he became pastor of St. Adalbert's parish, Milwaukee, Wisconsin. The author of many books and articles, including *Historya Polska w Ameryce* [*Polish History in America*], a massive, thirteen-volume pioneering history of Polish immigration in America, Kruszka was a strong advocate of the preservation of Polish heritage and supporter of equal rights for Polish clerics in America. Indeed, in an article titled "Polyglot Bishops for Polyglot Dioceses," he argued the right of immigrants in America to be served by priests and bishops who spoke their own language, a concept of ethnic pluralism that was much in advance of its time. In 1901 he was selected by the second national Polish convention in Buffalo to present the grievances of Polish clerics and laity in America to the pope. He undertook the trip in 1903–04, returning in the belief he had secured Pope Pius X's agreement to intercede on the Poles' behalf. When no action was taken, however, Kruszka lashed out at the Catholic hierarchy in an exchange of newspaper articles in the Polish press in Milwaukee. Despite these sometimes acrimonious exchanges, Kruszka remained loyal to Roman Catholicism while continuing his efforts to promote equity for Polish clergy within the Church. He died in Milwaukee on February 28, 1937.

See also POLISH CATHOLICS IN AMERICA.

JAMES S. PULA

KU KLUX KLAN, THE

In reality two societies would bear the name "Ku Klux Klan," the first lasting from 1865 to 1871, and the second founded in 1915. Whereas the purpose of the first Klan was to resist radical Reconstruction in the post-Civil War South, the second possessed a broader scope and engaged in nationwide activities.

After the last outburst of anti-immigrant and anti-Catholic activity in the early 1890s, nativist attention began to be focused on the national origins of immigrants. Orientals were the first to be restricted. By the mid-1890s, southern and eastern European immigration threatened to overcome newcomers of "Nordic stock." Whereas in earlier times all immigration was alleged to be a threat to the Republic, by the turn of the twentieth century, "racial purity" became the chief concern. Agitation before the Congress by nativist groups would lead, by the early 1920s, to restrictive legislation governing all immigration.

The reorganized Klan was founded by William J. Simmons at Atlanta, Georgia, in the fall of 1915. Imitating the old Know-Nothings in adopting a hierarchical structure, the Klan divided the entire nation into eight "domains." All national officials were to be named by the Imperial Wizard. Only local officers could be elected.

The movement was aided substantially by the immensely popular D. W. Griffith film *Birth of a Nation* which also appeared in the fall of 1915. The film presented a highly romanticized picture of the first Klan as the guardian of Southern civilization.

In the years immediately following its reestablishment, the Klan moved from being a fraternal association of Southern Protestant men dedicated to Southern "ideals" to being aggressively anti-alien, anti-Jewish, and anti-Catholic as well as asserting Caucasian supremacy over all other races. In addition, the Klan advocated a return to traditional moral values, claiming that these had been corrupted by the immigrant and by other undesirables.

World War I and its aftermath generated ideal conditions for Klan growth. Wartime fears over potential saboteurs and traitors were intensified by the successful Bolshevik Revolution in Russia. In addition, hordes of refugees were expected from Europe after the cessation of hostilities.

Ongoing migration of Southern blacks into Northern cities aggravated race relations and touched off riots, such as that in East St. Louis in 1917, which claimed the lives of twelve whites and five blacks. Between May and September of 1919, twenty additional outbreaks of interracial violence occurred.

The government seemed incapable of maintaining the peace or of administering its own laws. In January of 1920, ten thousand foreign-born radicals were rounded up, but the courts prevented their deportation. With the Volstead Act, Prohibition became the law of the land. Yet enforcement seemed lacking.

The national mood welcomed the Klan as an organization dedicated to action and to "100 percent Americanism." From a handful of members in 1915, numbers grew to 100,000 in 1921 and to 2,000,000 by 1925, with the Klan spreading to nearly all parts of the country.

The Klan eventually plunged into politics and was successful in electing legislators at the local and national level. With the Immigration Act of 1924, many Klan aims found themselves enshrined in federal law. European immigration was reduced to 150,000 per year, with the southern and eastern European numbers being cut the most drastically. Paradoxically, this legislative success deprived the Klan of some of its former relevance.

Internal and external conflicts combined to remove the Klan from the national stage by the end of the 1920s. Infighting broke out between founder Simmons and his would-be successor, Hiram Wesley Evans. Charges of financial impropriety were aimed at the national leadership. Political payoffs by the Klan were revealed and documented in 1925, after the Indianapolis Grand Dragon David C. Stephenson failed to receive a jail pardon from the state's Klan governor. The shallow moral leadership of the Klan became increasingly apparent, while lynchings and other mob violence came to be a regular feature of Klan gatherings. By 1929 the Klan lost much of its popular support. While it continued in existence, its numbers were severely reduced. It would not experience a resurgence in popularity until the onset of the civil rights movement.

Nativist sentiment in America did not end with the passing of the Klan from national politics in the late 1920s. Anti-Catholicism continued to make its voice heard, most notably during the election campaigns of Al Smith and John F. Kennedy.

See also AMERICAN PROTECTIVE ASSOCIATION; NATIVISM.

Bennett, David H. *The Party of Fear*. Chapel Hill: University of North Carolina Press, 1988.

Chalmers, David M. *Hooded Americanism*. New York: Doubleday, 1965.

Curran, Thomas J. *Xenophobia and Immigration, 1820–1930*. Boston: Twayne, 1975.

Jackson, Kenneth T. *The Ku Klux Klan in the City, 1915–1930*. New York, 1967.

Moore, Leonard. *Citizen Klansmen: The Ku Klux Klan in Indiana, 1921–1928*. Chapel Hill: University of North Carolina Press, 1996.

Wade, Wyn Craig. *The Fiery Cross*. London: Simon and Schuster, 1987.

ALBERT H. LEDOUX

L

LABOR MOVEMENT AND AMERICAN CATHOLICS, THE

In 1886 a group of American bishops led by Cardinal James Gibbons of Baltimore succeeded in heading off a Vatican condemnation of the Knights of Labor, the premier labor organization of the time. That intervention by the Gibbons bishops would prove to be a fateful one in the history of Church-labor relations. The Catholic Church in the United States proceeded to form close ties with the American labor movement. During the 1930s and 1940s, Church leaders offered their moral and material support to the great industrial campaigns of organized labor. In recent decades, cooperation between the Church and organized labor has become more sporadic, at times contentious. Yet, with new problems in the workplace have come renewed interest in Church-labor cooperation.

European and American Labor Unions

Collaboration between religion and labor appears to be a uniquely American phenomenon, at least from a historical view. This aspect of American exceptionalism has as much to do with the unhappy experience in Europe as it does with the situation in the United States. Beginning in the nineteenth century and for decades thereafter, there was a cleavage in many parts of the Continent between the labor movement and religion—between, especially, the Roman Catholic Church and Marxist-dominated labor movements. Many Christian workers felt they could not in good conscience take part in Marxist unions (and in-

deed they were frequently warned against doing so by ecclesiastical authorities). Meanwhile, many militant workers looked upon the Church and organized religion in general as bastions of reaction. These hard feelings, evident through much of prewar European labor history, had caused a partitioning of the union movement. In Germany, to cite one example, a socialist federation had coalesced on one side, countered by a Christian federation of Protestants and Catholics on the other. The German Christian Federation of Labor, abolished by the Nazis, was not revived after World War II.

In contrast to the European experience, there were no religious or denominational divisions in the American labor movement, no series attempts to establish a Catholic or Protestant or generically Christian labor federation. The social and cultural conditions that had triggered a separate Christian labor movement in Europe did not exist in the United States. No significant atheistic or antireligious movement had taken hold in the American trade union movement, or in American society at large. The U.S. movement, for the most part, honored the principle of trade-union "neutrality," that is, neutrality toward religion and questions of ultimate value; American unions limited themselves to collective bargaining, property redistribution, and other practical matters of economic wellbeing. European unions, on the other hand, generally chose the sectarian option during these formative stages. Christian unions affirmed religious doctrines; Marxist unions often took aggressively anticlerical and antireligious positions as part of their official ideology.

Church-labor relations have improved on the Continent in recent decades, but still, even the common forms of cooperation in the United States—joint statements by national religious and labor leaders, for example—would seem remarkable in many parts of Europe.

Knights of Labor

Within the American Catholic fold, a critical moment came during the heyday of the Knights of Labor. The idiosyncratic Knights predated modern trade unionism, and in many ways operated more like a fraternal association. They took ceremonial vows of secrecy and exchanged secret passwords to guard against labor's numerous enemies. This was the rub for the Catholic Church, which harbored a deep suspicion of secret societies, mainly as a result of the Church's experience with the Masons and other societies that had antireligious overtones. In Quebec, the French-Canadian bishops had prevailed upon the Vatican to condemn the Knights in Canada, and Rome was prepared to extend this ruling to the United States.

The prospects of condemnation alarmed Gibbons and the American bishops, particularly the liberal-minded "Americanists," as they were known. In 1886 they drafted a memorandum signed by Gibbons, who, as the only cardinal and spokesman for the Catholic Church in the United States, happened to be in Rome to make their case. In the memorandum, the bishops made clear their feeling that American workers needed an organization like the Knights, and that a condemnation would lead many Catholic workers to become alienated from the Church. In short, they urged Rome to drop the matter, and Rome agreed. Msgr. George Higgins, an internationally respected authority on Catholic social teaching and the Church's social tradition, has described the Gibbons' memorandum as one of the "neglected classics" of American Catholic social history. It reads, in part:

> Since it is acknowledged by all that the great questions of the future . . . (are) the social questions, the questions which concern the improvement of the condition of the great masses of the people, and especially of the working people, it is evidently of supreme importance that the church should always be found on the side of humanity, of justice toward the multitudes who compose the body of the human family. . . . In our country, especially, this is the inevitable program of the future, and the position which the Church must hold toward the solution is sufficiently obvious.

Msgr. Higgins has considered what might have happened if the Holy See had rejected the pleas of the Gibbons' bishops. He writes in his memoir: "Had the Vatican gone the other way and condemned the Knights of Labor, as the French-Canadian bishops had urged, a split would have occurred in the American labor movement, as it had in Europe. In that case, some Catholics would have remained loyal to the Church and joined an inconsequential Catholic union, while others would have fallen away from the Church to one degree or another. This would have proved disastrous for not only the Church but the workers, who needed solidarity."

With the blessings of Church leaders, Catholics began entering the ranks of the American labor movement. The Church, however, did not become instantly engaged in labor and social concerns. It had other things on its institutional mind—namely, the phenomenal influx of Catholic immigrants into the United States during the late nineteenth and early twentieth centuries. The Church went about the business of building schools, parishes, hospitals, and orphanages, ministering to millions of penniless workers, assimilating them into their new and strange surroundings. This was an all-absorbing mission; there remained little time for serious examination of the larger, structural issues of social and economic justice.

Msgr. John A. Ryan

It was during this period, however, that individual Catholics began sowing the seeds of the American Catholic social action movement. The name that towers above all others is that of Msgr. John A. Ryan, who drew inspiration from papal social teaching (enunciated in Pope Leo XIII's 1891 encyclical *Rerum Novarum*) as well as the American Protestant "Social Gospel" movement. Ryan received worldwide attention in 1906 with the publication of his first book, *A Living Wage,* written as his doctoral dissertation in moral theology at The Catholic University of America in Washington, D.C. It was one of the first books in any language to propose a federally mandated minimum wage.

Some years later, Ryan's program was adopted by the Catholic hierarchy in the United States. He drafted, in 1919, the *Bishops' Program of Social Reconstruction,* an ambitious statement that endorsed a minimum wage, subsidized housing, labor participation in industrial management, child labor laws, social insurance for the jobless, sick, and old-aged, and other reforms—basically, the New Deal program, thirteen years before the election of President Franklin Delano Roosevelt. "The employer has a right to get a reasonable living out of his business, but he has no right to interest on his investment until his employees have obtained at least living wages. This is the human and Christian, in contrast to the purely commercial and pagan, ethics of industry." The program served as the vehicle of American Catholicism's formal entry into the social arena.

The era of massive industrial organizing, beginning in the 1930s, marked the most intensive period of Church-labor interaction. During the Great Depression, millions of workers were asserting their right to organize and bargain collectively. Many of these workers were immigrants, and many, if not most, were Catholic. This convergence of social and cultural forces, involving the faithful at a moment of struggle in the Church's urban strongholds, demanded a response from Catholic clergy and institutions. The most impressive leadership came from the so-called "labor priests" who made the working person their apostolate.

Labor Priests and Labor Schools

Across the industrial map of America, priests opened "labor schools" for rank-and-file workers. These night schools gave ordinary workers basic training in labor organization: how to speak in public, run a meeting, and hold fair union elections, to cite a few of the rudiments. The workers also received a dose of Catholic social teaching, as interpreted by labor-friendly priests who tended to emphasize industrial cooperation whenever possible and confrontation when necessary to protect human rights and dignity in the workplace. At their highpoint in the 1950s, the number of Catholic labor schools climbed to over one hundred nationwide, with some of them functioning as extensions of Jesuit colleges and universities.

Labor priests were not confined to the classroom. In Pittsburgh, Msgr. Charles Owen Rice became known during the 1930s as "the chaplain of the CIO" for his direct involvement in strikes by the newly formed Congress of Industrial Organizations. In 1936 he and Fr. Carl Hensler formed the Catholic Radical Alliance that had its roots in Dorothy Day's Catholic Worker movement. Rice walked the picket line during such actions as the 1937 strike against the Pittsburgh-based Heinz corporation, and spoke to overflow crowds in churches, union halls, and immigrant meeting houses. (He remained active in local affairs, six decades later). In New York, the Rev. John "Pete" Corridan became nationally known as the "waterfront priest" after he navigated a successful rebellion of rank-and-file dock workers against labor racketeering in New York's maritime industry. Corridan's crusade inspired author and screenwriter Budd Schulberg's 1953 motion picture, *On the Waterfront.* A Jesuit priest, Corridan worked through the Xavier Labor School in Manhattan; he died in 1984.

ACTU and Revisionist Historians

During this age of robust unionism, many lay Catholics marched under the banner of the Association of Catholic Trade Unionists. Launched in the 1930s by former members of the Catholic Worker (notably John Cort, a Catholic convert and early organizer of the International Ladies Garment Workers Union), ACTU defined its mission broadly as spreading the Church's teachings on labor. The movement found its mandate in Pope Pius XI's 1931 encyclical *Quadragesimo Anno,* which encouraged Christian workers to form associations of Catholic workers (parallel to, though not necessarily in competition with, unions).

Quickly, ACTU branched out from New York, spawning independent chapters across the country as well as a number of popular newspapers including *The Wage Earner* in Detroit. With little or no national coordination, these chapters pushed on a number of fronts—from rallying support for striking workers to, especially in the 1940s and 1950s, fighting the leaderships of Communist-controlled unions and rooting out organized crime.

That the Church had an impact on the American trade union movement during its key organizational phase is beyond dispute. There are, though, differing assessments as to the kind of influence exerted by the Church. Msgr. Higgins, the Church's most authoritative spokesman on labor issues, places much less importance on any particular undertakings—the labor schools, for example—than on the symbolic effect of the Church standing with workers in defense of collective bargaining. He writes that while the labor schools reached only limited numbers of workers, they did lend "a certain respectability to the union movement at a time of extreme resistance to its campaigns." In particular, the presence of the Roman Catholic Church in the labor movement complicated the conservative business strategy of branding labor as a socialist or Communist tool.

A wave of revisionism has come from historians with leanings toward labor's left wing, and in particular the old Communist guard of some CIO unions. Representative of this literature is Douglas Seton's 1981 book, *Catholics and Radicals: The Association of Catholic Trade Unionists and the American Labor Movement from the Depression to the Cold War,* which casts the Catholic Church as heavily responsible for what he considers the "conservative" direction taken by the industrial unions from 1937 to 1950. This claim (setting aside his contention that Catholic social teaching is basically conservative) appears to exaggerate the Church's control over events during this period. Seton and other writers have also maintained that the Church entered the labor movement primarily, if not exclusively, to resist Communism. This, though, is a reductionist finding, one that overlooks the diversity of Catholic prolabor activities, and the plain fact that the Church supported industrial unionism.

The tapering off of ties between the Church and organized labor began in the 1950s and continued in the following decades. To a large extent, this was a result of success. By the 1950s, the labor movement had fought and won the primary battles for recognition in the industrial workplace, and arrived as a powerful force in American society. No longer needing the Church's help, and able to take care of its own, the movement turned inward—toward matters of less obvious moral content, such as negotiating contracts and building institutions. For its part, the Church began to explore new areas of social action, notably civil rights, peace, and community organizing.

These decades also brought a gradual shift in American Catholic demographics. In no small part due to the accomplishments of organized labor, the children of Catholic immigrants began to move off the assembly lines and into the ranks of management and white-collar professions. The labor cause had less of an appeal to the upwardly mobile Catholic. For this and other reasons, namely lack of necessity, Catholic labor schools, the concrete symbols of Church-labor unity, began closing their doors. By the mid-1990s, there was only one labor school remaining (and also thriving)—the School of Industrial Relations, run by the Labor Guild of the Archdiocese of Boston, headed by Fr. Edward J. Boyle, S.J. The last one to shut down was Xavier Labor School in New York, operated for fifty years by another Jesuit, Fr. Philip Carey; when Carey died in July 1989, so did the school.

The 1950s and After

New social and political sensibilities contributed to the estrangement between labor and the Catholic social action movement. During the 1960s, Catholic activists began partaking in the culture of cynicism toward trade unions, an attitude fed by liberalism's revised image of organized labor as a stodgy institution of the American "establishment." In the field of international policy, many in the Catholic movement became disaffected by what they viewed as mainstream labor's excessive anticommunism. The Vietnam War was a harbinger of clashes to come, between labor's hard-hat foreign policy and the romantic internationalism of many liberal religious leaders, not only Catholics. By the 1980s, the grounds of argument had shifted to Central America, Nicaragua especially. Activist groups allied themselves with the left-wing Sandinista government while the American Federation of Labor and Congress of Industrial Organizations supported the free trade unions outlawed by the regime. Since then, the collapse of worldwide Communism has largely removed foreign policy as an obstacle to religion-labor cooperation.

Despite the disruptions, Catholics concerned about economic justice did not disengage from labor problems. Rather, they tended to gravitate toward areas left untouched by the earlier organizing efforts. For example, during the 1960s and 1970s, it was the agriculture and textile industries that provoked a religious response. Large numbers of priests, nuns, and Catholic laity joined in the farm-labor crusade of Cesar Chavez, founder of the United Farm Workers, and himself a Catholic who quoted Pope Leo XIII in calling for the initial strike against California grape growers, in 1965. In this struggle, the Church had returned to first principles: the right to organize and bargain collectively. Likewise, simple moral principle drew bishops and other Church leaders into a long-running controversy over the J. P. Stevens Company, which tried for years, and

ultimately failed, to keep unions out of the Southern textile industry. By and large, however, religion and labor were an alliance for special occasions during the post-CIO era.

The decline of organized labor, from its power peak in the 1950s, has helped generate concern about the need for a new Church-labor engagement. The weakening of labor has aggravated some worrisome trends, among them the erosion of real wages; increasing polarization along income lines; the necessity of two or more paychecks in many families; and the growing numbers of working people who live in poverty. Against this background, Church and union leaders have come together on behalf of legislative initiatives such as a higher minimum wage; a ban on the revived antilabor practice of firing (the euphemism is "permanently replacing") strikers; and the linking of U.S. trade preferences to human rights and global standards in the workplace. One signal event was a 1989–90 strike by the United Mine Workers against the Pittston Coal Company in southwestern Virginia, which featured extraordinary solidarity both among unions and between labor and the churches, and ended in a surprise victory for the labor movement. That was followed by a succession of strikes and other labor crises in which Catholic, Protestant, and Jewish groups, locally and nationally, assumed prominent roles of mediation and support.

Those pastors and laypeople who have been drawn into the recent conflicts believe the moral content has returned to the principal issues affecting labor and its future in America. In the resuming dialogue between the Catholic Church and organized labor, one problematic point is the labor record of some Catholic institutions, which—imitating their secular counterparts—have at times engaged in what are commonly known as union-busting tactics; Catholic hospitals, with their sizable staffs of nurses and service employees, have been the focal point of the most bitter disputes. Yet even aside from this distraction, Church-labor relations have moved unsteadily, continuing ad hoc, as a chain of reactions to postindustrial crises in communities. It remains to be seen whether the Church in the United States will renew the tradition started by Cardinal Gibbons, and reach out to a new class of struggling workers (including millions of Catholic immigrants from Asia and Latin America) in a creative and coordinated way.

See also CATHOLIC TRADE UNIONISTS, ASSOCIATION OF; CHAVEZ, CESAR; GIBBONS, JAMES CARDINAL; KNIGHTS OF LABOR; NEW DEAL AND AMERICAN CATHOLICS, THE; RYAN, JOHN A.

Abell, Aaron I. *American Catholicism and Social Action: The Search for Social Justice.* Garden City, N.Y.: Hanover House, Doubleday, 1960.

Betten, Neil. *Catholic Activism and the Industrial Worker.* Gainesville: University Presses of Florida, 1976.

Broderick, Francis R. *Right Reverend New Dealer: John A. Ryan.* New York: Macmillan, 1963.

Higgins, George G. and William Bole. *Organized Labor and the Church: Reflections of a "Labor Priest."* New York/Mahwah, N. J.: Paulist Press, 1993.

McShane, Joseph M., S.J. *"Sufficiently Radical": Catholicism, Progressivism, and the Bishops' Program of 1919.* Washington, D.C: The Catholic University of America Press, 1986.

O'Brien, David J. *American Catholics and Social Reform: The New Deal Years.* New York: Oxford University Press, 1968.

WILLIAM BOLE

LACKAYE, WILTON (1862–1932)

Actor. William Lackaye was born on September 30, 1862, in Loudon County, Virginia. He studied in Ottawa for two years and later in Georgetown. He also studied for the priesthood for six years and still later tried a brief stint studying law. Finally, he gravitated to the theater and found success with the Lawrence Barrett Dramatic Club in Washington, D.C. Among his thespian associations were the Carrie Swan Company in New York, Fanny Davenport's Company from 1886 to 1887, and in 1887 Augustin Daly's Company. Lackaye was extremely successful in the role of Svengali in "Trilby" in 1894, and as Sir Lucius Trigger in "The Rival" in 1898. Lackaye was instrumental in founding the Actor's Equity Association and the Catholic Actors' Guild in 1914. He died in Long Island City, New York, on August 22, 1932.

LISELLE DRAKE

LAETARE MEDAL, THE

The University of Notre Dame's Laetare Medal is that institution's highest honor and is commonly acknowledged as the most prestigious honor given to American Catholics. The award takes its name from the fact that its recipient is annually announced by the university's president on Laetare Sunday, the fourth Sunday in Lent, an oasis of celebration in the middle of that otherwise penitential season.

Origins

The award was the brainchild of James F. Edwards, a professor of history at Notre Dame and the university's first librarian, who headed a small faculty group convened to discuss the contributions of educated lay Catholics to American life. "Men and women who have added luster to the name of the American Catholic by their talent and virtues deserve good will and encouragement," he wrote in the proposal which emerged from the gathering. "It is my opinion that our university might well take some action in that regard—take the initiative, as it were, in acknowledgment of what is done for faith, morals, education and good citizenship." Rev. Edward Sorin, C.S.C., Notre Dame's aged founder, and Rev. Thomas E. Walsh, C.S.C.,

its president, both agreed, and the first Laetare Medal was given to John Gilmary Shea, the Catholic historian, in 1883.

Originally conceived as an American counterpart to the Golden Rose, a papal honor bestowed on Catholic aristocrats and nobles since before the eleventh century, the Laetare Medal consists of a solid gold disk suspended from a gold bar and bearing the inscription, "Laetare Medal." Inscribed in a border around the disk are the words *Magna est veritas et praevalebit* ("Truth is mighty, and it will prevail"). The medal's design also includes the name of the recipient, a rose, and the seal of the University.

In 1896 the medal was given to General William Rosecrans, the Union army military strategist who had become famous during the American Civil War for a tactical blunder which lost his side the Battle of Chickamauga. An excerpt from the citation accompanying Rosecrans' medal has become the most frequently quoted criterion for the award. "The Laetare Medal," the Rosecrans citation reads, "has been worn only by men and women whose genius has ennobled the arts and sciences, illustrated the ideals of the church, and enriched the heritage of humanity."

The recipient of each year's Laetare Medal is elected by a vote of the officers of the university. The medal was awarded exclusively to laypeople until 1968, when then president Rev. Theodore M. Hesburgh, C.S.C., decided to expand the pool of candidates to include all American Catholics regardless of ecclesial status. In 1973 Rev. John A. O'Brien, the pamphleteer and pioneer of the Newman Club movement, was named recipient. Since then, several priests and members of religious orders have been honored including Msgr. John Tracy Ellis, the historian (1978); Cardinal John Francis Dearden, the retired archbishop of Detroit (1982); Rev. Theodore M. Hesburgh, C.S.C., president emeritus of Notre Dame (1987); Sr. Thea Bowman, F.S.P.A., the poet, evangelist, gospel singer, and the medal's first posthumous recipient (1990); and Cardinal Joseph Bernardin, archbishop of Chicago (1995).

History

The list of Laetare Medalists has been said to provide a sort of history in miniature of Catholicism in America. Observing the centennial of the award in 1983, Fr. Hesburgh wrote, "One hundred years ago neither Notre Dame nor Catholics generally loomed very large on the national horizon. Although the University offered degrees in liberal arts, science, engineering and law, total enrollment was less than two hundred, and American Catholics for the most part were far removed from the mainstream of our national life."

General Rosecrans may have been an exception to the marginalization Fr. Hesburgh described. In any event, the names of Laetare Medalists following that Civil War celebrity increasingly blur the distinction between American and Catholic as the list advances into the twentieth century: Supreme Court Chief Justice Edward Douglass White (1914); unsuccessful Democratic presidential candidate Alfred Emmanuel Smith (1929); operatic tenor John McCormack (1933); actress Irene Dunne (1949); labor leader George Meany (1955); Ambassador Clare Boothe Luce (1957); President John Fitzgerald Kennedy (1961); poet Phyllis McGinley (1964); first Peace Corps director, Robert Sargent Shriver (1968); Supreme Court Associate Justice William Joseph Brennan (1969); playwrights Walter and Jean Kerr (1971); Catholic Worker foundress Dorothy Day (1972); novelist Paul Horgan (1976); former Senator Michael Joseph Mansfield (1977); actress Helen Hayes (1979); House Speaker Thomas Philip ["Tip"] O'Neill (1980); Secretary of State Edmund Muskie (1981); novelist Walker Percy (1989); and Senator Daniel Patrick Moynihan (1992).

Fr. Hesburgh, who was responsible for the selections of all Laetare Medalists from 1952–87 (the years during which he served as president of the university), wrote in 1983, "I have always insisted that receiving the medal is not a prelude to beatification, but it does signal a Catholic of uncommon dedication." This insistence notwithstanding, a chapel commemorating Laetare Medalists was installed in the Basilica of the Sacred Heart on the Notre Dame campus that same year. The apsidal chapel contains three bronze plaques inscribed with the names of the Laetare recipients as well as a leather-bound album providing biographical notes on each of them.

Laetare Medalists

1883 John Gilmary Shea, historian
1884 Patrick Charles Keeley, architect
1885 Eltza Auen Starr, art critic
1886 General John Newton, engineer
1887 Edward Preuss, publicist
1888 Patrick V. Hickey,
        founder and editor of the *Catholic Review*
1889 Anna Hansen Dorsey, novelist

1890 William J. Onahan,
        organizer of the American Catholic Congress
1891 Daniel Dougherty, orator
1892 Henry F. Brownson, philosopher and author
1893 Patrick Donahoe, founder of the *Boston Pilot*
1894 Augustine Daly, theatrical producer
1895 Mary A. Sadlier, novelist
1896 General William Starke Rosecrans, soldier
1897 Thomas Addis Emmet, physician
1898 Timothy Edward Howard, jurist
1899 Mary Gwendoline Caldwell, philanthropist

1900 John A. Creighton, philanthropist
1901 William Bourke Cockran, orator
1902 John Benjamin Murphy, surgeon

1903 Charles Jerome Bonaparte, lawyer
1904 Richard C. Kerens, diplomat
1905 Thomas B. Fitzpatrick, philanthropist
1906 Francis J. Quinlan, physician
1907 Katherine Eleanor Conway, journalist and author
1908 James C. Monaghan, economist
1909 Frances Tiernan (Christian Reid), novelist

1910 Maurice Francis Egan, author and diplomat
1911 Agnes Repplier, author
1912 Thomas M. Mulry, philanthropist
1913 Charles B. Herbermann,
        editor in chief of *The Catholic Encyclopedia*
1914 Edward Douglass White,
        jurist and chief justice of the United States
1915 Mary V. Merrick, philanthropist
1916 James Joseph Walsh, physician and author
1917 William Shepherd Benson,
        admiral and Chief of Naval Operations
1918 Joseph Scott, lawyer
1919 George L. Duval, philanthropist

1920 Lawrence Francis Flick, physician
1921 Elizabeth Nourse, artist
1922 Charles Patrick Neill, economist
1923 Walter George Smith, lawyer
1924 Charles D. Maginnis, architect
1925 Albert Francis Zahm, scientist
1926 Edward Nash Hurley, businessman
1927 Margaret Anglin, actress
1928 John Johnson Spalding, lawyer
1929 Alfred Emmanuel Smith, statesman

1930 Frederick Philip Kenkel, publicist
1931 James J. Phelan, businessman
1932 Stephen J. Maher, physician
1933 John McCormack, artist
1934 Genevieve Garvan Brady, philanthropist
1935 Francis Hamilton Spearman, novelist
1936 Richard Reid, lawyer and journalist
1937 Jeremiah Denis M. Ford, scholar
1938 Irvin William Abell, surgeon
1939 Josephine Van Dyke Brownson, catechist

1940 General Hugh Aloysius Drum, soldier
1941 William Thomas Walsh, journalist and author
1942 Helen Constance White, author and teacher
1943 Thomas Francis Woodlock, editor
1944 Anne O'Hare McCormick, journalist
1945 G. Howland Shaw, diplomat
1946 Carlton J. H. Hayes, historian and diplomat
1947 William G. Bruce, publisher and civic leader
1948 Frank C. Walker,
        Postmaster General and civic leader
1949 Irene Dunne, actress

1950	General Joseph L. Collins, soldier
1951	John Henry Phelan, philanthropist
1952	Thomas E. Murray, member U.S. Atomic Energy Commission
1953	I. A. O'Shaughnessy, philanthropist
1954	Jefferson Caffery, diplomat
1955	George Meany, labor leader
1956	General Alfred M. Gruenther, soldier
1957	Clare Boothe Luce, diplomat
1958	Frank M. Folsom, industrialist
1959	Robert D. Murphy, diplomat
1960	George N. Shuster, educator
1961	John F. Kennedy, President of the United States
1962	Francis J. Braceland, M.D., psychiatrist
1963	Admiral George W. Anderson, Jr., Chief of Naval Operations
1964	Phyllis McGinley, poet
1965	Frederick D. Rossini, scientist
1966	Mr. and Mrs. Patrick F. Crowley, founders of The Christian Family Movement
1967	J. Peter Grace, industrialist
1968	Sargent Shriver, diplomat
1969	William J. Bennan, Jr., jurist and associate justice of the Supreme Court of the United States
1970	Dr. William B. Walsh, physician
1971	Walter Kerr, drama critic; and Jean Kerr, author
1972	Dorothy Day, founder of the Catholic Worker Movement, journalist and author
1973	Rev. John A. O'Brien, author
1974	James A. Farley, business executive and former Postmaster General
1975	Sr. Ann Ida Gannon, B.V.M., educator
1976	Paul Horgan, author
1977	Mike Mansfield, United States Senator
1978	Msgr. John Tracy Ellis, historian
1979	Helen Hayes, actress
1980	Thomas P. "Tip" O'Neill Jr., Speaker of the House
1981	Edmund S. Muskie, former United States Senator and secretary of state
1982	Cardinal John Francis Dearden, retired archbishop of Detroit
1983	Edmund A. and Evelyn Stephan, chairman emeritus of the University of Notre Dame's Board of Trustees and spouse
1984	John Noonan, legal scholar
1985	Guido Calabresi, dean of Yale University Law School
1986	Thomas P. and Mary Elizabeth Carney, chairman of the University of Notre Dame's Board of Trustees and spouse
1987	Rev. Theodore M. Hesburgh, C.S.C., educator
1988	Eunice Kennedy Shriver, humanitarian
1989	Walker Percy, novelist
1990	Sr. Thea Bowman, gospel singer and evangelist
1991	Corinne C. "Lindy" Boggs, former United States Congresswoman
1992	Daniel Patrick Moynihan, United States Senator
1993	Donald R. Keough, chairman emeritus of the University of Notre Dame's Board of Trustees
1994	Sidney Callahan, psychologist and author
1995	Cardinal Joseph Bernardin, archbishop of Chicago
1996	Sr. Helen Prejean, prison chaplain

MICHAEL GARVEY

LaFARGE, CHRISTOPHER (1862–1938)

Architect. Christopher Grant LaFarge was born on January 5, 1862, in Newport, Rhode Island, the son of John LaFarge, the famous painter. The younger LaFarge studied at the Massachusetts Institute of Technology for two years and began work with the architectural firm of Henry Hobson Richardson. In 1883 he began architectural work in his father's New York City office, and in 1886 cofounded an architectural firm with a classmate, George Lewis Heins. The firm gained a reputation by its design of the Cathedral of St. John the Divine in New York City. However, the original design of the cathedral was scrapped when Heins died, and the only remaining part of the original design that belonged to LaFarge is the apse. Upon Hein's death in 1907, LaFarge became affiliated with LaFarge and Morris from 1910 to 1915. From 1926 to 1931 he was a member of the firm of LaFarge, Warren and Clark, and from 1931 to 1938 with LaFarge and Son. LaFarge was responsible for designing churches (St. Paul the Apostle Church in New York City, St. Matthew's Church in Washington, D.C.); chapels at West Point (New York) and Wellesley College (Massachusetts); libraries (Packard Library in Salt Lake City, Utah); hospitals (the U.S. Naval Hospital in Brooklyn, New York); many of the New York City subway stations; and the New York Zoological Garden, which he helped found. LaFarge served as the director and vice president of the American Institute of Architects. He died on October 11, 1938, in Saunderstown, Rhode Island.

LISELLE DRAKE

LaFARGE, JOHN (1880–1963)

Jesuit priest and civil rights activist. John LaFarge was born in Newport, Rhode Island, on February 13, 1880. One of the most prominent Roman Catholic clergymen of his time, he achieved recognition as a major civil rights activist in the years before and after World War II, and as an editor of *America,* the Jesuit weekly of opinion and current events, until his death at age eighty-three. His own writings are voluminous, including eleven books and more than one thousand signed articles.

John LaFarge

Early Life

LaFarge was the last of the seven surviving children of John LaFarge, the well-known nineteenth-century American artist. His mother, Margaret Perry LaFarge, was a descendant of Benjamin Franklin and Oliver Hazard Perry, hero of the Battle of Lake Erie during the War of 1812. Other important names abound in the LaFarge family, including those of his brother C. Grant LaFarge, one of the original architects of St. John the Divine Cathedral in New York City, and author-nephews Christopher and Oliver LaFarge, the latter a Pulitzer Prize-winning novelist.

According to his autobiography, *The Manner Is Ordinary,* he decided to become a priest when he was only twelve years old. Until he entered Innsbruck University in Austria, however, he had a strictly secular formal education, attending public schools in Newport, then graduating from Harvard in 1901. He originally intended to become a secular priest, but before his ordination at Innsbruck in 1905, he revealed a long-concealed desire to become a Jesuit.

In the fall of 1905 he entered the Jesuit seminary, St. Andrew-on-Hudson, in Poughkeepsie, New York. Following two brief teaching assignments, one at Canisius College in Buffalo, New York, the other at Woodstock College in Maryland, he spent nearly a year as hospital and prison chaplain on Blackwell's Island (now called Roosevelt Island) in New York City's East River. There,

for the first time, he came into close contact with large numbers of blacks and poor people. It was one of the defining experiences of his life. "Innsbruck and Woodstock," he wrote in his autobiography, "were schools of knowledge, but Blackwell's Island was a school of life and death."

LaFarge and Civil Rights

In 1911 he began a fifteen-year career as a Jesuit missionary in Charles and St. Mary's Counties in southern Maryland, between the Potomac River and Chesapeake Bay. During those years he ministered to the religious, educational, social, and sometimes even economic needs of mostly poor white and black parishioners. And there he witnessed, and deplored, extreme racial prejudice against blacks. One of his principal accomplishments while in Maryland was the creation of the Cardinal Gibbons Institute, a vocational boarding school for young black men.

By the end of his stay in Maryland he had already achieved a reputation as an astute, highly intelligent writer on racial problems. In 1926 he was called to New York City to become an assistant editor of *America,* eventually rising to be editor in chief during World War II.

In 1934 he helped to found the Catholic Interracial Council of New York, currently headquartered at 16 West 36th Street in that city. After his death the council instituted annual awards, in his honor, given to individuals who excel in advancing civil rights.

In 1937 LaFarge published his most important work on civil rights, *Interracial Justice: A Study of the Catholic Doctrine of Race Relations.* In this book he equated racism with evil and sin. In 1938, while touring Europe for *America,* he met with Pope Pius XI. The Pope had read his book and was so impressed with his arguments and conclusions that he asked LaFarge to compose an encyclical on racism. During that summer he and two other Jesuits, one German, the other French, finished the encyclical. LaFarge personally delivered it to the Vatican in September. By then, however, Pius had become very ill. He died before the encyclical could be issued. His successor, Pius XII, decided against its publication. The text of this document can be found in the Father John LaFarge collection at Georgetown University in Washington, D.C.

In a very real sense LaFarge, on the issue of civil rights, was a man ahead of his times, one who acted upon a deep concern for blacks as early as the years before World War I. Some of the points he raised in *Interracial Justice* were the same as those proclaimed by the Supreme Court in its 1954 decision *Brown v. The Board of Education.* That part of his life should interest anyone studying the civil rights movement of more recent times.

Until near the end of his life, he strongly believed that gains in civil rights required close cooperation between whites and blacks. By the early 1960s, however, he wondered if blacks might make more progress through all-black organizations. One of his last efforts in the movement came in August 1963, when he participated in the "March on Washington," and heard Martin Luther King's "I have a dream" speech.

Among LaFarge's other interests were music (he was an accomplished organist), languages (he spoke fluently more than a dozen), liturgy (he helped found the Liturgical Arts Society), farm problems, and international affairs, especially after the outbreak of World War II. His last major work, *Reflections on Growing Old,* was published just a few months before his death.

LaFarge died peacefully and suddenly in his bedroom at America House on November 24, 1963. Cardinal Richard Cushing of Boston, a close friend and admirer of LaFarge, celebrated his funeral Mass at the Church of Saint Ignatius of Loyola in New York City.

See also AMERICA; CIVIL RIGHTS MOVEMENT AND CATHOLICS, THE.

Hecht, Robert. *An Unordinary Man: A Life of John LaFarge, S.J.* Metuchen, N.J.: Scarecrow Press, 1996.

LaFarge, John. *Interracial Justice: A Study of the Catholic Doctrine of Race Relations.* New York: America Press, 1937.

_____. *The Manner Is Ordinary.* New York: Harcourt Brace, 1954.

_____. *Reflections on Growing Old.* Garden City, N.Y.: Doubleday, 1963.

Southern, David. *John LaFarge and the Limits of Catholic Interracialism.* Baton Rouge: Louisiana State University Press, 1996.

ROBERT HECHT

LAFAYETTE, MARQUIS DE (1757–1834)

French soldier and statesman. Lafayette was born in Auvergne, France, on September 7, 1757. Born into a wealthy noble family, he lost both his parents at an early age and inherited his grandfather's fortune in 1770. He joined the King's Musketeers at age fourteen and three years later was a captain in the French army. After convincing the American agent in Paris to give him a commission as major general in the Continental Army, he left for America in 1777, where he joined the staff of General George Washington. He served with distinction throughout the war, being present at the battles of Brandywine, Monmouth, and Yorktown. In 1779 he temporarily returned to France to promote U.S. interests, where he played a major role in persuading the king to lend his full support to the colonists' cause and acted as intermediary between U.S. and French commanders for the remainder of the war.

He returned to France after the war as a national hero and assumed a visible role in the events leading up to the French Revolution as a member of the Assembly of Notables and Estates General, where he proposed the Declaration of the Rights of Man and of the Citizen and organized the National Guard, in which he served as commander. He supported liberal reforms, but remained loyal to the monarch and was condemned as a traitor by the radical Jacobins in 1792. He left the country but returned in 1797, where he lived in retirement until the restoration of the Bourbons in 1814, when he once again assumed a public role. He died in Paris on May 20, 1834.

Bernier, Olivier. *Lafayette, Hero of Two Worlds.* New York, 1983.

TRICIA T. PYNE

LAFORTUNE, BELLARMINE (1869–1947)

Jesuit missionary. The Iñupiat Inuit (Eskimos) of Alaska's Seward Peninsula area called him *ataatazuuraq,* "the little Father." This referred to his short stature, but also carried overtones of affection. He soon learned to speak their language fluently and, pioneer missionary that he was, established numerous missions among them. During his active apostolate of forty-four years, he never once left the Seward Peninsula area.

Lafortune was born in Saint-Roch-de-l'Achigan near Montreal on December 11, 1869. He entered the Jesuit novitiate at Sault-au-Récollet on July 30, 1890. After the two-year novitiate and four years devoted to the study of the humanities, sciences, and philosophy, he taught the sciences at the Collège de Saint-Boniface in Winnipeg for two years. He spent the year 1898–99 studying higher mathematics at the Sorbonne in Paris. On July 27, 1902, after three years of theological studies, he was ordained a priest. Following the year of tertianship, made at Poughkeepsie, New York, he sailed for Alaska, never to see his native land again. (He became a U.S. citizen on September 11, 1918.) On July 16, 1903, he landed in Nome, Alaska, to take "the charge of the Eskimos."

Though the whites in Nome and in the outlying mining camps took much of his time during his first years in Alaska, Lafortune still made the evangelization of the Seward Peninsula Inuit his primary concern. In 1905 he built a combination chapel-workshop for the Nome Inuit. Even before establishing missions at widely scattered Inuit settlements, he brought into the Church many of those Inuit. This he was able to do in Nome itself, where during the summer many of them came to work, to trade, to buy provisions. He founded missions in places like Teller, Sinuk, Marys Igloo, Wales, Pilgrim Springs, and on Little Diomede Island. For the most part he served these out of Nome.

The name of Lafortune, however, is most intimately connected with that of the King Islanders. By the time he was able to visit their island home for the first time, in June 1916, he had brought almost all of them into the Catholic fold. This he did during their summer sojourns in Nome. It was not until 1929 that he was able to build a mission on the island and to overwinter there. He died, after a stroke on October 22, 1947.

LOUIS L. RENNER, S.J.

LAMBERT, JAMES (1838–1906)

Editor, civic leader, and lay Catholic. James William Lambert was born in New York State on June 2, 1838, the son of John Lambert and Mary O'Sullivan, Irish immigrants. Shortly afterwards, the family moved to Natchez, Mississippi. James Lambert served as assistant postmaster before the Civil War. He entered the Confederate army in April 1861; rose from private to captain; took part in numerous battles including Fredericksburg, Chancellorsville, and Gettysburg; was twice captured and spent the last ten months of the war as a prisoner at Fort Delaware. Lambert returned to Natchez where he was elected county assessor (1866–70), city alderman (1878–81), and later county sheriff (1881–96). In 1866 he became part owner of the Natchez *Democrat,* and sole owner in 1879; the newspaper became a major source of Southern Catholic news and commentary for almost a century.

Lambert married Rose Kelly in 1877; their son, James K., continued his father's work as editor and civic leader. Contemporaries praised Lambert as a model Christian husband and father. Lambert devoted himself to attracting railroads, new capital, and new industry to Natchez and freely shared his shrewd business acumen with others. His generosity was proverbial; a colleague recalled that Lambert counted as a loss each day "in which he had not performed a good deed for some one or some purpose." He served on numerous business and civic boards including those of the Natchez Charity Hospital and Jefferson Military College.

In 1900 James Lambert inaugurated the Poor Children's Christmas Tree to gather and distribute gifts to needy children, a tradition his family still continues. Lambert was a close associate and advisor of Natchez's bishops and rectors for forty years. He was a strong supporter of education, an active member of the Knights of Columbus, and a major participant in major parish functions.

James Lambert died in Natchez on December 17, 1906. A group of black Natchezians publicly paid tribute to him as "a friend to the friendless." At a meeting of Mississippi Freemasons in Natchez in February 1907, James Lambert was publicly honored as "a man of the largest intelligence, broad-minded, liberal in his views, although tenacious in his devotion to his own religious belief; he freely accorded to all others that freedom of thought, choice and affiliation that he demanded for himself, which is a distinguishing characteristic of all men who are really and truly great."

Natchez *Democrat,* 1866–1907.

Nolan, Charles E. *St. Mary's of Natchez: The History of a Southern Catholic Congregation, 1716–1988.* Natchez, 1992.
Tributes on the Life and Character of James William Lambert by Friends and Associations. Natchez, 1907.

CHARLES E. NOLAN

LAMBERT, LOUIS ALOYSIUS (1835–1910)

Priest, journalist. Lambert was born in Charleroi, Pennsylvania, on April 13, 1835. He was educated at St. Vincent College, Latrobe, Pennsylvania, and at the St. Louis archdiocesan seminary, Carondelet, Missouri. He was ordained a priest of the Diocese of Alton, Illinois, on February 11, 1859. Fr. Lambert did pastoral work at Alton, Shawneetown, and Cairo, Illinois, 1859–68, except for a term (1861–62) as a Civil War battlefield chaplain, with the 18th Illinois Infantry Volunteers.

Though inept at parish administration, Lambert had a brilliant mind and was a voracious and discerning reader in philosophy, theology, and many other fields. Thinking he might feel more at home in a religious community, he spent 1868–69 with the Paulists in New York City, teaching their novices philosophy and moral theology. In 1869, however, he decided not to join the community, and was incardinated into the new Diocese of Rochester, New York, by its founder, Bishop Bernard J. McQuaid. There he held village pastorates at Waterloo, New York (1869–88), and Scottsville, New York (1890–1910).

The Publicist

At Waterloo he launched his literary career, founding and editing a diocesan weekly, *The Catholic Times,* 1877–80. Later on, still from his rectory study, he founded and edited *The Catholic Times* of Philadelphia (1892–94). From 1895 until his death he was editor in chief of the prestigious independent weekly, *The Freeman's Journal* of New York City. Journalism was plainly his forte. While religion was his favorite topic, his broad intellectual interest enabled him to discourse on many subjects, with crisp logic and winning clarity.

In general, Lambert exhibited "broad views and abounding charity," even in debate, for which he had a flair; but when personally goaded he could strike back without mercy. Bishop McQuaid, who admired his priest's literary skills, learned that painfully when, on concluding that the editor was becoming factious, he tried to edge him out of the diocese. A bitter quarrel ensued, resolved only when the bishop lay dying. Lambert won on points, partly by unfair use of his columns, spurred on by Archbishop John Ireland, Bishop McQuaid's leading adversary.

Hammer of Infidels

The author's positive accomplishments far outweighed the negative. One of his several religious books was a translation of Paul Merz's *Thesaurus Biblicus,* the first Catholic concordance to be published in the U.S.A. (Waterloo, 1880). What brought him international attention, however, was his writings against free thought. His *Notes on Ingersoll* (Buffalo, 1883) so toppled the arguments of the popular but shallow Col. Robert Green Ingersoll (1833–99) that this "Great Agnostic" never replied. *Notes* went into many printings, and he followed it with the more scholarly *Tactics of Infidels* (Buffalo, 1887). The writer received no royalties from his "best sellers," but money meant little to him. He did come to be a popular figure on the lecture circuit.

The recompense he enjoyed was fame, at home and abroad. Catholics proposed this "American Newman" for the cardinalate, and in 1892 the University of Notre Dame bestowed on him an LL.D. Orthodox Protestants welcomed his help in their own campaign against agnosticism. His attractive public image (partly authentic, partly retouched) won him a world of friends. They admired him as a venerable cleric and sterling citizen, simple and accessible despite his "greatness."

While the parameters have changed since Lambert vs. Ingersoll in the contest with agnosticism, Louis A. Lambert still deserves attention as a secular priest of high culture in our immigrant Church, and as the first American Catholic thinker to exert an influence outside his own religious communion. He died in Newfoundland, New Jersey, on September 25, 1910.

McNamara, R. F. *The Diocese of Rochester, 1868–1968.* Rochester, N.Y., 1968.
Shuster, G. N. *Dictionary of American Biography.* 10:557–59.
Zwierlein, F. J. *Life and Letters of Bishop McQuaid.* 3 vols. Louvain and Rome, 1925–27.
____. *The Letters of Archbishop Corrigan to Bishop McQuaid.* Rochester, N.Y., 1946.

ROBERT F. McNAMARA

LAMY, JOHN BAPTIST (1814–88)

Archbishop of Santa Fe. Jean Baptist Lamy was born at Lempdes, in the Diocese of Clermont, France, on October 11, 1814, the son of Jean Lamy, a prosperous peasant, and Marie Dié (or Drynat). He was educated at the seminary of Clermont-Ferrand, in which city he was ordained on December 22, 1838. Assigned to a parish in his native diocese, he and his friend Joseph Projectus Machebeuf responded eagerly the following year to an appeal of Bishop John Baptist Purcell of Cincinnati, Ohio, to work in that diocese. With but a halting command of English Lamy began his American labors at Sapp's Settlement (Danville), Ohio. From there he established a number of missions for Americans, Irish, and Germans, erecting churches for most of these incipient parishes. In 1847 he was sent to St.

John B. Lamy

Mary's Church in Covington, Kentucky, where as pastor he was chosen by the American bishops as vicar apostolic of New Mexico, one of the territories recently acquired by the Mexican War. On November 24, 1850, he was ordained titular bishop of Agathonica in St. Peter's Cathedral in Cincinnati by Bishop Martin John Spalding of Louisville.

Vicar Apostolic of New Mexico

Lamy traveled to New Mexico by way of New Orleans and San Antonio, Texas, the longer but less dangerous route, to begin his second and more demanding cultural adjustment. A shipwreck and illness prevented his reaching Santa Fe until August, 1851, but allowed Fr. Machebeuf, who had agreed to be his vicar, to catch up with him. When Padre Juan Felipe Ortiz, the rural dean and former vicar of the bishop of Durango, questioned the new bishop's authority, Lamy made the eight-hundred-mile journey to Durango, where Bishop José Antonio Zurbiría wrote a letter enjoining his former clergy to submit to Lamy's authority. He persuaded Lamy, however, to recognize his own jurisdiction over certain villages in the area of El Paso, a claim that would become a bone of contention throughout Lamy's episcopacy.

The new vicariate, including not only New Mexico and Arizona but also parts of Colorado and Nevada, would be further enlarged in 1853 by the Gadsden Purchase. It counted by far the greatest number of Catholics in the West, some 68,000 according to Lamy's reckoning, mostly Hispanos but some 8,000 Pueblo natives and a handful of Americans. Although there were some sixty-five churches or chapels, there were only nine active priests, and the morals of several of them were notorious. From the start Lamy encountered hostility from the leaders of the native clergy, not only Ortiz but also José Manuel Gallegos, pastor of Albuquerque, and the formidable Antonio José Martínez, pastor of Taos, who had accomplished much but was unable to surrender power gladly. A running battle waged by the insurgents ended in the suspension of Ortiz and Gallegos and in 1856 the excommunication of Martínez and another of the disaffected priests.

The clash was in part a result of what the insurgents perceived as an attack on their way of life, their culture. In his early pastorals Lamy proscribed not only the exorbitant fees they charged but also the expenditure of parish funds for theatricals, dances, or "other profane diversions" popular with the Hispanos. Devoted to the Romanesque art and architecture of his native Auvergne, Lamy had little appreciation of adobe churches or the primitive images in them crafted by the *santeros.* He attempted not only to curtail the activities of the *penitentes,* a pious fraternity given to flagellation, but also to modify the *entriega,* a folk wedding. In his early years in Santa Fe he replaced many of the native clergy with French priests.

First Bishop of Santa Fe

Lamy badly needed help. To his native Auvergne especially he turned for priests and seminarians. Fifteen years after his arrival, thirty-one of the fifty-one members of the clergy in his diocese were from France and six more from other parts of Europe. He was also successful in recruiting religious. On his way back from the First Plenary Council of Baltimore, which created for him the Diocese of Santa Fe, he induced four Sisters of Loretto to return with him in 1853. In 1858 he welcomed four Christian Brothers from France to open a boys' academy, which would become St. Michael's College. In 1865 he recruited four Sisters of Charity of Cincinnati to begin the first Catholic hospital and orphanage in the Southwest. Others of their orders would join these pioneering religious. By January 1867 Lamy could report in Rome itself that the Lorettines conducted five schools and a novitiate, the Christian Brothers, three schools, and the Sisters of Charity, one school in addition to the hospital and orphanage. That same year he persuaded the Neapolitan Jesuits to send three priests and two brothers, who would go to Albuquerque and Las Vegas, New Mexico, where they would begin a Spanish newspaper in 1875 and a college in 1877.

In his report to Rome in 1867 Lamy also revealed that there were now 135 churches and chapels to serve 110,000 Hispanos and 15,000 Pueblo natives in New Mexico, 8,000 Mexicans and Americans in Colorado, and 7,000 Mexicans and native peoples in Arizona. To the Diocese of Santa Fe, created July 29, 1853, had been entrusted in 1860 all of Colorado. To the growing number of miners

and Mexicans there Lamy sent Machebeuf and a young French priest. To Arizona, which Machebeuf had served for a time, he sent another native of the Auvergne, John Baptiste Salpointe. The creation in 1868 of vicariates apostolic for the territories of Colorado and Arizona, with Machebeuf and Salpointe their respective bishops, relieved Lamy of the care of his most distant charges.

Lamy, however, throve on travel. He covered perhaps more miles than any other American bishop in the West, almost always on horseback. In addition to his many visitations in New Mexico, Colorado, and Arizona, he traveled three times to Europe as a beggar and once to attend the Vatican Council (leaving Rome before the vote on papal infallibility was taken). Three times he went to Baltimore for plenary councils, twice deep into Mexico, and once across the Southwestern deserts to Los Angeles. Most of the journeys were arduous and dangerous, especially those along the Santa Fe Trail, where in 1867 he was reported to have been killed by the Native Americans in one of their fiercest attacks on its caravans. He rarely, however, visited the lawless cattle country of southern New Mexico.

Archbishop of Santa Fe

In 1869 Lamy began the imposing Romanesque cathedral of St. Francis of Assisi, which was still unfinished at his death. On February 12, 1875, Santa Fe was made an archdiocese with Lamy its archbishop and Machebeuf and Salpointe his suffragans. Salpointe would become Lamy's coadjutor April 22, 1884, and the second archbishop of Santa Fe upon Lamy's retirement the following year. Machebeuf would be created bishop of Denver six months before Lamy's death on February 13, 1888. After his appointment as titular archbishop of Cyzicus on August 18, 1885, Lamy enjoyed a peaceful retirement at the Bishop's Lodge north of the see city puttering in his garden. A memorial resolution was passed by the territorial legislature of New Mexico soon after his death that gave evidence of the esteem in which Lamy was held by Catholics, Protestants, and Jews for the contributions he had made to the civic and cultural improvement of the territory.

In her fictional tribute to Lamy in *Death Comes for the Archbishop* (1927), Willa Cather put her finger perhaps on the secret of his success when she characterized such French missionaries as having "a sense of proportion and rational adjustment" (7). While criticized by later historians for his role in having supplanted one culture (Hispanic) with another (Gallic), in actuality Lamy was a transitional bishop, adjusting a local church to the universal Church of the nineteenth century. The simplicity, dedication, piety, austerity, and dignity of this tall, spare prelate were admired by the great majority of his Spanish-speaking subjects, who acquiesced with little complaint in the discipline he imposed upon them. While Lamy had little appreciation of the *santos*, he never ordered them removed from the churches. And he bemoaned the fate that must inevitably overtake his Hispanic charges with the influx of Americans.

Chavez, Fray Angelico. *Archives of the Archdiocese of Santa Fe.* Washington, D.C., 1957.

____. *My Penitente Land: Reflections on Spanish New Mexico.* Albuquerque, 1974.

De Aragon, Ray John. *Padre Martinez and Bishop Lamy.* Las Vegas, N.M., 1978.

Horgan, Paul. *Lamy of Santa Fe: His Life and Times.* New York, 1975.

Warner, Louis H. *Archbishop Lamy: An Epoch Maker.* Santa Fe, 1936.

THOMAS W. SPALDING

LANE, JOSEPH (1801–91)

U.S. Senator. Bright, aggressive, egotistical, and ambitious, Joseph Lane was born in 1801 in North Carolina. He entered politics in Indiana, served in the legislature, and led a company of Indiana Volunteers in the Mexican War. In 1849, President Polk, just before he left office, appointed him territorial governor of the newly organized Oregon Territory. The appointment was short-lived, but he became a leader of the state Democratic Party and so impressed Oregonians that in 1851 they elected him their delegate to Congress, where he served until 1859 when Oregon became a state and Oregonians chose him to be one of their first two senators.

As the Civil War approached, Lane supported Southern claims with regard to slavery, and when the Democratic Party split in 1860, he became vice-presidential candidate on the Southern Democratic ticket. He approved the South's secession, but Oregon supported the Union. Repudiated by Oregon Democrats, he spent the rest of his life in semi-retirement near Roseburg, Oregon.

In 1867 he was received into the Catholic Church by Archbishop Francis N. Blanchet, with whom he had begun a friendship when he first came to Oregon. Subsequently his wife, two sons, and a daughter were also baptized. It is not clear if he remained faithful, since eventually he rejoined the Masons, and when he died in 1891, he was buried (at his request) in the Masonic cemetery in Roseburg without a religious service.

He was the most prominent Oregonian of that period to embrace Catholicism, and his grandson, Arthur Lane, became the first native Oregonian to be ordained a priest.

Dodds, Gordon B., *Oregon, A Bicentennial History.* New York: W. W. Norton & Company, Inc., 1977.

Hendrickson, James E. *Joe Lane of Oregon, Machine Politics and the Sectional Crisis, 1849–1861.* New Haven: Yale University Press, 1967.

Kelly, M. Margaret Jean, S.N.J.M. *The Career of Joseph Lane, Frontier Politician.* Washington, D.C.: The Catholic University of America, 1942.

Schoenberg, Wilfred P., S.J. *A History of the Catholic Church in the Pacific Northwest, 1743–1983.* Washington, D.C.: The Pastoral Press, 1987.

LILLIAN A. PEREYRA

LANGE, MARY ELIZABETH (1784–1882)

Founder and first superior of the Oblate Sisters of Providence of Baltimore, Maryland, the oldest community of women religious of African American descent in the United States. Born around 1784 in Saint Domingue to a free family of color and one possessed of some means, she was educated in France, and fled to the United States during the 1793 revolution in Haiti, landing in Baltimore. With the support, encouragement, and spiritual direction of the Sulpician, Fr. James Hector Joubert, also a refugee from Saint Domingue, Mary Elizabeth Lange, together with Marie Balas, Rosine Boegue, and Almaide Duchemin resolved to form a congregation of women religious for "gens de couleur."

Mary Elizabeth Lange

Formal ecclesiastical sanction of the idea was given on June 17, 1828, when Archbishop James Whitfield of Baltimore, having studied the written proposal (and quoting Pope Paul III's words of approval of the Jesuit constitutions in 1540), declared: "The finger of God is here!" The sisters' canonical novitiate began on June 24, 1828. With

St. Frances of Rome, St. Joseph, and the Blessed Virgin Mary as patrons, the sisters professed the traditional vows of poverty, chastity, and obedience on July 2, 1829, subsequently recognized as the official date of the foundation. (In 1845 Sr. Marie Therese Duchemin withdrew from the Oblate Congregation and founded the Sisters, Servants of the Immaculate Heart of Mary.) Fr. Joubert had already appointed Mary Elizabeth Lange as mother superior of the infant community on June 24, 1829. At that time the school had eleven boarders and seven day scholars.

Mother Mary Lange's goal was "to show the Face of Providence to the world." The steady increase of religious vocations and of boarding students necessitated larger accommodations, and after several moves, the sisters settled at 501 East Chase Street, Baltimore, their fourth motherhouse. In addition to staffing the school, the sisters did fine needlework for liturgical vestments and for wealthy laypeople, nursed victims of the cholera epidemic at the Baltimore City Almshouse in 1832, assumed responsibility for domestic service at (the Sulpician) St. Mary's Seminary in 1835, and, in 1875, accepted a large group of unwanted colored orphans from New York's St. Vincent's Foundling Asylum.

In the middle decades of the nineteenth century, Mother Mary Lange and her Oblate Sisters faced formidable obstacles. The legal status of free blacks was uncertain in a racist society. The Dred Scott Decision of 1857 (the majority opinion written by the Catholic Chief Justice Roger B. Taney) declared that slaves did not possess rights of citizenship and avoided the issue of free persons of color. In spite of such obstacles as the anti-Catholic riots that sporadically swept Baltimore, and the attack by nativist Know-Nothings on St. Joseph's School for Boys in 1856, and the general ecclesiastical skepticism and indifference to the Negro (the hierarchy being preoccupied with a dire shortage of priests during a period of enormous Irish and German immigration), Lange persevered in her work of teaching and evangelization. On the other hand, during the First Provincial Council of Baltimore in October 1829, four of the five prelates attending the council visited the young Oblate community. Mother Mary Lange also won the enthusiastic support of the Redemptorist provincial, Fr. John Nepomucene Neumann (later bishop and saint), during a crisis in the Oblate community in the 1840s. Neumann acted as confessor for the sisters and provided his priests for retreats and spiritual direction.

Mother Mary Lange died at the Oblate motherhouse on February 3, 1882. An account of her death was given in the *Catholic Mirror*, February 4, 1882. In 1995 her Cause for Beatification was pending before the Sacred Congregation for the Causes of Saints.

See also AFRICAN AMERICAN CATHOLICS.

Boston, Mary Petra, O.S.P. *Blossoms Gathered from Many Branches.* St. Louis: Oblate Sisters of Providence, 1914.

Curley, Michael J., C.Ss.R. *Venerable John Neumann, C.Ss.R.* New York: Crusader Press, 1952.

Lannon, Maria M. *Response to Love.* Washington, D.C., 1992.

Sherwood, Grace H. *Oblates One Hundred and One Years.* New York: Macmillan, 1931.

M. REPARATA CLARKE, O.S.P.

LA SALLE, ROBERT CAVELIER (1643–87)

Explorer. La Salle was born in Rouen, France, in November 1643, to Jean Cavelier and Catherine Geest. His father was a burgher of Rouen, and the title "La Salle" was derived from the family's seigniory near Rouen. After studying at the Jesuit college in Rouen, La Salle entered the Society of Jesus after much prodding by his father. The disciplined life of the society ran contrary to La Salle's free spirit and wanderlust, and after his father's death, he asked to be dispensed from his vows. Since he lost all claim to any inheritance once he became a Jesuit, La Salle was dependent upon the generosity of his family for his livelihood after his departure from religious life.

In 1666 La Salle went to New France where his brother, a Sulpician, had already ventured. He received a tract of land from his brother's community, began farming it, and started trading with the local people. After talking with some Iroquois visitors about a great river to the west, La Salle sold his property and joined two Sulpician missionaries who were making their way westward. This band visited regions around Lake Ontario, and after the priests decided to change plans and head to the northwest, La Salle went his own way and may have found the Ohio River, which the Iroquois had told him led to the "great waters." He eventually returned to Quebec and befriended the new French governor, Frontenac. The governor sent him to Paris to ask the king for a monopoly on fur trading. La Salle was successful and returned from France with Louis Hennepin, a Franciscan priest, who later accompanied La Salle on some of his explorations. When he returned in 1678, he began exploring the Great Lakes regions while conducting fur trade along with his lifelong lieutenant, Tonty.

La Salle had grand designs for France and hoped to establish a French empire in the lands drained by the Great Lakes and the West. In 1679 La Salle launched the *Griffon,* which was the first European vessel built and launched above Niagara Falls. He eventually made his way down the Illinois River to Lake Peoria and built Fort Crèvecoeur. Despite some setbacks, in 1682 La Salle and Tonty began to explore the Mississippi and entered the Gulf of Mexico on April 9, 1682. He claimed the whole Mississippi River and its surrounding regions for the king of France. In 1682 Frontenac was replaced by Antoine Lefebre as governor, and with this appointment La Salle lost his favored position. He lost his command of the fort in the Illinois region and was called to return to Quebec to respond to some alleged crimes. La Salle ignored the new governor's order and returned to France to a great welcome. After hearing La Salle wax eloquent about his adventures, King Louis XIV restored him to his former status and outfitted him for a new journey to colonize the mouth of the Mississippi. La Salle was unsuccessful in this venture and landed on the Texas coast instead of his desired destination. Abandoned by the seamen who had brought them to the Gulf Coast, La Salle and his colonists tried to make their way by foot to the Mississippi. Some of his company mutinied, and La Salle was murdered on March 19, 1687, by his own men. Although he had high hopes for his native France, La Salle was unable to secure a lasting foothold for his country outside of Quebec.

ANTHONY D. ANDREASSI

LA SALLE UNIVERSITY

La Salle's identity and heritage have always been closely associated with that of the religious teaching congregation of the Brothers of the Christian Schools (De La Salle Christian Brothers). Its name honors the innovative St. John Baptist de la Salle, the Frenchman who founded the Christian Brothers in the early 1680s. Pope Pius XII proclaimed him "Patron of all teachers" in 1950.

La Salle College was chartered midway through the Civil War (1863). Its founders consisted of a partnership of Christian Brothers, diocesan priests, and laity. Bishop James F. Wood, fifth bishop of Philadelphia, lent his personal support to provide young men with more opportunities in higher learning. In the history of America's colleges, such a collaborative concept represented a new approach. German-born Br. Teliow is identified as La Salle's first president.

Enrollment quickly outgrew the spatial limits of the original building. La Salle moved sequentially to two Philadelphia sites before settling in 1930 at its current northwest Philadelphia location, near historic Germantown. It thereby occupied a portion of the original "Belfield" estate, once home of Charles Willson Peale.

La Salle survived the Great Depression largely because of administrative resourcefulness and the growth of La Salle College High School, which shared the campus. World War II depleted the enrollment to just ninety college students, but returning veterans reinvigorated La Salle. In 1946 La Salle established one of the first Evening Divisions in the East to confer baccalaureate degrees. The Evening Division became coeducational in 1967, followed by the Day Division in 1970. La Salle's hallmark has been continuing innovative outreach to the educational needs of Philadelphia's working- and middle-class populations.

See also CATHOLIC UNIVERSITIES AND COLLEGES.

JOSEPH GRABENSTEIN, F.S.C.

LATHROP, MARY ALPHONSA/ROSE HAWTHORNE (1851–1926)

Foundress of the Congregation of St. Rose of Lima (Servants of Relief for Incurable Cancer). Rose Hawthorne was born in Lenox, Massachusetts, on May 20, 1851. She established this Dominican congregation in New York City in 1900 and remained mother general until she died. The society operates institutions for care of the poor suffering from incurable cancer. In 1995 the ninety-six members were operating seven hospitals located in Rosary Hill, New York; Manhattan, New York; Philadelphia, Pennsylvania; Fall River, Massachusetts; Atlanta, Georgia; St. Paul, Minnesota; and Cleveland, Ohio. These sisters have provided dignity and loving care for over 100,000 unfortunate victims of cancer since Rose Hawthorne Lathrop's first patient in 1896.

Rose H. (Mother Alphonsa) Lathrop

Early Life

Her life had two distinct parts: first, as the much-loved youngest child of Nathaniel and Sophia Hawthorne, wife of George Lathrop, mother, author, Catholic convert and lecturer; second, as inspired minister to the poor with terminal cancer, initially as a laywoman, then as foundress and leader of a religious community devoted to this apostolate.

As the daughter of Nathaniel and Sophia Peabody Hawthorne, Rose was exposed to the literary intelligentsia of the day. The Wayside, the Hawthorne home in Concord,

Massachusetts, was a familiar setting for visits by such notables as Ralph Waldo Emerson, Henry Thoreau, Orestes Brownson, Louisa Alcott, and Peabody relatives. Sophia's sister Elizabeth is credited with founding the kindergarten movement in the United States while her other sister, Mary, was the wife and helpmate of Horace Mann, the "Father of the American Public School." Rose always assumed that she would have a literary career.

In 1853 Nathaniel moved the family to England where he acted as American Consul in Liverpool. One day while visiting a workhouse for sick destitute children, an awful-looking, sickly little child followed him about and finally placed itself in front of him in a mute appeal for affection. Despite his revulsion, Nathaniel picked up the child and held it tenderly, something he recounted in a fictional account in his journal that Sophia later admitted was Nathaniel himself. Rose always remembered the incident and loved her father even more for his compassion, considering his account the most beautiful he ever wrote. While on an extended visit to Italy, both Nathaniel and Sophia underwent a change in their Unitarian views about Catholicism, so much so that he was later accused of incorporating Catholic proclivities into his writings. However, neither Hawthorne converted to Catholicism.

After Nathaniel's death in 1864, Sophia sold the Wayside and moved the family to Dresden, Germany, where Rose studied painting and music. There she met her future husband, George Lathrop, whose family was touring Europe. Sophia moved her family to London in 1871, where she soon died. Rose and George married in London and returned to the United States to begin their literary careers. Over the years each experienced off-and-on success. Their only child, Francis, died at age five. The marriage became tenuous. In 1891 both converted to Catholicism, an action that occasioned considerable comment, positive and negative, in literary circles, forcing George to write and publish an *apologia.*

After much marital strain, generally attributed to George's drinking, and several trial separations, Rose left George permanently in 1895 with the approval of her spiritual advisor. She then wrote and published her final literary effort, *Some Memories of Hawthorne,* widely acclaimed as her best product. This marked the end of the first part of her life.

Care of Poor Cancer Patients

The second part began when a priest friend described Blackwell's Island, a miserable warehouse in New York City for housing the poor dying of cancer. He recounted the smells and scenes of despair, agony, and sadness reflected in the faces of the dying. This hit Rose like a bombshell. As she later wrote, "A fire was then lighted in my heart where it still burns. . . ." She determined to devote herself to aiding such victims. Her first move was to spend three months studying the treatment of cancer patients at New York City Cancer Hospital. She then rented a small flat on the Lower East Side, visited poor homes with cancer patients, and let it be known that her flat was open to any without available proper care. Her first boarder was a Mrs. Watson whose cantankerous behavior taught Rose not to expect gratitude except from God. With others seeking help, Rose turned to writing articles and paid advertisements seeking contributions and helpers to join her in this work of mercy. At that time it was commonly believed that cancer was contagious, a complicating factor in seeking helpers.

Rose's first permanent companion was Alice Huber, a beautiful young Kentucky woman who later helped establish the congregation, taking the religious name of Sr. Mary Rose. Early in 1897 Rose and Alice moved to a larger flat where more patients could be accommodated. Despite shortage of funds, hostility from neighbors, and overpowering needs of the sick, the two women persevered with hands-on care. George died on April 19, 1897, adding to Rose's losses of Nathaniel, Sophia, her sister Una, and child Francis. George's death, however, opened the door for Rose's latent desire to become a religious.

Rose, Alice, and Cecelia Cochrane (later Sr. Mary Magdalen) began the road to full religious life by cutting their hair and donning a severe outfit. Their spiritual advisor and mentor, Dominican priest Clement M. Thuente, encouraged a visit to Archbishop Michael Corrigan. He, however, questioned the viability of the group and withheld approbation for several years. Meanwhile, the ever-increasing patient load caused them once again to move to larger quarters. In 1899 Archbishop Corrigan finally approved their entry into religious life as tertiaries of the Dominican Order. In December 1900, the tiny community donned the full Dominican habit and became an official religious congregation.

The final move for Mother Alphonsa Lathrop was to a large building in Rosary Hill, New York, still the site of their motherhouse. She died peacefully in her sleep in Hawthorne, New York, on July 9, 1926, at age seventy-five, prior to the completion of their new fireproof hospital, a dream she had cherished and furthered, finally completed in 1926. The Hawthorne name will live on for more than literary accomplishments.

See also DOMINICANS (O.P.).

Dehey, Elinor Tong. *Religious Orders of Women in the United States.* Hammond, Ind.: W. B. Conkey Company, 1930.

Stewart, George C., Jr. *Marvels of Charity: History of American Sisters and Nuns.* Huntington, Ind.: Our Sunday Visitor Publishing Co., 1994.

Valenti, Patricia Dunlavy. *To Myself a Stranger: A Biography of Rose Hawthorne Lathrop*. Baton Rouge: Louisiana State University Press, 1991.

GEORGE C. STEWART

LAVANOUX, MAURICE (1894–1974)

Architect, liturgist. Maurice Lavanoux, an architect who was trained in Canada and France as well as in his native United States, led a movement to improve the quality of American ecclesiastical art and architecture. Lavanoux wrote on Church art and lectured in the United States and Canada. He was one of the founders of the Liturgical Arts Society in 1928 and served as its secretary. He also launched the *Liturgical Arts Quarterly* in 1932 and was its editor until it was discontinued in 1972 due to lack of funds. After his retirement from the *Quarterly*, he became editor of *Stained Glass* magazine and worked with the Contemporary Christian Art Gallery in New York City.

He was born in New York City on June 10, 1894, and was educated at Mt. St. Louis Institute, Montreal, from 1906 until 1911; Columbia University Extension from 1912 until 1917, and the Atelier Hirons, New York City, from 1915 to 1917.

After serving first as an interpreter for the American army in France from 1917 to 1918 and then as a lieutenant in the French army in 1919, Lavanoux continued his studies at the Atelier Laloux in Paris.

From 1920 until the mid-1930s he worked as a draftsman and researcher for Gustave E. Steinback in New York, and for Maginnis and Walsh in Boston. He was made a Knight of Commander of St. Gregory in 1967, and received an honorary citation of membership from the American Institute of Architects in 1966. Lavanoux died on October 21, 1974, in New York City.

See also LITURGICAL MOVEMENT IN AMERICA, THE.

STEPHENIE OVERMAN

LAWRENCE, DAVID (1889–1966)

Mayor of Pittsburgh, governor of Pennsylvania. David Leo Lawrence was born in Pittsburgh, Pennsylvania, on June 18, 1889. Reared in a middle-class family and the son of a teamster, he began a lifelong career in politics at an early age. In 1920 he was chairman of the Allegheny County Democratic Organization.

He went on to hold major political offices in the state, including Collector of Internal Revenue for Western Pennsylvania (1933–34) and secretary of the Commonwealth of Pennsylvania (1935–38). Although he was accused several times of using his position to negotiate contracts and solicit campaign contributions from state employees, he was acquitted each time.

From 1945 to 1957 Lawrence was elected mayor of Pittsburgh four times. The urban renewal campaign he undertook during those years focused a national spotlight on the city, which resulted in *Fortune* magazine in 1958 naming Pittsburgh one of the eight best-governed cities.

Lawrence was influential in national politics, engineering the nomination of Harry S. Truman for vice president in 1940 and assisting with the nomination of John Fitzgerald Kennedy in 1960 for president on the Democratic ticket. He also served as president of the U.S. Conference of Mayors (1950–52).

In 1958 he was the first Catholic elected governor of Pennsylvania. When his term expired in 1963, Lawrence continued his career in politics by resuming leadership of the state's Democratic Party, a post he held until his death in Pittsburgh on November 21, 1966.

MARIANNA McLOUGHLIN

LEADERSHIP CONFERENCE OF WOMEN RELIGIOUS, THE

The Leadership Conference of Women Religious (LCWR) is a national organization of the chief officers of Roman Catholic religious communities of women in the United States. Founded in 1956 as the Conference of Major Superiors of Women (CMSW), LCWR was canonically established in 1959 and the initial statutes were approved by the Congregation for Religious in 1962.

In its earliest years, CMSW focused almost completely on matters directly affecting its own membership or the religious life of women. However, the Second Vatican Council propelled the CMSW in new directions, in response to the mandate of the Church for renewal. In 1968 the conference sponsored the National Sisters Survey, directed by sociologist Marie Augusta Neal, S.N.D. The survey, a total population study of American sisters, was designed to provide individual congregations with data about their internal resources and the readiness of their members for change. It also generated a historic first—a comprehensive, empirical national picture of women's communities as a group.

In September 1971 the national assembly ratified new bylaws and changed the name of the conference to the current Leadership Conference of Women Religious. The bylaws provided for a rearticulated purpose statement, universal suffrage in the election of national officers, and an expansion in the number of regions. The bylaws determined LCWR's current organizational structure: a collaborative presidency, composed of the president, the vice president, and the past president; an executive committee; and a national board, composed of LCWR's officers and fifteen regional chairpersons.

In 1976 the conference engaged in a major goal-setting process and framed four priorities, which have continued to guide the work of the conference: articulation of the contemporary theology of religious life, education for justice leading to systemic change, women's issues, and maximum collaboration.

From the inception of the conference, collaboration has been a central value. LCWR has maintained strong ties with its male counterpart, the Conference of Major Superiors of Men (CMSM). The two conferences work closely in a small building in Silver Spring, Maryland, which they purchased jointly in 1982; they share some staff and programs.

Another key relationship is the InterAmerican network among the LCWR, the CMSM, the Canadian Religious Conference, and the Confederation of Latin American Religious. These organizations have held six InterAmerican Conferences of Religious: Mexico City, 1971; Bogota, Columbia, 1974; Montreal, Canada, 1977; Santiago, Chile, 1980; Hyattsville, Maryland, 1985; and Santiago, Dominican Republic, 1993.

In 1988, with the National Conference of Catholic Bishops and the Conference of Major Superiors of Men, LCWR formed the Tri-Conference Commission on Religious Life and Ministry. The purpose of the commission has been to foster collaboration between U.S. bishops and religious leaders, to work on issues of common concern, and to promote dialogue.

LCWR translates goals into reality through programs and publications. In 1996 LCWR published the results of a two-year task force study on the role of women in the Catholic Church in *Creating a Home: Benchmarks for Church Leadership Roles for Women*. Together with the national conferences of bishops and of men religious, LCWR addresses the problem of retirement funding for religious communities through the National Religious Retirement Office. In 1991 LCWR conducted a major survey of the ministries of women religious in the United States, gathering data on institutions sponsored by religious congregations and on the ministries of individual religious. As a result of that survey, the conference has offered a grant program to encourage collaborative ministries to meet the needs of poor women or of poor women and children.

In 1990 LCWR initiated a project to provide assistance to women religious in Central and Eastern Europe. Over $70,000 was collected; the funds have been used to sponsor formation programs and programs of ministry preparation for women religious in Poland, Hungary, and Lithuania.

LCWR regularly publishes a monthly newsletter, *Update*, and *The Occasional Papers*, a journal on issues of interest to religious leaders. In December 1996, LCWR membership was 1,004, which represented the leadership of approximately 400 active women's religious institutes.

See also WOMEN RELIGIOUS IN AMERICA.

Foley, Nadine, O.P., ed. *Claiming Our Truth: Reflections on Identity by United States Women Religious.* Washington, D.C.: Leadership Conference of Women Religious, 1988.

Gottemoeller, Doris, R.S.M., and Rita Hofbauer, G.N.S.H., eds. *Women and Ministry: Present Experiences and Future Hopes.* Washington, D.C.: Leadership Conference of Women Religious, 1981.

Munley, Anne, I.H.M. *Threads for the Loom: LCWR Planning and Ministry Studies.* Silver Spring, Md.: Leadership Conference of Women Religious, 1992.

Neal, Marie Augusta, S.N.D. *Catholic Sisters in Transition from the 1960s to the 1980s.* Wilmington, Del.: Michael Glazier, Inc., 1984.

MARGARET CAFFERTY, P.B.V.M.

LEOPOLDINE SOCIETY, THE

Missionary aid society. From its foundation in 1828 until its end in 1921, members of the Austrian missionary aid association, the Leopoldinen Stiftung, contributed significantly to the fledgling Church in the United States by their weekly membership dues, gifts of church goods, and support of missionary vocations. Its annual *Reports (Berichte der Leopoldinen Stiftung im Kaiserthume Oesterreichs)* detailing income and expenditure and containing extensive information about life in Catholic America continue to be a rich historical source.

In 1827, Fr. Frederick Résé, a German priest (then vicar general of Cincinnati, later to become first bishop of Detroit) at the request of his bishop, Edward Dominic Fenwick, O.P., traveled to Bavaria and Austria seeking vocations and financial aid. His persuasive accounts of the American missions (including a history of the Diocese of Cincinnati published in German) so impressed the archbishop of Vienna that he arranged an audience with the emperor, Francis I, who agreed to the establishment of this new society devoted to supporting the missions in America, and named it in honor of both his recently deceased (1826) daughter Leopoldina, the empress of Brazil, and St. Leopold, an Austrian margrave. The Leopoldinen Stiftung was to be under the patronage and protection of his brother, Archduke Rudolph, the cardinal archbishop of Olmütz, and was to exist only within the empire. Similar in structure to the recently formed (1822, Lyons) Society for the Propagation of the Faith, the association was approved by Pope Leo XII in *Quamquam Plura Sint* on January 30, 1829. Together with the Ludwig Missionsverein, these three would be mainstays of American mission support for many years.

One measure of its effective help to the Catholics of America may be judged from unwarranted nativist attacks, such as that of Samuel F. B. Morse. His 1835 pamphlet,

Imminent Dangers to the Free Institutions of the United States thru Immigration, and the Present State of Naturalization Laws, spoke of Jesuits as "soldiers that the Leopold Society has sent to this country" and as "emissaries" of Metternich. Morse asked, "Is there no danger to the Democracy of the country from such formidable foes arrayed against it?" All this occurred in the wake of the Monroe Doctrine of 1823.

By 1861 the Leopoldine Society had distributed over $430,000 to needy dioceses, missionaries (especially for transportation to the U.S.A.), and religious communities. Unrestricted grants assisted the building of seminaries, cathedrals, and parish churches, convent schools for girls, colleges and schools for boys, and helped missionaries reach out to dispersed Catholic communities. Between 1829 and 1838, almost $170,000 was distributed in varying amounts to Cincinnati, St. Louis, Bardstown, Charleston, Philadelphia, Baltimore, Mobile, Boston, Detroit, Vincennes, New York, Kingston (Canada), and New Orleans. Gifts of chalices, vestments, artwork, and other religious articles were regularly sent, and prayers were promised.

Inevitably, questions arose as to fairness, particularly concerning the use of these funds for non-German purposes. Correspondence flowed between the U.S.A., Vienna, and Rome. Reports were written, and at least one visitation (by Canon Joseph Salzbacher, editor of the annual *Berichte*) was made to assess the complaints *(Meine Reise nach Amerika im Jahre 1842)*. Such documents still provide exciting insights into recurring issues.

Perhaps the deepest thanks, however, are due for those missionaries whose arrival here was assisted by the Leopoldine Society, namely, St. John Neumann, Bishop Frederic Baraga, Frs. Caspar Rehrl, Joseph Salzmann, John Raffeiner, Francis Pierz, and many others.

See also GERMAN CATHOLICS IN AMERICA; LUDWIG MISSIONSVEREIN, THE; RÉSÉ, FREDERICK.

Barry, Colman, O.S.B. *The Catholic Church and German Americans.* Milwaukee, 1953.

Bleid, Benjamin. *Austrian Aid to American Catholics, 1830–1860.* Milwaukee, 1944.

Roemer, Theodore, O.F.M. Cap. *Ten Decades of Alms.* St. Louis, 1942.

_____. *The Leopoldine Foundation and the Catholic Church in the United States, 1829–1839.* New York, 1933.

Salzbacher, Josef. *Meine Reise nach Nord Amerika im Jahre 1842.* Vienna, 1845.

JOHN T. MONAGHAN

LERNOUX, PENNY (1940–89)

Author and journalist. An investigative journalist who interpreted Latin American affairs principally for English-reading audiences, Penny Lernoux was born in Los Angeles, California, on January 7, 1940. During the 1970s and 1980s she chronicled the "preferential option for the poor" that Latin America's Catholic bishops embraced at that time when they increasingly abandoned traditional alliances with powerful elites. She also critiqued the damage that U.S. government policies inflicted on poor Central and South Americans.

Growing up in Los Angeles, Lernoux listened to Latin American acquaintances' concerns. As a result, she studied Spanish and journalism at the University of Southern California, where she earned a B.A. (1961) and membership in the honor society Phi Beta Kappa. Beginning in 1962, she lived in South America, initially as a United States Information Agency foreign service officer. From 1964 to 1976 she was bureau chief, then South American correspondent for Copley News Service, reporting successively from Venezuela, Argentina, and Colombia.

In 1976 Lernoux received an Alicia Patterson Foundation grant for research on the Catholic Church in Latin America and became a freelance writer. Her first book, *Cry of the People,* reported U.S.-supported persecution and told stories of such twentieth-century martyrs as a peasant murdered for supporting a farmers' cooperative. The book earned the 1981 Sidney Hillman Foundation award. Lernoux also received Columbia University's Maria Moors Cabot Award and honorary doctorates from Kenyon College (1983) and Elm College (1986).

In a 1987 letter, she explained her switch from secular to faith-related journalism. Colombia's institutional Church had seemed wedded to the upper classes during the early 1960s. She wrote: "My experience of this near-feudal institution was so painful that for years afterward I was estranged from the Church. But in the early 1970s I came in contact with Maryknoll missioners in Chile, who showed me a different Church—the church of the poor." That gave her "new faith and a commitment as a writer to tell the truth of the poor," she explained. Lernoux's second book, *In Banks We Trust,* examined international banking crimes and the burden foreign debt imposed on Latin America's poor. In its wake, Lernoux taught at Macalester College, St. Paul, Minnesota, as Hubert Humphrey Professor (1983), then became a Poynter Fellow at Yale University (1984).

For fifteen years, Lernoux was Latin American affairs writer for the *National Catholic Reporter,* and she contributed to many other publications, among them *The Nation, Sojourners,* and *Newsweek.* Lernoux's *The People of God,* a sequel to *Cry of the People,* surveyed the developing struggle between progressive and conservative forces in the Church. She was working on a book about Maryknoll Sisters when she was diagnosed with lung cancer shortly before she died on October 8, 1989, at Mount Kisco, New York. She was buried in the Maryknoll Sisters' cemetery in Ossining, New York.

Lernoux posthumously received Catholic Press Association and Associated Church Press awards. Her unfinished Maryknoll book, completed by Arthur Jones and Robert Ellsberg, was published as *Hearts on Fire* in 1993.

See also NATIONAL CATHOLIC REPORTER.

Lernoux, Penny. *Cry of the People.* Garden City, N.Y.: Doubleday & Company, Inc., 1980.
____. *In Banks We Trust.* Garden City, N.Y.: Anchor Press/Doubleday, 1984.
____. *People of God: The Struggle for World Catholicism.* New York: Viking Penguin Inc., 1989.
____. *Hearts on Fire: The Story of the Maryknoll Sisters.* Maryknoll, N.Y.: Orbis Books, 1993.

DAWN M. GIBEAU

LIBERIA, FIVE MARTYRS OF (1992)

Barbara Ann Muttra, Mary Joel Kolmer, Shirley Kolmer, Agnes Mueller, Kathleen McGuire; five American religious women murdered during the Liberian civil war in 1992. They were members of a mission in the West African country of Liberia sponsored by the Ruma, Illinois, province of the Adorers of the Blood of Christ (A.S.C.). The A.S.C. sisters had first established a mission in southern Liberia in 1971, providing health care and primary education. In 1973 a second site was opened in the Gardnersville section on the outskirts of the capital city of Monrovia. A third site was developed in 1983 at Bomi Hills, northeast of Monrovia.

Samuel Doe's violent coup and assassination of President William Tolbert ushered instability in the country from 1980 onward. In 1989 the National Patriotic Front of Liberia (NPFL), led by former cabinet minister Charles Taylor, invaded from the Ivory Coast and set off a period of civil war. The sisters continued their work in education and health care, adding now aid and care for the many refugees. In August 1990 conditions worsened to the point that all the sisters had to leave the country and so returned to the United States.

In March 1991 a visit to Liberia led to the decision that some sisters might return. Four sisters returned in July of that year: Barbara Ann Muttra (b. 1923), trained as a nurse, who had helped found the Liberian mission in 1971; Agnes Mueller (b. 1929), who had first come to Liberia in 1987 to work in pastoral ministry and women's literacy programs; Shirley Kolmer (b. 1930), former provincial, who taught mathematics at high-school and university levels; and Mary Joel Kolmer (b. 1934), cousin of Shirley and high-school teacher. They were joined the following month by Sr. Kathleen McGuire (b. 1937), a teacher who also served as director of Archdiocesan Relief Services upon her return.

Fighting surged again in October 1992 when NPFL forces attacked Monrovia. During this conflict, Srs. Mut-tra and Mary Joel Kolmer were killed by NPFL forces on October 20, when their vehicle was ambushed. They were taking one of the mission personnel to visit a sick relative and had picked up two of the peacekeeping soldiers along the way. On October 23, Srs. Shirley Kolmer, Mueller, and McGuire were shot outside their convent by a soldier identifying himself as Commanding Officer Black Devil. The bodies were recovered from the two sites in November and January, respectively, and returned to the Ruma motherhouse for burial. A monument to their memory now stands before the Ruma motherhouse, depicting the five sisters with hands joined and raised, looking outward and upward. Having given their lives for the victims of Liberia's civil war, they are considered martyrs of charity.

Boehmer, M. Clare, A.S.C. *Echoes in Our Hearts.* Red Bud, Ill., 1994.

ROBERT SCHREITER, C.PP.S.

LIGUTTI, LUIGI G. (1895–1984)

Pastor of rural ministry. Born near Udine, Italy, on March 21, 1895, he emigrated to the United States in 1912 with his mother, and settled in Iowa. He enrolled in St. Ambrose College in Davenport, and finished his theological studies at St. Mary's Seminary, Baltimore. After his ordination on September 22, 1917, for the Diocese of Des Moines, he engaged in graduate studies at The Catholic University of America in Washington, D.C.

He performed pastoral duties in Woodbine, Iowa, in the early 1920s and then, in 1926, he was named pastor of Assumption parish in Granger, Iowa. It was here that

Luigi G. Ligutti

Ligutti honed his views of Catholic rural sociology. With John Rawe, S.J., he wrote *Rural Roads to Security* in 1939, which demonstrated his effective skills as a champion for the needs of rural life.

In 1937 he was named executive secretary of the National Catholic Rural Life Conference (NCRLC), and in 1940, resigned his pastorship in Granger, moved the headquarters to Des Moines, and became the NCRLC's first full-time executive secretary. For the next twenty years he worked tirelessly for the needs of rural people as he traveled around the country expressing his knowledge and concern to all who would listen. Through his work he became connected with leaders in the liturgical movement, the National Conference of Catholic Charities, and Catholic Relief Services. He also worked with his counterparts in other Christian Churches to promote his goals. He remained the executive secretary of the NCRLC until 1958 when he was named its director of international affairs.

Ligutti also promoted his goals to a worldwide audience. In 1948 he was appointed Vatican Observer to the Food and Agriculture Organization of the United Nations. It was in this capacity that he helped draft the section on agriculture for Pope John XXIII's *Pacem in Terris,* and was the inspiration behind some of *Mater et Magistra.* He served as a consultant to the conciliar commission on the laity of Vatican Council II. Statements of the council concerning rural life, agriculture, and migration, especially in paragraphs 71–72 of the Pastoral Constitution on the Church in the Modern World (*Gaudium et spes*), are chiefly the results of his work. He also influenced the drafting of Pope Paul VI's *Octogesima Adveniens.* In 1971 he established *Agrimissio,* an international organization headquartered in Rome to promote agricultural production among underprivileged people in developing countries.

From 1971 until his death on December 28, 1984, he lived in Rome and was a canon at Santa Maria Maggiore. After his death his body was returned to the United States and interred in Assumption parish cemetery, Granger, Iowa.

See also CATHOLIC RURAL LIFE MOVEMENT.

Miller, Raymond W. *Monsignor Ligutti, The Pope's Country Agent.* Lanham, Md.: University Press of America, 1981.
Yzermans, V. A. *The People I Love: A Biography of Luigi G. Ligutti.* Collegeville, Minn.: The Liturgical Press, 1976.

JOSEPH M. McLAFFERTY

LITHUANIAN CATHOLICS IN AMERICA

European Origin

Lithuanians came to the United States from the last European state to accept Christianity. Faint beginnings date from the mid-thirteenth century when the leading chieftain, Mindaugas, sought baptism and received the crown around 1251. Revivals of the faith date from 1386 when the Lithuanian Prince Jogaila accepted the hand of the Poles' Princess Hedwig together with baptism, and from 1417–21 when emissaries of the Council of Constance christened throngs of villagers. The Lithuanian majority has remained Catholic in the Latin Rite. For the next five centuries the fate of Lithuanians, politically and culturally, interwove with Polish history, despite the linguistic and ethnic differences between the two groups. Lithuanians were living under oppressive Tsarist rule in the 1860s when chiefly economic survival prompted them to leave their homeland.

Beginnings in the United States

Just as Poles initially affiliated with German parishes, Lithuanians gravitated toward Poles, forming joint mutual benefit societies and churches. Except for a failed effort in New York City in the 1880s, the origin of the Lithuanian religious network lies in Pennsylvanian coal mines. Sometimes mistaken as Eastern-rite Catholics, Lithuanians settled in towns like Shamokin, Shenandoah, Pittston, and Freeland, Pennsylvania, forming mixed ethnic organizations with Poles. Sooner or later, as nationalist sentiments stirred in Polish-Lithuanian enclaves, quarrels flared up. As a result, in some instances Poles retained the parish property, ousting Lithuanians, and in other cases the reverse was true. Both sides frequently resorted to civil courts to settle their disputes.

A large, unknown percentage of Polish-oriented Lithuanians, nevertheless, remained in Polish parishes. A smaller number of Poles remained in Lithuanian churches where bilingual pastors read the gospel and preached in Polish as well as in Lithuanian. As a result, bishops regularly faced interparish and intraparish language disputes. Meanwhile, alongside constant ethnic friction fanned by chauvinists in both circles, the two ethnic groups most often paraded in one another's festivities marking church dedications, and united in civic and labor rallies. Likewise, Lithuanian and Polish clergy invited each other to participate in the religious and social camaraderie of the eucharistic tradition of annual Forty Hours Devotions.

Parishes

Eventually, Lithuanians founded 123 of their own parishes in the United States. Pennsylvania alone accounted for forty-four of them, surpassing the thirty-nine in the rest of the East Coast. The Midwest parishes in Chicago, Detroit, Cleveland, Wisconsin, and a few beyond the Mississippi River, constituted forty more in the Lithuanian diaspora.

Male saints predominated in parish name-choice, often a pastor's patronal name or that of the founding mutual-aid society. St. Casimir ranked first with twenty-one selections, with St. George chosen sixteen times. Twenty-one parishes chose the Blessed Virgin Mary, under various titles, while the only other woman was St. Anne, with three parishes named after her.

Women's Religious Communities

Religious communities provided sterling support for parish life. Four communities of religious women have distinguished themselves in serving Lithuanian immigrants and their offspring. After a decade of discussion, several clergy launched the Sisters of St. Casimir in 1907. Originating in Mount Carmel, Pennsylvania, the women quickly relocated to the huge Lithuanian colony in Chicago. They regard Fr. Antanas Staniukynas (1865–1918) as their cofounder with Mother Maria Kaupas (1880–1940) whose cause for beatification is pending.

In 1922 a Lithuanian contingent of sisters seceded from the Polish Sisters of the Holy Family, after a painful ethnic division. Fr. Mykolas Krušas of Chicago and Pittsburgh priests Jonas Sutkaitis and Magnus Kazėnas spearheaded the new community that brought the separatists to Pittsburgh to start life anew under the auspices of the German Franciscans of Millvale, Pennsylvania.

Finally, a Passionist priest, Alphonsus Urbanavičius, of Scranton, Pennsylvania, established the Poor Sisters of Jesus Crucified and His Sorrowful Mother at nearby Elmhurst in 1924 to care for widows and orphans of coal mine tragedies. When circumstances permitted, the sisters entered the catechetical and teaching field.

Sisters of the Immaculate Conception, based in Putnam, Connecticut, arrived from Lithuania in 1936 to provide domestic service in nearby Thompson, Connecticut, for the Marian Fathers at their Marianapolis College Preparatory School. The women soon opened a retirement home in Thompson, and bought property for their motherhouse and novitiate in Putnam. The retirement facility evolved into the Matulaitis Nursing Home in Putnam. For a generation, the sisters' print shop accounted for much religious literature, including Sunday missalettes for the entire world outside the homeland during Soviet occupation. In the aftermath of World War II, a few refugee Benedictine sisters found their way to Bedford, New Hampshire. There they still sponsor a kindergarten.

Women's vocations flourished. For example, at least thirty-five sisters originated in St. Joseph parish, Scranton, Pennsylvania; and in Massachusetts, fifty came from St. Casimir, Worcester, and twenty from St. Peter, South Boston. Urgently deserving a separate study, these vowed women inspired many other vocations to the religious life, some to non-Lithuanian communities.

Men's Religious Communities

There were no indigenous male religious congregations. Marian Fathers from Lithuania first arrived in Chicago to staff St. Michael parish in 1913. Their labors soon expanded to journalism when they assumed charge of the local daily, *Draugas* [*Friend*], begun in 1909 and still publishing.

When World War II broke out, Fr. Justinas Vaškys, O.F.M. (1909–94), came to the United States to found a Franciscan branch in exile. The friars established major houses in Kennebunkport, Maine, and in Brooklyn, New York, reaching the public through their weekly *Darbininkas* [*Worker*] and devotional magazine *Varpelis* [*Little Bell*]. Refugee Jesuits regrouped in Chicago, building a Youth Center as the focus of religious and cultural events. *Laiškai lietuviams* [*Letters to Lithuanians*] has been their chief publication aimed at an educated readership. Roving clergy of all three communities crisscrossed throughout Lithuanian enclaves, preaching missions. One of the best known was the Jesuit, Fr. Jonas Kidykas (1905–).

High-ranking clergy have included Lithuanian-Americans such as: Archbishop Charles Salatka (1918–), ordinary of Marquette, Michigan (1968–77), and archbishop of Oklahoma City, Oklahoma (1977–92); Archbishop Paul Marcinkus (1922–), Vatican bank official; Msgr. Francis Statkus, chancellor, Archdiocese of Philadelphia; Msgr. Albert Olkovikas, chancellor, Diocese of Manchester, New Hampshire; Fr. Casimir Pugevicius, director, Lithuanian Catholic Religious Aid. In the late 1940s, the influx of displaced persons included many learned priests who already possessed doctoral degrees in canon law or theology, or acquired them here in America. Several dozen served in Spanish parishes of the Southwest and Far West.

Disunity

From the late 1880s a strong leftist movement of freethinkers and socialists, influenced by nineteenth-century rationalism, disrupted growth. Atheist physicians, lawyers, and editors traveled the lecture circuit, drawing away about one-fifth of the Lithuanians from their faith. Lacking sufficient clergy and lay leaders, Catholics rallied with a countermovement of various national associations only a few decades later as dates of origin indicate: Catholic Federation, 1906; Priest League (revived), 1909; Knights of Lithuania, 1913; Catholic Women's Alliance, 1915; Catholic Workers' Alliance, 1915. There were also networks of organists, temperance promoters, and college students.

Roman Catholic unity was also weakened by a separatist movement, affiliated mostly with the Polish National Church. At least fifteen independent parishes of varying longevity can be identified. Most of them lasted a year or so, a few extended a decade or more. Such congregations survive at this writing in Scranton, Pennsylvania, and in Lawrence, Massachusetts.

The 1990s

In recent decades, surviving Lithuanian enclaves have witnessed parish closings and mergers. Suburban flight, exogamous marriage, loss of language, and other assimilational factors have taken their toll. The demise of ethnic parishes has been hastened by a shortage of priestly vocations and the virtual end of new immigrants. In 1995 not one of the eight Lithuanian parishes in the Diocese of Pittsburgh, Pennsylvania, had survived. Only two of twelve in the Chicago archdiocese still function, as do two of five in the Diocese of Brooklyn, New York. Meanwhile, Bishop Paulius Baltakis, O.F.M. (1984 to present), keeps his worldwide watchful eye on the remaining parishes in his papal capacity as "Bishop for Spiritual Assistance to Lithuanians Living Outside Lithuania."

Kučas, Antanas. *Lithuanians in America*. Boston, 1975.

Wolkovich-Valkavičius, William. *Lithuanian Religious Life in America, A Compendium of 150 Roman Catholic Parishes and Institutions*. Vol. 1, *Eastern United States*. Vol. 2, *Pennsylvania*. Norwood, Mass., 1991, 1996.

____. *Lithuanian Pioneer Priest of New England: The Life, Struggles, and Tragic Death of Rev. Joseph Žebris*. Brooklyn, 1980.

____. *Lithuanian Fraternalism: Seventy-Five Years of U.S. Knights of Lithuania (1913–1988)*. Knights of Lithuania, 1988.

____. "Religious Separatism Among Lithuanian Immigrants in the United States and Their Polish Affiliation." *Polish American Studies*, Autumn, 1983.

____. "Lithuanian Immigrants and Their Irish Bishops in the Catholic Church of Connecticut." *The Other Catholics*. New York, 1978.

WILLIAM WOLKOVICH-VALKAVIČIUS

LITURGICAL CONFERENCE, THE

In 1940, at the continued bidding of Michael Ducey, O.S.B., the American Benedictine Liturgical Conference convened in Chicago, the first ever national Liturgical Week in the United States. By then, but only if we include the European experience, the modern liturgical movement was one hundred years old.

The First National Liturgical Week

The theme of the week was the Living Parish. Over 1,200 bishops, priests, and laypeople gathered, so we read in its *Proceedings,* in "serious" manner but with "enthusiasm and piety" to witness for themselves what the movement was recommending for parish worship. No doubt the names of the keynote speaker and the other presenters of prepared papers, including Msgrs. Reynold Hillenbrand and Martin Hellriegel and Dom Godfrey Diekmann, were part of the attraction.

Msgr. Hillenbrand made it clear that the Liturgical Week was a gathering of adherents. It would, he said, give them a clearer notion of their common objective, a clearer idea of the means at hand for achieving it, and focus on a particular theme of importance to Catholic life. There would be, he said, a series of worship services for their common prayer, six prepared addresses with time allotted for impromptu remarks, and from time to time special added features.

To the extent that the week had a call to action it can be gleaned from Msgr. Hellriegel's address. We are called, he said, to go back

to doing God's things, God's way—without slovenliness,
to a holier, worthier celebration,
to the Sunday high Mass,
to active participation, and
to more earnest preparation and joyful announcement of God's word through the homily, Sunday, and feast day Vespers, and other seasonal instructions.

In short, he said, we are called *sentire cum Ecclesia*.

Other speakers followed, and other weeks, but the Liturgical Conference—the sponsoring body of the weeks—though it moved in social awareness sometimes to the right, sometimes to the left, never deviated in forty years from the basic platform that Hellriegel had spelled out.

William Busch, who like Hellriegel had been associated with the movement since the beginning (in 1926), urged the first Liturgical Week not to act in undue haste by "urging various practices . . . sometimes called liturgical reforms . . . when people are not yet sufficiently prepared by understanding of the inner nature of the liturgy." Then, on behalf of the archbishop of St. Paul, he invited the gathering to hold another Liturgical Week like the first one, in his diocese in 1941. And so the tradition began. For over thirty years, the annual Liturgical Week was the chief work of the Liturgical Conference.

The Liturgical Conference

Although the American Benedictine abbeys acting through an advisory board had sponsored the first Liturgical Weeks, in 1943 a subcommittee on ways and means met to consider how best to continue the movement. It was decided that the American Advisory Committee for the Liturgical Week would "henceforth be known as the Liturgical Conference." This Liturgical Conference would consist of a fifteen-member board elected from the advisory committee with authorization to organize itself for the continuation of the Liturgical Weeks, and to incorporate under the laws of whichever of the states they might choose. In the same year, a subcommittee of the newly elected conference would meet to devise a governing plan, and a representative would "wait upon the several Benedictine abbots to see to what extent their cooperation may be secured for the work of the Conference."

Thus, the Liturgical Conference began its work, not too closely tied to any religious order, and indeed, not too closely linked to any place. It was to some extent a traveling show—moving its secretariat to whatever diocese had invited it for the week and passing the time in relative obscurity otherwise. It was a grassroots phenomenon, given more to education and formation than to experiments in either community or the liturgy. In 1946 some members of the conference began a new society—at first called the St. Jerome Society; it was renamed the Vernacular Society the following year (after the publication of Pius XII's *Mediator Dei*). Hardly a soul remained in the liturgical movement who was not convinced by then that Christians would be better served hearing the word in their own tongue, yet the Liturgical Conference stood apart from this new "movement." To a certain extent the members of the Liturgical Conference had only one mission: to seek the best ways to celebrate the liturgy as it then existed in parishes all across this land and Canada.

These are not disparaging remarks. The annual Liturgical Weeks were instrumental in fostering liturgical study and communal prayer. Above all, they made known the key leaders and spokespersons for the reform that was to come, among them: Godfrey Diekmann, Robert Hovda, Frederick McManus, Gerard Sloyan. The themes of the weeks themselves stand out as signposts for an age just dawning: the parish, the family, social justice, Sunday, Holy Week, education, the liturgy, and unity. H. A. Reinhold, the author of so many Timely Tracts in *Orate Fratres*, had this to say about a talk given by Mary Perkins Ryan at the 1946 Liturgical Week:

> You can be an American and liturgical without becoming touchingly weird and strange. The hundreds of sisters and priests who heard the full doctrine and liturgical richness must have realized how much there is to do to free our teaching from the pseudo-claustral anemia which besets so much of our catechesis on this great sacrament. There was a member of the articulate laity—putting us clerics to shame—the only hope for any Catholic Action. Married people all over the United States ought to know what took place as this first "penetrative" Liturgical Week that broke with spiritual isolationism.

And of worship at the same gathering:

> Have you ever seen and heard a cathedral full of priests, sisters, and lay people sing an archbishop's Mass as one man? In Denver it happened, though fortunately not for the last time. In the evening hundreds chanted the psalms and hymns of Compline together. Remembering your own parish church you will believe me: there is spiritual spring in the air right now in our own country.

Evolution of the Liturgical Conference

Events in the American hierarchy and on the continent were fodder for the Liturgical Weeks, and eventually changed the face of the Liturgical Conference. The reforms of Holy Week and the first Mass in English were celebrated at Liturgical Weeks. In 1958 the American bishops established the first standing Bishops' Committee on the Liturgy, and in 1959, Pope John XXIII announced the Second Vatican Council. First McManus, and then also Godfrey Diekmann, was named a *peritus*—an expert—to advise the conciliar liturgical commission. The Liturgical Conference opened a corporate office in Washington, D.C., and in addition to the annual weeks began publishing a series of practical guides to bring the new liturgy to the people. It published among other titles: *A Manual of Celebration, Liturgy Committee Handbook, Commentaries on the Rite of Penance,* a lenten program called *From Ashes to Easter,* and arguably the best book on presiding, Robert Hovda's *Strong, Loving and Wise.*

The annual weeks drew large crowds in the 1960s. They came to learn the new liturgy or to protest it, inflating expectations of what had always been a modest movement. When they quit coming in such droves, it seemed to many that the Liturgical Conference was no longer needed. In fact, however, we are always going to need practice and improvement in our common prayer, and our prayer together is always going to challenge us to deeper involvement in the Church. And so it has happened. Liturgical renewal has taught us to see Christ in the Eucharist as sign and reality of the Church's unity. The Liturgical Conference has rewritten its constitution to affirm that its concern for the life and worship of the Christian Churches cannot cease until the Church is one.

This goal is not a modest undertaking. Yet now, as always, the conference has but meager ways and means. It continues to publish *Homily Service* and *Liturgy* magazine, striving thereby to encourage a full participation in the liturgy which it continues to preach as Christ's life for the world.

See also LITURGICAL MOVEMENT IN AMERICA, THE.

RACHEL REEDER

LITURGICAL MOVEMENT IN AMERICA, THE

The history of the Catholic liturgical movement in America is in some ways an easy story to tell: it has a datable beginning and quite obviously a briefer span than its forebears in Europe. Its main characters are memorable, likable, and strong, if somewhat curmudgeonly eccentric, while its main and somewhat mundane events—educational conferences, publications, and liturgical weeks—seem almost to belie its intensity of purpose and significant accomplishment. The wave crested shortly after Vatican Council II, and the movement evanesced, but hasty attempts to assign an ending date have not been successful.

Prologue in Europe

The liturgical movement in its modern form began in Europe as early as the mid-nineteenth century (1840s) in

Dom Prosper Guéranger's pioneering efforts to understand the origins and history of liturgical texts, revive Gregorian chant, and restore the Benedictine abbey of Solesmes. By the early 1900s the center of the movement had shifted to Beuron and then to the abbeys of Maredsous and Mont César in Belgium, where Dom Lambert Beauduin became the voice of the movement. Before entering the monastery, Beauduin had been a labor chaplain, and under his influence, the movement took on a distinctly pastoral character.

Beauduin wrote only one book, *Liturgy, the Life of the Church,* but his presence at Liturgical Weeks and his university teaching influenced many, including young priests from the United States and Germany who would later bring the movement to this country.

America's turn had not yet come, however, when the center of the movement shifted yet again—this time going south to the Benedictine abbey of Maria Laach and to the Augustinian monastery of Klosterneuberg (in Austria). At the latter, Pius Parsch began a popular liturgical apostolate that sought to explain both the Bible and the liturgy to the laity; at the former, Dom Ildefons Herwegen encouraged young educated Germans to participate actively in the life of the Church by praying the *missa recitata* and attending liturgical conferences. The abbey's *Jahrbuch für Liturgiewissenschaft* in which Dom Odo Casel's mystery theology first appeared and its *Ecclesia Orans* series, which published Romano Guardini's *The Spirit of the Liturgy* in 1918, carried the movement far beyond Germany—and for many years. H. A. Reinhold (1940) was speaking as much for two generations as for himself when he said: "When I read [*The Spirit of the Liturgy*], the restrictions and commandments that had seemed to be the essence of Catholicism and that I had defended in fierce and dull despair, vanished before the vision of Christ's Mystical Body and the incredible beauty of His mystical Life among us through His sacraments and mysteries."

The Early Years

Benedictines in America—at Conception Abbey in Missouri, and at the Abbey of St. John the Baptist in Collegeville, Minnesota—were probably connected to the movement, chiefly through Beuron, as early as the 1890s. But one man, Virgil Michel, a monk of St. John's Abbey, is generally accepted as founder of the liturgical movement in America. At St. Anselm's College in Rome, Michel met and studied with Dom Lambert Beauduin; and in visits to Maria Laach and other European monasteries, he observed and absorbed the liturgical movement in its monastic setting and pastoral orientation.

If Beauduin taught Michel liturgy as the life of the Church and introduced him to the notion of the Church as the body of Christ, so the monasteries in Germany and Austria immersed him in the experience of worship as a communal act. In the sung or recited Mass (the dialog Mass), Michel saw what it was like to participate actively in the Church's prayer. When he returned to Minnesota, he had not only resolved to bring this movement to America, he had also conceived how it might be transformed and put to work in a new and quintessentially different culture.

Michel's plan was threefold. He proposed to publish (1) "a popular liturgical library," a series of pamphlets and leaflets that would be available in churches throughout America; (2) a series of translations that would bring the best of European liturgical scholarship to this country; and (3) a periodical that would serve to educate and unify those whose interest in the liturgical revival had so far occurred only sporadically and in vastly different settings. The popular liturgical library and the translations project became The Liturgical Press, which Michel directed most of his life; the periodical, called *Orate Fratres* when it first appeared in 1926, was renamed *Worship* magazine in 1948.

Michel's leadership was part inspiration, part cooperation. He had an appreciation close to genius for recognizing those whose gifts were complementary to his own. From the beginning, he assembled a formidable roster of associate and contributing editors, among them the young Jesuit Gerard Ellard. Ellard's letter to the periodical *America,* in which he advocated liturgical education and "why not a journal of liturgical studies?" brought him to Martin Hellriegel's notice. Hellriegel, a chaplain to the Precious Blood Sisters in O'Fallon, Missouri, introduced Ellard to Michel, and the three of them, on the night before Christmas 1925, planned the journal that would become *Orate Fratres/Worship* magazine. Other early associates were Donald Attwater, Wales; William Busch, St. Paul, Minnesota; Mother Mary Ellerker, Duluth, Minnesota; Leo F. Miller, Columbus, Ohio; Richard E. Power, Springfield, Massachusetts; and Justine B. Ward, Washington, D.C.

The diversity of these editors and the simplicity of their objective helps explain the later movement as it no doubt contributed to the magazine's success. The aim, according to that first issue, was to better understand the "spiritual importance of the liturgy" because a "sympathetic understanding of the liturgy would affect" the life of Catholics and the corporate life of the Church's "natural social units." This emphasis on the spiritual dimensions of the liturgy was not expected to lead to neglect of its literary, musical, artistic, or historical aspects, but to keep these elements—or any one of them—"from breaking away from the rest."

Similarly, though many on hearing of the new venture praised it for its faithfulness to the Benedictines' traditional liturgical charism, the first issue made clear that "the present liturgical enterprise is Catholic in the full sense of the word." It was not addressed to monks or even to the clergy, but "to Christians who have a zeal for the liturgy."

The earliest issues of *Orate Fratres* included catecheses on the seasons of celebration, popular explanations of the liturgy's theological depths, and sections on the apostolate that helped bring the practical aspects of the liturgical movement into prominence.

The liturgical movement in America retained its popular appeal for many years; it was, above all else, an ecclesial movement. It originated in, and served, parish life and the needs of a population growing more and more committed to Catholic Action. For example, both Michel and Ellard continued their catechetical work; Michel as editor of the *Christ-Life* series of religious texts and dean of St. John's College, Ellard as the author of the immensely popular *Christian Life and Worship*. In print from 1933 to 1963, and with later editions illustrated by Adé Bethune, this text introduced generations of young Catholics to the idea of the Church as the Mystical Body of Christ, and to the Bible and liturgy as a single source of unity and truth.

Liturgy and Social Justice

Equally important to the liturgical movement in America was Michel's lifelong commitment to social justice, which he not only shared with others—most notably, perhaps, with Reynold Hillenbrand—but which he also made, to some extent, the goal of the movement. Ellard's *Men at Work at Worship: America Enters the Liturgical Movement,* was published soon after Michel's untimely death on November 20, 1938. Though vastly different in style from the liturgical and Church commentary we have grown accustomed to since Vatican Council II, its central premise is convincing, namely, that the social or "mystical body" Catholicism that impelled the liturgical movement was likewise the solution to "the social question." He quotes Catherine de Hueck: "Through all the immense network of Catholic Action moves and breathes the liturgical movement, forming as it were the basis of its whole spirit."

Ellard's survey of Catholic Action was global, but his appeal was equally to "the manifold activities of the American laity." The liturgical movement was essential nourishment for, and was itself strengthened by, the cooperative movement. The Rural Life Conference, early labor organizers, the legions and sodalities, even the National Council of Catholic Women were influenced by the movement. The latter resolved in council (in 1936) to encourage "the adoption of courses in public worship and plainsong," at colleges and schools nationwide, and "to second all efforts . . . inducing the laity to cooperate . . . with true liturgical practice."

From such a vantage point, it would be tempting to assume that the liturgical movement in this country had moved confidently forward inspired by universal approbation and its own impressive agenda. In fact, as Godfrey Diekmann was later to say, the movement evoked more in-

difference than encouragement. Pius X's felicitous acknowledgment in 1903 that active participation in the liturgy was the true font of the Church's life was the only *bon mot* the movement had for several decades, "and we did find ways to use it," Diekmann said, "on nearly all occasions."

The movement was, to say the least, many-faceted, rather than seamlessly united, and quite lacking in consensus for what ought to be done to secure its primary aim of "restoring all things in Christ." There were, in addition to *Orate Fratres,* other currents at work—sometimes in tandem with, sometimes independent of each other's notice or cooperation.

In 1928, for example, Maurice Lavanoux had begun publication of a periodical called *Liturgical Arts.* Lavanoux, a layman and architect, founded the Liturgical Arts Society and served for five decades as its only secretary and editor. This magazine embodied the liturgical movement's commitment to a suitable art and architecture for public worship.

Lavanoux and his followers advocated a style in church architecture that would support the public and participatory nature of the liturgy—free-standing altars, hospitable yet suitably festive spaces (not domestic in the sense of mundane), and redolent of symbolic unity and simplicity with the baptismal font and altar on a single axis. Such style distinguished the liturgical buildings wrought by architects and artists in the movement and delighted the magazine's readers.

Officially, however, *Liturgical Arts* was somewhat neglected and eventually its founder was passed over altogether. Lavanoux won respect for a modern and living religious art, but the magazine ceased publication in 1972, and Lavanoux was unable to muster the financial resources to revive it.

Another current was at work in Justine Ward's work to revive Gregorian chant. For a time at least and for many parishes, the revival of chant was the only way a parish had of becoming liturgically active. A convert and laywoman, Ward was one of Michel's original associates. Prior to that, she and a colleague, Thomas Shields, had originated the "Ward method" for teaching Gregorian chant to school children; and in 1916, she had, with Mother Georgia Stevens, founded the Pius X Institute of Liturgical Music at Manhattanville College. For two decades, her method and the Pius X Institute enabled adults and children to immerse themselves in the Mass through the beauty of the chant.

The introduction of the vernacular promulgated in the wake of Vatican II caused the chant to fall into disuse. Ward felt that the progressives in all countries—and the Ward method had been used in many countries—were abandoning the liturgy to "the most ignorant elements."

Separate though their endeavors were, both Lavanoux and Ward accomplished a renaissance in the liturgical arts that cannot be forgotten or disparaged. Their subsequent eclipse, if anything, underlines the wisdom of Michel's original vision that had subordinated these cultural elements in the liturgy to its spirit. Indeed, at the first Liturgical Week, John LaFarge spoke eloquently of having taught schoolchildren the chant, not properly by the Ward method, but *pro modus clamandi.* It seems to depend, he said, "not so much on musical ability as on the right point of view." Eric Gill, Maurice Lavanoux, Adé Bethune, Frank Kacmarcik, and Justine Ward were artists whose names live on in the movement.

Another signal event in the life of the Church in America that had a far-reaching effect on the movement—and on the universal Church as well—was the publication in 1936 of Joseph Stedman's *My Sunday Missal.* More than half a century has now passed since missals became the common possession of the laity, and the change in the liturgy from Latin to the vernacular that followed Vatican Council II makes it nearly impossible for younger Catholics to appreciate the singular accomplishment of the Stedman missal.

Stedman's missal was more than a translation of the Mass; it was a paint-by-number missal, in which the parts of the Mass were numbered and the numbers tied to illustrations that gently guided the user into understanding the various parts of the Mass. Only thirty years ahead of Vatican Council II, *My Sunday Missal* fulfilled the mandate that Trent had issued and the ages ignored—to see that all people were instructed in the prayer of the Church. More than thirty million copies of the missal were in print when Stedman died of a brain tumor in 1946. More than 25,000 people attended his wake.

From 1940 to the Second Vatican Council

A final surge in the movement occurred in 1940 when the first National Liturgical Week took place in Chicago. Liturgical days, and local liturgical missions had, of course, occurred before 1940. But in 1940 the Benedictine Liturgical Conference was prevailed on to hold the first National Liturgical Week in Chicago, Illinois. About 1,200 bishops, priests, and laypeople attended the event.

The first and therefore subsequent Liturgical Weeks were in some sense prepared for and were even an outgrowth of various liturgical days and catechetical meetings, not to mention the summer schools of social action that Ellard and Hillenbrand had engaged in for so long. Certainly, the overwhelming interest in sessions devoted to the liturgy at the 1939 meeting of the National Catholic Education Association in Cincinnati at least signaled that the time had come to hold such a meeting.

Nevertheless, the Liturgical Weeks were from their inception unique. They were retreats, in-service training, and networking venues at which bishops, clergy, and laity

had an opportunity not only to learn together but to pray together—to model the full active participation that the liturgical movement was certain would eventually replace all partial notions of religion with a truly transforming life in Christ. Virgil Michel, H. A. Reinhold said, "created a genuinely American movement, and [Liturgical Weeks are] its natural sequel and the organ for further propaganda."

Close associates of Michel, Reynold Hillenbrand and Joseph Morrison were cochairs of the first week, and for many years afterward, Hillenbrand chaired the program committee for the Liturgical Weeks and oversaw the publication of the proceedings. Also on the first week's program, and frequently thereafter, was Godfrey Diekmann who not only succeeded Michel as editor of *Orate Fratres,* but succeeded him too as guide and friend of a new generation—for example, Kathryn Sullivan, Frederick McManus, Gerard Sloyan, Robert Hovda—and close behind them, Virginia Sloyan and Gabe Huck.

Godfrey L. Diekmann

Events in Europe continued to influence the American scene—most notably the tradition of *semaines liturgiques,* which led eventually to international conferences and papal endorsement. In 1943 Pius XII published the encyclical *Mystici Corporis,* thereby authenticating the theology of the movement; and in 1947 the "guarded" approval (and new *bon mot*) that the movement had been looking for arrived: the same Pope's *Mediator Dei* officially recognized the movement while yet reserving to itself the question of any changes in the liturgy.

Gradually, the reforms began: of the calendar and breviary, the restoration of Paschal Vespers and Holy Week, permission for bilingual translations of the ritual books, the call for an ecumenical council—and, at last, on December 7, 1963, ratification of the Constitution on the Sacred Liturgy. The general reforms of the liturgy that the constitution had previewed were virtually complete by 1978.

Evaluating the Movement

From the perspective of Vatican Council II, it is clear that, to some extent, the roots of the modern liturgical movement are not in Guéranger's scholarship but deep within the Church's own character inasmuch as the Church itself is a movement that is always being reformed. Thus, in some ways, the sources of the liturgical movement are as old as the gospel. We may, however, for convenience, trace them only as far back as the Council of Trent—and that far simply to explain how truly remarkable the accomplishments of the liturgical movement have been in our time.

This much maligned council assured the preservation of the Roman Rite in its simplicity and purity—at least as it had been celebrated in the thirteenth century in the papal court. Its insistence on the objective celebration of this rite began the reform that restored order, uniformity, and decorum to the worship act. But in codifying the best that was known at the time, it allowed elements that had been lost from earlier ages to remain lost, and misdescribed the changing, ephemeral elements of the rite as part of the divinely ordained, unchanging core.

The Tridentine missal was too lean and too Latin to overcome the dichotomy that had begun during the Middle Ages between private prayer and the liturgy. The people's understanding and participation in the Mass/Eucharist were not expected or required for an objective and valid celebration of the Mass; and the Latin language, no longer the people's tongue but the language of tradition, was not understood in the many countries now using the missal.

By the nineteenth century, popular prayers to Mary and the saints, prayers that had become increasingly less biblical, filled the void. As a result, the importance of Sunday was lost on people and sympathy with the sufferings of Christ and the sorrows of Mary overshadowed the wholeness of the death and resurrection of Jesus as the formative event of Christian faith. The liturgical movement, wherever it is active, and especially in America, is the Church's "natural response" to this situation (Bouyer, 1955).

Liturgical reforms similar to those advocated in the twentieth century and finally introduced at Vatican Council II were sometimes put forward during these ages—immediately after Trent, and again in the 1700s—but they were, not surprisingly, associated with secular, nationalistic, modernist movements, secularity, and nationalism that seemed so antithetical to the Church at the time. The times, if not the Tridentine liturgy itself, called more for submission than celebration.

Under such circumstances, the Mass became the hierarchy's privilege and function—something the laity watched or heard them do. The priest, it could be said, opened and closed a vertical channel between ourselves and God, and for this service we revered them as we loved God, but from a distance.

Such a liturgy could have had little or no relation to the work people did on the land or in the city and not much influence on their devotion or piety, and it is against this backdrop that the history of the liturgical movement has to be judged. To the extent that the reforms of Vatican Council II have destroyed the very circumstances that made the movement meaningful (i.e., the silent Mass, the private Mass, the substitution of seeing for doing, of yearning for action), we may judge that it has been a success. But to the extent that the corporate meaning of worship in the body of Christ still eludes us, we must pray that the spirit of liturgical renewal will not cease to billow and blow in our midst. To some extent, the "strangeness of the Roman liturgy" remains in the reformed rites. H. A. Reinhold should be heeded today as he was in 1958:

> Saying that the liturgy is sober and chaste and superior in content is not to be understood as an attempt to reserve the whole field of prayer, individual and communal for the liturgy only. . . . Its very sobriety and profundity are a challenge: the individual . . . as well as the congregation, has to fill these void vessels with his own personal contribution. Liturgy is either work, challenge, personal *"engagement"* or it remains an empty house.

Between the individual and the communal is still a great abyss; the liturgical movement simmers in all the Churches.

See also HILLENBRAND, RAYMOND; LAVANOUX, MAURICE; MICHEL, VIRGIL; REINHOLD, HANS.

Bouyer, Louis. *Liturgical Piety.* University of Notre Dame Press, 1955.

Ellard, Gerard. *Christian Life and Worship.* Milwaukee: The Bruce Publishing Co., rev. ed., 1941.

Franklin, R. W., and Robert L. Spaeth. *Virgil Michel: American Catholic.* Collegeville, Minn.: The Liturgical Press, 1988.

Hall, Jeremy. "The American Liturgical Movement: The Early Years." *Worship* 50 (6) (1976) 474–89.

Marx, Paul. *Virgil Michel and the Liturgical Movement.* Collegeville, Minn.: The Liturgical Press, 1957.

Michel, Virgil. "The Scope of the Liturgy." *Orate Fratres* 10 (1936).

Reinhold, Hans Ansgar. *Bringing the Mass to the People.* Baltimore: Helicon Press, 1960.

____. "Past and Present in the Liturgical Movement in the Catholic Church." *Worship* 26 (4) (1952) 176–86.

Simms, David McDaniel. "Liturgical Movement in the Roman Catholic Church." *Journal of Religious Thought* 19 (2) (1965) 141–55.

Tuzik, Robert L., ed. *How Firm a Foundation: Leaders of the Liturgical Movement.* Chicago: Liturgy Training Publications, 1990.

RACHEL REEDER

Related Document

DOM MICHEL EXPLAINS THE ORIGINS OF THE LITURGICAL MOVEMENT IN THE UNITED STATES, FEBRUARY 24, 1929

One of the most serious lacunae in the literature of American Catholicism is that pertaining to the inner life of the Church. Yet every historian must recognize the importance that forms and methods of worship and devotion play in the spiritual life of the people. In that connection the liturgical movement of the twentieth century has been of special significance. The movement, which has sought through the doctrine of the Mystical Body to bring all Catholics into active participation in the official worship of the Church, is now over a century old in Europe. But it was only in the 1920's that it began to take shape in the United States with the establishment of the Liturgical Press of St. John's Abbey, Collegeville, Minnesota, and its monthly journal, *Orate Fratres* (now called *Worship),* the first number of which appeared in November, 1926. The movement owed its origin to a number of persons scattered throughout the country, as the following document makes clear, but its successful launching was due to none more than to Virgil Michel, O.S.B. (1890–1938), first editor of *Orate Fratres,* and to the active support of his superior, Abbot Alcuin Deutsch (1877–1951). In a letter to a fellow religious Dom Michel fixed the date of the efforts at St. John's when he said, "The first ideas of our plans were penned in February 1923, and by dint of slow correspondence the plans grew until they are now full-fledged."

(*Source: Archives of St. John's Abbey*, Michel to Francis Augustine Walsh, O.S.B., Collegeville, January 25, 1926, copy.)

IT WAS ONLY RECENTLY WE RECEIVED TWO FALL NUMBERS of the "midweek" section of an excellent Catholic paper. One number contained an article in which St. John's Abbey was spoken of with enthusiasm as the "source of the Liturgical Movement." The unnamed author is evidently a very good friend. In the second number there was an answer to the first article, written by two intimate friends of ours. The second article briefly describes earlier European "sources" of the Liturgical Movement, mentions the fact that the spirit of the movement began to manifest itself "almost simultaneously in various sections of the United States some seven or eight years ago," and that various promoters of it were at work independently and, at first, even unknown to each other, until a number of them were brought together. Their deliberations and plans finally resulted in an organized liturgical apostolate, the founding of the Liturgical Press at St. John's Abbey, and the publishing of *Orate Fratres* by the monks of St. John's with the assistance of fellow editors outside the monastery. In the interest of truth we are glad to add a few facts that

happen to come to mind at the present writing, especially since no written record of the beginning of the movement exists.

There were various "sources" of liturgical movement in the United States quite independent of St. John's Abbey, and antedating the public apostolate in which the latter is now engaged. Foremost among these must be mentioned well-known O'Fallon (Mo.), where Father Hellriegel and the late Father Jasper commenced activities that have been a great inspiration to many. From O'Fallon—in part at least, unless we are mistaken—came the spark that grew to a live flame among some of the Jesuit Fathers of St. Louis, at whose University lectures on aspects of the liturgy have been given for some years, and where the recent National Students Spiritual Leadership Convention took place. . . . Over a decade ago the late Dr. Shields, as head of the Education Department of the Catholic University of America, was seeking to imbue a complete program of Catholic primary education with the spirit of the liturgy. More recently, Dr. George Johnson has done excellent work in directing efforts along the same line. It was at least under the encouragement of Dr. Shields that the work of Mrs. Justine B. Ward grew into an extensive program of gregorian revival, and with the co-operation of the Religious of the Sacred Heart resulted in the influential Pius X Institute of Liturgical Music, soon to enter upon its thirteenth flourishing year. At the St. Paul Seminary the Reverend William Dush *[sic]* was working quietly but perseveringly for many years, and the results of his inspiration are now showing themselves in the zeal and efforts for a more liturgical formation of the people on the part of many young priests that caught the divine spark from him. His translation of Father Kramp's *Eucharistia* [St. Paul, 1926] antedated *Orate Fratres* by some months, as did also the translation of Father Kramp's *The Sacrifice of the New Law* [St. Louis, 1926] by Rev. Leo F. Miller. The translations of the Latin sacramental texts by the Reverend Richard E. Power, published in our Popular Liturgical Library and known everywhere for their excellent qualities, are the result of years of study engaged upon when The Liturgical Press was not even existing in any human dream-world. There were many other centers of liturgical life carrying on unknown to each other, quietly preparing the way for a more conscious general revival.

Not only were our Associate Editors, among others, so many independent "sources" of liturgical awakening. They have also been co-operators in organizing and developing the work that centers in our abbey; and this, first of all, by their active part in the plans and discussions preceding the launching of our ventures; and then by their continued advice, and their free contribution of efforts—which later assistance is of no mean importance for a new journalistic undertaking, especially in our own day when money rules the day and is all-decisive. Some of our contributors have also helped us in a similar way, notably Miss Ellen Gates Starr, whose articles on the Breviary received special mention from many of our correspondents.

All of these are doing their own part towards what is now consciously a common cause, one which it is also our privilege to promote to the best of our abilities. All of them have their efforts and intentions recorded in the Book of Life and they are not seeking for recognition of this work here below. Yet we have mentioned the above facts here, not so much for their sake—for we know their good will and desires—but for our own sake, lest in any way we should appear willing to receive credit beyond our desert. God forbid! It is from Him and Him alone that all sufficiency comes.

The liturgical apostolate is bigger than any individual, than any abbey, than any order, than any larger group of men, than the entire body of those who are spending their efforts in its promotion throughout the world. For it is in truth a spiritual ferment destined to permeate the entire body mystic of Christ according to the words of its official inaugurator. Its aim is to imbue the members of this body more thoroughly with "the true Christian spirit," and through this renewed vigor to institute also a renewed growth of that mystic body unto an ever greater attainment here on earth of the "fullness of him who is filled all in all."

(*Source*: John Tracy Ellis, ed. *Documents of American Catholic History*. Vol. 2:1866–1966. Wilmington, Del.: Michael Glazier, 1987, 621–24.)

LOCHTEFELD, MELCHIOR (1905–84)

Religious and pastor. Melchior Lochtefeld was born on January 4, 1905, to John and Catherine Hoying Lochtefeld in St. Rose, Ohio. In 1919 he entered the Society of the Precious Blood in Burkettsville, Ohio. He made his perpetual profession in the community on December 5, 1926. On May 14, 1931, he was ordained to the priesthood.

His first assignment was at Our Lady of Good Counsel parish in Cleveland. On June 22, 1937, Lochtefeld was named pastor of the nearly bankrupt parish of Our Lady of the Blessed Sacrament, Cleveland's only African American parish. Lochtefeld began working to serve both the spiritual and material needs of his parishioners. The parish became a hub of activity with vocational training programs, dances, and various activities for children and youth. Under Lochtefeld's direction the parish began a perpetual novena to St. Martin de Porres. Emphasizing self-help, the parish began a credit union in 1940. That same year the parishioners established a chapter of the National Catholic Interracial Federation.

Aware of the challenges of ministry in the African American community, Lochtefeld and several pastors organized the Midwest Clergy Conference on Negro Welfare in 1938.

The organization provided both support and education for those in ministry. Lochtefeld served as its first secretary-treasurer and later as its president in 1947.

In 1941 Lochtefeld began an outreach to those African Americans living in the near east side neighborhood of Cedar-Central. This mission outreach continued until 1943 when Bishop Joseph Schrembs designated St. Edward parish as the second parish for Cleveland's African Americans and named Lochtefeld as its pastor.

During his tenure at Our Lady of the Blessed Sacrament, over four hundred African Americans were received into the Church. He would continue this successful evangelization at St. Edward. As usual, he organized numerous activities and organizations, including a girls' high school.

In 1957 his community transferred him to the Toledo diocese where he became pastor of the growing rural church of St. Michael in Kalida. In 1969 his next assignment took him to St. Anthony parish in St. Anthony, Ohio. He was next stationed in Ottawa, Ohio, where he served until illness forced his retirement in 1978. He resided at St. Charles Seminary in Carthagena, Ohio, until his death on July 27, 1984.

Blatnica, Dorothy A. "'In Those Days': African-American Catholics in Cleveland, 1922–1961." Ph.D. dissertation, Case Western Reserve University, 1992.

Clip file on Rev. Melchior Lochtefeld, Archives of the Society of the Precious Blood.

Mossing, Lawrence A. *History of the Diocese of Toledo, Volume II, Northern Ohio West Section*. Toledo, 1984.

Papers of Our Lady of the Blessed Sacrament Parish, 1922–60, Archives, Diocese of Cleveland.

Papers of St. Edward Parish, 1943–60, Archives, Diocese of Cleveland.

CHRISTINE L. KROSEL

LONGSTREET, JAMES (1821–1904)

Civil War general. Longstreet was born in Edgefield District, South Carolina, on January 8, 1821. The son of James Longstreet and Mary Ann Dent, he was raised on a cotton plantation in the piedmont section of Georgia, until his father's death in 1833. He was then sent to be raised by his uncle, Judge Augustus B. Longstreet, in Richmond, Georgia. He graduated from West Point Military Academy in 1842 and shortly after began his career as a military officer. He was awarded two brevets for his service in the Mexican War and had attained the rank of major in the Paymaster Corps when he resigned his commission in June 1861.

He was appointed a brigadier general in the Confederate army two weeks later and fought at First Manassas in July. After being promoted to major general in October

1861, he served in the Peninsular Campaign, the Second Manassas, and Antietam. He was promoted to lieutenant general in October 1862 and given command of the First Corps of the Army of Northern Virginia. He was present at the battles at Fredericksburg, Gettysburg, Chickamagua, Knoxville, the Wilderness, and Richmond. After the war he invested in a number of business ventures, including an insurance company and a cotton brokerage. He alienated fellow Southerners when he joined the Republican Party, but went on to hold a number of political appointments, including that of U.S. minister to Turkey, U.S. railroad commissioner, and U.S. marshal for Georgia. He published his memoirs, *From Manassas to Appomatox,* in 1869 and became a member of the Catholic Church in 1877. He died in Gainesville, Georgia, on January 2, 1904.

See also CIVIL WAR AND CATHOLICS, THE.

TRICIA T. PYNE

LOOTENS, LOUIS ALOYSIUS (1827–98)

Vicar apostolic. Lootens was born in Bruges, Belgium, March 17, 1827. Upon completion of courses in philosophy and theology in St. Nicholas Seminary, Paris, he was ordained on June 14, 1851, for the missions on Vancouver Island, Canada. Owing to poor health he transferred to San Francisco in 1860.

He was named first vicar apostolic of Idaho, March 3, 1868. At that time there were four diocesan priests and three Jesuits in the vicariate. His home consisted of two rooms added to a small mission church in the mining village of Granite. His cathedral was in the neighboring village of Idaho City. Before leaving for the First Vatican Council in late 1869, he approved building plans for the first Catholic church in Boise.

Not much is known about the bishop's life. He kept few records; his letters were chiefly appeals for financial aid. Showing the effects of his primitive living conditions, lack of proper food, the cold winters, and travel on horseback or on foot, he entered a period of deep depression and frustration. The closing of the mines in southern Idaho, the exodus of thousands of miners and their families, the departure of the Sisters of the Holy Names who had stayed only two years, and a vicariate in debt, contributed to the decline of the bishop's health. He remained in the vicariate until October 25, 1875, then returned to Vancouver Island.

Relieved of his heavy burdens, he gradually regained some of his earlier energy. His last years were devoted to writing and to working among the native peoples. He wrote commentaries on the *Imitation of Christ,* articles for the *London Tablet,* and a book on Gregorian chant in French. He died on January 12, 1898, and according to his request was buried in the Island's Saanichton Indian cemetery.

Bradley, Cyprian A., O.S.B., and Edward J. Kelly. *History of the Diocese of Boise 1863–1953.* Boise, Idaho, 1953.

Schoenberg, Wilfred, S.J. *History of the Catholic Church in the Pacific Northwest 1740–1983.* Washington, D.C.: The Pastoral Press, 1987.

Walsh, Nicholas E. *The Catholic Church in Idaho: An Overview.* Boise, Idaho, 1990.

✠ NICHOLAS E. WALSH

LORAS, MATHIAS (1792–1858)

First bishop of Dubuque, Iowa. Mathias Loras was born in Lyons, France, on August 30, 1792. He was ordained a priest in Lyons on November 12, 1815, and was ordained bishop of Dubuque in Mobile, Alabama, on December 10, 1837. He was the tenth of eleven children born during the French Revolution into a devoutly Catholic, wealthy bourgeois family. When he was ten weeks old, his father Jean, a city councilor of Lyons, was guillotined, the first of seventeen relatives who were victims of the Reign of Terror.

Mathias Loras

As a boy in the presbytery school of Rev. Charles Balley at Ecully, Loras began a lifelong friendship with a schoolmate, (St.) John B. Vianney. At the major seminary of St. Irenaeus in Lyons, he was taught by Ambrose Maréchal and was a fellow student of the Englishman James Whitfield, both future archbishops of Baltimore, Maryland.

During the great revival of the Church in France after the defeat of Napoleon I, Loras headed first the minor seminary at Meximieux and then the larger one at l'Argentière, founded in 1805 by Cardinal Fesch, archbishop of Lyons and uncle of Napoleon I. In 1827 he became a home missioner but then the next year left for the United

States with the Lyonnais, Michael Portier, first bishop of Mobile, Alabama.

First Bishop of Dubuque

After nine years in Mobile, where he acted as vicar general and was involved in the foundation of Spring Hill College there, Loras was named the first bishop of Dubuque. Following Portier's example, he returned, after ordination as bishop by Portier, to Lyons and Europe in search of clergy and funds. Loras arrived in Dubuque on April 18, 1839, accompanied by two Lyonnais priests, Joseph Crétin, later first bishop of St. Paul, Minnesota, and Anthony Pelamourges, along with four seminarians, and the Dominican priest, (the Venerable) Samuel Mazzuchelli, O.P., who had in 1835 and following years built at Dubuque a small stone church, the later Cathedral of St. Raphael, and a two-story brick "episcopal palace." Immediately Loras undertook the formation of the seminary of St. Raphael, which later was moved into stone buildings on the Table Mound south of the see city and renamed St. Bernard's. It eventually evolved into Loras College.

Beginning in 1839 Loras undertook missionary voyages up and down the Mississippi River by steamboat and canoe, and then overland into Wisconsin and into the Iowa Territory. During the 1840s and 1850s, when the public land in Iowa was being first offered for sale through the U.S. land offices at Dubuque and Burlington, Loras shrewdly purchased numerous town lots along with farm and timber land for future parishes and institutions, using funds generously supplied by the mission society of Lyons but also by those in Vienna and Munich. Especially Irish and German immigrants were encouraged to settle in Iowa, particularly around Dubuque, and promised, as soon as feasible, priests of their ethnic background or who spoke their language. The government policy of the removal of indigenous peoples and Protestant opposition ended missionary efforts to the Native Americans begun by Mazzuchelli, especially among the Winnebago.

In 1843 the Irish Sisters of Charity B.V.M., who had been burned out in Philadelphia during nativist riots, accepted the invitation of Loras to come to Dubuque, and in 1849 Trappist monks from Mount Melleray, Ireland, founded the priory, later abbey, of New Melleray on land southwest of Dubuque given them by Loras; one of them, the prior Clement Smyth, became the coadjutor and then successor of Loras as bishop, and another, James O'Gorman, became the first vicar apostolic of Omaha in 1859. During 1849–50 Loras made a second successful journey to Europe in search of priests, seminarians, and funds.

When the walls and roof of Mazzuchelli's St. Raphael's Church gave way, a new St. Raphael's was begun beside it. On Christmas Day 1857 Loras offered the first Mass in the new cathedral, when his final illness was already upon him. He died in Dubuque on February 19, 1858. During the nineteen years Loras was resident in Iowa the four priests and three churches had grown to fifty churches, forty-seven mission stations, with thirty-eight priests and three religious orders. To the hardships of the frontier born by his priests Loras sought too avidly to join the austerities he practiced in his own life. His gracious manners and pronounced accent were always those of a Frenchman, but his breadth of view and directness of approach were those of the American frontier.

See also IOWA, CATHOLIC CHURCH IN.

Auge, Thomas E. "This Savage Land" *Seed/Harvest, a History of the Archdiocese of Dubuque.* Ed. M. K. Gallagher. Dubuque, 1987, 1–23.

____. "The Dream of Bishop Loras, a Catholic Iowa." *Palimpsest* 61 (1980) 170–79.

WILLIAM E. WILKIE

LORD, DANIEL ALOYSIUS (1888–1955)

Jesuit priest, writer, and educator. Daniel Lord was born to George Douglas Lord and Iva Jane Lord on April 23, 1888, in Chicago, Illinois. He was one of two sons. He attended Catholic schools for his elementary and secondary education as well as for his college education (St. Ignatius College, Chicago). Lord entered the Society of Jesus at Florissant, Missouri, in 1909, received an M.A. degree from St. Louis University in 1915, and was ordained on June 24, 1923. Lord taught English at St. Louis University and its high school from 1917 to 1920. He also cofounded, administered, and taught in the university's Department of Education. From 1925 until 1948, Lord served

Daniel A. Lord

as editor of the *Queen's Work,* the primary means of communication for the Sodality of the Blessed Virgin. During that same period, he served as director of the sodality and revived that organization into a viable national movement.

Daniel Lord was dedicated to serving young Catholics. His primary concern was to raise their level of religious, social, and ethical consciousness that they might act in socially responsible ways. He acted on this commitment through his leadership of the Sodality of the Blessed Virgin, the largest Catholic youth organization in the country. Lord transformed the Jesuit organization by linking spiritual development with Catholic Action. In the summer of 1928, he organized the first national Leadership School. Three years later he held the first Summer School of Catholic Action (SSCA) on a national level. Along with the summer schools, he used lectures, retreats, and national sodality conventions to encourage development of the habits of reading and writing as well as to foster moral and spiritual life.

Lord believed that literature, motion pictures, and the performing arts were effective means of communicating moral values in society. Consequently, he continually worked to establish moral codes for producing, reading, and viewing these arts. Indeed, he helped draft the Motion Picture Production Code. Lord was himself an accomplished writer. He published thirty books, almost three hundred pamphlets, sixty-six booklets, fifty plays, twelve musicals, and six pageants. His talents were such that he was consulted for advice by movie producers, including Cecil B. DeMille. His own literary models included G. K. Chesterton and Hilaire Belloc.

Lord died of cancer on January 15, 1955, in St. Louis, Missouri.

Faherty, W. B. "A Half-Century with *Queen's Work.*" *Woodstock Letters* 92 (1963) 99–114.

——. "A Revival Is Organized: Daniel A. Lord and the Sodality Literary Campaign." *To Promote, Defend, and Redeem,* Arnold Sparr. New York, 1990, 31–50.

Lord, Daniel Aloysius. *Armchair Philosophy.* New York, 1918.

——. *Six One-Act Plays.* New York, 1925.

——. *Religion and Leadership.* Chicago, 1933.

——. *Storm-tossed: If Communists Had the Truth, or Catholics Had the Zeal.* St. Louis, 1936.

——. *Some Notes on the Guidance of Youth.* St. Louis, 1938.

——. *The New Sodality Manual.* St. Louis, 1945.

——. *Our Part in the Mystical Body.* St. Louis, 1955.

——. *Played by Ear.* Chicago, 1956.

McGloin, J. T. *Backstage Missionary.* New York, 1958.

PATRICIA DeFERRARI

LOUGHLIN, JOHN (1817–91)

First bishop of Brooklyn. John Loughlin, born in Clonduff, County Down, Ulster, emigrated with his parents, John and Mary McNulty Loughlin, to Albany about 1830. He attended Albany Academy, St. Peter's College at Chambly, south of Montreal, Nyack Seminary, Mt. St. Mary's College, Emmitsburg, and St. Mary's Seminary, Baltimore. Bishop John Hughes ordained Loughlin at old St. Patrick's Cathedral, New York City, on October 18, 1840. After brief assignment at St. John parish, Utica, he returned to the cathedral, becoming rector in 1844 and also vicar general in 1849. Loughlin attended the First Plenary Council of Baltimore

John Loughlin

as theologian to Hughes who proposed that Long Island become a distinct diocese. On July 29, 1853, Pope Pius X announced the erection of the Brooklyn diocese with Loughlin as its bishop. Consecrated by Archbishop Gaetano Bedini on October 30, 1853, Loughlin was installed at historic St. James Church in Brooklyn on November 9. Twenty-five priests in thirty-three parishes or missions were then ministering to fifty thousand Catholics. Loughlin attended the Second and Third Plenary Councils of Baltimore and the First Vatican Council. Although recommended for other sees, he remained in Brooklyn where, in 1890, 184 diocesan priests ministered to 300,000 Catholics. He died on December 29, 1891.

See also NEW YORK, CATHOLIC CHURCH IN.

Donnelly, Francis B. "Erection of the Diocese of Brooklyn: A Providential Afterthought." *U.S. Catholic Historian* 1 (4) (Fall 1981) 106–32.

One Hundredth Anniversary of Roman Catholic Diocese of Brooklyn 1853–1953. Supplement to *The Tablet* XLVI (October 31, 1953).

Sharp, John K., ed. *Priests and Parishes of the Diocese of Brooklyn, 1820–1944.* New York, 1944.

_____. *History of the Diocese of Brooklyn, 1853–1953: The Catholic Church on Long Island*. 2 vols. New York: Fordham University Press, 1954.

MARGARET M. QUINN, C.S.J.

LOUISIANA, CATHOLIC CHURCH IN

French Colonial Period

The 1699 presence of the French fleur-de-lis on the northern shore of the Gulf of Mexico, a Spanish preserve, was born of competition for empire and was effectively terminated by the 1759 British victory at Quebec. It was the will of his Most Christian Majesty Louis XIV (1643–1715), who thought of himself as a supervisor of bishops, that the cross would be a twin symbol of his authority. French political fate and the life of the Church were intertwined. Thus chaplains were assigned to the exploratory voyage of the Canadian brothers, Pierre Le Moyne d'Iberville and Jean-Baptiste de Bienville, and missionaries among the Native American nations were an integral component of the Le Moyne strategy. An alliance with the natives was essential for blocking the advance of the English deerskin traders from Carolina and the presence of missionaries in native villages was a necessity for winning the loyalty of the nations to the French Sun King and the one, true religion.

The military colony first planted at Biloxi and then at Mobile Bay, despite the grand strategy, experienced a constant struggle for survival. The timing could not have been worse. While the Treaty of Ryswick (1697) provided the opportunity for the French Gulf venture, the War of the Spanish Succession (1700–13) meant years of waiting for ships that did not arrive. Thanks to Bienville's skillful Native American diplomacy and the food supplied by the natives, the colony was barely able to maintain a foothold. When the Treaty of Utrecht brought peace to Europe, a war-exhausted king asked a financier rich from war profiteering, Antoine Crozat, to become proprietor of Louisiana. With Laumet of Cadillac as governor this arrangement continued until 1717. From the beginning, Louisiana was a part of the Diocese of Quebec. From 1704, when the few Jesuit missionaries withdrew, it was staffed by priests of the Society of Foreign Missions from Paris and Quebec. The ecclesiastical situation foreshadowed problems which would plague the Church throughout the French period: a bishop at an impossible distance, conflict between the Jesuits and the Capuchins over an exclusive vicar general, bickering with colonial authorities, and too few priests, inadequately supported, for such a vast and difficult mission. The bishop of Quebec erected, in July 1703, a parish at Mobile which survived the turmoil.

As returns on his investment were not forthcoming, Crozat surrendered his proprietorship that John Law's Company of the Indies inherited. The company at once made the fateful decision that the Mississippi valley was to be exploited by slave labor. A flurry of activity followed, some of which was in response to the regent's instruction: "We look particularly to the glory of God, in procuring the salvation of the settlers, the Indians, the Savages and the Negroes, whom we wish to be instructed in the True religion." The Superior Council of Louisiana promulgated a *Code Noir*. Concessionaires received huge land grants, purchased slaves in large numbers, and employed chaplains, the names of eight of whom are known. Contracts were signed with the Capuchins, the Jesuits, and the Ursulines. The friars were responsible for parishes and missions for the settlers; the Jesuits for the native missions; and the Ursulines, who arrived in 1727, for a hospital, care of orphans, and for the education of girls. A degree of tangible and permanent Church presence was at hand. In 1728 twenty-two priests were ministering in Louisiana. The next year, at Natchez, disaster struck. Two Jesuit missionaries were among those massacred. Lower Louisiana was traumatized. The company ceased importing slaves and surrendered its charter. The focus of the company on the Mississippi is indicated by the location of parishes erected from 1718–28: La Balize, New Orleans, Chapitoulas, the German Coast, Pointe Coupée. A parish at Natchitoches on the Red River, near the border with New Spain, was the exception. As a Royal colony, 1731–60s, Louisiana was stable but stagnant. The population of slaves and settlers lingered at 7,000 and, significantly, no new parishes were established.

Spanish Colonial Period

Once the defeat at Quebec in 1759 ended the French presence on the North American continent, Louis XV (1715–74) had to consider the disposition of Louisiana. He looked across the Pyrenees to his Bourbon cousin, His Most Catholic Majesty Charles III (1759–88), who accepted, not without hesitation, the huge and empty territory as a borderland or buffer against British expansionism. Indeed, only in 1769 with the arrival of General Alexandro O'Reilly with two thousand troops did Spanish governance become firm. After exterminating remnants of the Creole Revolt, O'Reilly ruled with a light hand and instituted extensive reforms. Given that Church and state still remained inseparable (Catholicism was the glue of the Spanish empire), ecclesial reform was included in his plans. The real *patronato* gave the Spanish king authority over all Church appointments. O'Reilly saw the need for eighteen additional priests and the establishment of parishes in strategic locations: between 1765 and 1798 fourteen were erected. Spanish Capuchins were recruited, the first band, with Cirillo de Barcelona as superior, arriving in 1772. A decade later Cirillo was nominated by Charles III to be auxiliary bishop of Santiago with residence in New Orleans. A zealous, if unbending reformer, his episcopal career was not a happy one. He returned to Cuba when a diocese was erected. A more famous, if controversial, friar, Antonio de Sedella (Père Antoine), arrived in 1781, remaining in New Orleans, except for a five-year exile in Spain and Cuba, until his death in 1829.

The most dramatic change in the Spanish years was demographic. As a consequence of international wars the population grew from 7,000 to over 50,000. Many of the Acadians exiled at the beginning of the Seven Years War eventually came to Louisiana, welcomed first by interim French authorities and then by Spanish governors, who erected for them parishes on the Acadian coasts of the Mississippi and on Bayou Lafourche. At the end of the American Revolution both east and west Florida, which for the preceding twenty years had been British, became Spanish territory, but with English-speaking subjects in interior west Florida. Irish missionaries from Salamanca were recruited to minister to them. And in the Saint Bernard delta a parish for emigrants from the Canary Islands was established. At the end of the century refugees from Saint Domingue literally doubled the population of New Orleans. And the free Louisiana Negro population increased from 1,300 in the Spanish census of 1785 to 8,000 in the first American census of 1810. For the most part, the new cathedral was their parish church.

Linked with the dramatic demographic changes was a definitive ecclesiastical organization in 1793. A need for a diocese could no longer be ignored. Finally, the efforts of Governor Baron de Carondelet prevailed and Charles IV (1788–1808) nominated Luis Peñalver y Cardenas (1749–1810) as bishop of the new Diocese of Louisiana and the Floridas. Peñalver, a talented native of Havana, took possession of his see August 2, 1795, his newly rebuilt cathedral (the old St. Louis Church was destroyed in the fire of 1788) was a gift of the philanthropist and builder Andres Almonester y Roxas, and had been consecrated the previous Christmas Eve by one of the Irish missionaries from Salamanca, Fr. Patrick Walsh. Although the bishop suffered from Louisiana's humidity, in his short administration he made four official visitation tours visiting his whole diocese with the exception of Upper Louisiana and east Florida. He established two new parishes, one in Avoyelles, west of the Mississippi, where Acadians had settled; and one in New Feliciana, east of the Mississippi, where Anglos had settled. At the end of the century, Peñalver asked to be transferred; and in 1801 he became the sixth archbishop of Guatemala.

At this time Napoleon was redrawing maps and Louisianans were once more treated as pawns. Napoleon took Louisiana in 1800 only to sell the territory to the young Republic of the United States in 1803. Having learned a lesson, unhappy residents resisted rebellion and opted to adjust to a new situation. Bishop John Carroll was advised, probably unnecessarily, by Pierre Clément de Laussat, the interim French colonial prefect, that the American government would take little interest in religious affairs.

1803–1835

An unfortunate result of Napoleonic European mischief and consequent shifting sovereignties in the Mississippi valley was jurisdictional chaos and searing discord in the "widowed" new American see with Franco-Spanish roots. The infant Church of Louisiana and the Floridas would remain without a bishop until DuBourg's consecration in 1815. Church personnel were lost, e.g., sixteen of the twenty-three Ursuline nuns left for Havana. When in March 1805 Sedella (Père Antoine), frustrated by the behavior of two French assistants, resigned as rector of St. Louis Cathedral, Fr. Patrick Walsh, who claimed to be vicar general, appointed himself rector. When the people rebelled and elected Sedella as pastor, a two-year schism followed. On September 20, 1805, Propaganda Fide in Rome extended Bishop Carroll's jurisdiction to the Louisiana Territory. Carroll, in turn, appointed Jean Olivier and Louis Sibourd, successively, as vicar general, and Louis William DuBourg as an apostolic administrator; each, upon arrival in New Orleans, was opposed by the church wardens. Indeed, when DuBourg returned to the United States in 1817 after his consecration in Rome, unwilling to face their hostility, to a certain extent based on his friendship with the restored Bourbons, he opted for an episcopal residence in St. Louis. This dispute over *jus patronatus* endured until a decision of the Louisiana Supreme Court in 1844.

Despite the early chaos and subsequent rapid succession of bishops—DuBourg resigned in 1826; Joseph Rosati, C.M., administrator, 1826–29; Leo de Neckère, C.M., 1829–33; and Antoine Blanc and Pierre Ladavière, S.J., coadministrators, 1833–35—remarkable initiatives were undertaken. DuBourg was a successful European recruiter for his frontier diocese. Vincentians established a seminary in Missouri; the Congregation of the Sacred Heart, under the leadership of Philippine Duchesne, began an educational apostolate; Italian missionaries founded parishes in Grand Coteau, Thibodaux, and Vermilionville (Lafayette). He had the Society for the Propagation of the Faith, founded in Lyons in 1822, allot a significant portion of its funds to the Louisiana Mission.

Rosati was influential in bringing the first contingent of Sisters of Charity from Emmitsburg to New Orleans in 1830. De Neckère invited the Sisters of Mount Carmel from Tours and established a second parish, St. Patrick's, in the see city. He also convinced a band of Jesuits on their way to Bardstown, Kentucky, to remain in his diocese for a year giving retreats and missions. The huge diocese of 1793 became, with the erection of the vicariate apostolic of Alabama and the two Floridas in 1825, and of St. Louis as a separate see for Upper Louisiana in 1826, a diocese coterminous with the state. Nonetheless, statistics are indicative of the missionary challenge. The population of the state had increased from 50,000 in 1803 to 215,739 in 1830; however, there were only twenty-four priests in Louisiana when de Neckère became a victim of yellow fever in 1833.

1835–1860

Bishop Louis William DuBourg never lost interest in his former see. From Montauban, his new see in France, he articulated New Orleans' need—a robust, hands-on leader. And being DuBourg, he had his candidate, his 1817 recruit from the Lyons seminary, Antoine Blanc, a forty-two-year-old veteran of the American Mission. DuBourg did not live to see Blanc wear the miter, but his protégé was, from 1835 until his death in 1860, the bishop DuBourg foresaw, and New Orleans needed. Like DuBourg, Blanc knew that his first task was to visit France to recruit priests and religious. And also, like his predecessor, he was eminently successful.

This success was the necessary ground of the hallmark of the Blanc administration: growth. Forty-seven parishes were established. The huge Redemptorist complex of three national churches for the Germans, the Irish, and the French, located near the Mississippi docks in the old City of Lafayette, was just the most notable. Twenty-four parishes in rural areas were added to the already existing seventeen. Legendary diocesan priests emerged in centers outside of New Orleans: the Raymond brothers, Gilbert and J. François, in Opelousas for southwestern Louisiana; Charles M. Menard in Thibodaux as the Apostle of Bayou Lafourche; Ange Marie Felix Jan in St. Martinville on Bayou Teche; and August Marie Martin in Natchitoches for the area north of the Red River.

Most satisfying for Blanc was that he had fulfilled DuBourg's dream of founding a seminary in Lower Louisiana. Staffed by the Vincentians, the Seminary of the Assumption was located in Plattenville on Bayou Lafourche and opened in 1838. The Jesuits established three colleges, two of which, one in Grand Coteau and one in New Orleans survived. The one in Baton Rouge closed when the faculty was wiped out by an epidemic. The number of academies for young ladies increased to eight. New Orleans's sword of pestilence was yellow fever; in 1853 at least nine thousand died, the majority recently arrived Irish and German immigrants. Thus there was an obvious need for care of parentless children; and the 1860 *National Catholic Directory* enumerates thirteen orphanages in the archdiocese and lists the religious congregations of men and women who staffed them. The Little Sisters of the Poor and the Sisters of the Holy Family, founded in

1842 in New Orleans by Henriette Delille with the encouragement of Vicar General Etienne Rousselon, provided care for the elderly. At Blanc's death there were some fifteen congregations, twelve of which were female, ministering in parochial, educational, and charitable apostolates.

Blanc had responsibilities beyond the boundaries of the diocese even prior to New Orleans' elevation to an archdiocese in 1850. Baltimore continued to ask the bishop of New Orleans to serve as vicar general in the state of Mississippi until in 1841 a bishop arrived in Natchez. Rome asked Blanc to undertake the diplomatic task of regularizing the ecclesiastical situation in the new Republic of Texas, which he accomplished by co-opting two outstanding Vincentians from St. Louis, John Timon and Jean Marie Odin, for refounding the Church in Texas. After 1850, as archbishop of the province of New Orleans, it was Blanc's responsibility to convoke and prepare provincial councils. And it was at his suggestion that Propaganda erected in 1853, for the northern part of the state, the Diocese of Natchitoches with his friend Auguste Marie Martin as the first bishop (1853–75). The French-born Martin strove valiantly to implant the Church in this strictly missionary territory north of latitude 31. Prior to his recruiting trips to France there were only four priests and seven churches, five of which were on the Red River, in his diocese; twenty years later, when among the 1873 yellow fever epidemic victims were five priests in Shreveport, there were twenty-nine priests, three religious communities of women, and twenty-six churches and chapels. A remarkable growth in a frontier diocese.

Nativism and trusteeism were twin demons commonly confronted by the early American Catholic bishops; however, the Louisiana experience, as in many other areas, was *sui generis*. For instance, while the Irish Catholic governor Edward Douglass White (1835–39) was scared by the customary attacks by the Native American politician William H. Christy, Blanc, as a "foreign" Frenchman, was attacked by the *ancienne population,* whose instrument was the Fabrique of St. Louis Church, for failure to respect Louisiana's colonial traditions. The confrontation became full blown when, following the death on August 3, 1842, of Fr. Louis Moni, Blanc appointed Etienne Rousselon as rector of the cathedral, an appointment that the church wardens declared null and void. Arguments in the press (Blanc's apologist was Abbé Napoleon Perché, editor of *Le Propagateur Catholique*) and courts continued until the summer of 1844 when the Louisiana Supreme Court decided that the *jus patronatus,* as a relic of colonial Church-state relationships, was not relevant in an American context. Toward the end of his episcopacy, in September 1858, Blanc broke his leg in an accident on the levee in Donaldsonville. The health of this previously energetic archbishop was never the same. He died of a heart attack on June 20, 1860.

1860–1905

Elected administrator of the archdiocese after Blanc's death, Jean-Marie Odin, C.M., bishop of Galveston, was appointed by Propaganda as archbishop at the beginning of 1861. Thus the experience of New Orleans as an Occupied City would be his. Nonetheless, aware as DuBourg and Blanc had been that recruiting was an imperative, he departed in the summer of 1862 for France. When he returned the following April on the chartered *Ste. Genevieve,* on board were thirty-six clerics for Louisiana, including Marist priests to staff Jefferson College in St. James parish, and another fifteen for Texas. Although Odin was remembered by his clergy for tightening the financial administration of the archdiocese, he erected parishes in settlements as far apart as Buras near the mouth of the Mississippi, Montegut in Terrebonne parish, and Lake Charles at the southwestern corner of the state.

An initiative of enduring impact was the invitation of the Sisters of Mercy to staff schools in the Redemptorist complex. Odin died in France in 1870, having gone to Rome to attend the First Vatican Council. He was succeeded by his recently consecrated coadjutor, Napoleon Joseph Perché, who had been in New Orleans since 1842 and was well known as the editor of *Le Propagateur Catholique,* as a staunch defender of Blanc against Know-Nothings and the church wardens, and as an ardent Confederate. Unfortunately, he was not an administrator. Rapid expansion of both rural parishes and parochial schools, in addition to unwise loans to friends, resulted in a staggering debt of $600,000. The panic of 1873 aggravated the situation and bankruptcy loomed. Frantic appeals were made to Propaganda through Archbishop James Gibbons of Baltimore with the result that in 1879 Bishop Francis X. Leray of Natchitoches was appointed coadjutor bishop and administrator of temporalities. Managing the debt remained a crippling concern of subsequent archbishops and, worse, soured relationships with pastors and religious until completely redeemed by Archbishop Chapelle in 1904.

When Perché died on December 27, 1883, Leray automatically became archbishop. Leray's unhappy tenure ended with his death in 1887 with the debt reduced by a quarter and bankruptcy avoided, but with angry disputes over his succession in the air. The two leading candidates, Fr. Placide Louis Chapelle and Bishop Francis Janssens, were well known in New Orleans. French-born Chapelle, pastor of St. Matthew's Church in Washington, D.C., and an intimate of diplomats and statesmen, had visited New Orleans with Gibbons. He was the candidate of the so-called French wing which saw New Orleans as a French see. Dutch-born Janssens, a protégé of Gibbons and bishop of Natchez since 1881 and thus a member of the province of New Orleans, was a proven administrator. After much

delay, possibly because Gibbons was a supporter of both prospects, Propaganda opted for the administrator, appointing Janssens on August 7, 1888.

A confident administrator, Janssens worked to decrease the debt without allowing it to consume him. He not only founded new parishes, but had each parish incorporated as a distinct legal entity, a most important initiative in the Americanizing of the archdiocese. Aware, however, of immediate needs, he recruited a band of Dutch priests and stationed many of them in the southwestern part of the archdiocese. The Lake Charles area became known as the "Dutch Deanery." Sensing that there would not be local vocations without a minor seminary, he invited monks from St. Meinrad to establish a Benedictine monastery and seminary on a two-thousand-acre plantation north of Lake Pontchartrain.

To minister to the numerous immigrants from Sicily, he invited both Mother Frances Xavier Cabrini, foundress of the Missionary Sisters of the Sacred Heart, and Scalabrini Fathers to work in the old French Quarter where the Sicilians had settled. To better serve black Catholics, he induced Mother Katharine Drexel to underwrite the erection of St. Katharine parish on Tulane Avenue in 1895. He also invited Josephites to work in black communities in rural Louisiana. Of special significance was Janssens' realization that evangelization of African Americans depended on a clergy of African American descent. He argued for a preparatory school for promising candidates, making his case, as early as 1887, in the *Catholic World.* This remarkably balanced Church leader died enroute to a vacation in the land of his birth. His successor was the other candidate of a decade earlier, Louis Placide Chapelle.

The new archbishop arrived on the eve of the Spanish-American War. At once his linguistic and diplomatic skills, as well as his old Washington friendships, were needed by the Church on the international scene. To protect Church interests he served as apostolic delegate to the Philippines until 1901 and to Cuba and Puerto Rico until 1905. He was also called on to attend the peace conference in Paris. Although these absences caused grumbling among the clergy, Chapelle had the pleasure of announcing at Midnight Mass, on Christmas Eve 1904, that the cursed debt had been liquidated. Finally free from both overseas travels and the debt, Chapelle dedicated himself to archdiocesan administration. Visiting Lake Charles in late July 1905 he was informed of a yellow fever epidemic in the French Quarter and returned to New Orleans. On August 9 he was a victim. And an era ended.

1905–1945

It was ironic that the one destined to be identified as the last French-born bishop of New Orleans would be an untimely victim of the last yellow fever epidemic to plague

Louisiana. A conjunction of additional events marked a new era: on a national level, the Church of the United States was removed from the jurisdiction of the Congregatio de Propaganda Fide; on a local level, engineer Albert Balwin Wood was perfecting his wood-screw pump which would drain the back-of-town swamps and alter the landscape of New Orleans. After both World Wars parochial restructuring followed radical residential changes.

Chapelle's successor was James Hubert Blenk, S.M., a Marist priest thoroughly identified with the Church in south Louisiana. Raised in the neighborhood of the Redemptorist complex, he became, after ordination in 1885, president of Jefferson College in St. James parish, and was pastor of Holy Name of Mary in Algiers and chairman of the board of studies for the Catholic Winter School when selected by Chapelle, in 1899, to be bishop of San Juan, Puerto Rico. Fittingly, the former college president is remembered as dedicated to educational reforms. Blenk established a school board and appointed Fr. Leslie J. Kavanagh, a former member of the Jefferson College faculty, as superintendent of Catholic education; St. Mary's Dominican became a normal school for Catholic teachers; Loyola College, in a new Uptown location, received a state charter as a university in 1912; and in 1915 the Sisters of Blessed Sacrament founded a school for blacks which would evolve into a high school, a normal school, a college and, in 1925, Xavier University of Louisiana. He reopened the preparatory seminary at St. Benedict, and laid plans for a future major seminary.

Blenk also established five separate parishes for blacks, thereby elevating into a policy what Janssens had introduced as an experiment, a policy that would not be successfully challenged until after World War II. In 1912 a council of the Knights of Peter Claver was organized in New Orleans. Blenk realized that, despite improving rail services, the archdiocese was too extensive and encouraged the erection of a diocese in southwestern Louisiana with Lafayette as the see. Blenk died of a heart attack on April 20, 1917, before Jules B. Jeanmard, his secretary and chancellor, was installed on December 12, 1918, as the first bishop of Lafayette.

Jeanmard, a native of the Acadian village of Breaux Bridge, knew the needs of his diocese. With the aid of Katharine Drexel, he founded twenty-seven rural schools for isolated Catholic blacks. In New Orleans Blenk's successor was John William Shaw, a native of Mobile, and bishop of San Antonio since 1911. Shaw saw the plans for a major seminary to fulfillment; and Notre Dame Seminary, staffed by the Marist Fathers, received its first students in 1923. In New Orleans population growth and new residential developments beyond the natural levees demanded new parishes; Shaw oversaw the erection of thirty-three new parish plants. Congregations with which Shaw was familiar in San Antonio, the Oblates of Mary Im-

maculate, the Teresian Sisters, and the Sisters of the Incarnate Word, were invited to help with staffing. In 1924, following a national trend, Shaw had Msgr. Peter M. Wynhoven centralize the social services and charities by setting up Associated Catholic Charities. In 1932, again using the multiple talents of Wynhoven, publication of the *Catholic Action of the South* was initiated. Shaw died on November 2, 1934, in the depths of the depression.

It was Wynhoven who masterminded the welcome of new archbishop, Joseph Francis Rummel, a New York priest who had been bishop of Omaha since 1928. He came to New Orleans with a reputation as a reformer, an orator, and a thorough administrator. Ordained in Rome in 1902, Rummel had taken his theology in an atmosphere fearful of theological Modernism and imbued with what the rector William O'Connell called *Romanità*. Rummel's sense of dignity, with a touch of triumphalism, earned him the affectionate title of Sir Noble. Both the depression and World War II limited the physical initiatives of the first decade of his administration. In the prewar years he directed the establishment of the Confraternity of Christian Doctrine in every parish and urged a thorough Christian formation. A strong believer in public profession of the faith, Rummel hosted in 1938 the Eighth National Eucharistic Congress, which, thanks to his own methodical genius, the skills of Wynhoven, and multiple committees, merited national praise. A suspicious cardinal archbishop even thought that Cardinal George Mundelein of Chicago was grooming Rummel for New York. The election of Pope Pius XII and World War II brought that talk and an era in American Church history to an end.

1945–1995

Unlike Chapelle, who died on the eve of the previous turning point in the history of the Church in Louisiana, Rummel administered the archdiocese until Vatican Council II, thus witnessing, as a Church leader, the end of the immigrant Church, the flourishing of the struggle for civil rights, and the emergence of white flight. World War II massively integrated American Catholics into the United States mainstream; and the G.I. Bill of Rights produced a generation of college-educated Catholics. As a Church leader Rummel was a crusader for social justice and, to a certain extent, the spokesman for racial integration, issuing, in 1953, a pastoral entitled "Blessed Are the Peacemakers," and publishing, in 1956, "The Morality of Racial Segregation."

His efforts were met by hysterical opposition in the state legislature and mass meetings of the White Citizens Council, and resistance by a segment of his clergy. His prophetic voice was never silenced, although liberals complained that his articulated stance was never implemented. Despite the tensions Rummel calmly continued to supervise multiple building programs: forty new parishes, mostly in suburban areas; a philosophy hall on the campus of Notre Dame Seminary in 1953; a new St. Benedict Seminary and a new chancery in the late 1950s; and finally a drive for four Catholic high schools in the burgeoning suburban Jefferson civil parish. On the sixtieth anniversary of his ordination to the priesthood in 1962, Rummel handed over the administration of the archdiocese to Coadjutor Archbishop John Patrick Cody (Rummel died November 20, 1964), who administered the see until he was transferred to Chicago, June 16, 1965. Cody's New Orleans years were marked by a flurry of building activities, specifically, the erection of twenty-five new parishes. He proceeded with the total racial integration of Catholic schools and centralized archdiocesan finances.

The appointment of Cody as coadjutor, July 20, 1961, was accompanied with the news of the erection of the Diocese of Baton Rouge, consisting of twelve civil parishes in southeastern Louisiana. After Vatican II additional jurisdictional divisions were forthcoming: Houma-Thibodaux (1977), comprising two civil parishes in southeastern Louisiana; Lake Charles (1980), comprising five civil parishes in southwestern Louisiana; and Shreveport (1986), comprising sixteen civil parishes in north Louisiana. These small dioceses were a consequence of the ecclesiology of Vatican II with its emphasis on the bishop as pastor of the local church. The divisions were contemporaneous with the emergence of the laity in supervisory positions and a rapid decrease in vocations to the priesthood and religious life. Long before the third millennium, the post-Vatican II Louisiana local churches had a new face. The change was most striking in parochial schools, where lay staffs became the rule; for example, in 1994 the ten elementary schools in Houma-Thibodaux engaged only four sisters, three in one school.

The Congregation of Bishops did not delay in appointing a successor to Cody. On September 29, 1965, Philip M. Hannan became the eleventh archbishop of New Orleans. The Roman-trained auxiliary bishop of Washington, D.C., was not unknown to the archdiocese as he had won fame as a paratrooper chaplain in World War II, as a friend of the Kennedys, and as a defender of American interests at Vatican II. He thus had personal experience with the three most significant components in twentieth-century American Catholicism. During his long administration (1965–89) Hannan earned recognition as a superb crisis manager and for his strong belief in the pastoral value of his personal presence. These talents were in demand at once, for Hannan arrived in the aftermath of Hurricane Betsy, the most destructive tropical storm ever to strike southeast Louisiana.

The fact that by the time of his resignation Hannan was the episcopal founder of thirty parishes is evidence of the resilience of the Church in New Orleans. Concurrent with the establishment of new suburban parishes was the decay of the inner city and new needs of senior citizens. Hannan's response to these was a social apostolate with which he personally identified, especially in fundraising. He was also instrumental in the emergence of Associated Catholic Charities as an agency for certain federal programs, and the construction of apartments for senior citizens, likewise with the help of government funds.

In addition, there was response to the immediate needs of Latin American and Vietnamese refugees and appropriate offices for long-term apostolates. Black Catholics had been a presence in Louisiana since the founding of the colony and their evangelization a challenge not adequately met, although called for as early as the *Code Noir* of 1724. A bold initiative was taken when Archbishop Hannan, having returned to the final session of Vatican II, announced in Rome, October 3, 1965, that the Divine Word priest Harold R. Perry, a Lake Charles native, would become his auxiliary. Perry was the first African American Catholic bishop in the twentieth century. He would be followed by a dozen others, six of whom are natives of Louisiana. A Black Catholics Office provides leadership in facilitating activities that involve the African American Catholic community. Two moments were particularly satisfying to Hannan. During the 1984 Louisiana World Exposition, the Vatican Pavilion was a state-of-the-art exhibit. And in 1987 from September 11–13, Archbishop Hannan was the host of the visiting Bishop of Rome, Pope John Paul II. The constant need of recruiting priests and religious was met by Hannan's personal recruiting visits to Ireland and by vocations from the local Vietnamese community. One-third of the diocesan priests ordained since 1989 were of Vietnamese descent.

In terms of overall Church organization, the province of New Orleans became coterminous with that of the state of Louisiana when Oklahoma City (1973) and Mobile (1980) became metropolitan archdioceses. In 1973, to formulate public policy positions and to speak more effectively in the public square, the Louisiana Catholic Conference was incorporated, the bishops of the province constituting the board. In 1993, the twelfth archbishop of New Orleans, Francis Bible Schulte, presided over the celebration of the Bicentennial of a Catholic Diocese.

Baudier, Rodger. *The Catholic Church in Louisiana.* New Orleans, 1939.

Conrad, Glenn, ed. *Cross, Crozier, and Crucible: A Volume Celebrating the Bicentennial of a Catholic Diocese in Louisiana.* Lafayette, 1993.

Curley, Michael J. *Church and State in the Spanish Floridas (1783–1822).* Washington, D.C., 1940.

Davis, Cyprian. *The History of Black Catholics in the United States.* New York, 1991.

Kasteel, Annemarie. *Francis Janssens, 1843–1897: A Dutch-American Prelate.* Lafayette, 1992.

Melville, Annabelle M. *Louis William DuBourg: Bishop of Louisiana and the Floridas, Bishop of Montauban, and Archbishop of Besançon, 1766–1833.* 2 vols. Chicago, 1986.
Muldrey, Mary Hermenia. *Abounding in Mercy: Mother Austin Carroll.* New Orleans, 1988.

EARL F. NIEHAUS, S.M.

LOYOLA COLLEGE IN MARYLAND

Loyola College in Maryland is a Catholic comprehensive university, under the aegis of the Society of Jesus, and more recently in collaboration with the Institute for the Sisters of Mercy of the Americas. Established in 1852, Loyola College was the first Jesuit college in the U.S.A. to bear the name of St. Ignatius Loyola and ninth among today's Jesuit collegiate institutions in the country.

Fr. John Early and eight of his Jesuit confreres opened Loyola's doors to the young Catholic laity of Baltimore—and also to a wider circle of non-Catholics—who sought a liberal education without the commitment of joining the priesthood. Less than a year later, the college petitioned the Maryland legislature for a charter, and on April 13, 1853, the Associated Professors of Loyola College in the City of Baltimore were incorporated. The charter permitted the granting of university-level degrees.

The original course of studies at Loyola followed the consensus of that time on what subjects were necessary to the formation of a liberally educated gentleman. The classical curriculum ranged from the rudiments of Latin, Greek, and English grammar, the humanities and rhetoric, to mathematics, the natural sciences, philosophy, and religion. In 1996, with 222 full-time faculty, the college had 3,000 undergraduate and 3,000 graduate students representing thirty-four of the fifty states and several foreign countries.

See also CATHOLIC UNIVERSITIES AND COLLEGES.

LOYOLA MARYMOUNT UNIVERSITY

Loyola Marymount University in Los Angeles is a Catholic independent university emphasizing undergraduate liberal arts in the educational traditions of the Society of Jesus (Jesuits) and the Religious of the Sacred Heart of Mary, and offering selected graduate professional degrees.

The university was founded in 1911 as an outgrowth of St. Vincent's College, the first college in Los Angeles. St. Vincent's had flourished into the early twentieth century. However, Bishop Thomas J. Conaty sought to expand, something which the Vincentians found of little interest. Bishop Conaty invited the Jesuits into the diocese and in 1911 the Vincentians withdrew and the Jesuits opened classes in the fall of 1911.

In 1926 Fr. Joseph Sullivan became the fifth president of the school and two years later decided that the high school and college should be physically separated. In 1928 the then Loyola College moved to its current location on the Westchester bluffs in the western portion of Los Angeles and two years later became Loyola University. The new location of the campus came about in part through the generosity of Harry Culver, movie industry executive, who donated one hundred acres on the condition that two buildings would be put up on the site within two years.

In 1973 the university merged with Marymount College to become Loyola Marymount University. Marymount College had been opened as a Junior College by the Religious of the Sacred Heart of Mary in 1933. In 1966 its president, Mother Raymunde McKay, approached then Loyola president Fr. Charles Cassasa to discuss an affiliation. The college physically moved to the Westchester campus in 1968 and the merger took place five years later. In 1996 the university enrolled more than 6,000 students at its Westchester campus and its Loyola Law School, located in downtown Los Angeles.

See also CATHOLIC UNIVERSITIES AND COLLEGES.

LOYOLA UNIVERSITY CHICAGO

Loyola University Chicago was founded as St. Ignatius College on September 5, 1870, by Arnold Damen, a member of the Society of Jesus who opened the college on the grounds of Holy Family Church, the first Jesuit parish in Chicago and, by the 1890s, the largest English-speaking parish in the city.

At the time of its opening, the college had four professors and thirty-seven students. The course of studies was the traditional six-year classical program favored by the Jesuits, which mirrored the model of the French *lycée*.

The college completed its first year of existence in 1871, just as the Great Chicago Fire swept the city on October 7. A change in the wind's direction spared the college, which served during the fire as both a shelter for the homeless and a distribution center for provisions. The college reopened two weeks after the great fire, but attendance decreased during the winter months due to a smallpox epidemic that had hit the city.

By 1895, the year of the college's silver anniversary, nearly five hundred students were enrolled, and some 1,500 students had matriculated at the school during its first twenty-five years.

In 1906 the college bought twenty-five acres at Devon Avenue and Sheridan Road on the North Side of Chicago, along Lake Michigan; this marked the beginning of what is today's Lake Shore Campus. In 1907 the college was renamed Loyola University; its current name, Loyola University Chicago, was adopted in 1970.

In 1908 Loyola established its first professional school in law; its second professional school, medicine, was initiated in 1909. In 1914 Frederic Siedenburg, S.J., opened the School of Social Work, the first of its kind established at a Roman Catholic institution of higher learning in the United States.

Since the 1960s, Loyola has continued to expand and enhance its commitment both to higher education and to health care. In 1962 Loyola became the first American university to establish a study center in Rome, Italy, and this international campus continues today as the Rome Center of Liberal Arts. In 1968 Loyola's Stritch School of Medicine was moved from its downtown Chicago location to a new campus in suburban Maywood, Illinois, west of Chicago.

In 1991 Mundelein College, a former women's college under the direction of the Sisters of Charity of the Blessed Virgin Mary, affiliated with Loyola.

In 1996 Loyola University Chicago had nearly 14,000 students from 50 states and 74 foreign countries enrolled in its nine schools and colleges. More than 104,000 Loyola alumni live and work in all 50 states and in some 120 countries around the world.

See also CATHOLIC UNIVERSITIES AND COLLEGES.

LOYOLA UNIVERSITY, NEW ORLEANS

The Jesuits were among the earliest settlers of New Orleans and Louisiana. A Jesuit chaplain accompanied Iberville on his second expedition and they are credited with introducing the growing of sugar cane to Louisiana, paving the way for one of the state's prime industries. The city's leaders, including Bienville, had long hoped for a Jesuit college and implored the Jesuits in France to come to the city. In 1837 seven Jesuit priests arrived. After weighing several sites, they decided that Grand Coteau, in St. Landry parish, was a better site for their boarding college than the fever-ridden city. In 1849 the College of the Immaculate Conception opened its doors at the corner of Baronne and Common Streets in downtown New Orleans. This college became a well-established and beloved institution. As the city grew, however, it became obvious to Rev. John O'Shanahan, S.J., superior general of the province, that the downtown area would become too congested for a college. He began looking for a suburban site.

In 1904 the long-planned Loyola College, together with a preparatory academy, opened its doors on St. Charles Avenue. The first president was the Rev. Albert Biever, S.J. The college grew steadily. In 1911 the Jesuit schools in New Orleans were reorganized. Immaculate Conception College became exclusively a college preparatory school. On July 10, 1912, the governor signed a legislative act authorizing Loyola to grant university degrees. Under the direction of the dynamic Fr. Biever and with the advice and financial support of New Orleans business leaders, the new university grew dramatically. The School of Law was also established in 1914. The College of Music

was incorporated into Loyola in 1932 from its previous existence as the New Orleans Conservatory of Music and Dramatic Art.

From 1926 to 1947, a four-year degree program leading to a bachelor of science degree in economics was offered by the College of Arts and Sciences. In 1947 the Department of Commerce of the College of Arts and Sciences expanded into the full-fledged College of Business Administration granting a bachelor of business administration degree. In 1950 the college was admitted to associate membership in the American Assembly of Collegiate Schools of Business, and in 1957, to full membership. In 1983 the college was renamed the Joseph A. Butt, S.J., College of Business Administration in honor of the Jesuit priest who taught generations of Loyola business students.

The university thus has a colorful and distinguished history marked by the zeal and scholarship of the Jesuits and the valued advice and support of leading citizens of New Orleans. Hundreds of the city's top leaders received their education from the Jesuits at Loyola University New Orleans, or its predecessor, the College of the Immaculate Conception. Teachers, scientists, attorneys, pharmacists, musicians, and business executives call Loyola their alma mater. Today, there are 33,000 total alumni.

Total enrollment in 1995 was 5,500 including 3,500 undergraduates. Fifty-nine percent were women, 41 percent were men, from 50 states and 59 countries, with 25 percent ethnic minorities. There were 261 full-time and 198 part-time faculty with 89 percent holding terminal degrees. There were sixty undergraduate degree programs and five colleges: Arts and Sciences, Business Administration, Music, City College (evening division), and School of Law.

JULIA McSHERRY

LUCE, CLARE BOOTHE (1903–87)

Author, member of Congress, ambassador. The multifaceted career of Clare Boothe Luce included a stint as editor of *Vanity Fair* magazine, the writing of hit Broadway plays, and public service, as both a Republican member of Congress from Connecticut and U.S. ambassador to Rome. She was later appointed ambassador to Brazil, but amid furor over a sharp-tongued remark she made at the time, she declined to accept the nomination even though it had been confirmed by the Senate. "She had enough careers to satisfy the ambitions of several women, but none tied her down for long," wrote Albin Krebs in the *New York Times* upon her death.

Clare Boothe, the daughter of a violinist and a chorus girl, was reared in lace-curtain poverty after her parents separated and until her mother married a physician from Greenwich, Connecticut, in 1919. As a young adult Clare Boothe became active in the woman's suffrage movement,

Clare Boothe Luce

then married the millionaire playboy, George Tuttle Brokaw, twenty-three years her senior. He was a heavy drinker and abusive, and the marriage ended in divorce.

Clare Boothe then landed a job as a magazine editor, first at *Vogue* and then at *Vanity Fair,* where she wrote satirical pieces at first and political pieces as she rose in influence and position. She left the magazine in 1934. A year later, her first play was produced on Broadway. *Abide with Me* (1935) concerned a drunken, abusive husband who is shot in the last act. Although her play flopped, the glamorous playwright received star billing in the society event of the year: she married the tycoon publisher of *Time* and *Fortune,* Henry R. Luce. Reportedly, it was Clare who suggested that her husband publish a new picture magazine. He did and called it *Life.*

Her second Broadway play, *The Women,* met with raves and earned her two million dollars. The story revolved around a wife trying to retrieve her husband from the clutches of an admiring saleswoman. The enterprising Clare Boothe Luce then lost no time cashing in on the success of Margaret Mitchell's Pulitzer Prize-winning novel, *Gone With the Wind.* Luce's comic play, *Kiss the Boys Goodbye,* was based on the Hollywood hoopla surrounding the search for the lead actress to play opposite Clark Gable in the film version.

With the outbreak of World War II, Clare Boothe Luce strove to make a more substantial mark on history. In 1940, she wrote a book about her recent travels, *Europe in the Spring,* which received mixed reviews. She also began to criticize President Roosevelt's handling of the war. On the platform, "Let's run a hard war instead of a soft war," Luce ran for Congress in Connecticut's Fourth

District in 1942, the same district where her stepfather had once been elected a representative. She ousted the Democratic incumbent in a close race, but won reelection handily the following year. Serving as the only female member of the House Military Affairs Committee, the freshman Congresswoman attracted an unusual amount of newspaper publicity.

When her nineteen-year-old daughter was killed in an automobile accident, Luce met the popular radio preacher, the Rev. Fulton J. Sheen, and reportedly asked him, "Listen, if God is good, why did He take my daughter?" "In order that you might be here in the faith," Sheen replied, setting her on the road to conversion. Luce became a Roman Catholic in 1946. She published a series of articles about her religious conversion in *McCall's* magazine and wrote several religious works, including *Saints for Now,* an edited volume with contributions by Evelyn Waugh, Rebecca West, and Whitaker Chambers. Her screenplay for the film *Come to the Stable,* starring Loretta Young and Celeste Holme as two Catholic nuns, was nominated for an Oscar as best motion picture of the year.

Luce actively campaigned for the election of Dwight D. Eisenhower, and, in return, the successful candidate offered her a cabinet post as secretary of labor. When she declined, the president appointed her ambassador to Italy (1953-57). She was the nation's second female ambassador, following Rheta Child Dorr's appointment to Denmark.

In a short tribute to Luce appearing on the *New York Times* editorial page after her death, the author wrote that what eludes print is "how she was able to disarm those she well knew were disposed to dislike her, especially males determined not to be taken in by a woman they believed to be too smart and ambitious to be up to any good." What, exactly, was her technique? The author concluded: "She would ask a question, and, wonder of wonders . . . she listened. Then she would ask another question and do the same. She gave what was most unlikely: her ear."

The recipient of several honorary doctorates, frequently appearing on lists of the nation's "ten most admired women," Luce also received the Presidential Medal of Freedom in 1983. She died of cancer on October 9, 1987, while living at the Watergate in Washington, D.C.

New York Times, October 10 and 12, 1987.

KAREN SUE SMITH

LUCEY, ROBERT EMMET (1891–1977)

Archbishop. Robert Emmet Lucey was born on March 16, 1891, in Los Angeles, California, the fourth of nine children of John and Mary Nettle Lucey. Following an education at St. Vincent's College in Los Angeles and St. Patrick's Seminary, Menlo Park, Lucey was sent to the

North American College in Rome to complete his theological studies. In May 1916 he was ordained a priest. A month later he was awarded a doctorate in theology. In July 1916, Fr. Lucey sailed for home to commence a priestly vocation which led him—within the next few years—to serve in several parishes, act as Newman Club chaplain at U.C.L.A., work on a number of boards and commissions related to welfare programs, initiate Confraternity of Christian Doctrine courses in the Diocese of Los Angeles, and found the radio program, "The St. Anthony Hour." He was, by the early 1930s, viewed by many people as an activist priest.

Robert E. Lucey

A Texas Prelate

On May 1, 1934, Robert Emmet Lucey was consecrated bishop of Amarillo, Texas. Lucey, who had been named the ordinary of Amarillo on February 10 of that year, was consecrated at St. Vibiana's Cathedral in Los Angeles, by Archbishop Amleto Giovanni Cicognani, apostolic delegate to the United States. Such an ecclesiastical appointment seems to have been made in anticipation of the churchman's ultimately receiving the episcopal miter for the archbishopric of San Antonio, where his work on behalf of the poor and oppressed people would serve the Church and humanity well.

A bishop who focused on applying Catholic social teaching especially to the Mexican-Americans throughout his diocese, Lucey often ran into opposition from within and outside of the Church. He persevered in his efforts and accomplished much good. In this context, Lucey emerged as an outspoken supporter of labor unions, not only in his diocese, but throughout the United States.

With the death of Archbishop Arthur Drossaerts of San Antonio on September 8, 1940, Lucey appeared a natural choice as his successor. And so he was named and consecrated on January 21, 1941. In San Antonio, Lucey quickly initiated a Confraternity of Christian Doctrine program. He displayed his interest in ecumenism by involving non-Catholic students in that program. It should be remembered that that was two decades before the Second Vatican Council.

Archbishop Lucey was involved in virtually every major issue that confronted the Catholic Church during the almost three decades that he labored as archbishop. In 1969 he retired as archbishop of San Antonio, and on May 23 of that same year was named titular archbishop of Taormina. Named archbishop emeritus of San Antonio in 1970, Lucey died at San Antonio on August 2, 1977.

See also TEXAS, CATHOLIC CHURCH IN.

Bronder, Saul. *Social Justice & Church Authority: The Public Life of Archbishop Robert E. Lucey.* Philadelphia: Temple University Press, 1982.

Privett, Stephen A., S.J. *The Catholic Church and Its Hispanic Members: The Pastoral Vision of Robert E. Lucey.* San Antonio: Trinity University Press, 1988.

PATRICK FOLEY

LUDWIG MISSIONSVEREIN, THE

King Ludwig I of Bavaria on December 12, 1838, gave his name and formal approval to the Ludwig Missionsverein. Its purposes included aid to German Catholics in the United States. Ten years earlier, Fr. Frederick Résé, a German priest (then vicar general of Cincinnati) had unsuccessfully petitioned the king in Munich to create a society for support of the young American Church similar to both the Leopoldine Society (Vienna, founded 1828) and the Society for the Propagation of the Faith (Lyons, founded 1822). The king did, however, permit the collection of alms in Bavaria, which during the next decade were sent to Cincinnati and Detroit. Various reports of missionary needs and successes, and continued requests from Résé (now bishop of Detroit), persuaded the king to create a mission aid society which was to assist the Church in America, as well as in Asia and the Holy Land. Ten thousand promotional copies of its statutes were used to attract members who were organized in groups of ten, made weekly contributions, prayed the Our Father and the Hail Mary (without obligation in conscience), and could receive indulgences granted to members of other mission societies.

Although associated in its beginning years with the Society in Lyons for reports *(Annales)*, requests, and distribution of collected funds, by 1844, after considerable turbulence concerning inappropriate disposition of funds to non-German causes, the Ludwig Missionsverein had severed these connections and was channeling its gifts first through the Congregation for the Propagation of the Faith in Rome, and then directly to recipients.

The king resigned his throne in 1848, but continued until his death in 1868 as enthusiastic Protector of the expanding mission society, by then extensively devoted to the United States. On May 19, 1852, Archbishop Francis Kenrick, on behalf of the assembled bishops of the First Plenary Council of Baltimore, wrote, "We extend renewed thanks for the many kind donations, which the worthy Ludwig-Missionsverein has sent during so many years to the missions of this country, and also for the prayers. . . . By these means it has become possible to accomplish much that would otherwise have remained a pious wish."

The central council in Munich decided their first priority should be to supply German-speaking priests, and from 1845 many efforts of varying success were supported: a planned general seminary; Bishop John Martin Henni's *Salesianum* (Milwaukee, 1856) that received large sums from 1862 through 1879; various preparatory schools for young seminarians; theological study in Europe for American seminarians; for example, with the Redemptorists in Altötting, Bavaria, or at The American College (Louvain, 1857). Interestingly, Bishop Michael Domenec of Pittsburgh declined assistance offered on condition of European study, saying he would train his own seminarians, and in 1863 he ordained one priest exclusively for work with German-speaking Catholics, with one other seminarian then not yet of canonical age.

The Redemptorists were the principal beneficiaries for many years through 1864. Funds were also supplied to the Benedictines, starting with Abbot Boniface Wimmer and St. Vincent's Abbey at Latrobe, the Abbey of St. Louis on the Lake at Collegeville (named after the king, but later called by the name of its college, St. John's), St. Meinrad's, Conception Abbey, St. Benedict's at Mt. Angel, Oregon (which received 45,700 marks between 1882 and 1901), and many other Benedictine foundations. The Franciscans, Carmelites, Capuchins, Vincentians, Jesuits (especially in the missions among the Native Americans of the West) also received help.

The Austrian Jesuit, Fr. Francis Xavier Weninger, came to America in 1848, worked principally among German-speaking Catholics, traveled and preached widely, received (between 1852 and 1887) 45,699.02 gulden and 24,621.43 marks, ended the schism at St. Louis' parish in Buffalo, and was instrumental in starting the annual national collection for missions among African American and Native American Catholics. Assistance ($4,000) was given through Fr. Weninger to establish a school for black American children in Cincinnati staffed by the Sisters of Notre Dame de Namur. German Ursuline Sisters, Benedictines, Dominicans, Sisters of the Poor of St. Francis, and other communities of religious women received significant assistance, as did many bishops for their parishes, schools, and dioceses.

Following the movement of German-speaking immigrants, donations of varying amounts and duration were recorded (separately from gifts to religious in the same areas) for many bishops and dioceses including Burlington, Richmond, Charleston, Buffalo, Newark, and Pittsburgh. On the Upper Peninsula of Michigan, Bishop Frederic Baraga received a special gift to acquit diocesan debts before his death, and Bishop Ignatius Mrak, because of his poverty, received a gift for episcopal vestments on his way to Rome. Bishop Henni received generous help for Milwaukee, as did the Dioceses of La Crosse and Green Bay. Until retirement at age ninety, Fr. Pierz in Minnesota received help, as did the Dioceses of Leavenworth and Wichita, dioceses in Idaho and Texas, and elsewhere. Gifts were described in the *Annalen* of the following year.

Documents in many archives and the Munich *Annalen* (published between 1848 and 1918) detail a proud, if sometimes turbulent, story of effective Bavarian help for the young American Church.

See also GERMAN CATHOLICS IN AMERICA; LEOPOLDINE SOCIETY, THE; RÉSÉ, FREDERICK.

Barry, Colman, O.S.B. *The Catholic Church and German Americans*. Milwaukee, 1953.

Bleid, Benjamin. *Austrian Aid to American Catholics, 1830–1860*. Milwaukee, 1944.

Roemer, Theodore, O.F.M. Cap. *Ten Decades of Alms*. St. Louis, 1942.

_____. *The Ludwig-Missionsverein and the Church in the United States (1838–1921)*. New York, 1933.

JOHN T. MONAGHAN

LUSK, HALL S. (1883–1983)

Jurist. Hall Stoner Lusk was born in Washington, D.C., in 1883. He graduated from Georgetown University with an A.B. degree in 1904, and from its Law School in 1907. He moved to Oregon and was admitted to the bar there in 1910.

He joined a private practice in Portland, was assistant United States attorney for Oregon from 1919 to 1921, and became active in various Catholic organizations, serving on the board of trustees of the University of Portland and the advisory board of Marylhurst College, among others. In 1922 Oregon voters passed an initiative measure that would have required all children to attend public schools, and Archbishop Alexander Christie appointed him one of the four attorneys to challenge the law's constitutionality on behalf of the Sisters of the Holy Names. When the state appealed a lower court's adverse ruling, he helped to write the brief which led the United States Supreme Court to confirm its unconstitutionality.

In 1930 he was appointed a state circuit judge, and in 1937 he became a justice on the State Supreme Court, served as chief justice for the 1949–51 term, and continued as justice until 1960. Then-Governor Mark Hatfield appointed him to the United States Senate to fill out the last six months in the term of Richard Neuberger who had died earlier that year. In 1961 he was recalled to the State Supreme Court as a pro-tem justice and continued in that position until 1968.

He was highly regarded by his fellow barristers, and his reputation as a stylist led his colleagues on the State Supreme Court often to choose him to write decisions demanding precise language. He was cited in 1951 by the National Conference of Christians and Jews for his contribution to interfaith understanding, and he also served in many civic organizations, including the governing councils of the Portland Symphony Society and the Boy Scouts. He died in 1983, six months short of his one-hundredth birthday.

The Oregonian, Portland, Oregon, October 8, 1972; May 16, 1983.

Schoenberg, Wilfred P., S.J. *Defender of the Faith. The History of the Catholic Sentinel, 1870–1990,* Portland: Oregon Catholic Press, 1993.

JOSEPH A. SCHIWEK, JR.

LYKE, JAMES P. (1939–92)

Franciscan friar and archbishop. James Patterson Lyke was born February 18, 1939, in Chicago, Illinois, the youngest child of Amos and Ora Sneed Lyke. Lyke's parents separated during his childhood and he was reared in Chicago's housing projects. Desiring an excellent education for her children, his mother enrolled them in Catholic schools. Most of the Lyke family converted to Catholicism during Lyke's childhood.

In 1959 James entered the Franciscan novitiate at Teutopolis, Illinois, and was ordained to the priesthood on June 24, 1956. His first assignment in Ohio was teaching at Padua Franciscan High School in a Cleveland suburb. An African American, Lyke found time to organize voter registration drives and to assist with Dr. Martin Luther King's "Operation Breadbasket" in Cleveland's predominantly African American East Side.

His next appointment took him to Memphis, Tennessee, where he served at St. Thomas Church and convinced his parishioners to involve themselves in organizations that sought peace and justice. His next pastoral assignment brought him to St. Benedict the Black Church in Grambling, Louisiana. Here Lyke continued his work and convinced his parishioners to work for the poor and oppressed.

Pope John Paul II appointed Lyke auxiliary bishop of Cleveland and titular bishop of Fornos Maggiore on June 30, 1979. Cleveland's ordinary, Bishop James A. Hickey, named Lyke Vicar of the Urban Region which encompassed the city of Cleveland. Lyke began the Urban Region Planning Process where Cleveland parishes met in clusters and began planning for a sharing of personnel, resources, and ministries. Lyke participated in numerous civic organizations such as the Cleveland Commission on Poverty, the Cleveland Roundtable, and a special commission to review charges of police brutality.

Lyke recognized the necessity for African American Catholic leaders to work together nationally. In 1984 he was one of the conveners in writing the African American bishops' pastoral letter on evangelization, "What We Have Seen and Heard." Lyke was specially concerned about melding the African American heritage into Roman Catholic liturgy. He was the coordinator for *Lead Me, Guide Me,* the African American hymnal published in 1987, which gained a worldwide audience.

A prolific writer and gifted speaker, Lyke testified before congressional panels on behalf of tuition tax credits, housing for the poor, and the need to combat hunger. As a social critic he spoke out against those trends which threatened and debased African Americans. He pointed out that the trivialization of sex contributed to the destruction of families.

On July 10, 1990, he was appointed apostolic administrator of the Archdiocese of Atlanta. His first pastoral letter in Atlanta was a poem on the dignity and value of human life. Pope John Paul II named Lyke archbishop of Atlanta on April 30, 1991, and he was installed on June 24, 1991. Lyke became ill with cancer and died in Atlanta on December 27, 1992.

Bishop James P. Lyke, Public Information File, Archives, Diocese of Cleveland.

Catholic News Service. January 5, 1993.

Catholic Universe Bulletin. January 15, 1993.

Chicago Tribune. April 27, 1980.

CHRISTINE L. KROSEL

LYNCH, DOMINICK (1754–1825)

Merchant and philanthropist. Lynch was born in Galway, Ireland, in 1754. He was the son of James Lynch, a successful merchant, and Anastasia Joyce, a prominent Galway family. After marrying his distant cousin, Jane Lynch, in 1780, he went to Bruges, Flanders, to open a commercial house for his father. There he made his fortune in trading flax seed to Ireland. In 1783 he formed a partnership with Thomas Stoughton, a merchant with Spanish and French connections, to open a commercial house in America. Stoughton immediately left for New York and Lynch emigrated with his family in 1785. Disagreements between the two men over the management of the firm led to its dissolution in 1795. Lynch continued to add to his fortune through numerous business ventures, including land speculation. By 1800 he had purchased close to 2,000 acres in the Fort Stanwix region of upstate New York that he laid out into village lots. It eventually became the city of Rome.

Lynch immediately assumed an active role in New York's Catholic community. Appealing to his friends and family in Ireland, it was largely due to the funds raised and contributed by Lynch that New York's first Catholic church, St. Peter's, was built. In 1790 he was asked to be one of five signers to the "Address of Congratulations from the Catholics of the U.S." to George Washington after he became president. Lynch contributed generously to Catholic causes throughout his life, with his final act being the donation of his country estate in Clason Point (now part of the Bronx) to the Christian Brothers after his wife's death.

Meehan, Thomas F. "Some Pioneer Catholic Laymen in New York: Dominick Lynch and Cornelius Heeney." *Historical Records and Studies* 4 (1906) 285–301.

TRICIA T. PYNE

LYNCH, KILIAN (1902–85)

Carmelite friar. Kilian Lynch was born in Ballymanus, County Wicklow, Ireland, in 1902. After entering the Carmelites and professing his vows (1922), he was sent to Rome for studies. Ordained there on June 17, 1828, he also received a doctorate from the Academy of St. Thomas in 1926, the *laurea* in theology from the Venerabile Collegium Vaticanum, and the lectorate in theology from Collegio San Alberto. From the Gregorian University he received a doctorate in theology and the honor *Magister Aggregatus*. Lynch was the vicar prior for a short period of time at the Carmelite Roman center of studies, San Alberto. In the fall of 1931 he was sent to the United States to teach philosophy at Marymount College, Tarrytown, New York. He was prior of the Tarrytown Carmelite community (1934–43) and pastor of Transfiguration Church there (1937–43). Having served as a provincial consultor, he was elected provincial of the New York province of St. Elias in 1943 and served until 1947 when he was elected general of the order in a chapter delayed by World War II.

During his term, he repaired the ravages of war to those provinces not under communist domination, reestablished provinces in Portugal and in England where he secured the repossession of the ancient monastery of Aylesford, and inaugurated it as a center of pilgrimage. Using himself as an example, Lynch insisted on regular observance, and promoted vocations and education in the order. In his term the membership of the order increased by 767 and this trend continued until 1963 when it reached 2,760.

He provided liturgical texts for the Carmelite Rite, established a heremitical house at Wolfnitz, Austria, and opened a Carmelite house at Fatima, Casa Beato Nuno. To promote studies within the order, Lynch began the Institutum Carmelitanum for the publication of monographs and the scholarly periodical, *Carmelus*.

Together with the Discalced Carmelites, he planned the celebration of the seven-hundred anniversary of the scapular in 1950–51, commemorated the centenary of the Immaculate Conception in 1954 with an international congress, and celebrated the fifth centenary in 1952 of the membership of women in the order.

After completing twelve years as general (1959), Lynch was briefly prior of Aylesford and then provincial of the English province. He served (1972–85) at the retreat house in Hazlewood, England, where he died on October 11, 1985.

ALFRED ISACSSON, O.CARM.

LYNCH, PATRICK NEISON (1817–82)

Bishop. He was born in Clones, County Monaghan, Ireland, on March 10, 1817, the son of Conlaw Peter Lynch and Eleanor MacMahon Neison. The Lynch family immigrated to America in 1819 and settled in Cheraw, South Carolina.

At twelve years of age, Patrick Lynch entered the Seminary of St. John the Baptist in Charleston, South Carolina. Because of his academic abilities, Bishop John England sent him and James A. Corcoran to study in Rome. Lynch entered the College of the Propaganda where he studied philosophy and theology. He excelled in his studies and

Patrick N. Lynch

received many honors and awards, placing first in his class for Arabic and Hebrew studies. Lynch was ordained on April 4, 1840, by the Cardinal Prefect of the Propaganda. On September 4 he received a doctorate in sacred theology.

After returning to the Diocese of Charleston, Lynch acted as secretary to Bishop John England. He was also assigned as editor of the *U.S. Catholic Miscellany* and remained as editor until 1845. In 1845 Lynch was appointed rector of St. Mary's Church, Charleston, and he also taught Church history at the Seminary of St. John the Baptist until its closure in 1851. Upon Bishop Reynolds' death on March 9, 1855, Lynch was made the administrator of the Diocese of Charleston. He was appointed bishop on December 11, 1857. Under his leadership the diocese continued to develop. By 1860, the diocese, which included both North and South Carolina, had nineteen churches, forty stations, and fifteen priests.

On the issue of slavery and the Civil War, Bishop Lynch proved to be a loyal son of the South. Following the theological position of Bishop England, Lynch did not approve of the slave trade, but he accepted the practice of slavery as it existed in the South. Lynch did support freeing the slaves, but only after they had been educated and prepared for freedom. Lynch himself bought at least one slave and the diocese paid taxes on nine slaves. After the Civil War, Lynch established several programs to educate the former slaves.

When the South severed itself from the Union, Bishop Lynch approved of the separation and blamed the Republicans for the breakup. In 1863 Lynch issued a pastoral letter to the faithful of the diocese asking all to pray for an end to the violence and the establishment of a just and honorable peace. He was invited by the South Carolina House of Representatives to a seat on the floor of the House. Lynch stayed through the August bombardment of Charleston which saw 2,500 shells fall on the city. The diocese had previously suffered severe property losses in the 1861 fire. After the bombardment the only Charleston facility left standing was St. Patrick's Church. In 1864 Lynch was commissioned by Confederate President Davis to go to Europe on a confidential mission to seek support for the Confederate government. After visits to Halifax, England, and France, Bishop Lynch arrived in Rome where his efforts to have Pope Pius IX recognize the Confederate government failed. Earlier in the Civil War, assurances were received through the efforts of Archbishop Hughes that the Vatican would not intervene in the American war. Consequently, Lynch was only received in Rome as a bishop on an *ad limina* visit. When Lynch learned of Lee's surrender on April 9, 1865, he made arrangements to return home. In Paris, he encountered difficulty with American officials and was refused papers to return to the U.S.A. Through the efforts of Archbishops Martin Spalding and John McCloskey, Lynch received a pardon from President Johnson. After taking the required oath of allegiance to the United States, he was able to sail for New York.

Bishop Lynch spent the remainder of his years in the diocese working to rebuild the devastated churches. Strapped with a large debt, estimated at $385,000 in the gold values of 1860, and constantly in need of funds, Lynch spent considerable time outside the diocese seeking support.

He died in Charleston on February 26, 1882.

See also CIVIL WAR AND AMERICAN CATHOLICS, THE.

Madden, Richard C. *Catholics in South Carolina: A Record.* Lanham, Md., 1985.

O'Connell, Jeremiah J. *Catholicity in the Carolinas and Georgia.* New York: D & J Sadlier, 1879.

EDWARD LOFTON

M

MACHEBEUF, JOSEPH (1812–89)

The first Catholics to enter what is now the state of Colorado were Spanish missionaries. To minister to these and to other Catholics who came to the region following the discovery of gold in 1858, the archbishop of Santa Fe, New Mexico, Jean Baptist Lamy, who had ecclesiastical jurisdiction over the territory of Colorado, chose a frail-looking Frenchman, Joseph Projectus Machebeuf, who was born in Riom, France, on August 11, 1812. In 1860

Joseph P. Machebeuf

Machebeuf was assigned his new parish—all of what is now Colorado and Utah. Fr. Machebeuf traveled in a wagon outfitted with a square canvas top so he could sleep inside. When he wished to offer Mass, he lowered the tailgate of the wagon, which served as his altar.

Machebeuf arrived in Denver on October 29, 1860. A handful of Catholics welcomed him with the news that they had acquired two lots on what is now the corner of Fifteenth and Stout Streets. The first church in Denver was completed on this site in time for Christmas Mass, 1860. The church was named St. Mary in honor of Our Blessed Mother, to whom Machebeuf dedicated all of his ministry. He was consecrated bishop of the vicariate on August 16, 1868. To his great relief, the huge vicariate of Colorado was cut in half in 1871 when Utah was transferred to the Archdiocese of San Francisco.

Machebeuf founded Colorado's first Catholic charity, the St. Vincent de Paul Society, on April 1, 1878. By the 1880s, the society had raised and spent several thousand dollars each year on Colorado indigents. On September 1, 1882, Machebeuf opened Mt. St. Vincent Orphanage for over two hundred children under the guidance of the Sisters of Charity of Leavenworth, Kansas. This was the institution in which Pope John Paul II offered Mass for the children during World Youth Day in August 1993.

In 1876, when the Colorado Constitution was adopted, Bishop Machebeuf and others fought successfully to exempt churches and church schools from state taxation. He also argued that tax money should follow students to the school of their choice, but he was unsuccessful. On August 16, 1887, Pope Leo XIII elevated the vicariate of

Colorado to the Diocese of Denver. Because of his failing health, Bishop Machebeuf was assigned at this time a coadjutor with the right of succession, the Rev. Nicholas C. Matz. Machebeuf died on the morning of July 10, 1889, having received the last sacraments from the hands of Bishop Matz.

The lasting influence of Machebeuf has been well documented by the Rev. William J. Howlett, Colorado's first native-born priest and the author of *Life of Bishop Machebeuf.* Howlett wrote:

> When Father Machebeuf came to Colorado in 1860 he was alone with Father Raverdy, without a single church, or a roof over his head; when he was made bishop, he had but three priests; when he died the Diocese of Denver counted 64 priests, 102 churches and chapels, 9 academies, one college, one orphanage, one house of refuge, ten hospitals, and over 3,000 children in Catholic schools. This was primarily the work of one man, and that man was Bishop Machebeuf. He was truly: The Apostle of Colorado.

Howlett, William J. *Life of the Right Reverend Joseph P. Machebeuf.* Pueblo, Colo.: Franklin Press, 1908.

Noel, Thomas J. *Colorado Catholicism and the Archdiocese of Denver, 1857–1989.* Niwot: University of Colorado Press, 1989.

WILLIAM JONES

MacRAE, GEORGE WINSOR (1928–85)

Biblical scholar. MacRae entered the Society of Jesus in 1948 and was ordained a Catholic priest in 1960. In addition to his undergraduate studies at Boston College, philosophical studies at Louvain, and theological studies at Weston Jesuit School of Theology, he received a master of arts degree in Semitics from Johns Hopkins University and a Ph.D. in New Testament studies and the history of religion from the University of Cambridge. After teaching at Weston from 1966 to 1972, he became the Stillman Professor of Roman Catholic Studies at Harvard Divinity School in 1973. He was acting dean of Harvard Divinity School at the time of his sudden death in 1985.

MacRae lectured and wrote on various New Testament books (especially John's Gospel), the Coptic gnostic documents from Nag Hammadi, and Catholic biblical interpretation. He was associated for many years with *New Testament Abstracts,* and served as executive secretary of the Society of Biblical Literature (1973–76) and on many editorial and university boards. He was regarded as a brilliant lecturer and preacher, as well as a leader in American biblical scholarship, theological education, and ecumenism. A selection of his essays and a bibliography of his writings appeared in the posthumous *Studies in the New Testament and Gnosticism* (Wilmington, Del.: Glazier, 1987).

DANIEL J. HARRINGTON, S.J.

MAGINNIS, CHARLES DONAGH (1867–1955)

Architect. Famous for the design of churches, hospitals, seminaries, schools, and monuments, Maginnis was born on January 7, 1867, in Londonderry, Ulster, Ireland. He studied architecture in Dublin and migrated to the United States in 1884. Settling in Boston, Maginnis joined the architecture firm of Edmund Wheelwright. By 1898 Maginnis had his own architecture firm, Maginnis and Walsh. His work reached all parts of the United States, but his most famous works are to be found on the East Coast, with such magnificent designs as the Shrine of the Immaculate Conception and the chapel of Trinity College, both in Washington, D.C. Maginnis' firm won the Architects' Gold Medal for Ecclesiastical Architecture in 1927 for his work on the chapel at Notre Dame. Examples of his work in the academic setting can be found at Boston College, Marymount Seminary, and Holy Cross College. During his career, Maginnis won many awards, including the Laetare Medal in 1924. He won the gold medal of the American Institute of Architecture three times, was made a Knight of Malta, and was awarded numerous degrees. He served as the president of the American Institute of Architecture in 1937–38 and was the first president of the Liturgical Arts Society. Maginnis died on February 15, 1955, in Brookline, Massachusetts.

LISELLE DRAKE

MAGNIEN, ALPHONSE (1837–1902)

Seminary rector, educational reformer. Born in Mende, France, in 1837, and ordained for the Diocese of Orleans in 1862, Alphonse Magnien developed his ecclesiastical vision in accord with the liberal Catholicism of his bishop, Félix Dupanloup, and the prominent lay leader Charles de Montalembert. After entering the Society of St. Sulpice in 1865 he volunteered to teach at St. Mary's Seminary in Baltimore. Some twelve years later (1878) he became superior of the seminary. The appointment of the liberal, urbane Magnien represented a departure from the austere French conservatism that had dominated the society in the United States. Indeed, Magnien was a vigorous Americanizer, which involved adjustments in Sulpician traditions to accommodate the needs of American seminarians.

The desperate need for native vocations to the society led to a movement for an American Solitude (Sulpician year of formation following the ordination of the candidate) and for greater self-government among the Sulpicians in the United States. Americanization also entailed opening of the seminary to contemporary intellectual and social trends. He hosted the Third Plenary Council of Baltimore at the seminary with a blend of American openness and French savoir-faire.

Magnien endorsed a climate of trust within the seminary. He said that Americans "have a taste for freedom

Alphonse Magnien

and are used to it; appealing to their reason, their conscience and their heart is the means to teach them gradually how to use that freedom responsibly and to be able to give up some of it in the matter of our Rules. . . . Teaching them with a broad mind and trust, we have a great advantage of seeing them open to us, and thus letting us know them as they are." Such a prescription would be considered liberal in the 1990s.

However, Magnien went even further. He placed newspapers and journals in the student reading room, allowed the best students to attend classes at Johns Hopkins University, and initiated extracurricular "academies" in Scripture studies and moral theology in which seminarians were introduced to the finest secular and religious scholarship in those areas. Such reforms fostered Sulpician vocations among the brightest students, which allowed the Sulpicians to expand into Boston, New York, and San Francisco. Magnien appointed young American Sulpicians to leadership positions in Boston and New York as well as in the minor seminary, St. Charles in Ellicott City, Maryland.

As secretary, friend, and confidant of Cardinal James Gibbons, Magnien was a behind-the-scenes participant in the controversies associated with Americanism. According to one of the most impassioned Americanists, Denis O'Connell, rector of the North American College, later rector of The Catholic University of America and bishop of Richmond, Magnien was "the heart and head of the whole movement in America." Americanism may be viewed as a blend of ecclesiology and spirituality that extolled the development in American Catholic ethos of democracy as *the* model for Catholic adaptation to the forces of modernity throughout the world. Based upon a positive

anthropology and an incarnational spirituality, Americanism became associated with events in France which led to its condemnation in 1899 in the apostolic letter *Testem benevolentiae.* One of the Americanist errors was that the Church should "shape her teachings in accord with the spirit of the age."

Though Magnien was distressed with this setback, he wrote to his close friend, the leading Americanist prelate Archbishop John Ireland of St. Paul, during the heat of the controversy:

> You stand before the public as a representative of views which are sure to win and to rule, though you may not live long enough to see their triumph. Bishop Dupanloup and M. Montalembert fought to the end and died apparently conquered; today their names are glorified and their policy rules the church. So, I suppose it will be in America. Let us have confidence in the future. . . . Your labors will be reaped in the American Church.

Alphonse Magnien died in 1902, five years before the condemnation of Modernism; anti-Modernist measures led to the demise of his American reforms and imposed an arid manualist conformity upon the intellectual and academic life of the seminary. Magnien's prophecy on the long-range success of the ideals of John Ireland proved to be on the mark as Vatican Council II fostered an ecclesiology and an intellectual climate congenial to movements analogous to Americanism and Modernism.

Kauffman, Christopher J. *Tradition and Transformation in Catholic Culture: The Priests of St. Sulpice in the United States: 1791 to the Present.* New York: Macmillan, 1988.

Papers of Alphonse Magnien are located at the Sulpician Archives, Baltimore and Paris.

White, Joseph M. *The History of Catholic Seminaries in the U.S.* University of Notre Dame Press, 1990.

CHRISTOPHER J. KAUFFMAN

MAGUIRE, CHARLES BONAVENTURE (1768–1833)

Franciscan friar. Born in County Tyrone, Ireland, on December 16, 1768, Charles Bonaventure Maguire entered the Irish province of the Franciscan friars as a young man and was sent to study at The Catholic University of Louvain, Belgium. Following his ordination to the priesthood, he taught theology at the College of St. Isidore, the Irish Franciscan school in Rome. Subsequently, while ministering to Germans in the Netherlands, Fr. Maguire narrowly averted an almost certain death at the hands of Napoleon's troops. In 1817 he arrived in the United States with an appointment as "missionary apostolic" from the Roman Congregation for the Propagation of the Faith. Ambrose Maréchal, the archbishop of Baltimore, sent him to western Pennsylvania, where he established the church in Ebensburg. Three years later, he was appointed pastor of St. Patrick's Church in Pittsburgh.

During the 1820s in that city, Maguire zealously preached the gospel and witnessed a dramatic increase in the Catholic population. In 1825 he published an apologetic for the faith, *A Defense of the Divinity of Jesus Christ and of the Mystery of the Real Presence.* He also served as a professor at the academic institution now known as the University of Pittsburgh. His foresight led to the establishment of Pittsburgh's second Catholic Church, St. Paul the Apostle. On June 29, 1829, he laid the cornerstone for the new church at the corner of Fifth Avenue and Grand Street. Although he did not live to see the completion of the edifice, the church was dedicated on May 4, 1834, and became the cathedral of the newly erected Diocese of Pittsburgh on August 11, 1834. At the time of his death on July 17, 1833, Maguire's erudition and faith had merited the esteem of the entire city of Pittsburgh.

See also FRANCISCAN FRIARS.

Lambing, Andrew A. *A History of the Catholic Church in the Dioceses of Pittsburgh and Allegheny From Its Establishment to the Present Time.* New York: Benziger, 1880.

JOHN COUGHLIN, O.F.M.

MAINE, CATHOLIC CHURCH IN

The Catholic Church in Maine began with the French settlement of Sainte-Croix Island where Nicholas Aubry offered the first Mass in New England in 1604. Subsequently, the Jesuits founded a mission on Mount Desert Island in 1613 prior to the arrival of the Franciscans in 1619. Later, in 1648, the Capuchins, who had established themselves in the area of Penobscot Bay by 1635, set up a chapel at what is now Castine. However, eventually the whole region became the responsibility of the Jesuits who had founded the Assumption Mission on the Kennebec River in 1646 and who, thereafter, served the inhabitants on all the major rivers of Maine.

With France and England struggling for the control of North America (1689–1763), most of the Jesuit missions were destroyed, including St. Anne's, which had been founded among the Penobscots on Indian Island in 1688. Certainly, the martyrdom of Sebastian Râle (August 23, 1724), the defeat of the French at Quebec (September 18, 1759), and the suppression of the Jesuits (August 16, 1773) weakened the growth of the Catholic Church in Maine.

Nineteenth Century

However, after the American Revolution, in which the Catholic Native Americans of Maine played a vital role, there were encouraging signs. John Carroll, the nation's

first Catholic bishop, sent priests like John Cheverus, later first Catholic bishop of Boston, to care for the Penobscots near Old Town and the Passamaquoddy natives at Pleasant Point. Then, with the coming of the Irish, what is now the oldest Catholic Church in New England, St. Patrick's at Newcastle, was formally opened on July 17, 1808, the year that Maine was included in the newly established Diocese of Boston. And, on August 11, 1833, due to the efforts of Fr. Charles Ffrench, old St. Dominic's, the first Catholic Church in Portland, was dedicated.

When the Diocese of Portland was established on July 29, 1853, Catholics were an isolated minority in Maine with roots deep in the past. However, they increased in numbers in Benedicta, Madawaska, and North Whitefield, while, at the same time, attracting converts elsewhere. This growth came about despite such examples of bigotry as the burning of Catholic Churches at Bath and Ellsworth and the tarring and feathering of John Bapst, the Jesuit pastor of the Bangor area.

After Henry B. Coskery (1808–72) of Baltimore refused the appointment, David W. Bacon became the state's first Catholic bishop (1855–74) and dedicated the cathedral, designed by the renowned Catholic architect Patrick J. Keeley, on September 8, 1869. Bacon was followed by James Augustine Healy, the first black American Catholic bishop, whose episcopate (1875–1900) witnessed the arrival of many immigrants, especially the French-Canadians who settled in Biddeford, Lewiston, and elsewhere, thereby raising the Catholic population close to 100,000.

Twentieth Century

Healy's successor, William H. O'Connell (later cardinal archbishop of Boston), was a new bishop (1901–06) in a new century. O'Connell sought to improve relations among Catholics of different ethnic groups as well as with those of other faiths. Louis S. Walsh (1906–24), his energetic successor, set his own imprint on the diocese by establishing parishes, including national ones for Italians and Poles, and building schools. John G. Murray, the fifth bishop (1925–31; later archbishop of St. Paul), gifted with a command of languages that endeared him to many immigrants, experienced the increasing financial threat to the diocese. With the Great Depression absorbing much of the Church's revenues, Joseph E. McCarthy, the next bishop (1932–55), a lovable shepherd, labored generously for close to a generation to stabilize the serious fiscal distress of the diocese.

Eventually, building on McCarthy's achievements, Daniel J. Feeney, the first native son to serve as bishop of Portland (1955–69), brought the diocese out of debt and attuned it to the reforms of the Vatican Council II. His immediate successor, Peter L. Gerety (1969–74), later archbishop of Newark, was a forward-looking innovator who emphasized social action. Edward C. O'Leary, a second Maine native, followed Gerety as the ninth bishop (1974–88), and proved himself to be a friendly and popular leader. With Joseph J. Gerry, a Benedictine and the third native of Maine to become bishop of the Diocese of Portland (1988), now assisted by Michael R. Cote, his new auxiliary bishop, the Catholics of Maine have been blessed with a devoted teacher of the word of God in a diocese with some 140 parishes.

Certainly, the Catholic Church in Maine is more than its bishops and priests, even though it can claim as native sons Josue M. Young, who became bishop of Erie (1854–66); Donald E. Pelotte, S.S.S., bishop of Gallup (since 1990), who became the first Native American ordained a bishop in 1986; and Armedee Wilfrid Proulx, whose whole episcopal career was unique in the diocese as auxiliary bishop of Portland (1975–93). Though the diocese includes many different religious groups such as Dominicans, Franciscans, Jesuits, and Ursulines, among others, the involvement of the Sisters of Mercy throughout the diocese has been paramount.

Likewise, the contributions of laypersons cannot be overlooked. Edward Kavanagh, the first Catholic to serve as Maine's governor (1843–44), was followed in that office by other Catholics such as Edmund S. Muskie (1955–59), James B. Longley (1975–79), and Joseph E. Brennan (1979–87). Though Muskie has been regarded as the first Catholic to serve as secretary of state (1980–81), he was actually preceded in that office by James G. Blaine (1881, 1889–92) of Maine and James F. Byrnes (1945–47) of South Carolina, who had been baptized Catholics, not unlike Margaret Chase Smith (1897–1995), a Maine Republican who was the first woman to serve in both houses of the U.S. Congress. And, finally, lay organizations like the Knights of Columbus, Daughters of Isabella, St. Vincent de Paul Society, Holy Name Society, and Legion of Mary have also added to the lives of Maine Catholics, who presently number about 235,000 out of 1,230,000 inhabitants.

Lord, Robert H., John E. Sexton, and Edward T. Harrington. *The History of the Archdiocese of Boston in the Various Stages of Its Development.* 3 vols. New York: Sheed and Ward, 1944.

Lucey, William L. *The Catholic Church in Maine.* Francestown, N.H.: M. Jones Co., 1957.

Young, Edmund J. A. "The Diocese of Portland." *History of the Catholic Church in the New England States,* ed. William Byrne and others. Boston: Hurd & Everts Co., 1899. 2:465–561.

VINCENT A. LAPOMARDA, S.J.

MALONE, SISTER STANISLAUS (1863–1949)

Religious, hospital administrator. Catherine Malone was born on December 24, 1863, near Marysville, California, the daughter of Francis Malone and Brigid Collins Malone. Raised by the Daughters of Charity in Virginia City, Nevada, she entered that community on November 15, 1883, and professed her first vows on November 21, 1888, as Sr. Stanislaus. She received her early professional and religious training at Mount Hope Retreat House and Emmitsburg novitiate in Maryland, worked briefly at St. Agnes Hospital in Baltimore, and was assigned to Charity Hospital in New Orleans (1884).

Sr. Stanislaus was among Charity Hospital's first class of graduating nurses (1895) and one of the state's earliest registered nurses. Her many positions at the hospital included supervisor of outpatient services, operating room supervisor, director of nursing, and local superior. She was influential in establishing Charity Hospital's School of Anesthesia (1916) and affiliating the nursing school with Louisiana State University (1932). She attracted more than three million dollars in donations to the hospital.

For more than sixty years, Sr. Stanislaus unselfishly ministered to New Orleans' needy and afflicted, "regardless of race or creed," during every major local epidemic and catastrophe. She received an honorary doctorate of science from Loyola University (1936) and the New Orleans *Times-Picayune* Loving Cup (January 13, 1945) for her "exemplary humanitarian work" and her contribution to the development of Charity Hospital. The announcement mentioned that she was often called "New Orleans' Most Beloved Woman."

Sr. Stanislaus died at Charity Hospital on June 8, 1949, and was buried in Soniat Cemetery in New Orleans.

Catholic Action of the South, August 6, 1936; January 18, 1945; June 9, 1949.

Doherty, Eddie. *Nun with a Gun: Sister Stanislaus, A Biography.* Milwaukee: Bruce Publishing Co., 1960.

Lancaster, Vincentine. *Katie Malone.* St. Louis, Mo.: Marillac Provincial House, 1963.

New Orleans *Times-Picayune,* January 13, 1945.

Personnel Files, Archives of the Daughters of Charity, Marillac Provincial House, St. Louis, Missouri (courtesy of Patricia Garland, D.C.).

CHARLES E. NOLAN

MALONE, SYLVESTER (1821–99)

Priest and social activist. Malone was born in Trim, County Meath, Ireland, on May 8, 1821, to Catholic parents, Laurence Malone and Marcella Martin Malone. He was educated in a school with both Protestant and Catholic students. In 1839 Malone emigrated to the United States and began studies for the priesthood in the Diocese of New York at St. Joseph's Seminary, Fordham. He was ordained a priest by coadjutor Bishop John McCloskey in 1844. His first assignment was pastor of St. Mary's Church in Williamsburg on Long Island. Malone became a priest of the newly formed Diocese of Brooklyn in 1853 and remained pastor of this same Williamsburg parish for fifty-five years, during which time he built a new church and renamed the parish SS Peter and Paul.

Malone soon became known to a wider circle than his parishioners. One of the rare Catholic abolitionists, he strongly supported the north in the Civil War and evoked criticism for his "negrophily" from Bishop John McGill of Richmond. Malone also believed strongly in ecumenism and spoke out publicly against religious prejudice. In 1868 he appeared at a civic event with Protestant and Jewish clergy—an action considered radical for its day. Malone associated with progressive New York priests who were known as the "Accademia," and he suffered criticism and suspicion because of this association. He supported Dr. Edward McGlynn after his excommunication, and even spoke out strongly against Archbishop Michael Corrigan for his treatment of McGlynn.

Though Malone was kept at arm's length by Church authorities, he was enormously popular with the public, and in 1894 he even defeated Bishop Bernard McQuaid of Rochester for a seat on the Board of Regents of the University of New York. While popular, Malone still had his critics. Even Dr. Richard L. Burtsell, a close friend of Malone's and a fellow member of the Accademia, complained about him. In Burtsell's famous diary, which chronicled clerical life in New York during this period, Burtsell criticized a statement Malone had made about Bishop John Loughlin of Brooklyn and remarked that Malone "never had any brains" (July 23, 1865).

In 1895 Malone hosted a fete in his own honor celebrating the golden anniversary of his priesthood. At this ostentatious event, Archbishop John Ireland of St. Paul praised Malone and predicted that "the future success of the Catholic Church in America will be measured by its fidelity to the lines suggested by the record and lifework of Father Malone." Malone was much like Ireland in that they shared a love for being the center of attention and would speak publicly to claim the limelight. They also realized that old models of Church-state relationships would not work in the new American republic. While keeping to the Catholic tradition, Malone, and other liberal-minded priests, tried to forge a new way for the Church in the United States, an effort that led to the condemnation of "Americanism" in *Testem benevolentiae,* Pope Leo XIII's letter to Cardinal James Gibbons of Baltimore, dated January 22, 1899. Malone died in Brooklyn on December 29, 1899.

Memorial of the Golden Jubilee of the Reverend Sylvester Malone. Brooklyn, N.Y., 1895.

O'Brien, Denis R. "The Centenary of Rev. Sylvester Malone, Great Catholic and Great Citizen." *The Journal of the American Irish Historical Society* 20 (1921)179–92.

ANTHONY D. ANDREASSI

MANHATTAN COLLEGE

Manhattan College traces its origin to four Christian Brothers who arrived in New York City on July 26, 1848, from LeHavre, France. They were received and supported by Fr. Annet Lafont, pastor of the French parish of St. Vincent de Paul, who wanted the brothers' services in staffing his newly established parochial school.

The Christian Brothers quickly succeeded in attracting many students to their classrooms at 16 Canal Street. In fact, they found it necessary to move to a more ample location where they could also open their first novitiate, with the welcome approval of the bishop. Br. Stylien secured a new site at West 131 Street in Manhattanville. Manhattan College had its beginnings in this newly founded school in 1854, which was then called the Academy of the Holy Infancy. Br. Paulian Fanning succeeded Br. Stylien as director of the academy in 1861 and changed the name of the institution to Manhattan Academy "in honor of the historic island in which it stands." In the same year, Br. Paulian was joined by Br. Patrick Murphy, who had spent his previous six years as the founding president since obtaining accreditation from New York state.

Another important figure in the founding of Manhattan Academy was Dr. Levi Silliman Ives, a former Episcopalian bishop. Dr. Ives and his friend Br. Patrick incorporated Manhattan College in 1863 with the help of "prominent and sympathetic laymen." The first catalog of Manhattan College states as one of its goals a certain "prominence to the higher mathematics and natural sciences not hitherto received in any similar institution in this country; thus combining the advantages of a first-class College and Polytechnic Institute." The catalog of 1864–65 listed twenty-one faculty members, including seven brothers, one priest, and nine laymen.

Manhattan College received its permanent charter on February 12, 1891. By that time, it had four identifiable schools in existence: Arts and Sciences, Engineering, Business, and an Evening School, which eventually became the School of Teaching Preparation. In 1923 the campus was moved to the Riverdale section of the Bronx.

Manhattan College became coeducational with the acceptance of its first women undergraduates in 1973. The current number of students averages about 3,500, including 2,835 undergraduates and 665 graduates. The present mission statement of Manhattan College recognizes the founding spirit of John Baptist de La Salle as it identifies the school as a "private independent institution of higher learning which embraces qualified men and women of all faiths, races and ethnic backgrounds."

Costello, Gabriel. *The Arches of the Years: Manhattan College, 1953–1979.* New York: Manhattan College, 1980.

____. *The Tree that Bore Fruit: Manhattan College, 1853–1953.* New York: Manhattan College, 1953.

THOMAS A. LYNCH

MANOGUE, PATRICK (1831–95)

Founding bishop of the Diocese of Sacramento, California. Patrick Manogue's life has a heroic quality about it. He stood six feet four inches tall and was both handsome and intelligent—a "man's man." In addition, he is forever associated with the discovery of gold in California and silver in Nevada, since he was a miner during the early days of the gold rush.

Manogue was born March 15, 1831, in County Kilkenny, Ireland. Because of famine and foreclosure—and the fact that both his mother and father had died, he emigrated to the United States to look for work to support his family. He was eighteen years old. In a letter written in 1885 to a possible relative living in Grass Valley, Manogue recalled that "I left Ireland in 1849 from school and went on my arrival to Virginia in quest of my uncle who used to write to the old country. . . . Not finding him or seeing any encouragement in Virginia I left for the Northern States and after some time I entered the University of St. Mary's of The Lake, Chicago. . . ." Patrick Manogue wanted to be a priest; yet, in 1853 he left the university and crossed the country to California and gold. In the hills above Grass Valley he worked blasting rock. Manogue soon made enough money to buy a share in the mine and a good education at one of the best seminaries in the world, St. Sulpice in Paris. Manogue had never given up his idea of becoming a priest. In fact, even while he worked as a miner he continued his studies. He was a remarkably self-possessed man, a quality well respected and rarely tested by the miners.

Missionary Priest in Nevada

Ordained in Paris in 1860, he was sent by Archbishop Joseph Alemany, O.P., to Virginia City, Nevada, a raw little town some six thousand feet above sea level, unknowingly perched upon the Comstock silver lode. One of Manogue's closest mining friends, John Mackay, later discovered the silver, and supported Manogue's efforts at building churches, hospitals, and the present cathedral in Sacramento.

Manogue lived in Virginia City for twenty years. In 1861 the area was organized into the vicariate apostolic of Marysville, and in 1868 it became the Diocese of Grass Valley. Manogue described his life in one of his earlier letters: "This state of Nevada [part of the Marysville vicariate, 167,000 square miles, which included northern California and Nevada] contains 98,000 square miles, and for several years I have been the only priest to attend to [the] spiritual wants of the people dispersed over its vast surface." He was, however, made for the job and relished it. He was the right man not only for the city and the territory, but for that time in the history of the Church in the United States. Like any far-seeing leader, he saw the need for and built not just churches, but hospitals, schools, and orphanages. And he organized huge societies that helped the underprivileged. In the late nineteenth century, he was already encouraging priests hoping to work in the Diocese of Grass Valley to learn Spanish before they arrived. His priests loved the man with genuine affection.

Because of his temperament, a web of myths and stories gradually accumulated around the things he did—and these stories stuck with him. There is a story about the time he went out at night on a sick call to a dying woman. When he arrived at the cabin, the woman's husband, a non-Catholic, was waiting for him—with a gun in his hand. No "priest" was going to enter his house! Manogue calmly got off his horse, "decked" the husband, took his gun away, then went in to anoint the woman and pray with her. When he left the cabin, he returned the gun to the stunned husband and rode off for Virginia City.

First Bishop of Sacramento

On January 16, 1881, Manogue was named coadjutor to Bishop Eugene O'Connell of Grass Valley, but he continued to live in Virginia City. On March 17, 1884, Manogue succeeded O'Connell as bishop of Grass Valley, but that same year the diocesan boundaries were reorganized and the see city was relocated in Sacramento with Manogue as the first bishop.

Manogue was an impressive, well-known, and well-educated figure during his time. He read French, Latin, Greek, Hebrew, and studied all his life, yet he had a genuine and effective concern for the poor. Fortunately, he never lost sight of his origins. Nor did he use his authority to brow-beat or diminish a person. However, it is true to say that men brought up solely on the lines of ecclesiastical authority were probably intimidated by Manogue because of his ability and strength: he was not poured into a narrow mold, and those who were instinctively gave him a wide berth. Still, he was just as liable as not to answer the doorbell dressed in an apron carrying a dust mop.

Those who knew him best loved him and genuinely grieved when he died in Sacramento on February 27, 1895. What he said about his own death reveals this: "When I die I do not wish to be buried in the Cathedral, but out at the graveyard among my people."

See also CALIFORNIA, CATHOLIC CHURCH IN.

Breault, William, S.J. *The Miner Was a Bishop: The Pioneer Years of Patrick Manogue, California-Nevada, 1854–1895.* Rancho Cordova, Calif.: Landmark Enterprises, 1988.

BILL BREAULT, S.J.

MARÉCHAL, AMBROSE (1768–1828)

Archbishop of Baltimore. Ambrose Maréchal was born of fairly prosperous parents at Ingré in the Diocese of Orléans, France, on December 4, 1768. Although destined by his parents to study law, he chose instead the priesthood. He entered the Society of St. Sulpice and was ordained in Paris in 1792. He immediately left to join the Sulpicians at the recently established St. Mary's Seminary in Baltimore. Initially assigned to the Maryland missions, he eventually taught at both St. Mary's Seminary and Georgetown College before he was recalled to France in 1803. In 1812 he returned to teach at St. Mary's Seminary until his appointment as coadjutor to Archbishop Leonard Neale of Baltimore. After Neale died, Maréchal was raised to the episcopacy as archbishop of the oldest American archdiocese on December 14, 1817.

Ambrose Maréchal

To the Holy See he submitted the first truly comprehensive report on the Catholic Church in the United States. The most serious problem, he confided, was the number of schisms provoked by rebellious trustees. Maréchal had to contend with the schisms of Norfolk, Virginia, and Charleston, South Carolina, until 1820, when the Dioceses of Richmond and Charleston were created. To their creation, however, he objected strongly, having not been consulted in the process. He also contested the power of

the Jesuits in Maryland, who refused to continue a subsidy provided the two previous archbishops.

In 1821 Maréchal decided to make an *ad limina* visit to Rome to settle these and other affairs. There he practically dictated the terms of the papal brief *Non sine magno* of 1822, by which American bishops would be guided in their future dealings with trustees. He was awarded a substantial portion of the Jesuits' most productive estate in Maryland in lieu of a subsidy and was given a voice in the creation of future sees and the appointment of bishops. The Maryland Jesuits, however, refused to honor the Roman decision and the quarrel continued into the administrations of the next two archbishops. The Roman visit, nevertheless, established the archbishop of Baltimore as the principal spokesman for the Catholic Church in the United States.

While Maréchal displayed a decided boldness in his dealings with the Roman officials and the Jesuits, as well as with the Sulpicians who refused to close Mount St. Mary's College and Seminary of Emmitsburg, he was cowed by his suffragan, the dynamic Bishop John England of Charleston. From the day he arrived in Charleston until Maréchal's death, England importuned the archbishop of Baltimore to hold a provincial council to resolve the difficulties that beset the Church in America, a step Maréchal stubbornly refused to take. He also resented England's intrusion into the affairs of his suffragan sees.

Although considered by many of his suffragan bishops a man of mediocre talents, especially when compared to England, Maréchal proved an efficient, though sometimes querulous, administrator in his own archdiocese. Although a product of the *ancien régime,* he readily embraced such American principles as religious liberty and the separation of Church and state and moved as easily among the lowly as the elite. He died January 29, 1828, in Baltimore.

See also MARYLAND, CATHOLIC CHURCH IN.

Guilday, Peter. *The Life and Times of John England: First Bishop of Charleston (1746–1842).* 2 vols. New York: The America Press, 1927.

Murtha, Ronin J. "The Life of the Most Reverend Ambrose Maréchal: Third Archbishop of Baltimore, 1768–1828." Ph.D. dissertation, The Catholic University of America, 1965.

Spalding, Thomas W. *The Premier See: A History of the Archdiocese of Baltimore, 1789–1989.* Baltimore: Johns Hopkins University Press, 1989.

THOMAS W. SPALDING

MARGIL, ANTONIO DE JESÚS (1657–1726)

A Missionary from Spain

Fray Antonio Margil de Jesús, O.F.M., has been called the "Apostle of Texas," comparing his importance to the Catholic missionizing of Texas with that of Fray Junípero Serra,

O.F.M., regarding the evangelization of California. The son of Juan Margil Salumaro and Esperanza Ros, Antonio Margil de Jesús was born on August 18, 1657, in Valencia, Spain. He was baptized into the Roman Catholic Church two days later in Valencia's Church of San Juan del Mercado (known later as the Church of Los Santos Juanes Bautista y Evangelista).

Ven. Anthony Margil of Jesus

At the age of fifteen, on April 22, 1673, Margil entered the Friars Minor—Franciscans—at the Convent of La Corona de Cristo in Valencia. When he turned eighteen, Margil matriculated at the Convent of San Antonio, located in Denía, to study for the priesthood. Six years later, in 1681, Margil was ordained a priest. The new cleric's first assignment sent him to the town of Onda, where he served as confessor and preacher. It was not long, however, until he volunteered as a missionary to the Americas.

Sailing with a number of other missionaries from the port of Cádiz in the spring of 1683, Margil arrived at Vera Cruz, Mexico, on June 6 of that year. Immediately he was assigned to what was to become the new apostolic Colegio de Santa Cruz at Querétaro, Mexico, arriving at his destination on August 13, 1683. For the next fourteen years, however, Margil de Jesús mainly labored among the Catholics and indigenous peoples of the Yucatán and Central America, especially Guatemala, Costa Rica, and Nicaragua. In March 1697 the Spanish Franciscan assumed the responsibilities of guardian at the college in Querétaro. After serving his three-year term as guardian, Margil spent an additional five years working back in Central America before returning to Mexico to establish an-

other apostolic college, this one situated in the foothills on the outskirts of Zacatecas.

The Zacatecan Missionaries and Texas

In 1704 King Felipe V of Spain (1700–46) issued a royal *cédula* (decree) that authorized the renovation of the hospice of Nuestra Señora de Guadalupe at Zacatecas into an apostolic college. Under Margil's direction such was ultimately accomplished in 1707. It would be this apostolic college, in conjunction with the college at Querétaro, that would provide the Franciscans for the evangelization of Texas for the next several decades.

The Zacatecan and Querétaran missionaries entered Texas as a part of the Domingo Ramon expedition, reaching the east Texas locale of the Hasinai in June 1716. Margil de Jesús had been delayed because of illness, but rejoined the group in time to direct the establishment of the missions Nuestra Señora de los Dolores and San Miguel de los Adaes, both in 1717. Several considerations eventually forced the Franciscans to withdraw from east Texas and focus their energies on San Antonio, where between 1718 and 1731 they founded—or relocated—five missions: San Antonio de Valero (the famous Alamo), San José y San Miguel de Aguayo, Purísima Concepción, San Juan Capistrano, and San Francisco de Espada.

In his preface to *San Antonio's Mission San José* (1968), by Fr. Marion Habig, O.F.M., Archbishop Robert E. Lucey of San Antonio wrote what is a very appropriate tribute to Antonio de Jesús, stating that "the Venerable Fray Antonio Margil, O.F.M., was one of the early heroes of the pueblo of Saint Anthony and he founded old San José Mission here in 1720. Very early in its history this structure was called the 'Queen of the Missions' and the 'Glory of New Spain.'" Venerable Fray Antonio Margil de Jesús, after laboring as a missionary for forty years, died from pneumonia on August 6, 1726, at Mexico City's Convento Grande de San Francisco. His last words were, "It is time to go to God" (Habig, 22). He was initially buried in the cathedral at Mexico City, but later his mortal remains were removed to Zacatecas.

See also FRANCISCAN FRIARS; TEXAS, CATHOLIC CHURCH IN.

Almaráz, Félix D., Jr. *The San Antonio Missions and Their System of Land Tenure.* Austin: University of Texas Press, 1989.

Cruz, Gilberto R. *Proceedings of the Second Annual Mission Research Conference.* San Antonio: San Antonio Missions National Historical Park, 1984.

Forrestal, Peter P. *Preliminary Studies of the Texas Catholic Historical Society: The Venerable Padre Fray Antonio Margil de Jesús.* Reprinted from *Mid-America* 3 (4) (April 1932).

Habig, Marion A. *San Antonio's Mission San José: State and National Historic Site, 1720–1968.* San Antonio: The Naylor Company, 1968.

PATRICK FOLEY

MARIANISTS (S.M.)

The Society of Mary, i.e., the Marianists, was founded in Bordeaux, France, in 1817 by William Joseph Chaminade (1761–1850), a priest who had initiated a distinctive sodality movement in postrevolutionary France. He also cofounded the Daughters of Mary (Marianist Sisters) in 1816 together with Adèle Trenquelléon. The history of the Marianists in the United States falls into three periods: foundation and expansion in primary education (ca. 1850–1900); modernization, professionalization, and the predominance of the high school (1900–60); reform, renewal, and the rise of Marianist lay communities (1960–95).

Foundation and Expansion

The foundation period opened in July 1849. Francis X. Weninger, S.J., an Austrian Jesuit familiar with the Marianist schools in Alsace, wrote to the superior general in Bordeaux on behalf of two pastors of German-speaking parishes in need of Marianists to staff the parish schools in Cincinnati. Leo Meyer, an Alsatian Marianist priest eager to be missioned to the United States, arrived in Cincinnati in July; the following December four brothers arrived to take charge of the parish schools and assist Meyer, who had purchased property in Dayton upon which was built St. Mary's Institute. With accommodations for postulants and novices, Nazareth, as the Marianist center in Dayton was called, was adjacent to St. Mary's (later University of Dayton) and housed a normal school. With the establishment of the U.S. province in 1855 Nazareth was the provincialate as well as the motherhouse where Marianists would make their annual retreat and receive their teaching assignments.

Bishop (after 1850, Archbishop) John B. Purcell, who had witnessed ethnic rivalry between German and Irish Americans, promoted German national parishes such as Holy Trinity in 1834 and St. Mary's in the Over-the-Rhine area of Cincinnati in 1840. During the 1850s the Marianists staffed these schools, and taught catechism in German illustrative of the prevailing principle: the German language preserves the faith of the people.

The French-born bishop of Galveston, J. M. Odin, made two visits to Bordeaux searching for Marianists to staff a school. In 1852 three brothers arrived in San Antonio, where they met Br. Edel from Cincinnati, to form a community that laid the foundation of St. Mary's College, today called St. Mary's University.

Another French bishop, Amadeus Rappe of Cleveland, successfully sought brothers to teach at St. Patrick's, the school of the Irish parish. Rappe was a self-styled Americanizer who alienated both the German-American and Irish-American communities. Eventually these ethnic conflicts led to his removal in 1870; he never administered another diocese. The Marianists, who had made a sig-nificant impact upon the school, remained at St. Patrick's for several years.

Expansion into Pittsburgh, New York, Baltimore, Chicago, and New Orleans occurred principally in response to Redemptorist pastors of German-speaking parishes. Br. Damian Litz taught in several of these schools and was a frequent contributor to the conservative German-language press. In 1880 the Marianists opened a school in Winnipeg, Manitoba, and as a result of a request from the community for missions in the Hawaiian Islands in 1882 the brothers opened schools in Honolulu, Wailuku (1883), and Hilo (1885). In 1884 the brothers responded to a call from a priest of the Archdiocese of San Francisco and opened a school in Stockton, California. The provincial associated with this national expansion was Fr. John N. Reinbolt; by the end of his twenty-year administration in 1886 there were 40 Marianist houses with 350 brothers and priests. With a few exceptions, the houses were attached to primary schools; classes were limited to boys usually of the upper grades through eight, but occasionally a higher grade included a commercial course. Generally, the brothers were responsible for incorporating the boys into the liturgical life of the parish, preparing them for First Communion, and being role models as dedicated religious men. Even after the development of secondary education the primary schools remained the major source of vocations.

Modernization and Professionalization

In 1897, at the request of the German-American pastor, the Marianists opened their first high school at SS Peter and Paul parish, which represented their entrance into the St. Louis area where they established several high schools. The three-year high school included both academic and commercial courses. Another high school was established in 1889 when the Marianists opened Spalding Academy in Peoria, Illinois, named after John Lancaster Spalding, the bishop who invited them into the diocese. Many of their parish schools evolved into high schools such as St. Michael's in Chicago. Several of the primary schools where Marianists taught boys' classes, such as St. Martin's in Baltimore, were turned over entirely to sisters whose salaries and expenses were less than the brothers; most of the constitutions governing sisters' communities prohibited women religious from teaching boys of high school age. Many of those schools in strongly German-American parishes, such as St. Michael's in Chicago and St. Michael's and St. James in Baltimore, remained single-sex classes. Hence, the Marianists' tradition as primary-school teachers persisted until the 1950s.

With the growth of the society by more than fifty schools and over five hundred members—from New York to California, Texas to Manitoba—a western province centered in St. Louis was established in 1908. This province included those houses west of 87 degrees longitude, except for the Hawaii and California houses that were still dependent upon the eastern province.

While provincials were priests, the inspectors of schools, a position first created in 1869, were brothers. During the first third of the twentieth century, John Waldron was inspector of the western province and a dominant presence in the early years of the National Catholic Education Association (NCEA). Under his leadership the Marianists successfully met the rising standards of teacher training and school administration established by the various state and regional accrediting agencies. Br. Eugene Paulin, inspector during the 1930s and 1940s, was also active in the NCEA and a pace setter in educational policies for the society. Both inspectors were associated with the society's adaptation to the development of diocesan school systems, particularly its central Catholic high school movement. During this period the University of Dayton and St. Mary's College in San Antonio achieved modernization and professionalization. Illustrative of the significance of education in the provinces of the United States, American brothers have dominated the position of assistant superior general in charge of instruction from the late nineteenth century to the 1990s. The Marianist Sisters opened their first house in the United States in 1949; their continuous growth led to the establishment of a U.S. province in 1969.

In 1946 the general chapter elected its first American superior general, Sylvester P. Jurgens, former provincial of the western province. In 1948 he announced the creation of the Pacific province with houses in California and Hawaii. Though by this time there was a trend to remove brothers from primary education, the Pacific province was in the vanguard of that movement. Also during the early phase of this period of modernization the sodality movement was revitalized in tandem with the renewed devotion to the founder, William Joseph Chaminade.

The continuous growth of the Marianists during the 1950s led to the foundation of the New York province in 1961, which included St. John's Boys' Home in Brooklyn, Chaminade High School in Mineola (Long Island), other high schools, and Colegio San Jose, Rio Padres, Puerto Rico. In 1961 there were about 1,500 Marianists in the North American provinces, which represented nearly a 100 percent growth in twenty-five years.

Vatican II and After

The third period, 1960 to 1995, followed a pattern etched into the post-Vatican II trends in renewal and reform: the composition of a new constitution based upon the principles of collegiality, subsidiarity, personal responsibility, and a scripturally based spirituality. Though provincials are not elected but appointed, a brother may hold that position; there were two brothers provincial in the United

States in 1995. Some of the missions that were founded between the 1930s and the 1950s in Latin America and Africa are flourishing today.

The general decline in traditional vocations has entailed removing brothers and priests from several schools in each of the provinces. However, the rise of Marianists' lay communities dedicated to a way of life infused with the society's spirituality is a positive force on the horizon. Subsidiarity was severely tested in a conflict between the Marianists of the community of Chaminade High School in Mineola, eager to maintain traditional structures in the school and community life, which they perceived as in accord with the best in Marianist life, and the New York province with its commitment to renewal infused by the spirit of Vatican II and based upon contemporary anthropological and ecclesiological understandings of freedom, authority, and subsidiarity. The dispute, which originated in 1968, was resolved by the Vatican Congregation of Religious in 1976; Mineola became an independent province with self-determination to pursue its own identity within Marianist traditions. However, all provinces still claim the original charism of the founder; the Marianist lay communities are new forms in a family whose origin was in a lay-sodality movement based upon a spirit of ecclesial equality.

Garvin, John E. *Centenary Book of the Society of Mary*. Dayton, Ohio: Brothers of Mary, 1917.

Paulin, Eugene, and Joseph A. Becker. *New Ways: The History of the Brothers of Mary (Marianists) in Hawaii, 1883–1958*. Milwaukee, Wisconsin, 1959.

Schmitz, Joseph W. *The Society of Mary in Texas*. San Antonio, Texas, 1951.

Schnepp, Gerald J. *Province of St. Louis 1908–1983, The First Seventy-Five Years*. St. Louis, Missouri, 1985.

CHRISTOPHER J. KAUFFMAN

MARIST FATHERS (S.M.)

The Society of Mary (S.M.), also known as the Marists, includes priests and brothers, although it is a distinct religious congregation from the Marist Brothers of the Schools and is distinct from another religious community of priests and brothers that shares the name "Society of Mary," known as the Marianists.

Origins of the Marists

The Marist community originated in France following the social and religious upheavals of the French Revolution. In the major seminary of the primatial see of Lyons, a small group of seminarians began to discuss a project of reviving Catholic faith and piety in their future priestly ministry. In 1815, during his last year of theology studies, Jean-Claude Courveille (1787–1866) disclosed to some classmates a profoundly moving experience he had had four years earlier during which the Virgin Mary communicated to him her desire to gather into one fold all those dispersed by the forces of the Revolution. To bring lost souls back to her merciful son, Jesus Christ, Mary asked for a religious community that would enjoy her special protection and motherly care and to which she would bestow as a singular grace her own most holy name.

Courveille understood this message as a clear invitation to provide for the Church and for Mary what St. Ignatius of Loyola had provided three centuries earlier. Just as the Society of Jesus had come into existence at a time when the Church had suffered the ravages of the Protestant Reformation, so in a parallel fashion the Society of Mary would fulfill Mary's wish to renew the Church as if by a new Pentecost, re-creating in the "last times" the same spirit and zeal of the first times, particularly a community of "one mind and one heart" (Acts 4:32).

On July 23, 1816, seven newly ordained priests and four seminarians consecrated themselves in the ancient Marian shrine of Fourvière, which looks down on the city of Lyons, promising to do all in their power to establish the religious congregation for which Mary was calling. As diocesan priests, however, they owed obedience to their bishops, and thus they were scattered as each one received his own individual diocesan assignment. Courveille himself eventually left the diocesan priesthood and entered the recently reestablished Benedictine abbey of Solesmes, where he died in 1866.

Jean-Claude Colin (1790–1875), a member of the early group of seminarians and among those who made the Fourvière pledge, started his priestly ministry in the small village of Cerdon in southeastern France. Colin found the inspiration and the time to pursue the goal of fulfilling Mary's wish of establishing the Marist Society. Writing various drafts of the future rule; encouraging a classmate, Blessed Marcellin Champagnat (1789–1840), to get the Marist Brothers started; helping in the formation of the Marist Sisters; developing a band of priests who preached missions and renewals in remote country parishes; aiding the bishop of Belley by bringing priests to teach in the diocesan minor seminary; and traveling to Rome to negotiate with the Holy See about pontifical approval for the Society of Mary, Colin proved to be a real religious founder.

The Society of Mary

Pope Gregory XVI gave canonical approbation to the branch of priests on April 29, 1836, with the understanding that the Marists would then undertake the evangelization of the islands of the South Pacific, known collectively as Western Oceania. Before the year ended, the first missionary group of priests and brothers set sail from Le Havre. One of the priests, St. Peter Chanel (1803–41), would become the first martyr of Oceania. Thus, in the first decades of its existence, the Society of Mary engaged in the ministries of foreign missions, of preaching parish renewals (also called "home missions"), of teaching in seminaries and secondary schools.

Marists in the United States

At the request of Archbishop John Mary Odin of New Orleans, two Marist priests arrived in the United States in 1863 in Convent, Louisiana, sixty miles upriver from New Orleans, to take up the pastoral care of St. Michael's parish. More Marists came the following year to staff nearby Jefferson College, where the sons of local planters and farmers could receive a higher education in their native French language. From their first apostolic labors in Louisiana, in fact, the Marists proved to be of great service to French-speaking people. The Society of Mary spread in the United States, accepting a parish in New Orleans (1865), parishes for French-speaking faithful in Lawrence, Massachusetts (1882), Boston (1883), Van Buren, Maine (1881), Haverhill, Massachusetts, San Francisco (1885), and St. Paul, Minnesota (1886).

Toward the end of the century, Marists began to take on works of a more missionary character: a high school in predominantly Mormon Salt Lake City, parishes in southern and northern Georgia, a high school in Atlanta, parishes in rural Idaho and West Virginia, and the establishment of a mission band, that is, itinerant preachers who conduct parish renewals and retreats. During the twentieth century, the Society of Mary has taken on the pastoral care of suburban parishes, the administration of diocesan seminaries, the staffing and teaching in high schools, and, more recently, ministry in the inner city, along the Mexican border in southeastern Texas, and on a reservation in South Dakota. There are three provinces of the Marist Fathers in the United States, headquartered in Washington, D.C., Boston, and San Francisco, numbering approximately 220 priests, brothers, and seminarians.

PHILIP GAGE, S.M.

MARKOE, WILLIAM MORGAN (1892–1969)

Jesuit priest and civil rights activist. Markoe was born in St. Paul, Minnesota, on May 11, 1892, one of seven children of Dr. James Cox and Mary Prince Markoe. After two years at St. Thomas College in Minnesota, he enrolled at the Jesuit-conducted St. Louis University in 1912. The following year he entered the Society of Jesus at Florissant, Missouri. He was convinced of his vocation to serve the poor black population of the area and was permitted to take a private vow dedicating himself "for the work of the salvation of the Negroes in the United States" after his perpetual vows as a Jesuit in 1915.

From 1921 to 1931 Markoe authored some twenty-four articles or letters in the Jesuit periodical *America,* calling for widespread Catholic evangelization of the black population in the United States. As a scholastic, he was able to help establish the Peter Claver Association for the education of black children, an organization that did not last long. He also established the Knights of Peter Claver and its Ladies' Auxiliary, a fraternal organization for black people.

Markoe was convinced that interracial cooperation on an equal basis was the only way by which racial justice would be achieved. To this end, he became involved with the Federated Colored Catholics in the United States, which he felt needed to be transformed from a segregated "Jim Crow organization" to a biracial effort for equality. He gave over the *St. Elizabeth's Chronicle,* which he had founded earlier, to the federation in order to express these goals. This journal eventually became the *Interracial Review,* which the New York Jesuit priest John LaFarge helped establish. Under growing pressure from his superiors, Markoe transferred control of the journal to LaFarge in 1934. After a brief assignment in Denver, Markoe returned to service in the black community in the Midwest until 1951, when he was assigned to teach theology at Marquette University in Milwaukee. He continued to preach the message of interracial justice in the classroom until his retirement in 1966. Markoe died in Milwaukee on December 6, 1969.

Nickels, Marilyn Wenzke. *Black Catholic Protest and the Federated Colored Catholics 1917–1933.* New York: Garland, 1988.

RICHARD G. SMITH

MARQUETTE, JACQUES (1637–75)

Jesuit missionary, priest, and explorer. Marquette achieved celebrity in Europe and North America for exploration and missionary activity in Canada and the United States during a nine-year period from 1666 to 1675. Marquette's journal account of his 1673 exploration of the lower Wisconsin and upper Mississippi Rivers, in co-leadership with

Fr. Marquette and Jolliet on the Mississippi River (engraving).

Louis Jolliet, gained a large readership in France, England, Canada, and the United States. Marquette's first-person narrative, "Recueil de Voyages" was published by Thevenots in 1681.

The 2,500 mile odyssey began in St. Ignace, Michigan, led south to the junction of the Arkansas and Mississippi Rivers. The return voyage north was on the Mississippi to the Illinois River to Lake Michigan and to St. Francis Xavier Mission near Green Bay. There the explorers separated and Jolliet reported to the governor in Quebec.

The Young Missionary

Born at Laon, France, June 1, 1637, Marquette entered the Society of Jesus at Nancy in 1654 at age seventeen. His university studies were at Pont-à-Mousson and he fulfilled teaching assignments at Rheims and Charleville. On March 7, 1666, he was ordained at Toul, France. His request to go to the missions brought an assignment to Quebec, Canada, and his Jesuit superiors sent him to Three Rivers to study the Algonquin and Huron languages.

In 1668 Marquette was assigned to Sault Ste. Marie to work with Fr. Dablon, and a year later he was sent farther west to replace Fr. Allouez at La Pointe on Madeline Island, Lake Superior. That Ottawa Mission of the Holy Spirit on Chequamegon Bay was adjacent to Ashland, Wisconsin. Marquette explored the south shore of the lake as far west as the Bois Brule River. Numerous languages and dialects such as Ojibwe, Cree, Huron, Menomonee, Pottawattomi, Sac, Fox, Winnebago, Miami, Dakota, and Illinois were spoken in that area. Information of an endless river to the sea was repeatedly related to Marquette by members of the Illinois.

Marquette, assisted by Br. Louys Le Boeme, baptized a chief and eighty members during one summer when six hundred Native Americans visited Holy Spirit Mission. Warring Dakota tribesmen drove Marquette from La Pointe and the mission was closed in 1671. Marquette then established a mission for the Hurons at Point St. Ignace on Mackinac Straights, on the western shore of Lake Michigan.

News of the huge Illinois Nation to the south and additional stories of a great river peaked Marquette's interest. Governor Frontenac in Quebec heard similar accounts and appointed Louis Jolliet, a fur trader, to explore the great river with Marquette. The two men spent the winter of 1673 at St. Ignace preparing for a spring departure.

The Discovery of the Mississippi

On May 17, 1673, with five French companions, Marquette and Jolliet embarked from St. Ignace. They followed the western shore of Lake Michigan into Green Bay and visited the Mission of St. Francis Xavier on the Fox River, the present De Pere, Wisconsin. Descending the Fox, the explorers came to a Maskouten village. Marquette wrote: "The village consists of three nations who have gathered there—Miamis, Maskoutens and Kickabous. The former are the most civil, the most liberal, the most shapely." On June 10, two Miami guides portaged the French "2,700 paces" to the Wisconsin River.

The journal continues:

> The river on which we embarked is called the Meskousing. It is very wide; it has a sandy bottom, which forms various shoals that render navigation very difficult. . . . On the bank one sees fertile land, diversified with woods, prairies and hills. . . . We saw there neither feathered game nor fish, but many deer and a large number of cattle. . . . Our route lay to the southwest, and, after navigating about 30 leagues, we saw a spot presenting all the appearances of an iron mine. . . . After proceeding 40 leagues on this same route, we arrived at the mouth of our river; and, at 42 and a half degrees of latitude, we safely entered Missisipi [*sic*] on the 17 of June, with a joy that I cannot express.

Marquette's narrative reads:

> Here we are, then, on this so renowned river, all of whose features I have endeavored to note carefully. The Missisipi [*sic*] River takes its rise in various lakes in the countries of the northern nations. . . . To the right is a large chain of very high mountains, and to the left are beautiful lands. . . . We saw only deer and cattle, bustards, and swans without wings, because they drop their plumage in this country. . . . From time to time we come upon monstrous fish, one of which struck our canoe with such violence that I thought it was a great tree, about to break the canoe in pieces.

The journal continues with detailed descriptions of the physical geography, the aquatic, animal, and plant life. Distances are reported in leagues and latitude by degrees and minutes.

> On the 25th of June we perceived on the water's edge some tracks of men, and a narrow and somewhat beaten path leading to a fine prairie. . . . We therefore left the two canoes under the guard of our people, strictly charging them not to allow themselves to be surprised, after which Monsieur Jollyet and I undertook this investigation—a rather hazardous one for two men who exposed themselves, alone, to the mercy of a barbarous and unknown people.

The French are peacefully received by "an Illinois village of 300 cabins." There follows a series of ceremonial dinners and dances and the Illinois ask for more information about Christ. The Illinois elders give Jolliet and Marquette an elaborate "calumet," a sign of peace, designed to defuse attacks from nations to the south. With a promise to return, the French embark with a send-off from six hundred Illinois.

Down river huge pictographs of fierce animals are sighted on a bluff. A river of considerable size, the "Pekitanoui" (the Missouri River), enters the Mississippi from the north-west. Marquette hopes it leads to the "vermillion or California sea." The explorers encounter mosquitoes in abundance and some Indians armed with guns near their village called Mitchigamae. The French are saved by displaying the calumet. At "33 degrees latitude" the Europeans learn they are ten days from the great sea. Manners and customs, flora and fauna are described. Marquette and Jolliet continue south until met by "Akamesa" people who display a calumet. At the Arkansas River they realize the Mississippi enters the Gulf of Mexico in Spanish territory, where they might be captured. "Finally, we had obtained all the information that could be desired in this discovery," Marquette wrote.

Return Trip

On July 17 the French begin their return trip, paddling against a swift current. In Illinois territory they are advised to navigate the easier Illinois River, which brings them to the southern shore of Lake Michigan, called Lake of the Illinois. At the Kaskaskia portage, "a village of 74 cabins," the French are warmly welcomed and Marquette promises to return and catechize. At the end of September he is stronger and seeks permission to return to the Illinois Nation. On October 25, with companions Pierre Poteret and Jacques (unnamed), Marquette paddles up Green Bay to Sturgeon Bay and travels across the peninsula to Lake Michigan. This is known as the "second voyage." Canoeing south along the western shore of Lake Michigan on November 23, the threesome are met by friendly Maskoutens at the Milwaukee River. On December 4, Marquette and the *"donnés"* arrive at the Chicago River and make winter camp where Chicago is now located. Pierre and Jacques build a log hut and hunt for food, but Marquette's health weakens drastically. Confined to bed, he is visited by Illinois delegates, who bring food and entreat the Jesuit to visit them.

On March 30 the French canoe down the Illinois River and are warmly greeted by a village of three thousand Illinois. The Kaskaskia Mission is established. During Easter week Marquette instructs the eager catechumens and visits each cabin. His illness worsens and the party begins the trip back to St. Ignace. Upon reaching Lake Michigan the *donnés* decide the east shore of Lake Michigan is a shorter route home. On May 18, 1675, Marquette dies at the location of present-day Ludington, Michigan, and is buried there. Two years later his skeletal remains are transferred to the chapel at St. Ignace, Michigan, on June 8, 1677.

Hedges, Samuel. *Father Marquette: Jesuit Missionary and Explorer.* New York: Christian Press Association, 1903.

Repplier, Agnes. *Père Marquette: Priest, Pioneer and Adventurer.* Garden City, N.Y.: Doubleday, Doran and Co., 1929.

Steck, F. B. *The Jolliet-Marquette Expedition 1673*. Quincy, Ill.: Franciscan Fathers, 1928.

Thwaites, R. J., ed. *The Jesuit Relations and Allied Documents*. Vols. 1, 22, 37, 50, 60–62, 70–71. New York: Pagent Book Co., 1959.

BERNARD McGARTY, S.T.D.

MARQUETTE UNIVERSITY

Marquette University is an independent, coeducational institution of higher learning founded in 1881 by members of the Society of Jesus. The university is named after Fr. Jacques Marquette (1637–75), who was part of an expedition that traveled the Mississippi River and was one of the first Europeans to visit the area that is now Milwaukee.

The origins of Marquette University lie in the desire of the first bishop of Milwaukee, John Martin Henni, to start a Catholic college in his diocese. While on a fundraising trip to Europe (1848–49), he obtained a pledge of sixteen thousand dollars from Guillaume DeBoey, a Belgian businessman, and Henni asked the Jesuits to open a school in Milwaukee. Mindful of Jacques Marquette's work as a missionary and explorer in the Midwest, Henni proposed that the institution be called Marquette College. But the Jesuits lacked the personnel to staff such an institution for decades, and Marquette College did not open until 1881.

Marquette remained a small liberal arts college for men until 1907, when it obtained a university charter from the state of Wisconsin. Between 1907 and 1913, Marquette expanded to include divisions of medicine, dentistry, nursing, pharmacy, law, business, engineering, music, and journalism. In 1909, influenced by requests from local Catholics and the archbishop of Milwaukee, as well as the needs of Catholic parochial schools for certified teachers, the president of Marquette decided the university would conduct a summer school (itself an innovation for Catholic colleges and universities) and admit female students. By 1917, 375 women attended Marquette. Today, men and women attend Marquette in about equal proportions.

Following World War II, enrollment at Marquette increased dramatically, as happened at other American colleges and universities. Demand for graduate and professional education grew, and the university's student body became more national in its composition. In the 1960s and 1970s Marquette introduced doctoral programs in various fields, including religious studies, biology, history, and chemistry. Since its founding, Marquette has graduated over 100,000 men and women.

Marquette University has a campus of approximately eighty acres and fifty buildings located on the western edge of downtown Milwaukee. Its 1994–95 enrollment was 10,651, with students in 12 colleges, schools, and programs: Arts and Sciences, Business Administration, Communication, Dental Hygiene, Dentistry, Education, Engineering, Graduate, Law, Medical Laboratory Technology, Nursing, and Physical Therapy.

See also CATHOLIC UNIVERSITIES AND COLLEGES.

Hamilton, Raphael N. *The Story of Marquette University*. Milwaukee: Marquette University Press, 1953.

MARTIN, AUGUSTE (1803–75)

First bishop of Natchitoches. Auguste Marie Aloysius Martin was born on February 1, 1803, at Saint-Malo, France, the son of Pierre-François Martin and Marie-Françoise Gautier. He was educated at the College of Rennes and ordained at Rennes on May 31, 1828. Martin successively engaged in pastoral and administrative work in the Dioceses of Rennes (1828–39), Vincennes (1839–46), and New Orleans (1846–53). He was pastor and vicar forane at Natchitoches when he was named the first bishop of the newly established diocese in north Louisiana (July 18, 1853). He was consecrated at New Orleans on November 30, 1853. His 22,000-square-mile diocese included only five priests, six churches, three mission chapels, and one convent school.

"My one goal is the salvation of souls, who in turn will themselves contribute to the salvation of others. We are fishermen just as the first Apostles were," Martin wrote in 1852 (McCants, 7–8). Martin greatly expanded the Catholic presence in a mission territory restricted by poverty, devastated by droughts, and decimated by regular epidemics. He successfully recruited priests and religious from Europe, principally France. He also established a seminary at Natchitoches in 1854 and opened the diocese's first school for free children of color at Isle Brevelle in 1857.

At the beginning of the Civil War, Martin's August 21, 1861, pastoral letter defended slavery and secession. On December 30, 1864, the Congregation of the Index decided to require Martin "to correct the [letter's] errors and inaccuracies." It is not known if this decision was implemented (Caravaglios, 69–70). Catholic communities in north Louisiana suffered extreme want during the war; many witnessed armed conflict and suffered property destruction during the 1864 Red River Campaign.

Martin attended and kept a personal journal of the First Vatican Council (1869–70). He died on September 29, 1875, at Natchitoches and was buried in his cathedral. At the time, sixteen priests were serving about fifty-five parishes, missions, and stations, while three religious communities, diocesan priests, and lay teachers staffed nineteen schools.

See also CIVIL WAR AND CATHOLICS, THE; SLAVERY AND AMERICAN CATHOLICS.

Baudier, Roger. "The Catholic Church in Louisiana." Unpublished manuscript. New Orleans, 1939.

Caravaglios, Maria Genoina. "A Roman Critique of the Pro-Slavery Views of Bishop Martin of Natchitoches." *Records of the American Catholic Historical Society of Philadelphia* 83 (June 1972).

"Cinq mois à Rome au Concile Oecumenique du Vatican, 1869–1870 . . . Auguste Marie Martin, Évêque de Natchitoches." Unpublished manuscript, 1870.

Code, Joseph B. *Dictionary of the American Hierarchy (1789–1965)*. New York: J. F. Wagner, 1964.

Copies of all unpublished manuscripts, including Martin's Vatican journal, in Archives of the Archdiocese of New Orleans.

D'Antoni, Blaise C. "Msgr. Auguste Martin de Natchitoches." Unpublished manuscript, 1957.

Doyle, Elisabeth Joan. "Bishop Auguste Marie Martin of Natchitoches and the Civil War." *Cross, Crozier and Crucible: A Volume Celebrating the Bicentennial of a Catholic Diocese in Louisiana*. New Orleans: Archdiocese of New Orleans in cooperation with the Center for Louisiana Studies, 1993.

Harrington, Carolyn. "Bishop Auguste Marie Martin." Unpublished manuscript, 1994.

Martin Correspondence in Diocese of Alexandria, Archdiocese of New Orleans, and New Orleans Collection in the University of Notre Dame Archives.

McCants, Dorothea Olga, ed. and trans. *They Came to Louisiana: Letters of a Catholic Mission, 1854–1882*. Baton Rouge: Louisiana State University Press, 1970.

CHARLES E. NOLAN

MARTÍNEZ, ANTONIO JOSÉ (1793–1867)

Priest, politician, and writer. Martínez was born in the frontier town of Abiquiú, New Mexico, on January 17, 1793. His Spanish-Mexican family moved to Taos when he was still a boy, and he married in young manhood only to be widowed at the birth of their first child. Leaving the infant girl (who died at age twelve) with her mother's family, Martínez entered the Tridentine Seminary of the Diocese of Durango in 1817. At this period, he seems to have taken as his great ideal Miguel Hidalgo, priest, revolutionary leader, and executed hero of Mexican independence. Furthermore, Martínez's seminary studies instilled in him a passion for the life of the mind, a passion he never lost.

Pastor of Taos

Ordained in declining health in 1822, the young priest traveled to Taos a year later for his first solemn Mass and to rest and recuperate at his parents' hacienda. Then, after spending a few years as pastor at Tomé and Abiquiú, he returned to Taos to spend the rest of his long life. He opened a school for boys and girls and a minor seminary to prepare young men for the Durango seminary. Eighteen of his pupils were ordained by Bishop José Antonio Zubiría of Durango, four by Bishop Jean Baptist Lamy of Santa Fe, and many others became noted lay leaders of the New Mexico Territory.

Martínez bought the first printing press to have arrived in New Mexico, turning it to the intellectual uses of school and Church as well as to politics, in which he and many other priests were then involved. Martínez's major political concerns were getting the Mexican government to cease enforcing the Church's tithing laws and to leave Church support to the people's free will (made national law in 1833); to mandate religious toleration; to defend New Mexico against marauding tribal nomads; and to prevent fraudulent land grants.

After the United States Army's bloodless conquest of New Mexico in 1846, Martínez appears to have decided that the United States offered a better chance than did Mexico for the concrete realization of the ideals of Hidalgo's Mexican Revolution. He did not incite or approve the Taos uprising of 1847 when Governor Charles Bent was assassinated. For seven years after the 1848 peace treaty, Martínez was a dominant figure in the conventions and legislative sessions that constructed the new political order of the territory.

In 1851 Martínez was initially in favor of the new ecclesiastical order at Santa Fe, supporting Bishop Lamy, until the publication of his letter of January 1854 that mandated withholding the sacraments from Catholics who did not tithe. In the spring of 1856, Martínez resigned his pastorate for reasons of health and age.

Conflict with Bishop Lamy

The new pastor, Spaniard Dámaso Taladrid, was insultingly uncooperative with his predecessor, subjecting him and members of his family to continual harassment. Martínez admitted the parishioners of Taos to the private chapel in his home, which stood in the immediate vicinity of the church, and began their unauthorized care, and so on October 27, 1856, Lamy suspended him. Several months later, Taladrid foolishly got Kit Carson to summon the U.S. Army on the false charge that the old priest was fomenting rebellion; the ensuing fiasco caused a major scandal, and Lamy removed Taladrid. But Martínez fought with the new pastor, Fr. Eulogio Ortiz. He also continued writing annoying and insulting letters to Lamy and publishing some in the Santa Fe newspapers, and he drew a neighboring pastor, Fr. Mariano de Jesús Lucero of Arroyo Hondo, into his orbit. The result was that about one-third of the people in the two parishes followed Martínez and Lucero. Therefore, on Sunday, April 11, 1858, Vicar General Joseph P. Machebeuf pronounced Martínez's solemn excommunication in Taos, and the next Sunday in Arroyo Hondo he did the same for Lucero. Back in the 1830s and 1840s, Martínez had begotten some children, but the affair was so covert that the bishop seems never to have learned of it.

Fr. Martínez had been cordial to non-Catholic clergymen from the time they had come into New Mexico with the invading army, but now he flirted with Episcopalianism without ever committing himself to it. From 1858 to 1862, Martínez wrote a series of polemical tracts and published them on his press (which one of his sons was running). But mainly he continued his unauthorized ministry to his third of the parishioners and working with the penitential Brotherhood of Our Father Jesus the Nazarene.

On July 27, 1867, death came for Padre Antonio José Martínez, who, despite his faults, was the most impressive New Mexican to the time of this writing. The penitential Brotherhood of Our Father Jesus turned out in force for his funeral, as did most of the people of Taos. About a year and a half later, Italian Jesuit Fr. Donato Gasparri preached a parish mission that brought Fr. Lucero and the vast majority of the disaffected Taoseños back to the Church, led by most of Martínez's relatives.

See also LAMY, JEAN BAPTIST; NEW MEXICO, CATHOLIC CHURCH IN.

Chávez, Fray Angélico. *But T & C: The Story of Padre Martínez of Taos, 1793–1867*. Santa Fe: Sunstone, 1981.

Francis, E. K. "Padre Martínez: A New Mexican Myth." *New Mexico Historical Review* 31 (1956) 265–89.

Mares, E. A., ed. *Padre Martínez: New Perspectives from Taos*. Taos, N.Mex.: Millicent Rogers Museum, 1988.

Sánchez, Pedro. *Memorias sobre la Vida del Presbítero don Antonio José Martínez*. Santa Fe: Nuevo Mexicano, 1903. Reprinted in David Weber, ed. *Northern Mexico on the Eve of the United States Invasion*. New York: Arno Press, 1976.

THOMAS J. STEELE, S.J.

MARTY, MARTIN (1834–96)

Bishop. Born in Schwyz, Switzerland, on January 13, 1834, Aloys Marty attended the local Jesuit school. After the Society of Jesus was expelled from Switzerland, he transferred to the Benedictine school at Maria Einsiedeln and was ordained a Benedictine priest on September 14, 1856.

Highly intelligent and exacting in his religious observance, Marty arrived in St. Meinrad, Indiana, on September 28, 1860. He became that abbey's first abbot in 1870. Fr. J.B.A. Brouillet, treasurer of the Catholic Indian Missions, appealed to Marty to send workers from the abbey to the Dakota (Sioux) Indians of the Standing Rock Agency in the Dakota Territory. Marty himself set out on the feast of St. Benedict, July 11, 1876. He arrived in Yankton, a site in Dakota on the Missouri River, where the local pastor refused him the privilege of offering Mass because Marty had no *celebret*.

Abbot Marty was confronted by the heat, cold, rain, and snow of Dakota. Often, he had little food and poor lodging; the distances he traveled were extreme. The language

Martin Marty

of the Native Americans was difficult to learn. Nevertheless, he persevered and was responsible for the administration of the sacraments and the religious instruction of Native American adults and children alike. Although he pined for the solitude of the abbey, he resigned himself to the divine will. He wrote:

> I have not yet formed a definite resolution as to what is to be done in Dakota because everywhere the task is to make something—something good at that—out of nothing. . . . If I can stay where I am and the conversion of the Indians will be adopted as the work of the order (instead of that of St. Meinrad alone), then my wish is fulfilled. God will provide.

On August 5, 1879, Pope Leo XIII published a decree naming Marty bishop of Tiberius. In a subsequent bull, the pontiff made Marty the vicar apostolic of the Dakota Territory. He was consecrated at St. Ferdinand Church in Ferdinand, Indiana, on February 1, 1880. The new bishop labored with as much zeal as he had previously. He continued his hectic pace and traveled often to outlying posts in his far-flung territory.

On September 19, 1889, Pope Leo XIII created the Diocese of Sioux Falls, then extending throughout all of present-day South Dakota. President Benjamin Harrison, on November 2, signed the declaration that made North and South Dakota the thirty-ninth and fortieth states of the Union, respectively. Bishop Marty—or "Black Robe Lean Chief" as he was saluted by the Native Americans—was transferred to the Diocese of St. Cloud, Minnesota, in December 1894. Ill health continued to plague the bishop, who died in St. Cloud on September 19, 1896, at the age of sixty-two.

After the Solemn Pontifical Requiem Mass, Archbishop John Ireland of St. Paul hailed the deceased bishop: "As we knew Bishop Marty he was a saint, and we feel today that a saint has passed from this earth, because he was a man of absolute obedience to his conscience."

Duratschek, M. Claudia. *Builders of God's Kingdom: The History of the Catholic Church in South Dakota.* Yankton, S.Dak.: Sacred Heart Convent, 1979.

Karolevitz, Robert F. *With Faith, Hope and Tenacity: The First One Hundred Years of the Catholic Diocese of Sioux Falls, 1889–1989.* Mission Hill, S.Dak.: Dakota Homestead Publishers, 1989.

CHARLES M. MANGAN

MARY IN AMERICAN CATHOLICISM

Colonial Period

The earliest image of Mary associated with American Catholicism is Columbus sailing to the New World in 1492 in his lead ship the *Santa María.* The second island he discovered in the Caribbean he named *Santa María de la Concepción.* His patroness, Queen Isabella, gave the first gold she received from America to build the ceiling of the west apse of the Basilica of Santa María Maggiore in Rome. Mary thus became a link between the Old World and the New.

In 1531, Juan Diego, an Aztec peasant recently converted to Christianity, had the extraordinary experience of meeting a beautiful woman on the hill of Tepeyac in northeastern Mexico. The image of her that appeared on his cloak when he was presented to the Spanish bishop of Mexico, Juan de Zumarraga, depicted Mary as an Aztec maiden. Devotion to Our Lady of Guadalupe, now so powerful among Central Americans and Hispanics in the United States, was born in the sixteenth century.

A century later, the first large group of Catholics arrived in the English colony of Maryland, named in honor of the wife of King Charles I, Henrietta Marie. The ships, the *Ark* and the *Dove,* reached their destination on March 25, 1634, the feast of the Annunciation. It was there that Fr. Andrew White, S.J., celebrated the first Eucharist in what was to become the thirteen original colonies. Leonard Calvert founded St. Mary's City as the first capital, and also named the river St. Mary's. Both honored the queen of heaven rather than the queen of England.

French missionaries and explorers in Canada, in the Louisiana Territory, and along the Mississippi River saluted Mary in various forms. Jacques Marquette, S.J., named the Mississippi River the "River of the Immaculate Conception" in 1673. Jesuit influence, with its strong devotion to Mary, left its mark on Native American missions and shrines in Spanish and French territories.

John Carroll

In the newly founded United States, no person influenced devotion to Mary as much as John Carroll. After a brief stay at the Jesuit school in Maryland, Bohemia Manor, he and his cousin Charles Carroll were sent for further Jesuit education at St. Omer's in French Flanders. John Carroll stayed on, joined the Society of Jesus, was ordained in 1769, and made final vows as a Jesuit in 1771. After the papal suppression of the Jesuits in 1773, he returned to America and was largely responsible for establishing the Catholic Church in the newly founded republic. Jesuit emphasis on devotion to Mary continued to be a strong element in Carroll's spirituality.

When John Carroll was elected the first bishop of Baltimore and the see was formally established (November 6, 1789), he chose the feast of the Assumption (August 15, 1790) as the date for his episcopal consecration and selected Mary under that title as patroness of his diocese, which included all of the United States. The cathedral that Carroll began, where the many Provincial and Plenary Councils of Baltimore were later held, is dedicated to the Assumption of Our Lady. The Assumption has always been a holy day in both our colonial and our national histories.

Devotion to Mary under the title of the Immaculate Conception blossomed in the nineteenth century. At the Sixth Provincial Council of Baltimore in 1846, the U.S. bishops requested that the Blessed Virgin Mary under the title of the Immaculate Conception be named patroness of the Roman Catholic Church in the United States. The decree was confirmed by Pope Pius IX the following year. The proclamation of the dogma of the Immaculate Conception in 1854 and the apparitions at Lourdes in 1858 underscored the appropriateness of the decision.

Nineteenth Century

Religious congregations devoted to Mary abounded in the nineteenth century. The Jesuits at Georgetown were the first to introduce May as the "Month of Mary" and to encourage the Sodality of the Blessed Virgin Mary in the United States. The Sulpicians established the first seminary, St. Mary's, in Baltimore. Many religious congregations of women devoted to Mary went to the Midwest to teach the native peoples and the immigrants (e.g., the Sisters of Charity of the Blessed Virgin Mary of Dubuque, Iowa, the Dominicans of the Most Holy Rosary of Sinsinawa, Wisconsin, and the School Sisters of Notre Dame, Milwaukee province). Mary became identified with a kind of frontier spirituality—saying "yes" to the seemingly impossible challenges in a new land. Devotion to her clearly identified Catholics as distinct from their Protestant brothers and sisters in the midst of nativist riots in the mid-nineteenth century.

Devotional renewal that centered on Mary received new emphasis with the arrival of Catholic immigrants from southern and eastern Europe after 1880. The Italian *festa* and Polish customs associated with devotion to Mary brought a new dimension to a Catholic spirituality where Irish and German immigrants were praying the rosary or being exhorted by Jesuit or Redemptorist mission preachers to attend novenas in her honor. For all of the immigrants, however, Mary was the loving mother to whom they could go in time of need. The building of the National Shrine of the Immaculate Conception on the campus of The Catholic University of America—first suggested in 1913—became a symbol of Mary's import in the U.S. Catholic Church in our nation's capital.

Twentieth Century

In the period between the World Wars and for the decade after, the neo-Thomistic revival created an atmosphere where a resurgence of devotion to Mary reflected the medieval period with its chivalric images. Rosary processions, the crowning of Mary as Queen in the month of May, novenas to the Sorrowful Mother and Our Lady of Perpetual Help, litanies, and the Family Rosary Crusade all contributed to a Catholic culture in which a statue of Mary was found in every home and classroom, and a rosary in every purse and pocket was the norm. The Sodality movement, with its magazine, *The Queen's Work*, inspired by Daniel A. Lord, S.J., was also a moving force behind the Legion of Decency, which pushed for censorship of films. Being "Mary-like" was the ideal. Marian hymns (e.g., "Mother Beloved," the Lourdes Hymn) were familiar to all. Marian conferences were popular.

Anticommunism, at a new high in the cold war era, found in devotion to Our Lady of Fatima an expression of both fear and hope. Statues of "the Pilgrim Virgin" toured parishes where Catholics gathered to pray for peace.

Vatican Council II and After

With Vatican Council II it appeared to some that devotion to Mary was a "casualty" of the liturgical changes that followed. Mary was not forgotten, but the council's teaching on her, included in the last chapter of *Lumen gentium* (The Dogmatic Constitution on the Church), emphasized her role as mother of Christ and mother of the Church. Although she was affirmed as Mediatrix, the document explicitly states that Christ is the one mediator and Mary's role derives from his. Theologians and preachers were exhorted to "carefully and equally avoid the falsity of exaggeration on the one hand, and excess of narrow-mindedness on the other" (LG 67).

The post-Vatican II period experienced a variety of responses to the image and role of Mary in the Catholic Church in the United States. With advances in scriptural studies, some feminist groups discovered a more assertive Mary willing to speak up. Developments in Jewish-Christian relations allowed for a new appreciation of Mary as a committed, prayerful Jewish woman. Advocates of social justice found in the Magnificat a model of "putting down the mighty from their thrones and exalting the humble." The concept of freedom—especially religious freedom—found a certain congeniality with Mary under the title of the Immaculate Conception, which emphasized her freedom from sin. Those with more traditionalist orientations mourned the absence of daily recitation of the rosary, novenas, and other devotions.

Claims of Mary's appearances in various parts of the world from Arizona to Medjugorje continue to encourage pilgrimages in her honor. John Paul II's devotion to Mary has been an inspiration for young and old. Appreciation of Mary by liberals and conservatives, feminists and traditionalists, young and old, and those of every ethnic group is part of the diverse responses of American Catholics to the mother of Jesus.

See also AMERICAN CATHOLIC SPIRITUALITY.

Athans, Mary Christine. "Mary in the American Catholic Church." *U.S. Catholic Historian* 8 (4) (Fall 1989) 103–16.

MARY CHRISTINE ATHANS, B.V.M.

MARYKNOLL

Maryknoll is the popular name of three canonically and juridically distinct organizations: the Catholic Foreign Mission Society of America (Maryknoll Fathers and Brothers), the Congregation of the Maryknoll Sisters of St. Dominic, and the Maryknoll Mission Association of the Faithful (laypersons, clergy, and religious sisters and brothers under temporary contract). However, all three branches of the Maryknoll family are bonded by a common foundation in the American Church; a shared missionary charism and spirit; and a long tradition of collaborative apostolic ministry across cultures, religions, and national boundaries, especially among the poor and marginalized peoples of the world.

The Society

The principal purpose of the Maryknoll Society is overseas mission ministry. Conceived as an evangelizing outreach on behalf of the U.S. Church, the society received the unanimous endorsement of the U.S. archbishops on April 27, 1911, and formal authorization by the Congregation for the Propagation of the Faith on June 29, 1911. Two diocesan priests, James A. Walsh of Boston and Thomas F. Price, originally from Wilmington, North Carolina, acquaintances since 1904, cofounded and organized the society. Walsh had been director of the Society for the

*(L. to R.) James E. Walsh, Thomas F. Price,
Francis X. Ford; standing: Bernard Meyer*

Propagation of the Faith in Boston since 1903. From 1907, he edited *The Field Afar,* a mission magazine. Price, for many years an itinerant missionary in North Carolina, also promoted home and foreign missions through a national magazine called *Truth.*

Patterned on the Paris Foreign Missionary Society, the Mill Hill Fathers (England), and similar societies of secular priests, the society emphasized development of a local clergy, rather than recruiting candidates from mission lands into their own ranks. Continuing in the tradition of both Walsh and Price, Maryknoll committed itself to publishing educational materials as a means of raising awareness of global mission among American Catholics.

In 1912 the society established its permanent headquarters near Ossining, New York, on a hilltop dedicated to the Virgin Mary ("Maryknoll"). A small group of lay women led by Mary Josephine Rogers became known as the "Secretaries," volunteering their services to continue *The Field Afar* as a means of mission education and fundraising.

In 1918 the society's first four missioners, with Price as superior, initiated mission work in Yeungkong, China. Although Price died the following year, the work continued, and additional ecclesiastical territories in southern China, Manchuria (1925), Korea (1923), and Japan (1937) were accepted. In 1926 the first Maryknoll priests were assigned to the Philippines. The society also undertook ministry among Asians in Seattle, Los Angeles, Hawaii, and in Chinese parishes in Chicago and New York.

In 1936, following the death of Bishop James A. Walsh, one of the pioneer China missionaries, Bishop James E.

Walsh became superior general. During the war years, despite death and displacement, Maryknollers continued to work in southern China. Concurrently, new mission territories were accepted in Latin America: Bolivia in 1942 and Peru, Chile, Ecuador, Guatemala, and Mexico in 1943. In 1946, under the superior general Bishop Raymond A. Lane, work was begun in Tanganyika (now Tanzania) and the Philippines. By 1949, with the expulsion or forced withdrawal of many missioners from China and North Korea, the society took up pastoral, educational, and social work in Hong Kong, Taiwan, and South Korea. New seminary facilities were opened to accommodate increased numbers of candidates and a more comprehensive program was initiated for the brothers. At this time, monthly circulation of *Maryknoll* (formerly *The Field Afar*) exceeded one million copies. Following Vatican Council II, the society accepted invitations to serve in churches of the Middle East and additional countries of Asia, Africa, and Latin America.

In 1971 the society expanded its publishing program, establishing Orbis Books, Inc., to promote new theological thinking emerging in local churches around the world. Today the society collaborates with the Maryknoll Sisters as cosponsors of the Maryknoll Mission Institute, and other formational programs for cross-cultural ministry, continuing the cofounders' early commitment to mission education of the U.S. Church.

In 1966 the society established an Associate Program whereby diocesan and religious priests and brothers could serve overseas through temporary contract with the society. In 1972 the first lay associates were received. In 1994 a distinct organization of associates was formally established.

The Congregation

The Maryknoll Sisters of St. Dominic, Inc.—a pontifical institute since 1953—traces its foundational inspiration to the emergence of a global missionary consciousness in the American Churches at the turn of this century. Mary Josephine Rogers, who became the foundress of the Congregation (Mother Mary Joseph), was inspired by Protestant students at Smith College involved with the Student Volunteer Movement. Her own missionary zeal was joined with that of the other cofounders of Maryknoll through collaboration from 1906 on the work of *The Field Afar* with Fr. James A. Walsh.

Early Foundations. Arriving at Hawthorne, New York, in 1912, Rogers assumed leadership of the group of women known as "Secretaries" who associated themselves with the new foundation for missionary work of the U.S. Church. Committed to supply crucial literary, clerical, and domestic supportive services to the fledgling society, these women also shared a common desire for religious life and direct engagement in the missionary apostolate abroad. Initially inspired by St. Teresa of Avila as a missionary model of contemplation in action, the Secretaries, later known as Teresians, incorporated elements of Carmelite spirituality into their daily routine. In 1932 this early orientation of the Maryknoll women found its most visible expression in the establishment of a contemplative community within the congregation.

Eventually, due largely to the influence of Archbishop John T. McNicholas, O.P., a patron and friend of the founders, the women became Dominican Tertiaries. They received their formal religious training under the Sinsinawa Dominican Sisters and adopted the more flexible Rule of St. Dominic as the basis of their constitutions. In 1920 the Maryknoll Sisters were canonically recognized as a diocesan religious institute known then as Foreign Mission Sisters of St. Dominic, Inc.

Missionary Outreach. In 1921 the first Maryknoll sisters, led by Sr. Mary Paul McKenna, arrived in Hong Kong, with the goal of joining the priests already at Yeungkong. Challenged from the beginning by financial and other practical needs, the sisters immediately took up educational work and initiated domestic arts projects with local women—even as they made the necessary arrangements to begin their work in South China. This pattern was to inform the future apostolic ministries of the congregation, both institutional works (educational, medical, and social) and community-based pastoral ministries (religious formation and promotion of women). From the beginning, the congregation was open to membership for Catholic women of all nationalities seeking to follow a call to cross-cultural mission, as well as to mission and ministry among social and cultural minority peoples in the United States.

Growth and Expansion. From China the congregation extended its missionary presence to North Korea (1923), the Philippines (1925), Japan (1937), and among Chinese and Japanese peoples in the United States. In 1946, Mary Columba Tarpey, a long-time confidant of the foundress, and gifted with the strong skills of administration and organization that were now demanded of the rapidly growing community, became the second mother general. The post-World War II boom in vocations also enabled expansion in Latin America, Africa, and the Pacific Islands. In recognition for her leadership of some 1,600 Maryknoll Sisters, then constituting "the largest, most active Roman Catholic Missionary Order" in the United States, Mother Columba was featured in a cover story article in *Time* magazine in 1957.

New Challenges. In the Vatican Council II era (1958–72), Mother Mary Coleman led the congregation as it faced the challenges before all religious orders to adapt the decrees of renewal in the spirit of their founders. This period was characterized by strong emphasis on education and professional preparation of the members through the Sister Formation movement. Maryknoll Teacher's College, established in the 1930s, was upgraded to a full liberal arts college. Simultaneously, those post-Vatican II years also brought an end to the rapid growth of the congregation as some members withdrew and new candidates were fewer in number.

Renewal and Refounding. Paradigm shifts in mission and in religious life necessitated creative adjustments and new orientations in the congregation to meet the demands of the times. When Sr. Barbara Hendricks assumed the presidency of the congregation in 1970, she brought to the task the dynamic experience of change and reorientation in mission of the Latin American Church. Leading efforts for renewal and refounding in the spirit of Mother Mary Joseph, Hendricks gave impetus to new commitments and new mission priorities for the Maryknoll Sisters: the "option for the poor"; promotion of women in all cultures; serious commitment to interreligious dialogue; and energies focused on a more effective evangelization through an integrated witness of life, word, and work in service of the gospel.

The Association

The Maryknoll Mission Association of the Faithful was founded on August 15, 1994. The association's vision statement affirms it as "a Catholic community called by the Holy Spirit to mission through our baptism and our on-going journeys of faith . . . crossing boundaries of culture, nationality and faith to join our lives to those of the poor, marginated and oppressed peoples of the earth."

The association, an ecclesial response of the U.S. Church to mission, is open to membership by laity, priests, and religious sisters and brothers. In the previous three decades, some five hundred associate missioners (priests, brothers, and laity) had already served in mission through associate programs of the society and congregation.

The Maryknoll Lay Mission Program begun in 1974 originally provided opportunities for lay Catholics to give short-term service in mission. Eventually, some lay missioners began to give longer term service, assuming institutional responsibilities such as fundraising and other administrative and professional services for the society. Concurrently, these missioners also sought a more active participation in the policy and decision-making processes of the society. Since the structures of canonical religious institutes did not provide adequate opportunities for such participation, the society was advised by the Congregation for Evangelization of Peoples to retain a clear distinction between priests and brothers bound under oath and associate members (lay, religious, and clerical) under temporary contract with the society. In 1992 a committee composed of representatives of society, congregation, and the Lay Missioner Program, was commissioned to develop a new mission association within the Maryknoll family.

In 1993 a consensus of the society and congregation led to the founding of the jointly sponsored Maryknoll Mission Association of the Faithful. The founding assembly of the MMAF was held at Maryknoll, New York, in August 1994, which approved the vision statement and statutes and elected the leadership.

By 1995 some 135 members of the association were serving in mission together with over 1,200 Maryknoll priests, brothers, and sisters in more than 30 countries of Africa, Asia, the Pacific Islands, Latin America, the Middle East, and the United States. Since 1982, coming full circle to its fundamental missionary outreach, more than thirty Maryknollers have returned to educational and social ministries in the Peoples Republic of China.

See also PRICE, THOMAS; ROGERS, MARY JOSEPHINE; WALSH, JAMES.

Kennedy, Camilla. *To the Uttermost Parts of the Earth: The Spirit and Charism of Mary Josephine Rogers.* Maryknoll, N.Y.: Maryknoll Sisters, 1980.

Lyons, Jeanne Marie. *Maryknoll's First Lady: The Life of Mother Mary Joseph, Foundress of the Maryknoll Sisters.* Garden City, N.Y.: Echo Books, 1967.

Molineaux, David J., and Mary J. Ress. *Maryknoll in Chile: The First Fifty Years.* Santiago, Chile, 1993.

Nevins, Albert J. *The Meaning of Maryknoll.* New York: McMullen Books, 1954.

Powers, George C. *The Maryknoll Movement.* Maryknoll, N.Y.: Catholic Foreign Mission Society of America, 1926.

Wiest, Jean-Paul. *Maryknoll in China: A History, 1918–1955.* Armonk, N.Y.: M. E. Sharpe, 1988.

JANET CARROLL, M.M.

Related Document

THE LAUNCHING OF THE CATHOLIC FOREIGN MISSION SOCIETY OF AMERICA (MARYKNOLL), MARCH 25, 1911

On June 29, 1908, the constitution *Sapienti consilio* of Pope Pius X removed the Church of the United States from the jurisdiction of the Congregation de Propaganda Fide and thus officially declared that its missionary status was at an end. Long before this date, however, the American Church had attained a position of strength in both numbers and resources and, in fact, by 1910 there were an estimated 16,363,000 Catholics in the country. Throughout the nineteenth century American Catholics had done relatively little for the foreign missions, although in 1904 their monetary contributions passed the $100,000 mark and rose steadily in the years thereafter. As yet, however, no full-fledged effort had been made to enlist American personnel for the foreign-mission field. In September, 1910, two American priests, James Anthony Walsh and Thomas Frederick Price, who had long thought and planned for this cause met at the In-

ternational Eucharistic Congress in Montreal, and from that meeting there stemmed the founding of the first distinctly American Catholic foreign-mission society. Walsh and Price secured the sponsorship of Cardinal Gibbons and the Apostolic Delegate, and at the annual meeting of the archbishops of the United States on April 27, 1911, at the Catholic University of America approval was given for the opening of a seminary for this purpose. Maryknoll, as it is popularly known, began modestly in 1911 and today the society numbers over 600 priests, more than 100 brothers, and nearly 750 students studying for either the priesthood or brotherhood in eight training centers. Other American religious orders and congregations meanwhile increased their participation in the work and by December, 1953, there was a total of 4755 American priests, brothers, and sisters serving abroad in mission stations all over the world.

(*Source*: Archives of Maryknoll Seminary, copy.)

To the Most Reverend Archbishops of the United States:

VENERABLE BRETHREN:

At the request of His Excellency, the Apostolic Delegate,[1] I submit to your consideration a plan to establish an American Foreign Mission Seminary.

That such a Seminary is needed, and urgently, seems daily more evident. The prestige of our country has become wide-spread; and Protestants, especially in the Far East, are profiting by it, to the positive hindrance of Catholic missioners. I understand that even the educated classes in China, misled by the almost complete absence of American Catholic priests, believe that the Church of Rome has no standing in America.[2]

Conscious that we are still short of priests in many dioceses, I would cite the words of Cardinal Manning referring to the foundation of Mill Hill:

> It is quite true that we have need of men and means at home; and it is BECAUSE we have need of more men and more means, by a great deal, than we as yet possess, that I am convinced we ought to send both men and means abroad. . . . If we desire to find the surest way to multiply immensely our own material means for works at home, it is by not limiting the expansion of Charity and by not paralyzing the zeal of self-denial.[3]

The priests of the United States number more than 17,000 but I am informed that there are hardly sixteen on the foreign missions. This fact recalls a warning which the late Cardinal Vaughan gave in a kindly and brotherly letter addressed to me twenty-two years ago, urging us American Catholics not to delay participation in foreign missions, LEST OUR OWN FAITH SHOULD SUFFER.

[1] Diomede Falconio, O.F.M. (1842–1917), was the third Apostolic Delegate to the United States, having served from 1902 to late in the year 1911.

[2] Between 1881–1888 five Franciscans had gone to China from the United States but only one of them was a native-born American; there were also two American-born Sisters of Charity in China in the late years of the nineteenth century.

[3] Gibbons took the Manning quotation from a letter he had received from Herbert Vaughan (1832–1903), Bishop of Salford and after 1892 Archbishop of Westminster. Vaughan's letter dated Mill Hill, October 28, 1889, used the occasion of the centennial of the American hierarchy to urge upon the Catholics of the United States participation in the foreign missions of the Church. "A Challenge to the American Church on Its One Hundredth Birthday," *Catholic Historical Review,* XXX (October, 1944), 297.

(*Source*: John Tracy Ellis, ed. *Documents of American Catholic History.* Vol. 2:1866–1966. Wilmington, Del.: Michael Glazier, 1987, 576–77.)

MARYLAND, CATHOLIC CHURCH IN

Maryland had its beginning in the vision of George Calvert (1580–1634), first Lord Baltimore, of Catholics and Protestants living in peaceful communion in a small corner of the New World. Out of this vision came the Maryland tradition in American Catholicism, one of interfaith harmony, public service, and attachment to such American principles as religious liberty and separation of Church and state. Fully articulated by Archbishop John Carroll, it would, in large measure, be replaced by attitudes and institutions that developed with the immigrant Church. Twice, however, the Maryland tradition would be revived within the Catholic Church in the United States by cardinal archbishops of Baltimore born in that city, James Gibbons and Lawrence Joseph Shehan. Today the tradition largely prevails.

The Colonial and Revolutionary Period

Though counting but twenty or so among the two hundred or more adventurers who landed at St. Clement's Island on March 25, 1634, Catholics provided the leadership of the new colony. They were accompanied by three Jesuits, Fr. Andrew White the superior. The task of implementing the plans of his father devolved upon Cecil Calvert (1605–75), second Lord Baltimore, who never saw his colony. His brother Leonard was the first governor. The Catholics who settled in St. Mary's County and spread to the adjoining Charles and Prince George's Counties would constitute the "cultural nucleus" of the Catholic Church in the United States. Several families constituted a Catholic elite, such as the Brents, Darnalls, Digges, Brookes, Sewalls, and Neales, to mention the most prominent, who were joined by a member of the beleaguered Irish gentry on the eve of the Glorious Revolution in England in 1689, Charles Carroll. By then the Jesuits had established sizable plantations and mission centers at St. Inigoes and Newtown in St. Mary's County, St. Thomas Manor in Charles County, White Marsh in Prince George's County, and Bohemia Manor in Cecil County. But Catholics went to Mass more often than not in the homes of well-to-do Catholics nearby.

It was, to a great extent, the favor shown by Charles Calvert (1637–1715), third Lord Baltimore, to relatives and wealthy Catholics that precipitated a revolt in Maryland that coincided with the Glorious Revolution in England and that ushered Maryland Catholics into their penal age. From a position of power they were reduced to a distrusted and persecuted minority. Despite the political ostracism and other legal penalties visited upon them—a double tax in 1756, for example, because they were barred from the militia—they clung tenaciously to their faith. Descendants of the Catholic core of 1689 remained about 12 percent of the population, despite few accretions from abroad thereafter. Many even prospered economically. The third Charles Carroll (1737–1832) was accounted the richest man in Revolutionary America. Charles Carroll of Carrollton, in fact, would lead his coreligionists into the patriots' camp.

The prejudice and distrust visited upon Maryland "papists," in fact, diminished after England's defeat of France in 1763. Separate churches (aside from private chapels) began to be built on land acquired for that purpose: near Tuckahoe in Talbot County, at Frederick in Frederick County, at Pomfret in Charles County, at or near Newtown, Leonardtown, Medley's Neck, and Bushwood in St. Mary's County, and in Baltimore Town, where land was acquired in 1764 and a modest church that would become the first cathedral in the United States was built about 1770. Something close to parish life developed in this period.

Catholics played a prominent part in revolutionary Maryland, the militia, the Maryland Line, county committees of observation, and the new state legislature. From 1774, when he was the first Catholic elected to office since 1689, until 1790, when he was sent to New York as one of Maryland's two senators, Charles Carroll was chosen by his state to play a number of important roles, including that of signing the Declaration of Independence.

In the period between the Peace of Paris (1783) and the adoption of the federal Constitution, the Maryland clergy (all former Jesuits) played a dominant role in laying the groundwork for the Catholic Church in the United States. John Carroll (1736–1815), a distant cousin of Charles, was the most prominent. In 1783 he drew up a tentative but democratic constitution for the Catholic clergy of Maryland. The body petitioned Rome in 1784 for spiritual faculties for a superior. Carroll was chosen superior of the American mission. Four years later the Holy See also allowed the clergy to elect a bishop. On November 6, 1789, John Carroll was named bishop of Baltimore, a diocese that then included the entire United States.

The Early National Period

Bishop Carroll held his only synod in 1791 mainly to provide a uniform administration of the sacraments and the support of churches. Carroll promoted the trustee system for the building of new churches, in effect the creation of new parishes. In Maryland, in all but Baltimore's German congregation, it worked well. Carroll also established the nation's first Catholic institution of higher learning, what would become Georgetown University, and its first seminary, St. Mary's in Baltimore, the latter under the Sulpicians. Both began classes in 1791. In 1790 Carmelite nuns in Belgium were invited by Carroll to establish a monastery in Charles County. In 1799 he approved the establishment of an academy in Georgetown by a group of religious women under Leonard Neale who soon adopted the Visitation Rule. In 1808, under his direction, Elizabeth Seton (1774–1831) opened an academy in Baltimore and organized a sisterhood that would become the Sisters (later Daughters) of Charity. In 1809 they moved to Emmittsburg, where the Sulpicians were in the process of establishing their second seminary and college, Mount St. Mary's. Carroll also took the initiative in the restoration of the Society of Jesus in the United States in 1805.

In 1808, when four dioceses were carved from that of Baltimore, Carroll became an archbishop and Baltimore a metropolitan see. It was the beginning of a process of ecclesiastical mitosis that would by 1822 reduce the Archdiocese of Baltimore to the state of Maryland and the District of Columbia.

Carroll's greatest role, perhaps, was as architect of the Maryland tradition. He was active in organizing secular colleges, humane societies, a library company, a dispensary, and other such evidences of his strong sense of public service. His sedulously cultivated friendship with non-Catholics won for him high esteem and for the Catholic body great respect. He instilled in Maryland Catholics a high degree of patriotism and an unwavering devotion to American principles, even those at variance with the Catholic theology and ecclesiology of the age, such as religious freedom and the separation of Church and state.

The traditions he established continued under his immediate successors, Leonard Neale (1746–1817); Ambrose Maréchal (1768–1828), a Sulpician; and James Whitfield (1770–1834), a student of Maréchal. Though Neale had little use for trustees, he valued the services of those of the cathedral, who were largely responsible for the magnificent Basilica of the Assumption begun by Carroll in 1806 but not completed until 1821. In 1816 Neale also entrusted to the Jesuits forty of the fifty or more parochial congregations in Maryland and the District of Columbia, a grant strongly contested by his successor. Maréchal's struggle with the Jesuits over an annuity also marked a decline of Jesuit power in Maryland and a rise of the Sulpicians. Under Whitfield, a black sisterhood, the Oblates of Providence, was founded in Baltimore by a Sulpician in 1829, and the Carmelites moved from Charles County to open a school in the see city in 1831. In 1829 Whitfield convoked the first of the triennial provincial councils of Baltimore. The archbishop of Baltimore had

Cathedral of the Assumption, Baltimore

by this time become the Holy See's principal conduit for American affairs.

The Immigrant Church: Part One

The episcopacies of Samuel Eccleston (1801–51), a Sulpician, and Francis Patrick Kenrick (1796–1863), from 1834 to 1863 witnessed the reappearance of antipopery in Maryland. Beginning with the "nunnery riot" at the Carmelite convent in 1839 and climaxing with the Know-Nothing triumph in Maryland in the 1850s, it was largely in response to the rapid influx of Irish and German immigrants. In this period the Catholic population of the archdiocese rose from 80,000 to over 140,000, of which Baltimore alone claimed 60,000. In the 1850s its German Catholic population grew from nineteen thousand to almost thirty-three thousand, double that of the Irish.

It was a period marked by the establishment of institutions designed to meet the needs of these immigrants: the national parish, the parochial school, the hospital, the orphanage, and a militant press whose principal purpose was to instill a sense of self-esteem. Eccleston invited the Redemptorists and School Sisters of Notre Dame to serve the Germans and the Christian Brothers to staff mostly Irish schools. Although a member of the eastern shore gentry, he proved more attuned to the needs of the immigrants than his Irish-born successor. Eccleston also helped establish a variety of charitable, mutual-aid, and devotional societies shaped to meet the physical and psychic needs of his immigrant charges. In 1851 the Jesuits opened Loyola College in Baltimore. Under Kenrick the archdiocese, though denied primatial status, was granted "prerogative of place" in 1858.

Under Martin John Spalding (1810–72), of Maryland descent, immigrant Catholics fared even better. He established, in addition to a great number of the same kinds of institutions mentioned above, reformatories for boys and girls, old-age homes, and the first parish in the United States, St. Francis Xavier in 1864, to serve exclusively African Americans. For these and other needs he brought in the Sisters of the Good Shepherd, Little Sisters of the Poor, Xaverian Brothers, Mill Hill Fathers (later the Josephites), Passionists, and Carmelites (later replaced by the Capuchins). At the Second Plenary Council of Baltimore—more than any other of the national synods the work of one man—he crafted what was, in effect, a *corpus juris* for the immigrant Church. A consequence of the council was the detachment of the eastern shore of Maryland from the archdiocese, which became on March 3, 1868, a part of the newly created Diocese of Wilmington, with Thomas A. Becker (1832–99), a friend of Spalding, as its first bishop. On the occasion of the twenty-fifth anniversary of the coronation of Pius IX in 1871, Spalding staged, perhaps, the most spectacular celebration Baltimore had ever seen. Characteristic of the immigrant Church in Baltimore were the endless parades that boasted almost numberless bands and banners, usually on the occasion of the laying of cornerstones and dedications of new churches.

Though poor health prevented the next archbishop, James Roosevelt Bayley (1814–78), from establishing many new institutions, his episcopacy witnessed an explosion of parish societies, particularly branches of the national organizations in whose foundation or expansion Baltimore played a significant role: the Irish Catholic Benevolent Union, the Catholic Total Abstinence Union, the Catholic Young Men's National Union, and the Knights of St. John. The knighthoods became a particularly popular feature of Baltimore Catholicism. Picnics, excursions, fairs, and balls, many of which Spalding had banned, reached a peak under Bayley. By his death in 1878 the oldest archdiocese was still one of the most richly endowed in the United States counting (excluding the District of Columbia) 120 churches, 69 with resident pastors, 252 priests, 174 of whom were members of nine different orders. Thirteen sisterhoods and three orders of brothers staffed a variety of parochial schools, academies, orphanages, hospitals, reformatories, and homes for the aged.

The Gibbons' Era

James Gibbons (1834–1921) reigned for forty-three years in Baltimore, for most of which Maryland Catholics reveled in their golden age. After presiding over the Third Plenary Council (1884), he was named a cardinal in 1886. A true patriot, public servant, and ecumenist, Gibbons' popularity among non-Catholics was even greater than that of John Carroll, whose traditions he sought consciously to revive. He became the spokesman for a group of bishops and religious labeled Americanizers, which embroiled

him in a number of controversies. His popularity remained unimpaired even after the condemnation of the heresy of "Americanism" in 1899 directed against these liberal bishops. In Baltimore he was especially popular with the perduring Catholic elite, which had given not only Charles Carroll and Roger B. Taney, but also Charles J. Bonaparte, a member of President Theodore Roosevelt's cabinet.

Not an institution builder, Gibbons' principal energies as archbishop of Baltimore were directed perforce toward the needs of the "new immigrants," for whose sensibilities he showed little appreciation, urging them to Americanize as soon as possible. He had to provide not only churches and schools for the Bohemians, Poles, Lithuanians, Ukrainians, and Italians of the see city and national capital, but he also had to find the priests and religious to staff them and to settle many of their internal quarrels himself. Most of their churches he entrusted to religious orders.

Lay Catholics, with but little encouragement from their cardinal, often took the initiative in these years in founding a variety of societies. The Ancient Order of Hibernians, the Knights of Columbus, and other national organizations spread throughout the archdiocese. Women also formed auxiliaries. A Catholic lyceum movement produced a host of young men's literary associations, some of which evolved into dramatic societies, some into sports clubs. Catholic building-and-loan societies and banks were established. The Sodality of the Blessed Virgin Mary, League of the Sacred Heart, the Holy Name Society, and other pious associations proliferated in these years.

As Gibbons' fame grew, his archdiocese shrank in relative strength. At the end of his long tenure the Catholic population (276,000) was hardly one-fourth of the other large archdioceses. Parishes scarcely kept pace. There were only ninety-seven parochial schools. There were few new major institutions and none for which he was responsible. In 1896 Notre Dame of Maryland was chartered as the first Catholic college for women. After Gibbons, the premier see would never quite recapture the leading role it had played since 1789.

The Immigrant Church: Part Two

Under Michael Joseph Curley (1878–1947), the Archdiocese of Baltimore experienced a twenty-five-year period of aggressive leadership. In his first few years it underwent its period of consolidation, centralization, and Romanization. An Office of Education, Catholic Charities, and the Propagation of the Faith were run with an efficiency heretofore unknown in the oldest archdiocese. Though he discouraged the proliferation of parish societies, Archbishop Curley gave full support to the Holy Name Society, Sodality, Knights of Columbus, and Catholic Daughters of America, the organizations he most often employed to spearhead his several crusades, those against the godless regime of Mexico, communism, and "dirty" movies being the most publicized. He encouraged members of national parishes to cherish their ethnic roots, lavished a special attention upon the poor, and ignored the dwindling elite. His outspokenness stirred an unaccustomed militancy among most Maryland Catholics until he was finally silenced by Rome as a result of an incautious remark about Pearl Harbor.

Curley also encouraged the League of the Little Flower for the support of rural schools, the Big Brothers Association, the Evidence Guild, and the Ladies of Charity. An institution builder and schoolman, his greatest achievement was the number of well-run parochial schools. He also taxed his parishes for a new and capacious St. Mary's Seminary.

On July 22, 1939, Curley was named archbishop of Washington, D.C. The double title was merely in preparation for another dismemberment of the archdiocese. On December 15, 1947, soon after the appointment of Francis Patrick Keough (1890–1961) as eleventh archbishop of Baltimore, the five southernmost counties of Maryland—St. Mary's, Charles, Prince George's, Calvert, and Montgomery—were made part of the Archdiocese of Washington under Archbishop Patrick Aloysius O'Boyle (1896–1987). The latter would be succeeded in 1973 by William Wakefield Baum, who was in turn succeeded in 1980 by James Aloysius Hickey. All three would be named cardinals. In 1967 the Maryland Catholic Conference was created by the archbishops of Baltimore and Washington and the bishop of Wilmington as a legal and lobbying agency to effect favorable legislation by the Maryland Assembly on such matters as school funding and abortion.

Archbishop Keough encouraged the growth of the CYO (Catholic Youth Organization) and CCD (Confraternity of Christian Doctrine). Another builder, he succeeded in providing a high-school education and health care for young and aged Catholics who had moved from the lower to the middle class. To Keough fell the task of erecting the cathedral (Mary Our Queen) made possible by a legacy of 1919 that Curley refused to honor.

Succeeded by still another builder in 1961, Lawrence Joseph Shehan (1898–1984), who conducted its most successful fundraising campaign, the archdiocese witnessed the replacement of a dozen or more antiquated institutions and motherhouses with new and costly ones, plus new high schools, hospitals, and a large Catholic Center to house the growing number of diocesan agencies. His even greater achievements, however, were pastoral and largely the result of the Vatican Council II, particularly in the areas of ecumenism, the liturgy, empowerment of the laity, and racial justice. In these he set an example not only for Maryland Catholics, but for the nation as a whole. Made a cardinal in 1965, he conducted special visitations of all his parishes to lead both priests and laity into the postconciliar world. Shehan set in motion the process of creating an archdiocesan pastoral council and regional and parish councils, a work that would be completed by his successor. His last years were saddened, however, by a series of crises in faith (Humanae vitae), vocations, education, finances, and racial conflict that beset the two archdioceses of Maryland. Under Daniel and Philip Berrigan and other activists, Baltimore became a center of the pacifist movement.

A measure of emotional and fiscal stability was achieved by Archbishop William Donald Borders, Shehan's successor in 1974, who also set in place the collegial structures and central services Shehan had envisioned. Under Archbishop Borders a variety of prayer and Bible-study associations, mutual-support groups, social outreach programs, and charismatic communities would develop. His successor was William Henry Keeler, whose administrative and diplomatic talents won for him not only the presidency of the National Conference of Catholic Bishops in 1992, but also the red hat in 1994, suggesting a return to Baltimore of the leadership to which it was long accustomed. In his interfaith collaboration and public service Cardinal Keeler represented certainly a perpetuation of the Maryland tradition, but the oldest archdiocese, no less than any other see, would continue to suffer the tensions of the postconciliar Church.

Beitzell, Edwin W. *The Jesuit Missions of St. Mary's County, Maryland.* Abell, Maryland, 1976.

Corrigan, Owen B. *History of the Catholic Schools in the Archdiocese of Baltimore.* Baltimore, Maryland, 1924.

Ellis, John Tracy, and Robert Trisco. *A Guide to American Catholic History.* 2nd ed. Santa Barbara, Calif.: ABC-Clio, 1982.

Guilday, Peter. *A History of the Councils of Baltimore 1791–1884.* New York: Arno Press, 1969.

Kauffman, Christopher J. *Tradition and Transformation in Catholic Culture: The Priests of St. Sulpice in the United States from 1791 to the Present.* New York: Macmillan, 1988.

Riordan, Michael J. *Cathedral Records from the Beginning of Catholicity in Baltimore to the Present Time.* Baltimore, Maryland, 1906.

Shehan, Lawrence. *A Blessing of Years: The Memoirs of Lawrence Cardinal Shehan.* University of Notre Dame Press, 1982.

Spalding, Thomas W. *The Premier See: A History of the Archdiocese of Baltimore, 1789–1989.* Baltimore: Johns Hopkins University Press, 1989.

_____. "'A Revolution More Extraordinary': Bishop John Carroll and the Birth of American Catholicism." *Maryland Historical Magazine* 84 (1989) 195–222.

_____. *St. Vincent de Paul of Baltimore: The Story of a People and Their Home.* Baltimore: Maryland Historical Society, 1995.

Stanton, Thomas J. *A Century of Growth, Or the History of the Catholic Church in Western Maryland.* 2 vols. Baltimore, Maryland, 1900.

THOMAS W. SPALDING

Related Documents

THE STATE OF CATHOLICISM
IN MARYLAND, 1638

In the first years of their mission in the colony of Maryland the Jesuits were hampered from carrying out their desire to convert the Indians by the hostile acts of neighboring tribes and of the Puritans from Virginia, the reluctance of the colonial officials to run the risk of losing their priests, and the necessity of establishing themselves on the land as their sole source of income. But their religious ministrations to the colonists bore fruitful results as can be seen from the following account embodied in the *Annual Letter* for 1638 which reveals a healthy state of religion among the Maryland Catholics, progress in converting some Protestants, and comfort afforded to a number of Catholics among the indentured servants of Virginia. At the time the letter was written there were three Jesuit priests in Maryland: Andrew White, John Altham, and Thomas Copley. If the original letter carried the name of the author it was eliminated by the Jesuit editor in England before it was sent on to the Jesuit headquarters in Rome.

(*Source*: E. A. Dalrymple, ed. *Narrative of a Voyage to Maryland by Father Andrew White, S.J. An Account of the Colony of the Lord Baron of Baltimore. Extracts from Different Letters of Missionaries, from the Year 1635 to the Year 1677*. Baltimore: Maryland Historical Society, 1874, 54–62.)

FOUR FATHERS GAVE THEIR ATTENTION TO THIS MISSION, with one assistant in temporal affairs; and he, indeed, after enduring severe toils for the space of five years, with the greatest patience, humility, and ardent love, chanced to be seized by the disease prevailing at the time, and happily exchanged this wretched life for an immortal one.[1]

He was also shortly followed by one of the Fathers,[2] who was young indeed, but on account of his remarkable qualities of mind, evidently of great promise. He had scarcely spent two months in this mission, when, to the great grief of all of us, he was carried off by the common sickness prevailing in the Colony, from which no one of the three remaining priests has escaped unharmed; yet we have not ceased to labor, to the best of our ability among the neighboring people.

And though the rulers of the Colony have not yet allowed us to dwell among the savages, both on account of the prevailing sickness, and also, because of the hostile disposition which the barbarians evince towards the English, they having slain a man from this Colony, who was staying among them for the sake of trading, and having also entered into a conspiracy against our whole nation; yet we hope that one of us will shortly secure a station among the barbarians. Meanwhile, we devote ourselves more zealously to the English; and since there are Protestants as well as Catholics in the Colony, we have labored for both, and God has blessed our labors.

For, among the Protestants, nearly all who have come from England, in this year 1638, and many others, have been converted to the faith, together with four servants, whom we purchased in Virginia, (another Colony of our Kingdom), for necessary services, and five mechanics, whom we hired for a month, and have in the meantime won to God. Not long afterwards, one of these, after being duly prepared for death, by receiving the sacraments, departed this life. And among these persons hardly anything else worth mentioning has occurred. . . .

Besides these, one of us, going out of the Colony, found two Frenchmen, one of whom had been without the sacraments of the Catholic Church for three entire years; the other, who was already near death, having spent fifteen whole years among Heretics, had lived just as they do. The Father aided the former with the sacraments and confirmed him in the Catholic faith as much as he could. The latter he restored to the Catholic Church, and, administering all the sacraments, prepared him for dying happily.

As for the Catholics, the attendance on the sacraments here is so large, that it is not greater among the Europeans, in proportion to the number of Catholics. The more ignorant have been catechised, and Catechetical Lectures have been delivered for the more advanced every Sunday; but, on Feast days sermons have been rarely neglected. The sick and the dying, who have been very numerous this year, and who dwelt far apart, we have assisted in every way, so that not even a single one has died without the sacraments. We have buried very many, and baptized various persons. And, although there are not wanting frequent occasions of dissension, yet none of any importance has arisen here in the last nine months, which we have not immediately allayed. By the blessing of God, we have this consolation, that no vices spring up among the new Catholics, although settlements of this kind are not usually supplied from the best class of men.

We bought off in Virginia, two Catholics, who had sold themselves into bondage, nor was the money ill-spent, for both showed themselves good Christians: one, indeed, surpasses the ordinary standard. Some others have performed the same duty of Charity, buying thence Catholic servants, who are very numerous in that country. For every year, very many sell themselves thither into bondage, and living among men of the worst example, and, being destitute of all spiritual aid, they generally make shipwreck of their souls.

In the case of one, we adore the remarkable providence and mercy of God, which brought a man encompassed in the world with very many difficulties, and now at length living in Virginia, almost continually without any aid to his soul, to undertake these exercises, not long before his death. This design a severe sickness prevented, which he bore with the greatest patience, with a mind generally fixed on God; and at length having properly received all the sacraments in the most peaceful manner, beyond what is usual, renders back to the Creator the breath of the life that remained, which had been so full of troubles and disquietudes. . . .

[1] Brother Thomas Gervase (1590–1637), who had come out with the original colonists.

[2] John Knowles (1607–1637).

(*Source*: John Tracy Ellis, ed. *Documents of American Catholic History*. Vol. 1:1493–1865. Wilmington, Del.: Michael Glazier, 1987, 108–10.)

MARYLAND'S ACT OF RELIGIOUS TOLERATION, APRIL 21, 1649

Among the famous documents of American religious liberty Maryland's bill of April, 1649, entitled "An Act Concerning Religion," deserves a prime place, even though it was not included among the documents carried on the Freedom Train in 1947. From the very beginning of the colony Cecilius Calvert, the second Baron of Baltimore (1606–1675), and his lieutenants had maintained religious freedom for all the inhabitants; thus the assembly's action of 1649 in no way constituted a new policy for Maryland. But with the current running strongly in favor of Cromwell in England, the Puritans who had found a refuge in Maryland from oppression in Virginia and elsewhere grew bolder in attacks upon their Catholic neighbors. Baltimore sought, therefore, to insure religious peace by a specific enactment. The fact that he acted from motives of expediency, as well as from personal conviction, should not be permitted to deprive the lord proprietor and his assembly of credit for a remarkably broad grant of religious toleration for the mid-seventeenth century; nor should it be forgotten that the Protestants in the assembly joined with their Catholic colleagues to pass the measure.

(*Source*: William Hand Browne, ed. *Archives of Maryland. Proceedings and Acts of the General Assembly of Maryland, January 1637/38–September 1664*. Baltimore: Maryland Historical Society, 1883, I, 244–47.)

FFORASMUCH AS IN A WELL GOVERNED AND XPIAN COM̄ON Weath matters concerning Religion and the honor or God ought in the first place to bee taken into serious consideratōn and endeavoured to bee settled. Be it therefore ordered and enacted . . . That whatsoever pson or psons within this Province . . . shall from henceforth blaspheme God . . . or deny our Saviour Jesus Christ to bee the sonne of God, or shall deny the holy Trinity the ffather sonne and holy Ghost, or the Godhead of any of the said Three psons of the Trinity or the Unity of the Godhead . . . shalbe punished with death and confiscatōn or forfeiture of all his or her lands and goods to the Lord Proprietary and his heires. . . . And bee it also Enacted by the Authority and with the advise and assent aforesaid. That whatsoever pson or psons shall from henceforth use or utter any reproachfull words or Speeches concerning the blessed Virgin Mary the Mother of our Saviour or the holy Apostles or Evangelists or any of them shall in such case for the first offence forfeit to the Lord Proprietary and his heires . . . the sume of ffive pound Sterling or the value thereof to be Leveyed

on the goods and chattells of every such pson soe offending. . . . And be it also further Enacted by the same authority. . . . that whatsoever pson or psons shall from henceforth uppon any occasion of Offence or otherwise in a reproachful manner or Way declare call or denoninimate any pson or psons whatsoever inhabiting . . . within this Province . . . an heritick, Scismatick, Idolator, puritan, Independant, Prespiterian popish prest, Jesuite, Jesuited papist, Lutheran, Calvenist, Anabaptist, Brownist, Antinomian, Barrowist, Roundhead, Sepatist, or any other name or terme in a reproachfull manner relating to matter of Religion shall for every such Offence forfeit and loose somē or tenne shillings sterling or the value thereof to bee leveyed on the goods and chattels of every such Offender. . . . And whereas the inforceing of the conscience in matters of Religion hath frequently fallen out to be of dangerous Consequence in those commonwealths where it hath been practised, And for the more quiett and peaceable government of this Province, and the better to pserve mutuall Love and amity amongst the Inhabitants thereof. Be it Therefore . . . enacted (except as in this psent Act is before Declared and sett forth) that noe person or psons whatsoever within this Province, or the Islands, Ports, Harbors, Creekes, or havens thereunto belonging professing to beleive in Jesus Christ, shall from henceforth bee any waies troubled, Molested or discountenanced for or in respect of his or her religion nor in the free exercise thereof within this Province or the Islands thereunto belonging nor any way compelled to the beleife or exercise of any other Religion against his or her consent, soe as they be not unfaithfull to the Lord Proprietary, or molest or conspire against the civill Governemt established or to bee established in this Province under him or his heires. And that all & every pson or psons that shall presume Contrary to this Act and the true intent and meaning thereof directly or indirectly either in person or estate willfully to wrong disturbe trouble or molest any person whatsoever within this Province professing to beleive in Jesus Christ for or in respect of his or her religion or the free exercise thereof within this Province other than is provided for in this Act that such pson or psons soe offending, shalbe compelled to pay trebble damages to the party soe wronged or molested, and for every such offence shall also forfeit 20[s] sterling in money or the value therof. . . . Or if the ptie soe offending as aforesaid shall refuse or bee unable to recompense the party so wronged, or to satisfy such ffyne or forfeiture, then such Offender shalbe severly punished by publick whipping & imprisonmt during the pleasure of the Lord Proprietary, or his Lieuetenāt or cheife Governor of this Province for the tyme being without baile or maineprise. . . .

(*Source*: John Tracy Ellis, ed. *Documents of American Catholic History*. Vol. 1:1493–1865. Wilmington, Del.: Michael Glazier, 1987, 112–14.)

DISFRANCHISEMENT OF CATHOLICS
IN MARYLAND, OCTOBER 20, 1654

For years William Claiborne (c. 1587–c. 1677), a leader of the Puritan element in Virginia, has been feuding with the Calvert regime in Maryland over the possession of Kent Island and other matters. The victory of Cromwell, therefore, gave Claiborne and his followers a pretext for an all-out assault in which they succeeded in overthrowing the government of Governor William Stone (c. 1603–c. 1660) and imposing their own rule upon Maryland. Claiborne was, of course, bitterly anti-Catholic and one of the first things which he did was to put through the assembly an act disfranchising Catholics. Thus the toleration practiced since 1634, and made the subject of special legislation in 1649, was abolished.

(*Source*: William Hand Browne, ed. *Archives of Maryland. Proceedings and Acts of the General Assembly of Maryland, January 1637/38–September 1664*. Baltimore: Maryland Historical Society, 1883, I, 340–41.)

It is Enacted and Declared in the Name of his Highness the Lord Protector with the Consent and by the Authority of the present Generall Assembly That none who profess and Exercise the Popish Religion Commonly known by the Name of the Roman Catholick Religion can be protected in this Province by the Lawes of England formerly Established and yet unrepealed . . . but are to be restrained from the Exercise thereof, Therefore all and Every person or persons Concerned in the Law aforesaid are required to take notice

Such as profess faith in God by Jesus Christ (though Differing in Judgment from the Doctrine worship & Discipline publickly held forth shall not be restrained from but shall be protected in the profession of the faith) & Exercise of their Religion so as they abuse not this Liberty to the injury of others The Disturbance of the publique peace on their part, Provided that this Liberty be not Extended to popery or prelacy nor to such as under the profession of Christ hold forth and practice Licentiousness

(*Source*: John Tracy Ellis, ed. *Documents of American Catholic History*, Vol. 1:1493–1865. Wilmington, Del.: Michael Glazier, 1987, 114–15.)

MASSACHUSETTS, CATHOLIC CHURCH IN

Colonial and Revolutionary Period

Massachusetts, chartered in 1628 as the Massachusetts Bay Colony, was settled by religious dissenters from England. These dissenters, known collectively as Puritans, arrived in the greatest numbers during the Great Migration of 1630–40. Earlier in the century another dissenting group, the Pilgrims (or Separatists), established Plymouth Colony, which remained a separate colony until annexed to Massachusetts in 1691.

Puritanism, of which Separatism was a variant, held that the Church of England under the Elizabethan Settlement had not completed the Protestant Reformation in eliminating all traces of Catholicism from its polity and liturgy. Thus in England and later in America the Puritans developed a strenuous resistance to Catholics and Catholicism. Colonial laws and ordinances made it unlawful for Catholics to participate in political life or openly practice their religion. In 1647 an antipriest law passed the general court, making it a criminal offense for a Catholic priest to enter Massachusetts upon pain of banishment for the first offense and death for the second.

To the north, in present-day Maine and Canada, French Catholics had been establishing settlements for almost a generation. The presence of France, the traditional enemy of England, and Catholicism, the adversary of Protestantism, provided the settlers of Massachusetts with sufficient reason to maintain their stiff resistance to a perceived Catholic threat.

Throughout the seventeenth century and into the eighteenth, the government of Massachusetts remained steadfast in its anti-Catholic stance. Additional laws were passed further restricting civil and religious rights of Catholics. The Massachusetts Charter of 1691 denied religious liberty to Catholics, and a second antipriest law was passed in 1700 declaring life imprisonment as a penalty for any Catholic priest found residing in the colony.

Most of these measures seemed directed toward keeping Catholics away from Massachusetts rather than inhibiting the few already there. During the early and middle part of the eighteenth century, the Irish began an influx into Massachusetts. While predominantly Protestants from Ulster, some of the immigrants may have been at least nominally Catholic. Still, anti-Catholic sentiment prevailed, and it remained in place until the necessities of the American Revolution relaxed that sentiment.

Realizing that intercolonial unity against England required attitudes that encompassed broader views on religion, the Massachusetts Revolutionary leaders made the effort to reduce, at least outwardly, their anti-Catholic biases, especially toward French in Canada and Catholic Native Americans, whose aid they sought in the conflict with Great Britain. It remained necessary to secure the same liberties for all Catholics in Massachusetts. This was eventually done through the Massachusetts Constitution of 1780, which permitted all Catholics the practice of their religion, but at the same time prevented them from holding office and required them to pay taxes to support Protestant ministers.

Although it is difficult to state with any precision how many Catholics resided in Massachusetts at this time, it is generally agreed that they were in significant enough strength to need a priest. These Catholics, mostly French and Irish, had to rely on chaplains from the French fleet in Boston for their services. It was not until 1788 that Massachusetts Catholics had their own resident priest.

The Abbé de la Poterie, a former French naval chaplain who remained in Boston, took over a Huguenot chapel, renamed it Holy Cross Church, and celebrated the first public Mass on November 2, 1788. Although Poterie and his next two successors proved unsatisfactory, the Catholic presence in Massachusetts had begun.

This presence was reinforced with the arrival in 1792 of a French priest, Fr. Francis Anthony Matignon, a refugee from the French Revolution. Matignon inherited a church divided by strife between French and Irish parishioners and regarded with suspicion by Protestant Boston. Fr. Matignon immediately embarked upon healing the rift between the French and the Irish by dividing temporal control of the parish between the two groups, favoring neither side over the other. Equally important, Fr. Matignon used his considerable tact to gain the respect not only of his congregation, but of Protestants as well.

With his pastoral cares mounting because of an increasing Catholic population and his missionary activities among the Native Americans in Maine, Matignon requested as an assistant Fr. Jean Louis Lefebvre de Cheverus, his friend and former student. Fr. Cheverus, a fellow refugee from revolutionary France, arrived in Boston in 1796. Initially required by Matignon to minister to the Passamaquoddy and Penobscot in Maine, Cheverus was soon providing missions to Massachusetts communities. Both priests earned respect for themselves and for the Church through their pastoral care and their charitable efforts during the yellow fever epidemic of 1798.

In 1799 Cheverus and Matignon solicited funds for a new church in Boston. Contributions came from the entire community, including President John Adams. The Church of the Holy Cross, consecrated in 1803, became the seat of Catholicism in New England. Five years later it became a cathedral church when Boston was elevated to diocesan status and Fr. Cheverus was consecrated as the first bishop of Boston.

The See of Boston

The new bishop traveled extensively in his diocese, which covered all of New England, continuing his missionary efforts as well as exercising pastoral care. Bishop Cheverus made some modest institutional advances, including the founding of St. Augustine Cemetery in 1818 to honor his friend and mentor, Fr. Matignon, who died that year, and the introduction of the Ursulines into the diocese and the foundation of a convent for their use.

Cheverus' greatest accomplishment, however, was his continuing work in improving relations between Catholics and Protestants, prompting several Protestants to join with Catholics in petitioning King Louis XVIII of France against Cheverus' removal. However, in 1823 he was recalled to France, becoming bishop of Montaubon and later archbishop of Bordeaux. Elevated to the College of Cardinals in 1826, Cheverus died in July of that year.

After two years without an ordinary, Benedict Fenwick, S.J., of Maryland was named as the second bishop of Boston. Under Fenwick Catholics would witness the establishment of Holy Cross College in Worcester, founded 1843; a Catholic newspaper, the *Jesuit,* later the *Pilot,* founded 1829; St. Vincent's Asylum, opened in 1832 when Fenwick asked the Sisters of Charity to undertake charitable work in the diocese. Several new parishes were also established in Massachusetts to accommodate a growing Catholic population. There remained, however, an entrenched anti-Catholicism. This culminated in the destruction of the Ursuline convent in Charlestown by a nativist mob in 1834. Of necessity Fenwick devoted a great deal of his energy toward presenting positively the Catholic position to a largely hostile public.

When Bishop Fenwick died in 1846, the diocese had become large enough to require subdivision, resulting in the creation of the Diocese of Hartford in 1843. Additional churches and services were established to meet the needs of a growing Catholic population. Amidst the turmoil and uncertainty Bishop Fenwick had brought the beginnings of organization to Catholicism in Massachusetts.

Bishop John Fitzpatrick assumed episcopal care of the Diocese of Boston on August 16, 1846. The diocese in his charge continued to grow and change; immigration brought to Massachusetts many new Catholics, including Irish fleeing the famine of the late 1840s.

It was necessary once again to divide the diocese. The Dioceses of Burlington, Vermont, and Portland, Maine, were created in the 1850s, leaving Massachusetts as the sole territory comprising the Diocese of Boston.

Parish foundations accelerated greatly throughout Massachusetts. During his episcopate Fitzpatrick increased manifold the number of churches. Recent immigrants apart from the Irish also needed churches. German Catholics in Boston saw the dedication of Holy Trinity Church in October of 1846, while national parishes and missions were set up to care for Canadians, Italians, and others who had settled in Massachusetts. To further the educational needs of the diocese, Fitzpatrick presided over the establishment of a parochial school system and supported the founding of Boston College.

As the Church in Massachusetts grew so did anti-Catholicism. The Know-Nothing Party, anti-immigrant and anti-Catholic, controlled the executive and legislative branches of state government. Fitzpatrick, as bishop, had to work carefully to maintain conditions favorable to Catholics until the influence of the Know-Nothings abated in the late 1850s. By the time of Bishop Fitzpatrick's death in 1866 the Catholic Church in the Diocese of Boston, although reduced geographically, grew in population and in the number of its parishes and institutions. Catholics survived continued displays of intolerance and proved themselves loyal and patriotic by supporting the Union during the Civil War. But challenges remained for Fitzpatrick's successor.

When John J. Williams became the fourth bishop of Boston in 1866, Boston lacked a seminary, Catholic education was only in the formative stages, hospitals and orphanages were few, and, despite the building program of his predecessor, a paucity of churches existed for a Catholic population estimated at over 300,000.

Over the next forty-one years, Williams presided over many changes. Several churches were added, including a new Cathedral of the Holy Cross, dedicated in 1875. St. John's Seminary opened in 1884. Parochial schools multiplied. Several hospitals and charitable institutions were founded. New religious orders were introduced. Geographically and administratively the diocese was again transformed. In 1870 and 1872 the Dioceses of Springfield and Providence were erected, thus leaving Massachusetts divided among three dioceses. This development culminated in the elevation of Boston to a metropolitan see in 1875; John Williams was appointed archbishop.

The Twentieth Century

By 1900 the number of Catholics had again increased dramatically. Over 30 percent of the population of Massachusetts in 1900 was foreign-born, with southern and eastern Europe now the predominant places of origin. Many of the newer immigrants went to the newly formed Dioceses of Springfield and Providence, whose Massachusetts portion became the Diocese of Fall River in 1904.

Like his predecessors, Williams found these positive developments tempered by a persistent anti-Catholicism. Campaigns against Catholics and immigrants spread in the late nineteenth century. Archbishop Williams counseled patience and restraint in response. Williams coordinated efforts among the other dioceses in the state and worked with government officials to gain limited recognition and support for Catholic institutions in Massachusetts. In 1906 Archbishop Williams allowed the appointment of a coadjutor bishop, William H. O'Connell. It would remain to O'Connell to build upon and to improve upon Williams' work. When Williams died the following year he left a developing archdiocese to his successor. However, many things still needed attention in order to sustain the achievements of Catholics and Catholicism in Boston and Massachusetts.

Archbishop (Cardinal after 1911) O'Connell immediately began reorganizing the archdiocese. He placed tight financial controls over all the parishes and institutions to put the see on a sound fiscal footing. Still in an age of expansion, the Church required more parishes and priests to accommodate the spiritual needs of a growing Catholic population. O'Connell erected over one hundred new parishes and increased the number of priests from six hundred to fifteen hundred. He enlarged St. John's Seminary and greatly increased the enrollment. In addition, the archbishop introduced more religious communities into the see, bringing the number to sixty-three at the time of his death.

Boston also saw the founding of three colleges for women, the move of Boston College to its present location in Chestnut Hill, and a substantial augmentation of the parochial school system.

Upon his death in 1944, Cardinal O'Connell left to his successor, Richard J. Cushing, a Church whose membership approached one-half of the total population in the area comprising the archdiocese and whose parishes and institutions had grown steadily in the attempt to keep pace with the need. Catholics now generated a real influence within Massachusetts. Catholic mayors, members of Congress, and governors were no longer an anomaly. As Richard Cushing assumed his office he would preside over a Church and a membership that were visible and viable in Massachusetts life.

Archbishop Richard Cushing (elevated to the cardinalate in 1958) was known for many things. Among these was the building program embarked upon soon after becoming archbishop. In his twenty-six-year episcopate, Cushing established over eighty churches, a great many of these in the suburbs, to serve a Catholic population moving away from the city of Boston. Included in this building program were hospitals, colleges, a school for disadvantaged children, and a national seminary for older candidates for the priesthood.

During these years Catholics became more self-assured and integrated more easily into American life. This was borne out by the election of Massachusetts Senator John F. Kennedy to the presidency in 1960. In addition, Vatican Council II placed greater emphasis on modernization and ecumenism. In Boston and throughout Massachusetts, Cushing led much of this ecumenical activity.

Cardinal Cushing resigned in 1970. His successor, Humberto S. Medeiros, assumed control over a see more than forty-two million dollars in debt, a debt that required ten years to retire. It also fell to Medeiros (who was elevated to the cardinalate in 1973) to implement the bulk of Vatican II directives. The continued growth of the archdiocese slowed, and many social challenges faced the Church and its members. The thirteen years of Medeiros' episcopate saw the Church coping with change. Vocations declined, abortion was legalized in Massachusetts, a school busing controversy divided opinion both within and outside the Church. Several Catholic schools closed and creation of new parishes came to a standstill. Cardinal Medeiros died unexpectedly in September 1983, leaving behind a Church emerging from financial burden but confronted with new challenges. The new archbishop, Bernard F. Law, who would be made cardinal in 1985, was named in 1984.

Diocese of Springfield

The Diocese of Springfield, erected in June of 1870, contained the five western and central Massachusetts counties. In 1950 Worcester County was detached and became a separate diocese.

No church existed in this area, nor did it have a resident priest until Fr. James Fitton founded Christ Church in Worcester in 1836. In 1843 Fr. John D. Brady founded a church in western Massachusetts, in what is now Chicopee, and became the first priest resident there. By 1870 the Catholic population had grown to one hundred thousand, mostly Irish canal and railroad workers. Thirty-eight parishes and over forty priests served them.

Over the next eighty years, led by Bishops Patrick Thomas O'Reilly (1870–92), Thomas Daniel Beaven (1892–1920), and Thomas Mary O'Leary (1921–49), the diocese continued to grow, fed like Boston, with immigrants not only from Ireland, but from Canada, Poland, Lithuania, Italy, and other European countries. When Christopher Weldon was appointed bishop of Springfield in 1950, the diocese (now minus Worcester County) contained a Catholic population of 285,000; there were 133 parishes, 413 priests, and 26 religious communities. Springfield also had a Catholic college, charitable institutions, and a newspaper, the *Catholic Mirror,* a monthly publication succeeded by the weekly *Catholic Observer* in 1954.

When Bishop Weldon resigned in 1977, he left a Church that had grown in population but remained stable in number of parishes, institutions, and priests. His successors, Bishop Joseph E. Maguire (1977–91) and Bishop John A. Marshall (1991–94), have witnessed a decline in the number of priests and in Catholic population. Thomas L. Dupre was named in 1995 to succeed Bishop Marshall.

Diocese of Fall River

The Diocese of Fall River was erected in March 1904. It comprises most of southeastern Massachusetts. From 1872 it had been part of the Diocese of Providence, Rhode Island. Virtually no Catholics settled in this region until the 1820s. As the textile and whaling industries began to grow, large numbers of Catholics, mostly Irish and Portuguese, moved into the area. After the Civil War, immigrants of other nationalities entered southeastern Massachusetts. Italians, Poles, Germans, and Lebanese joined the Irish, Portuguese, and French-Canadians already in residence.

At the end of the first year as a separate diocese, Fall River had 49 churches, 110 priests, 5 charitable institutions, and 11 religious communities serving a Catholic population well in excess of 100,000. In its first fifty years in existence the diocese, under Bishops William Stang (1904–07), Daniel Feehan (1907–34), James E. Cassidy (1934–51), and James L. Connolly (1951–70), grew to 99 parishes with 318 priests serving a Catholic population of more than 235,000. The diocese also included eight charitable institutions, thirty religious communities, and a college.

Since 1954, Bishop Connolly, Bishop Daniel A. Cronin (1970–91), and Bishop Sean O'Malley (since 1992) have seen a modest increase in the number of parishes, a growth in charitable institutions, and a dramatic increase in Catholic population. The over 350,000 Catholics amount to nearly 50 percent of the total population of the diocese, including the largest Portuguese community in the United States.

Diocese of Worcester

Worcester, the newest diocese in Massachusetts, was established in January 1950 when Worcester County was detached from the Diocese of Springfield. John J. Wright, auxiliary of Boston, was named as the first bishop of Worcester and served until 1959.

Since Worcester had functioned for many years as a Catholic center of the Diocese of Springfield, a strong Catholic tradition already existed. At the time it was established Worcester had 97 parishes and 375 priests. Twenty-four religious communities, 2 colleges, and 6 charitable institutions served 242,500 Catholics. The original Irish, plus French-Canadians, Poles, Slovaks, Italians, and Syrians, made up a large proportion of the Worcester Catholic population.

Since the creation of the diocese, three other bishops have served as ordinaries: Bernard J. Flanagan (1959–83), Timothy J. Harrington (1983–94), and Daniel Reilly (since 1994). In the 45 years of its existence the diocese has increased in Catholic population to 314,873. Serving them are 127 parishes, 196 priests, 36 religious communities, 3 colleges, and the diocesan newspaper, the *Catholic Free Press,* founded in 1951.

Catholics in Massachusetts have made great strides since 1808 when the newly formed Diocese of Boston included all of New England. Catholics, then a barely tolerated minority, now comprise nearly half of the Massachusetts population of six million. An archdiocese and three dioceses encompassing 771 parishes and over 2,000 priests serve the needs of Massachusetts Catholics. Colleges and universities, charitable institutions, and schools are spread across the state. Catholics are active participants in all aspects of life, public and private. What problems remain have not deterred Catholics from playing a valuable part in Massachusetts life.

Kane, Paula M. *Separatism and Subculture: Boston Catholicism, 1900–1920.* Chapel Hill: University of North Carolina Press, 1994.

Lord, Robert H., John E. Sexton, and Edward T. Harrington. *History of the Archdiocese of Boston in the Various Stages of Its Development, 1604–1943.* 3 vols. Boston: Pilot Publishing Company, 1944.

Merwick, Donna. *Boston Priests, 1848–1920: A Study of Social and Intellectual Change.* Cambridge, Mass.: Harvard University Press, 1973.

New Catholic Encyclopedia. New York: McGraw-Hill Book Company, 1967.

The Official Catholic Directory. Place and imprint vary.

O'Toole, James M. *Militant and Triumphant: William Henry O'Connell and the Catholic Church in Boston, 1859–1944.* University of Notre Dame Press, 1992.

Sullivan, Robert E., and James M. O'Toole, eds. *Catholic Boston.* Boston, Massachusetts, 1985.

ROBERT JOHNSON-LALLY

Related Documents

MASSACHUSETTS BAY PASSES AN ANTI-PRIEST LAW, MAY 26, 1647

It did not need the example of Virginia in 1642, the religious bitterness of the Thirty Years' War in Europe, and the proximity of the French Catholics with their missionaries in present-day Maine and Nova Scotia to alarm the Puritans of Massachusetts Bay over the prospects of what might happen if a Catholic priest were to settle in their midst. Actually some of the Puritans believed that were were disguised priests at work in the colony. These circumstances served, therefore, as an occasion for the passage of a law in May, 1647, that would bar the presence of priests in the future.

(*Source:* Nathaniel B. Shurtleff, ed. *Records of the Governor and Company of the Massachusetts Bay in New England.* Boston: William White, 1854, III, 112.)

THIS COURT, TAKING INTO CONSIDERATION THE GREAT WARRS & combustions which are this day in Europe, & that the same are obserued to be chiefly raysed & fomented by the secrit practises of those of the Jesuiticall order, for the prevention of like euills amongst o^{r}selues, its ordred, by the authorities of this Court, that no Jesuit or ecclesiasticall pson ordayned by ye authoritie of the pope shall henceforth come wthin o^r jurisdiction; & if any pson shall give any cause of suspision that he is one of such societie, he shalbe brought before some of the magists, & if he cannot free himselfe of such suspitiõ, he shalbe comitted or bound on to the next Court of Assistants, to be tried & proceeded with by banish^{nt} or otherwise, as the Court shall see cause, & if any such pson so banished shalbe taken the 2d time wthin this jurisdiction, he shall vppon lawfull triall & conviction, be put to death; pvided this law shall not extend to any such Jesuit as shalbe cast vppon o^r shores by shippwrack or other accydent, so as he contynew no longer then he may haue opptunitie of passage for his departure, nor to any such as shall come in company wth any messenger sent hither vppon publick occasions, or any marchant or master of any shipp belonging to any place not in enmitie wth the state of England or o^{r}selues, so as they depart agayne wth the same messenger, marchant, or m^r, & behaue themselues inoffenciuely duringe their abode here.

(*Source:* John Tracy Ellis, ed. *Documents of American Catholic History.* Vol. 1:1493–1865. Wilmington, Del.: Michael Glazier, 1987, 111–12.)

AN ACT AGAINST JESUITS AND POPISH PRIESTS IN MASSACHUSETTS, JUNE 17, 1700

The Treaty of Ryswick in September, 1697, brought no settlement of the rival claims of England and France in North America, and in the interval which led up to England's renewal of war against France in May, 1702, the border warfare between the two powers took an increasing toll in lives and property. In 1697 Richard Coote, the Earl of Bellomont (1636–1701), a son of the notorious Richard Coote who had committed so many outrages against the Catholic population of Ireland under Cromwell, was appointed Governor of New York, Massachusetts, and New Hampshire. Bellomont was himself fiercely anti-Catholic, and the widespread belief that Catholic missionaries were stirring up the Indians to attack the English made it an easy matter for him to put through anti-priest laws in both Massachusetts and New York within a few months' time. The Massachusetts law of 1700 was broader in application than that of 1647 and its terms were more severe.

(Source: *The Acts and Resolves, Public and Private, of the Province of the Massachusetts Bay.* Boston: Wright & Potter, 1869, I, 423–24.)

WHEREAS DIVERS JESUITS, PRIESTS AND POPISH MISSIONARIES have of late come, and for some time have had their residences in the remote parts of this province, and other his majesty's territories near adjacent, who by their subtile insinuations industriously labour to debauch, seduce and withdraw the Indians from their due obedience unto his majesty, and to excite and stir them up, to sedition, rebellion and open hostility against his Majestie's government; for prevention whereof,—

Be it enacted by His Excellency the Governour, Council, and Representatives in General Court assembled, and it is enacted by the authority of the same

[Sect. 1] That all and every Jesuit, seminary priest, missionary, or other spiritual or ecclesiastical person made or ordained by any authority, power or jurisdiction derived, challenged or pretended from the pope or see of Rome, now residing within this province or any part thereof, shall depart from and out of the same at or before the tenth day of September next, in this present year one thousand and seven hundred.

And be it further enacted by the authority aforesaid,

[Sect. 2] That all and every Jesuit, seminary priest, missionary or other spiritual or ecclesiastical person made or ordained by any authority, power or jurisdiction, derived, challenged or pretended, from the pope or see of Rome, or that shall profess himselfe or otherwise appear to be such by practising and teaching of others to say any popish prayers, by celebrating masses, granting of absolutions, or using any other of the Romish ceremonies and rites of worship, by or of what name, title or degree soever such person shall be called or known, who shall continue, abide, remain or come into this province, or any part thereof, after the tenth day of September aforesaid, shall be deemed and accounted an incendiary and disturber of the publick peace and safety, and an enemy to the true Christian religion, and shall be adjudged to suffer perpetual imprisonment; and if any person, being so sentenced and actually imprisoned, shall break prison and make his escape, and be afterwards re-taken, he shall be punished with death.

And further it is enacted

[Sect. 3] That every person which shall wittingly and willingly receive, relieve, harbour, conceal, aid or succour any Jesuit, priest, missionary or other ecclesiastical person of the Romish clergy, knowing him to be such, shall be fined two hundred pounds, one moiety therof to be unto his majesty for and towards the support of the government of this province, and the other moiety to the informer; and such person shall be further punished by being set in the pillory on three several days, and also be bound to the good behaviour at the discretion of the court. . . .

And further be it enacted by the authority aforesaid,

(*Source*: John Tracy Ellis, ed. *Documents of American Catholic History*. Vol. 1:1493–1865. Wilmington, Del.: Michael Glazier, 1987, 118–19.)

MATHEVON, LUCILE (1793–1876)

Religious of the Sacred Heart. Lucile Mathevon was born near Lyons, France, and was educated at home. In 1813 she entered the Society of the Sacred Heart in Grenoble, where she made her final profession in 1818. Those early years were spent in the same house where St. Philippine Duchesne lived and which was often visited by St. Madeleine Sophie Barat.

In 1822 Lucile Mathevon was sent to America, fulfilling her strong desire to follow Philippine Duchesne and to serve the Native Americans. She spent twenty-nine years working in the early foundation houses in Missouri: Florissant, St. Charles, St. Louis. She was named superior and finally, in 1841, her longing to serve the Native Americans was fulfilled. Fr. Pierre De Smet requested that the Religious of the Sacred Heart establish a school for girls of the Potawatomi along Sugar Creek in Kansas. Lucile Mathevon was charged with this foundation. She was to remain with the Potawatomi for the next twenty-one years. In 1847 she moved the school to St. Mary's, Kansas, accompanying the tribe when they moved to new lands in the Valley of the Kansas. Her courage and determination to accompany the tribe renewed hope among the leaders discouraged by the prospect of creating a new life for the tribe on the prairie.

In 1868 Mother Mathevon was recalled to St. Charles out of concern for her failing health. Though she submitted in obedience to her superiors, the Potawatomi were outraged and demanded the return of their holy woman.

They appealed to her superiors and, at their insistence, she was allowed to return in 1871 to St. Mary's, where she died on March 11, 1876, at the age of eighty-three.

Mother Mathevon is remembered for her strong and simple faith, deep piety, and burning zeal for souls. She was possessed of tireless energy, resourcefulness, and great joy.

Callan, Louise. *Philippine Duchesne*. Westminster, Md.: Newman Press, 1957.

____. *The Society of the Sacred Heart in North America*. London: Longmans, Green and Co., 1937.

Documents in the Society of the Sacred Heart, National Archives, U.S.A.

MARGARET PHELAN, R.S.C.J.

MATTHEWS, ANNE (1732–1800)

Carmelite prioress and foundress. Anne Matthews, one of three children, was born in Charles County, Maryland, to Joseph Matthews and Susanna Craycroft in 1732. Her great grandfather, Dr. Thomas Matthews, emigrated from England to Maryland between 1636 and 1638. Anne's family played a significant role in the foundation of Carmel in America. Her two Carmelite nieces were cofoundresses with her. Ignatius, her Jesuit brother, wrote the invitation urging his sister's return to Maryland: "Now is your time to found in this country for peace is declared and religion is free."

Accompanied by John Carroll's cousin, Ann Hill, Matthews sailed for the Low Countries in 1754 to join the Carmelites at Hoogstraten, where she was professed as Sr. Bernardina a year later. Exceptionally gifted, she was soon appointed mistress of novices and, in 1771 at age thirty-nine, elected prioress of the community. The Hoogstraten tradition makes it clear that Bernardina was deeply loved as prioress, respected as a capable administrator, and revered as a wise spiritual guide graced with unusual contemplative insight.

Perhaps her greatest contribution was a Teresian spirituality characterized by openness to contemplative prayer with strong emphasis on Christ's humanity. Her devotion to the Sacred Heart places her firmly within the more moderate humanistic tradition typical of Anglo-American Catholics reared in Maryland under the guidance of the Jesuits and educated in the Lowlands' recusant community. She was, writes Joseph Chinnici, the inheritor of a "muted mysticism" and a practical, dignified, restrained piety with definite ecumenical overtones. Grounded in respect for the movement of the Spirit in each person, her spirituality correlated well with her inherited position of political liberty and rights of conscience. In her abhorrence of coercion and hardness in a superior, she portrayed an uncommon gentility, humility, and mutual respect that spoke both of a spirituality akin to Francis de Sales and Teresa of Avila and also of her upbringing among the Catholic gentry of British America. Through Bernardina Matthews, the foundress of Carmel in America and the first community of religious women in the U.S.A., the tradition of colonial Maryland Catholicism and Carmelite spirituality was passed into religious life in the United States. She died in Port Tobacco on June 12, 1800.

See also DICKINSON, FRANCES; DISCALCED CARMELITE NUNS.

Beitzell, E. W. "Natives of Maryland in Religious Houses and Seminarians Abroad from 1684–1788." *Jesuit Missions of St. Mary's County, Maryland.* Abell, Maryland, 1976, 313–21.

Carr, Lois Grenne. "Notable American Women." *A Biographical Dictionary,* ed. E. T. James. Cambridge, Mass.: Belknap Press, 1971, 1:509–10.

Curran, R. M. *American Jesuit Spirituality, The Maryland Tradition, 1634–1900.* New York: Paulist Press, 1988.

FitzGerald, C. *The Carmelite Adventure.* Baltimore: Carmelite Sisters, 1990.

Hardman, A. *English Carmelites in Penal Times.* London: Burns, Oates and Washbourne, 1936.

Hennesey, J. "'Several Youths Sent From Here': Native-Born Priests and Religious of English America, 1634–1776." *Studies in Catholic History in Honor of John Tracy Ellis,* ed. N. H. Minnich and others. Wilmington, Del.: Michael Glazier, 1985, 1–26.

Spalding, T. *The Premier See, A History of the Archdiocese of Baltimore, 1789–1889.* Baltimore: Johns Hopkins University Press, 1989, 1–5.

CONSTANCE FITZGERALD, O.C.D.

MAURIN, PETER (1877–1949)

Lay activist. Aristode Pierre Maurin, later known as Peter Maurin, was cofounder with Dorothy Day of the Catholic Worker movement and is chiefly responsible for the movement's visionary qualities. He was born into a peasant family in Oultet, a village in the Languedoc region of southern France, on May 9, 1877. At sixteen he entered the Christian Brothers, a teaching order that stressed simplicity of life, piety, and service to the poor. In 1898–99, his community life was interrupted by obligatory military service, in the course of which Maurin perceived a tension between religious and political duties. In 1902, when the French government closed many religious schools, Maurin left the order and became active in *Le Sillon,* a Catholic lay movement that advocated Christian democracy and supported cooperatives and unions. In 1908, disenchanted with the movement's increasingly political character, Maurin resigned from *Le Sillon.*

Early Years in America

In 1909 he emigrated to Canada, where there was no military conscription. For two years he homesteaded in Sas-

Peter Maurin

katchewan. After the effort failed, he took whatever work he could find, first in Canada, then in the United States: digging ditches, quarrying stone, harvesting wheat, cutting lumber, and laying track. He worked in brickyards, steel mills, and coal mines. At times he traded French lessons for his necessities. He was jailed for vagrancy and for riding the rails. He never married. In 1932 he was handyman at a Catholic boys' camp in upstate New York, receiving meals, use of the chaplain's library, and living space in the barn.

Through his years of reflection and hard labor, Maurin came to embrace poverty as a gift from God. His unencumbered life offered time for study and prayer, out of which a vision had taken form of a social order instilled with basic values of the gospel "in which it would be easier for men to be good."

As often as his work allowed, he made his way to New York City, staying in Bowery flop houses. His days were spent either at the public library or expounding his ideas to anyone who showed interest. After all, he reasoned, "The way to reach the man on the street is meet the man on the street." He was a born teacher, lively, insightful, and good humored, and found willing listeners, among them George Shuster, editor of *Commonweal* magazine, who gave him the address of Dorothy Day, a Catholic convert supporting herself as a freelance journalist. Maurin introduced himself to Day in December 1932.

Maurin and Dorothy Day

To many Maurin would have seemed just one more street-corner prophet. Day quickly came to regard him as an answer to her prayers, someone who could help her discover what she was supposed to do. Maurin saw Dorothy Day as a new St. Catherine of Siena, the medieval reformer and peace negotiator. Maurin believed Day could "move mountains, and have influence on governments, temporal and spiritual." But first she needed a truly Catholic education. Maurin wanted her to look at history in a new way which centered not on the rise and fall of nations, but on the lives of the saints. She had to understand that sanctity was what really mattered and that any program of social change must emphasize sanctity and community.

Maurin proposed that Day start a newspaper to publicize Catholic social teaching and promote steps to bring about the peaceful transformation of society. Day responded positively, though unsure how she would ever find the money for such a venture. "In the history of the saints," Maurin assured her, "capital is raised by prayer. God sends you what you need when you need it. You will be able to pay the printer. Just read the lives of the saints." The name Maurin proposed for the paper was *The Catholic Radical.* The radical—from the Latin word *radix,* meaning root—is someone who does not settle for cosmetic solutions, he said, but goes to the root of personal and social problems. Day felt that the name should refer to the class of the readers she hoped the paper would have, so she named it *The Catholic Worker.* "Man proposes and woman disposes," Maurin responded meekly.

However, when the first issue of was ready for distribution May 1, 1933, Maurin was disappointed and asked that his name not be included among the list of editors. He found the paper short on ideas, principles, and a strategy for a new social order. Apart from his own blank verse "Easy Essays" and a few quotations from the Bible and papal encyclicals, the rest of the paper struck him as just one more journal of radical protest.

Maurin's Originality

A radical even among radicals, Maurin thought protest would do little to bring about real change. "Strikes don't strike me," he said, arguing that the old order would die from neglect, not censure. What was needed first of all was a vision of a future society, and with this a program of constructive steps with which to begin realizing bits of the vision in one's own life. *The Catholic Worker,* Maurin said, should not just be one more group of complainers. It should work for what he called "the green revolution."

He saw no point in struggling for better hours or more pay in places where the work was dehumanizing. It was time, he said, "to fire the bosses." But where, he was asked, could they go? How would they live? "There is no unemployment on the land," Maurin replied. *The Catholic Worker* should stand for a decentralized society stressing cooperation rather than duress, with artisans and craftsmen in worker-owned small factories and agricultural communities. Coming together in agricultural communities, worker and scholar could both sweat, think, and pray together and in the process develop "a worker-scholar synthesis."

Maurin was often accused of being a utopian romantic longing to travel backward rather than forward in time. But Day gradually became more open to his critique of assembly-line civilization and came to share his view that improved, unionized industrialism was not enough, that community was better than mass society.

In his *Catholic Worker* essays, Maurin repeatedly advocated renewal of the ancient Christian practice of hospitality:

> People who are in need
> and are not afraid to beg
> give to people not in need
> the occasion to do good
> for goodness' sake.
> Modern society calls the beggar
> bum and panhandler and gives him the bum's rush.
> But the Greeks used to say
> that people in need
> are ambassadors of the gods.
> Although you may be called
> bums and panhandlers
> you are in fact the ambassadors of God.
> As God's ambassadors
> you should be given
> food, clothing and shelter
> by those who are able to give it.

Every home, Maurin said, should have its "Christ Room" and every parish a house of hospitality ready to receive the "ambassadors of God." Within a year of its founding, the Catholic Worker movement was known as much for its houses of hospitality as for its newspaper. A strong believer in education through dialogue, Maurin advocated "round table discussions for the clarification of thought." Friday night meetings quickly became a tradition of the Catholic Worker community.

Catholic Workers also took up his call to start farming communes, which Maurin preferred to call "agronomic universities." In 1938 Maurin moved to Mary Farm, a ten-acre property the Catholic Worker community bought in Easton, Pennsylvania. Unfortunately there was always a surplus of people who preferred a discussion of theology or politics to work on the fields or the repair of a hinge. "It seemed," Day noted, "that the more people there were around, the less got done." Small matters took on divisive significance. Maurin alone seemed to look after basic chores. In 1944 part of the farm was sold, another part given away to a cantankerous group that regarded themselves as "the true Catholic Workers." Other "farms" were set up, but they were more rural houses of hospitality than agricultural communities.

From the founding of the Catholic Worker movement in 1933 until 1944, Maurin often traveled, speaking in church halls and on street corners to anyone who cared to listen. In 1944, following what appeared to be a minor stroke, Maurin slowly began losing his memory. His last five years were lived quietly and humbly at the Catholic Worker's Maryfarm Retreat Center near Newburgh. His death in 1949 was reported by *The New York Times* and the Vatican newspaper, *L'Osservatore Romano. Time* magazine noted that Maurin was buried in a "castoff suit and consigned to a donated grave," appropriate arrangements for a man who "had slept in no bed of his own and worn no suit that someone had not given away." After his death, a Catholic Worker farm located on Staten Island was named in his honor. Today the Peter Maurin Farm continues in Marlboro, New York.

See also CATHOLIC WORKER MOVEMENT, THE; DAY, DOROTHY.

Ellis, Marc. *Peter Maurin: Prophet in the Twentieth Century.* Ramsey, N.J.: Paulist Press, 1981.

Maurin, Peter. *Easy Essays.* Chicago: Franciscan Herald Press, 1984.

Miller, William. *A Harsh and Dreadful Love.* New York: Liveright, 1973.

Sheehan, Arthur. *Peter Maurin: Gay Believer.* Garden City, N.Y.: Hanover House/Doubleday, 1959.

JIM FOREST

MAYNARD, THEODORE (1890–1956)

Historian, poet, biographer. Maynard was born in Madras, India, on November 3, 1890. He received a bachelor of arts degree from Fordham University, a master of arts degree from Georgetown University, and a Ph.D. from The Catholic University of America. The son of Protestant missionaries Henry Maynard and Elizabeth Teague Maynard, he was raised in both India and England. He began his career as a writer at the *New Witness,* an independent general review founded by Hilaire Belloc, where he worked under G. K. Chesterton, a man who greatly influenced Maynard's thought and writing. During World War I he worked at the Ministry of Munitions, but continued his writing, publishing five works before the war's end.

His interest in religion led him to several Protestant churches before he converted to Catholicism in 1913. He began a lecture tour of the United States in 1920 and was offered a teaching position at the Dominican College, San Rafael, California, where he remained until 1925. Over his career, Maynard taught at a number of Catholic institutions, including Fordham University in New York, Georgetown University in Washington, D.C., and Mt. St. Mary's College in Emmitsburg, Maryland, while coterminously working on his three postsecondary degrees, as well as continuing to both publish and lecture widely. He pub-

Theodore Maynard

lished forty works in all, including *St. Francis Xavier* (1936), *Orestes Brownson* (1943), *The Last Garland: A Sequence of Sonnets* (1949), *The Story of American Catholicism* (1941), and his autobiography, *The World I Saw* (1938). He served as president of the Catholic Poetry of America Society in 1948. He died at Port Washington, New York, on October 18, 1956.

TRICIA T. PYNE

MAZZUCHELLI, SAMUEL (1806–64)

Dominican missionary. Samuel Mazzuchelli ministered to peoples of many cultures on the frontiers of the Old Northwest in the mid-nineteenth century. These included the French-Canadian fur traders, natives of four tribes of Woodland Native Americans, and American pioneers and civic leaders in nascent towns of the Mississippi valley. Among them, working with the first bishops of six Midwestern dioceses, he formed the Church, parish by parish. He brought to the service of the people several needed and lasting institutions: Dominican friars and sisters to strengthen their faith, and schools to educate their children. In return, the people he served have kept his memory alive for nearly seven generations.

Early Life and Call to Ministry

Samuel Mazzuchelli was born on November 4, 1806, in Milan, capital of Lombardy, to Luigi Mazzuchelli and Rachele Merlini Mazzuchelli. Their large family lived in a home on the Piazza Fontana, facing the great Duomo with its multiple spires and statues. After the death of Samuel's mother in 1812 he was sent to school at the

Samuel Mazzuchelli

Collegio Sant'Antonio in Lugano, Switzerland, north of Milan. There the Somaschi Fathers, founded by St. Jerome Aemilian to offer boys a caring education, provided excellent schooling, which Samuel completed when he was seventeen.

In 1823 Samuel entered the Order of Preachers at Faenza near the Adriatic Sea, in one of the few remaining houses of the Province of Lombardy. A year later, with his novitiate completed, he made his religious profession "even unto death," pronouncing the single Dominican vow of obedience for mission. Immediately afterward he was sent to Rome for further studies.

At Sta Sabina on the Aventine the Lombard province of the friars was opening a restored *studium* following the order's many years of moribund existence. The French Revolution and Napoleonic conquests had subjected all religious orders to widespread confiscation of their houses and scattering of their members, accompanied by their loss of spiritual vitality. At the Roman house of studies the Milanese youth fully enjoyed classes in Scripture, theology, and the literature of writers like his contemporary Alessandro Manzoni. Courses were given by professors of extraordinary competence, gathered to promote the renewal of the order through its essential element, study.

During his third year at Sta Sabina, Samuel learned of the dire need for missionaries on the American frontier, especially in the wilderness areas of Ohio and Michigan Territory, including "Ouisconsin." These were part of the Diocese of Cincinnati, of which a brother Dominican, Edward Dominic Fenwick, was made bishop. Calling his diocese "the poorest in the world" Fenwick sent his vicar general, Frederic Résé, to Rome in order to describe his

need for all kinds of resources, but chiefly personnel. The student Mazzuchelli, now a subdeacon, asked to volunteer for that mission. His superiors agreed with joy, as one of them, Iacinto Cipolletti, later recalled.

Journey to New Lands and Cultures

In June 1828 the neophyte set out for the United States with the vicar general of the Cincinnati diocese, Frederic Résé. He stopped en route for family farewells in Milan, then continued by stagecoach to Paris. There Résé suddenly left for Germany, leaving Mazzuchelli waiting for him at the Petit Séminaire. After waiting two months Mazzuchelli resumed the journey alone on a small sailing vessel to New York, and then on to Ohio. In November, just after his twenty-second birthday, he completed the winding journey on the Ohio River and arrived at Cincinnati to receive a warm welcome from Bishop Fenwick. A year later the bishop sent him, now a deacon, to St. Joseph parish in Somerset, Ohio. There, in a log cabin priory and Ohio's first church, he learned from a community of four Dominican missionaries the rugged lessons of an itinerant ministry in the forested wilderness.

Samuel Mazzuchelli was ordained a priest at Cincinnati on September 5, 1830. He was assigned by the bishop to the most remote region of his vast diocese, extending south from the Canadian border to the northern boundary of Illinois. He arrived at Mackinac Island, his "principal residence," in late October, before his twenty-fourth birthday, and began the winter in a rented room provided for traveling missionaries. The first resident priest in nearly sixty years, he succeeded the French Jesuits who had been withdrawn in 1773 by papal decree. Now he alone had the spiritual care of inhabitants of Upper Michigan and all of present-day Wisconsin. In 1831 came the Slovenian priest from Austria, Frederic Baraga, who assumed the Michigan portion of his mission and shared with him a holy friendship.

First Mission

From 1830 to 1835 Mazzuchelli ministered to the French-Canadian fur traders, responded to the assaults of anti-Catholic bigotry, and traveled through the forests to serve the native peoples. He invited the French-Canadians back to their Catholic faith and practices by celebrating the Eucharist and other sacraments, preaching in French, explaining Catholic beliefs and practices to Protestant objectors, and restoring the parish church of St. Anne.

In the spirit of Bishop Fenwick, who loved the Native Americans "above all others," Mazzuchelli came to know the natives of four Woodland tribes in his region: the Ojibwe and Ottawa, Menominee and Winnebago. By directive of the bishop, the latter two tribes were his special concern. The Menominee natives lived around Green

Bay and traded at the settlement of the same name at its foot. The Winnebago were found in western and south central "Ouisconsin," so-named by the French, but belonging until 1836 to the Michigan Territory. The Winnebago, unlike the Menominee, were reluctantly moving westward as a result of the Indian Removal Act of 1830.

To learn about these native peoples and offer them his ministry, the missionary traveled by snowshoe and canoe through the wilderness between Lake Michigan and the Mississippi River. He learned, along with such traits as hospitality, their way of life and customs, their belief in the Great Spirit. With the help of native catechists and translators he preached the gospel, baptized and instructed many, and published a prayer book for the Winnebago and a liturgical calendar for the Menominee. Each of these was the first item printed in their language. For the children of both tribes the missionary opened schools, but he could obtain none of the funds set aside for education. As treaties multiplied for the benefit of land-seeking Americans, Mazzuchelli protested vigorously to Congress about injustice to the natives, but to no avail.

To the Mississippi Valley

In 1835 the missionary became the only priest in the upper Mississippi valley, first serving the lead miners around Dubuque, Iowa, and Galena, Illinois, and then the families who came to settle up and down the river valley. With the people he laid the foundations for forty parishes, working with the bishops of six new dioceses: Cincinnati, Detroit, St. Louis, Dubuque, Milwaukee, and Chicago. Because of his concern for the welfare of all the citizens, they recognized his civic leadership as well, naming him chaplain of the first legislature of the territory of Wisconsin in 1836.

As priests and bishops slowly multiplied in regions he first served alone, Fr. Mazzuchelli could undertake another needed ministry: providing education for the pioneer families. At Sinsinawa Mound in southwestern Wisconsin he established a Dominican center of religious life and education. There he founded a province and novitiate of friars and Sinsinawa Mound College for men in 1845. These he conveyed to the original Dominican province, which gained a number of vocations from the Sinsinawa region. Province officials closed the college in 1865.

Meanwhile, in 1847 Mazzuchelli received into the order four young women of the region who became the first Sinsinawa Dominican Sisters, incorporated by the first Wisconsin legislature in 1848. With their founder they taught in one-room district schools, then established St. Clara Academy in 1853.

While directing and teaching in the Academy at Benton, Wisconsin, Mazzuchelli continued his pastoral and preaching ministry, having charge of five parishes in southwestern Wisconsin. During the cholera epidemic of 1849–50, his heroic care of the sick and dying increased the affection of the citizens, Catholic and Protestant, for the priest who spoke of them as the people whom he loved. The same people cherished his preaching and series of instructions on the Bible, Church history, and spiritual life. He was called frequently to preach in other towns along the Mississippi, even as far north as St. Paul. There the pioneers gathered to hear him in the log-cabin cathedral of Bishop Joseph Crétin.

Death came suddenly to Samuel Mazzuchelli in the midst of his pastoral ministry. Answering the calls of two dying parishioners in frigid weather, he fell ill with pneumonia and died on February 23, 1864, mourned by people near and far. Their mourning turned into rejoicing as they reviewed the life of a beloved missionary and pastor. They circulated memories of his many virtues: kindness and courage, humility and voluntary poverty, strength to proclaim justice, and the grace of powerful preaching of the gospel. The Dominican Sisters joined their memories to those of the people and recorded them. Bishops of three of the dioceses served by Samuel Mazzuchelli petitioned the Holy See in 1965 to consider the virtues of this American Dominican. Official recognition of his holiness was encouraged by Pope John Paul II in 1993 when he declared "Venerable" the apostolic missionary, Samuel Mazzuchelli, O.P.

See also DOMINICANS (O.P.).

Congregation of Causes of Saints. *Positio super vita, virtutibus et fama sanctitatis: Samuelis Mazzuchelli O.P.* Rome: The Vatican, 1989.

Crépeau, Rosemary. *Un Apôtre dominicain aux Etats-Unis: Le Pére Samuel-Charles-Gaëtan Mazzuchelli.* Paris: J. de Gigord, 1932.

Mazzuchelli, Samuel. *The Memoirs of Father Samuel Mazzuchelli.* Trans. Michele Armato and Mary Finnegan. Chicago: Priory Press, 1967.

McGreal, Mary Nona. *Samuel Mazzuchelli O.P.: A Kaleidoscope of Scenes from His Life.* Sinsinawa, Wisc.: Mazzuchelli Guild, 1994.

MARY NONA McGREAL, O.P.

Related Document

SAMUEL MAZZUCHELLI, O.P., ON THE CATHOLIC TEMPERANCE SOCIETIES, 1844

Although the evangelical trends in American Protestantism of the early nineteenth century had little in common with American Catholicism, except, perhaps, during the preaching of the parish mission, they shared an interest in the eradication of the evils of intemperance. Beginning in the late 1830's Catholic temperance societies spread rapidly. The American tour (June, 1849–November, 1851) of the famous Irish Capuchin temperance crusader, Theobald Mathew (1790–1856), gave them fresh impetus, and when a national union of these groups was formed at Baltimore in February, 1872, the meeting drew delegates from over 200 societies. One of those who had great admiration for the work of the temperance societies was the remarkable missionary, Samuel Charles Mazzuchelli (1806–1864). This Italian-born Dominican came to the United States in 1828 and for nearly forty years labored tirelessly in behalf of the Indians of the Middle West, in establishing parishes for the new settlers in Iowa, Illinois, and Wisconsin, in founding a teaching sisterhood of Dominican nuns, to say nothing of building the bishop's residence in Dubuque, designing the first capitol at Iowa City, and serving as chaplain to the first territorial legislature of Wisconsin. In 1843 he made his only visit home to Milan, the city of his birth, and there in the following year he published a volume of memoirs of his American experiences with a view to acquainting Italians with the progress of the Church in the United States and of preserving certain documentary materials for its history. Mazzuchelli's appreciation of the American Catholic temperance societies was deep and sincere, even if it was too optimistic about the permanency of the results obtained.

(*Source: Memoirs Historical and Edifying of a Missionary Apostolic of the Order of Saint Dominic among Various Indian Tribes and among the Catholics and Protestants in the United States of America*, translated by Sister Mary Benedicta Kennedy, O.S.D. Chicago: W. F. Hall Printing Co., 1915, 282–84; copyright The Dominican Sisters of Sinsinawa, Wisconsin.)

VERY FEW PERSONS IN THE UNITED STATES cultivate the vine or make wine to any extent, so this beverage forms one of the objects of commerce with France, Spain and Italy, while the distance, imposition of duties, etc., render it not only costly, but also very scarce. But to supply the lack of the vine in America, extensive use is made of strong spirits extracted from Indian corn, which grows there in prodigious quantities and can be had at a very low price. Many of the people are addicted to the abuse of this strong liquor to such a degree as to fall unhappy victims of intoxication.

A great number of the emigrants from Ireland, notwithstanding the Faith, the generosity, the honesty, the industry and all the other virtues that so eminently distinguish the race, were often too weak upon this one point, giving themselves up in bondage to the vice of intemperance. The more zealous among the Protestants, especially the Presbyterians, took occasion from this to hurl bitterest reproaches and invectives against the Catholic Church, which they accused of being far from the Evangelical sanctity she professed, while she held within her own bosom so many leading scandalous lives. But God who often makes use of His very enemies as instruments to carry out the inscrutable designs of His grace, raised up our far-famed Father Matthew [sic] in Ireland to banish the demon of drunkenness from that island, and to enroll millions of his compatriots in the Temperance Societies by virtue of which they pledged themselves to taste no beverage that could intoxicate.

The Irish who comprise more than half of the Catholics of the United States, followed the example of their brethren in Europe, and Temperance Societies were founded in every city and village of the land. It could be asserted now that these children of that Saint Patrick to whom Ireland owes her conversion to the Faith are now with very few exceptions models of temperance. The Catholic Clergy exerted themselves to the utmost in America, to bring about a change so marvelous and so necessary to the advancement of the Faith; the Faith that had retrograded among many Catholics through the vice of intemperance. A number of the Bishops and nearly all of the Priests are zealous members of this Society. . . .

If the tree is to be judged by its fruits, there is no doubt as to the Religious influence exerted by the Temperance Society,—in truth we must ascribe thereto these wonderful effects, the conversion of a great number of sinners hardened in vice for years, who approached the tribunal of penance only after they had promised to give up entirely the use of intoxicating liquors. From the year 1839 when the Societies had become established in the various Missions recorded in these Memoirs, piety actually made visible progress from day to day, in proportion as the virtue of Temperance won its blessed victories among the people; peace and plenty reigned in the families, Catholicity won the respect and reverence of its very enemies, and the Faith spread among the more sincere of those outside the Church. Many of the Catholic Irish abandoned entirely the dangerous traffic in intoxicating drink and sought more honorable means of subsistence. . . .

(*Source*: John Tracy Ellis, ed. *Documents of American Catholic History*. Vol. 1:1493–1865. Wilmington, Del.: Michael Glazier, 1987, 272–74.)

McAULIFFE, MAURICE F. (1875–1944)

Bishop. Born on June 17, 1875, Maurice F. McAuliffe is the only Hartford-born priest to serve as the bishop of Hartford. Educated at Mt. St. Mary Seminary, Emmitsburg, as well as in Paris and Eichstätt, McAuliffe was ordained a priest in 1900 and taught at St. Thomas Seminary for a number of years. He continued as rector of the seminary after his consecration as auxiliary bishop of Hartford in 1926, and guided the construction of the new seminary building in Bloomfield.

McAuliffe succeeded Bishop Nilan as the ordinary in 1934, guiding the Diocese of Hartford until his death ten years later. During his tenure, McAuliffe worked to bolster family life, establishing the Legion of Decency to protect Catholic youth from the damaging effects of violence, marital infidelity, and divorce portrayed and glamorized by the motion picture industry. He also established diocesan-wide Catholic Youth Organization and parish clubs to guide high school youth. In order to assist young

Maurice F. McAuliffe

families and mothers in the academic, religious, and moral education of their children, Mothers' Circles and Parent-Educator groups were established throughout the parishes of Connecticut during the early 1940s.

McAuliffe wanted to extend the Church's influence further into the educational formation of the state's young people. There already existed two Catholic women's colleges within the state. Wanting to open a Catholic high school and college for young Catholic men of Connecticut, McAuliffe invited the Jesuits to engage in the work. Fairfield College Preparatory School was founded in 1942, and Fairfield University of Saint Robert Bellarmine in 1945.

McAuliffe supported labor rights, establishing the Diocesan Labor Institute to promote papal social teachings. To expand the Church's work for black Americans, Bishop McAuliffe opened two interracial centers in the diocese: the Blessed Martin Center in New Haven in 1942 and the St. Benedict Center in Hartford in 1944.

During World War II, Bishop McAuliffe led the Catholic effort in Connecticut. McAuliffe was appointed to the state committee of the War Fund Campaign of the USO and helped to establish USO clubhouses in the larger Connecticut cities. He was the first American bishop to permit Masses to be celebrated within factories during the war.

The Diocese of Hartford celebrated its centenary in 1943, and counted approximately 667,000 Connecticut residents—one third of the state's population—as Catholic. Bishop McAuliffe died on December 15, 1944.

See also CONNECTICUT, CATHOLIC CHURCH IN.

DiGiovanni, Stephen M. *The Catholic Church in Fairfield County, 1666–1961.* New Canaan, Connecticut, 1987.
Duggan, Thomas S. *The Catholic Church in Connecticut.* New York: States History Co., 1930.

STEPHEN M. DiGIOVANNI

McAVOY, THOMAS TIMOTHY (1903–69)

Historian and educator. McAvoy was born in Tipton, Indiana, on September 12, 1903, and educated at Notre Dame University (B.A. 1925). He joined the Congregation of the Holy Cross in 1925. He continued studies at the College of the Holy Cross in Washington, D.C., and was ordained in 1929. In 1930 McAvoy received his master of arts degree from Notre Dame, and in 1940 he received a Ph.D. from Columbia University.

Thomas T. McAvoy

McAvoy is most noted for his scholarly works on American Catholic history, his work at the Notre Dame University Archives, and his editorship of the Notre Dame-based *Review of Politics*. His *Great Crisis in American Catholic History, 1895–1900* (1957), which dealt with the late-nineteenth-century Americanist controversy within the Church, remains one of the most systematic and thorough treatments of that conflict. This work, along with his *Roman Catholicism and the American Way of Life* (1960) and *A History of the Catholic Church in the United States* (1969) are illustrative of broader tendencies present in the liberal Catholic historical accounts of the period in that they sought to reconcile American Catholicism and modernity. In this sense, McAvoy's work, while not theologically liberal, helped fashion an intellectual groundwork for Catholic liberals of the 1960s by placing events such as the Americanist controversy in a broader historical context.

He also wrote a detailed biography on one of the most prominent members of his own community, *Father O'Hara of Notre Dame: The Cardinal-Archbishop of Philadelphia* (1967). He died at Notre Dame on July 7, 1969.

MARIA MAZZENGA

McCARRAN, PATRICK ANTHONY (1876–1954)

U.S. Senator. Patrick Anthony McCarran was born on August 8, 1876, in Reno, Nevada, to Patrick and Margaret Shea McCarran, Irish immigrants. He studied at the University of Nevada, working as a janitor to cover expenses. In 1903 he married Martha Harriet Weeks and began a quarter-century of service in Nevada politics by being elected to the Nevada legislature.

While serving in the legislature, he supported his family through farming and sheep raising. At the same time, he pursued the study of law and was admitted to the Nevada bar in 1905. From 1907 until 1909 he served as district attorney for Nye County and then opened a private law practice in Reno (1909–13). McCarran returned to the political arena in 1913 with his election to the Nevada supreme court, where he served as chief justice from 1917 until 1918. He also served as president of the Nevada Bar Association (1920–21), vice president of the American Bar Association (1922–23), and chairman of the Nevada State Board of Bar Examiners (1931–32).

In 1932 McCarran was elected U.S. senator for Nevada; he was reelected in 1938, 1944, and 1950. Although he was a Democrat, he often disagreed on policy issues with Presidents Franklin D. Roosevelt and Harry S. Truman. He opposed lend-lease aid to England in 1941 and other New Deal measures. He served on the Senate judiciary committee, Internal Security subcommittee, and the committee on foreign cooperation. He harshly criticized communism and what he saw as communist influence in government, as well as the United States' abandonment of China to communism.

McCarran sponsored the 1938 bill creating the Civil Aeronautics Authority and promoted an independent air force as a separate military entity. He was cosponsor of the McCarran-Walter Immigration and Nationality Act of 1952, which was passed over Truman's veto.

He died in Reno on September 28, 1954. In 1960 his statue was placed in National Statuary Hall in Washington, D.C., to represent Nevada.

MARIANNA McLOUGHLIN

McCARTHY, JOSEPH RAYMOND, AND AMERICAN CATHOLICS

Few politicians have so covered themselves with controversy as Senator Joseph R. McCarthy of Wisconsin. Fewer still have had so divisive, if short-lived, an impact on American political life. In the first half of the 1950s, when McCarthyism become a national issue, debate swirled principally around his so-called "methods." His armory of political tactics included his habit of accusing his opponents of being "soft on Communism" (as the Republican rhetoric of the cold war era put it), his slippery use of documents, and his habit of smearing his adversaries by innuendo.

Underlying all these questions was the matter of the senator's religion. Though commonly known as a Catholic because he had been baptized in the Church and had attended Marquette University, a Jesuit college in Milwaukee, little else in his life suggested he was Catholic. One might better call him an "indifferent" Catholic, but certainly not a leading Catholic layman in any acceptable sense of the term.

His religious ambiguity notwithstanding, his campaign against Communists-in-government quickly became a religious one. The belief that Catholics had lined up *en bloc* behind him quickly became widespread, even though the numerous opinion polls taken during the period failed to show any such massive support among Catholics.

Beginning of the Anti-Communist Campaign

The idea of waging a campaign against Communists in the government first came to him, so the story goes, on the night of January 7, 1950, when he met with a small group of supporters at the Colony Restaurant in Washington to discuss possible topics for his reelection campaign then two years away. He rejected suggestions that he talk about the economy, the growing conflict with North Korea, or foreign policy. When Fr. Edmund Walsh of Georgetown University, a noted Russianist and expert on Communism, suggested that he wage a crusade against Communist-sympathizers in the government, McCarthy leaped at the idea. Yes, he said enthusiastically, that was the issue that he needed. A month later he took his issue to the public, and in the next four years gained far more publicity, and, in some quarters, far greater praise, than he had probably imagined possible.

So the story goes. When word of the meeting hit the press, Fr. Walsh exploded in wrath (though privately so), insisting that he had never been present at such a meeting. The more the tale spread, however, the more it seemed to gain credibility. The supposed presence of Fr. Walsh, moreover, cemented a connection in the minds of many: it was a Catholic priest who had given McCarthy the idea in the first place.

Whether the meeting took place or not, less than a month later McCarthy gave a much-publicized speech to the Women's Republican Club in Wheeling, West Virginia, denouncing the Communist menace in America and saying that he had "a list" of the Communists working at that precise moment in the State Department. His accusations attracted so much national attention, and his battering-ram tactics quickly became so hotly controversial, that the Senate formed a special committee to look into his charges. Its investigations revealed no Communists in the State Department, but it helped solidify McCarthy's hold on public attention.

McCarthy and American Catholics

Soon the *Brooklyn Tablet,* the most strident of the right-wing Catholic publications, carried his crusade to Catholic readers on the East Coast, as did the slightly less shrill *Boston Pilot.* Early polls, including some taken a month after the Wheeling address, showed that nearly half (49 percent) of Catholics interviewed believed McCarthy when he said that Communists were active in the State Department, while only 28 percent thought that he was "just playing politics." Largely unnoticed was the fact that the numbers for non-Catholic respondents were almost the same as for Catholics. Virtually alone among Catholic publications in condemning McCarthy was the liberal weekly *Commonweal,* which vehemently criticized his now-familiar tactics of guilt by association, smear, and innuendo. As the former Speaker of the House John McCormack told the author somewhat timidly twenty years later, "McCarthy wasn't very charitable." (McCormack had studiously avoided taking a position on the senator while McCarthyism raged as a public issue.)

The national elections of 1952 gave McCarthy a priceless opportunity to project himself onto the national scene. He smeared the Democratic candidate for president, Adlai Stevenson, by referring to him as "Alger—I mean Adlai" Stevenson, thus linking Stevenson to Alger Hiss, a former State Department employee who had been convicted, amid fierce national debate, of giving secret documents to a Communist agent. Ever the opportunist, McCarthy would later announce, "We got Alger Hiss," though he had taken no part in the investigation at all.

The Republican candidate, Dwight D. Eisenhower, tried to sidestep the McCarthy issue, but when the two men showed up on the same platform together, Eisenhower warmly greeted McCarthy, an act that served only to enrage the former general's liberal followers. In the election, it took Eisenhower's coattails to give McCarthy the narrowest possible victory in Wisconsin. Attempts made at the time and in the years since to find a "Catholic vote" for McCarthy have failed. Quite the contrary, studies conducted at the time showed that Catholic labor, for instance, voted overwhelmingly against him. The rural areas of the state, plus burgeoning Wisconsin republicanism and the Eisenhower sweep, all combined to put McCarthy into the Senate for the second time. The *Tablet,* not surprisingly, interpreted his victory as a triumph for Catholic

anti-Communism, while *Commonweal* bitterly lamented his reelection.

Army-McCarthy Hearings

Undeterred by his narrow escape from defeat, McCarthy soon launched a fierce attack against the Army, accusing it of harboring Communists, Communist-sympathizers, and Communist spies to boot. The famous "Army-McCarthy" hearings, flung across the nation by a massive television hookup, would bring McCarthy his greatest moment in the spotlight. They would also lead to his undoing, however, since many of his fellow senators, and much of the public, came to the conclusion that he had finally gone too far with his usual tactics.

McCarthy's furious campaign against Communists and Communist sympathizers in the federal government also served to strengthen the bitter conflicts between Catholics and Protestants that so marred the 1950s. Protestant liberals worried, for instance, that McCarthy would run for president and thus become the first Catholic in the White House. When McCarthy hired a conservative Methodist minister, J. B. Matthews, to head his investigations unit, Matthews committed a mindless act that immediately antagonized the nation's Protestant ministers. Matthews published an inflammatory article in the *American Mercury,* saying that the largest single group supporting Communism in the country was the Protestant clergy. The nation's ministers responded with fury, and succeeded in extracting a telegram from Eisenhower condemning Matthews, whom McCarthy was eventually forced to discharge.

The article, however, helped to widen the chasm between Catholic and Protestant leaders. Many Protestants feared that Matthews had, by some secretive and circuitous path, become a pawn of anti-Protestant Catholics, and was now doing their bidding. They noted both that McCarthy had refused to repudiate Matthews, and was a Catholic besides, and thus concluded that the Catholic Church had somehow maneuvered McCarthy's man to write the article. It did not help that Catholic conservatives openly, and in print, gloated over the Matthews' piece. Catholic liberals expectedly denounced the article, but to little effect.

Nor did either side pay much attention to the polls taken during the Army-McCarthy hearings, which showed that, though a slightly larger number of Catholics supported McCarthy than did the rest of the country, his truly committed support among Catholics was quite small, and virtually the same as the rest of the country.

McCarthy's Downfall

By now, McCarthy's reckless behavior during the Army hearings had become so offensive to his fellow senators that they appointed a special committee, headed by Senator Arthur Watkins, Republican of Utah, to examine his treatment of the Army. McCarthy proved no match for Watkins, a stern, rigorous parliamentarian who quickly whipped McCarthy into submission and forced him to abide by the committee's rules. After swift and most un-McCarthyite hearings, the committee recommended that McCarthy be "censured" for his actions, but not expelled. The full Senate agreed overwhelmingly, and only three years later McCarthy passed away, a victim of a broken heart and a well-documented case of alcoholism. He was buried with the full honors of the Marine Corps, in which he had served in World War II, as well as with the complete burial ritual of the Catholic Church.

The man whose fractious tactics and obsessive drive for publicity had so dominated American politics in the first half of the 1950s is known today mostly for the "-ism" that ends his name. "McCarthyism," defined by one encyclopedia as "the practice of using innuendo and unsubstantiated accusations against adversaries," has come to stand for much that is objectionable and little that is positive in American political practice. McCarthy did little good either to the United States Senate or to the religion with which he was so curiously associated. Yet he bequeathed much that has since become standard practice in political life. Joe McCarthy was hardly the first political figure to dissemble the truth or to slur his opponents. Yet it was McCarthy who turned such practices into an art form, and who taught his successors, at least by his example, how to treat the truth as a plaything and one's enemies as convicted criminals.

However, something of value did emerge from the convulsive period that bears his name: it forced the Catholic Church to deepen its commitment to its historic practice of denying its official imprimatur to any political figure, even one who supported so genuinely a Catholic stance as anti-Communism. In the process, it fashioned itself into a more stable institution, as well as a Church that was more determined than ever to remain faithful to itself.

Crosby, Donald F. *God, Church and Flag: Senator Joseph R. McCarthy and the Catholic Church, 1950–1957.* Chapel Hill: University of North Carolina Press, 1978.

Gannon, Robert I. *The Cardinal Spellman Story.* Garden City, N.Y.: Doubleday, 1962.

_____. "Catholics, Non-Catholics and Senator McCarthy." *Commonweal* 59 (April 2, 1954) 639–40.

DONALD F. CROSBY, S.J.

McCLOSKEY, JOHN CARDINAL (1810–85)

Archbishop, first American cardinal. John McCloskey was born in Brooklyn, New York, on March 10, 1810, the son of Patrick McCloskey and Elizabeth Harron McCloskey, who emigrated to Brooklyn from Dungiven, County Derry, Ireland, in 1808. Young John received his

John Cardinal McCloskey

early education in private schools in Brooklyn and New York City, where the family lived after 1817. Following the death of John's father in 1820, Cornelius Heeney, a wealthy Catholic merchant in New York City, became his guardian. In 1821 John entered Mt. St. Mary's College in Emmitsburg, Maryland, and returned there in 1827 to attend the seminary. He was ordained a priest by Bishop John Dubois in old St. Patrick's Cathedral on January 12, 1834, the first native New Yorker to be ordained a diocesan priest.

Priest in New York

Fr. McCloskey's first assignment was to the faculty of the seminary that Bishop Dubois was building in Nyack, New York. In 1834 the institution was temporarily located in an old farm house on the property while the permanent structure was under construction. The enrollment consisted of five students; McCloskey and the rector, Fr. John McGerry, constituted the total faculty. Within a year, McCloskey prudently exchanged his unpromising seminary professorship for three years of study in Rome, which also gave him the opportunity to travel in Europe.

Upon McCloskey's return to New York in 1837, he was made pastor of St. Joseph's Church in Greenwich Village where the lay trustees had been quarreling with Bishop Dubois. McCloskey defused the situation through his patience and forbearance. In 1841 Bishop John Hughes named McCloskey the first president of St. John's College (the future Fordham University), a post he held for only one year. Temperamentally the quiet, peace-loving McCloskey was the exact opposite of the assertive and confrontational Hughes, but Hughes had a high regard for

McCloskey. In 1844, when McCloskey had been ordained for only ten years, Hughes selected him as his coadjutor with the right of succession. He was ordained titular bishop of Axiere on March 10, 1844.

Bishop of Albany

On May 27, 1847, McCloskey was named the first bishop of the newly established Diocese of Albany, which then comprised about half the area of New York state. McCloskey remained in Albany for seventeen years during which period the Catholic population increased from approximately 60,000 to 290,000. The number of priests grew from 38 to 95, and the number of churches increased from 47 to 120. McCloskey was also responsible for beginning the construction of the Cathedral of the Immaculate Conception although it was not completed until later in the century.

Archbishop of New York

After the death of John Hughes in 1864, McCloskey succeeded him as the second archbishop of New York. He was appointed on May 6, 1864, and was installed in old St. Patrick's Cathedral on August 21, 1864. One of McCloskey's main priorities was the completion of the new St. Patrick's Cathedral. Construction had been started under Hughes in 1858, but had been suspended during the Civil War. McCloskey resumed work on the unfinished building and dedicated it on May 25, 1879. He also rebuilt the old St. Patrick's Cathedral, which had been heavily damaged by fire in 1866.

On March 15, 1875, Pope Pius IX named McCloskey a cardinal, the first American to be so honored. In 1878 he arrived in Rome too late to take part in the conclave that elected Pope Leo XIII, but he was present at the coronation of the new Pope and finally received the cardinal's red hat from him on March 28, 1878. Two years later, as McCloskey's health began to fail, he received as his coadjutor Michael Augustine Corrigan, the former bishop of Newark.

Corrigan once said of McCloskey that "it was [his] privilege to grow up with Catholicity in this diocese and to . . . witness . . . a progress and development unparalleled in history." McCloskey was born two years after the Diocese of New York was established when there were only two churches, a half-dozen priests, and approximately fourteen thousand Catholics in the whole state of New York. At McCloskey's death in 1885, in the Archdiocese of New York alone, there were approximately 1,000,000 Catholics, 139 parishes, 279 priests, and 2,136 women religious. Two of New York's most famous Catholic charitable institutions date from the McCloskey years: Sr. Irene Fitzgibbon's New York Foundling Hospital and Fr. John Drumgoole's Mission of the Immaculate Virgin.

Corrigan also claimed that McCloskey's most conspicuous virtue was prudence. It was a virtue that enabled McCloskey to handle successfully such volatile characters as Dr. Edward McGlynn, but it sometimes prevented him from taking needed pastoral initiatives. In 1865, when two New York priests told him that fifty additional parishes were needed in the archdiocese, he refused to believe them. For twenty years he dismissed complaints about the deplorable living conditions in St. Joseph's Provincial Seminary in Troy. When a New York pastor, Fr. Thomas Farrell, left five thousand dollars in his will to establish a black parish in Manhattan, McCloskey waited three years before accepting the legacy. At the Second Plenary Council of Baltimore in 1866, he even opposed efforts to take up an annual collection for black Catholics.

McCloskey died on October 10, 1885, at Mount St. Vincent on the Hudson, the motherhouse of the Sisters of Charity, and was buried under the high altar of St. Patrick's Cathedral. He was immediately succeeded by his coadjutor, Michael Augustine Corrigan.

See also CARDINALS IN THE AMERICAN CHURCH; McGLYNN, EDWARD; NEW YORK, CATHOLIC CHURCH IN.

Becker, Martin J. *A History of Catholic Life in the Diocese of Albany, 1609–1864*. New York: U.S. Catholic Historical Society, 1975.

Cohalan, Florence D. *A Popular History of the Archdiocese of New York*. Yonkers, N.Y.: United States Catholic Historical Society, 1983.

Farley, John Cardinal. *The Life of John Cardinal McCloskey*. New York: Longman's, Green and Co., 1918. Ghost-written by Peter Guilday and eviscerated by Patrick J. Hayes, Farley's secretary and successor as archbishop.

THOMAS J. SHELLEY

McCLOSKEY, WILLIAM (1823–1909)

Bishop. William George McCloskey was born in Brooklyn, New York, on November 10, 1823, the son of George and Ellen Kenny McCloskey. Two of his brothers also became priests. Having attended Mt. St. Mary's Seminary in Emmitsburg, Maryland, he was ordained priest of the Archdiocese of New York on October 6, 1852. After serving as professor and rector at his alma mater, McCloskey was named first rector of the North American College in Rome in 1860. He left this post in 1868 after several American bishops criticized his financial abilities.

In March 1868, Pope Pius IX appointed McCloskey bishop of Louisville. He would hold this office until his death in 1909, by then "dean and nestor"—the oldest member—of the American hierarchy. Nearly one hundred new churches were built in the diocese during his lengthy tenure. His piety and personal virtue were never disputed, but his style of governance marked him as one of the most authoritarian Catholic bishops in nineteenth-century America. For his studious attention to detail of dress, historian

William McCloskey

James Hennesey has called McCloskey "the Lord Chester-field of the American Church."

The Louisville bishop was often embroiled in controversy with priests and sisters in his diocese, most notably with the former during a period in 1875 called simply "The Troubles" by contemporaries. Usually at issue were diocesan finances and his often sudden reassignment of clerics, moves that these gentlemen considered to be arbitrary. When appeals were made to Rome, McCloskey's judgments were often overturned. An investigator was appointed by the Vatican as early as 1871, but the prelate was exonerated and never removed from office.

McCloskey often interfered with the internal regulations of religious communities of women, once requiring that sisters not be permitted to leave the diocese to teach elsewhere until all of his own schools had been supplied with instructors. At times such disputes ended with a compromise, but at least one community left the diocese entirely rather than submit. McCloskey provides a case study of the growing phenomenon of a Roman, centralized, magisterial style of leadership among the Catholic hierarchy in the America of the Gilded Age and early twentieth century. He died in Louisville on September 17, 1909.

Crews, Clyde F. "American Catholic Authoritarianism: The Episcopacy of William George McCloskey." *The Catholic Historical Review* 70 (4) (October 1984) 560–80.

CLYDE F. CREWS

McCORMICK, ANNE O'HARE (1880–1954)

Journalist. Anne O'Hare was born on May 16, 1880. In the summer of 1936, McCormick became the first woman to join the prestigious editorial board of *The New York Times,* an institution averse to such promotion of a woman journalist until then. For fifteen years before her appointment, she had been sending freelance dispatches to the newspaper from Europe. From her position on the *Times* board, McCormick would, over the next eighteen years, write hundreds of editorials, including many stirring leads in the weeks before the outbreak of World War II.

McCormick became the newspaper's first foreign affairs columnist in 1937, appearing with a byline on the editorial page three times each week, alternating with the influential national correspondent Arthur Krock, a placement that gave her views special clout. Later that year, she became the first professional woman ever to win the Pulitzer Prize for journalism. She received it for the entire previous year's work, at a time when only one winner was selected from among both national and international correspondents.

Since McCormick had cultivated a lifelong interest in European affairs and had traveled to Europe both before World War I and nearly every year after it, she was able to bring long-term perspective to her chronicle of the rise and fall of Fascism. In describing Mussolini's first speech in the Italian Chamber of Deputies, McCormick showed characteristic prescience in noting how appealing he was to his countrymen. "Italy has heard its master's voice," she wrote.

McCormick showed an uncanny knack for being at the place where news was breaking and at obtaining interviews. Not only did she know Franklin D. Roosevelt well, but she also interviewed Mussolini, Hitler, Stalin, and Churchill. She met with Popes Pius X, Benedict XV, Pius XI, and Pius XII, not to mention most other European heads of state and their secretaries. A group of women, compiling a slate of possible female candidates for high government posts, once proposed her name to President Roosevelt as assistant secretary of state; Dorothy Thompson's assessment was that McCormick should have been secretary of state.

It was a well-kept secret that, before the United States declared war against the Axis, McCormick accepted an appointment to a confidential State Department committee that met each weekend for more than a year, advising the president on postwar planning. She also covered several domestic trends, including the rise of the new South, the phenomenon of Hollywood and the rise of the motion picture industry, the Florida real estate boom, and every presidential convention—Democratic and Republican—from the nomination of Calvin Coolidge to that of Dwight D. Eisenhower.

What brought McCormick such wide acclaim was a combination of "objective" reporting and compassion for the common people caught up in the forces of world politics. "Why should the young blood of Europe be shed over Danzig and the Corridor? Why should playgrounds be dug up for air shelters? Why should railway stations be crowded with weeping mothers and boys doomed to death if the guns go off?" she wrote on the eve of Germany's march into Poland, concluding, "There is no reason except that Hitler wills it." Although McCormick patriotically supported the war effort, she pronounced the war itself a "preventable catastrophe, depending on human choice."

In her day McCormick was the most celebrated woman in journalism. She was inducted into the prestigious American Institute of Arts and Letters and won numerous awards, including the Overseas Press Club award, the University of Notre Dame's Laetare Medal, and sixteen honorary doctorates. She was also voted Woman of the Year at the 1939 New York World's Fair by a coalition of women's groups. The theme of the fair—"The World of Tomorrow"—had an ironic twist: as record crowds swelled the exhibits, Britain and France declared war on Germany.

Born in England and brought to the United States by her Irish Catholic parents while she was still an infant, McCormick was educated at a finishing school, St. Mary of the Springs Academy in Columbus, Ohio. She obtained her journalistic skills during ten years as an editor of the Cleveland diocesan newspaper the *Catholic Universe.* She also published fiction in such national magazines as the *Saturday Evening Post* and *Colliers,* and poetry in *The New Republic* while living in Ohio.

For the first ten years of her marriage to Francis J. McCormick, a wealthy businessman from Dayton and a relative of Cardinal Gibbons, she held no paying job. McCormick could have remained a small town wife respected for her philanthropic and community activities, but she did not. Instead, her future changed dramatically in 1920, when, at age forty-one, she wrote to *The New York Times,* asking to send reports from Europe. "Try it," was the famous reply she received. Her first article, "The New Italy of the Italians," made the front page of the Sunday magazine and book review section, launching her career as the preeminent *Times* woman. Although McCormick had no children and was a full-time professional, she was esteemed as a model Catholic woman at the time.

She wrote only one book, *The Hammer and The Scythe: Communist Russia Enters the Second Decade,* though she was hounded by publishers for decades to write more. Two collections of her columns were published posthumously: *The World at Home* (introduction by James Reston) and *Vatican Journal* (introduction by Clare Boothe Luce). McCormick supported the League of Nations and the United Nations and served on the organizing committee of UNESCO. Her last column was published several weeks before her death on May 29, 1954, from lung cancer at age seventy-four.

KAREN SUE SMITH

McCORMICK, STEPHEN (1829–91)

Businessman, editor, legislator. Stephen James McCormick was born in Dublin, Ireland, on December 20, 1829, the son of well-to-do parents who sent him, at the proper age, to Castlenock College for a privileged education. At the age of twenty he married Ann Clark, and a year later sailed with her to New York to seek his fortune. He soon became engaged in the newspaper business. Another year following, he left New York for Oregon, where his priest-brother Patrick was pastor at the pro-cathedral in Oregon City.

In Portland, McCormick opened a job-print business. Combining printing with publishing one of the first magazines on the Pacific Coast, then adding a bookstore to the other enterprises, he soon became a local celebrity. He was elected Portland's mayor in 1858, no mean feat because of the voters' well-known hostility toward Catholics and the Irish. He lasted only one year, which was not uncommon in those lusty times. He then turned his attention to the care of his family and to his writing and publishing business. He and Ann had twelve children, five of whom died in infancy. His magazine project collapsed for lack of support. His bookstore burned to the ground at a critical time. But McCormick plunged on, justly achieving a fame surpassed only by one other Oregonian layperson, Dr. John McLoughlin.

Some of his accomplishments were as follows: editor of the *Portland Commercial;* editor and publisher of the *Franklin Advertiser,* editor of the *Daily Advertiser,* Portland's first evening paper; delegate to the Oregon Constitutional Convention; member of the state legislature; director of Portland schools; commissioner of the county; publisher of Portland's first city directories; publisher of the most important early Catholic books; editor of the *Catholic Sentinel,* a pioneer West Coast Catholic paper; and most able and dedicated "defender of the faith" in Oregon. A devout Catholic, he supported the poor and became Archbishop Francis Norbert Blanchet's loyal friend and ally.

Much attracted to San Francisco, which epitomized the glamour and excitement of the West Coast for many people from Ireland, he finally left Portland in 1880 to assume editorship of the Catholic *San Francisco Monitor.* He retained this position until his death after a long illness, on August 20, 1891. He was buried in grand style, as he deserved.

Schoenberg, Wilfred P., S.J. *Defender of the Faith: The History of the Catholic Sentinel 1870–1990.* Portland: Oregon Catholic Press, 1993.

WILFRED P. SCHOENBERG, S.J.

McCRORY, ANGELINE (1893–1984)

Foundress of the Carmelite Sisters of the Aged and Infirm. Mother Angeline was born Bridget Teresa McCrory on January 21, 1893, in Mountjoy, County Tyrone, Ireland. While she was still quite young, her family emigrated to Scotland. In 1912 the young Bridget McCrory entered the Little Sisters of the Poor and received her religious formation at the motherhouse at LaTour, St. Joseph, France. Known as Sr. Angeline, then Mother Angeline, she spent the next fourteen years serving the elderly in various homes in the United States.

As time passed, the charismatic Mother Angeline became increasingly convinced that the elderly of the United States needed a new kind of care, in harmony with American customs and in keeping with their position in society. Unable to effect the changes she felt necessary, and after much prayer, she turned to the archbishop of New York, Patrick Cardinal Hayes, for advice and counsel. With his blessing and support, Mother Angeline and six other sisters withdrew from their congregation in 1929, and, with the permission of the Roman authorities, began a new community dedicated to the care of the aged and infirm that would put Mother Angeline's ideals into practice. In 1931 the new group was affiliated to the Ancient Order of Carmel, where Angeline found the spirituality that nurtured her ideal: dedication to Mary, the Mother of God, and the mixed life of prayer and service that was the charism of the prophet Elijah, the spiritual father of the Carmelite Order.

The Carmelite Sisters for the Aged and Infirm, as they became known, had their first motherhouse at St. Patrick's Home in the Bronx. From there, the congregation spread rapidly with the blessings of many vocations. Mother Angeline Teresa's philosophy was simple, extraordinary for her time, yet timeless. With a deep respect for the sacredness of life, the sisters were to run modern residences where there would be a true home-like atmosphere. Mother Angeline envisioned the elderly spending their final years with dignity, with respect for their independence, and with the spiritual consolation of Mass and the sacraments. To her beloved Carmelite daughters she once wrote: "Try to see Christ in each of the old people entrusted to our care. Be kind to them as you would be to Christ Himself, and endeavor to meet their needs with all the love Mary must have shown in caring for her new born Babe in Bethlehem."

Mother M. Angeline Teresa died on her ninety-first birthday, January 21, 1984, at St. Theresa's motherhouse in Germantown, New York. At the time of her death, there were over three hundred professed religious serving over thirty homes for the aged in the United States and Ireland. The Cause for the Beatification and Canonization of Mother Angeline was introduced in 1989.

See also CARMELITE NUNS AND SISTERS (O.CARM.).

De Lourdes, Bernadette. *Woman of Faith: Mother M. Angeline Teresa, O.Carm.* Germantown, N.Y., 1984.

Mead, Jude. *The Servant of God: Mother M. Angeline Teresa, O.Carm.* Petersham, Mass.: St. Bede's Publications, 1990.

McDONALD, BARNABAS (1865–1929)

Edward Patrick McDonald became a Christian Brother at age twenty, receiving the name Barnabas Edward. He taught elementary school for a few years, then was assigned to vocation and formation work. In directing teenage retreats he became aware of the plight of dependent children, and for the next twenty years he was involved with the care of delinquents and orphans. He became supervisor of Lincoln Hall in Lincolndale, New York, where he introduced a plan of family-like living units known as "the cottage system," which heretofore had been employed only in exclusive boarding schools. Because of this and other innovations, Lincoln Hall became a model for child-care institutions throughout the country.

The Knights of Columbus, asked to work with recreation programs for city youths, accepted a plan put forward by Br. Barnabas, and appointed him executive secretary of a special committee charged with its implementation. This resulted in his establishing a graduate course in "Boyology" at the University of Notre Dame in 1924. He organized courses in adolescent guidance for volunteer welfare workers and summer school programs in leadership training. He also organized the junior order of the Knights of Columbus, now known as the Columbian Squires.

His reputation as an expert on adolescent development became known nationwide, so much so that he was in constant demand as an adviser and lecturer. Presidents Theodore Roosevelt and Calvin Coolidge sought his advice on child welfare. He was active in the Boy Scout movement and numerous other groups. At his death on April 22, 1929, he received tributes in newspapers and periodicals throughout the country. He was buried in New York under a headstone donated by the Columbian Squires.

Battersby, William J. *Brother Barnabas.* Winona, Minn.: St. Mary's College Press, 1970.

WILLIAM QUAINTANCE, F.S.C.

McGEE, THOMAS D'ARCY (1825–68)

Journalist, poet, politician. Thomas D'Arcy McGee was born on April 13, 1825, in Carlingford, County Louth, Ireland. He spent a decade in the United States, then moved to Canada, where he was assassinated on April 7, 1868. He was the fifth child of Dorcas (Morgan) and James McGee of Ireland's Coast Guard Service. An alumnus of Leinster "hedge schools," McGee was an early, enthusiastic, and lifelong devotee of Ireland's repeal movement.

McGee came to the United States in 1842, sailing from Wexford to Quebec, Philadelphia, and Boston, where he often revolutionary views on Irish questions, plus his holding that Catholicism and democracy were incompatible, earned him the hostility of both Church and state. When he urged the American Irish to quit the urban East for Catholic-Celtic colonies in the West or in Canada, he met more Church animosity, which worsened when McGee claimed the hierarchy opposed him because it feared losing the immigrants' monetary support for diocesan projects.

Persuaded that his fortunes would improve among Canadian sympathizers, McGee (who was never naturalized) moved to Montreal in 1857, where his opinions moderated considerably. In his *New Era* he backed French-Canadian identity, railway expansion, colonization of Inuit outposts, an indigenous literature that would benefit by tariff cuts for local publishers, and even a "Kingdom of the St. Lawrence" for a son of Queen Victoria. McGee's zeal attracted the attention of local politicians who helped him get elected to the legislative assembly representing Montreal. His parliamentary career, though erratic, advanced. Despite hurtful confrontations with the Church, McGee was elected to the Royal Irish Academy and various Canadian ministries, retaining constituent favor by touting a nation comprised of four Canadian provinces. When he applied his confederation theories to Ireland—self-government within an imperial embrace—incensed Fenians branded McGee a traitor. On April 7, 1868, a week shy of his forty-third birthday, McGee was ambushed and slain in Ottawa, apparently by a fervent Fenian (hanged within a year) disgruntled that McGee would not back the brotherhood's plan to invade British North America.

McGee is honored with a memorial in Carlingford, statuary at Ottawa, portraits in national collections, and in Canadian postage issued in 1927 to mark the sixtieth anniversary of Confederation. Three countries remember him for his significant contributions to Irish, U.S., and Canadian culture. He is buried in Montreal.

Cullen, James Bernard. "Thomas D'Arcy McGee." *The Story of the Irish in Boston.* Boston: J. B. Cullen, 1889.

Lord, Robert H., and others. *History of the Archdiocese of Boston in the Various Stages of Its Development 1604–1943.* 3 vols. Boston: Pilot Publishing Co., 1945.

Potter, George. *To the Golden Door: The Story of the Irish in Ireland and America.* Boston: Little Brown, 1960.

Ryan, George E. *Figures in Our Catholic History.* Boston: St. Paul Editions, 1979.

——, ed. *The Pilot at One-Fifty.* Special edition of the official newspaper of the Archdiocese of Boston published to mark its sesquicentennial. September 14, 1979.

GEORGE E. RYAN

McGILL, JOHN (1809–72)

Third bishop of Richmond. John McGill was born in Philadelphia on November 4, 1809, and practiced law

Thomas D'Arcy McGee

became New England accounts agent and correspondent for the *Boston Pilot.* In two years, McGee was recognized as an articulate spokesman for Irish causes, which prompted *Pilot* owner Patrick Donahoe to appoint the nineteen-year-old as editor. With the paper his rostrum, McGee continued to espouse Irish independence and almost any other issue that would antagonize Anglophiles, including the proposed federation of Canada and the United States into an entity extending from Labrador to Central America. During his editorship, McGee wrote books about the United Irishmen and Daniel O'Connell, also vexing Boston's "Yankee" elite with "ferocious" editorials alleging their ethnoreligious bigotry against Irish Catholic immigrants. To calm interfaith waters, Bishop Benedict J. Fenwick canceled his subscription in 1844.

Beginning in 1845, McGee crisscrossed the Atlantic, pursuing his peeves in Dublin, London, Scotland, and the United States as correspondent or editor of journals he himself founded. He contributed two volumes to Young Ireland's "Library" and married Mary Theresa Caffrey, with whom he had a son and five daughters. Badgered by sedition charges stemming from his role in the 1848 rebellion, he returned to the United States, soon alienating New York Bishop John Hughes by attacks on the Irish clergy, whom he faulted for not overtly supporting the insurrection. McGee founded *The Nation* in Manhattan, using it to promote Canadian-American unity. When he appealed for an Irish peace with the United Kingdom, republicans fumed and McGee left for Boston, where he founded *American Celt* and *Adopted Citizen,* later removed to Buffalo and New York. Between 1851 and 1857, he published four more Ireland-related books, none without some controversy. His before entering the seminary in Bardstown, Kentucky, where he was ordained in 1835. As a priest he served as assistant at St. Louis Cathedral and was editor of *The Catholic Advocate* in Louisville from 1840 to 1848. His Sunday sermons, lasting a hour and a half (short by the standards of the day), gained him a reputation as a preacher and controversialist.

John McGill

In 1850 he was appointed to Richmond when Richard Vincent Whelan was transferred to the new Diocese of Wheeling. When McGill arrived in his diocese, he found only seven priests, six of whom were Irish-born. In Richmond, moreover, he found no provisions for the support of a bishop. Immediately upon his arrival, he entered into a dispute with the pastor, Timothy O'Brien, who had served the diocese for eighteen years and had almost single-handedly built up the Church in Richmond at great personal expense. Within a week of McGill's arrival, O'Brien departed to join his brother, Fr. John O'Brien, in Lowell, Massachusetts. A committee of bishops subsequently recommended that the priest be reimbursed for his personal expenditures.

Reflecting his earlier career in Louisville, McGill engaged in newspaper disputes, particularly during the Know-Nothing campaign of 1855, when he imprudently implied that the yellow fever epidemic that struck Norfolk and Portsmouth may have been a divine punishment for the campaign. He opposed abolition, defended Virginia's secession, and even threatened to refuse faculties to the chaplains accompanying Union troops. He personally blessed the "Montgomery Guards," a company of Irish parishioners raised in Richmond, and ordered all churches to pray for Confederate authorities. This order later led to the imprisonment of Thomas Becker, the pastor in Martinsburg and later bishop of Wilmington and of Savannah, who insisted on reciting the prayer even in the presence of Union authorities. Toward the end of the Civil War he published an apologetical work, *Our Faith, Our Victory,* but its style prevented its widespread use. McGill was a rigid disciplinarian and dismissed any priest who did not reach his standards, including John Teeling, who had served as vicar general and chaplain in the Confederate army and had provided one of the legal precedents for the secrecy of the confessional.

Although McGill, against the advice of Archbishop Martin John Spalding of Baltimore, sought Lincoln's permission to go to Rome to make his official *ad limina* visit to Pius IX, he ultimately postponed this until 1868, when he used the opportunity to recruit for the diocese the first of many priests from The American College, Louvain, including Francis Janssens, who later became successively bishop of Natchez and archbishop of New Orleans, and Augustine van de Vyver, who became bishop of Richmond. He attended the First Vatican Council, but made little contribution and left before the council ended. He died in Richmond on January 14, 1872.

Bailey, James H. *A History of the Diocese of Richmond: The Formative Years.* Richmond: The Chancery Office, 1956.

GERALD P. FOGARTY, S.J.

McGINLEY, PHYLLIS (1905–78)

Writer. Born in Ontario, Oregon, on March 21, 1905, McGinley moved with her family to Colorado and then to Ogden, Utah, where she was educated at the Sacred Heart Academy. After graduation from the University of Utah in 1928, McGinley taught school in Utah and then in New York. She later worked as an advertising copywriter and a poetry editor at *Town and Country* magazine, while writing freelance poetry and prose pieces. She married Charles L. Hayden in 1937; they had two daughters.

McGinley's first book of poetry, *On the Contrary,* was published in 1934. She published seven other collections, including *The Love Letters of Phyllis McGinley* (1944) and *Times Three* (1960), for which she won the Pulitzer Prize for poetry in 1961. McGinley wrote light verse, in which her religious beliefs, family background, and suburban lifestyle were often reflected. She also wrote several children's books. *Wonderful Time* was named one of the best of the year by *The New York Times.* Elected to the National Academy of Arts and Letters in 1955, McGinley received many other awards, including the Catholic sorority Theta Phi Alpha's St. Catherine of Siena Medal in 1956. She died in New York City on February 22, 1978.

Phyllis McGinley

Wagner, Linda Welshimer. *Phyllis McGinley*. New York: Twayne
    Publishers, 1971.
Walker, Nancy. "Humor and Gender Roles: The Funny Femi-
    nism of the Post World War II Suburbs." *American Quarterly*
    37 (1) (1985) 98–113.

K. N. McCARTHY

McGIVNEY, MICHAEL J. (1852–90)

Diocesan priest, founder of the Knights of Columbus. The
Knights of Columbus originated as a result of the interaction between this young priest and a small group of
Irish-American laymen. Michael J. McGivney was a curate at St. Mary's Church, New Haven, Connecticut, and
was well known among the young men of the city. His
ministry to youth, expressed in his chaplaincy of the St.
Joseph's Young Men's Society of the parish, sharpened
his awareness of the need to establish a Catholic society
in accord with the strong fraternal movement of the day.

McGivney was concerned not only with the benefits of
fraternal fellowship but also with the death-benefit features common to most of these societies. He realized the
value of insurance protection from the early death of his
own father and from his ministry to families suffering
from the loss of the breadwinner.

Recognized as the founder of the K of C, Michael J.
McGivney was born in Waterbury, Connecticut, the oldest of thirteen children, four of whom died in infancy. Between graduating from elementary school and entering
the seminary he worked in a spoon factory to help support the family. After completing theology at St. Mary's
Seminary in Baltimore, he was ordained in December

1877 and was immediately assigned to St. Mary's parish.
On October 2, 1881, he chaired the first meeting in the
church basement of what officially became the Knights
of Columbus on March 29, 1882, the date of the order's
incorporation in Connecticut.

Fr. McGivney deeply believed in the compatibility of
Catholicism and American fraternalism. No doubt the
priest was motivated by the wish to keep young Catholics from entering the ranks of condemned secret societies
and by the need to protect families during sickness and
death; yet he was equally persistent in his aim to establish a Catholic fraternal society imbued with zealous pride
in the American Catholic heritage.

As the first supreme secretary, McGivney was entrusted
with daily management of the infant order, a position in
accord with his role as founder, organizer, and ambassador. San Salvador Council was founded in May 1882,
but it was not until April 23, 1883, that Silver City Council No. 2 was instituted in Meriden. After the founder had
written a long letter to the editor of the *Connecticut Catholic* in August 1883, in which he outlined the benefits of
the order, new councils were instituted in Middletown, a
second in Meriden, and in Wallingford during the following six months.

With expansion of the order assured, McGivney announced at the Supreme Council meeting of June 15,
1884, that he would not be a candidate for supreme secretary. However, he was elected Supreme Chaplain, an office that removed him from daily business concerns and
was more compatible with his other priestly duties. The
following November, Bishop Lawrence McMahon of
Hartford appointed McGivney pastor of St. Thomas

Michael J. McGivney

Church, Thomaston. The people of St. Mary's presented him with a testimonial resolution of deep fondness: "The Rev. M. J. McGivney has, by his courtesy and kindness, by the purity of his life, and by the faithful discharge of his duties . . . secured the love and confidence of the people of St. Mary's."

The priest-founder continued to promote the expansion of the order. He personally was involved in the formation of Atlantic Council in Thomaston, and must have taken great pride in the institution of Sheridan Council in his hometown, Waterbury. Never a man of robust health, McGivney was afflicted with pneumonia in January 1890. After traveling south on two occasions and after treatment in New York, the thirty-eight-year-old priest died on August 14, 1890.

On the feast of the Assumption, the day after he died, the *Waterbury Republican* simply stated: "Father McGivney was well-known throughout Connecticut. His conception and successful execution of the idea of organizing the Order of the Knights of Columbus brought him great prominence. Unassuming in manners, he was full of vitality and energy. His efforts were uniformly successful."

Although the various funeral eulogies went unrecorded, less than a year later Edward Downes, who was master of ceremonies at a gathering honoring the deceased members of the order, eulogized the founder in these words:

> He was a man of the people. He was ever zealous for the people's welfare and all the kindliness of his priestly soul asserted itself most strongly in his unceasing efforts for the betterment of their condition. . . . Our Reverend Founder, if [naught] else in all thy holy priestly career merited for thee heavenly rest, that act alone of thine, which gives life to the Knights of Columbus, has surely secured for thee everlasting joy and eternal peace.

See also KNIGHTS OF COLUMBUS.

Kauffman, Christopher J. *Faith and Fraternalism, The History of the Knights of Columbus.* Rev. ed. New York: Simon & Schuster, 1992.
____. *Columbianism and The Knights of Columbus.* New York: Simon & Schuster, 1992.

CHRISTOPHER J. KAUFFMAN

McGLYNN, EDWARD (1837–1900)

Priest and social activist. Born in Manhattan on September 27, 1837, Edward McGlynn was one of eleven children born to Peter McGlynn, a prosperous contractor, and Sarah McGlincy McGlynn. Baptized at old St. Patrick's Cathedral, McGlynn attended public schools and went to Rome in 1851 at the age of thirteen to study at the Urban College of the Propagation of the Faith (Propaganda Fide). A tall man, powerful in appearance and fluent in speech,

Edward McGlynn

McGlynn was a brilliant student and became the vice-rector of the North American College when it opened in late 1859. Michael Augustine Corrigan, later to be archbishop of New York, was a first-year student at the time. Ordained on March 24, 1860, McGlynn returned to New York in the fall of that year.

His first assignment was to St. Joseph's Church, Greenwich Village, where the liberal and outspoken Thomas Farrell was the pastor and instilled in McGlynn a dedication to social issues. Stationed there a little over six months and in three other parishes in the next year and a half, McGlynn was appointed the chaplain of the military hospital in Central Park (1862), where his tenure ended in August 1865. That October, he was appointed assistant to Jeremiah Cummings at St. Stephen's, then the largest parish in Manhattan. When Cummings died in January 1866, McGlynn became pastor. He completed the enlargement of the church, established St. Stephen's Home for Children, and developed a large Sunday school.

Early Controversies

Since the building of grammar schools was promoted by successive Plenary Councils of Baltimore, this was McGlynn's first area of conflict with archdiocesan authorities. Having received a good education in the public schools, McGlynn felt his time and the parish's funds should rather be devoted to religious instruction. There is no record beyond the general instructions of his ever being ordered to begin a parochial school, although Archbishop Corrigan frequently complained that he had none.

Beginning in late 1869, Msgr. Thomas Preston delivered a number of lectures on Catholic and public schools.

Pastor of St. Ann's and chancellor of the Archdiocese of New York, Preston praised New York City politicians for providing eight dollars per child to the students in the city's parochial schools. McGlynn told the *New York Sun* that such financial aid to religious schools was a violation of the separation of Church and state. He also said that acceptance of such funds involved nesting with corrupt Tammany Hall politicians and led to the possible creation of inferior schools. In McGlynn's view, education was the realm of the state and religious instruction belonged in Sunday schools. A copy of this article was sent to Propaganda Fide, and Preston forwarded to McCloskey in Rome a protest of McGlynn's position composed at a meeting of New York priests. Though McCloskey did show the protest to Cardinal Barnabò at Propaganda Fide, he did nothing to forestall or censure McGlynn.

McGlynn belonged to the Accademia, a group of New York priests who had formed a theological society modeled on that of Cardinal Manning in London. The group met monthly for the reading and discussion of original papers. The date of the group's beginning is lost in obscurity, but it met monthly at Thomas Farrell's Greenwich Village rectory. The group was generally abolitionist and supported Radical Reconstruction. They espoused Fenianism, questioned the inerrancy of Scripture, papal infallibility, and clerical celibacy. Opposed to national parishes, they favored the gradual assimilation of immigrants and felt the American Church had to take the initiative in social reform. Because some members considered the group an elitist clique of abolitionists and Roman-educated clerics, the Accademia voted to dissolve itself intending to form a society that would include all New York priests. Though this effort floundered, Thomas Farrell later resumed weekly meetings at his rectory.

McGlynn and Henry George

McGlynn participated in colonization schemes for Irish immigrants in the Midwest (1879–82) and supported the Irish Land League of Michael Davitt. He also became enamored with Henry George's single tax theory. The heart of George's theory was a single tax imposed on the income from rents using the logic that the value of land and buildings was created by workers whose compensation did not reflect the value they gave to property by their labor.

McGlynn's speeches at a New York rally for Michael Davitt and for the Land League in Cleveland were reported to the Roman authorities, who made McCloskey extract from McGlynn a promise to abstain from future political activity. Corrigan, then coadjutor archbishop of New York, felt that an 1883 speech of McGlynn on behalf of Irish charities violated this promise and McGlynn was forced to print a counter article, which he couched in a cagy fashion.

Corrigan succeeded McCloskey as archbishop of New York on the latter's death on October 10, 1885. The following year, Henry George was proposed by the General Labor Union as mayoral candidate for New York. At George's formal nomination on October 1, McGlynn spoke after having been forbidden by Corrigan to do so without the explicit permission of Propaganda Fide. McGlynn maintained that he had been advertised as speaking and could not withdraw, but this excuse did not sway Corrigan. Corrigan privately suspended McGlynn from priestly functions for two weeks. Though it cannot be proven, some would attribute the suspension to the efforts of Tammany Hall politicians from whose Democratic Party Henry George would draw votes. McGlynn spoke no more during the campaign, but he did make appearances with George.

Archbishop Corrigan and McGlynn's Suspension

After the election (in which George was defeated), Corrigan issued a pastoral letter on the rights of private property condemning socialistic theories. McGlynn did not speak directly against this pastoral letter but gave an interview to the New York *Tribune* (November 26, 1886) in which he condemned in one paragraph "temporary measures for the relief of social distress" and the preaching of contentment to the poor while doing nothing for them. The remaining three paragraphs concerned his opinion on the condition of working women and he expressed the need for abolition of private property and the reading of Henry George's *Progress and Poverty*. On that very day, Corrigan suspended McGlynn for the rest of the year.

In a cable dated December 4, 1886 (the authenticity of which has been questioned), Propaganda Fide ordered McGlynn immediately to come to Rome. McGlynn replied to Corrigan on December 20, saying it was impossible for him to go to Rome for reasons of health, finances, and his responsibility to his recently deceased sister's children. Corrigan was meanwhile sending anti-McGlynn material to Rome and Propaganda Fide was investigating his career as a Roman student. Corrigan suspended McGlynn's suspension until further instructions were received from Propaganda Fide. A plea from Leo XIII did nothing to change McGlynn's decision. In January 1887, Fr. Arthur Donnelly was appointed temporary pastor of St. Stephen's, and his presence caused rallies in support of McGlynn and a boycott of the parish.

In January 1887, John Moore, bishop of St. Augustine and a Roman student compatriot of McGlynn, entered the picture. He sent letters to Rome pleading in the case of McGlynn. At this time, Ella Edes, a Roman agent for Corrigan and other bishops of his persuasion, also entered the picture. It is through her that almost all Corrigan's correspondence was sent to Rome. In most cases original copies did not survive, but the translations of Edes, subject to suspicion, do. On January 21, Leo XIII took the case into his own hands; in New York, both Corrigan and McGlynn held press conferences to expound their views. The appointment of Fr. Charles Colton as pastor of St. Stephen's brought some measure of calm to the parish. From Rome Cardinal Gibbons sent a letter to McGlynn via his close friend Richard Burtsell urging McGlynn to come to Rome, and, in turn, Burtsell tried vainly to employ Gibbons' services in the cause of his friend.

On March 26, the Anti-Poverty Society was organized at the offices of *The Standard,* Henry George's newspaper. McGlynn was made president of the Anti-Poverty Society and three days later delivered his most famous speech, "The Cross of a New Crusade," promoting the single tax theory and better conditions for workers. Petitions of support for Corrigan were extracted from the German-speaking clergy of New York, the religious clergy, and finally from the diocesan clergy of the archdiocese. March and April of that year saw a clipping war in which both sides sent newspaper articles to Rome defending their positions.

Excommunication of McGlynn

On May 4, McGlynn was ordered to come to Rome within forty days or be excommunicated. McGlynn was on a speaking tour at the time, which he continued after receiving this ultimatum. On July 3, he was automatically excommunicated and received notice of this on July 8. Because Corrigan was fearful of the decision being overturned (due to McGlynn's large following and those interceding for him), he sent Fr. Charles McDonnell to Rome with evidence charging McGlynn with promiscuous behavior and heresy concerning sex. This material seems to have been accepted by the Holy Office but rarely mentioned in documents. Through the petitions of Bishop John Moore the case was reviewed, but on January 23, 1887, the original decision was reaffirmed; it was ratified by Leo XIII eight days later. McGlynn's response was an attack on the leadership of the Church.

Henry George was nominated by the United Labor Party at their 1887 convention as a candidate for New York secretary of state. McGlynn spoke for the ticket, which lost badly in the election. During 1888, McGlynn preached his message throughout the country. In January 1889 Corrigan made membership in the Anti-Poverty Society a reserved sin. In October 1889, Theresa Kelly, a parishioner of Richard Burtsell at Epiphany, died and was refused Christian burial because she belonged to the Anti-Poverty Society. She still lies buried in nonsectarian Woodlawn Cemetery. Burtsell was transferred from his city parish of the Epiphany to upstate Rondout.

Archbishop Francesco Satolli, on his way home from attendance at the dedication of The Catholic University, stayed with Corrigan in New York and telegraphed McGlynn to see him. McGlynn was on a lecture tour and when he returned home and received the message, Satolli had left for Rome.

In January 1890, Corrigan sailed for Rome and visited the Holy Land just before Lent. While there he wrote McGlynn seeking his reconciliation. McGlynn replied courteously and said that he would write in a few weeks. Corrigan responded that he would seek to have the censure withdrawn provided McGlynn cooperated, and he even offered to approach the Holy Father in company with him. McGlynn's response was that he could not go to Rome at that time. Henry George's works were condemned by Rome in 1891 but the decision was not to be published. In July, Archbishop John Ireland, on his way home from Rome, visited McGlynn in New York under instructions from the Holy See. What transpired is not known.

McGlynn's Reconciliation to the Church

In November 1892, Archbishop Francesco Satolli arrived in the United States as papal ablegate to the Columbian Exposition in Chicago. He also had instructions to reconcile McGlynn. Richard Burtsell saw Satolli in New York and briefed him on the McGlynn case. The outcome was that McGlynn had to compose an exposition of his political and economic theory. When finally done, Satolli examined it and found it "not adverse to the Catholic faith." Fr. Thomas Bouquillon, professor of moral theology at The Catholic University of America, suggested it should be complemented by McGlynn's acceptance of Leo XIII's recent encyclical *Rerum Novarum.* With Burtsell acting the role of intermediary, the statement went through several reviews and a promise on McGlynn's part to go to Rome. On December 23, 1892, McGlynn was received by Satolli at The Catholic University of America. He was absolved of his censures and restored to good graces. Two days later, he offered Christmas Mass at St. John's College, Brooklyn.

Corrigan was quite disturbed that he was not part of the reconciliation and complained to Satolli and to Cardinal Ledochowski, the prefect of Propaganda Fide. The Holy Office was confused because of the moral charges and wondered where Satolli had obtained the faculties to restore McGlynn while the case was still pending. It was not until June 1893 that McGlynn went to Rome, where he spent five days and saw Leo XIII.

Corrigan continued pressuring for a public retraction of McGlynn's theories, public penance, and the disposition of the moral case before the Holy Office. Through Satolli's efforts, Corrigan's efforts were squashed. However, McGlynn was not assigned to a parish by Corrigan. While Burtsell was in Rome in 1894, pleading his own cause of unjust transfer, he visited numerous prelates to help the cause of his friend. Corrigan and McGlynn finally met on December 21, 1894, and the latter was then assigned to the pastorate of St. Mary's Church, Newburgh, New York.

McGlynn arrived in Newburgh on December 31 and celebrated Mass on New Year's Day. He was active in speaking at civic celebrations and to labor organizations, as well as lecturing various groups. He also wrote articles and was active in the single tax movement. He made his last great speech at the funeral of Henry George on October 31, 1897, where he uttered those famous words, "There was a man sent from God, and his name was Henry George."

Edward McGlynn suffered from heart trouble, Bright's disease, and an abscess in his thigh. He took a bad turn in November 1899 and became bedridden. He died January 7, 1900, in Newburgh.

See also CORRIGAN, MICHAEL.

Bell, Stephen. *Rebel, Priest and Prophet: A Biography of Dr. Edward McGlynn.* New York: The Devin-Adair Co., 1937.

Curran, Robert Emmet. *Michael Augustine Corrigan and the Shaping of Conservative Catholicism in America, 1878–1902.* New York: Arno Press, 1978.

Fogarty, Gerald P. *The Vatican and the American Hierarchy from 1870 to 1965.* Wilmington, Del.: Michael Glazier, 1985.

Isacsson, Alfred. *The Determined Doctor: The Story of Edward McGlynn.* Tarrytown, New York: Vestigium Press, 1996.

Scibilia, Dominic. "Edward McGlynn, Thomas McGrady and Peter C. Yorke: Prophets of American Social Catholicism." Ph.D. dissertation, Marquette University, 1990.

———. "Edward McGlynn: American Social Catholic." *Records of the American Catholic Historical Society of Philadelphia* 101 (Fall 1990) 1–16.

Shanaberger, Manuel Scott. "Jeff," "A Missionary Priest and his Social Gospel." *U.S. Catholic Historian* 13 (Summer 1995) 23–47.

ALFRED ISACSSON, O.CARM.

McGRADY, THOMAS (1863–1907)

Priest, social activist. Thomas McGrady was born in 1863 in Lexington, Kentucky. He was a socialist priest who argued forcibly that the Church should end its support of capitalism. Ordained in 1887, he did pastoral work in Galveston, Texas, until 1891, when he became pastor of the Lexington, Cynthiana, and Bellevue areas of Kentucky. In the latter assignment, he saw firsthand the deleterious effects of industrial labor, leading him to examine the theoretical basis of laissez-faire capitalism and other forms of political economy. He read some of the leading works of political economy—including Henry George's *Progress and Poverty* (1879), Edward Bellamy's *Looking Backward* (1888), and Karl Marx's *Kapital* (1867, 1885–95)—and concluded that "collective ownership and administration of capital for the benefit of all people was the only rational solution of the industrial problem."

Though he considered socialism and Catholicism complementary, he found Catholic teaching on these issues—notably Pope Leo XIII's encyclical *Rerum Novarum* (1891), with its upholding of profit-driven capitalism—misguided and devoid of a practical solution to the problems created by industrialization. He wrote books and pamphlets criticizing Catholic views toward socialism and Catholic leaders' acceptance of a free-market system that caused great economic disparities. He traveled around the United States promoting socialism and supporting local socialist party leaders.

He was widely condemned for his views by his fellow priests, including his bishop, Camillus Paul Maes, who gave him poor marks as a pastor. McGrady, frustrated with what he considered shallow and political claims against him, resigned from the priesthood in 1902. He began preparing himself for a new career practicing law, and moved to San Francisco in 1903. He continued working as a lawyer there until his death in 1907 of chronic myocarditis.

Debs, Eugene V. "Obituary of Thomas McGrady." *Christian Socialist* (January 1, 1908) 4–5.

McGrady, Thomas. *Beyond the Black Ocean.* Terre Haute, Ind.: Standard Publishing Co., 1901.

———. *City of Angels: Review of Bishop Montgomery's Christian Socialism.* Terre Haute, Indiana, 1901.

———. "How I Became a Socialist." *Comrade* 2 (October 1902) 74–76.

———. *The Mistakes of Ingersoll.* Cincinnati: Curtis and Jennings, 1898.

———. *Socialism and the Labor Problem: A Plea for Social Democracy.* Terre Haute, Ind.: Debs Publishing Co., 1901.

———. *The Two Kingdoms.* Cincinnati, Ohio, 1899.

Scibilia, Dominic. "Edward McGlynn, Thomas McGrady, and Peter C. Yorke: Prophets of American Social Catholicism." Ph.D. dissertation, Marquette University, 1990.

Terrar, Toby. "Catholic Socialism: The Reverend Thomas McGrady." *Dialectical Anthropology* 7 (1983) 109–35.

———. "Thomas McGrady: American Catholic Socialist." *Ecumenist* 21 (November and December 1982) 14–16.

JOSEPH QUINN

McGRANERY, JAMES P. (1895–1962)

U.S. Attorney General. Born in Philadelphia, Pennsylvania, on July 8, 1895, to Irish immigrants, McGranery was educated in parochial schools and at Maher Preparatory School. Following service during World War I as an Air Force observation pilot, he studied law at Temple University in Philadelphia, earning his degree in 1928. He then practiced law privately and married fellow attorney Regina T. Clark in 1939; they had three children.

Interested in politics, McGranery headed Governor Al Smith's presidential campaign in Philadelphia. After an unsuccessful congressional bid in 1934, McGranery was elected to the House of Representatives in 1936. Reelected three times, McGranery was a loyal New Dealer and a militant anti-Communist. He resigned from Congress in 1943 to become assistant to the United States Attorney General. McGranery served until 1946 when he was named a federal judge for the Eastern District of Pennsylvania. He gave up his judgeship in 1952 when President Harry Truman appointed him United States Attorney General. He resigned after less than a year and resumed his private law practice in Philadelphia and Washington, D.C. McGranery received many honors and awards during his life, including several for his service to the Catholic Church: he was made Knight Commander of St. Gregory the Great, Knight Commander of the Holy Sepulchre, and Private Chamberlain of the Cape and Sword to Pope Pius XII and Pope John XXIII. He died in Palm Beach, Florida, on December 23, 1962.

K. N. McCARTHY

McGROARTY, SUSAN (1827–1901)

Religious. Susan McGroarty was born in Donegal, Ireland, on February 13, 1827; her family later emigrated to the United States. Sister Superior Julia, as Susan became known in the Sisters of Notre Dame de Namur, made training the sisters as teaching professionals her first goal as supervisor, a role she held for twenty-five years. She began a practice of sending circular letters to the sisters containing educational information and methodology. These letters became the book Sister Julia called the Sisters of Notre Dame "scheme of education."

Titled *The Course of Studies,* the book was compiled by sisters actually teaching in classrooms in Ohio and on the East Coast. It contained in outline form a curriculum to be followed from kindergarten through the primary and grammar grades, as well as secondary education. Much of the information was in German to accommodate the sisters and students in German parishes.

At the time of the book's publication in 1895, Sister Superior Julia was engaged in the establishment of Trinity College in Washington, D.C. This great undertaking, ten years in planning, was overshadowed by misunderstandings and disputes for Superior Julia. The completed college, however, was destined to become a great educational institution for women. She died on November 12, 1901.

See also SISTERS OF NOTRE DAME DE NAMUR (S.N.D.deN.).

Keenan, Angela Elizabeth. *Three Against the Wind: The Founding of Trinity College, Washington, D.C.* Westminster, Md.: Christian Classics, 1973.

Nugent, Helen Louise. *Sister Julia (Susan McGroarty).* Cincinati: Benziger Brothers, 1928.

O'Mahoney, Katherine A. O'Keeffe. *Famous Irishwomen.* Lawrence, Mass.: Lawrence Publishing Company, 1907.

LOUANNA ORTH, S.N.D.deN.

McHUGH, ANTONIA (ANNA) (1873–1944)

Catholic college founder and educator. Anna McHugh was born May 17, 1873, in Omaha, Nebraska, the oldest of seven children, five boys and two girls. Her parents, Patrick McHugh and Rose Welch McHugh, were both Irish. Anna had an itinerant frontier childhood following a move from Nebraska to Deadwood, South Dakota, when she was three, and, after a year's interlude in Chicago, to Langdon, North Dakota, where the family finally settled. Her father was influential in establishing new towns along the railroad as the tracks were extended beyond Langdon; he won election to the territorial, and later to the state legislature.

In the absence of Catholic schools or parishes, her parents sent Anna at the age of twelve to St. Paul, Minnesota, where she made her First Communion at St. Joseph Academy, conducted by the Sisters of St. Joseph. She was next sent to Winnipeg, Manitoba, to complete her high school studies with the Sisters of the Holy Name (Grey Nuns) at St. Mary's Academy. She joined the Sisters of St. Joseph in 1890, began teaching the elementary grades at St. Joseph's, and made permanent vows in 1898. The congregation, then headed by Mother Seraphine Ireland, arranged for her and several other sisters to begin studies toward their college degrees in the 1890s, first through summer courses at the University of Minnesota, and then, in the early 1900s, through correspondence and summer courses at the University of Chicago. She earned a bachelor of philosophy degree there in 1908, and, after a year in residence, a master of arts degree.

In 1905 Sr. Antonia and twenty-six other Sisters of St. Joseph opened Derham Hall preparatory high school and the College of St. Catherine on common premises in the rapidly developing Randolph Heights section of St. Paul. She was a gifted teacher and administrator who challenged young women to reach high. "Fill your minds with great things and there will be no room for trivialities," she liked to say. "She who would be a woman must avoid mediocrity."

Under her influence, a sister-faculty was recruited and educated in the best universities of the United States and Europe. Philanthropic support was secured to help pay for science, physical education, humanities, and residential buildings which, along with Our Lady of Victory Chapel and library, brought the college into the depression years with a fine physical plant free of debt. In 1936 St. Catherine's became the first Catholic college or university in the United States to be awarded a chapter of the prestigious national honor society Phi Beta Kappa.

Her educational leadership was recognized by invitational participation in the White House Conference on Child Health and Protection (1930), papal honors in the form of the *Pro Ecclesia et Pontifice* decoration (1931), presidency of the Minnesota Association of Colleges, chairing of the National Catholic Educational Association, an honorary doctorate from the University of Minnesota, and the University of Chicago Distinguished Alumni citation (1943).

She died October 11, 1944, after suffering a series of strokes.

College of St. Catherine Archives, manuscript collection of recollections and talks, "Addresses and Writings of Sister Antonia McHugh," and other sources.

Hurley, Helen Angela. *On Good Ground*. Minneapolis: University of Minnesota Press, 1951.

Kennelly, Karen M. "The Dynamic Sister Antonia and the College of St. Catherine." *Ramsey County History* 14 (1) (Fall/Winter 1978) 3–18.

KAREN M. KENNELLY, C.S.J.

McHUGH, JOHN AMBROSE (1880–1950)

Theologian and writer. John McHugh's name is almost always associated with that of his fellow Dominican and lifelong friend Charles Jerome Callan, O.P., with whom he produced a variety of biblical, theological, and devotional works.

A native of Louisville, Kentucky, he entered the Dominican novitiate not far from there at St. Rose in Springfield in 1897. Having demonstrated exceptional intellectual abilities, he was selected to pursue two years of additional studies in Latin before going on to philosophy. The delay resulted in his beginning philosophical studies at the same time as Callan, who had just completed his novitiate year. They were ordained priests together in 1905 by Bishop James Hartley of Columbus.

After obtaining the degree of lector in sacred theology at the University of the Minerva in Rome, McHugh was assigned in 1908 to the faculty at the Dominican House of Studies in Washington. There, over the course of the next seven years, he taught Church history, logic, and moral and dogmatic theology. Callan was likewise appointed to the faculty and taught Scripture. In 1915 both were reassigned to the parish of the Holy Rosary in Hawthorne, New York, where they served alternating terms as pastor over the next several decades and began a fruitful teaching career at the recently established Maryknoll seminary. Despite the fact that neither one of them enjoyed good health while being fully occupied as seminary professors and parish priests, they nevertheless found the time and energy for a prolific writing career that gained them an honored place in American Catholic intellectual life. Their rise to prominence began in 1916 when they embarked on what would be a tenure of thirty-four years as joint editors of the *Homiletic and Pastoral Review*. During this same period they also coauthored and coedited over thirty works.

Of the two, Callan was the motivating power behind their immense literary output. McHugh, however, possessed the finer intellect. Although both were awarded the degree of master of sacred theology in 1931 after completing the rigorous examination with distinction, McHugh slightly outshone Callan, capturing all twenty-five votes from the board of five examiners, compared to Callan's twenty-three votes. Yet, he produced very little of significance on his own. Without Callan, he probably would not have carried to completion the various projects he conceived.

Among their more important collaborative efforts was the four-volume *A Parochial Course of Doctrinal Instructions* (1920), which provided outlines and sermons linking the basic doctrines of the faith as presented in the Tridentine catechism with the readings for each Sunday and holy day of the year. A decade later, they produced the two-volume *Moral Theology* (1930) based on the teachings of St. Thomas Aquinas. In addition, they edited several prayer books for the laity and provided a new translation, in 1936, of *The Catholic Missal*. The following year, they finished editing a previously unpublished translation of the New Testament from the original Greek completed in 1913 by their deceased confrere, Francis Aloysius Spencer.

The appearance of the Spencer translation coincided with work already being done on a translation of the Scriptures from the Latin Vulgate proposed by the American bishops in 1935. Both McHugh and Callan had been invited by Bishop Edwin O'Hara to serve along with other biblical scholars on the editorial board overseeing the translation. The board itself soon evolved into the Catholic Biblical Association of America. In October 1938, McHugh was elected president of the association for a one-year term. He was also asked to serve as a theological revisor for the bishops' proposed revision of the Baltimore Catechism.

Years of overwork combined with poor health took their toll on McHugh, who died on April 9, 1950, at the age of sixty-nine. At the request of the Maryknollers, he was buried on the seminary grounds in recognition of his thirty-five years of devoted service to the society.

See also CALLAN, CHARLES JEROME; DOMINICANS (O.P.); MARYKNOLL.

JOHN LANGLOIS, O.P.

McINTYRE, JAMES FRANCIS CARDINAL (1886–1979)

Cardinal archbishop of Los Angeles. James Francis Aloysius McIntyre was born in New York City on June 25, 1886, the son of James F. and Margaret "Molly" Pelley McIntyre. He was baptized on July 11 at Saint Stephen's Church in Midtown Manhattan. He attended local public schools and later became a "runner" for the New York Curb Exchange. Meanwhile, he studied at Columbia University on

Morningside Heights and became office manager for the H. L. Horton Company.

Early Years in New York

Following his father's death in 1915, McIntyre entered Cathedral College as a clerical aspirant for the Archdiocese of New York. He completed his courses at Saint Joseph's Seminary, Yonkers, and was ordained to the priesthood by Archbishop Patrick J. Hayes on May 21, 1921, in Saint Patrick's Cathedral. After a brief stint as curate at Saint Gabriel's parish, Fr. McIntyre was assigned to the chancery office, where he served as liaison between Cardinal Hayes and chancery officials. He was named chancellor in 1934 and later that year was made a papal chamberlain by Pope Pius XI. Two years later he was made a domestic prelate.

James Francis Cardinal McIntyre

In 1939 McIntyre was renamed as chancellor by Francis J. Spellman, the newly appointed archbishop of New York. In that capacity, his duties expanded. He established a reciprocal loan fund, streamlined the business operations of the archdiocese, and renegotiated existing loans at reduced costs. Late in 1940, McIntyre was informed that he had been named to the titular see of Cyrene and made auxiliary bishop of New York. He was consecrated on January 8, 1941. In 1945, he was named vicar general and, in July of the following year, he was appointed coadjutor archbishop of New York without the right of succession. As chancellor and as auxiliary bishop of New York, McIntyre was a solidly conservative prelate open to changes and innovations.

Archbishop of Los Angeles

Early in 1948, McIntyre was appointed second archbishop of Los Angeles and was installed on March 19 of that year. The 9,508-square-mile archdiocese, stretching over 4 counties and numbering 232 parishes with 400,000 Catholics, was lineally descended from the jurisdiction established in 1840 by Pope Gregory XVI under the title of Ambas Californias.

During the first fifteen years of his tenure in the Golden State, McIntyre built a new church every sixty-six days and a new school house every twenty-six. By the time he retired, the two million Catholics in Los Angeles were served by 318 parishes, 350 schools, and 18 hospitals, an expansion record unparalleled in American ecclesial annals. McIntyre also reorganized the archdiocesan curial offices, erected a new chancery facility, expanded the local Catholic newspaper, built a separate educational headquarters, and refurbished Saint Vibiana's Cathedral. In 1952–53, he spearheaded a successful statewide campaign to remove the burden of taxation from the Catholic school system. The archbishop established the Youth Education Fund, which increased the enrollment in the Catholic schools by 73 percent in the first four years. He also initiated the Archbishop's Fund for Charity to provide for needs not covered by existing agencies.

First California Cardinal

In late 1952, McIntyre was named to the College of Cardinals by Pope Pius XII, only the twelfth American to achieve that distinction and the first west of the Mississippi River. He received the scarlet galero during a secret consistory at the Vatican on January 12, 1953. In 1953 the Cardinal launched a campaign to expand the archdiocesan seminary system, a program that eventually brought about the erection of Queen of Angels Seminary at Mission Hills and Saint John's College Seminary at Camarillo.

In keeping with the needs of an expanding and vital unit of the American Church, McIntyre initiated a series of outreach programs designed primarily to benefit the massive influx of peoples migrating to the West Coast. In 1965, he established a Job Finding Bureau and expanded the role of the Catholic Welfare Bureau. In addition to founding a Commission of Ecumenism and a Liturgical Commission, he totally reorganized the archdiocesan network of insurance coverage. He expanded the Confraternity of Christian Doctrine, opened the Kennedy Child Study Center, reorganized the St. Vincent de Paul Society, and established the Catholic Information Center in downtown Los Angeles where Mass is offered daily for the convenience of local workers. Earlier programs for people with disabilities were combined and amplified in 1967 into a new Department of Special Services.

Always mission-minded, Cardinal McIntyre encouraged the founding of the Lay Mission Helpers program in 1955 and, a few years later, he enthusiastically supported the establishment of the Mission Doctors Association, both of which groups were and still are unique in the American Church.

The statistics for the McIntyre era are truly phenomenal. He built a total of 192 schools, established 97 parishes, and opened 78 centers for the training of adult catechists. He endorsed the concept of middle schools, an innovative concept for the late 1960s.

Cardinal McIntyre was conservative in his theology and sociology. At the Second Vatican Council he argued against liturgical changes, he spoke for the original schema on divine revelation, sought the retention of Latin, and opposed giving juridical status to episcopal conferences. But he carefully implemented the council's decrees, even though some in the archdiocese felt that he was overly cautious in an era of unprecedented change.

Cardinal McIntyre retired on January 21, 1970, and spent the last years of his life serving as a parish priest at Saint Basil's in midtown Los Angeles. He died at Saint Vincent's Hospital on July 16, 1979.

McIntyre's papers are on file at the Archival Center, Archdiocese of Los Angeles in Mission Hills, California. See *Calendar of Documents and Related Historical Materials in the Archival Center: Archdiocese of Los Angeles for the Most Reverend J. Francis A. McIntyre, 1948–1971.* 3 vols.
Weber, Francis J. *Eulogy for a Cardinal.* Los Angeles, 1979.
____. *His Eminence of Los Angeles.* Santa Barbara, Calif.: McNally & Loftin, 1997.

FRANCIS J. WEBER

McKENNA, CHARLES HYACINTH (1834–1917)

Dominican friar. Known as "the apostle of the Holy Name," Charles McKenna achieved national recognition as a mission preacher and devoted his life to propagating throughout the country both the Confraternity of the Rosary and the Holy Name Society.

Born near Maghera, County Derry, Ireland, he emigrated to the United States at the age of seventeen and labored for several years as a stonecutter. After studying at the Dominican college in Sinsinawa, Wisconsin, he joined the Dominican province of St. Joseph and was ordained to the priesthood by Archbishop John Purcell of Cincinnati in 1867.

Appointed master of novices shortly after his ordination, he was soon recognized by his superiors as a gifted preacher and was transferred in 1870 to the parish of St. Vincent Ferrer in New York City, where he joined the provincial mission band. He was named head of the province's eastern mission band in 1880, a position he held for twelve years. Further acknowledgment of his eloquence in the pulpit came in 1881 when he was numbered among the first group of American Dominicans to be honored with the order's title of preacher general.

In 1892 he asked to be relieved of his position as head of the mission band in order to devote his energies to a work in which he was already engaged, the propagation of the Holy Name Society. McKenna saw the society as the most appropriate way of combating the use of profanities, which he believed to be one of the principal vices among Catholic men of the time. The spread of the society, however, was hampered by a papal restriction dating back to 1604, when Clement VIII forbade the establishment of more than one branch of the society in a given city. Largely through McKenna's efforts during visits to Rome, a dispensation from this restriction was granted by Leo XIII in 1896, allowing the society to be established in every parish.

Among his written works are several manuals, including *How to Make the Mission* (1873) and *St. Dominic's Tertiaries Guide* (1880). He also produced devotional works such as *The Crown of Mary* (1900) and *The Treasures of the Rosary* (1913).

Upon his death in 1917, McKenna was buried in St. Patrick's Cathedral in New York at the request of Cardinal John Farley as a tribute to the national stature the Dominican preacher had achieved.

See also DOMINICANS (O.P.); HOLY NAME SOCIETY IN AMERICA.

Coffey, Reginald. *The American Dominicans.* Washington, D.C.: Mt. Vernon Publishing Co., 1970.
O'Daniel, Victor. *Very Rev. Charles Hyacinth McKenna, O.P.* New York: Holy Name Bureau, 1917.
____. *Dominican Province of St. Joseph.* New York: National Headquarters of the Holy Name Society, 1942.

JOHN LANGLOIS, O.P.

McKENNA, JOSEPH (1843–1926)

Associate justice of the United States Supreme Court. Born in Philadelphia, Pennsylvania, on August 10, 1843, Joseph McKenna studied for the priesthood at St. Joseph's College. Turning from the priesthood to law, he graduated in 1865 from the local public college in Bernicia, California, where his family had moved in 1854. He began practicing law in Fairfield, California, and served two terms as county district attorney from 1866 to 1870. In 1869 McKenna married Amanda Frances Bornemann; they had four children.

Elected to the state assembly in 1875, McKenna lost three congressional races in 1876, 1878, and 1880, in part because of his Catholicism. However, he was elected in 1884 and served three subsequent terms. In Congress, McKenna supported railroads and high tariffs, and California issues like anti-Chinese legislation, free silver, and veteran's pensions. He voted against the establishment of the Interstate Commerce Commission in 1887. McKenna resigned in 1892 to become U.S. circuit judge for the ninth circuit. In 1897 President McKinley appointed him U.S. Attorney General. McKenna served eight months before McKinley nominated him for associate justice of the Supreme Court, where he spent twenty-seven years. Not guided by any particular legal philosophy, McKenna did not speak often for the Court. His few decisions, however, were marked by a practical vision of political and social arrangements. McKenna died in Washington, D.C., on November 21, 1926.

McDevitt, Matthew. *Joseph McKenna: Associate Justice of the United States.* New York: Da Capo Press, 1974.

Noonan, John T., Jr. "The Catholic Justices of the United States Supreme Court." *Catholic Historical Review* 67 (3) (1981) 369–85.

K. N. McCARTHY

McKENNA, MARY PAUL (1888–1984)

Missionary. Grace Anselma McKenna, known in religion as Sister Mary Paul, was born of Irish ancestry on September 21, 1888, in Reading, Pennsylvania. In 1917, at the age of twenty-eight, she joined the women auxiliaries at Maryknoll only five years after its foundation. Evident gifts of nature and grace and her missionary hopes were fulfilled when she was assigned to lead the first group of Maryknoll Sisters to China in 1921.

Without knowledge of Chinese language and culture, or any background and experience, and with very little money, the new missioners were strangers in a totally new environment. Mary Paul would later remark they had nothing to guide them save "faith and simplicity." Much of the success of the Maryknoll Sisters' missions in China can be attributed directly to Mary Paul's character and strong personality. She was a born leader, a gifted and resourceful administrator, forthright and fair in her dealings with others, and unhesitating in her decisions.

Immediately upon arriving in Hong Kong, McKenna acquired a library of Chinese books to help the sisters familiarize themselves with the Chinese culture. By 1924, the necessity of securing a reliable source of revenue for the missions was paramount. With characteristic energy, McKenna began a sewing enterprise in the convent dining room—producing liturgical vestments to be sold abroad. This at once provided jobs and skills for poor Chinese women and income to sustain the mission. The next year a kindergarten was opened in the convent garage, a venture that later developed into the prestigious Maryknoll Convent School. At the same time, a number of new mission houses were opened in the interior of China. Traveling the waterways, railroads, and dusty roads of China in the early part of the twentieth century was not only inconvenient and unhealthy, but dangerous. Undaunted, Mary Paul confronted each situation with her customary zeal and commanding demeanor.

In 1934, when Bishop Francis X. Ford, M.M., invited the sisters to work among the Hakka people in a radically different kind of apostolate—the direct evangelizing of women—he received warm support. McKenna was also an early advocate of the reception of Chinese women into the Maryknoll Sisters' Congregation.

McKenna traveled incessantly, visiting the missions all over southern China, and in Shanghai, Kunming, and Manchuria in the north, continuing her visits even during much of the Sino-Japanese War (1937–41). Shrewdly assessing each situation, she would manage to move the sisters from one location to another just in time to elude the advancing armies.

On Christmas Day 1941, when Hong Kong fell to the Japanese, the Maryknoll Convent School was commandeered as their headquarters. The military moved in, confining the sisters to a small area of the school. As Mary Paul's presence had often inspired awe from clergy and bishops alike, she now managed to awe the intruding Japanese military. Every evening she visited the commanding officers, chatting with them on just about anything, and thereby ensuring the well-being of her sisters. Her zeal and enthusiasm seemingly gave her the daring and courage necessary to cope with the most difficult and dangerous situations.

In January 1942, all American citizens in Hong Kong were interned on the grounds of the Stanley Prison, Mary Paul and other Maryknollers among them. Once interned, she immediately began to negotiate the release of the sisters. Claiming Irish ancestry, she was released in April 1942. Learning of the prisoner exchange ship, *Asama Maru,* she seized the opportunity to begin repatriation of the American sisters from June of that year.

McKenna returned to the United States for the 1946 general chapter, at which she was elected vicar general and served for two successive six-year terms. She later directed Maryknoll's work among the Chinese Catholic community in Chicago for almost a decade. In 1968, McKenna returned to Hong Kong where her keen intellect kept her active researching and reading about developments in missions and ministry. Those who knew her well said that she had adapted so completely in her use of Chinese facial expressions and gestures that she "began to look Chinese." She retired in 1978 and died at the Maryknoll Sisters Center on January 11, 1984.

See also MARYKNOLL.

BETTY ANN MAHEU, M.M.

McKENZIE, JOHN L. (1910–91)

Biblical scholar. A pioneer of critical biblical scholarship in North American Catholicism, John L. McKenzie was born in Brazil, Indiana, on October 9, 1910. He joined the Jesuits and was ordained to the priesthood in 1939. Because of World War II, he was deprived of the opportunity to pursue a doctorate in Rome. Instead, he went to Weston College, but enjoyed only one year of doctoral studies before he was called to teach at the new Jesuit seminary of the Chicago province in West Baden, near French Lick, Indiana. He taught at West Baden from 1942 until 1960.

John L. McKenzie

McKenzie served as book review editor of the *Catholic Biblical Quarterly* and wrote on Theodore of Mopsuestia as well as on biblical subjects. His first book, *The Two-Edged Sword: An Interpretation of the Old Testament,* was published in 1956. This was a landmark publication, as it was the first biblical study by a North American Catholic to win wide acclaim from Protestants and Catholics alike. It was translated into German, Spanish, Italian, and Portuguese, and was later reissued by Doubleday (Garden City, N.Y.: Image Books, 1966). Subsequent publications included *Myths and Realities* (collected essays, 1963), *Dictionary of the Bible* (1965), which he regarded as his *magnum opus, The Power and the Wisdom: An Interpretation of the New Testament* (1965), *Authority in the Church* (1966), *The World of the Judges* (1969), *The Roman Catholic Church* (1969), *Did I Say That?* (1973), and *A Theology of the Old Testament* (1974).

In 1960 he moved to Loyola University, where he taught in the History Department. From 1965 to 1966 he was vis-

iting professor at the University of Chicago Divinity School. He taught at the University of Notre Dame from 1966 to 1970, and concluded his teaching career at DePaul University (1970–78). In 1967 he became the first Roman Catholic president of the Society of Biblical Literature. He served as president of the Catholic Biblical Association in 1964.

Noted for his caustic wit, McKenzie was often at odds with his religious superiors. His career at West Baden was allegedly terminated because his midafternoon typing interrupted the silence of siesta. In the fifties and sixties he was often involved in controversies with conservative churchmen who questioned the orthodoxy of his work and that of Catholic biblical scholars in general. In the period during and following Vatican Council II he was a frequent, outspoken commentator on the exercise of authority in the Church. (A characteristic and much-publicized comment in "The Critic," to which he contributed a column, was, "Come off it, Your Holiness.") He eventually left the Jesuits, but was incardinated into the Diocese of Madison, Wisconsin, and remained a priest until the end of his life. His enduring legacy, however, was his lifelong insistence on the right of Catholic biblical scholars to pursue their research unhindered by dogmatic constraints and Church authorities. He died in Madison on March 2, 1991.

See also CATHOLIC BIBLICAL ASSOCIATION (CBA); CATHOLIC BIBLICAL SCHOLARSHIP IN AMERICA.

Flanagan, James W., and Anita Weisbrod Robinson. *No Famine in the Land: Studies in Honor of John L. McKenzie.* Biographical sketch by Thomas N. Munson. Missoula, Mo.: Scholars Press, 1989.

Fogarty, Gerald P. *American Catholic Biblical Scholarship.* San Francisco: Harper and Row, 1989.

McKenzie, John L. "American Catholic Scholarship 1955–80." *The Biblical Heritage in Modern Catholic Scholarship,* eds. John J. Collins and John Dominic Crossan. Wilmington, Del.: Michael Glazier, 1986.

JOHN J. COLLINS

McLOUGHLIN, JOHN (1784–1857)

John McLoughlin was born on October 19, 1784, in Rivière du Loup, Quebec, Canada, the son of John McLoughlin and Angélique Fraser. Since both of his parents were Catholic, he was baptized in the parish in the village of Mamouraska. However, after his father's death, he was raised by his mother's family, which was Protestant. He studied medicine in Scotland, and after completing his training he returned to Canada and practiced medicine among the members of the Northwest Fur Company. He soon tired of this and became a trader and later a partner in the company, eventually being put in charge of Fort William on Lake Superior.

John McLoughlin

The Hudson's Bay Company

When the Northwest Fur Company merged with the Hudson's Bay Company in 1821, McLoughlin was one of the negotiators. In 1824, as a chief factor of the Hudson's Bay Company, he was given direct supervision of the Columbia District, which consisted of the entire Columbia River valley and (after 1825) British Columbia. Besides being the representative of the Hudson's Bay Company in the region, he also had civil and criminal jurisdiction, since there was no civil government. He was an imposing figure, over six feet tall, with a herculean air about him, and a prematurely white, thick, and bushy head of hair that led the Native Americans to call him the "White Eagle." He had piercing blue eyes that could be kindly, cold, or flashing when he lost his temper, which happened easily if a slight was uttered against his person or family.

When he arrived, there was no major American presence in the Northwest, despite the 1818 treaty providing for joint occupation of the Pacific Northwest. McLoughlin's duty as company manager was to monopolize the fur trade as completely as possible and exploit it so that maximum annual returns could be realized for as long as possible. To this end, it was necessary for McLoughlin to make peace with the Native Americans and show them how to collect furs. Also, he was supposed to keep out rival traders and prevent agricultural settlement of the country. To satisfy his employers' demands and assuage his own conscience proved oftentimes to be a difficult task.

In 1825 he moved to present-day Vancouver, Washington, and made Fort Vancouver his headquarters for the next twenty-one years. The fort included a farm, gardens, orchards, dairies, a sawmill, and a flour mill. McLoughlin had at his disposal a small empire that grew to include some twenty forts and posts by 1839. He was an astute businessman, and by ruthlessly underselling and overbidding, controlling the Native Americans, and shipping out furs, flour, and lumber to various ports, McLoughlin realized profits of from $100,000 to $150,000 per year for the Hudson's Bay Company.

When the Americans began to arrive in the late 1830s and early 1840s McLoughlin was courteous to them, and, despite his Catholic background, he encouraged and gave aid to the Presbyterian and Methodist missionaries who came with them. He did likewise when the Catholic missionaries, Frs. Francis N. Blanchet and Modeste Demers, arrived in 1838. He was equally benevolent to settlers, in spite of Hudson's Bay Company rules against encouraging settlement, and many times he provided provisions and credit to help them survive their first winter. Believing the Columbia River would eventually be the boundary between British and American territories, he encouraged settlement south of the river. When it became apparent that the forty-ninth parallel would be the boundary, he quietly prepared to move company headquarters to Fort Victoria on Vancouver Island.

Last Years in Oregon

McLoughlin retired from the company in 1846, after the treaty drawing the boundary was concluded, and settled in Oregon City, Oregon, where he became an American citizen in 1849. McLoughlin's final years were not his happiest. He filed a land claim with the Oregon Provisional Government for land at the falls of the Willamette River, but, when Congress in 1850 passed the Donation Land Law, some of his enemies saw to it that an amendment was added limiting the right to file land claims to American citizens only. Since McLoughlin had been a British subject at the time he filed his claim it was not considered valid, and he spent the rest of his life fighting to regain his land. In 1862 the state of Oregon restored the land to his heirs for a nominal sum.

McLoughlin ruled the Native Americans with a firm yet just hand, which caused them to consider him a good chief. He was considerate of the beliefs of the various missionaries. Baptized a Catholic but raised by Protestant relatives, he practiced tolerance at Fort Vancouver, and even after he returned to the Catholic fold by making his profession of faith in 1842 he remained open-minded, going as far as to warn Dr. Marcus Whitman to be cautious in dealing with the Cayuse tribe prior to the Whitman Massacre. His generosity toward the American settlers may have influenced his resignation from the English-controlled Hudson's Bay Company. He married twice, had a son by his first wife and four more children by his second wife, Margaret Wadin McKay. In 1847 he was made a Knight of St. Gregory by the pope, one of the few Americans to receive such an honor. He died in Oregon City on September 3, 1857.

After his death, McLoughlin became known as "The Father of Oregon," and a statue of him was placed in the U.S. Capitol. His home is a national historic site in Oregon City, and he and his wife are buried in the park next to the house.

Clark, Malcolm, Jr. *Eden Seekers: The Settlement of Oregon 1818–1862.* Boston: Houghton Mifflin, 1981.

Fogdall, Alberta B. *Royal Family of the Columbia.* Fairfield, Wash.: Ye Galleon Press, 1978.

Montgomery, Richard G. *The White Headed Eagle.* New York: MacMillan, 1934.

JOSEPH A. SCHIWEK JR.

McMAHON, BRIEN (1903–53)

U.S. Senator. Brien McMahon was born on October 6, 1903, in Norwalk, Connecticut. After earning his B.A. (Fordham, 1924) and L.L.B. (Yale, 1927), McMahon practiced law in Norwalk until he was named to the Norwalk City Court in 1933. Later that year he began six years of public service, first as assistant to U.S. Attorney General Homer S. Cummings and then as assistant attorney general, criminal division, Department of Justice. Upon his return to private practice, he married Rosemary Turner in 1940. McMahon's return to private practice was short-lived, however, since he served as U.S. Senator from Connecticut from 1944 until his death in 1953.

Brien McMahon

McMahon was particularly interested in keeping civilian control of atomic energy, and in 1945 he became the chair of the special Committee on Atomic Energy. His efforts led to the establishment of the Atomic Energy Commission in 1946. From 1946 until 1949 he sat on the Joint Committee on Atomic Energy, serving as chair twice. McMahon also had an interest in foreign affairs and arms reductions, and was a civil rights champion. Connecticut Democrats put his name forward as a vice-presidential candidate in 1952, but a serious illness forced him to withdraw. He died soon after in Washington, D.C., on July 28, 1953.

In 1994 the United States Courthouse in Bridgeport, Connecticut, was designated the Brien McMahon Federal Building.

COLLEEN J. MATAN

McMASTER, JAMES ALPHONSUS (1820–86)

Journalist. James Alphonsus McMaster was born on April 1, 1820, in Duanesburg, New York, the son of the Reverend Gilbert McMaster, pastor of the Reformed Presbyterian Church of Duanesburg, and Jane Brown McMaster. He attended Union College, Schenectady, New York, but left after two years to study law at Columbia College, New York City. After practicing law for a time, he began studies at Union Theological Seminary, New York City. However, he was requested to leave after protesting the seminary's surveillance of professors and students in an effort to control "Romanizing influences."

At that time, McMaster became interested in the Catholic Church. In 1845 he converted and was accepted by the Redemptorist Order to study for the priesthood. He was sent with Isaac Thomas Hecker and Clarence Augustus Walworth to the Redemptorist college in Louvain, Belgium. On the way, they stopped at Littlemore, England, to visit John Henry Newman.

A year later, McMaster and the Redemptorists mutually agreed that he did not have a religious vocation. He returned to New York and began a career in journalism, writing for the *New York Tribune* and the *Freeman's Journal and Catholic Register,* the official newspaper of Bishop John Hughes, edited by James Roosevelt Bayley. In 1847 McMaster bought the bishop's interest in the newspaper and became its editor. In 1850 he married Gertrude Fetterman of Pennsylvania and they had four children: Alphonsus, who also became a journalist after trying a religious vocation, and three daughters who entered religious orders.

Under McMaster's direction, the *Freeman's Journal* became an authoritative voice of Catholicism in the United States. While he supported Hughes' stance on Catholic schools, McMaster never hesitated to spare the Church's highest dignitaries. His frankness and aggressiveness aroused controversy, in both civic and religious matters.

McMaster supported state rights and opposed abolition of slavery. When he criticized President Abraham Lincoln's appeal for troops after the attack on Fort Sumter, the paper was labeled treasonable and seditious, and mailing privileges were withheld by the U.S. Postmaster General. McMaster was imprisoned without an indictment at Fort Lafayette on August 24, 1861, and finally freed without a trial on April 19, 1862.

McMaster resumed publication of the *Freeman's Journal* without changing its editorial policy. He supported the temporal power of the pope but questioned the bishops' advocacy of papal infallibility. Beginning in 1870, after Vatican Council I, he used the newspaper to discuss the decentralization of Church authority, which would give the clergy an administrative voice, including the selection of bishops, a stance that antagonized members of the hierarchy.

McMaster also inaugurated the first American pilgrimage to Rome. Firm in his faith and aggressive in his religious beliefs, McMaster was once described by a Philadelphia prelate as "a Scotch Highlander with a touch of Calvinism not yet sponged out of him." As more diocesan newspapers were founded, the *Freeman's Journal* began to lose its influence. However, McMaster's editorials continued to demand attention up to the end. Not until his death on December 29, 1886, in Brooklyn, New York, was it learned that as penance he had worn a hair shirt.

See also FREEMAN'S JOURNAL AND CATHOLIC REGISTER; SLAVERY AND AMERICAN CATHOLICS.

Egan, M. F. "A Slight Appreciation of James Alphonsus McMaster." *Historical Records and Studies* 15 (1921) 7–18.

Kwitchen, M. A. *James Alphonsus McMaster: A Study in American Thought.* Washington, D.C.: The Catholic University of America Press, 1949.

McMaster Papers, Archives of the University of Notre Dame.

MARIANNA McLOUGHLIN

McNICHOLAS, JOHN T. (1877–1950)

Dominican friar, archbishop of Cincinnati. Timothy McNicholas (John was his name in religion) was born on December 15, 1877, in Kilitmagh, County Mayo, Ireland. His family came to the United States in 1881 and settled in Chester, Pennsylvania. McNicholas entered the Dominican Order at St. Rose's Priory in Springfield, Kentucky, in 1894 and made his simple profession of vows on October 10, 1895, followed by his solemn profession three years later. After taking his philosophical and theological studies at St. Joseph's Priory in Somerset, Ohio, McNicholas was ordained by Bishop Henry Moeller of Columbus on October 10, 1901. He would succeed Moeller as archbishop of Cincinnati twenty-four years later. After ordination McNicholas spent three years as a student at the

John T. McNicholas

Minerva University in Rome, where he received the lectorate in sacred theology in 1904. Returning to the United States he held various teaching and administrative positions at St. Joseph's, Somerset, and later at the new Dominican House of Studies in Washington, D.C.

In 1909 McNicholas was named the national director of the Holy Name Society and continued in this position while also serving as pastor of St. Catherine of Siena parish in New York City from 1913 until 1916. In 1916 he was recalled to Rome to serve as the English-speaking *socius* or counsellor at the order's headquarters. In such a position he renewed influential contacts and made new ones, which led to his appointment as the bishop of Duluth, Minnesota, on July 18, 1918, with episcopal consecration taking place on September 8 of that year. In Duluth he particularly devoted himself to the work of clerical education. In May 1925 McNicholas was named bishop of Indianapolis, although he never occupied that see because on July 8 he was appointed the fourth archbishop of Cincinnati.

McNicholas proved to be an active and energetic archbishop during his nearly twenty-five years in Cincinnati. Among other accomplishments he founded fifty new parishes, established a convert program and apostolate for African Americans, built up the educational facilities of the archdiocese, encouraged postgraduate studies among his priests, promoted lay retreats and the organization of the Holy Name Society, strongly supported the rights of labor, founded the Athenaeum of Ohio in Cincinnati, and, in 1935, opened the Institutum Divi Thomas as a graduate school of science.

On the national level McNicholas also proved to be an important figure. Along with Edward Mooney of Detroit and Samuel Stritch of Chicago, he dominated the affairs of the National Catholic Welfare Conference (NCWC) for many years. He served as episcopal chairman of the Department of Education from 1930 to 1935 and again from 1942 to 1945. He was chairman of the administrative board of the NCWC from 1945 to 1950. In addition to this work with the NCWC, McNicholas also served on numerous other committees: from 1933 to 1942 he was a member of the episcopal committee on motion pictures, which founded the National Legion of Decency; he was president general of the National Catholic Educational Association from 1946 to 1950; he was national chairman of the Catholic Students Mission Crusade; and he spent thirteen years as a member of the episcopal committee for the Confraternity of the Christian Doctrine.

McNicholas frequently served as a Catholic spokesman on the national level. During the depression he was a strong advocate for solving American farm problems through the application of Catholic principles. In 1938 he vigorously condemned the persecution of Jews in Germany and elsewhere and vigorously opposed the spread of Russian Communism in the postwar world. He had a strong influence on the annual statements issued by the American Hierarchy.

McNicholas died of a heart attack on April 22, 1950.

Avella, Steven M. "John T. McNicholas in the Age of Practical Thomism." *Records of the American Catholic Historical Society of Philadelphia* 97 (1986) 15–25.

Fogarty, Gerald P. *The Vatican and the American Hierarchy from 1870 to 1965*. Wilmington, Del.: Michael Glazier, 1985.

McNicholas, John T. *Mosaic of a Bishop*. Designed by Maurice E. Reardon. Paterson, N.J.: St. Anthony Guild Press, 1957.

THOMAS W. TIFFT

McQUAID, BERNARD JOHN JOSEPH
(1823–1909)

Bishop, educator. Bernard McQuaid was born in New York City on December 15, 1823, to Bernard and Mary Maguire McQuaid, from County Tyrone, Ireland. Bereft by 1832 of both parents, he was placed in the New York Roman Catholic Orphan Asylum. Mothered into manly virtues and a priestly vocation by its superior, Sr. Elizabeth Boyle, S.C. (1788–1861), he went on to Chambly College, Quebec, and St. Joseph's Seminary, Fordham, and was ordained a priest by Bishop John Hughes on January 16, 1848.

The New Jersey Years

Because of his "weak chest," Fr. McQuaid was assigned to a rural New Jersey parish, St. Vincent's, Madison. Vigorous care of his twenty-eight mission stations restored his health. Already a convert to Bishop Hughes' drive for

Bernard J. J. McQuaid

parochial schools, McQuaid opened New Jersey's first parish school at St. Vincent's and was its teacher for six months (1849).

In 1853 Pope Pius IX formed the Diocese of Newark out of all New Jersey, naming as its bishop Fr. James Roosevelt Bayley of New York. Bayley, able but timid, wisely chose for his aide Fr. McQuaid, who knew no timidity. McQuaid, as pastor of the cathedral, set up a St. Vincent de Paul Conference and built an ambitious center for young men. In 1854 he withstood a Know-Nothing riot. In 1861 he rallied Catholics to the Union cause, serving briefly as a Civil War chaplain in 1864. Bayley authorized, but McQuaid actually founded, Seton Hall College and Seminary (1856) and the Sisters of Charity of St. Elizabeth (1859). In 1866 he was named vicar general.

The First Bishop of Rochester

When Pius IX created the Diocese of Rochester, New York, on March 3, 1868, he picked Fr. McQuaid to head it. McQuaid was well qualified: a devout priest, voluntarily poor; a skilled preacher of sound doctrine; a creative and experienced financier and builder; a man born to command. Archbishop John McCloskey consecrated McQuaid in old St. Patrick's Cathedral, New York, on July 12. When installed on July 16, he told his new flock, "I come here without fear, knowing what is to be done." Nor would he ever leave Rochester for proffered promotions, eager as he was to perfect his small but "ideal" diocese.

As that diocese grew, he set up sixty-nine parishes, in which the liturgy was celebrated well, doctrine taught without fudging, solid devotion promoted, and good order maintained. He provided facilities for orphans, youth, the ailing, and the aged. He founded, to teach and nurse, the Rochester Sisters of St. Joseph (1868). He laid out a great, gardenlike cemetery, and planted a vineyard to provide pure altar wine. When disciplining was called for, whether of priests or laity, he was no respecter of persons.

Proud to be a native-born American, Bishop McQuaid fostered patriotism in his growing multinational flock, although he favored gradual rather than pressured Americanization. While opposed to priests' engagement in party politics, to the extent of never even voting himself, he served commendably for thirty-one years as an appointive member of the Park Commission of Rochester. For his time, he was relatively ecumenical, admired by many non-Catholic citizens, and on cordial terms with some non-Catholic clergymen.

As a bishop of the province of New York, he engineered the appointment of priests as state-paid chaplains in penal and welfare institutions. He was active in the Fourth Provincial Council of New York (1883) and the Third Plenary Council of Baltimore (1884). A junior bishop at the First Vatican Council (1869–70), he voted against the proposed definition of personal papal infallibility because it did not specify that a pope, before defining a doctrine, must consult with the bishops. Once the council had accepted the definition, however, he proclaimed his adherence on August 28, 1870.

In the great pastoral controversies that split the American hierarchy of his day, McQuaid sided strongly with the "conservatives" under Archbishop Michael A. Corrigan of New York, against the "liberals" under Archbishop John Ireland of St. Paul. At one point he publicly denounced the latter for harmful intervention in New York state politics. Fortunately, he and Ireland were personally reconciled in 1905.

McQuaid the Educator

Broadly cultured, Bishop McQuaid, a national publicist for parochial schools, delighted most in his own twoscore parish schools, which, for quality control, he put under the New York State Board of Regents. His innovative seminaries (St. Andrew's Preparatory, 1870–1967, and St. Bernard's, 1893–1981) furnished the diocese with an ample, loyal, "home-grown" presbyterium. Fascinated, as a natural pedagogue, by inquiring young minds, he backed the growing trend to college-level education, among his laity as well as his nuns. Pastoral concern made him hesitate to permit attendance at non-Catholic colleges, especially to young laywomen, but in his last years he almost succeeded in founding a Catholic "college" affiliated with Cornell University. While scarcely a feminist, he piloted the unusual editorial career of Katherine E. Conway. To her he prophesied with approval that American law would soon grant woman suffrage, and that even the nuns would vote.

Bernard McQuaid, in sum, won a secure place in American Catholic history. He was a progressive conservative who exercised a constructive, moderating influence in our turbulent immigrant Church. He died January 18, 1909.

See also AMERICANISM; NEW YORK, CATHOLIC CHURCH IN; VATICAN COUNCIL I, AMERICAN PARTICIPATION IN.

Akin, William E. "The War of the Bishops: Catholic Controversy on the School Question in New York State in 1894." *New-York Historical Society Quarterly* 50 (January 1966) 41–61.

Browne, Henry J. "The Letters of Bishop McQuaid from the Vatican Council." *Catholic Historical Review* 41 (1956) 408–41.

DAB 12:163–4.

DARB 279–80.

Janus, Glen. "Bishop Bernard McQuaid: On 'True' and 'False' Americanism." *U.S. Catholic Historian* 11 (3) (Summer 1993) 53–76.

McNamara, Robert F. *The Diocese of Rochester, 1868–1969.* Rochester, N.Y.: Diocese of Rochester, 1968.

NCAB 12:141–3.

NCE 9:44–5.

Zwierlein, Frederick James. *Letters of Archbishop Corrigan to Bishop McQuaid and Allied Documents.* Rochester, N.Y.: Art Print Shop, 1946.

_____. *The Life and Letters of Bishop McQuaid.* 3 vols. Rochester, N.Y.: Art Print Shop, 1925–27.

ROBERT F. McNAMARA

McSORLEY, JOSEPH (1874–1963)

Religious superior, retreat master, and author. McSorley was born in Brooklyn, New York, on December 9, 1874, and was educated at St. John's Preparatory School and College, receiving a bachelor of arts degree at age sixteen. He entered the Paulist community at St. Thomas College (adjacent to The Catholic University of America) in 1891. There he was awarded the S.T.B. (1895) and the S.T.L. (1897). He was ordained through special dispensation at age twenty-two by Bishop (later Cardinal Archbishop) John Farley of New York in October 1897. Assigned for two years as curate at the Paulist motherhouse, St. Paul the Apostle in New York City, he returned to St. Thomas as professor of dogmatic theology (1899–1907) and master of novices (1901–07), leaving at the height of the Modernism crisis.

McSorley returned to St. Paul's in New York where he distinguished himself in his work with Italian immigrants. Returning from service as an Army chaplain in World War I, he became pastor at St. Paul's before being elected superior general of the Paulists in 1924. Known to be a leader who restored community rigorism, he served as general until 1929. During his administration the Paulists established radio station WLWL, a pioneering effort in Catholic broadcasting, started St. Peter's College in Baltimore,

Joseph McSorley

and founded the novitiate at Oak Ridge, New Jersey. After a short assignment at St. Peter's in Toronto, he returned to St. Paul's in 1932 where he remained until his death on July 3, serving in administrative capacities as assistant to the superiors general and as contributing editor to the Paulist monthly, the *Catholic World.*

McSorley was an accomplished author, completing twelve books, twenty-six pamphlets, forty four-page leaflets, as well as entries for *The Catholic Encyclopedia* (1963), *Encyclopedia Britannica,* plus essays for learned and popular periodicals. Among his books, *A Primer of Prayer* (1934), *An Outline History of the Church by Centuries* (1943), and *Father Hecker and His Friends* (1952) have enjoyed continued popularity and several editions.

See also PAULISTS (C.S.P.).

RICHARD GRIBBLE, C.S.C.

MEADOWCROFT, MARY ELLEN (1893–1966)

Dominican sister. Mary Ellen Meadowcroft was born on April 16, 1893, in Mahony City, Pennsylvania. After high school she became a private secretary, but a career in business was not her goal. At twenty-five she entered the Dominican Monastery at Catonsville, Maryland.

In 1939 the great work of her life began: she founded the first interracial cloister. In Mother Mary Dominic's view, this was simply the right thing to do. Civil rights, protest marches, and sit-ins had not yet been heard of. At the invitation of Bishop Thomas J. Toolen of Mobile, Alabama, and with the assistance of Fr. Harold Purcell, founder of the City of St. Jude, the Dominican Monastery of St.

Jude was established in rural Marbury on August 17, 1944. With very limited funds Mother Mary Dominic built a permanent monastery in 1953. The building was simple, monastic, well suited to the contemplative life.

Mother Dominic's last years held much physical misery. It was only in death that the sisters could see the marks pain had drawn line by line on her face. She died on July 20, 1966.

See also DOMINICANS (O.P.).

MARY AIMEE, O.P.

MEAGHER, JOSEPHINE (1840–1925)

Religious superior and foundress. Josephine Meagher, born in Ireland in 1840, entered the Dominican Sisters in Kentucky in 1856. In 1873 she was appointed the first superior of a pioneer band of sisters sent to establish a new Dominican foundation in Illinois. In 1893 the congregation moved its motherhouse from Jacksonville to Springfield, Illinois, becoming known as the Springfield Dominicans, with Mother Josephine the center of its team of founding sisters.

In 1874 some thirty thousand people gathered in Springfield for the dedication of the newly completed monument to President Lincoln. President Ulysses S. Grant had requested that the statue of Lincoln that crowned the monument be unveiled by two sisters as a public expression of gratitude to all the "Nuns of the Battlefield" who had served during the Civil War. Learning the night before the ceremony that his request could not be met, since the only sisters in Springfield were cloistered Ursulines, the president and General Sherman were nonplused. Sherman, remembering the devotion of the Kentucky Dominicans during the war, exclaimed that he knew they would not disappoint him if only they were near. On hearing this, the pastor from Jacksonville declared that he had Kentucky Dominicans at his school. "Sherman," shouted the president, "order a special train, while I wire the Bishop." Thus it was that on October 15, 1874, Sr. Josephine Meagher and Sr. Rachel Conway unveiled the bronze image of the slain President.

When Sr. Josephine died in 1925, a flood of tributes testified to the extraordinary respect accorded her religious and educational leadership. Her unique role in Illinois history was acknowledged by the military salute fired as her coffin was lowered. The Illinois Historical Society enrolled her among the noted pioneer women of Illinois, and a wax figurine of her is preserved at the Illinois State Museum.

Graham, James M. *Dominicans in Illinois: A History of Fifty Years, 1873–1923.* Springfield, Ill.: Edward F. Harman, Co., 1923.

Winterbauer, Thomas Aquinas. *Lest We Forget: The First Hundred Years of the Dominican Sisters, Springfield, Illinois.* Chicago: Adams Press, 1973.

LINDA TONELLATO, O.P.

MEAGHER, THOMAS FRANCIS (1823–67)

Irish patriot, American lawyer, editor, general. Thomas Francis Meagher was born in Waterford, Ireland, the son of Thomas Meagher, a wealthy merchant and former member of Parliament; he lost his mother in infancy. His father sent him to the Jesuit College at Clongowes Wood, Kildare (1833–39), and then to Stonyhurst College in Lancashire (1839–43). While a student there Meagher did not come to love England, but rather the reverse. He returned to Ireland in 1845 and joined Young Ireland, a revolutionary group agitating for Irish independence. Daniel O'Connell, "the Liberator," gave the talented young orator a chance to speak at the gigantic national meeting in Kilkenny in 1846, but Meagher soon moved beyond O'Connell's parliamentary reforms. He visited France in 1848, soon after the revolution there, and returned home with an Irish tricolor (orange, white, and green), which he displayed in Dublin during a speech that the British considered seditious. He was arrested in June 1848, tried in October, and received the death sentence, which was commuted to exile to Tasmania in July 1849.

He married in 1851, then escaped from Tasmania in January 1852, making his way to the United States in May of that year. He became an American citizen and was admitted to the bar (1855). As an editor *(Irish News)* and orator, he became a leader of the sizeable Irish community in New York City. At the death of his wife in 1855, he remarried.

In 1861 he abandoned his law practice and organized a regiment of volunteers for the Union. He organized a second regiment in 1862, the Irish Brigade, which he commanded. He fought in the Peninsula Campaign, Second Bull Run, Antietam, Fredericksburg, and Chancellorsville—an astounding record of campaigning. But by 1863 his brigade had lost so many men that it had to be disbanded. Meagher resigned his commission and returned to a hero's welcome in New York. The army soon called him out of retirement; he received a military governorship, and he accompanied Sherman to Savannah. After the war President Andrew Johnson appointed him territorial secretary and temporary governor of the Montana Territory. On July 1, 1867, he fell from the deck of a Missouri River steamer near Fort Benton and drowned; he was forty-four years old. He had lived an extraordinarily full life, fulfilling occupations (orator, revolutionary, convict, escapee, editor, attorney, and military hero) well beyond the conventional.

Athearn, Robert G. *Thomas Francis Meagher: An Irish Revolutionary in America.* Boulder: University of Colorado Press, 1949.

DAB 6:481–2.
NCE 9:525–6.
Sifakis, Stewart. *Who Was Who in the Civil War.* New York: Facts on File, 1988.

JOSEPH F. KELLY

MEANY, WILLIAM GEORGE (1894–1980)

Labor leader. William Meany was born in New York City on August 16, 1894, to Michael Joseph Meany, a plumber, and Anne Cullen. He was the second of eight children. Meany was heavily influenced by the principles and the institutions fostered in his home and neighborhood—integrity, Irish ethnicity, politics, unions, and the Roman Catholic Church. After his family moved to the Bronx, Meany graduated from public elementary school, then dropped out of high school at age fourteen. He became an apprentice plumber in 1910, studied at night trade school at his father's insistence, and became a journeyman plumber in 1915, joining the United Association of Plumbers and Steam Fitters of the United States and Canada (UAPSF) in 1917. After Meany's father died in 1916 and his older brother John enlisted in the Army in 1917, Meany became the family's sole provider. Work as a journeyman plumber was unsteady and highly competitive. Meany supplemented his income by playing catcher on a semiprofessional baseball team until 1918.

Labor Union Official

On November 26, 1919, he married Eugenia A. McMahon, a clothing worker and member of the International Ladies' Garment Workers' Union; they had three children. Their sixty-year marriage was unusually close. That same year Meany began his career as a labor organizer. He ran for and was elected to the executive board of UAPSF New York City Local 463 in 1919. He was elected business agent for Local 463 in 1922, and also served as a delegate to the New York City Central Trades and Labor Council. During the 1920s, Meany's interest in the labor movement blossomed. He was profoundly influenced by Samuel Gompers' vision of labor. In 1932, at the age of thirty-eight, he was elected one of thirteen vice presidents of the New York State Federation of Labor, and from 1934 to 1939 he served as the federation's president.

Meany was shrewd, articulate, and adept at organizing, bargaining, and understanding the complex legal concepts involved in organized labor. As the New York Federation of Labor's president, Meany lobbied the state legislature effectively, testified before committees, made speeches, promoted membership, and, despite the depression, he established a sound financial base for the federation. Meany skillfully wielded federation promises for campaign funding and endorsements on both the national and state level, securing federal work relief programs, workers' compensation, unemployment insurance, and health and safety laws. He also served on the New York State Industrial Council and on the State Advisory Council on Unemployment Insurance.

In 1939 he was unanimously elected as secretary-treasurer of the American Federation of Labor (AFL) to replace eighty-year-old Frank Morrison. Meany was frustrated by the conservatism of the AFL's aging and ill president, William Green. But Green relied heavily on him, and Meany assumed greater decision-making responsibilities in the federation. In 1941 Meany was appointed by President Franklin Roosevelt to the National Defense Mediation Board and served as the AFL's permanent representative on the National War Labor Board. Meany also served as AFL fraternal delegate to the British Trades Union Congress in 1945, was a member of the executive board of the International Confederation of Free Trade Unions in 1951, and was appointed to the National Advisory Board on Mobilization Policy and the Contract Compliance Committee in 1952. After Green's death in November 1952, Meany served as acting president of the AFL until he was elected and affirmed in 1953.

President of the AFL-CIO

Meany was committed to merging the AFL with the Congress of Industrial Organizations (CIO). After the merger in 1955, he was elected as the new federation's first president, a post he held until his retirement in 1979. Meany worked to remove corrupt affiliates—chiefly the Teamsters and the International Longshoremen's Association—from the federation. He also served as a delegate to the United Nations in 1957 and 1959.

Meany led the AFL into a new direction after the passage of the antilabor Taft-Hartley Act by creating Labor's League for Political Education (LLPE) in 1947. As the political arm of organized labor, the LLPE worked to unseat legislators who voted for Taft-Hartley and, in 1948, Meany became its first director. After the merger of the AFL and the CIO, Meany maintained labor's involvement in partisan politics by creating a permanent body to influence political candidates, the Committee on Political Education (CPE). The CPE helped elect liberals to Congress and John Kennedy, Lyndon Johnson, and Jimmy Carter to the presidency.

In the 1960s, Meany exerted considerable political influence upon Democratic leaders, but seemed unwilling to compromise his principles. Though the AFL-CIO was generally supportive of civil rights legislation, Meany disapproved of affirmative action. He was also opposed to environmental legislation and wage-control policies. In 1972, Meany broke with the Democrats due to their affiliation with groups and positions he considered destructive of traditional values, and the AFL-CIO refused to endorse the Democratic candidate, George McGovern.

Meany was outspokenly anticommunist. In 1945 he led an AFL boycott of the World Federation of Trade Unions (WFTU) because it included trade unions from the Soviet Union. He also helped sponsor the International Confederation of Free Trade Unions as a rival of the WFTU. Meany was a vocal supporter of American intervention in Korea and the Vietnam War, and he opposed the Nixon-Kissinger policy of détente.

Forced by severe arthritis to resign in November 1979, Meany turned over leadership to his chosen successor, Lane Kirkland. He concluded his retirement speech with the prayer: "To my God go my prayers—prayers of thanks for granting me more than one man's share of happiness and rewards, and prayers for His continued blessing on this nation and on this movement and on each of you." Meany died in Washington, D.C., on January 10, 1980.

See also LABOR MOVEMENT AND AMERICAN CATHOLICS, THE.

Robinson, Archie. *George Meany and His Times: A Biography.* New York: Simon and Schuster, 1981.
Zieger, Robert H. "George Meany: Labor's Organization Man." *Labor Leaders in America,* eds. Melvin Dubofsky and Warren Van Tine. Urbana: University of Illinois Press, 1986.

DONALD STELLUTO

MEDEIROS, HUMBERTO CARDINAL (1915–83)

Cardinal archbishop of Boston. Humberto Sousa Medeiros was born on October 6, 1915, in Arrifes, São Miguel (Angra), Azores, and died in Boston, Massachusetts, on September 17, 1983. Coming to this country during the Great Depression, he labored in the Sagamore Mills of

Humberto Cardinal Medeiros

Fall River. After learning English, this Portuguese immigrant was able to move ahead by graduating as an honor student from B.M.C. Durfee High School (1937) and by becoming an American citizen (1940). Then, having undertaken studies at The Catholic University of America, where he earned a master's (1942) and a licentiate degree (1946), he was ordained a priest on June 15, 1946.

As a young priest, Medeiros continued his graduate studies while serving different parishes in his home diocese at Somerset (St. John of God), Fall River (St. Michael's, Our Lady of Health, and Holy Name), and New Bedford (Mount Carmel). His theological research in Washington and Rome between 1949 and 1950 led to his doctorate from The Catholic University of America in 1952. Meanwhile, having served as assistant and vice chancellor, Fr. Medeiros was selected by Bishop James L. Connolly as the chancellor of the Diocese of Fall River in 1953. Appointed a monsignor in 1958 and pastor of St. Michael's Church in 1960, he continued as chancellor until he was named bishop of Brownsville, Texas, on April 14, 1966, by Pope Paul VI.

After he was ordained bishop, on June 9, 1966, in the Cathedral of the Assumption in Fall River, Medeiros forged an exceptional record as one of the nation's upcoming bishops by leading a diocese of a quarter of a million Catholics, largely Mexican-American migrant workers. His reputation as a champion of the poor led Pope Paul VI to name him, on September 8, 1970, archbishop of Boston, an archdiocese that was much larger and far more complex than the Diocese of Brownsville.

Archbishop of Boston

In Boston, Medeiros faced a number of challenges. Foremost among them was an overwhelming debt of millions of dollars left by his popular predecessor, Richard Cardinal Cushing, who died shortly after Medeiros' installation on October 7, 1970. However, equally serious, in the aftermath of the cultural revolution of the 1960s, was a number of pastoral issues. In addition to the growth in defections from the clergy, Archbishop Medeiros had to deal with the unique problem of priests in politics before he was elevated, on March 5, 1973, to the Sacred College of Cardinals.

But far more serious was the challenge to the Church's teaching authority on such issues as abortion, contraception, homosexuality, and racism. The latter became a particularly disturbing problem that attracted national attention due to the radical opposition by Catholics of South Boston to the integration of the city's high schools through the busing ordered by the federal court in *Morgan v. Hennigan* on June 21, 1974. The Cardinal publicly apologized to those Catholics on May 8, 1976, for the frustration that he had expressed in an interview in the previous Sunday's *Herald Advertiser* about their resistance to the federal law.

However, Medeiros' own stand in upholding the law was completely consistent with what he had set forth earlier (August 15, 1972) in his pastoral letter, "Man's Cities and God's Poor."

Equally frustrating to Cardinal Medeiros was his failure to win a majority to his side when, a few days prior to a state primary election, he had urged his flock, through the archdiocesan weekly, the *Pilot* (September 12, 1980), to vote against candidates who favored public funds for abortion. Though the victory of the latter might indicate just how ineffective the voice of Boston's Cardinal had become in politics compared to the influence of his immediate predecessors, Medeiros did make a difference in an archdiocese that numbered 1,914,350 Catholics, 2,433 priests, and 401 parishes when he took office, compared to 1,936,146 of the faithful with 2,343 priests and 408 parishes at the end of his episcopacy. Actually, he effectively implemented a new governmental structure that gave a greater role to his auxiliary bishops for the three individual regions into which he originally divided the archdiocese. At the same time, he brought the Catholic Church closer to the laity by authorizing eucharistic ministers in all parishes. And, very significantly, Medeiros almost wiped out the vast financial debt that he had inherited on coming to Boston as its archbishop.

Though he was the first archbishop of Boston to participate in the election of two popes (John Paul I and John Paul II) and to welcome a pope to Boston (October 1, 1979), Cardinal Medeiros reflected a childlike simplicity that eventually impressed even his critics. Known for his fluency in languages (French, German, Italian, and Spanish, in addition to English and Portuguese), Medeiros exhibited a genuine piety, once revealing to the press that he would pray in these same tongues to empathize with those who had been raised in those languages. Though his gentle handling of serious problems was often interpreted as weakness, the Cardinal could exhibit firmness. When, for example, wealthy parishioners in St. Mary's in Scituate opposed the use of church land for housing for the poor in 1978, he declared: "I don't have two sets of rules, one for the wealthy, one for the poor."

Throughout his priestly life, Humberto Medeiros had sought to place himself at the service of the People of God in accord with his episcopal motto (*"Adveniat Regnum Tuum"*). He died the day after he had undergone a triple bypass open-heart surgery near the end of his thirteenth year as Boston's archbishop. His grave, in St. Patrick's Cemetery, Fall River, at the site where his parents, Antonio Sousa and Maria de Jesus Sousa Massa (Flor) Medeiros, are also buried, underscores the humility which characterized his saintly life.

See also MASSACHUSETTS, CATHOLIC CHURCH IN.

See the archives of the Archdiocese of Boston as well as those of the Diocese of Brownsville and the Diocese of Fall River. See also the Boston *Pilot,* October 1970 to September 1983.

Ellis, John Tracy. *Catholic Bishops: A Memoir.* Wilmington, Del.: Michael Glazier, 1983.

Lescault, Michael W. "In Season and Out of Season: The Boston Years of Humberto Cardinal Medeiros, 1970–1983." Ph.D. dissertation, Providence College, 1992.

Lukas, J. Anthony. *Common Ground: A Turbulent Decade in the Lives of Three American Families.* New York: Random House, 1985.

Patkus, Ronald D., compiler. *The Archdiocese of Boston: A Pictorial History.* Boston: Quinlan Press, 1989.

VINCENT A. LAPOMARDA, S.J.

MEEHAN, THOMAS (1854–1942)

Journalist, historian. Thomas Francis Meehan was born in Brooklyn, New York, on September 19, 1854, the eldest of eleven children of Patrick and Mary Jane Butler Meehan. Both parents were Irish immigrants, and his father was editor and owner of the *Irish American* from 1857 to 1906. Young Meehan was educated at a private elementary school, Xavier High School, and St. Francis

Thomas F. Meehan

Xavier College, where he received a bachelor of arts degree in 1873 and a master of arts degree in 1874.

Meehan began his career in journalism upon graduation from college, when his father appointed him managing editor of the *Irish American,* a post he retained until 1904. He also acted as the New York correspondent for several newspapers, including the Baltimore *Sun.* He served briefly on the editorial board of the New York *Herald* and was a contributor to the New York *Sun,* New York *Star,* Brooklyn *Eagle,* and Brooklyn *Citizen.*

Although Meehan had no formal training in history, he was an avid student of American Catholic history and wrote widely on the subject. He served as an assistant editor for the first five volumes of *The Catholic Encyclopedia* and wrote over one hundred articles for the encyclopedia, probably more than any other contributor. He was a member of the editorial staff of *America* from the first issue of the magazine on April 17, 1909, until his death in 1942. He served briefly (1919–20) as president of the Catholic Writers' Guild and was elected to the executive board of the American Catholic Historical Association in 1928. He was closely associated with the United States Catholic Historical Society from 1898 until his death, acting as assistant editor of publications (1905–16), editor of publications (1916–42), and president of the society (1939–42). As editor of publications, he was responsible for most of the USCHS' thirty-two volumes of *Historical Records and Studies* and for the sixteen volumes in the monograph series.

Meehan wrote only one book, *Thomas Maurice Mulry* (New York, 1917), but he was an editor and contributor to the five-volume *Catholic Builders of the Nation* (Boston, 1923), wrote over three dozen articles for the *Historical Records and Studies,* and contributed to the *Catholic Historical Review, North American Review, Catholic World, Commonweal,* and the *Encyclopedia Britannica.* In 1939 his friend Msgr. Peter Guilday referred to Meehan as one "who has not only given to American historical scholarship a treasury of data on Catholic life in this country, but has also been the inspiration of many students during the past two generations."

In 1881 Meehan married Molly O'Rourke; they had five children. A self-effacing man who shunned the limelight, he did like to boast that he knew every archbishop of New York from John Hughes to Francis J. Spellman. He died in New York City on July 7, 1942.

Farrelly, M. Natalena. *Thomas Francis Meehan (1854–1942): A Memoir.* New York: United States Catholic Historical Society, 1944.

Talbot, Francis. "A Noble Catholic Layman Passes from Our Midst." *America* 67 (July 18, 1942) 398–9.

THOMAS J. SHELLEY

MÉGRET, ANTOINE (1797–1853)

Antoine Désiré Mégret was born in the Diocese of Coutances, France, on May 23, 1797. He was ordained on September 22, 1822. While in France Fr. Mégret became associated with Félicité de Lamennais and wrote articles for his newspaper, *L'Avenir.* When the Ultramontanist movement and the newspaper were condemned by the pope, Fr. Mégret withdrew and decided to go to the mission country of Louisiana. It is unknown exactly when Mégret arrived in New Orleans, but it was at the time that Bishop Antoine Blanc was engaged in controversy with the church wardens over the governance of St. Louis Cathedral. In the rural districts of Louisiana, church wardens mimicked their city counterparts, contesting the appointment of pastors without consent of the wardens and raising issues designed to subject pastors to the will of the wardens.

In Vermilionville (now Lafayette, Louisiana), the wardens had been engaged in bitter controversy with several pastors over a period of years. In 1842 Bishop Blanc sent Mégret to Vermilionville to attempt to end the wrangling, but the outspoken Mégret only enflamed the arrogance of the wardens and became the victim of their abuse, both verbal and physical. At that point Mégret stopped celebrating Mass in the church controlled by the wardens, built a new church in Vermilionville, and turned his attention to the various mission chapels of the parish.

After failing to buy some land at Perry's Bridge, about twenty miles south of Vermilionville, Mégret succeeded, in 1845, in acquiring forty acres about three miles to the north. On this land he established the chapel of St. Mary Magdalene. The land surrounding the chapel was laid out in town lots and sold, thus giving birth to the town named for the Abbé—Abbeville. Mégret's time was now divided between his flocks in Vermilionville and at Abbeville. When a long and sometimes bitter struggle between the townspeople of Abbeville and Perry's Bridge began concerning the location of the courthouse, Mégret took a leadership role on behalf of the residents of Abbeville, offering to donate the land on which the courthouse was built. He also offered to build the courthouse at his expense. The issue was not resolved until 1854 when Governor Paul Hébert established Abbeville as the permanent seat of justice.

Fr. Mégret would not savor the fruits of his victory. He died on December 6, 1853, a victim of the yellow fever epidemic.

GLENN R. CONRAD

MEN, RELIGIOUS ORDERS AND CONGREGATIONS OF

(Sources: *Official Catholic Directory;* Catholic Almanac survey.)

Africa, Missionaries of (M. Afr.): Founded 1868 at Algiers by Cardinal Charles M. Lavigerie; known as White Fathers until 1984. Generalate, Rome, Italy; U.S. headquarters, 1624 21st St. N.W., Washington, DC 20009. Missionary work in Africa.

African Missions, Society of, S.M.A.: Founded 1856, at Lyons, France, by Bishop Melchior de Marion Brésillac. Generalate, Rome, Italy; American province (1941), 23 Bliss Ave., Tenafly, NJ 07670. Missionary work.

Alexian Brothers, C.F.A.: Founded 14th century in western Germany and Belgium during the Black Plague. Motherhouse, Aachen, Germany; generalate, Signal Mountain, TN 37377. Hospital and general health work.

Assumptionists (Augustinians of the Assumption), A.A.: Founded 1845, at Nimes, France, by Rev. Emmanuel d'Alzon; in U.S., 1946. General house, Rome, Italy; U.S. province, 330 Market St., Brighton, MA 02135. Educational, parochial, ecumenical, retreat, foreign mission work.

Atonement, Franciscan Friars of the, S.A.: Founded as an Anglican Franciscan community in 1898 at Garrison, N.Y., by Rev. Paul Wattson. Community corporately received into the Catholic Church in 1909. Generalate, St. James Friary, P.O. Box 5, Graymoor, Garrison NY 10524. Ecumenical, mission, retreat and charitable works.

Augustinian Recollects, O.A.R.: Founded 1588: in U.S., 1944. General motherhouse, Rome, Italy. Missionary, parochial, education work.

St. Augustine Province (1944), 29 Ridgeway Ave., W. Orange, NJ 07052.

St. Nicholas Province: U.S. Delegates, 2800 Schurz Ave., Bronx, NY 10465 (New York); P.O. Box 310, Mesilla, NM 88044 (South).

Augustinians (Order of St. Augustine), O.S.A.: Established canonically in 1256 by Pope Alexander IV; in U.S., 1796. General motherhouse, Rome, Italy.

St. Thomas of Villanova Province (1796), P.O. Box 338, Villanova, PA 19085.

Our Mother of Good Counsel Province (1941), Tolentine Center, 20300 Governors Hwy., Olympia Fields, IL 60461.

St. Augustine Province (1969), 1605 28th St., San Diego, CA 92102.

Good Counsel Vice-Province, St. Augustine Preparatory School, Richland, NJ 08350.

U.S. Address of King City, Ont., Canada, Province: 3103 Arlington Ave., Bronx, NY 10463.

U.S. Vicariate of Castile, Spain, Province (1963), Vicar, 3648 61st St., Port Arthur, TX 77642.

Barnabites (Clerics Regular of St. Paul), C.R.S.P.: Founded 1530, in Milan, Italy, by St. Anthony M. Zaccaria; approved 1533; in U.S., 1952. Historical motherhouse, Church of St. Barnabas (Milan). Generalate, Rome, Italy; North American province, 1023 Swann Rd., Youngstown, NY 14174. Parochial, educational, mission work.

Basil the Great, Order of St. (Basilian Order of St. Josaphat), O.S.B.M.: General motherhouse, Rome, Italy; U.S. province, 31-12 30th St., Long Island City, NY 11106. Parochial work among Byzantine Ukrainian Rite Catholics.

Basilian Fathers (Congregation of the Priests of St. Basil), C.S.B.: Founded 1822, at Annonay, France. General motherhouse, Toronto, Ont., Canada. U.S. addresses: 445 King's Hwy., Rochester, NY 14617 (East); 106 Fifth

St., Sugar Land, TX 77478 (West). Educational, parochial work.

Basilian Salvatorian Fathers, B.S.O.: Founded 1684, at Saida, Lebanon, by Eftimios Saifi; in U.S., 1953. General motherhouse, Saida, Lebanon; American headquarters, 30 East St., Methuen, MA 01844. Educational, parochial work among Eastern Rite peoples.

Benedictine Monks (Order of St. Benedict), O.S.B.: Founded 529, in Italy, by St. Benedict of Nursia; in U.S., 1846.

• American Cassinese Congregation (1855). Pres., Rt. Rev. Melvin J. Valvano, O.S.B., Newark Abbey, 528 Dr. Martin Luther King Blvd., Newark, NJ 07102. Abbeys and Priories belonging to the congregation:

St. Vincent Archabbey, 300 Fraser Purchase Rd., Latrobe, PA 15650; St. John's Abbey, P.O. Box 2015, Collegeville, MN 56321; St. Benedict's Abbey, Atchison, KS 66002; St. Mary's Abbey, Delbarton, Morristown, NJ 07960; Newark Abbey, 528 Dr. Martin Luther King, Jr., Blvd., Newark, NJ 07102; Belmont Abbey, 100 Belmont - Mt. Holly Rd., Belmont, NC 28012; St. Bernard Abbey, Cullman, AL 35055; St. Procopius Abbey, 5601 College Rd., Lisle, IL 60532; St. Gregory's Abbey, Shawnee, OK 74801; St. Leo Abbey, St. Leo, FL 33574; Assumption Abbey, P.O. Box A, Richardton, ND 58652;

St. Bede Abbey, Peru, IL 61354; St. Martin's Abbey, 5300 Pacific Ave. S.E., Lacey, WA 98503; Holy Cross Abbey, P.O. Box 1510, Canon City, CO 81215; St. Anselm's Abbey, 100 St. Anselm Dr., Manchester, NH 03102; St. Andrew Abbey, 10510 Buckeye Rd., Cleveland, OH 44104; Holy Trinity Priory, P.O. Box 990, Butler, PA 16003; St. Maur Priory, 4615 N. Michigan Rd., Indianapolis, IN 46208; Benedictine Priory, 6502 Seawright Dr., Savannah, GA 31406; Woodside Priory, 302 Portola Rd., Portola Valley, CA 94028; Mary Mother of the Church Abbey, 12617 River Rd., Richmond, VA 23233; Abadia de San Antonio Abad, P.O. Box 729, Humacao, PR 00661; Benedictine Monastery of Hawaii, P.O. Box 490, Waialua, Hawaii 96791.

• Swiss-American Congregation (1870). Abbeys and Priory belonging to the congregation:

St. Meinrad Archabbey, St. Meinrad, IN 47577; Conception Abbey, Conception, MO 64433; Mt. Michael Abbey, 22520 Mt. Michael Rd., Elkhorn, NE 68022; Subiaco Abbey, Subiaco, AR 72865; St. Joseph's Abbey, St. Benedict, LA 70457; Mt. Angel Abbey, St. Benedict, OR 97373; Marmion Abbey, Butterfield Rd., Aurora, IL 60504;

St. Benedict's Abbey, Benet Lake, WI 53102; Glastonbury Abbey, 16 Hull St., Hingham, MA 02043; Blue Cloud Abbey, Marvin, SD 57251; Corpus Christi Abbey, HCR2, Box 6300, Sandia, TX 78383; Prince of Peace Abbey, 650 Benet Hill Rd., Oceanside, CA 92054; St. Benedict Abbey, 252 Still River Rd., P.O. Box 67, Still River (Harvard), MA 01467.

• Congregation of St. Ottilien for Foreign Missions: St. Paul's Abbey, Newton, NJ 07860; Christ the King Priory, Schuyler, NE 68661.

• Congregation of the Annunciation, St. Andrew Abbey, Valyermo, CA 93563.

• English Benedictine Congregation: St. Anselm's Abbey, 4501 S. Dakota Ave. N.E., Washington, DC 20017; Abbey of St. Gregory, Cory's Lane, Portsmouth, RI 02871; Abbey of St. Mary and St. Louis, 500 S. Mason Rd., St. Louis, MO 63141.

• Houses not in Congregations: Mount Saviour Monastery, Pine City, NY 14871; Conventual Priory of St. Gabriel the Archangel, Weston, VT 05161.

Benedictines, Camaldolese Congregation, O.S.B. Cam.: Founded 1012, at Camaldoli, near Arezzo, Italy, by St. Romuald; in U.S. 1958. General motherhouse, Arezzo, Italy; U.S. foundation, New Camaldoli Hermitage, Big Sur, CA 93920.

Benedictines, Olivetan, O.S.B.: General motherhouse, Siena, Italy. U.S. monasteries, Our Lady of Guadalupe Abbey, Pecos, NM 87552; Holy Trinity Monastery, P.O. Box 298, St. David, AZ 85630; Monastery of the Risen Christ, P.O. Box 3931, San Luis Obispo, CA 93403.

Benedictines, Subiaco Congregation, O.S.B.: Independent priory, 1983. Monastery of Christ in the Desert, Abiquiu, NM 87510; St. Mary's Monastery, P.O. Box 345, Petersham, MA 01366.

Benedictines, Sylvestrine, O.S.B.: Founded 1231, in Italy by Sylvester Gozzolini. General motherhouse, Rome, Italy; U.S. foundations; 17320 Rosemont Rd., Detroit, MI 48219; 2711 E. Drahner Rd., Oxford, MI 48051; 1697 State Highway 3, Clifton, NJ 07012.

Blessed Sacrament, Congregation of the, S.S.S.: Founded 1856, at Paris, France, by St. Pierre Julien Eymard; in U.S., 1900. General motherhouse, Rome, Italy; U.S. province, 5384 Wilson Mills Rd., Cleveland, OH 44143. Eucharistic apostolate.

Brigittine Monks (Order of the Most Holy Savior), O.Ss.S.: Monastery of Our Lady of Consolation, 23300 Walker Lane, Amity, OR 97101.

Camaldolese Hermits of the Congregation of Monte Corona, Er. Cam.: Founded 1520, from Camaldoli, Italy, by Bl. Paul Giustiniani. General motherhouse, Frascati (Rome), Italy; U.S. foundation, Holy Family Hermitage, Rt. 2, Box 36, Bloomingdale, OH 43910.

Camillian Fathers and Brothers (Order of St. Camillus; Order of Servants of the Sick), O.S.Cam.: Founded 1582, at Rome, by St. Camillus de Lellis; in U.S., 1923. General motherhouse, Rome, Italy; North American province, 10213 W. Wisconsin Ave., Wauwatosa, WI 53226.

Carmelites (Order of Our Lady of Mt. Carmel), O. Carm.: General motherhouse, Rome, Italy. Educational, charitable work.

Most Pure Heart of Mary Province (1864), 1317 Frontage Rd., Darien, IL 60559.

St. Elias Province (1931), P.O. Box 868, Middletown, NY 10940.

Mt. Carmel Hermitage, Pineland, R.D. 3, Box 36, New Florence, PA 15944 (immediately subject to Prior General).

Carmelites, Order of Discalced, O.C.D.: Established 1562, a Reform Order of Our Lady of Mt. Carmel; in U.S., 1924. Generalate, Rome, Italy. Spiritual direction, retreat, parochial work.

California-Arizona Province, Central Office (1983), 926 E. Highland Ave., P.O. Box 2178, Redlands, CA 92373.

St. Therese of Oklahoma Province (1935), P.O. Box 26127, Oklahoma City, OK 73126.

Immaculate Heart of Mary Province (1947), 1233 S. 45th St., Milwaukee, WI 53214.

Polish Province of the Holy Spirit (1949), 1628 Ridge Rd., Munster, IN 46321.

Carmelites of Mary Immaculate, C.M.I.: Founded 1831, in India, by Bl. Kuriakose Elias Chavara and two other Syro-Malabar priests; canonically established, 1855. Generalate, Kerala, India; North American headquarters, Holy Family Church, 21 Nassau Ave., Brooklyn, NY 11222.

Carthusians, Order of, O. Cart.: Founded 1084, in France, by St. Bruno; in U.S., 1951. General motherhouse, St. Pierre de Chartreuse, France; U.S. charterhouse, R.R. 2, Box 2411, Arlington, VT 05250. Cloistered contemplatives; semi-eremitic.

Charity, Brothers of, F.C.: Founded 1807, in Belgium, by Canon Peter J. Triest. General motherhouse, Rome, Italy: American District (1963), Triest Hall, 7720 Doe Lane, Laverock, PA 19038.

Charity, Servants of (Guanellians), S.C.: Founded 1908, in Italy, by Bl. Luigi Guanella. General motherhouse, Rome, Italy; U.S. headquarters, St. Louis School, 16195 Old U.S. 12, Chelsea, MI 48118.

Christ, Society of, S.Ch.: Founded 1932, General Motherhouse, Poznan, Poland; U.S.-Canadian Province, 3000 Eighteen Mile Rd., Sterling Heights, MI 48311.

Christian Brothers, Congregation of, C.F.C. (formerly Christian Brothers of Ireland): Founded 1802 at Waterford, Ireland, by Edmund Ignatius Rice; in U.S., 1906. General motherhouse, Rome, Italy. Educational work.

American Province, Eastern U.S. (1916), 21 Pryer Terr., New Rochelle, NY 10804.

Brother Rice Province, Western U.S. (1966), 9237 S. Avalon Ave., Chicago, IL 60619.

Christian Instruction, Brothers of (La Mennais Brothers), F.I.C.: Founded 1817, at Ploermel, France, by Abbé Jean Marie de la Mennais and Abbé Gabriel Deshayes. General motherhouse, Rome, Italy; American province, Notre Dame Institute, P.O. Box 159, Alfred, ME 04002.

Christian Schools, Brothers of the (Christian Brothers), F.S.C.: Founded 1680, at Reims, France, by St. Jean Baptiste de la Salle. General motherhouse, Rome, Italy; U.S. Conference, 4351 Garden City Dr., Suite 200, Landover, MD 20785. Educational, charitable work.

Baltimore Province (1845), Box 29, Adamstown, MD 21710.

Chicago Province (1966), 200 De La Salle Dr., Romeoville, IL 60441.

New York Province (1848), 800 Newman Springs Rd., Lincroft, NJ 07738.

Long Island-New England Province (1957), Christian Brothers Center, 635 Ocean Ave., Narragansett, RI 02882.

St. Louis Province (1886), 2101 Rue de la Salle, Glencoe, MO 63038.

San Francisco Province (1868), P.O. Box 3720, Napa, CA 94558.

New Orleans-Santa Fe Province (1921), De La Salle Christian Brothers, 1522 Carmel Dr., Lafayette, LA 70501.

St. Paul-Minneapolis Province (1963), 807 Summit Ave., St. Paul, MN 55105.

Cistercians, Order of, O.Cist.: Founded 1098, by St. Robert. Headquarters, Rome, Italy.

Our Lady of Spring Bank Abbey, Rt. 3, Box 211, Sparta, WI 54656.

Our Lady of Dallas Monastery, 1 Cistercian Rd., Irving, TX 75039.

Cistercian Monastery, 564 Walton Ave., Mt. Laurel, NJ 08054.

Cistercian Conventual Priory, St. Mary's Priory, R.D. 1, Box 206, New Ringgold, PA 17960.

Cistercians of the Strict Observance, Order of (Trappists), O.C.S.O.: Founded 1098, in France, by St. Robert; in U.S., 1848. Generalate, Rome, Italy.

Our Lady of Gethsemani Abbey (1848), Trappist, KY 40051.

Our Lady of New Melleray Abbey (1849), 6500 Melleray Circle, Peosta, IA 52068.

St. Joseph's Abbey (1825), Spencer, MA 01562.

Holy Spirit Monastery (1944), 2625 Hwy. 212 S.W., Conyers, GA 30208.

Our Lady of Guadalupe Abbey (1947), Lafayette, OR 97127.

Our Lady of the Holy Trinity Abbey (1947), Huntsville, Utah 84317.

Abbey of the Genesee (1951), Piffard, NY 14533.

Mepkin Abbey (1949), HC 69, Box 800, Moncks Corner, SC 29461.

Our Lady of the Holy Cross Abbey (1950), Rt. 2, Box 3870, Berryville, VA 22611.

Assumption Abbey (1950), Rt. 5, Box 1056, Ava, MO 65608.

Abbey of New Clairvaux (1955), Vina, CA 96092.

St. Benedict's Monastery (1956), 1012 Monastery Rd., Snowmass, CO 81654.

Claretians (Missionary Sons of the Immaculate Heart of Mary), C.M.F.: Founded 1849, at Vich, Spain, by St. Anthony Mary Claret. General headquarters, Rome, Italy. Missionary, parochial, educational, retreat work.

Western Province, 1119 Westchester Pl., Los Angeles, CA 90019.

Eastern Province, 400 N. Euclid Ave. Oak Park, IL 60302.

Clerics Regular Minor (Adorno Fathers) C.R.M.: Founded 1588, at Naples, Italy, by Ven. Augustine Adorno and St. Francis Caracciolo. General motherhouse, Rome, Italy; U.S. address, 575 Darlington Ave., Ramsey, NJ 07446.

Columban, Society of St. (St. Columban Foreign Mission Society, S.S.C.): Founded 1918. General headquarters, Dublin, Ireland. U.S. headquarters, P.O. Box 10, St. Columbans, NE 68056. Foreign mission work.

Comboni Missionaries of the Heart of Jesus (Verona Fathers), M.C.C.J.: Founded 1867, in Italy by Bp. Daniel Comboni; in U.S., 1939. General motherhouse, Rome, Italy; North American headquarters, Comboni Mission Center, 8108 Beechmont Ave., Cincinnati, OH 45230. Mission work in Africa and the Americas.

Consolata Missionaries, I.M.C.: Founded 1901, at Turin, Italy, by Bl. Joseph Allamano. General motherhouse, Rome, Italy; U.S. headquarters, P.O. Box 5550, 2301 Rt. 27, Somerset, NJ 08875.

Crosier Fathers (Canons Regular of the Order of the Holy Cross), O.S.C.: Founded 1210, in Belgium by Bl. Theodore De Celles. Generalate, Rome, Italy; U.S. Province of St. Odilia, 3470 Vivian Ave., Shoreview, MN 55126. Mission, retreat, educational work.

Cross, Brothers of the Congregation of Holy, C.S.C.: Founded 1837, in France, by Rev. Basil Moreau; U.S. province, 1841. Generalate, Rome, Italy. Educational, social work; missions.

Midwest Province (1841), Box 460, Notre Dame, IN 46556.

Southwest Province (1956), St. Edward's University, Austin, TX 78704.

Eastern Province (1956), 85 Overlook Circle, New Rochelle, NY 10804.

Cross, Priests of the Congregation of Holy, C.S.C.: Founded 1837, in France; in U.S., 1841. Generalate, Rome, Italy. Educational and pastoral work; home missions and retreats; foreign missions; social services and apostolate of the press.

Indiana Province (1841),1304 E. Jefferson Blvd., South Bend, IN 46617.

Eastern Province (1952), 835 Clinton Ave., Bridgeport, CT 06604.

Southern Province (1968), 2111 Brackenridge St., Austin, TX 78704.

Divine Word, Society of the, S.V.D.: Founded 1875, in Holland, by Bl. Arnold Janssen. North American Province founded 1897 with headquarters in Techny, IL General motherhouse, Rome, Italy.

Province of Bl. Joseph Freinademetz (Chicago Province) (1985, from merger of Eastern and Northern provinces), 1985 Waukegan Rd., Techny, IL 60082.

St. Augustine (Southern Province) (1940), 201 Ruella Ave., Bay St. Louis, MS 39520.

St. Theresa of the Child Jesus (Western Province) (1964), 2737 Pleasant Ave., Riverside, CA 92507.

Dominicans (Order of Friars Preachers), O.P.: Founded early 13th century by St. Dominic de Guzman. General headquarters, Santa Sabina, Rome, Italy. Preaching, teaching, missions, research, parishes.

St. Joseph Eastern Province (1805), 869 Lexington Ave., New York, NY 10021.

Most Holy Name of Jesus (Western) Province (1912), 5877 Birch Ct., Oakland, CA 94618.

St. Albert the Great (Central) Province (1939), 1909 S. Ashland Ave., Chicago, IL 60608.

Southern Dominican Province (1979), 3407 Napoleon Ave., New Orleans, LA 70125.

Spanish Province, U.S. foundation (1926), P.O. Box 279, San Diego, TX 78384.

Edmund, Society of St., S.S.E.: Founded 1843, in France, by Fr. Jean Baptiste Muard. General motherhouse, Edmundite Generalate, Fairholt, S. Prospect St., Burlington, VT 05401. Educational, missionary work.

Eudists (Congregation of Jesus and Mary), C.J.M.: Founded 1643, in France, by St. John Eudes. General motherhouse, Rome, Italy; North American province, 6125 Premiere Ave., Charlesbourg, Quebec G1H 2V9, Canada; U.S. community, 71 Burke Dr., Buffalo, NY 14215. Parochial, educational, pastoral, missionary work.

Francis, Brothers of Poor of St., C.F.P.: Founded 1857. Motherhouse, Aachen, Germany; U.S. province, P.O. Box 187, Burlington, IA 52601. Educational work, especially with poor and emotionally disturbed youth.

Francis, Third Order Regular of St., T.O.R.: Founded 1221, in Italy; in U.S., 1910. General motherhouse, Rome, Italy. Educational, parochial, missionary work.

Most Sacred Heart of Jesus Province (1910), 215 57th St., Pittsburgh, PA 15201.

Immaculate Conception Province (1925), P.O. Box 29655, Brookland Sta., Washington, DC 20017.

Commissariat of the Spanish Province (1924), 301 Jefferson Ave., Waco, TX 76702.

Francis de Sales, Oblates of St., O.S.F.S.: Founded 1871, by Fr. Louis Brisson. General motherhouse, Rome, Italy. Educational, missionary, parochial work.

Wilmington-Philadelphia Province (1906), 2200 Kentmere Parkway, Box 1452, Wilmington, DE 19899.

Toledo-Detroit Province (1966), 2056 Parkwood Ave., Toledo, OH 43620.

Francis Xavier, Brothers of St. (Xaverian Brothers), C.F.X.: Founded 1839, in Belgium, by Theodore J. Ryken. Generalate, Twickenham, Middlesex, England. Educational work.

Sacred Heart Province, 10318-B Baltimore National Pike, Ellicott City, MD 21043.

St. Joseph Province, 704 Brush Hill Rd., Milton. MA 02186.

Franciscan Brothers of Brooklyn, O.S.F.: Founded in Ireland; established at Brooklyn, 1858. Generalate, 135 Remsen St., Brooklyn, NY 11201. Educational work.

Franciscan Brothers of Christ the King, O.S.F.: Founded 1961. General motherhouse, 3737 N. Marybelle Ave., Peoria, IL 61615.

Franciscan Brothers of the Holy Cross, F.F.S.C.: Founded 1862, in Germany. Generalate, Hausen, Linz Rhein, Germany; U.S. region, 2500 St. James Rd., Springfield, IL 62707. Educational work.

Franciscan Brothers of the Third Order Regular, O.S.F.: Generalate, Mountbellew, Ireland; U.S. region, 2117 Spyglass Trail W., Oxnard, CA 93030.

Franciscan Friars of the Immaculate, F.F.I: Founded 1990, Italy. General motherhouse, Benevento, Italy. U.S. addresses, 600 Pleasant St., New Bedford, MA. 02740; 22 School Hill Rd., Baltic, CT 06330.

Franciscan Friars of the Renewal, C.F.R.: Community established under jurisdiction of the archbishop of New York. Central House, St. Crispin Friary, 420 E. 156th St., Bronx, NY 10455.

Franciscan Missionary Brothers of the Sacred Heart of Jesus, O.S.F.: Founded 1927, in the St. Louis archdiocese. Motherhouse, St. Joseph Rd., Box 39, Eureka, MO 63025. Care of aged, infirm, homeless men and boys.

Franciscans (Order of Friars Minor), O.F.M.: A family of the First Order of St. Francis (of Assisi) founded in 1209 and established as a separate jurisdiction in 1517; in U.S., 1844. General headquarters, Rome, Italy. English-speaking conference: 3140 Meramec St., St. Louis, MO 63118. Preaching, missionary, educational, parochial, charitable work.

St. John the Baptist Province (1844), 1615 Vine St., Cincinnati, OH 45210.

Immaculate Conception Province (1855), 147 Thompson St., New York, NY 10012.

Sacred Heart Province (1858), 3140 Meramec St., St. Louis, MO 63118.

Assumption of the Blessed Virgin Mary Province (1887), Pulaski, WI 54162.

Most Holy Name of Jesus Province (1901), 58 W. 88th St., New York, NY 10024.

St. Barbara Province (1915),1500 34th Ave., Oakland, CA 94601.

Our Lady of Guadalupe Province (1985), 1350 Lakeview Rd. S.W., Albuquerque, NM 87105.

Holy Cross Custody (1912), 14246 Main St., P.O. Box 608, Lemont, IL 60439.

Most Holy Savior Vice-Province, 232 S. Home Ave., Pittsburgh, PA 15202.

St. John Capistran Custody (1928), 209 E. 83rd St., New York, NY 10028.

Mt. Alverna Friary, 517 S. Belle Vista Ave., Youngstown, OH 44509.

Holy Family Croatian Custody (1926), 4848 S. Ellis Ave., Chicago, IL 60615.

St. Casimir Lithuanian Vice-Province, P.O. Box 980, Kennebunkport, ME 04046.

Holy Gospel Province (Mexico), U.S. foundation, 2400 Marr St., El Paso, TX 79903.

Saints Francis and James Province (Jalisco, Mexico), U.S. foundation, 504 E. Santa Clara St., Hebbronville, TX 78361.

Commissariat of the Holy Land, Mt. St. Sepulchre, 1400 Quincy St. N.E., Washington, DC 20017.

St. Mary of the Angels Custody, Byzantine Slavonic Rite, P.O. Box 270, Sybertsville, PA 18251.

Academy of American Franciscan History, 1712 Euclid Ave., Berkeley, CA 94709.

Franciscans (Order of Friars Minor Capuchin), O.F.M. Cap.: A family of the First Order of St. Francis (of Assisi) founded in 1209 and established as a separate jurisdiction in 1528. General motherhouse, Rome, Italy. Missionary, parochial work, chaplaincies.

St. Joseph Province (1857), 1740 Mt. Elliott Ave., Detroit, MI 48207.

St. Augustine Province (1873), 220 37th St., Pittsburgh, PA 15201.

St. Mary Province (1952), 30 Gedney Park Dr., White Plains, NY 10605.

Province of the Stigmata (1918), P.O. Box 809, Union City, NJ 07087.

Western American Capuchin Province, Our Lady of the Angels, 1345 Cortez Ave., Burlingame, CA 94010.

Sts. Adalbert and Stanislaus Province (1948), 2 Manor Dr., Oak Ridge, NJ 07438.

Province of Mid-America (1977), 3553 Wyandot St., Denver, CO 80211.

Vice-Province of Texas, 2601 Singleton Blvd., Dallas, TX 75212.

St. John the Baptist Vice-Province, 216 Arzuaga St., P.O. Box 21350, Rio Piedras, Puerto Rico 00928.

Franciscans (Order of Friars Minor Conventual), O.F.M. Conv.: A family of the First Order of St. Francis (of Assisi) founded in 1209 and established as a separate jurisdiction in 1517; first U.S. foundation, 1852. General curia, Rome, Italy. Missionary, educational, parochial work.

Immaculate Conception Province (1852), Immaculate Conception Friary, Rensselaer, NY 12144.

St. Anthony of Padua Province (1906), 12300 Folly Quarter Rd., Ellicott City, MD 21043.

St. Bonaventure Province (1939), 6107 Kenmore Ave., Chicago, IL 60660.

Our Lady of Consolation Province (1926), 101 Anthony Dr., Mt. St. Francis, IN 47146.

Our Lady of Guadalupe Custody (vice-province), Holy Cross Friary, P.O. Box 158, Mesilla Park, NM 88047.

St. Joseph of Cupertino Province (1981), P.O. Box 820, Arroyo Grande, CA 93420.

Glenmary Missioners (The Home Missioners of America): Founded 1939, in U.S. General headquarters, P.O. Box 465618, Cincinnati, OH 45246. Home mission work.

Good Shepherd, Little Brothers of the, B.G.S.: Founded 1951, by Bro. Mathias Barrett. Foundation House, P.O. Box 389, Albuquerque, NM 87102. General headquarters, Hamilton, Ont., Canada. Operate shelters and refuges for aged and homeless; homes for handicapped men and boys, alcoholic rehabilitation center.

Holy Eucharist, Brothers of the, F.S.E.: Founded in U.S., 1957. Generalate, P.O. Box 25, Plaucheville, LA 71362. Teaching, social, clerical, nursing work.

Holy Family, Congregation of the Missionaries of the, M.S.F.: Founded 1895, in Holland, by Rev. John P. Berthier. General motherhouse, Rome, Italy; U.S. provincialate, 210 El Rancho Way, San Antonio, TX 78209. Belated vocations for the missions.

Holy Family, Sons of the, S.F.: Founded 1864, at Barcelona, Spain, by Bl. Jose Mañanet y Vives; in U.S., 1920. General motherhouse, Barcelona, Spain; U.S. address, 401 Randolph Rd., P.O. Box 4138, Silver Spring, MD 20904.

Holy Ghost Fathers, C.S.Sp.: Founded 1703, in Paris, by Claude Francois Poullart des Places; in U.S., 1872. Generalate, Rome, Italy. Missions, education.

Eastern Province (1872), 6230 Brush Run Rd., Bethel Park. PA 15102. Western Province (1964), 919 Briarcliff, San Antonio, TX 78213.

Holy Ghost Fathers of Ireland (1971), U.S. delegates: 4849 37th St., Long Island City, NY 11101 (East); St. Dunstan's Church, 1133 Broadway, Millbrae, CA 94030 (West); St. John Baptist Church, 1139 Dryades St., New Orleans, LA 70113.

Holy Spirit, Missionaries of the, M.Sp.S.: Founded 1914, at Mexico City, Mexico, by Felix Rougier. General motherhouse, Mexico City; U.S. headquarters, Our Lady of Guadalupe, 500 N. Juanita Ave., P.O. Box 1091, Oxnard, CA 93030. Missionary work.

Immaculate Heart of Mary, Brothers of the, I.H.M.: Founded 1948, at Steubenville, Ohio, by Bishop John K. Mussio. Motherhouse, 609 N. 7th St., Steubenville, OH 43952. Educational, charitable work.

Jesuits (Society of Jesus), S.J. Founded 1534, in France, by St. Ignatius of Loyola; received papal approval, 1540; first U.S. province, 1833. Generalate, Rome, Italy; U.S. national office, Jesuit Conference, 1424 16th St. N.W., Suite 300, Washington, DC 20036. Missionary, educational, literary work.

Maryland Province (1833), 5704 Roland Ave., Baltimore, MD 21210.

New York Province (1943), 501 E. Fordham Rd., Bronx, NY 10458.

Missouri Province (1863), 4511 W. Pine Blvd., St. Louis, MO 63108.

New Orleans Province (1907), 500 S. Jefferson Davis Pkwy., New Orleans, LA 70119.

California Province (1909), 300 College Ave., P.O. Box 519, Los Gatos, CA 95031.

New England Province (1926), 775 Harrison Ave., Boston, MA 02118.

Chicago Province (1928), 2050 N. Clark St., Chicago, IL 60614.

Oregon Province (1932), 2222 N.W. Hoyt, Portland, OR 97210.

Detroit Province (1955), 7303 W. Seven Mile Rd., Detroit, MI 48221.

Wisconsin Province (1955), PO Box 08277, Milwaukee, WI 53208.

Province of the Antilles (1947), U.S. address, 13339 S.W. 9 Terrace, Miami, FL 33184.

John of God, Brothers of the Hospitaller Order of St., O.H.: Founded 1537, in Spain. General motherhouse, Rome. Italy; American province, 2425 S. Western Ave., P.O. Box 77627, Los Angeles, CA 90018; Irish Province of Immaculate Conception, 532 Delsea Dr., Westville Grove, NJ 08093. Nursing work and related fields.

Joseph, Congregation of St., C.S.J.: General motherhouse, Rome, Italy; U.S. vice province, 338 Grand Ave., San Pedro, CA 90731. Parochial, missionary, educational work.

Joseph, Oblates of St., O.S.J.: Founded 1878, in Italy, by Bl. Joseph Marello; in U.S., 1929. General motherhouse, Rome, Italy. Parochial, educational work.

Eastern Province, Route 315, Pittston, PA 18640.

California Province, 544 W. Cliff Dr., Santa Cruz, CA 95060.

Josephite Fathers, C.J.: General motherhouse, Ghent, Belgium; U.S. foundation, 989 Brookside Ave., Santa Maria, CA 93455.

Josephites (St. Joseph's Society of the Sacred Heart), S.S.J.: Established 1893, in U.S. as American congregation (originally established in U.S. in 1871 by Mill Hill Josephites from England). General motherhouse, 1130 N. Calvert St., Baltimore, MD 21202. Evangelization in African American community.

LaSalette, Missionaries of Our Lady of, M.S.: Founded 1852, by Msgr. de Bruillard; in U.S., 1892. Motherhouse, Rome, Italy.

Our Lady of Seven Dolors Province (1934), 915 Maple Ave., Hartford, CT 06114.

Immaculate Heart of Mary Province (1945), 947 Park St., Attleboro, MA 02703.

Mary Queen Province (1958), 4650 S. Broadway, St. Louis, MO 63111.

Mary Queen of Peace Province (1967), 1607 E. Howard Ave., Milwaukee, WI 53207.

Lateran, Canons Regular of the, C.R.L.: General house, Rome, Italy; U.S. address: 2317 Washington Ave., Bronx, NY 10458.

Legionaries of Christ, L.C.: Founded 1941, in Mexico, by Rev. Marcial Maciel; in U.S., 1965. General headquarters, Rome, Italy; U.S. headquarters, 393 Derby Ave., Orange, CT 06477; novitiate, 475 Oak Ave., Cheshire, CT 06410.

Little Brothers of St. Francis, L.B.S.F.: Founded 1970 in Archdiocese of Boston by Bro. James Curran. General fraternity, 785-789 Parker St., Roxbury (Boston), MA 02120. Combine contemplative life with evangelical street ministry.

Marianist Fathers and Brothers (Society of Mary; Brothers of Mary), S.M.: Founded 1817, at Bordeaux, France, by Rev. William-Joseph Chaminade; in U.S., 1849. General motherhouse, Rome, Italy. Educational work.

Cincinnati Province (1849), 4435 E. Patterson Rd., Dayton, OH 45430.

St. Louis Province (1908), PO Box 23130, St. Louis, MO 63156.

Pacific Province (1948), PO Box 1775, Cupertino, CA 95015.

New York Province (1961), 4301 Roland Ave., Baltimore, MD 21210.

Province of Meribah (1976), 240 Emory Rd., Mineola, NY 11501.

Mariannhill, Congregation of the Missionaries of, C.M.M.: Trappist monastery, begun in 1882 by Abbot Francis Pfanner in Natal, South Africa, became an independent modern congregation in 1909; in U.S., 1920. Generalate, Rome, Italy; U.S.-Canadian province (1938), Our Lady of Grace Monastery, 23715 Ann Arbor Trail, Dearborn Hts., MI 48127. Foreign mission work.

Marians of the Immaculate Conception, Congregation of, M.I.C.: Founded 1673; U.S. foundation, 1913. General motherhouse, Rome, Italy. Educational, parochial, mission, publication work.

St. Casimir Province (1913), 6336 S. Kilbourn Ave., Chicago, IL 60629.

St. Stanislaus Kostka Province (1948), Eden Hill, Stockbridge, MA 01262.

Marist Brothers, F.M.S.: Founded 1817, in France, by Bl. Marcellin Champagnat. General motherhouse, Rome, Italy. Educational, social, catechetical work.

Esopus Province, 1241 Kennedy Blvd., Bayonne, NJ 07002 (office).

Poughkeepsie Province, 26 First Ave., Pelham, NY 10803.

Marist Fathers (Society of Mary), S.M.: Founded 1816, at Lyons, France, by Jean Claude Colin; in U.S., 1863. General motherhouse, Rome, Italy. Educational, foreign mission, pastoral work.

Washington Province (1924), 815 Varnum St., N.E., Washington, DC 20017.

Boston Province (1924), 27 Isabella St., Boston, MA 02116.

San Francisco Western Province (1962), 625 Pine St., San Francisco, CA 94108.

Maronite Monks, Congregation of (Cloistered Penitents of St. Francis), **O. Mar.:** Most Holy Trinity Monastery, 67 Dugway Rd., Petersham, MA 01366; Holy Nativity Monastery, Bethleham, S.D. 57708.

Maronite Lebanese Missionaries, Congregation of, C.M.L.M.: Founded in Lebanon 1865; established in the U.S., 1991. U.S. foundation, St. George Maronite Church, 6070 Babcock Rd., San Antonio, TX 78240.

Mary Immaculate, Oblates of, O.M.I.: Founded 1816, in France, by Bl. Charles Joseph Eugene de Mazenod; in U.S., 1849. General house, Rome, Italy. U.S. consulate, 290 Lenox Ave., Oakland, CA 94610. Parochial, foreign mission, educational work; ministry to marginal.

Southern U.S. Province (1904), 7711 Madonna Dr., San Antonio, TX 78216.

Our Lady of Hope, Eastern Province (1883), 391 Michigan Ave. N.E., Washington, DC 20017.

St. John the Baptist, Northern Province (1921), 61 Burns Hill Rd., Hudson, NH 03051.

Central Province (1924), 267 E. 8th St., St. Paul, MN 55101.

Western Province (1953), 290 Lenox Ave., Oakland, CA 94610.

Maryknoll (Catholic Foreign Mission Society of America), M.M.: Founded 1911, in U.S., by Frs. Thomas F. Price and James A. Walsh. General Center, Maryknoll, NY 10545.

Mekhitarist Order of Venice, O.M.Ven.: Founded 1701; transferred to Venice, 1717. U.S. address: 110 E. 12th, New York, N.Y. 10003. Promote ecclesial community among Armenians.

Mekhitarist Order of Vienna, C.M.Vd.: Established 1773. General headquarters, Vienna, Austria. U.S. address, 4900 Maryland Ave., La Crescenta, CA 91214. Work among Armenians in U.S.

Mercedarians (Order of Our Lady of Mercy), O. de M.: Founded 1218, in Spain, by St. Peter Nolasco. General motherhouse, Rome, Italy; U.S. headquarters, 3205 Fulton Rd., Cleveland, OH 44109.

Mercy, Brothers of, F.M.M.: Founded 1856, in Germany. General motherhouse, Montabaur, Germany. American headquarters, 4520 Ransom Rd., Clarence, NY 14031. Hospital work.

Mercy, Brothers of Our Lady, Mother of, C.F.M.M.: Founded 1844, in The Netherlands by Abp. Jan Zwijsen. Generalate, Tilburg, The Netherlands; U.S. region, 2336 S. C St., Oxnard, CA 93033.

Mercy, Congregation of Priests of (Fathers of Mercy), C.P.M.: Founded 1808, in France, by Rev. Jean Baptiste Rauzan; in U.S., 1839. General mission house, South Union, KY 42283. Mission work.

Mill Hill Missionaries (St. Joseph's Society for Foreign Missions), M.H.M.: Founded 1866, in England, by Cardinal Vaughan; in U.S., 1951. International headquarters, London, England; American headquarters, 12101 Gravois Rd., St. Louis, MO 63127.

Minim Fathers, O.M.: General motherhouse, Rome, Italy. North American delegation (1970), 3431 Portola Ave., Los Angeles, CA 90032.

Missionaries of St. Charles, Congregation of the (Scalabrinians), C.S.: Founded 1887, at Piacenza, Italy, by Bishop John Baptist Scalabrini. General motherhouse, Rome, Italy.

St. Charles Borromeo Province (1888), 27 Carmine St., New York, NY 10014.

St. John Baptist Province (1903), 646 N. East Ave., Oak Park, IL 60302.

Missionaries of the Blessed Sacrament, M.S.S.: Regional headquarters, P.O. Box 4337, Corpus Christi, TX 78469. Promotion of Perpetual Eucharistic adoration.

Missionaries of the Holy Apostles, M.Ss.A.: Founded 1962, Washington, D.C., by Very Rev. Eusebe M. Menard. North American headquarters, P.O. Box 7188, New Haven, CT 06519.

Missionary Fraternity of Mary, F.M.M.: General headquarters, Guatemala; U.S. foundation 340 Pine St., Seaford, DE 19973.

Missionhurst—CICM (Congregation of the Immaculate Heart of Mary): Founded 1862, at Scheut, Brussels, Belgium, by Very Rev. Theophile Verbist. General motherhouse, Rome, Italy; U.S. province, 4651 N. 25th St., Arlington, VA 22207. Home and foreign mission work.

Montfort Missionaries (Missionaries of the Company of Mary), S.M.M.: Founded 1715, by St. Louis Marie Grignon de Montfort; in U.S., 1948. General motherhouse, Rome, Italy; U.S. province, 101-18 104th St., Ozone Park, NY 11416. Mission work.

Mother Co-Redemptrix, Congregation of, C.M.C.: Founded 1953 at Lein-Thuy, Vietnam (North), by Fr. Dominic Mary Tran Dinh Thu; in U.S., 1975. General house, Hochiminhville, Vietnam; U.S. provincial house, 1900 Grand Ave., Carthage, MO 64836. Work among Vietnamese Catholics in U.S.

Oblates of the Virgin Mary, O.M.V.: Founded 1815, in Italy; in U.S., 1976; Generalate, Rome, Italy; U.S. provincialate: 65 Father Carney Dr., Milton, MA 02186.

Oratorians (Congregation of the Oratory of St. Philip Neri), C.O.: Founded 1575, at Rome, by St. Philip Neri. A confederation of autonomous houses. U.S. addresses: P.O. Box 11586, Rock Hill, SC 29731; P.O. Box 1688, Monterey, CA 93940; 4040 Bigelow Blvd., Pittsburgh, PA 15213; P.O. Drawer ii, Pharr, TX 78577; 109 Willoughby St., Brooklyn, NY 11201.

Pallottines (Society of the Catholic Apostolate), S.A.C.: Founded 1835, at Rome, by St. Vincent Pallotti. Generalate, Rome, Italy. Charitable, educational, parochial, mission work.

Immaculate Conception Province (1953), P.O. Box 573, Pennsauken, NJ 08110.

Mother of God Province (1946), 5424 W. Blue Mound Rd., Milwaukee, WI 53208.

Irish Province (1909), U.S. address: 3352 4th St., P.O. Box 249, Wyandotte, MI 48192.

Queen of Apostles Province (1909), 448 E. 116th St., New York, NY 10029.

Christ the King Province, 3452 Niagara Falls, Blvd., N. Tonawanda, NY 14120.

Paraclete, Servants of the, s.P.: Founded 1947, Santa Fe, N.M. archdiocese. Generalate and U.S. motherhouse, Via Coeli, Jemez Springs, NM 87025. Devoted to care of priests

Paris Foreign Missions Society, M.E.P.: Founded 1662, at Paris, France. Headquarters, Paris, France; U.S. establishment, 930 Ashbury St., San Francisco, CA 94117. Mission work and training of native clergy.

Passionists (Congregation of the Passion), C.P.: Founded 1720, in Italy, by St. Paul of the Cross. General motherhouse, Rome, Italy.

St. Paul of the Cross Province (Eastern Province) (1852), 80 David St., South River, NJ 08882.

Holy Cross Province (Western Province), 5700 N. Harlem Ave., Chicago, IL 60631.

Patrician Brothers (Brothers of St. Patrick), F.S.P.: Founded 1808, in Ireland, by Bishop Daniel Delaney; U.S. novitiate, 7820 Bolsa Ave., Midway City, CA 92655. Educational work.

Patrick's Missionary Society, St., S.P.S.: Founded 1932, at Wicklow, Ireland, by Msgr. Patrick Whitney; in U.S., 1953. International headquarters, Kiltegan Co., Wicklow, Ireland. U.S. foundations: 70 Edgewater Rd., Cliffside Park, NJ 07010; 19536 Eric Dr., Saratoga, CA 95070; 1347 W. Granville Ave., Chicago, IL 60660.

Pauline Fathers (Order of St. Paul the First Hermit), O.S.P.P.E.: Founded 1215; established in U.S., 1955. General motherhouse, Czestochowa, Jasna Gora,

Poland; U.S. province, P.O. Box 2049, Doylestown, PA 18901.

Pauline Fathers and Brothers (Society of St. Paul for the Apostolate of Communications), S.S.P.: Founded 1914, by Very Rev. James Alberione; in U.S., 1932. Motherhouse, Rome, Italy; New York province (1932), 6746 Lake Shore Rd., Derby, NY 14047; Los Angeles province, 112 S. Herbert Ave., Los Angeles, CA 90063. Social communications work.

Paulists (Missionary Society of St. Paul the Apostle), C.S.P.: Founded 1858, in New York, by Fr. Isaac Thomas Hecker. General offices, 86 Dromore Rd., Scarsdale, NY 10583. Missionary, ecumenical, pastoral work.

Piarists (Order of the Pious Schools), Sch.P.: Founded 1617, at Rome, Italy, by St. Joseph Calasanctius. General motherhouse, Rome, Italy. U.S. province, 363 Valley Forge Rd., Devon, PA 19333. New York-Puerto Rico vice-province (Calasanzian Fathers), P.O. Box 118, Playa Sta., Ponce, PR 00734. California vicariate, 3951 Rogers St., Los Angeles, CA 90063. Educational work.

Pius X, Brothers of St.: Founded 1952, at La Crosse, Wis., by Bishop John P. Treacy. Motherhouse, P.O. Box 217, De Soto, WI 54624. Education.

Pontifical Institute for Foreign Missions, P.I.M.E.: Founded 1850, in Italy, at request of Pope Pius IX. General motherhouse, Rome, Italy; U.S. province, 17330 Quincy Ave., Detroit, MI 48221. Foreign mission work.

Precious Blood, Society of, C.Pp.S.: Founded 1815, in Italy, by St. Gaspar del Bufalo. General motherhouse, Rome, Italy.

Cincinnati Province, 431 E. Second St., Dayton, OH 45402.

Kansas City Province, P.O. Box 339, Liberty, MO 64068.

Pacific Province, 2337 134th Ave. W., San Leandro, CA 94577.

Atlantic Province, 540 St. Clair Ave. West, Toronto M6C 14A, Canada.

Premonstratensians (Order of the Canons Regular of Prémontré; Norbertines), O. Praem.: Founded 1120, at Prémontré, France, by St. Norbert; in U.S., 1893. Generalate, Rome, Italy. Educational, parish work.

St. Norbert Abbey, 1016 N. Broadway, DePere, WI 54115.

Daylesford Abbey, 220 S. Valley Rd., Paoli, PA 19301.

St. Michael's Abbey, 19292 El Toro Rd., Silverado, CA 92676.

Priestly Fraternity of St. Peter, F.S.S.P.: Founded and approved Oct. 18, 1988. U.S. headquarters, Our Lady of Guadalupe Seminary, Griffin Rd., P.O. Box 196, Elmhurst, PA 18416.

Providence, Sons of Divine, F.D.P.: Founded 1893, at Tortona, Italy, by Bl. Luigi Orione; in U.S., 1933. General motherhouse, Rome, Italy; U.S. address, 111 Orient Ave., E. Boston, MA 02128.

Redemptorists (Congregation of the Most Holy Redeemer), C.Ss.R.: Founded 1732, in Italy, by St. Alphonsus Mary Liguori. Generalate, Rome, Italy. Mission work.

Baltimore Province (1850), 7509 Shore Rd., Brooklyn, NY 11209.

St. Louis Province (1875), Box 6, Glenview, IL 60025.

Oakland Province (1952), 3696 Clay St., San Francisco, CA 94118.

New Orleans Vice-Province, 1527 3rd St., New Orleans, LA 70130.

Richmond Vice-Province (1942), 313 Hillman St., P.O. Box 1529, New Smyrna Beach, FL 32170.

Resurrectionists (Congregation of the Resurrection), C.R.: Founded 1836, in France, under direction of Bogdan Janski. Motherhouse, Rome, Italy.

U.S. Province, 2250 N. Latrobe Ave., Chicago, IL 60639.

Ontario Kentucky Province, U.S. address, 338 N. 25th St., Louisville, KY 40212.

Rogationist Fathers, R.C.J.: Founded by Bl. Annibale (Hannibal) di Francia, 1887. General motherhouse, Rome, Italy. U.S. addresses: St. Mary Church, Box 335, Sanger, CA 93657; 9815 Columbus Ave., Sepulveda, CA 91343. Charitable work.

Rosary, Brothers of Our Lady of the Holy, F.S.R.: Founded 1956, in U.S., Motherhouse and novitiate, 1725 S. McCarran Blvd., Reno, NV 89502.

Rosminians (Institute of Charity), I.C.: Founded 1828, in Italy, by Antonio Rosmini-Serbati. General motherhouse, Rome, Italy; U.S. address, 2327 W. Heading Ave., Peoria, IL 61604. Charitable work.

Sacred Heart, Brothers of the, S.C.: Founded 1821, in France, by Rev. André Coindre. General motherhouse, Rome, Italy, Educational work.

New Orleans Province (1847), 4540 Elysian Fields Ave., New Orleans, LA 70122.

New England Province (1945), 685 Steere Farm Rd., Pascoag, RI 02859.

New York Province (1960), P.O. Box 68, Belvidere, NJ 07823.

Sacred Heart, Missionaries of the, M.S.C.: Founded 1854, by Rev. Jules Chevelier. General motherhouse, Rome, Italy; U.S. province, 305 S. Lake St., Aurora, IL 60507.

Sacred Heart of Jesus, Congregation of the (Sacred Heart Fathers and Brothers), S.C.J.: Founded 1877, in France. General motherhouse, Rome, Italy; U.S. provincial office: P.O. Box 289, Hales Corners, WI 53130. Educational, preaching, mission work.

Sacred Hearts of Jesus and Mary, Congregation of (Picpus Fathers), SS.CC.: Founded 1805, in France, by Fr. Coudrin. General motherhouse, Rome, Italy. Mission, educational work.

Eastern Province (1946), 73 Adams St. (Box 111), Fairhaven, MA 02719.

Western Province (1970), 15201 Rinaldi St., Mission Hills, CA 91345.

Hawaii Province, Box 797, Kaneohe, Oahu, Hawaii 96744.

Sacred Hearts of Jesus and Mary, Missionaries of the, M.SS.CC.: Founded 1833, in Naples, Italy, by Cajetan Errico. General motherhouse, Rome, Italy; U.S. headquarters, 2249 Shore Rd., Linwood, NJ 08221.

Salesians of St. John Bosco (Society of St. Francis de Sales), S.D.B.: Founded 1859, by St. John (Don) Bosco. Generalate, Rome, Italy.

St. Philip the Apostle Province (1902), 148 Main St., New Rochelle, NY 10802.

San Francisco Province (1926), 1100 Franklin St., San Francisco, CA 94109.

Salvatorians (Society of the Divine Savior), S.D.S.: Founded 1881, in Rome, by Fr. Francis Jordan; in U.S., 1896. General headquarters, Rome, Italy; U.S. province, 1735 Hi-Mount Blvd., Milwaukee, WI 53208. Educational, parochial, mission work; campus ministries, chaplaincies.

Scalabrinians: See Missionaries of St. Charles.

Servites (Order of Friar Servants of Mary), O.S.M.: Founded 1233, at Florence, Italy, by Seven Holy Founders. Generalate, Rome, Italy. General apostolic ministry.

Eastern Province (1967), 3121 W. Jackson Blvd., Chicago, IL 60612.

Western Province (1967), 5210 Somerset St., Buena Park, CA 90621.

Somascan Fathers, C.R.S.: Founded 1534, at Somasca, Italy, by St. Jerome Emiliani. General motherhouse, Rome, Italy; U.S. address, Pine Haven Boys Center, River Rd., P.O. Box 162, Suncook, NH 03275.

Society of Our Lady of the Most Holy Trinity, S.O.L.T.: Headquarters, St. Anthony Parish, 204 Dunne St., P.O. Box 152, Robstown, TX 78380.

Sons of Mary Missionary Society (Sons of Mary, Health of the Sick), F.M.S.I.: Founded 1952, in the Boston archdiocese, by Rev. Edward F. Garesché, S.J. Headquarters, 567 Salem End Rd., Framingham, MA 01701.

Stigmatine Fathers and Brothers (Congregation of the Sacred Stigmata), C.S.S.: Founded 1816, by St. Gaspar Bertoni. General motherhouse, Rome, Italy; North American Province, 554 Lexington St., Waltham, MA 02154. Parish work.

Sulpicians (Society of Priests of St. Sulpice), S.S.: Founded 1641, at Paris, by Rev. Jean Jacques Olier. General motherhouse, Paris, France; U.S. province, 5408 Roland Ave., Baltimore, MD 21210. Education of seminarians and priests.

Theatines (Congregation of Clerics Regular), C.R.: Founded 1524, at Rome, by St. Cajetan. General motherhouse, Rome, Italy; U.S. headquarters, 1050 S. Birch St., Denver, CO 80222.

Trappists: See Cistercians of the Strict Observance.

Trinitarians (Order of the Most Holy Trinity), O.SS.T.: Founded 1198, by St. John of Matha; in U.S., 1911. General motherhouse, Rome, Italy; U.S. headquarters, P.O. Box 5719, Baltimore, MD 21208.

Trinity Missions (Missionary Servants of the Most Holy Trinity), S.T.: Founded 1929, by Fr. Thomas Augustine Judge. Generalate, 1215 N. Scott St., Arlington, VA 22209. Home mission work.

Viatorian Fathers (Clerics of St. Viator), C.S.V.: Founded 1831, in France, by Fr. Louis Joseph Querbes. General motherhouse, Rome, Italy. Province of Chicago (1882), 1212 E. Euclid St., Arlington Hts., IL 60004. Educational work.

Vincentians (Congregation of the Mission; Lazarists), C.M.: Founded 1625, in Paris, by St. Vincent de Paul; in U.S., 1818. General motherhouse, Rome, Italy. Educational work.

Eastern Province (1867), 500 E. Chelten Ave., Philadelphia, PA 19144.

Midwest Province (1888), 13663 Rider Trail North, Earth City, MO 63045.

New England Province (1975), 1155 Prospect Ave., W. Hartford, CT 06105.

American Italian Branch, Our Lady of Pompei Church, 3600 Claremont St., Baltimore, MD 21224.

American Spanish Branch (Barcelona, Spain), 234 Congress St., Brooklyn, NY 11201.

American Spanish Branch (Zaragoza, Spain), Holy Agony Church, 1834 3rd Ave., New York, NY 10029.

Western Province (1975), 650 W. 23rd St., Los Angeles, CA 90007.

Southern Province (1975), 3826 Gilbert Ave., Dallas, TX 75219.

Vocationist Fathers (Society of Divine Vocations), S.D.V.: Founded 1920, in Italy; in U.S., 1962. General motherhouse, Naples, Italy; U.S. headquarters, 90 Brooklake Rd., Florham Park, NJ 07932.

Xaverian Missionary Fathers, S.X.: Founded 1895, by Archbishop Guido Conforti, at Parma, Italy. General motherhouse, Rome, Italy; U.S. province, 12 Helene Ct., Wayne, NJ 07470. Foreign mission work.

MERRICK, MARY VIRGINIA (1866–1955)

Founder of the Christ Child Society. Mary Virginia Merrick was born on November 2, 1866, in Washington, D.C. She was the second of eight children born to Washington lawyer Richard Merrick and his wife, Nannie McGuire Merrick. In her midteens, Merrick was paralyzed by a fall. Despite her injuries she continued a practice she had begun with her friends of sewing layettes for poor infants. The group then began preparing Christmas gifts for the children of the poor neighborhoods in honor of the Christ Child.

Mary V. Merrick

Merrick had great devotion to the Christ Child and Catholicism. She envisioned an organization whose volunteers would visit, instruct, and meet the spiritual and material needs of the poor. Using a network of friends and acquaintances, Merrick created the Christ Child Society in 1886. Many of her volunteers were college students, and they were instrumental in introducing the society to other cities.

Under Merrick's direction, the Washington society, which operated on a shoe string, opened a settlement house, summer camps, and youth clubs, in addition to providing directly for the needs of the poor. Several parishes directly resulted from Christ Child Society efforts.

Merrick closely monitored the progress of the Christ Child Society. In 1916 she set up a national organization composed of all local societies. Her procedure for chartering new organizations was to ensure that each society would emphasize direct service based on Christian principles. The whole development of every child, both spiritually and materially, was to be the goal of each volunteer. Funds were provided through volunteer efforts that bespoke much creativity. The society began thrift stores both to assist the poor and raise funds.

All chapters were expected to participate in the biennial convention where Merrick assessed their works. She allowed a great deal of local initiative, but insisted on fidelity to the society's mission. In later years Merrick received much recognition for her work, including the Laetare Medal from the University of Notre Dame in 1915 and the pontifical medal *Pro Ecclesia et Pontifice* in 1937. She died in Washington, D.C., on January 10, 1955.

Christ Child Society. *Annual Report.* Washington, D.C., 1922, 1926.

Correspondence of Mary V. Merrick, 1942–47. Papers of Christ Child Society, Cleveland. Archives of the Diocese of Cleveland.

Murray, Ann, and Agnes B. Blake. "History and Activities of the Christ Child Society." Papers of Christ Child Society in Cleveland. Archives of the Diocese of Cleveland. Unpublished manuscript.

CHRISTINE L. KROSEL

MERTON, THOMAS (1915–68)

Monk, author. Thomas Merton, who was later given the monastic name of Mary Louis, was born in Prades, France, on January 31, 1915, the first son of Owen Merton, an artist from New Zealand, and his American wife, Ruth Jenkins Merton. His life is conveniently divided into halves, each of twenty-seven years. The first half was completed just a few weeks short of his twenty-seventh birthday, when he entered Our Lady of Gethsemani Abbey, near Bardstown, Kentucky, on December 10, 1941. Exactly twenty-seven years later, on December 10, 1968, his life suddenly ended when he fell victim to a heart attack at the Red Cross Center outside of Bangkok, Thailand.

Thomas Merton

Both halves were blessed at the beginning with the presence of a strong motherly figure who, each in her or his own way, appreciated Merton's potential and encouraged him in the development of his literary talents. Ruth Jenkins Merton was the daughter of an Ohio newspaper man. She is not remembered as the most affectionate of mothers, but she appreciated writing and with a certain maternal intuition set her son to it at a very early age. She died when Tom was six years and eight months old. When Merton entered Gethsemani and began the second half of his life, the monastery was shepherded by a strong, motherly abbot who also came from Ohio from a family in publishing. Dom Frederic Dunne recognized the talent in the young monk and, after assigning him some translation projects and some pious biographies to write, put him to work on the book that would change his life, his autobiography, *The Seven Storey Mountain*. Coincidentally, Abbot Dunne died when Merton had been in his new life six years and eight months, just as the autobiography was published.

"Free by Nature"

Merton's life can be seen as a continuous quest for true freedom; indeed we can speak of the "seven freedoms" of Thomas Merton. In the second sentence of his autobiography he speaks of his being "free by nature. In the image of God," he says, "I was nevertheless the prisoner of my own violence and my own selfishness, in the image of the world into which I was born." As a young person Merton knew an exceptional amount of freedom. After the early death of his mother he traveled with his father on painting expeditions and was often left on his own in boarding houses for long periods. He knew some real discipline in a French *lycée* but as he rode away from that school with his father on his way to England he heard the horses' hoofs on the cobblestones saying: "Liberty, liberty, liberty. . . ." Life was much less disciplined in the English schools he then attended: Ripley Court and Oakham Public School, Rutland.

His father died two weeks before Merton's sixteenth birthday. The previous year his mother's father had given him financial independence through a trust fund. His English guardian was very liberal and trusting. Merton traveled widely: he was a barker for a strip show at the Chicago World's Fair, encountered young Nazis in Hitler's Germany, explored Rome. Before he was twenty he had crossed the Atlantic nine times. Winning a scholarship to Clare College, Cambridge, he lived a dissolute life, rarely attended classes, stayed up all night partying, fathered a child. In the end he was sent in disgrace to his grandparents then living in Douglaston, New York.

The Freedom of the Faith

Merton learned from his mistakes, though gradually. He entered upon a more serious college career at Columbia University. He devoted himself to literary concerns, edited the yearbook and the college literary magazine, the *Jester,* and studied medieval philosophy. He was searching for solid ground on which to stand. Working his way through the prejudices that were bred into him by his French men-

tors and his grandfather, aided by an influential teacher, Daniel Walsh, and his own broad and voracious reading, he embraced the Catholic faith in the fall of 1938. He now had something solid on which to take a stand.

The Freedom of Asceticism

To accept the faith and to live it can be two very different things, as Merton painfully experienced in the dissolute summer of 1939. Old habits were not easily shaken. In the fall he turned toward religious life to find support for the discipline he knew he very much needed. After an unsuccessful attempt to join the Franciscans, some experience teaching, and much soul-searching (which included a time with Catherine de Hueck at Friendship House in Harlem), as the Second World War broke out Merton took a train to Gethsemani.

Free to Be to the World

With the Trappists Merton found the ascetical discipline he needed and the support of a community to live it. But he fell into the snare of what he labeled "a dream of separateness, of spurious self-isolation in a special world, the world of renunciation and supposed holiness"—an idealization of "monk," the creation of a false self, that almost caused him his life. A wise abbot set him on the course toward freedom by having him teach—the best way to learn—the Greek Fathers with their healthy balance of finding God not only in the wholly other, but also in every other. A Jungian experience, described by Merton in a letter to Boris Pasternak, made this notion a reality in his life. Speaking in one of his journals of this experience, which took place on the crowded corner of Fourth and Walnut (now Ali Mohammed), he writes: "I was suddenly overwhelmed with the realization that I loved all those people, that they were mine and I theirs, that we could not be alien to one another even though we were total strangers." There was unleashed in him a tremendous flow of compassion which expressed itself in powerful social writings, deepened by the fruit of his contemplative theology. He had indeed become a free man, a man of the world, loving the whole world, embracing all its concerns even though he lived apart from that world.

"A Life Free from Care"

This is the title of the talk Merton gave to his monastic community the day he left community life to enter into full-time living in the hermitage he had built on the hill overlooking the abbey. No longer would he be burdened by the responsibilities of novice master that he had carried for ten years, or any other of the day-to-day concerns of living in community. Free now from the need of the structures of asceticism he could move ever deeper into contemplative prayer and being under the guidance of the

Holy Spirit. "It certainly is wonderful to wake up suddenly in the solitude of the woods and look up at the sky and see the utter nonsense of *everything*" (letter to Catherine de Hueck).

Free from care but not free from caring. He cared more than ever. His hermitage became a center of world care, where leaders of concern were welcomed and from which flowed powerful and healing words.

The Freedom of Final Integration

Merton's last week in India, just prior to his flight to Thailand and eternity, epitomized the freedom he arrived at which enabled him to find God and the fullness of God in all and in everything. At the beginning of the week he was flying into Madras, the excited, very Catholic pilgrim, with eleven relics in his pocket, on his way to the tomb of his patron, Saint Thomas. At the end of the week, walking barefoot in the great Buddhist shrine at Polonnaruwa, he had one of the great aesthetic experiences of his life: "I don't know when in my life I have ever had such a sense of beauty and spiritual validity running together in one aesthetic illumination. . . . I don't know what else remains but I have now seen and have pierced through the surface and have got beyond the shadow and the disguise" (*The Asian Journal of Thomas Merton*). In between these great experiences he enjoyed his Scotch-on-the-rocks at the finest hotel in Colombo and sought out the best jazz band in town. It all fitted together. And what remained?

The Eternal Freedom of the Kingdom

A certain amount of perhaps unnecessary mystery has hung around the death of Merton. He was in the midst of perhaps the longest journey of his life, certainly of his monastic life. He was responding to an invitation to address the first Pan-Asian Monastic Conference. He delivered his paper on the second morning of the conference and promised to answer questions in the afternoon. After lunch he retired to his room for a siesta. A few hours later he was found in the locked room lying on the floor with an electric fan across him, burning into his side. Merton had a heart condition. He had seemingly just taken a shower. Perhaps he went to turn on the fan and a faulty wire gave him a shock that caused the heart attack. Or perhaps he had a heart attack and fell against the fan bringing it over on top of him. We do not know, but it seemed to fulfill his own prophecy: "That you may become the brother of God and learn to know the Christ of the burnt men" (*The Seven Storey Mountain*).

Merton's Influence

While Thomas Merton's books, beginning with *The Seven Storey Mountain,* have sold in the millions and he has been more widely read than any other modern Catholic author, his contribution or perhaps his challenge to the current articulation of Catholic thought in America has not been fully recognized, even though Catholics proudly claim him and the American bishops readily acknowledge his extensive influence on their Peace Pastoral. Nor has he been generally recognized as the profound philosopher that he is, offering a new conception of the human person as well as developing the extensive social consequences of such an understanding of the person.

Merton was born in southern France. Although he spent part of his youth and all of adult life in the United States, French remained for him a primary language and he kept abreast of the thought of the philosophers and theologians writing in that language. He thought of himself primarily as a writer and more especially as a poet, though his greater influence was through his prose. He was a masterful letter writer. He became familiar with scholastic philosophy during his years as a student at Columbia University (1935–39), but it was his voracious reading that continued unflagging after his entry into the monastic life in 1941 that put him in touch with existentialism and other schools of philosophical thought. He did not hesitate to inaugurate a correspondence with the authors he read, and he attracted many of them to visit him in his monastery in Trappist, Kentucky. This constant rich dialogue with the thinkers of his time enabled him to present traditional Catholic thinking in a new and effective way. The fact that he more than any other has effectively brought the message of traditional Catholicism to the American people and continues to do this through his writings challenges the leaders and theologians of our tradition to question if they effectively fulfill their teaching mission by insisting on medieval scholasticism as the philosophical basis for their theological investigation and elaboration.

Merton's Basic Teaching

That the fulfillment of the human person or, as Merton would express it, sanctity, consists in discovering our true identity is one of the central themes that weaves its way through his writings. A necessary preliminary to this discovery of the true self is the realization that our true identity is not the one on the surface. The exterior self that we think ourselves to be and which we show to others is not the deep inner self that alone is real in us. We must therefore lose this false exterior self in order to find the true self. But we cannot even begin to do this until we come to the realization that we are lost in the realms of unreality, as in the density of a forest out of which we must find our way.

In *Seeds of Contemplation* (1949), where Merton first began to articulate his conception of the human person, he brings out that we cannot find our way out of this maze of unreality on our own. The secret of our identity is hidden, paradoxically, more in God than in ourselves. God makes us who we are. And God does it by identifying God's self with us. We become our true selves not in separateness and isolation, but in becoming identified with God in whom is the reason and fulfillment of our existence. God is present in us not simply as our creator, but as our "other and true self." Since, therefore, it is God who bears in God's self our true identity, we cannot hope to find our true selves anywhere except in God. The quest for the true self, therefore, is a quest for God.

The false or external self is a human construct which we bring into being by our own actions. It is made up of what we do and what we have (according to our own estimation) and what we think others think of us, the complex of all that we see in ourselves that is not God, and, therefore, of all that is ultimately destined to disappear. This false self is incapable of transcendent experience. It has a biography and a history, both of which end at death. The true self, on the other hand, is the self that sleeps silently in our depths, waiting to be awakened. It is the openness of our spirit to the call of God. It is what Merton, in a later work, *The New Man,* calls "the white hot-point of mystical receptivity," present in all of us, but dormant in most of us most of the time. The true self is beyond observation and reflection. It is our own subjectivity that can never be known as an object or a thing. It has no history or biography. It simply is—in hiddenness and in God.

The awakening of the true self in us must not be confused with the awakening of the rational consciousness that makes a human being responsible for his action as an individual. It is rather a deep spiritual consciousness, what Merton calls "that insatiable diamond of spiritual awareness" *(The New Man),* which takes us beyond the level of the individual ego. It awakens in us that centripetal force that changes us from within and yet tells us at the same time that change is a recovery of that which is deepest, most original, most personal in us.

This awakening of our inner identity does not mean the loss of any relations to external reality. The inner self is in contact with the world of objects but it does not see that world in bewildering complexity, separateness, and multiplicity, nor does it see the objects in it as things to be manipulated for pleasure or profit. There is a direct and immediate view of reality in which the experience of subject-object duality is destroyed. The inner self simply sees and does not take refuge behind a screen of conceptual prejudices or verbal distortions.

According to Merton, through this side of eschatological awakening it is possible for us to realize our true self only in contemplation. In the experience of contemplation we are able to answer God's call to become one with God. In contemplation the false self recedes and the true self awakens. Contemplation is the journey from the realms of unlikeness to God to the realms of likeness. It is the return from exile to paradise. The unity of contemplation brings us back from a state of disunity and self-alienation, from the domination of a false self that wants to live in isolation and separateness, in a self-constructed illusion that seeks to take over the functions of the inner self.

Contemplation is possible only by going beyond the external false self to the real self that is identified with God. Only then do we discover who we truly are. This discovery is a return to our original identity that was never fully lost. It is "not that we discover a new unity. We recover an older unity" *(The Asian Journal).* In contemplation we do not become something we were not. We become what we are and what we are called to be. We do not really become contemplative; we discover that in the depths of our being we are and always have been contemplative.

The journey into the land of contemplation begins where we are right now and goes on to where we should be. But the wonder of the journey is that when we arrive at our destination we discover that we were there all the time and did not know it.

> The human soul is still the image of God [an idea Merton draws from the Bible as it is developed in the writings of Augustine of Hippo and, more immediately for Merton, in those of his Cistercian forebear, Bernard of Clairvaux] and no matter how far it travels away from him into the regions of unreality, it never becomes so completely unreal that its original destiny can cease to torment it with the need to return to itself in God and become, once again, real *(New Seeds of Contemplation).*

> In returning to God and to ourselves, we have to begin with what we actually are. We have to start from our alienated condition. We are prodigals in a distant country, the "region of unlikeness," and we must seem to travel far in that region before we seem to reach our own land (and yet secretly we are in our own land all the time!) *(The New Man).*

Merton constantly developed his understanding of the human person in his many articles and books, but 1961 was the key year. In that year he published an expanded version of his earlier seminal work, *Seeds of Contemplation. New Seeds of Contemplation* contained all that is found in the earlier work, but showed a remarkable development in his thought. However, *The New Man,* published in the same year, is Merton's strongest philosophical and theological work. Daniel Walsh, who first opened Merton to scholastic philosophy at Columbia, exclaimed upon reading the volume: *"The New Man—the new Merton!"*

The Social Implications

After the publication of these volumes Merton devoted himself more and more to the social implications of his understanding of the human person and the human solidarity flowing from it. And he did not remain in the realm of theory. His powerful practical pronouncements on racial integration in his own South, on the Holocaust, and on the Vietnam War won him a new hearing and expanded the consciousness of many even while it alienated some of the traditional Catholics who had idolized him since the publication of *The Seven Storey Mountain*. But Merton never succumbed to the glamour of being an activist or lost his deep moorings. In *The Climate of Monastic Prayer,* the final book he prepared for publication before his untimely death in 1968 at the age of fifty-three, Merton restated in a highly personal way the basic struggle we must each face in order to recover our true self and find the integration and true freedom of the children of God. In the final pages of the book he wrote:

> Prayer [contemplation] must penetrate and enliven every department of our life, including that which is most temporal and transient. Prayer does not despise even the seemingly lowliest aspects of man's temporal existence. It spiritualizes all of them and gives them a divine orientation. . . . The most important need in the world today is this inner truth nourished by this Spirit of contemplation (*The Climate of Monastic Prayer*).

See also ABBEY OF GETHSEMANI; AMERICAN CATHOLIC SPIRITUALITY.

Finley, James. *Merton's Palace of Nowhere: A Search for God through Awareness of the True Self.* Notre Dame, Ind.: Ave Maria Press, 1978.

Hart, Patrick, ed. *The Message of Thomas Merton.* Kalamazoo, Mich.: Cistercian Publications, 1981.

Merton, Thomas. *The Climate of Monastic Prayer.* Kalamazoo, Mich.: Cistercian Publications, 1973.

____. *The New Man.* New York: Bantam Books, 1981.

____. *New Seeds of Contemplation.* New York: New Directions, 1972.

____. *The Seven Storey Mountain.* New York: Harcourt Brace, 1978.

Mott, Michael. *The Seven Mountains of Thomas Merton.* Boston: Houghton Mifflin, 1984.

Pennington, M. Basil. *Thomas Merton Brother Monk: The Quest for True Freedom.* San Francisco: Harper & Row, 1987.

M. BASIL PENNINGTON, O.C.S.O.

MESPLIE, TOUSSAINT (1824–95)

Missionary. Born in France in 1824, Toussaint Mesplie became famous for his work among the Native Americans along the Columbia River in Oregon and in Idaho, for his work as a pioneer missionary in Oregon and Idaho, and for his services to the Army and the government as a volunteer Army chaplain without pay for twenty-three years. According to Thomas Donaldson's *Idaho of Yesterday,* Fr.

Mesplie was short and stout with keen black eyes and closely cropped hair, a genial man and a "general favorite."

Mesplie did not start his missionary labors in Idaho until he was almost forty years old. When he arrived in the Boise Basin in the early 1860s he was surprised to find well over 10,000 gold seekers in the district, many of them Irish Catholics fresh from the exhausted California mines. He immediately started working with other priests in the area to raise funds to build churches in Idaho City, Placerville, Centerville, and Pioneerville. All four churches were built and dedicated within months of each other in 1863–64.

When his good friend Bishop Louis Lootens, first vicar apostolic of Idaho, was summoned to attend the Vatican Council in Rome in 1869, Fr. Mesplie was named administrator of the vicariate during his absence. In that capacity, he decided to build a church in Boise City. He wasted no time raising money, and by Christmas 1870 St. Patrick Church was dedicated. A year later it was destroyed by fire. By 1876, even with his missionary work and appointment as an Army chaplain in August 1872, he succeeded in building another church—St. John's.

Mesplie never forgot the Native Americans who were so close to his heart and for whom he labored much in Oregon. He continued to evangelize them in Idaho and fight for their rights. Edwin V. O'Hara relates in *Pioneer Catholic History of Oregon* that Mesplie "gathered more than two hundred of them [Native Americans] on the parade ground of Fort Boise [near Boise City] and baptized them all on a single day. It is reliably asserted that none of these Indians who was converted by Mesplie ever again bore arms against the whites." Mesplie proved himself an "indefatigable pioneer priest of the Catholic Church in Idaho. . . . He was revered and respected by all who came in contact with him; even his few political enemies respected him" (*History of the Diocese of Boise*).

Mesplie died November 20, 1895, in Grass Valley, California, where he was visiting his nephew. He was buried in the Grass Valley Cemetery where Bishop Edward Kelly of Boise erected a monument over his grave in 1950.

COLETTE COWMAN

MESSMER, SEBASTIAN (1847–1930)

Educator and archbishop. Sebastian Gebhard Messmer was born in Goldach, Switzerland, on August 27, 1847, and he began his studies for the priesthood at the University of Innsbruck, Austria, in 1866. He was ordained on July 23, 1871, by Bishop Athanasius Edward Zuber in Innsbruck. In October 1871 at the behest of Bishop James Roosevelt Bayley of Newark, Messmer emigrated to the United States and began teaching theology and canon law at Seton Hall College in South Orange, New Jersey. Dur-

Sebastian Messmer

ing his eighteen-year tenure at Seton Hall, he also served as a pastoral assistant to St. Mary's Orphanage in Newark.

Messmer served as a consulting theologian at the Third Plenary Council of Baltimore in 1884, and as a reward Pope Leo XIII conferred on him an honorary doctorate in divinity. In 1889 he was appointed to the faculty of the newly opened Catholic University of America. He spent a year of preparation at the Apollinaire College in Rome, where he earned a doctorate in canon law. In 1891 he was appointed bishop of Green Bay, Wisconsin, and was consecrated March 27, 1892, in Newark by Bishop Otto Zardetti. Despite the press of his episcopal duties Messmer retained his love for scholarship and published widely.

He served ten years in Green Bay, building schools and social welfare institutions. His reputation in the hierarchy was as a conservative and a "Germanizer." Messmer was an outspoken defender of the rights of Germans in the American Catholic Church and pleaded for the existence of distinctive German parishes and schools. Messmer was also critical of Prohibition, women's suffrage, and socialism. His disagreements with American socialists attracted a good deal of attention when he became archbishop of Milwaukee in 1904 and contended with rising socialist political influence in the city.

Together with Bishop James McFaul of Trenton, Messmer became an important force in the American Federation of Catholic Societies (AFCS). This organization, begun in 1901, attempted to coordinate the activities of lay Catholic organizations. It prospered briefly and collapsed in 1919.

In 1904 Messmer was transferred to the Archdiocese of Milwaukee, where he effected a major centralization of archdiocesan offices. Messmer continued to be pro-German, but in view of difficulties he had with Milwaukee's Polish community, he reversed his earlier support of ethnic diversity. Violent clashes with Fr. Wenceslaus Kruszka and his brother, newspaper editor Michael Kruszka, over the appointment of a Polish auxiliary bishop nearly caused a schism. Eventually tempers cooled and calm was restored. Messmer had two eastern European auxiliaries, Joseph Koudelka (a Bohemian), who became bishop of Superior, and Edward Kozlowski (a Pole), who died a year after his consecration.

Messmer favored formation of the National Catholic Welfare Conference and played a role in the formation of the Catholic Hospital Association. His efforts on behalf of higher education were considerable. He reorganized the archdiocesan seminary, encouraged the efforts of the Jesuits at Marquette University, and welcomed into the archdiocese Mt. St. Mary's College, a women's school operated by the School Sisters of Notre Dame. He also established a Catholic chaplaincy at the University of Wisconsin in 1904.

Messmer's health had deteriorated badly throughout the 1920s. When he traveled to Switzerland in 1930, Apostolic Delegate Pietro Fumasoni-Biondi suggested that he accept a coadjutor. He died in Switzerland on August 3, 1930, and was buried in his native Goldach.

See also GERMAN CATHOLICS IN AMERICA; WISCONSIN, CATHOLIC CHURCH IN.

Blied, Benjamin. *Three Archbishops of Milwaukee: Michael Heiss (1818–1890), Frederick Katzer (1844–1903), Sebastian Messmer (1847–1930)*. Milwaukee, Wisconsin, 1955.

Ede, Alfred J. *The Lay Crusade for a Christian American: A Study of the American Federation of Catholic Societies*. New York: Garland, 1988.

Kuzniewski, Anthony. *Faith and Fatherland*. University of Notre Dame Press, 1980.

STEVEN M. AVELLA

MEŠTROVIĆ, IVAN (1883–1962)

Sculptor, Yugoslavian nationalist. Meštrović was born in Vrpolj, Croatia, on August 15, 1883. Born into a peasant family, he first learned to carve from his father and was apprenticed to the marble cutter Pavle Bilinic at age thirteen. At age seventeen he went to Vienna to study at the Academy of Fine Arts under Edmund von Hellmer. By 1910 he had exhibited throughout Europe and is credited with inspiring a national artistic movement among Croats and Serbs. Meštrović spent World War I in Britain helping to create postwar Yugoslavia, but later refused a seat in the Provisional National Assembly. He served as rector at the Academy of Fine Arts in Zagreb, Croatia, from 1925 until 1941, when he was imprisoned by the Fascists

Ivan Meštrović

for his pro-Allied sympathies. He was released through Vatican intervention after four and a half months and took refuge in Switzerland for the remainder of the war. After the war he voluntarily exiled himself from his homeland when it was placed under Communist rule. He emigrated to the United States in 1947 and became a citizen in 1953. He was professor of fine arts at Syracuse University from 1947 until 1955, when he left to join the faculty at the University of Notre Dame, where he held the position of resident sculptor until his death.

Meštrović was the first living sculptor to be honored with a one-man show at the Metropolitan Museum of Art in New York and was known internationally for his modern religious sculptures, including *My Mother at Prayer* and *A Monument to Gregory, Bishop of Nin.* He died in South Bend, Indiana, on January 16, 1962, and was buried in his home village of Otavice in the family mausoleum he designed.

TRICIA T. PYNE

MEYER, ALBERT CARDINAL (1903–65)

Educator and cardinal archbishop. Albert Gregory Meyer was born in Milwaukee, Wisconsin, on March 9, 1903, the son of Peter and Mathilda Thelen Meyer. In 1917 he entered St. Francis Seminary in Milwaukee and began his preparation for the priesthood. In 1921, he was dispatched to Rome by Archbishop Sebastian G. Messmer for theological studies at the Propaganda College. There he completed a doctorate in theology and was ordained to the priesthood on July 11, 1926. Roman education left a deep impress on young Meyer and inculcated in him a reflex-

ive obedience to the papacy. In his years in the hierarchy virtually no speech or writing that issued from him lacked a lengthy quote from a papal document.

Early Years

He remained in Rome for additional studies at the Pontifical Biblical Institute and completed work on his licentiate in 1930. In that year he was assigned to a parish in Waukesha, Wisconsin. The following year, Archbishop Samuel A. Stritch appointed him to the faculty of St. Francis Seminary where he was a professor of dogma, biblical geography, ascetical theology, and religion. In 1937 he was appointed rector of St. Francis Seminary. Although his administrative duties left him little time for scholarship, he did participate in the translation work for the Confraternity of Christian Doctrine version of the Bible by translating and commenting on the three Johannine epistles. He left seminary work in 1946 when he was nominated to the Diocese of Superior, Wisconsin. He was consecrated a bishop by Archbishop Moses E. Kiley in Milwaukee's St. John the Evangelist Cathedral on April 11, 1946, and was formally installed as the sixth bishop of Superior on May 8, 1946. Meyer was a taciturn and introverted man, highly uncomfortable with public roles, yet he accepted episcopal responsibilities as a matter of dutiful obedience.

The Diocese of Superior comprised the sixteen northernmost counties of Wisconsin. A remote and underpopulated area with a scattered Catholic population, Meyer's episcopate (1946–53) was spent largely building up the ranks of the diocesan clergy and fostering a sense of dioce-

Albert Cardinal Meyer

san unity. He inaugurated some modest building projects and established a Catholic newspaper, a diocesan council of Catholic women, and a branch of the Serra Club to promote vocations to the priesthood.

In July 1953 he was appointed to succeed Moses E. Kiley as archbishop of Milwaukee and was installed on September 21, 1953. His administration saw a rapid growth in the Catholic population of southeastern Wisconsin, especially in the suburbs ringing the major cities of the see. Under Meyer, twenty-five new parishes were established. Moreover, thirty-five new grade schools, four new high schools, and new facilities for all the major institutions of higher education were built as well. Meyer issued a major pastoral letter entitled "Modesty and Decency" in 1956 that won national attention.

Archbishop of Chicago

In September 1958 he replaced Cardinal Samuel Stritch as the Archbishop of Chicago. He was formally installed in Chicago's Holy Name Cathedral on November 15, 1958. At that time the Archdiocese of Chicago had the largest concentration of Catholics in the United States (about two million). For Meyer the fast pace of the largely urban diocese, replete with economic and racial tensions, was a distinct departure from the relative calm of rural Superior or even Milwaukee. This came home to Meyer shortly after his installation, when a tragic fire at Our Lady of Angels school killed over ninety children and three teachers. Investigations of the fire brought a deluge of unfavorable publicity on the archdiocese, including Meyer, who attempted to reply to the horrendous tragedy with pious statements about "the will of God." The aftermath of the incident brought major changes in the construction codes for school buildings nationwide and mandated the upgrading of fire-safety procedures and equipment. Meyer dutifully implemented these in archdiocesan facilities.

Public issues related to race, especially the rapidly accelerating national civil rights movement, also required new forms of leadership from Meyer. To this he responded unambiguously. With the urging of priests who worked in Chicago's interracial movement and in African American parishes, Meyer departed from the policies of his predecessor and placed the full prestige of his office behind effort to integrate Chicago's Catholic schools. This came in the form of a firmly worded instruction to his priests in 1961 wherein Meyer forbade racial discrimination in Catholic schools and parishes. Privately, he confronted pastors and school administrators who attempted to circumvent his orders. He also pressured suburban pastors to welcome African American families to their parishes. In 1963, while serving as a host to a national conference on religion and race that met in Chicago, he publicly de-

cried racism as a "pathology." With these actions he joined the growing number of American bishops who spoke out forcefully on racial justice.

Meyer's work in racial issues brought him into an uneasy alliance with community organizer Saul D. Alinsky and his Industrial Areas Foundation. Seeking to stabilize changing Chicago neighborhoods afflicted by "whiteflight," Meyer gave support to Alinsky's organizers who were able to establish the Organization of the Southwest Community and a community organization on the city's near north side. Archdiocesan funds were also committed to the Woodlawn Organization, and all-black community group on Chicago's south side. In all these endeavors he was advised and supported by a cadre of activist priests in his archdiocese, especially Msgr. John Egan, head of the Archdiocesan Office of Urban Affairs. Ultimately, these efforts at neighborhood integration were unsuccessful, and Catholic institutions in those areas either accommodated new African American majorities or withered away.

Vatican Council II

Meyer was appointed to the College of Cardinals in 1960 and played a prominent role in the planning and administration of the Vatican Council II. At the council he joined the progressive bishops who eventually came to dominate the proceedings. With help from his theological advisors Barnabas Mary Ahern, C.P., and Francis McCool, S.J., Meyer made major interventions related to such documents as *Dei verbum, Gaudium et spes,* and *Lumen gentium.* Personally transformed by the experience of the council, the once-cautious Meyer became a forceful advocate for ecumenical amity and issued a pastoral letter to his archdiocese in 1964 encouraging interdenominational cooperation. Meyer, like many other American bishops, favored a strong conciliar statement in defense of religious liberty. As such he took a keen interest in the document prepared by Jesuit John Courtney Murray and others which would later emerge as the Declaration on Religious Liberty. When council president Cardinal Eugene Tisserant announced a delay in a critical preliminary vote on the document in late November 1964, Meyer, one of the council presidents, carried a hastily drafted petition to Pope Paul VI requesting a reversal of the decision. Although the Pontiff upheld the delay, Meyer and others redoubled their efforts to rework the document, which eventually passed in the council's final session. By the time of his death Meyer was considered the leading American prelate at the council.

Unfortunately, Meyer did not live to witness the passage of the document. In February 1965 he was diagnosed with a malignant brain tumor and, although he submitted to surgery, he never recovered. He died in Chicago on

April 11, 1965, and was buried in St. Mary of the Lake Cemetery in Mundelein, Illinois.

See also CIVIL RIGHTS MOVEMENT AND CATHOLICS, THE; ILLINOIS, CATHOLIC CHURCH IN; VATICAN COUNCIL II AND AMERICAN CATHOLICS; WISCONSIN, CATHOLIC CHURCH IN.

Avella, Steven M. "The Era of Confidence: Albert G. Meyer and the Transitional Church." *U.S. Catholic Historian* 7 (Winter 1988) 91–111.
____. *This Confident Church.* University of Notre Dame Press, 1992.

STEVEN M. AVELLA

MICHEL, VIRGIL (1890–1938)

Liturgical pioneer. Virgil Michel, Benedictine monk of St. John's Abbey in Collegeville, Minnesota, deserves more than anyone else the title of founder of the American Catholic liturgical movement. In the thirteen short years from 1925 to his untimely death in 1938 at the age of forty-eight, he set in place a number of the structures that would prosper the work of other liturgical pioneers—structures which exist to the present day.

Virgil Michel

Early Life and Education

George Michel was born on June 26, 1890, into a large Minnesota family of German extraction. After high school and two years of college at schools run by the Benedictines of St. John's Abbey, he entered the novitiate there at the age of nineteen. Ordained a priest in 1916, he immediately began a doctoral program in English at The Catho-

lic University of America in Washington, D.C., which took him only two years to complete.

From 1918 to 1924 he held various administrative and teaching positions at St. John's until his abbot sent him to Rome to study scholastic philosophy as a preparation for teaching seminarians. Little did the abbot realize that scholastic philosophy was soon to cede its place in Michel's interests to the Roman Catholic liturgical movement as it had developed in Europe during much of the nineteenth century and on into the twentieth. Michel would return to Collegeville a year and a half later prepared to alter the apostolic course of St. John's Abbey and, indeed, of Roman Catholic piety in the United States.

One of the principal influences felt by Michel during his eighteen months in Europe came in the person and work of his fellow Benedictine, Lambert Beauduin, monk of the Belgian monastery of Mont-César. From Beauduin Michel learned enthusiasm for the liturgy and for the doctrine of the Church as the Mystical Body of Christ, the foundation which gives meaning to active liturgical participation. Beauduin had himself extended the European liturgical movement from its nineteenth-century life within the walls of Benedictine monasteries to a wider appreciation by lay men and women of active participation in the liturgy as essential to their own spiritual life.

With his abbot's permission Michel abandoned plans to pursue a doctorate in philosophy, and decided instead to further work in that discipline with private study and conversation with leading figures in the field. This refocusing gave him time to acquaint himself in much more detail with the European liturgical movement, its leaders and centers. He traveled to the Benedictine abbeys of Solesmes, Maredsous, Beuron, Maria Laach, and Mont-César, his eyes and ears open to what was happening, imagining how this transformation of piety could be transplanted and flourish in American Catholicism.

Michel saw even further possibilities for the American Church. He understood how a sense of the Church as the body of Christ and enactment of this sense in active participation in the liturgy could become the basis of a renewed sense of the need for social reform in his country. Transforming the dominantly individualistic piety of American Catholics into a corporate spirituality could enable them to meet the ethical challenges of the time with new motivation and enthusiasm.

Michel's grasp of the larger possibilities never prevented him from imagining the details of how this transplanting could take place. During his stay in Europe he envisioned his abbey in Collegeville taking the lead in popularizing liturgical reform through translation and publication of works by European liturgical scholars, along with original writing at a more popular level and the foundation of a journal to support interest in the movement. All these plans would materialize in the years ahead and transform St.

John's Abbey into the center of inspiration of what would become the American Catholic liturgical movement.

The Beginning of the American Liturgical Movement (1925–30)

Once back at Collegeville, Michel began the work he had conceived during his months in Europe. Through the newly founded Liturgical Press he published several important European works on the liturgy in English translation, among them *Liturgy and the Life of the Church* (1926) from the French of his mentor Dom Lambert Beauduin. He developed the "Popular Liturgical Library," designed to present a series of pamphlets on liturgical topics. Then, with the advent of 1926, America saw the first issue of the journal *Orate Fratres,* which lives today under the title *Worship,* as the major journal of liturgical studies in the English-speaking world. The Liturgical Press and *Orate Fratres* became the vehicle for rallying and focusing the work of other American liturgical pioneers, Martin Hellriegel, William Busch, and Gerald Ellard, among others.

As with any new movement, the liturgical movement often found itself poorly understood and even suspect. The fathers and mothers of the American movement were aware of their task: to speak with commitment and prudence. They also realized the scope of their work: to educate American Catholics to understand their relation to God and to one another in a new way. Virgil Michel had given them a press and a journal to spread the word. And spread the word they did, to an often unknowing and sometimes hostile audience over the next forty years until the final seal of approval of their work came with the Constitution on the Liturgy of the Second Vatican Council.

Paul Marx, Michel's biographer, describes the scope and influence of Michel's personal dealings in the cause of liturgical renewal:

> His unusual ability, by conversation or letter, to initiate projects and keep them going; to win the cooperation of others; of enthusing co-workers, arousing their interest and setting them to action. . . . There could hardly have been a liturgical project in this country for which Dom Virgil did not dispense advice, or in which he did not play some role.

While The Liturgical Press did not yet have the equipment or staff to take on publication of what would become the *Leaflet Missal,* Michel offered his suggestions and support to the publishers of this pioneering effort and, in January 1930, Catholics had available this modest but effective resource to follow the Mass each Sunday.

While the range of Michel's interests and talents was unusually wide, he devoted a generous amount of his time and energy in particular to the field of religious education. He understood that changing the vision of American Catholics meant working with the young people to whom the future belonged. He pioneered an approach to catechetics that engaged the learners in a dialogue based in their experience and level of sophistication rather than the dry routine of rote memory prevalent in Catholic school classrooms of that era. He tried as well to relate the classroom learning to the worship experience of the students as the liturgical cycle turned each year.

Michel set out his theories of religious education in *Orate Fratres* and journals of education such as *The Catholic Educational Review* and the *Journal of Religious Instruction.* In 1934–35 he collaborated with Basil Stegmann, O.S.B., and the Dominican Sisters of Grand Rapids in producing *The Christ-Life Series* for grade school students. By 1938, at the time of his death, he had published *The Christian Religion Series for High School* in collaboration with Jane Marie Murray, O.P. With monks of his own abbey and, once again, with the Grand Rapids Dominicans, he published *The Christian Religion Series for College.*

The Development of the Liturgical Movement (1930–1938)

Between 1925 and 1930, in addition to founding The Liturgical Press and *Orate Fratres,* writing and speaking in support of the infant American liturgical movement, Michel edited some twenty publications, organized a liturgical summer school, and began this new series of religion texts along with his many duties as a teacher and administrator at St. John's Abbey and its schools. But his prodigious energy finally gave out at the turn of the decade when overwork nearly ruined his eyesight and brought him close to a nervous breakdown.

After a lengthy stay in the hospital to recover his strength, Michel was sent to northern Minnesota to do some minimal missionary activity with the Ojibwe tribe of Native Americans. The hope was to reduce the pressures of his previous regime and stabilize his physical and mental health. Michel, limited though he was in strength, turned his talents and attention to this new work and exercised significant leadership with the tribe over the next three years.

Called back to St. John's in 1933, Michel entered what would be the final five-year phase of his career. With the background of the depression in American life he moved *Orate Fratres* more in the direction of emphasis on the spiritual basis for social reform. His constant theme was that only when men and women come to see themselves as members of the Mystical Body of Christ with relations to God through Jesus and with relations to one another in the body of Jesus would they be able to set aside their inclination to a selfish individualism and realize their responsibilities to one another. Active participation in the liturgy would set the pattern and nourish the life of the

Mystical Body. In 1935 Michel constructed a syllogism that became the shorthand version of his message: Pius X tells us that the liturgy is the primary and indispensable source of the true Christian spirit; Pius XI says that the true Christian spirit is indispensable for social regeneration. Therefore, the liturgy is the indispensable basis of Christian social regeneration.

With the perspective of fifty years on the work of Virgil Michel, Kenneth Himes, O.F.M., wrote this assessment in 1988:

> In the end, then, Michel's great contribution to liturgical renewal was his effort at linking liturgy to social justice. His contribution to the movement of social reform was tying it to the center of Catholic life, the Church's liturgy. . . . At present there is great interest among social activists for developing a spirituality for social ministry. Among liturgists there is a resolve that the prayer of our communities offer ways of more deeply entering into the mission of the church in the world. As these two trends converge we may come to meet at the place where Virgil Michel stood fifty years ago.

Worn out with his many and complex labors, Michel fell fatally ill with pneumonia in late November 1938 and died a few days later at the age of forty-eight. Tributes poured in from all over the country, evidence of the widespread effect of his apostolate and of the far-flung network of his colleagues as well as the many clerics, religious, and laity for whom he had been a mentor.

Indeed, so effective had his leadership been that his sudden and early death left a shocked hush among those with whom he had worked. Gradually, however, they rallied in memory of the dynamo who in the short space of thirteen years had succeeded in laying the foundation for a new American Catholic piety. The results of his labors live decades after his death.

Conclusion

Paul Marx closes his biography of Michel by quoting Cardinal Emmanuel Suhard's description of a zealous priest:

> Like Christ, the priest brings mankind a priceless good, that of worrying it. He must be the "minister of restlessness"; the dispenser of a new thirst and a new hunger. . . . The revolt which the priest must advocate is the insurrection of consciences, the order which he comes to disturb is the apparent calm which covers up disorders and hatreds. . . . Eternally unsatisfied . . . he rejects the calm . . . to start a ferment.

And, as Marx concludes, "Dom Virgil Michel, it seems, was this kind of priest and caused this kind of ferment."

See also LITURGICAL MOVEMENT IN AMERICA, THE.

Franklin, R. W., and Robert L. Spaeth. *Virgil Michel: American Catholic.* Collegeville: The Liturgical Press, 1988.

Marx, Paul B. *Virgil Michel and the Liturgical Movement.* Collegeville: The Liturgical Press, 1957.

Worship 62 (3) (May 1988). This issue is devoted to an assessment of Virgil Michel's life and work fifty years after his death.

J. LEO KLEIN, S.J.

MICHIGAN, CATHOLIC CHURCH IN

The Mission Era

Two French Jesuits, Charles Raymbaut and Isaac Jogues, made the first missionary visit to Sault Ste. Marie in 1641. Then the Iroquois war in the 1640s depopulated Michigan. Fr. René Ménard resumed the delayed mission activity on the Keweenaw Bay in 1660, disappearing the next year in Wisconsin. In 1665 Fr. Claude Allouez reestablished the Keweenaw site. Following the Iroquois war, Fr. Jacques Marquette and Br. Louis de Boesme established a mission at Sault Ste. Marie in 1668. Fr. Claude Dablon replaced Marquette in 1669 and also established the Mission of St. Ignace on Mackinaw Island in 1670. The next year, Marquette moved the mission to its current site in the Upper Peninsula. Here Marquette was buried. Dablon noted that this spot was "the great resort of all Nations going to or coming from the north or the south."

In late 1675, Fr. Henri Nouvel rendered the first ministries in the Lower Peninsula at Thunder Bay and celebrated the first Mass in the interior near Saginaw. A cabin and chapel were built farther inland (in Isabella County) to pass the winter.

In early 1670, Fr. François Dollier and a deacon, René de Galine, were the first clerics to set foot in the Detroit area. In 1679 Fr. Louis Hennepin sailed aboard the *Griffon* to Green Bay. He continued by canoe to the St. Joseph River in southwest Michigan where a temporary fort was built and services were held. It is conjectured that Fr. Claude Jean Allouez established another mission on the St. Joseph just south of Niles, Michigan, and died there in 1689. This mission seems to have lasted until the destruction of Fort St. Joseph in the Pontiac uprising of 1763. By then many of the Potawatomi had been initiated into the Church.

The French established a fort at Detroit to secure the interior and to centralize the trade with the Native Americans. This drew them from the Jesuit Missions and quickly made Detroit the largest settlement in Michigan, serviced by Franciscan Recollects. St. Anne parish, the second oldest continuous parish in the United States, dates its origin from July 26, 1701, two days after the founding of the fort.

The British annexed this French territory in 1763, ending much of the French mission work among the Native Americans. They maintained control until the American takeover in 1796, which allowed Bishop John Carroll to appoint Gabriel Richard to St. Anne in 1798, to assist its pastor, Michael Levadoux. Richard made noteworthy contributions to the region in education and religion. He was the second founder of the settlement after its disastrous fire of 1805, served as the first priest in the United States Congress, and was named the first bishop of Detroit (though his letters of appointment were never sent from Rome), and died serving his flock in a cholera epidemic in 1832. It was in Richard's time, during the middle 1820s, that the population of Detroit began to shift from its mixture of French Catholics and American Protestants to one including Irish Catholics and others due to increased immigration. One early priest who served these newcomers was the Swiss-born Martin Kundig (1805–79). Kundig came to the city in 1833 and was instrumental in helping it organize its first hospital, orphanage, and benevolent society. He left the state in 1842 for Milwaukee, having incurred a great debt.

Diocesan Structures

The first bishop of Detroit (established as a diocese on March 8, 1833) was Frederic Résé (1833–71), who lived in Europe after 1839 due to a number of conflicts. His diocese covered Michigan and Wisconsin (lost to Milwaukee in 1843), as well as Iowa, Minnesota, and parts of the Dakotas (all lost to Dubuque in 1837). On November 24, 1841, Peter Paul Lefevere (1804–68) was consecrated coadjutor bishop and administrator of Detroit. His major accomplishments included restoring the fiscal state of the diocese; promoting temperance; erecting a new cathedral by 1848 (SS Peter and Paul) to free himself from trustee controls at St. Anne; gaining legal right under new Michigan law (1867) to hold all property in "fee simple"; instilling discipline through diocesan synods (1859 and 1862); opening the Seminary of St. Thomas (1846–54) in his residence; visiting his far-flung missions (almost yearly starting in 1842).

Lefevere also recruited Sisters of the Holy Cross (1843); Redemptorists (1844); many clergy from Belgium; Daughters of Charity (1844), who founded Providence Hospital in Detroit (origins in 1869) and St. Mary's Hospital in Saginaw (1874); Sisters, Servants of the Immaculate Heart of Mary in Monroe (1845) under Mother Teresa Maxis Duchemin; Brothers of Christian Schools (1851); Religious of the Sacred Heart (1851); and School Sisters of Notre Dame (1852). He also helped to found The American College in Louvain (1857), sending the college its first four rectors. He was unsuccessful in seeking public funds for Catholic schools (1852–53). He saw the Catholic population increase from under 25,000 to over 150,000 and the number of parishes grow from 30 to 80.

The Upper Peninsula was separated from the jurisdiction of Bishop Lefevere on July 29, 1853, with the creation of the vicariate apostolic of Sault Ste. Marie. Frederic Baraga (1797–1868) was consecrated its first vicar apostolic on November 1, 1853. On November 30, 1855, his vicariate became a diocese that was transferred to Marquette on October 15, 1867. This saintly man was noted for his extensive missionary journeys to serve his people, especially the Native Americans.

Growth and Development

Casper Henry Borgess (1826–90) was ordained coadjutor of Detroit on April 24, 1870. This humble bishop came to serve a people who were now predominantly German and Irish with mostly Belgian (thirty-nine of eighty-eight) and German clergy. His desire for discipline, efficiency, and a native clergy meant conflicts with nationalities and eccentric clergy. These conflicts included the Legel-Bunbury Affair (1871–73) over sloppy clerical financing in St. Augustine parish, Kalamazoo; the uncanonical transfer of Fr. Desiderius Callaert (1879) for which Borgess submitted his resignation (January 31, 1879; it was not accepted); the final termination of the trustees' control of St. Anne parish (1883) involving the closing of Fr. Richard's old church on June 27, 1886; and the fight against several attempts by the state legislature to impose lay trusteeism on Catholic Church properties.

The death of Bishop Résé on December 30, 1871, made Borgess the second bishop of Detroit. Borgess conducted five synods (1873, 1878, 1881, 1885, and 1886). He also gave his cathedral to the Jesuits to open the state's first Catholic College in 1877 (moved in 1926 to the McNichols campus as the University of Detroit). This necessitated using St. Aloysius as a pro-cathedral. Borgess brought in the Little Sisters of the Poor (1874); Dominican Sisters (at Adrian from 1878); Felician Sisters (1880; motherhouse moved to Detroit in 1881); Mercy Sisters who opened their hospital in Big Rapids in 1879; and Order of Friars Minor Capuchins (St. Bonaventure Monastery 1883). He began the diocese's first school board (1886).

Borgess also opened the Seminary of St. Francis in Monroe (1886–89) and dedicated the national Polish seminary, SS Cyril and Methodius, in December 1886 in Detroit (transferred to Orchard Lake in 1910). Borgess gave diocesan approval to the *Western Home Journal* (founded in 1872) in 1878. This newspaper took a new name, the *Michigan Catholic,* in 1883 when William Henry Hughes became owner and editor, his position until his death in 1917. The precipitating cause of Borgess' retirement was his dispute with the Polish over his suspension of Fr. Dominic Kolasiński (1885). A schism ensued that was only resolved by Rome in 1893. These conflicts added to the burden of his heart ailment and Rome acceded on April 16, 1887, to his request to retire to his home on Lake St. Clair. The Diocese of Detroit, now reduced in size, had

120,000 Catholics with 99 diocesan and 32 religious priests serving 90 churches.

On May 19, 1882, the Lower Peninsula was divided with the establishment of the Diocese of Grand Rapids. A Cincinnati priest, Henry Joseph Richter (1838–1916), was ordained the first bishop on April 22, 1883, to serve a Catholic population of about fifty thousand with almost forty priests. Richter proved a prudent bishop, not desiring to build until he had the funds to do so. He held Grand Rapids' first synod in 1903. He opened the minor seminary of St. Joseph in 1909 in Grand Rapids. Dominican sisters from New York began ministering in Traverse City in 1877 and opened Aquinas College (1886) and a motherhouse in Grand Rapids (1889). On September 8, 1915, Michael Gallagher (1866–1937) was ordained the coadjutor bishop, in time for Richter's death a year later.

Baraga's successor in Marquette was Ignatius Mrak (1818–1901). In 1845 he traveled to America where he served the Native Americans in the northwestern Lower Peninsula. He reluctantly agreed to be ordained the second bishop of Marquette on February 7, 1869, to serve twenty thousand Catholics with fourteen priests. He soon left for Rome to attend the First Vatican Council. In 1875 Marquette was removed from the province of Cincinnati and placed in the province of Milwaukee. Due to poor health, Mrak resigned in 1878.

John Vertin (1844–99), like his two predecessors a Slovene from the Carniola province of the Austro-Hungarian Empire, became the third bishop of Marquette on September 14, 1879. His was the first episcopal ordination in the Upper Peninsula. He had been the last priest ordained by Baraga on August 31, 1866. He was confronted with the burning of his cathedral (his new one was consecrated in 1890) and the Irish objection to his transfer of the cathedral's pastor, John C. Kenny, to Mackinaw. The bishop sought a uniform discipline in the diocese, holding a pro-synodal conference in 1889. Frederick Eis (1843–1926) was ordained the fourth bishop of Marquette on August 24, 1899. In 1905 he held the second synod. He resigned his see on July 8, 1922.

John Samuel Foley (1833–1918), a good friend of Cardinal James Gibbons and an Americanist, was named the third bishop of Detroit over the objections of the Congregation for the Propagation of the Faith; he was ordained on November 4, 1888. The first ten years of this charming man's long tenure were marked by a series of conflicts: with the Polish followers of Fr. Dominic Kolasiński, with two priests over the Church farm property, with Fr. Peter Baart in several canonical suits, and with German farmers in the North Dorr Church property dispute. Under his tenure the Knights of Columbus established its first branch in Detroit (1898); the Sisters of St. Joseph came to Kalamazoo (1889); the Immaculate Heart of Mary Sisters opened St. Mary's College, Monroe (1910; became

Marygrove College in Detroit in 1927); the charitable society of the Weinman Settlement Association began in 1906 (predecessor of the League of Catholic Women under its foundress, Mrs. Charles Casgrain, 1915); and the "Foley Guild" at the University of Michigan in 1889 began the foundations of the Catholic Chaplaincy.

In 1906 Josephine VanDyke Brownson laid the foundations of the largely female Catholic Instructional League (1916) that promoted modern methods of catechesis, although it reached only a small percentage of those who needed it. The first-ever mission to non-Catholics in Michigan was held in 1893–94 by the Detroit-born Paulist Walter Elliott. This was expanded to Grand Rapids in 1897. The first Catholic mayor of Detroit was William B. Thompson (1906). Fr. Frank Kelley, a pastor in Lapeer, served as a chaplain in the Spanish-American War. Later, Fr. Patrick Dunnigan was decorated four times as a chaplain in World War I. Foley's poor health limited the effectiveness of his administration during his last twenty years. By his death, the population of Detroit, due to the automobile industry, was approaching one million. The Catholic population of the diocese had outpaced the number of priests (318).

The Twentieth Century

The third bishop of Grand Rapids, Edward Kelly (1860–1926), had taught English at St. Francis Seminary, Monroe, and was consecrated an auxiliary bishop of Detroit on January 26, 1911. Expecting to succeed Foley, he was transferred instead to Grand Rapids on January 16, 1919. He oversaw a period of growth and development during which he built a new St. Joseph Seminary (1920). Together with Bishop Gallagher of Detroit and Bishops Eis and Nussbaum of Marquette, Kelly fought the two anti-Catholic school amendment campaigns of 1920 and 1924. He was succeeded by Joseph Gabriel Pinten (1867–1945) on June 25, 1926. Pinten resigned this see on November 1, 1940, due to poor health. Pinten curtailed the extensive building campaign of Bishop Kelly. Having paid off many of the latter's debts, he prepared the diocese to survive the upcoming depression.

Paul Joseph Nussbaum (1870–1935) was appointed the fifth bishop of Marquette on November 14, 1922. He had to confront the serious decline of the economy and population of his diocese that followed World War I, as well as a shortage of clergy. Nussbaum sought to foster a native clergy but also relied on assistance from the Passionists. Joseph Casimir Plagens (1880–1943), the first bishop ever consecrated in Detroit (an auxiliary), was transferred to Marquette on November 16, 1935 (and again to Grand Rapids on December 16, 1940). He arrived in his diocese to see the charred ruins of his cathedral. He started a successful Catholic Youth program.

Michael Gallagher's first ten years as the fourth bishop of Detroit were noted for a doubling of the Catholic population (386,000 to 725,000); a heavy recruitment of clergy from outside the diocese; the establishment of Sacred Heart Seminary (1919) with a nine-million-dollar fundraising campaign; the erection of numerous parishes and schools guided by a Diocesan Building Committee (1920); the purchase of the *Michigan Catholic* (1920); the origins of ministry to Mexican migrants (1920); the ordination of Fr. Norman Dukette, the first African American priest for the diocese (1926); the building of a chancery and episcopal residence; the naming of Fr. Carroll Deady as superintendent of schools (1934–57); the organization of the Society for the Propagation of the Faith in the diocese (1927); the Catholic Church Extension Society's mission experiment in Lapeer County (1923–25); and the general tightening of administration after the relative laxity of the Foley years.

The Adrian Dominicans incorporated St. Joseph's College in 1919 and the Sisters of St. Joseph opened Nazareth College near Kalamazoo in 1924. Gallagher saw his latter years tied up by the activities of the "Radio Priest," Fr. Charles Coughlin, and the financial crisis of the depression. He died on January 20, 1937. The Catholic mayor, Frank Murphy (1930–34), led the city's efforts to assist victims of the depression. He became the state's first Catholic governor in 1937 and mediated the sit-down strikes by automobile workers at General Motors and Chrysler. Murphy was named the U.S. Attorney General (1939–40) and then an associate justice of the Supreme Court.

The Diocese of Lansing was established on May 22, 1937, and its first bishop, Joseph Albers (1891–1965), was named to this see on August 4, 1937, the day after Detroit was made an archdiocese incorporating the whole state of Michigan in its province. Albers had been awarded the Silver Star as a chaplain in World War I. He oversaw an increase of 268 buildings and witnessed the Catholic population grow from 68,000 to 204,000 with 204 priests. He was succeeded by Alexander Zaleski (1906–75) on December 1, 1965, and by Kenneth J. Povish (born in 1924), who was transferred to Lansing on October 8, 1975. Povish's resignation was accepted on November 7, 1995, and Carl Frederick Mengeling (born in 1930) was named the fourth bishop of Lansing on the same day, being consecrated a bishop on January 25, 1996.

The Diocese of Saginaw was established on February 26, 1938. Its first bishop was William F. Murphy (1885–1950). This canon lawyer established the organization of the new diocese, holding its first synod in 1945. He started a Spanish-speaking migrant worker ministry and began the diocesan paper, the *Catholic Weekly* (1942). Murphy saw the Catholic population increase from 77,000 to 108,000. His successor was Stephen Woznicki (1894–1968), who was appointed to Saginaw on March 28, 1950. Woznicki was

responsible for erecting 158 new buildings, including St. Paul Seminary (1960). He strengthened other diocesan organizations before poor health forced his resignation on October 30, 1968, when there were 173,000 Catholics and 196 priests. Francis F. Reh (1911–94) was appointed to Saginaw on December 11, 1968, and retired April 29, 1980. Kenneth Untener (born in 1937) was ordained the fourth bishop of Saginaw on November 24, 1980.

The seventh bishop of Marquette, Francis J. Magner (1887–1947), was consecrated on February 24, 1941. He founded the diocesan paper, *Northern Michigan*. Thomas L. Noa (1892–1977) was appointed to Marquette on August 25, 1947. He organized Catholic Social Services for the Upper Peninsula, established the Lay Apostolate, erected over one hundred buildings, conducted the 1950 synod, and convinced the Sisters of St. Paul of Chartres to establish their United States motherhouse in Marquette in 1963. He retired on January 5, 1968, from serving his 100,000 Catholics and 170 priests. Charles A. Salatka (born in 1918) was appointed to Marquette on January 5, 1968, and transferred to Oklahoma City on October 11, 1977. He was followed by Mark F. Schmitt (born in 1923) on March 15, 1978, who retired on October 6, 1992, and by James H. Garland (born in 1931), appointed on October 6, 1992.

The fifth bishop of Grand Rapids was Joseph Casimir Plagens, transferred from Marquette on December 16, 1940. He suffered several heart attacks and very poor health, leading to his death on March 31, 1943, when there were 80,000 Catholics in the diocese. His successor was the labor mediator Francis Haas (1889–1953). Haas had taught at St. Francis Seminary in Milwaukee and at The Catholic University of America. He served as President Roosevelt's first chair of the Fair Employment Practices Committee. President Truman named him to the fifteen-member Committee on Civil Rights in 1945. In the diocese, he founded the diocesan paper, the *Western Michigan Catholic,* promoted adult education in the Church's social teachings, and held the second synod (1948). At the time of his death, the diocese had grown to 127,000 Catholics. Allen J. Babcock (1898–1969) was appointed Haas' successor on March 23, 1954. Joseph M. Breitenbeck (born in 1914) was appointed to Grand Rapids on October 6, 1969, and retired on June 24, 1989. The current (1997) ordinary, Robert J. Rose (born in 1930), was named the same day.

Detroit received its fifth ordinary in the person of Archbishop Edward Mooney (1882–1958) on August 3, 1937. He was elevated to the cardinalate on February 18, 1946. In Detroit, Mooney faced difficulties with finances (a twenty-two-million-dollar diocesan-wide debt), for which he rearranged financing in 1941 (eliminated by 1945), established a central "bank" for all parish deposits and borrowing, and began the Archdiocesan Development Fund

(1943). Mooney also faced problems with organization, for which he had chancery visitations conducted (1940, 1948, 1954), held the eighth and ninth synods (1944 and 1954), opened the Provincial Theologate of St. John's Seminary, Plymouth (1949–88), and supplanted the small Catholic Instructional League with the Confraternity of Christian Doctrine (1938, under Fr. John Ryan). Mooney also had difficulties with labor, for which he began the Archdiocesan Labor Institute (1939) and a Department of Social Action (1938), and supported the Association of Catholic Trade Unionists (1938) under Paul Weber and labor priests like Raymond Clancy. Perhaps Mooney's biggest problem was with Coughlin, whom he restrained, and eventually, with government pressure, silenced.

Mooney's era saw the beginnings of the Home Visitors of Mary (1949) for work among African Americans; the Catholic Worker's St. Francis House under Louis J. Murphy (1937); Mercy College (1941); Madonna College (1947); the Sister Formation under Sr. Mary Emil Penet, I.H.M. (1954–60); the Michigan Catholic Welfare Committee (predecessor of the Michigan Catholic Conference) in 1944; the ministry of Msgr. Clement Kern (Holy Trinity parish, 1945–77); and the liturgical leadership of Fr. Leo Trese (1950s). He also designated a new cathedral, Blessed Sacrament (1937), invited Guest House to operate in the diocese (1956), and saw the Catholic population of the diocese grow to 1.3 million.

Post-Vatican Council II

John Francis Dearden (1907–88) was transferred to Detroit on December 18, 1958. His primary mode of renewal in Detroit was diocesan-wide adult education. He conducted the tenth synod (1969). With the defeat of the campaign to allow state funds for Catholic schools (Proposition "C" in 1970) he closed one-fifth of the Catholic schools. He was outspoken on behalf of civil rights, earning some enmity by his financial support of urban projects after the riots of 1967. He was entrusted by his fellow bishops with organizing the American Bicentennial celebration that culminated in the Call to Action Conference of Detroit (1976). He was created a cardinal on April 28, 1969. He retired on July 15, 1980.

On December 19, 1970, the Diocese of Kalamazoo was erected and its first bishop, Paul Donovan (born in 1924), was consecrated on July 21, 1971, to serve over 80,000 Catholics and about eighty priests. He resigned his see in November 1994 when he was replaced by Alfred John Markiewicz (born in 1928), who died January 7, 1997.

The Diocese of Gaylord was created the same day as Kalamazoo. Edmund C. Szoka (born in 1927) was consecrated the first bishop on July 20, 1971, to serve 70,000 Catholics and about 77 priests. He was transferred to Detroit on March 21, 1981. Robert Rose (born in 1930) was ordained bishop of Gaylord on December 6, 1981, and was transferred to Grand Rapids on June 24, 1989. Patrick Cooney (born in 1934) was named to Gaylord on November 6, 1989.

Edmund Szoka came to Detroit as its seventh ordinary. He was involved in a number of controversies: the Sr. Agnes Mary Mansour case, the dispute over general absolution, the closing of St. John's Seminary and the beginning of a Theologate at Sacred Heart Major Seminary (1988), the initiation of the Catholic Services Appeal, and the closing of a number of urban parishes. Szoka reformed the Tribunal, the archives, and the telecommunications office. He welcomed Pope John Paul II to Detroit (September 18–19, 1987). On June 28, 1988, he was elevated to the cardinalate. He resigned his see on April 28, 1990, having been named the president of the Prefecture of the Economic Affairs of the Holy See.

The current (1997) archbishop of Detroit is Adam Maida (born in 1930), appointed on April 28, 1990. Maida initiated a successful one-hundred-million-dollar endowment campaign for the archdiocese. He was created a cardinal on November 26, 1994.

In January 1996 statistics for the Church in Michigan showed a total of 2,185,242 Catholics (23 percent of the state's population) served by 1,165 diocesan priests and 357 religious priests in 799 parishes and 60 missions. There were 291 permanent deacons, 95 religious brothers, and 2,568 female religious serving in the state.

Boyea, Earl. "Father Kolasinski and the Church of Detroit." *Catholic Historical Review* 74 (July 1988) 420–39.

McGee, J. *The Catholic Church in the Grand River Valley, 1833–1950.* Grand Rapids, Michigan, 1950.

Michalek, G. *Golden Jubilee: Diocese of Lansing Parish Historical Sketches.* Lansing, Michigan, 1987.

Paré, G. *The Catholic Church in Detroit, 1701–1888.* Detroit: Wayne State University Press, 1983.

Rezek, A. *History of the Diocese of Sault Ste. Marie and Marquette.* 2 vols. Chicago: M. A. Donohue & Co., 1906.

Tentler, L. *Seasons of Grace: A History of the Catholic Archdiocese of Detroit.* Detroit: Wayne State University Press, 1990.

EARL BOYEA

MIÈGE, JOHN BAPTIST (1815–84)

Jesuit missionary, bishop. John Baptist Miège, a native of Savoy, was born on September 18, 1815, the twelfth of fourteen children. Most of his early training in letters and piety he owed to his older brother Urban, first at the college of Conflans and then at the college and minor seminary of Moûtiers, where Urban was professor of grammar and belles-lettres. For a while John Baptist toyed with the idea of making the military his vocation in life; much to the relief of Urban, he decided instead to become a sol-

John B. Miège

dier of Christ in the Society of Jesus. After his novitiate in Milan, followed by further studies in philosophy, he taught for a while at Chambéry and then at Milan. In 1844 he was sent to the celebrated Roman College for his theological studies, and was ordained to the priesthood in 1847. When the Jesuit houses in Rome were closed during the Revolution of 1848, Miège asked for permission to work among the Native Americans in the United States. Reaching St. Louis, Missouri, in the fall of 1849, he taught moral theology for a while and worked briefly in a nearby mission. Then in 1850 the Holy See appointed him first vicar apostolic of the "Indian Territory" east of the Rocky Mountains. In a spirit of humility he declined the honor, only to receive a formal order from Rome to assume it. He was consecrated bishop at St. Louis on March 25, 1851, by Archbishop Peter Kenrick.

Bishop Miège's first "cathedral" was a log-constructed building at St. Mary's Potawatomi Mission in Kansas. There and among the Osage to the south, he proved to be a true father to his beloved Native Americans. Then, in 1854, the Kansas-Nebraska Act opened the grasslands to white settlers. In August 1855, amid changing conditions, Bishop Miège moved to Leavenworth, Kansas, where he established the cathedral parish of the Immaculate Conception. From Leavenworth, driving an old St. Louis milk wagon with a pair of swayback mules, he continued to move about his vast diocese, administering the sacraments, starting mission stations, founding parishes and schools. After attending the First Vatican Council (1869–70), he spent about a year in South America collecting funds for the superb cathedral he had built in Leavenworth. Bishop Miège resigned his episcopal dignity in 1874 and as a

simple religious made his way to Woodstock College, Maryland, where he became spiritual father for the scholastics studying there.

From 1877 until 1881 he was at Detroit, Michigan, serving as first rector-president of the newly established Jesuit college. Returning to Woodstock, he again took up his duties as counselor for the young Jesuits. When, on his deathbed, the Father Provincial asked him whether he had any special message for the students, he replied: "Tell them to be charitable." Bishop Miège was ever a humble man. His love of God and the Blessed Mother was the driving force in life. His love for his parishioners and for his fellow priests was amply attested at the time of his resignation. He had a heart as big as his 250-pound body. He died at Woodstock on July 21, 1884, and lies at rest in the old college cemetery there.

Carmen, J. Neale. "The Unwilling Bishop." *Kansas Magazine* (1952) 17–22.

Muller, Herman J., S.J. *Bishop East of the Rockies: The Life and Letters of John Baptist Miège, S.J.* Chicago: Loyola University Press, 1994.

Wand, Augustine C. "Pioneer Bishop of the Prairies." *The Benedictine Review* (Summer 1949) 5–11, 46–59.

HERMAN J. MULLER, S.J.

MILES, RICHARD PIUS (1791–1860)

Bishop. Richard Miles, O.P., who became the first bishop of Nashville, was born in Prince George's County, southern Maryland, May 17, 1791. With his parents, Nicholas and Ann Blackloc Miles, he migrated at the age of four to Kentucky, where they settled near Bardstown.

Richard P. Miles

In his youth Miles enrolled at St. Thomas College, established by the Dominican friars at St. Rose, Kentucky, in 1806. From there he entered the Order of Preachers, taking the religious name Pius, and made his profession on May 13, 1810. After six additional years of study, he was ordained to the priesthood by Bishop Benedict Flaget in 1816.

Richard Miles was described as six feet tall, a well-built man whose gracious, warm-hearted, and sympathetic manner won him many friends. After ordination he served in many capacities on the Kentucky frontier, teaching at St. Thomas College and serving parishes in the surrounding settlements. His varied musical talents were a gift to the nascent Church, especially in the conduct of the first church choirs. His preaching was particularly effective in responding to the prevalent accusations against Catholics. After 1822, when the first American Dominican Sisters were established at St. Catharine's, Kentucky (then St. Magdalen's), Miles became their chaplain and spiritual director. In 1828 he was called by Bishop Edward Dominic Fenwick, O.P., to be pastor in Zanesville, Ohio, and surrounding missions. In April 1837 the Dominican friars chose Miles as their American provincial; this short-lived responsibility ended when Miles was named bishop of Nashville, Tennessee.

Bishop of Nashville

Miles was consecrated by Bishop Joseph Rosati of St. Louis at Bardstown on September 16, 1838, over a year after the original appointment. His new diocese, which embraced forty-two thousand square miles, had not a single resident priest to serve an estimated three hundred Catholics. His challenge was to build a diocese from nothing.

Shortly after taking up his responsibilities in Tennessee, Miles and Elisha J. Durbin, seasoned missionary to Tennessee, began a systematic visitation of the new diocese. They rode horseback, using every available space to preach in the many small pockets of scattered Catholics. They assembled in non-Catholic churches, courthouses, or the open air. When they returned to Nashville, they estimated they had traveled five hundred miles. Each year thereafter, health permitting, Miles went alone to visit his diocese.

In a letter dated May 20, 1839, Miles told Bishop Anthony Blanc of New Orleans of his need for everything: "My great poverty deprives me of means of offering a competent salary to a clergyman . . . in default of this I am doomed to struggle alone among the frightful difficulties of every species that surround me!" The bishop's greatest need was "a good, zealous, active priest."

Appeals for clergymen in the diocese brought little return. Some priests could not obtain permission to leave their dioceses while others who came remained for only a short time. A greater degree of stability materialized after Miles invited his Dominican brethren to staff St. Peter's Church in Memphis. The first friar preacher to be pastor there was Joseph Alemany, later the first archbishop of San Francisco. Other friars served the diocese for many years and still staff St. Peter's.

The bishop had greater success in obtaining the assistance of women religious than in finding priests. The first to journey to Tennessee were the Sisters of Charity of Nazareth, Kentucky. In 1842 they opened St. Mary's Academy in Nashville. When they were recalled to Kentucky in 1851, six remained to form a new community of Sisters of Charity, later identified with Leavenworth, Kansas. In 1851 six Dominican sisters, three from St. Catharine's, Kentucky, and three from St. Mary's, Somerset, Ohio, formed a new community in Memphis to conduct St. Agnes Academy and, later, St. Peter's Orphanage.

Under adverse circumstances, in an area of much anti-Catholic sentiment, Bishop Miles built the church in Tennessee. Although progress was slow he chose his projects wisely. With grants from the Society for the Propagation of the Faith, he built a rectory that served as his residence, as a seminary, and as a home base for his itinerant missionaries. He also erected a fitting cathedral dedicated to Our Lady of Sorrows. In August 1847 Miles sent a ten-year report to Propaganda Fide in Rome in which he noted that from having not a single priest in 1838, there were six priests serving six churches and three chapels. In addition, the diocese had a free school for blacks, an academy for boys, and a school for girls. The Catholic population had increased fivefold.

In addition to his various journeys throughout the state, Miles attended five provincial councils and the First Plenary Council of Baltimore in 1852. In the decade of the 1850s, the health of the bishop failed gradually. He died on February 21, 1860, at the age of sixty-nine after serving as Tennessee's bishop for twenty-two years. In 1967 his body was placed in a special chapel in the present cathedral of Nashville.

This pioneer itinerant bishop of Tennessee left the diocese a legacy of perseverance under adversity. At his death, the diocese boasted twelve thousand Catholics, thirteen clergy, fourteen churches, six chapels, thirty mission stations, a theological seminary, two communities of sisters, one academy for girls, and an orphanage.

See also DOMINICANS (O.P.).

Code, Joseph. *Dictionary of the American Hierarchy*. New York: Longmans Green & Co., 1940.

O'Daniel, V. F. *The Father of the Church in Tennessee*. New York: Frederick Pustet Co., 1926.

Stritch, Thomas. *The Catholic Church in Tennessee*. Nashville: The Catholic Center, 1987.

Webb, Ben. *The Centenary of Catholicity in Kentucky*. Louisville, Ky.: Charles Rogers, 1884.

LORETTA PETIT, O.P.

MINNESOTA, CATHOLIC CHURCH IN

In 1655 Native Americans were the first to hear the gospel in what became Minnesota, which they called "Land of Sky-Tinted Waters." That year, Groseilliers and Radisson built a chapel, preached, and baptized Dakota children near the present city of Hastings. Two decades later, at Fond du Lac, Daniel Greysolon DuLuht helped to fashion peace among sixteen warring tribes. Fort Beauharnois, near Frontenac, supplied the setting for the first Mass in the region, celebrated on November 4, 1721, by the Jesuit missionary Michael Guignas. During the 1820s, Dakota natives near Lac Qui Parle read the Bible in a translation by Joseph Renville. In the 1830s, Pierre Cotte and his wife used Fr. Frederic Baraga's Ojibwe catechism to evangelize at Fond du Lac and Grand Portage; Fr. Francis Pierz ministered along the North Shore of Lake Superior before setting up his far-flung mission to the Ojibwe at Crow Wing. He joined Augustine Ravoux, who began preaching to the Dakota in 1841. That year, near the Mississippi River, Fr. Lucien Galtier built a little chapel in honor of St. Paul, the name adopted by the city that grew up around it.

Meanwhile, beginning in 1819, pioneers began farming along the Mississippi. In the years that followed, Jean Baptiste Faribault drew up treaties that opened the Minnesota River valley to white settlement. Territorial status arrived in 1849. During the next decade, steamboats from the south and oxcarts from the north delivered over 150,000 settlers, who in 1858 helped to turn Minnesota into the thirty-second state. This changed the original mission of the early laity and priests from evangelizing the tribes to caring for the new arrivals from Europe and Canada.

Catholic Development

On July 19, 1850, Pope Pius IX erected the Diocese of St. Paul from the northern reaches of the Dioceses of Dubuque and Milwaukee. St. Paul's territory, about 166,000 square miles, stretched between the borders of Iowa and Canada from the St. Croix River and Lake Superior west to the Missouri. A papal brief of February 12, 1875, denominated the upper two-thirds of this area as the vicariate of northern Minnesota, with headquarters at St. Cloud. On August 12, 1879, the portion between the Red River and the Missouri became the vicariate apostolic of the Dakotas, with headquarters at Yankton. Two Benedictines served as vicars—Rupert Seidenbusch, abbot of St. John's Abbey, Collegeville, Minnesota, and Martin Marty, abbot of St. Meinrad's Abbey, Indiana.

These subdivisions of St. Paul reflected the rapid growth of the region. Six thousand settlers in 1850 swelled to over 170,000 ten years later, 50,000 of whom were Catholic. Colonization efforts by Fr. Pierz and Joseph Crétin, St. Paul's first bishop (1851–57), account for much of this increase. Pierz also encouraged Crétin to invite Benedic-

tine monks from Latrobe, Pennsylvania, to open a foundation near St. Cloud. St. John's Abbey became the site of a seminary, a university, and the base from which the Benedictines founded parishes and took over Native American missions. Crétin also welcomed the Sisters of St. Joseph of Carondolet to St. Paul. They were first among dozens of orders of religious women who founded and ran schools, hospitals, and orphanages. In 1871, Crétin's successor, Bishop Thomas Grace, O.P., invited the Christian Brothers to conduct the cathedral school for boys. This was the first of several commitments to the education of men at the secondary and collegiate levels throughout the state.

Cathedral of St. Paul, St. Paul, Minnesota

In the 1880s Minnesota's population reached one million, of which about a quarter were Catholics. Colonization efforts by coadjutor Bishop John Ireland accounted for much of this increase. Recognizing this rapid expansion, the Holy See, on May 4, 1888, elevated St. Paul to archdiocesan status, appropriately naming Ireland its first archbishop. The influx continued. In 1871 railroads connected St. Paul to Chicago and Duluth, providing an easy way to western farmlands. Settlers filled up the Red River valley in the northwest corner of the state, while lumbering and mining sites became towns north of the ports appearing on Lake Superior.

In 1889 Catholicism in Minnesota took a "quantum leap." Within the span of sixty-five days the Holy See erected five new dioceses: St. Cloud (September 22), Duluth (October 3), Sioux Falls and Jamestown (later Fargo; November 12), and Winona (November 26). Apparently, the January solar eclipse, visible over the northern part of the archdiocese, was a good omen. "Never perhaps in the history of the Church has a province bloomed as rapidly as St. Paul's," wrote Cardinal Gibbons. One other early subdivision followed. Crookston was erected out of Duluth on December 31, 1909.

Dynamics of Development

Without the laity, this growth would have been impossible. Faribault's sons accompanied and provided housing for missionaries in the south, as did Joseph Jourdain and his wife in the north. Dillon O'Brien and John Sweetman joined Ireland in colonization. John Crosby Devereaux, Francis Fassbind, and Anton Murnik began the first Catholic newspapers. The earnest devotion of Mary Theresa Mehegan moved her non-Catholic husband, James J. Hill, to donate a quarter of a million dollars to Archbishop Ireland for building the Saint Paul Seminary. Ignatius O'Shaughnessy led the way in Catholic philanthropy. The names of donors on stained-glass windows and statues in countless churches symbolize thousands of unnamed faithful who sang in choirs, served as trustees, cooked parish breakfasts, and organized dozens of pious societies.

These self-sacrificing laity helped clerical leaders worthy of their generosity. Among these was the newly ordained Fr. Valentine Sommereisen, in 1856 the first resident pastor in Mankato. He ministered to thirty-six communities scattered across fourteen counties. In the 1870s and 1880s, Fr. Alexander Berghold visited sixteen communities from his parish in New Ulm, and was loved as a church builder who sometimes worked along with construction crews. Between 1888 and 1922 Msgr. Joseph F. Buh left his footprints in virtually every parish of the Duluth diocese. He published a Slovenian newspaper and helped to set up the Slovene Catholic Union with members in forty-two lodges around the country. Near the turn of the century in Crookston, Fr. Ellie Theillon studied the latest farming techniques, organized a dairy cooperative, and helped his parishioners to transform the poorest township of Polk County into one of the most prosperous.

The 1880s may have been the most turbulent for Minnesota's Catholics. Historian Henry Steele Commager noted "the Catholic Church was . . . one of the most effective of all agencies for democracy and Americanization." This was certainly true in Minnesota. Archbishop Ireland was probably the most vigorous of the Americanizers, Catholic leaders who believed in a fundamental harmony between American political ideals and Catholicism. They encouraged their coreligionists from Europe to shed foreign ways, especially languages, that would keep them from participating fully in American life. But many newly arrived immigrants feared that loss of the mother tongue led to loss of faith, and they conducted campaigns to thwart the Americanizers. The outcome was

ambiguous, despite Leo XIII's 1899 letter that condemned "false Americanism."

Consolidation and Expansion

In 1908 Pope Pius X decreed that the United States was no longer "missionary territory." Minnesota Catholic statistics presented a mixed picture. On the positive side, a total of 596 priests served over 425,000 Catholics in 402 churches with resident pastors and 164 missions. The state had two seminaries. Seven religious orders of men and fifteen of women operated three colleges and universities, sixteen secondary schools, eighty-four primary schools, sixteen hospitals, and six homes for children. By comparison with their "ecclesiastical parents," however, Minnesota Catholics may still have been in mission status. In Dubuque, which covered a territory of about 30,000 square miles, the ratio of priests to laity stood at 1 to 473. In Milwaukee, with an area of 13,000 square miles, the ratio was 1 to 631. Minnesota, an area of 85,000 square miles, had a ratio of 1 to 715.

The years between the two world wars witnessed much consolidation of the work of pioneering laity and clergy. In 1918 the Code of Canon Law went into effect. It provided universal standards for Catholic leaders in reforming, expanding, or going beyond earlier development. These years also witnessed the emergence of diocesan newspapers in St. Cloud and Duluth (*The Register* system), Winona (*Our Sunday Visitor* system), and Crookston, which published its own independent, *Our Northland Diocese*. Earlier, these dioceses had access to St. Paul's *The Northwestern Chronicle* (1866–1900) and *The Catholic Bulletin* (1910). In the years following World War II, Minnesota's Catholic population increased by over 150,000. This led to an extraordinary expansion of suburban parishes and parochial schools. The erection of the Diocese of New Ulm from the western half of St. Paul in 1957 reflected this growth.

Beyond Minnesota

Some Minnesota Catholics have contributed significantly to religious and cultural life outside their state. In 1889, Mother M. Alfred Moes, of the Sisters of St. Francis, opened St. Mary's Hospital in Rochester; this was the beginning of the internationally acclaimed Mayo Clinic. Thomas O'Gorman of St. Paul taught Church history at The Catholic University of America until appointed second bishop of Sioux Falls in 1895. Fr. Thomas Edward Shields of Mendota developed a progressive form of Catholic education, and in 1909 he founded the Department of Education at The Catholic University of America. In 1911 he founded the Sisters College at The Catholic University of America. Fr. John A. Ryan of Dakota County taught Catholic social thought at the university and drafted the

1919 "Bishops' Program of Social Reconstruction"; of twelve major proposals, eleven became law under President Franklin D. Roosevelt. In 1921 Sr. Mary Carmela, C.S.J., of St. Paul's Cathedral School, conceived the idea of the first school traffic safety patrol.

During the early 1930s, Sr. Olivia Gowan, O.S.B., of Duluth, played a key role in setting up the School of Nursing at The Catholic University of America. About the same time her fellow diocesan, Fr. Patrick J. Lydon, began to teach and write on canon law at St. Patrick's Seminary, Menlo Park, California. Halfback Bruce Smith of Faribault led the University of Minnesota football team to three national championships, won the Heisman Trophy in 1941, and later starred in the movie, *Smith of Minnesota.* During the 1950s and 1960s, the University of Minnesota Newman Center ranked among the leaders of this apostolate; the Newman Club of Hibbing Junior College earned national recognition as a premier small college organization.

In 1968 Minnesota's poet-senator, Eugene McCarthy, ran for the Democratic presidential nomination on a platform challenging the morality of U.S. involvement in the Vietnam War. In 1983 Archbishop John Roach of St. Paul-Minneapolis chaired the episcopal committee that wrote *The Challenge of Peace,* a pastoral letter that examined modern warfare in light of the Catholic just-war theory. Meanwhile, through decades of publishing the monthly journal *Worship,* the monks of St. John's Abbey helped to lead the twentieth-century liturgical revival.

On the Threshold of the Third Millennium

One the eve of Vatican Council II, Minnesota's 892,000 Catholics were about 27 percent of the state's population. They worshiped in 718 parishes and 99 missions where they received the ministrations of 1,465 priests. Nearly 5,900 sisters and 360 brothers conducted eight colleges, 70 secondary schools, 329 primary schools, and 29 hospitals. Four seminaries were instructing 1,100 students. Comparable figures for 1990 showed about 1,124,000 Catholics (26 percent of the state's total) worshiping in 713 parishes and 49 missions where they were served by 1,242 priests. Over 3,000 sisters and 178 brothers carried on the educational and healing apostolates in seven colleges, 22 high schools, 214 grade schools, and 21 hospitals. At 1 to 904, the priest/laity ratio was higher than it had been in 1908.

New statistics shaped a new picture. Laypersons, at 85 percent, dominated the ranks of parochial school teachers. Enrollment in the Confraternity of Christian Doctrine classes was up 30 percent. Enrollment in the four seminaries stood at 113. Throughout the state, permanent deacons numbered 173. Nearly everywhere, officials and lay leaders were thinking about reshaping traditional forms of ministry.

Ahern, Patrick H., ed. *Catholic Heritage in Minnesota, North Dakota, South Dakota.* St. Paul, Minn.: Diamond Jubilee Committee, 1964.

Barry, Colman J., O.S.B. *The Catholic Church and the German Americans.* Milwaukee: Bruce Publishing Company, 1953.

Hurley, Helen Angela. *On Good Ground.* Minneapolis: University of Minnesota Press, 1951.

O'Connell, Marvin R. *John Ireland and the American Catholic Church.* St. Paul, Minn.: Minnesota Historical Society Press, 1988.

Rauche, Annabelle, and Ann Marie Biermaier. *They Came to Teach.* St. Cloud, Minn.: North Star Press, 1994.

Reardon, J. M. *The Catholic Church in the Diocese of St. Paul.* St. Paul, Minn.: North Central Publishing Company, 1952.

JOHN WHITNEY EVANS

MINTON, SHERMAN (1890–1965)

Associate justice of the U.S. Supreme Court. Born in Georgetown, Indiana, on October 20, 1890, Minton was educated at Indiana University and Yale Law School. In 1916 he began to practice law in New Albany, Indiana. Milton married Gertrude Gurtz, a Catholic, in 1917; they had three children. After service in World War I as an infantry captain, Minton resumed his law practice in New Albany and in Miami, Florida. From 1933 to 1934, he served as public counselor for the Public Service Commission of Indiana, and in 1934 was elected to the U.S. Senate. A senator for six years, Minton strongly supported President Roosevelt's New Deal legislation and his "court-packing" bill in 1937. Defeated for reelection to the Senate in 1940, Minton was appointed an assistant to President Roosevelt and was responsible for liaison between the legislative and executive branches.

Minton's judicial career began in 1941 when Roosevelt appointed him to the U.S. Court of Appeals for the Seventh Circuit, where he was considered a liberal. In 1948 he served on a board to investigate the coal strike of 1948; the following year, President Harry Truman nominated him an associate justice of the U.S. Supreme Court. Serving for seven years, Minton voted most often with the Court's conservative majority, despite his liberal reputation. He resigned in 1956 because of ill health, but was briefly a judge on the U.S. Court of Claims in 1957. Converting to Catholicism in 1961, Minton died in New Albany on April 9, 1965.

Atkinson, David. "From New Deal Liberal to Supreme Court Conservative." *Washington University Law Quarterly* (Fall 1975).

____. "Justice Sherman Minton and the Balance of Liberty." *Indiana Law Journal* (Fall 1974).

Corcoran, David H. "Sherman Minton: New Deal Senator." Ph.D. dissertation. University of Kentucky, 1977.

K. N. McCARTHY

MISSIONARIES (ABROAD), AMERICAN CATHOLIC

European Mission Legacy

From the late fifteenth through the eighteenth centuries, the Spanish missionary efforts of Franciscans and Jesuits influenced the inhabitants of the western and southeastern tip of what would become the United States. Because the Church in the United States increased extensively in the nineteenth and early twentieth century due to a large influx of immigrants, much of the pastoral efforts of women religious, clergy, and bishops addressed the spiritual and corporal needs of these newly arrived Catholics.

Some of these notable Church leaders included Bishop John Neumann, Bishop John Martin Henni, and Mother Frances Xavier Cabrini. Pastoral letters of the American Bishops in 1866 and 1884 addressed the needs of immigrants. Attention was also given to missions among Native Americans and African Americans, much of it through the work of the Josephite Fathers and of Katherine Drexel, whose considerable finances and formation of her religious congregation, the Sisters of the Blessed Sacrament for Indians and Colored People, aided these persons with schools and various forms of pastoral care. The Oblate Sisters of Providence of Baltimore were one of the three congregations of women religious founded by African Americans. Noteworthy among the clergy's work with Native Americans were the effects of the Jesuits, the Dominican Samuel Mazzuchelli, and Bishop Frederic Baraga of Marquette, Michigan.

Nineteenth-Century U.S. Missionaries Abroad

With pastoral energies devoted to these groups, the U.S. Catholic Church had a late start in sending missionaries abroad. During this period, overseas missions were considered a matter of geographical location. Thus, some of the land masses that were to form the fifty states were considered "foreign" until the territory came into the Union. Such was true of Hawaii, for example. The work of Mother Marianne Cope (1838–1918) among the lepers of the native population of Hawaii was identified as mission work abroad.

Overseas missions were often pioneer, sporadic, and short-lived. They frequently resulted from personal piety or from a change of episcopal jurisdiction. In 1841 Denis Pindar, a lay catechist from Baltimore, and two clergymen, Edward Barron, Philadelphia, and John Kelly, New York, labored on the west coast of Africa for two years. Pope Pius IX through Propaganda Fide asked the bishop of Charleston, South Carolina, to take the Bahamian missions under his jurisdiction in 1858. "Mission" here was mainly to the few Catholics on the islands. In 1885, jurisdiction went to Archbishop Michael A. Corrigan of New York. Since the American Civil War, New York diocesan priests had taken annual pastoral trips to the Bahamas to minister to the Catholics. Rev. Charles George O'Keefe became the first resident missionary there. He organized the first Catholic parish, St. Francis Xavier, thanks to Lady Georgeanna Ayle-Curran, who provided the largest financial sum for the Church and who laid the cornerstone of this building, which became the cathedral for the Nassau diocese.

Somewhat more concerted and sustained mission efforts came through religious congregations, who often joined their European confreres. In 1852 the first U.S. Catholic missionaries were sent from the Holy Cross Congregation to teach in India: Sr. Mary of St. Victor, Br. Benedict Fitzpatrick, and Fr. Louis Etienne Barroux. The mission work in China of Sr. Xavier Berkeley (1861–1944), a Daughter of Charity, became well known to American readers through the pages of *Catholic Missions* and *The Field Afar.* She left for China in 1890 to work in a hospital and dispensary with the English Daughters of Charity. James A. Walsh, cofounder of Maryknoll, saw her mission houses as his ideal: simple buildings for the sisters and poor Chinese all around them.

Sisters of Charity from Mt. St. Vincent's on the Hudson, New York, arrived in 1889 in the Bahamas and opened a free school for poor children and, later, a nursery and clinic. In 1891 Fr. Chrysostom Schreiner, O.S.B., a "Tractarian" in apologetic preaching, was sent to Nassau, the beginning of the Benedictine men's ministry in these islands. Early mission efforts concentrated on establishing and preserving Catholic presence in a predominantly Protestant environment.

After the settlements that followed the Spanish-American War, the United States was asked to supply religious and clergy to Puerto Rico, Cuba, and the Philippines. The future cardinal archbishop of Philadelphia, Dennis Dougherty, was among those who went to the Philippines.

1908–18

Technically, Propaganda Fide removed the United States from the status of mission territory in 1908. While statistics are not available for this period, there were probably seventy U.S. Catholic missionaries overseas. By this date, however, the national office of the Society of the Propagation of the Faith and especially active archdiocesan offices in New York and Boston provided monies for "foreign" mission work, as it was then called. First thoughts about a possible seminary for U.S. missionaries abroad came when Paulist Frs. Walter Elliott and Andrew Doyle gathered missionaries together for discussion of the problems and potential of the missions to non-Catholics. The conferences, sponsored by their Catholic Missionary Union, started in 1896.

At one of these meetings in 1904, James A. Walsh (1867–1936), director of the Society for the Propagation of the Faith in Boston, and Thomas F. Price (1860–1919), missionary to non-Catholics in North Carolina, met and briefly discussed such a possibility. After their further conversations and with the support of James Cardinal Gibbons, the U.S. bishops approved of the foundation of the Catholic Foreign Mission Society of America (later popularly known as Maryknoll) in their April 1911 meeting. The Maryknoll men, who eventually settled in Ossining, New York, sent their first four missionaries, including Thomas Price, to China in 1918. Twelve women associated with the Catholic Foreign Mission Society, under the leadership of Mary Josephine Rogers, translated letters from French missionaries, edited *The Field Afar*, and helped to publish the magazine, which promoted the work of the newly formed missionary society. Originally called the Teresians, these women became the Foreign Mission Sisters of St. Dominic, later known as the Maryknoll Sisters. They worked with the Japanese in Seattle and Los Angeles in 1920 and went to South China in 1921. They also provided the largest number of U.S. Catholic women missionaries overseas.

In 1906 the Chicago province of the Society of the Divine Word opened St. Mary's Mission House after initial efforts in New Jersey in 1895 by Br. Wendelin Meyer, S.V.D., to obtain subscriptions to their mission magazine. This group of priests and brothers inherited a scientific approach to missions from their founder, Arnold Janssen. Their Mission Press at Techny published English translations of several major European mission texts from this tradition. In this same vein, Fr. William Ross, S.V.D., the first American S.V.D. assigned to New Guinea in 1926, learned and transcribed the language of the Highlanders there. The Holy Spirit Missionary Sisters, also founded by Janssen, formed an American province at Techny, Illinois, in 1901. They worked mainly in the missions in the southern part of the United States and sent their first missionaries to Papua New Guinea in 1921.

Further interest in missions at home and abroad came through two mission congresses (Chicago 1908, Boston 1913) organized by Francis Clement Kelley, the founder of the Catholic Church Extension Society of America. At the Boston conference, participants heard returned missionaries talk about the Church in the Philippines, Jamaica, and Puerto Rico.

Mission work was seen in this period primarily as pastoral or educational work carried out in a geographic locale different from one's birthplace. World War I, however, provided the circumstances for even greater impetus for missions abroad. European missionaries, accused of nationalism, were evicted from many of their missions and the demand for English-speaking missionaries focused attention on the United States.

1919–50

At the 1919 Catholic Education Association annual meeting, Walsh, Kelley, and Peter Janser, S.V.D., spoke about the importance of seminaries and mission awareness for the Catholic Church in the United States. A significant step toward this consciousness was taken when Clifford King and Robert Clark, Divine Word seminarians at Techny, Illinois, organized the Catholic Students Mission Crusade the year before. Initially inspired by these men reading articles from *The Field Afar* and by the work of American Protestant missionaries, the fledgling organization soon involved thousands of college and high school students across the country. The headquarters moved to Cincinnati to the "Crusade Castle," where the group published *The Shield* mission magazine. The CSMC raised funds for missions overseas, held large mission conferences, educated students about mission work around the world, published statistics about U.S. Catholic missionaries, and was the springboard for many vocations to missionary communities. King, while still a seminarian, went to South Shantung, China, in 1919 to secure the Divine Word mission, because the German S.V.D.'s were being expelled from China. He was the first American priest ordained in China.

Greater mission interest and the American foundation of provinces of other mission congregations, such as the Columban Fathers (1920) and Columban Sisters (1930), led to the publication of more magazines and fundraising efforts, sometimes in competition with the Society for the Propagation of the Faith and the Catholic Church Extension Society. In the hope of unifying and organizing these mission groups, a Bishops' Committee, under the chairmanship of Archbishop Henry Moeller of Cincinnati and Fr. Francis Clement Kelley, was instrumental in the formation of the American Board of Catholic Missions. Though efforts toward coordination had begun in 1919, the board began to function only in 1925 due to objections from Rome, the death of Benedict XV, and internal struggles among various mission groups that were to be on the board.

China was of particular interest in the 1920s and was the location of many American missionaries, who often took over former French or German missions. While religious orders and congregations such as the Maryknollers, the Franciscans, and the Jesuits sent missionaries to the Far East, many other American congregations not traditionally established for overseas missions began to send some of their members to China to teach or to establish clinics during the 1920s and 1930s. Such work was seen as an effective way to make friends with the Chinese. As it took a long time to learn the language, much of the work of these groups was done with children in orphanages or schools. Missionary brothers, often referred to as the "St.

Josephs" of the mission, provided invaluable service in constructing housing and other buildings, laying roads, running mission presses, and assisting where needed. Congregations consisting mainly of brothers, such as the Brothers of Christian Instruction (Fall River, Massachusetts), a group who had two brothers in China in 1942, started schools for boys or catechized young men.

Civil war in China during this period and the Japanese invasion of China created further difficulties for these missions. Some groups were placed under house arrest, while others, such as the Sisters of Providence (St. Mary-of-the-Woods, Indiana), left the country and opened missions in Korea. Several missionaries were killed in China during these unstable times. Among them were Passionist Frs. Walter Coveyou, Clement Seybold, Gregory Holbein, and Maryknoll Fr. Gerard Donovan.

In spite of these difficulties, three significant developments arose from American involvement in the China Mission: the Direct Apostolate of Sisters, the formation of trained lay catechists, and the foundation of indigenous congregations of religious. This first emphasis, advocated particularly by Bishop Francis X. Ford, M.M., dedicated sisters to specific evangelization of Chinese women. This was a change in prevailing mission thought, which held that women, though "equal in their sphere," were the auxiliaries of men. Popular mission books, such as Paulo Manna's *Conversion of the Pagan World* (Boston: Society for the Propagation of the Faith, 1921), recognized the importance of women's mission work, especially in the area of education, which was identified as the source of the "elevation of women" in non-Christian countries. However, the primary intent of mission work was the foundation of the parish church and the main function of the clergy was sacramental. All other mission activity, including hospitals, clinics, and schools conducted by women, were secondary to the establishment of the church where these sacraments could be performed.

The Direct Apostolate was also a change in prevailing mission practice. Sisters (and sometimes clergy as well) lived in China in mission compounds, that is, a walled series of buildings grouped around the church. This gave the Church an institutional aspect. In the Direct Apostolate, sisters lived among the people and so grew close to them and to their needs. Rather than wait for the Chinese to come to the Church, the Church would go to the Chinese. This form of mission work further emphasized the importance of women working directly with women in evangelization, a fact true in medical work in Muslim countries as well.

The second development, lay formation for catechists, was especially the work of Bernard Meyer, M.M. (1891–1975), who, even before he gained language facility, saw the importance of a more thorough formation program for the lay catechists, who could more readily touch the masses

of Chinese. After his expulsion from China, Meyer applied many of these principles of the lay apostolate in the 1960s in the United States through several publications.

The third development, the formation of native congregations of religious, had been an important focus for Pope Pius XI, who ordained the first Chinese bishops in modern times in 1926. Among the women's groups who established native sisterhoods were the Sisters of Loretto, the Sisters of Providence, and the Maryknoll Sisters. The Sisters of Charity (Cincinnati) and the Sisters of St. Francis of Assisi (Milwaukee) were among the congregations having novitiates in China.

Another geographic area of "mission" was Latin America, toward which laity directed their energies as part of the U.S. Catholic Revival in the 1930s and 1940s. While they themselves did not go overseas in traditional missionary fashion, these persons did see their contacts with the educated of the Southern Hemisphere as a work of the apostolate. Through the leadership of the Social Action Commission of the National Catholic Welfare Council, educated laypersons in the U.S.A., especially women, sought to increase knowledge about Latin America and to influence its political elite to employ Catholic action principles in their social and political lives. The growing interest in this area led to the initial formation of the Latin American Bureau of the NCWC in 1931. This lay apostolic movement aimed at persons overseas emphasized lay formation through study, action, prayer, and, though it did not understand the deeper causes of unrest in Latin America, highlighted the reconstruction of social structures in those countries through Catholic social principles.

Anticlericalism and unsettled political conditions in Mexico meant that the Church there could not conduct its seminaries. In 1935 the Montezuma Seminary for Mexican seminarians was opened in New Mexico, supported over the years by Mexican and U.S. bishops, until its closure in the 1980s. By 1955, 20 percent of the Mexican clergy had been educated at Montezuma Seminary.

The earliest U.S. women's congregation to be sent to South America was the Immaculate Heart of Mary Sisters (Philadelphia). In 1922 seven sisters left for Lima to teach, partially to combat the "leakage" of Catholics to Protestant groups. A notable breakthrough for Catholic medical missions came in 1936 when the Holy See, after much petitioning by Dr. Agnes McClaren and others, permitted women religious to become doctors. Medical mission work, long a staple among Protestants, had been prohibited for women religious. The Medical Mission Sisters, founded in the United States by Anna Dengel (1890–1980) in 1925, were finally able to send their personnel for further medical training. They were assisted with supplies and sometimes with personnel in the missions through the work of the Catholic Medical Mission Board, formed by Fr. Edward F. Garesché, S.J., in 1929.

Theological mission themes used by missionaries and those in the international apostolate in this period both in China and in Latin America were rooted very distinctly in the ecclesial image of the Mystical Body and the principles of social action.

1950–71

Another World War again impacted on the missionary situation. Several problems arose that required coordination among mission-sending groups: escalation of costs for sending supplies to missionaries, compensation and indemnity of mission properties in Japan, China, and Manchuria, passport assistance, contacts with the State Department, and legislation that affected social and religious questions in the Philippines and Latin America. At the bishops' annual meeting in 1949, a Mission Secretariat was approved to deal with such issues. Fr. Frederick McGuire, C.M. (1905–83), recently returned from China, was appointed executive secretary and worked at the secretariat from 1950 until 1969. This organization held annual meetings at which hundreds of religious and secular institute members heard talks on current mission problems and sought ways to work together. In 1969 the Mission Secretariat dissolved and subsequent reorganization led to the formation of the U.S. Catholic Mission Council (from 1970–1981) and the U.S. Catholic Mission Association (from 1982 to the present).

The expulsion of missionaries from China and the rapid rise of Communism around the globe had a significant impact on U.S. Catholic missionaries. Many were under house arrest or interned with other "foreign" missionaries. By 1950, when the Communist leaders controlled much of China, most foreigners were evicted. Maryknoll Bishop Francis X. Ford (1892–1952) died in prison. Sr. Joan Marie Ryan, M.M., his secretary, was held in solitary confinement for many months. Others who remained imprisoned were Harold Rigney, S.V.D. (1900–80), the former president of Peiping University, and James E. Walsh, M.M. (1891–1981), bishop of Kongmoon. Their release in 1956 and 1970 respectively gained significant attention from the U.S. media. For Walsh, remaining with the people, even under persecution, emphasized the witness value of a missionary's life.

Bishop Fulton J. Sheen (1895–1979), national director of the Society for the Propagation of the Faith from 1950 to 1966, and a popular figure known for his compelling radio and television programs, emphasized Communism as an ideology. Arguing from a neo-Thomist perspective, he portrayed the Antichrist, the "forces of godless materialism," pitted against the values of Western, presumably Christian, civilization. Rigney's memoirs of his imprisonment in Communist China, *Four Years in a Red Hell* (1956), captured this same tone. Ultimately, reason would guide persons toward truth. As editor of *Worldmission,* Sheen had another forum for discussion of these issues and their effects on the missionary. Sheen claimed to have raised three-fourths of all the Propagation of the Faith money through his media appearances. In 1959 the Latin American Bureau was reestablished at the National Catholic Welfare Conference. Fr. John J. Considine, M.M. (1897–1982), was asked to be the director, a position he held until 1966. Ordained in 1923, Considine was sent to Rome in 1924 to take care of the arrangements for the Maryknoll Exhibit at the Vatican Mission Exposition the following year. He worked at one of the offices of the Propaganda Fide until 1934, initiated an international religious news service (FIDES) in five languages, and traveled to missions all over the world. His *Call for Forty Thousand* (1946), a book compiled from such travels, drew the attention of North Americans to the mission needs in the Southern Hemisphere. As director of the Latin American Bureau, Considine was a respected figure whose advice was sought by anyone wishing to send persons to Latin America. Along with Jesuit anthropologist J. Franklin Ewing, Considine was one of the persons who inaugurated the Fordham Mission Institute in the 1950s and 1960s, was a member of the Peace Corps Board, and was one of the organizers of the Mission Secretariat.

In the 1950s, for the first time in its history, the U.S. Catholic Church sent significant numbers of diocesan clergy overseas. This was done primarily through the St. James Society, founded by Archbishop Richard Cushing of Boston in 1957. By 1963 forty dioceses were sending at least one priest to Latin America.

During the Korean War, several U.S. missionaries acted as chaplains in that country and were helpful as interpreters for the U.S. armed services. The Maryknoll and Columban areas in the northern part of the peninsula were especially affected after the division of the country. Agneta Chang, a Korean Maryknoll Sister, and several from her community were apparently killed in the north. After this war, other U.S. groups sent missionaries to start health facilities, education, and catechetical programs. Many of these personnel came through the efforts of Columban Bishop Harold Henry (1909–76), originally from Minnesota. The Seton Hill Sisters from Pennsylvania, the Adorers of the Precious Blood, and the Poor Clare Nuns from Minneapolis began local religious communities, which, in turn, became autonomous provinces in Korea. Maryknoller Mercy Hirschboeck, one of the first female graduates of Marquette's Medical College, became well known for her dispensary work. Her colleague, Sr. Gabriella Mulherin, began flourishing cooperative credit unions across South Korea.

The first U.S. Catholics received their doctorates in missiology in the late 1940s and 1950s. Among them were Frs. Ronan Hoffman, O.F.M. Conv., Edward L. Murphy,

S.J., and Ralph Wiltgen, S.V.D. Anthropologist Louis Luzbetak, an S.V.D. priest, wrote *The Church and Cultures: An Applied Anthropology for the Religious Worker* (1963), which became a classic in the field.

Lay mission vocations were on the rise in the 1950s. The Lay Mission Helpers of Los Angeles had a training program in their archdiocese and sent their first five missionaries to Africa in 1957. Other lay groups that trained and sent personnel overseas were the Grail, the Association for International Development, and the Catholic Lay Mission Corps. Probably the most well-known group was the Papal Volunteers for Latin America (PAVLA), founded in 1960 after Pope John XXIII had issued a call for more service to the Church in the Southern Hemisphere. Through a program administered by the Latin American Bureau, over seventy dioceses were sending four hundred volunteers to fourteen countries by 1965. These men and women received their formation at one of a number of centers, including the University of Ponce, Puerto Rico, the Institute of Intercultural Studies, Petropolis, Brazil, and perhaps the most controversial school, the Center for Intercultural Formation at Cuernavaca, Mexico, whose director was Msgr. Ivan Illich.

The 1950s and 1960s were also filled with racial tension in the United States. Trying to deal with segregation in this country, Americans were not as interested in African missions as they had been in the Chinese experience. Nevertheless, the number of U.S. missionaries who went to Africa rose from 108 in 1940 to 1,025 in 1964. Two groups who sent notable numbers of personnel were the Holy Ghost Fathers (New York) and the Sisters of the Holy Names of Jesus and Mary (Albany, New York). Considine addressed the issue of racism in the United States by reflecting on the experience of missionaries in other cultures and highlighting the equality of all persons before God and their inherent dignity. The most critical ecclesial event of the time, Vatican Council II, addressed the mission world in the Dogmatic Constitution on the Church and the Dogmatic Constitution on the Church in the World, and more specifically in the Dogmatic Constitution on the Missionary Activity of the Church. Bishop Fulton Sheen, as a member of the Propaganda Fide Commission, gave a talk at a plenary council session. The council commission originally placed a set of propositions before the bishops on which to vote yes or no. Strong opposition to this procedure led to the presentation and eventual approval of a document on missionary activity in 1965. Fr. Eugene Hillman, C.S.Sp., secretary to the East African bishops in their preparations for the council and noted for his work calling the Church to reexamine its position on polygamy in Africa, provided some leadership toward the formation of the African contribution to the mission document.

Mission themes of this period critiqued earlier theological themes, but continued to be related to social ac-

tion. "Civilization" had been closely aligned with salvation in previous years. Seeing parishioners and friends face dire economic realities and injustices, missionaries realized that in order for any type of "civilization" to occur in a people, a certain amount of subsistence and economic security needed to be in place. In the latter part of this period, the theme of development, later explicated in Pope Paul VI's encyclical, On the Development of Peoples (1968), took a more central place for many missionaries, particularly those in Latin America. Tensions about such a strong emphasis on social development led to the U.S. bishops' December 1971 Statement on the Missions that reminded missionaries of the need for the transcendental and spiritual.

Missionaries experienced many of the same strains in their work as did the U.S. Church in the 1960s. Self-doubt about the nature of missionary work and strong divergence in the same community over the approach to take in missions sapped much of the energy of mission communities. The peak number of missionaries occurred in 1968 and the crisis was further reflected in fewer numbers entering mission congregations after that time. The Catholic Students Mission Crusade ceased as a national organization in 1971.

1972–86

In addition to the theological tensions in the late 1960s, other developments such as the war in Vietnam, urban riots, and the murders of John F. Kennedy, Robert F. Kennedy, and Martin Luther King, Jr., had turned the focus of Americans to the home front. But U.S. black theology and Hispanic theology conveyed some of the same themes found in Latin American experience and expression, especially that of the social structures of oppression and liberation.

Mission theology showed a significant shift in understanding the role of mission not primarily in terms of "church implantation," but as providing conditions for the reign of God to appear. In addition to liberation, dialogue, and a theology of presence, missionaries stopped using the term "missions" and spoke more of "mission." With the importance of the local churches stressed after Vatican II, the wealth of missionaries' experience with "culture" was brought to bear on the theological issue of "inculturation." This led to an appreciation for the positive values in particular cultures and the recognition of God's work of grace in all peoples. Mutuality in mission shifted the emphasis on the missionary as one who primarily gives to that of receiving, as well.

Orbis Books, a corporation under the auspices of the Catholic Foreign Mission Society of America, remains a key publisher that promotes the work of Third World theologians and the fruits of missionary thought. Notable Americans who have published through this press are Robert

Schreiter, C.P.P.S, Stephen B. Bevans, S.V.D., and Vincent Donovan, C.S.Sp. This company has also provided an ecumenical dialogue through publishing authors from various religious traditions. This reflects the ecumenical cooperation of mission groups through the establishment of the American Society of Missiology in 1972.

Missionaries were still suffering imprisonment and death. In 1975 Conventual Franciscan Fr. Casimir Cypher was killed in Honduras. In 1980 lay missioner Jean Donovan, Ursuline Sr. Dorothy Kazel, and Maryknoll Srs. Ita Ford and Maura Clarke were killed by National Guardsmen on their way from the airport in San Salvador, El Salvador. In 1990 Agnesian Sr. Maureen Courtney was killed by the Sandinistas in Nicaragua. The impetus for these and many other similar deaths of missionaries was their work with the poor, which remained a threat to existing political structures.

In 1986 the U.S. bishops published *To the Ends of the Earth: A Pastoral Statement on World Mission.* After noting the missionary roots of the U.S. Church, the bishops commended the work of its missionaries since then and issued a call for mission vocations. Citing Jesus as *the* missionary, the bishops, in support of the Vatican decree on missionary activity, placed mission at the heart of the Church's life. The document also noted "reverse mission," i.e., persons from countries to which the United States had sent missionaries were now sending men and women apostles to the United States and to other parts of the world.

Recent Developments

Once again, wars and political events have affected the fate of missions. New areas of mission have again been reopened in Eastern Europe (after the fall of Communism in that part of the world) and in Cambodia, Thailand, and Vietnam.

The intersection of mission, World Christianity, and World Religions is now part of an international dialogue at the heart of which is the uniqueness of Jesus. Among American Catholics, Paul Knitter, former Divine Word missionary, opened the discussion in his *No Other Name?* (1985).

After reaching a plateau, since 1973 lay overseas missionaries have been on the rise, with service for as short a time as six weeks or as long as five years. In 1992 there were 406 lay missionaries overseas. The Maryknoll Associates, a group of lay men and women, formed a separate organization in 1994. Lay organizations such as the Holy Cross Associates, the Jesuit International Volunteers, and the Voluntary Missionary Movement continue to train and send persons abroad.

Returned missionaries have always given talks to parishes, mission clubs, and other organizations, often with the hope of raising money for particular projects where they worked. Today their expertise is called upon for cross-cultural and multicultural programs on educational, diocesan, and pastoral agendas. Such is the case, for example, of the Midwest Mission Task Force. This theme, arising from the issue of culture and gospel, will probably continue to be seen in new forms in the future, as its theological foundation, the incarnation, is central to Christianity.

Missionary Statistics:
Total Number of Missionaries Overseas

Year	Number
1940	2,222
1949	4,123
1960	6,612
1968	9,447
1970	8,283
1980	6,343
1990	5,702
1992	5,441

During the above years, the number of men missionaries was generally about 52 percent and women missionaries 48 percent, with the exception of Oceania, where more women served than did men.

Geographic Focus of U.S. Catholic Missionaries Overseas:

Three Highest Areas of Concentration

1940	China (740); West Indies (267); Philippines (231)
1954	Africa (901); West Indies (800); Pacific Islands (686)
1962	South America (684); Philippines (647); Japan (427)
1970	South America (2,080); Africa (1,141); West Indies (1,067)
1980	Asia (1,576); South America (1,556); Africa (909)
1990	South America (1,413); Asia (1,253); Africa (945)
1993	South America (1,296); Asia (1,163); Africa (949)

Five Religious Congregations Who Have Sent the Largest Number of Missionaries Overseas

Women	Men
Maryknoll Sisters	Jesuits
School Sisters of Notre Dame	Maryknoll Fathers and Brothers
Sisters of St. Joseph of Carondelet	Franciscans
Marist Missionary Sisters	Divine Word Fathers and Brothers

Daughters of Charity   Oblates of Mary
                              Immaculate
(Source: Catholic Students Mission Crusade and U.S. Catholic
Mission Association)

Fischer, Edward. *Journeys Not Regretted: The Columban Fathers' Sixty-five Years in the Far East.* New York: Crossroad, 1986.

Kelley, Francis Clement, ed. *Second American Catholic Missionary Congress, 1913.* Chicago: Hyland Company, 1913.

Lernoux, Penny. *Hearts on Fire: The Story of the Maryknoll Sisters.* Maryknoll, N.Y.: Orbis Books, 1993.

To the Ends of the Earth: The U.S. Catholic Bishops' Pastoral on Missionary Activity of the Church. Washington, D.C.: NCCB/USCC, 1986.

Wiest, Jean-Paul. *Maryknoll in China: A History, 1918–1955.* Armonk, N.Y.: M. E. Sharpe, 1988.

Wolf, Ann Colette. *Sisters of Providence: Mission to the Chinese.* St. Mary-of-the-Woods, Indiana, 1990.

ANGELYN DRIES, O.S.F.

MISSIONARY-AID SOCIETIES IN AMERICA

The great influx of immigrants from Europe during the nineteenth century threatened very early to overwhelm the financial resources of the Church in the United States. Church buildings, schools, and hospitals were urgently needed, as were the funds to build them and the clerical and religious personnel to staff them. The Church in the United States benefited mightily during this period from the financial and material assistance of the European missionary societies. The three organizations most responsible for assisting the infant Church were the Society for the Propagation of the Faith, the Leopoldinen Stiftung, and the Ludwig Missionsverein.

The first of these organizations was founded at Lyons, France, in 1822, and resulted from the merging of two recently founded mission societies in the textile city, the "Réparatrices du Coeur de Jésus," founded by Pauline Jaricot among working-class women, and the "Association de la Propagation de la Foi dans les Deux Mondes," founded by a pious widow, Mme. Petit, and dedicated to the collection of missionary alms among the well-to-do. Patterning itself on the Jaricot group, members of the new society were grouped by tens and hundreds, each contributing weekly a penny or *sou.* Since the society inherited much of its structure from the Jaricot group, Pauline Jaricot has been popularly termed the foundress of the Society for the Propagation of the Faith.

The movement struck the popular imagination, for thousands of members were soon enrolled in France, in neighboring countries, and ultimately worldwide. The first allocation of monies was made in 1822 and consisted of $4,583, divided into three portions among the Foreign Mission Seminary in Paris, the Asian missions, and the Dioceses of New Orleans and Bardstown, which split the remaining third. Although the initial American beneficiaries were dioceses headed by French-born prelates, all dioceses in this country eventually benefited from the largesse of the society. During its first century of existence, the society contributed some six million dollars to building up the Church in the United States. By 1922 American Catholics had returned some eleven million dollars to the coffers of the society.

Political differences between France and the Austro-Hungarian Empire prevented the implantation of the Society for the Propagation of the Faith in the imperial domains. In 1828 Rev. Frederick Résé, representing Bishop Edward Fenwick of Cincinnati, proposed to the Austrian Emperor Francis I that a parallel society be founded to channel monies to the American missions, most especially to those north of the Ohio River. The emperor acceded to the priest's request and named the new society for his favorite daughter, the late empress of Brazil and wife of Pedro I. Pope Leo XII affirmed the action on January 30, 1829, with the bull *Quamquam Plura Sunt.* Thus was born the Leopoldinen Stiftung.

The structure and constitution of the new society were patterned directly on the French original, although membership was limited to imperial subjects. The Austrian society lasted into the twentieth century, finally falling victim to the turmoil of World War I. After an initial period where monies were directed to German-speaking recipients, alms were subsequently offered irrespective of ethnic group. By the time of its demise, the Leopoldinen Stiftung sent to the American missions some $700,000, as well as a wealth of church furnishings, vestments, Mass vessels, and other liturgical articles.

The Ludwig Missionsverein owed its existence to the same Fr. Résé who helped found a mission society in Austria. During the same year of his visit to Francis I in Vienna, he determined to introduce the missionary movement into the German states. He received a sympathetic hearing from the Bavarian king, Ludwig I, although nothing substantial resulted until 1838. On December 12 of that year, the king approved the constitution of a society to which he gave his own name. The Ludwig Missionsverein was to be patterned on the French society in structure and constitution, but limited in membership to Bavarians. All funds raised were destined for the North American and Asian missions.

The Bavarian society functioned for several years as a de facto arm of its French counterpart, before a royal decree of 1844 reaffirmed its independence. Its assistance to the missions consisted of both money and personnel. Seminary formation in Europe of future missionaries was generously subsidized. Numerous German religious communities of men and women were introduced into the United States through the activity of the Ludwig Missionsverein. Among these were Ursuline, Dominican, and

Benedictine sisters, the School Sisters of Notre Dame, and the Benedictine monks. Before the Bavarian society ceased to exist in 1917, it would send nearly $900,000 to the American missions.

Hickey, Edward John. *The Society for the Propagation of the Faith.* Washington, D.C.: The Catholic University of America Press, 1922.
Roemer, Theodore. *The Leopoldine Foundation and the Catholic Church in the United States, 1829–1839.* New York: United States Catholic Historical Society, 1933.
____. *The Ludwig-Missionsverein and the Church in the United States.* Washington, D.C.: The Catholic University of America Press, 1933.

ALBERT H. LEDOUX

MISSIONS IN COLONIAL AMERICA, ENGLISH

Before the American Revolution Catholics were most numerous in Maryland and less so in Pennsylvania; they were also active in New York for a brief period.

Maryland. The founder of Maryland, George Calvert (ca. 1580–1632), had been a principal secretary of state and a privy councillor under King James I, had sat in Parliament, and by virtue of a royal charter had founded a colony in Newfoundland. In 1625 he resigned his public offices, perhaps because of his conversion to Catholicism, but was created baron of Baltimore by King Charles I. Preferring a warmer climate, he petitioned the king for land in the area of the Chesapeake Bay. Since he then died, the royal charter for Maryland was granted to his son Cecil(ius) Calvert, the second baron of Baltimore, making him a proprietor or lord palatine with extensive power. In that way he could afford sanctuary to Catholics, who were subject to fierce penal laws in England. However, he also sought Protestant settlers, partly because the English government would not have allowed an officially or exclusively Catholic colony, partly because he needed more participants for the economic development of the colony, and partly to prove that English people of different religions could live together harmoniously under a tolerant government.

Lord Baltimore engaged two Jesuit priests, Andrew White and John Altham, and a lay brother, who were to accompany the first colonists aboard the *Ark* and the *Dove.* They were granted land on the same terms as other settlers and received no direct support from the proprietor. Although a majority of the colonists were Protestants, because of the limited suffrage the greater number of those who from the beginning had a voice in the government of the colony were Catholics, most notably the first governor, Leonard Calvert (the proprietor's brother), and the first commissioners. The colonists made their first landing on the territory granted to Lord Baltimore at St. Clement's

Island, where Fr. White celebrated the first Mass on March 25, 1634. A total of nine Jesuit priests and two lay brothers labored in Maryland up to 1641, though not all simultaneously. Some of them were missionaries to the Indians, especially the Piscataways, but most of them ministered to the English Catholics and converted some of the Protestants.

Religious liberty existed in the colony in the early years, although no formal law was enacted lest hostile attention be attracted in England. Before the first voyage the proprietor instructed the governor to prevent the Catholics from giving any offense to the Protestants, to have Catholic worship practiced as privately as possible, and to treat the Protestants with mildness and favor. In 1636 he required the governor to swear under oath not to "trouble, molest or discountenance any person professing to believe in Jesus Christ for or in respect to religion," but rather to treat all Christians equally "in conferring offices, favors or rewards." Instances of the enforcement of religious liberty— the verdict of a trial and a decision of the assembly—may be cited within the first decade. According to an ordinance passed by the assembly of freemen and signed by the governor in the name of the proprietor in 1639, the inhabitants of the province, slaves excepted, were to have and enjoy all such rights, liberties, immunities, and free customs as any natural-born subject of England.

Catholics and Puritans. During the English Civil War a Protestant Englishman and tobacco trader, Richard Ingle, authorized by letters of marque from Parliament, arrived with an armed ship, *The Reformation,* in the winter of 1644–45 and seized control of the colony in the absence of the governor and with the support of many Maryland Protestants (mostly servants, former servants becoming planters, and a few free immigrants). For two years his men pillaged the plantations and impressed farm products and household goods; posing as the champion of the Protestant cause, he primarily attacked prominent Catholics and even sent some of them back to England. The Jesuits suffered most during this "plundering time." Three of them fled to Virginia, where they died under unknown circumstances in 1646; Frs. White and Thomas Copley were sent back to England in chains to be tried for treason simply for being Catholic priests and were condemned to perpetual banishment.

White, "the Apostle of Maryland," eventually returned to England, was arrested and imprisoned again, but was set free three years later and died in 1656. Copley made his way back to America, first to Virginia and then to Maryland in 1648, and ministered until his death in 1652. Toward the end of 1646 Leonard Calvert regained possession of the colony but died the following June at the age of thirty-nine. Lord Baltimore then appointed William Stone (a Protestant of Virginia and supporter of Parliament) governor, a Protestant secretary, and three Protestant councillors (out of five). The proprietor required that the governor swear under oath not to "molest any person in the province professing to believe in Jesus Christ and in particular no Roman Catholic for or in respect of his or her Religion nor in his or her free exercise thereof" as long as they were loyal to the proprietor and his government. The governor was also to avoid religious discrimination in conferring offices, rewards, and favors and to use his power and authority to protect Christians in the free exercise of their religion from molestation by any other officer or person in the province.

These principles were embodied in the Act concerning Religion of 1649, the first law prescribing religious toleration. The act ordained death and confiscation of all lands and goods for blasphemy and denial of the doctrines of the divinity of Christ and of the Holy Trinity, prohibited religiously offensive language, and provided for a Puritan Sabbath. In its most famous section it ordered:

> no person or persons whatsoever . . . professing to believe in Jesus Christ shall . . . be any ways troubled, molested or discountenanced for or in respect of his or her religion nor in the free exercise thereof . . . nor any way compelled to the belief or exercise of any other religion against his or her consent, so as they be not unfaithful to the Lord Proprietary, or molest or conspire against the civil government established or to be established in this province under him or his heirs.

Offending persons were to be punished by fines or forfeitures or whipping and imprisonment. Lord Baltimore had sent over for the assembly's assent a somewhat different draft, hoping to preserve his experiment by legislating the new idea of liberty of conscience and apparently making concessions (such as the disabilities against Unitarians and Jews) to the Protestants who formed a majority of the population. There is no record of the death penalty ever having been inflicted for blasphemy or of a fine ever having been imposed for violation of any provision of this act.

In the same year at Governor Stone's invitation hundreds of nonconformists who were being harassed because of their religion in Virginia came to Maryland with their movable goods. The assembly called by the governor in 1650 elected a Puritan speaker. The governor, members of the council and of the assembly, and other colonists signed a declaration of their enjoyment of "all fitting and convenient freedom and liberty in the exercise" of their religion under Lord Baltimore's government. In 1651 Parliament passed an act for the reduction of rebellious plantations and authorized the sending of a fleet for that purpose. Lord Baltimore had acknowledged the new Commonwealth and had had his colony excluded from the commission directed against Virginia, but since "all plantations"

in the Chesapeake were specified, the commissioners claimed the right to assert their authority in Maryland also. Thus they ejected Stone and his council and appointed another council under themselves, but soon they were compelled by public opinion to reinstate a part of the former government. Lord Baltimore then ordered Stone to issue a proclamation in which his rights under the charter were reaffirmed.

The Puritans then appealed to the commissioners, who had left Maryland but now returned and in August 1654 deposed Stone and placed the government in the hands of a Puritan council. An election was ordered but all who had borne arms in war against Parliament or professed the Roman Catholic religion were disfranchised. After the commissioners withdrew, the new assembly, exclusively Protestant in membership, first recognized Oliver Cromwell's title to and authority over the colony and repudiated the proprietor's rights; then it repealed the Act concerning Religion and passed a new act that omitted the extreme provisions against blasphemy and declared: "That none who profess and exercise the Popish Religion commonly known by the name of the Roman Catholic Religion can be protected in this Province by the laws of England formerly established and yet unrepealed . . . but are to be restrained from the exercise thereof." In this way those who had themselves fled from persecution and were welcomed into Maryland and who had taken an oath of fidelity to the proprietor responded to those who had given them asylum. The historian Sanford H. Cobb wrote that the Maryland Puritan "played the part of a viper stinging the bosom that had warmed him and made the most disgraceful chapter in the history of Puritanism and religious liberty."

Cromwell, however, restored Lord Baltimore's charter to its original validity, and the proprietor then ordered Stone to resume the government of the colony. Since some of the Puritans and Parliamentarians refused to take the oath of fidelity, Stone, with 130 Protestant and Catholic men, attempted to surprise the Puritan stronghold of Providence (later renamed Annapolis) but was defeated in the battle of the Severn in 1655. One-third of his force was killed or wounded on the field, and four, of whom three were Catholic, were executed afterwards. The Jesuits lost all their property and escaped to Virginia, where they could barely sustain life. Instead of supporting the Puritans, Cromwell submitted their dispute with Lord Baltimore to a commission. In 1657 an agreement was reached whereby the government of the colony was to be surrendered to the proprietor and the inhabitants were to take the oath of fidelity and to give due obedience and submission to his authority in matters of administration and the exercise of justice. In return Lord Baltimore guaranteed immunity to all offenders in the recent rebellion and promised never to give his assent to the repeal of the Act concerning Religion. He also had to appoint another Protestant (Josias Fendall) governor; he instructed him that the act "be duly observed." Though the Puritans were permitted to leave the colony if they wished, most of them remained and were restored to all their former rights and privileges. Shortly after Charles II returned to England in 1660 as king, he confirmed Lord Baltimore's proprietary rights. When the baron appointed his son Charles governor in 1661, he ordered him also to reinstate the Toleration Act of 1649.

Maryland during the Stuart Restoration. There followed a period of peace and growth, though Catholics still comprised only a small portion of the population during the latter part of the seventeenth century. Between 1667 and 1674 a total of 260 Protestants were converted or lapsed Catholics were restored to the Church by the Jesuit missionaries, but such activity caused much dissatisfaction and complaint. Lord Baltimore did little to provide for the religious needs of the Catholics. Between 1660 and 1674 nine or ten Jesuits had come to Maryland, but most of them had not remained long, and at times there were only two in the whole colony. Lord Baltimore complained that the Sacred Congregation of Propaganda Fide had failed to heed his plea for more missionaries, and he lamented that his efforts to secure secular priests had been thwarted by the reservation of Maryland for the Jesuits. Accordingly, he was asked in 1670 to submit the names of priests of proven merit to whom the congregation might issue faculties for the colonial missions. Consequently, he invited the English Franciscans, whose superiors decided in 1672 to send two priests to Maryland. The Jesuits welcomed them the following year. Usually there were only three or four Franciscans at any one time, although sometimes as many as six. The Franciscan mission lasted until 1720, when the last friar died.

When the second Lord Baltimore died in 1675, Charles Calvert became proprietor as well as governor. Although he was benevolent and paternal, he did not intend to yield any of the rights guaranteed him by the charter. He was criticized mainly for insisting that he retain complete review and an absolute veto over the legislation passed by the assembly, which by 1660 had become a bicameral body, with a lower house of elected representatives predominantly Protestant and commoner and an upper house of which usually at least half of the members were Catholic and attached to the Calvert family through consanguinity or marriage. The council was also dominated by Catholics with the support of a few Protestant relatives of the Calverts. Many of the colonists believed that they were being taxed for the benefit of the Calverts and their adherents. The third Lord Baltimore took some politically unpopular measures and made himself vulnerable to attack in England, where anti-Catholic sentiment was intense.

The Anglicans in particular, hardly more numerous than the Catholics but increasing through immigration, blamed the proprietor for not supporting their church and tried but failed to have their ministry established. They disliked having to maintain their institutions by voluntary contributions. In December 1676 or January 1677 they complained to the English authorities about the proprietary government, even asserting that the Catholics would join with the French and their Native American allies to drive out or destroy the poor Protestants. They attributed the weakness of the Anglican Church in Maryland to the proselytizing activities of the Jesuits and the Catholic priests and asked the king to take the government of the colony into his own hands, appointing a Protestant governor and ministers who would follow English customs. An Anglican minister, John Yeo, also complained to the archbishop of Canterbury in 1676 that the Protestant religion was being neglected, while Catholicism and Quakerism were growing. His letter stirred up hostile feelings against Lord Baltimore on both sides of the Atlantic.

In order to protect some of the rights of the charter that were being challenged and to settle a boundary dispute with Pennsylvania, the baron returned to England in 1684 and remained there during the reign of the Catholic king, James II. He defended himself against most of the charges but had to contend with others for years. When in 1688 he understood that he would not be able to leave England, he sent William Joseph over as president of the council, which was acting in his name and on behalf of his son, Benedict Leonard, a minor, the titular governor. Joseph, an advocate of high prerogative, as chief deputy governor, antagonized the lower house.

After the Revolution of 1688 occurred in England, for some reason the deputy governors, all but one of whom were Catholic, failed to proclaim William and Mary the rightful successors to the throne. Some of the Protestants accused the Catholics of being Jacobites, and feared that Roman Catholicism would be established. Some of the anti-Catholics formed a group called the Association in Arms for the Defense of the Protestant Religion; they alleged that Catholics were plotting with the native peoples against the Protestants. Although sixteen respected Protestants declared that they had investigated the circumstances surrounding the government's renewal of the annual treaty of peace with the native inhabitants and had found no evidence of any plot, the majority of Protestants still wanted a change of government. A former Anglican minister, John Coode, who had been elected to the lower house of the Assembly in 1676 and had been indicted in 1681 as a blasphemer and a man of flagitious life and conversation but had been acquitted by a provincial court, gathered an armed force of about 250 men and seized the capital of the colony, St. Mary's City, in July 1689. The proprietor's deputies were put to flight and soon surrendered to the rebels.

The rebels, calling themselves the Protestant Associators, called an elected assembly or convention, from which Catholics were excluded, to take control. The convention requested royal aid for the advancement of the Protestant cause and asked that Maryland be made a royal province. The associators also issued a declaration in which they attempted to justify their uprising and bitterly indicted the proprietary government for its allegedly discriminatory policy against Protestantism. Actually, religious freedom had not been restricted by Lord Baltimore, and Protestantism as a whole was growing. Since most of the revolutionaries were Anglicans, that is, adherents of the smallest sect in the colony, it seems that they exploited the anti-Catholic bigotry prevalent in all the English colonies and posed as defenders of all Protestants. Hence, it can be concluded that genuine religious grievances were not causes of the revolution.

Catholics in Eighteenth-Century Maryland. In response to the rebels' petition, King William made Maryland a royal colony and appointed the first royal governor, Sir Lionel Copley, in 1691. The commission and instructions given to this staunch Anglican marked the end of the era of religious toleration in Maryland. The crown ordered him to receive the oath of supremacy and the test oath, both impossible for Catholics to take in good conscience, from all officeholders, thereby excluding Catholics from the Assembly and local office. It was not until 1702, however, that the Assembly passed an act which received the royal assent to establish the Church of England in the colony; it remained the established church until the American Revolution. While some measure of toleration was granted to Protestant Dissenters, Catholics were excluded from both voting and holding office and were forbidden to worship in their own chapels. Although "An Act to prevent the growth of Popery within this Province," which would have made it a crime for any papist bishop, priest, or Jesuit to say Mass or exercise other religious functions or to convert non-Catholics, was passed by the Assembly and signed by the governor in 1704, the governor and legislature soon decided under pressure to suspend the prosecution of priests for celebrating Mass provided that such religious acts were performed in a private Catholic family. Since the priests were property owners, they could use their estates and homes for private worship. The Queen (Anne) in Council in 1706 ordered an indefinite suspension of the law without vetoing it outright, and in 1707 the Maryland legislature dutifully passed an act suspending it during the queen's pleasure. The Act against Popery was eventually repealed in 1717, because a subsequent act of Parliament to prevent the growth of popery was considered binding in Maryland. Meanwhile, however, other repressive laws had been enacted. In 1717 the tax on indentured Irish Catholic servants to be paid by masters of ships transporting them was doubled in order to hinder the growth of the Catholic population through immigration. The fifth Baron of Baltimore, Charles Calvert, who had been reared a Protestant, was invested by George I with the rights of the original charter in 1715 (though the absolute lordship was not revived), but he and his successors did not protect Catholics.

Catholics continued to be suspected of favoring the Stuarts, especially in 1715 and 1745; the Jesuits were constantly watched and sometimes arrested. In July 1746 the governor, Thomas Bladen, issued a proclamation warning Marylanders of the activities of the priests, whom he accused of alienating the affections of some from the British crown possessed by the House of Hanover.

The defeat of General Edward Braddock, the commander in chief of the British forces in North America, by the French and their Native American allies at Fort Duquesne in 1755 necessitated increased support for the army. In 1756 the Assembly imposed a tax of one shilling on every hundred acres of land and doubled it for Catholics (eighteen years of age and older) on the grounds that they did not serve in the militia, from which they were excluded, and that they were politically unreliable. Widespread false accusations against their loyalty provoked this unjustified discrimination, even though they had promoted the subscription raised to defend the frontier and had subscribed generously and had paid their pledges honorably beyond their proportion, as Charles Carroll of Annapolis argued in vain. The double-tax bill was a critical turning point in the history of Maryland Catholics. Previously they had sustained Baltimore's claims and depended on him for their safety; thereafter they lost confidence in the proprietor. The Catholics were oppressed enough to keep them politically powerless but not so much as to induce them to emigrate to French or Spanish colonies in North America. When the fourth Lord Baltimore became an Anglican, many prominent Catholic families of Maryland followed his example, as well as the majority of their dependents. These losses were permanent, for any attempt at conversion to Catholicism was illegal and dangerous.

According to a census taken in 1708, there were 2,974 Catholics out of a total population of 33,833, or less than 9 percent. Some of the Catholics, however, were wealthy plantation owners, such as Charles Carroll, who had arrived in 1688 as attorney general and had succeeded in establishing himself in the colony in spite of grave obstacles. Families such as the Carrolls, the Darnalls, and the Brookes, who remained Catholic, could afford to maintain chapels in their manor houses, such as Doughoregan Manor near Ellicott City in Howard County, where they provided facilities for celebrating Mass, catechizing children, and administering the sacraments not only to family members, but also to tenants, servants, and slaves. These wealthy families, moreover, sent their children abroad to be educated in schools such as the Jesuit College of St. Omer in northeastern France. Children of less affluent families were often taught by Irish indentured servants who had been hedge-school masters. The majority, however, grew up more or less illiterate. Eventually, around 1745, a clandestine school was opened at Bohemia Manor in Cecil County (near the Pennsylvania border), an estate that the Jesuits had bought in 1706. There boys such as Charles Carroll of Carrollton, the signer, his cousin John Carroll, the first bishop, and the sons of other eminent Catholic families received good elementary instruction before going overseas for higher studies.

The Jesuits continued to provide spiritual ministry for the Catholics until the end of the colonial period. They lived on the income from their plantations, on which they used slaves. By 1727 they owned a total of 9,133 acres, and two years later James Carroll bequeathed to the Society of Jesus the estate of Whitemarsh, a tract of 2,000 acres near the Patuxent River in Prince Georges County. They had long since forgone any missionary work among the indigenous peoples, which was strictly forbidden them by law. Most of them had to travel great distances regularly on horseback in order to visit the scattered congregations. They were often in danger of arrest; in fact, two of them were arrested in 1756, when fear of the French and Indians was widespread and intense, but they were both acquitted. When the Society of Jesus was suppressed in 1773, the ex-Jesuit priests were placed under the jurisdiction of the vicar apostolic of the London District, Bishop Richard Challoner, who appointed their former superior, Fr. John Lewis, his vicar general for the colonies. The American Revolution in effect terminated their dependence on any ecclesiastical authority in England.

Pennsylvania. In Pennsylvania the Catholics were even fewer but enjoyed greater toleration. Although the founder and proprietor, William Penn, held many Catholic beliefs and practices in contempt, he was a friend of certain Catholics, most notably King James II, and was even accused of being a papist. It was mainly for his fellow Quakers and other persecuted Protestants that he requested a colony large enough to become a sanctuary. When William and Mary drove James out of England, the governor appointed by Penn during his protracted absence from the province, Captain John Blackwell, and the council not only proclaimed the new sovereigns but also excluded Catholics from office, though it is unlikely that any Catholics actually held office. In 1693, when the royal Governor Col. Benjamin Fletcher summoned an assembly, he imposed on the members the usual oaths, thus excluding any Catholics who might have been elected in their counties. After Penn, reinvested with his proprietary rights, returned to the colony, he tried to restore religious liberty, but in 1706 the legislature, obeying the instructions of the British government, passed an act requiring office holders to take the usual oaths and test; thus Catholics were again excluded from office.

Under the mild Quaker rule, nevertheless, the Catholic population slowly grew, mainly through immigration of Catholics from Maryland and Germany. They built churches and chapels, imparted religious instruction to their children, and carried on public worship without hindrance. However, they were often subject to manifestations of extreme prejudice by the Anglicans and Presbyterians. After Penn died in 1718, the anti-Catholic bigots continued to allege collaboration between Catholics and Quakers. The English Protestants feared the increasing foreign immigration, and the Assembly placed a duty on the importation of "Irish servants and Persons of Redemption." During England's frequent wars against Catholic countries, especially Spain and France and the latter's native allies, the Catholics were thought to threaten the internal security of the colony. The Protestants exaggerated the number of Catholics, who actually constituted only .06 percent of the total population. After 1740 rumors of popish plots proliferated; even Benjamin Franklin contributed to the bigotry. After the outbreak of the French and Indian War the Catholic Irish and Germans were suspected of being ready to support the enemy in order to impose popery on the inhabitants. The 454 Acadians who had been deported from their homeland by the British and deposited in Philadelphia in November 1755 were treated with special harshness. With the help of Quakers the Catholic church in that city, St. Joseph's, was narrowly saved from destruction by a mob of enraged Presbyterians. In December 1760 the Catholic church in Lancaster was completely destroyed by furious Protestants. Under popular pressure the legislature in 1757 enacted the Militia Act, which excluded Catholics from the force, prescribed the confiscation of all arms, gunpowder, and ammunition found in the possession of a papist, and taxed all papists between the ages of seventeen and forty-five twenty shillings. Catholics were registered in order that their movements might be observed. Spies strove to win the reward offered to informers by having unoffending citizens summoned before the courts.

As the Catholic population in Pennsylvania increased, Jesuits came from Maryland to provide spiritual care. From St. Xavier Mission (later called Bohemia Manor) priests from time to time made trips into the neighboring areas of Pennsylvania. After serving as an itinerant missionary in the 1720s, Joseph Greaton, S.J., opened a Catholic chapel in Philadelphia around 1734 and became the first resident priest in the colony, though in 1740 St. Joseph's had to be protected against axe-wielding Presbyterians, to whom it symbolized the inroads of popery. Generally, nevertheless, the Jesuits were not molested in the exercise of their ministry, though in 1745 Fr. Richard

Molyneaux was arrested for having been present in Lancaster while a treaty was being negotiated between the English and the Native Americans.

From the outset the majority of the Catholics in the colony were German immigrants, mainly from the Palatinate. In 1727 a large number of them arrived. Most of the Catholics in rural areas were German. In 1741 Frs. Theodore Schneider and William Wappeler, both Jesuits, came from Germany and founded establishments at Goshenhoppen (now known as Bally) and Conewago, where the Sacred Heart mission was begun. Nine more German Jesuits expanded the work. By the time of the Revolution the Germans had become one of the most flourishing groups of Catholics in America.

On the eve of the Revolution there were approximately six thousand Catholics—German, Irish, and English, born in America—in Pennsylvania. At the same time there were about twenty thousand in Maryland, where they were even more commonly settled in the country, since they were unwelcome in Annapolis and since Baltimore began to grow only after 1760.

Between 1634 and 1776, 113 Jesuit priests, 1 Jesuit scholastic, and 30 Jesuit brothers ministered to colonial Catholics in Maryland, Pennsylvania, and Virginia. Forty-three Americans became Jesuits, one a Benedictine monk, one (a dubious case) a Franciscan, and three, secular priests. Twenty-one American Jesuits, including the future archbishop of Baltimore, John Carroll, and his coadjutor and successor, Leonard Neale, worked in America.

New York. North of Pennsylvania, the colony of New Netherland was taken over and renamed New York by James, Duke of York, to whom his brother, King Charles II, had issued a charter making him absolute proprietor in 1664. In the following year the duke sent over a body of laws, among which was a provision guaranteeing religious freedom to Christians; no congregation was to be disturbed in its private meeting, nor was any Christian to "be molested, fined, or imprisoned, for differing in judgment in matters of religion." The Dutch briefly recovered the colony in 1673, but the Duke of York, who had converted to the Catholic Church around 1668, took it back the following year and instructed his new governor to permit all persons of any religion to inhabit the territory without any disturbance because of "their differing opinions in matter of religion."

In 1683 he appointed Colonel Thomas Dongan, an Irish Catholic from a distinguished family, governor. The Test Act, which would have excluded him in England, did not apply in the colony. At the proprietor's behest Dongan convoked a general Assembly of Freeholders chosen by the inhabitants in 1683. Its first act, the Charter of Liberties and Privileges, which the duke was expected to confirm, included an enactment of religious liberty for all persons

professing "faith in God by Jesus Christ." All the Christian churches then existing in the colony were confirmed and from then on were to be held and reputed as privileged churches and to enjoy all their former freedoms in divine worship and church discipline. Thus New York became one of the four colonies, along with Maryland, Pennsylvania, and Rhode Island, where freedom of worship was permitted at least at some time. Although the Duke of York signed the charter in 1684, he had not yet promulgated it by the time that he became king (James II) in 1685. Following his accession, the status of New York was changed from that of a proprietary colony to that of a royal province subject to the Committee of Trades and Plantations. This committee disapproved of the charter with its claim of representative government; moreover, the Lords of Trade had advised James to consolidate the American colonies in the Dominion of New England, in which the New York "charter" would be superfluous. Nevertheless, James ordered Dongan to maintain religious liberty and even to extend it "to all persons of what religion soever," provided (as usual) they gave no disturbance to the public peace and did not molest others in the free exercise of their religion.

During Dongan's administration English Jesuits labored in New York. Before the new governor sailed from England, the Duke of York had obtained from the Jesuit superior one priest, Thomas Harvey, who accompanied Dongan to the colony. Although he does not seem ever to have been appointed an official chaplain, Dongan did later make a yearly payment of £60 to "Two Romish priests." A chapel was prepared in Fort James, and there Mass was said and the sacraments administered. Two other Jesuits joined Fr. Harvey—one in 1685 and the other in the following year. With Dongan's support they established a school in 1687; the building, located at the corner of what is now Broadway and Wall Street, had formerly been used by the Anglicans for a similar purpose.

The French in Canada, knowing that Dongan was Catholic, attempted to secure his collaboration against the Iroquois, who had treated the Jesuit missionaries so savagely. Dongan, however, suspected that the French were simply playing on his religious sympathies for political purposes, that is, to separate the English from their Native American allies. Hence, he promised only to try to protect the Jesuits from harm, and he kept his word, but he also prevented the French from gaining any political benefit from the labor of the missionaries. Intending to promote the preaching of the gospel among the natives and at the same time to retain their allegiance, Dongan planned to replace the French Jesuits with English Jesuits. None of the three Jesuits who came to New York, however, undertook missionary work among the Iroquois, probably because the Iroquois did not want them.

When the Dominion of New England, which included New York, was created in 1688, Edmund Andros was appointed captain general and governor in chief, and Dongan was recalled. James ordered Andros "to permit a liberty of conscience in matters of religion to all persons, so that they be contented with a quiet and peaceable enjoyment of it," pursuant to his Declaration of Indulgence of 1687. Some of the inhabitants, however, feared for the safety of the Protestant religion under a Catholic king and some Catholic officials in the province. Actually, the number of Catholics was very small in comparison with the Protestants of various denominations. Dongan, who had retired to his estates at Hempstead, was believed to be the center of Catholic plots, and even Andros was accused of sympathizing with the Catholics. The popular excitement and agitation, at times bordering on delusion, made the province ripe for revolt. Hence, when news of the Revolution of 1688 reached America, the colonists rose up and restored the old form of government under the charters of the several colonies. Since the lieutenant-governor of New York, Nicholson, who had previously been charged with secretly being a Catholic, hesitated to proclaim William and Mary the new sovereigns, a German merchant, Jacob Leisler, a coarse, vulgar, vain, ignorant, overbearing, but incorruptible man, and other bigots convinced the Protestant colonists that the Catholics and James II were conspiring with the French to seize New York, crush Protestantism, and establish Catholicism.

Exploiting the anti-Catholic sentiment, they raised the cry of "No Popery" and took over the government in 1689. They declared their entire opposition to papists and their religion, and denied them the right to hold office or to vote; prominent Catholics were thrown into prison. Leisler, considering all acts of a papist governor to be null and void, revoked all commissions and appointments made under Dongan, but found only three Catholic officials in the colony, and these were in inferior posts. He pursued Dongan himself, who fled from his estates and ultimately returned to England. The Jesuits too fled in haste. Fr. Harvey went to Maryland but later quietly returned to New York, where he ministered to the scattered and proscribed Catholics until 1696. The little chapel in Fort James and the school were closed.

When the new governor, Henry Sloughter, arrived in March 1691, the legislature passed an act declaring the rights and privileges of their majesties' subjects, which required that before anyone could hold any office, civil or military, he must take the oaths and subscribe the test which excluded Catholics. It specifically denied "liberty for any persons of the Romish religion to exercise their manner of worship contrary" to English law. The next governor, Benjamin Fletcher, in 1693 induced the assembly to pass a measure gradually establishing the Church of England in four of the most important counties; thus any Catholic living there would have to pay taxes for the support of Anglican clergy. Very few Catholics, however, remained in the royal colony.

The Protestants' continuing fear of the French and their native allies produced the act of 1700 against Jesuits and popish missionaries, which banished all Catholic priests from the province and threatened those who would remain or would come into it later with perpetual imprisonment. It provided that anyone sentenced to prison who escaped and afterwards was captured would be punished with death as a felon, and that anyone who wittingly aided such a priest would be fined £200, half of which was to be paid to the informer, and would be set in the pillory for three days; it also empowered any justice of the peace to apprehend any person suspected of being a priest and, if necessary, to try him. It even authorized any private person to apprehend without a warrant any priest and to bring him before the governor or any two members of the council to be examined and imprisoned in order to stand trial. Finally, in 1701 an act regulating elections of representatives for the several cities and counties definitively disfranchised Catholics. Consequently, during the rest of the eighteenth century up to the Revolution, hardly a Catholic was left in New York. For Catholics driven out by Leisler's Rebellion and for those who fled subsequently, Pennsylvania became a haven.

See also MISSIONS IN COLONIAL AMERICA, FRENCH.

Carr, Lois Green. "Sources of Political Stability and Upheaval in Seventeenth-Century Maryland." *Maryland Historical Magazine* 79 (Spring 1984) 44–70.

Casino, Joseph J. "Anti-Popery in Colonial Pennsylvania." *Pennsylvania Magazine of History and Biography* 105 (July 1981) 279–309.

Curran, Francis X. *Catholics in Colonial Law.* Chicago: Loyola University Press, 1963.

Ellis, John Tracy. *Catholics in Colonial America.* Baltimore: Helicon, 1965.

Gleissner, Richard A. "Religious Causes of the Glorious Revolution in Maryland." *Maryland Historical Magazine* 64 (Winter 1969) 327–41.

Graham, Michael. "Popish Plots: Protestant Fears in Early Colonial Maryland, 1676–1689." *Catholic Historical Review* 79 (April 1993) 197–216.

Hanley, Thomas O'Brien. *Their Rights and Liberties: The Beginnings of Religious and Political Freedom in Maryland.* Westminster, Md.: Newman Press, 1959.

Hardy, Beatriz Betancourt. "Papists in a Protestant Age: The Catholic Gentry and Community in Colonial Maryland, 1689–1776." Ph.D. dissertation, University of Maryland at College Park, 1993.

Hughes, Thomas. *History of the Society of Jesus in North America: Colonial and Federal.* 4 vols. New York: Longmans, Green and Co., 1907–17.

Kennedy, John H. *Thomas Dongan, Governor of New York (1682–1688).* Washington, D.C.: The Catholic University of America, 1930.

Koning, Gretchen Z. "The Transformation of the Catholic Community: Maryland, 1750–1840." Ph.D. dissertation, Harvard University, 1993.

Krugler, John D. "Lord Baltimore, Roman Catholics, and Toleration: Religious Policy in Maryland During the Early Catholic Years." *Catholic Historical Review* 65 (January 1979) 49–75.

____. "'With Promise of Liberty in Religion': The Catholic Lords of Baltimore and Toleration in Seventeenth-Century Maryland, 1634–1692." *Maryland Historical Magazine* 79 (Spring 1984) 21–43.

Ray, Mary Augustina. *American Opinion of Roman Catholicism in the Eighteenth Century.* New York: Columbia University Press, 1936.

ROBERT TRISCO

MISSIONS IN COLONIAL AMERICA, FRENCH

French Colonies: Extension of a Broad Arc. New France embraced not only Canada but also Upper Louisiana (the "Illinois Country") and Lower Louisiana, that is to say the entire Mississippi valley in the broadest sense. Lower Louisiana also included Biloxi, founded in 1699 (now in the state of Mississippi), and Mobile, founded in 1711 (now in the state of Alabama), along the northern coast of the Gulf of Mexico. The southern line of French colonial Canada, moreover, dipped into present-day New England, western Pennsylvania, and the area that came to be known in U.S. history as the Old Northwest.

The French Catholic presence in North America began with Jacques Cartier, discoverer of the St. Lawrence River, but his three voyages between 1534 and 1541 left no permanent settlements. In 1611 on the peninsula known as Acadie (England's Nova Scotia) two Jesuits launched a mission, but an English raid destroyed it two years later. In 1613 a short-lived Jesuit mission was set up on Mount Desert Island (in the present-day state of Maine); only a place-name relic remains: Saint Sauveur Mountain.

An enduring presence began in Quebec only when Samuel Champlain, a devout believer, established the town in 1608. Champlain invited the Franciscans to come to Quebec in 1615, but, after the Kirk brothers' raid (1628) removed all Catholic clergy, the Franciscans delayed their return.

Jesuits came back to New France in 1632 under the régime of the Compagnie des Cents Associés. To this association of one hundred shareholders, chartered in 1628, the royal government entrusted the colonizing of New France. The planning for this company and its role came from Franciscans and Jesuits who had reflected on the matter in Canada, but it was Fr. Philibert Noyrot, the Jesuit missions' agent and fundraiser in France, who won the interest and cooperation of Cardinal Armand de Richelieu. The basic aim of the enterprise was to establish settlements of Catholics from France and, from these settlements, reach out to evangelize the native population. From 1632 into the 1660s, when Jean-Baptiste Colbert supplanted the company, it worked consistently, although with little financial gain, toward its several idealistic goals of settlement, religious living, and spread of the faith.

West of Quebec lay the attractive lands of the island of Montreal. Jérôme de La Dauversière hoped to plant a missionary settlement there that would lead the nomadic Algonquins to take up a sedentary life and Christianity as well. Out on this dangerous frontier the devout founders of the future city of Montreal, like Paul de Maisonneuve and Jeanne Mance, while awaiting a propitious period of peace for their missionary enterprise, created on the island of Montréal in 1642 Ville Marie (Mary Town), which they intended to be a city that would live according to the high ideals of seventeenth-century French Catholicism. This intention was reinforced when the original colonizing company, the Société de Notre-Dame de Montréal, was succeeded by the Sulpicians (1662).

Like the English Puritans in New England, these French Catholics in New France yearned for a purer society than they had known in Europe, but they were less severe in judging Old France than the Puritans were in judging Old England. In general, the Canadian Catholics, especially their leaders and thinkers, saw themselves as renewing the life of the primitive Church in the forests of North America. They sought to build a New Jerusalem as they reenacted the Acts of the Apostles in spreading the faith to the pagans. The settlers and their descendants did in fact, according to witnesses of those centuries, live a remarkably good religious, civil, and social life. No society, of course, is sinless, and, even prescinding from the notorious *coureurs de bois,* one cannot canonize all who lived in New France.

In the farther west, a century and a third after Hernando de Soto reached the Mississippi River, the French Jesuit missionary and mapmaker Jacques Marquette (born in Laon, France) accompanied the Canadian-born explorer Louis Jolliet in a search for the great river spoken of by the tribes of the Great Lakes. In 1673 Jolliet and Marquette entered the Mississippi River from the Wisconsin River, and Marquette, in devotion to Mary, named the great stream "River of the Immaculate Conception," but his pious intention had no more lasting effect than the ambitious intention of those who wanted it to be called Colbert River.

An early death prevented Marquette from fulfilling his promise to the Illinois—the French pronounced the name ee-lee-nwa—that he would teach them the gospel; he had begun at Kaskaskia on the Mississippi River in 1674, but he died in 1675. By 1689, though, a fellow Jesuit, Jacques Gravier, arrived to live among the Illinois, a number of whom embraced Christianity.

In 1682 Robert Cavelier de La Salle, who in his youth had hoped to go to China as a Jesuit missionary, canoed down the Mississippi River to its mouth, where, in a ceremony complete with notarial recording, he claimed for the French King Louis XIV all the lands watered by the great river and its tributaries; La Salle's *"Louisiane"* extended from the Appalachians to the Rockies. As soon as European peace permitted, France sent Pierre Le Moyne d'Iberville to find the mouth of the Mississippi River from the open sea; he succeeded in 1699. The Franciscan Anastase Douay, who had been with La Salle, accompanied Iberville.

With Quebec and Montreal on the St. Lawrence, Detroit and Michilimackinac on the Great Lakes, Biloxi and Mobile in Lower Louisiana, the French had established a broad arc that extended for thousands of miles. The immigrant population that came was as thin as the indigenous population scattered along the waterways. The arc was never densely settled by French-born Catholics, except at its northern base. Hence a day eventually came when the arc was broken up, with the result that in the nineteenth and twentieth centuries mere remnants of French Catholicism remained in the scattered areas where once the vast arc had extended.

Diocese of Quebec. Catholic canonical discipline calls not only for assured episcopal succession, but also for clear diocesan boundaries. Seventeenth-century New France, however, lay in an ecclesiastical no-man's land. The Archdiocese of Rouen (from 1647) claimed jurisdiction because the Jesuit missionaries of Canada and their canonists in France had asked the archbishop of Rouen to be the ecclesiastical ordinary who was needed for validity of the vows of religious sisters and for marriage dispensations of the laity. Many, however, in France, New France, and Rome found Rouen's position to be an obstacle when the time came to create a Canadian diocese. Solution of the question was difficult because Gallican lawyers were determined to control Rome's activity within the domains of France, and the archbishop of Rouen could count on the support of his fellow French bishops in facing king and pope. Some, moreover, wanted the see city to be not the colonial capital (Quebec) but rather Montreal, with perhaps a Sulpician as first bishop.

In 1657 the royal court of France was ready to provide a resident bishop for Canada, and singled out François de Laval, a diocesan priest who enjoyed the respect of the court and of the Jesuits. In 1658 Pope Alexander VII, upon advice of the Congregation de Propaganda Fide and with the consent of the French monarchy, named him vicar apostolic, i.e., a bishop who was directly dependent on the Holy See and who had no residential claim to his area of jurisdiction. The reason for selecting this form of prelacy was to avoid the delays that were inevitable in the creation of a new French diocese, but Roman canonists and French jurists recognized the juridical implications. Although over the centuries popes had sent temporary vicars on specific missions, Laval was a pioneer among the permanent vicars apostolic in Catholic history. The French hierarchy and the royal tribunals were displeased with this

innovation, but the king and the queen regent supported Laval.

The anomalous situation lasted only a decade and a half, and, while Rouen definitively lost its claims, Laval was named residential bishop of Quebec in 1674. Already with his arrival in Canada in 1659 he provided ordination for Canadian-born priests; previously, candidates had to cross the Atlantic Ocean to receive Holy Orders in France. (Germain Morin was the first colonial ordained in New France.) A half century had passed since the founding of Quebec; canonically the Church in Canada entered upon a new era.

The vast region of Louisiana was part of the diocese of Quebec. A vicar of the bishop of Quebec, residing in Paris to transact the affairs of the Canadian diocese, cared for the Louisiana portion of the flock, for correspondence between France and Louisiana was easier than between Quebec and New Orleans. The regency of the Duke of Orleans did consider the question of setting up a separate diocese in Louisiana (1722), but nothing came of the proposal. At no time, therefore, during the French regime did a bishop visit Upper or Lower Louisiana.

Laval's successors in the see of Quebec were dutiful clergymen, but none equaled the zeal of the exemplary first bishop of Quebec, who, despite extremes of climate and conditions of travel, visited wide swathes of his huge diocese. In the case of one later bishop, on the contrary, officials of Church and state had trouble getting him to leave Paris for Quebec. None in the series, though, was insignificant or scandalous. Henri de Pontbriand, the last bishop of the French colonial régime (he died in 1760), was a model of dedication. His successor, Jean-Olivier Briand, had to cope with the problematic situation that resulted from the English conquest of French Canada.

In the seventeenth and eighteenth centuries colonial New France produced over three hundred priests, most of them for the Diocese of Quebec, and hundreds of religious sisters and several brothers. Louisiana, however, although part of the Diocese of Quebec, gave the Church only one priest and several sisters during the French colonial era, and was similarly weak in religious vocations during the Spanish period.

Ordinary Life of French Colonial Catholics. After the creation of the Diocese of Quebec the provisional missionary ministry among the French-Canadians became a parochial system much as in France. Among the parish clergy the Seminary of Quebec was a center of reference and a base of operations. In Canada, precisely because of the structure arranged by Laval, the Seminary of Quebec exercised a role greater than that of the diocesan seminaries in France.

Throughout the diocese, which extended from the Atlantic Ocean in the north to the Gulf of Mexico in the south,

Sunday Mass brought together the inhabitants of towns and rural areas. In fact, it may have been the only occasion in the week when people gathered together. Hence the civil authorities took advantage of the event, and, after Mass, promulgated decrees and made announcements. During the Mass the priest blessed bread, a tasty leavened bread that was different from the Eucharist and which was distributed at the end of the service in recollection of the *agape* of the early Christians. Thus the Lord's Day worship was the weekly reminder of religious and secular relationships.

The liturgical feast days of France were observed in Canada and the Mississippi valley. In addition to Easter, Pentecost, and Christmas, special devotion was shown on Corpus Christi Day, when usually there were processions in honor of Jesus in the Eucharist, the "Holy Sacrament," in French, *le Saint Sacrement.*

Devotion to Mary, the mother of Jesus, flourished, with Assumption Day, August 15, the day of the vow of King Louis XIII, receiving particular attention without becoming a holyday of obligation. As early as 1635 one finds devotion to Mary under the title of the Immaculate Conception. Subsequently many churches and chapels were given a Marian name.

The number of holydays of obligation varied over the centuries, but usually there was at least one per month. On a holyday the faithful attended Mass and abstained from hard labor, unless the season required the farmer's urgent attention to the fields. Games and sports, though, were allowed.

The local parish held a procession or some other festive rite on the feast day of its patron saint. All Canada nurtured devotion to St. John the Baptist, but the commemoration of June 24, his feast day, tended to become civilly traditional more than religiously devotional. Canadians were devoted to Saint Anne, mother of Mary, to St. Joseph, foster-father of Jesus, and to the Holy Family (Jesus, Mary, and Joseph). The repeated use of the name of St. Louis, particularly in Upper and Lower Louisiana, is not to be taken as a sign of a special cult of the medieval saint, King Louis IX, but rather of respect for the living king whose patron saint he was.

Major attention was given to receiving the sacraments of penance and the Eucharist during the Easter Season. Whoever did so was recognized as a practicing member of the Church. Whoever did not was looked upon with suspicion. Parish priests were expected to know their flocks and to provide certificates of practice. Inevitably, though, the parish clergy and the religious-order priests contended over their respective rights in matters of ministry and certification. This tension affected the exempt, nonparochial churches of the religious orders, whose members, on the other hand, might willingly, when invited, accept responsibility for a parish, or, when asked, give a parish over to the diocesan clergy.

In New Orleans, where there were no diocesan priests in the eighteenth century, the tension was rather between two groups of religious, namely between the Capuchins and the Jesuits. The Capuchins continued to invoke the agreements of 1726, which had the approval of the king and of the Company of the Indies. By these documents the Capuchins were assured of certain rights; for example, no one could exercise ministry in the region assigned to Capuchins without their express consent. The Jesuits could have a plantation next to the capital of Lower Louisiana as a way station for missionaries en route to their destination up the Mississippi River, and the Jesuit superior could reside there, but without Capuchin consent they could not function as priests in the New Orleans area.

In 1741, however, when the Jesuit superior in New Orleans was obliged by Bishop Henri Dubreuil de Pontbriand, the sixth bishop of Quebec, to accept the role of vicar general in place of a Capuchin, a legal struggle began that ended only with the 1764 exile of the Jesuits just when Louisiana was coming under Spanish rule. The Capuchins argued that what the king had decided could only be revised by the king, but the bishop of Quebec did not agree with the friars. In Lower Louisiana a short-lived Carmelite mission had functioned in the 1720s, but had ended when, as the Capuchin coadjutor bishop of Quebec (who lived in Paris) pointed out, the Carmelites in treating with Rome had not followed French procedure.

Lenten fast and abstinence were rigorous. In the northern regions, with the cold of Canada, these practices were more of a hardship than they were in a warmer climate like Louisiana's. Seafood, moreover, was easily obtainable in the streams near the Gulf of Mexico; thus it was easier to go without meat there.

The parishes were formed by united families whose tranquil tenor may have been marred by no vice other than rare drunkenness. Children were many, perhaps ten or twelve. The family routine included group prayer, often the rosary. Even the demanding bishop Jean-Baptiste de St. Vallier recognized the virtue and piety of the Canadian family.

The solid family of Canada, though, was the exception in Lower Louisiana. In the southernmost area of New France, which was sometimes referred to as Mississippi because of the great river, the French monarchy at first brought soldiers but not enough wives. Concubinage with native women followed. Then, to provide more women from France, the royal government shipped prostitutes who had been arrested in Paris and other French cities; the policy lasted only a year. Thus in Louisiana family-centered morality suffered; it flourished mainly among the Germans who settled up river from New Orleans (1720). Decades later, when Acadian refugee families came to Louisiana, they brought with them the stability and piety of their homeland, which the British called Nova Scotia.

In 1724 Jean-Baptiste Le Moyne de Bienville, observing the newly arrived slaves, applied to Lower Louisiana the "Black Code" that French law had developed for the Caribbean islands. One of its provisions required slave owners to have slaves instructed in the Catholic faith. Fr. Raphael de Luxembourg, the Capuchin pastor of New Orleans, later stated that slave owners were not observing that provision.

In general terms one can say that French colonial Canada was a devout Catholic society all during the seventeenth century, but less so in the course of the eighteenth; the shift was due more to immigration for merely secular purposes than to any loss of faith and piety among the residents. The population of the Illinois country (Upper Louisiana) held steadily to its religion and values. Lower Louisiana, however, was Catholic in name but less so in practice; this southern colony, where the immigrants and their descendants never numbered at any given time more than five thousand, began its existence with moral problems that continued to be obstacles to faith and piety. Actually, Louisiana probably improved religiously in the later decades of the eighteenth century; in this way its evolution was the opposite of Canada's.

Parish revenues came from collections, from pew rent (with the more prestigious paying more), and from some ceremonies like weddings and funerals, with various grades of services available and no charge for the poor. As in France the parish priests of Canada received support from a tax, the dîme, but since the missionary Franciscans and Jesuits had not had the parochial structure, Laval and the diocesan clergy had the embarrassing task of inaugurating the tithe, which in reality was less than a tenth—it was one-twenty-sixth. Louisiana never had the tithe or dîme; there parish priests received meager support from the king or, in the 1720s, from the proprietary company. In both Canada and Louisiana the clergy had personal title to a few stipends or fees.

A lay board called the *fabrique,* whose members were known as *marguilliers,* was periodically elected within the parishes to administer parochial temporalities. The parish priest, who presided over the meetings of the *marguilliers,* was appointed by the bishop and answered to him rather than to the *marguilliers,* except in matters of parish finances. The parish accounts, approved by the local pastor and *marguilliers,* were presented annually to the bishop.

Some Protestants made their way into the French colonies even though after 1685 they were technically excluded by law. In Louisiana the non-Catholic population during the French regime was probably around 10 percent. The percentage was lower in Canada, where the Protestants were few and, usually, after a time, converted to Catholicism.

Fr. Pierre François-Xavier de Charlevoix, who published a history of New France (1744) and recorded his travel (1720–23) through Canada and Louisiana, testified to the high quality of Canadians' religious practice.

Religious Instruction. Principally it was the parents who imparted religious instruction to their children. In Quebec City and other population centers north and south where priests were present, parents learned from sermon-lectures. The sermon on Sundays and holydays lasted at least an hour, enlightening the faithful surely, entertaining them perhaps, but probably testing their endurance in the harsh winter of Canada and the steamy summer of Lower Louisiana.

For many of the laity the catechism served also as a primer wherein they first learned to read. Clergy, religious, and lay teachers used catechisms shipped from the mother country. At the beginning of the eighteenth century Bishop St. Vallier of Quebec issued his own diocesan catechism, but after a few decades it yielded to a popular catechism brought over from the Archdiocese of Sens in France.

Laval, the first bishop of Quebec, who was nurtured in the French spirituality of his period, gave himself and his possessions for the instruction of his diocese. Through the Seminary of Quebec, a sister institution of the Séminaire des Missions Étrangères in Paris, Laval drew his clergy into collegial sharing of goods. Subsequently his successor changed the role of the Séminaire, made the clergy independent of the association, and eliminated the sharing of funds. In any case Laval had not only taught but implanted among Canada's clergy a lasting ideal of surrender of worldly goods.

Although in the Seminary of Quebec there were some rigorists who were of a mind like St. Vallier's, neither he nor they ever embraced Jansenism as such. The Jesuits were positively anti-Jansenist. In summary, Canada's Catholics received the equivalent of France's Catholic instruction, with the same mingling of currents then common in the mother country. Upper Louisiana and Lower Louisiana, however, were less well educated than the northeastern regions of the diocese.

In Quebec City the Jesuits founded a *collège* as early as 1635. When Laval later established the Séminaire de Québec, the seminarians who resided there went to the Jesuit school for courses in the humanities, philosophy, and theology.

The Ursulines, who arrived in Quebec in 1639, taught the daughters of settlers: boarders, whose families could afford to pay the *pension,* and day students, whose schooling was free. The nuns also instructed Native American girls. At the other end of the French colonial arc the Ursulines reached New Orleans in 1727, where they taught French girls and black and Native American women as well; they cared for orphans and served in the royal hospital. Lower Louisiana had no school for boys after the bankruptcy of the short-lived parochial school in New Orleans (1725).

The libraries of Quebec possessed abundant material for instruction in piety and study of theology. The libraries of New Orleans, though, given the few inhabitants, were more poorly endowed. Books arrived from France bringing the latest controversies of the mother country, for example, the question of the Chinese Rites, the issue of Jansenism, the theory of moral probabilism, and so on. Clergy and laity discussed these matters in the towns and even in the frontier missions, like the Illinois country, where one would have expected to find only basic evangelization.

Conversion of the North American Natives. Once Europeans came into contact with the native peoples of North America, interchange was inevitable. In commerce they traded reciprocally what they possessed for what they wanted. In material civilization each group borrowed tools, remedies, and methods. Quite naturally, they presented to each other their views of the origin of the world, the destiny of human beings, and the values of religion.

The missionary of New France sought to Christianize but not to "Frenchify" the native population. Therefore more than one French government official in the colony and in the mother country reproached the missionaries precisely because they were not as zealous in teaching French language and customs as they were in evangelizing. What officialdom condemned as a fault was then and later seen by others as a virtue.

The missionaries, who generally were well educated, gave up the comforts not only of old France but even the rugged amenities of New France in order to accompany the tribes in their migrations, which were not chosen freely but were imposed by the life of the hunt. The observable dedication of the missionary to the welfare of the North American native was evidence of an inner love and the beginning of an evangelical dialogue.

The missionaries brought pictures and medals, which they found to be helpful teaching tools and reminders of teaching. Similarly they invited the neophytes to place a cross over the entrance of their cabins as an expression of faith.

Soon after the Jesuits began their Canadian missions, Fr. Jérôme Lalemant recruited lay auxiliaries, called *donnés,* who accompanied the missionary and went hunting for food, performed other chores, and taught catechism. In this program the volunteers did not become members of the religious order, in which capacity they would not have carried firearms for hunting; they were not Jesuit lay brothers, but remained lay coworkers. They made a contract for life service, but without vows; they were free to leave and subject to being sent away. (René Goupil and Jean Lalande went to the missions as *donnés,* suffered martyrdom, and were canonized in 1930. Goupil, in danger of being killed, was admitted by Isaac Jogues to Jesuit vows.) The *donné* program was a noteworthy example of lay missionary service.

The frightening torture of eight missionaries captured by the Iroquois in the 1640s in their war upon the Hurons can be understood as a sort of ritual. The martyrs' suffering did not halt the flow of vocations; on the contrary, it gave rise to a veneration that inspired Christians in the Old World and the New and culminated in the canonization (1930) of the "Canadian" or "North American" martyrs (Jean de Brébeuf, Isaac Jogues, and six others). Three of them—Jogues, Goupil, and Lalande—laid down their lives in what is now New York State.

Even when allowance is made for the edifying literary genre of missionaries' reports, it is striking to read of the depth of faith and prayer among the converted Hurons. These neophytes were not superficial in their embracing and living of Christianity. Nonetheless, in facing the Iroquois enemy, the Christian Hurons stood solidly with their fellow tribesmen. In a sense, the Huron nation, which tried to live peacefully in western New France, showed a model of a religiously pluralist society.

To the southwest, in the Illinois country, Church-blessed marriage between the French and the Amerindian was common. The law of France recognized the juridical equality of the baptized natives with the France-born settler, and, while the French colonists felt a cultural superiority, they showed no attitude of racial superiority. The clergy cooperated in blessing these unions, for every such marriage diminished concubinage and profligacy. Civil officials complained, though, when the French settler went to live totally in native surroundings, for, given the fewness of immigrants, the loss of any one was a blow to the colonial enterprise.

The question of how many of the native peoples accepted the Christian faith can be answered only with a few statistics and a few surmises. In mid-seventeenth-century New France probably one-third of the baptisms of natives were given at their deathbeds. An estimate, made in the period, judged that there were somewhat more than ten thousand living indigenous North American Christians.

As the frontier moved to the Great Lakes, then to the Illinois country and Lower Louisiana, the missionaries (who were few) reported living among tribes—the missionaries called them "nations"—that were small in numbers. Perhaps the most numerous group in the southern region of New France were the Choctaw, who numbered about twenty thousand; the French missionary presence among them was enduring, and there were Choctaw converts. The Apalachee refugees, who fled from northern Florida to French protection near Mobile (in present-day Alabama), were probably all Catholics, but they numbered barely a thousand. Hence, in the Mississippi valley, French Catholic evangelization, brought by missionaries who averaged a mere dozen, reached only tens of thousands, and, of these, only a few thousand Christians could have been counted at any given time.

In later generations the indigenous population intermarried with white and black. Just as it would be difficult to establish a statistic for the number of living North Americans who have some Native American ancestry, it would be impossible to establish a statistic for the number of those who in some way draw their heritage of faith from that ancestry.

But, the question has been asked at times, were the conversions of native people to Christianity sincere? If no device can be found to measure the faith and piety of living present-day believers, the historian cannot *a fortiori* measure such qualities in individuals long dead. Two considerations, though, may be helpful. First, the conscience of the missionary, whose faith was strong enough to lead him to give up all for missionary service, would not permit him to baptize an adult unless he was convinced of the neophyte's sincerity. Second, the native convert could be expected to understand the basic doctrines of the Christian creed, but not to think in the terms of European scholastic theology with its Greco-Roman philosophical tradition. When these considerations are carefully weighed, one can cut through much discussion and accept the integrity of the procedure of catechesis and conversion. But to ask of historiography a clear, precise formulation of native peoples' Christian orthodoxy would be to ask for documents that do not exist and have never existed.

Church and State. The king of France personified the state, and, since the king was a Catholic, the fully loyal subject was one who shared the king's religion. This reasoning, recognized in various ways by other European states and rulers, applied to New France, especially in the later years of the reign of Louis XIV.

Clergymen were expected to lead prayers for the king, his family, and their welfare. The bishop of Quebec sat *ex officio* on the governing council of New France. Civil officials were expected to practice the Catholic religion. Clergy and government officials were expected to show respect toward one another. The interests of Church and state were so intertwined that one cannot speak of one being subject to the other; rather did the leaders of each look to the interests of both.

Exceptions to harmony led to controversy, indeed stark confrontation. Since the pre-Columbian North American population had not possessed a strong alcoholic beverage, the arrival of European brandy led to drunkenness, which often resulted in violent fighting. For moral reasons, therefore, in these circumstances the bishop of Quebec banned as evil the selling of brandy to the native peoples. French colonial government officials, however, knew that the English had no such scruples, and that hence the French traders needed to barter brandy for furs in order to keep their trade going on the frontier. When the matter came to Louis XIV's court, a decision favored the ethical ideal, but it was couched in such terms and applied with such flexibility that the brandy traffic and the fur trade did not suffer. On this point Church and state remained at odds in what was their most serious conflict in New France.

Louis XIV tended to promote bourgeois professionals as part of his policy of weakening the political position of the higher nobility. Jean-Baptiste Colbert was an outstanding example. When these professionals or their protegés made decisions regarding New France, they tended toward autocratic treatment of the Church while, of course, not ceasing to be practicing members. Although they still operated under the personal feudal title of the king, they were developing the modern impersonal state.

Church and state cooperated in providing social services. Religious orders taught school, tended hospitals, and cared for the indigent. The monarchy's responsibility to fund these welfare institutions at least in part was accepted, as well as the religious orders' responsibility to create them and serve in them.

Marriage was a matter of concern to both Church and state. After due pastoral counseling the couple contracted matrimony in church, usually at Mass. Civil authorities on their part set specific conditions which, if not followed, could result in a judicial declaration of nullity. Church authorities strongly favored parental consent before a marriage took place, and royal authorities made parental consent a *sine qua non* condition. Moreover, soldiers who wished to marry had to obtain the consent of their captain and of the royal governor. Banns announcing the forthcoming marriage were published in the parishes of both bride and groom on three successive Sundays; the normal way was to read the announcement at the time of the sermon. The priest who witnessed the marriage wrote a record of it in the parish register, which served simultaneously as state documentation. It was the royal government of France which, in harmony with the Council of Trent's opposition to clandestine marriages, had as of the sixteenth century initiated what became the modern vital statistics bureau.

In 1731 the Company of the Indies retroceded Louisiana to the king. Thus the care of religious affairs passed from company officials to royal officials. The change, however, had little effect on church affairs. As stated above, the area remained part of the Diocese of Quebec.

After the tribunals of France decided upon the suppression of the Society of Jesus in their respective jurisdictions (1762–63), the Superior Council of Louisiana, sitting in New Orleans, followed suit one year later and expelled the Jesuit missionaries from the colony (1764). Canadian-born Michel Baudouin was allowed to remain in New Orleans because his homeland had fallen to the British; as stated below, Sebastien Meurin was permitted to return to the Illinois country.

After the "Conquest" of 1759. The Treaty of Paris of 1763 radically altered the future of French Catholics in North America, for Canada and then the eastern bank of the Mississippi River passed definitively under British control. By a parallel treaty France ceded Louisiana west of the Mississippi River to Spain. When hopes that the mother country would reassume its role in America came to nought, Canadians and Louisianians had to adjust to their new overlords.

After the "conquest"—Quebec fell in 1759—the initial British attempts to anglicize and protestantize the French Catholics of Canada were unsuccessful. The earlier half century of dealing with Acadians, which ended in failure and violence, suggested that it would be better to proceed by diplomacy. (Henry Wadsworth Longellow's *Evangeline: A Tale of Acadie,* a classic of American literature, recalls the tragedy of the Acadian exiles.) So by the Quebec Act (1774) the British Parliament gave French-Canadians certain guarantees regarding their religion, language, and law code. Hence, when the Anglo-Americans of the thirteen colonies declared their independence, the French-Canadians opted to stay with the King of England rather than to ally themselves with the Congress of Philadelphia. The Congress, with patent duplicity, invited the Canadians to join the independence movement at the same time that it denounced the King of England for "establishing" Catholicism in his newly acquired Canadian colony. When the Congress sent a delegation to Canada, the bishop of Quebec made it clear to his clergy and flock that he preferred the British to the *Bostonnais.*

However, the French-speakers around Vincennes (in present-day Indiana) followed the lead not of Bishop Jean-Olivier Briand, but rather of their parish priest Pierre Gibaut (or Gibault), and rallied to the cause of the rebels and independence. Indeed it was due to these French Catholics and to the Spanish-tolerated financial support supplied from New Orleans that the Anglo-American revolutionaries were able to win with relative ease what was called the Northwest (present-day states of Ohio, Indiana, and Illinois).

Tardily and in the face of local opposition, Spain took possession of ceded Louisiana as a buffer to protect the rest of Spanish America against Anglo-American expansion. In the towns and missions Spanish Capuchins gradually replaced French Capuchins. The best known was "Père Antoine" (Friar Antonio de Sedella). As mentioned above, the French regime had expelled the Jesuits, but one of them, Sebastien Meurin, was allowed to stay in Upper Louisiana; eventually, under the Spanish, he crossed over to the Mississippi River's east bank in the years before Gibaut came to that area. (And the elderly Canadian-born Jesuit Michel Baudo[u]in was allowed to live out his last years in New Orleans.)

Spanish eyes viewed the French Catholics of Louisiana as lax, indeed profligate. What with widespread concubinage, the number of baptisms of infants was all out of proportion to the number of marriages. Royal authorities cooperated with churchmen to arrange for an auxiliary bishop of Havana to reside in Louisiana, which under Spain had been cut away from the Diocese of Quebec and depended ecclesiastically on Cuba, but the Spanish clergy never succeeded in reforming the Louisianians. The Spanish monarchy introduced Irish diocesan priests to minister to the Anglo-Americans in Louisiana.

Upon recommendation of the Capuchins of Louisiana and the bishop of Havana, King Charles IV of Spain petitioned Pope Pius VI to confirm his decision—made according to the royal *patronato*—to set up a diocese with New Orleans as the see city. Rome gave approval in April 1793. Thus, under the auspices of the Spanish king, the French-speaking Catholics of Louisiana received a Cuban-born bishop (Luis Peñalver y Cárdenas) merely a decade before Napoleon reacquired the colony for France and sold it to the English-speaking United States of America.

Thus in 1803 Louisiana was again French, from November 30 to December 20. Colonial Prefect Clément Laussat might have wished to implement the French Republic's religious policy and in particular give back to the French language the place it had yielded to Spanish, but what can one do in twenty days?

Leaders and Models. In the Canadian portion of New France the following persons were outstanding as religious leaders and models:

Among the native peoples the best-known saintly person is an Iroquois girl, Kateri [=Catherine] Tekakwitha [which means "who gropes her way because of weakened eyesight"], the "lily of the Mohawks," who awed French and native peoples with her extraordinary piety before dying in 1680 at the age of twenty-four. Her tomb at Caughnawaga/Kahnawake, across the St. Lawrence River from Montreal, remains a shrine to this day. She was beatified in 1980.

Paul Le Jeune, a Jesuit who went to Canada in 1632, was an energetic pioneer missionary planner.

Marie de l'Incarnation [Mary of the Incarnation], whose maiden name was Marie Guyart and married name was Martin, came to Canada as an Ursuline in 1639, and for the remaining three decades of her life exercised deep influence by her presence and her correspondence. It was she who introduced the Ursulines into Canada. She was beatified in 1980.

Jeanne Mance, 1606–73, was foundress of the Hôtel-Dieu of Montreal and a cofoundress of the town of Montreal.

François de Laval, first bishop of Quebec, who was revered in life and after death (he died in 1703), was beatified in 1980.

Marguerite Bourgeois, 1620–1700, went as a lay teacher to Canada, where she founded the Congregation of Sisters of Notre Dame for the education of the native peoples, schooling of the colonial girls, and service of the poor. She was canonized in 1982.

Canadian-born Marguerite Dufrost de Lajammerais, Widow d'Youville, 1701–71, was widowed in her twenties; she founded the Sisters of Charity, the "Grey Sisters." She was beatified in 1959 and canonized in 1991.

The high tone of Canadian spirituality was not equaled in the Illinois country or in Lower Louisiana. No individual was preeminent in religious example or leadership, but two persons may be singled out as highly significant amid Catholics in the lower Mississippi valley:

Madeleine Hachard, an Ursuline who came to Louisiana as a novice with the first group of nuns in 1727, exemplified the uplifting dedication of these religious women; her teenage freshness, cheerful spriteliness, and religious optimism come forth in her letters to her father about boarding the ship, about the transatlantic voyage, and about the town of New Orleans—in contrast with the reality of that rather unfortunate colonial port. Faithful to her missionary vocation, she died in New Orleans in 1760.

Etienne Viel was born in New Orleans in 1736. Young Etienne studied in France and was ordained there—the only priest to come from French colonial Louisiana. He was the first native of the Mississippi Valley to receive a full European education, to teach in a French *collège,* and to author a drama, which was in fact the first literary creation of a Louisiana-born writer. During the French Revolution he returned for priestly ministry in his native Louisiana, which was then under the Spanish monarchy. He died at Juilly, France, in 1821.

Conclusion: Nowadays? What remains of French colonial Catholicism at the end of the twentieth century in the regions that once comprised New France? Quebec has continued to be an identifiably Catholic area despite a self-consciously secularizing trend in the 1970s. Elsewhere pockets of Catholicism traceable to French colonial origins can be found in such diverse and widespread areas as Maine and New Hampshire, Michigan and Indiana, Missouri and Illinois, Louisiana and Mississippi. Yet, of course, only meticulous genealogical research and statistical surveys could show exactly how many present-day inhabitants have inherited from ancestors the religion of French colonial Catholics.

On the surface of things, on maps and *in situ,* geographical nomenclature has a way of reminding us of history. Thus place names recall the French Catholic piety of the colonial era. Towns of Canada and the United States bear saints' names; so too rivers and lakes. For example, there is the Saint Lawrence River in the east, and the city of Saint Louis, Missouri, in the Midwest. In some cases the old French name found on early maps is gone, replaced by a newer English name; for example, in upper

New York state Lac Saint-Sacrement became Lake George. Louisiana, alone among the fifty states, calls its counties parishes because when the new American government set up counties after the Louisiana Purchase, their area was too large, but, when the counties were divided, the new jurisdictions were about coequal with the rural church parishes of colonial days. So in Louisiana a county is a parish, and among the civil-parish names in the southern part of the present-day state are Ascension (of Jesus), Assumption (of Mary), and St. John the Baptist.

On a deeper level a literature remains: in the (edited) letters of the *Jesuit Relations* (edited by R. G. Thwaites, with an English translation), in the pastoral letters of the bishops of Quebec, and in the correspondence and devotional writings of outstanding French colonials. This body of writings has both historical and inspirational significance for Canada, the Illinois country, and the lower Mississippi valley.

Another effect, although recognizable, is more difficult to measure and define. English rule brought to its North American colonies an element of anti-Catholicism, which evolved in both Canada and the United States. In some of these regions and some of these times the Catholic immigrant was made to feel unwanted. In those regions, however, where French colonial presence was and still is recalled, later generations of Catholics felt more at home than elsewhere. Interestingly, also, even though the majority of present-day residents in some of those areas may be Protestant and of an ethnic-linguistic heritage other than French, they tend to recall with nostalgia the French Catholic colonials who preceded them and tend to be better informed than others elsewhere concerning the faith and piety that inspired the pioneers amid hardships and rugged living.

Baillargeon, Noël. *Le Séminaire de Québec de 1685 à 1760.* Québec: Presses de l'Université Laval, 1977.

____. *Le Séminaire de Québec sous l'épiscopat de Mgr de Laval.* Québec: Université Laval, 1972.

Baudier, Roger. *The Catholic Church in Louisiana.* New Orleans: A. W. Hyatt, 1939.

Campeau, Lucien. *Les Cent-Associés et le peuplement de la Nouvelle-France (1633–1663).* Montréal Editions Bellarmin, 1974.

____. *L'Evêché de Québec (1674). Aux origines du premier diocèse érigé en Amérique française.* Quebec: Société Historique de Québec, 1974.

____. *La Mission des Jésuites chez les Hurons.* Rome: Institutum Historicum S.I., 1987.

Conrad, Glenn R., ed. *Cross, Crozier and Crucible: A Volume Celebrating the Bicentennial of a Catholic Diocese in Louisiana.* New Orleans and Lafayette: Archdiocese of New Orleans, 1993.

Delanglez, Jean. *The French Jesuits in Lower Louisiana (1700–1763).* Washington, D.C.: The Catholic University of America Press, 1935.

Douville, Raymond, and Jacques-Donat Casanova. *La Vie quotidienne en Nouvelle France. Le Canada de Champlain à Montcalm.* Paris: Hachette, 1964. (Chapter VI: "La Vie religieuse.") [ET: *Daily Life in Early Canada: From Champlain to Montcalm.* Trans. Carola Congreve. London: Allen & Unwin, 1968.]

Heaney, Jane Frances. *A Century of Pioneering: A History of the Ursuline Nuns in New Orleans, 1727–1827.* New Orleans: Ursuline Sisters of New Orleans, 1993.

Nolan, Charles E. *Manifestations of the Spirit: Religion in Louisiana.* Vol. 19 in the Louisiana Purchase Bicentennial Series in Louisiana History, Lafayette Center for Louisiana Studies, forthcoming.

O'Neill, Charles Edwards. *Church and State in French Colonial Louisiana: Policy and Politics to 1732.* New Haven, Conn.: Yale University Press, 1966.

____. "Tamaroa: Mission Microcosm of Worldwide Debate in 1700." *Ecclesiae Memoria. Miscellanea in onore del P. Joseph Metzler, Prefetto dell' Archivio Segreto Vaticano.* Ed. Willi Henkel. Rome, Freiburg, Wien: Herder, 1991.

Têtu, H., and C.-O. Gagnon, eds. *Mandements, Lettres Pastorales et circulaires des évêques de Québec.* 6 vols. Québec: Coté et Cie, 1887–88.

Thwaites, Reuben Gold, ed. *Jesuit Relations and Allied Documents: Travels and Explorations of the Jesuit Missionaries in New France, 1610–1791.* 73 vols. Cleveland: Burrows Bros. Co., 1896–1901.

Vogel, Claude L. *The Capuchins in French Louisiana (1722–1766).* New York: Wagner, 1928.

CHARLES EDWARDS O'NEILL

MISSIONS IN COLONIAL AMERICA, SPANISH

This article will survey the Spanish missions in the United States from the sixteenth to the nineteenth centuries. It will begin by tracing the development of Spanish missionary policy in both theory and practice. Then it will survey five specific areas of evangelization: Florida (the southeast), Texas, New Mexico, Arizona, and Alta California.

Spanish Missionary Policy. In the Spanish concept of empire, Christianity accompanied conquest and was the only true justification for it. The earliest papal approvals of the Iberian penetration of the New World did so only on condition that the missionary enterprise be paramount. The two papal bulls *Inter Caetera* of 1493 created a type of religious vicariate for the Habsburg rulers of Spain. It was an obligation that, despite the unevenness of implementation, the crown took seriously. The Royal Orders for New Discoveries in 1573 stated that "preaching the holy gospel . . . is the principal purpose for which we order new discoveries and settlements to be made" (Weber, *The Spanish Frontier in North America,* 95). One result of this was encroaching royal control on the life of the Church. By 1700 the Spanish crown had reduced the Church to a department of state, but within that structure the Church still had a measure of control and influence. Government in Habsburg Spain was a balancing act among various special interest and pressure groups, a corporate state in the full sense of the term, and the Church was an essential part of that corporation.

The mission methods employed by the Spanish in what is now the United States were developed and perfected in New Spain (modern Mexico) in the sixteenth and seventeenth centuries. With adaptations to local needs these methods were used throughout the colonial period in all the Spanish possessions in the New World. The missions were primarily the work of friars, later joined by the Jesuits, and the Church in New Spain has been called a "Church of friars." The diocesan Church structure was not usually involved in missionary work, with the exception of a few mission stations in Florida. Bishops and the diocesan structure came after the evangelization by the friars and Jesuits. In North America it was the latter two that dominated the missionary endeavor.

The preeminent mission facility was the presidio/mission, which combined a group of friars with a limited military presence to protect them. In the sixteenth and seventeenth centuries the friars and Spanish government made use of Christianized Native Americans, especially the Tlaxcalans, to act as a penetrating factor and to win the confidence of the other natives. In the initial stage, or *misión,* the missionaries made use of elaborate ritual, rich vestments, and external panoply to capture the minds and imaginations of the natives. They also made use of gifts, such as bells and mirrors. When a large number of conversions had been effected, the *misión* became a *doctrina,* the equivalent of a parish of neophytes. The question of control over the *doctrinas* caused bitter disputes between friars and bishops in New Spain.

The friars, especially the Franciscans, also took the lead in preparing missionaries for their work. Since 1555 official missionary policy required that the indigenous peoples be evangelized in their own languages, and so the friars took the lead in linguistic studies, including the production of dictionaries and grammars. This carried over to North America. In 1612 the Franciscan Francisco de Pareja published both a catechism and confessional guide *(confesionario)* in Spanish and Timucuan, one of the native languages of Florida. Friars in Texas and California studied the native languages and produced devotional works, though most remained in manuscript form. A major difficulty was translating Christian theological terms into languages that lacked exact equivalents. The Spanish missionaries and the native peoples were separated by a major cognitive and theological gap. As in New Spain, the Franciscans often incorporated the Spanish terms, which then became part of the indigenous language. Evangelization in the native languages proved especially difficult in North America because of their bewildering variety. Although demands were made that the natives learn Spanish or that it be a form of *lingua franca,* no serious attempt at such linguistic uniformity was made until the eighteenth century, and then it failed.

Other methods included audio-visual aids, including plays, and the use of special ceremonies and devotions that were suited to the native cultures. There was not, however, any conscious effort at syncretism on the part of the missionaries. Though it is sometimes asserted that the missionaries consciously substituted Christian saints for local deities or Christianized prehispanic devotional practices, this was never official policy. On the contrary, most of the friars, at least in their writings, strongly condemned any form of syncretism. It was the natives themselves who blended the Christian and pagan elements into a new religious form, with or without the conscious assistance of the friars.

The presidio/mission system sought to bring the natives together from their seminomadic or isolated form of life into a more urbanized environment. Spaniards were incapable of understanding any life that was not led in cities. In their worldview there were two ways of living, *políticamente* and *bárbaramente.* The first, derived from the Greek word for city, meant an urban life, lived under rational political structures, with all that was associated with the well-regulated city. To live *bárbaramente* was to live nomadically, without fixed habitations, laws, or civic officials. The city was the apex of culture and civilization. Hence many missionaries sought to enforce a policy of *reducción (congregación)* whereby the natives were relocated from their small villages or wandering lifestyles into Spanish-inspired cities. This policy was opposed by many of the friars in New Spain because it favored control by the bishops. In New Mexico and Florida the natives already had a settled or at least semi-urban style of life, and so resettlement was unnecessary. The policy of *congregación* was implemented primarily in California. Unfortunately, this policy also facilitated the spread of European diseases.

As in New Spain the friars centered most of their efforts on the children. Because adults were often resistant or set in their ways, conversion was more difficult. By indoctrinating the children at an early age, they believed they could rear new generations of Christians. The negative side of this approach was the destructive impact it had on native cultures, pitting one generation against another and reducing respect for native elders and parents.

The missionaries sought to teach the Indians arts and crafts and the European lifestyle, but they also viewed contact with Spaniards as harmful and corrupting. The presence of soldiers, moreover, often proved an obstacle to evangelization. The friars were also oblivious to the culture shock caused by the forced gathering of the natives. In addition, the exposure to European diseases often proved disastrous. The policy of *congregación* provided an environment in which such diseases could spread with greater ease. The missionaries, like the Spanish in general, were completely convinced of the superiority of western European culture and Christianity. Their worldview was dominated by a European and Hispanic ethnocentrism. Missionaries of the "root and branch" school were convinced that all native religions and cultures were diabolically inspired and so should be extirpated immediately. Others took a gradualist approach, but both agreed that ultimately the natives should be incorporated into Spanish culture and mores. In the interim, before that goal was reached, the natives would be regarded as minors under the paternal supervision of the missionaries. The goal was never reached in the colonial period and the natives were kept in a state of tutelage.

The situation changed drastically in the eighteenth century, with the consolidation of the Bourbon monarchy in Spain after the Treaty of Utrecht in 1713. The change of dynasty from Habsburg to Bourbon helped to popularize French Enlightenment thought in Spain and the New World. "Reason" became the measuring rod for governmental policies, and efficiency and order were imposed on all aspects of imperial rule. This meant an increasing centralization and control, particularly of the Church. Impelled in part by chronic financial difficulties, the crown removed the colonial Church from any vestige of control over finances. Monarchy in the Spanish empire became absolute in a way that it had never been before. The enlightened royal ministers were particularly unsympathetic to the various expressions of popular religiosity, including confraternities, and sought to curtail them. More than their predecessors, they sought to create a true state Church, virtually independent of the papacy, and without any real power within the absolutist state.

Enlightenment thought was unsympathetic to religious orders, which were regarded as archaic and unnatural. A special hostility was reserved for the Jesuits, who were suspect because of their involvement with politics and their international status with its close relationship with the papacy. Their educational system was viewed as archaic and stultified. The reductions of Paraguay, in which large populations of natives were under the direct rule of Jesuits who were not primarily accountable to the king, were viewed as a state within a state. The reductions, like the haciendas and sugar plantations of New Spain, were believed to hide enormous wealth and thus were tempting targets to chronically indebted monarchs. On June 25, 1767, in a move of Machiavellian secrecy and stunning brutality, all Jesuits were expelled from the Spanish dominions. The harm done to both missions and education throughout the Americas was incalculable.

Distrustful of the independence of the friars and their control over the natives, the crown favored the diocesan clergy and attempted to "secularize" the Indian parishes, that is, turn them over to the direction of the more pliable diocesan clergy. Because so few of these priests knew the native languages, both civil officials and bishops believed that the natives should be compelled to learn Spanish. It was also believed that this would hasten their incorporation into a more civilized, European form of life. It was impossible to enforce such a scheme. In fact, as the Franciscan experience in New Mexico showed, some of the friars themselves had failed to learn new native languages. Still, the Franciscans did not lose their tradition of linguistic studies. In Florida, Texas, and California they produced grammars and confessional guides (confesionarios), though most of these remained in manuscript form. The bewildering variety of native languages hindered such studies, unlike New Spain where Nahuatl (Aztec) had served as a lingua franca.

At the same time, however, the Franciscans established three important missionary colleges. The famed Antonio Margil de Jesús founded the Franciscan missionary college of Our Lady of Guadalupe at Zacatecas for creoles (Spaniards born in the New World). Santa Cruz in Querétaro was for peninsular Spaniards. An offshoot of Santa Cruz, the hospice of San Fernando in Mexico City, founded in 1731, was converted into a missionary college in 1733. The first two colleges divided Texas between them but were unable to supply the men and material goods that were required. In 1749 the Zacatecas college had five mission stations in Texas with eight resident priests, centered in San Antonio, and was far more successful than its peninsular counterpart, Santa Cruz of Querétaro.

The Spanish missions in North America were on the fringe of the Spanish empire and were frontier institutions in the full sense of the term. They also were founded at a later period, at a time when the missionary fervor had declined somewhat in New Spain. They offered an opportunity for the missionaries, particularly the Franciscans, to recapture some of the glory days of the sixteenth-century missionary enterprise.

The work of the missions laid a heavy financial burden on the Spanish crown. The missionary enterprise was possible only when supported by a stable financial base. That such a base was found or proved adequate was one of the major accomplishments of Spain in the New World. This was all the more true in view of the precarious nature of the royal finances throughout most of the colonial period. Monarchs found themselves compelled on occasions to suspend the payment of interest on their debts, the equivalent of bankruptcy. Usually the debts were renegotiated, but the crown habitually faced extreme financial difficulties. A major source of support for all ecclesiastical institutions was the tithe, an ecclesiastical tax on agricultural products, which was collected by the crown and redonated to the Church according to a complex formula. Another source of support was the Pious Fund of the Californias.

When the crown proved unwilling to sponsor the Jesuit missionary enterprise in Baja California, it permitted in 1697 the establishment of a fund based on gifts of money and land. These were used as capital and the interest used to sustain the missions. The Jesuits administered the fund, and at their expulsion in 1767 the crown took it over. It was then used to support the Dominican missions in Baja California and the Franciscan ones in Alta California. After Mexico achieved its independence, the government of the new republic assumed administration.

The entire Spanish Empire in the New World depended ultimately on the labor of the natives, especially since the Indians were exempt from paying the tithe. The missions were no exception, especially in the case of those that tried to be self-supporting. Under the guidance of both Jesuits and Franciscans these missions could and did become thriving business enterprises whose revenues supported not only the individual mission but others as well. These revenues were administered by the missionaries, not by the Indians. Indian labor built the churches and residences, the ovens and olive presses, and raised the food that supported the missionaries and their neophytes. They tended the pigs, cattle, and sheep, and drove them to market. This use of native labor all too easily became exploitation, though some missions, such as the Jesuit reductions, were noted for the mildness of their administration. Though many Indians accepted and perhaps even liked mission life, others voted with their feet and fled. They were forcefully returned and punished for their apostasy.

The first areas to be evangelized by the Spaniards were present-day Florida and New Mexico.

Florida. In the sixteenth century the term Florida included not only the modern state but also most of Georgia, Alabama, and South Carolina. The principal groups of natives were the Apalachees, Apalachicola, Guale, and Timucua. These peoples shared a number of common characteristics, including social structure, culture, and, with the possible exception of the Timucua, language, though these were mutually unintelligible. The indigenous peoples led a settled way of life and had a well-regulated political system, but they were also fierce and warlike. They were agricultural but supplemented their diet of grains by hunting, fishing, and gathering. The Apalachees, whose center was near present-day Tallahassee, were particularly noted for their fearsome skills with the long bow with which they easily pierced Spanish armor. The Timucua were made up of at least fifteen different tribes in modern Georgia and northern Florida.

The Spaniards touched that area early in the period of conquest. In 1513 Juan Ponce de León made his famous voyage to Florida, where he landed on Easter Sunday (Pascua Florida), hence the name. His commission was not just to explore but also to colonize. This expedition, however, which failed and resulted in de León's death, had no priests with it.

Another serious attempt at colonization was that of Lucas Vázquez de Ayllón, who in 1523 received a royal license to settle a large expanse of the Atlantic coast in the area of the Carolinas. Three years later his expedition, consisting of six hundred colonists, including some women and children, three Dominican priests, some slaves, and captured native interpreters, reached modern-day South Carolina. One of the Dominicans was Antonio de Montesinos, who in 1511 had preached a fiery sermon on the island of Española that launched the humanitarian movement in favor of the natives. Eventually Ayllón established a small settlement at Winyah Bay. Sickness and the severe climate devastated the colony, and after Vázquez de Ayllón's death the 150 surviving and bickering settlers, including Fr. Montesinos, returned to Española.

In 1528 Pánfilo de Narváez, a veteran conquistador who some years earlier had lost an eye in a skirmish with Fernando Cortés' men, led an expedition to conquer and establish a settlement at Tampa Bay. He was accompanied by a number of priests, including five Franciscans, one of whom bore the optimistic title of bishop-elect of Florida. The Apalachees were initially friendly to the Spaniards, but, as so often happened, the arrogance and bungling of the intruders turned the natives against them. The results were disastrous and the survivors attempted to return to Mexico by sailing along the Gulf Coast in makeshift boats. Only four survived, including the redoubtable and famous Alvar Núñez Cabeza de Vaca. Posing as holy men and healers, they were able to make their way from Galveston, Texas, to Sinaloa in New Spain in one of the epic journeys of the colonial period. The tales they brought back of the lands they had been through gave rise to the famed expedition of Francisco Vázquez de Coronado in 1536–42. The expedition gained no riches except in geographical knowledge.

In 1537 Hernando De Soto was authorized to conquer and settle Florida. His expedition, which included several priests, landed there in 1539. There was very little in the way of positive settlement and very much destruction, pillage, and wanton slaughter of the natives. Almost nothing was done in the way of missionary activity, except to baptize native women whom the Spaniards had seized as slaves and concubines.

In 1549 the Dominican Luis de Cáncer de Barbastro and several companions sought to implement Bartolomé de las Casas' idea of peaceful evangelization unaccompanied by military conquest. When they landed on the Florida coast Cáncer was almost immediately killed by Calusa Indians. Ten years later Tristán de Luna y Arellano led an armada of thirteen ships, five hundred soldiers, a thousand colonists, five Dominican priests, and one lay brother to found settlements in Alabama and the Carolinas. Shortly after the expedition landed at Pensacola, it was devastated by a hurricane. Again, the missionary effort was frustrated. Two of the Dominicans on this expedition later became bishops: Pedro de Feria in Chiapas (New Spain) and Domingo de Salazar in Manila.

The catalyst for definitive Spanish occupation of Florida, as was so often the case, was the presence of foreign interlopers, in this instance, French Protestants in the Carolinas. To counter this threat the crown commissioned the capable but brutal sea captain Pedro Menéndez de Avilés to stop the French. His expedition was better planned than most and included four diocesan priests. In 1563 he established a presidio and municipality at San Agustín, present-day St. Augustine, the oldest continuously inhabited city in the United States. In 1566 two Dominicans came and were sent north to Chesapeake Bay, but their vessel apparently lost its way.

Between 1566 and 1572 the area was evangelized by Jesuits, who had come at the request of Menéndez de Avilés. They founded ten mission stations between Miami and Jamestown in Virginia on the Atlantic side and Tampa on the Gulf Coast. In 1570 eight Jesuits under the leadership of Fr. Juan Bautista Segura sailed to the mouth of the James River and established a precarious mission station but without any military presence. Their interpreter, an Algonquin-speaking native named Luis de Velasco, in honor of the viceroy of Mexico, who was also his godfather, deserted them. In the following year he led a group of natives that killed the defenseless Jesuits, and as a result the Florida missions were abandoned. At the same time most Spanish garrisons and mission stations were abandoned or destroyed. Because of the lack of gold and other precious metals, the Spaniards quickly lost interest in Florida. The natives proved particularly hostile and resistant. They resented the depredations of the soldiers and the perceived insults to their religion by the missionaries.

In 1573, a year after the Jesuits left, the Franciscans inaugurated their own missionary effort in Florida. By that time there were only two Spanish settlements. At first there were only a few missionaries. In 1587 thirteen Franciscans, led by Fray Alonso Reinoso, arrived at St. Augustine. The missions were still precarious until 1595 when the arrival of a new group, under Fray Francisco Marron, marked the beginning of an ambitious missionary program. From the financial point of view, however, Florida was a drain on the Spanish exchequer. In 1606 the crown decided that St. Augustine had lost its strategic value and should be abandoned. Because the native converts and their priests still needed protection, the crown devised a plan of stupefying impracticality: to move all the Christian Indians to Española. The strenuous opposition of the Franciscans decided the crown in favor of retaining Florida in 1608.

In 1612 the Franciscan Mission became an independent province, and the Florida missions entered their most prosperous period. By the mid-seventeenth century they had a flourishing series of mission stations that reached from north Florida to Georgia and on the Gulf Coast to the end of west Florida. By 1655 there were seventy Franciscans serving in Florida. Two decades later the number had been reduced to forty, but these cared for an extensive system of missions on the east coast of northern Florida and southern Georgia, as well as in the Florida panhandle. By the end of the seventeenth century the mission area consisted of four mission provinces: Guale, Timucua, Apalachee, and Apalachicola, corresponding to the different cultural and linguistic zones.

The Franciscans had begun the evangelization of the Guales in the 1570s. From there they expanded their efforts to the north, toward present-day South Carolina. By the mid-seventeenth century, however, native resistance had forced them to retreat to Guale country. At the same time that they began their work among the Guales the Franciscans had also begun missions among the eastern Timucuans, and early in the seventeenth century they did the same among the western Timucuans. By 1674 eleven Timucua missions extended westward from St. Augustine. The Franciscans began the evangelization of the Apalachee in 1608, but they did not establish any permanent missions until 1633. Within forty years this was the most prosperous and flourishing of the Florida missions. The latest and most precarious of the missions were those among the Apalachicola.

Although on the surface the missionary enterprise seemed to be stable and flourishing, it was not. Some of the native tribes, like the Apalachicola, Calusas, and Tocobagas, proved resistant to evangelization. For many of the indigenous peoples Catholicism was a veneer, and there was a brewing discontent with Spanish rule. The disorder and depredations of Spanish soldiers, the demands of an insistent bureaucracy, the perceived insults to the native religions on the part of the missionaries provided fuel for unrest. The natives were decimated by European diseases. Similarly, the attempt to make the natives live like Europeans met resistance, passive at first, but later violent. In 1647 the Apalachees rebelled against Spanish exploitation, and three missionaries were killed. The revolt was brutally suppressed, a factor that made the natives even more hostile to the missionaries. In 1645 the Timucuas and Apalachees, again in reaction to Spanish exploitation, revolted and again the insurgents were ruthlessly suppressed. In 1647 the English presence to the north began to have an impact on the Spanish territories. As the English extended their settlements to the south, they were able to profit by the natives' hostility to the Spaniards. In the 1680s the Guales abandoned Catholicism and joined the English. The Treaty of Paris (1763), which ended the Seven Years War (the French and Indian War in Anglo-America), put an end to Catholicism in that area.

It should be noted that at its height the Franciscan missions in Florida were far more numerous than their later ones in California. Though they seemed to be models of successful evangelization, their success was superficial. The natives had no genuine attachment to Catholicism, and most abandoned it at the first opportunity. The oppression and exploitation of the Spanish authorities and settlers exacerbated an already unstable situation.

New Mexico. The Spanish occupation of New Mexico leapfrogged the intervening area between it and Mexico City. The Spaniards were drawn there by the lure of mineral wealth, the hope of finding a strait to the Pacific Ocean. The native peoples the Spaniards encountered and evangelized were sedentary and agricultural. Despite some common characteristics, they were quite diverse. The Hopi lived by farming and herding, as did the Pueblos, of whom the Zuni formed a part. The Navajo lived in the same way but lacked any centralized tribal political organization. The Spaniards perceived the Pueblos as receptive to Christianity, at least initially.

The pioneer Spanish explorer of New Mexico was Juan de Oñate. About the year 1600 Juan de Oñate established his headquarters at San Gabriel, about halfway between Santa Fe and Taos. Oñate was accompanied by Franciscans, who immediately undertook a program of evangelization. The new colony proved precarious and would have been abandoned altogether, had it not meant deserting the newly converted natives. The New Mexico mission had a great deal of initial success, even if it proved temporary and superficial. After the capital was moved to Santa Fe in 1610, Tlaxcalan natives were brought from New Spain to help with church construction and to advertise the benefits of Christianity and Spanish civilization. By the 1630s there were twenty-five missions, serving fifty thousand natives, including Pueblo, Zuni, and Hopi.

All this came to a sudden end in 1680. The natives grew resentful of Spanish exactions and demands. The Franciscans did not have the same zeal and learning as their predecessors in New Spain and in particular do not seem to have learned the indigenous languages or become closely identified with the natives. The old religious ideas had not died, and for many Christianity was little more than a veneer. Under the leadership of a Pueblo medicine man, Popé, the natives staged a carefully planned revolt in 1680. With all the advantage of surprise, they killed at least four hundred Spaniards and thirty-two friars—twenty-one Franciscans were killed in one day. Some Spaniards managed to escape to El Paso, laying the foundations for a civilian settlement in what had been, until that time, a military garrison.

Spanish attempts to reconquer New Mexico failed until 1688 when Diego de Vargas, a skilled administrator and military tactician, was named governor. He began the re-occupation in 1692 and it was more or less complete by 1696, though the Hopi and Zuni continued to be independent and hostile. The later development of New Mexico followed a process that was isolated from that of New Spain. The European population have regarded themselves as Spanish, not Mexican. There has also been a notable Jewish element to the Catholic population of the state.

Kino and the Jesuit Missions in the Southwest. Eusebio Kino was one of the most notable of the missionaries who worked in Spanish territories of what is now the United States. He was not, however, Spanish by nationality, having been born in Trent in northern Italy in 1645. He studied at the Jesuit College of Hall, near Innsbruck, Austria, when he became seriously ill and vowed to enter the Society of Jesus if cured. After his recovery he joined the Jesuits in 1665 and was ordained to the priesthood eleven years later. Although the original intention was that he would go to China, he ended up going to New Spain in 1681. He was cosmographer and Jesuit superior on the unsuccessful expedition of Isidro de Atondo y Antillón to explore and missionize California in 1683.

In 1687 his superiors sent him north again to the Pimería Alta, an area that included present-day Sonora, Mexico, and southern Arizona. The native inhabitants included the Pima, Pápago, Sobaipuri, and Yuma. Establishing his headquarters at Nuestra Señora de Dolores, he undertook an extensive exploration of the vast territory that comprised his mission. In addition to evangelizing the Pima, he promoted cattle raising and agriculture—he was responsible for the introduction of wheat into the area. Under his guidance the Pima were remarkably successful as ranchers and exported livestock to neighboring areas. He also engaged in geographic exploration and cartography (he was an accomplished mapmaker). His explorations convinced him that Baja California was a peninsula, not an island, as the Spaniards had believed since it was first discovered. In 1689 he was named superior of the missions and brought in more missionaries to evangelize those areas that were only partly evangelized.

In 1691 he was joined by another Italian Jesuit, Juan María Salvatierra, who became almost as famous a missionary as Kino himself. His presence helped Kino through some difficult times. In 1695 the Pima revolted, in part as a reaction to harsh Spanish reprisals for the murder of a missionary. Kino was able to restore peace and then rode twelve hundred miles to Mexico City to lobby against the abandonment of the mission. Within the Jesuit order there was criticism of Kino because of his lifestyle, which was rather nomadic, and the accusation of hasty baptisms without sufficient catechesis. Some of his fellow Jesuits regarded him as idealistic and individualistic. One modern Franciscan critic referred to him as "the rancher who rarely

celebrated Mass" (Antonine Tibesar, *The Americas* 33 [3] [January 1967] 318).

Kino died at the mission of Magdalena in 1711. By that time that missions were beginning to decline, in part because of the financial problems of the Spanish crown caused by European wars. There were conflicts with civil authorities and with fellow Jesuits. Kino's headquarters at Dolores had no missionaries after 1738. The Jesuits continued to evangelize the northern areas but without the effort and results of an earlier period. After the expulsion of the Jesuits from all Spanish dominions in 1767, the Franciscans took over the missions of Baja and Alta California.

Texas. As has been mentioned above, in the Spanish outlook missions were an essential accompaniment to conquest and occupation. As a result the missionary enterprise tended to follow Spanish strategic interests. In two major missionary areas, Texas and California, the friars accompanied or followed the soldiers who went north to meet real or fancied threats to Spain's borderland empire. In Texas Native American settlements were rather sparse and distant from one another. In the eastern part of Texas a large number of tribes were gathered together in the Caddo confederacy. These peoples were successful agriculturalists and consequently sedentary. Their territory, however, lay between the conflicting claims of France and Spain.

The Spanish first went to Texas to counter the intrusion of the French under the leadership of Robert Cavelier, Sieur de la Salle. In 1689 a Spanish expedition entered Texas to locate the French but found that the French settlement had been destroyed by the natives. The expedition included a Franciscan friar, Damian Massanet, who left an account of it. He attempted to work among the Hasinai people (whose word for greeting gave us the name Texas) but was prevented by their hostility. Armed with a commission to establish four mission stations among the Kadohadachos, Hasinai, and one tribe outside the confederation, Domingo de Terán de los Ríos accompanied a second expedition to northeast Texas in 1690 and established two mission stations on the Neches River. Because there was no further threat from the French and the Caddoes proved resistant to conversion, the Spanish abandoned that area of Texas.

When the French renewed their penetration in the early eighteenth century, the Spanish reacted quickly and made plans to occupy east Texas. In 1716 they sent an expedition that included eight Franciscan priests and three lay brothers from the missionary college of Querétaro. They established a presidio along the Neches and then four mission stations. In 1718 another was established at San Antonio. Evangelization proved difficult because the Indians were nomadic, and the Spaniards were not strong enough to enforce *Congregación.*

These missionaries were soon joined by one of the most famous of the Franciscans of that period, Fray Antonio Margil de Jesus (1657–1726). A peninsular Spaniard of great asceticism and holiness, he joined the Franciscans in Spain in 1673 and was ordained to the priesthood in 1682. In the following year he came to New Spain and in 1684 was placed in charge of the missionary college of Santa Cruz in Querétaro. Subsequently he founded two other missionary colleges, Cristo Crucificado in Guatemala City (1701) and Our Lady of Guadalupe in Zacatecas (1708). He also did missionary work in New Spain and Central America before going to Texas. On the whole the missions in Texas were ineffectual, in part because of the resistance of the natives. By 1794 the missions had been secularized and their work effectively ended.

Alta California. There were a bewildering variety of native ethnic and language groups in Alta California. Until recent times it was common to view them as at a very low cultural level, little more than primitive hunter gatherers, "digger" Indians, and even as apathetic and brutish. More recent and sympathetic research is revising that view. The Chumash, in particular, are now seen as having had a vital culture, advanced technical skills, and a lifestyle in harmony with their environment. They dwelt in villages along the southern California coastline and made their living from the sea. They were skilled artisans, especially in the construction of boats.

Alta California was the scene of the final great Spanish missionary effort. The California missions were the last outpost of the Spanish empire in what is now the United States, and again it was a perceived foreign threat that drew the Spanish there. Though Juan Rodríguez Cabrillo had explored the coast in 1542 and Sebastián Vizcaíno in 1602, the Spanish made no effort to colonize or evangelize the area until the latter half of the eighteenth century. It was fear of Russian expansion in the northern part of Alta California that brought the Spanish there. Lured to the New World by the fur trade, the Russians first occupied Alaska and then began to work their way down the coast. In 1769 the *visitador general* of New Spain, José de Gálvez, ordered the occupation of California in order to block Russian expansion. The command of the expedition was given to Gaspar de Portolá, while the missionary enterprise was entrusted to the Franciscans of the apostolic college of San Fernando in Mexico City, who had replaced the Jesuits in Baja California after the expulsion of the latter. Fray Junípero Serra was named president of the missions. The first foundation was San Diego (1769). Within a year another expedition laid claim to Monterey Bay, and in 1776 a land expedition led by Juan Bautista de Anza discovered San Francisco Bay. Many of the Spanish foundations were precarious because of illness and the difficulty of bringing in supplies. Eventually

the Spanish were able to negotiate the withdrawal of Russia from California, but further north they ran into a determined wall of British resistance.

Serra's name is inextricably linked with the California missions. He was born at Petra, Majorca, Spain, in 1713. Baptized José Miguel, he adopted the name Junípero when he joined the Franciscans in 1730. He was ordained to the priesthood in 1738 and later received a doctorate in theology from the Lullian University in Palma de Majorca. After some years of teaching philosophy in Palma, he went to New Spain where he entered the missionary college of San Fernando in Mexico City. For eight years (1750–58) he worked as a missionary in the Sierra Gorda, where he learned the Otomí language. After his return to Mexico City he spent nine years in administrative posts at San Fernando and in missionary work in the central valley. After the expulsion of the Jesuits he was appointed president of the missions for Baja California. When the Spanish began the occupation of Alta California in 1769, he accompanied Portolá and founded his first mission at San Diego in that same year. In 1770 he made his permanent headquarters at San Carlos Mission in what is now Carmel, California. He founded nine of the twenty-one missions: San Diego (1769), San Carlos Borromeo (1770), San Antonio de Padua (1771), San Gabriel Arcángel (1771), San Luis Obispo de Tortosa (1772), San Francisco (1776), San Juan Capistrano (1776), Santa Clara (1777), and San Buenaventura (1782). Contrary to a romantic legend, these missions were not founded one day's journey apart, but where the native inhabitants were.

Serra's missions were the final and finished examples of the mission system first devised by the friars in sixteenth-century New Spain. The mission system required all natives to live in the missions. Those who refused were forcibly congregated while those who ran away, a not infrequent occurrence, were brought back and punished. The regimen was paternalistic, and in fact in 1773 Viceroy Antonio María de Bucareli decreed that the Franciscans held the place of parents over the natives. There was also a military presence, centered in the presidios of San Diego, Monterey, San Francisco, and Santa Barbara. This often hindered the missionary endeavor more than it helped. Serra and his successors had difficulty in controlling bored soldiers and intrusive bureaucrats, and as a result conflicts were frequent. There were disputes over jurisdiction, the right of asylum, and clerical appointments. As president Serra visited all the missions by land and sea, but not, as legend has it, on foot. At his death on August 28, 1784, he was buried with full military and naval honors at Mission San Carlos. He was beatified by Pope John Paul II in 1988, a controversial move that will be discussed in the conclusions.

Although Serra is the more famous as a mission founder, his successor Firmín Francisco de Lasuén may be equally important. He was born in Vitoria, Spain, in 1736 and joined the Franciscan Order in 1751. As a volunteer for the New World missions, he arrived in New Spain in 1759 and entered the apostolic college of San Fernando. After serving five years in the missions in the Sierra Gorda, he went to Baja California in 1767 and stayed there until 1773. In that same year he went to San Diego and then was assigned to Mission San Gabriel for two years. Serra sent him to found Mission San Juan Capistrano, but he was hindered by a native revolt in San Diego. When peace was restored, he was placed in charge of Mission San Diego until 1785, when after Serra's death he was named president of the missions of Alta California. He personally founded nine missions, bringing the total to eighteen. During his presidency the missions of California reached a high point in numbers and effectiveness. He died at Carmel, California, in 1803 and is buried in the mission chapel. Three more missions were founded after his death.

In 1780 Alta California became part of the newly erected diocese of Sonora, though no bishop actually visited the territory until 1840. The administrative structure of the missions was reorganized in 1812. The office of commissary prefect was established to handle temporal and business matters. In 1833 the administration of the northern missions was given to the missionary college of Our Lady of Guadalupe of Zacatecas. After Mexico gained its independence of Spain in 1821, California became part of the new republic. For a number of reasons, principally uncertain financial support after the republic assumed control of the pious fund, the missions went into decline. When the Mexican congress secularized the missions in 1833, temporal control was placed in the hands of lay commissioners, and the natives were free to leave. This effectively spelled their end.

There was a short-lived attempt to establish missions along the Colorado River at Yuma, but the hostility of the natives caused it to fail. The Franciscan missions of California are the best-known example of Spanish evangelization in North America, and their history has been greatly romanticized. In part this was the result of California boosterism at the beginning of this century. Yet these missions never equaled in number or importance those of Florida or the Jesuit missions of the Pimería Alta.

Overview. The Spanish missionary enterprise in the New World was of unprecedented magnitude and scope. At its height it extended from the tip of Argentina to northern California. Such an undertaking demanded enormous resources in personnel and finances. In approaching this incredible task, the missionaries had little tradition or experience to fall back on. The first missionary endeavors were improvisations, creative responses to peoples, languages, and cultures that were entirely new to the missionaries. The fact that they were able to develop programs,

pursue language and ethnographical studies, and achieve what success they did is a tribute to their zeal, intelligence, and creativity. These programs were not universally successful. The results of the missionary endeavor varied widely from one geographical area to another and from one people to another.

This task was made all the more challenging by the bewildering variety of languages and peoples the missionaries encountered. In the present-day United States alone, the different languages, dialects, and cultures were a major obstacle. In Florida and California languages varied dramatically in small areas. Some natives were nomadic or seminomadic, some were sedentary and agricultural, others were hunters and gatherers. The missionaries had to adapt themselves to these differences, and they were not always successful in doing so.

The principal agents of the Spanish missionary effort were the Franciscans and the Jesuits. After the expulsion of the latter from the Spanish dominions, the task fell primarily to the Franciscans. The system that they brought to North America required a military presence for the protection of the missionaries. Experience had shown that without it the friars faced grave dangers, including death. While the military presence safeguarded the missionaries, it was also in conflict with their work. It brought the natives into contact with the more brutal and venal aspects of Spanish society, especially in those areas where the natives were congregated into large, self-sustaining mission stations. This same concentration also exposed the indigenous peoples to European diseases and the impact of culture shock.

This leads to the important, and controversial, question of the impact of the missions on the natives. The question has been brought to the fore in recent times by the reaction to the beatification of Junípero Serra. The mission system is now criticized for uprooting the native cultures and exposing the natives to European diseases. In the case of the California missions, it has been shown that these contributed to the demographic decline of the indigenous peoples, not only through disease, but through unsanitary and unhealthy conditions, and an increase in miscarriages and abortions. Likewise, the system has been criticized for exploiting native labor and for the use of harsh punishments. One basis for these criticisms is found in the number of indigenous inhabitants who fled the missions.

Although the level of these criticisms has been intensified by the political correctness of the times, it is beyond doubt that to a great extent they are justified. Europeans, especially Spanish Christians, were absolutely convinced of the innate superiority of their culture and religion. The missionaries sincerely believed that the natives were under the control of the devil and that without Christianity they were condemned to eternal damnation. The ultimate purpose of the missions was to integrate the natives into Spanish civilization, while, contradictorily, keeping them isolated from that civilization. The result was that the natives, the "new plants," were kept in a state of tutelage.

Europeans of that age were also oblivious to the effects of culture shock. The jolting transfer from a familiar life and religion to something alien was often devastating to the natives. It was strange that after two centuries of experience the missionaries did not realize this. Again, however, the ethnocentrism of so many of them probably blinded them to this fact.

An additional factor was a change in the missionaries themselves and in Spanish colonial policies. In sixteenth-century New Spain the Franciscans had dedicated themselves in a special way to the study of native languages and cultures. In the following century the Jesuits took the lead in these studies. One result was that the missionaries often came to have a deep sympathy and understanding for their charges. Similarly, royal policies left the native languages intact and often imposed a minimum of change on local social and political structures. The picture was different from the late seventeenth century to the wars of independence. The crown became hostile to the missionaries' use of native languages because of their perceived sympathy with the natives. Under the Bourbon Dynasty in the eighteenth century there was an effort, ultimately unsuccessful, to compel the natives to learn Spanish and use it as the language of religion, law, and everyday life. The Franciscans in New Mexico and California either did not know or made little effort to learn the native languages, in part because they were too numerous.

Whatever the shortcomings, the missionaries did stand between the natives and the encroachment of predatory and gold-hungry Europeans. The goal of the mission was to preserve the natives' lives, not destroy them, even if it forced them into a European mold. This, unhappily, did not rule out the use and even exploitation of native labor. The missions never succeeded in turning the natives into Spaniards but rather tended to keep them in a state of tutelage. Still, the missionaries often had the best interests of the natives at heart, even if this was sometimes misguided and paternalistic. The friars endured their own culture shock in the form of loneliness, opposition, strange languages, strange food, and new customs. As vanguards of Spanish conquest and settlement, the missions also had uneven success. It is noteworthy that the missions in New Mexico in 1680 and those in Florida into the following century fell apart with astonishing speed once the Spanish military presence was absent or neutralized.

It should be emphasized that, in spite of their shortcomings, the missions provided the natives with a level of protection, at least temporarily, against the looming threat of aggressive and racist societies. The fate of the natives of California was far more dire after the secularization and destruction of the mission system than before.

In the nineteenth century the native populations suffered far more at the hands of the Mexican republic than they had under the Spanish or the friars. Just as in Mexico it was during the dictatorship of Porfirio Díaz (1876–80; 1884–1911) that the greatest attacks were made on the native lands and polity, so too in the American Southwest it was the coming of the American that spelled the total or partial destruction of these peoples.

Bolton, Herbert Eugene. *Rim of Christendom: A Biography of Eusebio Francisco Kino, Pacific Coast Pioneer.* New York: Macmillan, 1936.

Gannon, Michael. *The Cross in the Sand: The Early Catholic Church in Florida, 1513–1870.* Gainesville: University of Florida Press, 1965.

Geiger, Maynard. *Life and Times of Fray Junípero Serra, O.F.M.* 2 vols. Washington, D.C.: Academy of American Franciscan History, 1959.

Gutiérrez, Ramón A. *When Jesus Came, the Corn Mothers Went Away.* Stanford, Calif.: Stanford University Press, 1991.

Weber, David J. *The Spanish Frontier in North America.* New Haven, Conn., and London: Yale University Press, 1992.

STAFFORD POOLE, C.M.

MISSISSIPPI, CATHOLIC CHURCH IN

Mississippi is located in the heart of the South. The Mississippi River and the Gulf of Mexico, as well as Alabama, Arkansas, Louisiana, and Tennessee, form its borders. The diverse soil and topography of the state's 47,716 square miles contributed greatly to its economic diversity and political sectionalism. State historian John Ray Skates, looking beyond Southern myths, Northern stereotypes, and government statistics (on widespread illiteracy and rural poverty), noted "the eccentricities of Mississippi history . . . white and black, wealth and poverty, paranoia and pride, egalitarianism and racism, individualism and forced white unity, radicalism and reaction, honor and chicanery, political sterility and cultural fertility" (Skates, 17). Mississippi became "the last stronghold of the greatest American subculture, the South" (Skates, xi).

Native American and Colonial Periods

Mississippi was inhabited by an estimated 30,000 Native Americans when the first European explorers arrived. The Choctaws were the largest tribe, followed by the Natchez and Chickasaws. In 1699 missionaries from the Foreign Mission Seminary in Quebec began working among the natives near the future Natchez settlement with little long-lasting fruit. European immigration, a series of broken treaties, and government policies of displacement to Indian Territory left Mississippi with only 2,300 Native Americans by 1900. Through the initiative of Bishop Francis Janssens (1881–88), a small, strong Catholic Choctaw community, now centered in the Philadelphia area, developed in the late nineteenth century and remains a vital part of Mississippi Catholicism. By 1990 the number of Mississippians of Native American ancestry had grown to about 8,500.

Mississippi initially formed part of the France's Louisiana colony. During La Salle's 1682 expedition, Fr. Zenobious Membre celebrated the first recorded Mass in the state near present-day Fort Adams. The first European settlement was established near Ocean Springs in 1699; Old Biloxi, as it was called, was abandoned soon after New Orleans was founded in 1718. Throughout the French, Spanish, English, and early American periods, clusters of Gulf Coast Catholic families such as the Ladners and Nicaises maintained their Catholic identity and faith with only rare priestly visits from New Orleans or Mobile. Mississippi's oldest Catholic families reside along the Gulf Coast.

Fort Rosalie, a more permanent European settlement, was established at Natchez in 1716. The Cross and Crown worked poorly together at this outpost, with the lone priest sometimes living in abominable conditions at the whim of "godless" local commandants. The Natchez settlement was briefly obliterated after the 1729 massacre, which also resulted in the virtual extinction of the attacking Natchez tribe. A small military settlement was reestablished with the sacraments administered at neighboring Pointe Coupée or New Orleans or by passing clergy.

In 1788 Spain established the parish of San Salvador del Mundo at Natchez, a parish at nearby Coles Creek, and a mission chapel at the military post of Nogales (Vicksburg). The missions were staffed by Spanish-trained Irish clergy. Two churches were built, a cemetery established, a vigorous sacramental life was fostered (highlighted by the state's first administration of confirmation in May 1796 by Bishop Luis Peñalver y Cárdenas), and a nucleus of Catholic families formed. When the Natchez area was transferred to the newly emerging United States in 1798, the Spanish clergy withdrew.

Territorial and Antebellum Periods

After the Spanish withdrawal, the Mississippi area became a hierarchical no-man's land for Catholics. For four decades, residents wrote in vain to the bishops of Baltimore, St. Louis, and New Orleans for clergy. At Natchez, a core of devoted Catholic families, soon supplemented by European and transplanted colonial immigrants, incorporated (using a Protestant model), formed an effective board of trustees, supervised the church's property and buildings, and maintained a sense of community for forty years with only occasional resident pastors. A Catholic community also developed at Vicksburg.

The Mississippi Territory, including the future Alabama, was organized in 1798. Congress enlarged the territory in

1804 and 1813, and then split off the eastern (Alabama) section. Mississippi was admitted to the Union on December 10, 1817, as the twentieth state. Baptist and Methodist congregations quickly formed (and remain) the state's two largest religious denominations.

Mississippi's economy and culture were molded during the 1830s when former Native American lands were opened to settlement. Cotton-based agriculture, mainly worked first by black slaves and later by sharecroppers, created a distinctive political, social, and economic society that endured until World War II. Manufacturing workers did not outnumber agricultural laborers until the mid-1960s. The most regressive consequence of the cotton economy was the "race question," which became "the central theme of Mississippi history" (Skates, 173).

The dependence on agriculture created a society that remained significantly more rural than mainstream America. Eighty-five percent of the state's residents were still classified as rural in 1940. Most Catholic communities in Mississippi were located in small, rural areas until the urban and suburban expansion of the post-World War II years. More recently, the rapidly growing number of rural-dwelling urban workers has significantly changed Mississippi's demographic profile and the patterns of Catholic parish development.

Postcolonial Mississippi was successively part of the Diocese of Baltimore, the proposed (1822) but not implemented vicariate of Alabama and Mississippi, the Diocese of Louisiana, and, in 1826, the Diocese of New Orleans. Although the Diocese of Natchez was established on July 28, 1837, Bishop John Chanche, the first ordinary, was not consecrated until March 14, 1841. When he arrived in Mississippi on May 19, he found two sizable Catholic communities at Natchez and Vicksburg, a large number of families and small communities along the Gulf Coast, and an unknown number of families and individuals scattered throughout the state. The state had no Catholic churches or institutions and only two priests.

Mississippi Catholicism grew both in numbers and organization under the antebellum leadership of Bishops John Chanche (1841–52), James Oliver Van de Velde, S.J. (1853–55), and William Henry Elder (1857–80). By 1861, the diocese "presented a picture of sound organization" (Pillar, 149): about ten thousand Catholics served by one bishop and eighteen diocesan priests; thirteen parishes with resident priests and twenty-eight mission stations; fifteen churches with several more under construction; five parochial schools, two day schools, three boarding schools, and two orphanages staffed by five religious communities and several lay teachers; numerous parish devotional, altar, and charitable societies; and regular parish missions and clerical conferences. An imposing cathedral, viewed by Bishop Chanche as "the needed stimulus to the whole mission" (Nolan, 120), was built (though not consecrated until 1886).

Civil War, Reconstruction, and the Turn of the Century

Mississippi was a major battleground during the Civil War. Natchez, Vicksburg, Jackson, Meridian, Okalona, and Corinth were among the Catholic communities that witnessed battle and/or physical destruction. The Catholic church at Jackson was destroyed three times by federal troops. Bishop William Henry Elder was briefly sent into exile in July 1864 for his refusal to allow the local federal military commander to dictate specific prayers for Northern civil authorities at Mass.

The war left the state devastated politically, economically, and socially; it brought ruin to numerous families whose fathers were killed or disabled; it depleted the already meager resources of Mississippi Catholicism. The greatest postwar challenge was the peaceful, productive incorporation of newly freed slaves into Mississippi life. This challenge was met, after a brief reconstruction period, by a political-economic-social structure of sharecropping, segregation, and disenfranchisement that closely mirrored antebellum slave society.

Bishop Elder worked among the camps for freed slaves outside Natchez during the final years of the war and struggled to find the resources to address the challenge of evangelizing the freed slaves. By 1884 Mississippi numbered 1,500 African American Catholics. Bishop Janssens, lamenting the ineffectiveness of existing evangelization programs, proposed a fresh approach modeled on the missions in pagan countries—small chapel-schools overseen by priests but staffed by trained black catechists. In 1890, Holy Family parish, the state's first parish for African Americans, was established at Natchez. Between 1906 and 1914, seven additional parishes were founded at Vicksburg, Pascagoula, Jackson, Meridian, Pass Christian, Greenville, and Biloxi; all were staffed by Josephites or Divine Word Fathers. The latter established a seminary for African American students at Greenville in 1920; in 1923, the seminary was moved to Bay St. Louis, "a more Catholic neighborhood" (Gerow, 352).

Despite the upheavals of reconstruction and its aftermath, Mississippi Catholicism took on a new vigor in the late nineteenth and early twentieth centuries under the leadership of Bishops Francis Janssens, Thomas Heslin (1889–1911), and John Gunn, S.M. (1911–24). More than 250 Catholic communities, many short-lived, existed in the state between 1865 and 1910. The Society for the Propogation of the Faith and later the Catholic Church Extension Society provided essential financial resources for this growth.

Between World Wars

By 1917 more than 28,000 Catholics were scattered across the state in 41 parishes, 69 missions, and 54 stations; 11 percent were African Americans. Forty-two schools and 2 orphanages had a combined enrollment of 4,736; 29 percent of the students were African Americans; 0.8 percent, Choctaws. Upon his arrival in 1911, Bishop Gunn had observed, "I have found that with the Archdiocese of Philadelphia as the only exception, Natchez had provided more educational facilities for its Catholic children than any diocese in the country" (Nolan, 182).

Mississippi Catholics participated patriotically in World War I as they did in all previous and subsequent wars. Catholics constituted 1,355 (2.4 percent) of the state's military inductees or enlistees. The blunt, colorful Bishop John Gunn was one of the state's most vocal supporters, urging all to sacrifice "to win the war, which I declared to be emphatically a just war" (Nolan, 190).

Bishop Gunn set as one of his primary goals to establish chapels throughout the state. With generous aid from the Catholic Church Extension Society, more than thirty new churches and chapels were built between 1912 and 1924 alone. Despite this growth, at Bishop Gunn's funeral in 1924, Bishop John Morris of Little Rock observed that Natchez, like other Southern dioceses, was still a pioneer missionary territory "where the hardships of the missionaries are just as real today as they were seventy-five years ago" (Nolan, 209).

When newly consecrated Bishop Richard O. Gerow (1924–66) arrived, Catholicism was Mississippi's third largest religious denomination, after the Baptists and Methodists. The state had 31,387 Catholics served by 60 priests. Only 42 of the state's 149 churches and chapels had a resident pastor; 5,829 children were being educated in 41 Catholic schools. The state had no Catholic hospitals.

Catholic parishes and institutions suffered the harsh effects of the depression. At the end of 1932 Bishop Gerow agreed with his many knowledgeable episcopal colleagues that "a parish or institution today that can pay interest alone on its debt is considered very fortunate." During the 1930s, many pastors told Bishop Gerow they could no longer afford to house and feed assistant priests and asked to serve their parishes alone (Nolan, 210).

Recent Era

By 1958 Mississippi's Catholic population had almost doubled to 60,753. One hundred seventy-one priests served the state's 82 parishes, 65 missions, and 21 mission stations. The 74 Catholic elementary and high schools were educating 13,476 children; another 4,883 public school children were attending catechism programs. Mississippi had three Catholic hospitals in Jackson, Vicksburg, and Meridian.

Although the largest concentration of Mississippi Catholics continued to live along the Gulf Coast, the most dramatic Catholic growth in the post-World War II years took place in the state capital, Jackson. Between 1945 and 1958, five new parishes were opened in the capital; each had its own school. In 1954 a new St. Dominic's Hospital building was completed. The diocesan administration was moved from Natchez to Jackson in 1948. On December 18, 1956, the name of the diocese was changed to Natchez-Jackson; on June 6, 1977, the name was changed to Jackson. In 1980, Mississippi became part of the newly established province of Mobile.

Bishop Gerow consistently fostered increased lay activity in Church life. He participated in the Knights of Columbus organization, established the Mississippi branch of the National Council of Catholic Women in 1931, encouraged the lay retreat movement, asked adults to become involved in education and youth organizations such as the Catholic Youth Organization and scouting, and officially recognized outstanding lay leaders such as Margaret Pitchford of Natchez with Church honors.

Bishop Gerow, like other southern bishops, worked quietly and within the existing legal and social structure to expand Catholic parishes, schools, programs, and opportunities among the region's African American population. The Church concentrated on establishing parishes and strong schools with sisters in urban areas. The issue of desegregating Catholic schools surfaced in the wake of the 1954 Supreme Court decision. The violence with which some Mississippians opposed integration, particularly the 1963 murder of Medgar Evers, prodded the mild-tempered Bishop Gerow to order the initial desegregation of all Catholic schools in 1964; the following year, all grades were integrated.

Bishop Joseph B. Brunini (1966–84) became the first native son to guide the diocese. He established an open, participative style of leadership, fostered lay participation and ministry, expanded the Church's social ministry, led the state's efforts to break down racial barriers, and worked to establish closer bonds with other denominations. During his tenure, Catholic services to the needy, poor, and elderly rapidly expanded.

On March 1, 1977, the Diocese of Biloxi, comprising the seventeen southern counties, was established with Bishop Joseph L. Howze as the first ordinary. Bishop Howze was the country's first twentieth-century African American ordinary.

Bishop William B. Houck of Jackson (1984–present) established spiritual renewal as one of his first priorities. More than eight thousand Catholics soon participated in the RENEW program, which led to an ongoing program of spiritual renewal and the adoption of a diocesan pastoral plan.

In 1995 Mississippi Catholics numbered only 4 percent of the state's population. There were 108,000 Catholics forming 118 parishes (107 with residents priests) and 38 missions; 59 percent of the Catholics resided in the smaller Gulf Coast Biloxi diocese. Of the 21,000 children receiving Catholic instruction, 48 percent attended Catholic schools.

According to retired Bishop Brunini, the main challenge facing Mississippi Catholicism as the third millennium approaches is the same as it was when Bishop John Chanche first arrived in 1841—to become a more dynamic evangelizing presence in a multicultural, multidenominational society, particularly among the state's African Americans.

Archives, Dioceses of Biloxi and Jackson.

Gerow, Richard O. *Catholicity in Mississippi.* Natchez, Miss.: Diocese of Natchez, 1939.

Nolan, Charles E. *St. Mary's of Natchez: The History of a Southern Catholic Congregation, 1716–1988.* Natchez, Miss.: St. Mary's Parish, 1992.

Pillar, James J. *The Catholic Church in Mississippi, 1837–1865.* New Orleans: Hauser Press, 1964.

Pillar-Nolan research notes for "The Catholic Church in Mississippi, 1865–1911" (in preparation).

Skates, John Ray. *Mississippi: A Bicentennial History.* New York: Norton, 1979.

CHARLES E. NOLAN

MISSOURI, CATHOLIC CHURCH IN

Catholicism first touched what was to become the state of Missouri on June 17, 1673, when the Jesuit missionary and explorer Fr. Jacques Marquette and his companion, Louis Jolliet, entered the Mississippi River from the mouth of the Illinois River. Through Marquette's efforts a program of evangelization was inaugurated among the various Native American groups in the area and at the mission of the Immaculate Conception on Kaskaskia Island. The region was then under the ecclesiastical authority of the bishop of Quebec. For the next hundred years the number of French settlements in the Mississippi valley increased, as did the population. These settlements were all on the east bank of the river; not until around 1735 was the first settlement made on the west bank, at Ste. Genevieve. A parish was established there and the first church was built in 1659 by Jesuit missionaries.

The Treaty of Paris is 1763 drastically changed the political and thus the religious climate on both sides of the Mississippi. The great river was to be the boundary between the English on the east and the Spanish on the west. France was eliminated as a colonial power in North America. Religious jurisdiction was transferred from the bishop of Quebec to the bishop of Havana. In February 1764, the trading post of St. Louis was established just south of the mouth of the Missouri River on the west bank of the Mississippi. The post received an immediate influx of French settlers from the settlements on the east bank of the river. These French Catholics felt it was better to live under Catholic Spanish rule than under that of Protestant England.

Within a few years St. Louis boasted a population of over one thousand permanent residents.

The founder of the trading post laid out a village with three streets, and the center block in the third street was given to the Church. This block is the only one of the original designated by Pierre Laclede that has never changed hands. The Basilica of Saint Louis, King, still stands on this ground.

As long as the area west of the Mississippi remained under either French or Spanish sovereignty, the Catholic Church was the only recognized religion. Settlers from the east were required to affirm that they were Catholics. This privileged status of the Catholic Church came to an end with the sale of Louisiana to the United States. The formal transfer of Upper Louisiana to the United States took place in St. Louis in 1804. At that time Missouri was under the ecclesiastical jurisdiction of the bishop of Louisiana and Florida, who resided in New Orleans. The diocese was vacant in 1804, but the first bishop, Luis Peñalver y Cárdenas, had sent a vicar general to Upper Louisiana in the person of a Spanish-educated Irish priest, James Maxwell, who settled in Ste. Genevieve and attempted to administer the Church in the vast area from that location.

In 1812 the distinguished Sulpician educator and former president of Georgetown College, Louis William DuBourg, was appointed apostolic administrator of the Diocese of Louisiana. He was later appointed bishop and consecrated in Rome on September 24, 1815. His first goal was to recruit priests and religious for his missionary diocese. He was successful in bringing to the diocese a group of Vincentian priests and seminarians led by Fr. Felix DeAndreis and Fr. Joseph Rosati. Their first task was the establishment of the seminary of St. Mary's of the Barrens in what is now Perryville, Missouri, some eighty miles south of St. Louis. Bishop DuBourg also received a promise from Mother Madeleine Sophie Barat that she would send him a contingent of her Religious of the Sacred Heart. In 1818 four of them arrived in St. Louis under the guidance of Mother Rose Philippine Duchesne. They immediately moved west to the village of St. Charles where they founded an academy for young women.

Diocese of St. Louis

The Diocese of St. Louis was formally established by Pope Leo XII on July 14, 1826, when he divided the Diocese of Louisiana into the Diocese of New Orleans and the Diocese of St. Louis. The Diocese of New Orleans retained jurisdiction over the southern portion of the former Diocese of Louisiana, while the new Diocese of St. Louis comprised the vast area between Illinois and the Rocky Mountains, from which no fewer than sixteen new dioceses were to be created in the later nineteenth century. The exact limits (especially the western boundaries) of the new diocese were never defined with much exactitude, but basically the diocese extended from the Indiana border on the east to the Rocky Mountains on the west, and from the Arkansas River in the south to the Canadian border in the north.

Joseph Rosati was named the first bishop of St. Louis. He continued to recruit priests and religious from Europe and from elsewhere in the United States. The Sisters of Charity came to St. Louis to establish the first Catholic hospital in the United States. Jesuits of the Maryland province also came to St. Louis to establish the school that eventually became St. Louis University. In addition they opened a novitiate in Florissant, Missouri. Under the direction of Bishop Rosati, they sent Fr. Peter John De Smet and his companions into the Upper Missouri to establish missions among the Native Americans.

On January 30, 1847, St. Louis was raised to the status of an archdiocese, and Bishop Peter Richard Kenrick became the first archbishop. Kenrick had been made coadjutor bishop of St. Louis in 1841 and had succeeded Rosati as bishop of 1843. He ruled the Church in St. Louis as administrator, bishop, and archbishop for fifty-four years, until 1893 when the pastors petitioned Rome for the appointment of a coadjutor. The Holy See named John J. Kain, former bishop of Wheeling, administrator of St. Louis on December 14, 1893, and appointed him archbishop of St. Louis on May 21, 1895. Kenrick was then made titular archbishop of Marcianopolis and died the following year.

When St. Louis was made a metropolitan see in 1847, the suffragan sees were Dubuque, Nashville, Chicago, Milwaukee, and St. Paul. With the growth of the Church in the Midwest, new dioceses continued to be established from the original diocese of St. Louis. In 1996 there were forty-five archdioceses and dioceses that had once been part of the Diocese of St. Louis. In 1847 there were three main centers of Catholicism in Missouri. The city of St. Louis itself was strongly Catholic. South of the city along the Mississippi there were Catholic settlements, principally around Ste. Genevieve. In the Missouri River valley west of the city there were also Catholic settlements clustered around the German-American town of Herman.

Racial tensions have played a recurring role in Missouri history from the very beginning. In 1720 the French settlers made no objection when François de Renault's company brought a large contingent of black slaves from Saint Domingue to exploit the lead mines in the territory. Prior to that many Native Americans had been enslaved in order to provide cheap labor. The introduction of black slaves became a divisive issue for Catholics for several generations. When Missouri entered the Union in 1820, it entered as a slave state under the Missouri Compromise of that year. During the Civil War Missouri Catholics were to be found in both the Confederate and Union armies.

The first black priest in the United States who was recognized as such, Augustus Tolton, was an ex-slave from Hannibal, Missouri, who was ordained in Rome in 1886 for the Diocese of Alton, Illinois.

New Dioceses

In 1868 a diocese was established in St. Joseph, Missouri, to care for Catholics in the western part of the state. In 1880 a second diocese was created in western Missouri with its see in Kansas City. In 1956 two additional dioceses were created in the state: Jefferson City and Springfield-Cape Girardeau. At that same time the Diocese of St. Joseph was merged with that of Kansas City as part of a general realignment of diocesan boundaries in the state. As a result of these changes, St. Louis emerged as the smallest of the four Missouri dioceses in area, but the one with the largest Catholic population.

The history of the Catholic Church in Missouri is basically the history of the Archdiocese of St. Louis, which included most of the state's Catholics until 1956. The temper of Catholicism in St. Louis and the surrounding suburbs differs greatly from the temper of Catholicism in the rest of the state. The original French heritage was followed by the influence of Irish and German immigrants, outstanding clergy and bishops, numerous religious communities, and many lay Catholic organizations, all of which have combined to give a distinct flavor to St. Louis, and thus, to Missouri Catholicism.

In 1995 the Catholic population of the state was 841,226 out of a total population of 5,221,822; 558,880 Catholics lived in the Archdiocese of St. Louis. The percentage of Catholics in the general population ranged from a high of 27 percent in the Archdiocese of St. Louis to a low of 5 percent in the Diocese of Springfield-Cape Girardeau. In the state as a whole there were 836 diocesan priests, 591 religious order priests, 308 permanent deacons, 310 brothers, 2,951 sisters, 472 parishes, 4 colleges and universities, and 292 elementary and high schools.

Faherty, William. *Dream by the River: Two Centuries of St. Louis Catholicism.* St. Louis: Piraeus, 1973.

Hogan, John J. *On the Mission in Missouri, 1857–1868.* 1892; repr. Westminster, Md.: Christian Classics, 1972.

Rothensteiner, John. *History of the Archdiocese of St. Louis.* 2 vols. St. Louis: Blackwell Wielandy Co., 1928.

MARTIN G. TOWEY

MITTY, JOHN JOSEPH (1884–1961)

Fourth archbishop of San Francisco. John Joseph Mitty was born on January 20, 1884, in Greenwich Village, New York City, to Mary Murphy and John Mitty, one of four sons. Mitty's mother died in 1894, as did his father in 1898, leaving Mitty an orphan at the age of fourteen. He was schooled at St. Joseph's Grammar School, De La Salle High School, and Manhattan College, all in New York City, graduating from the latter in 1901. The same year he entered St. Joseph's Seminary in Dunwoodie, New York, to study for the priesthood for the Archdiocese of New York. He was ordained a priest on December 22, 1906, by Archbishop John Farley at Dunwoodie. He pursued graduate studies at The Catholic University of America, where he received a bachelor of sacred theology degree in 1907. The following year he studied in Rome, where he received a doctorate in sacred theology from the Lateran Seminary (1908). He did additional study in psychology at the University of Munich during the summer of 1908.

John J. Mitty

Early Years

In 1909 Mitty returned to New York, where he served a brief time as assistant pastor at St. Veronica's Church before being appointed to teach dogmatic theology at his alma mater, St. Joseph's Seminary. His eight-year tenure as professor ended in 1917 with the U.S. entry into World War I. Mitty left the seminary faculty to serve as a military chaplain to the 49th and 101st regiments of the U.S. Army, at Camp Merrit, New Jersey, and in France, where he participated in the famed Meuse-Argonne offensive. Following the war, in 1919, he was appointed pastor of Sacred Heart Church in Highland Falls, New York, where he served until 1922. In that year, he was appointed pastor of St. Luke's Church in the Bronx, New York. On June 21, 1926, Pope Pius XI named Mitty bishop of Salt Lake City, Utah. He was consecrated bishop at St. Patrick's Cathedral in New York by Cardinal Patrick Hayes, and was installed in Salt Lake on October 7. For six years he labored in the Mormon heartland, struggling to place the diocese on a firm financial basis, which he did, and stepping up evangelization efforts by revitalizing the diocesan newspaper, *The Intermountain Catholic,* and by sponsoring radio talks. On January 29, 1932, Mitty was appointed coadjutor archbishop of San Francisco with the right of succession. He succeeded Archbishop Edward Hanna upon Hanna's resignation on March 2, 1935, and was invested with the pallium on September 4, 1935. He served as archbishop until his death in 1961.

Archbishop of San Francisco

Mitty's episcopate began while San Francisco (jolted by a general strike the previous year) and the rest of the nation remained mired in the Great Depression. His episcopate spanned World War II, in which San Francisco served as a major debarkation point for American servicemen and was the site of the initial meeting of the United Nations, and culminated in the explosive population growth that began during the war and carried into the postwar era, making California the most populous state in the union by 1962. Mitty's thirteen-county archdiocese grew from 405,000 Catholics in 1935 to 1,125,000 in 1961. Despite these challenges, Mitty ushered in what many consider to be the golden age of Catholicism in the San Francisco Bay area. Mitty responded to the rapid growth by creating 85 new parishes (1935, 171 parishes; 1961, 256), sponsoring 563 major building projects, and overseeing the explosive growth of Catholic schools, religious education programs, and charitable agencies and institutions.

Though regarded as a stern, aloof man, Mitty was an able administrator and financial genius, qualities that placed him in stark contrast to his predecessor, Edward Hanna, who was widely regarded for his kind, loving demeanor, but who was a poor administrator. Mitty effectively organized and centralized the administration of the archdiocese, streamlining and energizing the Church's bureaucratic agencies. He revolutionized archdiocesan finances. Mitty was one of the national pioneers in the creation of a central archdiocesan banking system. Parishes that previously had established their own bank accounts were now required to deposit all surplus funds with the archdiocesan chancery. All parish loans had to be obtained through the archdiocesan bank. The new system gave the archbishop a better understanding and some control over the entire financial situation of the archdiocese. The central banking system is now standard in most dioceses throughout the United States.

Mitty's greatest achievement, and the one in which he took the most pride, was the creation of a highly motivated and well-trained diocesan clergy, which Mitty asserted was the equal of any religious order of priests. During Mitty's episcopate, clerical morale reached an all-time high. Priests chosen to head archdiocesan agencies were first sent to pursue postgraduate studies at The Catholic University of America in Washington, D.C., and elsewhere to assure that his leaders were well-trained in their fields. The various agencies of the archdiocese, especially the Catholic Youth Organization and the various branches of Catholic Charities, were the beneficiaries of this policy. Though seemingly authoritarian, Mitty was an able delegator, providing ample support with a minimum of meddling to the leaders he had placed in charge. Mitty also encouraged specialized, innovative apostolates, most significantly the Spanish Mission Band—a group of priests freed from parochial ministry to minister to the bracero and migrant workers in the fields of California. From this program emerged Cesar Chavez, Dolores Huerta, and the United Farmworkers (UFW) movement.

One final note of importance: Mitty's experience in Salt Lake City made him sensitive to ecumenical issues. He worked to make the experience of marriage between Catholics and non-Catholics ("mixed marriages") more dignified and less opprobrious to the non-Catholic party. At the national level, he succeeded in establishing the practice of having mixed marriages occur within the parish church instead of in the rectory.

Mitty succeeded in creating a positive, dynamic archdiocese in San Francisco. He was beset by a variety of illnesses his last few years, and spent much of his time at St. Patrick's Seminary in Menlo Park, California, where he died in 1961.

No biography has yet been written of Mitty. His personal papers are housed in the Archdiocesan Archives of the Archdiocese of San Francisco in Menlo Park, California. Several biographical articles include:

"Archbishop Mitty Dies." *San Francisco Examiner.* October 16, 1961.

"Archbishop Mitty Mourned." *San Francisco News Call Bulletin.* October 16, 1961.

Tappe, Walter. "Our Archbishop." *San Francisco Monitor.* September 4, 1953.

JEFFREY M. BURNS

MODERNISM IN AMERICA

Modernism was a short-lived phenomenon—one would err to call it a movement—probably involving no more than two dozen Roman Catholic priests in the United States. From 1895 to 1908, however, these priests were strategically located in North American seminaries and universities, where they attempted to disseminate the writings—and critical methods—of European Modernists such as Alfred Loisy, the French Catholic priest and biblical exegete; George Tyrrell, the English Jesuit who was rethinking the categories of revelation, dogma, and sacrament; and Baron Friedrich von Hügel, the Anglo-Austrian layman and expert on mysticism who was the correspondent, friend, and confidante of the leading European Modernists, but who was never censured.

The American priests dabbling in Modernism included few original theological or philosophical thinkers, but they embodied the link between Americanism—a liberal Catholic outlook that entailed the acceptance of religious voluntarism and pluralism, Church-state separation, and religious liberty—and Modernism which, from a different vantage, also implied consequences for the way Catholics understood the nature and proper function of external religious authority. In short, the Modernists taught that God revealed divine truth through, and not apart from, history and the experience of ordinary people. "We know what the American Spirit is in the political and social order," the Paulist priest William L. Sullivan wrote. "Translate it into the religious order and you have modernism at its best and purest."

The Modernist episode in American Catholicism occurred at approximately the same time that American Protestants struggled with their own company of seminary and university professors who were promoting a brand of theological Modernism, defined by historian William R. Hutchison as a cluster of related beliefs—in cultural immanentism, religiously based progressivism, and the adaptation of religious ideas to modern culture. These Protestant Modernists, active from about 1870 to 1930, differed from other Protestant liberals by the level of self-awareness with which they appropriated modern ideas and methods. Protestant Modernists were fully aware of the radical implications of their common enterprise, Hutchison notes.

In that respect, at least, their American Catholic counterparts, with one or two dramatic exceptions, were not full-fledged Modernists. The American Catholic priests—scientists, seminary professors, litterateurs, and missionaries—who absorbed the new learning from Catholic Europe did not see themselves as radicals bent on revolutionizing the Church according to the demands of modernity, but they did hope to fashion a new Catholic apologetic that would speak more effectively to the democratic, scientific worldview of their fellow Americans. To do so required them to question the relevance of Roman neoscholasticism as the encompassing framework for all forms of contemporary Roman Catholic thought.

Evolution and Divine Providence

In 1888 the bishop of Peoria, John Lancaster Spalding, proclaimed, at the dedication of The Catholic University of America, that a new generation of Catholic thinkers should "stand on the shoulders of St. Thomas Aquinas" and explore horizons he could not have known, using methods he could not have imagined. American priests like John Zahm took the challenge to heart.

The Modernist episode in the U.S. Catholic Church began with Zahm's public lectures and writing on "theistic evolution." In the 1880s Fr. Zahm, a Holy Cross priest and scientist at Notre Dame, seeking to upgrade the university's chemistry and biology laboratories, traveled frequently to Europe to acquaint himself with the newest scientific technology. While abroad he became absorbed in the details of the controversy over the various attempts to modify and Christianize Darwin's theory of evolution by means of natural selection. An ally of the Americanists, who affirmed the compatibility of Catholic teaching with modern science, Zahm decided to demonstrate that Catholics could accept an understanding of evolution that preserved Divine Providence and allowed for the immediate creation of the human soul by God. In this effort Zahm was joined by Fr. John Gmeiner, a seminary professor in St. Paul, Minnesota, the diocese presided over by Archbishop John Ireland.

In the 1880s and early 1890s Gmeiner and Zahm each published treatises and texts defending the general theory of biological evolution. Zahm became a popular but controversial lecturer on the Catholic summer school circuit in the mid-1890s, where he boldly and eloquently advanced the argument that St. Augustine, St. Thomas Aquinas, and other orthodox Roman Catholic theologians had embraced a form of theistic evolution. With the 1896 publication of his masterwork on the subject, *Evolution and Dogma*, Zahm went a step further and reinterpreted the Catholic doctrine of Divine Providence in light of theistic evolution.

Just as *Evolution and Dogma* was about to be issued in Italian and Spanish editions, however, the Vatican Congregation of the Inquisition, also known as the Holy Office, let it be known that the book would be condemned—listed on the Index of Forbidden Books—unless Zahm withdrew it immediately from publication. Rather than bring censure upon himself and his religious community, Zahm recanted any errors contained in the book, stopped its publication, and abandoned his efforts to promote theistic evolution. At issue, according to the Roman Jesuit Salvatore Brandi, was Zahm's misreading of the "mind of the Angelic Doctor" (Aquinas).

The New York Review: *Rethinking Revelation and Dogma*

In 1902, six years after Zahm was silenced, a group of priests teaching at St. Joseph's Seminary in Yonkers, New York, initiated a progressive program of studies at Dunwoodie, as the seminary was called. Fr. James F.

Driscoll, S.S., the new rector of Dunwoodie, had become familiar with Modernist thought during his studies in Canada and Europe, and he was in regular correspondence with the leading French Catholic Modernist, biblical critic Alfred Loisy. Driscoll believed that the new European methods of Bible study and historical criticism held great potential for reshaping Catholic philosophy so as to prepare the Church to enter into mutually corrective dialogue with modern scientists and philosophers. Thus he revamped the Dunwoodie curriculum, replacing courses in medieval studies and Latin with courses in "the new apologetics" and the higher criticism of the Bible, the latter taught by Francis E. Gigot, S.S. Driscoll also invited noted Protestant liberals, including Episcopalian Scripture scholar and erstwhile Presbyterian "heretic" Charles A. Briggs, to lecture at Dunwoodie. Driscoll's predecessor, Edward Dyer, had already set up exchange programs with Columbia University and Union Theological Seminary so that Dunwoodie seminarians could take occasional courses at those institutions. This was all quite radical for its day, but Driscoll was able to convince Archbishop John M. Farley to support the program and to incardinate (formally incorporate) him and four of his fellow Sulpicians into the Archdiocese of New York, in order to escape the circumspect Sulpician censors in Paris, who were quite suspicious of Driscoll's and Gigot's designs.

In 1905 Francis Duffy and another Dunwoodie professor, John Brady, suggested to Driscoll the establishment of a learned periodical best described as "A journal of the Ancient Faith and Modern Thought." The editors of *The New York Review* published some articles written by European Modernists and American progressives which attempted to demonstrate that their modern epistemology (theory of knowledge) and ecclesiology (theory of the Church) were inimical only to Roman neoscholasticism, not to the broader and richer Catholic intellectual tradition. According to the Modernists, the neoscholastics were passing themselves off as the sole inheritors and interpreters of the great Catholic tradition—a claim the Modernists denounced as a regressive position. Like Zahm, the American progressives who published in *The New York Review* argued that their ideas had already been taught, in somewhat different form, by Catholic luminaries such as St. Augustine, Duns Scotus, Blaise Pascal, and Cardinal John Henry Newman.

The journal balanced articles advocating reform with middle-of-the-road discussions of historical consciousness, vital immanence, and critical methods of inquiry. A number of articles, including those authored by the Paulist apologist Joseph McSorley, built on the optimism of Isaac Hecker and described the twentieth century as a "new age of the Holy Spirit" in which the Church would turn to its advantage the modern notion that all human institutions

and ideas had evolved. *The New York Review* circulated among American priests and influenced other Catholic periodicals such as the Paulist *Catholic World* and the *Catholic University Bulletin,* which ran their own (rather mild) endorsements of the new ideas emanating from Catholic Europe. Meanwhile, Driscoll and his associates on the Dunwoodie faculty were busy contributing to the *Catholic Encyclopedia,* which would become an authoritative reference source for American Catholic scholars.

In July 1907 Pope Pius X issued the encyclical *Pascendi Dominici Gregis,* which condemned Modernism as "the synthesis of all heresies." Six months later an embarrassed Archbishop Farley, reputedly chastised by Pope Pius X for allowing Modernists to invade his diocese seminary, ordered the closing of *The New York Review* and transferred Driscoll to a parish in September 1909. Gigot and other professors remaining at the seminary were required to take an oath against Modernism and to replace their "progressive" textbooks with the traditional scholastic manuals. The "modern" curriculum was indefinitely suspended. *Catholic World* and the *Catholic University Bulletin* printed endorsements of Pope Pius and his stand against modern heresies.

Modernism as the Final Phase of Americanism

In the work of two priests—the Paulist William L. Sullivan and the Josephite John R. Slattery, both of whom eventually left the priesthood and the Church—American Catholic Modernism reached its full expression. These two men concluded that the European Modernist program of theological updating, spiritual renewal, and institutional reform demanded a revision of the very categories of Christian thought. When Pope Pius X condemned Modernism in 1907, Sullivan and Slattery made their repudiation of Roman Catholicism a point of honor, and accused their fellow progressive priests of cowardice for buckling under ecclesiastical pressure.

Slattery was committed to expanding the Catholic apostolate to American blacks. He lobbied repeatedly before fellow Americanists Cardinal James Gibbons of Baltimore and Archbishop John Ireland of St. Paul, seeking more missionaries and funds to support the work among unchurched blacks. Struggling to overcome the bitterness that welled up inside him when his efforts failed, Slattery turned to the writings of Loisy and other European Catholics who were criticizing the Roman Catholic hierarchy for its inflexible attitudes. By 1905 Slattery had concluded that the Church would not break free of the racism, authoritarianism, and theological exclusivism stifling its vital religious impulses. In "How My Priesthood Dropped From Me," an article published in *The Independent* several years after he left the Catholic Church, Slattery describes the "dawning modernism" that impelled him away from "the ancient faith."

Sullivan's public break from the Church was even more controversial and scandalous. He had attended St. John's Seminary in Brighton, Massachusetts, where the abbé John B. Hogan, S.S., introduced him to the new theories of revelation, inspiration, and biblical exegesis. The precocious Sullivan became determined to author "a great apologetic work in defense of Christian Revelation." Yet Sullivan found his Paulist colleagues at The Catholic University of America "muddy, vagrant, and ill-equipped with [modern] erudition" and, after completing his S.T.L. thesis, he left Washington for two years (1899–1900) of mission preaching in Tennessee. He considered this assignment to be part of "the grandest work before the church in this country," but soon discovered that the traditional neo-scholastic approach, which stressed metaphysical arguments, was ineffective in the American towns and villages he visited. Accordingly, Sullivan began to craft a new message for Americans, who loved democratic values such as freedom of speech and liberty of conscience above all else.

At about the same time Sullivan began to research the First Vatican Council, Archbishop Ireland and Bishop Thomas S. Byrne of Nashville recommended that he read the postconciliar correspondence between Lord Acton and Archbishop Peter Richard Kenrick of St. Louis. Thus began Sullivan's obsession with the Inquisition and papal infallibility, two dark moments in Roman Catholic history for which Catholic Americanism was the antidote, Sullivan felt. By arousing the moral indignation of American Catholics, Sullivan came to believe, he would open the way for reform of the Church and the end of "Vaticanism, ultramontanism, and religious imperialism." Only after confronting these prior moral questions could the reformer proceed effectively to a critical examination and reconstruction of Catholic doctrine.

Thereafter Sullivan studied the new critical sciences and allied himself with other Americanists, becoming an occasional contributor to The *New York Review*. From 1901 to 1906 he saw himself as an orthodox Catholic crusader, even though his favorite authors were the Europeans Tyrrell, Loisy, and von Hügel. In 1906 Sullivan accepted what he later called "the key to the whole original Modernist movement," the notion that Catholic scholars should respect the facts established by critical scientific investigation of the Bible and of history, evaluating the evidence for themselves without prior restrictions from the Vatican. "The Church had been my Absolute," he wrote in his autobiography, *Under Orders*, "now the Moral Law was becoming my Absolute."

To this position of moral absolutism Sullivan wedded an increasing dependence on the "inner leading" of the Holy Spirit. He criticized the hierarchical exercise of authority which, he said, obstructed the creative work of the Spirit in the Church. "I began to see," Sullivan wrote in 1906, "that from the very nature of a personality or soul, we incur moral disaster in submitting it without reserve to any institution whatever, civil or ecclesiastical. . . . I was fated, no doubt, to take position with the Modernists." He began "to grasp the idea of the more radical Modernists, that Catholicism, in its essence, was capable of living its abundant life under different formulations."

In 1907 Sullivan was stunned when his fellow Americanists retracted their opinions or made similar "obscene" gestures of obeisance to Rome. He characterized his former colleagues as "moral cowards" devoid of integrity, and accused the Church of destroying "personality" by demanding an idolatrous moral submission of individual consciences. In 1908 Sullivan requested a transfer to Austin, Texas, far away from the controversies raging in Washington and New York. In 1910 he anonymously published *Letters to His Holiness, Pope Pius X,* a shrill polemic indicting Rome for immoral, inquisitorial behavior; the book was a naive bid to arouse the moral indignation of American Catholics in the face of what Sullivan saw as the papacy's persistent violation of basic human rights, including liberty of conscience and freedom from state coercion in matters of belief.

Letters to His Holiness depicted Pius X's Church as the reincarnation of the Inquisition, a conspiracy of Jesuit intellectuals and curialists seeking to preempt the direct experience of Christ. The Modernist, by contrast, sought to return religion to the people and thus sought political and social structures that would facilitate that return. Naturally, therefore, the eyes of many Modernists turned to the United States: "Whence could a more zealous advocacy of Modernism have rightly been anticipated?" Sullivan asked. "Americanism is a word that connotes patriotism," he wrote. "It seems to embrace all that is indigenous to this republic and is typical of it; and whatever becomes of Biblical criticism or the philosophy of dogmatic conformity, the mass of Catholics in this country will not be un-American." Ironically, Sullivan basically agreed with the Pope's assessment of the modern conflict within the Church. On one side stood the Modernists, adherents of liberalism, democracy, progress, and individual liberty. Adamantly opposed to them were the Romanists, defenders of the Church-controlled state.

Sullivan felt that Americans would never fully accept a system in which "the will of people, priests and bishops counts, as such, for nothing." "A courageous and intelligent laity is the sole hope for a better day," he wrote. Free-thinking American Catholics would ultimately reject the pretensions of papalism, along with the distortions they introduced into the Catholic tradition. In 1911, however, he joined the Unitarian Church in Cleveland, Ohio; in 1912 he was admitted to the Unitarian ministry, serving All Soul's Unitarian Church in Schenectady, New York.

The Significance of American Catholic Modernism

In 1907 the Roman Catholic Church officially declared itself anti-Modernist; thus it responded to the central institutional question raised by historical consciousness—the question of religious authority—by invoking the neoscholastic, absolutist habit of mind that had informed the decrees of the First Vatican Council. The European Modernists refused to submit to this response to historical consciousness, evolution, and biblical criticism. Although they were not directly implicated by the encyclical, the Americans, too, were commanded by their religious superiors to suspend original research, to eschew new scriptural approaches, to abandon seminary curriculum reform, to renounce theistic evolution, and to take an anti-Modernist oath. Although the magisterium actually singled out for condemnation a small number of Modernists, it became clear, from the scope of the vigilance and repression that ensued, that it intended to inhibit or abort the projects of a far greater number of scholars.

The American Catholics suspected of Modernism thereby came to understand the power of what sociologists of religion call the "elective affinity" between a system of thought (in this case, Roman neoscholasticism) and the entrenched system and rigidly conservative structure it served to buttress (the turn-of-the-century Roman Catholic hierarchy and Curia). When the Vatican followed its 1899 condemnation of Americanism with the 1907 condemnation of Modernism, Sullivan contended that both "movements" were denounced as heresies not because they violated biblical or spiritual truths, but because their major tenets, such as "vital immanence" (the emphasis on the indwelling of the Holy Spirit as the primary locus of spiritual authority for the individual), undermined the absolutist claims of the Roman Catholic hierarchy. However, the main legacy of the Modernist controversy was the advent of a censorious atmosphere of suspicion which stultified Catholic intellectual life, especially in scriptural and theological studies, for the next half-century.

See also AMERICANISM; HECKER, ISAAC; *NEW YORK REVIEW;* SLATTERY, JOHN R.; SULLIVAN, WILLIAM L.

Appleby, R. Scott. *"Church and Age, Unite!" The Modernist Impulse in American Catholicism.* University of Notre Dame Press, 1992.

Gannon, Michael V. "Before and After Modernism: The Intellectual Isolation of the American Priest." *The Catholic Priest in the United States: Historical Investigations,* ed. John Tracy Ellis. Collegeville: The Liturgical Press, 1971.

Shelley, Thomas J. "John Cardinal Farley and Modernism in New York." *Church History* 61 (3) (September 1993) 350–61.

Sullivan, William Laurence. *Under Orders: The Autobiography of William Laurence Sullivan.* Boston: Beacon Press, 1944; rev. ed., 1966.

Zahm, John A. *Evolution and Dogma.* repr. New York: Arno Press, 1978.

R. SCOTT APPLEBY

MOELLER, HENRY (1849–1925)

Archbishop of Cincinnati. Henry Moeller was born in Cincinnati on December 11, 1849. After attending St. Xavier College he was sent to Rome for theology and was ordained there on June 10, 1876. Returning to Cincinnati, he engaged in pastoral work for a year and then was appointed to the faculty of the Seminary of Mt. St. Mary of the West. In 1879 he was granted a leave of absence to serve as secretary to Bishop Chatard of Vincennes, but after a few months he was recalled to Cincinnati to assume the same position as secretary to Archbishop Elder. In 1886 he was appointed chancellor of the archdiocese. He was partially responsible for the organization of the administrative structure of the archdiocese and assisted Archbishop Elder in coping with the effects of the Purcell administration's financial failure.

Henry Moeller

Appointed bishop of Columbus, Ohio, on April 6, 1900, he received episcopal consecration on August 25 of that year. Although his stay in Columbus was brief, he paid off a large diocesan debt and placed the diocese on a solid financial foundation. Appointed coadjutor archbishop of Cincinnati on April 27, 1903, Moeller succeeded Archbishop Elder on the latter's death on October 31, 1904. During the next twenty years he worked to improve diocesan schools, founded a number of new parishes, engaged in several building projects including a new Mt. St. Mary

Seminary and Saint Rita School for the Deaf, and founded a diocesan bureau of Catholic Charities. On the national level he was active in the work of the NCWC and helped to found the American Board of Foreign Missions, of which he was chairman. Under Moeller, Cincinnati became the national headquarters for the Catholic Students Mission Crusade. He died on January 5, 1925.

Lamott, John. *History of the Archdiocese of Cincinnati.* New York: Frederick Pustet Co., 1921.

THOMAS W. TIFFT

MOLLOY, MARY ALOYSIA (1880–1954)

Catholic college founder and educator. Mary Molloy was born in Sandusky, Ohio, June 14, 1880, the only child of Patrick John Molloy and Mary Lambe Molloy. Her only formal Catholic education was at Saints Peter and Paul parochial school in Sandusky, where she attended the elementary grades. The religious piety imparted by her devout Irish immigrant parents and Madame Fitzgerald's Ladies (religious in secular clothing who staffed the parish school) stayed with her through the rest of her formal education: public high school in Sandusky; Ohio State University for her bachelor's and master's degrees; and Cornell University, where she became one of few women of her day to earn a doctorate (1907).

A few months after completing her doctoral studies, she answered an appeal publicized by an East Coast teachers' agency to initiate college courses for the Sisters of St. Francis in Winona, Minnesota. Working closely with the community superior, Mother Leo Tracy, she shaped the College of St. Teresa into a premier liberal arts college for women, first as dean (1912–28) and then as president. She developed a classical curriculum and challenged women to reach for high goals of scholarship and public service. With Mother Leo's firm support, she fostered the doctoral studies of a distinguished sister-faculty and saw the completion of an ambitious building program.

Molloy's courage and decisiveness in taking on unpopular causes set her apart from the crowd. She worked constantly to improve the quality of Catholic education and to counter prejudice in the larger society. In 1914 she secured a court injunction to block the anti-Catholic agenda of the American Protective Association and the Guardians of Liberty in southeastern Minnesota. She argued before the National Catholic Educational Association against the proliferation of Catholic colleges: "We have too many small, struggling, inefficient and useless so-called colleges." Women, particularly, were being short-changed by the system. "Only thirty-three per cent of college graduates find their place in the home," she said. "Can we at the present ignore the claims of the sixty-seven percent who may wish to pursue work other than that bearing directly on the home?" It was time, she felt, to take women's rightful ambitions seriously and prepare them "to become specialists in higher mathematics, in the classics, or in history or sociology" or law or medicine, if such was their ambition.

She joined the Franciscan community in 1922 and continued her career without pause, functioning in 1923 as the sole woman on the North Central States Accrediting Association's ad hoc commission on standards. She also accepted appointment as the first woman on the executive committee of the NCEA's college and university department. She died on September 27, 1954, after a brief illness.

Kennelly, Karen M. "Mary Molloy: Women's College Founder." *Women of Minnesota: Selected Biographical Essays,* eds. Barbara Stuhler and Gretchen Kreuter. St. Paul: Minnesota Historical Society Press, 1977.
Molloy, Mary Aloysia. *A Teresan Ideal in Service and System.* Winona, Minn.: College of St. Teresa, 1928.

KAREN M. KENNELLY, C.S.J.

MOLLOY, THOMAS (1884–1956)

Bishop. Thomas E. Molloy, son of John and Ellen Gaffney Molloy, was born in Nashua, New Hampshire, on September 4, 1884. He attended St. Anselm College, Manchester, New Hampshire, and graduated from St. Francis College, Brooklyn. After a year at St. John's Seminary, Molloy transferred to the North American College, Rome. Ordained on September 19, 1908, he continued his studies in Rome until 1909. Assigned to St. John's Chapel, Brooklyn, he was also secretary to auxiliary Bishop George W. Mundelein, whom he accompanied to Chicago in 1915. Returning after ten months, Molloy was appointed to Queen of All Saints parish and served also as spiritual director at Cathedral College and philosophy professor at St. Joseph's College for Women.

Consecrated auxiliary bishop on October 3, 1920, Molloy became administrator after Bishop Charles E. McDonnell's death on August 8, 1921, and was named ordinary on November 21, 1921. Pope Pius XII honored Molloy with the title archbishop *ad personam* on April 7, 1951. As leader of the growing Catholic population, Molloy established parishes, schools, and administrative agencies. Increased priestly vocations caused the diocesan clergy, numbering 628 in 1928, to more than double. The bishop dedicated Immaculate Conception Seminary, Huntington, debt-free, in 1930. Eighty-eight new parishes, some located in the eastern counties of Long Island, brought the total to 330. Religious women and men in greater numbers staffed the expanding educational system. Three colleges were enlarged and Molloy Catholic College for Women was opened. Diocesan high schools and additional private academies doubled the number of secondary schools. On the elementary level, 102 new parochial schools raised the total to 226. Diocesan normal schools for teachers were opened in 1926. The Catholic Schools Office administered this extensive educational system.

In 1930 Molloy established the chancery, which included existing agencies for parish services, central purchasing, and the Diocesan Building Commission. The Diocesan Commission for Catholic Charities, instituted in 1931, assumed responsibility for family welfare, youth, children in need, the aged, and the sick. Parish collections at Christmas and Easter supported the child-caring institutions. The Catholic hospitals and nursing schools were expanded. Additional offices, such as the Social Action Department, made Catholic Charities responsive to current needs.

Through pastorals and circular letters published regularly in *The Tablet* and eloquent sermons preached at parish, school, and diocesan celebrations, Molloy exhorted the laity to generosity and fidelity to Catholic principles. Organizations such as the Society for the Propagation of the Faith, the Confraternity of Christian Doctrine, and the Apostolate for the Instruction of non-Catholics flourished on the diocesan and parish levels. Molloy's benefactors included Catholics prominent in business and the professions. During the diocesan centenary in 1953 the bishop emphasized the accomplishments of others, not his own. He greatly preferred personal privacy to public acclaim. At his death on November 26, 1956, Molloy had completed thirty-five years as leader of the largest diocese in the United States.

Culkin, Henry M., ed. *Priests and Parishes of the Diocese of Brooklyn 1820–1990.* Vol. 1, 3d ed., rev. and expanded. W. Charles Print Co., 1990.

One Hundredth Anniversary Roman Catholic Diocese of Brooklyn 1853–1953. Supplement to *The Tablet,* October 31, 1953.

Sharp, John K. *History of the Diocese of Brooklyn 1853–1953: The Catholic Church on Long Island.* 2 vols. New York: Fordham University Press, 1954.

MARGARET M. QUINN, C.S.J.

MONAGHAN, JOHN P. (1889–1961)

Priest, educator, social activist. John Monaghan was born in County Tyrone, Ireland, on February 12, 1890. As a young man he emigrated to New York City, where he eventually studied at St. Joseph's Seminary in Yonkers after completing his studies at St. Francis College in Brooklyn. He finished his theological training at the North American College in Rome where he was ordained on June 2, 1917. He was subsequently assigned to St. Peter's parish on Staten Island. While serving as a parish priest for five years, he taught in both St. Peter's girls' and boys' High

John P. Monaghan

Schools while he earned a doctorate in English literature at Fordham University.

From 1922 until 1938, Monaghan was assigned to Cathedral College, the archdiocese's minor seminary where he taught religion, English, and history. It was during his sixteen years at Cathedral College that Monaghan influenced a whole generation of New York diocesan priests. Many of his students later recalled how Monaghan's cajoling style of teaching aroused their interest in such areas as the social teaching of the Church and induced them to pursue postgraduate studies.

Seminary Teacher and Liturgist

Monaghan's influence spread far beyond the seminary classroom. While teaching at Cathedral College from 1922 to 1938, he resided at Corpus Christi Church in Morningside Heights in Manhattan where he was influenced by the pastor, George Barry Ford, who was a pioneer in liturgical reform and ecumenism. Faculty and students alike came to Corpus Christi Church from the adjacent academic institutions such as Columbia University and Teachers' College. They were drawn to a celebration of the liturgy that featured innovations such as a priest in the pulpit translating the Latin liturgy into English—innovations that were considered highly suspect by the chancellor of the archdiocese, J. Francis McIntyre, the future cardinal archbishop of Los Angeles. Many others attended Corpus Christi Church simply to hear Monaghan preach, especially about social concerns during the worst years of the Great Depression. While the erudite were drawn to Monaghan, so too were the poor, who found in him a real friend.

Monaghan and ACTU

On February 27, 1937, Monaghan, along with eleven laymen, including John C. Cort, founded the Association of Catholic Trade Unionist (ACTU). The purpose of ACTU was to inform Catholic trade unionists of the Church's social teaching, especially the tenets of the papal encyclicals *Rerum Novarum* and *Quadragesimo Anno*. Another purpose of ACTU was the establishment of labor schools that trained Catholics for leadership roles in trade unions. In this way, Monaghan and his associates, including several of his former students, helped Catholic trade unionists to influence the American labor movement in general. As ACTU expanded beyond New York, it sought and usually received the approval of local bishops who appointed priests to serve as chaplains. Monaghan promoted the work of ACTU not only in the classroom, but also in speeches at labor conventions, on the radio, or at St. Patrick's Cathedral during the annual Labor Day Mass where he was often called upon to preach. Under the pseudonym "Don Capellano," Monaghan published a regular column in the ACTU's newspaper, *The Labor Leader*. One of his consistent and pervasive themes was the sacredness of human work.

While serving as chaplain to ACTU, Monaghan incurred the disapproval of his ordinary, Francis Cardinal Spellman. The occasion was the notorious Calvary Cemetery Strike of 1949. For its role in supporting the strikers, ACTU received criticism from prominent Catholics such as Patrick Scanlan, editor of the *Brooklyn Tablet*, who helped to convince Spellman that ACTU was supporting Communism. The settlement of the strike occurred only after Spellman challenged the ecclesiastical loyalty of ACTU, its chaplains, and in particular, Monaghan, which—needless to say—was a severe blow to him.

Pastor

While serving as the founding chaplain to ACTU, in 1939 Monaghan was assigned as pastor of St. Margaret Mary's Church in Midland Beach, Staten Island. Upon his arrival, he promised the people, "We are a poor parish and we are going to great things as a poor people." Monaghan's dedicated leadership, his interest in the liturgy, as well as his explanations of the Church's teaching and practical advice in the Sunday bulletin highlighted the energy and insight for which he was remembered. Monaghan served as pastor of St. Margaret Mary from 1939 until 1954, when he was reassigned as pastor of St. Michael's parish on West 34th Street in Manhattan, where he remained until his death on July 26, 1961. His assistant priests recalled how Monaghan frequently played host to prominent guests, such as the ambassador of Ireland, while he maintained the approachable simplicity of a parish priest who truly loved the people he served. One of the assistants said that Monaghan "made, without effort, the rectory a home for the priests and visitors—and they were legion."

At the time of Monaghan's death on July 26, 1961, one admirer called him a "benign agitator." Monaghan would have been pleased with such an epitaph, for he once wrote in his "Don Capellano" column:

> [A] priest who didn't often speak and work against the degradation of our slums, against the impersonal tyranny of union-hating corporations, against the human belittlement of old workers, foreign workers and underpaid workers, had little awareness of the world he lived in and less awareness of the world he was trying to reach.

See also SPELLMAN, FRANCIS CARDINAL.

Lynch, Thomas A. "Above All Things the Truth: John P. Monaghan and the Church of New York." *Dunwoodie Review* 16 (1992–93) 109–65.

Monaghan, John P. *A Christian Social Order*. Washington, D.C.: National Council of Catholic Men, 1939.

THOMAS A. LYNCH

MONASTICISM IN AMERICA

The evolution of monastic life in the United States has been, from its inception, closely connected to the historical development of the American Catholic Church. As an ecclesiastical institution, it migrated from Europe, went through an assimilation process, exemplified the diversity of a pluralist culture, and left a distinctive imprint upon the American religious scene.

It is interesting to note that the first Catholic bishop of the United States, John Carroll, expressed a desire to have a monastic foundation in his Diocese of Baltimore. Though this proposed English monastic community was never realized, it anticipated the desire on the part of many early bishops to draw upon the ancient monastic order to assist in the growth of the fledgling American Church.

Origins of American Monasticism

Two historical causes merged to help bring about the arrival of the monastic order in the United States. The first was the persecution of the Catholic Church in Europe. Beginning with the French Revolution, and continuing with the Communist revolutions of the twentieth century, there were a number of antireligious movements that precipitated the migration of monastic communities to North America. The first of these was a group of French Trappists who came to Kentucky in the first decade of the nineteenth century. Though this first group of monks (after an odyssey that took them from Kentucky to Illinois, to Canada and to Manhattan Island) had to return to Europe, they laid the groundwork for a later group of French monks who founded the Abbey of Gethsemani, Kentucky, in 1848.

By that same time, repression by the Swiss government against religious houses led the monastic communities of Einsiedeln and Engelberg in Switzerland to consider starting American foundations as a type of political refuge for their monks in case of dissolution.

Monks and Care of German Immigrants

The decade of the 1840s also coincided with the increasing migration of German-speaking Catholics to the United States and points to the second major cause of monastic migration to the New World: the pastoral care and Catholic education of the immigrant. This is exemplified in the life and work of the person known as the patriarch of American Benedictine monasticism, Boniface Wimmer. Wimmer, a monk of the Bavarian Abbey of Metten, conceived a plan to establish a monastery in Pennsylvania that would serve as a liturgical, educational, and cultural center for the German immigrant. That plan was realized when Wimmer came to the United States in 1846 and founded the monastery of St. Vincent in Latrobe, Pennsylvania. Wimmer believed that conditions on the North American continent in the nineteenth century were analogous to those on the European continent in the early Middle Ages. Just as the Anglo-Saxon monks of that earlier epoch had evangelized northern Europe, so would the European monks of the nineteenth century help to evangelize and catechize the emerging nation of the United States. Wimmer's monastic vision had a decidedly missionary character. This is seen in the rapid expansion of his monasteries, encompassing in his lifetime the American west (St. John's, Minnesota; St. Benedict's, Kansas; St. Procopius, Illinois) and south (Belmont, North Carolina; St. Bernard's, Alabama; Richmond, Virginia). Wimmer's monastic model came to grow out of its ethnically centered attention on German-speaking Catholics and included Native Americans, African Americans, and other ethnic groups. The legacy of Wimmer's leadership is seen in the formation of the first American Monastic Congregation, the American Cassinese, founded in 1855. This congregation was to continue the growth cycle of Wimmer and eventually encompass over twenty Benedictine communities and over one thousand monks in its membership.

Another monastic development in the United States that initially concerned itself with German-speaking immigrants was the Swiss-American Congregation. The congregation came into being in 1881 as a result of American monastic foundations from the Swiss abbeys of Einsiedeln and Engelberg. Einsiedeln first sent monks to St. Meinrad, Indiana, in 1854. This monastery too had a missionary orientation, committing itself to work with the Native American in the Dakotas and founding houses in Arkansas (1878) and Louisiana (1891). Engelberg, meanwhile, sent monks to Missouri to found Conception Abbey in 1873. In 1882, shortly after it became an independent house, monks of Conception founded Mount Angel Monastery in Oregon. Both of these Engelberg foundations began the work of seminary education, which they continue to this day.

Women Religious

Even as increasing numbers of monks were coming into North America from Europe in the mid-nineteenth century, they were joined by Benedictine women. These came first from the Bavarian convent of Eichstätt in 1852. Wimmer's original plan was to have the sisters work in tandem with the monks, assisting in work of education and pastoral care for Catholic immigrants. At the expense of their contemplative and cloistered identity, the sisters did this. The German sisters were later joined by sisters sent from the Swiss convents of Maria Rickenbach, Melchtal, and Sarnen. Their geographic expansion was as wide and rapid as the monks, and they increased in number even more rapidly than the monks. After prolonged and problematic efforts to attain their canonical independence, they formed themselves into the Federations of St. Gertrude, St. Scholastica, and St. Benedict. These federations focused on more active apostolic ministries of education, medical care, and missionary work. The Congregation of Perpetual Adoration was a more contemplative network of women's monastic communities. In the twentieth century, the quilt of monastic women became even more diverse. A number of Trappistine houses were founded in various parts of the United States. Contemplative monasteries were also founded from new European motherhouses (Boulder, Colorado; Greensburg, Pennsylvania; Bethlehem, Connecticut; and Petersham, Massachusetts).

Development of American Monasticism

The influence of American monasticism developed along with American Catholicism. The educational and evangelizing efforts of the nineteenth century gradually gave way in the twentieth century to involvement in the liturgical and ecumenical movements. The fascination of Americans with monasticism is perhaps best seen in the appeal of the writings of the Trappist monk Thomas Merton. From the time of his best-selling autobiography, *The Seven Storey Mountain,* in 1948, until his sudden death in 1968, Merton articulated a vision of monasticism that was both prophetic and persuasive. This more contemplative aspect of monasticism was also made evident in a whole new set of monastic foundations made in the latter half of the twentieth century. These foundations were far smaller in size than their predecessors and emphasized the dimensions of prayer and solitude. Mt. Saviour, New York; Christ in the Desert, New Mexico; Weston, Vermont; Sand Springs, Oklahoma; and Windsor, New York, are only a few examples of this.

The provincial character of American monasticism in its early stages was also replaced by a more cosmopolitan and variegated composition at the end of the second millennium. Within the United States, there were monasteries with ties to England and Ireland, France and Italy, Germany and Switzerland, Hungary and Belgium. There were also communities of Anglicans and Byzantines, Carthusians and Camaldolese, and Cistercians of Common and Strict Observance. American monasteries had made over twenty foundations in Latin America and had also set down roots in Taiwan, Japan, the Bahamas, and Puerto Rico. The composition of monastic houses of men and women was equally variegated. Hispanics and Asians now joined the traditional European melting pot of ethnic groups. The educational level of monastics had advanced in turn, with graduate degrees and specialized skills becoming the rule rather than the exception. Leadership was also provided by Benedictines in the area of renewal after Vatican Council II. The Leadership Conference of Religious Woman had Joan Chittister and others influence its vision of religious life. The American hierarchy had Archbishops Rembert Weakland, Daniel Kucera, Daniel Buechlein, and Jerome Hanus serve in leadership positions. Individual monastics also left their stamp on particular movements and groups: Cyprian Davis with African American Catholics; Thomas Keating with the centering prayer movement.

There is little doubt that monasticism in the United States has enriched the Catholic Church. Apart from its Gregorian chant and model of communal liturgical life, it has brought a spiritual tradition that has adapted well to a culture that at once needs stability and promotes change. In the relatively short span of its American history, it has also proven itself capable of acquiring a unique identity, faithful to its rich past and open to the demands of an ever-changing Church.

"Aspects of Monasticism in America." *Word and Spirit* 14 (1992).

Barry, Colman, O.S.B. *Worship and Work.* 3rd ed. Collegeville: The Liturgical Press, 1993.

Hollermann, Ephrem, O.S.B. *The Reshaping of a Tradition: American Benedictine Women, 1852–1881.* Winona, Minn.: St. Mary's Press, 1994.

Knowles, David. *Christian Monasticism.* New York: McGraw Hill, 1969.

Merton, Thomas. *The Waters of Siloe.* New York: Harcourt, Brace, 1949.

Oetgen, Jerome. *An American Abbot, Boniface Wimmer, O.S.B., 1809–1887.* Washington, D.C.: The Catholic University Press of America, 1997.

Rippinger, Joel, O.S.B. *The Benedictine Order in the United States.* Collegeville: The Liturgical Press, 1990.

_____. "The History of American Catholic Monasticism." *Perspectives on the American Catholic Church 1789–1989,* eds. Stephen Vicchio and Virgina Geiger. Westminster, Md.: Christian Classics, 1989.

JOEL RIPPINGER, O.S.B.

MONTANA, CATHOLIC CHURCH IN

Montana is the fourth largest state. Two dioceses, Helena and Great Falls-Billings, minister to the Catholic population of approximately 17 percent of the total population of 823,697.

Missionaries

During the first decades of the nineteenth century Catholic Iroquois natives traveled west into the mountains and introduced the Flatheads to Catholicism. Subsequently, the Flatheads requested Blackrobes from St. Louis and in 1840 the intrepid Fr. Pierre Jean De Smet, S.J., visited and then returned a year later to establish St. Mary's Mission in the Bitterroot valley. St. Ignatius Mission (1854) and St. Peter's Mission (1859) followed through the labors of Jesuits such as Hoecken, Point, Ravalli, Giorda, Zerbinatti, Mengarini, Imoda, Magri, and Palladino. Religious women were also pioneers. The Order of the Sisters of Providence of Montreal, Canada (S.P.), came to St. Ignatius Mission in 1864. Five years later the Sisters of Charity of Leavenworth (S.C.L.) arrived in Helena. The Ursuline nuns made three foundations in Montana in 1884, at Miles City, St. Labre Mission, and St. Peter's Mission.

Administration

From 1803 to 1883 this area was divided in half, joined to various vicariates apostolic. Montana became a territory in 1864 as fur trappers, then gold seekers and settlers arrived in western Montana. The first church for white settlers was built of logs at Hellgate in 1863. In 1883 Montana was named a vicariate apostolic and a year later Pope Leo XIII established Helena as a diocese embracing the whole of present-day Montana with the Rt. Rev. John B. Brondel (1884–1903) as the first bishop. His episcopacy laid the foundation for a strong Church in Montana.

Emerging State and Dioceses

Newly arrived Catholics played leadership roles in politics. General Thomas Francis Meagher was the first territorial governor and James M. Cavanaugh, Martin Maginnis, and Thomas Carter were delegates to Congress. After Montana became a state in 1889, Carter, Thomas C. Power, and later Thomas J. Walsh were U.S. senators who supported the Church legislatively and financially.

In 1903 the diocese was split with the eastern two-thirds becoming the Diocese of Great Falls under Bishop

Mathias Lenihan (1904–30), while the remainder continued as the Diocese of Helena under Bishop John P. Carroll (1904–25). Bishop Lenihan obtained more priests and religious and dedicated a new stone Cathedral of St. Ann in Great Falls in 1907, the first permanent cathedral to be completed in the Northwest. With the assistance of the Catholic Church Extension Society (1904), he formed parishes in the prairie communities beginning to experience the homestead boom. In Helena, Bishop Carroll founded churches for mining towns that had ethnic enclaves such as Anaconda and Butte, where the Church saw its greatest development. The Knights of Columbus began a long history of fellowship and public service with ten councils started by 1910. In both dioceses religious women built schools, hospitals, and orphanages.

Intent on making Helena a true see city, Bishop Carroll, with donations from mining magnates Thomas Cruse and Peter Larson, laid the cornerstone in 1904 for a magnificent cathedral (completed 1914). In 1909 he founded Mt. St. Charles College as a source of vocations for the diocese.

War and Depression Years

The Church responded to new waves of Catholic immigrants and attacks on those of German descent by founding churches for minority groups such as the Slavs and Poles in Black Eagle and the Belgians in Valier-Cut Bank and Shelby. After Bishop Carroll's death in 1925, Mt. St. Charles College was renamed Carroll College in his honor. Bishop George J. Finnigan (1927–32) succeeded him and established *The Register: Western Montana,* which would be the official diocesan newspaper for forty years. He also set up the women's counterpart to the Knights of Columbus, the Daughters of Isabella, in Helena in 1928.

The second bishop of Great Falls, Edwin O'Hara (1930–39), sought to meet the need for religious education for families struggling against drought and depression by establishing in Great Falls what he had earlier organized in Oregon, the Confraternity of the Christian Doctrine (CCD). Helena followed suit in 1932. Bishop O'Hara also founded the Great Falls Junior College in 1932 with a faculty of Ursulines and Providence (S.P.) Sisters who would later incorporate the Columbus School of Nursing. His successor, Bishop William J. Condon (1939–67), continued to support education at all levels and dedicated what became the College of Great Falls at its new campus in 1960.

Growth

The fifth bishop of Helena was Ralph L. Hayes (1933–35), succeeded by Bishop Joseph M. Gilmore (1936–62), who took on the task of rebuilding parishes damaged in the 1935 earthquake. In 1938 he established the first formal social services organization in Butte, the Catholic Social Services Bureau, which also worked with the Society of St. Vincent de Paul. He confronted government allotment cutbacks for Native Americans and the worsening financial problems for the Holy Family Mission, which the Jesuits and the diocese were forced to close in 1940. Bishop Gilmore realized the goals of Bishops Brondel and Carroll in providing native clergy. Carroll College also developed a School of Nursing during World War II.

Second Vatican Council

The sixth bishop of Helena, Raymond G. Hunthausen (1962–75), a native son of the diocese, participated in all four sessions of the council (from 1962–65). He started a diocesan mission to Guatemala and worked to implement the council's directives by forming a Diocesan Pastoral Council, a permanent diaconate program, and a Diocesan Ecumenical Commission. With Great Falls Bishop Eldon Schuster (1968–77), Bishop Hunthausen organized the Montana Catholic Conference on Social Welfare, which led to the statewide formation of the Catholic Charities of Montana, whose leaders also played an active roll in Montana's 1972 Constitutional Convention. When both bishops faced school closures, they placed greater emphasis on CCD programs. They also confronted some dissension to the council from traditionalist or Tridentine Catholics. In 1975 Bishop Hunthausen became the archbishop of Seattle.

In Great Falls Bishop Thomas J. Murphy (1978–87) consolidated schools and parishes and reorganized the priest's senate under the presbyteral council. In 1980 St. Patrick Church in Billings was elevated to the status of co-cathedral and the diocese became Great Falls-Billings. The present Bishop Anthony M. Milone (since 1988) and Helena Bishop Elden F. Curtiss (1976–93) countered continuing problems of fewer clergy and declining school enrollments with emphasis on the Renew programs. Seeking unity and growth, in the early 1980s Bishop Curtiss started an Office of Religious Education, a Diocesan Council on Women Religious, a program for lay ministry, and the Diocesan Pastoral Council. In 1988 he called a diocesan Synod, the first in eighty years, which committed the diocese to collaborative ministry. In 1993 Bishop Curtiss was named archbishop of Omaha. Bishop Alexander J. Brunett was installed in Helena in 1994.

Arts and Architecture

Jesuit Br. Joseph Carignano's fifty-eight murals painted in the St. Ignatius Mission Church in the late nineteenth century are an early example of inspiration. In recent decades in Great Falls, Ursuline Mother Raphael Schweda's paintings in the Chapel of the Ursuline Centre and Sr. Mary Trinitas Morin's (S.P.) glass, woodcarvings, and mosaics at the chapel at the College of Great Falls attest to their skill, as well as their dedication as art teachers. In and near Anaconda, Fr. James Barry's stained glass and Sr. Joann Daley's (O.P.) etchings are well known, as is Fr. Victor Langhan's (Frenchtown) stained glass. Fr. Michael Freze, whose parish is in Deer Lodge, is a prolific writer on Catholic spirituality. From Carroll College, Fr. Peter D. Hillen, a teacher, is known nationally for his stained glass and is sought for his expertise in the restoration of windows.

In 1995 Catholics constituted 15 percent of the population of Montana, 125,320 out of a total population of 823,904. They were served by 169 diocesan priests and 27 religious priests in 111 parishes and 113 missions. There were also 163 sisters, two brothers, and 29 permanent deacons.

Flaherty, Cornelia M. *Go with Haste into the Mountains: A History of the Diocese of Helena.* Helena, Mont.: Falcon Press, 1985.

Palladino, L. B. *Indian and White in the Northwest: A History of Catholicity in Montana, 1838–1891.* 2nd ed. Lancaster, Penn.: Wickersham Publishing Co., 1922.

Schoenberg, Wilfred P. *A History of the Catholic Church in the Pacific Northwest, 1843–1983.* Washington, D.C.: Pastoral Press, 1987.

———. *Jesuits in Montana, 1840–1960.* Portland: Oregon Jesuit, 1960.

Schrems, Suzanne. "God's Women: Sisters of Charity of Providence and Ursuline Nuns in Montana, 1864–1900." Ph.D. dissertation, University of Oklahoma, 1993.

Small, Lawrence F., ed. *Religion in Montana.* Vol 1. Helena, Mont.: Falcon Press, 1992.

JOAN BISHOP

MOONEY, EDWARD FRANCIS (1882–1958)

Cardinal archbishop of Detroit. Edward Francis Mooney was born May 9, 1882, in Mt. Savage, Maryland, the son of Thomas and Mary Heneghan Mooney. He attended St. Charles College, Ellicott City, Maryland, St. Mary Seminary, Baltimore, Maryland, and North American College, Rome. He was ordained on April 10, 1909, by Pietro Cardinal Respighi, vicar of His Holiness. Mooney served on the faculty of St. Mary Seminary, Cleveland, Ohio, from 1909 until 1916. He was also founding president of Cathedral Latin School, Cleveland, Ohio (1916–22), was involved in pastoral work for the Diocese of Cleveland (1922–23), and was spiritual director at North American College, Rome (1923–26). Mooney was elected to the archiepiscopal see of Irenopolis on January 18, 1926, and was appointed apostolic delegate to India. He was ordained bishop on January 31, 1926, by William Cardinal Van Rossum, C.Ss.R., assisted by Bishop Guilio Serafini, titular bishop of Lampsacus, and Archbishop Francesco Marchetti-Selvaggiani, titular archbishop of Seleucia. On February 25, 1931, Mooney was appointed apostolic delegate to Japan. He was appointed to the see of Rochester, New York, on August 28, 1933, and promoted to the metropolitan see of Detroit on May 31, 1937. He received the sacred pallium on December 16, 1937. In January 1946 he was created cardinal.

Edward F. Cardinal Mooney

Papal Diplomat

It was in India that Mooney first manifested his superb diplomatic skills. There he received into communion with Rome Mar Ivanios, Mar Theophilus, and eight Bethany monks, members of the Catholicos Party of the Jacobite Church. In 1930 he helped to solve the dispute between the Indian bishops of the native dioceses and the Portuguese missionaries on the east coast of India; he also ended Portuguese ecclesiastical control over some of India's Catholics, a problem that had festered for four centuries. Mooney helped to establish eleven new missionary territories and transferred three dioceses to native Indian bishops. In Japan in 1932 he ended a dilemma facing Japanese Catholics by deciding Catholics could attend Shinto shrines that were mandated by the civil government when he ruled that rites celebrated at these shrines were civil and not religious.

Role in the U.S. Church

Upon returning to the United States, Mooney served as a leader in many organizations of the Catholic hierarchy, including membership on the administrative board as chairman of the Social Action Department of the National Catholic Welfare Conference. In 1937 he became chairman of the Administrative Board of the NCWC, serving until 1945. At this post he was spokesman for the Catholic Church in the United States. He was first chairman of the Bishops' War Emergency and Relief Committee, first president of the National Catholic Community Service, and co-chairman of the Clergy Committee of the United Services Organization (USO).

Mooney's appointment to the metropolitan see of Detroit on May 31, 1937, coincided with the strife, intense for that time, in the automobile plants of the city caused by efforts to organize the workers into a union. Strongly supporting unionization with his statement that Catholics had an obligation to join unions, Mooney soon became a champion of the rights of the working class and of social justice.

Another major issue Mooney faced when he arrived in Detroit concerned the activities of Fr. Charles E. Coughlin, pastor of the Shrine of the Little Flower in Royal Oak, Michigan. Fr. Coughlin had gained a tremendous following with a weekly radio program and the publication of a weekly newspaper, *Social Justice*. At first it seemed Coughlin was devoted to social reform, but by 1937 he had become anti-Semitic, pro-Nazi, and a caustic critic of the policies of President Franklin D. Roosevelt. Coughlin drew widespread criticism from countless sources, yet is was this stance against the policies of the President that led to his silencing by the archbishop of Detroit and the Attorney General of the United States, acting in consort. Coughlin discontinued his radio program and his connection with *Social Justice*.

After World War II, Mooney greatly expanded the services and facilities of the archdiocese. During the first ten years of his episcopate, the Catholic population of the archdiocese went from one-half million people to one and one-third million people. He established one hundred new parishes, built schools and catechetical centers, social service centers, hospitals, and homes for persons in need. He opened St. John Provincial Seminary in 1949.

St. John Seminary had its own private golf course for the priests of the archdiocese. Mooney justified its construction by saying that a priest with a high score was neglecting his golf game—too low a score meant he was neglecting his priestly duties. Cardinal Mooney, unlike many of his brother bishops, was a trained theologian with an earned doctorate from the Propaganda College in Rome. In September 1935 he gave one of the major addresses at the National Eucharistic Congress held that year in his home diocese of Cleveland. His topic was "The Mystical Body of Christ and Its Implications for All Believers." This address, delivered seven years before Pope Pius XII's encyclical on the same subject, was filled with so many aspects of the encyclical, given in the same phrasing as the encyclical, that many have wondered whether the two documents were somehow connected.

Mooney died on October 25, 1958, in Rome during the conclave that elected Pope John XXIII.

See also COUGHLIN, CHARLES EDWARD; MICHIGAN, CATHOLIC CHURCH IN; NATIONAL CATHOLIC WELFARE CONFERENCE.

Tentler, Leslie Woodcock. *Seasons of Grace: A History of the Catholic Archdiocese of Detroit.* Detroit: Wayne State University Press, Great Lakes Books Edition, 1990.

NELSON J. CALLAHAN

MOORE, THOMAS VERNER (1877–1969)

Priest, ethicist, religious founder, psychiatrist, and writer. Thomas Verner Moore was born in Louisville, Kentucky, October 22, 1877.

Early Career

Thomas Verner Moore entered the Paulist community at St. Paul's College in Washington, D.C., in 1896 and was ordained a priest in 1901. He received permission from his superiors to study psychology at The Catholic University of America in Washington, D.C.; he received his Ph.D. from the university in 1903 and began to teach there under Dr. Edward A. Pace. In 1904–05 Moore studied in Leipzig in the Psychological Institute of Wilhelm Wundt. He began the study of medicine at Georgetown Medical School in 1910 and then did further medical and psychological studies in Munich under Oswald Kulpe. He received his M.D. from Johns Hopkins University in 1915. During World War I Moore served as an officer in the medical corps; he also ministered as chaplain to Catholic troops. After the war he resumed teaching at The Catholic University of America.

Founder of St. Anselm's Abbey

Moore was convinced of the value of psychiatry for improving the human situation, but he also recognized that psychiatry, as it was generally practiced, neglected the religious dimension of the human make-up and lost much of its power to be effective in the process. This recognition no doubt contributed toward his dream of founding a community of priest-scholars who should work in conjunction with The Catholic University of America—men whose religious lives would be integrated with the scientific research in various fields that they would pursue. He judged that the Benedictines, and precisely the English Benedictine Congregation (E.B.C.), would be the order best suited for this kind of life. He was able to find other men to share this vision and began laying plans to see it realized. But finding an E.B.C. community that would allow a group to enter together, go through the novitiate, and be professed to that community, with the previous intention of returning to America, was no easy task. After being turned down by some of the major E.B.C. houses in England, Moore and his group were accepted by St. Benedict's Abbey, Fort Augustus, Scotland. After their profession they returned to America with some members of the Fort Augustus community and founded, in 1924, St. Anselm's Priory (later Abbey) in Washington, D.C.

Psychiatry and Religion

Moore resumed his teaching at The Catholic University of America. Altogether he taught there for almost fifty years and eventually became chairman of the Department of Psychiatry and Psychology. In addition to teaching and lecturing, Moore carried on much of his apostolate through his writings. Although he was an accomplished scholar in the field of his specialization, a field he entered only after ordination, it was his religious interests that led him to the desire to combine the forces of science and religion to cure the ills of the mind; thus many of his specialized works relate mental health to religion. Given the areas of his special studies and teaching, it is not surprising that the lion's share of his publications relate to psychiatry, psychology, and psychoanalysis, but his explicitly religious concerns also surface in his writings, for much of his attention was turned directly to prayer and ethics, areas in which he published major works. An area of special interest was child psychology, and Moore founded at The Catholic University of America a center for the treatment of children with mental or emotional problems. He was also instrumental in founding St. Gertrude's School, operated for many years by the Benedictine sisters from the Duluth community, for developmentally disabled girls.

Benedictine and Carthusian Life

Moore's ideal of combining prayer and scholarship in one life, which had led to the founding of St. Anselm's, was amply realized in his own life. His scholarly research, teaching, and writing did not hinder his living the full monastic schedule in the monastery he had been instrumental in founding. In 1939 he became prior there and so combined the administration of this religious community with his many other activities; his conferences on prayer to the monks there are proclaimed memorable by all who heard them. Moore's deeply contemplative spirit led him in later years to join the Carthusians. He resigned his position at The Catholic University of America, effective October 1947, but already in January of that year, at the age of seventy, Moore left for Spain. He taught a semester at the University of Madrid (his *Conferencias de psicologia dinamica* was published in 1948) and immediately afterward entered the Charterhouse at Mira Flores. He returned to the United States in 1950 and helped found the first charterhouse in America. He returned to Mira Flores

in 1960 and continued living the Carthusian life until his death on June 5, 1969, at the age of ninety-one. He is buried there and is commemorated in a cenotaph in the cemetery of St. Anselm's Abbey.

Writings

As was intimated above, Moore was a prolific writer; he authored more than twenty books and nearly one hundred articles in the areas of his specializations. His published works appeared over at least fifty-nine years, beginning in 1904. Several of his titles (especially *Historical Introduction to Ethics, Dynamic Psychology, Cognitive Psychology, Principles of Ethics,* and *Driving Forces of Human Nature*) were used extensively as textbooks. His latest works appeared after he had become a Carthusian; one of them does not bear his name but is attributed simply to "A Carthusian Monk."

Diamond, R. "Moore, Thomas Verner." *New Catholic Encyclopedia.* Vol. 16. *Supplement 1967–1974.* New York: McGraw-Hill, 1974.

Knapp, Terry J. "T. V. Moore and His *Cognitive Psychology* of 1939." *Psychological Report* 57 (1985) 1311–6.

Misiak, Henryk, and Virginia M. Stout. *Catholics in Psychology: A Historical Survey.* New York: McGraw-Hill, 1954.

Roth, Bruce M. "Development of Psychology at the Catholic University of America." *Journal of the Washington Academy of Sciences* 82 (September 1994) 133–59.

JOSEPH JENSEN, O.S.B.

MORAN, MARY CONCILIA (1930–90)

Religious superior. Anne Amelia (Mary Concilia) Moran was born August 7, 1930, in Altoona, Pennsylvania. She and her twin brother, Joseph, were baptized three days later. Her parents, Elmer and Velma Ivory Moran, were first-generation Irish-Americans whose own parents had come from County Cork, Ireland, in the nineteenth century. Anne Moran entered the Sisters of Mercy of the Union, Scranton province, in the fall of 1948 and pronounced final vows in that congregation six years later on August 16, 1954.

A woman of many talents and warm personality, Concilia Moran taught elementary students, served as director of nursing, and, later, as a hospital administrator. The Scranton Sisters of Mercy, recognizing her vision and leadership qualities, elected her in 1970 to shepherd their eight-hundred-member province in the challenging years of post-Vatican II renewal. One year later, however, she was elected the youngest administrator general of the six-thousand-member congregation of the Sisters of Mercy of the Union. She served in that position from 1971 until 1977.

Concilia Moran's most visible contributions can be found in Catholic health-care arenas where she challenged both institutions and religious congregations to reevaluate the role of religious sponsors and the fundamental purpose of Catholic health care. "We need to remember," she wrote, "that the inspiration for all ministry is ultimately the Gospel. We are beginning to hear the Gospel differently today. . . . [T]he ultimate call to ministry is essentially the call to change society." She urged collaboration among Catholic health-care providers and identification of mission and values. Within her own congregation she was instrumental in the creation of Mercy health-care systems. After her leadership service, Concilia Moran joined the staff of one such system (Sisters of Mercy Health Corporation in Farmington Hills, Michigan), where she created a system-wide program of ministerial development. This program has became a model for mission effectiveness in the United States and abroad.

Concilia Moran died on January 7, 1990, after a long and courageous struggle with cancer. She was eulogized as an improvisor—as one generous, undismayed, and careful not to say anything too final.

See also SISTERS OF MERCY OF THE AMERICAS (R.S.M.).

HELEN MARIE BURNS, R.S.M.

MORANVILLÉ, JOHN (1760–1824)

Missionary, pastor. John Moranvillé was sent to Guiana in 1784, where he worked mostly among slaves and Native Americans until the French Revolution reached that colony. Then the people elected him to the colonial assembly, which elected him as its president. As no one elected was allowed to refuse, he accepted, hoping to prevent excesses. But in 1793 the assembly imposed a schismatic oath. He took it and committed excesses himself. Then, coming to his senses, he repudiated his oath and fled in December 1794, via Surinam to Baltimore. Throughout his life he did severe but voluntary penance for his aberration. In 1804 he became pastor of St. Patrick's Church, Baltimore, serving both whites and blacks. He built a beautiful church and opened the first parochial school in the diocese.

He gave most of his salary to poor families; he rose at 4:00 A.M. for three hours of prayer and never allowed his room to be heated. Sick calls received immediate attention, regardless of weather or distance. When yellow fever struck his parish, he was the only clergyman who stayed, caring for the sick. Twice he contracted the disease. The second attack left him permanently weakened, so that he resigned in 1823.

When his physician prescribed "native air," he dutifully traveled to France. Fearing for Moranvillé's life, Archbishop Maréchal wrote: "His loss would be a greater calamity than that of twenty ordinary priests." Moranvillé died in May 1824 in "the odor of sanctity," as the ancient phrase goes. Yesteryear's "shepherd in the mist" has grown to full stature and is revered as a distinguished member of the Congregation of the Holy Ghost.

Campbell, Bernard U. "Memoir of Reverend J. F. Moranvillé." *The United States Catholic Magazine* (1842) 434.
Koren, Henry J., C.S.SP. *The Serpent and the Dove: A History of the Congregation of the Holy Ghost in the United States, 1745–1984.* Pittsburgh: Spiritus Press, 1985.

HENRY J. KOREN, C.S.SP.

MORIARTY, PATRICK EUGENE (1805–75)

Friar, pastor, educator. Patrick Eugene Moriarty was born on July 4, 1805, in Dublin, Ireland. He entered the Order of St. Augustine in 1822 and was ordained in Rome in January of 1828. After returning to Ireland in July of 1829, he was appointed procurator of the Dublin community. In 1835 he went to serve at Madras, India, until 1838, when he was appointed vicar, prior, and pastor of St. Augustine Church, Philadelphia.

Patrick E. Moriarty

A great orator, Moriarty was frequently in demand up and down the Atlantic seaboard for preaching engagements. He also accomplished much good at St. Augustine's, establishing societies to deal with alcoholism and to expand the intellectual and cultural horizons of his parishioners. In 1842, seeing the need for educating future Augustinians as well as the laity, Moriarty purchased the land for Villanova College.

Between 1844 and 1850 he held several high-ranking offices in the order, as well as engaging in the reform of the Irish province. When he returned to the United States, among other things, he became commissary general of the order, served as president of Villanova College, and lent his considerable rhetorical and polemical gifts to the cause of the Fenian Brotherhood in Ireland against the British presence there. Moriarty lived all but the last few months of his life as a pastor, contributing to the Philadelphia *Catholic Record* and writing a biography of St. Augustine. He died at Villanova July 10, 1875.

See also AUGUSTINIANS (O.S.A.).

Ennis, Arthur J. *No Easy Road: The Early Years of the Augustinians in the United States 1796–1874.* New York: Peter Lang Publishing, 1993.

EDWARD ENRIGHT, O.S.A.

MORLEY, HUGH (1908–78)

Capuchin journalist. Hugh Morley, O.F.M. Cap., was born Michael Joseph Morley in upper Manhattan, New York, on October 17, 1908, to Michael Morley and Bridget Leonard, one of five children. After attending All Saints Grammar School and All Hallows High School, he completed his secondary education at Mary Immaculate Seraphicate, Glenclyffe, Garrison, New York. In August 1928 he entered the Capuchin novitiate where he was given the religious name Hugh; one year later he professed his temporary vows. His philosophical and theological formation took place at St. Anthony Friary, Marathon, Wisconsin. He professed final vows on November 23, 1932. Three years later, on June 16, 1935, he was ordained to the priesthood.

During his formation, Morley was so involved in journalistic projects that his superiors sent him to Sacred Heart Friary, Yonkers, New York; from there he traveled each day to New York's Columbia Graduate School of Journalism. After receiving a master's degree in journalism, he began his editorial career. Between 1937 and 1974 he was editor of *The Seraphic Chronicle, The Mission Almanac, The Cowl,* and *View,* and was a frequent contributor in the Catholic press and an active member of the Catholic Press Association. He was appointed to the board of directors of the association from 1952 to 1960 and was its treasurer from 1958 to 1960. In 1962 Dr. Raimondo Manzini, editor of *L'Osservatore Romano* and president of the International Catholic Union of the Press, appointed Morley the permanent representative at the United Nations of the International Catholic Union of the Press, a position he held until his death in 1978. In this role he became actively involved in UNESCO and the Conférence des Organisations Internationales Catholiques. As a member of the union's council, he attended its European meetings and was eventually elected American delegate to the World Congresses of the Catholic Press in New York, Berlin, Luxembourg, Buenos Aires, and Vienna. He became a widely known figure at the United Nations, promoting the views and interests of the Catholic Church in the area of communications in the international community. Throughout these commitments, Morley served his Capuchin brothers for nine years as provincial councilor and, in 1970, narrowly missed being chosen their provincial.

Shortly before his death, Morley was appointed the executive director of the Information Centers of the International Catholic Organizations at the United Nations in Paris and New York. In this position he effectively gathered and disseminated information for and about various international Catholic organizations at the United Nations and was continuously praised for bringing the spirit of St. Francis to the United Nations' institutions. On January 30, 1978, he was hospitalized with a severe case of blood poisoning, which doctors were unable to treat. He died on March 8, 1978, and was buried in the Capuchin cemetery at Sacred Heart Friary, Yonkers, New York. Knowledge of his death brought widespread recognition of his untiring and unassuming efforts at the United Nations and praise of his honest and responsible presentation of gospel values in the spirit of Francis of Assisi.

See also FRANCISCANS (CAPUCHINS).

REGIS J. ARMSTRONG, O.F.M. CAP.

MOUNT SAINT MARY'S COLLEGE AND SEMINARY

The second-oldest Catholic college and theologate in the United States, Mount Saint Mary's of Emmitsburg, Maryland, dates from the year 1808. Founding father and first president Fr. John Dubois had previously fled revolutionary France in 1791 and had been appointed by Bishop John Carroll as circuit-riding missionary in central Maryland and the Blue Ridge.

Founding Father John Dubois

In what is present-day Frederick County, Maryland, Fr. Dubois acquired a small tract of land on the side of a mountain, which local residents had already named Mount Saint Mary's. It was here, at his intended retreat, that he first built a parish church (1806) and conducted a school for local children. He founded a *petit séminaire* in 1808 at the urging of the Baltimore Sulpicians with whom he wished to affiliate himself.

Mother Seton arrived at Mount Saint Mary's in the summer of 1809 and resided in Fr. Dubois' log cabin while her sisters' own stone farmhouse in the valley below was being put into order. Because of the priest's experience with the work of the Daughters of Charity in France, it was a modified version of their rule that Mother Seton's Sisters of Charity eventually adopted as their own.

Mount Saint Mary's second founding father, Simon-Gabriel Bruté de Rémur, came to Emmitsburg in 1812, and, with the exception of the years 1814–18, remained there until he was named bishop of Vincennes, Indiana, in 1834. An expatriate Frenchman like Dubois, Bruté arrived in the United States in 1810 to engage in Sulpician seminary work in Baltimore. In Emmitsburg he became chaplain to the sisters, spiritual confidant of Mother Seton, parish priest, and teacher of theology and philosophy.

Although the express purpose of the *petit séminaire* was the preparation of young men for entrance into the Sulpician theologate in Baltimore, Dubois was forced by precarious finances to accept any paying student who presented himself. While officially titled Mount Saint Mary's Seminary until it was chartered as a college by the state of Maryland in 1830, the institution, from its earliest days, trained students for both ecclesiastical and secular careers.

As a measure of economy, Dubois adopted the policy whereby older boys helped teach the younger. While lessening the need for university-trained faculty, this necessitated retaining students beyond the point when the Sulpicians of Baltimore were prepared to accept them. Although essential for the survival of the *petit séminaire,* this policy resulted in considerable animosity between Dubois and his Sulpician superiors. It was not until after 1820 that Dubois received permission from Archbishop Ambrose Maréchal of Baltimore to offer a full theological course to seminarians. With the departure of Dubois in 1826 to head the New York diocese, and of Bruté in 1834, the period of Mount Saint Mary's infancy came to a close.

Later Developments

In the decades preceding the Civil War, Mount Saint Mary's began drawing more and more of its students from beyond the borders of Maryland and Pennsylvania. By the 1850s, the port cities of the South as well as those of the Caribbean furnished a significant portion of the enrollment.

While the seminary population remained largely intact during the Civil War, the college student body shrank substantially. Older boys served in uniform, while their younger brothers were increasingly kept home by parents who feared for their safety. The war ruined many Southern families and prevented the payment of their accumulated debts to the college. College finances teetered on the brink of disaster for the ensuing decade and a half, and led to the entire institution's being placed into receivership in 1881.

After liquidating the last of its debts, Mount Saint Mary's entered its second century with a new seminary building, large new campus chapel, and a sports facility that was the envy of many larger schools. In spite of the closing of the high school or "prep" section in 1936, expansion of student numbers continued until the outbreak of World War II. While most of the student body enlisted in the armed

services, Mount Saint Mary's remained open to train naval officers as part of the V-5 and V-12 programs.

The decades of the 1950s and 1960s were marked by further building projects and a corresponding increase in student numbers. With the closing of St. Joseph's College in Emmitsburg at the end of the 1971–72 school year, Mount Saint Mary's welcomed full-time women students to its classrooms for the first time. By the 1990s, enrollment in the liberal arts college and its graduate school of business administration stood at approximately 1,650. At this time the seminary was training some 150 men for the priesthood.

The National Shrine Grotto of Our Lady of Lourdes stands on the mountainside behind the college and seminary. Originally a place of private meditation for students and faculty, the site was embellished with a replica of the Lourdes Grotto in 1879. It was much esteemed by the late Amleto Cardinal Cicognani, former apostolic delegate to the United States, who urged that it be opened to pilgrims in time for the centenary of the Lourdes apparitions in 1958. It now draws many thousands of visitors annually.

By the end of the nineteenth century Mount Saint Mary's Seminary earned for itself the title "Cradle of Bishops." Despite the modest numbers of its seminarians, it succeeded by 1900 in giving twenty-nine bishops to the Church, including John Hughes, graduate of 1826 and first archbishop of New York, and John McCloskey, first American cardinal, a graduate of 1834. Since its inception, the seminary has furnished over two thousand priests to the Church in this country. Approximately half of these are presently (1995) alive and laboring in the ministry.

See also SEMINARIES (DIOCESAN).

Ledoux, Albert H. *A Walking Tour of Mount Saint Mary's College and Seminary.* Emmitsburg, Md.: Mt. St. Mary's, 1988.

Meline, Mary M., and F. X. McSweeney. *The Story of the Mountain.* Emmitsburg, Md.: Weekly Chronicle, 1911.

Shaw, Richard. *John Dubois: Founding Father.* Yonkers, N.Y.: United States Catholic Historical Society, 1983.

ALBERT H. LEDOUX

MOUTON, JEAN BAPTIST (1831–78)

Missionary. John Baptist Mouton was born in Maumusson, Département of the Loire Atlantique, France, on March 7, 1831. He studied at the seminary in Nantes and was ordained on January 31, 1859.

Mouton arrived in Natchez, Mississippi, on May 2, 1859, and initially was assigned to Sulphur Springs. From 1861 to 1878 he served as pastor in the vast area of northeastern Mississippi, residing at different times in Jackson, Columbus, Macon, Meridian, Aberdeen, Corinth, and finally Yazoo City, and "visiting distant and difficult missions and most successfully bringing souls to the knowledge and practice of the truth" (Bishop William Elder, October 2, 1873).

Mouton assisted the wounded at Corinth following the battle of Shiloh (April 6–7, 1862). His commission as a Confederate chaplain to the military hospitals along the Mobile and Ohio Railroad in eastern Mississippi was dated August 4, 1862; he served these hospitals throughout the remainder of the war.

Mouton designed and/or built, completed, improved (sometimes with his own hands) churches at Aberdeen, Columbus, Corinth, Iuka, Macon, Meridian, and Yazoo City. He possibly designed St. Francis Xavier's Academy (1869) and the rectory (1870) in Vicksburg. "He saw the church building as an indispensable catalyst for inspiring parishioners" (Fazio, 2).

In 1876 Bishop Elder proposed Mouton to fill the vacant episcopal see at neighboring Natchitoches, Louisiana. In 1877 Mouton became pastor of St. Mary's in Yazoo City. He died there on August 31, 1878, during a virulent yellow fever epidemic that also took the lives of three local Sisters of Charity. "Held in the highest esteem by all denominations, this great missionary laid the foundations of the Catholic Church in Northeastern Mississippi" (Gerow, 216).

See also MISSISSIPPI, CATHOLIC CHURCH IN.

Elder Correspondence and History Files, Archives, Diocese of Jackson (ADJ).

Fazio, Michael. "Father John Baptist Mouton; Builder-Priest of Mississippi." Sesquicentennial lecture, Natchez, September 21, 1987 (copy in ADJ).

Gerow, Richard O. *Catholicity in Mississippi.* Natchez, Miss.: Diocese of Natchez, 1939.

Pillar, James L. *The Catholic Church in Mississippi, 1837–1865.* New Orleans: Hauser Press, 1964.

Vally, Louis. "An East Mississippi Pastor." *Messenger of the Sacred Heart* 3, New Series (January 1888) (copy in ADJ).

CHARLES E. NOLAN

MOYLAN, STEPHEN (1737–1811)

General, businessman. Stephen Moylan was born in County Cork, Ireland. The son of John Moylan, a successful merchant, he entered the shipping business after settling in Lisbon, Portugal, in 1765. He emigrated to Philadelphia in 1768 where he soon prospered as a merchant. Assuming an active role in Philadelphia's growing Irish community, he helped to found the Friendly Sons of St. Patrick, serving as its first president in 1771.

When war was declared in 1775, Moylan was named muster master of the Continental Army, largely through the influence of his friend John Dickinson. By the following spring, he had been appointed Washington's aide-de-camp. In June 1776 Moylan was named quartermaster general by the Continental Congress with the rank of colonel. He resigned his commission the following September and returned to Washington's staff as a volunteer. In January 1777 he was commissioned to raise a regiment of light Dragoons from Pennsylvania that was placed under the command of Polish officer Count Casimir Pulaski. Quarreling between the two men ended with Moylan being brought up on court-martial charges of insubordination and disrespectful language. He was acquitted on all charges and returned to serve with the main army for the rest of the war, being present at both Valley Forge and Yorktown. He was awarded a brevet as brigadier general for his service.

Moylan returned to Philadelphia after the war to resume his career. He acted as recorder of Chester County, Pennsylvania, in 1792, and was appointed Pennsylvania commissioner of loans by Washington in 1793. He died in Philadelphia on April 13, 1811.

TRICIA T. PYNE

MUDD, SAMUEL (1833–83)

Physician. Samuel Alexander Mudd was born at Oak Hill Farm, Maryland, on December 21, 1933. A member of a distinguished Maryland Catholic family, he studied at St. John's College, Frederick, Maryland, and graduated from Georgetown University, Washington, D.C., in 1854. He then pursued the study of medicine at Baltimore Medical College of the University of Maryland and began practicing medicine after graduating in 1856.

The following year he married Sarah Frances Dyer and built a home, Rock Hill Farm, on land adjacent to his father's farm near Bryantown, Maryland. Mudd owned

Samuel Mudd

slaves who worked in his tobacco fields and, consequently, was sympathetic to the Confederacy during the Civil War.

Mudd's path into historical annals began on November 20, 1864, during a chance encounter with John Wilkes Booth at St. Mary Church, Bryantown. Booth supposedly was interested in purchasing land, and Mudd invited him to stay at his home. On December 23, Mudd and Booth also happened to meet in Washington, D.C.

On April 15, 1865, Booth stopped at Mudd's home while fleeing authorities after having killed President Abraham Lincoln. Mudd treated Booth's broken leg and was later arrested for complicity in the assassination plot.

Mudd swore that he had not recognized Booth, who, he claimed, was wearing a false beard. Mudd was arrested and arraigned with the other alleged conspirators. The testimony of Louis J. Weichmann was instrumental in convicting Mudd of involvement in the conspiracy. He was sentenced to life imprisonment on June 30, 1865, and sent to Fort Jefferson, Dry Tortugas, in the Gulf of Mexico.

Although he was treated inhumanely by the prison staff, Mudd used his medical skills during a yellow fever epidemic in 1867 after the army surgeons had died. After news of his heroic efforts leaked to family members and friends, a campaign was initiated to gain his freedom. In 1869 he was granted a pardon by President Andrew Johnson.

Mudd returned home and resumed his medical practice. However, while visiting patients during the winter of 1882, he contracted pneumonia and died on January 10, 1883, at Rock Hill Farm. He was buried at St. Mary Church Cemetery, Bryantown. His trial and conviction continue to be a source of contention among scholars, and his descendants remain steadfast in their belief of his innocence and that his conviction was a miscarriage of justice.

Mudd, Nettie, ed. *Life of Samuel A. Mudd.* New York and Washington, D.C.: Neale Publishing Co., 1906.

Sifakis, Stewart. *Who Was Who in the Civil War.* New York: Facts on File Publications, 1988, 461–62.

MARIANNA McLOUGHLIN

MUDSE, LEONARD (1901–78)

Capuchin lay brother. Leonard (Anthony Joseph) Mudse was born on September 19, 1901, in Troy, New York, the son of Mitro (Matthew) Mudse and Mary Hopkins (nee Hopko), both of Ukrainian origin. Poverty and the sudden accidental death of his father forced the two-year-old boy to be brought up by the Christian Brothers, who raised him until his graduation from Troy's LaSalle Institute. As a young man, Mudse did clerical work for the New York Central Railroad, *The New York Times,* Western Electric, General Motors, and Bell Telephone. Throughout these years, he continually developed his skill in playing base-

ball and, in 1931, was accepted by the farm team of the Cleveland Indians. At the same time, Anthony met the Capuchins of St. John's Church on West 31st Street, New York, and asked to become a lay brother. Suspecting that their brother would find happiness only among the friars, Anthony's sisters delayed informing him of his acceptance by the Cleveland Indians and rejoiced when, in 1932, he was invested with the Capuchin habit and received the name Leonard.

During the following forty-six years, "Joe" Leonard lived in Detroit, Milwaukee, New York, Brooklyn, and Interlaken, New York, and held many of the positions traditionally fulfilled by Capuchin lay brothers: sacristan, cook, maintenance man, and, above all, porter. As a porter he met a large number and wide variety of people and developed friendships with employees of many of the firms he had served as a young man, inspiring many to become Catholics or, like himself, to enter religious life. Throughout these years, Mudse's passion for baseball was rivaled only by his love for opera in that he developed an encyclopedic knowledge of batting and pitching averages as well as of the identities of the best performers for the best operas. He was a well-known figure not only at New York's Yankee and Shea Stadiums, but also at its opera houses and concert halls. Managers, stars, and, more frequently, ushers and maintenance personnel of both the sports' and musical worlds considered themselves his friends.

Because of countless hours as porter and his engaging personality, Mudse raised large sums of money for Capuchin missionaries throughout the world. His own province of New York-New England was the primary recipient of Mudse's dedication and was therefore able to sustain missions in Japan, the Mariana Islands, and Central America. Missionaries of many religious congregations, however, benefited from his zeal, as well as the countless poor and homeless who begged at the friary doors.

Plagued by a weak heart, Mudse spent his last years in the Capuchin formation fraternity in Garrison, New York, where he colorfully inspired the young friars with a love of the joyful side of the Capuchin Franciscan life. He died there on July 26, 1978, and was buried in the Capuchin cemetery at Sacred Heart, Yonkers, New York.

See also FRANCISCANS (CAPUCHINS).

REGIS J. ARMSTRONG, O.F.M. CAP.

MUENCH, ALOISIUS JOSEPH (1889–1962)

Cardinal archbishop, papal diplomat. Aloisius Joseph Muench was born in Milwaukee, Wisconsin, on February 18, 1889, to German immigrants Joseph and Theresa Kraus Muench. He attended St. Francis Seminary and was ordained on June 8, 1913. He was engaged in pastoral work until 1919 when he earned an M.A. degree at the Uni-

Aloisius Joseph Cardinal Muench

versity of Wisconsin. In 1921 he earned a doctoral degree *summa cum laude* from the University of Fribourg in Switzerland. After auditing classes at Oxford, Cambridge, Louvain, and the Sorbonne, he returned to St. Francis Seminary as professor of dogmatic theology in 1922, and served as rector from 1929 to 1935.

On August 10, 1935, Pius XI appointed Muench third bishop of Fargo; his consecration took place on October 15 of that year. He set up the Catholic Church Expansion Fund, founded a diocesan paper, *The Catholic Action News,* began the Priests Mutual Aid Fund, and in 1941 convened the first diocesan synod. Muench also served two terms as president of the Rural Life Conference.

His 1946 pastoral letter, "One World in Charity," insisted on mercy and compassion for the people of the defeated nations of Germany and Japan because charity, not revenge, was civilization's most successful builder. That year Pope Pius XII appointed Muench apostolic visitor to West Germany, where he also headed the Papal Commission for Displaced Persons. Muench also served as military vicar for the NCWC. In 1950 he became titular archbishop of Selembryia, and from 1951 to 1959 was papal nuncio to West Germany and dean of the diplomatic corps. When named cardinal in 1959, Muench resigned as bishop of Fargo to become the first American to hold office in the Curia. He died in Rome on February 15, 1962.

See also GERMAN CATHOLICS IN AMERICA.

Barry, Colman J., O.S.B. *American Nuncio.* Collegeville: The Liturgical Press, 1969.

JOHN WHITNEY EVANS

MULDOON, PETER (1862–1927)

Bishop. Peter Muldoon was born in the mining town of Columbia, California, on October 10, 1862. Later the family settled in Stockton. Muldoon received his college education at St. Mary's College in Lebanon, Kentucky, where his uncle, a priest, was on the faculty. During the summers he stayed with his uncle in Tennessee, where he met Bishop Patrick Feehan of Nashville. When Feehan became the first archbishop of Chicago, Muldoon's uncle joined the Chicago clergy. Peter, a student at St. Mary's Seminary, Baltimore, also asked to join the archdiocese. Archbishop Feehan accepted him. He completed his seminary training and was ordained on December 18, 1886. Archbishop Feehan assigned the new priest to St. Pius parish. Within a few months, Feehan made Muldoon his secretary and later named him as chancellor.

Peter Muldoon

In addition to his normal pastoral duties, Muldoon played a prominent role in archdiocesan activities. He was the chairman of the board of directors for the archdiocesan newspaper, *The New World.* He worked on the Catholic education exhibit for the 1893 Columbian Exposition. His experience and his close association with Archbishop Feehan made Muldoon a potential candidate for the episcopacy.

Auxiliary Bishop of Chicago

Because of Archbishop Feehan's age and ill health, Fr. Alexander McGavick was named as the first auxiliary for Chicago. When McGavick also became ill, Feehan requested that Rome name Muldoon as a second auxiliary.

The appointment of Muldoon created a controversy in Chicago. A number of Irish-born priests in the archdiocese resented Muldoon's advancement. Three Chicago priests, Thomas Cashman, Thomas Hodnett, and Hugh Smyth, wrote a letter to the apostolic delegate in January 1901 accusing Muldoon of immorality and drunkenness. Another twenty Irish-born priests in the archdiocese also signed the letter. Although one of the signers, Jeremiah Crowley, presented the case against Muldoon to the apostolic delegate, the charges were dismissed. Crowley then resigned his parish in protest over Muldoon's appointment. In this rancorous atmosphere, Muldoon was consecrated on July 25, 1901. Muldoon later confided to a friend that he expected some act of violence because of threats made against him.

The controversy left some bishops wondering if Feehan had lost control. Bishop John Lancaster Spalding (Peoria) reported to Rome that ecclesiastical affairs were in terrible shape in Chicago. He urged an investigation by the apostolic delegate. Although Feehan was exonerated, he did not live long after the investigation. After Feehan's death on July 12, 1902, the selection of a replacement occupied the attention of the American bishops. Muldoon's close association with Feehan made the new auxiliary bishop a potential candidate for the see. However, many archbishops considered Muldoon either too young and inexperienced or incapable of restoring peace among the clergy. With Muldoon's candidacy lacking episcopal support, the bishop of Buffalo, James Quigley, was chosen as Feehan's successor. Peter Muldoon served the new archbishop in the same capable manner as he had served Feehan. The new archbishop and the auxiliary played a crucial role in the establishment of the Catholic Church Extension Society in 1905. On September 28, 1908, Muldoon was named the first bishop of Rockford.

Bishop of Rockford

Education and social issues occupied Bishop Muldoon's attention in his first few years. The new bishop was a strong supporter of labor unions from his time in Chicago. In Rockford, he supported the social center established by the Catholic Women's League. He also continued his work with the Social Service Commission of the American Federation of Catholic Societies and his association with Fr. Peter Dietz on the commission.

After Archbishop Quigley's death in 1915, Muldoon was again a candidate for Chicago. Although he received strong support from Cardinal James Gibbons, the appointment went to George Mundelein. Although disappointed at not being selected, the following year Muldoon received word that he was to become the bishop of Monterey-Los Angeles. The Rockford priests petitioned Rome to have Muldoon stay. In June 1917 Muldoon received word from Rome that he would remain as the bishop of Rockford.

Muldoon and the NCWC

When the United States entered World War I in 1917, the American hierarchy organized the National Catholic War Council to coordinate Catholic efforts to support Catholic soldiers. Bishop Muldoon was named the chairman of the council and succeeded in gaining federal funds for Catholic support services. After the war Muldoon was one of the strongest episcopal voices arguing for the permanent establishment of a national Catholic organization to coordinate action on political matters. Muldoon persuaded Cardinal Gibbons and many American bishops to support a permanent organization at the September 1919 episcopal meeting that debated the question. Even with the approval of Pope Benedict XV and the support of Cardinal Gibbons, Cardinal William O'Connell (Boston), Archbishop Sebastian Messmer (Milwaukee), and Bishop Charles McDonnell (Brooklyn) strongly opposed the idea. Despite such opposition, the majority of the hierarchy wanted a permanent organization. Bishop Muldoon was named to the executive committee of the National Catholic Welfare Council (NCWC).

The vision of the permanent council was best expressed in the 1919 letter on "Social Reconstruction." The letter became a blueprint for Catholic social justice efforts in subsequent decades. Yet, the opposition to the council expressed in 1919 never really died out. By 1922 Cardinal O'Connell and others gained enough support in Rome so that a decree from the Holy See was issued that suppressed the council. The newly elected pope, Pius XI, had been persuaded to complete the unfinished business of his predecessor. The decree of suppression was one of those pieces of business. The administrative committee of the NCWC immediately sent a petition to Pius XI asking that he not publish the decree until they could present their case. Although Bishop Muldoon did not go to Rome to present the case, he played a key role in organizing the American hierarchy to protest the dissolution. He was part of the episcopal committee that drafted the petition to Pius XI to revoke the decree. By April 1922 their efforts succeeded in convincing Pius XI that the decree of suppression should be revoked. Bishop Muldoon's efforts on behalf of the NCWC showed his courage and dedication in service to the American Catholic Church.

With the NCWC's existence secured, Muldoon was able to turn his attention to some of the conference's activities. He served as the chairman of the important Social Action Department. One activity of the Social Action Department was the Catholic Conference on Industrial Problems that organized regional conferences to address various social and economic issues. Muldoon became the honorary president of this conference. Over the next few years, Muldoon attended to diocesan matters and promoted the work of the NCWC.

He participated in the 1926 Eucharistic Congress held in Chicago. A few days after the Eucharistic Congress ended, Bishop Muldoon suffered a burst appendix while attending the dedication of the new cathedral in St. Louis. He remained hospitalized in St. Louis until March 1927. Even when he returned to Rockford, he was confined to his bed. Since doctors could do little, his condition worsened. He died on October 8, 1927. Cardinal Mundelein officiated at his funeral, and his friend Archbishop Austin Dowling (St. Paul) preached the homily.

See also BURKE, JOHN JOSEPH; ILLINOIS, CATHOLIC CHURCH IN.

McKeown, Elizabeth. "The National Bishops' Conference: An Analysis of Its Origins." *Catholic Historical Review* 66 (October 1980) 565–83.

McManamin, Francis G. "Peter J. Muldoon, First Bishop of Rockford, 1862–1927." *Catholic Historical Review* 48 (October 1962) 365–78.

Miller, Robert R. *That All May Be One: A History of the Rockford Diocese.* Rockford, Ill.: Diocese of Rockford, 1976.

Shanabruch, Charles. *Chicago's Catholics: The Evolution of an American Identity.* University of Notre Dame Press, 1981.

Sheerin, John B. *Never Look Back: The Career and Concerns of John J. Burke.* New York: Paulist Press, 1975.

Slawson, Douglas J. *The Foundation and First Decade of the National Catholic Welfare Council.* Washington, D.C.: The Catholic University of America Press, 1992.

Sweeney, David Francis. *The Life of John Lancaster Spalding.* New York: Herder and Herder, 1965.

MARTIN ZIELINSKI

MULRY, THOMAS MAURICE (1855–1916)

Businessman, philanthropist, and first president of the Superior Council of the U.S. Society of St. Vincent de Paul. Thomas Maurice Mulry was born in New York City on February 13, 1855, the second of fourteen children born to Thomas and Parthenia Crolius Mulry. Following his education in New York at De La Salle Academy and old Cooper Union, Mulry became a business associate with his father as a building contractor. He was a successful businessman, and in 1906 became president of the Emigrant Industrial Savings Bank.

Mulry joined the Society of St. Vincent de Paul at the age of seventeen and was an active member his entire life. He took his vocation as a Catholic layperson very seriously and dedicated much of his time and money to charitable works. He was the first Catholic member of the Charity Organization Society, a group founded in 1882 that helped organize the work of 138 charitable groups. He was on the New York State Board of Charities (1907–16) and was one of three persons appointed by President Theodore Roosevelt to the first White House Conference on Children. Mulry became president of the Superior Council of the St. Vincent de Paul Society in 1915, which,

Thomas M. Mulry

under his leadership, helped unify the movement in the United States. He helped to establish the Catholic Home Bureau, the Fordham University School of Social Service, and the St. Elizabeth's Home for Convalescent Women and Girls.

Mulry's concern for charitable works for children was an extension of his family life. In 1880 Mulry married Mary E. Gallagher; the couple had thirteen children, of whom four sons entered the Society of Jesus and one daughter entered the Sisters of Charity. He died in New York City on March 10, 1916. In 1919 New York Archbishop Patrick Hayes described Mulry as "one who had done more in the interest of Christian Charity than any other American layman in his generation."

Cohalan, Florence D. *A Popular History of the Archdiocese of New York.* Yonkers, N.Y.: United States Catholic Historical Society, 1983.

Helmes, J. W. *Thomas M. Mulry: A Volunteer's Contribution to Social Work.* Washington, D.C.: The Catholic University of America Press, 1938.

Meehan, Thomas F. *Thomas Maurice Mulry.* New York: Encyclopedia Press, 1917.

RICHARD G. SMITH

MUNDELEIN, GEORGE CARDINAL (1872–1939)

Archbishop of Chicago and first American cardinal west of the Atlantic seaboard. George Mundelein was a consolidating bishop who centralized the administration of his archdiocese and set it on a firm financial footing, while tying it more closely to Rome. It was often remarked that he "put the Catholic Church of Chicago on the map."

George Cardinal Mundelein

Mundelein was born in New York City on July 2, 1872, the son of Francis Mundelein, a laborer, and Mary Goetz Mundelein, a housewife. Educated at Catholic elementary and secondary schools and at Manhattan College in New York, he pursued his seminary studies at St. Vincent's Archabbey in Latrobe, Pennsylvania, then at the Urban College of the Propaganda in Rome. He was ordained to the priesthood in Rome on June 8, 1895, and served first in the Diocese of Brooklyn. He received rapid promotion from his bishop, Charles McDonnell, becoming chancellor of the diocese after just two years as a priest, a monsignor at age thirty-four, and an auxiliary bishop at thirty-seven. At one time he simultaneously held ten different positions in the Brooklyn diocese.

Third Archbishop of Chicago

On December 9, 1915, Pope Benedict XV appointed Mundelein third archbishop of Chicago. He was installed in that city on February 9, 1916, the youngest Catholic archbishop in the United States at that time. Chicago was an important archdiocese, with the largest Catholic population in the United States, but it had a record of uncertain episcopal leadership and a rebellious clergy. Mundelein's assignment in Chicago was to assert papal and episcopal authority, discipline the clergy, centralize the administration, and increase fundraising. He succeeded in all these tasks and was widely noted for his business skills. One businessman remarked to him: "There was a great mistake in making you a Bishop instead of a financier, for in the latter case Mr. Morgan would not be without a rival in Wall Street."

Though a striking individual, Mundelein was also typical of a whole generation of Catholic bishops in the United States early in the twentieth century. In the years surrounding World War I, a number of American-born but Roman-trained bishops came to power in the largest urban dioceses of the United States. These men (some of the more notable, besides Mundelein, were William O'Connell in Boston and Denis Dougherty in Philadelphia) were consolidating bishops who, like their counterparts in American business and government, were searching for order in the administrations they headed. Simultaneously, they attempted to gain new respect for the American Catholic Church, both in Rome where their financial support became the mainstay of the Vatican, and in the United States where their business ability and political influence bolstered the self-image of their religious community and earned a sometimes grudging respect from non-Catholics.

In Chicago, Mundelein served as archbishop from 1916 until his death in 1939. He pursued a number of building projects, most notably Quigley Preparatory Seminary in downtown Chicago, completed in 1918, and St. Mary of the Lake Major Seminary in a rural location about forty miles north of the city. St. Mary of the Lake typifies Mundelein's attempt to make Catholic institutions first class in their fields. At a time when most Catholic seminaries were ramshackle affairs, Mundelein's architect laid out a lavish thousand-acre campus surrounding a small lake. All the buildings were of early-American design, with the main chapel a copy of a Congregational meetinghouse in Old Lyme, Connecticut, and the bishop's own residence modeled on George Washington's Mount Vernon. Mundelein attempted to show in brick and mortar that his Church could be both truly Catholic and truly American.

First Cardinal of the West

In 1924 Pope Pius XI named Mundelein to the College of Cardinals, the first American Cardinal from a city west of the Appalachians. Two years later, Cardinal Mundelein hosted the Twenty-eighth International Eucharistic Congress in Chicago. First held in France in 1881, the biannual congress had become a massive pilgrimage of priests, prelates, and laypeople. This devotional gathering had come to the Western Hemisphere only once before (to Montreal in 1910), and never to the United States. Over 800,000 people attended the final day's procession on the grounds of St. Mary of the Lake Seminary. This once-in-a-lifetime event is a good example of how Mundelein put the Catholic Church of Chicago on the map. Boosterism and civic pride overcame any anti-Catholic feelings on the part of non-Catholic Chicagoans, who took pride in the media attention lavished on their city in 1926.

Though Mundelein was similar to the other consolidating bishops in his financial prowess and his quest for publicity, he was more politically and socially liberal than most. His auxiliary bishop, Bernard J. Sheil, the founder of the Catholic Youth Organization, exercised considerable influence on Mundelein, and together they gave Chicago a reputation as a stronghold of liberal Catholicism. Mundelein reorganized and expanded the work of Catholic Charities in Chicago, encouraged Sheil in his wide-ranging social work projects, and appointed a liberal intellectual priest as rector of St. Mary's Seminary. Mundelein supported industrial union organizing at the time of the sit-down strikes in Detroit's auto plants, and Bishop Sheil addressed a rally of Chicago packing house workers in person.

Mundelein became a friend and supporter of President Franklin D. Roosevelt. The two met about a dozen times between 1933 and the time of the Cardinal's death, and they kept in close contact through personal couriers, most notably Roosevelt aide Thomas Corcoran. By chance, Corcoran happened to be at the Cardinal's residence the night Mundelein died. Mundelein hosted Roosevelt himself in Chicago on October 8, 1937, after the president delivered his "quarantine address" on foreign policy. The Mundelein-Roosevelt relationship was a useful one for both parties. The cardinal's support helped neutralize Catholic suspicions that the New Deal was radical or communistic, and Roosevelt's friendship gave Catholics a feeling of pride and self-confidence.

Though the Catholic Church was America's largest religious denomination as early as 1850, it lacked status and respect, both in Rome and in the United States. The leadership of Cardinal Mundelein and his generation of big-city bishops raised the status of American Catholics, giving them self-confidence and clout both at home and in the Vatican. Mundelein died in Chicago on October 2, 1939.

See also ILLINOIS, CATHOLIC CHURCH IN; NEW DEAL AND AMERICAN CATHOLICS, THE.

Mundelein's papers, consisting mostly of official administrative documents, are at the archives of the Archdiocese of Chicago.

Kantowicz, Edward R. *Corporation Sole: Cardinal Mundelein and Chicago Catholicism.* University of Notre Dame Press, 1983.

Shanabruch, Charles. *Chicago's Catholics.* University of Notre Dame Press, 1981.

EDWARD R. KANTOWICZ

MUNDELEIN SEMINARY

Mundelein Seminary is the major seminary and graduate school of theology for the Archdiocese of Chicago. In the last fifteen years, Mundelein Seminary has begun serving dioceses throughout the United States, as well as dioceses in Africa, South Africa, South Korea, and China. Since it opened its doors in 1921–22, the seminary has prepared over two thousand candidates for the priesthood. The seventy-five-year history of the seminary is a record of the development and achievement of great visions of the first cardinal of Chicago, George Cardinal Mundelein, and all of his successors, especially the late Joseph Cardinal Bernardin.

University of St. Mary of the Lake

The seminary has its beginnings in an earlier institution, the University of St. Mary of the Lake, founded in 1844 by William J. Quarter, the first bishop of Chicago. This earlier institution was originally located in the central area of Chicago and was staffed and administered by priests of the Holy Cross Congregation from Notre Dame, Indiana. This first institution of higher learning in the state of Illinois had an erratic history due to persistent financial problems and various administrative difficulties in establishing a full university. By 1868 the university had ceased to function as a major seminary. Its charter, however, was maintained and its board of directors was kept intact.

After James E. Quigley became archbishop of Chicago in 1902, he filed an application with the Illinois secretary of state for a reactivation of the seminary charter under the same title, University of St. Mary of the Lake. At that time, Archbishop Quigley sent five priests to Rome for advanced study to prepare to become the core faculty for the future university. Due to a number of circumstances, including financial concerns, no progress was made in reopening the University of St. Mary of the Lake until Archbishop Quigley's successor, George Mundelein, was promoted to the see of Chicago in December of 1915.

George Cardinal Mundelein

One of Archbishop Mundelein's earliest concerns when he arrived in Chicago was the establishment of an entire seminary system. In May 1916 Archbishop Mundelein announced plans to build a minor seminary in memory of his predecessor. At the same time, he expressed an interest in establishing a major seminary in the near future. By March 1918 Archbishop Mundelein had purchased several parcels of farmland in a town north of Chicago that later would bear his name. The land for the future seminary comprised nearly one thousand acres. Archbishop Mundelein hoped to establish a seminary that would be unequaled by any other seminary in the world.

On October 4, 1921, the new seminary opened its doors to its first students. The seminary was named St. Mary of the Lake Seminary and operated under the charter of the University of St. Mary of the Lake. It included a complex of fourteen major buildings that were constructed in the classic Georgian architecture often referred to as early American or colonial. The complex included private accommodations for 475 seminarians.

The course of studies at the new seminary embraced six years, the first two years being devoted to undergraduate studies in arts and sciences and the last four years being devoted to the study of theology. The teaching faculty consisted of Jesuit priests and the administration of the seminary was conducted by diocesan priests. The first rector of the seminary was J. Gerald Keeley, D.D., and the first director of studies was John B. Furay, S.J.

In September 1929, Cardinal Mundelein obtained from the Sacred Congregation of Seminaries and Universities in Rome a five-year grant for the theological faculty to confer the baccalaureate, the licentiate, and the doctorate in theology. In September 1934 this temporary grant was made permanent and the seminary faculty became the first American institution to be honored as a pontifical theological faculty under the new apostolic constitution, *Deus Scientiarum Dominus.*

Contemporary Developments

In 1961 Albert Cardinal Meyer redesigned the seminary system in the Archdiocese of Chicago. The University of St. Mary of the Lake opened a second campus in Niles, Illinois. The Niles campus offered a liberal arts program for the first two years of college, while the Mundelein campus program encompassed the last two years of college studies in philosophy, followed by a four-year theology curriculum.

Several years later, under the direction of John Cardinal Cody, the undergraduate program separated itself from the University of St. Mary of the Lake and became affiliated with Loyola University of Chicago.

The University of St. Mary of the Lake (now exclusively a school of theology and a seminary) and the ecclesiastical faculty began a revision of the graduate program and its theological curriculum. The program that resulted from that revision continued to be implemented for more than a decade.

In April of 1986, Cardinal Bernardin announced a new and exciting development for the University of St. Mary of the Lake. The university would not only include the major seminary that was serving nearly forty dioceses throughout the country, but it would now include a new Center for Development in Ministry, the sole purpose of which would be the ongoing development of those who were active in ministry. The University of St. Mary of the Lake would become an even more significant resource for those in ministry.

With the arrival of the Center for Development in Ministry, St. Mary of the Lake Seminary was renamed Mundelein Seminary to give it a clearer identity on the campus of the University of St. Mary of the Lake.

Presently, the University of St. Mary of the Lake is under the guidance of the chancellor. Mundelein Seminary is under the direction of the rector, the Rev. John Canary. The Center for Development in Ministry is under the directorship of the Rev. Wayne Prist. The entire campus is under the guidance of the board of advisors of the University of St. Mary of the Lake.

In September 1995 Mundelein Seminary began the academic year with an enrollment of 175 students, coming from thirty-seven dioceses throughout the United States, as well as dioceses in Uganda and China.

See also SEMINARIES (DIOCESAN).

MURPHY, FRANK (1890–1949)

Associate justice of the U.S. Supreme Court. Born in Harbor Beach, Michigan, on April 13, 1890, Murphy was educated in local public schools and at the University of Michigan, where he earned an A.B. degree in 1912 and L.L.B. degree in 1914. He became a law clerk and taught at Detroit College of Law before serving as a lieutenant and infantry captain during World War I. While in Europe, Murphy studied law at Lincoln's Inn, London, and at Trinity College, Dublin. Returning to Detroit in 1919, he became assistant U.S. attorney, taught law at the University of Detroit, and was elected judge of the Recorders' Court for two terms. In 1930 Murphy was elected mayor of Detroit. He was a strong supporter of President Roosevelt's New Deal. Murphy's support was rewarded two years later when Roosevelt appointed him governor general of the Philippine Islands; when the islands became autonomous in 1935, he was made high commissioner. In 1936 Murphy was elected governor of Michigan and served for three years. His settlement of the automobile workers' sit-down strike in Flint, Michigan, in 1937, in which he refused to enforce a court order compelling the strikers to return to work, brought Murphy national recognition, and one year after being defeated for reelection in 1938, he was named U.S. Attorney General by Roosevelt.

Murphy was an activist attorney general whose accomplishments included setting up a civil rights division in the Department of Justice. In 1940 he was nominated by Roosevelt to the Supreme Court where he served nine years and voted most often with the Court's liberal bloc. Never married, Murphy died in Detroit on July 19, 1949.

See also UNITED STATES SUPREME COURT AND CATHOLICS.

Fine, Sidney. *Frank Murphy.* Vol. 1, *The Detroit Years.* Vol. 2, *The New Deal Years.* Vol. 3, *The Washington Years.* Ann Arbor: University of Michigan Press, 1975–84.

Howard, J. Woodford. *Mr. Justice Murphy: A Political Biography.* Princeton, N.J.: Princeton University Press, 1968.

Lunt, Richard D. *The High Ministry of Government: The Political Career of Frank Murphy.* Detroit: Wayne State University Press, 1965.

K. N. McCARTHY

MURRAY, JANE MARIE (1896–1987)

Scholar, author, educator, and pioneer in religious education. Mary Winifred Murray was born in Freeport, Michigan, on March 18, 1896. She was orphaned at an early age and her education was subsequently entrusted to the Dominican Sisters of Grand Rapids. This association encouraged her own bent toward the intellectual life. As a young woman she chose to join the Dominican community in 1914. Murray's education continued amid teaching responsibilities. She completed a bachelor's degree at Michigan Central State College in 1925 and earned a master's degree in English from the University of Michigan in 1932. Her teaching and writing career spanned over fifty years, influencing high-school, college, and graduate students. In 1950 she became the first American woman to be awarded a licentiate in theology from the Pontifical Institute of Medieval Studies in Toronto.

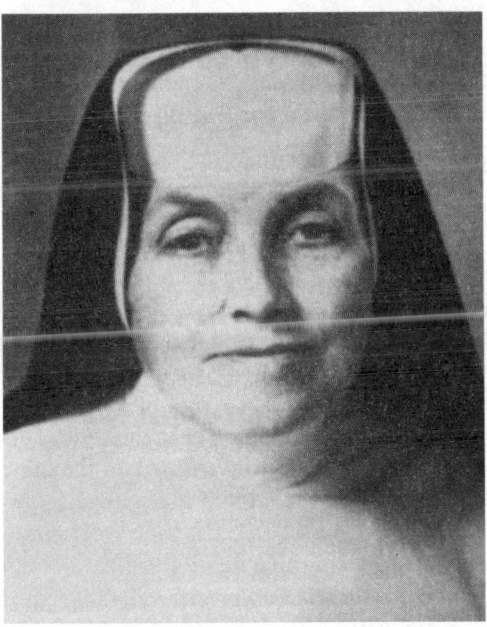

Jane Marie Murray

Murray identified the turning point of her life as a dialogue Mass celebrated in 1928. As a result she studied the writings of the liturgical movement and recognized the authenticity of its understanding of the mystery of Christ in the Church and in the Christian life. Her concern was to communicate that vision to young people in the Church. She and an experienced author, Estelle Hackett, O.P., approached Virgil Michel, O.S.B., a leader in the liturgical movement, about the need for catechetical materials in which the theology of Church was consistent with the Church's self-expression in the liturgy.

Within a year, *With Mother Church,* a series of supplementary books designed to involve students actively in the liturgy, was published for the elementary and secondary levels. Murray and Hackett, with Michel and Basil Stegmann, O.S.B., went on to publish *The Christ Life Series in Religion* (1934–35). It was recognized as launching a new stage in religious education by leaving the catechism genre and rediscovering the doctrinal, educational, and formational riches of the liturgical cycle.

Their original plan also envisioned a textbook series for students in high school and college, for which Murray wrote *The Life of Our Lord* (1942), *Living in Christ* (1946), and *Christ in His Church* (1952). In 1956 the National Liturgical Conference commissioned Murray to write *Full Measure of Grace* and *One Week of Grace* to introduce students to the newly restored liturgy of Holy Week. She went on to publish a high-school series, *The Christian Life Series* (1957–60).

Murray saw the connections between liturgy and life, between religion and culture. In the post-Vatican II era and at the age of seventy-five, she was actively involved in prison reform and was appointed to a state-level criminal council. In later years Murray received awards and recognition of her persistent effort to educate the Christians about liturgy and its integral connection to the Christian life. She died in Grand Rapids, Michigan, on July 22, 1987.

Murray, Jane Marie. "Involvement in the Liturgical Movement." Archives of Grand Rapids Dominicans, Oral History Audio Tape.
____. "The Liturgy the Way of Instruction." *Journal of Religious Instruction* 4 (1933) 245–54.
____, and Paul Marx. "The Liturgical Movement in the United States." *The Catholic Church U.S.A.,* ed. Louis Putz. Chicago: Fides Press, 1956, 301–14.
Oosdyke, M. K. "The Christ Life Series in Religion (1934–35): Liturgy and Experience as Formative Influences in Religious Education." Ph.D. dissertation, Boston College, 1987.

MARY KAY OOSDYKE

MURRAY, JOHN COURTNEY (1904–67)

Jesuit priest, theologian. John Courtney Murray was born in New York City on September 12, 1904, the son of Michael John and Margaret Courtney Murray. Murray attended high school at St. Francis Xavier in Manhattan and entered the Society of Jesus in 1920. He received a bachelor of arts degree from Weston College in 1926 and a master of arts from Boston College in 1927. For the next three years he taught Latin and English literature at the Ateneo de Manila in the Philippines. In 1930 he went to Woodstock College, Maryland, where he was ordained on June 25, 1933, and earned the S.T.L. degree in 1934. He then studied at the Gregorian University in Rome, where he earned the S.T.D. degree in 1937. From 1937 to 1967 he was professor of dogmatic theology at Woodstock College.

John Courtney Murray

From 1941 to 1967 he was editor of the Jesuit journal *Theological Studies.* He was a visiting professor of philosophy at Yale University in 1951–52. A *peritus* at the Second Vatican Council, 1963–65, he died in New York City on August 16, 1967.

Murray and Interreligious Cooperation

Murray studied in Europe at a time of acute crisis, when a series of important Catholic intellectuals were attempting to show the relevance of Catholic faith and life to a society and culture in mortal danger. Although his duties at Woodstock assigned him the treatises on grace and the virtues and on the doctrine of God, he very quickly demonstrated a great interest in articulating a similar vision of an engaged Catholicism for the United States. In 1940 he gave a series of lectures on "The Construction of a Christian Culture," which were echoed two years later at a symposium on "Religion and Society" sponsored by the Jewish Theological Seminary in New York, with whose director, Louis Finkelstein, Murray was to remain in close association for many years. The basis for the Church's involvement in society set out in these early lectures was strictly theological, a consequence of basic Christian doctrines: Trinity, incarnation, atonement. This vision also underlay his proposals for a theology to equip laypeople to undertake a redemptive role in society and history.

Shortly after becoming editor of *Theological Studies,* Murray, convinced that the Catholic Church could not accomplish a redemptive purpose in the world by itself, began to promote what was then known as "inter-religious cooperation." This involved him in his first controversy when he had to defend himself to some bishops and theo-

logians against the charge that such cooperation would run the risk of promoting indifferentism. On the other hand, many Jews and Protestants were suspicious of Catholic motives in this undertaking, particularly because of their fear that Catholics were pursuing a plan whose fulfillment would include infringements on the religious freedom of non-Catholics. It was the frustration of his vision, it seems, that led Murray to turn his attention to the questions that would largely define the work of the rest of his life: Church-state relations and religious freedom.

Writings on Church and State

After an abortive initial essay in 1945, Murray began in 1948 to outline a historical interpretation and systematic rethinking of the Church's relationship to society and state. In doing so, he had to address two audiences. Many of his fellow Catholics, both in the United States and in Rome, were convinced of the irreformable character of the teaching set out by the modern popes from Pius IX to Pius XII that defined as an ideal (the "thesis") that Church and state be harmoniously united, with the state assisting the one true Church and entitled to place restrictions on the activities of all other religious bodies. On this view, "toleration" was only legitimate under certain circumstances (the "hypothesis") and in order to prevent a greater evil.

In contrast, Murray presented an interpretation of the Church's teaching, particularly as stated by Leo XIII, which explained it as a necessary and legitimate response to the aggressive, secularizing liberalism of the European continent that considered religion a purely private matter and assigned near-totalitarian power to the state. This doctrine was not applicable, Murray argued, to the quite distinct liberal tradition in the United States, which was remotely dependent on the classic Catholic differentiation of the realms of the spiritual and the temporal, both of whose claims were clearly and properly distinguished in the First Amendment to the U.S. Constitution. A historically-aware interpretation of the papal teaching, he argued, could permit one to maintain that the American solution was not contrary to Catholic teaching and need not be considered only a *pis-aller.*

At the same time, Murray was aware that continental liberalism was beginning to make inroads in the United States. In the late 1940s two Supreme Court decisions (Everson and McCollum) interpreted the First Amendment to forbid any governmental support for any religion. Murray, who had assisted the U.S. bishops in preparing their supportive briefs for the Court, vigorously criticized the decisions reached. In 1948, when a new organization, Protestants and Other Americans United for Separation of Church and State, was formed to promote the Court's position, Murray was severely critical of what he saw as a new nativism, articulated in the hugely successful book by Paul Blanshard, *American Freedom and Catholic Power.* A series of articles, particularly in *America,* where Murray served briefly as associate editor, demonstrated his considerable skills as a polemicist.

While Murray's views were broadly accepted by important U.S. bishops who welcomed his assistance to their efforts to obtain governmental support for Catholic schools, they earned him much criticism from some U.S. theologians, most notably Francis Connell, C.Ss.R., Joseph Clifford Fenton, and George Shea. While the public controversy was carried on in the pages of the *AER* and *TS,* Connell and Fenton multiplied private attempts to have his views censured by Rome. Already in 1950, while in Rome for an ecumenical meeting, Murray was asked by Msgr. Giovanni Battista Montini to submit a statement of his views on Church-state relations in the United States.

In the early 1950s Murray's views began to become known in Europe. While considerable agreement was registered in Belgium, France, and Germany, theologians in Italy and particularly in Spain, where Church-state tensions were acute and the Vatican was in the process of elaborating a concordat with Franco's government, began to take issue with his views. An indication of Vatican suspicions was an article in *Civiltà Cattolica* that was quite critical of Murray's views.

The Holy Office and Murray

The suspicion became a crisis on March 5, 1953, when Cardinal Ottaviani, secretary of the Holy Office, urged the traditional doctrine in a lecture on the duties of a Catholic State toward religion. Ottaviani mentioned the U.S. controversy and, without naming him, referred to Murray's views as "liberalizing." Upon inquiry Murray was assured by Pius XII's private secretary, Robert Leiber, S.J., that Ottaviani's views were merely private and had no official character. In December 1953, Pius XII gave a speech on tolerance, which, Murray was told by Roman sources, was a diplomatic rejection of Ottaviani's views.

Armed with this assurance, Murray gave a talk at The Catholic University of America in March 1954 in which he departed from his own customary tact and publicly stated that the Pope had repudiated the views of the head of the Holy Office. Informed of this talk by Connell and Fenton, Ottaviani initiated a Holy Office inquiry into Murray's views, for which he enlisted the aid of two reports written by Fenton. At a session on July 7, 1954, the Holy Office found that Murray's views could not safely be held. Four propositions, considered to represent his views, were rejected as "erroneous." These were communicated to Murray by the Jesuit father general in August 1954. The Holy Office also approached the superior general of the Congregation of Holy Cross and attempted to halt the publication of a book by the University of Notre Dame Press that contained the essay of Murray that had just been found objectionable. When this effort failed, the Holy Office instructed Murray to correct his errors by inserting an explanatory paragraph in any future editions. In October 1954, Murray's two chief American critics, Fenton and Connell, were given copies of the erroneous propositions and informed of the measures taken against Murray; but, they were told, these measures were not to be made public. Connell and Fenton found this restriction frustrating, and they continued privately to press Roman authorities for a public repudiation of Murray's views.

Murray was placed under direct prior censorship by the Jesuit Curia in Rome. In 1955 an article in which he attempted to clarify and defend his position was rejected by the Roman censors, and his Jesuit superiors advised him to withdraw from this area of inquiry. An effort to return to the question in 1958 was also refused. In fact, the Holy Office at the time was preparing a formal document in which the views of Murray, Maritain, and others on Church and state were to be rejected. It appears that it was only the death of Pius XII that prevented the publication of this decree.

Meanwhile, Murray continued to explore what he called a "public philosophy," a set of principles, derived from the natural law, that could serve as the spiritual substance of a pluralistic society, provide criteria for addressing social problems and for discriminating between law and morality, and help prevent society from being handed over to the control of technocrats. His essays gained him a reputation as a leading U.S. Catholic intellectual, and he was invited to participate in a large number of ecumenical and secular conversations, as, for example, in the National Conference of Christians and Jews, The Foundation for Religious Action in the Social and Civil Order, and the Fund for the Republic (later the Center for the Study of Democratic Institutions). In 1960 a selection of his essays was published as *We Hold These Truths: Reflections on the American Proposition,* which became something of a public event when Henry Luce, with whom and with whose wife, Clare Boothe Luce, Murray was friendly, placed him on the cover of *Time* magazine. At the same time Murray continued to urge Catholics to bring their religious convictions to bear upon contemporary developments by the construction of a Christian humanism to be mediated to their world by a well-educated laity. His insistence on the religious dimension of education, even in public schools and universities, was matched by an emphasis on the educational and cultural responsibilities of the Church. He played major roles in such organizations as the Catholic Theological Society of America, the Catholic Association for International Peace, and the Catholic Commission on Intellectual and Cultural Affairs.

Vatican Council II

Roman suspicion of Murray remained great enough that he was not invited to assist in either the preparatory commissions for Vatican Council II or at the first session of the council. In fact, a first draft on Church and state, prepared by the Theological Commission, repudiated Murray's views. In 1963, however, Cardinal Spellman secured his appointment as an official expert at the council, and from then on he was the U.S. bishops' chief adviser on Church-state issues. He assisted them in making sure that the question of religious freedom remained on the conciliar agenda. Appointed to the subcommission of the secretariat for Christian Unity on the subject, he was one of the main architects of the council's Declaration on Religious Freedom.

Murray's contribution to the elaboration of the conciliar text was twofold. Summarizing his historical work of a decade earlier, he explained how a theory of doctrinal development could permit the council to make an acknowledgment of religious freedom without contradicting modern papal teaching. In the text itself, Murray urged that the issue be placed in the context of modern political and constitutional developments. This emphasis distinguished his position from that of several of his European colleagues on the subcommission who stressed rather the biblical basis for the right of religious freedom. In the end *Dignitatis humanae* reflects both emphases, with Murray's position reflected chiefly in the first section and that of the others in the second. The conciliar declaration made official Catholic teaching the position for which Murray had been censured only a decade earlier.

After the council Murray published many articles explaining and interpreting *Dignitatis humanae*. He also returned to larger issues that had always interested him. At Woodstock he continued to teach the course on the Trinity; his approach to the question can be seen in the set of lectures published in 1964 as *The Problem of God*. He became interested in the dialogue with atheists and with Marxists. He served on official commissions studying the problem of racism and the question of selective conscientious objection. In the confusion of the immediate postconciliar period, he urged on Catholics "the will to community." In 1966 he was appointed to head the John LaFarge Institute in New York.

Since the early 1950s Murray had suffered from recurrent heart problems, and it was a heart attack that killed him on August 16, 1967, in a taxicab in New York City.

The Significance of Murray's Work

Generally considered the finest theologian the Catholic Church has produced in the United States, Murray's writings are marked by clarity, rigor, and a quite distinctive style. His greatest contribution to scholarship is the series of essays, still widely cited today, on the teaching of Leo XIII. His work is best seen as a distinctively American effort to bring the Church into a more open and more effective dialogue with modern society and culture.

Murray's thought is today the subject of continued study and discussion. While there is fairly unanimous appreciation of his ideal and example of civil conversation, interpretations and evaluations of his work vary considerably. Substantively, Murray's work is invoked in support both of the progressive and vaguely liberal social agenda illustrated by the U.S. bishops' pastoral letters on war and on the U.S. economy, and of the neoconservative project conceived as the way to respond to what is sometimes called "the Catholic moment." Methodologically, criticism has been registered of Murray's reliance on natural law both to mediate biblical and dogmatic truths to social questions and to serve as a basis for cooperation among people of various faiths. Where some critics propose a public *theology* where Murray had advocated a public *philosophy,* others reply that his use of a mediating discipline was itself theologically motivated and grounded. Most radically, some critics think that Murray's whole agenda was flawed from the beginning by his desire to accommodate Catholicism and Americanism. A small minority, unreconciled to the council's teaching on religious freedom, blame Murray for his part in redirecting Catholic teaching on the subject. Where ideological passions do not drive the controversies, resolution of the differences will have to await the fuller publication of his talks and essays, and, especially, of his correspondence.

See also THEOLOGICAL STUDIES; VATICAN COUNCIL II AND AMERICAN CATHOLICS.

Gonnet, D. *La liberté religieuse à Vatican II: La contribution de John Courtney Murray.* Paris: Cerf, 1994.

Hooper, J. L. *The Ethics of Discourse: The Social Philosophy of John Courtney Murray.* Washington, D.C.: Georgetown University Press, 1986.

McElroy, R. *The Search for an American Public Theology: The Contribution of John Courtney Murray.* New York: Paulist Press, 1989.

Murray, John Courtney. *Bridging the Sacred and the Secular: Selected Writings,* ed. J. L. Hooper. Washington, D.C.: Georgetown University Press, 1994.

____. *The Problem of God Yesterday and Today.* New Haven, Conn.: Yale University Press, 1964.

____. *Religious Liberty: Catholic Struggles with Pluralism,* ed. J. L. Hooper. Louisville: Westminster/John Knox Press, 1993.

____. *We Hold These Truths: Catholic Reflections on the American Proposition.* New York: Sheed & Ward, 1960.

Pelotte, D. *John Courtney Murray: Theologian in Conflict.* New York: Paulist, 1976.

JOSEPH A. KOMONCHAK

MURRAY, THOMAS EDWARD (1891–1961)

Engineer, inventor, business executive, nuclear expert. Thomas Murray was born in Albany, New York, on June 20, 1891. After receiving his B.S. degree in mechanical engineering from Yale University, he joined his father's engineering firm where he soon distinguished himself as an inventor, receiving more than two hundred patents during his career. He took over as president of Metropolitan Engineering Company and as chair of Thomas E. Murray, Inc., when his father died in 1929. He later founded Murray Manufacturing Company and was named receiver of the Interborough Transit Company of New York City in 1932. Murray served as a member of the finance committee of the Chrysler Corporation and as a trustee of the welfare fund of the United Mine Workers.

Thomas E. Murray

He resigned from all his positions in 1950 when he was appointed to the newly formed U.S. Atomic Energy Commission. For the next seven years he was outspoken in calling upon the United States to unilaterally suspend thermonuclear testing. He opposed the testing and stockpiling of large hydrogen bombs, instead favoring the development of small, tactical weapons. Murray advocated public-private cooperation in the development of industrial nuclear power. He questioned the accuracy of the data on fallout for nuclear testing and stood alone when he tried to interject a moral argument into the development of the country's nuclear program.

Murray was the recipient of numerous honorary degrees and awards, including the Laetare Medal of the University of Notre Dame, and he was a Knight of Malta and a Knight of St. Gregory. He died in New York City on May 26, 1961.

TRICIA T. PYNE

MUSIC, CATHOLIC CHURCH IN THE U.S.A.

The history of music in the American Catholic Church may be divided conveniently into four periods: the colonial period and early immigration (1787–1871); the period of first American indigenous hymnals (1871–1926); the era of first American liturgical reforms (1926–65); and, finally, the Vatican II era (1965–present).

Within each period, three considerations will be given: the music, the musicians and their associations, and the theories about music for the Church during that period.

Prior to the music of the English colonies on the East Coast, the Franciscan and Jesuit missions in the Southwestern United States and northern Mexico were filled with music brought from Spain, together with music written by indigenous composers in Mexico and California. At the Mission San José, for instance, for twenty-five years, the Catalonian Padre Narciso Durán (1776–1846) composed Masses and hymns for boy choirs composed of Native Americans. As *presidente* of the California Missions, this Franciscan priest did much to spread the influence of music among the missions.

The Colonial Period and Early Immigration (1787–1871)

From the colonial period until 1870, the American Catholic music scene was dominated by the fact the Catholic Church was a minority immigrant community. Hymnals were largely dependent on "borrowings" from European models: Latin texts or translations from Latin, and tunes taken from English, French, Polish, and especially German collections. There was little need for vernacular hymnody during this time, since the use of these hymns was restricted to devotional services and occasionally to "low" Mass, but hymnals kept appearing nonetheless.

The Music. The first American hymnal for Catholic use in the United States, called *A Compilation of the Litanies and Vespers, Hymns and Anthems as they are sung in the Catholic Church: Adapted to the Voice and Organ,* was published in Philadelphia in 1787 by John Aitken.

The first attempt at publishing a truly national hymnal came in 1805. It was entitled *Masses, Vespers, Litanies, Hymns, Psalms, Anthems & Motets, Composed, Selected, and Arranged for the Use of the Catholic Churches in the United States of America.* Other early hymnals included text-only collections, such as *A Collection of Psalms, Hymns, Anthems . . . with the Evening Office* (1830).

The early publications reflected the need for music for popular devotions and for services such as lauds and vespers. Among these were *The Morning and Evening Services of the Catholic Church, for the use of the Diocese of Boston,* compiled by Richard Garbett (1840), and *Cantate, Contains the Vespers for all the Sundays and Festivals of the Year . . . and English Hymns,* edited by Anthony Werner.

Hymnals published in German during this period reflected the rise of "national churches" that were forming in the early 1850s. Among such hymnals were the *Katholisches Gesang-und-Gebetbuch* in 1858 and the *Katholisches Gesangbuch* in 1859.

Vernacular music sung at religious devotions already was popular and was compiled in collections such as *The Complete Sodality Manual and Hymn Book* (1863). Music directed toward and edited for children appeared in *Cantica Sacra or Hymns for the Children of the Catholic Church* in 1865.

The Musicians. Most musicians were volunteers, bringing the gift of making music with them from Europe. No organizations or associations were needed as music was seen as part of the inherited culture.

Music Theory and Liturgy. In many major cathedrals and churches, music for the liturgy was considered an accompaniment to Mass, providing a holy atmosphere for the sacred service and providing an appropriate setting for High Mass. The funeral liturgy was sometimes sung.

The First American Indigenous Hymnals: 1871–1926

The initial movement toward a reform of Church music was begun in Europe and was carried to the United States, to some extent, through the singing schools of Singenberger, the Alverno School of Music, the Pius X School, the Ward Method, and the Caecilian and St. Gregory Societies. Interest in renewing Catholic Church music was stimulated through the clash between two proponents or "schools" of Gregorian chant, which was being reintroduced to Catholic worship in the 1870s as an antidote to Church music based on the romantic musical traditions utilizing operatic styles, which was then in wide use.

The first move came in 1871 in Passau, Germany, when Friedrich Pustet published what came to be known as the Pustet Chant Book (also called the "Ratisbon edition"), edited by Franz Xavier Haberl. This edition received from Pope Pius IX an exclusive thirty-year noncompetitive "privilege" as the official chant book of the Roman Rite. That privilege—and Haberl's interpretation of chant—came under challenge from the Benedictine monks of St. Peter's Monastery in Solesmes, France, refounded in 1833 by Dom Prosper Guéranger. The French monks, while enthusiastic about chant, perceived the Pustet chant to be fundamentally flawed, and began major studies to demonstrate their position.

The controversy culminated in the publication, in 1903, by Pius X, of the first major document on liturgical music, *Tra le sollecitudini,* which encouraged congregational singing as well as other aspects of Church music.

The period ended with the beginning of the American liturgical movement by Dom Virgil Michel at St. John's Abbey, Collegeville, Minnesota. These twin movements—the revival of chant and the rise of the liturgical movement—are reflected in the repertoire published between 1871 and 1926.

The Music. The German immigrant community in the United States continued to swell and, with it, the need for carrying to the new land some form of the German singing tradition. The publishers issued hymnals for this market: in 1872 came *Gebet-und-Gesangbüchlein für die Schule und die katholische Jugend,* compiled by Wilhelm Becker, S.J.; in 1874 there was the *Katholisches Gesang-und-Gebet-Buch,* by B.H.F. Hellebusch; and in 1889 there appeared *Die Himmelsleiter, eine Sammlung von Kirchenliedern,* by F. J. Bauer.

Friedrich Pustet opened a publishing house in Cincinnati and soon expanded beyond the German Church music. In 1878 came *Cantiones Sacrae* by Joseph Mohr, S.J.; in 1884, the twentieth edition of the *Roman Hymnal,* compiled and arranged by John B. Young, S.J., was published, and in 1898 *Caecilia katholisches Gebet-und-Gesangbuch,* edited again by Joseph Mohr, was published. And in 1912 Pustet presented *Cantate, A Collection of English and Latin Hymns,* compiled by John Singenberger.

In New York, J. Fischer Publishing, an American-based publishing house, attempted to serve the American Catholic musical market with its *Manual of Select Catholic Hymns and Devotions* (1885), the imported English hymnal, *The Catholic Church Hymnal* (1898–1905), the *St. Mark's Hymnal,* published in 1911, as well as the German market with *Lobet den Herrn, Gesangbuch für alle Zeiten des Kirkenjahres.*

By the end of this period, the German hymnals had clearly become German-American, such as the *Catholic Hymns from the German Collections,* compiled by Rev. John Rothensteiner (St. Louis, 1922), which drew from the earlier collections of Mohr, Hellebusch, Dreves, and Rhode. In 1924 the *St. Mary's Hymnal,* edited by Christian Zittel (Catholic Book Company, New York), epitomized the German-American tradition. The German texts in this collection were freely translated into English, and many melodies were taken from the *Gesangbuchs* of Wilhelm Becker and Joseph Mohr, S.J.

With the expansion of Catholic schools, the "americanization" of the young, and the increasing number of religious communities serving them, the variety of hymnals and musical resources for the educational market grew rapidly. Hymnals were published by the Christian

Brothers, such as the *Catholic Youth's Hymn Book* (1871), by the Sisters of Notre Dame of Cleveland, by the Sisters of Notre Dame of Philadelphia, and by the Marist Brothers in 1913. Following Pius X's directive regarding frequent Communion and the age for First Communion, Justine Ward published volume I of the *Hymnal* in the Catholic Education Series in Washington, D.C.

The first *St. Basil Hymnal* appeared in 1889, with subsequent printings of this edition until 1935, edited by the Basilian Fathers. With the publication of *Tra le sollecitudini* in 1903, music publishing was influenced toward a more assembly oriented music, as illustrated by the *Parish Hymnal* (1915) and *Catholic Hymns for the People* (1919).

The summit of this period, however, was the *St. Gregory Hymnal and Choir Book,* compiled and edited by Nicola A. Montani in 1920. This landmark hymnal was published by the St. Gregory Guild, Philadelphia.

During this period the repertoire began to move from imported Latin and European vernacular hymns to collections that could be described as authentic American hymnals. This period also opened and closed with significant developments in the organization of musicians.

The Musicians. The first U.S. organization for Catholic musicians was the American Caecilian Society, founded in 1873 by John B. Singenberger (1848–1924). Born in Switzerland and educated in Regensburg, Singenberger came to Milwaukee in 1870, teaching at St. Francis Seminary. He began singing schools throughout the Midwest. One of the most influential of all the teaching musicians, he edited the periodical *Caecilia* for fifty years (1873–1923). The foundational roots of the St. Caecilia Society were in the Regensburg movement encouraged by Haberl and Pustet.

The period ended with the founding of the St. Gregory Society in 1923 by Nicola (or Nicholas) A. Montani (1880–1948). The St. Gregory Society attempted to follow the reforms initiated by Pius X in *Tra le sollecitudini,* specifically a revitalization of Gregorian chant and music of quality for the liturgy. It was an American movement. Montani was born in Utica, New York, served as organist at St. John the Evangelist Church, Philadelphia, and later at the Paulist Church, New York City. He served as editor of the society's periodical, *The Catholic Choirmaster,* for twenty-five years (1923–48). In 1920 he edited the first edition of the *St. Gregory Hymnal and Choir Book.* It was acclaimed as "a landmark in American Catholic hymnody" and set the standard that inspired others to achieve. Tunes from Slovak and Polish hymnals were introduced.

The first version of the "White List" was published by the St. Gregory Society. It was a list of music considered acceptable for use at Catholic weddings. By exclusion, it restricted some of the major abuses of the period, but it created the image of the musician as enforcer of a specific repertoire.

Music Theory and Liturgy. In this period the renewal of the liturgy became wedded to the Gregorian chant movement. That "wedding" became the foundation for two related educational efforts promoted by Justine Ward. With Mother Georgia Stevens, R.S.C.J., in 1916, Ward founded the Pius X Institute of Liturgical Music at Manhattanville College of the Sacred Heart. In 1920 Ward, Stevens, and others organized an International Congress of Gregorian Chant in New York that brought Dom Mocquereau from Solesmes. Justine Ward also developed a method for teaching music to school children that was rooted in Gregorian chant.

The First American Liturgical Reforms: 1927–65

Dom Virgil Michel, O.S.B., a monk of St. John's Abbey in Collegeville, Minnesota, initiated the American liturgical movement with the publication of the first issue of *Orate Fratres* (later renamed *Worship*) in 1926. American musicians and hymnal publishers generally ignored the movement that was to transform the Catholic Church at the Second Vatican Council.

The Music and Musicians. Those musicians interested in liturgical renewal invested in promoting the revival of Gregorian chant. In the 1920s, the Rev. Ermin Vitry, O.S.B., arriving from Maredsous, Belgium, spread an interest in chant, as music director at the motherhouse of the Precious Blood Sisters in O'Fallon, Missouri, as a presenter in Church music programs in Los Angeles and St. Louis, as a lecturer in the liturgical summer school at the University of Notre Dame, and at the liturgical music institutes at Boys Town in Nebraska.

The Caecilian Movement continued on through a number of pupils of John Singenberger. One such student, M. Cherubim Schaefer, O.S.F. (b. 1886), founded the Alverno School of Music in Milwaukee. As editor of the *Alverno Hymnal* (1948, 1951, 1953) she combined the classical European tradition with American culture, composing tunes for a number of texts. The Alverno School of Music influenced a wide range of modern liturgical musicians and composers, especially through the work of Theophane Hytrek, O.S.F. (1915–92), and Mary Hueller, O.S.F.

In 1949 Rev. Carlo Rossini (b. 1890) of Pittsburgh became executive director of the Caecilia Society. Born in Italy, he served as organist at Epiphany Church, Pittsburgh, in 1921, and later at the Cathedral of Sts. Peter and Paul, while composing his famous collection, *The Parochial Hymnal* (1936).

Until this time, the liturgical movement had encouraged a renewal of the "spirit of the liturgy." But with the documents of Pius XII's liturgical renewal (focused on the

Triduum) in the 1950s, music publishers responded to the possibility of ritual reform. The three-part *Alverno Hymnal* ushered in modern hymnal publications. Following the *Alverno Hymnal* was *The Gregorian Institute Hymnal* (1954, officially titled *Catholic Hymns*), edited by John C. Selner, S.S., the first publication of the Gregorian Institute, Toledo, Ohio, which was to become GIA Publications. The Gregorian Institute then published the *Mediator Dei Hymnal* in 1955. Edited by J. Vincent Higginson (pen name Cyr de Brandt), this hymnal revived some older tunes that had fallen out of use. The listing of tune names and meters in this hymnal began a trend for later Catholic hymnals.

In 1955 Omer Westendorf published the first English-language hymnal in the United States designed to be used for singing the "four-hymn" Mass, an adaptation of the German Sung Mass, for which permission had been granted to Germany in 1943. Promoting the use of the "dialogue Mass," Westendorf published, through World Library of Sacred Music in Cincinnati, *The Peoples Hymnal,* compiled by an ad hoc hymnal committee at the Theological College in Washington. World Library of Sacred Music published the *Parish Mass Book* in 1958, prepared and endorsed by a Committee of The Liturgical Conference (an enlarged edition appeared in 1961).

In 1959 The Liturgical Press published *Our Parish Prays and Sings,* complied by a committee led by Irvin Udulutsch, O.F.M. Cap.

Just as the council was beginning, Theodore Marier, an active proponent of chant and the classical style, sought to reinforce the earlier aims of the liturgical renewal by publishing *Cantus Populi, Hymns and Chants for the People's Participation in the Holy Mass* through McLaughlin and Reilly, Boston.

The beginning of this third period of musical development in the United States may be characterized by noting that some music publishers were aware of the seeds of the liturgical movement taking place in the 1920s; the period ended with some clear leadership being offered to the development of sung worship by the repertoire publishing industry.

Music Theory and Liturgy. In regard to understanding the role of music in the liturgy, a major shift was taking place. Briefly stated, for many years the liturgy had been seen as a ceremony to be done. Music accompanied the ceremony. As the liturgy came to be understood as an act of worship in which to participate, music came to be accepted as *the* principal instrument through which such participation was to occur. Music moved from being icing on the cake to the very center of the ritual action.

And not only did the understanding of music change, but the sense of who was to do the music changed. Prior to the council, music was often delegated to choir members or occasionally to the presider. Following the conciliar renewal, it became increasingly clear that music was to be done by the whole assembly, not only the appointed ministers. A "pastoral" musician became a person who loved the sound of a singing congregation above all other sounds.

That shift may be exemplified by the changes in the approach of the Rensselaer Program of Church Music and Liturgy, founded by Rev. Lawrence Heiman, C.PP.S., and Rev. Eugene Lindusky, O.S.C., in 1960 at St. Joseph's College in Rensselaer, Indiana. Their initial aim was to provide an American Church music program modeled on the approach of the Pontifical Institute of Sacred Music in Rome. By 1965 the program had more than doubled in size, but the demands of the conciliar liturgical reform caused the people at Rensselaer to shift their approach to a more contemporary, nonchant orientation focused on the needs of students who planned to lead the congregation in song.

The Vatican II Era: 1965 to the Present

The Second Vatican Council (1963–65) did not direct itself to the renewal of liturgical music. In fact, Chapter VI on sacred music in the Constitution on the Sacred Liturgy repeats with little change the ideas first presented by Pius X in 1903.

The force that brought about the change in music was the decision to use vernacular languages in the liturgy. That decision was somewhat tentative at first, with the use of living languages being introduced in sections, and with little realization of all the ramifications this decision would have in the areas of ritual, communication, music, and other aspects of worship. In short, the field of liturgical music, which had seemed so fixed at the beginning and even at the midpoint of the twentieth century, was set adrift by the decision to use contemporary languages, and little explicit direction was provided by Rome or the local bishops.

The Music. "God Is Love" sang Clarence Rivers at the 1965 Liturgical Week utilizing an African American rhythm and jazz overtones. C. Alexander Peloquin soon followed with the "Glory of the Bells" and liturgical music in English was launched. Susanne Toolan added "I Am the Bread of Life."

Music publishers at first followed the trends that had been developing before the council, especially in the use of hymnody at four points in the Order of Mass. After the council, the major publishers quickly stepped into the vacuum left by the Vatican and the bishops by publishing hymnals for this type of service: the *Peoples Mass Book* (World Library Publications, 1964) and *Our Parish Prays and Sings* (The Liturgical Press, 1966).

The Liturgical Conference, influenced by David Mc-Manus of Helicon Press, published *The Book of Catholic Worship* in 1966. The first printing was a success, but the decision to order a large reprinting was a critical mistake and drove The Liturgical Conference into major debt and limited its effectiveness in the important educational years of the liturgical renewal.

Disposable worship aids ("missalettes") used hymn texts and tunes that were in the public domain, supplemented by "house" composers. Quality control and the range of liturgical music provided in any one missalette were determined primarily by user demand.

There were five or six waves of development between 1965 and 1990 in the effort to develop a vernacular musical liturgy in the United States. From 1965 to 1972, the urgency to "get the people to sing" as a sign of full, conscious, active participation coincided with a rise in the popular culture of a ballad, storytelling style, which was labeled "folk" music. This music was popularized within the Catholic Church by the works of Joe Wise, Ray Repp, and the FEL *Hymnal for Young Christians.*

Between 1972 and 1975, this musical style was refined and redefined by compositions of John Foley, Dan Schutte, and Bob Dufford, Jesuit seminarians studying in St. Louis who, together with Tim Mannion and Roc O'Connor, were affectionately dubbed by their publishers, Dan Onley and Ray Bruno of NALR, the "St. Louis Jesuits." This style was further refined and popularized by J. Michael Joncas, David Haas, and Marty Haugen.

In 1969 the U.S. bishops authorized the use of hymnody traditionally identified with Protestant communities.

Compositions that had been developed as part of the European liturgical renewal were imported during these first years, including the psalm tones of Joseph Gelineau, the acclamations of Lucien Deiss, and the more radical liturgical forms of Bernard Huijbers.

In 1985 a second wave of European composers was introduced, including the St. Thomas More Group from England, which included Paul Inwood, Christopher Walker, and Bernadette Farrell, and the Taizé music of Jacques Berthier from France. The Iona Community in Scotland had collected a folk-style music of many Third World countries that was popularized by John Bell.

Gradually, hymnal publication grew in popularity. Through the guidance of Bob Batastini of GIA, *Worship* quickly went through three editions, together with Oregon Catholic Press's *Breaking Bread* worship aid, developed by Owen Alstott, and WLP's *Missalette* developed by Nick Freund.

Music for Spanish Catholic musicians appears in *Flor y Canto* (OCP) and for African American communities in *Lead Me, Guide Me* (GIA). Vietnamese, Korean, and other Pacific rim musicians are growing in publishing a Catholic repertoire in the United States.

In addition to postconciliar developments in repertoire, developments in two other areas should be mentioned: the way associations connected with musicians changed after the council, and the shifts in the ideas about music, including those in official documents.

The Musicians' Associations. In 1969, under the joint sponsorship of the Consortium Internationale Musicae Sacrae and The Liturgical Conference, American and European musicians met in Milwaukee and Chicago. The American delegation was led by C. Alexander Peloquin and Abbot Rembert Weakland, O.S.B. Public challenges between the European contingent who were hesitant about the use of contemporary, poorly crafted music in the liturgy, and the American group, who insisted that quality music could be developed in the vernacular languages, left a permanent division among the participants.

Following this meeting, the Caecilian Society and St. Gregory Society merged into the Church Music Association of America led by Msgr. Richard Schuler, publishing *Sacred Music,* which advocates the return of Latin and classical repertoire in the liturgy.

In 1976 the National Association of Pastoral Musicians was founded by Virgil C. Funk, a Richmond, Virginia, diocesan priest. Trained in community organizing, Funk had served as executive director of The Liturgical Conference and as diocesan director of music. NPM was to be a membership organization of musicians and clergy dedicated to fostering the art of musical liturgy. As an association, NPM concentrated its attention on the emerging ministry of musicians, rather than on repertoire, through its publications *Pastoral Music* and *Catholic Music Educator.* Its first national convention was held in Scranton, attracting more than 1,500 musicians. Subsequent national conventions were held in Chicago (1979), Detroit (1981), St. Louis (1983), Cincinnati (1985), Minneapolis (1987), Los Angeles (1989), Pittsburgh (1991), St. Louis (1993), and Cincinnati (1995), with over 10,000 members. Chapters of the NPM have been formed in more than seventy dioceses in North American and overseas, with divisions for full-time musicians and music educators. Week-long summer programs provide skill training for choir directors, organists, guitarists, cantors, as well as liturgical training in sacramental celebrations.

In 1986 the Conference of Roman Catholic Cathedral Musicians was established by Richard Proulx, Leo C. Nestor, and Gerald Mueller to serve the special liturgical programs for cathedral musicians.

Music Theory. What the Constitution on the Sacred Liturgy had to say about music was a compromise position that melded, without unifying, two schools of thought on the kind of music to be used in worship and its role as part of liturgy. These contrasting positions may be summarized in the terms "treasury of sacred music" and *"munus ministrale."* The treasury of sacred music school looked toward the preservation and development of classical musical forms begun with Palestrina in the 1570s, and to other parts of the Church's treasury, including Martin Luther's contribution to congregational hymn singing and Bach's cantatas. The *munus ministrale* school emphasized the position that music serves the liturgical elements of the rite not as an aesthetic adornment, but as a ministerial gift.

The *munus ministrale* approach was developed after the council by European musicians connected with Universa Laus, especially Helmut Hucke and Gino Stefani, in reimaging music as "functioning" in the liturgical rite. In the United States, two scholars have further clarified the terminology for English-speaking countries. John Gallen, S.J., began using the term "musical liturgy," and rejected such terms as music-and-liturgy, sacred music, and even liturgical music as misleading for the role of music in the liturgy. Edward Foley, Capuchin, has suggested a further clarification of these terms, using "ritual music" as the most accurate description of the way that music functions in the liturgy.

Conclusion

As we reach the twenty-first century, our history points out the three areas that challenge our future: repertoire, the role of musicians, and musicology.

In repertoire, the key issues are (1) the development of inculturated music in the vernacular(s) of the United States while maintaining a link to the universal Church; (2) the need to resist certain musical trends in the culture (e.g., the notion that music is to be listened to rather than performed) while continuing to develop indigenous musical forms; and (3) maintaining the tension between "quality" music and genuine participatory "folk" traditions.

For musicians, the key role-related issues are (1) the development of musical and liturgical skills in combination, (2) the financing of musicians, simultaneous with (3) the sustaining of the volunteerism so essential to a ministerial spirit.

In the area of musicology, the key issue remains the tension between resisting musical styles that are trendy and developing authentic repertoire that speaks the prayer of the contemporary assembly at worship.

See also LITURGICAL MOVEMENT IN AMERICA, THE.

Fellerer, Karl Gustav. *The History of Catholic Church Music.* Baltimore: Helicon Press, 1961.

Higginson, J. Vincent. *Handbook for American Catholic Hymnals.* New York: The Hymn Society of America, 1976.

———. *History of American Catholic Hymnals, Survey and Background.* New York: The Hymn Society of America, 1982.

Pastoral Music Magazine. National Association of Pastoral Musicians, 1976–95.

VIRGIL C. FUNK

MUSKIE, EDMUND SIXTUS (1914–96)

Politician. Edmund S. Muskie was born on March 28, 1914, in the small town of Rumford, Maine. His father, Stephen Muskie, was a Polish immigrant who changed his name from Marciszewski and married a Polish-American from Buffalo. Edmund Muskie worked his way through Bates College and went on to earn his law degree from Cornell University in 1939. He practiced law in Waterville, Maine, until he joined the Navy during World War II. He started on his political career when he left the service in 1946.

Muskie served in the state House of Representatives, and his integrity, charm, and bluntness won him the confidence of the people, who in 1954 elected him the first Democratic governor in twenty years. After two terms as governor he was elected to the U.S. Senate, where he served until he became secretary of state in the last year of the Carter administration, when Cyrus Vance resigned in a policy dispute with President Carter involving the American hostages in Iran.

In 1968 Hubert Humphrey chose Muskie as his presidential running mate, but Richard Nixon and Spiro Agnew won the election by a slim margin. In 1972 Muskie was enthusiastically nominated for the presidency, but when he allegedly wept publicly during the New Hampshire primary after the conservative Manchester *Union Leader* printed planted stories about his wife and him, his campaign faltered and he withdrew on April 27, just six weeks after the primary season had begun. After leaving the Senate he practiced law in Washington, D.C.; he also served with distinction on the commission investigating the Reagan administration's involvement in the Iran-Contra affair. Edmund Muskie built a durable reputation on his intelligence and the high standards he set for himself and others in political life. In 1981 he was awarded the Laetare Medal. He died at Georgetown Medical Center on March 26, 1996.

MICHAEL GLAZIER

N

NAGLE, URBAN (1905–65)

Dominican friar. Born Edward John Nagle in Providence, Rhode Island, on September 10, 1905, Nagle attended Providence College where he earned a B.A. degree, joined the Dominicans, and adopted the name "Urban" in 1924. He studied at the Dominican House of Studies in River Forest, Illinois, and at the Dominican House of Studies in Washington, D.C., and was ordained in 1931 in Washington. In 1932, with his colleague, Thomas Carey, Nagle cofounded the Blackfriars Guild, which was dedicated to the principle of producing plays in the Catholic tradition and would eventually establish chapters in twenty cities.

Nagle earned a Ph.D. at The Catholic University of America in 1934, and that same year returned to Providence College where he taught English and drama. While in Providence, Nagle founded the Providence chapter of the Blackfriars Guild in 1935 and cofounded the Catholic Theater Conference in 1937. In 1940 he was assigned to work on the *Holy Name Journal* in New York City. He became the editor and worked in that capacity until his departure in 1946. While in New York, Nagle established an affiliation with the New York Chapter of the Blackfriars Guild in 1940 and served as the moderator and coproducer until 1951. During this tenure, he also wrote plays for the Blackfriars Theater including *Lady of Fatima* (1948) and *City of Kings* (1949). In 1951 he published his autobiography, *Behind the Masque.* The end of Nagle's career of service to the Church was as chaplain of St. Mary's of the Springs in Columbus, Ohio. He died in Cincinnati on March 11, 1965.

See also DOMINICANS (O.P.).

LISELLE DRAKE

NATIONAL CATHOLIC EDUCATIONAL ASSOCIATION (NCEA)

The NCEA traces its founding to St. Louis, Missouri, in July 1904, when the Educational Conference of Seminary Faculties, the Association of Catholic Colleges, and the Parish School Conference formed the Catholic Educational Association of the United States. "National" was added in 1927. Bishop Thomas J. Conaty, the rector of The Catholic University of America, was the principal organizer of each of the groups. In its ninety-plus years the NCEA has had seven general secretaries (presidents).

The first secretary general (1904–29) was Fr. Francis W. Howard, later bishop of Covington, Kentucky. During his term these diverse groups were unified, a constitution was adopted, and it attained its autonomy from the bishops. Additionally, the Section of Catholic Colleges for Women was established.

Bishop Howard was succeeded by Msgr. George Johnson (1929–44), executive secretary of the NCWC Education Department. Johnson was an advocate of curricular reform and expanded the NCEA's relationships by developing partnerships with other American educators and agencies. In his term the association moved its office from Columbus, Ohio, to Washington, D.C.

Msgr. Frederick G. Hochwalt (1944–66), a student of Johnson's at The Catholic University of America, took over after Johnson's sudden death. He, too, headed the NCWC Education Department and the NCEA. During his time as general secretary of the Special Education Department, the Sister Formation Section, and the Adult Education Commission were initiated, and there was a remarkable growth in both the membership and financial base of the organization. Its membership increased from 3,455 institutions in 1944 to 14,788 in 1965.

Thereafter, enrollment began to decline as more and more schools began to close. The Rev. C. Albert Koob, O. Praem., Secondary Department associate secretary, was selected as general secretary. He faced the crisis of decline and made it a time of professional growth by convening a "Symposium on Catholic Education" to address the challenges of Vatican Council II. The symposium resulted in a rewritten constitution establishing a broadly representative governing board and changing the general secretary's title to president, establishment of a Department of Religious Education, the National Forum of Religious Educators, and the National Association of Boards of Education (NABE). The superintendent's department became the Chief Administrators of Catholic Education (CACE), and the Sister Formation Section left the NCEA to become the Leadership Conference of Religious Women (LCWR). The Data Bank on Catholic Education was started. In 1972 Koob was severely injured in an accident and Rev. John F. Meyers, executive director of CACE, was appointed acting president.

In 1974 Meyers became the fifth president, serving until 1986. Under his leadership, a second symposium on Catholic Education was held and new services were initiated including the National Forum of Catholic Parent Organizations, the curriculum project, "Vision and Values," the Religious Education Outcomes Inventory, and the McGivney Fund for New Initiatives in Catholic Education. He also addressed the need to continue serving the poor and minorities and promoted development as another school income source.

Sr. Catherine McNamee, C.S.J., succeeded Meyers and emphasized collaborative efforts in the educational community which led the NCEA to establish partnerships with the National Federation of Priests' Councils, the American Forum on Global Education, and the Catholic Health Association. The association held its first international convention in Toronto, Canada. Finally, she continued the NCEA's involvement in the Inter-American and International Catholic Educational Associations.

In 1996 Dr. Leonard DeFiore assumed the leadership of the organization succeeding Sr. Catherine McNamee. Dr. DeFiore had previously served as Superintendent for the Diocese of Metuchen and the Archdiocese of Washington.

Hochwalt, Frederick G., ed. *National Catholic Educational Association/60th Annual Convention: Catholic Education: Progress & Reports.* Washington, D.C.: NCEA, 1963.

Horrigan, Donald C. *The Shaping of NCEA.* Washington, D.C.: NCEA, 1979.

____. "NCEA Retrospective (1904–1966)." *Momentum* 25 (1) (February/March 1994) 33.

Koob, C. Albert. "NCEA: Meeting Crisis with Confidence (1967–1974)." *Momentum* 25 (1) (February/March 1994) 34–37.

McNamee, Catherine T. "NCEA: Forging the Future (1986–1994)." *Momentum* 25 (3) (August/September 1994) 40–44.

Meyers, John F. "NCEA: A Dramatic Renewal (1974–1986)." *Momentum* 25 (2) (April/May 1994) 60–64.

JOHN J. AUGENSTEIN

NATIONAL CATHOLIC REPORTER

The Second Vatican Council was well underway in Rome and the winds of reform were everywhere in the air when the *National Catholic Reporter* published its first issue dated October 28, 1964. Its price was fifteen cents.

The feisty newsweekly was quick to stake out new terrain. It would have a justice edge and would not dodge Church controversy. To the contrary, it fueled it, opening up for the first time public dialogue on Church issues. This, in effect, brought controversy to U.S. Catholic journalism, in stark contrast to traditional diocesan newspapers which purposely eschewed conflict.

Volume one, number one, a ten-page broadsheet, went right to the task: "Report Negroes Leaving Church"; "Ask Dramatic Council Action for World Attack on Poverty"; and, "Confessors 'Pinned to the Wall' by Pill Question, says Jesuit expert," all told new *NCR* readers this would not be like other Catholic publications they had seen.

Robert Hoyt, First Editor

NCR's first editor was Robert G. Hoyt, an energetic and creative journalist with a history in Catholic journalism. The National Catholic Reporter Publishing Company, a not-for-profit corporation in Kansas City, Missouri, was headed by publisher Michael J. Greene. The Second Vatican Council had called for the coming of age of Catholic laity; *NCR*'s birth should be viewed in the light of a new assertiveness by lay Catholics to establish a voice in the Church and by journalists to bring their professional skills to reporting Church affairs. The idea was to cover the Church as journalists would cover any other organization, with reasonable detachment and independent judgment.

The idea caught on. Catholics throughout the Church were amazed to find information in a newsweekly—debates on birth control, celibacy, papal decisions—they had simply never witnessed before. And, of course, the Second Vatican Council and the introduction of council reforms provided a large framework for reporting and debate. *NCR* encouraged readers' letters and many responded. As word spread, readership shot up. While no firm figures are available, the paper's circulation shot up to the 90,000 to 100,000 range in just a few years.

NCR's independent stance did not sit well with many U.S. bishops who viewed it as detrimental to the Church, which had traditionally insisted that the hierarchy control the discussion, if there was any discussion. Thus, the paper was banned in many seminaries, but was smuggled in clandestinely, often by rectors themselves.

When *NCR* helped break the story of Pope Paul's June 1968 encyclical *Humanae vitae* (reporting the secret results of the papal commission), and then provided a platform for the widespread criticism of the encyclical by the faithful, it proved too much for local Bishop Charles Helmsing who, in October 1968, issued "an official condemnation." He asked the editors to remove the word "Catholic" from the masthead. Both the board and editors declined.

By the early 1970s, with postconciliar and post-*Humanae vitae* disillusionment setting in, and with priests and women religious, *NCR* mainstays, fleeing their ministries, the paper's circulation was in a nose-dive. In May 1971, the board of directors announced Hoyt's firing. Both professional and personal reasons were apparently involved. Hoyt had divorced his wife in 1970 and remarried a few months later. But Hoyt's editing, too, was seen to be too critical and combative.

Decline and Recovery

The following years were not easy for the paper; it went through several successive executive editors as publisher and editor Donald Thorman largely called the shots and set the paper's general tone. Thorman, a more moderate reformer, tried to raise the circulation, in the words of board member Frank Brennan, by "bringing back many of those people who left us and who feel a strong commitment to the church." But the task proved elusive and circulation by the mid-1970s hovered just over 30,000.

NCR suffered from a lack of strong editorial leadership until January 1975 when Arthur Jones took over as executive editor. A decisive editor, he set out to reestablish *NCR*'s reporting and investigative credentials. He was also responsible for hiring two *NCR* notable foreign correspondents, the paper's first Latin American Affairs writer, Penny Lernoux, and its first full-time Vatican correspondent, Peter Hebblethwaite.

With those additions, the paper began to expose Catholic readers to unprecedented Latin American Church coverage and Vatican analysis. Jones also hired Michael Farrell who since 1980 has guided the paper's arts and opinions sections and since January 1997 has been the paper's executive editor.

When Thorman died after a short illness in November 1977, Jones assumed the roles as both publisher and editor. The paper's circulation, meanwhile, was again on the rise, but Jones, British by birth and only after a few years in Kansas City, was longing to return to England.

Jones was responsible for hiring both Jason Petosa, an inactive priest and later *NCR* national affairs writer, as the

company's next publisher in July 1979, and Thomas Fox, the next editor, in June 1980. Jones then moved to London to become the paper's London correspondent. Since then, he has continued to work in other capacities for the paper, primarily as Washington correspondent.

Fox has held the post of *NCR* editor since 1980. He guided the paper's early coverage of the moral issues involved in the U.S. nuclear buildup, the U.S. bishops' peace pastoral in 1983, and the justice pastoral in 1986.

By the mid-1980s the paper's circulation had risen to nearly 50,000 and it has fluctuated around that number since. In the mid-1980s, *NCR* became the first national publication to draw attention to the disturbing growth of child sex abuse cases by Catholic priests. The paper was criticized by some for its coverage, but within five years the story had entered the mainstream media. By then cases were being reported in virtually every diocese in the nation.

In November 1985 William L. McSweeney succeeded Petosa as publisher. In January 1997 McSweeney retired and Fox assumed the post of publisher in addition to his post as editor of the paper.

Since the early 1980s, *NCR* has supported the Church's renewal agenda and has often been an isolated voice in doing so during the pontificate of Pope John Paul II, who has resisted such moves.

While the mood of the country grew conservative in the 1980s and again in the mid-1990s, *NCR* has maintained its progressive voice on social issues. On Church matters, the paper has been an outspoken critic of Vatican moves to clamp down on what it has labeled "dissent" in the Church.

In the political arena, the paper has been a strong human rights supporter, has called for dialogue on abortion while advocating a consistent life ethic in social and political affairs. While exercising a strong voice in these areas, the paper nevertheless tries, when possible, to be an open forum for as many points of view as possible.

See also CATHOLIC PRESS (NEWSPAPERS), THE.

TOM FOX

NATIONAL CATHOLIC WELFARE CONFERENCE

The National Catholic Welfare Conference (NCWC) was established in 1919 under the name National Catholic Welfare Council, an organization whose purpose was "to unify, coordinate, encourage, promote and carry on all Catholic activities in the United States; to organize and conduct social welfare work . . . ; to aid in education; to care for immigrants, and generally to enter into and promote by education, publication and direction the objects of its being" (Certificate of Incorporation, copy, Archives of the United States Catholic Conference [AUSCC]). The idea for the organization coalesced from four diverse impulses: the example of the American Federation of Catholic Societies (1901) in unifying and energizing the laity; the success of the National Catholic War Council (1917) in coordinating the Church's effort in the First World War; the need for a Catholic committee in Washington, D.C., to counterbalance the political influence of the Protestant Federal Council of Churches; and the desire of Pope Benedict XV, expressed through his legate Archbishop Bonaventura Cerretti, for "America to be the leader in all things Catholic and to set the example to other nations" (quoted in *Report of the General Committee on Catholic Affairs and Interests Presented to the Catholic Hierarchy of America Assembled at The Catholic University, Washington, D.C., September 24, 1919, His Eminence, Cardinal Gibbons, Presiding* [n.p. (1919)] 1). In order to implement the wishes of the Pope, the American Board of Archbishops decided to hold annual meetings of the hierarchy and to form a standing committee of bishops to represent the hierarchy in matters of general Catholic interest.

Origins of the NCWC

At the first general meeting of the hierarchy (September 1919), the bishops constituted themselves in annual assembly as the National Catholic Welfare Council. To carry out the decisions of the NCWC, the hierarchy established an Administrative Committee of seven bishops, later expanded to ten, elected annually. (From 1954 onward, American cardinals became *ex officio* members of the committee, in addition to the ten elected bishops.) This committee met periodically throughout the year and operated a five-branch secretariat, located in Washington. Consisting of a committee of clerics and laypersons, chaired by a bishop of the Administrative Committee, each of the secretariat's five departments designed policies and programs to be carried out by the department director and Washington staff. The on-site supervision of the secretariat belonged to a general secretary, representing the chairman of the Administrative Committee. Rev. John J. Burke, C.S.P., a founder of the War Council and chairman of its Committee on Special War Activities, became the NCWC's first general secretary (1919–36) and in many ways gave shape and substance to the organization. While the NCWC was, technically speaking, the hierarchy in annual assembly, the name was applied by extension to the Administrative Committee and the Washington secretariat.

Functions of the Secretariat

The functions of the NCWC secretariat were as follows. Operating directly under the general secretary were the Immigration Bureau and the Motion Picture Bureau, the former stationed agents at ports of entry to offer immigrants technical and social assistance, the latter fostered decency in the movie industry. The Social Action Department promoted civic education, industrial relations, and rural welfare through publications, a speakers bureau, the Catholic Conference on Industrial Problems, and the Rural Life Bureau. The Department of Education tutored the public on the nature and aims of Catholic education, examined state and federal legislation on schools to recommend a course of Church action, and fostered parochial education by urging the establishment of state associations of Catholic education. The Legal Department scrutinized state and federal legislation with a view to either eradicating features harmful to the Church or injecting Catholic principles into proposed measures. The Press Department provided subscribing newspapers with a weekly service of articles covering national and international events of Catholic interest. The Department of Lay Activities organized the Catholic people countrywide into the National Council of Catholic Women (NCCW) and the National Council of Catholic Men (NCCM). By far the more successful of the two, the NCCW established a service bureau that found placements for social workers, published information on social work and legislative matters relating to Catholic interest, and maintained contact with government agencies to arrange for Catholic representation when necessary. The NCCW also ran the National Catholic School of Social Service for Women in Washington, D.C., and for a time conducted a series of settlement houses around the country. The NCCM, on the other hand, proved to be a rather feckless organization whose signal achievement was a weekly radio broadcast called "The Catholic Hour," begun in 1930 and given a new format in 1951 when it was added to television. The NCCM also operated the Narberth Movement, which furnished articles on Catholicism to secular newspapers and periodicals.

Suppression and Restoration

Very early in the NCWC's existence, the organization faced a serious challenge, which, while nearly spelling its ruin, led to important clarifications. Opposed to the NCWC from its foundation and viewing it as a threat to his prestige as the dean of the hierarchy, Cardinal William O'Connell of Boston sought to minimize the Welfare Council. At the 1921 meeting of the hierarchy, with the support of Cardinal Dennis Dougherty of Philadelphia, O'Connell attempted to reduce the NCWC simply to the Administrative Committee and the Washington secretariat. Having failed in that effort, he secured in the next year, again with Dougherty's support, the Vatican's suppression of the entire organization: the annual assembly of the hierarchy, the Administrative Committee, and the secretariat. The two American cardinals had convinced certain Vatican officials that the NCWC was something of a standing plenary council, introducing parliamentary government into the Church and legislating for American Catholics, thereby undermining the authority of individual bishops. Through Archbishop Henry Moeller of Cincinnati, Bishop William Turner of Buffalo, and especially Bishop Joseph Schrembs of Cleveland, the American hierarchy—the NCWC proper—lobbied Pope Pius XI and Vatican cardinals for the restoration of the organization. In June 1922 Pius XI had the NCWC reinstated under specific guidelines. Principally among them, the NCWC was to be a voluntary organization of the American bishops, without power to legislate; since the name National Catholic Welfare Council had caused misunderstanding among several bishops, the title was to be changed to "Welfare Committee" or some other variant (Sacra Congregatio Consistorialis, Instructiones S. Congregationis Consistorialis Circa Conventum Episcoporum Statuum Foederatorum Americae Septentrionalis mense Septembri A. 1922 Habendum, AUSCC). At the 1922 meeting of the hierarchy, the bishops clarified that the NCWC was a voluntary association of the entire American hierarchy, not to be confused with the canonical hierarchy of the United States. In order to make clear that the NCWC was neither the Administrative Committee nor the secretariat but a free association of the hierarchy for mutual conference about Church welfare, the bishops, at their 1923 meeting, altered the organization's name to National Catholic Welfare Conference, rather than the Vatican-suggested "committee." To drive the point home, the articles of incorporation were amended to name all the bishops of the United States and their successors as the NCWC, with the Administrative Committee acting as the board of trustees.

Although the NCWC's existence continued to have troubled moments for more than a decade after the crisis of suppression and reinstatement, the institution survived and expanded. In 1933 the hierarchy added a Department of Catholic Action Study to serve as a clearing house through which a bishop could find out what his colleagues were doing in their dioceses regarding Catholic Action, an international movement initiated by Pius XI, who had summoned the laity to labor for the Church under the direction of the hierarchy. This department was discontinued in 1954. In 1940 the hierarchy created a Youth Department, which included the National Council of Catholic Youth, the National Federation of Catholic College Students, and the National Newman Club Federation. In 1953 the Immigration Bureau was given departmental status. Finally, in 1960 the hierarchy set up the Latin American Bureau to place the resources of the U.S. Church at the disposal of the Pontifical Commission for Latin America. In 1967 the NCWC was reorganized and renamed the United States Catholic Conference.

Fogarty, Gerald, S.J. *The Vatican and the American Hierarchy from 1870 to 1965.* Wilmington, Del.: Michael Glazier Press, 1985.

——. "The Authority of the National Catholic Welfare Conference." *Episcopal Conferences: Historical, Canonical, and Theological Studies,* ed. Thomas J. Reese, S.J. Washington, D.C.: Georgetown University Press, 1989, 85–103.

McKeown, Elizabeth. "The National Bishops' Conference: An Analysis of Its Origins." *Catholic Historical Review* 66 (October 1980) 565–83.

——. "The 'National Idea' in the History of the American Episcopal Conference." *Episcopal Conferences: Historical, Canonical, and Theological Studies,* ed. Thomas J. Reese, S.J. Washington, D.C.: Georgetown University Press, 1989, 59–84.

——. *War and Welfare: American Catholics and World War I.* New York: Garland, 1988.

Sheerin, John B., C.S.P. *Never Look Back: The Career and Concerns of John J. Burke.* New York: Paulist Press, 1975.

Slawson, Douglas J. *The Foundation and First Decade of the National Catholic Welfare Council.* Washington, D.C.: The Catholic University Press, 1992.

DOUGLAS J. SLAWSON

NATIONAL FEDERATION OF PRIESTS' COUNCILS

The National Federation of Priests' Councils (NFPC) is a membership organization that represents, networks, and serves more than one hundred councils of priests, associations of priests, and religious institutes of men. The NFPC fosters the continuing professional development of presbyteral councils and individual priests by promoting fraternity and communication, providing a national forum for pastoral concerns, developing written materials and resources, and working with other national groups to serve the needs of the entire Church. As one of the first organizations to provide a national voice for priests, the NFPC continues to express a pastoral and prophetic message from the presbyterate of the United States.

The NFPC was founded in May 1968 in Chicago amid the profound ecclesiastical and social changes of Vatican Council II, the civil rights movement, the Vietnam War, and the assassinations of Martin Luther King, Jr., and Robert Kennedy. The federation was formed in response to the Second Vatican Council, which encouraged all members to participate in constructing a collegial Church, and called for a representative body of priests in each diocese. Delegates at the NFPC's first constitutional meeting agreed that the new organization should be one of the councils rather than individual priests.

The early years of the NFPC were marked by an energetic agenda that spoke forthrightly on issues of due process, continuing education, just wages, women in Church leadership, justice and peace, and accountability. National attention came when several priests from the Washington, D.C., archdiocese were suspended for signing a public statement protesting the rigid stance of *Humanae vitae.* The NFPC's effort to secure due process for the suspended priests was perceived by many bishops as adversarial.

In 1989 the NFPC attempted to resolve this lingering tension and adopted a working style that emphasized collaboration, not confrontation. The House of Delegates, the NFPC's decision-making body, no longer focuses on making resolutions at the national convention, but instead uses a process that surfaces and prioritizes areas of concern. The goal is to produce insights and reflections, not solutions, that lead to dialogue and cooperation with bishops, religious, and laity in addressing the needs of the Church. In this way, the collective wisdom of priests is brought to bear on matters of substance such as HIV/AIDS, pastoral leadership development, clergy sexual misconduct, and multiculturalism.

The NFPC has given birth to several organizations that are now part of the American Church landscape. These include NOCERCC (National Organization for the Continuing Education of Roman Catholic Clergy), NACPA (National Association of Church Personnel Administrators), CATH (Catholic Association of Teachers of Homiletics), the Catholic Church Personnel Group Benefit Trust, and the Parish Evaluation Project.

The structure of the NFPC consists of an Executive Committee, the National Board, the House of Delegates, and the national staff. The National Board of the NFPC is made up of representatives from religious communities, the twenty-eight ecclesiastical provinces of the United States, and the National Black Catholic Clergy Caucus. The House of Delegates, which meets annually, is the policy-setting body of the NFPC and is comprised of representatives of each member council. The staff of the national office, based in Chicago, includes a president, an executive director, and several administrative-support personnel.

BERNARD F. STRATMAN, S.M.

NATIONAL SHRINE OF THE IMMACULATE CONCEPTION

The Basilica of the National Shrine of the Immaculate Conception is the Western Hemisphere's largest Catholic church and the eighth largest in the world: its length is 459 feet, its area is 77,500 square feet, and its height reaches 329 feet above the ground. Under her title of the Immaculate Conception, Mary's status as patroness of the United States was prompted by an 1847 petition of American bishops to Pope Pius IX. The Catholic University of America's fourth rector, Bishop Thomas J. Shahan, won Pius X's moral and monetary support to honor Mary with a shrine on the university's campus.

The 1913 official designation and donation of the site of land by the board of trustees of The Catholic University of America elicited donations from across the nation. As chief architect of the design, Charles Maginnis (1867–1955), of the firm Maginnis and Walsh, with Frederick V. Murphy associate (the firm was later renamed Maginnis and

National Shrine of the Immaculate Conception

Walsh and Kennedy), sought to infuse ancient Byzantine tradition with contemporary American style. The completion of this design allowed for the laying of the cornerstone by James Cardinal Gibbons, archbishop of Baltimore, on September 23, 1920.

The Crypt Church was completed in 1926 and features a main altar of carved Algerian onyx, dedicated to Our Lady of the Catacombs and donated by more than thirty-thousand women who share the name of the shrine's patroness. Masses have been celebrated in the Crypt Church continually since 1927. The Crypt Church, at a length of 200 feet and a width of 160 feet, seats 400 persons. Resumption of the erection of the Great Upper Church occurred after the end of the Great Depression and World War II, in the Marian Year of 1954. The dedication Mass of the Great Upper Church was celebrated on November 20, 1959, by Francis Cardinal Spellman of New York, with four other cardinals, two hundred bishops and archbishops, and thousands of Catholics in attendance.

The enormity of the Great Upper Church is evidenced by its 399 foot length, seating capacity of 3,500 persons and total capacity of 6,000 persons. Continual additions were made to the shrine thereafter, including the numerous chapels reflecting American Catholics' international heritage, stained glass windows, mosaics, and polished stone sculptures. The one striking vertical architectural feature is the bell tower, or Knights' Tower, named for its Knights of Columbus donors who made the donation in 1963. At 329 feet, the Knights' Tower is the Federal City's second highest structure (after the Washington Monument) and home for a French-cast carillon of fifty-six bronze bells, activated by a wooden keyboard at its base.

On October 12, 1990, Pope John Paul II named the National Shrine a basilica. Although basilicas originated as public buildings in ancient Greece and Rome, their function evolved in the fourth century to places of worship, and then finally to a designation of historical (or other) significance bestowed only by the pope. The National Shrine enjoys the status of an active spiritual and musical community for the nation. It has a resident professional music director, cantors, chorus, and orchestra which regularly augment the shrine's four organs in the Great Upper Church and Crypt Church. The shrine also offers daily and weekly Masses, daily sacrament of penance, daily rosary, guided tours, other services expressly for pilgrims and visitors, and a regular publication entitled *Mary's Shrine.*

McKenna, Bernard. *Memoirs of the First Director of the National Shrine of the Immaculate Conception, Washington, D.C., 1915–1933.* N.p., 1959.
Warsaw, Michael P. *The National Shrine of the Immaculate Conception.* Washington, D.C., 1990.

LISELLE DRAKE

NATIVE AMERICANS AND THE CATHOLIC CHURCH

Methodology

This study presupposes that there is no "unbiased" history that purely and simply recounts the "facts just as they happened," whether these accounts come from eyewitness observation or from recorded documents. While the historian must of course seek to recount history as accurately as possible, one must be aware of one's own biases and cultural conditioning, as well as that of one's sources. At the present time, the history of missions is especially vulnerable to criticism as conditioned by a certain perspective—that of the missionaries rather than of the peoples of the cultures in which they have served. The history of missions to aboriginal North Americans has come under some of the heaviest fire for not considering the perspectives of the aboriginal people themselves. At the same time, there has been no dearth of historians who derive a certain glee from castigating, from a present-day perspective, the missionaries of another era.

The development of cultural anthropology, of the history and phenomenology of religion, of revisionist historical methods, and thus of an analysis of the cultural conditioning of the Church itself, has deeply affected the way in which we now appraise missionary activity. Within the Church itself, such terminology as inculturation, contextualization, indigenization, and adaptation has greatly altered missiology and mission historiography. In this essay, we shall try to be continually conscious of both a European Catholic and a Native American perspective on the events and attitudes we discuss. Thus, the selected bibliography given at the end includes some works, especially by native authors, that are at times polemical assaults on the Church that are not always unwarranted. In sum, then, the present article is as much missiological analysis as historical summary.

A brief mention must be made on terminology to describe the aboriginal people (or peoples, when discussing whole tribes). There is such extensive argument today over proper appellation that no clear usage exists, given the need for more general terms. Thus, this essay will vary usage among terms like native peoples, aboriginal peoples, natives, Native Americans, and even "Indians" (since many native people today simply employ that title for themselves). The precontact experience, of course, would be simpler, since each tribe had its own name (usually some form of "the people"), though not entirely simple even then, since tribes often gave names to one another based on ethnic peculiarities.

In focusing on Catholic mission among native peoples of the present continental United States, including Alaska, and, in its earliest periods, those areas sharing a common border with the present countries of Canada and Mexico, we shall seek to understand the elements that shaped this history. In the same spirit, this discussion attempts to avoid both facile hindsight criticism and a naive acquiescence in many policies that can expect no justification from any sense of authentic morality. But we shall likewise avoid railing against earlier practices in the self-deluded belief that the modern historian would have responded with any greater degree of enlightenment to the same situations. History, including Church history, is a story of many false starts, errors, injustices and sin, as well as one of creativity, insight, achievement, heroism, and even sanctity. Thus, a fitting image for this essay might be that of a laboratory pathology, which seeks for causal understandings of both health and disease. A theological description for the Church in this history might well be borrowed from Martin Luther: we are all both justified and sinners.

There are five major divisions to this article: (1) The period of direct mission from Europe, spanning common areas with what are now Canada and Mexico. (2) Mission work within the boundaries separating the continental United States (including Alaska) from present-day Canada and Mexico. Roughly speaking, these cut-off dates were 1783 and American independence from Britain, and 1848, with the Treaty of Guadalupe-Hidalgo setting most of the present border with Mexico, supplemented by the 1854 Gadsden Purchase. (3) A special section on schools. (4) A section on aboriginal "revitalization movements" as one important outcome of mission activity. (5) A final section on contemporary Catholic reevaluation and "praxis" since Vatican Council II, including especially a history of the Tekakwitha Conference and related issues.

In the sections on historical periods, the essay will discuss each under three general headings: (1) a description of the spread of missionary activity; (2) a description of missionary attitudes towards aboriginal people and mission among them; (3) an analysis of missionary methodology in these periods.

European Missions: Hispanic Missions from 1529–1848

Earliest Contacts. The earliest missionaries in what is now the continental United States left brief records about their experiences in the colony of Florida, which then included the area from the southern tip of the Atlantic Coast, along the Gulf of Mexico, and what was to become the territory of the Louisiana Purchase. There are some records of Franciscan friars accompanying Hernando De Soto on his penetration into the territory of present-day Texas, and of Franciscan missions in the eastern Gulf Coast areas, but there is little surviving account of missionary activity. An early narrative by the Franciscan Toribio Motolinia describes some initial impressions of aboriginal peoples as basically gentle and humble, living peacefully in what the friar saw to be great poverty. Motolinia took pains to contrast these people with his fellow Spaniards' pride and arrogance, and, in the spirit of his contemporary, Bartolome de Las Casas, he defended the Indians against accusations and depredations by the Spanish. At this time, thanks to earlier protests by Dominicans and Franciscans in Central America, Queen Isabella of Spain had already ordered reforms in the treatment of indigenous peoples, however poorly these reforms were implemented. In any case, as might be expected, the missionaries necessarily found themselves categorized with the Spanish political and military system, to which they were in so many ways bound.

Roughly two decades after the incursions of De Soto deeper into Florida territory, the Jesuit Juan Rogel, sailing from Havana in 1570, explored as far north as present-day South Carolina, making some unsuccessful attempts to missionize, although he apparently had acquired at least the rudiments of one native language (which one we are not told). Rogel recorded some narrative of his experiences and noted some impressions of aboriginal people; he was most deeply impressed by what he saw to be lofty moral standards, including monogamy. Employing the debating method of his era (the word "dialogue" being anachronistic for these times), he tried to conduct some conversation, and records that he was frequently ridiculed by native conversation partners. Many misunderstandings occurred because of linguistic problems. However, he wrote, when he offered to depart should they choose to reject his invitation to become Christians, the natives' feelings were hurt. Rogel, much like Motolinia, blames the conduct of the soldiers for many problems, also mentioning, as would so many future missionaries, the problem of the native

peoples' nomadic life patterns as obstacles to cross-cultural communication and to an eventual acceptance of Christianity. During this abortive Jesuit mission, it is recorded that several Jesuits suffered death at the hands of aboriginal people, again, apparently, because of their being associated with the conquistadors.

During this early period, a second wave of Spanish exploration and conquest advanced northward around 1540 from Mexico under Coronado, appealing to the "right of discovery" as it was understood under the "law of nations," and made incursions into present-day Kansas. The Friars Minor accompanied Coronado on this expedition and obtained some conversions among native people, many of whom seem to have made a connection between Christianity and European technology (a phenomenon that would appear in many early exchanges such as this). Efforts at conversion of the Indians seem again to have highlighted widespread misunderstanding of symbols on both sides: e.g., technological products seen as implements related to spiritual power, and lengthy debates about whether God dwells in the heavens or beneath the earth. Here, for the first time, one sees how those earliest proselytes, especially the Pueblos, developed a "compartmental" outlook on religion. For whatever the motive, most likely the very practical one of employing whatever might have the "power" to "work," they practiced both Christian and indigenous rites without seeking to synthesize them. This practice would become typical of the encounters between Christianity and aboriginal religion even to the present. Religion has always been intricately woven into indigenous "cultural systems" (C. Geertz), so that people lived within and by intertwining systems, all of them integral to cultural wholeness. Each symbol or complex of symbols had its place in a system—a point of continuous and often tragic misunderstanding between indigenous and European religious representatives. It is the source of constant debate about the value or disvalue of "syncretism" in the current dialogue between members of different systems. The problem of syncretism continues today in the argument over the nature of "essential Christianity" or of "pure Catholicism."

Missions into "Northwest New Spain." The Spanish period from 1533 on saw large movements of Franciscan and Jesuit missionaries northward into the areas of present-day northern Mexico, Arizona, New Mexico, and the territory of Upper and Lower California. The Franciscans labored among the Yaqui and the southern Athabascan tribes now known as Navajo and Apache as early as 1533, and among the eastern Pueblos during the Coronado expedition. These latter two tribes, however, were of so strong a nomadic culture that evangelization among them accomplished nothing at that time. The Jesuits began to experience some positive if highly tentative response to their evangelization efforts among the Tarahumaras of northern Mexico between 1590 and 1616, when a revolt took place within the Spanish dominions. The Jesuits were to return to the Tarahumaras in the nineteenth century to find many remnants of the Christian faith among the Tarahumara people, where current missionaries now embrace a facilitative approach to the way the native people live these practices. Although this account belongs outside the boundaries of the Church in the United States, it may be noted that the early Tarahumara period gives considerable evidence on mission theory and praxis of the time prior to the Jesuit expulsion in 1767. Further, there is a parallel, both in history and in present pastoral praxis among the Yaqui, Papagos, and Pueblos north of the border in Arizona. There, Jesuits, Franciscans, and others currently carry on pastoral presence and service alongside traditional native ways of living the Catholic faith imparted three to four centuries ago.

At this point, it is important to describe mission attitudes and methodology among the Franciscans and the Jesuits during this period of influence. The two orders shared many attitudes and methods, and both of course shared the same identification in the minds of the aboriginal peoples with the conquistadors whom they accompanied. Spicer has given the missionaries some favorable marks by noting that, contrary to popular belief, they did not practice "conversion by the sword," even though Spanish rule of the Indians was characterized by extreme forms of discipline and outright cruelty. Complicating this was the "law of nations" position that force might be employed should aboriginals hinder the spread of Christianity. It is thus difficult to grasp just how, in the perspective of the native people, conversion to Christianity was understood. That is, to submit to Spanish conquest was to submit to Spanish religion, which the native people no doubt saw to be part of the entire cultural system to which they were submitting. Their perspective on this seems to differ little from that of the Europeans of the time.

Spicer further assigns a favorable mark to the religious for defending native people against depredations and cruelty by "the secular arm," even though secular authorities also accused the religious of cruelty. However, this basically passing grade is qualified by the fact that, after the Inquisition was established in Mexico in 1616 (initially as a tribunal to settle ecclesiastical-civil litigation), permission was granted to the religious to impose severe punishments for specifically religious transgressions. This fact leads to a discussion of more particular attitudes and methods.

The fundamental theology of missions of the period of the Conquest, if it can be called a formal theology, was shaped by a number of sociopolitical cultural elements, as well as by distinctly religious viewpoints. Theologically, the patristic thought of St. Augustine, which dwelt on the absolute necessity of baptism for salvation, figured mightily in mission practices and in a spirituality of saving pagan souls from hell. Likewise, Augustine's argument that, although pagans may be found to have many good things in their cultures, they have no right to these goods, had its effect on missionary theory prior to Las Casas. Perhaps more critical than this somewhat obscure position of Augustine, however, was the powerful influence held by Aristotle, who taught the basic inferiority of "barbarians" (as well as of women), and this led to the argument of the right of European "free men" to expropriate such peoples, until the historic Valladolid debates of 1555 between Las Casas and the Aristotelian humanist Sepulveda.

The unsystematized third-century ecclesiology of Cyprian, which argued that there is "no salvation outside the Church," was now being applied far more extensively than the bishop of Carthage had likely intended it to be in dealing with the problems of his period. Added to the above, the positions of the later periods of the Council of Trent and of the burgeoning Inquisition, all intended to buttress the Church against heresy and especially against Protestantism, came to dominate the encounter with non-Christian peoples as well.

Sociopolitically, the Spanish Empire was flexing the muscles developed in its "reconquest" of Spain from the Muslims, long a "pagan" threat to their homeland. This sense of triumph, along with the Renaissance, gave Europeans the first of many reasons they would develop for the superiority of their culture, even though Jesuits in China at roughly the same time were arguing that Chinese culture was superior to European. Into this picture must also be etched the fact that, ever since the establishment of the Christian Church in the Roman Empire by Theodosius, the Church became increasingly Romanized and later Europeanized through an unreflective historical process that was not officially confronted until Vatican Council II.

In such a thought context, virtually all missionaries, Jesuit and Franciscan alike (and even the very justice-conscious Dominicans to the south) held a "replacement" theology of mission: pagan superstition, as well as the culture that supported it, must yield to a European form of Christianity. Consequently, there was little effort to search for common ground for dialogue in this atmosphere nourished by the adversarial and disputatious techniques of the universities. The missionaries, no doubt with all sincerity in most cases, believed that the greatest good they could do for aboriginals was to assimilate them slowly into a saving environment, with the result that missions became dynamic centers for cultural change. The journals of Jesuits in the late sixteenth and seventeenth centuries reveal numerous denunciations of and expressions of disgust for native behavior, although there were exceptions to this attitude, most notably on the part of the famous Eusebio Kino. In sum, civilization and evangelization were two sides of the same coin, although there was later to be a divergence of methods between Catholics and Protestants, the former civilizing in order to Christianize, and the latter Christianizing in order to civilize.

However, another dimension of mission policy must be examined here: that is, the more prudent stance towards aboriginal cultures that most missionaries eventually adopted, that the gospel and baptism are not magical endowments that will be embraced without gradual and free opportunity for acceptance. Thus, the evangelists of this period generally found themselves in conflict with the military and with settlers over the rights of Indians, whom the Europeans wanted either to absorb immediately into their ways, and if they resisted, to obliterate from their path to frontier conquest. It is in this light that the "reduction" principle, first made famous by the Dominican (and later bishop) Bartolome de Las Casas, and then adopted by the Jesuits in Paraguay, should be understood. The "reduction" principle was implemented in the Southern Hemisphere first, and then in the north toward the end of the sixteenth century, eventually in the missions of the French Jesuits, and finally in the efforts of nineteenth-century missions. The basic motives for this method were two. First, there was the conviction, harshly questioned today by revisionist history, that native culture in its aboriginal form could not survive and that the gospel must have a central environment in which to flourish. Second, there was the realization among the missionaries that most colonists could be nothing but a bad influence on the native people, who must therefore be kept separate from them. In such centers, the gradual process of acculturation could be followed, proper methods of catechesis could be implemented, and the native language could be learned and employed in mission work (even though the goal of hispanization of language was already an ideal).

Thanks to the previous campaigns of the indefatigable Las Casas, there was general papal support for enlightened policies at least in the area of social and economic development, and this support was seconded by the Spanish monarchs through Philip II. Certainly, in the light of late twentieth-century mission theory, and of the current experience of physical and sexual abuse, the disciplinary policies of the missions read badly, corporeal punishment being common and even de rigeur in the mission compounds and in the reductions. But even these more severe styles of order were far milder than secular practices, and the missionaries generally rejected the death penalty except for cases of open rebellion. There is much here to shock the modern or postmodern reader, especially anyone who expects to find a stable and perfect practice of a universal enlightenment morality, or of any developed capacity to distinguish between Christianity and culture.

Aboriginal religion and spirituality received little or no recognition as possible channels of grace, even though a few of the Jesuits (e.g., the aforementioned Kino), were inclined to have a tolerance for traditional ceremonial and festive practices, a tolerance they shared with the many of the later Franciscans and upon which they thought to construct Christianity. In any case, especially in the Spanish domains, the native leaders took their deeper tribal religious practices "underground," often to bequeath them only piecemeal to their descendants.

One important aspect of mission method that deserves special mention, however, is the Jesuit insistence on effective communication, and on the accommodation of the faith to the native idiom. The Jesuit founder, Ignatius of Loyola, had written into his "annotations" to the *Spiritual Exercises* that they must always be adapted to the needs and capacities of those undergoing them. The same principle came to characterize certain rules of the order's constitutions. A study of Jesuit mission precepts (especially by Polzer), reveals a very severe requirement placed upon all Jesuits in the missions: no one unable to learn the native language could be admitted to final vows, and those who failed to so learn must not be allowed to preach or catechize. Likewise, later decrees by provincials and official visitors in the late seventeenth and early eighteenth centuries prescribed numerous codes of conduct, no doubt legislated to counteract previous abuses that appeared in the missionizing process. Examples were: (1) Jesuits were not to cooperate in recapturing Indians who had fled from a master's severe treatment; (2) The primary recipients of alms must be the Indians; (3) Indians must be allowed sufficient time off from labor to look after their own plots; (4) Confessional practice must be characterized by gentleness; (5) Forms of the old culture not "explicitly religious" (admittedly a very European distinction) should not be forbidden. All of this, however enlightened, was, of course, still at best a benevolent despotism. But it was the age of despotism.

Franciscans in California. In closing this examination of the Spanish period, special mention must be made of the Franciscan missions in Lower and Upper California. Apparently, the friars were less inclined than the Jesuits to record their own histories or to develop articulated "methodologies," but it is possible to glean a great deal from historical writings. The Franciscans moved into Lower California as early as 1596, and seem to have gained the favor of many native people, largely because of the missionaries' efforts to defend the rights of the Indians against the military, and because the friars generally practiced a liberal acceptance of what they saw to be nonreligious cultural practices. Invariably, however, as has been noted, the missionaries also depended on the military for sustenance, and thus were forced to depart with them after only a few years, to return again in 1603, assisted by a small company of Discalced Carmelites. Eventually, the Dominicans were to assume charge of the Baja California peninsula in 1772, as the Franciscans migrated northward.

The continuing history of Franciscan missions in the area begins with the expulsion of the Jesuits from all Spanish domains in 1767, and the mandating of the friars to replace them in what was then the territory of Sonora. It is at this time that Junipero Serra figures so prominently, especially in the conflicts between Church and secular authorities. This period features the establishment of numerous missions whose names now read like a tour guide to the cities of California: San Diego, Los Angeles, Santa Barbara, San Francisco, and San Jose are only a few of the larger ones.

This period of expansion features a familiar "symbolic form" that would appear again in French Canada and elsewhere, which expressed the deep tribal dimension of European Catholicism, and was to affect profoundly the responses of native peoples as well to the Church. Minute details are recorded of the ceremony of "taking possession" by a European governor of some "new world" territory—a practice encouraged by the current interpretation of the "law of nations," by which the concept of *terra nullius* ("no one's land") denied recognition of aboriginal ownership. During the possession ceremony, a solemn *Te Deum* was sung, accompanied by drums and cannon; the new governor, assisted by a missionary sermon, stood alongside two juxtaposed symbols—the escutcheon of the conquering nation, and the Cross, while the land was claimed in the name of the king. The rhetoric of the ritual seems often to have left considerable ambiguity as to who the "great monarch" was.

The Franciscans, even while expressing (no differently than the Jesuits) many ethnocentric condemnations of native appearance and behavior, nonetheless were not devoid of self-criticism. Thus, Serra could record the lament that the main reason for the failure to Christianize the natives was due to ignorance of their language. Several Franciscans are cited as blaming their close identification with Spanish authority for the inability to be truly evangelical or prophetic, even though the natives, ironically, came to respect the missionaries only insofar as they shared the power of the military.

It is in this complex situation that the place of the Franciscans, and especially the recently controversial Serra, should be examined. The missions metamorphosed into tight systems of paternalistic and severe government, with the friars standing *in loco parentis* for the native people, who were, of course, viewed as either children or "savages" who could only "regress" apart from Church surveillance. Defenders of Franciscan policy point out that the Indians were treated far worse with the introduction of secularization of the missions by the Mexican government around 1835. It is once again wise to apply the image of the laboratory pathology here: in the light of contemporary critique of missions, such practice by both state and Church representatives are guilty—whether subjectively or objectively—of a grave "insult," (that is, both a deep wound and a social slur) to native culture, the consequences of which are even now only beginning to emerge. For this, the several apologies by Church representatives to late twentieth-century native groups are most appropriate (if perhaps overly guarded), and the anger of native persons should be understood always in this light. However, such a critique should produce, not orgies of self-righteous homilies by contemporary critics, but rather sober evaluations and discernment of new directions and proper reparations, undertaken in a mode of collaboration with modern native peoples, whether Christian or not.

European Missions: Catholic Missions in the Territories of "New France"

This section follows a development similar to the study of Spanish missions, first briefly describing the growth of French missions from the late sixteenth century to the close of the period of the common boundary areas between the United States and Canada in 1783, after which the two countries show a separate development of mission. This period is seminal for the understanding of later missions in the United States.

The earliest Catholic missionaries in New France date back to the sixteenth century in the person of the Franciscan Recollets, who labored mostly in the area of Acadia (the present-day maritime provinces) and the province of Quebec. Being seriously restricted in numbers and resources, they sought assistance from the Jesuits, who first arrived in Acadia in 1611. This point marks the beginning of the records called the *Jesuit Relations,* covering roughly a century and three-quarters of mission among the various Algonquin language tribes of Acadia and Quebec, the Hurons in Quebec and later in what is now Ontario, and the Mohawks in Quebec and the present upper New York state. The successes of the reduction method in Paraguay inspired the French Jesuits to introduce it, first, at Sillery in Quebec in 1637, where they experimented with developing an agricultural community that was to experience many severe hardships.

As with the Spanish settlements, the purpose of the reductions was twofold: to begin the process of assimilation of the native people and to introduce them to the faith in a gradual manner, as well as to segregate them from the bad influences of French settlers. The goal of this form of acculturation, however, was envisioned as a process leading to intermarriage between French *voyageurs* and native women. Of other such reductions, the best known are the former Ossernenon in upper New York state, Kahnawake near Montreal (the eventual home of Blessed Kateri Tekakwitha), and the doomed settlement of Ste. Marie among the Hurons, near present-day Midland, Ontario. In the Quebec missions, the services and contributions of the Ursuline Sisters under Mère Marie de l'Incarnation, as well later as the Notre Dame Sisters under Marguerite Bourgeois and the Hôtel Dieu Sisters under Jeanne Mance, were essential to the survival of missionary activity.

Somewhat later, contacts were made with the Ojibwe, and missions were established among them, especially after the destruction of Ste. Marie in 1649. The mission of New France extended into what is now the Upper Midwest of the United States, where the most famous name is that of Jacques Marquette, the short-lived but prolific missionary best known to secular history for his navigation of the Mississippi River with Louis Jolliet as far as present-day Arkansas. Marquette established missions among the Ottawa and Illinois, whose language he spoke fluently, having learned the related Algonquin tongue among the Algonquins, Ojibwe, and Pottowatomis.

As with the missions of "New Spain," those of "New France" should be examined under the same lens: the attitudes of the missionaries towards the natives, their mission methods, their relations with secular forces, and (because the Jesuits did record them!) the sentiments of many aboriginals towards the missionaries. The French, already experiencing the first thrill of mercantilism, were less fanatically religious and less interested in conquest than in trade and commerce, and, there being no vast deposits of precious metals in this territory, the lust for gold and silver did not figure in their dealings with the native peoples. The fur trade, however, should be seen as an analogy to that interest.

Certainly, nationalism was equally weighty as a motive; the *Relations* records a ritual strikingly similar to the Spanish practice—the "taking possession" of new territory by the French governor. Again one hears the verses of the *Te Deum*, the rumble of drums, and the roar of the cannon. Side-by-side on a large platform stand the cross and the insignia of French royalty mounted on a pole. A long harangue is delivered by a Jesuit, employing the style of militant rhetoric used by native orators, exalting the power of the monarch, as the greatest of captains. The aboriginal perspective, for which religion and culture were also part of a "cultural system," may be surmised, although one Jesuit records it as "astonishment."

It is impossible to categorize clearly the attitudes and methods of all the Jesuits towards the native people, so many diverse testimonies being found. It may be said, however, that the eventual conversion from aboriginal ways to those French ways not contaminated by sexual license and abuse of alcohol was the goal of mission. Moreover, the missionaries and the natives shared a mutual tendency to judge each other, with each side voicing criticism of the character and customs of the other: the natives saw the French as soft and self-indulgent, indi-

vidualistic and greedy, and the French considered the natives coarse and cruel. One of the most admirable traits of the early Jesuits should be noted: their readiness to travel with native parties during the worst periods of winter, to suffer hardships to which they were unaccustomed, and the humiliations of struggling with the language and culture.

Nearly all the Jesuits writing about native people agreed on one point: that the natives were intelligent and shrewd, their equals in bargaining and in debates about religion and worldviews. In the *Relations* one meets a variety of impressions about native spirituality: basically it was seen as superstitious, and at times symbolic of "the kingdom of Satan." The Jesuits, in their encounters with native *jongleurs* (today historians use the Siberian word *shaman*), sought to refute their "errors," while the "savages" repaid the compliment by asserting frequently that the missionaries "had no sense." The Jesuits were seen, further, as being shamans with dangerous powers. From today's culture-conscious perspective, it can be seen how profoundly culturally conditioned were the spiritualities of all parties concerned.

The Jesuits, aided by their classical training, did not hesitate to seek for what are now called "points of contact" between the Christian and native worldviews. Thus, one can find some accounts of native origin myths, native feasts such as the "feast of the dead" or burial custom, the rite of the sweat lodge, and other usages recounted without condemnation. The place some of these held in the life of the Jesuits' most famous convert and lay preacher, Joseph Chiwatenhwa, was fully acknowledged and accepted. There are also many tributes to the moral virtues of the native people, as the missionaries saw them—excelling the French in hospitality, family solidarity, loyalty, and the spirit of sacrifice. In sum, it may be argued that the Jesuits did not hold a theory of "radical discontinuity" (in the modern evangelical sense) between native spirituality and Christianity. Some of the Jesuits, especially Brébeuf and Marquette, sought to "Christianize" some native practices.

Again, methodology followed attitudes. The Jesuits sought to create a system of reductions, where they could influence the natives apart both from the traditional nomadic life, and from the deleterious influence of the French. They saw the native children as the hope of the Church, holding regular instruction for them, and building schools in which the children could be trained by the Ursuline Sisters. Brébeuf, in particular, also dreamt of a native spiritual leadership and clergy—a dream that has never been realized to the present day.

In summation of the attitudes of French Jesuits, one observes certain similarities to the views expressed at least in the letters of higher superiors in the Spanish missions. Brébeuf composed at least one set of instructions on how to relate to the people, emphasizing gentleness and courtesy, learning local languages, the surrender of one's own biases, and readiness to undergo the harsh conditions experienced by the natives. There are also self-critical reevaluations of mission attitudes and practices by Jesuit leaders, who acknowledge previous mistakes and excessive harshness of judgment.

The relationships between the missionaries and the French secular powers are even today a source of great controversy. Unfriendly critics argue that the Jesuits made a cynical use of the fur trade, as conducted especially by those expert entrepreneurs, the Hurons, in order to secure economic power that would buttress the Church. There are Jesuit testimonies even at the time denying this charge, although it is recognized that missions had to do business with the fur trade, and thus follow the French system. Accordingly, it must be admitted that the French had the opportunity to make pragmatic use of the missionaries for their own purposes.

Secular alliances were the source of severe tension, hostility, and eventually tragedy, especially in relation to the various tribes of the Iroquois Confederacy, of whom only some Mohawks became Catholic. The Iroquois, whose powerful political influence was threatened by the French and the British, while trying to play these off against each other, came to see the Jesuits as leagued not only with these powers but with their hereditary enemies, the Hurons. This would lead to the violent deaths of Brébeuf and several other Jesuits, while the deaths of Isaac Jogues and his companions to the south seem to have been more for actions conflicting with native religious beliefs. One may justly if guardedly grant the title of "martyr" to these men, whose Christian sanctity seems well-attested, but it would be superficial to insist that the natives killed them "primarily out of hatred for the faith." The reality is far more complex than that.

Missions within the United States

The fall of New France to the British in 1763, followed by the separation of Canada and the United States in 1783, mark the departure of this essay from the Canadian scene, where a vigorous mission westward was to be conducted from mid-nineteenth century on by the young order of Oblates of Mary Immaculate. The aforementioned dates, along with the year of 1848, marking the definitive separation of Mexico and the United States, set the boundaries for the remainder of this narrative.

Given the existence of smaller sporadic missions, the most significant mission enterprise in the former Spanish domains was and is that of the Franciscans in what was now the "American Southwest." In the Pueblo revolt of 1680, the missionaries too had been driven out or killed, but they began to return before the end of the century (un-

fortunately to some quarrels with the Jesuits over jurisdiction). Eventually, Franciscan missions dominated the entire area of present-day New Mexico and Arizona among the Navajo, Pueblos, and Papagos, featuring large mission compounds. The boarding schools, established by the Franciscans and conducted especially by the Sisters of the Blessed Sacrament, were to become part of an elaborate Catholic education campaign, which shall be discussed below. The eventual entry of Archbishop Jean Baptist Lamy into this territory from Colorado is a significant part of American Church and frontier history as well.

The nineteenth century saw extensive Catholic missionary activity move from the East into the Midwest, and from as far northeast as Quebec out into the American Northwest. Limitation of space allows only a summary of this vast territorial outreach, although the themes employed above may still serve as a valid form of analysis. The earliest initiatives in missions within the new American republic were taken in 1795 by Bishop John Carroll, who sent a small party to Indiana. The Sulpicians established a mission near Detroit early in the nineteenth century, without significant results. However, Bishop Frederic Baraga carried on energetic work among the Ojibwe in Michigan, and became fluent in their language, developing grammars and native language prayer forms as far as the liturgy of his day would allow.

One of the most notable accounts of episcopal outreach is that of the mission of Francis Norbert Blanchet (d. 1883) from Quebec to Oregon Territory beginning in 1819, where he was appointed vicar general, eventually bishop, and then archbishop. With impressive aid from Mother Katherine Drexel, Blanchet established missions among many of the plateau and coastal tribes. He also founded the Association for the Propagation of the Faith in his jurisdiction.

Through the efforts of the frontier bishops, religious orders began to circulate west of the Mississippi: the Oblates of Mary Immaculate worked in Washington state, the Dominicans moved into Wisconsin, the Benedictines into North and South Dakota to found the present abbeys of Assumption and Blue Cloud. At a later point, the Capuchins opened a mission among the Cheyenne of Montana, and eventually, in the mid-twentieth century, assumed responsibility from the Jesuits of a mission among the Crow. These missions have become significant centers of cultural dialogue and "inculturation" experiments.

The most widely recognized and documented activity began with the apostolate of Bishop William Louis DuBourg, who was appointed bishop of "Louisiana and the Floridas," in which vast domain he labored to attract missionaries for native tribes in the early nineteenth century. DuBourg saw the welfare of the native peoples as his highest priority, eventually arranging for the entry into these parts of the Jesuits and the Religious of the Sacred Heart. This period between DuBourg's initial efforts and the

American Civil War was one of immense missionary energy, but also of much frustration, and it intertwines with the beginning of the grim catastrophe of the frontier in its effects on native tribes.

It seems accurate to say that, by the third decade of the nineteenth century, all the mission groups considered schools for native children to be their most important project. Native leaders, in many instances, came to agree with the viewpoint, realizing that they had no choice but to prepare their children to deal with runaway American frontier expansion. There was universal agreement among secular and religious leaders that assimilation was the only possibility for Indians. A significant project to accomplish this process began when DuBourg's initiatives gained the response of the Jesuits in the East, and a party led by Charles Van Quickenborne (and including the young novice Peter John De Smet) traveled into the Mississippi valley and westward, where missions were either established or attempted among the Sauk, Osage, Kickapoo, and Pottowatomi tribes in Illinois, Missouri, Iowa, and Kansas.

Van Quickenborne's attitudes and methods were to characterize the general approach of Jesuits to their Midwestern missions. The typical Catholic attitude of "civilizing in order to convert" was motivated by the general conviction that native culture was inferior to the Euro-American culture, and must therefore give way to expansion and cooperate with it. The Jesuits' other principle was, again, the value of education, which led the missionaries to enter into alliances with a federal government whose motives they suspected, but with whom they were prepared to "sup with a long spoon." Van Quickenborne's belief, an enlightened one for his time, was in disagreement with the view of most of American society, in his assertion that the native people could indeed "be civilized" and Christianized. This tension was to give way to further disaster when expansion burst all existing restraints and assimilation gave way to a brutal roughshod conquest of native territories. An interesting irony has developed in contemporary native commentary on this period: this argument is that the Indians were indeed "unassimilable," but that this trait manifested a definite superiority over Euro-American culture, and that the native people would have proved this if they had been let alone.

Records of mission method are not as numerous as among earlier missions, but they do show certain policies. Van Quickenborne, following the order of his general superior, Jan Roothan, envisioned a local version of the Paraguay Reductions among the Osage and the Kickapoo tribes, with the same intention as his predecessors to separate the natives both from their traditions and from European secular influence. There seems to be some oral tradition among the Osages recalling earlier Jesuit missions on the upper Mississippi. With the reductions there were to be schools which would wean the native children away from "barbarism," and Van Quickenborne conducted these with his usual grim form of discipline.

These policies, as much pragmatic as idealistic, were to fail, as American expansion, and the grim specter of that most deadly of imported diseases, alcoholism, were to bring the missions to destruction. Whatever criticisms post-Vatican II insight might level at mission policies, this overwhelming onslaught of settlers and the traffic in fermented beverages (for which tribes north of the Rio Grande seem to have had no cultural preparation), may arguably be seen as the basic cause of the mission failure.

The Kansas-Nebraska Act of 1854, setting up a vast corridor for settlers, further made the Indians outcasts in their own territories. An 1861 treaty, which allotted land to the Pottowatomis, also called for land to be granted to Catholic and Baptist missionaries; this led to a Pottowatomi mission being founded near Council Bluffs, Iowa, eventually moving to Sugar Creek, and finally ending up in east-central Kansas, with the Kickapoos slightly to the north of this area. The Kansas Mission at St. Mary's did manage to thrive for about a generation.

The earlier failure of the Kickapoo mission features an encounter of considerable symbolic significance. Van Quickenborne recounts his dealings with a Kickapoo leader named Kennekuk, whom the natives considered a prophet, but whom Van Quickenborne saw as a charlatan. The Jesuit wrote of besting Kennekuk in an argument and seeming to have persuaded him of the value of Catholic Christianity. The anthropologist James Mooney, however, himself a Catholic, never mentions this, but describes how Kennekuk had tried to defend his people against removal from their lands in northern Illinois, and later accompanied them into exile. This history may explain why the Kennekuk Prophet Church survived the Jesuit mission and continues to exist even today. Kennekuk represented for his people a promise that they would sooner or later end their forced pilgrimage and find their ancestral "place" once again. For all their dedication, the Jesuits could never fulfill such a promise. The Kennekuk Indian Church remains one Native-Christian syncretic community among others that will be discussed below.

Some space in this essay must be given to mission from the Midwest to the West beyond the Rocky Mountains, especially to the life and work of Peter De Smet. De Smet was still a young priest working among the Pottawatomis when in 1837 Flathead delegates arrived from the Far West to request blackrobes to come and minister to them. Accordingly, De Smet, accompanied by a Jesuit brother, responded and undertook the first of his astounding history of journeys that had so much missionary and political significance. In his mission to the Flatheads and related tribes, De Smet envisioned a reduction, where the native people could live in peace and grow at their own pace, and (as he hoped at least at that time) not be separated from their traditional culture, to which De Smet was especially sensitive. This experiment too was to be short-lived, mostly because the very nomadic life of the buffalo cultures of the plateau defied settlement into sedentary living arrangements. So too, his initial contacts with the Arapaho and the Dakota tribes would lead eventually to missions among them by future Jesuits in Wyoming and South Dakota, only after their forced consignment to reservations.

In spite of this setback, De Smet was to become an almost universally admired figure among the aboriginal people. Although his constant travels, and perhaps a lack of linguistic skill, prevented language fluency, his physical vigor and his love of the rugged frontier life typical of the native people endeared him to them. His personal integrity made him one of the very few whites whom they believed they could trust. His devotion to peacemaking and treaty negotiation, even though it was to result in deep discouragement and bitter disappointment, requires far more space than one article can discuss. From another viewpoint, De Smet has not lacked his critics, who argue that he was at best a dupe of the government, at worst a cynical bargainer. However, John Killoren's recent study puts forth impressive evidence that De Smet struggled constantly against depredations against the Indians, and that he strove to convince them to make peace because he realized the futility of resistance. In his final years he carried with him a profound sadness, and continued to level devastating criticism at the expansionist practices that showed no compassion or justice for the first nations of the land.

Further developments in the Northwest after the earlier missions must at least be given mention. These may best be illustrated by the work of Joseph Cataldo, S.J. (1837–1928), who was to become perhaps the foremost representative of the Jesuits' Oregon province in his missions to the Nez Perces and the Spokanes, and briefly to the Alaskan natives. Not only did he know the Kalispell language fluently, but he was an early pre-inculturation practitioner of the principle of accommodation to native culture. Not only would wider-ranging missions open up around the Northwest, but his brief mission to Alaska in 1896 was part of another venture that flourishes today. The year 1886 saw the first expedition of Jesuits into Alaska to work among the Yup'iks and Inupiuts, Aleuts, and Athabascans, where Russian Orthodox missionaries had left some understanding of Christianity. By the time Fairbanks became a diocese in 1948, the Jesuits and women of several orders had established a recognizable methodology. Pastoral work was carried out in an itinerant mission style, first by dogsled, and eventually by air. Beginning about this time, Alaska was also to feature a radio apostolate through station KNOM in Nome, and also became the center of the now thriving Jesuit Volunteer Corps. Many of the missionaries learned the Yup'ik language and developed a system of orthography, although they followed the prevailing pattern of secular authority by promoting assimilation and forbidding the native languages in their schools and orphanages. As with nearly all pre-Vatican II missions, considerable energy was devoted to the gradual wearing-away of traditional religious practices.

Catholic Schools

The importance of schools, both in the eyes of the Church, and, once they saw the inevitability of massive cultural change, of the aboriginal leaders, deserves special notice. It is of course unfortunate that the history of schools among native peoples should have been so deeply tainted by the scandal of Christian division—which the Indians have always wryly recognized as one more example of European tribalism. But this problem is perhaps just as deeply rooted in the soil of ethnic identity beneath the outward persona of religious zeal. The Roman Catholic Church found itself at the center of the burgeoning problem of the "melting pot," as recent immigrants strove to "fit in" with the earlier dominant Anglo-Saxon culture. This created the tension of somehow maintaining a very strict and exclusivist brand of Christianity even while Catholics strove to blend into the American scene. In the long run, at least prior to 1965, the ecclesiastical exclusiveness endured, but the Church found itself yielding to the same policies of cultural meltdown as mainstream America. Hence, the history of the century between the Civil War and roughly 1970 was characterized by cultural-political conflict between the Bureau of Catholic Indian Missions (founded 1874, present title 1879) and the generally Protestant Indian Rights Association. In all these struggles, the native people themselves were mostly "objects" of history rather than "subjects" making and recording their own history.

The present analysis, once again, should be done with a minimum of hindsight condemnation, but with the earnest desire to learn the lessons of history. The Catholic approach to the contest, however unaware it was of its own cultural conditioning, saw missions and schools as agencies competent to serve the most pressing long-range needs of the native people. (Relief from sheer starvation was the most pressing short-range need in the late nineteenth century!) Catholics actually shared with Protestants a certain victimhood to national expansionist plans and pragmatic legislation, typified first by the Grant Peace Policy of 1869, and then by the Dawes Allotment Act of 1887. Under the Grant Policy, missionaries, most of them Protestant, were employed indiscriminately as Indian agents in a program riddled with corruption typical of the Grant regime. The later Dawes Act, which divided up Indian land for individual ownership and thus rapid transfer into the hands of settlers by the desperate Indians, was a natural sequel to the Kansas-Nebraska Act in the process of destroying any intratribal strength and intertribal solidarity.

The Catholic Church saw itself as combating some of these abuses. Once the Bureau of Catholic Indian Missions was recognized as an official Church agency by the Third Plenary Council of Baltimore in 1884, it gained the boldness to engage the federal government (and, inevitably and sadly, the Protestant churches) in battle over the control of Indian education. The Bureau began to maneuver for its full share of the policy of granting government contracts to fund schools, begun in 1870. The Protestants, seeing the logic of their own position of separation of Church and state, soon withdrew from the system, as well as from the running of schools, and that contract system was abandoned by the turn of the century. However, the Catholic Bureau continued its battles, largely under the strong personalities of Fr. William Ketcham, the polemical Fr. Joseph Stephan, and the more flexible and conciliatory Fr. Henry George Ganss, through such organizations as the Society for the Propagation of the Faith and the Marquette League.

Events subsequent to this would lead to a new policy of granting contracts at least for rations between 1904 and 1906, but the operation of schools would become almost the exclusive burden of religious orders, with help from some dioceses and special financial support from the Blessed Sacrament Sisters. The schools, especially residential ones, carried on perseveringly, though continuing to cultivate the policy of assimilation, often through severe disciplinary practices.

By the 1970s, however, some mission educators had come to see the necessity of placing education into the hands of the native people, this spirit of indigenization being considerably encouraged by dwindling finances. Simultaneous with this new mentality, Congress passed the Indian Education Act in 1972, which was intended to implement the earlier Johnson-O'Malley Act providing for self-determination for native tribes. The new contracts were awarded directly to the tribes, and many Catholic Schools were sold to them for a nominal figure, with many Catholic mission teachers and administrators then becoming employees of the tribes, and religious education generally conducted on released time. This policy remains in effect, and, though not without problems, continues in a hopeful spirit, especially with the growing number of native persons assuming the reigns of administration.

Aboriginal Revitalization Movements

No essay on the current relationship of the Church to indigenous peoples anywhere on the globe can afford to ignore the influence of native religious movements, whether traditional or modern, and often a synthesis of the two. (The focus here is on native-founded movements rather than on the tribal continuations of mission Catholicism such as we found in the Southwest.) The phenomenon of "revitalization movements" was introduced into ethnological literature by Anthony F. C. Wallace in 1956 to describe movements that had already been flourishing for some time, mostly under the inspiration of charismatic native prophets. The best-known eighteenth-century leaders were: the one known mysteriously only as "The Delaware Prophet" (from the Lenni Lenape tribe, renamed for some reason for Lord de la Ware), the Shawnee prophet Tenskwatawa, brother of the great general Tecumseh, and Handsome Lake, or Ganiyodayo, a visionary of the Iroquoian Seneca tribe.

Common to such leaders was a vision that told them to reform their own lives (often from drunkenness) as well as to restore the cultural dignity of their people. In the case of the Delaware and Shawnee prophets, their vision led to military action and eventually to the death of the religious movements with the founders. But with Handsome Lake, whose vision was partly Quaker-inspired and more irenic in tone, there was not only reform of his own life, but he was to found a renewal of the Iroquois longhouse which thrives today.

Farther to the west, a similar figure appeared in the person of the Kickapoo prophet Kennekuk, whom we have already met. Kennekuk's powerful vision for his people came to him even before the tribe's forced removal, and was proclaimed to his people by means of a type of "spiritual geography" etched onto a bark map—later ridiculed by Van Quickenborne. For this people, ousted from its sacred space by faceless hordes of migrants and by government policy, such a prophecy promised, albeit vaguely and mysteriously, some hope of a dwelling place secure. It is not difficult to understand how such a prophecy might endure even when the Church, seen as a tool of cultural destruction, passed from the scene. The Kennekuk Indian Church continues today in Kansas, still praying a Sunday liturgy that symbolizes the pilgrimage to the homeland.

We may liken the above to a more famous movement, begun with a vision to the Payute prophet Wovoka in Nevada around 1880. Wovoka too was given to understand that all Indian people must renounce all white ways and separate themselves from the Europeans. He taught them a version of the traditional "round dance," practiced to the point of vision-inducing exhaustion, which would eventually cause the disappearance of the whites and restore the long-dead ancestors and the native culture. This movement spread rapidly across the plains, acquiring greatest strength among the Dakota and Arapaho. The still militant Dakota gave the movement a tone of resistance, and continued to oppose consignment to reservations. But the movement ended with the massacre of some two hundred unarmed Dakota at Wounded Knee Creek on December 30, 1890.

This movement, however abortive, created the occasion for another movement, a peaceful one, known variously as the peyote religion, the peyote church, or, more officially after it incorporated to gain protection under the First Amendment, as The Native American Church. While the mild hallucinogenic cactus peyote had been used religiously from time immemorial by Mexican tribes, it was discovered through a vision, especially by the Winnebago leader John Rave around the turn of the century, and later spread through the efforts of the Comanche Quannah Parker. The ritual and prayer movements that developed called for spiritual healing, moral reform, sobriety, family wholeness, tribal solidarity, and peaceful coexistence with white society, featuring a ceremony that is deeply "Indian," if indeed a syncretism of many native and Christian elements. There are many practicing Christian Indians today who also share in peyote services. It continues to thrive alongside more traditional native ceremonies, sharing with them the value of both religious vision and cultural and social resistance to white society. The existence of such movements as the above leaves contemporary Christians to discern between mission, on the one hand, and ecumenism or interreligious dialogue. This observation leads into a discussion of the important Catholic-Indian revitalization movement known as The Tekakwitha Conference.

The Tekakwitha Conference and Related Issues

The present Tekakwitha Conference bears little resemblance to the small group of missionary priests and brothers first called together in 1939 by Bishop (later Cardinal) Aloysius Muench of Fargo, North Dakota, to form a discussion group and later a support group for missionaries, giving it the name of the Mohawk-Algonquin woman (now Blessed) Kateri Tekakwitha. The organization continued for nearly forty years in this form, led especially by the Benedictines. However, in 1976 the first stirrings of change took place in the form of discussions among missionary men and women and native representatives about the meaning of aboriginal culture for Catholic Indians. With many voices of discontent being heard, in 1977 the members agreed to appoint Fr. Gilbert Hemauer, O.F.M. Cap., a catechetical pioneer at St. Labre Mission in Ashland, Montana, to consult with native leaders and to redirect the conference.

With increased financial support from the Bureau of Catholic Indian Missions under Msgr. Paul Lenz, Hemauer formed a committee with two native consultants, Sr. Genevieve Cuny and (later Deacon) Francis Hairy Chin. This committee contacted other leaders from both mission and native communities, to construct a plan for a dramatically revised annual meeting. In August of 1978 the attendance increased from roughly forty to over two hundred, at least fifty of these native people. Lectures, workshops, and liturgies were devoted to native culture and to and experiments in native forms.

The next five years saw a dramatic growth both in numbers and focus. The growing interest of bishops led to many of them attending conference gatherings, and this involvement helped bring about a number of public episcopal pronouncements on issues of culture and social justice. A new humility characterized this assembly of clergy, following a rebellion by a group of native persons at the Yankton, South Dakota, gathering in 1979, which insisted on more active involvement and more native control. This began to happen with the still larger (ca. 600) gathering in Denver in 1980, with over half of the membership now native, including delegates from the eastern United States and areas in Canada. The growing number of workshops featured increased concentration on the issues discussed in this essay, and on native leadership.

The thousand-plus who assembled in Albuquerque in 1981 saw further innovations, including a full day's sharing in the name day feast of Santo Domingo Pueblo, where the traditional Catholic Mass was celebrated early in the morning, followed by the even more traditional native ceremony for good harvest and tribal empowerment—much of this still inside the secret kivas. The conference featured a survey of delegates as to the future of the Church among native people, which helped to lay down an agenda for future projects. Among these would be a native catechetical task force, an orientation workshop for non-Indians working in native settings, and the strengthening of the Association of Native Religious. Issues of chemical dependency, family problems, social and political empowerment, land rights, and tribal government began to receive special attention.

Steady growth of the conference was to see it pass into the hands of native and lay control in 1989. Since this time, the conference has continued to grow and to create new regional groups. Though not without conflicts, it has become a dramatic symbol of "revitalization" in which the hierarchical Church can hope to be involved without being in control. The conference currently advertises its goals as the following: (1) To unify Native American Catholics while respecting tribal differences; (2) To empower Native American Catholics to live in harmony with their Catholic and native spirituality; (3) To promote and maintain ongoing communication and involvement between tribes, the Tekakwitha Conference, and the hierarchy of the Catholic Church in America; (4) To pray for the canonization of Blessed Kateri Tekakwitha, to share the story of her life, and to follow the example of her holiness (It should be noted that this goal is subordinate to or shares the spotlight with those accompanying it, and was not the primary intention for the founding or revitalization of the conference, as has been alleged.); (5) To encourage the development of local Kateri circles; (6) To cooperate with local, regional, and national groups to realize this vision.

Conclusion

The problems that we have seen growing from the times of the earliest missions continue in some form today to call the Church, as well as secular government to sober self-examination and action. While the original policy of assimilation and imposition of foreign culture has been abandoned, much of the basic intent of these policies has already happened. The intimidating array of social problems that accompany cultural invasion and the aftermath of colonialism remains: alcoholism in devastating proportions; dysfunctional and single-parent families and the breakup of traditional extended families; high dropout rates from school; unemployment; and local tribal government conflicts. Catholic theology finds itself called to deal with such issues as "syncretism," inculturation, and interreligious dialogue, along with the vexing question of Church leadership, especially ordained priesthood, and clerical celibacy.

Native leadership has nevertheless grown, in the area of youth leadership, alcoholics anonymous, Alanon and Alateen, Adult Children of Alcoholics, and other Twelve-Step programs conducted often with a vivid aboriginal ritual setting. Bishops and clergy have worked for political advocacy for native people, all the while dealing with the ravages of boarding school abuse and sexual abuse problems. Problems posed by these issues defy easy conservative-liberal categorization, and those who work to resolve them face an intimidating barrage of pressures from all sides. Thus we end where we began: we acknowledge the very human quality of the Church, its dysfunctions and its sins, as well as its heroism and hope and ability to renew itself. We have come to recognize the Church more deeply through the models of communion and servanthood and People of God. The Church continues to remain as a strong (if less hierarchical) presence in many native communities, where it struggles to proclaim, in its members, a truly "native Christ" (Pope John Paul II, Midland, Ontario, 1984).

See also FRANCISCAN FRIARS; FRONTIER CATHOLICISM; JESUITS IN AMERICA, THE; MISSIONS IN COLONIAL AMERICA, ENGLISH; MISSIONS IN COLONIAL AMERICA, FRENCH; MISSIONS IN COLONIAL AMERICA, SPANISH.

Axtell, James. *The Invasion Within: The Contest of Cultures in Colonial North America.* New York, 1985.

Bowden, Henry Warner. *American Indians and Christian Missions.* Chicago, 1981.

Deloria, Vine, Jr. *Behind the Trial of Broken Treaties.* New York, 1974.

____. *Custer Died for Your Sins.* New York, 1969.

____. *God is Red: An Indian Manifesto.* New York, 1973.

Engelhardt, Zephyrin, O.S.F. *The Franciscans in California.* Harbor Springs, Mich., 1897.

Garraghan, Gilbert J., S.J. *The Jesuits in the Middle United States.* 3 vols. New York, 1938.

Grant, John Webster. *Moon of Wintertime: Missionaries and Indians of Canada in Encounter Since 1534.* Toronto, 1984.

Harrod, Howard W. *Mission Among the Blackfeet.* Norman: University of Oklahoma Press, 1971.

Hennesey, James, S.J. *American Catholics: A History of the Roman Catholic Community in the United States.* New York, 1981.

Jaenen, Cornelius J. *Friend and Foe: Aspects of French Amerindian Culture Contact in the Sixteenth and Seventeenth Centuries.* New York, 1976.

Killoren, John J., S.J. *Come, Blackrobe: DeSmet and the Indian Tragedy.* Norman, Okla., 1994.

Latourette, Kenneth Scott. *A History of the Expansion of Christianity.* Vol. 3. London, 1941.

Milner, Clyde, and Floyd O'Neil. *Churchmen and the Western Indians, 1820–1920.* Norman, Okla., 1985.

Mooney, James. *The Ghost Dance Religion and the Sioux Outbreak of 1890.* Lincoln, 1991.

Polzer, Charles. *Rules and Precepts of the Jesuit Missions in Northwest New Spain.* Tucson, 1976.

Prucha, Francis Paul. *A Biographical Guide to the History of Indian-White Relations in the United States.* Chicago, 1977.

____. *The Church and the Indian Schools, 1888–1912.* Lincoln, 1979.

Shea, John Gilmary. *History of the Catholic Missions Among the Indian Tribes of the United States, 1529–1854.* New York, 1857; repr. New York, 1969.

Spicer, Edward H. *Cycles of Conquest: The Impact of Spain, Mexico and the United States on the Indians of the Southwest, 1533–1960.* Tucson, 1962.

Thwaites, Ruben Gold, ed. *The Jesuit Relations and Allied Documents.* 73 vols. Cleveland, 1896–1901.

Tinker, George. *Missionary Conquest: The Church and Native American Cultural Genocide.* Minneapolis, 1993.

Trigger, Bruce. *Natives and Newcomers: Canada's "Heroic Age" Reconsidered.* Toronto, 1985.

Washburn, Wilcomb, ed. *The Indian and the White Man.* Garden City, N.Y., 1964.

CARL F. STARKLOFF, S.J.

Related Document

THE BULL *SUBLIMIS DEUS* OF POPE PAUL III, JUNE 2, 1537

To combat the charge that the Indians were not capable of receiving the Catholic faith, Paul III (1534–1549), following representations by the Dominicans, Bernardino de Minaya and Julian Garcés, Bishop of Tlaxcala in New Spain, issued on June 2, 1537, the bull *Sublimis Deus.* By this action the pope reaffirmed the traditional teaching of the Catholic Church concerning the spiritual equality and brotherhood of all men. This is a key document in the lengthy controversy over the intellectual capacities of the American Indians. Although it is impossible to say how many of the Spanish *conquistadores* really believed the Indians to be animals *[bruta animalia],* there is no doubt that some held this view. If it had prevailed without challenge it would have enabled the Spaniards to use the lives and properties of the defenseless natives unchecked by the protecting hand of the Church, and thus the task of the missionaries would have been rendered much more difficult than it actually was.

Emperor Charles V became so concerned over the effect of the *Sublimis Deus* in the Spanish dominions that he brought pressure to bear on Paul III to revoke it. As a consequence, the pope issued another bull on June 19, 1538, which revoked all previous papal briefs and bulls that might prejudice the power of Charles V in his colonial empire. In the latter document the pope did not take back what he had said in the *Sublimis Deus* concerning the Indians' capacity for conversion, but he did declare all ecclesiastical censures and penalties imposed by the missionaries on the *conquistadors* to be null and void. This action seriously hampered the missionaries' efforts to check the rapacity of the Spaniards, but as one scholar has stated, "the bull Sublimis Deus lived on as a force to be reckoned with in the endless disputes over the true nature of the American Indians because the nullification was not widely known." Lewis Hanke, "Pope Paul III and the American Indians," *Harvard Theological Review*, XXX (April, 1937), 97.

(*Source*: Francis Augustus MacNutt, *Bartholomew de Las Casas.* New York: G. P. Putnam's Sons, 1909, 427–31.)

PAUL III POPE. TO ALL FAITHFUL CHRISTIANS TO WHOM THIS writing may come, health in Christ our Lord and the apostolic benediction.

The sublime God so loved the human race that He created man in such wise that he might participate, not only in the good that other creatures enjoy, but endowed him with capacity to attain to the inaccessible and invisible Supreme Good and behold it face to face; and since man, according to the testimony of the sacred scriptures, has been created to enjoy eternal life and happiness, which none may obtain save through faith in our Lord Jesus Christ, it is necessary that he should possess the nature and faculties enabling him to receive that faith; and that whoever is thus endowed should be capable of receiving that same faith. Nor is it credible that any one should possess so little understanding as to desire the faith and yet be destitute of the most necessary faculty to enable him to receive it. Hence Christ, who is the Truth itself, that has never failed and can never fail, said to the preachers of the faith whom He chose for that office 'Go ye and teach all nations.' He said all, without exception, for all are capable of receiving the doctrines of the faith.

The enemy of the human race, who opposes all good deeds in order to bring men to destruction, beholding and envying this, invented a means never before heard of, by which he might hinder the preaching of God's word of Salvation to the people: he inspired his satellites who, to please him, have not hesitated to publish abroad that the Indians of the West and the South, and other people of whom We have recent knowledge should be treated as dumb brutes created for our service, pretending that they are incapable of receiving the Catholic Faith.

We, who, though unworthy, exercise on earth the power of our Lord and seek with all our might to bring those sheep of His flock who are outside into the fold committed to our charge, consider, however, that the Indians are truly men and that they are not only capable of understanding the Catholic Faith but, according to our information, they desire exceedingly to receive it. Desiring to provide ample remedy for these evils, We define and declare by these Our letters, or by any translation thereof signed by any notary public and sealed with the seal of any ecclesiastical dignitary, to which the same credit shall be given as to the originals, that, notwithstanding whatever may have been or may be said to the contrary, the said Indians and all other people who may later be discovered by Christians, are by no means to be deprived of their liberty or the possession of their property, even though they be outside the faith of Jesus Christ; and that they may and should, freely and legitimately, enjoy their liberty and the possession of their property; nor should they be in any way enslaved; should the contrary happen, it shall be null and of no effect.

By virtue of Our apostolic authority We define and declare by these present letters, or by any translation thereof signed by any notary public and sealed with the seal of any ecclesiastical dignitary, which shall thus command the same obedience as the originals, that the said Indians and other peoples should be converted to the faith of Jesus Christ by preaching the word of God and by the example of good and holy living.

(*Source*: John Tracy Ellis, ed. *Documents of American Catholic History.* Vol. 1:1493–1865. Wilmington, Del.: Michael Glazier, 1987, 7–8.)

NATIVISM

The antipathy which many nineteenth-century Americans felt toward the "foreigner" and toward Catholics dated from the colonial period, and was rooted in the political and religious intrigues of sixteenth- and seventeenth-century Britain. British nationhood coalesced around the Protestant cause, an interconnectedness which many Americans transferred to their own national experience and came to regard as indispensable.

In colonial times, non-Anglo-Saxon Protestants did not exist in numbers large enough to cause public alarm. By contrast, Irish (as well as German and English) Catholics, although small in number, inspired considerable dread among the colonists, and were thought to warrant special penal legislation. Concentrations of Catholics could only be found in two colonies, Maryland and Pennsylvania, and their numbers did not exceed 35,000 or about one percent of the American population in 1790.

Catholic Immigrants and the Nativists

The relative homogeneity of American society in 1800 would not endure. While 143,000 immigrants arrived between

1820 and 1830, more than 2.5 million made the journey between 1851 and 1860. This last figure equaled 13 percent of the total white population of the United States in 1850.

Waves of nativist feeling would rise and break around particular issues such as convents and convent schools, the "invasion" of the Mississippi valley by foreigners, the threat to the exclusive use of the King James Bible in public education, and the ever-growing numbers of foreign-born voters.

Certain "monuments" in the struggle are to be noted. Among these are the burning of the Ursuline convent at Charlestown, Massachusetts, on the night of August 11–12, 1834, and the appearance, two years later, of the wildly successful *Awful Disclosures of the Hôtel-Dieu Nunnery of Montreal* by Maria Monk.

In 1842, responding to the demands of Bishop John Hughes of New York for a share of public education funds, the state legislature removed control of the city schools from the Public School Society and vested it in local boards. Henceforth, and to the eternal regret of the nativists, the Protestant Scriptures and sectarian textbooks would no longer find an automatic home in the city classrooms.

Two years later, after Philadelphia had allowed Catholic children to use their own Bibles and had dispensed them from Protestant religious exercises, the Kensington and Southwark riots broke out. By midsummer, numerous Irish properties had been put to the torch, two Catholic churches lay in ashes, and scores of people were dead or injured. Public opinion recoiled from the violence, and organized nativism slipped into a short period of decline.

The Know-Nothings

The movement did not become altogether dormant. Journalistic and speaking careers continued to be made. Fraternities embodying nativist principles were founded. New York's "Order of United Americans" and Philadelphia's "United Sons of America" dated from the end of 1844. The most successful of the secret societies, the "Order of the Star-Spangled Banner," was founded in 1849, reorganized in 1852, and nicknamed the "Know-Nothings" by the press in 1853.

The country would soon witness a resurgence in overt anti-Catholic and anti-immigrant feeling. The ex-priest Alessandro Gavazzi arrived in America on March 23, 1853, and began a successful speaking tour. The arrival in the same year of Archbishop Gaetano Bedini, the papal nuncio to Brazil and extraordinary envoy to the United States, was seen as tangible proof of Rome's growing hegemony in American domestic affairs. In his travels, the archbishop was frequently greeted by hostile mobs and was burned in effigy.

By the 1850s, nativism was ready to delve into American politics. Besides its historic attractions, many thought that nativism had the potential to surmount the divisions wrought by slavery. The Know-Nothing cause enjoyed remarkable success in the spring elections of 1854, and even more stunning results in the fall when several state governments were captured. Many minor parties crowded the electoral stage, and allowed candidates with mere pluralities to win office.

Once in control, Know-Nothings revealed themselves to be inept legislators. Massachusetts found that it had placed itself in the hands of men who had never held office and who were quite incapable of governing. Legislative results were few. In Washington, Know-Nothing lawmakers could achieve a coalition with neither the Democrats nor the Whigs. The established parties had no desire to alienate the immigrant or the Catholic vote.

The great test of Know-Nothing power came in the presidential election of 1856. Millard Fillmore, their favored candidate, ran on the American Party ticket. By this point, however, party unity had been sapped by the slavery issue. While Know-Nothingism seemed poised to capture the White House by 1855, two years later its power lay in ruins. Fillmore carried only one state, Maryland. Slavery and war would supplant nativism, if only temporarily, as the burning issue of the day.

See also KU KLUX KLAN.

Anbinder, Tyler. *Nativism and Slavery*. New York: Oxford University Press, 1992.

Billington, Ray Allen. *The Protestant Crusade*. New York: Macmillan, 1938.

Curran, Thomas J. *Xenophobia and Immigration, 1820–1930*. Boston: Twayne, 1975.

Knobel, Dale T. *Paddy and the Republic*. Middletown, Conn.: Wesleyan University Press, 1986.

Shaughnessy, Gerald, S.M. *Has the Immigrant Kept the Faith?* New York: Macmillan, 1925.

ALBERT H. LEDOUX

Related Document

THE LAUNCHING OF THE AMERICAN PROTESTANT ASSOCIATION AGAINST THE CATHOLIC CHURCH, NOVEMBER 22, 1842

After 1820 the numerical strength of the Catholic Church in the United States rose rapidly by reason of immigration, and by 1840 there were estimated to be 663,000 Catholics out of a total population of 14,195,805 white Americans. This increase alarmed many American Protestants who disliked the Church and who feared, too, lest native Americans be supplanted in their jobs by the cheaper labor of Irish and German immigrants, so many of whom were Catholics. The result was an organized effort against Catholics under the banner of American nativism. The nativists needed only a very slender excuse to go into action and when

Francis P. Kenrick (1796–1863), Bishop of Philadelphia, on November 14, 1842, respectfully petitioned the board of the city's public schools for redress against Catholic children having to use the King James Bible and to be present at Protestant religious exercises in the schools, an excuse was at hand. A group of the city's Protestant leaders met and on November 22 ninety-four ministers, representing twelve denominations, signed the constitution of what they called the American Protestant Association. The association was responsible for arousing antagonism between Protestants and Catholics and its agents were in good measure to blame for the public riots in May and July, 1844, in which thirteen citizens were killed, over fifty wounded, and two of Philadelphia's Catholic churches burned. The constitution of this association which follows was typical of the numerous organizations of this kind which were actively at work against the Church throughout the country up to the Civil War.

(*Source*: Ray Allen Billington, *The Protestant Crusade, 1800–1860: A Study of the Origins of American Nativism*. New York: The Macmillan Co., 1938, 438–39; reissued in 1952 by Rinehart & Co., New York.)

WHEREAS, WE BELIEVE THE SYSTEM OF POPERY TO BE, IN its principles and tendency, subversive of civil and religious liberty, and destructive to the spiritual welfare of men, we unite for the purpose of defending our Protestant interests against the great exertions now making to propagate that system in the United States; and adopt the following constitution:—

Article I. This Society shall be called the American Protestant Association.

Article II. The objects of its formation, and for the attainment of which its efforts shall be directed, are—

1. The union and encouragement of Protestant ministers of the gospel, to give to their several congregations instruction on the differences between Protestantism and Popery.

2. To call attention to the necessity of a more extensive distribution, and thorough study of the Holy Scriptures.

3. The circulation of books and tracts adapted to give information on the various errors of Popery in their history, tendency, and design.

4. To awaken the attention of the community to the dangers which threaten the liberties, and the public and domestic institutions, of these United States from the assaults of Romanism.

Article III. This Association shall be composed of all such persons as agree in adopting the purposes and principles of this constitution and contribute to the funds by which it is supported.

Article IV. The officers of the Association shall be a President, three Vice-Presidents, a treasurer, a corresponding secretary, a recording secretary, and two lay directors from each denomination represented in the Association, to be elected annually; together with all the ministers belonging to it; who shall form a Board for the transaction of business of whom any seven, at a meeting duly convened, shall be a quorum. The stated meetings of the Board to be quarterly.

Article V. The Board of managers shall, at the first meeting after their election, appoint an executive committee, consisting of a minister and layman from each of the denominations represented in the association, of which the secretaries and treasurer shall be ex-officio members. This committee to meet as often as they may find necessary for the transaction of the business committed to them, and to report quarterly to the Board of managers.

Article VI. The duties of the Board shall be, to carry out, in every way most expedient in their view, the ends and purposes for which this Association is organized; and to aid and encourage the formation of similar associations in the various parts of the United States; and to render an annual report of their proceedings to the Association, at their annual meeting on the second Tuesday in November.

Article VII. The Board of managers shall have power to enact such by-laws as may not be inconsistent with this constitution, and to fill all vacancies that may occur between the annual meetings.

Article VIII. This constitution shall be subject to amendments only at the annual meetings of the Association, by a vote of two thirds of the members present at such meeting.

(*Source*: John Tracy Ellis, ed. *Documents of American Catholic History*. Vol. 1:1493–1865. Wilmington, Del.: Michael Glazier, 1987, 263–65.)

NEALE, LEONARD (1746–1817)

Second archbishop of Baltimore. Leonard Neale was born in Port Tobacco, Maryland, on October 15, 1746, the son of William and Ann Brooke Neale, both descendants of old Maryland Catholic families. Neale received a Jesuit education in France and Flanders, entered the Society of Jesus on September 7, 1767, at Ghent, and was ordained a priest on June 5, 1773, in Liège. He served as a missionary in England and in British Guiana, then returned to Maryland due to ill health in 1783 and was assigned to the mission in his native Port Tobacco.

In 1793 Neale left Port Tobacco to go to St. Mary's Church in Philadelphia where Bishop John Carroll had appointed him vicar general. In Philadelphia he met Alice Lalor and was instrumental in helping her to found the first community of Visitation Sisters in the United States. In 1798 Neale was appointed president of Georgetown Academy which developed into Georgetown College in 1801. On December 7, 1800, Neale was consecrated as John Carroll's coadjutor and succeeded Carroll as the second archbishop of Baltimore upon Carroll's death on December 3, 1815. Almost seventy years of age when he became archbishop, Neale had to face difficulties with lay

Leonard Neale

trustees in both Norfolk, Virginia, and Charleston, South Carolina. He died in Georgetown on June 18, 1817, and was buried in the chapel of the Visitation convent.

See also MARYLAND, CATHOLIC CHURCH IN.

Brislen, Bernetta, O.S.F. "The Episcopacy of Leonard Neale." *Historical Records and Studies* 34 (1945) 20–111.
Spalding, Thomas W. *The Premier See: A History of the Archdiocese of Baltimore, 1789–1989.* Baltimore, 1989.

LISELLE DRAKE

NEBRASKA, CATHOLIC CHURCH IN

Although it was a popular belief among Nebraskans well into this century that the Spanish explorer Coronado visited the area that would become their state during his search for the wealth of the fabled kingdom of Quivera, historians today agree that his expedition went no farther north than central Kansas. The first European entrance into the area to be known as Nebraska was the visit by Lieutenant Colonel Pedro de Villasur in 1720, whose party of over a hundred included a Franciscan chaplain, Juan Mingues. Probably incited by the rival French explorers, the Pawnee attacked the Spanish at their encampment beside the fork of the Platte River, and Villasur and Fr. Mingues were among the many killed. In 1739 the brothers Pierre and Paul Mallet, French-Canadians, made a more extensive tour of the area; their expedition escaped violence, and for nearly a century afterward, the area was the site of extensive fur trading. In the early 1800s Manuel Lisa, Peter Sarpy, and Lucien Fontenelle stood out among the traders with their posts along the river near today's

cities of Omaha and Bellevue, and they were connected with the foundations of the Catholic Church in St. Louis.

Catholic ecclesiastical authority over the area had begun in 1493 with Spanish control of most of North America. In 1682 the area came under the rule of France and Church supervision by the bishop of Quebec. Spanish control resumed in 1763 with Church administration by the bishop of Santiago, Cuba. The Louisiana Purchase of 1803 made the region part of the United States, with Catholic direction by Bishop John Carroll of Baltimore. Authority was transferred to New Orleans in 1815, and to St. Louis in 1827. In 1850 Pope Pius IX created the apostolic vicariate of the territory east of the Rocky Mountains with Jean Baptist Miège, S.J., as vicar apostolic. Miège was made a bishop and assumed his duties in 1851.

Three years after the United States government opened Nebraska Territory to non-Native American settlement in 1854, the vicariate of Nebraska was established. The ecclesiastical division was reduced with the formation of the vicariate of Dakota in 1880, and the vicariate of Montana in 1883.

First Missionary Activity

In the winter of 1822–23 Bishop Louis DuBourg of New Orleans went to Washington, D.C., to request government financial support from the secretary of war, John C. Calhoun, for missionaries who would minister to the Catholics at Fort Atkinson, the original Council Bluff of Lewis and Clark, as well as to the indigenous peoples in the Upper Missouri River area. Fort Atkinson was closed before a priest could be sent there, but St. Joseph's Mission to the Potawatomi in what is now Council Bluffs, Iowa, across the Missouri River from the future site of Omaha, was established on September 12, 1837, with three Jesuits in charge, Frs. Felix Verreydt, Andrew Mazella, and Peter Jean De Smet. De Smet would become the most traveled and most famous of Jesuit missionaries in nineteenth-century North America, working with both Native Americans and Europeans through the Plains and Rocky Mountains. He is credited with generously assisting Mormon leader Brigham Young in finding the best route to the Salt Lake. St. Joseph's Mission was not a success, however, because most of the Potawatomi moved away from the region under pressure from the hostile Dakota, and the mission was closed in 1841.

First Catholic Settlers

With the support of his bishop, Matthias Loras of Dubuque, Irish-born Fr. Jeremiah Trecy in 1856 led a wagon train of fellow immigrants across Iowa to found the St. Patrick's Colony in Dakota County in northeast Nebraska. Although the colony's town, St. John's Fountain Bluff, was abandoned after only a few years, many of these first Catholic settlers in Nebraska remained on the farms they had claimed, and their descendants are still among the most prominent residents of the state. One such descendant, Daniel Sheehan, became archbishop of Omaha in 1972.

In the 1870s, another Irish colony was established on the empty grassland of Holt County; it was named O'Neill after General John O'Neill, notorious for leading three Fenian raids into Canada in an attempt to end British rule over Ireland. The town of O'Neill flourished, and today considers itself the Irish capital of the state.

Later in the decade, a final Irish colony was located in Greeley County, sponsored by the Irish Catholic Colonization Association, promoted by Thomas D'Arcy McGee, Bishop John Ireland of St. Paul, and Bishop John Lancaster Spalding of Peoria. The towns of O'Connor (named after the Omaha bishop) and Spalding were developed, but always remained small in population.

Discovery of gold in Colorado in 1859 caused tens of thousands of Easterners to cross Nebraska, and the location of Omaha made it the principal outfitting center and a major gateway to the West. Many of the freighters and outfitters were Irish Catholics, and these formed the nucleus of the Church in the state's first urban area.

The building of the Union Pacific immediately after the Civil War as the nation's first transcontinental railroad not only guaranteed the development of Nebraska as one of the nation's most important agricultural states and Omaha as a major transportation center but also brought the largest number of Irish to the state, as laborers and often as contractors. Most of these eventually settled in Omaha, giving a particularly Irish cast to many of the city's social, business, and cultural institutions.

Construction of the Burlington Railroad, which principally served that part of Nebraska south of the Platte River, followed soon after the Union Pacific. Again, the Irish were leaders. John Fitzgerald, contractor for much of the Burlington Route, first settled in Plattsmouth, but in the early 1870s moved to Lincoln, where through extraordinary business acumen he became the state capital's first millionaire. He was the foremost patron of the Church in the city, funding a convent and an orphanage, and assumed a nationally visible role as president of the Irish National League, the American branch of Charles Stewart Parnell's Land League.

The Irish were hardly the only visible Catholic ethnic group however. Germans nearly rivaled them in numbers among pioneer Catholics in Nebraska. In 1858 a group of laborers from Buffalo, New York, founded a Germany Colonization Society which established a settlement on the Missouri River in southern Nebraska which they named Arago, after a French explorer. While this town was not successful, in 1861 Benedictine Fr. Emmanuel Hartig began the development of an already established parish in Nebraska City into one of the first major centers of Catholicism in the state; the parishioners were primarily German. Hartig developed numerous other parishes among the pioneers; these were mostly south of the Platte; north of that river Fr. John Daxacher was charged with the care of Germans, with the highest concentration in Cuming County, where even today the town of West Point exhibits a definite German character.

The Burlington Railroad brought Bohemians to the farms in the interior of the state. Their experiences on the harsh frontier are vividly described in Willa Cather's novels *My Antonia* and *O Pioneers!* Between 1866 and 1879 approximately five hundred families settled in Saline County alone. One-fifth of all Czech immigrants who remained to farm in the United States lived in Nebraska. The greatest concentration was in Butler, Colfax, Saline, and Saunders Counties, where at the turn of the twentieth century five thousand Bohemian families resided. For many years parts of South Omaha had a distinctly Bohemian flavor.

Growth of the Church

The first bishop, James M. O'Gorman, an Irish-born Trappist, was vicar apostolic from May 8, 1859, to his death July 4, 1874. His problems were the usual ones for a man heading a diocese in the American West. There were few priests to serve an enormous, sparsely populated geographical territory, and many of the priests he had were poorly educated and often headstrong individuals adverse to accepting authority. The laity were mostly poor, and suspicious of and occasionally hostile to Catholics of other ethnic groups.

These problems were still present when O'Gorman was succeeded by another Irish-born bishop, James O'Connor, who was consecrated vicar apostolic on August 10, 1876. By the time the erection of the Diocese of Omaha on October 2, 1885, with James O'Connor as the first bishop, and of the Diocese of Lincoln under the leadership of Thomas W. Bonacum on October 2, 1887, the state was more heavily populated, but throughout the 1890s severe drought and a national economic depression kept the Church in both rural and urban areas in a precarious financial situation.

By the beginning of the twentieth century, however, standards of living reflected those of most of the nation, and with the exception of the years of the Great Depression, a general prosperity has been characteristic of the state's people and institutions. The Diocese of Kearney was erected on May 8, 1912, comprising western Nebraska north of the Platte, with James A. Duffy as bishop; the name and seat were changed to Grand Island April 8, 1917.

In Omaha Richard Scannell, who was transferred from the Diocese of Concordia, Kansas, in 1891, is principally remembered as the builder of St. Cecilia's Cathedral, designed in the Spanish renaissance style by Thomas Kimball, a future president of the American Institute of Architects, and one of the ten largest cathedrals in the United States. The bishop of Omaha from 1928 to 1935 was Joseph Rummel, who went on to head the Archdiocese of New Orleans and achieve lasting national distinction for desegregating that city's Catholic schools. In Omaha his special accomplishment was hosting the Sixth National Eucharistic Congress in September 1930. Under James Hugh Ryan, a former rector of The Catholic University of America, Omaha became an archdiocese on August 7, 1945. Archbishop Gerald R. Bergan from 1946 to 1972 presided over the tremendous growth of physical facilities, especially of parochial schools. Daniel E. Sheehan, (1972–94) participated with his brother Nebraska bishops in the sessions of the Second Vatican Council and implemented the council's decrees. In 1995 retired bishop John L. Paschang of Grand Island was, at one hundred years, the oldest bishop in the world.

Religious Communities

Benedictines have been in the state since the arrival of Fr. Emmanuel Hartig in Nebraska City in 1858; today their principal residence is at Mt. Michael Abbey in Elkhorn, where they administer a boarding school for boys. They also operate Christ the King Priory in Schuyler. Jesuits have operated Creighton University since its founding in 1878, and also direct Creighton Preparatory School. Bellevue is the location of the American headquarters of the Columban Fathers in the United States.

The Sisters of Mercy arrived in Omaha in 1864, and since then have engaged in teaching and hospital work. The Poor Clares were established in Omaha in 1878, and the Religious of the Sacred Heart in 1881. The later group operated Duchesne College in Omaha until its closing in 1968. Other religious communities prominent in Nebraska have been the Servants of Mary, the Sisters of Charity of the Blessed Virgin Mary, the Dominicans, the School Sisters of St. Francis, and the Sisters of Notre Dame.

Catholic Institutions

Creighton University was founded in 1878, with a bequest from Edward and Mary Lucretia Creighton, and placed by Omaha bishop James O'Connor under the direction of the Jesuits, who still are in charge of the institution. In addition to the liberal arts and sciences, Creighton offers degrees in law, medicine, nursing, pharmacy, dentistry, and business administration. In 1995 enrollment stood at 6,600. The Sisters of Mercy established the College of St. Mary in Omaha in 1923. Today eleven hundred students are studying for associate and bachelor's degrees in twenty-six programs; the college is the only women's college in a five-state area.

The most famous charitable institution in the state, and undoubtedly one of the most famous in the world, is Boys Town, located in Omaha. In 1917 Fr. Edward Flanagan, an Irish immigrant with ninety dollars, rented an old mansion to house a dozen homeless boys. Flanagan's philosophy of caring for youth at risk won the support of community leaders and, within a short period, of national philanthropists as well. In 1938 an Oscar-winning film, *Boys Town,* starring Spencer Tracy and Mickey Rooney told the story of the institution's early years. Executive director since 1985, Fr. Val J. Peter has vastly increased the scope of Boys Town's work. Besides the main nine-hundred-acre facility in Omaha, home to 556 boys and girls, there are fourteen satellite facilities across the United States from Rhode Island to southern California, and on a separate Omaha campus the Boys Town National Research Hospital, which specializes in communication disorders.

Blessed Katharine Drexel, foundress of the Sisters of the Blessed Sacrament, established St. Augustine's Indian School in Winnebago, Thurston County, in 1908. In 1995 this was the principal residential educational facility for Native Americans in Nebraska.

While not strictly charitable institutions, two of the more prominent organizations with Catholic affiliation in Nebraska are the New Covenant Center for Justice and Peace, and the Pope Paul VI Institute for the Study of Human Reproduction.

Economic and Social Condition of Catholics

Although most pioneer Catholics in the state were poor, most of the Protestant pioneers were, too, and thus unlike their fellow church members in the eastern United States, Catholics generally started out on an equal footing with non-Catholics. The Irish, German, and Czech Catholics progressed socially and economically at approximately the same pace as Anglo-Saxon Protestants in the area.

In the early twentieth century, Italians, Poles, Hungarians, and Ukrainians joined the earlier groups of European immigrants to Nebraska. At first concentrated in the poorer districts of Omaha, often working in the meatpacking plants, they were soon assimilated into the mainstream of the community and frequently took leadership in the city's businesses and government. Nebraska African Americans in the state generally did not belong to the Catholic Church, but in 1947 Jesuit Fr. John Markoe of Creighton University organized the DePorres Club to work for integration and racial justice. Although the club no longer exists, various Catholic agencies in Omaha and especially Sacred Heart parish in the city's north side endeavor to put the faith into action regarding matters of race. After the Vietnam War, many parishes in Nebraska sponsored the immigration of Vietnamese and Hmong refugees. Currently, many Hispanic Catholics from Mexico and the Southwestern U.S.A. are settling in the state, having been attracted by jobs in the meatpacking plants of Omaha, South Sioux City, Columbus, and other smaller cities. The Church serves as a primary agency for efforts for integration and social welfare.

Catholic Involvement in Political Life

Historically, Nebraska has been a Republican state, and most of its Catholic residents have been Democrats. Because of their heavy concentration in the city of Omaha, however, they have been from very early times able to wield considerable political influence. John McShane was the first Nebraska Catholic elected to Congress, in 1886. James E. Boyd was an Irish immigrant who had achieved success in various businesses and, with McShane and John Creighton, was among the founders of the meatpacking industry in Omaha; elected mayor of Omaha in 1881, he was the first of many Catholics to hold the office. Boyd was governor of the state in 1893, but whether or not he had actually become an American citizen and thus eligible for the governorship became an issue seized upon by his opponent, the incumbent, who was also a prohibitionist. The opponent accused Boyd of winning the election through fraud and the collusion of Irish saloon-keepers. For a while Boyd was prevented from entering the state house by armed militia, but the Supreme Court affirmed the citizenship and he was able to serve his term.

Arthur Mullen of O'Neill first attracted notice as an attorney successful in overturning Nebraska's anti-German language legislation in 1919; he went on to become a Democratic National Committeeman, and was one of the leaders on the pro-Roosevelt delegation at the presidential nominating convention in 1932. Charles F. McLaughlin, a Democratic representative from Omaha, cast the deciding vote in Congress in favor of continuing the draft in 1941, when, before Pearl Harbor, national sentiment against American involvement in a world war was still strong. McLaughlin went on to become a federal judge in Washington, D.C., handing down decisions in several major cases.

Ideologically, Catholics in Nebraska have tended to be middle-of-the-road. An early political issue in the state was Prohibition. With their Irish or continental ethnic roots, Catholics offered no support to the opponents of saloons and alcohol who early in the century, well before the national passage of the Volstead Act, succeeded in making Nebraska a dry state. Despite some bitter strikes, first in Omaha at the turn of the century in the smelting and meatpacking industries, and in recent decades at the large meatpacking plants in smaller communities, there has been no strong labor movement, and attitudes on the government's role in education, health policy, business regulation, social justice, and military and international affairs tend to resemble in their moderation the national consensus. Institutionally, the Church maintains an office in the state capital, Lincoln, to monitor and advise upon legislation with clear ethical implications, such as civil rights issues, support for and regulation of education, and measures concerning welfare, abortion, and euthanasia. The Center for Rural Affairs, in Walthill, while not officially a Catholic organization, has for two decades had the support of the Church in its research and lobbying in the area of preservation of the family farm and improved use of agricultural land.

Catholic Involvement in the Arts

In the past, Nebraska Catholics focused their interests on agriculture and commerce, and their artistic output was minimal in quantity as well as in quality. Until recently, there were no nationally known artists from the state who were Catholic, nor were there interesting experiments in any artistic media. This is changing with the award-winning photography of Don Doll, S.J., and the ceramics of Jerry Horning, both of whom are faculty members in the Fine Arts Department at Creighton University. The Omaha-born Ron Hansen has won acclaim for his novels, especially *Mariette in Ecstacy* (1991), the story of a nun's experience with the stigmata. Hansen's 1996 novel, *Atticus*, is a contemporary retelling of the Prodigal Son story. Both Creighton University and the College of St. Mary have galleries which regularly present shows of important creative artists, and the Creighton theater mounts impressive dramatic performances, cosponsoring each summer outdoor performances of Shakespeare. Christian Brother William Woeger, liturgist for the Omaha archdiocese, inaugurated the Cathedral Arts Project in 1985, using St. Cecilia's for performances in instrumental music, opera, and dance involving the state's leading art groups in those fields; a highlight of the year attracting many thousands is the annual flower festival in the cathedral. Across the state, the arts are now strongly emphasized in Catholic elementary and secondary schools.

Prominent Laypeople

In the 1860s the Ohio-born brothers Edward and John Creighton were responsible for the development and construction of the transcontinental telegraph system; from this and from successful investments including banks and cattle ranches, they acquired a large fortune, much of which was devoted to Catholic philanthropy. In the 1870s, Gen. John O'Neill, a former Fenian leader, led the settling of the Holt County colony mentioned above. In Omaha, Edward Cudahy, a nationally prominent meatpacker, supported the cause of Irish home rule, while Valentine Peter published a national chain of German-language newspapers. Francis P. Matthews became Secretary of the Navy under President Truman and later served as ambassador to Ireland. Three generations of Leo A. Dalys have directed an architectural firm bearing their name which does a worldwide business. Army General Alfred Gruenther became Supreme Commander in Europe of NATO, and later president of the American Red Cross; his brother Homer was Chief of Protocol at the White House under four presidents.

Present total population of state: 1,591,838
   Catholic population: 341,122
   Omaha, Catholics: 206,186, out of total: 784,747
   Lincoln, Catholics: 82,931, out of total: 516,662
   Grand Island, Catholics: 52,005, out of total: 290,429
   Percentage of Catholics in the State: 21%

Casper, Henry W., S.J. *History of the Catholic Church in Nebraska.* Milwaukee: Bruce Publishing Co. Vol. I: *The Church on the Northern Plains,* 1960; Vol. II: *The Church on the Fading Frontier,* 1966; Vol. III: *Catholic Chapters in Nebraska Immigration,* 1966.

Garraghan, Gilbert J., S.J. *The Jesuits of the Middle United States.* 3 vols. New York: American Press, 1938.

Sister Loretta, C.PP.S. *History of the Catholic Church in the Diocese of Lincoln, Nebraska, 1887–1987.* Lincoln, Nebr.: The Catholic Bishop of Lincoln, Inc., 1986.

Luebke, Frederick C. *Nebraska: An Illustrated History.* Lincoln: The University of Nebraska Press, 1995.

Olson, James C. *History of Nebraska.* Lincoln: The University of Nebraska Press, 1955.

Szmrecsanyi, Stephen. *History of the Catholic Church in Northeast Nebraska.* Omaha, Nebr.: Catholic Voice Publishing Co., 1983.

1994 Official Catholic Directory. New York: P. J. Kenedy & Sons.

THOMAS A. KUHLMAN

NERINCKX, CHARLES (1761–1824)

Missionary priest. Charles Nerinckx was born in Herffelingen, in the Austrian Netherlands, on October 2, 1761. He was educated at Louvain and ordained a priest in 1785. After a decade of parochial ministry, he was forced into hiding for many years by anticlerical forces of the French Revolution. Resolving to become a missionary to the U.S.A., he arrived in Baltimore in November 1804. After a year of language study, Nerinckx was sent by Bishop John Carroll to assist in the Kentucky missions.

Nerinckx arrived in Kentucky in 1805, joining the pioneer missionary priest Stephen Badin. A man of stern morality and strong physical stature, Nerinckx was to build fourteen churches during his nineteen years in Kentucky. He was a leading force in the successful establishment of the Sisters of Loretto at the Foot of the Cross in 1812. Two other Nerinckx attempts at the founding of communities did not succeed: one for religious men, and another for African American religious women.

Charles Nerinckx

After disputes with his bishop—especially a quarrel over the rules of the Sisters of Loretto—Nerinckx left for Missouri in 1824. There he hoped to work as a missionary among Native Americans, but death overtook him that same year at Ste. Geneviève, Missouri, on August 12, 1824. He was later reburied at the Loretto motherhouse in Kentucky.

Howlett, W. J. *The Life of Charles Nerinckx.* Techny, Ill., 1915.
Wolff, Florence. *With Captain Dogwood.* Loretto, Ky., 1986.

CLYDE F. CREWS

NEUMANN, ST. JOHN (1811–60)

Saint, missionary, Redemptorist priest, fourth bishop of Philadelphia. John Nepomucene Neumann was born on March 28, 1811, in the village of Prachatitz, Bohemia, which was then part of the Hapsburg Empire. His father, Philip Neumann, a native of Bavaria, was a weaver and his mother, Agnes Lebis, was the daughter of a Czech harness maker. Young John received his early education at the village school in Prachatitz, and then attended the gymnasium in Budweis from 1823 to 1831. Budweis was a German-speaking city, and Neumann himself was culturally a German and received his education in that language, although he was also fluent in Czech.

In November 1831 Neumann entered the diocesan seminary in Budweis, and two years later won a scholarship to the seminary in Prague where he completed his studies for the priesthood in 1835. While in the seminary, Neumann developed a desire to become a missionary in America as a result of reading the descriptions of missionary activities that were published by the Leopoldinen Stiftung,

St. John Nepomucene Neumann

the Austrian missionary-aid society. He was also encouraged to pursue this missionary vocation by his spiritual director, Canon Hermann Dichtl, of the Budweis cathedral. Although Neumann passed the canonical examinations for priesthood in the Budweis diocese, the bishop decided to postpone temporarily the ordination of new priests because of the surplus of priests in the diocese. In February 1836 Neumann left for America with only two hundred francs in his pocket, without saying farewell to his parents, without dimissorial letters from the bishop of Budweis, and without a firm commitment from any American bishop to accept him into his diocese.

Missionary in America

Neumann arrived in New York City on June 1, 1836, and made contact with Bishop John Dubois, who was trying to provide priests for his sprawling diocese, which included all of New York state and the northern half of New Jersey. Within a month of his arrival in the United States, on June 25, 1836, Neumann was ordained a priest by Dubois, and he celebrated his first Mass the following day in the German church of St. Nicholas. Two days later, he left for his first assignment, in Buffalo, New York, where he served in the outlying villages of Williamsville and North Bush.

In the summer of 1840 Neumann's health broke down. His problems may have been as much emotional as physical, for he complained of loneliness and may also have suffered from scrupulosity. Among other things, he worried about the liceity of his ordination, since he had been ordained without dimissorial letters from the bishop of Budweis. In September 1840 Neumann applied for admission

to the Congregation of the Most Holy Redeemer (the Redemptorists). He informed Bishop John Hughes, administrator of the Diocese of New York, of his decision. When Neumann failed to receive a response from Hughes, he simply left the parish in October 1840 to join the Redemptorists in Pittsburgh.

At the time, the Redemptorists had been established in the United States for only eight years, and Neumann was their first American novice. In fact, his novitiate was a pious fiction, since he changed his residence that year no fewer than eight times and traveled 3,000 miles. After six weeks of a real novitiate, he made his religious profession in Baltimore on January 16, 1842. Neumann's first assignment as a Redemptorist was to the Church of St. James in Baltimore, a German national parish. From 1844 to 1847 he was pastor of another German national parish, St. Philomena's in Pittsburgh. In March 1847 he was appointed superior of the Redemptorists in the United States, with the title first of vice regent and later of vice provincial. He held the post for twenty-two months, but he was unhappy dealing with financial and personnel problems, and he repeatedly asked to be relieved of the position. In 1851 he received a more congenial assignment when he was made pastor of the still-unfinished Church of St. Alphonsus, the main Redemptorist parish in Baltimore, which also included responsibility for two mission churches, St. James and St. Michael's in Fells Point. One of his major accomplishments as pastor was to obtain the services of the School Sisters of Notre Dame for the parochial schools of all three churches.

Bishop of Philadelphia

On February 1, 1852, Neumann was appointed the fourth bishop of Philadelphia. Some American bishops objected to the appointment on the grounds that Neumann was not an effective public speaker in English and that he lacked the social graces that would be expected of a bishop in a sophisticated city like Philadelphia. The decisive factors in his appointment appear to have been the desire to give the Germans a greater representation in the American hierarchy and the influence in Rome of Archbishop Francis Patrick Kenrick of Baltimore (who had been Neumann's predecessor in Philadelphia). Neumann was consecrated in St. Alphonsus Church on March 28, 1852, his forty-first birthday. Only two bishops were present at his consecration; not one appeared at his installation in Philadelphia.

The Diocese of Philadelphia (which has since been subdivided into six additional dioceses) then contained some 170,000 Catholics spread over 35,000 square miles with 113 parishes and 100 priests to serve them. Like most German-American clerics, Neumann was a strong advocate of parochial schools, but the claim that he established one hundred parochial schools in Philadelphia seems to be a pious exaggeration. At the time of his death in 1860, according to the *Metropolitan Catholic Almanac and Laity's Directory,* the diocese contained only thirty-seven parochial schools of which nine had fewer than sixty students and nineteen had only one teacher.

Neumann was responsible for bringing seven religious communities to the Diocese of Philadelphia, and he was instrumental in establishing a flourishing local community of Franciscan sisters. However, he showed the same distaste for administrative duties that he had displayed as a religious superior. Twice (1855, 1858) he suggested that the diocese should be divided, and on both occasions he volunteered to become bishop of the newer and smaller diocese. He told the Congregation de Propaganda Fide that Philadelphia "needs someone else instead of myself, who am too plain and not sufficiently talented." "Besides," he said, "I love solitude."

Archbishop Gaetano Bedini, after his American tour, recommended in 1855 that Neumann be replaced as bishop of Philadelphia. Archbishop Kenrick was also critical of Neumann's management of his diocese. As a result, Neumann was given a coadjutor, James F. Wood, who was appointed on December 9, 1856, and consecrated on April 26, 1857. The relationship between the two bishops was somewhat strained, since Wood was under the impression that Neumann would retire shortly after his appointment, but Neumann showed no disposition to do so.

Even as bishop of Philadelphia, Neumann continued, as far as possible, to lead the life of a parish priest, devoting much of his time to hearing confessions, attending to sick calls, and teaching catechism to children. On one occasion, he made a trip of twenty-five miles over mountain roads in order to administer the sacrament of confirmation to a single child. A gifted linguist, he was fluent in German, Czech, English, French, Italian, and Spanish, and he even learned enough Irish to be able to hear the confessions of Irish-speaking immigrants in that language.

As a bishop, Neumann also continued his daily round of religious devotions, especially those that were focused on the expiation of sin. He was fond of the Forty Hours Devotion and promoted it in his diocese. Although his confessor denied it, Neumann may also have suffered from scrupulosity. On one occasion, for example, he refused to give Holy Communion to an adult convert after baptizing him for fear that the grains of salt placed on the man's tongue had broken the eucharistic fast. His confessor also revealed (after Neumann's death) that he had worn "a girdle of iron wire that had penetrated his flesh" and had "chastised his innocent body with a scourge which he had armed with a sharp nail."

In his own lifetime, Neumann's indifference to personal honors and to his own comfort was legendary. As bishop

of Philadelphia, he sometimes spent his free days at the local Redemptorist house where he would assist the lay brothers with the kitchen chores. At the age of forty-nine, Neumann collapsed suddenly on a street in Philadelphia and died, apparently of a heart attack, on January 5, 1860. He was buried in the Redemptorist Church of St. Peter the Apostle, Philadelphia. He was beatified on October 13, 1963, and canonized by Pope Paul VI on June 19, 1977. His feast day is celebrated on January 5.

See also AMERICAN CATHOLIC SPIRITUALITY.

The Autobiography of St. John Neumann, C.Ss.R. Boston, 1977.

Curley, Michael J., C.Ss.R. *Venerable John Neumann, C.Ss.R.* Washington, D.C., 1952.

Rush, Alfred C., C.Ss.R., and Thomas J. Donaghy, F.S.C. "The Saintly John Neumann and his Coadjutor, Archbishop Wood." *The History of the Archdiocese of Philadelphia,* ed. James F. Connelly. Philadelphia, 1976, 209–70.

THOMAS J. SHELLEY

NEVADA, CATHOLIC CHURCH IN

The state of Nevada was admitted into the Union in 1864 making it the thirty-sixth state. Geographically it lies in the Great Basin between the Rocky Mountains to the east and the Sierra Nevada to the west. There was no Catholic missionary work among Native American peoples living in the area until the nineteenth century, although Spanish missionaries traveling from New Mexico traversed the area.

The area came under U.S. jurisdiction in 1848 through the Mexican Cession. The first recorded Mass was celebrated in 1858 in Carson Valley, and shortly thereafter priests began accompanying miners leaving California for newly discovered silver mines in Nevada. The population increased rapidly because of prospecting, and the Church grew along with the population. Fr. Patrick Manogue, later the first bishop of Sacramento, built the first church in Virginia City and is credited with establishing the Church in Nevada. The Diocese of Reno, which once comprised the entire state, was not established until 1931, and before that, Catholics were under the jurisdiction of the bishops of Sacramento and Salt Lake City. Prior to that, Church organization was slow to develop due to the transitory life of miners.

Thomas K. Gorman, a priest of the Diocese (later Archdiocese) of Los Angeles, was named the first bishop of Reno in 1931, and he had about 10,000 Catholics in his new diocese, about one-tenth of the entire population of Nevada. The diocese was made a suffragan see of the Archdiocese of San Francisco. The state enjoyed rapid growth after the 1950s due mainly to tourism and legalized gambling. Because of this, in 1976 Pope Paul VI redesignated this diocese the Diocese of Reno-Las Vegas, and later in 1995, Pope John Paul II split off Las Vegas from the original see to create two separate dioceses: Reno and Las Vegas. Bishop Daniel F. Walsh was appointed the new diocese's first ordinary.

The federal government owns almost 85 percent of the state. The state contains both Native Americans (living mostly on reservations) and Hispanics, but the population is over 90 percent white. The Catholic Church in Nevada remains quite small with fewer than 60 diocesan priests for about 50 parishes with approximately 175,000 Catholics. The two dioceses operate no more than fifteen schools. However, the Church is growing quite rapidly with a statistically high number of both infant and adult baptisms. Nevada has liberal laws with both legalized prostitution and quick and easy divorces that create an unusual challenge for the Church compared to the situation in the rest of the U.S.A.

ANTHONY D. ANDREASSI

NEW DEAL AND AMERICAN CATHOLICS, THE

The decade of the 1930s, the years of the Great Depression and Franklin Delano Roosevelt's New Deal, marked the golden age of Catholic social action. With one-fourth of American wages earners unemployed by 1933, the nation's farm economy all but destroyed, its banks collapsing and many of its factories closed, Catholics, like all Americans, demanded change.

The Catholic bishops had among their responsibilities oversight of a complex array of social service agencies and institutions, not least their parishes. They knew better than most the inadequacy of private charity to cope with the emergency, and they became early and effective champions of federal action to relieve the suffering of the unemployed and correct the ills of the economy. In a series of public statements, concluding with the comprehensive "The Church and the Social Order" of 1940, the Catholic bishops endorsed the reforms of the New Deal, including federally sponsored relief and public works, old age pensions, unemployment insurance, support for the disabled and for families with dependent children, and the National Labor Relations Act, with its backing of the right of workers to form independent trade unions.

The bishops found theoretical support for this activism from two sources. One was Pope Pius XI's encyclical *Quadragesimo Anno* of 1931. While they shared little of that encyclical's enthusiasm for a "Christian social order," they found backing for their own instinctive support for the cause of social reform in its criticism of unrestrained capitalism and its endorsement of government responsibility. The second, related source was the work of Msgr. John A. Ryan, director of the Social Action Department of the Bishops' National Catholic Welfare Conference,

who drafted many of their statements on public policy. Ryan had much earlier worked out a Catholic understanding of social policy which corresponded to many of the positions adopted by the Roosevelt administration. So strong was Ryan's support that he became known as "The Right Reverend New Dealer."

Catholic voters, whose allegiance to the Democratic Party nationally was strengthened by the 1928 presidential campaign of Alfred E. Smith, gave Roosevelt and his party their strong support. Once quite divided in national politics, Catholic voters became an important and dependable component of the so-called New Deal coalition that dominated national politics from 1932 until the 1980s. Roosevelt recognized the importance of Catholic, blue collar voters, and he regularly added Catholics to his administration and courted Catholic leaders.

The New Deal years also saw the emergence of vigorous work for social justice among priests, religious, and laypeople. As the American Federation of Labor and the Congress of Industrial Organizations moved to unionize the mass production industries, they enjoyed the support of the bishops and of many "labor priests" who took up their cause. Later a number of priests established labor schools to educate Catholic workers about their rights and about the evil of communism. In 1933 convert author Dorothy Day and itinerant French agitator Peter Maurin launched the Catholic Worker movement, with its engaging newspaper. Its soup kitchens soon appeared in most major cities. Fr. Charles E. Coughlin, the famous radio priest of Royal Oak, Michigan, offered a far less benign version of Catholic social action with his bitter attacks, first on bankers and capitalists, then on Roosevelt, later on the Jews, as he became one of the country's most notorious anti-Semites.

Catholics were less enthusiastic about New Deal foreign policy. Even Roosevelt's stoutest Catholic backers disliked his recognition of Communist Russia in 1933 and his administration's support for the anticlerical Mexican government. When the threat of war arose again in Europe, Catholics and their leaders were divided. Some, like Chicago's George Cardinal Mundelein, actively supported Roosevelt's internationalist initiatives, while others openly supported the isolationist cause, their intensity rising after the outbreak of war in 1939. Still, Catholic voters remained loyal in 1940.

Flynn, George Q. *American Catholics and the Roosevelt Presidency, 1932–1936.* Lexington, Ky., 1968.

____. *Roosevelt and Romanism: Catholics and American Diplomacy, 1937–1945.* Westport, Conn., 1976.

O'Brien, David. *American Catholics and Social Reform: The New Deal Years.* New York, Oxford University Press, 1968.

DAVID O'BRIEN

NEW HAMPSHIRE, CATHOLIC CHURCH IN

Beginnings

New Hampshire has a proud and venerable history—ancient by American terms, at least. It was one of the thirteen original colonies, and the ninth state to ratify the Constitution. Catholicism did not take root easily in its 9,305 square miles of generally rocky soil. The first shoots of the faith sprouted in the hearts of some of the Native Americans converted by the French missionaries of neighboring New France. By the time of the American Revolution most of the Native Americans had been eliminated, generally by war, massacres, and disease. Some sought refuge on the reservations of New France where their descendants live today.

Most likely, the first Masses celebrated in what is now the state of New Hampshire were at Oyster River (now Durham) on July 18, 1694. These were celebrated by two Jesuits who accompanied a French-sponsored war party that ravaged Oyster River during King William's War (1689–97). One of the captives of that raid, Mary Ann Davis, was taken to New France where she was converted and subsequently became an Ursuline nun. Thus she became the first inhabitant of New Hampshire, and one of the first in New England, to enter religious life.

Except for the relatively small number of war prisoners of the French who became Catholics, bigotry was the overwhelming sentiment, an attitude strongly reciprocated by the Catholic French. Romanism was not tolerated by law in New Hampshire. For many years Catholics were even denied the rights of free citizens, and a religiously unacceptable "test-oath" was required under pain of fine or imprisonment. For a time after 1647, a Catholic priest, under certain specific conditions, found on the territory of the colony, could be put to death. This law was never enforced.

In fact, the state and any official Protestant church selected by the voters of a town were not legally separated until 1819, some forty-three years after the Declaration of Independence and a good thirty years after the passage of the Federal Constitution. Provisions disbarring Catholics from holding the offices of governor, state senator, or representative were not stricken from the state constitution until 1877. The final provision of the state constitution, perceived as anti-Catholic, which allowed certain civic entities to employ public Protestant teachers of piety under specified conditions, was not eliminated by the people until 1968.

New Hampshire was not regularly visited by Catholic priests until the 1790s. Among the first were Frs. Francis Matignon and Jean-Louis Cheverus, two heroic missionaries of much of New England. In addition to the few scattered Catholics reached by these early missionaries, there were an equally small number of converts. Among these were Thomas Goffe, his wife and children, who walked sixty miles from Bedford, New Hampshire, to Boston in the fall of 1831, to receive instructions and be admitted into the Catholic Church.

Certainly the most spectacular conversion of that period was that of Virgil Barber, his wife and their five children. Virgil Barber was an Episcopal priest. With unusual dispensations from Rome, he was allowed to be ordained a Jesuit, and his wife to become a Visitation nun. All five children eventually embraced religious life. Three daughters became Ursulines, another joined her Visitation mother, and the only son was eventually ordained a Jesuit, like his father.

After ordination on December 3, 1822, Fr. Virgil Barber was assigned to Claremont, New Hampshire, where he joined his father, a convert like himself, and for twenty-four previous years the rector of the Episcopal church in that town. Assisted by his father, Virgil Barber established St. Mary's parish, brought more than one hundred persons into the Catholic community, built the first Catholic church on the soil of New Hampshire, and opened the first secondary school for boys in New England. Unfortunately, Fr. Barber was withdrawn in 1828, after which most of the results of his ministry faded away.

Early Nineteenth Century

Indicative of how slowly Catholicism expanded in New Hampshire is the fact that it is estimated that there were only 387 Catholics in the state by 1835. In fact by the time Maine and New Hampshire were separated from Boston to found the Diocese of Portland, on July 29, 1853, there were only three parishes—Dover, Manchester, and Portsmouth—and three resident priests in the entire Granite State. Prior to the establishment of Portland, New Hampshire had been a part of the Diocese of Baltimore, 1789–1808, and then of Boston, 1808–53.

As the nineteenth century progressed, the number of Catholics in New Hampshire began to increase and eventually, toward the end of the century, to grow phenomenally. The first to arrive in numbers were the French-Canadians who began crossing the border from Quebec beginning in 1837. This immigration did not slow down appreciably until 1928, with the passing of federal anti-immigration legislation. Next came the Irish, who trickled in until the famine of 1846, and then arrived in almost uncountable numbers until the end of the century. The French-Canadians and the Irish were followed by German, Polish, Lithuanian, Syrian, and Ukrainian Catholics. Few Italians and even fewer Portuguese settled in New Hampshire. Negligible numbers of Catholics from other nations chose the state as their home. Those who chose New Hampshire were originally attracted by the cotton mills, the construction of the canals and railroads, and a few other industries.

In the spirit of the times, the arrival of Catholics in New Hampshire instigated an occasional outbreak of anti-Catholicism. The nativist outbursts of the 1830s and 1840s had little impact, other than an unsuccessful attempt to burn the Catholic church in Dover; the American Party, the Know-Nothings of the 1850s, created anti-Catholic disturbances in several towns, including a nearly successful one to burn down St. Anne's in Manchester on the Fourth of July 1854; the American Protective Association of the 1890s produced some unpleasantness, and the Ku Klux Klan of the 1920s created even less public antipathy.

One major factor in the expansion of Catholic institutions in New Hampshire was the arrival of five Sisters of Mercy in St. Anne parish, Manchester, on July 16, 1858, under the leadership of Mother Frances Xavier Warde, a strong and extraordinary woman. This community, the first group of religious to settle in the state, eventually expanded to all borders of New Hampshire, and served as the beacon and vanguard to some forty additional orders of religious women, and to more than twenty of men who followed them here. In the year of their arrival (1858) the Sisters of Mercy opened evening classes for adults, free schools for girls, and Mount St. Mary, a boarding school, one of the first for girls in New England. A school for boys was begun at St. Anne's, Manchester, in January 1859. Its first teacher and principal was Mr. Thomas Corcoran, recognized as one of the ideal educators of his day.

Diocese of Manchester

New Hampshire achieved majority status in the Church with the creation of the Diocese of Manchester on April 15, 1884. Its first ordinary was Denis Mary Bradley who presided over what can be called the golden years of Catholicism in New Hampshire. Based on the tide of immigration between 1884 and 1903, the Catholic population grew from roughly 45,000 to 100,000. This was accompanied by the founding of thirty-four parishes, twenty-nine elementary schools, five secondary schools, and an impressive number of additional educational, social, charitable, and cultural organizations. Many of these new institutions were in the hands of five newly arrived congregations of women and four of men.

Bishop Bradley also negotiated for the introduction of the first monastic order of men into New Hampshire, the Order of St. Benedict; the first monks arrived in 1888. In 1893 the Benedictines opened St. Anselm College, an educational institution still flourishing today. With the stated objective of having a religious community to pray for the spiritual welfare of the diocese, Bishop Bradley introduced the Sisters, Adorers of the Precious Blood, a contemplative order, into the see city in 1898. These nuns are at the same task one hundred years later.

Another significant, but too frequently unpleasant and agitated period of local church history occurred during the bishopric of the Most Rev. George A. Guertin (1907–31). Among the elements of progress during his tenure were an increase of thirty-eight diocesan priests and sixteen parishes, a growth in Catholic population of 28,000, and a notable rise of 10,000 students in Catholic schools. In 1919, he appointed the first layperson in the United States as superintendent of Catholic schools, Attorney Wilfrid J. Lessard. On a less provincial plane, a laywoman, Miss Irene Farley, founded in 1922 the Missionary Rosebushes of Saint-Therese, which has raised over four million dollars for the education of native clergy in the Third World. As a result, over 2,000 recipients of scholarships from the organization have been ordained to the priesthood.

On a sadder note, this period, 1907–31, was plagued by a series of adversities, personal, ecclesial, and national. Among these were World War I, the influenza epidemic of 1918 in which 2,000 to 2,500 residents of New Hampshire died, including seven diocesan priests; the Americanization program of the government which greatly upset national parishes and their members; the activities of the K.K.K., especially during the presidential campaign of Alfred E. Smith in 1928; and Prohibition, woman's suffrage, child labor, as well as a number of strikes. As a mediator in the Amoskeag strike of 1922, Bishop Guertin did not succeed.

During most of his episcopacy Bishop Guertin, the first ordinary of French-Canadian ancestry in New Hampshire, was both witness and participant in an Irish-French conflict that had been smoldering for years previously. This struggle is known in New England as "The Sentinelle Movement." Bishop Guertin was unable to cope with it. In a more serious ethnic conflict with the Catholic Poles, a large segment of them left the Catholic Church in 1915, and eventually became part of the Polish National Catholic Church. Culminating Bishop Guertin's episcopacy was the Great Depression, triggered by the stock market crash on Black Thursday, October 29, 1929.

Coping with the depression and its effects upon the Church was entrusted to the fourth bishop of Manchester, the Most Rev. John B. Peterson (1932–44). Archival evidence points to the fact that Bishop Peterson, the clergy, and the laypeople were primarily focused on the effects of the depression, both for the community at large and the Church in particular. Bishop Peterson, a one-time teacher of economics, was able to reduce diocesan and parish indebtedness to the point that he could announce a financial improvement as early as 1936. Despite the bleak economic picture and an actual drop in Catholic population in New Hampshire, the number of diocesan priests increased by forty-five between 1932 and 1944.

On the civic level, the skills of Bishop Peterson were needed to mediate strikes and to serve on various government bodies created to study the economic problems of the city of Manchester and the state.

One most encouraging sign in the area of ecumenism during this period was the election of Francis X. Murphy, a Catholic, as Republican governor of New Hampshire; he served for two terms (1937–41). Some fifty-eight years earlier he would have been barred from service in this office by the constitution of the state.

In addition to the depression, the American people were sadly burdened by World War II (1941–45). It is estimated that some 19,200 Catholic young men and women from the state served in the armed forces, and that perhaps as many as 510 gave their lives.

Catholics in New Hampshire, along with their coreligionists across the nation, entered a new phase of American Church history after World War II. Presiding over this new period of expansion was Bishop Matthew F. Brady (1945–59).

Responding to a postwar pent-up demand for material goods created by the depression and the shortages caused by the war, the enormous production capacity of the United States and the new prosperity, the country at large entered another period of expansion. This growth was fueled by a high birth rate, an impressive return to religion nationwide, and by a general increase in the educational level of the citizens, largely the result of the G. I. Bill of Rights.

For example, between 1945 and 1959, the Catholic population of the diocese increased by over 51,800. This was accompanied by the creation of twenty-nine new parishes, the building of forty-seven new churches, eleven elementary schools, and a corresponding number of other institutions. Catholic Charities was founded in 1945 and has developed into the largest and most active private social agency in New Hampshire.

Catholic elementary school population rose to 23,000, and that of high schools from 1,903 to 4,370. During this period (1945–59), a new emphasis was placed on the Confraternity of Christian Doctrine with many positive results.

Vatican Council II and After

During the 1960s there began the greatest discontinuity with the past experienced by the Church since the establishment of the first Catholics in what is now the United States. The generally linear and undisturbed continuity of the Church in the areas of theology, liturgical language and practice, prayers and devotions, as well as in almost all areas of Church life was questioned, argued, and often changed.

This new era of disturbance, disquiet, and confusion for many was set in motion by the Second Vatican Council, which was held in four sessions from 1962 to 1965.

New Hampshire played more than an ordinary role in the preparation of the council, its sessions, and its early implementation. The sixth bishop of Manchester, the Most Rev. Ernest J. Primeau, served on a body preparing the council, that of the Discipline of the Clergy and the Faithful (1962–65), as a participant in the council itself (1962–65), and as an elected member, chosen by his peers, on the Secretariat for Promoting Christian Unity (from 1963). During the council Bishop Primeau was one of only 5 percent of the American bishops to address the body orally in general congregation. This he did on three occasions. In addition, Bishop Primeau communicated two additional written presentations to the appropriate commissions.

Based on the sixteen documents promulgated by the Second Vatican Council, an intensive period of renewal began in the diocese in late 1964, a process that slowed down dramatically some ten years later.

Unshakably convinced of the essential role of the laity in the Church and the need for consultation, Bishop Primeau mandated the establishment of such bodies at all levels of the diocese. Some succeeded; some failed outright, such as the Council of Religious; others were allowed to lapse, but were subsequently reviewed, such as the Diocesan Pastoral Council and the Boards of Conciliation and Arbitration. Another massive attempt at consultation was built into the preparation of a diocesan synod, which extended from 1964 to 1968. Despite the participation of several thousand persons, the convening of hundreds of meetings, and the distribution of some one million pieces of educational materials, the synod was never completed nor officially approved.

Equally energetic and extensive efforts were made to establish lay ministries, focus on adult religious education, discern priorities at all levels, encourage cooperative planning, renew the liturgy, foster ecumenism, and to participate more actively in missionary work in Latin America. In the last two endeavors, the diocese was particularly successful. Ecumenical encounters begun in 1964 resulted in the Church becoming a full member of the New Hampshire Council of Churches in 1984; and the diocese has had a comprehensive affiliation with a parish in Cartago, Columbia, since 1963.

In addition to the disruptions in the Church mentioned earlier, rightly or incorrectly attributed to the Second Vatican Council, there occurred a partial collapse in some religious beliefs and practices normally associated with being a good Catholic. Mass attendance fell to roughly 50 percent from a high of 71 percent in the late 1950s; acceptance of birth control rose to nearly 90 percent of the faithful, including perhaps two-thirds of the clergy; and the tolerance of abortion and other immoral forms of behavior became rather common.

This post-Vatican II period also saw an alarming number of departures from the priesthood and from the religious orders of women and men. The number of diocesan seminarians dropped from some 110 in 1966 to only fourteen in 1994. Attendance at Catholic schools, once a strong indicator of Catholic faithfulness, had a similar fate. From a high of 24,400, elementary school attendance fell by roughly 50 percent to 12,431 students, and high schools lost about 1,400 students. Registration in Confraternity of Christian Doctrine programs did not increase nearly as rapidly as the Catholic schools lost students. As a consequence, there were roughly 6.6 million grammar and high schools not receiving Catholic religious education in the United States by 1976. Another casualty of this turbulent period was Bishop Primeau who resigned on January 30, 1973, the first to do so in the history of the diocese. Among the reasons cited for his withdrawal were the physical and emotional stresses of the previous years.

The Contemporary Era

A new phase in the history of Catholicism in New Hampshire was begun in the mid-1970s. The intensive phase of the implementation of the Second Vatican Council was followed by one of trying to regain normalcy, a period still in effect to the present (1996). Many programs were instituted by the two ordinaries and two auxiliary bishops who succeeded Bishop Primeau. Those two ordinaries were Bishops Odore J. Gendron and Leo E. O'Neil. Some of these programs included extensive visitations of the parishes and institutions; a collaborative setting of goals and the establishment of diocesan planning, a myriad of opportunities for the clergy's spiritual and educational growth, including the Emmaus Program; the creation of the permanent diaconate, resulting in twelve ordinations on December 10, 1983; the expansion of lay ministries; the flowering of charismatic renewal; the further development of religious education programs for adults, youth, and children; an outward thrust to minister to refugees and immigrants, such as Hispanics and Southeast Asians; the organization of a number of soup kitchens; and so on. This pattern of post-renewal development is similar in essence to that in virtually all the dioceses across the country.

While a certain level of stability has been achieved in the diocese, a good number of uncertainties and problems still remain. Omitting those at the theological, moral, and religious-observance levels, among the more critical are the growth in Catholic population and the shrinking number of diocesan clergy. Catholic population had grown from 387 in 1835 to 45,000 in 1884 (the year of the creation of the diocese) to 321,914 in 1996. At the same time, the number of active diocesan clergy increased from three in 1855 to 254 in 1959, and then fell to 167 who were still active in 1996. Compounding the diocesan clergy problem was the aging of those who were still involved in ministry. This situation was even more critical among religious women.

Another major casualty of the post-Vatican II period were the Catholic schools. From a peak of 30,230 elementary and secondary students in the 1964–65 academic year, in 1996 the system now educated 9,767 boys and girls. The six Catholic colleges in New Hampshire showed an opposite trend with increased enrollment. In 1996 they educated 6,690, with St. Anselm College being the largest and best known.

In summary, Catholicism in New Hampshire has gone through three major historical periods since the mid-seventeenth century: a long, linear period of development to the beginning of the Second Vatican Council; a brief, exciting, and frequently controversial period of renewal; and, finally, the current situation which seems to be one of consolidation, and despite the existing complex problems, one of hope.

Kegresse, M. St. L. "A History of Catholic Education in New Hampshire." Ph.D. dissertation, Boston, 1955.
Lord, R. H. and others. *History of the Archdiocese of Boston in the Various Stages of Its Development, 1604–1943.* 3 vols. New York, 1944.
Paradis, Wilfrid H. *Catholicism in New Hampshire: A Historical Summary, A Community of Faith.* Tabloid newspaper format, 1985, 28 pp.

WILFRID H. PARADIS

NEW JERSEY, CATHOLIC CHURCH IN

Colonial Era

Although there is some evidence of Catholics in New Jersey as early as 1680, organized Catholicism first developed in the mid-eighteenth century. German and Irish glassworkers in Salem County were first visited by Jesuit priests from nearby Philadelphia in 1743. At the opposite end of the state, German ironworkers, brought to Ringwood along the New York border in 1764, were first visited by Fr. Ferdinand Farmer (Steinmeyer), S.J., in the following year. Farmer, the "apostle of New Jersey," was particularly zealous and made frequent visits from Philadelphia to the southern New Jersey glassworks, as well as semiannual tours of the northern New Jersey ironworks, until his death in 1786. Some sense of the number of New Jersey Catholics in this period can be gained from the 385 baptisms Farmer recorded in northern New Jersey in the years 1765–86. Farmer brought Fr. John Carroll, the superior of the American missions, to administer the sacrament of confirmation at Ringwood in 1785.

Early Nineteenth Century

In the post-Revolutionary period Catholicism developed slowly, and the scattered Catholics in the state were ministered to sporadically from Philadelphia and New York. Pastoral ministry in New Jersey was formally divided between these two cities when they became the seats of new dioceses in 1808. The first Catholic church in the state was built at Trenton, then in the Philadelphia diocese, in 1814. Other early churches were built in Paterson (1821); by French emigrants in Madison (1825); at the bog-iron forge in Pleasant Mills in present Atlantic County (1827); in Newark (1828); and by the descendants of the ironworkers in Macopin in present-day Passaic County (1829). The first resident priest in the state was Fr. Richard Bulger, sent to Paterson by Bishop John Connolly of New York in 1820.

Diocese of Newark: James Roosevelt Bayley

In the mid-nineteenth century canals and railroads crossed New Jersey, and waves of Irish and German workers began to swell the state's Catholic population. On July 29, 1853, Pope Pius IX separated New Jersey from its neighboring sees, and erected the Diocese of Newark encompassing the entire state. Named as first bishop was James Roosevelt Bayley, secretary to Archbishop John Hughes of New York, and, like his aunt, St. Elizabeth Ann Seton, a convert to Catholicism. Bayley was installed in St. Patrick's Cathedral, Newark, on All Saints Day, 1853. Upon his arrival in Newark, Bayley found thirty-three churches in the state served by thirty priests. The see city had three churches and Trenton had two, including a German congregation in each city. Seven of the state's twenty-one counties had no Catholic church. The number of Catholics was estimated at 40,000.

Bayley set out systematically to visit his new flock, and to provide for its needs. In August 1856, Bayley conducted the first diocesan synod to tie the diocese together, and to provide uniformity in discipline, sacramental practice, and church administration. One of the synodal decrees, on the establishment of parochial schools, reflected Bayley's concern for Catholic education. It was Bayley's hope to have "every Catholic child in the State in a Catholic school."

Bayley felt that teaching religious sisters were essential to the identity and growth of the parochial schools. With this in mind, Bayley recruited five candidates for a New Jersey sisterhood. With assistance from the New York and Cincinnati Sisters of Charity, this group was organized at Newark as the Sisters of Charity of St. Elizabeth in 1859 under the leadership of Sr. Mary Xavier Mehegan of New York. In 1860 the motherhouse was moved to the former Seton Hall property in Madison. The long-term leadership of Mother Xavier (1859–1915) helped the Sisters of Charity to grow from five members to nearly five hundred by the time of the community's silver anniversary in 1884. This, together with Bayley's encouragement, had the desired effect. By the time of Bayley's departure for Baltimore in 1872, there were nearly 20,000 students in New Jersey Catholic schools.

To further bolster Catholic education, and to augment the numbers of diocesan clergy, Bayley founded Seton Hall College which opened at Madison with five students in 1856. Moved to South Orange in 1860, Bayley envisioned Seton Hall as a place where local candidates could be trained for the priesthood, and as a center of Catholic learning for the wider population. A theologate, Immaculate Conception Seminary, developed from the college, and the first alumnus was ordained a priest in 1863. Religious priests were also recruited and during Bayley's nineteen years as bishop: Benedictines, Passionists, Carmelites, Franciscans, and Jesuits were introduced into the state.

The growth of the Catholic community during the Bayley years was not entirely peaceful. Anti-Catholic sentiment grew apace, and at times rose to the surface. During the ascendancy of the Know-Nothing Party in 1854, anti-Catholic demonstrations were held in Jersey City, Hoboken, Perth Amboy, and Elizabeth. St. Mary's German Church in Newark was ransacked in a melee which left one Catholic dead and four injured.

Bayley was named archbishop of Baltimore in July 1872. One of his last acts in Newark was to secure the property for a new Sacred Heart Cathedral.

Michael Augustine Corrigan

Bayley was succeeded by a Newark native, Michael Augustine Corrigan, the first alumnus of the North American College to reach the episcopacy. During Corrigan's tenure (1873–80), despite the difficulties of the 1870s economic depression, Catholic growth continued. Religious persecution in Germany brought several new religious orders to the state. In 1880 the state's first contemplative community, a cloistered Dominican convent, opened at Newark. To offset anti-Catholic measures at the state reformatories, Catholic protectories were established for boys at Kearny, and for girls at Newark. Corrigan also encouraged the formation of the Catholic Union, a lay group, to help defend the rights of New Jersey Catholics against bigotry. Both Bayley and Corrigan were strong supporters of the Catholic Temperance Union and other societies formed to help combat alcoholism.

In a report prepared for his 1876 *ad limina* visit to Rome, Corrigan listed 123 churches in the state, staffed by 142 priests. There were 77 parochial schools, and nearly 700 sisters. Immigration had helped to swell the number of Catholics to 187,500, 18 percent of the state's population. Corrigan left Newark to become coadjutor archbishop of New York in November 1880. Because of the growth of the state's Catholic community, Newark was divided eight months later, and a new see erected at Trenton encompassing the fourteen central and southern counties of the state.

Immigration and New Jersey Catholicism

In the 1880 census, New Jersey had a population of 1,131,000. Over the next forty years the state would absorb some 517,000 immigrants into its population. Many of these "new immigrants" were Catholics from southern and eastern Europe and they greatly expanded and changed the nature of New Jersey Catholicism. The first challenge was to provide religious services for the immigrants in their own language. Ethnic, or "national" parishes proliferated across the state. The first of these parishes were: St. Anthony's, Jersey City, established for Poles (1884); Holy Rosary, Jersey City, for Italians (1886); SS Peter and Paul, Jersey City, for Ukrainians (1886); St. Joseph's, Bayonne, for Slovaks (1888); St. Michael's, Passaic, for Ruthenians (1891); SS Peter and Paul, Elizabeth, for Lithuanians (1895); Holy Trinity, Passaic, for Austrians (1900); Our Lady of Hungary, Perth Amboy, for Hungarians (1902); and St. Ann's, Paterson, for Syrians (1919). While these parishes were heavily concentrated in the state's urban areas, no part of the state was untouched by the new immigration. Thus the Cumberland County farming community of Vineland had an Italian parish by 1909, and the Delaware River town of Philipsburg had a Slovak parish by 1913.

The sudden growth of national parishes also brought tensions. Providing adequate clergy was a problem, especially among the Italians. Lack of understanding of ethnic customs and discipline by the Americans, and failure to accommodate European parochial structures to American diocesan practices by the new immigrants caused tensions which led to the formation of schismatic parishes among the Poles, Slovaks, Italians, and Ruthenians. While many of these situations were ultimately resolved, New Jersey became a center for the development of independent church bodies which emerged among the Poles in 1897, and the Ruthenians in 1936.

Tensions also arose, particularly in the 1890s, among those clergy and people who objected to the national parishes. They felt that the continuation of ethnic customs was divisive in the American Church. Newark's third bishop, Winand M. Wigger (1881–1901), suffered greatly from attacks from the "Americanists" among his own clergy. In particular, Fr. Patrick Corrigan of Hoboken consistently accused Wigger in the press of favoritism toward the new immigrants.

Twentieth-Century Developments

In the first third of the twentieth century, New Jersey Catholicism experienced not just numerical growth, but also an expansion of facilities and a deepening of Catholic life. Catholic education was expanding, especially on the high-school level. St. Peter's Jesuit College reopened at Jersey City in 1930, and Catholic colleges for women were opened at Convent Station (1899), Lakewood (1908), and Caldwell (1939) and Lodi (1942). Catholic social services were expanded and professionally organized with the establishment of the Mount Carmel Guild in Trenton (1920) and Newark (1930). Many new religious communities came into the state, and new motherhouses, novitiates, and retreat houses appeared in the state's rural areas. New Jersey became a center for the liturgical movement which found expression in several beautiful churches erected in the 1930s. Catholic lay movements also proliferated in the state. Trenton's second bishop, James A. McFaul (1894–1917), was instrumental in the formation of the American Federation of Catholic Societies in 1901.

This steady growth was recognized by the Holy See in 1937 with the formal separation of New Jersey from the New York province. On December 10, Newark was raised to the status of a metropolitan see, with Bishop Thomas J. Walsh (1928–52) as first archbishop. The previous day both existing dioceses had been divided. Newark relinquished three northwestern counties to the new Diocese of Paterson; Trenton gave up its six southernmost counties to the new Diocese of Camden.

Two movements greatly changed New Jersey Catholicism in the post-World War II era. The signing of the G.I. Bill in 1945 transformed New Jersey Catholicism from a largely urban to a suburban community. As improved transportation systems transformed rural western villages and summer shore communities, over 150 new parishes were opened between the end of World War II in 1945, and the end of Vatican II in 1965. Many of these new parishes constructed combination church-school buildings at the same time. Existing facilities were also expanded to meet the growth. Seton Hall became the largest diocesan college in the country and achieved university status in 1951. Throughout the 1960s, *The Advocate*, diocesan newspaper for Newark and Paterson, carried annual "construction" issues to enable its readers to keep up with the expansion.

Because of this continued growth the Trenton diocese was again divided in 1981, and a new see for the state's four central counties was established at Metuchen. Metuchen is the only new diocese created in the American northeast in the last quarter-century. The considerable presence of Eastern-rite Catholics in the state was recognized in 1963 when Passaic was chosen as the see city for a new diocese embracing Ruthenian Byzantine Catholics on the East Coast, and again in 1995 when Newark became the seat for the only Syrian-rite diocese in the Western Hemisphere.

The other growth factor was the unparalleled immigration of Hispanics, first from Puerto Rico, then, in the Castro era, from Cuba, and then from all Latin America. By 1995, 20 percent of the state's Latin-Rite parishes offered at least one Sunday Mass in Spanish.

The Contemporary Scene

Today, New Jersey Catholicism is marked by strength and diversity. The state's 3,250,000 Catholics constitute 41.9 percent of the state's population, the third highest concentration of Catholics in the nation. They are served by 2,521 priests, 709 deacons, 238 brothers, and 4,189 sisters in some 750 parishes. There is still a steady flow of Catholics from New Jersey's traditional centers of immigration, and also from newer centers of immigration such as Haiti, Portugal, Korea, Vietnam, India, Philippines, and the Middle East. Each Sunday liturgy is celebrated in New Jersey in all six rites of the Catholic Church in twenty-five different languages. Over five thousand religious men and women add to the rich diversity of Catholic life in the state which includes three abbeys, forty general and provincial headquarters, twelve hospitals, twenty-six retreat houses, ten cloistered convents, and a laura of hermits.

Many New Jersey laity have made significant contributions to the life of the Church, nationally and internationally. John Baptist Sartori of Trenton was named first U.S. consul in the Papal States in 1797, and later represented the Holy See in America, 1829–41. Nineteenth-century intellectuals Orestes A. Brownson, and John Gilmary Shea, "the father of American Church history," both lived in Elizabeth. Catholic publishers and apologists Frank Sheed and Maisie Ward made their home in Jersey City for forty years. Nicola Montani, author of the *St. Gregory Hymnal,* taught at Seton Hall and Immaculate Conception Seminary. Catholic Relief Services administrator James J. Norris of Rumson was the only layman to participate in the debates of the Second Vatican Council.

Prominent New Jersey Catholics in public life include Supreme Court Justices William Brennan and Antonin Scalia, Treasury Secretaries William Simon and Nicholas Brady, and Labor Secretaries James Mitchell, Raymond Donovan, and Ann Dore McLaughlin. Among New Jersey's Catholics in Congress were Peter Rodino, Judiciary Committee chair during the Nixon impeachment hearings, and Mary Norton, who in 1932 was the first woman to chair a congressional committee. Two powerful New Jersey Catholic politicians were Woodrow Wilson's private secretary, Joseph P. Tumulty, and Dwight Eisenhower's appointments secretary, Bernard Shanley.

New Jersey Catholics in the music field run the gamut from Major Edward Bowes of the 1930s "Original Amateur Hour" radio program, to Fr. Joseph P. Connor, a west New York pastor who wrote film scores under the pseudonym Johnny Oppenshaw, to jazz composer Mary Lou Williams, to Frank Sinatra and Bruce Springsteen.

Other famous New Jersey Catholics include poets Joyce and Aline Kilmer, submarine inventor John P. Holland, "Moody's Magazine" founder John Moody, and philanthropist Charles Englehard.

Flynn, Joseph M. *The Catholic Church in New Jersey.* New York, 1904.

Giglio, Charles J., ed. *Building God's Kingdom. A History of the Diocese of Camden.* South Orange, N.J., 1987.

Kupke, Raymond J. *Living Stones. A History of the Catholic Church in the Diocese of Paterson.* Clifton, N.J., 1987.

New Jersey Catholic Historical Records Commission. *The Bishops of Newark, 1853–1978.* South Orange, N.J., 1978.

Shenrock, Joseph C., ed. *Upon the Rock. A New History of the Diocese of Trenton.* Trenton, 1993.

RAYMOND J. KUPKE

NEW MEXICO, CATHOLIC CHURCH IN

In 1539, acting on hearsay from survivors of an expedition that came to disaster, the Spanish government sent a small party north to find the legendary seven golden cities of Cíbola. A Moorish survivor served as advance guide to a group under the command of a Franciscan priest. When they entered the western edge of present-day New Mexico, the natives of Zuni Pueblo killed the Moor, and the friar retreated south with exaggerated tales of what he had seen from afar—the simple town of some sedentary agriculturists.

Exploration and First Settlements

The very next year, Francisco Vásquez de Coronado led a major expedition northward to examine the entire region. He and his men found dozens of adobe and stone towns and villages of sedentary Pueblos living in architectural dwellings in agricultural villages, enjoying a well-developed culture featuring pottery and weaving and based on a complex religion with an elaborate ceremonial system. After spending nearly two years examining everything from the Grand Canyon to central Kansas, Coronado led his men back south, leaving behind three Franciscans who insisted on remaining with the Pueblo people.

For forty years, the Spanish left New Mexico alone, but then in 1581 other explorers, usually with Franciscan leaders or chaplains, began to probe the northern frontier. The Franciscans had hoped that they could lead the natives of New Spain into a millennial kingdom founded on evangelical poverty, and after that dream perished under the heel of greed, they may have thought that this *New* Mexico would prepare the world for the Second Coming. Perhaps alarmed by the loss of the Spanish Armada in 1588 and rumors of the English "Virginia Dare" Colony in the 1590s, the Spanish crown decided to push a "distant early warning" salient northward. Hence in 1598 Juan de Oñate led a military and missionary enterprise northward to live

El Santuario de Chimayo, Chimayo, New Mexico

off the settled Pueblo farmers. What Spain called New Mexico was much larger than the present state of New Mexico, but most Catholic activity happened in what is now the state.

During the eighty-two years this experiment endured, the Spanish founded only one town (Santa Fe, in 1608), governing the Pueblos by means of *encomiendas,* feudal grants of towns and of the people—serfs—who lived in them. The tribute the people owed was slight enough during the prosperous years that blessed the beginning of European New Mexico. In our terms, it was the equivalent of four cents on a hundred dollars, but as European diseases shriveled the population and years of drought shriveled the corn, the exactions of the *encomenderos* became intolerable. Furthermore, for the first sixty years of recorded New Mexican history, the military and the missionaries bickered and fought over what the dominant character of the northern colony was to be and over who was to benefit from native labor. The governor-general and his lieutenants, the feudal lords, wanted the Pueblos to work for them gathering piñon nuts, weaving serapes and rugs, herding sheep, and growing corn, while the friars wanted them to build more spacious *conventos* and more impressive churches of fieldstone, adobe, and rough timbers. (The Pueblos seem to have been willing accomplices in this last enterprise, pueblo competing with pueblo to have a more spectacular church.) So long as times were good and the Spanish fought among themselves, the Pueblos seem to have found a certain space in which they could live their own lives, practicing both the native religion in which they continued to trust along with the new religion of their conquerors. But when Church and civil government, missionary and military, appeared to gang up on the Pueblos (as happened when the governor and the Franciscan *custos* were blood brothers and as happened when another governor executed three Pueblo leaders for witch-

craft and scourged forty-three others), the Pueblo people decided to do something desperate.

Rebellion of 1680 and After

That was the Rebellion of 1680, the most successful native uprising in the history of North America. The Pueblos overcame barriers of language diversity and joined in a concerted attack on their rulers. They killed twenty-one friars and four hundred other Spanish—all they could catch—and drove the rest south to El Paso (today's Ciudad Juárez), where they remained for a dozen years.

As had happened ninety years before, changes in England may have tipped the Spanish scales: the friendly semi-Catholic Stuarts gave way to the bitterly antagonistic King William of Orange and Queen Mary, who came to power in the "Glorious Revolution" of 1688–89. Moreover, other tribes along the ragged northern frontier of New Spain began to entertain the idea that they too could rebel against Spain and get away with it. So the crown recruited Don Diego de Vargas, outfitted him with an army and a promise of settlers, and sent him up the Rio Grande to make peace with the Pueblos. In 1692 de Vargas convinced them to permit the Spanish to return, arguing that they were nicer to have around than the nomadic tribesmen who kept dropping by uninvited.

And de Vargas asserted that the Spanish had learned something and offered the Pueblos a "New Deal." They had to receive a Franciscan missionary and accept Catholicism, but otherwise they might live their own lives without interference except for matters of mutual advantage such as common defense against tribal nomads and shared irrigation systems. The Pueblos reneged on their agreement when de Vargas returned the next autumn with hundreds of settlers, but a few bitter battles and a few failed rebellions later, the two peoples settled into a successful entente. The Pueblos picked up their religious life where they had left off: converted *to* Christianity but not converted *from* their native religion, holding the two religions separate and unconfused as if in separate compartments, juxtaposing them but not mingling them.

The new colony was principally a settlers' and soldiers' enterprise, with the missionaries a weak third. Franciscans once more completely staffed the churches in New Mexico, the twenty or so Pueblos missions and three Spanish parishes—the reoccupied Santa Fe, Santa Cruz (founded 1695), and Albuquerque (founded 1706). They resisted adding more parishes for the settlers because they continued to think of themselves as missionaries to the Native Americans, not as pastors to the Spanish, and they remained locked into this pattern even when the demographics changed dramatically.

The number of Pueblos continued to decline, mainly due to disease, while the settlers experienced rapid and sustained growth. Some immigrants moved up from the south, and Native Americans of three sorts joined the Spanish villages: individual Pueblo natives too free-spirited to be happy in the extremely regimented Pueblo theocracies, where they were controlled by the priests of the indigenous religion; Native American nomads who came into the colony by capture, barter, or purchase; and some nomads who volunteered to adopt Spanish ways. These detribalized and acculturated Native Americans, called *genízaros,* composed between a quarter and a third of the Spanish population by the end of the eighteenth century.

As that century went on, the Diocese of Durango began to assert its jurisdiction over the Franciscan missionaries of New Mexico, and a few diocesan priests even moved up to the northern frontier. Meanwhile, the Spanish settlers and the detribalized natives of numerous nations who joined them had to move out of the three Spanish parishes and away from places near the Pueblo mission churches. They sought farmland and ranchland beyond the former limits of the colony or in the small gaps in the lovely mountain valleys, and they founded dozens and hundreds of little villages. The friars seldom visited these outlying settlers, remaining instead in the depopulating pueblos, sustained by the government stipend and by their increasingly anachronistic sense of vocation. The Franciscans lost the power over civil officials that the Inquisition had afforded them in the seventeenth century, and even the Pueblos for whom the friars were sacrificing their lives looked more often to civil officials and less often to their own pastors to right any wrongs they suffered.

It is one of the many cautionary ironies of history that the most beneficial work of Catholic New Mexico transpired exactly during those years and exactly in those little *placitas.* The people of these villages accomplished the acculturation into Spanish Catholicism of the numerous *genízaros* mentioned above. It was people's memory of Franciscans rather than the Franciscans themselves which guided the formation of the traditional Hispanic religious culture of northern New Mexico during the second half of the eighteenth century. The major components of this culture were: (1) the *santos,* a vernacular tradition of religious art of pictures and statues representing the divine persons, Mary, the angels, and the ordinary saints; (2) passion plays based on the fourteen Stations of the Cross as reinforced by the five Sorrowful Mysteries and the last four of the Seven Sorrows of Mary; (3) the *alabados,* narrative hymns about the passion; and (4) the penitential Brotherhood of Our Father Jesus the Nazarene. In these four main components is enshrined the mainstream late medieval spirituality of Bernard of Clairvaux and Francis of Assisi with its tender focus on the humanity of the Incarnate Word. By effectively acculturating the *genízaro* component of the Hispanic villages to their new life, this popular religious culture

evangelized far more Native Americans than the Franciscans in their own persons did.

Era of Transition

In 1833 Bishop Zubiría of Durango launched a frontal attack on *santos* and on the penitential Brotherhood, and the first two archbishops, the Frenchmen Jean Baptist Lamy and Jean Baptiste Salpointe, continued the latter campaign; but fortunately, the traditional religious culture survived and sustained the people through the relentless series of changes that totally altered the face of their world. The principal transitions were these:

(1) Franciscans were replaced by Durango diocesan priests, who increasingly staffed the colony from the turn of the eighteenth century through the first three decades of the nineteenth. These new priests for the first time got New Mexican men to enter the Tridentine seminary in Durango, perhaps because they were modeling themselves on the activist Padre Don Miguel Hidalgo y Costilla, the great hero-martyr of the Mexican Revolution. Padre Antonio José Martínez of Taos remains the best known of these New Mexican diocesan priests. In 1848 the last blue-robed Franciscan in New Mexico died.

(2) The Spanish Empire yielded to the Mexican Republic when Hidalgo's independence movement finally came to fruition in 1821.

(3) With the opening of Santa Fe Trail in that year of independence, New Mexico switched from the closed borders of colonial mercantilist economic theory, which had left New Mexican settlers in a tribe-dominated backwater, to the open borders of economic liberalism (free-market capitalism).

(4) After a mere quarter century of independence from Spain, the Mexican Republic lost New Mexico and the rest of the Southwest to the United States. New Mexican Catholics began to learn the odd ropes of U.S. nineteenth-century Church-state relations, staffing public schools with brothers, nuns, and priests—just as back East, Protestant ministers taught school during the week to supplement their meager church salaries.

(5) The Durango diocesan priests gave way to Bishop Lamy's European-born French diocesan priests, who began to arrive in 1851 and were supplemented after 1867 by Italian Jesuits, who helped to stabilize regional Catholicism by preaching parish missions, publishing the weekly newspaper, *Revista Católica,* and opening the College of Las Vegas (now Regis University and Regis Jesuit High School in Denver). Lamy arrived in 1851 and immediately set to work trying to improve the quality of the clergy and of education and health care, introducing mostly American Sisters of Loretto (1852; they were the first women religious ever to work in New Mexico), the Christian Brothers (1859; their school in the capital has become

Saint Michael's High School and the College of Santa Fe), and the Sisters of Charity of Cincinnati (1865).

Under Lamy's hands, the adobe parish church of Santa Fe underwent a gradual transformation into a French Romanesque stone edifice he deemed worthy to be a cathedral. Lamy was certainly a leading citizen of the territory. He became archbishop in 1875, and after his resignation in 1885 he was followed by four other Frenchmen, Jean Baptiste Salpointe (1885–94), Placide Chapelle (1895–97), Pierre Bourgade (1899–1908, at whose installation the first brown-robed Cincinnati Franciscans appeared), and J. B. Pitaval (1909–18). These Franciscans have done especially good work in southeastern New Mexico and with the Native Americans of the Gallup diocese. The majority of the clergy of New Mexico were European-born until about the Second World War.

(6) With the arrival of the railroad in 1879–80, New Mexico began to move from a village-based world of agriculture, herding, and barter to an urban industrial consumer-capitalist pluralism. The Hispanic Catholic village culture was no longer "the offer that nobody could refuse," for now there was the real choice between "Old Town" and "New Town" best exemplified in Albuquerque and Las Vegas, New Mexico. Individual Protestant Americans had of course visited New Mexico beginning in 1821, and in 1846 they arrived in force to run things. With the railroad, they began to transform the culture. The Presbyterians and the Congregationalists, most especially, operated schools that taught English, a good knowledge of which was mandatory for anyone who chose the new wage-work commercial world.

Recent Developments

During the nineteenth century, the Diocese of Santa Fe spun off two major diocesan sees. To the north, in 1868, Lamy's friend and first vicar general, Joseph P. Machebeuf, was named to head the vicariate apostolic of Colorado in the gold-mining towns of the Pike's Peak region. To the west and south, in 1869, Jean Baptiste Salpointe, later the second archbishop of Santa Fe, administered the vicariate apostolic of Arizona, which originally included El Paso and the southern quarter of the New Mexico Territory. Southern New Mexico continued to be part of the Diocese of Tucson until 1915, when it was split off to form part of the Diocese of El Paso; then in 1982, Ricardo Ramírez, C.S.B., was named to head a new diocese having its see in Las Cruces and comprising the ten counties in the southern part of the state, including two counties and part of a third county that had previously been part of the Archdiocese of Santa Fe.

In like manner, northwestern New Mexico was separated in 1939 to form the Diocese of Gallup under the guidance of Bernard T. Espelage, O.F.M.; besides Navajo and Hopi reservation land in Arizona, this diocese also includes non-reservation counties. Espelage was followed in 1969 by Jerome J. Hastrich and in 1990 by Donald E. Pelotte, S.S.S.

In Santa Fe, the Church found continuing leadership from Archbishops Albert Daeger, O.F.M. (1919–32), Rudolph Gerken (1933–43), Edwin V. Byrne (1943–63, a great builder during New Mexico's World War II and cold-war atomic-weapons boom and a staunch proponent of Marian and eucharistic devotions), James Peter Davis (1964–74, who led the archdiocese through the changes mandated by Vatican II), and Robert F. Sánchez (1974–93), a very pastoral native New Mexican.

The major men's orders to come into the state since the French era include the Benedictines, Norbertines, Servites, Dominicans, and Basilians and the Blessed Sacrament and Holy Family Fathers.

Congregations founded in New Mexico include the Missionary Catechists of Our Lady of Victory, the Little Brothers of the Good Shepherd, the Servants of the Paraclete, and the Handmaids of the Precious Blood. In 1887 Katherine Drexel founded St. Catherine's Indian School in Santa Fe, run by the Sisters of the Blessed Sacrament for Indians and Colored People (of Bensalem, Pennsylvania), and in the 1930s the Sisters of Saint Francis of Perpetual Adoration (of Colorado Springs) began a teachers' college that eventually became the University of Albuquerque, only to cease operation in the 1980s.

When Archbishop Sánchez resigned following accusations of personal misconduct, Bishop Michael J. Sheehan of Lubbock, Texas, became first the apostolic administrator and then the new ordinary, being installed on September 21, 1993, as the eleventh archbishop of Santa Fe. In 1995, Catholics were 26.2 percent of the total state population of one and two-thirds million.

Benavides, Fray Alonso de. *Memorial, 1630.* Ed. and trans. Charles F. Lummis and others. Chicago: R. R. Donnelly, 1916; repr. Albuquerque, N.Mex.: Horn and Wallace, 1965.

Burke, James T. *"This Miserable Kingdom."* Las Vegas: Our Lady of Sorrows Church, 1973; repr. Santa Fe: Cristo Rey, 1974; repr. Albuquerque: Our Lady of Fatima, 1994.

Cather, Willa. *Death Comes for the Archbishop.* New York: The Modern Library, 1931.

Chávez, Fray Angélico. *The Archives of the Archdiocese of Santa Fe.* Washington: Academy of American Franciscan History, 1957.

———. *My Penitente Land.* Albuquerque: University of New Mexico Press, 1974; repr. Santa Fe: William Gannon, 1979; Santa Fe: Museum of New Mexico Press, 1993.

Defouri, James H. *Historical Sketch of the Catholic Church in New Mexico.* San Francisco: McCormick Brothers, 1887.

Domínguez, Fray Francisco Atanasio. *The Missions of New Mexico, 1776.* Ed. and trans. Eleanor B. Adams and Fray Angélico Chávez. Albuquerque: University of New Mexico Press, 1956; repr. 1975.

Horgan, Paul. *Lamy of Santa Fe.* New York: Farrar, Straus and Giroux, 1975.

Howlett, William. *Life of Bishop Machebeuf.* Pueblo: Franklin Press, 1908; repr. Denver: Denver *Register,* 1953; Denver: Regis College, 1987.

Kessell, John. *The Missions of New Mexico Since 1776.* Albuquerque: University of New Mexico Press, 1979.

Salpointe, J. B. *Soldiers of the Cross.* Banning: St. Boniface's Industrial School, 1898; repr. Albuquerque: Calvin Horn Publisher, 1967.

Simmons, Marc. *New Mexico.* New York: W. W. Norton, 1977; repr. Albuquerque: University of New Mexico Press, 1988.

THOMAS J. STEELE, S.J.

Related Documents

THE ADVENT OF BISHOP LAMY TO THE SOUTHWEST, JUNE 29, 1851

One of the most attractive missionary bishops of the nineteenth century was John Baptist Lamy (1814–1888). He had come originally from France in 1839 to the Diocese of Cincinnati where his success recommended him to his superiors and on November 24, 1850, he was consecrated as first Vicar Apostolic of New Mexico. It was Lamy's colorful career in the Southwest that inspired Willa Cather's charming novel, *Death Comes for the Archbishop* (New York, 1926). Following his consecration he left for New Mexico by way of New Orleans and Texas, and after being laid up some months in San Antonio as the result of an accident, he reached Santa Fe in the summer of 1851. New Mexico had formerly been part of the Diocese of Durango in Mexico and some of the Mexican clergy were not disposed to bow to Lamy's authority. He decided to settle the question of jurisdiction by a personal visit to Bishop José A. Laureano de Zubiria at Durango, traveling the more than 1,000 miles each way by mule pack. In the letter that follows Lamy described for Antoine Blanc, Archbishop of New Orleans, his experiences, on his first trip to the Southwest.

(*Source: American Catholic Historical Researches,* XV [April, 1898] 136–137.)

El Passo del Norte, Mexico, June 29,1851.

Monseigneur:

After a journey of six weeks on the plains we arrived here. The country we saw has nothing very interesting— barren plains, barren mountains—with the exception of a few places. The last week there was a great scarcity of water and grass. Then we generally travelled at night. We had beautiful weather, some days rather too warm, but the nights were delightful; we generally preferred to sleep out than in our tent. We did not use it much except for Mass. We had the consolation to offer the Divine Sacrifice, at least one of us, almost every day. The first week I felt rather stiff from lying on a mere blanket, but I soon got use *[sic]* to it, and I never enjoyed my rest better.

There are three fine villages near El Passo on the Texas side. When the people heard of my arrival, they came several miles to meet us. In one place particularly, called Suc-

coro, I had a grand reception with music, national guards, arks of triumph, etc. Circumstances obliged me the next morning to make *mon premier debut* in public *en la langua de Dios* to a crowded congregation. We are now at the house of the cura d'El Passon, who kindly offered us hospitality. This village of El Passo is truly a beautiful spot. They have here all kinds of fruits; they make good wine. It rains very seldom; it has not rained to any consequence these two years, but irrigation supplies the want of rain water. This is a place very much scattered. It contains at least eight thousand inhabitants. The people seem to be good and docile. Their houses are mud; they call it, I think, adobe, but very clean inside; it is so warm that many go half naked. The few churches that I have seen are of the same materials as the houses, but they might be kept in better order with very little trouble.

I have yet four hundred miles to go; but after I have traveled one-third of it. I will get in the pueblos of New Mexico, and see at least the half of my district before I reach Santa Fé. From what I have heard, and the little I have seen here, no doubt I may expect to meet with serious difficulties and obstacles, but my hope is in the God of power. Please, Monseigneur, to remember me in your prayers, and also to recommend me to the prayers of the Ursuline Sisters who have been so kind to me. I hope my little niece is well and doing well. I received news from her parents; they are all well. I expect to start this week for Santa Fé.

Your most obedient serv't and devoted friend,

✠ JOHN LAMY, Vic. Ap. of N. Mexico.

A MISSIONARY BISHOP ON THE EDGE OF THE GREAT PLAINS, AUGUST 6, 1852

John Baptist Lamy, who served the Church with distinction in the Southwest from 1851 to his death in 1888, was named first Archbishop of Santa Fe in February, 1875. He was one of only three American bishops to have been in attendance at all three of the plenary councils of Baltimore. He used his presence in the East and the Middle West for the council of May, 1852, to good advantage in recruiting personnel and supplies for the missions of New Mexico. But upon his return journey to his vicariate that summer he encountered more than the ordinary number of vicissitudes, and in the following letter to Archbishop Blanc of New Orleans he told of the losses he had sustained, indicating as well the hazards of travel in the trans-Mississippi West.

(Source: *American Catholic Historical Researches,* V [April, 1898] 137.)

Blue River Camp [Mission], August 6, 1852.

Monseigneur:

I am writing to you from under a tree twenty miles west from Independence. The first time I went to New Mexico I met with some *contretemps;* but it seems that the Divine Providence has been pleased to send me this time more severe trials, disappointments and troubles than at my first start. A good priest from the diocese of Cleveland was coming with me to share the labor of our mission in New Mexico, but he died of the cholera at St. Louis on the 11th of July. His name was Rev. Mr. Pendesprat [sic].[1] From St. Louis to Independence the Mother Superior of the Sisters of Loreto died also of the cholera, on board the steamboat *Kansas*, the 16th of July; the same day another Sister was taken sick and is yet very low. I have been obliged to leave for Independence to my great regret. Two more Sisters were also attacked by the same dreadful epidemic, but thank God, they got over it. My Mexican priest has been very sick, and now he is just able to travel in a carriage; besides, I have lost nine of my best animals. You know that we have to travel through the plains with caravans, and that everything has to be brought by wagons. Besides some animals I had here, I bought a few more, but I have lost a great number of them. I have been very much fatigued myself, but still God has given me the grace to bear all with patience, and my strong constitution has stood the labor and the care I had on my mind. I hope to take a fair start tomorrow for the plains; we are only two or three miles from the boundaries between the State of Missouri and the Indian Territory. I have twenty-five persons in my company, ten wagons or other conveyances. My expenses are very great; but still, with God's help, I hope to meet all in one or two years. Recommending myself to your prayers, I have the honor to be,

Your most grateful friend and ob't serv't,

✠ JOHN LAMY, Vic. Ap. of N. Mexico.

[1] Father Peter Pandeprat had been a professor at St. Mary's Seminary, Cleveland.

(*Source*: John Tracy Ellis, ed. *Documents of American Catholic History*. Vol. 1:1493–1865. Wilmington, Del.: Michael Glazier, 1987, 301–04.)

NEW THEOLOGY REVIEW

New Theology Review first appeared in February 1988 as a collaborative venture between Michael Glazier, Inc., and the faculties of the Catholic Theological Union (Chicago), and the Washington Theological Union in Silver Spring, Maryland. The first editor was Robert Schreiter, C.PP.S., of the Catholic Theological Union, with Kenneth Himes, O.F.M., serving as the assistant editor. From the outset the journal's goal was to integrate contemporary pastoral concerns with solid theological and biblical scholarship. A thematic format has prevailed since the journal's inception with the focus on issues such as aging, the seven deadly sins, God, ecclesiology, and communications. The focus of the journal has been on the Catholic scene in the United States, but interreligious and international concerns and perspectives have also been treated on occasion. The Liturgical Press assumed responsibility for the publication of the journal in May 1990 and in February 1991 John T. Pawlikowski, O.S.M., replaced Robert Schreiter as editor. Subsequently, James Wallace, C.Ss.R., took over the position of assistant editor from Kenneth Himes.

JOHN T. PAWLIKOWSKI, O.S.M.

NEW YORK ACCADEMIA

The New York Accademia was an informal association of priests in the Archdiocese of New York founded in 1865. Modeled after a similar group founded by Cardinal Henry Manning of Westminster, the association was principally begun to provide ongoing theological reflection for New York priests who had done their seminary training in Rome. However, membership was open to all New York priests. The association soon dissolved itself because many priests found it elitist and dominated by Roman-trained priests with avant-garde ideas.

In late 1866, Fr. Thomas Farrell, the controversial and influential pastor of St. Joseph's Church in Greenwich Village, began hosting regular meetings of the clergy in his rectory. Among those in attendance were Edward McGlynn, Richard Burtsell, and other noteworthy New York clerics. A diary kept by Burtsell is the principal source for the topics discussed in these gatherings. According to Burtsell, these clerics challenged the importance of mandatory celibacy, Latin in the liturgy, contemporary notions of scriptural inerrancy, and the temporal power of the pope. They questioned the superiority of Catholic schools over public schools, and suggested that infallibility was to be found not in the person of the pope, but in the Church as a whole. They marveled over American-style democracy and wondered whether the Catholic Church could adopt more democratic modes of government. They also favored a strict separation of Church and state, an idea that the Roman authorities and many American bishops found unthinkable.

Soon after the beginning of the Accademia, word spread of this group's meetings. Archbishop John McCloskey suspected its members of subversive and unorthodox opinions. It is not clear how long this group lasted. Some members later fell into difficulties with ecclesiastical authorities, most notably Edward McGlynn, who was excommunicated in 1887. Another casualty was Richard Burtsell, who in 1890 was removed as pastor from Epiphany Church in Manhattan which he had founded in 1868. At least some of the innovations discussed by the members of the Accademia—for example, a vernacular liturgy—were adopted by the Church at the time of Vatican Council II (1962–65). Some historians have regarded the members of the Accademia as forerunners of the "Americanists" who were condemned by Pope Leo XIII in 1899.

See also McGLYNN, EDWARD.

Callahan, Nelson J., ed. *The Diary of Richard L. Burtsell, Priest of New York.* New York, 1978.

Curran, Robert E. "Prelude to 'Americanism': The New York Accademia and Clerical Radicalism in the Late Nineteenth Century." *Church History* 47 (March 1978) 48–65.

ANTHONY D. ANDREASSI

NEW YORK, CATHOLIC CHURCH IN

Colonial and Revolutionary Period

There were few Catholics in New York during the period of Dutch rule (1609–64), or immediately after the English conquest of the colony in 1664. The first evidences of Catholicism stem from the evangelizing efforts of French Jesuit missionaries between 1642 and 1709 among the Iroquois in upstate New York. Three of the French missionaries were martyred—René Goupil in 1642, Isaac Jogues, and Jean de Lalande in 1646—at Ossernenon (present-day Auriesville). They were canonized with the other North American Martyrs in 1930. In 1643, after his initial rescue from the Iroquois by the Dutch, Isaac Jogues passed through New York City where he found only two Catholics, an Irishman and a Portuguese woman. Other Jesuits who worked in upstate New York include Claude Dablon, Pierre Chaumonont, and Simon LeMoyne. They made few converts among the Iroquois; the most notable was Kateri Tekakwitha, who was baptized in 1676, died in Canada in 1680, and was beatified in 1980.

Neither the Dutch nor the English tolerated the practice of Catholicism. The one brief exception (1674 to 1688) occurred during the proprietorship of the Duke of York, a convert to Catholicism, who in 1685 became King James II. Two years earlier, Thomas Dongan, an Irish Catholic who was governor from 1682 to 1687, sponsored the passage by the colonial assembly of a Charter of Liberties and Privileges, giving religious toleration to all Christians. Dongan also brought to the colony three English Jesuit priests (Thomas Harvey, Henry Harrison, and Charles Gage) and two lay brothers, who opened a small school and celebrated the first Mass in New York City on October 30, 1683. Dongan's purpose was not only religious but also political, for he wished to use English Jesuits to counteract the activities of the French Jesuits in upstate New York.

This brief period of religious toleration came to an end with the Glorious Revolution in England in 1688 which toppled James II from the English throne. Catholicism was again legally proscribed in New York. In 1696 the royal governor reported that happily there were only nine Catholics in the colony. In 1700 an antipriest law outlawed the presence of Catholic priests under penalty of life imprisonment, and in 1709 the French Jesuits abandoned their missions among the Iroquois. Thereafter Catholic life in the colony became virtually extinct. In 1741 a nonjuring

Anglican priest named John Ury was mistaken for a Catholic priest and executed for his supposed involvement in a slave uprising in New York City. Apparently no Catholic priest appeared in the colony until the late 1770s when Fr. Ferdinand Steinmeyer ("Father Farmer"), a German-born Jesuit, made surreptitious visits to New York from his residence in Pennsylvania.

The triumph of the Patriot cause in the American Revolution resulted in religious freedom for Catholics everywhere in the new American Republic, but Catholics enjoyed full civil rights in only five states. The New York State constitution, for example, required officeholders to renounce all foreign allegiances, religious as well as political. Ironically, the person responsible for this law was John Jay, whose Huguenot ancestors had been welcomed to New York by Governor Dongan. The law was not changed until 1806, when it was successfully challenged by Francis Cooper, the first Catholic elected to the state assembly.

At the end of the American Revolution there was a Catholic community of approximately two hundred in New York City, which for a brief period was both the national and state capital. On June 10, 1785, the lay leaders formed a corporation ("The Roman Catholic Church in the City of New York"), purchased land from Trinity Episcopal Church, and erected St. Peter's Church on Barclay Street, a small-frame building that was the first Catholic church built in New York. The cornerstone was laid on October 5, 1785, and the unfinished building was dedicated on November 4, 1786. Among the lay leaders were merchants Dominick Lynch and Thomas Stoughton, the French consul, Hector St. John de Crèvecoeur, and the Spanish minister to the United States, Don Diego de Gardoqui, who donated one thousand dollars on behalf of King Charles III of Spain.

It was easier to erect a church building than to find a suitable pastor. The first two pastors of St. Peter's Church, Charles Whelan and Andrew Nugent, were Irish Capuchins who fought with one another and with the lay trustees. It was only the third pastor, an Irish Dominican named William O'Brien, who for the next two decades brought peace to the troubled congregation. However, lay trusteeism would remain a problem in the parish well into the nineteenth century. Historian James A. Reynolds said: "St. Peter's was to be the prototype in a half century of trustee difficulties for the American Church." On March 14, 1805, a young widow, Elizabeth Ann Seton, was received into the Catholic Church in St. Peter's. She subsequently founded the American Sisters of Charity and in 1975 became the first-native born American to be canonized.

At the height of the difficulties among Catholics in New York in the 1780s, Fr. John Carroll, the Superior of the Mission for the nascent American Church, twice was refused admission to St. Peter's Church by partisans of Nugent. Carroll's experiences in New York convinced him of the need for the appointment of a bishop with authority to deal with such situations. The Holy See agreed and appointed Carroll bishop of Baltimore in 1789 with jurisdiction over the whole United States (whose western boundary was then the Mississippi River).

On April 8, 1808, Pope Pius VII made Baltimore a metropolitan see and created four new American dioceses, one of which was the Diocese of New York, comprising all of New York state and the northern half of New Jersey. Carroll failed to recommend a candidate for the new diocese with the result that the Holy See appointed as first bishop of New York Richard Luke Concanen, a sixty-one-year-old Irish Dominican who had long been resident in Rome. Concanen was ordained bishop of New York in Rome, but, because of the Napoleonic Wars, he never got closer to his see than Naples where he died on June 19, 1810, awaiting passage to the New World. No successor was appointed until 1815 due to Napoleon's imprisonment of the pope.

St. Patrick's Cathedral, New York City

Since the Diocese of New York had no resident bishop between 1808 and 1815, Archbishop Carroll appointed as his vicar general in New York Anthony Kohlmann, an Alsatian-born Jesuit, who proved to be a splendid choice. Kohlmann erected New York City's second Catholic Church, now St. Patrick's Old Cathedral, which was dedicated by Bishop Jean Cheverus of Boston on May 4, 1815. Kohlmann organized the city's first Catholic "college," the New York Literary Institute, which lasted from 1809 to 1813, when most of the Jesuit teachers were reassigned to Maryland. During Kohlmann's brief stewardship, both French Trap-

pists and Irish Ursulines arrived in New York, but neither remained for more than a few years. Kohlmann also became involved in a celebrated court case about the seal of confession in which the civil authorities recognized the inviolability of confessional secrets.

Early Nineteenth Century, 1815–65

The end of the Napoleonic Wars made possible the resumption of European emigration to the United States. Between 1815 and 1865, some five million European immigrants crossed the Atlantic. Perhaps as many as half of them were Catholics, principally from Ireland and Germany. Since New York became the principal port of entry, many of the immigrants remained in the city, swelling the size of the Catholic community. Others migrated north, attracted by construction work on the Erie Canal (which was built between 1817 and 1825) and later by construction work on the railroads.

New York's first resident bishop, John Connolly, appeared on the scene in 1815. Like his predecessor, Connolly was an Irish Dominican who had lived for many years in Rome where he received episcopal ordination on November 6, 1814. His diocese included some 15,000 Catholics spread over New York State and northern New Jersey. To care for their pastoral needs, Connolly had two churches in New York City and one in Albany (St. Mary's, founded in 1798). His clergy consisted of seven priests, most of whom soon left. The sole diocesan priest was Michael O'Gorman whom Connolly had recruited and ordained in Ireland. There were no religious communities or charitable institutions, and only one Catholic school, which was attached to St. Peter's parish in New York City. Msgr. Peter Guilday said: "It may well be doubted if, in the entire history of the Catholic Church in the United States, any other bishop began his episcopal life under such disheartening conditions."

During his ten years as bishop, Connolly found it impossible to keep pace with the increase in the Catholic population, which grew to approximately 100,000. Most of the newcomers were poor Irish immigrants. Many remained in New York City; others provided the manual labor for the construction of the Erie Canal and brought Catholicism to upstate cities like Auburn, Syracuse, and Buffalo. There was also a considerable influx of German Catholics and sprinkling of French Catholics from France and the Caribbean. Among the latter was Pierre Toussaint, a slave who came to New York from Saint Domingue (Haiti) in 1787 and who eventually won his freedom and became a successful businessman and generous benefactor of the poor.

Two of Bishop Connolly's greatest handicaps were the poverty of the Catholic laity and the scarcity of vocations to the priesthood. He complained in a letter to Rome in

1816 that "American Catholics have absolutely no inclination to become ecclesiastics." Another major difficulty was the assertiveness of the lay trustees and their supporters among the local clergy, notably Peter Malou and William Taylor. The situation deteriorated to the point that in 1820 the Congregation de Propaganda Fide deputed Bishop Joseph Plessis of Quebec to visit New York and make a report to Rome.

Nonetheless, there were signs of progress. In 1816 a second Catholic school was opened in the basement of St. Patrick's Cathedral. The following year Mother Seton's Sisters of Charity came from Emmitsburg to establish a Catholic orphan asylum in New York City. Not all of the city's Catholics were poor immigrants; Cornelius Heeney was a wealthy businessman who had once been a partner of John Jacob Astor. Elsewhere in New York parishes were established in Syracuse (1819), Brooklyn (1823), Rochester (1823), Carthage (1825), and Buffalo (1829). In 1824 an exhausted Connolly asked the Holy See to appoint Michael O'Gorman as his coadjutor, but O'Gorman died that same year shortly before Connolly himself, who died on February 6, 1825.

Almost two years elapsed before the appointment of a successor to Connolly. In the interval, the diocese was governed by Connolly's former vicar general, the popular Irish-born Fr. John Power, who had been pastor of St. Peter's Church since 1819. In 1825 Power founded New York's first Catholic newspaper, *The Truth Teller,* and in 1826 he established New York City's third Catholic Church, St. Mary's. That same year the Holy See selected as third bishop of New York John Dubois, a French-born priest and émigré from the Revolution, who had founded Mount St. Mary's College and Seminary in Emmitsburg, Maryland. Dubois, who was ordained a bishop in Baltimore on October 29, 1826, inherited all of Connolly's problems plus several additional ones. The Catholic population doubled to perhaps 200,000, most of them poor immigrants. Their numbers and poverty triggered an outburst of anti-Catholic bigotry, which was especially severe in New York City where, in 1836, professional bigots published the *Awful Disclosures of the Hôtel Dieu Nunnery,* a salacious account of convent life supposedly written by the improbably named Maria Monk.

New York's Catholic community continued to be riven by internal disputes. Lay trustees not only controlled the finances of the parishes, but they also claimed the right to appoint and remove pastors. They clashed with Dubois even over the administration of his own cathedral. When Dubois suspended Fr. Thomas Levins, a curate at the cathedral, the lay trustees hired Levins to supervise the Sunday school and terminated Dubois' salary. Moreover, the fact that Dubois was French, and spoke English with a pronounced accent, caused widespread resentment among New York's Irish Catholics, who had expected John Power, not John Dubois, to have been named bishop of New York. Another successful pastor, who was equally popular with his Irish parishioners and less of a rival to Dubois, was Fr. Felix Varela, the Cuban-born founder of Transfiguration parish in Manhattan.

In 1837 the aging Dubois requested and received a coadjutor in the person of John Hughes, a Philadelphia priest who had once been student under Dubois at Mount St. Mary's Seminary. Hughes was ordained a bishop in St. Patrick's Cathedral on January 7, 1838. He became apostolic administrator of the diocese in 1839 and succeeded Dubois as fourth bishop of New York upon the latter's death on December 20, 1842. He was to become the most significant figure in the history of the Catholic Church in New York State in the nineteenth century.

Hughes quickly achieved national prominence because of two issues. First he unsuccessfully lobbied for government subsidies for Catholic schools, an effort that was used to depict him as an enemy of American public schools. Secondly, in 1844, he responded to threats of nativist violence against Catholic churches in New York City by surrounding them with armed guards, thus averting a repetition of the anti-Catholic riots that had rocked Philadelphia earlier that year.

Hughes was the first bishop of New York with the strength of character to be an effective leader. He held the first diocesan synod, created one hundred new parishes throughout the state, began the parochial school system in New York, and introduced into the diocese ten religious communities. He established St. Joseph's Seminary in 1840 and St. John's College (present-day Fordham University) in 1841. He encouraged the Sisters of Charity to begin St. Vincent's Hospital during the cholera epidemic of 1849. He effectively ended the trusteeism problem in the state, with the notable exception of St. Louis Church in Buffalo. One of his proudest moments occurred on August 15, 1858, when he laid the cornerstone for the new St. Patrick's Cathedral, which was not completed until 1879. He was enormously popular with his largely immigrant flock because he identified with them so naturally and defended their interests so vigorously. Recognition of his stature in the American Catholic Church came from the highest level when the United States government asked him to visit France during the Civil War on behalf of the Union cause.

Twice in Hughes' administration the original Diocese of New York was subdivided into new sees. In 1847 new dioceses were established in Buffalo for northwestern New York, and in Albany for the northeastern part of the state. In 1853, two more dioceses were created in Newark and Brooklyn for New Jersey and Long Island respectively. Three of the four new bishops were close associates of Hughes: James Roosevelt Bayley in Newark, John McCloskey in Albany, and John Loughlin in Brooklyn. Only the first bishop of Buffalo was an outsider, John Timon, a Vincentian who had been a missionary in Texas. Not one of the four new dioceses had more than thirty-four priests. Buffalo, which covered twenty counties and almost one-third of the total area of the state, had only eighteen priests in 1847.

On July 19, 1850, John Hughes became the first archbishop of New York when New York was made a metropolitan see. At the time of Hughes' death on January 3, 1864, the Archdiocese of New York had been reduced to only one-tenth of the size of the original diocese but, during Hughes' episcopate, the Catholic population of the archdiocese doubled to about 400,000. Catholics probably constituted a majority of the population of New York City, which was then coterminous with Manhattan. In 1861 the northern boundary of the Archdiocese of New York was adjusted to conform to the county lines. Since then, it has been one of the few metropolitan sees in the United States whose boundaries have remained unchanged.

Late Nineteenth Century, 1865–1908

Immigration continued to swell the number of Catholics in New York. Beginning in the 1880s, there was a large influx of Slavic and Italian Catholics. By 1900 there were an estimated 400,000 Italian immigrants in the Archdiocese of New York alone. Archbishop Corrigan brought Italian priests and sisters to New York, the most famous of whom was Mother Frances Xavier Cabrini, who founded Columbus Hospital (now Cabrini Medical Center) in Manhattan in 1895. She was canonized in 1946, the first (naturalized) American citizen to be so honored. By the turn of the century the Diocese of Buffalo could boast of a large Polish population. Not all the immigrants came from Europe. Many French-Canadians left rural Quebec to find work in upstate cities like Cohoes and Plattsburg. Like the rest of the American hierarchy, the bishops of New York responded to this pastoral challenge by establishing national parishes for the various ethnic groups. To meet the needs of the growing Catholic population in central and northern New York, new dioceses were also established in Rochester (1868), Ogdensburg (1872), and Syracuse (1886).

Several important charitable institutions date from the nineteenth century. In 1847 the Sisters of Mercy founded a House of Mercy in New York City which provided shelter and job training for thousands of immigrant girls. Archbishop John Hughes established the Catholic Protectory in New York City in 1863 to care for homeless and delinquent children. The first director of the institution was Levi Silliman Ives, the former Protestant Episcopal bishop of North Carolina. In 1870 Sr. Irene Fitzgibbon of the Sisters of Charity of Mount St. Vincent organized the New York Foundling Hospital. In 1881 Fr. John Drumgoole founded the Mission of the Immaculate Virgin, which became one of the largest orphanages in the United States.

John McCloskey, first bishop of Albany (1847–64), and archbishop of New York from 1864 to 1885, became the first American cardinal in 1875, an appointment which reflected the Holy See's recognition of the importance of the Archdiocese of New York. McCloskey's successor, Archbishop Michael Corrigan (1885–1902), was one of the leaders of the conservative wing of the American hierarchy. In that role he was ably assisted by Bernard J. McQuaid, first bishop of Rochester (1868–1909), a dynamic diocesan administrator who founded sixty-nine parishes, some forty parochial schools, and a model major seminary, St. Bernard's. Historian James Hennesey described him as "that most progressive of conservatives."

In the late nineteenth century both the clergy and laity in New York showed signs of emerging from the Catholic immigrant ghetto. In 1872, under "Honest John" Kelly (whose wife was Archbishop McCloskey's niece), Irish Catholics gained control of Tammany Hall, the New York City Democratic organization. Eight years later the city elected its first Catholic mayor, William R. Grace. The intellectual restlessness of the clergy found expression in the New York "Accademia," a loose association of "progressive" priests who discussed such issues as the advantages of a vernacular liturgy, the relevance of traditional religious orders, and the need for social welfare legislation. The most prominent member was Fr. Edward McGlynn, pastor of St. Stephen's Church in Manhattan, whose involvement in municipal politics led to his temporary excommunication (1887–92). Other members of the "Accademia" included canon lawyer Richard Burtsell and Brooklyn pastor Sylvester Malone. In the Diocese of Rochester, Fr. Louis Lambert conducted a long public dispute with Bishop McQuaid. In Poughkeepsie, in the Archdiocese of New York, Patrick McSweeny, pastor of St. Peter's Church, negotiated an agreement with the local school board in 1873 which resulted in public funding of his parochial school for almost thirty years. The "Poughkeepsie Plan" had the approval of Cardinal McCloskey, but its success was an embarrassment to Archbishop Corrigan, who feared that it would undermine Catholic support for the parochial school system.

The late nineteenth century also witnessed a revival of anti-Catholic bigotry in the United States. In 1884 in New York City, Dr. Samuel Burchard, a prominent Presbyterian minister speaking on behalf of Republican presidential candidate James G. Blaine, denounced the Democratic Party as the party of "Rum, Romanism and Rebellion." Blaine failed to repudiate the remark and subsequently lost New York State to Grover Cleveland by a margin of 1,200 votes.

Another example of anti-Catholic bigotry was the success in many states of the A.P.A., the American Protective

Association. The A.P.A. was weak in New York, but New York Catholics had a powerful adversary in a more genteel version of the A.P.A., the National League for the Protection of American Interests whose membership included the WASP establishment of the state. A major goal of anti-Catholic activists throughout the nation at that time was to deprive the Catholic Church of any government funds for its schools and charitable institutions. The N.L.P.A.I. spearheaded this effort in New York at the Constitutional Convention of 1894. The New York state bishops made the wise tactical decision not to seek government funds for Catholic schools, but to fight only for the continuation of funding for their charitable institutions, a battle which they won thanks to the efforts of several outstanding Catholic laymen, especially George Bliss and Frédéric Coudert.

In the second half of the nineteenth century, most New York diocesan priests were educated at St. Joseph's Provincial Seminary in Troy. Between 1864 and 1896 this seminary, whose core faculty consisted of six Belgian priests from the Diocese of Ghent, trained over seven hundred priests. However, appalling living conditions led to a high morality rate among the students and a demand for seminary reform. Bishop McQuaid of Rochester responded by establishing St. Bernard's Seminary in 1893, and, in 1896, Archbishop Corrigan founded the much larger St. Joseph's Seminary in the Dunwoodie section of Yonkers. During the next dozen years, Dunwoodie established itself as one of the intellectual centers of American Catholicism. From 1905 to 1908, it sponsored the *New York Review,* the leading American Catholic theological journal of its day. However, the papal condemnation of Modernism in 1907 put an end to this promising intellectual development.

In 1908 the Catholic Church in the United States officially ceased to be regarded as a missionary Church by the Holy See. That same year New York state Catholics celebrated the centenary of the diocese in New York City with a parade up Fifth Avenue that was widely interpreted as a demonstration of Catholic power. The Catholic population of the state numbered approximately 2,500,000, and the archbishop of New York had become such an influential figure in local politics that his residence at 452 Madison Avenue was often referred to as "The Powerhouse."

Twentieth Century, 1908–Present

Between 1912 and 1916 Catholic charitable institutions in New York came under scrutiny and criticism from several New York city and state investigative committees. As a consequence, Patrick J. Hayes, archbishop of New York from 1919 to 1938, established the Catholic Charities of the Archdiocese of New York under the direction of Fr.

Robert F. Keegan. It set new standards for professionalism in social welfare work and was widely imitated by other American dioceses. As a result of American entry into World War I, the Holy See created the Military Ordinariate for Catholics in the armed forces and attached it to the Archdiocese of New York, a connection that continued until 1985. On November 24, 1917, Hayes, then auxiliary bishop, was named Bishop Ordinary of United States Army and Navy Chaplains, a title that he retained when he became archbishop of New York on March 10, 1919. By the end of World War I, there were over 1,500 Catholic chaplains in the armed forces.

The Catholic population of the state continued to grow despite the restrictive immigration laws of the 1920s. The ethos of New York Catholicism remained very much that of "The Immigrant Church." In 1920, for example, 51 of the 113 parishes in Manhattan were "national parishes," representing 18 different ethnic groups. Until 1936 the Archdiocese of New York remained the most populous American see, and reputedly the wealthiest. Both Brooklyn and Buffalo also ranked among the most populous dioceses in the country. Francis Cardinal Spellman, archbishop of New York from 1939 to 1967, was the best-known American prelate of his era. A friend of both President Franklin D. Roosevelt and Pope Pius XII, Spellman wielded wide influence in national and international affairs from the moment that he was appointed archbishop of New York on April 15, 1939. An effective diocesan administrator, Spellman restored the financial health of the archdiocese, created a diocesan high school system, spent almost six hundred million dollars on expansion of diocesan facilities, and showed imaginative pastoral leadership in responding to the huge influx of Puerto Ricans into the archdiocese after World War II. During the war and after, Spellman used his role of military vicar to epitomize Catholic patriotism through well-publicized visits to American troops throughout the world.

New York City was an important intellectual center for American Catholics. It was the home of Jesuit-owned *America,* the older Paulist publication *Catholic World,* and lay-owned *Commonweal. The Brooklyn Tablet,* under the editorship of its conservative editor, Patrick J. Scanlan, attracted readers from across the country. In the middle of the Great Depression, on May 1, 1933, Dorothy Day and Peter Maurin launched the Catholic Worker movement in New York City. Fr. Philip Carey, S.J., organized the Xavier School of Industrial Relations to train Catholics for leadership roles in the labor movement. Another New York priest, Msgr. John P. Monaghan, promoted the Social Gospel among the diocesan clergy and helped to establish the Association of Catholic Trade Unionists. Fr. George Barry Ford made Corpus Christi Church in Manhattan an early center of liturgical renewal and ecumenism. Under the leadership of Fr. John LaFarge, S.J., the

Catholic Interracial Council of New York City did pioneer work in fostering better race relations among Catholics.

After World War II, the growth of the suburbs had a profound impact on the Catholic Church throughout the United States. In New York state, it was especially noticeable on Long Island, where in 1957 it led to the establishment of the new Diocese of Rockville Centre with its see "city" located in a small commuter village. During the first dozen years of the diocese's existence, the Catholic population almost doubled from 497,000 to 926,397, and the incredible sum of $233,000,000 was spent on new construction. "Nothing but euphoria was visible on the horizon in 1958," said one diocesan priest. As a result of the creation of the Diocese of Rockville Centre, the Diocese of Brooklyn was reduced in size to two New York City counties (Brooklyn and Queens), leaving it a totally urban diocese that is the smallest in area (179 square miles) but one of the largest in population in the United States. As a result of the flight of the white middle class to the suburbs, many of the large urban parishes in the old industrial cities of the state found themselves with dwindling congregations and declining financial resources. In the Archdiocese of New York, during the 1970s, the Catholic population remained approximately the same (1,800,000), but only because of the influx of large numbers of Hispanic immigrants. Terence Cardinal Cooke, archbishop from 1968 to 1983, levied an assessment on all parishes and used the income to subsidize poorer parishes. As a result most inner-city parishes were able to continue to provide religious and educational services for their new parishioners.

The Contemporary Scene

In 1994 the Catholic population of the state was 7,331,820 out of a total population of 18,246,019. More than two-thirds of the Catholics lived in the Archdiocese of New York (2,286,187) and in the Dioceses of Brooklyn (1,630,013) and Rockville Centre (1,340,279). Nationally those same three sees ranked third, fifth, and eighth respectively in population among all American archdioceses and dioceses. The overall percentage of Catholics in the general population of New York state was 41 percent, with the highest percentage in the Diocese of Rockville Centre (50 percent) and the lowest percentage in the Diocese of Rochester (27 percent). There were 1,692 parishes in the state, which varied greatly in size and distribution. In the largely rural Diocese of Ogdensburg, there were 122 parishes for 161,722 Catholics; in the Diocese of Rockville Centre, there were 133 parishes for eight times as many Catholics (1,340,279). There were 3,798 diocesan priests, 1,859 religious priests (more than half of them in the Archdiocese of New York), 1,009 permanent deacons, 994 brothers, and 11,904 women religious. Other statistics were less reassuring. In 1994 only

two new parishes were established in the state, and only 34 diocesan priests were ordained.

One of the most impressive features of New York Catholicism has been the development of the Catholic educational system in the state. In 1994 there were 29 Catholic universities and colleges with 109,060 students, 129 high schools with 73,804 students, and 736 elementary schools with 221,758 students. However, during the previous thirty years, there had been a drastic decline in the size of the Catholic elementary school system. In 1965 there were 1,114 elementary schools with almost three times as many students (639,723) as in 1994. In that same period the number of teaching sisters declined from 14,370 to 2,068. There was an even more precipitous decline in the number of seminarians, from 6,712 in 1965 to 347 in 1994.

Becker, Martin J. *A History of Catholic Life in the Diocese of Albany.* New York: U.S. Catholic Historical Society, 1975.

Carthy, Margaret. *A Cathedral of Suitable Magnificence: St. Patrick's Cathedral.* Wilmington, Del.: Michael Glazier, 1984.

Cohalan, Florence D. *A Popular History of the Archdiocese of New York.* Yonkers: U.S. Catholic Historical Society, 1983.

Curran, Robert Emmett. *Michael Augustine Corrigan and the Shaping of Conservative Catholicism in America, 1878–1902.* New York: Arno Press, 1978.

Diaz-Stevens, Ana Maria. *Oxcart Catholicism on Fifth Avenue: The Impact of the Puerto Rican Migration upon the Archdiocese of New York.* University of Notre Dame Press, 1993.

Dolan, Jay P. *The Immigrant Church: New York's Irish and German Catholics, 1815–1865.* Baltimore: Johns Hopkins University Press, 1975.

Guilday, Peter. "Trusteeism in New York." *Historical Records and Studies* 18 (1928) 44–74.

Leonard, Joan de Lourdes, C.S.J. *Richly Blessed: The History of the Diocese of Rockville Centre.* Rockville Centre: Diocese of Rockville Centre, 1991.

McNamara, Robert F. *History of the Diocese of Rochester, 1868–1968.* Rochester: Diocese of Rochester, 1968.

O'Brien, David J. *Faith and Friendship: Catholicism in the Diocese of Syracuse, 1886–1986.* Syracuse: Diocese of Syracuse, 1987.

Reynolds, James A. "Archdiocese of New York." *NCE* 10:398–406.

Sharp, John K. *History of the Diocese of Brooklyn, 1853–1953.* 2 vols. New York: Fordham University Press, 1954.

Shaw, Richard. *Dagger John: The Unquiet Life and Times of Archbishop John Hughes of New York.* New York: Paulist Press, 1977.

Shelley, Thomas J. *Dunwoodie: The History of St. Joseph's Seminary.* Westminster, Md.: Christian Classics, 1993.

____. "Dean Lings' Church: The Success of Ethnic Catholicism in Yonkers in the 1890s." *Church History* 65 (1) (March 1996) 28–41.

Smith, John Talbot. *The Catholic Church in New York.* New York: Hall and Locke, 1905.

Taylor, Mary Christine, S.S.J. *A History of the Foundations of Catholicism in Northern New York.* New York: U.S. Catholic Historical Society, 1976.

THOMAS J. SHELLEY

NEW YORK REVIEW

A scholarly journal published at St. Joseph's Seminary, Dunwoodie, from 1905 to 1908. In the opinion of John Tracy Ellis, it was "one of the most learned reviews ever undertaken under American Catholic auspices." The initiative for the journal came from two New York diocesan priests on the Dunwoodie faculty, Francis P. Duffy (later famous as a chaplain in World War I) and John F. Brady. They took their proposal to James F. Driscoll, the Sulpician rector of Dunwoodie, who brought it to the attention of Archbishop John M. Farley, who gave the proposal an enthusiastic endorsement.

The first issue of the *New York Review* appeared on June 21, 1905, with the subtitle: "A Journal of the Ancient Faith and Modern Thought." As promised in the prospectus, the tone of the journal was scholarly and constructive rather than polemical. Over the course of the next three years, about half of the articles were written by the members of the Dunwoodie faculty; the rest by American, British, and European writers of the caliber of Wilfrid Ward, George Tyrrell, Vincent McNabb, O.P., Joseph Turmel, and M. J. Lagrange, O.P. The review made available to American readers the latest developments in Scripture studies, philosophy and theology, especially apologetics. Driscoll was the editor and Duffy the associate editor; Brady served as managing editor and handled the finances.

In 1907 the appearance of two Roman documents sealed the fate of the *New York Review*. In July the Holy Office published *Lamentabili Sane Exitu,* a list of sixty-five condemned propositions said to be found in the writings of Modernist scholars; in September, Pope Pius X issued the encyclical *Pascendi Dominici Gregis,* denouncing Modernism in the strongest terms. The editors of the *New York Review* claimed that the Pope was not directing his criticism at them. "The teaching authority has condemned only extreme views," they said, and warned against "extending the condemnation to include, it would seem, everyone who has studied biology or Hebrew."

Despite this optimistic forecast, the *New York Review* never recovered from the papal condemnation of Modernism. In the June 1908 issue the editors announced that they were suspending publication because of the lack of subscribers. They denied newspaper reports that the review had been suppressed and asserted that neither the review itself nor any article in it "has ever been made the object of official condemnation or censure." However, the editors came closer to revealing the real reasons for the review's demise when they also declared: "At its inception three years ago its editors promised to present the best work of Catholic scholars at home and abroad on theological and other problems of the present day. It is the keeping of that promise, not the breaking of it, that is the cause of the suspension of the *Review.*"

See also DUFFY, FRANCIS PATRICK; MODERNISM IN AMERICA.

Appleby, R. Scott. *"Church and Age, Unite!" The Modernist Impulse in American Catholicism.* Notre Dame, 1992, 91–168.

DeVito, Michael J. *The New York Review, 1905–1908.* New York, 1977.

Gannon, Michael V. "Before and After Modernism: The Intellectual Isolation of the American Priest." *The Catholic Priest in the United States: Historical Investigations,* ed. John Tracy Ellis. Collegeville, Minn.: The Liturgical Press, 1971, 293–384.

Shelley, Thomas J. *Dunwoodie: The History of St. Joseph's Seminary.* Westminster, Md., 1993, 133–70.

————. "John Cardinal Farley and Modernism in New York." *Church History* 61 (3) (September 1992) 350–61.

THOMAS J. SHELLEY

NEWMAN MOVEMENT, THE

Catholic Campus ministry emerged from the Newman Movement. The latter was inspired by the life and writings of John Henry Newman (1801–90). It tried to provide pastoral care and religious education in U.S. non-Catholic colleges and universities. Its story unfolds in four stages.

Early History

The first appeared around the turn of the century, and was diocesan-based. Bishops provided leadership for professors, students, and priests who were organizing "the chaplain movement" in state universities. Even skeptics termed this innovation a "new link" in the evolution of American Catholic life.

The second stage appeared with the series of student organizations that emerged after 1910. These sought to regain lost episcopal leadership in a time that called for a delicate apologetic. On one side, Newman Clubs tried to defend their members against campuses sometimes hostile to Catholicism. On the other, Newman leaders struggled to validate their movement for sometimes unsympathetic Catholic educators and churchmen. This latter effort culminated in the formation of the National Newman Apostolate in 1962.

A third stage began in 1967, when a commission of chaplains and students redesigned the Newman Apostolate in "light of Vatican Council II and changes in the university world." The fourth stage began in 1985. That year the bishops issued a pastoral letter on campus ministry that endorsed progress made during the third stage.

The Newman Movement began in 1883 at the University of Wisconsin, when Catholics, seeking social and intellectual companionship, formed the Melvin Club. Ten years later, one of its members, Timothy L. Harrington, was a medical student at the University of Pennsylvania. He invoked the Melvin Club as a model for the first Newman Club. This became the inspiration for the Catholic student movement that flowered after 1915.

Twentieth-Century Development

Meanwhile, in 1905, Pope Pius X issued an encyclical letter on religious education, *Acerbo Nimis,* which commanded that "schools of religion" be set up at every college and university that did not teach about God. The first American bishop to respond was Archbishop Sebastian G. Messmer of Milwaukee. In 1906 he appointed Fr. Henry C. Hengell to the University of Wisconsin as full-time chaplain, and authorized a chapel and educational hall to be named "The Catholic College." By 1910, seventeen dioceses had announced full-time chaplaincies that included chapels, club houses, or educational buildings.

This initial development soon ended. The Catholic Educational Association claimed that "the chaplain movement" would destroy church colleges, and even endanger parish schools. In 1907 the bishops did not entirely agree with this position, and refused to excommunicate parents who sent their offspring to state universities. By the 1920s, however, the hierarchy endorsed the Catholic colleges collectively. They denoted the Newman Movement as something each bishop should care for individually according to the circumstances of his diocese.

So Catholics in nonsectarian colleges were largely on their own. In 1908 they had formed the Catholic Student Association of America. In 1915 the Federation of College Catholic Clubs (renamed the National Newman Club Federation in 1938) replaced it. For over two decades Fr. John W. Keogh of the University of Pennsylvania Newman Club almost single-handedly led the new organization. Ceaselessly citing *Acerbo Nimis* to bishops and Newman's example of intellectual honesty to students, Keogh organized more than six hundred clubs and brought dozens of priests into the cause.

By 1950 Newman Clubs enrolled 80,000 of the 310,000 Catholics attending non-Catholic colleges; Catholic institutions registered 293,000 students. Aware that this gap would increase and with it the need for spiritual leadership, campus priests organized the National Newman Chaplains Association.

Led chiefly by Cleveland Intercollegiate's Fr. Paul J. Hallinan, national chaplain 1952–54, and bishop of Charleston in 1958, chaplains joined students in developing liturgical and educational programs. In 1936 the students had set up the John Henry Cardinal Newman Honorary Society. Now three more auxiliary units, each bearing the "National Newman" prefix, followed: the Alumni Association (1957), and the Foundation and the Association of Faculty and Staff (1960). In 1962 these six units joined with the Youth Department of the National Catholic Welfare Conference at the "Ann Arbor Summit" to form the National Newman Apostolate. The bishops mandated it to do "the work of the Catholic Church in the secular campus community."

After Vatican Council II

Two years after the close of Vatican II, the Apostolate's leaders believed that its focus on the national student federation was out of date. A commission of chaplains and students successfully recommended a return to the original diocesan-based arrangement. Leaders also accepted a new description of their ministry as "a searching, believing, loving, worshiping . . . presence of the Catholic Church in the campus community." Feeling marginalized, the federation joined with the University Christian Movement. When this ecumenical experiment collapsed in 1969, the federation fell apart. Meanwhile, in 1969 the Chaplains Association became the Catholic Campus Ministry Association (CCMA), and included religious men and women, and lay leaders in its ranks.

In 1985 the bishops issued a pastoral letter, "Empowered by the Spirit." It termed campus ministry "vitally important for the future of Church and society," and named "all the baptized members of the campus community," as campus ministers. It specified that "professional campus ministers [were] called to lead the faith community." That benchmark year also witnessed the birth of the National Catholic Student Coalition. This united the National Federation of Catholic College Students (1938) with elements of the former Newman Student Federation.

Approaching the year 2000, Catholic campus ministry shows the following profile. About 200 diocesan directors, who have their own national association, coordinate the ministry of nearly 2,000 priests, deacons, brothers, sisters, and laypersons. These serve upwards of three million Catholics on the 2,500 campuses of the nation. Affiliated with the United States Catholic Conference, the CCMA enrolls about 55 percent of campus ministers, has members at work on 60 percent of public colleges and universities, and collaborates with the student coalition. It continues to conduct the yearly chaplains' training schools begun in the 1960s by the Newman Apostolate.

Evans, John Whitney. *The Newman Movement: Roman Catholics in American Higher Education.* Notre Dame, 1980, passim.

JOHN WHITNEY EVANS

NOGAR, RAYMOND JUDE (1916–67)

Dominican friar, educator, and philosopher. Nogar was born in Monroe, Michigan. After receiving his B.A. degree from the University of Michigan, he began his graduate work in sociology there, but withdrew from the program when he decided to convert to Catholicism in 1939. The following year he entered the Dominican novitiate in River Forest, Illinois, where he studied at the Aquinas Institute of Philosophy and Theology, earning his S.T.L. and Ph.D. degrees in the philosophy of science, and was ordained.

Raymond J. Nogar

He remained at River Forest, where he taught on the faculty at the institute and was cofounder and executive secretary of the Albertus Magnus Lyceum, an organization dedicated to advancing the dialogue between philosophers and scientists.

An expositor of a holistic approach to understanding man and nature, he questioned the scientific foundations of evolutionary thought by presenting evidence for an integral philosophy of evolution. He distinguished himself from the work of Pierre Teilhard de Chardin by rejecting Teilhard's cosmic optimism and convergence-theology in favor of a more chaotic view of the relationship between nature and religion. He lectured widely and published numerous scholarly articles. His works include *The Wisdom of Evolution* (1963) and *The Lord of the Absurd* (1967).

See also DOMINICANS (O.P.).

TRICIA T. PYNE

NOLL, JOHN (1875–1956)

Archbishop and publisher. John Francis Noll was born in Fort Wayne, Indiana, on January 25, 1875, the son of John G. Noll, a Fort Wayne haberdasher, and Anna Ford Noll. He was educated in Fort Wayne and at St. Lawrence College, Mount Calvary, Wisconsin. After studies at Mt. St. Mary's Seminary in Cincinnati, Ohio, he was ordained a priest of the Fort Wayne diocese on June 4, 1898.

From 1898 until 1925, he served in several Indiana parishes, the last being St. Mary's parish, Huntington, of which he became pastor in 1910. Two interests were very important to him as a parish priest: the conversion of non-Catholics to the Catholic Church, and anti-Catholicism which was in-

creasingly an issue especially in Indiana, on the way to becoming the national center for the Ku Klux Klan.

Noll's first publishing effort was in 1904 when he wrote a booklet, *Kind Words from Your Pastor,* designed to introduce Catholic beliefs to persons unfamiliar with the Catholic Church. In 1908 he organized *The Family Digest,* his first venture into Catholic periodical publishing. Four years later, he founded *Our Sunday Visitor,* chiefly to combat anti-Catholicism. Soon, *Our Sunday Visitor* was distributed across the country to hundreds of thousands of subscribers.

John Noll

Pope Pius XI appointed Noll bishop of Fort Wayne on May 12, 1925; Cardinal George Mundelein of Chicago consecrated the new bishop in Fort Wayne on May 12, 1925. Bishop Noll maintained an active interest in *Our Sunday Visitor* and its subsidiaries, and was a strong advocate of Catholic education and evangelization. On September 2, 1953, Pope Pius XII conferred on Bishop Noll the personal title of archbishop. He died in Huntington, Indiana, on July 31, 1956.

See also OUR SUNDAY VISITOR.

OWEN CAMPION

NORRIS, JAMES JOSEPH (1907–76)

Lay activist. James Joseph Norris was born August 10, 1907, at Roselle Park, New Jersey. While still in high school, Norris became acquainted with the charismatic Fr. Thomas A. Judge, C.M. After graduation in 1924, Norris joined Judge's fledgling religious community, the Missionary Servants of the Most Holy Trinity. Although he never took formal vows, Norris spent the next decade as Judge's assistant and treasurer, taking courses intermittently at The Catholic University of America where he received a B.A. degree in 1933. Feeling himself more in the business than religious world, Norris left the Trinitarians in 1934 and worked briefly for Automatic Electric Company.

Norris's four decades of Church work began in December 1936 when he was hired by Fr. (later Cardinal) Patrick O'Boyle as executive assistant at the Mission of the Immaculate Virgin, a large (1,100 children) child-welfare center on Staten Island. Here Norris was in charge of fundraising and public relations, as well as controller. During this time, Norris also took courses at the Fordham School of Social Service, and did street preaching with the Catholic Evidence Guild. With the outbreak of World War II, Norris joined the staff of the newly organized National Catholic Community Services, the Catholic branch of the U.S.O. organization, serving as assistant director (1941–42), and executive director (1942–44). From 1944 to 1946 he served on active duty as a Commander in the U.S. Navy Armed Guard.

Upon Norris's release from the Navy, O'Boyle hired him for the newly created post of European Director of War Relief Services–NCWC (later Catholic Relief Services–NCWC). Fluent in four languages, Norris organized nineteen offices in Europe for the processing of some 130,000 refugee emigrants to the United States. He helped to found both the Conference of Voluntary Agencies Working for Refugees, and the International Conference of Nongovernmental Agencies Interested in Migration. At the request of Pope Pius XII, he participated in intensive negotiations at the Vatican with Msgr. Giovanni Battista Montini (later Pope Paul VI), which resulted in the formation of the International Catholic Migration Commission in 1951. Norris served as president of ICMC from 1951 to 1974, and honorary president thereafter until his death.

As the focus of CRS activity moved from European emigration to Third World socioeconomic development, Norris was brought home from Geneva to New York in 1959 to serve as executive assistant to CRS executive director, Bishop Edward Swanstrom. In this post, which he held until his death, Norris had a wide range of responsibilities and traveled to every corner of the world, supervising personnel, inspecting projects, and networking with Church, government, nongovernment, and ecumenical groups. In 1963 Paul VI named Norris one of the first lay auditors at the Second Vatican Council. On November 4, 1964, Norris became the only layperson to participate in the conciliar debates, delivering a *relatio,* in Latin, on "World Poverty and the Christian Conscience," introducing a section of Schema XIII, "On the Church in the Modern World."

After the council's close, Norris, together with Luigi Ligutti, Barbara Ward, Gerald Mahon, Arthur McCormack, and Joseph Gremillion, lobbied at the Vatican for the establishment on an organism of the universal Church to deal with world poverty and social justice as called for in paragraph ninety of the conciliar pastoral constitution, *Gaudium et spes.* In 1966 Paul VI appointed Norris to a *Gaudium et spes* Ninety Working Group, which resulted in the formation of the Pontifical Commission on Justice and Peace (later Pontifical Council) in January 1967. Norris was named a founding member of the Justice and Peace Commission, and, in 1971, of the pontifical council "Cor Unum," the coordinating body for Church-aid societies. Norris represented the Holy See at the funeral of Dr. Martin Luther King, and at the depositing of the Holy See's accession to the Nuclear Test Ban Treaty. In 1969 he was part of the official suite that accompanied Paul VI on his one-day visit to the International Labour Office and the World Council of Churches in Geneva.

Norris married the former Amanda Tisch in 1941 and was the father of four sons. He received honorary doctorates from Georgetown, Seton Hall, St. John's (New York), and The Catholic University of America. In addition to several decorations from the Holy See, he was honored by the governments of the Netherlands, Germany, Greece, and Spain.

Norris died at Newark, New Jersey, on November 17, 1976, and is buried in Washington. Three weeks before his death, the U.N. High Commissioner for Refugees announced that Norris had been named the first American recipient of the Nansen Medal. The High Commissioner stated at the time that "he [Norris] was instrumental in creating more awareness of the plight of refugees, and throughout his life has wholeheartedly devoted his efforts to humanitarian causes." The medal was accepted by Norris's wife three weeks after his burial.

Egan, Eileen. *Catholic Relief Services. The Beginning Years.* Baltimore: Catholic Relief Services, 1988.

Kupke, Raymond J. "James J. Norris: An American Catholic Life." Ph.D. dissertation, The Catholic University of America, 1995.

RAYMOND J. KUPKE

NORTH AMERICAN COLLEGE

The North American College in Rome has three divisions: the seminary, 1859, founded by Pius IX; the graduate house (the Casa Santa Maria), 1933; and the Institute for Continuing Theological Education, 1970, a semiannual program for priests resulting from the renewal movement following Vatican Council II. The first and the third divisions are located not far from St. Peter's Basilica on the Janiculum hill, part of the extraterritoriality of Vatican

First-year students at the North American College, Rome (1859)

City State. The graduate division that also houses the Bishops' Office for U.S. Visitors to the Vatican, is on the Via dell'Umiltà, close to the Trevi Fountain, across from the Gregorian University and the Pontifical Biblical Institute. Modern theological graduate study in Rome dates from 1931, when Pius XI in the apostolic constitution *Deus Scientiarum Dominus* decreed major revision of requirements for advanced degrees at Roman theological universities. In conformity with this, the North American College graduate house of residence was established in 1933, first in the Villa San Giovanni on the Janiculum property and after World War II in the original refurbished College foundation on the Umiltà. The students attend Roman theological universities, from which they take their degrees. The American bishops had been sending students to study in Rome since 1790, but it was not until 1859 that they acceded to the wish of Pius IX and opened the North American College. This had been recommended to Pius IX by his diplomat Archbishop Gaetano Bedini, who had undertaken an extensive survey of the growing Catholic Church in America. Bedini saw in an American seminary in Rome the means of strengthening the theological education of the clergy and of binding U.S. Catholics more closely to the Holy See.

The formal opening of the college took place on December 8, 1859, in the Via dell'Umiltà in a former Dominican-Visitation convent dating from 1598. Twelve students from eight dioceses were enrolled, the first student being a grandson of Elizabeth Ann Seton, another being the future archbishop of New York, Michael A. Corrigan. The college was dedicated to the Immaculate Conception. National college seminarians wore a distinctive dress; that of the *Nordamericani* gained for them the name "Bacarozzi," a Roman dialect word for a black beetle; from its origin as a kind of insult, it was adopted as a title of honor, and college alumni call themselves "Bags."

Enrollment grew slowly for the first half century. This period saw the end of the Papal States in 1870, thirteen seminarians writing to Pius IX in that year to volunteer for the Papal Zouaves to fight Garibaldi, a gesture appreciated but refused by the Pope. The seizure of the Umiltà property was prevented by the official intervention of President Chester Arthur, spurred on by Cardinal McCloskey and his coadjutor Archbishop Corrigan. Leo XIII in 1884, by the papal brief *Ubi Primum,* granted the college pontifical status, but Propaganda Fide retained legal ownership until 1948, when Pius XII granted it to the college corporation as a tribute to the American hierarchy.

Much of the history of the Church in the U.S.A. in the nineteenth century was associated with the North American College. Before the establishment of the apostolic delegation in Washington in 1893, it served as a kind of Roman agency for American bishops, the position of its rector demanding impartiality as their agent. The brilliant Denis J. O'Connell, fourth rector (1885–95), was too favorable to the so-called "progressives" in the American hierarchy and was forced to resign. He was followed by William H. O'Connell, later cardinal archbishop of Boston, one of the two former rectors who became cardinals, the other being James A. Hickey (1969–74), presently cardinal archbishop of Washington.

The college continued through World War I, but expansion was deemed necessary. In 1926 Propaganda Fide and the American bishops jointly purchased the twenty-six acres of the Villa Gabrielli on the northern slope of the Janiculum hill as the future site of the Urban College and the North American College. The construction of the present seminary, built for three hundred occupants, was undertaken from 1946–53 under the rectorship of Bishop Martin J. O'Connor, Cardinal Francis J. Spellman being chairman of the episcopal board. Pius XII dedicated it on October 14, 1953.

Candidates for the Seminary Department must have a college bachelor degree and be sponsored by an American diocese. Seminary training leading to priesthood and the bachelor/license degrees demands four, five, or six years of residence. From 1858–1933 the American seminarians attended the Urban College. In 1933 they were switched to the Gregorian University. Today they may go to either the Gregorian or the Angelicum for their bachelor of theology degree. A wider choice is permitted for the license. In its 135 years of existence, the seminary has enrolled 4,428 students, most of whom were eventually ordained.

Basic support for the college is provided by the American bishops and gifts from benefactors. Among the latter are the American Knights of Columbus, who have established an endowment to honor their long-time Roman representative, the late Count Enrico Galeazzi, who is buried in the crypt of the college of which he was the architect.

See also SEMINARIES (DIOCESAN).

Brann, Henry A. *History of the American College of the Roman Catholic Church of the U.S.* Rome, Italy/ New York, 1910.

Doherty, Martin W. *The House on Humility Street.* New York, 1942.

McNamara, Robert F. *The American College in Rome, 1855–1955.* Rochester, 1956.

RANDAL RIEDE, C.F.X.

NORTH AMERICAN MARTYRS

In 1609 Samuel Champlain had incurred the lasting hatred of the Iroquois when he led his Algonquin allies down the lake named for him and attacked them near Ticonderoga. Champlain himself fired the first shots, killing two of their chiefs and wounding another. Thirty-two years later when other Frenchmen in black robes, the Jesuit missionaries, crossed the path of the Iroquois, they were to bear the brunt of their fury.

Of the eight Jesuit missionaries canonized by Pope Pius XI on June 29, 1930, three died a martyr's death in what is now New York State: René Goupil (1642), Isaac Jogues, and Jean La Lande (1646); the others were martyred in present-day Ontario: Antoine Daniel (1648), Jean de Brébeuf, Gabriel Lalemant, Charles Garnier, and Noël Chabanel (1649).

Goupil arrived in Canada in 1640, and spent two years as a *donné* assisting the Jesuit Fathers at Quebec. When Fr. Jogues arrived there with some Christian Hurons, he recruited Goupil and another lay volunteer to return with him to his mission. Soon after they began their journey, a party of Mohawk Iroquois captured them and took them to their villages. There they were condemned to slavery and tortured. On September 29, Goupil was killed at Ossernenon, near the present Auriesville, New York, because he had made the sign of the cross over a Mohawk child. He died with the name of Jesus on his lips. On his journey to Ossernenon he had taken vows as a lay brother in the Society of Jesus.

Isaac Jogues had arrived in Canada in 1636 after ordination as a Jesuit priest in France. Shortly after his arrival he undertook the arduous journey to a Huron mission recently established south of Lake Huron. From there in 1641 he traveled three hundred miles to the north to Sault Ste. Marie (so named by him and his Jesuit companion, Fr. Raymbault). There they instructed two thousand in the faith, but in 1642 he had to return to Quebec because of Raymbault's ill health.

With Goupil and Couture, Jogues headed westward again on August 1, 1642. But his party was captured by Mohawks and subjected to enslavement and torture. For a year he used every opportunity to instruct his captors and baptize the dying, before he and Couture were able to escape with the help of the Dutch Commander at Fort Orange (Albany). He arrived in New Amsterdam (New York City) as the first priest to set foot there, and after several months sailed for France, landing at Christmas 1643. At first he was forbidden to say Mass because his hands had been mangled by torture, but Pope Urban VIII gave special permission, saying: "It would be unjust that a martyr for Christ should not drink the blood of Christ."

In 1644 he sailed once more for New France to resume his missionary labors, particularly among the Mohawks. At first he participated in a peace conference between the Iroquois and the Hurons in 1645 at which the Mohawks of Ossernenon were conspicuously absent. Nevertheless he obtained permission to return to that village (now Auriesville, New York) in 1646. As it happened, an epidemic had struck the area along with a poor harvest, and the hostile Mohawks blamed it on a box of religious articles left there by Jogues. When Jogues, his lay volunteer Jean La Lande, and several Huron converts were still far from Ossernenon, they were captured and taken to that village. The council of the tribe determined after long consultation to free the prisoners, but members of the Bear Clan secretly planned to murder him. On the evening of October 18, they treacherously invited Jogues to a meal. He was tomahawked as he entered their cabin. The next day La Lande and a loyal Huron guide met a similar fate.

The killing of Jogues and his companions ended all hopes for peace between the Hurons and the Iroquois. The latter began attacking Huron villages, pillaging them, and sparing no one. At Teanaustaye on July 4, 1648, Fr. Antoine Daniel, after baptizing all those he could, went out to meet the attackers alone. Surrounded on all sides, he was struck by a hail of arrows and fell dead. They threw his body into the church and set it on fire.

Frs. Jean de Brébeuf and Gabriel Lalemant met death at the hands of the Iroquois on March 16, 1649, after particularly atrocious tortures. Brébeuf continued to exhort the Christians around him in the midst of his sufferings. Later in the same year, Fr. Charles Garnier was struck down while hastening to absolve Christians and baptize children and catechumens when his village came under Iroquois attack, and a short time later Fr. Noël Chabanel was killed by a Huron apostate after urging his followers to escape while there was time.

In the following decades Jesuit missionaries continued the efforts of Isaac Jogues and his companions among the Iroquois. One of the major obstacles to these missions was the liquor traffic, a vital part of the fur trade with the natives. Yet, although a majority of the Iroquois never accepted the Catholic faith as a permanent commitment, many of them did, and some like the Mohawk girl Kateri Tekakwitha, born of an Algonquin mother, were examples of extraordinary virtue. A large shrine was constructed in the 1930s at Auriesville to commemorate the heroic martyrdom of Isaac Jogues and his companions. It sits high on a hill and can seat several thousand people. In the wooded valley below, cabins and other historical artifacts present a picture of Iroquois culture at the time of the martyrdoms.

Talbot, Francis X., S.J. *Saint Among Savages: The Life of Isaac Jogues.* New York, 1935.

____. *Saint Among the Hurons: The Life of Jean de Brébeuf.* New York, 1949.

____. "The Torture Trail of St. Isaac Jogues." *Historical Records and Studies* 23 (1933) 7–86.

Thaites, Reuben, ed. *Jesuit Relations and Allied Documents.* 73 vols. Cleveland, 1896–1901.

JAMES HALEY

NORTH CAROLINA, CATHOLIC CHURCH IN

Catholicism came late to North Carolina. The first attempts at colonization date from 1584 and the first permanent settlement was made around 1653, but there were few Catholics until the nineteenth century. William Gaston (1778–1844) of New Bern was the only prominent Catholic during the colonial period. He served in the state legislature where in 1835 he authored the declaration on religious liberty in the new state constitution. Gaston also served two terms in the U.S. Congress and was a justice of the North Carolina Supreme Court.

Early Ecclesiastical History

In 1820 North Carolina became part of the newly established Diocese of Charleston, South Carolina. Bishop John England reported to the Society for the Propagation of the Faith in 1829 that there were only two churches in the whole state of North Carolina—at Washington and Fayetteville—and that the total Catholic population was about 150. In 1868 North Carolina was separated from the Diocese of Charleston and erected into a separate vicariate apostolic under the thirty-four-year-old James Gibbons. He had about seven hundred Catholics in the state with three priests to serve them. Gibbons became administrator of the Diocese of Richmond in 1872, and bishop of Richmond the following year, but he continued as administrator of the vicariate apostolic of North Carolina until going to Baltimore in 1877.

When John J. Keane succeeded Gibbons as bishop of Richmond in 1878, he also served as vicar apostolic of North Carolina. In the fall of 1879 Mark S. Gross was appointed vicar apostolic, but declined the position after keeping the letter of appointment in his possession for several months. In 1880 Keane offered to resign Richmond in favor of North Carolina, but his offer was refused in Rome. Then, in January 1882, Henry P. Northrup, a native of Charleston, South Carolina, was consecrated vicar

apostolic of North Carolina. A year later, however, he became bishop of Charleston while continuing as administrator of North Carolina until 1887. Thus, for only five of the first nineteen years of its existence did the vicariate apostolic of North Carolina have a resident bishop.

The solution was finally found by entrusting the vicariate to the care of the Benedictines, who had first come to North Carolina from St. Vincent's Abbey in Latrobe, Pennsylvania, in 1876 at the invitation of James Gibbons. In that year they had established Maryhelp Priory, and in 1884 the priory was raised to the status of an abbey, commonly known as Belmont Abbey from the name of the town where it is located, with Leo M. Haid as the first abbot. In 1887 Haid was appointed vicar apostolic of North Carolina and was consecrated a titular bishop the following year.

In 1910 the Holy See detached eight counties from the vicariate apostolic and erected them into the *abbatia nullius* of Belmont, the first and only instance of an *abbatia nullius* in American Catholic history. From 1910 until his death in 1924, Haid was both vicar apostolic of North Carolina and abbot-ordinary of Belmont Abbey. Moreover, the bull erecting the *abbatia nullius* of Belmont gave the monastic chapter of the abbey the right to nominate all future vicars apostolic of North Carolina. The diocesan clergy were so outraged by the terms of Haid's appointment that, under the leadership of Thomas Frederick Price (the future cofounder of Maryknoll), they unanimously petitioned the Holy See for the immediate erection of a diocese in the state. Cardinal Gibbons, conveniently forgetting that he had recommended the establishment of the *abbatia nullius,* asked Rome for the establishment of a diocese, but the request was denied.

At Haid's death in 1924, the two jurisdictions were separated. The vicariate apostolic of North Carolina (the last vicariate apostolic east of the Mississippi) was replaced by the Diocese of Raleigh while the abbot of Belmont retained jurisdiction over the eight counties of his *abbatia nullius,* which was subsequently reduced to a single county in 1944, to the 827 acres of the monastery grounds in 1960, and finally suppressed in 1977.

Diocese of Raleigh

At the time of its establishment in 1924, the Diocese of Raleigh comprised the whole state of North Carolina with the exception of the eight counties subject to Belmont Abbey, an area of 48,450 square miles with only 8,000 Catholics. Many of the parishes, especially in the eastern part of the state, were organized by Lebanese Catholics who emigrated into the state around the turn of the century. The early churches were often the living rooms of the laypeople. It was into this climate that Bishop William J. Hafey, the former chancellor of the Archdiocese of Baltimore, came in June 1925 as the first bishop of Raleigh. He and his successor, Eugene J. McGuinness of Philadelphia (1937–44), made slow progress as they planted the faith in this mission land. Under their guidance an effort was made to reach the African Americans of the state by establishing "black" parishes for them in all of the larger cities and inviting religious orders to staff them. The Passionists, Redemptorists, and Franciscans were among the first to respond to this challenge.

Bishop Gibbons had been instrumental in bringing the Sisters of Mercy of Charleston to North Carolina where they established houses in Wilmington, Hickory, and Belmont. Under Bishops Hafey and McGuinness other communities of women religious came to the state, including the Dominican Sisters of Newburgh, New York, and the Sisters, Servants of the Immaculate Heart of Mary of Scranton, Pennsylvania. Catholic hospitals were established by the Sisters of Mercy, the Daughters of Charity of Emmitsburg, Maryland, and the Sisters of St. Joseph of Newark, New Jersey.

Bishop Vincent Waters

Vincent S. Waters, third bishop of Raleigh (1945–74), a native of Roanoke, Virginia, who had received his early education at Belmont Abbey, brought a new missionary zeal to the diocese, which still contained only 13,000 Catholics, less than one percent of the total population. Waters tried to establish a parish in every county seat as well as to increase the number of Catholic elementary and high schools. Like his predecessors, Waters also toured the country seeking funds for the missions and seminarians of this "China of America." He also organized a summer school of Christian humanism which attracted scholars from around the country.

Waters also established the North Carolina Laymen's Association to promote unity among the scattered Catholic population of the large diocese. This organization brought together black and white Catholics for the first time. Dr. Norman Cordice, a Durham dentist, was the first African American elected to the board of directors of the association and later served two terms as the first African American president of the association. With the help of this organization, Bishop Waters established a diocesan newspaper, the *North Carolina Catholic,* and fostered the work of Christian education through the Confraternity of Christian Doctrine.

Perhaps Waters' finest hour occurred in 1953 when he, a Southerner by birth and upbringing, ordered the desegregation of all Catholic churches, schools, and institutions in the diocese. Some irate whites threatened to stone him when he inaugurated this policy in the small town of Newton Grove, but Waters did not cave in to pressure or threats. Integration proved to be a long, slow, and painful process,

but it was initiated thanks to the courageous leadership of Bishop Waters.

The Catholic population of North Carolina continued to grow with the result that Waters requested the Holy See to establish a second diocese for the state in Charlotte. The new see was erected in January 1972, comprising 20,000 square miles in the western half of the state. Bishop Waters died less than three years later, on December 3, 1974, after thirty years of guiding the growth and development of the Church in North Carolina.

The Contemporary Scene

Bishop Francis Joseph Gossman, auxiliary bishop of Baltimore, was appointed the fourth bishop of Raleigh and installed in the Raleigh Memorial Auditorium on May 19, 1975, at a ceremony attended by a large delegation of federal, state, county, and city officials, led by the chief justice of the North Carolina Supreme Court. During Bishop Gossman's twenty years in Raleigh the Catholic population grew from 38,000 to 105,000. In 1995 the diocese contained 70 parishes, 67 diocesan priests, 48 religious order priests, 13 permanent deacons, 9 brothers, and 82 sisters in a total population of 3,400,000.

Michael J. Begley served as the first bishop of Charlotte from 1972 until his retirement in 1984 when he was succeeded by John F. Donoghue who was bishop of Charlotte from 1984 to 1993 when he was appointed archbishop of Atlanta. William F. Curlin, auxiliary bishop of Washington, became the third bishop of Charlotte in February 1994. In 1995 the diocese contained 66 parishes, 70 diocesan priests, 68 religious order priests, 45 permanent deacons, 5 brothers, and 155 sisters. There were 97,000 Catholics in a total population of 3,500,000.

Baumstein, Paschal, O.S.B. *My Lord of Belmont: A Biography of Leo Haid.* Belmont, N.C., 1985.
____. "A Conflict of Mitres: The Diverse Polities and Cathedral Abbey of Bishop Leo Haid." *Word and Spirit* 14 (1992) 76–95.
O'Connell, Jeremiah J. *Catholicity in the Carolinas and Georgia, 1820–1878.* New York, 1878; repr. Spartanburg, S.C., 1972.

GERALD LEWIS

NORTH DAKOTA, CATHOLIC CHURCH IN

Official Catholic life began in North Dakota with the building of a little church at Pembina (1821). The far northeastern corner of the state was settled by French-Canadians, among whom the most famous clergyman was Fr. George Belcourt. From his parish at Walhalla (St. Joseph) he reached out far and wide to the Métis (mixed Native American and white) people, whom he encouraged to settle down to farming. He also founded an order of Métis nuns, but his handling of their affairs resulted in his expulsion from the territory in 1861.

The influx of the Dakota native peoples into the region after the Blue Earth massacre in Minnesota coincided with Catholic ministry to the Native American people. The Grey Nuns of Montreal arrived at Fort Totten in 1874, where they taught for the next century. At Fort Yates on the Missouri River, Abbot Martin Marty came in 1876 to evangelize the indigenous peoples. He later became the bishop of the vicariate of Dakota (1879–89), with headquarters in Yankton.

Catholic population only came to North Dakota in any quantity with the building of the Northern Pacific and Great Northern Railways (1873–88). From that point on, the Church was hard pressed to supply enough clergy to keep up with the movement of population toward the west. Many of the men who built the railroads were new immigrants from Ireland who were glad for the ministrations of their native Catholic religion.

Diocese of Fargo

In 1889 the Dakota Territory was divided into the states of North and South Dakota. At the same time, the Holy See created the Diocese of Fargo, to be presided over by thirty-seven-year-old John Shanley, a priest of St. Paul. He found things in a primitive state, with but a handful of clergy and frame shacks for churches. Nevertheless, good crops after 1898 led to a booming economy, which in turn triggered explosive immigration. The population of the state grew from 320,000 to 577,000 in the first decade of the twentieth century. The Catholic population grew to 65,000. And so Bishop Shanley was kept busy consecrating churches in his diocese until his death in 1909.

Part of the great growth of Catholicism in North Dakota was due to the immigration of the Germans from South Russia (1890–1910), who came to form the nucleus of the Church in the central and southwestern sections of the state. When the Diocese of Bismarck was created in 1910, it was natural to place over it Fr. Vincent Wehrle, the Benedictine abbot of Richardton. He had founded his monastery there to minister to the Germans, and was indefatigable in doing so until his death in 1941.

In the 1920s and 1930s, social conditions began to decline in North Dakota because the population never reached the projected levels, and serious drought conditions in the 1930s brought the state to virtual paralysis. In addition, control by outside banks and grain cartels made the state an economic colony. In these years, local politicians attempted to counteract these problems by innovative measures such as a state bank, a state mill, and a law prohibiting corporate farming. There is little evidence, however, that the official Church played any part in these efforts.

When Aloysius Muench came to Fargo as bishop in 1935, he found most of the parishes and the clergy impoverished. On the basis of his graduate education in economics, he created the Catholic Church Expansion Fund, which was eventually to be copied by virtually every diocese in the country. He also created a Priests Mutual Aid Fund. In 1946 he became Pius XII's personal envoy to West Germany; his efforts for that devastated nation earned him the cardinalate in 1959, but he never returned to Fargo.

Following Muench's lead, priests like Vincent Ryan of Fargo saw that, unless the family farm could be placed on a sounder economic footing, the entire society of this rural state would remain in jeopardy. As bishop of Bismarck (1940–51), Ryan continued to work at these issues. He was joined by Fr. Joseph Hylden of Grafton, among others, but, except for the 1940s, small-scale farming on the Plains has not prospered.

One of the glories of Catholic life in North Dakota has always been its large body of women religious, many of them members of indigenous convents. Their presence (especially the Benedictines in the west and the Presentations in the east) has made it possible to have many Catholic schools, even in small rural towns. In addition, these sisters often taught in public schools when lay teachers were in short supply. Consequently, a law prohibiting the wearing of religious garb in public schools (1948) was a strange and troubling episode.

There was an irony to the Anti-Garb Law, since many of the same sisters voluntarily put aside their habits after Vatican Council II. Now, however, their dwindling numbers made the future of even the Catholic schools questionable. For example, the school census of the Fargo Diocese dropped from 9,166 to 3,500 during the years 1964 to 1980. Yet by 1990 lay teachers had taken over for the sisters and most of the schools continued.

Vatican II and After

Another major challenge that the Church faced after Vatican II was permissive legislation concerning abortion. Although North Dakota voters turned it down by two to one in 1972, the U.S. Supreme Court disagreed. In order to fight this pernicious evil, the two North Dakota dioceses joined forces in the North Dakota Catholic Conference. Although the law has not yet been changed, this structure has made it possible for the Church to exercise concerted moral and political influence in North Dakota.

In the wake of the openness of Vatican II to the other Christian churches, ecumenism has flourished in North Dakota. Both of the dioceses were founding members of the North Dakota Conference of Churches in the early 1970s. The conference struggles economically, but its very existence is a powerful symbol of local attitudes. Since the Lutherans are so numerous in the state (35 percent of the total population, the Catholics having 25 percent), it helps very much that they are friendly to the Church.

Finally, the clergy shortage has hit North Dakota in recent years. Unlike many western states, North Dakota had a sufficiency of native vocations after 1930, but that has all changed. The building of Cardinal Muench Seminary in Fargo (high school and college) in the 1960s was an attempt to face a massive problem that seems to affect the continued existence of the Catholic Church as we know it.

Ahern, Patrick, ed. *Catholic Heritage in Minnesota, North Dakota, South Dakota.* St. Paul, 1964.

Kardong, Terrence. *Beyond Red River.* Diocese of Fargo, 1989.

____. *Prairie Church.* Diocese of Bismarck, 1985.

TERRENCE G. KARDONG, O.S.B.

NOTRE DAME OF MARYLAND, COLLEGE OF

The College of Notre Dame of Maryland was the first Catholic college for women in the United States chartered to grant a four-year baccalaureate degree. Founded by the School Sisters of Notre Dame, the college accepted its first students in September 1895 and held its first graduation in June 1899. In his address to the students at the first graduation in that year, Charles Bonaparte, grandnephew of Napoleon Bonaparte, commented, "Here for the first time in America a Catholic college for the education of young ladies bestows the bachelor's degree."

From 1873 until 1895 Notre Dame of Maryland Collegiate Institute offered postsecondary studies and a "degree" of Mistress of English Literature and of Liberal Arts. In 1895 Sr. Mary Meletia Foley, S.S.N.D., directress and later dean of the college, had the foresight to realize that, with the opening of The Catholic University of America for lay graduate students in 1889, there was a need for a Catholic college for women, if they were also to pursue graduate study. She applied to the General Assembly of Maryland for an amendment to the 1864 charter to authorize a four-year undergraduate college granting the bachelor of arts degree. Governor Lloyd Loundes of Maryland signed the act of the legislature on April 2, 1896, and the College of Notre Dame of Maryland began its century of educating young women in a strong liberal arts tradition.

The first class to complete a degree consisted of six graduates from five different states. In 1996 the College of Notre Dame of Maryland had more than 3,000 students representing different races, religions, and nationalities. There are fifteen departments and twenty-two majors.

See also CATHOLIC UNIVERSITIES AND COLLEGES.

Cameron, Mary David, S.S.N.D. *The College of Notre Dame of Maryland 1895–1945.* The Declan X. McMullen Company, Inc., 1947.

Engelmeyer, Bridget Marie, S.S.N.D. "A Maryland First." *Maryland Historical Magazine* 78 (3) (Fall 1983) 186–204.

Philbin, Anne Marie Scarborough. *Past and Promised.* Baltimore: College of Notre Dame of Maryland, 1959.

Report of the Commissioner of Education for the Year 1899–1900. Vol. 2. Washington, D.C.: Government Printing Office, 1901.

VIRGINA GEIGER, S.S.N.D.

NOTRE DAME, UNIVERSITY OF

The University of Notre Dame du Lac was founded near South Bend, Indiana, in 1842 by a band of eight members of the Congregation of Holy Cross. Four of the founders were French immigrants and four were Irish-born. In 1843, four members of the women's branch of the congregation came to the new foundation from France. The leader of the community and president of the university for its first twenty-three years was Rev. Edward F. Sorin.

Early Years

Although chartered by the state of Indiana as a university in 1844, the institution was primarily a middle, secondary, and trade school with a few college students for much of the nineteenth century. With the opening of St. Mary's College for Women on an adjacent property in 1854, the whole complex functioned as an apostolic center for the Catholic Church in northern Indiana and southwestern Michigan through the 1850s. Orphans and boarders were received and educated, the Holy Cross priests rode a circuit to provide pastoral care for scattered Catholic families, and young men and women were trained as Holy Cross Brothers and Sisters and sent out to conduct schools.

In the decades after the Civil War, the university began to expand. Courses in the study of law were begun in 1869 and the training of engineers, the first such program at any Catholic school in the United States, commenced in 1873. Although originally modeled on the French *lycée*, Notre Dame's curriculum came increasingly to resemble the American college, reflecting Sorin's admiration for the educational system of his adopted country.

Modernization and Professionalization

Rev. John A. Zahm was appointed director of studies in the Holy Cross Congregation in 1895 and immediately began a reform in the education of young priests in the community which ultimately effected the university. Seminarians were sent to The Catholic University of America for their theological studies and, while so engaged, were also expected to earn an advanced degree in some other branch of learning, which they would be expected to teach. When Zahm began his reform, no member of the congregation had an earned doctorate. By 1920, there were twenty men with earned doctorates from The Catholic University. At the same time the University of Notre Dame, during the presidencies of Revs. Andrew Morrissey and John W. Cavanaugh (1893–1919) slowly increased the number of college preparatory students while reducing the number in the commercial course.

The presidency of Rev. James A. Burns (1919–22) produced a major reform at Notre Dame. Burns closed the preparatory school, reorganized the university into four distinct colleges, and began systematic fundraising and the expansion of a qualified lay faculty. Summer course offerings at the graduate level leading to an M.A. degree, begun in 1918, became a regular fixture. During the 1920s the program in chemistry under Rev. Julius Nieuwland (d. 1936), renowned for his discovery of synthetic rubber, won respect in academic circles while a series of highly successful football teams under Coach Knute Rockne (1918–31) generated immense publicity for the school. The arrival of several émigré European scholars in the 1930s enhanced the faculty.

World War II and After

Like many American colleges, Notre Dame survived World War II by becoming the site for a training program for naval officers. In 1944 the program in graduate studies was reorganized into a graduate school and government funding for research, especially in the sciences, resulted in steady growth in this sector of the university. The postwar presidency of Rev. John J. Cavanaugh (1946–52) saw an undergraduate enrollment of over 5,000, the inauguration of an Institute of Medieval Studies and a center for liturgical studies, the development of the Lobund Institute for scientific research with germ-free animals, and the creation of the Notre Dame Foundation, a mechanism for fundraising which over the next forty years would increase the university's endowment to over $450,000,000.

The long presidency of Rev. Theodore M. Hesburgh (1952–87) saw Notre Dame become one of the leading Catholic universities in the world and possibly the best known. Enrollment increased to around ten thousand, more than thirty-five new buildings were erected, the annual operating budget increased from $9,000,000 to $200,000,000, and the academic credentials of both incoming students and faculty improved appreciably. A new university library, completed in 1964, was at the time the largest academic library building in the world. The university became host to several research institutes and doctoral programs in theology and liturgical studies. Women undergraduates were admitted for the first time in 1972. In 1967 Hesburgh arranged a change in the governance of the university whereby ownership passed from the Congregation of Holy Cross to a Board of Fellows, half of whose members were members of the congregation. Notre Dame thus became the first Catholic university in the country to effect the change to lay control.

In 1987, Rev. Edward A. Malloy, like all his predecessors a priest of the Congregation of Holy Cross, became president of the university. The upgrading of both students and faculty, the construction of new facilities, and the development of new programs have continued apace. With more than 80 percent of its students being Catholics as of 1995, Notre Dame continued to be, as it had for much of its history, a center of education for Catholics where other faith traditions were also represented. It continued to fulfill the vision of its first president, Edward Sorin, that amidst the forests of northern Indiana, Providence had designed to bring into being a great university.

See also CATHOLIC EDUCATION, HIGHER; HOLY CROSS, CONGREGATION OF; LAETARE MEDAL, THE.

Hope, Arthur J. *Notre Dame, One Hundred Years.* University of Notre Dame Press, 1943.

Sorin, Edward F. *Chronicles of Notre Dame du Lac.* University of Notre Dame Press, 1992.

Weber, Ralph E. *Notre Dame's John Zahm.* University of Notre Dame Press, 1961.

JAMES T. CONNELLY, C.S.C.

Related Document

A BROADSIDE ON THE INFANT UNIVERSITY OF NOTRE DAME, JANUARY 1, 1847

Among American Catholic institutions of higher learning none has found a more secure place in the hearts of all Americans, and none has had a brighter record of achievement in education for Christian manhood, than the University of Notre Dame. Like most universities, its origins were humble and obscure. A generous gift of land from Father Stephen Badin to the Bishop of Vincennes, the latter's determination to have a college for boys, but above all the zeal and resourcefulness of Edward Sorin (1814–1893), American founder of the Congregation of Holy Cross, were the principal factors that brought it into being. Sorin came to Notre Dame in November, 1842, and the following year he and his little community of Holy Cross priests and brothers began classes with two students on a site hallowed by the missionary labors of priests like Badin and Louis Deseille. In January, 1844, the school received a university charter from the legislature of Indiana. Less than a week after his arrival at Notre Dame the founder had outlined the prospect he entertained for its future to Basile-Antoine Moreau, Superior-General of Holy Cross, and in his letter of December 5, 1842, he predicted, "This college will be one of the most powerful means of doing good in this country. . . ." (*Circular Letters of the Very Reverend Edward Sorin* [Notre Dame, 1885], I, 261). The ensuing century fully justified the prediction for the university that today enrolls some 5,500 students taught by a faculty of nearly 600 teachers. The following broadside—a way of attracting students used by all schools of the period—was printed when the college was three years old; it gives a picture of the conditions and rules of student life in the days of its infancy.

(*Source*: Archives of the University of Notre Dame.)

UNIVERSITY OF NOTRE-DAME-DU-LAC,
St. Joseph County, Indiana.

UNDER THE DIRECTION OF THE PRIESTS OF THE HOLY CROSS.

THIS INSTITUTION COMMENCED UNDER THE AUSPICES OF THE Rt. Rev'd Bishop of Vincennes who presented to the priests of the Holy Cross, the beautiful and elegant site upon which the buildings are erected, is now in full operation.

Notre-Dame-du-Lac is at a distance of 1 mile from South Bend, the County seat; 80 miles from Chicago, Illinois; 180 from Detroit, Mich. with which there is direct communication by railroad, and 80 from Fort Wayne, Ia.

The edifice is of brick, four and half story [*sic*] high and not inferior in point of style or structure to any of the colleges of the United States, and is situated upon a commanding eminence on the verge of two picturesque and commodious Lakes, which, with the river St. Joseph and the surrounding country, present a most magnificent prospect. The rooms are spacious, well ventilated and furnished, with every thing conducive to regularity and comfort.

The Infirmary is intrusted to Sisters similar in their Institute to the Sisters of Charity; their well known kindness and skill are a sufficient guarantee, that the invalids will be attended to with all the diligence and care, which devotion and affection can suggest.

The disciplinary government is mild, yet sufficiently energetic, to preserve that good order, so essential to the well-being of the Institution. The morals and general deportment of the pupils are watched over with the greatest assiduity and solicitude; their personal comfort receives the most paternal attention, and no pains are spared to prepare them for fulfilling their respective duties in society. In their daily recreations, they are always accompanied by a member of the Institution; all books in their possession are subject to the inspection of the Prefect of Studies; and none are allowed circulation without his approval. Corporal punishments will never be inflicted, but more conciliatory and effective means of correction are judiciously used; should a pupil prove refractory, and incorrigible, he will be dismissed.

The faculty is formed of the priests of the Holy Cross: a member is annually sent to Europe to complete whatever contingent circumstances may require. In the reception of pupils no distinction of creed is made, and the parents of those, not professing the Catholic faith, may rest assured that there will be no interference with their religious tenets; they are required only to attend to the religious exercises with decorum, this being in conformity with the rules of all the catholic colleges in the United States.

TERMS,

Board, washing and medical attendance, with the English Course, embracing all the branches of a practical education; Orthography, Reading, Writing, Arithmetic, Grammar and Composition, to which particular attention is paid; Geography, Ancient and Modern History; the most approved methods of Book-keeping, Surveying, Mensuration, Mathematics, Astronomy, the use of the Globes, Rhetoric, Vocal Music, &c. Free admittance to the Museum, lessons of natation and

Equestrian exercises &c.	$100 per ann.
Half Boarders,	40 " "
Day scholars in the above course.	20 " "
The same in the preparatory School,	16 " "
The classical course of Latin, and Greek an additional sum of	20 " "
The French, German languages are taught at an extra charge of	12 " "
Instrumental Music and Drawing.	20 " "
Piano.	40 " "

Class books, Stationary [*sic*], and Medicines furnished at the usual rates.

The payments must be made semi annually in advance; from this rule there can be no deviation whatever, as the charges are based upon the lowest estimate, the object of the Institution being to increase the facilities of instruction, without any view to pecuniary reward.

The distribution of Premiums takes place on the 1st Tuesday of August, and the commencement of the scholastic year is irrevocably fixed on the 1st Friday of October.

The Institution being in possession of all the powers and privileges of a University: degrees will be conferred after the public examination.

No boarder will be received for a shorter term than half a year, and no deduction made for absence, except in case of sickness or dismission.

Examinations take place at the end of each Quarter, and reports are forwarded semi-annually to parents, informing them of the progress, health, &c., of their children. Public examinations, before the distribution of premiums, will take place in the last week of July in every year.

DIRECTIONS FOR PARENTS.

Each pupil must be provided with bed and bedding, (if furnished by the Institution, they form an extra charge,) six shirts, six pair of stockings, six pocket handkerchiefs, six towels (all of which must be marked,) a knife and fork, a table and tea spoon, a hat and cap, two suits of clothes, an over-coat, a pair of shoes and a pair of boots for winter; three suits of clothing and two pair of shoes for summer. No advances will be made by the Institution for clothing or other expenses.

The pupils will not be allowed to have money in their possession; their pocket money must be deposited in the Treasurer's hands, in order to guard against abuses, and to enable the Institution to apply the money as an incentive to virtue and industry. When parents wish to have their children sent home, they must give timely notice, settle all accounts, and supply means to defray their traveling expenses.

Visitors cannot be permitted to interrupt the pupils during the hours of study. The mid-day recreation commences at half past 12 and ends at half past one o'clock. This is the most appropriate time for the visits of parents and friends.

☞ All letters to pupils or members of the Institution must be post paid.

Rev. E. SORIN, President
Notre Dame du Lac, St. Joseph   )
County, Indiana, January 1st, 1847.)
References to the Rt. Rev. Bishop of Vincennes and to the Rt. Rev. Bishop of Detroit Rev. Mr. Benoit, Fort-Wayne, Ia. [*sic*].

(*Source*: John Tracy Ellis, ed. *Documents of American Catholic History*. Vol. 1:1493–1865. Wilmington, Del.: Michael Glazier, 1987, 291–94.)

O

OBLATES OF MARY IMMACULATE (O.M.I.)

A religious congregation of priests and brothers founded at Aix-en-Provence, France, in 1816 by St. Charles Joseph Eugene de Mazenod (d. 1861). Success in parochial mission work led to a rapid expansion of the institute. A rule, written by the founder, received episcopal approbation in November 1818 and Roman approval on February 17, 1826.

Although the first objective of the Oblates was the preaching of missions to the poor of the rural areas, other apostolic works soon followed. In 1824 the congregation accepted the task of improving the clergy by the establishment of seminaries, and two years later the Oblates assumed charge of the major seminary at Marseilles. Seminary work was extended to Canada, the United States, Asia, and Africa.

In 1831 a general chapter of the society sensed the need for working in foreign missions. The first mission foundations were made in Canada in 1841 and then in the U.S.A., Sri Lanka, and Africa. Teaching was added to the original works because of the need in mission countries. In 1848, the University of Ottawa, Canada, was founded. Parochial work was later also accepted as a part of the congregation's apostolic service. When the Oblates arrived in Montreal in 1841, they lost no time in taking over the care of the Native American missions, a work that led them to the remotest regions of James Bay and Labrador. The conquest of western Canada for the Church was accomplished largely by Oblates who preached the gospel as far as Alaska, the shores of the Arctic Sea, and Hudson Bay. By 1860 the Oblates had covered the entire expanse of Canada and many Oblates served as bishops, especially in the West.

From Canada, the Oblates spread to the United States, where they preached their first mission in New York in 1842. While still based in Canada, they established foundations in Oregon, Buffalo, New York, and as far south as Texas. By 1858 this southern expansion had reached across the Rio Grande into Mexico.

The first American province was founded in 1883 under the leadership of Fr. James McGrath. Today, the Oblate Region of the U.S.A. is divided into five provinces (with present headquarters): the eastern in Washington, D.C.; the southern in San Antonio, Texas; the northern in Hudson, New Hampshire; the central in St. Paul, Minnesota; and the western in Oakland, California.

From their start in the U.S.A., and like the early Oblates in France, the preaching apostolate made the Oblates known all over the country. Parishes were also accepted, often for immigrants. This included four hundred mission stations in Texas and ministry to Native Americans in the Midwest.

In the United States at present there are almost six hundred Oblates serving in thirty-eight states. Their first apostolate of preaching the gospel to the poor still endures. Oblates who serve as bishops are: Bishop Michael Pfeifer in San Angelo, Texas; Bishop Roger Schwietz in Duluth, Minnesota; and Archbishop Francis George in Chicago, Illinois. Oblates staff some 150 parishes that extend from the large urban centers along the East and West Coasts to isolated villages of Alaska and the Midwest. Others serve full-time as prison and hospital chaplains and continue in the educational ministry.

In keeping with their name and the tradition of the society, Oblates staff and assist in Marian shrines, including ministry at Our Lady of Grace in Colebrook, New Hampshire, Our Lady of the Snows in Belleville, Illinois, and Our Lady of San Juan in San Juan, Texas. The Oblates also provided pastoral service at the Basilica of the National Shrine of the Immaculate Conception in Washington, D.C., and staff St. Jude's International Shrine in New Orleans.

American Oblates have been sent as missionaries to Mexico, Haiti, South Africa, Lesotho, Japan, the Philippines, Laos, Chile, Bolivia, Northern Canada, Sweden, Brazil, Puerto Rico, Tahiti, and Zambia. Oblate missionaries have been named as bishops in the Philippines, Haiti, and Sweden.

Doyon, Bernard, O.M.I. *The Calvary of Christ on the Rio Grande, 1849–1883*. Milwaukee, 1956.

Wild, Joseph C., O.M.I. *Men of Hope: The Background and History of the Oblate Province of Our Lady of Hope (Eastern American Province)*. Boston, 1967.

RAYMOND A. PRYBIS, O.M.I.

O'BOYLE, PATRICK ALOYSIUS (1896–1987)

Cardinal archbishop of Washington, D.C. Patrick Aloysius O'Boyle, the first resident archbishop of Washington, is often characterized as an uneasy combination of progressive reformer and conservative disciplinarian. His lengthy episcopal career certainly reveals a personality

Patrick A. O'Boyle

that embraced the outlook of a serious social crusader, especially in the area of race relations and social justice, with a unswerving adherence to a traditional discipline in a Church undergoing startling change. But the suggestion of contradiction would no doubt have puzzled the man himself, who thought in terms of loyalty rather than reform or discipline. Indeed, in a sense, uncompromising loyalty was the central force in his career: his own total and exacting loyalty to the Holy See and the social class from which he had sprung, and, no less exacting, the loyalty he expected from clerical and lay subordinates.

Social Activist

The future cardinal, the only child of working-class Irish immigrants, was born on July 18, 1896, in Scranton, Pennsylvania, where his father toiled in the steel mills. Scranton at that time was near the epicenter of the intense economic turmoil rocking the nation, and the O'Boyles were firsthand witnesses to the struggle against brutal conditions and unjust wages in the coal and steel industries. When his father died in 1906, Patrick's mother became a housekeeper for two priest-professors at a local college while he supplemented their income with part-time jobs, including that of clerking in a stock brokerage house and running a streetcar. At the insistence of his mother's employers he returned to school, eventually graduating at the top of his class from St. Thomas College (now the University of Scranton) in 1916. Sure of a vocation to the priesthood, he successfully applied to the Archdiocese of New York, where he was ordained in 1921.

For five years Fr. O'Boyle served as a curate at St. Columba's parish in Manhattan's notorious "Hell's Kitchen." There the poverty, disease, and crime that haunted the lives of the urban underclass instilled in the immigrant's son an abiding concern for the problems facing America's ethnic minorities. In 1926 he returned to school, for five years following the graduate program at the New York School of Social Work (now part of Columbia University), and between 1932 and 1936 teaching social work at Fordham University.

During this period the archdiocese made good use of his organizational and financial skills. In 1933 he became assistant director of the children's division of New York's Catholic Charities. In 1936 he assumed the added responsibility of operating two orphanages, Mount Loretto on Staten Island and St. Benedict's Home in Rye, that cared for more than a thousand children. In 1941, now a monsignor, O'Boyle became director of Catholic War Relief Services and in 1943 its successor agency, the War Relief Services of the National Catholic Welfare Conference. Under his management this agency became the focal point of Catholic charity for war victims, dealing in vast sums of money and distributing more than 60,000 tons of food, clothing, and other supplies in forty-eight nations. In May 1947 Cardinal Francis Spellman named O'Boyle executive director of New York's Catholic Charities, but shortly after assuming that post, Pope Pius XII appointed him to head the Archdiocese of Washington. Consecrated bishop by Spellman on January 14, 1948, O'Boyle was installed in Washington's St. Matthew's Cathedral on January 21, 1948.

Accomplished Administrator

By 1948 Washington had finally shed the image, if not the social customs, of a sleepy southern city. During the next twenty-five years the capital and its sprawling suburbs would continue to grow in wealth and numbers. The new archdiocese, which included five counties in Maryland, would experience an even greater transformation, its population rising from 165,000 to almost 400,000. It was a diverse group. In addition to government employees and those attracted to local industries spawned by government were thousands of Catholics in rural southern Maryland, many of whom could trace their religious heritage to the Anglo-Catholic founders of the Church in America. Almost 25 percent of the diocese was African American, one of the highest concentrations of black Catholics in the country.

The orderly management of such a diverse and burgeoning Catholic community underscored O'Boyle's administrative gifts. During his twenty-three years as archbishop he established forty-six new parishes and constructed more than three hundred church buildings. Much of this was achieved at bargain prices because of his financial acumen. He used to jokingly call the real estate section of Washington's papers his "other Bible." O'Boyle was also a primary influence on the long-awaited completion of Washington's most imposing Catholic edifice, the National Shrine of the Immaculate Conception. ("Let's finish the building or fill in the hole," he dared his fellow bishops.) When parochial schools experienced severe difficulty in the 1960s, O'Boyle subsidized many from central archdiocesan funds, particularly those in the inner city unable to support themselves.

With his affable Irish temperament, the archbishop enjoyed good conversation and a good cigar. He genuinely enjoyed mixing with people, although the reality of an increasingly educated laity was somewhat at variance with his persistent notion of a largely unsophisticated flock easily scandalized and confused by theological debate and sudden change. At the same time his strong social instincts did not extend to a ready association with political figures. Throughout his career he remained especially sensitive to the need for maintaining, in appearance as well as in substance, the separation of Church and state. He only reluctantly accepted appointment as chairman of a presidential commission because it gave him special advantages in the fight to protect housing for the inner-city poor.

Civil Rights Champion

O'Boyle's profound sense of loyalty was especially manifest in the two defining events of his career as archbishop. The first concerned his championship of racial justice and civil rights. Within weeks of his installation, he informed his consultors that segregation in the churches and charitable institutions of the diocese was going to end, beginning immediately. He recognized that the more difficult task of integrating the schools, especially those in southern Maryland, would take special patience because of widespread opposition, but he was adamant that it would be done. A carefully orchestrated plan, beginning with schools in the District of Columbia in 1949, brought about complete integration in less than a decade.

From the schools O'Boyle proceeded to broader issues concerning racial justice. In terms that reflected his experiences in Scranton and Hell's Kitchen, he reminded his diocese: "Unless the full resources of the Church are placed at the disposal of every single member of the church and made available to every man, there is no Catholicism worthy of the name." He spoke out frequently as the nation's civil rights revolution gathered force in the 1960s. He chaired Washington's influential Interracial Committee on Race Relations that lobbied city officials for open housing and equal opportunity in employment and training. He joined in the historic 1963 March on Washington and supported the participation of priests in demonstrations for racial justice around the country. On an applied level, he organized the Urban Rehabilitation Corporation in 1967 which funneled diocesan support to urban renewal projects. He was entirely sincere when he interpreted his elevation to the College of Cardinals in June 1967 as an expression of papal gratitude for the ecumenical battle waged by Washingtonians of all faiths against racial and social injustice.

Humanae Vitae *Controversy*

Cardinal O'Boyle's uncompromising defense of the Church's magisterium also touched on his sense of loyalty. In 1968 a group known as the Association of Washington Priests (more than fifty clergymen, not all from the Archdiocese of Washington) issued a "Statement of Conscience" dissenting from Pope Paul VI's encyclical, *Humanae vitae,* which upheld the Church's traditional condemnation of all forms of artificial contraception. Strongly influencing these priests was the widely publicized opinion of a group of Catholic University theologians who said that the encyclical was not infallible and that couples might in good conscience decide that birth control was sometimes permissible and even necessary. Cardinal O'Boyle strongly defended the encyclical as binding in conscience, adding that no one was free to preach or counsel to the contrary.

Positions quickly hardened. The dissenters' appeals to the hierarchy for arbitration were rejected, and, although the Cardinal met individually with the dissenters to discuss their position, he stood firm. In October 1968 he deprived thirty-nine priests of various faculties: some were forbidden to preach or teach, others were barred from all priestly duties, including public celebration of Mass.

In succeeding months many dissenters simply drifted away, but nineteen priests, counseled by experts from the Canon Law Society of America, decided to appeal the Cardinal's action on the grounds that he had not observed the norms of canonical procedure. Their appeal was finally considered by the Vatican's Congregation for the Clergy, at whose hearings proxies for the dissenters and the archbishop presented their respective positions. In April 1971 the prefect of the congregation, Cardinal John Wright, announced that all parties had agreed that there was no basis for a canonical case against the Cardinal and then went on to outline the congregation's theological and pastoral findings in the case. It reaffirmed *Humanae vitae* as the authentic teaching of the Church, the archbishop's duty to defend this teaching, and the clergy's responsibility to abide by it. But the findings also discussed the role of a properly formed conscience and sound pastoral counseling which, though not undermining the stand taken by O'Boyle, nevertheless made reconciliation easier.

The congregation added that it was the wish of the Holy Father that those dissenters who agreed to these findings be reinstated without public recanting. Cardinal O'Boyle believed that those who dissented in public should recant in public, but he loyally agreed, and the nineteen priests, who all accepted the congregation's findings, were quietly reinstated.

Cardinal O'Boyle reached mandatory retirement age that same year. The Vatican, however, did not accept his resignation, arranging instead for him to remain as administrator of the Church in Washington, a move widely interpreted as a mark of gratitude for the doughty warrior's loyal defense of papal teaching. The Cardinal finally retired in May, 1973, spending his last years in Washington, where he died at the age of ninety-one on August 10, 1987.

Abel, William S., ed. *Patrick Cardinal O'Boyle As His Friends Know Him.* Washington, 1986.
Conley, Rory T. "'All One in Christ': Patrick Cardinal O'Boyle, the Church of Washington and the Struggle for Racial Justice, 1948–1973." M.A. thesis, The Catholic University of America, 1992.

MORRIS McGREGOR

O'BRIEN, HIERONYMO (1819–98)

Religious. Two congregations claim Sr. Hieronymo O'Brien as their own. Her life exemplifies each of them: the devotion to the sick poor characteristic of the Sisters of Charity, and the quiet, creative response to contemporary needs that mark the Sisters of St. Joseph.

As a young Sister of Charity she trained and worked as a nurse. There was no hospital in western New York in the mid-nineteenth century. In 1857 young Sr. Hieronymo announced to the citizens of Rochester that the Sisters of Charity would begin a hospital there which would be open to all without distinction of race, religion, or ability to pay. This was a rare gesture of tolerance in a city that was sternly Yankee and decidedly anti-Catholic. St. Mary's Hospital and its foundress became strong, familiar symbols of unity in the civic community.

After thirteen years, her superiors assigned her to another city. The city fathers were furious; the Rochester community demanded her return. She did leave Rochester, but when her annual vows expired that year, she left the Sisters of Charity and entered the young diocesan congregation of the Sisters of St. Joseph.

As a Sister of St. Joseph, Sr. Hieronymo devoted her life to ministry to women. She established a Home of Industry: a safe residence for working women, an industrial school where single women learned marketable skills, and a secure home for elderly women. With her contacts in the community, her ability to pinpoint real needs, and her talent for quiet persuasion, the Home of Industry became a model for similar programs throughout the country.

Sr. Hieronymo's service crossed religious and social lines in a day when these lines were tightly drawn, affording her a trust that could never be given to any Roman Catholic churchman. She is still revered as one of the seminal forces for social welfare in Rochester, New York. Her image stands next to those of Frederick Douglass, Susan B. Anthony, and George Eastman in permanent display of notable Rochesterians.

Beales, Irene. *Genesee Valley Women 1743–1985.* Geneseo, 1985.
Kelly, Gerald M. *The Life of Mother Hieronymo.* Rochester, n.d.
McNamara, Robert F. *The Diocese of Rochester 1868–1968.* Rochester, 1968.
Zweirlien, Frederick J. *The Life and Letters of Bishop McQuaid.* 3 vols. Rochester, 1926.

O'BRIEN, JOHN ANTHONY (1893–1980)

Priest, author, and educator. Born in Peoria, Illinois, on January 20, 1893, O'Brien was educated at the Spalding Institute there, at Holy Cross College in Worcester, Massachusetts, and at St. Viator College, Bourbonnais, Illinois (B.A., M.A.). He continued his studies at The Catholic University of America in Washington, D.C., was ordained

John A. O'Brien

a priest in 1920, and received the Ph.D. in psychology from the University of Illinois in 1920.

O'Brien was the center of much criticism in 1920's debate over the nature of Catholic higher education in America. For O'Brien, effective Catholic education could take place in secular institutions provided they possessed a "Catholic foundation"; other educators sought to promote Catholic education through wholly Catholic institutions. O'Brien was a strong figure in the Newman Club movement, advocated changes in Church law to permit priests to marry, and became a strong voice in Catholic family planning discussions. *Family Planning in An Exploding Population* (1968) attempts to delineate a Catholic position on family regulation in a pluralistic society. In 1968 he sought unsuccessfully to convince Pope Paul VI to rescind his condemnation of artificial birth control. O'Brien was prolific, writing some forty books and pamphlets, a number of which became extremely popular, such as *The Faith of Millions* (1938) and *The Road to Damascus* (1949). After teaching at the University of Illinois for twenty-two years, O'Brien became professor of theology at Notre Dame University in 1940, where he was awarded the Laetare Medal in 1973 and died on April 18, 1980.

See also NOTRE DAME, UNIVERSITY OF.

MARIA MAZZENGA

O'BRIEN, WILLIAM VINCENT (1740–1816)

Dominican. William Vincent O'Brien was a highly regarded preacher who came to the United States in 1787 to work as a missionary in the nascent American Church.

His priestly and religious formation took place in Italy. He entered the order in Rome at the Irish Dominican pri-

ory of San Clemente in 1760 and completed his studies in Bologna. Shortly after his ordination, he returned to his native Dublin where he spent approximately seventeen years in the preaching apostolate. In 1785 he was honored with the order's title of preacher general.

Upon his arrival in the United States, he was sent by Fr. John Carroll, then superior of the American missions, to work in Philadelphia. This first assignment, however, proved to be temporary. Within a few months, he was sent north to New York City where disorder was reigning in the congregation at St. Peter's.

The problems at St. Peter's originated in a rivalry between Charles Whelan and Andrew Nugent, two Capuchins who had been ministering to the congregation. Whelan had arrived first, in October of 1784, and was the first resident priest in the city. His confrere, Nugent, arrived the following year. Almost immediately, the newcomer began exploiting the dissatisfaction which some members of congregation had towards Whelan. By the end of 1785, the community was split into two factions.

Another aspect of the brewing controversy was the claim being made by the lay trustees that they had a right to choose their own pastor. Nugent's supporters among the trustees were threatening recourse to the civil courts if Carroll did not formally appoint him pastor in place of Whelan. Whelan, wearied by the factionalism, left New York in February of 1786 and Carroll, although with reservations, appointed Nugent in his place. Peace, however, was not forthcoming. When Nugent began demanding a higher salary, the trustees came to regret the appointment.

As a result of the renewed strife between pastor and congregation, Carroll finally decided to remove Nugent and appoint O'Brien as pastor in 1787. The appointment proved to be a wise one as O'Brien quickly endeared himself to the congregation and was able eventually to restore peace, although Nugent continued to stir up trouble for another two years.

In 1790 O'Brien traveled to Mexico City to solicit funds and decorations for the newly completed parish church. There he managed to collect close to five thousand dollars, thanks to the assistance of the archbishop, Alonzo Nuñez de Haro y Peralta, a former classmate from Bologna. He also returned with several paintings for the adornment of the church.

Among other accomplishments during his tenure as pastor was the establishment in 1800 of St. Peter's Free School, New York's first Catholic school. But he is best remembered for his heroic service to the sick and dying during the various epidemics of yellow fever which struck the city between 1795 and 1805.

He also proved to be a valuable assistant to Carroll when ecclesiastical problems arose in Boston over the pastor, Claude Florent Bouchard, who styled himself the Abbé de la Poterie. At Carroll's request, O'Brien traveled there in 1788 to depose the troublesome priest for his reckless spending and deception concerning his earlier suspension by the archbishop of Paris.

A recurring and acute rheumatism forced O'Brien to resign his position as pastor in 1806. In gratitude for his selfless devotion to St. Peter's, the trustees of the parish voted to provide him with a yearly pension until death. He died ten years later on May 14 and is buried in the cemetery by the side of the church.

Carey, Patrick. *People, Priests, and Prelates.* Notre Dame, 1987.

Curran, Francis X., S.J. *The Return of the Jesuits: Chapters in the History of the Society of Jesus in Nineteenth-Century America.* Chicago, 1966.

Ellis, John Tracy. *Catholics in Colonial America.* Baltimore, 1965.

O'Daniel, Victor, O.P. *Dominican Province of St. Joseph.* New York, 1942.

Ryan, Leo R. *Old St. Peter's: The Mother Church of Catholic New York, 1785–1935.* New York, 1935.

JOHN LANGLOIS, O.P.

O'CONNELL, DENIS (1849–1927)

Bishop of Richmond. Denis J. O'Connell was born in Donoughmore, County Cork, Ireland. When he was a young child, his family moved to Columbia, South Carolina, where three priest uncles were already working. After the Civil War, the family moved to Charlotte, North Carolina, from where he began his seminary studies at St. Charles College, Ellicott City, Maryland, as a student for the vicariate apostolic of North Carolina, with whose bishop, James Gibbons, he formed a long-lasting friendship. When Gibbons

Denis O'Connell

was named bishop of Richmond in 1872, he transferred O'Connell to that diocese and sent him to the North American College in Rome, where he was ordained in 1877, just as Gibbons was named coadjutor archbishop of Baltimore.

When Gibbons succeeded to Baltimore, he immediately dispatched O'Connell back to Rome to obtain his *pallium,* the sign of metropolitan office. Immediately after Gibbons' installation, he assigned O'Connell to accompany Bishop George Conroy of Ardagh on a visitation of the American Church. From 1878 to 1883 O'Connell served in pastoral ministry in the Diocese of Richmond, but was then summoned by Gibbons to accompany him to Rome for a meeting of archbishops in preparation for the Third Plenary Council. He assisted Gibbons in preparing the agenda for the council and was secretary to the council in 1884. After the conclusion of the council, he accompanied the delegation of bishops to Rome to gain approval for the conciliar decrees.

In 1885 he became rector of the North American College and unofficial agent for the American hierarchy. For him, however, the hierarchy meant primarily Gibbons (who was named a cardinal in 1886), and John Ireland. In 1888 Gibbons supported his nomination as bishop of Richmond, but Leo XIII personally intervened to retain him in his Roman post. In the 1890s, he took a leading role in the controversies which divided the hierarchy and in which he consistently sided with Ireland's positions on parochial education, the Knights of Labor, the case of Fr. Edward McGlynn, and the German question. In 1892 he accompanied Archbishop Francesco Satolli to the U.S.A. Satolli came originally to discuss the school question but remained as the first permanent apostolic delegate, the establishment of which O'Connell and Ireland had engineered.

In 1895 O'Connell was forced to resign as rector by Leo XIII because of complaints from other bishops, notably Archbishop Michael A. Corrigan of New York, about his partisanship in the earlier controversies. Remaining in Rome as vicar of Gibbons' titular church, he became one of the leading theoreticians of Americanism and delivered an address in 1897 arguing for the advantage to the Church of the American separation of Church and state. Although Americanism was condemned in 1899, O'Connell regained the favor of Roman authorities by 1903 and was named rector of The Catholic University of America. Unfortunately, he alienated the faculty and led the campaign against Modernism, even at the cost of the reputation of a distinguished and loyal Scripture professor, Henry Poels. In 1908 he was named auxiliary bishop of San Francisco. In 1912 he became bishop of Richmond, where he engaged in many civic activities, guided the diocese through the growth occasioned by World War I, and helped thwart the anti-Catholicism of the Ku Klux Klan in the 1920s. In 1926 he resigned because of ill health and became titular archbishop of Mariamne. He died on January 1, 1927.

See also AMERICANISM; IRELAND, JOHN; NORTH AMERICAN COLLEGE.

Fogarty, Gerald P., S.J. *The Vatican and the Americanist Crisis: Denis J. O'Connell, American Agent in Rome, 1885–1903.* Rome: University Gregoriana, 1974.

____. *The Vatican and the American Hierarchy from 1870 to 1965.* Collegeville: The Liturgical Press, 1985.

GERALD P. FOGARTY, S.J.

O'CONNELL, WILLIAM CARDINAL (1859–1944)

Cardinal archbishop of Boston. William Henry O'Connell was born in Lowell, Massachusetts, on December 8, 1859. The youngest of eleven children born to Irish immigrant parents, O'Connell was raised in Lowell, where his father and brothers worked in trades associated with the many textile mills of that city. After a primary education in the public schools and a brief, unhappy period at a minor seminary in Maryland, he enrolled at Boston College, where he graduated with the class of 1881. Thereafter, he studied for the priesthood at the North American College in Rome, and he was ordained there in 1884. On his return home, he served as a curate for two years in a small parish in Medford, Massachusetts, and then for nine years in a busy parish in the heart of downtown Boston. There he began to acquire a wider reputation in Church circles, especially as a preacher and lecturer.

William H. Cardinal O'Connell

O'Connell and Romanità

A giant step of advancement came in 1895 with his appointment to the position of rector of the North American College, Rome, as successor to the sometimes controversial Denis O'Connell, who was no relation to him. The American hierarchy was at this time divided into two factions: those who sought a distinctive national expression of Catholicism (known as "Americanists") and those who pressed for a more thoroughgoing reliance on the resurgent papacy in all Church matters (known as "Ultramontanes"). Though he was apparently intended as a compromise choice between these two groups, William O'Connell quickly aligned himself with the Ultramontanes. He was committed throughout the remainder of his career to promoting what was identified as *Romanità*—literally, "Roman-ness"— eagerly becoming an agent for the consolidation of papal authority in the Church in America.

This loyalty brought its rewards, and O'Connell returned to this country in 1901, serving for five years as bishop of Portland, Maine. His administrative duties there absorbed some of his attention, but he spent most of his time in this period actively lobbying among his Roman contacts for appointment to the more important position of archbishop of Boston. Each faction within the hierarchy hoped to have one of its supporters receive this promotion, and O'Connell quickly emerged as the candidate of the conservative Ultramontanes. In January 1906, while he was in Rome on his way home from a brief diplomatic mission to Japan for the Holy See, he was designated coadjutor of Boston. He became archbishop in August 1907 on the death of his predecessor, Archbishop John J. Williams. He was elevated to the cardinalate in 1911 by Pope Pius X, only the third American churchman to receive that honor.

Archbishop of Boston

O'Connell sought to introduce a greater degree of central control in overseeing the administrative affairs of the Boston church. He established procedures for the tighter management of archdiocesan and parish finances, and he reorganized important church institutions, including St. John's Seminary, Brighton, and the archdiocesan newspaper, the *Pilot*. He increased the number of local parishes by half, and vocations to the priesthood and religious life grew to impressive numbers. Never particularly popular with his priests, he faced significant opposition to this centralizing program from many powerful pastors and from the superiors of some women's religious orders. Even so, he created a powerful public image as a shrewd and efficient manager of church affairs, an image which became characteristic of many of his contemporaries in the American hierarchy.

O'Connell also helped define a wide public role for a self-assertive form of American Catholicism. He was quick to rebut any perceived slight against the loyalty and participation of Catholics in American life, pointing proudly to examples of material success among second-generation

Catholics. He believed that Catholic culture was a stronghold for the defense of traditional values whose power was loosening elsewhere, and he thought the Church had to assume the responsibility, previously entrusted to Protestant elites, for protecting broad moral and cultural standards in America. "The Puritan has passed," he said in a famous epigram in 1908, "the Catholic remains." Eagerly playing the role of a widely recognized public figure with noteworthy opinions on every subject, O'Connell was outspoken on a range of matters, embracing modern science, international affairs, popular entertainment, and women's fashions.

As part of this larger public role, O'Connell emerged as a powerful force in secular politics. Completing a trend begun a generation earlier, Catholics were taking final control of elective and appointive office in Boston and Massachusetts during his tenure as archbishop, with local bosses such as James M. Curley, John F. Fitzgerald, and David I. Walsh emerging as significant wielders of power. Publicly, O'Connell maintained correct and nonpartisan relations with these and other politicians, but privately their association was often stormy. Some of these political leaders seemed always to be dogged by suggestions of scandal, and most of them inclined toward a more expansive view of the role of government than that of the archbishop. More practically, they often were in effect his rivals for influence within the Catholic community. His position gave him many advantages, and local political leaders seldom dared to disagree with him. In 1924, for example, both Curley and Walsh had to make an abrupt about-face in the midst of a campaign on the question of restricting child labor. Each had initially supported a constitutional amendment restricting the practice, but when O'Connell denounced the measure—he was not in favor of child labor, but he thought the proposal concentrated in the hands of government authority best entrusted to the family and the Church—they both declared their opposition as well. More broadly, O'Connell was known to state legislators and city councilors simply as "Number One," a designation which expressed both their assessment of his influence and their unwillingness to cross him.

O'Connell as a National Figure

Within the American Church as a whole, O'Connell sought to exert a broad influence. Briefly successful at this during the reign of Pius X (d. 1914), changing political conditions at the Vatican thereafter generally left him on the losing side. His imposing personality and the conflicted circumstances of his designation as archbishop left him largely without friends and supporters in the American hierarchy. More seriously, in the early 1920s he was embarrassed in clerical circles by a financial and sexual scandal involving his nephew, Msgr. James P. E. O'Con-

nell, the chancellor of the Boston archdiocese, who was also secretly married and embezzling money from archdiocesan accounts to support his elaborate double life. O'Connell was aware of the scandal for several years before taking action to remove his nephew, finally acting only when forced to do so by the Vatican. Threatened with removal from office himself for his handling of the matter, he managed to hold on to his position but his wider influence was at an end. While the scandal never became widely known to the public at large, it was common knowledge among Catholic churchmen and, understandably, intensified O'Connell's isolation from them.

In spite of these troubled private matters, O'Connell nonetheless helped to articulate a confident public style for twentieth-century American Catholicism that was marked by its self-assurance. Never doubting that the Church was an authoritative stronghold for enduring values amid the confusing changes of modern life, he was unafraid to state what he considered the definitive truth and to stick by it. In the process, he offered Catholic immigrants and their children a means for achieving self-respect in a society previously inclined to view them with suspicion. O'Connell's religious and personal style was rendered generally obsolete by the changes of the Second Vatican Council and the ongoing movement of Catholics into middle-class respectability. For his own times, however, he provided Catholics with a visible symbol for their full participation in American life.

See also MASSACHUSETTS, CATHOLIC CHURCH IN.

O'Connell, William Henry. *Sermons and Addresses*. (1911–38).
____. *Recollections of Seventy Years*. 1934.
O'Toole, James M. *Militant and Triumphant: William Henry O'Connell and the Catholic Church in Boston*. Notre Dame, 1992.
Wayman, Dorothy G. *Cardinal O'Connell of Boston*. New York, 1955.

JAMES M. O'TOOLE

O'CONNOR, EDWIN (1918–68)

Author. Edwin Eugene O'Connor was born in Providence, Rhode Island, on July 29, 1918. He attended public elementary school, LaSalle Academy (Christian Brothers), and Notre Dame University where he received his B.S. degree in English *cum laude* in 1939. He was influenced by Frank O'Malley whose course in Modern Catholic Writers made a lasting impression. In later years, after O'Connor dedicated *The Last Hurrah* to his mentor, he returned to Notre Dame to speak to O'Malley's classes.

After a brief start in Notre Dame's graduate program in English, O'Connor worked as a radio announcer in Providence, West Palm Beach, Buffalo, and Hartford to finance his real vocation—writing fiction. He enlisted in

Edwin O'Connor

the Coast Guard in 1942 and served three years. Part of his duty involved public relations where he reported to Lt. Louis J. Brems, vaudevillian turned greeter for Mayor Maurice Tobin. Brems's stories of Boston's politicians and personalities introduced O'Connor to Irish-American urban politics and to the world that would be the background for *The Last Hurrah.* Cuke Gillan was based on Brems.

O'Connor returned briefly to broadcasting after his Coast Guard service before devoting himself to freelance writing. His "Roger Swift" column, a review of contemporary radio and television, appeared three times a week in the *Boston Herald.* Four essays satirizing the radio programs of the day appeared in the *Atlantic* in 1946 and 1947. O'Connor's experience in broadcasting and interest in the importance of radio as a medium provided the theme of his first novel, *The Oracle* (1951), a satire about a pompous broadcaster, the oracle of the network, who finds himself at a point of personal as well as professional crisis. The book received mixed reviews and was a commercial failure; however, its theme of the private and public behavior of men who exploit the power of words prepared O'Connor to write *The Last Hurrah.*

Arthur Schlesinger, Jr., said in his Introduction to *The Best and Last of Edwin O'Connor* (1970) that he recalled O'Connor commenting, "I would like to do for the Irish in America what Faulkner did for the South." Critics agree that he accomplished that ambition with *The Last Hurrah* (1858), the last campaign of a seventy-two-year-old Irish-American mayor, an old-fashioned political boss who is flamboyant, politically corrupt, but generous and benevolent. O'Connor fought the idea that Skeffington was based on Boston's Mayor Curley, though many, including Cur-

ley, linked the mayors. O'Connor did not lament the end of Irish urban machine politics, but he wrote an affectionate elegy to the colorful Irish-American political characters of the Skeffington era. *The Last Hurrah* made O'Connor's reputation and his fortune. It sold more than a million copies; it was selected by the Book of the Month Club, and abridged by the *Reader's Digest.* Columbia Pictures bought the film rights.

O'Connor's third novel, *The Edge of Sadness* (1961), was his personal favorite. Another story of the passing of Irish America, *The Edge of Sadness* describes the rehabilitation of Fr. Hugh Kennedy, an alcoholic priest in an inner-city parish whose search for grace ends not only with his rehabilitation but with his coming to terms with his vocation and with his faith. A Pulitzer Prize winner, *The Edge of Sadness* won the Thomas More Association Award in 1963, and was selected by the Book of the Month Club, *Reader's Digest* Condensed Books, the Catholic Book Club, the Catholic Literary Foundation, and the Thomas More Book Club.

O'Connor wrote two more novels with terrible old men protagonists. *I Was Dancing* (1964), which appeared first in play form and ran for seventeen performances on Broadway, is an entertaining contest between an old vaudevillian who schemes to stay with his son after deserting him years earlier. *All in the Family* (1966) treats the public and private lives of the politically ambitious Irish-American Kinsella family. Its publication in the aftermath of the Kennedy assassination and its treatment of Irish Catholic sexual puritanism drew criticism from Catholic periodicals.

O'Connor was working on two manuscripts, "The Cardinal" and "Boy," when he died of a cerebral hemorrhage in Boston on March 23, 1968, at the age of forty-nine. He left a wife of nine years, Veniette Caswell O'Connor, and a stepson. In 1970 *The Best and Last of Edwin O'Connor* appeared with an introduction by Arthur Schlesinger, Jr.

See also CATHOLICS AND AMERICAN LITERATURE.

Jones, Howard Mumford. "Politics, Mr. O'Connor and the Family Novel." *Atlantic* 218 (October 1966) 117–19.

Kelleher, John V. "Edwin O'Connor and the Irish American Process." *Atlantic* 222 (July 1968) 48–52.

Rank, Hugh. *Edwin O'Connor.* New York, 1974.

Schlesinger, Arthur M., Jr. *Introduction to the Best and the Last of Edwin O'Connor.* Boston, 1970.

Wilson, Edmund. "The Great Baldini: A Memoir and a Collaboration by Edmund Wilson and Edwin O'Connor." *Atlantic* 224 (October 1969) 64–75.

MAUREEN MURPHY

O'CONNOR, MARY FLANNERY (1925–64)

Author. First and foremost, Flannery O'Connor was a superbly gifted and disciplined writer. A native of Georgia,

Flannery O'Connor

a committed and widely read intellectual Catholic, she set her fiction mostly in the South and grounded it in her rock-solid faith in the mysteries of incarnation and redemption.

But there is nothing pious about her fiction, nor edifying about her characters and settings—a salesman who steals a crippled girl's wooden leg, a killer called "the misfit," a backwoods, hell-fire preacher, a man with an obsession for tattoos. As writer Patricia O'Connor put it succinctly in a 1982 article in *The Visitor:* "She wrote about people as she saw them—self-centered, misled, silly, sometimes brutal, often ignorant, crude, mean—ordinary people who refuse grace and remain unredeemed, get into all sorts of devilment, and people who struggle and finally accept grace." All of my stories, Flannery O'Connor said, "are about the action of grace on a character who is not willing to support it."

O'Connor's Life

The "physical" dimensions of her life are as ordinary as her talent was remarkable. Born on March 25, 1925, in Savannah, she grew up in the town of Milledgeville, Georgia. She attended Georgia State College for Women there, graduating in 1945. She then earned her Master of Fine Arts degree from the State University of Iowa and attended that school's highly regarded Writer's Workshop, studying under Paul Engle. After a brief residence at the writer's colony at Yaddo, she spent a few months in New York City and then went to live with writer/scholars Sally and Robert Fitzgerald at their farm in Connecticut. In 1950 she experienced her first major attack of disseminated lupus erythematosus, the dangerous disease (incurable but controllable to some extent by steroid drugs) that would cause

her death in fourteen years (and which had killed her father at about the same age).

From 1951 on, she lived with her mother, Regina, on a working farm (Andalusia) not far from Milledgeville. Here she continued to write, read, handle an ever-growing correspondence, and undertake an occasional trip (all complicated by her growing dependence on crutches) to lecture, give a reading or accept an honorary degree.

Of this forced retreat to Andalusia, Sally Fitzgerald, who selected and edited O'Connor's correspondence, writes in her introduction to *The Habit of Being:* "Her return was for good, in more ways than one. She herself acknowledged this, describing it in one of her letters as not the end of all work she had thought it would be but only the beginning. Once she had accepted her destiny, she began to embrace it, and it is clear from her correspondence that she cherished her life and knew that she had been brought back exactly where she belonged and where her best work would be done.

"Here her mature growth began. When she learned how matters really stood, and when her health had been more or less stabilized and meticulous treatment worked out to control her illness, she sat about building a life with her mother. . . . Her living and working habits were established so as to ensure that her diminished strength could go almost entirely into her writing. She wrote us that she was able to work at her fiction no more than two or three hours a day. If she had a long struggle accepting loneliness, and the reality of a permanently curtailed life, or if she felt resentment or self-pity (and how could she have failed to suffer these and much more, to some degree?), she gave no sign of such feeling to any of us. There is no whining. A characteristic description of how she stood is contained in a 1953 letter to Robert Lowell and his wife: 'I am making out fine in spite of any conflicting stories . . . I have enough energy to write with and as that is all I have any business doing anyhow, I can, with one eye squinted, take it all as a blessing. What you have to measure out, you come to observe more closely, or so I tell myself.'"

Her Place in American Literature

In 1963 her story "Everything That Rises Must Converge" won first prize in the annual O. Henry Awards. She was ever more painfully afflicted by lupus and in 1964, after winning another O. Henry First ("Revelation"), she died on August 3, 1964, in the Milledgeville Hospital.

Flannery O'Connor's impact on the American literary scene has grown since her death. Her talent bloomed very early, which, given her brief lifespan, was fortunate. She was appreciated first simply for her aesthetic skills, her vivid, terse descriptions, her dead-on-target ear for dialect and idiom, her irreverent humor, her use of the grotesque to arrest attention and frame moral and physical tragedies. It was evident to both critics and serious readers of fiction that it was almost impossible not to finish one of her stories and it was also evident that she was an original, highly creative voice.

Much has since been written about the deeply Christian and biblical underpinnings of her work. She would appreciate the irony in the fact that now many more words about what she wrote have come to roost on library shelves than those she actually banged out on her own typewriter. It is also ironic that many people never saw, nor much cared about this deeper side of her art. Catholics, who have since come to treasure her as one of the first and relatively few writers who openly avowed her faith as being central to her work and who thus made Catholic fiction "respectable," at first had trouble (if they were honest) in seeing what her novels and stories about Southern rural zealots and oddballs and "misfits" had to do with Catholicism, or Christianity, for that matter.

And if Catholics had trouble understanding her, so did others. I once asked her if she was pleased with the critical reception given her novel *The Violent Bear It Away,* not in a vain sense, but simply with regard to the measure of understanding she saw evidenced. I mentioned Orville Prescott's review for *The New York Times* in which he had said that while her talent for fiction was "so great as to be almost overwhelming," he had been unable to see any evidence of the Christian and biblical relationships she intended to convey (according to her own intentions set down in an article he had read in a symposium called "The Living Novel," edited by Granville Hicks).

O'Connor and Christianity

What she had written for Hicks was this: "I see from the standpoint of Christian orthodoxy. This means that for me the meaning of life is centered in our redemption by Christ and that what I see in the world I see in relation to that. I don't think that this is a position which can be taken halfway or one that is particularly easy in these times to make transparent in fiction."

As for the lack of biblical understanding, she told me, in an interview for *The Critic:* "The fact that Catholics don't see religion through the Bible is a deficiency in Catholics. And I don't think the novelist can discard the instruments she or he has to plumb meaning just because Catholics aren't used to them. You don't write only for now. The biblical revival is going to mean a great deal to Catholic fiction in the future. Maybe in fifty years, or a hundred, Catholics will be reading the Bible the way they should have been reading it all along. I can wait that long to have my fiction understood. The Bible we share with all Christians, and the Old Testament we share with the Jews. This is sacred history and our mythic background.

If we are going to discard this we had better quit writing at all."

I cited one of her college talks in which she had said that "for the modern reader, moral distinctions are usually blurred in hazes of compassion; there are not enough common beliefs to make this a fit age for allegory; and as for anagogical realities, they either don't exist at all for the general reader or are taken by him to be knowable by sensation." Did she think that this was the basic problem confronting the Christian novelist? Could this eventually be so limiting that such a writer will have to be content writing for only a few?

"One of the Christian novelist's basic problems is that she is trying to get the Christian vision across to an audience to whom it is largely meaningless," O'Connor agreed. "Nevertheless, she can't write only for a select few. The work will have to have value on the dramatic level, the level of truth recognizable by anybody. The fact that Mr. Prescott or anybody else can't see anything Christian about my novel doesn't interfere with many of them seeing it as a novel which does not falsify reality." "Still," she added, "there were enough Catholic reviews which shared my own interpretation of it for me to feel I succeeded well enough in doing what I intended to do."

I asked if she would amplify something she had said to the effect that there are ages when it is possible to woo the reader and other times when something more drastic is necessary. Did she deliberately set out to be more drastic in her fiction?

"I don't consciously set out to be more drastic," she said, "but this happens automatically. If I write a novel in which the central action is a baptism, I know that for the larger percentage of my readers, baptism is a meaningless rite; therefore I have to imbue this action with an awe and terror which will suggest its awful mystery. I have to distort the look of the thing in order to represent as I see them both the mystery and the fact."

Faith and Freedom

In an essay in *Mystery and Manners,* Flannery O'Connor stressed her conviction that a writer's commitment to a set of beliefs is actually a source of freedom, not constraint: "I have heard it said that belief in Christian dogma is a hindrance to the writer, but I myself have found nothing further from the truth. Actually, it frees the storyteller to observe. It is not a set of rules which fixes what the writer sees in the world. It affects his (her) writing primarily by guaranteeing respect for mystery. . . . A belief in fixed dogma cannot fix what goes on in life, or bind the believer to it. It will, of course, add a dimension to the writer's observation which many cannot, in conscience, acknowledge exists, but as long as what they *can* acknowledge is present in the work, they cannot claim that any freedom has been denied the artist. A dimension taken away is one thing, a dimension added is another."

We all live under sentence of death, but Flannery O'Connor had her certificate presented to her sooner than most—at age twenty-six, with her first serious attack of lupus. Thus she lived—not without hope, for there was the possibility of a cure being discovered—but with death very much a dark companion for all of her creative life. She was not cheerless or morbid—far from it—but knowing you are most likely going to die in a few years has a wonderful way of focusing the mind. Just as it made her take her faith most seriously, it evidently intensified and refined her perceptions. In such a context one wants to make every moment count, to savor things with intensity. Live this way for a few years and you become a special sort of person—particularly if you have a fine mind and a first-rate talent to begin with.

I didn't know Flannery O'Connor well but I saw that quality in her, and I read it large in everything written by people who did know her well—that she had a way of making every word count, of having a "condensed" presence, of being—well—more pulled together than perhaps anyone you've ever met.

Immediately after Flannery O'Connor's death, I wrote to novelist Katherine Anne Porter to see if she would pen an appreciation of her for *The Critic* (which had originally published her story, "The Partridge Festival"). She responded in terms which help to flesh out this special personal quality. The author of such classics as *Pale Horse, Pale Rider* and *Ship of Fools* was not easily impressed, especially by other writers, but she was candid in her admiration: "I saw our lovely and gifted Flannery O'Connor only three times over a period of about three years or more. But each meeting was spontaneously an occasion; and I want to write about her just as she impressed me. By what means she came to it so early I do not know, but she was at the center of the vortex, the great stillness that comes of tensions balanced against each other until perfect equilibrium is reached. And I do not know what her secret was, but that she had one I do not doubt. She was a genius, there is no question."

Thomas Merton was overawed, and he never met her face-to-face: "When I read Flannery O'Connor, I do not think of Hemingway, or Katherine Anne Porter, or Jean Paul Sartre, but rather of someone like Sophocles. What more can you say for a writer? I write her name with honor, for all the truth and all the craft with which she shows humankind's fall and dishonor and—redemption."

But for all her seriousness of faith, and her long walk holding death's hand, it should not be supposed that Flannery O'Connor was a person who went around with downcast eyes and her thumb inserted in the Bible. As any who knew her will testify, and as many of her stories and her lively letters confirm at every turn, she was warm, wise, witty, laconic, marvelously well informed and fully up to date with her times.

She was also tough-minded and candid. I will always remember fondly her answers to three rather fatuous questions I put to her: What did she think of Tennessee Williams? "Not much"; what was her opinion of Harper Lee's novel, *To Kill a Mockingbird* (which had just won the Pulitzer Prize for fiction)? "A wonderful book for children"; about William Faulkner's reputation as the master of Southern American fiction? "Everybody gets off the track when the big train comes through." And I will never forget the wonderfully sardonic, unabashedly deep Southern drawl with which she responded to my asking her what she planned to do when she finished her next novel: "An awful lot of porch-settin'."

See also CATHOLICS AND AMERICAN LITERATURE.

O'Connor, Flannery. *Wise Blood.* New York, 1952.
____. *A Good Man is Hard to Find.* New York, 1955.
____. *Everything That Rises Must Converge.* New York, 1956.
____. *The Violent Bear It Away.* New York, 1960.
____. *Mystery and Manners.* New York, 1969.
____. *The Complete Stories of Flannery O'Connor.* New York, 1971.
____. *The Habit of Being: Letters of Flannery O'Connor.* New York, 1980.

JOEL WELLS

O'CONNOR, MICHAEL (1810–72)

First bishop of Pittsburgh. O'Connor was born on September 27, 1810, in Queenstown, Ireland. His academic gifts took him from his native Ireland to the Urban College of Propaganda in Rome where he was ordained on June 1, 1833, and received his doctorate of sacred theology on the twenty-seventh day of the following month. After brief sojourns at the Irish College in Rome and in his home diocese of Cloyne and Ross, he was appointed in 1838 to the faculty of St. Charles Seminary in Philadelphia by Bishop Francis Patrick Kenrick.

In 1841 O'Connor was appointed vicar general and given the pastorship of St. Paul's Church in Pittsburgh. After several unsuccessful attempts on Kenrick's part, Rome finally erected a new diocese at Pittsburgh and named O'Connor its bishop on August 7, 1843. Already in Rome, the new prelate was consecrated by Cardinal Fransoni in the chapel of the Irish College eight days after the nomination.

During O'Connor's tenure, the Religious Sisters of Mercy (1843), the Benedictine monks (1846), the Brothers of the Third Order of St. Francis (1847), and the Passionists (1852) made their first American foundations in the Pittsburgh diocese. O'Connor's tenure was troubled by nativist agitation but was marked by tremendous growth in Catholic numbers.

Michael O'Connor

Failing health led to his resignation, which was accepted by Rome on May 20, 1860. After obtaining necessary permission from the pope and from Jesuit superiors, O'Connor fulfilled a long-held dream and was accepted into the Society of Jesus. He died a Jesuit and was buried in the community cemetery at Woodstock, Maryland.

See also PENNSYLVANIA, CATHOLIC CHURCH IN.

Lambing, Andrew A. *A History of the Catholic Church in the Dioceses of Pittsburgh and Allegheny*. New York: Benziger, 1880.

Szarnicki, Henry A. "The Episcopate of Michael O'Connor, First Bishop of Pittsburgh, 1843–1860." Ph.D. dissertation, The Catholic University of America, 1971.

ALBERT H. LEDOUX

O'CONOR, CHARLES (1804–84)

Lawyer. Charles O'Conor was born in New York City on January 22, 1804, to Thomas and Margaret O'Connor O'Conor. His family was unable to provide him with a higher education and so he began an apprenticeship to a tar and lampblack manufacturer following his mother's death in 1816. In 1817 he began his legal education as an errand boy in a law office; he eventually graduated to clerk and then law student and was admitted to the New York State bar in 1824. That year, at the age of twenty, he opened his own office with a capital of only twenty-five dollars.

O'Conor, a Democrat, had a lifelong ambition to hold political office, a desire which he believed was hindered by his Irish Catholic background. He was elected to the New York State constitutional convention in 1846, but failed in the campaign for lieutenant governor two years later. In 1853 he was appointed United States Attorney for the southern district of New York. He was also treasurer and president (1869) of the New York Law Institute, and served as vice president of the New-York Historical Society. Because of his support of the institution of slavery, he was popular among Southern Democrats, and served as counsel for Jefferson Davis after his indictment for treason following the Civil War.

As a lawyer, the two cases that brought him most fame were the Tweed litigation and the Forrest divorce suit. In the former, O'Conor represented the state of New York in abolishing the notorious "Tweed ring" of New York City. His account of this case is recounted in *Peculation Triumphant* (1875). O'Conor died in Nantucket, Massachusetts, on May 12, 1884.

Walsh, J. C. "Charles O'Conor." *Journal of the American Irish Historical Society* 27 (1928) 285–313.

RICHARD G. SMITH

O'DANIEL, VICTOR FRANCIS (1868–1960)

Dominican friar, archivist, Church historian. Victor Francis O'Daniel, son of Richard J. and Nancy Hamilton O'Daniel, was born on February 15, 1868, in Washington County, Kentucky. He died on June 12, 1960. His birth in the heartland of Kentucky affected his life and writings. At the age of eighteen, he entered the province of St. Joseph of the Dominican Order and completed his studies for the priesthood at St. Rose Priory near Springfield, Kentucky, and St. Joseph Priory near Somerset, Ohio. He was ordained a priest in the cathedral in Columbus, Ohio, on June 16, 1891, by Bishop John Watterson. His study of theology after ordination took him in 1893 to Louvain, Belgium, for two years.

When he returned to the United States he held teaching positions at St. Rose and St. Joseph and at the Dominican Houses of Study in Benicia, California, and Washington, D.C. In 1907 he became the first archivist of the province of St. Joseph and from 1913 until his death he devoted his time and talents to historical writings to make known the contributions of the Order of Preachers to the growth of the Church and the religious development of the United States. In 1915 he joined a group of faculty members under the direction of Peter Guilday at The Catholic University of America to launch the *Catholic Historical Review*. He was associate editor of that journal, and contributed many articles to its early numbers.

Among his books on the Order of Preachers in the United States, his earliest biography appeared in 1920. It was the life of Edward Dominic Fenwick, founder of the province of St. Joseph and first bishop of Cincinnati. Other biographies of Dominicans included those of Samuel Thomas Wilson, Matthew O'Brien, Charles McKenna, founder of the Holy Name Society in the United States, and Richard Pius Miles, first bishop of Nashville, Tennessee. His general history, *The Dominican Province of St. Joseph,* was published in 1942. O'Daniel's greatest contribution to historians was his collection of original documents concerning the life and mission of American Dominican friars. Researchers praise his inexhaustible efforts to obtain and preserve the earliest letters and other documents needed for writing authentic history. Seventy years after his first publication, the resources gathered by Victor O'Daniel, O.P., are still valuable to historians of the Order of Preachers in the United States.

See also DOMINICANS (O.P.).

Coffey, Reginald. *Pictorial History of the Dominican Province of St. Joseph.* New York, 1946.

LORETTA PETIT, O.P.

O'DEA, EDWARD JOHN (1856–1932)

Bishop. Edward John O'Dea was born in Boston, Massachusetts, on November 23, 1856. The O'Dea family moved to Portland, Oregon, in 1866. The son of a tailor, O'Dea eventually attended St. Michael's College, Portland, and entered the *grand séminaire* in Montreal in 1876. He was ordained by Archbishop Edouard-Charles Fabre in Montreal on December 23, 1882. He returned to Portland and was celebrated as the first resident of Oregon to become a priest. O'Dea served three different archbishops in various diocesan and pastoral positions throughout the Pacific Northwest. On June 13, 1896, he was named third bishop of Nesqually, and consecrated by Archbishop William Gross on September 8, 1896, at St. James Cathedral, Vancouver, Washington. By 1904 O'Dea had transferred the seat of the diocese to Seattle and had begun construction of the present St. James Cathedral.

O'Dea became bishop at a young age and presided over a diocese in the midst of rapid growth. During his episcopate, the number of parish and mission churches increased from eighty-nine to nearly two hundred, while the Catholic population increased from 40,000 to approximately 100,000. Hospitals, orphanages, and schools increased as did the number of women religious, and religious and diocesan priests attending the diocese. O'Dea promoted the grandeur of the institutional Church and recognized the need for a strong Catholic educational system. He established St. Edward's, the first seminary in Washington State, and in 1924, successfully fought Initiative No. 49, an antiprivate school bill sponsored by the Ku Klux Klan. He died on December 25, 1932, shortly after

the celebration of his golden jubilee, and is buried in Holyrood Cemetery, Seattle, Washington.

CHRISTINE TAYLOR

ODERMATT, ADELHELM (CHARLES) (1844–1920)

Abbot. Adelhelm (Charles) Odermatt, O.S.B., was born on December 10, 1844, at Enetmoos, near Stans, Nidwalden, Switzerland. On September 29, 1866, he made monastic vows at the Swiss Benedictine monastery at Engelberg where he had attended school. He was ordained a priest in 1869. In 1873, after teaching at Engelberg for several years, he departed with Fr. Frowin Conrad, O.S.B., to establish Engelberg's first foundation, in Missouri. He was made pastor of Maryville, Missouri, about twenty miles from the new monastery of the Immaculate Conception. He became a U.S. citizen in 1880.

In 1881 Fr. Adelhelm traversed the Western United States seeking a site for a second Engelberg foundation. He visited several sites in the Archdiocese of Portland, where he served briefly in the parish at Gervais, before returning to Switzerland. In 1882 he was appointed prior of a group of monks, who with some Benedictine sisters under Sr. Bernardine Wachter, O.S.B., and some laypeople, set out for Oregon. Monastic life was begun in Gervais, in November 1882. In 1884 the men's community transferred to Mt. Angel, where they opened a school in 1887. After a fire destroyed their monastery and seminary in 1892, Fr. Adelhelm spent a great deal of time traveling throughout the U.S.A., preaching and raising money for rebuilding. He was relieved of his duties as prior in 1894, but returned to that office 1899–1901. He was prior under Abbot Thomas Meienhofer, O.S.B., 1904–10; administrator in 1910; and prior again under Abbot Placidus Fuerst, O.S.B., 1910–16. He was declared a titular abbot in 1916. He died on November 6, 1920.

Abbot Adelhelm was a rotund and energetic person, cheerful and charming, zealous to serve the German-speaking Catholic settlers in America. People liked and trusted him; he was a very good preacher. These were qualities that made him a successful catalyst and fundraiser, but not a steady administrator. He observed the monastic horarium faithfully, raising regularly around 3:00 A.M. to say the rosary for the poor souls.

See also BENEDICTINES (O.S.B.).

Bauman, Albert, O.S.B. "Adelhelm Odermatt, The Founder of Mount Angel Abbey," *Mount Angel Letter.* April 1984, Supplement, 1–8; June 1984, 2–5.
Murphy, Bernard, O.S.B. "Rt. Rev. Adelhelm Odermatt, O.S.B." *Pacific Star.* St. Benedict, Oreg., vol. 11, no. 1 (1920) 8–10.

HUGH FEISS, O.S.B.

ODIN, JEAN-MARIE (1800–70)

A Missionary from France

Archbishop. Jean-Marie Odin, C.M., was a French Vincentian missionary priest who became successively vice prefect apostolic of Texas, vicar apostolic of Texas, first bishop of Galveston, and second archbishop of New Orleans. Odin was born in February 25, 1800, in the tiny French hamlet of Hauteville, a settlement existing within the parish boundaries of nearby St. Martin d'Ambierle Church. Ambierle was situated in the western reaches of the Archdiocese of Lyons. He was the seventh of ten children of Jean Odin and Caludine-Marie Odin.

Jean-Marie Odin

Baptized on the day of his birth, likely in his home, Jean-Marie early on in his life took advantage of what elementary schooling and tutoring was available to him in and about the Hauteville-Ambierle region. At age thirteen, Odin received the sacrament of confirmation from Joseph Cardinal Fesch, archbishop of Lyons and uncle of the emperor Napoleon Bonaparte. Fesch was to become a strong supporter of the future missionary to Texas until the cardinal-archbishop's death in the mid-1830s. In 1814 Jean-Marie Odin commenced his seminary training in the *petits séminaires* of the Archdiocese of Lyons. Subsequently, in 1820 he entered the Sulpician *grand séminaire* of St. Irenaeus at Lyons, where in the spring of 1822 he was raised to the subdeaconate.

Shortly thereafter, in May of that same year, he left his native France to labor as a missionary in the American Diocese of Louisiana and the Floridas. Bishop Louis William DuBourg, ordinary of that vast see, assigned Jean-Marie to the new St. Mary's of the Barrens Seminary, which the Congregation of the Mission (the Vincentians) had established at Perryville, Missouri, back in 1818. Raised to the deaconate at the Barrens Seminary on October 12, 1822, Odin was ordained to the priesthood by Bishop DuBourg at the Barrens Seminary on May 4, 1823. In the meantime, Odin had joined the Vincentians, taking his final vows in 1825.

Fr. Odin labored for the next seventeen years at the Barrens Seminary as a professor of theology, secretary to the rector, and ultimately rector himself. He also acted for a time as pastor of the local parish and confessor to a community of Sisters of Loretto established near the seminary. With all of this, he engaged in regular missionary activities throughout Missouri and Arkansas.

Texas and New Orleans

Called to Texas in May 1840, Odin arrived there (at Linnville on Lavaca Bay) with three other Vincentians on July 13. For more than twenty years, from the date of his disembarking at Linnville until early February 1861, Odin served the Catholics of that area. In the process, he built the base for the future of the Catholic Church in Texas. Named as vice prefect apostolic of Texas as he departed the Barrens Seminary for his new assignment in the spring of 1840, Odin was named vicar apostolic and bishop of Claudiopolis *in partibus infidelium* on July 16, 1841. Subsequently, in 1847, he was named bishop of Galveston, taking the reins of the new Diocese of Galveston that had been erected on May 4, 1847.

After spending those two decades bringing the Church's sacraments and catechesis to literally thousands of Catholics in Texas, building churches and assigning pastors, founding a college and a seminary, and recruiting priests, brothers, and nuns to his diocese, Odin was named to succeed the late Archbishop Antoine Blanc as the second archbishop of New Orleans in February 1861. He died back in France at his boyhood family home at Hauteville on May 25, 1870. He is buried at St. Martin d'Ambierle Church.

Bayard, Ralph, C.M. *Lone-Star Vanguard: The Catholic Re-Occupation of Texas (1838–1848).* St. Louis, 1945.

Castaneda, Carlos Eduardo. *Our Catholic Heritage in Texas, 1519–1936: Supplement, 1936–1950.* 7 vols. Austin, 1936–58.

Foley, Patrick. "Jean-Marie Odin, C.M., Missionary Bishop Extraordinaire of Texas." *Journal of Texas Catholic History and Culture* 1 (1990) 42–60.

Moore, James Talmadge. *Through Fire and Flood: The Catholic Church in Frontier Texas, 1836–1900.* College Station, 1992.

PATRICK FOLEY

O'FARRELL, JOHN ANDREW (1823–1900)

Businessman and Catholic activist. O'Farrell was born in County Tyrone, Ireland, on February 13, 1823, the second son of Andrew and Ellen O'Flaherty O'Farrell. John was educated in common schools, then went to sea when he was only fifteen years old. For many years he sailed over all the seas of the globe and "visited nearly every port in the civilized and barbarous nations of the world." He was in San Francisco when California was admitted to the union and by virtue of his presence there, became a citizen of the United States.

By this time, through his friendship with John Sutter, he became a prospector for gold. When mining was slack because of severely cold weather, he took to the sea again, was wounded in the Crimean War, then returned to California in 1853 to seek gold. Later he moved to Colorado where he discovered gold in 1860 in what became Leadville, one of the West's most famous mining camps.

In 1861 he was married to Mary Ann Chapman in Louisville, Kentucky. His bride remained in Philadelphia while John moved to Idaho Territory, where he built a log cabin home in what is now Boise, the state capital. When the cabin, which still stands as a local monument, was completed, Mary Ann moved to Idaho. There, in this primitive home, the devout couple welcomed priests coming and going in their missionary work. Boise's first Mass was offered there and plans for a church were made there. O'Farrell donated land for this church and willing soldiers at Fort Boise, many of whom were Catholics, assisted in building the church and providing money for its furnishings.

In the course of time, O'Farrell acquired vast sections of desert land, which were converted into farms by irrigation, which he promoted. As the principal founder of the city, he assisted in its design and growth. As a Catholic, he was always generous to the Church and to the poor. After nearly forty years of happy marriage, Mary Ann died. Her death hastened the end of John, who died on May 22, 1900.

Catholic Sentinel, November 8, 1900.

French, Hiram T. *History of Idaho.* Chicago, 1914, 2:662–65.

WILFRED P. SCHOENBERG, S.J.

O'GARA, CUTHBERT (1886–1968)

Passionist missionary and bishop of Yuanling, China. Martin O'Gara was born April 1, 1886, in Ottawa, Canada, to Judge Martin and Margaret Bowes O'Gara. He received an A.B. degree in 1910 from Ottawa University and a baccalaureate in canon law from the Grand Séminaire in Montreal in 1913. Given the name Cuthbert on his October 18, 1914, Passionist profession, he was ordained on May 26, 1915, as a member of St. Paul of the Cross province in West Hoboken, New Jersey.

O'Gara taught theology, canon law, and sacred Scripture to Passionist seminarians (1917–24). In 1921, responding to the 1919 mission encyclical *Maximum Illud,* the Passionists established a mission in Hunan, China.

O'Gara's life exemplifies the challenge of being a foreign Catholic missionary in twentieth-century China. Sent in 1924 as a member of the third missionary band, he directed the minor seminary in Shenchow, Hunan (1925–27), served as vicar delegate (1925–29), and was missioned to Wuki, Hunan (1927–30). Exhibiting administrative and pastoral leadership, on February 12, 1930, he was appointed prefect apostolic of Shenchow [later Yuanling]. He was named vicar apostolic of Yuanling and titular bishop of Elis on May 28, 1934. On October 28, 1934, he was consecrated a bishop by apostolic delegate Marius Zanin.

Chinese political insecurity, competing warlords, Nationalist-Communist anti-Western sentiments, and Japanese encroachment forced the Yuanling diocese to emphasize refugee work, medical care, and catechetical outreach from the 1930s until 1945. O'Gara coordinated the efforts of approximately sixty Passionist priests, Sisters of Charity of Convent Station, New Jersey, and Sisters of St. Joseph of Baden, Pennsylvania, in some fifteen mission stations, several schools, two hospitals, and thirteen refugee camps serving some 100,000 people. *Sign,* a Catholic magazine published by the Passionists, promoted the mission effort.

He was imprisoned by the Japanese in Hong Kong in 1941. Later, *Sign* gave him the title "stretcher-bearer bishop" for his aid to victims of Japanese bombings in Yuanling. On May 15, 1947, O'Gara became bishop of the new Yuanling diocese. His priority was to develop a native clergy. In 1948 Fr. John Nien was ordained (he died under the Communists in 1960). In 1950 Fr. Bede Chang was ordained (in 1995 he was still a priest in Yuanling). By 1950, the Communists controlled Yuanling. They arrested O'Gara in 1951. In 1953 the Canadian government helped gain his release; the Chinese expelled him and *Hsin Hunan Pao* [*New Hunan Paper*], Changsha, Hunan, declared him an "imperialist."

Many Passionists and Catholics respected O'Gara because he endured Japanese and Communist imprisonment. Upon O'Gara's return to the United States, Bishop Fulton J. Sheen proclaimed O'Gara "a dry martyr"—one who had suffered martyrdom without shedding blood. After 1953, O'Gara became a strident anti-Communist and a participant in the American Catholic China Lobby: a loosely defined interest group with a pro-Nationalist, anti-Communist agenda. On November 29, 1954, O'Gara gave the invocation at the pro-Joseph McCarthy rally at Madison Square Garden, New York, three days before the senator was censured by the United States Senate. O'Gara remained a popular speaker at Catholic religious events, rallies, and banquets. He died on May 13, 1968, in Union City, New Jersey, and Bishop Sheen preached at his funeral.

See also PASSIONISTS (C.P.).

Caulfield, Caspar, C.P. *Only a Beginning.* Passionist Press, 1990.

Rev. Cuthbert O'Gara, File: 17 AEV-40, Record Group 25, Volume 2251, in the National Archives of Canada.

Pendergast, Carita, S.C. *Havoc in Hunan.* College of St. Elizabeth Press, 1991.

Sheen, Fulton J. "Wet Martyrs and Dry Martyrs." *Worldmission* 4 (Fall 1953) 259–75.

Sign magazine (1921–82).

ROBERT E. CARBONNEAU, C.P.

O'GORMAN, THOMAS (1843–1921)

Second bishop of Sioux Falls, South Dakota. Thomas O'Gorman was born on May 1, 1843, in Boston, Massachusetts. His family moved to Chicago shortly thereafter where his father, John, met Richard Ireland, the father of the future archbishop of St. Paul, John Ireland. Both families moved to St. Paul, then the capital of the Minnesota Territory, in 1852.

Thomas O'Gorman

O'Gorman was introduced to Bishop Joseph Crétin of St. Paul who arranged for O'Gorman's enrollment in the minor seminary in Meximieux, Ain, France. The seminarian continued his studies at the Marist Fathers' novitiate house in Montbel, France, and was later ordained in St. Paul by Bishop Thomas Langdon Grace on November 5, 1865.

The young Fr. O'Gorman, twenty-two years old, was assigned to Rochester, Minnesota, where he took charge of a churchless parish and several missions. He quickly developed a national reputation as an outstanding preacher and was invited to preach in various churches along the East Coast, including St. Patrick's Cathedral, New York.

O'Gorman became instructor at The Catholic University of America in Washington, D.C. In 1895 his much-touted volume—*A History of the Roman Catholic Church in the United States*—was published.

Just a year earlier, O'Gorman had written a draft of *Longinqua Oceani,* the encyclical of Pope Leo XIII concerning Catholicism in the U.S.A. Pope Leo told one American cardinal: "O'Gorman helped me a great deal. He gave me many notes, but now I must go over them and make them my own. I shall give them another coloring, but the substance will be there."

On May 3, 1896, O'Gorman was installed as successor to Bishop Martin Marty as bishop of Sioux Falls. He worked diligently to secure additional priests to minister on the prairie. The new bishop's diocese extended throughout all of South Dakota until July 28, 1902, when Pope Leo created the Diocese of Lead.

O'Gorman was well known for his ability as pastor, preacher, historian, and churchman. His tenure saw the erection of schools and churches, including St. Joseph Cathedral in Sioux Falls, which was designed by the Paris-trained architect (who was also the master builder of the magnificent St. Paul Cathedral), Emmanuel L. Masqueray.

O'Gorman served as bishop of Sioux Falls for over twenty-five years. In 1920 he petitioned the apostolic delegate for an auxiliary bishop; the request was denied. O'Gorman died on September 13, 1921. Former President William Howard Taft sent condolences, while the editor of the local newspaper praised O'Gorman, stressing that the prelate possessed an "abiding love and respect he had won from all citizens without regard to class or creed."

The relationship of Thomas O'Gorman and John Ireland is still noted today. From childhood friends to seminarians to brother bishops, the two men remained close. O'Gorman was thought to have been generally sympathetic to many of the viewpoints of Ireland.

See also SOUTH DAKOTA, CATHOLIC CHURCH IN.

Duratschek, M. Claudia, O.S.B. *Builders of God's Kingdom: The History of the Catholic Church in South Dakota.* Yankton, 1979.

Karolevitz, Robert F. *With Faith, Hope and Tenacity: The First One Hundred Years of the Catholic Diocese of Sioux Falls 1889–1989.* Mission Hill, 1989.

CHARLES M. MANGAN

O'GRADY, JOHN (1886–1966)

Priest, educator, social reformer. John O'Grady was born at Annagh Feakle, County Clare, Ireland, on March 31, 1886. Raised in Ireland, he attended All Hallows College in Dublin beginning in 1902. Ordained on June 24, 1909, for service in the Diocese of Omaha in the United States, he served three years as an assistant pastor at the Cathedral in Omaha and then in the fall of 1912 was sent for graduate studies to The Catholic University of America. There he studied under Msgr. William Kerby, one of the leading Catholic social reformers of the day. Receiving his doctorate in 1915, O'Grady was immediately appointed an instructor in economics at the university. He remained on the faculty of The Catholic University of America until his retirement and served as the first dean of the School of Social Work from 1934 to 1938.

A prolific writer, O'Grady produced numerous articles for the leading Catholic journals of the day and five books, including a history of Catholic Charities in the United States. He served as the editor of *Catholic Charities Review* from 1920 until his retirement in 1961. As secretary of the Committee on Reconstruction and After War Activities of the National Catholic War Council, he persuaded John A. Ryan to produce the document known as *The Bishops' Program for Social Reconstruction* (1919). In 1920 O'Grady became the secretary of the National Conference of Catholic Charities and held this position for the next forty-one years. He traveled widely throughout the United States, helping to develop many of the diocesan agencies and training their leaders. He felt strongly that Catholic Charities should play an important role in achieving social reform. While a proponent of the principle of subsidiarity, he nevertheless believed that there were areas which demanded the intervention of the federal government. He served as a lobbyist for the National Conference of Catholic Charities for slightly more than forty years, and in such a position he not only defended Catholic interests but provided Catholic input and support for such legislation as social security, public housing, and national health insurance. Arthur Altmeyer, the writer of the social security legislation that was passed in 1935, called O'Grady "one of the most valuable supporters of the bill," and expressed his belief that O'Grady "influenced a great many members of Congress to support the bill who otherwise would have opposed it." In the post-World War II period O'Grady was active in the settlement of refugees and played an important role in the founding of the International Conference of Catholic Charities in 1951, serving as vice president of this organization for ten years. In such a capacity he was the conference's representative to the United Nations and served as a consultant to the Economic and Social Council of the U.N. He represented the International Conference in a number of African countries and was personally commended by Pope John XXIII in 1959 for the leadership that he had given to the foundation and development of a number of projects in Africa. He died in Washington, D.C., on January 2, 1966.

Tifft, Thomas W. "Towards a More Humane Social Policy: The Work and Influence of Monsignor John O'Grady." Ph.D. dissertation, The Catholic University of America, 1979.

THOMAS W. TIFFT

O'HARA, EDWIN (1881–1956)

Bishop, educator, social activist. Edwin Vincent O'Hara was born on September 6, 1881, to Irish immigrant parents Owen and Margaret Nugent O'Hara in Lanesboro, Minnesota. The youngest of six children, he attended local public schools until the age of seventeen, when he matriculated at the College of St. Thomas in St. Paul, Min-

Edwin O'Hara

nesota (which had been founded by Archbishop John Ireland in 1885 primarily to educate future clergy). In the fall of 1900, O'Hara entered St. Paul Seminary under the sponsorship of the Diocese of Winona. At the seminary, he excelled academically, publishing two articles in the *Catholic University Bulletin* of 1903 and translating from the German, Eberhard Dennert's *At the Deathbed of Darwinism,* which was reviewed in *The New York Times* in 1904. The reviewer referred to the translator as "Doctor O'Hara of St. Paul's Seminary." He later wrote a précis of Dennert's work that appeared in *Catholic World.* In that same year, O'Hara transferred to the Archdiocese of Oregon City on the recommendation of a close priest friend in that archdiocese and his own brother John, who edited Oregon City's diocesan newspaper. O'Hara was ordained to the priesthood by Archbishop Ireland on June 10, 1905.

Priest and Educator

For his first assignment, O'Hara was appointed by Archbishop Alexander Christie as assistant pastor of the pro-cathedral of the Immaculate Conception in Oregon City. He was extremely dedicated to his pastoral duties, which included teaching in a local high school, serving as a part-time hospital chaplain, forming the Catholic Educational Association of Oregon in 1907, conducting the first Diocesan Teachers' Institute, and serving as diocesan superintendent of schools from 1906 to 1920. In addition, O'Hara became known for his apologetical writings against the anti-Catholic bigotry which flourished in Oregon at that time. In 1911 his *Pioneer History of Oregon* demonstrated that Catholics were among the first settlers of Oregon and were neither newcomers nor threats to the state's heritage. He also contributed entries to the *Catholic Encyclopedia*. After a period of recovery from bronchitis, O'Hara spent one semester at The Catholic University of America, and, upon returning to Oregon, was appointed rector of the pro-cathedral in Oregon City.

O'Hara soon gained national prominence as a promoter of social justice. In 1912 the Oregon Consumers' League established a committee, with O'Hara as its chairman, to study the working conditions of women in Oregon and to lobby for corrective legislation. The committee drafted a bill (written, after much consultation, by O'Hara himself) which became Oregon's minimum wage law for women, and he was appointed the chairman of the Oregon Industrial Welfare Commission to enforce the provisions of the law. The law was upheld as constitutional by the Oregon State Supreme Court in the case *Stettler v. O'Hara* in 1914 and also by the United States Supreme Court in 1917. For his work, O'Hara was granted an honorary doctorate of laws from the University of Notre Dame.

In 1922, under the sponsorship of the Scottish-rite Masons, a referendum was placed on the ballot that would have required all children to attend public schools. O'Hara, as archdiocesan superintendent of schools, organized the Catholic Civil Rights Association to attack the bill as a denial of basic American rights. After the measure passed by 14,000 votes, he advised Archbishop Christie to conduct legal proceedings (among many possible courses of action), as he was convinced the bill was unconstitutional. A team of lawyers, with O'Hara as its priest-counselor, argued the case in the United States District Court in Oregon, which declared the Oregon Compulsory School Law to be unconstitutional in 1924. The state appealed the decision, and the United States Supreme Court upheld the lower court's decision in the case *Pierce v. Society of Sisters* the next year, declaring the child as "not the mere creature of the state."

Rural Life Bureau

O'Hara became best known for his work in the area of rural sociology. Upon returning from service as an Army chaplain in France in World War I, he was appointed pastor of a rural parish in Eugene, Oregon. He supported the Newman Club at the University of Oregon at Eugene, offering needed social and religious activities for Catholics at the secular university. O'Hara also worked to provide religious education for the many children who lived in remote areas and could not attend the parish school. He opened summer religious vacation schools, where children received two weeks of intensive religious instruction. During the regular school months, O'Hara prepared and mailed catechism lessons, exercises, and tests which families living in remote areas completed and returned to the church. They were then corrected by the pastor's staff and sent back to the families along with the next lesson.

In addition, in 1920, at the National Catholic Welfare Conference, he proposed the establishment of a Rural Life Bureau to provide dioceses with information and advice concerning rural economic and social work and became its first chairman in 1921. He also published *A Program of Catholic Rural Action* (1922) and *The Church and the Country Community* (1927), both of which gained national attention for his analysis of rural life and his proposals for the Church's ministry in these areas.

Bishop

On October 28, 1930, O'Hara was consecrated the second bishop of Great Falls, Montana, where he devoted much time to promoting the Confraternity of Christian Doctrine. He also established a Rocky Mountain and Pacific Coast Confraternity and was instrumental in the foundation of a national headquarters for the confraternity at The Catholic University of America. O'Hara's interest in catechetics involved him in the areas of biblical translation and catechetical reform. In 1936 he organized a committee of theologians and biblical scholars to discuss a revised English translation of the Bible, helped form the Catholic Biblical Association, and was instrumental in the establishment of the publication of the *Catholic Biblical Quarterly* in 1939. In addition, O'Hara chaired the committee of bishops which revised the Baltimore Catechism in 1941.

On April 15, 1939, O'Hara was appointed bishop of Kansas City, Missouri, where he led the expansion of the diocese by building forty-two churches, fourteen convents, sixteen grade schools, six high schools, and two colleges. He also opened the first racially integrated health facility in Kansas City in 1955. The previous year, on June 29, 1954, he was made a personal archbishop. O'Hara died on September 11, 1956, in Milan, Italy, while traveling to the International Congress of the Restored Liturgy in Assisi, Italy.

See also CATHOLIC RURAL LIFE MOVEMENT.

Dolan, Timothy M. *Some Seed Fell on Good Ground.* Washington, D.C., 1992.

Shaw, J. G. *Edwin Vincent O'Hara, American Prelate.* New York, 1957.

KEVIN J. O'REILLY

O'HARA, GERALD P. (1895–1963)

Bishop and papal diplomat. Gerald P. O'Hara was born in Green Ridge, Pennsylvania, on May 4, 1895, the son of Dr. Patrick J. and Margaret Carney O'Hara. O'Hara grew up in Philadelphia and attended its parochial schools. He also attended St. Charles Borromeo Seminary in Overbrook. He was ordained in Rome on April 3, 1920, while studying for a doctorate in canon and civil law at the Pontifical Roman Seminary. Upon completion of his studies in 1924, he returned to Philadelphia as secretary to Dennis Cardinal Dougherty.

He was appointed auxiliary bishop of Philadelphia in 1929 and was installed as bishop of Savannah on January 15, 1936. During his Savannah episcopate his accomplishments were many, including the establishment of fifteen parishes and missions; building of churches, schools, and rectories; and improving recreational facilities for children. Our Lady of Perpetual Help Free Cancer Home in Atlanta and the St. Mary's Hospital in Athens were opened. Religious orders of men and women were brought to the diocese to assist with the growing population. A trailer-chapel was purchased to serve the vast rural areas of the state.

On January 5, 1937, the Diocese of Savannah became the Diocese of Savannah-Atlanta with the new Atlanta parish of Christ the King designated as co-cathedral. In 1956 Georgia would become two dioceses with the canonical erection of the Diocese of Atlanta on November 8. Thereafter, O'Hara continued as bishop of Savannah, while Francis E. Hyland became the first bishop of Atlanta. Hyland had been auxiliary bishop of the Diocese of Savannah-Atlanta since 1949.

In 1947 Pope Pius XII appointed Bishop O'Hara regent of the apostolic nunciature in Rumania. Outspoken against Communism, O'Hara was placed under house arrest and finally expelled from Bucharest July 4, 1950. The personal title of archbishop was given to him eight days later. From 1951 to 1954 he served as papal nuncio to Ireland. He was then appointed apostolic delegate to England. He resigned as bishop of Savannah November 11, 1959, and died in London on July 16, 1963.

See also GEORGIA, CATHOLIC CHURCH IN.

"Archbishop O'Hara: Death Claims Prelate in England." *The Georgia Bulletin,* July 18, 1963.

"Bishop O'Hara Elevated to Rank of Archbishop." *St. Anthony's Catholic News,* August 1950.

"Most Rev. Gerald P. O'Hara, D.D., J.U.D." *St. Anthony's Catholic News,* April 1945.

Savannah, Georgia. Diocese of Savannah Archives. Diocesan History Files.

____. Georgia Historical Society. M. H. and D. B. Floyd Papers.

"Warm 'Welcome Home' Is Extended to His Excellency." *St. Anthony's Catholic News,* October 1950.

ANTHONY R. DEES

O'HARA, JOHN FRANCIS CARDINAL (1888–1960)

Cardinal, archbishop. O'Hara was born in Ann Arbor, Michigan, on May 1, 1888, the son of teacher, newspaper editor, and lawyer John Walter O'Hara and Ellen Thornton. He attended St. Charles parochial school in Peru, Indiana, where the family had relocated. He then continued his education at the Jesuit Collegio de Sagrado Corazon when his father was appointed United States consul in Montevideo, Uruguay. Two years later, O'Hara was serving as secretary to his father in Santos, Brazil.

John F. Cardinal O'Hara

In 1909 O'Hara was tutoring students in Spanish at Notre Dame University in return for tuition and board waivers. He entered the Holy Cross Father's novitiate three years later and was ordained a priest on September 9, 1916. At The Catholic University of America he studied history, spent a summer at the Wharton School of Commerce in Philadelphia, and ended up back at Notre Dame as dean of the Commerce Department, dormitory counselor, and prefect of religion in 1917.

Early Years

At Notre Dame, O'Hara insulated the students from books he considered objectionable, railed against jazz music, and prohibited students from frequenting South Bend dance parlors and movie theaters. In 1933 he became the vice president, and then in the following year, president of the university. He was instrumental in bringing famous scholars in many fields from Europe to teach at his school. He founded institutes, museums, and laboratories. In 1935 he sponsored a convocation to celebrate the inauguration of Philippine president Manuel Quezon at which Carlos Romulo, Cardinal George Mundelein, and President Franklin D. Roosevelt were guest speakers.

Through his friendship with Archbishop Francis Spellman, O'Hara was made auxiliary bishop of the Military Ordinariate on January 12, 1940. After he took up his new residence at St. Cecilia parish in New York City, O'Hara became involved in a neighborhood settlement house for Puerto Ricans called Casita Maria. During World War II, O'Hara was busy visiting military installations, supervising the chaplains corps, and keeping an eye on the religious life of the servicemen.

When O'Hara became bishop of Buffalo in May 1945, his energies became concentrated on the expansion of Catholic school facilities there, but he took time to exhort Catholics to refrain from reading books on the Index of Forbidden Books and from viewing morally objectionable movies. His staunch anti-Communism was evident in his 1946 condemnation of Henry Wallace, Truman's secretary of commerce, who was in favor of ignoring Soviet conquests in Eastern Europe. O'Hara also was cool to labor demands, anything which smacked of socialized medicine, and federal aid to education.

Archbishop of Philadelphia

In November 1951 O'Hara became archbishop of Philadelphia. O'Hara was a big change from his predecessor, Dennis Cardinal Dougherty. He was an outsider in a diocese where most of the priests, and the last two ordinaries, had been products of the local diocesan seminary. Also, he was not a secular priest like most of them. Unlike Dougherty, he was never in good health and he had an unusual ability of putting people at ease.

In many ways, O'Hara liberalized policies at the diocesan seminary. He allowed seminarians to smoke on campus, to drive cars, and to take summer jobs—all of which had been forbidden by Dougherty. He also opened the seminary to dioceses other than Philadelphia and Harrisburg, built a new swimming pool, and began in 1952 to host an annual open house.

As in Buffalo, O'Hara relied a great deal on the diocesan Board of Consultors for advice. He retained many of Dougherty's appointees, the most notable of whom was auxiliary Bishop J. Carroll McCormick, Dougherty's nephew, who remained in Philadelphia until 1960 when he was promoted to the Diocese of Altoona. O'Hara continued episcopal support for the Confraternity of Christian Doctrine, and he expanded the operations of the

Catholic Youth Organization. O'Hara was ideologically similar to Dougherty in his resistance to movies which contained obscenity or glorified crime.

In many ways, O'Hara was an innovator and a centralizer. He created the Archbishop's Committee for Christian Home and Family, which promoted motherhood as a spiritual vocation and supported family efforts in the religious education of children. In 1953 he inaugurated the annual blessing of the babies and set aside the feast of the Holy Family as Family Communion Sunday. He brought all of the women's charitable organizations into the Ladies of Charity. All appeals for missionary aid were centralized. He opened a Catholic Information Center in Philadelphia, merged parish banking into a centralized system, and created in 1954 the Institutional Procurement Service, a centralized purchasing agency, which provided schools, parishes, and diocesan employees with discounts on a wide variety of commodities.

O'Hara showed special concern for Native Americans, Hispanics, and African Americans. He served on the national Catholic Board of Negro and Indian Missions and supported the work of the Marquette League for Catholic Indian Missions. In 1954 he began the practice of sending two Philadelphia priests each year to Puerto Rico to prepare them for work among Philadelphia's growing Spanish-speaking population. That same year he opened the new center, Casa del Carmen. Auxiliary bishop Joseph McShea was named Archdiocesan Coordinator of Puerto Rican Affairs. O'Hara supported parish programs designed to evangelize among African Americans, and he encouraged the activities of the Catholic Interracial Council, the Martin de Porres Foundation, and Mercy Technical Institute.

Expanding Philadelphia's Catholic institutional system was an important part of O'Hara's agenda. He feared the influence of secular society on Catholics. Accordingly, he rejected any kind of federal influence on Catholic education or social institutions. He created 55 new parishes, built 61 new parochial schools, and renovated many others. He built 14 new diocesan, and 5 private high schools, and 2 new colleges. Two new wings were added to Fitzgerald-Mercy Hospital in Darby; a new hospital, Holy Redeemer, was opened in 1959 in Meadowbrook; Sacred Heart Hospital in Chester was dedicated in 1959; and new quarters for St. Edmund's Home for Crippled Children, founded in 1917, were dedicated in 1957. From 1953 to 1956, O'Hara battled Pennsylvania State Department of Welfare attempts to change adoption procedures that he thought would jeopardize the religious upbringing of the adoptees.

Cardinal

O'Hara was made a member of the College of Cardinals on December 15, 1958, even though his fondest wish had been to be allowed to retire and spend his last years at

Notre Dame. At the Second Vatican Council, O'Hara's interventions were always in line with tradition. He emphasized the doctrine of the Mystical Body of Christ as the key to Christian unity. He urged the continued explanation of infallibility. He held up the Church as a universal institution which should serve all the world's people with their varying needs, customs, and languages. This Church, he argued, should speak plainly on modern colonialism and imperialism, as well as on Communism and other false philosophies. It should be candid on relations with non-Catholics both in Catholic and pluralistic countries. It should state unequivocally what it believed to be proper Church-state relations, especially in countries where separation was a requirement of civil law.

O'Hara recommended that Pope Pius X's decree against Modernism, *Lamentabili,* be reviewed and confirmed so that it could be used against modern errors. Yet, he also proposed that the *Index of Forbidden Books* be adjusted to today's requirements and bishops be given wider power to permit the reading and owning of prohibited books. He wanted Latin kept in the Mass and the breviary, but he also wanted wider permission for celebrating Mass in places other than churches. He wanted the Church's teaching on birth control and the evil of divorce reemphasized and artificial birth control rejected.

O'Hara suffered from many physical maladies during his years in Philadelphia. He was frequently incapacitated from fulfilling public functions. On August 28, 1960, after painful surgery during which general anesthesia could not be administered, Cardinal O'Hara died. His will directed that he be buried in the Holy Cross community cemetery at the University of Notre Dame.

See also NOTRE DAME, UNIVERSITY OF; PENNSYLVANIA, CATHOLIC CHURCH IN.

Cardinal O'Hara Papers, Philadelphia Archdiocesan Historical Research Center, Wynnewood, Pennsylvania.

Carroll, Daniel B. "The O'Hara Years." *The History of the Archdiocese of Philadelphia,* ed. James F. Connelly. Philadelphia, 1976, 419–72.

_____. "John F. O'Hara, C.S.C., Military Delegate." *Records of the American Catholic Historical Society of Philadelphia* 64 (March 1953) 23–28.

McAvoy, Thomas T. *Father O'Hara of Notre Dame, the Cardinal-Archbishop of Philadelphia.* Notre Dame, Indiana, 1967.

_____. "John F. O'Hara, C.S.C., and Notre Dame." *Records of the American Catholic Historical Society of Philadelphia* 64 (March 1953) 3–22.

O'Donnell, George E. "John F. O'Hara, C.S.C., Archbishop of Philadelphia." *Records of the American Catholic Historical Society of Philadelphia* 64 (March 1953) 35–42.

Smith, Leo R. "John F. O'Hara, C.S.C., Bishop of Buffalo." *Records of the American Catholic Historical Society of Philadelphia* 64 (March 1953) 29–34.

JOSEPH J. CASINO

OHIO, CATHOLIC CHURCH IN

Ohio was originally settled by various tribes of Native Americans such as the Eries and the Iroquois. The Treaty of Paris of 1763 gave the territory to the British who in turn ceded it to the United States in another Treaty of Paris twenty years later. It was only then that white settlers established permanent settlements in the state near Cincinnati, Chillicothe, Marietta, Cleveland, and Toledo. These early settlers were New Englanders, Scots, Germans, and Marylanders. Ohio was admitted to the Union in 1803 as the seventeenth state.

Catholic Beginnings

There were sporadic efforts of French missionaries to minister in the area prior to 1800. The Jesuit Joseph de Bonnechamps accompanied Celeron de Blainville on an expedition into the area in 1749, and another Jesuit, Armand de la Richardie, built a chapel in the Sandusky area in 1751. In 1790 French Catholics settled at Gallipolis in southwestern Ohio and were served for very short periods by such priests as Peter Joseph Didier, Stephen Badin, and Peter Barrières. In 1795 Fr. Edmund Burke of Quebec opened a short-lived mission at Maumee (near Toledo).

The first permanent roots of Catholicism are associated with the arrival of Jacob Dittoe who together with his brother-in-law, John Finck, settled in the town of Middleton, between Zanesville and Lancaster, in 1805. They renamed the town Somerset and soon petitioned Bishop John Carroll of Baltimore for a priest to be sent to the area. Dittoe even went so far as to offer to donate 320 acres of land for a chapel and parish house. The Dominican priest Edward Fenwick, who would eventually be called the "Apostle of Ohio," located the Dittoe clan in October 1808 and found that there were about ten Catholic families in the area. Fenwick continued to visit the area periodically after 1808 and built the first permanent Catholic chapel in the state at Somerset on December 6, 1818. The chapel was dedicated to St. Joseph.

Diocese and Archdiocese of Cincinnati

Because of the increasing number of Catholics in the Ohio region, the Diocese of Cincinnati was created on June 19, 1821, with Edward Fenwick as the first bishop. The territory of the new diocese was contiguous with the civil boundaries of the State of Ohio. Michigan and the eastern part of the Old Northwest Territory were temporarily attached to the new diocese for purposes of administration. Approximately 6,000 Catholics were scattered across this broad territory. Fenwick proved to be quite energetic as a bishop and, in addition to engaging in considerable missionary work himself, he built the first cathedral, opened a seminary, and even founded a newspaper, the *Catholic Telegraph,* to combat anti-Catholic propaganda.

When Fenwick died in 1832, he was succeeded by the president of Mt. St. Mary Seminary in Emmitsburg, Maryland, John Baptist Purcell, who would serve as bishop until his death on July 4, 1883, although he would resign all administration to his coadjutor, William H. Elder, in 1880. It was during the latter years of Purcell's reign that the archdiocese underwent a severe financial crisis as a result of a banking operation run by Purcell's brother, the Rev. Edward Purcell. Legal action ensued in state and local courts and, in order to supplement the means for paying creditors, voluntary donations were solicited from priests and people of the archdiocese and from other dioceses throughout the United States. The crisis was a source of grave scandal to many and not only hindered evangelization efforts but limited the growth of the archdiocese down to the First World War. Steady growth has occurred since that time. In 1996 the Archdiocese of Cincinnati comprised nineteen counties in the southwestern part of Ohio and had a Catholic population of 542,000 out of a total population of 2,886,700.

New Dioceses

The Diocese of Cincinnati was raised to the status of a metropolitan see in 1850 and in 1996 there were five suffragan sees:

(1) The Diocese of Cleveland was erected on April 23, 1847, with Amadeus Rappe as the first bishop. In 1996 the diocese comprised eight counties in the north-central part of the state. Cleveland is the largest of Ohio's dioceses in terms of the number of Catholics. Out of a total population of 2,795,813 there were 813,460 Catholics.

(2) The Diocese of Columbus came into existence on March 3, 1868, and the auxiliary bishop of Cincinnati, Sylvester H. Rosecrans, a convert to the faith, was appointed as the first bishop. Although Columbus is the second smallest diocese in the province in terms of population, it covers the largest geographical area, embracing twenty-three counties and 11,310 square miles. In 1996 there were 207,036 Catholics out of a total population of 2,145,693.

(3) A split-off from the Diocese of Cleveland, the Diocese of Toledo was created on April 15, 1910. It covers nineteen counties in northwestern Ohio. Originally the diocese was administered by Bishop James Farrelly of Cleveland until Joseph Schrembs was appointed the first bishop on August 11, 1911. In 1996 there were 319,778 Catholics out of a total population of 1,479,041.

(4) Also, split off from the Diocese of Cleveland, the Diocese of Youngstown was formed on May 15, 1943, and comprises six counties in the northeastern part of the state. The auxiliary bishop of Cleveland, James A. McFadden, became the first bishop. The Catholic population of the diocese was 276,395 out of a total population of 1,224,866.

(5) The smallest of Ohio's dioceses, the Diocese of Steubenville, was erected in November 1944. Formerly part of the Diocese of Columbus, the Diocese of Steubenville covers thirteen counties and presently has a population of 46,724 Catholics out of a total population of 511,607. John King Mussio, the chancellor of the Archdiocese of Cincinnati, was appointed the first bishop on March 16, 1945, and served as the ordinary until his retirement on October 11, 1977.

In summary, in 1995 Roman Catholics composed almost 20 percent of the population of the state of Ohio—2,205,339 out of a total population of 11,048,720.

In addition to Latin-Rite Catholics, the state of Ohio has a considerable number of Eastern-rite Catholics, especially in the Cleveland area. On March 22, 1968, the Holy See erected the Byzantine Eparchy of Parma which embraces most of the Byzantine Ruthenian-rite Catholics in Ohio and throughout the Midwest. The chancellor of the Byzantine Diocese of Passaic, New Jersey, the Rev. Emil J. Mihalik, was appointed the first bishop, a position which he held until his death on January 27, 1984. The Catholic population of the diocese is 13,500, many of whom live in the state of Ohio.

Several of Ohio's bishops have moved on to larger sees and have eventually been raised to the rank of cardinal, namely, Samuel Stritch of Chicago (bishop of Toledo, 1921–30), James Hickey of Washington (bishop of Cleveland, 1974–80), and Joseph Bernardin of Chicago (archbishop of Cincinnati, 1972–82). In addition, several Ohio priests have also been created cardinals: Edward Mooney and John Dearden of Detroit, and John Krol of Philadelphia were all priests of the Diocese of Cleveland. Several Ohio bishops have made important contributions on the national level. Archbishop Karl Alter served as the chairman of the Administrative Board of the National Catholic Welfare Conference, and Bishops James Malone of Youngstown and Anthony Pilla of Cleveland have been presidents of the National Conference of Catholic Bishops. When the National Catholic Welfare Conference was temporarily suppressed in 1922, it was Bishop Joseph Schrembs of Cleveland who played a vital role in the restoration of the organization.

Education

The province of Cincinnati has always been very supportive of Catholic education. Perhaps because of the strong Germanic influence in the state, the province's early bishops stressed the building of parochial schools and were strong backers of the education legislation of the Third Plenary Council of Baltimore. This commitment to Catholic education continues to this day. In 1995 Ohio had 456 Catholic elementary schools with 143,357 pupils and 79 high schools educating 43,831 students. In addition,

143,087 elementary and high school students were receiving religious education in other programs. There are also eleven Catholic colleges and universities in the state, the largest of which are John Carroll University in Cleveland, Xavier University in Cincinnati, and the University of Dayton which is also located in the Archdiocese of Cincinnati. Both the Archdiocese of Cincinnati and the Diocese of Cleveland have their own theological seminary and Columbus is the site of the Pontifical College Josephinum which is a seminary directly under the governance of the Holy See.

Numerous religious orders of both men and women have made and continue to make substantial contributions to Catholic life in Ohio. As early as 1826 three Colletine Poor Clares from Belgium conducted a school in Cincinnati and in 1829 Bishop Fenwick secured the services of four Sisters of Charity of Emmitsburg and four Dominican sisters for work in the diocese. The Sisters of Notre Dame de Namur, the Ursulines, the Sisters of Notre Dame of Cleveland, the Franciscans, the Sisters of the Humility of Mary, and numerous others have staffed schools and charitable institutions throughout the state. Religious orders of men such as the Jesuits, the Franciscans, the Marianists, the Marists, the Benedictines, and others have conducted universities, colleges, and high schools and have taken on parishes as part of their ministry.

During the nineteenth century Ohio was frequently the site of nativist activity. For example, it was in Cincinnati in December 1853 that an effort was made to lynch Archbishop Gaetano Bedini, the papal nuncio to Brazil, who was visiting the United States. The newspaper of the Archdiocese of Cincinnati, the *Catholic Telegraph,* was founded in 1831 to combat such anti-Catholic feeling. In Cleveland, *The Catholic Universe* (now *The Catholic Universe Bulletin*) was begun by Bishop Richard Gilmour in 1874 for the same purpose. The Ku Klux Klan was active in Ohio during the 1920s and beyond. Today Catholics hold a number of important elected positions in local and state governments and on the state's congressional delegation. Frank J. Lausche, a Catholic from Cleveland, served as governor of the state from 1945–47 and again from 1949–57. He was later a United States Senator. The present governor of Ohio, George Voinovich, is also a Catholic.

Like many "rust-belt" states Ohio has undergone its share of economic woes in recent years and this has impacted the state's dioceses to varying degrees. The Diocese of Steubenville has long struggled with severe economic problems and in recent years the Diocese of Youngstown has been particularly affected by changes in the steel industry. Ohio's bishops have traditionally been noted for their social consciousness and for their strong support for labor unions. In the same way, the dioceses of the province of Cincinnati have had a proud record of ministering to the poor, the unemployed, and those harmed by economic dislocation. Such ministry to the poor and commitment to social justice continue today.

See also FENWICK, EDWARD; PURCELL, JOHN BAPTIST; STRITCH, SAMUEL CARDINAL.

Brown, Francis F. *A History of the Roman Catholic Diocese of Steubenville, Ohio.* Volume I: *The Mussio Years (1945–1977).* Lewiston, New York, 1994.

The Church in Cincinnati, 1821–1971. Sesquicentennial booklet containing articles reprinted from the *Catholic Telegraph.*

Hamilton, Albert. *The Catholic Journey through Ohio.* Columbus, 1976.

Hartley, J. J., ed. *The Diocese of Columbus: History of Fifty Years, 1868–1918.* Columbus, 1918.

____. *History of the Diocese of Columbus, 1918–1943.* Columbus, 1943.

Hynes, Michael J. *History of the Diocese of Cleveland, 1847–1952.* Cleveland, 1953.

Jurgens, W. A. *A History of the Diocese of Cleveland.* Volume I: *The Prehistory of the Diocese to its Establishment in 1847.* Cleveland, 1980.

Lamott, J. H. *History of the Archdiocese of Cincinnati, 1821–1921.* New York, 1921.

THOMAS W. TIFFT

OKLAHOMA, CATHOLIC CHURCH IN

Early History

The Coronado expedition probably crossed through western Oklahoma in 1541, and a succession of Spanish and French explorers visited various parts of the present state from then until the nineteenth century. The Jesuit Charles Van Quickenborne, seeking contact with a part of the Osage tribe, was in the northeastern region in 1830. After 1850 missionaries from Kansas, Texas, and especially Fort Smith, Arkansas, made short forays into what by then was designated the Indian Territory. The first resident missionaries, however, were French Benedictine monks, refugees from the aftermath of the Franco-Prussian War, who arrived in 1875 by way of Louisiana.

The following year Roman officials created the prefecture apostolic of the Indian Territory. This appears to be the only prefecture ever established in what was at the time a United States territorial possession. Dom Isidore Robot, O.S.B., whom Pope Leo XIII named honorary abbot in 1878, was the first prefect (1876–87). The Benedictines established Sacred Heart Mission in the Potawatomi Nation in 1877. (Today this institution is St. Gregory's Abbey, at Shawnee, Oklahoma.)

The tribes that had originally counted the Oklahoma area as part of their homeland were the Osages, who were centered in western Missouri, and the Quapaws, who chiefly lived on the lower reaches of the Arkansas River; and both of these had had earlier contact with Catholic missionaries. The Osages were evangelized on their reservation in

Kansas by Jesuits from 1847 until 1872, when the tribe moved to its final home in what is now Oklahoma. The Quapaws, much reduced in numbers, settled south of the Kansas line in 1852, and some of their children also attended the Jesuit school at Osage Mission, Kansas.

Pressure from the expanding white population of the United States drove many Native American tribes west of the Mississippi, where they were assigned homes in the Indian Territory. This entity, created by Congress in 1834, at first comprised most of the region between the Mississippi and the Rockies; it steadily shrank, however, as new states and territories were carved from it, until by 1870 it consisted only of modern-day Oklahoma, minus the Panhandle. Sixty-seven tribes, or remnants of them, were eventually settled in the region.

Significant white settlement began on April 22, 1889, when some 50,000 home seekers poured onto a million acres that had not yet been assigned to any tribe. Other land runs followed as the government maneuvered, first to reduce the size of the reservations, and then to extinguish tribal title altogether. Oklahoma became the twentieth century's first newly admitted state on November 16, 1907.

Among those who flocked to this last frontier were a small number of Catholics. No ethnic group predominated among them, although small pockets of Italians, Poles, Germans, and Czechs developed over time. In 1891 the entire Catholic population was generously estimated at five thousand, or about 2 percent of the total.

Bishop Meerschaert

In 1891 the Benedictine prefecture was elevated to the rank of a vicariate, and a Belgian diocesan priest working in Mississippi, Theophile Meerschaert, was named bishop and vicar apostolic of the Indian Territory. His assigned residence was Guthrie, capital of the Oklahoma Territory—the area newly populated by white homesteaders.

Bishop Meerschaert faced three principal challenges: in personnel, finances, and the sheer physical distances he had to travel. He recruited priests and begged money in his homeland; in thirty-two years he made eleven trips to Europe. (He did little, however, to encourage native vocations. Only one Native American was ordained in his lifetime, and the first two white Oklahoma-born diocesans were not ordained until 1928, four years after his death.) As to distance, in 1894 a pastoral visit to a single mission at the western end of the Oklahoma Panhandle involved a round-trip of sixteen hundred miles by train and buckboard through Kansas, Colorado, and the New Mexico Territory.

Although Native American evangelization was a nominal priority, lack of missionary manpower, uncertainty as to aims and methods, and the cultural disorientation of the tribes themselves resulted in few lasting conversions. A sizable chain of Indian mission schools, begun by the Benedictines, was carried on under Meerschaert. Many of these were funded by Mother Mary Katharine Drexel, a major benefactor of the Oklahoma Church, through the Catholic Bureau of Indian Missions. Enrollments at the schools were small—never more than a hundred—and by 1930 most of them had closed or been taken over by adjacent white parishes.

The Oil Industry

Oil exploration in Oklahoma began on the Osage reservation in 1896, and massive oil fields opened in the Tulsa area in 1901. Pennsylvania had until this time been the home of the oil industry, and many Pennsylvania oilmen who came to Oklahoma were Catholics, chiefly Irish. Because of the wealth oil brought to its developers, the Catholic population of Oklahoma tended to have political influence in the state that was disproportionate to its numbers.

Sacramental Wine Case

During the Meerschaert episcopate, an issue of national importance was what came to be known as the Sacramental Wine Case. This stemmed from the state legislature's decision in 1917 to ban manufacture or import of alcoholic beverages. No religious exemption was made, nor was one applied for. Not until priests found themselves actually unable to obtain altar wine for Mass, in fact, did the diocese appeal for relief from the courts. The state supreme court decided in the Church's favor in May 1918 in a case that was closely watched on both sides of the then-developing national debate over Prohibition.

In 1905, two years before statehood, the local church was given full status as the Diocese of Oklahoma, and Oklahoma City was named its diocesan seat. Bishop Meerschaert continued to lead the new jurisdiction until his death in 1924. Under his successor, Bishop Francis Clement Kelley, and with the spur provided by the rapid development of the oil industry in Oklahoma, plans were laid to create a separate diocese of Tulsa. These were frustrated, however, by the 1929 stock market crash and the onset of the Great Depression. To compensate, the Oklahoma Church was restyled in 1930 the Diocese of Oklahoma City and Tulsa.

Bishop Kelley

Bishop Kelley (1924–48) was Oklahoma's best-known prelate. As founder and president of the Catholic Church Extension Society (1905–24), he had been a highly influential churchman. He attended the Versailles Peace Conference on behalf of the exiled Mexican hierarchy and, through conversations there with the foreign minister of Italy, was instrumental in breaking the impasse between the Vatican and the Italian government over the Roman Question, leading to the creation ten years later of the

Vatican City State. He was a prolific author (seventeen books, dozens of articles in *Extension* magazine and elsewhere), and a superb orator.

This undeniable talent, however, proved inadequate to the realizing of his main program in Oklahoma, which was the increase of Catholic population through evangelization. At his death in 1948, Oklahoma Catholics were estimated to be approximately 73,000, out of a total population of two and a quarter million, or about 3 percent. This modest increase from 1891 appears largely based on the birthrate. The predominant culture of the state, expressed in its populist philosophy, had proven resistant to Catholic missionary inroads.

Bishop McGuinness

Bishop Kelley was followed in office by Bishop Eugene J. McGuinness, who had served as Kelley's vice president at the Extension Society. Consecrated bishop of Raleigh, North Carolina, in 1937, he came to Oklahoma in 1945 as apostolic administrator following Kelley's decline in health. Recognizing that there was no hope of evangelizing the state without a significant increase of Oklahoma-born vocations, he made recruitment to the priesthood and religious life the chief focus of his episcopate. Helped in part by the optimistic atmosphere of the postwar years, and by his own infectious enthusiasm, he achieved considerable success in this effort. In 1945 the diocese had but five seminarians. At McGuinness' death in December 1957 there were twenty-six, and ordination classes of ten or twelve a year were becoming commonplace. Given the comparatively large number of adult converts during this same period, it may be said that the 1950s marked an institutional high point of Oklahoma diocesan development.

Bishop Reed

Oklahoma's fourth bishop was the urbane and affable Victor J. Reed (1958–71), born in Indiana but an Oklahoman from the age of five. He inherited a diocesan church that was buoyed by its recent achievements and looking forward to further successes. These rising expectations, unrealistic to a degree and inflated further by the promised reforms of the Second Vatican Council, were severely affected by the presidential assassination and the country's involvement in Vietnam. By the middle 1960s, men and women were defecting from Catholic ministry in Oklahoma at a rate seemingly higher than in the country as a whole. (This phenomenon, however, came nearly to a stop in Oklahoma several years before it did in the rest of the nation.) Bishop Reed trusted and encouraged his priests and laity. Perhaps inevitably, he was hurt by the failure of many of them to meet his own expectations. He demonstrated his moral leadership on several occasions, most notably in 1967, when he became the first Catholic bishop publicly to protest the Vietnam War.

At forty-two, Bishop John R. Quinn was the American Church's youngest ordinary when he took office in Oklahoma City as fifth bishop in January 1972. He quickly showed himself to be a meticulous theologian and prudent administrator, deftly handling challenges from both ends of the spectrum of ecclesiastical and civil politics. It was no surprise that after only five years in Oklahoma, he was named archbishop of San Francisco. He was installed there in April 1977. A few months later he was elected president of the National Conference of Catholic Bishops.

New Province and Diocese

On December 19, 1972, it was announced that the long-awaited division of the Oklahoma diocese had taken place, and moreover, that a new ecclesiastical province had been created. Bishop Quinn was named the first archbishop of Oklahoma City, in which post he was installed on February 6, 1973. The Diocese of Little Rock (established in 1843) and the Diocese of Tulsa were designated as suffragan sees of the new province.

The founding bishop of the Diocese of Tulsa was Msgr. Bernard J. Ganter, ordained in 1952 as a priest of the Diocese of Galveston-Houston and, at the time of his appointment, chancellor of that see. He was ordained bishop by Cardinal-elect Luigi Raimondi, apostolic delegate to the United States, in Holy Family Cathedral on February 7, 1973. On the same day the new diocese, comprising some 51,000 Catholics in thirty-one of Oklahoma's seventy-seven counties, was formally established.

Bishop Ganter's nearly five years in eastern Oklahoma were spent principally in establishing the structures of the diocese. Under his direction a chancery was set up with departments to oversee the Church's educational mission, charitable functions, and programs of pastoral care. In 1975 he began a biweekly diocesan newspaper, *The Eastern Oklahoma Catholic*. Bishop Ganter became the third bishop of Beaumont, Texas, in December, 1977. He died in that office on October 9, 1993.

Archbishop Salatka

The second archbishop of Oklahoma City was Most Reverend Charles A. Salatka, born in Grand Rapids, Michigan, and ordained a priest of the Grand Rapids diocese in 1945. He had been auxiliary bishop of Grand Rapids (1962–68) and bishop of Marquette (1968–77) prior to his appointment in Oklahoma. As archbishop he initiated a planning process which led to a list of diocesan priorities (family life, youth ministry, and ministry to Hispanics were the first three), the sale of disposable property, and the consolidation of diocesan offices at the former seminary. He would gain a reputation for his stewardship of church assets, his compassion for troubled priests, and his opposition to the death penalty. When his resignation was announced in November 1992, he was the senior bishop, in years of ordination, in the United States.

Archbishop Beltran

Bishop Ganter was followed in Tulsa by Msgr. Eusebius J. Beltran, vicar general of the Archdiocese of Atlanta, Georgia. Bishop Beltran, a priest since 1960, was ordained bishop in Tulsa on April 20, 1978, by Archbishop Salatka. Bishop Beltran is credited with a significant expansion in the work of Catholic Charities, with maintaining the diocesan system of Catholic schools, and with a successful program of vocations recruitment. By 1993 the Diocese of Tulsa had seen thirty-five priests and forty-seven permanent deacons ordained for its service. In 1980 he established the Catholic Foundation of Eastern Oklahoma as a separate entity to provide for the future financial needs of the diocese. On January 22, 1993, Bishop Beltran was installed as third archbishop of Oklahoma City. His successor in Tulsa was Bishop Edward J. Slattery, a veteran, like Bishops Kelley and McGuinness, of the Catholic Church Extension Society. He was ordained by Pope John Paul II in Rome on January 6, 1994.

Notable Clergy

Three other bishops have roots in the diocese. Bishops Stephen A. Leven (auxiliary of San Antonio, Texas, 1957–69, ordinary of San Angelo, Texas, 1969–79, died 1983) and Charles A. Buswell (ordinary of Pueblo, Colorado, 1959–79) were Oklahoma natives. Bishop John J. Sullivan (ordinary of Grand Island, Nebraska, 1972–77, and of Kansas City, Missouri, 1977–93) was ordained an Oklahoma priest in 1944.

Another Oklahoma priest of note was Fr. William Henry Ketcham, director of the Bureau of Catholic Indian Missions, Washington, D.C., from 1901 to 1921, and a forceful advocate of Native American rights to Catholic education. Msgr. John J. Walde was the first Catholic priest in the United States to use radio as a forum for preaching Catholic doctrine; the weekly feature began in October 1925 and was broadcast uninterruptedly for forty-five years. Msgr. Don J. Kanaly organized the first American chapter of the Young Christian Workers in Ponca City, Oklahoma, in 1939; he was also instrumental in developing the program at the national level. Fr. Stanley F. Rother served thirteen years in the diocesan mission at Santiago Atitlan, Guatemala, culminating in his murder by forces of the Guatemalan regime on July 28, 1981.

Religious Orders

Among the more important religious communities to have labored in Oklahoma are the Benedictines: the monks of St. Gregory's Abbey, Shawnee, and the nuns of St. Joseph's Monastery, first located in Guthrie and now in Tulsa. St. Gregory's College, at present a coeducational junior college, has operated since 1877. The Benedictine nuns formerly ran secondary and collegiate institutions in Guthrie and Tulsa.

The Mexican revolution brought Carmelite priest refugees to Oklahoma in 1914. A diocesan sisterhood, the Carmelite Sisters of St. Therese, developed from their efforts in 1917. Also notable are the Sisters of Mercy, who established themselves in Oklahoma in 1884; their motherhouse is in Oklahoma City. Numerous other communities of religious men and women have ministered in the state. At present Oklahoma City and Tulsa are served by two Catholic high schools apiece.

Politics and the Arts

Catholic involvement in political life has centered around two time periods, the turn of the century and the present. Among important figures of the earlier period are James Bigheart, chief of the Osage tribe; Dennis Flynn, first congressional delegate from the Oklahoma Territory; Kate Barnard, a reformer who was elected Oklahoma's first commissioner of charities and corrections; Matthew Kane and Thomas Doyle, both high-ranking members of the Oklahoma judiciary (Kane was chief justice of the state supreme court at the time of the Sacramental Wine Case); and Peter Hanratty, an early labor organizer on behalf of Oklahoma's coal miners.

More recent Catholic political figures include Dewey Bartlett (governor 1967–71, U.S. senator 1972–79), Don Nickles (U.S. senator 1977–), James R. Jones (U.S. representative 1972–86, ambassador to Mexico 1992–), David Walters (governor 1991–95), and Frank Keating (governor 1995–).

Oklahoma Catholics in the arts have included poet John Berryman, actress Jennifer Jones (who made her screen debut in the title role of The Song of Bernadette), and ballerinas Maria and Marjorie Tallchief and Yvonne Chouteau. Fr. Gregory Gerrer, O.S.B., painted the official portrait of Pope St. Pius X in 1904. Fr. John Walch is a liturgical artist and designer whose works date chiefly from the 1950s and 1960s. Also of note are agronomists Joseph Danne and Fr. H. B. Mandelartz, who developed important new strains of wheat and corn, respectively.

Population

Oklahoma's population was estimated in 1992 to be 3,100,003. Catholics accounted for 132,568 of this number, or 5 percent. 84,761 Catholics were counted in the Archdiocese of Oklahoma City, and 47,807 in the Diocese of Tulsa.

Brown, Thomas Elton. *Bible-belt Catholicism: A History of the Roman Catholic Church in Oklahoma, 1905–1945.* Vol. 33. New York: United States Catholic Historical Society, 1977.

Gaffey, James P. *Francis Clement Kelley and the American Dream.* 2 vols. Bensenville, Ill.: The Heritage Foundation, Inc., 1980.

Monahan, David F. *One Family: One Century: A Photographic History of the Catholic Church in Oklahoma 1875–1975.* Archdiocese of Oklahoma City, 1977.

Murphy, Joseph F., O.S.B. *Tenacious Monks: The Oklahoma Benedictines, 1875–1975: Indian Missionaries, Catholic Founders, Educators, Agriculturists.* Shawnee, Okla.: Benedictine Color Press, 1974.

White, James D. *The Souls of the Just: A Necrology of the Catholic Church in Oklahoma.* Tulsa, Okla.: The Sarto Press, 1983.

———. *Diary of a Frontier Bishop: The Journals of Theophile Meerschaert.* Tulsa, Okla.: The Sarto Press, 1994.

———. *Getting Sense: The Osages and Their Missionaries.* Tulsa, Okla.: The Sarto Press, 1997.

JAMES D. WHITE

ONAHAN, WILLIAM JAMES (1836–1919)

Businessman, lay activist. He was born into a poor family in Carlow, Ireland, in 1836. In his early teens he worked in England and in 1851 he emigrated to America. In Chicago he worked as an office clerk and became active in politics. He married Margaret Duffy in 1860. During the Civil War he was civilian secretary for the Irish Brigade and recruited for the Union army. He became very active in public affairs and served as a member of the Chicago Board of Education, as city tax collector, as president of the public library, and as president of a savings bank. He was self-educated, widely read, and a talented organizer who devoted

William J. Onahan

much time and money to Catholic causes. As a friend of Archbishop John Ireland and Bishop James O'Connor, he promoted Irish colonization projects in Minnesota and Nebraska. He helped to organize the first Catholic Congress in Baltimore in 1889, and served as chairman of the second Catholic Congress that met in Chicago in 1893 in conjunction with the Columbia Exposition and World Parliament of Religions in that year. He was the Chicago correspondent for *Freeman's Journal* and wrote several books including *The Religious Crisis in France* and *The Influence of the Catholic Layman.* He was awarded the Laetare Medal in 1890, and Leo XIII made him a papal chamberlain in 1895. He died in Chicago on January 12, 1919.

MICHAEL GLAZIER

O'NEILL, THOMAS P., JR. (1912–94)

Speaker of the House of Representatives. Thomas P. ("Tip") O'Neill, Jr., was born on December 9, 1912, in Cambridge, Massachusetts, and died on January 5, 1994. The son of Thomas P. (Sr.) and Rose Anne (Tolan) O'Neill, he never forgot his working-class roots, maintaining contact with his local neighborhood and Barry's Corner until the end of his life. Thus, he exemplified the axiom that propelled him into public life, namely, "All politics is local," as he was fond of saying.

A graduate of St. John's High School and of Boston College, O'Neill had expressed interest in politics during the presidential campaigns of 1928 and 1932. He launched his own career in politics by winning a seat in the Massachusetts General Court in 1936 and rose to become Speaker of that body in 1949, the first Catholic to hold this position. Having become involved in the insurance business, he married Mildred Anne Miller, on June 17, 1941, and they had five children: Rosemary, Thomas III, Susan, Christopher, and Michael. After World War II, he won a seat on the Cambridge School Committee in 1946 and in 1949.

When John F. Kennedy ran for the United States Senate in 1952, O'Neill, who lived in that congressman's Eleventh Congressional District (it later became the Eighth) ran for the seat (earlier it had been held by James Michael Curley). Winning in the Eisenhower landslide of that year, O'Neill's political career was fixed to represent Massachusetts in every Congress from the Eighty-Third through the Ninety-Ninth. Thereafter, O'Neill's political progress was steadily upward, becoming majority whip of his party in 1971, its majority leader in 1973, and Speaker of the United States House of Representatives in 1977, a position that he held for the next ten years under Presidents Jimmy Carter and Ronald Reagan.

Although O'Neill easily projected a caricature of the Democratic politician, he was far from that with the charm and grace of a true statesman. Like many Democrats of his generation, he had become enamored early in his own career with the ideology of the New Deal. However, that did not prevent him from standing up against the abuse of presidential power whether it was in the Democratic Party or in the Republican Party. With respect to his own party, his independence became shockingly evident to President Lyndon B. Johnson when, on September 14, 1967, the press announced his opposition to the Vietnam War, and when, during Jimmy Carter's early months in office, he taught the new President how necessary it was for the White House to work together with his party in Congress if he wanted to be successful with that body. As for the Republicans, O'Neill worked as majority leader to bring about the resignation of Richard M. Nixon in the Watergate scandal, after Rev. Robert F. Drinan, S.J., a member of his own delegation, filed articles of impeachment on July 31, 1972. He was also a principal player in depriving President Ronald W. Reagan of funds for arms for conservative forces in Nicaragua during the Iran-Contra Controversy.

Though both Democrats and Republicans praised his genius for compromise in fashioning legislation, O'Neill did not abandon his liberalism even when it had become unfashionable. Yet, perhaps the genius of O'Neill was best exemplified in his strategy as Speaker by following a policy of including the younger generation in the activities of the various committees of the United States House of Representatives. These democratic reforms, along with live television coverage of its proceedings, helped to rid the nation's legislative body of its image as a body of political hacks.

Recipient of many honors, including the Laetare Medal from Notre Dame University (1980), the Legion of Honor from France (1984), and the Medal of Freedom (1991) from the United States, he was given a total of thirty-five honorary degrees. Understandably, of all these doctorates, he particularly treasured the one from Boston College, his alma mater and the repository of his papers, which named its library in his honor. Having come under the influence of the Dominican Sisters in his primary and secondary education, he never forgot the women religious who touched his life (in the controversy over El Salvador, the Speaker relied on the Maryknoll Sisters for his information) after his mother had died early in his own life. Though two earlier Speakers of the United States House of Representatives, James G. Blaine (1869–75) and Joseph W. Martin, Jr. (1947–49 and 1953–55), had been baptized Catholics, O'Neill was, like John W. McCormack (1962–71), his political mentor, and Thomas S. Foley (1989–95), one of his successors, among the few known Catholics to be Speaker of the House (1977–87). Before O'Neill died of cardiac arrest, his famous face was easily recognized as he appeared on television to participate in comedies, in adver-

tisements, and in the sale of his books. He was buried at Mt. Pleasant Cemetery in Harwichport, Massachusetts.

Clancy, Paul and Shirley Elder. *Tip, A Biography of Thomas P. O'Neill, Speaker of the House.* New York, 1980.
The O'Neill Papers are housed at Boston College, his alma mater, where one can find a replica of his office as Speaker.
O'Neill, Thomas and William Novak. *Man of the House.* 1987.
O'Neill, Thomas and Gary Hymel. *All Politics is Local.* New York, 1993.

VINCENT A. LAPOMARDA, S.J.

O'REILLY, JOHN BOYLE (1844–90)

Poet, novelist, and editor. John Boyle O'Reilly impacted on three continents. He was born in Drogheda, Ireland, in County Meath, on June 24, 1844, and attended a National School conducted by his father before entering journalism first as a printer with the *Drogheda Argus,* then a writer for *The Guardian* in Preston, England. At age nineteen, he joined the Tenth Hussars as a trooper, intending to work from within its ranks on behalf of the patriotic Irish Fenian movement. Betrayed to authorities, O'Reilly was court-martialed for treason against the Crown and sentenced to death. The sentence was commuted to life imprisonment, then twenty year's penal servitude in Australia, where O'Reilly was assigned to a road gang cutting roads through the western Australian forests.

John Boyle O'Reilly

O'Reilly was a sensitive man with a deep love of nature, and both qualities were manifest throughout his lifetime, including the period of his incarceration. As a prisoner he pleaded on one occasion for the sparing of a particularly magnificent tree that laid in the path of a projected imperial roadway. The plea was amusing enough to the work-detail's commander for him to tell the story to his wife. She asked to be shown the tree and, on seeing it, shared O'Reilly's concern. Wondrously, the road was detoured and the tree saved.

After several failed efforts, O'Reilly escaped from Australia with the help of Captain David R. Gifford of the whaling ship *Gazelle* out of New Bedford, Massachusetts, and in a blizzard of newspaper headlines he made his way to the United States by a circuitous route that at one time actually had him back in England. He arrived in Boston on November 23, 1869, a man famous for his exploits, and took out naturalization papers the same day.

After only a year in America, O'Reilly became editor of the *Pilot,* a Boston weekly devoted to Catholic and Irish interests. Together with Boston's Archbishop John Williams, he purchased the paper in 1876 to save it from bankruptcy, putting up one-quarter of the $29,000 purchase price himself, and Williams the remainder. O'Reilly, in full editorial control, continued the *Pilot's* Catholic and Irish focuses, but broadened its scope so that the paper became a major force in the wider community and the most famous "Irish" paper in the land. He brought to the paper literary excellence, crusading zeal and progressive editorial views that added to his fame and celebrity.

O'Reilly shunned political life, but not political issues. He crusaded against many forms of tyranny and injustice, calling for prison reform, denouncing inhuman working conditions, and championing the rights of immigrant groups, not just those of the Irish. He also spoke out strongly for the Native Americans, Jews, and African Americans. When eight blacks were lynched on December 28, 1889, in Barnwell, South Carolina, he wrote: "The black race in the South must face the inevitable, soon or late, and the inevitable is—DEFEND YOURSELF." He said that "unless the Southern blacks learn to defend their homes, women, and lives, by law first and by manly force in extremity, they will be exterminated like the Tasmanian and Australian blacks." To charges that he was inciting blacks to open rebellion, O'Reilly responded, "We have appealed only to the great Catholic and American principle of resisting wrong and outrage, of protecting life and home and the honor of families by all lawful means, even the extremest, when nothing else remains to be tried."

On the matter of women's rights, however, O'Reilly was very much a man of his times. He was decidedly antisuffragist, for instance, calling it "a hard, undigested, tasteless, devitalized proposition."

O'Reilly was perhaps most influential in easing the assimilation of immigrant Irish into the American milieu, a sensitive and challenging task given his own Fenian background and the intense republican activities taking place in Ireland, for which the Irish in America were being constantly rallied. O'Reilly was an ardent advocate of Irish Home Rule, but he repeatedly stressed to Irish Americans, "We can do Ireland more good by our Americanism than by our Irishism."

O'Reilly was preeminently a journalist, but he was also in demand as a lecturer and orator. His talents as a poet (appreciated more by contemporaries than by history) made him the choice to compose verses for the commemoration of the Daniel O'Connell Centenary and for the dedications of the Crispus Attucks Monument on Boston Common and the national monument to the Pilgrim Fathers at Plymouth. He wrote four volumes of poetry—*Songs from the Southern Seas* (1873), *Songs, Legends, and Ballads* (1878), *The Statues in the Block* (1881), and *In Bohemia* (1886)—and a novel based on his Australian experiences, *Moondyne* (1875). He collaborated on other books, including *Ethics of Boxing and Manly Sport* (1888) with Edward A. Moseley.

The University of Notre Dame awarded him a Doctor of Laws degree in 1881. That same year he was elected an honorary member of Phi Beta Kappa of Dartmouth College.

O'Reilly died at the height of his fame on August 10, 1890, at his summer home in Hull, a shore community south of Boston. He was only forty-six. A 1944 history of the Archdiocese of Boston says he "died suddenly of heart failure." The actual cause was an overdose of a sleeping medication prescribed for his wife. O'Reilly, who suffered from insomnia, reportedly was told by the doctor to take some of his wife's medicine for his own condition. Current histories refer to his death as a "possible suicide." Soon after his death, ownership of the *Pilot* was returned to its previous owner.

See also CATHOLIC PRESS (NEWSPAPERS), THE; IRISH CATHOLICS IN AMERICA.

McManamin, Francis G. *The American Years of John Boyle O'Reilly, 1870–1890.* New York, 1976.

Roche, James J. *Life of John Boyle O'Reilly, Together with His Complete Poems and Speeches.* New York, 1891.

Schofield, William G. *Seek for a Hero: The Story of John Boyle O'Reilly.* New York, 1956.

JOHN DEEDY

O'REILLY, MARY BOYLE (1873–1939)

Journalist. A writer and humanitarian in the tradition of her father, John Boyle O'Reilly, Mary Boyle O'Reilly was born in Charlestown, now part of Boston, on May 18, 1873, and educated at a Sacred Heart convent school in Providence and the Gilman School for Girls in Cambridge. A Radcliffe education had to be forgone for reasons of health. She went on, nonetheless, to a life of adventure and social service.

O'Reilly held the post of Prison Commissioner of Massachusetts from 1907–11, at the same time involving herself in a number of public issues. In 1910, in the disguise of a mill worker, she exposed the "baby farms" of New

Hampshire—facilities operating under the mantle of foster homes and hospitals that accepted unwanted children for a fee, then warehoused them. The children often suffered neglect, abuse, or worse. O'Reilly's investigations resulted in corrective legislation effectively ending "baby farms."

As a journalist, O'Reilly reported from Europe during World War I, syndicating accounts of the zeppelin raids on London and the burning of Louvain, among other military operations. She had smuggled herself into Belgium in 1914, this time in the disguise of a peasant. She came under surveillance on suspicion of being a spy, and was imprisoned for a time by the Germans. After the war she engaged in relief work in England, France, and Russia.

O'Reilly was a feminist, though hardly a radical one. She did not initially favor women's suffrage, for instance. She ultimately believed in the measure, but felt women should be educated up to the responsibilities suffragism entailed.

Overall, hers was a life dedicated to underprivileged women, and she had disdain for privileged female peers for their quickness to ostracize "the woman of today who has made a mistake." A concern for "working girls" led to her involvement in the 1912 Lawrence mill strike. Later, with three friends, she founded St. Elizabeth's Settlement House in Boston's South End for women in distress and their children. The *Boston Globe* saluted her activism, saying she was no "pink tea philanthropist."

O'Reilly, who never married, lectured widely on her war experiences and a range of social questions. She contributed to many magazines and newspapers, and amassed a large collection of propaganda and other materials relating to World War I that she presented to the Boston Public Library. She died on October 21, 1939.

Kane, Paula M. *Separatism and Subculture: Boston Catholicism, 1900–1920.* Chapel Hill, North Carolina, 1994.
The Boston Globe, October 22, 1939.
The New York Times, October 22, 1939.

JOHN DEEDY

O'REILLY, THOMAS (1831–72)

Priest. Thomas O'Reilly was born in County Cavan, Ireland, in 1831. He was educated at All Hallows College in Dublin and ordained to the priesthood there in 1857. O'Reilly arrived in Savannah in 1857 and was assigned to the Cathedral of St. John the Baptist. Following a bout of yellow fever he was assigned to the healthier locations of Macon and Albany, Georgia. In 1861 he became pastor of Atlanta's Immaculate Conception parish.

It was not long after his arrival in Atlanta before Catholics and non-Catholics alike grew to love this gentle priest. As the Civil War progressed, O'Reilly labored tirelessly to assist the wounded, suffering, and displaced people in Atlanta. When the battles neared Atlanta, Fr. O'Reilly was at the train depot to give aid to the wounded being transferred from the battlefields to the hospitals.

Bishop Augustin Verot requested that O'Reilly visit the Andersonville Prison Camp to aid the prisoners there which he did with regularity. In 1864 he was appointed a Confederate chaplain; however, he assisted Union soldiers as well. After a two-month siege, General William T. Sherman claimed Atlanta on September 2, 1864. His plan was to destroy this transportation and supply hub to cripple the Confederacy. He issued an order for all civilians to vacate the city. The Union soldiers left Atlanta in flames on November 15, 1864.

Fr. O'Reilly had welcomed the Union soldiers to his church and was known for the assistance he gave to many of the wounded and dying soldiers. When he heard of Sherman's plan to burn the city, he went to Major General Henry Slocum, who was stationed near Immaculate Conception Church, to intercede. O'Reilly reminded General Slocum that many of his soldiers were Catholic and would consider it sacrilege to burn a church. Slocum agreed not to burn the area around the five churches (Catholic, Episcopal, Methodist, Presbyterian, and Baptist) which included the City Hall, the courthouse, and several homes. Guards were posted to prevent them from being torched. Thus Fr. O'Reilly is credited with saving a portion of Atlanta from destruction. In appreciation of this deed, a monument to Fr. O'Reilly was unveiled in 1945 on the grounds of Atlanta's City Hall.

Following the war, the small Immaculate Conception Church was in a state of disrepair from its use as a hospital. Also the congregation was increasing as a result of Atlanta's population boom. O'Reilly engaged a leading architect, W. H. Parkins, to draw plans for a magnificent new brick church. The cornerstone was laid on September 1, 1869, by Bishop Augustin Verot.

The strain of the war years had taken its toll on Fr. O'Reilly's health, so he spent several months at Chalybeate Springs, Virginia, to rest and restore his health. It was there that he died on September 6, 1872. The body was returned to Atlanta by train and was met in Chattanooga, Tennessee, by an honor escort to accompany it into Atlanta. The largest crowd ever assembled at the Union depot paid tribute to him.

On September 10, 1872, Bishop Ignatius Persico presided at Fr. O'Reilly's funeral. In his eulogy he described O'Reilly as "affable, generous, gentle, patient, moderate, meek, unobtrusive and energetic." He also stated that through his zeal and energy he had established and erected churches at Albany and Dalton as well as having built the new convent and church in Atlanta. Fr. O'Reilly was then laid to rest in a specially prepared crypt under the altar of the new Immaculate Conception Church.

See also CIVIL WAR AND CATHOLICS, THE.

Colley, Van Buren. *History of the Diocesan Shrine of the Immaculate Conception.* Atlanta: Diocesan Shrine of the Immaculate Conception, 1955.

"Father's O'Reilly, Cleary—Missionary Frontiersmen." *The Georgia Bulletin,* January 13, 1982, 8–9.

Otis, Robert R. "High Lights in the Life of Father Thomas O'Reilly." *Atlanta Historical Bulletin* 8 (30) (October 1945).

Savannah, Georgia. Georgia Historical Society. Walter C. Hartridge Papers.

ANTHONY R. DEES

OREGON, CATHOLIC CHURCH IN

The Catholic Church in Oregon consists of the Archdiocese of Portland in Oregon, founded in 1846, and the Diocese of Baker, founded in 1903. The archdiocese embraces the western third of the state, an area of 29,717 square miles from the ridge of the Cascade Mountains to the Pacific Ocean. The Diocese of Baker, the eastern two-thirds of the state, has an area of 55,826 square miles, extending from the ridge of the Cascade Mountains to the border of Idaho. The western third has a population of 2,596,900 with a Catholic population of 269,774, approximately 11 percent. The eastern two-thirds has a population of 382,100, only 27,168 of whom are Catholic, approximately 8 percent. The population disparity is explained by the dissimilarities of geography and climate between the two areas. In 1995 the province of Portland in Oregon had jurisdiction over the Archdiocese of Portland, and the Dioceses of Baker, Boise (Idaho), and of Great Falls and Helena (Montana).

Early History

Catholicity came slowly to Oregon. The first missionaries, Francis Norbert Blanchet and Modeste Demers, arrived in 1838. The only Catholics in the area were French-Canadian fur trappers and a few members of the Lewis and Clark Expedition. Both of these groups were concentrated in the Willamette Valley where they became farmers. Blanchet was appointed bishop of this area in 1843 and archbishop in 1846. He established his see in Oregon City. In 1928 this was transferred to Portland. Blanchet encountered numerous challenges: the vastness of the territory, exiguous Catholics, governmental interference in the Native American missions, troubles with Protestant missionaries, unfounded accusations against Catholics, and numerous native wars. The California gold rush of the early 1850s drained the country of its population and placed a heavy financial burden on the Church. During the late 1850s and following, conditions began to improve. Financial aid was obtained from South America. Catholic education (begun in 1843 and abandoned in 1854) was reestablished in 1859

and began to flourish. The size of the archdiocese was reduced by the creation of the vicariate of Idaho. A diocesan newspaper, the *Catholic Sentinel,* was established in 1869. In 1875 a Catholic hospital, St. Vincent's, was opened. European volunteers joined the ranks of the clergy, and Catholic societies were founded.

Bishops and Clergy

Nine archbishops have served in the Archdiocese of Portland: Frances N. Blanchet, 1846–80; Charles J. Seghers, 1880–84; William H. Gross, C.Ss.R., 1885–98; Alexander Christie, 1898–1925; Edward D. Howard, 1926–66; Robert J. Dwyer, 1966–74; Cornelius Power, 1974–86; William Levada, 1986–95; and Francis E. George, O.M.I., 1995–96. Four bishops have served the Baker diocese: Charles J. O'Reilly, 1903–18; Joseph F. McGrath, 1919–50; Francis Leipzig, 1950–71; Thomas J. Connolly, 1971– . In 1995 the Archdiocese of Portland had 106 active incardinated priests, 44 retired diocesan priests, 209 religious order priests, and 18 permanent deacons. The Diocese of Baker had thirty active priests, seven retired priests, seven religious order priests, and two permanent deacons. Portland had 123 parishes with priest pastors, three parishes with lay administrators, and twenty-five missions. Baker had thirty-six parishes with priest pastors, and twenty-eight missions.

Religious Communities

Thirteen religious communities of men serve in the Archdiocese of Portland, four in the Diocese of Baker. Prominent among these communities, by numerical count and/or ministerial impact are: Benedictines (O.S.B.); Dominicans (O.P.); Franciscans (O.F.M.); Holy Cross (C.S.C.); Jesuits (S.J.); Redemptorists (C.Ss.R.); Servites (O.S.M.); and Trappists (O.C.S.O.). Twenty-six religious communities of women are engaged in various ministries in the Archdiocese of Portland, twelve in the Baker diocese. Prominent among these by numerical count and/or ministerial impact are: Benedictines (O.S.B.); Carmelite Sisters Discalced (O.C.D.); Sisters of the Holy Names of Jesus and Mary (S.N.J.M.); Sisters of Mercy (R.S.M.); Sisters of Providence (S.P.); Sisters of St. Francis of Philadelphia (O.S.F.); and Sisters of St. Mary's of Oregon (S.S.M.O.).

Education—Various Ministries

Catholic education has from the beginning been given a high priority in Oregon. Begun in 1843, it continues in vigor. There are within the two dioceses a total of three priestly formation programs, the most noted of them at Mount Angel Seminary. Other educational institutions include the University of Portland, Marylhurst College for Lifelong Learning, eight high schools (seven of them coeducational), forty-four grade schools, seventeen Catholic campus ministries on secular college and university campuses, and nine retreat houses and centers.

Catholic health care, social service, and welfare agencies are numerous. The Providence Health System, administered by the Sisters of Providence, has widespread facilities throughout the state in hospitals, medical centers, and related areas. The Sisters of Mercy maintain several residential care centers and nursing homes. The Benedictine Nursing Center in Mount Angel has extended services for the ill and elderly. Other agencies ministering to the needs of the Catholic population include: Catholic Charities, Catholic Community Services, St. Vincent de Paul Society, mental health and counseling centers, pregnancy and maternity services, and chaplain services to state and veterans' institutions. With the recent increase of Hispanic and Asian peoples, more attention and assistance has been channeled into services for these segments of the population.

Problems and Difficulties

Oregon has experienced a long history of anti-Catholic sentiment and feeling. Prejudice and bigotry are no strangers to the Catholic population of the state. In the early missionary days (1838–83) there were difficulties with Protestant missionaries, e.g., Jason Lee and the Methodist missionaries; Marcus Whitman and the aftermath of the Whitman Massacre. In the early 1920s anti-Catholic feeling, fanned by the activities of the Ku Klux Klan, was rampant. The infamous Oregon School Bill was passed in 1922, but declared unconstitutional by the United States Supreme Court in 1925. In 1923 the Oregon Religious Garb Bill prohibited anyone wearing a religious habit from teaching in public-related schools. That bill was still in effect in 1995. Separation of Church and state has been felt in other areas too. The use of state-owned textbooks and buses is denied to religious schools. Chief proponents in the above cases, besides the Ku Klux Klan, have been the American Civil Liberties Union (ACLU) and the Protestants and Other Americans United for Separation of Church and State (POAU).

Catholic Involvement

Despite the obstacles to its growth, the Catholic Church has had a deep and lasting influence on the political, educational, and social development of Oregon. Among those who have had a notable impact may be cited: Dr. John McLoughlin whose aid to early settlers and missionaries insured the continuance of the Church in the Northwest; Judge J. P. Kavanaugh who helped the defeat of the Oregon Compulsory School Bill; Sr. Miriam Theresa Gleason, S.N.J.M., whose work for wage reform was largely responsible for the first minimum-wage law in the state; Mother M. Joseph of the Sacred Heart, S.P., foundress of

the first Catholic hospital in Oregon; Mother M. Flavia, S.N.J.M., who established three normal schools in the Northwest and figured largely in the opposition to the Oregon School bill; and Bishop Edwin V. O'Hara, noted for his social reform legislation through the Catholic Rural Life Bureau, and for his catechetical program that developed into the nationally recognized Confraternity of Christian Doctrine (CCD).

Bagley, Clarence B. *Early Catholic Missions in Old Oregon.* 2 vols. Seattle, 1932.

Bolduc, Jean Baptiste Zacharie. *Mission of the Columbia,* ed. Edward T. Kowrach. Fairfield, Washington, 1979.

Laidlaw, John R. *The Catholic Church in Oregon and the Work of Its Archbishops.* Smithtown, N.Y.: Exposition Press, 1977.

Lyons, Mary Letitia. *Francis Norbert Blanchet and the Founding of the Oregon Missions, 1838–1848.* Washington, D.C., 1940.

O'Connor, Dominic, O.F.M., Cap. *A Brief History of the Diocese of Baker City.* Diocesan Chancery, Baker, Oregon, 1930.

O'Hara, Edwin V. *Pioneer Catholic History of Oregon.* Centennial Edition. Paterson, N.J.: St. Anthony Guild Press, 1939.

Oregon Catholic Directory. Portland: Oregon Catholic Press, 1995.

Saalfeld, J. *Forces of Prejudice: The Ku Klux Klan in Oregon, 1920–1925.* Portland, 1984.

Schoenberg, Wilfred P., S.J. *A History of the Catholic Church in the Pacific Northwest 1743–1983.* Washington, D.C.: The Pastoral Press, 1987.

Shelley, Thomas J. "The Oregon School Case and the National Catholic Welfare Conference." *Catholic Historical Review* 75 (July 1989) 439–57.

BEATRICE WEISNER, S.N.J.M.

OREGON SCHOOL LAW OF 1922, THE

The Oregon School Law of 1922 was one of the most serious challenges ever mounted against freedom of education in the United States. It was directed especially at Catholic schools, but the law backfired on its proponents and ironically proved to be of enormous benefit to the Catholic Church throughout the United States.

The Oregon Compulsory Education Act of 1922 became law, not through an act of the state legislature, but through the "initiative petition" process, which had been a favorite tactic of progressive reformers a decade earlier. In the early 1920s, however, a wave of xenophobia swept across the United States and affected even the usually liberal voters of Oregon. On a single day in June 1922 volunteers from the Masonic Lodges collected enough votes to put the proposition on the ballot. On election day, November 7, 1922, by a margin of 107,498 to 97,204, the voters of the state approved the proposal, which declared that, after September 1, 1926, every child in the state between the ages of eight and sixteen would be obliged to attend a public school. The success was due not only to the Masons, but even more to the Ku Klux Klan, which wielded considerable political power in Oregon between 1922 and 1924.

The Role of the NCWC

The Catholics of Oregon organized a Catholic Civic Rights Association to defend their schools, but they did not have the financial resources to challenge the law in the courts. Therefore, they appealed to the bishops of the whole country to share the burden with them. "Our case today will be theirs tomorrow," warned Alexander Christie, archbishop of Oregon City. In Washington, D.C., the newly established National Catholic Welfare Council had already turned down one request for funds. In January 1923, however, the Administrative Committee of the NCWC reversed itself and agreed to raise $100,000 from the American bishops in order to contest the law in the United States Supreme Court.

For the NCWC, the Oregon School Law was an opportunity to demonstrate the value of the organization to skeptical American bishops and suspicious officials in Rome. Day-to-day operations were in the hands of two extremely competent staff members: John J. Burke, C.S.P., general secretary of the NCWC, and James Hugh Ryan, chairman of the Education Department of the NCWC. Over the next two years, Burke and Ryan raised the necessary funds, hired the lawyers, mediated between the NCWC and the Oregon Catholics, and organized what was probably the most extensive and professional public relations campaign ever undertaken until that time by the Catholic Church in the United States.

Legal proceedings got under way in federal court in Portland in December 1923. The NCWC decided to contest the law in the name of the Sisters of the Holy Names of Jesus and Mary, a community which operated a number of schools in Oregon. The attorney for the NCWC asked for an injunction against the law, which was granted by a panel of three federal judges on March 31, 1924. Three months later the state filed an appeal against the injunction, setting the stage for a decision by the U.S. Supreme Court. Chief counsel for the NCWC was to be William D. Guthrie, a prominent New York attorney, who was to be assisted by Judge John P. Kavanaugh of Portland.

Interest in the case ran high because of the basic civil liberties that were involved. Roger Baldwin of the American Civil Liberties Union offered to obtain counsel for the NCWC, and John Dewey said that the Oregon Law struck "at the root of American toleration." Three groups filed *amici curiae* briefs on behalf of the NCWC: the Domestic and Foreign Missionary Society of the Protestant Episcopal Church, the North Pacific Union Conference of the Seventh Day Adventists, and the American Jewish Committee—an unusual array of allies in a case involving parochial schools. In the summer of 1924, when Guthrie went to Europe, he discussed the case in Rome with Cardinal Pietro Gasparri, the papal secretary of state.

U.S. Supreme Court

The U.S. Supreme Court heard the case *(Pierce v. Society of Sisters)* on March 16 and 17, 1925. Guthrie and Kavanaugh used the same arguments that Kavanaugh had used earlier in Federal District Court. They did not challenge the law on the basis of the First Amendment, but used three other arguments, namely, that the Oregon Law (1) violated the contract between the state and the sisters arising from the incorporation of their schools under Oregon law; (2) violated the Fourteenth Amendment by depriving the sisters of their property; and (3) violated the right of parents to determine the education of their children.

The Supreme Court decided the case on June 1, 1925. In a unanimous decision, the justices sustained the decision of the Federal District Court and nullified the Oregon Compulsory Education Law. Justice McReynolds, in delivering the opinion of the Court, said: "The child is not the mere creature of the state." Editorial opinion throughout the country was overwhelmingly favorable. Louis Marshall, a New York attorney who had written the *amicus curiae* brief for the American Jewish Committee, told Burke: "I do not think that the importance of this decision can be exaggerated. It will prove a landmark in our constitutional history."

Curiously, Burke himself did not share the elation of his colleagues, for he feared that the Supreme Court decision had left open the possibility of future government interference in Catholic education. Fortunately, his fears proved to be groundless. Never again has there been a serious legal challenge to the existence of private and parochial schools in the United States. Leo Pfeffer, an attorney not noted for his sympathy for parochial schools, called *Pierce v. Society of Sisters* "the Magna Carta of the parochial school system." A historian of American education (Willis Rudy) went further and said: "The case was a victory not for Catholic parochial schools alone, but for the principle of cultural pluralism in America."

See also BOUQUILLON, THOMAS; FARIBAULT-STILLWATER SCHOOL PLAN; POUGHKEEPSIE SCHOOL PLAN.

Holsinger, M. Paul. "The Oregon School Bill Controversy, 1922–1925." *Pacific Historical Review* 37 (1968) 327–42.

Jorgenson, Lloyd P. "The Oregon School Law of 1922: Passage and Sequel." *Catholic Historical Review* 54 (1968) 455–66.

The Oregon School Cases. Baltimore, 1925. A volume published by the NCWC which contains a complete transcript of the legal proceedings.

Pfeffer, Leo. *Church, State and Freedom.* Boston, 1953.

Rudy, Willis. *Schools in an Age of Mass Culture.* Englewood Cliffs, 1965.

Saalfeld, Lawrence J. *Forces of Prejudice: The Ku Klux Klan in Oregon, 1920–1925.* Portland, 1984.

Shelley, Thomas J. "The Oregon School Case and the National Catholic Welfare Conference." *Catholic Historical Review* 75 (1989) 439–57.

Slawson, Douglas J. *The Foundation and First Decade of the National Catholic Welfare Council.* Washington, 1992, 191–202.

Tyack, David B. "The Perils of Pluralism: The Background of the Pierce Case." *American Historical Review* 74 (1969) 74–98.

THOMAS J. SHELLEY

Related Document

THE SUPREME COURT AFFIRMS THE RIGHT OF PRIVATE RELIGIOUS SCHOOLS, JUNE 1, 1925

The right of private schools has more than once been questioned in the United States but never, perhaps, more seriously than by an Oregon law of November, 1922, which would have compelled all children in the state between the ages of eight and sixteen to attend the public schools. The constitutionality of the law was challenged by the Sisters of the Holy Names of Jesus and Mary who had many schools in Oregon, an action in which they were joined by the Hill Military Academy as a defendant. The case was ultimately appealed to the Supreme Court of the United States, and in the following unanimous decision in *Pierce v. Society of Sisters* handed down by Justice James C. McReynolds (1862–1946) the state was forbidden to deny the right of parents to choose a private school for their children as a violation of the fourteenth amendment.

(*Source: Pierce v. Society of Sisters*, 268 U.S. 510, 529–536).

THESE APPEALS ARE FROM DECREES, BASED UPON UNDENIED allegations, which granted preliminary orders restraining appellants from threatening or attempting to enforce the Compulsory Education Act adopted November 7, 1922, under the initiative provision of her Constitution by the voters of Oregon. They present the same points of law; there are no controverted questions of fact. Rights said to be guaranteed by the federal Constitution were specially set up, and appropriate prayers asked for their protection.

The challenged Act, effective September 1, 1926, requires every parent . . . of a child between eight and sixteen years to send him "to a public school for the period of time a public school shall be held during the current year" in the district where the child resides; and failure to do so is declared a misdemeanor. . . . The manifest purpose is to compel general attendance at public schools by normal children between eight and sixteen, who have not completed the eighth grade. And without doubt enforcement of the statute would seriously impair, perhaps destroy, the profitable features of appellees' business, and greatly diminish the value of their property.

Appellee, the Society of Sisters,[1] is an Oregon corporation, organized in 1880, with power to care for orphans, educate and instruct the youth, establish and maintain academies or schools, and acquire necessary real and personal property. It has long devoted its property and effort to the secular and religious education and care of children, and has acquired the valuable good will of many parents and guardians. It conducts interdependent primary and high schools and junior colleges, and maintains orphanages for the custody and control of children between eight and sixteen. In its primary schools many children between those ages are taught the subjects usually pursued in Oregon public schools during the first eight years. Systematic religious instruction and moral training according to the tenets of the Roman Catholic Church are also regularly provided. All courses of study, both temporal and religious, contemplate continuity of training under appellee's charge; the primary schools are essential to the system and the most profitable. It owns valuable buildings, especially constructed and equipped for school purposes. The business is remunerative—the annual income from primary schools exceeds thirty thousand dollars—and the successful conduct of this business requires long-time contracts with teachers and parents. The Compulsory Education Act of 1922 has already caused the withdrawal from its schools of children who would otherwise continue, and their income has steadily declined. The appellants, public officers, have proclaimed their purpose strictly to enforce the statute.

After setting out the above facts the Society's bill alleges that the enactment conflicts with the right of parents to choose schools where their children will receive appropriate mental and religious training, the right of the child to influence the parents' choice of a school, the right of schools and teachers therein to engage in a useful business or profession, and is accordingly repugnant to the Constitution and void. And, further, that unless enforcement of the measure is enjoined the corporation's business and property will suffer irreparable injury.

No question is raised concerning the power of the State reasonably to regulate all schools, to inspect, supervise and examine them, their teachers and pupils; to require that all children of proper age attend some school, that teachers shall be of good moral character and patriotic disposition, that certain studies plainly essential to good citizenship must be taught, and that nothing be taught which is manifestly inimical to the public welfare.

The inevitable practical result of enforcing the Act under consideration would be destruction of appellees' primary schools, and perhaps all other private primary schools for normal children within the State of Oregon. Appellees are engaged in a kind of undertaking not inherently harmful, but long regarded as useful and meritorious. Certainly there is nothing in the present records to indicate that they have failed to discharge their obligations to patrons, students, or the State. And there are no peculiar circumstances or present emergencies which demand extraordinary measures relative to primary education.

Under the doctrine of *Meyer v. Nebraska,* 262 U.S. 390,[2] we think it entirely plain that the Act of 1922 unreasonably interferes with the liberty of parents and guardians to direct the upbringing and education of children under their control. As often heretofore pointed out rights guaranteed by the Constitution may not be abridged by legislation which has no reasonable relation to some purpose within the competency of the State. The fundamental theory of liberty upon which all governments in this Union repose excludes any general power of the State to standardize its children by forcing them to accept instruction from public teachers only. The child is not the mere creature of the State; those who nurture him and direct his destiny have the right, coupled with the high duty, to recognize and prepare him for additional obligations.

The suits were not premature. The injury to appellees was present and very real, not a mere possibility in the remote future. If no relief had been possible prior to the effective date of the Act, the injury would have become irreparable. Prevention of impending injury by unlawful action is a well recognized function of courts of equity.

[1] The Sisters of the Holy Names of Jesus and Mary, founded in Canada, first came to Oregon in October, 1859, at the invitation of Francis Norbert Blanchet (1795–1883), first Archbishop of Oregon City. They were the first religious congregation of women to make a permanent settlement in Oregon where they still conduct numerous schools.

[2] In 1923 the Supreme Court in *Meyer v. Nebraska* declared unconstitutional a law forbidding the teaching of any language other than English to any child below the eighth grade by any teacher in a public or private school. The court upheld the right of the plaintiff, an instructor in a Lutheran parochial school, to teach a foreign language, as well as the right of the parents to engage him to instruct their children, both as being within the liberty of the fourteenth amendment.

(*Source*: John Tracy Ellis, ed. *Documents of American Catholic History*. Vol. 2:1866–1966. Wilmington, Del.: Michael Glazier, 1987, 613–16.)

ORTYNSKY, STEPHEN SOTER (1866–1916)

Bishop. Born in Ortynytski, Galicia, January 29, 1866, Stephen Ortynsky entered the Basilian Order in 1884, taking the religious name Soter. After studies at the University of Graz, he was ordained a priest January 19, 1891. During a varied career as teacher, administrator, and missionary, Ortynsky earned a reputation as a talented preacher and ardent Ukrainian patriot. Ortynsky was named titular bishop of Daulia and ordinary for American Byzantine Catholics on March 8, 1907. After episcopal ordination at Lviv on May 12, he arrived in America on August 27, the first Eastern-rite bishop in the Western Hemisphere.

Among the problems initially encountered by Ortynsky were clerical and parochial discipline, proselytization by the Russian Orthodox, factional disputes between Galicians and Transcarpathians, and misunderstandings with the Latin hierarchy, who were generally opposed to his appointment. These difficulties were exacerbated by the apostolic letter *Ea Semper,* which withheld ordinary jurisdiction from Ortynsky, outlined his duties and powers as an auxiliary bishop to all Latin-Rite bishops in whose territory the Byzantines lived, and abrogated several Byzantine practices in the United States including confirmation at baptism and a married clergy. Ortynsky was unaware of *Ea Semper* until after his arrival in the United States, and protested its provisions.

Despite these setbacks, Ortynsky's administration was marked by growth in the American Byzantine Church. He called a meeting of the clergy and parish delegates for October 15–16, 1907, at which financial and administrative structures were established. Basilian sisters were brought from Europe to staff a new orphanage. Ortynsky also founded a printing press, a newspaper, *Ameryka,* and *Provydinia,* a Catholic mutual assistance association. Many of these endeavors were grouped on North Franklin Street in Philadelphia, around a former Episcopal church that Ortynsky renovated in 1909 as Immaculate Conception Cathedral. On May 28, 1913, Pope Pius X granted Ortynsky ordinary jurisdiction, creating an exarchate for the American Byzantine Catholics. By the time of Ortynsky's death, the number of Catholics in the exarchate numbered nearly 500,000 gathered in 196 churches served by 220 priests.

Ongoing disputes with his Transcarpathian parishioners, who mistrusted him both as a Ukrainian nationalist and as a Latinizer, were a source of frustration for Ortynsky. Some of these parishes refused to acknowledge his jurisdiction, remaining under Latin ordinaries. Others defected to Orthodoxy. His health broken by these disputes, Ortynsky succumbed to pneumonia on March 24, 1916. After his death, separate apostolic administrators were appointed for the Ukrainian and Transcarpathian parishes, resulting in a permanent division into two exarchates in 1924.

Dyrud, Keith P. "The Establishment of the Greek Catholic Rite in America as a Competitor to Orthodoxy." *The Other Catholics,* eds. Keith P. Dyrud, Michael Novak, and Rudolph J. Vecoli. New York: Arno Press, 1978.

Fogarty, Gerald P., S.J. "The American Hierarchy and Oriental Rite Catholics, 1890–1907." *Records of the American Catholic Historical Society of Philadelphia* 85 (March–June 1974) 17–28.

Procko, Bohdan P. "Soter Ortynsky: First Ruthenian Bishop in the United States, 1907–1916." *Catholic Historical Review* 58 (January 1973) 513–33.

____. "The Establishment of the Ruthenian Church in the United States, 1884–1907." *Pennsylvania History* 42 (April 1975) 137–75.

Simon, Constantin, S.J. "The First Years of Ruthenian Church Life in America." *Orientalia Christiana Periodica* 60 (1994) 187–232.

RAYMOND J. KUPKE

O'SULLIVAN, JOAN ADELAIDE (1817–93)

Foundress. Born in Yonkers (New York) on October 8, 1817, Joan O'Sullivan was baptized an Anglican, became a Catholic at age four, and in 1830 made her First Communion. After her father's death, the family moved (1835) to Washington, D.C., where she completed her education at the Academy of the Visitation in Georgetown. In 1837 she entered the Georgetown Visitation monastery, and at the time of her profession (1839) received the name Sr. Mary John.

In the Georgetown convent she became familiar with the writings of St. Teresa of Jesus; these impressed her so deeply that from that time on she was convinced that she had to be a Carmelite. With her spiritual director's assistance, she transferred (1840) to the Carmel in Havana (Cuba). When Spain's anticlerical government decreed the suppression of all religious orders in Spain and its colonies, including Cuba, the novices at the Havana Carmel were forbidden to take vows. Unable to become a Carmelite in Cuba, Adelaide was encouraged to transfer to the convent in Guatemala City. She arrived there on September 8, 1843, and on the following October 4, received her habit, taking Adelaide of St. Teresa as her name in religion.

Fourteen years after her profession in Guatemala City, she was appointed (1858) mistress of novices, and in 1868 was unanimously elected prioress. She was again elected in 1871. In 1874 the Guatemalan Revolutionary Junta decreed the closing of all convents and gathered all nuns into one convent. When this convent was closed, the nuns sought shelter with family or friends. Adelaide and four sisters, responding to an invitation, went (November 1875) to Havana, and after a two-year sojourn there, answered the bishop of Savannah's request to start a Carmelite foundation in Georgia. After another two years it was evident to Adelaide that Savannah was not to be her permanent home and, thus, she and her sisters moved (1879) to Yonkers and later (1880) to Toronto (Canada).

Despite these failures, she would not set aside her plan to seek a permanent home for her foundation. While in Savannah she had become acquainted with the wife of the Spanish vice consul, who was also the niece of the bishop of León in Spain. The woman wrote to her uncle describing Adelaide's sufferings and wanderings. The bishop's response was quick and positive; he would accept them in his diocese. Thus, Adelaide and her fellow sisters left New York on May 18, 1881, and arrived in Spain on June 5. The bishop met them in Madrid on June 10, and took them to his diocese. In Grajal de Campos, Adelaide purchased an abandoned Franciscan monastery, supervised the renovations, and her new foundation was formally dedicated on December 18, 1882. She guided that community as prioress for ten more years and witnessed it grow and flourish. She died with a reputation for holiness on April 15, 1893. The cause for her beatification was begun in 1923.

Florencio del Niño Jesús, O.C.D. *La pasionaria de Nueva York. Vida, virtudes y escritos de la R. M. Adelaida de Sta. Teresa, Carmelita Descalza (1817–1893)*. Madrid, 1935.

Rodriguez, Otilio, O.C.D. "Yankee Courage in a Carmelite Nun: Mother Adelaide of St. Teresa, O.C.D. (1817–1893)." *Portraits in American Sanctity*, ed. Joseph N. Tylenda. Chicago: Franciscan Herald, 1982, 210–20.

Valerson, A. F., O.C.D. *Mother Adelaide of St. Theresa*. Oklahoma City, Okla.: Prompt Publishing Co., 1928.

JOSEPH TYLENDA, S.J.

O'SULLIVAN, MARY KENNEY (1864–1943)

Labor organizer and social reformer. Mary Kenney O'Sullivan was born in Hannibal, Missouri, in 1864, and was educated in both Catholic and public schools. After the death of her father in 1878, she worked as a bookbinder, and after four years was promoted to forewoman. When the bindery relocated to Iowa, she went with it, taking her mother with her. She witnessed the Burlington Railroad strike of 1888, and as a result became a firm believer in organized labor.

Mary Kenney O'Sullivan and children

When the bindery failed, she moved to Chicago in search of work, and encountered for the first time the dissipation of urban life, "the tragedies of meagerly paid workers, the haunting faces of undernourished children, the filth, the everlasting struggle, and then the whole thing over again. . . ." (Autobiography, 750). One way to break the cycle, she felt, was to organize the women laborers of her occupation; her effort resulted in the Chicago Women's Bindery Workers Union, a subsidiary of Ladies Federal Labor Union No. 2703, American Federation of Labor (AFL).

She was subsequently elected to the Chicago Trade and Labor Assembly, of which she became a leader, and which—together with Florence Kelley and other members of Jane Addams' Hull House—studied and prepared a report on the labor conditions in Chicago's sweatshops. The report, along with their lobbying of the Illinois legislature, resulted in a factory law passed in 1893 regulating employment of women and children, and creating a Factory Inspection Department. Kenney was then appointed inspector under Florence Kelley.

In 1892 she was appointed by Samuel Gompers to be the national organizer of women for the AFL, the first person to hold that post. Despite her vigorous efforts to organize women workers in New York City, upstate New York, and Massachusetts, the AFL eliminated her position five months later. During a trip to Boston, she met John F. O'Sullivan, labor editor of the *Boston Globe* and himself an AFL representative. They were married in 1894, settled in Boston, and had four children: Kenney, Mortimer, Roger, and Mary Elizabeth.

She remained active in the cause of organized labor, serving on the board of directors of the Women's Educational and Industrial Union of Boston and as executive secretary of the Union for Industrial Progress. In 1902 John O'Sullivan was killed in a train accident. Though devastated for a time by his loss, she continued in her reform efforts. Together with William English Walling, she cofounded in 1903 the National Women's Trade Union League, which became an influential voice for reform throughout the Progressive era.

O'Sullivan worked as a Massachusetts factory inspector between the years 1914–34, supporting her family and speaking out for the "full citizenship" of working women, voting rights for women, and organized labor. She was a delegate at the national conference of the League of Women Voters in 1922. Strongly opposed to U.S. involvement in World War I, she traveled to New York City to prevent one of her sons from enlisting, and joined the Women's International League for Peace and Freedom. She died in 1943 of heart disease in West Medford, Massachusetts, and her passing was marked with a solemn high requiem Mass.

Kenneally, James K. *Women and American Trade Unions*. Montreal, 1981, 20–22, 42–44.

_____. "Catholic and Feminist: A Biographical Approach." *U.S. Catholic Historian* 3 (Spring 1984) 229–53.

"The Labor War at Lawrence." *Survey* 28 (April 1912) 72–74.

JOSEPH QUINN

OUR SUNDAY VISITOR

Our Sunday Visitor was founded in 1912 by a priest of the Diocese of Fort Wayne, Indiana, Fr. John F. Noll, who was worried about the wave of anti-Catholic literature in the country at the time, and who fortuitously was offered a printing press in Huntington, Indiana, virtually as a gift.

Fr. John F. Noll, Founding Editor

Fr. Noll, who was born in 1875 in Fort Wayne and was ordained a priest in 1898, was pastor of St. Mary's Church in Huntington when the newspaper began publication. He was the founding editor and remained the publication's chief executive for many years, even after his own appointment as bishop of Fort Wayne in 1925. He died in 1956.

It was Fr. Noll's plan to establish a newspaper that would have national circulation primarily through distribution in the nation's Catholic parishes. Almost overnight, *Our Sunday Visitor,* published weekly, became a great success.

Responding to anti-Catholicism was a high priority in the early years. In 1913, one year after its first appearance, *Our Sunday Visitor* offered a reward of $10,000 to anyone who could prove the anti-Catholic charges then circulating. These charges most often dealt with the papacy and a supposed conspiracy of world domination, but they not uncommonly contained charges against bishops, priests, and nuns attacking not only their patriotism but their morality as well.

Our Sunday Visitor became an especially familiar periodical among Catholic Americans in the period between the First World War and the Great Depression. It was the time that the Ku Klux Klan became such a strong fixture in American politics, and it also was the time when Governor Alfred E. Smith of New York was seeking the U.S. presidency. Smith, a Catholic, campaigned for the Democratic presidential nomination in 1924 and was the Democratic nominee in 1928. Opposition to him very often was stridently anti-Catholic. While vigorously confronting the anti-Catholic slurs against Smith, *Our Sunday Visitor* studiously avoided any endorsement of his candidacy. The early years of *Our Sunday Visitor* were dominated by the wish to assure Americans that Catholic citizens indeed could be, and were, loyal to the country.

The newspaper also aggressively championed the needs of the poor and American blacks. When the U.S. bishops in 1919 called for sweeping changes in American public policy and attitudes about the poor, the newspaper supported them boldly. *Our Sunday Visitor* also editorially asked American Catholics to support Christian education for blacks.

In 1929 the Great Depression befell America, and many Catholics suffered the loss of jobs, of homes, and of confidence. In his editorials in *Our Sunday Visitor* of those years, by then Bishop Noll said that the greatest peril to American culture was its loss of religious values.

All these themes have been strong interests for *Our Sunday Visitor* over the years, and throughout the decades of its presence editorials have continually reflected these ideals.

Also highly important to the newspaper has been evangelization in the United States itself. Over the years, the newspaper has made countless monetary grants to missions in the United States. It is an activity still underway through the Our Sunday Visitor Institute, a philanthropy formed from publishing profits to assist Catholic missionary and religious causes in the United States.

Fr. Noll noticed that Protestant churches in Indiana in the early 1920s usually received donations in envelopes, distributed among regular members. As an adjunct of *Our Sunday Visitor,* he founded the envelope department, and this department was the first to supply American Catholic parishes with offertory envelopes.

Other Publications

In 1944, to reach priests in the United States, *Our Sunday Visitor* established *The Priest,* a monthly magazine for the clergy. Later, to reach other specified audiences, *Our Sunday Visitor* founded *Our Daily Visitor,* a bimonthly magazine of spiritual meditations for every day of the year; *Catholic Heritage,* a magazine devoted to the traditions of the Church; *The Catholic Answer,* a magazine to explain and clarify particular points of Catholic doctrine; and *Catholic Parent,* a magazine for Catholic spouses and parents.

By acquisition, *Our Sunday Visitor* also became the publisher of *The Pope Speaks,* a compendium of papal statements and addresses; the *U.S. Catholic Historian,* a scholarly review for American Catholic historians; and the *New Covenant,* a general religious magazine for Catholic adults.

Our Sunday Visitor also publishes annually about twenty-five books pertaining to Catholicity, and it is the publisher of catechetical materials, both in print and in various electronic forms.

Of the thirty-nine Catholic journalists in America to receive the St. Francis de Sales Award, the highest professional recognition conferred by the Catholic Press Association of the United States and Canada, up to 1994, six have been members of the staff of *Our Sunday Visitor.* The newspaper itself, and its companion publications, have consistently been recognized for professional excellence over the years.

OWEN CAMPION

P

PACE, EDWARD ALOYSIUS (1861–1938)

Priest, scholar, educator. Edward Aloysius Pace was born to George Edward and Margaret Kelly Pace on July 3, 1861, in Starke, Florida. He attended the public elementary school in Starke and Duval High School in Jacksonville before entering St. Charles College in Ellicott City, Maryland (1876–80) to study for the priesthood. He then studied at the North American College in Rome, where he was ordained on May 30, 1885. In 1886 he was awarded a doc-

Edward A. Pace

torate in sacred theology and returned to St. Augustine, Florida, to serve as rector of the cathedral and as chancellor. In 1888 he was selected for the faculty of the projected Catholic University of America and returned to Europe for graduate studies in psychology. In 1891 he was awarded a Ph.D. from the University of Leipzig, where he had studied experimental psychology under Wilhelm Wundt.

Pace was keenly interested in the dialogue between Thomistic philosophy and theology and the natural sciences, a dialogue that required comprehensive knowledge not only of Thomist principles and conclusions but also of contemporary scientific principles, method, and achievements. Pace dedicated his professional life to promoting that dialogue on the institutional as well as the intellectual level.

At The Catholic University, Pace served as professor of psychology (1891–94) and of philosophy (1894–1935), founder and dean of the School of Philosophy (1895–99; 1906–14; 1934–35), general secretary (1917–25), vice rector (1925–36), and founder (1899) and first director of the Institute of Pedagogy, which later became the School of Education. Pace was a founding associate editor of the *Catholic Encyclopedia* (1907–12), editor and cofounder with Thomas Edward Shields of the *Catholic Educational Review* (1911), first editor of *Studies in Psychology and Psychiatry* (1926), founder and first president of the American Catholic Philosophical Association (established at The Catholic University of America in 1926), and with James Hugh Ryan edited its journal, *New Scholasticism*.

Pace was elected president of the American Council on Education in 1925 and four years later was appointed by President Herbert Hoover to the National Advisory

Committee on Education. He was also one of the first leading figures in experimental psychology, establishing a psychology laboratory at The Catholic University of America, the second such facility in the U.S.A. His publications included his doctoral dissertation, *Das Relativitaets–prinzip in Herbert Spencer's psychologische Entwicklungslehre* (1891), *The Mass for Every Day in the Year* (Washington, D.C., 1916), and numerous scholarly articles on philosophy, religion, and education, all notable for their originality, clarity, and precision. Pace died in Washington, D.C., on April 26, 1938.

Nuesse, C. Joseph. *The Catholic University of America, A Centennial History.* Washington, D.C., 1990.

PATRICIA DeFERRARI

PALLADINO, LAURENCE BENEDICT (1837–1927)

Jesuit missionary. The last of the Northwest's pioneer missionaries, Laurence Benedict Palladino was born in a small village not far from Genoa, Italy, on August 15, 1837. As a missionary to the indigenous peoples of the Northwest, he arrived at St. Ignatius Mission in Montana Territory in September 1867, via the Isthmus of Panama and Santa Clara Mission, California.

Laurence B. Palladino

In 1873 he was assigned to the Helena Mission for whites, where he built the church which ten years later became Montana's first cathedral. He was reassigned to St. Ignatius Mission in December 1883 and in the spring of 1887 returned to Helena. In 1889 Bishop John B. Brondel appointed him the first diocesan director of schools, and in 1892 he became the bishop's right-hand man as chancellor and vicar general. In *Indian and White in the Northwest* (published in 1894), Palladino wrote of the development of the religious faith in the former wilds, and recorded with painstaking details both the brilliant and the foreboding acts of the invaders of the natives' territory. The book became, and still is, a classic in the Northwest.

In late 1894 he became the fifth president of Gonzaga College, and pastor of Spokane's St. Aloysius parish. In addition to time in Helena and two assignments in Missoula, Montana, he served briefly in Seattle and North Yakima, Washington, and in Lewiston, Idaho; but the greater portion of his more than sixty years devoted to the Church were as a zealous missionary. He knew the native peoples as few other men had the opportunity to know them. He was a man of faith who believed in miracles and questioned coincidences. He died in Missoula on August 19, 1927.

LUCYLLE EVANS

PALÓU, FRANCISCO (1723–89)

Franciscan, missionary. Palóu was born in Palma, Majorca, on January 22, 1723. He entered the Franciscan Order in 1739 and studied at Lullian University on Majorca under Junípero Serra. Palóu was ordained in 1747, and two years later he was sent with Serra to the missionary Apostolic College of San Fernando in Mexico City.

From 1750 to 1767, Palóu ministered to the mission natives of the Sierra Gorda and San Sabas (now Texas). After that he accompanied Serra to the missions of the Lower California Peninsula to replace the ousted Jesuits. There he eventually became missionary president. In 1773, Lower California was transferred to the Dominicans, and Palóu was assigned to the Upper California missions. On his way there, he marked the boundary between the Upper and Lower California missions. That demarcation was used to determine the border between the United States and Mexico in 1848.

While serving as temporary superior, he began his *Noticias de la Nueva California* (1774), a four-volume history of the early period of California's colonization. In 1776 he founded Mission San Francisco (also known as Mission Dolores), where he ministered for most of his remaining years. When Serra died in 1784, he transferred his authority to Palóu who again served as temporary president until he himself was recalled to San Fernando in Mexico City in 1785. The following year, he was chosen as superior of the college, a function which he held until his death. During that period he completed a biography of Serra (1787), which also serves as a history of the first nine California missions. Palóu died in Mexico City on April 6, 1789.

KEES-JAN WATERMAN

PANDOSY, CHARLES (1824–91)

Oblate of Mary Immaculate, missionary to the native peoples of the Northwest. Born in Margerides, France, on November 21, 1824, Pandosy attended Oblate seminaries in France. He was among four religious clerics Fr. Pascal Ricard recruited to become missionaries to the indigenous peoples of the Northwest. They left Le Havre on February 4, 1847, on the sailing ship *Zuric,* reaching New York on April 2, 1847. From St. Louis they prepared for the hazardous journey over the Oregon Trail, arriving at Fort Walla Walla on October 4, 1847. Pandosy and Fr. Chirouse were ordained on January 2, 1848, the first priests ordained in what is now Washington State.

Their first mission was at Yakima. During the Yakima Indian War, 1855–58, the mission was burned. Pandosy and the native converts fled to the mountains to escape the fury of American volunteers. After the Yakima War in 1859, he was moved to British Columbia. He founded a mission in Okanogan Valley, ministering throughout the area for forty years. He continued his missionary work, baptizing, marrying, burying, and teaching the natives to live peacefully among whites, to garden, grow wheat, raise animals, and plant apple trees. During severe winters when he was forced to stay indoors, he studied. He produced a native-language grammar, a dictionary, and hymns that were published by the Smithsonian Institution in 1862. He devoted his life to caring for the native peoples. He died in Penticton, British Columbia, on February 6, 1891.

EDWARD J. KOWRACH

PAPAL INFALLIBILITY AND AMERICAN CATHOLICS

Ultramontanism was one of the most notable movements of the nineteenth century. Confronted with the need for identity and stability in a rapidly changing world, the Catholic Church offered the answer of authority, personified in the pope. Generally treated as a European phenomenon, Ultramontanism significantly shaped Catholic culture and theology in the United States, where an ecclesiological and devotional revolution shaped patterns of prayer and religious sensibility from the middle of the nineteenth century until the dawn of Vatican Council II.

Nineteenth-Century Neo-Ultramontanism

The neo-Ultramontane attitude of the nineteenth century, unlike its predecessor of the same name (which was primarily a political and ecclesiastical power struggle), idealized the papacy and eventually made it the touchstone of infallibility for the entire Church. It was simply absent from American Catholic thought well into the nineteenth century. John Carroll held a typically eighteenth-century ecclesiology: while recognizing papal primacy, he saw the

Church not as a rule of absolute monarchy, but as a communion of churches centered on Rome. He believed infallibility to reside "in the body of bishops united and agreeing with their head, the bishop of Rome," and he considered the infallibility of the pope alone mere theological speculation. American bishops upheld a similar ecclesiology as late as the Second Plenary Council of Baltimore (1866).

During the long papacy of Pius IX (1846–78), the Catholic Church became identified with *Romanità,* in particular with the person of the pope. A chief factor precipitating this change was the need for security and identity caused by massive social upheaval—defined for American Catholics in the challenge of immigration, nativist reaction, and the trauma of the Civil War. In face of these, a centralized Church and a papacy endowed with certain truth afforded a rock of stability, a sense of unshakable certitude and justifiable pride. Roman centralization was achieved, in addition to personal feeling for the Pope, thorough standardization of ritual, education of seminarians, and direct papal influence in national churches. As the century progressed, appointment of bishops was increasingly appropriated by Rome, papal nuncios became direct channels of authority between pope and the local church, and Roman titles like *monsignor* were widely distributed. National seminaries founded or reestablished in Rome (the North American College in 1859) became a seedbeds for Ultramontane theology. Fostered by Dom Prosper Guéranger, the Roman Rite and Gregorian chant stood for the romantic ideal of a return to medieval Christendom united under the pope. Endorsed in the United States by the Third Plenary Council of Baltimore in 1884, this new "Gregorian reform" soon became normative for the universal Church.

From the 1840s, American Catholics were deeply affected by the new Ultramontane spirit developing in Europe. While freely acknowledging the spiritual supremacy of the pope, American Catholics remained aloof from the political aspects of Ultramontanism. American Ultramontane apologetics launched by the 1838 publication of Francis Patrick Kenrick's *The Primacy of the Apostolic See and the Authority of the General Councils Vindicated,* was further distinguished from the European by its claim that nineteenth-century popes actually affirmed American values, particularly liberty and social progress. A strong image of the papacy served, moreover, as a center of identity for the widely divergent elements of an immigrant Church.

For the majority of Catholics, the most consequential element in the process of Romanization was the emergence of a devotional piety which invoked symbols both spiritually powerful and uniquely adaptable to the new ecclesiology. Ultramontane piety, although thin on scholarly content and reliant on a pervasive emotionalism, did focus

Catholic spirituality on a God of love. The new devotionalism included recitation of prayers with papal indulgences attached and a strong rise in Marian piety—from the miraculous medal to the papal definition of the Immaculate Conception by Pius IX in 1854. Immensely popular, the Lourdes apparitions were interpreted as divine confirmation of the pontiff's decree. Eucharistic adoration, linked with devotion to the Sacred Heart in a theme of reparation, became widespread during the 1850s, and fit admirably the campaign to elicit loyalty to a papacy embattled in mid-nineteenth-century Italy. Devotionally inspired loyalty to the institutional Church in the person of the pope proved a strong lever for reinforcing the position of the proinfallibilists at Vatican Council I and played a large part in American response to the council's decrees.

U.S. Bishops at Vatican I

The United States bishops at Vatican Council I were deeply divided in their views; collectively, they embraced an entire spectrum of opinion. Bishop Edward Fitzgerald of Little Rock, for reasons that remain obscure, cast one of the two negative votes out of 535 for *Pastor Aeternus*. Peter Richard Kenrick, archbishop of St. Louis, stood out among the anti-infallibilists at Vatican Council I by his blunt and persistent opposition. There were also infallibilists, like Augustus Martin of Natchitoches. The true unifying theme behind the American bishops' activities at the council was pastoral concern: those who opposed the definition did so for reasons which were chiefly pragmatic and rooted in American experience, such as Archbishop Martin Spalding of Baltimore. In general, the United States Catholic press was moderately pro-infallibilist, although sometimes, as in the case of Orestes Brownson and James McMaster, stridently so. Opposition to the definition in the United States was swept away in a tide of sympathy and concern for the besieged pope when Italian troops invaded Rome. The defensive and devotional tenor of late nineteenth-century Catholicism was fused in ardent loyalty to the papal monarch whose authority was now absolute and unassailable. For American Catholics, the new image of the papacy provided a sense of unity among themselves and of moral superiority which allowed them to envision their Church in a leading role, bringing the American republic to the realization of its own true values. Paradoxically, a persecuted minority had found identity and a triumphal sense of mission in the very institution which made them so despised.

After Vatican Council I, American bishops ceased to govern their Church in the relatively collegial procedure of national councils. Baltimore III (1884) was the last plenary council to be held in the United States. By 1893, there was an apostolic delegation in Washington which promoted centralization of Church life under a compre-

hensive papal monarchy, and at the turn of the century, the Ultramontane Church was a *fait accompli*. Following the council, the pope was increasingly identified with the Church, and the aura of infallibility counted more than the actual definition or its explicit exercise. The codification of canon law, pontifical status for numerous religious orders, and Catholic Action (considered as participation of the laity in the apostolate of the hierarchy) underscored Roman centralization. The American Catholic press strongly affirmed Pius IX's *Casti connubii* (1930), with its traditional teaching on marriage, which included a prohibition of contraception. The beatification of Pius X in 1951 and his subsequent canonization in 1954 added enormously to papal prestige, placing an image of pope-as-saint to the fore.

Pius XII is the transitional figure in the history of Ultramontane feeling. While his era inaugurated the path to Vatican Council II, it also modeled the quintessence of papal devotionalism. His popularity among Americans was reinforced by a vigorous anti-Communist policy. In response to his *Humani generis*, American Catholic theologians offered only the most veiled distinctions.

Vatican II and After

After the Second Vatican Council, and in part because of it, Paul VI's *Humanae vitae* (1968), essentially reaffirming *Casti connubii*'s prohibition of contraception, created a storm of controversy. In the United States, six hundred theologians signed a statement of protest, and lay members of the Pontifical Study Commission on Family, Population, and Birth Problems expressed significant difficulty with the encyclical's conclusions. Directly or indirectly, the entire controversy regarding *Humanae vitae* reflected Catholics' attitudes toward the papacy, and for numerous Americans it spelled their disenchantment with the Ultramontane, authoritarian paradigm of Church government. What had served American Catholics as a universally binding ideology was shattered, and the Ultramontane papacy, instead of a rallying point and center of identity, became a touchstone of dispute. Questions regarding the nature of papal teaching authority set in motion at Vatican Council I were heightened in 1995, when the Vatican Congregation for the Doctrine of the Faith declared that the prohibition of the ordination of women by John Paul II in his apostolic letter, *Ordinatio Sacerdotalis* (May 22, 1994), had been "set forth infallibly by the ordinary and universal magisterium" (*Responsum ad dubium*, October 28, 1995). The issue highlighted unresolved tensions regarding how the pope speaks for the Church as well as the ecclesiological significance of such tensions.

For over a hundred years, Ultramontane Catholicism addressed profound issues of identity for American Catholics. In the United States, where Catholicism developed in a hostile environment, the Ultramontane ethos provided immense security and emphasized the distinction of the Catholic community. But as the separatist status of Roman Catholics disappeared, so did their separate, devotional, Ultramontane culture. The demise of devotionalism in Catholic life over the past twenty-five years is no accident. It is not the result of Vatican Council II, but symptomatic of the passing of a strong and largely successful worldview.

See also VATICAN COUNCIL I AND AMERICAN PARTICIPATION.

Byrne, Patricia, C.S.J. "American Ultramontanism." *Theological Studies* (June 1995) 301–26.

Costigan, Richard F., S.J. "Tradition and the Beginning of the Ultramontane Movement." *Irish Theological Quarterly* 48 (1981) 27–46.

Hennesey, James, S.J. *The First Council of the Vatican: The American Experience.* New York: Herder and Herder, 1963.

Holmes, J. Derek. *The Triumph of the Holy See: A Short History of the Papacy in the Nineteenth Century.* Shepherdstown, W. Va.: Patmos Press, 1978.

Mize, Sandra Yocum. "The Papacy in Mid-Nineteenth Century American Catholic Imagination." Ph.D. dissertation, Marquette University, 1987.

PATRICIA BYRNE, C.S.J.

PAPAL REPRESENTATION IN AMERICA

Early Contacts

"Congress will probably never send a Minister to His Holiness who can do them no service, upon condition of receiving a Catholic legate or nuncio: or, in other words, an ecclesiastical tyrant, which, it is to be hoped, the United States will be too wise ever to admit into their territories."

These words of John Adams, addressed to the Continental Congress in 1779, were destined to be ignored more than two centuries later when, in 1984, President Ronald Reagan accepted the credentials of the Most Reverend Pio Laghi as the first apostolic pronuncio to the United States.

Although it was only after it entered its third century of existence that the United States accepted an accredited ambassador, or nuncio, from the Holy See, it had, during its first century, maintained consular relations with the Papal States for seventy-five years and sent an accredited representative to the Papal Court for twenty years.

The Holy See initiated diplomatic dialogue when the papal nuncio at Versailles, Archbishop Doria-Pamphili, wrote, on July 28, 1783, to Dr. Benjamin Franklin, the United States Minister in France. He informed Franklin that Rome had decided to establish an episcopal office in the United States. He also requested that, if no suitable American could be found for the office, Congress might consent to the appointment of a citizen from a "friendly" country, meaning France. On May 11, 1784, the Continental Congress resolved:

That Doctor Franklin be desired to notify the Apostolical Nuncio at Versailles that Congress will always be pleased to testify their respect to his sovereign and State; but that the subject of his application to Doctor Franklin, being purely spiritual, is without the jurisdiction and powers of Congress, who have no authority to permit or refuse it, these powers being reserved to the several states individually.

Thus began the bumpy and erratic diplomatic correspondence between the United States of America and the Holy See.

Consular Relations

From 1797 until 1870, eleven consuls would serve American interests in Papal Rome. Papal consular representation in the United States began in 1826 and continued, oddly enough, more than twenty years after the demise of the Papal States. Consuls, whose chief care is the welfare of their fellow citizens and the promotion of commerce, are not diplomatic agents. Nonetheless, the Holy See granted the American consuls at Rome unusual diplomatic privileges and favors, seeing to it that they were received at formal functions on the same footing as diplomatic representatives of other nations.

Ministerial Relations

In 1848 the United States appointed a minister and opened a legation in the Papal States. A minister, although ranking beneath an ambassador, is accredited to a particular government. In the nineteenth century it was normal to send diplomats of ministerial rank to smaller nations. The major activity of the American Legation took place during the War Between the States when the United States Minister worked to assure papal support for the Union cause or, at least, nonrecognition of the Confederate States of America.

During this time there was never a question of reciprocity, of the United States accepting a papal diplomatic representative. In 1867, two years after the close of the Civil War, the legation's budget was eliminated by the United States Congress and the last "United States Minister Near the Holy Seat" (as the official stationary was imprinted) left Rome. However, the legation was not officially suppressed.

Rome Strives for Diplomatic Relations

The first official report to the Holy See from one of its own agents which recommended the establishment of a permanent representative in the United States was the report of Archbishop Gaetano Bedini after his American sojourn in 1853. Bedini believed that a nunciature would help the American Church to remedy the defects he perceived and to grow stronger on a firm foundation. The Catholic population was growing rapidly due to immigration chiefly from Ireland as well as the inclusion of many Catholics in the lands recently annexed from Mexico. He saw a nunciature as necessary to protect expanding Catholic interests in the United States.

Bedini emphasized a theme which would be continually repeated in official Roman deliberations concerning this question. He stressed that a nuncio would serve to keep the American bishops united to the Holy See. Many in the Roman Curia believed that the American bishops were affected to an unhealthy degree by American ideals of independence and liberty. The themes emphasized by Bedini, unity with Rome, selection of reliable bishops, clerical discipline, and financial stability, would be found in all subsequent Roman discussions concerning the American Church.

In 1861 and again in 1877, the Sacred Congregation for the Propagation of the Faith (Propaganda Fide, the Roman office charged with oversight of the Church in the United States until 1908), recommended sending a delegate to the United States to assure the flow of unbiased information necessary in the nomination of bishops. Bishop George Conroy of Ardagh, Ireland, sent as temporary apostolic delegate to Canada in 1878, made a similar recommendation on his return. The cardinals of Propaganda Fide, in discussions preparatory to the Third Plenary Council of Baltimore (1884), called for a permanent apostolic delegate who would obtain exact information on candidates proposed for the episcopate, gain better knowledge of the clergy, inform Propaganda Fide on questions disputed between bishops and priests, and solve the many questions and complaints which deluged the Roman offices. Finally, he would act as a brake on bishops and force them to proceed more regularly so that their priests would have less reason to complain.

In 1889 Archbishop Francesco Satolli represented the Holy See at the centennial celebrations of the establishment of the American hierarchy and the founding of The Catholic University of America. Upon his return to Rome, Satolli presented a report stating that "more direct means of communication between the Holy See and the American Church were desirable."

The apparent disunity of the American hierarchy over the "school question," continuing public strife between priests and bishops, and the machinations of various American prelates combined to offer Rome the opportunity it had long sought to send and establish a permanent apostolic delegate in the United States. Although almost all the archbishops and bishops opposed a permanent delegate, Archbishop John Ireland of St. Paul worked to bring to the United States a delegate whom he believed would support his views on parochial schools and other questions.

Archbishop Francesco Satolli returned to the United States on the pretext of representing the Holy See at the World Columbian Exposition of 1892–93. Arriving in Baltimore, Satolli told a taciturn Cardinal James Gibbons of the plan to establish a permanent apostolic delegation.

The opposition of Gibbons and the other archbishops, except Ireland, served to confirm Rome's view that a delegate was needed and on January 14, 1893, the establishment of a permanent apostolic delegation was announced. The apostolic delegate was to represent the Holy See to the Catholic Church in the United States but would not have diplomatic status before the government of the United States. In the words of Pope Leo XIII, "We cheerfully sent one who would represent Our Person. . . ." It had taken more than a century to establish a permanent representative of the Holy See in the United States. Reciprocity would not be achieved for almost another century.

The Apostolic Delegates and Nuncios

The first apostolic delegate, Francesco Satolli (1893–96), firmly established the delegation. Initially, Satolli supported the faction of the hierarchy represented by Archbishop John Ireland of St. Paul. By the end of his term he had switched his favor to the more conservative wing of the episcopate represented by Archbishop Michael A. Corrigan of New York. Created a cardinal in 1895, he returned to Rome the following year to become Prefect of the Sacred Congregation of Studies and Archpriest of the Basilica of St. Mary Major.

Satolli's successor, Sebastiano Martinelli, O.S.A. (1896–1901), began to exercise more vigilance over recommendations leading to the appointment of bishops. Named a cardinal, he returned to Rome to become Prefect of the Sacred Congregation of Rites.

Diomede Falconio, O.F.M. (1901–11), had been apostolic delegate to Canada and Newfoundland when he was named to succeed Martinelli in Washington. Known for his aggressive investigation of suspected Modernists in the seminaries of New York and Baltimore, he became cardinal bishop of Velletri in 1911.

The fourth delegate, Giovanni Bonzano (1912–22), had been a missionary in China and rector of the Urban College in Rome. During his tenure, he sought to reduce tensions stemming from the resentment of Cardinals William O'Connell of Boston and Dennis Dougherty of Philadelphia towards the nascent National Catholic Welfare Council, later the National Catholic Welfare Conference (NCWC). Named a cardinal in 1922, he returned to Rome.

Pietro Fumasoni-Biondi (1922–33), the fifth delegate, was a career diplomat. While apostolic delegate, he was involved in overtures by American Catholic leaders to ease the persecution of the Church in Mexico. In 1933 he was created a cardinal and served as Prefect of the Sacred Congregation for the Propagation of the Faith.

Amleto Giovanni Cicognani (1933–58) served the longest tenure as delegate. He held the post during the difficult years of World War II and the cold war which followed. Although lacking official diplomatic status, he engaged in frequent communications with the government of the United States in a variety of sensitive issues of international policy. The growing interest of the United States in communication with the Holy See was exemplified in 1939 by President Franklin D. Roosevelt's appointment of Myron Taylor as his personal representative to Pope Pius XII. Taylor remained in this post until 1950. In 1951 President Harry Truman nominated General Mark Clark as ambassador to the Holy See. The resulting controversy led Clark to withdraw his nomination. Receiving the red hat in 1958, Cicognani soon thereafter received the most prestigious appointment in the Vatican, Secretary of State.

Egidio Vagnozzi (1958–67), the seventh delegate, had been apostolic delegate and nuncio in the Philippines. He served in Washington when it was becoming popular to question Church authority in the period during and immediately after the Second Vatican Council. Recalled to Rome in 1967, he was elevated to the cardinalate and became head of the Prefecture of Economic Affairs.

Luigi Raimondi (1967–73) was apostolic delegate to Mexico when he was named to Washington. He served during an era made controversial by the war in Vietnam, civil rights turmoil, and the dissent subsequent to *Humanae vitae*. He worked behind the scenes to facilitate the opening of peace discussions between the United States and North Vietnam. Created a cardinal in 1973, he was named Prefect of the Sacred Congregation of the Saints.

Jean Jadot (1973–80), a Belgian, served in several diplomatic posts, coming to Washington from Cameroun. His informal style and his penchant for the appointment of men thought more "pastoral" and collegial, left its mark on the Church in the United States. The only non-Italian to hold the post of apostolic delegate to the United States, he was also the only delegate not to be appointed to the College of Cardinals. Upon his return to Rome he was named President of the Secretariat for Non-Christians.

Pio Laghi (apostolic delegate 1980–84, pronuncio 1984–90) was a career diplomat who had served in many posts. His approachable personality and fondness for American ways made him a popular figure in the United States. During his tenure, the United States established formal diplomatic relations with the Holy See (1984) and Laghi became the first pronuncio, the equivalent of an ambassador. Created a cardinal in 1990, he was named Prefect of the Congregation for Catholic Education.

Agostino Cacciavillan (1990–) served as pronuncio to India before coming to the United States. In 1991 the appellation "pronuncio" was abolished and Cacciavillan's title was changed to nuncio.

The Role of the Nuncio and the Nunciature

An apt description of the role of the nuncio was provided by Pope Paul VI, speaking in Manila in 1970:

> The role of Nuncios is also evolving. Until now, the Nuncio was little more than the Pope's representative to governments and churches. His activity with regard to the churches was above all of a hierarchical and administrative nature; in a certain sense he remained a stranger to the local church.
>
> Today, the Nuncio must place a more pronounced pastoral accent on his work. He too is at the service of the Kingdom of God as it goes forward in the land.

The role of the nuncio or the apostolic delegate is further spelled out in canon 364 of the revised Code of Canon Law. He is to serve as a liaison between the bishops of a given country and the central government of the Church, keeping Rome up to date on the situation in the host country. Further he is to assist the bishops while respecting their prerogatives and rights. One way he accomplishes this is by collaborating with the local conference of bishops. A very important, perhaps the most important, duty of a nuncio is to transmit names of candidates for the episcopacy after consulting with the bishops of the particular province and the officers of the episcopal conference.

The Holy See and the United States each maintain diplomatic relations with well over one hundred governments. Their relations with each other are mutually beneficial. Official diplomatic relations provide the United States with a listening post and an opportunity to influence the actions of the Holy See, a significant player in international affairs. They provide the Holy See with a channel of information and an opportunity to influence the most powerful player in international affairs.

See also POPES AND AMERICA.

Jean Jadot

Cardinale, Hyginus E. *The Holy See and the International Order.* Toronto: Macmillan of Canada, 1976.

Fogarty, Gerald P. *The Vatican and the American Hierarchy from 1870–1965.* Wilmington, Del.: Michael Glazier, 1985.

Graham, Robert A. *Vatican Diplomacy: A Study of Church and State on the International Plane.* Princeton, N.J.: Princeton University Press, 1959.

U.S. Catholic Historian 12 (2) (Spring 1994). Special Topic Issue: "The Apostolic Delegation/Nunciature 1893–1993."

ROBERT J. WISTER

PARISEAU, ESTHER (1823–1902)

Architect and religious. First superior of the Sisters of Providence in the Pacific Northwest. Mother Joseph was born Esther Pariseau, in Montreal, Canada, on April 16, 1823, the daughter of Joseph and Françoise Pariseau. She entered the Sisters of Providence in Montreal on December 26, 1843, taking the name of Joseph of the Sacred Heart, and made profession on July 21, 1845. Bishop Augustine Blanchet requested the services of the sisters for the Diocese of Nesqually from his colleague, Bishop Ignace Bourget, of Montreal. The bishop sent Mother Joseph and four sisters in response and on December 8, 1856, they arrived at Fort Vancouver located near the mouth of the Columbia River, Washington Territory. The sisters had been given a mandate to educate the young, care for the poor and sick, and to minister to the Native Americans in the region. Mother Joseph was skilled in carpentry and woodcarving, as well as the domestic arts, and used these abilities throughout her life in the Northwest. By early 1857, Mother Joseph had turned a fur storage building into a convent. This became part of a small complex of cabins known as the "Providence enclosure" that served as school, orphanage, bakery, laundry, and hospital. On June 7, 1858, St. Joseph Hospital, Vancouver, opened as the first permanent hospital in the Northwest.

During her tenure as superior, Mother Joseph oversaw the design, construction, and fundraising for nearly all Providence institutions in the Northwest. She designed and supervised construction of the permanent Providence Academy complex in 1873, St. Vincent Hospital, Portland, Oregon, in 1875, and Sacred Heart Hospital, Spokane, Washington, in 1886. To support projects such as these, she traveled by stagecoach and horseback to the mining camps in Idaho and Montana to beg for financial assistance. Mother Joseph was self-reliant and determined, and enjoyed a deep spiritual life and a special devotion to the Sacred Heart. By 1902 she had established twenty-nine institutions including schools, hospitals, orphanages, homes for the aged, and a mental asylum in Washington, Oregon, Idaho, Montana, and British Columbia. She died of a brain tumor in Vancouver, Washington, on January 19, 1902, and is buried in St. James cemetery, Vancouver, Washington. Mother Joseph is recognized as one of the state's first architects and is represented in Statuary Hall in Washington, D.C.

Gleason, Mary, S.P. *He Has Given Me a Flame: A Sketch of the Life of Mother Joseph of the Sacred Heart, 1823–1902.* Montreal, 1992.

Lentz, Dorothy, S.P. *The Way It Was in Providence Schools.* Montreal, 1978.

McCrossen, Mary, S.P. *The Bell and the River.* Palo Alto, 1956.

CHRISTINE TAYLOR

PASSIONISTS (C.P.)

Paul of the Cross and the Foundation of the Community

The tradition and spirit of the Passionist Congregation are rooted in the unique charism given to Paul Francis Daneo, known as Paul of the Cross, born at Ovada, Italy, January 3, 1694. From early experiences of mystical prayer and charitable service, Paul identified the ultimate sign of God's love for the world as the passion of Jesus. A forty-day retreat (November 23, 1720–January 1, 1721), during which he kept a spiritual diary and composed a first *Rule,* marks the birth of his congregation. Initially called 'The Poor of Jesus,' its mission would be to promote a living remembrance of the passion as a way to seek personal union with God and to reflect upon the meaning of human suffering. With others who shared his vision, Paul pursued this mission through a life structured around prolonged periods of prayer, solitude, and apostolic service. He unfailingly gave priority to the apostolate of the word by proclaiming the Gospel of the Passion, especially to the neglected and the poor.

Following the founder's death (October 18, 1775), the growth of the congregation until 1840 was confined to the area of present-day Italy. It was principally the political situation in Europe which delayed further expansion during this peninsular period. With the leadership of Anthony Testa (1839–62), recognized as the second founder, the congregation began to experience a period of universal growth, extending its mission "to Belgium, England, France, Holland, Australia and the United States" (Yuhaus, 29).

The First Foundation in America

When Michael O'Connor, first bishop of Pittsburgh, traveled to Rome with the *Acta* of the First Plenary Council of Baltimore and his diocesan report to Propaganda, he formally requested that the congregation be established in his diocese. The bishop assumed financial responsibility for the passage and lodging of the religious as well as their language study. They, in turn, were to live the rule and to work for the "spiritual advantage" of others. In the aforementioned areas and with regard to providing land for the first monastery, Bishop O'Connor was exceedingly generous, becoming the "first benefactor of the Order in America" (Yuhaus, 16–17, 22).

Frs. Anthony Calandri (superior), Albinus Magno, and Stanislaus Parczyk, and Br. Lawrence di Giacomo arrived in Pittsburgh in the fall of 1852. Calandri and Magno, both missionaries, were practically opposite in temperament. The former was exacting in regard to the observance of the rule and to his office, failing to appreciate differences in attitude and culture. Magno possessed "a stronger, more assertive and better balanced personality, kept himself open to discussion, adaptation and, if necessary, change." Testa had intended that such diversity would prove to be complementary (Yuhaus, 57).

Calandri first worked among the orphans who were being cared for by the Sisters of Mercy. In the course of fundraising, he reconciled lapsed Catholics, "rectified marriages, pacified families and won converts. . . . the city witnessed Father Anthony's heroic charity during the cholera epidemic in 1854," when he endeared himself to people of all denominations. Magno, the first to learn English, helped out in various congregations throughout the diocese and instructed some of the order's postulants (Yuhaus, 212–15).

At the request of Bishop John Neumann, Parczyk, who was fluent in German, worked for a brief period as an agent of reconciliation at Holy Trinity German Church in Philadelphia, the scene of long-standing tension over the issue of trusteeism. Shortly after arriving in Pittsburgh, he began to minister to the German people of St. Michael's parish in Birmingham, assisted by Br. Lawrence, the youngest of the group (Yuhaus, 43–44). It was these same German people who contributed generously toward the building of the first monastery. Contributions from local Catholics and Protestants enabled its completion in the spring of 1854. By that time, the religious had become widely known for their ministry as confessors.

Following these initial endeavors, the organization of life and apostolate was primarily due to the arrival of John Dominick Tarlattini from Italy in 1854 and Gaudentius Rossi from England. Tarlattini succeeded Anthony Calandri as superior and "was singularly responsible for the development of the Passionist life in the United States. Its shape, its vision, its spirit, the attitudes it adopted and the adaptations it accepted were his responsibility" (Yuhaus, 70).

The community's preaching apostolate began with the arrival of Rossi in December 1855. Following a special series of discourses on the passion which he delivered at the Pittsburgh cathedral, a mission campaign was inaugurated throughout the diocese. Lasting until the end of the following year, it brought "the spiritual exercises of a parish retreat or mission" to rural areas for the first time (Yuhaus, 256).

Subsequently, requests from outside the diocese brought the preaching ministry to Brooklyn (St. Joseph's, Pacific and Dean Streets), St. Louis, the Diocese of Hartford, Boston (St. Joseph's, Chambers St.), and Baltimore. The mission in Brooklyn, at which many Protestants were in attendance, was accompanied by the testimony of cures, arousing controversy "in the Protestant and Catholic press" (Yuhaus, 266). Most lasting in effect were the three missions held in Baltimore, after which a new foundation was initiated at the request of Archbishop Martin John Spalding in 1865.

Ministry to converts was an expressed concern of the congregation for its mission in America. After the opening of the monastery in Birmingham, this apostolate "was given a more definite form" in the more distinct preparation of mission sermons. The "first recorded instance of a fully organized mission for Protestants" was at St. Joseph's in Boston (March 1864) (Yuhaus, 278, 280).

Expansion and Adaptation

During the period 1854–60, dioceses in the East, Midwest, and the Northwest expressed interest in the establishment of Passionist foundations. It was in Dunkirk, Chautauqua County, New York, however, that the Passionists, with some uncertainty, established their second retreat. Bishop John Timon, C.M., based his request on an earlier promise of consideration by the Passionist general, and Magno strongly encouraged the new foundation. In April 1860, the latter assumed his duties as pastor of St. Mary's parish and by July 20, 1862, a small monastery had been built for the community. In 1877 the visitor general directed that it be converted into a preparatory school.

Following a mission given by Rossi and Calandri at Our Lady of Mercy, West Hoboken (now, Union City, New Jersey), Fr. Anthony Cauvin (a primary organizer of the Church in this area) offered to help to establish the community in the new diocese. James Roosevelt Seton Bayley, first bishop of Newark, was pleased with the proposed foundation, and, with the general's approval, the religious arrived in West Hoboken on April 16, 1861. In the years that followed, the Passionists founded parishes and schools and conducted numerous retreats and parish missions, thus contributing to the organization and growth of the Church in northern New Jersey.

During these early years, the founders were quickly presented with the growing needs of the local church in a new political and religious context. The American mentality was characterized by a concern for practicality. The nation was experiencing increased immigration and nativism; most importantly, it was deeply affected by the unrest and division which erupted into the Civil War. There was a pressing need for parish organization and ministry and new vitality was being sought through parish missions and retreats for the clergy.

The religious adapted to their new situation, dispelling concerns that their strict rule of life would be incompatible with other settings. Addressing the community's cautious approach to the acceptance of parishes, Anthony Testa determined that judgments in this regard would be made locally. He wisely admonished the founders, first in Belgium and then in America, to emphasize the spirit of the Passionist Rule, especially in the training of novices, while adapting to the national character. That they accepted his advice is confirmed in the observations of Cardinal Gibbons, who acknowledged that he had known the founders personally, praising them as "international men" who "identified themselves" with the country and "became Americans. Their work proves," he said, "that the rule and spirit of St. Paul of the Cross are adapted to every clime and every age" (Ward, 7).

Beginning in the 1870s, four new foundations were established in the Midwest, the first at the invitation of Archbishop John Purcell of Cincinnati. "The Immaculata" on Mt. Adams, the site of a popular Good Friday pilgrimage and a part of the "religious history" of the city (Ward, 350), was entrusted to the care of the Passionists in May 1871. Later, the community purchased and remodeled the Old Cincinnati Observatory for use as a monastery, and erected a church under the title of Holy Cross.

Following a clergy retreat preached by Charles Lang in the summer of 1877 and a mission at the cathedral, Bishop William McCloskey invited the Passionists to work in the Louisville diocese at the parish of St. Cecilia. A community residence soon opened in July 1880, with chaplaincies at St. Agnes Academy and St. Vincent's Orphanage.

In the Diocese of St. Louis, a plan for a new foundation was approved by Archbishop Peter Kenrick after a series of missions in 1883–84. When work on the new Passionist retreat at Normandy stopped for lack of funds, Fr. David Phelan, editor of the *Western Watchman,* organized a benefit, at which parishes and several religious congregations worked for its successful completion.

After giving retreats to religious in 1893, the Passionists saw the former Jesuit mission at Osage, southern Kansas, as a possible site for their own ministry and began work there in 1894. Later, the name of Osage Mission was changed to St. Paul, Kansas, in honor of the Passionist founder.

Adaptations in Preaching

Adaptation to the American context called for new approaches to preaching. The method adopted in America was based largely upon the experience of the Passionists in England, exemplified in the work of Gaudentius Rossi. Departing from certain traditional elements of style, he favored a more intellectual (and less emotional) content and less elaborate ceremonies. Greater conformity to the American setting and to local needs involved a change in the daily schedule, a simplified (and less public) opening

ceremony, and the introduction of catechetical instruction for children, especially as preparation for first confession and Communion. As in England, the renewal of baptismal promises replaced "the former acts of detestation of sin and the oath of perseverance in virtue" (Yuhaus, 247). Finally, a large mission cross was placed near the church at the close of the mission. Although Rossi had wanted to exceed "the accommodations granted in England and looked toward a far greater independent development of the apostolate much more in accord with American culture, ideas, and temperament" (Yuhaus, 252), it was not until 1884 that the congregation allowed particular mission directories for each province.

By the turn of the century, two missionaries were creating a distinct impact upon the preaching apostolate. James Kent Stone, formerly an Episcopalian priest and president of Hobart College, was ordained as a Paulist in December 1872 and later entered the Passionists as Fidelis of the Cross. Soon known for his eloquence, he was requested by Cardinal Gibbons to conduct a mission at the Baltimore cathedral and to preach at the requiem for Pius IX. He also preached at the inauguration of The Catholic University of America.

Fr. Xavier Sutton, born in Tiffin, Ohio, in 1852, was also very successful as a preacher. In 1899, at St. Raphael's Church in New York City, he began to develop a program of missions which reflected his interest in a ministry to the wider Christian community. Working almost exclusively in the Midwest, he became renowned in his preaching to Protestants, and, with the early Paulists, may be regarded as a pioneer in the development of this apostolate. His adapted mission format often included a one-week mission for Catholics and a second week for Protestants, followed by programs of instruction for those who were interested. Fr. Xavier's courtesy and charity did much to overcome anti-Catholic sentiment.

The Province of Holy Cross

The increasing territorial expansion of the American province at the turn of the century prompted the provincial chapter of 1906 to recommend unanimously that the province be divided. Consequently, beginning July 30, communities at Cincinnati, Louisville, St. Louis, St. Paul, Kansas, and Chicago became the first foundations of the new province of Holy Cross. All were not in agreement with this decision, expressing concerns about personnel, finances, and the existing structures. An acceptable resolution of these matters was reached by both provincial councils during the summer of 1908.

An opportunity for collaboration occurred with the appointment of a Passionist as the first bishop of the Diocese of Corpus Christi. Paul Joseph Nussbaum, who had served for seven years in Buenos Aires, arrived in the new diocese in June 1913. At the time of his installation, thirty-five priests were serving in nineteen churches and fifty-four missions, and more than seventy thousand of the eighty-two thousand Catholics were Mexican.

The bishop's plan for the spiritual development of the diocese involved the organization of parish societies, a regular program of spiritual exercises, and Catholic education. Becoming aware of anti-Catholic sentiment, he called upon the services of Frs. Camillus Hollobough and Isidore Dwyer, whose mission at the cathedral parish in 1915 was attended by many Protestants. Their lectures on the Catholic faith were well received and contributed to overcoming bigotry. Bishop Nussbaum submitted his resignation in 1920 and was appointed to the Diocese of Marquette in 1922, where he again received apostolic assistance from both provinces.

New Ventures: 1920–45

Beginning around 1920, important developments began to take place with regard to retreats for the laity, new mission endeavors, and the printed word. Novenas became popular forms of devotion and were conducted in honor of the Passionist saints at many of the monastery churches. At Scranton the weekly devotion in honor of St. Ann culminated in the celebration of the solemn novena each summer, attended by thousands of the faithful.

The Lay Retreat Movement. From the beginning, American foundations continued the Founder's tradition of providing opportunities for other religious, clergy, and laity to make the 'spiritual exercises.' Retreats were made at West Hoboken prior to 1869, and records at Pittsburgh show that more than five hundred laymen and clergy had made retreats between 1860 and 1920. Thus, a tradition had long been established prior to the first 'closed' retreat at Brighton, Massachusetts, in 1911.

Both American provinces, recognizing the importance of retreats for the laity, built new facilities for this purpose. The first separate retreat house for laymen was dedicated in Pittsburgh on November 21, 1920. In the East, this apostolate also developed at West Springfield, Massachusetts, and Jamaica, New York. In Holy Cross province, vision and perseverance guided the movement from a first retreat in July 1926 to the dedication of the first monastery-retreat center at Sierra Madre on May 1, 1932. Fr. Eugene Creegan, who had sustained the Passionist vision for Sierra Madre from the beginning, directed the first program at this new facility.

New Mission Endeavors. Responding to one of the expressed goals of the general chapter, the Twentieth Chapter of St. Paul of the Cross Province voted unanimously to establish a mission in China. Early in 1922, six missionaries arrived in Yuanling (formerly Shenchow) in north-

east Hunan province. Other groups followed in the summers of 1922 and 1923.

It was not long before this new venture exemplified an outstanding spirit of generous service and collaboration in mission. In 1924 four missionaries from Holy Cross province were among the new arrivals. During the next two years the Sisters of Charity from Convent Station, New Jersey, and the Sisters of St. Joseph from Baden, Pennsylvania, brought expertise in nursing, administration, and education. These religious and those who followed worked tirelessly to provide food, medical assistance, and hospital care for those in need, while caring for orphans and providing for catechetical instruction and education. Their efforts were challenged by the rugged environment of the land, famine, sickness, bandit raids, and war. During the Sino-Japanese War, care was provided for an estimated 100,000 refugees.

All of the missionaries did not return to their homeland. Sickness claimed the lives of some, and on April 24, 1929, Frs. Walter Coveyou, Clement Seybold, and Godfrey Holbein were brutally murdered by bandits. With the Communist takeover in 1949, the missionaries endured house arrest, imprisonment, and expulsion. Cuthbert O'Gara, C.P., first bishop of Yuanling, was imprisoned on July 2, 1951. After his release from Yuanling prison on March 20, 1953, the release of other missionaries followed. Finally, Frs. Justin Garvey and Marcellus White crossed into Hong Kong on November 19, 1955, the last of their community to depart.

At the initiative of Frs. Victor Koch and Valentine Lehnerd in 1922, the congregation was introduced into Germany and Austria. Both American provinces contributed personnel to this mission which had forty-three religious at the outbreak of World War II. Among the contributing pioneers were Leonard Barthelemy, Fidelis Benedik, and Br. Valentine Rausch.

The years 1928 to 1938 mark the beginning of an apostolate among black Americans in North Carolina and Alabama. From chapel-car missions, Eastern Passionists eventually worked toward building parish communities in New Bern, Washington, and Greenville, in the newly formed Diocese of Raleigh. The growth of these congregations was accompanied by the foundation of grammar schools and fully accredited high schools, directed by the I.H.M. Sisters from Scranton and the Sisters of Christian Charity. At Greenville, Fr. Maurice Tew began convert work, built a catechetical center for children from public schools, preached on TV, and was a popular speaker at school gatherings and before Protestant congregations. After Bishop Vincent Waters directed that all churches and schools be integrated, the consolidation of missions and parishes under diocesan personnel followed during the 1960s.

In 1938, at the invitation of Bishop Thomas J. Toolen of the Mobile diocese, the Passionists of Holy Cross province began a ministry to the black community in Ensley, Alabama. Organization and building began with the opening of the first school at Holy Family Mission in September, staffed by the Felician Sisters of Chicago, and continued when the Sisters of Charity of Nazareth began teaching at Holy Family High School in 1943. The Sisters of Charity also directed the development of a hospital facility in several stages. A second mission was begun at Fairfield, where the Church of St. Mary was dedicated in March 1943. A small elementary school staffed by the Franciscan Sisters of Joliet, Illinois, was dedicated in March 1949.

The Printed Word. Publication of the *Sign* magazine by the Eastern province began during the summer of 1921. Reporting on various aspects of Catholic life and issues of social concern, the *Sign* attempted to present a solid guide to Christian living by examining topics from local, national, and international perspectives. Articles, photographs, and personal accounts sent by the missionaries in China provided something of a mission diary for American readers. The *Sign* enthusiastically promoted the lay retreat movement during the 1920s, followed international developments prior to and during the Second World War, reflected upon aspects of the 'cold war,' presented issues of concern to American Catholics following the Second Vatican Council, and continued to comment upon developing social issues until publication was discontinued in 1982.

Religious Formation and Education. During this period religious formation and education was an internal ministry of the community with personnel who had often completed university studies in Rome, Jerusalem, or at The Catholic University of America. A program of religious formation and professional training for brother candidates was developed under the direction of Brs. Daniel Smith and Simon West. Their initiative provided a foundation for future training in fields of increasing specialization.

1945–1970: Postwar Years— Toward the Renewal of Vatican II

Following the war, there was increasing interest in the study of Passionist history and spirituality. *The Passionist,* published by Holy Cross province, responded to this interest by printing letters of the founder, articles relating to the spirituality of the congregation, and news from provinces around the world. This period also witnessed a remarkable development of and commitment to the lay retreat movement. By the late 1960s, retreat facilities were newly established at ten locations. Besides serving as centers for personal spiritual renewal, they offered formation in lay leadership prior to and following the Second Vatican Council.

During the 1950s the Passionists were able to extend their apostolate of the word through the media. A local radio program begun by Fidelis Rice in 1954 was later broadcast internationally and a TV ministry began to develop at West Springfield under the theme of "The Chalice of Salvation."

In 1955 Passionists of the Eastern province began a ministry among black Catholics in the Diocese of Atlanta. While serving at the parish of St. Paul of the Cross, the community also envisioned a ministry of evangelization conducted within a wider geographical area. An elementary school was staffed by the Sisters of St. Joseph of Baden.

Passionists from the American provinces had been involved in Spanish-speaking ministry at St. Joseph's Church, Tacubaya, Mexico (beginning in 1865), and in the Diocese of Corpus Christi. With the establishment of a foundation in California, however, Spanish missions (begun by Casmir DiCristina and Isidore Dwyer) and retreats to the Spanish-speaking clergy of the Los Angeles diocese were conducted regularly. This apostolate grew with the arrival of Edward Viti in 1939 and continued to develop in the 1950s with the ministry of Henry Vetter. From the latter's work, Passionists assumed the pastoral care of parishes in Tijuana and, in the 1970s, organized a volunteer program of apostolic outreach in Baja California and Mexico.

Following the expulsion of the Passionists from China, new missions were established by Holy Cross province in Japan (1953) and Korea (1964), and by St. Paul of the Cross province in Jamaica, West Indies (1955), and the Philippines (1958). As in previous mission endeavors, the religious would seek, as an integral part of their mission, to establish the congregation locally.

The arrival of five Passionists in Japan in 1953 was soon followed by the beginning of a retreat ministry. Within four years, the lay retreat movement, near Osaka, had hosted more than one hundred groups, and a second retreat center was established at Fukuoka. The parish at Ikeda, with a pastoral outreach to shut-ins, orphans, the elderly, and hospital patients, later included a day-care nursery, directed by the Sisters of St. Joseph of Wichita. A new foundation in Korea was begun by three Passionists in 1964; retreat centers were established at Kwangju (1969) and Seoul (1977).

At the invitation of John J. McEleny, S.J., V. A., the first Passionists departed for Jamaica in March 1955 to continue the missions begun by the Jesuits at Manchester, St. Elizabeth, and Kingston. The needs of the local church, as outlined by the bishop, focused on the development of parishes and educational programs. From parish settings, the missionaries began to address these needs through religious instruction, hospital ministry, and an outreach to the poor. A retreat center was established at

Mandeville in 1973. In recent years, the Passionist Sisters have become coworkers in these ministries.

Since 1958 the Passionist mission in the Philippines has extended to the territory of Mindanao and a large section of the Diocese of Cotabato. Through parishes and special mission programs, assistance has been offered to some of the most poor and neglected people of the islands. At Calumpang, a retreat ministry has been developed at Holy Cross Spiritual Center.

The Response to Vatican II

With all religious congregations, the Passionists entered into the spirit of *aggiornamento* encouraged by Vatican Council II. American participants at the council included Barnabas M. Ahern, a noted Scripture scholar, consultor, and adviser to the American bishops, Malcolm Lavelle (superior general), and Theodore Foley, a member of the Commission for Religious. Later, as superior general, Theodore encouraged members "to move with the Church" in its "pilgrimage toward God" while seeking first the gift of "personal and interior renewal." During the Chapter of Renewal of 1968–70, he and James Patrick White (former provincial of Holy Cross province) served as bridge-builders to the respect and unity which produced the Chapter Document of 1970. As the foundation for the revised *"Rule"* completed in 1982, this document placed the Passion of Jesus "at the very heart of the Congregation," the source of "authentic unity" for Passionists everywhere (see Mercurio, *The Passionists,* ch. 22, esp. 152–55).

Principles articulated at the council and during the extraordinary general chapter guided the process of internal renewal, formation and education, and reflection on ministry. Local communities attempted to foster increased dialogue and planning while province commissions directed work in liturgical development, historical research, and the preaching apostolate. The House of Solitude, established first at Birmingham (September 14, 1969), and later at Bedford, Pennsylvania, provided the opportunity for prolonged reflection in the context of the forty-day retreat. Religious formation began to combine the experience of a university education with internal programs of study and preparation for ministry.

In 1967 the Passionists of Holy Cross province joined with the Servites (Eastern province) and Franciscans (Sacred Heart province) to form Catholic Theological Union at Chicago. Paul Bechtold, C.P., elected as the first president, described this venture as an opportunity to create a "theological school with a greater depth of faculty, a larger student body, and in ecumenical contact with seminarians of other faiths." With a focus on the Master of Divinity program, the school's expressed purpose has been to prepare "men and women for ministry in the Roman Catholic tradition." With the formation of an interprovince

novitiate and theologate in 1981, students from St. Paul of the Cross province now participate in the theology program offered at CTU (Paul I. Bechtold, *Catholic Theological Union at Chicago: The Founding Years, 1965–1975,* Chicago: Catholic Theological Union, 1993).

Educational ministry has also been represented in the research and writing of such scholars as Carroll Stuhlmueller and Donald Senior (sacred Scripture) and John Francis Kobler (the study of Vatican II). Thomas Berry, formerly director of the Center for Religious Research at Riverdale, New York, is a noted authority on creation spirituality and issues of environmental concern. In the years following Vatican II, Passionists of both provinces offered various programs directed toward the renewal of religious life.

Ministry directly related to social justice has taken many forms. A mission to Honduras (with an outreach to Haiti), begun in the fall of 1987, has served the needs of the sick and poor, provided care for orphans and a hospice for dying children, and developed parish communities with an emphasis on the development of lay leadership. The *Casa Pasionista* has provided a home for the dying and those living with AIDS. A collaborative program in Detroit entitled "Life Directions" has encouraged high school students to focus upon developing their personal gifts in community. STAUROS: USA has attempted to relate the mystery of the passion of Jesus to the experience of human suffering. Stewardship regarding investments has been fostered through membership in the Interfaith Center for Corporate Responsibility. In various locations, Passionists have been committed to ministries which seek to bring assistance and hope to the alienated, the chemically dependent, and those suffering from serious illness. Since the early 1970s, Passionists have sponsored and worked in volunteer programs in Baja California, Appalachia, Mississippi, and Alabama. The ongoing commitment of the laity to these programs has been inspiring.

Present and Future

Together with these endeavors, the Passionists have continued to develop their established ministries, especially the preaching of missions, retreats, and renewals. Local communities also continue to provide apostolic assistance to neighboring parishes, and to provide opportunities for spiritual direction and the sacrament of reconciliation.

Both provinces have encouraged participation in leadership and planning through regional programs, membership on various boards, and open chapters. Interprovince collaboration has enriched apostolic endeavors and programs of initial and ongoing formation. Present objectives of the American provinces include continued collaboration with the local church, and ongoing collaboration with laity, religious, and clergy in the fulfillment of the Passionist mission.

See also COUVEYOU, WALTER; PASSIONIST NUNS (C.P.); PASSIONIST SISTERS OF THE CROSS AND PASSION (C.P.); STONE, FIDELIS KENT; STUHLMUELLER, CARROLL; SUTTON, XAVIER.

Mercurio, Roger. *The Passionists.* Collegeville: The Liturgical Press, 1992.

Rooney, Gerard. *The Passionist Heritage: A Circular Letter.* Union City, N.J.: St. Michael's Monastery, 1963.

Ward, Felix. *The Passionists: Sketches Historical and Personal.* New York: Benziger Brothers, 1923.

Yuhaus, Cassian J. *Compelled to Speak: The Passionists in America—Origin and Apostolate.* Westminster, Md.: Newman Press, 1967.

GERALD LABA, C.P.

PASSIONIST NUNS (C.P.)

The Religious of the Most Holy Cross and Passion of Jesus Christ (commonly known as the Passionist nuns) were founded in 1771 at Corneto (now Tarquinia), Italy, by St. Paul of the Cross (1694–1775). Early on in his religious life, St. Paul of the Cross envisioned the foundation of the Passionist nuns. The idea began to mature in his mind as early as 1734, while giving spiritual direction to two Italian laywomen (Agnes Grazi and Lucy Burlini) and a Poor Clare nun from Piombino, Sr. Cherubina Bresciani. However, the foundation was delayed for several reasons: controversies with the mendicant orders, failure to obtain solemn vows from the Holy See, and serious economic difficulties. But St. Paul of the Cross did not lose hope and continued to prepare young women for entrance when God's time came. In 1737 Paul met the future cofoundress and superior in the person of a Benedictine nun. While preaching a retreat to the Benedictine nuns in Corneto, Paul met Mother Mary Candida Constantini, who was drawn deeply to the mystery of the passion. Some thirty years later she began the foundation with ten postulants as Mother Mary Crucified. They opened the first convent on May 3, 1771, and one year later professed their vows on May 20, 1772.

Purpose and Nature

The Passionist nuns are totally dedicated to contemplation. They seek to remain continually united with Christ in silence. Besides the traditional vows of poverty, chastity, and obedience, the Passionist nuns make a vow to promote devotion to and grateful remembrance of the passion and death of Jesus, as well as a vow of enclosure that obliges only by virtue of the rule and constitutions.

Rules and Constitutions

The *Rule* of the nuns was written by St. Paul of the Cross, assisted by his consultor Frs. Giovanni Maria Cioni and Marcaurelio Pastorelli, and the procurator general, Fr.

Candido Costa. Paul began to write it around 1766 and it was approved on September 3, 1770, by Pope Clement XIV. Some modifications were made in the *Rule* and approved in 1790. A further updating took place after the new Code of Canon Law was promulgated. The changes made in the *Rule* then were approved by the Sacred Congregation in 1926. After the Second Vatican Council, the Sacred Congregation for Religious and Secular Institutes approved an experimental *Rule* for the nuns for seven years (1971–78). An international meeting of Passionist nuns was held in Lucca, Italy, from May 27 to July 4, 1978, to make a definitive revision of their *Rule.* The first part was the primitive *Rule of St. Paul of the Cross;* the second part was a new text expressing the understanding of the Passionist contemplative vocation and its actualization today. This text was approved by the Church on April 28, 1979.

Spirituality

By the charismatic grace of the Spirit, the Passionist nuns consecrate themselves totally by vow to the mystery of the passion which gives inspiration and unity to their lives. Mindful that their passion vow is rooted in a theology of remembering, of devotion, and of mourning, they promote devotion to the sacred passion by meditation on the passion; by offering to God their life of prayer, community, self-denial, and work; by teaching others how to contemplate the passion; by revealing the light of Christ's charity to one another as living witnesses to the crucified; and by praying for the conversion of sinners to whom Passionist missionaries preach.

Growth and Expansion

After the first foundation in Corneto, Italy, there was no expansion for a hundred years. Between 1810 and 1814, the nuns had to leave their monastery because of the Napoleonic suppression. The second foundation was made at Mamers in France in 1872.

Today the Passionist nuns have thirty-seven monasteries in fourteen countries. They are as follows: Italy (11 monasteries), France (3), Belgium (2), United States of America (5), Spain (4), Brazil (4), Netherlands (2), Japan (1), England (1), Philippines (1), Korea (1), Colombia (1), Indonesia (1), and Mexico (1).

Foundation of Passionist Nuns in the United States

A foundation of the Passionist nuns in the United States was considered as early as 1860. The American provincial, Fr. John Dominick Tarlattini, C.P., wrote to the Passionist general, Most Rev. Anthony Testa, C.P., to request a foundation in the United States. At first the general was amenable but later he forbade the provincial to begin such a foundation for financial reasons. Only fifty years later would this dream become reality.

In 1908 the Provincial Chapter of the American Passionists unanimously approved the invitation to Passionist nuns to make a foundation in Pittsburgh, Pennsylvania. The chapter requested the American general consultor, Very Rev. Joseph Amrhein, C.P., together with the American provincial, Very Rev. Stanislaus Grennan, C.P., to implement the decision. The general consultor conferred with the Passionist nuns in Corneto (now Tarquinia), Italy, the Passionist general, the appropriate Roman congregations, and Bishop J. F. Canevin of Pittsburgh, Pennsylvania. Bishop Canevin gave his hearty approval on May 6, 1909. Pope Pius X gave his blessing on this endeavor.

Five nuns were chosen for this foundation. They arrived in New York on April 14, 1910, and stayed with the Dominican Nuns of the Perpetual Rosary in Union City, New Jersey, until May 5. On that day they proceeded to Pittsburgh and stayed with the Franciscan sisters on Pius Street until July 9, when they moved into their first convent. This convent was dedicated to Our Lady of Sorrows. The first retreat for women began on July 24, 1911. From that year until 1968, over 23,000 women made retreats with the nuns. Presently the nuns have a House of Prayer where women and men may come to spend periods of time in prayer and solitude. The nuns have published material on Passionist spirituality.

The Pittsburgh community made the following four foundations: Scranton, Pennsylvania, in 1926; Erlanger, Kentucky, in 1947; St. Louis, Missouri, in 1940; and Osaka, Japan, in 1957.

The Passionist nuns of St. Gabriel's Convent, Clarks Summit, Pennsylvania, were founded from the Pittsburgh community in 1926. They first settled in Dunmore, Pennsylvania. In 1970 they moved to a new convent and retreat house in Clarks Summit, Pennsylvania. This community has done important translations from French on Passionist spirituality.

This community made two foundations. The first one was made in Owensboro, Kentucky, in 1946, the Monastery of St. Joseph. In 1969 a second foundation was made in Marbel, Philippines. This convent was dedicated to Our Lady of Hope and now has native vocations.

The Passionist nuns of Owensboro, Kentucky, were founded from the Scranton community in 1946. This new Monastery of St. Joseph also provided retreats for women. In 1995 this community moved to a new location in Whitesville, Kentucky, where they built a new monastery and retreat house. This community has published translations of valuable works on Passionist spirituality.

In Erlanger, Kentucky, a Passionist nuns' community was founded from the Pittsburgh convent in 1947 and is known as the Monastery of the Sacred Passion. This community has published valuable material on Passionist spirituality and formation.

The Erlanger community made a new foundation in Daventry, England, in 1964. This foundation is known as the Monastery of Our Lady of the Passion.

The St. Louis community of Passionist nuns was founded by the Pittsburgh community in 1948. They were first located in Kirkwood, Missouri. The community built a new monastery in Ellisville, Missouri, in 1959, dedicated to the Immaculate Conception. This community has published significant translations on Passionist spirituality.

Giorgini, Fabiano, C.P. *History of the Passionists.* Edizioni ECO, 1987, 1:537-61.

Grennan, Stanislaus, C.P. "Account of the First American Foundation of Passionist Nuns in America." Archives of Passionist Nuns, Our Lady of Sorrows Convent, Pittsburgh, Pennsylvania.

Mead, Jude, C.P. *Dove in the Cleft.* New York, 1971.

SILVAN ROUSE, C.P.

PASSIONIST SISTERS OF THE CROSS AND PASSION (C.P.)

On March 25, 1851, Elizabeth Prout and two young women moved into a house on 69 Stocks Street in the parish of St. Chad's in Manchester, England. They called it St. Joseph Convent. On November 21, 1852, the first seven sisters received the religious habit. This was the beginning of the Sisters of the Cross and Passion.

The foundation of the Sisters of the Cross and Passion was a direct outgrowth of the Passionist Mission to England in the mid-nineteenth century. The purpose of their foundation was twofold. The goal of the Passionists in England was to win converts to the Catholic Church and to inject new life into the Catholicism already present. The Passion Sisters were intended from the beginning to participate in this mission, especially in their work with women; they were also founded to make religious life available to poor, hard-working women who could not become nuns in other communities because they lacked the necessary dowry. The first Sisters of the Cross and Passion were unique in England because they combined a contemplative lifestyle with an active apostolate and they earned their own living, some in factories.

From the beginning, Elizabeth Prout, now Mother Mary Joseph, met with opposition from people who thought nuns who went out to work were a contradiction in terms. However, the bishop and many of the clergy were very pleased to have sisters who would teach not only day classes and Sunday school, but evening classes, instruct converts, care for sodalities, and go out to the homes to visit the lapsed and the sick.

In North America

The first four Sisters of the Cross and Passion arrived in the United States on March 6, 1924, at the invitation of

Bishop William A. Hickey of Providence, Rhode Island. The sisters established themselves in Providence teaching in the Assumption parish school. In 1932 they opened a novitiate in Bristol, Rhode Island. The community grew slowly and was able to accept invitations to staff other parish schools in Rhode Island, Connecticut, New York, and Maryland. The sisters also became involved in retreat work, opening their own retreat house, Our Lady of Calvary, in Farmington, Connecticut, in 1858. In 1985 three sisters began work with the Passionists at their mission in Jamaica, West Indies.

Today, in response to the changing needs of the Church, the Sisters of the Cross and Passion in North America engage in a variety of ministries. In addition to education and ministries of spirituality such as retreat work, preaching, and spiritual direction, many sisters do pastoral work in parishes and hospitals. In imitation of their foundress, Elizabeth Prout, much of the sisters' work is with the poor and aims at improving the lives of women.

MARY ANN STRAIN, C.P.

PASTORELLI, LOUIS (1873–1956)

Religious superior. Louis Bartholomew Pastorelli was born on July 10, 1873, in Genoa, Italy, the son of David and Christina Pastorelli. In 1876 the family moved to Boston where they attended St. James Church. After eight years of public school, Louis entered Epiphany Apostolic College in Baltimore on February 12, 1890. In Wilmington, Delaware, on September 11, 1898, he was ordained as a Josephite. In 1899 he established missions in Chastang and Mobile, Alabama. Administrative work lay in front of him the rest of his life. He was rector of St. Joseph Industrial School in Clayton, Delaware, 1902–12, and advisor to the superior; rector of St. Joseph Seminary, Baltimore, and advisor to the superior; superior general, 1918 to 1942.

While superior, Pastorelli built a new minor seminary in Newburgh, New York, and a new major seminary in Washington, D.C. In 1932 he had the Josephites raised to the status of a pontifical institute, and as part of that process, he instituted a novitiate. His care, patience, and diplomacy, as advisor in his early days, helped to bring the society through the trauma of John R. Slattery's departure and the near end of the society at that time. It was an experience he remembered all the rest of his life. He became rector of St. Joseph Seminary in Washington, as well as consultor, from 1942 to 1948. From 1948 until his death in 1956, he was once again rector of St. Joseph Industrial School in Clayton, Delaware. When Pastorelli became superior in 1918, there were sixty-five priests caring for thirty-eight parishes and twenty-four missions. In 1942 there were 162 priests with seventy-seven parishes and thirty-four missions.

See also JOSEPHITES, THE (S.S.J.); SLATTERY, JOHN R.

The Colored Harvest. 1888–1960.
The Josephite Harvest. 1960–95.
Ochs, Stephen J. Desegregating the Altar: The Josephites and the Struggle for Black Priests. Baton Rouge: Louisiana State University Press, 1990.
Pastorelli Papers, Josephite Archives, Baltimore, Maryland.

PETER E. HOGAN, S.S.J.

PAUL OF ST. PETER (1746–1826)

Missionary. Paul of St. Peter, O.C.D., one of the most important early missionaries along the Mississippi, was born Michael Joseph Plattner in Dettelbach, Germany (near Würzburg), on June 21, 1746. He made his religious profession as a member the Lower German province of Discalced Carmelites in 1767, and was ordained to the priesthood in 1769. He first came to North America in 1780 as military chaplain to the Duke of Zweibrücken's troops, who served with Rochambeau's "Régiment de Comte de Deux-Ponts" under George Washington's command at the Battle of Yorktown. Back in Europe after the war, he returned to the United States at the urging of the French envoy in Philadelphia, and approached John Carroll in Baltimore for permission to minister to French-speaking Catholics along the Mississippi. Unsure of Fr. Paul's faculties or his own jurisdiction, Carroll nonetheless sent the German missionary into Illinois Territory.

There, Fr. Paul first served at Holy Family parish in Cahokia and rebuilt the Native American Mission of Tamarois; at nearby Kaskaskia he also successfully defended the settlers' property rights against an exploitive land firm. In the wake of disagreements between John Carroll and the bishop of Quebec over jurisdiction of the Illinois missions, and conflicts with Carroll's vicar general, Fr. Paul obtained permission to move to the Spanish side of the Mississippi, where he served as pastor of Ste. Geneviève from 1789 to 1797, later moving to Natchez. In December 1803 he was appointed pastor of historic St. Gabriel's in Iberville, Louisiana, where "le brave and bon de saint Pierre" (as the people called him) remained until his death on October 15, 1826.

See also CARMELITE FRIARS, DISCALCED (O.C.D.).

Lenhart, J. "Notes on the Biography of Paul de Saint Pierre." Catholic Historical Review 21 (1935–36) 322–29.
Lickteig, F.-B. "The Propaganda Fide Archives and Carmel in the United States." Part II, The Sword 36 (June 1976) 17–25.
Rohrbach, P.-T. Journey to Carith: The Story of the Carmelite Order. Garden City, N.Y.: Doubleday & Co., 1966, 329–31.
Rothensteiner, J. "Paul de Saint Pierre, the First German-American Priest in the West." Catholic Historical Review 5 (1919–20) 195–222.

STEVEN PAYNE, O.C.D.

PAULISTS (C.S.P.)

Founded in 1858, the Missionary Society of St. Paul the Apostle, popularly known as the Paulist Fathers or Paulists, was the first religious community of Catholic priests to be established in the United States. The founders of the community were five priests—Isaac Thomas Hecker, Augustine Hewit, Francis Baker, Clarence Walworth, and George Deshon—all of whom were native-born American converts to Catholicism. All of them had originally been members of the Redemptorists, an order of priests devoted to parish missions and concerned mainly with care of German immigrants in America. The five priests desired to expand this work to include the evangelization of native-born Americans, both Catholic and non-Catholic.

Hecker in particular wished to present Catholicism in a more popular light to that portion of the American population, and his four companions possessed the same desire. In this way, they hoped to achieve their ultimate goal of converting America to Catholicism. The five wanted permission to open a Redemptorist house, but failed to receive it from their superiors in America.

Hecker journeyed to Rome in August 1857 to petition the Redemptorist rector major, Nicholas Mauron, for the establishment of an American house. Hecker, however, soon found himself expelled from the order for having made the journey without the official approval of his American superiors. Appealing the decision to Pope Pius IX, he and the four other Redemptorists obtained a release from their vows in March 1858. The Pope suggested to Hecker, in a private audience, that he and his companions should found their own community to evangelize non-Catholics in America.

Foundation and Early Years

Upon his return to the United States in 1858, Hecker met with Baker, Hewit, Walworth, and Deshon to plan a community. They drew up a Programme of Rule, approved by Archbishop John Hughes of New York in July of that year. Hecker was elected first superior of the Missionary Priests of St. Paul the Apostle in June, even before the community had drawn up its constitution. He continued in that post until his death in 1888.

To educate their candidates for the priesthood, the Paulists established their novitiate and studentate at the parish of St. Paul in New York City. In 1889 the community became the first to establish a house of studies, St. Thomas Aquinas College, on the campus of the newly established Catholic University of America. In 1914 they erected a new house adjacent to the campus, which they named St. Paul's College. In 1923 the novitiate was established as a separate edifice in Ridgefield, Connecticut, and was later moved to its present site in Oak Ridge, New Jersey.

The Paulists opened their first parish, St. Paul the Apostle, in New York City in 1859. St. Paul's is considered the motherhouse of the Paulist community, and it was the only Paulist parish until the community assumed responsibility for Old St. Mary's Cathedral, San Francisco, in 1894. The number of Paulist houses expanded in the following years as the congregation took on parishes in Chicago, Oregon, and elsewhere. In addition, the Paulists became involved in the growing campus ministry apostolate for non-Catholic colleges. Among their earliest endeavors were those in Berkeley, California, Austin, Texas, and Toronto, Canada, starting in the early twentieth century.

Hecker had sought specific means of evangelizing America, among these being lecture tours and missions to non-Catholics, but one of the most innovative and effective approaches was the Paulist involvement with communications. In 1865 Hecker founded the *Catholic World,* a magazine encompassing theological, social, literary, and scientific issues, and in 1866 he started the Catholic Publication Society to disseminate Catholic pamphlets and leaflets.

The year 1892 saw the establishment of the Catholic Book Exchange, now known as the Paulist Press, which marked the community's entry into the field of book publishing. At the Chicago World's Fair in that same year, Paulist Fr. Bertrand Conway introduced the "Question Box." This evangelizing technique allowed non-Catholics to drop their written questions about Catholicism into a box. A priest would then provide answers. In 1903 Conway gathered the questions and responses into a volume entitled *The Question Box.*

The Twentieth Century

In 1902 Frs. Walter Elliott and Alexander P. Doyle organized the Catholic Missionary Union to further the apostolate among non-Catholics. In 1903 they started the Apostolic Mission House, located on the campus of The Catholic University of America, where the Paulists offered homiletics and evangelization courses to priests and seminarians involved in the field. In 1924 the community established WLWL, the first privately owned Catholic radio station in the United States, which was based in New York City.

A number of Paulists made substantial contributions to the American Church early in this century. In 1905 Frs. Lewis O'Hern and Alexander Doyle organized the Catholic Army and Navy Chaplain Bureau, an organization designed to work with the government on chaplain affairs. It lasted until World War I, at which time the Military Ordinariate was established. Even more important was the work of Fr. John J. Burke in the founding the National Catholic War Council (1917), the ancestor of the present-day National Conference of Catholic Bishops.

Paulists had been working in parishes and campus ministry in Canada since 1914. In addition, the community took on overseas parishes for the first time in 1922, at the Church of Santa Susanna in Rome. The primary thrust of their pastoral work in Rome was geared toward American residents and visitors to Rome. In 1939 they took up parish work in Johannesburg, South Africa, where they would remain until 1969. The main thrust of the community, however, remained focused, as it does to the present, on the American apostolate.

Isaac Hecker and Americanism

One of Hecker's main goals in founding the Paulists was to show the American public that there was no essential incompatibility between the Roman Catholic religion and the American democratic way of life. At the time, he had few supporters in this endeavor. Throughout the nineteenth century, the main thrust of the Church's activity was directed toward the care of the newly arriving immigrants.

Hecker's ideas were picked up again in the 1890s by a number of prominent American bishops, among them James Cardinal Gibbons, Archbishop John Ireland, and Bishop John J. Keane. This group, known as the "Americanists," sought to realize many of Hecker's goals. They were strongly opposed, however, by another group in the hierarchy espousing a separatist approach. Among these were Archbishop Michael Augustine Corrigan of New York and Bishop Bernard J. McQuaid of Rochester, New York.

In 1891 Paulist Fr. Walter Elliott wrote a biography entitled *The Life of Father Hecker.* A French translation of the book became an issue between French Catholic liberals and conservatives, with the conservatives criticizing the book as an example of the "heretical" tendencies of the liberals. Among these were included an overemphasis on personal experience and a diminished emphasis on hierarchical authority and ecclesiastical institutions. In 1899 Pope Leo XIII condemned what he considered the heretical tendencies of "Americanism" in the apostolic letter *Testem benevolentiae.*

If *Testem benevolentiae* hurt the Americanist cause, it also cast suspicion on the very purpose for which the Paulist community had been founded. As a result, Paulists had to be careful to avoid actions or activities that might cast doubt on their orthodoxy. They had to avoid being seen as too concessionary in their relationship to American culture and life. Between 1907 and 1911, after Pope Pius X had condemned the Modernist movement, four American priests found themselves unable to accept the condemnation and left the community. The most famous of these was Paulist Fr. William L. Sullivan, later a famous Unitarian minister. In the subsequent years, Paulists continued their work with non-Catholics, but there was a marked shift toward parochial work.

By the time of the Second Vatican Council (1962–65), the conditions seemed ripe to espouse Hecker's vision on a fuller basis, since a more positive understanding of the relationship between the Church and the world had taken place. Hecker had preached this during his lifetime, and in a sense Vatican II vindicated his vision. Paulists continue to implement this vision up to the present in their work with non-Catholics, campus ministries, parishes, and media communications. In the 1960s Fr. Ellwood Keiser started Paulist Productions, the community's successful foray in visual media, while Fr. John Mulhall continued the radio work of the defunct WLWL with Paulist Communications.

In recent years, the Paulist mission has received its strongest elaboration in the work of the community's 1986 General Assembly. At that time the community stated its three main goals: evangelization, ecumenism, and reconciliation. In the first area, the Paulists seek to preach the gospel to those who have not yet heard it. By ecumenism, they strive toward dialogue and unity with other faiths. Finally, they attempt to bring back into the life of the Church those Christians who feel alienated from their community. At present there are 228 Paulists involved in these various ministries in 26 foundations in the United States and abroad.

See also AMERICANISM; CATHOLIC BOOK PUBLISHING; ELLIOTT, WALTER; HECKER, ISAAC.

O'Brien, David J. *Isaac Hecker: An American Catholic.* New York: Paulist Press, 1992.

Robichaud, Paul G., C.S.P. "'The Very Reverend Superior': A History of Paulist Leadership from Isaac Hecker to Thomas Stransky." *Paulist History* 4 (1) (May 1994) 3–29.

PATRICK J. McNAMARA

Related Document

FATHER HECKER SKETCHES HIS PLANS AND HOPES FOR THE PAULISTS, JULY 24, 1859

One of the most important figures in nineteenth-century American Catholicism was Isaac Thomas Hecker (1819–1888). Hecker became a Catholic in August, 1844, after a lengthy search for truth that had led him in 1843 to Brook Farm and Fruitlands. During this time he became very well acquainted with Orestes Brownson, Bronson Alcott, Henry Thoreau, and other New England religious thinkers. After a novitiate in Belgium he became a member of the Congregation of the Most Holy Redeemer in 1846, returning to the United States in 1851 where for some years he was engaged in giving missions with several other convert Redemptorists. Since the order's principal concern was for the German Catholic immigrants, Hecker and his missionary companions were convinced that it would benefit the missions if the Redemptorists would open an English-speaking house which would be a center for the English missions. With this in mind, and with the encouragement of Bishop Bayley of Newark and Archbishop

Hughes of New York, Hecker went to Rome in August, 1857, as the spokesman for his associates, to lay the proposition before the Redemptorist rector major. Three days after his arrival, he was expelled without a hearing for having made the journey without the necessary permission. Hecker found a defender in Alessandro Cardinal Barnabò, Prefect of the Congregation de Propaganda Fide, who took his case to Pius IX. It was thus that the Paulist Fathers came into existence in July, 1858, and from that time until his death thirty years later Hecker remained the superior general. He was an intensely active man who wrote several books, e.g., *Questions of the Soul* (New York, 1852) and *Aspirations of Nature* (New York, 1857), founded the *Catholic World* in 1865, organized the Catholic Publication Society the following year, acted as theologian for Archbishop Spalding of Baltimore at the Vatican Council—in all of which he kept uppermost in his mind the dominant motive of his priestly life, the winning of American Protestants to the Catholic faith. Three years after his death one of his confreres, Walter Elliott, C.S.P., published *The Life of Father Hecker* (New York, 1891) which appeared in a French translation in 1897 and became the center of a theological controversy on both sides of the Atlantic under the name of the so-called heresy of Americanism. The following letter, written a year after the establishment of the Paulists, to Father Adrien-Emmanuel Rouquette (1813–1887), poet, writer, and Indian missionary of Louisiana, gives an excellent picture of Hecker's plans and aspirations for the future of his new congregation.

(*Source*: Archives of the Paulist Fathers, photostat of original in the archives of the Archdiocese of New Orleans.)

New York, July 24, 1859

Rev. Dear Friend.

Six months and more have elapsed since the reception of your last letter so full of kindred sympathy and hope. In it you say: "I will write to you soon my end, my means, & the degree of success which I have already attained." And also that "you would write to me more at length and intimately" & you throw out the suggestion that "one day we might meet in the same vocation." Your letter has been lying on my table ever since, & I had but to glance at it to awaken my sympathies and enkindle my enthusiasm. I will not disguise to you that your last suggestion has more than once also occurred to my thoughts. For I cannot refuse to recognize the same aims, thoughts, & sentiments which occupy your mind also occupy mine. Apparently our ways differ, but as you remark, they are not so different in reality.

Your attrait *[sic]* for solitude, silence, prayer, contemplation is no greater than my own. There was a time when my Superiors hesitated whether it were not better for me to change my state, & enter a contemplative order. During my years of study the greater part of my time was given to such a life, & one year of this period was wholly given to it and the care of the sick. Not as a matter of choice but of inability to apply myself to scientific studies. Among the so many pressing occupations at present, I cherish the same attrait, & act always with reluctance & from a sense of duty. But when unable to study & my attention ab-

sorbed in contemplation I was at the time aware that the grace of God was preparing me only for a more intensive & extensive action than all studies could have done. While most helpless and by others regarded as a fool, it was my most intimate conviction that God's Providence was preparing me for a great work, the conversion of our countrymen. And when compelled under obedience at the time to give in writing an explanation of my state, I did not hesitate to express this conviction. The same conviction prompted subsequently *Questions of the Soul* and *Aspirations of Nature*. The position in which I am at present placed I cannot regard in any other light than in view of this conviction, & as a special providence of God.

The conversion of the American people to the Catholic faith has ripened into a conviction with me which lies beyond the reign of doubt. My life, my labours, and my death is *[sic]* consecrated to it. No other aim as an end outside of my own salvation and perfection can occupy my attention a moment. But all other things in view of this,—art, science, literature, etc. etc. enter in as a part of the means, and command my interest, & demand all the encouragement within my reach. In the union of Catholic faith and American civilization a new birth awaits them all, and a future for the Church brighter than any past. That is briefly my "Credo."

Individually the faith has been identified with American life. Our effort is to identify Catholicity with American life in a religious association. I feel confident of its practicability. I entertain the hope of our opening a door to our young men who aim at consecrating their lives to God & Religion, and of our Institution becoming in the hands of Divine Providence a means of spreading the Faith among our people.

Thus far God's blessing have *[sic]* accompanied our labors, never were they more successful. The location secured for our community could not be more suitable, its value has increased doubly since its purchase. Our house is large and now almost ready for its roof; & in October we expect to occupy it. A few applications by priests to join us have been made; and several by young men, but these we are *not yet prepared* to receive. A few days ago I received from Cardinal Barnabò the permission to increase our numbers.

Our institution is based on the voluntary principle, with the idea of practicing all the religious virtues in the same degree of perfection as those under the vows. These are our practical measures.

You will perceive My Dear Friend, that I have taken up your offer "to write to me more at length & intimately" & fulfilled it in respect to yourself, which I trust will suggest a reciprocal confidence.

With great esteem

Your devoted friend & Servant in Xt.

I. T. HECKER

(*Source*: John Tracy Ellis, ed. *Documents of American Catholic History*. Vol. 1:1493–1865. Wilmington, Del.: Michael Glazier, 1987, 339–42.)

PAX CHRISTI U.S.A.

Pax Christi U.S.A., the national Catholic peace movement founded in 1972 by Gordon Zahn, Eileen Egan, and others, strives to create a world that reflects the Peace of Christ. Pax Christi U.S.A. rejects war, preparations for war, and every form of violence and domination. It advocates primacy of conscience, economic and social justice, and respect for creation.

Pax Christi U.S.A. has approximately 12,000 dues-paying members, including 120 bishops. Members elect a National Council that establishes the movement's priorities and oversees its operations. The National Council elects a bishop president. A full-time national staff implements policies and services members' needs.

Pax Christi U.S.A. is a national section of Pax Christi International, which began in France in 1945, as World War II was ending. The cofounders, Mme. Dortel-Claudot and Bishop Theas (himself a concentration camp survivor), were concerned for the reconciliation of the French and German peoples. Today the international movement includes sections in more than twenty-two nations around the world and has consultative status at the United Nations, UNESCO, and the Council of Europe.

Pax Christi U.S.A. members meet in local groups for prayer and reflection, believing that action must be rooted in prayer and study. The flow of publications from the national office to members is motivational as well as informational. Publications include a quarterly magazine, Advent and lenten reflections, process books, topical books and brochures, prayer services, bulletin inserts, and prayer cards.

Pax Christi U.S.A. sponsors demonstrations, petitions, advocacy campaigns, prayer vigils, overseas delegations, and other events to educate the public and change structures.

When the Catholic bishops of the United States released *The Challenge of Peace: God's Promise and Our Response* in 1983, Pax Christi U.S.A. was a dedicated promoter of the peace pastoral, but also a critic of the bishops' failure to condemn nuclear deterrence.

At the time of the Persian Gulf War, Pax Christi U.S.A. supported UN sanctions, opposed military intervention, and raised conscience issues about the "just war" theory. During and after the conflict, Pax Christi questioned the reluctance of the United States bishops to apply their own principles and condemn the war. Simultaneously, Pax Christi became deeply involved in efforts to recognize and support the conscientious objectors who were punished for refusing to fight.

In 1992, for the bicentennial anniversary of the first Columbus landing, Pax Christi published materials and sponsored programs honoring the indigenous peoples who were the victims of that "discovery." Members were encouraged to recognize the historical roots of racism and ethnocentrism in our culture.

In 1994–95, when people of the United States were recalling and often celebrating the events of World War II, Pax Christi U.S.A. declared a Year of Nonviolence to critically and prayerfully evaluate the violence in our national heritage.

Members have been repeatedly present in such troubled countries as Nicaragua, Guatemala, El Salvador, and Haiti. During the exile of Jean Bertrand Aristide, the elected president of Haiti, Pax Christi U.S.A. led a collaborative effort (Cry for Justice) with other peace organizations to establish a sustained presence of unarmed volunteers in Haiti to defuse the violent atmosphere.

Pax Christi's stances and actions arise, not from politics, but from a deep commitment to the Christian message as articulated by the teachings of the Catholic Church. Pax Christi is energized by the Gospels, the earliest Christian traditions, and the social encyclicals of the past hundred years.

Pax Christi U.S.A. commits itself to peace education and, with the help of its bishop members, promotes the gospel imperative of peacemaking as a priority in the Catholic Church in the United States. It strives for gospel nonviolence and collaborates with other groups committed to nonviolent peacemaking.

See also CATHOLIC PEACE MOVEMENT, THE.

McNeal, Patricia. *Harder than War: Catholic Peacemaking in Twentieth Century America.* New Jersey: Rutgers University Press, 1992.
Pax Christi U.S.A. 17 (1/2) (Spring/Summer 1992).

JIM DINN

PEGIS, ANTON (1905–78)

Philosopher. Anton Pegis was born on August 24, 1905, in Milwaukee, Wisconsin. He received both a bachelor's degree and a master's degree at Marquette University, Milwaukee, and a doctorate at the University of Toronto.

Baptized into the Greek Orthodox Church, he converted to Roman Catholicism in 1930. The following year, after receiving his doctorate, he began teaching philosophy at Marquette University (1931–37), moved to Fordham University's Graduate School (1937–40), and went on to the University of Toronto where he taught the history of philosophy at the Pontifical Institute of Medieval Studies.

A follower of Etienne Gilson's school of thought, Pegis was influential in reviving Thomistic philosophy in the United States. He was president both of the American

Anton Pegis

Catholic Philosophical Association (1946–47) and the Pontifical Institute of Medieval Studies (1946–54).

After serving as editorial director of the Catholic textbook division of Doubleday and Company in New York City from 1954 to 1961, he returned to the Pontifical Institute. During his academic career, Pegis wrote and lectured extensively on the teachings of St. Thomas Aquinas.

His works include a translation and edited version of *On the Truth of the Catholic Faith* by St. Thomas Aquinas. He also edited the two-volume *Writings of St. Thomas* (1945), *Introduction to St. Thomas* (1948), and *The Wisdom of Catholicism* (1949). Pegis' writings include: *St. Thomas and the Greeks* (1939), *Christian Philosophy and Intellectual Freedom* (1955), *The Middle Ages and Philosophy* (1963), and *St. Thomas and Philosophy*. He died in Toronto, Canada, on May 13, 1978.

MARIANNA McLOUGHLIN

PEÑALVER Y CÁRDENAS, LUIS IGNACIO (1749–1810)

Colonial bishop of Louisiana. Luis Ignacio Maria Peñalver y Cárdenas was born in Havana, Cuba, on April 3, 1749, son of Diego Peñalver Angulo y Calvo de la Puerta and María Luisa de Cárdenas Vélez de Guevara y Sotolongo. He studied at the Colegio de San Ignacio and the Universidad de San Jerónimo, both in Havana; he received his doctorate in theology at the latter on May 4, 1771. He was ordained to the priesthood on April 4, 1772. He served as the vicar general of Diocese of Santiago de Cuba and the newly created (1787) Diocese of San Cristóbal de La Habana.

On April 25, 1793, Pope Pius VI established the vast Diocese of Louisiana and the Floridas; on September 14, 1794, King Charles IV of Spain named Peñalver y Cárdenas as the colonial diocese's first bishop. He was consecrated at Havana on April 26, 1795, and took formal possession of his new see on July 24, 1795.

Peñalver y Cárdenas worked closely with local governors under the *patronato real* to provide the needed clergy, facilities, and resources for his widespread flock. He established ecclesiastical parishes in Avoyelles (1797) and Bayou Sara (ca. 1798); strove to uplift the colony's moral climate and to improve Church discipline, with special emphasis on fulfillment of one's annual Easter duty; worked with Bishop John Carroll of Baltimore to minister to Catholics on both sides of the Mississippi River regardless of political borders; required annual parish census reports and accurate, detailed sacramental and financial record-keeping. His long pastoral visits brought confirmation to outlying communities for the first time.

Luis I. Peñalver y Cárdenas

In 1801 he was appointed the sixth archbishop of Guatemala. His departure left a void in ecclesiastical authority in the Lower Louisiana Church that lasted for thirty years. Poor health forced Peñalver y Cárdenas to resign from Guatemala in 1805; he retired to Havana where he died on July 17, 1810.

See also LOUISIANA, CATHOLIC CHURCH IN.

Baudier, Roger. *The Catholic Church in Louisiana*. New Orleans, 1939.

Code, Joseph B. *Dictionary of the American Hierarchy (1789–1964)*. New York, 1964.

Curley, Michael J. *Church and State in the Spanish Floridas, (1783–1822)*. Washington, D.C., 1940.

O'Neill, Charles Edwards. "A Bishop for Louisiana." *Cross, Crozier and Crucible: a Volume Celebrating the Bicentennial of a Catholic Diocese in Louisiana.* Lafayette, 1993.

Peñalver y Cárdenas Papers in New Orleans Collection at the University of Notre Dame Archives.

Rodriguez, Josefina Alonso de. *El Ilustrimo Don Luis de Peñalver y Cardenas [sic] Sexto Arzobispo de Guatemala: El hombre, el sacerdote y su tiempo.* Guatemala, 1972.

CHARLES E. NOLAN

PENNINGS, BERNARD HENRY (1861–1955)

Abbot. Pennings was born on June 9, 1861, in the village of Gemert, Holland. He entered the novitiate of the Abbey of Berne in Heeswijk on October 26, 1879, and made his first profession as a canon regular of Prémontré on June 5, 1881. He was ordained a priest on June 19, 1886. In 1889 Abbot Augustine Bazelmans of Berne appointed him circator, as well as professor of theology and philosophy. The following year he was appointed master of novices.

Bernard H. Pennings

On July 20, 1893, Bishop Sebastian Messmer of Green Bay, Wisconsin, petitioned the abbot of Berne for priests to work among the Belgian immigrants northeast of Green Bay. Negotiations proceeded rapidly and on November 1, 1893, Pennings, age thirty-two, with Fr. Lambert Broens and Br. Servatius Heesakkers, set sail from Rotterdam, arriving in Hoboken, New Jersey, on November 13. Proceeding directly to Green Bay, the little mission band was assigned by Bishop Messmer to serve in the Belgian parishes. Between 1893 and 1912, twenty-five members of the Berne community followed Pennings to America.

Pennings assumed responsibility for St. Joseph parish in De Pere on September 28, 1898. He immediately established St. Norbert Priory and St. Norbert College as well as assuming responsibility for the Shrine of St. Joseph and the Archconfraternity of St. Joseph.

On November 5, 1902, by papal brief, St. Norbert Priory, De Pere, gained its independence from the mother abbey of Berne. Within the next decade, Pennings sent missionaries to Manitoba, Canada, and preachers on mission bands to Louisiana. He early on sent community members to The Catholic University of America and the University of Wisconsin to earn doctorates in order to teach at St. Norbert College.

In 1936 Pennings celebrated his golden jubilee of ordination, continuing to preside over the growing community and its ministries. On August 12, 1947, he accepted a coadjutor abbot, Sylvester M. Killeen. Academic and international honors recognized his educational and immigration efforts. He died on March 17, 1955, after having served the American Church, the Diocese of Green Bay, and the members of St. Norbert Abbey for sixty-one years.

Traeger, Adrian C., O. Praem. *A Survey of the Norbertine Fathers in the United States.* De Pere, Wisconsin, 1986.

BENJAMIN MACKIN, O. PRAEM.

PENNSYLVANIA, CATHOLIC CHURCH IN

The story of the colonial Catholic community in Pennsylvania has been called, "the most pleasant and positive of any of the original thirteen colonies" (J. T. Ellis, *Catholics in Colonial America,* 370). Though barred from holding public office by the Test Oath (1693–1775), Catholics were accorded a wide scope of religious liberty in keeping with William Penn's vision of his colony as a "holy experiment."

Missionary Era

Jesuit missionaries first visited Pennsylvania as they made their way north from their farm at Bohemia Manor, Maryland, a location chosen for its proximity to Philadelphia. Bohemia was established in 1704, and already by 1708 Governor Logan was complaining to Penn of the "scandal of the Mass." By the year 1720 missioners were celebrating Mass in the Wilcox homestead in Ivy Mills, near Chester, but it was not until 1733 that Fr. Joseph Greaton purchased a plot of land on Walnut Street and erected a small chapel and residence. St. Joseph's Church was the first urban foundation in the colonies, and the first place of public Catholic worship since the chapel at St. Mary's City in Maryland had been demolished in 1704. Catholicism flourished in Philadelphia, necessitating a larger church in 1757, followed in 1763 by a second, St. Mary's, used for Sunday worship.

From Philadelphia the Jesuits' ministry extended northwest to the Catholics living in Berks County. In 1742 Greaton bought a parcel of land at Goshenhoppen and Theodore Schneider, a Jesuit university professor from Heidelberg turned missionary, was assigned to care for the foundation. Work was begun on St. Paul's Chapel in 1743, with Schneider particularly concerned for the education of the local children, both Catholic and Protestant. From Goshenhoppen, Schneider and his successors journeyed to Reading (where a Roman Catholic "meetinghouse" existed by 1753), Lebanon, Pottsville (a log church by 1827), Bethlehem, Easton (the first "parish church" in Northampton County would be built here in 1836), Tamaqua, Sunbury, and Williamsport. It was at Goshenhoppen that in 1757 a Corpus Christi procession was mistaken by Protestant observers for a military drill, resulting in a law that barred Catholics from bearing arms.

Despite this flurry of activity in the eastern third of the state, the central and western sections were not ignored. Already by 1725 Maryland Catholics were migrating into south-central Pennsylvania in search of land and greater religious freedom, soon to be joined by groups of German immigrants. A mission chapel was established in 1730 at Conewago, ten miles from Gettysburg. In 1742 William Wappeler, who had arrived with Schneider, began work among the Germans of the region, and the mission flourished throughout the surrounding area. In 1742 land was purchased for a chapel in Lancaster (Old St. Mary's); St. Patrick's in York followed in 1750.

In the central and eastern sections of the colony, the earliest missionary work was that of English and German Jesuits; in the west it was French missionaries who accompanied their country's military expeditions of the early eighteenth century. The first place of public worship was the chapel of Fort Duquesne, built in 1754 at the confluence of the Allegheny and Monogehela Rivers (present-day Pittsburgh), and dedicated to the "Assumption of the Blessed Virgin Mary of the Beautiful River." Denys Baron, a Recollect friar, was the fort chaplain and his baptismal register survives as a testimony to his four years' labor, until the destruction of the fort by the British in 1758.

Early Growth and Turmoil in Philadelphia

During the Revolutionary War the majority of colonial Catholics supported the war effort, though 180 men from St. Mary's Church in Philadelphia did form "Clifton's Regiment" to fight for the British. A number of Catholics, buried in St. Mary's churchyard, were prominent patriots, including Commodore John Barry (1745–1803, "the Father of the American Navy"), Thomas FitzSimmons (1741–1811, banker, merchant, delegate to the Constitutional Convention and United States Congressman), and Stephen Moylan (1734–1811, merchant, cavalry commander, and aide-de-camp to Washington).

By 1790 there were, by Bishop John Carroll's estimate, at least two thousand Catholics in Philadelphia alone, with another five thousand scattered throughout the state of Pennsylvania. The Church was flourishing, thanks to the efforts of such zealous priests as Ferdinand Farmer, who traveled throughout Pennsylvania and New Jersey, and showed an equal concern for both the needy of Philadelphia as well as the city's intellectual life, and Lorenz Grässel, who was stricken as he cared for the victims of the city's yellow fever epidemic in 1793.

The number of Catholics continued to grow, and soon St. Mary's and St. Joseph's could no longer contain the burgeoning number of worshipers. St. Augustine's was begun by Irish Augustinians in 1796, counting George Washington among its benefactors. Upon its dedication in 1801, it was Philadelphia's largest church. German Catholics, led by two Capuchin priests, John and Peter Helbron, incorporated in 1788 as the "German Religious Society of Roman Catholics" and established Holy Trinity Church in November of 1789. Bishop Carroll struggled with this, the country's first "national" church, for over a generation, denying their alleged right to appoint pastors of their own choosing.

In 1808 Carroll, moved not only by the size of his diocese but also by the complexities he had encountered in shepherding it, obtained the erection of four new dioceses. One was erected in Philadelphia, which by now numbered 10,000 faithful in the city alone. On April 8, 1808, Michael Egan, an Irish Franciscan, was appointed its first bishop. The diocese included the entire states of Pennsylvania and Delaware and the western and southern regions of New Jersey, with St. Mary's as the cathedral church.

Egan, a pious, peaceable, and humble man, though easily manipulated and plagued by ill health, was beleaguered during his brief tenure as bishop by financial conflicts with the trustees of his cathedral. At his death on July 22, 1814, he left the diocese in turmoil. The situation was so problematic that the see remained vacant for five years, as the best candidates were either unavailable or refused it. In the interim, Louis de Barth administered the diocese from Conewago, though he rarely visited the city. Finally, in 1819 Rome appointed Henry Conwell, an Irish priest from the Archdiocese of Armagh.

The appointment could hardly have been more unfortunate. Conwell was seventy-three at his arrival in Philadelphia, a stern, uncompromising man with an exalted sense of his own position, and unfamiliar with the Church in America. Soon after his arrival the trustee troubles at St. Mary's flared up again, aided by William Hogan, a flamboyant priest whose oratorical skills—which Conwell lacked—had earned him a devoted following. Hogan challenged Conwell publicly from the pulpit, and in the ensuing conflict many trustees sided with Hogan, dividing the congregation. Numerous charges and countercharges were leveled against both Conwell and Hogan, damaging the Church's reputation. The crisis prompted the letter *Non sine magno* from Pius VII, setting strict limits to the power of the lay trustees and precipitating a decline in Hogan's popularity, leading to his departure in November of 1823.

Unhappily, the struggles continued when Conwell signed an agreement with the trustees in 1826, which seemed to concede the right of veto over the bishop's pastoral appointments. The pact was denounced to Rome, which proceeded to indicate its disapproval in 1827. In 1830 Conwell, confused and desperate over his situation and weakened by the onset of senility, was given Francis Patrick Kenrick as his coadjutor and administrator of the diocese, while he himself was allowed to remain in the city until his death in 1842.

Kenrick dealt swiftly with the trustees at St. Mary's, placing the church under interdict when conflicts continued. In 1832 he established a new church, St. John the Evangelist, and founded St. Charles Seminary; there were now over 100,000 Catholics in the diocese, with fifty churches and thirty-eight priests. Kenrick realized the diocese had become unwieldy, and from 1835 to 1843 worked to have another diocese erected in Pittsburgh. Finally, on August 11, 1843, in the brief *Universi Dominici*, the Diocese of Pittsburgh was established, with Michael O'Connor as the first bishop. The new diocese encompassed some 21,000 square miles and 45,000 Catholics.

Catholicism in Western Pennsylvania

During the years of Philadelphia's trials, the Church had been growing throughout the state. In 1789 Theodore Brouwers, a Franciscan from the West Indies, arrived in the United States and heard of the need for priests in western Pennsylvania. He purchased a three-hundred-acre farm in Westmoreland County, "Sportsman's Hall," on April 16, 1790, and before his death that August willed the land to whoever succeeded him in his ministry. In 1799 Peter Helbron, who had earlier been involved in the struggles at Holy Trinity, arrived to take up residence at the Hall, extending his missionary labors throughout the region. In this he was joined by Demetrius Gallitzin, son of a Russian count and a German princess (the first student to complete his seminary training and be ordained in the United States), who soon after began ministering to Catholics at McGuire's settlement where he opened a mission and school, renaming the town Loretto.

In 1808 Pittsburgh gained its first resident pastor in the person of William O'Brien, who established St. Patrick's Church in August of 1811. In 1820 St. Paul's Church was begun by Fr. Charles Maguire, O'Brien's successor, which upon its completion was the largest church in the country. This became O'Connor's cathedral church upon his arrival in Pittsburgh.

Before returning from his consecration in Rome, however, O'Connor had traveled throughout Europe seeking clergy and religious for his new diocese. In Dublin he recruited seven members of the Sisters of Mercy, who arrived with him in Pittsburgh and proceeded to found Saint Xavier's Academy in 1844 and Mercy Hospital in 1846. (However, their arrival, and O'Connor's patronage of them, led to the departure of the Sisters of Charity, who had been in Pittsburgh since 1835, operating an academy, orphanage, and school.) The Sisters of Mercy would later establish foundations in the Archdiocese of Philadelphia (Merion), and in the Dioceses of Erie and Scranton (Dallas).

In 1846, Boniface Wimmer, a Benedictine monk from St. Michael's Abbey in Metten, Bavaria, established a monastery at St. Vincent's parish (the former Sportsman's Hall farm)—the first Benedictine monastery in the United States. Wimmer founded a seminary the same year and a college in 1849, and though he and O'Connor would feud continually over the goals and methods of his community, the Benedictines would play a major role in the growth of the Church in western Pennsylvania. O'Connor also managed to attract the Passionists to Pittsburgh in 1852, when three priests and one brother arrived to found their first community in the United States.

Nativist Troubles

Anti-immigrant prejudice led to the growth of nativism, which spawned a wave of violence up and down the Eastern seaboard. In Philadelphia, tensions over increasing Irish immigration, exacerbated by Catholic concerns with the exclusive use of the King James Bible in the public schools, exploded in early May 1844, when riots in the Kensington section of the city resulted in the burning of two Catholic churches (including St. Augustine's and its valuable library). On July fifth and sixth, a mob of nativists clashed with a regiment of state militia guarding St. Philip Neri Church. Over twenty people were killed and at least one hundred injured in these violent encounters.

In Pittsburgh, plans of the Protestant Association to burn Mercy Hospital in 1850 were thwarted after Bishop O'Connor ordered Catholic property guarded around the clock. The Church, though, remained a target for Joseph Barker, a virulent anti-Catholic who became mayor of the city in 1850 (while in prison!) and proceeded to have O'Connor arrested.

In the context of nativist violence, the founding of St. Mary's in Elk County in 1842 is notable. Organized by German families in Philadelphia and Baltimore as an alternative to the growing violence and prejudice of the cities, 35,000 acres of land were purchased to provide for the founding of a Catholic colony. Thirty-five families arrived on December eighth and named their settlement "St. Mary's." Soon the community was a flourishing settlement with developed mills, mines, and various small industries.

An Era of "Saintly" Expansion

Despite the nativist troubles, the Church in Philadelphia continued to grow. St. Joseph's, the first Catholic hospital in Philadelphia, was opened in June of 1849 staffed by the Sisters of St. Joseph, who had arrived in the city in 1847 (and would soon be caring for a boy's orphanage, a widow's asylum, and a private academy). Two colleges were founded in the diocese: Villanova, begun by the Augustinians in 1842, and St. Joseph's, founded in 1851 by the Jesuits. Kenrick left Philadelphia that year to become archbishop of Baltimore, leaving behind 92 churches, 43 seminarians, 101 priests, and 170,000 Catholics.

John Nepomucene Neumann was consecrated the fourth bishop of Philadelphia on March 28, 1852. A Bohemian, he had emigrated to the United States and was ordained for the Diocese of New York in 1836. He entered the Redemptorist Order in 1842, and was assigned to St. Philomena's parish in Pittsburgh. As bishop of Philadelphia he pushed for the establishment of parochial schools (the number of students increased twentyfold), made yearly visitations of the diocese, inaugurated the Forty Hours devotion, and established the first church for Italian Catholics, St. Mary Magdalen de Pazzi, in 1853. He founded a religious community, the Sisters of the Third Order of Saint Francis, in 1855, and welcomed the Sisters, Servants of the Immaculate Heart of Mary to the diocese in 1858. Neumann, despite the aid of his coadjutor James Wood—appointed in 1857—grew increasingly frail from his labors, and died on January 5, 1860. He was beatified in 1863, and canonized in 1977.

New Dioceses for Pennsylvania

In 1852 the Fifth Provincial Council of Baltimore recommended that the Diocese of Pittsburgh be split in two; accordingly, on April 29, 1853, Pius IX established the Diocese of Erie comprising thirteen counties in northwestern Pennsylvania. Michael O'Connor was named the first bishop, but the faithful of his diocese were so distraught at his departure that in seven months he was returned to Pittsburgh, replaced in Erie by Josue Moody Young, a New England convert. Young was succeeded by Tobias Mullen, bishop from 1868–99, who witnessed the religious and industrial expansion of the diocese.

All was not well in Pittsburgh, though, even with O'Connor's return. The bishop had long desired to enter the Society of Jesus (the pope had personally forestalled his request in 1843), and in 1860 he resigned to pursue his dream. The Spanish Vincentian Michael Domenec (lately on the faculty of St. Charles Seminary) was appointed his successor on September 23, 1860. Domenec was plagued first by struggles with pro-O'Connor priests in his chancery, and later by the financial machinations and intrigue of his cathedral rector, John Hickey. Because of these and other difficulties in the diocese, Domenec traveled to Rome in 1875 to recommend its division. On January 16, 1876, Domenec was appointed the first bishop of the newly erected Diocese of Allegheny, and on March 19, 1876, John Tuigg, from St. John's Church in Altoona, was appointed the third bishop of Pittsburgh. Tuigg was overwhelmed as his realization of Pittsburgh's indebtedness grew (insolvent parishes were clustered in his share of the divided diocese), and he asked Rome to investigate after a local audit failed to clarify matters. The two priests he chose to represent him to the Holy See offered detailed presentations, to which Domenec was unable to offer a coherent response. The Congregation for the Propagation of the Faith asked for Domenec's resignation and reunited the Diocese of Allegheny to Pittsburgh. Domenec became seriously ill while returning to the United States and died in his native Spain on January 7, 1878.

Bishop James Frederic Wood, who succeeded Neumann in 1860 as the fifth bishop of Philadelphia—though a quiet, reserved man, known as the "Shadow" even by his contemporaries—was a vigorous and talented administrator. He presided at the dedication of the new Cathedral of Saints Peter and Paul on November 20, 1864, and worked to build a larger seminary on the outskirts of the city at Overbrook ("Wood's Folly"). The size of the burgeoning diocese was so great that in June of 1867, while on a visit to Rome at the invitation of Pius IX, Wood requested assistance in its governance. The Holy See replied to his appeal and the recommendations of the Second Plenary Council of Baltimore, by erecting three new dioceses on March 3, 1868. Delaware was separated from Philadelphia and a Diocese of Wilmington was established. Ten counties of northeastern Pennsylvania were detached to form the Diocese of Scranton, where Bishop William O'Hara was called to build on foundations that stretched back to the royalist refuge at French Azilum in Bradford County (where in 1793 a colony of exiles built fifty dwellings and a chapel, hoping to provide a refuge for Queen Marie Antoinette), and the pastoral work of Jeremiah O'Flynn, who in 1825 had the entire region for his parish. Eighteen counties in the central region of the state became the Diocese of Harrisburg under the care of Bishop Jeremiah F. Shanahan. With the state now encompassing five dioceses, it seemed appropriate that on March 15, 1875, the Diocese of Philadelphia was raised to the rank of a metropolitan see.

A Church of Immigrants

The second half of the nineteenth century saw vast numbers of immigrants from eastern and southern Europe flood the dioceses of Pennsylvania, attracted by jobs in the coal, steel, and petroleum industries. National parishes were established for various ethnic groups, some of which were the first of their kind in the country: e.g., St. Joseph's Slovak Church in Hazelton (Scranton) and St. Nicholas Croatian Church in Pittsburgh. Religious communities were established for ministry to the ethnic communities, e.g., the Daughters of Saints Cyril and Methodius in 1909.

Sometimes these efforts were too little too late, as in the case of the schism that occurred among Polish Catholics. In 1897 the Polish parishioners of Sacred Heart Church in Scranton sought to retain control of their newly completed church. When Bishop O'Hara refused, Fr. Francis Hodur and 250 families built a new church over which they were determined to retain governance. Despite an unsuccessful appeal to Rome, Hodur and his flock refused to yield, even after his excommunication. In 1904 they joined with other dissatisfied Polish Catholics to form a synod, electing Hodur as bishop of the Polish National Catholic Church, which was distinguished by its use of Polish in the liturgy and lay control of church property.

Bishop O'Hara was also involved in the controversy over secret societies, many of which were formed to protect the rights of workers. The Knights of Labor, the first national labor union, was led by a Catholic from Scranton, Terrence Powderly (1879–93), who attempted to use his influence to make the rituals and practices of his organization acceptable to the Church. Through his contact with O'Hara, Archbishop Ryan of Philadelphia, and others, Powderly succeeded in gaining the Church's toleration of his organization (1887).

It was the influx of immigrant labor into the mills and industries in the mountainous regions of western Pennsylvania that led to the erection of yet another diocese. In 1899 Bishop Phelan of Pittsburgh met with Archbishop Ryan to discuss the increasing pastoral burden of caring for his diocese. A first petition of the bishops of the province to Rome for the erection of a new diocese with its see in Altoona produced no response, and so on February 26, 1901, Ryan and his suffragans repeated their request. This time Rome acted, announcing the erection of the see of Altoona, and appointing Eugene A. Garvey of the Scranton diocese as the first bishop. The diocese consisted of the counties of Cambria, Blair, Bedford, Huntingdon, Somerset, Center, Clinton, and Fulton. In 1957 it was redesignated the Diocese of Altoona-Johnstown.

Catholic Benefaction

The new diocese had only one Catholic college within its boundaries, Franciscan College of Loretto, which would grow and expand thanks to the generosity of Charles Michael Schwab (1862–1939), a Loretto native who became the first president of U.S. Steel. Schwab made many donations to the Church in Pennsylvania; indeed, the early years of the twentieth century saw numerous wealthy Pennsylvania Catholics who shared their fortunes with a wide range of Church institutions, and were rewarded with awards and papal knighthoods. These included Martin Maloney (a papal marquis in 1903), Nicholas Brady, benefactor of the novitiate of the Maryland Jesuit province at Wernersville (recipient of the "Supreme Order of Christ"), his wife Genevieve Garvan Brady (a papal duchess), and John J. Sullivan, a banker who pioneered the retreat movement for laymen in Philadelphia and left millions of dollars to the black and Native American missions.

Certainly one of the state's most generous Catholics was Katharine Drexel (1858–1955) who used her inheritance for similar purposes. Born into a wealthy banking family, Katharine was inspired by the Third Plenary Council of Baltimore's call in 1884 for missionary aid to Native Americans and blacks. Upon being told by Pope Leo XIII that she could best assist the cause by becoming a missionary religious herself, she founded the Sisters of the Blessed Sacrament for Indians and Colored People in 1891. By the end of her life she had spent more than twelve million dollars of her own money, founding numerous missions and a college. Katharine Drexel was beatified in 1988.

Other Catholics made their mark in different ways in the new century. Writers Maurice Francis Egan (1852–1924) and Agnes Repplier (1855–1950) were well-known and respected literary figures, along with such clerical authors as Herman Heuser (1851–1932), editor of the *American Ecclesiastical Review,* and Peter Guilday (1884–1947), a pioneer in the field of American Catholic Church history. Pennsylvania Catholics could also mark out with pride such leaders in the medical field as John M. Keating (1852–93), a well-known pediatrician, Ernest Leplace (1861–1924), one of the foremost surgeons of his day, and Lawrence F. Flick (1856–1938), who dominated the field of tuberculosis research. In the field of sacred music, Nicola A. Montani (1880–1948), choirmaster of St. John the Evangelist Church from 1906–23, was known throughout the country for his *St. Gregory Hymnal* (1920) as well as his dedication to the restoration of Gregorian chant. The lawyer Walter George Smith, president of the American Bar Association, was also on the boards of numerous Catholic organizations, including The Catholic University of America. Charles G. Fenwick (1880–1973), who specialized in international law, was a well-known activist in the Peace Movement in the 1920s and 1930s.

The growth of Catholic higher education in the state continued apace, especially women's colleges: notably, Immaculata (1920), Rosemont (1921), and Chestnut Hill

(1924) in the Archdiocese of Philadelphia; Marywood (1915) and College Misericordia (1924) in Scranton; Villa Maria (1925) and Mercyhurst (1926) in Erie; and Seton Hill (1918) and Mount Mercy [Carlow] (1929) in Pittsburgh.

Cardinal Dougherty and his Age

Three dioceses in Pennsylvania had the same bishop for much of the first half of the century. In Philadelphia, Dennis Dougherty had a long-lasting influence in the archdiocese over the forty years of his incumbency, from 1918 to 1951. A formal and demanding administrator who reveled in the title "God's bricklayer," Dougherty worked zealously to establish parishes and schools, dispel racial discrimination, and raise the level of clerical education, overseeing the foundation of 112 parishes, 145 schools, 4 colleges, and 12 hospitals, and ordaining over two thousand priests. Dougherty was named Pennsylvania's first cardinal on March 7, 1921.

Erie was also blessed in these years with a dynamic and long-lived ordinary, John Mark Gannon, who shepherded his diocese from 1920 to 1966. Given the personal title of archbishop in 1953 in recognition of his manifold labors, Gannon oversaw a robust growth in schools and parishes, as well as the founding of Gannon College in 1933.

In Pittsburgh, Bishop Hugh Boyle (1921–50) added to this stability in diocesan leadership; during his tenure, Pittsburgh grew to become the eighth largest diocese in the United States. This increase in population was due in large part to the continuing industrial expansion in the region, on which the Church cast a critical eye. Pittsburgh priests George Barry O'Toole, Carl Hensler, and Charles Owen Rice, members of the Catholic Radical Alliance, gave their enthusiastic support to labor unionism. It was not accidental that Philip Murray, Patrick Fagan, and John J. Kane, all prominent union organizers in the steel and mining industries, were Catholics influenced by the Alliance.

New Dioceses for Pennsylvania

Pittsburgh's growing population led to the formation of the Diocese of Greensburg in May of 1951, removing four eastern counties from Pittsburgh's jurisdiction (Westmoreland, Armstrong, Indiana, and Fayette). Bishop Hugh L. Lamb, who had been administrator of Philadelphia, became the first bishop.

In February of 1961 it was Philadelphia's turn to be trimmed. Bishop Joseph McShea, administrator of the archdiocese upon the death of Cardinal O'Hara (1952–60), had recommended the formation of a diocese in either Allentown or Bethlehem. On February 15, it was announced that a new Diocese of Allentown would be formed with McShea as its first bishop. John Krol was named the tenth ordinary of Philadelphia on the same day. Soon after his appointment Krol left to attend the Second Vatican Council, where he took an active role in the deliberations, as did his suffragan, John J. Wright of Pittsburgh. Although Wright (who was subsequently named a cardinal, serving as Prefect of the Congregation for the Clergy in Rome) remained in Pittsburgh only until 1969, Krol, who became a cardinal in 1967, would guide the archdiocese through the turmoil following the council with a firm but steady hand until his retirement in 1988, when Anthony Bevilacqua was moved from Pittsburgh to succeed him.

One of the most sensitive issues facing the Church in Pennsylvania at the end of the century has been the reorganization of parishes in light of changes in population and a decline in the number of priests. Both Pittsburgh (with its program of Reorganization and Revitalization begun in 1989 under the guidance of Bishop Donald Wuerl) and Philadelphia (in the Catholic Faith and Life 2000 program) have attempted to situate any changes in parish configuration within the broader context of a renewal of Catholic life.

Statistical Summary

According to the 1995 *Catholic Directory,* Roman Catholics in the state of Pennsylvania numbered 3,613,052 out of a total population of 11,979,750, making the state approximately 30 percent Catholic. Figures for each diocese follow (total population/Catholic population/ percentage of Catholics): Philadelphia: 3,777,995/1,438,564/38 percent; Pittsburgh: 2,022,057/768,381/38 percent; Erie: 874,074/229,259/26 percent; Scranton: 1,025,488/362,415/35 percent; Harrisburg: 1,867,124/227,242/12 percent; Altoona-Johnstown: 643,493/129,124/ 20 percent; Greensburg: 685,335/200,492/29 percent; Allentown: 1,084,184/257,575/24 percent.

Connelly, James F., ed. *The History of the Archdiocese of Philadelphia.* Philadelphia, 1976.

Fink, Leo Gregory. *Old Jesuit Trails in Penn's Forest.* New York, 1936.

Gallagher, John P. *A Century of History, The Diocese of Scranton: 1868–1968.* Scranton, 1968.

Glenn, Francis A. *Shepherds of the Faith, 1843–1993, A Brief History of the Bishops of the Catholic Diocese of Pittsburgh.* Pittsburgh, 1993.

JOSEPH C. LINCK, C.O.

PERCY, WALKER (1916–90)

Author. When Walker Percy, M.D., died on May 10, 1990, in his home in Covington, Louisiana, just north of Lake Pontchartrain, the United States lost a philosophic and creative man of letters. Born in Birmingham, Alabama, on May 28, 1916, of a prominent family involved in the legal side of producing coal and steel, young Walker attended the Birmingham University School, the first of a number of schools where he had the advantage of having an excellent education. His parents, LeRoy and Martha Susan ("Mattie Sue") Phinizy Percy, were part of the social elite of the Birmingham community.

Early Years and Education

After his father died at the age of forty of self-inflicted wounds on July 9, 1929, a traumatic event that not only deeply affected the entire family but is significant in understanding Percy's fiction, young Walker and his mother and two brothers, LeRoy and Billups Phinizy ("Phin"), moved to Athens, Georgia, to live with Walker's grandmother. In Athens, a lovely university town that tried to live up to the ideals of its namesake, the Percy family dealt with their grief for approximately a year, until William Alexander Percy (affectionately called "Uncle Will"), a noted lawyer, plantation owner, poet, author of several works, including his popular autobiographical *Lanterns on the Levee* (1941), and first cousin of Walker's father, invited Mattie Sue Percy and her three sons to move to Greenville, Mississippi, and live with him.

Life with Uncle Will in this quiet Delta town gave stability to the four Percys until, on April 2, 1932, Mrs. Percy died in a tragic car accident. Again, the Percy boys were plunged into grief, from which they gradually emerged when Uncle Will legally adopted them. Walker graduated from Greenville High School in 1933 and entered the University of North Carolina at Chapel Hill where he majored in chemistry. His four years in college, which included a brief, but important, trip to Germany during the summer of 1934 with some fellow classmates, provided the opportunity to read the classics in literature, study biology and chemistry in particular, see movies in the local theater, and prepare for medical school. In the fall of 1937, Percy moved to New York City and started classes at the College of Physicians and Surgeons of Columbia University, and graduated in 1941 a full-fledged medical doctor. Soon after, while a pathology intern at Bellevue Hospital in New York City, Doctor Percy acquired tuberculosis and was sent to Trudeau Sanatorium in Saranac Lake, New York, to rest and recuperate.

Now under medical care himself, Percy had little to do but sit in the open air and read. Starting with his days in Saranac Lake, Percy began to immerse himself continuously in the works of Kierkegaard, Sartre, Camus, Marcel, Heidegger, Buber, Charles Sanders Peirce, and other semiotic, literary, theological, and philosophical writers; like a transplanted Thomas Mann, Percy explored the inner world of his own "Magic Mountain," as expressed in his unpublished novel *The Gramercy Winner.* Once cured of tuberculosis, Percy realized that his days in the sanatorium had changed his life and that he would probably never practice medicine himself. And, thus, he eventually returned to the South, moving to New Orleans where he made four important decisions that were to change the course of his life: (1) He proposed to Mary Bernice ("Bunt") Townsend, a medical technician who had worked in a clinic in Greenville and whom Percy had come to know during summer visits there while in medical school; (2) he and his wife converted to Catholicism (they simply walked up to the Jesuit rectory at Holy Name Church and asked to talk to a priest, and eventually were baptized conditionally on December 13, 1947); (3) he decided to eke out an existence by becoming a writer; (4) he and his wife moved to Covington (an hour's drive north of New Orleans on the other side of Lake Ponchartrain), which was known in those days as a quiet sleepy town where the ozone in the air created a healthy environment to live and work.

Literary Works

For Walker Percy as a writer, Covington provided a perfect place to write; it was one of the last outposts in the Deep South and far enough away from New Orleans that he could enjoy The Big Easy's culture, traditions, and mores without being totally absorbed by them. As Percy explains in his April 1980 essay in *Esquire* entitled "Why I Live Where I Live," Covington is a cheerfully anomalous town with an "admirable tradition of orneriness and dissent." Percy sought a place where the terrors he faced as a writer would not be neutralized, but "rendered barely tolerable." In short, in Covington, Percy could sniff the clean air, eat crawfish étouffé, write when he pleased, enjoy his family life, visit friends on occasion, and feel about as good as he could on this green earth.

Percy wrote six novels that were published (*The Moviegoer* [1961], *The Last Gentleman* [1966], *Love in the Ruins* [1971], *Lancelot* [1977], *Love in the Ruins* [1980], *The Thanatos Syndrome* [1987]), as well as two works of nonfiction (*The Message in the Bottle* [1975]; *Lost in the Cosmos* [1983]). To a great extent, Percy's novels depict men and women, often on the fringes of society, searching in a concrete time and place for salvific meaning in their lives. In *The Moviegoer,* for example, Binx Bolling, a resident of Gentilly, wanders about New Orleans in an effort to search for a direction in his life. Like Leopold Bloom in James Joyce's *Ulysses* or Quentin Compson in the second section of William Faulkner's *The Sound and the Fury,* Binx has the sensation of dominating space and time when he is in motion.

As a thirty-year-old stockbroker, an average citizen with few ambitions, a fatherless son with only a step-family and some relatives to comfort him, Binx finds limited solace in movies and in chasing after women, particularly his secretaries, Marcia, Linda, and Sharon. He makes a connection between movies and place, what he calls "certification": "Nowadays when a person lives somewhere, in a neighborhood, the place is not certified for him. More than likely he will live there sadly and the emptiness which is inside him will expand until it evacuates the entire neighborhood. But if he sees a movie which shows his very neighborhood, it becomes possible for him to live, for a time at least, as a person who is Somewhere and not Anywhere." The overall effect, however, is clear: New Orleans assumes ever-so-subconsciously the dimensions of a mythic city, as is true likewise in *The Last Gentleman* with the fictional Ithaca, Mississippi, and Santa Fe, New Mexico. The result is that Binx's search, which culminates in his marriage with Kate Cutrer, becomes to some extent the search of Everyman in Everycity. In 1962, *The Moviegoer* won the National Book Award for Fiction.

Percy's lecture, "The Fateful Rift: The San Andreas Fault in the Modern Mind," delivered on May 3, 1989, in Washington, D.C., as the Annual Jefferson Lecture in the Humanities for the National Endowment for the Humanities, contains a helpful synthesis of his views on language, literature, and semiotics. Percy begins with two propositions: (1) The view of the world that we obtain from science, either consciously or unconsciously, is radically incoherent, and (2) modern science is itself radically incoherent not when it seeks to understand subhuman organisms and the cosmos, but when it analyzes an individual person as such. Were this coming from someone other than a medical doctor, who, parenthetically, always excelled in his studies, such propositions might be rejected quickly. Percy explains that he is not raising the standard humanistic objection to science, namely that it is too abstract, detached, impersonal, and does not take into consideration art and faith, but he challenges science in the name of science itself.

In analyzing the gap that exists in scientific theories, Percy notes that while Darwin, for his part, studied the origin of the species and Freud tracked the struggle between the id and the superego, both were revolutionaries who ironically were not revolutionary enough for neither could account for his own activity by his own theory: "For how does Darwin account for the 'variation' which is his own species and its peculiar behavior—in his case, sitting in his study in Kent and writing the truth as he saw it about evolution? And if Freud's psyche is like ours, a dynamism of contending forces, how did it ever arrive at the truth about psyches, including his own?" Percy proposes to bridge the gap that science cannot deal with by looking primarily to the theories of the American scientist, logician, philosopher, and semiotician, Charles Sanders Peirce (1839–1914), who realized that language could mend the rift between mind and matter, particularly as proposed in his analysis of triadic events in this world.

In referring to the paradigmatic experience of Helen Keller touching water, Percy places great emphasis on the knowing subject, the object in question, and the verb that relates the two—the copula. "We now know," Percy said, "at least an increasing number of people are beginning to know, that a different sort of reality lies at the heart of all uniquely human activity—speaking, listening, understanding, thinking, looking at a work of art—namely Charles Peirce's triadacity. It cannot be gotten around and must sooner or later be confronted by natural science, for it is indeed a natural phenomenon. Indeed it may well turn out that consciousness itself is not a 'thing,' an entity, but an act, the triadic act by which we recognize reality through its symbolic vehicle." Peirce had named this entity that throws together words and things "interpreter," "asserter," "mind," "I," "ego," and "soul," though each of these words carries with it historical and semiotic baggage that might hinder a fresh appreciation of the acts of understanding and communication. In attempting to create a new anthropology by fusing, in part, Peirce's triadic creature with its named world, Percy contends that "one might even explore its openness to such traditional Judeo-Christian notions as man falling prey to the worldliness of the world, and man as pilgrim seeking his salvation."

Walker Percy added a distinctive, fresh voice to American literature, one with strong theological and philosophic undertones, due in part to the fact that in most of his fiction he never wandered far from what he knew of the world directly within his geographical purview. This explains, in large measure, the authentic ring to his fiction that Louisianans—and non-Louisianans, for that matter—find so appealing.

See also CATHOLICS AND AMERICAN LITERATURE.

Percy, Walker. *The Moviegoer.* New York: Knopf, 1961.

____. *The Last Gentleman.* New York: Farrar, Straus & Giroux, 1966.

____. *Love in the Ruins.* New York: Farrar, Straus & Giroux, 1971.

____. *The Message in the Bottle.* New York: Farrar, Straus & Giroux, 1975.

____. *Lancelot.* New York: Farrar, Straus & Giroux, 1977.

____. *Love in the Ruins.* New York: Farrar, Straus & Giroux, 1980.

____. *Lost in the Cosmos.* New York: Farrar, Straus & Giroux, 1983.

____. *The Thanatos Syndrome.* New York: Farrar, Straus & Giroux, 1987.

____. *Signposts in a Strange Land,* ed. Patrick Samway, S.J. New York: Farrar, Straus & Giroux, 1991.

____. *A Thief of Peirce: The letters of Kenneth Laine Ketner and Walker Percy,* ed. Patrick Samway, S.J. Jackson: University Press of Mississippi, 1995.

Samway, Patrick, S.J. *Walker Percy: A Life.* New York: Farrar, Straus & Giroux, 1997.

PATRICK SAMWAY, S.J.

PERMANENT DIACONATE IN THE U.S.A.

On November 21, 1964, Pope Paul VI promulgated the Dogmatic Constitution on the Church. In Article 29 of that document it is decreed that "the diaconate can in the future be restored as a proper and permanent rank of the hierarchy. It pertains to the competent territorial body of bishops . . . with the approval of the Supreme Pontiff, to decide whether and where it is opportune for such deacons to be established for the care of souls." On June 18, 1967, Pope Paul VI published his apostolic letter *Sacrum Diaconatus Ordinem* by which he began the restoration of the permanent diaconate. The following year the National Conference of Catholic Bishops requested restoration of the diaconate. The Holy Father approved the U.S. request in August 1968.

The Bishops' Committee on the Permanent Diaconate came into existence in November, 1968. Its principal responsibilities were: (1) to offer diocesan bishops recommendations concerning concrete details of and questions about the diaconal vocation; (2) to establish the basic requirements for a formation program including doctrinal, pastoral, and spiritual aspects of training; and (3) to review and approve diocesan plans for the formation and ministry of deacons in a diocese. Within two months of its inception, the Bishops' Committee received four proposals for the training and formation of deacons. By 1971 thirteen diocesan programs with 430 candidates were in operation. In the next 25 years nearly 12,500 deacons, formed in 155 diocesan centers, were ordained for a lifetime of service.

In 1971 the National Conference of Catholic Bishops published *Guidelines* which provided the necessary norms for the formation and ministry of deacons. In 1984, based upon the experience of the first generation of the renewed diaconate by bishops, deacons, wives of deacons, and supervisors of deacons' ministry, and conforming to the pertinent provisions of the 1983 revised Code of Canon Law, the Conference of Bishops published a revision of these *Guidelines*. Criteria by which a man is called to the diaconate are cited by the Apostle Paul in his first letter to Timothy (1 Tim 3:8-13). In deacons, the Church expects to find emotional maturity, personal integrity, Christian holiness, generosity for service, and a demonstration of the gifts needed for the diaconal ministry.

In developing a profile of the deacon in the United States, the following statistics are helpful: In 1995 the median age of deacons was 60; 83 percent were Caucasian, 13 percent were Hispanic, 4 percent were African American; 45 percent were college graduates, of these 19 percent had advanced degrees; 4 percent of the deacons were retired from active ministry; 94 percent of the deacons were married, 4 percent were celibate, 2 percent were widowers.

In the documents of Vatican Council II and in the two decrees of Pope Paul VI implementing the restoration of the diaconate (*Lumen gentium* 29, *Ad Gentes* 16, *Sacrum Diaconatus Ordinem* V, 22, and *Ad Pascendum,* Introduction), several lists of diaconal tasks are given, none of which is exhaustive. From these it is possible to distinguish three general areas of diaconal ministry: love and justice, the Word, and liturgy.

Pope John Paul II, on September 19, 1987, in Detroit, Michigan, addressed 3,000 deacons and wives of deacons. The Holy Father enumerated the ministries in which deacons were engaged: "to the ill, the abused and battered, the young and old, the dying and bereaved, the deaf, blind and disabled, those who have known suffering in their marriages, the homeless, victims of substance abuse, prisoners, refugees, street people, the rural poor, the victims of racial and ethnic discrimination, and many others." The deacon's ministerial efforts show how the obligation of family, work, and ministry can be harmonized in the service of the Church's mission, an encouragement to all others who are working to promote family life. The service of the deacon is the Church's service sacramentalized.

From its beginning and particularly during the first three centuries of the life of the Church, the diaconate has been primarily a ministry of love and justice. The early description of the deacon as "the eyes and ears, the mouth, heart and soul of the bishop" (*Didascalia Apostolorum,* II, 44,4) refers to the duty of the deacon to identify those in need, report this to the bishop, and direct the Church's loving service to the needy. Pope Paul VI described the deacon as the animator and promoter of the Church's service or *diaconia* in the local community of faith.

At present (1997) there are about 11,500 active deacons in the U.S.A., but as the Church moves into the third millennium, it is anticipated that the diaconate will continue to grow at an annual rate of 5 percent. Increasing emphasis will be placed on the deacon's ministry to respond to the real needs of the local church. There will be more intensive recruiting of candidates from minority communities and among younger age groups. The average length of deacon formation programs will continue at four and a half years.

National Conference of Catholic Bishops. *Permanent Deacons in the United States Guidelines on Their Formation and Ministry 1984 Revision.* Washington: USCC Office of Publishing and Promotion Services, 1985.

Pope Paul VI. *Sacrum Diaconatus Ordinem.* June 18, 1967.

Taub, Deacon Samuel. *The Permanent Deacon in the Church Today.* Collegeville: The Liturgical Press, 1989.

U.S. Bishops' Committee on the Permanent Diaconate. *Permanent Deacons in the United States Guidelines on Their Formation and Ministry.* Washington: USCC Publications Office, 1971.

SAMUEL MICHAEL TAUB

PETER, CARL J. (1932–91)

Priest, theologian. Carl J. Peter, the son of Carl and Anna Marie Peter, was born on April 4, 1932, in Omaha, Nebraska. An internationally acclaimed theologian and educator, Carl Peter was ordained a priest of the Archdiocese of Omaha on July 12, 1957.

Peter received a doctorate in sacred theology from the Pontifical Gregorian University in Rome in 1962 and a Doctor of Philosophy degree from the University of St. Thomas Aquinas in 1964. He served as vice rector of the North American College in Rome from 1960 to 1964, when he joined the faculty of The Catholic University of America.

He served as chairman of the Department of Theology at The Catholic University of America from 1975 to 1977. He was appointed dean of the School of Religious Studies in 1978 and served in that capacity until 1985. Later, Peter was named Shakespeare Caldwell-Duvall Professor of Theology at the university. Peter is considered one of the most eminent scholars in the university's history.

Peter served as *peritus* for the bishops of the United States during the Roman synods of 1971, 1983, and 1985. In 1980 he was appointed to the International Theological Commission by Pope John Paul II. He won worldwide acclaim as a member of the commission and as a member of the Lutheran-Roman Catholic Dialogue. He also served as a member of the Faith and Order Commission of the National Council of Churches and as a member of the Presbyterian/Reformed Catholic ecumenical consultation.

Following his death on August 20, 1991, The Catholic University of America established the Carl J. Peter Chair in Theology on March 14, 1995. He was awarded the prestigious John Courtney Murray Award by the Catholic Theological Society of America in 1975.

See also CATHOLIC UNIVERSITY OF AMERICA, THE.

Phan, Peter C., ed. *Church and Theology: Essays in Memory of Carl J. Peter.* Washington, D.C.: Catholic University of America Press, 1995.

VAL J. PETER

PETER, VALENTINE J. (1875–1960)

Journalist and publisher. Valentine Joseph Peter, one of America's most successful publishers of German-language newspapers, was born in Bavarian Franconia in 1875 and arrived in America as a boy with his family in 1889. They settled in Rock Island, Illinois.

The decade of the 1880s brought the last great wave of migration from Germany of almost 1.5 million people. These newcomers created ethnic churches and social organizations of every kind. German newspapers flourished and comprised the most impressive journalistic structure developed by any American immigrant group.

Peter began his career in German journalism as a reporter for *The Rock Island Volkszeitung* and quickly became city editor of *The Daily Peoria Sonne.* In 1904 he purchased the *Volkszeitung.* After his marriage in 1905 to Margaret Reese, he looked for a place to settle down and raise his family. He selected Omaha, Nebraska, and in 1907 purchased his first paper, *The Westliche Presse,* and in 1908, *The Omaha Tribune,* and combined both into the *Omaha Tribune Westliche Presse.* In March 1912 he published the first issue of *The Daily Omaha Tribune.* The *Tribune* continued to be the centerpiece of Peter's newspaper enterprise until his death in 1960.

Peter fast became a leading spokesman of German immigrants across America and continued to acquire more newspapers, including the *Baltimore Correspondent* (1929), the *Toledo (Ohio) Express* (1933), the *Buffalo (New York) Volksfreund* (1935), and a Catholic newspaper in Chicago, *Katholisches Wochenblatt* (1931).

In 1955 Peter received the Officer's Cross of the Legion of Merit from the Federal Republic of Germany, the nation's highest civilian award. The honor was in recognition of his work to help refugees escape persecution in Germany before and during World War II. Peter, in 1950, became a Knight of St. Gregory, and in 1953 he was awarded an honorary Doctor of Laws degree from Creighton University after all twelve of his children graduated from that Jesuit institution. His proudest boast was that he was an American and every year he celebrated on April 17—the day he became a citizen.

See also GERMAN CATHOLICS IN AMERICA.

VAL J. PETER

PEYTON, PATRICK (1909–92)

Holy Cross priest, radio and television evangelist. Born in Carracastle, Ballina, County Mayo, Ireland, on January 9, 1909, Peyton and his brother, Thomas, emigrated to the United States and lived with relatives in Scranton, Pennsylvania. Both entered Holy Cross Seminary at Notre Dame, Indiana, in 1929, professed vows in the Congregation of Holy Cross in 1933, and were ordained priests in 1941. Patrick contracted tuberculosis during his studies and promised that if cured he would spend his life spreading devotion to the Blessed Mother, especially the recitation of the rosary by families.

Assigned as chaplain to a high school in Albany, New York, in 1942, Peyton began preaching his message in parishes pulpit by pulpit. In 1945 he persuaded the Mutual Radio Network to let him broadcast a special program for Mother's Day and in 1947 he established the Family Theater, Inc., in Hollywood, California, and launched the Family Theater radio series which aired over a national network for the next twenty-two years. In 1950 Family Theater also began producing television programs and films.

In 1947 Peyton held his first diocesan-wide Family Rosary Crusade in London, Ontario. Using the slogan, "The family that prays together stays together," Peyton conducted these crusades over the next forty-five years throughout the United States and Canada and on every continent. In 1985 he conducted a nationwide crusade in the Philippines that drew two million people to its closing rally in Manila. An award-winning communicator, Peyton built up an organization that came to specialize in adult catechesis and formation, especially in Third World countries. He died in New York City on June 3, 1992, and is buried in the Holy Cross Cemetery on the campus of Stonehill College in North Easton, Massachusetts.

Arnold, Jeanne Gosselin. *A Man of Faith.* Colonie, N.Y.: Crest Lithographing, 1983.

Peyton, Patrick. *The Ear of God.* London: Burns and Oates, 1954.

———. *All For Her.* Garden City, N.Y.: Doubleday, 1967.

JAMES T. CONNELLY, C.S.C.

PHELAN, MARY GERARD (1872–1960)

Religious, educator. She was born in Kilkenny, Ireland, on January 17, 1872, and was named Anastasia. She was educated by the Religious of the Sacred Heart of Mary, and later joined the congregation in 1883, taking the name Gerard at her profession. She continued her education at Cambridge and taught for some years in England. In 1907 she came to America, and with Mother Mary Butler founded Marymount College in Tarrytown, New York. She worked diligently to expand the work of her congregation in the United States and in England. She also resumed her studies at Oxford, the Sorbonne, and Fordham University. She was elected superior general of her congregation in 1946 and again in 1952. During her terms as superior general, her congregation established twenty-eight colleges and schools—including Marymount College in New York City—in eleven countries. She died in Tarrytown on March 22, 1960.

MICHAEL GLAZIER

PILOT, THE

Newspaper of the Archdiocese of Boston since 1908, was established in 1829 by the see's second bishop, Benedict J. Fenwick, S.J. In tribute to his order, Fenwick called his paper *The Jesuit,* one of four names it had before being titled the *Boston Pilot* in 1836. The weekly was established, Fenwick wrote in his September 5 "Prospectus," to serve New England's growing number of Catholics, to explain "the Doctrine of the Holy Catholic Church," and to repudiate "the crying calumnies and gross misrepresentations . . . heaped upon" the Church of his day.

After five years of episcopal ownership, *The Jesuit* was sold to two laymen, publisher Henry Devereaux and Patrick Donahoe, of the editorial staff. It would remain in lay hands for more than forty years, until Donahoe sold the paper to Archbishop John J. Williams in 1876. In turn, it was acquired (again from lay owners) by Boston's fifth ordinary, William H. O'Connell, who declared it his official organ. Meanwhile, under Donahoe, it began its climb to eminence as the best-known Catholic journal in the country. In 1890, it had a circulation of 1,500,000.

Patrick Donahoe

Donahoe launched the era by naming his paper for the *Pilot* of Dublin, that "most popular and patriotic" journal, the foremost champion in Ireland of Daniel O'Connell and Catholic Emancipation. Donahoe's commitment was wisely made: as immigration from Ireland increased and then peaked around midcentury's Great Famine, the *Pilot* (it deleted "Boston" in 1858) became the emigrant's key link with "the old country." Donahoe ran a "missing persons" section that helped families reunite after being scattered at the threshold of "the golden door." He published Irish county and ecclesiastical news, kept up with British politics affecting Ireland, ran marriage and death notices, and featured the newest poems, theater, and fiction reflecting Irish Catholic life here and abroad. Its coverage of U.S. wars and domestic affairs, though apt to focus on an Irish brigade or heroine, was meticulous and is of continuing value to U.S. historiography. From the 1830s until well into the twentieth century, the *Pilot* was popularly styled "the Bible of the American Irish," an image it strove to blur during and after World War II.

Beginning with Donahoe, the paper boasted an unusually distinguished masthead—writers, editors, and publishers, but contributors, too. Donahoe hired Thomas D'Arcy McGee, a teenage firebrand whose editorship lasted less than three years but preceded a career in letters and Canadian politics that numbered him among the Dominion's founders. Then came John Boyle O'Reilly, the most charismatic of the paper's nineteenth-century celebrities, who built a gracious bridge between Catholics and their neighbors. Next was James Jeffrey Roche, who succeeded O'Reilly and was his first biographer. Last of this talented line was Katherine E. Conway, first woman editor (of two) and a novelist of note, whose tenure ended when O'Connell bought the paper and named priests to conduct it. Though Donahoe was a businessman primarily (banker, bookseller, travel agent, founder of *Donahoe's Magazine*), all his immediate successors were creative and literary, publishing hundreds of poems, histories, biographies, works of fiction, essays, and editorials that fix for them a firm place in U.S. Catholic history. At their instance, Irish luminaries like Oscar Wilde, Lady Gregory, Douglas Hyde, William Butler Yeats, and Dion Boucicault were *Pilot* byliners, as were the Americans, Frs. John Bannister Tabb and Abram Ryan, Fannie Parnell, Louise Imogen Guiney, James Whitcomb Riley, Orestes Brownson, Rose Hawthorne, and Mary Blake. Writings by three English cardinals, Wiseman, Newman, and Manning, were frequently serialized.

Official Diocesan Newspaper

After the *Pilot* was declared official, it became what the cardinal archbishop wished it to be—the chronicler of "events of importance to the Church as they occurred in any part of the world with special reference to Catholic life in the Archdiocese." The paper's readership area and circulation fluctuated as new New England dioceses were erected, many establishing their own newspapers. The Boston Archdiocese, with a 1990s Catholic population of nearly two million, embraces 2,500 square miles of eastern Massachusetts.

Richard J. Cushing, O'Connell's auxiliary and successor in 1944, sparked a resurgence of vitality in the *Pilot* by the force of his vivid personality. Coming to his office as World War II was ending, Cushing expanded the Church into suburbia, welcomed an avalanche of vocations, educated and housed huge student populations, and introduced scores of religious orders and communities to the see. He built millions of dollars worth of hospitals, schools, churches, convents, and other institutions, meanwhile seeing to it that his newspaper reported the news and reflected the *aggiornamento* decreed by John XXIII. To achieve his goals, Cushing appointed urbane priest-editors educated in the artistic and social sciences as well as the Church's higher disciplines. By utilizing new journalistic techniques, by hiring trained professionals (including photographers and art critics), and by employing "secular" as well as Catholic resources, he brought his paper to heights repeatedly hailed by the Catholic Press Association and acknowledged by peers in the general media.

In the 1980s, in step with a newspapering vogue, the *Pilot* switched from broadsheet to tabloid, from "good gray" editions to ones of arresting illustration and color, from a product born of "hot lead" and its own roaring presses to one edited and "poured" by a handful of people using computer technology. Following a practice urged by Vatican Council II and mandated by the vocation crisis, the *Pilot* also experimented with a lay editorship. Cardinal Cushing's successors, Humberto Medeiros and Bernard F. Law, revamped the administrative structure of the see and authorized hiring laypersons for ministries hitherto the province of religious. The practice extended to the

Pilot when two laypersons were engaged in succession, their editorships within the competence of the Secretariat of Community Relations, a new cabinet department responsible for several media and interfaith programs. Neither appointment (nor a brief attempt to publish select articles in Spanish) succeeded. As the 1990s began, the editor's chair had reverted to a priest of the archdiocese, a theologian who had previously served as director of the Archdiocesan Office of Communications.

See also CATHOLIC PRESS (NEWSPAPERS), THE.

Harris, Ruth-Ann, Donald M. Jacobs, and B. Emer O'Keefe, eds. *The Search for Missing Friends: Irish Immigrant Advertisements Placed in the Boston 'Pilot.'* Boston: New England Historic Genealogical Society, 1989 and following years.

Lord, Robert H., and others, eds. *History of the Archdiocese of Boston in the Various Stages of Its Development 1604–1943.* 3 vols. Boston: Pilot Publishing Co., 1945, passim.

O'Toole, James M. *From Generation to Generation: Stories in Catholic History from the Archives of the Archdiocese of Boston.* Boston: St. Paul Editions, 1983, 34, 40–42.

Patkus, Ronald D. *From Generation to Generation II.* Hanover, Mass.: Christopher, 1992.

Ryan, George E., ed. *The Pilot at One-Fifty.* Boston: Pilot Publishing Co., 1979. Special 98-page edition, 150 (37) (September 14, 1979).

GEORGE E. RYAN

PITASS, JOHN (1844–1913)

Priest, spokesman for Polish-American Catholics. John Pitass [Jan Pitass] was born in Piękary, Poland, on July 3, 1844. A student of theology at the Collegium Romanum in Rome from 1868 to 1873, he came to the United States in May 1873 and settled in Buffalo, New York, where he was ordained on June 7, 1873. Appointed founding pastor of St. Stanislaus, Bishop and Martyr, parish on the same day, the cornerstone for the new church was laid in September, 1873, and the church was dedicated on January 25, 1874. Pitass founded the first Polish school in Buffalo in 1874, and by 1881 the parish boasted some 1,000 families, eventually reaching a peak of about 30,000 parishioners. In 1887 he founded the influential newspaper *Polak w Ameryce* [*The Pole in America*] to minister to the needs of Polish Catholics in their own language.

Appointed dean of the Polish clergy in Buffalo (*vicarius foraneus*) by Bishop Stephen Ryan in 1894, Pitass maintained a strong interest in Polish heritage and in protecting the rights of Polish clergy and laity in America. In keeping with this, he hosted the first national convention of Polish immigrants held in Buffalo in 1896, and chaired the second such convention in Buffalo in 1901. Ostensibly organized to discuss national concerns of Polish-Americans, the second meeting focused extensively on the rights of Polish clergy in America. The second convention passed a resolution to send two representatives to Rome to present the concerns of Polonia to the pope. Pitass and Rev. Wacław Kruszka were selected as the emissaries, but Pitass had to withdraw before the trip. Nevertheless, his energy and organizational expertise were largely responsible for both the growth of his parish and the national conversations that eventually led to increased opportunities for Poles within the American Catholic Church. He died in Buffalo on December 11, 1913.

See also POLISH CATHOLICS IN AMERICA.

JAMES S. PULA

PITCHFORD, MARGARET (1884–1967)

Catholic lay activist. Margaret Pitchford was born in Natchez, Mississippi, on October 22, 1884, daughter of Frederick F. Pitchford and Catherine Lynch. She graduated from local Catholic schools and pursued a successful, lifelong business career with James J. Cole and Company.

Pitchford worked tirelessly "for every worthwhile charitable and civic welfare program that her generous and lovable spirit permitted." She served four years as president of the St. Joseph's Alumnae Association and two terms as president of the Children of Mary Sodality; she also served on the local Catholic school board. In 1931 she helped Bishop Richard Gerow organize the Mississippi branch of the National Council of Catholic Women and served three times as president (1941–43, 1945–46, and 1950–51).

In 1931 she was chosen governor of the Mississippi Federated Catholic Alumnae. She also served as governor of the Mississippi Chapter of the International Federation of Catholic Alumnae (1932–36), two terms as trustee for the organization's Third District, and twice as its International Mary's Day chairperson. She was a board member of the local United Givers Fund and the Adams County Tuberculosis Association.

On July 1, 1950, Pope Pius XII honored Margaret Pitchford as one of the first three Mississippi women to receive the *Pro Ecclesia et Pontifice* Medal.

Pitchford also kept a constant "little list of prayers" which she offered for bishops, priests, sisters, parishioners, and especially for converts. At her death on March 22, 1967, she was praised as "a faithful and untiring worker among the laity of her faith."

Catholic Action of the South, September 14, 1950.
Natchez *Democrat,* November 26, 1950; March 23, 1967.
Nolan, Charles E. *St. Mary's of Natchez: The History of a Southern Catholic Congregation, 1716–1988.* Natchez, 1992.

CHARLES E. NOLAN

PITTINI, RICCARDO (1876–1961)

Archbishop, Salesian missionary. He was born on April 30, 1876, in Tricesimo (Udine), Italy. As a teenager Richard Pittini came to Don Bosco's Salesians with the desire of becoming a missionary. After his religious profession in 1893, he was sent to Uruguay, where he was ordained, worked in youth centers and schools, and served as master of novices and provincial. He also opened up a new mission in Paraguay.

Appointed provincial of the Salesian province in the eastern United States in 1927, Fr. Pittini encouraged his confreres to inculturate themselves and the immigrant populations whom they served in eleven parishes and three schools. He faced problems of insufficient personnel and inadequate finances. He traveled and spoke extensively to raise money and publicize the Salesians and their founder, and he sponsored Don Bosco's first American biography.

In 1928 Pittini established a formation house in Newton, New Jersey. Despite the depression, it thrived, as did the province. When Pittini arrived there were fewer than 100 Salesians in his province; when he left there were over 130. The house at Newton opened with 47 seminarians; by 1933 there were 76. He opened orphanage-trade schools in Tampa, Florida, and Marrero, Louisiana, and summer camps at all five schools and the seminary. His friendship with Archbishop Cushing helped bring the Salesians to Boston in 1945.

In 1933 the rector major sent Pittini to inaugurate Salesian work in the Dominican Republic. In 1935 he was named archbishop of Santo Domingo. Although he went blind during the 1940s, he remained a dynamic pastor. He died on December 10, 1961.

See also SALESIANS (S.D.B.).

Hurley, James. *Service for the Young.* Columbus, Ohio, 1972.
Pittini, Riccardo. *Memorie salesiane di un Arcivescovo cieco.* Turin: LDC, 1948; Eng. trans. Paul Aronica, *Memories in My Blindness.* Paterson, New Jersey, 1952.

MICHAEL MENDL, S.D.B.

PLASSMANN, THOMAS (1879–1959)

Franciscan friar, scholar, and educator. Born in Averwedde, Westphalia, Plassmann left Germany in 1894 to join the U.S. missions of the Franciscan friars. He received his classical education in Quincy, Illinois, and was received into the Friars Minor in Paterson, New Jersey, in 1898. By the time he was ordained in 1906, he was completing his Ph.D. degree at The Catholic University of America. His dissertation, *The Significance of Berakah,* was a seminal biblical study. He then pursued a doctorate in theology in Rome.

In 1910 he was assigned to St. Bonaventure's College and Seminary, Allegany, New York, where he spent practically the rest of his life. In 1919 he organized the Franciscan Educational Conference, serving as its president until 1957. Its annual meetings did much to retrieve the Franciscan intellectual and spiritual heritage for the English-speaking world. He became the president of St. Bonaventure's College in 1920, leading a small college of 300 students to a university with an enrollment of over 2,200 by 1950. He also was responsible for the founding of the noted Franciscan Institute there and the establishment of Siena College outside Albany, New York, in 1937.

Plassmann exerted a wide influence in ecclesiastical circles. He served as provincial of Holy Name province from 1949 to 1952, when he returned to St. Bonaventure's as rector of the seminary there until his death. For almost five decades, he had a great impact on the many diocesan and religious priests he educated. Author of numerous scholarly and devotional works, including *The Priest's Way to God* (1938), he was in constant demand as a speaker. In the words of Cardinal Cushing of Boston, "he was one of the greatest priests of our generation."

See also FRANCISCAN FRIARS.

The Provincial Annals, Holy Name Province (1959).

DOMINIC V. MONTI, O.F.M.

POELS CONTROVERSY, THE

The Dutch-born priest Henry Poels (1868–1948) began teaching the Old Testament at The Catholic University of America in September 1904. In June 1906, the Pontifical Biblical Commission promulgated its decree upholding the "substantial" Mosaic authorship of the Pentateuch. Troubled by the decision, Poels went to Rome in the summer of 1907 and met with Pope Pius X. According to Poels' own recollection of the audience, the Pope advised him to consult with two leading Roman biblicists, both of whom urged him to continue at the university.

In the summer of 1908, the university's rector, Denis J. O'Connell, had an audience with the Pope during which O'Connell denounced an unnamed theology professor for corrupting students. The Pope took him to be referring to Poels and stated that he had already instructed the offending professor to resign. Basing himself on the Pope's words, O'Connell forbade Poels to resume teaching until Cardinal James Gibbons, chancellor of the university, had pronounced on his case. Gibbons did eventually permit Poels to resume teaching, and at their spring 1909 meeting the university trustees voted to retain him on the faculty.

Matters, however, did not rest there. In the summer of 1909, Thomas J. Shahan, the university's new rector, saw Pius X. At their meeting, the Pope vented his displeasure that Poels was still teaching at the university. He also gave Shahan a memorandum concerning the 1907 meeting be-

tween himself and Poels at which he had (purportedly) told Poels that he must resign if he could not accept the Biblical Commission's decree. As a follow-up to the Shahan audience, Cardinal Rafael Merry del Val, the secretary of state, sent Gibbons the text of an oath which Poels would have to sign in order to continue at the university. Gibbons forwarded the text of the oath to Poels who proceeded (September 1909) to Rome where he informed Merry del Val of the conditions for his signing it. In Rome Poels also met the Jesuit Leopold Fonck, rector of the Biblical Institute, who intervened with the Pope on his behalf. Following his interview, Fonck wrote Poels to tell him that the Pope wanted him to resume teaching and did not require that he resign at the end of the current academic year. Nevertheless, Merry del Val, on his own initiative, wrote Gibbons that the Pope did indeed expect Poels' resignation within the year, although shortly afterwards he rescinded this statement at the urging of Fonck.

The long-running Poels drama reached its culmination at the trustees' meeting in November 1909. When called on to take the oath, Poels refused to do so unless he could put his own construction on its terms. In response, the trustees decided not to take final action until Gibbons wrote once again to Rome. In his subsequent letter to Merry del Val, Gibbons, going beyond the motion actually adopted by the trustees, informed the Cardinal that they that had decided to dismiss Poels in June of 1910, pending the requested papal approval of this decision. On December 8, 1909, Merry del Val answered Gibbons that the Pope did so approve. The trustees met again in April 1910, after having received a lengthy statement by Poels entitled *A Vindication of My Honor.* Unmoved, they resolved to terminate him that June.

Following his dismissal, Poels returned to Holland where he assumed a leading position in the Dutch Catholic labor movement.

See also MODERNISM IN AMERICA.

Colsen, J. *Poels.* Roermond: J. J. Romen & Zonen, 1955.

Fogarty, G. P. *American Catholic Scholarship.* San Francisco: Harper & Row, 1989, 78–119.

____. "Dissent at Catholic University: "The Case of Henry Poels." *America* 155 (9) (October 11, 1986) 180–84.

Poels, H.A. *A Vindication of My Honor,* ed. F. Neirynck. Leuven: Leuven University Press/Peeters, 1982.

CHRISTOPHER BEGG

POINT, NICHOLAS (1799–1868)

Jesuit missionary. Point was born of humble parents on April 10, 1799, in Rocroi (Ardennes), France. He was eleven years old when he was obliged to find full-time work as a clerk in an army supply store to support his widowed mother and two siblings. Marshal Michel Ney (1769–1815) noticed the boy's fine handwriting and recognized in his sketches an unusual talent. He offered to find a place for him and support him at a Paris art academy, but Point's mother refused the offer.

Instead, the boy was tutored by the local priest, and after reading the life of St. Francis Xavier and accounts of the seventeenth-century Jesuit Reductions in Paraguay, he entered the novitiate of the Society of Jesus in September 1822, but left the following May. Until October 1826, when he reentered the order, he taught catechism in army barracks and was an assistant to Jean-Nicolas Loriquet, S.J. (1767–1845), the architect of the plan of studies in Restoration Jesuit schools.

When the order was expelled from France in 1830, Point took refuge in Switzerland, where he was ordained (Sion, 1831), and where he taught at the Jesuit *collège* in Fribourg. In 1833 he was assigned to a *collège* in Spain, but when the Jesuits were expelled the following year, he returned to France, made his tertianship, and was granted his request to be sent to North America (1836) to work among the native people.

Because had been designated "the man for the colleges," he was appointed principal at St. Mary's College, Lebanon, Kentucky. In 1837 he founded St. Charles College, Grand Coteau, Louisiana, where he introduced the Fribourg curriculum of studies. In 1841 he accompanied Peter De Smet (1801–73) in founding St. Mary's "Reduction" for the Flatheads in present-day Montana. The following year, he built the first church in Idaho, among the Coeur d'Alenes, and he was the first missionary to this tribe and to the Blackfeet.

Point is best known for his sketches and paintings of Native Americans and trappers, but he was also a talented architect, naturalist, writer, director of souls, and a missionary far ahead of his times. He hired Pierce Connelly (1804–73) to teach at Grand Coteau and became spiritual director to his wife, Cornelia Connelly (1809–79). Some contemporaries considered him neurotic, but he was also a victim of misunderstanding, even vindictiveness on the part of his fellow Jesuits, and from 1839 to 1847, he lived in morbid fear of being expelled from the Society. In 1847 he was transferred to work with the French Jesuits in Canada. He died July 4, 1868, at Quebec, and was interred in the basilica.

Buckley, Cornelius Michael, S.J. *Nicolas Point, S.J.: His Life and Northwest Indian Chronicles.* Chicago: Loyola University Press, 1989.

Schoenberg, Wilfred P., S.J. *A History of the Catholic Church in the Pacific Northwest, 1743–1983.* Washington, D.C.: The Pastoral Press, 1987.

_____. *Paths to the Northwest: A Jesuit History of the Oregon Province.* Chicago: Loyola University Press, 1982.

CORNELIUS BUCKLEY, S.J.

POINTS, MARIE LOUISE (1863–1931)

Journalist. One of the first women editors of a Catholic newspaper in the United States, Marie Louise Points was born in 1863. She became an editor of the *Morning Star,* New Orleans archdiocesan newspaper, in 1907. She was the daughter of George Washington Points and Delphine Stuart Points, who had moved to New Orleans from Virginia. Points attended local schools and taught for a while before joining the *New Orleans Picayune* in the women's department. She eventually became editor of the department.

Following the departure of James Randall (renowned composer of "Maryland, My Maryland") as editor of the *Morning Star* in 1907, Archbishop James Blenk drafted Points to become editor. For four years she served as managing editor or coeditor of the paper, which had a priest editor. Without fanfare, in the issue of July 8, 1911, her name began appearing alone as editor.

An article in the 1918 golden jubilee history of the *Morning Star* (probably written by Points) stated that "for nine years she has directed its policy and tone. She alone has written every editorial that appeared in its columns during all this long period, her only assistant has been her younger sister, Miss Marie Marguerite Points."

Often beset with financial problems, the *Morning Star* folded in 1930. Points herself died on September 28, 1931, at the age of sixty-eight. Roger Baudier called her "one of the leading Catholic women writers that Louisiana has produced."

Baudier, Roger. *The Catholic Church in Louisiana.* New Orleans, 1939.

FLORENCE HERMAN

POLISH CATHOLIC IMMIGRANTS: HISTORICAL BACKGROUND

Poland lies along the Central European plain bordered on the west by Germany and on the east by Russia. To the north is the Baltic Sea, while on the south rest the Carpathian Mountains. The Polish people are generally considered to be descended from the *Polanie,* a Slavic tribe whose name is thought to derive from the word *pole* meaning "field," probably a reference to the fact that the tribe lived in the plains area as an agricultural society. Legend has it that Lech, a ruler of the *Polanie* tribe, formed the first united "Polish" government at Gniezno when he found an eagle's nest on that spot and determined that it would be a good place for his people to settle.

Medieval and Early Modern Poland

The Poles first formed a modern nation state in 966 when Mieszko I agreed to accept Christianity as a means of protecting his people from the Teutonic Order's relentless invasions, launched on the pretext of converting the "pagans" to Christianity. His conversion inaugurated the Piast dynasty which established formal ties between Poland and western Europe. Under Mieszko's successor, Bolesław the Brave, Poland sent missionaries to promote Christianity, built a large cathedral in Gniezno, and churches and monasteries proliferated, creating a bond between Poles and Catholicism that endures to this day.

During the Piast era Poland was beset by military threats from the Prussians and Lithuanians to the north and the Muscovites and Tartars to the east. Immersed in a long series of wars lasting some 150 years, the bond between Poland and Christianity became more profound because of the peoples' reliance on the solace and hope afforded by their religion in times of constant danger and deprivation. Indeed, Polish knights rode into battle singing the *Bogurodzica* [*Oh Mother of God*], a hymn that is still regarded as an expression of Polish patriotism. The bond between nation and religion was further strengthened in 1241 when a greatly outnumbered Polish army under Henry the Pious halted a Tartar advance into Europe, prompting the Polish nation to consider itself the protector of Christian Europe.

In 1331 Polish forces under Władysław the Short ended a series of Germanic incursions by soundly defeating the Teutonic Knights at Płowce. The voluntary union of Poland and Lithuania in 1386 brought the latter nation under the influence of Rome, while the decisive military victory of the Polish-Lithuanian Commonwealth under King Władysław Jagiełło over the Teutonic Knights at Grünwald in 1410 broke the crusading power of the knights.

Poland's national attachment to Catholicism was further solidified by the defense of the small monastery at Jasna Góra against an invading Swedish army in the seventeenth century. Regarded as a miracle of national salvation by the Poles, the victory was ascribed to the influence of the "Black Madonna" housed in the monastery. Since that time, Our Lady of Częstochowa has been regarded as the "Queen of Poland." When, in 1683, King Jan III Sobieski led a multinational European army to victory over the invading Ottoman army at Vienna, Poles considered this yet another proof that their long history of sacrifice on behalf of Christianity placed them in a special position among European nations.

Despite the traditional adherence of Poles to Catholicism, however, the nation proved liberal in granting equal civil and religious rights to minorities as long as they maintained their allegiance to the Polish crown. By the sixteenth century, when religious warfare tore western Europe asunder, the principle of religious toleration was already long established in Poland. In fact, when the warring factions called upon King Zygmunt August to choose sides in the conflict he declined, affirming instead: "I am the king of the people, not the judge of their consciences."

Because of this spirit of tolerance, by the end of the eighteenth century Poland had become a truly multireligious nation. In 1791, for example, the Polish state included 53.2 percent Roman Catholics, 29.2 percent Uniates, 10.5 percent Jews, 3.2 percent Disuniates, 1.7 percent Protestants, 1.1 percent Russian Orthodox, 0.6 percent Muslims, and a few smaller groups.

German Poland

The attachment of most Poles to Catholicism was affirmed and strengthened during the nineteenth century when they found themselves under the control of foreign powers. In 1772, Austria, Prussia, and Russia began a series of three partitions that eventually erased Poland from the map of Europe in 1795. The German-occupied section of Poland was the most industrialized and prosperous of the three sections, yet it was also the section from which Poles first began migrating in large numbers. During the early years of occupation the Prussian government assumed that given time the Poles would assimilate. In the late 1840s, however, the authorities began to reevaluate their policy when much of the Polish gentry supported the Mierosławski Revolt in 1846 and the revolutions that swept through many of the German states in 1848. Bad harvests in 1848 and in 1853–56 led to economic recession that exacerbated Prussian impatience with the Poles. Taking advantage of the poor economic conditions during the next decade, the Prussians established a land bank in 1858 to purchase land from Poles and resell it to Germans.

With Bismarck's unification of Germany in 1870, conditions for Poles became decidedly worse. As Thomas Michalski explained, "Bismarck's attitude towards the Poles was essentially feudal. To him . . . the 'Polish problem' was essentially a problem generated by a few 'meddlesome priests' and disgruntled gentry. If only a few radical clergy could be muzzled, the problem would go away." To this end, the new German Constitution of 1871 contained no provision whatever for the protection of minority rights. To the German nationalists, Poles were nothing but *Reichsfeinde* (enemies of the Reich). To discourage the use of Polish they sought to force Polish newspapers to print in German, accused the Polish clergy of polonizing Germanic names, and sought to prevent the use of Polish in any official capacity. The German postal system, for example, refused to deliver mail if it was addressed with the Polish name *Gdańsk* instead of the German *Danzig,* or if the sender used the Polish word *ulica* (street) instead of the German *Strasse.* By 1912 about 7,500 towns, villages, and other places had their Polish names officially changed to German, and in 1908 the Association Act made the use of German mandatory at all public meetings. Further, in 1874 the Association for Advancement of the German Nationality in the Eastern Marches demanded expulsion of the Poles. By 1885, some 1,250,000 acres of land passed from Polish to German ownership in Poznania and West Prussia alone, while further actions begun in the following year displaced 35,000 Poles over the following decade.

Viewing the Polish clergy as major opponents of his germanization campaign, Bismarck began a systematic attack on the Catholic Church in January 1872 that sought to secularize education and replace Polish clergy with Germans. Polish clergy were ordered not to engage in any political activity, the Polish religious and patriotic hymn *Boże cos Polskę* [*God, Protector of Poland*] was banned, and priests who disobeyed Bismarck's edicts were jailed. As a result of his failure to "control" Polish clergy, the Germans arrested Archbishop Mieczysław Ledóchowski of Poznań-Gniezno and eventually exiled him to Rome when the Vatican interceded to secure his release from custody. The diocese remained unoccupied for twelve years, leaving the Poles without strong leadership.

The blatantly discriminatory policies of the German government, combined with economic dislocation in the German industrial areas, resulted in the emigration of a growing number of Poles to the United States. Between 1840 and 1910, some 1,575,000 people migrated from the German partition of Poland, forming the first large wave of Poles arriving in America and dominating Polish immigration into the 1880s.

Austrian Poland

Located in the southern regions of Poland along the Tatra Mountains, the Austrian partition, generally referred to as Galicia, was the poorest agricultural region of the segmented nation. In 1882 the average family landholding was 14 acres, a figure that declined precipitously to a mere six acres by 1900. Further, the land was so poor that it became increasingly difficult to feed the traditionally large agrarian families on the dwindling acreage. One estimate suggests that by 1900 some 50,000 people were dying of starvation in Galicia each year, while the average male life expectancy was only twenty-seven years.

For those who sought to support their families through paid labor, the average daily wage for agricultural laborers in Galicia in 1891 was only one-eighth as much as in the United States, while wages for unskilled industrial laborers were but one-twelfth those in America. Exacerbating this economic situation was the policy of the Austrian government which, according to historian Victor Greene, purposely retarded industrial and commercial development in Galicia to protect a major source of grain needed in the more industrialized and urbanized areas of the Austro-Hungarian Empire, particularly Bohemia and Silesia. Not until 1910 did the Austrians finally establish an industrial bank to support economic development in Galicia. As a result of these policies, the agricultural population in Galicia in-

creased from 77 percent of the total in 1890 to 90 percent by the beginning of World War I, making it the least urbanized and least industrialized of the three partitions.

Although the exodus from southern Poland did not surpass that of the German section in number until the 1890s, by the 1870s it was substantial enough that both Austrian and Roman Catholic authorities feared an increase in economic dislocation and societal upheaval because of the movement. As early as 1876, the bishop of Tarnów sought to restrain the tide of emigration with a pastoral letter in which he cautioned that, "Deceived by dishonest speculators, the inhabitants of our country are selling their homes and farms, are leaving [their] native fields, and are setting off to America." It was the responsibility of the parish priests, he counseled, to "bring to the parishioners' attention this criminal assault on the pocketbook, on the sweat, and on the blood of the Polish people." Galician migration to America peaked during the period between 1890 and 1910, supplanting by a wide margin the earlier migration from the German partition.

Russian Poland

The Russian-occupied partition of Poland was the most multiethnic of the three areas. Data for 1897 indicate that the area included 64.6 percent Poles, 12.1 percent Jews, 6 percent Russians, 1 percent Germans, 3 percent Lithuanians, and lesser numbers of Tatars, Bohemians, Rumanians, Estonians, Gypsies, and Hungarians. Beginning in the 1850s the Russians permitted some local self-government in the form of a *gmina* ruled by a council consisting of landowners. This movement toward political liberalism abruptly halted in 1870 when the czar's government instituted a policy of russification that prohibited the use of Polish as a language of instruction, repressed Polish cultural expression, and, although somewhat less vigorously, engaged in religious oppression.

Economically, the Russian partition was more industrialized than Galicia, but less so than the German zone. Łódź developed into a leading textile center and a stimulus for industrial and commercial development in the surrounding areas. Yet, the wages for unskilled labor in 1900 remained only one-fourth those in industrial America and, despite the movement toward industrialization, the northern areas of Suwalki, Łomza, and Płock remained generally poor agricultural areas where conditions closely resembled those in Galicia. No doubt for this reason, most of the Polish emigration from the Russian partition originated in these three provinces, with one-third of all Russian Poles originating in Suwalki as late as 1905.

It is estimated that between 1875 and 1914 some 9,000,000 Poles migrated either internally or externally, and by 1900 one-third of all adult Poles born in agricultural areas no longer lived and worked where they were born, a startling statistic for what had heretofore been a very stable agrarian society. Of those who migrated to the United States between 1899 and 1913, approximately 49 percent were from Russian Poland, 47 percent were Galicians, and 4 percent were from German Poland. As World War I approached, the percentage from the Russian areas increased to 66 percent in 1913, with 32 percent from Galicia and 2 percent from the German partition.

To promote economic and cultural advancement, Poles in the German-controlled areas began forming mutual-aid societies as early as 1850, a movement referred to as "organic work." This self-help movement spread to the other partitions so that by the beginning of the twentieth century Poles migrating to the United States not only sought economic opportunity, but possessed a recent history of banding together in pursuit of mutual goals.

Polish Catholicism

Perhaps the single most important factor common to Poles from each of the partitions was their commonly held allegiance to Roman Catholicism. A century of national trauma shaped Roman Catholicism in Poland into a very distinct ethnic experience. During the 1830s, the Vatican's recognition of the partitions inflamed Polish nationalists, causing patriotic partisans like the respected Romantic poets Adam Mickiewicz and Juliusz Słowacki to create what John Bukowczyk described as a "distinctly Christian" but "decidedly anti-clerical" tradition of religious nationalism called "Polish messianism" which "endowed the Polish nation with the mission of a chosen people whose tribulations and sufferings would redeem Poland and earn its resurrection. The resurrected Poland would

Our Lady of Czestochowa

herald the moral regeneration of the Universe and thus become the 'Christ of Nations.'" Although the more overt anticlerical tendencies of Polish messianism declined in subsequent decades, the image of Poland as a martyr nation found popular acceptance among the general population.

While the Church hierarchy often appeared passive in the struggle between Poles and their occupiers, the local parish priests were frequently staunch supporters of Polish heritage. Through a century of occupation, the local parish became a center of not only religious and social life, but cultural renewal and patriotic expression. By the mid-nineteenth century there developed a growing trend toward religious vocations among Polish women seeking inspiration for social and religious service under the auspices of the Virgin Mary. Polish Marianism formed a very strong impetus to the formation of sisterhoods between 1850 and 1890. Foremost among these in terms of its later impact on Polish immigrants in America was the Felician Sisters (Sisters of St. Felix) founded by Mother Angela (Sophia Camille) Truszkowska in Warsaw in 1855. Transplanted to the United States in 1874, this example of women's religious "organic work" was a mainstay in the development of Polish parochial schools in America and did much to shape the religious, cultural, and social values of Poles during their first century in America.

By the end of the nineteenth century, the values of patriotism and Catholicism melded in the Polish national consciousness to a degree that Polish immigrants in America looked to the Church as a source of solace, protection, and mutual support in the new socioeconomic environment of North America. Roman Catholicism became the initial impetus to Polish "organic work" in America, and the primary bulwark for an immigrant generation struggling to preserve its religious and national heritage while at the same time seeking economic and social opportunity.

See also POLISH CATHOLICS IN AMERICA; POLISH ROMAN CATHOLIC UNION OF AMERICA (PRCUA).

Davies, Norman. *God's Playground: A History of Poland.* 2 vols. New York, 1982.

Halecki, Oskar. *A History of Poland.* New York, 1943; new ed. London, 1978.

JAMES S. PULA

POLISH CATHOLICS IN AMERICA

Establishing Polish Parishes in America

Although individual Poles migrated to the Jamestown colony as early as 1608, and several small groups of political exiles or economic settlers arrived in the United States between 1830 and 1860, large-scale Polish migration to America did not begin until the 1870s, a time when Poles in each of the partitions had been suffering under varying degrees of foreign occupation for nearly a century.

Given the immediacy of the Old World ties between Roman Catholicism and Polish patriotism, it is not difficult to understand why one of the most pervasive and important values that Poles brought with them to the United States was their deep religious faith. In America, early Polish settlers usually attended Irish or German parishes until they could form their own. To begin the process they generally created lay committees to raise funds and lobby with the bishop for the establishment of a parish. When sufficient numbers and funds were present, the request was usually granted, a parish officially approved, and a priest appointed to lead the flock. Founding of the parish led to the creation of other voluntary societies. Chief among these were organizations providing financial insurance for illness and death, fundraising for the establishment of a school or other parish activities, promoting religious observances, sponsoring youth activities, or addressing other parish needs.

Father blesses the food

The Polish parish in America was both a reflection of Polish religious conviction and group pride. Polish historian Andrzej Brożek suggests that individual contributions to the local parish "became as important a source of prestige as land holdings had been in the Old Country." By 1908 per capita church support among Poles in Chicago was $3.51, or $17.55 for the average family of five. This was about one and one-half week's wages for an unskilled worker, or about two months' rent in a tenement. The rate of Polish contributions was among the highest in the city.

In fact, the very proliferation of Polish parishes was also evidence of their importance in community life. In 1870 there were approximately 15 "Polish" parishes in America, a number that rose quickly to 75 in 1880, 170 in 1890, 330 in 1900, over 500 by 1910, about 760 in 1920, and more than 800 in the 1930s.

Because of the multifaceted role of the parish in Poland and among Polish settlements in America, the role of the priest as both religious and civic leader was usually undisputed in the immigrant generation. The local priest functioned as spiritual father, temporal leader, priest, teacher, legal counselor, business advisor, and intermediary with the unfamiliar ways of American society.

In America the parish took on new importance as a means of transmitting traditional religious and cultural values to a community otherwise surrounded by foreign and generally Protestant beliefs and customs. In this, the parish school became particularly important. Polish immigrants tended to view American public education with suspicion, considering it both antireligious and anti-Polish. Consequently, they were willing to contribute their meager resources to support parish schools as guardians of their traditional values. Classes were generally taught in Polish and the curriculum emphasized religious education and Polish history. English was taught as a foreign language. Though limited in its scope and purpose, the Polish parish school was a key factor in preserving Polish heritage, religious values, and social and family discipline.

Research indicates that Polish-Americans traditionally place high value on "security, stability, order, and respectability." Through the development of ethnic parishes and schools they fulfilled these needs. In the self-sustaining ethnic communities they found a degree of security from overt discrimination, while at the same time being able to maintain their own culture, religious values, and social organization.

Nationalism vs. Religion

By the mid-1860s Chicago was already the largest Polish settlement in America. Because of this, some of the early efforts to unify Poles into a single umbrella organization began there. These efforts were frustrated because of a division between nationalist and clerical factions, a division mirrored throughout Polonia. Led by Ladislas Dyniewicz, head of the *Gmina Polska* [The Polish Commune] society, the nationalists were a secular group who believed that *all* Poles should be organized into a central association to work for the independence of the homeland. The clerical faction, led by Piotr [Peter] Kiołbassa, head of the St. Stanislaus Kostka Society, also favored independence for the homeland, but they equated *Polskość* [Polishness] with Catholicism and objected to the nationalists' inclusion of socialists, Jews, schismatics, and nonbelievers.

Bitter quarrels raged between the two groups as each attempted to gain control of Chicago Polonia. In the early years the nationalists predominated, but in 1871 the Congregation of the Resurrection negotiated an agreement with Bishop Thomas Foley to administer all nondiocesan Polish parishes for ninety-nine years. The Resurrectionists became a strong ally of Kiołbassa's clerical faction, providing it with the authority and resources to displace the nationalists as the more influential group. Under Rev. Wincenty Barzyński's leadership, nineteen Polish parishes were established in the Chicago area between 1874 and 1899. In further moves to consolidate the clerical position, Barzyński established a parish bank that held savings deposits, issued loans, and assisted in founding the influential *Dziennik Chicagoski* [*Chicago Daily News*] in 1889 to support clerical and Resurrectionist positions.

The lack of any lay organizational structure beyond the parish level was a detriment to the solidification of religious influence over the immigrant community. To remedy this and spread clerical influence even further, Rev. Teodor Gieryk founded in 1873 the *Zjednoczenie Polskie Rzymsko-Katolickie* [Polish Roman Catholic Union; PRCU] to promote *Polskość* on the national level. Gieryk envisioned this organization as open to all. His primary supporters, Resurrectionist Rev. Wincenty Barzyński and his brother Jan, lay editor of *Pielgrzym* [*The Pilgrim*], insisted that membership be restricted to Poles loyal to Roman Catholicism. Initially, the debate between exclusiveness and inclusiveness continued within the PRCU. In 1875, at its third congress, the PRCU formally voted to remain "Roman Catholic," fusing religion and nationalism in its constitution as reflected in the motto *"Bóg i Ojczyzna"* ["God and Fatherland"]. The constitution called for maintenance of the faith, mutual aid, cultural improvement, and loyalty to parish priests and bishops. Because of this, the organization lacked the central focus of "inclusive nationalism" required to maintain a truly national Polish-American organization.

With its headquarters in Chicago, the PRCU organization was closely tied to local parishes. In its early years it promoted the founding of schools, supervised the establishment of loan associations, and assisted with the beginning of parish libraries. On the national level it funded a hospital, seminary, and convent, and published a weekly Catholic newspaper, *Gazeta Katolicka* [*Catholic Gazette*].

As the dominance of the clerical element in Chicago spread under the influence of the Resurrectionists and the Polish Roman Catholic Union, the nationalist faction became increasingly determined to regain its former position of dominance. Encouraged by growing discontent with exclusive clerical control of the PRCU, a meeting of nationalist leaders in 1880 led to formation of the *Zwiazek Narodowy Polski* [Polish National Alliance; PNA]. The fundamental question that divided the PRCU and PNA was

the definition of *Polskość*. While the PRCU maintained that Polishness and Catholicism were inextricably linked, the PNA held that *anyone* who supported the Polish national cause should be admitted to membership regardless of their religious or political views. Its leaders were laymen, its policies at least mildly anticlerical, and its membership open to socialists, Jews, schismatics, nonbelievers, and others whose beliefs were antithetical to the PRCU.

The PNA grew rapidly after its founding. By 1894 it included over 200 lodges in 21 states. Largely because of its popular insurance programs, PNA membership rose to over 600 lodges in 25 states by 1905. By comparison, in the same year the PRCU numbered only 250 lodges in 18 states. The success of the PNA thwarted the aspirations of the PRCU to gain hegemony over American Polonia. To counter the growing dominance of the PNA, the PRCU initiated in the 1880s a major structural reorganization, creating both a federation of local parish societies akin to the PNA lodges and creating its own insurance program. The PRCU also began publishing two official organs, *Wiara i Ojczyzna* [*Faith and Fatherland*] in 1887 and *Naród Polski* [*The Polish Nation*] in 1897. After these changes the PRCU grew during the 1890s, but it suffered from the depression of 1893-97, low dues, and other financial difficulties. Thus, despite its willingness to adopt a new structure, the PRCU remained unable to overtake the PNA as the principal national Polish-American organization.

The struggle for dominance between the PNA and PRCU in the 1880s and 1890s was a bitter fight punctuated by vicious editorials, legal actions, and sometimes violence. The clerical forces, led by Rev. Wincenty Barzyński of Chicago and Rev. Jan Pitass of Buffalo, attacked the PNA repeatedly over its inclusive definition of *Polskość*, labeling it a godless organization and at one time threatening to excommunicate any Catholic who joined its ranks. The PNA struck back, arguing in its weekly organ, ironically named *Zgoda* [*Harmony*], that the PRCU was not committed to supporting the Polish national cause, only promoting Catholicism. In 1908 the PNA began publishing the daily *Dziennik Zwiazkowy* [*Alliance Daily News*]. The PRCU followed with the daily *Dziennik Zjednoczenia* [*Union Daily News*] in 1923.

The vicious attacks and counterattacks eventually led the moderate Polish Catholic clergy who hitherto supported the PNA to withdraw their support. Led by Rev. Dominic Majer, the moderates founded the Polish National Union in 1889 as an alternative to the PNA and PRCU. This organization eventually split into the Polish Union of the United States, with headquarters in Wilkes-Barre, Pennsylvania, and the Polish Union of America headquartered in Buffalo. Further defections occurred with the secession of the eastern Poles to form the Polish National Alliance of Brooklyn in 1903. Thus, the debate over inclusiveness prevented Polonia from developing a unified national representative organization and somewhat weakened the traditional bonds between Poles and Roman Catholicism.

Attempts to Maintain Immigrant Loyalty to Catholicism

As immigration increased, the Catholic hierarchy recognized that the Poles formed a large and growing percentage of Catholics in America, and that some effort to retain their religious loyalty was in order. This became critical as organized labor and other secular movements eroded the influence of the Church. Rev. Wacław Kruszka estimated that through this "leakage" the Church lost as many as one-third of the immigrants. At the Third Plenary Council of Baltimore in November 1884, Church authorities attempted to solidify their control over immigrants by decreeing that all American Catholics "should educate their children in parochial schools in order to protect them from Protestant and secular influences." John J. Bukowczyk notes that as a result of this the number of Polish-American parochial schools increased between 1887 and 1914 from about 50 to almost 400, with student enrollments rising from 14,150 to 128,540. By the 1920s approximately two-thirds of all Polish-American children were enrolled in parochial schools.

In addition to mandating a parochial school education for Catholic youth, Church leaders took other actions to maintain the loyalty of their Polish flock. In 1887 Victor Zaleski and Jan Radziejewski founded a Roman Catholic newspaper in Chicago entitled *Wiara i Ojczyzna* [*Faith and Fatherland*] to promote the view that the nature of *Polskość* inseparably linked Roman Catholicism and national identity. Soon, other periodicals followed in most major immigrant communities.

Another policy adopted by the Church to maintain its influence over the ethnic communities was the creation of "national parishes." The Catholic hierarchy in America was organized into parishes and dioceses on a geographical basis. Thus, the national parish was an exception. But it was an exception with some precedent. So-called "nonterritorial" parishes were first sanctioned in the Fourth Lateran Council in the thirteenth century and later reaffirmed by the Council of Trent in the sixteenth century. Under this principle parishes could be organized according to the "particular character" of the people. In America, the "particular character" was usually language.

By 1912 there were almost 1,600 "official" national parishes including 346 German, 336 Polish, and 214 Italian parishes. Bukowczyk, Kruszka, and others maintain that these numbers are vastly understated, with Kruszka citing a figure of 517 Polish parishes by 1900. Whatever the truth, from the perspective of the Catholic hierarchy, the movement to national parishes was designed specifically to preserve the faith among immigrant communities. To the immigrants, however, the creation of the national parishes provided "a focus of group activity, preserved the group's ethnoreligious identity, and provided a means of passing on its language and culture to succeeding generations. The national parish was thus a compromise between the Church's interest in preventing the loss of adherents, and immigrants' concern with sustaining their religious and cultural heritage."

Religious Schism

Many Poles, however, were not satisfied with the largely symbolic nature of the national parish. Church authorities exerted strict control over the parishes, demanding title to all property, assigning priests, and otherwise denying lay participation in decision-making. This conflicted with the Poles' concept of lay involvement and the ideals of democracy and property ownership they equated with America. In partitioned Poland, the Roman Catholic Church provided both a unifying factor and a haven for the expression of Polish nationalism. In America, immigrants unfamiliar with the language or culture of their new environment relied upon their religious convictions and institutions as a stabilizing element in their lives.

In Poland there was a tradition of lay involvement in the founding of parishes. The *ius patronatus* was a long-established "right of patronage" under which a member of the gentry whose ancestors endowed a parish might nominate a pastor to that parish. Although this right did not directly involve the parishioners, it was well known among Polish immigrants and established a precedent of lay involvement in parish affairs. As a result, most of the early Polish parishes in America were begun by lay initiatives rather than by religious authorities.

Polish Catholics often believed the American Catholic hierarchy and local priests displayed little understanding of the new arrivals, choosing instead to ignore them, or in some instances make them the focal point for derision and discrimination. As their protests grew, Bishop Ignatius Horstmann of Cleveland asked, "Why is it that only the Poles cause trouble in this regard?" The answer lay in the historical and cultural perspectives that Poles brought from the old country and their concept of American democracy. J. David Greenstone maintains that "the Poles were the most ethnically assertive among the Roman Catholic immigrant groups, since they found on arrival that 'their' Church, in practical terms the most important Polish institution before 1918, was controlled in America by a foreign, particularly Irish, clergy and hierarchy."

Most of the Poles' complaints involved their desire for democracy and equality in parish and Church governance. Since most parishes began through lay initiative, the Poles, relying for justification on both the Polish precedent of lay involvement and their view of American democracy, sought some control over parish finances, the right of parish councils to hold title to property purchased with the parishioners' money, and increased authority for the parish councils. In addition, Polish priests, often frustrated by lack of career mobility in the national parishes, voiced their own complaints over inequities in assignments and promotions. These grievances crystallized around the demand for appointment of Polish bishops. Not all of the Polish clergy supported this, but few opposed it.

In 1896 the first Polish Catholic congress convened in Buffalo under the leadership of Rev. Jan Pitass to discuss concerns about the American Catholic Church. Deeply concerned about the lack of recognition and sensitivity on the part of Church leaders in America, the meeting brought together religious and lay leaders whose reaction ranged from those who advocated schism to those who counseled patience and change within the Church.

A second congress met in Buffalo in 1901, attended by representatives of several important Polish organizations including both the Polish National Alliance and the Polish Roman Catholic Union. Chief among their concerns was the movement to appoint a Polish bishop to minister to the immigrants in America. If there could be national parishes, they reasoned, why not a bishop to serve the needs of different cultural and linguistic groups?

Rev. Wacław Kruszka, a strong voice for Polish rights within the Church, made an emotional appeal for "unity in diversity," a view of cultural pluralism within the American Catholic Church that was clearly ahead of its time. Largely through Kruszka's influence, the conference decided to send letters of appeal to the apostolic delegate, Archbishop Francisco Satolli, to Cardinal James Gibbons, and to the American bishops. In the letters the Poles asked for the creation of Polish-speaking auxiliary bishops in twelve dioceses whose population numbered between 25 percent and 50 percent Polish-Americans.

When their letters were ignored, the Poles sent delegates to plead their case directly with the Vatican. Thus, Kruszka and Buffalo Congressman Rowland B. Mahaney left for Rome in July 1903. There the Polish priest met with Pope Pius X whom he claimed promised that "something in the near future will be done according to your wishes." Following additional appeals, Pius X dispatched Archbishop Albin Symon, himself of Polish ancestry, to the United States in 1905 to investigate the situation. After an extensive review, Symon recommended the appointment of a Polish bishop in areas where Poles formed a large percentage of the Catholic population. As a result, Rev. Paul Rhode was appointed auxiliary bishop of Chicago in 1908, the first Polish-American to attain that status.

Despite Rhode's elevation, Kruszka and his supporters were clearly unhappy. They did not view the position of auxiliary bishop, with its limited influence and lack of real authority, as in any way fulfilling their desire for equality. When no further action was forthcoming to redress their grievances, the sentiment for independentism increased dramatically.

While most Poles attempted to work within the Church to secure equality, by the mid-1890s a serious movement toward the establishment of "independent" parishes had already begun. The complaints of these local parishioners were emphatically articulated in *Kuryer Polski* [*The Polish Courier*]: "The founders and benefactors of Polish churches in America are not priests nor American bishops. The founders and benefactors of Polish churches in America are the Polish parishioners. Polish parishioners give their hard-earned pennies for the founding and support of the churches. . . . In the old country, the founders and benefactors had a voice not only in the running of church affairs, but in the selection of the pastor. Here in America, the founders and benefactors of the Polish churches, that is, the Polish people, should certainly have the same rights and privileges."

Early dissent appeared in Chicago and Buffalo but soon spread to other communities as lay trusteeship and the appointment of Polish bishops became the focal issues representing equality and Polish nationalism. Church authorities responded quickly and dramatically against the "independents," equating "lay rights" with heresy and labeling them pagans, heathens, atheists, revolutionaries, lawbreakers, and worse. In a concerted effort to crush growing dissent, bishops used discipline and excommunication to enforce obedience from parishioners and priests alike.

Gradually, the independent movement crystallized around Rev. Franciszek Hodur, a strongly nationalistic priest in Scranton, Pennsylvania. Serious trouble began when Hodur demanded that property in his parish be held by the laity, and that the laity have a voice in the appointment of pastors, classic demands of those advocating "trusteeism." When Hodur refused to relent he was excommunicated, but even this failed to sway him. In 1897 he founded the newspaper *Straż* [*The Guard*] to disseminate his views, a move quickly countered by Roman Catholic publication of *Przegląd* [*The Review*].

As support for Hodur increased, he moved to consolidate his position by organizing the independent parishes into the Polish National Catholic Church. The new church's constitution, adopted in 1904, provided the following rationale for separatism: "Should we Poles renounce today our rights and our national character given to us by God? Should we disinherit our souls, and deprive ourselves of independence, in order that we might please the Pope and the Irish bishops? No, never! If our nation has any mission in humanity's reach for higher goals, then it must also have its own distinct, Polish faith, its National Church, as all creative peoples of the world have. Our Polish National Church in America is the first step in the work of forming an independent life in emigration, and, God grant, for the future of our entire people."

Hodur's movement retained much of Roman Catholic tradition and belief, including the hierarchical Church organization. The liturgical language changed from Latin to Polish and the Church calendar expanded to include many additional feast days commemorating events in Polish history. Hodur, elected bishop of the new Church at its general synod in 1904, characterized his Church as "republican" in comparison to the "monarchical" Roman Catholics. This strategic move symbolically aligned Hodur's Church with the ideals of American democracy.

PNCC membership rose steadily to between 60,000 and 85,000 in more than fifty parishes by 1926. By the time of Hodur's death in 1953, it numbered more than 130,000 members, but this was less than 5 percent of the membership of organized Polonia. Although numerically small, the PNCC movement provided an outlet for Polish religious nationalism and eventually influenced the Roman Catholic Church to adopt a more conciliatory attitude toward its ethnic minorities in America. In 1946 the PNCC entered into intercommunion with the Protestant Episcopal Church, but it was terminated in the 1970s over the issue of Episcopal ordination of women. In the 1990s efforts were renewed to develop intercommunion with Rome and a general reconciliation has since occurred which many PNCC leaders feel will eventually lead to a complete *rapprochement* between their movement and Roman Catholicism.

The Second Generation

A major factor in the rise of Polish ethnic identity and cohesion between 1920 and 1940 was the work of the Polish-American clergy. It was the parish that provided the legitimacy of underlying ethnic values and early socialization into the psychological makeup of Polish youth in the second and third generations. It was, according to Stanislaus A. Blejwas and M. B. Biskupski, the traditional duty of the Polish-American clergy "to transmit a Polish identity to an increasingly Americanized and secularized Polonia." In this, the clergy were faced not only with encroaching secularization and Protestant appeals, but also with a Catholic hierarchy that sought Americanization of the immigrants as a means of maintaining their religious loyalty.

The decade of the 1920s was particularly pivotal as a new generation of Polish-American clergy grew to maturity. The younger clergy were born and raised in America. "At the heart of their commitment as Christian pastors," noted Daniel Buczek, "was *salus animarum suprema lex* [the salvation of souls is the highest law]." With this, the preservation of *Polskość* became clearly secondary in importance. Further, the Polish-American clergy had to face the conflict in philosophy between the authority of the priest and the democratic principles of America. As Buczek explains, the Catholicism of the Polish peasant village was complete. In America, the dominant society was Protestant and the Church was controlled by Irish and Germans. This difference was significant because during the interwar period the Roman Catholic hierarchy vigorously pursued its belief that "to Catholicize America we must Americanize the immigrants." Between the wars many states adopted laws requiring that classroom instruction be in the English language, thus supporting the Americanization of Polish parochial schools. In the face of these forces, the Polish-American clergy were faced with the often contradictory demands of parishioners and the Church hierarchy.

That Poles remained committed to Catholicism during this period can be seen in the fact that the number of official "national" parishes within the Roman Catholic Church continued to increase and the enrollment at Orchard Lake Seminary, an institution designed to produce priests to minister to Polish parishes, continued to rise until it peaked at 540 in 1929.

Chief among the forces acting to maintain *Polskość* were the Polish parochial schools and their complement of teaching nuns. By 1927 there were more than five hundred Polish Roman Catholic grade schools. According to Thaddeus Radzilowski, the various sisterhoods made a tremendous contribution to "defining Polish American identity through their schools and textbooks, in shaping its institutions, channeling its human resources and surplus capital into educational and charitable endeavors, tying together its neighborhoods and educating its youth."

Much has been written about the Polish parochial school and there is still a debate among historians and sociologists about the effects of the system on second- and third-generation Polonians. A study of the problem by Polish historian Józef Miąso concluded that, while the parochial system may have "saved the young Polish generation not only from denationalization, but above all from illiteracy," the education itself was adequate only for living within the restricted environment of the Polish ethnic community. In comparison with the public school system, or for that matter the non-Polish parochial schools, "the majority of these [Polish] schools remained for a long time . . . far behind in both their educational level and in their teaching methods." Thus, the argument goes, the Polish parochial schools and parishes may have been a significant deterrent to entry into the mainstream of American socioeconomic life.

The opposite point of view is taken by Daniel Buczek who argues that "the Polish ethnic parish was, in the 1920s and 1930s, an intelligent transition from the Polish immigrant parish-community before World War I to the American community of Polish ancestry after World War II." The truth probably lies somewhere between these two extremes. It seems likely that the Polish parochial school was a significant factor in assisting in the transition from Poland to America and in preserving Polish history and culture. It also seems likely that by the end of the second generation the low academic standards and focus on Polish issues did not prepare students adequately to compete in mainstream America.

Post-World War II Changes

While church attendance remained high among Polish-Americans in the generation following World War II, religious life nevertheless underwent significant change. The Polish nature of many parishes became very suspect as migrations and changing demographics reduced the Polish presence in many of the traditional urban neighborhoods. By 1970, many of the smaller Polish parishes had already undergone a dramatic change, conducting services in English and catering to new ethnic groups. Even in the larger city parishes, urban renewal and changing demographics made the future viability of Polish parishes problematical.

Stanislaus A. Blejwas, who studied parishes in Connecticut, noted that the more enlightened Polish pastors viewed education as a road to both socioeconomic progress and "transmission of cultural values." The continued observance of Polish Masses and traditional holidays, and the sponsoring of "Polish schools" for children, often after actual parish membership had changed dramatically, no doubt provided a source of ethnic identification to Polish-American suburbanites that was otherwise unavailable. This explanation is supported by Paul Wrobel who concluded from his study of Detroit Polonia that "the parish performs an important social function by providing an opportunity for Polish Americans to interact with one another. As a result of that interaction, linkages among nuclear families are established and maintained, and an ethnic community is formed and sustained."

In a study of the persistence of ethnic parishes, Roger Stump compared the national parishes in existence in 1940 with those recognizably ethnic in 1980. He found that, of the two largest groups of national parishes in 1940, only 38 percent of German parishes were still functioning in 1980, whereas 76 percent of Polish parishes were still active. Other evidence suggests that Polish ethnic parishes have not only survived, but flourished. A study of Italian and Polish neighborhoods in Detroit, Baltimore, and Providence (Rhode Island) by John Carlisi in 1978–79 indicated that Polish families "scored strongly on both church affiliation and the desire to send their children to parochial schools," while studies of other Polish ethnic parishes in Buffalo, Chicago, Los Angeles, New Britain (Connecticut), Pittsburgh, and Rochester (New York) support the same conclusions.

Yet, despite the documented persistence of Polish religious allegiance, as the original urban immigrant communities began to dwindle in numbers, an interesting phenomenon began to occur as Poles living in suburban areas often traveled into the cities, many driving some distance, to attend services and celebrate holidays in the old Polish parishes with which they now had no other link. Documented by several scholarly studies, this phenomenon clearly suggests the continued interest in ethnic heritage and religious values among Polish Americans in the postwar generation. Research by John Simpson suggests that 80 percent of second-generation Polonians attended church services regularly, a figure nearly equaled by the 79 percent attendance rate of the third generation. This conclusion is supported by Donald Pienkos who, in a study of Milwaukee Polonia, found that 74 percent of those surveyed considered themselves to be "strongly religious," compared with only 41 percent of non-Poles. Two studies by Andrew Greeley suggest a similar conclusion. In 1973 he found that "among Catholics in the academic profession, Polish Americans ranked highest in weekly church attendance, with ninety-one percent claiming they performed this religious function." In another study in the following year he found "Polish respondents to be the most likely to stress loyalty to the Catholic Faith." Together, the results of these studies, as Pienkos notes, "point to the persistence of Polish ethnic culture" in America.

The Polish parish, then, despite changing neighborhoods and the movement of the third and fourth generations to the suburbs, continues to serve as a link among Polish-Americans who wish to preserve their heritage. Yet, Ewa Morawska found that the rationale for attending ethnic parishes differed noticeably between the immigrant and subsequent generations. The immigrants "usually point to a sense of *national duty*" to explain their attendance, while second-, third-, and fourth-generation ethnics indicate they maintain ties with the ethnic parish for "religious and/or *social-relational* reasons." Morawska's findings appear to support the general conclusion that later generations of Polish-Americans continue to exhibit high instances of church attendance primarily as a means of continuing their religious traditions and maintaining social relationships with other Polonians.

Yet, as the nature of the parish underwent change, the role and status of the priest also underwent a metamorphosis. In the early part of the century the priest's standing within the Polish community was very high. The Church served as a center of both religious and social life, with the pastor being consulted on any major decision from potential marriages to industrial strikes. By 1970, while the priest was still looked upon as a religious leader, his role in the secular lives of his parishioners, and consequently his socioeconomic status, declined seriously. The rise of parish councils further diluted the authority of the parish priest, and a serious decline in the number of new seminarians resulted in an increasingly aging clergy. Where replacements were available, they were often third-generation Polonians who no longer felt the preservation of Polish culture was a special aspect of their religious mission.

Another casualty of the changing times was the Polish parochial school system. In 1953 the Felician Sisters, the largest of the Polish teaching orders, operated 250 elementary schools, 28 high schools, 3 junior colleges, and one senior college with a total enrollment in excess of 85,000 students. Two years later, the Sisters of the Holy Family of Nazareth reported operating 10 hospitals, 81 elementary schools, 15 secondary schools, 7 postsecondary schools, and two colleges. The contribution of these and other orders to the socialization of incoming immigrants into American society, the education of immigrant children, and the preservation of cultural and social values was inestimable during the early years of the twentieth century. The influence of parochial schools continued to be significant in the postwar era as seen in a national study by Andrew Greeley and Peter H. Rossi in 1966. They concluded that 73 percent of children of Polish extraction had some parochial school background. By then, however, the decline of Polish parochial school education was already at hand. As Poles gradually moved out of the urban ethnic enclaves and away from their traditional parish schools, the changing demographics of traditional neighborhoods altered the ethnic nature of many schools and the declining number of religious vocations decreased the number of priests and nuns available as teachers. With this, Polish parochial schools found it increasingly difficult to staff classrooms. Many began hiring laypersons to fill the gaps, but qualified lay teachers increased expenses leading in many cases to unbalanced budgets and steady economic decline to the point where schools were no longer viable. Some parishes resorted to hiring unqualified teachers, but as educational standards declined because of this dubious expedient, enrollments also declined as parents sought a better opportunity for their children in suburban public schools.

The decline of the Polish parish school was a significant change for Polonia. As Wrobel eloquently explained in his analysis of Detroit, the fears of those worried about the future of the Polish ethnic community crystallized around the issue of the parochial school. "Many believe the future of this Polish-American community is dependent on what happens to the school in the years to come. If it remains open, people argue, current residents with children will stay, and the neighborhood will attract young Polish-American families. But if the school closes, parents will move to the suburbs, where their children can get a Catholic education, and the neighborhood will lose its appeal for Polish Americans with school-age youngsters."

Ironically, while the size and influence of the Polish-American ethnic parish began to decline, the hierarchy of the Roman Catholic Church began to respond to some of the issues that split Poles into anticlerical and independent movements earlier in the century. In 1952 the apostolic constitution *Exsul Familia* guaranteed, for the first time, "the rights of immigrants to proper pastoral care in their own language and traditions." Further, the Church became much more receptive to Polish-American priests. One tangible symbol of this was the elevation of John Joseph Krol, auxiliary bishop of Cleveland, to the Archdiocese of Philadelphia in 1961. The eleventh Polish-American bishop, he became the first to lead a major Roman Catholic diocese in America. Eight years later, he gained elevation to the College of Cardinals.

Further evidence of the Poles' growth in status within the Church, and within American society, came during the celebration of the millennium of Poland's existence as a nation in 1966. On that occasion, President Lyndon Johnson issued a proclamation on May 3 commemorating the occasion and the U.S. Postal Service issued a special commemorative stamp. Although the Polish government refused to allow the Polish Primate, Stefan Cardinal Wyszyński, to visit the United States because of cold war tensions, a crowd of 135,000 attended the dedication of the Polish Catholic shrine at Doylestown, Pennsylvania. President Johnson delivered the major address on this occasion, "emphasizing the heritage of freedom for Poles and other minorities in America."

Buczek, Daniel S. "Polish-Americans and the Roman Catholic Church." *Polish Review* 21 (1976) 39–61.

Bukowczyk, John. *And My Father Did Not Know Me: A History of the Polish-Americans.* Bloomington, Indiana, 1987.

Domanski, F. *The Contribution of the Poles to the Growth of Catholicism in the United States. Sacrum Poloniae Millenium.* Rome: Gregorian University Press, 1959.

Galush, William. "Both Polish and Catholic: Immigrant Clergy in the American Church." *Catholic Historical Review* 70 (1984) 407–27.

Kuzniewski, Anthony J., S.J. *Faith & Fatherland: The Polish Church War in Wisconsin, 1896–1918.* University of Notre Dame Press, 1980.

Liptak, Dolores, R.S.M. *Immigrants and Their Church.* New York: Macmillan, 1989.

Mocha, Frank, ed. *Poles in America: Bicentennial Essays.* Stevens Point, Wisconsin, 1978.

Orton, Lawrence D. *Polish Detroit and the Kolasinski Affair.* Detroit, 1981.

Parot, Joseph J. *Polish Catholics in Chicago, 1850–1920: A Religious History.* DeKalb, Ill.: Northern Illinois University Press, 1981.

Pula, James S. *Polish Americans: An Ethnic Community.* New York, 1995.

Renkiewicz, Frank, ed. *The Polish Presence in Canada and America.* Toronto, 1982.

Znaniecki, Lopata. *Polish Americans: Status Competition in an Ethnic Community.* Englewood Cliffs, 1976.

JAMES S. PULA

POLISH ROMAN CATHOLIC UNION OF AMERICA (PRCUA)

In an effort to create a national organization that would maintain religious influence over Polish immigrants in America, Rev. Teodor Gieryk, with strong support from Rev. Wincenty Barzyński and the Congregation of the Resurrection in Chicago, founded the *Zjednoczenie Polskie Rzymsko-Katolickie* [Polish Roman Catholic Union] in 1873. Taking as its motto the Polish slogan *"Bóg i Ojczyzna"* ["God and Fatherland"], the organization's constitution stressed maintenance of the faith, mutual self-help, and cultural improvements as its primary goals, while requiring that all members be loyal to their priests and bishops. The organizational structure was closely tied to local parishes, and in its early years it promoted the establishment of parish schools, libraries, and loan associations. Nationally, it sponsored a hospital, seminary, convent, and published the weekly newspaper *Gazeta Katolicka* [*Catholic Gazette*].

In its early years the PRCUA was locked in an acrimonious struggle with the Polish National Alliance, a secular Chicago-based national organization, for control of the Polish immigrant community. While the PRCUA maintained that Catholicism and Polish patriotism were inseparable, the PNA argued that anyone loyal to the recreation of an independent Poland—including religious and ethnic minorities such as the Jewish, Orthodox, Protestant, and Uniate populations of the old Polish-Lithuanian Commonwealth—should be welcomed to membership. In 1887 the PRCUA began publishing *Wiara i Ojczyzna* [*Faith and Fatherland*], a newspaper later replaced by *Naród Polski* [*The Polish Nation*] in 1897. In 1923 it established the influential daily, *Dziennik Zjednoczenia* [*Union Daily News*]. In 1898 the PRCUA incorporated as a fraternal insurance company in the state of Illinois in order to better compete with the popular insurance programs offered by the PNA. Regardless, the PRCUA was not able to overtake the PNA in membership and influence within the Polish-American community. PRCUA membership rose to a peak in the 1920s with 900 local groups in 24 states; yet, it continued to lag behind the PNA which counted 1,670 lodges in 32 states in the same decade. In 1980 the PRCUA numbered 104,254 members with assets of $59,097,000 and insurance policies amounting to $111,346,000.

See also POLISH CATHOLICS IN AMERICA.

JAMES S. PULA

POLITICS AND AMERICAN CATHOLICS

The American political tradition has allowed the United States to survive the myriad of social, demographic, religious, and economic changes for four centuries. Catholics' participation in American politics, however, has been circumscribed by the American religious tradition of anti-Catholicism. From colonial times to John F. Kennedy's election in 1960, anti-Catholicism banned or impeded Catholic involvement in local, state, and federal offices and elections. The radical Protestantism of the Puritans and the deistic principles of the Founding Fathers portrayed the Catholic Church as the enemy of freedom and tolerance and all Catholics as anti-American in both their religious and political ideals. This subtext of bigotry and discrimination undermined the American Catholic political tradition and determined the limited role of this cultural subgroup in the political life of the United States. Such a paradoxical wedding of this political tradition of reform and of this religious tradition of intolerance has dramatically taken this Catholic minority on an interesting political journey between 1633–1995. Eventually, this minority has become the largest religious denomination in the United States. The numbers speak for themselves: 30 in 1633; 25,000 in 1776; 60,000 in 1820; two million in 1850; eight million by 1900; 20 million in 1920; 27 million in 1945; and today nearly 60 million. Catholics and the presidency, Catholic assimilation and power, and the Catholic crusades of the twentieth century represent the three major stages of American Catholic political life during these substantial demographic changes.

Catholics and the Presidency

Individual triumphs in overcoming anti-Catholicism dominate the history of American politics. In spite of this hostile host culture, Catholics played a role in the political life of colonial and revolutionary as well as progressive and modern America. The most important symbolic individual Catholic achievement in the overcoming of this religious animosity was a Catholic running for, and eventually winning, the presidency. The first attempt to challenge this tradition of "No Catholic in the White House" was made by Charles O'Conor in 1872. He only received 29,000 votes in his third-party bid to defeat Ulysses S. Grant who garnered 3.5 million votes to Horace Greeley's 3 million votes. Because he was never a serious contender, O'Conor did not encounter the ugly head of religious bigotry during this presidential campaign. The next Catholic candidate ran nearly fifty years later; he was Al Smith, a former governor of New York. Because he was the viable presidential candidate of the Democratic Party, Smith did encounter widespread anti-Catholic attacks, which made the "Popish Plot" an important factor in this presidential election. Although Smith received 15 million votes in the

1928 election, he was still not able to defeat the Republican presidential candidate, Herbert Hoover, who had won a plurality of 21.5 million votes. Catholic Americans were convinced that Smith lost the election because of the bigoted attacks against his religion. Subsequently, historians have concluded that Smith did not lose because of anti-Catholicism but because he was a wet urban-ethnic who could not possibly defeat the Republican record of "prosperity."

In spite of this tradition of losing and of religious bigotry, John Fitzgerald Kennedy sought the presidency of the United States in 1960. Like Smith, Kennedy was an Irish Catholic who was the presidential candidate of the Democratic Party. Unlike Smith, he was able to end, and some scholars would argue, bury the anti-Catholic issue in American politics during his presidential campaign and election. Kennedy directly confronted and attacked the anti-Catholic invective and suspicions throughout the campaign. His most effective response concerning this religious issue was contained in his speech before the Houston Ministerial Association in September 1960. In this speech, he addressed and allayed the fears most non-Catholics had concerning a Catholic in the White House. He told his audience of Protestant ministers that he believed in an America that promoted separation of Church and state and religious tolerance and liberty; that he was not a Catholic candidate for the presidency but a Democratic candidate who happened to be Catholic; and that he promised that his Catholic beliefs would not impede nor would they be incompatible with his constitutional duties contained in the presidential oath.

Kennedy won with a slight edge in the popular vote. With over sixty-eight million Americans voting, only 112,000 votes separated the two candidates, giving Kennedy that slim but necessary margin of victory. In terms of the electoral votes, Kennedy received 303 to Richard Nixon's 219. Kennedy's victory at least symbolically meant that Catholic participation in the American political system would no longer be circumscribed and that Catholics had become first-class American citizens.

Catholic Politics of Assimilation and Power

Catholic immigrants to America first looked to family and then to the Church for assistance in the process of emigration and immigration. Family usually provided the money for the fare of passage, while the local parish church provided financial assistance as well as religious comfort in America. The church eventually became the social, cultural, and ethnic center of a particular neighborhood. It was in these Catholic ethnic enclaves in the urban centers that Catholics began to participate in the American political process in the nineteenth century. Catholics had a decisive advantage in the political arena because a large

number of Irish Catholics had immigrated to the United States before and after the Civil War, bringing with them knowledge of, and experience with, the democratic process due to the great work of Daniel O'Connell in Ireland. Not surprisingly, Irish Catholic immigrants began to politically organize American Catholic communities into urban districts for the local Democratic Party. They believed that such political activism and organization would give Catholics the power to improve their neighborhoods, to demand respect from the rich, powerful, and anti-Catholic, and to achieve full assimilation and acceptance.

By 1890 most of the country's major cities had an Irish Catholic for mayor or had a city government that was heavily influenced by the Catholic vote. These big-city bosses began to use local government to help their own kind. They built better schools, improved the physical conditions of the neighborhoods, and provided jobs to Catholics. The hope was to transform these Catholic ghettos into respectable, middle-class, American neighborhoods. Such a parochial use of local power led to rampant graft and corruption. One of the most celebrated examples of this democratic nepotism and paternalism was Mayor James Michael Curley's administration in Boston, but, of course, such a tradition can be traced back to the days of Boss Tweed and Tammany Hall of New York. Some scholars have also argued that such a personal use of power led to Catholics, in particular Irish Catholics, being tied to the lower levels of the working class and middle class. Instead of advancing, they held on to these secure city jobs of policeman, fireman, garbage collector, and numerous others generation after generation.

Despite its shortcomings, this local political tradition thrived in the Catholic community, creating an American Catholic political class and contributing to the emergence of President Franklin Delano Roosevelt's New Deal and social welfare measures. Historians have argued that the last Catholic political machine was Richard Daley's in Chicago and that now African American bosses are taking over the country's cities. Yet, the Catholic tradition in American politics has continued on the national level. Consistently, there has been an Irish Catholic Speaker of the House. The last two were of this tradition, Tip O'Neill and Tom Foley. Even in 1995, there was a total of 145 Catholic members in Congress, 20 in the Senate and 125 in the House of Representatives.

The Twentieth-Century Crusades of the American Catholic Political Tradition

While winning first-class citizenship, Catholics engaged in three political crusades in the twentieth century: the establishment of economic and racial justice, the defeat of Communism, and the inculcating of Catholic morality in the body politic. Fr. John A. Ryan, Bishop Francis Haas,

Peter Maurin, Dorothy Day, and Michael Harrington were leaders of the Catholic social justice movement in this century who sought to rid American society of its social and economic inequities. Daniel and Philip Berrigan, Fr. Theodore Hesburgh, and Robert F. Kennedy represented a few of the Catholic leaders to seek racial justice and end segregation and inequality during this country's civil rights movement. In short, Catholics who joined this crusade perceived the United States as being economically and socially immoral because of the existence of poverty, segregation, and discrimination.

The crusade of anti-Communism also became a major feature within the American Catholic political tradition. In the 1930s, Fr. Charles Coughlin, "the radio priest," told millions of Catholic listeners and other Americans that Communism was going to subvert freedom and faith in the United States. Catholics must be vigilant, he admonished, while Communist oppression and atheism threatened the country, but eventually this message was replaced by Coughlin's more demagogic thrust of Fascism and anti-Semitism. After World War II, Coughlin's anti-Communist crusade was led by another Catholic, Senator Joseph McCarthy. At the height of the Red Scare in the beginning days of the cold war, 1950–55, McCarthy instigated and led the attacks against suspected Communists in American society. A majority of American Catholics embraced McCarthyism because he was a coreligionist, and because they believed they were proving their 100 percent Americanism by leading the country in this life-and-death struggle against communism.

The final Catholic political crusade actually began during the cold war. After becoming a major part of middle-class suburbia, Catholics left the Democratic Party and turned to the anticommunist rhetoric and social conservatism of the Republican Party and Dwight Eisenhower. This was the beginning of the strange death of Democratic Liberalism as the dominant political tradition in the American Catholic community. With a temporary return in the 1960 election to one of their own kind, John F. Kennedy, the majority of Catholic Americans began to join the rank and file of the Republican Party during the 1960s and 1970s. Seeking a restoration of law and order, the winning of the cold war, and the establishment of economic stability, Catholics overwhelmingly supported the Republican president, Ronald Reagan, and his successes solidified the Catholic transition to the conservative side in American political life. This conservative Catholic majority also found appealing Reagan's attempt to interject religious values into the nation's public policy decisions. For them, this was the beginning of their current Catholic political crusade for a morally and socially conservative America. The issues of family, divorce, illegitimacy, and abortion have become the major concerns of Catholic conservatives, who think that by addressing these is-

sues in a Catholic moral framework, American society will be renewed. Ironically, those previous anti-Catholic forces of Protestant America have presently joined with Catholic America to effectuate this socially conservative agenda in the 1990s.

Allitt, Patrick. *Catholic Intellectuals and Conservative Politics in America, 1950–1985*. Cornell, 1993.

Byrnes, Timothy. *Catholic Bishops in American Politics*. Princeton, 1991.

Crosby, Donald. *Senator Joe McCarthy and The Catholic Church, 1950–1957*. Chapel Hill, 1978.

Erie, Steven P. *Rainbow's End: Irish-Americans and the Dilemmas of Urban Machine Politics, 1840–1985*. Berkeley and Los Angeles: University of California Press, 1988.

McCaffrey, Lawrence. *Textures of Irish-America*. Syracuse, 1992.

O'Brien, David. *American Catholics and Social Reform*. Oxford, 1968.

Sarbaugh, Timothy J. "John F. Kennedy, the Catholic Issue, and Presidential Politics in 1960." Ph.D. dissertation, Loyola University of Chicago, 1988.

TIMOTHY J. SARBAUGH

PONTIFICAL COLLEGE JOSEPHINUM

In the 107 years of its existence, the number of priests who have studied at the Josephinum comes close to 1,400. In 1995 the alumni directory listed 868 living alumni who were active in 130 dioceses of the United States and in 24 foreign countries. Among these alumni, twenty religious communities are represented, among whom are more than a hundred Salesians of Don Bosco. The 1995 student directory listed 92 in the School of Theology and 52 in the College of Liberal Arts. These students came from 45 different dioceses and the Salesians of Don Bosco. Foreign countries represented among the student body were Latvia, Hungary, Vietnam, Uganda, Nigeria, China, and Myanmar. The largest number of students at the Josephinum was 430 during the time when it also consisted of a high-school department.

First an Orphanage

That the Pontifical College Josephinum exists at all has been termed either an accident or an act of God. Its founder, Joseph Jessing, was born in 1836 in Münster, Westphalia, Germany, the eldest of three children whose father was a common laborer. Jessing's father died when he was only four years of age. As soon as young Jessing had finished elementary school, he found it necessary to find employment in order to support his mother and his younger brother and sister. After working twelve hours a day in a printery, he spent long hours in private study with a view to eventually studying for the priesthood, a goal which he had in mind from his earliest years. At the age of twenty, in 1855,

Jessing had to fulfill military service in the Prussian army. His military obligations ended in the year 1866 during which year his mother also died. No longer obliged to support his mother, and fearing that new conflicts would impede his dream of studying for the priesthood, Jessing emigrated to the United States in July 1867. Thanks to the generosity of lay friends and helpful clergy, he entered St. Mary's Seminary in Cincinnati, Ohio, and there completed his studies in the year 1870. After ordination he was appointed pastor in Pomeroy, Ohio. His earlier experience in a printery in Germany induced Jessing to begin publishing a newspaper for German Catholic immigrants to the United States. He named his paper *Ohio*. Because he had suffered the loss of his father at the age of four, he felt the need to found an orphanage in 1873. With the proceeds of his weekly newspaper and with the generous help of his subscribers throughout the United States, Jessing found support for his orphanage and renamed his publication the *Ohio Waisenfreund (Orphans' Friend)*. In 1877 he resigned as pastor of Pomeroy and relocated his orphanage to a square city block in Columbus, Ohio.

Then a Seminary

Because many of his readers wrote to him asking what he could do by way of furnishing German-speaking priests for German-Americans, he printed a short notice in the July 4, 1888, issue of the *Waisenfreund* stating that, if there were any boys of German descent who would be interested in studying for the priesthood, they should contact him and he would finance their seminary education. However, since forty boys responded to his call, twenty-three of whom he considered fit applicants, Jessing could not afford to pay their tuition in a seminary; he, therefore, decided to start his own. As new groups of freshmen arrived each year, additional buildings and faculty became necessary. Since as yet he had neither asked for nor received ecclesiastical recognition for his seminary, Jessing embarked upon a bold venture. Since the purpose of the Josephinum was to furnish German-speaking priests for German immigrants, and since the United States was at that time still considered to be a mission country, through friends in Europe Jessing offered the Josephinum to the Holy See as a missionary seminary for the whole United States. As a result, in 1892 notice was received by Jessing from the Cardinal Prefect of the Sacred Congregation of the Propaganda to the effect that "the Josephinum College in Columbus, Ohio, is from now on subject to this same Congregation, and that this decree has been ratified by Pope Leo XIII."

In recognition of his work as a priest, Jessing was elevated to the rank of domestic prelate in 1896. The years of his intense labors had taken their toll and he realized his days on earth were numbered. In order for Jessing to enjoy the first fruits of his seminary, the first class of Josephinum-trained priests was ordained a year ahead of schedule, on June 29, 1899. On November 2 of the same year, Jessing died quietly at the age of sixty-three.

The "New" and Present Josephinum

Because of the influx of students and the lack of space in downtown Columbus, in 1924 the Josephinum purchased a one-hundred-acre farm north of Worthington, Ohio. Between 1929 and 1931 the present main building and powerhouse were built. The students and a handful of orphans moved to this new location in the fall of 1931. In 1932 the orphanage was officially discontinued. Increases in the student body necessitated the building of a facility for the college department in 1958. Because of a decline of applicants for the high-school department, it was officially discontinued in the fall of 1967. The high-school building was remodeled in 1980 and 1982 to become an education center housing the Wehrle Memorial Library and four classrooms used by the students of the School of Theology. For about ten years the Josephinum has joined with Trinity Lutheran Seminary of Columbus and the Methodist Theological Seminary of Ohio in a consortium, enabling its students to attend elective courses offered at these two other seminaries. The *Josephinum Journal of Theology* is published twice a year and provides a forum for theological and pastoral essays. The Josephinum is accredited by the state of Ohio, the North Central States Accrediting Agency, and the Association of Theological Schools.

See also SEMINARIES (DIOCESAN).

Annuario Pontificio, 1992. Libreria Editrice Vaticana, 1992.

Fick, Leonard J. *The Jessing Legacy.* Columbus, Ohio: The Pontifical College Josephinum, 1988.

Miller, Leo F. *Monsignor Joseph Jessing.* Columbus, Ohio: Carrol Press, 1936.

MUELLER KOMP

POOR CLARES (P.C.; O.S.C.; P.C.C.; P.C.P.A.)

Poor Clares, the popular name for the Order of St. Clare, founded by her and Francis of Assisi in 1212. Clare created a unique synthesis of contemplative monastic life and Franciscan values. She called her community "the Poor Sisters of San Damiano," after the church in Assisi where they began. The rapidly spreading order was given canonical recognition when a stable form of life was drawn up by Hugolino, cardinal bishop of Ostia (later Gregory IX), in 1219. These "Damianites" were like traditional monastic orders in that each local house was totally autonomous. Clare managed to have her own rule approved in 1253, which emphasized her distinctive Franciscan values of a sisterhood of equals and the renunciation of all property by the community. However, this rule was a concession to the monastery of San Damiano itself; almost all of the other houses adopted a mitigated rule issued by Urban IV in 1263. It was at this time that the Poor Sisters were first referred to as the Order of St. Clare. A powerful reform movement, analogous to the Observants among the Franciscan friars, was begun by Colette of Corbie in 1410. Colette restored the Rule of Clare and formulated a set of rigorous constitutions to safeguard its observance. Other reform movements followed in the sixteenth century, notably the Capuchin Poor Clares, founded in Naples in 1535. Although there are no Urbanist Poor Clares in the United States, the other branches of the order mentioned above have established themselves in the country.

First Attempts to Bring Clares to America

The Poor Clares were not able to find a permanent home in the United States until the last quarter of the nineteenth century. Two previous attempts at establishing the order had proven unsuccessful. The first Clares to come to the United States were three French nuns who had been expelled from their convent in Amiens late in 1792. Since they also belonged to aristocratic families, they decided to flee the country, and like many émigré clergy, sought refuge in the United States. This little group, headed by Mother Genevieve de la Marche, arrived in Charleston early in 1793. Making their way to Baltimore, they were welcomed by Bishop John Carroll. For a short time they conducted a girls' school; then, persuaded that a more congenial life awaited them in Spanish territory, they journeyed to New Orleans. There they spent several years of continual hardship. Returning to Baltimore in 1797, the Clares were urged by Fr. William DuBourg, president of Georgetown College, to open a girls' school adjacent to it in order to support themselves. The school struggled on for several years, hampered by the fact that the sisters believed that such a ministry was inimical to their contemplative vocation. Following the death of their abbess in 1804, the disheartened nuns returned to France. However, the school founded by the Poor Clares continued, conducted by several laywomen who had assisted them; these women later became the Georgetown (D.C.) community of Visitation nuns.

A second attempt at bringing the Clares to the United States followed two decades later. In 1823 Bishop Edward Fenwick of Cincinnati visited the Colettine Poor Clare convent in Bruges, speaking of the needs of his vast new diocese. Two nuns responded, coming to Cincinnati in 1826 to begin a community of the order. After a number of misunderstandings, the sisters eventually resettled in Pittsburgh. But the prejudices of the rapidly expanding American Church were against their establishing a contemplative form of religious life. Instead these Clares were also charged with "the instruction of young girls, for the honor and glory of God." Under the circumstances, the sisters were willing to mitigate their observances: they petitioned Rome for permission to adapt the regulations of cloister, the right to possess property in common, and other dispensations from Clare's Rule. Young American women entered the order, and new foundations were established in 1833 in Detroit and Green Bay. However, severe differences soon emerged between the various bishops who sought jurisdiction over the nuns and among the Clares themselves. Some, backed by their European superiors, thought the accommodations they had made had sacrificed too many essentials of their contemplative religious life. The sisters, along with five of their American vocations, returned to Belgium in 1839.

Establishment of the Order

The permanent establishment of the Poor Clares in the United States was due to a petition to Pius IX by Mother Ignatius Hayes, an Anglican religious who had joined the Catholic Church and come to the United States to found the Franciscan Missionary Sisters of the Immaculate Conception in 1872. The Pope was very willing to accede to this request due to the current political situation in Italy, especially since the government of the newly unified nation had enacted measures suppressing the religious orders. The Pope approached the sisters of the ancient Poor Clare monastery of San Lorenzo in Panisperna, who had been restricted to one small section of their cloister, to obtain volunteers for this new venture. Pius personally selected two blood sisters, Maddalena and Constanza Bentivoglio, members of a noble Roman family. Although the community at San Lorenzo observed the mitigated Urbanist Rule, the Bentivoglio sisters were instructed by Bernardine of Portugruaro, general minister of the Order of Friars Minor, to establish monasteries in the United States that would follow the Rule of Clare. After several weeks in France immersing themselves in the Primitive Observance, the sisters set sail for America, arriving in New York in October 1875. What followed was a frustrating three-year odyssey for the Bentivoglio sisters, as they sought a diocese that would welcome a foundation of contemplative nuns. After vainly attempting to found convents in New York, Cincinnati, and Philadelphia, in 1876 Mother Maddalena was finally invited to settle in New Orleans by Archbishop Napoleon Perché. However, that same year the general minister had placed the nuns under the supervision of Gregory Janknecht, O.F.M., superior of the German Franciscans settling in the Midwest due to the *Kulturkampf.* When Fr. Gregory visited the New Orleans foundation in 1877, he was dismayed at the sisters' living arrangements and ordered them to move to Cleveland, Ohio, where he could place them under the care of his friars.

And so, accompanied by two postulants, the Bentivoglio sisters founded the little Monastery of St. Mary of the Angels in Cleveland in August 1877.

But the odyssey of Mother Maddalena had not yet ended. A monastery of Colettine Poor Clares in Düsseldorf, which had been directed by Fr. Gregory, had also fallen victim to the *Kulturkampf* in 1875, and the community had taken refuge in the Netherlands. Later in 1877, Fr. Gregory wrote these Colettines, asking for sisters to come to help in establishing the new Cleveland monastery. Five German nuns arrived there in December. It quickly proved impossible to merge the two communities, divided by both nationality and religious observance. In February 1878, with the permission of the general minister, the Bentivoglio sisters and the American novices left Cleveland. Another frustrating search for a home followed, until the philanthropist John Creighton of Omaha offered to establish a monastery for the sisters in that city. Meanwhile, Fr. Gregory selected Mother Mary Veronica von Elmendorff as abbess of the Colettine community in Cleveland. Thus the two motherhouses of the largest observances of the Order of St. Clare in the United States were established: the Colettine Poor Clares (P.C.C.) in Cleveland, and the Primitive Observance (O.S.C.) in Omaha.

Clares of the Primitive Observance

The Omaha community lived in two temporary dwellings until their new monastery of St. Clare was completed in 1881. Several Poor Clares from Marseilles arrived the next year to assist the group, and more American vocations entered. By 1885 Mother Maddalena felt the Omaha monastery was sufficiently stable to found its first daughter house. She returned to New Orleans with two other nuns, one of whom she selected as abbess of the new community, a postulant who had entered there seven years earlier, Mary Francis Moran. A third foundation followed in 1897, when Bishop Silas Chatard of Vincennes (later Indianapolis), who had years earlier met Mother Maddalena in Rome, welcomed her into his diocese. A young woman from Evansville, Indiana, had joined the Omaha monastery several years earlier, pledging her future inheritance for the construction of a house in that city. And so Mother Maddalena, with seven sisters from the Omaha community, settled in Evansville; she herself became the first abbess. This monastery proved to be the poorest of her foundations, and the early years in Evansville were filled with hardships. This time was also saddened by the loss of her sister, Constanza, who had remained with the Omaha monastery, in 1902. But she remained ever the pioneer: more sisters entered the community, and in 1905, shortly before her death, Mother Maddalena received permission to found her last monastery, in Boston. Nine sisters from Evansville opened the latter house in 1906. Over the course of the century,

an additional sixteen monasteries of the Primitive Observance were established in the United States, four others before 1920, seven between 1920 and 1960, and four since 1960. In addition, the American Poor Clares have founded houses in Canada, Japan, Brazil, Bolivia, and Korea.

In 1950 Pius XII promulgated an apostolic constitution, *Sponsa Christi,* in which he strongly recommended that cloistered nuns form federations for mutual support. Since there was very little response to this suggestion, Rome prodded the Franciscan friars who were largely responsible for visitation of the monasteries. The issue was addressed at the meeting of the American Franciscan provincials in 1955. Finally in 1957, Fr. Pius Barth, O.F.M., minister of the Sacred Heart province, addressed a letter to all the Poor Clare monasteries in the U.S.A. in the name of the Franciscan Order and the apostolic see, asking them to initiate a discussion of the topic. The initial response on the part of the Clares was almost unanimously negative when delegates from eleven monasteries met in Evansville in 1958. In the words of one sister, federation was "unsought, undesirable, but probably inevitable." As discussions progressed over the years, the sentiment gradually changed. In view of the large number of houses of Regular Observance, it was decided to form two units. Holy Name Federation was established on the East Coast (1963); most of the other monasteries joined the Mother Bentivoglio Federation (1964). Over the years, the federated monasteries have assisted one another financially, fostered initial and continuing formation programs, and agreed on common regulations of life.

Colettine Poor Clares

Meanwhile, the Cleveland community of the five German Colettines also prospered, despite initial obstacles. The first American postulant, Mary Murray, entered in 1878. The fact that she was nicknamed "Deutschverderber" ("one who spoils the German") reveals the fact that most of the other new vocations were from German immigrant families. By 1885 the monastery numbered twenty; in 1887 Mother Veronica initiated perpetual adoration of the Blessed Sacrament. Fr. Kilian Schloesser, O.F.M., the devoted chaplain of the Cleveland community, had been transferred to Chicago in 1885, and eventually bought property near the Franciscan parish in the area known as "Back of the Yards" to found a new monastery. Six sisters, headed by Mother Veronica, moved from Cleveland in 1893 to establish this first daughter house. Nine other U.S. Colettine monasteries have sprung from these first two foundations in the twentieth century; the Chicago monastery was forced to close in 1986.

Although the Colettines were never under the jurisdiction of the Franciscan general minister, they were included in the 1957 letter of Fr. Pius Barth mentioned above, urging that the Poor Clares initiate discussions which might lead to eventual federations. Since the Colettines already shared a set of constitutions, in a sense they were ready-made for federation; indeed, the Cleveland monastery had already informally investigated this possibility. In any case, they moved towards this end much more quickly than their sisters of the Primitive Observance. The very first meeting of abbesses and delegates at the Cleveland motherhouse in March 1958 drew up statutes for the Colettine Poor Clare Federation of Mary Immaculate.

Other Poor Clare Foundations

In 1884 Bishop William Gross, C.Ss.R., of Savannah, invited a group of Poor Clares from York, England, to his diocese. Three sisters from the community responded; upon their arrival, Bishop Gross assigned them to Skidaway Island, off the Georgia coast, to open a trade school for black girls. This foundation was doomed to failure; the bishop, who did not establish adequate financial support for the community, was transferred to Oregon early in 1885; the English nuns did not have adequate training to pursue a successful active ministry, and they soon fell hopelessly into debt. Gross's successor, Thomas Becker, dismissed the nuns from his diocese in 1887.

In 1921 a small group of Austrian sisters, Franciscan Nuns of Perpetual Adoration, founded a monastery in Cleveland. They belonged to a congregation of cloistered Franciscan Third Order Regular nuns founded in France in 1854 who had adoration of the Blessed Sacrament as a special charism. Over the years, this congregation changed its affiliation from the Third Franciscan Order to the Second, deciding to follow the Rule of Clare, thus becoming Poor Clares of Perpetual Adoration (P.C.P.A.). This congregation has flourished in the United States, founding four other monasteries from the original Cleveland motherhouse. In recent years Mother Angelica, abbess of the monastery in Birmingham, Alabama, has become arguably the most prominent woman religious in the United States thanks to her activities as director of the Eternal Word Television Network.

When the revolution of Fidel Castro took control of Cuba, the nuns of an Urbanist Poor Clare monastery in Havana were forced to seek refuge in the United States, living temporarily with the New Orleans community. The Cuban nuns, assisted by several of the New Orleans Clares, managed to found a new monastery in Brenham, Texas, in 1965. This community has since adopted the Primitive Observance and become a member of the Mother Bentivoglio Federation.

The Capuchin Poor Clares (O.S.C. Cap.) are the latest branch of the order to establish themselves in the United States. Sisters from Mexico founded a house in Amarillo, Texas, in 1981. Blessed with a large number of Hispanic

vocations, they have spread rapidly, and now have two other monasteries, in Denver and Wilmington, Delaware.

See also FRANCISCAN SISTERS IN AMERICA; WOMEN RELIGIOUS IN AMERICA.

Cicognani, Amleto. *Sanctity in America.* Paterson, New Jersey, 1941.
Koester, Mary Camilla. *Into This Land.* Cleveland, 1980.
Short, William. *The Franciscans.* Wilmington, 1989.
Private publications of individual houses and federations collected at the library of the Franciscan Institute, St. Bonaventure University.

DOMINIC V. MONTI, O.F.M.

POPES AND AMERICA

Since Europe's first contact with the New World, Catholicism has maintained a role of crucial importance in America. That role, however, has not always been successful or positive, and has been complicated by the Holy See's challenge to exert its control over the American churches. More often than not, furthermore, Roman aims were contravened by suspicious state authorities, local clergies and hierarchies, or by the people themselves.

Papal interest in the New World was ignited upon Christopher Columbus' first voyage there in 1492. That year also witnessed the elevation of the Spaniard, Alexander VI Borgia, to the throne of St. Peter, an event which determined the political fate of much of the Americas. Pope Alexander justified his interest in the New World by the "omni-insular doctrine" of the fraudulent "Donation of Constantine" that gave the papacy jurisdiction over countless islands from Sicily to Britain and beyond. Under the assumption that the new territory was an archipelago, and thus covered by the "omni-insular doctrine," the Pontiff assumed an active role in disputes concerning it. In 1493, on the suggestion of Spain's King Ferdinand, the Holy See appointed Bernal Buyl as the first vicar apostolic in America, an act instructive only as a revelation of Rome's intent and not of any real accomplishment by the envoy, who reached the New World but returned to Europe within a year after arguments with Columbus. The Pope also issued the two (sometimes cited as three) Alexandrine bulls, *Inter caetera,* of May 3 and 4, 1493, to rationalize Christian Europe's first contacts with the new lands and to settle political and jurisdictional disputes over them between Spain and Portugal. Alexander agreed to all of the former's territorial claims and largely excluded the latter from the Americas by a "Line of Demarcation" which separated their spheres of influence by a north-south line across the globe situated one hundred leagues west of the Azore islands. One year later, in the Treaty of Tordesillas, Spain and Portugal agreed to shift the line to 370 leagues west of the Cape Verde islands. Alexander reaffirmed

Spain's privileges in the New World in his letters, *Examine devotionis* of July 2, and *Dudum siquidem* of September 25 or 26, 1493.

Spanish and Portuguese Empires

In Alexander VI's bull of November 16, 1501, and one of Pope Julius II in 1508, Rome consented further to Spanish royal control over ecclesiastical administration in America if the crown reciprocated by introducing, protecting, and maintaining the Church there and by sanctioning the conversion of the Native Americans. This arrangement was eventually known as the *patronato real.* Similar concessions to the Portuguese, the *padroado,* had been granted earlier, during the pontificate of Martin V in 1418. The Spanish modified the *patronato real* during the first decades of their American empire. By Charles I's royal decree of 1530, the Spanish crown nominated American archbishops, bishops, and abbots for the Pope's approval. Canons and other members of cathedral chapters were nominated by the king to a council of American prelates. Curates and *doctrineros* (priests in Indian parishes) were nominated by the crown's viceroy or governor to local prelates. Ecclesiastical tithes and revenues of vacant benefices were awarded to the government. State permission was needed to remove ecclesiastics, for clerics to travel to the New World, and for the publication and circulation of Roman bulls. Only rarely did papal veto curb royal power, most notably over Madrid's unsuccessful attempts to secure a Catholic patriarch for the Indies. By the sixteenth and seventeenth centuries, the *patronato real* was reinforced by the strong Spanish presence in Rome itself and, in the eighteenth century, by the ascension to the Spanish throne of Bourbon monarchs who brought with them Gallican traditions. The Spanish Bourbons even claimed the *patronato real* by virtue of their authority as kings and not as the result of papal largesse.

It cannot be said, however, that the *patronato real* on the whole divorced the Church in America from papal control and influence. As problems arose in the daily function of Church business, arguments could pit clergy obedient to Rome against royal authority. The Holy See, furthermore, circumvented some restrictions of the *patronato real* in at least two ways: the Inquisition and the missions to the native peoples. Like most other aspects of Catholicism in the New World, the Inquisition was characterized by confused administrative lines which ran through the episcopal authorities and Madrid, as well as the papacy and the Holy Office in Rome. Most of the Inquisition was launched and administered by Spanish clerics in close collaboration with the royal government. It was introduced in 1517 by Cardinal Ximenes de Cisneros and, in 1569, coordinated by King Phillip II with courts in Mexico City, Lima, and Cartagena. But into this royal picture must appear some papal involvement through the Holy Office and, somewhat less, through the role of the Dominican Order which enjoyed administrative rights. The movement was so complex, furthermore, that the titles of inquisitor-general, archbishop, and viceroy could be held by the same person.

While the crown stood between the papacy and the secular clergy in America, its screen was not as effective between Rome and the religious orders which initially administered missions to the Native Americans. Whereas the orders' major superiors (or vicars general or commissaries general) were subject to a vicar general at the Spanish court, some, particularly the Jesuits, maintained strong ties with Rome. The Holy See reciprocated and supported an important role for the orders through the 1522 grant of *Omnimoda* allowing them ample rein in their evangelization of the non-European population.

The tension between Madrid and Rome might best be examined in arguments over the dignity of the native peoples wherein the papacy often maintained their human worth, whereas the Spanish sought to subjugate them through forced labor and enslavement. In his 1537 bull, *Sublimis Deus,* Pope Paul III declared the natives to be rational and capable of accepting Catholicism. While such measures were greeted with hypocrisy by many Europeans, they carried enough weight to prompt the Spanish government to issue the "New Laws" in 1542 which, although largely ineffectual, sought to protect the rights of the Native Americans. That hypocrisy, nevertheless, also extended to the European clergy in America who banned the ordination of native people. After a petition from mestizo clergy to Rome, however, Pope Gregory XIII in 1588 pressured Madrid into canceling the ban. *Sublimis Deus,* furthermore, was incorporated into the final statements of the Third Provincial Council at Lima in 1584 and approved by the Council of the Indies in 1591. Unfortunately, neither *Sublimis Deus,* nor the "New Laws," nor the 1588 decree were much observed in America. Furthermore, by the late sixteenth century, decline in the Native American population and arguments that evangelization had at least nominally fulfilled its goals facilitated measures by the Spanish monarchy to restrict the influence of the missionary orders and favor the secular clergy. The *Junta Magna* of 1568 that effectively abolished the *Omnimoda* and tightened royal control over the orders, and the *Ordenanza del Patronazgo* of 1574, were the key manifestations of this.

French and British Empires

North of Spain's New World empire, Rome encountered other difficulties from the French and British crowns. The problems were different in part because, while Catholic France founded a North American empire, it was not as extensive as was Spain's, it was established later, and it did not endure as long. The other power, Great Britain, was an avowed enemy of the papacy.

During the first decades of French activity in the New World, the crown permitted Huguenot pastors to accompany some explorer-merchants to Canada but conversion of the Native Americans was reserved only for Catholic missionaries. In 1627, however, Cardinal Richelieu disbanded the old "Company of Merchants" and established a "Company of One Hundred Associates" to rule Quebec with directions to render it exclusively Catholic. In 1674 Pope Clement X established the first Canadian see at Quebec with the proviso, over the protests of King Louis XIV, that it be responsible directly to Rome and not a suffragan of any French diocese. After their 1763 victory over the French, however, the British appropriated Jesuit property, disallowed any new recruitment by that order, and severed ties between the Canadian Church and the pope. In 1766 London nevertheless secretly permitted the consecration in Paris of a Canadian bishop, Joseph Olivier Briand, by the papal nuncio. The Quebec Act of 1774 also allowed some Catholic freedoms and replaced the obligatory and offensive renunciation of the faith by a simpler oath of loyalty to the English Crown.

Papal connection with what is now the United States of America was negligible before the American Revolution. While the Catholic presence in Florida, the Gulf Coast, the Louisiana Territory, and the Southwest was tied to the Spanish or French empires, only the palatinate and proprietary colony of Maryland possessed any vague status as a Catholic land, and then, only in the seventeenth century. British Catholics on the Atlantic seaboard were subject to the vicar apostolic in London even after the Revolution. By the early 1780s, however, infighting among the clergy prompted the U.S. Church to petition Pope Pius VI for a superior who would be elected by the priests. Pius instead appointed John Carroll of Baltimore as superior of the mission in 1784. In 1789, however, Pius VI allowed the American priests to select Carroll as the first bishop of Baltimore. In 1808 Pius VII reorganized the Church by establishing the Dioceses of New York, Philadelphia, Boston, and Bardstown, Kentucky, with Baltimore as metropolitan see. Carroll became an archbishop in 1808. Trusteeism, the election of priests, threatened papal and episcopal authority in the early U.S. Church, but an alliance between Rome and the bishops brought it under control by 1829 at the First Provincial Council in Baltimore.

Latin America after Independence

Napoleon's conquest of Spain and Portugal in 1808 triggered the independence movement in Latin America which pitted the Church against itself: those who supported the crown, primarily the Holy See and much of the American episcopate, against those with strong sentiments for liberation, mostly the lower clergy. After the collapse of French power in Madrid, Pope Pius VII issued the encyclical, *Etsi longissimo,* in January 1816, that directed the Church and the faithful in America to submit to the restored king of Spain, Ferdinand VII. Between 1814 and 1820, moreover, Rome confirmed royal nominations to the sees of Santiago de Chile, Charcas, Arequipa, Merida, and Puebla. But military victories by Simon Bolivar and other insurrectionists and a liberal and moderately anticlerical revolution in Spain prompted the Holy See by the 1820s to distance itself from Madrid and consider most of the new regimes as legitimate and permanent.

First steps toward working relations between Rome and the new nations, however, proved difficult. As late as 1824, for instance, Pope Leo XII spurned a request for recognition of Mexico's president, Guadalupe Victoria, with another encyclical calling for obedience to Spain's monarch.

Matters were made worse by difficult conditions within the Latin American Church. Being cut off from Spain meant reduced numbers of new priests, sees which remained vacant for years, and the total abandonment of native missions (a process that had begun with a royal decree in 1752 and King Charles III's expulsion of the Jesuits in 1767). Neither of the separate delegations to Rome of the Chilean archdeacon Jose Ignacio Cienfuegos in 1821–22 and the Mexican canon Pablo Vazquez in 1822, nor the papal venture to South America of Archbishop Giovanni Muzi (which included the young Giovanni Mastai Ferretti, later Pope Pius IX) in 1823–25, yielded fruit. Only in 1829 did the cautious Pius VIII appoint Pietro Ostini to Rio de Janeiro as nuncio to all of Latin America.

Papal initiative and diplomatic activity accelerated after 1831 during the pontificate of Gregory XVI and his successor, Pius IX. Gregory committed himself to the cultivation of relations between Rome and the states of the former Spanish empire. He named six Latin American bishops in his first consistory and oversaw the return of the Jesuits to Argentina in 1836, New Granada in 1842, and Chile in 1843. Pope Pius IX continued this work, establishing what became known as the Collegio Pio Latino-Americano in Rome, negotiating concordats with Guatemala, Costa Rica, Honduras, Nicaragua, San Salvador, Haiti, and Equador between 1852 and 1862, and initiating discussions with Bolivia, Peru, and Argentina. Pius IX also sent the first apostolic delegate to Mexico City in 1851.

Renewal of ties was complicated by philosophical and political questions. Upon independence, most new Latin American leaders assumed that revived versions of the *patronato real* would continue in force. This new system of state interference in Church affairs (or government resistance to Roman interference) was usually and subsequently termed "national patronage" or "regalism." The problem was compounded by strong veins of anticlerical and Masonic liberalism and positivism which influenced policy in many of the new nations. In Mexico, for example, after particularly intense attacks on the Church, President Benito Juarez expelled Pius IX's apostolic delegate in 1861. On the other hand, Rome and much of the clergy had embraced the philosophy of Ultramontanism, popularized by the Italo-French writer, Joseph de Maistre. In Latin America this Ultramontane faction was often referred to as the *apostolicos*. As a result, arguments over episcopal appointments between Latin American governments and Rome erupted frequently and continued well into the twentieth century. Important clashes occurred in Brazil in 1833 and 1844, Paraguay in the 1850s, Venezuela in 1870, and Argentina in 1822, 1832, 1923, and 1952.

Church-state conflicts involving the papacy, however, played differently from case to case. In Brazil, for example, a bitter argument between episcopal authorities and Masonic lodges resulted in the imprisonment of the country's two most outspoken anti-Masonic bishops, Vital Maria Gonçalves de Oliveira and Antonio de Macedo Costa. In 1873 Emperor Pedro sent the Baron of Penedo to Rome to negotiate a solution with Pius IX and Cardinal Giacomo Antonelli. The mission backfired and the Holy See accused Brazil of duplicity, resulting in a face-saving amnesty for the two bishops. For his part, Pius ordered the pair to rescind their interdictions against the Masons. The end of Brazil's monarchy in 1888 led to improved relations with Rome and, by 1905, Pope Pius X rewarded the nation with the elevation of the archbishop of Rio de Janeiro as Latin America's first cardinal.

Guatemala's dictator, Rafael Carrera (1839–65), handled events quite differently. He rescinded anticlerical laws from an earlier regime, restored ecclesiatical privileges, and returned confiscated lands to religious orders. Carrera also promoted the abolition of anticlerical legislation in neighboring states, thus earning the gratitude of Pius IX who bestowed on him the Grand Cross of the Order of Saint Gregory the Great in 1853. Nevertheless, as in most of the American nations, Guatemala also witnessed ruptures with Rome. Soon after Carrera's regime, liberal and harshly anticlerical governments forbade clerical dress in public, banished the Jesuits, exiled the archbishop in 1887, and constructed a Temple to Minerva for the celebration of a civic cult.

By the turn of the century, relations between Rome and America had improved or had at least reached a tolerable status quo in most places, so that a certain optimism marked the Latin American Plenary Council, convened by Pope Leo XIII in 1899, which reemphasized the authority of the papal nuncio over each nation's episcopacy.

The United States

Compared to Latin America, relations between the United States and the Holy See were not as volatile for most of the nineteenth and early twentieth centuries. This was in large part due to the absence of formal diplomatic relations after a congressional budgeting decision canceled American representation to the Papal States in 1867. The fact that Rome sent no nuncio permitted the U.S. Church to develop in relative freedom from Roman control. That situation changed, however, in 1893 with the appointment of Archbishop Francesco Satolli as the first apostolic delegate to the United States.

Pope John Paul II at the National Shrine, Washington, D.C.

The freedom enjoyed by the American Catholic Church had its limits, and by the late nineteenth century Rome questioned and condemned some of its most noteworthy manifestations. Leo XIII's apostolic letter, *Testem benevolentiae,* in 1899, was the most famous censure of "Americanism," particularly the notions of American particularism associated with Isaac Hecker and archbishop John Ireland. The letter, however, written in part by Satolli, was directed as much or more to French Catholics as it was to Americans.

In the twentieth century, some friction persisted in such dilemmas as the Holy See's disdain for the writings of John Courtney Murray in the 1950s and Charles Curran in the 1980s. The most noteworthy working connection between the United States government and the Holy See developed during and immediately after the Second World War when President Franklin Roosevelt discerned a community of interest with Pope Pius XII and sent to the Vatican an unofficial personal envoy, Myron Taylor. President Richard Nixon revived the practice of sending a personal representative to the pope, a custom which would continue into the Ronald Reagan administration. Full diplomatic relations, however, waited until 1983 when U.S. Congressman Clement Zablocki sponsored State Department appropriations that enabled Washington to send an ambassador to the Holy See. At the same time the apostolic delegate to the United States received formal diplomatic recognition as a papal nuncio.

Persecution in Mexico

In Latin America, despite the generally improved relations with Rome, the twentieth century witnessed confrontations more dramatic and violent than those encountered in the north or almost anywhere else. In 1913 one of the worst persecutions of the Church in modern history began in Mexico. Schools were shut, Masses were prohibited, and, in 1914 and 1915, many priests were imprisoned. The February 1917 *Constitution* formalized this assault in Articles 3, 5, 24, 27, and 130, by curtailing Church property rights and canceling all political and civil freedoms for priests. The Mexican government, however, did not strictly enforce these measures until 1926 when they were challenged by the bishops, who were encouraged to do so in a letter from Pope Pius XI. President Plutarco Calles launched an attack without quarter against all Catholic activity and pushed many of the faithful into an armed rebellion, the *Christeros* War. A truce was negotiated in 1929 and the ferocity of the persecution ceased for a while, but Pope Pius XI's encyclical, *Acerba animi anxietudo,* of September 1932, deplored the government's many violations of the accords. The election of President Lazaro Cardenas in 1934, furthermore, reinstituted anticlerical measures. Although less violent than during the Calles years, the situation was bad enough in 1937 for Pius XI to issue an apostolic letter that urged the faithful not to lose hope in Mexico. Pius and the U.S. bishops also aided Mexican students for the priesthood by establishing a *Seminario Nacional Pontifico* across the border in Montezuma, New Mexico. The regime of General Manuel Avila Camacho (1940–46) ended the persecution but did not rescind the anticlerical laws. Rome, furthermore, later confronted more anticlerical persecutions in Latin American regimes of all political colors, from Daniel Ortega's Sandinista regime in Nicaragua and Fidel Castro's Communist dictatorship in Cuba, to Juan Peron's regime in Argentina, and at the hands of right-wing death squads in El Salvador.

Contemporary Developments

The Second Vatican Council (1962–65), its aftermath, and the first papal visits to the Western Hemisphere in 1965 and 1968 indicated a new, more activist, role for the Holy See in America. Pope John XXIII's call for a "Church of the Poor," the pastoral constitution, *Gaudium et spes,* Pope Paul VI's creation of a Pontifical Commission for Justice and Peace, his 1967 encyclical, *Populorum progressio,* and his 1971 "call to action," *Octogesima Adveniens,* assigned to the Holy See new tasks on behalf of the Third World which inspired many progressive members of the American clergy, both north and south. In 1965 Pope Paul undertook the first papal visit to the Western Hemisphere. Before the United Nations General Assembly in New York, he urgently emphasized the need to end war in the nuclear age. Before the Medellín, Colombia, meeting of the Latin American Episcopal Conference (CELAM) in 1968, Paul aligned Rome with the struggle for liberation and justice among Latin America's poor. Rome's relations with some Latin American governments suffered as a result; and Pope John Paul II's visit to the 1979 CELAM conference at Puebla, Mexico, was characterized by a more ambiguous position on the question of liberation theology. He nevertheless reaffirmed papal support for the movement in his 1980 visit to Brazil, his lifting of a ban of silence on its leading exponent, Leonardo Boff, in 1986, and in Cardinal Joseph Ratzinger's *Libertatis Conscientia.* Although John Paul's identification with the Church of the Poor was viewed with suspicion by many progressive Catholics, the Pope continued to express familiar concerns over the developed world's materialism and its lack of commitment to the Third World, particularly during travels in the United States and Canada in 1979, 1987, 1993, and 1995.

Fogarty, Gerald P. *The Vatican and the American Hierarchy from 1870 to 1965.* Stuttgart: Hiersemann, 1982.

Gibson, Charles. *Spain in America.* New York: Harper and Row, 1966.

Handy, Robert T. *A History of the Churches in the United States and Canada.* New York: Oxford University Press, 1977.

Haring, Clarence H. *The Spanish Empire in America.* New York: Oxford University Press, 1947.

Mecham, J. Lloyd. *Church and State in Latin America, A History of Politico-Ecclesiastical Relations.* Chapel Hill: The University of North Carolina Press, 1966.

ROY DOMENICO

Related Document

THE BULL *UNIVERSALIS ECCLESIAE* OF POPE JULIUS II, JULY 28, 1508

By the bull *Universalis ecclesiae* of July 28, 1508, Pope Julius II (1503–1513) conceded to the Spanish crown universal patronage over all ecclesiastical benefices in its New World possessions. Whether or not this bull granted for the first time the *real patronato,* or whether it merely reconfirmed rights already bestowed by the Holy See, it continued to be regarded as the principal documentary evidence of the legal right of the Spanish sovereigns to exercise jurisdiction over the Catholic Church in the New World down to the nineteenth century.

(*Source*: J. Lloyd Mecham, *Church and State in Latin America.* Chapel Hill: University of North Carolina Press, 1934, 18–20.)

JULIUS, BISHOP, SERVANT OF THE SERVANTS OF GOD. WE, PRESIDING by divine choice, although unworthily, over the government of the Universal Church, do concede voluntarily to the Catholic kings principally those things that augment their honor and glory, and contribute effectively to the benefit and security of their dominions. Since our beloved son in Christ, Ferdinand, illustrious king of Aragon, and also of Sicily, and Isabella, of cherished memory, Queen of Castile and León, after having expelled the Moors from Spain, crossed the ocean and planted the Cross in unknown lands, and subjugated many islands and places, and among these being one very rich and extremely populous named New Spain, thereby fulfilling to the extent of their ability the saying *in omnem terram exivit sonus eorum*—Therefore, we, in order that it (New Spain) might be purged of false and pernicious rites, and the true religion be planted there, have acceded to the most urgent requests of the king and queen, and do hereby erect for the greater glory of the name of Christ, a metropolitan church in Ayguacen, and two cathedrals in Maguen and Bayunen,[1] and if the converts imbued by the new faith should attempt to found any church or pious place, they should do so in such a way as not to injure the new religion or the temporal dominions of the king.

In view of the fact that the said Ferdinand, who is also at present governor-general of the kingdoms of Castile and León, and our most cherished daughter in Christ, Juana, queen of the same kingdoms and daughter of the aforementioned Ferdinand, wish that no church, monastery, or pious place be erected or founded either in the islands and lands already possessed, or in those subsequently acquired, without their express consent and that of their successors; and considering that since it is convenient to those kings that the persons who preside over churches and monasteries be faithful and acceptable to them, they desire that they be conceded the right of patronage and of the cathedral churches already erected, or to be erected in the future, and for all the other ecclesiastical benefices inside of a year of their vacancy, and also for inferior benefices; and in case the ordinary should refuse without legitimate cause to grant the one presented with canonical institution inside of ten days, any other bishop, at the request of the king should grant it. We, appreciating that these privileges increase the honor, beauty and security of those islands, and also of the said kingdoms, whose kings are always devout and faithful to the Apostolic See, and heeding the reiterated demands made on us by King Ferdinand and Queen Juana, after mature deliberation with our brothers the cardinals of the Holy Roman Church, and with their advice, by these presents we concede with apostolic authority, other constitutions, ordinances, and laws to the contrary notwithstanding, to the said Ferdinand and Juana, and to the future kings of Castile and León, that nobody without their consent can construct or build in the above mentioned islands, now possessed or to be possessed, large churches; and we concede the right of patronage and of presenting qualified persons to cathedral churches, monasteries, *dignities,* collegiates, and other ecclesiastical benefices and pious places in this manner: respecting benefices that are

instituted in the consistory, the presentation is to be made to Us, or Our successors, within one year after the vacancy occurs; and respecting the other benefices, presentation will be made to the respective ordinaries, and if these refuse without cause to give institution inside of ten days, any bishop in those lands, on the petition of King Ferdinand or of Queen Juana, or the king ruling at that time, can bestow, under those conditions, free and legal canonical institution on the person presented. Nobody should deign to infringe on or act contrary to this concession, and if any one attempts to do so, let him know that he will incur the indignation of God Almighty and of the blessed apostles Peter and Paul. Given in Rome, etc., July 28, 1508.

[1] The Archdiocese of Ayguacen (Hyaguata) and the suffragan Sees of Maguen (Magua) and Bayunen (Bayuna) never existed except on paper. After the impracticality of their sites had become known, and after Ferdinand of Aragon had objected strenuously to assigning to the bishops a part of the tithes on gold, silver, and precious stones, Julius II issued a brief on August 8, 1511, that suppressed these jurisdictions and in their place erected three new dioceses at San Domingo and Conception de la Vega in Española (Haiti) and at San Juan in Puerto Rico, all made suffragans of the Archdiocese of Seville.

(*Source*: John Tracy Ellis, ed. *Documents of American Catholic History.* Vol. 1:1493–1865. Wilmington, Del.: Michael Glazier, 1987, 4–6.)

PORTIER, MICHAEL (1795–1859)

Missionary and bishop. Portier was born at Montbrison, France, on September 7, 1795, and studied for the priesthood in nearby Lyons. There he responded to a missionary appeal for workers for Missouri and Louisiana by Louis William DuBourg (1766–1833): "We offer you: No

Michael Portier

salary, No Recompense; No Holidays; No Pension. But: Much Hard Work; A Poor Dwelling; Few Consolations; Many Disappointments; Frequent Sickness; A Violent or lonely Death; An Unknown Grave." Portier, a subdeacon, returned with DuBourg, briefly stayed with Charles Carroll, and studied English at Mt. St. Mary's College, Emmitsburg, before departing for Louisiana. Ordained a priest on September 29, 1818, in St. Louis, Portier was assigned to the cathedral in New Orleans, successfully undertook direction of a boys' school there, occasionally served the Gulf Coast missions, and later acted as treasurer for the seminary at the Barrens, Missouri. Appointed as a missionary bishop to the newly established vicariate of Alabama and the Floridas, he was consecrated by Joseph Rosati (1789–1843) in St. Louis on November 5, 1826.

In Alabama and the territory of Florida the new bishop founded parishes in Mobile, Pensacola, and St. Augustine. The latter was without a priest, and within a year the two other pastors returned to New Orleans. Portier used the year to renew parish life and become familiar with the region. In October 1827 a fire destroyed a large part of Mobile, including the Catholic church. After six months alone trying to care for the vicariate, Portier left for Europe to seek help.

The Society for the Propagation of the Faith in France responded generously and would continue its support throughout Portier's life. The Congregation de Propaganda Fide at Rome offered a four-year subsidy, and one of its cardinals, Joseph Fesch, an uncle of Napoleon and former archbishop of Lyons, supported the establishment of the Diocese of Mobile in 1829. Michael Portier returned to Alabama in 1830 having secured the services of four priests and six seminarians.

That same year Spring Hill College, the oldest in Alabama, was founded, and in 1833 the Visitandines from Georgetown, D.C., started a girls' school in Mobile. Education was a high priority and by 1850 Catholic schools in the Mobile area served 1,000 students, including a unit for "creole" children—the first recorded effort for nonwhite children in the state. The Jesuits staffed the college after 1847 and the Daughters of Charity as well as the Brothers of the Sacred Heart provided care for orphans. The sisters assumed charge of the City Hospital in 1852, but "Know-Nothing" political ascendancy in 1854 forced them out. This led to the founding of Providence Hospital under the sisters' direction.

Priests visited central and northern Alabama and parishes were established in Tuscaloosa and Montgomery. Florida remained a part of the diocese until 1850 when the peninsula was detached. Pastors were provided for Tallahassee, Key West, and Apalachicola, and a new parish was founded near Pensacola. In Mobile two additional parishes were founded and a fifteen-year labor resulted in the consecration of a monumental cathedral in 1850. Shortage of clergy remained constant. The first and last priests ordained by Portier died within a year. Two outstanding priests became bishops: Mathias Loras (1792–1858) for Dubuque in 1837, and Stephen Bazin (1796–1848) for Vincennes in 1847. Portier is credited with the institution of diocesan consultors, a practice later adapted worldwide.

The Catholic population grew but slowly. Slavery and almost annual outbreaks of yellow fever discouraged immigration, the principal factor in Catholic growth elsewhere. An estimated census of Catholics in 1826 of 2,000 had increased by 1859 to 10,000. Michael Portier attended all of the provincial councils of Baltimore except the first, and he also attended the first plenary council there in 1852. At the time of his death at Mobile on May 14, 1859, he was considered the dean of the American hierarchy.

See also ALABAMA, CATHOLIC CHURCH IN.

Kenny, Michael J., S.J. *Catholic Culture in Alabama.* New York, 1931.
Lipscomb, Oscar H. "The Administration of Michael Portier, Vicar Apostolic of Alabama and the Floridas, 1825–1829, and First Bishop of Mobile, 1829–1859." Ph.D. dissertation, The Catholic University of America, 1963.
_____. "The Administration of John Quinlan, Second Bishop of Mobile, 1859–1883." *Records of the American Catholic Historical Society of Philadelphia* 78 (March–December 1967) 3–163.

+ OSCAR H. LIPSCOMB

POUGHKEEPSIE SCHOOL PLAN

One of the most successful efforts at cooperation between public and parochial schools in the United States took place in the small Hudson River city of Poughkeepsie, New York, between 1873 and 1898. The originator of the plan was Fr. Patrick F. McSweeny, pastor of St. Peter's Church in that city. McSweeny, who had been ordained in Rome in 1862, was a friend of Thomas Farrell, Edward McGlynn, Richard Burtsell, and other progressive New York priests who formed the so-called New York Accademia. In June 1873, two years after his arrival in Poughkeepsie, McSweeny made an offer to the local public school board, which he knew was hard pressed to provide adequate classroom space for all of the city's children.

McSweeny offered to rent his two parochial school buildings to the city for an annual fee of one dollar each. He also agreed to accept non-Catholic students, to refrain from religious exercises or instructions during school hours, and to allow the city to inspect the schools and to examine both the teachers and students. In return he wanted the city to pay the teachers' salaries and fuel bills, to allow him to select the teachers, and to permit him to use the school buildings outside of class hours. The city balked at only one of the proposed conditions, namely, McSweeny's request that he should be allowed to choose the teachers. Instead, the city insisted that they should be selected by the board of education. McSweeny agreed to that stipulation and secured the approval of Archbishop John McCloskey. On August 21, 1873, McSweeny signed a ten-year lease with the president of the board of education, and the Poughkeepsie Plan went into effect on September 1, 1873.

St. Peter's two parochial school buildings became Public School Eleven and Twelve. Enrollment hovered around six hundred students, at least a few of whom were Protestant or Jewish. The annual city expenditures on the two schools averaged about $8,000. All of the teachers were Catholics, most of them Sisters of Charity. The religious atmosphere was more pronounced than one might expect. Since state law fixed the school hours as 9:00 A.M. to 12:00 P.M. and 1:30 P.M. to 3:00 P.M., prayers and religious instruction took place, not only before and after the school day, but also between noon and 1:30 P.M. In 1877 McSweeny was succeeded as pastor by his friend, Fr. James Nilan, another alumnus of the Accademia, who gave the plan his enthusiastic support.

Not everyone shared Nilan's enthusiasm. Conservative critics such as Bishop Bernard McQuaid of Rochester and the *New York Freeman's Journal* disliked the element of government supervision and feared that the Poughkeepsie Plan would undermine Catholic determination to build their own parochial school system, a policy which was mandated by the American bishops at the Third Plenary Council of Baltimore in 1884. On the other hand, Archbishop John Ireland mentioned the Poughkeepsie Plan with approval during his famous address to the National Education Association of the United States at its convention in St. Paul in 1890, and advocated its adoption elsewhere. Shortly thereafter, the Poughkeepsie Plan was implemented (with minor variations) in two parishes in John Ireland's own archdiocese, at Faribault and Stillwater, Minnesota. In neither place did the arrangement last for more than two years, but the Faribault-Stillwater Plan created far more controversy than the Poughkeepsie Plan, and ever since it has attracted considerably more attention from historians.

The most curious aspect of the Poughkeepsie Plan was the attitude of Archbishop Michael Corrigan (McCloskey's successor), who tolerated it for thirteen years despite his outspoken opposition to the Faribault-Stillwater Plan. The Poughkeepsie Plan came to an end as a result of the New York State Constitutional Convention of 1894, which prohibited the use of public funds for denominational schools. On December 23, 1898, the State Superintendent of Public Instruction ordered the arrangement terminated on the grounds that it violated the new state constitution because of the religious habits worn by the school teachers. Similar arrangements in four other New York state school districts were also declared illegal.

See also BOUQUILLON, THOMAS; CATHOLIC EDUCATION, PAROCHIAL; FARIBAULT-STILLWATER SCHOOL PLAN; OREGON SCHOOL LAW OF 1922, THE.

Connors, Edward M. *Church-State Relationships in Education in the State of New York.* Washington, 1951.

Ireland, John. "State Schools and Parish Schools." *The Church and Modern Society.* Chicago, 1896, I:198–214.

McSweeny, Edward. "A New York Pastor in the Latter Half of the Nineteenth Century." *Records of the American Catholic Historical Society of Philadelphia* 19 (1908) 42–58.

_____. "Christian Public Schools." *Catholic World* 44 (March 1887) 788–97.

Morrisey, Timothy H. "Archbishop John Ireland and the Faribault-Stillwater School Plan of the 1890's: A Reappraisal." Ph.D. dissertation, University of Notre Dame, 1975.

Pratt, John Webb. *Religion, Politics and Diversity: The Church-State Theme in New York History.* Ithaca, 1967.

THOMAS J. SHELLEY

POWDERLY, TERENCE V. (1849–1924)

Labor leader. Terence Vincent Powderly was born in Carbondale, Pennsylvania, January 22, 1849, the eleventh of twelve children born to Terence and Margery Walsh Powderly, immigrants from County Meath, Ireland, who settled in the Lackawana Valley, Pennsylvania, around 1829. Powderly attended Carbondale public school until age thirteen when he joined thousands of other Irish immigrants and their children as a railroad worker. During the next four years he worked as switch tender, car inspector, and brakeman for the Delaware and Hudson Railway Company. At age seventeen he became a machinist apprentice in the same company's shops.

Terence Powderly

His first exposure to labor disputes came as he ended his apprenticeship in 1869. A local miners' strike forced Powderly to seek employment in nearby Scranton. The Delaware, Lackawanna, and Western Railroad hired him as a machinist. Working during the day, he studied mechanical engineering at night.

Early Labor Union Activities

Despite the personal difficulties caused by the strike, Powderly found inspiration especially in John Siney, the powerful spokesperson for the miners' union. Young Terence wrote to the Machinist and Blacksmith Union in Cleveland, Ohio, for assistance in organizing a local in Scranton. The union came to Scranton in 1869, but Powderly himself had to wait until 1871 to meet the membership age requirement. The new member quickly took leadership positions as secretary in 1872, and then president later that same year. September 19, 1872, marked the beginning of his twenty-two-year marriage to Hannah Deyer who died in 1901. Powderly married Emma Fichenscher in 1919.

Powderly continued grassroots organizing activity among workers guided by a vision of all workers uniting into a single association. Early efforts at national organizing included his 1874 involvement in the short-lived Industrial Brotherhood. The same year, during a trip to Philadelphia, Terence qualified for initiation into the Knights of Labor. Founded by nine Philadelphia garment workers, the Knights operated as a fraternal order with elaborate initiation rituals and secrecy among members. Its leader, Uriah Stephens, a trained Baptist minister, informed the rites of induction with biblical quotes reflecting strong Protestant commitments.

Powderly's journals written during this period depict him as an active Catholic parishioner who recognized the Church's condemnation of secret societies. He also indicates the existence of a certain confusion over the official Catholic position on labor unions. Certain priests and bishops recognized the need for secrecy as a means of protecting members who sought economic justice. His journals indicate contact with clergy sympathetic to the formation of labor unions, while his autobiography suggests animosity-dominated Church contacts.

For two years, Powderly had little contact with other Knights of Labor members until a local of the Stationary Engineers admitted him in 1876. That same year, Powderly increased the Knights' local presence in Scranton by starting Local No. 222. He became master workman of the new local, primarily made up of machinists. Other newly founded locals in the area made possible the formation of a District Assembly for which Powderly served as corresponding secretary.

The burgeoning Knights of Labor organization began to experience rivalries between certain districts, and the leaders determined on the need for a clarification of the union's purpose. At a general convention held in 1878 at Reading, Pennsylvania, Powderly served on the constitutional committee. The final document emphasized worker solidarity transcending divisions by skills and trades. A national governing body was created to foster this solidarity.

Powderly's activism in local and national social reform made him a well-known figure in Scranton. In 1878 the city elected the twenty-nine-year-old its mayor, representing the Greenback-Labor ticket. He held that office for two more terms, stepping down in 1884. The year after his local political success, Powderly enjoyed victory in two national Knights of Labor elections. He became the Grand Worthy Foreman (vice president), and then later that same year, 1879, his fellow workers made him the Grand Master Workman, the highest office of the Knights of Labor. He remained Grand Master Workman until 1893.

The Knights of Labor

Powderly, consistent with his desire to found a national labor association, made a concerted effort to transform the Knights of Labor into an organization representing a diverse constituency. He successfully eclipsed the influence of Uriah Stephens, the Knights' founder, who had insisted on maintaining the absolute secrecy and the Protestant-inspired initiation rituals. Both features had deterred Catholic laborers from joining the Knights. Powderly also lowered the age of admission and opened membership to African Americans, women, and new immigrants, excepting the Chinese, officially excluded in 1880. Despite the racially biased decision against Asian immigrants, the Knights of Labor could point with pride at racially integrated locals in the South. As a result of Powderly's policies, membership rose from the 9,000 in 1879 to 700,000 in 1886. The rapid growth may also be attributed to early Knights' victories for labor, especially in the 1885/1886 strike against Jay Gould. The organization's equally rapid decline in the second half of the 1880s came in part from a series of failed strikes including another one against Jay Gould.

Terence Powderly's struggle on behalf of laborers took shape within an encompassing vision of social reform. In addition to the labor battles, Powderly fought for land reform and supported Henry George's single tax proposal. During his entire adult life, the Irish-American also supported the temperance movement as crucial to improving the workers' lot. Powderly had very specific long-term goals for economic reform. Central to his plan was replacing the wage system with worker-owned producer cooperatives that would sell to consumer cooperatives. Some 135 such cooperatives came into existence under Powderly's leadership, but all quickly failed. He also fought for government intervention to manage public utilities, oversee trusts, reform currency, and abolish child labor.

In Powderly's plan, the Knights of Labor served as an educational system that would introduce laborers to cooperative means of economic and social reform. He remained reticent to promote strikes as a means of gaining workers' rights even after the success against Jay Gould. He preferred boycotts and arbitration to the volatile situations precipitated by strikes. Even though he held a political office for three terms, he discouraged Knights' official engagement in political activities.

Powderly's popularity came in part from his effective speaking and his clear commitment to the cause of labor. His talents and hard work made him labor's national voice during the 1880s. However, his grand vision of reform obscured the desires of the rank-and-file members who sought very practical gains, higher wages, and shorter hours. Terence Powderly's refusal to take these demands seriously precipitated Samuel Gompers' departure from the Knights of Labor to found the American Federation of Labor in 1886. Powderly's personal weaknesses also undermined his effectiveness. He seemed unable to delegate responsibilities and interpreted all criticism as disloyalty. Western farmers joined with eastern seaboard socialists to remove him from office in 1893.

Powderly and the Catholic Church

Powderly's leadership did, however, come at a crucial time in the formation of Catholic Church's official position on the faithful's membership in labor unions. Begun as secret societies in large part out of practical necessity, labor unions bore the hostility of bishops and priests who identified them with quasi-religious secret societies, most notably, the Masons. Powderly's success in minimizing the secrecy and anti-Catholic flavor of initiation rituals helped mitigate clerical hostility. In 1884, when Quebec's Archbishop Taschereau petitioned Rome and received a desired decree prohibiting Catholic membership in the Knights, U.S. prelates hesitated to follow suit.

Despite denials in his autobiography, Powderly's journals and extant letters from 1886 indicate sincere efforts to work with the Catholic hierarchy, especially Baltimore's prelate, James Gibbons, to overturn the Quebec decision. Especially important to Gibbons' case was a Powderly letter promising to amend the Knights' constitution in accordance with any episcopal objections. Whatever the intended limits of the Roman memorial of 1887, its expression of tolerance for the Knights removed the onus of condemnation and provided a starting point for official U.S. Catholic support of the labor movements, a support further bolstered with Leo XIII's *Rerum Novarum.*

Hierarchical approval came ironically enough just as the influence of the Knights of Labor had begun to wane.

In the midst of factional fighting, Powderly tendered his resignation in 1893. In 1894 he was admitted to the bar. In 1897 he was appointed U.S. Commissioner General of Immigration as a reward for campaigning on behalf of William McKinley. Theodore Roosevelt dismissed him from the post in 1902. In 1906 Powderly served in the Department of Commerce and Labor and later in the Division of Information at the Bureau of Immigration. From 1921 until his death in 1924 he worked as Commissioner of Conciliation at the Department of Labor.

In his later years he remained disaffected from the institutional Church though he maintained close friendships with such Catholic notables as Archbishop John Ireland and The Catholic University of America professor, William Kerby. His autobiography, *The Path I Trod,* published posthumously, indicates a deep bitterness toward the Church's attitude to labor. He had in fact trod a difficult path between the anti-labor forces among clergy and capitalists as well as the anti-Catholic forces among his pro-labor allies. He remained to the end of his life a believer in the Jesus who cared for the poor and the outcast. He died in Washington, D.C., on June 24, 1924.

See also KNIGHTS OF LABOR; LABOR MOVEMENT AND AMERICAN CATHOLICS, THE.

The Catholic University of America possesses the Powderly papers.

Browne, Henry, J. *The Catholic Church and the Knights of Labor.* Washington, D.C., 1949.

Grob, Gerald N. *Workers in Utopia: A Study in Ideological Conflict in the American Labor Movement, 1865–1900.* 1961.

———. *Dictionary of American Reformers.* 1985.

Powderly, Terence Vincent. *Thirty Years of Labor.* New York, 1899.

———. *The Path I Trod: The Autobiography of Terence V. Powderly.* New York, 1940.

SANDRA YOCUM MIZE

POWERS, JESSICA (1905–88)

Poet and Carmelite nun. Jessica Powers was born Agnes Jessica Powers on February 7, 1905, the third of four children of John Powers II and Delia Veronica Trainer. As a child she changed the order of her name to Jessica Agnes, and years later as a Carmelite nun she was given the name Sr. Miriam of the Holy Spirit. But to the countless readers of her lyric poetry she was always known as Jessica Powers who, in her lifetime, published hundreds of poems in newspapers, literary journals, anthologies, and several volumes of verse. She began writing in childhood and continued until her death at age eighty-three. Her vocation was as much to poetry as it was to prayer, and she lived out the poetic quest in different settings: the farmlands of Wisconsin, the cityscapes of Chicago and New York City, and for forty-seven years the austerity of a Carmelite monastery.

Early Life—Cat Tail Valley

Jessica Powers was born and raised in Juneau County near Mauston, Wisconsin, in a small lumber and farming community called Cat Tail Valley. That name will not be found on any official map, but it is part of the oral history of the locale. Sweeps of cattails border the stream that cuts through the region (a branch of the Lemonweir River), undoubtedly suggesting the colorful name.

Cattails appear over and over again in Powers' work. In one poem she writes, "My songs are cattails in a swamp."

Cat Tail Valley was settled by immigrants fleeing Ireland's potato famine in the 1840s. They brought with them their love for the land and for their Catholic religion. After building their homesteads, they built their church, St. Patrick's, whose steeple is visible from many points in Cat Tail Valley.

Jessica Powers' grandparents, maternal and paternal, were among the first settlers in Juneau County, all Irish except for her maternal grandfather, James Trainer. He and his brother Daniel emigrated from Scotland in 1850, bringing with them road-building skills and a small volume of poetry by Robert Burns, a distant cousin. The book remained in the family and is today part of the archives at Mother of God Carmelite Monastery in Pewaukee, Wisconsin. James became a Catholic after his marriage to Catherine Keena in 1852.

Juneau County did not escape the agony of the country's Civil War. Like many of his neighbors, James Trainer joined the Lemonweir Minute Men to fight with the Union army. These "pioneers," as they were called, were with General Sherman in his merciless march through the South. Trainer led the pioneers in constructing corduroy roads that allowed the army to move through a severely muddy terrain in North Carolina. But war repelled him and he wrote his wife that "I have seen more than I wish to see again." He returned to his family before the end of the Civil War. Delia, Jessica's mother, was born a few years after his return.

Jessica Powers attended the one-room school across the road from her family's farm until she was eleven when she became a student at the parish school, the "Sisters' School," as it was called. This required that she board with other children in Mauston. She did so from grade six through twelve, returning home to the farm on weekends.

These elements of her ancestry—Irish Catholicism, the pioneer experience, close association with nature, the communal bonds of Cat Tail Valley—all were kneaded into her life and her art. Even more central was death, ever present. Jessica's sister, Dorothy, died at age sixteen of tuberculosis; many other Cat Tail Valley children also succumbed to the disease; and when Jessica was thirteen her beloved father, John, a farmer-politician, suddenly died of a heart attack. Her sense of profound loss and her deep

need of God were translated into her "songs," reflecting Patricia Hampl's insight that death, not lyrical flights, is the real intimate of poetry.

Milwaukee and Chicago

In 1922 Jessica Powers left the familiar place and people of Cat Tail Valley to study at Marquette University in Milwaukee. She enrolled in the School of Journalism, the only school of the Jesuit university open to women at that time. The *Milwaukee Sentinel* published a number of her poems, sparking a correspondence with Jessie Pegis, also a writer and the wife of philosopher Anton Pegis. It would be years before the two Jessicas would meet in New York City.

Lack of money forced her to leave Marquette after one semester. She then went to Chicago where she worked as a secretary. Her real work, however, was the cultivation of the inner life. She read (mostly in the public library); she wrote (prodigiously); she published (in newspapers and literary journals); and she enjoyed the intellectual and spiritual stimulation of an informal literary salon. The latter met regularly at the Dominican priory at River Forest outside Chicago. There, laity mingled with seminarians and friars to read plays and poetry and discuss art. Urban Nagle, O.P., founder of the Blackfriars Theater in New York, was part of the group.

The Farm Years: Loss and Revival

Her Chicago experience ended abruptly when incipient tuberculosis flared up, and she returned home to Cat Tail Valley for rest and recovery. She intended to go to New York as soon as she was strong enough, but again, her plans were altered when her mother died unexpectedly. She mourned this latest loss in poetry.

> *Since she is gone,*
> *This spring I cannot bear*
> *To walk beneath the weight of lilac scent*
> *That presses on my nostrils and my heart*
> *With ill intent.*
>
> *Since she is lost*
> *But lately unto me, I am not strong*
> *Enough without the armor of her love*
> *To brave the daggers in a robin's song.*

This Maytime, published in *Commonweal,* May 26, 1926.

Jessica, age twenty, took on the tasks of homemaking for her two unmarried brothers who were farming the land, the only security for the family as the country headed into the Great Depression of the 1930s. She remained on the farm for ten years, remembered in her later life as years of poverty and inner desolation. Yet they were productive years. She wrote a great deal, continued to be published, and during that period Ruth Mary Fox, the Wisconsin writer and Dante scholar, introduced her to the works of

John of the Cross to whom she has been compared by Carmelite scholars.

She had given up her dream of living in New York when suddenly everything changed. Both brothers married within a six-month period, and Jessica felt free to leave Cat Tail Valley. She arrived in New York City in 1937, a woman without financial means, few business skills, no urban sophistication, but eager to participate in the Catholic literary revival underway there. She immediately connected with the Catholic Poetry Society and attended both the small-group work sessions where writers critiqued each other's work, and the larger gatherings often held at the Waldorf Astoria Hotel. Her poem, *The Terminal,* was composed after a walk through New York streets on her way to a meeting.

During her New York years Jessica Powers lived with Anton and Jessie Pegis and their three children. The women took turns caring for the children, allowing each of them free time for writing. Clifford Laube, a *New York Times* editor and a leader of the Catholic Poetry Society, had established his own publishing company called Monastine Press after SS Monica and Augustine. He had long admired Jessica Powers' poetry and he offered to publish her first book. She asked the well-known Wisconsin writer August Derleth to read her manuscript. He suggested the name, *The Lantern Burns.* It was published in 1939 and received favorable reviews.

In 1941, just when her poetic vocation was gaining recognition in the secular as well as religious literary arenas, Jessica Powers entered a newly established Carmelite monastery for women in Milwaukee, Mother of God Carmel, undertaking a lifetime of prayer and penance. (The monastery was later moved to Pewaukee.) She fully expected to give up her writing, but that was never required of her. Instead, she continued to weave remembrances of Wisconsin and New York into the discoveries of the cloister, creating new poems. As a Carmelite nun she explored the secrets of the soul, secrets of solitude and suffering, shaping poems which delighted the readers of *Commonweal* and *America* for decades. She also produced five more books of poetry, including one for children. Six weeks before her death she worked with Sr. Regina Siegfried, A.S.C., and Bishop Robert Morneau in revising and editing her most extensive collection, *Selected Poetry of Jessica Powers,* which was published posthumously. Jessica Powers was faithful to her poetic call throughout her lifetime, into elderhood, unto death. Her papers are in the Marquette University archives. She died on August 18, 1988.

See also CATHOLICS AND AMERICAN LITERATURE.

Kappes, M. *Track of the Mystic: Carmelite Influence on the American Poet Jessica Powers.* Kansas City: Sheed & Ward 1994.

Leckey, D. R. *Winter Music: A Life of Jessica Powers. Poet, Nun, Woman of the 20th Century.* Kansas City: Sheed & Ward, 1992.

Morneau, R. *Mantras From A Poet.* Kansas City: Sheed & Ward, 1991.

Powers, J. *Mountain Sparrow.* Reno Carmel, 1972; illustrated by Sr. Marie Celest, O.C.D.

____. *Journey to Bethlehem.* Pewaukee, Wisconsin, 1980.

____. *The House At Rest.* Pewaukee, Wisconsin, 1984.

____. *Selected Poetry of Jessica Powers.* Kansas City, 1989; includes a bibliography of secondary sources.

DOLORES R. LECKEY

PRECIOUS BLOOD, MISSIONARIES OF (C.PP.S.)

The Missionaries of the Precious Blood is a religious institute of priests and brothers organized as a society of apostolic life. It was founded in the Papal States in 1815 by St. Gaspar del Bufalo, a Roman priest. Its purpose was to renew the Christian life of the clergy and the laity. In 1838 the missionaries accepted their first non-Italian member, a Swiss priest seeking a missionary congregation after the dissolution of his monastery in France. This priest, Francis de Sales Brunner (1795–1859), was then sent to begin a foundation in Canton Graubünden in Switzerland.

In 1842 Bishop John Purcell of Cincinnati requested priests to serve the German immigrant population. Brunner arrived in Cincinnati on December 31, 1843, with seven priests and seven seminarians. The group set out almost immediately to take charge of a mission at Peru, Ohio, that had been established by the Redemptorists. Up to the time of the death of Brunner, pastoral work centered in the rural regions of northern and western Ohio.

In 1861 headquarters were moved to Carthagena in Mercer County, Ohio. Work expanded beyond Ohio in the subsequent decades. Parishes were served for over two decades in southern Tennessee. In the 1870s an attempt was made to establish a college in northern California, but it failed. In the late 1880s, the missionaries assumed responsibility for an Indian school in Rensselaer, Indiana, that was to become St. Joseph's College.

In the first part of the twentieth century, the missionaries expanded their parish work through the Midwest, into Missouri, Wisconsin, Minnesota, Iowa, and Nebraska. They also undertook hospital chaplancies and the preaching of parish missions. They moved into work with the African Americans moving north to cities such as Cleveland and later Detroit. In 1947 they began missionary work in Chile, followed by Peru in 1962, and Guatemala in 1975.

By the later 1950s the missionaries' membership was over four hundred. This led to the division of the American province into three provinces in 1965, with headquarters in Cincinnati, Kansas City, and the Bay area of San Francisco. In the latter part of the twentieth century, the Cincinnati province began extensive work with the expanding population in Florida, and the Kansas City province worked with Hispanic communities in Texas.

The two members who have made perhaps the most notable contribution to American Church life were Bishop Joseph Dwenger (1837–93), whose program for a parochial school system in his Fort Wayne, Indiana, diocese was adopted by the Third Council of Baltimore in 1884; and Fr. Edward Siegman (1908–67), pioneer in the modern Catholic biblical movement.

In 1995 missionaries working in the United States numbered about three hundred priests and brothers.

Knapke, Paul J. *History of the Society of the Precious Blood in the United States*. 2 vols. Carthagena, Ohio, 1958, 1968.

Robbins, Charles J. *The American/Cincinnati Province of the Society of the Precious Blood: A Chronicle Account 1843–1984*. Carthagena, Ohio, 1985.

ROBERT J. SCHREITER, C.PP.S.

PRENDERGAST, EDMOND (1843–1918)

Archbishop. Edmond Francis Prendergast was born in Clonmel, County Tipperary, Ireland, on May 3, 1843. At the age of sixteen, he came to Pennsylvania and entered St. Charles Borromeo Seminary. On November 17, 1865, he was ordained to the priesthood in the newly dedicated Cathedral of Saints Peter and Paul.

For nine years after his ordination, Prendergast served in several parishes in the archdiocese. In 1874 he became pastor of St. Malachy parish in Philadelphia, where he remained for the next thirty-seven years. During his pastorate,

Edmond F. Prendergast

Prendergast served on a number of committees, boards of consultors, and advisory groups.

In 1896 Prendergast became vicar general of the archdiocese; and on February 24, 1897, he was consecrated auxiliary bishop of Philadelphia. With the death of Archbishop Patrick Ryan, Prendergast became archbishop of Philadelphia on July 16, 1911. With forty-five years as a Philadelphia priest, Prendergast came to his new position with more experience in his diocese than any previous ordinary.

Many things planned by Archbishop Ryan were actually accomplished under Prendergast. It was Prendergast who laid the cornerstone of Catholic Girls' High School on October 1, 1911. The Newman Club movement, moribund since 1906, was revived and spread to universities outside the Archdiocese of Philadelphia. The Archbishop Ryan Memorial Institute for the Deaf was opened by Prendergast in May 1912. He blessed the newly completed Ryan Memorial Library at St. Charles Seminary, Overbrook, on October 9, 1911. Prendergast continued Ryan's support for the American Catholic Historical Society of Philadelphia, founded in 1884, attending many of its monthly meetings and encouraging the publication of Catholic historical sources in the society's publication, *Records*.

Prendergast showed the same interest as Ryan in providing the expanding Catholic population with churches and schools. Prendergast established nineteen new territorial parishes located mostly in areas of greatest Catholic population growth or migration. Twenty-three new national parishes were established: ten Italian, five Lithuanian, three Polish, two Hungarian, two Slovak, and one German. In 1912 a church for Spanish-speaking seamen, Our Lady of the Miraculous Medal, was opened.

Many of Prendergast's accomplishments, while in line with the thinking of his predecessor, were his ideas from the start. West Philadelphia Catholic High School for Boys was opened in 1916 to serve the rapidly expanding Catholic population in the western part of Philadelphia, and the new school building was dedicated the following year. A new Catholic hospital (Misericordia) was also opened in that part of the city, and one (Sacred Heart) was begun in Allentown. Prendergast opened a home for crippled children and a home for the children of derelict or destitute parents. The work begun at Madonna House among Italian immigrant children was expanded with the opening of L'Assunta House in 1912. St. Charles Seminary saw a new dormitory, St. Edmond's Hall, and a new service building, added between 1914 and 1917. The Laymen's Weekend Retreat League of Philadelphia, founded in 1913, received enthusiastic support from Archbishop Prendergast. He also acted as spiritual director of several lay guilds. Between 1914 and 1915, Prendergast undertook the first major renovation of the Cathedral of Saints Peter and Paul.

Prendergast died on the evening of February 26, 1918. On March 5 he was buried in the cathedral crypt amid great public mourning.

See also PENNSYLVANIA, CATHOLIC CHURCH IN.

Archbishop Prendergast Papers, Philadelphia Archdiocesan Historical Research Center, Wynnewood, Pennsylvania.
Consuela, Mary, I.H.M. "The Church of Philadelphia (1884–1918)." *The History of the Archdiocese of Philadelphia,* ed. James F. Connelly. Philadelphia, 1976, 271–338.

JOSEPH J. CASINO

PRESENTATION SISTERS (P.B.V.M.)

The Sisters of the Presentation of the Blessed Virgin Mary in the United States trace their beginnings from the days of Nano Nagle, a young woman, native of Ballygriffin, Ireland. Educated in France because of English government restrictions on education for Irish Catholic families, this daughter of a nobleman became more and more aware of what was happening in her home country. She decided to use some of the resources of her affluent family to do something about the situation.

Nano began her ministry to the poor and uneducated in Cork long before she formally established the religious community which has developed into the Sisters of the Presentation. Education was her primary goal and the original title she chose for her little community was "Sisters of the Sacred Heart of Charitable Instruction."

Thousands of Presentation Sisters over 220 years have followed Nano's spirit and are today in almost every nation on the globe.

West and Southwest

San Francisco was the first Presentation foundation in the United States. It was made by five sisters under the leadership of Mother M. Joseph Cronin and Sr. M. Terese Comerford. Cloistered nuns, these early sisters came from Ireland to San Francisco by way of New York on boat, railroad, and muleback. On their arrival, Archbishop Joseph S. Alemany, who had invited them, was out of town. When he returned, the original plans for them to locate in Sacramento were changed and they took over a school for girls, receiving salaries from the state until 1856 when funding was cut. They continued to teach, relying on benefactors rather than resorting to charging tuition. In 1857 they opened the first Catholic school in California for African American girls. Native American girls were also numbered among their pupils. Today, the San Francisco sisters work in education and diocesan ministries.

In 1952 a new surge of Presentation missionaries from Ireland came when small groups arrived in the Southwestern part of the United States. These sisters formed the United States Province of the Union in 1989 and re-

tained their headquarters in Ireland. Members of the province, while regarding education as their primary work, regard any social need as part of their ministry. In 1995 they were serving in seven states.

Eastern Areas

Although the first Presentation foundation to be established outside Ireland was the one in St. John's, Newfoundland, the first invitation to the sisters to minister in New York came from the pastor of St. Michael's parish in New York City. In August 1874, sisters from three convents in Ireland—Teranure, Clondelkin, and Tuam—came to teach in the parish school. Eventually, three separate congregations developed from this beginning. The summer home, provided by St. Michael's for the sisters, was located on Staten Island. It became the site for another ministry, a home for destitute children. The group of sisters who remained at St. Michael's formed an autonomous congregation in 1890, and today their headquarters are located on Staten Island. Their ministries include education from elementary to university levels, campus ministry, and religious education.

The second group of sisters whose congregation was an outgrowth of St. Michael's was invited to St. Bernard parish in Fitchburg, Massachusetts, in 1886. Their first assignment was to staff a school in the parish. Through the years they have expanded their educational ministry, and today they work in various services including health and pastoral care. Missionary activity has taken them to West Africa and Ghana.

From St. Michael's in New York City also came the sisters now located in Newburgh, New York. The first mission house which remained attached to the St. Michael's foundation was opened in Our Lady of Solace parish in the Bronx in 1916. Because of expanding numbers, the sisters found it necessary in 1921 to purchase property in Newburgh, New York. Later a new motherhouse, novitiate, retreat center, and boarding school were built and the congregation became autonomous. Like other Presentation Sisters, they continue their work in education but are also active in social services, pastoral ministry, prison ministry, and retreat work.

The foundation of St. Colman's Presentation Convent and St. Colman's Home in Watervliet, New York, dates back to 1881 when, at the invitation of Rev. William F. Sheehan, five sisters came from Fermoy, Ireland. Because of a tragic event in his own ministry, he saw the need for a home for children deprived of their natural homes. The sisters helped him to establish St. Colman's Home where, from that time until the present, they have sought to meet the needs of the children at every level of their development. The Home is especially recognized for its program for autistic persons.

Midwest Centers

The Second Plenary Council of Baltimore was held in 1866. At that council a clear message was enunciated by the bishops in attendance, encouraging parochial schools to be established in all parishes. Pastors were urged to support competent teachers from parish revenues. John J. Hennessy, bishop of the Diocese of Dubuque, invited the Presentation Sisters from Mooncoin, Ireland, to Dubuque in 1874. After finding no house or school in the intended site outside Dubuque, the sisters started a school in the newly established St. Joseph parish in Key West, Iowa.

In 1879 Bishop Hennessy asked the sisters to open a school for the poor working people on the west border of Dubuque. This time there was no parish, no school, and no convent. Part of the alms collected by the diocese during the 1878 Holy Year were allocated to build a school and convent, and in December 1879 the school which would evolve into St. Vincent Academy opened in the area now known as St. Columbkille parish. Bishop Hennessy requested the sisters immediately to move to Dubuque to establish their headquarters. Within two months Mother Vincent Hennessy, the foundress, died, but the young community continued to flourish. The ministry of the sisters spread throughout Iowa and other Midwest states where they helped set up elementary and secondary schools in many rural parishes. Today the presence of the Dubuque Presentations is found not only in education but also in pastoral ministry, catechetics, prison ministry, and varied forms of social service in the economically depressed areas of the United States. They also engage in mission activity in Central and South America.

In 1880 when Church authorities were seeking to meet the needs of the pioneers and Native Americans in the huge tract of land known as the Dakota Territory, Bishop Martin Marty, O.S.B., invited two Presentation Sisters to come to the vicariate of the Dakotas. Mother John Hughes came from George's Hill, Dublin, with her sister, Mother Agnes Hughes, from Doneraille. After some disappointments in their early efforts, the two sisters and three novices arrived in Fargo to open a parish school there. In 1886 they opened a school in Aberdeen. Again the Presentation Sisters were seen as being dedicated to the ministry of teaching.

The Dakota Territory was divided in 1889 to form the states of North and South Dakota. The sisters divided their resources also, and the result was the development of two autonomous congregations, one in Fargo, the other in Aberdeen.

As the years passed, the Fargo sisters were challenged to serve the needs of the people among whom they lived: caring for the homeless, offering religious education, helping the seasonal migrant workers, and serving the ill and elderly in rural communities in the eastern part of North Dakota. Today they continue to address contemporary needs not only in education but also in health care, in retirement centers, in hospices, in Partners in Housing, and in their Presentation Prayer Center.

The sisters in Aberdeen also remained faithful to Nano Nagle's dream for education, but as early as 1900 they felt the need to begin hospital work. Their Presentation Health System now includes four hospitals and two nursing homes. Presentation College in Aberdeen is owned and operated by the sisters. The courses offered not only promote their hospital work but also include training for a variety of programs. The Aberdeen sisters are involved in diocesan and pastoral work, the Diocesan Office of Education, Marriage Tribunal, and also have charge of a mission in Mexico.

Seven motherhouses of the Presentation Sisters in the United States and St. John's of Newfoundland form the North American Conference of Presentation Sisters, an integral part of the International Presentation Association formed in 1987.

See also IOWA, CATHOLIC CHURCH IN; WOMEN RELIGIOUS IN AMERICA.

Bannon, Francis, P.B.V.M., and Benedict Murphy, P.B.V.M. Annals of the Sisters of the Presentation, Dubuque, Iowa, 1874–1949. Unpublished.

Driscoll, Justin A. *With Faith and Vision.* Dubuque, 1966.

Halliday, Therese, P.B.V.M. and Pius O'Farrell, P.B.V.M. *Nano Nagle, a Story of Faith and Courage.* Strasbourg: Sadifa, 1983.

Walsh, T. J. *Nano Nagle and the Presentation Sisters.* Dublin: M. H. Gill, 1959.

ANGELA FEENEY, P.B.V.M.

PRESTON, THOMAS SCOTT (1824–91)

Convert, priest, vicar general of the Archdiocese of New York. Thomas Scott Preston was born on July 23, 1824, in Hartford, Connecticut, where he attended Washington (Trinity) College. While attending General Theological Seminary in New York, Preston was heavily influenced by the Oxford Movement, and, because of these beliefs, was refused ordination by the Episcopal bishop of New York. He was eventually ordained by the Episcopal bishop of Western New York in 1847.

After a brief stint as an Episcopal clergyman in St. Luke-in-the-Fields in Greenwich Village, Preston was received into the Catholic Church on November 14, 1849, by James Roosevelt Bayley, who was himself a convert Episcopal clergyman. In November 1850 he was ordained a priest by coadjutor bishop John McCloskey and shortly thereafter was appointed pastor of St. Mary's Church in Yonkers. Chancellor of the Archdiocese of New York from 1853 to 1891, as well as vicar general from 1873 until his

Thomas S. Preston

death, Preston also served as pastor of St. Ann's Church in Manhattan from 1863 until his death. He was influential in diocesan circles under three archbishops, Hughes, McCloskey, and Corrigan. He was known for his theological conservatism and extreme Ultramontanism.

Dr. Richard L. Burtsell, Preston's assistant at St. Ann's and captious commentator on the archdiocese, detailed a story in his diary highlighting Preston's rigidity. Burtsell reported that Preston continually refused absolution to a young girl for her insufficient resolve to desist from lying. Burtsell said that Preston simply "did not know his theology." Although Burtsell questioned Preston's understanding of theology, Preston had confidence in his own scholarship and in 1871 published a book on papal infallibility, *The Vicar of Christ; or Lectures upon the Office and Prerogatives of our Holy Father, the Pope.* In a letter dated January 5, 1872, John Henry Newman thanked Preston for the gift of this book but carefully avoided endorsing it and never said that he had actually read it. In a letter dated just two weeks later, on January 19, 1872, Cardinal Henry Manning of Westminster praised the book and agreed wholeheartedly with Preston's thesis on infallibility, remarking that "Catholic and ultramontane are convertible."

In 1886 Preston cofounded a religious community, the Sisters of Divine Compassion, with a fellow convert, Mother Veronica Starr. A prolific writer and influential churchman, Preston embodied a wing of the American Church that was becoming increasingly fearful and hostile to American-style democracy and its influence on the Catholic Church. In an article for the *American Catholic Quarterly Review,* Preston warned Catholics that they must not transfer to the Church the democratic ideals embodied in the American system of government. Preston argued that the true American Catholics were those who "maintain the rights and liberties which our constitution guarantees to us [but who] are obedient to the divine voice which speaks to man through the Catholic Church."

Preston, Thomas S. *The Vicar of Christ; or Lectures upon the Office and Prerogatives of our Holy Father, the Pope.* New York, 1871.

———. "American Catholicity." *American Catholic Quarterly Review* 16 (1891) 396–408.

Wilson, Robert Kent. "The Oxford Movement and the Church of New York." *Dunwoodie Review* 15 (1991) 34–66.

ANTHONY D. ANDREASSI

PREUSS, ARTHUR (1871–1934)

Journalist and editor. Preuss was a native of St. Louis, Missouri, of German extraction who for over forty years was one of the most influential Catholic journalists in the United States. After completing his studies for a master's degree in philosophy in June 1890, at St. Francis Solanus College (now Quincy College) in Quincy, Illinois, Arthur Preuss followed his father, Edward Preuss, into the field of Catholic journalism. For eighteen months Preuss wrote for the German-language Catholic daily, *Die Amerika,* of St. Louis and also contributed articles to a Catholic weekly journal of that city, the *Church Progress.* In early 1892, just prior to his twenty-first birthday, Preuss was hired by William Kuhlmann of Chicago to be the editor of his two Catholic weeklies, *Katholisches Sontagsblatt* and *Die Glocke.*

Arthur Preuss

Two years later, on April 1, 1894, Preuss launched his own journal, the *Review* (later the *Fortnightly Review*), and thus became a pioneer in the transformation of the ethnocentric German-language press into the English-language medium of conservative Catholics. Although Preuss would be closely involved in the publication of other Catholic journals, including stints as the editor of *Die Amerika* (1902–05, 1920–21), and as editor of the *Echo* of Buffalo (1919–34), it was through his own *Review* that he established a reputation as the leading journalistic voice of both German and conservative Catholics in America during the years from 1894 until 1934.

Preuss enjoyed tremendous stature among the educated Catholics of his day. Among his friends and associates were Peter Paul Cahensly, Archbishop Michael Corrigan, Frederick Kenkel, Msgr. John A. Ryan, Msgr. Peter Guilday, Patrick H. Callahan, and Fr. Virgil Michel, O.S.B. Preuss appears often in historical studies of the issues listed above as the spokesman for an element in the American Church which contested, often unsuccessfully, the direction in which Catholicism in America was developing. Specific issues that Preuss was involved in as a commentator included the controversy surrounding German Catholic ethnicity and "Americanization," the foundation of The Catholic University of America, the crisis over "Americanism," the "social question," the formation of the American Federation of Catholic Societies, the German Catholic experience of World War I, the establishment of the National Catholic Welfare Conference, the presidential campaign of 1928, the depression, and the first years of the Roosevelt administration.

In addition to his career as a journalist, for nearly forty years Arthur Preuss was the literary editor for the B. Herder Publishing Company of St. Louis, Missouri, and in that capacity was responsible for the adaptation into English of numerous German-language works on theology and spirituality. Perhaps the most famous of these was his ten-volume adaptation of Joseph Pohle's *Lehrbook der Dogmatik,* which was published in English between 1910 and 1918 as the "Pohle-Preuss" series on dogmatic theology. These neo-Thomistic volumes became standard texts of American seminary education prior to the Second Vatican Council and were still being published forty years after their first appearance. Arthur Preuss died in 1934 in Jacksonville, Florida.

See also GERMAN CATHOLICS IN AMERICA.

Abell, Aaron. *American Catholicism and Social Action.* Garden City, N.Y.: Doubleday & Company, 1960.
Appleby, R. Scott. *Church and Age Unite! The Modernist Impulse in American Catholicism.* University of Notre Dame Press, 1992.
Barry, Colman, O.S.B. *The Catholic Church and German Americans.* Milwaukee: Bruce Publishing Company, 1953.
Conley, Rory T. "Arthur Preuss, Journalist and Voice of German and Conservative Catholics in America, 1871–1934." Ph.D. dissertation, The Catholic University of America, 1996.
——. "Arthur Preuss, German Catholic Exile in America." *U.S. Catholic Historian* 12 (Summer 1994) 41–62.
Gleason, Philip J. *The Conservative Reformers: German-American Catholics and the Social Order.* University of Notre Dame Press, 1968.
McAvoy, Thomas T. *The Great Crisis in American Catholic History 1895–1900.* Chicago: Regnery, 1957.
Slawson, Douglas J. *The Foundation and First Decade of the National Catholic Welfare Council.* Washington, D.C.: The Catholic University Press, 1992.

RORY T. CONLEY

PREUSS, EDWARD F. (1834–1904)

Convert journalist and editor. Preuss was born in 1834 in Königsburg, East Prussia. Raised as a devout Lutheran, he earned a doctoral degree in philosophy from the University of Königsburg in 1853, and a doctoral degree in theology from the University of Berlin four years later. He then spent the next ten years as a tutor at the University of Berlin, numbering among his students some members of the Prussian royal family. He was also well acquainted with some of the most prominent men in Berlin, including Otto von Bismarck and the historians, Theodor Mommsen and Leopold von Ranke.

As an orthodox Lutheran, Preuss published a polemical book refuting the Catholic dogma of the Immaculate Conception of the Blessed Virgin Mary in 1865. Ironically, this work soon involved Preuss in theological controversies with liberal Protestant contemporaries over the rationalistic theology which divided the evangelical churches. His vehement defense of Lutheran orthodoxy alienated him from his colleagues at the University of Berlin and by December 1868 he felt compelled to resign his position. Shortly thereafter, Preuss left Germany for America to take a teaching position at the theologically conservative Concordia Lutheran Seminary in St. Louis where he was assigned to teach courses in exegesis, Church history, and Hebrew.

However, Preuss's previous involvement in controversies with liberal Protestant theologians had undermined his faith in Lutheranism and he began to see it as simply the transitional stage between the true faith of Catholicism and the outright apostasy of the rationalists. After an intense personal struggle, Preuss resigned his position at Concordia Seminary on December 1, 1871, and seven days later, on the feast of the Immaculate Conception, left behind the Lutheran fold forever. Preuss was baptized into the Roman Catholic Church by the German vicar general of the Archdiocese of St. Louis, the Rev. Henry Muehlsiepen, on January 26, 1872. Also at this time, Preuss's infant son, Arthur, was received into the Church.

Edward Preuss's talents were soon put to use by the German Catholics in St. Louis as the assistant editor of their daily Catholic newspaper, *Die Amerika,* which began publication on October 17, 1872. Edward Preuss did not formally take over the job of editor of *Die Amerika* until January 17, 1878; however, he had been in fact the real editor from the start.

Under Edward Preuss's editorship, *Die Amerika* became the largest and most successful German Catholic daily in the United States. Approximate circulation figures indicate that *Die Amerika* started with 3,000 subscribers, and had reached a circulation of 13,000 subscribers by 1895. Recognized as the central organ of the German Catholics in the United States, *Die Amerika* was actively involved in the "Abbelen Memorial" and "Cahensly" controversies of the 1880s and 1890s which concerned the continued use of the German language in the Church in the United States. In recognition of his contribution to Catholicism in America, Edward Preuss was chosen by the University of Notre Dame to be the recipient of its Laetare Medal in 1887. However, keeping with a repentant vow that he had made upon his conversion to Catholicism, Preuss respectfully declined the honor and his medal remains at the university. He remained the editor of *Die Amerika* until ill health forced him to retire in 1902. He died in St. Louis in 1904.

See also GERMAN CATHOLICS IN AMERICA.

Barry, Colman, O.S.B. *The Catholic Church and German Americans.* Milwaukee: Bruce Publishing Company, 1953.

Conley, Rory T. "Arthur Preuss, Journalist and Voice of German and Conservative Catholics in America, 1871–1934." Ph.D. dissertation, The Catholic University of America, 1996.

____. "Arthur Preuss, German Catholic Exile in America." *U.S. Catholic Historian* 12 (Summer 1994) 41–62.

Gleason, Philip J. *The Conservative Reformers German-American Catholics and the Social Order.* University of Notre Dame Press, 1968.

RORY T. CONLEY

PRICE, THOMAS (1860–1919)

Missionary, cofounder of the Maryknoll Fathers and Brothers. Thomas Frederick Price was born August 19, 1860, in Wilmington, North Carolina. His father, Alfred Price, was editor of the Wilmington *Daily Journal.* An Episcopalian, the elder Price became a Catholic near the end of his life. Price's mother, Clarissa Bond, had been raised a Methodist but became a Catholic at age eighteen. Dispossessed by her parents, she had found hospitality in the Catholic family of Thomas F. Gallagher. There were ten Price children; two of the women became Sisters of Mercy and conducted the local Catholic grammar school that their brother Thomas attended. The pastor in Wilmington during those years and the vicar apostolic of North Carolina was Fr. James Gibbons, the future cardinal archbishop of Baltimore. It was he who encouraged young Price in his inclination to become a priest.

Price completed his studies at St. Charles Seminary, Ellicott City, Maryland, and St. Mary's Seminary in Baltimore. While traveling to Baltimore during his first year the ship on which he was a passenger was wrecked in a storm. Lives were lost, but Price survived, convinced that the Virgin Mary had appeared to him in the water and directed him to floating debris. His devotion to Mary would henceforth be the most striking aspect of his spirituality and eventual mysticism.

Missionary in North Carolina

Price was ordained June 30, 1886, becoming the first native North Carolinian Catholic priest. He served as pastor in New Bern to 1896, regularly journeying by horseback to scattered settlements of Catholics. In 1896 Gibbons' successor as vicar apostolic, Bishop Leo Haid, O.S.B., authorized Price to devote his full time to an itinerant mission ministry throughout North Carolina, work that he continued for fifteen years. He made his base in Raleigh where he acquired land and established an orphanage under the direction of his sister, Sr. Agnes, and a training center, "Regina Apostolorum," for seminarians and priests whom he recruited for temporary assistance in his missions. He hoped that eventually he might be able to create a community of priests for North Carolina and other mission areas even overseas.

In 1897 Price founded *Truth,* a national monthly magazine offering Catholics and interested non-Catholics reliable information about the Catholic faith and its contemporary implications. Price was editor and publisher, and the quality varied from month to month, but Gibbons gave it strong commendation in 1900: "*Truth* is the most instructive periodical published in the whole country," he said. "There is none which effects more real good." There were more than 17,000 subscribers by 1905.

In 1904 Price attended a meeting in Washington, D.C., of the Catholic Missionary Union, an organization of priests involved in missionary activity in the U.S.A. Among the speakers was the recently named director of the Society for the Propagation of the Faith in Boston, Fr. James A. Walsh. Walsh urged that the U.S. Church be encouraged to extend its missionary interest to overseas mission fields. Price shared Walsh's view that mission work in the U.S.A. would be further stimulated by a similar commitment to the foreign missions. It was the first meeting of the two priests who would be cofounders of the Catholic Foreign Mission Society of America (Maryknoll). Price made the linking of home and foreign missions the subject of several editorial comments in *Truth,* and was in occasional correspondence with Walsh.

The Founding of Maryknoll

In September 1910 Price attended the International Eucharistic Congress in Montreal. On the final day he learned that Walsh was also present and arranged to meet him. He urged that the two join efforts to establish a national mission-sending society. Price subsequently secured the encouragement of his friend Cardinal Gibbons and the apostolic delegate, Archbishop Diomede Falconio; he also interceded with Archbishop William O'Connell of Boston, onetime classmate of Price at St. Charles Seminary, for the release of Walsh for the new work. It was Price who then visited many bishops to explain the project and was on hand in Washington when it was approved at the annual meeting of the archbishops (April 27, 1911). Price and Walsh together proceeded to Rome where they received formal authorization for the new society from the Congregation for the Propagation of the Faith (June 29, 1911).

Before leaving Europe, Price made two visits to Lourdes. It was at this time that his devotion to the Virgin Mary became profoundly linked with that of Bernadette Soubirous. He was drawn to a sense of mystical union with Christ through Mary and Bernadette, a union he later celebrated at the tomb of Bernadette in Nevers and which he commemorated on a silver ring which he wore until his death. The depth of this relationship is documented in the daily letters that he addressed to Mary, 3,087 of which have been preserved.

Price was disappointed that his North Carolina project for home missions was not to be incorporated into Maryknoll; he also felt the new society should include the Philippines and Latin America among its mission fields. At that time, however, Walsh judged that Maryknoll should focus on overseas missions under the jurisdiction of the Congregation for the Propagation of the Faith. This difference nearly resulted in Price's withdrawal from Maryknoll to establish another society in 1914 and again in 1916. In the end, however, he continued to work with Walsh and committed himself in the early years to seeking support for Maryknoll by visiting parishes especially in the East and Midwest. When not on the road, he provided spiritual direction and conferences to the seminarians at Maryknoll Seminary.

In 1918 Price accepted from Walsh appointment as superior of the first group of Maryknoll missioners assigned to work in Yeungkong, China. He immediately developed a great affection for the Chinese: "The more I see of the Chinese, the more I love them," he wrote. Price's ministry in China was, however, cut short by illness. Following surgery for an infected appendix, he died at St. Paul's Hospital in Hong Kong, September 12, 1919. His tomb is beside that of Bishop James A. Walsh in the crypt of the Society Chapel at Maryknoll, New York.

See also MARYKNOLL.

Murrett, John C., M.M. *Tar Heel Apostle: Thomas Frederick Price Cofounder of Maryknoll.* New York: Longmans, Green, & Co., 1944.

Seddon, John T. "The Spirituality of the Reverend Thomas Frederick Price, M.M." Ph.D. dissertation, Fordham University, 1989.

Sheridan, Robert E., M.M. *The Founders of Maryknoll: Historical Reflections.* Maryknoll, 1981.

WILLIAM D. McCARTHY, M.M.

PROHIBITION AND CATHOLICS

Between 1865 and 1919, Americans were confronted by moral and social reformers who attempted to prohibit the sale and consumption of alcohol. While the National Prohibition Party was formed in 1869, the Women's Christian Temperance Union and the Anti-Saloon League were established by 1893. These groups were fighting what they considered to be the major source of immorality, criminality, and indolence in American society. They believed, according to their social gospel, that society would go through a moral regeneration if the evil of drink were excised. They were particularly hopeful about transforming communities such as San Francisco and New York, where in 1900 there existed one saloon for every two hundred residents. Success in this campaign to create a "Dry America" first came on the state level when by 1914 one half of the country's population resided in Prohibition territory. The final victory came when World War I's demands for grain and other foodstuffs as well as its spirit of self-sacrifice brought Americans to the altar of Prohibition, with the ratification of the Eighteenth Amendment in 1919, and the congressional passage of its legislative counterpart, the Volstead Act.

Catholic participation in this crusade against liquor took two forms: moral persuasion and prohibitory legislation. Leaders of the Church promoted this campaign for a "Dry America" in an attempt to help Catholics overcome second-class citizenship status and to become accepted middle-class Americans. Catholic respectability and social acceptance would only come with total abstinence along with hard work. In 1872 and 1903 respectively, the Catholic Total Abstinence Union of America and the Priests' Total Abstinence League were established. By 1919 the Catholic Prohibition League of America and the Catholic Clergy Prohibition League of America existed in order to organize Catholics to campaign for the Eighteenth Amendment. Fr. John J. Curran, Fr. George Zucker, Bishop John Lancaster Spalding, and Montana Senator Thomas J. Walsh were some of the prominent Catholic leaders in this assault on "Wet America." The Catholic clergy also played a prominent role in the Anti-Saloon League by regularly providing a priest to serve as vice president. Perhaps the most famous cleric to hold this position between 1896 and 1901 was Archbishop John Ireland. Lastly, Catholic children at parochial schools were admonished by nuns about the dangers of drink and were encouraged to take the teetotaler pledge.

Most Catholics, nonetheless, ignored the calls of abstinence and opposed Prohibition. Prohibition was especially troubling because of the use of government to coerce such behavior and because the movement's leaders seemed to espouse intolerant Puritanism. Most Catholics thought such a decision not to drink should be made by the individual voluntarily. A large number of Catholic immigrants also perceived Prohibition as a direct attack upon their cultural traditions brought from the old country which usually saw drinking as both a social and cultural tradition and not as a moral issue. Catholic working men and women, of course, resented this attack on their local saloons and discerned it as an attempt by the middle class to impose its values upon them. Al Smith, himself, a Catholic, urban-ethnic of the working class who was "wet," ran as the Democratic candidate for the presidency in 1928. His defiance of Prohibition was one factor that helped to explain his loss to Herbert Hoover by a margin of nearly six million votes. Catholic veterans of World War I were as defiant as Smith; they found solace in the bottle during the war and were not about to embrace Prohibition after Armistice Day. Even some Catholic Church leaders spoke out against Prohibition. Cardinal James Gibbons thought that the Prohibition law was essentially hypocritical and ineffectual in thought and implementation. Fr. John Ryan came to the same conclusion about the inability of government to enforce Prohibition toward the end of the 1920s.

Ryan was correct in his observations. The Prohibition amendment had failed miserably. Drinking did not cease in the 1920s. The illicit liquor traffic controlled by the criminal element kept everyone very wet, and the saloon was replaced by the speakeasies as a gathering place for those men and women who drank. Because of this profuse consumption of alcohol, the beginning of the depression, and the election of Franklin Delano Roosevelt to the presidency, Prohibition was repealed. In the final analysis, Catholic historian James Hennesey appropriately concluded the following about American Catholics and Prohibition: "Except in a negative sense, Prohibition was never a Catholic issue."

See also SMITH, ALFRED EMANUEL.

Bland, Joan. *Hibernian Crusade: The Story of the Catholic Total Abstinence Union of America.* Washington, 1951.

Hennesey, James. *American Catholics.* Oxford, 1981.

Ryan, John. *Questions of the Day.* Reprint 1931; Freeport, 1967.

Timberlake, James H. *Prohibition and the Progressive Movement.* New York, 1970.

TIMOTHY J. SARBAUGH

PROPAGATION OF THE FAITH, SOCIETY FOR THE

The *New Catholic Encyclopedia* contains two articles on the Propagation of the Faith with different subtitles: a Congregation and a Society. The first, created in 1622 as the Sacred Congregation of the Propaganda Fide, is now known as the Congregation for the Evangelization of Peoples. It oversees four missionary associations including since May 3, 1922, the Society for the Propagation of the Faith.

Background

In 1818, Pauline Jaricot, later officially designated as the founder of the society in 1881, began collecting money in Lyons for her brother and his friends who were missionaries in Asia. Volunteers formed groups of ten associates, each willing to give one French *sou* per week and to find ten more members who were willing to keep looking for new associates.

There was no formal organization until Bishop Louis William DuBourg sent Angelo Inglesi, a man whom he trusted too much, to visit devoted friends of his in Lyons, the Petits, who had already sent some money to Louisiana. The minutes of the first five meetings, held in Fr. Inglesi's home beginning on May 3, 1822, for a small group of men who were willing to form an association of pious people motivated as he was, make it clear that DuBourg's envoy really established the first organization. The funds were collected as Pauline's associates had done, the society was under the control of lay directors, and it was decided that the sums would be divided equally for Asia, Louisiana, and "Kentuki."

During the next ten years, the United States received 42 percent of the society's total allocation. In all, more than $7,000,000 had been given to the United States by 1861. While giving money to the dioceses, the society also asked them to contribute for others. In 1884 the Third Plenary Council of Baltimore endorsed Cardinal Gibbons' suggestion for a National Organization of the Society of the Propagation of the Faith. It became a reality in 1897 with Henry Granjon as the first national director; he was soon followed by Joseph Freri, who remained until the creation of the Pontifical Society on May 3, 1922. The American branch had already given many times more than the amount that it had received.

More important than the financial help given by the society is the historical value of the thousands of letters sent by the bishops asking for assistance, who presented their needs, their problems, and their hopes. Some of these documents have been published in the *Annals* of the society, but even after the studies of Fr. Edward Hickey in 1922 and the attempts made by three different groups to microfilm them in the 1950s, they were not always available.

From 1987 to 1992, all documents from the archives in Paris and Lyons were photocopied in triplicate and sent to the United States, to the Pontificia Università Urbaniana in Rome, and to the Lyons archives where the entire collection is now housed. A total of 83 dioceses appear in 163 files from Paris and 99 files from Lyons.

The true importance of these documents might be summarized in the words of the Rettore Magnifico of the Pontificia Università Urbaniana: "These documents are of enormous richness. They concern the foundation and the development of the Church in the United States . . . there will be scholars, as well as students in our various Roman universities, who will find here the beginnings of exciting historical research."

Hickey, Edward J. *The Society for the Propagation of the Faith: Its Foundation, Organization and Success, 1822–1922*. Washington, D.C., 1922.

Jammes, Jean-Marie. "Correspondence from the United States Dioceses in the Propagation of the Faith Archives in Paris and Lyon." *Catholic Historical Review* 75 (2) (April 1989) 264–67.

JEAN-MARIE JAMMES

PROVIDENCE COLLEGE

Providence College is a coeducational, four-year, primarily undergraduate college of liberal arts and science. Its main objective is the intellectual development of its students through the disciplines of the sciences and humanities, equipping them to become productive and responsible citizens of a democratic society.

Providence College was established in 1917 under an Act of Incorporation approved by the General Assembly of the State of Rhode Island. Founded by the Order of Preachers of the Province of St. Joseph, more commonly known as the Dominicans, a seven-hundred-year-old Catholic teaching order, Providence College continues to be the only institution of higher education in North America conducted by Dominican friars under the auspices of the Dominican Order.

The college has continued to grow, and presently (1997) boasts an enrollment of approximately 3,600 full-time undergraduates, 1,500 School of Continuing Education students, and 780 graduate students. More than 31,000 graduates have left to make lasting contributions to society.

See also CATHOLIC UNIVERSITIES AND COLLEGES.

PROVINCIAL AND PLENARY COUNCILS OF BALTIMORE

The oldest consistent witness to collegial tradition in the Catholic Church in the United States of America is the Provincial and Plenary Councils (1829–84). Bishop John Carroll had convened a synod of his nascent Diocese of Baltimore in 1791. Some twenty-two priests attended. In November of 1810 the archbishop met for two weeks with his coadjutor and three of his suffragans. Serious plans were in motion for a provincial council in 1812, but John Carroll's declining health and the looming war with England caused its cancellation.

It remained for the Irish-born John England, bishop of Charleston, to father the provincial council phenomenon. There was stern opposition from his metropolitan archbishop, Ambrose Maréchal, S.S., of Baltimore. After Maréchal's death, his protégé, James Whitefield, succeeded him as archbishop. He lacked the stomach for battle and acceded to the wishes of Bishop England.

The Provincial Councils

The First Provincial Council of Baltimore was convened at Benjamin Latrobe's recently completed Cathedral of the Assumption on October 3, 1829. Twenty-two bishops, religious superiors, and theologians attended the sessions. Three lawyers including the future chief justice, Roger Taney, were invited to attend certain sessions. Territorial jurisdiction of the various dioceses occupied much of the deliberations. A rather complex system of nominating bishops for vacancies was also established. Every bishop of the province was to compose a list of worthy candidates for a see that became vacant. It was made clear that these were only recommendations for appointment. The pastoral letter that came out of the Second Provincial Council was of excellent quality. Note was made of the increasingly anti-Catholic spirit of the day, goaded by "some of the conductors of the press."

The Third Provincial Council met in the spring of 1837, opening on April 16, 1837. It was a particularly harmonious meeting, presided over by the new archbishop of Baltimore, Samuel Eccleston, S.S. This was in contrast to American society at that time which was showing a marked hostility toward Catholicism. Over thirty participants, bishops, religious superiors, and theologians drafted legislation requesting new dioceses at Dubuque, Nashville, Natchez, and western Pennsylvania. Legislation was issued requiring the exclusive use of the Roman Ritual. An English ceremonial composed by Joseph Rosati, C.M., bishop of St. Louis, was also approved. To mark the end of the council, eight of the bishops traveled fifty miles west to consecrate the impressive Jesuit Church of St. John the Evangelist in Frederick, Maryland. The council's pastoral letter was a strong appeal for the defense of Roman Catholicism in the face of the current nativist bigotry.

By 1840 the Catholic population in the United States was estimated at one million. On May 17 of that year, American bishops with their theologians and the superiors of the major religious orders gathered for the Fourth Provincial Council. This would prove to be Bishop John England's last council, as death would claim him in 1842. This council's legislation forbade Catholic participation in secret societies and warned against mixed marriages. The pastoral letter again denounced the libels against Catholics current in the country. Interestingly, Catholics were reminded of their serious duty to vote in all elections. It was made very clear, however, that the Church was not to enter partisan politics.

The Archdiocese of Baltimore had fifteen suffragan dioceses in 1843 when the Fifth Provincial Council met. The prelates and theologians began their meeting on May 13, 1843, at the archbishop's house behind the Cathedral of the Assumption. One of their first concerns was the establishment of new dioceses at Chicago, Hartford, Little Rock, Milwaukee, Pittsburgh, and a vicariate apostolic for Oregon. The eleven decrees of the council dealt with the holding of church property, annual parochial reports, the required use of the confessional, and penalties for marriage after civil divorce. The pastoral letter following this council was the briefest of all coming from the seven provincial councils. It made interesting note of the Oxford Movement, the Liberian Mission, and the Total Abstinence Crusade.

By 1846 the Catholic Church in the United States was putting out some fourteen periodicals on a weekly or monthly basis. Despite some harrowing confrontations with nativist violence, the Church grew stronger and more confident. Twenty-three bishops joined Archbishop Samuel Eccleston on May 9, 1846, to open the Sixth Provincial Council. Much of the council's work was routine. The sole exception was the placing of the United States under the patronage of the Immaculate Conception. This was not yet a defined dogma of the Church universal, and this activity of the American bishops won great favor in Rome. Only four decrees were enacted, but this council is perhaps the best remembered of the seven provincial meetings because of the alliance of the Church in the United States with strong Marian patronage.

In a sense, the Seventh Provincial Council, convened in Baltimore on May 5, 1849, could have been the First Plenary Council. In July of 1846 Pius IX had created the Archdiocese of Oregon City with suffragans both in the United States and Canada. In July of 1847 St. Louis had been raised to the archepiscopal rank. The question of St. Louis' suffragan dioceses was to be left to the next provincial council. The Seventh Provincial Council requested that additional archdioceses be erected at Cincinnati, New Orleans, and New York. The assembled bishops also petitioned the Holy See that Baltimore be recognized as the primatial see in the United States with respective rights and privileges. The last request was repeated twice again but never granted. The council decreed that an annual collection be taken up in every parish for the Holy Father, then in exile. Requests were passed for new dioceses at St. Paul and Wheeling, and for new vicariates apostolic in the Indian Territory and New Mexico.

First Plenary Council, 1852

Something of a new era began with the opening of the First Plenary Council of Baltimore on May 7, 1852. Hundreds of priests joined the procession of archbishops and twenty-four bishops entering the Baltimore Cathedral for the solemn Mass that opened the council. The learned Francis Patrick Kenrick, newly appointed archbishop of Baltimore, had been named apostolic delegate for the council. Appropriately, the future St. John Nepomucene Neumann served on the Committee for the Education of Catholic Youth.

The twenty-five decrees that came out of this First Plenary Council were geared toward consolidating the various legislation that had come from the provincial councils. There was an emphasis on unity in conscious counterpoint to the mainline Protestant Churches that were breaking up along sectional lines. This was done, sadly, at the cost of silence over the slavery question.

Banns of marriage were to be called in all parishes, every pastor was to see to the catechetical instruction of the parish children, where possible Catholic schools were to be established, and religious rights of soldiers and sailors were to be sought. All bishops were encouraged to set up boards of consultors to meet monthly. Each diocese was to have a seminary. If poverty made this impossible, each metropolitan province was to have a seminary. Even the perennial problems of trusteeism and wandering priests were treated. The Holy See approved all the decrees, but in a private communication to Archbishop Francis Patrick Kenrick warned against even the appearance of an American National Church.

Second Plenary Council, 1866

It is hard to exaggerate the damage done to a society by civil war. It would take decades for the nation and the Catholic Church to recover from the American Civil War. The Second Plenary Council of Baltimore was convened to address these problems and meet the challenges of a growing yet wounded Church. Archbishop Kenrick had died in the summer of 1863, and so Rome appointed his successor, Martin John Spalding, as apostolic delegate to the council. This Second Plenary Council opened on October 2, 1866. Archbishop Spalding envisioned the council's work as compiling an American *corpus juris* in harmony with pertinent Roman legislation. Seven committees were formed including not only the bishops but over one hundred priests. Some 534 pieces of legislation grouped under fourteen titles were passed. Included were support for the temporal power of the papacy, decrees on clerical dress and occupations, sacramental regulations, rules for Mass stipends and Perpetual Mass Funds, and encouragement given for soldalities and confraternities.

Archbishop Spalding had hoped to launch plans for a Catholic University of America at the council, but the time was not ripe. More tragically, his appeal for the evangelization and spiritual care of the four million newly emancipated African Americans received a cool reception. Very few of his fellow bishops realized that this prime opportunity once ignored would never return. The closing ceremony and solemn Mass on October 21 was attended by President Andrew Johnson. The pastoral letter coming from the council urged cheerful obedience to Church authority. The entire proceedings had been altogether too Ultramontane for Archbishop Peter Richard Kenrick of St. Louis who pushed for a radical revision of the council's work just before its conclusion. His Gallican convictions were surely in the minority at this council. By 1884, however, there would be a sea change.

Third Plenary Council, 1884

The Third Plenary Council of Baltimore convened on November 9, 1884. The opening Mass was celebrated by Archbishop Peter Richard Kenrick. Although John Cardinal McCloskey was still archbishop of New York, he was of advanced years. Pope Leo XIII therefore appointed James Gibbons, archbishop of Baltimore, as apostolic delegate to the council. Gibbons had served in a minor capacity at the Second Plenary Council. It is indicative of the remarkable growth of the Church in the United States that in attendance at the Third Plenary Council were 14 archbishops, 57 bishops, 7 archabbots, and 31 religious superiors. In legislation, the Third Plenary Council followed the format instituted by the Second Plenary Council. Much work was done under section 11, *Ecclesiastical Persons*. At this time, many clerics had found themselves in conflict with the local bishop. Appeal to Rome was costly and beyond the scope of many. It was hoped that the council would facilitate some resolution. In reality, not much was done to resolve this at the council.

Many issues were addressed, however. Temperance societies were praised. The six standard holy days were appointed for the United States. The time had come for the establishment of a central Catholic university for the nation. Whenever possible, parochial schools were to be erected and parents were commanded to send their children there, though not under pain of sin. Only slightly more famous than the council's dramatic support for Catholic education was the commissioning of a common catechism

for the United States. Its parentage is not clear, but the Baltimore Catechism that emerged from the Third Plenary Council became the standard work for seventy-five years. The Baltimore Ritual, also a child of the Third Plenary Council, gained even wider usage, spreading through much of the English-speaking world. Some attention was given to the spiritual needs of African Americans and Native Americans. The Commission for Catholic Missions among the Colored People and the Indians was established as a permanent board by the council. An annual collection that continues today was mandated.

Although James Gibbons would find himself in the Americanist camp in the next decade, Rome was very pleased with his work at the Third Plenary Council. Propaganda recommended to the Scottish and Canadian hierarchies that they follow the model of Baltimore's Third Plenary Council. Archbishop Gibbons' masterful directing of the council was thought to be a major consideration in Rome's bestowing of the red hat on him.

No further plenary councils would be held. Regular meetings of the archbishops would take their place. Only in the wake of World War I with the establishment of the National Catholic War Council (which evolved into the National Catholic Welfare Conference) did such broad-based episcopal collegiality come into being again. In 1966 that collegiality would see a fuller flowering in the establishment of the National Conference of Catholic Bishops. The civil entity would be known as the United States Catholic Conference, Inc.

Fogarty, Gerald P., S.J. "Church Councils in the United States and American Legal Institutions." *Annuarium Historiae Conciliorum* 4 (1972) 83–105.

Guilday, Peter. *A History of the Councils of Baltimore, 1791–1884.* New York, 1932.

Hennesey, James, S.J. "The Baltimore Conciliar Tradition." *Annuarium Historiae Conciliorum* 3 (1971) 71–88.

———. "The Baltimore Council of 1866: An American Syllabus." *Records of the American Catholic Historical Society of Philadelphia* 76 (1965) 157–73.

MICHAEL J. ROACH

PUBLIC SCHOOLS AND AMERICAN CATHOLICS

American Catholics have been involved in the development of public education since the 1840s. Some Catholics were ardent supporters of public schools from their origins. But others—particularly the bishops—opposed the Protestant tone and later the sectarian content of public schooling. Little did the bishops realize, however, that the changes they demanded would make public schools increasingly popular with Catholic parents. By 1997, an estimated 80 percent of American Catholic children would enroll in public schools.

Catholics and the First Public Schools

Catholic dissatisfaction with public education in the middle decades of the nineteenth century was textual, catechetical, and cultural. The textual issue focused on which version of the Bible would be used to teach Catholic children. Public school officials were insulted that Catholics would not accept the King James Bible and resisted any accommodation with Catholic requests to use the Douay version.

A second disagreement was catechetical. Public school officials insisted that reading the Bible without note or comment was nonsectarian. Catholic leaders disagreed and charged that Bible reading without guidance was a Protestant practice and therefore unacceptable for the education of Catholic children.

But the major Catholic dissatisfaction with public education in the nineteenth century was cultural. Catholic bishops and prominent laypeople accused public school officials of a subtle campaign to win the allegiance of Catholic children and at the same time denigrate the Catholic Church and ethnic cultures. The end result, noted Catholic leaders, was a generational conflict between these "Americanized" children and their immigrant parents.

Not surprisingly, Catholic leaders regularly spoke out on the "evils" of public education. Beginning in 1829, the bishops published periodic pastoral letters that warned Catholic parents about the dangers of public schooling. Catholic novelists and editors dramatized the negative impact of public education on Catholic children. But, in spite of these exhortations, large numbers of Catholic parents continued to send their children to public schools because parish schools were either unacceptable or unavailable. For many Catholic parents, the choice was between public school or no school at all.

Tax-Supported Parish Schools

For some Catholic families, public and parochial schools were one and the same. From 1831 to 1916, Catholics in at least twenty-one communities in fourteen states bridged the gap between parochial and public school education. The specific terms of the agreements varied slightly; but in almost every community where the experiment took place, the school board leased a building from a local parish for a small sum and paid all the expenses of running the school. The teachers were selected jointly by the school board and the local pastor. The board regulated the curriculum, selected the schoolbooks, and conducted periodic examinations, but the local pastor had the right to insure that all elements of the curriculum were acceptable to the Church. Most important, however, was the fact that the school day at these tax-supported parish schools was the same as at any public school. No religious instruction was conducted until after classes were dismissed.

These schools were experimental, and in most communities the experiments were short-lived. But in three communities—Lowell, Massachusetts, from 1831 to 1852; Savannah, Georgia, from 1870 to 1916; and Poughkeepsie, New York, from 1873 to 1898—tax-supported parish schools educated several generations of Catholic children. Even though the total number was small, the tax-supported parish school was an important grassroots effort to resolve outstanding differences that separated many Catholics from public education.

The Appeal of Public Education

During the 1870s and 1880s, Catholic leaders mounted a campaign to pressure Catholic parents to abandon public schools. The campaign was led by James A. McMaster, a Catholic convert and editor of *The Freeman's Journal* of New York. In February 1874, McMaster sent a formal memorandum to the Vatican asking if Catholic parents could send their children to public schools. In an effort to influence the answer, he sent along several articles on the "evils" of public education in the United States.

The Vatican responded quickly by sending a formal inquiry to the archbishops of the United States regarding public education. Specifically, the Vatican wanted to know why some Catholic parents sent their children to public schools. Was there an effective way to reverse this trend? Why did some Catholics advocate the denial of the sacraments to parents who sent their children to public schools?

The archbishops answered by noting that most public schools were not opposed to Catholicism, "but are proudly secular." The archbishops further argued against denying the sacraments to Catholic parents with children in public schools. Many rural communities had no Catholic schools, and in many large cities, parish schools were inferior to public schools. Through a formal "instruction," the Vatican called on all American bishops to do everything in their power to prevent Catholic children from attending public schools. The bishops agreed in principle, yet few had the economic resources to provide a desk in a parish school for every Catholic child in their diocese. It was not possible for every Catholic child to attend a Catholic school and the "instruction" was largely ignored.

The Public/Parochial School Controversy

The bishops never gave up the hope that every Catholic child would attend a Catholic school. In 1884, when they met in plenary council in Baltimore, they articulated this hope. "No parish is complete," they wrote, "until it has schools adequate to meet the needs of its children." They further noted that "all Catholic parents are bound to send their children to parochial schools" unless they "otherwise provided for their Christian education." But as with the Vatican instruction, these education decrees had little impact and Catholic parents continued to send their children to public schools in record numbers.

Archbishop John Ireland of St. Paul had his own plan in mind when he addressed the National Education Association in 1890. Quite simply, he proposed the merger of the public and parochial school systems. "I would have all schools for the children of the people be state schools," he said.

Ireland's speech—and his plan—caused havoc within the American Church. Attacked by conservatives, Ireland defended himself and the public schools. More important, he enlisted the support of Cardinal James Gibbons of Baltimore, who wrote to the Vatican on Ireland's behalf. Pope Leo XIII sent Archbishop Francesco Satolli to resolve the matter and Satolli suggested a compromise that infuriated the conservatives. The controversy died with bitter feelings on both sides as did Ireland's efforts to find a Catholic compromise with public education. What did not vary was the continued support of public schools by many Catholic families.

Catholic Views of Progressive Education

Given the rapid changes in the American economy, the nation's leaders argued that the substance of formal schooling needed to be more relevant to the promise and the problems of an increasingly urban and industrial society in the twentieth century. The progressive education movement, as fostered by famed educator John Dewey, was a formal effort to respond to these concerns.

But Catholic leaders were suspicious of these new educational ideas—ideas that would make the public school curriculum increasingly secular and materialistic. What good was it for a Catholic child to gain a good job but lose his or her soul? Many conservative educators attacked Dewey and his progressive ideas not only from the pulpit, but also at the annual meetings of the National Catholic Educational Association.

This did not mean that Catholic educators completely rejected progressive ideas. In fact, many Catholic educators looked for ways to adapt elements of the public school curriculum for their own purpose. Their goal was to make parish schools both Catholic and progressive. These educators realized that Catholic parents would want the best secular and religious education for their children. They should not be forced to choose one or the other. Progressive educational ideas gradually and quietly found their way into the parish school curriculum by 1940.

Public and Parochial Education and the Courts

What is the proper relationship between Church, state, and school under the Constitution? This question was at the center of a number of court debates in the decades from 1920 to 1950. In the 1920s, the federal courts decreed that the states could regulate parochial school education by establishing reasonable standards, but could not abolish these institutions. The court later went so far as to say that the state could provide free schoolbooks to children attending parochial schools.

The 1930s and 1940s were decades of crisis in the United States and throughout the world. Ten years of economic depression followed by a decade of world war and international tension made conflicts over education seem insignificant. Compromise became possible, even logical. Thus by the mid-1930s, with closure imminent, nearly 350 parochial schools across the country received public funds to keep their doors open.

Recalling the tax-supported parish schools of old, local school boards took over the former parish schools on an emergency basis and employed members of Catholic religious orders to teach the children assigned to the new "public" schools. In most ways the new schools were conducted exactly like other public schools; the course of study and school books were the same, and all teachers, including the nuns, were state certified.

There were a few differences, however. Pastors were permitted to use the schools for religious instruction before and after the school day; there was no prohibition of religious pictures or statues; and the women religious who taught in these schools were permitted to wear their habits. It is doubtful that the young students were even aware that they were attending tax-supported schools.

The public partnerships with Catholic education were local responses to economic crisis. Few public officials or citizens opposed these short-term, temporary plans until a few communities attempted to make these arrangements permanent.

Setting Limits for Public Aid to Education

In 1947, after a century of debate and experimentation, the Supreme Court decided to clearly define the constitutional relationship between Church, state, and school. In *Everson v. Board of Education,* the Court allowed state governments to provide bus transportation to parochial school students, but little else. The Court broke new ground with a test to be applied to all future programs of public aid to parish schools, and had every expectation that the matter was closed.

Two other Supreme Court decisions defined the limits of state cooperation in the religious education of public school students. In 1948 the Court ruled that it was unconstitutional for school boards to allow local clergy to use public school classrooms to offer religious education to children who had their parents permission to attend such classes. But four years later the Court allowed school districts to release their students during the school day to attend religious education classes in local church buildings.

"We are a religious people," noted the Court, "whose institutions presume a Supreme Being."

By the mid-1950s, the relationships between Church, state, and school were clear. School districts were free to provide limited aid such as school books and transportation to parish school students and public school students could be released from school to attend religious education classes. But that was all. The justices hoped they had decided this thorny matter once and for all.

John F. Kennedy and Public Education

Beginning in the middle of the 1950s and culminating in the election of John F. Kennedy as president in 1960, a climate of mutual respect grew in both the Catholic and public school communities. Thus the stage was set for a renewed discussion of federal aid for public education, a part of the Kennedy administration's legislative proposals.

The campaign was rejoined a month after Kennedy was inaugurated in January of 1961. The President proposed a program of financial aid to public schools, but made mention of parochial schools only to exclude them from the program. It was a position that disappointed the American Catholic community coming as it did from the nation's first Catholic president.

Catholics, who made up 25 percent of nation's population, seemed united in their opposition to the bill.

The congressional hearings were tense and opened old wounds. As is often the case in legislative conflict, Congress looked for a compromise but could not find one. As the education bills moved through the appropriate committees, public opinion shifted against any federal aid to either public or private schools. By the summer the Kennedy education aid package was "as dead as slavery," in the words of one veteran congressman.

Lyndon B. Johnson and Parochial Education

It would take the exceptional legislative skills of Lyndon B. Johnson to achieve any measure of federal aid for education. What assured victory for the Elementary and Secondary Education Act of 1965 was the unprecedented support for the bill by education groups that had previously opposed specific elements of the Kennedy legislation. Knowing that Johnson had the votes to pass any bill he wanted, many groups feared that they would be shut out of the congressional debate if they opposed all assistance.

Thus public and parochial education advocates joined together to support a program that would be administered by the public schools for the benefit of all children including those enrolled in parochial schools. It was a historic achievement. For the first time in American history, poor children received federal aid for their education. It also is the first time that such aid was provided to parochial school students. It remains an unprecedented piece of legislation.

Catholics, Public Schools, and a New Century

Catholic parochial school enrollments reached a peak in 1965 when about 12 percent of all the children attending the nation's schools were enrolled in parochial schools. Yet even at this level of enrollment, a majority of Catholic children attended public schools. It was a harbinger of a further Catholic shift to public schools.

Catholic parents have been attracted to public schools because of the quality of their facilities, teachers, and course of instruction. The principal concern of most parents—Catholic as well as non-Catholic—is the future careers and economic security of their children. Unlike their parents and grandparents, contemporary Catholic parents have not valued the spiritual development of their children as highly as they have their career development.

But the most powerful reason for the current generation of Catholic parents abandoning parish schools is that there is no social and denominational pressure to support these institutions. Their grandparents and parents saw parochial schools as a form of protection and security for their children against a frequently anti-Catholic society. In an increasingly ecumenical world, discrimination against Catholics is a distant memory. For many contemporary Catholics, parochial schools seem unnecessary.

When Catholic leaders first established parish schools—especially in the century between 1830 and 1930—their stated goal was to serve both their faith and their nation. By all accounts and measures, parish schools did an extraordinary job of meeting those stated goals. But by 1997, many questioned the relevance of these schools to the larger Catholic community. Catholics had, for the most part, embraced public education.

See also CATHOLIC EDUCATION, PAROCHIAL.

Buetow, Harold A. *Of Singular Benefit: The Story of U.S. Catholic Education.* New York: Macmillan, 1970.

Dolan, Jay P. *The American Catholic Experience: From Colonial Times to the Present.* Garden City, N.Y.: Doubleday, 1985.

Greeley, Andrew M., William C. McCready, and Kathleen McCourt. *Catholic Schools in a Declining Church.* Kansas City, Mo.: Sheed and Ward, 1976.

Morgan, Richard E. *The Supreme Court and Religion.* New York: Free Press/Macmillan, 1972.

Walch, Timothy. *Parish School: American Catholic Parochial Education from Colonial Times to the Present.* New York: Crossroad/Herder, 1996.

TIMOTHY WALCH

PUERTO RICO, CATHOLIC CHURCH IN

The presence of the Catholic Church in Puerto Rico dates back to the end of the fifteenth century when Christopher Columbus discovered the island on his second voyage.

On November 19, 1493, he and his crew landed in Borikén, the native name of the island, and renamed it San Juan Bautista (St. John the Baptist). The island was claimed in the name of the Castilian Crown and the Catholic Church. But some years would pass before a systematic occupation, conquest ("pacification," as it came to be called), and evangelization of the island would occur.

The first attempt at colonization took place in 1505, but only a couple of animals were brought. Then, in 1508, Don Juan Ponce de León, conqueror of Higüey, in Hispaniola, became interested and asked permission to colonize Borikén. After exploring the place, one of the first things he requested was friars to evangelize the natives and keep alive the faith of the first European settlers. This was conceded and a small community of Franciscans established two convents, one in Caparra, the island's first city, and another on the western side of the island. It seems that the latter community suffered martyrdom at the hands of the native inhabitants. The other community in Caparra lasted only a short while longer.

The first dioceses in the new colonies were established by Rome in 1511 under the terms of the Royal Patronage (*patronato real*) which granted the crown the right to interfere in religious affairs. The papal bull of Julius II erected the Dioceses of Santo Domingo and Concepción de la Vega in Hispaniola, and San Juan Bautista in Puerto Rico. Alonso Manso was the first bishop to set foot in the New World and take possession of his Diocese of St. John the Baptist. He was a man of letters, chaplain at the Royal Court, and rector of the University of Salamanca. Although he was accustomed to palace life, he soon found himself administering to the poorest diocese he could imagine with very few attending services. During these first years the colony was very poor and little was allotted for Church needs. Under these circumstances, Manso went to Spain to look for more economic aid. He returned to his see in 1519 where he remained until his death in 1539. Upon his return from Spain, Alonso Manso, along with Pedro de Córdova, vice provincial of the Dominican friars, was named Inquisitor General of the Indies.

Conditions where the first city was established were not good. Soon the settlers found that Caparra was not the best place to live. It was decided to move to an adjacent small island that was healthier. The settlers finally moved to Puerto Rico (name given to the capital during these first decades) in 1521. At this time the bishop started building the cathedral. To assist him in the administration of the diocese and in the liturgy, a chapter of canons was established. This chapter, along with the secular clergy and the Dominican friars who came in 1522, were the only personnel the bishop could count for the evangelization of the flock.

When Manso returned in 1519, the crown extended the territory of the diocese to include all the Windward Is-

lands of the Lesser Antilles from Santa Cruz to Dominica. Again, in 1541 the islands of Margarita and Cubagua were added. Finally, in 1588 the diocese was further extended to embrace the island of Trinidad, and that tract of mainland in Venezuela which comprises Cumana and the region between the Amazon and the Upper Orinoco. Of course, this addition of territories (*anejos* as they were called) increased the bishop's pastoral burden.

Religious Orders

The Franciscans and the Dominicans were the first religious orders to come to the island. However, the sons of St. Francis left shortly and only the Dominicans remained to evangelize and teach. They returned in 1634 to stay and help in the education and the care of souls, especially of the poor people of the city of San Juan.

The first convent was established due to the desire of some hidalgo families to have a convent where girls could spend the rest of their lives, safe from the dangers of the world. This is how the foundation of a cloistered convent was born. The project was made possible by a rich widow, Dona Ana de Lanzós, who donated her inheritance. She wanted to spend her last days as a cloistered nun. After getting the approval from Rome, the Convent of San José of the Carmelite nuns was founded in 1651. The foundation of this convent solved a social problem in the colony.

In the second half of the nineteenth century educational and social needs required additional prepared personnel. In 1863 Bishop Benigno Carrion, O.F.M. Cap., invited to the island the Daughters of Charity of St. Vincent de Paul. The Religious of the Sacred Heart came in 1880 to take care of the education of well-to-do girls. The Servants of Mary, invited in 1887, specialized in the work with sick people in their own homes. Four years later the Little Sisters of the Poor arrived to establish homes for the care of the poor and homeless elderly.

The presence of communities of religious men also increased during the nineteenth century. Bishop Benigno Carrion invited the Jesuits to the island in 1858 to take care of the education of young men. Also, in 1895, the Piarist Fathers were called for the same purpose. In 1896 came the Augustinian friars.

Church Development During the Spanish Colonial Period

Of the three synods that apparently took place during this period, we have documentary evidence for only one of them, the one convoked by Bishop-Friar Damián López de Haro in 1645. This synod is very important for its description of Church work. With some changes, it established the norms for the Church until the synod of 1917.

López de Haro's synod is interesting on the subject of the indigenous peoples. Although none remained in Puerto

Rico by that time, the other territories *(anejos),* which were part of the diocese until 1791, needed pastoral norms for guidance of the various tribes within their local jurisdictions.

At the end of the eighteenth and during the nineteenth century, Puerto Rico's economic condition improved. Commercial improvements transformed the island into an important producer and exporter of sugar, coffee, and tobacco. Furthermore, the colony's importance was recognized by the Spanish crown.

The Church also benefited from this progress and many pastoral projects were developed. The documentation for this period shows bishops making pastoral visits from one side of the island to the other. The *anejos* were split from the diocese in 1791. Concentrating on pastoral needs of the island's faithful, and with more funds in their coffers, the prelates were able to construct better churches and they established new parishes to better facilitate the presence of the Church among the people.

This was a time when the pastoral need of religious instruction, as witnessed in the pastoral visits of bishops, led to the publication of catechisms. They were important since the fundamentals of the faith were taught not only to the children, but also to the adults. It is significant that these catechisms were adapted to the particular needs of the Puerto Rican Catholics of the time.

Nevertheless, many pastoral problems remained, even during this period of economic and religious development. Bishops did not have enough personnel. Roads were not good and it was hazardous for the faithful to attend even the closest church. The towns were deserted most of the time since practically everyone, rich or poor, went to the mountains to work the fields. This absence of priests and the inability of the people to attend church were the cause of pastoral problems. Many couples lived together without their union being blessed by the Church. Children were not baptized, or instructed in the fundamentals of faith. Social ills included drunkenness and gambling, superstition and self-indulgence.

This situation gives us a picture of the difficult task faced by the bishops and priests. Further, there was the ever-present tension between the Church and the local civil administration. In many instances the bishop and the governor of the island were at odds. One of the quarrels best remembered in the history of the island occurred during the time of the first and only Puerto Rican bishop during the Spanish government.

He was Bishop Juan Alejo Arizmendi y de la Torre, a native of San Juan. He was bishop from 1803 to 1814. Spain was invaded by Napoleon in 1808. The emperor installed his brother José as king of Spain, keeping the true king, Ferdinand VI, as his guest in Paris. As soon as these events took place a loyal government was formed in Cádiz and the Cortes gathered there to establish a new consti-

tution. In the meantime, the Latin American colonies gave their support to Ferdinand, but shortly thereafter revolts began against Spain. Arizmendi had studied in Venezuela where he had many friends and connections. Venezuela was a center of conspiracy. Governor Salvador Melendez was very suspicious of any ties with that country, which was enough to make the bishop's position very uncomfortable. He was falsely accused by the governor of being disloyal to the mother country, although the evidence indicates he was loyal to both Spain and King Ferdinand. However, the governor gave him a very hard time, although he was unable to prove any of his accusations. After Arizmendi died, no other Puerto Rican was named as bishop of the island during the Spanish administration.

1898: Americans Arrive, Effect on the Church

On the July 25, 1898, American troops landed in Puerto Rico, almost at the close of the Spanish-Cuban-American War. This move was made in order to act before Spain surrendered, for then Puerto Rico would have been lost to the Americans. At this point the see of San Juan was vacant. The bishop who had been named in 1897, Don Francisco J. Valdés, O.S.A., had declined the see in view of the outbreak of the war.

As soon as Spain surrendered and signed the Treaty of Paris of 1898, the relations between Church and state that existed between Spain's colonies and Rome were severed. Under the American Constitution there was no place for such a status. That complicated things for the local church. For the first time in four centuries the Church had no ties with the civil administration and the areas of education, health, marriage, and even cemeteries were no longer controlled by Church authorities. This brought friction at the beginning between the two spheres of influence.

To make matters worse for the Church, many priests left for Spain at the war's outset, and those who remained were left without income. This was due to the fact that the wages for the religious personnel had been paid by the Spanish crown. Besides, after the war, the American administration, together with some of the municipalities, claimed that some properties which were in the hands of the Church belonged to them. They said that since they were in the hands of the Spanish government at the time of the invasion, they belonged now to the new masters, or to the people of Puerto Rico.

Circumstances caused much trouble and confusion for the Church. To alleviate problems Rome took two important steps. The Vatican named Archbishop Placide Chapelle of Louisiana as new apostolic delegate for Cuba and Puerto Rico. He was present, as an observer, at the Treaty of Paris negotiations in 1898 to protect the Church's interests. He was to be instrumental in the finding of a satisfactory solution for the Church's claims. The second step was the nomination of an American bishop to the see of Puerto Rico. A secretary of Archbishop Chapelle, Bishop James Humbert Blenk, S.M., was named bishop of the ancient see of San Juan in 1899.

An American bishop could more easily facilitate the sorting out of all the difficulties the Church was facing. Bishop Blenk was an American, not by birth, but by heart. He was born in Bavaria and was brought to the United States by his parents, who were Protestants, when he was a little boy. Surrounded by a strong Catholic environment, he converted and was baptized when he was twelve years old. One of the first things he had to handle as the new bishop was a natural disaster that came to Puerto Rico in 1899. Hurricane San Ciriaco literally devastated the coffee and sugar plantations, leaving the economy in ruins. Lives were lost and property destroyed and Bishop Blenk now faced the more immediate need of traveling back to the United States to ask for support, knocking desperately at any door that was willing to offer assistance to the stricken island. When he returned to Puerto Rico, the American government named him coordinator of all the aid received for the victims of the hurricane.

It was Bishop Blenk who brought the Church's claims of her property rights before the island's courts. Also, facing personnel shortages, he invited different congregations of men and women to come to the island for missionary work.

His Protestant family background was a good preparation for someone who had to deal with the hostility of the different religious denominations that came to the island after 1898. At the end of the Spanish occupation, only one Protestant Church existed in Puerto Rico. The Anglican Church had established two churches, one in Ponce and another in Vieques in 1873 with the crown's permission, after a petition by Queen Victoria of England was granted.

When the Americans came, the doors were open for any denomination that wanted to come to the island. Soon hostility grew between Catholics and Protestants. The Commissioner of Education for many years was a Protestant. Nurses, teachers, officials, and civil administrators were Protestants, invited by the government, or sponsored by it, to come to work in the island to help Americanize the people.

In 1906 Blenk was named archbishop of New Orleans, and the vacant see of Puerto Rico was filled by Bishop William Ambrose Jones, O.S.A. When the new bishop arrived on the island he found the diocese, and the country in general, in very poor condition. Being a man of action and a good administrator, Jones was instrumental in changing drastically the old Spanish Church he found into a Church modeled after the American Catholic pattern. One of the things he did along this line was to eliminate the chapter of canons, an institution the American Church never developed. In 1917 the bishop called a synod. Through the legislation enacted in this ecclesiastical meeting the Puerto Rican Catholic Church broke its links with the Spanish past. Bishop Jones died on February 18, 1921.

Toward a Puerto Rican Church

At the time of the American occupation, Puerto Rico was part of the ecclesiastical province of Santiago de Cuba. On February 20, 1903, by the brief *Actum Praeclarae,* the diocese was severed from Santiago and made subject immediately to the Holy See. From that time on the Catholic Church on the island responded not to the American Church or any Church in the Western Hemisphere, but to the Vatican. In 1924, for the first time, the island was divided into two dioceses, the new one in Ponce, in the southern part of the island. Both were to be headed by American bishops.

In the 1960s the two sees of the island were occupied by Bishops Peter Davis in San Juan, and James McManus, C.Ss.R., in Ponce. The governor of Puerto Rico at the time was Luis Munoz Marín, a very charismatic politician, loved and admired deeply by the people. When the *jíbaro* (Puerto Rican peasant) was dying of hunger, jobless and sick, Don Luis was able to rise in politics. He became senator and then governor, and through his ability and personal dedication was able to improve greatly the *jíbaro*'s condition. Before Operation Booststrap, a program of economic reconstruction for the island designed by Munoz Marín and his associates in 1947, these *jíbaros* constituted the majority of the population.

At that time, most Puerto Ricans were Catholics. As the island's economic condition was improving, there was the feeling that the moral conditions were not. People were becoming more materialistic. Davis and McManus started a crusade to ask the government to set aside time during the last hour of the school day to let the children go to the church of their preference to be instructed in morality and religion. But the civil authorities rejected the prelates' claims. Another problem that worried both bishops was the use of the women of the island in experiments with contraceptives. According to some people in the American and Puerto Rican government, economic progress would not be possible if the population growth was not stopped.

In 1960 the tension between Church and state led to a formation of a political party supported by the bishops. The Christian Action Party (*Partido Acción Cristiana* or PAC) caused trouble both in the United States and on the island. It was formed at the time John F. Kennedy was running as presidential candidate. Since he was a Catholic, many Protestants brought back to life the old accusation of popery and the fear that the pope was going to interfere in the political life of the United States through the presence of a Catholic president. To make things worse in Puerto Rico, the Catholic bishops appeared to be getting into politics.

The truth is that neither McManus or Davis were interested in getting into politics. They backed the party as an instrument through which they could bring pressure on the government to make their point clear. However, the PAC did not win the elections. The number of votes the party won was too small to have an impact. The whole issue not only left the Church split, but through the influence of Don Luis, eventually both bishops were removed from the island.

After failing to win the elections of 1960, the PAC survived until the next election year of 1964. In the meantime some changes were made in the Catholic hierarchy. Already, on October 12, 1960, Bishop Luis Aponte Martínez, the second Puerto Rican bishop, was consecrated and made auxiliary bishop of the Diocese of Ponce. As the electoral year of 1964 approached, radical changes took place. In 1963 Bishop McManus was removed and Aponte Martínez took his place in the see of Ponce on October 18. On November 4, 1964, San Juan was elevated to the status of an archdiocese. Archbishop Davis was promoted to the see of Santa Fe in New Mexico and Aponte Martínez was promoted to San Juan. The same date saw the creation of the Diocese of Caguas with Msgr. Rafael Grovas as its bishop. Archbishop Aponte Martínez was made a cardinal on March 5, 1973. Finally, on March 1, 1976, the Diocese of Mayagüez was created and Bishop Ulises Casiano Vargas placed in charge of the new see. From this time on all the bishops were Puerto Ricans. An exception to this rule was to take many by surprise. The vacant see of Arecibo witnessed a Spaniard, Bishop Inaki Mallona Txertudi, promoted to it on January 26, 1992. It seems that, in view of the many priests and sisters in Puerto Rico from Spain, the nomination of a Spanish bishop was a sign of thanksgiving for their presence. Having won the esteem of his fellow bishops, Mallona was elected president of the Episcopal Conference of Puerto Rico in November of 1994.

Popular Religiosity

Like other Latin American countries, Puerto Rico has a rich popular religiosity which is the mixture of different elements. Official Catholic doctrine and devotion had been for centuries influenced by the Native American and African heritage of its ethnic components. These neophytes did not always convert fully to the Christian faith. And even after they were evangelized, there were aspects of their previous beliefs they did not find to be in opposition with the new by acquired or imposed religion.

The birth of popular religiosity was also influenced by the long distances between the rural areas where most people lived and the centers of the official religion. Christian families were loyal to their faith. But it was practically impossible to attend church in order to participate in the Eucharist, to receive the sacraments, or to be taught Christian doctrine. Long distances, bad roads (if any), bad weather, work in the haciendas, were all obstacles to get to the town church, and also obstacles for the priests to reach the people.

Another aspect of the problem was insufficient personnel. Throughout the Spanish colonial period the shortage of priests was a serious problem. Even though there were friars of St. Dominic, and, later in the seventeenth century, Franciscans, most of their time was spent working within the walls of the city of San Juan. Sometimes they visited other parts of the island to preach missions or to assist the bishop in his pastoral visit.

What did people do in the absence of the official Church? They developed their own domestic rituals to keep their faith alive. Statues or pictures of the saints of their preference that they venerated when they went to the parish church were very expensive and difficult to get. Beginning in the middle of the eighteenth century, they carved saints in wood. These saints (santos), which included their most cherished apparitions of Our Lady, were put in little rustic shrines. At the time of their feast, they made a religious domestic celebration for them where all the community gathered. Sung rosaries during a period of nine days (novena) were one popular form of domestic ritual.

One of the most important expressions of this popular religiosity in Puerto Rico was the devotion to Our Lady of Monserrat of Hormigueros. The legend is that at the end of the sixteenth century some miraculous manifestations of Our Lady under the title of Monserrat took place in the small town of Hormigueros in the western side of the island. First a hermitage, and later a sanctuary, was built on top of a hill where the miracles occurred. From the time of the miracles until the present, thousands of people have visited the shrine imploring divine help through the intercession of Our Lady. On February 12, 1995, an old image of Our Lady of Monserrat and its child was canonically crowned by Luis Cardinal Aponte Martínez as an official recognition by Rome of the importance of Hormigueros as a center of faith and popular religiosity. That day the cardinal stated that Our Lady of Monserrat was the people's patroness of the island. Puerto Rico has also Our Lady of Divine Providence in San Juan, a devotion that was brought to the island in 1851 by Bishop Gil Esteve y Tomás. Our Lady of Divine Providence became the official patroness in 1970.

Laity

From the beginning of the Spanish colonial period to the present day many laypeople have contributed to the life of the Church. Some of them were in positions of power or influence; some of them were in very humble positions.

The widow Dona Ana Lanzós, who founded the convent of the Carmelites in San Juan in the seventeenth century, was among them. In the same century two Spanish governors also became very famous because of their religious fervor. One of them, Agustín de Silva y Figueroa, worked hard and even begged alms personally for the construction of a convent and a church for the Franciscans.

In the eighteenth century the painter José Campeche (1751–1809) became well known; he received commissions from as far as Venezuela and Cuba. He was also a musician who played the organ in the cathedral and taught music to the Carmelites. He belonged to the Third Order of St. Dominic and was a very pious man. Every morning he attended Mass in the church of the Dominicans, and in the evening returned for the recitation of the rosary. As a Dominican tertiary, he was under the obligation to recite the Little Office of the day. On Sundays and holidays he refrained from work of any kind. He ate sparingly and was an enemy of strong drink.

At a time when it was very difficult to attend school because there were few teachers, Rafael Cordero, a humble tobacco artisan, dedicated his spare time teaching the boys in San Juan. Some of the most prominent figures in the Puerto Rican history of the nineteenth century were his students. Also in this century Dona Filamena Quinones, a rich widow from San Germán, used her fortune for the benefit of the poor and part of it was dedicated to the construction of a school for poor children.

At the beginning of the twentieth century, just after the Americans took over the island, a religious group started to do missionary work in the central part of Puerto Rico. All began with José de los Santos Morales, a deeply religious Catholic layman who, seeing the advance of Protestantism among the *jíbaros,* decided, under the guidance of the Holy Spirit, to start preaching the Catholic religion. Soon another José followed in his steps. That is why they are called the Hermanos Cheos (Cheo Brothers), since "Cheo" is a nickname for José. The movement spread quickly through the mountain region and many Catholics went to listen to their preaching. A very important fact about this movement is that there were also women preaching the word of God. The Hermanas Cheas is a very important presence in the life of the Church of that time, since women were limited in their public expression of faith in the Catholic Church.

The most famous layman in the history of the Puerto Rican church is Carlos Manuel Rodríguez Santiago (1918–63). Charlie was a student of the University of Puerto Rico, Rio Piedras campus, during the 1950s. He was very interested in liturgy and was a very pious man. He attended the Catholic University Center in the same city of Rió Piedras, under the guidance of the Jesuits. There he gathered a group of friends and together they reflected on the life of the Church and ways of being bet-

ter Christians. Also, in Caguas, the city where he was born, he developed an extraordinary apostolate. He was a young man when he died in 1963. His cause for canonization was introduced in 1992 before the Sacred Congregation for the Causes of the Saints.

Berbusse, Edward J. *The United States in Puerto Rico, 1898–1900.* Chapel Hill: The University of North Carolina Press, 1966.

Curbelo de Díaz, Irene. *El Arte de los santeros puertorriqueños— The Art of the Puerto Rican Santeros.* Bilingual ed. San Juan: Instituto de Cultura Puertorriqueña, 1986.

Dolan, Jay P. and Jaime R. Vidal, eds. *Puerto Rican and Cuban Catholics in the U.S., 1900–1965.* University of Notre Dame Press, 1994.

Hauptly, Denis J. *Puerto Rico, An Unfinished Story.* New York: Macmillan Publishing Company, 1991.

Julián de Nieves, Elisa. *The Catholic Church in Colonial Puerto Rico, 1898–1964.* Río Piedras: Editorial Edil, Inc., 1982.

Lange, Yvonne. *Santos de Palo, The Household Saints of Puerto Rico.* New York: The Museum of American Folk Art, 1991.

Morales Carrión, Arturo. *Puerto Rico: A Political and Cultural History.* New York: W. W. Norton & Company, Inc., 1983,

Picó, Fernando. *Historia general de Puerto Rico.* Río Piedras: Ediciones Huracán, 1986.

Ramírez de Arellano, Annette B. and Conrad Seipp. *Colonialism, Catholicism, and Contraception: A History of Birth Control in Puerto Rico.* Chapel Hill: University of North Carolina Press, 1983.

Taylor, René. *José Campeche and His Time.* Ponce: Museo de Arte de Ponce, 1988.

FLOYD McCOY

PULASKI, CASIMIR (1748–79)

Polish officer and patriot. Pulaski was born in Winiary, Poland, on March 4, 1748. The son of Count Jozef Pulaski and Maria Zislinska, he was born into a wealthy noble family. At age nineteen he served as an officer in the Confederation of Bar (1768), a revolt to gain Polish independence that was quickly put down by the Russians. He escaped to Turkey and continued to fight from abroad for the next four years, earning a reputation as an aggressive military commander. In 1771 he was implicated in a plot to kidnap King Stanislaw August. He left the country as an exile, eventually making his way to Paris, where he was introduced to Benjamin Franklin.

He arrived in Boston, Massachusetts, in 1777, where he joined General George Washington's staff as a volunteer and served with him at the Battle of Brandywine. He received his commission as brigadier general and Commander of the Horse four days later. In October he led an unsuccessful attack at Germantown, Pennsylvania. He was sent next to Trenton, New Jersey, but refused to serve under General Anthony Wayne and tendered his resignation. With Washington's support he formed the Pulaski Legion, an independent corps of mixed infantry and cavalry.

Casimir Pulaski

They were ambushed by the British in October 1778 at Egg Harbor, New Jersey, in their first military outing and suffered high casualties. In February 1779 he was ordered to serve under General Benjamin Lincoln in South Carolina, where he participated in the defense of Charleston. He was mortally wounded in the attack on British-occupied Savannah and died two days later, on October 11, 1779, aboard the U.S. warship, *Wasp.*

TRICIA T. PYNE

PURCELL, JOHN BAPTIST (1783–1883)

Archbishop. Purcell was born on July 4, 1783, in Mallow, Ireland, the third of four children of Edward and Johanna Keefe Purcell. At the age of eighteen, John emigrated to the United States to seek the education he could not obtain in Ireland. He eventually tutored (1818–20) in Queen Ann County, Maryland, before attending Mt. St. Mary's College, Emmitsburg (1820–23). He then studied with the Sulpicians in Paris (1824–27) and was ordained on May 20, 1827, at Notre Dame Cathedral by the archbishop of Paris. He returned to Emmitsburg as a professor (1827–29) and president (1829–33) before being consecrated the second bishop of Cincinnati on October 13, 1833. He seems to have been chosen over the more highly recommended Jesuit, Peter Kenny, because the mostly Dominican clergy in Cincinnati would have found it difficult to work with a Jesuit.

Purcell's long tenure, first as bishop (1833–50), then as archbishop (1850–83), saw tremendous growth in the diocese with churches increasing from 16 to 500 and clergy from 14 to 480, with the addition of thirty schools, three colleges, three seminaries, six hospitals, ten communities of women religious, and eight monastic orders, the holding of three provincial councils (1855, 1858, and 1861), and the creation of two suffragan dioceses: Cleveland in 1847 and Columbus in 1868. Purcell avoided ethnic conflicts with the Germans by establishing the first German parish west of the Alleghenies, Holy Trinity Church, in 1834, and the periodical *Der Wahrheitsfreund,* three years later. Purcell also gave the property of St. Francis Xavier Seminary (founded in 1829) to the Jesuits in 1840 and laid the foundations of a new seminary on Price Hill in 1848, dedicating it as Mount St. Mary's of the West in 1851.

Purcell was a man of strong opinions. He held a week-long debate with a Protestant minister, Alexander Campbell, in February 1837, publicly defending the faith. He invited Archbishop Gaetano Bedini to his see and defended him in 1853. He also was a strong supporter of the Total Abstinence movement. He supported the Union and opposed slavery during the Civil War. At Vatican Council I he saw the decree on infallibility as inopportune and left Rome before the final vote. However, he accepted it once it was defined.

His last years were marred by a financial disaster. The diocese had been receiving parishioners' deposits in the wake of the Panic of 1837, and Purcell had given his younger brother, Edward, power of attorney in 1838 after ordaining him. Total deposits exceeded twenty-five million dollars over the next forty years. It seems some of these funds helped pay for the new cathedral, St. Peter in Chains. Poor investments and management, plus a panic in 1878 caused a run on the bank, revealing a $2.5 mil-

John B. Purcell

lion debt. The seminary had to close (1879–87) due to the difficulties. Embarrassed by this crisis, Purcell accepted a coadjutor, William Elder, in 1880, and died on July 4, 1883, in Brown County, Ohio. He is buried in the cemetery of the Ursuline convent at St. Martin's.

See also OHIO, CATHOLIC CHURCH IN.

Hussey, M. E. "The 1878 Financial Failure of Archbishop Purcell." *The Cincinnati Historical Society Bulletin* 36 (1978).
Trisco, R. *The Holy See and the Nascent Church in the Middle Western United States, 1826–1850.* Rome: Gregorian University Press, 1962.

EARL BOYEA

PUTNAM, CAROLINE CANFIELD (1921–93)

Social worker, Religious of the Sacred Heart. Caroline (Carol) Putnam was born in Springfield, Massachusetts, on April 26, 1921, the first of six children of Roger L. Putnam and Caroline Jenkins. In 1942 she graduated from Manhattanville College of the Sacred Heart and entered the Society of the Sacred Heart in Albany, New York. She made her final profession in Rome in 1950, and pursued graduate work in philosophy (aesthetics) at The Catholic University of America.

From 1968 to 1971 Putnam served on the Urban Task Force of the Archdiocese of Boston which began her work on behalf of immigrants, refugees, and migrant workers in Florida and California. Her vision of education regarded all races and cultures as mutually enriching; such an education she saw not as a privilege, but as belonging to each person by right.

In Indiantown, Florida, Putnam established Hope Rural School, the first full-time school in the country dedicated to the needs of migrant children. In 1986 the school was left in the hands of the Sinsinawa Dominicans. She went

Caroline Canfield Putnam

to California to search out the needs of migrant farmworkers there. After consulting with Cesar Chavez and other leaders, she focused on the Coachella Valley town of Mecca as the place of greatest need. In 1990 Putnam and another religious moved into a trailer in Mecca and began developing a "skills bank" among the women, supporting herself by cleaning houses in Palm Springs. These contacts led to the creation of a house-cleaning cooperative among the women. By recognizing and encouraging their creativity, the people began to find alternative sources of income. Putnam trained community leaders, began youth groups, and offered a compassionate outreach to any and all who needed help. She died in Menlo Park, California, on April 16, 1993.

MARGARET PHELAN, R.S.C.J.

Q

QUARTER, WILLIAM (1806–48)

Bishop. The first Irish-born bishop of Chicago was trained at St. Patrick's Seminary (Maynooth) and Mt. St. Mary's Seminary (Emmitsburg). Ordained on September 19, 1829, by Bishop John Dubois (New York), Quarter worked for fourteen years in New York. He was remembered for his educational, spiritual, and charitable contributions to the growing Catholic community.

William Quarter

With the expansion of the Catholic Church in the nineteenth century, the need for new dioceses was discussed at various provincial councils of Baltimore. Quarter was selected as bishop for the newly erected see of Chicago in November 1843. Two of the prominent bishops of that era, Joseph Rosati (St. Louis) and Francis Kenrick (Philadelphia), were not strong in their support for Quarter (Trisco, 88). Despite the reservations by some fellow bishops, William Quarter arrived in Chicago on May 5, 1844, after his consecration by Bishop John Hughes.

Two issues facing any new bishop of that era were the lack of clergy and the potential for disputes with lay trustees. Bishop Quarter addressed these issues, after his first pastoral visit of the new diocese, by seeking a charter from the Illinois state legislature for the University of St. Mary of the Lake and having himself declared a corporation sole for church property. In 1845 Quarter returned to New York to visit friends and raise money. His friends were surprised by his appearance. Sarah Kerrigan, daughter of a New York friend, noted: "We were very sorry to look upon his whitened hair, sunken eye, and hollow cheek, for they were so many indications of the trials he had undergone" (Meehan, 145). The conditions in Chicago and Illinois did not deter Bishop Quarter from pastoral visits, establishing new churches, attracting the Mercy Sisters to Chicago, holding a diocesan synod (1846), and from conducting semiannual clergy conferences. He maintained his support for new immigrants through his activity in the Chicago Hibernian Benevolent Emigrant Society. He died on April 10, 1848, exactly twenty-six years after his arrival in America from Ireland.

See also ILLINOIS, CATHOLIC CHURCH IN.

Garraghan, Gilbert J., S.J. *The Catholic Church in Chicago.* Chicago: Loyola University Press, 1921.

Meehan, Thomas F., ed. *Historical Records and Studies* 28 (1937) 145.

Trisco, Robert Frederick. *The Holy See and the Nascent Church in the Middle Western United States, 1826–1850.* Rome: Gregorian University Press, 1962.

MARTIN ZIELINSKI

QUASTEN, JOHANNES (1900–87)

Priest, patristics scholar, liturgist. Johannes Quasten was born in Homberg across the Rhine from Duisburg, Germany, on May 3,1900. After a traditional classical education at the *Gymnasium* of nearby Moers, he entered the University of Münster in 1921. Following his priestly ordination in February 1926, he pursued higher studies in the area of ancient Christian literature and archeology under the direction of Franz Joseph Dölger. In line with the interests of his director, Quasten developed a special love for liturgical history. His doctoral dissertation on *Music and Worship in Pagan and Christian Antiquity* was completed in 1927 and published in 1930 (English translation, 1983).

Having completed his second doctoral dissertation on the Good Shepherd in early Christian art, he began his university career as an instructor at the University of Münster in 1931. The new Nazi regime made his life increasingly difficult, and in the fall of 1937 he was forbidden to teach. This led to his acceptance of an invitation to come to The Catholic University of America in Washington where he joined the theology faculty in 1938. Thus began an association of nearly forty years. He retired in 1970 but stayed on, offering patristic seminars until 1977. In that year he returned to Germany, living near Freiburg where he died on March 10, 1987.

Quasten's best-known work is his three-volume *Patrology,* a detailed survey of the lives, writings, and theological teachings of the postbiblical authors of the early Church. These volumes appeared in English in 1950, 1953, and 1960. French, Spanish, and Italian translations quickly followed. Over the years, these volumes became a standard reference work, valuable especially for their wealth of bibliographical data. A fourth volume covering the golden age of the Latin Fathers was published in Italian in 1978 (English translation, 1986). Conceived of as completing the work of Quasten, this was a joint venture of eight scholars from the Augustinianum Institute in Rome.

Over the years, Johannes Quasten published many studies in the area of patristics, especially in the field of liturgy. While still working in Germany, he edited a series of fascicles in the collection *Florilegium Patristicum,* containing Latin and Greek selections of the most significant texts bearing on the early Eucharist *(Monumenta eucharistica et liturgica vetustissima, 1935–37).* His activities in the United States were not confined to teaching and publishing his own research. In the mid-1940s he, together with a faculty colleague, Joseph Plumpe, launched a collection of patristic translations in English, *Ancient Christian Writers* (1946–). This series is especially noted for its extensive theological commentary. On his seventieth birthday, a two-volume collection of essays was published in his honor.

Johannes Quasten's love for the history of worship made a noteworthy contribution to the progress of the liturgical movement leading up to the Second Vatican Council. He was a member of the council's Preparatory Commission on the Liturgy. His writings were instrumental in stirring greater interest in the heritage of the early Church among American Catholics and his teaching helped to prepare a new generation of specialists to carry on his work in this country.

Granfield, P. and J. Jungmann, eds. *Kyriakon.* Festschrift Johannes Quasten. 2 vols. Münster: Asehendorff, 1970.

Quasten, Johannes. *Music and Worship in Pagan and Christian Antiquity.* Trans. Boniface Ramsey. Washington: National Association of Pastoral Musicians, 1983.

____. *Patrology.* 4 vols. Vol. 4 trans. Placid Solari. Westminster, Md.: Christian Classies, 1950–86.

ROBERT B. ENO, S.S.

QUEBEC ACT, THE (1774)

In 1763 the British acquired Canada from France, and the Quebec Act of 1774 represented an effort on the part of the British to successfully integrate this territory into the British Empire. Originally the British had intended to introduce into Quebec the colonial pattern of representative government and British law. The problems of administering a territory that contained a large French Catholic population, however, soon made this system unworkable. In the compromise drawn up by Parliament, as represented in the Quebec Act, the Test Acts, which debarred Catholics from participating in public life, were suspended, the Catholic Church was recognized as the state religion. French civil law was incorporated into the legal system, and representative government was replaced with a royal governor and an appointed legislative council. To help stabilize the frontier region, the southwestern boundary of the territory was extended to the Ohio River.

Colonial reaction to the Quebec Act was vocal and vituperative, unleashing a virulent anti-Catholicism not seen since the Seven Years War (1756–63). The American colonists accused the British of establishing an arbitrary government in Quebec, with the intent of suppressing individual liberties there, as seen through the establishment of the Catholic Church. Rumors of an impending attack against the colonies by Quebec's Catholic and Native American inhabitants immediately began to circulate, and fears that representative government in the colonies was to be abolished next became real. The colonists viewed British actions in Quebec, then, not as those of a benevolent ruler, but of a tyrannical government intent on attacking the rights and liberties of her colonial subjects. It confirmed suspicions of a British conspiracy and acted as a rallying call to unite the colonists in their opposition to British rule.

For Catholics living in the colonies at that time, the Quebec Act confirmed the prejudice and hatred that had been directed at their community throughout the colonial period and further underscored the tenuous position they held in that society. Incidents of anti-Catholic violence can be pointed to, but they were isolated and few. They included the vandalizing of a school operated by John Heffernan in Baltimore, Maryland; the harassment of a Catholic settlement of recently arrived Scottish Highlanders the in Mohawk Valley, New York, and that of John Maguire and his wife in Delaware. All were so threatened by the actions taken against them that they left the colonies. The attacks against Catholics were principally political in nature. For future generations of Catholics, however, the implications of this act were far greater. American political identity was born out of conspiracy and defined by its reaction to the threat of tyranny. In the minds of most colonists, and successive generations of Protestant Americans, no institution embodied the threat of tyranny more than the Catholic Church. Viewed as an authoritative institution that imposed its will over the lives of its followers, the Catholic Church came to represent the antithesis of the republican principles on which the country was founded. The political rhetoric of the Revolutionary period actively promoted the association of the Catholic Church with the corruption of the British government, erupting in anti-Catholic hysteria after issuance of the Quebec Act, and from that point on colonists defiantly proclaimed: "No King, No Popery."

See also AMERICAN CATHOLICS: 1492–1815.

Metzger, Charles, S.J. *The Quebec Act.* New York, 1936.
____. *Catholics and the American Revolution.* Chicago, 1962.

TRICIA T. PYNE

QUIGLEY, JAMES EDWARD (1855–1915)

Archbishop. James Edward Quigley was born in Oshawa, Ontario, Canada, on October 15, 1855. The Quigley family settled in Buffalo when he was ten. His college education and initial seminary training were in the Buffalo diocese. Quigley finished his education in Europe at the University of Innsbruck and the Urban College of Propaganda in Rome where he received his doctorate in theology. He was ordained on April 13, 1879. His pastoral work in Buffalo included being the rector of the cathedral and president of the diocesan school board. Any American diocese at the end of the nineteenth century needed priests who spoke more than one language. Quigley spoke German and Italian and understood French and Polish. When Bishop Stephen Ryan died, Quigley was selected to succeed Ryan. Quigley was consecrated on February 24, 1897, by Archbishop Michael Corrigan of New York.

In the last decade of the nineteenth century, socialists were making a strong appeal to American workers. Quigley was not unsympathetic to the plight of the workers. He acted as a successful mediator in the 1899 Buffalo dock strike. However, he opposed the socialist philosophy and wrote a pastoral letter (1901) against the socialist-dominated labor unions in the city. He not only took up his pen against the socialists but also spoke to Catholic German-American workers in Buffalo about the false claims of the socialists.

The death of Archbishop Patrick Feehan (Chicago) in the summer of 1902 created an opportunity for Quigley to become an archbishop. The last years of Feehan's life were troubled by ethnic disputes among priests and parishioners. The most likely candidates to succeed Feehan were his former chancellor and auxiliary bishop, Peter Muldoon, or John Lancaster Spalding of Peoria. Quigley's name made it on the priests' terna, but a number of American bishops had their doubts about his suitability for the post. Cardinal James Gibbons (Baltimore) thought Quigley did not have enough experience to lead Chicago. Archbishop John Williams (Boston) thought that Quigley was still needed in Buffalo. As the discussion developed, Muldoon was rejected because of some doubts about his personal conduct, the danger that his selection would divide the archdiocese, and his inexperience. Bishop Spalding's name was removed because of charges brought against him by Elizabeth Caldwell. When another candidate withdrew his name and a fourth candidate's health problems eliminated him from contention, Quigley was named to Chicago on January 8, 1903.

The second archbishop of Chicago came to a local church racked by many troubles. Would he be able to stop the divisions which had arisen between Irish-born priests and American-born priests of Irish descent at the time of the selection of Muldoon as auxiliary? Would he be able to reconcile some of the Polish Catholics who had left the church at the time of Rev. Anthony Kozlowski's excommunication? Early in his episcopal tenure, Quigley decided not to accept any more Irish-born clergy into the archdiocese. In 1908 he presided over the election of the first Polish bishop in the United States, Paul Rhode. Between 1908 and 1911 Quigley also helped to clarify procedures with Rome to readmit schismatic Polish Independents to the Roman Catholic Church. While these actions did not immediately eliminate the ethnic bitterness, Quigley helped to ease some of the tension.

The new archbishop was able to take a number of positive actions that helped the archdiocese. Shortly after his arrival, Quigley took the necessary steps for the establishment of a minor seminary, Cathedral College of the Sacred Heart (named changed to Quigley Memorial Seminary under Cardinal Mundelein), which opened in October 1905. That same month Fr. Francis Clement Kelley met at the residence of the archbishop to discuss the founding of the Catholic Church Extension Society. The new archbishop also assumed personal responsibility for the pastoral needs of the growing Italian Catholic community in Chicago. He asked the Scalabrini Fathers to undertake this pastoral work. Within two years, five parishes were established for Italian Catholics. In 1909 he asked the Sisters of St. Casimir to come to Chicago to work with Lithuanian Catholics. He encouraged and supported the establishment of two schools of higher education, Loyola University and DePaul University.

Although many of Quigley's efforts would benefit the Church of Chicago, his interest and support for the Catholic Church Extension Society would have far-reaching effects for the whole American Catholic Church. After the establishment of the society in 1905, Quigley continued to take an active interest in the work of the group. When the society faced challenges from Eastern bishops and the apostolic delegate, Quigley gave his full support to the organization and its founder. He advised Fr. Francis C. Kelley to seek papal approval for the new society. In 1908 he suggested that a national conference on missions be held to promote the goals and aims of the society.

In the spring of 1915 Quigley suffered a stroke. With his ability to administer the archdiocese impaired, he returned to New York to convalesce at his brother's home in Rochester. It was there he died on July 10, 1915. He entered an archdiocese which was in a state of turmoil after the death of Feehan. Although reserved and shy, he provided stable, competent leadership for more than a decade.

See also EXTENSION SOCIETY, CATHOLIC CHURCH; ILLINOIS, CATHOLIC CHURCH IN.

Gaffey, James P. *Francis Clement Kelley and the American Catholic Dream.* Bensenville, Ill.: The Heritage Foundation, Inc., 1980.

Kelley, Francis Clement. "Archbishop Quigley: A Personal Tribute to Our First Chancellor." *Extension Magazine* 10 (August 1915) 1–12.

Parot, Joseph John. *Polish Catholics in Chicago, 1850–1920.* DeKalb: Northern Illinois University Press, 1981.

Shanabruch, Charles. *Chicago's Catholics: The Evolution of an American Identity.* University of Notre Dame Press, 1981.

Skerrett, Ellen, Edward R. Kantowicz, and Steven Avella. *Catholicism, Chicago Style.* Chicago: Loyola University Press, 1993.

MARTIN ZIELINSKI

QUIGLEY, MARTIN JOSEPH (1890–1964)

Editor and publisher. He was born in Cleveland, Ohio, May 6, 1890, the son of Hugh C. and Ellen Daly. After attending Niagara University (1906–08) and The Catholic University of America (1908–09), he married Gertrude Schofield; the couple had four children. Work as a newspaper reporter (1910–13) in Cleveland, Detroit, and Chicago was followed in 1915 by his founding the *Exhibitors' Herald,* a motion picture trade publication. Between 1917 and 1931 Quigley acquired several other publications, including *Motography* (1917), *The Moving Picture World* (1928), and *Motion Picture News* (1931). Combined into the renamed *Motion Picture Herald,* the publication became one of the most influential movie trade papers. Other Quigley publications included *Motion Picture Daily, Motion Picture Almanac, Fame, International Television Almanac,* and *Better Theaters.*

Concern about the perceived decline in motion picture morality in the 1920s led Quigley to an active though largely unofficial role in nearly every major development in motion picture censorship. With Daniel A. Lord, S.J., Quigley devised the 1930 Motion Picture Production Code and persuaded Will Hays and the Hollywood studio heads to accept the code's authority. Subsequently exasperated with Hays' inability to enforce the code, Quigley then helped to engineer the compromise between Hays' office and the U.S. bishops that resulted in the 1934 establishment of the Production Code Administration, headed by Joseph I. Breen. Quigley was also instrumental and vocal in the founding of the Legion of Decency, in establishing its national headquarters in New York City, and in many disputes over the Legion's ratings of controversial films. The recipient of numerous papal honors, Quigley remained active in motion picture publishing and in the debate over movie decency until his death in New York City on May 4, 1964.

See also CENSORSHIP.

Black, Gregory D. *Hollywood Censored: Morality Codes, Catholics and the Movies.* New York: Cambridge University Press, 1994.

Quigley, Martin Joseph. *Decency in Motion Pictures.* New York, 1937.

Quigley's papers are at Georgetown University.

Skinner, James M. *The Cross and the Cinema: The Legion of Decency and the National Catholic Office for Motion Pictures, 1933–1970.* Westport, Conn.: Praeger, 1993.

Walsh, Frank. *Sin and Censorship: The Catholic Church and the Motion Picture Industry.* New Haven: Yale University Press, 1996.

UNA M. CADEGAN

R

RAFFEINER, JOHN (1785–1861)

Pioneer German priest. In the early and middle years of the nineteenth century large numbers of immigrants came to the shores of the United States from countries in Europe. Among them was a goodly number from Germany. Care for the spiritual needs of the Catholics among these German immigrants was a great concern of the American bishops at the time. John Raffeiner, destined to become "apostle to the German immigrants," was one of the priests from Germany who answered the call.

This zealous young cleric had already had an interesting life. He was born December 26, 1785, of a well-to-do family in the Austrian Tyrol. After preparatory education in a Benedictine monastery, he went to Rome to be ordained there. The imprisonment of Pius VII by Napoleon ended this hope. His mind then turned to medicine, a more possible career at that moment. After receiving his degree in medicine on May 4, 1813, Raffeiner served as a surgeon in the Austrian army and later in private practice in Switzerland.

Raffeiner in New York

The priesthood was, however, his dream. After completing the required studies John Raffeiner was ordained priest on May 1, 1825, at the age of forty. Five years later he responded to the call for German missionaries in the New World. Raffeiner arrived in New York harbor on January 1, 1833. Although it was the plea of Bishop Fenwick of Cincinnati that had brought him to the New World, it was his contact with Bishop John Dubois, head of the vast New York diocese, that persuaded the new cleric to remain in the New York area where there were many new German immigrants. Fr. Raffeiner was a gift to Bishop Dubois!

Raffeiner's subsequent travels brought him to lower New York City; to Williamsburg in Brooklyn; to several cities in upper New York State. In fact, wherever there were German Catholics, there was John Raffeiner. The plan of destiny for this zealous missionary was the Williamsburg area in Brooklyn. Here he established the Most Holy Trinity parish which could eventually claim the distinction of having a school, an orphanage, a cemetery, a hospital. This giant of a missionary even began a preparatory seminary.

Fr. Raffeiner was ever alert to the call of Divine Providence in his life. Toward the end of August 1853 he went to the Redemptorist church in New York City, probably for confession as was his custom. Here he learned that four Dominican nuns from Regensburg, Bavaria, had arrived in New York on August 26, 1853. They had come expecting to meet a Benedictine abbot who would bring them to Pennsylvania to teach the children of German immigrants. Stranded and knowing nothing of English, the concerned religious were open to the suggestion of Raffeiner to become part of his parish for his school. He made all the necessary arrangements and brought the four nuns across the East River to Most Holy Trinity. It was September 2, 1853. The nuns had met their first benefactor in the New World in John Raffeiner, their *landsmann*. His concern and generosity impressed the Dominicans. Then they began to wonder!

Raffeiner and the Dominican Sisters

The residence the pastor gave them was the basement in the rectory, with barely enough room. After a short time the basement of the school became their second "home." To add to this, Raffeiner arranged to have the sisters cook for the priests, thus saving a salary. Also the domestic chores for the rectory were the obligation of these four nuns just arrived from a well-organized monastery. The pastor also hired a woman to make the beds in the rectory, with the sisters paying her salary!

To add to these strange and unexpected arrangements Raffeiner took the money the sisters had brought with them from Germany, and put it in a bank, and took one percent interest as his commission. All these unexpected and uncalled for circumstances, especially the dark and damp living quarters, called forth all the stamina these women could muster. And when tuberculosis struck, they knew they were paying a price! One of their group died of this disease May 22, 1855, only two years after their arrival.

This zealous, almost ascetic, priest seemed to think that he could make any and all decisions unilaterally. It took the sisters a while to understand this man who had, as it were, rescued them and seemed very anxious to have them for his school. Raffeiner was certainly energetic, zealous, interested in the good of his parish, willing to give of himself in his missionary tours. But, in his dealings with these cloistered nuns, he was frequently niggardly, stern, unconcerned that these women were giving their days to teaching in his school, and spending any free time in embroidery and art work to try to support themselves. He seemingly had forgotten that the twenty-five-cent tuition, frequently unpaid by many, was hardly sufficient to support them. The few times he was "father" to them were overshadowed by his evident lack of compassion on too many other occasions.

Despite this the parish grew, and the group of four nuns slowly developed into a large congregation, the Dominican Sisters of Amityville, New York, which became a vital part of the life of the Church on Long Island.

Fr. Raffeiner began to suffer from the effects of his strenuous life as a traveling missionary and from his responsibilities as a pastor among immigrants who themselves required all kinds of services. Assisted by a young capable priest who just a few months before had arrived from Germany, John Stephen Raffeiner was ready to answer God's call. He died July 16, 1861. He was buried in Holy Trinity cemetery, and later his body was transferred to the lower level of the parish church.

A few months before his death, at the beginning of the Civil War, the pastor had ordered the American flag to be raised over Holy Trinity and encouraged his people to answer the call to defend the Union. It was a final act that helped the Dominican sisters of the parish to see the heart of the patriot in their pastor.

Meehan, Thomas F. "Very Rev. Johann Stephan Raffeiner." *Historical Records and Studies* 9 (1916) 161–75.

FRANCIS MAUREEN CARLIN, O.P.

RÂLE, SEBASTIAN (1652–1724)

Jesuit missionary, martyr. Sebastian Râle, a native of Pontarlier, France, was baptized on January 28, 1652, and died in what is now Norridgewock, Maine, on August 23, 1724. Following his arrival in Quebec on October 13, 1689, Fr. Râle (there are various spellings of his family name) remained in North America and, except for his mission to the Illinois Native Americans (1692–95) and to the Abenakis of Becancour (1705–11), his ministry was mainly among the Abenakis of the Kennebec River valley in what is now the state of Maine. However, at the same time, he did not neglect the other Native Americans outside this river valley in New France and New England.

Since Râle's life was lived amidst the rivalry between France and England for the control of North America, his career was not free from conflicts, such as King William's War (1689–97) and Queen Anne's War (1702–13), which marked that development. During that struggle, which would continue after his death, the Jesuit consistently opposed the English who were seeking to entice the Abenakis away from their Catholic faith and to separate them from their alliance with the French.

At that time, the Native American forts, situated on the major rivers of Maine, were mission centers cared for by the Jesuits, and they constituted a defensive perimeter between the French centered in Quebec and the English centered in Boston. Realizing how effective were Râle's efforts in protecting the Abenakis and in keeping them aligned with the French, the English placed a bounty on the priest's head, hoping thereby to eliminate him as a major obstacle to their expansionist goals.

Shortly before his death, Fr. Râle, conscious of the dangers that he was confronting, wrote to his nephew (October 15, 1722) back in France that he would never abandon his flock. Though previous attempts to capture the Jesuit had failed, the English eventually succeeded. That the news of his death occasioned much rejoicing throughout Protestant New England, especially in Boston, indicates how notorious the Jesuit was in colonial New England. Râle's legacy is preserved today in the Maine Historical Society in Portland, which houses a few artifacts from his mission, and in the Houghton Library at Harvard University, which treasures his Abenaki dictionary.

The circumstances of his death (recorded in a letter of October 29, 1724, by Pierre-Joseph de La Chasse, superior general of the missions of New France), in a war that was not devoid of religious hatred, testify how Râle died a martyr. So meaningful was the Jesuit's life that it is celebrated annually, in conjunction with the anniversary of his death, at Madison, Maine, not far from the site where he was killed. That he was listed among 116 candidates proposed for beatification, in a letter directed to the Sacred Congregation of Rites, on September 23, 1941, by Dennis Cardinal Dougherty of Philadelphia, affirms Râle's exceptional stature in the history of Catholicism in New England.

Calvert, Mary R. *Black Robe of the Kennebec*. Monmouth, Maine: Monmouth Press, 1991.

Dragon, Antonio. *Le Vrai Visage de Sébastien Râle*. Montreal: Editions Bellarmin, 1975.

Lapomarda, Vincent A. "The Jesuit Missions of Colonial New England." *Essex Institute Historical Collections* 126 (1990) 91–109.

VINCENT A. LAPOMARDA, S.J.

RAPPE, LOUIS AMADEUS (1801–77)

First bishop of Cleveland. Rappe was born on February 2, 1801, in Audrehem, France, the tenth child of farmers Eloi and Marie Rappe. After completing his studies at Boulogne-sur-Mer and Arras, he was ordained on March 14, 1829. He served as a parish priest and as chaplain to the Ursuline sisters at Boulogne-sur-Mer where he was recruited by Bishop John B. Purcell of Cincinnati for missionary duty in Ohio. Rappe arrived in America in October 1840.

Purcell named him pastor of St. Francis de Sales Church in Toledo, Ohio. As pastor Rappe was responsible for the additional Catholic settlements. Experience with the havoc alcohol caused among the Irish canal workers made Rappe become a fervent advocate of the temperance movement.

On April 23, 1847, the Diocese of Cleveland was established as comprising all the territory of the Archdiocese of Cincinnati which lay in northern Ohio. Rappe became Cleveland's first bishop on October 10, 1847. He quickly began the necessary infrastructure for his diocese, constructing a seminary, cathedral, orphanages, and a hospital. Many parishes and schools were also established. Rappe himself stressed the importance of schools for the young.

Rappe made several trips to France to raise funds and recruit missionaries. His episcopate was marred by conflicts over parochial administration and ethnic tensions. He was accused of favoring various nationalities. His selection of seminarians for their language skills sparked controversy.

False charges were brought against him in Rome. Though he was found innocent, Rappe resigned in 1870. Despite his age and failing eyesight, he spent his last years as a missionary in Vermont. He died in St. Albans, Vermont, on September 8, 1877. His body was returned to Cleveland for burial.

Hynes, Michael J. *History of the Diocese of Cleveland: Origin and Growth (1847–1952)*. Cleveland, 1953.

Jurgens, W. A. *A History of the Diocese of Cleveland, Volume I: The Prehistory of the Diocese to its Establishment in 1847*. Youngstown, 1980.

____. "Bishop Rappe and His Diocese." Unpublished manuscript. Cleveland, 1982.

CHRISTINE L. KROSEL

RASKOB, JOHN JAKOB (1879–1950)

Financier and philanthropist. John Jakob Raskob was born on March 19, 1879, in Lockport, New York, the oldest of four children of John and Anna Frances Moran Raskob. He grew up in a close-knit, devoutly Catholic family. His paternal grandfather, a cigar maker, had emigrated from France in 1845, and his maternal grandparents, from Dublin, Ireland.

He studied accounting and stenography at Clark's Business College in Lockport and worked at area firms and in a steel company in Nova Scotia, Canada, before being hired by Pierre S. du Pont, who was managing a real estate and interurban railroad company in Ohio, as his personal secretary.

Raskob's financial skills were invaluable when in 1902 du Pont and two cousins took control of the family firm,

Louis A. Rappe

E. I. du Pont de Nemours and Company in Wilmington, Delaware. Through financial arrangements devised by Raskob, the du Ponts bought out their competitors and became the leading black powder and dynamite manufacturer in the United States.

During reorganization of the new company, Raskob assisted in modernizing the accounting and auditing departments, as well as in developing procedures for stockholders' return on investments. In 1909 when du Pont became acting president of the company, Raskob assumed the tasks of treasurer and received the title officially in 1914, eventually becoming a company vice president. During World War I, Raskob directed financing for the Du Pont Company's rapid growth.

Du Pont and Raskob also had invested in the General Motors Corporation. In 1915 they owned enough stock so that when a rift developed between General Motors' founder, William Durant, and his bankers, du Pont was named chairman of the board and Raskob a director. In 1918 Raskob was named chairman of the company's finance committee. In that position, he introduced modern accounting procedures and formed the General Motors Corporation, which allowed customers to purchase automobiles for the first time on an installment plan.

In 1928 Raskob left General Motors to become chairman of the Democratic National Committee at the request of his friend, Alfred E. Smith, who was running for president. Raskob concentrated on raising campaign funds and reorganizing the committee. However, techniques he initiated led to Smith losing the 1932 nomination to Franklin D. Roosevelt, and Raskob was replaced as chairman by James A. Farley. Opposed to the New Deal, Raskob in 1934 cofounded the Liberty League that campaigned against Roosevelt's nomination in 1936.

The year 1932 was a turning point in Raskob's life. His investments did poorly and he had to sell his estate, Archmere, on the Delaware River at Claymont, Delaware. From the organization of Empire State, Inc., in 1930 until his death, Raskob was vice president and a director of the organization that operated the Empire State Building in New York City. He remained a director of General Motors until 1946 and maintained an office in the Empire State Building.

For his contributions to civic and charitable causes, Raskob was made a knight of the Order of St. Gregory the Great and a papal chamberlain. He was a member of the Knights of Columbus and a charter member of the American branch of the Knights of Malta.

On June 18, 1906, Raskob had married Helena Springer Green of Galena, Maryland, in Wilmington, Delaware. They had thirteen children. He and his wife separated but never divorced; she moved to Arizona and he lived in New York, often spending weekends at his Eastern Shore farm near Centreville, Maryland. Most of his estate was left to the Raskob Foundation for Catholic Activities. He died in Centreville, Maryland, on October 15, 1950.

See also FARLEY, JAMES; SMITH, ALFRED EMANUEL.

Chandler, Alfred D., Jr., and Stephen Salsbury. *Pierre S. du Pont and the Making of the Modern Corporation.* New York, 1971.
Collection of Raskob Papers at the Eleutherian Mills Historical Library, Greenville, Delaware.
Winkler, J. K. *The Du Pont Dynasty.* New York, 1935.

MARIANNA McLOUGHLIN

RAVALLI, ANTHONY (1812–84)

Jesuit missionary. Anthony Ravalli was born in Ferrara, Italy. At age fifteen he entered the Society of Jesus, and, beginning in 1833, taught biology at Jesuit universities in Nizza, Novara, and Turin. In 1837 he returned to Rome for ordination to the priesthood, and for three years studied medicine at the University of Rome. In 1843, as a recruit of Pierre J. De Smet, he crossed the Atlantic to become a missionary among native tribes of the Northwest.

Anthony Ravalli

The winter of 1844–45 he spent at St. Ignatius Mission in present-day Washington, going in the spring to build a chapel for the Colvilles at Kettle Falls. Upon completion of that project he became the assistant at St. Mary's Mission among the Flatheads in the Bitterroot valley of present-day Montana. There, in addition to duties of priest, physician, surgeon, and pharmacist, he built the first grist mill and sawmill. Also, he drew plans for the Mission of the Sacred Heart (today known as Cataldo) among the Coeur d'Alenes. When St. Mary's was temporarily closed in

1850, he went to the Coeur d'Alenes to supervise completion of the church and priests' chapel.

In 1858 Ravalli returned to Kettle Falls as the superior, where he built a larger church. When that had to be abandoned, he was sent to Santa Clara Mission, California, to be an instructor. In 1862 he was confessor of the house, prefect of health, and admonitor to the rector. In 1863 he was master of novices when recalled to St. Ignatius Mission at its new location in Montana. During that assignment he, together with Br. William Claessens and native helpers, built the first church for whites, St. Michael's at Hellgate. He spent the next three years at St. Peter's Mission among the Blackfeet, east of the mountains, returning to St. Mary's Mission at the time of its reestablishment in the Bitterroot valley in 1866. Ravalli designed and supervised the building of churches, painted Stations of the Cross, carved statues, and built altars which he painted to resemble marble. Following the discovery of gold and the resultant influx of whites, accidents were of frequent occurrence, and Fr. Ravalli became the good Samaritan of all western Montana. He died at St. Mary's Mission on October 2, 1884.

Schoenberg, Wilfred P., S.J. *A History of the Catholic Church in the Pacific Northwest, 1743–1983.* Washington, D.C.: The Pastoral Press, 1987.
_____. *Paths to the Northwest: A Jesuit History of the Oregon Province.* Chicago: Loyola University Press, 1982.
LUCYLLE EVANS

RAVOUX, AUGUSTINE (1815–1906)

Missionary. Ravoux was born in Langeac, Auvergne, France, in 1815. He entered the minor seminary at Le Puy, France, in 1834 and in 1837 was recruited as a missionary by the recently ordained bishop of Dubuque, Iowa, Mathias Loras. He accompanied Loras on the journey back to America, completing his studies at Mt. St. Mary's, Emmitsburg Seminary, Maryland, and at Dubuque. He was ordained at the cathedral in Dubuque in 1840 and was immediately assigned to minister to the peoples at Prairie du Chien, Wisconsin.

In 1841 he was sent to work with the Santee Dakota in northern Iowa (now Minnesota), and by 1843 had translated a catechism and hymnal entitled *Wakantanka Ti Ki Chanku (Path to the House of God)* into Dakota. He labored as the sole missionary in the vast Minnesota territory for the next seven years, until the Diocese of St. Paul was created in 1851.

Ravoux worked closely with St. Paul's first bishop, Joseph Crétin, as his vicar general, a position he held until his retirement 1892. In 1868 Pope Pius IX, in recognition of Ravoux's contributions as both a missionary and administrator, appointed him the first vicar apostolic of the

Augustine Ravoux

newly erected vicariate of Montana, an honor he was forced to decline due to ill health. He was later elevated to domestic prelate by Pope Leo XIII 1887.

Ravoux lived in residence at the cathedral rectory in St. Paul's during his retirement, where he wrote on his experiences as a missionary, including *Reminiscences, Memoirs and Lectures* (1890; French ed., 1892) and *Labors of Monsignor A. Ravoux at Mendota, St. Paul and Other Localities* (1899).

TRICIA T. PYNE

REDEMPTORISTS (C.Ss.R.)

The Congregation of the Most Holy Redeemer (C.Ss.R.; the Redemptorists) is a religious congregation of priests and brothers founded in 1732 by St. Alphonsus Liguori (1696–1787). Alphonsus was moved by the plight of rural peasants in southern Italy to found a congregation "to follow Christ the Redeemer in preaching the gospel to the poor," especially by means of parish missions and retreats. Alphonsus had international aspirations for his congregation. The first non-Italian member of the congregation, Clement Hofbauer (1751–1820; canonized 1909), attempted to extend the Redemptorists outside of Italy, first in Poland and later in Austria. Clement had little success in establishing a permanent foundation of the Redemptorists in Northern Europe because of civil unrest and the anticlerical climate of the early nineteenth century. Clement looked to North America as a possible refuge for the Redemptorist Congregation. Under Joseph Passerat (1772–1858), Clement's successor as superior of the Redemptorists outside Italy, the dream of an American foundation would become a reality.

In 1827 Bishop Edward Fenwick, O.P., of Cincinnati sent his vicar general, Fr. Frederick Résé, to Europe to raise funds and recruit personnel for his diocese which comprised the states of Ohio, Michigan, and part of Wisconsin. This trip led to the foundation of two mission societies dedicated to the American Mission—the Leopoldine Foundation in Austria and the Ludwig Missionsverein in Bavaria. These two societies were very influential in providing funds for the American missions and for raising consciousness in Europe about the needs of the Church in North America. While in Vienna, Résé met Passerat and invited him to send Redemptorist missionaries to Ohio. Passerat was favorable to the idea while having reservations because of lack of personnel and because of Résé's request that the Redemptorists undertake the running of parishes and schools, activities prohibited by the Redemptorist Rule.

U.S. Foundation

After a number of attempts, six men were chosen as the pioneers of the American Mission, three priests and three brothers: Fr. Simon Saenderl, the superior, Fr. Francis Tschenhens, Fr. Francis Haetscher, Br. James Kohler, Br. Aloysius Schuh, and Br. Wenceslaus Witopil. The six pioneers arrived in New York harbor on June 20, 1832. Nearly one hundred years after their foundation, the Redemptorists arrived in the New World. The differing expectations of the Redemptorists and Fenwick caused almost immediate problems. Fenwick's main concern was providing priests for his far-flung diocese. His plans often conflicted with the Redemptorist desire to maintain religious community life by the establishment of a permanent foundation. For seven years the Redemptorists traveled extensively through Ohio, Michigan, and Wisconsin ministering to the spiritual needs of the immigrant populations and, to some extent, with Native Americans. Several early attempts to establish a permanent foundation proved unsuccessful.

The arrival of the Redemptorists in the U.S.A. coincided with the waves of German immigration and because the majority of the Redemptorists were German-speaking their attention soon turned from the Midwestern frontier to the immigrant enclaves in the Eastern urban centers. This proved to be a much more successful ministerial strategy. The first permanent foundation in the United States was St. Philomena's Church, a German parish in Pittsburgh, Pennsylvania (1839). A notable event of the pioneer years was the first profession of vows in the United States in 1842 of the diocesan priest John Neumann, later bishop of Philadelphia (1852–60) and the first American man canonized (1977).

Development and Expansion

The last half of the nineteenth century was to be a time of rapid expansion and development for the Redemptorists as they accepted parishes in the major urban centers of the United States: Rochester (1839), Baltimore (1840), New York (1842), Philadelphia (1843), Buffalo (1845), Detroit (1847), New Orleans (1847). The direction of parishes was forbidden by the Redemptorist Rule and the heavy investment of personnel in parochial ministry made the American Redemptorists unique. It was also to be a source of periodic conflict between the American Redemptorists and their European superiors. The characteristic ministry of the Redemptorist was the preaching of parish missions. Parish or popular missions are brief (several weeks in length) courses of preaching and spiritual exercises directed toward strengthening religious belief and practice among baptized Catholics. The missions were highly successful and were influential in forming a style of devotional Catholicism in the United States that endured until the Second Vatican Council. The Redemptorist Mission Book, a prayer book of readings and devotions, was one of the most influential religious texts of nineteenth-century American Catholicism. Missions were preached in the United States by the Redemptorists from the beginning, but they took on new vigor with the formation of an organized mission band in 1851. The Redemptorists were also enthusiastic supporters of the parochial school system and enlisted the School Sisters of Notre Dame and other congregations of religious women for the schools in their parishes. The Redemptorist parish was noted as a center of immigrant life, offering a number of social and cultural services as well as religious ones—orphanages, welfare societies, musical and dramatic organizations.

Establishment of the American Province

In 1841 the Redemptorist Congregation was divided into five provinces, and from 1844 to 1850 the American Mission was under the jurisdiction of the Belgian province. The American Mission was governed by a superior: Simon Saenderl from 1832–35; Joseph Prost from 1835–41; Alexander Czvitkovicz from 1841–45; Peter Czackert from 1845–47; John Neumann from 1847–49. All important decisions had to be referred to the provincial in Europe which often resulted in misunderstanding and frustration. This situation was resolved in 1850 when the United States became a province itself. In January of 1851 Fr. Bernard Hafkenscheid became the first provincial superior and the provincial headquarters were located in Baltimore. The greater autonomy of the American province resulted in an expansion of missionary work and an increase in American-born vocations. Hafkenscheid organized an English mission band among whose members was the newly ordained convert Isaac Hecker. Hecker, in later years, impatient with the Redemptorist focus on ministry to foreign immigrants and anxious to devote more attention to the conversion of Protestant America, left the Redemptorists in order to found the Congregation of St. Paul (Paulists) in 1858. Hafkenscheid and his English-speaking mission band gave its first mission in 1851 in St. Joseph's Church in New York City. It was widely publicized and highly successful. By 1869 the Redemptorists had given missions in twenty-eight of the fifty-two dioceses in the country. Many invitations to make permanent foundations resulted from the wide exposure the Redemptorists received from their missions. By the end of the century the Redemptorists had established houses in Annapolis, Maryland (1853), Chicago (1860), Boston (1871), St. Louis, Missouri (1872), Quebec (1874), Kansas City (1876), Toronto (1880), Detroit (1880), Brooklyn, New York (1893), and several other places. Formation houses were established as well: St. Mary's Seminary (1881), a minor seminary in North East, Pennsylvania; and a major seminary in Ilchester, Maryland (1868), which was replaced in 1907 by the new major seminary, Mount St. Alphonsus, Esopus, New York.

Our Lady of Perpetual Help

Promotion of devotion to the Blessed Virgin Mary was a part of Redemptorist spirituality and ministry from the time of St. Alphonsus. This devotion received a new impetus when the image of Mary under the title of "Our Lady of Perpetual Help" was confided to the Redemptorists by Pope Pius IX in 1866. Redemptorist churches became centers of devotion to Mary under this title and the image of Perpetual Help became one of the most popular Marian images in the United States. The novena to Perpetual Help became a weekly feature in many American parishes. At its height the novena devotion attracted thousands every week to Redemptorist churches dedicated to Perpetual Help in Boston, Brooklyn, and St. Louis.

Division of the American Province

The Redemptorists followed the westward expansion of the United States and it became increasingly difficult for the provincial superior in Baltimore to administer such a large province. Various plans were discussed with the superior general in Rome, Fr. Nicholas Mauron, and in November 1875 the United States was divided into two provinces, the Baltimore province and the St. Louis province.

The new St. Louis province consisted of four houses with thirty-five priests and twenty-one brothers. Nicholas Jaeckel (1834–99) was appointed the first provincial. The St. Louis province grew in autonomy, established its own formation system, and made foundations in the Midwestern and Western states. The St. Louis province continued to make a large investment of personnel in parochial ministry although every large house had an itinerant mission band attached to it. The Redemptorist ministry in the United States took on a new dimension in 1913 when

some members of the faculty of the major seminary in Oconomowoc, Wisconsin, undertook the publication of a monthly magazine named the *Liguorian,* in honor of St. Alphonsus. The publication of the magazine was moved in 1947 to a new foundation in Liguori, Missouri, which developed over the years into a publishing center of books, pamphlets, and parish bulletins, and more recently to video production as well.

Foreign Mission Activity

In the twentieth century the Redemptorists in the United States began to respond to requests for pastoral ministry outside the United States. In 1902 the Baltimore province sent men to Puerto Rico. The first foundation was made in that same year in Mayaguez. The Redemptorist presence in Puerto Rico grew over the years until the new province of San Juan was erected in 1984. The province of San Juan also included the houses in the Dominican Republic where American Redemptorists had been working since 1948. Hundreds of members of the Baltimore province worked in Puerto Rico and the fluency in Spanish of the returning missionaries proved to be a valuable asset in ministry among the Spanish-speaking immigrants in the large urban centers of the United States. In 1918 the Baltimore province also assumed responsibility for a mission in the American Virgin Islands in the West Indies. In 1930 Redemptorists of the Baltimore province began to work in Mato Grosso in the south of Brazil. This mission flourished as well and became the independent province of Campo Grande in 1989. In 1934 a foundation was made from Brazil in neighboring Paraguay which became the vice province of Asuncion. The St. Louis province also accepted a mission in the Amazon region of Brazil in 1943 which became a vice province in 1947. In 1949 the St. Louis province began a mission in Thailand, the first mission of the American Redemptorists to a country that was not predominantly Catholic. The vice province of Bangkok was established in 1969.

Modern Developments

Like most religious congregations, the Redemptorists enjoyed a large number of vocations in the first half of the twentieth century and grew to number over a thousand in the United States. In 1952 the province of Oakland, California, was established from the St. Louis province. In the same year the vice province of New Orleans which comprised the houses in the Southwest of the United States was established. The Redemptorists of the Baltimore province had been working in the Southeast since 1926, largely in areas with very few priests and in the African American community. The houses in the Southeast were established as the vice province of Richmond in 1942. The central ministries of the American Redemptorists continued to be parochial ministry, preaching of parish missions and retreats, and foreign mission work. During World War II, when travel to the missions became impossible, 188 American Redemptorists served as chaplains to the armed forces.

The Redemptorists shared in the dramatic changes in the American Church following the Second Vatican Council. Parish mission preaching sometimes failed to integrate new theological insights. Traditional Catholic devotions lost much of their appeal with the advent of the vernacular liturgy. The once thriving Redemptorist parishes in the large cities of the United States struggled to adapt to the social and economic fluctuations of the sixties and seventies. The decrease in vocations after the council resulted in dramatic changes in Redemptorist formation. By the end of the 1980s all the Redemptorist seminaries were closed and the American Redemptorists joined in collaborative ventures with other religious congregations for the academic and theological formation of their members. In more recent years Redemptorist chapters and assemblies have struggled to reclaim the charism of St. Alphonsus for the next millennium. Mission preaching has undergone a revival and missions are again popular and well attended. The Redemptorists direct over a dozen retreat centers in the United States which offer a wide variety of programs. In fidelity to the mission of St. Alphonsus to spread the love of Jesus the Redeemer to those who have the least access to the Church's ministry, Redemptorists in the United States have committed themselves to ministry among the economically poor and marginal groups. In an effort to make better use of personnel and resources the St. Louis and Oakland provinces merged, and resulted in the formation in 1996 of one new province with its headquarters in Denver.

Byrne, John F., C.Ss.R. *The Redemptorist Centenaries*. Philadelphia: The Dolphin Press, 1932.

Curley, Michael J., C.Ss.R. *The Provincial Story—A History of the Baltimore Province of the Congregation of the Most Holy Redeemer*. New York: The Redemptorist Fathers, 1963.

Dolan, Jay P. *Catholic Revivalism: The American Experience 1830–1900*. University of Notre Dame Press, 1978.

Skinner. Thomas L. *The Redemptorists in the West*. St. Louis: Redemptorist Fathers, 1933.

Wallace, James A., C.Ss.R. "Reconsidering the Parish Mission." *Worship* 67 (4) (July 1993) 340–51.

Wuest, Joseph, C.Ss.R. *Annales Congregationis Ss. Redemptoris, Provinciae Americanae*. Ilchester, 1888–1924.

TERRENCE J. MORAN, C.SS.R.

REDEMPTORISTINES (O.Ss.R.)

The Redemptoristines (Order of the Most Holy Redeemer, O.Ss.R.), a contemplative order, were founded in Scala (Naples), Italy, in 1731 by Maria Celeste Crostarosa (1696–1755) with the collaboration of St. Alphonsus Liguori. Maria Celeste was a mystic and gifted writer of a number of works of deep spirituality. Maria Celeste reformed a small Visitation convent in Scala according to a new rule. The nuns of the order aspired to be a *viva memoria*—a living memory to the life, death, and resurrection of Jesus the Redeemer. The habit is a deep red to symbolize divine love. The order existed only in Italy until 1831 when a foundation was made in Vienna from which the Redemptoristines expanded to various parts of the world. The order has two foundations in the United States. The Monastery of Our Mother of Perpetual Help was founded in Esopus, New York, on the grounds of the Redemptorist Major Seminary, in 1957. The Monastery of St. Alphonsus was founded in Liguori, Missouri, in 1960. The Liguori community made a flourishing foundation in the Philippines in 1980.

TERRENCE J. MORAN, C.SS.R.

REEDY, JOHN L. (1925–83)

Priest, editor. John L. Reedy was born in Newport, Kentucky, on October 16, 1925. He entered the Congregation of Holy Cross at Notre Dame, Indiana, in 1944 and was ordained to the priesthood in 1952. After a year of graduate studies in journalism at Marquette and Notre Dame Universities, Reedy was appointed assistant editor of the *Ave Maria,* a weekly magazine for Catholic families published by the Holy Cross Fathers at Notre Dame since 1865 with a circulation of 60,000. In 1955 he became the editor of the magazine and the director of Ave Maria Press, a printing plant that employed seventy workers and that annually printed and distributed one and one-half to two million religious pamphlets.

Under Reedy's editorship, the *Ave Maria* focused less on spiritual and devotional themes and emphasized the application of the social teachings of the Church to problems facing contemporary Catholics. When declining circulation forced the magazine to cease publication in 1970, Reedy published a biweekly bulletin, *A.D. Correspondence,* in which he explored issues of relevance to the post-Vatican II Church. In the 1960s, he had already begun to establish Ave Maria Press as a publishing house for spiritual books and religious education materials and this became its mission after the demise of the magazine.

In 1966 Reedy received the Catholic Press Association's award for outstanding contributions to Catholic journalism. After 1970, he became a syndicated columnist for Catholic diocesan newspapers and for the national edition of *Our Sunday Visitor*. In his last column, published a week after his death, he recalled the many who had visited or written during his last few months and described them as "an incomplete but representative snapshot album touching all the years of my priestly life. . . . My presence to them, at special moments in their lives, had been more than the support of a caring friend." He died at Notre Dame, December 2, 1983.

See also AVE MARIA.

John L. Reedy file, Indiana Province Archives Center, Notre Dame, Indiana.

JAMES CONNELLY, C.S.C.

REID, RICHARD (1896–1961)

Newspaper editor, attorney, lay leader. Reid was born in Winchester, Massachusetts, on January 21, 1896, to Michael William and Catherine Dee. He graduated from Holy Cross College in 1918 and went to New York City to begin graduate studies at Fordham University and Columbia University. After a brief teaching stint at St. Francis Xavier High School in Manhattan, he took a position as writer and reporter for the *Daily Chronicle* and the *Daily Herald,* both of Augusta, Georgia. In 1921 Reid became the executive secretary of the Georgia Catholic Layman's Association and editor of the *Bulletin,* a Catholic newspaper for the Southeast. In 1923 he married Catherine O'Leary, and the two had five children. In 1919 Reid was admitted to the Georgia bar, and was a member of the firm of Mulherin and Reid (1930–40).

Reid became a national lay leader in the Church, and he held prestigious posts such as president of the Catholic Association (1932–34), general counsel of the National Council of Catholic Men (1937–40), and he taught as a guest professor at the University of Notre Dame. In 1940 he was appointed editor of the New York *Catholic News,* the unofficial newspaper of the Archdiocese of New York, a post that he held until his death. As editor Reid vigorously supported interracial justice and the right of Catholics to participate fully in all aspects of civic and public life. In 1946 he was recognized by the papacy for his work and received the Hoey Interracial Justice Medal. He also received the Laetare Medal of the University of Notre Dame in 1936. He died in New Rochelle, New York, on January 24, 1961.

See also CATHOLIC PRESS (NEWSPAPERS) IN AMERICA.

Cashin, Edward J. "Thomas E. Watson and the Catholic Laymen's Association of Georgia." Ph.D. dissertation, Fordham University, 1962.

Mulherin, Mary Jeanne, R.S.M. "The First Years of the Catholic Laymen's Association of Georgia, 1916–1921." M.A. thesis, The Catholic University of America, 1954.

Powers, Felicitas, R.S.M. "Prejudice, Journalism, and the Catholic Laymen's Association of Georgia." *U.S. Catholic Historian* 8 (3) (Fall 1989) 201–12.

ANTHONY D. ANDREASSI

REINHOLD, HANS (1897–1968)

Priest, liturgist. Hans Ansgar Reinhold was born in Hamburg, Germany, on September 9, 1897, to devout parents who introduced him at an early age to the beauty of sacred music and church architecture. Young Reinhold excelled at his studies and took a keen interest in languages, history, art, and architecture. Throughout his life he suffered from bouts of melancholy and depression. In 1914 he joined the German army, was wounded in action, and was assigned to an army intelligence unit translating French and English codes.

Hans Reinhold

After the war, Reinhold studied at the University of Freiburg where he became acquainted with Romano Guardini's *The Spirit of the Liturgy,* which had a profound effect on his theological thinking. In 1920 Reinhold entered the Jesuit seminary at Innsbruck to begin preparation for the priesthood. In 1922 he spent some time at the monastery of Maria Laach, where he met the abbot, Ildefons Herwegen, and the famous liturgist Dom Odo Casel. At Maria Laach, Reinhold had his first experience of the "dialogue Mass" and was deeply impressed by the participation of the people in the celebration of the liturgy. He decided to dedicate the rest of his life to furthering the cause of liturgical reform.

Reinhold was ordained a priest of the Diocese of Osnabruck on December 19, 1925. Three years later he was sent to Rome for further studies at the Pontifical Institute of Archaeology. In 1929 he became secretary of the Seamen's Apostolate in Germany, a post that helped to make the connection between liturgical reform and social justice.

In 1930 he was instrumental in founding the International Council of the Apostolate of the Sea.

In 1935 he was forced to leave Germany because of his criticism of the Nazi government. He went first to the Netherlands, then to England, and finally to the United States, settling in New York City where he worked for the Catholic section of the Protestant Refugee Committee. Such activities created friction between him and the Archdiocese of New York. Consequently, Reinhold moved to Long Island, and then in 1937 he accepted a teaching position at Portsmouth Priory in Rhode Island. The following year he moved to Seattle, Washington, to serve as port chaplain. Eventually he was named pastor of a church in Yakima, Washington. In 1944 he became an American citizen, and was named pastor of St. Joseph's Church in Sunnyside, Washington, where he remained for the next twelve years.

In 1956 Reinhold requested a leave of absence from Bishop Joseph Dougherty of Yakima for health reasons. Disagreements with Bishop Dougherty and his own deteriorating health caused him great distress in those years. Bishop John Wright of Pittsburgh accepted Reinhold into his diocese and afforded him every kindness, including the right to speak and write. In 1957 Reinhold was diagnosed with the early stages of Parkinson's disease and died in Pittsburgh on January 26, 1968.

From 1938 to 1957 Reinhold wrote a popular column called "Timely Tracts" for *Orate Fratres* and its successor, *Worship.* He was also author of seven books: *The Soul Afire: Revelation of the Mystics* (New York, 1944); with P. F. Anson, *Churches: Their Plan and Furnishings* (Milwaukee, 1948); *The American Parish and the Roman Liturgy* (New York, 1958); *Bringing the Mass to the People* (Baltimore, 1960); *The Dynamics of the Liturgy* (New York, 1961); *Liturgy and Art* (New York, 1966); *H.A.R: The Autobiography of Fr. Reinhold* (New York, 1968).

Reinhold spent his entire adult life advocating liturgical reform. He emphasized the celebration of Mass on the parish level, focusing on the celebratory manner of worship moving the people away from an exclusive preoccupation with pietistic adoration of the Reserved Sacrament. The original understanding of Eucharist as an action of the entire Church, which necessitated full and active participation on the part of all, was Reinhold's lifelong goal.

See also LITURGICAL MOVEMENT IN AMERICA, THE.

Garner, Joel Patrick. "The Vision of a Liturgical Reformer: Hans Ansgar Reinhold, American Catholic Educator." Ed.D. dissertation, Columbia University, 1972.

Tuzik, Robert L. "H. A. Reinhold: The Timely Tract to the American Church." *How Firm a Foundation: Leaders of the Liturgical Movement.* Chicago, 1990, 174–183.

STEPHEN M. RYAN

RELIGIOUS OF JESUS AND MARY (R.J.M.)

The Religious of Jesus and Mary, an apostolic congregation of pontifical right, was founded in 1818 at Lyons (France), by Claudine Thévenet (1774–1837), the daughter of a silk merchant, and André Coindre (1787–1826), a diocesan missionary who later founded the Brothers of the Sacred Heart (1821). The congregation is marked by its Ignatian spiritual heritage, devotion to the Hearts of Christ and Mary, commitment to educational service, and a missionary tradition.

Origins

Having witnessed the brutal death of two of her brothers during the French Revolution, Ms. Thévenet dedicated her life and resources to alleviating the moral and physical ravages left in its wake. She believed that the greatest misfortune was to live and die without knowing God. Thus, she gathered friends around her to offer shelter and basic education for poor girls, whom she considered the "weakest, the most shameful, the most deprived" of post-Revolutionary French society.

Originally a parish-based pious association of laywomen, with the foundress as its president, the sisters began to assist orphans and the daughters of impoverished silk weavers of the Lyons region in workschools known as *providences,* and later undertook boarding schools for young ladies of more affluent families. At Claudine's death in 1837, her institute seemed to be in decline: of the five establishments she had founded, only three remained, all within a thirty-mile radius of Lyons. Yet, by 1842, a small band of sisters left for Agra, India, inaugurating the international and missionary character of the congregation, and thus ensuring papal approbation of its constitutions in 1847.

Growth and Expansion

Foundations followed in Spain (1850), Eastern Canada (1855), England (1860), the U.S.A. (1877), Switzerland (1893), Italy (1896), Mexico/Cuba (1902), Ireland (1912), Argentina (1913), and Germany (1922). A second wave of expansion occurred in the 1950s, and by 1968 the congregation's membership reached a peak of over 2,600 sisters in 142 establishments worldwide. In 1959 it absorbed a small Belgian institute, the Sisters of St. Juliana of the Blessed Sacrament. At the time of Vatican Council II, Religious of Jesus and Mary had expanded their apostolic presence to include Latin America (Colombia, Bolivia, Uruguay), Africa (Algeria, Gabon, Equatorial Guinea), Lebanon, and New Zealand.

Religious of Jesus and Mary in the U.S.A.

The American experience of Religious of Jesus and Mary mirrors this nation's evolution within a multicultural and heterogeneous population. In 1877 four sisters from Quebec, Canada, arrived at Notre Dame parish in Fall River, Massachusetts, where they opened an elementary school, an orphanage, and a night school to meet the educational needs of a growing population of French-Canadian mill workers. From there, they branched out to staff other parochial schools, and to direct private boarding schools at elementary and secondary levels in New Hampshire (1881), Rhode Island (1884), and New York (1904), where they had already opened a residence for working women in Lower Manhattan (1902).

With the expulsion of religious congregations from Mexico during its decades of persecution and civil war (1917–39), sisters arrived in the Southwestern U.S.A. to start a boarding school in El Paso, Texas (1926). They moved into border towns of New Mexico and southern California, where they ministered to Hispanic communities, staffed a women's residence in San Diego (1937), and taught in several parish schools. The expatriates also opened a novitiate for Mexican candidates to the congregation.

Communities in the eastern U.S.A. formed part of the Canadian-American province until 1948–49, when they became autonomous as the Eastern-American province. The postwar influx of novices and other circumstances led the provincial, Mother Vincent Ferrer Ducharme (1895–1955), to move the province's headquarters from Highland Mills, New York, to Hyattsville, Maryland, in the newly formed Archdiocese of Washington, D.C. In August of 1955, sisters took up residence in yet-unfinished buildings, and opened a private girls' high school on the property, where the novitiate and infirmary were also housed. Communities in the Southwest were dependent on Spain and Mexico until 1960, when they were established as the Western-American province. In 1968 both U.S. provinces were united, bringing together 341 sisters in sixteen educational institutions. Throughout the twentieth century, sisters have been sent from the U.S.A. to Europe and Canada, as well as to missions in India, Pakistan, Lebanon, Colombia, and Bolivia.

Postconciliar Development

Since Vatican Council II, the congregation has experienced institutional decline and numerical diminishment, while extending its services to broader educational and pastoral needs. Sisters in the U.S.A., numbering 160 in 1996, have closed many schools and convents. But they have multiplied their ministries by collaborating with other religious congregations, lay colleagues, and associates at every level. Since 1971 they have sponsored and directed QUEST, a project of volunteer communities in service to the urban poor. In 1977 they initiated the first of several "Christian communities" in the province,

where sisters and young adults share prayer, life, and ministry. The charism of the foundress, threatened with extinction at its origin, seems to have found new life once again in a flourishing lay association, the Family of Jesus and Mary, which numbers over one thousand members worldwide.

Claudine Thévenet was beatified in Rome by Pope John Paul II on October 4, 1981, and canonized on March 21, 1993.

Farnham, Janice, R.J.M., ed. and trans. *Letters of Claudine Thévenet.* New York: Jan Press, 1977.

Farnham, Janice, R.J.M., and Rosemary Mangan, R.J.M. *Claudine Thévenet: A Spiritual Profile.* Hyattsville, Md., 1974.

Hugon, Eugénie. *History of the Congregation of the Religious of Jesus and Mary According to Contemporary Witnesses.* Trans. Thomas More Borrell, R.J.M. Orig. 1896. Pune: Anand Press, 1992.

JANICE FARNHAM, R.J.M.

RENGGLI, MARY BEATRICE (1848–1942)

Benedictine sister. Rose Renggli was born in Entlebuch, Canton Lucerne, Switzerland, January 1, 1848. She took the name of Sr. Mary Beatrice on entering religious life as a Benedictine sister. After teaching in the local academy at Maria Rickenbach for some years, she was sent to America as a representative of her institute, the Olivetan Benedictine Sisters. One of the five sisters sent to Clyde, Missouri, she was cofoundress and assistant superior of the first Swiss community established by Maria Rickenback in America.

Later she was sent to Pocahontas, Arkansas, as superior of the little group of four to begin a new foundation in the swampy, malaria-infested wilderness. They had a cash fund of eighty-three cents. When the sisters arrived in Pocahontas on December 13, 1887, there were no paved roads. Deep rivers served as main arteries of travel, and the dirt roads were impassable in rainy seasons. Fr. Eugene Weibel, the pastor, voiced his satisfaction in these words: "With the arrival of the sisters on December 13, 1887, a new era began in the history of Catholicism in Northeast Arkansas." On July 5, 1900, the sisters opened St. Bernard's Hospital. In January 1902 Mother Beatrice fell and broke her hip. The help she received from the newly founded hospital completely won her over to this new apostolate. From the day it first opened, St. Bernard's grew and developed into the magnificent operation it is today, now known as St. Bernard's Regional Medical Center, serving all the people of northeast Arkansas as well as surrounding states. After many years of serving the Lord, Mother Beatrice celebrated her diamond jubilee, the seventy-fifth, on August 15, 1942. She died on September 7, 1942.

REPPLIER, AGNES (1855–1950)

Author. Repplier was born to John and Agnes Matthias Repplier on April 1, 1855, in Philadelphia. Although she started her education by attending convent schools, she finished her education under the guidance of her mother, who recognized and nurtured her daughter's talent for writing. Agnes began publishing short stories as a teenager, contributing to both the *Catholic World* and *Young Catholic*. By the mid-1880s, she was writing for the *Atlantic Monthly* and had begun to establish herself as a respected essayist.

Agnes Repplier (engraving)

Although few of her essays deal with religion directly, the deep influence of her faith is evident throughout the wide range of topics she addressed. Repplier advocated the basic equality of the sexes and set forth the fundamental dynamics of spiritual commitment. On occasion, she also criticized the individualism and materialism in American culture and the superficial spirituality of certain segments of American Catholicism. Although Repplier affirmed the basic human equality of men and women, she did not support women's suffrage. In fact, she viewed the vote as irrelevant to attaining social equality and objected to those who argued for it on purely emotional bases, such as the claim that women are morally superior to men. She believed that such a position betrayed both the cause and women. Repplier was thus a traditionalist in terms of women's suffrage and, indeed, supported many of the social conventions of her era.

Throughout her fifty-five-year writing career, Repplier published a total of seventeen volumes, which included collected essays and three historical biographies written later in life. Several universities granted her honorary degrees, and the University of Notre Dame awarded her the Laetare Medal. Repplier was also elected to the National Institute of Arts and Letters. She died on December 15, 1950, in Philadelphia.

Stokes, George S. *Agnes Repplier: Lady of Letters*. Philadelphia, 1949.
Witmer, E. Repplier. *Agnes Repplier: A Memoir*. Philadelphia, 1957.

PATRICIA DeFERRARI

RÉSÉ, FREDERIC (1791–1871)

Bishop. Résé (pronounced Ray-zay) was born into poverty on February 6, 1791, in Viennenburg, Hanover, the son of John Gotfried Résé and Caroline Altruz. He soldiered against Napoleon at Waterloo. He studied at the Urban College in Rome and was ordained in 1822. Poor health ended a brief mission stint in Africa. In Rome, Bishop Edward Fenwick enlisted him in 1824 for Cincinnati. Résé gained funding for Cincinnati from the Lyons Society for the Propagation of the Faith and from the Leopoldine Stiftung, which he helped found in 1827–29.

On March 8, 1833, Rome named Résé the first bishop of Detroit. Résé would have preferred the vacant see of Cincinnati but he was judged to be more fit for Detroit where a lower level of culture prevailed. Résé argued with the bishop of Cincinnati over European mission funds and the governance of the Toledo, Ohio, area. Résé, as provincial authority of the Poor Clares in Detroit and Pittsburgh, opposed their 1835 rejection of a sister which led to later financial disputes. At the Third Provincial Council of Baltimore (1837), Résé resigned. Archbishop Samuel Eccleston cited the problem of Résé's heavy drinking. Résé changed his mind and, in Rome, obtained a papal reversal of Propaganda's acceptance of his resignation.

During 1838 Résé raised funds in Europe, helping to found the Ludwig Missionsverein in Munich. Rome, alarmed at his unauthorized mission appeals, ordered him back from Detroit. He came to Rome in early 1839 and from there witnessed the economic collapse of his diocese. Seeing he could not return to Detroit, Résé in late 1840 accepted a coadjutor bishop and promised to stay in Europe. John-Marie Odin, C.M., rejected the position and in 1841, Peter Paul Lefevere was named. Résé was falsely reported in the American press to have been imprisoned in Rome. Instead, he was traveling, finally being entrusted to the Sisters of Charity in Hildesheim in 1859 due to a deteriorating mental condition. He died on December 31, 1871, and is buried beside the cathedral in Hildesheim.

See also MICHIGAN, CATHOLIC CHURCH IN.

Canfield, F. "A Diocese So Vast: Bishop Résé in Detroit." *Michigan History* 51 (1967) 202–12.
Paré, G. *The Catholic Church in Detroit, 1701–1888*. Detroit: Wayne State University Press, 1983.

Tentler, Leslie Woodcock. *Seasons of Grace: A History of the Catholic Archdiocese of Detroit.*

Trisco, R. *The Holy See and the Nascent Church in the Middle Western United States, 1826–1850.* Rome: Gregorian University Press, 1962.

EARL BOYEA

RHODE ISLAND, CATHOLIC CHURCH IN

First Catholic Settlers

Although Roger Williams, one of the founders of the colony of Rhode Island and Providence plantations, championed religious liberty for dissenters within the Church of England, neither he nor his fellow Puritans in Rhode Island believed that Catholics should have the right to worship publicly in the colony. The few Catholics among colonial Rhode Islanders lived for the most part in Newport among the foreign merchants who settled in the city.

The first Mass celebrated publicly in Rhode Island was the funeral Mass of the commander of the French fleet, then in Newport harbor, Admiral de Ternay, in 1780. Various priests stationed in Boston visited Rhode Island after the United States gained its independence. By 1813 there were enough Irish and French Catholics in Providence to rent an old wooden schoolhouse to use for Mass. This group of Catholics disappeared during the depression that settled on many cities after the War of 1812, and it was not until the late 1820s that there was again a significant number of Catholics in the state. In 1828 a newly ordained priest of the Diocese of Boston, Fr. Robert D. Woodley, set up mission stations in Newport and Pawtucket to serve mainly Irish congregations. By 1832 the largest number of Catholics was settled in Providence, which soon became the center for missionary work among the Irish attracted to the state by its expanding industries.

Rhode Island under the Diocese of Hartford

The commercial and industrial growth of Rhode Island was matched by that of Connecticut. In 1844 the Holy See erected the Diocese of Hartford and chose a native New Englander and convert, Rev. William Tyler of Boston, as the diocese's first bishop. After looking over the situation in Hartford, which was centrally located in the new diocese, Bishop Tyler chose to settle in Providence which had the larger Catholic population. Rome declined to change the seat of the diocese to Providence but gave Tyler permission to reside there.

After Bishop Tyler's death in 1849, the American bishops nominated and Rome confirmed Irish-born Fr. Bernard O'Reilly as the second bishop of Hartford. An energetic but impulsive man, Bishop O'Reilly ministered to a Catholic population swollen by famine emigration from Ireland. In 1851 he arranged to bring the Sisters of Mercy under Frances Warde to Providence where they opened an orphanage in their convent and took over the task of teaching in the cathedral parish school opened in 1848 with lay teachers. In March 1855, Bishop O'Reilly confronted a crowd of nativists which had gathered in front of the sisters' convent on Broad Street to demand the "release" of a girl who was reportedly being held in the convent. The mayor of Providence stood with the bishop against the crowd and a few hours later the crowd peacefully dispersed. After Bishop O'Reilly's untimely death at sea in 1856, the much beloved Francis B. McFarland took up the duties of bishop.

The Diocese of Providence

In 1871 Bishop McFarland asked Rome to divide his diocese, whose population had increased to approximately two hundred thousand souls, and to create a new diocese encompassing Rhode Island and southeastern Massachusetts, with its see city at Providence. Pope Pius IX approved the petition in February 1872 and appointed a priest of the Diocese of Hartford, Fr. Thomas F. Hendricken, the first bishop of Providence.

Bishops Hendricken and Harkins

Within a few months of taking up his duties, Bishop Hendricken announced that he would undertake the building of a new cathedral church which Bishop McFarland had himself hoped to build. Hendricken chose Patrick C. Keely to design and supervise the construction of a neo-Gothic church, which, when completed, would be among the finest in the country.

Among the pastoral concerns which Bishop Hendricken addressed during his years as bishop was the particular spiritual needs of the increasing number of French-Canadians who had begun settling in Rhode Island and Massachusetts in the 1850s. In 1884, when Bishop Hendricken sent a priest of mixed Irish-French ancestry to be pastor of Notre Dame de Lourdes parish in Fall River, he inadvertently provoked a dispute with the Canadians which had national importance. The Canadians asserted that a bishop was *obligated* to appoint a pastor of the same nationality as his parishioners. Rome's initial response was that a bishop was so obligated. When Hendricken and other American bishops pointed out the practical impossibility of this obligation, the Congregation for the Propagation of the Faith revised its response and asked that the bishops do all they could to provide pastors of the same nationality.

Bishop Hendricken's years witnessed the advent of politically and economically prominent Catholics in Rhode Island. The diocese and the Holy See recognized one of the former, Joseph D. Banigan, an important rubber manufacturer and philanthropist, by conferring on him knighthood of the Order of St. Gregory the Great in 1885. When

Bishop Hendricken died in June 1886, his funeral Mass was the first Mass celebrated in the new cathedral to which he had devoted so much of his energies.

During his thirty-four years as bishop, Matthew Harkins, Bishop Hendricken's successor, would create over eighty territorial and ethnic parishes and mission stations for a diocese which grew to be one of the largest in the country. Beside the Irish and French-Canadians, large numbers of Italian, Polish, and Portuguese immigrants settled in the diocese along with smaller numbers of Lithuanians, Germans, Austrians, Carpatho-Rusyns, and Syrians. In addition to increasing the number and diversity of parishes and of the clergy, both diocesan and religious, Bishop Harkins also directed the expansion of institutions dedicated to the material and spiritual care of the people of the diocese so that few if any dioceses in the country rivaled Providence in providing for orphans and the sick. Harkins' years also saw the founding and growth of numerous lay organizations dedicated to the service of the peoples' material, social, and spiritual needs. Some of the organizations served all the peoples of the diocese, while others were organized on strictly ethnic lines. The growth of the diocese was such that in 1903, Bishop Harkins asked that his diocese be divided. In February 1904, Rome acceded to his request, creating the Diocese of Fall River from the Massachusetts part of the diocese. Although rheumatism in his later years forced him to give over the administration of the diocese to his assistants, Bishop Harkins took a personal interest in the founding of the first Catholic college in the diocese, Providence College, opened in 1919 by the Dominicans and the establishing of a small community of Benedictines in Portsmouth also in 1919.

Bishops Hickey and Keough

In 1918 Bishop Harkins asked for and received a coadjutor, Bishop William A. Hickey, to whom Harkins turned over the administration of the diocese following Hickey's episcopal ordination in April 1919. Two years after Bishop Harkins' death in May 1921, Hickey announced his intention of conducting a three-year-long drive to raise a million dollars to expand existing diocesan high schools and to establish new ones. The drive proved a success as did later annual Catholic Charity Fund appeals aimed at replacing existing buildings that housed diocesan charitable institutions and providing funds for their operations. Hickey also initiated an annual drive to support the diocesan newspaper, the *Providence Visitor,* which in those years, claimed to have the largest circulation of any Catholic newspaper in the United States. Ultranationalists among the French-Canadians in the diocese, however, regarded these endeavors as threats to the continuation of their distinct Catholic and Canadian traditions. The Sentinellists contested Bishop Hickey's fundraising procedures before both

Church and civil courts to the point where in 1927 sixty-five men prominent in the movement were excommunicated for causing public scandal and the French-language newspaper, *La Sentinelle,* was placed on the Index. Within two years all sixty-five were reconciled to the Church, but the scars of the dispute remained for many years.

Bishop Hickey died of a heart attack in October 1933, and his successor, Bishop Francis P. Keough, provided strong, positive leadership for both the Church and the state as the citizens of Rhode Island struggled to cope with the impact of the depression. Through his leadership of the Catholic Charity Appeal, Bishop Keough provided the diocesan charitable institutions with a solid financial footing. He also encouraged the founding of the Catholic Youth Organization in the diocese and vigorously supported the *Providence Visitor* and its campaigns against indecent movies and literature.

Bishops McVinney, Gelineau, and Mulvee

In December 1947 Bishop Keough was appointed archbishop of Baltimore, and, in July 1948, Providence-born Fr. Russell J. McVinney, the rector of the minor seminary Bishop Keough had opened in 1941, became the fifth bishop of Providence. In the 1950s and 1960s both the Catholic population of the diocese and the number of its institutions increased substantially. Bishop McVinney skillfully directed both the material and the spiritual growth of the diocese into the postwar suburbs. Although conservative in his own thinking, he sought to implement faithfully the vision of the Church that emerged from the Second Vatican Council. Possessing a deep and sincere interest in social justice issues, he encouraged the clergy, religious, and laity of the diocese to devote themselves to care of the poor and the oppressed. His last years were saddened by the resignation of a number of priests and religious, among them his own auxiliary, Bishop Bernard M. Kelly.

Following Bishop McVinney's death in August 1971, the Holy See appointed Msgr. Louis E. Gelineau as the next bishop of Providence. Bishop Gelineau, after his ordination in January 1972, oversaw a Church which was forced by a decline in the number of religious and clergy to reorganize and reprioritize both the human and financial resources of the diocese. Changes in the immigration laws in the 1960s led to a renewed influx of immigrants from the Cape Verdes, Southeast Asia, and especially from Latin America and the Caribbean. Rather than create new ethnic parishes for the Southeast Asian and Hispanic immigrants, the diocese chose to integrate them into the existing parishes in the cities where they settled. In order to minister to the new immigrant populations and to provide ministers to serve the diverse spiritual needs of the people, the diocese recruited and trained increasing numbers of laymen as lay deacons. The diocese also recruited both lay men and women to serve in a multitude of ways after being trained in a Lay Ministry Program. Many of these volunteer ministers in the post-Vatican II Church were motivated by their experiences in the Christian Family, Cursillo, Renew, and Charismatic movements.

In February 1995 Bishop Gelineau announced the appointment of Robert E. Mulvee, bishop of Wilmington, Delaware, as coadjutor bishop of Providence with the right of succession. At the time of his appointment, the 645,643 Catholics of the diocese made up 64 percent of the state's population, one of the highest percentages in the nation.

Conley, Patrick T., and Matthew J. Smith. *Catholicism in Rhode Island: The Formative Era.* Providence, R.I.: Diocese of Providence, 1976.

Cullen, Thomas F. *The Catholic Church in Rhode Island.* Providence, R.I.: The Franciscan Missionaries of Mary, 1936.

Hayman, Robert W. *Catholicism in Rhode Island and the Diocese of Providence, 1780–1886.* Providence, R.I.: Diocese of Providence, 1982.

____. *Catholicism in Rhode Island and the Diocese of Providence 1887–1921.* Providence, R.I.: Diocese of Providence, 1995.

ROBERT W. HAYMAN

RHODE, PAUL (1870–1945)

Bishop. The first Polish bishop in the United States was born in Werowo (Prussian Poland) on September 16, 1870. He came to the United States in 1879 and settled in Chicago with his mother. His early education was at St. Stanislaus Kostka, the first Polish parish in Chicago. As was true for

Paul Rhode

many Chicago seminarians at that time, he attended St. Francis Seminary (Milwaukee). On June 16, 1894, he was ordained by Archbishop Frederick Katzer of Milwaukee. Rhode returned to Chicago and began his pastoral work at St. Michael's parish on the southeast side of the city.

Divisions in the Polish Community

The Chicago Polish Catholic community was one of the largest ethnic groups in the city. Although the priests of the Congregation of the Resurrection had been given charge of the Polish parishes under Bishop Thomas Foley, the authoritarian style of Rev. Vincent Barzynski alienated many Polish Catholics who wanted non-Resurrectionists as their pastors. Religious and political differences contributed to the establishment of two ethnic organizations in the city, the Polish Roman Catholic Union and the Polish National Alliance. By the 1890s, Polish Catholics in Chicago were battling one another in street fights, church occupations, rectory invasions, and attacks on priests.

All these tensions finally erupted at St. Hedwig's parish. Many of the parishioners wanted Archbishop Patrick Feehan to name a popular associate, Fr. Anthony Kozlowski, as the pastor of St. Hedwig. He was to replace the Resurrectionist priest whom Feehan had named over the objections of the parishioners. The continuing confrontations between the archbishop and the parishioners lead to Kozlowski's dismissal. The young priest then decided to form his own parish and asked the archbishop to consecrate the new church. When Feehan refused, Kozlowski himself consecrated the church. After his excommunication, Kozlowski was consecrated a bishop by an Old Catholic bishop. He then established a Polish Independent Catholic Church. Not only did he attract a thousand families from St. Hedwig's to his church, but he also toured the country to gain additional members. Kozlowski's schism was not the only sign of Polish dissatisfaction. Stefan Kaminski (Buffalo) and Francis Hodur (Scranton) also attracted a number of Polish Catholics to their independence movements.

By the turn of the century, Polish Catholic priests were urging members of the American hierarchy to name Polish bishops to their dioceses. In 1903 Fr. Wenceslaus Kruszka arrived in Rome to present a petition on behalf of the Polish Catholic Congress seeking the nomination of Polish priests to the episcopacy. Not until April 1904 was Kruszka able to meet with Pope Pius X. The new pontiff promised that the Poles in America would receive Polish bishops. Before the actual selection of bishops, Rome sent Archbishop Francis Symon (Plock) to visit the Polish Catholic communities in the United States. After his tour, Symon wrote two reports for the Vatican. In his 1906 report, Symon recommended that Buffalo, Pittsburgh, Chicago, Milwaukee, Detroit, and Philadelphia receive

Polish bishops. Despite these reports, Rome did not take action until 1907 when the followers of Anthony Kozlowski joined with Francis Hodur's Polish National Catholic Church after Kozlowski's death. Finally, Archbishop James Quigley of Chicago was instructed by Rome to convene all the Polish pastors of Chicago for the election of an auxiliary bishop. Since the Archdiocese of Chicago had the largest Polish Catholic population in the United States, the choice of Chicago to have the first Polish bishop made sense. All these events were the background to Paul Rhode's election.

Bishop in Chicago and Green Bay

On August 16, 1907, Archbishop Quigley met with all the Chicago Polish pastors for the election. Of the thirty-two pastors who voted, twenty-six cast their ballot for Paul Rhode. Four years earlier, when the Association of Polish Priests had canvassed their members on possible episcopal candidates, Paul Rhode came in last. In selecting Paul Rhode as auxiliary bishop of Chicago, the Polish pastors chose a man who appealed to first-, second-, and third-generation Polish immigrants. He also was respected by both the Polish Roman Catholic Union and the Polish National Alliance. Given the division within the Polish Catholic community and the loss of Catholics to the Polish National Catholic Church, the first Polish bishop needed to be a reconciler. Rhode received notice of his election in May 1908 and was consecrated on July 28, 1908. Shortly after this, Rhode began the task of reconciliation. Within a couple of months, he helped Polish parishes in Cleveland, Duluth, and St. Louis return to the Roman Catholic Church.

During the next seven years, Rhode continued to support the religious and charitable projects of Polish Catholics. He remained on good terms with Archbishop Quigley. However, on July 10, 1915, the Vatican announced that Paul Rhode was named the bishop of Green Bay. The announcement came on the same day as Quigley's death. The Polish clergy in Chicago made an appeal in late July 1915 to the apostolic delegate, John Bonzano, not to leave the Polish Catholics in Chicago without a bishop. That same year George Mundelein was named the new archbishop of Chicago.

The desire of Polish Catholics to have Rhode named an archbishop became the subject of a 1920 memorial written by the General Union of the Polish Clergy in collaboration with the Polish legation at the Vatican. In many ways, this memorial was the Polish version of Cahenslyism. Archbishop Mundelein, the major writer of the American bishops' response, warned the Vatican of the serious consequences if the government of the United States became aware of the appeal by Polish priests in the United States to the Polish government. The charge of Catholic disloyalty to the government and Catholic allegiance to foreign powers were favorites themes of anti-Catholic groups. The actions of the Polish clergy only served to validate those themes. In the end, the Holy See took no action on the petition. Bishop Rhode remained as bishop of Green Bay until his death there on March 3, 1945.

See also ILLINOIS, CATHOLIC CHURCH IN; POLISH CATHOLICS IN AMERICA.

Kantowicz, Edward. *Corporation Sole.* University of Notre Dame Press, 1983.

Kuzniewski, Anthony J. *Faith and Fatherland: The Polish Church War in Wisconsin, 1896–1916.* University of Notre Dame Press, 1980.

Parot, Joseph John. *Polish Catholics in Chicago, 1850–1920.* DeKalb: Northern Illinois University Press, 1981.

Shanabruch, Charles. *Chicago Catholics: The Evolution of an American Identity.* University of Notre Dame Press, 1981.

MARTIN ZIELINSKI

RICHARD, GABRIEL (1767–1832)

Missionary priest, congressman. Gabriel Richard was born on October 15, 1767, at Saintes, in Saintonge, France, the third of six children, of François Richard and Marie-Geneviève Bossuet. He attended college at Saintes from 1778, and studied philosophy and theology at the Sulpician Seminary in Angers (1784–90), declaring education "the most precious possession" his father could give him. He appreciated the Sulpician image of God as kind and loving in contrast to the more severe Jansenist one. Joining the Society of St. Sulpice, he completed his novitiate at Issy (1790–91) and was ordained on October 9, 1791.

Gabriel Richard

Richard fled the French Revolution with his fellow Sulpicians, François Ciquard and Ambrose Maréchal, and arrived in Baltimore in June 1792.

After serving in the Illinois missions (1792–98), the young priest was transferred by Bishop John Carroll to St. Anne parish, Detroit. He was responsible for religious activity in the Lower Peninsula and in Green Bay. Richard remodeled the old church, despite opposition from the parish trustees. The isolated life did not suit this teacher and in 1805 he was prepared to return to France. After fire destroyed Detroit on June 11, 1805, however, Richard committed himself to the town and its future, providing its motto, *ex cineribus resurgat*. The trustees opposed the rebuilding of their church in the town and the dismantling of their cemetery. The local bishop forced a resolution in 1817 and Richard's church was completed in 1828. Richard also opened a seminary (1804), a school for Native American and French children at Spring Hill (1808), and a school for the blind. All failed due to lack of funding or students. In 1817 he and the Presbyterian minister, John Monteith, laid the foundations of the University of Michigan.

Seeking to advance his ideas for education and the Native Americans in Michigan, Richard was elected a territorial delegate to the United States Congress in 1823. This first priest in Congress was jailed in Detroit in 1824 when an old lawsuit against his excommunication of an irregularly married parishioner was resolved with a fine on Richard for defamation of character, a fine he refused to pay on principle. Released only to return to Congress, where he lobbied successfully for the authorization of the Chicago-Detroit Road (Michigan Avenue), he was vilified by his political opponents in Detroit who rigged his defeat in 1825. The rest of his life was spent in "house arrest" in Wayne County.

From 1820, Rome considered making Detroit a diocese with Richard as its first bishop. Briefs for the diocese and new bishop were dated in Rome on March 20, 1827, but never sent. Letters from Stephen Badin and a visit by Frederic Résé to Rome raised concerns about the small number of Catholics in Michigan, its low income, and Richard's debts, lack of decorum, and past imprisonment.

In June 1832, the steamboat *Henry Clay* brought cholera to Detroit. Caring tirelessly for his people, Richard died of the epidemic on September 13, 1832. His body currently rests at St. Anne Church in a separate chapel.

Coombs L., and F. Blouin, Jr. *Intellectual Life on the Michigan Frontier: The Libraries of Gabriel Richard and John Monteith.* Ann Arbor: University of Michigan Press, 1985.

Mast, D. *Always the Priest: The Life of Gabriel Richard, S.S.* Baltimore: Helicon, 1965.

Woodford, F. *Gabriel Richard: Frontier Ambassador.* Detroit: Wayne State University Press, 1958.

EARL BOYEA

RIEPP, BENEDICTA (SYBILLA) (1825–62)

Benedictine. The Bavarian tradition of Benedictine women in the United States owes its origin to Benedicta (Sybilla) Riepp, O.S.B. Sybilla was born in Waal, in the old Swabian province of the kingdom of Bavaria, on June 28, 1825. She attended elementary school in Waal until the age of twelve, and then studied at the Franciscan convent in Kaufbeuren until 1842, the year in which she successfully completed the examinations for teacher certification in Germany.

In 1844 Sybilla entered the Benedictine monastery of St. Walburg in Eichstätt, Bavaria, where she later professed first vows in 1846 and perpetual vows in 1849. During the eight years she lived at St. Walburg, she taught in the girls' school of Eichstätt and served as the mistress of novices from 1849 until her departure for North America in 1852.

Imbued with the missionary zeal so characteristic of the postsecularization Catholic revival in Bavaria, Benedicta volunteered to go to America when the request came to Prioress Edwarda Schnitzer to send nuns to teach the children of the German immigrants who had settled in Pennsylvania. Benedicta and her companions arrived in the wilderness clearing of St. Marys, Pennsylvania, on July 22, 1852, and established there the first monastery of Benedictine women in North America. The six years she spent as superior there were plagued with physical hardship and misunderstandings between herself and local churchmen, most notably Abbot Boniface Wimmer, O.S.B., of St. Vincent Abbey in Latrobe, Pennsylvania. She resisted his interference in the internal matters of the fledgling community, as well as his efforts to thwart her authority in her role as the legitimate superior of the earliest monasteries of Benedictine women in North America. Nonetheless, her leadership during those years resulted in the establishment of three new monasteries in Erie, Pennsylvania (1856), Newark, New Jersey (1857), and St. Cloud, Minnesota (1857).

In 1857 Benedicta Riepp returned to Europe, confident that her superiors in Eichstätt and Rome could help her resolve the controversial issues surrounding the threatened autonomy of the newly established communities in the United States. She and her companion were not favorably received in Eichstätt, and were prevented from traveling to Rome where she was prepared to present her case before Pope Pius IX.

Broken in spirit and failing in health, Benedicta returned to the United States in 1858, and was closed out of the monasteries she had founded in the East. Ostracization had been the price of her efforts to resolve the issues that were threatening the autonomy of the newly established monasteries of women in the United States. Upon the invitation of Prioress Willibalda Scherbauer in St. Cloud, Minnesota, Benedicta Riepp took up residence there in the spring of 1858, until she died of tuberculosis on March 15, 1862, at the age of thirty-seven. In 1884 her remains were transferred from St. Cloud to the cemetery of the Sisters of the Order of St. Benedict, St. Joseph, Minnesota, which has become a pilgrim site for Benedictine women nationwide.

The only extant writings of Benedicta Riepp are fifteen letters which she wrote between the years 1852 and 1861. These letters reveal her conviction that the Benedictine vocation was privileged and graced, that gratitude was the only appropriate response to the providential workings of God, and that the goal of Benedictine life was the search for God in unity and mutual love.

See also BENEDICTINES (O.S.B.); GERMAN CATHOLICS IN AMERICA.

Baska, R., O.S.B. *The Benedictine Congregation of St. Scholastica: Its Foundations and Development, 1852–1930.* Washington, D.C.: The Catholic University of America, 1935.

Drey, E., O.S.B. *Die Abtei St. Walburg (1035–1935): 900 Jahre in Wort und Bild.* Eichstätt: St. Walburg Abbey, 1934.

Girgen, I., O.S.B. *Behind the Beginnings.* St. Joseph, Minn.: Sisters of the Order of St. Benedict, 1981.

Hollermann, E., O.S.B. *The Reshaping of a Tradition: American Benedictine Women, 1852–1881.* St. Joseph, Minn.: Sisters of the Order of St. Benedict, 1994.

Mathäser, W., O.S.B. "Koenig Ludwig I von Bayern und die Gründung der Ersten Bayerischen Benediktinerabtei in Nordamerika." *Studien und Mitteilungen* 35 (1926) 123–82.

EPHREM HOLLERMANN, O.S.B.

RIOBÓ/RIOBÓO, JUAN ANTONIO GARCÍA (1740–ca. 1805)

Missionary. Riobó was born in Malpica, Spain, received his training at the Convento de San Francisco, Salamanca, Spain, and became a Franciscan in 1760. He was sent to the Colégio de San Fernando, Mexico, in 1769 and arrived in Lower California in 1771, where he labored as a missionary near Cape San Lúcas until 1773. According to the diary kept by Riobó, he and his fellow Franciscan Matías Noriega served as chaplains for the third Spanish expedition in search of a Northwest passage in 1779. Departing from San Blas, Mexico, aboard *La Princesa* and *La Favorita,* the expedition sailed along the Pacific Coast, going as far north as Alaska. Riobó's diary was later discovered among some papers stored in the library at Santa Clara University. It was translated by William Thornton, S.J., and published under the title "An account of the voyage made by Fr. John Riobo . . ." in *Historical Records and Studies* 12 (1918) 76–89. He returned to Lower California in 1783. At the request of the dying Fray Junipero Serra, superior of the California Mission, he went to mission headquarters at San Carlos, Monterey-Carmel, with fellow Franciscan Fray Diego Noboa, to act as Serra's supernumeraries. Riobó then sailed with Serra to San Diego and accompanied him on an overland trip back to San Carlos. He was then sent to head the mission at San Buenaventura in early 1784. The records show he labored at San Gabriel from 1784 to 1785. From there he went to the mission at San Diego, where he remained until 1786, when it is believed he returned to Mexico.

TRICIA T. PYNE

RIORDAN, PATRICK (1841–1914)

Archbishop of San Francisco. Patrick William Riordan was born on August 27, 1841, in Chatham, New Brunswick, Canada, of Irish immigrants, Matthew Riordan, a ship carpenter, and Mary Dunne. In 1848 the family moved to Chicago. Patrick attended school at St. Mary's of the Lake Academy, and entered the University of Notre Dame in 1856, where he studied for two years. In 1858 he decided to study for the priesthood for the Archdiocese of Chicago, and was sent to Rome to study at the Congregation for the Propagation of the Faith's Urban College. He was selected to be one of the first students at the newly established North American College, but poor health forced him to withdraw after less than a year. He studied briefly in Paris before he enrolled at The American College at Louvain, Belgium, in October 1861. He was ordained to the priesthood in Mechlin, Belgium, on June 10, 1865, by Cardinal Englebert Sterckx. The following year he received his licentiate in sacred theology.

In 1866 Riordan returned to Chicago, where he was assigned to teach canon law and ecclesiastical history in the Seminary Department at St. Mary's of the Lake. After several brief pastoral assignments, in 1871 he was appointed

Patrick Riordan

pastor of St. James parish in Chicago, where he remained until 1883. Riordan distinguished himself as an excellent administrator, builder, and fundraiser, qualities that led to his appointment in 1883 as coadjutor archbishop for the Archdiocese of San Francisco, with the right of succession. He was consecrated bishop by Archbishop Patrick Feehan on September 16, 1883, in Chicago, and succeeded Joseph Alemany as archbishop of San Francisco on December 28, 1884.

Archbishop of San Francisco

As archbishop, Riordan distinguished himself as an aggressive builder, a competent businessman, and a promoter of Catholic education. Distressed by the poor quality of the buildings in his archdiocese, Riordan began a massive building and restoration program to upgrade wooden churches and structures to brick and stone buildings. His most significant building project was the erection of a new cathedral, St. Mary's of the Assumption, dedicated on January 11, 1891, to replace the old cathedral that was located in an increasingly unseemly part of town. Riordan's efforts suffered a devastating blow from the great earthquake and fire of 1906 that leveled large sections of the city, including twelve parish churches and numerous other Catholic institutions. Archdiocesan property damage was estimated at six million dollars. Mercifully, Riordan was not in San Francisco at the time of the disaster; he was notified of it while in Omaha, Nebraska. Upon his return, Riordan rallied the city in an emotional speech to the Citizen's Committee of San Francisco, in which he asserted in the words of St. Paul, "I am a citizen of no mean city, although it is in ashes," and he vowed, "We shall rebuild." Though personally devastated by the tragedy, Riordan rallied his people, and within two years, all the earthquake damaged parishes, save one, were reopened.

Riordan also distinguished himself as a businessman. In November 1906 he successfully supported a state referendum that amended the California state constitution to exempt church buildings from taxation. He also successfully concluded the archdiocese's dispute with the government of Mexico over the Pious Fund. Riordan brought the case before the Permanent Court of Arbitration at the recently established Hague Tribunal, the first case argued before this body. The court decided in favor of Riordan, though the Mexican Revolution of 1910 disrupted the payment schedule that the court had dictated.

Riordan was also an enthusiastic supporter of Catholic education. After his arrival in San Francisco, the parochial school system expanded significantly, with total enrollment doubling to eight thousand students within five years of his arrival. He also supported Catholic college students attending non-Catholic institutions by establishing Newman Centers at the University of California at Berkeley, at Stanford University, and at San Jose State College. Most significantly, Riordan sought to provide for the needs of a local clergy by establishing his own archdiocesan seminary, St. Patrick's Seminary in Menlo Park, which opened in September 1898.

For the last fifteen years of his episcopate, Riordan, burdened by the heavy demands of his missionary archdiocese, sought to obtain a coadjutor bishop to assist him in his work. On February 8, 1903, George Montgomery was appointed, but after serving impressively for four years, he died prematurely on January 10, 1907, forcing Riordan to resume his search for an assistant. His nomination of Edward Hanna of Rochester resulted in a long and bitter dispute with the Vatican; it denied Hanna's appointment on the grounds that Hanna was a "Modernist." Ultimately, Hanna was appointed as an auxiliary in 1912 and succeeded Riordan as archbishop in 1915; however, the whole episode left a bitter taste in Riordan's mouth. Riordan's distance from Rome allowed him to assert his independence from Rome on occasion by inviting several suspect figures to his archdiocese, most notably the English Modernist George Tyrrell.

Riordan's thirty-year episcopate had been one of enormous growth for the archdiocese, even with the earthquake. Parishes increased in number from 50 to 120, the number of clergy grew from 100 to 350, and numerous charitable and educational institutions had been established. By the time of his death on December 27, 1914, the Church in San Francisco was firmly established.

See also CALIFORNIA, CATHOLIC CHURCH IN.

Gaffey, James. *Citizen of No Mean City: Archbishop Patrick Riordan of San Francisco.* Consortium, 1976.

JEFFREY M. BURNS

RITTER, JOSEPH ELMER (1892–1967)

Cardinal archbishop of St. Louis. Joseph Elmer Ritter was born on July 20, 1892, in the small farming town of New Albany, Indiana, on the banks of the Ohio River. His parents were Nicholas Ritter and Bertha Luette. Nicholas Ritter was the town baker. He was one of six children: two brothers became physicians; one brother became a dentist; and a fourth brother became a businessman. His only sister became a religious of the Sisters of Charity of Nazareth, Kentucky.

Early Years

Joseph Ritter attended St. Mary's elementary school in New Albany, graduating with honors. He then entered St. Meinrad's Seminary and upon completion of his studies was ordained as a priest of the Diocese of Indianapolis on May 30, 1917. It was Ritter's desire immediately to begin graduate studies in Rome, but Bishop Chartrand felt his talents

Joseph Cardinal Ritter

were needed in the diocese and assigned him as assistant priest at the cathedral parish of SS Peter and Paul. In 1925 he was appointed pastor of the cathedral parish and shared the rectory with Bishop Chartrand. One problem that plagued the young Fr. Ritter was the rise of a strong Ku Klux Klan movement in Indiana. He spoke out frequently from the cathedral pulpit condemning the anti-Catholic sentiments of the Klan. He was influential in having the Indiana newspapers publish the names of Klan members, thus causing a rapid decline in its membership.

On March 28, 1933, Fr. Ritter was ordained auxiliary bishop of Indianapolis by Bishop Joseph Chartrand. Upon Chartrand's death one year later, Ritter was named bishop of Indianapolis. Ten years later, when the diocese was raised to metropolitan status, he was named the first archbishop of Indianapolis. As ordinary of Indianapolis, Ritter followed a much beloved predecessor. While Bishop Chartrand was a deeply spiritual person, his administrative and business talents left much to be desired. As auxiliary and then ordinary, Archbishop Ritter was able to create a sound fiscal base for the archdiocese and bring efficiency to its administrative operations.

On his fifty-fourth birthday, July 20, 1946, Archbishop Ritter was selected by the Holy See as archbishop of St. Louis, succeeding the late John Cardinal Glennon. Again, he followed in the footsteps of a beloved prelate. He was installed as the fourth archbishop, fifth ordinary of the archdiocese, in October 1946.

Archbishop of St. Louis

In St. Louis, Ritter found not only a segregated city, but a segregated Church as well. African American young men were not allowed in the diocesan seminaries, and the parish schools as well as the parishes themselves were segregated. African Americans had only one parish to attend in the entire city. In the late spring of 1947, the archbishop issued an order integrating all Catholic schools, churches, and agencies. The integration of all schools was to begin with the 1947 school term in September. The order stirred up a storm of protest, many from prominent and wealthy Catholic laymen. A protest committee was formed and took their cause directly to the apostolic delegate in Washington. When he rejected their petition, they threatened to seek to ban the order in civil court.

The archbishop became aware of the protest committee's plans on a Saturday and immediately sent telegrams to all pastors with the text of a letter to be read at all Sunday Masses on September 21, 1947. The pastoral letter threatened with excommunication any Catholic who openly opposed the edict on integration. The committee immediately dissolved. It was a great victory for Ritter and the Church, and it occurred six and a half years before the U.S. Supreme Court decision ending segregation.

To stabilize the financial situation and provide for the future growth of the archdiocese, Ritter began the Archdiocesan Development Appeal, a capital improvements appeal that raised millions of dollars each year for program development and buildings. One significant result of this appeal was the erection of Cardinal Glennon Children's Hospital, the only Catholic hospital for children in the nation. He also established a diocesan bank into which parishes and agencies could deposit surplus funds and earn interest, and from which other parishes could borrow at low interest rates for building, repairs, and expansion. This fiscal stability allowed for the building of four diocesan high schools and numerous suburban parishes.

The Archbishop Ritter Worldmission Exhibition, held in St. Louis in May 1953, centered the attention of the community and the religious world on the missionary movement of the Catholic Church. A direct outcome of this was the fact that the Archdiocese of St. Louis became the first diocese in the United States to establish a foreign mission in Bolivia. The mission was staffed by diocesan clergy and religious men and women, and supported by the archdiocese.

Cardinal

Archbishop Ritter was the only American among four prelates named to the cardinalate in late 1960 by Pope John XXIII. The red hat was conferred by the pontiff on January 16, 1961. In October 1962 he returned to Rome to participate in the Second Vatican Council. He went with three major concerns: the liturgy, religious freedom, and the nature of the Church. He was appointed to the Central Commission that set much of the agenda for the meetings and served as a steering committee. He was one of the first prelates to reject the schema on revelation and was instrumental in having that document completely revised. Throughout the sessions of the council, Cardinal Ritter championed the cause of religious freedom and ecumenism. In the second session of the council, Ritter spoke about the importance of the restoration of the order of deacon and the importance of preaching within liturgical ceremonies. He assumed a growing leadership position among the American hierarchy. This often placed him at odds with more conservative East Coast prelates. He was also a strong advocate for the establishment of national episcopal conferences with the authority to enforce their decisions. He felt that this would promote the total welfare of the Church in a given country.

Following the council, Cardinal Ritter began the process of putting the council's decisions into practice within his own archdiocese. He sponsored a National Liturgical Week in order to introduce the changes in the liturgy. He established a Commission on Ecumenical Affairs and a Council of the Laity. He also formed the Office on Human Rights and organized Catholic Charities to coordinate the various charitable activities of the archdiocese.

Just before his seventy-fifth birthday, Cardinal Ritter suffered a heart attack. Within days he suffered another that took his life on June 10, 1967.

See also MISSOURI, CATHOLIC CHURCH IN; VATICAN COUNCIL II AND AMERICAN CATHOLICS.

MARTIN G. TOWEY

ROBINSON, PASCHAL (1870–1948)

Franciscan friar, scholar, diplomat, archbishop. Born in Dublin, Ireland, Charles Robinson was the son of Nugent Robinson, a prominent Catholic author. He received his early education in London and New York, and took up a career in journalism. A brilliant writer, at the age of twenty-two he became foreign correspondent and associate editor of the *North American Review*. Robinson entered the Franciscans at St. Bonaventure's College, Allegany, New York, in 1896, receiving the name Paschal; he completed his theological studies in Rome in 1902. Teaching in the internal schools of his order, he came into academic prominence through his work "The Real St. Francis of Assisi" (1903), a refutation of the Protestant Paul Sabatier's portrait. Robinson soon became known as the leading scholar of Franciscana in the English-speaking world, and contributed extensively to the *Catholic Encyclopedia* and various reviews. In 1913 he was appointed professor of medieval history at The Catholic University of America, and in 1914 was named a fellow of the Royal Historical Society.

Robinson served on the U.S. Educational and Economic Mission at the Versailles conference of 1919, where his diplomatic skills became apparent. He increasingly was called into service by the Holy See, being named consultor to several Vatican congregations in 1924. After several missions to the Middle East, he was named titular archbishop in 1927. In 1929 he successfully mediated a conflict between the British governor of Malta and the hierarchy there. That same year he was chosen as the first papal nuncio to the Irish Free State, an office he filled with distinction until his death in 1948 in the city of his birth.

See also FRANCISCAN FRIARS.

The Provincial Annals, Holy Name Province (1948).

DOMINIC V. MONTI, O.F.M.

ROCKNE, KNUTE KENNETH (1888–1931)

Notre Dame football coach. Rockne was born in Voss, Norway, and at the age of five migrated to Chicago with his family. He went to the University of Notre Dame and earned a bachelor's degree in 1914. As a student Rockne played on Notre Dame's football team and was a member of the famous team that defeated Army in 1913. After graduation he became a chemistry teacher at Notre Dame and began his coaching career as assistant coach. In 1918 he was named head coach, made Notre Dame into a powerful national team, and came to be regarded as one of the greatest coaches in the history of American college football. Rockne held his position for thirteen years and achieved the prestigious record of 105 victories in 122 games. His contributions to the sport included the introduction of the "precision backfield" and the perfection of line play. In addition to his accomplishments on the playing field,

Knute K. Rockne.

Rockne authored several books on football. In 1925 he became a Catholic. Tragically, Rockne died in a plane crash in Bazaar, Kansas, on March 31, 1931, at the age of forty-three. Part of Rockne's fame is due to the film made in his memory, *The Knute Rockne Story,* that starred Pat O'Brien. That same movie featured a young actor named Ronald Wilson Reagan, who in 1980 became the fortieth president of the United States.

ANTHONY D. ANDREASSI

ROGERS, ALICE (1880–1961)

Foundress. Alice Rogers was born of Irish immigrant parents February 18, 1880, in Billerica, Massachusetts, and after graduation from a local high school attended Lowell State Normal School for two years (1899–1901). She then taught for three years—two in Billerica and one in Ayer. On September 12, 1904, she entered the Discalced Carmelite monastery in Boston and when she received the religious habit in January 1905, she also received the name Aloysius of the Blessed Sacrament.

Superior

Nine years after her profession she was chosen (1914) subprioress of the Boston Carmel, and in 1918 prioress of the same. When her three-year term was over, she served as a member of the monastery's council and was once more elected prioress in 1924 and again in 1927 and 1930. In answer to a special request in 1934 from M. Ignatius, prioress of the Seattle Carmel, M. Aloysius spent sixteen months there as subprioress and mistress of novices. She had been asked for by name so that she could instruct the Seattle community in liturgics and to instill in its members the Teresian spirit of community life.

Founder

On M. Aloysius' return to Boston, she was again elected superior of her community. In 1945 Bishop Matthew Brady of Concord (New Hampshire) invited the Boston Carmelites to found a monastery in his diocese. M. Aloysius and five nuns left for Concord and took up residence (June 1946) in a small house. As founder, she purchased land for a new convent and supervised its construction. The community moved into its new home on March 19, 1952. With increasing age, M. Aloysius' health began to weaken and she died on April 16, 1961. In view of her reputation for holiness, her cause for beatification is under consideration.

See also CARMELITE NUNS, DISCALCED (O.C.D.).

Cooney, Adrian James, O.C.D. "Give All—and Ever: Mother Aloysius of the Blessed Sacrament, O.C.D. (1880–1961)." *Portraits in American Sanctity,* ed. Joseph N. Tylenda. Chicago: Franciscan Herald, 1982, 360–72.

Fragrance from Alabaster: Thoughts of Reverend Mother Aloysius of the Blessed Sacrament, Discalced Carmelite. Concord, N.H.: Discalced Carmelite Nuns of Concord, 1961.

JOSEPH TYLENDA, S.J.

ROGERS, MARY (1882–1955)

One of the three founders of Maryknoll. Mary Josephine Rogers, was born in Boston, Massachusetts, on October 27, 1882. In 1912 she became the leader of the first group of women to commit themselves to this pioneer American Catholic missionary movement. A dynamic, compassionate, and faith-filled apostolic leader, Mary Josephine Rogers was the first American Catholic woman to found a religious congregation of women solely dedicated to the global mission of the Church.

Mother M. Josephine Rogers

Early Mission Interest

Always known as Mollie, Mary Josephine was brought up in a strong Catholic family of eight children whose parents, Abraham Rogers and Josephine Plummer, were deeply interested in foreign missions. The Rogers family subscribed to the only available mission publications in English (i.e., those published by the Propagation of the Faith and the Holy Childhood Association). Their concern for the Church's universal mission was unusual for this period, which predated the awakening of the foreign mission consciousness of U.S. Catholics in the late nineteenth century.

Mollie attended Smith College from 1901–05. In her senior year, Rogers became the sustaining spirit of an organization of Catholic students that promoted the frequent reception of the sacraments, generosity to Catholic missions, and encouraged involvement of Catholics in "Christian Work." Mother Mary Joseph often said that Smith College was the place where she found her mission vocation.

After graduation, Rogers accepted a teaching fellowship at Smith College in the Zoology Department. In 1906 her efforts to organize the first 'Mission Study Class' for Catholic students led her to seek the advice of Rev. James Anthony Walsh, then director of the Society of the Propagation of the Faith in Boston.

Coworker with James A. Walsh

Rogers soon became a collaborator with Walsh, translating mission materials from French and writing mission articles for *The Field Afar*. In the spring of 1908 she left her academic post at Smith, and began teaching in Boston public schools in order to be more closely involved in mission education at the Propagation of the Faith Office.

When Walsh, together with Thomas Frederick Price, began the actual organization of the Catholic Foreign Mission Society of America in the fall of 1911, they were joined at Hawthorne, New York, on January 6, 1912, by a group of women auxiliaries. Rogers became the leader of this small band later known as "Teresians," all of whom also dreamed of going to the foreign mission field. The permanent home of Maryknoll—a missionary movement for priests, brothers, and sisters—later was relocated to Ossining, New York. With Teresa of Avila as their model and Mollie Rogers as guide, the "Teresians" set to work as secretaries, editors, translators, and sometimes as cooks, seamstresses, and receptionists at Maryknoll.

In 1920 the 'Teresians' received canonical recognition as the "The Foreign Mission Sisters of St. Dominic," and Rogers was formally elected mother general, taking the name Mary Joseph. At the time, the community numbered only thirty-five sisters, yet Rogers courageously decided to launch out into mission by sending sisters to work among the Japanese immigrants in Los Angeles and Seattle. The following year the first group of six Maryknoll Sisters sailed for China under the leadership of Sr. Mary Paul McKenna.

By 1937, impelled by the missionary spirit and charism of their foundress, the congregation of 560 sisters had established missions with a wide spectrum of educational, medical, social, and pastoral ministries in Hong Kong, China, Korea, Japan, Manchuria, Philippines, and the Hawaiian Islands. In the formation and leadership of her sisters, Rogers held out the ideal that every Maryknoll Sister should be a contemplative in the midst of unflagging missionary work. She emphasized the uniqueness of each sister's gifts and the importance of individuality as part of the charism and spirit of the new missionary commu-

nity. Identifying wholeheartedly with the mission vision and creative leadership of Bishop Francis Xavier Ford, one of Maryknoll's first martyrs in China, Rogers permitted the sisters under Ford's direction to develop a new model for women religious in mission in South China. Living in small groups of two or three, the sisters traveled to remote villages where they stayed for weeks at a time doing evangelical work and sharing directly their faith, hope, and love amongst the poor, especially women in rural areas.

Final Years, 1947–1955

In January of 1947, despite having been unanimously re-elected to a fourth term as mother general, Rogers graciously acceded to the decision of ecclesiastical authorities that she retire, retaining the title of "Mother Foundress." At that time she wrote to her sisters, "God has yet a great work for us to do, but the realization of this vision depends on you and me as individuals and on our cooperation. Do we love enough, do we work enough, do we pray enough, do we suffer enough? Maryknoll's future depends on our answer."

At her death on October 27, 1955, there were 1,127 Maryknoll Sisters present in mission in nineteen countries in Africa, Asia, Latin America, the Central Pacific Islands, and the U.S.A.

See also MARYKNOLL.

Kennedy, Camilla. *To the Utmost Parts of the Earth: The Spirit and Charism of Mary Josephine Rogers.* Maryknoll, N.Y.: Maryknoll Sisters, 1980.

Lyons, Jeanne Marie. *Maryknoll's First Lady: The Life of Mother Mary Joseph, Foundress of the Maryknoll Sisters.* Garden City, N.Y.: Echo Books, 1967.

Rogers, Mary Josephine. *Discourses of Mother Mary Joseph Rogers, M.M., Foundress, Maryknoll Sisters.* Compiled by Sister Mary Coleman, M.M., and staff. 4 vols. Maryknoll, N.Y.: Mission Archives, 1982.

Wiest, Jean-Paul. *Maryknoll in China: A History, 1918–1955.* Armonk, N.Y.: M. E. Sharpe, Inc., 1988.

BARBARA HENDRICKS, M.M.

ROSARY COLLEGE

A small liberal arts university originally founded as St. Clara College in Sinsinawa, Wisconsin, by the Very Reverend Samuel Mazzuchelli, O.P., in 1901. Under the leadership of Sr. Mary Samuel Coughlin, this college for women was moved to River Forest, Illinois, where it opened in the fall of 1922 as Rosary College and was incorporated in the state of Illinois. The library science school was established as a coeducational entity in 1930, and the whole college followed suit in 1970.

The university was a pioneer of study abroad programs, opening the Villa des Fougeres in Fribourg in 1925 under the leadership of Sr. Hyacintha Finney. The study abroad programs expanded to include Florence in 1948, London in 1971, Strasbourg in 1987, and Salamanca and Heidelberg in 1993. At one time the university had a Dublin program as well.

Rosary College supports three graduate schools. The Graduate School of Library and Information Science, founded in 1930, offers master's degrees in library and information science. The Graduate School of Business, founded in 1981, offers master's degrees in business administration, accounting, management information systems, and organizational administration. The Graduate School of Education, founded in 1981, offers master's degrees in learning disabilities, special education, educational administration, and teaching.

The college, known for its thirty-acre wooded campus with its original buildings designed by Ralph Adams Cram, has a library that houses a collection of over 250,000 volumes and several special collections, including the Berenice Lawler O'Brien collection of Evelyn Waugh materials, History of Print collection, including books from many Catholic presses, and the Historic Children's Literature Collection.

See also CATHOLIC UNIVERSITIES AND COLLEGES.

Kantowicz, Edward R. *Corporation Sole: Cardinal Mundelein and Chicago Catholicism.* University of Notre Dame Press, 1983.

O'Rourke, Alice, O.P. *Your Will Be Done: A Biography of Sister Mary Samuel Coughlin.* Dubuque, Iowa: Kendall/Hunt Publishing Co., 1995.

THERESA A. ROSS-JONES

ROSATI, JOSEPH (1789–1843)

First bishop of St. Louis. Joseph Rosati was born on January 12, 1789, in Sora, Naples, Italy, the son of John and Vienna Senese Rosati, both of whom were of the lesser nobility. He was ordained a priest of the Congregation of the Mission on February 10, 1811. His first assignment was in the city of Rome giving retreats and parish missions. Rosati was among a group of Vincentian Fathers selected by Bishop William Louis DuBourg to staff his new Diocese of Louisiana. He and his companions arrived in the United States in 1816 and at once set out for the territory of the upper Mississippi valley. Immediately, Rosati was appointed rector and ordered to establish a seminary at Perryville, Missouri, a village some sixty miles south of St. Louis. He was also appointed superior of the order for the region.

In 1823 Rosati received a mandatory appointment from the Holy See as coadjutor bishop to DuBourg. He was consecrated by Bishop DuBourg in Donaldsonville, Louisiana, on March 25, 1824. On March 20, 1827, the Diocese of Louisiana was divided and the Diocese of St. Louis was established with Rosati as its first bishop. At that time the diocese had twenty-one priests and twenty-five seminarians. The boundaries of the new diocese began at the Arkansas River on the south, the Wabash River on the east, the Canadian border on the north, and the Rocky Mountains on the west.

As bishop, Rosati initiated missionary activity to the Native American nations in the West, established a college at St. Louis, built the first hospital in that city, and invited the Religious of the Sacred Heart under the direction of Mother Philippine Duchesne to establish a convent and an academy for young women. He also built the first cathedral for the diocese along the riverfront. He established the first diocesan newspaper, *Shepherd of the Valley,* in 1832. The paper was printed in both English and French, reflecting the fact that Rosati himself was fluent in seven languages.

Rosati attended both the First and Second Provincial Councils of Baltimore. He was an outspoken critic of lay trusteeism in parishes and supported the position of the pastor. He was also instrumental in having the catechism of Cardinal Bellarmine translated into English. The work of translating the catechism was given to Bishops John England of Charleston and Rosati. In 1839 he convoked the first diocesan synod setting decrees for the direction of the diocese. Many of his decrees were adopted later by the Baltimore Provincial Council of 1840.

In September of 1839, Bishop Rosati returned to Europe in order to raise funds for his diocese and recruit priests and religious. While in Rome in the spring of 1841, Pope Gregory XVI named him apostolic delegate to Haiti to negotiate a concordat between the Holy See and the new troubled republic. On his trip to Haiti, he visited Philadelphia and there consecrated Peter Richard Kenrick as his coadjutor with right of succession.

Upon the successful completion of the concordat with Haiti, Bishop Rosati returned to Rome. There he died on September 25, 1843. In 1954 his remains were moved from Rome to be interred in the Cathedral of St. Louis.

See also MISSOURI, CATHOLIC CHURCH IN.

Easterly, Frederick J., C.M. *The Life of the Rt. Rev. Joseph Rosati, First Bishop of St. Louis, 1789–1843.* Washington, D.C., 1942; repr. New York, 1974.

MARTIN G. TOWEY

ROSS, XAVIER (1813–95)

Foundress. Mother Xavier Ross, founder of the Sisters of Charity of Leavenworth, Kansas, was born Ann Ross on November 17, 1813. At age fifteen, she converted to Catholicism, a move which alienated her from her father, a Methodist minister. A year later, Ann left home to enter the community of the Sisters of Charity of Nazareth, Kentucky. On August 22, 1832, Ann was received into the community and received her name in religion: Sr. Xavier. She professed vows on March 25, 1834. Between 1834 and 1851, she taught at several schools and orphanages in Louisville, Kentucky, and Nashville, Tennessee.

In 1851 Bishop Richard Miles of Nashville asked sisters from the Nazareth community to form a new community in his diocese. Six responded to his call to form the Sisters of Charity of Nashville. Sr. Xavier was one of the six. She was elected mother superior in 1852. In 1857 a dispute between Rev. Ivo Schacht, the spiritual director of the young community, and the bishop resulted in the bishop's decision to withdraw his support for the sisters.

Mother Xavier, at the urging of her sisters, went to St. Louis to see if another bishop would accept the sisters in his diocese. Through the mediation of Fr. Pierre De Smet, S.J., she met Bishop John B. Miège, S.J., vicar apostolic of the Indian Territory. He urged the sisters to come to Leavenworth, his see city, as soon as possible. Sixteen sisters and three orphan girls came to Leavenworth, the first arriving on November 11, 1858.

The community opened schools for boys and for girls in Leavenworth within months of their arrival. St. John Hospital in Leavenworth, the first civilian hospital in Kansas, was opened in 1864. In 1868 the sisters opened missions in Montana in response to the request of Fr. De Smet. Over the years, the community established schools, hospitals, and orphanages in Kansas, Missouri, Nebraska, Wyoming, Colorado, Montana, New Mexico, and California.

Mother Xavier served as mother superior after the move of the community to Kansas, from 1858 to 1861, and again from 1864 to 1877. She was a woman ahead of her time. With the move to Leavenworth, she elicited a promise from the bishop that all property purchased by the sisters would remain in their name, rather than in the name of the diocese. She insisted on accurate property surveys. She resisted the attempt by Fr. Schacht in Nashville to have the community affiliated with the French Daughters of Charity, desiring instead to confirm the American origin of the community. The first novitiate for the community was opened July 26, 1859. Mother Xavier gave regular conferences to the novices, and was a retreat director for the sisters for many years. An early decision of Mother Xavier was to accept missions in the West rather than in the more settled areas of the East. When debt threatened the ownership of community property, Mother Xavier sent sisters to beg funds in Ireland, and throughout the United States.

Following her terms as mother superior, Mother Xavier served as superior of St. Vincent's Academy in Helena, Montana, and St. Mary's Academy, Independence, Missouri. Fluent in French, she translated the *Conferences* of St. Vincent de Paul for her sisters. She wrote to the sisters and visited the community houses throughout her term as superior. The last retreat she gave was to novice Sr. Basilissa Dowling in January 1895. Over the next several months Mother Xavier's health deteriorated, and she died at the motherhouse on April 2, 1895. She had been a religious for sixty-three years. At her death, the community had grown to number close to three hundred sisters. She left a legacy of concern for the poor, especially for the orphan; and of deep spirituality tempered by American practicality.

Buckner, Mary, S.C.L. *History of the Sisters of Charity of Leavenworth, Kansas.* Kansas City, Mo.: Hudson-Kimberly Publ. Co. 1898. Repr. 1985.
Fitzgerald, Mary Paul, S.C.L. "History and Spirit of the Community: The Sisters of Charity of Leavenworth." Manuscript, motherhouse, Leavenworth, Kansas, 1959.
Gilmore, Julia, S.C.L. *We Came North: Centennial Story of the Sisters of Charity of Leavenworth.* St. Meinrad, Ind.: Abbey Press, 1961.
———. *Come North: The Life Story of Mother Xavier Ross.* New York: McMullen Books, 1951. Repr. 1985.

MARY LENORE MARTIN, S.C.L.

ROUQUETTE, ADRIEN EMMANUEL (1813–87)

Missionary, priest, and author. Adrien Emmanuel Rouquette was born in New Orleans, Louisiana, on February 13, 1813. He spent his childhood in New Orleans and in St. Tammany Parish (county) across Lake Ponchartrain from the city. Here he lived with his maternal relatives and spent much time with members of the Native American Choctaw tribe in the area. He attended the Collège d'Orléans, New Orleans, and Transylvania University, Lexington, Kentucky. In 1829, at the age of sixteen, he made the first of several extended visits to France, attending the Collège Royal in Nantes. Four years later he returned to New Orleans, uncertain about a career. He chose to study law in Paris, but on completing his studies decided against a legal career. His ardent love of nature and poetry and a growing interest in religion led him to change his goals.

He now wanted to join the ranks of genuine "American" poets and to minister as a priest. He was ordained on July 2, 1845, the first native diocesan priest since Louisiana attained statehood. Bishop Antoine Blanc immediately appointed Rouquette his secretary and an assistant at St. Louis Cathedral in New Orleans. Within a few years, however, he felt called to leave the city, live in solitude as a hermit in St. Tammany Parish, and found an order of hermits. When these efforts failed, he sought permission to become a hermit missionary among the Choctaw across the lake. The bishop reluctantly gave his permission in 1859.

As a full-time missionary, Rouquette set out to master the Choctaw tongue and win acceptance with the Choctaw in their largest village, Buchuwa. A rich and detailed account of these early efforts is preserved in a series of long letters to the New Orleans *Catholic Standard,* written as the events took place. His work met with great success and the Choctaw named him "Chahta-Ima" (like a Choctaw), a title he cherished. During the Civil War the village was destroyed and he spent the war years ministering to the material and spiritual needs of his beloved flock as they hid in the swamps and woodlands. Later he established small mission chapels along the bayous of the area. He became a legend and a recognized authority on the Choctaw language, folk tales, and way of life.

Rouquette continued writing throughout his missionary years. His desire to be a genuine "American" poet led him to correspond with such authors as Thoreau, Longfellow, Bryant, and Isaac Hecker and to send them copies of his works. Because most of his books are in French, Rouquette has never received the recognition he deserves as an important author of Romantic literature in nineteenth-century America.

———————————

D'Antoni, Blaise A. *Chata-Ima and St. Tammany's Choctaws.* St. Tammany Historical Society, Inc., 1986.

LeBreton, Dagmar Renshaw. *Chahta-Ima, the Life of Adrien Emmanuel Rouquette.* Baton Rouge: Louisiana State University Press, 1947.

Rouquette, Adrien Emmanuel. *Les Savanes, poésies américaines* (1841).

_____. *Wild Flowers* (1848).

_____. *Le Thébaïde en Amerique ou Apologie de la vie solitaire et contemplative* (1852).

_____. *La Question Américaine* (1855).

_____. *Catherine Tegahkwitha, the Saint of Caughnawaga* (1873).

_____. *La Nouvelle Atala* (1879).

DOMINIC BRAUD, O.S.B.

RUDD, DANIEL (1854–1933)

Journalist, lecturer, publisher, civil rights leader. Daniel Rudd was a leading figure in the development of a religious and spiritual foundation for African American Catholics in the late nineteenth century. Born in Bardstown, Kentucky, in 1854 to Robert and Elizabeth Rudd, both slaves on estates in the Bardstown area, he was one of twelve children. Following the Civil War, he went to live with his older brother, Robert, in Springfield, Ohio, where he attended secondary school.

In 1886 he founded the weekly newspaper, the *Ohio Star Tribune,* which he renamed the *American Catholic Tribune* later that year. The paper focused on issues concerning African Americans; Frederick Douglass's resignation as minister to Haiti, for example, and it had correspondents in a number of major cities to report on news in the African

Daniel Rudd

American communities there. Philosophically, the paper's strong pro-Catholic stance mirrored Rudd's unequivocal commitment to his Church. In his feature articles and editorial comments, he advocated racial equality and religious unity between African American Catholics and those of other races and creeds. Rudd made known to his readers the trend of increasing violence against blacks in the South, and he criticized the continual efforts to expand and add to existing segregation laws.

He published a translation of Pope Leo XIII's encyclical, *Rerum Novarum,* in 1891, considering it to have direct bearing on the plight of black persons in America. Of it he wrote: "In its treatment of the rights of rich and poor it has not been equaled by any writer upon this subject, besides it comes with the teaching authority of the teaching Church." He traveled to France in 1899 to meet Cardinal Lavigerie, founder of the White Fathers and White Sisters—now the Society of Missionaries of Africa and the Missionary Sisters of Our Lady of Africa—and a great opponent of the slave trade, and to attend an international congress on slavery (postponed until 1890). Lavigerie subsequently appointed Rudd his emissary in the U.S.A., to assist him in his campaign against slavery. Rudd relocated the office of the *American Catholic Tribune* to Detroit in 1894, though it did not prosper there and its publication appears to have ceased within five years of the move.

Rudd's major contribution to the furtherance of religious cohesion among African American Catholics was probably his establishment of a national lay congress for them. Five congresses were held between 1889–94, with delegates present from black parishes and black Catholic societies all over the country. Addresses were given by prominent members of the African American community, and by various priests, bishops, and archbishops. There were discussions about the establishment of Catholic high schools, trade schools, and colleges for African Americans, racism in the Church, and missionary work among African Americans. Ideologically, the members postulated the inalienable "rights of man" before the Church universal, and asserted a certain black Catholic theology, which incorporated into its foundation the notion of the equality of all peoples before God. The historical consciousness of the African American community was also demonstrated at the congresses. Records show regular references to the historical black Church, namely that of North Africa, with such luminaries as SS Augustine, Monica, Cyprian, and Perpetua acknowledged as its founders.

The congresses achieved in large measure what Rudd had envisioned. They brought together, and provided a forum for, a community that was proud, eloquent, and devoted. Rudd lived in Detroit for about five years, after which he lived in Mississippi and Arkansas. He continued to work for racial equality and justice in the Church and in the secular culture throughout the next three decades, though in a local context. He died on December 3, 1933, at the age of seventy-nine.

Davis, Cyprian, O.S.B. *The History of Black Catholics in the United States.* New York, 1990, 164–72, 214.

Spalding, David. "The Negro Catholic Congresses, 1889–1894." *Catholic Historical Review* 55 (April 1969) 337–57.

Three Afro-American Congresses. Cincinnati, 1893; repr. New York, 1978.

JOSEPH QUINN

RUMMEL, JOSEPH FRANCIS (1876–1964)

Archbishop and social leader. Joseph Francis Rummel was born in Steinmauern, Baden, Germany, on October 14, 1876, son of Gustave Rummel and Teresa Bollweber. The family immigrated to New York City in 1882; Rummel became a naturalized U.S. citizen on February 2, 1888.

He attended St. Boniface Elementary School; St. Anselm's College in Manchester, New Hampshire (B.A., 1896). He studied at St. Joseph Seminary in Yonkers, New York, and the North American College in Rome (S.T.D., 1903).

Rummel was ordained to the priesthood in Rome on May 24, 1902. He spent his early priestly years in pastoral work and administration in Archdiocese of New York in New York City, Kingston, and the Bronx (1902–28). He took an early interest in social problems and first gained national prominence through German relief efforts, serving as executive secretary of the German Relief Committee (1923–24).

Rummel was consecrated bishop of Omaha, Nebraska, in New York City, on May 29, 1928. In Omaha, he directed

Joseph F. Rummel

the rapid expansion of parishes, schools, and other diocesan institutions; encouraged the formation of rural ministry; encouraged greater lay participation in diocesan life; and hosted the Sixth National Eucharistic Congress (1930).

Archbishop of New Orleans

Rummel was appointed the ninth archbishop of New Orleans on March 9, 1935. He directed a period of rapid Catholic growth in southeast Louisiana as the number of local Catholics increased almost 75 percent by 1962 to 630,000. More than 680 building projects were completed; forty-eight new parishes were established. He guided an expansion program for Catholic education that included more than seventy new school buildings. The number of elementary and secondary school children rose from 40,000 to 85,000. Social service facilities and programs were likewise expanded. The Diocese of Baton Rouge was carved from the archdiocese on July 20, 1961.

Rummel served on numerous national Catholic boards and committees, i.e., as episcopal chairman of Catholic Committee on Refugees (1936–47), and on the board of trustees of National Catholic Community Services-USO (1940–44).

He was a strong advocate of increased lay involvement in Louisiana Church life, promoting the establishment of many local units of national organizations, such as the Confraternity of Christian Doctrine (1935); Archdiocesan Council of Catholic Women (1936); Catholic Youth Organization (1936); Christian Family Movement (1953); and Young Christian Workers (1954).

He promoted frequent public expressions of faith, including the Eighth National Eucharistic Congress (1938), the first such congress in the South.

Rummel encouraged local clergy to educate their parishioners in social justice issues and consistently supported their efforts to implement social programs. He sponsored the South's first Catholic Conference on Industrial Problems (1940). He exhorted generous, self-sacrificing service to country in his December 7–8, 1941, pastoral letter, "The Nation at War," and encouraged wholehearted Catholic support throughout the war. After the war, he encouraged equally generous support for relief efforts, worked for a temporary extension of rent control, and established a local resettlement bureau to assist (and sometimes resettle) more than 33,000 displaced persons who entered the U.S.A. via New Orleans between 1949 and 1952.

Rummel vigorously supported the rights of the working class. He publicly opposed Louisiana's right to work laws and actively supported the efforts of Louisiana agricultural workers, particularly sugar cane workers, to organize in the 1950s. He supported the unsuccessful 1953 sugar cane workers' strike.

Rummel and Desegregation

Rummel labored patiently for over a quarter century to create a community atmosphere conducive to full racial equality and to foster the growth of Church organizations, facilities, and activities among African American Catholics and, eventually, to achieve integration of Catholic parishes, schools, organizations, and institutions. In 1939, at Rummel's urging, Xavier University in New Orleans began a Catholic Action School for African Americans. In 1951, Rummel established the archdiocese's first secondary school for black youth—St. Augustine High School—where numerous national and local black leaders have been educated.

On March 15, 1953, his pastoral letter, "Blessed are the Peacemakers," ordered the desegregation of all Catholic parish activities and organizations. He suspended all Catholic services at Jesuit Bend Mission (1955–58) after an African American priest was prevented from celebrating Mass there. In his pastoral letter of February 11, 1956, he declared racial segregation morally wrong and sinful. He was also influential in preparing and gaining support for the 1958 U.S. Catholic bishops' statement condemning racism. On March 27, 1962, working closely with Archbishop John Cody and key clergy advisors, he ordered all Catholic schools within the archdiocese desegregated, leading to international news stories of confrontations with the local self-proclaimed Association of Catholic Laymen and vocal segregationists.

Rummel turned over administration of the archdiocese of New Orleans to Archbishop John P. Cody on June 1, 1962. He died in New Orleans on November 8, 1964, and was interred in St. Louis Cathedral.

See also CIVIL RIGHTS MOVEMENT AND CATHOLICS, THE; LOUISIANA, CATHOLIC CHURCH IN.

Becnel, Thomas. *Labor, Church, and the Sugar Establishment Louisiana 1887–1976*. Baton Rouge, 1980.

Catholic Action of the South, March 14 and 21, and May 16, 1935; April 4, 1940; July 29, 1943; May 14, 1953; May 20, 1960; passim.

Clarion Herald, November 12, 1964.

Grant, Philip A., Jr. "Archbishop Joseph F. Rummel and the 1962 New Orleans Desegregation Crisis." *Records of the American Catholic Historical Society of Philadelphia* 91 (March–December 1980) 59–66.

Rummel Papers, Archives, Diocese of Omaha.

Rummel Papers, Roger Baudier Collection, and taped interviews with Msgr. Charles J. Plauche and Bishop Joseph G. Vath of Birmingham, August 30 and October 11, 1980, Archives, Archdiocese of New Orleans.

CHARLES E. NOLAN

RUSSELL, MARY BAPTIST (1829–98)

Religious superior. Katherine Russell was born in County Down, Ireland, on April 18, 1829. At the age of twenty-two, she entered the Order of the Sisters of Mercy in Kinsale and took the name Mary Baptist. She served in an area still struggling with the effects of cholera and famine. In 1854, Joseph Alemany, the first archbishop of San Francisco, invited the Irish Sisters of Mercy to come to his new diocese. Mother Mary Baptist led a group of eight nuns and novices to the new country. They arrived on December 8, 1854, and immediately began working with the sick and the poor. In 1855 the city suffered an outbreak of cholera and, because of their experience in caring for the afflicted, the Sisters of Mercy were given complete charge of the county hospital. Mother Mary Baptist reopened this institution in 1857 as St. Mary's Hospital, the first Catholic hospital on the West Coast. That same year she opened a second convent in Sacramento. The Sisters of Mercy established many charitable institutions, including a night school for adults, a home for unemployed women, a reform shelter for former prostitutes, homes for the aged, and primary schools for girls and boys. In 1894 Mother Mary Baptist convened a meeting of Catholic schoolteachers in the San Francisco archdiocese, the first meeting of its kind in the United States. When she died on August 6, 1898, the *San Francisco Bulletin* acclaimed her the "best known charitable worker on the Pacific Coast."

Evans, Mary E. *The Spirit is Mercy: The Story of the Sisters of Mercy in the Archdiocese of Cincinnati, 1858–1958*. Westminster, Md., 1959, 61–67.

McArdle, Mary Aurelia. *California's Pioneer Sister of Mercy: Mother Mary Baptist Russell, 1829–1898*. Fresno, California, 1954.

Morgan, M. E. *Mercy, Generation to Generation.* San Francisco, 1957.

Russell, Matthew. *The Life of Mother Mary Baptist Russell, Sister of Mercy.* New York, 1901.

PATRICIA DeFERRARI

RUSYN CATHOLICS IN AMERICA

The relationship of Rusyns to the Catholic Church in the United States is intimately connected with the history of the Byzantine Ruthenian Catholic Metropolitan Archdiocese of Pittsburgh. Today, that archdiocese, with suffragan dioceses in Passaic, New Jersey; Parma, Ohio; and Van Nuys, California, contains nearly 245,000 faithful in 251 parishes that are served by 261 priests (1991). The vast majority of the archdiocesan faithful are descendants of Slavic immigrants who came to the United States during the four decades before World War I from the southern slopes of the central ranges of the Carpathian Mountains in the heart of east-central Europe. In terms of linguistic and ethnonational background, most of the immigrants were Rusyns, or Carpatho-Rusyns.

Rusyns in Europe

When the Rusyns (also known in English as Carpatho-Russians, Carpatho-Ruthenians, or simply Ruthenians) left their European homeland, it was part of the Hungarian Kingdom within the Hapsburg-ruled Austro-Hungarian Empire. After World War I, that homeland was united with the new state of Czechoslovakia, where Rusyns enjoyed a degree of self-government in a province called Subcarpathian Rus' (Carpatho Ruthenia). About one-quarter of the estimated 600,000 Rusyns lived north of the Carpathians in an area popularly known as the Lemko Region of southeastern Poland. International boundaries changed on the eve of and then again after World War II when Communist rule was imposed in all countries where Rusyns lived. At the present time, the Rusyn homeland is found within the borderland regions of three countries: in far western Ukraine (the Transcarpathian oblast); in northeastern Slovakia (the Prešov Region); and in southeastern Poland (the Lemko Region). There is also a small community in Yugoslavia (Serbia's Vojvodina) and in eastern Croatia.

The Rusyns are an East Slavic people who trace their Christian roots back over 1,100 years to the Byzantine missionaries SS Cyril and Methodius. During the second half of the ninth century, either those two missionaries or their disciples brought Christianity to the Carpatho-Rusyn homeland, at which time a diocese was ostensibly established at Mukachevo (today in Ukraine's Transcarpathian oblast), the mother diocese of the Archdiocese of Pittsburgh. From the time of their conversion, Rusyns were of the Eastern, or Byzantine Rite and under the ultimate jurisdiction of the Orthodox ecumenical patriarch in Constantinople.

In 1646 the Orthodox bishop of Mukachevo and several priests signed the Union of Uzhhorod, placing themselves under the jurisdiction of the pope. Within a century, all former Orthodox Rusyns had become Uniates or, as they were known after 1771, Greek Catholics. As part of the agreement that led to the union, the Rusyns were permitted to retain several of their Eastern-rite practices, including the liturgy of St. John Chrysostom, use of Church Slavonic instead of Latin as the language of the liturgy, reception of the Eucharist under both species, married as well as celibate priests, and the Julian calendar, which by the twentieth century was, for fixed feasts, two weeks "behind" the Western Gregorian calendar. It was as Greek Catholics following the Eastern Rite with the above-mentioned religious practices that Rusyns arrived in the United States during the four decades preceding World War I. Initially, they did not have their own Eastern-rite churches and so attended Latin-Rite parishes, if possible those served by a Polish or Slovak priest who spoke languages that were related but nonetheless different from Rusyn. Many of these early Rusyn immigrants remained Latin-Rite Catholics.

Immigration to the United States

By the 1880s, individual immigrant communities, most especially in the industrial towns and cities of the northeastern United States, began requesting their bishops in Europe to send them Greek Catholic priests. Priests were sent and the first parishes were established in eastern Pennsylvania—Shenandoah (1884), Freeland (1886), Hazleton (1887), and in Minneapolis, Minnesota (1887). Such immigrant lay initiative, to which Greek Catholic bishops in the homeland responded favorably, was not welcomed by the Latin-Rite American Catholic hierarchy and by many priests in the United States. The 1880s and 1890s was a period when the American Catholic Church was in the midst of the Americanization movement led by bishops like John Ireland of St. Paul who wished to minimize ethnic differences so that Catholics could become "full-fledged" Americans in what was still a Protestant-dominated United States.

In such an environment, it is not surprising that Greek Catholic priests who were invited by laypersons and who followed a "strange" rite—many were even married—were at best tolerated and more often openly rejected by local Latin-Rite priests and bishops. Nevertheless, Rusyn immigrants continued to arrive in the United States in ever larger numbers (as many as 250,000 before World War I), and more and more Greek Catholic parishes were established in which committees of laypersons paid for the ocean trip of the priest and built (as well as held the property rights to) a church.

As a result of this clash of religious cultures, the first seven decades of the Rusyn presence in the United States

(1880s through the 1940s) were marked for the most part by strained relations with the Catholic Church. One side felt it had a duty to uphold the order and authority of the Holy See as embodied in the Catholic *communitas;* the other side felt that, while remaining true to the Catholic Church, it also had a duty and right to maintain its own religious traditions. At the same time, those traditions became for Rusyns a matter of cultural survival and self-respect in an otherwise linguistically, politically, and culturally alien American world. The manner in which Greek Catholics adapted their religious culture to American circumstances and accepted compromise in the face of papal authority is what, in essence, forms the history of Rusyns and the Catholic Church in the United States.

As early as 1890, the Vatican, in response to complaints lodged by Latin-Rite bishops in the United States, issued its first regulatory decree regarding Greek Catholic priests in America. It specified that each newly arriving Greek Catholic priest had to report to and receive jurisdiction from the local Latin-Rite bishop. Moreover, all new priests had to be celibate and married ones were to be recalled to Europe. A supplemental decree issued in 1895 stipulated that in areas where there were no Greek Catholic parishes, the faithful could become Latin-Rite Catholics. While these decrees did not achieve what they set out to do, they did succeed in alienating even further both parties. The very existence of such decrees seemed to Rusyns a threat to their centuries-old traditions and rite which had long ago been recognized by the Catholic Church in Europe. On the other hand, American Roman Catholic prelates remained unhappy because the decrees were disregarded by the Rusyns and were not enforced by the Vatican.

One practical result of Rusyn discontent was a movement to leave the Catholic Church altogether. The movement was promoted by secular and clerical patriots as a "return to Orthodoxy"—the "true" Rusyn faith. It began in March 1891, when the Greek Catholic priest, Alexis Toth, responding in part to what he considered insulting treatment by Archbishop Ireland of St. Paul, brought his entire Minneapolis parish into the Russian Orthodox Church. Fr. Toth then turned to other Greek Catholic parishes in Pennsylvania and the neighboring northeastern states, so that by the time of his death in 1907 he had "brought back" to Orthodoxy over 25,000 Rusyns. As a result of Toth's efforts, he became known as "the father of Orthodoxy" in the United States, and in 1994 he was canonized by the Orthodox Church in America.

Rusyn relations with the Catholic Church at the outset of the twentieth century were strained for another reason—national differentiation. Initially, Greek Catholic parishes consisted of Rusyn immigrants from both parts of Austria-Hungary, the northeastern counties of the Hungarian kingdom and the province of Galicia in the "Austrian half" of the empire. Most of the Rusyns from Galicia (excepting those from the Lemko Region) began to adopt a Ukrainian national identity. In contrast, Rusyn immigrants from south of the Carpathians in Hungary maintained their identity as the people of Rus', that is, as Rusyns. Many even began to identify themselves as Russians, or Carpatho-Russians.

Hierarchical Organization

The nationality question became entangled with the Greek Catholic demand for their own bishop. When, in 1907, the Vatican appointed Soter Ortynsky, a priest from Galicia, to be the first Greek Catholic bishop in America, he was considered a Ukrainian and therefore was unacceptable to the Rusyns from Subcarpathia. To make matters worse, the new bishop was expected to enforce the latest decree *(Ea Semper)* issued by the Vatican in 1908, which reiterated that Greek Catholic priests must be celibate, that church property must be transferred from lay committees to the Latin-Rite bishop, and that children of mixed marriages born in the United States should be baptized in the Latin Rite (a requirement if the father was of the Latin Rite; by choice if he was of the Ruthenian Rite). The bishop himself had "no ordinary jurisdiction" but, like any other Greek Catholic priest he was subordinate to the local Latin-Rite bishop.

Once again, this latest papal decree did not resolve the problems it addressed. Married Greek Catholic priests continued to arrive, recently married seminary graduates were ordained, and most property remained in the hands of lay church committees. Papal policy did, however, continue to assist inadvertently the growth of Orthodoxy, since Rusyns who felt their religious and national identity was being undermined by unfair decrees and by a "Ukrainian" Greek Catholic bishop continued to join the Russian Orthodox Church.

In response to the "nationality" problem, the Vatican set up in 1916 two separate administrations, one for Greek Catholics from Hungary (Rusyns), the other for Greek Catholics from Galicia (Ukrainians). Then, in 1921, the administrations were replaced by exarchates (dioceses), each with its own bishop. At the time of its establishment, the Ruthenian Exarchate of Pittsburgh had 155 churches, 129 priests, over 288,000 faithful, and its first bishop was Basil Takach. With the separation of the Greek Catholic parishes into two jurisdictions, Rusyn relations with the Catholic Church stabilized and defections to Orthodoxy decreased. And despite the various papal decrees going back to 1890, much church property still remained in lay hands, and married seminarians were still being ordained by the new bishop, Basil Takach.

This relatively tranquil period was interrupted after 1929, when the Vatican issued the *Cum Data Fuerit* decree. Its purpose was to regulate Greek Catholic practices that for decades had remained lax in the United States. Once again celibacy for priests was reiterated and all existing church property was to be turned over immediately to the bishop. Added to these previous regulations were two new ones: that no newly arriving Greek Catholic priest would be recognized in the United States unless he were previously authorized by the Sacred Congregation for Oriental Churches in Rome; and that neither priests nor the faithful should be members or be associated with organizations that were not under "lawful ecclesiastical authority." The reference here was to the Greek Catholic Union, the powerful Rusyn fraternal organization which since the 1890s had forcefully criticized Vatican policy toward America's Greek Catholics.

During the decade following the *Cum Data Fuerit* decree of 1929, Rusyn relations with the Catholic Church reached a nadir. In cooperation with the Greek Catholic Union fraternal society, numerous laymen and priests refused to accept what was considered "illegal" Vatican interference in their Church affairs. Several legal battles over church property were initiated and fought out in United States federal and state courtrooms, and several priests together with about 30,000 faithful led by Fr. Orestes Chornock of Bridgeport, Connecticut, left the Catholic Church. Arguing that only they were maintaining the Eastern Rite, the defectors eventually formed, in 1937, what became known as the American Carpatho-Russian Orthodox (i.e., "true") Greek Catholic Church under the jurisdiction of the ecumenical patriarch in Constantinople. Throughout the 1930s and into the 1940s, Greek Catholic Rusyn parishes and even families were torn apart between supporters of "the bishop" (who was obliged to enforce the decrees) and defenders of the traditional Eastern Rite who joined the new Carpatho-Russian Orthodox Greek Catholic jurisdiction.

Contemporary Developments

By the 1950s, tensions gradually began to decrease and Rusyn-Catholic relations improved. This was in large part the result of the policies of Bishop Takach's successors, Bishop Daniel Ivancho and Bishop Nicholas T. Elko. Celibacy was by then strictly enforced (although remaining married priests were allowed to function until retirement or death), and all church property not lost to the Orthodox in court battles was in the hands of the bishop. The Greek Catholic Union had made its peace with the bishop and even contributed heavily to the establishment of the first Byzantine Catholic seminary in the United States, opened in Pittsburgh in 1950. As part of its attempt at accommodation, the Byzantine Catholic Church, as it was now known, under Bishops Ivancho and Elko even outwardly tried to become more like the rest of the Catholic Church. Thus, English steadily replaced Church Slavonic

in the liturgy, the Western Gregorian calendar was adopted, and the traditional icon screens that stood before altars were removed from many existing churches and often not even installed in newly built sanctuaries. There was also some discussion in the mid-1950s that the Byzantine Ruthenian and Ukrainian (Greek) Catholic dioceses might be merged, but the potential threat of new conflicts over national identity canceled all such projects.

Instead, the Vatican created in 1963 two fully self-governing Byzantine Ruthenian dioceses (Pittsburgh and Passaic, New Jersey), and then in 1969 a third diocese (at Parma, Ohio) which together formed the Byzantine Ruthenian Metropolitan Province of Pittsburgh. This new ecclesiastical jurisdiction seemed to guarantee the future of a distinct Byzantine Catholic Church in the United States whose roots went back to the pre-World War I Rusyn immigrants and, through them, to the 1,100 year-old Greek Catholic Eparchy of Mukachevo in east-central Europe.

The eventual creation of a self-governing Byzantine Catholic archdiocese did not come without cost, however. In order to survive in the United States, the Greek/Byzantine Catholics had to surrender many of the traditions which were and still are practiced in the European homeland. After World War II, Byzantine Catholic leaders also felt that, in order to survive, their Church had to become fully "Americanized." This included a down-playing of its association with a Rusyn or any other ethnicity.

These factors, together with the creation in 1969 of an archdiocesan structure, began a period in which relations between Byzantine Catholics (Rusyns) and the Catholic Church in the United States have been better than ever before. Also, during the 1970s and 1980s, most especially as a result of the policies of Archbishop Stephen Kocisko and Bishop Michael Dudick of Pittsburgh, the Church began to appreciate its own value and the uniqueness of the Eastern Rite within the larger Catholic world. While still considering itself an "American" and not "ethnic" Church, and now using English almost exclusively in all parishes, there nonetheless began in the 1970s a movement to establish heritage museums, to publish books about Greek/Byzantine Catholicism and about Rusyns, to establish music programs for instruction in Carpathian plainchant *(prostopinie)*, and to restore icon screens *(iconostases)* and other Eastern-rite representational elements in church architecture. Finally, as a result of the Revolution of 1989 and the fall of Communism in east-central Europe and the Soviet Union, American Byzantine Catholics, who for nearly half a century had been cut off from the European homeland of their forefathers, were once again able to normalize relations through travel, family contacts, and renewed relations between Church hierarchs and seminarians.

For their part, the attitude of many Latin-Rite Catholics toward Byzantine Catholics has changed since Vatican

Council II from one of suspicion and condescension to one of respect for the Eastern Rite which is accepted as equal to any other. Ironically, that same council, whose decisions resulted in the replacement of Latin with English and the introduction of "Protestant-like" congregational hymn-singing, has prompted some Latin-Rite Catholics to join the Byzantine Catholic Church where they are attracted because the "old traditions" are still being maintained. Thus, in little over a century, the status of relations between Rusyns/Byzantine Catholics and the Catholic Church in the United States has been transformed from one of suspicion and antagonism to one of mutual respect and equality.

Gulovich, Stephen C. "The Rusin Exarchate in the United States." *Eastern Churches Quarterly* 6 (1946) 459–85.

Magocsi, Paul Robert. *Carpatho-Rusyns in America.* New York and Philadelphia: Chelsea House Publishers, 1989.

____. *Our People: Carpatho-Rusyns and Their Descendants in North America.* 3rd rev. ed. Toronto: Multicultural History Society of Ontario. 1994.

Pekar, Athanasius B. *The History of the Church in Carpathian Rus'.* New York: Columbia University Press/East European Monographs, 1992.

Slivka, John, ed. *Historical Mirror: Sources of the Rusin and Hungarian Greek Rite Catholics in the United States of American, 1884–1963.* Brooklyn, N.Y., 1978.

Warzeski, Walter C. *Byzantine Rite Rusins in Carpatho-Ruthenia and America.* Pittsburgh: Byzantine Seminary Press, 1971.

PAUL ROBERT MAGOCSI

RUTH, GEORGE HERMAN "BABE" (1895–1948)

Baseball player. Ruth was born in Baltimore on February 6, 1895, and was orphaned. He was placed at St. Mary's Industrial School to be cared for and early on showed an ability to play baseball. In 1914 he was signed by the minor league Baltimore Orioles and soon picked up the nickname "Babe" because he pitched left-handed. In 1915 he made the major leagues by pitching for the Boston Red Sox, but his pitching prowess did not gain him fame. In 1919 Ruth broke the home run record by hitting twenty-nine home runs in one season and soon established his reputation as a great hitter. In 1920 he was traded to the New York Yankees, played the outfield, and began breaking a series of batting records. While he was with the Yankees, Ruth gained a colorful public image and became a darling of the press and the public, and helped to restore baseball's tarnished image after the "Black Sox" scandal of 1919. After a few more trades, in 1935 Ruth retired from his playing career with the Boston Braves after hitting three home runs in his last game. He died of cancer in New York City on August 16, 1948.

ANTHONY D. ANDREASSI

RYAN, ABRAM JOSEPH (1838–86)

Priest, poet. Matthew Abram Ryan was born in Hagerstown, Maryland, on February 5, 1838, son of Matthew Ryan and Mary A. Coughlan. He received the name "Joseph" at confirmation and later dropped Matthew. The family migrated to Missouri in the early 1840s and eventually settled in St. Louis.

Ryan was educated at Christian Brothers' School, St. Louis, Missouri; St. Mary's of the Barrens Seminary, Perryville, Missouri; and Our Lady of Angels Seminary, Niagara Falls, New York. He entered the Vincentian novitiate in 1854, taking his vows on November 1, 1856. He was ordained to the priesthood in St. Louis on September 20, 1860, according to the St. Louis Archdiocesan Archives.

Ryan led a peripatetic priestly life. Due partially to poor health and partially to his ardent Confederate sympathies, he moved back and forth from New York to Missouri to Illinois between 1860 and 1862. On September 1, 1862, he was dispensed from his vows as a Vincentian. He served as an uncommissioned chaplain to the Confederate troops and was in Augusta, Georgia, at the war's end. He was deeply affected by the 1863 battlefield death of his younger brother, David, whom he memorialized in two poems.

"Always a man of restless nature, Father Ryan found no peace even after Appomattox" (Dillard, 64). He remained in Georgia, engaged in pastoral work, writing, and assisting with the *Banner of South*, until June 8, 1870, when he moved to the Mobile diocese where he served as assistant at the cathedral, briefly as the bishop's secretary, and, after 1877, as pastor of St. Mary's in Mobile. He also edited from Mobile *New Orleans' The Morning Star and Catholic Messenger* (1872–75). He was a frequent preacher, lecturer, and essayist. In October 1881 he retired to Biloxi, Mississippi, "to attend to some religious literary work" (*Sadlier's Catholic Directory, 1883*). Ryan died on retreat at the Franciscan monastery in Louisville, Kentucky, on April 22, 1886, and was buried in Mobile.

His published works include *Father Ryan's Poems* (Mobile, 1879); *Poems, Patriotic, Religious, Miscellaneous* (Baltimore, 1880); *A Crown For Our Queen* (Baltimore, 1882). Ryan is most frequently honored as the Poet of the Confederacy for his many tributes to the Confederate dead, including "The Sword of Robert E. Lee," "The Lost Cause," "Sentinel Songs," and especially "The Conquered Banner." He also wrote of laughing brooks, approaching death, and praying, playing children. He wrote of liturgical feasts and priestly life. Much of his poetry reflects the loss, melancholy, suffering, and sadness of the postwar Confederacy. "Time is measured by tears," he wrote ("The Rosary of My Tears"). And again, "Father, I kneel, 'mid ruin, wreck, and grave—A desert waste, where all was erst so fair ("The Prayer of the South").

Ryan was "an open, manly character, in which there was no dissimulation. His generous nature and warm heart were ever moved by kind impulses and influenced by charitable feelings, as became his priestly calling" (Moran, xxx). He served selflessly during the many epidemics that struck regularly in the South. Writing of himself as author in the preface to the 1880 edition of his poems, Ryan wrote, "His feet know more of the humble steps that lead up to the Altar and its Mysteries than of the steps that lead up to Parnassus and the Home of the Muses. And souls were always more to him than songs. But, still, somehow—and he could not tell why—he sometimes tried to sing. Here are his simple songs." Ryan was honored by monuments in Augusta and Mobile and a stained glass window in New Orleans' Confederate Museum.

See also CIVIL WAR AND CATHOLICS, THE.

Dictionary of American Biography; New Catholic Encyclopedia, s.v., "Ryan, Abram Joseph."

Dillard, I. "Father Ryan, Poet-Priest of the Confederacy." *Missouri Historical Review* 36 (October 1941) 61–66.

"Father Abram Ryan," address by Roger Baudier, Confederate Memorial Hall, New Orleans (October 21, 1950). Baudier Historical Collection, Archives of the Archdiocese of New Orleans.

Lipscomb, Oscar H. "The Administration of John Quinlan, Second Bishop of Mobile, 1859–1883." *Records of the American Catholic Historical Society of Philadelphia* 78 (March–December 1967) 104–107

Moran, John. "Memoir of Father Ryan," in 1896 edition of *Poems, Patriotic, Religious, Miscellaneous,* xxv–xxxviii.

CHARLES E. NOLAN

RYAN, JAMES HUGH (1886–1947)

Archbishop, educator. James Hugh Ryan was born in Indianapolis, Indiana, on December 15, 1886, to John Marshall Ryan and Brigid Rogers Ryan. His higher education began at Holy Ghost College in Pittsburgh (later Duquesne University), where he played intercollegiate football. He went on to Mt. St. Mary of the West Seminary, Cincinnati, and to Rome, to the North America College and the College of Propaganda. From the last he received the degrees of S.T.B. (1906) and S.T.D. (1909). He received a Ph.D. from the Roman Academy in 1908. Ryan's ordination as a priest took place in the Lateran Basilica on June 5, 1909; only twenty-two years of age, he was ordained under a special dispensation because of his outstanding academic record.

From 1911 to 1920 he taught psychology at St. Mary of the Woods College in Terre Haute, Indiana. In his final year there he was chosen president, but within a month resigned to serve as executive secretary for the National Catholic Welfare Conference in Washington, a post he held until 1928.

James H. Ryan

The Catholic University of America

He joined the Philosophy Department of The Catholic University of America in 1922, his record of publications having begun with a dictionary of Catholic colleges in 1921. This was followed by *A Catechism of Catholic Education,* and in 1924, *An Introduction to Philosophy.* An edition of the encyclicals of Pope Pius XI followed in 1927. He founded the theological journal *The New Scholasticism,* in 1927, and edited it for the next decade. That year he was made a domestic prelate, and in 1929, a prothonotary apostolic. Appointed on July 12, 1928, as rector of The Catholic University, he was installed on November 25 in a ceremony at which William Cardinal O'Connell of Boston presided and U.S. President Calvin Coolidge was awarded an honorary degree.

As the youngest rector of the university up to that time, Ryan had three main concerns for the institution: financial stability, academic reorganization, and faculty improvement. In each area he found obstacles or opposition. Despite his vigorous fundraising efforts (those among the alumni were a first for the university), because of the Great Depression he achieved financial soundness only through effecting an unwelcome austerity. Ryan also found that setting up clear standards by which to distinguish graduate and undergraduate programs annoyed department heads content with the status quo of admissions and course requirements. Finally, his strict enforcement of a "publish or perish" policy alienated those professors accustomed to a more leisured academic life, and his efforts to eliminate cliques within the faculty were also resented.

While in Washington, Ryan involved himself actively not only in academic matters but also in the capital's social and cultural life. He was a frequent guest at foreign embassies and at the White House, enjoying the respect and confidence of presidents from Coolidge to Roosevelt. He became a member of the Medieval Academy and the American Academy of Arts and Sciences, and for his promotion of Italian culture was made a Knight Commander of Italy by King Victor Emmanuel III.

His relations with the faculty, other administrators, and board of the university, however, grew from cool to bluntly hostile. His frequent disagreements on policy matters with Cincinnati archbishop John T. McNicholas ultimately led the latter to turn to Rome with a demand for Ryan's dismissal. The Vatican acceded to McNicholas's request while making the firing actually seem a promotion. On July 23, 1935, the apostolic delegate, Amleto Cicognani, informed Ryan that he had been appointed bishop of Omaha, Nebraska. Having been designated titular bishop of Modra in 1933, he was installed as ordinary of the Omaha diocese on November 21, succeeding Joseph Rummel, who had been appointed archbishop of New Orleans.

Bishop of Omaha

Ryan was warmly welcomed in Nebraska, but first the depression and then World War II prevented growth of the diocese in population, institutions, and financial wealth, a growth his postwar successors would know. In Omaha there was no friction of the severe nature he had encountered at The Catholic University, but it was clear to all that Ryan's affections and interests remained with the national and international leaders with whom he had dealt back in Washington.

He spoke out on issues of social justice, but assured Pope Pius XI that there was little reason to fear communism in the United States because American workers on the whole, despite the depression, enjoyed decent wages and living and working conditions compared to their counterparts in Europe. He expressed strong opposition to Hitler, and condemned the radical right-wing and anti-Semitic pronouncements of radio priest Charles Coughlin. Ryan criticized the American Medical Association for its support of birth control, and also opposed the widening of state medical services on the grounds that Christian ethical traditions might be compromised.

Nevertheless, he backed President Roosevelt on many New Deal issues, and while at first an isolationist, became an enthusiastic supporter of the President's international policies. He harshly scolded Ireland for its neutrality during World War II, and worked with his friend, Under-Secretary of State Sumner Welles, and with others in Washington to assist victims of Axis power persecution to escape from Europe.

In 1938, with Fr. Maurice B. Sheehy, chair of the Department of Religious Education at The Catholic University, he was sent by Roosevelt on an 18,500 mile fact-finding trip through South America. Visiting Venezuela, Brazil, Argentina, Chile, and Peru, Ryan drew up recommendations for cultural exchange and a propaganda blitz to use motion pictures and radio to promote "spiritual and cultural unity" in the countries of the Pan-American Union.

Ryan also gave considerable attention to efforts of fellow members of the American hierarchy to crusade against what they perceived to be immorality in Hollywood movies. At the same time, he had cordial relations with some of the most famous motion picture actors and executives, especially when Louis B. Mayer, Spencer Tracy, and Mickey Rooney made the movie *Boys Town* in Omaha.

While changes among Catholics in Omaha were undramatic during his tenure, the see, organized in 1885, had definitely matured by the end of the war, and it was made an archdiocese in 1945. Ryan was installed as its first archbishop on October 10 of that year. He lived but two more years, however, dying in Omaha on November 23, 1947.

Correspondence and scrapbooks in the archives of the Chancery Office, Archdiocese of Omaha.

Nuesse, C. Joseph. *The Catholic University of America: A Centennial History.* Washington, D.C.: The Catholic University of America Press, 1990.

Smerczanyi, Roger. *History of the Catholic Church in Nebraska.* Vol. IV. Omaha, Nebr.: The Catholic Voice Publishing Company, 1971.

Willis, H. Warren. "The Reorganization of the Catholic University of America during the Rectorship of James Hugh Ryan (1928–1935)." Ph.D. dissertation, The Catholic University of America, 1972.

THOMAS A. KUHLMAN

RYAN, JOHN AUGUSTINE (1865–1945)

Priest, educator, social reformer. John Augustine Ryan was the foremost thinker and advocate on social issues for the Catholic Church in the United States during the period 1906–45. He emerged from a Church that had hesitantly (and not completely) embraced the labor movement, whose social vision seemed to extend no further than denunciations of socialism, that distrusted government power, and that had only recently begun to make use of information provided by the newly developing social sciences. Out of this milieu Ryan developed a specific Catholic agenda for social reform in the United States that was positive and practical, and that explored the middle ground between laissez-faire capitalism and socialism.

Though presenting an agenda compatible with Catholic teaching, Ryan did not present his argument in explicitly Catholic terms. Rather, he grounded his arguments in natural law theory which was accessible to both Catho-

John A. Ryan

lic and non-Catholic American reformers. Indeed, much of Ryan's analysis was in accord with the leading American progressive reformers of his day. Ryan argued that the economic order could not be left to some mystical "invisible hand" that would insure prosperity. Ryan believed that the social and economic problems were essentially moral problems, and that the ethical aspects of these problems had to be appropriately addressed if adequate solutions were to be developed. Or, as one historian commented, for Ryan, "Good ethics was good economics" (O'Brien, 150). Ryan's answers to social problems dominated American Catholic social thinking during the first half of the twentieth century.

Biographical Data

John Ryan was born in the rural, farming community of Vermillion, Minnesota, the eldest of eleven children of William and Mary Luby Ryan—Irish immigrants who had fled the potato famine in the 1850s. In 1887, John decided to become a priest, and entered St. Thomas Seminary in his home diocese of St. Paul, where he was ordained to the priesthood on June 4, 1898. The same year, he was sent for advanced study in moral theology to The Catholic University of America (CUA) in Washington, D.C. Though he did not complete his doctoral dissertation until 1906, in 1902 he returned to St. Paul's Seminary to teach moral theology and economics. In 1915 Ryan returned to CUA as a professor in the School of Sacred Theology where he remained until 1940 (though he spent his last three years as a professor in the School of Social Sciences). He also taught at Trinity College for women and later at the National Catholic School of Social Service.

From 1917 to 1921, Ryan served as the first editor of the *Catholic Charities Review,* which had been started by one of his mentors, Fr. William Kerby. While Ryan supported charities, he believed that charity did not replace the demand for justice. Echoing Henry George, he observed, "Charity is a poison when taken as a substitute for justice" (Broderick, 23). Like Kerby, Ryan believed that real charity called for changes in the root causes of poverty and not mere relief of the symptoms.

In 1919, at the urging of Fr. John O'Grady, Ryan reworked a speech he had intended to deliver to the Knights of Columbus of Louisville into a program of social reconstruction for the post-World War I world. Ryan's program was adopted with a few revisions and published by the Administrative Board of the National Catholic Welfare Conference as *The Bishops' Program of Social Reconstruction* in 1920. The program was the first major episcopal statement by the U.S. bishops on the economy, and represented a bold step by the American hierarchy. The program served notice that the U.S. bishops were no longer content with the "masterly inactivity" of the Gibbons era; the American Catholic Church would henceforth be actively involved in determining the direction of the American society and economy. The progressive tone of the program was met by many with a good deal of surprise, and was referred to by socialist Upton Sinclair as the "Catholic miracle" (Broderick, 107).

In 1919 Ryan was appointed director of the newly created Social Action Department (SAD) of the NCWC. With the able assistance of Fr. Raymond McGowan, Ryan served as director until 1944. SAD served as a platform from which Ryan could publicize his notions of social reform, and through which the general public could be educated as to the basic tenets of Catholic social teaching. To further this end, in 1923 Ryan initiated the Catholic Conference on Industrial Problems as a forum to discuss and disseminate information.

During the 1920s Ryan became an advocate of international peace through disarmament. In 1927 he assisted in the creation of the Catholic Association for International Peace. The association avoided pacifism, opting to propagate the Catholic theory of the just war. Ryan also belonged to the National Council for the Prevention of War, but resigned when the orientation of the council became too pacifist, and because the council sided with the anticlerical forces during the Mexican disputes of the 1920s and 1930s.

Ryan belonged to numerous secular organizations over the course of his lifetime, including the National Popular Government League, the Public Ownership League, the National Conference of Charities and Corrections, the National Consumers League, the National Child Labor Committee, and various others. Most controversial was Ryan's position on the board of the American Civil Liberties

Union. Ryan believed that Catholic isolation was self-defeating. Catholics needed to serve in these organizations to ensure that the Catholic viewpoint would be heard, and operate as a brake on the radical tendencies of these groups. Finally, Catholics could not achieve social reform alone—they had to work with other groups to attain their goals.

Ryan became a controversial figure during the 1928 presidential election that featured the first Catholic presidential candidate, Al Smith. Critics argued that Smith's Catholicism would prevent him from maintaining the constitutional separation of Church and state. Cited as evidence was a textbook Ryan had written with M.F.X. Millar entitled *The State and the Church,* published in 1922. Ryan and Millar had stated that, in ideal terms, Church and state should be united, with Catholicism as the established religion. They argued, however, that in real terms, no such state ever existed and would never exist, and so it offered no threat to the American notion of the separation of Church and state. Such distinctions were lost in the political rhetoric of 1928.

During the first years of the depression, Ryan was outspoken in his criticism of the Hoover administration. He argued that the depression was brought on by underconsumption that was created by a maldistribution of wealth. Real purchasing power had to be returned to the public, if the depression was to be reversed. Ryan, eschewing American Catholic fears of government power, urged federal and state governments to become more active, advocating minimum-wage laws, and public works programs.

Though initially lukewarm to Franklin Delano Roosevelt, Ryan became an ardent supporter of the New Deal, which he regarded as the closest approximation to Catholic social teaching. The New Deal, Ryan believed, provided a middle road between socialism and individualism. Ryan served on government panels, most notably the Industrial Appeals Board of the National Recovery Administration. In 1936, in response to the increasingly bitter attacks on FDR by the radio priest, Fr. Charles Coughlin, Ryan defended FDR and the New Deal in a nationally broadcast radio speech. Coughlin sarcastically called Ryan "Right Reverend New Dealer," and the title stuck. In 1937 Ryan became the first Catholic priest to deliver a benediction at a presidential inauguration. For the remainder of his life, Ryan supported FDR, even endorsing his infamous court-packing plan.

In 1940 Ryan retired from CUA but continued as director of SAD until 1944. He died in St. Paul on September 16, 1945.

Economic Thought

Ryan was influenced at an early age by the populist thinking of Ignatius Donnelly, and that of Patrick Ford, editor of the *Irish World,* as well as by the forthright stands of his archbishop, John Ireland. While studying at St. Thomas Seminary, he was exposed to Pope Leo XIII's great social encyclical, *Rerum Novarum,* on the condition of the working class. Ryan spent the rest of his life exploring the practical implications of the encyclical and applying them to the American scene. While at CUA, he studied under the great Catholic "scientific" social reformers, Thomas Bouquillon and William Kerby, who insisted that questions of social morality had to be grounded in precise observations of social reality and not just considered in abstract terms. They provided the tools by which Ryan analyzed and applied *Rerum Novarum.*

Ryan's basic economic thought was most clearly articulated in his two scholarly works: his doctoral dissertation, *A Living Wage: Its Ethical and Economic Aspects,* published in 1906; and *Distributive Justice: The Right and Wrong of Our Present Distribution of Wealth,* published in 1916. He considered the latter his "most important work" (Ryan, 136). Central to Ryan's thought were three basic principles: the worker's right to a living wage; the need for a better distribution of the world's material goods; and the right and duty of the state to promote the common good through social legislation. Ryan publicized these principles in countless articles, both scholarly and popular.

According to Ryan, each worker had a natural right to a wage that allowed the worker to live in accord with his or her dignity as a human being. This was a minimum of justice. The so-called "iron law of wages" that sought to pay the worker as little as possible was not only bad economics, it was also immoral. The worker had a *right* to a wage that enabled him to ensure the basic rights for himself and his family—food, shelter, clothing, and insurance against sickness, disability, and old age. In addition, in light of the requirements of human nature, the living wage also had to provide for the religious, recreational, and educational needs of the worker. Further, the living wage was "familial" as marriage was an essential part of a decent life. The living wage was a fundamental right; while acknowledging the right to private property and the right to a profitable return on an investment, Ryan denied that these were absolute rights. Both rights were subordinate to the worker's right to a living wage, which was grounded in a more fundamental right—the right to life.

Ryan endorsed unions and collective bargaining as a means of securing the living wage, but, when these failed, it was the duty of the state to step in and secure that right. Critics objected that Ryan's program violated the right of "free contract" between employer and employee, but Ryan exposed the lie of free contract which he saw as neither a right nor a reality. No worker freely consented to less than a living wage unless forced to do so by a superior economic force. "The name free contract is a misnomer. There can be no freedom of contract [for] laborers who must work or starve" (Ryan, 68). The worker's right to a living wage superseded all other economic rights, and served as the keystone to Ryan's economic thought.

Equally important was the proper distribution of wealth. Adopting the economic theory of John A. Hobson that depressions resulted from underconsumption and oversaving, Ryan argued that the central economic problem was one of distribution, not production. The United States was able to produce enough to supply all of its people with an adequate standard of living. Depressions resulted when supply exceeded demand, but the lack of demand was the result of a lack of purchasing power created by a maldistribution of wealth, or as Ryan observed, "speaking generally we may say that capital receives too much purchasing power and labor too little" (Ryan, 68).

To achieve a more equitable distribution of wealth, workers had to become more involved in what Ryan called "industrial management." While he affirmed the usefulness of unions, unions did not go far enough. Workers had to become involved in "the control of processes and machinery, the nature of product," and other fundamental concerns of the industry in which they worked (*Bishops' Program*, 342). He asserted that the majority of workers must "become owners, at least in part, of the instruments of production" (*Bishops' Program*, 345), though he acknowledged that this was a long-term goal.

In 1931 Pope Pius XI promulgated his important social encyclical *Quadragesimo Anno,* "On Reconstructing the Social Order," forty years after *Rerum Novarum.* Many heralded it in the United States as an endorsement of John Ryan's social agenda. CUA rector Fr. Thomas Shahan reportedly observed, "Well, this is a great vindication of John Ryan" (Broderick, 196). Papal approval was further suggested in 1933 when Ryan was named a domestic prelate.

Following QA, Ryan adopted Pius XI's call for a "vocational group system," similar to the medieval guild system in which labor and management worked together cooperatively directing their industry. The vocational group system intended to give the worker greater control over the industrial process but to maintain the right of individuals to private property.

While this remained a long-term goal, Ryan insisted on the right of the state to ensure immediate economic justice and order by guaranteeing the natural rights of the worker. The state was to provide for the common good by protecting the weak (the laborer) from the strong (the rich capitalist). Ryan was fond of quoting the following passage from *Rerum Novarum*: "Whenever the general interest or any particular class suffers, or is threatened with evils which can in no other way be met, the public authority must step in to meet them" (Ryan, 44). Whenever Ryan was accused of being too socialistic because of his heavy reliance on the state, he referred people to this passage from RN.

Ryan was beset throughout his career with accusations that he was a socialist. Early on in 1913 he had attempted to deflect these charges, by debating noted socialist Morris Hillquit. In a series of debates published in *Everybody's Magazine,* Ryan clearly delineated his views in contrast to the socialist vision. The debates were published in book form in 1914 as *Socialism: Problem or Menace?*

Practical Reform

Ryan was not content to argue abstractly over economic theory. He also proposed a detailed plan of social legislation and worked to see his agenda enacted into law. The ultimate test of any economic theory for Ryan was its social utility. Did it contribute to "human welfare?" (Curran, 32). Ryan believed in gradual, not radical reform. While upholding the ideal as the ultimate goal, he worked for short-term gains.

In 1909 he clearly articulated his short term goals in an article in the *Catholic World* entitled, "A Program of Social Reform by Legislation." His proposal included a call for a legal minimum wage; an eight-hour workday; protective legislation for women and children; the right to boycott and picket; unemployment insurance; employment bureaus; social security against sickness, accidents, and poverty in old age; public housing; public ownership of utilities, of mines, and of forests; control of monopolies; land taxes; and prohibition of speculation in the stock market (Broderick, 58–59). These proposals became the basis of his life's work. In 1919 most of these provisions (for example, minimum wage legislation, social security insurance, and public housing) were included in *The Bishops' Program for Social Reconstruction,* which he had authored. The document gave authority to Ryan's prescription for social change and buoyed Catholic social reformers.

In 1911 Ryan helped draft minimum wage legislation for the state of Minnesota as part of the Minnesota Committee on Social Legislation, and he lobbied hard for the bill. In the 1920s Ryan worked hard for an amendment to the United States Constitution prohibiting child labor. This amendment was vigorously opposed by William Cardinal O'Connell of Boston, who referred to it as "Soviet legislation," which allowed the government to usurp the rights of parents. This pernicious precedent, he believed, would ultimately lead to government interference in Catholic schools. Ryan contended that the greater danger was the continued abuse of the child in the workplace. After a bitter battle, the amendment was defeated.

During the 1930s Ryan became an avid supporter of the New Deal programs of Franklin Delano Roosevelt, which he believed to be in accord with the papal social program. Much of the legislation advocated by Ryan such as social security insurance was passed during the 1930s, much to Ryan's delight.

Conclusion

In an era in which Catholics were hesitant to address public policy issues that did not directly affect Church concerns, Ryan clearly enunciated Catholic social teaching. In an era in which American Catholic social thought was primarily negative, antisocialist, hesitant, and isolated, he presented a positive, practical agenda for social reform. Most importantly, he did so in a way that was understandable to non-Catholic Americans and reformers. Henceforth, the Catholic Church in the United States would be involved in the debate over public policy issues and on the economy. From 1906 until 1945, John Ryan was the leading Catholic voice in the United States on social issues. His principle of the "living wage" continues to be the basis for all Catholic economic thought.

Broderick, Francis. *Right Reverend New Dealer: John A. Ryan.* New York: Macmillan, 1963.

Curran, Charles. *American Catholic Social Ethics: Twentieth Century Approaches.* University of Notre Dame Press, 1982.

McShane, Joseph, S.J. *"Sufficiently Radical": Catholicism, Progressivism, and the Bishops' Program of 1919.* Washington, D.C.: CUA Press, 1986.

O'Brien, David. *Public Catholicism.* New York: Macmillan, 1989.

———. *American Catholics and Social Reform: The New Deal Years.* New York: Oxford, 1968.

Ryan, John A. *Social Doctrine in Action: A Personal History.* New York: Harper, 1941.

———. "The Bishops' Program of Social Reconstruction." *American Catholic Thought on Social Questions,* ed. A. Abell. New York: Bobbs-Merrill, 1968.

JEFFREY M. BURNS

RYAN, PATRICK JOHN (1831–1911)

Archbishop. Ryan was born in Thurles, County Tipperary, Ireland, on February 20, 1831, the son of Jeremiah Ryan and Mary Toohey. At an early age he exhibited a zeal for the priesthood and demonstrated an oratorical ability that would later earn for him the title "Chrysostom of the American Church."

In 1847 Ryan entered St. Patrick's College in Carlow to begin studies for the priesthood. When still only a deacon, he was invited to the Archdiocese of St. Louis and appointed to the faculty of the seminary at Carondelet, Missouri. Ordained to the priesthood on September 8, 1853, Ryan served as assistant at the cathedral until 1861 when he became the pastor of Annunciation parish which he built.

During the Civil War, he served as chaplain to a Confederate prison camp in St. Louis. In 1866 he accompanied Archbishop Peter Kenrick to the Second Plenary Council of Baltimore, where he delivered one of the main addresses. Two years later, Ryan became rector of the Church of St. John, and he also journeyed to Rome with

Patrick J. Ryan

Kenrick. Pope Pius IX selected Ryan to preach the English lenten sermons there. After his return, he became vicar general of St. Louis, and he acted as administrator of the diocese when Kenrick was in Rome during the First Vatican Council.

Ryan was consecrated coadjutor bishop of St. Louis with the right of succession on April 14, 1872. He served in that capacity for twelve years, during which he was frequently called upon to defend Catholicism from renewed anti-Catholic attacks.

On June 8, 1884, Ryan was appointed to the vacant see of Philadelphia, the second largest diocese in the United States. Hardly had he taken up residence in Philadelphia when he was called to attend the opening of the Third Plenary Council of Baltimore.

Immigration was a main topic at the council, and Ryan worked tirelessly as archbishop to hold the new immigrants in the Catholic Church. At times, he had to fight vigorously against Catholic ethnic minorities that claimed jurisdiction over church property and finances. At other times, he showed his concern for the immigrants by creating national parishes for them: 18 Polish, 17 Italian, 13 Slovak, 8 Lithuanian, 4 German, and 3 Hungarian. The first Greek Catholic (Ruthenian) cathedral in the United States was dedicated in Philadelphia on October 2, 1910.

Ryan supported St. Frances Xavier Cabrini and Mother Katharine Drexel in their work among immigrants, African Americans, and Native Americans. Madonna House, which provided religious instruction, medical services, and athletic activities to Italian immigrant youth, was opened in 1904 in Philadelphia. Ryan also created the first parish in the Archdiocese of Philadelphia for African Americans,

St. Peter Claver (1889). In 1902 President Theodore Roosevelt appointed Ryan to the Board of Indian Commissioners where he served until his death in 1911.

When he assumed editorship of the *American Catholic Quarterly Review* in May 1890, he noted that the periodical would address and refute attacks charging American Catholics with disloyalty. Ryan always maintained that there was no incompatibility between being a Catholic and being a good American citizen. Even during the Spanish-American War, when the United States fought against a Catholic country, Ryan led Philadelphia Catholics in supporting the American war effort.

Under Ryan's leadership, forty-five new parochial schools were created by 1903; and in new parishes, a parochial school was always a prime consideration. Ryan appointed the first diocesan school board (1887) and the first superintendent of schools (1889). Roman Catholic High School for Boys (which opened in 1890) was the first free Catholic secondary school in America, and it set the precedent for a Catholic secondary school system in Philadelphia that was unique in the world. Shortly before his death, Ryan donated the land for the first diocesan high school for girls in the United States.

Ryan was instrumental in the creation of a number of charitable institutions: St. Joseph's Protectory for Girls (1886), St. Agnes Hospital (1888), St. Francis de Sales Industrial School for Boys (1888), St. Joseph's House for Homeless Industrious Boys (1890), St. Magdalen's Asylum for Colored Girls (1892), St. Mary's House for Catholic Working Girls (1893), the Gonzaga Memorial House (1899), the expansion of St. Vincent's Home and Maternity Hospital (1885–92), and the Philadelphia Protectory for Boys (1898).

Ryan was always in demand as a speaker and as an arbitrator. In 1895 he served on a committee to arbitrate a dispute over wages and hours and union recognition between the Union Traction Company and the Amalgamated Association of Street Railway Employees of America. At the Republican national convention in 1910 in Philadelphia, Ryan was chosen to pronounce the benediction.

When Ryan died on February 11, 1911, the mourning in the city was considerable. He was buried five days later.

See also PENNSYLVANIA, CATHOLIC CHURCH IN.

Archbishop Ryan Papers, Philadelphia Archdiocesan Historical Research Center, Wynnewood, Pennsylvania.

Consuela, Mary, I.H.M. "The Church of Philadelphia (1884–1918)." *The History of the Archdiocese of Philadelphia,* ed. James F. Connelly. Philadelphia, 1976, 271–321.

Kirlin, Joseph J. *Life of the Most Reverend Patrick John Ryan, D.D., LL.D., Archbishop of Philadelphia.* Philadelphia, 1903.

JOSEPH J. CASINO

RYAN, THOMAS FORTUNE (1851–1928)

Financier and philanthropist. Ryan was born on October 17, 1851, in Lovington, Virginia. Orphaned at an early age, he went to Baltimore, Maryland, when he was fourteen years old to find work. He later married Ida M. Barry, his employer's daughter. At the age of twenty-two, he moved to New York City and joined the New York Stock Exchange.

Along with several well-known financial manipulators, he became involved in consolidating utility companies and, in 1892, formed the Metropolitan Street Railway Company, the first American holding company. In 1905 the company merged with August Belmont's Interborough Rapid Transit Company to finance a subway system for New York City.

Ryan accomplished most of his business deals in secrecy, among them the formation of the American Tobacco Company, the National Bank of Commerce, and control of the Seaboard Air Line Railroad. However, his acquisition methods aroused policyholders' protests when he purchased controlling interest in the Equitable Life Assurance Society. The firm was later turned over to trustees headed by Grover Cleveland.

Besides railroads and utilities, Ryan also owned interests in natural resources, such as coke, coal, oil, rubber, and lead, as well as diamonds in the Belgian Congo, the result of an invitation from Belgium's King Leopold II to form a syndicate to develop the Belgian Congo.

He owned one of the world's finest art collections. His charitable contributions, more than $20 million to Catholic causes, were made anonymously.

He died in New York City November 23, 1928.

Ryan, T. F. "Why I Bought the Equitable." *North American Review* 198 (August 1913) 161–77.

MARIANNA McLOUGHLIN

S

SACRED HEART, SOCIETY OF THE (R.S.C.J.)

The Society of the Sacred Heart is a religious order of women founded in Paris, France, by St. Madeleine Sophie Barat, November 21, 1800, with the assistance of Fr. Joseph Varin, superior of the Fathers of the Faith. Known publicly until 1815 as the "Association Religieuse des Dames de l'Instruction Chrétienne" for political reasons, the purpose of the society was "to glorify the Sacred Heart of Jesus by laboring for the salvation and perfection of its members through the imitation of the virtues of which this Divine Heart is the center and model, and by consecrating its members . . . to the sanctification of others, as the work dearest to the Heart of Jesus." The spirit of the society (marked deeply by the imprint of St. Madeleine Sophie who served as superior general for sixty-five years and whose extant correspondence numbers over 14,000 letters) is summarized in the *Constitutions* as *Cor unum et anima una in corde Jesu.* At once contemplative and apostolic, the institute was dedicated primarily to the education of youth, as expressed in a fourth vow, and centralized under the government of a superior general. The members observed a form of cloister and included choir and coadjutrix members, the former obliged to the Office of the Blessed Virgin in choir. However, since Mother Barat refused grilles in view of the educational aims of the order, the nuns did not make solemn vows, but substituted a vow of stability, or perseverance in the order. The *Constitutions,* written by Fr. Julien Druilhet, S.J., but inspired by Mother Barat and Fr. Varin, were adopted in 1815 and approved by Pope Leo XII in 1826.

The first school was opened at Amiens in 1801, followed by Grenoble (1804) and Poitiers (1806); by 1808 the society extended to Belgium. In 1818 five missionaries led by St. Philippine Duchesne (1769–1852) established the first American house at St. Charles, Missouri. By the death of the foundress (May 25, 1865), the Society of the Sacred Heart numbered 3,500 religious and was established in various European countries, North and South America, and Africa. In the 1880s, foundations were made in New Zealand and Australia; by 1908 the first Asian house was opened in Japan. Due to antireligious laws, forty-five houses were closed in France (1903–09), and the motherhouse was moved to Ixelles, Belgium. Since 1925 it has been located in Rome.

American Foundations

The first Sacred Heart foundations in the United States were in the Mississippi valley: St. Charles and St. Louis in Missouri; Grand Coteau, St. Michael's and Bayou La Fourche in Louisiana. In 1841 Mother Duchesne was among the band of four nuns missioned to the Potawatomi at Sugar Creek in Indian Territory (Kansas), and in the same year a house was opened at Houston and Mulberry Streets in New York City. The first Canadian convent followed in 1842 at St. Jacques de l'Achigan, near Montreal. From these houses, numerous foundations were made throughout the United States, eastern Canada, South America, Cuba, Mexico, and New Zealand. Each Convent of the Sacred Heart was an apostolic center, featuring an academy, and a free school, as well as the *oeuvres populaires,* such as orphanages, night schools, occupational training, and catechetical classes. Through retreats and various sodalities (notably the Children of Mary), the religious exercised a spiritual ministry, and the writings of Janet Erskine Stuart (1857–1914) on education and spirituality influenced women in many American congregations far beyond the Society of the Sacred Heart. The educational excellence of the Sacred Heart academies, the clientele they attracted and the graduates they produced, created an aristocratic reputation, which belies the fact that students in the free or parish schools during the late nineteenth and early twentieth centuries typically outnumbered those in the academies. Sacred Heart nuns also educated thousands of young boys in parish schools and in primary departments of their own. From 1914 the Society of the Sacred Heart established ten college-level institutions for women, of which Manhattanville College in New York became the best known. In 1933 the first meeting of the Associated Alumnae of the Sacred Heart was held in St. Louis, and by the mid-1960s there were thirty-five Convents of the Sacred Heart in five vicariates throughout the United States.

After 1964, when cloister was discontinued, Religious of the Sacred Heart rapidly undertook many extra-institutional works, sometimes in collaboration with other groups. Chiefly educational, such efforts were directed particularly at combating poverty and racism. The nuns formed smaller communities, more integrated with neighborhoods, often in poorer areas. Schools, under the control of boards of trustees, after 1975 were formed into the Network of Sacred Heart Schools, whose goals and criteria assure continuity with Sacred Heart philosophy. Since 1969, the society has adopted a less centralized form of provincial governance, and in 1982 the five U.S. provinces were united into one. At its peak in 1965, the society in the United States numbered over 1,000 members, and in 1995 numbered 545.

See also WOMEN RELIGIOUS IN AMERICA.

Callan, Louise. *The Society of the Sacred Heart in North America.* New York, 1937.

Charry, Jeanne de. *Histoire des Constitutions de la Société du Sacré Coeur.* 2 vols. Rome, 1975, 1981.

_____. *Dizionario degli Instituti di Perfezione,* s.v. "Società del Sacro Cuore di Gesù, S. Sophia Barat."

_____. *Philippine Duchesne, Frontier Missionary of the Sacred Heart, 1769–1852.* Westminster, Md.: Newman, 1957.

Stuart, Janet Erskine. *The Education of Catholic Girls.* London, New York, 1912.

_____. *The Society of the Sacred Heart.* London, 1914.

Williams, Margaret. *The Society of the Sacred Heart, History of a Spirit, 1800–1975.* London: Dartman, Longman & Todd, 1978.

PATRICIA BYRNE, C.S.J.

SADLIER, MARY (1820–1903)

Novelist. Mary Anne Madden Sadlier was born in Cootehill, County Cavan, Ireland, on December 30, 1820, the daughter of Francis Madden, a successful merchant. Mary Anne Madden received her education at home. Her writing talents emerged early, and the eighteen-year-old had verse published in *La Belle Assemblée.* The twenty-four-year-old Irish woman immigrated in 1844 to Montreal where she met James Sadlier, a leading Catholic publisher who, with his brother Denis, owned D. & J. Sadlier. Madden married Sadlier in 1845. Fifteen years and six children later, James and Mary Anne Sadlier moved to New York City.

Mary Sadlier

Mary Anne had already published six books in Montreal. In addition to producing more fiction, M. A. Sadlier became principal editor of the Sadlier-owned newspaper, *The Tablet,* in which she published both editorials and serial fiction. Over the next ten years she published twenty-three more books. After James's death in 1869, Mary Anne Sadlier ran the publishing company and wrote twelve more novels. Most of her novels dealt with specific questions of the day, particularly the difficulties faced by the Irish immigrants. *The Blakes and the Flanagans,* for example, dealt with the New York school controversy. Novels like *The Red Hand of Ulster* and *The Confederate Chieftains* reminded Irish immigrants of their homeland's history. She also translated devotional works including Orsini's *Life of the Blessed Virgin.*

As a Catholic philanthropist, Sadlier sponsored a Foundling Asylum, a Home for the Aged, and a Home for Friendless Girls. She returned to Montreal in 1885 after her nephew took over the publishing company. She remained in the Canadian city until her death on April 5, 1903.

See also CATHOLIC BOOK PUBLISHING; CATHOLICS AND AMERICAN LITERATURE.

Donnelly, E. C. *Round Table of Representative American Catholic Novelists* (1897).
Sadlier, Mary Anne Madden. *The Red Hand of Ulster* (1850).
____. *The Blakes and the Flanagans* (1855).
____. *Old and New; or Taste Versus Fashion* (1862).
____. *Bessy Conway; or The Irish Girl in America* (1863).
____. *Catechism of Sacred History and Doctrine* (1864).
____. *Confessions of an Apostate* (1864).
____. *The Old House by the Boyne* (1865).
____. *Aunt Honor's Keepsake* (1866).
____. *The Invisible Hand* (1873).
____. *Maureen Dhu, The Admirals's Daughter* (1870).
____. *Obyrne; or the Expatriated* (1898).
"Sadlier, Mary Anne." *Dictionary of Irish Literature* (1979).
"Sadlier, Mary Anne (Madden)." *The Feminist Companion to Literature in English* (1990).
Seraphine, M., O.S.U. *Immortelles of Catholic Columbian Literature* (1896).

SANDRA YOCUM MIZE

ST. AGNES, CONGREGATION OF (C.S.A.)

The Congregation of St. Agnes was founded in Wisconsin in 1858. Since 1845 an Austrian missionary priest, Fr. Caspar Rehrl, had been responsible for the missions on the eastern shore of Lake Winnebago. As German settlers moved into the Milwaukee diocese in significant numbers, Bishop Henni encouraged them to move into the Fox River valley where they could maintain their culture and faith at a safe distance from the "English" settlers in Milwaukee. Fr. Rehrl, trudging up and down the Fox River valley, building churches from Milwaukee to Green Bay, could devote little time to the parishes he was founding. The anticlerical sentiments many of the settlers brought over from Europe caused him deep distress. The children were getting little or no education as schools were few and the teachers only too frequently incompetent, alcoholic, or both. Fr. Rehrl, believing that a religious community working along with him could help him strengthen and preserve the Catholic faith of the people, wrote for assistance to congregations in Europe without success. Disheartened, he resolved to found his own sisterhood, a desperate but audacious move since other religious congregations had their roots in Europe.

Early Difficulties

Armed with the consent of Pius IX, he named his society after the young Roman martyr, Agnes. In 1858 three young women joined him in Barton, Wisconsin. They were followed by others, some as young as eleven years old. But the pressure of his own pastoral duties, his inability to provide religious formation, education, and even such necessities as food and warmth, drove the new recruits away. In 1861 there was only one sister left, and she was blind. Remarkably, however, more women came.

The arrival of Mary Hazotte of Detroit, Michigan, in 1863 gave Fr. Rehrl his "child of destiny." Nineteen months later she and two other candidates became the first professed sisters of St. Agnes. That same day, Mary, seventeen years old, became Mary Agnes and was elected first canonical superior of the community.

It was not long before the priest and the sister were battling over the direction of the community. Fr. Rehrl, inured to a life of hardship, had little idea of the needs of young women. He wanted the sisters in the classroom almost immediately. Mary Agnes, educated by the Notre Dame Sisters and influenced by the nearby Capuchin Franciscan community, wanted more preparation for her sisters and a traditional religious lifestyle. Matters came to a head in 1870, when, toward the close of the sisters' annual retreat, the vicar general of the Milwaukee diocese arrived with the startling announcement that the community was to be dissolved. Only when the Capuchin retreat master, Fr. Francis Haas, who had just completed a rule for the community, agreed to direct it was the community saved.

That same summer the break came. A few sisters remained with Fr. Rehrl; the majority followed Mother Agnes to Fond du Lac. Those twenty-six women taught in five public and ten Catholic schools in the area.

The next few years were ones of crisis. The separation had not been without suffering on both sides. Poor nutrition and austere living made the sisters vulnerable to illness and death. In the decade after 1872, thirteen young women died. Their average age was twenty-four. Pneumonia and tuberculosis took the lives of these daughters of German and Irish immigrants. Sisters had to go on begging expeditions to raise money to keep their work alive. One died of yellow fever on such a tour. Throughout it all, Agnes' indomitable strength sustained the group through their struggles.

As the little community became better known, bishops and pastors began to request the sisters to teach, play the organ, direct choirs—anything to help the overworked priests. As early as 1870, three sisters were sent to staff a school in Defiance, Ohio. By 1879 Mother Agnes was sending her sisters as far as Kansas and Texas. It was not without cost. The first two sisters sent to Kansas contracted typhoid fever. When one died, Agnes was torn between sending help to the remaining sister and fear that those sent would also succumb. She wrote:

> Dear Sister, you must not think that we have forgotten you or that we do not care for you. I grieve to think that you are there alone and if it would be possible, I would go immediately to you myself. . . . Dear Sister, I know it's hard for you to be alone, but . . . be resigned to the Holy Will of God. . . .

Later Development

In the following decades, the congregation grew in numbers and apostolates. By the time Agnes died in 1905, the sisters were staffing more than forty parochial schools and a house for German immigrants in New York. They established a hospital, sanitarium, and a home for the aged. Later they staffed orphanages, high schools, and established an academy, a school of nursing, and a college. In 1945 four sisters went to Waspam, Nicaragua, staffing a school, a dispensary, and a clinic.

The congregation realized a steady growth until, like other communities, it experienced the upheaval caused in the Church by the Second Vatican Council. But religious renewal opened new horizons for the sisters. Today they serve as pastoral associates, hospital chaplains, social workers, religious education directors, as well as in the traditional ministries of nursing and teaching. Embracing "the preferential option for the poor," sisters are working in black schools in Chicago's inner city and in the Deep South, on Native American reservations, in New York's Chinatown, as well as in East Harlem and Central America.

See also WOMEN RELIGIOUS IN AMERICA.

Lorimer, Margaret, C.S.A. "Mother M. Agnes Hazotte." *Wisconsin Women: A Gifted Heritage.* Wisconsin State AAUW, 1982.

Naber, Vera, C.S.A. *With All Devotedness.* New York: P. J. Kenedy & Sons, 1959.

Palen, Imogene, C.S.A. *Fieldstones: The Story of Caspar Rehrl.* Fond du Lac: Badger-Freund Printers, 1969.

____. *Fieldstones '76: The Story of the Founders of the Sisters of Saint Agnes.* Oshkosh: Oshkosh Printers, 1976.

LEANNE SITTER, C.S.A.

ST. BONAVENTURE UNIVERSITY

St. Bonaventure University was founded on October 4, 1858, when its first building was formally dedicated in Allegany, New York. This foundation was the result of planning that started in 1854 when Nicholas Devereux (1791–1855) and John Timon (1797–1867), the bishop of Buffalo, traveled to Rome to ask Pope Pius IX to establish a Franciscan community in the southern tier of the Diocese of Buffalo to carry out missionary and educational work. As a result of that meeting, Fr. Pamphilus da Magliano, O.F.M. (1824–76), led a small group of friars to America in 1855 to the western New York town of Ellicottville. On August 23, 1856, Bishop Timon presided over a crowd of 2,000 people who had gathered to witness the laying of the cornerstone of the first college building in Allegany. The dedication of that building took place in 1858, and the first classes of what was then St. Bonaventure College were held in 1859.

The college was under the care of the Franciscan Custody of the Immaculate Conception until 1901 when it was turned over to the newly formed Holy Name province. In 1875 a provisional charter was granted the college by the Board of Regents of the State of New York, and in 1883 a permanent charter of incorporation was given.

The first diplomas offered were for bachelor of arts degrees, but already in 1914 a master's degree program was formally put in place. By 1916 courses were established toward a bachelor of science degree. It was also in 1916 that courses started to be taught which later formed the basis of the School of Education.

The most prominent president in the history of the school was Fr. Thomas Plassmann, O.F.M. (1879–1959), who served from 1920 until 1949. During Fr. Plassmann's term of office the college went through an unprecedented time of development and growth.

The first steps toward making the college coeducational took place in the summer of 1922 when extension courses were begun for women. It was not until 1942 that women were admitted as undergraduate day students.

In 1932 the School of Commerce was started, which by 1948 had expanded into the School of Business. The Franciscan Institute began in the late 1930s with the teaching of a few classes and the creation of a separate collection of library materials. It was formally founded by Fr. Plassmann with the help of Fr. Philotheus Boehner, O.F.M. (1901–55), and Fr. Matthias Fause, O.F.M. (1879–1956), who was the provincial of Holy Name province.

The year 1949 saw the founding of the Journalism Department by Russell J. Jandoli (1918–91). That department is now a school named after its founder. It was also in 1949 that work was begun on a building for Christ the King Seminary, for the training of diocesan priests. The dedication of that facility took place in 1952 (the seminary moved in 1974).

With the growth in graduate programs over the years, the college was granted university status by New York State in 1950. The university's first woman president was Sr. Alice Gallin, O.S.U., who acted in an interim capacity in 1993. In 1994 the university appointed Dr. Robert J. Wickenheiser as president, the first Catholic layman to be given that office.

See also CATHOLIC UNIVERSITIES AND COLLEGES.

Angelo, Mark V. *The History of St. Bonaventure University.* St. Bonaventure, N.Y.: Franciscan Institute, 1961.

Callahan, Adalbert. *Medieval Francis in Modern America.* New York: Macmillan, 1936.

Hammon, Walter. *The First Bonaventure Men.* St. Bonaventure, N.Y.: St. Bonaventure University, 1958.

PAUL J. SPAETH

ST. CHARLES BORROMEO SEMINARY

Catholic seminary of the Archdiocese of Philadelphia located in Wynnewood, Pennsylvania, just outside the city of Philadelphia. The mission of the seminary is the formation of Catholic men of the Archdiocese of Philadelphia and of other dioceses and religious communities for the Roman Catholic priesthood.

Early History

Plans for a seminary for the Diocese of Philadelphia were announced by Bishop Francis P. Kenrick at the first diocesan synod of Philadelphia on May 15, 1832. On June 26, 1832, St. Charles Borromeo Seminary officially opened in the bishop's residence.

Since it was devoted solely to clerical education and did not accept lay students, St. Charles was the first seminary in the United States based exclusively on the model set forth in the decree on seminaries of the Council of Trent (1545–63).

Except for the period 1841–53, the seminary has been administered by the secular clergy of the Archdiocese of Philadelphia. In 1841, due to a shortage of diocesan priests, the seminary was administered by the Congregation of the Mission (Vincentian Fathers). In 1853, due to their own shortage of priests, the Vincentians ceased administration of the seminary and control reverted to diocesan clergy.

Recognizing the need for a steady income to support the seminary, Bishop Kenrick announced the establishment of an annual seminary collection in 1835. This collection still exists as a major source of support for the seminary.

On April 13, 1838, the seminary was chartered by the legislature of the Commonwealth of Pennsylvania with the power to grant degrees. On May 1, 1838, a board of trustees was established that consists of twelve members with the archbishop of Philadelphia as president.

In 1859 the bishop of Philadelphia, John Neumann, opened a preparatory seminary at Glen Riddle, Pennsylvania, to prepare young men still in high school for their theological studies. It exists today as the college division of the seminary. On September 16, 1871, the seminary moved to its present location. This allowed the combination of the preparatory and theology programs in the same location. The college and theology divisions are currently maintained in separate buildings on the same campus.

During the period 1876–1927, St. Charles Seminary was a major center of American Catholic cultural and intellectual life due to its association with two important Catholic periodicals of the period: the *American Catholic Quarterly Review* (1876–1924) and the *American Ecclesiastical Review* (1889–1975). Both were founded and operated during this period by seminary faculty.

Recent Developments

During the 1950s the seminary became more involved with the larger Catholic community of the archdiocese, offering its facilities for use by outside organizations. In October 1952 the seminary held its first annual open house in which the Catholic laity of the archdiocese were invited to tour the seminary.

In 1964 the seminary began its "Thursday Apostolate" for fourth-year theologians. This was the first field education program for Catholic seminarians in the United States. The program currently includes all seminarians in both the college and theology divisions.

The Second Vatican Council's Decree on Priestly Formation (October 28, 1965) had a tremendous effect on the seminary. Among the changes at St. Charles in the wake of Vatican II were more freedom for the seminarians, creation of a student council, revision of the curriculum, accreditation, improved library facilities, the creation of a formation program, and the expansion of the field education program. In 1964 the seminary reached its peak enrollment with 566 students in the college and theology divisions.

In 1969 a summer Religious Studies Division was established. Originally for women religious, it expanded to include laypeople. In 1973 the Religious Studies program expanded from a summer program to a year-round evening and summer program.

In 1970 the theology division was accredited by the American Association of Theological Schools. The following year, the Middle States Association of Colleges and Secondary Schools granted accreditation to both the college and theology divisions.

Since its founding, St. Charles Seminary has sent nearly three thousand seminarians into the priesthood. Including its founder, Bishop Francis Kenrick, the seminary has had sixty-one alumni, faculty, and administrators become bishops and four became cardinals.

See also SEMINARIES (DIOCESAN).

Connelly, James Francis. *St. Charles Seminary, Philadelphia: A History, 1832–1979*. Philadelphia: St. Charles Seminary, 1979.
———, ed. *The History of the Archdiocese of Philadelphia*. Philadelphia: The Archdiocese of Philadelphia, 1976.
"St. Charles Borromeo Seminary, 1832–1982: 150 Years of Service." Supplement to *The Catholic Standard and Times*, February 4, 1982.

SHAWN WELDON

ST. JOHN'S ABBEY (COLLEGEVILLE, MINNESOTA)

As a monastery, St. John's Abbey is a product of the Benedictine Order. Its traditions and stability are rooted in the *Rule* of St. Benedict, written by a monk who founded the monastery of Monte Cassino in Italy more that fourteen hundred years ago. The need for new communities of worship and culture led Augustine and his fellow monks to leave St. Andrew's in Rome in 596 at the behest of Pope Gregory the Great and to work for the conversion of England in the seventh century. This same need inspired the Englishman Boniface to go to the Germans in the eighth century and to begin the building of the great Benedictine monasteries that were to become centers of Christianity and civilization for all the northern European peoples. Among them was the monastery of Metten in Bavaria, still vigorous today after more than a thousand years of monastic life.

The pioneer monk, Boniface Wimmer, who laid the foundations for the growth of Benedictinism in the United States in 1846, established St. Vincent Abbey at Latrobe, Pennsylvania, near Pittsburgh. He was a monk from Metten. This monastery flourished, and in 1856, in answer to a plea from the bishop of St. Paul, Joseph Crétin, for missionaries to care for the spiritual needs of an increasing number of German immigrants in Minnesota, Abbot Boniface was able to dispatch five monks to develop a monastery in the Upper Midwest.

A site was finally selected in 1866 on a scenic elevation at the north end of Lake Sagatagan, about twelve miles northwest of St. Cloud, Minnesota. Here the monks built an expansive abbey, and here they still reside. In 1995 the community numbered 228 members. As a Benedictine institution, St. John's maintained the tradition of *ora et labora* (worship and work). It developed a thriving university and incorporated into its physical plant many new architectural features. In the 1950s the famed architect, Marcel Breuer, was commissioned to design a new abbey church and seven other buildings which have been widely acclaimed.

Since the 1920s the Benedictines at St. John's have helped to promote a worldwide movement for liturgical reform in the Roman Catholic Church, such as the use of the vernacular, popular participation, and the rearrangement of the sanctuary. Many liturgical changes advanced by St. John's theologians were later endorsed by the Second Vatican Council (1962–65). Since that time, St. John's monks have continued their leadership, seeking new and meaningful changes in worship—changes that meet contemporary needs yet recognize the importance of tradition. The sponsorship and development by the abbey of The Liturgical Press since 1926 has been a notable means for explaining and implementing liturgical matters in its numerous publications.

The Institute for Ecumenical and Cultural Research, founded by the monks of St. John's in 1967 as an independent corporation, links the Benedictine tradition of scholarship with the new openness of Christians to one another and to other religious groups. The institute, a residential center on the abbey grounds to which men and women from many religious traditions come to do research and writing, is committed to supporting careful

thought for the sake of mutual understanding and a more widespread, meaningful articulation of faith.

In 1995 monks of St. John's served in twenty-seven parishes, thirteen chaplaincies, one Native American mission in northern Minnesota, and also in priories in Tokyo and the Bahamas.

See also BENEDICTINES (O.S.B.); ST. JOHN'S UNIVERSITY (COLLEGEVILLE, MINNESOTA).

Barry, Colman J., O.S.B. *Worship and Work: Saint John's Abbey and University, 1856–1992.* 3rd ed. Collegeville: The Liturgical Press, 1992.

VINCENT TEGEDER, O.S.B.

ST. JOHN'S UNIVERSITY (COLLEGEVILLE, MINNESOTA)

St. John's University, founded in 1857 in central Minnesota by five Benedictine monks from St. Vincent Abbey in Latrobe, Pennsylvania, near Pittsburgh, to serve the needs of German immigrants, is one of the oldest institutions of higher education in the Midwest. It received its charter from the territorial legislature of Minnesota in 1857. Its stated mission was "the promotion of the instruction and education of youths." In 1869 the Minnesota State Legislature granted the St. John's administration the power "to confer degrees and grant such diplomas in their discretion as are usual in colleges and universities. . . ." Fourteen years later in 1883 the state legislature granted the title of "university" to St. John's.

Panorama of St. John's Abbey and University

From its inception the university has valued the liberal arts as a preparation for careers of leadership in Church and society. Its educational program is rooted in Catholic and Christian tradition and the guiding Benedictine principles of its founders.

On the undergraduate level since the 1960s, St. John's has developed a unique joint institutional program with the College of St. Benedict, a Benedictine college for women located four miles apart in central Minnesota. The students of these two colleges share in one common education, as well as coeducational, social, cultural, and spiritual programs. St. John's and St. Benedict's have a common core curriculum, identical major requirements, and a common academic calendar. Most departments are joint, and those which are unique to one college allow full enrollment to students of the other college.

In 1995 the colleges enrolled approximately 1,800 women and 1,800 men. The combined faculties include about 260 professors, among them Benedictines and lay professors with diverse backgrounds.

At the graduate level, the St. John's University School of Theology offers a master's degree in theology, religious education, liturgical studies, and liturgical music. The School of Theology also operates the St. John's Seminary which prepares men for the priesthood in the Roman Catholic Church.

See also CATHOLIC UNIVERSITIES AND COLLEGES.

Barry, Colman J., O.S.B. *Worship and Work: Saint John's Abbey and University, 1856–1992.* 3rd ed. Collegeville: The Liturgical Press, 1992.

VINCENT TEGEDER, O.S.B.

ST. JOHN'S UNIVERSITY (NEW YORK)

St. John's University, New York, the largest Catholic university in the United States, was founded in 1870 by priests of the Congregation of the Mission, popularly known as the Vincentians. This religious community, animated by the compassionate concern for the poor and disadvantaged that marked the life and work of St. Vincent de Paul, responded to the invitation of the first bishop of Brooklyn to provide education for immigrants and the children of immigrants within the city of New York. St. John's has been, since its beginnings, Catholic, Vincentian, and metropolitan.

Initially, the university offered education in the liberal arts and sciences to young men. Subsequently, it became coeducational and, while continuing to emphasize study in the liberal arts, added a number of professional schools and programs. Today the university is comprised of nine academic units that offer associate, baccalaureate, master's, and doctoral degrees in over one hundred major areas, including professional preparation in the fields of education, business administration, law, and pharmacy. Total enrollment is approximately 20,000.

In 1955 St. John's moved from its original location in downtown Brooklyn to its current main campus on 102 acres which were formerly the Hillcrest golf course in the borough of Queens. In 1970 it acquired the 16.5-acre site of the former Notre Dame College on Grymes Hill, Staten Island, and established a second campus.

See also CATHOLIC UNIVERSITIES AND COLLEGES.

ST. JOSEPH'S SEMINARY (DUNWOODIE)

St. Joseph's Seminary, Dunwoodie, takes its name from the Yonkers neighborhood in which it is located. It was the fifth and most successful major seminary established by the Archdiocese of New York. The first two attempts—at Nyack from 1833 to 1837, and at Lafargeville from 1838 to 1839—ended in failure. In 1840 Bishop John Hughes established the first St. Joseph's Seminary at Fordham, but he was forced to close it in 1860 due to lack of money and faculty. From 1864 to 1896, most New York diocesan priests were trained at St. Joseph's Provincial Seminary in Troy, an institution that educated over 700 priests in its brief existence. However, appalling living conditions and a high mortality rate led to a demand for seminary reform.

Archbishop Corrigan and Dunwoodie

In 1886 Archbishop Michael Augustine Corrigan announced his intention of providing New York with a modern seminary facility. The property at Dunwoodie was purchased in 1890; the cornerstone was blessed on May 17, 1891, at a chaotic ceremony attended by some 60,000 people. Construction began later that year and was completed in 1896 at a cost of approximately $1,000,000 with Archbishop Corrigan personally contributing $50,000 for the cost of the chapel. The building was dedicated on August 12, 1896, and the debt was liquidated in May 1898. Bishop Bernard McQuaid of Rochester described Dunwoodie as "the grandest seminary building in Christendom," and James Cardinal Gibbons of Baltimore told Corrigan that the new seminary would be "his grand crowning work."

In 1896 Dunwoodie represented the state of the art in seminary design and construction. Corrigan wanted a healthy environment in which to train future priests to be both gentlemen and scholars. Living conditions were so superior to those at Troy that the older priests in New York referred to the new seminarians as "Dunwoodie Dudes." Archbishop Corrigan entrusted the administration of the seminary to the Society of St. Sulpice despite vigorous opposition from his vicar general, auxiliary bishop John M. Farley, who wished to place New York diocesan priests in charge of the institution.

The Sulpicians assumed control of Dunwoodie at a time when progressive Sulpician superiors such as Alphonse Magnien and John Hogan were making major reforms in seminary education at St. Mary's Seminary in Baltimore and at St. John's Seminary in Boston. The same atmosphere prevailed in Dunwoodie under the first two rectors, Edward Dyer and James Driscoll. Dunwoodie was especially noted for the quality of its Scripture professors and for the publication of the *New York Review* between 1905 and 1908. In those years, in the opinion of John Tracy Ellis, Dunwoodie ranked second only to The Catholic University of America in its contribution to American Catholic intellectual life.

Cardinal Farley and the Sulpicians

However, friction developed between the more progressive Sulpician professors at Dunwoodie and their more conservative superiors in Paris, especially over the censorship of faculty publications. Archbishop John Farley (who had succeeded Corrigan in 1902) indicated a willingness to accept the Sulpician professors into the Archdiocese of New York. Five of the six Sulpicians accepted Farley's implicit offer in 1906, thus bringing the Sulpician era at Dunwoodie to a close.

Farley's promise of support proved to be illusory. After the papal condemnation of Modernism in 1907, the *New York Review* was suppressed and the rector, Scripture scholar James Driscoll, was forced to resign. Farley ordered the professors to teach their classes in Latin, and Dunwoodie—like seminaries everywhere—reverted to a pedagogical system of rote memorization that Peter Guilday aptly described as "an intellectual coma." Conditions further deteriorated under Patrick Cardinal Hayes (1919–38) whose cost-cutting economies reduced living standards to barely tolerable levels. In 1922 the rector, John P. Chidwick, resigned in protest. Nonetheless, enrollment boomed, reaching a peak of 303 students in 1932. Thereafter, Hayes deliberately reduced the enrollment by one-third because he felt that the Archdiocese of New York had a surplus of diocesan priests.

Cardinal Spellman and Dunwoodie

Under Francis Cardinal Spellman (1939–67), Dunwoodie enjoyed a renaissance. He renovated the neglected material fabric, installed modern lighting and plumbing, and erected a new library and gymnasium—earning the right to be considered the second founder of Dunwoodie. He also rebuilt the faculty by providing well-trained professors. Unlike Farley, Spellman came to the defense of his priests when they encountered opposition from reactionary critics, most notably Scripture professor Myles Bourke and Richard Dillon, student editor of the *Dunwoodie Review,* a scholarly student periodical which began publication semiannually in 1961.

Spellman also introduced an element of professionalism not seen since the departure of the Sulpicians. In 1961 Dunwoodie won accreditation from the Middle States Association of Colleges and Secondary Schools. In 1970 the two years of philosophy were transferred to a new college seminary and Dunwoodie became a four-year theologate. The turmoil that disturbed many seminaries in the wake of Vatican Council II was relatively muted at Dunwoodie. By the early 1970s, with a faculty that was stronger and better balanced than it had been in decades, Dunwoodie seemed poised for its second spring.

Unfortunately, the promise was never realized. Enrollment had already begun to plummet from 217 in 1966 to 97 in 1970 to 47 in 1973. Spellman's financial generos-ity did not continue under his successor, Terence Cardinal Cooke (1968–83), ironically the only Dunwoodie alumnus to become archbishop of New York. The faculty became increasingly polarized on ideological grounds, culminating in November 1973 in a public letter in the archdiocesan newspaper from five professors voicing alarm at the identification of orthodoxy with fundamentalism. As dissatisfied professors left Dunwoodie to accept university teaching positions elsewhere, by 1980 the core faculty had shrunk to the smallest size in its history. Efforts to increase student enrollment from outside the archdiocese met with little success. In 1977 the Archdiocesan Catechetical Institute (later renamed the Institute of Religious Studies) was established to offer laypeople and others the opportunity for graduate courses in theology leading to a Master of Arts degree in religious studies.

Under John Cardinal O'Connor (1984–), the faculty was enlarged and Dunwoodie reverted to the professionalism of the Spellman era in such areas as curriculum revision, library modernization, and the encouragement of graduate studies. On October 6, 1995, Dunwoodie was visited by Pope John Paul II who celebrated vespers in the seminary chapel and delivered an address on the priesthood. As Dunwoodie approached its centenary year, it could take credit for the education of almost 2,450 priests, approximately 2,125 of whom were ordained for the Archdiocese of New York.

See also HUGHES, JOHN; *NEW YORK REVIEW;* SEMINARIES (DIOCESAN); SPELLMAN, FRANCIS CARDINAL.

DeVito, Michael J. *The New York Review, 1905–1908.* New York: U.S. Historical Society, 1977.

Gannon, Michael V. "Before and After Modernism: The Intellectual Isolation of the American Priest." *The Catholic Priest in the United States: Historical Investigations,* ed. John Tracy Ellis. Collegeville: The Liturgical Press, 1971, 293–384.

Illo, Joseph. "'The Pride of My Early Episcopacy': Archbishop John Hughes and St. Joseph's Seminary." *Dunwoodie Review* 15 (1991) 91–97, a study of St. Joseph's Seminary, Fordham.

Scanlan, Arthur J. *St. Joseph's Seminary, Dunwoodie, N.Y., 1896–1921.* New York, 1922.

Shelley, Thomas J. *Dunwoodie: The History of St. Joseph's Seminary.* Westminster, Maryland, 1993.

____. "Francis Cardinal Spellman and His Seminary at Dunwoodie." *Catholic Historical Review* 80 (1994) 282–98.

____. "'Good Work in Its Day': St. Joseph's Provincial Seminary, Troy, New York." *Revue d'Histoire Ecclésiastique* 88 (1993) 416–38.

____. "John Cardinal Farley and Modernism in New York." *Church History* 61 (1992) 350–61.

THOMAS J. SHELLEY

ST. JOSEPH'S UNIVERSITY (PHILADELPHIA)

Philadelphia's growing Catholic population, enjoying the city's religious tolerance and economic prosperity, voiced the need as early as 1741 for a Jesuit educational establishment to meet the needs of the community. Felix Barbelin, S.J., and four other Philadelphia Jesuits ultimately met this demand and, on September 15, 1851, thirty young men enrolled in the first class at St. Joseph's College. The tradition of Jesuit education in Philadelphia began on Willings Alley—site of the Jesuit parish, Old Saint Joseph's, one block from Independence Hall.

Although the college's first decades were unstable—as enrollment fluctuated and the site of the college varied—a million-dollar fundraising campaign in 1922 led to the purchase of twenty-three acres on the western edge of the city and gave St. Joseph's the stability of a permanent home. Construction of St. Joseph's gothic Barbelin Hall was completed in 1927 atop Philadelphia's highest hill—"Hawk Hill"—where the institution stands today.

The college experienced great growth after World War II. An expanding student body saw the construction of resident and academic buildings and the creation of new academic programs. St. Joseph's opened its doors to women in 1970 and received university status in 1978. In the same year, a College of Business and Administration was added to complement the School of Arts and Sciences. In 1995 St. Joseph's University educated nearly 7,000 students on the undergraduate and graduate level.

See also CATHOLIC UNIVERSITIES AND COLLEGES.

Burton, David H., and Frank Gerrity. *Saint Joseph's College. A Family Portrait*. Philadelphia: Saint Joseph's College Press, 1977.

Talbot, Francis X., S.J. *Jesuit Education in Philadelphia: Saint Joseph's College 1851–1926*. Philadelphia: Saint Joseph's College, 1927.

MAUREEN H. O'CONNELL

ST. LOUIS UNIVERSITY

St. Louis University traces its history to the foundation of the St. Louis Academy by Bishop Louis William DuBourg, bishop of Louisiana, in 1818. The academy occupied a building within a few blocks of the Mississippi River in what is now downtown St. Louis. In 1827, at Bishop DuBourg's request, the Society of Jesus took over direction of the academy. The Jesuits were recent arrivals to the mid-Mississippi valley and had established missions and schools among the Native American populations in Missouri.

Soon the Jesuits moved what was then called St. Louis College a few blocks to the northwest to land then on the edges of wilderness. This property is now near Ninth Street and Washington Avenues, also in downtown St. Louis and less than one mile from the Mississippi. The school received its charter from the State of Missouri as St. Louis University in 1832, making it the first university established west of the Mississippi River. The university moved to its present location on Grand Boulevard in 1888.

St. Louis University is a private university under the auspices of the Catholic Church and the Society of Jesus. It is presently composed of eleven colleges on four campuses in two states and in one foreign country. The eleven colleges and the dates of their establishment are: College of Arts and Sciences (1818); Graduate School (1832); School of Law (1842); College of Philosophy and Letters (1889); School of Medicine (1903); School of Business and Administration (1910); School of Nursing (1928); School of Social Service (1930); Parks College (1946); School of Allied Health Professions (1979); and School of Public Health (1991).

The university currently (1996) enrolls more than 11,000 full- and part-time students, including 1,000 international students from more than 75 countries. St. Louis University has some 80,000 alumni around the world.

See also CATHOLIC UNIVERSITIES AND COLLEGES.

ST. MARY'S SEMINARY AND UNIVERSITY (BALTIMORE, MARYLAND)

When John Carroll traveled to England in 1790 to be consecrated first bishop of Baltimore, he met with representatives of the Sulpician Fathers from Paris, who were concerned about the closure of most of their French seminaries. They asked to transfer a seminary from France to the United States, and the bishop embraced the proposal when they promised to supply priests and seminarians and to pay their own expenses. Upon their arrival in Baltimore in July 1791, the first group under François Charles Nagot soon took possession of a former inn, the One Mile Tavern. Classes for the first four students began that October.

Early Years

Among the early additions to the faculty was Louis William DuBourg, who began St. Mary's College (1799–1852) for French- and Spanish-speaking refugees from the Caribbean. Soon he was able to get the new institution recognized by the Maryland legislature as a university. He also inspired Jean Dubois to begin a minor seminary at Emmitsburg, Maryland, to serve as a feeder for the Baltimore house; instead it developed into a second major seminary in the diocese. DuBourg was also able to raise funds for the erection of St. Mary's Chapel, which from 1808 served the seminary, the college, and the parish for French-speaking refugees. It was there that he and others invited Elizabeth Ann Seton, who founded the first U.S. Catholic elementary school, and the Sisters of Charity of St. Joseph (now the Daughters and Sisters of Charity). DuBourg went off to New Orleans in 1812 as Carroll's administrator and then as ordinary.

Early view of St. Mary's Seminary (1850)

Also prominent in this early period was Fr. Nagot, who spent 1807–09 at a house in Pigeon Hill, Pennsylvania, trying to train young German-Americans for the Baltimore seminary. While he was gone, John Tessier served as temporary (and later second) superior of St. Mary's. He took over the direction of the parish from Fr. DuBourg and passed it on to James H. Joubert, himself a refugee, who in 1829 helped Elizabeth Lange found the first community of African American religious, the Oblate Sisters of Providence. Others of these pioneers were Ambrose Maréchal, recalled to France in 1802, only to return to Baltimore as third archbishop and then obtain for St. Mary's the status of a pontifical university (1821); and Benedict Flaget, who reluctantly went to Bardstown in 1811 as first bishop and as founder of St. Thomas' Seminary there.

Though the number of ordained alumni remained small (only thirty-two between 1829 and 1849), the third superior, Louis R. Deluol, began the process of opening up the seminary and making it more American. So great was his success that his French superiors recalled him to Europe in 1849. His next two successors renewed the practice of a closed and separated seminary, with no lay college and no outside responsibilities.

The small number of students began to grow after the founding of St. Charles' College near Ellicott City, Maryland, in 1848. Coupled with the increasing number of alumni was the huge influx of Catholic immigrants to the United States, especially from Ireland and Germany (and later Poland and Italy), in the second half of the century. By 1900 there was hardly a U.S. state, territory, or diocese without priest-alumni of St. Mary's.

Americanization and Modernization

Another era of the seminary began in 1878 when Alphonse Magnien became the sixth superior of St. Mary's. He had a vision like that of Fr. Deluol. He encouraged the open-

ing of new Sulpician seminaries in Boston (1884), New York (1896), and San Francisco (1898). He was backed by the scholarship of John B. Hogan; by American-born superiors like Charles Rex, Edward Dyer, and James Driscoll; and by his close association with Cardinal James Gibbons and that prelate's allies in the U.S. hierarchy. By his studied moderation he brought the seminary through the troubled waters of Americanism and Modernism. He also saw the opening of St. Austin's College, a Sulpician house of studies in Washington, D.C., before he retired and died in 1902. His period also marked the beginning of publication of the famous theology manuals written by faculty member Alphonse Tanquerey.

Fr. Magnien's successor, Edward R. Dyer, who had been first rector of the Dunwoodie seminary, would become the first Sulpician vicar general and later the first U.S. provincial, while remaining St. Mary's superior. His time would see the loss of the seminaries of New York (1906) and Boston (1911) and the 1911 fire that destroyed St. Charles' College, soon to be relocated to Catonsville, Maryland. He would also succeed in opening the first U.S. Sulpician Solitude (or novitiate) in Washington in 1911; six years later he would initiate the effort that would establish the Sulpician Seminary (now Theological College) near The Catholic University of America, as an attraction for degree students and as a relief for the overcrowded seminary in Baltimore. He joined with Cardinal Gibbons' successor, Archbishop Michael Curley, to try to rebuild St. Mary's in a suburban location.

With Fr. Dyer's death in 1925, John F. Fenlon came from his previous work at the NCWC, at The Catholic University of America, and at the Sulpician Seminary to be superior of St. Mary's and U.S. provincial (until the two positions were separated in 1936). He brought the building of the Roland Park seminary to completion in 1929 and witnessed the separate status of the Washington seminary, which became the Theological College of the university in 1940. He trained his two successors as rector, John J. Lardner and James A. Laubacher, the latter of whom served as a *peritus* at the Second Vatican Council. All through these years the seminary staff taught full contingents of students (sometimes over four hundred in theology in a year), but they were confined to the bland content of theological and scriptural studies in the aftermath of Modernism. Only in the decade before Vatican II did a few faculty members (like James Laubacher, Raymond Brown, Eugene Walsh, Frank Norris, Peter Chirico, and others) begin to open up to their students the possibilities that the council eventually approved.

By the late 1960s, John Dede became president of the university and brought to completion the work of accreditation by the Middle States Association of Colleges and Secondary Schools and by the American Association of Theological Schools. That period also saw the closing of the undergraduate division of St. Mary's and the precipitous decline of the student population. Under the inspiration of Baltimore's then-archbishop, Cardinal Lawrence Shehan, St. Mary's provided direction, a place, and some of the staff for what has proved to be a very successful Ecumenical Institute, catering to clerics and laypeople of all faiths. New efforts are under way to fill in the void in the spiritual background of many present-day students, and construction finished in 1996 to make available suitable facilities for the Center for Continuing Studies for the benefit of priests, whether alumni or not—all indications of St. Mary's continued efforts to meet the needs of priests and future priests as it has done throughout its two centuries of existence.

See also SULPICIANS (S.S.).

Herbermann, Charles G. *The Sulpicians in the United States.* New York, 1916.

Kauffman, Christopher J. *Tradition and Transformation in Catholic Culture.* New York, 1988.

Ruane, Joseph William. *The Beginnings of the Society of St. Sulpice in the United States.* Baltimore, 1935.

JOHN W. BOWEN, S.S.

ST. MARY'S SEMINARY OF THE WEST (CINCINNATI, OHIO)

Early American bishops found the seminary college a practical way to launch higher education. Only one or two priests were needed for the seminary and one or two well-educated professors for the college. The seminarians had one or two classes in theology each day and spent their other working hours teaching the collegians whose tuition, in turn, supported their needs.

Edward Fenwick and Seminary Education

Edward Dominic Fenwick, the first bishop of Cincinnati, used this model in 1829 when he established St. Francis Xavier Seminary and the Athenaeum College. The theology professors were priests who served the cathedral and cared for the seminary only incidentally. But the daily association of the seminarians with their bishop and his hard-working priests was a valuable supplement to their minimal theological education.

In 1829 the city of Cincinnati already had a population of 30,000 and boasted of banks, schools, theaters, hospitals, industry, and a public landing crowded with steamboats. The Diocese of Cincinnati also experienced rapid growth as the interior of the state opened to new settlers. The old frame church which housed the bishop's residence and the seminary-college soon became inadequate. Alphaeus White, one of Cincinnati's early architects, designed new buildings which were completed by 1832 and were among the city's early architectural monuments.

Fenwick's successor as bishop of Cincinnati, John Baptist Purcell, recruited religious orders to provide a more professional teaching staff. In 1840 the Jesuits took over the Athenaeum College, renamed St. Francis Xavier College, and in 1842 the Vincentians agreed to operate the seminary which had been moved to Brown County, Ohio, but they departed within two years because Purcell retained complete control of the seminary and expected them merely to staff it under his supervision. The seminarians led a nomadic existence for several years, moving from Brown County back to the Jesuit College and then to the attic of the bishop's house at the new Cathedral of St. Peter-in-Chains.

Bishop Purcell and Mt. St. Mary's

In 1851 the seminary moved into a new and handsome four-story building on Price's Hill, just west of the city, with its name changed to Mt. St. Mary's of the West to avoid confusion with the Jesuit college and to honor Mt. St. Mary's Seminary in Maryland where Purcell had been a student and a professor. Purcell inaugurated an annual diocesan collection for the support of the seminary and built a faculty by recruiting theologians from Europe and sending seminarians to Europe for graduate studies.

The initial twelve students increased to 126 by 1870. They studied a broad range of theological subjects and used recently published Latin, English, and German texts. They were also encouraged to read widely and a catalogue of the library published in 1873 listed 14,168 volumes.

In 1879 an archdiocesan financial crisis closed the seminary for eight years. When it reopened, it adopted a curriculum designed at the request of the Third Plenary Council of Baltimore, which provided for two years of philosophy and four years of theology, specified the order in which the courses were to be taken, and suggested the textbooks to be used. The academic program acquired a routine quality and lost much of its vitality. But enrollment increased rapidly and in 1890 St. Gregory's Seminary was established for the college students.

Twentieth-Century Changes

Inclines to lift street cars out of Cincinnati's basin area enabled the city to crowd around the Price Hill seminary. Consequently, in 1904 Archbishop Henry Moeller moved the seminary to Mt. Washington at the southeast edge of the city, where it had a rather uneventful, two-decade history. The already lackluster quality of the theological curriculum was reinforced by the condemnation of Modernism in 1907. Students learned little more than the material in their texts and the bulk of the library from the Price Hill seminary remained unpacked. Nevertheless, the faculty included well-educated teachers and the student life was enhanced by liturgies, spiritual exercises, music, drama, and sports.

Enrollment continued to increase during the Mt. Washington years and so in 1923 the four-year theology program moved to suburban Norwood. The two years of philosophy remained in Mt. Washington as the nucleus of a revived St. Gregory Preparatory Seminary which quickly expanded to a four-year high school and a four-year college.

In 1927 the name of the first college, the Athenaeum, was revived for an umbrella organization chartered to grant degrees for the seminaries and for two newly established schools, a teacher's college, and a graduate school of science. In 1953 the Athenaeum applied for membership in the Ohio College Association, beginning a process of accreditation to bring the seminaries in line with other academic institutions. A catalogue of courses was published, faculty credentials were verified, a dean of studies was appointed, academic records were separated from sacramental records, degree requirements were clarified, and a librarian with professional certification was appointed.

However, the theological studies and the discipline of seminary life still remained untouched. The most insistent complaint about seminaries after the Second Vatican Council was their isolation. This remoteness was not merely a matter of location but also a distance from pastoral problems and from those engaged in pastoral work.

In the late 1960s the semimonastic life of the seminary was gradually replaced by an "open campus" giving students greater freedom to leave the grounds, to have visitors, and to use telephones and automobiles. The curriculum moved from an exclusive reliance on theological compendiums toward an increasing use of specialized treatises and journal articles. The new liturgical reforms were implemented and internships in parishes became an integral part of the curriculum.

This renewal of the seminary was accompanied, however, by a decline in vocations to the priesthood and, therefore, in the number of seminarians. The 1965–66 enrollment was 566 students. By the early 1980s St. Gregory Seminary had been closed and Mt. St. Mary Seminary of the West had returned to Mt. Washington with only seventy seminarians, a number that continues to decline. Currently (1996) the seminary is also finding a new role as the home of a lay pastoral ministry program and of other programs for the permanent diaconate and for the continuing education of priests.

See also SEMINARIES (DIOCESAN).

Hussey, M. Edmund. *A History of the Seminaries of the Archdiocese of Cincinnati, 1829–1979.* Norwood, Ohio: Mt. St. Mary's Seminary of the West, 1979.

Miller, Francis J. "A History of the Athenaeum of Ohio, 1829–1960." Ph.D. dissertation, University of Cincinnati, 1967.

White, Joseph M. *The Diocesan Seminary in the United States: A History from the 1780s to the Present.* University of Notre Dame Press, 1980.

M. EDMUND HUSSEY

ST. MICHAEL'S COLLEGE

St. Michael's College was founded in 1904 by the Society of Saint Edmund who came to the United States to escape the anticlerical laws of the French government. Previously, the society had taken charge of the famous abbey church of Mont-St-Michel off the coast of Normandy.

In 1913 the Vermont legislature authorized the granting of college degrees. At present, there are about 1,600 women and men students, most of whom reside on campus. St. Michael's grants baccalaureate and masters' degrees. There is a very active student volunteer movement. There is a Center for International Programs (English for foreign students). There are 126 full-time and 70 adjunct faculty. The Prevel School is for graduate and undergraduate *adult* learners. There is a large new sports center. St. Michael's is situated near Burlington, Vermont, close to Lake Champlain and within view of the Green Mountains. It is an hour and a half from Montreal.

See also CATHOLIC UNIVERSITIES AND COLLEGES.

Dupont, Gerald D., S.S.E. "The History of Saint Michael's College, 1970." TMs [photocopy]. Special Collections, Durick Library, St. Michael's College, Colchester, Vermont.

Maloney, Vincent B., S.S.E., and Jeremiah K. Durick. *Saint Michael's Through the Years.* St. Michael's College Press: Winooski Park, Vermont.

McLaughlin, Joseph M., S.S.E. *From Pontigny. A Chronicle of the Society of Saint Edmund.* Society of Saint Edmund: Winooski Park, Vermont, 1978.

Popecki, Joseph T. "A Chronicle of Saint Michael's College, 1992." TMs [photocopy]. Special Collections, Durick Library, St. Michael's College, Colchester, Vermont.

PAUL E. COUTURE, S.S.E.

ST. PATRICK'S SEMINARY (MENLO PARK)

Located some thirty miles south of San Francisco, St. Patrick's Seminary is the first successful school to train the diocesan clergy in the Far West. Earlier abortive efforts in clergy education had included small schools at several California missions, but each of these closed its doors either because of the difficulty in supplying trained faculty or because of the scarcity of promising candidates. Archbishop Patrick W. Riordan of San Francisco resolved these problems in 1898 when he founded a junior seminary in Menlo Park and arranged to have the Sulpician

Fathers oversee its growth into a full twelve-year institution, eventually combining high school, college, and theology programs.

Early Years

Riordan's purpose was to mold a native clergy not only for his own archdiocese but, in his own words, for "all districts west of the Rocky Mountains." For this reason he broke the West's dependence upon institutions in Europe and east of the Mississippi, and offered free scholarships to each diocese of the Pacific Coast. From these beginnings, the student body represented the diverse Catholic communities of the Far West. In the first forty years, candidates from San Francisco numbered slightly more that half of the students, and almost a third came from Los Angeles. The composition of the student body changed significantly when theologates opened in Seattle (1935) and in Los Angeles (1939). From this point on, St. Patrick's virtually became a provincial seminary, accommodating students largely from the metropolitan province of San Francisco and thereby focusing its vast service territory from Salt Lake City to Guam.

Before Vatican Council II, the threefold program of piety, studies, and discipline at Menlo Park was traditional. The almost exclusive route for spiritual formation was the French school of spirituality, which had flourished in the seventeenth century and numbered among its leading figures the founder of the Sulpicians, Jean-Jacques Olier. The academic program was limited to the scholastic manuals in theology and philosophy, and Latin continued to be the language used in textbooks, examinations, and many lectures. Outside the core of the curriculum, English and contemporary textbooks were used. The early importance of this seminary was celebrated at its seventy-fifth anniversary in 1943. That festive occasion acknowledged that, of the thirteen ordinaries serving in the existing dioceses of the three Far-Western states, eleven had been students at Menlo Park, and Patrician alumni were at work tending neighboring dioceses in Alaska, Arizona, and New Mexico.

Archbishop McGucken and the Sulpicians

Vatican Council II had an enormous impact on St. Patrick's Seminary. Several conciliar documents and others derived from them encouraged radical revision of all aspects of the program. Sulpician leaders joined with the student body in initiating several bold experiments that were intended to develop maturity and independence in the students but eventually alienated Archbishop Joseph T. McGucken (1962–77). Compulsory spiritual exercises and the wearing of traditional clerical dress were abolished. The curriculum was thoroughly revised, and instructors were allowed to use contemporary textbooks in theology and to search out alternative approaches to scholasticism. Students were permitted to possess radios and automobiles on campus. The most serious innovation, in McGucken's eyes, was a new plan to provide pastoral training for the deacon class by allowing them to reside in rectories during their final year and to return to the campus for occasional workshops.

Several factors brought McGucken into direct conflict with the seminary community. First, there were unexpected but dramatic losses in the enrollment. In 1966 the student body had crested at 191, but by the next year 30 percent had dropped out, a shocking rate of attrition that even attracted the attention of the apostolic delegate. The decline continued for several years; by 1972 there were only sixty resident students at Menlo Park, less than one-third of the student body six years earlier. Second, McGucken disapproved of the membership of clergy on the faculty and of the deacon class in the Association of Priests, a legitimate body of clergy that was a noncanonical and voluntary segment of the presbyterate. The Association of Priests in 1970 declared that no member, including deacons from St. Patrick's Seminary, would undertake an assignment to a pastor who failed to accept the spirit of Vatican II. McGucken questioned how this principle, which appeared to prevail at Menlo Park, could be reconciled with the promise of obedience at priestly ordination. Third, a series of Sulpician superiors found it increasingly difficult to work collaboratively with McGucken, a highly intelligent prelate of the old school who advocated a return to some aspects of the pre-Vatican seminary and called for a moratorium on further experimentation with student freedom. This chronic irritation rippled into the faculty and student body and became public in 1972 when the majority of the faculty delivered to Sulpician authorities in Baltimore an "open letter" in which they threatened to resign unless the archbishop met certain conditions.

Recent Developments

Reconciliation between the seminary and the archdiocese occurred with the appointment of John R. Quinn as the sixth archbishop of San Francisco (1977–95) and of Joseph Bonadio and Howard Bleichner as successive superiors. Under their leadership, the spiritual and academic reforms preserved the open spirit of Vatican II while instituting methods of assessing individual student progress through faculty advisers. The centerpiece of the new reforms was to offer as an option a complete "pastoral year" after the fourth semester in which students worked in parishes under seminary supervision. This approach did not dilute academic requirements and provided early exposure to parish life which motivated candidates to concentrate on specific pastoral skills during the remainder of their training on campus. Another striking feature of the current student body is its ethnic composition. While students with European antecedents had numerically dominated the community in the past, today the ascendant groups are men of Latino and Asian heritage. This development for the first time has required attention to arranging courses on "English as a second language."

St. Patrick's Seminary was incorporated by the State of California in 1891. The chairman of the corporation is the archbishop of San Francisco, who is guided by a corporate board of trustees. Half of the original estate of 84 acres was sold in 1995, and revenues from this sale were to pay for past subsidies from the archdiocese and make a substantial contribution to the endowment, which stands in 1996 at $5,500,000. After having suffered some recent decline in numbers, the student body has risen in 1996 to fifty-five, representing twelve dioceses and two religious communities.

See also SEMINARIES (DIOCESAN); SULPICIANS (S.S.).

Dubois, Leon L., S.M. "St. Thomas Seminary at San Jose, California." *Acta Societatis Mariae* 17 (August 15, 1955) 373–82.
Englehardt, Zephyrin. *Mission Santa Inés, Virgen y Martir; and Its Ecclesiastical Seminary.* Santa Barbara, 1932.
Gaffey, James P. *Men of Menlo: Transformation of an American Seminary.* Lanham, Maryland, 1992.
McDonough, John, S.S. "St. Patrick's Seminary, Menlo Park, California, 1898–1948." Unpublished manuscript.
Prendergast, John J. "The First Seminary of San Francisco." *Monitor* (San Francisco), September 17, 1898, n.p.

JAMES P. GAFFEY

ST. PAUL SEMINARY

The St. Paul Seminary, now the School of Divinity of the University of St. Thomas in St. Paul, Minnesota, was the dream of Archbishop John Ireland brought to fruition by railroad magnate James J. Hill. In 1890 the Methodist millionaire announced his contribution of one-half million dollars in honor of his Catholic wife, Mary Theresa Mehegan Hill, to build and endow an institution to educate men for the Roman Catholic priesthood in the Upper Midwest.

Archbishop Ireland and James J. Hill

James J. Hill was not only the benefactor but also the overseer of the project popularly known as "the Hill Seminary." He employed Cass Gilbert, architect of the Minnesota capitol, to design the buildings and supervise the planning and execution of the venture. The new six-building facility overlooked the Mississippi River. On September 6, 1894, sixty-five seminarians moved across the street from the St. Thomas Aquinas Seminary which, since 1885, had been educating both collegians and seminarians. Eighteen men were ordained to the priesthood in the spring of 1895.

The formal dedication of the seminary took place the following September.

Ireland's goal was a seminary where students studying for the diocesan priesthood in the United States would be taught by qualified faculty who were themselves diocesan priests. The Archbishop believed that, if Catholics were to become "at home" in American culture, they needed leaders among the clergy who were trained in America and who believed in an American model of the Church. For Ireland, moreover, the priest should be "a gentleman, a scholar, and a saint."

Msgr. Louis Caillet, a close friend of the Hill family and a mentor to Mary Hill, was appointed the first rector. Caillet's health was failing, however, and it was Ireland who made the major decisions, gave conferences to seminarians, and even presided at student examinations twice a year. Hill, however, continued to supervise financial matters.

In the fall of 1894, the St. Paul Seminary became the first seminary located at any distance, to affiliate with The Catholic University of America in Washington, D.C. (Several religious congregations had opened houses of studies near the university beginning in 1890—a different type of affiliation.) The rector, Bishop John J. Keane, described the relationship in his annual report of that year:

> An admirable example has been given to the Seminaries and Colleges of the country by the affiliation to the University of the Seminary of St. Paul, at St. Paul, Minnesota. In virtue of this affiliation, the University has the right to preside over and pass upon the examinations for degrees held in the Seminary; and the Seminary has the privilege of having the Baccalaureate of the University [S.T.B.] conferred on students who pass said examinations satisfactorily.

The program was in place until 1931. The recipient of the S.T.B. then had the option of enrolling at CUA with the possibility of receiving the S.T.L. degree after only one year of study.

St. Mary's Chapel, largely financed by the Hill family, was dedicated in 1905. By 1912 the seminary enrollment had reached two hundred and filled the newly constructed Grace Residence Hall. Before World War I, thirty-five different dioceses were represented in the student body. Although the majority were from the Upper Midwest, students came from Chicago and points west, as well as from Central Europe and Ireland.

Outstanding alumni of the school in the first half of the twentieth century include founder of the rural life movement Archbishop Edwin O'Hara, social ethicist Msgr. John A. Ryan, and Church historian Msgr. William Busch who was active in the liturgical movement in the 1930s.

In March 1946 the St. Paul Seminary became the first Catholic seminary to be accredited by the North Central States Association of Colleges and Universities. In 1947 the Bachelor of Arts and the Master of Arts in Church History were approved by North Central. The state of Minnesota had given the power to grant academic degrees to the board of trustees at the time of the incorporation (September 1895). However, the University of Minnesota also granted recognition to the M.A. degree in 1947.

The Post-Vatican II Era

In the post-Vatican II ecumenical era, the Association of Theological Schools of the United States and Canada invited Catholic theologates to apply for membership. The St. Paul Seminary became a member in 1974 and retains its accreditation with both North Central and the ATS to this day.

With the decline in enrollment from 350 students in the 1960s to approximately 100 students in the 1980s, the seminary opened a dialogue with the (then) College of St. Thomas whose mother institution had also been the St. Thomas Aquinas Seminary. In 1987 an affiliation took place in which the graduate programs in religious studies of the College moved to the St. Paul Seminary, and together they became the School of Divinity of the (now) University of St. Thomas. St. Thomas acquired three-fourths of the seminary property, but the seminary was entitled to first use of the buildings. A new seminary complex (residence hall and administration building) was built, conjoined to a renovated chapel and gathering space. These buildings were dedicated in 1989.

The School of Divinity offers the following degrees: the M.Div.; the M.A. in theology; the M.A. in pastoral studies; the M.A. in religious education; and the D.Min. degree in conjunction with the Minnesota Consortium of Theological Schools.

See also MINNESOTA, CATHOLIC CHURCH IN; SEMINARIES (DIOCESAN).

Ahern, Patrick Henry. "A History of the Saint Paul Seminary." M.A. thesis, The St. Paul Seminary, 1945.

Athans, Mary Christine, B.V.M. *To Work for the Whole People: The History of the Saint Paul Seminary.* St. Paul, Minn.: University of St. Thomas, 1998.

Connors, Joseph P. *Journey Toward Fulfillment: A History of the College of St. Thomas.* St. Paul, Minn.: The College of St. Thomas, 1986.

O'Connell, Marvin. *John Ireland and the American Catholic Church.* St. Paul, Minn.: The Minnesota Historical Society, 1988.

MARY CHRISTINE ATHANS, B.V.M.

ST. RAPHAEL SOCIETY

The St. Raphael Society was founded in New York City in 1883 as a German immigrant-aid society by Simon Peter Cahensly (1838–1923) with the support of Archbishop Michael A. Corrigan, and with Bishop Winand N. Wigger of Newark as its honorary president.

Cahensly, a shipping merchant from Limburg an der Lahn, Germany, founded the society as the American counterpart, and the first daughter society of "Der St. Raphaelsverein zum Schutze Katholischer deutscher Auswander," which he had established in Germany in 1871. The purpose of these societies was to assist German Catholic immigrants in every possible way, before, during, and after the completion of their voyage to the United States. Both organizations were lay-led, with Cahensly as their driving force, and they were funded by private contributions from German Catholics both in the Fatherland and in America. The society in Europe used paid agents to see that the immigrants were not charged exorbitant prices for their passage, or subjected to squalid or "immoral" living conditions during their ocean voyage. Having reached the United States they were met at the port, most often New York, by members of the American branch of the society who would protect them from "swindlers" and aggressive Protestant proselytism.

The society's assistance also included financial aid and temporary housing until the immigrants could be permanently resettled in the German Catholic communities to which they were guided. In 1888 the St. Raphael Society opened an immigrant settlement house in New York after raising $52,000 among German Catholics in America. This institution, the "Leo House," was named for Pope Leo XIII who had given his blessing to the various branches of the St. Raphael Society, and still exists as of this writing. While Cahensly himself would be embroiled in much controversy in the ensuing years, the immigrant-aid societies that he founded continued to multiply with Belgian, Austrian, and Italian branches all established by 1890.

See also CAHENSLY, SIMON PETER; GERMAN CATHOLICS IN AMERICA.

Barry, Colman J., O.S.B. *The Catholic Church and German Americans.* Milwaukee, 1953.

Festschrift zum Silbernen Jubilaüm des Leo-Hauses Gegründet zum Schutze Katholischer Einwanderer. New York, 1914.

Schaeffer, Joseph, and Charles Herbermann. "The Society of Saint Raphael and the Leo House." *Historical Records and Studies* 1 (1899) 111–29.

RORY T. CONLEY

Related Document

THE ST. RAPHAELSVEREIN PROTESTS THE NEGLECT OF IMMIGRANT CATHOLICS IN THE UNITED STATES, FEBRUARY, 1891

The addition of an estimated 2,475,000 immigrants from twenty or more countries to the Catholic population of the United States in the years 1880–1900 brought inevitable strains within the American Church. One of the most acute controversies among these varied national groups developed between the Irish and German Catholics over the demand of the latter for their own parishes, priests, and schools, and a higher proportion of bishops of German birth or extraction in the hierarchy. This situation led to a protest being lodged with the Holy See in November, 1886, by Father Peter Abbelen of the Archdiocese of Milwaukee which maintained that unless the demands were met there would be grave losses to the faith. In the succeeding years the question took on more serious proportions when it entered into the discussions of the various national branches of the St. Raphaelsverein, an organization founded in 1871 for the care of German Catholic emigrants. From an international conference of the St. Raphaelsverein held in Lucerne, Switzerland, on December 9-10, 1890, there emerged a document signed by officials of the society from seven different countries. This document, dated February, 1891, was presented to Pope Leo XIII on April 16, 1891, and on the following May 28 the full text was published in the New York *Herald*. Most of the American hierarchy protested vigorously against the implication that they had neglected the spiritual welfare of the immigrants and that there had been anywhere near the fantastic figure of ten million souls lost to the Church in this country.

(*Source*: Colman J. Barry, O.S.B., *The Catholic Church and German Americans*. Milwaukee: The Bruce Publishing Co., 1953, Appendix IV, 313–15.)

Most Holy Father,

The presidents, secretaries general, and delegates of the societies under the protection of the Holy Archangel Raphael for the protection of emigrants, encouraged by the benevolence which Your Holiness has shown them, assembled on December 9 of last year at an international conference in Lucerne to deliberate upon means best suited to serve the spiritual and material well-being of their Catholic compatriots who have emigrated to America, the number of which is in excess of 400,000 yearly.[1]

The above mentioned take the liberty to place before Your Holiness, with deepest respect, the fact that the numerous emigrants constitute a great strength, and could co-operate eminently in the expansion of the Catholic Church in the several states of America. In this way they could contribute to the moral stature of their new homeland, as well as to the stimulation of religious consciousness in the old European fatherlands.

Only the true Church, of which Your Holiness is the highest shepherd, can obtain these happy results because it is the true source of all progress and civilization.

But in order that European Catholics, in their adopted country, preserve and transmit to their children their faith and its inherent benefits, the undersigned have the honor to submit to Your Holiness the conditions, which in the light of experience and in the nature of things, appear to be indispensable for that purpose in the countries of immigration. The losses which the Church has suffered in the United States of North America number more than ten million souls.[2]

1. It seems necessary to unite the emigrant groups of each nationality in separate parishes, congregations, or missions wherever their numbers and means make such a practice possible.

2. It seems necessary to entrust the administration of these parishes to priests of the same nationality to which the faithful belong. The sweetest and dearest memories of their homeland would be constantly recalled, and they would love all the more the holy Church which procures these benefits for them.

3. In areas settled by emigrants of several nationalities who are not numerous enough to organize separate national parishes, it is desirable as far as possible, that a pastor be chosen to guide them who understands the diverse languages of these groups. This priest should be strictly obliged to give catechetical instruction to each of the groups in its own language.

4. It will be especially necessary to establish parochial schools wherever Christian public schools are not available, and these schools should be separate, as far as possible, for each nationality.

The curriculum of these schools should always include the mother tongue as well as the language and history of the adopted country.

5. It seems necessary to grant to priests devoting themselves to the emigrants all rights, privileges, and prerogatives enjoyed by the priests of the country. This arrangement, which is only just, would have the result that zealous, pious, and apostolic priests of all nationalities will be attracted to immigrant work.

6. It seems desirable to establish and encourage societies of various kinds, confraternities, charitable organizations, mutual aid and protective associations, etc. By these means Catholics would be systematically organized and saved from the dangerous sects of Freemasons and organizations affiliated with it.

7. It seems very desirable that the Catholics of each nationality, wherever it is deemed possible, have in the episcopacy of the country where they immigrate, several bishops who are of the same origin. It seems that in this way the organization of the Church would be perfect, for in the assemblies of the bishops, every immigrant race would be represented, and its interests and needs would be protected.

8. Finally the undersigned wish to point out that for the attainment of the objectives which they have enumerated, it would be very desirable, and this they vigorously urge, that the Holy See foster and protect in the emigration countries: a) special seminaries and apostolic schools for training missionaries for emigrants; b) St. Raphael societies for the protection of emigrants, and that it recommend to the Most Rev. Bishops that they establish such societies in the emigration countries where they do not yet exist, and that the Holy See place them under the protection of a Cardinal Protector.

The undersigned hope for the happiest and most immediate results from this organization and these measures. Emigration missionaries trained under the direction of a distinguished Italian Bishop have already gone to America.[3] Others, members of neighboring nations, are waiting, before entering, upon their important and holy calling, for the Supreme Shepherd of the Church, by a decree of his wisdom, to guarantee the free exercise of their mission. If the Holy See will lend its indispensable co-operation, wonderful results should follow. The poor emigrants will find on American soil their priests, their parishes, their schools, their societies, their language, and thus cannot fail to extend the boundaries of the Kingdom of Jesus Christ on earth.

In giving solemn testimony of their loyal devotion to the Apostolic See, the undersigned humbly beg Your Holiness to grant paternal approbation to the propositions which they have proposed for the salvation of souls and the glory of our holy mother, the Church, in the different American nations. With the most loyal devotion, Your most devoted, humble, and obedient sons: [There then follow the signatures of the boards of directors of the St. Raphael Society in Germany, Austria-Hungary, Belgium, and Italy, with the signatures of a single delegate each from Switzerland and France. A duplicate of the memorial was attached in the interests of the French-speaking Canadian Catholics in the United States and was signed by fifteen Canadian Catholics, including Prime Minister Henri Mercier of Quebec].

[1] If the memorialists had in mind Catholic immigrants solely to the United States this figure was a gross exaggeration. The best authority on the subject estimated that in the years 1881-1890 inclusive there was a total increase of 1,250,000 to the American Catholic population through immigration, a figure that included 119,000 from Canada, Mexico, and other non-European countries. From those European countries whose delegates signed the Lucerne Memorial there had been in the entire period 1881-1890 approximately only 700,000 Catholic immigrants (Gerald Shaughnessy, S.M., *Has the Immigrant Kept the Faith?* [New York, 1925], 165).

[2] The recklessness with which figures on Catholic leakage were used by the ill informed in these years may be gauged by the fact that at an international Catholic congress held in Liège, Belgium, in September, 1890, a French-Canadian priest of the Diocese of Albany, Alphonse Villeneuve, presented a paper which alleged that out of twenty-five million Catholic immigrants who had entered the United States twenty million had been lost to the Church.

[3] Giovanni Battista Scalabrini (1839–1905), Bishop of Piacenza, founded the Congregation of Missionaries of St. Charles Borromeo, the first of whose members had arrived in the United States in July, 1888, for work among the Italian immigrants.

(*Source*: John Tracy Ellis, ed. *Documents of American Catholic History*. Vol. 2:1866–1966.Wilmington, Del.: Michael Glazier, 1987, 480–83.)

ST. VINCENT DE PAUL, SOCIETY OF

Twelve years after the Society of St. Vincent de Paul was founded in 1833 in Paris, France, the American Conference of the society was formed in 1845 at the Basilica of St. Louis, King of France (Old Cathedral) in St. Louis,

Missouri. In 1995 the 60,000 American Vincentians marked one-hundred-fifty years of service to the poor. This international Catholic society of laypersons grew rapidly in Europe and in the United States during the lifetimes of its youthful founders. The principal founder was Venerable Frédéric Ozanam (1813–53).

What began as a challenge during a discussion among six university students of the role of the laity in the Church in nineteenth-century Paris, led to the founding of the Conference of Charity in April 1833. The conference became the Society of St. Vincent de Paul when the students chose St. Vincent de Paul as their patron saint, because his thinking and work inspired the young group. In a spirit of justice and charity and by person-to-person involvement of its members, the society seeks to help those who are suffering.

The conference, the basic unit of the society, is usually associated with a parish and derives its name from the name of the parish. In the United States, parish conferences average eight to ten members, which is considered ideal. The growth of the society resulted in the formation of multiple Paris conferences when the founding conference totaled one hundred members. During 1839, the first district council, a collection of conferences in a geographic area, was organized in France. In the United States, the first district council was the District Council of New York, instituted in 1857.

Society's Growth in the United States

As the society continued to develop in this country, the need for unifying structure beyond town and diocesan organizations led to the creation of several provincial councils. Because of the country's vast geographical dimension, the movement toward a single national Society of St. Vincent de Paul Council went slowly. The provincial councils dissolved under a reorganization plan that culminated in the institution on November 21, 1915, of the superior council of the United States, which received authority for the entire country. In 1946 the superior council, now called the national council, was legally incorporated under the laws of the state of Delaware. Charter and bylaws harmonize with and develop the organization's basic rule that is promulgated by the society's international governing body in Paris and are universally binding.

The Rule of the Society—Basic Principles

Development of the society from a single group into an organization with many units required regulations that would help preserve the objectives and spirit of the original foundation. In 1835 François Lallier (1814–86), a founder, wrote the society's *Rule,* a series of articles based upon practical experiences of the first Vincentians. With only a few major changes, this *Rule* continues as the guide and blueprint for the society. In 1973, at the international meeting of the society, the *Rule* was divided into three principal parts: Part I sets forth the characteristics of the society. A statement of thirteen items, this section applies to all members and Vincentian units throughout the world. Part I is a Vincentian charter. Part II concerns itself with conference and council structure and operations. Each national council is free to adopt its own regulations with respect to conference and council organization and activities. The U.S. Council adopted the international model of Part II in 1975. Part III of the current *Rule* concerns the organization, functioning, and authority of the council general, the international governing body of the society.

The Works of the Society

Vincentians provide assistance directly to the poor. The society cooperates with other organizations in serving the poor, but all Vincentian assistance results in person-to-person visitation, generally in the home of those in need. No work of charity is foreign to the society. There are more than 60,000 Catholic lay Vincentians, located in every region of the United States. They provide for the poor through 4,600 conferences. Vincentians serve the poor through home visitations, thrift stores, prison ministries, disaster relief, always person-to-person, and in every area because no work of charity is foreign to the society.

Society Membership

There are three types of membership in the society: active, associate, and contributing, according to the *American Manual of the Society of St. Vincent De Paul* (23).

St. Vincent de Paul

An active member must belong to the Catholic Church, accept the *Rule* and basic principles, bylaws, and charter of the society. The person is accepted as an active member by a conference or a council and enrolled in that Society of St. Vincent de Paul unit. The active member takes part in the life of the society to which the member is attached. Participation implies a reasonable degree of involvement in society meetings, charitable activities, and religious observances.

An associate member is one who accepts the society's basic principles but does not participate fully in the life of the conference or council. An associate member is one who sometimes—or "on call"—takes part in the meetings and charitable activities of the conference and who may provide financial support. In practice, almost all associate members are Catholic. Associate membership may, however, include those who, while they sincerely and publicly accept the society's basic principles, do not belong to the Catholic Church. An associate member is urged to attend the general meetings and festival observances of the society. A contributing member is the designation applicable to one who regularly or in a substantial way provides financial support but who does not engage in the work of the society.

ROBERT R. TROTTER

Related Document

THE INAUGURATION OF THE FIRST CONFERENCE OF THE SOCIETY OF ST. VINCENT DE PAUL IN THE UNITED STATES, NOVEMBER 20, 1845

One of the most important agencies of private charity in the United States is the Society of St. Vincent de Paul. Founded in Paris in 1833 by Frédéric Ozanam (1813–1853), a young professor of literature in the Sorbonne, it had an immediate appeal and rapidly spread throughout the Catholic world. Through John Timon, C.M. (1797–1867), first Bishop of Buffalo, who witnessed its beneficent results on a visit to France, the idea was brought to St. Louis while Timon was still working in Missouri. Father Ambrose J. Heim (1807–1854), a French-born assistant pastor in the old cathedral parish, took it up and won the immediate support of a small group of zealous laymen who held their first meeting in the schoolroom of the old cathedral on November 20, 1845. A week later on November 27 a second meeting—the minutes of which are given below—worked out the details as to the procedure they would employ in relieving the city's Catholic poor. From these humble beginnings the society fanned out across the country until today it is a recognized feature of numerous parishes and embraces thousands of Catholic laymen in its membership.

(*Source*: Minute Book, St. Louis Old Cathedral Conference, St. Vincent de Paul Society, p. 26, quoted in Daniel T. McColgan, *Century of Charity. The First One Hundred Years of the Society of St. Vincent de Paul in the United States.* Milwaukee: The Bruce Publishing Co., 1951, I, 79–80.)

AT A SECOND MEETING OF THE ST. VINCENT DE PAUL SOCIety held at the Cathedral School Room on the Thursday evening of the 27th ultimo, the minutes of the preceding meeting were read by the Secretary and approved.

Dr. Linton[1] on the part of the committee appointed to wait upon the right Reverend Bishop[2] to apprize him of the organization and purposes of the Society read a letter received by the committee from him fully approving of the organization and objects of it, being designed to relieve and alleviate the suffering and wants of those in a poor and destitute condition during the inclement season of the year.

The Visitors selected at the previous meeting to ascertain the particular cases in the neighborhood of their respective Parishes requiring immediate attention and assistance on the part of the Society, made their reports, in which several cases of suffering and destitution were portrayed that appealed thoroughly to the liberal and charitable feelings of the meeting.

On motion it was resolved and carried that a collection be immediately taken up in furtherance of the objects had in view in the formation of the society, in order to place funds in the hands of the visitors whereby individual suffering for want of means may be relieved to the extent at least of the means placed by the Society at the disposal of the visiting committee.

The collection amounted to the sum of twenty dollars forty seven and a half cents which added to the sum collected at the previous meeting, made the total sum of thirty seven dollars seventeen and a half cents was placed in the hands of the Treasurer.

On motion it was resolved and carried unanimously that half the funds collected should be equally divided among the different Parishes, giving to each an equal proportion: and that one-fourth be applied to the immediate relief of the cases just mentioned to the meeting, and the remaining fourth be kept on hand for contingency.

A motion was made and carried that a committee of three be appointed to draft a letter of communication to the parent Society in Paris, whereupon the President appointed the following gentlemen as that Committee— Judge Mullanphy,[3] Judge Manning, Revd. Mr. Heim.

A motion was made and carried that the fourth of the funds for present distribution be numerically divided among the visitors present who were acquainted with the locality where the distress was to be found whereupon the President appointed the following gentlemen as distributors of this fund:

Mr. Everhart
Mr. O'Neil
Mr. O'Keefe
Mr. Ridener (Reidener?)

A motion was then put and carried that the several visitors appointed should severally report themselves to the Priests and distribute the funds entrusted to their care according to their sense of propriety, taking into consideration those most in need of their assistance, whereupon the President appointed as the Visiting Committee (one Visitor for each of the following)—

1) For the Parish of St. Vincent de Paul
2) For the Cathedral
3) For the Parish of Saint Francis Xavier
4) For the Parish of Saint Patrick

[1] Moses L. Linton (1808–1872), first president of the society, was a convert to Catholicism and a professor of medicine in St. Louis University.

[2] Peter Richard Kenrick (1806–1896) was the second bishop and first Archbishop of St. Louis.

[3] Byran Mullanphy (1809–1851) was a judge of the Circuit Court who in 1847 became Mayor of St. Louis. He was the only son of the wealthy merchant and philanthropist, John Mullanphy (1758–1833), whose generosity brought about the first Catholic hospital in the United States at St. Louis in November, 1828, besides generous gifts to the Jesuits, the Religious of the Sacred Heart, and the Sisters of Loretto. Speaking of the elder Mullanphy's death in August, 1833, John E. Rothensteiner stated, "With him died the noblest Catholic layman St. Louis has ever known. . . ." (*History of the Archdiocese of St. Louis* [St. Louis, 1928], I, 450). At his death in 1851 the younger Mullanphy left one third of his estate, valued at about $200,000, as a trust fund to furnish relief to poor immigrants passing through St. Louis to settle in the West.

(*Source*: John Tracy Ellis, ed, *Documents of American Catholic History*. Vol. 1:1493–1865. Wilmington, Del.: Michael Glazier, 1987, 288–90.)

ST. XAVIER UNIVERSITY

Sr. Mary Frances Warde, R.S.M., and five Sisters of Mercy founded the school that was to become St. Xavier University in 1846. Called the St. Frances Xavier Academy for Females, it was located in what is now Chicago's Loop. When the school received its charter in 1847, it was one of the first institutions of higher learning in Illinois, and the first Mercy college of several in the United States.

The building housing St. Xavier Academy burned in the Chicago Fire on 1871. The school made its home at 29th Street and Wabash Avenue from 1875 to 1901, when a new campus was built on Cottage Grove Avenue at 49th Street, on the city's South Side.

St. Xavier moved to its present fifty-five-acre campus at 103rd Street and Central Park Avenue in 1956. The university became coeducational in 1969, opening new programs and schools. The continuing education program, created in 1970, attracts both degree and nondegree-seeking students. The Weekend College opened in 1978, offering flexible schedules for working professionals. The Graham School of Management, across 103rd Street from the main campus, was dedicated in 1985.

Today (1997), St. Xavier University offers 35 undergraduate majors and 27 graduate options to over 4,000 students of all ages.

See also CATHOLIC UNIVERSITIES AND COLLEGES.

SALESIANS (S.D.B.)

The Arrival

William Patrick Riordan, archbishop of San Francisco, requested Blessed Michael Rua, the superior general of the Salesians, to send priests to his archdiocese. Thus on March 11, 1897, under the leadership of Fr. Raphael Piperni, the first four Salesians arrived in the United States. On the East Coast, Archbishop Michael A. Corrigan of New York had also been asking for Salesians, and on November 28, 1898, his request was fulfilled with the arrival of three Salesians under the leadership of Fr. Ernest Coppo.

American Apostolates

The apostolate of the Salesians developed into five chief areas, the first being parishes. In San Francisco, the Salesians were given the parish of SS Peter and Paul to minister to Italian immigrants. In New York, Archbishop Corrigan gave the Salesians charge of Italian immigrants on the Lower East Side of Manhattan. There they founded the parish of Mary, Help of Christians. Not only in those cities, but also in Port Chester, New York; Paterson, Elizabeth, and Mahwah, New Jersey; Miami and Belle Glade, Florida; and in Oakland and Los Angeles, California, the Salesians have been ministering to other immigrants besides Italians.

Along with parish schools, the Salesians founded junior and senior high schools, beginning in 1917 in Ramsey, New Jersey; two years later in New Rochelle, New York. A grammar school followed in Goshen, New York, in 1925; an orphanage in Tampa, Florida, in 1928; another in Marrero, Louisiana, in 1933; and a high school and college seminary were opened in 1928 in Newton, New Jersey. In 1984 the Salesians accepted the administration of La Salle High School in Miami.

St. John Bosco's belief that technical schools were an excellent option for some youths has long been acknowledged as sound advice. Therefore, the Salesians opened a technical school in Boston, Massachusetts, in 1945, and another in Paterson, New Jersey, in 1948. In Rosemead, California, the Salesians opened a technical high school and junior college in 1955. A classical high school had been opened long before in Richmond in 1927, and in Bellflower in 1940, both in the golden state.

The Salesians have always envisioned youth centers as an essential ingredient of their apostolate. St. John Bosco's first work was what he called an "oratory." Today we call it a boys' and girls' club or youth center. The purpose is always the same; namely, to offer youth wholesome recreation and religious instruction with a family atmosphere of care and concern. In SS Peter and Paul parish in San Francisco, the Salesians have conducted a youth center since the early years of the twentieth century. Another was opened in East Los Angeles in the mid-1950s. The Salesians began one in East Boston, Massachusetts, in 1945, and another there in 1948. Other aspects of youth work carried on by the Salesians consist of summer camps, youth leadership training programs, and youth retreats. A youth apostolate is fostered in all Salesian parishes.

Foreign Missions and Communications

In doing missionary work, Salesians are following the example of St. John Bosco who sent eleven bands of missionaries to foreign countries, beginning in 1875 with a group of ten sent to Argentina. His successors have followed that lead through the years. Young Salesians have gone from the United States to foreign missions since 1945. Currently (1994), there are twelve Salesians from the United States working in Korea, Japan, Kenya, Sierra Leone, Liberia, Ethiopia, and Chile. The Salesian Mission Procure in New Rochelle, New York, promotes mission awareness and financial assistance for Salesian missions everywhere in the world. *Salesian Missions,* a quarterly magazine published by the Mission Procure, informs friends and contributors about the Salesian missionary apostolate. An important development since 1981 is the Salesian Lay Missionary movement. Since then 103 persons have worked in foreign and home missions. Currently (1994), twenty-five Salesian lay missionaries are in the field.

Since 1946 the Don Bosco Multimedia Center in New Rochelle, New York, has been carrying on this apostolate by spreading Catholic publications, wholesome films, religious, catechetical, and educational filmstrips, slides, video and audio cassettes. It has taken its cue from St. John Bosco, who wrote and published books for youth as well as periodicals for adults. *The Salesian Bulletin,* a monthly periodical begun by St. John Bosco in 1876 in Turin, informs Salesian Cooperators and the general public about the entire range of Salesian apostolic work. The periodical is now printed in all major languages. In the United States it is published bimonthly.

In 1995 the American Salesians had two provinces, an eastern province with its headquarters in New Rochelle, New York, and a western province located in San Francisco, California. The eastern province consisted of 169 priests, 13 professed clerics, and 52 brothers, who were stationed in 12 dioceses as well as in Canada and Nassau. The western province consisted of 85 priests, 6 professed clerics, and 33 brothers, who were stationed in 9 dioceses as well as in Canada and Sierra Leone.

PHILIP J. PASCUCCI, S.D.B.

SALPOINTE, JEAN BAPTISTE (1825–98)

Missionary and archbishop. The first bishop of the vicariate apostolic of Tucson was born February 25, 1825, in San Maurice de Poinsat, Puy-de-Dome, Clermont-Ferrand, France. He was educated at the Petit Séminaire of Agen, the preparatory College of Riom, and at the Seminary of Mont Ferrand. Ordained at twenty-six years of age by Bishop Louis Charles Feron of Clermont, he spent a short time as a parish priest and then became procurator and professor of natural sciences at the major seminary.

In 1859 Bishop John Baptist Lamy visited Clermont in search of volunteer missionaries for his widespread diocese of Santa Fe, New Mexico. Salpointe accepted the challenge and arrived in the Río Grande valley in 1860 where he was assigned to the parish church of Mora. The blend of Spanish, English, and Native American dialects complicated his ministry in this crossroads town east of the Sangre de Cristo Mountains.

Salpointe's prowess convinced Lamy that he would be the proper man as vicar general in the southern district. Obediently, Salpointe accepted the post and rode into Tucson in February 1866. There was need of schools, churches, hospitals, and general ministry, but everything was lacking. In 1868 the area was made a vicariate apostolic and Salpointe its bishop. He knew his need for help, and so he determined to be consecrated in Clermont where he too might successfully recruit missionaries as Lamy had done. Returning in 1870 after an *ad limina* visit to Pope Pius IX, Salpointe dedicated himself to building all the facilities the new diocese lacked. He was highly successful, but Archbishop Lamy chose him as his coadjutor successor in 1885, and so Bishop Salpointe left the desert for the upper Río Grande. He retired in 1891 and returned to his beloved Tucson where he spent the last years of his life writing the famous *Soldiers of the Cross,* the history of the Church in the Southwest. With proofs of his work hardly off the press, the humble and productive cleric died in 1898. He lies buried in St. Augustine Cathedral.

Salpointe, John Baptiste. *Soldiers of the Cross.* Ed. Odie B. Faulk. Tucson, 1966.

CHARLES POLZER, S.J.

SANSBURY, ANGELA (1794–1839)

Religious. Mariah Hamilton Sansbury was the first woman to become a Dominican Sister in the United States. Born in Prince George County, Maryland, in 1794, she became the foundress of the first Dominican sisterhood in this country. After the death of her father, Alexius Sansbury, the family migrated to Kentucky where Mariah and her mother, Elizabeth Hamilton Sansbury, purchased property in Washington County, a short distance from Springfield, Kentucky.

As a member of St. Rose parish, the first Dominican parish in the United States, Mariah was present when Fr. Samuel Thomas Wilson, O.P., invited young women to form a community of Dominican Sisters for the education of youth. Nine women responded. On the morning of April 7, 1822, in St. Rose Church, Mariah was the first one formally received, taking the name of Sr. Angela. Later in the day, Fr. Wilson received three others as novices, thus establishing the community of St. Mary Magdalen, later to be known as the Congregation of St. Catherine of Siena. Their first home was a crude log cabin belonging to the Dominican friars. After the death of her mother, Angela and her companions moved into the Sansbury homestead that she and her mother had purchased in 1820. An abandoned still house on the property became the first school with fifteen students in the opening class.

Fr. Wilson obtained a dispensation for Angela to make her profession before the expiration of her novitiate year. Since her companions indicated they wanted her as their leader, Wilson, as provincial, confirmed her as canonical prioress, June 6, 1823, in the presence of the communities of St. Mary Magdalen and St. Rose.

Unlike European cloistered foundations, the sisters in the New World had to support themselves for there were usually no endowments or generous sponsors. Extreme poverty, threats of disbandment, and crushing debts did not deter Angela and companions from their mission which was parish-based and action-oriented. They worked in the fields, taught school, studied for the apostolate, and maintained a rigorous prayer schedule.

Angela served two terms as prioress in Kentucky. After being transferred to St. Mary of the Springs, Ohio, she was elected prioress twice but died November 30, 1839, before the expiration of her second term. It was said of her that she was "like a flame" animating the others to pursue truth and to give to others the fruits of their contemplation. She is buried at St. Mary of the Springs, Columbus, Ohio. On her tombstone is inscribed:

Sister Angela Sansbury, 1794–1839
foundress of the Dominican Sisterhood
in the United States
1822

In fact, among active Dominican congregations it is agreed that Angela Hamilton Sansbury founded the first Dominican congregation of sisters in the world.

See also DOMINICANS (O.P.).

Crews, Clyde F. *An American Holy Land: A History of the Archdiocese of Louisville.* Wilmington, 1978.
Green, Patricia M. *The Third Order Dominican Sisters of the Congregation of St. Catherine of Siena, St. Catherine, Kentucky.* St. Catherine, Kentucky, 1978.

PASCHALA NOONAN, O.P.

SCANLAN, PATRICK FRANCIS (1894–1983)

Newspaper editor. Born in New York City on October 7, 1894, Patrick ("Pat") Scanlan was one of seven children born to Michael and Maria O'Keefe Scanlan. Three of his brothers became priests of the Archdiocese of New York. One of them, Arthur Scanlan, became rector of St. Joseph's Seminary, Dunwoodie, and *censor librorum* for the archdiocese. After the family moved to Philadelphia in 1901, Scanlan attended St. Elizabeth's grammar school and St. Joseph's High School in that city. In 1914 he received a bachelor's degree from the Jesuit-run St. Joseph's College in Philadelphia.

After graduation, Scanlan studied at St. Joseph's Seminary, Dunwoodie, for two years, leaving due to illness. Soon thereafter he took a teaching position at the newly established St. Peter's High School for Boys, Staten Island, New York. In 1917 he was hired as temporary managing editor of the *Tablet,* the official newspaper of the Diocese of Brooklyn, where he had recently taken up residence. He took the place of managing editor Joseph Cummings, who had been drafted into the Army during World War I.

The Brooklyn Tablet

After Cummings died in 1918, Scanlan received a permanent position at the *Tablet.* He remained there for a total of fifty-one years. During those years, Pat Scanlan achieved a reputation as the most vehement anticommunist in the American Catholic press. He also became famous for an opposition to anti-Catholicism wherever he saw it, a wariness of ecumenism, and a distrust of any expansion of governmental power.

One of the major issues of concern to Scanlan was the growth of anti-Catholicism in the 1920s. The rise of the Ku Klux Klan became a frequent topic of his editorials during that decade as he urged Catholics to band together in the defense of their common interests. During the 1928 presidential campaign, anti-Catholicism played a significant factor in the defeat of Democratic candidate Alfred E. Smith. The blatant prejudice displayed only confirmed Scanlan's beliefs that Catholics were still outsiders in America, and as such must remain militantly united against a hostile Protestant establishment.

By the end of the 1920s, Scanlan's fears of anti-Catholicism gave way to a larger concern with the onslaughts of economic depression. In his editorials he castigated President Herbert Hoover for his seeming inaction as millions starved and faced the terrors of unemployment. In the wake of the 1932 presidential election, Scanlan praised Franklin D. Roosevelt's active response to the country's woes.

As time went on, however, Scanlan became increasingly disenchanted with the Roosevelt administration. He distrusted what he saw as an increase in governmental bureaucracy prone toward inefficiency and wasteful spending. American diplomatic recognition of Soviet Russia in 1933 aroused his strong anticommunism. In addition, he interpreted Roosevelt's inaction on Catholic persecution in mid-1930s Mexico as a sign of the President's insensitivity toward American Catholic concerns. He said this in spite of the fact that Roosevelt had given more government appointments to Catholics than any previous executive.

Scanlan and Anti-Communism

On the domestic front in 1930s America, Scanlan berated the rise of domestic communism. Throughout the next three decades, he warned his readers, on an almost weekly basis, against Communist presence in government, the unions, politics, and the public schools. At times his anticommunism bordered on the obsessive. In fact, it became the predominant characteristic of the Brooklyn *Tablet* throughout Scanlan's tenure as managing editor.

By the mid-1930s, Scanlan was the biggest supporter of Fr. Charles E. Coughlin, the "radio priest," in the Catholic press. This support continued even after Coughlin turned to an overt anti-Semitism in 1938. Scanlan had several reasons for supporting Coughlin. The priest had become increasingly anti-Roosevelt after the 1936 election, and Scanlan himself had been moving in that direction for some time previous.

In addition, he was critical of what he perceived as a lack of Jewish concern for Catholic persecutions in Mexico, and Jewish support for the Loyalists in the Spanish Civil War. Finally, he resented the fact that New York City's Jewish community was not as hard hit by the depression as were the Irish. Although he never indulged in the same blatant anti-Semitism as did Coughlin, Scanlan continued to support Coughlin even after his withdrawal from public life in 1942.

As American entry into the Second World War became increasingly imminent, Scanlan espoused a strong isolationist stance. After the bombing of Pearl Harbor, however, he urged American Catholics to fulfill their patriotic duties and support the war effort. At the same time he did not cease to voice criticism of America's alliance with Russia. This was understandable, given Scanlan's belief that Communism constituted a far greater danger to the Church than Fascism.

In the postwar years, with the rise of the cold war, Scanlan wrote ceaselessly on the need to fight Communism both at home and abroad. Consequently, he strongly supported Senator Joseph R. McCarthy's campaign to root out domestic radicals. His stance on the Korean War, however, was more ambivalent. While he appreciated the effort to halt Communist expansion, he felt that the war could have been avoided if America had taken a tougher stance toward Russia in 1945.

Winds of Change

As the 1950s ended, great changes were taking place in both the Church and the world, and Patrick Scanlan was not entirely equipped to meet them. Although he praised the 1960 election of John F. Kennedy as a major step toward the erosion of anti-Catholicism, he was not overly enthusiastic about Kennedy himself. He felt that Kennedy was almost embarrassed to defend or espouse his religious affiliation.

Scanlan always publicly supported the Second Vatican Council (1962–65), but he was not prepared to take on a new understanding of Church. He had misgivings about the new ecumenism, liturgical changes, and a more general openness toward the modern world. Nor was he able to deal with changes in the American Church as clergy and laity joined the various popular movements of the 1960s.

Scanlan retired in June 1968, at the age of seventy-four. He spent his retirement years in his Long Island home with his wife and family. In 1974 he became incapacitated, spending his last years at the Belair Nursing Home on Long Island. He died there on March 27, 1983. He was survived by his wife of fifty-nine years, the former Mae Mannning, his son Patrick F. Scanlan, Jr., and his daughter Marie.

See also ANTI-COMMUNISM AND AMERICAN CATHOLICS; McCARTHY, JOSEPH RAYMOND.

McNamara, Patrick J. "A Study of the Editorial Policy of the Brooklyn *Tablet* under Patrick F. Scanlan, 1917–1968." M.A. thesis, St. John's University, 1994.

———. "Patrick F. Scanlan, The Brooklyn *Tablet,* and the New Deal." *New York Irish History* 8 (1993–94) 8–12.

PATRICK J. McNAMARA

SCHISMS (OR INDEPENDENCE MOVEMENTS) IN AMERICA

Canon 751 of the 1983 Code of Canon Law gives the Catholic view on schism as "the refusal of submission to the Roman Pontiff or of communion with the members of the church subject to him." Throughout U.S. Catholic history, a variety of splinter groups, sometimes called "underground" or occasionally "storefront" churches, have come under this definition. The many thousands of Ruthenians who transferred to communion with the Russian Orthodox Church under the guidance of Fr. Alexis Toth, though technically not schismatics, constituted the largest leakage and require a separate study. This article deals with the hitherto little-known but significant severance of what

became the Polish National Catholic Church. Smaller departures among Lithuanians, Slovaks, and Italians, sooner or later came under the patronage of the PNCC.

Polish National Catholic Church

The Polish alienation began in the late nineteenth century as a grassroots jurisdictional departure, led by clergy such as Dominik Kolasinski at Detroit, Franciszek Kolaszewski at Cleveland, Anton Kozlowski at Chicago, and Stephen Kaminski at Buffalo. Kozlowski, who became a bishop in 1897 at the hands of Old Catholics in Switzerland, founded as many as twenty-three parishes, ranging from New Jersey into Manitoba, Canada, while Kaminski, who became a bishop in 1898, eventually claimed fourteen congregations. Finally, these spontaneous efforts crystallized under Franciszek Hodur (1866–1953), who initiated separation at Scranton in 1897. During a decade of rivalry with Kozlowski and Kaminski, Hodur obtained episcopal rank at Utrecht on September 29, 1907. In subsequent years, numerous other independent parishes joined the PNCC ranks of more than one hundred parishes under Hodur and his four successors, Leon Grochowski, Thaddeus Zielinski, Francis Rowinski, and John Swantek, known as Prime Bishops. This American independence movement reached Poland where to this day there are some one hundred parishes in three dioceses. Several South American missions were also established. For a time, the PNCC practiced intercommunion with the Episcopal Church. In recent times, dissension in the Anglican Church over women's ordination and liturgical changes brought into PNCC ranks a separate Toronto parish, using the Anglican Missal Rite. A similar development occurred in an Episcopalian parish of Spartansburg, North Carolina.

Reasons for separation focused on real or perceived injustices centering around quarrels between hierarchy and clergy-laity over parish property ownership and lay control of pastors; Irish-Polish ethnic conflict; local pastor-parishioner strife; and Rome's refusal to set up a separate extraterritorial jurisdiction with a bishop for all Poles, and the long delay in gaining even a token appointment of a Polish bishop in the U.S.A., despite repeated requests. Only in 1908 did Paul Rhode (1871–1945) become an auxiliary bishop in Chicago and later the ordinary of Green Bay, Wisconsin, with its heavy Polish population.

In 1907 the PNCC organized its own Savonarola Seminary in Scranton, Pennsylvania, still training students at this date. Despite uncertainty of some Catholic observers, the PNCC always maintained that its clergy possessed valid orders. Eventually, this view was upheld by Rome when a PNCC priest and family in Rochester, New York, became Roman Catholics, without any question of the clergyman's ordination. Celibacy was modified at the Sixth General Synod at Buffalo, June 2–5, 1931, allowing a priest to marry only after two years of service. Over the years, a number of Roman Catholic clergy transferred to the PNCC.

As of 1990 the PNCC was divided into four dioceses with the following number of parishes: Canada, 14; Buffalo-Pittsburgh, 20; Central (Pennsylvania, New Jersey, New York, Maryland), 49; Eastern (New England), 29; Western (Illinois, Indiana, Minnesota, Ohio, Wisconsin, Florida), 31, with a dozen or so missions. Isolated parishes include Los Angeles, San Diego, California; and Denver, Colorado. A quadrennial General Synod of clergy and lay boards is the supreme governing authority, presided over by the Prime Bishop and parliamentarian. Through 1990, eighteen such assemblies have been held.

As early as 1900, Mass was offered in Polish, a practice which was made universal by mandate in 1921. English was later introduced, e.g., at Buffalo in 1961. Hodur retained seven sacraments, adding preaching, while numbering baptism and confirmation as one. Auricular confession became optional, replaced by general confession. The PNCC has preserved traditional eucharistic and Marian devotions.

Since 1984 a semiannual dialogue has taken place between Roman Catholic and PNCC officials. In the late 1970s activist Thomas A. Michalski spearheaded a "healing" service in Buffalo, the forerunner of the two 1992 "healing" services of mutual apology and forgiveness for past misunderstandings that took place in Scranton, Pennsylvania, and Buffalo, New York. In 1993 Rome granted intercommunion at the request of the PNCC.

Lithuanian National Catholic Church (LNCC)

As many as sixteen independent parishes arose, mostly in Pennsylvania and New England. Some were short-lived, others lasted a decade or more. At this writing, Divine Providence parish in Scranton is still a viable parish, while a remnant remains at Sacred Heart, Lawrence, Massachusetts. The fifth PNCC General Synod in Scranton, Pennsylvania, July 15–16, 1924, set up a diocese for the LNCC, consecrating Fr. Jonas Gritenas (1884–1928) as bishop, August 17, 1924. In 1927 he went to Lithuania in a vain attempt to inaugurate a separatist church. Among other reasons, lack of a charismatic priest impeded the movement, though the potential for widespread separatism existed.

Slovak National Catholic Church (SNCC)

Data on the Slovak National Catholic Church is sketchy at best on this complex Slovak-Hungarian-Polish mixture of conflict and accommodation. SS Cyril and Methodius, one of the first independent congregations, originated in Masontown, Pennsylvania, in 1909, lasting to at least 1926. Other such separatist units included St. John the Baptist,

begun in Cleveland around 1917, and others known in 1919 at Palmerton, Pennsylvania, and Youngstown, Ohio. In 1922, in Passaic, New Jersey, some three hundred families formed their own Holy Name of Jesus parish, coming into the PNCC fold in 1927. Others surfaced in Braddock and McKeesport, Pennsylvania, by 1931, both called Holy Name of Jesus, and both still extant in the late 1950s. A Slovak National Catholic Synod took place as late as February 1963, when the PNCC appointed Fr. Eugene Magyar as a bishop.

Italian National Catholic Church (INCC)

A hint of Italian separatism was found in Chicago in 1899 under Fr. Antonio d'Andrea and his St. Anthony parish sanctioned by a local independent Polish bishop, Anton Kozlowski. Another clue can be traced to a Roman Catholic, ex-priest, Paulo Miraglia-Gulotti who became a bishop at the hands of the independent Bishop Joseph Rene Vilatte in 1900 at Piacenza. After Gulotti's vain effort to expand his "Italian National Episcopal Church," he made further attempts in Brooklyn, New York, in 1908, and West Virginia in 1911, and finally left for Corsica. Apart from isolated instances of Italian separatism in Youngstown, Ohio, and Erie, Pennsylvania, the one identifiable organized movement arose in Hackensack, New Jersey, in 1915. There the excommunicated Fr. Antonio Giulio Lenza placed his independent St. Anthony congregation of some five hundred families under the jurisdiction of Villate and in 1919 shifted to the PNCC. Hodur designated Lenza as Vicar General for the Italian Diocese of St. Anthony. Under Lenza's authority, short-lived independent parishes arose in Garfield and Passaic, New Jersey, where 1,500 received confirmation in 1919; and in Marlboro, Massachusetts; Schenectady, New York; Duryea, Pennsylvania; and in North Dakota. Though the INCC briefly numbered at least twenty-four churches, this separatist movement, weakened by irresolute former Roman Catholic clergy, collapsed because of renewed Roman Catholic attention to Italian immigrants.

See also FEENEY, LEONARD; LITHUANIAN CATHOLICS IN AMERICA; POLISH CATHOLICS IN AMERICA; STALLINGS SCHISM, THE.

Anson, Peter. *Bishops at Large.* London, 1964.

Brzana and Rysz, eds. *Journeying Together in Christ: The Report of the Polish National Catholic-Roman Catholic Dialogue.* Huntington, Ind.: Our Sunday Visitor, 1990.

Grotnik, Casimir, ed. *Synods of the Polish National Catholic Church, 1904–1958.* East European Monographs. Boulder: Columbia University Press, New York, 1993.

PNCC Studies [an annual devoted to the PNCC and other separatist movements], 1980 to present.

Pruter and Melton. *The Old Catholic Sourcebook.* New York/London, 1983.

Ward, Persson, Bain, eds. *Independent Bishops: An International Directory.* Detroit: Apogee Books, 1990.

Wielewinski, Bernard. *Polish National Catholic Church Independent Movements, Old Catholic Church and Related Items: An Annotated Bibliography.* East European Monographs. Boulder: Columbia University Press, New York, 1990.

Wlodarski, Stephen. *The Origin and Growth of the Polish National Catholic Church.* Scranton, 1974.

Wolkovich-Valkavičius, William. "Religious Separatism Among Lithuanian Immigrants in the United States and Their Polish Affiliation." *Polish American Studies* (Autumn 1983) 93–123.

WILLIAM WOLKOVICH-VALKAVIČIUS

SCHMITZ, CARL (1917–88)

Missionary. Carl Schmitz was born in Chicago, Illinois, October 10, 1917, and baptized with the name of William. He was professed as a Passionist with the name of Carl, July 17, 1938, and ordained in Louisville, Kentucky, April 26, 1944. In the summer of 1948, Carl was on his way to China, one of the second group of Passionist missionaries to go to China after the Second World War. He was studying Chinese at Beijing, only to be rushed out of the country before the Red Army took all of mainland China. A year later he was working among the blacks in Alabama. Three years later, in 1953, he was sent to Japan to found the congregation in that country. In 1974 he asked to join the Passionists in the Philippines. There he served as pastor in a large parish on the island of Mindinao for several years. Finally he became the missionary to the B'laans, a minority people who had been driven out of their homelands. There, in front of his "convento" among his B'laan people, one whom Carl knew and had trained killed him with a gun which he fired repeatedly.

As a young boy he had been inspired by the martyrdom of Frs. Walter Coveyou, Godfrey Holbein, and Clement Seybold in China. In 1931 he entered the Passionist minor seminary in St. Louis, with the hope of one day following their example. He took his vows on July 17, 1938, including the passion vow proper to every Passionist. This mysticism of the passion was deepened by his apostolic ministries. He was in China long enough to experience the sufferings of refugee peoples; among the blacks of Birmingham to share the needs of the poor and segregated; from the Japanese to learn the pitfalls a prospering people face.

In his final years, Fr. Carl lived the life of the B'laans in his mission center in the mountains. He felt the injustices they experienced in being driven from their homelands. He defended their rights to their lands and way of life. But he also taught them the faith and its demands of Christian morals. It is no wonder that there were those who wanted to see him silenced, removed, murdered.

In his final letter dated March 1, 1988, he writes of "doggedly plugging on in this marathon of a life lived by 'faith in the Son of God who loved me and gave up his life for love of me.'" Carl Schmitz followed Christ even to death by an assassin's gun. It was Thursday in Easter Week, April 7, 1988.

See also PASSIONISTS (C.P.).

Clancy, Rian, C.P., and Roger Mercurio, C.P. *Father Carl—Passionist.* Chicago, 1990.

ROGER MERCURIO, C.P.

SCHOOL SISTERS OF NOTRE DAME (S.S.N.D.)

On November 17, 1985, School Sisters of Notre Dame around the world rejoiced as the Church beatified their founder, Mary Theresa of Jesus Gerhardinger. From the tiny mustard seed of three sisters in Neunburg vorm Wald, Bavaria, on October 24, 1833, grew an international congregation of more than 7,000 sisters serving in more than thirty countries and organized into twenty-one provinces and two regions united under a general superior residing in Rome.

Origins and Arrival in the United States

Mother Theresa founded her congregation for the purpose of "training and educating female youth." She believed that girls and women needed to be educated if the world were to become a better place. Because of the political situation in Bavaria in 1847, which raised the specter of secularization of religious, and the needs of German immigrants in the United States, Blessed Theresa of Jesus led the first band of S.S.N.D. missionaries to North America that summer. Included in that first group of five School Sisters who arrived in the United States on July 31, 1847, were Sr. Mary Barbara Weinzierl, one of the congregation's founding members at Neunburg vorm Wald and first provincial superior in Baltimore, and Sr. Mary Caroline Friess, the major superior in North America from 1850 until her death in 1892.

With the assistance of John Neumann, the Redemptorist provincial, schools were opened that fall of 1847 in St. Mary's, Pennsylvania; and at St. James, St. Michael, and St. Alphonsus, in Baltimore, Maryland. Before Mother Theresa returned to Munich, the site of the main motherhouse of the congregation from 1843 until 1957, a second group of ten S.S.N.D. missionaries arrived in Baltimore on March 25, 1848. Mother Theresa also accepted several American candidates during the year she lived in the United States. In January 1849 she sent to the United States one last missionary group of ten novices and candidates. All future growth in North American would depend on native vocations.

Educational Ministry and Growth

Although the School Sisters of Notre Dame came to the New World to educate the daughters of German immigrants, from the beginning they accepted new members of other national origins, taught in schools serving a variety of ethnic groups, and permitted boys into their classrooms and orphanages. The sisters rapidly gained a reputation as educators. They brought with them the *Volksschule* method of teaching from Bavaria and trained their new members in the Pestolozzian ideas which it incorporated, earning for themselves a reputation for using progressive teaching methods.

Stories abound of pastors and bishops demanding School Sisters of Notre Dame for their schools, one bishop going so far as to write to Mother Caroline in 1885, "I will not receive a negative reply from you." Other bishops counseled their pastors not to say that the children of their school were German, but rather that they were needy, as this was surely the most certain way to gain the services of the School Sisters. At Mother Caroline's funeral on July 27, 1892, Archbishop Frederick Katzer of Milwaukee said, "I fear little contradiction, if I maintain that the Catholic parochial school was [in 1847] an uncultivated field—a primeval forest of America, which scarcely any one thought of clearing or tilling." He then went on to credit the School Sisters of Notre Dame with changing all that.

By the turn-of-the-century, the School Sisters of Notre Dame formed the largest congregation of women religious in the United States, with more than two thousand members, teaching in nearly three hundred parochial schools and almost a dozen congregation-sponsored academies. In Baltimore in 1895 the College of Notre Dame of Maryland accepted its first freshman class and was chartered by the General Assembly of the State of Maryland in April 1896, making it the first Catholic college for women to be chartered in the United States. Moved to Milwaukee in 1929, Mount Mary College had its roots in St. Mary College in Prairie du Chien, Wisconsin. Both Notre Dame of Maryland and Mount Mary continue to be thriving women's colleges in 1997.

By the end of the nineteenth century the congregation's growing membership had necessitated the establishment of provincial motherhouses in Baltimore and St. Louis, with the main North American motherhouse located in Milwaukee. In the twentieth century further expansion meant the founding of provincial motherhouses in Mankato, Minnesota (1912); Waterdown, Ontario (1927); Wilton, Connecticut (1957); Dallas, Texas (1961); and Chicago, Illinois (1965). The growth of the congregation peaked in the 1960s when its membership totaled more than twelve thousand members, approximately half of whom were ministering in the United States. In the last fifty years, School Sisters from the United States have traveled to Sierra Leone, Ghana, Nigeria, Kenya, Japan, Guam, Yap, Ebeye, Chuuk, Mexico, Guatemala, Honduras, Bolivia, Peru, Chile, Paraguay, and El Salvador to minister to and with the people.

Post-Vatican II Era

In the 1960s, 1970s, and 1980s, following the directives of Vatican Council II, the congregation studied its charism and heritage, and rewrote its rule. Today, under the guidelines set forth in *You Are Sent,* more than three thousand School Sisters of Notre Dame in the United States continue to teach at the elementary, secondary, and college levels. Believing the words of *You Are Sent* that "education means enabling persons to reach the fullness of their potential," members of the congregation also minister to the homeless, the prison bound, adults who are illiterate, those who come to soup kitchens, children in "Head Start" programs, migrant workers, the unemployed, the abused, and the poor of Appalachia and the inner cities. In December 1993, in keeping with the words of *You Are Sent* that "As members of an international congregation, we recognize our obligation and opportunities to develop a world vision and a sense of global responsibility," the congregation received official nongovernmental status at the United Nations.

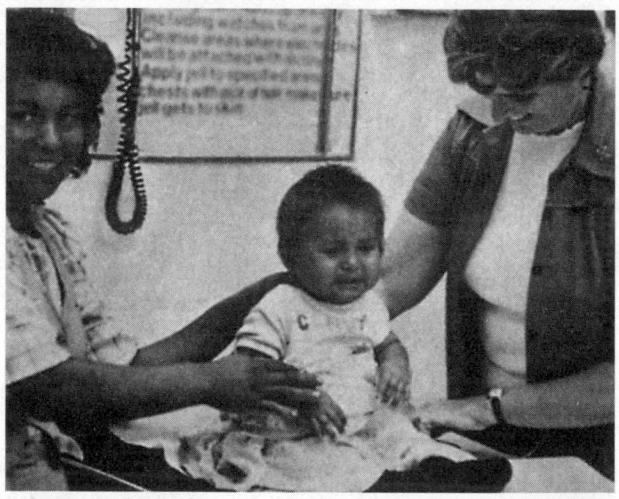

Sisters in social ministry

In 1992 the Nineteenth General Chapter of the School Sisters of Notre Dame challenged the congregation with the *Mandate for Action* to "risk in faith for a more just and truly human world." School Sisters around the world were called to reverence all creation, to prefer the poor and to seek solidarity with them, and to work against unjust structures. As the School Sisters of Notre Dame in the United States prepare for the challenges of the twenty-first century, they recall the words of Blessed Mary Theresa of Jesus Gerhardinger, "Let us continue to serve the Triune God all our lives with joy."

See also WOMEN RELIGIOUS IN AMERICA.

Friess, Mary Caroline, S.S.N.D. *The Letters of Mother Caroline Friess, School Sisters of Notre Dame.* Ed. Barbara Brumleve, S.S.N.D. Winona, Minn.: St. Mary's Press, 1991.

Gerhardinger, Mary Theresa, S.S.N.D. *The North American Foundations: Letters of Mother M. Theresa, SSND.* Ed. M. Hester Valentine, S.S.N.D. Winona, Minn.: St. Mary's College Press, 1977.

You Are Sent: Constitution and Directory of the School Sisters of Notre Dame. Milwaukee: Privately printed, 1986.

STEPHANIE MARY PILACHOWSKI, S.S.N.D.

SCHREMBS, JOSEPH (1866–1945)

Archbishop. Joseph Schrembs was born on March 12, 1866, at Wurzelhofen in Bavaria, the second youngest of sixteen children. His father was a blacksmith and his mother a homemaker. Schrembs attended the Catholic elementary school at Ratisbon. At age eleven he was introduced to Bishop Rupert Seidenbusch, O.S.B., who was visiting from the United States in search of vocations. Three years later Schrembs became a student at St. Vincent Archabbey at Latrobe, Pennsylvania, where he was united with his older brother, Fr. Rudicent, O.S.B., who had earlier emigrated to the United States. Eventually, Bishop Henry Richter, of the Diocese of Grand Rapids, sponsored Schrembs' entrance into the seminary in Montreal, Canada. On June 29, 1889, Schrembs was ordained to the priesthood by Bishop Richter. Twenty-two years later, in January 1911 Schrembs was named titular bishop of Sophene, as well as auxiliary bishop of Grand Rapids. In August of that same year, Schrembs was assigned to be the first bishop of Toledo, Ohio.

During his tenure in Toledo, Schrembs dedicated thirteen new parishes and created councils of men and women representing all parishes of the diocese. Perhaps his greatest achievement centered around his steadfast belief in Catholic education, a belief that emerged as the cornerstone of his administration in Toledo, where he established thirty-three schools.

Bishop of Cleveland

The final and most important leg of Schrembs' episcopal career commenced on September 8, 1921, with his installation by Archbishop Henry Moeller of Cincinnati as the fifth bishop of Cleveland. As in Toledo, Schrembs gave the Catholic community of Cleveland schools and colleges to educate its youth. His administration even waged a relentless but futile campaign for state aid to assist Ohio's parochial schools during the depression years. Among the European ethnic and African American communities of Cleveland, the Schrembs administration reconciled ethnic conflicts, advanced the spirit of assimilation, assisted African American Catholics in their struggles against a predominantly white Church, and attacked racist and anti-Catholic organizations. Schrembs also supported Dorothy Day's Catholic Worker movement, and assiduously fought for better working conditions, equal pay for men and women, and the right to organize unions.

Outside of his diocese, Schrembs emerged as one of the major promoters of the National Catholic War Council, and later, it was primarily his influence that prompted Pope Pius XI to accept the National Catholic Welfare Council (NCWC). Schrembs' prudent leadership on the NCWC was instrumental in organizing the National Council of Catholic Men (NCCM) and the National Council of Catholic Women (NCCW), and as a member of the NCWC's Administrative Committee, Schrembs was very much involved in addressing the anti-Church policies of the Mexican government and in confronting the dilemma of American recognition of the Soviet Union. Finally, Schrembs was not afraid to admonish the outspokenness of the controversial, but popular, Fr. Charles Coughlin. Nor did he allow secular pressures to interfere with official Catholic teaching on morality and family life as he campaigned against the birth control movement and condemned the making of indecent films.

The Schrembs administration brought new meaning to the concept "American Catholicism." His episcopal leadership demonstrated to the people of his diocese that the American Catholic Church was an important part of their lives, as it cultivated their physical and spiritual needs enabling them to practice and integrate their Catholic faith into the American culture.

On March 25, 1939, the manhood, the priesthood, and the episcopacy of Joseph Schrembs came to a dramatic climax when he was presented with the title of archbishop by Pope Pius XII. Unfortunately, despite his relentless energy to serve the faithful, Schrembs suffered through several years of poor health, dying of pneumonia on November 2, 1945.

"While my mission is, of course, primarily to Catholics," he said, "the scope of my work, of necessity, extends far beyond the limits of my own communion."

See also GERMAN CATHOLICS IN AMERICA; OHIO, CATHOLIC CHURCH IN.

Hynes, Michael J. *History of the Diocese of Cleveland: Origin and Growth (1847–1952).* Cleveland: World Publishing Company, 1953.

McKeon, Elizabeth. "Apologia for an American Catholicism: The Petition and Report of the National Catholic Welfare Council to Pius XI, April 25, 1922." *Church History* 43 (1974) 514–28.

Poluse, Martin F. "Archbishop Joseph Schrembs and the Twentieth Century Catholic Church in Cleveland, 1921–1945." Ph.D. dissertation, Kent State University, 1991.

Slawson, Douglas J. *The Foundation and First Decade of the National Catholic Welfare Council*. Washington, D.C.: The Catholic University of America Press, 1992.

MARTIN POLUSE

SCHRIECK, LOUISE (JOSEPHINE) VAN DER (1813–86)

Religious superior. Sr. Louise was born Josephine Van Der Schrieck in Bergen-Op-Zoon, Holland, on November 14, 1813. She was educated by the Sisters of Notre Dame de Namur in Namur, Belgium, and joined the community there in 1837. At Namur she studied German and English, choices that eminently qualified her for future work in America. In 1840, as one of eight sisters, she arrived in Cincinnati, Ohio, where German immigrants had already arrived who very much wanted a good education for their children.

The "French Ladies," as they were called, were well trained to educate the students who arrived at the academy at Sixth Street. Representing the sisters, Sr. Louise, as she was then known, articulated the system of education introduced by Sr. Julie Billiart and refined under the direction of Françoise Blin de Bourbon.

For thirty-eight years Sr. Louise saw the numbers of sisters and their works increase. Before her death, sisters were instructing twenty-three thousand students in parochial schools, many among the poorest in Ohio and on the East Coast. They also taught boarders and day students in the academies and thousands of Sunday school students. Of special concern to Sr. Louise were the twenty-four thousand sodalists associated with the sisters' work among the poor.

When Sr. Louise died in Cincinnati, Ohio, on December 3, 1886, Bishop Williams of Boston eulogized her by saying, "The work of Sister Superior Louise should be reckoned with that of the early bishops of the United States. A great woman . . . her death was a loss not only to you, but to the entire church."

Linscott, Mary, S.N.D.deN. *Quiet Revolution*. Glasgow, 1966.
Nugent, Helen Louise, S.N.D.deN. *Sister Louise (Josephine Van Der Schrieck)*. Cincinnati, 1931.

LOUANNA ORTH, S.N.D.deN.

SCRIPTURE AND CATECHETICS IN THE UNITED STATES

Roman Catholic catechetical literature in the United States published between 1795–1995 has utilized Scripture in various ways. Initially, Scripture was peripherally included as a means of proving doctrine or of demonstrating its source. Then gradually Scripture was written about, running parallel to doctrine and sometimes correlated with it. Later catechetical materials indicated a significant shift in the use of Scripture, and after Vatican Council II the Bible was accepted as the foundation of catechesis.

The first English catechism published in the United States carries the name of Archbishop John Carroll of Baltimore and cites and occasionally quotes biblical texts to "prove" doctrine. The oldest introductory text for Bible study was that of Joseph Reeve, *The History of the Old and New Testaments* (1780), and it was the principal text for the biblical education of American Catholics before 1840. Reeve's book continued to be printed through the nineteenth century. In 1810 the American bishops endorsed Richard Challoner's version of the Douay-Rheims Bible for use in the United States. Their goal was to provide an accurate English translation.

Scripture in Early Catechisms

French-born Jean Cheverus, Boston's first bishop, had Claude Fleury's *Short Historical Catechism of Sacred History and Christian Doctrine* revised and circulated. Fleury's catechism began with a summary of sacred history that served as a basis for doctrinal questions and answers. The German-language *Large Catechism* of Joseph Deharbe (1847) was translated into English and several other languages for use throughout the United States. Deharbe began with sacred history, quoted the words of Jesus as the source for various teachings in the doctrinal section, and he drew on Scripture to illustrate applications for Christian attitudes and behavior. The French-born Sulpician and third bishop of Savannah, Augustin Verot, continued but modified the Fleury tradition by adding an appendix on sacred history to his *General Catechism of Christian Doctrine* (1869).

Bible Histories

Bible histories became increasingly popular in the second half of the nineteenth century. The works of the English priest, Henry Formby, one of Fleury's translators, emphasized St. Augustine's catechetical dictum that sacred history be taught in an unbroken narrative from creation to the present time. Formby's 1858 *Pictorial Bible and Church History Series* was one of many illustrated Bible histories used in the U.S. Richard Gilmour, later bishop of Cleveland, published his widely used *Bible History* in 1869. Replete with typology (e.g., "David is a figure of Jesus Christ"), it contained maxims from the Scriptures and a table correlating Scripture with Christian doctrine. Another sacred history designated for catechetical use and translated from the German was Ignatz Schuster's *Illustrated Bible History* (1876) which rivaled Gilmour's in popularity. The Bible histories of Gilmour and Schuster continued to be printed until the eve of Vatican Council II.

The Baltimore Catechism and Scripture

The Baltimore Catechism of 1885 contained no direct references to Scripture itself, although it quoted Christ's words in nine of the 421 answers, but did not cite the scriptural source. Some effort was made to demonstrate the biblical basis for doctrine with the publication of books such as Thomas Cox's *Biblical Treasury of the Catechism* (1899).

Peter Yorke's graded textbooks, based on the Baltimore Catechism and used in several California dioceses, were published in 1898 and later revised. They combined Bible history and catechism questions in the same book, and a close connection between the two was sometimes established. The textbooks used by the Christian Brothers' schools incorporated events in sacred history within their own question-and-answer format. Their upper-level books were related to the *Manual of Christian Doctrine* published by McVey in 1904, and an accompanying table showed the relationship of the books to the lessons of the Baltimore Catechism.

Bishop Edwin O'Hara of the CCD

By 1936 Edwin O'Hara, chairman of the bishops' committee for the Confraternity of Christian Doctrine (CCD), had taken steps to revise both the Baltimore Catechism and the Douay-Rheims Bible to provide texts better adapted for use in religious education. The work achieved three results: the formation of the Catholic Biblical Association in 1936, the 1941 revision of the New Testament, and the 1941 revision of the Baltimore Catechism. The 1941 revision contained 499 questions and answers, referring to Scripture in twenty-four of them. An enlarged edition for adults, Baltimore Catechism Number Three, added scriptural quotations for each answer. In 1943 Pope Pius XII promulgated the encyclical *Divino Afflante Spiritu* which encouraged biblical translations based on the original languages; and it led to the publication of the *New American Bible,* completed in 1970.

The biblical renewal set in motion by the encyclical and the liturgical and catechetical efforts of Dom Virgil Michel and others came together in the 1957 publication of the *On Our Way Series* for public school elementary students. The series, inspired by the kerygmatic approach pioneered in the U.S.A. by Johannes Hofinger, aimed to present Christ as the "good news" of all catechesis, and it did so by integrating biblical stories and biblical history with liturgy, doctrine, art, and music.

Vatican II on Scripture in Catechetics

Vatican II's Dogmatic Constitution on Divine Revelation, *Dei Verbum,* emphasized the role of the Bible in the life of the Church. The *General Catechetical Directory,* mandated by the council, pointed to Scripture as the soul of catechetical formation (GCD no. 112; see also no. 14), drawing on *Dei Verbum*'s description of catechesis as a "ministry of the Word" (DV no. 24). *Sharing the Light of Faith,* the National Catechetical Directory for Catholics of the United States (1979), emphasized that "catechesis studies scripture as a source inseparable from the Christian message" (NCD no. 43). Noting the Bible's role in catechesis as "essential and indispensable" (NCD no. 60), *Sharing the Light of Faith* stipulated the use of the Bible as a text for study by older children, youth, and adults (NCD no. 264).

Textbook series in the post-Vatican II era gave great prominence to Scripture, quoting the Bible frequently throughout and paraphrasing biblical stories according to the reading level of the students. In most standard textbook series, the sixth-grade text gave a general introduction to the individual books of the Bible. Catholic secondary school curricula usually included a year of Scripture study.

Vatican II gave new impetus to introductory courses on the Bible at the college level, and parishes formed Scripture study groups for adults. Publishers began to supply biblical materials in various media for use in catechesis.

With the spread of the Rite of Christian Initiation of Adults, the lectionary became a source for catechesis. Lectionary-based catechesis is a form of biblical catechesis that focuses on the themes of the Old and New Testaments found in the Sunday readings.

Scripture, Catechesis, and the Catechism *of the Catholic Church*

The 1992 *Catechism of the Catholic Church* (CCC) makes extensive use of Scripture in its presentation of doctrine. It provides several guidelines on how to teach from Scripture, particularly in catechesis on creation (CCC nos. 279–421), on liturgy (CCC nos. 1093–1095), on the formation of conscience and the teaching of morality (CCC no. 1724, no. 1785, nos. 1961–1971, nos. 2052–2063), and on prayer (CCC nos. 2568–2619). The *Catechism* gives an extended treatment on Scripture (CCC nos. 101–141) in which it repeats Vatican II's statement that catechetics, as a ministry of the word is "healthily nourished and thrives in holiness through the Word of Scripture" (CCC no. 132). The *Catechism* also repeats Vatican II's exhortation that the Christian faithful "learn 'the surpassing knowledge of Jesus Christ' by frequent reading of the divine Scriptures" (CCC no. 133).

The Pontifical Biblical Commission's document, *The Interpretation of the Bible in the Church* (1993), declares that catechesis has "sacred Scripture as first source," and that "explained in the context of the tradition, Scripture provides the starting point, foundation and norm of catechetical teaching." It adds that the "correct understanding and fruitful reading of the Bible" is one of the goals of catechesis (*Origins,* 23 [January 6, 1994] 522, CNS Documentary Service).

Bryce, Mary Charles. *Pride of Place: The Role of the Bishops in the Development of Catechesis in the United States.* Washington, 1984.

_____. *The Influence of the Catechism of the Third Plenary Council of Baltimore.* Ann Arbor, Mich.: University Microfilms, 1971.

Carmody, Charles. "The Origins of the Roman Catholic Catechesis in the United States (1776–1799)." *Journal of the Midwest History of Education Society* 3 (1975) 1–13.

Fogarty, Gerald. *American Catholic Biblical Scholarship.* San Francisco: Harper and Row, 1989.

Marthaler, Bernard. *The Catechism Yesterday and Today: The Evolution of a Genre.* Collegeville, Minn.: The Liturgical Press, 1995.

CAROL DORR CLEMENT

SEATTLE, CHIEF (1786–1866)

Native American leader. Chief Seattle, son of Schweable, chief of the Suquamish of Puget Sound, and son of the daughter of Scholitza, chief of the Duwamish, a neighboring tribe, was born about 1786 near present Port Madison in Washington State. He stated later that as a boy he saw Captain George Vancouver's ship in Puget Sound in 1792. Described by a contemporary "as a man of more than ordinary ability, both physically and mentally," he succeeded in organizing Puget Sound tribes in "the Duwamish League" to protect themselves from factious natives dwelling east of them. He was elected as head chief of this league of Coast Indians.

At the approximate age of fifty-four, he was baptized as a Catholic, receiving the name of Noah. His new faith doubtlessly influenced his attitude toward white settlers, who arrived in 1851 at what is now West Seattle. He welcomed the newcomers and became their loyal friend.

In 1855, representing his people, he attended the historic Port Elliot Treaty Conference conducted by Governor Isaac Stevens. Convinced that his people were powerless to prevent whites from taking over tribal lands, he accepted terms of the treaty and allegedly made a speech which in recent years has become world famous. Noted authorities regard the speech as apocryphal. For his decision, Chief Seattle, who became more commonly known as Sealth, was considered a traitor by many native peoples. He did not turn his back on his people, however; he did what he could to help them.

When the hostile native groups living east and south of Puget Sound organized an army to make war on the whites during 1855–56, Chief Seattle kept his Coast tribes from taking part. Dr. David Maynard, one of the settlement's founders and the chief's closest white friend, described him at this time "as experiencing great mental distress during the attack. Loving his own race but counting the white men as his friends, he prayed the two groups might be reconciled." It was Dr. Maynard who convinced his associates to name the settlement in honor of the chief, whose indigenous name they could not pronounce. They used "Seattle" in its place, so the great city on the Sound today, named for him, is neither his native nor his baptized name.

Chief Seattle died on June 7, 1866. After two ceremonies, one Catholic and one native, both attended by crowds of respectful white people as well as by the indigenous people, he was buried in the churchyard at Suquamish, a mission across the bay from the city. Twenty-three years later his white friends built a monument over his grave.

One of the mourners at the funerals was Chief Seattle's daughter, who achieved a modicum of fame as did her father. Known to history as Princess Angeline, she survived her father by twenty years and was buried from the parish church in Seattle. Present were her many white friends who had provided her with a coffin in the shape of a canoe. Like her father, the princess had been a devout Catholic to the end.

Egan, Timothy. "Chief's 1854 Speech Given New Meaning," with text. *New York Times,* April 21, 1992.

Kaiser, Rudolf. "A Fifth Gospel: Almost Chief Seattle's Speech(es): American Origins and European Reception." *Indians and Europe,* ed. Chiniken F. Feest. Aachen, 1987, 505–26.

Metcalfe, Vernon. *The Life of Chief Seattle.* Seattle, 1970.

Rich, John M. *Chief Seattle's Unanswered Challenge.* Seattle, 1932.

WILFRED P. SCHOENBERG, S.J.

SEDELLA, ANTONIO DE (1748–1829)

Capuchin friar, pastor of St. Louis Cathedral in New Orleans, Louisiana. Sedella was the place in the Province of Granada, Spain, where he was born on November 18, 1748. In baptism he was Francisco Antonio Ildefonso Moreno y Arce. In the Capuchin Order he was Friar Antonio de Sedella, and later known as "Père Antoine."

A volunteer for the Louisiana Mission, he arrived in New Orleans in 1781. The auxiliary bishop and the governor cooperated in deporting him in 1790. Back in Spain the friar pursued his defense and produced a goodly number of favorable testimonial letters. The royal government eventually ordered that he be reinstated as pastor of St. Louis Church in New Orleans, which upon the creation of the bishopric in 1793 had become a cathedral.

A controversial figure, he has been accused by some historians (like John Gilmary Shea and Roger Baudier) of egocentric rebelliousness; he is said to have accepted election to the pastorate in a noisy mass meeting held in St. Louis Cathedral. Technically, Père Antoine always observed canon law and ecclesiastical procedures. He maintained to the end that he had been duly appointed to the pastorate by the bishop of the time.

Bred under the Spanish royal *patronato,* Friar Antonio (Père Antoine) thought of leaving Louisiana after the area was joined to the United States of America in the possession-changes of 1803. He remained at his post but did not lose his gratitude to the king of Spain. Suspicious American authorities obliged Père Antoine to take an oath of allegiance to the U.S.A. in 1806. Meanwhile, the trustees or *marguilliers* of New Orleans and their opponent, Fr. Patrick Walsh, engaged in controversy and legal skirmishes; but it was Walsh who took the initiative against Antonio, not the other way around. Walsh died in 1806, but during his life and after his death one could legitimately ask who was in charge of the Church in Louisiana and what canons were in force. In other words, there is something to be said in favor of Père Antoine.

The New Orleans in which Antonio de Sedella exercised his ministry was so tense that some thought of involving Emperor Napoleon because France, by the Louisiana Purchase document of 1803, was guarantor of religious rights in the region. Neither Washington nor Rome would have relished Napoleonic intervention.

Bishop Louis-Guillaume Dubourg, the Sulpician sent to Louisiana by John Carroll and by Rome, was puzzled over Friar Antonio (Père Antoine); actually, before turning against him, Dubourg thought of making the Capuchin his auxiliary bishop. So even the hostile Dubourg found something to be said in favor of Père Antoine.

Although Père Antoine may have been problematic for some of his contemporaries (and later historians), he remained a beloved pastor. When he died in New Orleans on January 22, 1829, his funeral was a triumphal procession; the Freemasons invited their members to take part in it.

Bruns, J. Edgar. "Annotating for Posterity: The Sacramental Records of Father Antonio de Sedella." *Cross, Crozier and Crucible, A Volume Celebrating the Bicentennial of a Catholic Diocese in Louisiana,* ed. Glenn R. Conrad. New Orleans and Lafayette, 1993.

———. "Sedella, Antonio de." *Dictionary of Louisiana Biography,* ed. Glenn R. Conrad. Lafayette, Louisiana, 1988, II: 726–27.

Melville, Annabelle M. *Louis William DuBourg.* 2 vols. Chicago, 1986, II. See index, under "Sedella."

O'Neill, Charles Edwards. "'A Quarter Marked by Sundry Peculiarities': New Orleans, Lay Trustees, and Père Antoine." *Catholic Historical Review* 76 (1990) 235–77.

CHARLES EDWARDS O'NEILL

SEELOS, FRANCIS XAVIER (1819–67)

Redemptorist priest. Seelos was born on January 11, 1819, in Füssen, Bavaria, and after grammar school in his hometown he attended St. Stephen's Academy in Augsburg and in 1839 entered the University of Munich. In 1842 he applied for admission to the Redemptorists (Congregation of the Most Holy Redeemer) and expressed his desire to work as a missionary among German-speaking immigrants in the United States. He arrived in New York City in April 1843 and began his noviceship at the Redemptorist parish of St. James in Baltimore. He was ordained to the priesthood in December 1844.

In August 1845 Seelos was assigned to St. Philomena's parish in Pittsburgh, where (St.) John Neumann was pastor. In 1851 he became pastor of the parish and three years later (March 1854) was transferred to Baltimore as pastor of the downtown St. Alphonsus Church and as superior of the Redemptorist community. In 1857 he was appointed pastor of SS Peter and Paul in Cumberland (Maryland) and was, at the same time, superior of the community, director of the Redemptorist students, and seminary professor. Because of the Civil War and the threat that Cumberland might become a battlefield, the seminary and seminarians moved in May 1862 to Annapolis. Though no longer director of students, Seelos was again pastor and continued as professor. He likewise ministered to the soldiers and prisoners of war in the Annapolis area.

In August 1863 he was appointed head of the Redemptorist Mission Band and for the next two years gave parish missions in more than a dozen states, as far west as Illinois and Missouri. In autumn 1865 he was subsequently assigned to Holy Redeemer parish in Detroit and after ten months was reassigned to St. Mary's parish in New Orleans, where he ministered to the English-, German-, and French-speaking inhabitants. When New Orleans was struck by a yellow fever epidemic in September 1867, he worked tirelessly among the sick and on September 17 he himself became its victim. He died on October 4, 1867. He was popular as a preacher, confessor, and spiritual guide. In 1860 Bishop Michael O'Connor of Pittsburgh wanted him named as his successor, but Seelos wrote to Pope Pius IX asking not to be appointed. The cause for his beatification has been introduced in Rome.

See also REDEMPTORISTS (C.SS.R.).

Artz, Thomas, C.Ss.R. "Redemptorist Preacher and Healer: Father Francis Xavier Seelos, C.Ss.R. (1819–1867)." *Portraits in American Sanctity,* ed. Joseph N. Tylenda. Chicago: Franciscan Herald, 1982, 168–78.

Cicognani, Amleto. "Francis Xavier Seelos, C.Ss.R., Redemptorist Preacher and Missionary." *Sanctity in America.* Paterson: St. Anthony Guild, 1945, 93–96.

Curley, Michael Joseph. *Cheerful Ascetic: The Life of Francis Xavier Seelos, C.Ss.R.* New Orleans: Redemptorist Fathers, 1969.

Elworthy, Joseph. "Father Seelos, Holy Man of New Orleans." *Ligourian* 70 (October 1982) 49–53.

JOSEPH TYLENDA, S.J.

SEGHERS, CHARLES JOHN (1839–86)

Archbishop. Charles John Seghers, sometimes called "the Apostle of Alaska," was one of many zealous missionaries in the Pacific Northwest. The fifth and last child of Paulina and Charles Francis Seghers, he was born in Ghent, Belgium, on December 26, 1839. His father and four siblings died of tuberculosis before his nineteenth birthday, and two years later his mother succumbed to the same disease, leaving him, at the age of twenty, with no member of his immediate family. He, too, was infected with tuberculosis. For the rest of his life he struggled for survival.

After completing his studies for the priesthood, he was ordained in Ghent in 1863. He volunteered for the North American Mission and was accepted by Bishop Modeste Demers of the Diocese of Vancouver Island in present-day British Columbia. He soon left Belgium, then arrived at Victoria by ship in November of the same year.

In Victoria his talents and zeal were quickly recognized. He was assigned to pastoral work in the city but was, in effect, the bishop's assistant in charge of the diocese during the bishop's many absences for raising funds or for caring for his fragile health. When Demers traveled to Rome for the First Vatican Council in 1869, he took Seghers with him. Both returned to Victoria in worse condition than when they had departed. Demers soon died, in 1871, after designating Seghers as temporary administrator of the diocese. Two years later, Seghers was appointed as his successor. He was consecrated as the second bishop of Vancouver Island on June 29, 1873. He was thirty-two years old, the youngest bishop in North America. A month later, he left for the wilderness of Alaska, which was part of his diocese. From this time on, his pastoral priority was Alaska.

Meanwhile, aging Archbishop Francis Blanchet of Oregon City (which is now called Portland in Oregon) requested Pope Leo XIII for a coadjutor. On July 18, 1878, Seghers was appointed with the title of titular bishop of Cana and coadjutor bishop of Oregon City. When Blanchet resigned on December 18, 1880, Seghers succeeded him as archbishop.

Seghers knew the archdiocese well. While coadjutor, he had traveled throughout Montana and Idaho Territories and eastern Oregon, all subject at this time to Oregon City. Now he concentrated on western Oregon, establishing parishes, promoting the beginnings of parochial schools, and preaching constantly on the need for good Christian lives. He brought in the Benedictines and helped them establish Mount Angel Abbey. He published pastoral letters and summoned Oregon's first synod. Alaska, however, was his first love, and when the see of Vancouver Island became vacant again after the departure of Bishop John Baptist Brondel for Helena in Montana Territory, he appealed to Rome to be assigned to it. In a personal audience with Leo XIII, he stated his reasons for wishing to resign as archbishop of Oregon City. The Pope, greatly edified, yielded to his request. Two days later, on March 9, 1884, he was formally appointed to his former Diocese of Vancouver Island with the title and privileges of an archbishop.

In July 1886, with two Jesuit priests, Paschal Tosi and Aloysius Robaut, and Francis Fuller, a layman, he left Victoria for his fifth tour of Alaska. Traveling via Skagway and the Chilkoot Pass, he and his companions entered the Yukon drainage. Directing the Jesuits to remain in its upper region until spring, he left with Fuller for a village called Nulato, far down the river. They traveled first by boat then by dog sled. In late November, some few miles from their goal, they stopped for the night in a primitive hut. Fuller had become increasingly erratic. Early the next morning, November 28, 1886, he awakened the archbishop, then killed him with the victim's rifle.

In the spring, the Jesuits arranged to move his body to St. Michael's on the coast. Later it was taken to Victoria and was placed in a tomb beneath the altar of St. Andrew's Cathedral, where it has been venerated by the faithful ever since.

DeBaets, l'Abbé Maurice. *Mgr. Seghers, L'Apôtre De Alaska.* Gand-Paris, 1896. Engl. trans. Mary Mildred, S.S.A., *The Apostle of Alaska: Life of the Most Reverend Charles John Seghers.* Patterson, New Jersey, 1943.

Steckler, Gerard G., S.J. *Charles John Seghers Priest and Bishop in the Pacific Northwest 1839–1866: A Biography.* Fairfield, Washington, n.d.

WILFRED P. SCHOENBERG, S.J.

SELTICE, ANDREW (? –1902)

Native American leader. Andrew Seltice served as administrative chief of the Coeur d'Alene Native American tribe in northern Idaho from the closing of hostilities against the U.S. government in 1858 until his death in 1902. For forty years he led his people's growth from a little-known group of Interior Salish natives to a prosperous and well-educated tribe by the opening of the twentieth century.

Missionary Peter De Smet, S.J., had founded Sacred Heart Mission among the Coeur d'Alenes in 1842. The tribe quickly converted to Christianity and by 1850 had built a magnificent mission church, still the oldest standing building in Idaho. But overwhelmed by immigrants and miners, the mission relocated southeast of Lake Coeur d'Alene in 1878. There the tribe and their missionaries built a new mission church, boarding schools for both boys and girls, mission camp houses, and extensive farming homesteads in their valleys of rich palouse soil.

It was Seltice's responsibility to reorganize the diverse family-based aboriginal villages into a centralized community that would become a modern Native American tribe. He led the Coeur d'Alenes to federal recognition with a final treaty agreement in 1889, developed a law and order program for his people, promoted the boys' and girls' boarding schools, and worked closely with the missionaries to help his people become a wealthy reservation community.

See also NATIVE AMERICANS AND THE CATHOLIC CHURCH.

Burns, Robert I., S.J. *Jesuits and the Indian Wars.* New Haven, Conn.: Yale University Press, 1966.

Seltice, Joseph. *Saga of the Coeur d'Alene Indians.* Eds. E. Kowrach and T. Connolly. Fairfield, Wash.: Ye Galleon Press, 1990.

THOMAS CONNOLLY, S.J.

SEMINARIES (DIOCESAN)

Origins

The Council of Trent (1545–63) addressed a needed reform of diocesan priests with the decree *Cum Adolescentium Aetas* (1563), the Church's first general legislation related to their training. The decree enjoins each bishop to sponsor a *seminarium* (seed bed) or seminary at his official church, the cathedral, to prepare poor youth as priests of his diocese. Without providing a detailed program of studies, the decree expects the youth to receive moral training, general education, and instruction in the tasks of ministry. The bishop was to address the organization, content, and length of seminary studies. The decree, then, gives primacy to local diocesan needs and resources in formulating a program. Seminary formation is not required as a condition for ordination thereby allowing affluent priesthood candidates recourse to theological studies at universities. The training of priests belonging to religious orders is not addressed. Despite its limitations, the decree signaled an end to informal practices of preparation for ordination and implanted the ideal that the priesthood requires formal training.

The Council of Trent did not articulate a model of priesthood as a basis of clerical formation. In filling this void, the seventeenth-century French School of Spirituality, associated with Pierre de Bérulle, Charles de Condren, Vincent de Paul, and Jean Jacques Olier, developed a spirituality for ministry stressing self-denial and daily mental prayer on aspects of Christ's life. By thus conforming to Christ, the seminarian prepared for the priest's role of imparting grace through the ministry of sacraments. For the training of seminarians, the French School produced clerical communities such as Olier's company of diocesan priests, the Society of St. Sulpice (Sulpicians), formed in 1641, and Vincent de Paul's Congregation of the Mission (Vincentians), founded in 1625, that was also active in evangelization. These major communities, based in Paris, along with smaller ones, conducted seminaries for French dioceses as did local diocesan clergy. While furnishing the model of shared responsibility of bishop and a clerical community in conducting seminaries, the French School's legacy for the entire Church is the primacy assigned to spiritual formation in preparing for priesthood.

Seminaries through the Nineteenth Century

In 1791 Sulpicians started the first diocesan seminary in the United States, later known as St. Mary's Seminary, at Baltimore, the seat of the country's first diocese. Its opening began the adaptation of Trent's ideals of clerical formation to the American Catholic community. An initial change related to the seminary's organizational form by adding lay education. Because seminarians were few, the Sulpicians opened an affiliated lay college in 1805 to secure tuition revenue for the seminary's support. Sulpicians initially sponsored Mt. St. Mary's College at Emmitsburg, Maryland (1808), as a minor seminary to prepare boys educated in the classics for theological studies at their Baltimore seminary, but it too was constrained to enroll boys who did not aspire to the priesthood and to add theological instruction for older seminarians who served as part-time teachers.

As new dioceses were formed across the country up to the 1850s, most bishops attempted seminaries and tried various institutional models as funds permitted by training seminarians in the bishop's residence, at the cathedral, or attached to a school for lay students. Seminarians often served as part-time teachers while studying theology. Most of these efforts failed because of insufficient funds, lack of seminarians, or lack of trained faculty.

After midcentury, Trent's ideal of each diocese having its own seminary gave way to the more realistic approach of larger dioceses with financial resources developing seminaries that enrolled students from several dioceses. This new type of seminary is today called 'freestanding,' that is, devoted exclusively to clerical formation without an affiliated enterprise needed for financial support. An early example of this trend, St. Charles Borromeo Seminary, had modest beginnings in downtown Philadelphia in 1838 before moving to a magnificent suburban campus in 1871. Other freestanding seminaries started on substantial campuses that separated their resident communities from urban life such as: Mt. St. Mary's Seminary of the West, Cincinnati (1851); St. Francis de Sales Seminary, Milwaukee (1856); and St. Joseph's Seminary, Troy, New York (1864–96). The Sulpicians' St. Mary's Seminary at Baltimore discontinued its lay college in 1855 to become freestanding. By contrast, the Newark diocese's Immaculate Conception Seminary (1861) with Seton Hall College, South Orange, New Jersey, exemplified the joining of lay and clerical education.

Religious orders also trained seminarians of local dioceses such as the Order of St. Benedict's seminaries at monasteries now known as St. Vincent Archabbey, Latrobe, Pennsylvania (1846); St. John's Abbey, Collegeville, Minnesota (1857); St. Meinrad Archabbey, Indiana (1854); and Mt. Angel Abbey, Oregon (1889). In 1818 Vincentians arrived at Perryville, Missouri, to open St. Mary's Seminary for the local diocese and soon started an affiliated lay college. They conducted seminaries linked to lay colleges at Cape Girardeau, Missouri (1859–94), and Niagara, New York (1863–1961). Franciscans joined a diocesan seminary to lay education at St. Bonaventure College, Allegany, New York (1859).

Priestly ministry for the country's burgeoning immigrant Catholic community influenced the content and length of seminary studies. With the ideal that the priest required just enough learning to administer sacraments, philosophical and theological studies varied as weaker seminaries offered a year or two, while freestanding seminaries provided four years by the 1870s. This brisk pace of learning was based on studying short topical treatises or 'tracts' as found in dogmatic and moral theology 'manuals.' Other subjects were either abbreviated or not offered.

To improve seminary learning, the American bishops framed decrees at their Third Plenary Council of Baltimore in 1884 to expand the curriculum for the six-year minor seminary (high school and junior college) and the six-year major seminary (philosophy and theological studies) with the latter to give more attention to biblical studies, Church history, and homiletics.

The council's higher standards were well timed for the opening of new major seminaries serving dioceses in their region. Sulpicians conducted Boston's St. John's Seminary, Brighton, Massachusetts (1884) and New York's St. Joseph's Seminary (Dunwoodie) at Yonkers (1896) until the early twentieth century when local diocesan priests replaced them. The Sulpicians also opened San Francisco's St. Patrick's Seminary at Menlo Park, California (1898). Vincentians staffed Kenrick Seminary, St. Louis, Missouri (1894). Diocesan priests conducted St. Paul Seminary, St. Paul, Minnesota (1894), and St. Bernard Seminary, Rochester, New York (1893–1981), as well as SS Cyril and Methodius Seminary for Poles in Detroit (1855) and the Pontifical College Josephinum for Germans in Columbus, Ohio (1892).

The Baltimore Council's attention to clerical learning stimulated a general discussion about the seminary and the American priest. Seminary founders, Archbishop John Ireland and Bishop Bernard McQuaid, advocated a liberally educated, theologically well-trained clergy capable of articulating Catholic beliefs in a pluralistic society. Sulpician John B. Hogan explained in *Clerical Studies* (1898) how each subject in the modern seminary curriculum should be taught. Reacting to outdated seminary ways, John Talbot Smith, a New York priest, proposed in *Our Seminaries: An Essay in Clerical Training* (1896) that the seminary aim to produce a priest who was an educated gentleman fitted for public life, physically sound, in sympathy with his environment, and imbued with the true missionary spirit. These views stimulated the writing of updated seminary textbooks and new pastoral theology literature by the 1890s.

This sustained discussion of clerical standards and learning diminished in the early twentieth century as the Holy See imposed greater control on Catholic thought. For ecclesiastical learning, Pope Pius X issued the condemnation of theological Modernism in 1907 and required seminary faculties to take an oath against Modernism in 1910. Though the presence of Modernism in American seminaries was unlikely, the new climate discouraged scholarship in theological and biblical studies among seminary faculties and the discussion of new standards of priestly ministry.

The Code of Canon Law and Its Age

The trend toward greater Roman direction and uniform practices in the entire Catholic Church culminated in the implementation of the Code of Canon Law in 1918. In its canons, the Code provided the Church for the first time with a blueprint for the internal organization of the diocesan seminary by naming its officers, listing courses, and setting the length of studies at six years each for minor and major seminaries. Seminary formation was made a prerequisite for ordination. Subsequently, the Holy See, through the Sacred Congregation of Seminaries and Universities, established in 1915, issued decrees on seminary life and learning based on the Code. In 1924 the congregation mandated that bishops submit triennial reports on their seminaries to demonstrate compliance to its canons. Thus, Trent's principle of the bishop as responsible for his diocesan seminary was transformed to make him the local agent of Roman authority.

Until the 1960s, the diocesan major seminary network grew as more institutions opened across the country. Sulpician activity expanded with the opening of: Sulpician Seminary, Washington, D.C., now Theological College (1919); Seattle's St. Edward (later St. Thomas) Seminary, Kenmore, Washington (1931–80); and the Michigan dioceses' St. John's Seminary, Plymouth, Michigan (1949–88), that they relinquished in 1970. Vincentians staffed: St. Thomas Seminary, Denver (1907–95); the Los Angeles archdiocese's St. John's Seminary, Camarillo, California (1940); and the Miami archdiocese's St. Vincent de Paul Regional Seminary, Boynton Beach, Florida (1965), relinquishing the latter in 1970. Diocesan clergy staffed San Antonio's St. John's (later Assumption) Seminary (1919), though Vincentians directed it from 1941 to 1967, and St. Mary's Seminary, Houston (1911), which Vincentians operated from 1951 to 1982. Jesuits and diocesan priests shared staffing of the Chicago archdiocese's St. Mary of the Lake Seminary, Mundelein, Illinois (1921), with the Jesuit presence diminishing by the 1970s. Notre Dame Seminary, New Orleans (1923), opened under the Society of Mary's direction. Diocesan priests conducted St. Mary's Seminary, Cleveland (1924), St. John's Home Missions Seminary, Little Rock, Arkansas (1911–67), and the Brooklyn diocese's Immaculate Conception Seminary, Huntington, New York (1930). Through the era several older major seminaries either expanded or relocated to new facilities. Though minor seminaries were attached to many major seminaries, some thirty-two dioceses lacking the latter opened freestanding minor seminaries.

From 1904 seminary educators shared ideas on clerical formation and studies at annual meetings of the National Catholic Educational Association. By the 1950s, they addressed concerns about the quality of the burgeoning minor seminary network, the need to improve standards, and to end the seminary's isolation from modern educational practices. Though Church authority was generally not involved in these issues, seminary educators themselves began to pursue administrative reforms and improve academic standards in their institutions that during the 1960s began to obtain accreditation with resulting recognition of their credits and degrees.

The Era of Vatican Council II

Vatican Council II (1962–65) set the course for a general reform of the diocesan seminary. The council's Decree on Priestly Formation, *Optatam Totius* (1965), directed each nation's bishops to devise a seminary program suitable for their country. The Congregation for Catholic Education (formerly Congregation of Seminaries and Universities) then formulated a *Basic Plan* (or *Ratio Fundamentalis*) for conducting seminaries. Based on this document and their Committee on Priestly Formation's consultations with seminary educators, the American bishops issued in 1971 the *Program of Priestly Formation* (PPF) to guide the country's diocesan and religious order seminaries at high school, college, and theology levels. The PPF outlined academic and administrative reforms that brought the seminary into conformity with modern educational practices. It introduced pastoral field education and ecumenical activities to seminary formation.

The PPF encouraged seminaries to discontinue the inherited plan of six-year minor and major seminary programs and to adopt the American standard of four years each for high school, college, and theology levels. As the college seminaries achieved accreditation with regional accrediting associations, the schools of theology obtained membership with the Association of Theological Schools, the major accrediting body for seminaries and divinity schools in North America. Accordingly, academic credits and degrees of accredited Catholic seminaries are recognized by other member institutions.

Through the 1970s and 1980s, as seminary learning responded to the renewal of Catholic theology, the bishops' Committee on Priestly Formation continued its responsibility for seminaries by issuing documents on spiritual formation, pastoral formation, and vocations personnel. In addition to sponsoring seminary evaluations, the conference updated the PPF in 1976 and 1981. Likewise, the Congregation for Catholic Education continued its oversight of all seminaries by issuing substantial documents on teaching philosophy, theology, canon law, liturgy, social communications, and other subjects.

The volume of seminary activities changed markedly in the wake of cultural changes during the post-Vatican II era. Enrollment of 26,762 diocesan seminarians at all levels among 48,992 diocesan and religious-order seminarians crested in 1965, then began falling. The decline produced a wave of seminary closings, mostly of high school and college programs and religious order seminaries that joined theological unions. Diocesan students at the theology level numbering 4,761 in 1966–67, declined to 2,069 by 1994–95. Despite the trend of closings, some thirty historic diocesan seminaries, now often referred to as 'theologates,' remain open.

In 1981, amidst these changes, Pope John Paul II mandated an apostolic visitation of all American seminaries. This process required each seminary to submit requested information, then to receive an examination team's visit. On-site visitations involved five-member teams drawn from a pool of 128 bishops, religious order representatives, and seminary educators. In 1986, following the team evaluations, Cardinal William Baum, Prefect of the Congregation for Catholic Education, issued a general evaluation of the country's freestanding theologates, then numbering thirty-eight, most of which trained diocesan clergy. He found them satisfactory. Some were excellent, and a few had selected deficiencies requiring correction. His major concern was the need to clarify the concept of ordained priesthood, especially at seminaries enrolling lay students preparing for ministerial positions.

After receiving the visitation's evaluations of freestanding seminaries, the religious orders' theological unions, and college seminary programs, the Committee on Priestly Formation drew additional ideas from the 1990 International Synod of Bishops and Pope John Paul II's apostolic exhortation, *Pastores Dabo Vobis* (1990), to formulate the PPF's fourth edition. Approved by the Congregation for Catholic Education in 1992, the latest PPF presently directs the ongoing renewal of all American Catholic seminaries.

See also SEMINARIES IN AMERICA.

Kauffman, Christopher J. *Tradition and Transformation in Catholic Culture: The Priests of Saint Sulpice in the United States from 1791 to the Present.* New York: Macmillan, 1988.

National Conference of Catholic Bishops. *Program of Priestly Formation.* 4th ed. Washington, 1993.

O'Donohoe, James A. *Tridentine Seminary Legislation: Its Sources and Its Formation.* Louvain, 1957.

Schuth, Katarina. *Reason for the Hope: The Futures of Roman Catholic Theologates.* Wilmington, Del.: Michael Glazier, 1989.

Shelley, Thomas J. *Dunwoodie: The History of St. Joseph's Seminary, Yonkers, New York.* Westminster, Md.: Christian Classics, 1993.

White, Joseph M. *The Diocesan Seminary in the United States: A History from the 1780s to the Present.* University of Notre Dame Press, 1989.

JOSEPH M. WHITE

SEMINARIES IN AMERICA

(Sources: Almanac survey; *Official Catholic Directory;* Catholic News Service.)

Information, according to states, includes names of archdioceses and dioceses, and names and addresses of seminaries. Types of seminaries, when not clear from titles, are indicated in most cases. Interdiocesan seminaries are generally conducted by religious orders for candidates for the priesthood from several dioceses. The list does not include houses of study reserved for members of religious communities. Archdioceses are indicated by an asterisk.

California: Los Angeles*—St. John's Seminary (major), 5012 Seminary Rd., Camarillo 93012; St. John's Seminary College, 5118 Seminary Rd., Camarillo 93012.

San Diego—St. Francis Seminary (college and pre-theology formation program), 1667 Santa Paula Dr., San Diego 92111.

San Francisco*—St. Patrick's Seminary (major), 320 Middlefield Rd., Menlo Park 94025.

Connecticut: Hartford*—St. Thomas Seminary (college formation program), 467 Bloomfield Ave., Bloomfield 06002.

Norwich—Holy Apostles College and Seminary (adult vocations; minor and major), 33 Prospect Hill Rd., Cromwell 06416.

Stamford Byzantine Rite—Ukrainian Catholic Seminary: St. Basil College Seminary (minor), 195 Glenbrook Rd., Stamford 06902.

District of Columbia: Washington*—Theological College (national, major), The Catholic University of America, 401 Michigan Ave., N.E. 20017.

St. Josaphat's Seminary, 201 Taylor St. N.E., Washington 20017. (Major house of formation serving the four Ukrainian Byzantine-rite dioceses in the U.S.)

Florida: Miami*—St. John Vianney College Seminary, 2900 S.W. 87th Ave., Miami 33165.

Palm Beach—St. Vincent de Paul Regional Seminary (major), 10701 S. Military Trail, Boynton Beach 33436.

Illinois: Chicago*—Archbishop Quigley Preparatory Seminary (high school), 103 East Chestnut St., Chicago 60611; St. Joseph Seminary (college), 6551 N. Sheridan Rd., Chicago 60626. Mundelein Seminary, University of St. Mary of the Lake, 1000 E. Maple Ave., Mundelein 60060.

Indiana: Indianapolis*—St. Meinrad Seminary, College and School of Theology (interdiocesan), St. Meinrad 47577.

Iowa: Davenport—St. Ambrose University Seminary, 518 W. Locust St., Davenport 52803.

Dubuque*—Seminary of St. Pius X (interdiocesan), Loras College, Dubuque 52001.

Louisiana: New Orleans*—Notre Dame Seminary Graduate School of Theology, 2901 S. Carrollton Ave., New Orleans 70118; St. Joseph Seminary College (interdiocesan), St. Benedict 70457.

Maryland: Baltimore*—St. Mary's Seminary and University, 5400 Roland Ave., Baltimore 21210; Mt. St. Mary's Seminary, Emmitsburg 21727.

Massachusetts: Boston*—St. John's Seminary School of Theology, 127 Lake St., Brighton 02135; St. John's Seminary, College of Liberal Arts, 197 Foster St., Brighton 02135; Pope John XXIII National Seminary (for ages 30–60), 558 South Ave., Weston 02193.

Newton—Melkite Greek Catholic—St. Gregory the Theologian Seminary, 233 Grant Ave., Newton 02159.

Michigan: Detroit*—Sacred Heart Major Seminary (college/theologate and institute for ministry), 2701 Chicago Blvd., Detroit 48206; Sts. Cyril and Methodius Seminary, St. Mary's College (theologate and college) independent, primarily serving Polish-American community, 3535 Indian Trail, Orchard Lake 48324.

Grand Rapids—Christopher House, 723 Rosewood Ave., S.E., East Gland Rapids 49506.

Minnesota: St. John's School of Theology and Seminary, St. John's University, P.O. Box 7288, Collegeville 56321.

St. Paul and Minneapolis*—St. Paul Seminary School of Divinity of the University of St. Thomas, 2260 Summit Ave., St. Paul 55105; St. John Vianney Seminary (college residence), 2115 Summit Ave., St. Paul 55105.

Winona—Immaculate Heart of Mary Seminary, St. Mary's College, No. 43, 700 Terrace Heights, Winona 55987.

Missouri: Jefferson City—St. Thomas Aquinas Preparatory Seminary (High School Seminary), 245 N. Levering Ave., P.O. Box 858, Hannibal 63401.

St. Louis*—St. Louis Roman Catholic Theological Seminary, Kenrick School of Theology, 5200 Glennon Dr., St. Louis 63119; Cardinal Glennon College (major seminary), 5200 Glennon Dr., St. Louis 63119.

Montana: Helena—Pre-Seminary Program, Carroll College, Helena 59625.

New Jersey: Newark*—Immaculate Conception Seminary—college seminary; major seminary; graduate school—Seton Hall University, 400 South Orange Ave., South Orange 07079.

New Mexico: Santa Fe*—Immaculate Heart of Mary Seminary (college level), Mt. Carmel Rd., Santa Fe 87501.

New York: Brooklyn—Cathedral Seminary Residence of the Immaculate Conception (college and pre-theology), 7200 Douglaston Parkway, Douglaston 11362; Cathedral Preparatory Seminary, 56–25 92nd St., Elmhurst 11373.

Buffalo—Christ the King Seminary (interdiocesan theologate), P.O. Box 607, 711 Knox Rd., East Aurora, 14052.

New York*—St. Joseph's Seminary (major), 201 Seminary Ave., Dunwoodie, Yonkers 10704; St. John Neumann Residence (college and pre-theology), 5655 Arlington Ave., Riverdale 10471. Cathedral Preparatory Seminary, 946 Boston Post Rd., Rye 10580.

Ogdensburg—Wadhams Hall Seminary College (interdiocesan), 6866 State Hwy. 37, Ogdensburg 13669.

Rockville Centre—Seminary of the Immaculate Conception (major), Lloyd Harbor, Huntington, L.I. 11743.

St. Maron Eparchy, Brooklyn—Our Lady of Lebanon Maronite Seminary, 7164 Alaska Ave. N.W., Washington, D.C. 20012.

North Dakota: Fargo—Cardinal Muench Seminary (interdiocesan high school, college and pre-theology), 100 35th Ave. N.E., Fargo 58102.

Ohio: Cincinnati*—Mt. St. Mary's Seminary of the West, 6616 Beechmont Ave., Cincinnati 45230 (division of the Athenaeum of Ohio).

Cleveland—St. Mary Seminary (graduate school of theology), 28700 Euclid Ave., Wickliffe 44092.

Columbus—Pontifical College Josephinum (national), theologate and college, Columbus 43235.

Oregon: Portland*—Mt. Angel Seminary (interdiocesan, college, pre-theology program, graduate school of theology), St. Benedict 97373.

Pennsylvania: Erie—St. Mark Seminary, P.O. Box 10397, Erie 16514.

Greensburg—St. Vincent Seminary (interdiocesan; pre-theology program; graduate program in theology; religious education), 300 Fraser Purchase Rd., Latrobe 15650.

Philadelphia*—Theological Seminary of St. Charles Borromeo, One Thousand East Wynnewood Rd., Overbrook 19096. (College, pre-theology program, theologate.)

Pittsburgh* (Byzantine-Ruthenian Rite)—Byzantine Catholic Seminary of Sts. Cyril and Methodius (college, pre-theology program, theologate), 3605 Perrysville Ave., Pittsburgh 15214.

Pittsburgh—St. Paul Seminary (interdiocesan, college and pre-theology), 2900 Noblestown Rd., Pittsburgh 15205.

Scranton—St. Pius X Seminary (college and pre-theology formation; interdiocesan), Dalton 18414. Affiliated with the University of Scranton.

Rhode Island: Providence—Seminary of Our Lady of Providence (House of Formation; college students and pre-theology), 485 Mount Pleasant Ave., Providence 02908.

Texas: Dallas—Holy Trinity Seminary (college and pre-theology; English proficiency and academic foundation programs), P.O. Box 140309, Irving 75014.

El Paso—St. Charles Seminary College, P.O. Box 17548, El Paso 79917.

Galveston-Houston—St. Mary's Seminary (theologate), 9845 Memorial Dr., Houston 77024.

San Antonio*—The Assumption-St. John Seminary (theologate and pre-theology, Hispanic ministry emphasis), 2600 W. Woodlawn Ave., San Antonio 78228.

Washington: Spokane—Bishop White Seminary. College Formation Program, E. 429 Sharp Ave., Spokane 99202.

Wisconsin: Milwaukee*—St. Francis Seminary, 3257 S. Lake Dr., St. Francis 53235; College Program, East Hall, 915 W. Wisconsin Ave., Milwaukee 53233. Sacred Heart School of Theology (interdiocesan seminary for second career vocations), P.O. Box 429, Hales Corners, Wis. 53130.

SERRA, JUNÍPERO (1713–84)

Franciscan friar, missionary, and founder of the California missions. Serra was the son of Antonio Nadal Serra and Margarita Rosa Ferrer, and was born at Petra, Majorca, Spain, November 24, 1713. That same day he was baptized at St. Peter's Church and given the name Miguel

Junípero Serra

José. He was confirmed at the age of two by the bishop of Palma. He received his primary education at a school conducted by the Franciscans at the friary of San Bernardino. When he was fifteen, he was placed in the charge of the canons of the cathedral in Palma and began to assist in philosophy classes held in the Franciscan San Francisco monastery. Thus his early life was deeply influenced by the Franciscans who were his teachers.

Young Friar

On September 14, 1730, at the age of sixteen, he was admitted as a novice at the Convento de Jesus located near Palma and made his profession the following year on September 15. On the occasion of his profession, he chose the name, Junípero, in memory of St. Francis of Assisi's brother companion.

The young friar studied philosophy from 1731 to 1734, followed by four years of theology at the Convento de San Francisco. Unfortunately, the date of his ordination to the priesthood is not known, but his biographer, Maynard J. Geiger, O.F.M., suggests that "it probably occurred during the Ember Days of December 1738." Prior to his ordination, Serra took the competitive examinations for his province's lectorate of philosophy and received the title.

The year following his ordination he served as friary librarian, but beginning in the fall of 1740 he taught philosophy at San Francisco for the ensuing three years. In the meantime, he earned his doctorate in theology in 1742 from Lullian University in Palma and was called to the Scotistic chair of theology at the university in January 1744. There he established a reputation as an excellent teacher and became a highly sought-after preacher, renowned for his pulpit style and religious zeal. But his local fame could not quench his burning desire to become a missionary. That wish was granted in early 1749.

Missionary in America

On April 13, accompanied by his former pupil, Francisco Palóu, who would later write the first biography of Serra, the companions sailed from Palma to America by way of Málaga and Cádiz. After a perilous voyage, Vera Cruz, Mexico, was reached on December 7, 1749. Refusing the horses provided to the new missionary, Serra and an unnamed companion walked the 250 miles to reach Mexico City and arrived at San Fernando College on January 1, 1750.

Six months later a call for volunteers to administer to the Sierra Gorda missions was answered by Serra and Palóu. Together they walked the 175 miles to Jalpan, the principal mission station which served the Pame natives. For the ensuing eight years Serra labored to enhance and enlarge the missions under his care, mastering the Otomí language so as to effectively reach the Pames. Not only did the Sierra Gordo missions prosper, but Serra also became a champion of native rights against obstinate white abuse.

In September 1758, he was summoned to San Fernando College in anticipation of being transferred to the San Sabá missions in Texas which had suffered from violent attacks from the indigenous peoples, but for a variety of reasons that posting never came about. Instead, he remained at the college until 1767 where he held a number of responsibilities, among them choir director, master of novices, college counselor, and a confessor within and without the college, as well as a commissioner of the Holy Office of the Inquisition, which dated back to 1752 when he was first appointed to that post.

As a home missionary Serra was immensely active in preaching missions in numerous areas of central Mexico, ranging from Oaxaca in the south to Valles in the north. That wide field experience was recognized when in 1767 he was appointed to the presidency of the ex-Jesuit missions in Baja California that were placed in the hands of the Franciscans after the Jesuit expulsion from Spanish dominions. Serra took up his new post at Loreto on April 1, 1768. It proved to be a short-lived appointment.

The California Missions

Acting on the orders of José de Gálvez, visitor general to New Spain (Mexico), the exploration and settlement of Alta California was to be implemented. Serra volunteered to undertake the evangelization of the new territory even though not in the best of health. Gálvez readily accepted. Thus the Franciscans were granted Alta California as their new mission field.

Serra set out on March 27, 1769, from Loreto to join the expedition led by Captain Gaspar de Portolá and arrived at San Diego on July 1. En route, Serra established his first mission at San Fernando de Velicatá on May 14, 1769. However, the overland journey proved arduous on Serra for he suffered from varicose ulcers in his legs which caused him acute pain. But he was not to be deterred by infirmities in his quest for native converts.

In the ensuing fifteen years of his life, Serra labored without surcease in his Alta California apostolate. He founded nine missions: San Diego, July 16, 1769; San Carlos at Monterey, June 3, 1770; San Antonio, July 14, 1771; San Gabriel, September 8, 1771; San Louis Obispo, September 1, 1772; San Francisco, October 12, 1777; San Juan Capistrano, November 1, 1776; Santa Clara, January 12, 1777, and San Buenaventura, March 31, 1782. At the same time, the founding of the first civilian settlements at San Jose, November 29, 1777, and Los Angeles, September 4, 1781, were effected.

During his apostolate, Serra traveled extensively in Alta California administering to the native peoples and his fellow Franciscans. His travels included a major trip to Mexico City to plead for the rights of the neophytes under his care as president of California's Franciscan Mission. This trip resulted in the famed *Regulamento* of 1773 that provided for the governance of the new province issued by Viceroy Bucareli. Although plagued by his varicose ulcers, compounded by recurring asthmatic attacks, Serra labored tirelessly in his efforts to bring Christianity to California's native people.

By the time of his death at Mission San Carlos, August 28, 1784, the nine California missions he had founded reported a total of 6,736 baptisms and 4,646 Christian Native Americans living at the missions. Maynard Geiger, his biographer, declared of Serra: "He remained a model religious despite his distractions and activity—a man of prayer and mortification. He had a consuming love for the Indians and ever defended them. . . . Considered a man of saintly qualities during his life by [his co-missionaries] . . . he has been thought so unbrokenly since his death."

His cause for beatification was introduced in the Diocese of Monterey-Fresno (now Monterey) in 1934 and was completed in 1949. The Sacred Congregation of Rites declared Serra Venerable on February 15, 1985. He was beatified by Pope John Paul II on September 25, 1988.

See also CALIFORNIA, CATHOLIC CHURCH IN; FRANCISCAN FRIARS.

Geiger, Maynard J., O.F.M., ed. and trans. *Palóu's Life of Junípero Serra.* Washington, D.C.: Academy of American Franciscan History, 1955.

_____. *The Life and Times of Fray Junípero Serra, O.F.M., or the Man Who Never Turned Back.* 2 vols. Washington, D.C.: Academy of American Franciscan History, 1959.

Tibesar, Antonine, O.F.M., ed. and trans. *Writings of Junípero Serra.* 4 vols. Washington, D.C.: Academy of American Franciscan History, 1945–65.

DOYCE B. NUNIS, JR.

Related Document

JUNÍPERO SERRA MAKES HIS FINAL REPORT ON THE MISSION OF SAN CARLOS DE MONTEREY, JULY 1, 1784

We previously met Junípero Serra as a young man of thirty-six on the eve of his departure for the New World in August, 1749 (No. 13). In the document that follows we find him signing his final missionary report. In the thirty-five years that had intervened this intrepid missionary had traveled thousands of miles on foot, founded nine of California's twenty-one missions, and brought hundreds of pagan Indians into the Catholic Church. This report on San Carlos de Monterey is one of the best factual surveys we possess of his efforts, illustrating as it does, the number of Indians who were made Christians with a description of the religious practices of the neophytes, the daily life as lived by the friars and Indians at the missions, and the hardships endured from the elements and from enemies. Eight weeks after

the document was signed the great missionary, worn out by his unremitting and exhaustive labor in behalf of the Indians of Mexico and of Lower and Upper California, died on August 28, 1784, at his beloved San Carlos de Monterey where his remains lie buried beneath the sanctuary floor of the mission church.

(*Source*: Manuscript in the possession of the Academy of American Franciscan History.)

Hail Jesus, Mary, Joseph!

ON THE MOST SOLEMN FEAST OF THE HOLY SPIRIT, PENTEcost Sunday, June 3, 1770, this mission of San Carlos de Monterey was founded to the joy of the sea and land expeditions. In a short time the rejoicing was shared by the entire kingdom and eagerly celebrated in both Spains.

On that day, after imploring the assistance of the Holy Spirit, the sacred standard of the cross was blessed, raised, and adored by all. The ground was blessed, an altar set up, and a sort of chapel formed with naval flags. The holy sacrifice of the Mass was sung, a sermon was preached, and, at the end, the *Te Deum* was intoned. With these (ceremonies), possession was duly taken of Monterey for (our) holy Church and the crown of Spain. A legal document covering all was drawn up and will be found where it belongs. All this occurred on the beach at the landing place of the said port, the same spot on which one hundred sixty-seven years before, as it is written, the expedition of Don Sebastián Vizcaino had celebrated Mass.[1]

The following day, after choosing the most likely spot on that plain, the construction of the presidio was enthusiastically begun by the men of both sea and land forces. By the fourteenth of the same month, the most solemn feast of Corpus (Christi), a chapel had been built, as well as it could be, at the spot in the presidio which it still occupies, and a high Mass was sung with the Blessed Sacrament exposed in its monstrance. After the Mass there was a procession, in which His Sacramental Majesty passed over the ground that till then had been so heathen and miserable. It was a day of great consolation for all of us who were Christians.

So the presidio was begun but the troop was too small to be divided into two bodies. Thus we, the religious, were forced to establish ourselves in and remain incorporated with this presidio until further arrangements [could be made], even though we knew that there we could do no sowing or any other kind of work.

We remained like this for one year, spending the time putting in order our residence and the most necessary storerooms for our supplies and in making friends with the Indians who were coming to see us; and we tried to win some children. In fact, within a short time, we baptized three and when the boat returned at the end of the year [1771], we had already twenty new Christians at Monterey. As ten religious came on this vessel, we were then twelve. We all dressed in rich chasubles and had a most solemn procession for Corpus (Christi). We had here the vestments for future missions, the men from the ship, and those of the land force, etc. Thanks be to God!

In August, 1771, with the express consent of His Excellency, Marquis de Croix,[2] at that time viceroy of New Spain, and of the Illustrious Inspector General, Don José de Gálvez,[3] both of whom officially informed me about this, San Carlos Mission was begun at the site it now occupies on the banks of Carmel River and in view of the sea at the distance of about a cannon shot where it forms the little bay south of Point Pinos. [The mission is] a little more than a league from the royal presidio, which is to the north in latitude 36°44". The next place to the south is San Antonio [Mission], about twenty-five leagues away. Santa Clara [Mission] is in the opposite direction and a little farther away.

On the twenty-fourth of the said month, the feast of St. Bartholomew, the apostle, the holy cross was set up at the site and the first Mass celebrated under a temporary arbor. For four months only one father stayed here with the personnel doing the building. The other priest with the two missionaries destined for the future San Luis [Obispo] Mission remained at the presidio until Christmas Eve that same year. After previously transferring everything belonging to the mission, we left the presidio on foot and arrived here with an escort of eight men: four soldiers, one muleteer, and three servants [who had been] sailors. When we received our share of the stock, after the division, there were great and small eighteen head of cattle; namely, nine cows, one bull, two heifers, and six small calves. That is all the cattle of that which the mission has and all which the mission has spent. I will write further on about the rest.

The eight remaining days of the year were spent in fiestas and in putting things in order.

1772

This mission's baptisms numbered twenty-three. In the last half of the past year, we added only three and in the whole of this year only eight, because the scarcity of provisions which had been severe during the two preceding, this year became even more critical for no boat reached [Monterey]. Neither of the two which came were able to proceed here and ported at San Diego.

We passed the time erecting around [the buildings] a stockade of stout, closely set palings, with ravelins in the corners of the square. We also finished the buildings, added some [new ones], and started a garden to help with its vegetables. No sowing at all was done in this whole year.

Before definitely establishing [the mission] here, the first concern was to have men familiar with farming see and state whether it would be easy or difficult to take water from the river for irrigating these lands. All agreed that it would be [easy]. Now when we tried to carry it out, they all reversed themselves and declared it impossible. This was the chief, if not the only, reason why there was a delay about the sowing for which we longed. Finally, in the next year, and thereafter, we determined to dry farm, which was both wise and fruitful as shall be seen from the harvests of the following years.

This year we got news of the arrival of both vessels at San Diego, at a time when scarcity had brought the greatest distress to the presidio and the two missions, this one and San Antonio, which had been founded one year earlier. Father President Fray Junípero Serra decided to accompany Commander Don Pedro Fages[4] on the trip to San Diego in order to use his influence also in procuring aid for the religious and missions.

He left this mission for that trip on St. Bartholomew's day, August 24, the first Anniversary of the first Mass at this site, as was stated above. On his way he founded, September 1, Mission San Luis Obispo, in the same place where it is today, under such circumstances of want of the necessary supplies that it should have been considered rashness had it not been justified by charity and trust in God, who in fact, did not abandon the agents of such a holy enterprise as He had promised everyone: "He who trusts in Him shall not be confounded."

When the commander and the father president arrived at San Diego, they sent by land what small aid the fewness of mules permitted and it was decided that one of the boats would return to San Blas, while the other would attempt to go on to Monterey. In fact, it reached there at the end of the same year.

The father president, considering that the state of things demanded better provision for the maintenance and advancement of these new establishments, sacrificed himself to the advice of the religious present, to go to Mexico to seek aid from His Excellency, the new viceroy.[5] He sent from there a religious, who would take his place here, and gave him strict orders to trust in the Lord and proceed with the work of God in things both spiritual and temporal, etc. The father [president] embarked in the middle of October and the other came up to take his place. The vessel arrived at the end of the year with the regular provisions.

1773

In this year, there were one hundred thirty-four baptisms, which with the thirty-one preceding total one hundred sixty-five. Twenty-six marriages of new Christians were celebrated. With the two that they had before, these made twenty-eight neophyte families belonging to this mission.

Towards the end of last year, three pecks and one quart of wheat had been sowed with great difficulty and on ground only half cultivated, because as yet there was no way to plow. Despite the entire absence of irrigation they harvested five bushels, four pecks, and three quarts of good wheat. From half a quart of barley, they gathered three pecks, and from two pecks of Indian corn, four and one-half bushels.[6] Horse beans, chick peas, and beans, a little of each were also sowed, but all [this] was lost. Such was the first sowing and harvest of this mission.

In this whole year, no boat at all came, even though His Excellency, the viceroy, had ordered one to set out from San Blas with the usual provisions, while better arrangements were being made. This was not carried out and since the number of religious was increased by those who had come from Lower California after they had turned their missions over to the Reverend Dominican Fathers, the privations which they suffered were most severe. Even so, the ministers of this mission kept intact the above-mentioned harvest in order to sow it all the following year, which they did.

While in this and the rest of the missions they were suffering such want, in Mexico provisions were being ordered with the greatest enthusiasm and being sent to San Blas for the prosperity of these new establishments. By December, the Father President, Fray Junípero, was again in San Blas for his return trip in the new frigate, *Santiago,* which was loaded with every good thing as no other boat that ever came to this land before or since.

1774

The frigate, *Santiago,* sailed from San Blas, January 25, 1774, and, having favorable stern winds for several days, it arrived at the port of San Diego, March 13, or in less than a month and a half. These circumstances could have brought the boat to Monterey, but it was better this way, for this place was thus succored en route as was the expedition of Don Juan de Anza,[7] which had just arrived, hungry and in great need at San Gabriel Mission.

The father president disembarked and made the rest of the trip by land, so that he could see the missions and his religious brethren. The frigate and his reverence arrived at Monterey at almost the same time to the great consolation of the entire land, for then the famine, privations, and shortages were ended. In fact, they have not returned since.

It would not be out of place to specify the provisions which, out of pure charity and without charge, His Excellency, the viceroy, sent on this occasion for these missions: corn, beans, flour, hams, clothing for the Indians, beads, etc., but suffice it to say that [the missions] were abundantly supplied and equipped to begin and to continue their spiritual and temporal labors as they did with great success. Thanks be to God!

In this mission they had one hundred two baptisms, which added to the preceding made a total of two hundred sixty-seven. There were six marriages for a total of thirty-four. Work on the land consisted in sowing the above-mentioned wheat harvest. From it, without irrigation, one hundred twenty-five bushels were gathered this year. From

three short pecks of barley, twenty bushels were reaped; from six pecks of beans, five bushels, seven pecks; from eight pecks of corn, one hundred fifty bushels, three pecks; and from one peck of horse beans, one bushel; total three hundred one bushels.

This year we began to profit by the help of the six servants granted to us by His Excellency, the viceroy. We got some capable farm hands from the boat, and oxen were broken; hence, more land was prepared for the year.

1775

The baptisms this year were one hundred one, which added to the preceding made a total of three hundred sixty-eight. The marriages were thirty-five, which also added to the preceding made a total of sixty-nine families.

The grain harvest this year reached a total of seven hundred nine bushels, six and one-half pecks. From one bushel of barley, one hundred seven bushels, ten pecks, and one quart were gathered and measured; from one bushel of fine wheat, sixty-three bushels, twenty and one-half pecks; from six bushels of [ordinary] wheat, three hundred fifty-three bushels, four and one-half pecks; from ten pecks of corn, after very severe damage, one hundred fourteen bushels; and the rest was garden vegetables: beans, lentils, horse beans, chick peas, and a few peas. The entire harvest came without any irrigation.

During this whole year, like last, this mission maintained seven religious and quite a few [Lower] California Indians destined for future missions. Though the king had assigned a double ration for each religious, during a five year period, to date this mission has not received this ration for even one day, nor for any religious. Though I suppose the gentlemen who have administered the royal property will have notified their superiors of the merit of this saving in their accounts, nevertheless, it is but fair that we also speak up that their honors may be increased! They also have other merits in this line. Now that the missions are on their feet we can give thanks to the gentlemen!

At the end of this year the destruction of San Diego Mission took place, a tragedy in which we all shared.[8] Blessed be God!

1776

There were seventy-one baptisms during this year, which added to the preceding made four hundred thirty-nine Christians. The marriages were twenty-two and with the preceding they made ninety. In this way, Christianity was gradually progressing in proportion to the means available in the following years, 1777, 78, 79, and 80. At the end of this last [year] we reached six hundred thirty-eight baptisms and one hundred sixty-two marriages.

During all this time we failed to get water for irrigation, even though we took extreme steps. On this account, the harvests were diverse since they depended on the rain.

There were two years in which we had scarcely harvested four hundred bushels of all grains, from which we had to take the seed which was to be sown in the following year. This left very little for so many people and in one year we had recourse to Mission San Luis [Obisp] to which this [mission] paid one hundred thirty pesos in cash.

In the other years the harvest was sufficient because even though the Indian corn was never abundant, since it was sowed too late for the rains, its place was taken by barley of which we regularly gathered from two hundred to four hundred and more bushels.

In the earlier years of this period, this mission had to transport and supply [grain] as best it could, for the fathers who founded the mission of our father, St. Francis, in the year 1776.

In the middle of this year, the father president embarked for the restoration of San Diego Mission and the reestablishment of San Juan Capistrano. Both were set up successfully because of the favorable provisions made by the Knight Commander, His Excellency Viceroy Bucareli may he be with God.

The following year, Mission Santa Clara was founded and its father ministers, too, quitted San Carlos where they had resided for more than two years. This mission did well while consuming the abundant supplies which the father president had brought for it from Mexico. But they served the purpose for which they came which was the propagation of our Catholic faith.

Meanwhile, noting the little security and the lack of protection afforded by the dwellings and other buildings no matter how much these were plastered with mud, we started to make buildings of adobes and gradually those were erected which are now in use and which are listed at the end of this report.

In 1778, the father president made another voyage to San Diego to administer confirmation there and, on his return trip, at the rest of the missions. The apostolic faculty to confirm had come to him this year on the same boat.

He started the voyage on St. Bartholomew's day, August 24, and he returned by land, after he had accomplished his task, December 23, the same year. During this and other similar trips, this mission had always had at least two religious.

The year after the destruction of San Diego, this mission also was menaced with several rumors that a similar misfortune was being prepared for it by the pagans known as Sanjones, old and powerful enemies of the natives of this territory. On one occasion the indications appeared so certain that on his own initiative the sergeant, who commanded the presidio in the absence of the captain at San Diego, came with quite a force and begged us religious to sleep in one place so that we could be more easily protected. They locked the seven of us in the adobe black-smith shop, the safest place, and there, packed together, we spent the night while the soldiers passed it in the saddle, patrolling the vicinity, but no enemy showed up, nor did any later evidence appear to prove that any such danger had existed. Those who were then painted to us as such enemies are almost all Christians today. So, we pass on to the year.

1781

The supplies from the preceding harvest, that were used in the beginning of this year, were sufficient and the planting of barley, wheat, and some garden vegetables promised a harvest in accordance with the amount of water. Nevertheless, the hope [persisted] of bringing water with all the possibilities of irrigation, especially for the corn which for lack of water was valueless as a crop. Father Juan Crespí,[9] now deceased, decided to try to get water. He realized through his surveys that at least for irrigating the land so far cultivated, he could get water from a point closer than the one he had until then considered. The enterprise was started with such confidence of success that corn was sown where it was thought it could be irrigated.

When there were but a few days left [of Father Crespí's work], the famous steward of San Luis Obispo came to our house offering to take the same job at this mission. He started May 1, at a salary of two hundred pesos in cash, etc. He saw and approved the work that the two fathers were doing toward extracting water and, after stating that within three days we would see the corn irrigated, he went out one morning and without saying anything to us, he took the people from the work and set them to digging another ditch a few yards further up the river, claiming that what had been done previously was valueless and, with that, the corn sown was lost and he spent seven months and used all the workmen in the new ditch.

Not a grain of corn was gathered and they got a little over four hundred bushels of barley. Because of the folly of this man, a great part of the wheat was lost in the fields. Less than four hundred bushels were obtained, when to be conservative we should have expected more than five hundred. But finally the water was extracted that same year in the month of December. From then on the mission has had irrigation. Thanks be to God!

This year there were only twenty-four baptisms and seventeen marriages. We sowed in a proper manner for the

Year 1782

Towards the end of the past year, thirty-one bushels of barley were sown and fifty-three of wheat. The barley was planted where the water could not reach it and as the drought was great, it was lost. This had never happened before in the case of this grain. We gathered only one hundred seven bushels.

The wheat which was irrigated did well but less was harvested than in the preceding year for the same reason and there were large stretches of sown land where [the major domo] did not attempt to gather a single head. There was a task that they were completing in less than an hour and, to make it shorter, they gathered only the tall ears and even so it took them a long time. A great many of the people got sick and the [steward] asked permission to betake himself to Mission San Luis Obispo, because they had sent to tell him that he was needed there. Leaving the wheat in the fields and the people down he departed and never returned.

The harvested wheat threshed out at four hundred fifty bushels. There were twenty-seven bushels of garden vegetables and one hundred sixty of Indian corn. These are the results of the first year of irrigation and such an intelligent steward.

In things spiritual it was better. We had one hundred and one baptisms and twenty-three marriages. The people gradually improved in health, even though some of them died, and without any steward, good or bad, we sowed for the

Year 1783

We can consider this the happiest year of the mission because the number of baptisms was one hundred seventy-five and of marriages thirty-six.

The sowing of all grains amounted to eighty-four bushels, eight pecks. This included one bushel and a half of wheat, half a bushel of corn, and two pecks of beans, which were sown for the [Lower] California Indians, who had moved here and were married in this mission.

And the harvest, less the amount of forty-seven bushels which belonged to these Indians and other concessions made to the people such as a portion of the barley which they might reap and some twenty bushels of wheat from the chaff of the threshing, which was stored in the mission granaries amounted to twenty-six hundred fourteen and a half bushels, that is, of measured barley six hundred seventy bushels, eight hundred thirty-five of wheat, only two hundred according to our estimate are kept in the ear. There were nine hundred seventy-one bushels of corn of both kinds according to our estimate, sixty-three bushels of peas, sixteen bushels of horse beans, four bushels of lentils, and fifty-three bushels of various kinds of beans.

Today the new Christians of this mission number six hundred fourteen living persons, even though some of them take a leave of absence from time to time. They have been maintained and are maintained without any scarcity and we supplied the quartermaster of the presidio of San Carlos with one hundred thirty bushels of Indian corn; because they did not ask for more, also with thirty bushels of beans. The escort of this mission, at the request of the ensign quartermaster, received rations in these two kinds

of grain. There have not been other deliveries of consequence so that in our prudent judgment of the two chief commodities, wheat and corn, about half the amount harvested may still remain.

The value of the food supplied to the presidio has been paid already in cloth, which now covers the Indians who grew the crops, but at that we are still distressed at the sight of so much nudity among them.

We do not get clothing now from the soldiers, as we did formerly, not even from those who have debts to us no matter how small. The wool, which in some of the missions is enough to cover Indian nakedness, here has not been any help to us so far, because the thefts of sheep are so numerous that already for more than three years, we can not exceed two hundred head between goats and sheep, and from shearing the few that we have we get nothing worthwhile.

The condition, then, of the Mission in things spiritual is that up to this day in this Mission:

Baptisms	1,006
Confirmations	936
And since those of the other missions belong in some way to this it is noted in passing that their number is	5,307
Marriages in this mission	259
Burials	356

The number of Christian families living at the mission and eating jointly, as well as widowers, single men, and children of both sexes, is evident from the enclosed census lists and so is omitted here.

They pray twice daily with the priest in the church. More than one hundred twenty of them confess in Spanish and many who have died used to do it as well. The others confess as best they can. They work at all kinds of mission labor, such as farm hands, herdsmen, cowboys, shepherds, milkers, diggers, gardeners, carpenters, farmers, irrigators, reapers, blacksmiths, sacristans, and they do everything else that comes along for their corporal and spiritual welfare.

The work of clearing the fields once, sometimes twice, or even three times a year, is considerable because the land is very fertile. When we clear new land great hardship is required. Altogether there is sufficient land cleared for sowing more than one hundred bushels of wheat, and it is sowed in that grain, barley, vegetables, and corn. Every year we clear a little more.

To the seven months' work required to take water from the river for irrigation, as mentioned above, we must add the labor of bringing it to the lagoon near the mission residence. In some years, this lagoon used to be dry. Now it is always full, making it a great convenience and a delight to the mission. Some salmon have been placed in the pool and so we have it handy.

The timber palisade was inadequate to protect the seed grain because they steal the paling for firewood. So we dug a circular trench many thousands of varas[10] long. This was a two years' labor and withal nothing sufficed to prevent losses every year.

Some of the land which we cleared for farming was not only covered with long tough grasses and thickets but also with great trees, willows, alders, and so forth, and it has been hard work, as we have already noted, but we hope that it will pay off at a profit. We also have a sizable walled garden [which produces] abundant vegetables and some fruit.

Mission Buildings

In the first few years, we worked hard and well on the church and the rest of the buildings. [They were made] of paling with flat earthen roofs to minimize fire danger, but no matter what we did they always leaked like a sieve and between that and the humidity everything would rot. So we decided to build of adobe and thus today all buildings are [of that material]. They are as follows:

An adobe church, forty by eight varas, with a thatched roof.

Likewise, the three-room residence of the three priests. One [room is] large, with an alcove for a bed. The floor is plain earth and the roof thatched.

Also, a granary about twenty varas long with several small compartments, a porch, and a thatched roof.

Likewise, another granary about thirty varas long with its porch and four wooden barred windows. The floor is plain earth and the roof thatched.

Also, another adobe house, thirty varas long, divided for the present into only three sections: one serves as a storeroom, another at the opposite end is used as a dormitory for the girls; the center section is a large room with two barred windows and doors. It is white-washed and clean and is used as a guest chamber for the ships' officers and for some other occasions. It is going to be divided into two rooms for which we already have the two doors with their hinges.

Likewise, another adobe building with an earthen roof and with its own shed and key. It houses the forge where the blacksmith works. It has a porch and window.

Also, next to this building is another which we call the carpenter shop. It has a room with a separate door and key for safeguarding the tools. It has two windows with bars and a door.

Likewise, another building next to the ones just mentioned where the women grind [grain], make cheese, and where different tools are kept.

Also, another building, larger than the preceding ones, where for the present the family of the Mexican blacksmith lives.

Likewise, four adobe buildings a little further on, which are [a place for] five carts, the wood shed, kitchen, and a hen house.

Also, there is a serviceable adobe corral with sections for sheep and goats and next to this a separate pen for pigs. The rest of the corrals for horses and cattle, with their corresponding stud and bull stalls, are all made of paling and from time to time give us quite a bit of repair trouble.

The Animals

number today:

Cattle, large and small	500
Sheep and goats, about the same number of each	220
Riding and draft mules	18
Tame and broken horses	20
Four herds of mares with their colts	90
Also with them, two young mules from the time we had a jack	
One old ass that may be with foal	1
Pigs	25

Accounts

Regarding the remainder of the status of the mission, [we note] that when the vessels arrive from Mexico with the supplies we know whether we have credits or debits from our stipends. This year the [boats] have not yet reached here, so we do not have this information.

We know of no local debts but there may be some hidden or unexpected debt like those we have had in the past.

The mission paid Lieutenant Ortega[11] eighteen pesos for a tent from the King's stores, which was given the father president for use when he was at San Buenaventura Mission, and while he assisted at the foundation of the new presidio of Santa Barbara. He did not think such a debt existed until they came to collect it.

Not long ago this mission paid fifteen pesos as a donation for the war, more than a year after the conflict ended,[12] as a result of misinformation given the commandancy general to the effect that the father president had excluded from the count some Indians who had run away from the mission after the lists had been completed. This was not true, for when we made the lists everyone of them had been apostates for at least two years and some for more than three. He mentioned them only as an incentive so that they might return them [to the mission] for me.

We did not even think about mentioning those who ran away, nor those who died, after the lists were made, nor did we discount them, but just the same we paid the fifteen pesos and the [entire] donation amounted to over one hundred pesos, the sum they finally asked for. At the beginning of the year when the governor showed me these [directions for] reports, inventories, and census lists, of the missions [that were] to be sent to the commandancy general, I told him that I would care for it gladly, since the reverend father guardian of my holy college[13] had given me the same order.

But, that it had to be on condition, that the papers and letters for those documents would be post free, for I had received a letter from the commander general of much less bulk than any of these reports and it bore the notation: eleven reales. What would so many papers cost?

He answered me that yes [they were post free] and, in fact, the ensign always urged me to accept [such] letters saying, even in writing, that the figures in question had reference to other accounts and that I would not have to pay it.

With that assurance, I went ahead certain that the envelope which came from San Gabriel entitled: "Reports, Inventories, and Census List of San Gabriel Mission" [was free even though] there was a notation, twenty reales, which I have kept by accident. Despite this, a few days ago we received a bill from the quartermaster for twenty-five pesos, two reales for [postage on] letters sent to the mission. They were the creditors and they collected. All we need now is some other arbitrary debt unknown to us.

What we get in the annual distributions purchased in Mexico with our stipends is known already. After using enough for our clothing, chocolate, wine, and candles for Mass, and some minor objects for the church, the rest goes for the Indians, especially for clothing to cover them. So far as we can see, nothing more need be said on this point.

If anything else should be made known about the administration and state of the mission, it can be asked of us specifically and with assurance that we will hide nothing, for thanks to the goodness of God we do not fear the light, and, since what has been said so far is true, we the ministers of the mission sign it, July 1, 1784.

Fray Junípero Serra—Fray Mathías Antonio de Santa Cathalina Noriega [rubrica].

[1] Don Sebastián Vizcaino (1550?–1615) and his exploring party entered Monterey Bay on December 16, 1602.

[2] Marquis Carlos Francisco de Croix served as Viceroy of New Spain during the years 1765-1771.

[3] Don José de Gálvez (1720–1787), an energetic explorer and administrator, was very helpful to Serra and the missionaries in his office of Inspector General of New Spain.

[4] Don Pedro Fages, commandant at Monterey, was later Governor of California.

[5] Don Antonio Maria Bucareli y Ursúa was Viceroy of New Spain from September, 1771, to his death in Mexico City on April 9, 1779.

[6] The original uses the Spanish terms: *fanega, almud,* and *quartillo,* for which there is no exact English equivalent. Each Spanish measure, however, was several times larger than the English measure given here.

[7] Don Juan Bautista de Anza (1735–1788), born in Sonora, led several expeditions from Mexico to California and was later Governor of New Mexico.

[8] San Diego was destroyed by fire by the Indians in November, 1775.

[9] Juan Crespí, O.F.M. (1721–1782), had been a student of Serra's; he was a favorite of the founder of the missions and had acted as assistant to him at Monterey and Carmel.

[10] The Spanish *vara* was equivalent to about 2.8 feet.

[11] José Francisco Ortega (d. 1798) was a Mexican-born soldier who rose to the rank of brevet captain in the Spanish colonial forces.

[12] The preliminary articles of peace between Great Britain and Spain were signed on January 20, 1783.

[13] The College of San Fernando in Mexico City had been formally established in 1733.

(*Source*: John Tracy Ellis, ed. *Documents of American Catholic History.* Vol. 1:1493–1865. Wilmington, Del.: Michael Glazier, 1987, 34–47.)

SETON, ELIZABETH ANN BAYLEY (1774–1821)

Early Years

Saint, foundress of the American Sisters of Charity. Elizabeth Ann Bayley Seton was born in New York City on August 28, 1774. She was of colonial descent and renowned family background: her father was Richard Bayley, a prominent physician and professor at King's College (later Columbia University), and the first public health officer of the Port of New York; her mother was Catherine Charlton Bayley, whose father was rector of St. Andrew's Episcopal Church on Staten Island, New York. She was less than three years of age when her mother died (May 8, 1777). Shortly thereafter (June 10, 1778), her father married Charlotte Amelia Barclay, daughter of the socially and financially successful Andrew and Helena Roosevelt Barclay. Her father's second family numbered seven half brothers and sisters for Elizabeth and her older sister, Mary. Passages in Elizabeth's "Dear Remembrances" (written in 1812) indicate that her father's second marriage was not always pleasant for her and her sister, and that while young and into their teenage years, they often lived with their Bayley relatives at New Rochelle, New York. Meanwhile, her father provided her and her

Mother Elizabeth Ann Seton

sister with a fine education; this included the study of French and piano at a private school known as "Mama Pompelion's" in New York City.

Some time in 1791 Elizabeth was introduced to William Magee Seton. His father was William Seton of the Parbroath branch of the famous Anglo-Scottish family, one of the founders and first cashier of the Bank of New York, and also the founder of Seton, Maitland, and Company which became one of New York's largest and most prosperous shipping firms; his mother was Rebecca Curson Seton of the baronets of that name (Curson) in Oxfordshire, England. Following a courtship conducted in accord with the standards for the upper class of the day, Elizabeth and William were married on January 25, 1794, by Bishop Samuel Provost, first Episcopal bishop of New York City (probably in the home of Dr. and Mrs. Wright Post, Elizabeth's brother-in-law and sister).

Marriage and Widowhood

The Setons made their home in New York City. Between 1795 and 1802, Elizabeth gave birth to five children (Ann Maria, William, Richard, Catherine Josephine, and Rebecca). Caring for the children and tending to other family responsibilities placed heavy demands on her time and energy. However, while her husband's fortunes prospered, the Seton household was well staffed with servants and fine conveyances for travel. Thus the young wife and mother was actively involved in social affairs, such as frequent attendance at the theater; in charitable works, especially as a member of the Society of Widows, an association founded to help destitute widows and children; and in reading and discussing in intellectual circles a wide variety of works, including Rousseau's *Emile.* As a devout Episcopalian and a member of Trinity Church, she was also immersed in matters of a spiritual nature, often under the guidance of a young clergyman of Trinity Church, Dr. John Henry Hobart.

In 1799 Elizabeth and William were confronted with a critical financial situation, the result of varied factors: the continuance of the "undeclared war" between England and France which threatened neutral American cargo vessels; William's rapidly declining health as a victim of tuberculosis; and his inability to adequately head Seton, Maitland, and Company since taking it over at the death of his father in the previous year. In December 1800 he was forced to file a petition of bankruptcy for his firm.

Until now he was not very interested in religion, and seemed content with being a nominal Christian. Elizabeth, working with Dr. Hobart, was mainly responsible for a spiritual conversion he experienced at this time of loss of fortune and worsening of health. In an attempt to forestall his death, William, Elizabeth, and their eldest child, Anna Maria, departed on a sea voyage for Leghorn (Livorno) Italy in the fall (October 2) of 1803, having been offered hospitality there by business friends, the Filicchi family. After seven weeks of travel, they were quarantined for a month (November 18–December 19) in a dungeon-like building called the *Lazaretto,* located several miles from Leghorn, because of recent outbreaks of yellow fever in New York. During that period of extremely difficult living, Elizabeth manifested admirable courage and faith in providing both physical and spiritual comfort to both daughter and husband. Following release from the *Lazaretto* on December 19, the three were provided with a comfortable house in Pisa by the Filicchis. William died there on December 27, and was buried in Leghorn on the following day.

Conversion to Catholicism

Elizabeth spent the early months of her widowhood with the Filicchi household in Leghorn where she became increasingly knowledgeable of and appreciative of the Catholic faith. By the time she returned to New York in June 1804, she was strongly convinced that she should embrace Catholicism. Despite opposition from her close friend and one-time spiritual adviser, Dr. Hobart, most family members, and other Protestant friends, she was received into the Catholic Church on March 14, 1805, by Fr. Matthew O'Brien, pastor of St. Peter's Church in New York City.

She was now in great financial need and depended on the help of such people as the Filicchis, her brother-in-law, Dr. Wright Post, and her close Protestant friend, Julia Sitgreaves Scott, widow of Lewis Allair Scott, former secretary of state of New York, until she could find the means to support herself and her children. For her few remaining years in New York, she undertook two projects to this end: a school and a boarding house for young children, both of which failed. She also seriously considered relocating to Montreal, Canada, to assume a teaching position in what she believed would be a more suitable climate than the anti-Catholic one in New York.

On June 16, 1808, at the invitation of the Sulpician, Fr. William DuBourg, founder of Baltimore's St. Mary's College, and with the encouragement of Bishop John Carroll, she arrived in Baltimore, where in the following September she opened a school for young girls. The school, her first successful one, was located on Paca Street, near St. Mary's Seminary. From the beginning of her stay in Baltimore, she manifested a desire to adopt a form of religious life. By early March of 1809 it was apparent that property purchased for her in Emmitsburg, Maryland (some fifty miles northwest of Baltimore), by Samuel Cooper, a wealthy convert and seminarian, would be the site for her religious community and new school for girls.

On March 25, 1809, she professed religious vows in the presence of Bishop John Carroll and received from him the title of "mother," thus becoming the foundress and first superior of the religious community to be established in Emmitsburg. In early June, four young women presented themselves to her as candidates for her community and donned habits similar to what she had been wearing as a widow: a black dress, short black shoulder cape, and a white cap (later, changed to black) which tied under the chin.

The Sisters of Charity

On July 31 of the same year, after several weeks of temporary residence in a log house given them by Fr. John Dubois on the mountain overlooking his recently founded (1808) Mt. St. Mary's College and Seminary in Emmitsburg, Elizabeth and the nucleus of her community, along with her sisters-in-law, Harriet and Cecilia Seton, her daughters (the sons were enrolled at Mt. St. Mary's), and two students from the Paca Street school, settled into their home—a four-room farmhouse, called the "Stone House," in nearby St. Joseph's Valley. That date, July 31, 1809, marked the commencement of regular community life for Mother Seton and her sisters. It is recognized as the beginning of her community, the Sisters of Charity of St. Joseph.

The rule for the community received final approval from Archbishop John Carroll and Fr. John Tessier, Sulpician superior, in Baltimore on January 17, 1812. It was based on St. Vincent de Paul's Rule for the Daughters of Charity, but with certain modifications, one of which allowed exceptions for the foundress in living out the vow of poverty in order to care properly for her children.

By the time the rule was approved, the sisters were successfully operating a free day school for young girls of the area and a boarding school for daughters of families whose homes were at a distance from Emmitsburg, and whose tuition and room-and-board fees were a vital source of income for the community. As early as February 1810, with the increased numbers in the sisterhood and school, the sisters and students moved into a new and larger building, known as the "White House." There, Mother Seton worked tirelessly to assure stability for her school and community. She observed classes, taught lessons, supervised the preparation of textbooks, conducted religious conferences and retreats for students and sisters, translated religious books from French to English, and authored spiritual treatises.

From the "White House," she and her sisters engaged in various other ministries in the neighborhood. They visited and cared for the poor and sick, gave religious instruction to children and adults, and served in domestic work and as infirmarians at Mt. St. Mary's. In 1814 she accepted an invitation to send sisters to direct an orphanage in Philadelphia; and in 1817 she responded in the same way to a similar request for New York City.

Mother Seton overcame vast obstacles in leading her community to growth and success: conflicts, especially of an administrative nature with clergy and sisters; financial issues of enormous proportions; and sickness and deaths of many sisters. At the same time, she provided loving care for her children; and she suffered the loss of two of them (Anna Maria and Rebecca) during their early years in Emmitsburg. Through it all, she manifested a deep spirituality, being directed for many years by the saintly Fr. Simon Bruté of Mt. St. Mary's. Following a lengthy period of intense suffering brought on by tuberculosis, Mother Seton died in Emmitsburg on January 4, 1821.

Mother Seton's Legacy

Following her death, Mother Seton's sisterhood underwent a remarkable expansion. Her sisters have been serving Church and society in practically every ministry of education and charity.

In 1850 her Sisters of Charity in Emmitsburg were affiliated with the Daughters of Charity in France, with Emmitsburg as the headquarters of the U.S. Province of the Daughters of Charity of St. Vincent de Paul. Later, four other U.S. provinces were established. They are: Albany, New York; Evansville, Indiana; Los Altos, California; and St. Louis, Missouri.

Five other congregations of the Sisters of Charity trace their origin in North America to Mother Seton. They are: Sisters of Charity of St. Vincent de Paul, New York; Sisters of Charity of Cincinnati, Ohio; Sisters of Charity of St. Vincent de Paul, Halifax, Nova Scotia; Sisters of Charity of St. Elizabeth, Convent Station, New Jersey; and Sisters of Charity of Seton Hill, Greensburg, Pennsylvania.

Elizabeth Ann Bayley Seton—wife, mother, widow, convert, and foundress—was declared venerable on December 18, 1959, beatified on March 17, 1963, and canonized on September 14, 1975. She was the first native-born citizen of the United States to be canonized.

Code, J. B. *Elizabeth Seton.* Baltimore, 1879.

Dirvin, J. I. *Mrs. Seton: Foundress of the American Sisters of Charity.* New York, 1962.

Kelly E., and A. Melville, eds. *Elizabeth Seton: Selected Writings.* New York, 1987.

Melville, A. M. *Elizabeth Bayley Seton, 1774–1821.* 3rd ed. New York, 1976.

Vincentian Heritage 14 (2) (1993), Papers from the Symposium, "Elizabeth Seton in Dialogue with Her Time and Ours." Dayton, Ohio, and Convent Station, New Jersey, 1992.

White, C. I. *Life of Mrs. Elizabeth A. Seton* 3rd ed. Baltimore, 1868.

ANN MIRIAM GALLAGHER, R.S.M.

Related Document

MOTHER SETON'S PLANS FOR HER RELIGIOUS COMMUNITY, FEBRUARY 9, 1809

The founder of the first American religious congregation of women, the Sisters of Charity of St. Joseph, was Elizabeth Ann Seton (1774–1821). This convert widow of a distinguished Protestant Episcopalian family of New York laid the foundations of her community at Baltimore in 1808 under the auspices of Archbishop Carroll and the Sulpicians. In the summer of 1809 she moved to Emmitsburg, Maryland, where the mother house was permanently established and where the school for small children which had been begun in Baltimore was continued. Mother Seton's sisters increased in number and within six months after her death they had schools in Philadelphia, New York, and Baltimore. In the following letter to Filippo Filicchi she described the plans of herself and her advisers for the future of the infant community. She was canonized on September 14, 1975, the first native-born American to be so honored.

(*Source:* Annabelle M. Melville, *Elizabeth Bayley Seton, 1774–1821.* New York: Charles Scribner's Sons, 1951, 145–46.)

MY DEAR FILICCHI,[1] YOU WILL THINK, I FEAR, THAT THE poor little woman's brain is turned who writes you so often on the same subject, but it is not a matter of choice on my part, as it is my indispensable duty to let you know every particular of a circumstance which has occurred since I wrote you last week relative to the suggestions so strongly indicated in the letters I have written both yourself and your Antonio[2] since my arrival in Baltimore. Some time ago I mentioned to you the conversion of a man of family and fortune in Philadelphia.[3] This conversion is as solid as it was extraordinary, and as *the person* is soon to recieve [*sic*] the Tonsure in our seminary, in making the disposition of his fortune he had consulted our Rd. Mr. Dubourg,[4] the Prest. of the College on the plan of establishing an institution for the advancement of Catholick female children in habits of religion and giving them an education suited to the purpose. He also desires extremely to extend the plan to the reception of the aged and also uneducated persons who may be employed in spinning, knitting, etc., etc., so as to found a Manufactory on a small scale which may be very beneficial to the poor. You see I am bound to let you know the disposition of Providence that you may yourself judge how far you may concur with it. Dr. Matignon[5] of Boston to whom Mr. Cheverus[6] the Bishop elect and Antonio referred me on every Occasion, [*sic*] had suggested this plan for me before the gentleman in question ever thought of it. I have invariably kept in the background and avoided even reflecting voluntarily on anything of the kind, knowing that Almighty God alone could effect it if indeed it will be realized. Father Mr. Dubourg has always said the same, be quiet, God will in his own time discover His intentions, nor will I allow one word of intreaty [*sic*] from my pen. His blessed will be done.

In my former letter I asked you if you could not secure your own property and build something for this purpose on the lot (which is an extensive one) given by Mr. Dubourg. If you will furnish the necessary expenditures for setting us off, and supporting those persons or children who at first will not be able to support themselves. Dr. Matignon will appoint a Director for the establishment which if you knew how many good and excellent souls are sighing for would soon obtain an interest in your breast, so ardently desiring the glory of God. But all is in his hands. If I had a choice and my will would decide in a moment, I would remain silent in his hands. Oh how sweet it is there to rest in perfect confidence, yet in every daily Mass and at communion I beg him to dispose of me and mine in any way which may please him. YOU are Our Father in him, thro your hands we received that new and precious being which is indeed true life. And may you in your turn be rewarded with the fullness of the divine benediction. Amen a thousand times.

MEA Seton

[1] Filippo Filicchi, a well-to-do merchant of Leghorn, Italy, had long been a friend of the Seton family. He had assisted and encouraged Mrs. Seton in becoming a Catholic.

[2] Antonio was the brother of Filippo Filicchi.

[3] Samuel Sutherland Cooper (1769–1843), a convert of means who became a priest, gave financial aid to Mother Seton's community in its early years.

[4] Louis W. V. Dubourg, S.S. (1766–1833), was at the time president of St. Mary's College, Baltimore. He died as Archbishop of Besançon.

[5] François A. Matignon (1753–1818) was a French-born priest who was pastor of what was soon to become the Cathedral of the Holy Cross in Boston.

[6] Jean Cheverus (1768–1836) was the first Bishop of Boston who died as Cardinal Archbishop of Bordeaux.

(*Source*: John Tracy Ellis, ed. *Documents of American Catholic History.* Vol. 1:1493–1865. Wilmington, Del.: Michael Glazier, 1987, 188–90.)

SETON HALL UNIVERSITY

Seton Hall University, located in South Orange, New Jersey, is an independent Catholic institution founded in 1856 and chartered by the state of New Jersey in 1861. It is the nation's oldest and largest diocesan Catholic university, and New Jersey's only Catholic university. Its charter makes it one of five New Jersey institutions of higher education not subject to the New Jersey Commission on Higher Education. Originally a liberal arts college, the university is now composed of eight schools. The College of Arts and Sciences, the W. Paul Stillman School of Business, the College of Education and Human Services, the School of Law, the College of Nursing, the Immaculate Conception Seminary School of Theology, the Graduate School of Medical Education, and University College are located on a fifty-eight-acre campus in South Orange, New Jersey, while the School of Law is located in Newark, New

Jersey. The Carnegie Classification for Seton Hall is as a Doctoral University II. The university is governed by two boards. The twelve-member board of trustees, chaired by the archbishop of Newark, maintains the essential character of the university as a Catholic institution of higher learning. The twenty-seven-member board of regents, which elects its own chair, is responsible for monitoring the operation of the university.

Seton Hall College was established in 1856 by James Roosevelt Bayley, first bishop of Newark, who named it after his aunt, Mother Elizabeth Ann Seton, a pioneer in Catholic education and the first American-born saint. From its original enrollment of a handful of students, Seton Hall grew rapidly. During its first twelve years, the college had enrolled over five hundred freshmen from seventeen states and six foreign countries. In the nineteenth century, in spite of setbacks, major fires, difficult economic times, and the War Between the States, the college continued to expand. By 1937 Seton Hall established a University College. This marked the first matriculation of women at Seton Hall, which became fully coeducational in 1968. The School of Law opened in 1951, the same year that the college was organized into a university. In 1984 Immaculate Conception Seminary returned to Seton Hall, its original home. The Recreation Center was dedicated in 1987 and four new residence halls were constructed between 1984 and 1988. In 1994 the university dedicated its $20,000,000 Walsh Library and in 1997 completed a $20,000,000 Academic Services Building.

The total number of students at the university is over 10,000, of whom more than 4,000 are undergraduate students. There are 60,000 Seton Hall alumni.

ROBERT J. WISTER

SHAHAN, THOMAS JOSEPH (1837–1932)

Bishop, educator. Shahan was born in Manchester, New Hampshire, on September 11, 1857, to Irish immigrant parents, Maurice Peter Shahan and Mary Anne Carmody Shahan. He attended public schools and in 1872 began studies for the priesthood at the Sulpician College in Montreal. In 1878 he went to the North American College in Rome, received a doctorate in theology from the Roman Seminary, and was ordained a priest on June 3, 1882. After doing pastoral work in Connecticut, in 1883 he became the chancellor of the Diocese of Hartford. In 1888 John J. Keane, the first rector of the newly founded Catholic University of America, invited Shahan to join the faculty. To prepare himself, he went to Europe to do advanced studies, first at the University of Berlin and then at the Institut Catholique in Paris. In 1891 he began teaching patristics and Church history at The Catholic University of America. Shahan was a prolific writer, and in 1895 he began publishing the *Catholic University Bulletin*. He was a

Thomas J. Shahan

major force in the publication of the *Catholic Encyclopedia* and personally contributed over two hundred entries.

Soon Shahan became a leader on the national scene. In 1909 he became rector of The Catholic University of America and held this post until 1928. As rector, he expanded both the faculty and the student body and added new buildings to the campus, including the John K. Mullen of Denver Library. He also started construction of the National Shrine of the Immaculate Conception. He had great designs for the fledgling university but was always hampered by the lack of funds. Shahan helped found Catholic Sisters College (1911), the National Conference of Catholic Charities (1910), and the American Catholic Historical Association (1917). He was instrumental in the founding of Trinity College, a women's college near The Catholic University of America and was president of the Catholic Educational Association from 1909 to 1928. A tireless leader in Catholic education and scholarship, Shahan retired in 1928 and took up residency at Holy Cross Academy near the university where he died on March 9, 1932.

Dixon, Blase. "The Catholic University of America, 1909–1928: The Rectorship of Thomas Joseph Shahan." Ph.D. dissertation, The Catholic University of America, 1972.

Nuesse, C. Joseph. *The Catholic University of America*. Washington, 1990.

ANTHONY D. ANDREASSI

SHANLEY, JOHN (1852–1909)

Bishop. The first bishop of Fargo was born in 1852 and ordained for the Archdiocese of St. Paul in 1874. Soon after North Dakota became a state in 1889, Shanley was named bishop of Jamestown. He soon moved his head-quarters to the larger town of Fargo, but even there he had a hard time convincing people that it was important to be part of the universal Church. For some years, Shanley had to preach retreats in the East to support himself, and to build St. Mary's Cathedral and rectory.

John Shanley

Eventually, the economy improved and immigration caused the Catholic census to shoot upward. But to serve this new population, an effective clergy was needed. As long as the frontier was in flux, North Dakota was plagued by priests with chequered pasts and crippling personal problems. Not only did Shanley deal firmly with this mot-ley crew (thirty priests suspended in the decade 1890–1900), but he succeeded in fostering native vocations. By 1930 North Dakota had abundant local clergy.

John Shanley was uniquely suited to the situation that existed in North Dakota at the turn of the century. By and large, leadership in the new state was Protestant and out-spokenly anti-Catholic. What the Church needed was a spokesman who could and would defend her in the pub-lic forum. In that role, Shanley had few peers. His role as a leader in the temperance movement in Minnesota had forged him into an effective debater, and he could charm the most hostile audience with his passion and wit.

When John Shanley died in 1909 at age fifty-seven, the cause was listed as pneumonia, but it was really overwork. Long, hard years moving about his huge diocese had worn him out in the Lord's service.

Kardong, Terrence. *Beyond Red River.* Fargo, 1989, 47–69.

TERRENCE KARDONG, O.S.B.

SHAUGHNESSY, GERALD (1887–1950)

Fourth bishop of Seattle, Washington. Gerald Shaughnessy was born in Everett, Massachusetts, on May 19, 1887. After graduating from Boston College in 1909, he taught in Maryland, Montana, and Utah. In Salt Lake City he came to know the Society of Mary, which ran a high school there. He entered the Marists, completing his novitiate and then theology studies, and was ordained a priest in Wash-ington, D.C., in 1920. After earning a doctorate in theol-ogy from The Catholic University of America, he taught there and at the seminary of the Marists, and he worked at the same time on the staff of the apostolic delegation in Washington (1919–32). During his academic career, he contributed various articles to the *Catholic Encyclopedia Supplement* and scholarly journals. At a time when the be-lief was gaining currency that the Catholic Church had been a failure in the United States, suffering enormous losses through defections, he produced an often quoted statistical study, *Has the Immigrant Kept the Faith?* (1925), chronicling the growth and vitality of the faith in Amer-ica. In 1933 he was appointed bishop of Seattle, Washington, and was ordained to the episcopate at the National Shrine of the Immaculate Conception by Archbishop Amleto Ci-cognani, at the time apostolic delegate to the United States. Shaughnessy began his pastoral leadership at the height of the Great Depression, but he brought the diocese through precarious financial straits and inaugurated a successful program of building and expansion. In 1935 he approved the association of Catholic men which began in his dio-cese seeking to foster priestly vocations, known later as Serra International. When the American religious congre-gation of Missionary Servants of the Most Holy Trinity began to experience financial difficulties and personnel shortages, running the risk of suppression, the Holy See put Shaughnessy in charge of the community. He aided and fostered the congregation so well that it considers him a second founder. Bishop Shaughnessy died in Seattle on May 18, 1950, after having suffered a severe stroke several years earlier from which he never completely recovered.

See also MARIST FATHERS.

Adaptations and translations of works by the French Marist, Julius Grimal: *To Die with Jesus* (1925), and *With Jesus to the Priesthood* (1932).

Shaughnessy, Gerald. *Has the Immigrant Kept the Faith?* New York: Macmillan, 1925.

PHILIP GAGE, S.M.

SHEA, JOHN GILMARY (1826–92)

Editor and historian. John Gilmary Shea has posthumously merited the title of the "Father of American Catholic Church historians" as he earned the reputation of being the most significant historian of American Catholicism in the nineteenth century. Born in New York City, July 22, 1824, Shea was the son of an Irish immigrant, James Shea, and Boston-born Mary Ann Flannigan. Shea attended Columbia College grammar school of which his father had been principal. Shea demonstrated an interest in Catholic history at an early age and quickly acquired fluency in the Spanish language. At the age of fourteen, he published a biographical article on Cardinal Alvarez Carilo in the *Young People's Catholic Magazine* in 1838.

John Gilmary Shea

Shea turned to a career in law and was admitted to the New York bar in 1846. He maintained a serious interest in the study of Catholic history and even published several articles. In 1848 Shea pursued a religious vocation and joined the Society of Jesus; he studied at St. John's College, Fordham, New York, and St. Mary's College, Montreal. At St. Mary's College Shea studied history under Felix Martin, S.J., who convinced him of the importance of reliable documentation and the need for collecting original source materials. In 1852 Shea left the Jesuit novitiate and returned to his native New York to pursue a career as an editor and writer.

Major Publications

His first major publication that caught the favorable attention of Catholic and non-Catholic scholars alike, was his *Discovery and Exploration of the Mississippi Valley,* published in 1852. In that work Shea instituted a "renaissance of interest" in the original narratives and events of the French North American missionaries. The contents of the book included original maps and documents that had not been previously accessible to scholars. Two years later, Shea's next important volume appeared, which appealed not only to critical scholars but to "every Catholic fireside." The result of ten years' collection of materials and historical research, this was his *History of the Catholic Missions among the Indian Tribes of the United States, 1529–1859.* The work was widely acclaimed as the most valuable volume that had been issued from the Catholic press up to that day. Even one of Shea's early critics, Orestes Brownson, declared that the work was of "solid merit, entitling the author to an honorable rank among our historical writers."

Shea was a frequent guest in social circles in New York as he pursued his career as a writer in historical studies. In 1854 he married Sophie Savage. The couple had two daughters, Ida and Emma Isabel. John Gilmary Shea contracted with several publishing companies, including Dunigan and Brother and J. Sadlier, to produce a number of school histories including *A General History of Modern Europe* and *The Catholic Church in the U.S.* Poverty was often a serious concern within the Shea family's home as he worked as editor of *The Catholic Directory* for over forty years while publishing companies wavered in their financial support. However, Shea remained determined to continue the tedious work of collecting the necessary statistics of each diocese in the United States. He pursued many literary ventures that could put food on the table including collections of Catholic Bibles and other parts of the Scriptures that had been printed in the United States. He also edited the *Historical Magazine* from 1859 to 1865 and the New York *Catholic News* from 1889–92. Because of his well-known ability to sustain a scholarly and credible reputation, Shea was saluted by Archbishop John Hughes of New York, who declared that "some unborn historian will pray for the prolongation of your life . . . for having contributed to leave behind data, from which he may complete his ecclesiastical history of the U.S. with less toil and more satisfaction than you have experienced in your attempts hitherto."

Shea gained a reputation for expertise concerning the Catholic missions among the indigenous peoples as he edited the fifteen-volume *Library of American Linguistics* and wrote many articles on the Jesuit explorations in North America. In 1884 Shea founded and became the first president of the U.S. Catholic Historical Society which committed itself to collecting and preserving sources for future historians. Perhaps his greatest work was his four-volume *History of the Catholic Church in the U.S.* which occupied the last six years of his life from 1886–92.

Father of American Catholic History

Contemporary historians have placed Shea's contributions in the "archivist school" of writing. Historians of the

Catholic Church in the United States owe no small debt to Shea's persistent and perhaps vexatious attachment to details of documents that served as credible history rather than apologetics. As an admirer and strong supporter of his bishops and Catholic Church, Shea worked with a steadfast determination to prove to non-Catholics the loyalty and good citizenship of Catholics. He dismissed nativist attacks that identified Roman Catholics as foreigners, providing examples of Catholic accomplishments and their importance in the founding of the United States.

Shea's contemporaries viewed him as a serious, scientific historian. While he certainly broke ground for the Catholic Church's entry into scientific methods of historiography, he also demonstrated his own theological bent as he selected and controlled documentation to support his strong, loyal convictions. Shea was very protective of his Church. When the accusations of "Cahenslyism" ignited public sparring among bishops, German Catholics and non-Catholics, Shea defensively blamed all of the problems on Peter Paul Cahensly for "mischievous conduct" that he predicted would "produce evil results by arousing public opinion against the Catholic Church."

The editor and writer of more than two hundred publications, John Gilmary Shea was a pioneer in his field and well deserved to be designated the "Father of American Catholic Historians." He died in Elizabeth, New Jersey, on February 22, 1892.

Guilday, Peter K. "John Gilmary Shea." *Historical Records and Studies* 17 (July 1926) 9–154.
_____. "Bibliography of Shea's Works." *Historical Records and Studies* 17 (July 1926) 155–71.
_____. *John Gilmary Shea: Father of American Catholic History, 1824–1892.* New York, 1926.
Thomas, J. Douglas. "A Century of American Catholic History." *U.S. Catholic Historian* 6 (1) (Winter 1987) 25–49.

THOMAS A. LYNCH

SHEED, FRANK (1897–1981)

Author, publisher, and apologist. Francis Joseph (Frank) Sheed was born in Sydney, Australia, on March 20, 1897, the son of a Presbyterian father and a Roman Catholic mother. His boyhood religious upbringing was shrouded in sectarian bickering and controversy. Perhaps the argumentation that permeated his spiritual formation oriented him toward a legal career early in life, and decisively directed his choice of publishing as a profession and apologetics as an avocation.

Determined to see England and Ireland before beginning law school, he arrived in London in 1920. Shortly after his arrival he became active in the Catholic Evidence Guild and through this association met his future wife, Maisie Ward (granddaughter of Oxford Movement convert, William Ward). He went back to Australia in 1924 to study for the bar, completed his studies, and returned to England to wed Maisie in 1926.

Publisher and Public Speaker

Sheed, with his wife, founded the publishing firm of Sheed and Ward in the same year that they were married. From London, the firm expanded and an office was opened in New York in early 1933. Sheed and Ward became the most influential Catholic publishing house in the English-speaking world. He cultivated, introduced, and disseminated the works of Catholic authors throughout the period that was often referred to by Sheed as the "Catholic Literary Revival."

Even though he was kept busy on both sides of the Atlantic by business concerns, Sheed and his wife remained active in the Catholic Evidence Guild, a group of lay apologists trained in both theology and public speaking. Sheed assisted the fledgling Guild affiliates in both England and the United States by participating in both the theological and oratorical training of their members. He took part in outdoor speaking throughout his life, ending his commitment to the work of the guild only when the ill health of advancing age prevented him from continuing. His erudition in theology was recognized by the Vatican when he was awarded a pontifical doctoral degree in that sacred science.

Theologian and Apologist

Sheed put his oratorical abilities to further use by booking lecture tours throughout the United States every year, effectively advancing the apologetic enterprise as well as promoting the works published by Sheed and Ward. Sheed himself had become a prolific author. In his first work, *Nullity of Marriage* (1931), the trained lawyer who never practiced his craft put his legal mind to work defending the Church's recent grants of annulment to the Duke of Marlborough and Guglielmo Marconi. This was followed by *A Map of Life* (1933), *Communism and Man* (1938), *Theology and Sanity* (1946), *Society and Sanity* (1953), *Theology for Beginners* (1958), and *To Know Christ Jesus* (1962).

The crisis within the Church that followed the Second Vatican Council precipitated a crisis in the Catholic publishing world as well. In the early 1960s, Sheed had turned over to others effective control of both the London and New York branches of the company he had founded. He returned to active management only briefly in order to organize the final sale of Sheed and Ward in 1973.

Following the council, Sheed continued to lecture and to write: *God and the Human Condition* (1966), *Is It the Same Church?* (1968), *Genesis Regained* (1969), *What Difference Does Jesus Make?* (1971), and his memoirs, *The Church and I* (1974).

Sheed the apologist and Sheed the businessman were not always free of conflict. After Vatican II, the acquisition of saleable theological titles became increasingly the object of great competition among Catholic publishers. There appears to have been a concern that he would fall out of intellectual favor with the theologians that he published, leading them to avoid association with his firm's name. Except for this anxiety, he might have been able to demonstrate that the breach that had developed between theology and apologetics was unnecessary. Regardless, what cannot be eclipsed is the immense contribution he made toward the development of a new apologetic where the methodology of exposition replaced that of argument.

Central to this apologetic was the need to stress that the Gospels had to reflect faithfully the personality and life of Jesus of Nazareth and, above all, to reject any notion of a cleavage between the Christ of history and the Christ of faith. He applauded the post-Vatican II dual theological focus on what revelation tells us of both God and humanity. Throughout his apologetic there remains, however, the primary concern that humanity acquire an accurate perception of God, lest it distort the truth about itself.

See also CATHOLIC BOOK PUBLISHING.

McLucas, James. *Frank Sheed: Apologist*. Rome, 1991.
Sheed, Frank. *The Church and I*. Garden City and New York, 1974.
Sheed, Wilfred. *Frank and Maisie*. New York, 1985.
Ward, Maisie. *Unfinished Business*. New York, 1964.

JAMES McLUCAS

SHEEHAN, LUKE (1873–1937)

Capuchin missionary, pioneer of the Church in Oregon. Francis Bernard Sheehan was born in Cork City, Ireland, on February 28, 1873. At the age of fifteen he entered the minor seminary of the Capuchins in Cork and, the following year, their novitiate where he took the religious name, Luke. He was ordained to the priesthood in 1896.

After six years of teaching philosophy in the Capuchin House of Formation in Kilkenny, Luke embarked upon the first phase of his missionary life by volunteering to work in Aden, the British colony on the southwestern coast of the Arabian peninsula. Shortly after his arrival, Sheehan was appointed pro-vicar apostolic and, from 1902 to 1908, ministered to the needs of the members of the British garrison and to the Goan seamen who passed through the port of Aden. Periodically he traveled to Somalia, to the remote islands of Aden, and to Bombay, India, to preach retreats and missions. Forced to leave Aden because of illness, Sheehan returned to Ireland. When he learned that his replacement had died of the same illness, Sheehan immediately returned and remained until he was too weak to continue his work. He returned again to Ireland where

he remained until 1910 when Bishop Joseph O'Reilly of the Diocese of Baker City, Oregon, asked the Irish Capuchins to come to the United States.

In 1910 Luke Sheehan, together with Thomas Dowling, arrived in Hermiston, Oregon. Within four months his companion returned to Ireland leaving Sheehan to explore the possibilities of developing the Church of eastern Oregon. When his Irish confreres sent Casimir Butler to help him, Sheehan left him to care for Hermiston and moved to minister to Crook County, Oregon, and the barely developed town of Bend where there were only one hundred and fifty Catholics scattered over an area of eight thousand square miles. After taking up residence in a small room over a wooden dance hall, the Irish Capuchin walked or rode on horseback thousands of miles to solidify the Church's presence. In 1916 the railroad came to Bend, bringing a large influx of Irish Catholics to the remote Western town. Four years later Sheehan built a new church and, shortly thereafter, brought the Sisters of St. Joseph of Tipton, Indiana, to staff the newly established St. Charles Hospital. In 1936 he succeeded in opening a parish school in which the Sisters of the Holy Names taught.

Throughout these years Luke Sheehan suffered not only innumerable physical hardships, he endured the more difficult bigotry of many of Crook County's residents, especially members of the Ku Klux Klan. Barriers were continually placed in his attempts at purchasing property for the church; once built, the windows of the new church were repeatedly broken, and Sheehan himself was often denounced and maligned. He never relented in his efforts to build the church. In 1935 he courageously challenged the Klan at one of their meetings and was thus instrumental in their decline in Oregon. Luke Sheehan died at Hood River, Oregon, on February 11, 1937, twenty-seven years after his arrival in Bend.

See also FRANCISCANS (CAPUCHINS).

REGIS J. ARMSTRONG, O.F.M. CAP.

SHEEN, FULTON JOHN (1895–1979)

Educator, author, radio and television apologist, archbishop. He was born Peter Sheen (May 8, 1895), the first of four sons, to Newton Morris Sheen and Delia Fulton Sheen on the second floor of the family hardware store, El Paso, Illinois. He died in New York City on December 9, 1979. Three grandparents were Irish immigrants, whose fluctuating economic circumstances shaped his earliest perceptions of outsiders struggling to move into the American mainstream. His uncle, Daniel R. Sheen, financially assisted Fulton's education which began in Peoria at St. Mary's Cathedral School (1901–09), where he took John as his confirmation name, and continued at Spalding Institute (1909–13), a Catholic high school run by the Brothers of

Fulton J. Sheen

Mary, where he enrolled as Fulton John Sheen, adopting his mother's maiden name.

Sheen received an A.B. (1916) and M.A. (1917) at St. Viator College and Seminary, Bourbonnais, Illinois, where his articles on Shakespearean drama in the school journal, *Viatorian,* and a triumphant string of debating contests displayed a promising aptitude for writing and oratory. Completing his studies at the Seminary of St. Paul, St. Paul, Minnesota, he was ordained to the priesthood (September 20, 1919) for the Diocese of Peoria, under Bishop Edmund M. Dunne. Sheen earned the S.T.L. and J.C.B. at The Catholic University of America (1920) and his Ph.D. at The Catholic University of Louvain, Belgium (1923), one of the foremost centers of scholastic studies in the Catholic world.

In 1925 Sheen received the *Agrégé en Philosophie* for his doctoral dissertation, "God and Intelligence in Modern Philosophy: A Critical Study in the Light of the Philosophy of Saint Thomas." While teaching dogmatic theology at St. Edmund's College, Ware, England, he met the renowned apologist G. K. Chesterton, whose weekly radio broadcasts over the BBC inspired Sheen's later work as the featured speaker on the NBC radio broadcast "The Catholic Hour" (1930–52). The published dissertation (1926), embellished by Chesterton's introduction, was acclaimed a philosophic masterpiece in which "the Catholic Church comes forward as the one and only real champion of Reason," and earned Sheen the distinction of being the first American to receive the Cardinal Mercier Prize for International Philosophy.

At the outset of *God and Intelligence,* his only thoroughly researched piece of writing, Sheen set the pattern

for what followed in his own career and, indeed, for most of the neo-Thomist movement in America. He saw his task as an attempt "to make St. Thomas functional, not for a school, but for the world . . . a remedy against the anarchy of ideas, riot of philosophical systems and breakdown of spiritual forces."

Professor at The Catholic University of America

After calling him back to his home diocese for a few months service at St. Patrick's Church, a poor inner-city parish, Dunne released Sheen to teach theology at The Catholic University of America in Washington, D.C. Within that first year (1926), altercations among the faculty concerning standards for seminary training forced his abrupt reassignment to the Philosophy Department and the chair of Apologetics. Recurrent disputes with academic theologians created skepticism concerning Sheen's scholarly reputation. A *Commonweal* review of *Old Errors, New Labels* (1931) complained that Sheen's historical inaccuracies indicated he was "more interested in imparting an effect than information." Virgil Michel, O.S.B., a prominent liturgical theologian, accused him of plagiarism and careless scholarship in a stinging review of Sheen's *The Mystical Body of Christ* (1938). Archbishop Francesco Laurdo, faculty of Canon Law, urged Sheen to discontinue his attempts at popularizing Catholic doctrine on radio and to restrict himself to the discipline of the classroom. Church historian and Sheen-confidant, John Tracy Ellis, reported that Sheen "consciously abandoned the life of a scholar for that of the preacher, realizing in a realistic way that it was impossible to serve both simultaneously."

Preacher and Convert-Maker

Sheen's intellectual status remains arguable, but the success of his apologetical career is indisputable. In this sphere, as Ellis observed, "[t]he contribution of Archbishop Sheen to the Catholic Church and to the general American public was incalculable." His wide-ranging preaching career included: annual lenten homilist at St. Patrick's Cathedral (1930–52) and Paulist Church (1926–31) in New York City; preacher at the Summer Conferences at Cambridge, England (1930–31) and Westminster Cathedral, London (1925–31); Cardinal Spellman's 1948 Pacific Tour; and countless retreats for priests and religious congregations, which, by his own report, were his most gratifying preaching experiences and occupied his agenda to the very end of his life.

His no fewer than ninety-two books were invariably repetitive reworkings of his public platform addresses and were "designed to foster one's spiritual growth rather than deepen intellectual enrichment." Most notable: *Peace of Soul* (1949), which rose to sixth place on the *New York Times* best-seller list and was considered by Sheen his finest next to *Preface to Religion* (1946), "my best popular presentation." His most financially successful *Life of Christ* (1958) was based on fifteen addresses given on "The Catholic Hour" (1952). By his own report, *Religion Without God* (1928) was "absolutely terrible and should never have been published."

Sheen's reputation as a convert-maker was well publicized. In Washington and New York City his courses of instruction drew people from all walks of life, but most notably congresswoman Claire Booth Luce, Henry Ford II, Heywood Broun (columnist for the New York *Telegram*), pro-Communist journalist Louis Budenz, and violinist Fritz Kreisler.

Television Personality

Sheen spoke on the first televised religious service on Easter Sunday, 1940. But it was the 129 broadcasts of "Life Is Worth Living" (commercially sponsored by the Admiral Corporation) on the Dumont (1952–55) and ABC (1955–57) television networks that established Sheen as the best-known Catholic priest in 1950s America. For many he represented the movement of Roman Catholicism into mainstream American life. His talks essentially redefined the Church within the larger society by telling stories of Catholics in terms of their own heritage, while claiming continuity with other Christian communions and Judaism, and asserting the social and political standing of Catholics within the American democracy. By design, his rhetorical aim was to mediate rather than maintain denominational division, a fact that accounts for the ecumenical appeal of his telecasts for both Catholic and non-Catholic audiences.

As a staunch neo-Thomist, Sheen emphasized the importance of reason in sorting out the problems of the day, especially the American confrontation of Communism. The infusion of anti-Communism into his talks recast its social meaning as a spiritual component of the postwar religious revival of 1950s America. In no fewer than forty-two programs he treated the evils of atheistic Communism, yet at the same time he argued the need for love of the Russian people. His program on "The Death of Stalin," aired live one week before Stalin's death (March 5, 1953), drew enormous media attention and clinched Sheen's role as the premier Catholic anti-Communist.

On another front, Sheen's attacks on Freudian psychology, a staple of his earlier radio and public platform talks, were noticeably tempered after Catholic psychologists publicly objected to his attacks in 1947. Sheen conceded, "If the modern soul wants to begin its quest for peace with psychology instead of our own metaphysics, we will begin with psychology." This type of accommodation brought Sheen's television talks into the realm of popular culture, where religious ideas and secular knowledge mingled easily, and effectively increased his diverse audiences' willingness to agree with him.

While Sheen was building his television audience of millions, he also served as auxiliary bishop of the Archdiocese of New York (1951–66) and as national director of the Society for the Propagation of the Faith (1950–66), a fundraising organization for Catholic missions around the world. The telecasts displayed the SPF logo (a corpus-less cross) on the studio set, and the SPF mailing address at the end of each program. Donations in 1955 had reached twenty-five million dollars, of which one million was Sheen's personal contribution of royalties and fees earned from his books and television appearances. His generosity was also regularly directed to Archbishop T. J. Toolen for mission work in poor black neighborhoods, such as the Martin de Porres Hospital in the diocese of Mobile-Birmingham.

Sheen and Cardinal Spellman

As director of SPF, Sheen had frequent confrontations with his superior, Francis Cardinal Spellman, over the disposition of funds. Most notable was the trouble ignited by Spellman's demand in 1957 that SPF reimburse the archdiocese for large quantities of powdered milk acquired by Spellman as head of the Military Ordinariate during the Korean conflict. Sheen, knowing that Spellman had not paid for the milk, balked at the idea of reimbursement and led his board of directors to refuse the Cardinal's assessment. At Spellman's request the matter was brought to the attention of the ailing Pope Pius XII, whose own investigation revealed the accuracy of Sheen's position. But repercussions for Sheen were severe. Spellman, who had direct responsibility for approving Sheen's television contract with the Admiral Corporation, notified its president that Sheen was no longer permitted to perform. In a terse announcement in *The New York Times* (October 19, 1957) Sheen explained that for "personal reasons" he was moving on to "other projects." After Spellman's death (1967), Sheen disclosed that he "could have gone higher" had he foregone principle in his clash with the Cardinal. Two later attempts (1964, 1966) to revive the television program failed to get the prominence of a network timeslot and faded quickly in syndication.

From 1958 to 1966, Sheen galvanized his work at SPF, traveling to Catholic missions around the world, editing the *Mission* and *World Mission* magazines, and serving on the Commission on the Missions at the Second Vatican Council in Rome (1962–65). Thoroughly taken with the spirit of conciliar reform, Sheen felt poised to create the model postconciliar diocese, a goal he set out to realize when installed as the sixth bishop of the Diocese of Rochester, New York (December 16, 1966).

Bishop of Rochester

His agenda to implement council decrees was ostensibly driven by a collegial approach to administrative and social justice issues. He immediately created territorial vicars, a diocesan priests' council, a board of counselors that included several laypersons, and a new Vicar for Urban Ministry. He spoke out against abortion legislation (pastoral letter, 1967), the Vietnam War, and alleged racial discrimination at Eastman Kodak Company. He instituted annual parish missionary appeals and a tax on new church construction to assist the poor in repairing housing units. His crowning ecumenical concept was the Rochester Center for Theological Studies (1968), a consortium of local seminaries including Colgate-Rochester (Baptist), Bexley Hall (Episcopalian), and St. Bernard's Seminary (Catholic).

Rochester Church historian Robert McNamara observed that in all of these projects Sheen was more a man of ideas than details. Their success was achieved by local individuals who followed them through to realization, as in the case of the accreditation of St. Bernard's Institute in 1971. In fact, Sheen seldom, if ever, consulted with his various committees, and compromised the reception of his innovations by consistently promoting them through *The New York Times* rather than the local Gannett papers. The most notable "failure" was Sheen's offer of St. Bridget Church property to the federal government (HUD) as a site for federal housing. Learning of the project from the national media, the parishioners picketed the Pastoral Office, diocesan officers were caught uninformed, and HUD pulled out of the deal. "One can gather from his autobiography that [Sheen] never realized himself that he had small skill as an administrator and had little sense of true collegiality, and that this was the real cause for at least several of his 'failures.'" Discouraged, Sheen resigned as ordinary (October 10, 1969) a full year short of seventy-five, the mandatory age for retirement.

Last Years

For the next ten years Sheen conducted countless retreats worldwide, until heart disease confined him to his Manhattan apartment. In 1969 Pope Paul VI appointed him to the Papal Commission for Nonbelievers and named him titular archbishop of Newport, Wales. Of all the awards and testimonials amassed during his career, Sheen cherished the words Pope John Paul II spoke to him personally two months before Sheen's death: "You have written and spoken well of the Lord Jesus, and you are a loyal son of the Church." He was buried in the crypt of St. Patrick's Cathedral (December 13, 1979).

At the end of the twentieth century, historians increasingly note the prophetic quality of Sheen's ecumenical ambition. To be sure, no other American Roman Catholic churchperson has matched the popularity and influence of this mediagenic bishop whose apologetic touched the lives of millions of Catholics and non-Catholics alike.

Ellis, John Tracy. *Catholic Bishops: A Memoir.* Wilmington, Del.: Michael Glazier, 1984.

Fields, Kathleen Riley. "Bishop Fulton J. Sheen: An American Catholic Response to the Twentieth Century." Ph. D. dissertation, University of Notre Dame, 1988.

Halsey, William M. *The Survival of American Innocence.* Indiana: University of Notre Dame Press, 1980.

McNamara, Robert F. *The Diocese of Rochester 1868–1968.* New York: Diocese of Rochester, 1968.

McSweeney, Thomas J. "The Rhetorical Fulton J. Sheen: 'Life Is Worth Living' (1952–57)." Ph.D. dissertation, University of Maryland, College Park, 1996.

Sheen, Fulton J. *Treasure in Clay: The Autobiography of Fulton J. Sheen.* Garden City, N.Y.: Doubleday, 1980.

THOMAS J. McSWEENEY

SHEERIN, JOHN BASIL (1906–92)

Priest, author, editor. John Basil Sheerin was born in Brooklyn, New York, on October 12, 1906—one of eight children of Frank and Margaret Sheerin. He graduated from Fordham University and from Fordham Law School, was admitted to the bar of the state of New York in 1932, and was licensed to practice before the Supreme Court of the United States in 1938. He would receive two honorary doctorates: in 1958, a Doctor of Law degree from Boston College; and in 1982, a Doctor of Humane Letters degree from St. Francis College in Brooklyn, New York. He entered the Paulist novitiate in 1933 and was ordained a Paulist priest in 1937. He received an M.A. degree from

John B. Sheerin

The Catholic University of America and taught English at St. Paul's College in Washington, D.C., until 1940. In 1945 he founded the Paulist Information Center on Park Street in Boston, Massachusetts.

From 1948 to 1972, he was senior editor of the *Catholic World,* the flagship journal of opinion of Paulist Press. He was ahead of his time on such issues as ecumenism, race relations, and civil rights. He advocated Church renewal and urged new approaches to the Catholic-Jewish dialogue. He was a vigorous and early opponent of U.S. policy in Vietnam. The Catholic Press Association of the United States and Canada presented him with the Saint Francis de Sales Award in 1975, and cited his courage in defending unpopular causes, civility in exploring controversial issues, and responsibility in respecting the complexity of issues. For many years Sheerin also explored these issues as a syndicated columnist. His column, "Sum and Substance," appeared in a score of diocesan Catholic newspapers.

In 1957 he and Gustave Weigel, S.J., were the first Catholics to serve as official Vatican observers at the World Council of Churches meeting in North America. He was a *peritus* at all the sessions of the Second Vatican Council from 1962 to 1965. During the 1960s he served on the steering committee of Clergy and Laity Concerned About Vietnam, an ecumenical antiwar group that included among its directors Dr. Martin Luther King, Jr., Rev. William Sloan Coffin, and Rabbi Abraham Heschel. From 1967 to 1975 Sheerin served as an advisor to the U.S. Bishops' Catholic-Jewish Secretariat. In 1974 he was appointed a general consultor to the Secretariat for Catholic-Jewish Relations at the National Conference of Catholic Bishops.

His writings appeared frequently in such periodicals as *America, Commonweal, The Ecumenist, American Ecclesiastical Review, Jubilee, Interracial Review, Lumen Vitae,* and *The Catholic Lawyer.* Among Sheerin's books are *The Sacrament of Freedom* (on confession), *Peace, War and the Young Catholic* (advocating selective conscientious objection for draft-age Catholic youth), and his last book, *Never Look Back: The Career and Concerns of Msgr. John J. Burke, CSP.*

After he finished *Never Look Back,* he found it increasingly difficult to look back at all. By 1983, Alzheimer's disease robbed Fr. Sheerin's mind of memory. He died nine years later on January 13, 1992.

See also CATHOLIC WORLD, THE; ECUMENISM IN AMERICA; PAULISTS (C.S.P.).

THOMAS E. COMBER, C.S.P.

SHEHAN, LAWRENCE JOSEPH (1898–1984)

Education and Early Ministry

Cardinal archbishop. He was born on December 18, 1898 in Baltimore and studied at St. Charles College, Catonsville, Maryland, St. Mary's Seminary, Baltimore, and at the Pon-

Lawrence J. Cardinal Shehan

tifical North American College, Rome, where he was ordained a priest on December 23, 1922. He completed his doctoral studies in theology the following year at the Urbaniana University in Rome, and returned as a curate in St. Patrick Church, Washington, D.C. Shehan was involved in pastoral work from 1923–47. He also served as assistant director of Catholic Charities from 1929–36, and director from 1936–45. He was appointed auxiliary bishop to the archbishop of Baltimore and Washington in 1945 and, in 1947, auxiliary to the archbishop of Baltimore, and served as vicar general from 1948 until his translation to the newly erected Diocese of Bridgeport, Connecticut, in 1953.

First Bishop of Bridgeport

During his nine years in Bridgeport, Shehan devoted himself to ensuring the adequate organization and functioning of the diocesan offices, approved the construction of twenty-four new churches and the establishment of eighteen new parishes, as well as numerous parish schools, and the founding of three diocesan high schools, in Bridgeport (1957), Stamford (1958), and Norwalk (1959) (DiGiovanni, 211–15).

Shehan also organized youth ministry in the diocese, improved vocation work for priestly and religious vocations, began parish ministry for the growing numbers of Hispanic, Portuguese, and Brazilian immigrants, and founded St. Joseph Manor in Trumbull for the care of the elderly, introducing the Carmelite Sisters for the Aged and Infirm to staff the facility in 1958. In order to complete the initial organization of the diocese and establish a uniform code of practice and discipline for the clergy,

Shehan celebrated the first synod of Bridgeport in October 1960.

Archbishop of Baltimore

In July 1961 Shehan was promoted to the titular archiepiscopal see of Nicopolis ad Nestum, and appointed coadjutor to the archbishop of Baltimore, Francis Keough. He succeeded to the see in December of that year, following the death of Keough and received the pallium March 29, 1962 (Shehan, 136).

In 1962, as the twelfth archbishop of Baltimore, Shehan began his official work in the field of ecumenism, with his nomination as a member of the Congregation for the Union of Christians (*Osservatore Romano,* September 3, 1984). In November 1964 he was chosen by the bishops as the head of the Episcopal Commission for Ecumenism, which was to inform the American hierarchy on the practical application of the decrees of Vatican II on dialogue with other Christians. During the Second Vatican Council, Shehan served as a member of the Conciliar Commission for the Discipline of the Clergy and of the Faithful, and was named a member of the Council of Presidency of Vatican Council II in July 1965. During the council he made a number of interventions concerning ecumenism and religious liberty. In 1965 Pope Paul VI named Shehan his representative at meetings with the Orthodox, which resulted in the lifting of the mutual excommunications by Constantinople and Rome.

Concerned about racism in America, and in his archdiocese, Shehan participated in the 1963 March on Washington with Doctor Martin Luther King, Jr. (*National Catholic Reporter,* September 7, 1984). In March 1963 Shehan issued a strong pastoral letter on racial justice, stating that "discrimination has no place in the Church." He made a study of racism in the Catholic institutions within the archdiocese, and formally requested the Catholic hospitals to approve and support a rule of nondiscrimination.

Shehan was not a supporter of the war in Vietnam, which he called "uncontrolled violence and senseless wholesale destruction of human life and moral values" (*National Catholic Reporter,* September 7, 1984). In the early 1970s Shehan supplied the bail for the Harrisburg Seven, which included Fr. Philip Berrigen, following one of their protests. Shehan visited them in jail and assigned an archdiocesan attorney to defend them in court. Throughout his years in Baltimore, Shehan supported nonviolent efforts for peace, social justice, and fair housing.

Cardinal Archbishop

Pope Paul VI created him a cardinal on February 22, 1965, the second of Baltimore's archbishops to receive the red hat. In 1973 he served as the papal legate to the Fortieth Eucharistic Congress in Melbourne, Australia, and retired in 1974.

Shehan has often been compared with the first cardinal of Baltimore, James Gibbons. He was the leader of the nation's premier see during years of social and ecclesial turmoil, striving to hold together both Baltimore society while teaching racial and social equality, and the Church in America, by encouraging moderation in the new and respect for the traditional. At a testimonial dinner for the retiring Cardinal Shehan on May 21, 1974, Bishop Joseph Grossman said, "Lawrence Shehan is a man who became a bishop in a world where everything was certain, and a cardinal in a world where nothing was" (Shehan, 291–92). He was a man who served the universal Church faithfully and loyally. He worked to strengthen Baltimore's bonds with the universal Church by his own faithful preaching and forceful leadership, giving life to Rome's legislation and instructions by his tireless efforts in the areas of ecumenism, race relations, equal rights, and education.

See also MARYLAND, CATHOLIC CHURCH IN; VATICAN II AND AMERICAN CATHOLICS.

DiGiovanni, Stephen M. *The Catholic Church in Fairfield County, 1666–1961.* New Canaan, 1987.

Shehan, Lawrence J. *A Blessing of Years. The Memoirs of Lawrence Cardinal Shehan.* Notre Dame, 1982.

National Catholic Register, June 24, 1990.

National Catholic Reporter, September 7, 1984.

Osservatore Romano, September 3, 9, 1984.

Spalding, Thomas W. *The Premier See: A History of the Archdiocese of Baltimore.* Baltimore: Johns Hopkins University Press, 1989.

STEPHEN M. DiGIOVANNI

SHEIL, BERNARD JAMES (1886–1969)

Archbishop, social activist. Sheil was born in Chicago on February 18, 1886. His early education was in the parochial schools of Chicago and at St. Viator's College in Bourbonnais, Illinois. After turning down an offer from the Chicago White Sox baseball team, he entered St. Viator's Seminary. He was ordained to the priesthood by Archbishop James Quigley on May 21, 1910. He served as a curate in Chicago parishes and performed chaplaincy services at the Great Lakes Naval Training Station during 1918–19. In the 1920s he became chaplain for the Cook County jail and was deeply affected by his work, especially among juvenile offenders. Youth work would become a centerpiece of his career.

Gregarious and hard-working, Sheil was appointed to various chancery posts by Archbishop George Mundelein, who made use of his organizational skills in arranging the mammoth International Eucharistic Congress held in Chicago in 1926. Sheil was appointed auxiliary bishop in 1928 and

Bernard J. Sheil

was consecrated by Mundelein on May 1, 1928, in Chicago's Holy Name Cathedral. He was later appointed pastor of St. Andrew's parish on the near north side of Chicago.

Catholic Youth Organization

Unaccustomed by temperament to sit in the shadows and with Mundelein's blessing, Sheil set to work developing the youth apostolate that he had committed himself to during his jail chaplaincy. By 1931 he had consolidated a variety of existing youth programs and combined them with some fundraising and social welfare operations run by the archdiocese to form the Catholic Youth Organization (CYO). Undoubtedly, the CYO was one of the most successful youth programs in American Catholic history. In its glory days, Sheil put together a mini-empire that consisted of CYO camps, educational programs, and summer schools. But the main emphasis of the organization was its extensive athletic program that welcomed Chicago youths of any creed or color. Tough Chicago teens competed vigorously in local boxing competitions that eventually worked up to a major tournament. Sheil stoutly defended his programs from critics who disliked boxing by maintaining that the morally dubious sport was the best way to rehabilitate impoverished young men who otherwise would have turned to gangs and a life of urban crime. Many dioceses imitated CYO programs and Sheil tried unsuccessfully to create a national CYO under the auspices of the Youth Department of the National Catholic Welfare Conference.

The CIO and National Politics

His CYO triumphs and his high public visibility in Chicago propelled him into national politics. He benefited espe-cially from the relationship between President Franklin D. Roosevelt and Cardinal Mundelein. With the assistance of his personal lawyer (and later federal judge), William Campbell, Sheil began to cultivate contacts in the Roosevelt administration, especially Thomas G. ("Tommy the Cork") Corcoran. He endeared himself to Roosevelt by publicly blasting Fr. Charles Coughlin, a bitter critic of his administration. He also earned the esteem of the labor movement in 1937 when he appeared on the dais of a huge public rally called by leaders of the CIO to organize Chicago's meat-packers. Despite threats to his life, he delivered a warm endorsement of John L. Lewis. Later, Sheil would attempt unsuccessfully to mend the strained relationship between the union chieftain and the President.

After the death of Mundelein in 1939, Sheil nurtured hopes that he would succeed to the Chicago see. Moreover, officials of the Roosevelt administration lobbied Roman officials on his behalf. Sheil was disappointed when the post went to Milwaukee archbishop Samuel A. Stritch, but turned his hopes for ecclesiastical advancement on programs of self-promotion under the auspices of the CYO. In the 1940s, with the assistance of a stable of bright young Catholic intellectuals, Sheil began a new career as a public spokesman for union rights, American democracy, and economic justice. He was one of the first American bishops to speak out against racism and denounced anti-Semitism with equal ferocity.

Even before Mundelein's death, Sheil was wearying of the athletic emphasis of the CYO and sought to give it more of an intellectual and academic direction. With the help of his "brains trust" he sought to augment his new role as social spokesman, and conceived an educational arm of the CYO called the Sheil School of Social Studies. The Sheil School, with its adult classes in theology, social issues, and art, lasted nearly a decade and thousands of Chicagoans visited the school, making it in the words of one observer "a kind of Catholic Times Square." Sheil also branched out into other endeavors, sponsoring an FM radio station, organizing the first ministry to Chicago's growing Puerto Rican community, and even running a polo field.

Much to Sheil's unhappiness, these efforts did not have the intended effect of making him a bishop of his own diocese. Despite a constant stream of rumors that he was to be appointed archbishop of Washington, D.C., or St. Louis, Sheil was never able to overcome the distrust of his superior, Cardinal Samuel Stritch, or the outright hostility of Cardinal Francis Spellman of New York. They interdicted his efforts at promotion and he never left Chicago.

Later Years

Growing disappointment with his failure to rise in the ranks of the hierarchy was aggravated by serious financial difficulties in the CYO. Although Sheil periodically reshuffled the CYO's administrators, the financial situation never seemed to improve. Continually popular with those outside his organization, many of Sheil's staffers regarded him with contempt, especially after he squelched an attempt on the part of his employees to unionize.

Beset by financial difficulties and growing increasingly bitter, Sheil nonetheless kept up his public speaking engagements. Having often jousted with conservatives in and outside the Church, he took relish in leveling a blast against the tactics of Senator Joseph McCarthy of Wisconsin at a speech at a labor convention in April 1954. In September of that year, Sheil dramatically resigned from the leadership of the CYO and determined to return to full-time parish life.

The timing of Sheil's departure with the McCarthy attack gave the appearance that Sheil was being punished for attacking the Senator. In fact, Sheil's deteriorating financial position compelled him to resign. After a brief flurry of press interest, Sheil resumed his pastorate of St. Andrew's parish and slowly faded from the scene. The Archdiocese of Chicago paid his debts and absorbed or terminated the various programs of the CYO. Sheil periodically reemerged from his self-imposed seclusion, securing for himself an honorary archbishop's title in 1961 and a place on a committee at Vatican Council II. But he never attended a session of the council and was largely a forgotten man. In 1967 Archbishop John Cody insisted on his retirement from the pastorate and he moved to Tucson, Arizona, where he died on September 13, 1969.

See also CODY, JOHN CARDINAL; ILLINOIS, CATHOLIC CHURCH IN; McCARTHY, JOSEPH RAYMOND.

Avella, Steven M. *This Confident Church: Chicago Catholicism 1940–1965.* Notre Dame, 1992.

Carroll, Mary Elizabeth. "Bishop Sheil: Prophet Without Honor." *Harper's* 211 (November 1955) 45–51.

Kantowicz, Edward. *Corporation Sole: Cardinal Mundelein and Chicago Catholicism.* Notre Dame, 1982.

Treat, Roger L. *Bishop Sheil and the CYO.* New York, 1951.

STEVEN M. AVELLA

SHERIDAN, PHILIP HENRY (1831–88)

General. The son of Irish immigrants, Sheridan served as a cavalry commander in the Civil War, was active in Native American campaigns in the West, and was elevated to the rank of general, the highest military office available in his lifetime. He was born in Albany, New York, on March 6, 1831, and was raised in the small town of Somerset, Ohio. He received an appointment to West Point, and he graduated in 1853 with average grades but with a reputation as an excellent horseman. After leaving the academy, Sheridan served in a variety of positions in the

General Philip H. Sheridan

Southwest and in the Washington Territory, where he led mounted infantry against an uprising by the Yakima on the Columbia River.

After the Civil War began, Sheridan was recalled from the Northwest to serve as chief quartermaster for General Curtis' Army of Southwest Missouri. It was in this position that then Lieutenant Sheridan first earned a reputation for being dedicated to the comfort and well-being of his men. This reputation followed him through the ranks, and was a great source of pride for Sheridan. In May of 1862 he accepted a commission from the governor of Michigan to head the newly organized Second Michigan Cavalry as a colonel. During 1862 and 1863 Sheridan's cavalry served in Mississippi, Kentucky, and Tennessee.

In November of 1863 he gained the notice of General Grant when he and his men helped the Union army to capture Missionary Ridge and Lookout Mountain near Chattanooga. In March 1864, when Grant was named to head the army of the Potomac, he chose Sheridan to be his commander of cavalry for the entire army. In the summer and fall of 1864 he drove Confederate General Jubal Early's forces out of the Shenandoah Valley of northern Virginia, which had previously been a stronghold for the Confederacy. At the Battle of Cedar Creek, he led his retreating forces back into their pursuers, turning a potential disaster into victory, and earned the respect of other military leaders as well as the American population at large. Soon after the Battle of Cedar Creek, Sheridan was promoted to the rank of major general in the regular army. His cavalry remained active until the very last campaigns of the war, pursuing the remainder of the army of northern Virginia from Petersburg to Appomattox Court House, where Lee eventually surrendered.

After the war ended, Sheridan served in Mexico and as military governor of the Fifth Military District, which encompassed Louisiana and Texas. He later returned to his antebellum mission of settling Native American disturbances in the West, where he served with another young general named George Custer. It was during this period that Sheridan was credited with the epithet: "The only good Indian is a dead Indian." Despite his reputation for harsh—often ruthless—treatment of his military foes, he was admired and respected by those who served under his command. The nickname "Little Phil," which he received from his men in the Second Michigan Cavalry, illustrates the friendly rapport he kept with his men. In 1884 he succeeded William T. Sherman as commander-in-chief of the U.S. Army, and on June 1, 1888, Congress elevated him to the rank of full general. He died only two months later, on August 5, in Nonquitt, Massachusetts.

Hoig, Stan. *The Battle of Washita: The Sheridan-Custer Indian Campaign of 1867–69.* New York, 1976.
Hutton, Paul Andrew. *Phil Sheridan and His Army.* Lincoln, Nebraska, 1985.
Lewis, Thomas A. *The Guns of Cedar Creek.* New York, 1988.
O'Connor, Richard. *Sheridan, the Inevitable.* New York, 1953.
Sheridan, Philip. *Personal Memoirs of P. H. Sheridan.* New York, 1888.
Stackpole, Edward J. *Sheridan in the Shenandoah.* New York, 1961.
Taggart, Joseph. *Biographical Sketches.* Kansas City, 1907.
MATTHEW LaFLAMME

SHERMAN, PASCHAL (1895–1970)

Native American leader. Paschal Sherman was born in 1895 on the homestead of his grandfather, Chief Wapato John, a leader of the Lake Chelan Native Americans in eastern Washington State. Sherman was educated at St. Mary's Mission, Omak, Washington, a protégé of its founder, Rev. Etienne DeRouge, S.J. Sherman went on to earn five college degrees, including a Ph.D. degree from The Catholic University of America and two law degrees. He made his career as a legal expert in "claims service regulations" for the Veterans' Administration, working in Seattle, Boise, and Washington, D.C. After nearly forty-four years of service, Sherman retired in 1962 and was honored in the *Congressional Record.*

Sherman was an activist in maintaining the status of Native American land law, a founding member of the National Congress of American Indians, the Affiliated Tribes of Northwest Indians, and chairman of the American Indian Civil Liberties Trust. He became a nationally noted figure during the effort to "terminate" the federal-tribal relationship in the 1960s. Often flying from Washington, D.C., to serve as consultant and legal advisor to his own Colville Confederated Tribes and other tribes throughout the country, he fulfilled the native name given to him in his youth of *Kwas-kway*—the bluebird, with magical powers to fly to distant places and bring back news for the people. With Sherman's persistent help, the tribes were able to turn back the congressional threat to their future.

Sherman passed away in 1970, and his body was flown home for burial at his beloved St. Mary's Mission, with many telegrams of tribute from the president, federal, and tribal leaders. In 1974 his old mission school was renamed Paschal Sherman Indian School.

See also NATIVE AMERICANS AND THE CATHOLIC CHURCH.

Ilma, Maria, P.P. *Blackrobes and Indians on the Last Frontier: A Story of Heroism.* Milwaukee, 1966.
THOMAS CONNOLLY, S.J.

SHIELDS, JAMES (1806–79)

Brigadier general, U.S. senator; the only man to represent three different states (Illinois, Minnesota, Missouri) in the U.S. Senate. Born in Altmore, County Tyrone, Ireland, on May 12, 1806, the son of Charles and Katherine McConnell Shields, he received training from hedge schools and private tutoring from a retired priest. His initial attempt at reaching America aborted in a shipwreck on the Scottish coast. Shields supported himself by tutoring until he obtained another passage. In the late 1820s he settled in Kaskaskia, Illinois, where he taught French, read law, and fought in the Black Hawk War. As a Democrat he served in the Illinois legislature and as state auditor. Shields, after receiving public criticism from certain Whigs (including Mary Todd), challenged Abraham Lincoln to a duel; however, the affair was settled amicably with the two principals becoming permanent friends.

Shields served on the Illinois Supreme Court (1843–45) and volunteered for the Mexican War. Commissioned a brigadier general of the Illinois volunteers, he received wounds at Cerro Gordo and distinguished himself at Churubusco. He served Illinois as U.S. senator from 1849–55. The late 1850s found Shields holding patronage positions in Minnesota where he encouraged and stimulated Irish immigration. When Minnesota became a state, Shields won election as U.S. senator. In 1859, after the end of this abbreviated term, Shields moved to California and, in 1861, married Mary Ann Carr, the daughter of an old friend from Armagh, Ireland. After Fort Sumter, Shields was appointed a brigadier general of U.S. volunteers. In 1862 he commanded a division in the Shenandoah Valley opposing the Confederate general, Stonewall Jackson. Shields defeated Jackson at Kernstown, March 23, 1862, the only Union general able to make that claim. Later in

May 1862, Jackson defeated Shields at Port Republic. Resigning his commission in March 1863, he returned to the West. Shields participated actively in politics in Missouri in the 1860s and 1870s as a Liberal-Republican which resulted in his third term in the U.S. Senate in 1879. He died in Ottumwa, Iowa, on June 1, 1879, while on a lecture tour and was buried in Carrollton, Missouri.

See also CIVIL WAR AND AMERICAN CATHOLICS, THE.

JOHN ALLEN

SHIELDS, THOMAS EDWARD (1862–1921)

Priest, psychologist, and educator. Thomas Edward was born on May 9, 1862, in Mendota, Minnesota. His parents were immigrants from Ireland. He studied at St. Francis Seminary in Milwaukee, Wisconsin, and at St. Thomas Seminary in St. Paul, Minnesota, where he published his first book, *Index Omnium* (1888). He was ordained on March 4, 1891. After ordination, he entered a doctoral program in psychology at Johns Hopkins University in Baltimore, Maryland. His dissertation, "The Effect of Odors Upon the Blood Flow" (1895), became an influential work in psychological research. In 1902 he became an instructor in psychology at The Catholic University of America.

At The Catholic University, Shields' attention turned to education. In 1905 he began a program of correspondence courses and diocesan summer institutes for sisters teaching in the rapidly growing Catholic school system. In addition to setting up the university's Department of Education in 1909 and serving as its first chair, Shields founded the *Catholic Educational Review* in 1910. The following year he ran the first Summer Institute for Catholic Sisters at the university and founded the Sisters College, for which he served as dean.

Thomas Shields was one of several progressive faculty members at The Catholic University (e.g., John A. Ryan in social thought, Edward Pace in philosophy, and William Kerby in sociology) who promoted the dialogue between Catholic theology and modern science and philosophy. Shields developed a Christian view of education shaped by discoveries of biology, experimental psychology, and the then-current, child-centered approaches to education. In opposition to those who emphasized the content of religious education, Shields maintained the importance of the method of teaching and the need for teachers to be aware of the learning readiness and psychological capacity of the student. He argued that rather than stressing memorization, religious education ought to correlate content with the stages of psychological growth of the student, a very innovative approach for the first decade of the twentieth century.

Shields provided a comprehensive exposition of his thought in *The Philosophy of Education* (1917), a work which incorporates the efforts of many thinkers of his day, including John Dewey. Shields believed that children learn best by doing and that they learn not only through books but also through music, signs, symbols, and liturgical activity. He also believed that students needed a center or framework for connecting the different subjects they studied; he believed that religion provided that integrating and directive center for all education. As part of his work to realize these educational goals in Catholic schools, Shields developed a series of four widely used texts in religion. Other works of his include *The Education of Our Girls* (1907) and *The Making and Unmaking of a Dullard* (1909), a depiction of his own youth.

Shields' continuing support for higher education for women, particularly sisters, and his innovative efforts in religious education were considered revolutionary in his day and were resisted by many. He died on February 5, 1921, in Washington, D.C.

Nuesse, C. Joseph. *The Catholic University of America, A Centennial History.* Washington, 1990.

Shields, Thomas Edward. *The Education of Our Girls.* New York, 1907.

____. *The Teaching of Religion.* Washington, D.C., 1907.

____. *The Making and the Unmaking of a Dullard.* Washington, D.C., 1909.

____. *Teachers Manual of Primary Methods.* Washington, D.C., 1912.

____. *The Philosophy of Education.* Washington, D.C., 1917.

Shields, Thomas Edward, and Edward A. Pace. *Catholic Educational Series of Primary Textbooks.* 6 vols. Washington, D.C., 1908–17.

Ward, Justine. *Thomas Edward Shields, Biologist, Psychologist, Educator.* New York, 1947.

PATRICIA DeFERRARI

SHUSTER, GEORGE NAUMAN (1894–1977)

Educator, author, editor. George Nauman Shuster was born on August 27, 1894, in Lancaster, Wisconsin, the eldest of three children of Anton and Elizabeth Nauman Schuster. (Shuster later changed the spelling of his family name.) His father, a stone mason, and his mother, a convert to Catholicism, spoke German at home until the children went to school. Shuster was educated in his parish grade school, St. Lawrence College (Mt. Calvary, Wisconsin) for high school, and the University of Notre Dame, graduating in 1915.

He enlisted in the Army in World War I, saw action at St. Mihiel and the Meuse-Argonne area, and, fluent in German, served for a time translating intercepted German communiqués. He remained in France for a year after the war and received a *Certificat d'Aptitude* in French culture from the University of Poitiers. On his return, he was offered a teaching position at Notre Dame and remained there for five years (1919–24), earning an M.A. degree in 1920 and chairing the Department of English from 1920 to 1924.

George N. Shuster

In 1924 Shuster married a former summer session student, Doris Parks Cunningham, and moved to New York where he enrolled in Columbia University's doctoral program in English and Comparative Literature, taught at St. Joseph's College for Women in Brooklyn, and joined the editorial staff of the newly founded Catholic periodical, *Commonweal*, that fall. He remained with the magazine for twelve years, serving as managing editor for eight years, and contributing numerous articles and book reviews himself, often under a pseudonym. He made three trips to Europe in the 1930s, became a close friend of former German chancellor Heinrich Bruening, and published three books on contemporary Germany. He resigned from *Commonweal* in 1937 over that magazine's support of General Francisco Franco in the Spanish Civil War.

Shuster received his Ph.D. degree in 1940 and, after a year as acting president (1939–40), was named president of New York's Hunter College, the world's largest college for women. He successfully adapted the curriculum to wartime conditions, presided over the admission of men into the formerly all-women's college, established a new School of Social Work, and inaugurated the widely acclaimed Hunter College Concert Series and Opera Workshop. He found time for service off-campus also: he served on a University of Chicago Committee on Freedom of the Press, interviewed German civilian and military leaders in 1945 as chairman of a War Department Historical Commission, was president of the American Council on Germany, served as land commissioner (governor) of Bavaria during the American occupation in 1950–51, and was United States representative on the executive board of the United Nations Educational, Scientific, and Cultural Organization (UNESCO) from 1958 to 1962.

Shuster resigned his position at Hunter College in 1960 and returned the next year to Notre Dame as assistant to the president, Rev. Theodore Hesburgh, C.S.C., and director of the newly established Center for the Study of Man in Contemporary Society. He helped procure outside funding for research in the humanities and social sciences, oversaw a major study of Catholic primary and secondary education in the United States, was instrumental in setting up a Latin American Studies program, and organized several conferences with Ford Foundation assistance to study world population problems. Continuing his work outside the university, he served as a board member of the Carnegie Endowment for International Peace, the Center for the Study of Democratic Institutions, and the National Conference of Christians and Jews.

Shuster remained a writer throughout his life, producing close to twenty books and three hundred articles, chiefly on education, international affairs, and religion. He was quick to praise the contributions of Catholics to American life and to defend Catholicism from attack, but he was also critical of the Church's authoritarianism and its strict prohibition of artificial contraception.

Shuster and his wife had one child, Robert, born in 1925, but at various times four foster children lived with them also. Shuster enjoyed walking for exercise and classical music, reading, playing bridge, and tending roses for recreation. He received numerous awards throughout his life, including the Insignis Medal from Fordham University, the Laetare Medal from Notre Dame, the Great Gold Medal of the Republic of Austria, and the Great Cross of the West German Federal Republic. His health gradually declined throughout the 1970s and he died in South Bend, Indiana, on January 25, 1977, at the age of eighty-two.

See also COMMONWEAL; NOTRE DAME, UNIVERSITY OF.

Blantz, Thomas E., C.S.C. *George N. Shuster: On the Side of Truth.* University of Notre Dame Press, 1993.

——. "George N. Shuster and American Catholic Intellectual Life." *Studies in Catholic History,* eds. Nelson Minnich and others. Wilmington, Del.: Michael Glazier, 1985, 345–65.

Lannie, Vincent P. "George N. Shuster: A Reflective Evaluation." *Leaders in American Education,* ed. Robert J. Havighurst. Chicago: The National Society for the Study of Education, 1971, 306–20.

Shuster, George N. *The Ground I Walked On.* 2nd ed. University of Notre Dame Press, 1969.

THOMAS E. BLANTZ, C.S.C.

SIEDLISKA, FRANCES (1842–1902)

Foundress. Frances Anna Siedliska was born in central Poland on November 12, 1842. Despite a series of national catastrophes that had left most of the people of Poland frustrated and poor, Frances and her family were far from underprivileged. Frances learned quickly and well under the tutorship of private scholars. She was artistic and had a seemingly insatiable intellect. However, as the years passed, she seemed more and more to shun the superficiality of the "social world" and riches around her. As she advanced in her study and personal love for God, so did her desire to serve God through others, and a whole new lifestyle dawned for her. After years of opposition from her parents, they finally consented to her wish to dedicate herself to God.

With the approval of Pope Pius IX on October 1, 1873, Frances Anna Siedliska began laying the foundation for a new congregation, the Sisters of the Holy Family of Nazareth. Two years later the congregation formally became a unit of the Roman Catholic Church, as Mother Mary Frances took up residence in Rome with a handful of other sisters who had chosen to adopt her way of life.

And so, the beginnings of the Sisters of the Holy Family of Nazareth, whose work today extends from Europe to North and Central America, Australia, and England. It is work that is totally devoted to the Christian education of youth and to the care of the sick, of dependent children and of the elderly.

Throughout the past century, the congregation spread, first to Poland, and ten years later—in 1885—to the United States. With eleven sisters, the foundress herself crossed the Atlantic to establish the first foundation in Chicago, which has since expanded to five provinces in the United States: Chicago, Connecticut, Pittsburgh, Philadelphia, and Texas. Her attachment to America is testified by the fact that she became a naturalized citizen of the United States on July 26, 1897. Currently, the congregation has nine provinces. There are convents in France, England, Italy, Australia, Poland, Russia, Nazareth (north Israel), the United States, the Philippines, and Puerto Rico.

Mother Mary of Jesus the Good Shepherd (her name in religion) died November 21, 1902, in Rome, after a life of total dedication to the service of God and to the spiritual and material welfare of families. On April 23, 1989, she was declared "Blessed" by Pope John Paul II.

See also POLISH CATHOLICS IN AMERICA.

DeChantal, M., C.S.F.N. *Out of Nazareth: A Centenary of the Sisters of the Holy Family of Nazareth in the Service of the Church.* New York: Exposition Press, 1974.

Gecewicz, Mary Michael, C.S.F.N. *Love Finds A Way: A Biography of Frances Siedliska.* Philadelphia: Pioneer Press, Inc., 1986.

Strzalkowska, Inez M., C.S.F.N. *Blessed Mary of Jesus the Good Shepherd (Frances Siedliska) Foundress of the Congregation of the Sisters of the Holy Family of Nazareth.* Rome: Romagrafic Press, 1989.

ANCILLA SOJKA, C.S.F.N.

SIEGMAN, EDWARD (1908–67)

Biblical scholar. Edward Ferdinand Siegman was born on June 4, 1908, in Cleveland, Ohio. He entered the Missionaries of the Precious Blood in 1922. He was ordained a priest at Carthagena, Ohio, in 1934, and went thereafter to The Catholic University of America in Washington, D.C., to study Scripture and Semitic languages. He earned an S.T.D. in 1937, with a dissertation on the false prophets of the Old Testament.

Edward Siegman

From 1937 to 1951 he taught Scripture at his congregation's seminary in Carthagena, Ohio, and served as dean of studies from 1945 to 1951. In 1951 he returned to The Catholic University of America as an assistant professor of Scripture, becoming associate professor in 1954. During a 1958–59 sabbatical leave, he earned an S.S.L. at the Pontifical Biblical Institute in Rome.

He was a charter member of the Catholic Biblical Association, and was from his early years at the forefront of the new Catholic scholarship that was emerging. He contributed many articles and reviews to the *Catholic Biblical Quarterly,* and became its editor in 1951. He was credited by many as having given that journal its scholarly stature and reputation. He remained editor until 1958.

His own scholarly contribution and the leadership of the *Catholic Biblical Quarterly* won him enemies who opposed the new biblical scholarship. In 1961 he suffered a heart attack that became the occasion for the president of The Catholic University to terminate his contract in 1962, ostensibly for reasons of health. Protests from Siegman himself, the School of Sacred Theology, and the Graduate School of Arts and Sciences were to no avail. The full story behind the dismissal has not been made known, but it was held by many to have been wrongful.

He spent the 1963–64 academic year in campus ministry at Yale University, and then returned to teaching at his congregation's seminary in Ohio. In 1966 he accepted an appointment at the University of Notre Dame, and died there of a heart attack on February 2, 1967.

Along with his articles and reviews, Siegman worked on the Old Testament translations for both the CCD version and the New American Bible. He was also New Testament area editor for the *New Catholic Encyclopedia.* He was elected president of the Catholic Biblical Association in 1966, but died before completing his term.

Siegman was known for his scholarship and collaboration in a variety of projects. He was also esteemed as a mentor to his many students. He is remembered as one of those who suffered to make modern biblical scholarship accessible and possible for Catholics.

See also CATHOLIC BIBLICAL ASSOCIATION (CBA); CATHOLIC BIBLICAL SCHOLARSHIP IN AMERICA.

Fogarty, Gerald P. *American Catholic Biblical Scholarship.* San Francisco, 1989.
"Siegman, Edward Ferdinand." *New Catholic Encyclopedia* 16:417–18.

ROBERT J. SCHREITER, C.PP.S.

SIGN, THE

The Sign, a national Catholic monthly published by the Passionists in West Hoboken (later Union City), New Jersey, from 1921–82, was founded to counter the anti-Catholicism of the 1920s. *The Sign* attempted "to disseminate truth; to combat the thousand and one errors confronting Catholics at every turn; to interpret from a Catholic viewpoint significant current events; to offset, in some measure, the pernicious influence of the lurid secular press." For over sixty years, this editorial policy was expressed by articles on Church doctrine, "industrial, social, and economic questions, refreshing and wholesome literary entertainment." In keeping with the Passionist charism, the magazine also promoted devotion to the passion of Jesus Christ.

All editors were Passionists. Managing editor Harold Purcell (1921–34) was the guiding force of *The Sign.* Subsequent editors were Theophane Maguire (1934–43), Ralph Gorman (1943–66), Augustine Paul Hennessy (1967–75), Arthur McNally (1976–79), and Patrick McDonough (1979–82). During the course of its existence, at least seventy Passionist priests or brothers were assigned as associate editors or business managers. Many laypeople were part of the production staff. Passionist preachers crisscrossed the country promoting the magazine and soliciting subscriptions in Catholic parishes.

In August 1921 there were 500 subscribers. By the early sixties it was the fourth most popular Catholic magazine in the country. In 1972 the circulation was 130,428; by 1981, it had dropped to 94,925. However, by the 1980s, inability to maintain a viable marketing structure, financial concerns, and a redefining of Passionist ministry priorities forced the magazine to cease publication.

The Sign style was eclectic, containing intellectual, literary, devotional, doctrinal, informative, and pastoral articles. Regular features were: an editorial page; "Current Fact" and "Comment," providing shorter editorial views on contemporary events; articles by feature writers, Catholic and secular; short stories; "Signpost"-readers' questions on Catholic culture and moral issues; movie and book reviews. Until the 1950s it published a sports column. From the 1920s to the 1950s, "With the Passionists in China" was a series which allowed subscribers to become armchair missionaries by following the foreign missionary activities of the Passionists in Hunan, China. In turn, readers contributed financial and spiritual support. This series retains importance in providing a history of Hunan province and represents a classic style of mission education given to American Catholics prior to the Second Vatican Council.

The Sign prose was direct and easy to read. Photos and artwork made the layout appealing and frequently balanced or enhanced thematic issues in the text. While Passionists were regular contributors to *The Sign,* the magazine gave a voice to many other writers. Prior to World War II writers included G. K. Chesterton, Hilaire Belloc, Enid Dinnis, Dorothy Day, and Daniel Lord, S.J. From 1933–69, *The Sign* featured "Woman to Woman," a woman's column by Katherine Kurz Burton. After World War II, Jerry Cotter was the drama critic; Don Dunphy and Red Smith were sports editors. Other writers were John F. Cronin, S.S., Fulton J. Sheen, Jim Bishop, Eileen Egan, and John C. Cort. After the Second Vatican Council some contributors were Rosemary Haughton, Andrew Greeley, Eileen Egan, Edward M. Hays, James H. Forest, and Pam Robbins. Gabriel Moran was "Stage and Screen" editor.

Proudly Catholic in the 1920s, isolationist in the 1930s, patriotic during World War II, pro-Palestinian in the late 1940s, the magazine was by the 1950s anti-Communist. Open to the changes of Vatican II from the mid-1960s until 1981, the magazine is best described as pastoral in its attempt to reconcile liberal and conservative movements in American and world Catholicism.

For sixty years *The Sign* promoted the sanctity of the American Catholic family by advocating adherence to Catholic social and moral principles. At the same time, development of sound family spirituality was a prominent theme. *The Sign* was an important contributor to American Catholic twentieth-century culture.

See also PASSIONISTS (C.P.).

Coffman, Mary Ruth, O.S.B. *Build Me a City: The Life of Reverend Harold Purcell, Founder of the City of St. Jude.* Montgomery, Ala.: Pioneer Press, 1984.

ROBERT E. CARBONNEAU, C.P.

SISTERS OF CHARITY OF OUR LADY OF MERCY (O.L.M.)

The Sisters of Charity of Our Lady of Mercy, one of the first eight permanent congregations of women religious founded in the United States, was established in Charleston, South Carolina, in December 1829 by John England, first bishop of Charleston. The first four members, Mary and Honora O'Gorman, their fifteen-year-old niece, Teresa Barry (all natives of Ireland), and the American-born Mary Elizabeth Burke, had met Bishop England in Baltimore while he was attending the First Provincial Council and expressed their willingness to form a religious community under his direction.

Bishop John England

Bishop England called the new institute "The Sisters of Our Lady of Mercy," but patterned it on the Sisters of Charity established by Mother Seton in Emmitsburg, Maryland.

The bishop gave the sisters a simple rule based upon the Rule of St. Vincent de Paul. Oral tradition maintains that the original habit came from Emmitsburg. This dress and bonnet, very similar to Mother Seton's, was worn by the sisters from 1830 until 1932. At the time of Bishop England's death, April 11, 1842, the community numbered nineteen who were conducting an orphanage, an academy for girls from middle-class homes, a free school for girls from poor families, and a school for free black children.

On several occasions before his death Bishop England spoke of writing a constitution for "his Sisters" based upon that of the "Sisters of Emmitsburg." The task, however, fell to Ignatius Reynolds, the second bishop of Charleston. This document guided the lives, prayer, and work of the sisters from 1844 until 1949. In that year (1949), the congregation adopted a new constitution and a new name, the Sisters of Charity of Our Lady of Mercy. The insertion of the word "charity" was intended to identify the congregation with other religious institutes whose lives are based upon the Rule of St. Vincent de Paul and its American adaptations.

Civil War and After

Mother Teresa Barry guided the community during the Civil War. Under her leadership sisters staffed a Confederate hospital in Montgomery White Sulphur Springs, Virginia. Others moved inland to Sumter, South Carolina, with the orphans and boarders while Charleston was being bombarded. There they founded St. Joseph's Academy, a day and boarding school that continued to operate until 1929. The remainder of the community stayed in Charleston, visiting Union soldiers in the prisons and hospitals, and teaching whenever possible.

In the second fifty years of its history, 1880–1929, the congregation doubled in membership and broadened the scope of its ministries. In 1882, as health care moved from home to hospital, the sisters established St. Francis Xavier Hospital in Charleston, and in 1900 opened a School for Nurses in conjunction with it. The establishment of parochial schools in the diocese led the community to close the academies in Charleston and Sumter and place more sisters in parish schools throughout South Carolina.

From the 1930s through the 1950s many sisters served in the summer vacation camps sponsored by the Diocese of Charleston that offered religious education to those Catholic children who did not attend parochial schools. During the academic year the sisters taught many of these children in Sunday school and CCD programs. In the 1940s and 1950s the community accepted invitations from the bishops of Trenton and Camden, New Jersey, to open missions in their respective dioceses. Sisters taught religion in Hightstown, New Jersey, from 1947 until 1954, and staffed parish elementary schools in Gibbstown and Middlesex, New Jersey, for twenty-one and thirty years respectively.

At the request of Bishop Emmet Walsh in 1938, the community opened Divine Saviour Hospital in York, South Carolina, to serve the rural poor in a predominantly non-Catholic area. Not only did the hospital grow, but the parish of Divine Saviour originated on its premises. In 1961 a nursing home was added. Simultaneously, St. Francis Xavier Hospital in Charleston grew and expanded its services. Among these was the establishment of a social service agency popularly called the Neighborhood House.

The Sisters of Charity of Our Lady of Mercy have always been a diocesan congregation. While Georgia and North Carolina were part of the diocese, sisters were sent to establish convents in Savannah and Wilmington. However, when these states were separated from Charleston to create new dioceses, the local convents became independent of the motherhouse in Charleston.

Contemporary Scene

At present there are thirty-eight Sisters of Charity of Our Lady of Mercy, all living and working in the Diocese of Charleston (which includes the whole state of South Carolina). The motherhouse is located on James Island on a tract of land overlooking Charleston Harbor. It is simultaneously a home, administrative headquarters, and a Center of Spirituality. In 1989 the congregation transferred sponsorship of its hospitals to the Bon Secours Sisters. However, sisters continue in health-care ministries by working in hospitals, and by visiting the sick and aged in their homes and institutions. In 1989 the congregation also established an Outreach Facility and program providing direct service to the poor and elderly on Johns Island, James Island, and Wadmalaw Island.

See also WOMEN RELIGIOUS IN AMERICA.

ANN FRANCES CAMPBELL, O.L.M.

SISTERS OF CHARITY OF THE BLESSED VIRGIN MARY (B.V.M.)

When Mary Frances Clarke and four of her friends left Dublin, Ireland, in 1833 for the United States, they did not intend to found a women's religious congregation. Instead they intended to teach the children of the other Irish immigrants working in the textile mills of Philadelphia. As a group of laywomen they had established a little school, Miss Clarke's Seminary, for the poor girls of Dublin who could not afford to attend the convent schools of the day. A missionary from Philadelphia, convalescing in Ireland, convinced the young women they were more needed as educators of the poor Irish children in the United States.

Mary Frances Clarke, Margaret Mann, Eliza Kelly, Catherine Byrne, and Rose O'Toole, all in their twenties, set sail for the U.S.A. They arrived at Old St. Joseph Church, Philadelphia, on September 7, 1833. A local parishioner introduced them to the former pastor, Rev. Terence J. Donaghoe. He, too, was a native of Ireland and he offered to assist the women in establishing a school for poor girls.

The Origins of the Congregation

Two months later, acting on the advice of Donaghoe, the women formed a pious organization called the Sisters of the Blessed Virgin Mary. They made an act of consecration on November 1, 1833, the date claimed as the foundation of the congregation later known as the Sisters of Charity of the Blessed Virgin Mary (B.V.M.). Although Donaghoe designated Margaret Mann as the "Mother" of the group, the women chose instead Mary Frances Clarke. Donaghoe and the sisters agreed that he was "superior" of the young community.

From Fr. Donaghoe, the community learned that it must provide for its own survival through the works of education. From Mother Clarke it imbibed a spirit of freedom in following the gospel of Jesus Christ. In the congregation's revised *Constitutions,* approved by the Church in 1989, the original mission is restated, "Being freed and helping others enjoy freedom in God's steadfast love. . . . Our mission finds expression in our traditional commitment to education and in ministries emerging from new needs in Church and society."

Life on the Frontier

In 1843 Bishop Mathias Loras, the first bishop of the Diocese of Dubuque, which encompassed the territories of Iowa, Minnesota, the Dakotas, and parts of Wisconsin and Illinois, invited the sisters to start schools for the Native American children and for those of the pioneer miners and farmers. The bishop had heard about the sisters from John Norman, a teacher on the frontier whom Donaghoe had trained in Philadelphia as a catechist. Five sisters traveled with Loras from Philadelphia to the Mississippi River town of Dubuque in the Iowa Territory, arriving on June 23, 1843. They began teaching at St. Mary's Academy, a log cabin located near the primitive cathedral of the diocese.

Because of the unrest in Philadelphia due to the nativist rioting against Irish immigrants, Loras convinced Donaghoe and the other members of the community to move also to the Iowa Territory. On September 8, 1843, the other fourteen sisters and Donaghoe settled in Dubuque. Loras provided the B.V.M.s with the canonical status they needed to become an official women's religious congregation. He added the word "Charity" to their title and he requested that they wear a religious habit. The sisters built their first motherhouse on the Iowa prairie ten miles outside the town.

Catholic Schools

While serving as Loras' vicar general, Donaghoe encouraged parishes to establish schools and he staffed them with B.V.M.s. He also purchased land and built boarding academies for girls which the sisters staffed. In 1867 he sent sisters to open a school in Holy Family parish, Chicago. After his death on January 5, 1869, Mary Frances Clarke assumed the roles of both "mother" and "superior."

Clarke incorporated the Sisters of Charity of the Blessed Virgin Mary as a not-for-profit corporation in 1869, obtained

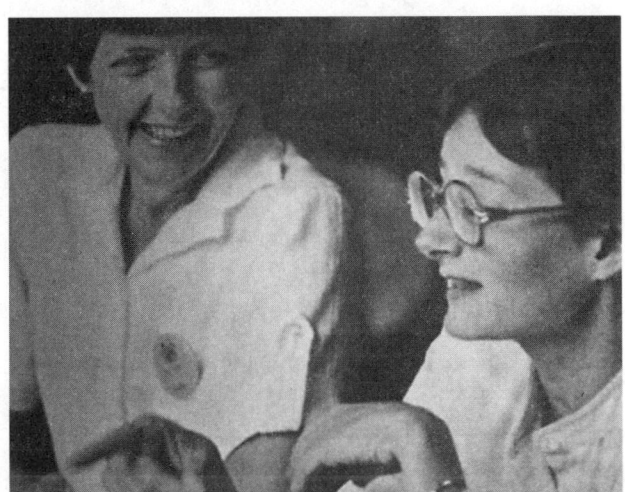

Sisters of Charity

papal approbation of the congregation in 1877, and continued to send the sisters to teach in newly opened parish schools and academies. From their early Midwest schools the B.V.M.s attracted other women with the pioneer spirit needed to follow the frontier westward along the railroad lines and the rivers. The sisters arrived in San Francisco in 1887 to begin a school in St. Bridget's parish. It was the last school to which Mary Frances Clarke sent sisters before her death on December 4, 1887.

Renewal and Expansion

The B.V.M.s elected Mary Gertrude Regan, who had been a student at the sisters' first Philadelphia school, to succeed Mary Frances Clarke as the mother superior. She moved the motherhouse from the prairie to its present site at Mt. Carmel on the Mississippi River bluffs in Dubuque. Six other mother superiors succeeded her in governing the congregation until 1968. Following the renewal of religious life prescribed by Vatican Council II, the governance has been directed by an elected president and two vice presidents. Since 1833 over 4,800 women have entered the congregation and they continue to travel to Dubuque to join the B.V.M.s In 1996 there were 1,010 sisters.

See also WOMEN RELIGIOUS IN AMERICA.

Coogan, Jane, B.V.M. *The Price of Our Heritage.* 2 vols. Dubuque, Iowa: Mt. Carmel Press, 1975.

Doran, Lambertina, B.V.M. *In the Early Days.* St. Louis: Herder, 1911.

Lawlor, Kathryn, B.V.M., ed. *Terence J. Donaghoe: Co-Founder of the Sisters of Charity, BVM.* Dubuque, Iowa: Mt. Carmel Press, 1995.

Smith-Noggle, Laura, ed. *My Dear Sister. Correspondence and Notes of Mary Frances Clarke.* Dubuque, Iowa: Mt. Carmel Press, 1987.

KATHRYN LAWLOR, B.V.M.

SISTERS OF LORETTO (S.L.)

The Sisters of Loretto, one of the first religious communities of women founded in the United States, began on the Kentucky frontier in 1812. Mary Rhodes had come to visit members of her family who had migrated from Maryland to settle in central Kentucky near Bardstown. Seeing a need for some kind of formal education for the children, she began to teach catechism and basic subjects to her brother's children.

News of her instruction spread quickly and soon other parents asked her to teach their children. As the number of pupils increased, Mary welcomed the assistance of Christina Stuart and Ann Havern. When space in the Rhodes' home became inadequate, the "school" was moved to an abandoned log cabin nearby.

Origins

The idea of dedicating their lives to the service of God and neighbor began to animate the lives of the three women. They presented their hopes and aspirations to their pastor, Fr. Charles Nerinckx, a Flemish émigré from the French Revolution, who had been serving the Kentucky missions since 1805. At the women's request and with their consultation, Fr. Nerinckx composed a simple rule as their way of life. On April 25, 1812, the three women took up residence together and announced their intention to dedicate their lives as women religious.

The original rule named the group *The Little Society of the Friends of Mary Under the Cross of Jesus.* At the suggestion of Nerinckx, their log cabin complex was designated *Little Loretto,* after the shrine in Italy which honors the house of the Holy Family at Nazareth.

On June 29, 1812, Mary, Christina, and Nancy received the veil as the first novices of the little frontier community. The same day two postulants, Ann Rhodes and Sarah Havern, younger sisters of Mary and Nancy, were admitted to the group. In July, Nellie Morgan joined them.

Expansion

The first house outside Kentucky was opened in 1823 at The Barrens in Perry County, Missouri. The following year Nerinckx, because of the disagreements which had arisen between himself and other Kentucky clergy, decided to leave Kentucky in the hope of easing the situation.

On June 16, 1824, he left Kentucky intending to visit the sisters in Missouri. When he arrived at Ste. Genevieve, Missouri, he became ill. There, on the morning of August 12, 1812, he received the last sacraments and died that afternoon.

Following the death of Nerinckx, the motherhouse of the Sisters of Loretto was moved from Little Loretto to its present location on St. Stephen's Farm. From there the westward expansion of the Sisters of Loretto continued.

In 1847 Loretto opened a school for members of the Osage tribe in southeastern Kansas. Five years later, at the request of Bishop Jean Baptist Lamy, six sisters began the arduous journey to Santa Fe to begin work with the Spanish-speaking children. By the end of the nineteenth century, Loretto foundations had also been established in Colorado, Texas, Alabama, California, Illinois, Ohio, and Arizona.

From the beginning of its existence, the primary focus of the apostolate of Sisters of Loretto was teaching. In the second decade of the twentieth century, two of the academies developed into senior colleges for women: Webster College in St. Louis and Loretto Heights College in Denver.

New calls for service came in 1923 with the opening of Loretto's first foreign mission in Han Yang, China. There and in Shanghai the Chinese missions flourished until interrupted by war and the sisters' final expulsion by the Communists in 1952. Eight years later the sisters opened a school in La Paz, Bolivia, and subsequently another school in Tacna, Peru, and a catechetical center in Santiago, Chile.

After Vatican Council II major changes occurred in the lifestyle and service of the sisters. Opportunities for additional ministries expanded to include health and social works, pastoral ministry, peace and justice projects, and retreat and contemplative prayer centers, to name only a few. Toward the end of the twentieth century the sisters and Loretto co-members are to be found working and praying in over thirty states as well as in other areas of the globe.

See also WOMEN RELIGIOUS IN AMERICA.

Barbour, Richard Marie, S.L. *Light in Yucca Land.* Louisville, Ky.: General Printing Company, 1982.

Howlett, W. J. *Life of Rev. Charles Nerinckx.* Techny, Ill.: Mission Press, SVD, 1940.

Maes, Camillus P. *The Life of Rev. Charles Nerinckx.* Cincinnati: Robert Clarke & Co., 1880.

Minogue, Anna C. *Loretto Annals of the Century.* New York: The America Press, 1912.

Sanders, Helen, S.L. *More Than a Renewal.* Nerinx, Ky.: Sisters of Loretto, 1982.

Ware, Ann Patrick, S.L., ed. *Naming Our Truth.* Inverness, Calif.: Chardon Press, 1995.

AURELIA OTTERSBACH, S.L.

SISTERS OF MERCY
OF THE AMERICAS (R.S.M.)

An apostolic religious congregation of women founded in Dublin, Ireland, in 1831. As beneficiary of the William Callaghan estate, fifty-year old Catherine Elizabeth McAuley determined to use her inheritance to provide assistance for poor persons, especially young working women. Her project attracted the support of friends and colleagues within the Catholic community of Dublin. Eventually other women began to join her in her effort to serve the poor, sick, and ignorant. Sisters of Mercy soon spread to England, Scotland, the Americas, Australia, New Zealand, and South Africa. In January 1995 the Sisters of Mercy of the Americas numbered 6,695 women serving primarily in the United States, Central America, Latin America, the Caribbean area, Guam, and the Phillipines.

Catherine's Ireland

The Ireland of Catherine's time was not a hospitable environment for many of its native sons and daughters. The repeal of the Penal Laws directed toward the practice of Catholicism in Ireland had begun only a few decades before Catherine's birth. Clergy, members, and practices of the Catholic Church were no longer subject to legal sanctions. Prejudicial attitudes, however, embedded in societal structures, continued to mark the experience of Irish Catholics well into the nineteenth century. A recent work on Catherine McAuley describes the situation of eighteenth-century Ireland for its majority Catholic population as a time in which "anti-Catholic measures [victimized] the Catholic population as regards religious practice, education, material wealth, business enterprise, social status and personhood . . . in a manner calculated to exclude the Irish Catholic majority from all positions of importance in their own country" (Bolster, 4).

Episcopal leaders in Dublin and elsewhere seized the moment to revitalize and renew Catholic identity, self-esteem, and influence. A significant piece of their plan for revitalizing the faith centered on caring for the basic needs of impoverished masses of the faithful and providing for the education of children. Angela Bolster, author of the *Proposito* prepared for the canonization of Catherine McAuley, links this activity in Dublin to Dr. Daniel Murray, friend and mentor of Miss McAuley: "[1820–30] was a decade of religious revival, spearheaded by Dr. Daniel Murray [archbishop of Dublin] . . . whose remedy for the spiritual malnutrition . . . was to revive the sacramental life of the people and to increase the number of clergy, churches and schools in his diocese" (*Proposito,* 66).

This was also a time of high unemployment in Ireland and of migration to urban areas of the country. Repeated crop failures forced farmers from their land. Rapid industrialization in the cities promised work and assistance. In reality, poor houses and work houses multiplied as fast as factories. Uneven educational opportunities, neighborhood decay, urban and rural tensions, resulted from both religious discrimination and rural migration.

This was the Ireland into which Catherine ("Kitty") McAuley was born on September 29, 1778, at Stormanstown House to the north of Dublin. She was the eldest of three children of James and Elinor (Conway) McAuley. Catherine's father was one of a strong Catholic middle class who managed to garner wealth and a certain degree of influence in eighteenth-century Dublin. Records indicate he was a wealthy gentleman at the time of his marriage to Elinor Conway and provided comfortable circumstances for his growing family. However, the death of James McAuley in 1783, combined with Elinor's inability to manage her financial matters, brought the McAuley family to the edge of destitution. Catherine and her siblings were separated as various relatives (mostly Protestant) opened their homes to the orphaned young people. At the age of twenty-five, Catherine accepted an invitation to be a companion for Mrs. William Callaghan and to assist in running the Callaghan household at Coolock House. This position afforded Catherine a degree of independence and an opportunity to utilize skills learned in caring for her mother during her lengthy illness. Catherine, caregiver and confidant, remained in the Callaghan household for twenty years, until both of her employers had died. As the sole residuary legatee of all the Callaghan estates and effects, Catherine found herself, at the age of forty-four, with the means to begin a project of service which had long been her dream.

Beginnings of the Sisters of Mercy

Catherine McAuley did not intend to found a congregation of women religious. Raised in largely Protestant households after her father's death, she was surrounded by an Anglo-Irish society whose prejudices relative to Catholicism and its institutions were as harsh as they were pervasive. Catherine maintained a staunch loyalty to the faith of her birth, but also internalized some of the biases of her environment. She was concerned that enclosed convents of women religious served little value in a world of acute human need and occasioned self-centered and bizarre lifestyles. When she found herself, at the age of forty-four, single and heiress of a large fortune, she determined to dedicate both her wealth and her person to addressing the needs of families living in the poorer neighborhoods of Dublin. She thought to do so as a single woman of independent means.

She gave her energies to projects sponsored by Archbishop Murray, to tutorial work in the Poor School of St. Mary's in Liffey Street, and to visitation of the sick poor in the area around Coolock House. However, she also began to design her own project: a residence on the edge of a wealthy section of Dublin which would house a school, an employment agency, a residence for working women, and a variety of other services. Friends and acquaintances from among Dublin's social set joined her as well as generous strangers who heard of Miss McAuley's work through a network of Catholic colleagues.

In 1827 the House of Mercy opened on Baggot Street. Over the course of time, the women who gathered to serve its residents adopted similar dress and a regular schedule of meals, common prayer, and spiritual reading. To outsiders the regime seemed very akin to a conventual lifestyle. Complaints began to arise concerning the nature of the residence on Baggot Street, the intentions of its occupants, and their boldness in undertaking service in the name of the Church without approval or sponsorship.

Over the next three years, Catherine struggled with the criticisms, the prejudices of her heart, and pressures from social and ecclesial acquaintances. Finally, in 1830, she yielded to the advice of many colleagues and to her own growing understanding of the importance of ecclesiastical approval for the stabilization of her work on behalf of the poor. Arrangements were made for Catherine and two companions to enter the novitiate of the Presentation Sisters at George's Hill.

On December 12, 1831, Catherine McAuley, Anna Maria Doyle, and Elizabeth Hartley took vows in the chapel of the Presentation Convent and became the first Sisters of Mercy. The House of Mercy on Baggot Street was designated the first Convent of Mercy the next day. In a letter to an associate some years later, Catherine recalled those early beginnings rather simply:

> I would find it most difficult to write what you say Mr. Clarke wishes [an account of the beginning of the order], for the circumstances which would make it interesting could never be introduced in public discourse. It commenced with 2, Sister Doyle and I. The plan from the beginning was such as is now in practice. In '27 the House was opened. In a year and a half we were joined so fast that it became a matter of general wonder. . . . Seeing us increase so rapidly . . . great anxiety was expressed to give it stability. We who began were prepared to do whatever was recommended and in September 1830 we went . . . to George's Hill to serve a novitiate for the purpose of firmly establishing it. In December '31 we returned and the progress has gone on as you know (Neumann, 154–55).

Growth of the Sisters of Mercy/Death of Catherine McAuley

The progress mentioned by Catherine included a growing reputation for good works and a steady effort to obtain recognition as a religious congregation. In 1832 a cholera epidemic struck Dublin. Suffering and death were widespread. The women from Baggot Street spent long hours in the cholera hospital comforting the dying, insuring the care of the living. The news of this labor and other works of the "Baggot Street Ladies" soon spread to other sections of the capital city and to points beyond the urban area. Meanwhile, in 1833, Catherine McAuley began the process to petition the Holy See to grant her and her companions official recognition as a congregation of women religious. The young sisterhood received such recognition with the 1841 approval of its constitutions. By that time, fourteen centers of service had been established from the Baggot Street House: twelve in Ireland and two in England. Requests for assistance had been received from Newfoundland and the United States.

Catherine accompanied the founding sisters to every new location. She stayed until a beginning was well secured, then returned to Baggot Street. Those left behind were responsible for all decisions relative to growth and development. It was in settling a founding group in Birmingham (England) that Catherine began to show clear signs of the imminent approach of her death. Tuberculosis, the disease which had already taken the lives of several young sisters, was now ravaging the body of the foundress. On November 11, 1841, she died in the House of Mercy in Baggot Street, surrounded by a grieving community. One of those present, in a circular letter informing the other members of the congregation of Catherine's death, spoke of her peace and her clarity: "Ten minutes before eight o'clock

. . . she calmly breathed her last sigh. I did not think it possible for human nature to have such self-possession at the awful moment of death, but she had an extraordinary mind in life and death" (Savage, 376–79).

Sisters of Mercy as Apostolic Religious Congregation

Catherine's legacy was not only the founding of a new religious congregation, but also the development of a new form of religious life in the Church. The Sisters of Mercy in nineteenth-century Ireland were known as "the walking sisters." This simple title signaled their link with an ongoing effort begun in the sixteenth century to establish apostolic religious life as a distinct form of consecrated life. In a time when cloistered life was the norm for women in religious congregations, Angela Merici, Jane de Chantal, and Mary Ward struggled to establish communities of women actively involved in serving the needs of God's people in the marketplace. John W. Padberg, S.J., in an article entitled "Memory, Vision and Structure: Historical Perspectives on the Experience of Religious Life in the Church," describes the circumstance for women quite succinctly: "In the sixteenth and seventeenth centuries, extraordinarily imaginative women and men tried to fashion specifically apostolic congregations of women, dedicated to work outside the cloister. . . . The problem lay with those who had to approve and make use of the orders. Every one of these religious congregations of women was forced back into the cloister, [except] the Daughters of Charity. . . . Only in the nineteenth century did externally apostolic orders of women come into being on a significant scale."

Even in the nineteenth century the struggle to authenticate a lifestyle shaped by the social and ecclesial order of the time and the pressing needs that reflect the absence of the reign of God was long and arduous, especially for women. In eighteenth- and nineteenth-century Ireland three names are remembered in this struggle: Mary Aikenhead (Irish Sisters of Charity), Nano Nagle (Presentation Sisters), and Catherine McAuley. These women benefited from their circumstances within an Irish culture possessing a long history in which the gifts of women had been recognized in social and political life. Even so, social mores relative to women's place in world order as well as an ecclesial atmosphere which favored cloister for women occasioned subtle but effective resistance. Catherine McAuley's petition to the Holy See in 1833 clearly maintains her intent that the women gathered in the Congregation of Mercy would be dedicated to service in the midst of the world. "The principal aim of this Congregation is to educate poor girls, to lodge and maintain poor young women who are in danger . . . and to visit the sick poor." Catherine also insisted that the schedule of prayer and common activities be shaped by the needs and customs of those among whom the sisters labored. "Every place," she wrote to her close friend, Francis Warde, "has its own peculiarities which must be yielded to when possible" (Neumann, 147).

Catholicism in the United States in the Nineteenth Century

This flexibility in service and quality of mobility was especially appreciated by local churches in frontier lands and in areas of social distress. The death of the foundress in 1841 seemed only to increase the demands for the services of the Sisters of Mercy throughout the world. Calls for assistance came to convents of Mercy in Ireland and England from various parts of the Americas. For the most part these requests reflected the movement of Irish immigrants in the New World, but there were exceptions to this pattern. Between 1843 and 1890, sixty-two women in nine different groups left from the various Mercy convents in Ireland and England to found the Mercy community in the Americas. The Church into which these women came was not unlike the Irish Church they were leaving. Of course, the United States Catholic Church was a much younger reality than the ancient Church of Ireland. Officially established in 1789 with the creation of the see of Baltimore, the vast mission territory of the United States consisted of only twenty-three dioceses when the first Sisters of Mercy arrived in Pittsburgh in 1843. The newest of these dioceses which were formed in 1843—Chicago, Hartford, Little Rock, Milwaukee, Pittsburgh, and Portland (Oregon)—provided a travel plan for the spread of the Congregation of Mercy in the United States.

Jay Dolan in *The American Catholic Experience* observes that even before masses of immigrants started coming to the United States—between 1820 and 1890—Roman Catholicism experienced a fundamental conflict in its relation to American society: "Some Catholics wanted a church that would be thoroughly American. . . . These Catholics were mostly American- or Irish-born people. Other Catholics . . . composed mainly of French-born clerics and German-born priests and lay people . . . wanted to transplant a European model of Roman Catholicism to the United States" (Dolan, 294). Episcopal leadership on both sides faced two major tasks: unification of the Catholic population and Americanization of diverse ethnic groups. They addressed these challenges through strategies similar to those of their counterparts in Ireland: education, charitable institutions, the Catholic press, and close contact with the people.

The Sisters of Mercy who came to the United States were well versed in such strategies. Within days of their arrival in the United States, wherever their destination and whatever the circumstances, the sisters began visitation of the sick, comfort of the distressed, and Christian education programs for adults and children. Various educational, health-care, and social-service institutions often followed in each location. Sisters of Mercy were soon found in service among diverse ethnic groups: Native Americans, Euro-Americans, African Americans, as well as Irish-Americans.

These same sisters also knew the violence of religious prejudice, the hardship of urban and rural poverty, and the oppression of racial discrimination. They were not easily daunted by the threats and/or violence which often characterized the Catholic as well as the early Irish immigrant experience in the United States in the eighteenth and nineteenth centuries. The Native American Party publicly denounced the establishment of the first Mercy Hospital in the world in Pittsburgh in 1847. They used every means possible in an unsuccessful attempt to convince the citizenry that the sisters intended proselytization and conversion rather than a healing ministry. Several hundred members of the Know-Nothing Party in Providence, Rhode Island, in 1855, threatened Frances Warde and her sisters in an attempt to free a Miss Rebecca Newell alleged to be held in the convent against her will. Armed men gathered on both sides of the convent walls to defend the right to freedom of association. In both instances, patience and steadfastness on the part of the Sisters of Mercy eventually brought reconciliation and understanding.

Original Sites in the United States

Between 1843 and 1872, six colonies of Mercy women journeyed from five convents in Ireland to establish the Congregation of the Sisters of Mercy in the United States. The situations into which they journeyed were remarkably similar: immigrant peoples overwhelmed by needs arising from poverty and ignorance sought assistance from religious women who could combine spirituality with practicality, initiative and independence. Although Mary de Sales Reddan (destined for San Francisco) was fifty-four years old, most of the Sisters of Mercy who came were under thirty years of age. Many were recently professed in the congregation and some were still novices or postulants.

As was true of many of their contemporaries, the stories of these early Sisters of Mercy are preserved through diaries, letters, house annals, and occasional news clippings. An observation made by Mary Austin Carroll regarding Teresa Maher (destined for Cincinnati) could have been applied to most of the sixty-two emigrants: "Nothing extraordinary came into her experience. . . . Performing uncommonly well the common duties of every day . . . she was . . . a shining light to her associates" (Carroll, 4:310). This quality of ordinariness, characteristic of the lives of many nineteenth-century women, may be attributed as much to the criteria by which such judgments are made as to the actual quality of their presence and/or contribution.

Frances Warde and seven companions were the first to make this journey. They departed from St. Leo's Convent in Carlow in November 1843, and arrived in Pittsburgh one month later, having set sail from Liverpool, England, aboard the *Queen of the West*. The diary of one of the travelers, Elizabeth Strange, records the circumstances of their voyage: "No ladies but ourselves which we are glad of. Cabins, rooms and c. very commodious. Found it very strange to substitute caps for coifs and veils and still more to appear at the general table which is very well kept. . . . All of us ill during the evening. The ship 'heaved' as they term it, remaining nearly on one side all night. The sea very rough—the sisters very sick."

The group disembarked in New York and quickly made their way by train and then by coach to Pittsburgh. On December 21, 1843, Frances Warde, Josephine Cullen, Agatha O'Brien, Aloysia Strange, Elizabeth Strange, Veronica McDarby, and Philodmena Reid established the first Mercy convent in the United States at 800 Penn Street. Frances Warde eventually left Pittsburgh to found over one hundred sites for Mercy ministry across the country.

The second colony departed from Dublin aboard the *Montezuma*. Agnes O'Connor, Angela Maher, Austin Horan, Monica O'Doherty, Camillus Byrne, Teresa Breen, Vincent Haire, and Marianne Byrne spent twenty-eight days enroute, anchoring in New York harbor on May 14, 1846. Bishop John Hughes was in Baltimore attending a council when they arrived, but the Sisters of Charity welcomed them to New York and extended hospitality in their convent until a house could be readied for the Sisters of Mercy. The immediate works of Mercy in New York included a lending library, Sunday School, and rescue of young immigrant girls directly from the ships docking in the New York harbor.

Foundations followed in 1851 from Naas to Little Rock; in 1854 and 1858 from Kinsale to San Francisco and Cincinnati, respectively; and in 1872 from Ennis to Meriden (Connecticut). The annals of the convent in Ennis describe the leave-taking which was a bittersweet mixture of expectation and regret:

> Eleven Sisters left Ennis, April 26, 1872, amid the greatest demonstrations of affection and reverence. The carriages which bore them from the convent to the train could scarcely move through the immense concourse of people of every age, rank and creed. . . . Though the people showed great sorrow at losing so many of their Sisters, still they were rather proud of the mission confided to the daughters of Erin.

Teresa Farrell and her companions on the way to the foundation at Little Rock, Arkansas, traveled with three hundred farmers and their families moving to the southern region of the United States at the invitation of Bishop

Andrew Byrne. Their ship was blown off course, which resulted in a two-month journey at sea. By the time the band of Sisters of Mercy traveled by riverboat from New Orleans up the Mississippi, most of the three hundred immigrants who had arrived a bit earlier had already moved on, embittered that houses promised for the new colonists had not been built.

Baptist Russell and the Sisters of Mercy enroute to California could not all get passage on the *Arctic,* and so they decided to wait a few days in Liverpool to book passage on the *Canada.* They learned later that the *Arctic* sank during the crossing and all aboard were lost. They anchored in San Francisco on December 8, 1854, the day of the proclamation of the dogma of the Immaculate Conception. As they were the first of their kind, they were viewed with suspicion and hostility.

While San Francisco, in 1854, was a gold-bust town of miners, sailors, and muddy streets, Cincinnati was an urban center of nearly 200,000 people when Teresa Maher and eight companions arrived in 1858. The employment bureau they were able to initiate placed over 4,000 women between the years 1858 and 1872.

Agnes Healy and Mary Teresa Perry and their companions, arriving in Connecticut in 1872, found a warm welcome but inadequate housing, scarcely sufficient income, and a severe climate. They began immediately, however, educational endeavors which flourished within a very short time.

Expansion and Stabilization

Catherine McAuley, in accounting for the beginnings of the Sisters of Mercy, recalled that "it commenced with two, Sister Doyle and I" (Neumann, 154). This sense of a relational enterprise and mutual endeavor marked the early congregation of Mercy. Clergy, appealing to Dublin for women to serve their faith communities, were readily referred to Carlow, Naas, Kinsale, or elsewhere. Agnes O'Connor was already "on loan" from Dublin to Bermondsey (England) when she received Bishop Hughes' request for help in the New York diocese, and mixed contingents of women from various Irish and English convents nursed soldiers in the Crimean War.

The women chosen for the westward treks to the United States were often not strangers to one another. Teresa Maher and Baptist Russell shared an early formation in the convent at Kinsale and, through long years of service in the United States, remained devoted letter writers to their mentor in Kinsale, Frances Bridgman. The convent on Houston Street in New York City often hosted traveling groups of Mercy Sisters moving westward from Ireland or returning there for recruitment or visitation. Excursions to found new sites for service were also occasions to renew Mercy acquaintances along the way.

The actual works of Mercy conducted by this sisterhood were as diverse as the circumstances required. "We ought then have great confidence in God in the discharge of all these offices of Mercy, spiritual and corporal, which constitute the business of our lives," Catherine McAuley had written in a small treatise entitled *Spirit of the Institute.* A variety of settings—urban and rural, Catholic and Protestant, Irish and non-Irish, poor and wealthy—shaped particular nuances in the works of Mercy, freely developed in response to the needs of the local church. The breadth and depth of these works is astounding: visitation of prisons, adult education, catechesis, homes for the aged, homes for working women, orphanages, vocational training centers, home health care, public and private schools, publication of manuals and books, employment agencies, social service agencies, musical education, public and private hospitals.

The period of expansion in the United States contains extraordinary events as well as daily responses to basic human needs for education, shelter, consolation, and support. Epidemics in several locations—Pittsburgh, San Francisco, Chicago, and Vicksburg, to name a few—claimed both the energy and the lives of many Mercy women in the last decades of the nineteenth century. In each instance, with courage and endurance, Sisters of Mercy nursed the ill, consoled the suffering, prayed with the dying, and buried the dead.

The Civil War also garnered a generous response from Sisters of Mercy in a variety of settings. Sisters in New York City, Cincinnati, Baltimore, and many other places opened their own institutions for the care of the wounded on both sides or traveled wherever they were needed to offer comfort and care. Abraham Lincoln, Ulysses S. Grant, and Jefferson Davis were among those acquainted with and inspired by the heroic efforts of the sisters. Jeane Heimberger Candido in an article in the October 1993 issue of *Blue and Gray Magazine* records a story involving President Lincoln. Frustration with military red tape fueled a long journey through the chain of command which ended with a personal directive from the President for Sisters of Mercy serving at the Douglas Hospital in Washington, D.C.:

To Whom It May Concern:

On application of the Sisters of Mercy in charge of the Military Hospital in Washington furnish such provisions as they desire to purchase and charge same to the War Department.

Abraham Lincoln

Membership within the congregation steadily increased through this period of expansion. According to Justine Sabourin, by 1929 the Mercy membership in the United States numbered 9,308 women in sixty independent motherhouses (Sabourin, 296–97). This expansion in numbers and works led to stabilization in the early decades of the twentieth century. These years witnessed the institutionalization of the congregation of the Sisters of Mercy as well as their works. Schools, hospitals, child-care agencies, colleges, and homes for women and children developed into complex institutions of education, health care, and social services. Visitation of the sick in their homes, prison work, catechetical programs, sheltering the homeless, and feeding the hungry became specialized activities of particular persons rather than common activities of the sisterhood.

The process of institutionalization within the congregation itself was seen in a gradual movement toward centralization. Although Francis Warde, as early as 1861, had proposed a centralized novitiate and centralized government for the Sisters of Mercy in the United States, the realization of that proposal occurred in increments of union and amalgamation throughout the twentieth century. "Between 1881 and 1928, at least sixteen unions occurred in the United States among communities of Sisters of Mercy. . . . Church authorities saw these unions affecting a stronger organization and a more uniform discipline" (Darcy, 51–52). In 1929, thirty-nine of the sixty existing Mercy motherhouses joined together in the Sisters of Mercy of the Union. The remaining twenty-one motherhouses soon formed the McAuley Conference, an association which convened annually and served as a conduit for information sharing and mutual enrichment. In 1965 both of these organizations joined in the establishment of the Federation of the Sisters of Mercy of the Americas.

The Contemporary Scene

This process of institutionalization in the congregation and in its works often saw flexibility, spontaneity, and diversity recede in favor of rigidity, predictability, and uniformity. Rules and regulations became the norm for faithful service. However, a watershed moment for the Catholic Church throughout the world was to change all of this. The Second Vatican Council, convoked in December 1961, challenged the institutionalization of the Church itself and set in motion processes which continue to affect the experience of Catholics worldwide. In his apostolic constitution *Humanae Salutis,* Pope John XXIII stated clearly that the council was to bring "the modern world into contact with the vivifying and perennial energies of the gospel."

In keeping with that purpose *Perfectae Caritatis,* the council's document relative to religious congregations, urged both "a constant return to the sources of the whole of the Christian life and to the primitive inspiration of the institutes, and their adaptation to the changed conditions of our time." Efforts to enter into this process of renewal led to significant changes in the structures and practices of religious congregations. The Sisters of Mercy were no exception.

Processes of renewal began with external concerns such as horariums, dress, placement processes, chapter formats, and local community structures. By the mid-1970s, the current of change flowed more deeply in participative processes which empowered members toward greater influence in decision-making and more intentional presence in ministry and local community. Commitments to justice, to individual freedom, to institutional works, and to unmet social needs resulted in points of tension and controversy within and without religious congregations. Membership declined, often dramatically, and the median age of most congregations advanced. Through the 1980s religious congregations in the United States were primarily concerned with strategic planning and the reallocation of limited resources and energy. Efforts were directed toward reclaiming the meaning and energy at the heart of their particular story as a religious congregation.

Such a journey of renewal culminated for the Sisters of Mercy in the United States in a ten-year process to realign their resources and energies in one unified congregational entity. The central governance envisioned by Francis Warde in 1861 became a reality in July 1991 with the proclamation of the decree granting permission for the establishment of the Institute of the Sisters of Mercy of the Americas.

In 1995 Mercy Sisters worldwide numbered over 15,000, half of whom were members of the Sisters of Mercy of the Americas. These latter Sisters of Mercy work in 202 cities, 46 of the states as well as the District of Columbia, and in 25 other countries. They are joined in their efforts by more than 1,300 Mercy Associates, men and women who by formal commitment share in various aspects of Mercy life and ministry. Since 1978 more than 30 men and women—of all ages and competencies—have been commissioned annually to Mercy Corps, a volunteer lay ministry program whose participants spend one or two years in service in Mercy ministry sites in the United States. The Institute Office for the Sisters of Mercy of the Americas is located in Silver Spring, Maryland. Twenty-five regional community offices are located in Albany, Brooklyn, Buffalo, Dobbs Ferry, and Rochester, New York; Auburn and Burlingame, California; Baltimore, Maryland; Cedar Rapids, Iowa; Chicago, Illinois; Cincinnati, Ohio; West Hartford, Connecticut; Dallas, Erie, Merion Station, and Pittsburgh, Pennsylvania; Farmington Hills, Michigan; Windham, New Hampshire; Watchung, New Jersey; Belmont, North Carolina; Omaha, Nebraska; Portland, Maine; Cumberland, Rhode Island; St. Louis, Missouri; and Burlington, Vermont.

Bolster, M. Angela. *Catherine McAuley: Venerable for Mercy.* Dublin: Dominican Publications, 1990.

Bourke, Carmel. *A Woman Sings of Mercy.* Sydney: E. J. Dwyer, 1987.

Carroll, M. Austin. *Leaves from the Annals of the Sisters of Mercy.* 4 vols. New York: P. O'Shea, Publisher, 1881–95.

Darcy, Catherine C. *The Institute of the Sisters of Mercy in the Americas.* Lanham, Md.: University Press of America, 1993.

Degnan, M. Bertrand. *Mercy Unto Thousands.* Westminster, Md.: The Newman Press, 1957.

Dolan, Jay P. *The American Catholic Experience.* New York: Image Books, 1985.

Neumann, M. Ignatia. *Letters of Catherine McAuley.* Baltimore: Helicon Press, Inc., 1969.

Sabourin, M. Justine. *The Amalgamation.* St. Meinrad, Ind.: Abbey Press, 1976.

Savage, Roland Burke, S.J. *Catherine McAuley: The First Sister of Mercy.* Dublin: M. H. Gill and Sons Ltd., 1949.

Werntz, M. Regina. *Our Beloved Union.* Westminster, Md.: Christian Classics, Inc., 1989.

HELEN MARIE BURNS, R.S.M.

SISTERS OF NOTRE DAME DE NAMUR (S.N.D.deN.)

The Sisters of Notre Dame de Namur were founded during the social, political, and economic upheaval following the French Revolution by St. Julie Billiart, who was born on July 12, 1751, in the small village of Cuvilly, France. Together with the support and encouragement of her good friend, the Vicountess Françoise Blin de Bourdon, Julie resolved that her congregation was to serve the poor in the most abandoned places. Together this peasant woman and the noble woman, who barely escaped the guillotine, began fashioning a rule for the sisters which was quite unusual for the times. As the young congregation began to grow, Julie's insistence on freedom of movement from diocese to diocese for herself and her sisters made confrontation with members of the hierarchy inevitable.

After her expulsion from the Diocese of Amiens by Bishop Demandolx in 1809, Bishop Pisani de la Gaude of Namur, Belgium, offered sanctuary and the name of his diocese to Julie and the first sisters of the congregation. That same year, Bishop de Broglie of Ghent, at first unsure of Julie's motives, prophesied her future. He told her, "Mère Julie, it is your vocation to go anywhere in the world; you are not meant to stay in only one diocese." That prophecy became reality in thirty-one short years. For in 1840, eight Sisters of Notre Dame under the leadership of Sister Superior Louis de Gonzague sailed from the great mission port of Antwerp to America. They were the first of many to realize that prophecy, a prophecy which Julie had written "was in my heart."

In America

When yet another bishop welcomed the eight Sisters of Notre Dame de Namur to his diocese at the great public landing of Cincinnati on October 31, 1840, neither Bishop John B. Purcell nor the sisters could have guessed what their future collaboration would mean for Catholic education in the United States. Unlike some of his brother bishops, Bishop Purcell had already decided to begin a diocesan school system. Now, with the Sisters of Notre Dame, he would work out a pattern for an elementary school system which would become standard in both the Midwest and New England. Together they fashioned a system which was typically Catholic but also typically American. It became the basis for the future educational works of the congregation in the United States. Within eight years, nine parish schools were begun in Cincinnati. In 1870 there were 103 parish schools scattered throughout the archdiocese, 14 in Cincinnati alone.

Although the term Manifest Destiny was coined in 1845, restless Americans and many immigrants were already on the move. The sisters, immigrants themselves, entered into this restless milieu with great enthusiasm. In three short months they had purchased their first Notre Dame Convent, the thirty-two-room Spencer Mansion on Sixth Street, and were ready to greet their new students. Those who came were exposed to a curriculum that had been well developed in the Notre Dame schools in Namur, Ghent, and other cities throughout Belgium. This course of studies the sisters transplanted almost in its entirety to the American scene. They also readily adapted it to American needs. Highly trained teachers, they did not hesitate to request teachers from Namur skilled in other disciplines when the need arose. Among their first requests were teachers trained in science in order to improve course offerings.

Notre Dame Academy, their first school in Cincinnati, which opened in January 1841, included the three divisions of a school with which the sisters were familiar in Belgium. All three, the boarding school, a day school, and a free school, were available from the very opening day of classes. The latter was a necessity so that the sisters could teach the poor, those who could not pay for their education. This academy was a significant educational establishment. It was designed to meet the needs of both elementary and secondary education, and its free school may be considered the first parish school in the city. After being housed in the convent building for years, the free school moved and became the parish school of St. Xavier's.

Expansion

As growth in Cincinnati and other Ohio cities continued, requests for the sisters multiplied from other parts of the country. It was the entreaty for sisters to come to Boston in 1849, however, which greatly strained their personnel. However, it also opened up many new ministerial opportunities. The sisters had been asked to come there because as the pastor of St. Mary's observed, "No one speaks for girls." The sisters not only spoke for the adolescent girls when they began teaching the poor of St. Mary's parish school, but they also soon found themselves involved in many ways with the Irish immigrants who were emigrating in large numbers. By 1890 there were twenty-one parish schools being staffed by the sisters in cities in and around Boston.

In all of the foundations the familiar pattern begun in Ohio was repeated over and over again—too few sisters for too many students who were housed in too small buildings. Hardships, however, did not keep the sisters from developing new and creative ways to reach out to the poor. They used the classrooms to teach the girls during the day, as well as establishing nursery schools for the youngest children. At night the mothers and aunts of the students used the same rooms for classes. When the women made it known that their own mothers were often at home during the day, sick and alone, one of the sisters began a nine-bed hospital which was later merged with the first "official" hospital in Lowell, Massachusetts.

This growing awareness of the needs of their time also led the sisters in Ohio to find other ways to reach out to the poor. When the sisters were asked by the Jesuits to teach at St. Ann's school, the annals note that every sister in the community volunteered. The school was being opened for the children of the freed slaves who had come to Cincinnati after the Civil War. Another important undertaking was the establishment of a school for the deaf in one of the classrooms of the academy. The success of this school which continued for thirty years was well known.

On the West Coast, too, the sisters in California became involved in many other ministries. Six Sisters of Notre Dame had arrived in Oregon at St. Paul's in 1844. The great Belgian missionary Fr. De Smet requested the sisters for his missions there. At St. Paul's the sisters struggled to catechize and teach secular subjects to the Chinook natives. However, the Namur-style approach to education employed successfully by the sisters in Cincinnati failed badly. In Oregon the sisters simply did not understand the needs of their students.

By 1851 thousands had left the Willamette region headed to California in search of gold. The sisters also left to search for another gold, their beloved poor. Although they first established an academy school in San Jose in 1851, shortly thereafter, a free school was begun for the poor Spanish-speaking girls.

Twentieth Century

With the arrival of the twentieth century, the sisters turned their sights to yet another educational endeavor. After years of service to thousands of students in academies and parish schools scattered throughout the country, as well as working in various social ministries and training thou-

sands more sodalists to aid them in those works, the sisters opted to do something about higher education for women. Assuming great financial burdens, the sisters succeeded in opening Trinity College in Washington, D.C., in 1900. In 1919 Emmanuel College opened in Boston, and in 1951, Belmont College in California reverted to full college status.

As with many religious communities, in the 1950s and 1960s, the sisters experienced growth both in personnel and ministries. Many newly established parishes increased the number of requests for sisters to staff the schools which seemed to multiply geometrically. This growth also occurred not only in cities where the sisters had been a part of the diocesan systems for a long time, but in other cities as well. At the same time, changes mandated by Vatican Council II began to be felt in the Church and in religious communities. Much of what might be called traditional growth came to a rather abrupt halt as some sisters left their communities and sought new ways to meet the needs of their times and serve the people of God.

This new emphasis on the signs of the times found many Sisters of Notre Dame rethinking St. Julie's work of education in a broader context outside of the traditional classroom. Others responded to the call to serve the poor in Kenya, Zaire, South Africa, Zimbabwe, Nigeria, Japan, Brazil, Peru, and recently Nicaragua. Today, with fewer members and greater diversity in ministries, the Sisters of Notre Dame de Namur serve in thirty-five states. In the spirit of St. Julie, they proclaim the message of God's goodness to all, especially the poor.

See also WOMEN RELIGIOUS IN AMERICA.

Gusweiler, Agnes Immaculata, S.N.D.deN. *New Apostolate in a New World, 1840–1886*. Privately Printed, 1967.
Linscott, Mary, S.N.D.deN. *Quiet Revolution*. Glasgow, 1966.
Murphy, Roseanne, S.N.D.deN. *Julie Billiart: Woman of Courage*. New York, 1995.
Nugent, Helen Louise, S.N.D.deN. *Sister Julia (Susan McGroarty)*. Cincinnati, 1928.
____. *Sister Louise (Josephine Van Der Schrieck)*. Cincinnati, 1931.

LOUANNA ORTH, S.N.D.deN.

SISTERS OF PROVIDENCE (S.P.)

The Congregation of the Sisters of Providence of Saint Mary-of-the-Woods, Indiana, has its origins in Ruillé-sur-Loire in the Diocese of Le Mans, France. In 1806 Fr. Jacques-François Dujarié (1767–1839), a country pastor, found two young laywomen to assist him by giving religious instructions to the Catholic children of the area, and by visiting the sick poor in their homes. Gradually, other young women were attracted to join the original two until the group developed into the nucleus of a religious congregation dedicated to the works of charity and to the Providence of God.

Call to America

In 1839 Célestine de la Hailandière, bishop of Vincennes, Indiana, asked the superiors at Ruillé to send sisters to his diocese where there was a pressing need among the settlers for teachers. Sr. Saint Theodore Guerin (1798–1856), with two other professed sisters and three novices, crossed the Atlantic by sailing vessel and then proceeded by canal boat, river boat, and stagecoach to a little clearing in the forest five miles from the frontier town of Terre Haute.

During the first winter, while their convent was being built, the sisters were sheltered by Joseph Thralls, a local farmer, and his family. Mother Theodore, as she was now called, and her companions spent the winter months studying the English language and preparing to open their academy. In July 1841, they welcomed the first five students to St. Mary's Female Institute in the building that Bishop de la Hailandière had intended for the sisters' convent, but which Mother Theodore found "too grand" for that purpose.

In September 1843 the American foundation became an autonomous religious congregation. By 1854 Mother Theodore could write to France that the sisters were already teaching more than a thousand children in the Vincennes diocese, many of these in young ladies' academies at St. Mary's, in Jasper, Vincennes, Madison, Terre Haute, and Fort Wayne. In addition to the academies, a number of parish schools and two orphanages were under the sisters' care. The congregation continued to grow after Mother Theodore's death, spreading throughout Indiana, Illinois, and Michigan. During the Civil War the sisters staffed military hospitals in Indianapolis and Vincennes.

A disastrous fire in February 1889 completely destroyed the convent built by Mother Theodore as well as the community chapel. Six months later Mother Euphrasie Hinkle, the fifth superior general, died, leaving Sr. Mary Cleophas Foley, her first assistant, in charge of a community which had lost in rapid succession its motherhouse, its church, and its superior.

Expansion in America and Abroad

When Sr. Mary Cleophas was elected superior general in July 1890, the community numbered about 450 members; when she left office in 1926, there were close to 1,200 sisters. The congregation continued to grow in Indiana and Illinois and had spread to Michigan, Missouri, Massachusetts, and the District of Columbia. The sisters were much in demand as pastors attempted to carry out the mandate of the Third Plenary Council of Baltimore (1884) to erect schools in every Catholic parish.

The academy at St. Mary-of-the-Woods evolved into a four-year liberal arts college for women awarding its first degree in 1899. Two college buildings, Anne Therese Guerin Hall and St. Cecilia Conservatory of Music, were completed in 1913, the year the first four-year graduates were awarded their degrees.

In 1920 Sr. Marie Gratia Luking (1885–1964) with five companions left St. Mary-of-the-Woods for Kaifeng, Hunan, China. This mission, the first established by an American congregation on the mainland of China, persisted despite civil war, Japanese invasion, and Communist takeover until finally in 1948 the sisters were forced to resettle on the island of Taiwan. In 1929 Sr. Marie Gratia founded a native congregation of sisters called Providence Sister-Catechists, especially dedicated to the religious education of Chinese women. These sisters became an autonomous congregation in 1962.

The Sisters of Providence gradually expanded into new areas of missionary work in the United States, sending sisters to California, North Carolina, Oklahoma, and Texas, and continued the ministry to the immigrant communities that began in the first days of the community, especially in such metropolitan centers as Boston, Chicago, Indianapolis, and Los Angeles. While still primarily engaged in education, the congregation has moved away from the ownership of large educational institutions in favor of more individualized ministries.

The apostolic process for the beatification of Mother Theodore was begun in 1907. The ordinarily lengthy process was further hindered by two world wars, but in July 1992 Pope John Paul II accorded the foundress the title Venerable in recognition of her dedication to the Church.

The congregation in 1995 numbered 723 professed sisters of whom 711 are perpetually professed, serving in 55 dioceses in the United States and in Taiwan.

See also WOMEN RELIGIOUS IN AMERICA.

Brown, Mary Borromeo, S.P. *History of the Sisters of Providence.* Vol. 1. New York, 1949.

Burton, Katherine. *Faith is the Substance.* New York, 1959.

Logan, Eugenia, S.P. *History of the Sisters of Providence.* Vol. 2. St. Mary-of-the-Woods, 1991.

Madden, Mary Roger, S.P. *The Path Marked Out: History of the Sisters of Providence.* Vol. 3. St. Mary-of-the-Woods, 1978.

Mug, Mary Theodosia, S.P., ed. *Journals and Letters of Mother Theodore Guerin.* St. Mary-of-the-Woods, 1937; repr. 1970.

____. *Life and Life-Works of Mother Theodore Guerin.* New York, 1904.

Sisters of Providence. *A Journey in Love, Mercy and Justice: A Pictorial History of the Sisters of Providence.* St. Mary-of-the-Woods, 1989.

Wolf, Ann Colette, S.P. *Against All Odds: The Chinese Mission of the Sisters of Providence.* St. Mary-of-the-Woods, 1990.

MARY ROGER MADDEN, S.P.

SISTERS OF ST. JOSEPH

Religious congregations of women tracing their origin to the foundation by Jean Pierre Médaille, S.J., in 1650, and given official recognition by Henri de Maupas, bishop of Le Puy. There are presently thirty-one congregations in the United States and Canada.

Origins

Sisters of St. Joseph were part of the spiritual movement in seventeenth-century France which gave rise to apostolic religious life for women, characterized by lack of cloister and service of the neighbor. Heralded in St. Francis de Sales' first plan for the Visitation (1610) and St. Vincent de Paul's Daughters of Charity (1633), it was realized in divers women's communities of the time.

Fr. Médaille, in his missions in the Massif Central, encountered women called to religious consecration, but lacking either dowry or vocation to monastic life. Through spiritual guidance and the formulation of rules, Médaille helped these women to realize what he termed the "little design": a life of union with God, dedicated to the salvation and perfection of the neighbor through loving service. Correspondence of Jesuit Father General Vincent Caraffa in 1647 shows that Médaille had already prescribed rules for a group of women, possibly as early as 1645. The first extant rules, *Règlement pour les Soeurs de Saint Joseph,* describe small groups of three to six, living a consecrated life in service of the neighbor, but without distinctive habit or dwelling. Allusions to a secret society, the works of mercy, and eucharistic emphasis may suggest influence of the *Compagnie du Saint-Sacrement.*

Surviving records reveal a small community established at Dunières in 1649, and another at Le Puy in 1650. Françoise Eyraud, first superior at Le Puy, was already at the hôpital de Montferrand, newly reorganized and devoted to orphan girls, early in 1647. The official foundation, according to the *Constitutions* of 1694, was October 15, 1650, when Bishop de Maupas assembled a group of widows and young women at the hôpital de Montferrand and gave them charge of the orphanage, placing them under the protection of St. Joseph. He prescribed a form of dress (that of widows, not a religious habit), and exhorted them to observe their rules. Official episcopal recognition of the *Filles de Saint-Joseph* followed on March 10, 1651, and a formal act of association on December 13, 1651, reveals their names: Françoise Eyraud, Clauda Chastel, Marguerite Burdier, Anna Chalayer, Anna Vey, and Anna Brun.

Constitutions

The *Constitutions,* written by Fr. Médaille in the early 1650s, bear a strong Ignatian stamp. They specify three simple vows of poverty, chastity, and obedience, accompanied by a protestation "to profess in all things and every-where the most profound humility and the most cordial charity toward the neighbor." Each house was under the authority of the local bishop. Approved by Armand de Béthune of Le Puy in 1665, the *Constitutions* were first printed at Vienne in 1694. Reissued at Lyons in 1730, 1788, and 1819, they were substantially the same as those diffused throughout the nineteenth-century congregations. Significantly altered during the first half of the twentieth century in compliance with newly codified canon law, the *Constitutions* regained more of their original orientation after Vatican Council II.

The primitive *Constitutions* imply a great deal of flexibility, revealed in diversity of structure within the congregation. In order to facilitate service of the neighbor and accommodate membership from different classes, there were three types of members in the principal houses: *demoiselles de service,* women who could give themselves full time to charity; *demoiselles de travaille,* who had to work part-time to earn a living; and women and widows *de basse condition,* who had to work full-time. There were also *agrégées* living in small communities in city and country, practicing the same exercises as the sisters, and united to the congregation by a vow of stability. *Associées,* who lived with their families, formed a type of third order for single or married women. Sisters did not recite Office in choir, nor were they cloistered, since they went out to do the works of mercy. Communities were organized in districts, in which country houses were affiliated with a larger city house. Each community, however, was juridically autonomous until the beginning of the nineteenth century, when Napoleon required diocesan centralization.

Spirituality

Informed by a trinitarian and christocentric spirituality, the congregation was ordered toward love and service of God in love and service of the neighbor, seen as one integral goal, rather than as primary and secondary ends. The profoundly incarnational tone is captured in a formula, "Summary of the Purpose of the Very Little Congregation of St. Joseph," used by Médaille four times in the early documents. In it the apostolic life of the congregation is seen to flow directly from the love of God ("the Uncreated Trinity"), and this divine union of love is exemplified on earth in the life of Jesus, Mary, and Joseph ("the Created Trinity"). The mission of the Sisters of St. Joseph is to make this love known and shared through "complete zeal and union with God, among themselves, and with every kind of neighbor" (*Règlement,* 17). As a means of working toward this union, the sisters were to practice all the spiritual and corporal works of mercy, especially those most needed or neglected by others, gradually becoming "all for God and the dear neighbor, nothing for self," in order to "contribute . . . to this total union among human beings . . . among themselves and with God" (*Lettre eucharistique,* 51) (See Vacher, "San Giuseppe," col. 528).

Historical Development

The congregation spread rapidly in the Massif Central and the southeastern quarter of France, with at least thirty-four houses in six dioceses by the death of Médaille (1669), and about 150 at the time of the French Revolution. Sisters of St. Joseph wore the dress of widows and lived in a section of the institution where they worked, or in houses little distinguished from those of their neighbors. They undertook any work "of which woman is capable": orphanages, care of the sick at home and in hospitals, elementary schools, catechetics, sacristy work in parishes, asylums for fallen women, and teaching manual skills. The unassuming edification of their life and the extraordinary utility of their works in the *ancien régime* earned Sisters of St. Joseph a secure footing, and their success was due largely to harmonious fit with the world in which they were.

During the French Revolution, Sisters of St. Joseph were known for their counterrevolutionary sympathies, grounded in religious principles. By 1793 almost every community was dispersed and many sisters were imprisoned. In the summer of 1794 at least five sisters were guillotined: Marie Anne Garnier and Jeanne Marie Aubert at le Puy (June 17), and Antoinette Vincent, Marie-Anne Sénovert, and Madeleine Dumoulin at Privas (August 5).

Following the Revolution, former communities sought to reconstitute themselves, and for the first time were organized into diocesan congregations with a superior general, the first at Clermont in 1811. By that time, the original structure had been modified: communities were divided into "choir" and "lay" members, and choir sisters wore a habit with veil and guimpe. Mother Saint-Jean Fontbonne, former superior at Monistrol who had been imprisoned during the Revolution and was reputed to have narrowly missed the scaffold, effected diocesan centralization in Lyons. The resulting congregation rapidly became one of the largest in France and also the source of the first American foundation. During the nineteenth century, French congregations saw extensive international development: Italy (1821), United States (1836), India (1849), Canada (1851), Denmark (1856), Brazil (1858), Switzerland (1862), Russia (1863), England (1865), Norway (1865), Argentina (1882), Algeria (1884), and Iceland (1896). Laws of secularization early in the twentieth century prompted further dispersal: Lyons, for example, added foundations in Lebanon, Armenia, Greece, and Egypt. By 1950, there were fifty to sixty thousand Sisters of St. Joseph in approximately sixty congregations throughout the world.

The United States

The first Sisters of St. Joseph arrived in North America at St. Louis, March 25, 1836. They were six volunteers from the Lyons congregation: Srs. Fébronie Fontbonne, Delphine Fontbonne, Marguerite-Félicité Bouté, Marie-Fébronie Chapellon, St. Protais Déboille, and Philomène Vilaine. On April 7, 1836, three sisters went to the French-speaking settlement in Cahokia, Illinois, which was finally abandoned in 1855. The remaining three formed the first permanent establishment at Carondelet, Missouri, on September 12, 1836. They were followed in 1837 by Srs. Celestine Pommerel and St. John Fournier, who had studied methods for teaching deaf persons at St. Etienne. The American foundation was prompted and partly financed by a devout, wealthy laywoman, Félicité de Duras, Countess de la Rochejacquelin. Inspired by the *Annales de la propagation de la foi,* she secured the cooperation of Bishop Joseph Rosati of St. Louis and Mother Saint-Jean Fontbonne, superior at Lyons (and also aunt of two missionaries), to bring Sisters of St. Joseph to the Missouri frontier.

Congregations

The thirty-one juridically independent Congregations of St. Joseph presently in the United States and Canada spring from three sources: (1) missions of six French congregations; (2) communities founded by Carondelet before 1860; (3) congregations established by those derived from Carondelet.

Date	Congregation	Origin
1836	Carondelet	**Lyons**
1847	Philadelphia	Carondelet
1851	Toronto	Carondelet\ Philadelphia
1851	Carondelet-St. Paul	Carondelet
1852	Hamilton	Toronto
1853	Wheeling	Carondelet
1854	Buffalo	Carondelet
1854	Rochester	Carondelet
1854	McSherrystown*	Philadelphia
1855	Bay St. Louis (Médaille 1977)	**Bourg**
1856	Brentwood	Philadelphia
1858	Carondelet-Albany	Carondelet
1860	Erie	Carondelet
1866	St. Augustine	**Le Puy**
1867	Savannah*	St. Augustine
1868	London	Toronto
1869	Baden	Brentwood
1870	Carondelet-Los Angeles	Carondelet
1872	Cleveland	Carondelet-St. Paul
1873	Boston	Brentwood

Date	Congregation	Origin
1873	Rutland	Brentwood
1880	Watertown	Carondelet-Albany/Erie
1883	Concordia	Rochester
1883	Springfield	Brentwood
1885	Chambéry-West Hartford	**Chambéry**
1888	Tipton	Cleveland/Watertown
1888	Wichita	Concordia
1889	Kalamazoo	Watertown
1890	Peterborough	Toronto
1892	Muskogee*	Brentwood
1899	La Grange	Concordia
1900	Belvidere*	La Grange
1902	Fall River-Le Puy*	**Le Puy**
1902	Lewiston*	La Grange
1903	Quebec-St. Vallier	**Saint-Vallier**
1906	Maine-Lyons	**Lyons**
1907	Superior*	Savannah
1912	Orange	La Grange
1917	Silver City*	Tipton
1921	Pembroke	Peterborough
1936	Sault-Ste. Marie	Peterborough
1956	Columbus*	Erie
1956	Corozal	St. Augustine

NB: The Congregation of Moûtiers sent thirty-nine sisters between 1854 and 1889 who became affiliated with Carondelet.

*Presently extinct or fused with another congregation

Ecclesiastical Identity

Congregations of St. Joseph have either diocesan or pontifical approbation. (1) *Diocesan.* According to their constitutions, Sisters of St. Joseph who came to Carondelet in 1836 were a congregation of diocesan rite, governed by a superior general and subject to the local ordinary. These constitutions did not envision a congregation with houses beyond diocesan boundaries. In 1847, however, Mother St. John Fournier made a foundation in Philadelphia, and by 1860 there were houses in at least ten dioceses. In this situation, Mother Celestine Pommerel, superior at Carondelet, acted informally as superior general (although without legal definition) until her death in 1857. By 1860 canonical centralization was planned with a motherhouse at Carondelet, but only St. Paul and Albany responded; the other groups derived from Carondelet chose local diocesan status. Save Carondelet, communities established after 1860 tended to became diocesan. Bishops, as well as being ecclesiastical superiors, were often the key to successful integration in a new area. Many, like John Ireland, came to consider Sisters of St. Joseph as "agencies that he might summon to his aid." Diocesan status often facilitated expansion, and lent a highly local color to congregations of St. Joseph in various geographic areas. (2) *Pontifical.* Following centralization, the far-flung congregation of Carondelet sought pontifical status, formally granted in 1877. The Sisters of St. Joseph of Chambéry, already highly international, had pontifical approbation when they came to the U.S.A. in 1885. A number of other American congregations eventually became pontifical either because of overseas missionary commitments, or to accommodate extradiocesan houses.

Historical Development

Sisters of St. Joseph came to the United States recommended by Countess de la Rochejacquelin as "ready for anything." Lack of restriction by rule on works they could undertake, such as care for boys, placed them in great demand, and a tendency toward rapid Americanization facilitated their access to a variety of settings. Sisters of St. Joseph of Carondelet and some other congregations worked extensively with Native Americans, beginning at Long Prairie; in Minnesota Territory with the Winnebago in 1852; and later through schools, orphanages, and other means in Wisconsin, New Mexico, California, Arizona, Idaho, Wyoming, and New York. St. Joseph's School for the Colored was the first house opened in St. Louis, where sisters taught between eighty and one hundred free children, including about twenty boys, and instructed enslaved African Americans for the reception of sacraments after school hours. When Bishop Augustin Verot of St. Augustine brought sisters from Le Puy in 1866, it was "for the Negroes, and for them almost exclusively." Although significant, works with Native and African American populations formed a scant part of the whole. Sisters of St. Joseph worked largely with immigrant ethnic groups representing their own backgrounds (particularly French, Irish, and German), often in urban parishes. Some congregations, however, particularly Concordia, Wichita, and Tipton, were distinctly rural. They, and the St. Paul Province of Carondelet, served in one- or two-room schools, sometimes as public school teachers in small settlements, or established boarding schools to provide education for girls from isolated farms or ranches.

Sisters of St. Joseph served primarily with working-class people, where they addressed, as they had in France, the unmet needs of a larger society. At Carondelet in the 1830s, Sisters of St. Joseph were the public school teachers. There was no school in Tucson when seven Sisters of St. Joseph arrived there by overland trek in 1870, and they opened the first hospital there in 1880. Sisters of St. Joseph served repeatedly in cholera and typhoid epidemics, and as nurses during the Civil and Spanish American Wars. Indispensable agents of education and poor relief within the immigrant Church, Sisters of St. Joseph were deeply integrated into parishes through schools and always by visiting sick and poor parishioners. They operated charitable hospitals and orphanages as well, supporting their works through paying academies, government grants, large doses of financial aid from European mission societies, and by whatever they could earn from needlework, taking in washing, and (in Florida) manufacturing the famous Le Puy lace.

Americanization

Adaptation to the American milieu included gradual abolition of the two-tiered membership of choir and lay sisters, offensive to democratic sensibilities. Sisters were subject to nativist hostility throughout the nineteenth century: for example, mob activity prompted Bishop Peter Kenrick to close the school for African American children in St. Louis in 1845; sisters had to be accompanied to Mass in Philadelphia; and in 1895 sisters in Gallitzin, Pennsylvania, were barred by a special act of the state legislature from teaching in the public schools because of their religious garb. Ethnic rivalries also played their part within communities: Mother St. John Fournier was resented by some Irish sisters in the Philadelphia congregation as "that French woman," and French Irish tensions underlay the eventual separation of St. Augustine from the Le Puy motherhouse. Cultural conflict seems to have been continuous and painful in the American branches of the Bourg congregation, which finally became independent in 1977.

Sisterhoods in the American milieu developed within the framework of the professionalization of women in the fields of teaching and health care. In keeping with the pioneer tradition at Carondelet, Sisters of St. Joseph were noted in several congregations for teaching deaf children in respected schools such as the Boston School Serving Deaf and Aphasic Children, St. Joseph's Institute for the Deaf in St. Louis, and the St. Mary's School for the Deaf in Buf-

falo. Nearly every congregation of St. Joseph operated hospitals or dispensaries at some point. With the transformation of health care in the late nineteenth and early twentieth centuries, communities opened nursing schools and some developed complex health-care systems; the largest at present are those of Orange, Wichita, Carondelet, and Kalamazoo. Increasing professionalization was also evidenced by the seventeen four-year colleges of Sisters of St. Joseph, beginning with the College of St. Catherine in St. Paul (1916), which in 1937 became the first Catholic college of any kind to have a chapter of Phi Beta Kappa.

The last permanent foundation in mainland United States was at Eureka, California, in 1912, and in Canada at Sault-Ste. Marie, Ontario, in 1936. While membership increased steadily until the mid-1960s, the number of congregations remained fairly constant. At the same time, overseas missions developed as the Baden Congregation began a mission in the Hunan province of China in 1926. Sisters from Brentwood went to Puerto Rico in 1930, and the Puerto Rican community of Corozal, established from St. Augustine, became an independent congregation in 1977. Orange began missions in the Solomon Islands in 1940; Wichita and Carondelet went to Japan in the 1950s. As a result of Pope John XXIII's appeal for Latin America, numerous congregations sent missions to South and Central America, where Concordia and Carondelet have significant membership in Brazil and Peru respectively. Americans also formed part of the large international extension of the Chambéry and Lyons congregations in Europe, the Mideast, Asia, Africa and South America. Following Vatican II, in addition to the places mentioned above, Sisters of St. Joseph from the U.S.A. have served as missionaries in Chile, Guatemala, Haiti, Nicaragua, Jamaica, Kenya, Liberia, Korea, the Philippines, New Guinea, and Australia.

The Federation of Sisters of St. Joseph, United States of America, was established in 1966 at the instigation of Mother Eucharista Galvin (Carondelet). A purely voluntary and not juridical organization, it includes every congregation of St. Joseph in the United States. In close cooperation with the Canadian Federation, it has sponsored intensive research on the history and spirituality of the Sisters of St. Joseph, offered formation and renewal programs for members, and fostered intercongregational ministries. In 1995 there were approximately 9,690 Sisters of St. Joseph in the United States and 1,070 in Canada.

Sisters of St. Joseph

Byrne, Patricia, C.S.J. "Sisters of St. Joseph: The Americanization of a French Tradition" *U.S. Catholic Historian* 5 (1986) 241–72.

Dougherty, Dolorita Marie and others. *Sisters of St. Joseph of Carondelet.* St. Louis: Herder, 1966.

Logue, Maria Kostka. *Sisters of St. Joseph of Philadelphia: A Century of Growth and Development 1847–1947.* Westminster, Md.: Newman, 1950.

Quinn, Margaret M. "Two Decades of the 'Dynamic Union': History and Achievements 1966–1986." Unpublished manuscript, Archives of U.S. Federation of Sisters of St. Joseph.

Soeurs de Saint-Joseph, Textes Primitifs. Clermont-Ferrand: Siman, S. A., 1981.

Vacher, Marguerite [Sr. Thérèse]. *Des "régulières" dans le siècle: Les soeurs de Saint-Joseph du Père Médaille aux XVIIe et XVIIIe siècles.* Clermont-Ferrand: Adosa, 1991.

Vacher, Thérèse and G. Rocca. *Dizionario degli istituti di perfezione,* s.v. "San Giuseppe del p. Jean-Pierre Médaille" 8:521-77.

PATRICIA BYRNE, C.S.J.

SISTERS OF THE GOOD SHEPHERD (R.G.S.)

The Sisters of the Good Shepherd were founded in Angers, France, in 1829 by St. Mary Euphrasia Pelletier, to minister to women who were victims of the social ills of their times. Originally a sister of Our Lady of Charity of the Refuge (founded for the same purpose by St. John Eudes in 1641), Mary Euphrasia was inspired by his words that "a person is of more value than a world" to extend their mission far beyond the four autonomous houses then in existence. By means of a centralized government that would send sisters wherever they were needed, she envisioned a community that would go where they were required.

The Generalate

Overcoming objections by the French bishops who wished the community to remain diocesan, Mary Euphrasia petitioned Rome to authorize her to found houses throughout France. One of the consultors at the assembly of cardinals, Anthony Kohlmann, S.J., suggested to Gregory XVI that they substitute "universe" for "France." There was unanimous agreement, and the generalate that would provide apostolic mobility for her sisters was approved in 1835 under the name and protection of the Good Shepherd.

Kohlmann had spent nearly a quarter of a century as a missionary under Bishop John Carroll in the U.S.A. when it was one diocese, working indefatigably among the Irish and German immigrants in New York and Pennsylvania. Before his recall to Europe in 1824 to teach at the Roman College, Kohlmann and Benedict Joseph Flaget, a French missionary himself and friend of Mary Euphrasia Pelletier, both taught at Georgetown University, where Kohlmann served as its tenth president.

The Call to America

Flaget, one of the first four bishops appointed by Bishop Carroll (founder of the American hierarchy), was assigned to the see of Bardstown, later Louisville, Kentucky. Louisville was a veritable seaport on the Ohio River and rife with corruption, gambling, and immorality. Flaget's concern for young immigrant girls at risk in the city inspired him to appeal to Angers for Good Shepherd Sisters to provide a desperately needed refuge for them. Five sisters set out for Louisville in 1842, and despite poverty and discrimination against Catholics and foreigners, they befriended vulnerable women longing for a better life, many of whom were worn out with illness, hard work, and exploitation. Others they prepared for a peaceful death after a wretched life.

From Louisville they spread to St. Louis (1849), Philadelphia (1850), Cincinnati and New York (1857), Baltimore (1864), and St. Paul (1868)—cities which became the nuclei of the five present-day provinces in the U.S.A. The Canadian foundation was made in Montreal in 1844. Houses continued to radiate from these cities to meet the needs of young women and their families marginalized in society.

The Contemplatives

In 1831, recognizing a desire among the young women in her care for a deeper spiritual life, Mary Euphrasia founded in Angers the Magdalen Sisters, known today throughout the world as Contemplative Sisters of the Good Shepherd. The first Contemplative Sisters in the New World entered from Louisville in 1852, and today, by their lives of prayer and work, which includes making altar breads, vestments, painting, ceramics, and handcrafts, they provide a powerhouse of prayer to support the work of the active sisters in their ministries.

Residential Treatment Centers/Group Homes

By timely interventions in the lives of the women in their care, the sisters not only provided them with an opportunity to renew their faith and self-esteem but to envision their stay, not as a final refuge, but as a steppingstone to a meaningful life, prepared by the vocational skills needed to be self-supporting. Always in touch with the 110 houses she had founded before her death in 1868, Mother Euphrasia, the first mother general of the congregation, was canonized on May 2, 1940. In the next two decades, the sisters would number 10,000 throughout the world.

During the 1960s a trend toward de-institutionalization swept the country and affected the existing model of care at the Good Shepherd residential treatment centers. Community-based group homes were established, some as satellites of the institutions, many of which continued to flourish, meeting the needs of those unable to profit from a more open setting. Some programs diversified, providing out-patient services for adolescents and their families.

Forging the Future

Once again the signs of the times challenge. As needs surface with fewer people to meet them, the Good Shepherd has extended its membership to three important groups known as the Associates of the Good Shepherd, the Companions of the Good Shepherd, and the Good Shepherd Volunteers. The associates include laypeople, both men and women. Some work directly in the ministry, others support the mission by their prayers and good works; all are dedicated to promoting respect for the dignity of the human person. The companions are a smaller group of women from the business world and the professions, who take private vows and strive to make visible the compassionate love of the Good Shepherd by bringing gospel values to the environment in which they live and work. The volunteers include college-age students who seek God in a shared experience of community while committing themselves to work in a Good Shepherd program for one year.

At the present time, the sisters work in 64 countries and number over 6,000 worldwide, 645 of whom are located in the United States.

See also WOMEN RELIGIOUS IN AMERICA.

MARY EILEEN FOLEY, R.G.S.

SISTERS OF THE HOLY CROSS (C.S.C.)

Origins

The Sisters of the Holy Cross were founded in 1841 in Le Mans, France, by Fr. Basil Anthony Moreau, a diocesan priest. He called them Marianites of Holy Cross. Their original apostolate was to provide domestic service for institutions staffed by the men of Holy Cross, both priests and brothers. In 1843 four of the sisters came to the United States to help the work of Holy Cross at the recently founded University of Notre Dame in Indiana.

Development in the United States

Soon the original purpose of the community began to disappear. The sisters started to conduct schools and care for orphans, while continuing to serve in laundry and infirmary at Notre Dame. Their own academy, begun in Bertrand, Michigan, in 1844, developed into St. Mary's College, Notre Dame, Indiana. It was the first of many academies and parochial schools staffed by the Sisters of the Holy Cross throughout the United States. While continuing to expand in the Midwest, in 1859 they opened their first permanent institution in the East, St. Patrick's School in Baltimore, Maryland. Many other institutions followed in Washington and other eastern cities. In 1875 Fr. (later Bishop) Lawrence Scanlon asked them to establish an academy in Salt Lake City, Utah. This was the first of many establishments in the Far West.

Because of the overwhelming number of Americans who entered, the dynamic nature of American life, and the slowness of communication with France, the sisters of the Indiana province (all the United States except Louisiana) separated from France in 1869 and became an autonomous congregation. Their general house became St. Mary's, Notre Dame, Indiana. No longer were they called Marianites, but Sisters of the Holy Cross. Their *Constitutions* were definitively approved by Rome in 1895.

Health Care

During the Civil War, in October 1861, at the request of Governor Morton of Indiana, six sisters, the first of many, were sent to nurse the sick and wounded primarily in Cairo and Mound City, Illinois, and in Memphis, Tennessee. By the end of the war approximately eighty sisters had spent time in the military hospitals. Those sisters who served on the hospital ship the *Red Rover* as it plied the Mississippi are considered by the U.S. Navy as forerunners of the Navy Nurse Corps.

Because of this service to the sick and wounded, they were asked by the local bishop to open a hospital in Cairo. St. Mary's Hospital, founded in 1869 in that city, was the first of eleven hospitals. Three of them have been closed. The other eight and their associated institutions are now part of the Holy Cross Health System Corporation founded in 1979.

Education

They did not neglect their apostolate of education. After the Third Plenary Council of Baltimore, the emphasis shifted from select schools to parochial ones. In the middle of the twentieth century, orphanages that had been founded in the previous century were closed as bishops made different arrangements for the care of orphaned children. Three more colleges were opened and subsequently closed: St. Mary-of-the-Wasatch in Salt Lake City, Utah; Dunbarton College in Washington, D.C.; and Cardinal Cushing College in Brookline, Massachusetts.

Missions Outside the United States

In 1853 the Sisters of the Holy Cross opened their first mission in Bengal, now Bangladesh. They were withdrawn in 1875, but went again in 1889. They were recalled in 1895 but returned once more in 1927. In 1995 there were fifty-two sisters in that country of whom most were Bangladeshi. In 1947 missionary activity began in Brazil and expanded to Peru in 1982. The sisters began work in Uganda in 1967 and in Ghana in 1983. Local formation programs were inaugurated. In 1974 the Sisters of the Holy Cross opened Mater Ecclesiae Center in Tiberias, Israel, to provide ongoing formation for sisters from Asia and Africa. In the 1960s, the congregation began to respond to emergency needs abroad, working first with Catholic Relief Services, then the Catholic Near East Welfare Association and the Pontifical Mission for Palestine. The greatest response was service to the Cambodian refugees in Thailand in 1979–80.

Status

The Sisters of the Holy Cross are a congregation of pontifical right, available for service to the entire Church. Their post-Vatican II *Constitution,* approved in 1982, says: "As a congregation whose missionary charism is to respond to the needs of the Church, we determine our types and places of service based on these needs." They participate in the Church's mission of evangelization through ministries of education, health care, and other pastoral services.

See also HOLY CROSS, CONGREGATION OF (C.S.C.); WOMEN RELIGIOUS IN AMERICA.

Brosnahan, M. Eleanore, C.S.C. *On the King's Highway.* New York: D. Appleton and Company, 1931.

Costin, M. Georgia, C.S.C. *Priceless Spirit, A History of the Sisters of the Holy Cross, 1841–1893.* University of Notre Dame Press, 1994.

____, ed. *Fruits of the Tree, Sesquicentennial Chronicles, Sisters of the Holy Cross.* Vols. 1–3. Notre Dame, Indiana, 1991.

SISTER CAMPION, C.S.C.

SISTERS OF THE HOLY FAMILY OF NAZARETH (C.S.F.N.)

The Sisters of the Holy Family of Nazareth, an international apostolic congregation, was founded in Rome by a Polish noblewoman, Frances Siedliska, known in religious life as Mother Mary of Jesus the Good Shepherd. In 1885 the congregation was granted the Decree of Praise by the Sacred Congregations of Bishops and Regulars, and on August 5, 1909, the definitive Decree of Approval by the Congregation of Religious. On July 4, 1885, the foundress with eleven sisters arrived in New York and in two days reached Chicago, Illinois, where they began their missionary work. During her years as superior general, Frances Siedliska crossed the Atlantic Ocean three times to visit the convents she had established and administered. Her attachment to America is testified by the fact that she became a naturalized citizen of the United States on July 26, 1897. At the time of her death in Rome on November 21, 1902, there were twenty convents in the United States. Pope John Paul II proclaimed her "Blessed" on April 23, 1989. The metropolitan curia of Warsaw, Poland, on September 18, 1991, began the cause of canonization for eleven of her sisters who were shot to death by the Nazis on August 1, 1943, in Poland.

The convents in the United States are geographically divided into five provinces to facilitate intracommunity solidarity and the efficacy of operation under the leadership of provincial superiors who work in collaboration with a superior general. The sisters are at work on three continents: North America, Europe, and Australia, and in the Philippines and Israel. Of the 1,780 members of the congregation, 741 are in the United States; of 143 convents, 65 are in this country.

In accordance with the wish of their foundress, the sisters promote the religious and moral development of families by organizing within their respective provinces a lay Association of the Holy Family.

Education

The sisters began their diversified work in the United States by responding to an invitation from Archbishop Patrick A. Feehan and the Polish clergy in Chicago. Besides work assigned them in an orphanage, they taught, held weekly discussion groups and prayer sessions with girls of all ages, and made home visits to the sick and dying. From Chicago and other parts of Illinois, the sisters were welcomed in Indiana, Scranton, Philadelphia, and Brooklyn, New York.

Teaching and evangelization extended to many cities in other states: Alabama, Connecticut, Florida, Maryland, Massachusetts, Michigan, Montana, New Jersey, North Dakota, Ohio, Pennsylvania, Puerto Rico, Texas, and Wisconsin. Prior to the days of racial integration, in 1933 the sisters accepted teaching positions in St. Joseph Mission in Chicago. In 1938 they assisted in ministry to the sick and dying in extreme conditions of poverty, and cared for spastic children in Montgomery, Alabama. When a shortage of public school teachers was experienced in South Heart, North Dakota, the sisters offered their services in that public school system in 1941. Nazareth sisters teach in diocesan/parish high schools in Philadelphia, Pennsylvania; Chicago and Burbank in Illinois; Danbury, Connecticut; Allen Park, Michigan; and Worcester, Massachusetts.

In 1885 the sisters were entrusted with the care of Polish orphans in Chicago and have been engaged in this apostolate in various parts of America for over a century. They have also been active in the care of the elderly, and since 1896 have been active in hospital work and management. In 1934 they expanded the variegated apostolate to fostering retreats for religious and laity, and established retreat centers and houses of prayer in Rockville Centre, New York; in Des Plaines and Schiller, Illinois; in Cleveland, Ohio; and in Philadelphia, Pennsylvania.

See also POLISH CATHOLICS IN AMERICA.

Dylewska, M. De Chantal, C.S.F.N. *Out of Nazareth.* New York: Exposition Press, 1974.

Ricciardi, Antonio, O.F.M. *His Will Alone.* Trans. Regis Barwig, O.S.B. Oshkosh, 1971.

Sisters of the Holy Family of Nazareth. *Covenant of Love.* Rome, 1983.

MARY MICHAEL GECEWICZ, C.S.F.N.

SISTERS, SERVANTS OF THE IMMACULATE HEART OF MARY (I.H.M.)

Numerous congregations of women religious were established in the United States in the mid-nineteenth century. Many came into being as foreign missions. Sisters were sent from Europe to accompany or serve among various immigrant groups. Some were founded here in the United States. The Sisters, Servants of the Immaculate Heart of Mary (I.H.M.) belong among the latter. In 1843 Louis Florent Gillet, a French-speaking Belgian Redemptorist priest, came to Michigan to minister to a French-speaking community in Grosse Pointe. Within a short while, Gillet went to the less settled area of Monroe, Michigan. There he established schools for young men and looked for sisters to educate young women.

While on an extended visit to the Redemptorist community in Baltimore, Maryland, Gillet met an Oblate Sister named Theresa Maxis Duchemin. Theresa, daughter of a Haitian woman and a British army officer, was a member of the Oblate Sisters of Providence. The Oblates were experiencing great difficulties at the time. They received no support from ecclesiastical sources, and their survival was in question. Theresa accepted Gillet's invitation to work with him in Monroe.

On November 10, 1845, three women (Theresa Maxis, Oblate Charlotte Schaaf, and Theresa Renauld from Grosse Pointe, Michigan) attended Mass celebrated by Fr. Gillet and then moved into their new home (a wooden cabin by the River Raisin). Theresa Maxis became the first superior of the Sisters of Providence (they took the I.H.M. name in 1858). As with so many acts of God, none of the four had any inkling of the suffering awaiting them.

Gillet was the first to know drastic change. Due to unfounded accusations and faulty communications, he was called back to Baltimore in April 1847, less than eighteen months after the founding of the I.H.M. Sisters. He eventually returned to Europe, left the Redemptorist Congregation, and died a member of a Cistercian community in Haute Combe, France. Decades passed before he learned what happened to the sisters.

The Redemptorist Congregation withdrew from Monroe in 1855. One consequence of their departure was that the local bishop, Peter Paul Lefevere, who was very unhappy with their departure, did little to support the works the Redemptorists had begun, including the I.H.M.s. Finally, in 1857, he appointed a young Belgian priest—Edward Joos—director and superior of the I.H.M. congregation. The authority of Theresa as superior of the congregation no longer existed. Joos was to remain superior of the congregation for forty-four years.

Theresa Maxis received what must have felt like a "God-sent" invitation in 1858. Redemptorist bishop John Nepomeucene Neumann asked the I.H.M. Sisters to establish a mission in Susquehanna, Pennsylvania. Theresa was given permission to send sisters there, and the new mission was successful. When, however, Bishop Neumann requested sisters for a second mission, Bishop Lefevere refused permission. When Theresa protested vehemently, Fr. Joos informed Bishop Lefevre. The bishop dismissed Theresa from office and sent her to Pennsylvania. Theresa Maxis was never allowed to return to the sisters in Monroe. She spent decades of her life as a guest of the Grey Nuns of Ottawa, was finally allowed to return to the I.H.M. Sisters in Scranton, Pennsylvania, and died there.

In 1859 the congregation was split in two. Twelve sisters remained in Pennsylvania with Theresa Maxis. Twelve were in Monroe. The I.H.M. Sisters of Scranton, Pennsylvania, developed from this beginning. They were to grow and become a distinct congregation. A year later the second mission in Reading, Pennsylvania, also became a separate congregation. Three religious congregations resulted from the insight and courage of Theresa Maxis and Louis Florent Gillet. Because of the orders of the hierarchy, these three congregations had very little contact with each other. Yet each wore the blue habit and each followed the same rule. All three were also devoted to education, and all three flourished. Thousands and hundreds of thousands of women and men in America were educated by the I.H.M. Sisters. Thousands of women and men have contributed to their society and their Church in response to the social consciousness that was given to them as integral to their education. After Vatican Council II, the Philadelphia, Scranton, and Monroe I.H.M.s were reacquainted with each other, their common heritage, their common charism. The year 1994–95 marked a common celebration of the sesquicentennial of the I.H.M.s. The three congregations numbered more than 3,000 sisters in 36 states and 15 countries.

See also WOMEN RELIGIOUS IN AMERICA.

Gannon, Margaret, I.H.M. *Paths of Daring, Deeds of Hope.* Scranton, Pa., and Monroe, Mich.: Sisters, Servants of the Immaculate Heart of Mary, 1992.

Kelly, Rosalita, I.H.M. *No Greater Service: The History of the Congregation of the Sisters, Servants of the Immaculate Heart of Mary.* Detroit: Sisters, Servants of the Immaculate Heart of Mary, 1948.

JULIANA CASEY, I.H.M.

SIUWHEEM, LOUISE (? –ca. 1850)

Native American Catholic laywoman. Louise Siuwheem (Saw-gée-heem) or *Sighouin,* as the French spelled the name, was a young Native American woman of the Coeur d'Alene Tribe in what is now Idaho, who was known for her zeal for the conversion of her tribe, her penitential spirit, and her ministry to the sick.

Fr. Pierre De Smet, S.J., who baptized Louise in 1842, said in his book, *New Indian Sketches,* that Louise was "rich in virtue and exalted. . . . She was an oasis amid a sterile waste; she was a light amid the shades of death."

De Smet added that, from the time of her conversion, Louise lived a life of poverty and spent the remainder of her days in service to the Lord, teaching the word to the members of her tribe, preparing young and old alike to receive the sacraments, tending the sick with care, patience, and interest, and even adopting a crippled, blind child whom she tended for several years until his death. Her life was an act of continual charity.

Louise had a great devotion to the Holy Cross, De Smet observed. Each year during sowing season, she would ask her spiritual director to bless the seed corn. Then she went through fields digging up a piece of ground in the shape of a cross and planting the corn there. Each year she did this, the crop was abundant and fine, even when the neighbors all around lost their grain.

Louise had learned, said De Smet, "that heaven and earth had been disunited, and that the Cross had reconciled them; that no one can enter into heaven except by the way of the Cross. She sowed her grain in the form of a cross, having implicit confidence that our Lord, who died on the cross, would fructify it." According to De Smet's accounts, when Louise died sometime in the 1850s, the Coeur d'Alenes deeply missed and remembered this person they called mother, guide, and true friend.

See also NATIVE AMERICANS AND THE CATHOLIC CHURCH.

COLETTE COWMAN

SLATTERY, JOHN R. (1851–1926)

Civil rights priest, pioneer in African American apostolate. John Richard Slattery was born in New York City on July 26, 1851, of Irish-American parents. He entered St. Charles College, Maryland, as a seminarian for the Archdiocese of New York, but eye problems forced him to leave within a year. In 1871 he entered Columbia College School of Law. As a member of the Paulist parish of St. Paul, he heard Herbert Vaughan preach there on the work of the newly formed English Foreign Missionaries (St. Joseph Society of the Sacred Heart for Foreign Missions) and their work in the black community of America. He entered Mill Hill in London in January of 1873. He was ordained on March 17, 1877. Protesting his original assignment as a teacher at Mill Hill, he was sent to America in October of 1877. He rapidly became pastor of St. Francis Xavier, Baltimore, and American provincial from 1878 to 1883. When he was phased out of authority, he was sent to establish the Richmond missions under Bishop John J. Keane. His success there in an extended and complex mission field, coupled with growing support from liberal members of the American hierarchy, balanced the continued con-

John R. Slattery

flicts with Mill Hill authority. Worried about possible problems of American candidates studying in England, Slattery received permission from Vaughan to establish a seminary in America. He opened St. Joseph's Seminary in Baltimore in 1888, followed by a minor seminary in 1889.

With Mill Hill sending more men to India, Borneo, and New Zealand, Slattery sought to have a separate American community. Beginning in 1892, Vaughan gave his men a year to choose their future positions. Two returned to Mill Hill, nine joined dioceses, and five, along with Slattery, formed the new American community. Among the founders was Charles Randolph Uncles, the first African American priest trained and ordained in the United States, and a protégé of Slattery. Expansion of the work took place under Slattery as superior general. Black vocations to the priesthood were encouraged, directly through the seminary, and indirectly through the development of St. Joseph's Catechetical College in Montgomery, Alabama. He promoted trade schools (St. Joseph's Industrial School, Clayton, Delaware). He encouraged social work through helping in the founding of the Mission Helpers of the Sacred Heart, as well as fostering vocations for the Franciscan Sisters of Glen Riddle.

As provincial, he had welcomed and helped to fit the Mill Hill Franciscans into the work of the missions. He welcomed and encouraged the efforts of the Drexels. In a time of liberal-conservative conflicts, he was involved in the fray as an Americanist. The 1899 *Testem benevolentiae* of Leo XIII undermined Slattery's confidence, especially when coupled with the opposition and frustration of the African American mission work. After Slattery's sermon at the first Mass of John Henry Dorsey, the second black priest ordained in the United States, in which Slattery attacked the racism especially of the clergy and Irish Catholics, he, in effect, withdrew from America to study in Germany under those who would be later considered as Modernists. In 1904 he resigned from the Josephites, and a short while later from the priesthood. On June 15, 1906, he married Adele Wingate of St. Louis in an Anglican church in London. In 1909 he returned to the study of law at Columbia and in 1915 was admitted to practice law in California. He wrote and translated works against celibacy of the clergy and submitted notes for his biography to Albert Houtin. Without any reconciliation to the Church, he died in Monte Carlo on March 6, 1926.

See also JOSEPHITES, THE; MODERNISM IN AMERICA.

Ochs, Stephen J. *Desegregating the Altar: The Josephites and the Struggle for Black Priests, 1871–1960.* Baton Rouge: Louisiana State University Press, 1990.

Portier, William L. "John R. Slattery's Vision for the Evangelization of American Blacks." *U.S. Catholic Historian* 5 (1) (1986) 19–44.

Slattery Papers, Josephite Archives, Microfilm, "Biographie de J.R. Slattery," Papiers Houtin, Bibliothèque Nationale, Paris, France.

PETER E. HOGAN, S.S.J.

SLAVERY AND AMERICAN CATHOLICS

Many Catholics are surprised to learn that their religious tradition has not always been opposed to what today is clearly judged a heinous social evil: slavery. Since the 1960s, when speaking of race relations, official Catholic teachings have articulated a consistent and unambiguous theme—that all human relationships must be directed by respect for the dignity of the person, not the color of the other's skin; by requirements of social justice, not the other's social status. Regrettably, Catholics have not always seen race relations in this light.

Catholics of earlier centuries were citizens of *their own age*, limited by their own worldview and moral horizon. "Justice" (and in particular "social justice" as we understand it today) is a fairly modern concept which slowly *evolved* over time. Understanding the demands of justice in any age, as a virtue or a religious practice championed by the Church, has varied from generation to generation depending on Catholics' sensitivity to the profound implications of the gospel dictum: "Love one another as I have loved you."

This article presumes familiarity with the baneful practices and history of slavery and will concentrate on American Catholics' relationship to it from the establishment of the first American diocese (1789) until the Second Plenary Council of Baltimore (1866) convened after the Civil War. Specifically, we will offer: (1) a synopsis of the Catholic theological tradition on the morality of slavery which shaped the American Church's understanding of the "peculiar institution"; (2) a presentation of the sociopolitical context in which American Catholics lived which gives a perspective to the Church's teaching on slavery; and (3) highlights of the relationships of American Catholics with slavery and slaves.

The Catholic Theological Tradition on Slavery

The "Catholic position" on slavery was rooted in (1) a literal reading of certain passages from the Old Testament (Gen 9:25-27; Exod 20 and 21:1-11; Lev 19 and 25; and Deut 5:14; 15:12-18; 20:10-14 and 23:15-16) and New Testament (Col 3:22-25 and 4:1; Eph 6:5-9; 1 Tim 6:1-2; Titus 2:9-10; 1 Cor 7:20-24; and all of Phlm); (2) canons of Church councils (the ecumenical councils of Chalcedon and Lateran III, and local councils of Gangra, Orleans IV, Toledo IV and IX); (3) writings of Church Fathers and theologians (including Ignatius of Antioch, Gregory of Nyssa, John Chrysostom, Augustine, Gregory the Great, and Thomas Aquinas); and (4) papal declarations of Pius II (1482), Paul III (1537), Urban VIII (1639), Benedict XIV (1741), and Gregory XVI (1839).

The law of Moses as found in the Pentateuch did not establish slavery for the Jews, but regulated and modified it. The Hebrew Slave Code in Exodus must be seen in this context. The Talmud, too, counseled slave owners to treat slaves with compassion. The Passover meal, a ritual liberation from slavery, decried the condition of servitude. During the Seder, the words of the Haggadah were recited by some Jewish lad: "We were Pharaoh's slaves in Egypt and the Lord Our God brought us from there."

It was observed that in the New Testament Jesus never condemned slavery. There were instances of pious and good men who had slaves, and in no case did Jesus accuse them of cruelty or immorality; nor did he require emancipation. In many of Jesus' parables, masters and slaves are used as illustrations without any condemnation of slavery. St. Paul, who claimed to have met the resurrected Christ, did nothing to abolish it; in fact, he did just the opposite when he acknowledged the right of the master to the services of his slaves. Masters were to be kind to slaves and slaves were to be obedient to masters. It seemed so obvious: from Genesis to Philemon one could find no condemnation of the practice.

Thus, Christians believed that Scripture sanctioned slavery. Various Church authorities confirmed and taught that theological view. Certainly, it was recognized that there were abuses in slavery, but *in se* it was not a moral evil. It was a condition brought about by human sinfulness that needed to be accepted and which could be transcended for spiritual betterment. It was no sin, therefore, to own slaves. Throughout the Christian centuries, bishops, priests, religious congregations, and laypersons were slaveholders.

Through the centuries, popes became more and more aware of the terrible immorality of enslaving the native peoples of the New World and repeatedly condemned it. From the fifteenth century onward, they recognized the horrors of the African slave trade and condemned it. Their condemnations were not heeded. The African trade was too lucrative and too useful in the colonization enterprise to be abandoned—even by the Catholic kings of Europe. American Catholics never read the popes' utterances as a condemnation of *domestic slavery* as it was practiced in the United States. If it was sanctioned by civil authority and did not violate divine commandments, Catholics could practice slavery or support it in principle without qualms of conscience. They did both.

However, Catholic teaching insisted on humane treatment of slaves. Slaves *were* rational human beings possessing souls (a point disputed by many slaveholders). Masters were warned not to take (sexual) advantage of the weakness, ignorance, dependence, or lowly position of slave women. The Church taught that masters were to permit and foster marriage and family life among slaves and said it was unchristian and immoral to separate (by sale) a husband from his wife and children. Slaves were to be provided with the means of knowing and practicing religion. This was called a sacred and indispensable duty. Masters were taught that they must provide food, clothing, and decent dwellings for their slaves. Finally, the civil rights of freed slaves were to be respected. Once manumitted, they were to be forever exempt from slavery. Testimonies of former slaves of Catholic masters indicate that some sincerely attempted to live within this code, others did not. All accepted the basic assumption, however, that slave-owning was a moral practice and that a master had the right to make a profit from the labor of slaves.

Sociopolitical Context of American Catholics

It is important to remember that slavery was established on American soil (1619) long before a Catholic nun ever visited these shores (1704) or a bishop was consecrated (1789). Catholics were a statistically insignificant minority. By 1830 they comprised a mere 5 percent of the population and by 1860 only about 14 percent.

Until the 1830s the vast majority of American Catholics lived in the Maryland-Kentucky area and in the rural South, in areas settled by Spain and France. Catholics had a presence in the Southern states but controlled no state legislatures and no governors' mansions. There were Catholic slaveholders, but they were always greatly outnumbered by the Protestants who owned 90 percent of all the slaves in the United States.

After 1830 Catholic immigrants from Germany and Ireland flooded the Northern cities and towns. They brought with them their allegiance to the Church, but they strained the limited resources of existing Catholic institutions. Catholic leaders focused most of their energies on the pastoral and temporal care of these new arrivals by creating dioceses, parishes, seminaries, orphanages, hospitals and schools to serve them. In the years preceding the Civil War, while the nation debated slavery and states' rights, Catholics in the North and South were absorbed in ecclesiastical matters brought on by the influx of immigrants.

The new immigrants did not add political influence to the Church. On the contrary, their arrival initiated resistance and hostility to all things Catholic. Many Protestants organized into "nativist" and "Know-Nothing" political and social action groups. These were designed "to protect America" from the "papist puppets" whose loyalties, they said, were to the pope and not the president. In an effort to turn back these attacks and to prove that Catholics were "good Americans," the Catholic hierarchy practiced a studied noninvolvement in politics and political issues, especially the most controversial issue of the times, slavery. This noninvolvement, however, must not be mistaken for neutrality on the issue. Catholics were tolerant of states rights and slavery. Some of the brightest lights among the American hierarchy (Bishops John England, Francis Kenrick, and Martin Spalding) had written extensive theological justifications of slavery. The Catholic press was also foresquare behind the legality and morality of slavery.

American Catholics and Slavery

As early as 1785 Fr. John Carroll of Baltimore decried Catholics' indifference to their slaves' faith and morals. Bishop James Whitfield, his successor, regretted the lack of priests to evangelize the slaves. The Catholic priest who traveled through the rural South was a transient figure to black and white alike and very often did not speak English. Besides, as Randall Miller observed, most blacks were attracted to the emotional riches of Afro-Protestantism where they could sing, dance, and listen to black ministers preach.

The American Catholic bishops encouraged the manumission of slaves and their voluntary resettlement to Africa. Although colonialization schemes were afoot since 1817, the issue did not get the attention of the Catholic hierarchy until the Second Provincial Council of Baltimore in 1833. There, the bishops recommended to Pope Gregory XVI that American Jesuits attempt to establish and care for a colony of freed slaves in Liberia. The Pope agreed but the Jesuits lacked the personnel to undertake the task. In 1841 some American clergy did establish a colony at Cape Palmas but it lasted only four years.

Catholic bishops, clergy, and religious were among slave owners. This means they were involved in the business of buying and selling slaves. They were supporters of the institution and benefited from it. However, it must also be noted that to be a "priest's slave" or a "nun's slave" was considered a fortunate circumstance for the slave as they were generally better treated than others. By 1840, after Pope Gregory's encyclical (*In Supremo Apostolatus*), Catholic religious orders began selling their slaves, in family units, to Catholic slave owners, and in the process helped some to escape.

American Catholics, regardless of region, supported slavery and regarded the black as their social inferior. Catholics also rejected Abolitionism because it was regarded as a Protestant (thus anti-Catholic) movement. Many Catholics, transplanted Europeans, interpreted antislavery as a species of continental liberalism which challenged political orthodoxy. There were no outstanding Catholic abolitionists and none gained any distinction in the Underground Railroad operation to aid fugitive slaves. There were a few voices among the bishops who saw slavery for what it was, most notably Archbishop John Purcell of Cincinnati, but even he was not agitating for a change in Church teaching as much as expressing his personal revulsion at the misery forced on slaves. In 1862 Fr. Claudius Maistre of New Orleans spoke out in favor of equal treatment for black Catholics. He was silenced by his bishop.

This is not to say that Catholics were indifferent to the plight of the slaves or that no one saw to their religious needs. Pastoral efforts were organized, especially among the religious orders. In 1791 the Sulpicians in Baltimore began to work among the blacks, teaching catechism and administering sacraments. In the 1820s, Bishop England of Charleston celebrated a second Mass and preached a sermon every Sunday exclusively for blacks. He opened a school for freed black children with the help of the Sisters of Mercy. In 1829 Archbishop Ambrose Maréchal of Baltimore endorsed the founding of the first community of black nuns, the Oblate Sisters of Providence. In 1842 Archbishop Anthony Blanc of New Orleans gave permission to Henriette Delille to found the Sisters of the Holy Family, a second group of black women devoted to serving the needs of blacks. In 1859 St. Francis Xavier Church in Baltimore became the first parish established exclusively for black Catholics. Bishop Augustin Verot of Florida brought the Sisters of St. Joseph to his diocese in 1866 to work with black children.

In 1866, after the horrors of the Civil War, 7 archbishops, 38 bishops, 3 abbots, and 120 theologians met at the Second Plenary Council of Baltimore. Here they drafted a pastoral letter which expressed no significant racial sensitivity but did call for organized efforts to evangelize the former slaves in the dioceses where they lived. While the council did not place the American Catholic Church in the vanguard of civil rights, it did mark the start of what would become a vibrant ministry to people of color.

See also AFRICAN AMERICAN CATHOLICS; CIVIL RIGHTS MOVEMENT AND CATHOLICS, THE; TANEY, ROGER BROOKE.

Davis, Cyprian, O.S.B. *Black Catholics in the United States.* New York: Crossroad, 1990.
Ewens, Mary. *The Role of the Nun in 19th Century America.* New York: Arno Press, 1978.
Hennesey, James, S.J. *American Catholics.* New York: Oxford University Press, 1981.
Miller, Randall and Jon Wakelyn, eds. *Catholics in the Old South.* Macon, Ga.: Mercer University Press, 1983.
Rice, Madeline H. *American Catholic Opinion in the Slavery Controversy.* New York: Columbia University Press, 1911.
Zanca, Kenneth J. *American Catholics and Slavery: 1789–1866.* Lanham, Md.: University Press of America, 1994.
KENNETH J. ZANCA

Related Document

FATHER PURCELL'S STAND IN BEHALF OF EMANCIPATION OF THE SLAVES, APRIL 8, 1863

The oldest continuous Catholic newspaper in the United States is the *Catholic Telegraph* of Cincinnati which began publication on October 22, 1831. Like its Catholic contemporaries, the *Telegraph* commented freely on political affairs and as the Civil War came on its editor, Father Edward Purcell (1808–1881), brother of John B. Purcell (1800–1883), first Archbishop of Cincinnati, became more outspoken in his opposition to slavery. It was not an easy policy to pursue in a border state like Ohio, and as a consequence Purcell had to pay dearly in loss of support from southern-minded Catholics in the area and in abuse from fellow Catholic editors like Courtney Jenkins of the Baltimore *Catholic Mirror*, McMaster of the *Freeman's Journal*, and John Mullaly of the New York *Metropolitan Record*, who charged him with being an abolitionist. But he did not retreat and, in fact, the *Telegraph* was the first Catholic paper in the country to come out clearly for emancipation of the slaves, a policy which Archbishop Purcell had publicly espoused as early as August, 1862. Lincoln's proclamation was formally issued on January 1, 1863, and caused widespread disagreement in the North. Two months after he published the uncompromising editorial which follows, Purcell announced that reaction had shown that many Catholics in all sections of the country had been brooding over "the multitudinous wrongs and anti-Christian proclivities of the 'peculiar institution.'" His mail proved that there were Catholics in every part of the United States who wished, as he said, "to express their satisfaction that there was a Catholic-Church-paper which was not afraid to raise its voice in favor of the most oppressed people on earth" (*Catholic Telegraph*, June 10, 1863).

(*Source*: Editorial, "The Church and Slavery," *Catholic Telegraph*, April 8, 1863.)

IN SOME REMARKS LATELY MADE ON THE EMANCIPATION OF the serfs in Russia, we observed that the Church and slavery could never get along well together. The New York *Freeman's Journal* condemns our remarks, quotes St. Paul and Church Councils, and says that we are ignorant of ecclesiastical history. The writer in the *Freeman* also observes that he does not wish for a controversy with us. As the *Freeman,* on this occasion, is mild and uses no very offensive language, we reply to his comments at some length.

We assure our cotemporary *[sic]* that we, too, have no desire to enter into a controversy. It would be useless now, because the subject of slavery is dead. The first canon fired at Sumter sounded its knell. It would be much easier to take Richmond or open the Mississippi, than restore slavery in the United States. The thing is gone forever.

But our cotemporary suggests that we are not acquainted with ecclesiastical history and that slavery and the Church have got along well together, and quotes St. Paul and certain Councils. Our cotemporary has a right to entertain any opinion he pleases about our ignorance. His opinion is his own. But without acrimony we can write on this subject of slavery. It must be discussed; there is no help for it—and whilst we accord to those who are its advocates all liberty of speech, we hope that some license will be extended to us when we give our reasons on the other side. It is not in a factious spirit or a fanatical spirit that we write, but under the strong conviction that a great change is at hand in the political welfare of the country, and that it is of some consequence to Catholics to decide wisely what part to take. This cannot be done by crying out "ignorance," "abolition," but by friendly discussion. Whether we like it or not, slavery is extinguished in the United States, and all that we have to do is to decide how we shall accommodate ourselves "to coming events."

We have said and we now repeat it, that slavery and the Catholic Church could never get along well together. The Church never tries to correct evils by revolutionary means. When she has not the legislative power in her hands she is patient, long-suffering, gentle. What she could not suppress she tolerated. But she found slavery little disposed to imitate her meekness. When the slave power predominates, religion is nominal. There is no life in it. It is the hard-working laboring man who builds the church, the schoolhouse and the orphan asylum, not the slaveholder, as a general rule. Religion flourishes in a slave State only in proportion to its intimacy with a free State, or as it is adjacent to it. There are more Catholics in the Cathedral congregation of this city than in North and South Carolina and Georgia! There are more Catholics in one of our second-rate congregations than in the whole State of Alabama! Louisiana ought to be a Catholic State, but it has never sent a Senator or Representative to Congress who identified himself with the Catholic cause, so far as we know. The slave-owners are not the zealous men of the Church in that State.

What help is Cuba, with all its riches, to the Catholic cause? The poorest Irish or German congregation in the free States does more for religion than Havana, if we can rely upon the representations of those who ought to know and whose character forbids deception. It appears to us, therefore, that slavery is not friendly to the propagation of the Catholic Faith—or to its charity and fervor when it happens to be professed. If for telling these plain truths any subscriber wishes to withdraw his patronage, we hope he will do so at once. And if for telling these truths the ladies of a community in a slave State choose to burn our Paper again, they have our liberty, if that be of any consequence, to prove their amiability and piety by doing so. The time is near at hand when they will wish that they had been more tolerant to the expression of an opinion.

But to our knowledge of ecclesiastical history: "No one now ventures to doubt," says Balmes, "that the Church exercised a powerful influence on the abolition of slavery: this is a truth too clear and evident to be questioned. . . . It did all that was possible in favor of human liberty; if it did not advance more rapidly in the work, it was because it could not do so without compromising the undertaking—without creating serious obstacles to the desired emancipation. Such is the result at which we arrive when we have thoroughly examined the charges made against some proceedings of the Church. . . . That slavery endured for a long time in presence of the Church is true; but it was always declining, and only lasted as long as was necessary to realize the benefit without violence—without a shock—without compromitting *[sic]* its universality and its continuation."[1] These few words from the fifteenth chapter of Balmes' incomparable work, show the exact position occupied by the Church in reference to slavery. To say that she ever favored the system is a calumny. She proclaimed men's fraternity with each other, and their equality before God, and therefore could not be the advocate of slavery.

With respect to the words of St. Paul, so often quoted, we find a full justification of our position. He writes to Philemon, commending his faith and charity, and he says— "wherefore, though I might have much confidence in Christ Jesus *to command thee that which is to the purpose,* for charity's sake I rather beseech, *thou being such a one,* as Paul the aged and now also a prisoner of Jesus Christ, I beseech thee for my son Onesimus, whom I have begotten in my chains—whom I have sent back to thee. And do thou receive him as my own bowels. . . . Not now as a servant, but instead of a servant a most dear brother, especially to me; but how much more to thee, both in the flesh and in the good?"[2]

Any one who can find anything in this in favor of slavery, must have piercing optics. Would St. Paul have sent him back to a Heathen master—or one who would have the power and the will to despise him—to sell his wife and children into slavery? The thought is not to be entertained of the blessed apostle?

If a fugitive slave in this country was to be sent back to some master in Mississippi or Texas by a Catholic Bishop of our days, bearing such an epistle as the above, how would the master mock and the world laugh at the Bishop? What a joke it would be considered in the South?

But what did the Popes think of slavery? This will probably throw some light on ecclesiastical history. Paul III. in 1537, and Urban VIII. in 1639, condemned in the strongest terms the crime of reducing men to slavery, separating them from their wives and children, or in any manner depriving them of their liberty, or upon any pretext to preach or teach that it is lawful. Pius II. in 1462, also denounces the system in the strongest terms. Gregory XVI., who, in his Apostolic Letter of the 3d of December, 1839, refers to the foregoing, uses this vehement language on the same subject—"Wherefore, we, desiring to turn away so great a reproach as this from all the boundaries of Christians, and the whole matter being maturely weighed, certain Cardinals of the Holy Roman Church, our venerable brethren being also called into Council, treading in the footsteps of our predecessors with Apostolic authority, do vehemently admonish and adjure in the Lord, all believers in Christ, that no one hereafter may dare unjustly to molest Indians, negroes or other men of this sort, or to spoil them of their goods or reduce them to slavery. We, therefore, with Apostolic authority do reprobate all the aforesaid actions as utterly unworthy of the Christian name; and by the same Apostolic authority do strictly prohibit and interdict that any ecclesiastic or lay person shall presume to defend that very trade in negroes *as lawful under any pretext or studied excuse,* or otherwise to preach, or in any manner, publicly or privately, to teach contrary to those things which we have charged in this, our Apostolic Letter."[3]

This is tolerably showy language. Its import, we think, is clear enough to any one who has a human mind. There can be "no pretext or studied excuse," says the good and great Pontiff. Are Catholics afraid or unwilling to read the admonition of the Vicar of Jesus Christ?

But it will be said that Gregory XVI. alluded to the foreign slave trade! This, however, is a pretext, and has not even the dignity of a "studied excuse." We have a word to say on the point.

Shortly before the appearance of this Apostolic letter, a religious order in the United States, by their close communication with Rome, received information of its existence and approaching publication. With more wit than piety the Superiors of that order collected together a large number of their slaves and sold them all to a Southern *gentleman,* we will call him so, who hurried them into Louisiana, and they were scattered over the South without reference to their relationship one to another. The whole Catholic community was shocked at the occurrence. Pope Gregory's letter appeared soon after, and it did not moderate the feeling of indignation. When the fact was known in Rome, such was the emotion felt by His Holiness, that the Superiors, on whom the responsibility rested, were ordered forthwith to proceed to the Eternal City and they did not return for years. Why they were detained it is unnecessary to discuss.[4]

This shows that slavery in every shape, is condemned and reprobated by the Church. In the meantime she did nothing violently. She only spoke the solemn words of admonition. Events have hurried on—what the Church would not or could not do the politicians have done. The door is now made open without any agency of Catholics, and those who wish to despise the venerable Pontiffs and be the jailors of their fellowmen, may endeavor to close and lock and bolt it. We take no part in any such proceeding.

[1] James Balmes, *Protestantism and Catholicity Compared in Their Effects on the Civilization of Europe* (Baltimore, 1851), pp. 91-94.

[2] Philemon 1:8–16.

[3] For the text of Gregory XVI's apostolic letter, *In supremo apostolatus,* cf. Antonius Maria Bernasconi (Ed.), *Acta Gregorii Papae XVI* (Rome, 1901), II, 387–388.

[4] Purcell was referring here to the sale in 1838 of forty-nine slaves for $25,000 by Thomas F. Mulledy, S.J., (1794-1860), then provincial of the Maryland province, to Henry Johnson (1783–1864) who had been Governor of Louisiana, 1824–1828, and was at the time serving his second term in the United States Senate. Cf. Mulledy to John P. Roothaan, S.J., General of the Jesuits, August 9, 1838, in Thomas Hughes. S.J., *History of the Society of Jesus in North America. Documents* (New York, 1910), I, 1122. The lasting effects of this episode on the Negroes of southern Maryland was commented upon by John LaFarge, S.J., *The Manner Is Ordinary* (New York, 1954), p. 184.

(*Source*: John Tracy Ellis, ed. *Documents of American Catholic History.* Vol. 1:1493–1865. Wilmington, Del.: Michael Glazier, 1987, 378–83.)

SLOVAK CATHOLICS IN AMERICA

Introduction

Of the 1,882,897 Slovak Americans recorded by the United States Census of 1990, approximately 80 percent are Roman Catholics, 15 percent are Lutherans, and the rest are Greek Catholics or Calvinists (Reformed). The Slovaks are the second-largest Slavic group (after the Poles) in the United States, and they probably rank second to the Poles in the number of Roman Catholic parishes built by Slavs, as well as having contributed the second-largest number of clergy and religious to the service of the Catholic Church by Slavs.

The Slovaks started to immigrate in search of work to the United States from their homeland in the ancient kingdom of Hungary in the 1870s and continued to do so until the early 1920s, when the United States Congress passed the Immigration Restriction Acts. Approximately 650,000 made the trip, and about 500,000 stayed for good. The

1920 federal census counted 619,866 first- and second-generation Slovaks in the United States. A second, and much smaller wave of political émigrés came after World War II and after the 1968 Warsaw-Pact invasion of Czecho-Slovakia.

Fraternal-Benefit Societies

The first concern of the earliest Slovak immigrants to the United States was survival. Coming largely from peasant or worker backgrounds, they found unskilled work in the coal mines, steel mills, and oil refineries of the Northeast. However, they found virtually no social services to help them survive accidents, illness, or to pay compensation to their families in case of death. Therefore, the first formal institutions that Slovak immigrants established were fraternal-benefit societies that provided for accident, illness, or death insurance. Fifty such fraternal-benefit societies, most named after a patron saint, were established by Slovak immigrants to the United States in the 1880s.

Slovak National Parishes

Having secured their material existence, Slovak immigrants also sought spiritual sustenance. The Roman Catholics among them initially worshiped in already existing Czech or Polish parishes, because of the similarity of their languages, or, less frequently, in Irish parishes, where they were barely tolerated, and consigned to the back of the church, or to its basement. Finding this situation intolerable, Slovak Catholic immigrants set out to build their own parish churches in the mid-1880s. The first to do so were the coal miners of Hazleton, Pennsylvania, and of Streator, Illinois, in 1885. By 1930 Slovak Roman Catholics had established 241 parishes in the United States. Their Greek Catholic brethren, meanwhile, built 155 churches, but these were ethnically mixed (Rusins and Slovaks), and it is impossible to estimate the number of Slovaks in them, or even the number of such parishes that the Slovaks controlled.

In establishing Roman Catholic parishes in America, Slovak laymen often ran afoul of canon law, and ended up quarreling with their pastors and/or bishops. Since laymen, particularly those organized in fraternal-benefit societies, most often led the way in establishing a parish by purchasing the land, constructing the building, and even sending for a priest, often without the knowledge or permission of the local bishop, they were astonished when the local bishop proceeded to assert his authority over their priest, and especially over parish property. It often took a whole generation for committees of parish trustees to submit to the authority of the local bishop to the point where their pastor could select his own church trustees, who then submitted to his (and the bishop's) authority. This thorny chapter in Slovak-American Church history has largely been forgotten by the third and fourth generations.

Ethnic Tensions and Nationalism

Another major problem that early Roman Catholic Slovaks faced was ethnic mixing and antagonism at the parish level. While Slovaks immigrated to America from the kingdom of Hungary first, their Magyar compatriots followed about ten years later. Finding no Magyar priests in America, these immigrants gravitated to the newly emerging Slovak parishes and asked the Slovak pastors to also serve them in the Magyar language. Most early Slovak pastors were willing to do so. However, the Slovak and Magyar laymen then began to quarrel over who would control the parish, with the result that those in the majority expelled those in the minority and the latter then had to build their own churches.

A further division that surfaced among Slovak Catholics was their region of origin. Most Slovaks migrated to the United States in village chains. If enough of them settled in a neighborhood (and the critical number hovered around two hundred), then they proceeded to establish a parish. However, if another group of Slovaks also migrated to the same locality in the United States, but they came from a different dialectical region, this group would also (if it were numerous enough) establish its own parish. Thus, in a large American city such as Cleveland, Ohio, one could find, until recently, eight Slovak Roman Catholic parishes scattered in various neighborhoods, whose parishioners had different regional origins in Slovakia. In a smaller American city, such as Bethlehem, Pennsylvania, one will find only one Slovak Roman Catholic parish, most of whose members trace their origins to eastern Slovakia. In neighboring Allentown, however, most of the Slovaks hailed from western Slovakia, and they built their own parish, rather than worship with the "easterners."

Slovak Roman Catholic parishes also reflected the nationalism (or lack of it) of their parishioners. In looking at the names of the 241 parishes established by Slovak Roman Catholics up to 1930, one will quickly discover that thirty-one carried the name of SS Cyril and Methodius. This was remarkable because not one parish in the kingdom of Hungary had this name before 1918. The Apostles of the Slavs had not been elevated to full sainthood in the Roman Catholic Church until 1880, and Magyar authorities forbade naming any churches after them, because such a practice might interfere with the desire of the Hungarian government to assimilate ("Magyarize") the subject nationalities, among them the Slovaks. The fact that American Slovaks named only ten parishes after specifically Magyar saints (Stephen and Elizabeth), thirty-one for the Apostles of the Slavs, and the rest after popular Roman Catholic saints (Peter, Paul, Joseph, John, etc.) shows that Slovak nationalism was alive and well in many Roman Catholic parishes in America.

Diocesan Priests

Shortly after the arrival of Slovak immigrants to America, a few clergy began to follow them. The earliest clergymen tended to be "Magyarones" from eastern Slovakia, such as the Rev. Ignác Jaškovič of St. Joseph's parish in Hazleton, Pennsylvania, and the Rev. Joseph Kossalko of St. Stephen's parish in Streator, Illinois. They had come on their own initiative to serve the early immigrants and, some said, to make money off them.

Later, most of the clergy who came were Slovak nationalists from central Slovakia who found working in Hungary under the supervision of Magyarone bishops too stressful. The outstanding example is the Reverend Štefan Furdek (1855–1915), who emigrated to the United States in 1882, initially to serve a Czech parish in Cleveland before the Slovaks arrived in large numbers. Once they did begin to appear in Cleveland, Furdek helped them to establish their parishes and other institutions. Dozens of such priests came before World War I and eventually staffed the ever-increasing Slovak parishes.

After the First World War, when second-generation Slovak-Americans began to graduate from grade and high schools, some started to enroll in American seminaries, and upon graduation began to staff the Slovak parishes. Large numbers came from St. Mary's Seminary in Cleveland, Ohio; St. Vincent's Archabbey in Latrobe, Pennsylvania; St. Charles Borromeo Seminary in Philadelphia, Pennsylvania; and St. Procopius College in Lisle, Illinois. These seminaries or colleges all provided instruction in the Slovak language, which was a prerequisite for being placed in a Slovak parish. While all of these second-generation Slovak-American priests were bilingual, they received most of their education in the English language, and felt more comfortable in it. Thus, while they initially celebrated Mass in Slovak, they also introduced services in English, much to the consternation of the "old timers" in their parishes. Once the immigrant generation died out, the American-trained priests switched to English-only Masses. This process started after World War II and gained speed after the reforms of Vatican Council II. Today only a minority of Slovak parishes still has one Sunday Mass in Slovak. These are usually for the post-World War II or post-Dubček Era (1968) immigrants.

Religious Orders of Men

The secular clergy, whether originating in Slovakia, or trained in American seminaries, has also been supplemented by several religious orders. The most important was the Slovak Benedictines of Cleveland, Ohio. They organized themselves in 1922 out of the Czech Benedictines headquartered at St. Procopius Abbey in Lisle, Illinois. In 1929 they became the independent priory of St. Andrew Svorad, and in 1934 an independent abbey. Meanwhile, in 1926 they established the Benedictine High School for Boys, and they also served as pastors of several Slovak parishes in the United States and Canada. Their work has been supplemented by the Slovak Franciscans, who first arrived in America in 1926, organized a monastery in Pittsburgh in 1927, became an independent commissariat in 1929, and established yet another monastery in Valparaiso, Indiana, that same year. They serve the Slovak community by conducting yearly missions, staffing two parishes, and assisting Slovak parish priests where needed.

Religious Orders of Women

Meanwhile, since about half of all Slovak Roman Catholic parishes in America established their own parochial schools, they needed Slovak-speaking teachers to staff them. Fr. Adalbert Kazinczy (1871–1947), pastor of St. Michael's parish in Braddock, Pennsylvania, took the initiative in 1902 when he invited the Vincentian Sisters of Charity, stationed in Satu Maru, Hungary, to send some teachers for his parochial schools. Five Slovak-speaking sisters responded in November of that year. By 1907 they were so successful in attracting other recruits to their order that their mission became an independent province, and in 1915 they built an impressive motherhouse in Perrysville, a suburb of Pittsburgh. In 1928 they established a second province in Bedford, Ohio, and in 1940 a mission in Marbury, and Phoenix City, Alabama, where they catered to poor blacks. By then they had broadened their mission from principally education to hospital work as well. Indeed, in 1943 they received St. Vincent Hospital in Monett, Missouri, as a gift from a wealthy physician, in addition to St. Jude's, which they already staffed in Montgomery, Alabama. By 1955 they had 357 members in their community, staffed thirty-one schools, two hospitals, two nursing homes, and several social and catechetical missions.

At almost the same time that Fr. Kazinczy was sending for teaching sisters from Hungary, the Rev. Matúš Jankola (1872–1916) decided to establish a Slovak religious order in America. In 1903 he managed to recruit three postulants for his proposed Community of SS Cyril and Methodius, and arranged for them to be temporarily accepted for their initial training by the Sisters, Servants of the Immaculate Heart of Mary at Mount St. Mary's in Scranton, Pennsylvania. In 1909 the new order of the Congregation of SS Cyril and Methodius was recognized by Rome, making it the only purely Slovak religious congregation in the world at that time. In 1919 the congregation made its permanent home in Danville, Pennsylvania, where it established its motherhouse, and in 1922 opened the first Slovak high school for girls in America (Danville Academy), and later a home for the aged as well. Meanwhile, from 1909 until it was closed in the 1980s, the Sisters of SS Cyril and Methodius also operated the orphanage of the First Catholic Slovak Union in Middletown, Pennsylvania, and later another home for the aged in Highland Park, Illinois. The sisters also staffed thirty-three Slovak parochial schools and three catechetical schools. By 1955 they had 351 professed members, twenty novices, and eight postulants.

In addition to these two large women's religious orders, Slovak-Americans also established four smaller ones. Among them are the Congregation of the School Sisters of the Third Order of St. Francis, which first appeared at St. Gabriel's parish on Pittsburgh's North Side in 1913, and which established a permanent home at Mount Assisi Academy in Bellevue, Pennsylvania, in 1928. By 1955 they had 203 members and had expanded their educational and other work into South America. Meanwhile, in 1923 the Slovak Sisters of the Third Order of St. Dominic established their motherhouse in Oxford, Michigan. By 1955 their one hundred members staffed two high schools and twelve grammar schools in the Midwest. In 1946 the Slovak Daughters of St. Francis of Assisi organized themselves and by 1948 they established their permanent home in Lacon, Illinois, where they operated a home for the aged. Finally, in 1953 the Slovak Benedictine Sisters were canonically established in Tinley Park, Illinois, to serve in Slovak parishes and schools in the Chicago region. By 1955 they had grown into a community of twenty. Today they call their convent the Slovak Catholic Cultural Center.

Slovak-American Bishops

Even though Slovak Catholics have lived in the United States in large numbers for over one hundred years, they have thus far produced only three diocesan bishops. The first was Joseph A. Durick (1915–94), who was of mixed Irish-Slovak parentage, and who was elevated to auxiliary bishop of Mobile, Alabama, in 1954, and later to bishop of Nashville, Tennessee, where he served until 1975, when he retired and devoted himself to pastoral work in federal prisons. The next was Andrew Grutka (1908–93), bishop of Gary, Indiana, from 1957 until his retirement in 1985, who was more active in the Slovak-American community, having helped establish the Slovak World Congress in New York in 1970. The third is Joseph Adamec (1935–), who was elevated to bishop of Altoona-Johnstown in 1987. As president of the Slovak Catholic Federation of America, which was founded in Wilkes-Barre, Pennsylvania, in 1911, Bishop Adamec is now the spiritual leader of Slovak-American Catholics.

Catholic Fraternals and Newspapers

As mentioned above, by 1890 Slovak-Americans had established fifty local fraternal-benefit societies. These started to federate into national bodies that year and by 1920 there were twelve large nationwide Slovak fraternals in America,

five of them Catholic. The most important were the First Catholic Slovak Union of the United States and Canada, headquartered in Cleveland, Ohio, and its sister organization the First Catholic Slovak Ladies Union, also of Cleveland. They were founded in 1890 and 1892, respectively. By 1985 they each had around 100,000 members.

Meanwhile, three smaller Slovak Catholic fraternals appeared in the next decade. In 1893 Slovaks in Pittston, Pennsylvania, founded the Pennsylvania Slovak Catholic Union, and in 1898 their wives established the Ladies' Pennsylvania Slovak Catholic Union in Hazleton. And, in 1905 Slovaks in Passaic, New Jersey, created the Slovak Catholic Sokol.

All of the above Catholic fraternals also published their own weekly or monthly newspapers. The most prominent is the *Jednota* (Middletown, Pennsylvania), official organ of the First Catholic Slovak Union. It (along with the FCSU) was established as a weekly by the Rev. Štefan Furdek, mentioned above, and with a circulation of around 40,000 (even though it recently became a biweekly), it remains the most important Slovak newspaper in America. Its nearest competitor is the weekly *Slovenský Katolícky Sokol* (Passaic, New Jersey), official organ of the Slovak Catholic Sokol, with a circulation of about 20,000. The women's fraternals publish the monthly *Fraternally Yours* (Cleveland, First Catholic Slovak Ladies Union) and the *Zornička* (*Morning Star*, Wilkes-Barre, Ladies' Pennsylvania Slovak Catholic Union) for their members. All of these newspapers can be considered to be a part of the Catholic press in America.

Future Prospects

Having surveyed the history of Slovak Americans and their religious institutions, it may be useful to speculate about their future. As Slovak-Americans enter into the third and fourth generations, they become less Slovak and more American. They have virtually lost the use of the Slovak language, and fewer and fewer join their fraternal-benefit societies. Cheap commercial insurance, plus the abundance and variety of mass entertainment, have made fraternals less relevant to most Slovak-Americans (and others). Furthermore, as Slovaks acquire more education and find better jobs, they increasingly abandon their old neighborhoods in the inner city and move to the suburbs. American bishops, faced by dwindling numbers of Slovaks attending Mass in their national parishes, have increasingly shut down (or consolidated with other parishes) the churches founded by the Slovak immigrants. In addition, with few exceptions, American bishops have not allowed Slovaks in the suburbs to build national parishes. Instead, they have been told to join already existing territorial parishes. Thus, the bedrock upon which Slovak-American Catholic life was built—fraternals and parishes—is coming apart. It will be interesting to see how (or if) Slovak-Americans will be able to maintain their ethnic identity in the United States of the future.

Alexander, June Granatir. *The Immigrant Church and Community: Pittsburgh's Slovak Catholics and Lutherans, 1880–1915.* Pittsburgh: University of Pittsburgh Press, 1987.

Hrobak, Philip A., ed. *Slovak Catholic Parishes and Institutions in the United States and Canada.* Cleveland: First Catholic Slovak Union, 1955.

Hrušovský, František. *Slovenské rehole v Amerike.* Cleveland: St. Andrew's Abbey, 1955.

Shelley, Thomas J. "Neither Poles nor Magyars nor Bohemians: The Slovak Catholics of Yonkers, New York." *Records of the American Catholic Historical Society of Philadelphia* 105 (1–2) (1994) 16–31.

Stolarik, M. Mark. *Growing Up on the South Side: Three Generations of Slovaks in Bethlehem, Pennsylvania, 1880–1976.* Lewisburg, Pa.: Bucknell University Press, 1985.

———. *Immigration and Urbanization: The Slovak Experience, 1870–1918.* New York: AMS Press, 1989.

M. MARK STOLARIK

SLOVENIAN CATHOLICS IN AMERICA

Slovenia, an independent Alpine Central European nation that won its independence in 1991, had for centuries been the westernmost Slavic province of the Austrian Empire and, between 1918 and 1991, the northernmost part of royal and (after 1945) of Communist Yugoslavia. The Slovenians, a staunchly Catholic people who in the Republic of Slovenia count only two million souls, have long been sending missionaries and priests to numerous countries of the world. Even in the 1990s, after forty-five years of ruthless Communist oppression when Christmas could not be celebrated as a work-free day, Slovenian missionaries and priests were laboring in no fewer than thirty-seven countries.

Missionaries and Bishops

The first North American missionary of mixed Slovenian-Croatian ancestry was Ivan Ratkaj (in Spanish, Juan Ratkay de Petau), born in the ancient Slovenian city of Petau or Ptuj (Ptooy), a Jesuit professor who reached Vera Cruz in 1680 (F. M. Picolo, *Informe del estado de la nueva Cristianidad de California,* 1702). He was followed, in 1687, by Mark Anton Kappus (Kapus), also a Jesuit, who labored (with Eusebio Kino) as a missionary, educator, explorer, and superior in the enormous territory of Sonora and Pimería Alta and was, in 1701, the first person to inform Europe that Baja California was not an island but a solid part of the American continent (Herbert E. Bolton, *Rim of Christendom,* New York: Russell, 1936).

The most famous Slovenian missionary, however, was Frederic Baraga (1797–1868), the "snowshoe priest" and apostle of the Native Americans of the Great Lakes, who labored in a vast territory of over eighty thousand square miles, and authored books and articles in Native American, Slovenian, German, French, and English languages. He was the first Catholic bishop to issue his pastoral letters also in Native American languages (his *Dictionary of the Ojibway Language* was reprinted as late as 1992 by the Minnesota Historical Society Press). The first bishop of Marquette, Michigan, Baraga was, according to the Vatican's *Enciclopedia Cattolica* (1949), "one of the greatest missionaries of North America in modern times." He is now a candidate for beatification. Baraga also put America on Slovenia's foreign aid list, as collection boxes for American missions were installed in churches throughout Slovenia and, in addition to money, religious objects, artworks, clothes, and seedlings were sent to American missions, not to mention the aid secured by him from Austria and other countries.

Four of Baraga's Slovenian compatriots became American bishops: Ignacij Mrak and Ivan Vertin, both bishops of Marquette; Jacob Trobec, the founding bishop of St. Cloud, Minnesota; and Ivan Stariha, the founder of the Diocese of Lead, South Dakota. While all five Slovenian nineteenth-century bishops were immigrants, the archives of the Slovenian Research Center of America include, for the 1970–95 period, four American-born bishops: James S. Rausch, of Slovenian-German parentage, who served as general secretary of the National Conference of American Catholic Bishops in the 1970s; Elden F. Curtiss, archbishop of Omaha, Nebraska, and Norman McFarland, bishop of Orange, California, both sons of Slovenian mothers and Irish fathers; and A. Edward Pevec, auxiliary bishop of Cleveland, Ohio, whose parents were immigrants from Slovenia.

Priests, Religious, and Laity

More than 350 missionaries and priests of Slovenian descent served the American Catholic Church, among them Francis Pirc (Pierz, after whom the town of Pierz, Minnesota, is named), a legendary missionary, linguist, author of books in several languages, and an expert on fruit culture and horticulture. Others include Msgr. Joseph Buh, one of the many Slovenian vicars general and the founder of the diocese of Duluth, Minnesota; Bernard Locnikar, abbot of St. John's Abbey and president of St. John's College in Collegeville, Minnesota; Bonaventure Bandi, abbot of Holy Cross Abbey in Canon City, Colorado; several Slovenian professors at St. Paul's Seminary in St. Paul, Minnesota, among them John Seliskar, also a noted author, and Francis Missia, acclaimed for his contributions to music; Francis T. Jager, internationally known bee expert at the University of Minnesota; Vendelin Spendov, O.F.M., and Becket G. Senchur, O.S.B., musical pedagogues and composers; Msgr. Antoine Rezek and Msgr. John Zaplotnik, historians; and George Trunk, Vital Vodusek, Kazimir Zakrajsek, Alexander Urankar, Bernard Ambrozic, Basil Valentine, Fortunat Zorman, and Bernardin Susnik, writers and/or editors.

The work of Slovenian missionaries and priests has always profited greatly from their remarkable linguistic skills. Indeed, an ability to converse, write, and preach in five or more languages was not unusual. Thus, in 1987, the *Catholic Outlook* of Duluth, while commemorating the contributions of many of Minnesota's Slovenian pioneers, wrote of Fr. John Chebul (Cebulj): "Parishioners and priests remembered the builder of Duluth's first Catholic church as a brilliant linguist who fluently spoke Slovenian, German, French, English, several Indian dialects, five Slavic languages, Latin, Greek, and probably Arabic. Father Chebul was also a musician who played several instruments and put Slovenian songs into the native dialects."

The same source suggests the immense sacrifices of these valiant missionaries. In a letter to his cousin in Slovenia, Fr. Chebul wrote: "The strings with which my snowshoes were tied to my moccasins froze and became as hard as iron. They cut into my feet, bruising and lacerating them. But I will go to Chippewa River as soon as my feet get a little better. Remember me as I start my long journey, as you are in your warm rooms, in soft beds, peacefully resting. I'll sleep in the woods, on cedar branches, roasting on one side before the fire and freezing on the other." Bishop Baraga and many others suffered great hardships on long trips of several days and even several weeks, when sweat from walking incredibly long distances turned into ice and there was only a little dried bread to eat. Somehow, they survived. Fr. Lawrence Lavtizar, who had just come from Slovenia to help the legendary missionary Pirc, was not so lucky. In 1858, when walking across the frozen Red Lake to attend to the sick, he froze to death. He was only thirty-eight years old (Edward Gobetz, "Culture of the Heart," *The World & I,* September 1989).

Slovenian Catholic Women

At least since the time of Baraga, when his sister Antonia had begun helping him and then, in 1840, established the Ladies' Institute in Philadelphia, many Slovenian women, too, served the American Catholic Church. Among them was Sr. Anastasia Ohmann (Oman) who became mother general of the Franciscan Sisters of the Immaculate Conception, built many schools and orphanages and, in 1971, received the papal medal, *Pro Ecclesia et Pontifice.* Sr. Diane Bergant, a professor of Old Testament Studies at the Catholic Union in Chicago, served as editor of the *Bible Today* and also edited the *Collegiate Bible Commentary,* volumes 13–25. Sr. Germaine Habjan is a singer,

guitarist, composer, and recording star, known for such albums as "Songs of Salvation," while Sr. Susanne Prebilic was a child prodigy on the piano, violin, and clarinet, and has become first violinist of the Duluth Symphony Orchestra, an educator, concertmaster, and composer, and is included in the *International Who's Who in Music.* Albina Aspell (nee Molek), was president of the Catholic Press Association of America and, in 1987, addressed the entire Synod of Bishops in the Vatican. Sr. Katherine Perko of Cleveland, Ohio, was, in 1994, elected to her second term as mother general of the Sisters of the Blessed Sacrament in Rome, Italy.

Practicing Their Faith

While most religiously active Slovenian Americans have been integrated into various American parishes, there have also been up to forty-five Slovenian-American national parishes, usually with their own parish schools and libraries. In 1924 Fr. Kazimir Zakrajsek established the Franciscan Custody of the Holy Cross in Lemont, Illinois, a favorite pilgrimage site and Catholic cultural center which also publishes *Ave Maria,* a Slovenian-language religious monthly magazine. By 1983 the Franciscans also published seventy volumes of *Koledar Ave Maria,* the Slovenian Catholic almanacs, filled with valuable historical and religious writings. The church is dedicated to Mary Help of Christians, with a replica of the famous painting from the basilica of Brezje (Bresyeh), Slovenia, which also hangs in the Slovenian chapel in the National Shrine of Immaculate Conception in Washington, D.C., and in many churches and countless homes throughout America. Among many other contributions, including those by numerous Catholic educators, artists, and journalists, let us here mention only Paul Sifler's composition, *The Seven Last of Christ,* and works by Dr. Frank A. Retzel, a Fordham University professor of music who was commissioned to compose both the opening and the closing hymn for the Mass by Pope John Paul II in Queens in 1996. Also of great importance are several Catholic-oriented fraternal societies, such as the American Slovenian Catholic Union (former K.S.K.J.), established in 1894, and the Slovenian Women's Union, founded in 1926. These groups, with lodges throughout America and with their own periodical press, *Amerikanski Slovenec* and *Zarja–The Dawn* respectively, continue to offer strong support to Slovenian Catholicism in America, as well as to other Catholic activities in U.S.A. to the missions around the world, and to the Catholic Church in Slovenia, the land of their roots.

Coleman, Bernard, and Verona LaBud. *Masinaigans: The Little Book, A Biography of Monsignor Joseph F. Buh* (with an appendix of over 60 biographical sketches of Slovenian American missionaries and priests). St. Paul, Minn.: North Central Publishing Co., 1972.

Furlan, William P. *In Charity Unfeigned: The Life of Father Francis X. Pierz*. St. Cloud, Minn.: The Diocese of St. Cloud, 1952.

Gobetz, Edward. *Slovenian Heritage*. Willoughby Hills, Ohio: Slovenian Research Center of America, 1980, 1:125–35; 386–93.

Rezek, Antoine Ivan. *History of the Diocese of Sault Ste. Marie and Marquette*. Vols. I and II. Houghton, Michigan, 1906.

Zaplotnik, John. *Janez Cebulj*. (Slovenian-language biography of John Chebul.) Groblje: Misijonska knjiznica, 1928.

EDWARD GOBETZ

SMITH, ALFRED EMANUEL (1873–1944)

Governor of New York, political reformer, presidential candidate. He was born on December 30, 1873, in the Lower East Side of Manhattan where poverty and racial diversity were taken for granted. He was named after his father, Alfred Emanuel Smith, whose parents were German and Italian, and he, at some unknown date, assumed the surname "Smith." It is possible he did so when he joined the Union army during the Civil War. He married Catherine Mulvihill, the daughter of an Irish father and an English mother, who had converted to Catholicism on her marriage. So the future politician personified the ethnicity of America: German, Italian, Irish, English.

He attended the local parish school and served as an altar boy at St. James' Church. He was an average student, and gradually displayed a flair for oratory and theater. At eleven he became a parish celebrity when he won a citywide oratory competition for his oration on Robespierre. But the following year his father, who owned a very small trucking business, died, and left his wife and two children on the border of poverty. Alfred Smith quit school at fourteen, the end of his formal education. He took a job as a messenger, and for the next four years he supported his mother and sister by working at unskilled jobs for long hours and meager payments. He was eighteen when he landed a job, at twelve dollars a week, as a clerk in the Fulton Fish Market, and when two years later he went to work for a boiler company in Brooklyn, Smith came to realize that politics was his only exit from dead-end jobs.

Into Politics

Local saloon keepers were men of some influence within the closely knit community and they stood in higher esteem when they had political connections. Tom Foley, whose bar was a political forum, befriended young Smith and taught him the political ropes of local affairs. In 1894 Foley successfully opposed Richard Croker's and Tammany Hall's selection for the Fourth District's congressional seat, and Smith's work and initiative won the confidence of Foley, who used patronage with finesse. The following year Smith was appointed process server for the commissioner of jurors with a salary of $800 a year, a comfortable salary for a young man at the time. Foley mended his fences with Tammany Hall, the Democratic nerve center in New York, and in 1903 he had Smith selected as a Democratic candidate for the state assembly of New York, and his winning was due to the benevolent influence of Tom Foley and the political muscle of Tammany Hall.

Tammany was originally a social and cultural club whose early membership included Aaron Burr and Andrew Jackson. When Jackson was elected president in 1828, Tammany Hall was transformed into a powerful political machine in New York City. Over the decades its social contributions were overshadowed by the corruption of some of its leaders, especially William Marcy "Boss" Tweed whose graft and fraud landed him in jail where he died in 1878. Again, during the leadership of Richard "Boss" Croker from 1896 to 1902, corruption became so flagrant that New Yorkers elected Seth Law as a reform mayor in 1901. Regardless of the probity of most of its leaders, Tammany Hall was a tarnished name in the public mind. Neither were the Republicans paragons of virtue when power came their way in upstate New York; but, as Alfred Smith was to learn, Tammany became a national synonym for political malfeasance.

With little formal education but with unusual mental acuity, Smith became an adept student of assembly procedures and the structures of state government. In this he was aided by Robert Wagner, a future governor and U.S. senator. He became Wagner's roommate and by instinct both sided with the interests of "the plain people." Gradually the studious Smith became one of the best-informed advocates of labor legislation and insurance reform. He also won the affection of his colleagues and the respect of his Republican opponents for his integrity and fairness. In 1911 he became the leader of the Democratic majority and chairman of the ways and means committee, and two years later he was chosen as Speaker of the Assembly. He became closely associated with humanitarian issues such as workmen's compensation, rent control, and decent working conditions for women and children. He became the ardent advocate of home rule for New York City and for a state conservation department.

Smith was a pragmatist and strove to rise above ideological and partisan bickering. He was not beholden to the dictates of Tammany Hall but he kept his connections and conferred regularly with its leader Charles F. Murphy and the men who dispensed favors and patronage. Reformers were drawn by Smith's unswerving commitment to social reform and decent government, and gradually he became the political friend of progressives and earned the support of the reformist Citizen's Union.

Tragedy brought Smith into wider prominence. In 1911, a fire at the Triangle Shirtwaist Company in Manhattan took 146 lives, most underpaid women and children. New Yorkers were appalled at the dreadful working conditions in too many factories in their city. Smith sponsored legislation for an investigating commission to examine working conditions in factories in New York State. Robert Wagner was chosen as chairman, and Smith became vice chairman. The commission brought together the brightest and the best among social activists and reformers. The inquiry lasted until 1915, and its findings shocked the nation and gave Smith the opening to launch sweeping legislation on health, sanitary, and fire laws, workman's compensation, and on the working conditions for women and children. Smith's reputation grew and his outlook broadened. He became a convert to women's suffrage; and at the constitutional convention Smith was in the forefront for government reforms and advanced the fight for home rule for New York City. His mastery for procedure and his knowledge of the intricacies of state government won him the plaudits of Republican stalwarts such as Henry Simpson and Elihu Root.

In the autumn of 1915 he was elected sheriff of New York City. He had sought the position as it offered an income of $60,000 a year. Smith needed some financial security, something he had rarely known. He had married Catherine Dunn, an Irish woman from the Bronx, and they had five children: Alfred Emanuel, Emily, Catherine, Arthur, and Walter. His new position gave him an opportunity to enjoy normal family life and to move out of the stress and bustle of the political maelstrom.

Governor

In 1917 the reality of New York politics was brought home to him. Friends urged him to run for mayor. But Tammany's leader, Charles F. Murphy, had other plans and he picked John F. Hylan of Brooklyn who won easily while Smith was elected president of the board of aldermen. But in the following year he was chosen over William Randolph Hearst to be the Democratic candidate for the governorship of New York. He attracted talented helpers, as he usually did, such as Frances Perkins, Joseph Proskauer, Belle Moskowitz, and many other able and versatile men and women flocked to Alfred E. Smith. It was a Republican year, but in the GOP sweep, Smith ousted Governor Charles S. Whitman with a plurality of 15,000 votes.

His agenda for the first of his four terms as governor of New York set his course and hopes. Despite unrelenting Republican and business opposition, he sponsored low-cost housing, the temporary extension of rent controls, control on milk prices, and the reorganization of state government. He opposed antisedition legislation which sought to curtail the civil liberties of socialist and other groups that disagreed with the rightist positions of the proponents. He ran into unexpected grassroots disagreement when he successfully sought to outlaw the Ku Klux Klan.

He sought reelection and lost to Republican Nathan L. Miller. Two years later he overwhelmed Miller; in 1924 he easily defeated Theodore Roosevelt, Jr.; and in 1926 he swamped Ogden Mills for his fourth term. Will Rogers wrote to him: "The man you ran against ain't a candidate, he is a victim." Smith is regarded as one of the great governors of New York. In the face of opposition from many quarters, his persistence reduced 152 unwieldy state agencies to a handful of cabinet posts. He made his mark for his staunch stand for social equality, conservation, safety regulations, bond issues for parks and recreation facilities, and the extension of state education. No governor before him matched his rapport between the people of New York and their governor.

National Politics

At the Democratic convention of 1920, Al Smith's name was mentioned as a possible candidate, but his supporters viewed their efforts as publicity to make his name more known and acceptable nationwide. James M. Cox was selected, with Franklin D. Roosevelt as his running mate. Warren G. Harding won a landslide victory for the G.O.P., and Smith set eyes on 1924.

The Ku Klux Klan was revived in Georgia in 1915 and spread rapidly in Southern and Western states. By 1924 it was a potent negative force with a virulent anti-Catholic, anti-Jewish, anti-immigrant agenda; and it became the focal issue in the Democratic convention in New York. The delegates failed to endorse a resolution to condemn the Klan, whose members were prominent in many Southern and Western delegations. Smith was taken by surprise as he had underestimated the undercurrent of bigotry in American life. The leading candidate, William McAdoo of California, refused to take a stand on this divisive issue, and Smith felt that his neutrality was a tacit endorsement of the Klan. McAdoo had wide Southern and Western support and accepted the backing of fundamentalist stalwarts such as William Jennings Bryan. Smith disliked McAdoo whose supporters felt that as the son-in-law of Woodrow Wilson and as a former secretary of the treasury he should be accepted as the heir apparent. Smith was nominated by Franklin D. Roosevelt whose speech is one of the memorable episodes of the tumultuous convention, and he closed with the famous Wordsworth couplet: "This is the happy warrior: this is he/ Whom everyman in arms should wish to be." In the long run, the speech and the convention benefited Roosevelt more than Smith.

The balloting began on June 30 and McAdoo led Smith all the way but was several hundred votes shy of what he needed for nomination. Day after day, in sultry heat, the balloting dragged on and delegates became more irascible. Smith held firm, and on July 9 McAdoo knew that he had lost in a deadlocked convention after 109 ballots. The weary delegates turned to John W. Davis of West Virginia and chose Charles Bryan, William Jennings' brother, for vice president.

In the presidential election, Calvin Coolidge had an overwhelming victory, polling over fifteen million votes to Davis's eight million. Robert M. LaFollette ran impressively as a Progressive Socialist and drew almost five million votes; and the Republicans won both houses of Congress. Smith won his fourth term as governor by a comfortable margin of over a million votes.

1928

As a sop to the South, Houston was chosen for the Democratic convention of 1928. Four years of planning and publicity and Smith's defeat of McAdoo in the California primary made Smith the unbeatable candidate. Again he was nominated by Franklin D. Roosevelt, but his nomination was never made unanimous. Four Southern states refused to vote for him, and the platform supported prohibition while Smith opposed it. The campaign begun with the hope that a Democrat would occupy the White House for the third time since the Civil War and a Catholic would be elected president of the United States, with Joseph T. Robinson—a dry and a Southern Protestant—as his running mate.

By tradition, the candidate selected the head of the Democratic National Committee, and against the advice of old friends and advisors he selected John J. Raskob, an industrialist, a Catholic, and a Republican. While Harry Byrd of Virginia, Scott Ferrio of Oklahoma, Nellie Taylor Ross of Wyoming, and other national and state Democrats joined the Smith camp, the power was vested not in them but in a select executive committee consisting of James Hoey, Franklin D. Roosevelt, George Van Namee, Herbert Lehman, Belle Moskowitz, and Peter Gerry (the only non-New Yorker).

The Republicans nominated Herbert C. Hoover, secretary of commerce, a staid, safe, experienced and conservative Republican, who felt that America with a booming economy would not take a chance on a Catholic with a Tammany background, a wet and a socialist. He was right. The campaign brought out the worst in American life. Prohibition, which Hoover called "the noble experiment," was a grassroots issue with support much wider than its fundamentalist base. Will Rogers got it right: "The voting strength of this country is dry." The Catholic question was the focal issue of vocal bigots, but it also dominated discussion and created reservations in academic and professional quarters. *The Atlantic Monthly* published an article by an eminent lawyer and Episcopalian Charles C. Marshall in April 1927 which questioned Smith's ability as a Catholic to be president. Smith was taken aback, avowing that as a devout Catholic he wasn't a theologian and "never heard of these bulls and encyclicals and books." Reluctantly, he responded, pained that anyone would or could see a conflict between his religion and his patriotism. Joseph Proskauer drafted a reply and had it vetted by Fr. Francis P. Duffy, Irving Lehman, and others. When Smith's rebuttal was published, it created national discussion, but it influenced few as the vitriolic campaign of the election year confirmed.

The business community, basking in the euphoria of a booming stock market and projecting endless prosperity, backed Hoover as a trustworthy guardian of free enterprise. In agricultural quarters, Smith was portrayed as the Tammany urbanite politician who knew little of rural America's problems and values.

When the votes were counted, Herbert Hoover was swept to the White House with some twenty-one million votes while Alfred E. Smith trailed with fifteen million votes. Hoover won 444 electoral college votes to Smith's 81. The loss of the election was a disappointment, but his rejection by the voters of his own state was the most painful episode of the campaign.

After the election Smith was a disillusioned man; his political career had come to an end, and power and influence ebbed away. Franklin Roosevelt had bucked the Republican sweep and won the governorship of New York. He quickly disengaged himself as neatly as possible from Smith whose disappointment festered into resentment. After the stock market collapsed in 1929, and the economy floundered, Roosevelt dubbed Hoover a do-nothing architect of economic disaster and set his course to oust Hoover in 1932. Smith was moved by the economic devastation and was appalled by the inaction of the government. But he resented Roosevelt and viewed his professed concern for "the forgotten man at the bottom of the economic pyramid" as political opportunism. He launched a futile attempt to stop Roosevelt who easily captured the 1932 Democratic nomination and swept to an outstanding victory.

Smith became a folk hero and celebrity and was the welcome guest at the leading social and socialite events. He took up residence in an exclusive Fifth Avenue apartment and moved in the best business circles. He became president of the Empire State Building Corporation (with the help of John J. Raskob, one of its powerful directors) with a salary of $50,000. He was welcomed on corporation boards and became a prominent speaker for executive gatherings. As chairman of a trust company, he took a critical view of the New Deal, and in a monthly column of the *New Outlook* he excoriated its policies. He joined the Liberty League, founded in 1934 for industrialists,

Alfred E. Smith

corporation lawyers, and conservatives of both major parties, and the League actively opposed such measures as the Wagner-Connery Labor Relations Bill and the Wealth Tax Bill. He pilloried the growth of the Washington bureaucracy and railed against many of the New Deal programs as socialistic. In 1936 he voted for Republican Alfred Landon and canvassed for Wendell Willkie in 1940. Many of his old friends and supporters felt a sense of sadness and betrayal.

He was feted as the leading Catholic layman, was patronized by bishops and clergy, and received a spate of honors and honorary degrees. Pius IX made him a Papal Chamberlain, the University of Notre Dame gave him the Laetare Medal, and he was welcomed into the Knights of Malta. In 1939 the clouds of war led Smith to support Roosevelt's Neutrality Act amendments and the lend-lease program. His enmity toward F.D.R. wilted, and he made two social visits to the White House. In May 1944 his wife died; and when he died in October the nation mourned his passing. He still awaits a full-scale biography.

Handlin, Oscar. *Al Smith and His America*. Boston, 1958.

Josephson, Matthew and Hannah. *Al Smith: Hero of the City*. New York, 1969.

Moore, E. A. *A Catholic Runs for President: The Campaign of 1928*. New York, 1956.

Moskowitz, Hapgood and Henry. *Up from the City Streets: Alfred Smith*. New York, 1927.

Perry, Elizabeth Israels. *Belle Moskowitz*. New York, 1987.

Smith, Alfred E. *Up to Now: An Autobiography*. New York, 1929.

_____. *Public Papers*. 8 vols. Albany, 1919–38.

MICHAEL GLAZIER

Related Document

GOVERNOR SMITH'S ANSWER TO THE RELIGIOUS BIGOTRY OF THE PRESIDENTIAL CAMPAIGN, SEPTEMBER 20, 1928

Following the decline of the A.P.A. in the late 1890's the American people were not again subjected to an organized outburst of religious and racial bigotry until the revival of the Ku Klux Klan. The second K.K.K. was founded in November, 1915, in Georgia by William J. Simmons and a group of associates for the purpose of opposing Catholics, Negroes, Jews, and the foreignborn. One of its principal targets was Alfred E. Smith (1873–1944), four times Governor of New York. Smith was a strong contender for the presidential nomination in the Democratic conventions of 1920 and 1924, and on June 28, 1928, he was nominated on the first ballot by the convention at Houston. Once the nomination had become an accomplished fact the K.K.K. concentrated all its fire on Smith with the result that his Tammany Hall connections, his opposition to prohibition, but, above all, his Catholic faith were made the objects of the most scurrilous attacks. As the campaign progressed the attacks on his religion became increasingly insidious, and on September 20 at Oklahoma City Smith brought the subject into the open. A recent work states that the hostility at Oklahoma City was so marked that there was "real concern for Smith's personal safety, and his eastern advisers were relieved when the telephone brought word that the Governor had reached his hotel safely after an emotion-packed evening" (Edmund A. Moore, A *Catholic Runs for President. The Campaign of 1928* [New York, 1956], p. 180). The same authority remarks, "At Oklahoma City, Smith neither invented nor introduced the issue. His address there stands beside his 'Reply' to Marshall as a great effort in the arduous struggle to extend freedom in the United States" (*ibid.,* p. 187). Yet his candor and straightforwardness, and his brilliant record as Governor of New York, had little effect on the final result, and on November 6 it was found that he had carried only eight states with an electoral vote of eighty-seven against 444 for his Republican rival. In spite of the abuse to which he had been subjected, Governor Smith spoke to the nation in a postelection address on November 13 with true magnanimity in which he called for the aid and co-operation of all citizens for the president-elect. The measure of the man's greatness was evident in his closing words when he said, "Regardless of the outcome, in a spirit of the deepest appreciation of the opportunities afforded me and of the loyal support given to me by upward of 15,000,000 of my fellow citizens, I pledge my unceasing interest and concern with public affairs and the well-being of the American people" (*op. cit.,* p. 322).

(*Source: Campaign Addresses of Governor Alfred E. Smith.* Washington: Democratic National Committee, 1929, 43–45, 49, 51, 53–58.)

. . . IN A PRESIDENTIAL CAMPAIGN THERE SHOULD BE BUT two considerations before the electorate: The platform of the party, and the ability of the candidate to make it effective.

In this campaign an effort has been made to distract the attention of the electorate from these two considerations and to fasten it on malicious and un-American propaganda.

I shall tonight discuss and denounce that wicked attempt. I shall speak openly on the things about which people have been whispering to you. . . .

Twenty-five years ago I began my active public career. I was then elected to the Assembly, representing the neighborhood in New York City where I was born, where my wife was born, where my five children were born and where my father and mother were born. I represented that district continuously for twelve years, until 1915, when I was elected Sheriff of New York county.

Two years later I was elected to the position of President of the Board of Aldermen, which is really that of Vice-Mayor of the City of New York.

In 1918 I was elected by the delegates to the State convention as the candidate of the Democratic Party for Governor and was elected.

Running for re-election in 1920, I was defeated in the Harding landslide. However, while Mr. Harding carried the State of New York by more than 1,100,000 plurality, I was defeated only by some 70,000 votes.

After this defeat I returned to private life, keeping up my interest in public affairs, and accepted appointment to an important State body at the hands of the man who had defeated me.

In 1922 the Democratic Convention, by unanimous vote, renominated me for the third time for Governor. I was elected by the record plurality of 387,000, and this in a State which had been normally Republican.

In 1924, at the earnest solicitation of the Democratic presidential candidate,[1] I accepted nomination. The State of New York was carried by President Coolidge by close to 700,000 plurality, but I was elected Governor. On the morning after election I found myself the only Democrat elected on the State ticket, with both houses of the Legislature overwhelmingly Republican.

Renominated by the unanimous vote of the convention of 1926, I made my fifth State-wide run for the governorship and was again elected the Democratic Governor of a normally Republican State.

Consequently, I am in a position to come before you tonight as the Governor of New York finishing out his fourth term.

The record of accomplishment under my four administrations recommended me to the Democratic Party in the nation, and I was nominated for the presidency at the Houston convention on the first ballot.

To put the picture before you completely, it is necessary for me to refer briefly to this record of accomplishment. . . . [Governor Smith then went into detail concerning the main legislative enactments, appointments, etc., of his administrations.]

One scandal connected with my administration would do more to help out the Republican National Committee in its campaign against me than all the millions of dollars now being spent by them in malicious propaganda. Unfortunately for them, they cannot find it, because the truth is it is not there. I challenge Senator Owen[2] and all his kind to point to one single flaw upon which they can rest their case. But they won't find it. They won't try to find it, because I know what lies behind all this, and I will tell you before I sit down to-night. . . .

I know what lies behind all this and I shall tell you. I specifically refer to the question of my religion. Ordinarily, that word should never be used in a political campaign. The necessity for using it is forced on me by Senator Owen and his kind, and I feel that at least once in this campaign, I, as the candidate of the Democratic Party, owe it to the people of this country to discuss frankly and openly with them this attempt of Senator Owen and the forces behind him to inject bigotry, hatred, intolerance and un-American sectarian division into a campaign which should be an intelligent debate of the important issues which confront the American people. . . .

A recent newspaper account in the City of New York told the story of a woman who called at the Republican National headquarters in Washington, seeking some literature to distribute. She made the request that it be of a nature other than political. Those in charge of the Republican Publicity Bureau provided the lady with an automobile and she was driven to the office of a publication notorious throughout the country for its senseless, stupid, foolish attacks upon the Catholic Church and upon Catholics generally.

I can think of no greater disaster to this country than to have the voters of it divide upon religious lines. It is contrary to the spirit, not only of the Declaration of Independence, but of the Constitution itself. During all of our national life we have prided ourselves throughout the world on the declaration of the fundamental American truth that all men are created equal.

Our forefathers, in their wisdom, seeing the danger to the country of a division on religious issues, wrote into the Constitution of the United States in no uncertain words the declaration that no religious test shall ever be applied for public office, and it is a sad thing in 1928, in view of the countless billions of dollars that we have poured into the cause of public education, to see some American citizens proclaiming themselves 100 per cent. American, and in the document that makes that proclamation suggesting that I be defeated for the presidency because of my religious belief.

The Grand Dragon of the Realm of Arkansas, writing to a citizen of that State, urges my defeat because I am a Catholic, and in the letter suggests to the man, who happened to be a delegate to the Democratic convention, that by voting against me he was upholding American ideals and institutions as established by our forefathers.

The Grand Dragon that thus advised a delegate to the national convention to vote against me because of my religion is a member of an order known as the Ku Klux

Klan, who had the effrontery to refer to themselves as 100 per cent. Americans.

Yet totally ignorant of the history and tradition of this country and its institutions and, in the name of Americanism, they breathe into the hearts and souls of their members hatred of millions of their fellow countrymen because of their religious belief. . . .

I would have no objection to anybody finding fault with my public record circularizing the whole United States, provided he would tell the truth. But no decent, right-minded, upstanding American citizen can for a moment countenance the shower of lying statements, with no basis in fact, that have been reduced to printed matter and sent broadcast through the mails of this country.

One lie widely circulated, particularly through the southern part of the country, is that during my governorship I appointed practically nobody to office but members of my own church.

What are the facts? On investigation I find that in the cabinet of the Governor sit fourteen men. Three of the fourteen are Catholics, ten Protestants, and one of Jewish faith. In various bureaus and divisions of the Cabinet officers, the Governor appointed twenty-six people. Twelve of them are Catholics and fourteen of them are Protestants. Various other State officials, making up boards and commissions, and appointed by the Governor, make a total of 157 appointments, of which thirty-five were Catholics, 106 were Protestants, twelve were Jewish, and four I could not find out about.

I have appointed a large number of judges of all our courts, as well as a large number of county officers, for the purpose of filling vacancies. They total in number 177, of which sixty-four were Catholics, ninety were Protestants, eleven were Jewish, and twelve of the officials I was unable to find anything about so far as their religion was concerned.

This is a complete answer to the false, misleading and, if I may be permitted the use of the harsher word, lying statements that have found their way through a large part of this country in the form of printed matter.

If the American people are willing to sit silently by and see large amounts of money secretly pour into false and misleading propaganda for political purposes, I repeat that I see in this not only a danger to the party, but a danger to the country. . . . [Here other instances of bigotry in the campaign were cited.]

I have been told that politically it might be expedient for me to remain silent upon this subject, but so far as I am concerned no political expediency will keep me from speaking out in an endeavor to destroy these evil attacks.

There is abundant reason for believing that Republicans high in the councils of the party have countenanced a large part of this form of campaign, if they have not actually promoted it. A sin of omission is some times as grievous as a sin of commission. They may, through official spokesmen, disclaim as much as they please responsibility for dragging into a national campaign the question of religion, something that according to our Constitution, our history and our traditions has no part in any campaign for elective public office. . . .

One of the things, if not the meanest thing, in the campaign is a circular pretending to place someone of my faith in the position of seeking votes for me because of my Catholicism. Like everything of this kind, of course it is unsigned, and it would be impossible to trace its authorship. It reached me through a member of the Masonic order who, in turn, received it in the mail. It is false in its every line. It was designed on its very face to injure me with members of churches other than my own.

I here emphatically declare that I do not wish any member of my faith in any part of the United States to vote for me on any religious grounds. I want them to vote for me only when in their hearts and consciences they become convinced that my election will promote the best interests of our country.

By the same token, I cannot refrain from saying that any person who votes against me simply because of my religion is not, to my way of thinking, a good citizen. . . .

The constitutional guaranty that there should be no religious test for public office is not a mere form of words. It represents the most vital principle that ever was given any people.

I attack those who seek to undermine it, not only because I am a good Christian, but because I am a good American and a product of America and of American institutions. Everything I am, and everything I hope to be, I owe to those institutions.

The absolute separation of State and Church is part of the fundamental basis of our Constitution. I believe in that separation, and in all that it implies. That belief must be a part of the fundamental faith of every true American. . . .

[1] John W. Davis (1873–1955) had been nominated on the 103rd ballot after a prolonged fight between the forces of Smith and William G. McAdoo.

[2] Robert L. Owen (1856–1947) had served three terms as United States Senator from Oklahoma, 1907–1925. He left the Democratic Party in 1928 to go over to the Republicans on the score that Smith was the creature of Tammany Hall.

(*Source*: John Tracy Ellis, ed. *Documents of American Catholic History*. Vol. 2:1866–1966. Wilmington, Del.: Michael Glazier, 1987, 616–21.)

SMITH, CHARLES (1877–1958)

Priest and newspaper editor. Charles Smith was born and baptized in 1877 in Chicago, Illinois, but he had to teach himself about his Catholic faith, and after high school he put himself through business school. In 1900 he left a promising business career to attend college and enter the seminary. He was ordained in 1910 for the Archdiocese of Oregon City (now the Archdiocese of Portland in Oregon).

In 1922, after Oregonians passed a law hostile to Catholic schools, Oregon's Catholic Truth Society was started with Smith as one of the initiators and a board member. He then took charge of its activities and wrote most of its publications. In 1928 the society bought from its lay owners the diocesan newspaper, the *Catholic Sentinel.* Described as "a small human dynamo" and a workaholic, Smith became publisher and editor of the newspaper, along with his duties as executive secretary of the Catholic Truth Society, parish pastor, radio lecturer, and preacher on the chapel railroad car which traveled throughout western Oregon. Almost single-handedly he wrote the columns and headlines of the *Catholic Sentinel,* taking items from *The New York Times* and the National Catholic News Service.

He changed the nature of the Catholic Truth Society from being primarily an organization to defend and explain the faith to non-Catholics to one that met the sacramental needs of Catholics, starting with the publication of Sunday missals in pamphlet form in 1934. Eventually it became the Oregon Catholic Press. In recognition of his work, he was elevated to the rank of monsignor in 1953, and died in 1958.

See also CATHOLIC PRESS (NEWSPAPERS), THE.

Archives, Archdiocese of Portland in Oregon, Smith Folder.
Brandt, Patricia, and Lillian A. Pereyra. "History of the Archdiocese of Portland in Oregon." Unpublished manuscript.
Schoenberg, Wilfred P., S.J. *Defender of the Faith. The History of the Catholic Sentinel, 1870–1990.* Portland: Oregon Catholic Press, 1993

LILLIAN A. PEREYRA

SMITH, JOHN TALBOT (1855–1923)

Priest, writer, historian. John Talbot Smith was born in Saratoga, New York, on September 22, 1855, the son of Bernard and Brigid Smith Talbot. He attended a Christian Brothers school in Albany, New York, and then moved to Toronto, Canada, to attend St. Michael's College and Seminary. He was ordained a priest in Canada but returned to New York State to serve in the Diocese of Ogdensburg. Smith served first in the industrial city of Watertown; he later became a pastor in the town of Rouses Point. The young priest had literary ambitions that manifested themselves as early as 1880 with the publication, à la Dickens, of a novel, *A Woman of Culture,* in serialized form in the *Catholic World;* the novel dealt with life in Toronto. Next came *A History of the Diocese of Ogdensburg* (1885). Fortunately for Smith, his bishop acknowledged his talents; in 1889 he allowed the priest to leave the diocese and move to New York City, a center not only of literary life in general but also of Catholic intellectual life. Smith supported himself as a chaplain, first to a Christian Brothers house, and then to a convent of nuns.

John Talbot Smith

His comparatively light duties allowed him time to write. He became editor of a weekly Catholic newspaper, *The Catholic Review,* and he wrote several poorly received novels and some better received short stories. The stories dealt largely with local color and culture in northern New York State, particularly of the Adirondack and Lake Champlain regions and of the French-Canadian and Irish Catholics trying to adapt to life in the United States. He returned to historical writing in 1906 with his *History of the Catholic Church in New York* in honor of archdiocese's centennial. In his day he was best known for *In Our Seminaries* (1896), which a contemporary issue of the *Catholic World* (vol. 64, March 1897) said "is . . . exciting attention in ecclesiastical circles for the candor of its utterances and the high standard advocated for the education of the clergy." In fact, Smith's stringent and pointed criticisms of seminary education caused great resentment, but the book remained in print for years and caused some rethinking of the seminary educational system. Concerned with the state of the arts in the Church, Smith founded the Catholic Writers Guild and the Catholic Actors Guild, organizations which brought together creative Catholics for mutual support. In 1908 he became a pastor again, in Dobbs Ferry on the Hudson River, where he spent the remainder of his life. He died on September 24, 1923.

Catholic World 64 (May 1897) 419–20.
Catholic World 118 (November 1923) 218–20.
Curtis, G. P. *The American Catholic Who's Who.* St. Louis, 1911, 611–12.
New Catholic Encyclopedia 13:304.

JOSEPH F. KELLY

SMITH, LUCY EATON (1845–94)

Promoter of retreat movement. On May 24, 1880, Lucy Eaton Smith, who chose later to be known as Sr. Maria Catherine de'Ricci, inaugurated a new form of spiritual ministry in the United States. Born in Brooklyn, New York, on March 22, 1845, Lucy's background in a financially comfortable and close-knit family did not prevent her from being aware of her time and her place in it. Her deep spiritual hunger made her sensitive to others' needs, especially those of women. Although religious influence was minimal in her early years, in her late teens she was drawn by the music of the High Mass at St. Vincent de Paul Church in New York, and she was received into the Catholic Church there in 1865. After her conversion, Lucy spent some years in Europe where she became a lay Dominican. She was attracted to the retreat work of the Sisters of the Cenacle and wished to join them, but her spiritual director insisted that her own country needed this ministry.

Lucy's attempts to introduce this new ministry on her return to the United States met with little enthusiasm and support. Family financial reverses took her to Fort Edward, New York, where she met Fr. Louis St. Onge, a pastor in nearby Glens Falls, who gave her an opportunity to begin her work. In 1880 she and a small community of women who shared her vision began retreat and parish ministry there. As patron of the new congregation, Lucy chose St. Catherine de'Ricci, a sixteenth-century Dominican mystic, known for contemplation of Christ's passion and active involvement in ministry to the laity.

Throughout her life, Lucy carried on a continuous correspondence with her younger sister, Lilly. These letters provide a rich source of information concerning Lucy, giving her congregation constant inspiration, encouragement, and challenge to "see God's will and our work in the circumstances of the hour." She died at age forty-nine in 1894.

See also DOMINICANS (O.P.).

Brennan, Mary Joseph, O.P. *A Place of Springs.* Elkins Park, Pa: Dominican Retreat House, 1980.

Carroll, Mary James, O.P. *An American Pioneer in Retreat Work.* Elkins Park, Pa: Dominican Retreat House, 1949.

Dominican Sisters of St. Catherine de'Ricci. *Rejoice and Remember That You May Tell Others.* Media, Pa: Dominican Congregation of St. Catherine de'Ricci, 1980.

Krebs, Carolyn, O.P. *Listening in Loneliness for Love.* Schenectady, N.Y.: Dominican Retreat House, 1982.

CAROLYN KREBS, O.P.

SNYDER, MITCHELL ("MITCH") (1943–89)

Activist and agitator on behalf of the homeless in the 1970s and 1980s. He was born on August 14, 1943, in the Flatbush section of Brooklyn, New York. His father deserted his family when Mitch was a child. Years later, he too left his own wife and two sons to pursue an activist career. His life took direction when in prison for car theft. There he met Jesuit Daniel Berrigan and his brother Philip, an ex-Josephite priest, both of whom were imprisoned for civil rights disobedience and antiwar activities. Snyder was impressed by the dedication of the Berrigans, shared their peace philosophy, and began reading the Bible and formulating views to counter the indifference to the needs of the poor.

His life became a long confrontation. He went on an unsuccessful hunger strike to get the Jesuit-run, 127-year-old Holy Trinity Church in the upscale Georgetown area of Washington to divert its $400,000 building fund to meet the needs of the poor instead of repairing the old church. He was sentenced to prison for two months for unlawful entry into St. Matthew's Cathedral and Washington National (Episcopal) Cathedral hoping to draw attention to the needs of the street people. He and two others fasted for sixty days on water and forced the Reagan administration to back off naming a nuclear submarine *Corpus Christi* (Body of Christ). President Reagan ordered the name to be changed to *City of Corpus Christi.* Snyder attracted Hollywood's attention and Martin Sheen played the title role in "Samaritan: The Mitch Snyder Story," aired on CBS. No individual of his generation did more to focus attention on the wretched lives of the street people than Mitch Snyder. At the age of forty-six he ended his own life, by hanging, in his bedroom in a shelter he had convinced the federal government to give to the poor.

L. FRANKLIN CARTER

SORIN, EDWARD F. (1814–93)

Religious superior, founder of the University of Notre Dame. Born February 6, 1814, in Ahuillé, France, Sorin was ordained a priest for the Diocese of Le Mans in 1838. He joined the recently organized Congregation of Holy Cross in 1839, professed vows in 1840, and was sent in 1841 with six Brothers of Holy Cross to Vincennes, Indiana, the congregation's first mission in North America. As the only priest in the group, Sorin was appointed superior. He would be the community's highest authority in the United States for the rest of his life, serving as provincial superior until 1866 when he was elected superior general of the congregation, an office he held until his death.

In 1842 Sorin led the community's move to property near South Bend, Indiana, which he named Notre Dame du Lac. He and the brothers opened a school there that was chartered in 1844 as the University of Notre Dame du Lac. Sorin served as president until 1865. He promoted the expansion of his congregation's work in schools and in 1876, as superior general, he directed the foundation of what became St. Edward's University in Austin, Texas.

Edward F. Sorin

In 1865 he founded *Ave Maria,* a weekly Catholic magazine, which continued until 1970.

From their arrival in the United States in 1843, the Holy Cross Sisters were under Sorin's authority until 1860 when they became an autonomous congregation, the Marianites of Holy Cross. When the sisters in the Midwestern states became an autonomous community in their own right in 1869 as the Sisters of the Holy Cross, Sorin served as their ecclesiastical superior and directed their expansion into Texas, Utah, and California. During the Civil War, Sorin sent eighty sisters and eight priests as nurses and chaplains to the Union forces. He died at Notre Dame, Indiana, on October 31, 1893.

See also HOLY CROSS, CONGREGATION OF (C.S.C.).

Hope, Arthur. *Notre Dame: One Hundred Years.* University of Notre Dame Press, 1943.

Lemarié, Charles. *De la Mayenne à l'Indiana: le Père Edouard Sorin (1814–1893).* Angers, France: Université Catholique de l'Ouest, 1978.

Sorin, Edward F. *The Chronicles of Notre Dame du Lac.* University of Notre Dame Press, 1992.

JAMES T. CONNELLY, C.S.C.

SOUTH CAROLINA, CATHOLIC CHURCH IN

Catholicism came to Carolina with the Spanish explorations around 1521. A settlement was established in Wingaw Bay, and it was there the first Mass was celebrated. This colony and others that followed failed. The Spanish vanished with the coming of the English.

In 1788 Fr. Matthew Ryan, the first priest, came to Charleston. He was replaced by Fr. Keating who built St. Mary's, the first Catholic church in the Carolinas and

Georgia. Problems occurred when church authority was taken over by the vestry, causing the Charleston schism. This schism moved Rome on July 11, 1820, to establish the Diocese of Charleston, consisting of North Carolina, South Carolina, and Georgia.

John England, a native of Cork, Ireland, was appointed the first bishop. When he arrived, Bishop England found only two churches, one in Charleston and one in Augusta. His twenty-two-year episcopate put the diocese on a sound footing. He established fourteen churches, forty-seven missions, the first national Catholic weekly newspaper, *The United States Catholic Miscellany,* and a seminary. Bishop England died on April 11, 1842.

Ignatius A. Reynolds was consecrated the second bishop of Charleston on March 19, 1844. Under his administration a cathedral was built and the state of Georgia was erected as the Diocese of Savannah in 1850. The third bishop of Charleston, Patrick N. Lynch, was consecrated on March 14, 1858. Bishop Lynch was a strong supporter of the Confederacy and served as an emissary for the Confederate States. Following the Civil War, he was not permitted to return to the U.S.A. until he received a presidential pardon. Lynch returned to the diocese and found only one church standing in Charleston. Bishop Lynch spent the remainder of his episcopacy seeking support from other dioceses to repay the debt and rebuild the diocese. In 1886 the state of North Carolina was established as a vicariate. At Bishop Lynch's death in February 1882, the diocese still suffered serious economic effects from the war.

Henry P. Northrop was consecrated the fourth bishop of Charleston in 1883. During his episcopate the diocese

Henry P. Northrop

finally began recovering from the war. The cathedral was rebuilt, two convents were constructed, St. Francis Xavier Hospital was built in Charleston, and fifteen parishes were established throughout the diocese. Bishop Northrop died on June 7, 1916.

Bishop William T. Russell, a native of Baltimore and former secretary to Cardinal Gibbons, was consecrated the fifth bishop of Charleston on March 15, 1917. Russell was one of the organizers of the National Catholic War Council, later renamed the National Catholic Welfare Conference. Seven churches and one high school were built during his episcopacy. After his death in March of 1927, Emmet M. Walsh, a South Carolina native, was appointed the sixth bishop.

Bishop Walsh served the diocese during the important World War II years which saw significant Catholic population growth. Under his leadership four Catholic hospitals were established. Several religious groups of men and women came to the diocese to care for the African American people. The Monastery of Our Lady of Mepkin was established in 1949 by the Trappists. After spending twenty-two years in the diocese, Walsh was transferred in 1949 to the Diocese of Youngstown.

John J. Russell was installed as bishop on March 28, 1950. During his eight years in office the Confraternity of Christian Doctrine was developed. The Catholic population grew from 17,500 to 30,000. The number of parishes grew from forty-two to fifty-seven. Russell was named bishop of Richmond in September 1958. Paul J. Hallinan was named bishop in September, consecrated in October, and installed in Charleston on November 25, 1958. He began to deal with racial justice in parochial schools in 1961. His time in the diocese was short lived; he was named archbishop of the newly erected Atlanta archdiocese. Francis F. Reh was named bishop and consecrated on June 29, 1962. In 1964 he was appointed rector of the North American College in Rome. The auxiliary bishop of Richmond, Ernest L. Unterkoefler, was appointed bishop and consecrated on December 16, 1964.

Bishop Unterkoefler's episcopate was to last twenty-five years. During that time the churches were fully integrated, and Unterkoefler spoke out strongly for the poor. He attended Vatican Council II, serving on the International Committee for the Restoration of the Permanent Diaconate and as co-chairman for the Anglican-Roman Catholic Sub-Committee on the Theology of Marriage. Unterkoefler served on numerous committees for the National Conference of Catholic Bishops and the United States Catholic Conference. Bishop Unterkoefler hosted the pastoral visit of Pope John Paul II to the diocese in September 1987. During Unterkoefler's episcopate the number of Catholics increased from 42,000 to 79,000. Bishop Unterkoefler retired in February 1990. David B. Thompson was consecrated the eleventh bishop of Charleston.

See also ENGLAND, JOHN.

Guilday, Peter. *Life and Times of John England, 1786–1842.* 2 vols. New York: The American Press, 1927.

Madden, Richard C. *Catholics in South Carolina: A Record.* Lanham, Maryland, 1985.

O'Connell, Jeremiah J. *Catholicity in the Carolinas and Georgia, 1820–1878.* New York, 1879; repr. Westminster, Maryland, 1964.

Shelley, Thomas J. *Paul J. Hallinan, First Archbishop of Atlanta.* Wilmington, Delaware, 1989.

EDWARD LOFTON

SOUTH DAKOTA, CATHOLIC CHURCH IN

The first contact with present-day South Dakota by those other than Native Americans was probably made in the 1670s by Frenchmen who pushed westward. Although no missionaries accompanied these explorers, the possibility of evangelization was aroused among the supporters of the expeditions.

Augustine Ravoux, born in Langeac, Auvergne, France, on January 11, 1815, heeded the request for missionaries to North America. He left his homeland in 1838 and, after a forty-five day voyage across the dangerous Atlantic Ocean, made his way to Dubuque and was ordained to the priesthood in 1840. In 1841 he was entrusted with the task of evangelizing the Dakota (Sioux) natives in the northern section of the Minnesota vicariate. Pierre Jean De Smet, born in Belgium in 1801, was a Jesuit missionary who found his way to Fort Vermillion on May 11, 1839. He persuaded the Yankton Dakota to reconcile with the Pottowatomie, the latter having been viciously attacked by the former. That very night, Fr. De Smet delivered instructions on the Apostles' Creed through an interpreter and baptized twenty-nine persons, twenty-six of whom were children, and three of whom were adults in danger of death.

Fr. De Smet made fourteen trips to Dakota between 1839 and 1870; he reported 1,500 baptisms during the summer of 1851. Fr. Ravoux, who died in 1906 at age ninety-one, continued his efforts despite the long and harrowing trips through the Upper Midwest. On April 19, 1858, the chiefs of the Yankton Dakota people, led by Struck-by-the-Ree, a leading chief of the End-Village group, ceded fourteen million acres of land between the Missouri and Big Sioux Rivers. Struck-by-the-Ree or Padanniapapi and his wife Mazaitzashanawi were presumably baptized by Fr. De Smet.

In 1860 August Bruyer, a former tailor from France, erected, along with his wife Josephine and a few of their neighbors, a tiny dirt-floored log building to be used for religious purposes. Eventually dedicated to Our Lady of the Rosary, this structure is recognized as the first Catholic church in what would become the Diocese of Sioux Falls.

March 2, 1861, witnessed the creation of the Dakota Territory by President James Buchanan. The Homestead Act, enacted May 20, 1861, granted 160 acres to qualified persons who would improve the land for a period of five years. Both acts did not initially entice many adventurers to the region. Benedictine abbot Martin Marty arrived in the Dakota Territory in 1876. He was to become the vicar apostolic of this area in August 1879 by decree of Pope Leo XIII. He worked strenuously to establish the Catholic faith on the prairie.

President Benjamin Harrison declared North and South Dakota the thirty-ninth and fortieth states of the Union on November 2, 1889. More than a month earlier, Pope Leo XII established the Diocese of Sioux Falls, which then encompassed the entire state. Bishop Marty then became the first bishop of Sioux Falls and served in that capacity until his transfer to the Diocese of Saint Cloud in 1894. The other bishops of Sioux Falls were: Thomas O'Gorman (1896–1921), Bernard J. Mahoney (1922–39), William O. Brady (1939–56), Lambert A. Hoch (1956–78), Paul V. Dudley (1978–95), and Robert J. Carlson (1995–).

Bishop O'Gorman, convinced that his diocese was much too large, shared his concern with Archbishop John Ireland of St. Paul who, in turn, petitioned the Holy See to create a second diocese in South Dakota. On July 28, 1902, Pope Leo XIII created the Diocese of Lead, an area of 42,000 square miles, existing west of the Missouri River in South Dakota. John N. Stariha was appointed the first bishop of Lead, serving until 1909.

Joseph F. Busch (1910–15) was the second bishop of Lead, while John J. Lawler (1916–48), the third bishop, saw the transfer of the see from Lead to Rapid City in 1930. Bishop Lawler's successors as bishop of Rapid City were: William T. McCarty, C.Ss.R. (1948–69), Harold J. Dimmerling (1969–87), and Charles J. Chaput, O.F.M. Cap. (1988–97). The Catholic population of the Diocese of Rapid City in 1995 was 39,000 in a total population of 211,000, while the Catholic population of the Diocese of Sioux Falls was 118,000 in a total population of 500,000.

Duratschek, Claudia, O.S.B. *Builders of God's Kingdom: The History of the Catholic Church in South Dakota.* Yankton: Sacred Heart Convent, 1979.

Karolevitz, Robert F. *With Faith, Hope and Tenacity: The First One Hundred Years of the Catholic Diocese of Sioux Falls 1889–1989.* Mission Hill, S. Dak.: Dakota Homestead Publishers, 1989.

CHARLES MANGAN

SPALDING, CATHERINE (1793–1858)

Cofoundress of the Sisters of Charity of Nazareth, Kentucky. Catherine Spalding was born in Charles County, Maryland, on December 23, 1793. She was elected the first mother superior of this third American-founded community of women religious, a position she filled for four different six-year terms. Despite extreme poverty in the early years of the community, it gradually expanded, opening schools and orphanages in Kentucky and Tennessee. There were 142 members in 14 convents when Mother Spalding died. In 1995 the motherhouse was still in Nazareth, Kentucky, and the 853 members were serving in health care, education, and various charitable apostolates in eight archdioceses and twenty-four dioceses in the U.S.A., and overseas in India, Nepal, and Belize.

Mother Catherine Spalding

Catherine was baptized by Fr. John Baptist David (1761–1841), a Sulpician priest. She moved with her family from Maryland to Kentucky as a child and upon the death of her mother, she and her younger sister lived with her aunt, Elizabeth Elder. Because of the numerous Catholics who had migrated to Kentucky in the so-called Maryland diaspora (ca. 1785), Rome designated Bardstown a diocese in 1808 along with New York, Philadelphia, and Boston. Benedict Joseph Flaget (1763–1850), also a Sulpician, became first bishop but did not arrive until 1811, accompanied by Fr. David.

During 1812 and 1813, at the suggestion of Bishop Flaget, Fr. David preached sermons calling on women to devote their lives to the service of God and the Church by forming a religious community based on the precepts of St. Vincent de Paul. First to respond were Teresa Carrico, Elizabeth Wells, and Catherine Spalding. Their first convent was a log cabin in Nelson County where Fr. David undertook to train them as teachers, assisted by Ellen O'Connor who soon joined the community. In 1814 the original seven sisters adopted a habit and opened a school, the first of many the community would operate over the next 180 plus years.

Like most early American foundresses, Mother Catherine's religious life was marked by struggles. Money was always a problem, yet she managed to purchase property at Nazareth for the permanent motherhouse in 1822, establish St. Vincent's Orphanage in Louisville in 1832, and St. Thomas Orphanage in Bardstown in 1850. When Bishop Flaget directed the community in 1841 to join the Sisters of Charity of Emmitsburg and change their habit, Mother Catherine composed a petition signed by fifty-two of the fifty-six members pleading for continuance as they had been established. After hearing the appeal, he acquiesced. In 1841 Bishop Pius Miles of Nashville sought to establish a diocesan community using Sisters of Charity of Nazareth serving in his diocese. Six of the fourteen sisters agreed while the other eight returned to Nazareth. The Nashville community was short lived as such, with the remaining members later moving to Leavenworth, Kansas, to form the Sisters of Charity of Leavenworth. Mother Catherine was determined that the rules of the community be followed and insisted on the election of another superior when each of her six-year terms expired. The untimely death of one superior combined with chaotic record-keeping by the treasurer created yet another crisis challenging Mother Catherine's competence.

Catherine Spalding died as she lived, serving others. Going out in winter weather to visit a poor family in distress, she contracted a cold and died two weeks later. Spalding University in Louisville is named in her honor, one of the great antebellum women religious leaders.

McGann, Agnes Geraldine, S.C.N. *SCN's Serving since 1812.* Indiana: St. Meinrad Press, 1985.

Stewart, George C. Jr. *Marvels of Charity: History of American Sisters and Nuns.* Huntington, Ind.: Our Sunday Visitor Press, 1994.

GEORGE STEWART

SPALDING, JOHN LANCASTER (1840–1916)

Bishop, author, educator. Born in Lebanon, Kentucky, on June 2, 1840, Spalding was educated at a succession of schools: St. Mary's College in Kentucky, Mt. St. Mary's in Maryland, Mt. St. Mary's of the West in Ohio, and The American College of Louvain in Belgium. He was ordained a priest at Malines on December 19, 1863, and briefly studied canon law at Rome before returning to America and his home diocese of Louisville in 1865. The young cleric threw himself into an array of tasks, serving as bishop's secretary, assistant at the cathedral, diocesan newspaper editor, chancellor, and founding pastor of the diocese's first African American parish.

Louisville's bishop in the late 1860s was the authoritarian William George McCloskey, a successor to Martin John Spalding (uncle of John Lancaster Spalding), who had been appointed archbishop of Baltimore from Louisville in 1864. Clerical disputes racked the Kentucky diocese under McCloskey; additionally, the latter maintained ongoing quarrels with the elder Spalding in Baltimore. When Martin John Spalding died in 1872, the nephew left Louisville behind, moved to New York City, and there published his illustrious uncle's biography the following year. Spalding remained in New York and from there was appointed first bishop of Peoria, Illinois, in 1877. He would remain in this post until illness caused his resignation in 1908.

Writer and Activist

Spalding's administrative energies, agile mind, and literary skills were almost constantly engaged throughout his long career. Hailed as "the Catholic Emerson," Spalding was a prodigious writer of books and essays. These included *Education and the Higher Life* (1890), *Things of the Mind* (1894), *Aphorisms and Reflections* (1901), *Religion, Agnosticism and Education* (1902), *Socialism and Labor* (1902), and *Glimpses of Truth* (1903). Spalding also produced such books of poetry as *America and Other Poems* (1885), and *The Poet's Praise* (1887).

In the realm of education, Spalding not only wrote prodigiously, but pressed insistently for a Catholic research institution of higher learning to enhance the intellectual standing of Catholic leadership in America. With the assistance of a major financial donation from his friend, Mary Gwendolyn Caldwell, Spalding led in the foundation of The Catholic University of America in Washington.

Spalding declined an offer to become the first rector of The Catholic University, but preached a notable sermon when the cornerstone was placed on May, 24, 1888. In an address of October 13, 1899, titled "The University: A Nursery of the Higher Life," the bishop repeated his frequent theme that Catholicism would fail to become a major force in the modern world unless its adherents were possessed of intellectual and moral vitality.

Spalding served on the committee of bishops that oversaw the composition of the Baltimore Catechism in 1885 as a direct consequence of the Third Plenary Council of Baltimore that had met the previous year. Ever a proponent of increased educational opportunities for women, Spalding encouraged the establishment of Trinity College (1900) for women near The Catholic University in Washington.

The "Americanist" Issue

The bishop of Peoria was imbued with an intense affection for America and its freedoms. Thus he would be a frequent ally of the "Americanist" wing of the late nineteenth-century hierarchy in its enthusiastic support for political democracy, separation of Church and state, and cautious ecumenical engagement. But the aristocratic Spalding was not outspokenly supportive of lay initiative or democracy inside the Church. Nor was Spalding's love of the nation unconditional. Immediately after the Spanish-American War of 1898, he resolutely and publicly opposed the imperialistic instinct then ascendant in America, most notably in a lecture before the Anti-Imperialist League of Chicago.

Spalding's address, "Education and the Future of Religion," delivered at the Church of the Gesù in Rome, March 21, 1900, was widely considered his most outspoken support of the Americanist cause. Coming over a year after the cautionary papal letter *Testem benevolentiae*, it was a clear call for self-criticism within Catholicism, for free and academically disciplined inquiry, understanding of the views of intellectual opponents, involvement of Catholic leaders in the public realm, and of openness to "the vital movements of the age."

At the time of President William McKinley's assassination, Spalding delivered an oration entitled "A National Calamity," that received widespread attention across the country. Americans, the Peoria bishop said, seek facile solutions to the great problems. In the midst of his critique of America, though, he maintained that the nation still remained "dedicated to securing the largest freedom, the fullest opportunity, the completest justice to all, to men and women, to the strong and the weak, to the rich and the poor" (*Socialism and Labor*, 145).

After the death of Chicago's Archbishop Patrick Feehan in 1902, Spalding was under serious consideration by Rome to be named as his successor. Ultimately, in the face of charges by the Baroness von Zedtwitz (sister of Mary Gwendolyn Caldwell) against Spalding's integrity, the Holy See put aside the Spalding nomination. In 1908, three years after a debilitating stroke had impaired him, Spalding was given the honorary title of archbishop by Pope Pius X. He died in Peoria on August 25, 1916.

See also AMERICANISM; CATHOLIC UNIVERSITY OF AMERICA, THE; ILLINOIS, CATHOLIC CHURCH IN.

Ellis, John T. *John Lancaster Spalding*. Milwaukee, 1962.
Sweeney, David F. *The Life of John Lancaster Spalding*. New York, 1965.

CLYDE F. CREWS

Related Document

BISHOP SPALDING ON THE INTELLECTUAL WEAKNESS AMONG AMERICAN CATHOLICS, NOVEMBER 16, 1884

With the maturity of the Church in the twentieth century it has become increasingly evident that the principal weakness of American Catholicism lies in its lack of national influence and intellectual leadership. One of the keenest foreign observers of the Church in the United States has said, not without reason, that "in no modern Western society is the intellectual prestige of Catholicism lower than in the country where, in such respects as wealth, numbers, and strength of organization, it is so powerful" (D. W. Brogan, *U.S.A. An Outline of the Country, Its People and Institutions* [London, 1941], p. 65). No American Catholic spotted this weakness earlier, nor emphasized it more forcefully, than John Lancaster Spalding (1840–1916), first Bishop of Peoria. Spalding was easily the most intellectual American Catholic bishop of his lifetime, a man who had capitalized to the fullest extent on his training at the Catholic University of Louvain and his additional study at several German universities and in Rome. When he was only forty-four, he made a powerful plea to the hierarchy for an American Catholic university that would be worthy of the name in a sermon preached during the Third Plenary Council of Baltimore. In that sermon Spalding showed his awareness of the need for quality rather than quantity in higher education, while at the same time the optimism of the Gilded Age in which he lived and the deep love he had for the United States. It was this sermon which, in a sense, launched the Catholic University of America. The bishop's contribution to American life was well summarized in the citation for the honorary degree of doctor of letters conferred on him by Columbia University on June 11, 1902, which read: "Descendant of a house honored among two peoples; Christian priest and prelate, man of letters, orator, educator and patriotic citizen." Spalding's analysis of 1884 still has pertinence for those who believe that the intellectual life has in no way won the esteem and support among the more than thirty million American Catholics that might have been hoped.

(*Source*: John Lancaster Spalding, *Means and Ends of Education*. Chicago: A. C. McClurg and Co., 1897, pp. 219–223.)

. . . AND NOW, WHEN AT LENGTH A FAIRER DAY HAS DAWNED for us in this new world, what can be more natural than our eager desire to move out from the valleys of darkness towards the hills and mountain tops that are bathed in sunlight? What more praiseworthy than the fixed resolve to prove that not our faith, but our misfortunes made and kept us inferior. And, since we live in the midst of millions who have indeed good will towards us, but who still bear the yoke of inherited prejudices, and who, because for three hundred years real cultivation of mind was denied to Catholics who spoke English, conclude that Protestantism is the source of enlightenment, and the Church the mother of ignorance, do not all generous impulses urge us to make this reproach henceforth meaningless? And in what way shall we best accomplish this task? Surely not by writing or speaking about what the influence of the Church is, or by pointing to what she has done in other ages, but by becoming what we claim her spirit tends to make us. Here, if anywhere, the proverb is applicable—*verba movent, exempla trahunt*. As the devotion of American Catholics to this country and its free institutions, as shown not on battlefields alone, but in our whole bearing and conduct, convinces all but the unreasonable of the depth and sincerity of our patriotism, so when our zeal for intellectual excellence shall have raised up men who will take place among the first writers and thinkers of their day their very presence will become the most persuasive of arguments to teach the world that no best gift is at war with the spirit of Catholic faith, and that, while the humblest mind may feel its force, the lofty genius of Augustine, of Dante, and of Bossuet is upborne and strengthened by the splendor of its truth. But if we are to be intellectually the equals of others, we must have with them equal advantages of education; and so long as we look rather to the multiplying of schools and seminaries than to the creation of a real university, our progress will be slow and uncertain, because a university is the great ordinary means to the best cultivation of mind. The fact that the growth of the Church here, like that of the country itself, is chiefly external, a growth in wealth and in numbers, makes it the more necessary that we bring the most strenuous efforts to improve the gifts of the soul. The whole tendency of our social life insures the increase of churches, convents, schools, hospitals, and asylums; our advance in population and in wealth will be counted from decade to decade by millions, and our worship will approach more and more to the pomp and splendor of the full ritual; but this very growth makes such demands upon our energies, that we are in danger of forgetting higher things, or at least of thinking them less urgent. Few men are at once thoughtful and active. The man of deeds dwells in the world around him; the thinker lives within his mind. . . .

But the Church needs both the men who act and the men who think; and since with us everything pushes to action, wisdom demands that we cultivate rather the powers of reflection. And this is the duty alike of true patriots and of faithful Catholics. All are working to develop our boundless material resources; let a few at least labor to develop man. The millions are building cities, reclaiming wildernesses, and bring forth from the earth its buried treasures; let at least a remnant cherish the ideal, cultivate the beautiful, and seek to inspire the love of moral and intellectual excellence. And since we believe that the Church which points to heaven is able also to lead the nations in the way of civilization and of progress, why should we not desire to see her become a beneficent and ennobling influence in the public life of our country? She can have no higher temporal mission than to be the friend of this great republic, which is God's best earthly gift to His children. . . . If we keep ourselves strong and pure, all the peoples of the earth shall yet be free; if we fulfill our providential mission, national hatred shall give place to the spirit of generous rivalry, the people shall become wiser and stronger, society shall grow more merciful and just, and the cry of distress shall

be felt, like the throb of a brother's heart, to the ends of the world. Where is the man who does not feel a kind of religious gratitude as he looks upon the rise and progress of this nation? Above all, where is the Catholic whose heart is not enlarged by such contemplation? Here, almost for the first time in her history, the Church is really free. Her worldly position does not overshadow her spiritual office, and the State recognizes her autonomy. The monuments of her past glory, wrenched from her control, stand not here to point, like mocking fingers, to what she has lost. She renews her youth, and lifts her brow, as one who, not unmindful of the solemn mighty past, yet looks with undimmed eye and unfaltering heart to a still more glorious future. Who in such a presence, can abate hope, or give heed to despondent counsel, or send regretful thoughts to other days and lands? Whoever at any time, in any place, might have been sage, saint, or hero, may be so here and now; and though he had the heart of Francis, and the mind of Augustine, and the courage of Hildebrand, here is work for him to do. . . .

(*Source*: John Tracy Ellis, ed. *Documents of American Catholic History*. Vol. 2:1866–1966. Wilmington, Del.: Michael Glazier, 1987, 415–17.)

SPALDING, MARTIN JOHN (1810–72)

Archbishop of Baltimore. Martin John Spalding was born in rural Washington (later Marion) County, Kentucky, May 10, 1810, the son of Richard and Henrietta (Hamilton) Spalding, Maryland-born Catholics. He was educated at St. Mary's College and St. Joseph's Seminary in Kentucky before he was sent by Bishop Benedict Joseph Flaget of Bardstown to the Urban College of the Propaganda Fide in Rome to finish his theological studies. There he was ordained on August 13, 1834, after a brilliant defense of 356 theses for the degree of doctor of divinity.

In Kentucky he served as pastor of churches in Bardstown and Lexington and as president of St. Joseph's College in Bardstown before he was appointed vicar general of the Diocese of Louisville in 1844. He was unhappy in his administrative roles largely because of a temperamental incompatibility with Bishop Guy Ignatius Chabrat, coadjutor to Bishop Flaget. On April 18, 1848, after Chabrat's resignation, he himself was named coadjutor to Flaget and raised to the episcopacy September 10 by the old bishop, who immediately turned over to him the administration of the diocese. At Flaget's death on February 11, 1850, Spalding became bishop of Louisville.

A voracious reader with a scholarly bent, Spalding began in 1834 an almost monthly essay or review of popular works for Catholic periodicals. As a priest he published *D'Aubigné's "History of the Reformation" Reviewed* (1844), *Sketches of the Early Catholic Missions of Ken-*

tucky (1844), and *General Evidences of Catholicity* (1847). As a bishop he produced *Sketches of the Life, Times, and Character of the Rt. Rev. Benedict Joseph Flaget* (1852), *Miscellanea* (1855), and a two-volume *History of the Protestant Reformation* (1860). At the same time he built a reputation as a preacher and lecturer. Particularly acclaimed were the series of lectures he delivered at Tremont Temple in Boston, Cooper Union in New York, and the Smithsonian Institution in Washington, D.C., in 1860. Excepting Orestes Brownson, he was the most influential American Catholic apologist in the antebellum period, his efforts being particularly attuned to American audiences.

Bishop of Louisville

Spalding was bishop of Louisville during the golden years of that city. One of his first achievements was the impressive cathedral still standing. A begging tour of Europe in 1852–53 won a number of exceptional priests and the Xaverian Brothers. The tour also led to the foundation of The American College of Louvain in 1857, of which Spalding was regarded the principal founder and patron. He began in earnest after his return in 1853 to create a parochial school system, recruiting still more religious orders to staff them. Particularly during his years in Louisville, he was one of the most outspoken champions of the Catholic school system and critics of the "godless" public schools.

A check on the swelling tide of Catholic immigrants to his see city, however, occurred in August 1855 with an outburst of nativist violence called "Bloody Monday," whose severity Spalding sought to moderate. The Civil War also brought a halt to institutional growth. In the conflict Spalding sought to remain neutral, but the "Dissertation on the American Civil War" he composed for the enlightenment of his Roman superiors (published anonymously in the *Osservatore Romano*) made it clear that his sympathies were with the South. Such sympathies also caused him to denounce secretly to Rome his metropolitan, Archbishop John Baptist Purcell of Cincinnati, a staunch supporter of the Union.

A result of his Roman education, Spalding was one of the most proficient of the American bishops in canon law. He played a leading role at the First Plenary Council of Baltimore (1852) and at the three provincial councils of Cincinnati that followed (1855, 1858, and 1861). A recognition of his talents as legislator, as well as his fame as an author, induced a majority of the American bishops to recommend him as successor to his friend and mentor, Archbishop Francis Patrick Kenrick of Baltimore. To the oldest archdiocese he was translated on April 3, 1864, and installed on August 31. Though Spalding and others believed so, there had been no interference to his appointment on the part of the federal government.

Archbishop of Baltimore

Spalding immediately visited as much of the archdiocese as the Civil War permitted, taking careful note of its needs. He would establish more parishes and institutions per year and introduce more religious orders than any other archbishop of Baltimore. One of the institutions he founded was St. Mary's Industrial School, a home for wayward boys, a work in which he pioneered. One of the orders he introduced was the Mill Hill Fathers, whose ministry was directed exclusively to African Americans. Through the two diocesan synods he held he would bring greater system and regularity to the oldest see.

Martin J. Spalding

It was, however, as leader of the Church in the United States that Martin Spalding sought to make his greatest contribution. Although the archbishops of Baltimore had served as conduits for the Holy See in matters touching the American Church as a whole, Spalding was the first to exercise an unblushing and vigorous leadership. His greatest contribution was the Second Plenary Council of Baltimore of 1866. For its convocation he had to overcome the reluctance of a number of bishops. In the troubled period following the Civil War, he argued, a display of unity was necessary. "Four million of these unfortunates are thrown on our Charity," he told the archbishop of New York, referring to the emancipated slaves, "and they silently but eloquently appeal to us for help."

The 534 decrees of the council constituted a *corpus juris* for an immigrant Church that was rapidly achieving definition, providing as it did a distinctly American statement of doctrine and of discipline in such areas as diocesan organization, sacraments, worship, pious associations, and Catholic publications. No other council was so much the work of one man. Though its work would be overshadowed by the Third Plenary Council of 1884, the latter could never have accomplished what it did had not Spalding broken the pattern of piecemeal legislation and modeled the procedures it would follow. Much that Spalding was compelled to leave as exhortation the Third Plenary Council would mandate. The three great goals that Spalding had set the council in 1866 but failed to achieve—a uniform catechism, a Catholic university, and a process for addressing the needs of African Americans—would be realized in 1884. His attempt to do more in 1866 was to a degree thwarted by episcopal timidity and in at least one case, that of Archbishop Peter Richard Kenrick of St. Louis, outright hostility.

Another of Spalding's signal contributions, but one seldom recognized by historians, was his prevention of the condemnation of workingmen's unions by both the American hierarchy and the Holy See at a critical juncture of the labor movement. At the Second Plenary Council he succeeded in having the bishops exempt labor unions from a blanket condemnation of secret societies. When asked by Rome his opinion on such unions, Spalding observed that in commercial countries capital was a "despotic ruler" and the worker its slave. "This being the case, I say, leave the poor workers alone." He advised that the Church elsewhere follow the example of the Second Plenary Council.

Spalding took the lead in an unsuccessful attempt to prevent a Roman condemnation of the militant Irish and American Fenians but a successful one to prevent the formation of an American Battalion to fight for the Papal States. Initially sympathetic to many of the priests who complained against their bishops, Spalding set himself against a movement for priests' rights when informed of the radical views of some of the leaders, especially in New York, and rebuked those in Chicago when asked by Rome to investigate affairs in that diocese.

In Baltimore Spalding was not able to write as much as in Kentucky but did revise some of his earlier works and dashed off occasional pieces for the Catholic Publication Society and the *Ave Maria*. When the Syllabus of Errors with its apparent condemnation of such American principles as freedom of worship and separation of Church and state reached the United States in 1865, Spalding took it upon himself to issue a pastoral letter assuring Americans in general that the condemnations were not intended to extend to the United States. His attempt to extract a statement to this effect from the Roman authorities, however, was unavailing.

Fearful that the Vatican Council called for 1869 would attempt to legislate such condemnations, Spalding urged upon the preparatory commission the avoidance of any reprobation of the Church-state arrangement of countries like the United States. He also urged an implicit rather than explicit definition of papal infallibility. At the council itself Spalding attempted, unsuccessfully, to create a compromise party that favored an implicit definition. Drawn into a dispute with Bishop Félix Dupanloup of Orléans, who had the support of Archbishops Kenrick and Purcell and a small number of other Americans, Spalding came out in favor of an explicit definition of papal infallibility in which the concurrence of the bishops would not be required, a retreat from his earlier position. In a pastoral letter he wrote before leaving Rome, he explained that such a definition was necessary in order to eradicate forever the revived Gallicanism that his opponents clearly represented. At the prorogation of the council, Spalding worked, unsuccessfully, with Cardinal Henry Manning of Westminster and Archbishop Victor Deschamps of Malines, for a resumption of the council in the latter city. Upon his return to Baltimore and on the occasion of the twenty-fifth anniversary of the coronation of Pius IX, Spalding staged two of the most impressive demonstrations of papal support in the Catholic world.

Spalding's last year was troubled not only by illness (he had suffered severe attacks of gastritis throughout his life) but also by an acrimonious dispute with Bishop William McCloskey of Louisville, in which he sided with those in his former see who complained to Rome of their new bishop. McCloskey, however, had the support of his metropolitan, Archbishop Purcell. Spalding died on February 7, 1872, of bronchitis, and was buried in the crypt of the cathedral in Baltimore.

Assessment

Spalding was a popular bishop both in Louisville and Baltimore but was strict in such matters as dress, dancing, theater-going, mixed marriages, and abortion. He had an amazing capacity for work, a driving energy that contributed to his death three years before he would have received the reward he undoubtedly sought, that of being the first American to wear the red hat. Few, if any, American prelates surpassed Spalding in his range of interests and activities, whether as organizer, administrator, legislator, apologist, author, orator, or scholar. Perhaps to a greater degree than any other bishop at midcentury, John Hughes not excepted, he contributed to the shaping of the immigrant Church by articulating its attitudes, breathing life into its institutions, and systematizing its discipline. Though old-stock in birth and breeding, he came to identify with the immigrant poor. Ambitious, and possessed of a touch of vanity, he was, nevertheless, a caring bishop, his principal efforts being directed, as his nephew-biographer noted "to the orphan, to the negro, to the sinful, to the outcast, to the aged, to all who suffered and had none to pity them."

See also KENTUCKY, CATHOLIC CHURCH IN; MARYLAND, CATHOLIC CHURCH IN; VATICAN COUNCIL I AND AMERICAN CATHOLICS.

Crews, Clyde F. *An American Holy Land: A History of the Archdiocese of Louisville.* Wilmington, Del., 1987.

Fogarty, Gerald P., S.J. *Patterns of Episcopal Leadership.* New York, 1989.

Micek, Adam A. *The Apologetics of Martin John Spalding.* Washington, D.C., 1951.

Spalding, John Lancaster. *The Life of the Most Rev. M. J. Spalding, D.D., Archbishop of Baltimore.* New York, 1873.

Spalding, Thomas W. *Martin John Spalding: American Churchman.* Washington, D.C., 1973.

——. *The Premier See: A History of the Archdiocese of Baltimore, 1789–1989.* Baltimore, 1989.

THOMAS W. SPALDING

SPANISH CIVIL WAR AND AMERICAN CATHOLICS, THE

When the Spanish Civil War broke out in the summer of 1936, American Catholics were not at first disposed to support, or even to concern themselves with, either side. They had shown some moderate uneasiness with the actions of the liberal-socialist Spanish government which had in the previous five years since 1931 enacted anticlerical legislation separating Church and state, forbidding the religious orders to teach, and dissolving the Jesuits. There had been some apprehension over the government's condoning a few incidents of destructive anticlerical violence. But, while the American Catholics commiserated with their Spanish brethren, many saw the Spanish Church as backward and unaware of the needs of millions of poor and oppressed Spaniards. Many would agree that the Spanish clergy were reaping the results of decades of close alliance and dependence upon reactionary governments before 1931.

Anticlerical Atrocities

However, this perception changed rapidly by the end of the first month of the war. The war had been started by a military rebellion (later labeled Nationalist) backed by conservatives and Catholic groups (although no clergy were involved in the conspiracy to rebel) against an anticlerical government (later called Loyalist) made up of socialists and left-wing liberals and backed by anarchists. Within a few days after the outbreak of war there was such an outburst of anticlerical violence in Loyalist Spain that horrified Catholics throughout the world. Decades of pent-up tension between Spanish clericals and anticlericals erupted in a bloodletting unparalleled in Catholic history. Over 5,000 priests, monks, nuns, and seminarians were assassinated in the first dozen weeks of the war (and the number was to total nearly 7,000 by the end of the war in 1939). Thousands of Catholic laypersons were also killed, solely because they were identifiable practicing Catholics. Thousands of churches were burned, destroyed, or turned into stables and warehouses. Innumerable holy objects were profaned. The Loyalist government could not control this fury, which was led by common criminals as well as by anticlerical elements. In response, Catholics throughout the world came to support General Francisco Franco's rebel Nationalist government against the anticlerical Loyalist government.

American Catholics were no different. Still largely an immigrant or second-generation, working-class group, they supported their clergy, who were naturally sympathetic to the plight of their Spanish counterparts. The anticlerical fury dominated their response to the exclusion of all other issues raised by the Spanish war, despite the fact that working-class people elsewhere, even in some of the Catholic European countries, supported the Spanish Loyalists in a war which they viewed as a conflict between rich and poor, between fascism and democracy.

American Catholics and Protestants

The American Catholic stance, however, was not only a response to Spanish events. It was also influenced by decades of hostility between Catholics and Protestants in the United States. Once the anticlerical fury began, Catholics came to the defense of the Spanish Church and therefore the Nationalists as well. Protestants, on the other hand, downplayed the anticlerical fury and came to support the Loyalist government; they had long feared that Catholics wanted to establish a powerful and domineering American Church along the lines of the Spanish Church. Most Catholics defended the Franco uprising, blind to its repressive cruelties and its controlled assassination of thousands of Loyalists who were guilty of nothing more than supporting their government. They ignored its dependence on Nazi Germany and Fascist Italy. Bishops and laypeople alike lauded Franco as a modern-day George Washington and saw the war in simplistic terms as a communist-Masonic (and often Jewish) conspiracy to overthrow Catholic Christian civilization. Soviet Communist support of and aid to the Loyalists was proof of their beliefs.

American Protestants and secular agnostics in response argued that the Spanish clergy had participated in Franco's uprising and were bearing arms (which was not true, except in very isolated instances), and that, in any event, the Spanish people could hardly be blamed for rising up against an oppressive priesthood. They urged support for the Loyalists, whom they portrayed as progressive democrats fighting against a reactionary establishment. The mythologizing of the war made strange bedfellows: the WASPish DAR praised Spanish Loyalist proletarians who would have assassinated them on a class basis if they had been Spaniards. Neither Catholics nor Protestants in the United States knew much about the religious background of the Spanish war. Both constructed myths about the Spanish clergy in order to justify their beliefs. Thus the Spanish Civil War became, in the United States, a bloodless, but highly polemical war of words between Catholics and Protestants.

Their debate spilled over into politics and it had an effect on the course, if not the outcome, of the war. President Franklin Roosevelt was sympathetic to the Loyalist cause. His wife, Eleanor, actively supported the Loyalists and constantly urged the President to aid them. The Loyalist government wanted to purchase arms, an action marginally illegal according to the Neutrality Act passed in 1935, barring the sale of weapons to belligerents in foreign wars. The Act was amended in 1937 to include factions fighting in civil wars, a clear application to Spain. Roosevelt was not anxious to involve the United States in a foreign war under any circumstances; in the Spanish war he could not aid the Loyalists without alienating the Catholic bloc, one of the pillars of his New Deal coalition.

American Catholic Political Pressure

Catholic pressure prevented the administration from carrying out humanitarian endeavors. In 1937 the Loyalist Basques asked permission to send refugee children abroad to get them out of the combat zone. British and French Catholics responded and accepted them, but Catholic Congressman John McCormack of Massachusetts, acceding to his archbishop, Cardinal William O'Connell, and to his mobilized constituents, pressured the State Department to refuse them visas, arguing that Franco had promised not to harm the children. And, in late 1938, in the waning days of the war, the American bishops mounted a successful campaign to prevent the administration from sending a shipment of surplus wheat to the starving Loyalists (even though Roosevelt promised to send an equal amount to the Nationalists), arguing that such aid would simply prolong a war which the Loyalists had already lost.

At the local level, organized Catholic groups such as the Knights of Columbus worked to prevent expressions of sympathy for the Spanish Loyalists. Loyalist supporters were labeled as communists at worst or communist dupes at best. Theaters which showed pro-Loyalist movies were boycotted. When the Loyalists organized lecture tours by Spanish Loyalists to raise funds, Catholic pressure denied them the use of municipal auditoriums. Organized humanitarian relief campaigns for the Loyalists were picketed, protested against, or otherwise confronted, especially in the large cities where there were substantial numbers of Catholics. Pro-Loyalist newspapers were boycotted. Legitimate supporters of the Loyalists found themselves harassed and threatened, and in some cases even lost their jobs as a result of organized Catholic pressure.

Not all Catholics supported Franco's Nationalists. Bishop Edwin V. O'Hara of Kansas City and Cardinal George Mundelein of Chicago regarded the Nationalists as little better than Fascists or Nazis. Mundelein's diocesan paper, *New World,* stood out as a moderate voice in the polemical battle between Catholics and Protestants. But the rest of the Catholic press was vociferous in its support of the Nationalists. The diocesan papers got their news from the NCWC wire service, which daily reported instances of anticlerical violence in Spain, of clergy killed, of churches burned.

The Catholic periodical press was divided. The Jesuit-edited *America* early on took up the cause of the Nationalists. Much of the idealization of the Spanish Church, its leaders, and General Franco, stemmed from its pages. Differing with it were the lay-edited *Commonweal,* along with the Paulist *Catholic World* and the proletarian *Catholic Worker.* These journals supported neither side and instead called for a compromise peace. *Commonweal,* with the largest circulation of the three, stated that the communist-Masonic conspiracy theory as a rationale for the attack on the Spanish clergy was simplistic and that it ignored the immense social problem in Spain and the long history of anticlerical tension that went back to the eighteenth century. *Commonweal* published the articles of French Catholic laymen such as Jacques Maritain, François Mauriac, and Georges Bernanos, Catholic thinkers and writers who denounced the Nationalists for their repression of civil liberties and wholesale execution of innocent Loyalist soldiers and supporters. *Commonweal*'s editor, George Shuster, defended his journal's position and wrote articles for the leading pro-Loyalist periodical, *The New Republic,* as well.

Pastoral Letter of the Spanish Bishops

The conflict in America came to a climax in the late summer of 1937 when the Spanish bishops issued a joint pastoral letter to the world. In the letter, they justified their support of the Nationalists by citing the anticlerical fury and by recounting all of the anticlerical legislation passed by the prewar government. They issued the letter, they said, to answer criticism of their position on the war and to ask their fellow bishops throughout the world to help them to spread the truth about the war. They denied accounts that claimed they favored the wealthy and that they had provoked the anticlerical fury by engaging in combat themselves. When the letter was published in the United States, 150 American Protestant leaders responded with a public letter published in *The New York Times.* The Protestants charged that the Spanish clergy had ignored social and economic abuses in the years before the war and that, while the Spanish bishops condemned the Loyalist government for the anticlerical fury, those same bishops ignored atrocities committed by the Nationalist forces. They said that the Spanish bishops had made religion an issue in a war that was "a struggle between the forces of progress and democracy against special privilege."

Within two weeks, 175 Catholic leaders, including all American Catholic college and university presidents, responded to the Protestant letter. They defended the Nationalist uprising, comparing Spanish Catholics to the Americans who rose up against the British in 1776. They denied that the anticlerical fury was caused by "deep popular resentment created by social abuses," and pointedly asked the Protestants if they supported a regime that had carried on a ruthless persecution of Christians.

The war of words continued even after the end of the Spanish war in the spring of 1939, when the Loyalists surrendered to Franco's Nationalists. Four hundred fifty Protestant clergy and laymen sent an open letter to Pope Pius XII criticizing the Pontiff's blessing of Franco's victory and asking him to intervene to prevent reprisals against Loyalist supporters. By this time, many American Catholics were becoming more aware of the real issues of the war and they were chagrined when they thought back to the laudatory support they had given the Franco forces during the war. Most kept prudently silent about Spanish affairs thereafter.

In the final analysis, the Spanish Civil War was one of the most divisive elements in American religious life in the first half of the twentieth century. Relations between Catholics and Protestants, which had been tempered by the common struggle against the disaster of the Great Depression, deteriorated as the two groups now found themselves fighting again over the events of a foreign civil war. The war, in fact, had become a mirror which reflected back to Americans the hostility of generations of Catholics and Protestants against each other. Only the desperate need of national unity in the Second World War moderated this hostility in the years following the Spanish Civil War.

See also ANTI-COMMUNISM AND AMERICAN CATHOLICS.

Crosby, Donald F. "Boston's Catholics and the Spanish Civil War: 1936–1939." *New England Quarterly* 44 (March 1971) 82–100.

Guttmann, Allen. *The Wound in the Heart: America and the Spanish Civil War.* New York, 1962.

Sánchez, José M. *The Spanish Civil War as a Religious Tragedy.* Notre Dame, 1987.

Traina, Richard P. *American Diplomacy and the Spanish Civil War.* Bloomington, 1968.

Valaik, J. David. "American Catholic Dissenters and the Spanish Civil War." *Catholic Historical Review* 53 (January 1968) 537–55.

JOSÉ M. SÁNCHEZ

SPELLMAN, FRANCIS CARDINAL (1889–1967)

Cardinal archbishop. Spellman was born in Whitman, Massachusetts, on May 4, 1889, the oldest of five children of William and Ellen Conway Spellman. His parents were middle-class Americans of Irish ancestry (his father was a grocer) who were sufficiently well off to give their children a good education. The two youngest sons both became physicians. Frank, as he was always called, attended the local public schools in Whitman and Fordham College in New York City from which he graduated in 1911. Upon deciding to study for the priesthood for the Archdiocese of Boston, Spellman was sent to the North American College in Rome in September 1911.

Early Years in Rome and Boston

In that era students at the North American College attended classes at the Urban College of Propaganda Fide whose faculty was composed of Italian secular priests, many of whom rose to important positions in the Roman Curia and who were not loathe to advance the careers of their favorite students. In the words of historian Florence D. Cohalan, "This was well known to the students, and those among them who were ambitious for high rank set their sights accordingly. Not all succeeded, but among those who did, Francis Spellman was outstanding in his generation—and even among all the American priests who have ever studied in Rome." One professor with whom Spellman became especially friendly was Francesco Borgongini-Duca, a future nuncio to Italy and curial cardinal, who was to play a key role in Spellman's ascent of the greasy pole of ecclesiastical preferment.

In 1914 Spellman was hospitalized for almost six months with "a weakness of the lungs." He recovered and was ordained in Rome on May 14, 1916. As a priest in Boston from 1916 to 1925, Spellman incurred the displeasure of William Cardinal O'Connell, the autocratic archbishop, who assigned Spellman to such unglamorous positions as circulation editor of the archdiocesan newspaper and archdiocesan archivist (with his office in the basement of the chancery office). O'Connell had become coadjutor archbishop of Boston in 1906 by using his Roman connections, and in 1925 Spellman used the same means to escape from O'Connell's control. Capitalizing on his friendship with Borgongini-Duca, he wrangled an appointment as the director of the Knights of Columbus playgrounds in Rome and (more importantly) as an attaché at the Vatican Secretariat of State.

Spellman's second Roman sojourn lasted from 1925 to 1931. He continued his earlier practice of cultivating significant people who could advance his own career, among them American millionaire Nicholas Brady and his wife Genevieve, and Vatican architect Enrico Galeazzi. Through another former professor, Msgr. Giuseppe Pizzardo,

Spellman met Archbishop Eugenio Pacelli, who was to become Secretary of State in 1930. In 1931 Spellman won the gratitude of Pius XI by arranging for the publication in Paris of the Pope's anti-Fascist encyclical, *Non Abbiamo Bisogno*. The following year, Pius XI named him an auxiliary bishop of Boston. He was ordained titular bishop of Sila on September 8, 1932, by Cardinal Pacelli in St. Peter's basilica. The co-consecrators were Borgongini-Duca and Pizzardo.

Auxiliary Bishop of Boston

From 1932 until 1939, Spellman was an unwanted auxiliary bishop in Boston. O'Connell signaled his displeasure by assigning Spellman to residence in the seminary and then as pastor of a debt-ridden parish in Newton Center. At a clergy conference in September 1935, O'Connell scolded the Boston priests for attending funerals of people whom they barely knew. Spellman noted in his diary that "the priests naturally thought that the Cardinal was referring to [my] mother's funeral," which had taken place five weeks earlier. Spellman endured such humiliations stoically, always careful to observe the ecclesiastical proprieties. Meanwhile, he continued to cultivate his Roman connections and solidified his friendship with Joseph P. Kennedy through whom he secured access to the White House. In 1936 Spellman achieved national prominence when he escorted Cardinal Pacelli on his tour of the United States and arranged a meeting between Pacelli and President Franklin D. Roosevelt at Hyde Park on November 5, 1936. On March 2, 1939, Pacelli was elected pope. On April 12, 1939, Spellman was privately informed that he was to be the next archbishop of New York. The first person (outside his family) to whom he told the news was President Roosevelt. The formal announcement was made on April 24, and Spellman was installed as the sixth archbishop of New York on September 8, 1939.

Archbishop of New York

In New York, Spellman proved to be a capable and energetic administrator. His first order of business was to reorganize the chaotic financial situation. Under his predecessor, Patrick Cardinal Hayes, the archdiocese had incurred a debt of $28,000,000. With the help of Boston banks, Spellman refinanced the debt and saved $500,000 in interest payments in his first year as archbishop. Hayes had allowed wide autonomy to pastors. Spellman centralized power in his own hands through the introduction of such new agencies as the Archdiocesan Building Commission and a central purchasing agency. He remained aloof from the local clergy, dealing with them through a series of vicars general to whom he delegated wide authority. He also distributed papal honors among the priests of the archdiocese with unprecedented largesse and undiscriminat-

ing profusion. After World War II, Spellman embarked upon a major building program in New York. He spent over $500,000,000 on the construction or renovation of over 370 schools. He created a system of diocesan high schools whose minimal tuition was made possible by the large number of diocesan priests on the staff. He also refurbished the badly neglected diocesan seminary at Dunwoodie and provided it with a well-trained faculty. Spellman also took a deep interest in the social services of the archdiocese, spending over $92,000,000 on the expansion of hospitals and other institutions.

Military Vicar in World War II

Spellman was the most prominent archbishop of New York since John Hughes, and probably the best-known American prelate since Cardinal Gibbons. His friendship with Pope Pius XII gave him influence in Rome unmatched by any other American bishop or even by the apostolic delegate to the United States. He played a major role in the negotiations that led to the announcement by President Roosevelt on December 24, 1939, that he would appoint a "personal representative" to the Holy See. As Military Vicar for the Armed Forces, an appointment which he received on December 8, 1939, Spellman kept a high profile in World War II through his trips to American troops around the world. From 1942 to 1966, Spellman never missed a Christmas visit with American troops overseas. A mystery-shrouded visit to wartime Rome in 1943 aroused intense speculation in the American press. Thanks to such well-publicized activities, he came to personify the patriotism of American Catholics. In a nonideological way he achieved the synthesis of loyalty to both Church and country that had eluded the "Americanist" bishops of the late nineteenth century. In the words of Gerald P. Fogarty, Spellman was "the personification of Romanization and Americanization." On February 18, 1946, at the first postwar consistory, he was one of four American archbishops to receive the cardinal's red hat.

National Influence

After World War II, Spellman remained nationally prominent as an opponent of Communism both at home and abroad. He was particularly outspoken in denouncing the persecution of the Catholic Church in Eastern Europe and China. His anti-Communism led him to blame Communist influence for a gravediggers' strike at local Catholic cemeteries in 1949. In an action that dismayed many New York Catholics, Spellman broke the strike by using seminarians as substitute gravediggers. On April 4, 1954, Spellman attended a Communion Breakfast of the Holy Name Society of the New York City police department at which the principal speaker was Senator Joseph McCarthy. Spellman's presence was widely interpreted as a sign of support for the controversial senator. In 1949 Spellman became involved in one of the most acrimonious incidents in his career when he tangled publicly with Mrs. Eleanor Roosevelt over an issue that was dear to his heart, federal aid for Catholic schools. She had recently indicated her opposition to such aid. He accused her of "conduct unworthy of an American mother"—a remark for which he later apologized.

Spellman's influence was evident in a number of episcopal appointments. Patrick O'Boyle, who had headed Catholic Charities in New York, became the first archbishop of Washington in November 1947. James Francis McIntyre, who had been auxiliary bishop and coadjutor archbishop (without right of succession) in New York, became archbishop of Los Angeles in February 1948. John O'Hara, who had served as auxiliary bishop in the Military Ordinariate during World War II, became bishop of Buffalo in March 1945 and archbishop of Philadelphia in November 1951. In 1957, upon the death of Archbishop Thomas Molloy of Brooklyn, the new Diocese of Rockville Centre was created for Long Island. Both dioceses were filled by New Yorkers, Bryan J. McEntegart in Brooklyn and Walter P. Kellenberg in Rockville Centre.

After the death of Dennis Cardinal Dougherty of Philadelphia in 1951, Spellman was poised to assume the position once held by James Cardinal Gibbons of unofficial primate of the Catholic Church in the United States. In fact, as Gerald Fogarty has pointed out, Spellman was unable to achieve this goal because of three Midwestern prelates who dominated the inner workings of the National Conference of Catholic Bishops, namely, Stritch of Chicago, Mooney of Detroit, and McNicholas of Cincinnati. They combined to form what they called the "Hindenburg Line" to prevent the extension of Spellman's power beyond the eastern seaboard. With the exception of the appointment of McIntyre to Los Angeles, they were successful. After the death of Pius XII in 1958, Spellman's influence in Rome waned.

One of Spellman's finest pastoral initiatives in his own archdiocese stemmed from the influx into New York of several hundred thousand Puerto Rican immigrants in the 1950s and 1960s. Spellman responded to the challenge by organizing a Spanish Apostolate to provide pastoral care for the newcomers. According to sociologist Ana Maria Diaz-Stevens, Spellman's greatest contribution "was to recognize the missionary character of the situation." He abandoned the traditional practice of national parishes for integrated parishes, and insisted that his own diocesan priests, rather than religious orders, should assume the major responsibility. By 1958 the archdiocese had over two hundred Spanish-speaking priests, and approximately one-quarter of the parishes were providing services in Spanish.

Francis Cardinal Spellman

Vatican II and After

Spellman defied facile ideological classification. At Vatican Council II, he generally supported the conservatives, especially in matters of liturgical reform. Even in this area, however, he was not always consistent. He was adamant about keeping the Mass in Latin, but wanted priests to have the option of saying the breviary in the vernacular. He was responsible for the presence at the council of John Courtney Murray, S.J., and he strongly supported the Declaration on Religious Liberty and the council's statement on the Jews. He was surprisingly receptive to modern Catholic biblical scholarship and defended two of his priest-scholars, Myles Bourke and Patrick Skehan, when they came under attack from reactionary critics. He also defended the right of priests and religious to participate in the civil rights demonstrations of the 1960s.

The upheavals in the post-Vatican II Church disturbed Spellman greatly as did the turmoil in American society occasioned by the Vietnam War and the civil rights movement. "I am having a difficult time," he told his friend Galeazzi in 1965. "I do not think that things in Rome could be any more 'dizzy' than they are here in the United States." To the end, Spellman remained a staunch supporter of the Vietnam War, declaring in 1966 that "total victory means peace." Shortly before his death, antiwar demonstrators (including some sisters) were arrested for disrupting Sunday Mass in St. Patrick's Cathedral. It must have been an incomprehensible development for Spellman, who belonged to an earlier age where faith and patriotism were unquestioning allies. A notably ambitious man, Spellman wedded his ambition to the service of both his Church and his country and made outstanding contributions to both. He died in New York City on December 2, 1967.

See also NEW YORK, CATHOLIC CHURCH IN; O'CONNELL, WILLIAM CARDINAL; VATICAN COUNCIL II AND AMERICAN CATHOLICS.

Cohalan, Florence D. *A Popular History of the Archdiocese of New York.* Yonkers: U.S. Catholic Historical Society, 1983, 265–326.

Cooney, John. *The American Pope: The Life and Times of Francis Cardinal Spellman.* New York: Times Books, 1984.

Diaz-Stevens, Ana Maria. *Oxcart Catholicism on Fifth Avenue: The Impact of the Puerto Rican Migration upon the Archdiocese of New York.* University of Notre Dame Press, 1993.

Fogarty, Gerald P., S.J. "Francis J. Spellman, American and Roman." *Patterns of Episcopal Leadership.* New York: Macmillan, 1989.

Gannon, Robert I., S.J. *The Cardinal Spellman Story.* Garden City: Doubleday, 1962.

Shelley, Thomas J. "Francis Cardinal Spellman and His Seminary at Dunwoodie." *Catholic Historical Review* 80 (2) (April 1994) 282–98.

Van Allen, Rodger. "Cardinal Spellman: His Real Biography Is Still Needed." *Records of the American Catholic Historical Society of Philadelphia* 96 (1986) 93–100.

THOMAS J. SHELLEY

STALLINGS SCHISM, THE

George Augustus Stallings, Jr., who was ordained a Roman Catholic priest, founded the breakaway African American Catholic congregation in 1989 and was excommunicated the following year.

Five years later, the church claimed a membership of 4,200, with eight temples, one archbishop (Stallings), nine priests, and two deacons. The African American Church, also known as Imani Temple, allows optional clerical celibacy, women's ordination, birth control, abortion, rejects auricular confession, and permits divorced and remarried Catholics to receive Holy Communion.

Fr. Stallings was director of evangelization for the Archdiocese of Washington, D.C., and former president of the National Black Catholic Clergy Caucus when he announced his plans in June 1989 to form a black Catholic church to "address the needs and aspirations of African-American people." In meetings with James Cardinal Hickey of Washington, Stallings said the U.S. Roman Catholic Church was unresponsive to the cultural, social, and spiritual needs of blacks.

The African American Catholic Church was founded July 2, 1989, and two days later Fr. Stallings celebrated its first Mass before more than 2,000 people at a high school in Maryland. Cardinal Hickey suspended Fr. Stallings from his duties as a priest and forbade him from celebrating Mass. On a television talk taped in January and aired in nationwide syndication on February 5, 1990,

Stallings said that "as of today, the African-American Church is going independent" and that it would be "no longer under the pope or under the aegis of the Roman Catholic Church."

In a statement the same day, Fr. William Kane, vicar general of the Washington archdiocese, said Fr. Stallings had "excommunicated himself" when he "announced publicly his formal and complete break with the Roman Catholic Church." At the same time, one of Stalling's priests, Salvatorian Fr. Bruce E. Greening, sought reconciliation with the Catholic Church.

Later that year, May 14, Stallings was ordained bishop of his breakaway denomination. Ordaining Bishop Stallings was Archbishop Richard Bridges of the Independent Old Catholic Church of Southern California. Six other bishops, all from Old Catholic denominations, took part in the ceremony. Bishop Stallings ordained a former Roman Catholic nun, Rose Vernell, on September 8, 1991. The same day, he took the rank of archbishop in a ceremony presided over by two of the prelates from Old Catholic churches who had ordained him a bishop the previous year.

In 1992 Stallings initiated the Black Christ/Black Church Project, a campaign to replace white images of Jesus with a black image. "Jesus in his human nature was Afri-Asiatic and Black," he said in a 1993 news release. "This action will liberate the image of Jesus from the shackles of Eurocentric cultural hegemony."

Archbishop Stallings was born on March 17, 1948, and soon after was baptized at St. Joseph's Catholic Church, a black congregation in New Bern, North Carolina. After attending St. Joseph's Catholic School, he enrolled in a preparatory seminary in Asheville, North Carolina, to begin his studies for the priesthood. After college in Erlanger, Kentucky, and five years of theological training at the North American College in Rome, he was ordained a priest in 1974 in Washington, D.C. He was pastor of St. Teresa of Avila Church in Washington, D.C., and taught at Mt. Mary's Seminary, Emmitsburg, Maryland, and at the Washington Theological Union.

STEPHENIE OVERMAN

STARR, ELLEN GATES (1859–1940)

Teacher, social worker, social activist. Ellen Gates Starr was born on March 19, 1859, near Laona, Illinois. She practiced Unitarianism nominally as a child, and as a young adult became an Episcopalian. Some thirty years later, after the publication of the American Bishops' Program of Social Reconstruction in 1919, and influenced by her work with immigrants, she converted to Catholicism. She was also a member of the Socialist Labor Party, a prominent activist in the social settlement movement, and a strong supporter of organized labor. In 1894 she and others founded the Chicago Public School Art Society, and Starr served as first president. In 1897, together with Jane Addams, she founded Hull House in Chicago to provide for the needs of the desperate immigrants in the west side of the city.

For some thirty years, Starr served as director of cultural activities at Hull House. She used art as a way of raising the human spirit. The immigrants were taught English and the principles of democracy. Starr herself was quite active in the efforts of the labor movement to improve the living and working conditions of the workers. She was arrested many times for leading strikes. Her conversion only deepened her devotion to the poor. She remained at Hull House until 1929 when a spinal operation left her paralyzed. She retired to Suffern, New York, where she spent her final years confined to a bed in the convent of the Holy Child. She died at the convent on February 10, 1940.

See also LABOR MOVEMENT AND AMERICAN CATHOLICS, THE.

STEPHEN M. RYAN

STEVENS, GEORGIA LYDIA (1870–1946)

Religious of the Sacred Heart. Georgia Stevens was born in Boston, Massachusetts, the third daughter of Henry Stevens and Helen Granger Stevens. She attended Miss Gillian's School, Boston, and the Elmhurst Convent of the Sacred Heart in Providence, Rhode Island. Gifted for violin and cello, she studied at the Hoch Conservatory (Frankfurt), and with other German, Alsatian, and American professors. In 1894 she became a Catholic. After twelve years of travel, professional tours, and works of charity, she entered the Society of the Sacred Heart. A large part of her religious training was directed by the renowned educator, Mother Janet Erskine Stuart, R.S.C.J., in London and Ixelles, Belgium.

In 1916 she cofounded with Mrs. Justine Ward the Pius X Institute of Liturgical Music, later the Pius X School, associated with Manhattanville College in New York. They intended to form musicians and teachers for the restoration of the plainchant (Gregorian) in Catholic worship, in accordance with the *motu proprio* of St. Pius X (1903).

An inspiring and vivacious teacher, Mother Stevens trained children as well as adults to read music, sing, and even to compose. She asked perfection in vocal production from her choirs, and helped choirmasters and organists with the correct interpretation of ancient musical texts, relying greatly on the assistance of the Benedictine monks of Solesmes Abbey who often assisted on the faculty of the summer sessions. Those who observed her closely at work realized that in reality she was a woman of prayer. She died on March 28, 1946.

Carroll, Catherine A. *A History of the Pius X School of Liturgical Music, 1916–1969.* St. Louis: Society of the Sacred Heart, 1989.

Stevens, Georgia. *Tone and Rhythm Series.* 6 vols. New York: MacMillan, 1935–41.

_____. *Medieval and Renaissance Music.* Boston: McLaughlin & Reilly, 1940.

ELIZABETH FARLEY, R.S.C.J.

STONE, JAMES KENT (1840–1921)

Convert, Passionist priest. James Kent Stone was born in Boston, Massachusetts, on November 11, 1840, the son of Dr. John Seely Stone, dean of the Episcopal Theological School, Cambridge, Massachusetts, and of Mary Kent Stone, daughter of the jurist James Kent. Young James studied at Harvard University, spending a year at Göttingen University, Germany, and graduated from Harvard in the class of 1861. He served as a lieutenant in the Union army, seeing action in the battle of Antietam.

Later while teaching at Kenyon College, Gabier, Ohio, he studied theology and was ordained as an Episcopalian priest in June 1866. He had married Cornelia Fay in 1863. Three children blessed the family. For one year he was president of Kenyon College, and in 1868 he was president of Hobart College, Geneva, New York.

In convoking the First Vatican Council in 1869, Pope Pius IX invited all Protestants to study their own religious status. This the young president of Hobart College did. He was received into the Catholic Church on December 8, 1869, and wrote his reasons in a book entitled *The Invitation Heeded.* Convinced that God had called him to the priesthood, he was ordained as a Roman Catholic priest in the Paulist community. There he shared the dream of the founder, Fr. Isaac Hecker, of bringing Catholicism to this country.

In 1877 Stone transferred to the Passionist Congregation at Pittsburgh. He took his vows as a Passionist on August 11, 1878, receiving the name of Fidelis of the Cross. He continued his preaching ministry, and also fulfilled various offices in the congregation, especially when called to help found the congregation in Argentina. He was elected provincial superior in both the United States and in Argentina, also serving as a consultor to the general superior in Rome. As an old man he spent some time at a black parish in the new diocese of Corpus Christi, Texas. He also reedited his earlier book which was published with the title: *An Awakening and What Followed.* Finally, he retired to the Passionist monastery in Norwood Park, Chicago, Illinois.

All through his life there had been a deep hidden sorrow—his separation from his children. His wife had died shortly after the third child's birth in 1868. With the intention of being ordained as a Paulist priest, he secured the help of Mother Frances Warde. She promised to take care of his three daughters at the Sisters of Mercy Convent in New Hampshire. In order to enter the Passionist community, he arranged for a Catholic couple to adopt his two daughters (one had died earlier). Fidelis agreed not to contact his children. This enforced separation became a lifelong heartbreak for him.

Finally in 1921 the younger daughter learned of her father's sacrifice from his book. She visited him in Chicago. Eighty-one years old, he returned with her to California and died with his two daughters in their home in San Mateo. Fr. Fidelis of the Cross had made this supreme sacrifice to become a missionary of the passion. Unfortunately his sacrifice also meant a sacrifice for his children. Both he and his daughters were granted a foretaste of peace in those final weeks in San Mateo.

See also PASSIONISTS (C.P.).

Burton, Katherine. *No Shadow of Turning*. New York, 1944.
Healy, Kathleen. "Suffering and Resurrection: Frances Warde and Kent Stone." *Frances Warde: American Founder of the Sisters of Mercy*. New York, 1973, 320–51.
Smith, William George, and Helen Grace Smith. *"Fidelis of the Cross," James Kent Stone*. New York, 1926.
Stone, James Kent. *The Invitation Heeded*. New York, 1870.
——. *An Awakening and What Followed*. Notre Dame, 1920.

ROGER MERCURIO, C.P.

STRITCH, SAMUEL CARDINAL (1887–1958)

Cardinal archbishop of Chicago. Stritch was born in Nashville, Tennessee, on August 17, 1887. An extremely precocious youth, he finished grade school by the age of ten. Through the influence of Fr. John B. Morris, he became a seminarian for the Diocese of Nashville and studied at St. Gregory's Seminary in Cincinnati. When Stritch finished high school at the age of sixteen, his bishop, Thomas S. Byrne, sent him to Rome to complete his theological studies at the Urban College of the Propaganda. On May 21, 1910, he was ordained to the priesthood in the Lateran Basilica. He returned to Nashville and worked for a time as a pastor in Memphis and later served as the bishop's secretary, rector of the cathedral, chancellor, and superintendent of schools. Stritch was a bookish man, unfailingly courtly and easygoing, who never lost his light Southern drawl despite his many years in the North.

Toledo and Milwaukee

In August 1921, at the age of thirty-four, he was appointed to head the Diocese of Toledo, Ohio. He was consecrated in Toledo on November 30, 1921, by Archbishop Henry Moeller of Cincinnati. Stritch spent nine years in Toledo. Putting a high priority on education, he called for a greater professionalization of teaching sisterhoods and assisted in the founding of Mary Manse College by the Ursuline Sisters. He built a magnificent cathedral, based in part on the great cathedral of Toledo, Spain, which unfortunately saddled his successor with a heavy debt. In 1930 he was transferred to the Archdiocese of Milwaukee after the death of Sebastian G. Messmer. He arrived in Milwaukee just as the depression was beginning to affect this heavily industrialized archdiocese. Throughout the years of the depression, Stritch steadfastly adhered to rigid diocesan economies even to the point of refusing to rebuild the cathedral which had had been gutted in a destructive fire in early 1935. Faced with diminishing funds, the Milwaukee archdiocese felt the pinch of hard times, aggravated by the collapse of the diocesan bond agency. Several parishes begun during the prosperous 1920s were only spared collapse because of Stritch's personal efforts on their behalf. Shortfalls in funds for diocesan social welfare agencies led Stritch to inaugurate an emergency appeal in 1934. So successful was the drive that it was replicated every year afterwards.

As in Toledo, Stritch took a special concern for the condition of Catholic education. More specifically, he insisted on greater professionalization of teachers and adherence to state norms for teacher education. Early in his term, he urged the major teaching sisterhoods to open up teacher training institutes in their respective motherhouses. He also assisted Jesuit-run Marquette University which experienced a severe financial crisis in the 1930s.

In Milwaukee, Stritch became increasingly involved in the affairs of the National Catholic Welfare Conference. Together with Archbishops Edward Mooney of Detroit, and John T. McNicholas, O.P., of Cincinnati, he played an active role on the executive board of the organization. Indeed, the Stritch-Mooney-McNicholas trio dominated NCWC deliberations for many years. Stritch became particularly interested in the cause of Catholic Action popularized especially by Pope Pius XI. He strongly insisted that it be closely linked with the work of the clergy and under the firm direction of local bishops. In Milwaukee he coordinated the activities of many lay groups such as the Knights of Columbus and the Holy Name Society under the Catholic Action banner. Under an innovative Secretariat for Catholic Action which he established in 1937, Catholic Youth groups, devotional societies, archdiocesan athletics, adult education programs, and women's organizations were brought under one centrally directed enterprise.

Archbishop of Chicago

In 1940 Stritch succeeded Cardinal George Mundelein as archbishop of Chicago. He was formally installed on March 7, 1940, in Chicago's Holy Name Cathedral. Chicago was larger than Toledo or Milwaukee, but Stritch adapted himself nicely to his new home. Deliberately unpretentious, he shunned his predecessor's penchant for pomp and remoteness. He never stayed at Mundelein's home on the campus of the diocesan seminary and virtually ignored the institution which had been the late Cardinal's pride and joy. He quickly paid off the debts left by Mundelein and hewed to a more conservative fiscal line. He abhorred public controversy and confined his political activities to discreet discussions or correspondence with government officials.

His instinctive conservatism manifested itself in an uncharacteristically harsh way when he abruptly removed the social activist/liturgical pioneer, Msgr. Reynold Hillenbrand, from the leadership of the major seminary in 1944. Stritch would show the same coolness to other "liberal" groups in the diocese such as those who advocated liturgical change, devotees of "specialized" Catholic action which emphasized lay leadership, or those who engaged in interracial activities. Yet, at the same time he allowed such groups to operate in the archdiocese provided they did not trouble him or upset the faithful.

Mundelein's other holdover, auxiliary bishop Bernard Sheil, was also kept at a distance from the center of archdiocesan life. Sheil's episcopal status afforded him greater leeway than the hapless Hillenbrand and he managed to give Stritch some anxious moments. However, Sheil virtually ignored the archdiocese and immersed himself in the affairs of his mini-empire, the Catholic Youth Organization. When it collapsed under financial strain in 1954, Sheil retired to parochial life and Stritch graciously picked up the large indebtedness of the organization.

Stritch's administration of Chicago was greatly facilitated by two powerful clerics, Msgr. George Casey and Msgr. Edward Burke. Unlike other Mundelein holdovers, these two did not find themselves in exile, but were given wide latitude in conducting the day-to-day affairs of the diocese. This gave Stritch a respite from the desk work he despised and allowed him to appear frequently in public at confirmations, church dedications, and priests' funerals.

Stritch and the NCWC

His association with the National Catholic Welfare Conference continued and his status in the organization was enhanced when he and Mooney were named cardinals in February 1946. Indeed, when contact was cut off with Rome during the war, the NCWC assumed even greater importance as an intermediary between the Holy See and the American government. Through his leadership in the NCWC, Stritch would play an important role in the dissemination of the "papal peace points."

In a series of Christmas addresses early in the 1940s, Pope Pius XII enunciated "peace points" which called for the acceptance of the natural law as a basis for a universal law of nations that would preclude future conflict. The NCWC accepted the responsibility of publicizing these peace points and of lobbying American officials to use them as a basis for the postwar world order. Stritch, who was chairman of the executive board of the NCWC in 1942, accepted responsibility for raising public awareness of these principles and under his direction a compilation of all papal statements on peace was made by seminary librarian Harry Koenig and sent to all government officials, including President Roosevelt. Stritch also lobbied U.S. government officials on behalf of the points and took an especially keen interest in the formation of the United Nations organization which seemed to be an appropriate vehicle for the implementation of the papal viewpoint. Ultimately, the final shape of the U.N. charter displeased Stritch and others, and he turned away from international affairs to the concerns of Chicago.

Chicago after World War II

After the war several aligned issues confronted Stritch relating to the presence of the Church in the city. First of all, a rapid expansion of the suburban areas coupled with an explosion in the birth rate after the war required a massive building program to keep up with the needs of Catholics who now ringed the city. Stritch himself observed early in the 1950s: "As things are going now we are building a new archdiocese on the perimeter of Chicago."

With this suburban exodus, there remained the plight of city parishes, schools, and other institutions which had once been the hubs of thriving urban neighborhoods. Concerns for the devaluation or loss of church property and uncertainty about the direction of the Church in the suburbs led Stritch to cooperate, at least initially, with early urban renewal efforts that removed blighted housing and promised to protect key Catholic institutions.

Underlying both suburban flight and urban renewal was the issue of race. Chicago's sizable African American community, largely confined to the city's south and near west sides, began to grow rapidly after the war. Severe housing shortages in the ghetto literally pushed African Americans into all-white neighborhoods. The appearance of blacks in all-white communities was often met by violent resistance not only from residents, but also from Church officials who refused to admit black children to their schools and did not permit them to attend church services. Even some religious communities would not admit blacks in their private hospitals or if they did so placed them in segregated wards.

Reflecting his Southern roots, Stritch had ambiguous feelings about integration and did comparatively little to address these situations. Although he did privately upbraid pastors who openly discriminated against blacks from the pulpit or in direct dealings with African Americans,

Samuel Cardinal Stritch

he rarely spoke out publicly on racism in the Church despite the urgent pleas of African American Catholics, the example of other bishops and pleas from some of his own priests at work in the interracial apostolates of the archdiocese. The one initiative towards Africans Americans that Stritch did wholeheartedly endorse were the efforts of some Chicago priests and religious to convert them to Catholicism. He readily allowed priests who desired this work to be assigned to African American parishes.

Stritch's final days in Chicago are shrouded in mystery. In early 1958, while on vacation in Florida, he was appointed proprefect of the Congregation for the Propagation of the Faith. This required leaving Chicago and taking up residence in Rome in order to assist the existing prefect of the Congregation, the ailing Pietro Fumasoni-Biondi. Stritch attempted to be excused from the appointment but could not convince Roman officials to let him go. The reasons for appointing the seventy-year-old Stritch to the post are unclear to this day. Nonetheless, he departed Chicago in April 1958, and while in Rome suffered the amputation of his right arm. While recovering from this surgery he suffered a stroke and died on May 27, 1958. His body was shipped back to Chicago and he was buried in Mount Carmel Cemetery.

See also ILLINOIS, CATHOLIC CHURCH IN.

Avella, Steven M. *This Confident Church: Catholic Leadership and Life In Chicago, 1940–1965.* Notre Dame, 1992.
____. "Samuel Stritch and Milwaukee Catholicism, 1930–1940." *Milwaukee History* (Autumn 1990) 70–91.
Buehrle, Marie Cecelia. *The Cardinal Stritch Story.* Milwaukee, 1959.

STEVEN M. AVELLA

STUHLMUELLER, CARROLL (1923–94)

Passionist priest, biblical scholar. Carroll Stuhlmueller was born in Hamilton, Ohio. He was an internationally recognized biblical scholar, a revered teacher, lecturer, and preacher, and a leading figure in numerous Catholic Church movements. Actively involved in biblical scholarship throughout the United States and around the world, he was president of the Catholic Biblical Association of America (1978–79) and of the Chicago Society of Biblical Research (1982–83).

Carroll Stuhlmueller

His teaching ranged far beyond the classroom. He was one of the leading figures who made biblical scholarship accessible to the wider Catholic community. He organized and was the feature lecturer at biblical conferences for priests, religious, and laity that frequently drew hundreds of people.

His expertise and broad interests enabled him to assume an active role in progressive Church movements. He was the only male member of the steering committee of the first Women's Ordination Conference and spoke at its first national meeting. He was a long-time member of the Roman Catholic/Southern Baptist Scholars Dialogue, and was a consultant to such diverse bodies as the Faith and Order Commission of the National Council of Churches, the Lectionary Committee of the International Commission on English in the Liturgy, and the Pontifical Commission on Religious Life in the United States.

A prolific writer, he authored twenty-three books and scores of articles on biblical topics. He was the coeditor of *Old Testament Message,* a twenty-three-volume international commentary series on the Bible (Michael Glazier, 1981–84) and an associate editor of and contributor to *The Catholic Study Bible* (Oxford University Press, 1990). He contributed commentaries and chapters to almost all of the major Catholic and many of the Protestant dictionaries and series on biblical topics, including the *Jerome Biblical Commentary* (Prentice-Hall, 1965), the *Old Testament Reading Guide* (The Liturgical Press, 1986), the *New Testament Reading Guide* (The Liturgical Press, 1960), the *New Catholic Encyclopedia* (McGraw-Hill, 1967), the *New Dictionary of Theology* (Michael Glazier, 1987), the *Collegeville Bible Commentary* (The Liturgical Press, 1987), the *New Jerome Biblical Commentary* (Prentice-Hall, 1990), and the *Harper Bible Dictionary* (Harper & Row, 1988). He also recorded six major cassette series on biblical books and topics. Three major works had just been completed or were nearing completion at the time of his death: *The Collegeville Pastoral Dictionary of Biblical Theology, Biblical Spirituality of the Psalms,* and *The Writings of Barnabas Ahern, C.P.*

Some of his publications were especially characteristic of his interests and spirit: *The Prophets and the Word of God* (Fides, 1964; 2nd ed., 1966), a collection of essays on the prophets; *Thirsting for the Lord* (Alba House, 1977, and later reprinted in Doubleday Image Books, 1979), a collection of essays on biblical theology. His major scholarly work in book form was his dissertation on Deutero-Isaiah, *Creative Redemption in Deutero-Isaiah* (Biblical Institute Press, 1970). His contribution to *The Biblical Foundations for Mission* (coauthored with Donald Senior and published by Orbis Books, 1983) revealed another aspect of his biblical scholarship. His seven-volume series of *Biblical Meditations* published by Paulist Press (*Lent* [1978], *Easter Season* [1979], *Advent and Christmas* [1980], *Ordinary Time* [3 volumes, 1985]) were the fruit of his personal spirituality and biblical scholarship. The same blend of scholarship and vigorous piety led to his two-volume commentary on the *Psalms* (1983), published in the Michael Glazier series, *Old Testament Message.*

Stuhlmueller served as general editor of *The Bible Today,* a popular Catholic journal on the Bible (1981–85), and was on its editorial board from its beginning in 1965 until his death, serving as the Old Testament book review editor as well. He was also on the editorial boards of the *Journal of Biblical Literature* (1987–92) and the *Catholic Biblical Quarterly* (1973–77). He had almost completed his superb editorial work on *The Collegeville Pastoral Dictionary of Biblical Theology* when he died in Chicago on February 21, 1994.

See also CATHOLIC BIBLICAL ASSOCIATION (CBA); CATHOLIC THEOLOGICAL UNION; PASSIONISTS (C.P.).

Obituary notice, *National Catholic Reporter,* March 11, 1994, p. 14

DIANNE BERGANT, C.S.A.

SUFFRAGE MOVEMENT AND AMERICAN CATHOLICISM

By 1890 leaders of the American woman's movement had concluded that the greatest civil and political discriminations facing women were in the area of voting rights. Progressives were especially concerned because they had spent many hours testifying before local, state, and federal committees and believed that women could play an important role in the reform of society. They also reasoned that it was practical to give women the ballot. Many issues facing the country, especially those related to urbanization, industrialization, and immigration, dealt directly with the role of women in home and society. The passage and enforcement of legislation to ensure the safe building and maintaining of tenements, for instance, would allow wives and mothers to maintain a healthier environment for their families. The ultimate solution was the election of the appropriate officials. If women with a special interest in these issues could not vote, then the goals of the reformers would never be reached.

Women were granted suffrage in four states (Wyoming, Utah, Colorado, and Idaho) during the 1890s. Other states followed throughout the first two decades of the twentieth century. At the request of President Woodrow Wilson, the House of Representatives passed a constitutional amendment enfranchising women on June 5, 1919. On August 26, 1920, the amendment was ratified by the thirty-sixth state, and enacted into law.

Position of the Church

Although the Catholic Church in the United States generally opposed the movement aimed at guaranteeing women the right to vote, there was no official Catholic position on the issue. The hierarchy, however, tended to promote the idea that woman suffrage would challenge the teachings of the Church on the role of women in family and society. The dominant view of middle-class Catholics and their leaders was that the family was an educational institution; and the mother was the primary teacher of the faith. She was responsible for instructing children in prayers, catechism, and devotions. There was widespread fear that if women left the home to enter the workforce, the primary way by which faith was transmitted would be lost.

The traditional teaching of Catholicism asserted that men and women were not and could not be equal. The general argument of those opposed to passage of the Nineteenth Amendment claimed that women would be encouraged to leave the home to become involved in politics, and, by extension, business, economics, and other areas not suited to the "weaker sex." Other critics went further and alleged that suffrage would eventually lead to socialism and the legalization of birth control. They pointed to the fact that groups such as the National Birth Control League, led by Margaret Sanger, were ardent supporters of woman suffrage. Both movements were viewed by the American hierarchy as a threat to home and family.

The most prominent Catholic hierarchical opponent of extending the vote to women was James Cardinal Gibbons, archbishop of Baltimore. Gibbons believed that men and women should receive equal pay for equal work, and even supported the admission of women to the Johns Hopkins Medical School, but he thought that woman suffrage would damage the idea that the proper place for women was in the home. (He later came to the reluctant conclusion that passage of the Nineteenth Amendment was probably inevitable following a meeting with a group of Catholic proponents of suffrage.)

Although the magisterium never took an official position on this movement, the American bishops did speak to the issue in a 1919 pastoral. The bishops claimed that the role of women with respect to the public sphere was to touch the hearts of men. By teaching men right from wrong, women were playing an active role in public affairs and acting according to their nature.

Because most of the American hierarchy and many lay leaders opposed woman suffrage, they were often held responsible for any losses suffered by the movement. Catholics were blamed for the defeat suffered by the Massachusetts suffrage campaign in 1915 despite the fact that the issue had been brought to a vote by Governor David I. Walsh, who was a Catholic, and that the archbishop of Boston, William Cardinal O'Connell, refrained from speaking on the subject.

Attitude of Catholic Women

At least during the early years of the woman suffrage debate, several prominent Catholic laywomen spoke out against the proposed amendment. Katherine E. Conway (1853–1927) expressed her views on suffrage in both her fiction and in the editorials she wrote during her years managing the *Boston Pilot*. Conway supported the traditional teachings of the Church on women, and claimed that the ballot would cause women to move away from their natural role, a role that included merging their identities with those of their husbands. She was so vehemently opposed to woman suffrage that she became an active member of the Massachusetts Association Opposed to the Further Extension of Suffrage to Women.

As the movement to ratify the Nineteenth Amendment intensified, many Catholic women began to express support for this reform. These women tended to be members of the middle class with the freedom to spend time outside the home campaigning for woman suffrage. Like their non-Catholic counterparts, they believed that granting woman the vote would ensure the protection of those values central to the home and family (the values the antisuffragists claimed would be destroyed!), and allow the transmittal of these values to other areas of society, such as politics.

Among the Catholic proponents of suffrage was Jane Campbell (1845–1928), founder of the Philadelphia County Woman Suffrage Association. Campbell asserted that granting women the right to vote would not destroy the family; women would not be inspired to leave the domestic sphere for politics. But political parties would tend to nominate men with high moral standards to run for office, and this would improve the home. Other suffrage enthusiasts, such as Sara McPike (d. 1943), refused to accept the idea that a prosuffrage stance was against the teachings of the Bible and the Catholic Church, and she quoted St. Paul's message that in Jesus Christ there was neither male nor female.

The number of Catholic women who supported woman suffrage increased as more women began to be employed outside the home during World War I. They argued that women needed the vote to: support protective employment legislation; clean up corrupt political operations; and transmit the values of home and motherhood to the political sphere. This argument was eventually extended to the assertion that the right of women to vote was consistent with Catholic teaching; women would be the ones who would introduce Catholic values to the secular world. The most vocal member of the hierarchy who supported women's right to vote was Austin Dowling, bishop of Des Moines, Iowa.

As suffrage began to be granted at both the local and national levels, women were encouraged to vote by both the opponents and the proponents of the Nineteenth Amendment. The first arena in which the vote was extended to women was school committee elections, and they were urged to exercise their new right by Catholic leaders who thought Catholic children attending public schools needed protection from those who would indoctrinate them in the tenets of Protestantism. As woman suffrage amendments to state constitutions were ratified, Catholic bishops, including Gibbons (who even instructed nuns to vote), Archbishop Patrick W. Riordan of San Francisco, and auxiliary Bishop Paul Rhode of Chicago, reversed their public stance and began to encourage Catholic women to vote, since they could influence the creation of a more moral political realm. Leaders of the hierarchy, laity, and the Catholic press even began to advocate that women join political parties to lobby for reform in education, inflation, and child labor. Organizations such as the National Council of Catholic Women recommended that their members register to vote so that they could save the country from the secularists. Rev. John A. Ryan thought women could set an example for men by using their new right to vote in a constructive and responsible manner.

The passage of the Nineteenth Amendment did not end the controversy over woman's role in Church and society. Successors to those involved in both sides of the suffrage debate would find themselves dealing with other controversial issues such as the legalization of birth control, abortion rights, and the Equal Rights Amendment. The debate over the place of women in Church and society clearly will continue into the twenty-first century.

Dolan, Jay P. *The American Catholic Experience: A History from Colonial Times to the Present.* University of Notre Dame Press, 1992.

Hennesey, James. *American Catholics: A History of the Roman Catholic Community in the United States.* New York: Oxford University Press, 1981.

Kenneally, James. *The History of American Catholic Women.* New York: Crossroad, 1990.

Kennelly, Karen, ed. *American Catholic Women.* New York: Macmillan, 1990.

MARGARET McGUINNESS

SULLIVAN, WILLIAM L. (1872–1935)

Priest. William Sullivan was born on November 15, 1872, in East Braintree, Massachusetts. He earned his bachelor's degree from St. John's Seminary in Brighton, Massachusetts, in 1896. The following year he joined the Paulists. As a Paulist, he studied theology at The Catholic University of America, where he earned an S.T.B. in 1899 and an S.T.L. in 1900. From 1899 to 1901 he served as a Paulist missionary. He then returned to Washington, D.C., to teach at the Paulist College. In 1908 he left that post to become the pastor of a parish in Austin, Texas. Throughout his career, Sullivan worked to promote the dialogue between Catholic theology and modern science, to develop a rapprochement between American political and social institutions and Catholicism. Finding little success in this effort and much discouragement, particularly from Pius X's encyclical *Pascendi* (1908), which condemned Modernism, Sullivan left the Catholic Church in 1911 and joined the Unitarian Church. He served as a Unitarian minister in Schenectady, New York, and in Germantown, Pennsylvania.

As a Catholic, Sullivan worked to promote an intellectual renaissance in Catholicism. His goal was to develop a Catholic philosophy and theology that addressed the achievements of modern philosophical and scientific work. After *Pascendi* he despaired of ever achieving this. In 1910 he published *Letters to His Holiness Pope Pius X* in which he attacked Catholic scandals, certain past Catho-

lic practices, and the ideology that had spawned them. The Unitarian Church allowed Sullivan the religious and intellectual freedom he failed to find in Catholicism. As a Unitarian minister, he continued to preach, to do research, and to write scholarly essays as well as spiritual meditations and prayers. He died in Germantown, Pennsylvania, on October 5, 1935.

See also MODERNISM IN AMERICA.

Appleby, R. Scott. *"Church and Age Unite!" The Modernist Impulse in American Catholicism.* Notre Dame, 1992, 169–206.

Carey, Patrick W. *The Roman Catholics.* Westport, Conn.: Greenwood Press, 1993, 319–20.

Duclos, Warren E. "Crisis of an American Catholic Modernist: Toward the Moral Absolutism of William L. Sullivan." *Church History* 41 (1972) 369–84.

McGarry, Michael B. "Modernism in the United States: William Laurence Sullivan, 1872–1935." *Records of the American Catholic Historical Society of Philadelphia* 90 (March–December 1979) 33–52.

New York Times, October 7, 1935, 15.

Ratte, John. *Three Modernists: Alfred Loisy, George Tyrrell, and William L. Sullivan.* London, 1966, 257–337.

Sullivan, William L. "Catholicity and Some Elements in our National Life." *New York Review* 1 (1905) 259–67.

_____. *Letters to His Holiness, Pope Pius X.* Chicago, 1910.

_____. *The Priest: A Tale of Modernism in New England.* Boston, 1914.

_____. *From the Gospel to the Creeds: Studies in the Early History of the Christian Church.* Boston, 1919.

_____. *Under Orders: The Autobiography of William L. Sullivan.* Boston, 1944.

_____. *The Flaming Spirit: Meditations and Prayers of William L. Sullivan.* New York, 1961.

PATRICIA DeFERRARI

SULPICIANS (S.S.)

The Sulpicians, one of the smallest communities of priests in the Church, derived their name from the parish of St. Sulpice where their founder, Jean Jacques Olier, established a seminary (1641) based upon a spiritual renewal of the diocesan priesthood and reform of the parish. Accordingly, the Sulpician was not a member of a religious order but a diocesan priest, incardinated in his diocese, and living in a seminary community. The priests and seminarians lived a common life based upon the spiritual exercises and mental prayer. Each Sulpician was referred to as a director, symbolic of his role as a spiritual director of seminarians. This relationship was mediated in the sacrament of penance but manifested in a personalism as both director and penitent shared a common journey.

Pervading the seminary was the Sulpician ethos of priesthood, an *esprit ecclésiastique* representative of the priest's immersion into his role as a churchman and a maker of religious culture. Contrary to the Roman system of seminary governance, with the rector as superior and responsible for the initial call to orders, the Sulpician system was based upon collegiality as the seminary faculty (with the individual's director abstaining) held that responsibility. Also there was no one spiritual director since each faculty member was a director. By the latter decades of the seventeenth century there were nearly thirty Sulpician seminaries in France, while other French seminaries adopted the Sulpician system.

St. Mary's Seminary, Baltimore

St. Mary's Seminary in Baltimore, the nation's first Catholic theological school, was founded in 1791 as both a refuge from the French Revolution and as a secure foundation for the continuity of the Sulpician tradition. St. Mary's was not a missionary outpost; it was a replica of St. Sulpice, with its high spirituality, its tradition of learning associated with the University of Paris, and its Gallican ecclesiology, i.e., its openness to the local church and its deference to the local ordinary.

Throughout the nineteenth century Sulpicians were not only seminary directors, but also parish priests, vicars general, and archbishops in Baltimore (Ambrose Maréchal and Samuel Eccleston); founders of and collaborators with such communities of women religious as the Sisters of Charity of Emmitsburg, the Oblate Sisters of Providence and the Sisters of Charity of Nazareth, Kentucky; and they were notable priests and bishops in various missionary areas (Gabriel Richard, John B. David, Jean Dubois, William Louis DuBourg, Benedict Flaget, and Simon Bruté). Their blend of seminary idealism, missionary realism, and particularist ecclesiology was congenial to the Enlightened Catholicism of John Carroll with its cosmopolitan character, its openness to American culture, and its embrace of religious liberty and the separation of Church and state.

Eight years after the opening of the seminary, the Sulpicians founded St. Mary's College, intending it to be a feeder school for the seminary, but it actually had a student enrollment that was predominantly Protestant.

Jean Dubois, a French priest who founded Mt. St. Mary's College in Emmitsburg, Maryland, became a Sulpician shortly before he opened the college in 1808. With low enrollment at St. Mary's, the Sulpicians could not afford to run two seminaries in one archdiocese. Hence, they eventually withdrew from Mt. St. Mary's, closed St. Mary's College, and in 1848 opened a minor seminary, St. Charles, on land donated by Charles Carroll of Carrollton, adjacent to his plantation in the countryside outside Baltimore. By this time the impact of immigration fostered increasingly high enrollments in both the minor and major seminaries that were national as well as diocesan institutions.

Traditionalists and Transformationists

Sulpician leadership during the nineteenth century alternated between French traditionalists and American transformationists. The administration of François Nagot and Jean Marie Tessier (1791–1829) represented the continuity with French preservationism with its emphasis upon discipline, authority, and the relative isolation from local Baltimore society. Louis R. Deluol, superior of St. Mary's (1829–48), was a transformationist, flexible and adaptable to the peculiar needs of American seminarians, a proponent of St. Mary's College, an activist in the Baltimore community and the American Church. Because of his administrative style, a conservative superior general replaced him with two conservative superiors, François Lhomme and Joseph Dubreul (1848–78), who implemented a traditional code of French discipline and course of studies, one which earned them the enmity of some American bishops, particularly Martin John Spalding, archbishop of Baltimore.

Alphonse Magnien, who had been influenced by French Catholic liberals, including Bishop Félix Dupanloup of Orleans in whose diocese he was incardinated, succeeded Dubreul in 1878. During his administration (1878–1902) the Sulpicians opened seminaries in Boston (1884), New York (1896), and San Francisco (1898), a trend that was dependent upon the rise in American vocations. Magnien became the secretary to Cardinal James Gibbons and was close to Sulpician alumni of notable significance: John J. Keane, bishop of Richmond, rector of The Catholic University of America and archbishop of Dubuque; and Denis O'Connell, rector of the North American College, rector of The Catholic University, and bishop of Richmond. Archbishop John Ireland of St. Paul was closest to Abbé Magnien, as he was fondly called, and through these associations the Sulpician superior played a vital role behind the scenes in the dramatic controversy of Americanism. An ardent Americanizer, Magnien promoted a house of studies at The Catholic University of America as a means of training French Sulpicians for the American apostolate and as a first phase in the establishment of an American novitiate which finally materialized in 1911.

John Hogan, James Driscoll, Joseph Bruneau, and Francis E. Gigot were prominent Sulpician theologians and Scripture scholars on the liberal side of the ideological spectrum. Influenced by the contemporary scholarship on religion and culture, each of these men fashioned an apologetic based upon the historical development of Scripture, dogma, and religious culture. Hogan's work, *Clerical Studies,* marked him as a significant voice in tacit opposition to the prevailing neoscholastic synthesis. Joseph Bruneau promoted the "higher criticism" of Scripture and advanced notions of the theology of atonement; James Driscoll was a scholar of Scripture eager to become Alfred Loisy's agent in the U.S.A.; Francis Gigot was a scholar of the

Hebrew Bible and openly opposed the prevailing Catholic position on the Mosaic authorship of the Pentateuch. Driscoll and others at New York's St. Joseph's Seminary in Dunwoodie founded the *New York Review* (1904–08), a liberal scholarly journal aimed at adapting Catholic thought to the major intellectual trends of the day.

Crises in New York and Boston

In 1905, during the administration of Edward Dyer, the first vicar general and later the first provincial of the American Sulpicians, Driscoll, Gigot, and three other Sulpicians at St. Joseph's Seminary left the society with the support of Archbishop John Farley who removed the remaining Sulpician and placed the seminary in the hands of diocesan priests. This episcopal *coup d'état* was rationalized on the basis that the superior general and his council had so centralized authority that there was little hope for American autonomy, provincial status, and a local novitiate to attract vocations. Though Driscoll denied that the *New York Review* played a role in the decision to leave the society, the journal was so identified with him that it is difficult not to see it at least a factor in the decision. However, in the last analysis, Farley's desire to directly control the seminary by a rector and faculty chosen by him was the decisive factor. The removal of the Sulpicians from the archdiocesan seminary in New York was a severe blow to the society's status and prestige.

The San Francisco earthquake in 1906 resulted in the destruction of two-thirds of St. Patrick's Seminary, but that was reparable. Not so the rupture between the Sulpicians and Archbishop William Henry O'Connell of Boston over the control of St. John's Seminary, Brighton, Massachusetts. Former rector of the North American College and an Ultramontanist on the far right of the ecclesiological spectrum, O'Connell was opposed to Sulpician collegial governance and the individualized style of spiritual direction. He considered their Gallican tradition as conspiratorial "Sulpicianism" aimed at the demise of the "Christendom" and the anti-Modernist mentality infused into the papacy of Pope Pius X. Despite the fact that in 1909 he had negotiated a five-year contract, O'Connell expelled the Sulpicians in 1911 and later disinterred the grave of the one Sulpician buried in the cemetery; John Hogan's statue still stands at St. John's as a solitary witness to the Sulpicians' historical presence in the Archdiocese of Boston.

Twentieth-Century Developments

The society's prestige, strongly defended by Cardinal James Gibbons during these critical years (Gibbons was an alumnus of St. Mary's), was substantially restored with the establishment of the Sulpician Seminary in the orbit of The Catholic University of America. Owned and operated by the society, since 1940 it has been known as Theological College. It is a seminary residence on the Roman model for theological students enrolled at the university's theology program. Since 1922 it has also housed the Basselin scholars whose three-year program in philosophy was funded by an endowment, a bequest of Theodore Basselin with the stipulation that the students be well instructed in homiletics.

Edward Dyer, who had energetically developed the Sulpician presence in Washington, D.C., died in 1925. His successor, John Fenlon, had been assistant secretary of the National Catholic Welfare Conference, a position which placed him in a principal role as a defender of the conference in opposition to the strategy of Cardinals William H. O'Connell and Dennis Dougherty of Philadelphia who intended to convince the Vatican to dismantle the conference on the basis of its supposed threat to the ordinary authority of the bishops. Under Fenlon the society expanded into Seattle with the establishment of St. Edward's as a minor seminary in 1931 and as a major seminary four years later. He also presided at the opening of the new St. Mary's Seminary, a theologate located in Roland Park in 1929.

As a second-generation Americanist, John Fenlon possessed a Gallican skepticism toward Vatican centralization, but he was a traditionalist in the value that he attached to the spiritual exercises and institutional authority. Though not a forceful speaker, he was a recognized savant and spoke with authority on a wide variety of issues. Spiritual leadership was manifested in Francis Havey and Anthony Vieban, both directors of the Sulpician Solitude (novitiate). The former wrote on the formation of priests, while the latter had enormous influence as rector of Sulpician Seminary, later Theological College. Fenlon, Havey, and Vieban represent a generation that stretched back to the days of Magnien and Hogan; Fenlon died in 1943, while Havey and Vieban died in 1944. By that time the province had become Americanized; of the 123 Sulpicians, 114 were born in the United States.

Fenlon's successor, John Lardner, was provincial for only five years (1943–48) during which time the Sulpicians opened St. Stephen's minor seminary in Kaneohe, Hawaii. He also negotiated with Cardinal Edward Mooney and the bishops of the Detroit province for what became St. John's provincial seminary, opened in 1949. The postwar period witnessed the considerable institutional growth of the Catholic Church in the United States: between 1945–67 the number of parishes grew from 14,300 to 18,000; the number of priests went from 5,300 to 12,300, while student enrollment grew from 7,500 to 16,000 seminarians. Sulpicians numbered 126 in 1945; in 1967 there were 159 members. Hence, from the beginning their influence was considerably disproportionate to their numbers.

Catholic intellectual life during much of this period was still rather arid, but the Catholic Biblical Association was founded in 1936 and Edward Arbez, a Sulpician Scripture scholar, was its first president; in the 1950s Raymond Brown was emerging as a leading Catholic exegete. Eugene Walsh of St. Mary's Seminary, who had published his dissertation on the French School of spirituality, was influential in the liturgical movement; Frank Norris of St. Patrick's Seminary in San Francisco was introducing his students to Karl Rahner; and Peter Chirico was advocating the new ecclesiology of Ives Congar to his students at St. Thomas Seminary in Seattle. James Laubacher, rector of St. Mary's (1945–67), wrote his doctoral dissertation on the Modernist, George Tyrrell, and was conversant with the new developments in theology. Lloyd P. McDonald, the provincial who presided over the opening of St. Thomas minor seminary in Louisville in 1952, was primarily a preservationist, who, though provincial during Vatican Council II, was unable to stem the tide of adaptation, reform, and renewal.

The idealism associated with the early 1960s, ranging from John F. Kennedy and the New Frontier to Pope John XXIII and Vatican Council II, gave way to the disillusionment associated with the assassinations of Robert Kennedy and Martin Luther King, Jr., and the Vietnam War. By 1968 the priesthood and religious life reflected this disillusionment, and in these contexts seminary enrollment experienced drastic decline; thousands of men left the priesthood. Despite the highly regarded qualities of Paul Purta, the Sulpician's first *elected* provincial (1967–77), between 1971 and 1977 Sulpician seminaries shrank from eleven to four; enrollment fell from 1,400 to 575. When Edward Frazer was elected provincial in 1977, he established as his top priorities the restoration of morale, the appointment of strong rectors who had the confidence of the bishops, the spiritual and professional growth of the members, and promotion of continuing education for priests. Gerald Brown, provincial (1985–97), has been committed to these same goals but within a multicultural context. Able to delegate authority, Brown carries on the tradition of forming priests as if both Sulpician and seminarian are on a common transformationist journey.

Kauffman, Christopher J. *Tradition and Transformation in Catholic Culture: The Priests of St. Sulpice in the United States: 1791 to the Present.* New York: Macmillan, 1988.

Shelley, Thomas J. *Dunwoodie, The History of St. Joseph's Seminary.* Westminster, Md.: Christian Classics, 1993.

White, Joseph M. *The Diocesan Seminary in the United States, A History from the 1780s to the Present.* University of Notre Dame Press, 1989.

CHRISTOPHER J. KAUFFMAN

SUMNER, IGNATIUS (1826–95)

Mercy Sister. Frances Sumner was born to a Unitarian family related to Cotton Mather and Senator Charles Sumner, abolitionist. Her mother, widowed, converted to Catholicism and was disinherited by her family. Frances's two brothers became Jesuits in Maryland. Her younger sister nursed at Gettysburg and married the nephew of Jefferson Davis.

A well-educated socialite, Frances entered the Sisters of Mercy where she taught, nursed at the Washington Infirmary, and served as fundraiser and accountant. In 1860 she was selected as principal to join the group of six Mercies sent to establish a school in Vicksburg, Mississippi. The school educated boys and girls as well as adults of the community. After the first year, she and her faculty were enlisted as itinerant nurses for the Confederate army.

Her journal is an example of a sensitive religious woman's firsthand observation of the horrors of the Civil War. She describes vividly nursing the wounded from Shiloh at the University of Mississippi campus, spending nights comforting the dying, and wearing rabbit-skin shoes and a tattered habit at the end of the war.

Her journal also chronicles the yellow fever epidemic where six of her Mercy Sisters died while nursing the sick. One Mercy historian, Sr. Austin Carroll, wrote of the Vicksburg sisters, "Perhaps no other community ever had so many obstacles in its incipient stages, living through war, pestilence, pain and sorrow." Sr. Ignatius describes these masterfully in her journal, a legacy to the Sisters of Mercy.

See also SISTERS OF MERCY OF THE AMERICAS (R.S.M.).

Carroll, Teresa Austin, R.S.M. *Leaves from the Annals of the Sisters of Mercy.* Vol. 3. London, 1889.

Chronicles of the Sisters of Mercy, 1860–1990; letters and scrapbooks. Vicksburg, Miss.: Archives of the Sisters of Mercy.

Sumner, Ignatius, R.S.M. Handwritten Journal, 1860–95. Vicksburg, Miss.: Archives of the Sisters of Mercy.

M. PAULINUS OAKES, R.S.M.

SUTTON, XAVIER (1852–1926)

Passionist priest and preacher. Xavier Sutton was born in Tiffin, Ohio, September 22, 1852; baptized with name of William; professed as a Passionist religious with name of Xavier, December 1, 1873; ordained October 18, 1879. After ordination, Xavier Sutton was assigned to the Holy Cross Monastery in Cincinnati to prepare to preach parish missions. His first mission was at Big Rapids, Michigan, November 19–27, 1882. He continued this mission ministry of preaching until a year before his death. During this long career he specialized in parish missions to Catholics, retreats to religious, and other forms of preaching. In 1899 he conducted a four-week mission at St. Raphael's Church on West 41st Street, New York City, to be followed by a one-week mission to non-Catholics in the same parish, November 20 to 27. Thus he began twenty-five years of preaching missions to non-Catholics. His friend, John

W. Shanahan, bishop of Harrisburg, had him spend several years (1899–1901) in his diocese preaching non-Catholic missions. His last mission was at the new Servite church in Hillside, Illinois, November 29–December 6, 1925. Xavier preserved records of his missions in two loose-leaf folders which he called his "Book." He conducted 691 weeks of parish mission and 115 retreats and shorter preaching ministries.

He found time to write several books, including *Crumbs of Comfort for Single Girls* in 1899, and a *Life of St. Gabriel* in 1912. He also served as local superior of the Chicago monastery and one term as consultor to the provincial superior. Preaching missions, however, was his life!

Xavier offers an example of the work of many religious and diocesan priests in the United States since the 1830s. For him the parish mission ministry stirred the lapsed Catholics to return to the practices of their faith. It enabled the newly arrived immigrants to rediscover their Catholic heritage in this new and seemingly "Protestant" land. The parish missionaries stirred up the pride of poor and even "beaten down" Catholics. Xavier preached both in older parishes and in newly founded parishes, in the great cities and in the small towns and rural areas.

Also, Sutton's non-Catholic missions offered him the opportunity to explain the Catholic teachings to many who had never heard about the Church. He used the question-box to great advantage. He noted that "not one insulting question was received. . . . Walls of prejudice were broken down. [The] Catholics who were timid and almost ashamed of their faith became proud of it [and] were filled with a love for their religion . . . especially when they saw how easily objections could be brushed aside." As the years went by he realized that "the Catholics needed the lectures as much as the non-Catholics for many knew little of their faith, being few in numbers and isolated."

After a long career of constant preaching, Xavier Sutton died in Cincinnati on July 28, 1926.

See also PASSIONISTS (C.P.).

Mercurio, Roger, C.P. "Xavier Sutton: An American Passionist Missionary." *The Passionist* 5 (1977) 54–69.

Passionist Provincial Archives, Chicago. Xavier's "Book" (records of his missions) is preserved in these archives.

Ward, Felix, C.P. *The Passionist, Sketches Historical and Personal.* New York, 1923, 251–55.

ROGER MERCURIO, C.P.

SYBILSKA, MARY MONICA (1824–1911)

First superior of the Felician Sisters American foundation. She was born Eleanor Konwerska in Warsaw, Poland, in 1824, and entered the Felician Congregation in 1856 after the death of her husband, but left the community a short time later in order to arrange for her son's welfare before returning to religious life in 1860.

Mother Monica was fifty years old when she was appointed superior of the Felician Sisters American foundation. She and four other sisters were missioned to Polonia, Wisconsin, in 1874, in response to the request of the Rev. Joseph Dabrowski who asked for Felician Sisters to teach children of the Polish immigrants settling in his rural parish.

For twenty years Mother Monica administered the American foundation, serving as its first provincial superior with additional responsibilities of earlier years as director of novices, treasurer, and house superior. She was responsible for the acceptance of thirty schools and three institutions in nine states; for transfer of the American province's provincial house from Polonia, Wisconsin, to Detroit, Michigan, in 1882, and for its construction and subsequent building additions in 1884 and 1887.

At the conclusion of her term of office, membership in the American province which she began with five sisters had grown to 262 members who included 156 professed sisters, 27 novices, and 79 postulants. Mother Monica was then engaged in less arduous ministry until blindness and disability confined her to the provincial house infirmary where she died on September 15, 1911, at the age of eighty-eight.

See also FELICIAN SISTERS; POLISH CATHOLICS IN AMERICA.

Ziolkowski, Mary Janice. *The Felician Sisters of Livonia, Michigan: First Province in America.* Detroit: Harlo Press, 1984.

MARY JANICE ZIOLKOWSKI, C.S.S.F.

T

TAKACH, BASIL (1879–1948)

Bishop. Basil Takach was born October 27, 1879, into a priestly family in Vuchkovo, Ukraine. Following studies in Uzhorod, he was ordained there on December 12, 1902. After a nine-year pastorate in Kis Rakooz, he was transferred to Uzhorod where he was entrusted with ever greater responsibilities in the administrative and educational facets of the Mukachevo Eparchy.

After World War I, the Holy See decided to divide the American Byzantine Exarchate, troubled by ethnic factionalism, into two distinct exarchates, one for Ukrainians (from Galicia) at Philadelphia, and one for Ruthenians (from Transcarpathia) at New York. Takach was appointed titular bishop of Zela and first Ruthenian Exarch of the United States on May 20, 1924, and ordained in Rome on June 15. New York was deemed too remote from the center of the Ruthenian population, and Takach settled in Uniontown, Pennsylvania. In 1926 Takach received permission from Rome to locate in the Pittsburgh suburb of Munhall, and thereafter his jurisdiction was known as the Exarchate of Pittsburgh.

The new exarchate had 288,000 faithful organized in 155 churches served by 129 priests. For the next two decades, Takach worked tirelessly to organize the exarchate and to increase its pastoral effectiveness. He founded a diocesan press, and under his administration many schools were built, and the number of churches, clergy, and faithful increased.

Takach's episcopate was marred, however, by an intense period of trouble (1930–36) primarily resulting from the 1929 decision of the Holy See, contained in the decree *Cum Data Fuerit,* to enforce clerical celibacy in the Byzantine Rite in America. Takach tried unsuccessfully to dissuade Rome from taking this course, but strove faithfully to implement the decree. Difficulties resulting from clerical discipline and parochial trusteeism exacerbated the tension. As a result disgruntled clergy and faithful held Takach responsible for what they considered violations of their Byzantine traditions. The dispute ended unhappily in February 1936 when a number of clergy and parishes under the leadership of Fr. Orestes Chornock, severed union with Takach and formed the American-Carpatho-Russian Orthodox-Greek Catholic Church. An estimated 60,000 faithful were lost to the exarchate during this period.

Because of illness, Takach was granted a coadjutor bishop, Daniel Ivancho, in 1946. After a long battle with throat cancer, Takach died in Pittsburgh on May 13, 1948.

Greek Catholic Union of the U.S.A. *Opportunity Realized. The Greek Catholic Union's First One Hundred Years 1892–1992.* Beaver, Pa.: Greek Catholic Union of the U.S.A., 1994.

Pekar, Athanasius, O.S.B. M. *Our Past and Present. Historical Outlines of the Byzantine Ruthenian Metropolitan Province.* Pittsburgh: Byzantine Seminary Press, 1974.

Warzeski, Walter C. *Byzantine Rite Rusins in Carpatho-Ruthenia and America.* Pittsburgh: Byzantine Seminary Press, 1971.

RAYMOND J. KUPKE

TALBOT, FRANCIS X. (1889–1953)

Editor, author. Francis X. Talbot was born in Philadelphia on January 25, 1889, and after his high school education entered the Society of Jesus on August 14, 1906. Novitiate and classical studies were done at St. Andrew-on-Hudson (Poughkeepsie, New York), and philosophy (1913–16) at Woodstock College (Maryland). He taught English at Loyola School, New York City (1913–17), and religion at Boston College (1917–18). Theology was at Woodstock College (1918–22) with ordination in 1921.

In 1923 Talbot became literary editor of the Jesuit weekly *America,* and because of his interest in prose, poetry, drama, and criticism, as well his native inventiveness and organizing ability, he had great influence on the American Catholic literary scene. He launched the Catholic Book Club (1928) and helped start the Spiritual Book Associates (1932) and the Pro Parvulis Society (1934) for children's books. He formed the Catholic Poetry Society of America (1930) and helped organize the Catholic Theatre Conference and the Catholic Library Association. He was editor in chief of *America* (1936–44), and during the Spanish Civil War organized the *America* Spanish Relief Fund. He was likewise editor of *Catholic Mind* (1936–44) and *Thought* (1936–40). Because of his interest in films, he served for twenty years as chaplain to the Motion Picture Department of the International Federation of Catholic Alumnae (the reviewing body of the Legion of Decency).

Among his books are *The Eternal Babe* (1927), *Jesuit Education in Philadelphia* (1927), and *The America Book of Verse* (1928). His best-remembered works are his historico-biographical novels, *Saint among Savages* (1935), the story of St. Isaac Jogues, martyred in New York State, and *Saint among the Hurons,* the life of St. Jean de Brébeuf, martyred in Canada. While investigating this last book in Canada, he became interested in the plight of the Dionne quintuplets, who had been placed under the care of Dr. Dafoe, the physician who had brought the infants into the world. Convinced that the physician was exploiting them for his own benefit, he managed to induce Quebec authorities to restore the girls to their parents.

In 1944 he became assistant archivist at Georgetown University and continued writing. In 1947 he was appointed president of Loyola College, Baltimore. When his term was finished, he did parish work at St. Aloysius Church in Washington (1951–52), gave retreats at Manresa-on-the-Severn (1952–53), and then moved to Holy Trinity parish in Washington, where he died on December 3, 1953.

See also AMERICA; JESUITS IN AMERICA, THE.

LaFarge, John. "Father Talbot, S.J., 1889–1953." *America* 90 (1953–54) 317–18.

———. "Father Francis X. Talbot, 1889–1953." *Woodstock Letters* 85 (1956) 337–44.

JOSEPH TYLENDA, S.J.

TANEY, ROGER BROOKE (1777–1864)

Chief Justice of the U.S. Supreme Court. Roger Brooke Taney was born in Calvert County, Maryland, on March 17, 1777, to an eminent Maryland planter family that traced its lineage to a Michael Taney who arrived in Maryland as an indentured servant about the year 1660. Through shrewd business practices and because of the natural fertility of the southern Maryland soil, this first ancestor died wealthy, both in personal possessions and real estate. Although the first Taneys were Anglicans, their descendants converted to Roman Catholicism in the late seventeenth or early eighteenth century. Young Roger was born to the fifth Michael Taney, and his wife,1365 Monica Brooke, who was herself a member of a family that traced its ancestry to the time of the Norman Conquest.

Roger B. Taney

Early Years

The future chief justice was educated in local Calvert County, Maryland, schools and by tutors before enrolling at Dickinson College, in Carlisle, Pennsylvania, in 1792. He graduated from this institution in 1795 as valedictorian of his class.

After three years of private study in the law office of Jeremiah Townley Chase, one of the three judges of the general court at Annapolis, Maryland, Taney was admitted to the bar in 1799. His father had already served in the Maryland House of Delegates, and determined that his son should replace him. At the age of twenty-two, therefore, young Roger was elected to public office for the first time. He was defeated in 1800 as part of a general repudiation of Federalist Party policies that swept Thomas Jefferson into the presidency.

The following year, Taney moved his law practice to Frederick, Maryland, and on January 7, 1806, married Ann Key in a ceremony witnessed by Fr. John Dubois, the Catholic pastor of Frederick, future founder of Mt. St. Mary's Seminary, and future bishop of New York. Six daughters and one son would be born to the union. While the son died young, all the daughters attained adulthood and were reared in the Protestant faith of their mother.

Taney maintained his Federalist Party affiliation until the early 1820s, in spite of the party's waning fortunes. The Federalists chose him for presidential elector in 1808, and he received the greatest number of Federalist votes for senator in 1811. He served in the Maryland senate from 1816 to 1821.

Attorney General of the U.S.A.

Taney's increasing renown as a lawyer led to the removal of himself and his family to Baltimore in 1823. He argued his first case before the U.S. Supreme Court in 1825, and was appointed attorney general of Maryland in 1827. He held this post until June 21, 1831, when President Andrew Jackson named him Attorney General of the United States. He also served as interim secretary of war during July and August of 1831, pending the arrival in Washington of secretary-designate Cass.

Much political turmoil was then being generated by the Bank of the United States and the efforts to obtain an early renewal of its charter. The Jacksonian Party was of the opinion that the bank operated for the benefit of certain Eastern and foreign shareholders, to the detriment of the agricultural and mercantile classes of the South and West. The bank furthermore was sufficiently powerful to be able to manipulate currency supplies and credit on a nationwide basis. Jackson was determined to break the power of the bank, and in doing so, utilized many arguments formulated by Taney.

The battle for the renewal of the bank's charter pitted Jackson against the Congress. The President's veto of the renewed charter in 1832 led to eventual congressional retaliation on June 24, 1834. Taney, who had served as secretary of the treasury since the previous September without congressional approval, was rejected one day after Jackson formally submitted his nomination. While the attempt of the bank to have its charter renewed was rebuffed, it continued to operate under a Pennsylvania charter, manipulating credit and currency supplies to its advantage, and in Jacksonian eyes, precipitating the Panic of 1837.

Chief Justice of the U.S. Supreme Court

From 1834 to 1836 Taney was without a government appointment. He had given up his private law practice in Frederick and Baltimore, and now found himself in severe financial straits. An attempt by Jackson to place him on the Supreme Court was rejected by the Senate in 1835. One year later, on March 15, with the political complexion of the Congress somewhat changed, Taney was approved to succeed John Marshall as chief justice.

During the next twenty-eight years, Taney would participate in some three hundred decisions. He would help to define the relationship between individual and communal property rights, the legal rights of corporations, and federal versus state control of commerce. He was wary of federal attempts to interfere in the internal workings of the states beyond the powers specifically enumerated in the Constitution.

While much of Taney's judicial thinking was heavily criticized at the time, most of it has been recognized in hindsight as a proper application of constitutional law. One notable exception, the "Dred Scott Decision" of 1857, has never enjoyed this sort of rehabilitation.

The slave, Dred Scott, a resident of Missouri, had accompanied his master, Dr. John Emerson, to military outposts in Illinois and in the northern portion of the Louisiana Purchase commencing in 1834. At Fort Snelling he met and married a slave woman, Harriet, after Dr. Emerson purchased her from another army officer. A daughter was born to the couple at the fort, and another after their return to Missouri. Dred Scott alleged that his residence on "free soil" had rendered him free.

An initial lawsuit brought in the courts of Missouri had terminated with a decision by the state supreme court in 1852. Whatever his condition had been while in a free state or territory, his willing return to Missouri was deemed to have placed him under Missouri statutes. Dred Scott and his family were still to be regarded as slaves.

The now-widowed Mrs. Emerson married a Massachusetts abolitionist named Dr. C. C. Chaffee who determined to make a test case of the whole matter. Transferring ownership of Dred Scott to Mrs. Chaffee's brother-in-law, a resident of New York State, in the latter part of 1853, Chaffee arranged for suit to be brought in federal court, an avenue open to litigants who resided in different states. The court subsequently ruled that Dred Scott was not a citizen by virtue of his status as a slave, and therefore had no ability to bring suit before the court.

The matter was referred to the U.S. Supreme Court in December of 1854. A backlog in work resulted in the suit not being heard until February of 1856. Differences of opinion among the justices resulted in the case being reargued after the presidential elections of that year, this in spite of politicians on both sides who wished to use the Court's decision as ammunition in the campaign.

The decision, authored by Taney, was made public on March 6, 1857. Dred Scott was held to have no standing as a citizen based on the presumed fact that African slaves and their descendants were not regarded as citizens at the time the U.S. Constitution was written. The Missouri

Compromise of 1820, which forbade slavery in the northern portion of the Louisiana Purchase, was held to be an unconstitutional extension of congressional power into the internal affairs of the states and territories. Taney furthermore reiterated the opinion of the lower court, that whatever Dred Scott's status outside Missouri, his return to the state had reaffirmed his status as a slave and deprived him of the ability to sue in federal court. Reaction was swift to follow, with Southern papers praising Taney's wisdom, and abolitionist and Republican papers pointing to inaccurate historical assertions on which the decision rested.

Taney was destined to cross swords with the Lincoln administration over the constitutionality of various war measures. Taney doubted the legality of Lincoln's suspension of the writ of habeas corpus. In other pronouncements, Taney disputed the constitutionality of paper currency, military conscription, and regulation of intrastate commerce by the federal government.

In 1854 Taney commenced the composition of his memoirs. The following year, on September 29, his wife succumbed to yellow fever at the family's summer retreat at Old Point Comfort, near Norfolk, Virginia. Taney's own physical constitution deteriorated markedly in his later years. After his death in Washington on October 12, 1864, the body of the chief justice was buried in St. John's Cemetery in Frederick, next to the grave of his mother.

See also SLAVERY AND AMERICAN CATHOLICS.

Smith, Charles W., Jr. *Roger B. Taney: Jacksonian Jurist.* Chapel Hill: University of North Carolina Press, 1936.

Swisher, Carl Brent. *Roger B. Taney.* New York: Macmillan, 1935.

Tyler, Samuel. *Memoir of Roger Brooke Taney, LL.D.* Baltimore: John Murphy & Co., 1872.

ALBERT H. LEDOUX

Related Document

DRED SCOTT V. SANDFORD
19 Howard, 393
1857

Error to the U.S. circuit court for the district of Missouri. In 1834 Dred Scott, a negro slave, was taken by his master from Missouri, a slave state, to Illinois, a free state, and hence to Wisconsin Territory where slavery was forbidden by the Missouri Compromise of 1820. Subsequently Scott was brought back to Missouri, and in 1846 he began suit to obtain his freedom, on the ground that he had become free when taken into free territory. The case was eventually brought on appeal to the Supreme Court. Three major questions were involved: whether Scott was a citizen of the State of Missouri, so as to give the Federal courts jurisdiction; whether he had been set free by his sojourn in the free state of Illinois; whether he had been set free by his sojourn in the free Territory of Wisconsin, e.g., whether the Missouri Compromise was constitutional. The Court ruled that Scott was not a citizen of the United States or of the State of Missouri and therefore not competent to sue in the Federal courts. Having thus refused jurisdiction, the court went on to pass on the other questions presented, all of the judges giving separate opinions. Of the dissenting opinions, that by Justice Curtis dealt most elaborately with the question of citizenship.

This case, probably the most famous in the history of the Court, has been the subject of an extensive literature. See the discussion of the case and bibliographical notes in Warren, *Supreme Court,* Vol. II, ch. xxvi; C. B. Swisher, *R. B. Taney;* Hodder, "Some Phases of the Dred Scott Case," *Miss. Valley Hist. Rev.* Vol. XVI; Corwin, "Dred Scott Decision in the Light of Contemporary Legal Doctrines," A. H. R., Vol. XVII; Cattarall, "Some Antecedents of the Dred Scott Case," A. H. R., Vol. XXX; Cohn, "Dred Scott Decision in the Light of Later Events," 46 Am. Law Rev. 548.

TANEY, C. J. . . . There are two leading questions presented by the record:

1. Had the Circuit Court of the United States jurisdiction to hear and determine the case between these parties? And,

2. If it had jurisdiction, is the judgment it has given erroneous or not?

The plaintiff in error, who was also the plaintiff in the court below, was, with his wife and children, held as slaves by the defendant, in the State of Missouri, and he brought this action in the Circuit Court of the United States for that district, to assert the title of himself and his family to freedom.

The declaration is . . . that he and the defendant are citizens of different States; that is, that he is a citizen of Missouri, and the defendant a citizen of New York.

The defendant pleaded in abatement to the jurisdiction of the court, that the plaintiff was not a citizen of the State of Missouri, as alleged in his declaration, being a negro of African descent whose ancestors were of pure African blood, and who were brought into this country and sold as slaves.

To this plea the plaintiff demurred, and the defendant joined in demurrer. . . .

Before we speak of the pleas in bar, it will be proper to dispose of the questions which have arisen on the plea in abatement.

That plea denies the right of the plaintiff to sue in a court of the United States, for the reasons therein stated.

If the question raised by it is legally before us, and the court should be of opinion that the facts stated in it disqualify the plaintiff from becoming a citizen, in the sense in which that word is used in the Constitution of the United States, then the judgment of the Circuit Court is erroneous, and must be reversed. . . .

The question to be decided is, whether the facts stated in the plea are sufficient to show that the plaintiff is not entitled to sue as a citizen in a court of the United States.

This is certainly a very serious question, and one that now for the first time has been brought for decision before this court. But it is brought here by those who have a right to bring it, and it is our duty to meet it and decide it.

The question is simply this: Can a negro, whose ancestors were imported into this country, and sold as slaves, become a member of the political community formed and brought into existence by the Constitution of the United States, and as such become entitled to all the rights, and privileges, and immunities, guarantied by that instrument to the citizen? One of which rights is the privilege of suing in a court of the United States in the cases specified in the Constitution.

It will be observed, that the plea applies to that class of persons only whose ancestors were negroes of the African race, and imported into this country, and sold and held as slaves. The only matter in issue before the court, therefore, is, whether the descendants of such slaves, when they shall be emancipated, or who are born of parents who had become free before their birth, are citizens of a State, in the sense in which the word citizen is used in the Constitution of the United States. And this being the only matter in dispute on the pleadings, the court must be understood as speaking in this opinion of that class only, that is of persons who are the descendants of Africans who were imported into this country and sold as slaves. . . .

We proceed to examine the case as presented by the pleadings.

The words "people of the United States" and "citizens" are synonymous terms, and mean the same thing. They both describe the political body who, according to our republican institutions, form the sovereignty, and who hold the power and conduct the government through their representatives. They are what we familiarly call the "sovereign people," and every citizen is one of this people, and a constituent member of this sovereignty. The question before us is, whether the class of persons described in the plea in abatement compose a portion of this people, and are constituent members of this sovereignty? We think they are not, and that they are not included, and were not intended to be included, under the word "citizens" in the Constitution, and can, therefore, claim none of the rights and privileges which that instrument provides for and secures to citizens of the United States. On the contrary, they were at that time considered as a subordinate and inferior class of beings, who had been subjugated by the dominant race, and whether emancipated or not, yet remained subject to their authority, and had no rights or privileges but such as those who held the power and the government might choose to grant them. . . .

In discussing this question, we must not confound the rights of citizenship which a state may confer within its own limits, and the rights of citizenship as a member of the Union. It does not by any means follow, because he has all the rights and privileges of a citizen of a State, that he must be a citizen of the United States. He may have all of the rights and privileges of the citizen of a State, and yet not be entitled to the rights and privileges of a citizen in any other State. For, previous to the adoption of the Constitution of the United States, every State had the undoubted right to confer on whomsoever it pleased the character of a citizen, and to endow him with all its rights. But this character, of course, was confined to the boundaries of the State, and gave him no rights or privileges in other States beyond those secured to him by the laws of nations and the comity of States. Nor have the several States surrendered the power of conferring these rights and privileges by adopting the Constitution of the United States. Each State may still confer them upon an alien, or any one it thinks proper, or upon any class or description of persons; yet he would not be a citizen in the sense in which that word is used in the Constitution of the United States, nor entitled to sue as such in one of its courts, nor to the privileges and immunities of a citizen in the other States. The rights which he would acquire would be restricted to the State which gave them. . . .

It is very clear, therefore, that no State can, by any Act or law of its own, passed since the adoption of the Constitution, introduce a new member into the political community created by the Constitution of the United States. It cannot make him a member of this community by making him a member of its own. And for the same reason it cannot introduce any person, or description of persons, who were not intended to be embraced in this new political family, which the Constitution brought into existence, but were intended to be excluded from it.

The question then arises, whether the provisions of the Constitution, in relation to the personal rights and privileges to which the citizen of a State should be entitled, embraced the negro African race, at that time in this country, or who might afterwards be imported, who had then or should afterwards be made free in any State; and to put it in the power of a single State to make him a citizen of the United States, and endue him with the full rights of citizenship in every other State without their consent. Does the Constitution of the United States act upon him whenever he shall be made free under the laws of a State, and raised there to the rank of a citizen, and immediately clothe him with all the privileges of a citizen in every other State, and in its own courts?

The court think the affirmative of these propositions cannot be maintained. And if it cannot, the plaintiff in error could not be a citizen of the State of Missouri, within the meaning of the Constitution of the United States, and, consequently, was not entitled to sue in its courts.

It is true, every person, and every class and description of persons, who were at the time of the adoption of the Constitution recognized as citizens in the several States, became also citizens of this new political body; but none other; it was formed by them, and for them and their posterity, but for no one else. And the personal rights and privileges guarantied to citizens of this new sovereignty were intended to embrace those only who were then members of the several state communities, or who should afterwards, by birthright or otherwise, become members, according to the provisions of the Constitution and the principles on which it was founded. . . .

It becomes necessary, therefore, to determine who were citizens of the several States when the Constitution was adopted. And in order to do this, we must recur to the governments and institutions of the thirteen Colonies, when they separated from Great Britain and formed new sovereignties. . . . We must inquire who, at that time, were recognized as the people or citizens of a State. . . .

In the opinion of the court, the legislation and histories of the times, and the language used in the Declaration of Independence, show, that neither the class of persons who had been imported as slaves, nor their descendants, whether they had become free or not, were then acknowledged as a part of the people, nor intended to be included in the general words used in that memorable instrument.

It is difficult at this day to realize the state of public opinion in relation to that unfortunate race, which prevailed in the civilized and enlightened portions of the world at the time of the Declaration of Independence, and when the Constitution of the United States was framed and adopted. . . .

They had for more than a century before been regarded as beings of an inferior order; and altogether unfit to associate with the white race, either in social or political relations; and so far inferior that they had no rights which the white man was bound to respect; and that the negro might justly and lawfully be reduced to slavery for his benefit. . . . This opinion was at that time fixed and universal in the civilized portion of the white race. It was regarded as an axiom in morals as well as in politics, which no one thought of disputing, or supposed to be open to dispute; and men in every grade and position in society daily and habitually acted upon it in their private pursuits, as well as in matters of public concern, without doubting for a moment the correctness of this opinion. . . .

The legislation of the different Colonies furnishes positive and undisputable proof of this fact. . . .

The language of the Declaration of Independence is equally conclusive. . . .

This state of public opinion had undergone no change when the Constitution was adopted, as is equally evident from its provisions and language. . . .

But there are two clauses in the Constitution which point directly and specifically to the negro race as a separate class of persons, and show clearly that they were not regarded as a portion of the people or citizens of the Government then formed.

One of these clauses reserves to each of the thirteen States the right to import slaves until the year 1808, if he thinks it proper. And the importation which it thus sanctions was unquestionably of persons of the race of which we are speaking, as the traffic in slaves in the United States had always been confined to them. And by the other provision the States pledge themselves to each other to maintain the right of property of the master, by delivering up to him any slave who may have escaped from his service, and be found within their respective territories. . . . And these two provisions show, conclusively, that neither the description of persons therein referred to, nor their descendants, were embraced in any of the other provisions of the Constitution; for certainly these two clauses were not intended to confer on them or their posterity the blessings of liberty, or any of the personal rights so carefully provided for the citizen. . . .

Indeed, when we look to the condition of this race in the several States at the time, it is impossible to believe that these rights and privileges were intended to be extended to them. . . .

The legislation of the States therefore shows, in a manner not to be mistaken, the inferior and subject condition of that race at the time the Constitution was adopted, and long afterwards, throughout the thirteen States by which that instrument was framed; and it is hardly consistent with the respect due to these States, to suppose that they regarded at that time, as fellow-citizens and members of the sovereignty, a class of beings whom they had thus stigmatized; . . . More especially, it cannot be believed that the large slave-holding States regarded them as included in the word "citizens," or would have consented to a constitution which might compel them to receive them in that character from another State. For if they were so received, and entitled to the privileges and immunities of citizens, it would exempt them from the operation of the special laws and from the police regulations which they considered to be necessary for their own safety. . . . And all of this would be done in the face of the subject race of the same color, both free and slaves, inevitably producing discontent and insubordination among them, and endangering the peace and safety of the State. . . .

But it is said that a person may be a citizen, and entitled to that character, although he does not possess all the rights which may belong to other citizens; as, for example, the right to vote, or to hold particular offices; and that yet, when he goes into another State, he is entitled to be recognized there as a citizen, although the State may measure his rights by the rights which it allows to persons of a like character or class, resident in the State, and refuse to him the full rights of citizenship.

This argument overlooks the language of the provision in the Constitution of which we are speaking.

Undoubtedly, a person may be a citizen, that is, a member of the community who form the sovereignty, although he exercises no share of the political power, and is incapacitated from holding particular offices. . . .

So, too, a person may be entitled to vote by the law of the State, who is not a citizen even of the State itself. And in some of the States of the Union foreigners not naturalized are allowed to vote. And the State may give the right to free negroes and mulattoes, but that does not make them citizens of the State, and still less of the United States. And the provision in the Constitution giving privileges and immunities in other States, does not apply to them.

Neither does it apply to a person who, being the citizen of a State, migrates to another State. For then he becomes subject to the laws of the State in which he lives, and he is no longer a citizen of the State from which he removed. And the State in which he resides may then, unquestionably, determine his *status* or condition, and place him among the class of persons who are not recognized as citizens, but belong to an inferior and subject race; and may deny him the privileges and immunities enjoyed by its citizens. . . .

. . . But if he ranks as a citizen of the State to which he belongs, within the meaning of the Constitution of the United States, then, whenever he goes into another State, the Constitution clothes him, as to the rights of person, with all the privileges and immunities which belong to citizens of the State. And if persons of the African race are citizens of a state, and of the United States, they would be entitled to all of these privileges and immunities in every State, and the State could not restrict them, for they would hold these privileges and immunities, under the paramount authority of the Federal Government, and its courts would be bound to maintain and enforce them, the Constitution and laws of the State to the contrary notwithstanding. . . .

And upon a full and careful consideration of the subject, the court is of opinion that, upon the facts stated in the plea in abatement, Dred Scott was not a citizen of Missouri within the meaning of the Constitution of the United States, and not entitled as such to sue in its courts; and, consequently, that the Circuit Court had no jurisdiction of the case, and that the judgment on the plea in abatement is erroneous. . . .

We proceed, therefore, to inquire whether the facts relied on by the plaintiff entitled him to his freedom. . . .

In considering this part of the controversy, two questions arise: 1st. Was he, together with his family, free in Missouri by reason of the stay in the territory of the United States hereinbefore mentioned? And 2d, If they were not, is Scott himself free by reason of his removal to Rock Island, in the State of Illinois, as stated in the above admissions?

We proceed to examine the first question.

The Act of Congress, upon which the plaintiff relies, declares that slavery and involuntary servitude, except as a punishment for crime, shall be forever prohibited in all that part of the territory ceded by France, under the name of Louisiana, which lies north of thirty-six degrees thirty minutes north latitude, and not included within the limits of Missouri. And the difficulty which meets us at the threshold of this part of the inquiry is, whether Congress was authorized to pass this law under any of the powers granted to it by the Constitution; for if the authority is not given by that instrument, it is the duty of this court to declare it void and inoperative, and incapable of conferring freedom upon any one who is held as a slave under the laws of any one of the States.

The counsel for the plaintiff has laid much stress upon that article in the Constitution which confers on Congress the power "to dispose of and make all needful rules and regulations respecting the territory or other property belonging to the United States;" but, in the judgment of the court, that provision has no bearing on the present controversy, and the power there given, whatever it may be, is confined, and was intended to be confined, to the territory which at that time belonged to, or was claimed by, the United States, and was within their boundaries as settled by the treaty with Great Britain, and can have no influence upon a territory afterwards acquired from a foreign Government. It was a special provision for a known and particular territory, and to meet a present emergency, and nothing more. . . .

If this clause is construed to extend to territory acquired by the present Government from a foreign nation, outside of the limits of any charter from the British Government to a colony, it would be difficult to say, why it was deemed necessary to give the Government the power to sell any vacant lands belonging to the sovereignty which might be found within it; and if this was necessary, why the grant of this power should precede the power to legislate over it and establish a Government there; and still more difficult to say, why it was deemed necessary so specially and particularly to grant the power to make needful rules and regulations in relation to any personal or movable property it might acquire there. For the words, *other property* necessarily, by every known rule of interpretation, must mean property of a different description from territory or land. And the difficulty would perhaps be insurmountable in endeavoring to account for the last member of the sentence, which provides that "nothing in this Constitution shall be so construed as to prejudice any claims of the United States or any particular State," or to say how any particular State could have claims in or to a territory ceded by a foreign Government, or to account for associating this provision with the preceding provisions of the clause, with which it would appear to have no connection. . . .

But the power of Congress over the person or property of a citizen can never be a mere discretionary power under our Constitution and form of Government. The powers of the Government and the rights and privileges of the citizen are regulated and plainly defined by the Constitution itself. And when the Territory becomes a part of the United States, the Federal Government enters into possession in the character impressed upon it by those who created it. It enters upon it with its powers over the citizen strictly defined, and limited by the Constitution, from which it derives its own existence, and by virtue of which alone it continues to exist and act as a Government and sovereignty. It has no power of any kind beyond it; and it cannot, when it enters a Territory of the United States, put off its character, and assume discretionary or despotic powers which the Constitution has denied to it. It cannot create for itself a new character separated from the citizens of the United States, and the duties it owes them under the provisions of the Constitution. The Territory being a part of the United States, the Government and the citizen both enter it under the authority of the Constitution, with their respective rights defined and marked out; and the Federal Government can exercise no power over his person or property, beyond what that instrument confers, nor lawfully deny any right which it has reserved. . . .

The rights of private property have been guarded with equal care. Thus the rights of property are united with the rights of person, and placed on the same ground by the fifth amendment to the Constitution. . . . An Act of Congress which deprives a person of the United States of his liberty or property merely because he came himself or brought his property into a particular Territory of the United States, and who had committed no offense against the laws, could hardly be dignified with the name of due process of law. . . .

And this prohibition is not confined to the States, but the words are general, and extend to the whole territory over which the Constitution gives it power to legislate, including those portions of it remaining under territorial government, as well as that covered by States. It is a total absence of power everywhere within the dominion of the United States, and places the citizens of a territory, so far as these rights are concerned, on the same footing with citizens of the States, and guards them as firmly and plainly against any inroads which the general government might attempt, under the plea of implied or incidental powers. And if Congress itself cannot do this—if it is beyond the powers conferred on the Federal Government—it will be admitted, we presume, that it could not authorize a territorial government to exercise them. It could confer no power on an local government, established by its authority, to violate the provisions of the Constitution.

It seems, however, to be supposed, that there is a difference between property in a slave and other property, and that different rules may be applied to it in expounding the Constitution of the United States. And the laws and usages of nations, and the writings of eminent jurists

upon the relation of master and slave and their mutual rights and duties, and the powers which governments may exercise over it, have been dwelt upon in the argument.

But . . . if the Constitution recognizes the right of property of the master in a slave, and makes no distinction between that description of property and other property owned by a citizen, no tribunal, acting under the authority of the United States, whether it be legislative, executive, or judicial, has a right to draw such a distinction, or deny to it the benefit of the provisions and guarantees which have been provided for the protection of private property against the encroachments of the Government.

Now . . . the right of property in a slave is distinctly and expressly affirmed in the Constitution. The right to traffic in it, like an ordinary article of merchandise and property, was guaranteed to the citizens of the United States, in every State that might desire it, for twenty years. And the Government in express terms is pledged to protect it in all future time, if the slave escapes from his owner. . . . And no word can be found in the Constitution which gives Congress a greater power over slave property, or which entitles property of that kind to less protection than property of any other description. The only power conferred is the power coupled with the duty of guarding and protecting the owner in his rights.

Upon these considerations, it is the opinion of the court that the Act of Congress which prohibited a citizen from holding and owning property of this kind in the territory of the United States north of the line therein mentioned, is not warranted by the Constitution, and is therefore void; and that neither Dred Scott himself, nor any of his family, were made free by being carried into this territory; even if they had been carried there by the owner, with the intention of becoming a permanent resident. . . .

Upon the whole, therefore, it is the judgment of this court, that it appears by the record before us that the plaintiff in error is not a citizen of Missouri, in the sense in which that word is used in the Constitution; and that the Circuit Court of the United States, for that reason, had no jurisdiction in the case, and could give no judgment in it.

Its judgment for the defendant must, consequently, be reversed, and a mandate issued directing the suit to be dismissed for want of jurisdiction.

WAYNE, J., NELSON, J., GRIER, J., DANIEL, J., CAMPBELL, J., AND CATRON, J., filed separate concurring opinions. MCLEAN, J. and CURTIS, J. dissented.

(*Source:* Henry Steele Commager. *Documents of American History.* 9th ed. Englewood Cliffs, N.J.: Prentice-Hall, 1973. 1:339–45.)

TARPEY, ELIZABETH H. (1892–1979)

Religious superior. Elizabeth H. Tarpey was born on January 4, 1892, in Philadelphia, Pennsylvania, to an Irish mother and an English father and educated in Catholic elementary and high schools. After completing school, she was employed as a bookkeeper and records supervisor, and later placed in charge of the Special Services Department at Remington Arms, Inc.

Interested in religious life, Tarpey searched for an order that might draw her interest. In 1917 she was deeply moved by a talk about Maryknoll and immediately initiated inquiries. Through Maryknoll's magazine, *The Field Afar,* she came to know about the women auxiliaries at Maryknoll, known as "Teresians." Although she hoped to join them in 1918, due to a flu epidemic at Maryknoll, New York, their foundress, Mary Josephine Rogers, advised her to wait. Tarpey visited Maryknoll for the first time on May 30, 1919, and was interviewed by the cofounder, James Anthony Walsh. She entered the congregation on December 7, 1919, and was given the name of Sr. Mary Columba at profession on August 5, 1921.

Mary Columba's leadership and administrative gifts were at once recognized by Rogers. Their mutual appreciation for each other's gifts, led to a lifelong friendship between these two pioneer women of the Maryknoll Sisters. Tarpey was named to the first general council in 1921; and while Rogers was away on visitation to the missions, took her place, a leadership role she was to have almost all of her religious life.

Rogers confided in Walsh her sense that either Mary Columba Tarpey or Mary Paul McKenna would succeed her in leadership of the congregation. Therefore, though Tarpey was Walsh's secretary at the time, the foundress wished her to have mission experience. In 1927 Tarpey was missioned to the Philippines where she served as administrator of St. Paul's Hospital in Manila. Returning for the 1931 general chapter, she was again elected to the general council, and in 1936 visited the missions on behalf of Rogers. She was reelected to the general council in 1937, and elected to succeed the foundress as mother general in 1947.

It was Tarpey who met the challenges of the postwar and pre-Vatican II era at Maryknoll. Global realities were shifting as China was closed to foreign missioners. Many other external and internal factors coalesced at this critical time in the congregation's history. New opportunities for missionary presence and service throughout the world were on the horizon. Concurrently, the great postwar surge of vocations to the religious life saw Maryknoll receive hundreds of women into the congregation. Around the world, requests for personnel multiplied rapidly, placing heavy demands on the need to prepare missioners to respond.

Mother Columba had talents for organization and planning, indispensable at this time of rapid expansion. She oversaw the opening of large novitiates in Missouri and Massachusetts; initiated missions in East Africa, Micronesia, Chile, Peru, Mexico, Guatemala, and Taiwan; and fostered structures and policies essential to guide a congregation totally dedicated to the global mission of the Church. In 1955 Tarpey was featured on the cover of *Time* magazine. In extensive coverage of the "remarkable 20th century boom in monastic orders," this article commented on the appropriateness of Columba's title—"mother general"—as the leader of the "largest, most active Roman Catholic missionary order" and a symbol of this growth in the U.S.A. She died in Ossining, New York, on August 27, 1979.

See also MARYKNOLL.

Lyons, Jean Marie. *Maryknoll's First Lady.* New York: Dodd Mead, 1964.
Time Magazine 65 (April 11, 1957).

CAMILLA KENNEDY, M.M.

TEKAKWITHA, KATERI (1656–80)

The first Native American to be beatified. Kateri was the daughter of Kahenta (Flower of the Prairie), a baptized Algonquin Native American taken from Canada to New York during an Iroquois raid who became the wife of Kenhoronkwa (Beloved), a Mohawk chief, who conferred upon her all privileges belonging to a full member of the tribe. While living in the village of Ossernenon (now Auriesville, New York), the couple had a daughter, Kateri Tekakwitha, and a son who received the name Otsikehta.

Tekakwitha was only four years old when death took her parents and brother through a smallpox epidemic. Although she survived, Tekakwitha was left with a permanently disfigured face and impaired vision. The orphaned girl and another child were adopted by her uncle, Onsigongo, and two aunts. Tekakwitha lived a secluded life, doing household chores and remaining indoors most of the time because of her inability to tolerate bright sunlight.

In order to punish the Mohawks for their cruel attacks, the French invaded the Mohawk territory in 1666. To avoid further recrimination, the Mohawks agreed to maintain peace. They begged the French to send them the "Black Robes" (Jesuits) as missionaries. The first missionaries arrived, were assigned to live in the same dwelling as Tekakwitha's family, and after three days left to visit other Mohawk settlements without any noticeable effect on Tekakwitha.

Upon the arrival of other missionaries, many Mohawks were converted to Catholicism and moved from the village to a mission with other Christians. When Tekakwitha made known her desire for baptism, Onsigongo voiced his opposition, but finally consented with the stipulation that she would remain in the village afterwards.

Although a two-year period of catechumenate instruction was the rule, an exception was made for Tekakwitha because of her reputation of integrity. With great rejoicing among her people, Tekakwitha was baptized on Easter

Sunday, April 5, 1676, and given the name Catherine (in Iroquois, Kateri).

The rejoicing of her tribe soon turned to rancor. Because Kateri attempted to keep Sunday holy by not working, people judged her as lazy. Others ridiculed her strong devotion to Mary and the rosary. Kateri's celibate lifestyle produced intense hostility: her aunts attempted to trick her into marrying a young warrior; her uncle urged others to molest her; one aunt tried to destroy her reputation by insisting there was an incestuous relationship between Kateri and her uncle; a young man threatened to kill her with a tomahawk. Teasing, insults, mockery, and harsh treatment were common in her daily life. Throughout such adversity, Kateri remained cheerful and kind toward everyone.

In 1677 the catechist Louis Garonhiague (Hot Ashes), arrived at the village, captivating everyone with the story of his conversion and the glories of life at the mission, so much so that Kateri resolved to leave her village. While Onsigongo was at Ft. Orange on business, Kateri's brother-in-law and two others facilitated her escape. Onsigongo learned what happened, returned to the village, loaded his gun, and left in pursuit of his niece. On account of the cleverness of Kateri's three guides, Onsigongo noticed only a hunter and another person smoking a pipe. Failing to discover Kateri, he gave up the chase and returned home.

After Kateri arrived at the mission in the autumn of 1677, she resided with her adopted sister and brother-in-law, and a friend of her mother named Anastasia, who was one of the first Native American Iroquois to have been baptized. Under the guidance of Anastasia and with direction from a Jesuit missionary, her spiritual life continued to develop. That Christmas, over eighteen months after her baptism, Kateri made her First Communion.

Everyone acquainted with Kateri was aware of her goodness and thought her deserving of membership in the Confraternity of the Holy Family, an organization reserved for outstanding Catholics. Consequently, Kateri was received into the Confraternity on Easter Sunday and received Communion for the second time in her life.

Prayer became increasingly important to Kateri. Early writings disclose that at 4:00 A.M. each morning, no matter the weather, Kateri was at the church and remained several hours in prayer.

Although she lived an ordinary life, Kateri wanted to dedicate herself to God. Finally, she was permitted to make a vow of virginity on March 25, 1679. A deep friendship developed between Kateri and the widowed Marie Therese Tegaiaguenta. They became spiritual companions, encouraged one another to prayer and penance, and conversed about God and spiritual matters.

Kateri became seriously ill during Holy Week of 1680. It was customary for persons who desired to receive viaticum to be brought to church; however, because of Kateri's holiness, viaticum was brought to her. Kateri Tekakwitha died on Wednesday, April 17, 1680, at the age of 24. Those who saw her after death described a beautiful change in her features in that her facial disfigurement disappeared entirely. She was beatified by Pope John Paul II in 1980 and has the distinction of being the first Native American beatified by the Catholic Church.

As Tekakwitha, her name had been interpreted as "That which or who puts things in order" or "One who advances and who casts something before her." As Kateri, she became known as a lily among thorns, the Lily of the Mohawks, and "The Most Beautiful Flower that ever bloomed for the Indians."

See also NATIVE AMERICANS AND THE CATHOLIC CHURCH.

Coffey, Thomas J., S.J. *Kateri Tekakwitha.* Auriesville, N.Y.: Tekakwitha League, 1994.
Lecompte, Edward. *Glory of the Mohawks.* Trans. Florence Ralston Werum. Milwaukee: Bruce Publishing Co., 1944.
Lodi, Enzo. *Saints of the Roman Calender.* Trans. Jordan Aumann, O.P. New York: Alba House, 1992.

JUDITH DAVIES, O.S.F.

TEMPERANCE MOVEMENT AND AMERICAN CATHOLICS

"Demon rum" was the symbol of an ongoing problem in American Catholic culture during the nineteenth century. Millions of immigrant Catholics frequented saloons and used alcoholic drink as an escape from the troubles of the day. Some were moderate in their consumption, but far too many Catholics spent too much time in these taverns, which led to drunkenness, poverty, and misery for their families.

In response, the Catholic bishops established diocesan temperance societies. First endorsed by the bishops in council at Baltimore in 1840, these societies exerted social pressure on the laity to give up alcoholic drinks and the saloon and gave them moral support in their effort. The movement was invigorated by an 1849 visit to the United States from the Irish priest Theobald Mathew. Known as the "apostle of temperance," Mathew conducted a crusade across the country and many Catholics pledged to abstain from all alcoholic drinks after hearing Mathew preach. But after Mathew's return to Ireland, the movement fell into decline.

The Catholic Total Abstinence Union

A small but aggressive minority of Catholics led a renewed temperance effort in the 1870s. Arguing that abstinence from liquor and other strong drink was a religious duty for Catholics, these temperance advocates reorganized the diocesan and state societies and had a significant impact on the consumption of liquor, especially in urban areas. The movement was given a boost with the establishment of the Catholic Total Abstinence Union in 1872, a national confederation of the diocesan societies.

The union used "moral suasion" as its principal tool and worked to establish "young men's societies" as social alternatives to the saloon. In this effort, the CTAU distributed millions of tracts and booklets and organized countless religious missions. The organization received substantial support from a number of bishops, particularly James Roosevelt Bayley of Newark, John J. Keane of Richmond, and John Ireland of St. Paul.

The Bishops Take Up the Cause

As was the case with many social causes, Ireland was tireless in his temperance work. Although he seemed to favor prohibition, he never formally supported that position. Rather, he advocated the tight control of liquor through license and local option. Above all, Ireland believed that liquor was a hindrance to Catholic social progress in America as well as in St. Paul, and nothing should stand in the way of that progress.

Ireland's support and that of other bishops at the Third Plenary Council Baltimore in 1884 contributed to the success of the CTAU. By the mid-1890s, the Union had over 80,000 members, all deeply committed to the cause of abstinence if not prohibition. Yet in spite of this success, the CTAU could not carry its influence into the next century. Membership declined in the years after 1900 almost as quickly as it had grown in the 1890s.

But the decline of the CTAU did not end the Catholic temperance movement. Religious missions and revivals continued to be popular in urban parishes in the new century. A central feature of these missions was the condemnation of any Catholic father who spent his money on "a glass of poison . . . filled with the blood of your starving wife and children." Liquor brought poverty and destroyed the family and the saloonkeeper was depicted as the "doorkeeper of hell." It was a powerful message that scared many Catholic laymen into abstinence.

The Saloon as a Social Institution

Yet, in spite of these efforts, many Catholics continued to resist the call of the bishops to abstain from liquor. Try as they might, Catholic temperance advocates failed to provide an adequate substitute for the saloon as a social club, bank, employment office, and general respite from the workday world. Just as important, alcoholic drinks—particularly beer—was ingrained in the ethnic culture of many Catholics. Germans, for example, saw nothing wrong with an occasional glass of beer and many perceived the temperance campaign as an attack on their ethnic culture.

Catholics also were alienated by the Protestant fervor of the Anti-Saloon League, the Women's Christian Temperance Union, and other national organizations that aggressively advocated the total prohibition of alcoholic drink. Many Catholic leaders, including the revered Cardinal James Gibbons of Baltimore, regarded a federal prohibition law as a "national catastrophe." With the passage of the Eighteenth Amendment in January 1920, the Catholic temperance movement gradually faded away.

See also PROHIBITION AND CATHOLICS.

Abell, Aaron I. *American Catholicism and Social Action: A Search for Social Justice.* University of Notre Dame Press, 1963.
Bland, Joan. *Hibernian Crusade: The Story of the Catholic Total Abstinence Union of America.* Washington, D.C.: The Catholic University of America Press, 1951.
Dolan, Jay P. *Catholic Revivalism: The American Experience, 1830–1900.* University of Notre Dame Press, 1978.

TIMOTHY WALCH

TENNESSEE, CATHOLIC CHURCH IN

The Catholic Church in Tennessee was created out of a geographical quandary. Its parent diocese, Bardstown, Kentucky (1808), ranged from Michigan almost to the Gulf Coast. Early missionaries, like Fr. Stephen Badin, the first priest to be ordained in the United States, traversed this vast expanse as far south as Tennessee from where, he wrote to Archbishop John Carroll in 1810, "I found very few Catholics." Indeed, there were very few, and there were not many more when, as part of an effort to lighten the burden of Bardstown, the first bishop of Tennessee was appointed in 1837.

Bishop Richard Miles, O.P.

Richard Pius Miles, O.P., a Kentuckian by birth and education, who was also the only priest in the new diocese of Nashville. As bishop and priest rolled into one, he was mainly a missionary on horseback—his consecration gift from Bardstown was a horse. He traveled the breadth of his long horizontal state to minister to its tiny scattered Catholic population. But growth and expansion were in the very air of the trans-Appalachian West. Within ten years Miles attracted clergy, opened schools, set up a central administration, and built a beautiful cathedral halfway up Capitol Hill in Nashville.

What counted most in the early history of the Church was the coming of the railroads. These were, in Miles' time, a-building everywhere in Tennessee, bringing with them hundreds of mostly Irish immigrant workmen. Many of these Irish workers settled permanently in or near the towns and cities where they worked. These Irish were, of course, Catholic to the bone. They welcomed Miles with open arms and asked for more like him. Like practically all the missionary bishops, Miles worked and prayed hardest for a good native clergy. These came slowly, haltingly, almost the final fruit of a settled and thriving Church. The Irish, too few in number to create real ghettos, took kindly to the Southern culture they found in Tennessee. They acquired a flavor of their own, evidenced in the extraordinary number of bishops they contributed to the American Church, among them John P. Farrelly of Cleveland and Samuel Stritch, eventually the cardinal archbishop of Chicago.

Even so, the Catholic population of the state was always small, never more than 1.5–2 percent. They were mostly concentrated in cities. Despite the vigorous labors of all the nine bishops of the whole state, plus the important help of the Catholic Church Extension Society of America, rural Tennessee remained mostly non-Catholic. The huge immigration of Catholics from Europe in the second half of the nineteenth century and the first quarter of the twentieth, left most of the South untouched. The few efforts at plantation mostly fizzled; only two worked, the Germans at Lawrenceburg and the Irish at McEwen. In the cities, especially under the long episcopate (1893–1923) of the fifth bishop, Thomas S. Byrne, Catholicism became stable and well organized. Continued railroad building and dock construction in Memphis brought more Irish and new Italians into Memphis especially, but waves of new Catholics into the state did not come until the post-World-War-II period. These vivified the state's Catholic population, and was reflected in the creation of two new dioceses, Memphis in 1970 and Knoxville in 1988.

Tennessee Catholicism

This new Catholicism, a fusion of the old and the new, was full of vitality, action, and bustle, acutely conscious of the reforms of Vatican Council II. It builds on a rich historical heritage. Miles died in 1860. Tennessee, during the Civil War, was almost wholly occupied by federal armies with many Catholics in them who settled permanently in the state. The Church went through a troubled time as Confederate sympathizers mixed with Union ones. When Bishop Patrick Feehan arrived in 1865, things began to straighten out under his wise and prudent leadership. When he left in 1880 to become the first archbishop of Chicago, he left behind him a thriving establishment of new parishes and native clergy, foreshadowing his well-nigh incredible Chicago record of 140 new parishes. Feehan oversaw the heroic work of the Church during the horrors of the yellow fever plagues of the 1870s in Memphis, one of the proudest moments in the history of Tennessee Catholicism.

Memphis has long been an anomaly in Tennessee. The most populous city in the state, it is also the most Catholic. But the importance and prosperity of Memphis owes much to its being the commercial center for the Mississippi delta region, none of which is in Tennessee. Memphis Catholicism, with its sizeable Italian population, has contributed much to the city's religious and civil life. Its creation as a separate diocese affirmed a long-standing estrangement from middle Tennessee. By contrast, east Tennessee's two principal cities, Chattanooga and Knoxville, were, until after World War II, one-parish Catholic outposts.

Like so many other parts of the United States, Tennessee Catholics have known anxious periods of anti-Catholicism. But the Know-Nothing movement of the 1840s and its successor, the American Protective Association in the late nineteenth century, left no lasting impression in the state. The third manifestation of anti-Catholic feeling, the Ku Klux Klan of the 1920s, was a different story. Its most outspoken opponent was Catholic C.P.J. Mooney, the editor of the Memphis *Commercial Appeal,* who led the fight against the Klan not only in the state but in the South. Here, as in the national prominence of Alfred E. Smith, Catholic laymen took the offensive. It was a good omen for the future.

East Tennessee, now a brand-new diocese of its own based in Knoxville, is quite different from Nashville and Memphis. Never sympathetic to the old Civil War Confederacy, always Republican in politics rather than the normal Democratic affiliation of the rest of the state, its Catholicism too has the flavor of the Midwest rather than that of the South. Its future will be interesting to watch. The vitality is there, particularly in the industrialized northeast, for so long the preserve of the last of the horseback missionaries, but now full of the hum of industry and the tourism of the Great Smokies. The more southern part, headed by Chattanooga, is also more Southern in character. Like Caesar's Gaul, Tennessee is divided into three parts. Its new Catholic organization follows these three geographical and cultural sections. The future of Catholicism in all three seems brighter than ever before.

O'Daniel, Victor F. *The Father of the Church in Tennessee, or the Life, Times and Character of the Right Reverend Richard Pius Miles, O.P.* New York, 1926.
Stritch, Thomas. *The Catholic Church in Tennessee.* Nashville, 1987.

THOMAS STRITCH

TEXAS, CATHOLIC CHURCH IN

The Birth of Catholicism: The Franciscan Missions

The initial charge to bring the Roman Catholic faith to that vast region in the southwestern part of present-day United States that today makes up Texas, was given to the Franciscan Order. The impetus for the Franciscans' evangelization journeys to Texas was the sixteenth- and seventeenth-century *entradas* of the Spanish into the northernmost reaches of New Spain in search of the fabled lands of Cibola and Quivira. The latter proved significant to the future history of Texas, because it included the southern Great Plains area that formed a part of the Texas Panhandle. The years 1680–1794, however, marked the friars' great achievement of erecting a chain of thirty-six missions through which the Catholicization of portions of the Native American and Mexican populations of Texas occurred.

The Roman Catholicism which the Franciscans brought to Texas was that of the universal Church, as its history and catechesis evolved over a span of centuries in the Spanish regions of the Iberian Peninsula, blended with the Catholic legacy of Mexico. In addition to the intellectual and spiritual bases that were conveyed from Spain to the New World via the establishment of universities, such as the Dominican school that opened its doors to students in 1553 and eventually became known as the University of Mexico, seminary colleges also matured as prominent centers of formation for the missionaries as the Church expanded its proselytizing efforts from Mexico into Texas.

It was two such seminary colleges that trained the Franciscans who went forth to labor for souls in Texas. The Colegio de Santa Cruz de Querétaro was founded at Querétaro in 1683 as the Franciscans' first seminary college. Almost a quarter century later, in 1707, the Venerable Fray Antonio Margil de Jesús—considered the Apostle of Texas—led the effort to build the Colegio de Nuestra Senora de Guadalupe, situated on the outskirts of Zacatecas, Mexico.

At the same time, a Spanish-Mexican-Native American culture was in the process of developing in the province of New Spain then known as *Tejas* (Texas). A personalized and deeply pious Catholic religiosity matured among the peoples of *Tejas,* with its heritage maturing from the Valley of Mexico. A very important aspect of that piety was the cult of the Virgin of Guadalupe. While the narrative of the apparitions of the Virgin of Guadalupe to a mature Aztec Catholic convert named Juan Diego four times between December 9 and 12, 1531, is well known, it is significant that a number of scholars believe that the Blessed Mother's appearance to Juan Diego proved an immense influence on the wedding of the indigenous and Mexican peoples to the Roman Catholic religion. The Franciscans, in a number of ways, reinforced that *Culto Guadalupano* among the Mexicans of Texas and brought it also to the Native Americans in their mission environments.

Three clusters of mission activity emerged from the Franciscans' work: one that centered on the half dozen or so missions constructed in eastern Texas in the years 1690–93 and 1716–19; another which consisted of missions established inland from the Gulf of Mexico in the

Mission San Jose y San Miguel de Aguyo, San Antonio, Texas

vicinity of Matagorda Bay; and a third that focused on the several missions in and around the municipality of San Antonio de Béxar. The latter group included, among others, Mission San Antonio de Valero—the famous Alamo—which Fray Antonio de San Buenaventura y Olivares built in 1718, and Mission San José y San Miguel de Aguayo, erected under the watchful eye of Fray Margil de Jesús in 1720. The remaining three San Antonio missions all were constructed in 1731: La Purísima Concepción, San Juan Capistrano, and San Francisco de la Espada.

The "era of the Franciscan missions" came to a close with secularization between 1794 and the early 1830s. The missions originally were intended to serve as temporary frontier conduits of Catholic formation for the Native Americans until a more structured ecclesiastical organization came into being. It most cases, Church authorities determined that each mission would be required to operate for a decade or two, giving way to a regular diocesan-parish hierarchical conformation as the hinterlands were increasingly brought into the Spanish Catholic society.

By the mid-to-late eighteenth century, however, in most mission locales, such hoped-for ecclesiastical and societal maturation had not developed. The vastness of the territory and the aggressiveness of the bellicose indigenous peoples—especially the Comanches—combined with surfacing political complications in Mexico and Texas from the first decade of the nineteenth century on, undermined the Franciscans' efforts.

The most serious consequence of this situation was that the Catholic peoples of Texas of that time, Native American as well as Mexican, were for the most part denied the sacraments, catechesis, and other essential spiritual comforts of the Church. By the 1830s, a mere handful of priests served the Roman Catholics in that land from San Antonio de Béxar and the Nueces River north. South of San Antonio de Béxar, in the lower Rio Grande Valley, it appears that a strong Catholic faith survived, based on parish development and popular religious devotions.

During the 1820s and 1830s, nonetheless, the remainder of the missions were secularized. Then on March 2, 1836, the independence of Texas from Mexico was declared. In the context of that, religious freedom for all Texans was proclaimed. At the same time, though, the stage had been set for a revitalization of Roman Catholicism in that land as an integral aspect of the emerging immigrant populating of Texas from the United States to the north and east and from Europe as well.

The Nineteenth-Century Immigrant Church

As the Venerable Fray Antonio Margil de Jesús is viewed as Texas' outstanding religious figure during the era of the missions, Vincentian missionary and bishop, Jean-Marie Odin, C.M., is seen as the heroic religious leader and builder of the Catholic faith in Texas from 1840 on. A compendium of the historical circumstances that resulted in Fr. Odin's coming to Texas shows that Pope Gregory XVI (1831–46), in 1838, notified Bishop Francisco José María de Jesús Belaunzarán y Ureña of Monterrey, Mexico (formerly bishop of Linares, Mexico), that ecclesiastical jurisdiction over Texas was being transferred from his see to the Diocese of New Orleans. The bishop of the latter diocese, New Orleans, at the time was the highly respected Antoine Blanc. In turn, Bishop Blanc asked the Vincentian visitor (superior), Fr. John Timon, C.M., of St. Mary's of the Barrens Seminary at Perryville, Missouri, to offer the priests and brothers of his community for the mission field of Texas.

Fr. Timon, later named first bishop of Buffalo, New York (1847), made a quick reconnaissance of Catholic Texas from December 26, 1838, to January 12, 1839, and then reported his assessment back to Bishop Blanc. Several months later Fr. Timon was named prefect apostolic of Texas and charged with the leadership in reviving the Catholic presence in Texas. Inasmuch as it proved impossible for him at the time to personally go to Texas on a permanent basis, Timon named his fellow Vincentian and close friend, Fr. Odin, as vice prefect apostolic, and gave him the task of reinvigorating Catholicism there.

Fr. Odin headed the small contingent of Vincentians venturing to Texas, stepping ashore at Linnville on the banks of Lavaca Bay on July 13, 1840. Thus was inaugurated the beginning of a formal hierarchical organization and renewed missionizing effort that was to lay the foundation for the Church's growth in much of known Texas for decades to come.

Despite suffering hardships and deprivations that would try the heart and soul of the most dedicated missionary, Fr. Odin presided over a noticeable rejuvenation of Roman Catholicism where the Franciscans from Spain and Mexico had labored so diligently to lay a religious foundation earlier. Odin and his confreres focused first and foremost on bringing the sacraments of the Church and catechesis to the increasingly ethnically diversified Catholics of Texas. But pastorates were established and reestablished, the first two being at Victoria (Spanish Fr. Eudald Estany) and at San Fernando in San Antonio de Béxar (Spanish Fr. Miguel Calvo). Moreover, numerous churches were built where none had existed before.

On July 16, 1841, Pope Gregory XVI raised Texas to the status of a vicariate apostolic and elevated Jean-Marie Odin to the episcopacy as bishop of Claudiopolis *in partibus infidelium* and vicar apostolic of Texas. Six years later, on May 4, 1847, the new Pope Pius IX (1846–78) created the Diocese of Galveston, to include all of known Texas at the time. Seventeen days later, on May 21, Odin was named first bishop of Galveston. As the diocesan ordinary, Odin began to organize his diocese in a way that would eventually result in not only the establishment of a regular diocesan parish structure, but that would also lay the basis for Texas' second diocese (later archdiocese) erected at San Antonio in 1874.

Odin's years in Texas, 1840–61, increasingly witnessed the growth of the immigrant Church there. Making their way into Texas were Irish, Germans (including Wends), Belgians, Poles, French, Swiss, Alsatians, Czechs, Spaniards, and others. Germans inhabited New Braunfels in 1844 and Fredericksburg in 1846. The Irish settled the colonies of San Patricio de Hibernia and Refugio even earlier, in the early 1830s. Many of the Germans and virtually all of the Irish were Catholics. Belgians, French, and Swiss populated Henri Castro's colonies west of San Antonio in the 1840s, a majority of those settlers being Catholics. The Polish came to Panna Maria (the name means Virgin Mary) in 1854, establishing there the first Polish-American community in the United States. Like the Irish, these Poles were all Catholics. In fact, they were led to Panna Maria by a Polish Franciscan priest, Fr. Leopoldo Moczygemba. On September 29, 1856, Fr. Moczygemba dedicated the Church of the Immaculate Conception of the Virgin Mary at Panna Maria.

Bishop Odin traveled to Europe seeking help for his diocese, not only funds, but priests, brothers, seminarians, and nuns as well. He brought the diocese's first women religious, the Ursulines, to Galveston in 1847 (from Louisiana). A few years later, Odin enticed the Sisters of the Incarnate Word to follow the Ursulines to Texas. These congregations of women religious were just the first of many such communities that ventured to Texas to labor for the Church there.

Men's religious orders, congregations, and societies—in addition to Odin's own Vincentians—soon began to appear also. One of the earliest was the Oblates of Mary, who originally, in 1849, came to Texas from Montreal,

Canada, at the personal request of Bishop Odin. Although their initial effort of 1849 failed and they withdrew to Canada, the Oblates of Mary returned to Texas in 1852 and have been in the state ever since then.

So too came the Marianists, Jesuits, Franciscans, Benedictines, Cistercians, and others. It would be a grievous error to ignore commenting upon the point that it was in these days that the famous Oblate missionary, Fr. P. F. Parisot, O.M.I. (author of *Reminiscences of a Texas Missionary*), commenced his dedicated career in Texas as a beloved and imperturbable evangelizer.

In 1852 Bishop Odin founded Texas' first Roman Catholic institution of higher education, the college which today is located at San Antonio and is known as St. Mary's University. The Marianists eventually came to staff St. Mary's. In the meantime, Odin's Vincentians were withdrawn from Texas in 1847 to serve other mission fields. The bishop increasingly sought diocesan clergy in the absence of his congregation. Within that historical context, in or about 1854, Texas' first seminary was erected at Frelsburg (James Vanderholt, *Called to Serve . . . History of St. John's and Assumption Seminaries, San Antonio, Texas, 1915–1990*, 7). When he departed Texas to become the second archbishop of New Orleans in February 1861, Bishop Odin had left a legacy for the Diocese of Galveston that included, in addition to the seminaries, academies, the college, and other institutions, forty-five parishes, and forty-six priests.

Bishop Claude Marie Dubuis, like Odin, a Frenchman from the Archdiocese of Lyons, inherited the episcopal reins of the Diocese of Galveston. Dubuis continued efforts that Odin had initiated, Dubuis having served under Odin as a priest in the Galveston diocese for several years. Thanks to the foundation which Bishops Odin and Dubuis laid, the Church in Texas began to experience steady growth and development.

The Twentieth Century

The hierarchical structure in Texas began to expand with the erection of the state's third diocese, that of Dallas, in 1890. On August 3, 1926, the Diocese of San Antonio was raised to the status of an archdiocese, with four suffragan sees attached to it: Galveston, Dallas, Corpus Christi, and Amarillo. And in fact, the Archdiocese of San Antonio at that time also had ecclesiastical responsibility for the Diocese of Oklahoma City. Today Texas can count fifteen suffragan dioceses of San Antonio.

In the meantime, Catholic educational institutions multiplied. Incarnate Word College at San Antonio was founded in 1881. In 1885 the Holy Cross Fathers established St. Edward's University at Austin. The twentieth century has witnessed the building of four additional Catholic colleges or universities: Our Lady of the Lake University at San Antonio in 1911; the University of St. Thomas at Houston in 1947; the University of Dallas, refounded at Irving in 1956; and the College of Saint Thomas More erected in Fort Worth in 1981.

Given the nature of its universality, the Catholic Church has from its origin always embraced a diverse ethnic-national base. Nonetheless, in given areas the Church has had to address specific issues of racial demography to insure social justice according to its long-evolving teachings in that area. Important to Catholic Texas is that the twentieth century has stood witness to a large increase in the population of Catholics, numbering in 1995 more than three million. In Texas' case, this growth has been extraordinary among the Mexican Catholics especially. In response, the Church in Texas has refocused its emphasis on its ministry to Mexicans, Cubans, Puerto Ricans, and others. In addition to the Mexican-American archbishop Patrick Flores (currently serving as archbishop of San Antonio), a number of Texas dioceses enjoy the presence of Mexican or other Latin American bishops. In addition, the Church actively supports the Mexican-American Cultural Center located in San Antonio.

The laity are involved in various ministries throughout all of the dioceses in Texas. They serve as eucharistic ministers in parishes throughout the state; increasingly seek admission to ordination as deacons; support the multifarious social, health, and catechetical agencies of the Church in Texas; and so on. The prelature of Opus Dei has existed in the state for many years, with centers in Houston, Irving, and San Antonio.

Such is not to suggest that the Catholic Church in Texas has been immune to the spiritual, social, and economic challenges that face religion throughout the world. On the contrary, matters related to evangelization and spiritual growth among Catholics in Texas—especially declining numbers of ordinations to the priesthood and novices entering religious communities, male and female—persist in needing resolution. And as seems to always be the case, finances remain a major concern for the Church in Texas, as elsewhere in the United States. Nevertheless, from its first appearance in Texas with the Franciscan missionaries, through the nineteenth-century immigrant Church period, into the twentieth century and contemporary times, the Roman Catholic Church in Texas has continued to bring the "Good News" to countless of the faithful for more than four centuries.

Almaráz, Félix D., Jr. "The Legacy of Columbus: Spanish Mission Policy in Texas." *Journal of Texas Catholic History and Culture* 3 (1992) 17–36.

Bayard, Ralph, C.M. *Lone-Star Vanguard: The Catholic Re-Occupation of Texas (1838–1848)*. St. Louis: The Vincentian Press, 1945.

Castañeda, Carlos Eduardo. *Our Catholic Heritage in Texas, 1519–1936: Supplement, 1936–1950.* 7 vols. Austin, Tex.:

Von Boeckmann-Jones Company, 1936–58; repr. New York, 1976.

Foley, Patrick. "Jean-Marie Odin, C.M., Missionary Bishop Extraordinaire of Texas." *Journal of Texas Catholic History and Culture* 1 (1990) 42–60.

Hackett, Sheila, O.P. *Dominican Women in Texas: From Ohio to Galveston and Beyond.* Houston: D. Armstrong Company, Inc., 1986.

Moore, James Talmadge. *Through Fire and Flood: The Catholic Church in Frontier Texas, 1836–1900.* College Station: Texas A&M University Press, 1992.

Morkovsky, Mary Christine, C.D.P. "Challenges of Catholic Evangelization in Texas: The Response of Women Religious." *Journal of Texas Catholic History and Culture* 4 (1993) 65–96.

Wright, Robert E., O.M.I. "Pioneer Religious Congregations of Men in Texas Before 1900." *Journal of Texas Catholic History and Culture* 5 (1994) 65–90.

PATRICK FOLEY

Related Document

THE CHURCH IN THE REPUBLIC OF TEXAS, APRIL 11, 1841

Ever since the time when the Spanish Franciscans had begun their labors in Texas in 1690 that vast area had proved a difficult terrain for the Church's missionaries. In 1836 Texas broke from Mexico and declared its independence with the result that a new arrangement had to be made for spiritual care of the widely scattered Catholics. On October 24, 1839, the Holy See erected the Prefecture Apostolic of Texas and its care was entrusted to the Vincentian Fathers with John Timon (1797–1867) as first prefect. By reason of Timon's many preoccupations elsewhere the practical establishment of the Texas mission was delegated to Jean-Marie Odin (1800–1870) who was later first Vicar Apostolic of Texas, 1841–1847; first Bishop of Galveston, 1847–1861; and second Archbishop of New Orleans, 1861–1870. The following letter of Odin was written to Jean-Baptiste Etienne who was Superior-General of the Vincentians from 1843–1874. Besides the description of religious conditions, it demonstrates how primitive life was in large sections of Texas four years before it entered the American Union.

(*Source: Annales de la Propagation de la Foi,* XIV 1842, 453–60.)

Galveston, Texas, 11 April 1841

My dear Brother,

Last year the Holy See having conferred on our Congregation the spiritual direction of the Catholics of Texas, I left the seminary of the Barrens,[1] on May 2, 1840, in order to explore this new Mission in my capacity of vice-prefect apostolic. It was not without regret that I left Missouri; to separate myself from a people who had become very dear to me, and from flourishing establishments that I had seen born, was like expatriating myself a second time.

Texas, situated between the 26th and the 35th degrees of latitude and extending from the 93rd to the 102nd of longitude, possesses vast prairies, and more abundant pasturage than any other region of America. Woods are rare here, especially in the west. Several rivers irrigate the country, but they are not large or deep enough for navigation. Although the exact figure of the population of Texas is not known, it is rather generally agreed not to exceed thirty thousand souls.

When the first Spaniards settled in Texas more than a century and a half ago, some Franciscans came and founded several Missions in order to convert and civilize the savage tribes. The most celebrated of these were: *San Antonio, de la Conception de San Jose, del Refugio,* and *San Sabas* and *Nacogdoches;* they became very flourishing and soon counted a great number of fervent neophytes. Each year the Reverend Fathers plunged into the forests, earning by their gifts and their very affable manners the confidence of the Indians, and conducting them to the stations where they fashioned them little by little to piety and work. In 1812 these precious establishments were suppressed; today they are only heaps of ruins. For the poor savages, deprived of their Fathers, were dispersed: some returned to Mexico; several succumbed under the blows of the uncivilized tribes, and others returned to their primitive state. The fervor which I have found in the small number of those who still inhabit the country clearly indicates that they had been formed to virtue by capable hands. Two churches, the only ones that have resisted the assaults of time and of the recent wars, are of a beauty which does honor to the taste and zeal of the old Missionaries. . . .

From Liunville, a small seaport where we debarked, we proceeded to Victoria. I left in that post M. l'abbé Estany,[2] and I took the route to San Antonio with M. Calvo[3] and a coadjutor brother. The distance which separates the two towns is only fifty leagues, but the numerous bands of savage *Comanches* and *Tonakanies* who roam the country without ceasing make the trip extremely perilous: it is even pretty nearly certain that one will be massacred, if one does not travel in sufficient numbers to intimidate the Indians. We therefore joined a convoy of twenty-two wagons which were transporting some merchandise. All of our companions were very well armed; but, if on the one hand the force of the caravan reassured us against the attacks of the Indians, on the other, what miseries to endure! What slowness in our advance! The heat was excessive, and scarcely a bush offered itself in the shade of which we might enjoy a moment of repose. Toward sunset we moved forward; but often at first step one of our vehicles got out of order and it was necessary to pass a part of the night in repairing it. These accidents sometimes happened far from any springs or rivers; we then had to scour the wastes, very happy when after a lot of searching we found in a mudhole some drops of muddy and distasteful water. Moreover, we were very poorly provisioned, and yet we hastened to partake as brothers with our traveling companions, worse provided for than ourselves; it was even necessary to have recourse to hunting at the risk of attracting the savages by the noise of the guns.

To scarcity there was also joined the fever; I had several attacks, like the others; but some medicines which I had provided myself proved opportune, and they restored us little by little to health. The relief that I obtained for our poor sufferers gave me a reputation by which I was later often embarrassed; because some of our good wagoners recognized me under the name of the *"Father who knows how to heal,"* all the sick came to ask me for consultations and remedies. Several times along the way, the cry of *Los Indios* spread alarm in our midst: this was, I believe, only a mistake of our scouts, because we arrived at San Antonio without striking a blow.

That city, founded in 1678 by the Spaniards from the Canary Islands,[4] includes a population of two thousand souls: one notices there some houses of stone; the other houses are only miserable huts covered with rushes. It is irrigated on the east by the San Antonio river, on the west by a very small stream; in the center one finds a canal from which the abundant water fertilizes all the gardens; it was built by the Indians under the direction of the Missionaries. There is nothing more beautiful than the valley of San Antonio: agreeable climate, pure and healthful air, rich and fertile soil, all contribute to make it a delightful place, without the continual hostility of the savages, who up to the present have not permitted its immense resources to be exploited. There is not a family who does not mourn the death of a father, of a son, of a brother, or of a spouse pitilessly slaughtered by the *Comanches.* To the massacre of the colonists, these brigands add the devastation of the land and the kidnapping of the herds: thus poverty is extreme in the country, and if ever it would have been consoling to have some aid to distribute, it would undoubtedly have been at the sight of so many needy and unfortunate.

A few days after our arrival at San Antonio, there took place a ceremony which filled us with consolation in proving to us how much of the faith still lived among the Mexicans. A sick person, in danger of death, needed to receive holy viaticum; we judged it opportune to carry it to him publicly and with pomp. At the sound of the bell, the people hastened to the holy place in order to accompany Our Lord through the streets; many tears fell from the eyes of the old people who for forty years had not been witnesses of this homage rendered to our Religion. Some among them cried out that they did not fear death any longer now that heaven had sent them Fathers to assist them in their last moment.

After three months in San Antonio, seeing that, thanks to God, all went as we desired, I directed myself toward Seguin, Gonzales, and Victoria. My visit in these towns was very brief because I was not able to separate myself from my traveling companions without exposing myself to be killed by the Indians. Later I reascended alone the Lavaca river, which offers less danger, and I found on its banks seventy Catholics, formerly my parishioners at the Barrens. It was very consoling to me to see them again, and especially to convince myself that they had lost nothing of their faith and their early piety, because since their arrival in Texas they had been deprived of the aid of Religion. All of them went to confession and had the good fortune to receive holy communion.

I was able to remain with them only one week. From Lavaca I went to Austin, a powerful little town, recently designated to be the seat of the Texas government. The congress was then in session; I solicited from some of the legislators a decision which would confirm to the Catholic Church all the churches constructed by the Spaniards in former times. It is true that, with the exception of *Conception* and *San Jose,* these edifices are almost all in ruins; nevertheless they can be repaired, and considering the poverty and small number of the faithful, they can be turned to account while awaiting happier times that will give us the chance of constructing new ones. Thanks to the generous intervention of M. de Saligny,[5] chargé d'affaires of France, my request has been well received.

There still remains the eastern part of Texas to visit. What difficulties and obstacles present themselves on that long route! Sometimes it is a river there which it will be necessary to cross by swimming, sometimes a vast and desolate swamp where we will run the risk of losing our horses; here the famine and nothing to alleviate it; elsewhere torrents of rain and no shelter. Thus we proceeded from Montgomery to Huntsville, from Cincinnati to Crok and to Douglas, from Nacogdoches to San Augustine. It is true that we were well compensated for our fatigue by the eagerness to hear our instructions which was manifested by the inhabitants of these diverse localities; rarely have I seen the word of God heard with more joy and recollection. This visit, although short, has contributed not a little to dissipate the prejudice of the Protestants, and to awaken pious sentiments in the heart of the faithful.

Outside of the Catholic population of Texas, estimated to be about ten thousand souls, there are some savage tribes to which it will be urgent to apply ourselves: these are the *Comanches* to the number of 20,000; the *Tonakanies,* the *Lipans,* the *Tankanago,* the *Bidaïs,* the *Karankanags,* the *Nacoës,* etc. Most of these Indians like to eat human flesh; the feet and hands are their favorite parts. I have already made several approaches to the *Karankanags,* in order to unite them in a mission: M. Estany has also visited them, and they have expressed to him the desire to have a priest. The *Comanches* will be the most difficult to win over. From time immemorial this tribe has been constantly at war with the civilized inhabitants and the neighboring tribes. Clever horsemen, skillful thieves, they handle the spear and the lance with great dexterity; one sees them in bands of ten, twenty, thirty, or fifty, running about the country without ceasing. From the heights where they lie in wait for their prey, when they discover a convoy too feeble to resist them, they pounce on the travelers with the rapidity of lightning and they gorge themselves without pity. It would be impossible to say how many unfortunates have succumbed under their blows, how many women and children have been taken captive.

A short time after my arrival in Texas one party of five or six hundred *Comanches* penetrated almost to Liunville. The inhabitants, who were not expecting this visit, were obliged to hide themselves in the middle of the Labaca *[sic]* bay in order to protect themselves from their spears: there were eight victims; a young woman married only ten days became their prisoner after having seen her husband fall pierced in his sides. When the savages had plundered the stores and had made a minute search of all that might enrich them, they delivered the town to the flames. From Liunville they went to Victoria. The first house they attacked was the one where our confrère M. Estany lived: he had the good fortune to pass through a hail of spears without receiving any wound; but all that he possessed was taken: linens, ornaments, books, nothing was spared. There were again some murders; several women and children were carried off. Soon the alarm was spread, and they rushed forth in pursuit of the brigands and caught up with them near the *Plombereek* and *St. Marc* rivers. The battle was bloody; eighty-four *Comanches* lost their lives, without mentioning those who a short time after succumbed to wounds they had received. These unfortunates, at the approach of the Texans, sought to kill all the prisoners whom they had carried off. One poor mother who fell into their hands with her little infant, scarcely ten months old, had the anguish of seeing this innocent creature crushed under her eyes, and was herself finally pierced by several blows of the lance! I have counted, in the space of ten months, almost two hundred slaughtered by that tribe alone.

In spite of the devastation to which this country is prey, heaven has already begun to bless our feeble work. From August 1, 1840, to March 1, 1841 we have heard 911 confessions and administered 281 baptisms; there have been 478 communions. . . . The good of Religion will demand that there be erected immediately at least six chapels at the most important places of the republic; but where to find the funds? We are without resources, and the population is poor. In my travels, I pass part of the night in the woods in the open air; I cook my own food, nevertheless my traveling expenses are always considerable. Thus lately in order to have two armed men accompany me during three days of traveling, I was obliged to pay them twenty-four piasters. Schools are also necessary at San Antonio and Galveston: who will cover the first expenses? We are without lodgings, obliged to beg hospitality among the Catholics, often even with the Protestants. . . . Here one learns, indeed, how to lead the life of a Missionary: I thought that I had already made a long apprenticeship; but since my arrival in Texas I have discovered that I was not yet initiated.

Your devoted servant,
J.-M. Odin.

[1] St. Mary's Seminary, Perryville, Missouri (the Barrens), had been established by the Vincentians in 1818 at the little village about eighty miles south of St. Louis.

[2] Eudald Estany was a Spanish Vincentian who had accompanied Odin to Texas.

[3] Michael Calvo was another Spanish Vincentian who had come to Texas in May, 1840.

[4] Odin was wrong here. San Antonio had been founded in 1718 and the Canary Islanders did not arrive until 1730.

[5] Alphonse Dubois de Saligny was *chargé d'affaires* in Texas for the government of King Louis Philippe of France.

(*Source*: John Tracy Ellis, ed. *Documents of American Catholic History*. Vol. 1:1493–1865. Wilmington, Del.: Michael Glazier, 1987, 253–58.)

THEOLOGICAL STUDIES

Theological Studies began publication in February 1940. It was then, as it continues to be, a project of the Society of Jesus in the United States. In the latter part of 1937 the directors of the America Press in New York City thought it advisable for the Society of Jesus in this country to inaugurate the publication of a scientific journal of theology. Participating in the early meetings were representatives of the then five Jesuit faculties in the United States: Woodstock College (Maryland); Weston College (Massachusetts); St. Mary's College (Kansas); St. Mary of the Lake Seminary (Illinois); and Alma College (California). William J. McGarry, S.J., rector of Boston College, was chosen first editor in chief; editorial offices were in New York City.

With Fr. McGarry's death in 1941, John Courtney Murray, S.J., professor of dogmatic theology at Woodstock College, became editor. Editorial offices were at the same time transferred to the college in Maryland. It was during Fr. Murray's years as editor that the journal grew in size, importance, and prestige. Because of its in-depth articles on theological topics, surveys of trends in theology, investigations into current moral questions, together with a generous selection of critical book reviews, the periodical earned the reputation of being the leading American Catholic theological journal. Its authors were among the nation's leading theologians. For example, Fr. Murray wrote on Church-state relations; Gerald Ellard, S.J., on the liturgy; John C. Ford, S.J., and Gerald Kelly, S.J., on moral questions; Robert E. McNally, S.J., on Church history; Herbert Musurillo, S.J., on patristics; Cyril Vollert, S.J., on theology; Joseph A. Fitzmyer, S.J., on New Testament questions; and John L. McKenzie, S.J., dealt with those on the Old Testament. During the journal's early years the authors were principally Jesuits, but, with the increase of departments of theology in Catholic and non-Catholic institutions, the journal's list of contributors became as varied as the colleges and universities where the authors taught.

When Fr. Murray died in 1967, his successor was Walter J. Burghardt, S.J., professor of patristics at Woodstock College. He supervised the journal's operations until 1990. With Woodstock College's move to New York City in 1970, editorial offices likewise moved, but remained there only until 1974, when they were transferred to their present location on the campus of Georgetown University in Washington, D.C. At the time of Fr. Burghardt's retirement in 1990, Robert J. Daly, S.J., professor of theology at Boston College, took over as editor, and in 1996 he was succeeded by Michael A. Fahey, S.J., dean and professor of theology at St. Michael's College, Toronto, Canada.

THEOLOGY DIGEST

Cyril A. Vollert, S.J., first presented his vision of *Theology Digest* to the faculty and students at St. Mary's College (the Divinity School of St. Louis University at St. Mary's, Kansas) in the early 1950s. Beside making foreign-language theological literature available to readers of English, it would also be a way of broadening theological interests of the Jesuit students at St. Mary's.

Gerald F. Van Ackeren, S.J., professor of dogmatic theology at St. Mary's, became the first editor. After favorable response to a pilot issue, regular publication began in 1953 with three issues a year. Students under the supervision of the faculty did the work of surveying journals, indexing articles, and preparing translations and digests of such authors as Yves Congar, Karl Rahner, Joseph Fuchs, Bernard Häring, Jean Daniélou, Oscar Cullman, Edward Schillebeeckx, Hans Urs von Balthasar, Louis Bouyer, and Marie-Dominique Chenu. More than any other journal in the English-speaking world, *Theology Digest* played a unique role in introducing its readers to the most creative thinkers in Catholicism. *Theology Digest* inaugurated the Robert Cardinal Bellarmine Lecture series with Frank Sheed as first speaker in 1956, and a few years later (1962) the journal became a quarterly to accommodate publication of this annual lecture. Under Van Ackeren's leadership, several early participants in the work of *Theology Digest* translated significant sections of Denzinger (*The Church Teaches,* Herder, 1955).

When the Divinity School moved to St. Louis University (1967) the *Theology Digest* staff and seminars eventually broadened to include laity and scholars of other denominations.

ROSEMARY JERMANN

THEOLOGY IN AMERICA

Practical and Pastoral

The first century of the life of the Church in the United States was characterized by the all-absorbing necessity of keeping abreast of the immigrant tide. The Church's preoccupation with the practical problems resulting from immigration accounted in large part for the dearth of American achievement in theology and other intellectual spheres in this period. The theological enterprise was not formally organized but the application of theology was, not surprisingly, pragmatic and apologetic. In some of its themes, it presaged future theological inquiry in areas of religious freedom and ecclesiology.

The exponents of this theology were often bishops. John Carroll (1736–1815), archbishop of Baltimore, caring for a tiny flock in a pluralist society, supported religious freedom. His delineation of the subordination of the Church in America to Roman authorities in spiritual matters alone gave evidence of the compatibility of Catholicism and democracy.

John England (1786–1842), bishop of Charleston, established the first Catholic newspaper in America, the *United States Catholic Miscellany,* to explain the teachings of the Church in response to anti-Catholic polemics. He authored a constitution for his diocese which called for an annual convention of clergy and lay delegates representing the parishes.

Francis Patrick Kenrick (1796–1863), archbishop of Baltimore, was a noted apologist and author. He wrote four volumes of dogmatic theology and three of moral theology to provide textbooks for seminarians, and produced a translation of the Old and New Testaments. His brother, Peter Richard Kenrick (1806–96), archbishop of St. Louis, published several theological works, was a member of the minority at Vatican I opposed to the definition of papal infallibility as inopportune, and defended his position in a pamphlet which was condemned by the Congregation of the Index.

James Gibbons (1834–1921), cardinal and archbishop of Baltimore, was perhaps the greatest of the episcopal apologists. His book, *The Faith of Our Fathers,* proved to be the most successful work of its kind in the apologetical literature of American Catholicism.

The Councils of Baltimore, seven provincial and three plenary, while they dealt primarily with practical pastoral matters, demonstrated the collegial character of the episcopate in action. The Baltimore Catechism, produced at the direction of the bishops in 1885, provided basic instruction for Catholics for generations.

Orestes Brownson (1803–76), one of the most influential Catholic laymen of the nineteenth century, founded *Brownson's Quarterly Review.* A controversialist, he brought a Catholic perspective to bear on the political and social questions of the day. Brownson's central concern was to clarify the relation between Christianity and civilization, between Church and state, and to define the limits of freedom and authority.

Conversion of non-Catholics was uppermost in the writings of Isaac Hecker (1819–88), founder of the Paulists. He launched the *Catholic World* in 1865 in which he wrote in defense and explanation of the Church and its teachings.

Theological Education

Throughout the nineteenth and well into the twentieth centuries, the seminary was the principal, if not the only setting for the formal teaching of theology. Sulpicians, and later Jesuits, Vincentians, Benedictines, and diocesan priests conducted seminaries. Most of the professors were of European origin or had pursued their theological studies at Roman or other European universities. Until the Third Plenary Council of Baltimore (1884), there were no specifically American regulations governing the theological curriculum, its length or its content. This council established a four-year theological curriculum as the norm. The course of study followed the European system of "tracts" or theological topics and was divided into dogma, moral theology, Scripture, Church history, and canon law. European textbooks and manuals written in Latin were utilized, and classroom lectures were, in some institutions, in Latin for many years. The theology was, in method and content, European and neo-Thomist. Controversy was infrequent, except for occasional accusations against the Sulpicians for harboring "Gallicanist" tendencies.

The founding of The Catholic University of America (1889) gave the United States a national center for the professional study of theology. The *American Ecclesiastical Review*, founded in 1889, published articles which covered a wide range of theological and pastoral interest.

As the century ended, disputes surrounding Catholic schools and the adaptation of the Church to American society severely hampered the possibility of growth and development of theology in America. The French translation of Walter Elliott's biography of Issac Hecker helped bring about the apostolic letter *Testem benevolentiae* (1899) that condemned various errors under the rubric "Americanism." The resultant controversy placed the budding American theological enterprise under a cloud.

The condemnation of "Modernism," following closely on the heels of the Americanist controversy, brought further restrictions that hindered theological development. *Sacrorum Antistitum* (1910), which applied the restrictions of *Lamentabili* (1907) and *Pascendi* (1907) to seminaries, the chief locus of theological activity, reinforced "manual theology" and prohibited secular newspapers and theological journals in seminaries. Signs of the times were the failure in 1908 of the *New York Review,* the most learned ecclesiastical journal to be published under Catholic auspices up to that time; the forced resignation of Henry A. Poels, an Old Testament professor at The Catholic University of America; Rome's questioning the orthodoxy of Joseph Bruneau, S.S., professor at St. Mary's Seminary, Baltimore; and the general atmosphere of suspicion and distrust that pervaded Catholic intellectual centers. These were hardly calculated to encourage Americans who might otherwise have aspired to a career in theology.

Although this situation was admittedly injurious to intellectual pursuits, initiative was never completely destroyed, and it gradually revived. Signs of revival may be perceived in the founding of a series of scholarly journals. *Orate Fratres,* now *Worship,* produced its first issue in 1926. The *Catholic Biblical Quarterly* and *The Thomist* appeared in 1939, and were followed by *Theological Studies* in 1940.

In 1946 the Catholic Theological Society was founded in New York. Initially an association composed chiefly of seminary professors, it provided a national forum for scholarly discussion of fundamental and practical theological questions. It was at the meetings of this society and in the pages of *Theological Studies* that John Courtney Murray, S.J., expounded his theology of religious freedom which eventually resulted in the Declaration on Religious Freedom at the Second Vatican Council.

Theology Today

In the second half of the twentieth century, Catholic theology began to emerge from its European parentage and from its traditional setting in the seminary. Catholic colleges and universities, spurred by growth assisted by the G.I. Bill, raised their professional standards. Until the 1950s most Catholic colleges did not even offer courses in theology as an academic discipline. They were liberal arts institutions whose curriculum was centered on philosophy, not theology. Many now created departments of theology and these departments were held to the same professional standards as the other disciplines. To provide professors for these new departments, several American universities established doctoral programs in theology. Up until this time, doctoral programs in theology were limited to ecclesiastical degrees offered at The Catholic University and at a handful of seminaries. Ph.D.s in theology can now be earned at The Catholic University of America, Notre Dame, Boston College, Marquette, Duquesne, Fordham, St. Louis University, Loyola University of Chicago, and through Catholic schools affiliated with the Graduate Theological Union at Berkeley.

Reflecting this new situation, the Society of Catholic College Teachers of Sacred Doctrine was founded in 1954, providing a professional forum for professors of theology in undergraduate departments. In 1967, reflecting the move to a religious studies approach in many Catholic institutions, it changed its name to the College Theology Society.

The Second Vatican Council (1962–65) stimulated the study of theology. The council's focus on sacred Scripture and early Christian writers encouraged studies in these areas, hitherto neglected by most American scholars. The American theological community, for the most part, embraced the wide range of conciliar statements, and with great enthusiasm, engaged in the analysis and diffusion of its teachings. The Declaration on Religious Freedom affirmed the groundbreaking work of John Courtney Murray, S.J., and for many, vindicated the American Catholic experience in the midst of a pluralistic society. The Dogmatic Constitution on the Church gave impetus for deeper studies on ecclesiology. Other conciliar documents encouraged theologians to broaden their perspectives and the range of their investigations.

In 1968 Walter Burghardt, S.J., at the annual convention of the Catholic Theological Society of America, entitled his presidential address "Towards an American Theology." He called for a theology which would no longer be derivative but reflect the American experience, a theology which would be interdisciplinary as well as collaborative. Such a theology would apply traditional theological principles to the American experience, learning from it and contributing to the betterment of society as a whole.

That same year, Pope Paul VI's encyclical *Humanae vitae* precipitated a crisis among many American theologians. Significant numbers of theologians took exception to its prohibition of artificial methods of birth control. At The Catholic University of America, the Rev. Charles Curran led the public dissent against the encyclical. The decision (1986) of the Congregation for the Doctrine of the Faith that Curran "could no longer be considered suitable to exercise the function of a professor of Catholic theology" and his subsequent dismissal from the faculty of The Catholic University led to a lengthy contest in the civil courts that was resolved (1989) in favor of the university. The negative reaction of the hierarchy to the publication of *Human Sexuality* by Anthony Kosnick in 1977 also appeared to widen a gap between Catholic theologians and the American bishops. That same year theologians who believed that the Catholic Theological Society of America was taking too liberal a position formed the Fellowship of Catholic Scholars.

Intertwined with many issues was the definition of theology. As Catholic theology moved into the university world the traditional definition of theology as a discipline necessarily rooted in faith, *fides quaerens intellectum,* was debated. Some theologians opted for a phenomenological approach more akin to religious studies. Others continued to regard theology as an ecclesial discipline but maintained that the theological academy possessed a teaching role similar to that of the hierarchy. Many accepted the complementary role of the theologian and the hierarchy but insisted that authentic theology must probe and investigate with the concomitant risks involved. More conservative scholars saw the role of theology as the explanation of official positions of the hierarchical magisterium.

In spite of occasional tensions, theologians and bishops continued to work together. In 1989, the National Conference of Catholic Bishops, after lengthy consultation with theologians and other scholars, adopted a document on "Doctrinal Responsibilities: Approaches to Promoting Cooperation and Resolving Misunderstandings Between Bishops and Theologians." Throughout the 1980s and 1990s the Joint Committee of Catholic Learned Societies and Scholars has sponsored colloquies between bishops and scholars on a variety of basic theological issues.

Specific areas in which discussion continues include: the relationship of bishops and theologians, especially in Catholic institutions of higher learning; academic freedom; human sexuality; biomedical ethics; feminist theology; and the ordination of women.

Theology itself is more complex than in the past. Internally, the scholastic and neo-Thomist approach of the late nineteenth century has been replaced by a variety of methodologies. Contemporary theological systems are further specified by social, cultural, political, ethnic, and feminist critiques. This phenomenon has produced an increasing variety of specializations and approaches within the traditional areas of the discipline.

The widening and development of academic theology took place at the same time as Catholic colleges and universities were becoming autonomous institutions. These changes have since provoked an analysis of what constitutes a Catholic university. This self-definition is an ongoing process which will be affected by the implementation of the apostolic constitution on Catholic universities, *Ex corde ecclesiae.* Underlying this process, fundamental ecclesiological questions must be worked out, central to which is the role of theology in the Catholic university.

Today, the Catholic theological enterprise exists in a variety of locales. It exists in seminaries, in Schools of Theology, in clusters of theological schools, in Catholic colleges and universities, and in private and state colleges and universities, as well as in nondegreed institutes. Its personnel are priests, sisters, and lay women and men. The theologian is accountable to many publics: the local ordinary or superior, college and university authorities, rank and tenure committees, scholarly organizations, and accrediting agencies. Most experts in Catholic theology are Catholic, though this is not universally so.

The purpose of theological education is diverse. It educates candidates for the priesthood. It educates lay women and men, some of whom will enter the public ministry of the Church, others who will teach theology at the graduate, undergraduate, and secondary levels in Church-related and non-Church-related institutions, some of whom will simply form part of an increasingly theologically sophisticated laity.

The vitality of theology in the United States is demonstrated by the wide range of issues discussed at both very sophisticated and popular levels. Theological discussion is not limited to scholarly journals. It is a public discipline as never before. The public character of theology and the swiftness of communication bring complex issues before the public as soon as they arise. Weekly newsmagazines, television talk shows, and the Internet all take part in the contemporary theological conversation.

See also AMERICAN ECCLESIASTICAL REVIEW; CURRAN (CHARLES) CONTROVERSY, THE; THEOLOGICAL STUDIES; THOMISM IN AMERICA.

Carey, Patrick, ed. *American Catholic Religious Thought.* New York: Paulist Press, 1987.

Fogarty, Gerald. *American Catholic Biblical Scholarship: A History from the Early Republic to Vatican II.* San Francisco: Harper and Row, 1989.

The Proceedings of the Catholic Theological Society of America, vols. 1–50.

ROBERT J. WISTER

THOMAS MORE ASSOCIATION, THE

The association, a Chicago-based, lay-managed organization dedicated to fostering the best in Catholic thought and reading, came into being in 1940 when a small Catholic bookstore in Chicago went bankrupt. John C. Tully, a retired banker and manufacturer, purchased the assets of the store that he sustained through the war years.

Dan Herr

In 1948 Tully hired Daniel J. Herr and made him president of the newly formed Thomas More Association, chartered as a not-for-profit Illinois corporation under the direction of an unsalaried board of directors. Herr (1917–90), a graduate of Fordham University, served in the Army during World War II, rising from private to the rank of major, and was decorated with the Purple Heart and Silver Star Medals. In the years 1945–48 he worked as an editor of *Information Journal,* in Washington, D.C., as a reporter for the *New York Daily News,* and as a freelance writer who published articles in *Life, The Saturday Evening Post,* and other magazines.

The Thomas More Association was largely Dan Herr's creation and he devoted the rest of his life to generating and managing its many activities and sometimes exerting considerable influence on both the Catholic press and general publishing. He also served as president of the newly formed *National Catholic Reporter* from 1968–71 and as chairman of the board of Rosary College from 1970–72. Besides writing a feisty column called "Stop Pushing" for

the association's own, *The Critic,* he contributed articles and reviews to dozens of magazines and newspapers, was the author of two books, and coeditor of six anthologies of mystery and fiction. He received Marquette University's Père Marquette Award in 1957, and was awarded an Honorary Doctor of Letters degree by Rosary College in 1967. He won the Association of Chicago Priests Award in 1978.

Range of Activities

The Thomas More Association's main achievement was to search out, create, and make available readings, art, cultural, historical, and educational materials for the group of more educated, intellectual, and literate Catholics who emerged in the 1950s and whose interests and energies were part of the ferment and *aggiornamento* which would result in Vatican Council II.

To this end, the association sponsored a wide variety of activities. In Chicago's Loop it operated the world's largest Catholic bookstore, backed by a national mail-order service which offered good books for Catholic adults, clergy, religious, and laity all across the country and in many areas where it was difficult to hear about, much less acquire such reading. It operated the Thomas More Book Club that offered books by leading Catholic authors, historians, theologians, and novelists from both Europe and the U.S.A. It published a number of educational and resource newsletters, sponsored a lecture agency, recorded a substantial series of outstanding audiocassettes by these thinkers and speakers, sponsored annual lectures (by such theologians as John Courtney Murray, Hans Küng, and others) and symposia (in conjunction with Mundelein and Rosary Colleges), and made space in its store for a Center for Religious Art. In 1955 the first annual Thomas More Medal "for the most distinguished contribution to Catholic literature" was awarded. This later succeeded not only in drawing attention to, and honoring Catholic authors, but encouraged general publishers to include Catholic-interest titles on their lists. The award generated national publicity and was coveted even by internationally known authors. (When the somewhat controversial English Catholic novelist Graham Greene was awarded the medal, he wrote to me saying, "While I suspect that the headless corpse of St. Thomas More will spin in its grave, I am honored and happy to accept.")

The Critic

The association's influence was perhaps most effectively exerted by its award-winning Catholic literary and cultural magazine, *The Critic* (launched in 1942 under the title *Books on Trial;* it became *The Critic* in 1957), which grew to a circulation of some 33,000 in the 1960s and 1970s, and which could at one point boast of subscriptions being held by both the Vatican and the Kremlin.

While the magazine was decidedly liberal in bent, it was not rabidly so and often published articles on both sides of Church issues. It was known primarily, however, for the quality of its articles and fiction and for a fiercely independent, sometimes irreverent use of satire, parody, and cartoons at a time when Catholics needed to at least have the option of not taking themselves too seriously. Though it carried advertising, the magazine was heavily subsidized by the association's other activities, and had to be, since its list of contributors is a dazzling one by any standards, including such writers as T. S. Eliot, Graham Greene, Evelyn Waugh, Flannery O'Connor, Thomas Merton, Arthur Koestler, Brian Friel, J. F. Powers, Hans Küng, François Mauriac, Nelson Algren, John Courtney Murray, Paul Horgan, Andrew Greeley, Martin Luther King, Jr., Edwin O'Connor, Garry Wills, and many, many more. In those heady years (*"The Critic* is, as far as I know unique in character. I read it regularly and wish it all prosperity,"— Evelyn Waugh; "We have fought over *The Critic* when it arrived to see who would get to read it first. There has never been anything quite like it in the religious field."— Dorothy Day), the magazine was edited first by Paul Cuneo and then, from 1962 to 1978, by Joel Wells.

The Critic was nonetheless not spared the debilitating effects of the dwindling lack of interest in the more intellectual side of Catholicism which gradually developed in the decades following Vatican II. Its circulation (together with many other Catholic publications) fell, and it had to retrench to quarterly publication that continues today.

Thomas More Press

In 1970, at a time when so many old-line Catholic publishers were either going out of business or being absorbed by larger mainstream publishing houses, the association launched The Thomas More Press which was to eventually publish more than 250 hard- and soft-cover titles designed to serve a broad spectrum of Catholic reading needs. Authors included such well-known Catholic writers as Andrew Greeley, John L. McKenzie, John Shea, and Jack Deedy, but also the work of some fifty younger Catholic writers and thinkers whose first books might not otherwise have found a publisher. In January 1994 the Thomas More Press (only) was acquired by RCL Enterprises, Inc., of Allen, Texas.

Thomas (Todd) Brennan succeeded Dan Herr as chairman of the Thomas More Association, which still continues to operate from offices in Chicago.

Upon Dan Herr's death, Fr. Andrew Greeley, who preached his eulogy in Chicago's Holy Name Cathedral, said: "If there is such a thing as history in the years to come, and if anyone bothers to write about American Catholicism during the middle years of the twentieth century, a spe-cial chapter will have to be devoted to Daniel Joseph Herr and his Thomas More Association. His discovery of new Catholic writers and encouragement of established ones, may make him the most important man in Catholic publishing."

And Fr. Theodore Hesburgh, C.S.C., president emeritus of the University of Notre Dame, paid tribute, saying: "Anyone who is interested in the cause of Catholic culture and the best intellectual tradition of Catholicism can rightfully be happy for the existence of the Thomas More Association, which has indeed promoted Catholic reading and reading among Catholics in the most effective way."

JOEL WELLS

THOMISM IN AMERICA

The Beginnings of Thomism in America

By the 1920s, when Thomism began to make its major impact in North America—fifty years after Leo XIII had launched his campaign to make St. Thomas the theologian par excellence in the Catholic Church—European Thomism had moved beyond the restricted circles of the Church's religious orders and of her diocesan clergy. Lay philosophers favorable to the movement, such as Maurice de Wulf, Jacques Maritain, and Etienne Gilson, had won an international reputation through their publications.

Gilson's invitation to serve as a visiting professor at Harvard University led to his invitation by the Canadian Basilians to establish a medieval institute at St. Michael's College. The institute, already affiliated with the University of Toronto, became a Pontifical Institute in 1929. Under Gilson's direction, a whole generation of distinguished Thomists such as Gerald Phelan, Anton Pegis, Joseph Owens, Armand Maurer, Laurence Shook, Robert Henle, George Klubertanz, Gerald Smith, and Linus Thro, were formed there, and the institute's review, *Mediaeval Studies,* was recognized as a major journal for American medievalists.

Inspired by the significant contribution which their Dominican colleagues had made to the revival of St. Thomas in France, the Canadian Dominicans established a medieval institute of their own at Ottawa in 1930, a year after Laval University had opened its Ecole Supérieure de Philosophie at Quebec. At Laval, in its heyday under the direction of Charles de Konninck, another generation of American Thomists received their graduate education. The Catholic University of America, founded in 1887, had taken the University of Louvain for its model. Like Louvain, it had striven from the outset to insure that its higher instruction in philosophy and theology was kept in the hands of the diocesan clergy and free from the influence of any of the Church's religious orders. By the 1920s it had formed its own group of independent Thomists, many of whom had been trained at the university itself.

In 1926, aware of the need felt by the growing number of Catholic college teachers of a forum for scholarly discussion, a group of Catholic university professors founded the American Catholic Philosophical Association. The association, committed explicitly to promoting the philosophy of St. Thomas, remained a major force in Catholic college education for several decades, and its review, *The New Scholasticism,* provided Catholic professors of philosophy, most of whom considered themselves Thomists until the 1960s, with a much-needed vehicle for their publications.

American Thomism Reaches Its Maturity

From the end of World War I, Catholic education went through a period of continuous expansion, and, before Vatican Council II, philosophy played an extremely important role in Catholic colleges. It was the integrator of their liberal arts curriculum and it vindicated the Church's teaching on individual and social ethics. In the 1920s and 1930s, Thomism was still looked upon as a generalized scholasticism. That would change, however, when the growing professionalism of philosophy teaching and the presence of lay men and women on college faculties made a graduate degree a prerequisite for employment. Future college teachers went in increasing numbers to Toronto, Laval, Ottawa, The Catholic University of America, Louvain, and, a little later, to Notre Dame, Marquette, Fordham, and St. Louis University to equip themselves for their future work. College teachers then knew the difference between the philosophy of St. Thomas and generalized scholasticism, and they also knew the difference between the various types of Thomism which students encountered in different graduate institutions.

St. Louis University, many of whose Jesuit professors had been trained at Toronto, was sympathetic, on the whole, to Gilson's form of Thomism, although its outstanding historian of modern philosophy, James Collins, a layman trained at Catholic University, could be quite critical of it. Maritain's influence was very strong at Notre Dame, where Yves Simon, a distinguished disciple of Maritain, served on the faculty, and professors like Leo Ward and Joseph Evans helped to make Maritain's thought accessible to their fellow Americans. Nevertheless, there was variety in the Thomism taught at Notre Dame, and Gerald Phelan, who had worked closely with Gilson at Toronto and translated Maritain's *The Degrees of Knowledge,* joined the faculty there and established the Notre Dame medieval institute. There was variety in Fordham's Thomism as well. The Thomism of Joseph Maréchal, Louvain Thomism, and the independent Thomism of Norris Clarke were all represented there.

The type of scholarly research recommended by Leo XIII was carried on in America. The textual studies conducted at the Franciscan Institute at St. Bonaventure University, notably Philotheus Boehners's studies on Scotus and Ockham, were of a very high order. An American Branch of the Dominicans' Leonine Institute was set up at Yale and later at Toronto and the outstanding quality of the publications on St. Thomas by Dominicans associated with it, such as Ignatius T. Eschmann and James A. Weisheipl, was internationally recognized. Other publications by well-known Thomists helped to make St. Thomas better known. Among them were Anton Pegis's two selections of texts, *The Basic Works of St. Thomas* and *Introduction to St. Thomas,* and Vernon Bourke's *Aquinas' Quest for Wisdom.* A number of scholarly reviews were also published, such as *The New Scholasticism, The Thomist,* and *The Modern Schoolman.*

Thomism Since Vatican II

Changes in the Church since Vatican II and even more radical changes in the curricula of Catholic colleges deprived Thomism of the dominant place in Catholic education and culture which it had held in the first half of the century. Nonetheless, in the new forms which it has taken on, it has given evidence of continuing vitality. Building upon his historical studies of St. Thomas and employing the transcendental approach to Thomism pioneered by Joseph Maréchal, Bernard Lonergan worked out a revised form of Thomistic epistemology and metaphysics, justified by his own cognitional theory, and used both of them to ground his new method for theology. Norris Clarke has developed an original form of Thomism built upon the interpersonal activity of the free human subject. Alasdair MacIntyre, an internationally recognized authority on the history of ethics, has created a new version of Thomistic virtue ethics. The proportionalist position in contemporary moral theology owes a good deal to the transcendental Thomism of Rahner and the debates between its defenders and its opponents have stimulated historical research on St. Thomas's own ethics. At the end of the century the history of Thomism in America remains an ongoing one.

See also THEOLOGY IN AMERICA; *THOMIST, THE.*

Clarke, W. Norris, S.J. *Person and Being.* Milwaukee: Marquette University Press, 1993.

Crowe, Frederick E., S.J. *Lonergan.* Collegeville: The Liturgical Press, 1992.

MacIntyre, Alasdair. *Three Rival Versions of Moral Inquiry.* Notre Dame University Press, 1990.

McCool, Gerald A., S.J. "The Tradition of Saint Thomas in North America: at 50 Years." *The Modern Schoolman* 15 (March 1988) 185, 206.

Shook, Laurence K. *Etienne Gilson.* Toronto: Pontifical Institute of Mediaeval Studies, 1984.

GERALD A. McCOOL, S.J.

THOMIST, THE

The Thomist is a quarterly journal of philosophy and theology, based at the Dominican House of Studies in Washington, D.C., and published under the auspices of the Eastern province of the Dominican friars. Faithful to its Thomistic orientation, the journal features articles and reviews that focus directly on the thought of St. Thomas Aquinas. In addition, it seeks to support and promote critical discussion of central philosophical and theological issues, especially though not exclusively where such discussion can be advanced by creative use of the thought of Aquinas and of significant authors in the Thomistic tradition. In the years since its first issue in April 1939, *The Thomist* has sought to cultivate a fruitful dialogue between modern and contemporary philosophical systems and the classical tradition of philosophy and Christian theology. The journal also publishes textual and historical studies, especially as they bear on enduring speculative questions or as they illumine the intellectual setting of Thomistic thought.

St. Thomas Aquinas, painting by Carlo Crivelli, ca. 15th cent.

The Thomist was launched by a planning committee which met on February 17, 1938, at the Dominican House of Studies in Washington. With the authorization and support of the provincial council, Fr. Timothy McDermott, O.P., provincial of the province of St. Joseph, appointed four friars to constitute this planning committee: Frs. Walter Farrell (the Regent of Studies at the time and later popular Thomistic author); Arthur L. McMahon (former provincial of the Western province); Patrick A. Skehan (later, procurator general of the whole Dominican Order);

and Robert J. Slavin (later, president of Providence College in Rhode Island).

This meeting would bring to fruition a long-cherished dream among American Dominicans for the establishment of a Thomistic philosophical and theological review. The idea was first proposed in 1922 by the lifelong collaborators and coauthors, Frs. John A. McHugh, O.P., and Charles J. Callan, O.P. (editor of the *Homiletic and Pastoral Review* at the time). In 1926 the idea surfaced again when the provincial chapter approved the plan and appointed two editors, Frs. Edward G. Fitzgerald, O.P., and Ignatius Smith, O.P. Still nothing came of the project. Again, in 1933, Callan and McHugh made a more formal proposal for the foundation of what they called "The Thomistic Quarterly" to the provincial, Fr. McDermott, who, after a few false starts, at last commended the project to the friars at the Dominican House of Studies.

From the start, the planning committee wanted to appeal to a broad readership. In their "Editorial Notes" in the first issue, they stated that "the audience to whom *The Thomist* speaks . . . is made up not only of professional theologians and philosophers but also of the educated nonprofessional who has maintained an interest in the worthwhile things of life." This objective reflected the general determination among Thomists of the period to make "the ultimates of human thought and life," as the first editors wrote, accessible to all intelligent readers and not just "the exclusive possession of a caste." In line with this objective, the first issue contained both scholarly articles by Reginald Garrigou-Lagrange, O.P., and by Mortimer J. Adler, as well as more public-interest essays by Rudolf Allers and by Farrell himself.

As the years passed, however, the journal has increasingly become a forum for more purely scholarly discussion. Many of the best-known authors in the twentieth-century neo-Thomistic revival, as well as noted Catholic and non-Catholic authors, have appeared in its pages, including, in addition to those already mentioned, Jacques Maritain, Yves Simon, Maurice Blondel, Charles De Koninck, Eric Mascall, Paul Ramsey, Yves Congar, M.-D. Chenu, Edward Schillebeeckx, Avery Dulles, Peter Geach, Benedict Ashley, William Wallace, and Ralph McInerny.

The first issue was "edited by the Dominican Fathers," published by Sheed and Ward, and printed by the J. H. Furst Company of Baltimore. Although the Thomist Press subsequently assumed publication of the journal, Furst has continued uninterruptedly as its printer. The editors, who were not identified by name until 1965, were largely drawn from the Pontifical Faculty of the Dominican House of Studies. Since that time, the editors in chief have been Anthony D. Lee, O.P. (to 1970), Nicholas Halligan, O.P. (1970–76), William J. Hill, O.P. (1976–83), and J. A. Di Noia, O.P. (1983–).

See also THEOLOGY IN AMERICA; THOMISM IN AMERICA.

Callan, Charles J., O.P. Letters and papers on "The Thomistic Quarterly," *The Thomist* Archives.

Coffey, Reginald M., O.P. "The Way of the Eagle." Unpublished biography of Walter Farrell, O.P. (1960).

"Editorial Notes." *The Thomist* (1939) 123–26.

J. A. DI NOIA

TIERNEY, MICHAEL A. (1839–1908)

Bishop. Michael A. Tierney was born in Ballylooby, County Tipperary, Ireland, on September 29, 1839, and immigrated to the United States eight years later with his family, settling in Norwalk, Connecticut. They attended St. Mary parish, and Michael served as an altar boy.

Following his seminary studies in Bardstown, Kentucky, Montreal, and Troy, New York, Tierney was ordained a priest of the Diocese of Hartford, Connecticut, on May 26, 1866. Tierney served as chancellor to Bishop McFarland, and as rector in various parish assignments in Providence, Rhode Island, Norwich, New London, Stamford, Hartford, and New Britain until January 18, 1894, when he was appointed sixth bishop of the Diocese of Hartford, a position he held until his death fourteen years later (Duggan, 179).

The priests of the diocese had petitioned for "home rule" in Connecticut, attempting to elect their own bishop prior to Tierney's appointment. Rome's appointment of Tierney was made independently of the Hartford clergy, even though the choice was identical with that of the priests (DiGiovanni, 150).

Upon his consecration, Bishop Tierney found an estimated 150,000 Catholics, served by 122 priests in ninety-eight churches within the Diocese of Hartford. With a growing number of Catholics, especially immigrants, Tierney determined to improve the spiritual life, theological knowledge, and number of his clergy by establishing yearly, mandatory retreats for all his priests, yearly theological examinations for the younger clergy, and by founding Hartford's St. Thomas Seminary in 1897. He sought European clergy and religious, and sent numerous American-born students to study abroad, all to assist immigrant Catholics (Liptak, 60, and following).

The number of parishes increased to 167, and parish schools from forty-eight to eighty. He opened Catholic hospitals in Hartford, Waterbury, Bridgeport, Willimantic, and New Haven, and orphanages in New Haven and Hartford. Tierney also worked to ameliorate the lot of the Catholic laity outside the strictly religious sphere. Believing that the suffering of many Catholics was the fruit of alcoholism and near-slave work conditions, he strongly supported the Catholic Total Abstinence Union, and advocated strong labor unions and workers' rights

(DiGiovanni, 154 and following). He died in Hartford on October 5, 1908.

See also CONNECTICUT, CATHOLIC CHURCH IN.

DiGiovanni, Stephen M. *The Catholic Church in Fairfield County, 1666–1961.* New Canaan, 1987.

Liptak, Dolores A. *European Immigrants and the Catholic Church in Connecticut, 1870–1920.* Staten Island, 1987.

O'Donnell, James H. *The Diocese of Hartford.* Boston, 1900.

STEPHEN M. DiGIOVANNI

TIMON, JOHN (1797–1867)

The first bishop of Buffalo, New York (1847–67). John Timon was born in Conewago, Pennsylvania, on February 12, 1797. At the age of three he accompanied his family to Baltimore, Maryland, where his father became a merchant. Briefly enrolled as a day student at St. Mary's College, Baltimore, in 1811, John began working with his father, becoming a business partner by the time his family moved again, first to Louisville (1818), and then to St. Louis a year later. At that gateway town, Timon discerned his priestly vocation aided by Fr. Felix De Andreis, a member of the Congregation of the Mission (Vincentians).

John Timon

Timon began his formation in July 1822, attending St. Mary-of-the-Barrens Seminary, founded by the Vincentians at Perryville, Missouri. Pronouncing his vows as a Vincentian on June 10, 1825, Timon was ordained a priest at Perryville on September 23, 1826, by Bishop Joseph Rosati, a Vincentian who had recently been appointed apostolic administrator of the new see of St. Louis. Already involved in pastoral ministry, the new priest continued such work in Missouri and Illinois, while carrying out additional duties at the Perryville seminary. Timon soon gained a reputation as a strong defender of the Church who offered a compassionate hand to its members struggling to remain true to the faith in the wilderness. His innate abilities brought him recognition by his confreres and his ecclesiastical superiors.

In 1835 Timon was named the first superior of the newly independent Vincentian province in the United States; at the same time, he became Rosati's vicar general. Seven years later his name surfaced for the office of superior general of the Vincentians; by that time, he had reestablished the Church in the Republic of Texas, having become its first prefect apostolic in 1839. Considered for several episcopal positions (e.g., in St. Louis, and New Orleans), Timon steadfastly declined the honor. Finally, in 1847, he accepted appointment as the first bishop of Buffalo, doing so in part to avoid assignment to Louisville, Kentucky, because of his distaste for the institution of slavery. He was consecrated bishop in New York City by Bishop John Hughes on October 17, 1847.

John Timon was a man of action, possessed of an iron will and a strong temper. As a religious superior, while perhaps too quick to respond positively to numerous episcopal requests for assistance, he was most solicitous for the personal welfare of his confreres. As a bishop, he left admirable evidence of his pastoral care in the founding of not only parishes, colleges, and seminaries, but also numerous charitable institutions aiding all citizens of western New York. Becoming embroiled in a conflict with the lay trustees of Buffalo's St. Louis Church, he placed the parish under interdict in order to uphold episcopal rights outlined by the Councils of Baltimore. Timon's stand aided the recognition of the legal right of bishops to inherit ecclesiastical property in New York (1863), and in other states. As a member of the hierarchy, his native roots made him an important asset in a Church facing growing anti-Catholic sentiment; he was seriously considered for the post of archbishop of Baltimore in 1851 and 1863. During the Civil War, while not taking a militant stand against slavery, Timon maintained support for the Union. He contributed to the deliberations of the First and Second Plenary Councils of Baltimore; at the latter he called for greater care of the recently freed slaves.

Bishop Timon died on April 16, 1867. He was interred in Buffalo at St. Joseph's Cathedral which was built during his episcopacy.

See also NEW YORK, CATHOLIC CHURCH IN.

Deuther, C. *Life and Times of the Rt. Rev. John Timon, D.D.* Buffalo, 1870.

Mogavero, I. F. *Brief History of the Diocese of Buffalo.* Buffalo, 1956.
Riforgiato, L. "Bishop Timon, Buffalo, and the Civil War." *Catholic Historical Review* 73 (January 1987) 62–80.
Rybolt, J., C.M., ed. *The American Vincentians.* Brooklyn, N.Y., 1988.

JOSEPH G. HUBBERT, C.M.

TOBIN, MAURICE JOSEPH (1901–53)

Mayor of Boston, governor of Massachusetts, secretary of labor. Maurice Joseph Tobin was born in Roxbury, Massachusetts, on May 22, 1901, the son of Irish Catholic immigrants James and Margaret Daly Tobin, who settled in the Mission Hill section of Boston. He was educated at schools in the Boston area before he took courses in the study of law at Boston College.

Attracted by American Irish leaders like David I. Walsh, the first Catholic to be elected governor of Massachusetts (and later United States senator), and James Michael Curley, the colorful and controversial mayor of Boston, Tobin followed their careers as diligently as he followed the sports pages as a newsboy. Not unexpectedly, he cast his lot with the Democratic Party and became a Curley protégé early in his career. With the help of his brother, James G. Tobin, Maurice set his eyes on a career in politics.

Winning a seat in the state legislature in 1926, Tobin was in the minority party when the Republicans dominated both the legislative and executive branches of state government. Nevertheless, having been thus introduced to politics on the state level, he chose to run for a seat on the national level in 1928. Although he lost this bid for a seat in the United States Congress, he did not abandon politics even though he was, at that time, advancing to a managerial position in the New England Telephone and Telegraph Company. Certainly, his appeal as a candidate for public office became dramatically evident in 1931 when he won a seat on the Boston School Committee by topping a list of twelve candidates.

With Franklin Delano Roosevelt running for the presidency in the following year, Tobin, who had been at Houston for the nomination of Alfred E. Smith in 1928, joined Mayor Curley in supporting the man from Hyde Park. He became known for his exposure as a politician interested in local issues on the school committee and in national issues during the campaign. On November 19, 1932, Tobin married Helen Noonan, and they had three children (Helen Louise, Carol Ann, and Maurice, Jr.).

Tobin's ideological commitment to Roosevelt remained unshakable. After winning a second term on the Boston School Committee in 1935 by gathering more votes than any candidate running for that position, he set his sight on the city's highest office. He was propelled in this direction during the next two years, particularly by his disillusionment with Curley as governor of Massachusetts.

The latter, having been defeated in his bid for the United States Senate in 1936, sought to redeem his political reputation by running against Tobin for the office of mayor, a position he had previously held for three separate terms. Tobin, assisted by his brother, waged a campaign that appealed to younger voters and to Republicans as well as Democrats. Since he projected a fresh image in a very effective campaign against the old ward boss, Tobin defeated Curley decisively by a margin of 25,000 votes in 1937. Then, in 1941, when his former mentor continued his rivalry for that same office, Tobin defeated Curley by close to 10,000 votes.

As mayor of Boston between 1938 and 1945, Tobin forged a record of fiscal conservatism on the local level and of staunch support for the programs of the New Deal on the national level. While handling such disasters as the hurricane of 1938 and the Cocoanut Grove Fire of 1942, he restored confidence in Boston's ability to pay its debts and raised confidence in Roosevelt's ability to handle world problems. Running successfully for governor of Massachusetts in 1944, he was able to fashion a record of liberalism on the state level that drew attention to him in the upper echelons of the Democratic Party, especially for his opposition to racial discrimination.

Exhibiting the same loyalty to Harry S. Truman as he had to his predecessor, Tobin was called upon to bear the burden of a cabinet position and of a campaigner during the 1948 election.

Consequently, with Truman's election, Tobin was assured of his position as the first Catholic to occupy the office of United States Secretary of Labor. In this national office, he demonstrated, more than he had on the local and state level, that he was a transitional figure in politics from the old bossism of a person like James Michael Curley to the new frontiersman of John Fitzgerald Kennedy. Before Tobin died of a heart attack on July 19, 1953, in Scituate, Massachusetts, shortly after he left office, he had emerged as the Truman administration's staunchest supporter within the Catholic community.

The papers of Maurice J. Tobin can be found in the National Archives, Washington, D.C., and in the Boston Public Library.

Dinneen, Joseph F. *Young Man of New Boston: Maurice Tobin's Story. The Boston Globe,* November 4–13, 1937.

Lapomarda, Vincent A. *The Boston Mayor Who Became Truman's Secretary of Labor: Maurice J. Tobin and the Democratic Party.* 1995.

VINCENT A. LAPOMARDA, S.J.

TOLAN, PROVIDENCIA (1909–89)

Religious, teacher, writer, and political activist. She was born Denise Tolan in Anaconda, Montana, in 1909. She was educated at Holy Names College in Oakland, California, and earned a master's degree in sociology at The Catholic University in Washington, D.C.

In 1930 she made her profession with the Order of the Sisters of Providence of Montreal (S.P.). Thereafter she taught at schools in the Northwest and served as a missionary on Idaho's Coeur D'Alene Indian Reservation. In 1948 she moved to Great Falls, Montana, and in 1952 joined the faculty of the College of Great Falls, a Catholic coeducational liberal arts college.

Over the next two decades, Sr. Providencia lobbied extensively on behalf of Montana's off-reservation Native Americans (mainly Ojibwe and Cree bands), many of whom lived on nearby Hill 57 and at other Montana towns. She also served as a tribal consultant for six tribes on the Blackfeet, Crow, Flathead, and Rocky Boys' reservations. Ultimately, at the national level, she assisted Montana's United States Senators James J. Murray and Mike Mansfield, and Congressman Lee Metcalf, in opposing implementation of the 1953 House Concurrent Resolution 108, the "Termination Resolution." The National Congress of American Indians honored her with an award in 1955.

Sr. Providencia then sought passage of the Economic Opportunity Act (1964) and helped to organize some of the community projects it generated. She was also active locally as a member of the NAACP and worked for prison reform and alcoholic rehabilitation programs. At the state level, she was a leader of the 1960s' religious ecumenical movement.

In the late 1970s Sr. Providencia retired and wrote *A Shining from the Mountains,* a history of the Sisters of Providence at Montana's St. Ignatius Mission, which had been established in 1864. She died in 1989.

Bishop, Joan. "From Hill 57 to Capitol Hill: 'Making the Sparks Fly.'" *Montana Magazine of History* 43 (Summer 1993) 16–30.

JOAN BISHOP

TOLTON, AUGUSTUS (1854–97)

Ex-slave, first African American priest in the U.S.A. Augustus Tolton was born to Catholic slaves in Ralls County, Missouri, in 1854. During the Civil War, he escaped from slavery with his mother and settled in Quincy, Illinois, a haven to many refugee slaves. While attending Catholic schools, he began to discern a calling to the priesthood. Because no American seminary would accept him, he studied for the priesthood in Rome. He was ordained in 1886, the first fully African American priest in the United States.

Upon ordination, Tolton became pastor of St. Joseph's, a small African American congregation in Quincy, Illinois. He was well received by his congregation and by many

Augustus Tolton

whites who came to services at St. Joseph because of him. His fellow priests were not so welcoming. Many were openly racist in their comments to him, and one actively campaigned against him. Neither did he receive support from his bishop. He felt alienated and discouraged. In 1889 he requested a transfer to Chicago, where he became pastor of St. Augustine's, an African American congregation meeting in the basement of St. Mary's Church. Under his leadership St. Monica's Church was constructed. He remained there until he retired in 1894 for health reasons. During this same period (1889–94), Tolton was active in the first African American congresses. He died of a stroke on July 9, 1897, in Chicago, Illinois.

See also AFRICAN AMERICAN CATHOLICS.

Carey, Patrick W. *The Roman Catholics.* Westport, Conn.: Greenwood Press, 1993, 323–24.
Davis, Cyprian, O.S.B. *The History of Black Catholics in the United States.* New York, 1990.
____. "Black Catholics in Nineteenth Century America." *U.S. Catholic Historian* 5 (1986) 1–18.
Hemesath, Caroline. *From Slave to Priest: A Biography of the Rev. Augustine Tolton (1854–1897), First Afro-American Priest of the United States.* Chicago, 1973.
Ochs, Stephen. *Desegregating the Altar.* Baton Rouge, 1990.
"Rev. Augustus Tolton." *St. Joseph's Advocate* 4 (1886) 185–87; 5 (1887) 202–4, 245–46, 322–23, 326, 360.
Spalding, David, C.F.X. "The Negro Catholic Congresses, 1889–1894." *Catholic Historical Review* 55 (October 1969) 337–57.
Tolton, Augustus. *Three-American Congresses.* Cincinnati, 1893; repr. New York, 1978.

PATRICIA DeFERRARI

TOSCANINI, ARTURO (1867–1957)

Conductor. Toscanini was born on March 25, 1867, in Parma, Italy, to Claudio and Paolo Montani Toscanini. Although his father was a poor tailor, Claudio loved music and the opera and often took his son to performances. After studying the cello and musical composition for nine years and distinguishing himself for his virtuosity, the young Toscanini conducted one of his own compositions at the Parma Conservatory on May 25, 1884. While traveling and conducting through South America, he was unexpectedly called upon to conduct Verdi's *Aida,* and his performance won wide acclaim. He soon returned to Italy and his popularity and fame grew. In 1897 he married Carla DeMartini, a ballerina, and in the next year he was named principal conductor of the La Scala Opera House in Milan.

Arturo Toscanini

In 1908 Toscanini came to America and began conducting at the Metropolitan Opera House in New York. In 1915 he returned to his native Italy after the entry of Italy into the First World War, and in 1919 he reopened La Scala. In 1926 he returned to New York, began conducting the New York Philharmonic Orchestra, and was named its musical director in 1933. In 1937 he founded the NBC Symphony Orchestra for radio and achieved national fame for the numerous concerts he broadcasted over the new medium.

Toscanini was an outspoken critic of fascism and Nazism, and while in Italy under Mussolini, he was beaten up by the Blackshirts and was placed under house arrest. He was eventually allowed to leave and returned to the U.S.A., living in the Riverdale section of the Bronx. He never returned to Italy. He attacked Nazi anti-Semitic policies, and in 1936 he went to Palestine to conduct the Palestine Symphony Orchestra in support of the Jewish people. Toscanini strongly supported the Allied effort during the Second World War and put on many benefits to support the U.S.A. In 1954, at the age of eighty-seven, Toscanini faltered while conducting two separate concerts. Because of this he immediately went into retirement, and he died in Riverdale on January 16, 1957.

ANTHONY D. ANDREASSI

TOTH, ALEXIS (1853–1909)

Ruthenian priest, schismatic leader. Alexis Georgievich Toth was born near Presov, present-day Slovakia, on March 14, 1853, and was educated at Esztergom, Ungvar, and Presov. Following the example of his father, the dean of the Greek Catholic clergy in Saris County, Toth was ordained a priest at Presov in 1878. Following brief pastoral assignments, Toth was named chancellor of the Presov eparchy. In 1881 he was named director of the United Greek Catholic Seminary in Presov, as well as professor of canon law and Church history.

Acting on a request from Fr. Alexander Dzubay, Bishop John Valyi of Presov sent Toth as a "missioner" to America. By this time Toth, who had been a married priest following the Ruthenian tradition, had been widowed. Toth celebrated his first liturgy as pastor of St. Mary's Church, Minneapolis, on Thanksgiving Day, 1889. Toth's arrival coincided with the "Americanism" controversy that divided the American Catholic hierarchy over several issues, including the pastoral approach to immigrants. Archbishop John Ireland of St. Paul was the leader of those who advocated the rapid assimilation, or "Americanization" of the new immigrants.

Toth and Archbishop John Ireland

On December 19, 1889, Toth visited Ireland to request pastoral faculties. Toth's version of the stormy confrontation between the two volatile characters has been reprinted many times. Conversing in Latin, Ireland stated: "I have already written to Rome protesting against this kind of priest being sent to me!"

"What kind of priest do you mean?"

"Your kind."

"I am a Catholic priest of the Greek Rite. I am a Uniate and was ordained by a regular Catholic bishop."

"I do not consider that either you or this bishop of yours are Catholic; besides, I do not need any Greek Catholic priests here; a Polish priest in Minneapolis is quite sufficient; the Greeks can also have him for their priest."

Although there is no Ireland version of the meeting, Toth's account is not inconsistent with Ireland's views or temperament. The stalemate continued for over a year, during which Toth invited the other Ruthenian priests to a meeting on October 29, 1890, in Wilkes-Barre, Pennsylvania, under his chairmanship to organize and make representations concerning their grievances. Toth's frustration pushed him, "to do something which I carried in my heart for a long time, for which my soul longed: that is to become Orthodox." Toth and some 365 members of his Minneapolis congregation were received into the Russian Orthodox Church by Bishop Vladimir of Alaska and the Aleutian Islands on March 25, 1891.

"Father of Orthodoxy" in America

In November 1892 Toth was invited to take up the pastorate of St. Mary's, an independent Ruthenian parish in Wilkes-Barre, Pennsylvania, a center of Ruthenian immigration. Toth accepted, and the following month led his new parish into Russian Orthodoxy. Toth wrote a propaganda brochure, *Where to Seek the Truth?*, in Russian and Slovak, and over the course of the next decade was active in promoting Russian Orthodoxy among the Ruthenian immigrants. Toth's example encouraged several other Ruthenian clergy to embrace Orthodoxy, and as many as thirty-eight parishes were brought into the Russian fold.

Several factors contributed to Toth's success. Toth himself was a gifted man, a "man of the people," who had a magnetic personality and who related well to the flock he was leading. In addition, the immigrants, for the most part, lacked precision concerning their religious and national identity. The threat to their religious heritage was seen as a possible loss of identity which made the familiar rituals of Orthodoxy attractive. Finally, the insensitivity of many of the American bishops helped to pave the way for many Ruthenian immigrants to Russian Orthodoxy.

Toth's successes were not unqualified. A large part of his own Wilkes-Barre congregation returned to Catholic communion, and engaged Toth in protracted and successful litigation for the return of the church property. This allowed Toth to construct his own church which was dedicated in 1901. Of all the Ruthenian priests who followed Toth into Orthodoxy, every one eventually returned to Catholic communion, and in later years the Ruthenian parishes were served by Russian priests. Nevertheless, it is estimated that the movement begun by Toth is responsible for as much as half of the membership of the Russian Orthodox Church in America today.

Toth died at Wilkes-Barre on May 7, 1909, but he remains a somewhat controversial figure. In Ruthenian Catholic circles, mention is made of possible financial improprieties that made his immigration to America more desirable. There is also a long-standing tradition that, like his other Ruthenian brothers, he returned to Catholic union on his deathbed. Among the Orthodox, Toth is revered as the "Father of Orthodoxy" in America. In ceremonies conducted by Metropolitan Theodosius on May 29–30, 1994, Toth was canonized as a saint by the Orthodox Church in America.

Fogarty, Gerald P., S.J. "The American Hierarchy and Oriental Rite Catholics, 1890–1907." *Records of the American Catholic Historical Society of Philadelphia* 85 (March–June 1974) 17–28.

Hospodar, Robert J. "A Clash of Titans. Archbishop John Ireland and Reverend Alexis Toth." *Eastern Catholic Life* XXI (January 17, 1985) 5–9; (April 7, 1985) 5–7; (April 21, 1985) 5–9.

Procko, Bohdan P. "The Establishment of the Ruthenian Church in the United States, 1884–1907." *Pennsylvania History* 42 (April 1975) 137–75.

Russin, Keith. "The Right Reverend Alexis G. Toth." M.A. thesis, St. Vladimir's Seminary, 1971.

Simon, Constantin, S.J. "The First Years of Ruthenian Church Life in America." *Orientalia Christiana Periodica* 60 (1994) 187–232.

_____. "Alexis Toth and the Beginnings of the Orthodox Movement among Ruthenians in America (1891)." *Orientalia Christiana Periodica* 54 (1988) 387–428.

Tarasar, Constance J., ed. *Orthodox America, 1794–1976.* Syosset, N.Y.: The Orthodox Church in America, 1975.

RAYMOND J. KUPKE

TOUSSAINT, PIERRE (1766–1853)

Former slave, businessman, philanthropist. Pierre Toussaint was born into slavery in the French colony of Saint Domingue (Haiti) sometime in 1766. The identity of his father is unknown, but his mother and maternal grandmother were both house slaves on a plantation in the Artibonite

Pierre Toussaint

River valley, near the port of Saint Marc. The French-born plantation owner, Pierre Bérard, was a devout Catholic who treated his slaves in a relatively humane manner. Young Toussaint was spared the dehumanizing experience of a field slave and was employed instead as a domestic servant. He was even allowed access to his master's library and perfected his knowledge of French by reading the classical sermons of such seventeenth-century preachers as Bossuet and Massillon. It was from these sources, rather than from any contact with the notoriously corrupt local clergy, that Toussaint appears to have acquired his deep attachment to the Catholic faith.

Pierre Bérard retired to France, leaving the plantation to his son, Jean-Jacques Bérard. In 1787, as the political situation in Saint Domingue began to deteriorate, the younger Bérard left the island for an extended visit to New York City, bringing with him his wife and five slaves, one of whom was Pierre Toussaint, now twenty-one years of age. Like his master, Toussaint expected that his stay in New York would only be temporary. In fact, he was to remain in the city for the next sixty-six years.

In 1788 M. Bérard died suddenly during a visit to Saint Domingue where he had made a fruitless effort to regain his lost property. At the same time, his widow, Mary Elizabeth Bérard, found herself penniless in New York. It was Pierre Toussaint who saved her from total penury. He had already been taught the elements of hairdressing, and he was able to earn enough from this trade to support both his mistress and himself. In 1802 Madame Bérard married Gabriel Nicholas, a fellow refugee from Saint Domingue. She died in the summer of 1807. Shortly before her death, however, on July 2, 1807, she and her husband appeared at the French consulate and signed the formal papers giving Pierre Toussaint his freedom.

Toussaint's economic prospects improved steadily. In 1811 he purchased the freedom of his sister, Rosalie, so that she could marry Jean Noel in St. Peter's Church. He also purchased the freedom of another refugee from Saint Domingue, Mary Rose Juliette, and married her in the same church on August 5, 1811. In 1817 he was sufficiently wealthy to rent a house for $240 per year. In 1835 he offered $5,000 for the purchase of his own home but balked when the owner demanded $6,000. Nonetheless, a few years later, he was able to buy his own house in Manhattan.

Economically, Toussaint was far better off than most blacks in New York City, and far better off than most of the Irish immigrants who disliked the color of his skin. He became one of the best-known hairdressers in the city and numbered among his customers some of New York's wealthiest families such as the Livingtons, Schuylers, and Hamiltons. "As a hairdresser for ladies, he was unrivaled," said Hannah Sawyer Lee, a prominent socialite, "he was the fashionable coiffeur of the day." Toussaint also lived frugally and made wise investments. For example, he was a stockholder in the East River Bank. At the time that Toussaint was buying his own Manhattan house, a black newspaper editor complained that black ministers in New York City "have to follow low and vile servile occupations to get bread for themselves."

Toussaint's hairdressing business was financially lucrative but physically demanding. He spent sixteen hours on his feet each day and traveled throughout the city to the homes of his wealthy customers. The most convenient form of transportation would have been the city horsecars, but blacks were barred from using them. It was just one example of the humiliations that he encountered everyday because of his race. Moreover, as a black among Catholics, and a Haitian among blacks, Toussaint belonged to a minority within each of these minorities and was thus doubly disadvantaged.

Toussaint was a devout Catholic who was a pewholder in St. Peter's Church, New York's oldest Catholic parish. For over sixty years, he began every day by attending the 6:00 A.M. Mass at the church. He was also a generous benefactor of the Catholic Orphan Asylum and of the Church of St. Vincent de Paul, New York's first French parish, established in 1840. He and his wife Juliette, who were childless, also had the practice of taking into their home destitute black children whom they sheltered and educated until they were able to fend for themselves.

Toussaint's piety and charity did not protect him from the racial prejudice of his fellow Catholics. In 1842 he was insulted in St. Patrick's Old Cathedral by a white usher who objected to his presence in the congregation. The lay chairman of the board of trustees apologized to Toussaint for the incident, but even the apology revealed the unconscious racism of well-intentioned whites. "If God by his will has created you and your good wife with black skin," said the white layman, "by His grace He has also made your heart and soul as white as snow."

Toussaint played no role in the local Abolitionist movement, which is not surprising in view of the anti-Catholic sentiments of many Abolitionists. What is more puzzling, however, is his apparently total silence about the injustice of slavery at a time when it was becoming the outstanding moral issue of the day. His white admirers thought that they were paying him a compliment when they called him a "Catholic Uncle Tom." However, Toussaint was a man of peace who feared violent social change, a legacy perhaps of his own experience of the early stages of the Haitian revolution. He died in New York City on June 30, 1853. John Cardinal O'Connor introduced his cause for canonization in Rome in 1990. He was declared Venerable in 1997.

See also AFRICAN AMERICAN CATHOLICS; NEW YORK, CATHOLIC CHURCH IN.

The Pierre Toussaint Papers, consisting of some 1,200 items, are in the New York Public Library.

Binsse, Henry. "Pierre Toussaint: A Catholic Uncle Tom." *Historical Records and Studies* 12 (1918) 90–101.
Dorsey, Norbert M., C.P. "Pierre Toussaint of New York, Slave and Freedman: A Study of Lay Spirituality in Times of Social and Religious Change." Ph.D. dissertation, Pontifical Gregorian University, Rome, 1986.
[Lee, Hannah Sawyer] *Memoir of Pierre Toussaint, Born a Slave in Saint Domingue.* Boston: Crosby, Nicols and Company, 1854; repr. Sunbury, Pa.: Western Hemisphere Cultural Society, 1992.
Ryan, Leo R. "Pierre Toussaint: God's Image Carved in Ebony." *Historical Records and Studies* 25 (1935) 39–58.
Shelley, Thomas J. "Black and Catholic in Nineteenth-Century New York: The Case of Pierre Toussaint." *Records of the American Catholic Historical Society of Philadelphia* 102 (Winter 1991) 1–18.

THOMAS J. SHELLEY

TRADITIONALIST MOVEMENT, THE

An international movement of laity and clergy opposing the reform initiatives of the Second Vatican Council. Traditionalism in the United States arose in the context of uneasiness among conservative American Catholics with conciliar-inspired *aggiornamento.* This discontent derived from the perception of "excesses" and "novelties" associated with the implementation of the reforms, the destabilizing impact of the council on Catholic identity, and concerns over the resurgence of Modernism and liberalism in the Church. In particular, postconciliar dissent on the Catholic right galvanized around the liturgical changes inaugurated by the Constitution on the Sacred Liturgy *(Sacrosanctum Concilium).* With the introduction of the *Novus Ordo Missae* in 1967, this dissent intensified, creating a more ideologically self-conscious "traditionalist" movement. By the early 1970s, traditionalist repudiation of the New Mass *(Novus Ordo Missae)* had evolved into a radicalized repudiation of the council in general. Following the mandatory implementation of the New Mass in 1971, traditionalist Catholics began establishing a counter-Church organizational infrastructure consisting of a segmented network of associations, publishing initiatives, and chapel sites and Mass locations. By the late 1980s, more than three hundred of these locations had been established throughout the United States.

Origins of the Movement

The first American traditionalist initiative occurred in early 1965 when Fr. Gommar De Pauw, a professor of theology and academic dean at Mt. St. Mary's Seminary in Emmitsburg, Maryland, launched the Catholic Traditionalist Movement, Inc. (CTM) in New York. De Pauw subsequently established CTM headquarters in Ave Maria Chapel in Westbury, Long Island, from which he led an aggressive media campaign in defense of "truth and tradition." A second and more organizationally extensive traditionalist effort, the Orthodox Roman Catholic Movement, Inc. (ORCM), came eight years later in Bridgeport, Connecticut, through the initiatives of a priest/pastor and longtime John Birch Society apologist, Fr. Francis Fenton. The ORCM eventually established a network of traditionalist chapels around the United States but disbanded in the late 1970s over a series of internal conflicts. Fr. Fenton subsequently founded the Traditional Catholics of America in Pueblo, Colorado. A third American traditionalist initiative took the form of the Tridentine Latin Rite Church (now known as the Congregation of Mary Immaculate Queen or Mt. St. Michael's group). The TLRC was founded in Coeur d' Alene, Idaho, in 1967 by Francis Schuckardt, a layman and one-time head of the Blue Army of Mary. Schuckardt moved his center of operations to Mt. St. Michael's, a former Jesuit seminary northeast of Spokane, in 1977. In 1984, after years of internal turmoil, Schuckardt was ousted from Mt. St. Michael's. In 1984 the Mt. St. Michael's group reorganized itself as the Congregation of Mary Immaculate Queen (CMIQ).

In addition to the above efforts, traditionalist dissent among American Catholics also found expression in publications such as *The Voice* (Canandaigua, New York) and *The Remnant* (St. Paul, Minnesota), and in a growing number of anticonciliar books and pamphlets denouncing the New Mass, the Second Vatican Council, and the authority of Paul VI and his successors.

Traditionalist initiatives among American Catholics received a significant boost in 1973, when the first priests of French Archbishop Marcel Lefebvre (and his clerical Fraternity of St. Pius X [SPXX]) established chapel sites in the United States in Michigan, Texas, California, and New York. Lefebvre's SPXX eventually became the most media-visible representation of the traditionalist cause both here and abroad. Within two decades the society had established over one hundred chapel locations, including a seminary in Winona, Minnesota, and an educational complex in St. Mary's, Kansas.

In addition to the CTM, the ORCM, and the SPXX, traditionalist initiatives in the United States have also been undertaken by individual priests unaffiliated with any organization and by lay Catholic traditionalist organizations such as the Society of Traditional Roman Catholics (Charlotte, North Carolina). In addition, the Society of St. Peter (SSP), a priestly fraternity operating under the provisions of the May 5, 1988, Vatican protocol first signed and subsequently rejected by Archbishop Lefebvre, began serving American traditionalists in 1991 from headquarters in Scranton, Pennsylvania.

The traditionalist repudiation of Vatican II and establishment of chapels, Mass sites, and other institutional structures outside the channels of ecclesiastical authority brought the movement into conflict with the American hierarchy. American bishops generally avoided public confrontations with traditionalists, while warning of the schismatic dangers of the movement and admonishing Catholics not to attend traditionalist Mass locations. Hierarchical attempts to accommodate traditionalist dissent, particularly in conjunction with Vatican gestures of accommodation surrounding "reinstatement" of the Tridentine liturgy (1984 Indult), have varied from diocese to diocese.

Divisions Among Traditionalists

In addition to conflict with the American hierarchy, traditionalist Catholics have also been in dispute with conservative groups such as Catholics United for the Faith (CUF) who, while sharing many traditionalist concerns with the malaise in the postconciliar Church and the moral and cultural crisis in society at large, nevertheless eschew the movement's more radicalized sectarianism.

Typical of sectarian-like religious movements, traditionalism in the United States has been plagued from its inception with organizational infighting and fragmentation. These tensions have formed around issues of doctrinal rectitude, how to respond to hierarchical blandishments, and questions of leadership and authority within the movement itself. One of the more noteworthy of these conflicts occurred in 1983 when nine American priests of the SPXX were ousted from the society by Archbishop Lefebvre. Under the leadership of Fr. Clarence Kelly, the dissident priests founded the Society of St. Pius V (SSPV) in Oyster Bay, New York. Some of the most intense divisions among American traditionalists surround the question of "sedevacantism" (whether or not the see of Peter is vacant) and the canonical status of various sedevacantist "bishops" of dubious ecclesiastical lineage.

The roots of the traditionalist movement among American Catholics lie within the broader currents of Catholic integralism, a reactionary movement that arose in connection with the magisterial condemnation of Modernism. Traditionalist is also a Catholic analogue to American Protestant fundamentalism. Like Protestant fundamentalism, traditionalism is a reaction against the loss of the sacred, the loss of religious identity, the dissolution of religious social boundaries, and the perception of defilement and penetration. Traditionalist Catholics share Protestant fundamentalism's reactive/innovative character, selective appropriation of authority, literalistic and dogmatic cognitive orientation, tendencies toward extreme objectifying, elitism/exclusivism, and conspiracy action orientation.

Catholic traditionalism in the United States has had only limited media visibility due, in part, to the size and diffusion of the movement and to its characteristics as an introversionist sect. It has, however, assumed a distinctive place in American's sect and cult milieu while, itself, exemplifying a diffuse collection of religious subcultures.

By the later 1980s, traditionalist dissent in the United States was becoming a second-generational phenomenon while the leaders who first mobilized that dissent were passing away. American Catholics drawn to traditionalist enclaves found in them not only spiritual edification in a company of like-minded individuals along with "true Mass," but a social remedy to what is perceived as the chaos and moral degeneracy of society at large. Thus, the broader social breakdown that has stimulated the rise of other expressions of religious totalism, militant traditionalism, and fundamentalist apocalypticism in the latter twentieth century has also benefited the traditionalist cause among American Catholics.

Dinges, William D. "Catholic Traditionalism." *Fundamentalisms Observed,* eds. Marin E. Marty and R. Scott Appleby. Chicago: University of Chicago Press, 1991, 66–101.
____. "'We Are What You Were': Catholic Traditionalism in the Wake of Schism." *Conservative Catholics in America,* eds. Mary Jo Weaver and R. Scott Appleby. Indiana University Press (forthcoming).
Whitehead, Kenneth D. *The Pope, The Council, and the Mass: Answers to the Questions Traditionalists Are Asking.* West Hanover, Mass.: Christopher, 1981.

WILLIAM D. DINGES

TRINITY COLLEGE (WASHINGTON, D.C.)

Trinity College in Washington, D.C., is one of the oldest Catholic liberal arts colleges for women in the United States. Trinity was founded by the Sisters of Notre Dame de Namur in 1897 to offer women the opportunity for higher education within the Catholic intellectual and spiritual tradition. Trinity's founding was guided by the visionary leadership of Sr. Superior Julia McGroarty and Sr. Mary Euphrasia Taylor, with the encouragement of James Cardinal Gibbons.

Trinity was chartered by Act of Congress on August 20, 1897, and land for the new college was purchased that same summer. Construction of the first structure, Main Building, was begun in 1899 and completed in 1909; the building continues to be the main center of the campus. In November of 1900 the Sisters of Notre Dame welcomed students, and Trinity's first degrees were conferred upon the Class of 1904. Many of the traditions that continue today were established in Trinity's early years.

Trinity's Notre Dame Chapel was completed in 1924 and the chapel's designers, Maginnis and Walsh of Boston, were awarded the gold medal for ecclesiastical architecture in 1925. In 1979 Pope John Paul II celebrated an ecumenical prayer service in Trinity's chapel.

Master's degrees were awarded early in Trinity's history; however, the graduate program was formally established in 1966, and today offers both women and men degrees in education, counseling, administration, and other fields. In 1984 Trinity launched its Weekend College program to meet the educational needs of working women. Today (1997), Trinity enrolls more than 1,400 students in its undergraduate programs for women and coeducational graduate programs. Trinity also enrolls more than 2,000 nondegree students each year.

See also CATHOLIC UNIVERSITIES AND COLLEGES.

TRUSTEEISM

In many early nineteenth-century parishes, trusteeism (1785–1860) was a lay movement to adapt European Catholicism to American republican values by asserting the rights of lay governance and exclusive lay control of ecclesiastical temporalities. Catholic bishops and many pastors vigorously resisted the movement, insisting that congregational lay leaders had usurped episcopal and pastoral authority within the Church. These lay and clerical claims and counterclaims gave rise to a series of protracted congregational debates and hostilities.

Origins and Significance

Trusteeism was significant in American Catholicism because it represented an early attempt to Americanize the Catholic Church. The battles that ensued reflected conflicting understandings of the Church, its structures, and lay and clerical roles within those structures. The trustees' arguments for lay participation demonstrated a popular, democratically influenced theology that was, according to Nathan Hatch (*Democratization of American Christianity,* 1989), widespread among American Christians in the early nineteenth century. The clerical, episcopal, and even papal reactions this democratic tendency produced had profound influences upon the structures of the Catholic Church in the United States.

Lay trusteeism arose from a variety of sources, but it was legally grounded in the trustee system. According to American law, every congregation that wanted legal protection for its properties had to elect a board of trustees who were corporately responsible for church debts, pastors' salaries, and for hiring and firing ecclesiastical personnel (e.g., sextons, organists, teachers, building contractors). From Maine to Louisiana, lay Catholics formed new congregations according to this American legislation and thereby received legal sanction for many of their powers and responsibilities within the congregations. These legal sanctions, the general republican atmosphere in the country, the congregational practices of other Christian denominations, and the European Catholic practice of patronage combined to give many of the elected lay trustees ideological and practical support for their demands for lay initiative, leadership, and even lay control of their congregations.

The lay trustee system operated peacefully and successfully in a number of congregations, but in some of the most prominent antebellum congregations in the largest cities, it produced a series of notorious ecclesiastical conflicts between elected lay trustees who claimed extensive rights to govern the congregations, and their pastors and/or bishops who denied and rejected these rights. These particular conflicts tended to split the congregations into competing camps, some laity favoring the lay trustees and others siding with the bishops or pastors.

Parish Conflicts

The first major trustee dissensions arose in 1786 at St. Peter's congregation in New York City. Other late-eighteenth-century conflicts erupted in Boston and in German parishes in Philadelphia and Baltimore. Between 1815 and 1829, the most volatile period of trusteeism, congregational battles broke out in Norfolk, Charleston, and Philadelphia. Trusteeism in Philadelphia's St. Mary's, perhaps the wealthiest Catholic parish and the one with the most distinguished Catholic laity in the country at the time, became the most celebrated case in the nation. In 1820 a newly arrived Irish priest, William Hogan, siding with lay trustees in opposition to Bishop Henry Conwell's authority, supported lay demands for complete control of ecclesiastical temporalities and for lay participation in the selection of pastors and even bishops. Popularly known as Hoganism, trusteeism in Philadelphia created a schism that lasted from 1820 until 1829, when a new bishop, Francis Patrick Kenrick, was able to restore and enforce episcopal authority in Philadelphia. The Hogan affair had national implications. It represented in dramatic and very public ways what was going on in many Catholic congregations across the country where laypeople, clergy, and bishops struggled to define Catholic ecclesiology and ecclesiastical practices in the new environment of American democracy. In 1829 the American bishops responded to Hoganism by organizing at Baltimore a provincial council that established national policies reasserting exclusive episcopal authority to appoint and dismiss pastors and to supervise all ecclesiastical temporalities.

This episcopal legislation set the pattern for future congregational developments, but it did not bring trusteeism and congregational quarrels over lay responsibilities to an end. From 1829 to 1855, trusteeism, although not as widespread as previously, was volatile, especially in the cities of New Orleans and Buffalo, New York, where lay trustees between 1830 and 1855 engaged in protracted public debates with their bishops over their legal and ecclesiastical rights to control their own parishes. Even after the Civil War, trustee-like dissensions arose here and there in various ethnic communities that brought European traditions of lay participation and control with them to this country. These post-Civil War debates, however, did not have the same impact upon the entire American Catholic Church as did those of the antebellum period because by then most bishops had gained civil legal control of parish properties and therefore had civil support for their canonical legislation.

The Role of the Laity in the American Church

Prior to 1829 in particular, trusteeism was, among other things, a national ideological battle to determine the shape of the decision-making powers in the American Catholic Church. Lay trustees throughout the country argued, as did members of other ecclesiastical traditions, that the Church in the United States should be distinctively American in its manner of governing. Within the Church this meant that temporal ecclesiastical concerns should be under the laity's control and spiritual concerns under the clergy's. This division of powers within the Church corresponded to ancient Catholic as well as American distinctions. Many elected lay trustees asserted that they had the right and duty to select their pastors, establish a description of the pastoral role, and fire them when they proved incompetent or unacceptable in the congregation. The trustees' democratic aspirations were reflected in their frequent appeals to the republican shibboleth "the voice of the people is the voice of God" in Church as in state.

The trustees also appealed to the Catholic tradition to support their call for lay leadership in the Church and to show that the Catholic tradition was itself consistent with the American republican tradition. They claimed that the ancient Catholic practice of lay patronage should be instituted in the United States in a way that acknowledged the American practice of voluntarism. Lay patronage in the European Catholic legal tradition had acknowledged that those who built or financially supported congregations had the right to select and reject pastors. The Catholic people in the United States who supported their churches through their free-will offerings, therefore, should be acknowledged as legal patrons. In effect, the trustees' arguments were attempts to democratize the European ecclesiastical practice of patronage.

Those who joined the bishops in opposition to the trustees charged that the trustees' claims, if fully implemented, would destroy Catholic identity. The trustees had identified Catholicism with a republicanism and Protestantism that asserted that all authority, ecclesiastical as well as political, arose from the people. This was absolutely contrary to the Catholic view which held that all ecclesiastical authority arose from divine commission. The trustees' administration of congregational temporalities, most antitrustees asserted, could be tolerated as long as their authority was subordinate in all things to that of the pastors and bishops. They could not claim an independent authority within the congregations. To do so, the bishops argued, would be to create a republican, not a Catholic Church.

The antitrustees believed that the American separation of Church and state, which the trustees used to support their division of temporal and spiritual powers within the Church, provided a providential opportunity for the Church to be freed from excessive lay and governmental interference in ecclesiastical affairs. In Europe, lay interference had frequently impinged upon or even destroyed ecclesiastical freedom. Lay intervention in pastoral appointments represented the worst kind of tyranny, made pastors the slaves of congregational whim, and at times muffled the preaching of the gospel. Under trustee controls, not only was pastoral authority practically eliminated, but the Church's message was utterly dependent upon the congregation's cultural and political condition.

From 1829 to 1855, the bishops—through individual efforts, conciliar legislation, and papal support—were able to crush the republican lay assertiveness behind trusteeism and to gain for themselves new civil legislation that gave them legal control over ecclesiastical properties and temporalities. Lay trustees continued to function in many congregations after 1829, but they did so under the pastoral and episcopal arm.

The ecclesiastical tensions created by trusteeism had a significant impact upon the development of American Catholicism. The memories of the antebellum battles were almost indelibly etched upon clerical consciousness. Trusteeism unwittingly aided the formation of a strong, centralized episcopal authority in American Catholicism, made the subsequent nineteenth- and early twentieth-century episcopacy suspicious of lay participation in the Church, and supported American nativists' charges that Catholicism and republicanism were ideologically and practically incompatible. Because elements of republicanism were not appropriated in ecclesiastical government, American Catholicism after the Civil War was periodically disturbed by lay-clerical tensions, repeated calls for lay and clerical rights, and attempts to create a more effective constitutional balance of powers within the Church.

Carey, Patrick W. *People, Priests and Prelates: Ecclesiastical Democracy and the Tensions of Trusteeism.* University of Notre Dame Press, 1987.

Fecher, Vincent J. *A Study of the Movement for National Parishes in Philadelphia and Baltimore (1787–1802).* Rome: Gregorianae, 1955.

Gerber, David. "Modernity in the Service of Tradition: Catholic Lay Trustees at Buffalo's St. Louis Church and the Transformation of European Communal Traditions, 1829–1855." *Journal of Social History* 15 (1983) 655–84.

Tourscher, F. E. *The Hogan Schism and Trustee Troubles in St. Mary's Church, Philadelphia, 1820–1829.* Philadelphia: Peter Reilly Co., 1930.

PATRICK W. CAREY

Related Document

LAY TRUSTEEISM IN NEW YORK, JANUARY 25, 1786

The most serious trouble that confronted the Catholic Church in the United States after the Revolution arose from the abuse of lay trusteeism. The root causes of the difficulty were: an imperfect knowledge, on the part of both clergy and laity, of the canon law pertaining to the holding and administration of church property; small groups of laymen imbued with the heady wine of their newly won religious freedom, and the example of their Protestant neighbors who had the dominant voice in ruling their congregations; wayward priests who for selfish reasons abetted the laymen's ambitions to govern the congregations; and a mounting antagonism among Catholics of varying national backgrounds. All the principal elements were present at St. Peter's Church, New York City, in the 1780's, plus the frustration suffered by John Carroll as ecclesiastical superior due to his limited faculties to deal with situations of this kind. St. Peter's got its start with an Irish-born Capuchin, Charles Whelan, who arrived in 1784, but with the appearance of another Irish Capuchin, Andrew Nugent, in 1785, quarrels arose and the congregation was soon divided between warring factions with the trustees finally casting Whelan out and going over to Nugent as the better preacher. Carroll was appealed to and in his reply to the trustees he cogently set forth the chief issues involved. The ugly affair eventually resulted in schism and it was only with the coming of Father William V. O'Brien, O.P. (1740–1816), in October, 1787, that peace was restored. Carroll's letter is included here to illustrate the nature of an evil that would plague the American Church in one form or another until near the middle of the nineteenth century.

(*Source: American Catholic Historical Researches*, XVII [January, 1900] 1–4.)

R.C. [Rock Creek] near Georgetown, Jan. 25, 1786.

Gentlemen:

I was honored yesterday at the same time with your letters of Dec. 22, 1785, and January 11, 1786. You did me justice in supposing that the former was delayed on its way or had miscarried; for certainly I should not have failed in my duty of immediately answering so respectable a part of the congregation. You will however readily conceive, that this is not an easy nor, allow me to say, a very agreeable office in the present instance. One circumstance indeed gives me comfort; you profess to have no other views than for the service and credit of religion; and as I make it my endeavor to be influenced solely by the same motive, I trust that proposing to ourselves the same end we shall likewise agree in the means of obtaining it.

The first advices of any disturbances among you, were transmitted to me in letters from Messrs. Whelan and Nugent which I answered on the 17th and 18th inst. Both these gentlemen represented the steps taken as extreme and improper. I spoke of them therefore in the same manner in my answers, and the more freely as neither of them mentioned the name of one single person concerned. Having now received a communication of your sentiments, I shall likewise deliver mine with the respect due to your representations, and with the freedom and plainness becoming the responsible and burdensome office, of which I feel myself every day more unworthy, in proportion as the duties and the weight of it grow upon me.

But I must first state to you the previous information I had received: 1st, that the trustees denied having agreed to the articles, of which I left a copy with Mr. Whelan; and which to my best apprehension had been adopted at the meeting I had the honor of having with those gentlemen. 2d, that an opinion was formed and propagated of the congregation having a right not only to choose such parish priest as is agreeable to them, but discharging him at pleasure, and that after such election, the bishop or other ecclesiastical superior cannot hinder him from exercising the usual functions. 3dly, that two of the congregation (by whose orders I am not informed) on Sunday, December 18th, after Divine Service and in the face of all present in the chapel, seized in a tumultuary manner and kept possession of the collection then made. The first part of this intelligence shocked me very much both because it reflected on my veracity which in this instance I will steadily assert and because I considered the matters then agreed on as right in point of justice as the renewal of confidence and foundation of future union. The next point of intelligence was still more important. If ever the principles then laid down should become predominant, the unity and catholicity of our Church would be at an end; and it would be formed into distinct and independent societies, nearly in the same manner as the congregational Presbyterians of our neighboring New England States. A zealous clergyman performing his duty courageously and without respect of persons would be always liable to be the victim of his earnest endeavors to stop the progress of vice and evil example, and others more complying with the passions of some principal persons of the congregation would be substituted in his room; and if the ecclesiastical superior has no control in these instances, I will refer to your own judgment what the consequences may be. The great source of misconception in this matter is that an idea appears to be taken both by you and Mr. Whelan that the officiating clergyman at New York is a parish priest, whereas there is yet no such office in the United States. The hierarchy of our American Church not being yet constituted, no parishes are formed, and the clergy coming to the assistance of the faithful, are but voluntary laborers in the vineyard of Christ, not vested with ordinary jurisdiction annexed to their office, but receiving it as delegated and extra hierarchical commission. Wherever parishes are established no doubt, a proper regard (and such as is suitable (?) to our governments) will be had to rights of the congregation in the mode of election and representation; and even now I shall ever pay to their wishes every deference consistent with the general welfare of religion: of which I hope to give you proof in the sequel of this letter. The third article of my information was particularly mortifying; for I could not but fear, that a step so violent, at such a time and place, and probably in the presence of other religionists would breed disunion among yourselves and make a very disadvantageous impression, to the prejudice of the Catholic cause, so soon after the first introduction of public worship into your city.

I now return to the contents of your letters, and observe that after stating some censurable instances of Mr. Whelan's conduct, you desire me to remove him, and imply a desire that Mr. Nugent, as being very acceptable, may succeed to his office. I can assure you, Gentlemen, that I have a very advantageous opinion of Mr. Nugent's abilities, and he shewed me very good testimonials of his zeal and virtue. I repeatedly told him, as I did to many of yourselves, that nothing but my own want of sufficient authority prevented me from giving him every power requisite for the exercise of his ministry. I hoped before this to have that restriction of my authority removed, but as it is not, it remains still out of my power to employ him agreeably to your and my desires. If I am ever able to do it, I will certainly remember my assurances to him. But in the mean time what can I do? Can I revoke Mr. Whelan's faculties and leave so great a congregation without assistance? Can I deprive him, when neither his morals, his orthodoxy, or his assiduity have been impeached? especially while I am uncertain whether his removal be desired by a majority of the congregation? For I have received assurances very much to the contrary. But even if a considerable part are still attached to him, would the great object of unanimity be obtained by his removal? Would not his adherents consider Mr. Nugent as coming in upon the ruins of his predecessor and consequently would they not keep alive the spirit of discord? Upon these considerations I have taken a resolution which will, I hope, meet your wishes, as well as of every part of the congregation. As soon as I am at liberty to grant them, Mr. Nugent shall have powers from me [to] act as your joint-chaplain; for the idea of parish-priest is not admissible. He has repeatedly assured me he never will accept of an appointment to the exclusion of his brother: in his letter he says a sufficient maintenance of both may be obtained. In the mean time he has full authority to announce the word of God, and I promise myself he will do it with effect, especially by including the great duty of charity and unanimity. He and Mr. Whelan will concur in recommending this characteristic virtue of christianity, by their examples as well as advice. Educated in the same school of religion, and connected by special ties to the same order, they will assist each other in the work of the ministry and every part of the congregation will have it in their power to apply to him of the two, in which they have the greatest confidence. I must not omit taking notice of Mr. Whelan's address to the congregation inclosed in your last. I greatly disapprove it, and shall so inform him. When I wrote the letter to which he refers, I had heard nothing from New York concerning your uneasiness. I lamented that my hands being still tied, I was prevented from giving full employment to Mr. Nugent's zeal; and I must add, for Mr. La Valinère's[1] credit, that when I declined granting him leave to administer the Sacraments to the Canadian refugees, it was for the same reason, because I had no power to do it. Otherwise I have such a conviction of his many qualities, that I should gladly have indulged the wishes of those good people who solicited [this power] and of this I beg to inform him.

[At the close?] of your last letter you make some mention of eventually having recourse to legal means to rid yourselves of Mr. Whelan. The insinuation makes me very unhappy. I cannot tell what assistance the laws might give you; but allow me to say that you can take no step so fatal to that respectability, in which as a religious Society you wish to stand, or more prejudicial to the Catholic cause. I must therefore entreat you to decline a design so pernicious to all your prospects; and protesting against measures so extreme, I explicitly declare, that no clergyman, be he who he may, shall receive any spiritual powers from me who shall advise or countenance so unnecessary . . . [the copy breaks off at this point].

[1] Pierre Huet de la Valinière (1732–1806), a French-born Sulpician, who had incurred the displeasure of both Bishop Briand and the British authorities in Canada during the Revolution because of his flirtations with the Americans. He was a rather erratic fellow whose many wanderings seemed to bring him little peace of mind.

(*Source*: John Tracy Ellis, ed. *Documents of American Catholic History*. Vol. 1:1493–1865. Wilmington, Del.: Michael Glazier, 1987, 150–54.)

TUMULTY, JOSEPH (1879–1954)

Presidential secretary. Joseph Patrick Tumulty was born May 5, 1879, in Jersey City, New Jersey, the son of an Irish grocer. He graduated from St. Peter's College, Jersey City, in 1899, was admitted to the bar in 1902, and married Mary Catherine Byrne in 1903. Drawn into the liberal "progressive" wing of the Democratic Party, Tumulty was elected to the state assembly from Hudson County in 1906.

Like other progressives, Tumulty initially opposed the election of the president of Princeton University, Woodrow Wilson, as governor, fearing him to be a front for the old party bosses. But Tumulty was moved by the progressive ideals in Wilson's acceptance speech at the state Democratic convention, switched sides, and campaigned for Wilson. After his election, Wilson appointed Tumulty as his secretary, "in order that I may have a guide at my elbow in matters of which I know almost nothing."

Tumulty was a close advisor to Wilson as he broke with the state's political bosses and achieved a series of progressive reforms in the state, and was an early supporter of Wilson for the presidency in 1912. Having won election, Wilson brought Tumulty to Washington as presidential secretary, despite some opposition to his Catholicism. In this role, Tumulty was, in effect, Wilson's chief of staff, handling political strategy, speeches, publicity, press relations, and party patronage.

Tumulty was completely loyal to Wilson, and never lost his enthusiasm for the Wilsonian view of the world order. The aloof, patrician, cerebral Wilson and the genial, crowd-working, politically astute Tumulty were a complementary team who worked well together. But, as Wilson's second term became more and more occupied with international diplomacy, Tumulty was often out of his element. Increasing criticism from his political rivals and anti-Catholic bigots, and Tumulty's alienation from the new Mrs. Wilson, whose 1915 marriage to the President Tumulty he had opposed as inopportune, created a distance between the two men. Although Tumulty continued as secretary to the end of Wilson's term, relations were not the same after 1917. In 1920 Wilson broke completely with Tumulty when a message he delivered to the Democratic convention on behalf of the ailing President was misconstrued as support for the Cox nomination.

After the White House, Tumulty returned to the private practice of law in Washington. Tumulty was the first Catholic to hold the position of presidential secretary, and, with the possible exceptions of Chief Justice White and Justice McKenna, was the most influential Catholic in government of the day. Tumulty died at Olney, Maryland, on April 8, 1954.

Blum, John M. *Joe Tumulty and the Wilson Era*. Boston: Houghton Mifflin, 1951.

Heckscher, August. *Woodrow Wilson. A Biography*. New York: Charles Scribner's Sons, 1991.

Tumulty, Joseph P. *Woodrow Wilson As I Knew Him*. Garden City, N.Y.: Doubleday, Page & Co., 1921.

RAYMOND J. KUPKE

TURGIS, ISIDORE-FRANÇOIS (1813–68)

Missionary. Père Turgis, as he was invariably referred to in New Orleans, was born April 12, 1813, in the Normandy farming village of Carantilly, came of age in the France of the restored Bourbons, and was ordained priest in 1846. L'Abbé Turgis (his proper title as he was a priest of the Diocese of Evreux), was finally accepted in 1858, at the age of forty-five, into the Corps of Military Chaplains. During the remaining decade of his life, he served as chaplain on three continents.

Although Emperor Napoleon III declared that peace was his goal, he was determined to rebuild a French colonial empire which meant that wars were inevitable. Chaplain Turgis' *baptême du feu* was in Lombardy at Montebello on May 20, 1859. Later that year he was with French forces on the coast of Indo-China and in the following year in Beijing, the capital of Manchu China. The 1860 Treaty of Tientsin granted France its imperial commercial goals and the French troops and Chaplain Turgis returned to France.

Inspired by missionary literature and by *Uncle Tom's Cabin,* Turgis opted for the American Mission. His French biographer wrote, "He dreamed of leaving for America and of living there among the black slaves of America." Arriving in New Orleans on the eve of the War for Southern Independence, his chaplain career was to continue instead. His ordinary, Archbishop Jean-Marie Odin, granted him faculties for men in the Confederate army and Père Turgis went north with the Orleans Guards as part of the Army of Mississippi to block General Grant's incursion. The April 1862 battle of Shiloh resulted. It was in the midst of this battlefield carnage that Turgis won "immortal renown" for his priestly ministry and devotion to his men. Both Turgis and remnants of the Orleans Guards returned to occupied New Orleans in late April.

Turgis remained, impatiently it appears, as an assistant at St. Louis Cathedral until Archbishop Odin returned in April 1863 from a successful recruiting visit to France. Père Turgis' second stint as chaplain was with the Thirtieth Louisiana Infantry and began on June 20, 1863. He was with this regiment in the Eastern Theater for a few months prior to assignment to the Department of the Gulf in September. There he remained on the rolls until the end of April 1865. Brigadier General Randell L. Gibson, C.S.A., reported that during an end-of-the-war engagement, "The Reverend Father Turgis shared our dangers and our hardships, and gave the consolation of religion whenever the occasion offered along the trenches and in the hospital."

After the war, Père Turgis was in residence at the mortuary chapel of the cathedral where his apartment became a center for veterans. Prior to his death he established an asylum for orphans, earned universal praise for ministry during the yellow fever epidemic of 1867, and, in general, adopted an unassuming lifestyle. Turgis died on March 3, 1868. His funeral the following day was a demonstration of Confederate pride, Generals Beauregard and Gibson being two of the pall bearers. In the 1890s, at the height of Confederate nostalgia, Père Turgis became a local icon of the Lost Cause with a "portrait" being hung in the newly constructed Confederate Museum, and a monument erected at his grave. Later in the 1930s his memory as "Le Bon Père Turgis" was again evoked as the Con-

federacy's immortal hero who ministered wherever duty called to the heroic sons of Creole Louisiana.

EARL F. NIEHAUS, S.M.

TURNER, THOMAS WYATT (1877–1978)

Educator and civil rights leader. Thomas Wyatt Turner was born in Hughesville, Maryland, on March 16, 1877, to sharecroppers. His father died when he was eight years old, leaving his mother to raise him and his eight siblings alone. He attended a black Episcopalian secondary school, and studied biology at Howard University in Washington, D.C., receiving his bachelor's degree in 1901.

He continued his studies at The Catholic University of America in Washington, D.C., on a scholarship, but left after his funds ran out. He subsequently taught biology at Tuskegee Institute in Alabama (1901–02), Baltimore High and Training School (1902–10, 1911–13), and St. Louis High School (1910–11). He received his master's degree from Howard in 1905. In 1913 he was appointed professor of biology at Howard, and one year later was appointed acting dean of the School of Education there, a post he held until 1920. Increasing discrimination against African Americans during these years—together with a lack of educational opportunities for African American children—caused Turner to become an activist in the struggle by blacks to achieve equal status both in the Church and in secular American society.

He became active in the NAACP in Baltimore and Washington, D.C., and organized the group's first citywide membership drive in the latter city in 1915. Turner also joined others from St. Augustine's parish there in protest against racial discrimination in Catholic institutions, such as the Knights of Columbus and the Josephite seminary in Baltimore, and against the lack of Church-related services available to black Catholic soldiers during World War I. The parish group became the Committee Against the Extension of Race Prejudice in the Church, and evolved into the Federated Colored Catholics in 1924. It insisted to Church leaders that blacks be given more educational opportunities and equal access to the services provided by Catholic institutions; it also decried racial segregation within these bodies. In 1919 the group began a correspondence with the American Catholic hierarchy, on the occasion of the latter's first full meeting at The Catholic University of America. Its first letter, nearly twenty typewritten pages in length, identified the mission and goals of the committee as "the collection of data concerning colored Catholics, the protection of their interests, promotion of their welfare, and the propagation of the Faith among colored people."

Members of the committee, the letter stated, included "Catholic colored laymen . . . among its membership [are] teachers, doctors, lawyers, government employees, and others." The statement enumerated five principal areas in which segregation was keeping blacks isolated and constrained from achieving spiritual and social parity within the Church: education; Catholic organizations; The Catholic University of America—which by then had changed its original policy and refused admittance to African American students; insufficient training for black candidates for the priesthood; and racism within the Church. Between 1927–32 the FCC convened at national meetings, and wrote to the national hierarchy after each one—expressing similar concerns, insisting on redress, and thanking them for initiatives taken in these areas.

The FCC separated into two groups in 1933, the result of philosophical and administrative dissension between Turner and two white Jesuits, William Markoe and John LaFarge, both active allies of the group. Turner wanted the federation to retain its African American solidarity, while the two priests supported an interracial approach, with both African Americans and their white colleagues collaborating on the group's administration. Turner and his faction continued as the FCC until 1952, though after the split it lacked the cohesion and force it possessed during the earlier period.

Professionally, Turner served as head of the Biological Sciences Department at Hampton Institute from 1924–45, and continued teaching at the university level for several years after that at schools in Florida and Texas. He would remain active in matters of racial justice for the rest of his life. In 1976, at ninety-nine years of age, he received an honorary degree from The Catholic University of America for his efforts to secure equal rights for African Americans in the Church. He died in Washington, D.C., on April 21, 1978.

Davis, Cyprian, O.S.B. *The History of Black Catholics in the United States.* New York, 1990.

Nickels, Marilyn W. *Black Catholic Protest and the Federated Colored Catholics, 1917–1933: Three Perspectives on Racial Justice.* New York, 1988.

____. "Thomas Wyatt Turner and the Federated Colored Catholics." *U.S. Catholic Historian* 7 (Spring–Summer 1988) 215–32.

JOSEPH QUINN

TURPIN, MARY (1731–61)

Religious. Mary Turpin, born in 1731, was the first Native American woman to join a Roman Catholic religious order in what is now the United States. Her father, Louis Turpin, a French-Canadian and the guardian of the king's warehouses in Illinois, and her mother, Dorothy Mechiperousta, a free Native American member of the Illinois tribe, were married in 1724. After Mary's birth, Dorothy, inspired by Jesuit missionaries, raised the child in the Catholic faith. After Dorothy's death, the young Mary continued her religious education under the Jesuits and expressed a desire to commit herself to a life of sacrifice and prayer.

News of the arrival of the Ursuline Sisters in New Orleans was passed on to the mission community from travelers to the Midwest. But when Mary asked her father for permission to join the Ursulines, he was most reluctant to allow her to make the trip. He finally agreed that she could leave her home for the boarding school which the Ursulines conducted in New Orleans. After a year of residence in New Orleans, Mary again asked for her father's approval to enter the order. This time Louis Turpin granted the needed permission and his daughter began her novitiate on July 2, 1749. Five months later on December 7, 1749, she received the religious habit and the name Sr. St. Martha. Sr. Jane Frances Heaney notes in her history of the Ursulines that Mary Turpin was questioned very closely by the Rev. Baudouin, S.J., in his canonical examination, because the colonists were prejudiced against Native Americans and worried about their stability.

Sister St. Martha was a coadjutrix sister and therefore was responsible for tasks of cooking, sewing, and cleaning, as well as caring for the boarders and orphans who lived with the Ursuline community. She died on November 20, 1761, twelve years after her profession at the age of thirty, and many years passed before any other native-born women joined the Ursulines of New Orleans.

See also AFRICAN AMERICAN CATHOLICS; URSULINES (O.S.U.).

JOAN MARIE AYCOCK, O.S.U.

U

UHLENKOTT, JOHN J. H. (1833–1922)

Benefactor of the Benedictine Sisters. John Uhlenkott was born on February 16, 1833, in Ahaus, Germany. During his youth he was in the service of the Dutch nobility. At the age of twenty-one, he was smuggled out of the country to America by a Dutch nobleman.

In 1887 Uhlenkott migrated with his wife, Gertrude, and twelve of his thirteen children from New Munich, Minnesota, to settle on Camas Prairie, Idaho. He was brought in contact with the farmers of Colton and Uniontown, Washington, through trade and became acquainted with the people and the sisters. In 1892 one of his daughters became a member of the Benedictine community and another entered in 1894.

Within the next few years, the sisters outgrew the convent in Colton, and their thoughts turned to Cottonwood, Idaho. They recalled Mr. Uhlenkott's earlier offer to donate land, if the convent moved to the prairie. In 1906 the sisters bought a piece of farmland, and Uhlenkott donated one hundred acres to them. He later donated one of the bells in the convent tower and the fourteen Stations of the Cross in thanksgiving for the recovery of Sr. Augustine, his daughter.

The Uhlenkott family extended their generosity and concern not only to the sisters but also to the Keuterville community and were instrumental in initiating the first place of worship there. When the priest could not come on Sundays, one of the men, usually John Uhlenkott, led the prayers and music. By a special privilege granted at the request of John Uhlenkott, he and his wife were interred in the private graveyard of the convent upon their deaths.

CARM TERNES, O.S.B.

UKRAINIAN CATHOLICS IN AMERICA

Ukrainians are a Slav people whose native land is located in southeastern Europe north of the Black Sea. A nation of over fifty-two million people, Ukraine is the second largest country in Europe. From the earliest era of recorded history, developments in Ukraine have been greatly influenced by its geographical configurations. As a result of its location, Ukraine served as the gateway to Europe for millennia. As early as the tenth century, both the Roman and Byzantine Empires sought to establish religious, political, and economic ties with Kiev, the capital of Ukraine. Lacking natural barriers, the country became an easy target for hostile invaders, as various nomadic tribes, including the Tatars, poured out of the Asian subcontinent to exploit and ravage the fertile Ukrainian soil.

Ukraine's promising beginnings were put to an end during the thirteenth century as a result of internal discord and the attack of the Mongols who sacked Kiev in 1240. A new era had dawned in Ukraine—an era of foreign domination as the country began its long history of subordination to the rule of other states. The Ukrainian people and Ukrainian lands fell prey to neighboring countries who began to scramble for control of Ukrainian territory. Russia, Austria, Lithuania, Poland, Romania, Hungary, Czechoslovakia, and the Soviets, all occupied parts of

Ukraine at some point in history. Ukrainians were denied their own churches, schools, and freedom of the press. They were discriminated against and oppressed and were even forbidden to speak their own language. During the First World War, the country enjoyed a brief period of independence (1918–20); shortly afterwards, Soviet forces succeeded in occupying Eastern Ukraine and creating the Ukrainian Soviet Socialist Republic, which was actually dominated by Moscow. On August 24, 1991, one year after the collapse of the Soviet Union, Ukraine proclaimed its independence.

Christianity in Ukraine

Christianity came to Ukraine by the end of the first century C.E. from the East, by way of the Greek colonists who settled the northern coast of the Black and Azov Seas. In 988 Ukrainian Grand Prince Volodymyr the Great officially adopted Christianity from Byzantium as the state religion. At that time, the Church was united into one apostolic and universal Church. The Great Schism of 1054 that split the Church had no real effect on the Ukrainian Church, which never formally went into schism but was alienated from Rome because of political circumstances. Indeed, the Ukrainian Church continued to maintain contacts with the Holy See: in 1245 Archbishop Peter of Ukraine attended the First Council of Lyons, and Prince Danylo was crowned king of Ukraine by the papal legate in 1253. In 1596 the bishops of the Kievan Metropoly accepted the Union of Brest, which formally united the Ukrainian Church with Rome on the condition that it would retain the Eastern Rite, its hierarchy, traditions, and rights that included the right of married men to be ordained as priests.

The Ukrainian Catholic Church, also known as the Uniate Church, was persecuted and finally liquidated in Eastern Ukraine by the Russian Tsarist regime. In Western Ukraine (Galicia), which was under Austrian rule, the Ukrainian Church, which became known as the Greek Catholic Church to distinguish it from the Roman Catholic Church, flourished until 1939.

In 1939, when Galicia was occupied by the Communists and became incorporated into the Ukrainian Soviet Socialist Republic, all Church institutions including seminaries, monasteries, schools, and publishing houses were abolished or taken over by the state. Priests and laity were persecuted and arrested in large numbers and Church property was confiscated. The Church remained steadfast, however, under one of its greatest leaders, Metropolitan Andrew Sheptytsky, whose beatification process is now well under way. In April 1945 the Ukrainian Catholic Church was liquidated and subordinated to the Russian Orthodox Church. Stalin ordered the arrest of the entire Church hierarchy; the bishops were secretly tried and deported to Siberia where all, except Metropolitan Archbishop, later

Cardinal, Joseph Slipyj, died in concentration camps. Archbishop Slipyj was released in 1963 through the intercession of Pope John XXIII after eighteen years in Siberian exile. Hundreds of priests, monks, and nuns and thousands of faithful perished as martyrs in the concentration camps of Siberia. The Church went underground, where it existed for over four decades in the catacombs until its revival in 1989–90.

Ukrainian Immigration to the United States

Although individual Ukrainians were found in the United States in colonial times, large-scale immigration of Ukrainians to the United States did not begin until the 1880s. By the outbreak of World War I, nearly 500,000 Ukrainians had reached America's shores. The second wave of Ukrainian immigration (1920–39) was much smaller, only some 15,000 to 20,000, because of immigration restrictions imposed by the National Origins Act of 1924. The third or post–World War II wave reached close to 90,000 Ukrainians, the majority of whom were persons displaced by the war. While the first wave of immigrants was composed primarily of peasants and poorly educated people escaping overpopulation, poverty, and industrial underdevelopment, the second and especially the third immigration wave consisted mostly of the intelligentsia fleeing religious and political persecution.

Organization of Religious Life in the United States

The first Ukrainian immigrants in the United States attended liturgical services in already established churches belonging to other nationalities. As early as 1884, a group of Ukrainian Catholics who settled in Shenandoah, Pennsylvania, petitioned the archbishop of Lviv for a Ukrainian priest and permission to build a church. That same year, the Rev. Ivan Volansky was sent to minister to the Ukrainian faithful; the first liturgical service was offered on December 19, 1884. The first Ukrainian Catholic Church in the United States was consecrated two years later. Because he was a married priest, Fr. Volansky encountered hostility from the Latin-Rite clergy. At the insistence of the Latin hierarchy in the United States and Rome, he was recalled to Ukraine in 1889.

A circular letter from the Congregation de Propaganda Fide of October 1, 1890, written to the Ukrainian and Carpathian hierarchs in Europe, insisted that only celibate priests or widowers be permitted to serve in the United States. It also stipulated that the Ukrainian faithful would fall under the jurisdiction of the local Latin-Rite bishops. That same year, the Ukrainian clergy and laity in the United States petitioned the Holy See for a bishop of their own rite. It was only in 1907 that Rome answered the petition, appointing a Basilian monk, Soter Ortynsky, bishop for Ukrainians in the United States. Bishop Ortynsky, who settled in Philadelphia, Pennsylvania, on August 27, 1907, had no ecclesiastical jurisdiction, except that which he received by appointment as vicar general for Ukrainian Catholics from each individual Latin-Rite bishop at the latter's discretion.

On August 17, 1914, in its decree *Cum episcopo,* the Holy See granted Bishop Ortynsky full ordinary jurisdiction and independence of the local Latin-Rite ordinaries. After Bishop Ortynsky's untimely death in 1916, instead of designating a successor, the apostolic delegate directed the diocesan consultors to appoint two administrators, Rev. Peter Poniatyshyn for the faithful from the Galician region of Ukraine, and Rev. Gabriel Martiak for those from the Transcarpathian region and from Croatia. On May 20, 1924, Rome appointed two bishops for the Ukrainian Catholic Church, Constantine Bohachevsky for Ukrainians from Galicia and Basil Takach for Ruthenians from Transcarpathia, establishing a permanent division between the two groups. Both candidates were ordained in Rome on June 15, 1924. Bishop Bohachevsky, who was named archbishop in 1954, became the first metropolitan of Philadelphia in July 1958 with jurisdiction over all Ukrainian Catholics in the United States. Bishop Takach was named ordinary of the Apostolic Exarchate of Pittsburgh with jurisdiction over the Byzantine Slavic-rite Catholics from Transcarpathia, Slovakia, Hungary, and Yugoslavia.

On July 20, 1956, the apostolic constitution *Optatissimo unitatis* established the Exarchy of Stamford, Connecticut, for the faithful residing in New York and the New England states. Ambrose Senyshyn, O.S.B.M., the auxiliary bishop of Philadelphia, became the first Exarch of Stamford. On July 10, 1958, Pope Pius XII issued the apostolic constitution *Apostolicum hanc,* which established the Ukrainian Byzantine Rite Ecclesiastical Province of Philadelphia. The Ukrainian Catholic Church in the United States now consisted of the Archeparchy of Philadelphia, with Archbishop Bohachevsky as its metropolitan, and an Eparchy of Stamford with Bishop Senyshyn as its first eparch. After the metropolitan's death on January 6, 1961, Bishop Senyshyn became metropolitan archbishop of Philadelphia. Joseph Schmondiuk, auxiliary bishop of Philadelphia, was named bishop of Stamford. A third diocese for Ukrainians, the Eparchy of St. Nicholas of Chicago, was established by the decree *Byzantini ritus* of July 14, 1961. Jaroslav Gabro was named the first bishop of the new eparchy whose territory included all of the United States west of the western borders of Ohio, Kentucky, Tennessee, and Mississippi.

On May 25, 1971, John Stock, chancellor of the Diocese of Stamford, and Basil Losten, econome of the Archdiocese of Philadelphia, were named auxiliary bishops of Philadelphia. Bishop Stock suffered an untimely death on June 29, 1972.

Archbishop Senyshyn, who died on September 11, 1976, was succeeded by Bishop Schmondiuk as metropolitan-archbishop of Philadelphia. Bishop Losten was named the new bishop of Stamford on December 7, 1977. After Metropolitan Schmondiuk's untimely death on December 25, 1978, Msgr. Myroslav Lubachivsky was named the new metropolitan of Philadelphia. He was consecrated by Pope John Paul II, Cardinal Josyf Slipyj, and Metropolitan Maxim Hermaniuk of Canada in the Sistine Chapel on November 12, 1979, and installed by the apostolic delegate on December 4, 1979.

Metropolitan Lubachivsky was chosen coadjutor with right of succession to the major archbishop of Lviv in Ukraine, Josyf Cardinal Slipyj, at a Synod of Ukrainian bishops convened in Rome by Pope John Paul II. Stephen Sulyk, who was named metropolitan of Philadelphia on January 29, 1981, to succeed him, was consecrated in Rome on March 31, 1981, by Cardinal Slipyj. Innocent Lotocky, O.S.B.M., was consecrated on the same day to succeed Bishop Gabro of Chicago, who died on March 28, 1980.

A complete reorganization of the Ukrainian Catholic Church in the United States took place in 1983, when the Holy See established a fourth diocese for Ukrainian Catholics, the Eparchy of St. Josaphat in Parma, Ohio, with jurisdiction over the states of Ohio, Mississippi, West Virginia, Kentucky, Tennessee, Alabama, Georgia, North Carolina, South Carolina, Florida, and western Pennsylvania. Bishop Robert Moskal, auxiliary bishop of Philadelphia since October 13, 1981, was named the first bishop of the new diocese. All four eparchies are united in one Ukrainian Catholic Church headed by Archbishop-Major Myroslav Cardinal Lubachivsky who resides in Lviv.

All Ukrainian bishops in the United States are members of the Synod of the Ukrainian Catholic Church which meets every two years under the leadership of Cardinal Lubachivsky as head of the Ukrainian Catholic Church in Ukraine and the diaspora. During liturgical services, Ukrainian priests commemorate Cardinal Lubachivsky as His Beatitude Patriarch Myroslav, despite the fact that the Holy See has not yet officially granted him the title of "Patriarch." Ukrainians in the diaspora have organized a lay movement to promote the creation of a patriarchate. Besides petitions to the Holy Father and other activities, the organization publishes the monthly journal *The Patriarchate.*

Organization of Ukrainian Catholic Schools

The first Ukrainian Catholic elementary school, directed and staffed by the Sisters of St. Basil the Great, was established by Bishop Ortynsky in Philadelphia in 1910. This was followed by other elementary and secondary schools throughout the exarchy. In 1933 Bishop Bohachevsky founded St. Basil Preparatory School, the minor seminary in Stamford, and St. Basil's College in 1939. St. Josaphat's Major Seminary was founded in Washington, D.C., in 1941.

Candidates for the priesthood are sent to Washington, D.C., Innsbruck, or Rome to pursue their theological studies.

Currently, Ukrainian Catholic high schools are operating in New York City and Hamtramck, Michigan. Some parishes run full-time parochial schools and almost every parish offers religious instruction classes for children attending public schools.

In 1996 the four Ukrainian dioceses in the United States contained 125,520 people organized in 197 parishes served by 169 diocesan priests and 40 religious order priests.

Significant Commemorations in the History of the Ukrainian Catholic Church

The year 1988 marked the celebration of the Millennium of Christianity in Ukraine by Ukrainian Catholics in parishes throughout the United States. In 1996 the 400th anniversary of the Union of Brest marking the reunion with Rome was celebrated.

Ammann, Albert M., S.J. *Abriss der Ostslawischen Kirchengeschichte.* Wien: Thomas Morus Presse im Verlag Herder, 1950.

Byzantine Rite Archeparchy of Philadelphia. *Ukrainian Catholic Metropolitan See. Byzantine Rite U.S.A.* Philadelphia, 1959.

Pawliczko, Ann Lencyk. *Ukraine and Ukrainians Throughout the World.* Ontario: University of Toronto Press, 1994.

Procko, Bohdan P. *Ukrainian Catholics in America, A History.* New York: University Press of America, 1982.

Struk, Danylo Husar, ed. *Encyclopedia of Ukraine.* Vol. V. Ontario: University of Toronto Press, 1993.

WASYL LENCYK

UNGER, DOMINIC (1907–82)

Capuchin writer and scholar. Joseph Unger was born on March 30, 1907, in Herndon, Kansas, the son of Andreas Unger and Teresa Zivickls. After completing three years at Hays Catholic College, Hays, Kansas, he entered the Capuchin novitiate in Herman, Pennsylvania, on July 13, 1928, and took the religious name Dominic. On July 14, 1932, he professed his final vows. Five years later, June 3, 1934, Unger was ordained a priest, and began his final year of sacerdotal theological formation. In 1935 he began his studies at the Pontifical Gregorian University, Rome, Italy, where he obtained a licentiate in sacred theology, and then entered the Pontifical Biblical Institute to study under Augustine Bea. Within two years, he received *cum laude* a licentiate in sacred Scripture; by the time World War II broke out in Europe, he had completed all but the dissertation of his work toward a doctorate.

Upon his return to the United States in 1939, Dominic began teaching at St. Fidelis Seminary, Victoria, Kansas. In 1940 he moved to Washington, D.C., and throughout the 1940s, in addition to his responsibilities as director of

formation, he was a professor of theology and sacred Scripture and continued to refine the research skills he had acquired in Rome. During these years, he worked with James Kleist, S.J., and Joseph Lilly, C.M., on a proposed new Confraternity translation of the New Testament from the original Greek. Between 1950 and 1953, Unger was assigned to St. Conrad Friary, Annapolis, Maryland. During the following two years, 1953 to 1955, he worked as a member of the Capuchin Historical Institute in Rome, but was forced to return to Annapolis, Maryland, because of his health. From 1956 until 1965, Dominic resumed his teaching responsibilities in Washington, D.C., spent the following six years in the Midwest (one in St. Charles Borromeo, St. Louis, Missouri, and five in St. Mary's, Ellis, Kansas), then returned to Washington, D.C., for the last four years of his teaching career, 1971–75. The last seven years of his life were spent as a parochial assistant in St. Louis and Wentsville, Missouri, and Hays, Kansas. After a year's struggle with stomach cancer, Dominic Unger died in St. Anthony Hospital, Hays, Kansas, on July 11, 1982.

Throughout his life Dominic was known for his studies on the absolute primacy of Christ, Mariology, and the theology of St. Irenaeus of Lyons. In 1960 Pope John XXIII appointed him a consultor to the Theological Commission preparing for the Second Vatican Council. A preliminary bibliography of his published writings includes five books, including a critical edition and study of Irenaeus's *Adversus haereses,* 126 articles, 177 book reviews, and scores of pamphlets and leaflets. He contributed to such scholarly periodicals as the *American Ecclesiastical Review, The Catholic Biblical Quarterly, The Catholic Educational Review, Verbum Dei, Collectanea Franciscana, Laurentianum, Antonianum, Franciscan Studies, Marianum, Review for Religious, Theological Studies,* and *Marian Studies;* and to those of a more popular nature such as *Ave Maria, Homiletic and Pastoral Review, Franciscan Herald and Forum, The Priest,* and *Pastoral Life.* He was a regular speaker at the International Marian Congresses, a member of the Pontifical International Marian Academy, and the Mariological Society of America. In addition to being honored by the Mariological Society of America in 1956, Dominic Unger received a Citation of Achievement from the Franciscan Institute of St. Bonaventure University in 1982.

See also FRANCISCANS (CAPUCHINS).

REGIS J. ARMSTRONG, O.F.M. CAP.

UNITED NATIONS AND AMERICAN CATHOLICS, THE

At the end of World War II, the National Catholic Welfare Conference (NCWC) appointed "consultants" to the U.S. delegation at the 1945 United Nations Conference on International Organization (UNCIO) at San Francisco.

These international affairs specialists from NCWC, and those from the Catholic Association for International Peace (CAIP), attempted to modify the Dumbarton Oaks and Yalta Agreements along lines suggested by Pius XII's "Five Point Peace Program" and the U.S. hierarchy's statements *On International Order* and *On Organizing World Peace.*

At UNCIO Catholics saw many setbacks and disappointments but did achieve several things: cooperation among consultants from American religious organizations; Western Hemispheric solidarity among Latin American delegates; inclusion of Christian principles in the codification of international law; development of the Economic and Social Council (ECOSOC) as a UN body concerned with social and humanitarian endeavors, and acceptance in principle of an International Bill of Rights. Most important, the Catholic consultants helped secure approval of Article Seventy-One of the UN Charter, which accredited Non-Governmental Organizations (NGOs), permitting them to present statements and to attend sessions of UN bodies. In spite of these successes, NCWC's episcopal leadership was in 1945 divided on the issue of U.S. Catholic support for the UN. Its consultants, however, were unanimous in arguing that NCWC should endorse this world body, then try to transform it in the light of Catholic precepts.

UN Office of the NCWC

In October 1946 Samuel Cardinal Stritch, head of the Bishops' Peace Committee, persuaded the NCWC Administrative Board to establish an Office for United Nations Affairs in New York. The board appointed as assistant to the general secretary of NCWC for UN Affairs the layperson Catherine Schaefer, an NCWC Social Action Department expert who had been a CAIP consultant at UNCIO. What NCWC envisioned for its UN Office was some kind of observing and reporting office. It was to follow developments in various agencies, prepare summaries thereon, and generally make sure that Catholic viewpoints were advanced. It was also to attempt to enlist Catholics, particularly in the American delegation, and others whose viewpoints were marked by a regard for Christian principles. With the advent of the cold war and the rise of the Soviet Bloc at the UN, the NCWC Office moved in another direction: global activism, sometimes in conjunction with U.S. foreign policy, but always in accord with the internationalist objectives of the popes. Under Pius XII it advanced the power of the UN as a buffer against Soviet aggression. Later, under Popes John XXIII and Paul VI, it saw the UN as a instrument for detente and international social justice, in the spirit of the 1963 encyclical, *Pacem in Terris.*

From the beginning the UN Office developed a strategy not mandated by NCWC. Inspired by Catherine Schaefer, it evolved into a center where Catholic representatives at the UN and Catholics from the United States could meet

for social and policy-development purposes. A dynamic collaboration soon resulted among Catholic representatives from the two NGO categories—that is, International NGOs accredited to ECOSOC and National NGOs ("Observers") in consultative status with the Department of Public Information. This was possible because UN Office staff members functioned both as "Observers" from NCWC and as American representatives of an International Catholic Organization (ICO), the World Union of Catholic Women's Organizations (WUCWO), which had obtained ECOSOC Consultative Status A, the highest NGO level.

Some American Catholic "Observer" organizations with which NCWC's UN Office maintained particularly close contacts over the years included Catholic Relief Services (CRS), the National Council of Catholic Women (NCCW), and the National Catholic Educational Association (NCEA). It also helped other Catholic groups from the U.S.A. to gain UN accreditation. ICOs with whom it regularly collaborated were the International Federation of Christian Trade Unions, the Catholic Near East Welfare Association, the International Catholic Union of Press, the International Union for Catholic Social Service, Caritas Internationalis, and Pax Romana.

The UN Office helped all these Catholic organizations to cover and to report on General Assembly sessions and ECOSOC matters for the benefit of this "Catholic circle." The prototype for this concept had been developed at the League of Nations. Under the League, there was at Geneva a group of Catholic delegates and specialists who worked together to advance international Catholic social teachings. At the UN, assistance and training of this type was supplied by the UN Office staff. This entailed advice on preparing formal statements and organizing reports, briefing Catholic participants on UN projects, and frequent gatherings on UN issues, to which were invited representatives of Catholic groups and other coreligionists active in organization and public opinion, or with special competence or interest in world organization. The UN Office was used regularly for all these functions, and thereby was recognized as the convening agent and facilitator for Catholic UN enterprises in New York.

The UN Office disseminated information to Catholic organizations and media channels throughout the world. Reports were made on the activities of the UN General Assembly, Security Council, and especially ECOSOC. Monthly articles, summaries, and "news-notes" were submitted for inclusion in the NCWC publication, *Foreign Affairs.*

Over the years the UN Office worked with certain delegations, national envoys—most of them Catholic—and UN special agencies such as the Human Rights Commission. The staff kept in contact with members of the UN Secretariat and, of course, with members of the U.S. delegation. From 1964 it worked closely with the Permanent Observer Mission of the Holy See to the UN, on both routine and extraordinary operations. Concerning the latter, it helped arrange the visit of Pope Paul VI in 1965, during which the Pope addressed the General Assembly with his famous plea for peace.

End of the UN Office

In 1972 the Episcopal Committee on Research, Plans, and Programs of the United States Catholic Conference (USCC), the successor to NCWC, determined that because of fiscal shortfalls at USCC, and because the Holy See's Mission provided ample Catholic representation, the UN Office, which by that time had been renamed the Division for United Nations Affairs, was no longer needed. USCC concluded that it could deal directly with the UN and its agencies without benefit of a New York office. USCC was now seen as essentially a domestic organization serving the needs of individual dioceses in the U.S.A. and representing their interests at the national level. Involvement in foreign operations was therefore to be strictly limited.

This decision was steadfastly opposed by *Commonweal* magazine, and representatives of ICOs protested strenuously that the Holy See's mission could not replace the services of the UN Division. The Vatican's secretariat of state agreed, declaring that the division had been an effective means of ensuring Catholic presence at the UN, and that the Permanent Observer needed its expertise and facilities in order to carry out his work. All agreed that the educational services the division provided to the Church, the nation, and the world through its publications, informational services, and contacts, were irreplaceable. The U.S. hierarchy was unyielding, nevertheless, and on June 30, 1972, the UN Division shut its doors.

After the closing, CRS, as a U.S. organization with NGO status, led a group of International Catholic Organizations in establishing an ICO Information Center at the UN, which furnishes the support services once provided by the UN Division. Several U.S. Catholic NGOs have remained influential at the UN; these include CRS, Covenant House, the Catholic Near East Welfare Association, NCEA, and NCCW. Many Americans serve as representatives of major ICOs such as WUCWO, which was affiliated with the UN Office from the start.

Rossi, Joseph S., S.J. *American Catholics and the Formation of the United Nations.* Lanham, Md.: University Press of America, 1993.

JOSEPH S. ROSSI, S.J.

UNITED STATES CATHOLIC CONFERENCE

The United States Catholic Conference (USCC) is the civil successor of the National Catholic Welfare Conference (NCWC). In the decree *Christus Dominus* (October 1965), the Second Vatican Council called for the estab-

lishment of national episcopal conferences "so that by sharing their wisdom and experience and exchanging views [bishops] may jointly formulate a program for the common good of the Church" (Austin Flannery, O.P., ed., *Vatican Council II: The Conciliar and Post Conciliar Documents,* 587). As a civilly incorporated, voluntary association of the American hierarchy, the NCWC had already been fulfilling this role. In annual assembly, the bishops managed both the internal and external affairs of the Church, the execution of the latter being carried out through a secretariat located in Washington, D.C. Because the Second Vatican Council gave episcopal conferences canonical status and the authority to make binding decisions, the American bishops felt it necessary to restructure the NCWC to reflect that reality.

Origins of the USCC

In so doing, the bishops established two organizations: the National Conference of Catholic Bishops (NCCB) and the USCC, the former a canonical entity to effect the joint, authoritative exercise of the pastoral ministry of bishops, and the latter a civil corporation "to unify, coordinate, encourage, promote and carry on all Catholic activities in the United States; to organize and conduct religious, charitable and social welfare work . . . ; to aid in education; to care for immigrants and generally to enter into and promote . . . the objects of its being" (*Handbook: National Conference of Catholic Bishops, United States Catholic Conference,* 21). Thereafter, the American hierarchy met semiannually in two capacities, the one as pastors of the Church, the other as a corporation conducting the civic and religious work of the Church in America. This dual identity is further reflected in the fact that the same bishops compose both the Administrative Committee of the NCCB and the Administrative Board of the USCC. The distinction between the two organizations is embodied in the personnel. The committees of the NCCB consist entirely of bishops, while the departments of the USCC consist of bishops, clerics, and laypersons, all full voting members.

The USCC resembles the former NCWC in almost every respect. The corporation is the hierarchy in semiannual assembly, which implements its decisions through an Administrative Board of bishops (expanded from fourteen under the NCWC to fifty-two under the USCC) operating a secretariat in Washington, D.C. The USCC secretariat took over the various departments of the NCWC and in July 1968 reorganized them into the following: Education, Communications, Health Affairs, International Affairs, and Social Development. In 1972 these were again reorganized and streamlined into three: the Departments of Communications, Education, and Social Development and World Peace. The Department of Communications contains four divisions: the National Catholic News Service, the National Catholic Office for Information, Creative Services, and Film and Broadcasting. The Education Department contains five divisions: Elementary and Secondary Education, Higher Education, Religious Education, Family Life, and Youth Activities. The Department of Social Development and World Peace contains six divisions: Chaplains Services, Health Affairs, Justice and Peace, Rural Life, Spanish-Speaking, and Urban Affairs. Each department has a committee consisting of an equal number of episcopal and nonepiscopal members, chaired by a bishop of the Administrative Board. The responsibility of the departmental committee is to recommend and review objectives, policies, and programs implemented by the departmental secretary and the Washington staff. In 1969 the hierarchy added an Advisory Council to the USCC. Composed of sixty members—bishops, clerics, religious, and laypersons—the council offers advice both on matters referred to it by either the hierarchy or the Administrative Board and on matters resulting from initiatives taken by the USCC. It also reviews and comments on reports of the USCC departments.

USCC and NCCB

In actual operation, the distinction between the USCC and the NCCB often became blurred. The USCC Department of Education, for instance, was interested not only in state and federal support for Catholic schools but also in the doctrinal content of teaching in those institutions. The Pro-Life Committee of the NCCB, on the other hand, was deeply concerned not only about the morality of abortion but also about abortion legislation. The hierarchy further obfuscated matters by their public utterances. In order to emphasize the importance of some declarations, the bishops have issued pastoral letters from the NCCB on issues like peace and the economy, which are properly the province of the USCC. Because of the overlap, the blurring, and the cumbersomeness of maintaining two parallel structures, the hierarchy considered a plan, in 1995, to restructure the NCCB and amalgamate the USCC into it. The idea met stiff opposition in part from bishops who deplored the loss of priestly and lay participation in decision-making if the USCC were to cease.

Flannery, Austin, O.P., ed. *Vatican Council II: The Conciliar and Post Conciliar Documents.* Northport, N.Y.: Costello Publishing Company, 1975.

Handbook: National Conference of Catholic Bishops, United States Catholic Conference. Washington, D.C.: NCCB-USCC, 1982.

Reese, Thomas J., S.J. "Conflict and Consensus in the NCCB/USCC." *Episcopal Conferences: Historical, Canonical, and Theological Studies,* ed. Thomas J. Reese, S.J. Washington, D.C.: Georgetown University Press, 1989.

_____. "Collegiality in Action." *Collegiality Put to the Test,* eds. James Provost and Knut Walf. London and Philadelphia: Trinity Press International, 1990.

_____. "The Bishops' Conference: More Secretive, More Clerical, Less Vocal." *America* 172 (June 3, 1995) 14–18.

_____. "Bishops' Plan Would Reduce Laity Role." *National Catholic Reporter,* June 16, 1995.

_____. "Bishops Again Debate Liturgical Wording." *National Catholic Reporter,* June 30, 1995.

DOUGLAS J. SLAWSON

UNITED STATES CATHOLIC HISTORICAL SOCIETY

The United States Catholic Historical Society was founded in New York City two days after the conclusion of the Third Plenary Council of Baltimore, which was the inspiration for the creation of the society. In the pastoral letter issued at the close of the council, on December 7, 1884, the bishops had directed that "the history of the United States should be carefully taught in all our Catholic schools . . . and form a favorite part of the home library and home reading." One person who took this admonition to heart was John Gilmary Shea, one of the invited lay observers at the council and the country's premier Catholic historian.

In Baltimore, Shea and Richard H. Clarke (a New York lawyer) consulted Bishop John Ireland about the possibility of establishing an American Catholic historical society. Ireland encouraged them to pursue the project. They first obtained the approval of Cardinal John McCloskey of New York and his coadjutor, Michael Augustine Corrigan, and then issued invitations for a meeting in New York City on December 9, 1884. John Ireland came directly from Baltimore to preside at the meeting. The other participants were Fr. Richard Lalor Burtsell, Fr. James H. McGean, Cornelius O'Leary, Patrick Farrelly, Charles Carroll Lee, Charles G. Herbermann, Marc Vallette, Thomas Addis Emmett, and Franklin Churchill. They appointed Shea, Clarke, and Herbermann to draw up a constitution for the United States Catholic Historical Society which was adopted at a second meeting on December 17, 1884.

The stated purpose of the USCHS was not only to collect and publish material pertaining to American Catholic history, but also to establish a reference library to house this material. After the initial meetings in December of 1884, however, little was achieved. In 1887 the USCHS began publication of a quarterly journal, the *United States Catholic Historical Magazine,* but publication was discontinued in 1892, and thereafter the society became practically moribund. According to Charles Herbermann, "the principal cause of the trouble was the mistaken policy of starting with exaggerated pretensions."

In 1897, thanks in large measure to the interest of Archbishop Corrigan, the USCHS was revived, and Herbermann was elected president. Two years later, the USCHS began publication of its annual *Historical Records and Studies* with Corrigan himself contributing a series of articles on the pioneer clergy in New York. Between 1899 and 1964, fifty volumes appeared in the series, almost all of which were edited first by Herbermann and later by Thomas F. Meehan. In 1903 the USCHS also began publication of a monograph series which numbered thirty-eight volumes through 1984. As a replacement for the defunct *Historical Records and Studies,* in 1981 the USCHS sponsored a quarterly journal, the *U.S. Catholic Historian,* under the editorship of Christopher J. Kauffman, which devotes each issue to a specific topic. Publication of the journal was assumed by Our Sunday Visitor, Inc., in 1993, although it remains an official publication of the USCHS.

Reardon, Timothy J. "The Society's Golden Jubilee." *Historical Records and Studies* 25 (1935) 7–19.
Ridder, Charles H., and Timothy J. Reardon. "U.S. Catholic Historical Society: A Resumé of Its Record." *Historical Records and Studies* 33 (1944) 13–18.

JAMES HYNES

UNITED STATES SUPREME COURT AND CATHOLICS

Catholic Justices

The Supreme Court of the United States has had 108 justices since its establishment in 1789. All told, eight Catholics sat on the country's highest judicial bench. In fact, the first Catholic to become a Supreme Court justice was Roger B. Taney who was appointed to the Court by President Andrew Jackson in 1836 and who became the Court's chief justice sixteen years later. With the end of Taney's term at the close of the American Civil War in 1864, thirty years passed before the next Catholic justice was selected by President Grover Cleveland in 1894. Edward Douglass White was a Supreme Court justice between 1894 and 1910, and with him, a tradition began in which one Catholic was a member of the Supreme Court until President Harry Truman's administration: Joseph McKenna sat on the Court from 1897–1925, Pierce Butler from 1922–39, and Frank Murphy from 1940–49. This Catholic tradition resumed when President Dwight D. Eisenhower appointed William J. Brennan, Jr., in 1956, who remained a justice until 1990.

Today, the Court has three justices who are Catholic. They were Republican appointees. President Ronald Reagan selected Antonin Scalia in 1986 and Anthony Kennedy in 1988. Clarence Thomas, President George Bush's nominee in 1991 and perhaps the most controversial appointment to the high Court in the last three decades, was born a Baptist, raised a Roman Catholic, briefly enrolled in the Catholic seminary of the Immaculate Conception in 1967, attended Episcopalian services for a number of years, and in 1996 returned to the practice of the Catholic faith.

Catholics and Supreme Court Cases

The American Catholic community has been primarily concerned with the Supreme Court cases dealing with federal aid to parochial schools, with prayer in schools, and with the volatile issue of abortion. The Supreme Court case that received the most attention from American Catholics concerning prayer in school was *Engel v. Vitale* (June 1962) which ruled that public schools may not require pupils to "recite a state composed prayer at the beginning of each school day." The issue of federal aid to parochial schools was addressed in the *Lemon v. Kurtzman* case (June 1971) in which the Court established a three-part test to determine whether state aid would be permissible without violating the First Amendment's ban on government action "establishing" religion. The final Supreme Court case that still polarizes non-Catholic and Catholic Americans was, and is, *Roe v. Wade* (January 1973) which decided that the right to privacy guaranteed by the Fourteenth Amendment's due process clause "encompasses and protects a woman's decision whether or not to bear a child."

Because the Court has three Catholic conservatives on its bench, some have predicted that the Court is moving in a socially conservative direction, which might eventually restore prayer in American classrooms and permanently ban abortions in this country. Yet, there is also a Catholic liberal voice which focuses upon the Supreme Court's decisions concerning the death penalty and racism. Whatever the scenario, Catholic Americans for the first time in their history can have a major impact upon American life through the nation's highest judicial institution.

See also BUTLER, PIERCE; MCKENNA, JOSEPH; MURPHY, FRANK; TANEY, ROGER BROOKE; WHITE, EDWARD DOUGLASS.

Hall, Kermit, ed. *The Oxford Companion to the Supreme Court of the United States.* New York: Oxford University Press, 1992.
Witt, Elder, ed. *Guide to the U.S. Supreme Court.* Washington, D.C.: Library of Congress, 1979.

TIMOTHY J. SARBAUGH

UNIVERSITY OF DAYTON

The Society of Mary in 1850 founded St. Mary's School for Boys, the institution that was to become known as the University of Dayton. The Marianists, as members of the society are called, comprise both priests and brothers committed to community and to the education of the whole person.

In 1882 the institution was incorporated and empowered by the State of Ohio to confer degrees. Known at various times as St. Mary's School, St. Mary's Institute, and St. Mary's College, the school was incorporated in 1920 under its present name, the University of Dayton. In 1935 the university opened a College for Women that closed two years later when all divisions became open to women.

In 1960 most of the major units of the university assumed their present names: the College of Arts and Sciences and the Schools of Business Administration, Education, and Engineering. The School of Law, which had operated from 1922 to 1935, reopened in 1974. A Graduate School, created in 1994, assumed several coordinating functions for the graduate offerings of the schools and the college.

The Marian Library which originated in 1943 and in 1975 founded the International Marian Research Institute (incorporated in 1984 as a branch of the Marianum in Rome), holds the world's largest collection of materials related to Mary, the mother of Jesus.

University enrollment by the mid-1990s reached approximately 10,500 students, including 3,500 graduate students and 6,000 full-time undergraduates, with more than 90 percent of those undergraduates living on campus. The university, by the mid-1990s, also had an annual operating budget of nearly $200 million and an endowment of nearly $100 million.

See also CATHOLIC UNIVERSITIES AND COLLEGES.

UNIVERSITY OF SAN FRANCISCO

The University of San Francisco was established as the city of San Francisco's first institution of higher education by Jesuit priests in October 1855. The original college, first known as St. Ignatius Academy, was located in a simple frame building seventy-five feet long by thirty-five feet wide on Market Street. The academy opened its doors under the guidance of Fr. Anthony Maraschi, S.J., founder and first president.

On April 30, 1859, the State of California issued the academy a charter under the title of "St. Ignatius College," empowering the college to confer degrees "with such literary honors as are granted by any university in the United States." The curriculum included courses in Greek, Spanish, Latin, English, French, algebra, and arithmetic. In 1862 the college built a larger campus at the same location. In June 1863 the first bachelor of arts degree was conferred.

The college prospered and in 1880 moved to new buildings on Van Ness Avenue, the present site of the Louise M. Davies Symphony Hall. The 1906 San Francisco earthquake and fire, though, destroyed the campus and its art treasures. The campus relocated to temporary buildings on Hays and Shrader Streets in what became known as the "Shirt Factory Campus" because of their similarity to textile factories of the day.

In 1930, on the occasion of its diamond jubilee, the college was renamed University of San Francisco. In 1996 nearly 4,000 students were enrolled in the undergraduate programs, with another 3,900 engaged in graduate study.

See also CATHOLIC UNIVERSITIES AND COLLEGES.

UNIVERSITY OF SCRANTON (SCRANTON, PENNSYLVANIA)

The University of Scranton, founded as St. Thomas College, received its university charter in 1938 and became the twenty-fourth of twenty-eight Jesuit colleges and universities in the United States in 1942.

In August of 1888, lacking the necessary funds but nonetheless committed to his vision of a college that would serve the sons of laborers and miners in northeastern Pennsylvania's Lackawanna Valley, Bishop William O'Hara blessed a single block of granite as the cornerstone for the school he intended to build. St. Thomas College opened formally in 1892 with a solemn high Mass celebrated in the college chapel in "Old Main," the three-story building erected upon Bishop O'Hara's cornerstone. Administered first by the Diocese of Scranton and then for one year by the Xaverian Brothers, St. Thomas College was placed in the care of the Christian Brothers in 1897. Worthington W. Scranton, grandnephew of the founder of the city, donated his magnificent family home and adjoining properties some six blocks from "Old Main" in 1941. Almost simultaneously, the Society of Jesus was invited by the diocese to assume ownership and administration of the University of Scranton.

In 1956 the university began the move from "Old Main" to a new campus surrounding The Estate. The first women were admitted as undergraduate day students in 1972, although women had been receiving degrees since 1943 in the evening college. Today the University of Scranton is a comprehensive university offering more than sixty undergraduate and graduate programs of study through five schools and colleges: the College of Arts and Sciences, the School of Management, the College of Health, Education and Human Resources, Dexter Hanley College, and the Graduate School.

See also CATHOLIC UNIVERSITIES AND COLLEGES.

URSULINES (O.S.U.)

An order of nuns prominent in American Catholic history, especially noted for educating young women in academies. Their practice of admitting Protestant girls during the antebellum years was a factor in ameliorating anti-Catholicism among the upper classes. Ursuline nuns have also taught in parochial schools in many locations over the nation as well as performing missionary work in various foreign lands and among Native Americans, including Alaskan natives.

St. Angela Merici (1474–1540) founded the order in Brescia, Italy, in 1535, naming it for the martyred St. Ursula. St. Angela (sometimes called the Holy Maid of Dezenzano) and her "companions" began as a secular group seeking to train young women to be good Christian wives and mothers. She wrote a primitive *Rule* that is still used with modifications. Over time, the community grew in numbers and maturity prompting St. Charles Borromeo (1538–84) to give the group formal status as an order of independent nuns, not second order or associated with any male order. Their primary charism lay in teaching girls and young women.

Early in the seventeenth century, Church authorities sought to impose cloister, causing most Italian communities to disband as a result. However, the numerous French communities formed the Congregation of Paris in 1612 and secured a compromise solution: they would agree to cloister provided they could teach young women inside their convents. During the Reign of Terror, demonstrating great Christian courage, thirty-five Ursulines died under the guillotine. Following the restoration of religious liberty, they demonstrated great vitality in reestablishing numerous convents. Many American Ursulines trace their origins to nuns coming from France with lesser numbers coming from Ireland and Germany.

Ursulines in Colonial Louisiana

A number of unique incidents have marked the Ursuline American experience. Eight French Ursuline nuns under the leadership of Mother Marie Tranchepain sailed from France on the *Gironde* on February 23, 1727. Because of storms, pirates, and sandbars, the voyage took five months. Under contract with the Company of the Indies, they expected a convent and promised support, neither of which was provided on their arrival in New Orleans. Nevertheless, they persevered, taught young women, cared for orphans, and made the first permanent establishment of women religious in the present-day United States. Following the Battle of New Orleans in 1815, they nursed the sick and wounded of both sides; General Andrew Jackson expressed his gratitude then and again later as President. This community is still in existence and its convent on Chartres Street is the oldest standing building in the Mississippi Valley.

Over the decades the New Orleans community provided a haven for various displaced women religious, most recently nuns from Cuba. Ursulines are honored in New Orleans for heroically nursing the affiliated during vicious yellow fever epidemics. New Orleans sent founding nuns to Galveston, Texas, in 1844 who later refused to leave during the Civil War bombardments of 1861 and 1864 by Union naval forces. Instead, they remained to operate a small hospital in their convent after other hospitals had moved inland. New Orleans also sent founding nuns to San Antonio in 1855 who in turn furnished foundresses for Laredo, Texas. During persecutions in Mexico in 1916 and 1917, the Laredo community sheltered large numbers of refugee priests and women religious from various orders.

The Ursuline convent in New Orleans, Louisiana, 1745

Irish Ursulines

The second group of Ursulines arriving in the United States came from Ireland to New York City in 1812, but returned in 1814 due to lack of priests, funds, and vocations. Another group, also Irish in origin, established a convent and academy in Charlestown, Massachusetts, that operated successfully from 1822 to 1834 when a mob, aroused by fiery anti-Catholic preaching, burned the convent and sent the nuns fleeing for their own and students' lives. This resulted in the nuns' dispersal to other convents and ended the Massachusetts initiative. Many historians consider the Charlestown convent-burning to be the opening shot of the virulent anti-Catholicism of the Know-Nothing era.

Bishop John England (1786–1842) of Charleston, South Carolina, imported Irish Ursulines in 1835 who later dispersed to Ohio convents when his successor, Bishop Ignatius Reynolds, refused to reimburse the nuns for dowries spent in Charleston, an action for which he asked forgiveness on his deathbed in 1855. They later reestablished their community in Columbia, South Carolina. During the Civil War their convent was destroyed when Union troops put Columbia to the torch, causing these nuns to disperse once again to other Ursuline convents. They ultimately returned to Columbia.

Ursulines in Ohio

Two English-born Ursuline leaders from French convents made lasting Ohio establishments. Mother Julia of the Assumption (Julia Chatfield, 1809–78) led a group of eleven nuns from their convent in Boulogne-sur-Mer to Cincinnati, Ohio, in 1845 to await Archbishop John Baptist Purcell's (1800–83) directive for their permanent location. After much indecision, he sent them to St. Martin's in Brown County, far from any urban center and potential pupils. Despite poverty and isolation, the community persevered and gradually grew to become a fountainhead for other communities, including the first Ursuline foundation in California in 1880.

Julia's friend in France, Mother Mary of the Annunciation (Mary Beaumont, 1818–81), led the second founding group from Boulogne-sur-Mer to Cleveland in 1850. This group also suffered extreme poverty but persevered with financial assistance from the St. Martin's community to become yet another Ursuline fountainhead. In 1871 the community founded Ursuline College in Pepper Pike, Ohio's first chartered college for women and the first Catholic women's college in the United States. Subsequently, other Ursuline communities established three women's colleges and a junior college. The Cleveland community sent missionaries to Montana as early as 1883 to teach in parochial schools and minister on Native American reservations.

An Ursuline nun from the Toledo community, Sr. M. Amadeus of the Heart of Jesus (Sarah Theresa Dunne), remembered as Mother Amadeus, became a renowned missionary on Native American reservations and later ministered to the Inuits of Alaska, earning the title "Teresa of the Arctic." She also acted as provincial-superior of the northern United States communities of the Roman Union, established by Pope Leo XIII in 1900. He and his two successors held Mother Amadeus in high esteem. Sr. Dorothy Kazel, a member of the Cleveland community on missionary assignment in El Salvador, was ambushed, brutalized, and murdered in 1980 along with two Maryknoll sisters and a lay missionary, Jean Donovan.

Other American Foundations

Two German-speaking groups made antebellum foundations: one in St. Louis in 1848 and one in Kentucky in 1859. Mother Magdalene Stehlin led the Oldenburg nuns to St. Louis and Mother Mary Salesia Reitmeier led the Straubling nuns to Louisville, Kentucky. In 1874 five of these nuns went down the Ohio River by flatboat to make a foundation in the Owensboro, Kentucky, area. Brescia College is their contribution to higher education.

In 1878 Mother Clare Cornely led a group from Germany fleeing the *Kulturkampf* to Peoria, Illinois. This foundation sent out shoots to Nebraska and other locations. A French community, the Society of St. Ursula, established a province in New York City in 1902. A group of German Ursulines arrived in 1910 and settled in Belleville, Illinois, and in 1921 a group arrived from Belgium to establish their community in Ozone Park, New York.

In 1995 Ursuline Nuns of the Congregation of Paris numbered 1,175 members in eight congregations; Ursuline Nuns of the Roman Union numbered 633 members in four provinces; Ursuline Sisters of the Congregation of Tildonk, Belgium, numbered 78 members; and the Society of St. Ursula numbered 41 members—a total of 1,947 Ursulines in the United States.

Ursulines, first women religious in the present-day United States, have made enormous contributions to education and American Catholicism.

Dehey, Elinor Tong. *Religious Orders of Women in the United States.* Hammond, Ind.: W. B. Conkey Company, 1930.

Francis, M. Michael, O.S.U. *The Broad Highway: A History of the Ursuline Nuns in the Diocese of Cleveland, 1850–1950.* Cleveland: The Ursuline Nuns, 1951.

Life of the Rev. Mother Amadeus of the Heart of Jesus. New York: The Paulist Press, 1923.

Stewart, George C. Jr. *Marvels of Charity: History of American Sisters and Nuns.* Huntington, Ind.: Our Sunday Visitor Press, 1994.

GEORGE C. STEWART, JR.

Related Document

PRESIDENT JEFFERSON REASSURES THE LOUISIANA URSULINES ABOUT THEIR FUTURE UNDER THE AMERICAN GOVERNMENT, MAY 15, 1804

In August, 1727, a little band of eleven Ursuline nuns arrived in Louisiana from France to open the first convent of religious women in what was later to be the United States. All through the eighteenth century they persisted—often under the greatest handicaps—with their teaching the young, nursing the sick, and other works of charity. The sisters witnessed the colony change hands several times, and in 1803 they found themselves citizens of the United States. The anxiety which they felt about their property rights and status under the American regime were conveyed by their superior to both Bishop Carroll and President Jefferson. In his reply Jefferson set their fears at rest about the future and assured them of the appreciation which Americans of all religious faiths felt for the charitable labors which they had carried on in Louisiana for so many years.

(*Source*: Henry C. Semple, S.J., ed. *The Ursulines in New Orleans and Our Lady of Prompt Succor. A Record of Two Centuries, 1727–1925.* New York: P. J. Kenedy & Sons, 1925, facsimile facing p. 60.)

Washington May the 15, 1804

To the Soeur Therese de St. Xavier Farjon, Superior; and the Nuns of the Order of St. Ursula at New Orleans.

I have received, holy sisters, the letter which you have written me, wherein you express anxiety for the property vested in your institution by the former government of Louisiana. The principles of the Constitution and government of the United States are a sure guarantee to you that it will be preserved to you sacred and inviolate, and that your institution will be permitted to govern itself according to it's own voluntary rules, without interference from the civil authority, whatever diversity of shade may appear in the religious opinions of our fellow citizens, the charitable objects of your institution cannot be indifferent to any; and its furtherance of the wholesome purposes of society, by training up its younger members in the way they should go, cannot fail to ensure it the patronage of the government it is under. Be assured that it will meet with all the protection which my office can give it.

I salute you, holy sisters, with friendship and respect,

Th. Jefferson

(*Source*: John Tracy Ellis, ed. *Documents of American Catholic History*. Vol. 1:1493–1865. Wilmington, Del.: Michael Glazier, 1987, 184–85.)

UTAH, CATHOLIC CHURCH IN

Missionaries

Spanish Franciscan explorers Atanazio Dominguez and Silvestre Velez de Escalante brought the first Catholic presence into the lands within Utah's present borders. Sent in 1776 by the Spanish government in search of an overland route from New Mexico to California, their expedition represented the first entry of non-Native Americans into Utah. Traveling without military escort, the missionaries evangelized the peoples they met along the way. Christian names that Dominguez and Escalante gave to Utah mountains and rivers testify to Utah's Catholic heritage.

Early Settlers

The history of the early nineteenth century includes a few Catholic traders and trappers who viewed the Great Salt Lake or carved petroglyphs in rock near their Utah campsites. The Church of Jesus Christ of Latter-day Saints, the Mormons, colonized the Utah Territory in 1849. Catholics, often poor and transient, were to be found among the federal troops dispatched to Utah in 1862, among miners searching for the mineral wealth discovered in 1863, and among the railroad gangs completing the transcontinental railroad in 1869. The fledgling Catholic community, struggling for survival, did not enter into the political turmoil that preceded Utah's achievement of statehood in 1896.

Administration

The Holy See had assigned ecclesiastical responsibility for Utah Territory in 1853 to Archbishop Joseph S. Alemany of San Francisco, whose domain extended eastward to the Colorado River. Rev. Bonaventure Keller, a Franciscan en route from California to Philadelphia, offered the first known Mass in Utah in 1859 at Camp Floyd near Lehi. In 1866 Fr. Edward Kelly, ordained by Archbishop Alemany for the vicariate of Marysville, bought a lot in Salt Lake City at present-day First South and Second East Streets, Utah's first Catholic Church property.

Archbishop Alemany entrusted the approximately 800 Catholics among Utah's 87,000 inhabitants to Fr. Lawrence Scanlan in 1873. A Catholic identity began to form throughout his missionary outpost as small churches grew up in Salt Lake, Ogden, Silver Reef, Park City, and Eureka. The Sisters of the Holy Cross opened schools and hospitals. Named vicar bishop in 1886, Scanlan established *The Intermountain Catholic* newspaper in 1899, and completed construction of the Cathedral of St. Mary Magdalene in 1909.

The Diocese of Salt Lake City

On January 27, 1891, Pope Leo XIII created the Diocese of Salt Lake, embracing 157,657 square miles in Utah and eastern Nevada, the largest geographical entity of the Catholic Church in the United States. The Nevada segment was detached in 1931, forming contiguous boundaries for the Diocese of Salt Lake and the State of Utah.

The expanding role of Catholics in civic life was symbolized by the election of mining magnate Thomas F. Kearns to the United States Senate for the years 1901 to 1905. In Salt Lake in 1901, he and his wife, Jennie Judge Kearns, endowed Kearns-St. Ann's Orphanage; and the family of John Judge founded Judge Mercy Home and Hospital for miners, forerunner of today's Judge Memorial High School.

Bishop Scanlan's successor, Bishop Joseph S. Glass, enhanced Catholic culture with an artistic interior renovation of St. Mary's Cathedral, which he renamed the Cathedral of the Madeleine. The Catholic Woman's League was formed in 1916 at the same time that men throughout Utah were joining the Knights of Columbus, the League of the Sacred Heart, and the St. Vincent de Paul Society.

World War II and the efforts of Bishop Duane G. Hunt increased the diocesan population to 40,000 by 1960. Gradually a native clergy developed, supplemented today by religious orders of men and women from throughout the United States. Monasteries were founded by the Trappist monks at Huntsville, Utah, in 1947 and by the Carmelite Sisters in Salt Lake in 1952. The Benedictine Sisters, active in Utah since 1944, established an independent monastery in Ogden in 1994.

Challenges

Numbering 4 percent of the state's population, Utah Catholics experience an ongoing struggle to retain their cultural and religious values. In rural areas, which comprise much of the state, families have to travel considerable distances for Mass; their children have no opportunity to attend any of Utah's eleven Catholic schools. Since 1994 there have been no Catholic hospitals in Utah.

Having arrived in Utah as auxiliary bishop in 1951, Bishop Joseph Lennox Federal responded to such concerns by building religious education centers and parishes wherever feasible. Ushering in the era of the Second Vatican Council, he ordained twenty-three permanent deacons to minister throughout the state and opened an Office for Hispanic Ministry.

Building upon this work, Bishop William K. Weigand, champion of social justice, elicited ecumenical support for the 1993 restoration of the cathedral, a unique historical treasure in Utah. His successor, Bishop George H. Niederauer, who was ordained on January 25, 1995, as eighth bishop of the diocese, now leads 80,000 Utah Catholics into the twenty-first century of Christianity.

Dwyer, Robert J. "Pioneer Bishop: Lawrence Scanlan, 1843–1915." *Utah Historical Quarterly* 20 (April 1952) 135–58.

Fries, Louis J. *One Hundred and Fifty Years of Catholicity in Utah.* Salt Lake City, 1926.

Harris, William R. *The Catholic Church in Utah.* Salt Lake City, 1909.

Mooney, Bernice Maher. *The Story of the Cathedral of the Madeleine.* Salt Lake City, 1981.

Stoffel, Jerome C. "Hesitant Beginnings of the Catholic Church in Utah." *Utah Historical Quarterly* 36 (1) (Winter 1968) 41–62.

BERNICE MAHER MOONEY

V

VARELA, FELIX (1788–1853)

Scholar, Cuban patriot. Felix Varela was born in Havana, Cuba, on November 20, 1788, to a Spanish father and a Cuban mother. Felix became an orphan at the age of three. His grandfather raised him in St. Augustine, Florida, and at the age of fourteen he moved to Havana to enter San Carlos Seminary.

Educator in Havana

With the strong support of Bishop Díaz de Espada y Landas, Varela became the leader of an intellectual movement

Felix Varela

that renewed Thomistic philosophy from scholasticism, made learning more accessible through the use of the vernacular, and introduced empirical sciences into the curriculum. A prolific writer throughout his life, he published seven works in Havana on themes related to philosophy and social science. The most important one was *Lecciones de Filosofía* (three tomes) which was reedited five times

Parlamentarian in the Spanish Cortes

Elected to represent the Island for the 1822 sessions of the *Cortes,* Varela left Cuba on April 28, 1821. Through very carefully drafted interventions, Varela sought the abolition of slavery with an elaborate plan to accomplish it without disrupting the economy, and he presented a "Project for Colonial Autonomous Government." However, confronted by the new political forces in Europe, King Ferdinand VII dismantled the *Cortes* and persecuted the delegates who dared to oppose him. Varela had to flee to the United States of America, arriving in New York on December 17, 1823. On this period of transition he published Thomas Jefferson's *Manual of Parliamentary Practice,* in Spanish. He added extensive notes to this work and he also published Humphrey Davy's *Elements of Chemistry Applied to Agriculture.*

Editor of El Habanero

In 1825 Varela moved to Philadelphia and there he began the publication of a newspaper called *El Habanero* which, according to Paul J. Foix, was "the first Spanish Catholic magazine published in the United States [and] Varela subsequently became one of the most brilliant lights in Catholic journalism" (*Pioneer Catholic Journalism* [New York:

U.S. Catholic Historical Society, 1930] 65). *El Habanero* promoted the separation of Cuba from the Spanish government as an inevitable historical fact. Varela is widely recognized as the first one to call for Cuban independence. By promoting a peaceful political change ("war of reason"), he hoped to prevent unnecessary bloodshed and hate between the Spanish people and the residents in the Island of Cuba.

Vicar General and Pastor

In 1826, at the same time as the third bishop of New York, John Dubois, was installed, Varela moved to New York. As pastor first of Christ Church, and then Transfiguration Church, Varela was known for his care of Irish immigrants and for the creation of educational and social programs. He also became the vicar general of the diocese in 1829. In that capacity he represented the see of New York at the First and Third Provincial Councils of Baltimore. J. P. Dolan recognized that "strange as it may seem, the apostle of the Church in New York City, of the Catholic Irish, was a Cuban priest" (*The Immigrant Church* [Baltimore: Johns Hopkins University Press, 1975] 36).

Varela was the founder, publisher, and editor of *The Protestant's Abridger and Annotator* (1830), which was described by Willging and Hatzfield as "the first ecclesiastical or pastoral magazine in the United States" (*Catholic Serials of the Nineteenth Century in the United States. Descriptive Bibliography and Union List*, 2nd Serial [Washington: The Catholic University of America Press, 1968] 14–15:138). He also founded *The Catholic Expositor and Literary Magazine* (1841–43), described as "the first literary or learned magazine in U.S. Catholicism" (Willging-Hatzfield, 147). He also initiated a weekly newspaper, *The Catholic Observer* (1836–39). Then he became the editor of *The New York Catholic Register* (1839–40) until it merged with the *New York Freeman's Journal* at which point Varela ceased to be its editor but remained a close collaborator thereafter. As Eugene P. Willging and Herta Hatzfield stated, "It seems unbelievable what he wrote besides *The Habanero* in not completely 30 years in New York" (69). Furthermore, he was very involved in defending the Catholic faith in public debates and public lectures, at a time when the most intensive anti-Catholic bias existed in U.S. society.

Letters to Elpidio

His last and most important publication in Spanish was a series of essays on social evil organized in an interrelated trilogy, "impiety, superstition and fanaticism in relation to society," addressed to the youth with the symbolic name of *Elpidio* (*elpis,* hope). Inspired by Aquinas's *Summa* analysis of the vices he opposed to the virtue of religion: by excess, superstition; and by deficiency, impiety (II-II,

qq. 92–100), Varela added the vice of fanaticism. Regretfully, only two volumes were published and it is not known whether he wrote his essays on fanaticism. In spite of lacking methods of social analysis, he was searching with remarkable foresight for a model of involving Christian leaders in building a just society.

In 1850 Varela moved to St. Augustine, Florida, for reasons of health, where he died on February 25, 1853. At the request of the Episcopal Conference of the Bishops of Cuba the cause for his beatification was introduced in Rome (1986). He is also recognized as one of the most important founders of Cuban cultural national identity. One can also claim that Varela is a remarkable pillar of the founding generation of the Catholic Church in U.S.A.

Blakeslee, William F., C.S.P. "Felix Varela, 1788–1853." *Records of the American Catholic Historical Society of Philadelphia* 38 (1927) 15–46.

McCadden, Joseph and Helen. *Father Varela, Torch Bearer from Cuba.* New York: United States Catholic Historical Society, 1969.

Merrick, D. A., S.J. "The Cuban Apostle of New York." *Messenger* 38 (1898) 613–26.

Varela, Felix. *Letters to Elpidio.* Ed. Felipe J. Estevez. Sources of American Spirituality. New York: Paulist Press, 1989.

FELIPE J. ESTEVEZ

VATICAN COUNCIL I, AMERICAN PARTICIPATION IN

The First Vatican Council met in the north transept of St. Peter's Basilica, Rome, from December 8, 1869, until September 1, 1870. Pope Pius IX (1792–1878) had announced its convocation to cardinals in Rome on December 6, 1864, and a formal public announcement was made on June 19, 1867. That same summer preparatory commissions composed of Roman cardinals, bishops, and theologians began to meet on faith and dogma, politico-ecclesiastical relations, Eastern Churches and missions, Church discipline, and religious orders. In the event, only two draft constitutions were adopted by the council, both from the faith and dogma commission, *Dei Filius,* on faith (April 24, 1870), and *Pastor Aeternus* (July 18, 1870), which enunciated the solemn definitions of papal primacy and papal infallibility. After desultory summer sessions, the final meeting of the council occurred on September 1, 1870. Italian troops led by General Raffaele Cadorna occupied Rome on September 20, and the council was prorogued on October 20, never to resume. The council can be seen as the culmination of the neo-Ultramontane movement that had grown within the European Roman Catholic Church in reaction to the Enlightenment, the French Revolution, and the political and intellectual thrust of nineteenth-century rationalism and liberalism. Earlier highlights of Pius IX's counteroffensive against the secular spirit of the times included the 1854 definition as Catholic dogma of the Immaculate Conception of Mary, underlining the original sin and consequent moral frailty of the rest of the human race; the 1864 syllabus of eighty errors of contemporary liberalism; and assertion in 1863 of the authority of the pope's "ordinary magisterium," or teaching authority as normative for Catholic theologians.

Led by the theologians of the Jesuits' Roman College, theoreticians building on the thought of the Camaldolese monk Mauro Cappellari (the later Pope Gregory XVI, 1831–46), and antirevolutionary political thinkers like Count Joseph de Maistre (1754–1821), promoted the teaching of papal infallibility as a sure defense against liberal thought. That the pope, independently of an ecumenical council, might speak infallibly on matters of faith and morals, was a long-debated theological question, but, as Yves Congar has pointed out, it was at the outset of the nineteenth century held to be definable teaching by only a minority of theologians.

The Maryland Tradition

One part of the universal Church where papal infallibility was not taught as standard Catholic doctrine was the United States of America. The Catholic Church was first planted on U.S. shores in 1565 with the founding of St. Augustine, Florida. Structurally, the U.S. Church developed from the colony of Maryland, founded in 1634 by Lord Baltimore, a Catholic proprietor. Despite those Catholic auspices, Baltimore's settlement was never politically a "Catholic" colony. A majority of the population was always Protestant. But a Catholic financial, social, and political elite dominated for the first fifteen years. Roman Catholicism was never the state religion; Roman Catholic canon law had no legal status; but, as long as Catholics retained control, there was complete freedom of religious practice and complete separation of Church and state.

Even when Maryland Catholics lost political power and were subjected to penal laws like those prevailing throughout the rest of the British Empire, they held on to the "Maryland tradition" of religious toleration that became the hallmark of early American Catholicism. Lay leaders like the signer of the Declaration of Independence, Charles Carroll of Carrollton (1737–1832), and his cousin, John Carroll (1735–1815), first Catholic bishop in the United States, were unequivocal advocates of freedom of conscience, religious toleration, and a Church unencumbered by ties to the state. John Carroll was theologically formed in an ecclesiology that distinguished between a "mission" and a fully formed "Church," arguing that the latter had the right to elect its own bishop and then present his name to Rome for confirmation. The pope was head and Rome the center of the Catholic Church, but bishops were not papal appointees and local churches were not branch offices of a centralized papacy. John Carroll held that the Church's infallibility, in which he believed, rested in the pope *and* an ecumenical council, received by the Church. All else was mere theological opinion.

Bishop John England (1796–1842) of Charleston, prime mover in the series of provincial councils of Baltimore (which Eugenio Correcco has called "paradigmatic" for the nineteenth-century Church) stated in the constitution which he framed for his diocese that papal infallibility was not a matter of Catholic dogma. Debating Disciples of Christ founder Alexander Campbell in 1837, Bishop John Baptist Purcell (1800–83) declared the same. The American Church's leading nineteenth-century theologian, Bishop Francis Patrick Kenrick (1796–1863), emphasized in 1839 the existence of the worldwide episcopal college and argued that for an infallible papal statement its consent was demanded. Restating the common theme, Bishop Bernard J. McQuaid (1823–1909) of Rochester put it this way: "Somehow or other it was in my head that the bishops ought to be consulted."

John Carroll's visions of an "ordinary national Church" choosing its own bishops and operating autonomously, but in communion with Rome, had faded, and the U.S. Church was ruled from Rome by the Congregation for the Propagation of the Faith. One exception, at least theologically, was Archbishop Peter R. Kenrick (1806–96) of St. Louis. His was an inductive theology, drawing on Scripture and the way it had been understood in the life and thought of the Church down through the ages. The "monuments of tradition" were important to him. Emphasis on the authority of the pope at the expense of local bishops he thought contrary to the ancient constitution of the Church as found in tradition. In his reading of Church history, Rome's role as appellate court did not lead to the pope's having monarchical power over other bishops. But, he wrote, if one conceived of "the supreme pontifical authority in this fashion," then it was not surprising that its advocates wished to attribute infallibility to papal decrees. He accepted papal primacy in the Church, "but primacy, not domination." He accepted the Church's infallibility, but the agent that expressed it was the college of bishops acting with the pope, its "head and chief part."

Most U.S. bishops as the Vatican Council approached were preoccupied with the cares of administering a missionary Church. Contacts with Europe were limited to visits and correspondence soliciting funds and personnel. A dozen bishops, most of them of French-Canadian or French background, held strong neo-Ultramontane views. Another dozen bishops, like those mentioned above, were decidedly anti-Ultramontane. The rest expressed no opinions, considering the theological dispute a European affair. Church structures were not highly developed. Bishops had only rudimentary staffing, perhaps a priest-secretary. The summons to the council provoked a hurried effort by the bishops to equip themselves with episcopal paraphernalia that they did not use in the ordinary course of their ministry.

The first extended entry of American bishops into larger Church affairs came in 1854 in the proceedings leading to the dogmatic definition of Mary's Immaculate Conception. Several Americans played roles which foreshadowed the attitude of U.S. bishops at the council fifteen years later. Coming from a land of religious pluralism, they challenged careless citation of Scripture and patristic texts and doubtful theological deductions that would be rightly criticized by Protestants. Bishop Michael O'Connor (1810–72) asked that any dogmatic definition be made explicitly with the consent of the college of bishops. The 1864 Syllabus of Errors had a mixed American reception. Archbishop John McCloskey (1810–85) of New York wrote: "According to all rules of mere human prudence it was ill-timed," and would put the U.S. Church in conflict with American political institutions. He saw the papal document as indicative of the differing American and European political contexts. When the bishops met in the Second Plenary Council of Baltimore in 1866, they repeated none of the strictures of the Roman syllabus, but attempted a listing of contemporary American errors. They combined an affirmation of their collective episcopal authority with homage to the pope's prerogatives.

Initial U.S. involvement in the actual work of the council began with the arrival in Rome on November 1, 1868, of James A. Corcoran (1820–89), the theologian designated by the American bishops to share in the preparatory work already in progress. His reports spoke of a Roman "mania" for dogmatic definitions, many contrary to U.S. understanding of Church-state relations. By spring 1869 he saw the definition of papal infallibility as a foregone conclusion, although he thought that the question would be introduced cautiously.

The archbishop of Baltimore and unofficial primate of the American Church, Martin J. Spalding (1810–72), wrote to Rome on behalf of those "who live in a totally different state of things," suggesting that the hands-off approach of English and American civil authorities in religious affairs should be commended to other nations, that civil indifferentism should not be confused with theological indifferentism, that progress and human betterment should not be equated with materialism. If infallibility must be discussed, Spalding preferred an implicit, rather than an explicit, definition.

U.S. Bishops at the Council

Forty-nine U.S. prelates attended at least some sessions of the council. They represented a constituency of four million American Catholics, of whom three-quarters of a million were immigrants in the decade of the 1860s. Altogether, some 750 council fathers representing a world Catholic population of 731 million attended, most of them Europeans, either from sees on that continent, the Roman Curia, or colonial possessions. No native African, Indian, or East Asian prelates existed. Council membership was all-white and Eurocentric.

Peter R. Kenrick, a stickler for procedure at the recently finished Second Plenary Council of Baltimore, wasted no time in lodging a protest at the first general congregation of the council on December 10, 1869. He wanted more time and the opportunity to gather information on candidates for the conciliar committee on procedures. He spoke of the rights and responsibilities of bishops in council and asked that a preliminary committee be chosen to propose lists that would represent different nationalities and languages. Objections were overridden, and few Americans were chosen for council committees, all of them, as Bishop McQuaid recalled, conservatives picked by Archbishop Henry Manning of Westminster, leader of the pro-infallibility forces. Spalding and Archbishop Joseph Alemany, O.P., of San Francisco were on the doctrinal committee; Bishop Michael Heiss of La Crosse and Archbishop McCloskey on the one on Church discipline; Bishop Stephen Ryan, C.M., on religious orders; and Bishop Louis de Goesbriand of Burlington on Eastern Churches and missions.

U.S. bishops kept up a steady drumbeat of suggestions. Veterans of nine national councils, they asked for elected membership on the committee on proposals (the "rules" committee), they wanted committee meetings to be open to other bishops, and agenda thoroughly vetted in committee before presentation to the council. They urged relaxation of conciliar secrecy. They called for elimination of time-consuming, boring, and pointless debates and for shifting sessions to a hall with better acoustics. None of these suggestions were adopted. From home, James A. MacMaster, editor of the New York *Freeman's Journal*, urged the Americans to accept the arrangements made by the Roman Curia. Throughout the council he was a persistent gadfly of the "liberal" bishops.

In the eighty-six general congregations held between December and July, Bishop Augustin Verot of Savannah and then St. Augustine spoke eight times; Bishop Thaddeus Amat, C.M., of Monterey-Los Angeles, six; Bishop Richard Whelan of Wheeling, three; Archbishops Alemany and Kenrick, twice each; and Archbishops Purcell and Spalding and Bishop Michael Domenec, C.M., of Pittsburgh, once each. Most vocal was Verot, whose colorful style earned him the appellation of *"enfant terrible"* of the council. He called for reversal of the judgment on Galileo, admission that the world was indeed round, and he wanted no condemnation of geologists' views on the six days of creation or their duration. Fed up with philosophical discussion of the "human composite," he asked affirmation of the fact that Africans have souls and belong to the human race. He distinguished political opposition to the papacy from theological opposition to the pope. He spoke against racism and for modern science, reform of the Liturgy of the Hours, and of the spiritual life of priests.

Archbishop Purcell left a memorable, but undelivered speech in the archives of the council, in which

> I said that our civil constitution grants perfect liberty to every denomination of Christians; that it grants perfect liberty to them all; and that I verily believe this were infinitely better for the Catholic religion than were it the special object of the state's patronage and protection; that all we want is a free field and no favor.

Other Americans objected to frequent condemnations in the draft proposals. Catholics did not need them; nonbelievers mocked them. Some urged more frequent scriptural citations and deletion of tedious philosophical argumentation. Many objected to phraseology offensive to non-Catholics. Their overall approach was pastoral and reflected the milieu in which they carried on their ministry, and this was apparent in their observations on the Dogmatic Constitution on Faith voted by the council on April 24, 1870, with thirty-nine Americans among those approving it.

Papal Infallibility

The great debate on papal primacy and infallibility occupied the late spring and early summer of 1870, but polarization of the council fathers had begun long before. In a battle of petitions to have infallibility brought to the floor, twenty-one Americans were counted against and ten for in mid-January, while five, including Spalding, wanted only an indirect or implicit statement on the subject. A debate on including the adjective "Roman" in the name of the Church had undertones of opposition to neo-Ultramontane centralization.

In the debate on primacy, Spalding secured inclusion of a statement that the universal jurisdiction attributed to the pope did not replace the local jurisdiction of bishops. Whelan of Wheeling rejected the claim that membership in the Roman Catholic Church was necessary to participation in truth. He demanded that the role of bishops be made clear: *they* defined what Catholics were to hold doctrinally. He wanted less emphasis on the role of committees meeting in secret, and he was unwilling to discuss the papal relationship to infallible statements until the Church itself had been more adequately described with ample use of the rich imagery of Scripture.

Archbishop Kenrick was the most formidable U.S. opponent of a definition of papal infallibility, a teaching which he himself held as a theological opinion. Deprived of an opportunity to explain his position when cloture was invoked in the council, he evaded the papal ban on publications by having two pamphlets published at Naples. In the first he argued that a doctrine unknown for the first thousand years of the Church, then argued as a theological opinion for centuries, was not material for a solemn definition. It was moreover insufficiently grounded in Scripture and tradition, a statement he backed with examination of the "Petrine" texts and evidence from Church Fathers, conciliar documents, and Church history. The second pamphlet repeated many of the same arguments and refuted contrary opinions. He took a firm position: "I boldly declare that the opinion, as set down in the *schema* [draft], is not a doctrine of faith, and that it cannot become such by any definition whatsoever, even of a council." He summed up his own understanding: "We are custodians of the deposit of faith, not its masters. We are teachers of the faithful entrusted to our care just insofar as we are witnesses." Christ's injunction to "teach all nations" was addressed, Kenrick wrote, to all the apostles, "a sort of college of apostles."

Opponents of a definition generally used the same arguments. Purcell and Domenec wanted to emphasize the connection of the pope with the rest of the Church. McQuaid observed that there was no patristic evidence for attributing infallibility to the pope. Amat observed that the help of the Holy Spirit was promised to the whole Church, not just to the Bishop of Rome. The activities of these bishops were coordinated with those of other opponents through an international committee which met, among other venues, in the salon of the English historian, Lord Acton.

Cardinal James Gibbons of Baltimore, a bishop in North Carolina at the time of the council, remembered later that a majority of the U.S. bishops were "inopportunists" rather than outright opponents of the infallibility definition. They wondered how to explain to Protestants how a formerly freely disputed teaching could become an article of faith, and they feared worsening of relations with them. The half dozen who supported Spalding's hopes for an implicit or indirect definition were among these inopportunists.

A third American group was as ardent for the infallibility definition as the opposition was against it. They did not actively participate in conciliar debate, but they signed petitions and voted consistently with what was clearly the majority party in the council. Several expressed themselves strongly in private letters. This was the case with Archbishop Francis N. Blanchet of Oregon City, who exulted in the death of "the dirty snake of Gallicanism." Bishop William Elder of Natchez preferred a compromise, but, failing that, came down for the definitions of primacy and infallibility. Bishop John Baptist Miège of the Indian Territory aligned himself strongly with fellow-Jesuit supporters and both Abbot Boniface Wimmer, O.S.B., and Bishop Heiss sided with Bishop Ignatius Senestrey of their native Regensburg diocese, continental whip of the pro-infallibility forces. All these generally saw the anti-infallibilists as "liberal," "rationalistic," or "Gallican." They were strongly pro-central authority and did not argue their case or engage in debate with its opponents.

In mid-January, nearly half the U.S. bishops were counted as being to some degree opposed to a definition of infallibility. A mid-May survey counted ten opponents, thirteen in favor and ten doubtful. In a final test vote on July 13, eighteen Americans voted their approval, three did so conditionally, and seven were opposed. On the eve of the final balloting, fifty-five opposition bishops signed a protest against the definition and left Rome, among them Kenrick, Verot, and Domenec. Others had already departed for home. The constitution *Pastor Aeternus* was adopted by a vote of 533–2, with Bishop Edward Fitzgerald of Little Rock being one of the dissenting voters. Papal primacy of jurisdiction and infallibility were doctrines to be accepted by all Catholics. All the U.S. bishops eventually indicated their acceptance of the new dogmas, although some, like Kenrick, only after much soul-searching. The neo-Ultramontane cause had won the day, and centralization of the Church became the hallmark of the new era.

See also INFALLIBILITY AND AMERICAN CATHOLICS.

Browne, Henry J. "The Letters of Bishop McQuaid from the Vatican Council." *Catholic Historical Review* 41 (1956) 408–41.

Byrne, Patricia, C.S.J. "American Ultramontanism." *Theological Studies* 56 (June 1995) 301–26.

Fogarty, Gerald P., S.J. "Archbishop Peter Kenrick's Submission to Papal Infallibility." *Archivum Historiae Ponitificae* 16 (1978) 205–22.

Hennesey, James, S.J. *The First Council of the Vatican: The American Experience.* New York, 1963.

_____. "Papacy and Episcopacy in Eighteenth and Nineteenth Century American Catholic Thought." *Records of the American Catholic Historical Society of Philadelphia* 77 (September 1966) 175–89.

_____. "The American Church and Vatican I." *Annuarium Historiae Conciliorum* 1 (1969) 348–73.

_____. "James A. Corcoran's Mission to Rome, 1868–1869." *Catholic Historical Review* 48 (1962) 157–81.

Portier, William L. "Isaac Hecker and the First Vatican Council." *Catholic Historical Review* 71 (1985) 206–27.

JAMES HENNESEY, S.J.

VATICAN COUNCIL II AND AMERICAN CATHOLICS

The Catholic Church in the U.S.A. was not expecting Vatican Council II but it was not unprepared when the council was summoned. In fact its own historical development had well prepared the Church in the U.S.A. for the Second Vatican Council.

Prior to Vatican II

The first half of the twentieth century had been a time of tremendous progress for U.S. Catholicism. At the beginning of the century (1908) the Vatican Congregation for the Propagation of the Faith removed the Catholic Church in the U.S.A. from its list of missionary territories. By the middle of the century, the U.S. Church boasted an increasing Catholic population, a vibrant parish life, an expanding educational, health-care, and social system, high enrollment in seminaries and religious communities, dynamic movements and organizations of laypeople, and signs of growing influence in public life.

The readiness of the U.S. Catholic Church may be seen in three important areas.

1. *The Church and Society.* Catholics had always struggled for acceptance in the U.S.A. Their immigrant status and diverse ethnic composition had made it difficult to assimilate with the mainstream American Protestant majority. These same factors fostered a ghetto mentality that kept Catholics to themselves and made them self-conscious, if not defensive, about their religious heritage and identity. This began to change prior to Vatican II.

The turning point was World War II. As they did during World War I, Catholics supported the war effort through direct military service, priest chaplains, and hierarchical endorsement, especially that of Archbishop Francis Spellman of New York who was also the head of the Military Ordinariate. These facts dispelled any doubt about Catholics' loyalty to America despite the persistent opposition to the war of the Catholic Worker movement and the conscientious objection of individual Catholics.

After the war, Catholics were stalwart opponents of Communism. Prayer for the conversion of Russia was commonplace in Catholic churches, inspired by the stories of Cardinal Mindszenty, Archbishop Stepinac, and others who were imprisoned or martyred for their faith. Bishop Fulton Sheen frequently used his weekly television program to expose the ideological errors of Communism while Senator Joseph McCarthy, himself a Catholic, won widespread initial support for his efforts to purge the government of communists. When war was declared in Korea in 1950 to halt the advance of world communism, Catholics were once again prepared to join the fight.

Two other events after World War II increased Catholic acceptance in the U.S.A. and prepared them for Vatican II. The G.I. Bill of Rights enabled unprecedented numbers of Catholics to acquire college educations, many of them the first in their families to do so. The money to pay for higher education gave a great boost to Catholic colleges and universities, and Newman clubs on secular campuses increased to look after the spiritual and pastoral needs of Catholic students. College education also led to improved employment opportunities and a movement of Catholics from the cities to the suburbs. Improvement in lifestyle was accompanied by a more positive outlook on modern culture by younger Catholics compared to the cautious and self-defensive attitude of previous generations.

In both respects (education and suburban lifestyle) Catholics were becoming more conversant with diverse points of view and learning to think on their own while becoming more comfortable with the contemporary culture in which they lived.

These changes did not replace traditional Catholic care for its own immigrant population, still largely centered in the cities. The most prominent charitable organization in most parishes was the St. Vincent de Paul Society, while Catholic Charities coordinated services at the diocesan level. Papal social teaching in the twentieth century provided a firm foundation for this Catholic commitment to the social welfare of immigrants, workers, the poor, and the ill. The message of the popes was conveyed to American Catholics through the National Catholic Welfare Conference (NCWC), a reorganization of the National Catholic War Council established during World War I.

Through the NCWC, the *Bishops' Program for Social Reconstruction* (1919), crafted by John Ryan as an application of papal teaching to the American situation, contributed many ideas which anticipated the programs and social policies of the New Deal. At the same time the Catholic Worker movement, founded in 1933 by Peter Maurin and Dorothy Day, modeled a radical commitment to the poor and the value of nonviolence, while Friendship House, founded by Catherine de Hueck Doherty, promoted interracial understanding in centers across the country.

The area of social life where Catholics were most prominent and gave most direct leadership prior to Vatican II were the trade unions. This involvement grew out of service to Catholic immigrants who frequently worked the worst jobs with the least protection. Both clergy and laity were involved in the labor movement. Labor priests like John Boland (Buffalo), John Monaghan (New York), and Charles Owen Rice (Pittsburgh), supported the efforts of Catholic labor leaders in all the unions.

On a theoretical level, Catholics accepted the constitutional separation of Church and state and even defended it, in the case of John Courtney Murray, S.J., as a viable safeguard for religious liberty, a value which had often been denied in the countries from which Catholics had emigrated. At the same time Catholics worked for financial aid to parochial schools and tried to establish standards of morality in entertainment through the ratings of the Legion of Decency (1934). When John F. Kennedy was elected president, it was a symbolic victory which prepared Catholics to play a new and positive role in the social life of the country just as Vatican II was about to encourage Catholics to read the signs of the times and co-operate with people of good will to solve the problems of modern life.

2. *The Laity.* The Catholic Church prior to Vatican II was unmistakably a hierarchical organization, but this did not mean that the laity were completely passive or that their contributions to the Church were unwelcome. It is sometimes said that Catholics of that era were expected only "to pray, pay, and obey." In fact, most Catholics had a deep loyalty to the Church and were eager to help in any way they could. Their help was typically channeled through Catholic Action, the term applied to a form of lay activity initially proposed by Pope Pius X and actively encouraged by Pope Pius XI.

Catholic Action was formally defined as the participation of the laity in the apostolate of the hierarchy. In Europe this meant primarily bringing Christian principles to bear on the reform of society. In the U.S.A. it had a wider application. Catholic Action covered almost any activity or organization intended for the good of the Church that was approved by the hierarchy and governed (chaplained) by the clergy.

The clearest example of Catholic Action in the U.S.A. was the Confraternity of Christian Doctrine—CCD. Originally conceived by Pope Pius X as a total evangelization effort, under the leadership of Bishop Edwin O'Hara (Kansas City–St. Joseph) a national center for CCD was established at The Catholic University of America (1935) to concentrate on the religious education of Catholic youth who were not enrolled in Catholic schools.

Besides Catholic Action in the strict sense, other opportunities for lay participation were the St. Vincent de Paul Society with parish chapters for charitable work, the Holy Name Society with parish associations to foster devotion to the Eucharist, Serra International with diocesan clubs for encouraging vocations to the priesthood, and the Sodality of the Blessed Virgin Mary for spirituality, evangelization, and social action, especially under the leadership of Daniel Lord, S.J., and his Summer Schools of Catholic Action.

Some lay organizations which began independently eventually became fixtures of Catholic life throughout the U.S.A. Among these are the Knights of Columbus (1882), Young Christian Students (1925), Young Christian Workers (1925), Catholic Youth Organization-CYO (1930), Cana Conferences (1943) and later pre-Cana marriage preparation, and the Christian Family Movement (1943). Since 1920 the National Council of Catholic Men and of Catholic Women had represented lay societies at the bishops' National Catholic Welfare Conference.

Although these activities and organizations were usually under clerical control and adhered loyally to official Catholic teaching, they also provided laypersons with numerous opportunities to be active in the Church. When

Vatican II issued a still broader and more challenging invitation, the laity in the U.S.A. were prepared.

3. *Liturgy and Spirituality.* The groundwork for the modern liturgical movement was laid in Europe, beginning with the initiatives of Pope Pius X (restoration of Gregorian chant, encouragement of frequent Communion) and the liturgical experience of abbeys in Belgium, France, Germany, and Austria. The fruit of this work was brought to the U.S.A. by Virgil Michel, a Benedictine based at St. John's Abbey in Collegeville, Minnesota. Michel inaugurated the magazine *Orate Fratres* (now *Worship*), in which he consistently drew the connection between liturgy and social justice. In 1940 the annual National Liturgical Week conferences began which gave liturgical study a popular, pastoral outlet.

Pope Pius XII endorsed the theology of the liturgical movement with his encyclicals *Mystici Corporis* (1943) and *Mediator Dei* (1947), and promoted its popular implementation with a new Latin psalter, relaxation of the eucharistic fast regulations, and restoration of the Easter Vigil and the Triduum of Holy Week. Parishes in the U.S.A. began advocating use of the daily missal during Mass rather than private devotions. From this the "dialogue Mass" emerged, with priest and people reciting their respective parts (in Latin), and in some places congregational singing increased. Other changes were frequently discussed, especially the vernacular in the liturgy and Communion under both species. Overall, the liturgy was becoming more accessible to the people on the eve of Vatican II.

Closely connected with these liturgical developments was an increased interest in the spiritual life, motivated by the devastation of World War II and the fear of nuclear

Vatican II in session

destruction which followed. Thomas Merton's autobiography, *The Seven Storey Mountain* (1948), was a bestseller as were his subsequent spiritual writings. This spiritual fervor coupled with gradual liturgical changes was preparing the Church in the U.S.A. for the Second Vatican Council's call to spiritual renewal and a more participative liturgy.

Permeating all these developments were two distinctive features of U.S. Catholicism: a deep-seated loyalty to Rome and an American flair for organization and achievement. Influenced by the condemnation of Americanism by Pope Leo XIII (1899) and the sweeping indictment of Modernism by Pope Pius X (1907), Catholic clergy in the U.S.A. were extremely insistent on compliance with Vatican directives and imbued the Church at every level with a spirit of docility. On the one hand, this discouraged both critical and historically informed thinking on religious matters; on the other hand, it made the Catholic Church in the U.S.A. receptive to whatever was approved by the pope and hierarchy—such as Vatican II.

Complementing this spirit of loyalty was a vigorous desire to accomplish great deeds in the American style. Prior to Vatican II this meant visible signs of success and a penchant for organization. Parishes and dioceses prided themselves on their "brick and mortar" accomplishments. Catholic organizations held public rallies, parades, and demonstrations. Statistics, as compiled by P. J. Kenedy's *Official Catholic Directory,* were a standard barometer of success, measuring even sacramental participation. Every effective activity seemed to be replicated on a national scale (including such diverse groups as the Catholic Worker and the Knights of Columbus).

The dynamic activity of the Catholic Church in the U.S.A. prior to Vatican II was held together by a genuine allegiance to the hierarchy and a sense of belonging to a thriving, unified, well-coordinated organization. As the experience of Vatican II would show, Catholic dynamism was not dependent solely on these factors.

Vatican II and U.S. Catholics

When Pope John XXIII announced on January 25, 1959, his intention to convene an ecumenical council, few Catholics in the U.S.A. knew exactly what an ecumenical council was, much less why one should be summoned at that time. Nonetheless, when the first session began on October 11, 1962, the U.S. Catholic Church was ready to contribute through its participants and through the issues it advocated.

1. *Participants.* Vatican II was, of course, a hierarchical meeting. In fact, it was the largest gathering of bishops (over 2,600) in the history of the Church. Forty-three delegates from the U.S.A. served on preparatory commissions, twenty-three were appointed to committees dur-

ing the council, and over sixty attended as advisors (*periti*) to the bishops. There were three lay observers from the U.S.A.: Martin Work of the National Council of Catholic Men, Catherine McCarthy of the National Council of Catholic Women, and James Norris of Catholic Relief Services, who addressed a session of the council in 1964. Sr. Mary Luke Tobin, S.L., attended as head of the Conference of Major Superiors of Women.

The vast majority of U.S. Catholics, like Catholics in other countries, had no active part to play. They were simply the recipients of the deliberations and decisions of the council, to the extent they were informed at all about what was going on.

Although the U.S. delegation represented almost ten percent of all the bishops, they did not exert much initiative or leadership until the end of the council. Altogether, they submitted a little more than three hundred written and oral interventions and a third of those were delivered by Cardinal Francis Spellman of New York. Spellman, along with Cardinal Albert Meyer of Chicago (and after his death, Cardinal Lawrence Shehan of Baltimore), also served as presidents of the council.

Perhaps the most notable intervention by a U.S. bishop did not occur during the sessions but behind the scenes when reactionary opponents tried to prevent a vote on the Declaration on Religious Liberty. Cardinal Meyer gathered over eight hundred signatures on a protest petition and took it to Pope Paul VI who authorized the vote the following day which approved the declaration.

Among others, Archbishop Paul Hallinan of Atlanta was a strong advocate of liturgical reform; Cardinal Shehan was a proponent of ecumenism; Cardinal Joseph Ritter of St. Louis was a champion of race relations as was Cardinal Richard Cushing of Boston, who also offered to pay for translation equipment so everyone could understand the Latin speeches in modern languages.

Among the *periti,* Godfrey Diekmann, O.S.B., and Frederick McManus made valuable contributions to the discussion of the liturgy; Gustave Weigel, S.J., was instrumental in the field of ecumenism; George Higgins was expert on the role of the laity and social justice questions; and John Courtney Murray, S.J., was the chief architect of the Declaration on Religious Liberty.

These participants represented the experience and feelings of large segments of the U.S. Catholic Church, especially when they spoke on the following issues.

2. Issues.

a. RELIGIOUS LIBERTY. Within the universal Church, Catholics in the U.S.A. had a somewhat unique perspective on the constitutional separation of Church and state which was the opposite of Pope Pius IX's desire that Catholicism be the official state religion. It was also in tension with the so-called thesis-hypothesis view: ideally Catholicism should be the state religion (thesis) but practically speaking this was not always possible and the most appropriate accommodation should be made (hypothesis). U.S. bishops, especially Cardinals Spellman and Cushing, defended the practical benefits of the U.S. arrangement and supported the theoretical justification of it worked out by John Courtney Murray. As a result, the Declaration on Religious Liberty was approved—and acknowledged as a development of Church doctrine (no. 1).

b. LITURGY. The pioneering work of Virgil Michel had cultivated a number of liturgical scholars in the U.S.A. whose understanding of the liturgy was closely tied to pastoral life and the spiritual renewal of Catholics (somewhat to the detriment of Michel's insistence on social justice). This emphasis and the budding experience of liturgical change in the U.S.A. supported the governing principle of liturgical reform: the full, conscious, and active participation of the faithful. It also encouraged use of the vernacular, simplification of liturgical rites, and prudent use of experimentation and adaptation to local circumstances—the latter reflective of pluralistic conditions in the U.S.A.

c. ECUMENISM. Unlike the liturgy, there was not much ecumenical practice among Catholics in the U.S.A. prior to Vatican II. However, Catholics were well acquainted with religious bigotry and anti-Catholic stereotypes, most dramatically demonstrated in the presidential campaign of Alfred E. Smith (1928). On the whole, U.S. bishops welcomed changes that would improve relations with their Protestant neighbors as long as the changes did not compromise Catholic integrity or distinctiveness. This ecumenical sentiment was especially keen after the election of John F. Kennedy as president (1960) which seemed to open a new era of religious toleration for Catholics.

An area of special ecumenical interest in the U.S.A. was the Catholic relationship with the Jews. Because of the large Jewish populations in urban areas where there were also many Catholics, and because of the parallel history of ethnic prejudice and religious bigotry, U.S. bishops were sensitive to the evils of anti-Semitism. They supported the clarification of the traditional charge of deicide and welcomed a more positive statement of the historical and spiritual integrity of the Jewish people.

d. SOCIAL JUSTICE. In addition to the history of caring for Catholic immigrants and translating papal social teaching into public practice, U.S. bishops during the council were grappling with the modern civil rights movement in the U.S.A. and increasing polarization over the war in Vietnam. These practical concerns moved them to support the proposal, made at the end of the first session, for a document on the Church's relation to the modern world. The council's fundamental optimism about solving modern social problems resonated with the typical American spirit of confidence and action exemplified in the U.S. Catholic Church at that time.

These were the major issues which concerned Catholics in the U.S.A., but they did not exhaust the Church's receptivity to all that Vatican II initiated. When the council ended, the Catholic Church in the U.S.A. was prepared to receive and implement the full teaching of the council.

Post-Vatican II

The Catholic Church in the U.S.A. did not feel the effects of Vatican II all at once nor did it implement the changes of the council uniformly. As a result, the reception of Vatican II has been a complex process reflecting a full range of reactions and feelings. These are often reduced to the alternatives of conservative and liberal but this hardly does justice to the diverse experience of postconciliar Catholicism in the U.S.A.

The reception of Vatican II by the U.S. Catholic Church may be analyzed with regard to the documents it produced, the structures it generated, and the priorities it called for.

1. *Documents.* The sixteen documents of Vatican II are generally available in two English translations. The first, edited by Walter Abbott, S.J., appeared in 1966. The second, edited by Austin Flannery, O.P., appeared in 1975 (rev. ed. 1996). The Flannery translation is the most widely used at the present time.

Despite the availability of English translations, the documents were not read or studied in their entirety by many people. In part this was due to the patchwork nature of the texts which did not yield a smooth and coherent reading (but did allow individuals to find wording supportive of their viewpoints). In part it was also due to the technical vocabulary, the universal scope, and the complexity of issues covered by the documents. By 1985 the U.S. bishops were concerned that the documents themselves were being neglected and asked for a new catechetical presentation of their contents. The parish discussion program, *Vatican II—Act II,* published by The Liturgical Press, is one response to this appeal.

Most often, the contents of the documents were summarized or paraphrased according to major themes or compelling images. Among the themes most favored by U.S. Catholics were participation in the liturgy, collegiality between bishops and pope, community in the Church, biblical spirituality, ecumenical dialogue, lay ministry, religious renewal, service in the world, and religious liberty. Among the most familiar images were the People of God, separated brethren, signs of the times, pilgrim people, and domestic Church.

Although they were not read in their entirety and studied thoroughly, the documents of Vatican II still had a significant impact on the Catholic Church in the U.S.A. This may be seen in reference to the three types of documents Vatican II produced.

a. CONSTITUTIONS. The Dogmatic Constitution on the Church *(Lumen gentium)* provided the leading image of the People of God (chapter two) which harmonized with American democratic sentiment and reinforced the experience of lay involvement prior to Vatican II. The very use of images and models to describe the Church (no. 6) became common (especially after the influential book of Avery Dulles, *Models of the Church*). The universal call to holiness (chapter five) stimulated a spiritual renaissance among the lay faithful (initially channeled through the Cursillo and charismatic movement, later through RENEW and Marriage Encounter), while the positive description of the laity (chapter four) as called and gifted (the phrase used by the U.S. bishops in their 1980 reflection) supported a host of lay initiatives. The discussion of collegiality between pope and bishops (chapter three) provided the underpinnings for collaborative ministry in other areas of the Church, and the restoration of the deaconate (no. 29) was implemented in the U.S.A. to a greater degree than anywhere else in the world.

The Pastoral Constitution on the Church in the Modern World *(Gaudium et spes)* conveyed a positive orientation toward secular life without minimizing its problems and challenges. This gave fresh motivation to a new generation of Catholics, typified by John F. Kennedy, who saw their religious beliefs as compatible with the cultural values and public life of the U.S.A. It also prompted many Catholics to become more outspoken about civil rights, the Vietnam War, and the enduring poverty in the U.S.A. The Pastoral Constitution's treatment of marriage (nos. 47–52), economic issues (nos. 63–72), and peace (nos. 77–82) laid the groundwork for subsequent teachings by the U.S. bishops, and its commitment to read the signs of the times encouraged the formation of "think tanks" on social issues such as the Center of Concern, the Catholic Committee on Urban Ministry (now disbanded), and NETWORK.

The Constitution on Revelation *(Dei Verbum)* dealt with several technical biblical questions but its greatest impact on the Church in the U.S.A. was chapter six, which emphasized the centrality of the word of God in worship (concretized through the expanded Lectionary) and in the spiritual lives of Catholics, leading to Bible sharing groups and charismatic expressions.

The Constitution on the Liturgy *(Sacrosanctum Concilium)* had its greatest impact by calling for a revision of the sacramental rites and encouraging fuller participation of the faithful. As changes were introduced, Catholic laity filled new roles (lector, eucharistic minister) while serving on liturgical committees and implementing the Rite of Christian Initiation of Adults. When the number of priests sharply declined after Vatican II, vowed religious and laypersons were appointed to conduct Sunday Communion services and give pastoral leadership in parishes without a resident priest.

b. DECREES. Among the Decrees of the council, those on the Lay Apostolate *(Apostolicam Actuositatem)* and the Renewal of Religious Life *(Perfectae Caritatis)* affected the most Catholics in the U.S.A. Affirmation of the laity's charisms (no. 3) led to unprecedented involvement in Church life, including the emergence of a new, professional form of lay ministry and opportunities to give advice through consultations and leadership at every level of Church life.

The changes in the lifestyle and work of religious communities, especially of women, affected large numbers of Catholics. In many places women in religious communities were the most informed and the most innovative in implementing the teachings and spirit of Vatican II. They created new positions in religious education, Church administration, social outreach, and pastoral ministry which laypersons have subsequently filled.

The Decree on Ecumenism *(Unitatis Redintegratio)* reversed Catholic attitudes toward non-Catholics (no. 3), admitting partial responsibility for disunity and acknowledging that many of the most significant elements of the true Church are found in Protestant Churches. Just as important, this decree encouraged widespread ecumenical cooperation at the local level and called for official dialogues to foster common understanding (no. 4). This exhortation has been realized in the U.S.A. through bilateral dialogues, cooperative Bible translations, a common liturgical lectionary, and professional associations in theology (American Academy of Religion), seminary field education (Association for Theological Field Education), and chaplaincy training (Clinical Pastoral Education).

The Decree on Missionary Activity *(Ad gentes)* reoriented the goals and methods of missiology by placing greater stress on inculturation (no. 6, although the council did not use that word), and asserting that the Church by its very nature is missionary (no. 35). These themes not only guided American missionaries going to foreign countries but also stimulated a revival of evangelization efforts in the U.S.A., promoted especially by the Paulist Fathers through their national center for evangelization in Washington, D.C. Catholic evangelization in the U.S.A. is often tied in to the RCIA and includes welcoming back former Catholics as well as responding to the cultural needs of African American and Hispanic Catholics.

The Decree on the Pastoral Office of Bishops *(Christus Dominus)* initially led to more pastors being appointed to this office and affirmed the pastoral value of an episcopal conference (nos. 37–38) such as the National Conference of Catholic Bishops.

The Decree on the Training of Priests *(Optatum Totius)* has been adapted to the U.S.A. through four editions of the Program for Priestly Formation.

The Decree on the Life and Ministry of Priests *(Presbyterorum Ordinis)* has been the basis for a standing committee at the bishops' conference which has issued numerous practical publications and prepared the bishops for the 1990 Synod on Priestly Formation.

The Decrees on Oriental Churches *(Orientalium Ecclesiarum)* and Communications *(Inter Mirifica)* have had minimal direct impact on the Church in the U.S.A. since Vatican II, although the Eternal Word Television Network airs Catholic programs nationwide.

c. DECLARATIONS. The Declaration on Non-Christian Religions *(Nostra aetate)* has had the most relevance to the Church in the U.S.A. with regard to Catholic-Jewish relations. The key assertions of this declaration have been promoted by a special office for Catholic-Jewish Relations at the Bishops' Committee for Ecumenism and Interreligious Affairs. The declaration's position on other religions may become more pertinent to U.S. Catholics as members of these religions enter the country and as global contacts increase.

The Declaration on Religious Liberty *(Dignitatis Humanae)* essentially confirmed the arrangement of Church and state in the U.S.A. and has not had a major postconciliar impact, although specific issues of public policy (aid to parochial schools, the legality of abortion, reform of health care) remain vibrant. In addition, the general principles of religious liberty are often invoked when dealing with tensions and disagreements internal to the Church, such as public dissent from noninfallible teachings, remarriage and the sharing of the Eucharist, and the rights of homosexual persons.

The Declaration on Education *(Gravissimum Educationis)* has been largely forgotten, although the educational commitment of the Church in the U.S.A., channeled through the National Catholic Education Association, has continued to be strong and creative at all levels: parochial schools, parish religious education programs, seminary and ministry formation, and Catholic higher education.

2. *Structures.* In addition to the documents of Vatican II, new structures have been created and existing structures have been revised as a direct result of the council. The tendency to organize is part of the American ethos and the Catholic Church in the U.S.A. has utilized it with great success. The structural impact of Vatican II on the U.S. Catholic Church may be seen at the universal, national, and diocesan levels.

a. UNIVERSAL LEVEL. As a result of Vatican II, there are three new structural elements of the universal Church which affect the Church in the U.S.A.: the Synod of Bishops, the revised Code of Canon Law, and the *Catechism of the Catholic Church.*

The most council-like structure to emerge from Vatican II is the Synod of Bishops. Requested by Vatican II (Decree on Bishops, no. 5) and authorized by Pope Paul VI, the Synod is composed of a representative number of bishops proportional to the Catholic population of each country. It is convened by the pope approximately every three years to discuss topics which the pope proposes after consultation with the bishops. There have been ten ordinary Synods (1967–canon law and conciliar implementation; 1969–collegiality; 1971–priesthood, justice; 1974–evangelization; 1977–catechesis; 1980–the Christian family; 1983–penance and reconciliation; 1987–the laity; 1990–priestly formation; 1994–religious life) and one extraordinary Synod (1985–reception of Vatican II). U.S. bishops have been actively involved in the individual synods as well as the synodal structure in Rome.

Revision of the Code of Canon Law was a concomitant goal with Vatican II and it affects every national Church. Members of the U.S. hierarchy as well as the Canon Law Society of America were active contributors to the revised Code (1983) which seeks to implement the intent of Vatican II. Sections of the Code which have had special bearing on conditions in the U.S. Catholic Church are provisions for mixed marriages (canons 1124–1129), conditions for marital consent (canon 1095), the mandate to teach theological disciplines in any institution of higher learning (canon 812), and a list of the rights of the lay faithful (canons 224–231).

The *Catechism of the Catholic Church* was suggested by Cardinal Bernard Law of Boston, among others, at the 1985 extraordinary Synod of Bishops. It is an attempt to summarize Catholic teaching in light of Vatican II for the guidance of bishops and those responsible for catechetical programs and materials. The U.S. Church has been implementing the *Catechism* since its publication in English in 1994.

b. NATIONAL LEVEL. The most influential structural change on the national level has been the reorganization in 1966 of the National Catholic Welfare Council into the twin divisions of the United States Catholic Conference-USCC (to handle relations with public institutions and deal with social issues) and the National Conference of Catholic Bishops-NCCB (to handle internal Church affairs). The U.S. bishops were among the first to organize themselves into a national conference which has served as a model for other countries to follow.

The NCCB has been the primary guiding and coordinating agent for implementing the liturgy (including music and architecture), promoting religious education (especially through its Department of Education and the *National Catechetical Directory,* 1977), fostering ecumenism (especially through official bilateral dialogues with Protestant churches and numerous associations with other Christians and religions), overseeing seminary education (through the *Program for Priestly Formation,* fourth edition, 1991), and issuing episcopal statements on human life (1968), peace (1983), and economic justice (1986).

Paralleling the reorganization of the Bishops' Conference have been the revisions of the constitutions of religious communities in the U.S.A. These changes have directly affected the lifestyle and ministry of vowed religious and indirectly influenced all those they work for and with. The Conference of Major Superiors of Men and the Leadership Conference of Religious Women have been prominent contributors to the creative implementation of Vatican II in the U.S.A.

Also on a national level but independent of official Church connection are a variety of professional societies and organizations. Foremost among these are the Canon Law Society of America, the Catholic Theological Society of America, and the National Catholic Education Association, all of which predated Vatican II and have given leadership to its implementation.

Since the council, new professional organizations have come into existence such as the National Federation of Priest Councils (1968), the National Office of Black Catholics (1970), the National Assembly of Religious Women (1970), and the National Association for Lay Ministry (1981).

National movements, more or less structured, have also become a feature of U.S. Catholicism since Vatican II: the charismatic movement, RENEW, Cursillo, Marriage and Engaged Encounter, Dignity, and Separated and Divorced Catholics.

National Catholic publications cover the spectrum of opinion and range from preconciliar magazines like *America, Commonweal,* the *Homiletic and Pastoral Review,* and the *National Catholic Register* to new publications like the *National Catholic Reporter, Chicago Studies, Church,* and *Communio.*

c. DIOCESAN AND PARISH LEVEL. Diocesan and parish structures tend to complement each other and reflect the needs and resources of the local church. Since Vatican II there have been four noteworthy innovations.

Pastoral councils are well established as a permanent feature of Catholic life in the U.S.A. These councils are strongly recommended by canon law (canons 511, 536). They are consultative and allow laypersons to give input and leadership in all areas of Church life.

Presbyteral councils parallel pastoral councils. They are required by canon law (canon 495) as an advisory body to the bishop and give priests a forum to express the concerns of the diocese.

The Rite of Christian Initiation of Adults grew out of a proposal at Vatican II to restore the catechumenate (Constitution on the Liturgy, no. 64). In the U.S.A. it has become a major vehicle of evangelization and a source of parish renewal, especially for Catholics who act as sponsors or catechists.

The Marriage Tribunal has always been part of the diocesan structure. With the introduction of new principles for judging annulment cases, first on an experimental basis in the U.S.A., then on a permanent basis in the revised Code of Canon Law, the work of the Marriage Tribunal has expanded into more pastoral and spiritual services.

In all these ways the Second Vatican Council has had a structural impact on the Catholic Church in the U.S.A. These structural changes give form to the general directives of the council documents and the priorities that emerged from them.

Priorities

Vatican II was a reform council. It rearranged the priorities that govern the life of the Church without providing a detailed program for change. This shift of priorities has brought with it a new experience of being Catholic which has been welcomed by some and resisted by others. The priorities of Vatican II are less tangible than its documents and structures. Nonetheless, certain shifts have occurred since the end of Vatican II that are clearly distinct from the priorities and experiences of Catholics before the council. These are most evident in the following areas.

1. *Liturgy*. The first major change Vatican II called for was in the liturgy. The priority shifted from the priest's performance of the ritual (e.g., celebrating Mass) to the assembly's participation in the liturgy (over which the priest presides). The initial reform of the liturgy concentrated on the ritual books (Sacramentary, Lectionary) and led to increased liturgical roles for the laity (reader, acolyte, eucharistic minister) and eventually leadership of "priestless parishes." Informed participation of the whole assembly through prayer and singing has come more slowly.

The experience of the liturgy since Vatican II has been demystified. Some interpret this as a loss of reverence and a cause of ignorance, especially regarding the eucharistic Real Presence. Others interpret it as a growth of communal experience and a sign of the liturgy's incarnational character. Differences of opinion also exist regarding the role of women in the liturgy, especially as it pertains to ordination, the possibility of lay preaching, and the restriction of anointing to the priest when nonordained ministers exercise pastoral care of the sick.

2. *Parish*. The parish has remained the preeminent form of Catholic life in the U.S.A. and the primary structure for channeling the changes of Vatican II to most Catholics. The understanding of parish has shifted from a ju-

ridical territory governed by Church law to a community of the faithful whose charisms are coordinated by a pastoral team. Numerous resources and programs have been developed to support this shift led by the National Pastoral Life Center in New York.

One of the priorities of parish life since Vatican II has been the desire for community and one of the most significant developments in this respect has been the emergence of Small Christian Communities. In some instances these communities are a way to reorganize the territorial parish; in other instances they are an alternative to it. In contrast to the desire for increased community is the phenomenon of unchurched Catholics who consider themselves Catholic but do not participate in any of the communal experiences which characterize the Catholic Church (liturgy, parish, organizations).

The shift in priorities in parish life has opened up numerous opportunities for laypersons and vowed religious to contribute their talent and experience in leadership positions and through participation in parish pastoral councils and committees, periodic consultations, and forms of collaborative ministry. Some see this as detracting from the laity's primary role in society and prefer to promote the latter (e.g., the National Center for the Laity). Others see it as an appropriate enactment of the ecclesiology of Vatican II and seek to make it more professional (e.g., the National Association for Lay Ministry).

In contrast to the new opportunities for laypeople, the shift of priorities in parish life has created confusion about the traditional role and status of the parish priest. This issue has been complicated by the sharp decline in the number of priests and the revelation of sexual misconduct by a few. These developments in turn have sharpened the debate over the value of mandatory celibacy for parish priests and the most appropriate type of formation for seminarians.

3. *Outreach*. The Second Vatican Council consistently stressed the priority of the poor and focused attention in the Second Part of the Pastoral Constitution on the Church in the Modern World on the root causes of poverty and injustice. Following this lead, the priority in Catholic outreach has shifted from charitable responses and immediate needs to systemic change with a special focus on peace and justice. The purpose of this shift is not to displace charitable work but to correct a one-sided approach.

One of the first concrete signs of this shift in the U.S.A. was the establishment of the Campaign for Human Development (1969) that provides funding for educational and action programs in which the poor take an active part. Another sign was the nationwide grape boycott of the National Farm Workers Association led by Cesar Chavez in 1968 and supported by Catholics at all levels of the Church.

Since Vatican II, many parishes and dioceses have formed peace and justice committees while Catholic schools and colleges include social justice teachings in their curricula. A number of religious communities (Franciscan, Jesuit, Maryknoll, Holy Cross) have established associate programs for young people which involve them directly in the community's work for peace and justice, and some communities and dioceses use their investment portfolio as a way of effecting systemic change.

This shift of priority has an inevitable political implication. Catholic Conferences at the national and diocesan levels have provided guidance on public policy issues and organized Catholics to lobby their elected officials on a range of concerns, most notably abortion. The Bishops' Conference has produced a steady stream of teachings on current social issues, including major statements on peace and economic justice, and has advocated the "seamless garment" approach to human life issues. Some Catholics object to this activity, arguing either that the hierarchy should stay out of the public realm or that they are not competent to speak as they do. The majority of Catholics seem to welcome the input but make up their own minds on social issues, dispelling the notion that there is a unified Catholic position.

4. *Collegiality.* The Second Vatican Council was an exercise in collegiality. The formal and informal interaction of pope, bishops, advisors, and observers yielded dramatic results and symbolized a shift from centralized, autocratic authority to shared, consultative authority. This shift was very congenial to the American experience and the U.S. bishops were quick to capitalize on it by reorganizing their own conference in 1966 and authorizing nationwide consultations in preparation for the *National Catechetical Directory* (1972–77) and for the celebration of the U.S. Bicentennial through the Call to Action process (1976).

The shift to collegiality has raised contrasting expectations. Opponents sometimes claim that the appeal to collegiality is an attempt to turn the Church into a democracy or to define doctrine by popular vote; proponents sometimes act as if collegiality means that their opinion has to be followed. Some of the harshest disagreements and sharpest debates since Vatican II have revolved around the implications of collegiality for determining Church teaching and practice.

The most controversial postconciliar teaching in this category was the prohibition of artificial contraception by Pope Paul VI (*Humanae vitae,* 1968). Not only did this decision run counter to the informed consciences of many Catholics in the U.S.A., it seemed to violate the meaning of collegiality when it was learned that the special Papal Commission established to advise the Pope had counseled a more liberal position.

The Pope was not obliged to follow the recommendations of the Papal Commission, but his decision exemplified the tension accompanying the shift to collegiality. For some, it damaged the credibility of the magisterium itself and made it more difficult to accept subsequent decisions regarding the ordination of women, divorce and remarriage, the morality of homosexuality, and the possibility of public dissent from non-infallible teachings. For others, it clarified that there is one ultimate source of authority in the Catholic Church which a faithful Catholic has no choice but to obey.

Conclusion

Vatican II was the most significant religious event of this century, and the Catholic Church in the U.S.A. has been profoundly and irrevocably shaped by it. Ultimately, the meaning of the council will not be measured by its contrast with the past, but by its influence on the future through generations of Catholics whose only experience of Church is the result of the Second Vatican Council.

Alberigo, Giuseppe, Jean-Pierre Jossua, and Joseph A. Komanchak, eds. *The Reception of Vatican II.* Washington, D.C.: The Catholic University of America Press, 1987.

Hastings, Adrian, ed. *Modern Catholicism: Vatican II and After.* New York: Oxford University Press, 1991.

O'Connell, Timothy E., ed. *Vatican II and Its Documents: An American Appraisal.* Collegeville, Minn.: The Liturgical Press, 1986.

Yzermans, Vincent A., ed. *American Participation in the Second Vatican Council.* New York: Doubleday and Co., 1967.

ROBERT L. KINAST

VAWTER, BRUCE (1921–86)

Scripture scholar. Bruce Vawter was born in Texas and was a convert to Catholicism at age sixteen. He joined the Vincentians and was ordained to the priesthood in 1947. He studied in Rome at the Angelicum and at the Pontifical Biblical Institute. He taught at Kenrick Seminary in St. Louis (1952–56, 1962–67), St. Thomas Seminary in Denver (1958–62), and finally, from 1968, at DePaul University in Chicago, where he served as chairman of the Department of Religious Studies. He spent 1967–68 at the Eberhard-Karls University in Tübingen.

Vawter's first book, *A Path Through Genesis,* was published in 1956 before he returned to Rome to complete his doctorate. Like John McKenzie's *The Two-Edged Sword,* which appeared in the same year, this was a pioneering work of critical biblical scholarship by a North American Catholic. At this point he felt obliged to wrestle with the possibility of Mosaic authorship of the Pentateuch, and concluded somewhat evasively that "substantial Mosaic authorship may be seen to be of the order of quality rather than of quantity." Twenty-one years later he returned to the subject in another book, *On Genesis. A New Reading* (1977). By then he could say: "Mosaic authorship no longer forms a problem for practically anyone." The contrast between the two statements reflects the change in Catholic biblical studies brought about by the Second Vatican Council.

Vawter's scholarship ranged over both Testaments. In addition to his work on Genesis, his Old Testament contributions included books on the prophets, *The Conscience of Israel* (1961), and a commentary on *Amos, Hosea and Micah* (1981), and a study of *Job and Jonah* (1983). His most important New Testament contribution was his book *This Man Jesus* (1973), but he also contributed to Johannine studies and wrote important articles on divorce in the New Testament. He also addressed the theological role of the Bible. In an early work, *The Bible in the Church* (1959), he expounded "the Catholic position" on the need for a mediating tradition in biblical interpretation. In his later book on *Biblical Inspiration* (1972) he insisted on the role of tradition within the biblical corpus itself, so that the Sermon on the Mount could update the Law and the Prophets.

Vawter's greatest contribution to biblical scholarship may well have been in his editorial work. He served as editor of *The Catholic Biblical Quarterly* (1966–68) and of the *Catholic Biblical Quarterly Monograph Series* (1975–82), and he was the founding editor of *Old Testament Abstracts*. In 1980 he received the H. G. May award of the Society of Biblical Literature in recognition of his editorial work. He served as president of the Catholic Biblical Association in 1961.

Collins, John J., and John Dominic Crossan, eds. *The Biblical Heritage in Modern Catholic Scholarship.* Wilmington, Del.: Michael Glazier, 1986.

Fogarty, Gerald P. *American Catholic Biblical Scholarship.* San Francisco: Harper, 1989, passim.

Vawter, Bruce. *The Path of Wisdom: Biblical Investigations.* Wilmington, Del.: Michael Glazier, 1986.

JOHN J. COLLINS

VERMONT, CATHOLIC CHURCH IN

The statewide Diocese of Burlington (Vermont) was created by decree of Pope Pius IX on July 29, 1853. The Catholic presence in the state actually predated this by nearly 250 years. The French explorer Samuel de Champlain, traveling by canoe in 1609 down the lake which now bears his name, is said to have exclaimed *"Voilà les monts verts,"* thus unknowingly giving the future state its name.

Catholic Beginnings

In 1666 a French garrison was sent to construct Fort Sainte Anne on Isle la Motte, the southernmost French fort intended to block raids from the native inhabitants from the south. Here the first Mass was offered that year in the future state of Vermont. In 1668 Fort Sainte Anne hosted the first epis-

copal visitation in New England when Msgr. François de Montmorency Laval, vicar apostolic of Quebec, came to administer the sacrament of confirmation. After the fall of French Canada to the British, virtually all the remaining French settlers withdrew to Canada, leaving Vermont without a Catholic presence until the next century.

In 1815 Fr. François Matignon of Boston visited Burlington, finding roughly one hundred Catholics. Perceiving the need for spiritual care of these nearly forgotten souls, the bishops of Boston and Quebec agreed to have Fr. Pierre Marie Mignault, pastor of Chambly, Quebec, visit the settlements along Lake Champlain whenever possible, beginning in 1819. He continued these visits until 1853.

In 1830 Bishop Fenwick of Boston finally secured a priest he could spare to be resident in Vermont. This was Fr. Jeremiah O'Callaghan of Cork, Ireland. This intrepid, irascible cleric, outspoken in his opposition to taking interest on loaned money, among other things, attended mission stations throughout Vermont for more than twenty years. After 1837 he was assisted in the southern part of the state by Fr. John B. Daly, O.S.F. The following two decades saw increased French-Canadian and Irish Catholic immigration into Vermont as more farmland was cultivated, quarries opened, and railway lines developed. Smaller numbers of Poles and Italians also settled in the state in later years.

Diocese of Burlington

At the First Plenary Council of Baltimore it was decided to petition Rome for the establishment of several new dioceses, among them the state of Vermont. The new diocese, with the see city in Burlington, was formally erected on July 29, 1853. Appointed as first bishop was the French-born Louis de Goesbriand, then vicar general of the Diocese of Cleveland, Ohio. On his arrival in Vermont, he found five priests and ten churches serving a Catholic population of roughly 20,000. By the time of his retirement in 1892, de Goesbriand had increased the number of priests from 5 to 52, the number of churches from 10 to 78, and the Catholic population had more than doubled from 20,000 to 46,000.

In 1892 his successor was Fr. John Stephan Michaud, a native of Burlington, who served as the second bishop of Burlington until his death in 1908. Following a two-year *sede vacante* period, Fr. Joseph John Rice of the Diocese of Springfield, Massachusetts, was named third bishop. At his death in 1938, Fr. Matthew Francis Brady of the Diocese of Hartford became bishop until his transfer to Manchester, New Hampshire, in 1944. In 1945 Fr. Edward Francis Ryan of Boston became Burlington's fifth ordinary. In 1954 Fr. Robert Francis Joyce, a Vermont native, was consecrated Ryan's auxiliary, and installed as his successor on Ryan's death in 1956.

Bishop Joyce submitted his mandatory resignation at the age of seventy-five in 1971, and the following year Fr. John Aloysius Marshall, a priest of the Worcester, Massachusetts, diocese then stationed in Rome, succeeded him. Bishop Marshall ably served Vermont's Catholics for twenty years until his appointment as bishop of Springfield, Massachusetts, in 1992. His tragic death in 1994 was a great loss for the Church in New England.

The Contemporary Scene

The present bishop of Burlington, Kenneth Anthony Angell, a native of Providence, Rhode Island, was previously auxiliary bishop of Providence. He was installed in Burlington on November 9, 1992.

There are a number of religious women in the diocese, among them the Sisters of Mercy, whose motherhouse and Trinity College are in Burlington. The Sisters of St. Joseph have their motherhouse in Rutland. The Cloistered Benedictine Sisters have a new monastery in Barre. Several other orders have smaller convents in various locations around Vermont.

Male religious are represented by the Society of Saint Edmund, whose generalate is at St. Michael's College at Winooski Park, as well as a priory of Benedictine monks at Weston. High on Mount Equinox stands the only Charterhouse of the Carthusian Order in the Western Hemisphere.

The Diocese of Burlington, a suffragan of the metropolitan see of Boston, comprises an area of 9,135 square miles. In 1995 there were 95 parishes and 44 missions, 136 diocesan and 53 religious clergy. The Catholic population was 146,332 out of a total state population of 575,691.

De Goesbriand, Louis. *Catholic Memoirs of Vermont and New Hampshire.* Burlington, 1886.

WILLIAM W. GOSS

VEROT, AUGUSTIN (1805–76)

Bishop. Jean-Pierre Augustin Marcellin Verot, "rebel bishop" of Confederate Florida and Georgia during the Civil War, and *enfant terrible* of Vatican Council I, was born in Le Puy, France, on May 23, 1805. He studied for the priesthood at the Sulpician seminary in Issy, outside Paris, where his classmates included the future luminaries Lacordaire and Dupanloup.

In 1803 he joined the faculty of the Sulpician St. Mary's College in Baltimore, where, until the college closed in 1852, he taught mathematics and the physical sciences. Devoting himself thereafter to parochial work, he was consecrated bishop in 1858 and assigned to the new vi-

Augustin Verot

cariate of Florida, where, east of the Apalachicola River, there were six churches and chapels, three priests, and perhaps 3,000 Catholics. The largest concentration of Catholics (952 whites, 376 blacks) lived in the old Spanish city of St. Augustine, where the bantam (5 ft. 2 in.) prelate took up residence and began his ministry to the vast vicariate. In 1859 he recruited seven priests from France to assist him.

On January 4, 1861, Verot preached a sermon at St. Augustine that, later, in published form as a Confederate tract, earned him the sobriquet "rebel bishop" throughout the North. In it he made a biblically based defense of slavery and compared the institution favorably to the factory system in Northern states. At the same time, he called on the South to purge slavery of its patent abuses and to adopt a "servile code" for reforming and humanizing the system.

In 1861 Verot's responsibilities were doubled when he was named third bishop of Savannah while remaining vicar apostolic of Florida. During the war years, he actively ministered to soldiers of both North and South. He and five of his priests were the only ministers of any denomination to attend the unfortunate federal prisoners at Andersonville, Georgia. At war's end he advocated the rights of the freed slaves with a vigor that belied his earlier endorsement of their enslavement. Enlisting the help of Sisters of St. Joseph from his native Le Puy, he opened schools for children of the "freedmen" at St. Augustine, Savannah, and five other towns in his huge jurisdiction. No other Southern bishop matched his earnestness or success in this endeavor. In another educational undertaking, Verot arranged in 1870 for his two parochial schools in

Savannah to be supported wholly as public schools. The so-called Savannah Plan lasted until 1916.

When the First Council of the Vatican opened in 1870, Verot quickly established himself as one of its most vocal participants, delivering long lectures in Latin that, in their pastoral practicality, defied the prevailing theoretical interests of the council fathers, most of them Europeans. Stating, *"venio de America"*—"I come from America"—he urged that the council set aside its anathemas against obscure philosophical heterodoxies and concern itself with ministry; that it recognize the full equality of people of African descent; vindicate Galileo and pay attention to the findings of scientific research; cleanse the breviary and other Church manuals of patent historical errors; seek a friendly reconciliation with Protestant Christians; and forgo the council's intent to declare papal infallibility, which doctrine would hamper his pastoral mission in predominately Protestant America. His trenchant arguments against infallibility were greeted by laughter and rebukes from the floor. Though in the end he signed his adherence to the new dogma, Verot became remembered as the *enfant terrible* of the assembly; or, as his one-time classmate Bishop Félix Dupanloup, of Orléans, put it: *"Vérot—en voilà un!"* Many of his positions would be adopted at Vatican II (1960–65).

During the course of the council, on March 11, 1870, Pius IX transferred Verot from Savannah to the newly established see of St. Augustine, which then claimed 8,000 Catholics and eight priests. For the remainder of his life, Verot tirelessly traveled the length and breadth of Florida's thinly settled wilderness to preach the gospel and administer the sacraments. A priest companion described the bishop's travels as consisting of "sleepless nights, protracted fasts, exposure, long and interminable rides through roads often impassable, in wretched and incommodious stage-coaches." At the conclusion of one such trip, Verot died, at St. Augustine, on June 10, 1876.

See also SLAVERY AND AMERICAN CATHOLICS; VATICAN COUNCIL I, AMERICAN PARTICIPATION IN.

Gannon, Michael V. *Rebel Bishop: The Life and Era of Augustin Verot.* Milwaukee, 1964.

MICHAEL GANNON

VERRAZANO, GIOVANNI DA (1484–1528)

Explorer, navigator. Verrazano was born in Florence around 1484 and was raised there, in Egypt, and in Syria. Spurred on by Magellan's circumnavigation of the globe in 1522, Verrazona desired to find a westward water route to Cathay (China). Under the patronage of King Francis I of France, he embarked on an expedition in 1524 from Madeira to find such a route. Never accomplishing his original goal,

Giovanni da Verrazano

he and his crew wound up exploring the region of the North American coast from Newfoundland in the north to as far south as the Carolinas. Verrazano is remembered for his famous letter addressed to Francis describing New York Bay and other points on the East Coast. In 1528 Verrazano set sail for the Rio de la Plata looking for spices and was killed in an ambush by Carribeans in 1528. In 1529 his brother, Hieronimo, made and circulated a map showing his late brother's final explorations.

Recognizing his importance as navigator and explorer, in 1964, the then longest suspension bridge in the world, connecting Staten Island and Brooklyn, was named in Verrazano's memory. This bridge spans the "narrows," at the entrance to New York harbor that Verrazano had explored four and a half centuries earlier.

ANTHONY D. ANDREASSI

VESPUCCI, AMERIGO (1451–1512)

Explorer. Vespucci was born in Florence, Italy, on March 9, 1451. His father was a notary, and he was given a good education by his uncle, a Dominican friar. Embarking on a career as a clerk for the Medici family, Vespucci soon became involved in ship-chandlery and was involved in fitting out Columbus's second voyage in 1493. Soon Vespucci began sailing on voyages with European explorers, and between 1497 and 1502 went on four major expeditions across the Atlantic. In one of his many letters describing the lands he had seen, Vespucci coined the term "New World," although he, like Columbus, believed these areas were part of Asia. The Pacific Ocean was not fully explored before the voyage of Magellan in 1521. The German

Amerigo Vespucci

cartographer, Martin Waldseemüller, in a 1507 map, first used the term "America" in naming the areas now called "South America." Soon, both newly explored continents acquired the name "America," although Vespucci was not the original explorer of either continent. Vespucci died in Seville on February 22, 1512.

ANTHONY D. ANDREASSI

VIEL, ETIENNE-BERNARD-ALEXANDRE (1736–1821)

Priest and educator. Viel was born in French colonial New Orleans on October 3, 1736. His mother, Marie Trépagnier Viel, died before Etienne was two years of age. His father, one of the colony's earliest medical doctors, sent the child to France in 1743 for an education at one of the home country's finest schools, namely the Académie Royale de Juilly, which was conducted by the Congregation of the Oratory. (Juilly is about nineteen miles northeast of Paris.) Etienne himself entered the Oratorians in August of 1756, and was ordained a priest in September of 1774. He was the only priest born in French colonial Louisiana.

Young Viel was assigned to teach—his specialty was French composition—in more than one Oratorian school, but spent most of his years in France at the *collège* of Juilly, where he was named *préfet* or headmaster in 1775; he occupied the post for twelve years. As teacher and administrator, he left a reputation for kindness in an era not known for pedagogical benignity. In his temperament he probably resembled the late François de Salignac de la Mothe-Fénélon, whose *Télémaque* Viel translated into Latin verse. Viel admired Fénélon and probably imitated him.

During the series of revolutions in France that began in 1789, he exercised pastoral ministry in and around what became the town of St. Martinville, Louisiana. In sum, Viel spent about two decades (1792–1812) as a priest in his native Louisiana, which at the time of his return was a Spanish colony. Called back to France by his confreres and former students, he helped to reestablish the Oratorian school at Juilly, where he died at the age of 85.

Etienne Viel was the first formally educated native of the Mississippi Valley, and he was the area's first author. He wrote a school play entitled *Evandre,* a pastoral, moralistic play in French verse; in a classical Greek art form he preached gospel values.

In Louisiana in 1803 he saw the tricolor of revolutionary France replace the royal emblem of Spain, and he was there when the United States of America took possession of the colony; thus, he was one of the small number of persons to have lived under all the forms of Louisiana's colonial and territorial administration.

Viel died in Juilly, France, on December 16, 1821.

O'Neill, Charles Edwards. *Viel, Louisiana's Firstborn Author, with Evandre, the First Literary Creation of a Native of the Mississippi Valley.* Lafayette, 1991.

CHARLES EDWARDS O'NEILL

VIETNAMESE CATHOLICS IN AMERICA

The victory of Communist North Vietnam over South Vietnam in April 1975 provoked the largest ever exodus of Vietnamese, and in particular Vietnamese Catholics, to the United States of America. Vietnamese refugees settled in various parts of the world, in particular in Canada and Australia, but the country of choice was and remains the United States, partly because it had the best organized resettlement programs and partly because it was perceived as offering most opportunities for educational and economic advancement.

To date, there have been no exact statistics on the Vietnamese population in general and on Vietnamese Catholics in particular in the United States. The current number of Vietnamese is estimated to be one million, of whom a quarter are Catholic (whereas in Vietnam about 8 percent of the population is Catholic).

Immigration and Settlement

In general, there were three waves of Vietnamese immigration to the United States in the last twenty years: the first wave consisted of about 250,000 who arrived in the immediate aftermath of the fall of South Vietnam; the second wave consisted of hundreds of thousands of "boat people" who came after being temporarily sheltered in various refugee camps, mainly in Thailand, the Philippines, and Hong Kong; and the third wave consisted of a much smaller number of people who were reunited with their families through various official programs such as Orderly Departure Program and Humanitarian Operations.

Like most other recently arrived ethnic groups, the Vietnamese tend to settle close to each other. California has the largest number of Vietnamese and Vietnamese Catholics (Orange County and San Jose), followed by Texas (Houston, Dallas/Fort Worth, and Port Arthur), and Louisiana (New Orleans). As a whole, the Vietnamese have done well in the new country, as testified by the high educational achievements of their young and their economic successes.

In general, Vietnamese Catholics are deeply attached to their Vietnamese churches and hold their pastors in high esteem. They spare no resources to have their own churches and their own priests so as to be able to worship in their mother tongue and to preserve their religious and cultural customs. Most dioceses where there is a sizable number of Vietnamese Catholics have at least one Vietnamese parish (e.g., New Orleans, Dallas, Arlington, [Virginia], and Washington, D.C.). Even where there are no Vietnamese parishes, Vietnamese Catholics often have the opportunity to worship together, using the churches of the American parishes. Only extremely rarely has the relationship between the Vietnamese Catholic community and the local ordinary been marked by controversies (e.g., in San Jose and Port Arthur); otherwise, the collaboration between the Vietnamese clergy and the American hierarchy has been positive.

There are currently some four hundred Vietnamese priests, some fifteen permanent deacons, and several hundred sisters. Among the dozen of male religious orders, the most numerous are the Congregation of Mary Corredemptrix, whose founder is a Vietnamese priest, and is headquartered in Carthage, Missouri. Each August the order organizes a religious celebration in which some 30,000 people regularly take part. There are about twenty female religious congregations, the most numerous of which are the Lovers of the Cross, founded in Vietnam by Bishop Lambert de La Motte in the seventeenth century and divided into many groups according to the dioceses to which the members belong in Vietnam (e.g., Ha Noi, Hue, Thanh Hoa, Vinh, Cho Quan, Qui Nhon, and Phat Diem).

Two of the several official organizations for Vietnamese Catholics in the United States deserve mention: the Vietnamese Catholic Federation in the United States of America, whose general assembly meets every four years; and the Community of Vietnamese Clergy and Religious in the United States of America, whose general assembly meets every two years. There also exists a Vietnamese Pastoral Center that functions in collaboration with the United States Catholic Conference.

Achievements and Challenges

Like many other ethnic groups, Vietnamese Catholics are deeply concerned with preserving their language, culture, and religious traditions. To achieve this goal they publish numerous newspapers, magazines, and journals, among which the most important are *Dan Chua (People of God)*, *Duc Me Hang Cuu Giup (Our Lady of Perpetual Help)*, *Thoi Diem Cong Giao (Catholic Magazine)*, and *Hop Tuyen Than Hoc (Theology Journal)*. Other activities include Vietnamese language classes and catechetical instruction in Vietnamese (there is a well-attended biannual national catechetical conference). Occasions on which Vietnamese cultural traditions are particularly celebrated are weddings and funerals. Other more public occasions include the lunar New Year *(Tet)*, the commemoration of the fall of South Vietnam (April 30), and the feast of the martyrs in Vietnam (November 24). The Vietnamese Catholics also generously contribute to the Church in Vietnam, especially in the reconstruction of old churches or the building of new ones.

Interestingly, the greatest challenge for most Vietnamese Catholics in this country is not inculturation into the American sociopolitical and economic scene. By and large, the majority of them have adapted to the new culture and ethos quickly and have succeeded very well. This success, however, has a price to pay on the religious level. The Vietnamese youth, who tend to be more adaptive to the American way of life, find the traditional Vietnamese Catholic piety, which is heavy with devotional practices, strange and unhelpful. On the other hand, the highly individualistic slant of Vietnamese Catholicism, reinforced by the individualism of the American ethos, blinds them to the sociopolitical dimensions of the Christian faith.

The challenge for Vietnamese Catholics in the United States therefore lies in retrieving the deeply communitarian ethos both of their own culture and of the Christian faith, and suffusing their religious practices with this new spirit. This task is all the more urgent both because the Vietnamese Catholics in the United States have reached the stage where their traditional piety is powerless against the onslaught of consumerism and materialism and because, with the United States lifting the economic embargo against Vietnam and establishing diplomatic relations with the government, Vietnam is rushing to embrace capitalism with its market economy as the panacea to all the ills besetting its society.

PETER C. PHAN

VIETNAM WAR AND AMERICAN CATHOLICS, THE

In the 1960s and early 1970s, the American Catholic community was deeply divided over the Vietnam War, as was the nation as a whole. Yet the extraordinarily passionate debate among Catholics was rooted in a uniquely intimate relationship between the American Church and the Republic of South Vietnam. Since that involvement originated in the decade prior to the Second Vatican Council, American Catholic attitudes toward the war in Vietnam were inevitably linked to the tumultuous experience of the Church itself in the immediate postconciliar period.

The Diem Regime

In 1950 Ngo Dinh Diem, an ardent Vietnamese nationalist and devout Catholic, spent a brief time in self-imposed exile at Maryknoll seminaries in Lakewood, New Jersey, and Ossining, New York. During his stay in the U.S.A., Diem—the scion of a leading mandarin family and a staunch opponent of both Vietnamese communism and French neocolonialism—met with such prominent American Catholics as Francis Cardinal Spellman of New York, Ambassador Joseph P. Kennedy, and Senators John F. Kennedy and Mike Mansfield. In a widely publicized 1965 article in *Ramparts,* a formerly Catholic publication, journalists Robert Scheer and Warren Hinckle alleged that Diem's American coreligionists had conspired in 1954 with other members of the "Vietnam Lobby" to bolster Diem's quixotic effort to establish a democratic regime in South Vietnam, a new state created following the defeat of the French at Dienbienphu in April of that year.

Traditional American concerns over clerical involvement in policy decisions led many to greatly exaggerate the role of Spellman and others in winning support for Diem among U.S. legislators, though there is no question that well-placed American Catholics played an active role on Diem's behalf; especially in the early days of his fledgling administration, when the United States Navy relocated nearly one million Catholics from North Vietnam to the South. In the midst of the largest refugee operation in history, Lt. Col. Edward G. Lansdale of the Central Intelligence Agency "discovered" Thomas A. Dooley, an ambitious young American Catholic naval physician working in a Haiphong refugee camp. Dooley was authorized to speak on behalf of both Diem and the Navy, as part of Lansdale's ambitious campaign to provide his client with a Catholic constituency while assuaging American fears of sectarian politics. Dooley's best-selling account of the refugee operation, *Deliver Us From Evil* (1956), placed the travail of the Vietnamese pilgrims in the ecumenical context of American religious freedom: his book was the single most effective weapon unleashed by the "Vietnam Lobby" at a time when leading figures in the State Department remained dubious of Diem, and few Americans had any awareness of Indochina.

Largely as a result of this public relations campaign, Diem enjoyed broadly consensual support in the U.S.A. throughout the remainder of the 1950s. Although many of the secular liberals who had ardently supported Diem would grow disenchanted with his authoritarian rule by the end of the decade, American Catholics remained staunchly committed to his regime, from the liberal internationalists associated with *Commonweal* and *America* magazines to militant anticommunists who viewed South Vietnam as a bulwark of Christian civilization. A Columban priest from Ireland, Patrick O'Connor, produced highly partisan dispatches on Diem's behalf for the National Catholic News Service, the American bishops' official news agency. Given the paucity of journalists permanently assigned to Vietnam in the 1950s, Fr. O'Connor's reporting enjoyed great influence over readers of the diocesan press.

But in the autumn of 1963, America's first Roman Catholic president grudgingly yielded to advisers who insisted that the increasingly ruthless and unpopular dictator be forcibly removed from office. Since Kennedy had been an ardent Diem supporter (he proclaimed in 1956 that South Vietnam "is our offspring"), the decision to endorse the October 1963 coup was a painful one. Diem's ouster and subsequent assassination were completely overshadowed, of course, by the killing of Kennedy himself a month later. In the wake of his death many young, idealistic Catholics experienced a crisis of faith in the American political system. At the same time, the message of the Second Vatican Council was interpreted by many as a call to action and a challenge to established civil and ecclesiastical authority.

Catholic Pacifists and Protesters

By 1965 Catholics were in the forefront of opposition to increased American military involvement in Vietnam. In August of that year Christopher Kerns, a member of the pacifist Catholic Worker movement, burned his draft card in a public ceremony captured by a photographer from *Life* magazine. The ensuing uproar resulted in federal legislation mandating fines and jail terms for similar acts committed in the future. Thomas Cornell, a prominent peace activist, challenged radicals to defy the law in the September issue of Dorothy Day's *Catholic Worker* newspaper. On October 16, 1965, David Miller, a young member of the New York Catholic Worker community, climbed atop a sound truck in front of the Induction Center on Whitehall Street and burned his draft card in front of an audience consisting largely of the working media. The event produced such a "sensation," recalled Tom Cornell, that a larger event was organized for November 6, timed for coverage in Sunday newspapers across the nation. Cornell and several other Catholic Workers burned their draft cards on a platform set up at the northern end of Union Square: "Again it caused a sensation. . . . It made an enormous impact" (Meconis, 12).

While the Catholic Worker movement enjoyed a long tradition of pacifist resistance, the young radicals tended to be much less committed to Church orthodoxy than its foundress, Dorothy Day. On November 9, 1965, Roger

LaPorte, a young graduate of the Jesuit's Le Moyne College, set himself afire in front of the United Nations building in protest against the rapidly expanding American war effort. Before dying he explained: "I am a Catholic Worker. I am antiwar, all wars. I did this as a religious action." The Jesuit activist Daniel Berrigan, who had known and influenced LaPorte, preached that "[h]e gave his life, so that others might live." Berrigan was subsequently "exiled" to Latin America. This series of events, beginning with the draft card burnings by Catholic Workers, galvanized the Catholic Left and paved the way for more drastic actions yet to come. In the short term, however, Roger LaPorte's suicide provoked some harsh judgments on the fledgling Catholic antiwar movement, as the Trappist monk Thomas Merton, the columnist John Leo, and other generally sympathetic figures warned that the movement demanded a more substantial moral and intellectual foundation.

Highly publicized expressions of dissent notwithstanding, as of 1966 "the number of American Catholics opposed to the war in Vietnam constituted a distinct minority." In November of that year the American Catholic bishops concluded, in a joint statement on the war: "It is reasonable to argue that our presence in Vietnam is justified." During his Christmas visit to Vietnam, New York Cardinal Francis Spellman proclaimed that the conflict entailed "a war for civilization" (Meconis, 15). Ironically, many prominent Catholic conservatives now expressed dismay over the fledgling efforts of Pope Paul VI to promote negotiations between the North Vietnamese and representatives of Western democracies. As early as 1961, William F. Buckley and other conservatives associated with *National Review* had chided Pope John XXIII for allegedly neglecting communism's persisting threat in *Mater et Magistra*. John XXIII's 1963 encyclical, *Pacem in Terris,* was even more widely criticized by the Right for its apparent endorsement of pacifism and nonviolent civil disobedience.

The Catonsville Nine

In 1967 Paul VI embraced a neutralist position concerning the Vietnam War, perhaps due to his frustration over the unwillingness of President Lyndon B. Johnson to call a halt to American bombing of the North. Members of the American Catholic Left now sought to establish for themselves "the moral leadership which they felt the bishops had failed to provide" (Meconis, 16). In Baltimore, Philip Berrigan, a Josephite priest, conspired with several non-Catholic radicals to vandalize files of the local draft board by covering them with animal blood, purportedly a symbolic Christian form of protest. Berrigan's subsequent incarceration served to further divide the Catholic Left between radicals anxious for direct action and members of more traditional groups such as the Catholic Peace Fellowship. The Baltimore raid led to a more notorious ac-

tion against the draft board at Catonsville, Maryland. On May 17, 1968, nine Catholic activists, including Philip Berrigan and his brother Daniel, removed draft records from the facility while employees looked on in a mixture of shock and horror (a clerical worker who clung to some files in her charge was slightly injured by the pacifists). The raiders proceeded to a nearby parking lot, where they joined hands and prayed while dousing the records with homemade napalm. Moments later the "Catonsville Nine" were taken into custody.

The specter of priests being imprisoned and charged with committing felonies haunted the American Catholic community at a tumultuous moment in its history, as the antiwar activities of radical Catholics were inevitably, and with good reason, linked to the broader convulsions of the immediate post-Vatican II era. When a disgusted Catholic FBI agent told one of the Berrigans that he felt compelled to change his religion, he expressed a widely held view that the Church, in seeking "relevance" to the modern world, had undermined the faith of those who had looked upon it as the one unchanging edifice in a complex modern world. Many Catholics became more militantly patriotic than ever before: though reliable statistics are lacking, impressionistic evidence suggested that Catholics were overrepresented among the U.S. troops sent to Vietnam between 1965 and 1973. Catholics were also prominent among the so-called "hardhats" who countered antiwar demonstrations with displays of their own loyalty in numerous cities across the country.

Catholic antiwar activists were often viewed as bearers of a historical shift within the American Church, from a defensive parochialism to bold engagement with "the modern world," in the spirit of a celebrated document of the Vatican Council. Daniel Berrigan certainly achieved a postdenominational cult status in the late 1960s, especially when, as a fugitive from justice, he sought protection from elements of the nonreligious militant Left. Yet the occasionally self-congratulatory tone of Catholic radicalism belied its ambiguous relationship with the secular Left as well as its tenuous links with the Church itself. As one radical priest conceded: "Most of the student-Marxist Left had real troubles with the religious aspect of a lot of the actions and with the middle-class stuff, calling us 'mindless, moralistic masochists'—the '3-M Theory' of the Catholic Left" (Meconis, 38). At the same time, many Catholic antiwar activists left the Church during this period to face an uncertain future, especially the priests and religious whose vocations foundered on the rocks of the often apocalyptic militance of the era.

Divisions Among American Catholics

While Catholic radicals garnered extraordinary notoriety for their anti-Vietnam War activities, they clearly failed to win wide support within the American Church as a whole. The debate over the war did succeed, however, in deeply dividing that community and unleashing a rancorous wave of self-incrimination without precedent in American Catholic history. Some, including the philosopher Daniel Callahan, indicted their coreligionists for failing to transcend nationalism. Callahan wrote in 1968: "The overwhelming picture presented by American Catholicism is of a passive, unprotesting, faintly chauvinistic herd, satisfied to go along with the Administration. In this respect, American Catholics are much like the rest of the population, and if (according to some polls) they are somewhat more favorable toward the war than some groups, the difference is not all that striking" (Callahan, 61). Conservatives responded that the Catholic antiwar movement had tainted the Church with its uncivil and even blasphemous behavior that included disruptions of several ordination ceremonies.

The war was too divisive to sustain neatly defined, opposing camps constructed around the traditional liberal/conservative axis. The Catholic Left grew deeply divided over tactics, especially the decision of Daniel Berrigan and others to go "underground" in 1970 rather than to accept punishment, a traditional tenet of nonviolent resistance. Even at the presumed "center," within the American hierarchy itself, divisions became apparent in 1967 when several bishops, including Paul Hallinan of Atlanta and James Peter Davis of Santa Fe, joined a national coalition which, under the rubric "Negotiation Now," sought a political settlement of the war. Yet, while this position was initially viewed as highly controversial, by 1968 many leading American Catholics had concluded that support for and advocacy of a negotiated settlement represented the only just response to a war that threatened to drag on interminably.

The Catholic Left was seemingly vindicated by the growing support for peace within the Church. According to a student of the movement: "Much of what was once deemed rhetoric when uttered by the Catholic Left has in recent years become the official social teaching of the Catholic Church on both a global and a national level" (Meconis, 144). Yet this was a triumph laced with irony, for many prominent figures within the Catholic antiwar movement would later abandon the Church entirely, while others renounced their activism and took up the cause of neoconservatism in the 1980s, rejecting the Church's apparent embrace of pacifism for a militant advocacy of free market anticommunism. Perhaps the most enduring legacy of the Vietnam War for American Catholics entailed not issues of war and peace but authority and cohesion. Once the consensus bolstering American Catholic patriotism was shattered in the 1960s, it proved to be very difficult, if not impossible, to find the grounds for reconstructing a unified faith community in the United States.

Allitt, Patrick. *Catholic Intellectuals and Conservative Politics in America, 1950–1985*. Ithaca, N.Y.: Cornell University Press, 1993.

Au, William A. *The Cross, The Flag, and The Bomb*. Westport, Conn.: Greenwood Press, 1985.

Callahan, Daniel. "Renewing the Church in a Nation at War." *American Catholics and Vietnam*, ed. Thomas E. Quigley. Grand Rapids, Mich.: William B. Eerdmans Publishing Company, 1968.

Gray, Francine du Plessix. *Divine Disobedience: Profiles in Catholic Radicalism*. New York: Vintage Books, 1970.

Meconis, Charles A. *With Clumsy Grace: The American Catholic Left, 1961–1975*. New York: The Seabury Press, 1979.

JAMES TERENCE FISHER

Related Documents

WAR AND PEACE. A PASTORAL LETTER TO THE ARCHDIOCESE OF ATLANTA, OCTOBER, 1966

The plight of the world in the aftermath of World War II and the mounting peril of nuclear warfare, is well illustrated by the opening paragraph of the introduction to a volume of papal documents on peace, published in 1943, which read as follows:

At some future hour, known now only to God, a group of statesmen will take their places around a conference table and hammer out a treaty designed to settle the staggering problems of a world torn apart by years of bitter war. When that hour strikes, what role will the Pope play in forging that instrument which will decisively determine the character of the post-war world? [Harry C. Koenig, (ed.), *Principles for Peace. Selections from Papal Documents, Leo XIII to Pius XII* (Washington: National Catholic Welfare Conference, 1943), p. xv.]

Twenty-three years have passed since Monsignor Koenig wrote those lines and the statesmen have not yet taken their places around the conference table to negotiate a general peace treaty. Meanwhile the "staggering problems" of 1943 have multiplied and deepened in their complexity with the shadow of nuclear conflict. And the answer to the question concerning the role that the Pope will play in a final settlement is as uncertain as it was in 1943. During the early 1940's Pius XII issued a series of striking Christmas messages which, in the judgment of Thomas P. Neill of St. Louis University, constituted "the most profound consideration on the nature and requirements of peace in modern times." Yet, as he said, while most people in the free world received the Pope's words respectfully, they were generally dismissed as "impractical theorizing," whereas had his advice been followed, "the problems confronting statesmen today would not be as difficult as they are." ["The Practicality of 'Idealism,'" *Saint Louis Review,* October 7, 1966, p. 19.] The voice of American Catholics has not been nearly as strong in pursuit of world peace as one might rightly have expected. To remedy the deficiencies on that score, and to awaken the conscience of their coreligionists and of others as well, several bishops of the United States have issued formal statements on this pressing problem, but none with more balance and sound reasoning than that of

Archbishop Hallinan and Bishop Bernardin of Atlanta. The following document not only echoes Paul VI's piercing cry, "never war again," but it summons the conscience of American Catholics and all men of good will to serious reflection on this gravest of all problems that now face the world.

(*Source: War and Pence. A Pastoral Letter to the Archdiocese of Atlanta, October, 1966.* Distributed in pamphlet form by The Chancery, 2699 Peachtree Road, N.E., Atlanta, Georgia 30305.)

War and Peace

THE SLAUGHTER OF MEN AND THE DEATH OF VILLAGES ARE certainly not new to the history of mankind. Yet the passionate desire for true peace has never died in men's hearts. The tension created by the desire for peace and the realities of war has been brought into sharp focus by the current conflict in Viet Nam. But as Pope Paul reminded us in his encyclical two weeks ago,[1] this war is just one of many tragedies which severely threaten the peace and stability of the human family. "For instance," he stated, "there are the increasing race for nuclear weapons, the unscrupulous efforts for the expansion of one's nation, the excessive glorification of one's race, the obsession for revolution, the segregations enforced on citizens, the iniquitous plotting, the murder of the innocent."

1. The Five Questions

The Church cannot remain silent in the face of these grave disorders. True peace will not be brought about solely by military victory; it will not be achieved by maintaining a balance of power between enemies. Reflecting the thinking of Pope John XXIII as expressed in *Peace on Earth,* the Second Vatican Council has stated very clearly that, "peace results from the harmony built into human society by its Divine Founder, and actualized by men as they thirst after ever greater justice." All action and all talk about peace will be irrelevant unless it is cast in a moral context.

The Church, then, as the living voice of Christ must speak out. It must give an effective witness to the gospel message which provides a sure framework for universal brotherhood. This must be based on mutual respect and love so essential to the establishment of peace. For this reason, an American Catholic who has lost his moral perspective on war can hardly be considered a true Christian patriot.

As the great debate on war and peace gathers momentum, certain urgent questions demand that we respond:—

1. What are the demands of true patriotism?
2. Is it possible to speak of a "just war" today as we did in the past?
3. On at broader level, should nations try to maintain peace by a "balance of terror"?
4. Does universal disarmament (all sides) differ morally from unilateral disarmament (one side)?

5. What are our obligations in contributing toward a genuinely moral consensus regarding American involvement in Viet Nam?

2. Who Is the Patriot?

The well being of every nation depends on the patriotism of its citizens. The American Catholic—citizen, soldier, pacifist—has held an honorable place in our country's history, side by side with those *of* other faiths. The Bishops of Vatican II, however, clearly point out that there is a significant difference between *true patriotism* which is "living for God and Christ by following the honorable customs of one's own nation" and *false patriotism* which stems from "a narrowing of mind . . . racial prejudice and bitter nationalism."[2] True patriotism, in other words, does not end at a nation's borders. That American is truly patriotic who, while devoting himself to the legitimate needs and concerns of his country, also seeks "the welfare of the whole human family . . . a universal love for mankind." As Pope John stated in his last encyclical, *Peace on Earth:* "Individual countries cannot rightly seek their own interests, and develop in isolation from the rest."

This is not to say, of course, that a country cannot defend itself. While making it clear that all means short of force must first be employed, the Council restates the traditional teaching of the Church regarding the right of self-defense: "As long as the danger of war remains and there is no competent and sufficiently powerful authority at the international level, government cannot be denied the right to legitimate defense . . ." Moreover, the Council Fathers commend those in the military forces who serve as "agents of security and freedom on behalf of their people" as long as they fulfill this role properly.

In the light of our duty to examine the moral position of our country, another question remains: that of the right of a conscientious objector. The Church, after a brief warning that peace cannot exist "unless personal values are safeguarded" states clearly:

> It seems right that laws make humane provisions for the case of those who (for reasons of conscience) refuse to bear arms, provided however, that they accept some other form of service to the human community.

3. Limits and Illusions

If men are to remain human, there must be definite limits to the conduct of any war. The Council clearly defines these limits:

1. Any act of war aimed *indiscriminately at the destruction* of entire cities or of extensive areas along with their population is a crime against God and man himself. It merits univocal and unhesitating condemnation.

2. Those actions designed for the *methodical extermination* of an entire people, nation or ethnic minority must be vehemently condemned as horrendous crimes. . . . Blind obedience cannot excuse those who yield to them.

The Council also considered the massing of arms as a means of avoiding war. It pronounced such a method of deterrence a "treacherous trap for humanity." It is a trap because it is, without question, a dangerous way of maintaining peace. Moreover, the causes of war are actually intensified because the vast sums used for stockpiling weapons make it extremely difficult, if not totally impossible in some cases, to give attention to the human misery which is usually the root cause of war. For this reason the Bishops made an urgent plea for disarmament. But they realized that disarmament is a two-sided coin: it would have little meaning unless all sides agreed on it and unless there were effective means of enforcing it.

What bearing do these general principles have on our involvement in Viet Nam? What implications do they have generally for our efforts to promote world-wide peace?

4. The Only Alternative—?

As in every great human problem, there is no simple solution. American Catholics can put faith in the integrity of our government's aims in Viet Nam. There is surely abundant evidence of it in a number of areas: the recent large vote in South Viet Nam opening the door to local civilian government; the aid we have given to get such projects as the Mekong Delta improvements underway in Southeastern Asia; the support of the United States voiced in Washington last month by President Ferdinand Marcos of the Philippines; the total withdrawal of American troops from the Dominican Republic, leading the way to a constitutional government free of extremists, both left and right.

In the light of events rather than slogans, then, it can be argued that to the present course of action in Viet Nam there may be no visible alternative.

But we cannot stop here. It is the Christian duty to keep looking for *other alternatives*. We must know as much about the factual situation as possible, in order that these alternatives be realistic. To a limited extent our national security requires secrecy. Except for that, however, we must keep insisting that our leaders fully inform us of the facts and issues involved in the Viet Nam war.

We must help to enlarge the new climate of thought, based on Pope John's principle: in an age which prides itself on its atomic energy, it is unreasonable to hold that war is still a suitable way to restore violated rights. We can help by conversation, study, example, discussion groups and lectures.

Christians should advocate what they believe is the best way to bring about disarmament:—mutual agreements, safeguards and inspection; world federalism; the creation of a public authority empowered to negotiate toward peace.

We have the obligation to make sure that our government pursues, vigorously, wholeheartedly and repeatedly every opening which has even the slightest hope of peaceful settlement. Ambassador Arthur Goldberg's recent summary of the present American policy was such an opening. To the United Nations, he stated that we were ready to join in a phased withdrawal of all external forces, and a halt to bombing upon the assurance from North Viet Nam that it would halt its war effort.

As Cardinal Lawrence Shehan of Baltimore recently said in his splendid pastoral:

> Those who argue against restraint and against keeping a nation's warmaking acts within moral bounds are likely to win an even greater hearing . . . (But) if our means become immoral, our cause will have been betrayed.[3]

We must protest, therefore, whenever there is danger that our conduct of the war will exceed moral limits. A Christian simply cannot approve indiscriminate bombing, methodical extermination of people, nuclear arms designed for "overkill" or disregard for noncombatants.

In short, our dedication to the cause of peace must become so evident, so intense, so convincing that the old balance of mutual terror will be phased out to make way for a new balance of mutual trust. In Christian confidence, we can hope that if many nations come to trust each other, those who instead rely on war will reevaluate their own positions.

On a broader level, we must give our leaders a mandate to pursue the problem of disarmament. While no Catholic teaching demands that a nation disarm by itself, the whole Catholic momentum today is toward a disarmament that is complete, thorough and internal, resting on mutual agreement and workable safeguards. We cannot stand aside because such a solution is hard to visualize or difficult to achieve.

Moreover, we must never cease to do everything in our power to help make it possible for the poorer nations of the world to give their people what they need—educationally, culturally, materially, and socially—to live in a way that squares with their God-given human dignity. We must be strong for the working out of the social and economic programs that will heal, not inflame, the causes of war.

5. "Never War Again!"

Mankind longs for peace, and has tragically sought it through the inhuman process of war. The Church calls us all—especially parents, teachers and those who form public opinion—to make known "fresh sentiments of peace." Pope Paul, speaking of the purpose of his recent encyclical, asked, "What is the use of it?" and answered that all Christians should "speak out and pray."

We must speak out; we cannot remain silent. In his novel, *War and Peace,* Tolstoy asks how men can ignore the continued disasters in which "Christians, professing the law of love, murder one another." Christian consciences and voices must be raised against the savagery and terror of war. We must speak out—for justice, for truth, for freedom and for peace.

And we must pray with Christian minds and hearts until hope replaces anxiety, and love crowds out hatred. On October 11, we observe the Motherhood of Our Lady, mother of the Son of God and of all His brothers. Do we love them as brothers? The month ends with the Feast of Christ the King, patron of our Cathedral. The preface of that feast describes a world not stained with the blood of men, but marked by the blood of Christ, the Lamb of God—"a Kingdom of truth and life, of holiness and grace, a Kingdom of justice, of love and peace."

Through the courage and the prayers of each of us, may our country and every other sovereign state "beat their swords into plowshares, and their spears into pruning hooks. One nation shall not raise the sword against another, nor shall they train for war again." (Is. 2,4)

As people of God, let us reaffirm what Paul VI, His vicar on earth said a year ago to the United Nations:—"never war again!"

✠ Paul J. Hallinan
Archbishop of Atlanta
✠ Joseph L. Bernardin
Auxiliary Bishop of Atlanta

[1] *Christi Matri Rosarii,* September 15, 1966, *The Monitor* (San Francisco), September 29, 1966, p. 9.

[2] Reference to documents of Vatican Council II are generally to the "Pastoral Constitution on the Church in the Modern World," Walter M. Abbott, S.J., and Joseph Gallagher (Eds.), *Documents of Vatican II* (New York: Guild Press, 1966), pp. 183–316.

[3] *The Catholic Review* (Baltimore), July 1, 1966, p. 2.

(*Source*: John Tracy Ellis, ed. *Documents of American Catholic History.* Vol. 2:1866–1966. Wilmington, Del.: Michael Glazier, 1987, 696–702.)

PEACE AND VIETNAM. A STATEMENT BY THE CATHOLIC BISHOPS, NOVEMBER 18, 1966.

It is doubtful if any public policy of the Catholic bishops of the United States better illustrates the strikingly altered status of the American Catholic community than that relating to the issue of war and peace. In every conflict from the revolution of the 1770's up to and including World War II, the bishops stood stoutly behind the government, including the two armed conflicts of a gravely doubtful moral character, namely, the Mexican War (1846–1848) and the war against Spain (1898). It was a position that reflected Catholics' minority status in the midst of the traditional anti-Catholic bias of many Americans. In fact, this stance carried well into the war in Vietnam when as late as 1966 the bishops with, it is true, carefully nuanced reservations, yet maintained that "in the light of the facts as they are known to

us, it is reasonable that our presence in Vietnam is justified." The greatly enhanced position of Catholics in relation to the American mainstream was a significant factor in the changed attitude represented between this document and the view expressed in the one that follows.

(*Source*: Hugh J. Nolan, ed. *Pastoral Letters of the United States Catholic Bishops.* Washington: National Conference of Catholic Bishops. 1983. III, 74-7.)

1. OUR COMMON HUMANITY DEMANDS THAT ALL PEOPLE live in peace and harmony with one another. This peace will exist only if the right order established by God is observed, an order which is based on the requirements of human dignity. Everyone, therefore, must be vitally and personally concerned about correcting the grave disorders which today threaten peace. As Catholics, we are members of the Church that Pope Paul has called a "messenger of peace."

2. We, the Catholic bishops of the United States, consider it our duty to help magnify the moral voice of our nation. This voice, fortunately, is becoming louder and clearer because it is the voice of all faiths. To the strong words of the National Council of Churches, the Synagogue Council of America, and other religious bodies, we add our own plea for peace. Our approaches may at times differ, but our starting point (justice) and our goal (peace) do not.

3. While we cannot resolve all the issues involved in the Vietnam conflict, it is clearly our duty to insist that they be kept under constant moral scrutiny. No one is free to evade his personal responsibility by leaving it entirely to others to make moral judgments. In this connection, the Vatican Council warns that "men should take heed not to entrust themselves only to the efforts of others, while remaining careless about their own attitudes. For government officials, who must simultaneously guarantee the good of their own people and promote the universal good, depend on public opinion and feeling to the greatest possible extent."[1]

Peace and Modern Warfare

4. While it is not possible in this brief statement to give a detailed analysis of the Church's total teaching on war and peace, it seems necessary to review certain basic principle if the present crisis is to be put in its proper moral perspectives.

5. We reaffirmed at the Council the legitimate role of patriotism for the well-being of a nation, but a clear distinction was made between true and *false* patriotism: "Citizens should develop a generous and loyal devotion to their country, but without any narrowing of mind. In other words, they must always look simultaneously to the welfare of the whole human family, which is tied together by the manifold bonds linking races, peoples and nations."[2]

6. But these limits on patriotism do not rule out a country's right to legitimate self-defense. While making it clear that all means short of force must first be used, the Council restated the traditional teaching regarding the right of self-defense: "As long as the danger of war remains and there is no competent and sufficiently powerful authority at the international level, government cannot be denied the right to legitimate defense."[3] And what a nation can do to defend itself, it may do to help another in its struggle against aggression.

7. In the conduct of any war, there must be moral limits: "Any act of war aimed indiscriminately at the destruction of entire cities or of extensive areas along with their population is a crime against God and man himself. It merits univocal and unhesitating condemnation."[4] Moreover, as the Council also reminded us, the fact that a war of self-defense has unhappily begun does not mean that any and all means may be employed by the warring parties.

8. While the stockpiling of scientific weapons serves, for the present, as a deterrent to aggression, the Council has warned us that "the arms race in which so many countries are engaged is not a safe way to preserve a steady peace."[5] Indeed, it is a "treacherous trap for humanity." Far from promoting a sure and authentic peace, it actually fosters war by diverting resources which could be better used to alleviate the human misery which causes war. In their urgent plea for disarmament, however, the Council Fathers understood that it will be effective only if it is universal and if there are adequate means of enforcing it.

9. The Council commended those citizens who defend their nation against aggression. They are "instruments of security and freedom on behalf of their people. As long as they fulfill this role properly they are making a genuine contribution to the establishment of peace."[6]

At the same time, however, it pointed out that some provision should be made for those who conscientiously object to bearing arms: "It seems right that laws make humane provisions for the care of those who for reasons of conscience refuse to bear arms; provided, however, that they accept some other form of service to the human community."[7]

Principles Put to Work

10. In the light of these principles, how are we as Americans to judge the involvement of the United States in Vietnam? What can we do to promote peace?

11. Americans can have confidence in the sincerity of their leaders as long as they work for a just peace in Vietnam. Their efforts to find a solution to the present impasse are well known. We realize that citizens of all faiths and of differing political loyalties honestly differ among themselves over the moral issues involved in this tragic conflict. While we do not claim to be able to resolve these issues authoritatively, in the light of the facts as they are known to us, it is reasonable to argue that our presence in Vietnam is justified. We share the anguish of our government officials in their awesome responsibility of making life-and-death decisions about our national policy in Vietnam. We commend the valor of our men in the armed forces, and we express to them our debt of gratitude. In our time, thousands of men have given their lives in war. To those who loved them, we express our sorrow at their loss and promise our constant prayer.

12. But we cannot stop here. While we can conscientiously support the position of our country in the present circumstances, it is the duty of everyone to search for other alternatives. And everyone—government leaders and citizens alike—must be prepared to change our course whenever a change in circumstances warrants it.

13. This can be done effectively only if we know the facts and issues involved. Within the limits imposed by our national security, therefore, we must always insist that these facts and issues be made known to the public so that they can be considered in their moral context.

14. On the basis of our knowledge and understanding of the current situation, we are also bound always to make sure that our government does, in fact, pursue every possibility which offers even the slightest hope of a peaceful settlement. And we must clearly protest whenever there is a danger that the conflict will be escalated beyond morally acceptable limits.

15. On a broader level, we must support our government in its efforts to negotiate a workable formula for disarmament. What we seek is not unilateral disarmament, but one proceeding in the words of the Council, "at an equal pace according to agreement, and backed up by authentic and workable safeguards."[8] We commend the officials of our country and others for their contribution to the proposed Treaty against Nuclear Proliferation which, hopefully, will soon become a reality.

16. Moreover, we must use every resource available, as a nation, to help alleviate the basic causes of war. If the God-given human dignity of the people of poorer nations is not to become an illusion, these nations must be able to provide for the spiritual and material needs of their citizens. We must help them do this. The economically developed nations of the world, as Pope John insisted in his great encyclical, *Pacem in Terris,* must come to the aid of those which are in the process of developing so that every man, woman and child in the world may be able "to live in conditions more in keeping with their human dignity."[9]

"The Second Mile"

17. There is a grave danger that the circumstances of the present war in Vietnam may, in time, diminish our moral sensitivity to its evils. Every means at our disposal,

therefore, must be used to create a climate of peace. In this climate, prayer, personal example, study, discussion, and lectures can strengthen the will for peace. We must advocate what we believe are the best methods of promoting peace: mutual agreements, safeguards, and inspection; the creation of an international public authority to negotiate toward peace. Above all, in its peace-making efforts, we must support the work of the United Nations which, in the words of Pope Paul, marks "a stage in the development of mankind, from which retreat must never be admitted, but from which it is necessary that advance be made."[10]

18. We ask every person of good will to support with prayer the Holy Father's plea for a Christmas ceasefire. May it open the way to lasting peace. In the spirit of Christ, the Christian must be the persistent seeker in the Gospel, the man willing to walk the second mile (cf., Mt 5:42). He walks prudently, but he walks generously and he asks that all men do the same.

19. As Catholics we walk in good company. Pope Paul, in his recent encyclical on peace, cried out, in God's name, to stop war. We pray God that the sacrifices of us all, our prayers as well as our faltering efforts toward peace, will hasten the day when the whole world will echo Pope Paul's historic words: No more war, war never again!"[11]

[1] *Pastoral Constitution on the Church in the Modern World*, Part II, Chapter V, Section 1 (*The Documents of Vatican II*, Guild Press, New York, p. 296).

[2] Ibid., Part II, Chapter IV, p. 286.

[3] Ibid., Part II, Chapter V, Section 1, p. 293.

[4] Ibid., Part II, Chapter V, Section 1, p. 294.

[5] Ibid., Part II, Chapter V, Section 1, p. 295.

[6] Ibid., Part II, Chapter V, Section 1, p. 293.

[7] Ibid., Part II, Chapter V, Section 1, p. 293.

[8] Ibid., Part II, Chapter V. Section 1, p. 296.

[9] *Pacem in Terris* (NCWC, Washington, D.C., pp. 28, 29).

[10] *Address to the United Nations Assembly*, Oct. 4, 1965 (*Pope Paul VI in New York*, NCWC, Washington, D.C., p. 77).

[11] Ibid., p. 9.

(*Source*: John Tracy Ellis, ed. *Documents of American Catholic History*. Vol. 3:1966–1986. Wilmington, Del.: Michael Glazier, 1987, 703–07.)

VILLANOVA UNIVERSITY

Villanova University's 220-acre campus is located on the Philadelphia Main Line, some twelve miles west of downtown, in Radnor Township, Delaware County, Pennsylvania. Villanova University is a coeducational institution founded in 1842 by the Order of St. Augustine, one of the older religious teaching orders of the Catholic Church. The American Augustinian community was established in Philadelphia in 1796. It was this community that purchased the 197-acre Belle-Air estate of a wealthy Catholic merchant named John Rudolph as a site for the then Villanova College. In August 1843 this property was placed under the patronage of St. Thomas of Villanova, and on September 18 of that same year the first classes opened at Villanova College. Villanova achieved legal standing as a corporation on March 10, 1848, when the Pennsylvania state legislature granted an official charter under the name of "The Augustinian College of Villanova in the State of Pennsylvania," with the power to offer degrees in arts and sciences.

During its early decades Villanova was a small liberal arts college which featured a classical curriculum. There was also a secondary academy on campus until 1923 when it moved to Malvern, Pennsylvania, and became known as Malvern Preparatory School. At the beginning of the twentieth century the college curriculum was enlarged to include programs in engineering, premedical, and prelegal studies. At the same time Villanova launched an ambitious building project which included new laboratories, dining and residential facilities, gymnasium, library, auditorium, and a new building for the St. Thomas of Villanova Monastery. The former monastery, which included portions of the old Rudolph mansion, was now turned over for use as a seminary.

The 1920s was a prosperous time for the nation as well as for Villanova. Student enrollment increased nearly four times during this decade, requiring Villanova to erect two new dormitories, a new library, a commerce and finance building, and a field house. The accomplishments of this period were marred, however, by two disastrous fires: the burning of College Hall (later Tolentine Hall) in 1928, and of the St. Thomas of Villanova Monastery in 1932. By then Villanova was beginning to feel the full force of the Great Depression, which led to serious declines in enrollment. After rising again in the 1930s and early 1940s, enrollments were threatened by military enlistments during World War II. Villanova saved itself from even more serious enrollment problems by obtaining a Navy V-12 officers training unit.

The postwar period saw dramatic increases in students, as veterans took advantage of the G.I. Bill of rights. A new wave of construction was launched to meet their needs. Among these were dormitories, a free-standing library, chemical engineering building, Navy ROTC headquarters, and a commerce and finance building. Included in the postwar expansion were new academic programs, most importantly the College of Nursing and School of Law. These new divisions, in addition to the older engineering and commerce and finance schools and expanding graduate programs, led Villanova to obtain university status in 1953. Through an act of the state legislature and a decree from the Common Pleas Court of Delaware County, the college charter was amended and the name changed to Villanova University.

In 1994 the total enrollment was 10,760. Of these 6,274 were full-time undergraduate students. The remainder were graduate or law school students. The number of men and women in the undergraduate divisions were approximately equal.

See also CATHOLIC UNIVERSITIES AND COLLEGES.

Constosta, David R. *Villanova University, 1842–1992*. University Park, Pennsylvania, 1995.

DAVID R. CONSTOSTA AND DENNIS J. GALLAGHER, O.S.A.

VINCENTIANS (C.M.)

The Congregation of the Mission (C.M.), founded by Saint Vincent de Paul (1581–1660) in 1625 in Paris and approved by Pope Urban VIII in 1633, slowly increased in numbers and multiplied its apostolic endeavors. The earliest Lazarists, so-called because of the name of their motherhouse, Saint-Lazare, preached parish missions in the rural areas of France, established post-Tridentine seminaries at the request of the bishops, preached retreats to ordinands, and conducted weekly conferences for priests. During St. Vincent's lifetime these works took root in Italy and Poland. At the request of the Congregation for the Propagation of the Faith, Vincentians evangelized and catechized the people of Ireland and Scotland, ministered to the slaves in Algiers and Tunis, and set sail for Madagascar.

Vincentians in the U.S.A.

Sons of St. Vincent brought this same zeal and these same works to the United States. In 1815 Louis William DuBourg, the first American bishop of New Orleans, traveled to Europe to interest priests in the work of his diocese. He stayed at the Vincentian house in Rome and subsequently recruited Felix DeAndreis, C.M., for the American Mission. DeAndreis helped attract other Vincentians to this mission: Frs. Joseph Rosati and Joseph Acquaroni, Brs. Anthony Bobone, Francis Boranvaski, and Martin Blanka, and a seminarian, Leo Deys. These Vincentians, along with some other priests and seminarians recruited by Bishop DuBourg, arrived in Baltimore on July 26, 1816, traveled by wagon to Pittsburgh and flatbottom boat down the Ohio River to the Mississippi, and arrived in St. Louis in October 1617. Fr. Felix DeAndreis started a novitiate on December 3, 1618.

St. Mary's of the Barrens, a seminary established in Perryville, Missouri, became the center from which various apostolic works emanated: missionary parishes, parish missions, and seminaries. The American Mission of the Congregation of the Mission provided for the Church in America some of its needed bishops: Joseph Rosati in St. Louis (1826), Leo De Neckere in New Orleans (1829), John Mary Odin, apostolic vicar for Texas (1841) and later bishop of Galveston (1847), John Timon, first bishop of Buffalo (1847), and Thaddeus Amat in Monterey-Los Angeles (1853). John Timon had been named Visitor when

the first American province of the Congregation of the Mission had been erected (1835). Subsequent Visitors, among them Stephen Vincent Ryan, who became bishop of Buffalo in 1868, administered this province through some remarkable years of growth.

Between 1838 and 1842 the diocesan seminaries of New Orleans and Philadelphia were entrusted to the care of the Vincentians. In subsequent years the bishops of St. Louis, New York, Cincinnati, Bardstown, and Buffalo (at Niagara, New York) engaged the Vincentians for their seminaries; offers from others had to be declined for lack of personnel. Sometimes in conjunction with seminaries, at other times independently of them, an educational apostolate developed: St. Vincent's College, Cape Girardeau, Missouri; Niagara University, New York; St. Vincent's College, Los Angeles; and St. John's University, New York. During this same period a goodly number of parishes gave witness to Vincentian zeal. In Illinois alone some forty-eight rural parishes or missions experienced Vincentian care. Similar pioneering endeavors and growth were experienced in Louisiana, Mississippi, Missouri, California and Texas; Brooklyn, Philadelphia, and Chicago.

Growth and Organization

The growth of the American province was such that in 1888 two provinces were formed: the Eastern, centered in Germantown, Pennsylvania, and the Western, headquartered in St. Louis, Missouri. The two provinces continued the apostolates that their predecessors had initiated: seminaries: Brooklyn and Denver; colleges and universities: DePaul (1897) and Dallas (1906), along with a number of high schools and college preparatory schools; notable amidst the parish apostolate was the beginning and growth of the Alabama Mission and a number of parishes for black Catholics in New Orleans, Philadelphia, and Greensboro, North Carolina. Both provinces heard and answered the call to staff foreign missions. The Eastern province posted priests to Panama in 1914 and to China, Kanchow vicariate of Kiangsi province; the Western province assigned men to Yukiang vicariate of Kiangsi province. Although both missions were closed in 1951, missionary apostolic work continues on the island of Taiwan, and by individual confreres who have answered the call of the superior general for Madagascar, Iran, Vietnam, the Solomon Islands, Kenya, Ethiopia, etc.

Within all these works, the Vincentians have made popular the Confraternity of Charity, originally pioneered by St. Vincent, the propagation of the Miraculous Medal entrusted to St. Catherine Labouré in 1830, and the Miraculous Medal Novenas. They have also promoted the Confraternity Home Study Service which grew out of the "Motor Mission" apostolate in the rural South during the 1930s and 1940s.

In 1905 some Vincentians from Poland, on their way to a new mission in Brazil, stopped in New York. They never left the United States, since bishops in Hartford, Philadelphia, and Brooklyn convinced them to stay. They preached missions in Polish-speaking parishes, staffed "national" parishes, and opened a high school for boys in Erie, Pennsylvania (1912). Personnel from Poland continued to keep this mission alive. This Polish vice province (1920) became an American province in 1975. Like their Polish confreres, Vincentians from Spain, Portugal, Italy, and Mexico staffed a few parishes where their countrymen predominated.

At present (1994), the American Provinces of the Congregation of the Mission number five (divisions made in 1975), and some five hundred priests and brothers labor at works similar to those initiated by St. Vincent de Paul and, in the United States, by the sons of St. Vincent who began the American Mission.

Coste, Pierre, ed. *Correspondance, Entretiens, Documents de Saint Vincent de Paul.* 14 vols. Paris: Gabalda, 1920–25. An English translation is in progress: *Correspondence, Conferences, Documents.* Trans. and ed. Sr. Marie Poole, D.C., and annotated by Rev. John W. Carven, C.M. 5 vols. to date. New York: New City Press, 1985– .

_____. *The Life and Works of St. Vincent de Paul.* Trans. Joseph Leonard, C.M. 3 vols. Westminster, Md.: The Newman Press, 1952; repr. New City Press, 1987.

Rybolt, John E., ed. *The American Vincentians.* New York: New City Press, 1988.

JOHN W. CARVEN, C.M.

VIRGINIA, CATHOLIC CHURCH IN

Catholicism was slow in taking root in Virginia. In 1570, near the future site of Jamestown, Spanish Jesuits established a mission, but they were betrayed and massacred within a year. When Jamestown was settled in 1607, the colony was decidedly hostile to Catholics, a situation exacerbated when Maryland was settled under Catholic auspices in 1634. In 1642 Virginia passed laws prohibiting the exercise of Catholicism. Nevertheless, in the 1650s, Giles Brent, a Catholic, and his family, moved from Maryland and settled in Stafford County, between the Potomac and Rappahannaock Rivers. The Brent family was the only notable Catholic presence in Virginia before the Revolution.

Early Nineteenth Century

In the 1790s, Catholics settled principally in Alexandria and Norfolk. Both communities owed their foundation to laymen, but the church in Alexandria was owned by former Jesuits (the order had been suppressed in 1773 and was restored in the U.S.A. in 1805). Jean Dubois celebrated Mass for a small congregation in Norfolk in 1791 and then traveled on to Richmond where he taught school for over a year. One of the founders of Mt. St. Mary's College in Emmitsburg, Dubois became the third bishop of New York. By 1817, however, lay trusteeism had disrupted Norfolk. Though most of the parishioners were Irish, their leader was a Portuguese physician, Oliveira Fernandez, who opposed the authority of the French-born archbishop of Baltimore, Ambrose Maréchal. In 1820, against Maréchal's advice, the Congregation of Propaganda established the Diocese of Richmond, which comprised all of Virginia, which included West Virginia, but excluded Alexandria, then part of the District of Columbia.

The first bishop, Patrick Kelly, came from Ireland, but never reached his see city. After mollifying the trustees, he remained in Norfolk, where he taught school. After less than a year, he returned to Ireland to become the bishop of Waterford and Lismore. The Diocese of Richmond reverted to the administration of Baltimore.

In his final report to Propaganda, Kelly noted that out of a population of over a million, there were about one thousand Catholics, tended by five priests, and centered in three regions: Norfolk, Richmond, and the northwestern section around Martinsburg and Harpers Ferry. Each region developed in different ways. From Norfolk, a seaport, there sprang up Portsmouth, which at times threatened to eclipse its mother church, Richmond, the capital. It became a canal center, from which derived parishes in Lynchburg and the southern part of the Shenandoah Valley. Martinsburg, which had a small Catholic congregation by 1794, began as a farming village and then evolved into first a canal and then a railroad center. It was also the headquarters for missionary priests serving Harpers Ferry, Winchester in the northern Shenandoah Valley, and Bath (now Berkeley Springs, West Virginia).

In 1841, Richard Vincent Whelan, who had served in Martinsburg, became the second bishop. He established a short-lived seminary in Richmond, but, in 1846, moved to Wheeling where he unsuccessfully attempted to have the Jesuits establish a college. To staff his poor diocese, he begged from other dioceses, but then became the first Southern bishop to recruit from All Hallows College outside of Dublin. Irish priests were soon working with Irish immigrant laborers on the railroads, particularly around Harpers Ferry and in the Shenandoah Valley.

In 1851 the Holy See established the new Diocese of Wheeling for western Virginia and transferred Whelan there. John McGill, a priest of Louisville, then became the third bishop of Richmond. Unlike the North, Virginia never became the home for large numbers of immigrants. Many of the Irish who came to Richmond and Norfolk in the 1830s belonged to the merchant or professional classes. A small group of Germans also settled in Richmond, where in 1848 they founded the only national parish in the diocese; Jesuits were in charge of it until 1860, when they were replaced by Benedictines. In the 1830s and 1840s, there were also significant conversions, including the three daughters, wife, and son of Governor John R. Floyd, Sr. These converts and the Irish middle class helped create rapprochement with Virginia's establishment. In the 1850s, therefore, the Church in Virginia did not experience the nativism and political victories of the Know-Nothings that plagued the North. In Norfolk and Portsmouth, moreover, Catholic heroism in the yellow fever epidemic of 1855 won Protestant admiration. The Daughters of Charity from their school and orphanage in Norfolk began nursing the victims. The following year, they opened St. Vincent's Hospital (now DePaul), the result of a bequest of Anne Behan Plum Herron, who herself died in the epidemic.

Civil War and After

As the nation began to debate slavery, Virginia Catholics, though few were slave owners, opposed abolition. When Virginia seceded, they supported the Confederate cause, and many served in the Confederate army. Both McGill in Richmond and Whelan in Wheeling supported secession, but, while McGill now had the capital of the Confederacy in his see city, Whelan found himself in the capital of West Virginia which seceded from Virginia. The diocesan lines of both sees would cross state lines until 1974.

After the war, McGill recruited priests from The American College in Louvain to supplement his clergy diminished by death or departures from the diocese. Two of these Louvain recruits rose to the ranks of the hierarchy, Francis Janssens, who was successively bishop of Natchez and archbishop of New Orleans, and Augustine van de Vyver, who became bishop of Richmond and recruited both his nephew and great nephew for the diocese. In 1866, moreover, Sisters of the Visitation arrived from Baltimore to open Monte Maria Monastery and Academy for girls.

By 1870 Reconstruction ended in Virginia. Service in the Confederate army now provided the credentials for Catholics to assume prominent positions. In 1870 Anthony J. Keiley, born of Irish parents in New Jersey, but raised in Petersburg, became mayor of Richmond, served for many years as the president of the Irish Catholic Benevolent Union, and later became a judge of the international court in Cairo. James Dooley, son of an Irish merchant in Richmond, served in the state legislature and later became a millionaire through railroad and land speculation. In addition, John W. Johnston, whose wife, Niketti Floyd, was a convert and whose children were all Catholic, served two terms in the U.S. Senate.

In 1872 McGill died. His successor was James Gibbons, a Baltimore native, who was appointed the first vicar apostolic of North Carolina in 1868. In 1875 Gibbons thwarted the efforts of Bishop John J. Kain of Wheeling, a Martinsburg native, to have Rome realign the Dioceses of

Wheeling and Richmond to coincide with the new state lines, for, he said, this would take away the area around Martinsburg, then the fastest growing section of his diocese. Gibbons also initiated work among the freed African Americans, few of whom were Catholic.

In 1877 Gibbons became coadjutor archbishop of Baltimore and was named a cardinal in 1886. His successor, John J. Keane, was Irish-born, the first foreign-born bishop of Richmond since Kelly, and had served as a pastor in Washington. Deeply spiritual and a follower of Isaac Hecker, he sought to nourish the spiritual development of his clergy through semiannual conferences and monthly regional meetings. In the 1880s, the Shenandoah Valley was the focus of Catholic development. Founded in 1882, Roanoke, a railroad center, had a school and orphanage by 1892, staffed by the Sisters of Charity of Nazareth. Moreover, in the 1880s, the Josephites opened their first parish in Richmond. In 1888 Keane was named the first rector of The Catholic University of America, established by the Third Plenary Council in 1884.

The succession to Keane brought to the fore the ethnic tension characteristic of the American Church elsewhere. Although both the eligible Richmond priests and the bishops of the province of Baltimore had placed van de Vyver, then the vicar general and administrator of the diocese, on their lists of candidates, Gibbons sought to gain the appointment of Denis J. O'Connell, a priest of Richmond, who had been named rector of the North American College in Rome in 1885 and who appeared only on the bishops' list. Leo XIII, however, rejected O'Connell's appointment on the grounds that he was too valuable in Rome. Gibbons and Keane then attempted to prevent the appointment of van de Vyver, who was, however, named bishop in 1889.

Van de Vyver remained aloof from the controversies in which Gibbons, Keane, and O'Connell played major roles and which divided the hierarchy in the 1890s. Instead, he devoted himself to the internal development of the diocese. Under his administration, the Josephites expanded their work with African Americans to Norfolk, Lynchburg, and Alexandria. In addition, Louise D. Morrell and her sister, Mother Katherine Drexel, in 1895 and 1896 respectively, opened high schools for African American boys and girls at Rock Castle. The diocese was the recipient of other major benefactions. In 1906 the Cathedral of the Sacred Heart in Richmond was dedicated. It was built entirely from the donation of Mr. and Mrs. Thomas Fortune Ryan.

Twentieth Century

With van de Vyver's death in 1911, O'Connell, then auxiliary bishop of San Francisco, was finally named to Richmond. World War I brought the first major increase in the state's Catholic population as the U.S. Navy established the Norfolk Naval Operating Station, and the government located other installations in northern Virginia. The end of the war temporarily stifled Catholic growth, but these two regions were poised for the growth that followed World War II. In the postwar years, however, anti-Catholicism also experienced a resurgence, but the old style of Virginia Catholicism's accommodation with the political establishment held fast. In 1920 O'Connell advised against forming a Catholic Laymen's Association, similar to those in other states, since friendly Protestant legislators had prevented the passage of anti-Catholic bills. But, in 1924, the Ku Klux Klan launched a vociferous but unsuccessful campaign against the reelection of the incumbent state treasurer, John Purcell, a Catholic. In what may have been one of the earliest expressions of ecumenism in the period, the Episcopal Diocese of Virginia donated land to the Catholics the next year to build a church.

Forced by ill health to resign in 1925, O'Connell died the following year. His successor, Andrew J. Brennan, formerly auxiliary bishop of Scranton, had a short episcopate. In 1931 he opened St. Joseph's Villa, a model orphanage for girls made possible by a bequest of three million dollars from "Major" James Dooley in 1922. In 1934 Brennan suffered a massive stroke. Peter Leo Ireton, a priest of Baltimore, became coadjutor bishop and succeeded as ordinary upon Brennan's formal resignation in 1945. While Ireton left much of the diocesan administration to a series of able chancellors, he did encourage better race relations and a nascent ecumenical movement. World War II and the postwar years ushered in the period of greatest growth in Catholic population. Northern Virginia, long a rural outpost of the diocese, rapidly developed into a suburb of Washington. In the Norfolk area, military expansion and new housing turned Virginia Beach into one of the state's largest cities.

Ireton died in 1958 and was succeeded by John Russell, the bishop of Charleston and a native of Baltimore. Under Russell, the diocese realized a long-time dream and opened St. John Vianney minor seminary in 1961, only to have it close a decade later. Russell actively participated in the Second Vatican Council and immediately sought to implement its decrees. He established an ecumenical commission, the second in the U.S.A., and promoted racial justice. At his retirement in 1973, Walter F. Sullivan, the auxiliary bishop, was appointed administrator. In 1974 he became the bishop, and the new Diocese of Arlington was established with Thomas Welch as the first bishop—he was later transferred to Allentown to be replaced in Arlington by Thomas R. Keating. Those counties of West Virginia that had belonged to the Richmond diocese were transferred to Wheeling, while the counties of southwest Virginia, formerly in Wheeling, and the counties on the Delmarva Peninsula, formerly belonging to the Diocese of Wilmington, were ceded to Richmond. The Dioceses of both Richmond and Arlington now coincide with the state boundaries. In 1995 the Catholic population of both dioceses was 464,000 out of a total Virginia population of 6,394,600, with the majority, 294,101, in the Diocese of Arlington.

See also HECKER, ISAAC; McGILL, JOHN; O'CONNELL, DENIS.

Bailey, James H. *A History of the Diocese of Richmond, the Formative Years.* Richmond, Va.: The Chancery Office, 1956.

GERALD P. FOGARTY, S.J.

Related Document

VIRGINIA'S ACT AGAINST CATHOLICS AND PRIESTS, MARCH, 1642

From the foundation of Virginia as a colony a strong hostility toward Catholics had been evident. When the first Baron of Baltimore visited there in October, 1629, with a view to finding a place for his coreligionists to settle, he was at once confronted by a demand that he take the oath of supremacy recognizing the king as head of the Church. By 1640 matters had become critical again for the Catholics in England and in the years 1641–1642 eleven priests were put to death. This situation was reflected in Virginia with attacks upon the neighboring colony of Maryland, and the passage of an act by the Virginia assembly in March, 1642, which sought to seal off the colony from affording refuge to those who might secretly be Catholics by exacting the oath of supremacy, as well as from giving any stay or comfort to refugee priests.

(*Source*: William Waller Hening, ed. *The Statutes at Large; Being a Collection of all the Laws of Virginia* [Richmond: Samuel Pleasants, Jr., 1809] I, 268–69.)

WHEREAS IT WAS ENACTED AT AN ASSEMBLY IN JANUARY 1641, that according to a statute made in the third year of the reigne of our sovereign Lord King James of blessed memory, that no popish recusants should at any time hereafter exercize the place or places of secret councellors, register, comiss: surveyors or sheriffe, or any other publique place, but he utterly disabled for the same, And further it was enacted that none should be admitted into any of the aforesaid offices or places before he or they had taken the oath of allegiance and supremacy, And if any person or persons whatsoever should by sinister or corrupt meanes assume to himselfe any of the aforesaid places of any other publique office whatsoever and refuse to take the aforesaid oaths, he or they so convicted before an Assembly should be dismissed of his said office, And for his offence therein forfeit one thousand pounds of tobacco to be disposed of at the next Assembly after conviction, And it is further enacted by the authoritie aforesaid that the Statute in force against the popish recusants be duely executed in this government, And that it should not be lawfull under the penaltie aforesaid for any popish priest that shall hereafter arrive to remain above five days after warning given for his departure by the Governour or commander of the place, where he or they shall bee, if wind and weather hinder not his departure, And that the said act should be in force ten days after the publication thereof, at James City, this present Grand Assembly to all intents and purposes doth hereby confirm the same.

(*Source*: John Tracy Ellis, ed. *Documents of American Catholic History.* Vol. 1:1493–1865. Wilmington, Del.: Michael Glazier, 1987, 110–11.)

VISITATION NUNS (V.H.M.)

Beginnings

When a religious order takes root in a new land, it is usually founded by a motherhouse that sustains it until it is able to exist on its own. This was not the case with the Order of the Visitation in America. When the Visitation came to this country, it was through the efforts of Leonard Neale, second archbishop of Baltimore. He was born in southern Maryland in 1747, and like so many of his compatriots, he was sent abroad to study. He returned to this country a priest and a Jesuit.

Assigned to the city of Philadelphia in 1793, he learned he was to be the coadjutor of Bishop John Carroll. There in that city he met three women newly arrived from Ireland: Miss Alice Lalor, Mrs. McDermott, and Mrs. Sharpe, both widows. All three desired to become religious and sought direction from a priest. Bishop Neale satisfied their desires. At his suggestion, they lived in community and began a small school.

Georgetown

When the president of Georgetown College resigned in 1798, the position was given to Neale. He urged the three women to join him. A small house was all he could offer them. Here in 1799 they opened a school. Alice Lalor became the superior with the name of Mother Teresa. Known to the Georgetown natives as the "Pious Ladies," they began a school for the neighborhood's poor children.

An important question faced the group: what rule would they adopt? Recalling his interest in the writings of St. Francis de Sales in his student days, Bishop Neale decided upon the Order of the Visitation. Great interest had followed this order from its foundation by two saints: Francis de Sales and Jane Frances de Chantal in 1610 in Annecy, France. It had spread widely in the eighteenth century. Here, he thought, he would find the virtues he wanted his sisters to emulate: meekness, humility, and charity. A wonderful gift of a copy of the *Constitutions of the Visitation Order* came to them. The bishop translated it and taught it to the group.

When Archbishop Carroll died in 1815, Bishop Neale became Baltimore's second archbishop. One of his first acts was to write to Pope Pius VII to explain the presence of the nuns. He asked that their house be made a monastery of the Visitation, that they be permitted to make solemn vows, and that they might conduct a school. A papal indult granting all his requests reached America, November 10, 1816.

In 1817 Archbishop Neale wrote to the monastery of Annecy, France, telling of the Pope's approval of the American house, and of the great lack of religious instruction for girls in this country. His nuns were filling this need. He desired assistance from the French monasteries by way of instructional materials and a loan of sisters who would teach the new community the customs and ways of the older houses. Several European monasteries responded with supplies. All this led to a triumph for Archbishop Neale as he approached his life's end. He died June 18, 1817.

French Assistance and New Foundations

In response to the archbishop's request in 1829, three sisters came from Europe. The monasteries of Fribourg, Le-Mans, and Valence each sent a sister. Mother Magdalen Augustin, superior of the group, taught the Americans. She was anxious for spread of the order in the new world, and so she welcomed a request from Bishop Michael Portier of Mobile, Alabama, for a girls' academy in his diocese. She departed with five Georgetown nuns to fulfill the mission in 1832.

A second foundation was requested by Bishop Joseph Rosati of St. Louis in 1833 in Kaskaskia, Illinois, a town on a tributary of the Mississippi River. When a flood overwhelmed the town, the sisters had to move to St. Louis to join a community formerly established. They formed one house in St. Louis.

Here in the history of Georgetown there begins a series of new foundations. After St. Louis came Baltimore in 1837, then Frederick in 1846. Baltimore in turn founded Wheeling in 1848, Brooklyn in 1855, and Richmond in 1866; Washington, D.C., and Catonsville in 1852. The last was founded Parkersburg in 1864.

Immigration brought many people from Europe to the eastern part of the country and on to the West. In 1853 Bishop Loras of Dubuque, Iowa, wrote to a monastery in Monthuel, France, for sisters to staff a school at Keokuk, Iowa. Help, he knew, would come from the house in St. Louis. The *Georgetown Annals* tell of a correspondence with the monastery of Montuel relating that the French sisters promised to stop at Georgetown on their way to Keokuk. There they hoped to learn English before they proceeded any farther on their way. For some reason their itinerary was changed and they did not come. They moved across the country to St. Louis where some sisters from this house joined them. The St. Louis house, faced with overcrowding in 1873, became two. One remained in the city, while the other went to Springfield, Missouri. The St. Paul monastery was begun the same year.

The monastery of Keokuk, the only house in the country to be founded directly from France, grew too small for its numerous inhabitants, so it began to divide. In 1864 a group went to Ottumwa, Iowa, and in 1865 a second group moved to Maysville, Kentucky. The remaining sisters in 1865 departed for Suspension Bridge, New York. These moved to Wilmington, Delaware, in 1868.

Into the Twentieth Century

The twentieth century brought changes in the Visitation Order. Mother Alexandrine de Butler, superior of the monastery of Annecy, France, wrote a circular letter to the American houses, inviting them to give up their schools and become contemplative monasteries. Wilmington had a boarding school and a day school. In 1893 both were closed and Wilmington became the first house to imitate the European houses. Several other American monasteries followed: Washington-Bethesda in D.C.; Riverdale, New York; and Richmond, Virginia. In 1915, when a group of Georgetown sisters desired the same move, they founded a house in Toledo, Ohio. The remaining houses chose to retain their schools.

Sisters of the Visitation

Once a foundation was made from the beginning of the Visitation in America, it remained directly under the bishop of the diocese who requested it. When the sisters of a community sent a colony to establish a house, that community no longer had any responsibility for it; only, as the old chronicles state, a bond of love and charity.

While early monasteries and schools were forced to close because of a want of means, insufficient students, or unsuitable locations, closing meant movement to another diocese. Sisters were always numerous and apparently eager to go on new foundations. In more recent times, the dearth of vocations to the religious life has been the reason why houses have had to close. The sisters have joined other communities of the Visitation bringing their talents with them, enriching their new homes.

The American Visitation kept its status as a contemplative community with papal approval for various works from the time of Archbishop Leonard Neale's appeal to Pope Pius VII in 1816. Numerous documents state that the sisters had the right to pronounce vows, to conduct schools, and to maintain the kind of enclosure needed for the work.

Movements from Rome to unify contemplative monasteries resulted in the decree *Sponsa Christi* in 1950, which provided for major and minor papal cloister. For the Visitation it was proposed in 1951 that there be a federation of monasteries grouped into a confederation. A later arrangement was made when the houses were divided into first and second federations to provide for the activities of monasteries with or without apostolic works. Future documents ratified all the former provisions. Later statutes were approved to regulate enclosure and permit apostolic activities.

Recent developments in the Visitation Order in the United States include the building of a new monastery in Rockville, Virginia, by the sisters of Richmond in 1986. The sisters of Wilmington sold their city property and moved to a new monastery in Tyringham, Massachusetts. Sisters from St. Louis and St. Paul joined forces to begin a new venture—a monastery in an inner-city setting in Minneapolis, Minnesota, in 1989. Among other events is one that is unforgettable—the fire that destroyed the main building of the school at Georgetown Visitation in 1993 leaving a brick shell. Great effort and much charity have produced a new school and a restored chapel.

Opportunities for growth have come by way of diverse meetings of sisters from several monasteries. Past liturgy workshops at Conception Abbey in Missouri have offered training in singing the Liturgy of the Hours. Yearly Salesian conferences on the life and teachings of St. Francis de Sales in union with lay groups have provided means of inspiration, knowledge, and opportunities for communication among the participants.

By 1999 Visitation nuns in the United States will have served the Church for two hundred years. The labors of the past, kept alive by the spirit of their founders, will take them into the future.

See also WOMEN RELIGIOUS IN AMERICA.

"Annals of the Georgetown Visitation Convent." Unpublished Manuscript.

Burton, Katherine. *Bells of Two Rivers*. Milwaukee: Bruce, 1965.

Sisters of the Visitation. *The Silver is Mine*. Wilmington, Del.: Monastery of the Visitation, 1953.

Sullivan, Eleanore C. *Georgetown Visitation: Since 1799*. Washington, D.C.: Georgetown Visitation Convent, 1975.

MARY VIRGINIA BRENNAN, V.H.M.

W

WACHTER, BERNARDINE (1846–1901)

Foundress and educator. Mother Bernardine Wachter, O.S.B., was born Josepha Wachter in Isny, Germany, on August 25, 1846. Having been educated by her schoolmaster father, she went to Switzerland in 1865 to join the Benedictine Sisters at Maria Rickenbach. There she pronounced her vows as Sr. Mary Bernardine on August 20, 1867. She taught in the convent school until 1876 when she volunteered to join a group of missionaries going to Missouri. Here again she was engaged in teaching, first at Maryville, then at Fort Yates in the Dakota Territory. In 1882 Adelhelm Odermatt invited her to establish a community of Benedictine women in the West. With three sisters from the Dakota Mission, and four recruits from Europe, Sr. Bernardine left for Oregon, arriving in Portland on October 30, 1882. Their destination was Gervais, where the sisters opened St. Scholastica Academy, after living in an abandoned saloon until a convent and school building were complete.

The community, enlarged by recruits from Europe and America, chose Sr. Bernardine as their prioress at their first election held in 1887. Under her leadership, the sisters built a permanent home in Mt. Angel and opened an academy and normal school.

By the time of her death on June 3, 1901, Mother Bernardine had served as prioress of a flourishing Benedictine community for eleven years. Six schools had been established in Oregon parishes, as well as residential schools for Native Americans in Grande Ronde, Oregon, and Kakawis, British Columbia. She is honored as the foundress of Queen of Angels Monastery in Mt. Angel, Oregon.

ALBERTA DIEKER, O.S.B.

WAGNER, ROBERT FERDINAND (1877–1953)

United States Senator. Wagner was born in Nastatten, Germany, on June 8, 1877, to Reinhardt and Magdalene Schmidt Wagner. At the age of nine, he and his family emigrated to the United States to the Yorkville section of New York City, then a heavily German immigrant area. They lived in the basement apartment of a tenement building of which Wagner's father was the custodian, and his mother took in laundry to help support their seven children. Wagner, the youngest of the children, also helped the family financially by selling newspapers and candy in Central Park. Always hardworking, Wagner was able to attend City College and graduated from New York Law School in 1900 thanks to the financial help of his brother who worked as a cook.

Wagner began his political career in 1898 working for Tammany Hall, New York's Democratic machine. Wagner was an unlikely recruit for Tammany, since he was Methodist and Tammany was run by Catholics. Wagner's law practice prospered because of this association, and in 1904 he was elected to the New York Assembly from his home district in Yorkville. While in Albany Wagner was a loyal son of Tammany, but this cost him reelection. He voted against a lower gas rate at the urging of Tammany, and he was defeated by a Progressive in the next election.

In 1906 he regained his seat, but now he embraced a more reform-minded model of government and was successful in getting Tammany to back his new ideas. In 1911 he was elected to the state senate and began numerous investigations into working conditions in factories, child labor, and was a member of the commission that investigated the notorious fire at the Triangle Shirtwaist Company in which 147 women died. With the help of another powerful State Senator and future presidential candidate, Alfred E. Smith, Wagner was responsible for sponsoring more than sixty bills.

In 1908 Wagner married Margaret Marie McTague, a Catholic, and they had one child, Robert F. Wagner, Jr. In January 1946 Wagner was received into the Catholic Church by Msgr. Robert F. Keegan, a leader in social action in New York. Wagner attributed his conversion to both his wife and the many Catholics he had grown to work with and admire in New York. In 1918 Wagner was elected to the New York State Supreme Court, and in 1926 was elected to the U.S. Senate and served here until 1949 when he resigned because of illness. While in the Senate, Wagner vigorously supported many of the New Deal programs including Social Security and the beginning of public housing projects. In 1935 he helped pass the "National Labor Relations" or the "Wagner" Act which created the National Labor Relations Board. This board helped reestablish the rights of labor in the wake of the Great Depression, and new unions were formed for workers who were notoriously underpaid and poorly treated. A lifelong advocate for the poor and the working class, Wagner was awarded the Pope Leo XIII Award from the Sheil School of Social Service in 1947 for his work on behalf of the less fortunate. Wagner died in New York City on May 4, 1953.

See also SMITH, ALFRED EMANUEL.

O'Brien, John A., ed. *The Road to Damascus: The Spiritual Pilgrimage of Fifteen Converts to Catholicism.* Garden City, New York, 1955.

ANTHONY D. ANDREASSI

WALDRON, MARY PATRICIA (1834–1916)

Foundress of Philadelphia Sisters of Mercy. Anne Mary Waldron (born in 1834) entered the Convent of Mercy in Ballinrobe, County Mayo, Ireland on February 20, 1852. She attracted attention for her special leadership qualities very soon after her entrance.

In the U.S.A., Frances Warde (the first American foundress) was looking for women who could be inspiring leaders for the work of educating new members of the Mercy community in the ways and works of Mercy. Frances had an unrealized dream of uniting all the U.S. Mercies beginning with a common novitiate. She begged her Irish sisters to find the right woman. Mother Mary Gertrude O'Brien recognized Sr. Mary Patricia Joseph Waldron as the person to be sent. Her destination was Manchester, New Hampshire, and her ministry was mistress of novices.

After being in this country only about one year, Patricia was chosen by Frances to be part of a new Mercy community in Philadelphia. An English Mercy (Sr. Gertrude Ledwith) had been Frances's original choice for superior—probably a wise one since the pastor of the proposed parish, Assumption, was Charles Ignatius Hamilton Carter (a convert from the Episcopal Church). Sr. Gertrude never arrived, and on October 1, 1861, Sr. Patricia Waldron was named the founding leader of the Philadelphia community.

This woman with her nine Irish companions entered one of the largest cities of the world caught in the turmoil of war and just emerging from an era rocked with riots—anti-Irish, antiblack. In 1860 Philadelphia was the second largest city in the U.S.A. and possibly the fourth largest in the Western world. Population: 565,529. Of these, 169,430 were foreign-born—more than half Irish. Philadelphia had the largest black population in any Northern city—22,000. Irish moving in threatened black jobs.

On September 2, 1861, she opened the Assumption School (ninety students), a small academy in the convent (thirty students)—necessary for life upkeep of the sisters—and a night school for poor women in need of education. Visitation of the poor sick began immediately. In a few months the sisters began another mercy work: visitation of the prisoners. Her style is described by an early companion: "Spontaneous cooperation. . . . She never asked what others did. . . . She simply consulted her present resources and moved into action."

The sisters left Assumption parish after about a year and a half. The reasons were never recorded—at Mother Patricia's request. However, there were difficulties with the clergy and the sisters were taken in at nearby St. Malachy's parish where the Mercy works continued. Women in the area were most supportive, some contributing their salaries for the upkeep of the venture.

Possessing only $5.00, she gave it as a down payment to lease a house at Broad Street and Columbia Avenue, Philadelphia, where (much ahead of her time) Mother Patricia educated a most ecumenical student body. Of the first fifteen graduates, five list religion as Jewish, five as Protestant, and five as Catholic. When Mary Patricia Waldron died in 1916, the Sisters of Mercy had expanded greatly their educational and hospital apostolates and were deeply involved in work for the poor and the neglected sick.

See also SISTERS OF MERCY OF THE AMERICAS (R.S.M.).

PATRICIA J. CORKERY, R.S.M.

WALKER, FRANK COMERFORD (1886–1959)

Postmaster General. He was born in Plymouth, Pennsylvania, on May 30, 1886, and grew up in Montana. He attended Gonzaga University, took his law degree at Notre Dame, practiced law in Montana, and was elected to the legislature in 1913. He served in World War I and resumed his law practice after the war. In 1924 he moved to New York and became active in politics and business. He was a friend and active supporter of Franklin D. Roosevelt in his gubernatorial and presidential races. Walker was treasurer of the Democratic National Committee in 1932, and was secretary of the President's Executive Council in 1933–35. He was Roosevelt's Postmaster General from 1940–45. Throughout his career he was active in Catholic affairs and received the Laetare Medal in 1948. He died in Manhattan on November 18,1959.

MICHAEL GLAZIER

WALKER, JAMES (1881–1946)

Mayor of New York. James "Jimmy" Walker was born on May 1, 1881, in the western part of Greenwich Village, the son of William H. Walker and Ellen Roon. His father was an immigrant from Ireland who became a successful builder. He soon entered politics and was elected a city alderman and finally a member of the state assembly. The Walker house was a popular gathering place for neighborhood politicians big and small, and young Jimmy was schooled in the craft from an early age. While still at the parish school of St. Joseph's, the pastor nicknamed the youngster, "Jimmy Talker" for his ability to charm an audience.

Living close to the quarter where many theatrical performers lived, Walker was drawn to the entertainment world as well as to politics. In collaboration with songwriter Ernest Ball, he wrote the song "Will You Love Me in December as You Did in May?" The song was destined to become his theme song and had, in view of his subsequent career, almost prophetic content. Walker himself appeared as a performer of comic and heroic roles at small theaters and at parish entertainments. It was in these surroundings that he met his wife, the actress Janet Allen, a Christian Scientist who converted to the Catholic Church.

In 1910 Jimmy Walker succeeded his father in the state legislature. First as an assemblyman and from 1914 as a senator, Jimmy Walker continued to represent the same familiar neighborhood as his father had before him for the next sixteen years. His public acclaim was won by his espousal of a number of local and populist issues such as the removal of the surface railroad tracks from 11th Avenue and his long-standing opposition to the Volstead Act. Consequently, he sponsored a bill allowing the brewing of low-alcohol beer, which was nevertheless declared unconstitutional, and another bill withdrawing assistance to the federal authorities in the enforcement of Prohibition. A bill to allow Sunday sports, permitting professional baseball to be played on that day for the first time, made him an instant hero among the sports-minded residents of the city.

Walker had always been a stalwart of the Tammany political machine. By the mid-1920s he had a strong following who wanted to see him mayor of New York. He was a popular choice with the electorate as well, and after an easy election victory assumed office in January 1926. The first few years of his mayorship were almost idyllic. He was described as one of the most popular mayors in the history of the city and like visiting royalty made a triumphant European excursion in 1927 which was followed eagerly by the New York press.

A long series of disclosures beginning in 1928 soon tarnished the image of the handsome mayor. There would be no respite in the corruption charges involving initially his administration and then finally the mayor himself. Under the unfolding testimony of the Seabury Commission, Walker was forced to resign on September 2, 1932, vowing to run again in November. He fled to Europe, but his return trip was delayed, causing him to miss the nominating convention and a chance for another term.

Walker's decline from political power coincided with his pursuit of a young English-born actress, Betty Compton, whom he first met in 1926. Compton was his frequent companion at dinners and dancing clubs, but this behavior was strongly objected to by Governor Al Smith. After Walker's reelection in 1929, he openly flaunted his connections with Compton to the dismay of Catholic clergy and laity alike. In 1933 his wife sued him for divorce and in April of that year Walker married Compton at Cannes, France. They lived together in England for a time, but returned to New York in 1935. Following the death of Compton, Walker reconciled himself to the Church and made public pronouncements to that effect shortly before his death on November 14, 1946.

Finnegan, James E. *Tammany at Bay.* New York: Dodd, Mead & Co., 1933.

Fowler, Gene. *The Life and Times of Jimmy Walker.* New York: Viking Press, 1949.

Fuller, Hector. *Abroad with Mayor Walker.* New York: Shields Publishing Co., 1928.

Gribetz, Louis J., and Joseph Kaye. *Jimmy Walker: The Story of a Personality.* New York: Dial Press, 1932.

JOHN T. RIDGE

WALKER, MARY JOSEPH (1828–64)

Religious superior. Considered by many to have been the "true foundress" of the Immaculate Heart of Mary Congregation, Mary Phoebe Walker was born in Hamilton,

Ontario, in 1828. She entered the Grey Nuns Congregation, but remained there only a few months.

In 1854 Phoebe traveled to Monroe, Michigan, to visit her sister (Sr. M. Ignatius), who was already a member of the nine-year-old I.H.M. congregation. Phoebe never returned home. She joined the I.H.M. community and became Sr. Mary Joseph. Only five years later, Mary Joseph was appointed general superior and given the task of leading the congregation through its most painful and perilous times.

In 1859 the local bishop, Peter Paul Lefevere, dismissed the founding superior of the I.H.M. Sisters, Mother Theresa Maxis. Theresa was forced to leave Monroe. Three other sisters went to Pennsylvania to join those I.H.M.s who had gone before them to establish a mission in Susquehanna, Pennsylvania. Upon the dismissal of Theresa Maxis, Mary Joseph was appointed superior. Hers could not have been a more painful task.

The congregation was very young (founded in 1845) and very small (only eight professed sisters, four novices, and one postulant remained in Monroe). The separation and dismissal of Theresa Maxis were abrupt and acrimonious. Communication between the sisters in Monroe and those in Pennsylvania was forbidden by Bishop Lefevere. In a real sense, they died to each other.

Mary Joseph acted as peacemaker and restored relationships between the sisters, their appointed superior, Fr. Edward Joos, and the local bishop. Where Theresa had been fiery and had questioned authority, Mary Joseph was diplomatic and resilient. She gave the gift of stability and loving care to those who had stayed in Monroe. And she often did so from her own sick bed.

Frail and grieving herself, Mary Joseph kept together a small fledgling community, in the midst of the Civil War, the imposed separation of the community, and the loss of many she loved—including her own sister. Separations are always about those who go (or are sent) and those who stay and carry on. Mother Mary Joseph is witness and reminder of the pain and courage and grace involved in staying. She died on October 18, 1864.

See also SISTERS OF THE IMMACULATE HEART OF MARY (I.H.M.).

JULIANA CASEY, I.H.M.

WALSH, JAMES ANTHONY (1867–1936)

Missionary, religious superior, bishop. James Anthony Walsh was cofounder (with Thomas F. Price) and first superior general of the Maryknoll Fathers and Brothers. Walsh was born in Cambridge, Massachusetts, on February 24, 1867. He studied at Boston College and Harvard University, and completed his studies for the priesthood at St. John's Seminary, Brighton, Massachusetts. Sulpician priests John Hogan and Gabriel André of the seminary faculty were major influences in evoking in the young Walsh an

James A. Walsh

interest in "foreign missions." André, who had promoted the establishment of the Society for the Propagation of the Faith in the U.S.A., shared with him letters received from priests working in the Far East, and the two published articles about the missioners in the Boston *Sacred Heart Review.* The interest would mark the rest of Walsh's life.

He was ordained a priest of the Boston archdiocese May 20, 1892. For the next ten years he served as an assistant in St. Patrick's parish, Roxbury. In 1903 he became archdiocesan director of the Society for the Propagation of the Faith. In 1904, at a meeting in Washington, D.C., he met Fr. Price of North Carolina who shared Walsh's view that the time had come for U.S. Catholics to engage more vigorously in the world missionary activity of the Church. Both were convinced that missionary effort at home would be strengthened by a greater overseas commitment.

As a means of promoting nationally a greater knowledge of overseas missions, Walsh founded in 1906 a "Foreign Mission Bureau" which from 1907 would publish a new mission magazine, *The Field Afar.* Among the volunteers who assisted Walsh in the venture was Mary Josephine Rogers, future foundress of the Maryknoll Sisters. Walsh and Price met again by chance in 1910 at the Montreal Eucharistic Congress and agreed to work together to establish a national mission-sending society. With the endorsement of the U.S. archbishops (April 27, 1911) and authorization of the Congregation for the Propagation of the Faith, they founded the Catholic Foreign Mission Society of America (June 29, 1911). Walsh's *The Field Afar* became the society's publication.

Superior General of Maryknoll

During the next twenty-five years of his life Walsh served as superior of the society. In 1917–18 he visited the Orient to secure a missionary territory where the first Maryknollers could be assigned. He made subsequent visits to encourage the missioners who, in growing numbers, were serving in China, Korea, Japan, and the Philippines.

From the society's headquarters near Ossining, New York, Walsh directed the formation of the Maryknollers. His missiological vision included a sincere respect for non-Christian cultures: "The hallmark of a sterling missioner is his willingness to forget the customs of his own country and to enter sympathetically into the lives of those whom he would shepherd for Christ. . . . No single influence has injured the cause of worldwide evangelization so much as the attempts to force the habits of the West on the peoples of the East." In was in this spirit that Walsh directed that Maryknoll's headquarters and major seminary reflect Chinese architectural style.

In full accord with the directives of Popes Benedict XV and Pius XI urging the promotion of local church leadership, Walsh frequently declared, "We look forward to a native clergy, to a self-supporting Catholic body, to a day when the appointment of native bishops will mean the assignment of future Maryknollers to other fields. . . . We will always work toward this end which the Church wisely considers not only desirable but necessary."

Related to this missiology, Walsh's spirituality emphasized an open charity: "The love of Christ cannot be confined: like the flame, charity must expand or it will die." This charity should include a readiness for martyrdom if that be God's will. Like Ignatius Loyola, the prayer that he recommended for missioners was that of contemplation in action.

Throughout his years as superior, Walsh continued to edit *The Field Afar,* and to promote the publishing of books on missionary themes. He was convinced that "the hope of our foreign missions lies in a more widely diffused knowledge of them." His own works included: *Thoughts from Modern Martyrs; In the Homes of the Martyrs; A Modern Martyr* (an adaptation of a life of the French martyr Théophane Venard); and *Observations in the Orient.*

Though Walsh considered Maryknoll's principal work to be overseas missions, he did not regard the Church's work in the United States as less missionary. "Personally," he said, "I always fear to overemphasize a distinction [between home and foreign missions] that is largely geographical. As catholic Catholics, our interest should be in the extension of Christ's kingdom anywhere and everywhere on the earth."

Consistent with this view he maintained throughout his life a strong interest in current projects in the U.S. Church; he was a firm supporter of The Catholic University of America, and encouraged founding editor Michael Williams in the early years of the *Commonweal,* Fr. Paul of Graymoor in his movement for Church unity, and Maurice Lavanoux in the foundation of the Liturgical Arts Society.

In 1933, in recognition of his leadership in promoting missionary activity, Pius XI, at the recommendation of the bishops of the U.S.A., named Walsh titular bishop of Siene. He was ordained in Rome at the hands of Cardinal Fumasoni Biondi, prefect of the Congregation for the Propagation of the Faith. Walsh chose for his coat of arms the words he had made the motto of the society: "Seek first the Kingdom of God." As he explained, "This maxim is one of our foundation stones. The words, we know, are Christ's addressed to us. . . . Our privileged task is to find Christ enthroned in our hearts and then make him known to others."

Bishop Walsh died at Maryknoll, New York, April 14, 1936. His tomb is beside that of Fr. Price in the crypt of the Maryknoll Society chapel.

See also MARYKNOLL.

Lane, Raymond A., M.M. *The Early Days of Maryknoll.* New York: David McKay Co., 1951.

Powers, George, M.M. *The Maryknoll Movement,* Maryknoll, N.Y.: Catholic Foreign Mission Society of America, 1926.

Sargent, Daniel. *All Day Long: James Anthony Walsh, Cofounder of Maryknoll.* New York: Longmans, Green & Co., 1941.

Sheridan, Robert E., M.M. *The Founders of Maryknoll: Historical Reflections.* Maryknoll, N.Y.: Maryknoll Fathers, revised, 1981.

———, ed. "Discourses of James Anthony Walsh, M.M. (1890–1936)." Privately printed. Maryknoll, N.Y., 1981.

WILLIAM D. McCARTHY, M.M.

WALSH, JAMES EDWARD (1891–1981)

Religious superior, missionary, bishop. James Edward Walsh was born in Cumberland, Maryland, on April 30, 1891. A graduate of Mt. St. Mary's College at Emmitsburg, Walsh was among the first six students to enter the major seminary of the newly founded Catholic Foreign Mission Society of America in 1912. He was ordained on December 7, 1915. In 1918 he was one of the four first Maryknoll missioners assigned to China. In 1919 he became superior of the mission and in 1927 was ordained the first bishop of the newly established vicariate apostolic of Kongmoon in southeastern China.

Superior General of Maryknoll

In 1936, following the death of Maryknoll's cofounder, Bishop James A. Walsh, the younger Bishop Walsh was elected superior general, a position he held to 1946. From this time he was titular bishop of Sata. A major concern of Walsh during these years was to formulate the elements

James E. Walsh

of a spirituality related to the particular demands of missionary life as he and others experienced it. He had earlier expressed his own commitment to the poor ("Shine on, Farmer Boy"); he now further developed his reflections in a *Maryknoll Spiritual Directory* (1946) and his *Blueprint of the Missionary Vocation* which became basic formational guides for the society.

With national rivalries and racial hatred violently dividing the world in those years, the *Maryknoll* magazine gave heightened emphasis to themes of human solidarity. Walsh himself wrote nearly all of the monthly editorials during his term. During the fateful months of 1941, Walsh and his vicar general, Fr. James M. Drought, agreed to the request of some elements in the Japanese government to serve as unofficial channels for proposals for avoiding war with the U.S.A. Their role undertaken, in the interests of peace, was accepted by the U.S. secretary of state and the apostolic delegate to Japan. The effort, of course, proved fruitless, and it was later concluded that the Japanese proposals were unsupported by those then governing that country.

When war spread throughout the Far East, limiting areas open to missioners, Walsh and his council determined to respond to some appeals from Latin America. Walsh personally accompanied the first missioners to Bolivia in 1942, and visited several other countries to survey the needs. The severe shortage of priests and other apostolic personnel convinced him that, despite large Catholic populations, the Church in many areas of Latin America was not yet implanted and could be considered mission territory. The following year additional Maryknollers were sent to Bolivia, and others to Chile, Peru, Ecuador, Guate-

mala, and Mexico. He told them: "We are going to South America as missioners, but we are not going as exponents of any so-called North American civilization. We will endeavor to preach the Catholic faith in areas where priests are scarce and mission work is needed; but, as regards the elements of true civilization, we expect to receive as much as we have to give."

Missionary in China

In 1948 Walsh returned to China to serve as executive secretary of the Catholic Central Bureau in Shanghai, the new coordinating organization of the bishops of China. Following the establishment of the regime of Mao Zedong the bureau came under surveillance and from 1951 its activities were officially suspended. Walsh resisted government suggestions that he leave China, and was finally arrested on October 18, 1958. Held for a year and a half in a detention center and subjected to prolonged interrogations, Walsh was then tried on charges of espionage for the U.S.A. and sentenced to twenty years imprisonment. He was interned at Shanghai's Ward Road prison for the next twelve years. The only visit permitted him was that of his brother William in 1960. Bishop Walsh was suddenly deported from China on July 10, 1970. In August, Pope Paul VI received him warmly at the Vatican stating: "You have been a witness, authentic and simple, in joy and in sorrow, then in suffering and humiliation, and finally in separation from the people you loved so much. For all this, we thank you on behalf of the entire Church of Christ."

Walsh spent his final eleven years at Maryknoll, New York. He remained keenly interested in news of China and rejoiced that the situation of the Church there was being eased. He made no public pronouncements against his former captors. "I have no bitterness" he said, "toward those who tried and condemned me. I could just never feel angry with any Chinese. I felt that way almost from the first day I set foot in China in 1918 and it has grown stronger with the years, even during my imprisonment. I love the Chinese people." Though he had been uninformed of Vatican Council II prior to his release, he seemed to adjust readily to the liturgical and other changes. He died peacefully at Maryknoll July 29, 1981.

See also MARYKNOLL.

Butow, Robert J. C. *The John Doe Associates: Backdoor Diplomacy for Peace, 1941.* California: Stanford University Press, 1974.

Description of a Missioner. Maryknoll, N.Y.: Maryknoll Fathers, n.d. (a reprint); includes "Shine On, Farmer Boy," reprinted from *Maryknoll* (July–August 1942).

Sheridan, Robert E. *Bishop James E. Walsh as I Knew Him.* Maryknoll, N.Y.: Maryknoll Publications, 1981.

____, ed. *Zeal for Your House.* Huntington, Ind.: OSV Press, 1976.

Walsh, James E. *Blueprint of the Missionary Vocation.* Maryknoll, N.Y.: Maryknoll Publications, n.d. [ca. 1957].

Wiest, John-Paul. *Maryknoll in China: A History 1918–1955.* Armonk, N.Y.: M. E. Sharpe, 1988.

WILLIAM D. McCARTHY, M.M.

WALSH, JAMES JOSEPH (1865–1942)

Physician, historian, writer. James Joseph Walsh was born in Archbald, Pennsylvania, on April 12, 1865, son of Martin (a merchant) and Bridget Walsh. He received his B.A. and M.A. degrees from St. John's College, now Fordham University. He spent some years as a Jesuit novice but left to pursue his M.D. degree at the University of Pennsylvania (1895). Until 1898 he studied in Paris, Vienna, and Berlin; in 1900 he became a practicing neurologist in New York City, his home for the rest of his life. Always interested in education, he became an instructor in medicine at the New York Polyclinic School of Medicine in 1904, leaving to become dean of the Fordham University School of Medicine in 1907. Between 1912 and 1930 he taught at the College of New Rochelle, Georgian Court College, and Mt. St. Joseph's College in Philadelphia. From 1920 to 1932 he served as medical director of the Fordham School of Sociology. He also served as a fellow of the American Academy for the Advancement of Science and the New York Academy of Medicine; he was also an editorial writer for the *Journal of the American Medical Association.*

Yet Walsh's impressive career as a neurologist is not what made him famous. He lived in an era when anti-Catholic intellectualism was fashionable, and Walsh set out to refute the Church's critics. A conservative man, he believed that much supposedly modern knowledge was actually rediscovered older knowledge. To the charge that the Church opposed progress, Walsh countered that much progress was illusory, and even suggested that the popes did not get credit for their aid to science. He wrote forty-five books and more than five hundred articles; he also lectured constantly. The title of his best-known book, *The Thirteenth, Greatest of Centuries* (1907), conveys his views most succinctly.

His coreligionists appreciated his efforts, and he received honorary doctorates from Fordham University, Georgetown University, the University of Notre Dame, the University of San Francisco, and The Catholic University of America. Notre Dame also gave him its Laetare Medal in 1916. Other honors included being named a Knight Commander in the Order of Saint Gregory the Great (1908) and a Knight of Malta (1931). Although his historical views do not carry weight today, in his day he forced people to take seriously Catholicism's intellectual achievements. He married in 1915; his wife Julia and he had two children. He died in New York City on February 28, 1942.

Kirwin, H. W. "James J. Walsh, Medical Historian and Pathfinder." *Catholic Historical Review* 45 (1960) 409–35.

National Cyclopedia of American Biography 46 (1963) 349–50.

NCE 14:782–3.

JOSEPH F. KELLY

WALSH, ROBERT (1784–1859)

American journalist and author. Robert Walsh was born in Baltimore, Maryland, on August 30, 1784, the son of Robert Walsh, a wealthy merchant, and Elizabeth Steel Walsh, whose family was of Pennsylvania Quaker origin. Walsh was educated by the French Sulpicians at St. Mary's Seminary, Baltimore, and at Georgetown University. In 1806 he obtained both his bachelor's and master's degree from St. Mary's. He then studied law under Robert Goodloe Harper, and became an ardent Federalist. Walsh lived in Europe from 1806 until 1809, during which time he wrote for a number of British and French journals; while living in England, he served for a time as secretary to U.S. Minister William Pinkney.

Walsh returned to America, settled in Philadelphia, Pennsylvania, and was married to Anna Moylan, the niece of Stephen Moylan and Bishop Moylan of Cork; they had twelve children. For a brief time he practiced law, but his interests led him to journalism. In 1810 he published a brochure entitled *A Letter on the Genius and Dispositions of the French Government,* which drew from his knowledge of international affairs, and which was reprinted and favorably reviewed in England. In 1811 he founded the first American quarterly, *The American Review of History and Politics,* a journal which was published only for a short time due to its Federalist tone and the War of 1812. He founded the *American Register* in 1817, which survived a year. In 1819 he published *An Appeal from the Judgments of Great Britain Respecting the United States of America,* earning him praise from Thomas Jefferson, John Adams, and the Pennsylvania legislature, and denunciation from the British press. With William Frye, Walsh founded the *National Gazette and Literary Register,* a liberal triweekly which quickly became a daily Philadelphia newspaper. He edited the *Museum of Foreign Literature and Science* (1822–23) and several volumes of *The Works of the British Poets,* issued by Mitchell, Ames and Whits S. F. Bradford of Philadelphia. In 1827 he founded the *American Quarterly Review* which published articles from such American scholars as Joseph Story, George Bancroft, Washington Irving, and many others. He also gained a reputation as an educator, serving as professor of English at the University of Paris (1818–28) and as a trustee and manager of Rumford's Military Academy at Mt. Airy, Pennsylvania (1828–33).

He retired to Paris in 1837 due to poor health and political pressure. During these years, he regularly contributed to several French journals and served as foreign correspondent for the *National Intelligencer* (Washington, D.C.) and the *Journal of Commerce* (New York). From 1844 until 1851 he served as the U.S. consul-general in Paris. He died in Paris on February 7, 1859, and was buried in Versailles.

Lochemes, M. F. *Robert Walsh: His Story.* New York: American Irish Historical Society, 1941.
Walsh, H. C. *United States Historical Magazine* 2 (1889) 301–13.
Walsh, J. C. "Robert Walsh." *Journal of the American Irish Historical Society* 26 (1927) 207–27.

RICHARD G. SMITH

WALSH, WILLIAM THOMAS (1891–1949)

Author and educator. Born in Waterbury, Connecticut, on September 11, 1891, Walsh attended Yale (B.A. 1913), worked as a reporter for the *Waterbury American and Republican,* the Hartford *Times,* and the Philadelphia *Public Ledger* between the years of 1907 and 1917, and married Helen Gerard Sherwood in 1914. Following his years in journalism, Walsh served in the Connecticut State Fuel Administration, after which he taught English at Hartford High School and the Roxbury School in Cheshire, Connecticut (1917–33). He became professor of English at Manhattanville College of the Sacred Heart, New York City, in 1933, and remained there until 1947.

In 1930 he began a writing career that would span two decades, publishing books such as *Isabella of Spain* (1930), *Out of the Whirlwind* (1935), *Our Lady of Fatima* (1947), *Saint Peter the Apostle* (1948), and *Saints in Action.* He also published the plays *Shekels* (1936), *Citizens of Heaven* (1948), and *Lyric Poems* (1939). Walsh believed that the spirit of the Church could be seen in the lives of its heroes. This was especially valid, he thought, for the saints of the first six centuries of Christianity. All Catholics could learn from the problems confronting the apostles and early Christians. Walsh was named commander of the Order of Alphonso X in 1943, and received the Laetare Medal and a Catholic literary award in 1944. He died in White Plains, New York, on February 22, 1949.

MARIA MAZZENGA

WALWORTH, CLARENCE AUGUSTUS (1820–1900)

Priest, author, social activist. Clarence was born to Reuben H. and Mary K. Averill Walworth on May 30, 1820, in upstate New York. His father was a judge, a congressman, and the last chancellor of New York State. Both of his parents were Presbyterian. He attended Union College in Schenectady, New York, and was graduated in 1838. Three years later he was admitted to the bar. He practiced law for a year in Rochester, New York, before entering the Episcopalian General Theological Seminary in New York City to study for the ministry. At that time the seminary was in the midst of an Anglo-Catholic Romantic movement, a period Walworth later described in his book *The Oxford Movement in America* (1895).

Walworth became a Catholic in 1845 and was received into the German-American Congregation of the Most Holy Redeemer (Redemptorists). He was then sent to Europe to study for the priesthood. Upon ordination in 1848, he returned to the United States to work with Isaac Hecker and other young Redemptorists in leading a series of parish missions. During these years, Walworth became more and more frustrated with the seeming inability of the German-dominated order to adjust to American practices. He left the order in 1858 to become a diocesan priest. Three years later, however, he joined fellow ex-Redemptorists who had formed the Missionary Priests of St. Paul the Apostle (Paulist Fathers). He remained with them until 1865, when he left because of some disagreements with Hecker, the founder of the Paulists. He once again became pastor of a parish, St. Mary's Church in Albany.

As a pastor, Walworth advocated social justice and promoted the temperance movement. He decried industrial abuses, poor working conditions, and political corruption. He also labored to improve conditions at St. Regis Indian Reservation. Throughout his career as a Catholic priest, Walworth wrote many articles and several books. His pamphlets and tracts utilized both history and apologetics for the Catholic tradition. His efforts provided an intellectual leadership in the Catholic community that had been lacking prior to the mid-1840s. He emphasized community and authority as an antidote to the disintegrating effects of individualism in American religious, political, and economic life. For Walworth, Catholicism provided a viable defense against the increasing threat of historical relativism, atheistic evolutionism, socialism, and secularism. Walworth died on September 19, 1900, in Albany, New York.

See also PAULISTS (C.S.P.).

Elliott, Walter. "Father Walworth: A Character Sketch." *Catholic World* 73 (1901) 320–37.
McSorley, Joseph. *Father Hecker and His Friends.* St. Louis, 1953.
Walworth, Clarence Augustus. *The Doctrine of Hell.* New York, 1873.
____. *Andiatorocte and Other Poems.* New York, 1888.
____. *Early Ritualism in America.* New York, 1893.
____. *Reminiscences of Edgar P. Wadhams.* New York, 1893.

____. *The Oxford Movement in America.* New York, 1895.

____. *The Walworths of America.* Albany, New York, 1897.

____, ed. *Gentile Skeptic.* New York, 1863.

Walworth, Ellen. *Life Sketches of Father Walworth.* Albany, New York, 1907.

PATRICIA DeFERRARI

WANDERER, THE

The Wanderer, a national Catholic weekly journal of news, commentary, and analysis, has been publishing continually since 1867. Owned and operated by Catholic laymen, *The Wanderer* is independent of ecclesiastical oversight but maintains a fiercely loyal adherence to Catholic doctrine and discipline. The journal has published during the reigns of ten popes and has consistently looked to these pontiffs for teaching, guidance, and leadership. With its founding in St. Paul, Minnesota, as *Der Wanderer,* and published in German, the paper was intended to inform and strengthen the faith of German immigrants in Minnesota and the Dakotas who were being attracted to and influenced by Masonic and quasi-Masonic German-language newspapers and organizations.

As the years progressed, *Der Wanderer's* circulation and influence spread across the nation. It was a major opponent of the "Americanizing" tendency within the Church led by the archbishop of Baltimore, James Cardinal Gibbons, and the archbishop of St. Paul, John Ireland. That tendency was addressed by Pope Leo XIII in his 1899 apostolic letter, *Testem benevolentiae.*

Under the editorship of Joseph Matt (the present writer's grandfather), *Der Wanderer* was instrumental in promoting the principles of the Church's social teaching as set forth in Pope Leo XIII's great encyclical, *Rerum Novarum.* The paper was supportive of labor unions which organized with a sense of solidarity among their members, who usually belonged to a specific craft or trade. On the other hand, it was skeptical of the large industrial unions which often promoted their objectives with appeals to class conflict and ideology—an approach rejected in the social encyclicals.

In 1931 *Der Wanderer* was joined by *The Wanderer* published in English, and the two journals published concurrently until 1957 when the German-language *Der Wanderer* ceased publication.

During the 1930s and 1940s, *Wanderer* editors were much involved in the growing liturgical movement in the United States led by Dom Virgil Michel, O.S.B., of St. John's Abbey in Collegeville, Minnesota.

As the world watched the rise to power in Germany of Adolf Hitler with fear and fascination, *The Wanderer* was among the first to denounce Nazism as totalitarian and antithetical to Christian principles. In September of 1933, the newspaper was barred from Germany where it reached some 1,200 readers.

During World War II, its editor, Joseph Matt, monitored the course of the war each week, and published a series of brilliant and penetrating analyses of the long-range geopolitical effects of what he saw as an unholy alliance between the Western powers and Communist Russia. He rightly predicted the move by Josef Stalin to expand Soviet hegemony as Nazi power was crushed and the West hesitated to challenge the Soviets. Not surprisingly, as the war drew to a close in 1945, the official Soviet newspaper, *Pravda,* demanded that the U.S. government suppress *The Wanderer* "for urging the Allies to make war on the Soviet Union or expel her from the United Nations."

Joseph Matt, editor

Vatican II and After

The Wanderer's long history and "institutional memory" served it well with the opening of the momentous Second Vatican Council and the generation that has since followed. Breaking the Church out of what some observers termed a "siege mentality" into a fresh approach to evangelization and dialogue with the world, the council unleashed both positive and destructive energies.

The Wanderer itself suffered from the divisions and upheavals following the council. In 1967 editor Walter Matt left the newspaper over a dispute about the meaning of Vatican II. He saw it not so much as a reform and a renewal of the Church but as a revolution that threatened to undermine the Church herself. His brother, Alphonse J. Matt, Sr. (the present writer's father), took over the reins at *The Wanderer* and reminded its readers that the real intent of the council was a renewed evangelization of the world for Christ and a personal renewal of every individual Catholic.

For *The Wanderer,* the council was not a rejection or an abandonment of tradition, but a development of that tradition, safeguarded for 2,000 years by the Holy Spirit, to better enable the Church to continue to bring the gospel to all men.

The years since the council were turbulent ones both for the Church and *The Wanderer.* A spirit of dissent, experimentation, and innovation pervaded many members of the clergy, religious, and theologians. The effects on catechetics, liturgy, and traditional Catholic practices were significant. Even bishops were divided in their views of the council.

The single most divisive issue in the postconciliar Church was that of contraception (brought into sharp focus with the development of the "Pill" in the early 1960s), and it created renewed and controversial debates on sexuality. Pope Paul VI met this challenge and hoped to resolve the problem with the encyclical *Humanae vitae. The Wanderer* was unyielding in its defense of that encyclical and helped to mobilize support for *Humanae vitae* by joining some other Catholic leaders in organizing Catholics United for the Faith, now a leading Catholic lay group in the United States.

The Wanderer found itself more and more in opposition to the theologians, clerics, religious, and bishops who used the council as the pretext for advancing new and untraditional programs. The newspaper was a vigorous opponent of the Call to Action Program in 1976 which threatened to loosen the ties of the Church in the United States to the Vatican and to focus on social change with a left-wing bent. Some new catechisms, liturgies, and scriptural theories were frequent targets of *The Wanderer*'s writers and editorialists.

As the twentieth century draws to a close, the Church in the United States is slowly returning to a calmer, more traditional mode under the leadership of Pope John Paul II. His issuance of the *Catechism of the Catholic Church* and his appointment of increasing numbers of bishops loyal to the Vatican's views on doctrine and discipline were welcomed by *The Wanderer.*

See also CATHOLIC PRESS (NEWSPAPERS), THE; TRADITIONALIST MOVEMENT, THE.

ALPHONSE J. MATT, JR.

WARD, MAISIE (1889–1975)

Publisher, writer, street preacher, and social activist. Mary Josephine Ward's life represents in microcosm the changes in Roman Catholicism in the twentieth century. Daughter of Wilfrid and Josephine Ward (nee Hope-Scott) and granddaughter of William George Ward, she was born in Shanklin on the Isle of Wight on January 4, 1889. Maisie, eldest of five children, was educated at home and in a convent school in Cambridge run by the Mary Ward nuns. She was in-

Maisie Ward

fluenced by the intellectual elite of Catholic England and two great preachers, Frs. William Basil Maturin and Robert Hugh Benson. She worked as a secretary to her father and volunteered for the Red Cross during World War I. In 1919 she became a founding member of the Catholic Evidence Guild and remained active in it for almost fifty years. Through it she met her future husband, the Australian law student, Francis Joseph Sheed, whom she married in April 1926. In that same year they cofounded the publishing firm of Sheed and Ward with money given by Josephine Ward. Seven years later an American office was opened in New York. In 1927 a daughter, Rosemary, was born; a son, Wilfrid, was born in 1930.

Through her twenty-seven books and her work in the firm, Ward influenced several generations of educated Anglo-American Catholics. She edited *The English Way,* essays about English spiritual writers from Bede to Newman, and wrote *The Wilfrid Wards and the Transition,* a two-volume study of the Ward family.

During World War II, she and her children lived in the United States. *This Burning Heat, Gilbert Keith Chesterton,* her most popular book, and *The Splendor of the Rosary* were published during the war years. She returned to England after the war where she published her favorite book, *Young Mr. Newman,* and *Return to Chesterton.* Her interest in the priest-worker movement led to *France Pagan?* and efforts to bolster family life produced *Be Not Solicitous.* In the 1950s she turned to religious topics and wrote *They Saw His Glory; An Introduction to the Gospels and Acts* and *Saints Who Made History.* She commemorated the life of her friend Caryll Houselander in *The Divine Eccentric* and *Letters of Caryll Houselander.* Her final major work was a two-volume study entitled *Robert Browning and His World*. She wrote two autobiographies: *Unfinished Business* and *To and Fro on the Earth*.

Ward's writing life was paralleled by a commitment to social concerns. Influenced by Distributism, she operated several unsuccessful farms. She supported the Catholic Worker, Friendship House, the Marycrest Community, the Canadian maritime cooperatives, the priest-worker movement, and land reform in India. She was cofounder of the Catholic Housing Aid Society in England. From the 1940s until her death she traveled extensively to the Continent, the United States, Australia, and Asia. She taught Catholic doctrine on street corners in many cities, and lectured extensively in the United States to Catholic audiences.

She died January 27, 1975, at age eighty-six and was buried in Jersey City, New Jersey.

See also CATHOLIC BOOK PUBLISHING; SHEED, FRANK.

Sheed, Frank. *The Instructed Heart*. Huntington, Ind.: Our Sunday Visitor, 1979.

Sheed, Wilfrid. *Frank and Maisie: Memoir with Parents*. N.Y.: Simon & Schuster, 1986.

Ward, Maisie. *The Wilfrid Wards and the Transition*. 2 vols. London: Sheed & Ward, 1934, 1937.

———. *Unfinished Business*. N.Y.: Sheed & Ward, 1964.

———. *To and Fro on the Earth*. N.Y.: Sheed & Ward, 1973.

DANA GREENE

WARDE, MARY FRANCIS XAVIER (?1810–84)

Mercy Sister. Born in Queens County, Ireland, around the year 1810, Mary Xavier was the daughter of John and Jane Maher Warde. As a young woman, she met Catherine McAuley and worked with her at her Baggot Street center for children and needy women. In 1831 Mother McAuley founded the Sisters of Mercy with the mission of providing education and support for the sick and the poor. Mary Xavier joined the new order, helped to establish the community in Dublin, and opened several convents in other parts of Ireland. In 1843 she and several other sisters came to Pittsburgh at the request of Bishop Michael O'Connor to establish their community there. Their original mission was to establish a convent and boarding school for girls, but they soon became involved in the care of orphans and the sick. Within three years of its establishment, the convent was large enough to send out sisters to establish convents throughout the United States.

In 1850 Warde became superior of the mission to Providence, Rhode Island. Under her leadership, the Sisters of Mercy spread to Hartford and New Haven, Connecticut (1852), and to Rochester and Buffalo, New York (1857). From Providence, Mother Warde moved to Manchester, New Hampshire, where she served as superior for twenty-six years, during which time she promoted night schools for young mill workers. Success in these endeavors was anything but guaranteed. In New England Mother Warde met resistance from the Know-Nothings, who threatened her sisters, smashed windows, and harassed students. In Pittsburgh and Philadelphia she met the challenge of bishops who tried to weaken her community by placing separate motherhouses under diocesan control. In the midst of these controversies and others, Warde continued to advance the mission of the order by opening new schools, orphanages, and hospitals. She died in Manchester on September 17, 1884.

Carroll, M.T.A. *Leaves from the Annals of the Sisters of Mercy*. 4 vols. New York, 1881–95.

Garety, M. Catherine. *Rev. Mother M. Xavier Warde*. Boston, 1902.

Healy, Kathleen. *Frances Warde: American Founder of the Sisters of Mercy*. New York, 1973.

PATRICIA DeFERRARI

WASHINGTON, CATHOLIC CHURCH IN

The history of the Catholic Church in Washington State began with the arrival of the Heceta and Bodega y Cuadra expedition of 1775 to the Pacific Northwest. A Franciscan priest and others disembarked at what is currently known as Point Grenville, Washington, and erected a cross. Nearly seventy-five years later, missionaries went to the Northwest in response to the requests of settlers and fur traders in Oregon Territory. Frs. Modeste Demers and Francis Norbert Blanchet were the first to arrive in November 1838. Additional priests, including Blanchet's brother, Augustin Magloire Alexander Blanchet, traveled to the region throughout the 1840s. The missionaries appointed Native Americans and others as lay catechists to lead fledgling Catholic communities in prayer and to ensure the construction of churches. Missionaries such as Pierre De Smet, S.J., Louis Rossi, C.P., Eugene Casimir Chirouse, O.M.I., and Charles Pandosy, O.M.I., also contributed to the expansion of the Catholic Church in the Northwest. The Sisters of Notre Dame de Namur were the first women religious to arrive at Fort Vancouver in 1844; they moved into what is now Oregon State that same year. In July 1846, Francis Norbert Blanchet was named archbishop of Oregon City (later Portland) and Augustin Blanchet was named bishop of Walla Walla. These early years were marked by hostilities between Native Americans and settlers, the Whitman Massacre, and increased tension between Catholic and Protestant missionaries. By 1850 the mission at Walla Walla was closed and the diocese suppressed.

Archdiocese of Seattle

Established May 31, 1850, as the Diocese of Nesqually, its first bishop, Augustin Blanchet, arrived at Fort Vancouver on the Columbia River, October 27, 1850. Vancouver was designated the episcopal city for the Diocese of Nesqually. The diocese encompassed what is now Washington State. Mother Joseph and four other Sisters of Providence began work in health care and education in the diocese in 1856, and by 1864 there were thirty-one Providence Sisters, seven diocesan priests, five Jesuits, and two Oblate missionaries serving the diocese.

The growth of Catholic institutions and churches continued through the first part of the twentieth century. Diocesan priests such as John Boulet continued work begun by Jesuit and Oblate missionaries among Native Americans in eastern Washington and along Puget Sound. Sisters of the Holy Names, Sisters of Providence, and Sisters of St. Dominic opened schools, hospitals, and orphanages throughout Washington. The transfer of the see to Seattle in 1907 and the construction of St. James Cathedral marked the beginning of the urbanization of Catholicism in the state. By 1913, Spokane, a city on the eastern border of Washington, was elevated to a diocese. The Diocese of Seattle then consisted of all territory west of the Columbia River. The Catholic population of 100,000 reflected the tremendous growth of the Church in Washington, yet only 10 percent of the total population.

Between 1903–15, Mother Frances Cabrini and the Missionary Sisters of the Sacred Heart established a presence for Italian immigrants in Puget Sound, and built an orphanage, school, and hospital. The influx of German immigrants to southern Puget Sound led to the establishment of St. Martin's College by German Benedictines. The Maryknoll Sisters arrived in Seattle to educate Japanese and Japanese-American Catholics. Their kindergarten evolved into a Maryknoll parish for Asian Americans in the diocese.

The growth of lay Catholic organizations in the early twentieth century marked a renewal of lay involvement in Catholicism in Washington. The first Knights of Columbus Council in Washington was organized in Seattle in 1902. The Seattle Council of Catholic Women was created in 1919, and the first official St. Vincent de Paul Society was established in 1920 at St. Benedict parish, Seattle. The laity was an integral part in the fight against Initiative no. 49, an antiprivate school bill sponsored by the Ku Klux Klan in 1924. The Serra Club, founded by Catholic businessmen in Seattle in 1934, supported the advancement of vocations and financial assistance to seminarians.

Catholicism in the mid-twentieth century expanded in a region considered to be one of the most unchurched in the nation. In 1951 Yakima, a city in central Washington, became a diocese, and Seattle was elevated to an archdiocese. The Sisters Formation Program began and two diocesan high schools opened, as did St. Thomas, an Archdiocesan Seminary staffed by the Society of St. Sulpice. The Catholic Youth Organization (CYO) and Confrater-

nity of Christian Doctrine (CCD) programs grew, along with liturgical reform. Ecumenical programs, and multicultural and justice and peace ministries were established, reflecting a continuing commitment to the diverse populations of the archdiocese.

Diocese of Spokane

The Diocese of Spokane was created in response to the growth of the Catholic population in Washington. Catholicism was well established due to the missionary efforts of priests such as Pierre De Smet, S.J., Joseph Joset, S.J., Joseph Cataldo, S.J., Toussaint Mesplie, Emile Kauten, and Peter Poaps. Women religious, particularly the Sisters of the Holy Names and the Sisters of Providence, provided health care and education to Native Americans and Euro-Americans. The early twentieth century in the Spokane diocese was marked by the institutional growth of the Jesuits and the expansion of lay organizations such as the Knights of Columbus. A rural life program and a CCD program were created in 1932. By midcentury, the diocese increased its emphasis on vocations; Bishop White Seminary was built in 1956 and *Mater Cleri* Seminary in 1963. Hispanic ministry was formed, and the Guatemala missionary effort began in 1959. Recent demographic changes have caused the development of a large immigrant Mexican Catholic community in Okanogan County.

Diocese of Yakima

Oblate and Jesuit missionaries and Sisters of Providence and Sisters of St. Dominic were instrumental in the establishment of Catholicism in Central Washington. The development of the Columbia Basin into workable farmland and the influx of Hispanic migrant farm workers as well as other migrant populations during WWII created a region with special needs. The first years of the Diocese of Yakima were marked by the construction of churches and schools and the establishment of a diocesan high school. Mexican priests preached missions to the Latinos in the Yakima Valley, and by 1968 the "Spanish Speaking Apostolate" was created. The Catholic population of Central Washington is approximately half Hispanic. Pastoral initiatives stress evangelization and spiritual renewal.

In 1995 there were 519,101 Catholics in Washington out of a total population of 5,384,433. They were distributed among 256 parishes and served by 333 diocesan priests, 235 religious order priests, 139 permanent deacons, 47 brothers, and 1,200 sisters. The percentage of Catholics ranged from a low of 9 percent in the Archdiocese of Seattle to a high of 15 percent in the Diocese of Yakima.

Buerge, David, and Junius Rochester. *Roots and Branches.* Washington: Church Council of Greater Seattle, 1988.

O'Hara, Edwin V. *Catholic History of Oregon*. Portland, Oreg.: Catholic Book Company, 1925.

Rossi, Louis. *Six Years on the West Coast of America 1856–1862*. Fairfield, Wash.: Ye Galleon Press, 1983.

Schoenberg, Wilfred, S.J. *A History of the Catholic Church in the Pacific Northwest, 1743–1983*. Washington, D.C.: The Pastoral Press, 1987.

____. *Paths to the Northwest: A Jesuit History of the Oregon Province*. Chicago: Loyola University Press, 1982.

CHRISTINE TAYLOR

WASHINGTON, D.C., CATHOLIC CHURCH IN

Although the notion that the capital of the United States was important enough to merit consideration as a see surfaced as early as 1819, it was not until the eve of World War II that the city of Washington was erected as a separate archdiocese from the Archdiocese of Baltimore. This change was formalized on Columbus Day, October 12, 1939. The new Archdiocese of Washington was confined geographically to the territory of the District of Columbia, an area of only sixty-four square miles. At the time of its establishment, the archdiocese had thirty-four parishes, twenty-seven of which were staffed by diocesan priests and seven by religious orders, to serve a Catholic population of approximately 75,000 persons. The new archdiocese remained united to Baltimore with equal status under Archbishop Michael J. Curley, whose title became "Archbishop of Baltimore and Washington." Archbishop Curley was installed as the first archbishop of Washington at St. Matthew's Cathedral on Easter Monday, March 25, 1940.

Archdiocese of Washington

On November 15, 1947, following the death of Archbishop Curley, the Washington archdiocese was completely separated from the Archdiocese of Baltimore and was enlarged by the addition of five Maryland counties: St. Mary's, Charles, Calvert, Prince George's, and Montgomery. Thus the Archdiocese of Washington acquired the most historic area of Maryland with Catholic communities dating back to the first settlement of the colony in 1634. In 1947 the newly constituted Archdiocese of Washington included 81 parishes, 91 schools, and 127 diocesan priests, with a Catholic population of approximately 165,000.

Patrick A. O'Boyle of the Archdiocese of New York was installed as the second archbishop of Washington at St. Matthew's Cathedral on January 21, 1948. During the tenure of Cardinal O'Boyle (he was elevated to the Sacred College in 1967), the archdiocese experienced tremendous growth. The size of its Catholic population more than doubled, reaching a total of 389,000 in 1973. The number of Catholic institutions greatly increased as well with the number of parishes growing by 50 percent to 122

at the time of Cardinal O'Boyle's retirement. In 1965 the Archdiocese of Washington was elevated to the status of an ecclesiastical province with the assignment of the Virgin Islands as a suffragan see.

It was also under Cardinal O'Boyle that events in the Archdiocese of Washington captured the attention of outside observers. The first of these events was the archdiocese's successful integration of its parishes and schools prior to the Supreme Court decision of 1954 striking down the legality of racial segregation. Then, in 1968, the archdiocese became the focus of worldwide Catholic attention when the Catholic Church in Washington was plunged into turmoil following the publication of Pope Paul VI's encyclical *Humanae vitae*. After twenty-five years of service to the Church of Washington, Cardinal O'Boyle retired in 1973.

On May 9, 1973, William W. Baum, bishop of the Diocese of Springfield-Cape Girardeau, Missouri, and a national voice in ecumenism was consecrated the third archbishop of Washington. Archbishop Baum was appointed to the College of Cardinals in 1976. Under his leadership six more parishes were created in the archdiocese to meet the needs of Washington's ever-expanding suburbs, and new organizations were established to minister to the needs of local African American and Hispanic Catholics. One of the notable events of Cardinal Baum's tenure as the archbishop of Washington was the visit of Pope John Paul II to the nation's capital in the fall of 1979. Cardinal Baum left Washington for Rome the following year when Pope John Paul II named him Prefect of the Congregation for Catholic Education. At the time of Cardinal Baum's resignation as archbishop of Washington, the Catholic population of the archdiocese had reached 396,000.

Bishop James A. Hickey of Cleveland was installed as the fourth archbishop of Washington on August 5, 1980, and appointed to the College of Cardinals in 1988. During Cardinal Hickey's tenure the Archdiocese of Washington has met new challenges posed by the changing demographics of the Washington region and the suburbanization of once rural areas. Additionally, a threat to the unity of the local church occurred in 1989 when a schismatic movement, led by Rev. George A. Stallings, attempted to gain support from African American Catholics. However, through the adroit policies and pastoral care of Cardinal Hickey, this schismatic movement had no significant effect on the archdiocese.

Since approximately 1980, the Church of Washington, which had not known the tremendous ethnic diversity found in other urban areas, has been blessed and challenged with the arrival of thousands of immigrant Catholics from Latin America, the Caribbean, and Asia. The changing face of the archdiocese has led to the creation of twelve more parishes. Currently (1995) the archdiocese has 140 parishes, 101 schools, and 335 priests serving approximately 450,000 Catholics.

The Archdiocese of Washington has a unique place within the Catholic Church in America as it is home to numerous national Catholic institutions. Among these are the National Conference of Catholic Bishops, the United States Catholic Conference, the Archdiocese of the Military Services, The Catholic University of America, Georgetown University, and the Basilica of the National Shrine of the Immaculate Conception. The archdiocese is also the home of the apostolic nunciature to the United States.

The Catholic Historical Society of Washington, established 1976.

MacGregor, Morris J. *A Parish for the Federal City St. Patrick's in Washington, 1794–1994.* Washington, D.C.: The Catholic University of America Press, 1994.

Spalding, Thomas W. *The Premier See: A History of the Archdiocese of Baltimore, 1789–1989.* Baltimore: Johns Hopkins University Press, 1989.

Warner, William W. *At Peace with All Their Neighbors: Catholics and Catholicism in the National Capital 1787–1860.* Washington, D.C: Georgetown University Press, 1994.

RORY T. CONLEY

WATERS, VINCENT (1904–74)

Bishop. Vincent Stanislaus Waters was born in Roanoke, Virginia, on August 15, 1904. He attended high school at Belmont Abbey in North Carolina before beginning seminary studies at St. Mary's Seminary, Baltimore, Maryland. In 1927 he sailed to Rome to study theology at the North American College and the Gregorian University. There he was ordained priest in December 1931. Returning to the Diocese of Richmond, he served successively as associate pastor in Lynchburg, chancellor of the dio-

Vincent Waters

cese, director of the Diocesan Mission Band, and as auxiliary chaplain at the United States Army bases in Virginia.

He was named the third bishop of Raleigh and consecrated in the Cathedral of Richmond on May 15, 1945. His diocese included the entire state of North Carolina with a Catholic population of only 13,000, less than one-tenth of one percent of the population. He spent almost thirty years as a missionary bishop trying to establish the Catholic Church in every county of the state, striving to strengthen the faith of his small flock and to extend this faith to all who would hear. In 1953 Bishop Waters decreed the end of racial segregation in Catholic churches, schools, and institutions of the diocese. He inaugurated this policy in the small rural town of Newton Grove, where he was threatened with stoning by the local congregation. He prevailed, and segregation of the races slowly disappeared from Catholic churches in North Carolina. Bishop Waters lived to see the Catholic population of the state grow to 70,000, at which time he petitioned the Holy See to establish a second North Carolina diocese with its see in Charlotte. This was done in January 1973.

Bishop Waters died at his home in Raleigh on December 3, 1974, and was buried in the cemetery at Newton Grove, North Carolina, where twenty years earlier he had been rejected because of his courageous stand on behalf of racial justice.

GERALD LEWIS

WATTSON, PAUL (1863–1940)

Religious superior. Fr. Paul James Wattson was a cofounder with Sr. Lurana Mary White of the Society of the Atonement, a Third Order Franciscan community with roots in the Anglican tradition. Born in Maryland in 1863 during the American Civil War, the son of an Episcopal priest, Joseph Newton Wattson, Paul had been baptized as Lewis Thomas and had grown up in a devout Episcopal family with definite Anglo-Catholic leanings. He graduated from St. Steven's College at Annandale-on-the-Hudson before he enrolled in General Theological Seminary in New York City in preparation for the Episcopal priesthood. Upon ordination to the diaconate in 1885, Rev. Lewis Wattson became rector of St. John's Church, Kingston, New York, and was ordained presbyter the following year. From his youth, Lewis had the desire to found a religious community in the Episcopal Church and began to give serious consideration to it while still rector in Kingston in 1891. It was also during his tenure as rector in Kingston that he began to publish *The Pulpit of the Cross,* a parish bulletin in defense of High-Church Anglicanism in which he expressed views which, after a controversy over liturgical practices, led to his departure from Kingston in 1895.

With the idea of establishing a religious community, Lewis accepted a position as superior of a group of un-

Paul Wattson of Graymoor

married Episcopal clergymen leading a semimonastic life in Omaha, Nebraska. While he was in Omaha, he became thoroughly convinced of the universal ministry of the Roman Pontiff as successor of Peter and Vicar of Christ. From that time on, papal primacy as well as corporate reunion of the Anglicans with the Roman Catholic Church became the characteristic marks of Fr. Wattson's convictions for the next ten years. During his years in Omaha he had been in correspondence with an Episcopal religious, Lurana Mary White, who was also interested in founding a religious community of women in the Episcopal Church and one that was dedicated to corporate poverty. When they had finally met in 1898, they both realized that they held common convictions about the religious life and through prayer decided to move forward with their plans. Both Fr. Paul and Sr. Lurana decided that their new community should follow the Third Order Franciscan Rule.

The Society of the Atonement

Sr. Lurana arrived at a little mission church called St. John-in-the-Wilderness near Peekskill, New York, in 1898 to begin the new religious community. The patrons of this chapel had named it Graymoor and by so doing honored Dr. Albert Zabriskie Gray, the Episcopal rector of St. Philip's Church, Garrison, New York, who erected it, and William Moore, a vestryman and chief benefactor. Fr. Wattson then entered the novitiate of the Order of the Holy Cross in Westminster, Maryland, to learn the principles of the religious life. In July 1900 Fr. Wattson was professed as a religious with the name Paul James in the presence of Bishop Leighton Coleman of Delaware who was

also named official Visitor to the community by Bishop Henry Codman Potter of New York. In the summer of 1900, Fr. Wattson, now known as Fr. Paul, outlined the Christian unity vocation of his new community in which the members were to work toward the reunion of the Anglican and Roman Catholic communions. He believed that it was possible because, in his opinion, they both had valid orders and because a precedent had been set by the reunion of certain Eastern Churches with Rome.

Late in 1900 Fr. Paul explained to Bishop Coleman that he held to the doctrine of the Immaculate Conception, the infallibility of the pope, and the primacy of the Bishop of Rome as the successor of Peter. This brought on the deterioration of his relationship with his Church to the point where his opponents wished to have him charged with heresy. Eventually, Fr. Paul was condemned for his views and the pulpits of his own Church were closed to him, a truly intolerable situation for one who founded a preaching order. He then directed his energy to street preaching in New York City and to the publishing of *The Lamp* magazine. In the first issue, Fr. Paul stated that the magazine would be devoted to "the eternal principles of church unity" and professed: "We believe all that the Catholic Episcopate, in communion with the Apostolic See of Rome, believes, the dogmas of the Immaculate Conception and Papal infallibility not excepted. But we also believe in Anglican Orders and the perpetuity of the Anglican Church."

Reception into the Catholic Church

In 1909, the new Episcopal bishop of Delaware, Frederick Joseph Kinsman, told Fr. Paul that his position in regard to Roman claims and Anglican orders was an impossible one for an Episcopal clergyman and advised him to make a choice between the two Churches. The bishop advised him to "give up Anglican Orders, make an unqualified submission to the Latin Church, and be a good Roman Catholic." Fr. Paul believed that he had convincing evidence of God's will as to what he should do. Subsequently, he petitioned the pope for a corporate reception of the society into the Roman Catholic Church and asked for papal "sanction, protection and governance, in order that the name and institute (Society of the Atonement), which we believe we have derived from Our Lord Jesus Christ, may be confirmed to us by His Vicar." The response from Rome was to allow the first corporate reception into the Roman Church since the Reformation. Fr. Paul was required to take a course of studies at Dunwoodie, the Roman Catholic seminary in New York, and was ordained a Roman Catholic priest in 1911.

In the years that followed, Fr. Paul sought to build up his small community at Graymoor on the Hudson River. He endured immense trials in this endeavor, but his faith in a covenantal promise that his religious community would endure enabled him to stay the course. This same faith and the desire to proclaim the gospel of reconciliation and peace everywhere led him to develop original and creative ways to promote his message. From its inception, Graymoor had been a place of hospitality to all people, but especially the indigent. Fr. Paul eventually provided shelter for the homeless men who came to Graymoor, men whom he called "Christophers" or Christ-bearers in respect for their human dignity. This original shelter developed into St. Christopher's Inn where no restrictions about race, creed, or color were ever set. This effort symbolized Fr. Paul's great love for people and his deep desire that every person be reconciled with self, with society, and with God. This original effort led his community of Franciscan friars to a powerful commitment to the ministry of alcoholic and drug rehabilitation which continues to the present day.

The founder of the Franciscan Friars of the Atonement perceived the importance of employing every possible form of communication to propagate At-One-Ment among people. His passion for the unity of the Christian Churches did not restrict itself to the pen alone. In 1935 he gave his full support to the work of one of his friars, Anselm De Pasca, in developing a radio program called *The Ave Maria Hour* which would dramatize the lives of Christian saints. For Fr. Paul electronic journalism was one more way to break down the barriers erected by ignorance, prejudice, and hatred. This project was an immediate success and for thirty-five years, it brought a message of reconciliation to people of many faiths and none.

Fr. Paul died on February 8, 1940, at his beloved Graymoor in the foothills of the Catskills. His conviction and faith in the reconciling power of the Spirit enabled him to do much for the cause of Christian unity. He knew the difficulties and barriers to ecumenical progress but early in his career, while still an Anglican, he wrote: "Were the mountains of difficulty to be surmounted a thousand times higher and vaster than they are, God is able to cast them into the sea. Faith serenely rests her case with God."

TIMOTHY MacDONALD, S.A.

WEHRLE, VINCENT (1855–1941)

The first bishop of Bismarck, North Dakota. Vincent Wehrle was born in Berg, St. Gall, Switzerland, on December 19, 1855. As a Benedictine monk of Einsiedeln, he volunteered for a new foundation in Arkansas in 1882. Later, as an assistant to Bishop Martin Marty, O.S.B., in Dakota Territory, he was assigned to Devils Lake (1888), where his "parish" consisted of all the Catholic settlers along the Great Northern Railroad for two hundred miles.

Although he was indefatigable in his pastoral travels, Wehrle's ideal of Benedictine stability caused him to

Vincent Wehrle

found a small monastery as a base of operations. When the Germans from Russia and Hungary flooded into North Dakota after 1890, Bishop Shanley asked Wehrle to move his little community to Richardton in the German zone in Stark Country (1899). As abbot of St. Mary's, Wehrle built a huge European-style church and monastery that was eventually to bankrupt those who tried to pay for it (1924).

In his dealings with the German Catholics, however, Wehrle was extremely successful. He was so successful, in fact, that they began to invoke his name against Bishop Shanley. A potential crisis was defused when the latter died in 1909; moreover, Wehrle himself was named head of the newly created Diocese of Bismarck (1910). In his long career as bishop, Wehrle continued to function as a simple missionary, sometimes ignoring canon law and diocesan boundaries to the intense irritation of Bishop Reilly of Fargo.

While Wehrle was devoted to the small farmers of his diocese, he never understood the forces that conspired to keep them poor and dependent on outside bankers. When state politicians tried to counteract these oppressive conditions with innovative measures, Wehrle denounced their efforts as socialism (1919). No doubt because of his disastrous financial history at Richardton, Wehrle was never able to arrange financing for a new cathedral at Bismarck, but he is remembered as a selfless and ardent missionary in the pattern of his model, St. Boniface. He died in Bismarck on November 2, 1941.

Kardong, Terrence. *Prairie Church*. Bismarck, 1985, 52–76.

TERRENCE KARDONG, O.S.B.

WEIGEL, GUSTAVE (1906–64)

Jesuit priest and ecumenist. Gustave Weigel was born in Buffalo, New York, on January 15, 1906. His parents had immigrated to the United States from Alsace in 1902. Gustave was the second of three children, the first of whom died in infancy.

Gustave Weigel

He entered the Jesuit novitiate in 1922 at St. Andrew-on-Hudson near Poughkeepsie, New York, and studied for the priesthood at Woodstock College, Maryland, from 1926 until 1934. He became particularly interested in the works of Immanuel Kant and Joseph Maréchal.

Weigel did graduate studies in dogmatic theology at the Pontifical Gregorian University in Rome between 1935 and 1937. He received his S.T.D. degree after completing his dissertation on the fifth-century theologian Faustus of Riez. Because his scholarship was not judged completely satisfactory, Weigel, who had initially been considered as a potential member of the faculty at the Gregorian University, was instead assigned to teach dogmatic theology at The Catholic University of Chile in Santiago where he served from 1937 to 1948.

He reportedly charmed both Catholics and Protestants in the English and American communities in Santiago, but Weigel's extensive popularity led to his removal from Chile. He simply did not fit the mold of the Chilean Jesuits.

Weigel returned to the United States in 1948. A new impetus was given for his work when John Courtney Murray invited him to become the specialist in Protestant theology for *Theological Studies*. Weigel wrote extensive articles, analyzing the writings of Protestant theologians and Protestant ecclesial structures, becoming a major pioneer in the promotion of ecumenism in the United States.

He became professor of ecclesiology at Woodstock College in 1949 and of fundamental theology in 1951. He served there until his death in 1964.

His theology of the Church was considered traditional except for his emphasis on the Church as Mystery. He stressed that the Roman Catholic Church, as the Mystical Body of Christ, is a divinely instituted society and that the truth of that claim could best be demonstrated by the moral miracle of the Church's united and effective existences in the world.

From 1954 on, Weigel became an activist, speaking and writing extensively on behalf of ecumenism. Ecumenism for him was, above all, a conversation between differing brothers, leading to a type of unity which only God could give to the Church. Frequently, Weigel mentioned three solutions to unity: compromise, comprehension, and conversation.

Weigel served as a consultor to the Secretariat for Promoting Christian Unity during the preparatory period for the Second Vatican Council. He said he was not initially optimistic about the council's chances for Church renewal but that he took new hope from the positive, pastoral, and ecumenical approach of Pope John XXIII. The third session in 1963, under Pope Paul VI, brought a return of pessimism to Weigel, who was exhausted by the divisive debates and their meager results that were "not good enough but far better than we deserved."

He decided against returning for the fourth session. He died in New York City on January 3, 1964, shortly after returning from the council. He is buried at the Jesuit cemetery in Woodstock.

Collins, Patrick. *A Pioneer for Reform.* Collegeville: The Liturgical Press, 1990.

STEPHENIE OVERMAN

WENINGER, FRANCIS XAVIER (1805–88)

Missionary and writer. Weninger was born in Styria, Austria, on October 31, 1805. He studied theology at the University of Vienna, was ordained, and received a doctorate of divinity in 1830. While a professor at the University of Graz, he resigned in 1832 to enter the Jesuits. The 1848 suppression of the Society in Austria led Weninger to emigrate to the United States where he greatly boosted the sagging Jesuit mission band.

From a base in Cincinnati, he traveled widely and became a great influence in the German-American community. He was known for his direct style and was considered the premier Jesuit revivalist whom German, French, and Irish pastors called upon for missions. He often preached in three different languages at one mission, demonstrating his versatility. In his autobiography Weninger referred to the mission as an event "intended to produce repentance and to convert the contrite sinner." As a non-native himself, he incorporated the immigrant experience into his preaching with emphasis on the need for temperance. As an itinerant preacher, his appeal ran from the small rural community to the large urban parish. It is estimated that he traveled over 200,000 miles and preached over 800 missions in 40 years.

Weninger was a prolific writer on catechetics, apologetics, and liturgy. One collection of Jesuit writings lists fifty-six titles written in German, Latin, and English. He was active and preached missions until he was eighty. He died in Cincinnati on June 29, 1888.

RICHARD GRIBBLE, C.S.C.

WEST VIRGINIA, CATHOLIC CHURCH IN

Early Centers of Catholicism

The Diocese of Wheeling-Charleston, West Virginia, now includes the entire state of West Virginia, but, at its formation in 1850 it had another name and configuration. Founded before the state of West Virginia itself (1863), the Diocese of Wheeling-Charleston was originally part of the Diocese of Richmond, which had been established in 1820. Virginia had few early Catholic settlers because of the anti-Catholic atmosphere, but gradually the situation improved, and Catholic settlers, most of them Irish immigrants, began to trickle into the state.

Western Virginia had a natural mountainous barrier which separated it from the tidewater, and it developed along different lines. The two fastest growing regions in what is now West Virginia were the Northern and Eastern Panhandles, with Wheeling and Shepherdstown as key cities. Wheeling on the Ohio River was the terminus for the National Road in 1818 and this attracted industry, provided jobs, and drew immigrants, especially German and Irish Catholics. By 1822 a brick Gothic church was erected, said to be the first on Virginia soil, and served by a priest from Pittsburgh. In the Eastern Panhandle, Richard McSherry had settled near Shepherdstown and his home became the focus of the Catholic population there.

The 1830s saw a spurt of growth in both Panhandles and the emergence of a great priest, Richard Vincent Whelan of Baltimore. In 1841 he became head of the new Virginia diocese. Because of travel difficulties and the far-flung regions of his see, in 1846 Bishop Whelan took up residence at Wheeling, after Richmond, the second most industrialized city in the state. He built a new, larger church, St. James, and in 1848 he brought the Sisters of the Visitation to set up a girls' school. The bishop began a new church at Parkersburg, opened a local seminary, and begged money from Europe to finance his expansion.

New Diocese Created

Because of the vastness of the Richmond diocese, Bishop Whelan petitioned Rome to divide it along the natural barrier of the Alleghany Mountains, and on July 19, 1850, Pope Pius IX erected the Diocese of Wheeling, Virginia. Bishop Whelan chose to take over the new western see. It contained 29,172 square miles, 5,000 Catholics, 4 churches (Wheeling, Weston, Summersville, Wytheville), and 6 priests. In 1850 there was also the need for a hospital in heavily industrialized Wheeling, and so the bishop established Wheeling Hospital. In 1853 he brought in the Sisters of St. Joseph from Carondelet, Missouri, to staff the institution, and in 1860 set them up as the first diocesan religious congregation.

With the increased building of roads and railroads in the state, aided by the Irish potato famine and discontent in Germany, the Catholic population continued to increase. This was a difficult time for the Church in the United States because of the Know-Nothing movement, and in 1854 papal diplomat Gaetano Bedini journeyed to Wheeling as part of his American fact-finding tour. A mob gathered at the cathedral and Irish Catholics with guns protected Bedini.

With the outbreak of the Civil War in 1861, the Diocese and the State of Virginia were caught in a tug of war between Northern and Southern sympathy. Bishop Whelan worked to maintain his neutrality and hold the Church together. In June of 1863, President Lincoln proclaimed the new state of West Virginia, and the Wheeling and Richmond dioceses found themselves with parts of two states under their jurisdiction. It was not until 1974 that the two swapped counties, simplifying boundaries, and the Wheeling diocese added the capital city of Charleston to its name.

During the Civil War, Wheeling Hospital, the only medical facility between Pittsburgh and Cincinnati, played a prominent part in ministering to soldiers of both North and South. In 1864 the hospital was taken over by the United States government and six Sisters of St. Joseph were enrolled as army nurses.

In 1869–70, Bishop Whelan attended the First Vatican Council and addressed the assembly twice. He had been head of the diocese for twenty-four years when he died in 1874. At the time, there were 18,000 Catholics, 45 churches, and 29 priests. He and the other diocesan bishops are buried in a chapel at Wheeling's Mt. Calvary Cemetery.

Bishop Kain and Bishop Donohue

The second bishop of Wheeling was a thirty-four-year-old pastor from the Shenandoah Valley who had been active in ministering to those devastated by the war—John J. Kain. When appointed to the diocese in 1875, he was the youngest bishop in the country. Bishop Kain was called on to address the debt left by the needs of a rapidly expanding pioneer diocese and yet continue to meet the religious demands of an increasing population. In 1893 Bishop Kain was appointed archbishop of St. Louis where he served for ten years, dying in 1903.

The man who succeeded Bishop Kain was Patrick J. Donahue, rector of the cathedral parish in Baltimore where he often served as secretary to Cardinal Gibbons. A native of England, Bishop Donahue earned a law degree from Columbia University before entering the priesthood. For twenty-eight years he guided the Church in West Virginia through a time of booming industrial growth and an exploding immigrant population. The oil and gas industries, lumbering, and coal provided jobs. Towns and coal camps sprang up almost overnight. Slovaks and Poles, Hungarians and Italians immigrated in search of a better life, swelling the Catholic communities. The bishop brought in more priests and brothers—the Marists, Capuchin friars, Xaverian Brothers—to staff schools and new parishes. Religious orders of women—the Sisters of Our Lady of Charity of Refuge, the Carmelites, the Felicians, and the Pallotines—were invited to work among the people. Hospitals were established and orphanages opened. In 1904, Miss Sara Tracy, a wealthy woman from New York, left the diocese a sizable bequest which helped sustain the expanding programs and continues to provide important revenue to the present day.

Bishop Swint and Bishop Hodges

When Bishop Donahue died in 1922, the Catholic population had grown to 67,000. The man who succeeded him, John J. Swint, was a native West Virginian who would head the diocese for forty years. During his tenure the Catholic population expanded to 109,373. Of necessity, he too was a builder. New institutions or parishes were left untouched. In 1954 the bishop founded Wheeling College, staffed by the Jesuits, the only Catholic institution of higher learning in the state. In 1951 Bishop Thomas J. McDonnell of New York arrived to assist Bishop Swint as coadjutor, but McDonnell died suddenly in 1961. To replace him, a native West Virginian, Joseph H. Hodges of Harpers Ferry, then auxiliary bishop of Richmond, was appointed coadjutor with the right of succession. Bishop Swint died in 1962 and Bishop Hodges was to lead the Church of West Virginia through one of its most challenging and exciting periods. The bishop created diocesan offices and commissions to implement new conciliar directives. Lay involvement in Church affairs grew more vigorous and in 1968 the First Lay Congress was convened. To address problems of poverty and powerlessness, in 1975, at Wheeling College, the bishops of Appalachia promulgated their joint pastoral letter, "This Land is Home to Me." Bishop Hodges attempted to establish a Catholic presence in every county of West Virginia, and built four pastoral centers in strategic locations.

Bishop Schulte and Bishop Schmitt

When Bishop Hodges died in January 1985, he was succeeded by Francis Bible Schulte of Philadelphia. Installed in July 1985, Bishop Schulte vigorously supported the work of the diocesan schools and stressed the fostering of priestly and religious vocations. He also began a restructuring of diocesan offices. Schulte was assisted in his efforts by Bernard W. Schmitt, a native West Virginian, who was appointed auxiliary bishop on May 31, 1988. On December 13, 1988, Bishop Schulte was appointed archbishop of New Orleans, and on March 30, 1989, Bishop Schmitt was appointed seventh bishop of the Diocese of Wheeling-Charleston.

Evangelization has always been a key issue in West Virginia where almost 60 percent of the people are classified as "unchurched." In a 1995 population of 1,793,477, there were 106,779 Catholics, approximately 6 percent of the total. The diocese appointed a public affairs representative at the state capital to represent its interests in such areas as abortion and capital punishment legislation.

Ecumenism continues to be at the forefront of diocesan initiatives. The four bishops of West Virginia, Episcopal, Lutheran, Methodist, and Roman Catholic, meet several times a year to express a common voice on important matters. In 1994 they issued a pastoral, "Health and Wellness in Our Time." Mary Virginia DeRoo was the first Catholic to be elected president of the West Virginia Council of Churches.

The Catholic Church in West Virginia looks to the many social as well as spiritual needs of the people. The Office of Catholic Community Services is the second largest provider of social services in the state. A multiyear diocesan process of reorganization was begun to better utilize diocesan resources and revitalize parish life in view of decreasing resources and personnel. In 1995 there were 198 priests and 313 women religious serving in the state's 24,282 square miles. The Church sponsors four Catholic hospitals and eight high schools, together with many other institutions, rooting God's presence in the West Virginia hills.

Centennial: Diocese of Wheeling, 1850–1950. Wheeling: West Virginia Register, 1950.

Mauer, B. B., and Keith A. Mehleman. *Mission in the Mountain State.* Parsons: McClain Printing Company, 1981.

MARGARET BRENNAN

WHITE, ANDREW (1579–1656)

Jesuit missionary. White was born in or near London, England, on December 27, 1579. Educated at the English colleges in Valladolid and Seville, Spain, and Douai, Spanish Netherlands, he was ordained as a secular priest in 1605 and sent to work in the English Mission. In the aftermath of the failed Gunpowder Plot (1605), White, together with forty-five other priests, was arrested and banished from England. In 1606 he traveled to Louvain, Belgium, where he entered the Jesuit novitiate. He was sent back to the English Mission in 1609 and later taught theology for the Jesuits at their colleges in Valladolid, Louvain, and Liège.

He is credited with writing the *Declaratio Coloniae Domini Baronis de Baltimore,* a pamphlet that was later revised and published by Cecil Calvert, the second Lord Baltimore, to attract settlers to Maryland. Together with fellow Jesuits Fr. John Altham and Br. Thomas Gervase, he set sail in 1633 on the *Ark* and *Dove* with the original expedition. White built a chapel in the colony's first capital and founded the Jesuit Mission at St. Inigoes. By 1639 he had established a mission among the neighboring Native American tribes and translated a grammar, dictionary, and catechism into the Algonquian dialect. Political unrest in 1645 led to the temporary overthrow of Lord Baltimore's government. Catholic chapels were ransacked and White and his fellow Jesuit, Thomas Copley, were arrested and sent back to England in chains to be tried under English penal laws. Although acquitted of all charges, he was immediately banished. Unable to return to Maryland, White labored as a missionary in southern England under an assumed name until his death. He is referred to as the "Apostle of Maryland," and a statue to commemorate his labors was erected in St. Mary's City. He died in England on December 27, 1656.

Tierney, Richard H., S.J. "Father Andrew White, S.J., and the Indians." *Historical Records and Studies* 15 (1921) 89–103.

TRICIA T. PYNE

WHITE, EDWARD DOUGLASS (1845–1921)

Chief justice of the United States. Born in the parish of LaFourche, Louisiana, on November 3, 1845, White studied at Mt. St. Mary College, Emmittsburg, Maryland; Loyola College, New Orleans, Louisiana; and Georgetown College, Washington, D.C. He left school at fifteen to serve in the Confederate army during the Civil War. Captured in 1863, he was paroled until the war was over, when he studied law as an apprentice to Edward Bermudez. Admitted to the Louisiana bar in 1868, White practiced law privately and became involved in politics. Elected state senator in 1874 and 1876, he was named associate justice of the Louisiana Supreme Court in 1878. When the court was reconstituted and his term ended in 1881, White retired to his private practice, but remained active in civic projects, including the founding of Tulane University in New Orleans. Elected to the United States Senate in 1891, White served until 1894 when he was appointed to the U.S. Supreme Court by President Grover Cleveland. The same year he married Leita Montgomery Kent.

Edward D. White

White spent twenty-seven years on the Court, and was named chief justice in 1910 by President William Howard Taft. Considered a conservative, he wrote some seven hundred opinions, including those dealing with the Insular Cases and the Interstate Commerce Acts. Also significant were White's "rule of reason" decisions in the Standard Oil and American Tobacco Company cases. A recipient of the University of Notre Dame's Laetare Medal in 1914, White died in Washington, D.C., on May 19, 1921.

Highsaw, Robert B. *Edward Douglass White: Defender of the Conservative Faith.* Baton Rouge, 1981.
Klinkhamer, M. C. *Edward Douglass White: Chief Justice of the United States.* Washington, 1943.

K. N. McCARTHY

WILLIAMS, EDWARD BENNETT (1920–88)

Attorney. Edward Bennett Williams was born in Hartford, Connecticut, on May 31, 1920. He graduated *summa cum laude* from the College of the Holy Cross in 1941 and served in the Army Air Corps in World War II. He was also a graduate of Georgetown University Law School.

Williams was founder of the prominent Washington law firm of Williams & Connolly, an owner of the Washington Redskins football team, and was owner of the Baltimore Orioles baseball team at the time of his death.

Time magazine once called him "the country's top criminal lawyer." A guiding principle of his life was what he called "contest living," a system in which success depends only on winning, not just on doing one's best. Although the only public office he ever held was membership on the Foreign Intelligence Advisory Board, Williams was considered among the most influential people in the United States. He was on personal terms with every president from John F. Kennedy to Ronald Reagan and had important connections in business and in the press.

He was a national treasurer of the Democratic Party, and was one of the leaders of a move to deny the Democratic nomination to President Jimmy Carter in 1980. President Gerald Ford asked him to be director of Central Intelligence in 1975, and Reagan offered him the same job in 1987. He said he declined the first time because of ill health. But as a member of the Intelligence Advisory Board, since abolished, he was privy to an unlimited range of the country's secrets.

During his career in Washington, Williams attended Mass each morning at Trinity Church. After his death he left two million dollars to the College of the Holy Cross in Worcester, Massachusetts, two million dollars to Georgetown University, and one million dollars to the Archdiocese of Washington.

"He had a low tolerance for people who don't work hard," said Fr. John E. Brooks, who was president of the College of the Holy Cross when Williams was chairman of the board. "When we discussed building on campus, he would say, 'You're either churning up earth or you're standing still.'" He received honorary degrees from Fairfield University, Loyola University in Chicago, Mt. St. Mary's College, and St. Joseph's College, both in Emmitsburg, Maryland.

He began his law practice in Washington in 1944. Clients ranged from giant corporations such as The Washington Post Company to celebrities such as Frank Sinatra and William F. Buckley. He also represented some of the most notorious figures of the day, including Senator Joseph R. McCarthy, the Red-baiting Republican senator from Wisconsin; Frank Costello, the New York Mafia leader; James R. Hoffa, the president of the Teamsters Union; and stock swindler Robert Vesco.

Williams died on August 13, 1988, at Georgetown University Hospital at the age of sixty-eight.

Thomas, Evan. *The Man to See, Edward Bennett Williams.* New York, 1991.

STEPHENIE OVERMAN

WILLIAMS, JOHN (1822–1907)

Archbishop. John Joseph Williams was born in Boston, April 27, 1822, of Irish parents. After attending public school and Bishop Benedict Fenwick's "house seminary," he was sent to the Sulpician seminary in Montreal, and then to the major seminary in Paris where he was ordained a priest in 1845. When he returned to Boston, Bishop John Fitzpatrick made him vicar general and assigned him as rector of St. James Church where, in 1842, he established

John J. Williams

the first Conference of St. Vincent de Paul in New England. In January 1866 he was named coadjutor, and became the fourth bishop of Boston upon Fitzpatrick's death the following month.

At the time of Williams' accession, Boston had become the second largest diocese in the country, with 109 churches, 116 priests, and a Catholic population of some 300,000 souls. The new bishop separated the five western counties of the state into the new Diocese of Springfield, and turned the three southeastern counties into the Diocese of Providence. Nevertheless, Boston continued to grow at such a rate that in 1875 it was made an archdiocese with Williams as its metropolitan.

A quiet, conservative prelate, known best as an administrator, Williams presided over a Catholic population that expanded from 400,000 in 1887 to 600,000 in 1896. For the growing Irish population he dedicated at least eight to ten new churches each year, brought in nine religious orders of brothers and sisters, and in 1880 formally established a parochial school system. For French-Canadians moving into the areas of Lowell and Lawrence, he furnished French-speaking priests; for Portuguese and Cape Verdeans in the Fall River and New Bedford areas, he provided Portuguese priests. During the late 1880s and early 1890s, to accommodate new waves of immigrants from Italy, Poland, Lithuania, and Syria, he provided parishes in which their native languages were spoken.

In addition to his duties in Boston, Archbishop Williams traveled extensively throughout the United States and made many visits to Rome where his thoughtful and moderate views were often sought on troublesome questions. Early in 1905 Bishop William Henry O'Connell was named as coadjutor for the eighty-four-year-old Williams who was in poor health after an episcopacy of forty years. He was still attending to his official functions, however, until his death on August 30, 1907. He was buried in the crypt of the massive new cathedral he had completed in 1875 in Boston's South End.

See also MASSACHUSETTS, CATHOLIC CHURCH IN.

Corr, Bernard, ed. *Memoirs of the Twenty-Fifth Anniversary of the Consecration of the Most Rev. John J. Williams, D.D., Archbishop of Boston.* Boston, 1891.

Lord, Robert H., John E. Sexton and Edward Harrington. *History of the Archdiocese of Boston,* 3 vols. Boston, 1945. III:3–437.

THOMAS H. O'CONNOR

WILLIAMS, MARY LOU (1910–81)

Jazz pianist, composer, arranger. Mary Lou Williams was long considered to be the single most important woman musician in jazz. Her playing and her composing, moreover, had, by the later period in her career, brought her into the front rank of all jazz musicians, no matter what the category. She was fond of pointing out that she had lived and played through various eras in the history of jazz—playing the new music of each era, a claim that is difficult to dispute. She was entirely self-taught, had perfect pitch, was musically astute and advanced; announced that her mother had never allowed a teacher to interfere with her but had exposed her to actual musicians whenever they turned up; and often spent twelve hours at a stretch playing the piano when she was only a child.

Early Years

She was born in Atlanta, Georgia, on May 8, 1910. Her mother was Virginia Riser; her father Joseph Scruggs. There were seven Riser sisters. As part of the great black migration, all seven sisters traveled north—some fanning out to Philadelphia, Pennsylvania, and others in a slightly more westward direction to Pittsburgh. Family lore has it that Mary Lou made the journey in the horn of an RCA Victor victrola. Her mother played an old-fashioned pump organ, often holding Mary Lou on her lap to keep her out of mischief. One day while her mother was pumping up the organ, little Mary Lou's fingers beat hers to the keyboard and picked out a melody. Mary Lou was three. Later in life in her lectures and demonstrations, she would often point out the great value of learning through observation. "I watch," she would tell her students.

By the age of six, Mary Lou was professional enough to be known throughout Pittsburgh as "The Little Piano Girl" and was playing parties for white society people such as the Olivers and the Mellons. Gradually, she also played with the Union Band in Pittsburgh, as well as with Earl Hines' musicians, McKinney's Cotton Pickers with Don Redmond, or other musicians as they traveled through Pittsburgh. One day a black vaudeville unit, Buzz n' Harris' *Hits and Bits,* came to town. Its piano player was among the missing. The producer was told by a local, "I know someone who can play your show for you." He was taken out to East Liberty, the black suburb of Pittsburgh, and was told, "There she is," pointing to a little girl playing hopscotch. Incensed, Mr. Harris began to leave, but was persuaded to stay and to hum the score to Mary Lou, who played the show that night and also traveled with the unit that summer, mostly in the Midwest and South, on the TOBA circuit. She may have been as young as thirteen.

Professional Career

The pit band was led by John Williams who also played alto sax and baritone sax. Mary Lou Burley (after a stepfather) remained with *Hits and Bits* for a good while; wound up marrying John Williams in Memphis in 1926; traveled on the BF Keith Circuit with Seymour and Jeanette in Big Time vaudeville; recorded with John Williams' Syncopators in 1926 and 1927 in Chicago; stayed behind in Memphis to continue leading the band while her husband went to Tulsa, Oklahoma, to join Andy Kirk and His Clouds of Joy. After a short period she rejoined her husband and, again replacing a missing pianist, recorded with the Clouds of Joy in 1929 and 1930, though she was not yet an official member of the band. She wrote her first arrangements for these recording sessions, including *Messa Stomp* and *Mary's Idea,* and appeared, to full advantage, as a strong two-fisted swinging stride pianist with the band. She also made the first recording under her own name in 1930: *Nite Life* on one side and *Drag 'Em* on the other. She was not yet twenty.

Mary Lou Williams remained with Andy Kirk and His Clouds of Joy from 1929 to 1942—the bulk of the swing era in jazz. Not only did she play piano, appearing on more than 180 recordings with Kirk's orchestra, she also composed and arranged the music for many of those sides. Her most important compositions of the period include: *Walkin' and Swingin', Froggy Bottom, Little Joe from Chicago, What's Your Story Morning Glory?, Steppin' Pretty,* and the beautiful *Big Jim Blues.* During the same period she wrote two compositions for Benny Goodman's Big Band: *Camel Hop* and the boogie-woogie based *Roll 'Em* which became quite popular for Goodman. Decca also recorded Miss Williams separately as a pianist with rhythm accompaniment in 1936 and 1938. The title of one of them, *Swinging for Joy,* is just right.

Miss Williams left Andy Kirk in 1942, returning first to Pittsburgh to her sister's (Mamie Floyd's) house to rest.

She then formed a smaller musical group (seven pieces) that included Harold Baker, the trumpeter, who became Miss Williams' second husband, and a youthful Pittsburgh native, the drummer Art Blakey.

By 1943 Miss Williams was in New York, and from that time forward she developed into a highly skillful solo pianist who also wrote for various small combinations of musicians, and occasionally for big bands. In 1944 Duke Ellington recorded her arrangement of Irving Berlin's *Blue Skies.*

In 1945 Mary Lou Williams composed *The Zodiac Suite,* writing harmonically advanced music not formerly associated with jazz. She recorded the suite for Asch Records with piano, bass, and drums. Later in 1945 Miss Williams scored the suite for small chamber orchestra and jazz instruments, premiering the work at Town Hall on December 31, 1945. The following June, she scored three sections of the suite for seventy pieces and played those sections with the New York Pops Orchestra at Carnegie Hall.

At the same time, a great musical shift was taking place in jazz as a whole. Charlie Parker and Dizzy Gillespie and others were inventing a new musical language for jazz later described as Be Bop or Modern Jazz. Mary Lou Williams was one of the few major names from the previous eras of Stride and Swing to make the successful transition to Bop. In 1947 she wrote two Bop-influenced pieces for Benny Goodman: *Lonely Moments* and *Whistle Blues.* In 1949 she wrote the bop fairy tale *In the Land of Oo Bla Dee* for Dizzy Gillespie's Big Band.

For the next few years, Miss Williams remained in New York, continuing to appear in clubs, in concert, and to record and compose. In 1952 she left for Europe for the first time. She had been hired to go to England to play with British musicians, thus breaking a ban preventing American and British musicians from playing together. A nine-day engagement stretched out to two years. She played in England, and at length in France (at the Boeuf sur le Toit and at a club named for her, Chez Mary Lou). She recorded for six different companies and also toured the continent.

Mary Lou Williams and Catholicism

Then one night in Paris in 1954 she walked away from two different jobs (an earlier one at a theater, and a later one in a club), even leaving her money behind. She withdrew into the country to the home of the grandmother of a French drummer she knew. Earlier in England, she had been at a party where an American G.I. noticed that she seemed disturbed. He told her to read the Ninety-First Psalm. She remembered things in a different way. She thought he had said, "Read the Psalms," and so she read all of them. A significant new period in the life of Mary Lou Williams had begun. Mary Lou Williams returned to

New York in late 1954. In early 1955 she recorded an album for Jazztone and then went into a long period of seclusion and prayer.

During the beginning of this period, Miss Williams sought to pray in various churches. At one point she was a member of Adam Clayton Powell's Abyssinian Baptist Church in Harlem. In her search, she found that Our Lady of Lourdes, a Roman Catholic Church near her apartment in Harlem, remained open at all hours. She went there to meditate and pray, preferring the chapel in the lower church. Through Barry Ulanov, who was a jazz critic and had written the first serious booklength study of Duke Ellington, and who was also a theologian and serious Catholic, Mary Lou Williams met the Rev. Anthony S. Woods, S.J. He began to give Miss Williams and Lorraine Gillespie, the wife of the musician Dizzy Gillespie, instruction in the Catholic faith.

Mary Lou Williams was baptized into the Catholic Church in 1956 at the Church of St. Ignatius Loyola on Park Avenue in New York. Ulanov was her godfather. Fr. Woods remained her good friend, spiritual director, and guide. It was he, together with other priests, including Fr. John Crowley who had been a musician himself, who encouraged Mary Lou Williams to return to music. For more than two and a half years she had not struck a note or written a measure, as she turned deeply inward to respond to the grace of conversion. It should be noted that Miss Williams had never been a churchgoer prior to 1955; though she carried a small white leatherbound Bible all during the 1930s and beyond, she never opened it. Her mother did attend church occasionally, and even played the organ for the church, but Miss Williams did not. On the other hand, her older sister, Mamie, had been baptized a Catholic when a child.

Jazz and Sacred Music

In 1957 Mary Lou Williams appeared with the Dizzy Gillespie Big Band at the Newport Festival in Rhode Island playing three sections of her *Zodiac Suite* in new arrangements. She continued to appear and work intermittently during the next dozen years, all the while developing into an ever more mature artist. She formed her own recording company (Mary Records) in 1962, as well as a music publishing company (Cecilia Music Publishing, in honor of the patron saint of music). In 1963 she released an important album consisting of six piano works and four choral compositions with sacred themes. One was an *a capella* piece, *Black Christ of the Andes (Hymn in Honor of St. Martin de Porres),* with a short solo piano interlude. Harmonically dense, requiring singers with perfect pitch, and reverently moving, it had lyrics by Anthony S. Woods, S.J.

During this time Mary Lou Williams formed the Bel Canto Foundation. Ten percent of all her earnings from music went directly into this foundation. Its purpose was to help in rehabilitating musicians who were hobbled by alcohol or drugs. To raise funds Miss Williams operated a series of two thrift shops: the first was located on East 29th Street near Bellevue Hospital in New York City; when she lost that, she established a second on Amsterdam Avenue in Harlem. She ran the thrift shops herself, had a small piano installed, and could be found there by customers and musicians alike. She often took troubled people around the corner to Our Lady of Lourdes for meditation and prayer. She helped with cash, with prayer, and with encouragement, prodding musicians into playing with her in the store. Her life combined the deeply interior aspect of prayer and the deeply soulful experience of creating music. It was creative prayer in action.

She founded the Pittsburgh Jazz Festival at this time, sponsored by the Catholic Youth Organization of the diocese and her good friend, John Cardinal Wright, then bishop of Pittsburgh. In 1964 she met another Jesuit, Peter F. O'Brien, S.J., who was to remain her friend for the rest of her life and who became her personal manager, seeing to all the details of an active career in the professional world of music, in the Church, and also as an educator.

To the program of a concert held at Carnegie Hall in 1967 entitled *Praise the Lord in Many Voices,* Miss Williams contributed three stunning pieces: *Thank You, Jesus;* a brilliant version of the Lord's Prayer, *Pater Noster,* for solo voice, mixed chorus, and instruments; and a thunderous *Praise the Lord.* In early 1967 she wrote the first extended sacred composition: *Mass I.* She wrote and developed the music while teaching at Seton High School in Pittsburgh and the work received its premiere at St. Paul's Cathedral in Pittsburgh with Bishop Wright celebrating and the girls from Seton High School singing with Miss Williams at the piano.

In 1968 the Church of St. Thomas the Apostle in Harlem asked Mary Lou Williams to write some music for Lent. She responded with her second Mass: *Mass for the Lenten Season.* In addition to various texts, as well as the common, Miss Williams composed two motets using the words of Martin Luther King, Jr.: *I Have a Dream* and *Tell Them Not to Talk Too Long.* The music was performed by an instrumental ensemble with Miss Williams at the piano, together with a choir of teenagers from the church, and several jazz vocal soloists, for the six Sundays of Lent.

During 1968 and 1969, Mary Lou Williams returned to Europe on a number of occasions: to perform in concert in England; to open a club in Denmark where she remained for more than six months; and to live and tour in Italy for a period of time. Miss Williams wanted to play one of her Masses in a church in Rome. She also wanted to play for the pope to show him the spiritual contents of jazz, which, she pointed out, had been born of the suffering of a whole race of people, making it an apt music for praising God.

Things moved forward in Rome for a performance of the Mass, arranged with the help of Rev. Vincent T. O'Keefe, S.J., and the Benedictine abbot, Rembert Weakland. A chorus was assembled from the seminarians at the North American College in Rome. But news of the jazz Mass reached quarters in Rome that found the idea displeasing. The music was not heard at Mass but in a concert in the church—not the same thing. The cancellation and switch made news around the world. During that same visit in 1969, Msgr. Joseph Gremillion, who headed the Institute for Justice and Peace at the Vatican, handed the texts for the Votive Mass for Peace to Miss Williams. These texts and carefully expanded texts for the Common of the Mass formed the literary basis for Miss Williams' third and most well-known Mass, *Music for Peace,* which she recorded for her own label. The work was later renamed *Mary Lou's Mass* by the great choreographer Alvin Ailey who used the music for a series of dances of praise also called *Mary Lou's Mass.*

It is important to note that Mary Lou Williams' interior journey and conversion to Catholicism led to the composition of three complete Masses and more than a dozen other sacred works.

With Fr. Peter O'Brien, S.J., at her side, Miss Williams' involvement in her career became constant and intense. Extended engagements in clubs and in concert at universities or at jazz festivals were often mingled with preparation of choirs for performances of *Mary Lou's Mass.* A college appearance would often consist of a master class, a full concert with piano trio, a workshop demonstration with questions from the audience, radio appearances; all the while training the college glee club to sing the Mass, and then at the end a celebration of Mass by Fr. O'Brien with Miss Williams at the piano, and the chorus singing her music.

Later Years

Between 1971 and 1978 Mary Lou Williams recorded eight complete albums and contributed to three others. In 1977 she appeared twice at Carnegie Hall, once with the swing-era musician Benny Goodman, and three months later with the avant-garde pianist Cecil Taylor, giving some idea of her scope and versatility. Both concerts were recorded.

In the fall of that year Miss Williams entered the final period of her life and career. She accepted the position of artist-in-residence at Duke University in Durham, North Carolina. It was a deeply fulfilling period for her. She loved the students and they loved her. She received The Trinity Award, an award given directly by the vote of the students themselves to one faculty member. The period was active away from the campus as well: the recording of two fine albums for Pablo, one of them a live solo piano concert in Montreux, Switzerland; touring throughout the United States and in Europe; playing at the First White House Jazz Festival for President Carter in 1978; as well as the teaching and appearing in many North Carolina churches with her musical Masses.

Mary Lou Williams battled bladder cancer for the last two years of her life. She never complained. When she could no longer teach and play the piano, she continued to compose. Her last work remains incomplete—a work for a fifty-five-piece wind symphony plus piano trio called *The History of Jazz,* a history she largely lived and helped to create.

Mary Lou Williams died on May 28, 1981, in Durham, North Carolina. At her funeral in New York at the Church of St. Ignatius Loyola (where she had been baptized twenty-five years earlier), the musical world gathered. Dizzy Gillespie played, Benny Goodman and Andy Kirk were there. Fr. O'Brien celebrated the Mass, and excerpts from *Mary Lou's Mass* were sung. Her body was taken to Pittsburgh where another Mass was celebrated by Fr. O'Brien, with family and friends attending, in the Jesuit Church of SS Peter and Paul. She is buried in Calvary Cemetery in Pittsburgh, Pennsylvania.

See also AFRICAN AMERICAN CATHOLICS.

PETER F. O'BRIEN, S.J.

WILLIAMS, MICHAEL (1877–1950)

Author; editor. In any history of American Catholicism and the growing role of the laity, the layman and editor, Michael Williams, deserves a prominent place. He was born on February 5, 1877, in Halifax, Nova Scotia, and died in 1950 in Westport, Connecticut. A fine figure of a

Michael Williams

man, he excelled as a public speaker and as a firmly convinced editorialist. Several of his published books were widely read and appreciated. During a troubled quarter-century and more, Michael Williams' colorful career had an important impact on both Church and state.

As a youth Williams attended a Jesuit academy in New Brunswick, but his seafaring father's death forced him to leave school in order to support his family. It was while working in a warehouse in 1890 that he temporarily gave up the practice of his religious faith. But it was also during his five years' employment in the warehouse that he managed, with the help of a local bookseller, to become an avid reader.

Around the turn of the century Williams moved to Boston and began reporting for the *Boston Post* and later for the *New York World* and *Evening Telegram.* The next step in his rising journalistic career was his appointment as editor of the *San Francisco Examiner,* only to be thwarted by the catastrophic California earthquake of 1906.

By 1912 he and his family had moved to Carmel, California, where, thanks to his association with cloistered Carmelite nuns, he returned to the Church. In his 1918 *The Book of the High Romance,* Williams attributed his conversion to St. Thérèse, for whom thereafter he had a lifetime devotion. In 1919, in Washington, he was hired by the National Catholic War Council, which soon became the National Catholic Welfare Conference, and, in recent years, the National Council of Catholic Bishops. Under its auspices he brought out *American Catholics and the War* in 1921. The same year he was sent to Rome to cover the coronation of Pope Pius XI for the NCWC News Service.

In 1922 Williams began developing the idea of founding an intellectual weekly with a Catholic point of view, to parallel the influential *New Republic* and the *Nation.* Toward this objective he organized the Calvert Associates, a distinguished, articulate group of well-stationed supporters. At their meetings were four clergymen, including the future Bishop Francis C. Kelley of Oklahoma and Fr. Lawrason Riggs (who would serve as the Catholic chaplain at Yale), and several notable laymen, among them Professor Carlton J. H. Hayes of Columbia University and an Anglican, the distinguished Boston architect, Ralph Adams Cram.

These enthusiastic preliminaries led to the publication, in November 1924, of the first issue of *The Commonweal,* an independent, ecumenical, socially minded, lay-edited Catholic journal of opinion. The new weekly soon gained the respect of both the Catholic and the non-Catholic reading public, and, in the words of Rodger Van Allen, became "perhaps the most important symbol and achievement in the history of American Catholicism."

Williams served as editor of the magazine for fourteen years and attracted many notable authors such as G. K.

Chesterton, Walter Lippmann, Lewis Mumford, and Hilaire Belloc. He hired George N. Shuster who served as the managing editor until 1937 when he resigned over his differences with Williams on the Spanish Civil War. The magazine's recurrent need to appeal for funds hampered Williams' editorial efforts during his years as editor. Editorially, he consistently inveighed against such evils as the persecution of the Church in Mexico, the Catholic-bashing of his time, Communism, and the Nazis. After a mass meeting which he had convoked in May 1938 in Madison Square Garden in support of General Franco, *The Commonweal*'s editorial council dismissed Williams as editor, although he continued as a weekly columnist for five years more.

None of Michael Williams' zealous accomplishments and contributions to American Catholic history stand out in comparison with his founding of *The Commonweal,* which for over seventy years played a singular role in American Catholic journalism, providing an enduring Christian influence in American society. He died in Hartford, Connecticut, on October 12, 1950.

See also COMMONWEAL.

EDWARD SKILLIN

WILSON, SAMUEL, JR. (1911–93)

Architect, scholar, preservationist. Samuel Wilson, Jr., was born in New Orleans on August 6, 1911, the son of the senior Wilson and Stella Poupeney Wilson. Wilson grew up in the Carrollton section of the city and even as a youngster demonstrated a keen interest in architecture. At fifteen he entered Tulane University and received a degree in architecture in 1931. He first worked with Moise Goldstein on such projects as Dillard University. In 1934 Wilson formed a partnership with Richard Koch, a tie that lasted until Koch's death in 1971. Together the two men became leaders of the fledgling architectural-preservationist movement in the South.

Wishing to know more about the architectural gems of New Orleans, Wilson did extensive research in French archives during 1938. As a result, he began writing on the historical architecture of his city which over the span of his career produced 175 articles and books. Jean M. Farnsworth and Ann M. Masson compiled and edited many of Wilson's articles in a work entitled *The Architecture of Colonial Louisiana: Collected Essays of Samuel Wilson, Jr., FAIA* (Lafayette, La.: Center for Louisiana Studies, 1987). The book offers a complete bibliography of Wilson's scholarly production. Wilson is well known for his decades-long study of the life and work of Benjamin Latrobe, the architect of the U.S. Capitol and the White House. A reason for this interest may be found in the fact that Wilson married Latrobe's great-great-granddaughter, Ellen Elizabeth Latrobe, in 1951. The couple had no children.

Wilson's work as an architect can be seen throughout New Orleans and Louisiana. He is best remembered for his two restorations of the famed Cabildo, the Upper and Lower Pontalba Buildings, the French Market, the Pitot House, and his glorious restoration of St. Patrick's Church.

Wilson was the recipient of numerous awards, including the Order of St. Louis which was presented to him in recognition of his years of service to the Church in the Archdiocese of New Orleans. He was the cofounder of several preservationist organizations and was a fellow of the American Institute of Architects. Wilson died in New Orleans on October 21, 1993.

GLENN R. CONRAD

WIMMER, BONIFACE (1809–87)

United States archabbot, founder of first Benedictine community in the U.S.A. Wimmer was born on January 14, 1809, in Thalmassing, Bavaria, the son of Peter Wimmer and Elizabeth Lang Wimmer, and was baptized Sebastian. He was educated at the University of Munich and the Regensburg Seminary, and was ordained for the Diocese of Regensburg on July 31, 1831. After a year at the Marian shrine at Altötting, he entered the newly restored Benedictine monastery at Metten. He professed his solemn vows in 1833, taking the name Boniface, and held various positions in Bavaria for the next decade.

While a prefect at a Bavarian boardinghouse, he became interested in the missions among German immigrants in the United States. Peter Lemke, a German priest who had been working among German immigrants in Pennsylvania since 1834, offered Wimmer some land on which to

Boniface Wimmer

build a monastery. With a group of candidates for the priesthood and brotherhood, and some laity, Wimmer landed in New York in September 1846. In October the community moved to the Diocese of Pittsburgh, where Wimmer received from Bishop Michael O'Connor farmland in St. Vincent parish near Latrobe, Pennsylvania.

The community grew under Wimmer's direction and included a college, seminary—and a brewery. In 1852 it was made a priory, and in 1855 it was elevated to an abbey, with a community of 150 members. Wimmer was made abbot and the abbey was made the Cassinese Congregation of the Benedictine Order. This first Benedictine foundation in the U.S.A. evolved into the St. Vincent Archabbey, College, and Seminary.

Throughout his time as abbot (1855–83) and archabbot (1883–87), Wimmer sent priests throughout the country for missionary work among Germans. With support from King Ludwig I of Bavaria and the Ludwig Missionsverein, Wimmer established parishes and new Benedictine foundations. He was influential in fulfilling the desire of Leo XIII to unite all Benedictine houses into a single confederation. He did this by establishing or developing new communities in Collegeville, Minnesota (1856); Newark, New Jersey (1857); Atchison, Kansas (1857); Covington, Kentucky (1857); Texas (1859); Alabama (1875); and Belmont, North Carolina (1876). He also attended several of the provincial and plenary councils of Baltimore and Vatican Council I. He died at St. Vincent Archabbey on December 8, 1887.

Barry, Colman J., O.S.B. *Worship and Work: St. John's Abbey and University, 1856–1956.* Collegeville, Minnesota, 1956.

JOSEPH M. McLAFFERTY

WISCONSIN, CATHOLIC CHURCH IN

The development of Catholic life in the state of Wisconsin shares the characteristics of the emergence of organized Catholic life in other areas of the Upper Midwest. Indeed, its distinctive identity is coextensive with the emergence of the larger patterns of social and economic development in this region of the United States.

First Contacts

Wisconsin was Native American territory before the advent of Europeans. Ojibwe, Menominee, Winnebago, Sauk, Fox, and Miami all laid claim to parts of the land. Europeans patrolled the shores of Lake Michigan in search of water routes to the West. But it was the abundance of fur-bearing animals in the region that attracted French fur traders who established trading posts at Green Bay in the east and Prairie du Chien on the west, among other places. These traders came down the Fox River from Green Bay, portaged to the Wisconsin River, and traveled down to where it joined the Mississippi. Catholic missionaries, mostly Jesuits, would use these same commercial routes to spread the renewed Catholic faith of the Counter-Reformation to the indigenous peoples. It would be south of this Fox/Wisconsin axis, which ran diagonally down the state, that the majority of settlement would take place in Wisconsin and where the Catholic community would be planted and flourish.

The first European to enter Wisconsin was Jean Nicolet who appeared in 1634. In 1656 French fur traders began operations around Lake Superior and in 1660, Jesuit missionary René Menard arrived to take up work among the Hurons who had fled to Wisconsin. When Menard perished in the wilderness somewhere below present-day Goodrich, he was replaced by a fellow Jesuit, Fr. Claude Allouez, who arrived in October 1665. He resided at the trading base on Chequamegon Bay on Lake Superior and there established a chapel dedicated to the Holy Spirit a few miles east of present-day Ashland, Wisconsin. In 1669 Allouez left the Chequamegon Mission and moved south to establish a mission at present-day Oconto on Green Bay. In 1670 he opened a mission chapel dedicated to St. Francis Xavier at DePere. Two other missions were established at river intersections, taking advantage of these well-traveled, fur-trading sites. From these mission stations, succeeding Jesuits penetrated the interior of Wisconsin. Among these were Frs. Claude Dablon and Jacques Marquette.

It is difficult to ascertain the extent and ultimate success of the Catholic presence in Wisconsin in this period of initial contact. Jesuit missionaries worked with varying degrees of success with the native tribes. Moreover, they also provided essential ministry and the contours of organized Church life to the resident French-Canadians at Green Bay and Prairie du Chien. Apparently, the region's religious development suffered a severe setback in 1682 when the Fox War erupted. Moreover, the reconcentration policies of Antoine Cadillac and the commencement of rivalry between England and France that culminated in the French and Indian War of 1756–63 further jeopardized the condition of organized religion in the Wisconsin area. By 1728 only one solitary priest, John Baptist Chardon, S.J., remained in Green Bay. The suppression of the Society of Jesus in France in 1763 dealt an additional blow to the development of the Church in this region. Episodic visits from wandering clerics were about the only remnant of institutional Catholic life that remained from 1728 until 1823. However, the continued lucrative prospects of the fur trade in the region continued by the British, attracted a trickle of white settlers (including Charles de Langlade who settled in Green Bay in 1764) who represented a core group of mostly Catholic French-Canadians. Catholic life continued in some form by the whites and the native peoples, but lacking regular sacramental celebrations.

The Territorial/Early Statehood Period (1820–1870)

Wisconsin changed hands repeatedly both civilly and ecclesiastically. Originally part of the vast empire of New France, it was transferred to British control after the French and Indian War ended in 1763. It was to remain under British sovereignty until the United States gained right to the territory in 1783 after the American Revolution. In 1787 the Confederation congress laid down a pattern of governance for the area by terms of the Northwest Ordinance. Of the five states carved out of the Old Northwest, Wisconsin would be under multiple jurisdictions until it was created as a territory in its own right in 1836. It entered the federal Union in 1848.

Just as fur trading had provided the matrix for economic and ecclesiastical development in the first period, so economic and political realities dictated the development of Catholicism in Wisconsin in this period. The federal government took an active interest in the development of the region when in 1816 it established three strategic forts along its critical waterways: Fort Crawford at Prairie du Chien, Fort Winnebago at Portage, and Fort Howard at Green Bay. These federal installations brought protection and increased the desirability of the land for eastern settlers. The government also extinguished native claims and built military roads that facilitated internal development.

Critical as well to Wisconsin's development was its integration into the larger commercial economy of the region, one initially dependent on commercial agriculture. Wisconsin's fertile farmlands and desirable lakefront harbors were not easily accessible until the opening of the Erie Canal in 1825. The advent of quick and inexpensive lake travel, coupled with the extinguishing of Native American claims to choice sections of the Wisconsin lands, set off a rush of settlement that brought in its wake hundreds of Catholics to the region in the 1830s and 1840s. Despite a thriving lead industry in the southwestern corner of the state, Wisconsin's economy was fixed in this early period on grain farming, dairying, and lumbering.

Ecclesiastically, Wisconsin began under the jurisdiction of the Diocese of Quebec and remained under this control even after France was expelled from the region. In 1791 the area was formally transferred to the new see of Baltimore. In 1808 it came under the direction of Bishop Benedict Joseph Flaget of Bardstown. Flaget actually visited this far-flung area of his diocese and after the trip impressed on Roman officials that it was too far for him to ever go again. In 1821 Wisconsin was transferred to the see of Cincinnati and in 1833 given to the newly created Diocese of Detroit.

Pioneer Priests

Various priests had visited the territory and ministered to the remaining French-speaking Catholics at either Prairie du Chien or Green Bay. In 1816 Trappist Marie Joseph Dunand from Monks Mound near St. Louis organized the Prairie du Chien Catholics into a congregation. Gabriel Richard, the missionary and church organizer from Michigan, who visited in Green Bay in 1823 and again in 1826, noted that there were 1,224 Catholics in Green Bay and an additional 720 in Prairie du Chien. Richard laid plans for a church in Green Bay to replace the one burned in 1687. It was blessed in 1825 by yet another wandering missionary, Stephen Badin. While under the jurisdiction of Cincinnati, Dominican bishop Edward Fenwick visited the state and conducted a mission.

By 1830 a rising tide of interest in the Wisconsin Territory was beginning to build and the numbers of Catholics clamoring for priestly ministration and regular worship began to grow. In the critical last stage of Wisconsin's evolution from missionary dependency to a free-standing ecclesiastical entity, bishops and priests from Detroit played an important role.

In 1831 one of Wisconsin's most famous missionaries, the Dominican Samuel Charles Mazzuchelli arrived in the state, one year after his ordination by fellow Dominican Edward Fenwick of Cincinnati. An energetic and peripatetic soul, Mazzuchelli began his work in Wisconsin in Green Bay where he began the construction of a church and worked with local native peoples. In 1834 he moved south, arriving in Galena, Illinois, the heart of the lead mining region. He returned to Wisconsin in 1844 and there helped to establish a number of parishes in the southwestern corner of the state, a college for Catholic men (that failed), and a native sisterhood of Dominican Sisters that still exists today at Sinsinawa Mound. Until his death in 1864, Mazzuchelli was an important force for Catholic development and played a critical role in the shaping of the political and social life of the rapidly growing state of Wisconsin.

Mazzuchelli was in many ways typical of the kind of priest who came to Wisconsin. Not only was he an agent of spiritual ministry, but in the inchoate conditions of emerging community in Wisconsin, Mazzuchelli and other priests of the territorial period exercised an influence and role beyond the realm of the sanctuary and the sacristy. This highlights a critical aspect of this territorial period: namely, the interdependence of the Church with the emerging civil society. Later boundaries between Church and state were not as sharply drawn in this period. Indeed, Catholic institutions provided rudimentary social organization to the emerging state and Catholic priests played a role in the marketing of the state. Moreover, prominent lay figures, such as future territorial governor James Doty, viewed the Church as an important element of social order in Wisconsin and an important part of the image of the state as it sold itself to potential landowners in the East.

Wisconsin's organization as a territory in 1836 made possible the sale of federal lands and the settlement of existing settlers' rights. Although temporarily stymied by the Panic of 1837, the demand for Wisconsin land soared in the 1840s and brought hosts of land speculators and entrepreneurs to the state. The older cities of Green Bay and Prairie du Chien were already being eclipsed by the emergence of a chain of attractive cities that grew up around choice harbor locations along the shore of Lake Michigan. These included Southport (later Kenosha), Racine, and of course Milwaukee, the latter destined to become the population hub of the state and the leader in Catholic life. Milwaukee's hegemony as the leading city on the lake and the source of population made it a logical center for Catholic growth. The Detroit priest Florimond Bonduel offered the first Mass in the city in 1833, and land for a small chapel for the tiny Catholic community was donated by the city's putative founder, the French-Canadian Solomon Juneau. The swelling tide of population that swept the state raised the number of Catholics and increased the numbers of priests who worked in the scattered centers of Catholic population along the lake and in the agricultural hinterland.

Martin Kundig, a native of Switzerland ordained to serve in Cincinnati and Detroit, eventually appeared in Milwaukee and recognized the potential of the lakefront city as a center for Catholic life. He effectively propagandized on behalf of the state's swelling Catholic population, writing letters to eastern newspapers describing robust parochial growth and recounting the wonders of the region and its potential. Kundig's salesmanship bore fruit in 1842 when the bishops of the Fifth Provincial Council of Baltimore petitioned Rome to establish a see in Wisconsin. At the time of the petition it is estimated there were nearly 7,000 Catholics scattered throughout the state. On November 28, 1843, by the bull *In Suprema Militantis,* Pope Gregory XVI erected the Diocese of Milwaukee. He appointed the Swiss-born priest of the Archdiocese of Cincinnati, John Martin Henni, as its first bishop.

Bishop Henni of Milwaukee

Henni was born in Switzerland in 1805 and, together with Kundig, had been ordained for the Diocese of Cincinnati in 1828. In Cincinnati he devoted himself to the pastoral needs of the growing number of Germans migrating to the state. He received episcopal consecration on March 19, 1844, and appeared in his see city in company with Fr. Michael Heiss on May 5, 1844. At the time of Henni's arrival the number of Catholics in Wisconsin had dramatically increased to 19,000. Nineteen priests were available to serve this scattered flock. Five years later, Wisconsin would be admitted to the Union. Henni's reputation as an apostle to the Germans certainly played a role in attracting many German-speaking Catholics to the state and hence accelerating the processes of civil development. As in so many other portions of the Midwest, the Church and the community grew up together.

Upon his arrival, Henni immediately commenced a tour of the diocese, which comprised the entire state of Wisconsin and a small portion of present-day Minnesota east of the Mississippi. His journeys took him to the farthest extremities of the state, to the shores of Lake Superior where Fr. Frederic Baraga had restarted the mission on the shores of Lake Superior left long ago by Allouez. He visited native villages as well as the prospering farming communities of the hinterland and the growing cities of the lake coast. Wisconsin's Catholic (and general) population lay for the most part south of the Fox/Wisconsin axis. He discovered church-building going on in Oak Creek, Racine, Kenosha, Burlington, Brighton, Geneva, and Yorkville.

What Henni also discovered on this journey was the ethnic diversity of the Catholic population. In addition to the old French-Canadian settlers and the remaining Native American tribes, there were colonies of Dutch and Belgian Catholics in and around Green Bay, and a small but vibrant Irish community. But the largest single immigrant group were German-speakers, forging Wisconsin's place as the apex of a German triangle in the Midwest together with St. Louis and Cincinnati. By the end of Henni's years of service (1881), large-scale Polish immigration had begun. By 1853 the Catholic population had grown to 100,000 and the number of priests serving them had risen from nineteen in 1843 to sixty-four. But, despite this diversity and the growing number of English-speaking Catholics, Henni and his successors, Michael Heiss (1881–90) and Frederick X. Katzer (1890–1903), perpetuated the strong Teutonic flavor of Wisconsin Catholicism by encouraging the foundation of German-language parishes and parochial schools.

To serve the growing educational and social welfare needs of the swelling Catholic flock, Henni traveled to Europe in order to secure funds from missionary societies in France, Austria, and Bavaria. With these funds he erected a suitable cathedral, named for his patron, St. John the Evangelist, and designed in a handsome federal style by architect Victor Schulte.

Of even greater significance for the development of the Church in Wisconsin, Henni found money to build a seminary dedicated to St. Francis de Sales. The "Salesianum," as it was known throughout the region, opened its doors in 1856 and was headed by Fr. Michael Heiss. Thanks to the fundraising and advertising skills of Fr. Joseph Salzmann, St. Francis quickly acquired a national reputation as a seminary for German-speaking youth. It also was the major supplier of priests for the dioceses of Wisconsin and the Upper Midwest until the 1980s.

Henni also built orphanages and encouraged the development of a Catholic hospital run by the Daughters of Charity in Milwaukee. Since Catholic schools were a high priority to Henni and his coworkers, he vigorously recruited religious women from the German-speaking areas of Europe to teach in them. Mother Caroline Friess and the School Sisters of Notre Dame arrived in Milwaukee in 1850 where they established their motherhouse. The School Sisters would become one of the most powerful influences in Catholic education in the city of Milwaukee as well as in Prairie du Chien. The School Sisters of St. Francis, whose members fanned out across the Midwest, also established their general headquarters in Milwaukee in 1871. Dominican Sisters from Regensburg, Germany, under Mother Benedicta Bauer established themselves in Racine and opened an academy named for St. Catherine of Siena in 1864. A group of Franciscan tertiaries which would eventually evolve into a religious order, associated themselves with the care of the diocesan seminary, and were indeed the original owners of the land on which it would sit. A split in this community in 1871 created the Franciscan Sisters of Perpetual Adoration who would become prominent in La Crosse.

In St. Nazianz, a small farming village north of Milwaukee, Fr. Ambrose Oschwald attempted to create a Catholic communitarian society in the 1850s. The failure of this endeavor brought the lands into the hands of the Society of the Divine Savior (Salvatorian Fathers) and the Sisters of the Divine Savior in 1895. In 1896 the Salvatorian Fathers would open a monastery at the site. Associated with the first St. Nazianz project were the Franciscan Sisters of Charity who established themselves in Manitowoc. Capuchin Franciscan friars began their work in 1857, and opened a seminary at Mount Calvary, Wisconsin, in 1860. At Henni's invitation, the Society of Jesus began work in Wisconsin in 1849, settling first in Milwaukee. In 1879 they took over a boys' academy in Prairie du Chien that had been founded by the Christian Brothers and renamed it for St. Edmund Campion.

Relatively minor nativist disturbances broke out in the city in the mid-1850s, abetted by local Whigs who feared the potential political power of the largely immigrant flock and their affiliation with the Democrats. Henni spoke to these issues, but they never loomed large as a force in the identity of the Catholic community.

Wisconsin Catholicism

Catholic life in Wisconsin in this period took on the main contours of its subsequent existence. Catholic parishes and schools developed throughout the southern half of the state from the shore of Lake Michigan to the banks of the Mississippi. Interreligious rivalry existed not only with evangelical groups, but even more with numerous German Lutherans who seemed to match the Catholics church for church. Most Wisconsinites settled in rural areas and Catholic parishes dotted the farm landscape of the state. Cities, especially those along the lake, reflected as well the dominance of German ethnicity, rivaled weakly by Irish or English-speaking congregations. By 1850 Kenosha had two churches for Germans and Irish respectively. Milwaukee had three German parishes by midcentury, while the cathedral served the English-speaking population.

The fluidity of frontier social conditions and the ad hoc nature of early political arrangements allowed an easy symbiosis between Church and civil society. In many parts of the state Catholics dominated public school boards and could easily shape school policies to their liking. Catholic social welfare institutions served the general public, such as the case of the first Catholic hospital in Milwaukee staffed by Mother Elizabeth Seton's Daughters of Charity, which Milwaukee County officials used to house the county's sick poor until they built their own facilities in 1861. In 1845 Wisconsin's first public school was opened in the basement of St. Mark's Catholic Church in Kenosha. Indeed, cooperation between the Church and civil officials on educational matters was commonplace in nineteenth-century Wisconsin. Priests such as Mazzuchelli and Kundig took an active role in boosting the state and serving as agents of growth. Public officials and state boosters recognized the potential value of religion and the existence of religious institutions as important social anchors. Indeed, as some historians have noted, religion's social function on the Midwestern frontier was as an agency of community consciousness and an integral link in the development of "translocal" communities despite the remoteness of the settlements. Henni's careful planning, his longevity as bishop, the success of his seminary, and the growing economic prosperity of the region placed Milwaukee in the first rank of dioceses in the country.

As early as his venture of 1844, Henni realized that the broad expanse of his diocese would be too much for one man. In the 1850s the creation of the Diocese of St. Paul took away some of the territory in the northwest. In 1868, after representations at the Second Plenary Council of Baltimore two years earlier, Propaganda agreed to a split in the Wisconsin administration. Two dioceses with headquarters at each end of the Fox/Wisconsin axis were erected. Green Bay was created on March 3, 1868, and Austrian-born Joseph Melcher, a priest of the Diocese of St. Louis, was selected as its first bishop. At the time of Melcher's consecration there were 40,000 Catholics and 26 priests in the 15,738 square miles of his diocese. To the southwest, the growing city of La Crosse, founded in 1841, was chosen as the see city, and Henni's close friend and associate, Michael Heiss, was selected as its first bishop.

Heiss's domain extended over about 28,000 square miles and included 30,000 Catholics and fifteen priests. Green Bay had about sixty churches and mission stations, while La Crosse had around forty. In 1875 Milwaukee was raised to metropolitan status and Henni was named archbishop. The development of the La Crosse and Green Bay dioceses proceeded much more slowly than Milwaukee. Both had vaster and less populated areas in which to minister. Although each diocese had sizeable cities (Green Bay having that city and a chain of cities along the lakefront that prospered from lake trade, and La Crosse benefiting from river traffic), neither could match Milwaukee or even Racine and Kenosha as a magnet site for continual immigration. Later diocesan subdivisions with the creation of the Superior diocese in 1905 and Madison in 1946 would create new configurations of Catholic life in the state. Diocesan boundaries would be altered in 1905 and 1946 to adjust to these changes.

Catholicism in the Industrial Era (1870–1945)

A decisive shift in the development of Catholic life in Wisconsin came about when the economic base of the area shifted dramatically from commercial agriculture to industrial production.

Wisconsin's hegemony as a grain, dairy, and lumber-producing state had been well established by midcentury, and in 1873 most Wisconsin inhabitants lived in rural areas (under 2,500 people). By 1890 this would change and the preponderance of Wisconsinites would be urbanites. Catholics followed these patterns as well, but their urban numbers were always slightly higher. Significant changes in Wisconsin's economy began before the Civil War with the advent of the railroad. By 1857 rail expansion linked Milwaukee with Prairie du Chien. Aided by entrepreneurs and bankers, Wisconsin's rail lines increased their mileage and the consolidation of smaller lines into larger systems increased their efficiency. The railroad also linked Wisconsin even more securely to the emerging Midwestern industrial economy.

The social effects of industrialism brought about great changes in society as people moved to urban centers and shaped their lives around the demands of large-scale manufacturing. Indeed, the majority of Wisconsin's Catholics would either be industrial workers themselves or be associated with service industries that supported and were dependent on the industrial economy.

For Catholics, the social effects of industrialism coalesced with the centralizing and Romanizing tendencies in Catholic life worldwide to produce a qualitatively different Catholic experience in the state in the period from 1870 on. The Church grew in numbers, the ethnic urban parish became the dominant modality of Catholic life, the earlier cooperation between Church and state gave way to more clearly specialized spheres of influence for Church and state, and the organizational revolution of industrial life had an impact on the administration of the temporalities of Catholic institutions.

In the period 1870 to 1890 the Church underwent rapid growth. Milwaukee went from 155,000 to 280,000 Catholics; La Crosse went from ca. 40,000 to 67,000 and Green Bay from 50,000 to 100,000. Even the underpopulated northern reaches of the state began to feel the effects of industrial possibilities. Millionaire John D. Rockefeller laid plans to turn the distant city of Superior into a major shipping depot on the Great Lakes and even to locate some heavy industry in the area. In 1905, in response to the growing population, the Holy See created the Diocese of Superior and appointed a Milwaukee priest, Augustine Schinner, as its first bishop.

Ethnic Tensions

Ethnic tensions between German-speaking and English-speaking Catholics flared in Milwaukee over the succession to the ailing Henni. The aged prelate's choice for coadjutor had been his old friend Heiss, who intended to perpetuate Henni's devotion to the German cause. English-speaking priests vigorously opposed the nomination and succeeded in stalling it for two years until 1880. German-speaking bishops continued to be appointed to the sees of La Crosse and Green Bay into the twentieth century.

Milwaukee's, and by extension Wisconsin's national reputation in the latter years of the nineteenth century was as a bastion of Germanic conservatism. It was a Milwaukee priest, Peter Abbelen, who presented a petition to Pope Leo XIII (the Abbelen Memorial) in 1886 demanding better treatment of Germans in America. Indeed, Wisconsin bishops in general played an important role in opposing the so-called Americanizers in the U.S. hierarchy. Moreover, the active efforts of German-speakers in the state (including Lutherans) were successfully deployed in repealing the Bennett Law in 1890, which had attempted to curtail the use of foreign languages in schools.

But German hegemony was not to last. Industrial work attracted scores of Southern and Eastern immigrants. Polish Catholics who had begun to appear in larger and larger numbers after 1880 came mostly from the German-dominated area of the former Polish state. Large numbers lived in urban areas but also in rural areas. There may have been close to 200,000 first- and second-generation Poles in Wisconsin by 1900. Milwaukee's first Polish-ethnic congregation, St. Stanislaus, opened its doors in 1866. From this nucleus, the city's Polish community expanded rapidly on the city's south side dotting the urban landscape with numerous churches and schools.

Bohemians had already been on the scene since the 1860s, settling mostly in Racine. A Bohemian parish opened in Milwaukee in 1865 and in Racine in 1897. Slovaks as well began arriving in statistically measurable numbers in the late nineteenth century, adding to the medley of parishes in most cities. Between 1900 and 1910 Wisconsin's Italian community grew dramatically, settling in Milwaukee, Racine, Kenosha, Madison, and Beloit.

For all these newcomers, the ethnic urban parish became a mainstay of their religious identity. The domes and steeples of these churches began to be raised against the skyline of virtually every major city of Wisconsin, some of them, like St. Josaphat's Basilica in Milwaukee, of truly mammoth proportions. The ethnic church served not only as a spiritual center, but also offered an array of social services that eased the strains of urban life. German parishes had intricate networks of organizations (*vereine*) organized according to age and gender. Polish church life expended much energy on the issue of Poland's restoration as an independent country. Italian Catholics in Kenosha, Racine, Beloit, and Milwaukee replicated devotions from the *mezzogiorno* and withstood pressures to build Catholic schools which they distrusted. Urban parishes at their best created tendons of cohesion in neighborhoods. At their worst they overbuilt the urban landscape with facilities that later became too financially burdensome to carry.

German Catholic leaders held the reins of power well into the twentieth century and ethnic tension flared once again, this time from Polish Catholics. Like the English-speaking dissidents of the previous generation, they demanded representation in the Wisconsin hierarchy based on their numbers and the intensity of their Catholicism. These demands, fanned by the writing of Polish Catholic layman Michael Kruszka, in the pages of his *Kuryer Polski* as well as the heated pulpit oratory of his half-brother priest, Wenceslaus Kruszka, nearly created a schism within the large Polish Catholic community of Milwaukee. Milwaukee did have one Polish-speaking auxiliary bishop, Michigan priest Edward Kozlowksi (1914–15), who lived only a year after his consecration. Later, Chicago pastor Paul Peter Rhode was sent to Green Bay, beginning a series of Polish bishops that lasted in that see until the appointment of Robert Banks of Boston in 1990.

Eventually, the reality of Wisconsin's changing ethnic demography began to have effects. The hegemony of German Catholics had begun to wane already by the late nineteenth century. In the 1890s, school lessons became bilingual and the demands of Americanized Germans required the same policy in parish services, especially devotions, confessions, and sermons. By World War I, anti-German feelings gave the bishops of the state the necessary cover to curtail German-language services, religious instruction, and records keeping. Ultimately, as with the rest of America, congressional strictures on immigration in the twenties undercut the perpetuation of ethnicity in Wisconsin and propelled Catholics toward Americanization.

Growth and Organization

The steady growth of the urban churches continued. Moreover, the number of priests continued to increase apace as well. From 1870–90, the numbers of priests serving in the three Wisconsin dioceses rose from 197 to 432 (diocesan and religious). The number of Catholics in the state rose in the same time period from approximately 250,000 to nearly 450,000. From 1910 to 1940, the number of priests in the four dioceses of the state rose from 837 (diocesan and religious) to 1,494. The number of Catholics for the same time period spiraled from 532,217 to 828,140. Catholics in Wisconsin broke the one million mark in 1960, recording over 1.2 million adherents.

The heaviest concentrations of Catholics continued to be in the eastern dioceses of Milwaukee and Green Bay. Madison and La Crosse kept a slower pace and Superior, its early hopes of becoming a major port on Lake Superior and an industrial center dashed early in the century, always lagged well behind with fewer than 100,000 Catholics.

The reorganization of Catholic life in the dioceses of Wisconsin took the form of greater episcopal centralization and the reconfiguration of Catholic identity based on doctrinal distinction rather than ethnicity. Under the direction of Sebastian Messmer (1904–30) in Milwaukee, the diocesan administration was increasingly bureaucratized. A full-time chancellor, who functioned as an executive assistant to the bishop, was appointed, and the episcopal residence moved to a stately mansion on Milwaukee's most prestigious street. Messmer created a centrally directed social welfare agency and an education department that oversaw the development of the parochial school system. The diocesan seminary shed its status as a provincial and even regional institution and focused its attention on candidates from Milwaukee. Messmer's administrative reforms were reinforced by the issuance of the Code of Canon Law in 1918.

In La Crosse, energy for these reforms came from the auxiliary bishop William J. Griffin, (1935–44). Griffin, a Chicago priest, had been sent in 1935 to aid his old friend and fellow Chicagoan, the elderly and ailing Alexander McGavick (1921–48). McGavick outlived his auxiliary and was given a coadjutor in the person of John Patrick Treacy (1946–64), a priest of Cleveland. Treacy, an indefatigable builder and a strong authoritarian, came on the scene in 1946, and upon assuming the reins of leadership built extensively in the diocese, including a seminary which opened in 1951 and a new cathedral which was dedicated in 1962.

In Green Bay, Bishop Paul P. Rhode (1915–45) implemented reforms in diocesan life. He appointed a school superintendent in 1917 and in 1928 created a unified school department under the direction of Edward J. Wiestenberger, Ph.D. In 1918 he created a diocesan social welfare bureau to coordinate child welfare efforts.

The paucity of clergy and Catholics in the Diocese of Superior kept the pace of bureaucratization at a slower pace, but even it experienced a brief boomlet of expansion in the 1920s culminating in the construction of a magnificent cathedral by Bishop Joseph Gabriel Pinten (1921–26). Unfortunately, the economic collapse of the region with the depression left a terrible burden of debt under which the diocese struggled until the return of prosperity during the Second World War.

The decades of the 1920s and 1930s saw the waning of ethnicity as a defining feature of Catholic life. But it was replaced by a new form of Catholic mobilization that took place through a proliferation of Catholic organizations of lay men and women under the banner of Catholic Action. Designed to engage the laity in "the apostolate of the hierarchy," bishops encouraged membership in Catholic groups such as the Holy Name Society, the Sodality movement, and the associations of Catholic Men and Women. In Milwaukee, the Holy Name Society, under the leadership of layman Leo Dohn, enrolled hundreds of men in behalf of popular crusades against public profanity, developed adult education programs, and enlisted hundreds of Catholic professionals in a well-used speaker's bureau. A similar program was launched in Green Bay when Bishop Rhode began the Holy Name Society in his diocese in 1922. At the urging of the National Catholic Welfare Conference, diverse organizations of Catholic Women associated themselves with local councils of Catholic Women. Milwaukee's was organized in the 1920s under the direction of Katherine Williams, an attorney who would go on to head the National Council of Catholic Women. La Crosse began its diocesan council in 1934. These women's groups not only performed charitable works, such as providing housing for single working women in cities and catechetical instruction for children not enrolled in parochial schools, but also kept a vigilant eye on local and state government, especially on legislation that might affect Catholic interests.

Catholic Youth Activities became a leitmotif of the career of Auxiliary Bishop William Griffin of La Crosse, who in 1930 adapted the successful model of the Catholic Youth Organization of his native Chicago to the youth needs of the diocese. Milwaukee's Catholic athletic programs began under the auspices of the Holy Name Society and prospered under the direction of layman Peter Murphy. Griffin also pressed for the development of the sodality in the diocese, making Jesuit Daniel Lord, its national leader, a regular visitor to the diocese for speaking engagements.

One additional Catholic Action group that developed in all the Wisconsin dioceses in the 1930s were branches of the Catholic Rural Life Conference (Milwaukee, 1935; La Crosse, 1936) promoted by Bishop Edwin Vincent O'Hara. Devoted to the spiritual and educational needs of rural Catholics, it enjoyed great success in Wisconsin's agricultural areas. Yet another O'Hara initiative that was formally established in all Wisconsin dioceses in the 1940s was the Confraternity of Christian Doctrine that developed a program of religious education for children who did not attend parochial schools.

All of these multifarious enterprises were reported in the Catholic press. Catholic journalism had begun in Wisconsin at the behest of Henni who launched *Der Seebote,* a German-language paper in the 1850s. *Die Columbia* was its successor. English-language publications came and went until layman Humphrey J. Desmond took over as head of *The Catholic Citizen* in 1891. Desmond's career as a Catholic journalist propelled him to the leadership of an impressive chain of Catholic publications. In 1922 Archbishop Messmer of Milwaukee began an official diocesan weekly to compete with the lay-controlled *Citizen* called *The Catholic Herald.* The two merged in 1935 and *The Catholic Herald-Citizen* became the dominant Catholic newspaper in the state, spinning off special editions for the dioceses of Superior and Madison. It was renamed *The Catholic Herald* in the 1980s. Green Bay began *The Green Bay Register* in 1956 and La Crosse affiliated with the nationwide *Register* chain in 1935. In 1958 it began its own free-standing paper, *The Times-Review.*

The onset of the depression hit the economy of Wisconsin gradually, coming into full force in the latter part of 1931. Milwaukee, Racine, Kenosha, Fond du Lac, and other industrialized regions of the state were hit hard. Catholic social welfare agencies, such as the St. Vincent de Paul Society, tried valiantly to plug the dike of economic collapse, but were overwhelmed, especially in hard-hit Milwaukee, by requests for assistance. Each diocesan administration adopted economies that expressed sensitivity to the plight of the poor. For example in Milwaukee, Archbishop Samuel Stritch (1930–40) refused to purchase land for a new major seminary and delayed plans to rebuild the cathedral that had been gutted by fire in early 1935. In La Crosse, aging Bishop McGavick likewise forbade a subscription drive by the publisher of *The Catholic Daily Tribune,* citing "the financial condition of our parishes" and ordered the debt-encumbered parishes of the diocese to retire their outstanding liabilities. Plugging the drain on diocesan finances and precluding the financial collapse of parishes preoccupied the bishops of depression-era Wisconsin. Stritch inaugurated a special fund appeal that would shore up faltering diocesan agencies. Superior's bishop, Theodore Revermann (1926–41), spent his time trying to pay off the huge debt left by his predecessor for the cathedral.

Wisconsin Catholics entered the ranks of discussion on the causes of the depression. Of significant note were the writings and activities of two priests: Aloysius Muench (1889–1962) who wrote on social issues and publicly challenged Fr. Charles Coughlin's monetary theories, and Francis Haas (1889–1953) who served as a prominent labor mediator and advisor to the Roosevelt administration.

One other feature of Catholic life emerged at this time and that was the growing presence of Catholic higher education. Already in the nineteenth century, Henni had opened Holy Family Catholic Normal School behind the diocesan seminary (later renamed Pio Nono). This institution developed a national reputation as a center for the training of church musicians under the leadership of layman John Singenberger (1848–1924). Henni desired to have a Catholic college in Wisconsin, a dream that was fulfilled in 1881, the year of his death, when the Jesuits opened Marquette College. In 1893 St. Norbert's College in DePere under the direction of the Canons Regular of Prémontré opened its doors. Education for Catholic laywomen in the state was only realized by the opening of St. Mary's College in Prairie du Chien under the auspices of the School Sisters of Notre Dame. In 1928 this college moved to Milwaukee and was known as Mount Mary College.

Catholic higher education for women religious advanced considerably in the twentieth century. Many religious orders had academies at or near their motherhouses. In the 1930s, in part stimulated by the passage of teacher certification laws and the establishment of professional standards, communities of sisters began college programs at their motherhouses. Indeed, already in 1885, the Franciscan Sisters of Christian Charity had begun a normal school that reached a four-year status in 1939. In the 1930s as well the Franciscan Sisters of Penance and Charity in St. Francis opened St. Clare's College (later renamed Cardinal Stritch College) in 1932, while the Agnesian Sisters of Fond du Lac opened Marian College in 1936, and the Dominican Sisters of Racine had commenced St. Albertus College (later Dominican College) a year earlier. After desultory efforts to unite with Marquette University, the School Sisters of St. Francis opened St. Joseph's Teaching College (later Alverno) in 1936. In 1937 the Franciscans of La Crosse changed the name of their junior college to Viterbo College.

Catholics attending the University of Wisconsin were not forgotten. In 1908 Messmer founded a successful campus chaplaincy and staffed it with priests of high academic caliber, such as the aforementioned Aloysius Muench, who later became a seminary rector, bishop of Fargo, North Dakota, apostolic nuncio to Germany, and a cardinal.

The onset of the war and the return of prosperity to the nation ushered in new changes for Catholic life in Wisconsin. By 1945 the Church had come through its early foundational period and had settled itself as a prominent and visible urban presence.

Expansion, Suburbia, and Transition (1945–)

The historical proximity of this epoch of Wisconsin Catholic history makes it difficult to do much more than comment on general trends. The dominant motif of this period seems to be one of rapid expansion and a flowering of Catholic mobilization followed by a period after 1965 (the close of Vatican Council II) of unsettling social and ecclesiastical change and a general contraction of Catholic numbers and institutions.

The explosion of the birthrate among Catholics led to unprecedented expansion of existing facilities, especially schools, in all of the dioceses. In 1950 all five dioceses had 453 parochial elementary schools. Ten years later there were 536 schools. The proliferation of parishes told an even more dramatic story. Milwaukee added thirty new parishes in the decade of the 1950s; Green Bay, ten; La Crosse, nine; Madison, one; and Superior, twelve. Expansions of existing facilities also reflected the burgeoning growth. Total Catholic population in the decade broke the million mark, increasing from 934,048 to 1,256,147.

Everywhere, even in Superior, there were the traces of building, expansion, and Catholic vitality. Catholic secondary education, which had begun somewhat tentatively as the projects of different orders, now became diocesan projects enrolling hundreds of Catholic youth. Higher education possibilities were enhanced by the G.I. Bill. Catholic colleges experienced overnight expansion and many of the sisters' colleges formed in the 1930s evolved into four-year institutions that welcomed laywomen to their student bodies.

Catholic demographics were shifting as well. The long-dominant urban church surrounded by a school, a large hall, and nestled in a working-class neighborhood was starting to give way to the realities of suburban life. Aided by government loans and upward social mobility created by access to higher education, Wisconsin Catholics began emptying out into the suburban regions. Indeed, much of the tremendous parochial expansion in Milwaukee was in suburban areas of the diocese. The availability of the automobile and the construction of expressways made going and coming to the city easier than ever. The building of the latter also impacted negatively on urban neighborhoods. In Milwaukee it cut through the heavily Polish neighborhoods of the south side and caused the destruction of one of the older German parishes in the diocese. In other existing cities in the diocese, the parishes at the perimeter of the city often found themselves the recipients of accelerated growth, school enrollments, and demand for services.

Wisconsin's seminary also began to feel the need for expansion. Already in the 1940s, Milwaukee Archbishop Moses E. Kiley (1940–53) had separated the high school and junior college program from the major seminary. But, by the early 1950s, the old seminary building was crowded to the point where students had to be turned away. In 1956 a major expansion of the seminary was undertaken and opened in time for its centennial celebrations. On adjacent property, the archdiocese built a magnificent new high school and college seminary that opened its doors in 1962. Not to be outdone and fearing that their students would be excluded from the burgeoning seminaries of the archdiocese, La Crosse under John P. Treacy, and Green Bay under Stanislaus Bona (1945–67), built their own minor seminaries. Religious orders such as the Capuchins, Salvatorians, Redemptorists, and Cistercians also ran seminaries for their candidates. Ordination classes were large for every diocese, Milwaukee ordaining over fifty at one ceremony in 1955.

Yet another major phenomenon was the advent of large numbers of African Americans to the urban areas. Milwaukee saw its black population double between 1950–60. Racine, Madison, and Beloit all saw tremendous increases in the numbers of African Americans. Efforts to minister to African American Catholics had begun in Milwaukee as early as 1908 when a lay couple, Lincoln and Julia Valle, opened a chapel dedicated to St. Benedict the Moor in Milwaukee. This endeavor, eventually taken over by the Capuchins, became an important hub of African American Catholicism in Wisconsin. It soon acquired the old Marquette Academy and ran a successful boarding school for African American youth until the 1950s. Hispanic Catholics, largely of Mexican descent, began arriving in Milwaukee in the 1920s, and through the work of layman Frank Gross, a chapel for their ministry was opened in the 1920s.

The impact of African American migration, especially heavy in the 1950s and 1960s, changed the face of Catholic life in the urban centers of Wisconsin where the majority of Catholics lived. The north side of Milwaukee, once heavily German and dominated by fifteen predominantly German parishes, soon dwindled in Catholic population, requiring the consolidation of the nine parishes to two in the summer of 1994. Racine's downtown area as well, once dotted with a myriad of ethnic churches, saw a steep decline in the numbers attending Mass and once-thriving Catholic schools.

The impact of Vatican II on Wisconsin was largely favorable. All of the bishops of the state attended the council and returned home to implement reforms. Changes in liturgical practice, architecture, and the enhanced role of the laity in divine services, marked the most dramatic and visible changes brought about by the council in the Advent of 1964. Generally, the changes were well accepted by most Catholics, but pockets of dissatisfaction exist on both ends of the ideological spectrum that find liturgical practice as their flashpoint.

Equally as important has been the steady diminution of priests and religious women to serve in parishes and schools. Schools themselves have undergone a period of contraction, falling in number from 536 (elementary) in 1960 to 381 in 1990. The declining birthrate among Catholics, coupled with the heavy expense of maintaining these schools without the contributed services of women or men religious, is primarily responsible for their demise.

The changing role of religious men and women has also been a feature of the postconciliar Catholic landscape. Emerging from the fixed patterns of clerical and religious life into less defined and more mobile roles, Catholic priests and sisters in Wisconsin have become involved in a variety of different ministries and approaches to ministry. This first development became vividly evident in the racial politics of the late 1960s, when a Milwaukee priest, James Groppi, took a leading role in open-housing marches in 1965 and in helping to quell racial disturbances that wracked Milwaukee in 1968. Groppi's activities won him support and acclaim from many Catholics but also seriously alienated others, including Milwaukee's Catholic mayor, Henry Maier, who thought his political activities incongruent with his vocation. The commitment of women religious to social issues has been even more dramatic with numerous members of many congregations becoming more active in advocacy for the poor and homeless as well as using their corporate investment portfolios to challenge the practices of the companies in which they invest. Many Wisconsin motherhouses were declared "nuclear free zones" in the 1980s as a protest against the military build-up of the Reagan years. Even more lay and religious women in Wisconsin have been influenced by the winds of Catholic feminist thought and practice and have increasingly demanded a share in the leadership and governance of the Church. Women hold the key position of chancellor in some Wisconsin dioceses, and laywomen and women religious administer "priestless parishes" in Green Bay, Milwaukee, and Superior.

In recent years, Catholic life in Wisconsin has experienced the same vicissitudes as the general region, namely, a slowing or even reversal of the rate of growth due to a decline in the birthrate and the exodus of well-paying industrial jobs and continued concern about the viability of cities wherein most Catholics live. Internally, the declining numbers of priests and the increasing burdens of financing Church operations have also given rise to considerable anxiety.

Avella, Steven M., ed. *Milwaukee Catholicism: Essays on Church and Community*. Milwaukee: Knights of Columbus, 1991.

Fisher, Gerald Edward. *Dusk is My Dawn: The First Hundred Years of the Diocese of La Crosse, 1868–1968*. Wisconsin: Diocese of La Crosse, 1968.

Johnson, Peter Leo. *Crosier on the Frontier: A Life of John Martin Henni*. Madison, Wisc.: State Historical Society, 1959.

Kuzniewski, Anthony J. *Faith and Fatherland: The Polish Church War in Wisconsin*. University of Notre Dame Press, 1980.

Ludwig, M. Mileta. *Right Hand Glove Uplifted: A Biography of Michael Heiss.* New York: Pageant, 1968.

Rummel, Leo. *History of the Catholic Church in Wisconsin.* Madison, Wisc.: Knights of Columbus, 1976.

STEVEN M. AVELLA

Related Document

A REPORT TO THE LUDWIG-MISSIONSVEREIN ON CATHOLICISM IN WISCONSIN, APRIL 23, 1845

Among the most important agencies for financial assistance to the American Church was the Ludwig-Missionsverein, founded at Munich in December, 1838, under the patronage of King Louis I of Bavaria, from whom it derived its name. The special objects of this missionary society's benefactions in the United States were the German Catholic immigrants. No center of German Catholic activity was more prominent than the Diocese of Milwaukee which had been erected on November 28, 1843, and which included the entire state of Wisconsin with its 54,715 square miles. When John Martin Henni (1805–1881), the first Bishop of Milwaukee, arrived in his see city in May, 1844, he found only four priests to care for the 15,000 Catholics scattered throughout the state. The fact that by 1850 there were over 60,000 Catholics in Wisconsin with forty-three priests will give some idea of the rapidity of growth of the See of Milwaukee. Between 1838 and 1921 the Ludwig-Missionsverein gave nearly a million dollars to the American missions and the Diocese of Milwaukee was among its principal beneficiaries. Less than a year after his arrival Henni sent a report on religious conditions to the Reverend Joseph Mueller, general manager of the Munich society, in which he included some interesting observations on the secular scene, even to anticipating the St. Lawrence Waterway.

(*Source: Salesianum,* XXXVII [April, 1942] 82–5, translated by Augustine C. Breig and edited by Peter Leo Johnson.)

Milwaukee, April 23rd, 1845.
I received your letter of February 17th. You may imagine how anxiously I was waiting for it for some time. I am very grateful to you for having released at least to a certain extent the suspense I was in and still partly am in on account of some intervening "difficulties" as you remark. In the meanwhile you bid me to be of good cheer. In fact I am, especially since your esteemed letter assures me of your good will towards me and also of the sincere efforts of you and of the rest of the friends in Munich in behalf of my cause, in which no one can be indifferent who has the welfare of the church in this part of America at heart. This holds good especially as far as I am concerned, for I more than others must realize the importance of this cause. I shall therefore very anxiously wait for further developments. In the meanwhile I shall leave the matter entirely to God and to the efforts and prudence of my friends in Munich.

Complying with your advice I have sent a petition directly to the board of directors, as enclosure shows. But since I presumed that the lengthy report on my diocese and my mission journeys, especially among the Indians, which I have sent at the same time to Vienna and Einsiedeln[1] and also to the Catholics of Bavaria, would become known, I have purposely avoided all repetitions and mentioned only the most pressing needs. However I did not dare to ask for a definite sum fearing that such a request might be misinterpreted by some at least. I would prefer that one or the other of my benefactors would suggest this to the board of directors.

With regard to the German-English seminary I have nothing else to add than that the proposed plan appeals to me more day by day. The establishment of such an institute in Bavaria itself should certainly not be undertaken in order to spare the young men the slur of being emissaries because it is this slur the sly bigots yell continuously into our ears. They do not write any more so strongly against the truths of our religion because here they have overcome the strongest prejudices perhaps more than in Germany. But now these people accuse us as being anti-republicans, dangerous to the state. Nothing more than this lie arouses the American, who is generally broad minded, to follow without hesitation justice and truth wherever he finds them. Just this political lie especially invites the American of all classes to investigate our teachings and principles; they are the first ones who follow their conviction. For this reason, to be honest, I like them better than all other Protestants. Lately I received Dr. Hunt an excellent physician into the church. Several others are taking instructions. A good Catholic priest is certainly more respected than the numerous preachers. In spite of my poverty as bishop every one of our outstanding state officials wished to get acquainted with me.

At present I am about to arrange an old frame building for a temporary seminary. I have three seminarists, a German, an Irishman and an Italian, the latter of whom has studied for some time in America, and upon whom I will soon confer major orders. Three other clerics I expect towards the end of August from the Jesuit college in Cincinnati and a fourth one from Montreal, Canada.

Good Father Boeswald[2] is still waiting for a "German bishop" to carry out his grand plan as he lately wrote to Father Heiss.[3] Father Heiss whom I did not keep in the dark about my plans regarding the seminary made him acquainted with it. In the meanwhile I endeavor to get the Rev. Boeswald here if our plan should become a reality. I believe that he would come if he should realize that Covington has not more Germans than Milwaukee. South of the Ohio (river) among the Negroes Germans will never settle. Their main settlements in fact are in the northwestern states. Yes, the majority of the domiciled Germans are there; there only the poor farmer from Europe can acquire the desired land at a low price. It is also easier for him to come to Milwaukee from New York than to Cincinnati. Besides only two or three years may elapse till the English-shipping Welland canal will connect Quebec with Lake Erie. Then ships from Liverpool (and from the Rhein and Trieste, if you wish) shall enter the harbor of Milwaukee. Do not smile dear friend. The time when this shall happen is not far off.

However I do not wish that your box packed with the different church utensils should wait till then. Unfortunately I am not acquainted with anybody on one of the seaports to whom you could send the goods intended for me. For the present I have to ask to inquire [sic] of the Liguorians [Redemptorists] who certainly have shipping agents everywhere, how and to what place to send the goods. Even in New York their society might be the surest agent also for me. I shall inform the Rev. Rumpler of this.[4] But I kindly ask you not to send my goods with any belonging to them.

With joy we are looking for the arrival of the Rev. Schraudenbach.[5] Should you be able to find one or the other priest or theological student, I would be very well pleased. I need also two priests who speak French very well, for this reason I shall write to the bishop of Strassburg. Last fall I received at last from Lyons 15,000 francs. What help this was you may imagine. Perhaps you would do well to order for several 100 florins some vestments from the factory you spoke of. Should they be cheap and come up to our expectations some more could be ordered. Could you perhaps get a suitable mitre for me? For all this I authorize you to handle in my name the money granted by the board of directors.

We are informed that Europe had a very severe winter. We had hardly any snow. In fact I have never lived through a more pleasant winter. No doubt the climate here is the healthiest in the United States especially for Europeans. People who come sickly from southern regions grow here healthy and strong. I have also to confess that the spiritual life here is a comfort to me. Since the enlargement of my frame cathedral and a better arrangement of the divine services an excellent spirit manifests itself around me, even among the Protestants.

I have been informed that Miss Linder of Basle was received into the church and that she is living in Munich. Should this be the case kindly give her my best regards and tell her that that I still gratefully remember her kindness towards me. She gave me a beautiful painting representing Christ. Unfortunately I had to leave it at Cincinnati where it adorns a side altar in Holy Trinity church. If Miss Linder still devotes her time to painting I would like to ask her for a picture of St. Francis de Sales. Dear friend in doing so use your own good judgment.

May God bestow his blessing on us and grant that our friends in Munich, you yourself and canon Speth, may work for a long time for the distant missions.

[1] The Leopoldinen-Stiftung of Vienna, founded in April, 1829, was the Austrian counterpart to the Ludwig-Missionsverein. The Abbey of Our Lady of the Hermits at Einsiedeln, Switzerland, was generous in its help to German Catholic missions abroad; it was from Einsiedeln that several Benedictine monks founded the future St. Meinrad's Archabbey in southern Indiana in March, 1854.

[2] Charles Boeswald was pastor of Immaculate Conception Church in Louisville.

[3] The Bavarian-born Michael Heiss (1818–1890) was pastor of St. Mary's Church, Covington, Kentucky, when he volunteered to accompany Henni to Milwaukee in 1844. He later became the first rector of St. Francis Seminary, Milwaukee, 1856–1868; first Bishop of La Crosse, 1868–1880; and Henni's successor in the See of Milwaukee.

[4] The Redemptorists first came to the United States in June, 1832, from Austria and all through the nineteenth century they continued to be one of the leading religious congregations to devote its labors to the German immigrants. Gabriel Rumpler, C.SS.R., was pastor of St. Alphonsus Church in Baltimore at this time.

[5] Charles Schraudenbach was pastor of St. Ignatius Church, Racine, Wisconsin.

(*Source*: John Tracy Ellis, ed. *Documents of American Catholic History*. Vol. 1:1493–1865. Wilmington, Del.: Michael Glazier, 1987, 274–77.)

WOLFF, MADELEVA (1887–1964)

Author, educator, college president. She was born Mary Evaline Wolff on May 24, 1887, in Cumberland, Wisconsin, the second of four children and the only daughter of August and Lucy Arntz Wolff. Eva, as her family called her, grew up in a happy household where education was valued. Through her first year in college, her entire education occurred in the Wisconsin public school system. In 1905 she attended the University of Wisconsin in Madison where she helped found a Catholic student center, a

Madeleva Wolff

prototype of the Newman Centers established on state college campuses. After seeing a magazine advertisement for St. Mary's College, Notre Dame, Indiana, the independent Eva applied and was accepted.

The college opened Mary Evaline to a whole new world of intellectual challenge and spiritual commitment. Under the tutelage of an English professor and poet, Sr. Rita Heffernan, C.S.C., Eva discovered her love and talent for writing, especially poetry. She also found in Sr. Rita a more than capable mentor who inspired this high-spirited young woman to consider dedicating herself to the Holy Cross religious order. In 1908, only two years after her arrival, Mary Evaline took her first vows as Sr. Mary Madeleva. The following year she graduated from St. Mary's with an A.B. in English. Over the next nine years, she taught English in both the college's department and the girl's academy on campus. Her lifetime commitment to Holy Cross Sisters came with perpetual vows on August 14, 1915. She completed her master's degree in English at Notre Dame University in 1918 through a summer program opened to women in 1909.

The year after Sr. Madeleva completed her M.A. degree, her superior assigned her as principal of Sacred Heart Academy in Ogden, Utah, where she served from 1919 to 1922. In the fall of 1922 she became principal at Holy Rosary Academy in Woodland, California. The new assignment facilitated her other obligation, that of completing a doctorate in English at the University of California at Berkeley. In 1925 Sr. Madeleva Wolff became the first woman religious to receive a doctorate from Berkeley. Her dissertation, "Pearl: A Study of Spiritual Dryness," explicitly drew from her own experience as a woman religious in its literary analysis. Appleton-Century published the work the same year that she graduated. A collection of essays on various topics including Chaucer and nineteenth-century religious poetry appeared the same year.

Madeleva's own poetry rather than her analysis of others' verse won her national recognition. Her first collection of poetry, *Knights Errant and Other Poems,* appeared in 1923. Determined to place Catholic literary works before the general public, Madeleva, using her religious name, submitted her works to secular journals. Among those who accepted her verse were *Bookman, American Mercury, Saturday Review of Literature,* and *The New York Times.* She also published in Catholic periodicals like *Ave Maria, Commonweal,* and *America.* Her poetry expressed wonder over the presence of beauty whether in nature or sacrament and the deep and passionate mystery of love of God.

Educator and College President

With doctorate in hand, Sr. Madeleva took on the other task for which she is most noted: a college administrator.

From 1925 to 1933 she served as the first dean and president at the Holy Cross Sisters' new college in Utah, St. Mary's-of-the-Wasatch. These eight years prepared her for her longest assignment, twenty-seven years as president of her alma mater, St. Mary's College. Refreshed after a year's study at Oxford where she heard the lectures of such notables as C. S. Lewis, J.R.R. Tolkien, and Martin D'Arcy, S.J., Madeleva dedicated herself to her new position.

The published poet and essayist laid great plans for the small Catholic women's college with an enrollment in 1934 of only three hundred taught by dedicated Holy Cross Sisters. By 1961 the college enrollment had grown to 1,100 students with a broadly educated faculty of laypeople and religious. She raised money to build several new buildings, including science and fine arts facilities. The NBC opera performed for the 1956 dedication of the fine arts auditorium and gained national attention for St. Mary's College.

The enrollment increases and new facilities reveal little of the genuine educational innovations implemented under Sr. Madeleva's leadership. In 1935, the year after her arrival, she initiated a required course of study known as the Trivium. Inspired by the medieval course of studies, this program combined logic, rhetoric, and grammar with the intent of teaching students to write well by teaching them how to think clearly. In 1956, inspired by Christopher Dawson's vision of Christian Humanism, Madeleva established an interdisciplinary major known as "Christian Culture." Drawing upon the disciplines of history, literature, fine arts, philosophy, and theology, the program exposed students to the richness of Catholic intellectual traditions.

Madeleva's educational innovations affected not only St. Mary's undergraduates but also women educators across the nation. In 1943 Sr. Madeleva founded the Graduate School of Sacred Theology to provide women with an opportunity to receive advanced degrees in theological studies. The school modeled itself after seminary education and thus provided a unique opportunity for Catholic women. She took this bold step in response to a growing recognition among Catholic educators that high-school and college religion courses needed vast improvement.

Another major contribution to the education of women educators came from a proposal to reform the education of young religious teachers. Her 1949 talk entitled "The Education of Sister Lucy" argued convincingly for the careful intellectual and spiritual formation of young sisters to prepare them to cope with the demands of the modern classroom. Her summons to educate the whole person served as a major inspiration for the Sister Formation program of the 1950s.

Madeleva received recognition from many venues—six honorary doctorates, the Siena Medal, the Cum Laude

Poets' Corner Medal, the Campion Award of the Catholic Book Club, and the Woman of Achievement Award from Women's International Institute. Her leadership skills were drawn upon as vice president of the Indiana Conference on Higher Education, president of the Catholic Poetry Society of America, and member of the Catholic Commission on Intellectual and Cultural Affairs. Her essays on women's education reveal the vision which inspired such respect among her contemporaries. Convinced that God's grace can and does transform nature, Madeleva acted on the conviction that women educated in the full knowledge of their infinite potential in light of their supernatural ends should, could, and would transform their society. She died in Boston, Massachusetts, on July 25, 1964.

Sister Madeleva Wolff's papers are at St. Mary's College Archives and Holy Cross Sisters Provincial Archives, Notre Dame, Indiana.

Kennelly, Karen, C.S.J. "Wolff, Sister Madeleva (Mary Evaline)." *Notable American Women: Modern Period, A–Z.* Cambridge, 1980.

Klein, Mary Ellen. "Sister M. Madeleva Wolff, C.S.C., Saint Mary's College, Notre Dame, Indiana: A Study in Presidential Leadership 1934–1961." Ph.D. dissertation, Kent State University, 1983.

Mandell, Gail. *One Woman's Life.* New York, 1994.

Williamson, Susan. "Sister Mary Madeleva Wolff." *Women Educators in the United States.* Wesport, 1994.

Wolff, Madeleva, C.S.C. *Knights Errant and Other Poems* (1923).

_____. *Chaucer's Nuns and Other Essays* (1925).

_____. *Pearl: A Study in Spiritual Dryness* (1925).

_____. *Penelope and Other Poems* (1927).

_____. "Scholarship for Catholic Women." *The Catholic Educational Review* 30 (January 1932) 21–32.

_____. *A Question of Lovers and Other Poems* (1935).

_____. *The Happy Christmas Wind* (1936).

_____. *Four Girls* (1941).

_____. *Addressed to Youth* (1944).

_____. *Lost Language and Other Essays* (1951).

_____. *American Twelfth Night* (1955).

_____. *My First Seventy Years* (1959).

_____. *The Four Last Things* (1959).

_____. *Conversations with Cassandra* (1961).

SANDRA YOCUM MIZE

WOMEN RELIGIOUS IN AMERICA

Pioneer Beginnings 1723–1850

Religious congregations of women in the Roman Catholic tradition began contributing to the formation of the Church in the United States when nine Ursuline nuns came to French colonial New Orleans in 1727. They set a pattern for later congregations by opening an academy for girls, a free school for blacks and Native Americans, and an orphanage. Their acceptance of the practice of holding slaves, reinforced by most of the early nineteenth-century U.S. congregations, also set precedents which would affect attitudes toward African American women and religious life. After the Louisiana Territory was absorbed into the U.S.A. (1803), they assisted by their hospitality the French congregations who reached their destinations along the upper Mississippi valley by way of New Orleans.

Prior to Independence, hostility toward Catholics and restrictive laws precluded religious congregations from establishing foundations in the British colonies. Anglo-Catholic families in Maryland often sent their daughters to be educated in Belgian and French convents where eighteenth-century records show that thirty-six women from Maryland entered religious orders, including three members of the Matthew family who were professed as Carmelites in Hoogstraeten, Belgium. Ann Matthew, prioress of the house, along with her two Carmelite nieces and an English-born nun, established a Carmelite monastery in Port Tobacco, Maryland, in 1790, as the first house of women religious in what was then territorial U.S.A.

Bishop John Carroll, still a few months shy of his consecration as first and only bishop in the new republic, had prepared for the Carmelites' arrival by obtaining papal permission for them to teach despite the contemplative life enjoined by their rule. This unusual act reflected Carroll's concern that the nuns be able to justify their existence and earn their living in the midst of a largely Protestant population with a long colonial history of virulent anti-Catholicism. With only 30,000 Catholics in a population of 3.9 million, families who could endow or give alms to a cloistered community were few and critics abounded. There was, moreover, an urgent need for teachers and schools.

The women declined to make use of the permission and, aside from a brief period in the 1830s when they conducted a school to alleviate extreme poverty, dedicated themselves to a life of prayer. A forty-seven-year-old woman, Elizabeth Carberry, joined them a few months after their arrival, thus initiating a stream of American-born women who would either join immigrant communities or form their own during the decades to come.

A second important foundational contribution of the Matthew women and their companions was the permanent establishment of contemplative life for women. Several other groups were short-lived: neither the Poor Clares who came to Georgetown in 1794, nor the Trappistines who came to New York City in 1810, survived more than a few years. The Maryland Carmelites endured, eventually founding a number of daughter houses before successful initiatives later in the nineteenth century by the Poor Clares, Mexican Carmelites, Magdalens (the contemplative branch of the Good Shepherd Sisters), and contemplative Dominicans widened opportunities for American-born women desiring vowed contemplative life.

Even with the elaboration of Carmelite and related foundations, numbers of women choosing contemplative life remained very small in comparison to those choosing the active or apostolic life soon to be offered by an abundance of congregations. This was in marked contrast to women's experience in the Latin American countries colonized by Spain and Portugal. There, the Carmelite model, having persisted as the only way for women to live vowed religious life for much of a three-hundred-year colonial period, exerted an influence that persisted well into modern times, with a corresponding limit on women's roles in Church growth. The Canadian experience more closely resembled that of the U.S.A. with the introduction of the Ursuline way of life into Quebec in 1639. A succession of active congregations beginning with the Congregation of Notre Dame and the Grey Nuns facilitated the entry of middle-class women into groups engaged in an active apostolate.

A group of three "pious ladies" who came to Georgetown from Philadelphia in the mid-1790s to teach with the Poor Clares, and who stayed on to form their own religious group when the Poor Clares left a few years later, constituted a kind of transition from contemplative to active religious life in the United States. They adopted the Visitation Rule which bound them to a cloistered way of life but also placed stress on teaching as a ministry. Founded by Francis de Sales and Jane Frances de Chantal in the early seventeenth century, the order's original rule had allowed for an active apostolate without cloister but had been modified to conform to Tridentine reform ideals.

These defined cloister and solemn vows as a necessity for women's religious life, and forced modifications of early experiments, such as those by the Ursuline and Visitation founders, to open religious life to women seeking to exercise an active apostolate. Vincent de Paul and Louise de Marillac evaded these strictures by stipulating simple, annual vows for their Daughters of Charity in 1633. The Sisters of St. Joseph, formally established in 1650, accomplished the same end by securing letters patent from the king of France rather than papal approval.

Supported by the seventeenth-century Visitation Rule, the women promptly opened Visitation Academy for girls as the first of its kind in what was then territorial U.S.A. Twenty-nine others had joined the founders by 1816 when a papal indult finally allowed Archbishop Neale, an early friend of the women and Carroll's successor, to accept their solemn vows. The difficulties experienced by the Visitation group in securing permission to pronounce solemn vows were indicative of the rigid canonical stress on cloister at that time, and hesitancy in approving adaptations to the American environment.

A fresh impetus to the growth of religious life for women came when the convert and widow, Elizabeth Seton, came from New York to Emmitsburg, Maryland, in 1808. There a French Sulpician priest, Louis DuBourg, persuaded her to use the Daughters of Charity Rule to organize a religious way of life for herself and the four companions who had come with her. They took the name of Sisters of Charity of St. Joseph, later shortened to Sisters of Charity, and with the flexibility allowed for by the Vincentian Rule, began an academy-free school combination and took in orphans as their initial apostolate. Conditions were extremely primitive, but new women soon came along to swell their numbers, and income from the academy helped them support free schooling for children unable to pay anything. Within less than a decade, they had sent sisters to Philadelphia (1816) and New York City (1817), in response to urgent requests from bishops, to open orphanages.

Mother Seton's Sisters of Charity had acquired rudimentary nursing skills in the process of caring for their own members and boarders, as well as providing emergency care to the public when epidemics of cholera and yellow fever struck the port cities. Furthermore, they were following the rule of a congregation which already had an extensive commitment to hospital work in Europe. When doctors at the University of Maryland opened the country's first voluntary hospital in 1823, a fifty-bed infirmary in Baltimore, five Sisters of Charity agreed to manage and staff the institution.

Mother Seton, who died in 1823, was the catalyst for a growing number of vocations among American-born women. The dominance of American-born membership, a vital factor for growth and apostolic effectiveness, was in sharp contrast to the situation in Latin America where women born in Spain accounted for the majority of religious until well into the twentieth century.

The next several congregations to be founded in the U.S.A.—the Sisters of Loretto and the Sisters of Charity of Nazareth, both begun in Kentucky in 1812; and the Sisters of the Third Order of St. Dominic, also in Kentucky, in 1822—demonstrated traits similar to those of Mother Seton's Sisters of Charity. They were each formed around a nucleus of women, a generation or more removed from immigration, who embraced the vocation of teaching united by the bonds of religious vows. The few priests ministering to the Catholic community in Kentucky welcomed the offer by these women to open schools in their frontier parishes and advised them on how to organize themselves into religious communities.

The Sisters of Loretto, after an unsuccessful experiment following a very ascetic rule of life devised by their spiritual guide, Belgian priest Charles Nerinckx, adopted the Rule of St. Augustine which had proven its usefulness to apostolic communities of women in Europe. As suggested by their title, the Sisters of Charity adopted the rule and statutes of the Emmitsburg Sisters of Charity without, however, seeking any affiliation with them. Dominican priest Thomas Wilson adapted the contemplative Second Order of St. Dominic Rule to frontier conditions for the four women whose vows he received and to whom he gave the Dominican habit.

These groups quickly attracted more members and were generally able to establish daughter houses within a decade of being formed. The same rapid Americanization in terms of membership affected congregations sent to the U.S.A. from Europe beginning with the Society of the Sacred Heart which arrived in New Orleans in 1818, in the persons of Mother Rose Philippine Duchesne and four companions. The French-speaking group settled in St. Louis and received its first American postulant within two years. Others followed, permitting the congregation, with the help of some further members from France before Mother Duchesne's death in 1852, to establish six schools in the lower Mississippi valley; a motherhouse, orphanage, academy, and parish school in St. Louis; and a mission among the Potawatomi in Kansas.

The motherhouses of the earliest congregations were all located in slave-holding states, and most of the groups owned slaves who helped with farm and household work. The Sisters of Loretto received several African American women in the early 1820s in a kind of second-class capacity resembling that of lay sisters in the European tradition. The practice was abandoned after only a few years. Later that same decade, Elizabeth Lange, a mulatto immigrant to Baltimore from Saint Domingue, gathered several Haitian women about her for the purpose of teaching African American children. Maryland public schools were legally prohibited from teaching slave children and no exceptions were made for free immigrant Negroes. The women who dared to take up this cause did so in secret at considerable danger to themselves and with little or no support from the Catholic community in Maryland. By 1829 they professed vows as Oblate Sisters of Providence, adapting the rule of an older French congregation to the ministry of educating African American girls.

From this point on to midcentury the handful of indigenous and immigrant congregations that introduced religious life for women in the U.S.A. was swelled by sixteen new foundations. American-born women, or, in several cases, recently arrived immigrants from Ireland, formed five new congregations: the Sisters of Charity of Our Lady of Mercy, under Bishop John England in Charleston, South Carolina, 1829; another congregation just for African American women, the Sisters of the Holy Family, in New Orleans, 1842; the Sisters of Charity of the Blessed Virgin Mary in Philadelphia, 1843; Sisters, Servants of the Immaculate Heart of Mary in Monroe, Michigan, 1845; and the Dominican Sisters of Sinsinawa, Wisconsin, 1847. Eleven new groups came as missionaries to the U.S.A. from Europe during this twenty-year span: Sisters of St. Joseph from France; Sisters of Notre Dame de Namur from Belgium; Sisters of Providence from France; Sisters of the Good Shepherd and the Congregation of the Holy Cross, both from France; Sisters of Mercy from Ireland; Sisters

of the Precious Blood from Switzerland; and Ursulines, School Sisters of Notre Dame, Franciscans, and Dominicans from Germany.

Sisters in an Immigrant Church, 1850–1920

By the close of the Civil War in 1865 an additional thirty congregations, plus offshoots of the earlier groups, gave a definitive cast to the U.S. Church as one in which women, bound together by vows of poverty, chastity, and obedience, and pursuing a life of intensive prayer and the spiritual and corporate works of mercy enjoined by the Gospels, constituted a part of every diocese. Groups following the Franciscan Third Order Regular Rule were formed in Pennsylvania, New York, and Illinois, each originating with a few women who responded to the appeal of bishops or priests to meet the immigrant needs. The adaptability of this rule, which had evolved from that of the cloistered Second Order or Poor Clares, soon proved itself in the U.S.A. where seventy-seven congregations ultimately adopted it.

The remaining American foundations from this period, the Congregation of St. Agnes and the Sisters of Charity of Leavenworth, each exemplified the growth process typical of the period. The St. Agnes group formed around a small group of women in Wisconsin to teach children of German immigrants. The Nazareth Sisters of Charity had sent members to Tennessee in 1842; when this mission dispersed in the 1850s, some returned to the motherhouse in Kentucky while others went to the Kansas frontier. There, the founding group of six professed sisters, a novice, and a postulant lost no time opening an academy and a day school; they continued caring for an orphan girl brought with them from Tennessee, and were soon a common sight in the streets of Leavenworth caring for the sick from the numerous wagon trains passing through and meeting a myriad of other local needs.

The Leavenworth Charities pioneered hospitals in the West when Sr. Joanna Bruner, trained in nursing at their Nashville hospital, organized the first nonmilitary hospital in Kansas (1863). The 1870s and 1880s found the congregation establishing hospitals in Montana, Wyoming, Utah, and Colorado. Sr. Blandina Segale's letters to her sister in the Cincinnati Sisters of Charity record for posterity some of the more colorful of the women's exploits in the last-named state and in New Mexico.

The twenty-five European congregations who made foundations from 1850 to 1865 enriched the immigrant Church with their missionary zeal, their practical charity and expertise, and their experience with traditional and innovative forms of religious life. Among these groups were Benedictine women who brought monasticism from Germany; more Third Order Franciscans, from Germany and Italy; Ursulines from France; Sisters of Mercy and

Presentation sisters from Ireland; and more Sisters of St. Joseph from France.

Still other groups to come at this time from France, where an amazing religious revival would give rise to over five hundred new women's congregations in the nineteenth century, were Sisters of Charity of St. Augustine; Daughters of the Heart of Mary; the Congregation of the Incarnate Word and the Blessed Sacrament; the Daughters of the Cross; Sisters of Our Lady of Charity; and Sisters of the Humility of Mary. Isolated groups came from other European countries, including Mother Cornelia Connelly's Society of the Holy Child Jesus, from England; and the Sisters of St. Mary of Namur, from Belgium.

Canada made three U.S. foundations in the antebellum period: the Northwest became the scene of the missionary labors of the Sisters of the Holy Names of Jesus and Mary, and of the Sisters of Providence, the latter under the inspired leadership of Mother Joseph Pariseau. The Congregation of Notre Dame sent women to minister to French-speaking immigrants in Illinois.

The geographic spread of houses of women religious up to the time of the Civil War reflected both the growth of the Catholic population in the older states of Maryland, Pennsylvania, New York, Ohio, Kentucky, and Louisiana; but also the appeals of bishops and priests for religious to assist them in poor or frontier dioceses in South Carolina and West Virginia; Arkansas, Kansas, and Missouri; Texas; Iowa, Illinois, Michigan, Minnesota, and Wisconsin; California; and Washington and Oregon.

Although the massive waves of immigration that were to characterize the late nineteenth and earlier twentieth centuries—a phenomenon that affected Canada and the Latin American republics in relatively minor ways—had yet to create the immigrant Church, Irish and German Catholics were already arriving in large numbers. The Catholic population had begun the dynamic growth which would move it from less than one percent of the total population at the time of independence, to 10 percent at midcentury, to 16 percent by World War I. Women religious kept pace with the growth, with an estimated 6,000 by the Civil War; 32,000 by 1890; and 84,000 by 1917. The significance of this trend for the Church was heightened by the failure of clergy to match the sisters' growth: the priest-sister ratio, roughly equal in 1850 (1,109 priests to 1,344 sisters), had altered by 1900 to 3.5 sisters for every priest.

Two phenomena impelled the growth: vocations from among first-generation immigrants, and the constant influx of immigrant congregations. No fewer than 152 new European foundations came between the Civil War and World War I as Central and Eastern European motherhouses sent women to minister to immigrants from those regions, especially from Poland, and numerous German and French motherhouses made U.S. foundations. The waning number of new congregations from Ireland was more than compensated for by the growing number of Irish women entering U.S. congregations. As a result, they came to dominate many groups not of Irish origin.

Abatement of the anti-Catholic prejudice that threatened Church freedom in these years owed much to the visible example of sisters putting their lives at risk to attend to the sick during the epidemics and in the Civil War. During the Civil War, 617 sisters from twenty-one communities ministered to the sick and injured of both the Union and the Confederacy. The generic name of "sisters of charity" or of "mercy" by which nuns came to be called is indicative of the impression they made on the public as a result of ministry to the sick.

The largest number of Civil War sister-nurses was supplied by the Daughters of Charity, the first in the country to conduct hospitals. In all, 479 hospitals were founded by sisters up to World War I, 58 by the Daughters. Congregations following the Sisters of Mercy Rule founded 79 hospitals, followed by the various Franciscan congregations who together accounted for 57; and the Sisters of St. Joseph who established 35. The Sisters of Providence were particularly prominent in this work in the West and Northwest; and, in the South, the Sisters of Mercy, the Daughters of Charity, and the Sisters of the Incarnate Word. Still others organized health care for particular immigrant groups—various branches of the Franciscans among Germans in such cities as Baltimore, Philadelphia, Cincinnati, St. Louis, Milwaukee, and Cleveland; Felician Sisters among immigrants from Poland in Chicago and Manitowoc, Wisconsin; and Mother Cabrini's Missionary Sisters of the Sacred Heart among Italians in New York City, Chicago, and Seattle. Others, such as the Dominican Servants of Relief for Incurable Cancer, founded by convert Rose Hawthorne Lathrop in 1899, dedicated themselves to ministry to the sick poor.

Sisters conducting hospitals in this era exercised great resourcefulness to finance their care of impoverished patients. The practice of charging fees to those who could pay to balance free care was introduced in most early hospitals but never covered more than a third of hospital costs.

Impressive as was the work of the Catholic sisterhoods in hospitals, no activity equaled that of education in its importance for the Church in America. Most American congregations originated with a small group of women, often widows, who had associated with one another as teachers of young children. The clergy, who advised the women, and recruited others overseas, saw education as the Church's most pressing need. This conviction was heightened by development of a public school system with a pronounced Protestant bias during the years of massive immigration, circumstances which prompted bishops to mandate establishment of parochial schools (Third Plenary Council of Baltimore, 1884).

A partial "system" of parochial schools was in place by then, composed of the free schools established by nearly every congregation of women. By the Civil War, women were responsible for around 200 academies, income from which was usually applied to cover expenses of the nearly 1,500 free schools. An explosive growth occurred after the war, with an average increment by decade of over 100 parochial schools and nearly 40,000 pupils, the total by 1920 reaching 6,551 schools and 1,701,219 pupils in a Catholic population numbering 17,753,553.

The Third Plenary Council also concerned itself with educational standards, calling upon bishops to facilitate the establishment of normal schools by conferring with superiors of congregations (canon 205). This laudable concern was not backed up by resources, with the result that it fell to the sisterhoods to devise means whereby their members could meet the higher teacher certification standards being required in many states. They did so by incorporating teacher-training courses in novitiate programs, sending sisters to public normal schools and universities (Catholic universities did not admit women until 1911), and creating their own postsecondary institutions.

The uniqueness of the U.S. sisterhoods compared to those of Europe, South America, and Canada is especially remarkable in their creation of colleges. Beginning in the last quarter of the nineteenth century, a handful of women's congregations anticipated the extension of academy curricula into the baccalaureate level by securing state charters officially recognizing their right to award college degrees. The School Sisters of Notre Dame in Maryland, Ursulines in Ohio (Cleveland), Sisters of the Holy Cross in Indiana, Sisters of Charity in New Jersey, and Sisters of Notre Dame de Namur in the nation's capital, had taken this step by the turn of the century.

Others followed in quick succession, until by the time Catholic women's colleges were first identified on the Catholic Educational Association accreditation list (1918), ten additional groups were sponsoring colleges: Sisters of St. Joseph and Franciscans in Minnesota; Dominicans in Wisconsin; Sisters of Charity of the Blessed Virgin Mary in Iowa; Sisters, Servants of the Immaculate Heart of Mary in Michigan; Ursulines and Grey Nuns in New York; Sisters of Mercy in New Jersey; and Religious of the Sacred Heart in Ohio. Friction with bishops, which had earlier centered around diocesan control of congregations, was revived by the sisters' ambitious foray into higher education.

Undeterred by the opposition of some bishops who felt it was neither appropriate nor necessary for women, destined for domestic roles, to seek a college education, the sisterhoods grasped the implication of rising certification standards, and expanding employment opportunities for women, by founding colleges.

Similar concerns prompted the creation of schools of nursing in sister-owned hospitals by 1900—by which time 59 of the country's 393 such schools were operated by Catholic sisters.

The limited resources of the sisterhoods, always more abundant in personnel than in money, were somehow stretched to support the higher education of their members. There were isolated examples of sisters holding advanced degrees at the time of entrance or shortly thereafter. The Sisters of Notre Dame de Namur admitted a practicing physician in 1891, her M.D. having been earned at Boston University. Here and there, entrants came with baccalaureate or even master's degrees. The great majority had a high school diploma or less. Between 1890 and 1920 numerous congregations made a concerted effort to enable members to study for normal school or baccalaureate degrees and to send promising sisters on for advanced degrees.

A Sister of Charity (College of St. Elizabeth, Convent Station, New Jersey) was the first to earn a doctorate (1909), with others following in the next decade. At the College of St. Catherine, St. Paul, Minnesota, a group of eight newly professed sisters assigned to the college in 1921 (having already begun baccalaureate studies) had, within a decade, earned Oxford master's degrees (two, in English language and literature); doctorates from the University of Munich (two, in chemistry and German); advanced degrees from two top U.S. fine arts conservatories; and a doctorate in English from the University of Chicago where Mother Antonia McHugh, dean of St. Catherine's College, had earned her baccalaureate and master's degrees.

Obstacles in the form of scarce financial resources, unsympathetic or cautious bishops who feared exposure of sisters to secular tendencies in public or sectarian universities, or wanted more sisters assigned to parochial schools, and restricted opportunities to attend Catholic universities that were closed to women except for summer sessions, were formidable. Canonical barriers prohibiting women religious from pursuing medical degrees were successfully challenged by the Austrian immigrant, Anna Marie Dengel, when she founded the Medical Mission Sisters (1925) for work among women in India.

The enormity of the basic task confronting congregations striving to afford members wider educational opportunities is well illustrated by the action of the Sisters of Charity of the Blessed Virgin Mary of Dubuque, Iowa. The sum of $6,000 they budgeted to send six sisters for full-time baccalaureate study in 1911 was equivalent to the stipends paid to thirty teaching sisters! As a result of sisters' determination in the matter of women's education, their own as well as that of the laity, was that U.S. sisterhoods progressed into the twentieth century as a highly educated force in U.S. Church and society.

The Mature Years, 1920–1965

Immigration continued to exert decisive influence on sisters' roles in Church and society even as the country entered into a period of restrictive laws that slowed immigration to a trickle. Membership in congregations expanded at a remarkable rate, going from around 90,500 in 1920 to 209,000 by 1965. The increase came primarily from daughters of second-generation immigrants who found religious life, with its triple dimension of prayer, common life, and ministry, an attractive vocation. New congregations continued to be founded from motherhouses in Europe and elsewhere, with 145 groups from those sources coming to the U.S.A. during this period. Another 27 new congregations were founded within the U.S.A.

The accelerating demand for schools and hospitals, especially during the baby-boom years following World War II, gravitated around the same focal point of population growth among Catholics and the incorporation of suburbs into once urban dioceses.

The revised Code of Canon Law promulgated in 1918 incorporated the earlier (1900, *Conditae a Christo*) papal approval of active congregations with simple vows while also reinforcing for these groups aspects of cloister and a certain uniformity of custom and spirit. The Code lent greater force to episcopal authority over diocesan congregations, a status replaced by papal approbation for many of the larger congregations who had directly submitted their rules to the Vatican for approval in the late nineteenth and early twentieth centuries. Whether diocesan or papal, congregations had a keen sense of participation, in collaboration with the local bishop, in the life and work of the Church.

Contemplative groups, never more than a tiny fraction of the total of women religious in the U.S.A., nevertheless became a stable part of the Church in this country. Carmelites, the first and largest of the contemplative groups, numbered over 1,000 by 1965, followed by the Poor Clares and Second Order Dominicans, both of whom had around 650 members. In all, over 4,000 women belonged to contemplative communities by the end of this period and were present in 41 states.

Monastic communities also grew, best exemplified by the Benedictines who numbered 7,141 sisters by the close of this period. One of their monasteries, St. Benedict's in Minnesota, was the largest such house in the world with over 1,000 members inclusive of dependent priories in Japan and the Bahamas.

Willingness on the part of communities to undertake missions outside the U.S.A. had its beginnings during the last quarter of the nineteenth century when women's congregations sent individual members or groups to open missions in parts of Central and South America and the Caribbean, India, and South Africa; in the leper colonies of Hawaii; and to China. This trend was given greater thrust by the formation of the Maryknoll congregation specifically for foreign mission work. Maryknoll Sisters undertook their first missions to China in the 1920s, as did also several

other women's congregations. Others, including the Sisters, Servants of the Immaculate Heart (Philadelphia) opened missions in South America.

The vast majority of congregations concentrated their resources solely on meeting the needs of the U.S. Church until papal appeals in the 1950s and 1960s prompted numerous congregations to begin missions in parts of Asia, Africa, and Latin America. By 1965, approximately 3,000 women religious were engaged in foreign missions.

Within the U.S.A., the Sisters of the Blessed Sacrament for Indians and Colored people, founded in 1891 by the Philadelphia heiress, Katherine Drexel, worked alongside older congregations to maintain the Church's presence among Native Americans and African Americans. By the time of her death in 1955, 69 schools for Native Americans and African Americans either founded or supported by her were teaching 15,000 pupils. Xavier University, founded by Drexel in 1915 to give African Americans access to Catholic higher education, gained accreditation in the 1920s and continues to flourish as the only institution of its kind in the Western Hemisphere. Other groups such as the Home Mission Sisters of America (Glenmary, 1952), were founded to minister in rural regions of the U.S.A. having a sparse Catholic population.

Both foreign and domestic missionary activity were peripheral to the overriding concern of congregations to meet the educational and health-care needs of an increasingly urban, middle-class U.S. Catholic population. All sectors of the sisters' educational work saw growth and, by the end of this period, significant incorporation of lay teachers into parochial school, academy, and college faculties. As this period drew to a close, over 10,000 schools with 4.56 million pupils were staffed by around 100,000 sisters and 74,000 lay teachers. The number of women's colleges had grown to 168, with a similar sister-lay faculty ratio.

Congregations had to exert considerable pressure on bishops to accept the shift to greater lay involvement in parish schools, with a corresponding increase in salary expenses. The sisters' resolve in the matter had come from an awareness that the old system was breaking down. Assigning newly professed sisters to the classroom with minimal teaching credentials and expecting them to earn a baccalaureate degree through summer sessions, sometimes over the course of fifteen or twenty years or more, was no longer tolerable either in terms of sisters' health and prayer life, or in terms of educational standards. The Sister Formation Conference, organized in 1954 to promote and facilitate an education for women religious that would integrate academics and spirituality, captured the essence of a movement begun in the 1940s to address the issues. Sr. Madeleva Wolff, president of St. Mary's College (Indiana), created a master's degree program in theology in 1941 out of concern to meet the needs of sisters obliged to teach the subject without the appropriate advanced degree. St. Mary's offered then and for many years to come women's only opportunity to earn advanced degrees in theology at a Catholic institution.

Sisters in health care felt the same pressures as educators when rising standards and a surge of hospital construction following passage of the 1946 Hill-Burton Act intensified the need for more and better prepared personnel. Fifty-three congregations built 123 new hospitals during the postwar era alone, for a total of over 800 Catholic hospitals by the end of this period. Degree programs in nursing had been assumed by colleges in many instances, but hospital sisters were still responsible for 341 schools of nursing.

Attention to sisters' formation programs and the growing partnership with the laity reflected a changing theology of religious life which had its roots in such papal documents as *Mediator Dei* and *Mystici Corporis*. These texts, as well as the liturgical reform movement, moved away from the Tridentine emphasis on personal salvation and a hierarchy of states of perfection to stress a common baptismal call to holiness among the faithful. It was against this context that Pius XII convened assemblies of religious superiors in Rome (1950, 1952) and urged women religious to return to the spirit which had animated their founders and to adapt outmoded customs to the demands of the day. Saintly founders had incarnated Christ in their own time and country; now, superiors were to adapt nonessentials in the light of the same gospel imperative.

The Conference of Major Superiors of Women, formed in response to a papal recommendation in 1956, as well as the Sister Formation Conference and various associations or federations of autonomous congregations who shared the same rules (Sisters of Mercy, Benedictines, Sisters of St. Joseph, Ursulines, Franciscans, Dominicans, and others), brought religious together in national assemblies and workshops to study the latest trends.

Consequently, it was a very receptive group of women that heard the Belgian Cardinal Suenens' call to action on the eve of the Second Vatican Council. His central thesis, set forth in *The Nun in the World* (1962), was that all Christians, and certainly all religious—excepting the strictly contemplative—had an obligation to spread the gospel by direct personal action.

Religious and the Contemporary Church, 1965–1990

Few groups took the renewal message of the Second Vatican Council as seriously as U.S. women religious. Inspired by the vision of the People of God as the Church as set forth in *Lumen gentium* (1964), and urged by *Perfectae Caritatis* (1966) and other postconciliar documents to seek renewal by returning to the original spirit of their communities, studying the signs of the times, and re-

flecting on how to live the gospel in the contemporary world, communities subjected their life and ministry to prayerful scrutiny. A new revision of the Code of Canon Law (1983) offered further guidelines for a period of experimentation during which congregations revised their constitutions to reflect insights into what renewal meant for their life and ministry.

Despite their apparent preparation for assimilating the council's call to renewal, most communities went through a period of tension and dislocation before achieving internal consensus and Vatican approval for revised constitutions. Large numbers of women left religious life in the 1960s and 1970s, and diminishing numbers entered. The process of maintaining older ministries and beginning new ones was undermined by shrinking numbers of religious and the necessity, paralleled in society at large, of allocating substantial resources to the care of retired members.

Differences of opinion over renewal concepts and applications led to a resurgence of nineteenth-century episcopal-religious tensions, and resulted in some cases in irreconcilable divisions, as in the case of such diocesan communities as the Glenmary Sisters and Sisters of the Immaculate Heart of Mary (Los Angeles). On a national level, some congregations challenged the legitimacy of the Leadership Conference of Women Religious (the renamed Conference of Major Superiors of Women) and formed a rival group. More often, differences were resolved amicably though not without cost to the parties involved.

As a consequence of postconciliar trends, membership in women's congregations fell by nearly half, to 111,000 in 1990. At the same time, a subtle shift took place among religious away from a traditional concept of charitable work: having labored for years to carry out the works of mercy so as to alleviate ignorance, poverty, sickness, hunger, and homelessness, religious now began to reflect on the necessity for structural change and social activism if they were to be faithful to the spirit of their founders and the Church was to be true to its gospel mission.

Sisters continued to maintain traditional works. These included numerous free-standing hospitals as well as newly created health systems. The largest of these, conducted by Daughters of Charity (St. Louis), Sisters of Mercy (St. Louis), Sisters of the Incarnate Word (Houston), Sisters of Providence (Seattle), Sisters of Holy Cross (South Bend), and Sisters of St. Joseph (Carondelet, Orange), recalled the pioneer roster of women's congregations involved in caring for the sick and orphaned.

Large numbers of academies and colleges were still being conducted by women religious as of 1990, usually with the assistance of lay boards of trustees. Sisters retained an influential presence in parochial schools, while a growing number assumed other parish ministry roles and a variety of direct ministries among the poor.

Catholic women continue to found new congregations, exploring new ways of expressing gospel values and different structures of religious life. Congregations are still emigrating to the U.S.A., including Mother Teresa's Missionary Sisters of Charity from India. U.S. congregations, for their part, are still responding to the missionary call by sending members to parts of Africa, Asia, and Latin America. Some met a martyr's death, as with Maryknoll and Ursuline Sisters and their lay associate in El Salvador (1980), and Adorers of the Blood of Christ Sisters in Liberia (1992).

The process of empowering the laity to assume roles sisters once filled, already well underway before the council, has intensified. Many communities are forming associate programs whereby laypersons formally join themselves to sisters for prayer and ministry without making vows. New ministries typically involve religious with laypersons in collaborative partnership. New congregations often bring religious and laypersons together in a common commitment with or without seeking canonical recognition.

Whatever the tendencies, to preserve past structures or to change them, it is evident that the full implications of the conciliar challenge to renewal has yet to be fully realized. It is also clear that women have given new meaning to religious life by adapting its traditional forms to pioneer and immigrant conditions in the U.S.A., and by initiating new modes of religious commitment in contemporary times.

See also AMERICAN CATHOLIC WOMEN; CATHOLIC EDUCATION, PAROCHIAL; CATHOLIC HEALTH CARE; WOMEN RELIGIOUS IN AMERICA, DEMOGRAPHIC OVERVIEW; WOMEN, RELIGIOUS ORDERS AND CONGREGATIONS OF.

Ewens, Mary, O.P. *The Role of the Nun in Nineteenth Century America.* New York, 1978.

____. "Women in the Convent." *American Catholic Women: A Historical Exploration,* ed. Karen M. Kennelly, C.S.J. New York, 1989, 17–47.

Kauffman, Christopher J. *Ministry and Meaning: A Religious History of Catholic Health Care in the U.S.* New York, 1995.

Kennelly, Karen M., C.S.J. "Historical Perspectives on the Experience of Religious Life in the American Church." *Religious Life in the U.S. Church: The New Dialogue,* ed. Robert J. Daly, S.J., and others. New York, 1984, 79–97.

____. "Foreign Missions and the Renewal Movement." *Review for Religious* 49 (3) (May/June 1990) 445–63.

McNamara, JoAnn Kay. *Sisters in Arms: Catholic Nuns through Two Millennia.* Cambridge, Mass., 1996.

Misner, Barbara, S.C.S.C. *Highly Respected and Accomplished Ladies, Catholic Women Religious in America.* New York, 1988.

Neal, Marie Augusta, S.N.D.deN. *Catholic Sisters in Transition.* Delaware, 1984.

____. *From Nuns to Sisters: An Expanding Vocation.* Connecticut, 1990.

Stepsis, Ursula, C.S.A., and Dolores Liptak, R.S.M., eds. *Pioneer Healers: The History of Women Religious in American Healthcare.* New York, 1989.

Stewart, George C. Jr. *Marvels of Charity: History of American Sisters and Nuns.* Huntington, Indiana, 1994.

Thomas, Evangeline, C.S.J. *Women Religious History Sources.* New York, 1983.

KAREN M. KENNELLY, C.S.J.

WOMEN RELIGIOUS IN AMERICA, DEMOGRAPHIC OVERVIEW

General

A demographic historical study of women religious in the United States would examine such items as women religious population, numbers of orders, type of orders, ethnic composition, ages of members, geographical distribution, and other related matters. In this brief overview, such a complex subject must of necessity be incomplete and treated by generalities.

Historical Population of Women Religious

Total Women Religious and Number of Orders by Decade

Year	Number of Religious	Number of Orders
1830	448	10
1840	902	15
1850	1,941	31
1860	5,090	66
1870	11,424	82
1880	21,835	115
1890	32,534	141
1900	46,583	170
1910	61,944	212
1920	90,558	248
1930	134,339	290
1940	164,293	305
1950	179,657	334
1960	194,353	391
1970	194,941	415
1980	141,115	424
1990	111,481	427
1995	92,107	432

French Ursulines established the first order in the present-day United States in New Orleans in 1727 and American-born Carmelites established the first order in the original thirteen states in Maryland in 1790. By 1840 American women had established nine of the fifteen existing orders; the other six being French-founded. Beginning in 1848, potato famines in Ireland and revolutions throughout Europe propelled floods of immigrants and immigrant religious orders into the United States. American bishops and their agents roamed Europe and Canada seeking women religious to establish and operate schools. Following the

Civil War, the Age of Immigration witnessed burgeoning growth in the number of religious orders and their memberships. Thereafter, until 1965, population growth was based principally on domestic vocations.

At its zenith in 1965, the women religious population was approximately 209,000. Today, most orders are shrinking and many small ones are on the verge of extinction due to lack of vocations and deaths of aging members. The downward spiral since 1965 continues unabated in 1995; a reasonable prognosis puts the total close to 50,000 very early in the twenty-first century.

Number of Orders

The numbers of orders displayed on the chart are based solely on original foundations. Once firmly established, they traditionally dispatched members to make new foundations. In some orders these remained subordinate or co-equal components of the founding order. In other cases, these new foundations became fully autonomous once they were self-sustaining and in turn sent out foundresses to establish more communities. For example, there are thirty independent congregations of Dominican Sisters while Benedictine Sisters of Pontifical Jurisdiction have three federations with fifty-one different communities, and Discalced Carmelites have sixty-four independent monasteries. Thus the number of autonomous "orders" in the United States is far in excess of the original 432 foundations.

Type of Orders

Broad classifications include apostolic, semimonastic, and contemplative. Historically, the great majority of American women religious orders has been apostolic (e.g., the sixty-four Franciscan congregations), concentrating on teaching, health services, charitable works, and missionary endeavors.

Semimonastic orders (e.g., Visitadines) have constituted the second largest group. Often, orders coming from semimonastic communities in Europe had to adjust to the apostolic mode in order to function in the American milieu with its demands for apostolic work, for reasons of poverty, and because of hierarchal pressures. Conversely, at various times and places, some apostolic communities lived lives akin to the semimonastic lifestyle. Since Vatican Council II, many of the semimonastic communities have forgone traditional monastic practices.

Contemplative communities, with the smallest membership, were slow in establishing themselves in the United States. Carmelites of Maryland were the only purely contemplative order until 1875 when Poor Clares made permanent foundations after several failed attempts. Since then there has been a steady growth in the number of such communities. Membership among the contemplative communities shrank in the post-Vatican II years, but far less so than the apostolic and semimonastic communities; and, contrary to the general experience, contemplative communities are currently witnessing vocation increases.

Ethnic Composition

Anglo-American identity predominated among the earliest nineteenth-century American-founded orders. However, by midcentury Irish and Irish-American women had joined in such large numbers that they assumed ascendancy. Since then, Irish surnames have been prominent in most American-founded orders and in many of the immigrant-founded orders. The early French-founded orders "Americanized" only gradually, retaining their French character for decades with in-house French language and customs.

The two decades prior to the Civil War witnessed the arrival of large numbers of French- and German-speaking orders. These newer French orders were quicker to absorb American women and to dilute their French complexions. Conversely, German-speaking immigrant communities tended to locate where Germans had settled and where German-speaking women provided vocations. Some communities adamantly refused to drop their German language and customs, resisting change until forced by the anti-German propaganda generated by World War I; teaching in both German and English ceased while in-house German quickly faded.

Polish immigrant orders of the late nineteenth century retained their ethnic character for extended periods. Some required Polish ancestry for members until recent years. This practice was also true of the small Slavic orders of the early twentieth century. These ethnic groups have experienced fewer membership losses than the general experience.

Primarily because of language barriers, most Italian-founded orders of the late nineteenth and early twentieth centuries had difficulty drawing vocations from the general Catholic population, consequently retaining their Italian identities for considerable periods. Religious Sisters Philippini had this experience whereas Mother Cabrini's Missionaries of the Sacred Heart of Jesus often practiced ministry in areas with little Italian presence and consequently drew vocations from the general population.

Throughout American history immigrant orders have all undergone the Americanization process, some rapidly and others rather slowly. By the middle of the twentieth century there were only a few small orders that did not reflect the ethnic mix of the Catholic population.

Ages of Members

During most of the nineteenth century, the average age of entrants into the communities was markedly young, heavily weighted by teenagers and women in their early twenties.

During the first half of the century, early deaths resulting from consumption, poor diet, and harsh living conditions combined with young new members to maintain low community mean ages. During the latter part of the century and into the twentieth, higher educational levels of the Catholic population and entrants plus increased longevity gradually raised both the average and mean ages of women religious. By 1965 these reflected the general female population. Since 1965, the dearth of vocations, departures of women still relatively young, and the aging of remaining members have resulted in an unprecedented rise, with the average age in 1995 at sixty-seven years.

Geographical Distribution

Founding orders normally established themselves among concentrations of Catholics; this was especially true for ethnic orders situating themselves among ethnic enclaves. Thus, to this day, motherhouses and provincialates are usually found in clearly Catholic areas.

However, historically the geographical distribution of women religious over the nation has not been in ratio to Catholic population distribution; many areas with sparse numbers of Catholics have enjoyed the ministries provided by sisters. Beginning with missionary sisters moving into the West to serve on Indian reservations and in pioneer settlements, they have been willing to answer calls for help by bishops and priests in non-Catholic areas. The Deep South is a prime example. By mid-twentieth century hardly a city or town of any size was without a parochial school or hospital operated by women religious.

Many orders have participated in foreign missionary work, in addition to orders specifically founded for this purpose. The zenith of women religious in foreign missions was in 1968 with 4,105 recorded as serving in numerous countries in Central and South América, Africa, the Far East, and Oceania. Since then, numbers have dwindled by half.

Summary

This brief overview does not mention shifting historical economic status and educational levels, both proper subjects for a demographic study. The foregoing article merely suggests further study by those so interested.

Dehey, Elinor Tong. *Religious Orders of Women in the United States.* Hammond, Ind.: W. B. Conkey Company, 1930.
New Catholic Encyclopedia. Washington, D.C.: The Catholic University of America.
The Official Catholic Directory. New Providence, N.J.: P. J. Kennedy & Sons. Various years.
Stewart, George C. Jr. *Marvels of Charity: History of American Sisters and Nuns.* Huntington, Ind.: Our Sunday Visitor Press, 1994.

GEORGE C. STEWART, JR.

WOMEN, RELIGIOUS ORDERS AND CONGREGATIONS OF

(Sources: *Official Catholic Directory; Catholic Almanac* survey.)

Adorers of the Blood of Christ, A.S.C.: Founded 1834, in Italy; in U.S., 1870. General motherhouse, Rome, Italy. U.S. provinces: 2 Pioneer Lane, Red Bud, IL 62278; 1400 South Sheridan, Wichita, KS 67213; 3950 Columbia Ave., Columbia, PA 17512. Education, retreats, social services, pastoral ministry.

Africa, Missionary Sisters of Our Lady of (Sisters of Africa), M.S.O.L.A.: Founded 1869, at Algiers, Algeria, by Cardinal Lavigerie; in U.S., 1929. General motherhouse, Rome, Italy; U.S. headquarters, 3715 Williams Lane, Chevy Chase, MD 20815. Medical, educational, catechetical and social work in Africa.

Agnes, Sisters of St., C.S.A.: Founded 1858, in U.S., by Rev. Caspar Rehrl. General motherhouse, 475 Gillett St., Fond du Lac, WI 54935. Education, health care, social services.

Ann, Sisters of St., S.S.A.: Founded 1834, in Italy; in U.S., 1952. General motherhouse, Rome, Italy; U.S. headquarters, Mount St. Ann, Ebensburg, PA 15931.

Anne, Sisters of St., S.S.A.: Founded 1850, at Vaudreuil, Que., Canada; in U.S., 1866. General motherhouse, Lachine, Que., Canada; U.S. address, 720 Boston Post Rd., Marlboro, MA 01752. Retreat work, pastoral ministry, religious education.

Anthony, Missionary Servants of St., M.S.S.A.: Founded 1929, in U.S., by Rev. Peter Baque. General motherhouse, 100 Peter Baque Rd., San Antonio, TX 78209. Social work.

Antonine Maronite Sisters: Established in U.S., 1966. U.S. address, 2691 N. Lipkey Rd., North Jackson, OH 44451.

Apostolate, Sisters Auxiliaries of the, S.A.A.: Founded 1903, in Canada; in U.S., 1911. General motherhouse, 689 Maple Terr., Monongah, WV 26555. Education, nursing.

Armenian Sisters of the Immaculate Conception: U.S. address, 6 Eliot Rd., Lexington, MA 02173.

Assumption, Little Sisters of the, L.S.A.: Founded 1865, in France; in U.S., 1891. General motherhouse, Paris, France; U.S. provincialate, 214 E. 30th St., New York, NY 10016. Social work, nursing, family life education.

Assumption, Religious of the, R.A.: Founded 1839, in France; in U.S., 1919. Generalate, Paris, France; North American province, 227 N. Bowman Ave., Merion Sta., PA 19066.

Assumption of the Blessed Virgin, Sisters of the, S.A.S.V.: Founded 1853, in Canada; in U.S., 1891. General motherhouse, Nicolet, Que., Canada; U.S. province, 316 Lincoln St., Worcester, MA 01605. Education, mission, pastoral ministry.

Augustinian Nuns of Contemplative Life, O.S.A.: Established in Spain in 13th century; U.S. foundation, Convent of Our Mother of Good Counsel, 4328 W. Westminster Pl., St. Louis, MO 63108.

Augustinian Sisters, Servants of Jesus and Mary, Congregation of, O.S.A.: Generalate, Rome, Italy; U.S. foundation, St. John School, Brandenburg, KY 40108.

Basil the Great, Sisters of the Order of St. (Byzantine Rite), O.S.B.M.: Founded fourth century, in Cappadocia, by St. Basil the Great and his sister St. Macrina; in U.S., 1911. Generalate, Rome, Italy; U.S. motherhouses: Philadelphia Ukrainian Byzantine Rite, 710 Fox Chase Rd., Philadelphia, PA 19111; Pittsburgh Ruthenian Byzantine Rite, Mount St. Macrina P.O. Box 878, Uniontown, PA 15401. Education, health care.

Benedict, Sisters of the Order of St., O.S.B.: Our Lady of Mount Caritas Monastery (founded 1979, Ashford, Conn.), Seckar Rd., Ashford, CT 06278. Contemplative.

Benedictine Nuns, O.S.B.: St. Scholastica Priory, Box 606, Petersham, MA 01366. Cloistered.

Benedictine Nuns of the Congregation of Solesmes, O.S.B.: U.S. establishment, 1981, in Burlington diocese, Monastery of the Immaculate Heart of Mary, H.C.R. Box 11, Westfield, VT 05874. Cloistered, papal enclosure.

Benedictine Nuns of the Primitive Observance, O.S.B.: Founded c. 529, in Italy; in U.S., 1948. Abbey of Regina Laudis, Flanders Rd., Bethlehem, CT 06751. Cloistered.

Benedictine Sisters, O.S.B.: Founded c. 529, in Italy; in U.S., 1852. General motherhouse, Eichstätt, Bavaria, Germany. U.S. addresses: St. Emma's Monastery, Motherhouse and Novitiate, 1001 Harvey Ave., Greensburg, PA 15601; Abbey of St. Walburga, 6717 S. Boulder Rd., Boulder, CO 80303.

Benedictine Sisters (Regina Pacis), **O.S.B.:** Founded 1627, in Lithuania as cloistered community; reformed 1918 as active community; established in U.S. 1957, by Mother M. Raphaela Simonis. Regina Pacis, 333 Wallace Rd., Bedford, NH 03102.

Benedictine Sisters, Missionary, O.S.B.: Founded 1885. Generalate, Rome, Italy; U.S. motherhouse, 300 N. 18th St., Norfolk, NE 68701.

Benedictine Sisters, Olivetan, O.S.B.: Founded 1887, in U.S. General motherhouse, Holy Angels Convent, P.O. Drawer 130, Jonesboro, AK 72403. Educational, hospital work.

Benedictine Sisters of Perpetual Adoration of Pontifical Jurisdiction, Congregation of the, O.S.B.: Founded in U.S., 1874, from Maria Rickenbach, Switzerland. General motherhouse, 8300 Morganford Rd., St. Louis, MO 63123.

Benedictine Sisters of Pontifical Jurisdiction, O.S.B.: Founded c. 529, in Italy. No general motherhouse in U.S. Three federations:

• Federation of St. Scholastica (1922). Pres., Sister Regina Crowley, O.S.B., 5807 N. Kolmar Ave., Chicago, IL 60646. Motherhouses belonging to the federation:

Mt. St. Scholastica, 801 S. 8th St., Atchison, KS 66002; Benedictine Sisters of Elk Co., St. Joseph's Monastery, St. Mary's, PA 15857; Benedictine Sisters of Erie, 6101 E. Lake Rd., Erie, PA 16511; Benedictine Sisters of Chicago, St. Scholastica Priory, 7430 Ridge Blvd., Chicago, IL 60645; Benedictine Sisters of the Sacred Heart, 1910 Maple Ave., Lisle, IL 60532; Benedictine Sisters of Elizabeth, St. Walburga Monastery, 851 N. Broad St., Elizabeth, NJ 07208; Benedictine Sisters of Pittsburgh, 4530 Perrysville Ave., Pittsburgh, PA 15229; Red Plains Monastery, 1132 N.W. 32nd, Oklahoma City, OK 73118; St. Joseph's Convent, 2200 S. Lewis, Tulsa, OK 74114; St. Gertrude's Monastery, Ridgely, MD 21660; St. Walburga Monastery, 2500 Amsterdam Rd., Covington, KY 41016; Sacred Heart Monastery, Cullman, AL 35056; Benedictine Sisters of Virginia, Bristow, VA 22013; St. Scholastica Convent, 416 W. Highland Dr., Boerne, TX 78006; St. Lucy's Priory, 19045 E. Sierra Madre Ave., Glendora, CA 91741; Benedictine Sisters of Florida, Drawer H, St. Leo, FL 33574; Benet Hill Monastery, 2555 N. Chelton Rd., Colorado Springs, CO 80909; Queen of Heaven Convent (Byzantine Rite), 8640 Squires Lane N.E., Warren, OH 44484; Benedictine Sisters of Baltimore, Emmanuel Monastery, 2229 W. Joppa Rd., Lutherville, MD 21093; Queen of Angels Monastery, 2101 Hughes Rd., Liberty, MO 64068.

• Federation of St. Gertrude the Great (1937). Office: Sacred Heart Monastery, P.O. Box 364, Richardton, ND 58652. Pres., Sister Ruth Fox, O.S.B. Motherhouses belonging to the federation:

Mother of God Monastery, 120 SE 28th Ave., Watertown, SD 57201; Sacred Heart Monastery, 1005 W. 8th St., Yankton, SD 57078; Mt. St. Benedict Monastery, 620 E. Summit Ave., Crookston, MN 56716; Sacred Heart Monastery, P.O. Box 364, Richardton, ND 58652; Convent of St. Martin, 2110-C St. Martin's Dr., Rapid City, SD 57702; Monastery of Immaculate Conception, 802 E. 10th St., Ferdinand, IN 47532; Monastery of St. Gertrude, P.O. Box 107, Cottonwood, ID 83522; Monastery of St. Benedict Center, Box 5070, Madison, WI 53705; Queen of Angels Monastery, 840 S. Main St., Mt. Angel, OR 97362; St. Scholastica Monastery, P.O. Box 3489, Fort Smith, AR 72913; Our Lady of Peace Monastery, 1511 Wilson Ave., Columbia, MO 65201; Queen of Peace Monastery, Box 370, Belcourt, ND 58316; Our Lady of Grace Monastery, 1402 Southern Ave., Beech Grove, IN 46107; Holy Spirit Monastery, 22791 Pico St., Grand Terrace, CA 92324; Spirit of Life Monastery, 10760 W. Glennon Dr., Lakewood, CO 80226; St. Benedict's Monastery 225 Masters Ave., RR #1b, Winnipeg, Man. R3C 4A3, Canada; The Dwelling Place Monastery, 3450 Bucks Branch Rd., Martin, KY 41649.

• **Federation of St. Benedict (1947).** Pres., Sister Colleen Haggerty, O.S.B., St. Benedict's Monastery, 104 Chapel Lane, St. Joseph, MN 56374. Motherhouses in U.S. belonging to the federation:

St. Benedict's Monastery, St. Joseph, MN 56374; St. Scholastica Priory, 1200 Kenwood Ave., Duluth, MN 55811; St. Bede Priory, 1190 Priory Rd., Eau Claire, WI 54702; St. Mary Priory, Nauvoo, IL 62354; Annunciation Priory, 7520 University Dr., Bismarck, ND 58504; St. Paul's Priory, 2675 Larpenteur Ave., E., St. Paul, MN 55109; St. Placid Priory, 500 College St. N.E., Lacey, WA 98516; Mt. Benedict Priory, 309 E. 5450 South, Ogden, UT 84405.

Bethany, Sisters of, C.V.D.: Founded 1928, in El Salvador; in U.S., 1949. General motherhouse, Santa Tecla, El Salvador. U.S. address: 850 N. Hobart Blvd., Los Angeles, CA 90029.

Bethlemita Sisters, Daughters of the Sacred Heart of Jesus: Founded 1861, in Guatemala. Motherhouse, Bogota, Colombia; U.S. address, St. Joseph Residence, 330 W. Pembroke St., Dallas, TX 75208.

Blessed Virgin Mary, Institute of the (Loretto Sisters), I.B.V.M.: Founded 17th century in Belgium; in U.S., 1954. Motherhouse, Rathfarnham, Dublin, Ireland; U.S. address: 2521 W. Maryland Ave., Phoenix, AZ 85017.

Blessed Virgin Mary, Institute of the (Loretto Sisters), I.B.V.M.: Founded 1609, in Belgium; in U.S., 1880. U.S. address, Loretto Convent, Box 508, Wheaton, IL 60189. Educational work.

Bon Secours, Congregation of, C.B.S.: Founded 1824, in France; in U.S., 1881. Generalate, Rome, Italy; U.S. provincial house, 1525 Marriottsville Rd., Marriottsville, MD 21104. Hospital work.

Brigid, Congregation of St., C.S.B.: Founded 1807, in Ireland; in U.S., 1953. U.S. regional house, 5118 Loma Linda Dr., San Antonio, TX 78201.

Brigittine Sisters (Order of the Most Holy Savior), O.SS.S.: Founded 1344, at Vadstena, Sweden, by St. Bridget; in U.S., 1957. General motherhouse, Rome, Italy; U.S. address, Vikingsborg, Runkenhage Rd., Darien, CT 06820.

Canossian Daughters of Charity (Canossian Sisters): Founded 1808 in Verona, Italy, by St. Magdalen of Canossa. General motherhouse, Rome, Italy; U.S. provincial house, 5625 Isleta Blvd. S.W., Albuquerque, NM 87105.

Carmel, Congregation of Our Lady of Mount, O. Carm.: Founded 1825, in France; in U.S., 1833. Generalate, P.O. Box 476, Lacombe, LA 70445. Education, social services, pastoral ministry, retreat work.

Carmel, Institute of Our Lady of Mount, O. Carm.: Founded 1854, in Italy; in U.S., 1947. General motherhouse, Rome, Italy; U.S. novitiate, 5 Wheatland St., Peabody, MA 01960. Apostolic work.

Carmelite Community of the Word, C.C.W.: Motherhouse and Novitiate, 1304 13th Ave., Altoona, PA 16601.

Carmelite Nuns, Discalced, O.C.D.: Founded 1562, Spain. First foundation in U.S. in 1790, at Charles County, Md.; this monastery was moved to Baltimore. Monasteries in U.S. are listed below, according to states.

Alabama: 716 Dauphin Island Pkwy., Mobile 36606. *Arkansas:* 7201 W. 32nd St., Little Rock 72204. *California:* 215 E. Alhambra Rd., Alhambra 91801; 27601 Highway 1, Carmel 93923; 68 Rincon Rd., Kensington 94707; 1883 Ringsted Dr., P.O. Box 379, Solvang 93463; 6981 Teresian Way, Georgetown 95634; 5158 Hawley Blvd., San Diego 92116; 721 Parker Ave., San Francisco 94118; 530 Blackstone Dr., San Rafael 94903; 1000 Lincoln St., Santa Clara 95050.

Colorado: 6138 S. Gallup St., Littleton 80120. *Georgia:* Coffee Bluff, 11 W. Back St., Savannah 31419. *Hawaii:* 6301 Pali Hwy., Kaneohe, HI 96744. *Illinois:* River Rd. and Central, Des Plaines 60016. *Indiana:* 2500 Cold Spring Rd., Indianapolis 46222; 59 Allendale Pl., Terre Haute 47802. *Iowa:* 17937 250th St., Eldridge 52748; 2901 S. Cecilia St., Sioux City 51106. *Kentucky:* 1740 Newburg Rd., Louisville 40205. *Louisiana:* 1250 Carmel Ave., Lafayette 70507; 1611 Mirabeau Ave., New Orleans 70122.

Maryland: 1318 Dulaney Valley Rd., Towson, Baltimore 21204; 4035-A Mt. Carmel Rd., Port Tobacco 20646. *Massachusetts:* 61 Mt. Pleasant Ave., Roxbury, Boston 02119; 15 Mt. Carmel Rd., Danvers 01923. *Michigan:* 3800 Mt. Carmel Dr. NE, Ada 49301; 35750 Moravian Dr., Clinton Township 48035; U.S. 2 Highway, P.O. Box 397, Iron Mountain 49801; 3501 Silver Lake Rd., Traverse City 49684. *Minnesota:* 8251 De Montreville Trail N., Lake Elmo 55042. *Mississippi:* 2155 Terry Rd., Jackson 39204.

Missouri: 2201 W. Main St., Jefferson City 65101; 9150 Clayton Rd., Ladue, St. Louis Co. 63124; 424 E. Republic Rd., Springfield 65807. *Nevada:* 1950 La Fond Dr., Reno 89509. *New Hampshire:* 275 Pleasant St., Concord, 03301. *New Jersey:* P.O. Box 785, Flemington 08822; 189 Madison Ave., Morristown 07960. *New Mexico:* Mt. Carmel Rd., Santa Fe 87501. *New York:* 745 St. John's Pl., Brooklyn 11216; 139 De Puyster Ave., Beacon 12508; 75 Carmel Rd., Buffalo 14214; 1931 W. Jefferson Rd., Pittsford 14534; 68 Franklin Ave., Saranac Lake 12983; 428 Duane Ave., Schenectady 12304.

Ohio: 3176 Fairmount Blvd., Cleveland Heights 44118. *Oklahoma:* 20,000 N. County Line Rd., Piedmont 73078. *Oregon:* 87609 Green Hill Rd., Eugene 97402. *Pennsylvania:* 70 Monastery Rd., Elysburg 17824; 510 E. Gore Rd., Erie 16509; R.D. 6, Box 28, Center Dr., Latrobe 15650; P.O. Box 57, Loretto 15940; Byzantine Rite, R.R. No. 1, Box 1336, Sugarloaf 18249. *Rhode Island:* Watson Ave. at Nayatt Rd., Barrington 02806.

Texas: 600 Flowers Ave., Dallas 75211; 5801 Mt. Carmel Dr., Arlington 76017; 1100 Parthenon Pl., Roman Forest, New Caney 77357. 6301 Culebra and St. Joseph Way, San

Antonio 78238. *Utah:* 5714 Holladay Blvd., Salt Lake City 84121. *Vermont:* RR 2, Box 4784, Barre, 05641. *Washington:* 2215 N.E. 147th St., Seattle 98155. *Wisconsin:* W267 N2517 Meadowbrook Rd., Pewaukee 53072.

Carmelite Nuns of the Ancient Observance (Calced Carmelites), O. Carm.: Founded 1452, in The Netherlands; in U.S., 1930, from Naples, Italy, convent (founded 1856). U.S. monasteries: Carmelite Monastery of St. Therese, 3551 Lanark Rd., Coopersburg, PA 18036; Carmel of Mary, Wahpeton, ND 58075; Our Lady of Grace Monastery, 1 St. Joseph Pl., San Angelo, TX 76905; Carmel of the Sacred Heart, 430 Laurel Ave., Hudson, WI 54016. Papal enclosure.

Carmelite Sisters (Corpus Christi), O. Carm.: Founded 1908, in England; in U.S., 1920. General motherhouse, Tunapuna, Trinidad, W.I. U.S. address: Mt. Carmel Home, 412 W. 18th St., Kearney, NE 68847. Home and foreign mission work.

Carmelite Sisters for the Aged and Infirm, O. Carm.: Founded 1929, at New York, by Mother M. Angeline Teresa, O. Carm. Motherhouse, 600 Woods Rd., Avila-on-Hudson, Germantown, NY 12526. Social work, nursing and educating in the field of gerontology.

Carmelite Sisters of Charity, C.a.Ch.: Founded 1826 at Vich, Spain, by St. Joaquina de Vedruna. Generalate, Rome, Italy; U.S. address, 701 Beacon Rd., Silver Spring, MD 20903.

Carmelite Sisters of St. Therese of the Infant Jesus, C.S.T.: Founded 1917, in U.S. General motherhouse, 1300 Classen Dr., Oklahoma City, OK 73103. Educational work.

Carmelite Sisters of the Divine Heart of Jesus, Carmel D.C.J.: Founded 1891, in Germany; in U.S., 1912. General motherhouse, Sittard, Netherlands. U.S. provincial houses: 1230 Kavanaugh Pl., Milwaukee, WI 52313 (Northern Province); 10341 Manchester Rd., St. Louis, MO 63122 (Central Province); 8585 La Mesa Blvd., La Mesa, CA 92041 (South Western Province). Social services, mission work.

Carmelite Sisters of the Most Sacred Heart of Los Angeles, O.C.D.: Founded 1904, in Mexico. General motherhouse and novitiate, 920 E. Alhambra Rd., Alhambra, CA 91801. Social services, retreat and educational work.

Carmelites of St. Theresa, Congregation of Missionary, C.M.S.T.: Founded 1903, in Mexico. General motherhouse, Mexico City, Mexico; U.S. foundation, 9548 Deer Trail Dr., Houston, TX 77038.

Casimir, Sisters of St., S.S.C.: Founded 1907, in U.S. by Mother Maria Kaupas. General motherhouse, 2601 W. Marquette Rd., Chicago, IL 60629. Education, missions, social services.

Cenacle, Congregation of Our Lady of the Retreat in the, R.C.: Founded 1826, in France; in U.S., 1892. Generalate, Rome, Italy. Eastern Province: Cenacle Rd.,

Lake Ronkonkoma, L.I., NY 11779; Midwestern Province, 513 Fullerton Pkwy., Chicago, IL 60614.

Charity, Daughters of Divine, F.D.C.: Founded 1868, at Vienna, Austria; in U.S., 1913. General motherhouse, Rome, Italy. U.S. provinces: 205 Major Ave., Staten Island, NY 10305; 39 N. Portage Path, Akron, OH 44303; 1315 N. Woodward Ave., Bloomfield Hills, MI 48304. Education, social services.

Charity, Little Missionary Sisters of, L.M.S.C.: Founded 1915, in Italy by Bl. Luigi Orione; in U.S., 1949. General motherhouse, Rome, Italy; U.S. address, 120 Orient Ave., East Boston, MA 02128.

Charity, Missionaries of, M.C.: Founded 1950, in Calcutta, India, by Mother Teresa; first U.S. foundation 1971. General motherhouse, 54A Lower Circular Road, Calcutta 700016, India. U.S. address, 335 E. 145th St., Bronx, NY 10451. Service of the poor.

Charity, Religious Sisters of, R.S.C.: Founded 1815, in Ireland; in U.S., 1953. Motherhouse, Dublin, Ireland; U.S. headquarters, 10664 St. James Dr., Culver City, CA 90230.

Charity, Sisters of (of Seton Hill), S.C.: Founded 1870, at Altoona, Penn., from Cincinnati foundation. Generalate, Mt. Thor Rd., Greensburg, PA 15601. Educational, hospital, social, foreign mission work.

Charity, Sisters of (Grey Nuns of Montreal), S.G.M.: Founded 1737, in Canada by St. Marie Marguerite d'Youville; in U.S., 1855. General administration, Montreal, Que. H2Y 2L7, Canada; U.S. provincial house, 10 Pelham Rd., Lexington, MA 02173.

Charity, Sisters of (of Leavenworth), S.C.L.: Founded 1858, in U.S. Motherhouse, 4200 S. 4th St., Leavenworth, KS 66048.

Charity, Sisters of (of Nazareth), S.C.N.: Founded 1812, in U.S. General motherhouse, SCN Center, P.O. Box 172, Nazareth, KY 40048. Education, health services.

Charity, Sisters of (of St. Augustine), C.S.A.: Founded 1851, at Cleveland, Ohio. Motherhouse, 5232 Broadview Rd., Richfield, OH 44286.

Charity, Sisters of Christian, S.C.C.: Founded 1849, in Paderborn, Germany, by Bl. Pauline von Mallinckrodt; in U.S., 1873. Generalate, Rome, Italy. U.S. provinces: Mallinckrodt Convent, Mendham, NJ 07945; 1041 Ridge Rd., Wilmette, IL 60091. Education, health services, other apostolic work.

Charity, Vincentian Sisters of, V.S.C.: Founded 1835, in Austria; in U.S., 1902. General motherhouse, 8200 McKnight Rd., Pittsburgh, PA 15237.

Charity, Vincentian Sisters of, V.S.C.: Founded 1928, at Bedford, Ohio. General motherhouse, 1160 Broadway, Bedford, OH 44146.

Charity of Cincinnati, Ohio, Sisters of, S.C.: Founded 1809; became independent community, 1852. General motherhouse, Mt. St. Joseph, Ohio 45051. Educational, hospital, social work.

Charity of Ottawa, Sisters of (Grey Nuns of the Cross), S.C.O.: Founded 1845, at Ottawa, Canada; in U.S., 1857. General motherhouse, Ottawa, Canada; U.S. provincial house, 975 Varnum Ave., Lowell, MA 01854. Educational, hospital work, extended health care.

Charity of Our Lady, Mother of Mercy, Sisters of, S.C.M.M.: Founded 1832, in Holland; in U.S., 1874. General motherhouse, Den Bosch, Netherlands; U.S. provincialate, 520 Thompson Ave., East Haven, CT 06512.

Charity of Our Lady, Mother of the Church, S.C.M.C.: U.S. foundation, 1970. General motherhouse, Baltic, CT 06330.

Charity of Our Lady of Mercy, Sisters of, O.L.M.: Founded 1829, in Charleston, S.C. Generalate and motherhouse, 424 Fort Johnson Rd., James Island, Charleston, SC 29412. Education, campus ministry, social services.

Charity of Quebec, Sisters of (Grey Nuns), S.C.Q.: Founded 1849, at Quebec; in U.S., 1890. General motherhouse, 2655 Le Pelletier St., Beauport, Quebec GIC 3X7, Canada; U.S. address, 359 Summer St., New Bedford, MA 02740. Social work.

Charity of St. Elizabeth, Sisters of (Convent Station, N.J.), S.C.: Founded 1859, at Newark, N.J. General motherhouse, P.O. Box 476, Convent Station, NJ 07961. Education, pastoral ministry, social services.

Charity of St. Hyacinthe, Sisters of (Grey Nuns), S.C.S.H.: Founded 1840, at St. Hyacinthe, Canada; in U.S., 1878. General motherhouse, 16470 Avenue Bourdages, SUD, St. Hyacinthe, Quebec J2T 4J8, Canada; U.S. regional house, 98 Campus Ave., Lewiston, ME 04240.

Charity of St. Joan Antida, Sisters of, S.C.S.J.A.: Founded 1799, in France; in U.S., 1932. General motherhouse, Rome, Italy; U.S. provincial house, 8560 N. 76th Pl., Milwaukee, WI 53223.

Charity of St. Louis, Sisters of, S.C.S.L.: Founded 1803, in France; in U.S., 1910. Generalate, Rome, Italy; U.S. provincialate, 4901 S. Catherine St., Plattsburgh, NY 12901.

Charity of St. Vincent de Paul, Daughters of, D.C.: Founded 1633, in France; in U.S., 1809, at Emmitsburg, Md., by St. Elizabeth Ann Seton. General motherhouse, Paris, France. U.S. provinces: Emmitsburg, MD 21727; 7800 Natural Bridge Rd., St. Louis, MO 63121; 9400 New Harmony Rd., Evansville, IN 47712; 96 Menands Rd., Albany, NY 12204; 26000 Altamont Rd., Los Altos Hills, CA 94022.

Charity of St. Vincent de Paul, Sisters of, V.Z.: Founded 1845, in Croatia; in U.S., 1955. General motherhouse, Zagreb, Croatia; U.S. foundation, 171 Knox Ave., West Seneca, NY 14224.

Charity of St. Vincent de Paul, Sisters of, Halifax, S.C.: Founded 1856, at Halifax, N. S., from Emmitsburg foundation. Generalate, Mt. St. Vincent, Halifax, N. S., Canada. U.S. addresses: Commonwealth of Massachu-

setts, 125 Oakland St., Wellesley Hills, MA 02181; Boston Province, 26 Phipps St., Quincy, MA 02169; New York Province, 84-32 63rd Ave., Middle Village, NY 11379. Educational, hospital, social work.

Charity of St. Vincent de Paul, Sisters of, New York, S.C.: Founded 1817, from Emmitsburg foundation. General motherhouse, Mt. St. Vincent on Hudson, 6301 Riverdale Ave., Bronx, NY 10471. Educational, hospital work.

Charity of the Blessed Virgin Mary, Sisters of, B.V.M.: Founded 1833, in U.S., by Mary Frances Clarke. General motherhouse, Mt. Carmel, 1100 Carmel Dr., Dubuque, IA 52001. Education, pastoral ministry, social services.

Charity of the Immaculate Conception of Ivrea, Sisters of, S.C.I.C.: Founded 18th century, in Italy; in U.S., 1961. General motherhouse, Rome, Italy; U.S. address, Immaculate Virgin of Miracles Convent, R.D. 2, Box 348, Mt. Pleasant, PA 15666.

Charity of the Incarnate Word, Congregation of the Sisters of, C.C.V.I.: Founded 1869, at San Antonio, Tex., by Bishop C. M. Dubuis. Generalate, 4503 Broadway, San Antonio, TX 78209.

Charity of the Incarnate Word, Congregation of the Sisters of (Houston, Tex.), C.C.V.I. Founded 1866, in U.S., by Bishop C. M. Dubuis. General motherhouse, P.O. Box 230969, Houston, TX 77223. Educational, hospital, social work.

Charity of the Sacred Heart, Daughters of, F.C.S.C.J.: Founded 1823, at La Salle de Vihiers, France; in U.S., 1905. General motherhouse, La Salle de Vihiers, France; U.S. address, Sacred Heart Province, Littleton, NH 03561.

Charles Borromeo, Missionary Sisters of St. (Scalabrini Srs.): Founded 1895, in Italy; in U.S., 1941. American novitiate, 1414 N. 37th Ave.. Melrose Park, IL 60601.

Child Jesus, Sisters of the Poor, P.C.J.: Founded 1844, at Aix-la-Chapelle, Germany; in U.S., 1924. General motherhouse, Simpelveld, Netherlands; American provincialate, 4567 Olentangy River Rd., Columbus, OH 43214.

Chrétienne, Sisters of Ste., S.S.CH.: Founded 1807, in France; in U.S., 1903. General motherhouse, Metz, France; U.S. provincial house, 297 Arnold St., Wrentham, MA 02093. Educational, hospital, mission work.

Christ the King, Missionary Sisters of, M.S.C.K.: Founded 1959 in Poland; in U.S., 1978. General motherhouse, Poznan, Poland; U.S. address, 3424 W. Adams Blvd., Los Angeles, CA 90018.

Christ the King, Sister Servants of, S.S.C.K.: Founded 1936, in U.S. General motherhouse, Loretto Convent, Mt. Calvary, WI 53057. Social services.

Christ the King, Sisters of, S.C.K.: Hermitage of Christ the King, 6501 Orchard Station Rd., Sebastopol, CA 95472.

Christian Doctrine, Sisters of Our Lady of, R.C.D.: Founded 1910, in New York. Central office, 23 Haskell Ave., Suffern, NY 10901.

Christian Education, Religious of, R.C.E.: Founded 1817, in France; in U.S., 1905 General motherhouse, France; U.S. provincial residence, 14 Bailey Rd., Arlington, MA 02174.

Cistercian Nuns, O. Cist.: Headquarters, Rome, Italy; U.S. address, Valley of Our Lady Monastery, E. 11096 Yanke Dr., Prairie du Sac, WI 53578.

Cistercian Nuns of the Strict Observance, Order of, O.C.S.O.: Founded 1125, in France, by St. Stephen Harding; in U.S., 1949. U.S. addresses: Mt. St. Mary's Abbey, 300 Arnold St., Wrentham, MA 02093; Santa Rita Abbey, HCR Box 929, Sonoita, AZ 85637; Our Lady of the Redwoods Abbey, Whitethorn, CA 95489. Our Lady of the Mississippi Abbey, 8400 Abbey Hill Rd., Dubuque, IA 52001; Our Lady of the Angels Monastery, Rt. 2, Box 288-A, Crozet, VA 22932.

Clare, Sisters of St., O.S.C.: General motherhouse, Dublin, Ireland; U.S. foundation, St. Clare's Convent, 449 S. Pine Ave., Brea, CA 92621.

Claretian Missionary Sisters (Religious of Mary Immaculate), R.M.I.: Founded 1855, in Cuba; in U.S., 1956. Generalate, Rome, Italy; U.S. address, 9600 W. Atlantic Ave., Delray Beach, FL 33446.

Clergy, Congregation of Our Lady, Help of the, C.L.H.C.: Founded 1961, in U.S. Motherhouse, Maryvale Convent, 2522 June Bug Rd., Vale, NC 28168.

Clergy, Servants of Our Lady Queen of the, S.R.C.: Founded 1929, in Canada; in U.S., 1934. General motherhouse, 57 Jules A. Brillant, Rimouski, Que. G5L lXl Canada. Domestic work.

Colettines: See Franciscan Poor Clare Nuns.

Columban, Missionary Sisters of St., S.S.C.: Founded 1922, in Ireland; in U.S., 1930. General motherhouse, Wicklow, Ireland; U.S. region, 73 Mapleton St., Brighton, MA 02135.

Comboni Missionary Sisters (Missionary Sisters of Verona), C.M.S.: Founded 1872, in Italy; in U S., 1950. U.S. address, 1307 Lakeside Ave., Richmond, VA 23228.

Consolata Missionary Sisters, M.C.: Founded 1910, in Italy, by Bl. Giuseppe Allamano; in U.S, 1954. General motherhouse, Turin, Italy; U.S. headquarters, 6801 Belmont Rd., Belmont, MI 49306.

Cordi-Marian Missionary Sisters, M.C.M.: Founded 1921, Mexico City; U.S. foundation, 1926. General motherhouse, Mexico; U.S. address, 11624 FM 471, Apt. 402, San Antonio, TX 78253.

Cross, Daughters of the, D.C.: Founded 1640, in France; in U.S., 1855. General motherhouse, 1000 Fairview St., Shreveport, LA 71104. Educational work.

Cross, Daughters of, of Liege, F.C.: Founded 1833, in Liege, Belgium; in U.S., 1958. U.S. address, 165 W. Eaton Ave., Tracy, CA 95376.

Cross, Sisters of the Holy, C.S.C.: Founded 1841, at Le Mans, France, established 1847, in Canada; in U.S.,

1881. General motherhouse, St. Laurent, Montreal, Que., Canada; U.S. regional office, 377 Island Pond Rd., Manchester, NH 03109. Educational work.

Cross, Sisters of the Holy, Congregation of, C.S.C.: Founded 1841, at Le Mans, France; in U.S., 1843. General motherhouse, Saint Mary's, Notre Dame, IN 46556. Education, health care, social services, pastoral ministry.

Cross and Passion, Sisters of the (Passionist Sisters), C.P.: Founded 1852; in U.S., 1924. Generalate, Northampton, England; U.S. address: Holy Family Convent, One Wright Lane, N. Kingstown, RI 02852.

Cyril and Methodius, Sisters of Sts., SS.C.M.: Founded 1909, in U.S., by Rev. Matthew Jankola. General motherhouse, Villa Sacred Heart, Danville, PA 17821. Education, care of aged.

Disciples of the Lord Jesus Christ, D.L.J.C.: Founded 1972; canonically erected 1991. Address, P.O. Box 17, Channing, TX 79018.

Divine Compassion, Sisters of, R.D.C.: Founded 1886, in U.S. General motherhouse, 52 N. Broadway, White Plains, NY 10603. Education, other ministries.

Divine Spirit, Congregation of the, C.D.S.: Founded 1956, in U.S., by Archbishop John M. Gannon. Motherhouse, 409 W. 6th St., Erie, PA 16507. Education, social services.

Divine Zeal, Daughters of, F.D.Z.: Founded 1887 in Italy by Bl. Hannibal Maria DiFrancia; in U.S., 1951. Generalate, Rome; U.S. headquarters, Cabrini Convent, 234 Franklin St., Reading, PA 19602.

Dominicans

Nuns of the Order of Preachers (Dominican Nuns), O.P.: Founded 1206 by St. Dominic at Prouille, France. Cloistered, contemplative. Two branches in the United States:

• *Dominican Nuns having perpetual adoration.* First monastery established 1880, in Newark, N.J., from Oullins, France, foundation (1868). Autonomous monasteries:

St. Dominic, 375 13th Ave., Newark, NJ 07103; Corpus Christi, 1230 Lafayette Ave., Bronx, NY 10474; Blessed Sacrament, 29575 Middlebelt Rd., Farmington Hills, MI 48334; Monastery of the Angels, 1977 Carmen Ave., Los Angeles, CA 90068; Corpus Christi, 215 Oak Grove Ave., Menlo Park, CA 94025; Infant Jesus, 1501 Lotus Lane, Lufkin, TX 75901.

• *Dominican Nuns devoted to the perpetual Rosary.* First monastery established 1891, in Union City, N.J., from Calais, France, foundation (1880). Twelve autonomous monasteries (some also observe perpetual adoration).

Dominican Nuns of Perpetual Rosary, 14th and West Sts., Union City, NJ 07087; 217 N. 68th St., Milwaukee, WI 53213; Perpetual Rosary, 1500 Haddon Ave., Camden, NJ 08103; Our Lady of the Rosary, 335 Doat St.,

Buffalo, NY 14211; Our Lady of the Rosary, 543 Springfield Ave., Summit, NJ 07901; Mother of God, 1430 Riverdale St., W. Springfield, MA 01089; Perpetual Rosary, 802 Court St., Syracuse, NY 13208; Immaculate Heart of Mary, 1834 Lititz Pike, Lancaster, PA 17601; Mary the Queen, 1310 W. Church St., Elmira, NY 14905; St. Jude, Marbury, AL 36051; Our Lady of Grace, North Guilford, CT 06437; St. Dominic, 4901 16th St. N.W., Washington, DC 20011.

Dominican Sisters of Charity of the Presentation, O.P.: Founded 1696, in France; in U.S., 1906. General motherhouse, Tours, France; U.S. headquarters, 3012 Elm St., Dighton, MA 02715. Hospital work.

Dominican Sisters of Our Lady of the Rosary and of St. Catherine of Siena (Cabra): Founded 1644 in Ireland. General motherhouse, Cabra, Dublin, Ireland. U.S. regional house, 1930 Robert E. Lee Rd., New Orleans, LA 70122.

Dominican Sisters of the Roman Congregation of St. Dominic, O.P.: Founded 1621, in France; in U S., 1904 General motherhouse, Paris, France; U.S. province, 305 Oberlin St., Iowa City, IA 52245. Educational work.

Eucharistic Missionaries of St. Dominic, O.P.: Founded 1927, in Louisiana. General motherhouse, 1101 Aline St., New Orleans, LA 70115. Parish work, social services.

Marian Society of Dominican Catechists, O.P.: Founded 1954 in Louisiana. General motherhouse, P.O. Box 176, Boyce, LA 71409. Community of Alexandria, La., diocese.

Maryknoll Sisters of St. Dominic, M.M.: Founded 1912, in New York. Center, Maryknoll, NY 10545.

Religious Missionaries of St. Dominic, O.P.: General motherhouse, Rome, Italy. U.S. address (Spanish province), 2237 Waldron Rd., Corpus Christi, TX 78418.

Sisters of St. Dominic, O.P.: Thirty congregations in the U.S. Educational, hospital work. Names of congregations are given below, followed by the date of foundation, and location of motherhouse.

St. Catharine of Siena, 1822. 2645 Bardstown Rd., St. Catharine, KY 40061.

St. Mary of the Springs, 1830. 2320 Airport Dr., Columbus, OH 43219.

Most Holy Rosary, 1847. Sinsinawa, WI 53824.

Most Holy Name of Jesus, 1850. 1520 Grand Ave., San Rafael, CA 94901.

Holy Cross, 1853. Albany Ave., Amityville, NY 11701.

Most Holy Rosary, 1859. 320 Powell Ave., Newburgh, NY 12550.

St. Cecilia, 1860. 801 Dominican Dr., Nashville, TN 37228.

St. Mary, 1860. 580 Broadway, New Orleans, LA 70118.

St. Catherine of Siena, 1862. 5635 Erie St., Racine, WI 53402.

Our Lady of the Sacred Heart, 1873. 1237 W. Monroe St., Springfield, IL 62704.

Our Lady of the Rosary, 1876. Sparkill, NY 10976.

Queen of the Holy Rosary, 1876. P.O. Box 3908, Mission San Jose, CA 94539.

Most Holy Rosary, 1892. 1257 Siena Heights Dr., Adrian, MI 49221.

Our Lady of the Sacred Heart, 1877. 2025 E. Fulton St., Grand Rapids, MI 49503.

St. Dominic, 1878. Blauvelt, NY 10913.

Immaculate Conception (Dominican Sisters of the Sick Poor), 1879. 299 N. Highland Ave., Ossining, NY 10562. Social work.

St. Catherine de Ricci, 1880. 750 Ashbourne Rd., Elkins Park, PA 19117.

Sacred Heart of Jesus, 1881. 1 Ryerson Ave., Caldwell, NJ 07006.

Sacred Heart, 1882. 6501 Almeda Rd., Houston, TX 77021.

St. Thomas Aquinas, 1888. 935 Fawcett Ave., Tacoma, WA 98402.

Holy Cross, 1890. P.O. Box 280, Edmonds, WA 98020.

St. Catherine of Siena, 1891. 37 Park St., Fall River, MA 02721.

St. Rose of Lima (Servants of Relief for Incurable Cancer), 1896. Hawthorne, NY 10532.

Dominican Sisters of Great Bend, 1902. 3600 Broadway, Great Bend, KS 67530.

St. Catherine of Siena, 1911. Box 1288, Kenosha, WI 53141.

St. Rose of Lima, 1923. 775 Drahner Rd., Box 167, Oxford, MI 48371.

Immaculate Conception, 1929. 9000 W. 81st St., Justice, IL 60458.

Immaculate Heart of Mary, 1929. 1230 W. Market St., Akron, Ohio 44313.

Dominican Sisters of Spokane, 1925. West 3102 Fort George Wright Dr., Spokane, WA 99204.

Dominican Sisters of Oakford (St. Catherine of Siena), 1889. Motherhouse, Oakford, Natal, South Africa. U.S. regional house, 1965. 1855 Miramonte Ave., Mountain View, CA 94040.

(End, Listing of Dominicans)

Dorothy, Institute of the Sisters of St., S.S.D.: Founded 1834, in Italy, by St. Paola Frassinetti; in U.S., 1911. General motherhouse, Rome, Italy; U.S. provincialate, Mt. St. Joseph, 13 Monkeywrench Lane, Bristol, RI 02809.

Eucharist, Religious of the, R.E.: Founded 1857, in Belgium; in U.S., 1900. General motherhouse, Belgium; U.S. foundation, 2907 Ellicott Terr., N.W., Washington, DC 20008.

Family, Congregation of the Sisters of the Holy, S.S.F.: Founded 1842, in Louisiana, by Henriette Delille and Juliette Gaudin. General motherhouse, 6901 Chef Menteur Hway., New Orleans, LA 70126. Educational, hospital work.

Family, Little Sisters of the Holy, P.S.S.F.: Founded 1880, in Canada; in U.S., 1900. General motherhouse, Sherbrooke, Que., Canada; U.S. novitiate, 285 Andover St., Lowell, MA 01852.

Family, Sisters of the Holy, S.H.F.: Founded 1872, in U.S. General motherhouse, P.O. Box 3248, Mission San Jose, CA 94539. Educational, social work.

Family of Nazareth, Sisters of the Holy, C.S.F.N.: Founded 1875, in Italy; in U.S., 1885. General motherhouse, Rome, Italy; U.S. provinces: Sacred Heart, 353 N. River Rd., Des Plaines, IL 60016; Immaculate Conception BVM, 4001 Grant Ave., Torresdale, Philadelphia, PA 19114; St. Joseph, 285 Bellevue Rd., Pittsburgh, PA 15229; Immaculate Heart of Mary, Marian Heights, 1428 Monroe Turnpike, Monroe, CT 06468; Bl. Frances Siedliska Provincialate, 1814 Egyptian Way, Box 530959, Grand Prairie, TX 75053.

Filippini, Religious Teachers, M.P.F.: Founded 1692, in Italy; in U.S., 1910. General motherhouse, Rome, Italy; U.S. provinces: St. Lucy Filippini Province, Villa Walsh, Morristown, NJ 07960; Queen of Apostles Province, 474 East Rd., Bristol, CT 06010. Educational work.

Francis de Sales, Oblate Sisters of St., O.S.F.S.: Founded 1866, in France; in U.S., 1951. General motherhouse, Troyes, France; U.S. headquarters, Villa Aviat Convent, Childs, MD 21916. Educational, social work.

Franciscans

Bernardine Sisters of the Third Order of St. Francis, O.S.F.: Founded 1457, at Cracow, Poland; in U.S., 1894. Generalate, 403 Allendale Rd., King of Prussia, PA 19406. Educational, hospital, social work.

Capuchin Poor Clares (Madres Clarisas Capuchinas): U.S. establishment, 1981, Amarillo diocese. Convent of the Blessed Sacrament and Our Lady of Guadalupe, 4201 N.E. 18th St., Amarillo, TX 79107. Cloistered.

Congregation of the Servants of the Holy Child Jesus of the Third Order Regular of St. Francis, O.S.F.: Founded 1855, in Germany; in U.S., 1929. General motherhouse, Wuerzburg, Germany; American motherhouse, Villa Maria, P.O. Box 708, North Plainfield, NJ 07061.

Congregation of the Third Order of St. Francis of Mary Immaculate, O.S.F.: Founded 1865, in U.S., by Fr. Pamphilus da Magliano, O.F.M. General motherhouse, 520 Plainfield Ave., Joliet, IL 60435. Educational and pastoral work.

Daughters of St. Francis of Assisi, D.S.F.: Founded 1894, in Hungary; in U.S., 1946. Provincial motherhouse, 507 N. Prairie St., Lacon, IL 61540. Nursing, CCD work.

Eucharistic Franciscan Missionary Sisters, E.F.M.S.: Founded 1943, in Mexico. Motherhouse, 943 S. Soto St., Los Angeles, CA 90023.

Felician Sisters (Congregation of the Sisters of St. Felix), C.S.S.F.: Founded 1855, in Poland by Bl. Mary Angela Truszkowska; in U.S., 1874. General motherhouse, Rome, Italy; U.S. provinces: 36800 Schoolcraft Rd., Livonia, MI 48150; 600 Doat St., Buffalo, NY 14211; 3800 Peterson Ave., Chicago, IL 60659; 260 South Main St., Lodi, NJ 07644; 1500 Woodcrest Ave., Coraopolis, PA 15108; 1315 Enfield St., Enfield, CT 06082; 4210 Meadowlark Lane, S.E., Rio Rancho, NM 87124.

Franciscan Handmaids of the Most Pure Heart of Mary, F.H.M.: Founded 1916, in U.S. General motherhouse, 15 W. 124th St., New York, NY 10027. Educational, social work.

Franciscan Hospitaller Sisters of the Immaculate Conception, F.H.I.C.: Founded 1876, in Portugal; in U.S., 1960. General motherhouse, Lisbon, Portugal; U.S. novitiate, 300 S. 17th St., San Jose, CA 95112.

Franciscan Missionaries of Mary, F.M.M.: Founded 1877, in India; in U.S., 1904. General motherhouse, Rome, Italy; U.S. provincialate, 3305 Wallace Ave., Bronx, NY 10467. Mission work.

Franciscan Missionaries of Our Lady, O.S.F.: Founded 1854, at Calais, France; in U.S., 1913. General motherhouse, Desvres, France; U.S. provincial house, 4200 Essen Lane, Baton Rouge, LA 70809. Hospital work.

Franciscan Missionaries of St. Joseph (Mill Hill Sisters), F.M.S.J.: Founded 1883, at Rochdale, Lancashire, England; in U.S., 1952. Generalate, Manchester, England; U.S. headquarters, Franciscan House, 1006 Madison Ave., Albany, NY 12208.

Franciscan Missionary Sisters for Africa, O.S.F.: American foundation, 1953. Generalate, Ireland, U.S. headquarters, 172 Foster St., Brighton, MA 02135.

Franciscan Missionary Sisters of Assisi, F.M.S.A.: First foundation in U.S., 1961. General motherhouse, Assisi, Italy; U.S. address, St. Francis Convent, 1039 Northampton St., Holyoke, MA 01040.

Franciscan Missionary Sisters of Our Lady of Sorrows, O.S.F.: Founded 1939, in China, by Bishop Rafael Palazzi, O.F.M.; in U.S., 1949. U.S. address, 3600 S.W. 170th Ave., Beaverton, OR 97006. Educational, social, domestic, retreat and foreign mission work.

Franciscan Missionary Sisters of the Divine Child, F.M.D.C.: Founded 1927, at Buffalo, NY, by Bishop William Turner. General motherhouse, 6380 Main St., Williamsville, NY 14221. Educational, social work.

Franciscan Missionary Sisters of the Infant Jesus, F.M.I.J.: Founded 1879, in Italy; in U.S., 1961. Generalate, Rome, Italy; U.S. provincialate, 1215 Kresson Rd., Cherry Hill, NJ 08003.

Franciscan Missionary Sisters of the Sacred Heart, F.M.S.C.: Founded 1860, in Italy; in U.S., 1865. Generalate, Rome, Italy; U.S. provincialate, 250 South St., Peekskill, NY 10566. Educational and social welfare apostolates.

Franciscan Poor Clare Nuns (Poor Clares, Order of St. Clare, Poor Clares of St. Colette), P.C., O.S.C.,

P.C.C.: Founded 1212, at Assisi, Italy, by St. Francis of Assisi; in U.S., 1875. Proto-monastery, Assisi, Italy. Addresses of autonomous motherhouses in U.S. are listed below.

3626 N. 65th Ave., Omaha, NE 68104; 720 Henry Clay Ave., New Orleans, LA 70118; 6825 Nurrenbern Rd., Evansville, IN 47712; 1310 Dellwood Ave., Memphis, TN 38127; 920 Centre St., Jamaica Plain, MA 02130; 201 Crosswicks St., Bordentown, NJ 08505; 1271 Langhorne-Newtown Rd., Langhorne, PA 19047; 4419 N. Hawthorne St., Spokane, WA 99205; 142 Hollywood Ave., Bronx, NY 10465; 421 S. 4th St., Sauk Rapids, MN 56379; 8650 Russell Ave. S., Minneapolis, MN 55431; 3501 Rocky River Dr., Cleveland, OH 44111;

1671 Pleasant Valley Rd., Aptos, CA 95001; 2111 S. Main St., Rockford, IL 61102; 215 E. Los Olivos St., Santa Barbara, CA 93105; 460 River Rd., W. Andover, MA 01810; 809 E. 19th St., Roswell, NM 88201; 28210 Natoma Rd., Los Altos Hills, CA 94022; 1916 N. Pleasantburg Dr., Greenville, SC 29609; 28 Harpersville Rd., Newport News, VA 23601; 1175 N. County Rd. 300 W., Kokomo, IN 46901; 3900 Sherwood Blvd., Delray Beach, FL 33445; 200 Marycrest Dr., St. Louis, MO 63129; 6029 Estero Blvd., Fort Myers Beach, FL 33931; Rt. 7, Box 7504, Brenham, TX 77833.

Franciscan Sisters, Daughters of the Sacred Hearts of Jesus and Mary, O.S.F.: Founded 1860, in Germany; in U.S., 1872. Generalate, Rome, Italy; U.S. motherhouse, P.O. Box 667, Wheaton, IL 60189. Educational, hospital, foreign mission, social work.

Franciscan Sisters Daughters of Mercy, F.H.M.: Founded 1856, in Spain; in U.S., 1962. General motherhouse, Palma de Mallorca, Spain; U.S. address, 612 N. 3rd St., Waco, TX 76701.

Franciscan Sisters of Allegany, O.S.F.: Founded 1859, at Allegany, N.Y., by Fr. Pamphilus da Magliano, O.F.M. General motherhouse Allegany, NY 14706. Educational, hospital, foreign mission work.

Franciscan Sisters of Baltimore, O.S.F.: Founded 1868, in England; in U.S., 1881. General motherhouse, 3725 Ellerslie Ave., Baltimore, MD 21218. Educational work; social services.

Franciscan Sisters of Chicago, O.S.F.: Founded 1894, in U.S., by Mother Mary Therese (Josephine Dudzik). General motherhouse, 14700 Main St., Lemont, IL 60439. Educational work, social services.

Franciscan Sisters of Christian Charity, O.S.F.: Founded 1869, in U.S. Motherhouse, Holy Family Convent, 2409 S. Alverno Rd., Manitowoc, WI 54220. Educational, hospital work.

Franciscan Sisters of Little Falls, Minn., O.S.F.: Founded 1891, in U.S. General motherhouse, Little Falls, MN 56345. Health, education, social services, pastoral ministry, mission work.

Franciscan Sisters of Mary, F.S.M.: Established, 1987, through unification of the Sisters of St. Mary of the Third Order of St. Francis (founded 1872, St. Louis) and the Sisters of St. Francis of Maryville, MO (founded 1894). Address of general superior: 1100 Bellevue Ave., St. Louis, MO 63117. Health care, social services.

Franciscan Sisters of Mary Immaculate of the Third Order of St. Francis of Assisi, F.M.I.: Founded 16th century, in Switzerland; in U.S., 1932. General motherhouse, Bogota, Colombia; U.S. provincial house, 4301 N.E. 18th Ave., Amarillo, TX 79107. Education.

Franciscan Sisters of Our Lady of Perpetual Help, O.S.F.: Founded 1901, in U.S., from Joliet, Ill., foundation. General motherhouse, 201 Brotherton Lane, St. Louis, MO 63135. Educational, hospital work.

Franciscan Sisters of Peace, F.S.P.: Established 1986, in U.S., as archdiocesan community, from Franciscan Missionary Sisters of the Sacred Heart. Congregation center, 20 Ridge St., Haverstraw, NY 10927.

Franciscan Sisters of Ringwood, F.S.R.: Founded 1927, at Passaic, New Jersey. General motherhouse, Mt. St. Francis, Ringwood, NJ 07456. Educational work.

Franciscan Sisters of St. Elizabeth, F.S.S.E.: Founded 1866, at Naples, Italy, by Bl. Ludovico of Casorio; in U.S., 1919. General motherhouse, Rome, Italy; U.S. delegate house, 499 Park Rd., Parsippany, NJ 07054. Educational work, social services.

Franciscan Sisters of St. Joseph, F.S.S.J.: Founded 1897, in U.S. General motherhouse, 5286 S. Park Ave., Hamburg, NY 14075. Educational, hospital work.

Franciscan Sisters of St. Joseph (of Mexico): U.S. foundation, St. Paul College, 3015 4th St. N.E., Washington, DC 20017.

Franciscan Sisters of the Atonement, Third Order Regular of St. Francis (Graymoor Sisters), S.A.: Founded 1898, in U.S., as Anglican community; entered Church, 1909. General motherhouse, Graymoor, Garrison P.O., NY 10524. Mission work.

Franciscan Sisters of St. Paul, Minn., O.S.F.: Founded 1863, at Neuwied, Germany (Franciscan Sisters of the Blessed Virgin Mary of the Holy Angels); in U.S., 1923. General motherhouse, Rhine, Germany; U.S. motherhouse, 1388 Prior Ave. S., St. Paul, MN 55116. Educational, hospital, social work.

Franciscan Sisters of the Immaculate Conception, O.S.F.: Founded in Germany; in U.S., 1928. General motherhouse, Kloster, Bonlanden, Germany; U.S. province, 291 W. North St., Buffalo, NY 14201.

Franciscan Sisters of the Immaculate Conception, O.S.F.: Founded 1874, in Mexico; in U.S., 1926. U.S. provincial house, 11306 Laurel Canyon Blvd., San Fernando, CA 91340.

Franciscan Sisters of the Immaculate Conception, Missionary, O.S.F.: Founded 1873, in U.S. General motherhouse, Rome, Italy; U.S. address, 790 Centre St., Newton, MA 02158. Educational work.

Franciscan Sisters of the Immaculate Conception and St. Joseph for the Dying, O.S.F.: Founded 1919, in U.S. General motherhouse, 485 Church St., Monterey, CA 93940.

Franciscan Sisters of the Poor, S.F.P.: Founded 1845, at Aachen, Germany, by Bl. Frances Schervier; in U.S., 1858. Congregational office, 133 Remsen St., Brooklyn, NY 11201. Hospital, social work and foreign missions.

Franciscan Sisters of the Sacred Heart, O.S.F.: Founded 1866, in Germany; in U.S., 1876. General motherhouse, St. Francis Woods, 9201 W. St. Francis Rd., Frankfort, IL 60423. Education, health care, other service ministries.

Hospital Sisters of the Third Order of St. Francis, O.S.F.: Founded 1844, in Germany; in U.S., 1875. General motherhouse, Muenster, Germany; U.S. motherhouse, Box 19431, Springfield, IL 62794. Hospital work.

Institute of the Franciscan Sisters of the Eucharist, F.S.E.: Founded 1973. Motherhouse, 405 Allen Ave., Meriden, CT 06450.

Little Franciscans of Mary, P.F.M.: Founded 1889, in U.S. General motherhouse, Baie St. Paul, Que., Canada. U.S. region, 55 Moore Ave., Worcester, MA 01602. Educational, hospital, social work.

Missionary Sisters of the Immaculate Conception of the Mother of God, S.M.I.C.: Founded 1910, in Brazil; in U.S., 1922, U.S. provincialate, P.O. Box 3026, Paterson, NJ 07509. Mission, educational, health work, social services.

Mothers of the Helpless, M.D.: Founded 1873, in Spain; in U.S., 1916. General motherhouse, Valencia, Spain; U.S. address, Sacred Heart Residence, 432 W. 20th St., New York, NY 10011.

Poor Clares of Perpetual Adoration, P.C.P.A.: Founded 1854, at Paris, France; in U.S., 1921, at Cleveland, Ohio. U.S. monasteries: 4200 N. Market Ave., Canton, OH 44714; 2311 Stockham Lane, Portsmouth, OH 45662; 4108 Euclid Ave., Cleveland, OH 44103; 3900 13th St. N.E., Washington, DC 20017; 5817 Old Leeds Rd., Birmingham, AL 35210. Contemplative, cloistered, perpetual adoration.

St. Francis Mission Community, O.S.F.: Autonomous province of Franciscan Sisters of Mary Immaculate. Address: 203 S. Avondale, Amarillo, TX 79106.

School Sisters of St. Francis, O.S.F.: Founded 1874, in U.S. General motherhouse, 1515 S. Layton Blvd., Milwaukee, WI 53215.

School Sisters of St. Francis, (Pittsburgh, Pa.), O.S.F.: Established 1913, in U.S. Motherhouse, Mt. Assisi Convent, 934 Forest Ave., Pittsburgh, PA 15202. Education, health care services, and related ministries.

School Sisters of the Third Order of St. Francis (Bethlehem, Pa.), O.S.F.: Founded in Austria, 1843; in U.S., 1913. General motherhouse, Rome, Italy; U.S. province,

395 Bridle Path Rd., Bethlehem, PA 18017. Educational, mission work.

School Sisters of the Third Order of St. Francis (Panhandle, Tex.), O.S.F.: Established 1931, in U.S., from Vienna, Austria, foundation (1845). General motherhouse, Vienna, Austria; U.S. center and novitiate, P.O. Box 906, Panhandle, TX 79068. Educational, social work.

Sisters of Mercy of the Holy Cross, S.C.S.C.: Founded 1856, in Switzerland; in U.S., 1912. General motherhouse, Ingenbohl, Switzerland; U.S. provincial residence, 700 Riverside Ave., Merrill, WI 54452.

Sisters of Our Lady of Mercy (Mercedarians), S.O.L.M.: General motherhouse, Rome, Italy; U.S. addresses: Most Precious Blood, 133 27th Ave., Brooklyn, NY 11214; St. Edward School, Pine Hill, NJ 08021.

Sisters of St. Elizabeth, S.S.E.: Founded 1931, at Milwaukee, Wis. Address, 2005 Division St., Manitowoc, WI 53005.

Sisters of St. Francis (Clinton, Iowa), O.S.F.: Founded 1868, in U.S. General motherhouse, Bluff Blvd. and Springdale Dr., Clinton, IA 57232. Educational, hospital, social work.

Sisters of St. Francis (Millvale, Pa.), O.S.F.: Founded 1865, Pittsburgh, PA. General motherhouse, 146 Hawthorne Rd., Millvale P.O., Pittsburgh, PA 15209. Educational, hospital work.

Sisters of St. Francis (Hastings-on-Hudson), O.S.F.: Founded 1893, in New York. General motherhouse, Hastings-on-Hudson, NY 10706. Education, parish ministry, social services.

Sisters of St. Francis of Assisi, O.S.F.: Founded 1849, in U.S. General motherhouse, 3221 S. Lake Dr., Milwaukee, WI 53207. Education, other ministries.

Sisters of St. Francis of Christ the King, O.S.F.: Founded 1864, in Austria; in U.S., 1909. General motherhouse, Rome, Italy; U.S. provincial house, 13900 Main St., Lemont, IL 60439. Educational work, home for aged.

Sisters of St. Francis of Penance and Christian Charity, O.S.F.: Founded 1835, in Holland; in U.S., 1874. General motherhouse, Rome, Italy; U.S. provinces: 4421 Lower River Rd., Stella Niagara, NY 14144; 2851 W. 52nd Ave., Denver, CO 80221; 3910 Bret Harte Dr., P.O. Box 1028, Redwood City, CA 94064.

Sisters of St. Francis of Philadelphia, O.S.F.: Founded 1855, at Philadelphia, by Mother Mary Francis Bachmann and St. John N. Neumann. General motherhouse, Convent of Our Lady of the Angels, Aston, PA 19014. Education, health care, social services.

Sisters of St. Francis of Savannah, Mo., O.S.F.: Founded 1850, in Austria; in U.S., 1922. Provincial house, La Verna Heights, Box 488, 104 E. Park, Savannah, MO 64485. Educational, hospital work.

Sisters of St. Francis of the Congregation of Our Lady of Lourdes, O.S.F.: Founded 1916, in U.S. General motherhouse, 6832 Convent Blvd., Sylvania, OH 43560. Education, health care, social services, pastoral ministry.

Sisters of St. Francis of the Holy Cross, O.S.F.: Founded 1881, in U.S., by Rev. Edward Daems, O.S.C. General motherhouse, 3025 Bay Settlement Rd., Green Bay, WI 54301. Educational, nursing work, pastoral ministry, foreign missions.

Sisters of St. Francis of the Holy Eucharist, O.S.F.: Founded 1378, in Switzerland; in U.S., 1893. General motherhouse, 2100 N. Noland Rd., Independence, MO 64050. Education, health care, social services, foreign missions.

Sisters of St. Francis of the Holy Family, O.S.F.: U.S. foundation, 1875. Motherhouse, Mt. St. Francis, 3390 Windsor Ave., Dubuque, IA 52001. Varied apostolates.

Sisters of St. Francis of the Immaculate Conception, O.S.F.: Founded 1890, in U.S. General motherhouse, 2408 W. Heading Ave., Peoria, IL 61604. Education, care of aging, pastoral ministry.

Sisters of St. Francis of the Immaculate Heart of Mary, O.S.F.: Founded 1241, in Bavaria; in U.S., 1913. General motherhouse, Rome, Italy; U.S. motherhouse, Hankinson, ND 58041. Education, social services.

Sisters of St. Francis of the Martyr St. George, O.S.F.: Founded 1859, in Germany; in U.S., 1923. General motherhouse, Thuine, Germany; U.S. provincial house, St. Francis Convent, 2120 Central Ave., Alton, IL 62002. Education, social services, foreign mission work.

Sisters of St. Francis of the Perpetual Adoration, O.S.F.: Founded 1863, in Germany; in U.S., 1875. General motherhouse, Olpe, Germany; U.S. provinces: Box 766, Mishawaka, IN 46544; 7665 Assisi Heights, Colorado Springs, CO 80919.

Sisters of St. Francis of the Providence of God, O.S.F.: Founded 1922, in U.S., by Msgr. M. L. Krusas. General motherhouse, Grove and McRoberts Rds., Pittsburgh, PA 15234. Education, varied apostolates.

Sisters of St. Francis of the Third Order Regular, O.S.F.: Founded 1861, at Buffalo, N.Y., from Philadelphia foundation. General motherhouse, 400 Mill St., Williamsville, NY 14221. Educational, hospital work.

Sisters of St. Joseph of the Third Order of St. Francis, S.S.J.: Founded 1901, in U.S. Administrative office, P.O. Box 688, South Bend, IN 46624. Education, health care, social services.

Sisters of the Infant Jesus, I.J.: Founded 1662, at Rouen, France; in U.S., 1950. Motherhouse, Paris, France; Generalate, Rome, Italy; U.S. address: 20 Reiner St., Colma, CA 94014.

Sisters of the Sorrowful Mother (Third Order of St. Francis), S.S.M.: Founded 1883, in Italy; in U.S., 1889. General motherhouse, Rome, Italy; U.S. address: 17600 E. 51st St. S., Broken Arrow, OK 74012. Educational, hospital work.

Sisters of the Third Franciscan Order, O.S.F.: Founded 1860, at Syracuse, N.Y. Generalate offices, 2500 Grant Blvd., Syracuse, NY 13208.

Sisters of the Third Order of St. Francis, O.S.F.: Founded 1877, in U.S., by Bishop John L. Spalding. Motherhouse, St. Francis Lane, E. Peoria, IL 61611. Hospital work.

Sisters of the Third Order of St. Francis (Oldenburg, Ind.), O.S.F.: Founded 1851, in U.S. General motherhouse, Convent of the Immaculate Conception, Oldenburg, IN 47036. Education, social services, pastoral ministry, foreign missions.

Sisters of the Third Order of St. Francis of Penance and Charity, O.S.F.: Founded 1869, in U.S., by Rev. Joseph Bihn. Motherhouse, St. Francis Ave., Tiffin, OH 44883. Education, social services.

Sisters of the Third Order of St. Francis of the Perpetual Adoration, F.S.P.A.: Founded 1849, in U.S. Generalate, 912 Market St., La Crosse, WI 54601. Education, health care.

Sisters of the Third Order Regular of St. Francis of the Congregation of Our Lady of Lourdes, O.S.F.: Founded 1877, in U.S. General motherhouse, Assisi Heights, Rochester, MN 55901. Education, health care, social services.

(End, Listing of Franciscans)

Good Shepherd Sisters (Servants of the Immaculate Heart of Mary), S.C.I.M.: Founded 1850, in Canada; in U.S., 1882. General motherhouse, Quebec, Canada; Provincial House, Bay View, 313 Seaside Ave., Saco, Maine 04072. Educational, social work.

Good Shepherd, Sisters of Our Lady of Charity of the, R.G.S.: Founded 1835, in France by St. Mary Euphrasia Pelletier, in U.S., 1843. Generalate, Rome, Italy; U.S. provinces: 2849 Fischer Pl., Cincinnati, OH 45211; 82-31 Doncaster Pl., Jamaica, NY 11432; 504 Hexton Hill Rd., Silver Spring, MD 20904; 7654 Natural Bridge Rd., St. Louis, MO 63121; 5100 Hodgson Rd., St. Paul, MN 55112. Active and contemplative (Contemplative Sisters of the Good Shepherd, C.G.S.).

Graymoor Sisters: See Franciscan Sisters of the Atonement.

Grey Nuns of the Sacred Heart, G.N.S.H.: Founded 1921, in U.S. General motherhouse, 1750 Quarry Rd., Yardley, PA 19067.

Guadalupan Missionaries of the Holy Spirit, M.G.Sp.S.: Founded 1930 in Mexico by Rev. Felix de Jesus Rougier, M.Sp.S. General motherhouse, Mexico; U.S. delegation: 2483 S.W. 4th St., Miami, FL 33135.

Guardian Angel, Sisters of the Holy, S.A.C.: Founded 1839, in France. General motherhouse, Madrid, Spain; U.S. foundation, 1245 S. Van Ness, Los Angeles, CA 90019.

Handmaids of Mary Immaculate, A.M.I.: Founded 1952 in Helena, Mont. Address: Mountain View Rd., Washington, NJ 07882.

Handmaids of the Precious Blood, Congregation of, H.P.B.: Founded 1947, at Jemez Springs, N. Mex. Motherhouse and novitiate, Cor Jesu Monastery, Jemez Springs, NM 87025.

Helpers, Society of, H.H.S.: Founded 1856, in France; in U.S., 1892. General motherhouse, Paris, France; American province, 303 W. Barry Ave., Chicago, IL 60657.

Hermanas Catequistas Guadalupanas, H.C.G.: Founded 1923, in Mexico; in U.S., 1950. General motherhouse, Mexico; U.S. foundation, 4110 S. Flores, San Antonio, TX 78214.

Hermanas Josefinas, H.J.: General motherhouse, Mexico; U.S. foundation, Assumption Seminary, 2600 W. Woodlawn Ave., P.O. Box 28240, San Antonio, TX 78284. Domestic work.

Holy Child Jesus, Society of the, S.H.C.J.: Founded 1846, in England; in U.S., 1862. General motherhouse, Rome, Italy. U.S. province: 460 Shadeland Ave., Drexel Hill, PA 19026.

Holy Faith, Congregation of the Sisters of the, C.H.F.: Founded 1856, in Ireland; in U.S., 1953. General motherhouse, Dublin, Ireland; U.S. province, 12322 S. Paramount Blvd., P.O. Box 2085, Downey, CA 90242.

Holy Heart of Mary, Servants of the, S.S.C.M.: Founded 1860, in France; in U.S., 1889. General motherhouse, Montreal, Que., Canada; U.S. province, 145 S. 4th Ave., Kankakee, IL 60901. Educational, hospital, social work.

Holy Names of Jesus and Mary, Sisters of the, S.N.J.M.: Founded 1843, in Canada by Bl. Marie Rose Durocher, in U.S., 1859. Generalate, Longueuil Que., Canada. U.S. addresses: Oregon Province, Box 25, Marylhurst, OR 97036; California Province, P.O. Box 907, Los Gatos, CA 95031; New York Province, 1061 New Scotland Rd., Albany, NY 12208; Washington Province, 2911 W. Ft. Wright Dr., Spokane, WA 99204.

Holy Spirit, Community of the, C.H.S.: Founded 1970 in San Diego, Calif. Address: 1275 Nagle Ave., San Jose, CA 95126.

Holy Spirit, Daughters of the, D.H.S.: Founded 1706, in France; in U.S., 1902. Generalate, Bretagne, France; U.S. motherhouse, 72 Church St., Putnam, CT 06260. Educational work, district nursing, pastoral ministry.

Holy Spirit, Mission Sisters of the, M.S.Sp.: Founded 1932, at Cleveland, Ohio. Motherhouse, 1030 N. River Rd., Saginaw, MI 48603.

Holy Spirit, Missionary Sisters, Servants of the: Founded 1889, in Holland; in U.S., 1901. Generalate, Rome, Italy; U.S. motherhouse, Convent of the Holy Spirit, Techny, IL 60082.

Holy Spirit, Sisters of the, C.S.Sp.: Founded 1890, in Rome, Italy; in U.S. as independent diocesan community, 1929. General motherhouse, 10102 Granger Rd., Garfield Hts., OH 44125. Educational, social, nursing work.

Holy Spirit, Sisters of the, S.H.S.: Founded 1913, in U.S., by Most Rev. J. F. Regis Canevin. General motherhouse, 5246 Clarwin Ave., Ross Township, Pittsburgh, PA 15229. Educational, nursing work, care of aged.

Holy Spirit and Mary Immaculate, Sisters of, S.H.Sp.: Founded 1893, in U.S. Motherhouse, 301 Yucca St., San Antonio, TX 78203. Education, hospital work.

Holy Spirit of Perpetual Adoration, Sister Servants of the: Founded 1896, in Holland; in U.S., 1915. Generalate, Bad Driburg, Germany; U.S. novitiate, 2212 Green St., Philadelphia, PA 19130.

Home Mission Sisters of America (Glenmary Sisters): Founded 1952, in U.S. Glenmary Center, P.O. Box 22264, Owensboro, KY 42302.

Home Visitors of Mary, Sisters, H.V.M.: Founded 1949, in Detroit, Mich. Motherhouse, 356 Arden Park, Detroit, MI 48202.

Humility of Mary, Congregation of, C.H.M.: Founded 1854, in France; in U.S., 1864. U.S. address, Humility of Mary Center, Davenport, IA 52804.

Humility of Mary, Sisters of the, H.M.: Founded 1854, in France; in U.S., 1864. U.S. address, Villa Maria Community Center, Villa Maria, PA 16155.

Immaculate Conception, Little Servant Sisters of the: Founded 1850, in Poland; in U.S., 1926. General motherhouse, Poland; U.S. provincial house, 1000 Cropwell Rd., Cherry Hill, NJ 08003. Education, social services, African missions.

Immaculate Conception, Sisters of the, R.C.M.: Founded 1892, in Spain; in U.S., 1962. General motherhouse, Madrid, Spain; U.S. address, 2230 Franklin, San Francisco, CA 94109.

Immaculate Conception, Sisters of the, C.I.C.: Founded 1874, in U.S. General motherhouse, 4920 Kent Ave., Metairie, LA 70006.

Immaculate Conception of the Blessed Virgin Mary, Sisters of the (Lithuanian): Founded 1918, at Mariampole, Lithuania; in U.S., 1936. U.S. headquarters, Immaculate Conception Convent, 600 Liberty Hwy., Putnam, CT 06260.

Immaculate Heart of Mary, Missionary Sisters, I.C.M.: Founded 1897, in India; in U.S., 1919. Generalate, Rome, Italy; U.S. province, 283 E. 15th St., New York, NY 10003. Educational, social, foreign mission work.

Immaculate Heart of Mary, Sisters of the: Founded 1848, in Spain; in U.S., 1878. General motherhouse, Rome, Italy. U.S. province, 4100 Sabino Canyon Rd., Tucson, AZ 85715. Educational work.

Immaculate Heart of Mary, Sisters of the (California Institute of the Most Holy and Immaculate Heart of the B.V.M.), I.H.M.: Founded 1848, in Spain; in U.S., 1871. Generalate, 3431 Waverly Dr., Los Angeles, CA 90027.

Immaculate Heart of Mary, Sisters, Servants of the, I.H.M.: Founded 1845, at Monroe, Mich., by Rev. Louis Florent Gillet. Generalate, 610 W. Elm St., Monroe, MI 48161.

Immaculate Heart of Mary, Sisters, Servants of the, I.H.M.: Founded 1845; established in Scranton, Penn., 1871. General motherhouse, Marywood, Scranton, PA 18509.

Immaculate Heart of Mary, Sisters Servants of the, I.H.M.: Founded 1845; established in West Chester, Penn., 1872. General motherhouse, Villa Maria, Immaculata, PA 19345.

Incarnate Word, Religious of, C.V.I.: General motherhouse, Mexico City, Mexico. U.S. address, 153 Rainier Ct., Chula Vista, CA 92011.

Incarnate Word and Blessed Sacrament, Congregation of, C.V.I.: Founded 1625, in France; in U.S., 1853. Incarnate Word Convent, 3400 Bradford Pl., Houston, TX 77028.

Incarnate Word and Blessed Sacrament, Congregation of the, I.W.B.S.: Motherhouse, 1101 Northeast Water St., Victoria, TX 77901.

Incarnate Word and Blessed Sacrament, Congregation of the, I.W.B.S.: Motherhouse, 2930 S. Alameda, Corpus Christi, TX 78404.

Incarnate Word and Blessed Sacrament, Sisters of the, S.I.W.: Founded 1625, in France; in U.S., 1853. Motherhouse, 6618 Pearl Rd., Parma Heights, Cleveland, OH 44130.

Infant Jesus, Congregation of the (Nursing Sisters of the Sick Poor), C.I.J.: Founded 1835, in France; in U.S., 1905. General motherhouse, 310 Prospect Park W., Brooklyn, NY 11215.

Jesus, Daughters of, F.I.: Founded 1871, in Spain; in U.S., 1950. General motherhouse, Rome, Italy; U.S. address, 2021 Stuart Ave., Baton Rouge, LA 70808.

Jesus, Daughters of (Filles de Jesus), F.J.: Founded 1834, in France; in U.S., 1904. General motherhouse, Kermaria, Locmine, France; U.S. address, 4209 3rd Ave. S., Great Falls, MT 59405. Educational, hospital, parish and social work.

Jesus, Little Sisters of: Founded 1939, in Sahara; in U.S., 1952. General motherhouse, Rome, Italy; U.S. headquarters, 400 N. Streeper St., Baltimore, MD 21224.

Jesus, Servants of, S.J.: Founded 1974, in U.S. Central Office, 9075 Big Lake Rd., P.O. Box 128, Clarkston, MI 48016.

Jesus, Society of the Sisters, Faithful Companions of, F.C.J.: Founded 1820, in France; in U.S., 1896. General motherhouse, Kent, England. U.S. province: St. Philomena Convent, Cory's Lane, Portsmouth, RI 02871.

Jesus and Mary, Little Sisters of, L.S.J.M.: Founded 1974 in U.S. Address: Joseph House, P.O. Box 1755, Salisbury, MD 21801.

Jesus and Mary, Religious of, R.J.M.: Founded 1818, at Lyons, France; in U.S., 1877. General motherhouse, Rome, Italy; U.S. province, 3706 Rhode Island Ave., Mt. Ranier, MD 20712. Educational work.

Jesus Crucified, Congregation of: Founded 1930, in France; in U.S., 1955. General motherhouse, Brou, France; U.S. foundations: Regina Mundi Priory Devon, PA 19333; St. Paul's Priory, 61 Narragansett, Newport, RI 02840.

Jesus Crucified and the Sorrowful Mother, Poor Sisters of, C.J.C.: Founded 1924, in U.S., by Rev. Alphonsus Maria, C.P. Motherhouse, 261 Thatcher St., Brockton, MA 02402. Education, nursing homes, catechetical centers.

Jesus, Mary and Joseph, Missionaries of, M.J.M.J.: Founded 1942, in Spain; in U.S., 1956. General motherhouse, Madrid, Spain; U.S. regional house, 12940 Up River Rd., Corpus Christi, TX 78410.

Joan of Arc, Sisters of St., S.J.A.: Founded 1914, in U.S., by Rev. Marie Clément Staub, A.A. General motherhouse, 1505, rue de l'Assomption, Sillery, Que. G1S 4T3, Canada. U.S. novitiate, 529 Eastern Ave., Fall River, MA 02723. Spiritual and temporal service of priests.

John the Baptist, Sisters of St., C.S.J.B.: Founded 1878, in Italy; in U.S., 1906. General motherhouse, Rome, Italy; U.S. provincialate, Anderson Hill Rd., Purchase, NY 10577. Education, parish and retreat work, social services.

Joseph, Poor Sisters of St.: Founded 1880, in Argentina. General motherhouse, Muniz, Buenos Aires, Argentina; U.S. addresses, Casa Belen, 305 E. 4th St., Bethlehem, PA 78015; Casa Nazareth, 532 Spruce St., Reading, PA 19602; St. Gabriel Convent, 4319 Sano St., Alexandria, VA 22312.

Joseph, Religious Daughters of St., F.S.J.: Founded 1875, in Spain. General motherhouse, Spain; U.S. foundation, 319 N. Humphreys Ave., Los Angeles, CA 90022.

Joseph, Religious Hospitallers of St., R.H.S.J.: Founded 1636, in France; in U.S., 1894. Generalate, Montreal, Que., Canada; U.S. address, Holy Family Convent, 100 Mansfield Ave., P.O. Box 176, Burlington, VT 05401. Hospital work.

Joseph, Servants of St., S.S.J.: Founded 1874, in Spain; in U.S., 1957. General motherhouse, Salamanca, Spain; U.S. address, 203 N. Spring St., Falls Church, VA 22046.

Joseph, Sisters of St., C.S.J. or S.S.J.: Founded 1650, in France; in U.S., 1836, at St. Louis. Independent motherhouses in U.S.:

637 Cambridge St., Brighton, MA 02135; 1515 W. Ogden Ave., La Grange Park, IL 60525; 480 S. Batavia St., Orange, CA 92668.

St. Joseph Convent, Brentwood, NY 11717; 23 Agassiz Circle, Buffalo, NY 14214; Avila Hall, 7 Clement Rd., Rutland, VT 05701; 3430 Rocky River Dr., Cleveland, OH 44111; 1440 Division Rd., Tipton, IN 46072; Motherhouse and Novitiate, Nazareth, MI 49074; 1425 Washington St., Watertown, NY 13601; Mt. Gallitzin Academy and Motherhouse, Baden, PA 15005; 5031 W. Ridge Rd., Erie, PA 16502.

4095 East Ave., Rochester, NY 14610; 215 Court St., Concordia, KS 66901; Mont Marie, Holyoke, MA 01040; Pogue Run Rd., Wheeling, WV 26003; 3700 E. Lincoln St., Wichita, KS 67218.

Joseph, Sisters of St. (Lyons, France), C.S.J.: Founded 1650, in France; in U.S., 1906. General motherhouse, Lyons, France; U.S. provincialate, 93 Halifax St., Winslow, ME 04901. Educational, hospital work.

Joseph, Sisters of St., of Peace, C.S.J.P.: Founded 1884, in England; in U.S., 1885. Generalate, 1225 Newton St. N.E., Washington, DC 20017. Educational, hospital, social service work.

Joseph of Carondelet, Sisters of St., C.S.J.: Founded 1650, in France; in U.S., 1836, at St. Louis, Mo. U.S. headquarters, 2307 S. Lindbergh Blvd., St. Louis, MO 63131.

Joseph of Chambéry, Sisters of St.: Founded 1650, in France; in U.S., 1885. Generalate, Rome, Italy; U.S. provincial house, 27 Park Rd., West Hartford, CT 06119. Educational, hospital, social work.

Joseph of Chestnut Hill, Sisters of St., S.S.J.: Founded 1650; Philadelphia foundation, 1847. Motherhouse, Mt. St. Joseph Convent, Chestnut Hill, PA 19118.

Joseph of Cluny, Sisters of St., S.J.C.: Founded 1807, in France. Generalate, Paris, France; U.S. provincial house, Brenton Rd., Newport, RI 02840.

Joseph of Médaille, Sisters of, C.S.J.: Founded 1650, in France; in U.S., 1855. Became an American congregation Nov. 30, 1977. Central office, 1821 Summit Rd., Cincinnati, OH 45237.

Joseph of St. Augustine, Florida, Sisters of St., S.S.J.: General motherhouse, 241 St. George St., P.O. Box 3506, St. Augustine, FL 32085. Educational, hospital, pastoral, social work.

Joseph of St. Mark, Sisters of St., S.J.S.M.: Founded 1845, in France; in U.S., 1937. General motherhouse, 21800 Chardon Rd., Euclid, Cleveland, OH 44117. Nursing homes.

Joseph the Worker, Sisters of St., S.J.W.: General motherhouse, St. Joseph Convent, 1 St. Joseph Lane, Walton, KY 41094.

Lamb of God, Sisters of the, A.D.: Founded 1945, in France; in U.S., 1958. General motherhouse, France; U.S. address, 2068 Wyandotte Ave., Owensboro, KY 42301.

Life, Sisters of, S.V. (Sorores Vitae): Founded by Cardinal John J. O'Connor, 1991, to protect life. Address: St. Frances de Chantal Convent, Hollywood Ave., Bronx, NY 10465.

Little Sisters of the Gospel, L.S.G.: Founded 1963 in France by Rev. René Voillaume; in U.S., 1972. U.S. address, Box 305, Mott Haven Sta., Bronx, NY 10454.

Little Workers of the Sacred Hearts, P.O.S.C.: Founded 1892, in Italy; in U.S., 1948. General house, Rome, Italy; U.S. address, Our Lady of Grace Convent, 635 Glenbrook Rd., Stamford, CT 06906.

Living Word, Sisters of the, S.L.W.: Founded 1975, in U.S. Motherhouse, The Center, 800 N. Fernandez Ave., Arlington Heights, IL 60004. Education, hospital, parish ministry work.

Loretto at the Foot of the Cross, Sisters of, S.L.: Founded 1812 in U.S., by Rev. Charles Nerinckx. General motherhouse, Nerinx, KY 40049. Educational work.

Louis, Congregation of Sisters of St., S.S.L.: Founded 1842, in France; in U.S., 1949. General motherhouse, Monaghan, Ireland; U.S. regional house, 22300 Mulholland Dr., Woodland Hills, CA 91364. Educational, medical, parish, foreign mission work.

Lovers of the Holy Cross Sisters (Phat Diem): Founded 1670, in Vietnam; in U.S., 1976. U.S. address, Our Lady of Peace Convent, 902 Langdon Ave., Sepulveda, CA 91343.

Marian Sisters of the Diocese of Lincoln: Founded 1954. Motherhouse, Marian Center, R.R. 1, Box 108, Waverly, NE 68462.

Marianites of Holy Cross, Congregation of the Sisters, M.S.C.: Founded 1841, in France; in U.S., 1843. Motherhouse, Le Mans, Sarthe, France. North American headquarters, 1011 Gallier St., New Orleans, LA 70117.

Marist Sisters, Congregation of Mary, S.M.: Founded 1824, in France. General motherhouse, Rome, Italy; U.S. convents: St. Albert the Great, 4855 Parker, Dearborn Hts., MI 48125; St. Barnabas, 24262 Johnston, E. Detroit, MI 48021; Our Lady of the Snows, 4810 S. Leamington, Chicago, IL 60638; Marie, Madre de la Iglesia, 4419 St. James, Detroit, MI 48210.

Mary, Company of, O.D.N.: Founded 1607, in France; in U.S., 1926. General motherhouse, Rome, Italy; U.S. motherhouse, 16791 E. Main St., Tustin, CA 92680.

Mary, Daughters of the Heart of, D.H.M.: Founded 1790, in France; in U.S., 1851. Generalate, Paris, France; U.S. provincialate, 1339 Northampton St., Holyoke, MA 01040. Education, retreat work.

Mary, Missionary Sisters of the Society of (Marist Sisters), S.M.S.M.: Founded 1845, at St. Brieuc, France; in U.S., 1922. General motherhouse, Rome, Italy; U.S. provincial house, 349 Grove St., Waltham, MA 02154. Foreign missions.

Mary, Servants of, O.S.M.: Founded 13th century, in Italy; in U.S., 1893. General motherhouse, England; U.S. provincial motherhouse, 7400 Military Ave., Omaha, NE 68134.

Mary, Servants of (Servite Sisters), O.S.M.: Founded 13th century, in Italy; in U.S., 1912. General motherhouse, Our Lady of Sorrows Convent, 1000 College Ave., Ladysmith, WI 54848.

Mary, Servants of, of Blue Island (Mantellate Sisters), O.S.M.: Founded 1861, in Italy; in U.S., 1916. Generalate, Rome, Italy; U.S. motherhouse, 13811 S. Western Ave., Blue Island, IL 60406. Educational work.

Mary, Sisters of St., of Oregon, S.S.M.O.: Founded 1886, in Oregon, by Bishop William H. Gross, C.Ss.R. General motherhouse, 4440 S.W. 148th Ave., Beaverton, OR 97007. Educational, nursing work.

Mary, Sisters of the Little Company of, L.C.M.: Founded 1877, in England; in U.S., 1893. Generalate, London, England; U.S. provincial house, 9350 S. California Ave., Evergreen Park, IL 60642.

Mary, Sisters Servants of (Trained Nurses), S.M.: Founded 1851, at Madrid, Spain; in U.S., 1914. General motherhouse, Rome, Italy; U.S. motherhouse, 800 N. 18th St., Kansas City, KS 66102. Home nursing.

Mary and Joseph, Daughters of, D.M.J.: Founded 1817, in Belgium; in U.S., 1926. Generalate, Rome, Italy; American provincialate, 5300 Crest Rd., Rancho Palos Verdes, CA 90274.

Mary Help of Christians, Daughters of (Salesian Sisters of St. John Bosco), F.M.A.: Founded 1872, in Italy, by St. John Bosco and St. Mary Dominic Mazzarello; in U.S., 1908. General motherhouse, Rome, Italy; U.S. provinces, 655 Belmont Ave., Haledon, NJ 07508; 6019 Buena Vista St., San Antonio, TX 78237. Education, youth work.

Mary Immaculate, Daughters of (Marianist Sisters), F.M.I.: Founded 1816, in France, by Very Rev. William-Joseph Chaminade. General motherhouse, Rome, Italy; U.S. foundation, 251 W. Ligustrum Dr., San Antonio, TX 78228. Educational work.

Mary Immaculate, Religious of, R.M.I.: Founded 1876, in Spain; in U.S., 1954. Generalate, Rome, Italy; U.S. foundation, 719 Augusta St., San Antonio, TX 78215.

Mary Immaculate, Sisters of, S.M.I.: Founded 1948, in India, by Bishop Louis LaRavoire Morrow; in U.S., 1981. General motherhouse, Bengal, India; U.S. address, R.D. 5, Box 1231, Leechburg, PA 15656.

Mary Immaculate, Sisters Servants of, S.S.M.I.: Founded 1878, in Poland. General motherhouse, Mariowka-Opoczynska, Poland; American provincialate, 1220 Tugwell Dr., Catonsville, MD 21228.

Mary Immaculate, Sisters Servants of, S.S.M.I.: Founded 1892, in Ukraine; in U.S., 1935. General motherhouse, Rome, Italy; U.S. address, 9 Emmanuel Dr., P.O. Box 6, Sloatsburg, NY 10974. Educational, hospital work.

Mary of Namur, Sisters of St., S.S.M.N.: Founded 1819, at Namur, Belgium; in U.S., 1863. General motherhouse, Namur, Belgium; U.S. provinces: 250 Bryant, Buffalo, NY 14222; 909 West Shaw St., Ft. Worth, TX 76110.

Mary of Providence, Daughters of St., D.S.M.P.: Founded 1872, at Como, Italy; in U.S., 1913. General motherhouse, Rome, Italy; U.S. provincial house, 4200 N. Austin Ave., Chicago, IL 60634. Special education for mentally handicapped.

Mary of the Immaculate Conception, Daughters of, D.M.: Founded 1904, in U.S., by Msgr. Lucian Bojnowski. General motherhouse, 314 Osgood Ave., New Britain, CT 06053. Educational, hospital work.

Mary Queen, Congregation of, C.M.R.: Founded in Vietnam; established in U.S., 1979. U.S. region, 535 S. Jefferson, Springfield, MO 65806.

Mary Reparatrix, Society of, S.M.R.: Founded 1857, in France; in U.S., 1908. Generalate, Rome, Italy. U.S. province, 225 E. 234th St., Bronx, NY 10470.

Medical Mission Sisters (Society of Catholic Medical Missionaries, Inc.), M.M.S.: Founded 1925, in U.S., by Mother Anna Dengel. Generalate, London, Eng.; U.S. headquarters, 8400 Pine Rd., Philadelphia, PA 19111. Medical work, health education, especially in mission areas.

Medical Missionaries of Mary, M.M.M.: Founded 1937, in Ireland, by Mother Mary Martin; in U.S., 1950. General motherhouse, Dublin, Ireland; U.S. headquarters, 563 Minneford Ave., City Island, Bronx, NY 10464. Medical aid in missions.

Medical Sisters of St. Joseph, M.S.J.: Founded 1946, in India; first U.S. foundation, 1985. General motherhouse, Kerala, S. India; U.S. address, 3435 E. Funston, Wichita, KS 67218. Health care apostolate.

Mercedarian Missionaries of Berriz, M.M.B.: Founded 1930, in Spain; in U.S., 1946. General motherhouse, Rome, Italy. U.S. headquarters, 1400 N.E. 42nd Terr., Kansas City, MO 64106.

Mercy, Daughters of Our Lady of, D.M.: Founded 1837, in Italy, by St. Mary Joseph Rossello; in U.S., 1919. General motherhouse, Savona, Italy; U.S. motherhouse, Villa Rossello, RR 1, Box 159, Newfield, NJ 08344. Educational, hospital work.

Mercy, Missionary Sisters of Our Lady of, M.O.M.: Founded 1938, in Brazil; in U.S., 1955. General motherhouse, Brazil; U.S. address, 388 Franklin St., Buffalo, NY 14202.

Mercy, Religious Sisters of, R.S.M.: Founded 1973, in U.S. Motherhouse, 1835 Michigan Ave., Alma, MI 48801.

Mercy, Sisters of, Daughters of Christian Charity of St. Vincent de Paul, S.M.D.C.: Founded 1842, in Hungary; U.S. foundation, Rt. 1, Box 353A, 240 Longhouse Dr., Hewitt, NJ 07421.

Mercy, Sisters of, of the Americas: Formed in July, 1991, through union of 25 regional communities of Sisters of Mercy which previously were independent motherhouses or houses which formed the Sisters of Mercy of the Union. Mother Mary Catherine McAuley founded the Sisters of Mercy in Dublin, Ireland, in 1831; the first establishment in the U S., 1843, in Pittsburgh. Address of administrative office: 8300 Colesville Rd, No. 300, Silver Spring, MD 20910. Pres., Sr. Doris Gottemoeller.

Mercy of the Blessed Sacrament, Sisters of, H.M.S.S.: Founded 1910 in Mexico; in U.S., 1926. General motherhouse, Mexico. U.S. regional house, 222 W. Cevallos St., San Antonio, TX 78204.

Mill Hill Sisters: See Franciscan Missionaries of St. Joseph.

Minim Daughters of Mary Immaculate, C.F.M.M.: Founded 1886, in Mexico; in U.S., 1926. General motherhouse, Leon, Guanajuato, Mexico; U S. address, Our Lady of Lourdes High School, Box 1865, Nogales, AZ 85621.

Misericordia Sisters, S.M.: Founded 1848, in Canada; in U.S., 1887. General motherhouse, 12435 Ave. Misericorde, Montreal H4J 2J3, Canada; U.S. address, 820 Jungles Ave., Aurora, IL 60505. Social work with unwed mothers and their children, hospital work.

Mission Helpers of the Sacred Heart, M.H.S.H.: Founded 1890, in U.S. General motherhouse, 1001 W. Joppa Rd., Baltimore, MD 21204. Religious education, evangelization.

Missionary Catechists of the Sacred Hearts of Jesus and Mary (Violetas), M.C.: Founded 1918, in Mexico; in U.S., 1943. Motherhouse, Tlalpan, Mexico; U.S. address, 805 Liberty St., Victoria, TX 77901.

Mother of God, Missionary Sisters of the, M.S.M.G.: Byzantine, Ukrainian Rite, Stamford. Motherhouse, 711 N. Franklin St., Philadelphia, PA 19123.

Mother of God, Sisters Poor Servants of the, S.M.G.: Founded 1869, in London, England; in U.S., 1947. General motherhouse, Maryfield, Roehampton, London. U.S. addresses: Maryfield Nursing Home, Greensboro Rd., High Point, NC 27260; St. Mary's Hospital, 916 Virginia Ave., Norton, VA 24273. Hospital, educational work.

Nazareth, Poor Sisters of: Founded in England; U.S. foundation, 1924. General motherhouse, Hammersmith, London, England; U.S. novitiate, 3333 Manning Ave., Los Angeles, CA 90064. Social services, education.

Notre Dame, School Sisters of, S.S.N.D.: Founded 1833, in Germany; in U.S., 1847. General motherhouse, Rome, Italy. U.S. motherhouse, 1233 N. Marshall St., Milwaukee, WI 53202. Provinces: 6401 N. Charles St., Baltimore, MD 21212; 320 E. Ripa Ave., St. Louis, MO 63125; 170 Good Counsel Dr., Mankato, MN 56001; 345 Belden Hill Rd., Wilton, CT 06897; P.O. Box 227275, Dallas, TX 75222; 1431 Euclid Ave., Berwyn, IL 60402.

Notre Dame, Sisters of, S.N.D.: Founded 1850, at Coesfeld, Germany; in U.S., 1874. General motherhouse, Rome, Italy. U.S. provinces: 13000 Auburn Rd., Chardon, OH 44024; 1601 Dixie Highway, Covington, KY 41011; 3837 Secor Rd., Toledo, OH 43623; 1776 Hendrix Ave., Thousand Oaks, CA 91360.

Notre Dame, Sisters of the Congregation of, C.N.D.: Founded 1658, in Canada by St. Marguerite Bourgeoys;

in U.S., 1860. General motherhouse, Montreal, Que., Canada; U.S. province, 223 West Mountain Rd., Ridgefield, CT 06877. Education.

Notre Dame de Namur, Sisters of, S.N.D.: Founded 1803, in France; in U.S., 1840. General motherhouse, Rome, Italy. U.S. provinces: 400 The Fenway, Boston, MA 02115; 30 Jeffrey's Neck Rd., Ipswich, MA 01938; 468 Poquonock Ave., Windsor, CT 06095; P.O. Box 298, 5025 Ilchester Rd., Ellicott City, MD 21041; 305 Cable St., Baltimore, MD 21210; 701 E. Columbia Ave., Cincinnati, OH 45215; 14800 Bohlman Rd., Saratoga, CA 95070; Base Communities Province, 3037 Fourth St. N.E., Washington, DC 20017. Educational work.

Notre Dame de Sion, Congregation of, N.D.S.: Founded 1843, in France; in U.S., 1892. Generalate, Rome, Italy; U.S. province, 349 Westminster Rd., Brooklyn, NY 11218. Creation of better understanding and relations between Christians and Jews.

Notre Dame Sisters: Founded 1853, in Bohemia; in U.S., 1910. General motherhouse, Javornik, Czech Republic; U.S. motherhouse, 3501 State St., Omaha, NE 68112. Educational work.

Oblates of the Mother of Orphans, O.M.O.: Founded 1945, in Italy. General motherhouse, Milan, Italy. U.S. address, 20 E. 72nd St., New York, NY 10021.

Our Lady of Charity, North American Union of Sisters of, Eudist Sisters (Sisters of Our Lady of Charity of the Refuge), N.A.U.-O.L.C.: Founded 1641, in Caen, France, by St. John Eudes; in U.S., 1855. Autonomous houses were federated in 1944 and in May, 1978, the North American Union of the Sisters of Our Lady of Charity was established. General motherhouse and administrative center, Box 327, Wisconsin Dells, WI 53965. Primarily devoted to re-education and rehabilitation of women and girls in residential and non-residential settings.

Independent monasteries: 1125 Malvern Ave., Hot Springs, AR 71901; 620 Roswell Rd. N.W., Carrollton, OH 44615; 4500 W. Davis St., Dallas, TX 75211.

Our Lady of Sorrows, Sisters of, O.L.S.: Founded 1839, in Italy; in U.S., 1947. General motherhouse, Rome, Italy; U.S. headquarters, 9894 Norris Ferry Rd., Shreveport, LA 71106.

Our Lady of the Garden, Sisters of, O.L.G.: Founded 1829, in Italy, by St. Anthony Mary Gianelli. Motherhouse, Rome, Italy; U.S. address, 67 Round Hill Rd., Middletown, CT 06457.

Our Lady of Victory Missionary Sisters, O.L.V.M.: Founded 1922, in U.S. Motherhouse, Victory Noll, Box 109, Huntington, IN 46750. Educational, social work.

Pallottine Missionary Sisters (Missionary Sisters of the Catholic Apostolate), S.A.C.: Founded in Rome, 1838; in U.S., 1912. Generalate, Rome, Italy; U.S. provincialate, 15270 Old Halls Ferry Rd., Florissant, MO 63034.

Pallottine Sisters of the Catholic Apostolate, C.S.A.C.: Founded 1843, at Rome, Italy; in U.S., 1889. General motherhouse, Rome, Italy; U.S. motherhouse, St. Patrick's Villa, Harriman Heights, Harriman, NY 10926. Educational work.

Parish Visitors of Mary Immaculate, P.V.M.I.: Founded 1920, in New York. General motherhouse, Box 658, Monroe, NY 10950. Mission work.

Passion of Jesus Christ, Religious of (Passionist Nuns), C.P.: Founded 1771, in Italy, by St. Paul of the Cross; in U.S., 1910. U.S. convents: 2715 Churchview Ave., Pittsburgh, PA 15227; 631 Griffin Pond Rd., Clarks Summit, PA 18411; 1420 Benita Ave., Owensboro, KY 42301; 1151 Donaldson Hwy., Erlanger, KY 41018; 15700 Clayton Rd., Ellisville, MO 63011. Contemplatives.

Passionist Sisters: See Cross and Passion, Sisters of the.

Paul, Daughters of St. (Missionary Sisters of the Media of Communication), D.S.P.: Founded 1915, at Alba, Piedmont, Italy; in U.S., 1932. General motherhouse, Rome, Italy; U.S. provincial house, 50 St. Paul's Ave., Boston, MA 02130. Apostolate of the communications arts.

Paul of Chartres, Sisters of St., S.P.C.: Founded 1696, in France. General house, Rome, Italy; U.S. address, 1300 County Rd. 492, Marquette, MI 49855.

Perpetual Adoration of Guadalupe, Sisters of, A.P.G.: U.S. foundation, 2403 W. Travis, San Antonio, TX 78207.

Peter Claver, Missionary Sisters of St., S.S.P.C.: Founded 1894 in Austria by Bl. Maria Teresa Ledochowska; in U.S., 1914. General motherhouse, Rome, Italy; U.S. address, 667 Woods Mill Rd. S., Chesterfield, MO 63017.

Pious Disciples of the Divine Master, P.D.D.M.: Founded 1924, in Italy; in U.S., 1948. General motherhouse, Rome, Italy; U.S. headquarters, 60 Sunset Ave., Staten Island, NY 10314.

Pious Schools, Sisters of, Sch. P.: Founded 1829, in Spain; in U.S., 1954. General motherhouse, Rome, Italy; U.S. headquarters, 17601 Nordhoff St., Northridge, CA 91325.

Poor, Little Sisters of the, L.S.P.: Founded 1839, in France by Bl. Jeanne Jugan; in U.S., 1868. General motherhouse, St. Pern, France. U.S. provinces: 110-30 221st St., Queens Village, NY 11429; 601 Maiden Choice Lane, Baltimore, MD 21228; 80 W. Northwest Hwy., Palatine, IL 60067. Care of aged.

Poor Clare Missionary Sisters (Misioneras Clarisas), M.C.: Founded Mexico. General motherhouse, Rome, Italy; U.S. novitiate, 1019 N. Newhope, Santa Ana, CA 92703.

Poor Clare Nuns: See Franciscan Poor Clare Nuns.

Poor Handmaids of Jesus Christ (Ancilla Domini Sisters), P.H.J.C.: Founded 1851, in Germany by Bl. Mary Kasper; in U.S., 1868. General motherhouse, Dern-bach, Westerwald, Germany; U.S. motherhouse, Ancilla Domini Convent, Donaldson, IN 46513. Educational, hospital work, social services.

Precious Blood, Daughters of Charity of the Most: Founded 1872, at Pagani, Italy; in U.S., 1908. General motherhouse, Rome, Italy; U.S. convent, 1482 North Ave., Bridgeport, CT 06604.

Precious Blood, Missionary Sisters of the, C.P.S.: Founded 1885, at Mariannhill, South Africa; in U.S., 1925. Generalate, Rome, Italy; U.S. novitiate, New Holland Ave., P.O. Box 97, Shillington, PA 19607. Home and foreign mission work.

Precious Blood, Sisters Adorers of the, A.P.B.: Founded 1861, in Canada; in U.S., 1890. General motherhouse, Canada. U.S. autonomous monasteries: 54th St. and Fort Hamilton Pkwy., Brooklyn, NY 11219; 700 Bridge St., Manchester, NH 03104; 7408 S.E. Alder St., Portland, OR 97215; 166 State St., Portland, ME 04101; 1106 State St., Lafayette, IN 47905; 400 Pratt St., Watertown, NY 13601. Cloistered, contemplative.

Precious Blood, Sisters of the, C.Pp.S.: Founded 1834, in Switzerland; in U.S., 1844. Generalate, 4000 Denlinger Rd., Dayton, OH 45426. Education, health care, other ministries.

Precious Blood, Sisters of the Most, C.Pp.S.: Founded 1845, in Steinerberg, Switzerland; in U.S., 1870. General motherhouse, 204 N. Main St., O'Fallon, MO 63366. Education, other ministries.

Presentation, Sisters of Mary of the, S.M.P.: Founded 1829, in France; in U.S., 1903. General motherhouse, Broons, Côtes-du-Nord, France. U.S. address, Maryvale Novitiate, 11550 River Rd., Valley City, ND 58072. Educational, hospital work.

Presentation of Mary, Sisters of the, P.M.: Founded 1796, in France, by Bl. Marie Rivier; in U.S., 1873. General motherhouse, Castel Gandolfo, Italy. U.S. provincial houses: 495 Mammoth Rd., Manchester, NH 03104; 209 Lawrence St., Methuen, MA 01844.

Presentation of the B.V.M., Sisters of the, P.B.V.M.: Founded 1775, in Ireland; in U.S., 1854, in San Francisco. U.S. motherhouses: 2360 Carter Rd., Dubuque, IA 52001; 880 Jackson Ave., New Windsor, NY 12553; 2340 Turk Blvd., San Francisco, CA 94118; St. Colman's Convent, Watervliet, NY 12189; 1101 32nd Ave., S. Fargo, ND 58103; 1500 N. Main, Aberdeen, SD 57401; 99 Church St., Leominster, MA 01453; 419 Woodrow Rd., Staten Island, NY 10312.

Presentation of the Blessed Virgin Mary, Sisters of, of Union: Founded in Ireland, 1775; union established in Ireland, 1976; first U.S. vice province, 1979. Generalate, Kildare, Ireland. U.S. provincialate, 729 W. Wilshire Dr., Phoenix, AZ 85007.

Providence, Daughters of Divine, F.D.P.: Founded 1832, Italy; in U.S., 1964. General motherhouse, Rome,

Italy; U.S. address, 3100 Mumphrey Rd., Chalmette, LA 70043.

Providence, Missionary Catechists of Divine, M.C.D.P.: Administrative house, 2318 Castroville Rd., San Antonio, TX 78237.

Providence, Oblate Sisters of, O.S.P.: Founded 1829, in U.S., by Mother Mary Elizabeth Lange and Father James Joubert, S.S. First order of black nuns in U.S. General motherhouse, 701 Gun Rd., Baltimore, MD 21227. Educational work.

Providence, Sisters of, S.P.: Founded 1861, in Canada; in U.S., 1873. General motherhouse, Our Lady of Victory Convent, Gamelin St., Holyoke, MA 01040.

Providence, Sisters of, S.P.: Founded 1843, in Canada; in U.S., 1854. General motherhouse, Montreal, Canada. U.S. provinces: P.O. Box 11038, Seattle, WA 98111; 9 E. 9th Ave., Spokane, WA 99202; 353 N. River Rd., Des Plaines, IL 60616.

Providence, Sisters of (of St. Mary-of-the Woods), S.P.: Founded 1806, in France; in U.S., 1840. Generalate, St. Mary-of-the-Woods, IN 47876.

Providence, Sisters of Divine, C.D.P.: Founded 1762, in France; in U.S., 1866. Generalate, Box 197, Helotes, TX 78023. Educational, hospital work.

Providence, Sisters of Divine, C.D.P.: Founded 1851, in Germany; in U.S., 1876. Generalate, Rome, Italy. U.S. provinces: 9000 Babcock Blvd., Allison Park, PA 15101; 8351 Florissant Rd., St. Louis, MO 63121; 363 Bishops Hwy., Kingston, MA 02364. Educational, hospital work.

Providence, Sisters of Divine (of Kentucky), C.D.P.: Founded 1762, in France; in U.S., 1889. General motherhouse, Fenetrange, France; U.S. province, St. Anne Convent, Melbourne, KY 41059. Education, social services, other ministries.

Redeemer, Oblates of the Most Holy, O.SS.R.: Founded 1864, in Spain. General motherhouse, Spain; U.S. foundation, 60-80 Pond St., Jamaica Plain, MA 02130.

Redeemer, Order of the Most Holy, O.SS.R.: Founded 1731, by St. Alphonsus Liguori; in U.S., 1957. U.S. addresses: Mother of Perpetual Help Monastery, P.O. Box 220, Esopus, NY 12429; St. Alphonsus Monastery, Liguori, MO 63057.

Redeemer, Sisters of the Divine, S.D.R.: Founded 1849, in Niederbronn, France; in U.S., 1912. General motherhouse, Rome, Italy; U.S. province, 999 Rock Run Road, Elizabeth, PA 15037. Educational, hospital work; care of the aged.

Redeemer, Sisters of the Holy, C.S.R.: Founded 1849, in Alsace; in U.S., 1924. General motherhouse, Wurzburg, Germany; U.S. provincial house, 521 Moredon Rd., Huntingdon Valley, PA 19006. Personalized medical care in hospitals, homes for aged, private homes; retreat work.

Reparation of the Congregation of Mary, Sisters of, S.R.C.M.: Founded 1903, in U.S. Motherhouse, St. Zita's Villa, Monsey, NY 10952.

Resurrection, Sisters of the, C.R.: Founded 1891, in Italy; in U.S., 1900. General motherhouse, Rome, Italy. U.S. provinces: 7432 Talcott Ave., Chicago, IL 60631; Mt. St. Joseph, Castleton-on-Hudson, NY 12033. Education, nursing.

Rita, Sisters of St., O.S.A.: General motherhouse, Wurzburg, Germany. U.S. foundation, St. Monica's Convent, 3920 Green Bay Rd., Racine, WI 53404.

Rosary, Congregation of Our Lady of the Holy, R.S.R.: Founded 1874, in Canada; in U.S., 1899. General motherhouse, Rimouski, Que., Canada. U.S. regional house, 20 Thomas St., Portland, ME 04102. Educational work.

Rosary, Missionary Sisters of the Holy, M.S.H.R.: Founded 1924, in Ireland; in U.S., 1954. Motherhouse, Dublin, Ireland. U.S. regional mailing address, 5334 Vine St., Philadelphia, PA 19139. African missions.

Sacrament, Missionary Sisters of the Most Blessed, M.SS.S.: General motherhouse, Madrid, Spain; U.S. foundation: 1111 Wordin Ave., Bridgeport, CT 06605.

Sacrament, Nuns of the Perpetual Adoration of the Blessed, A.P.: Founded 1807 in Rome, Italy; in U.S., 1925. U.S. monasteries: 145 N. Cotton Ave., El Paso, TX 79901; 771 Ashbury St., San Francisco, CA 94117.

Sacrament, Oblate Sisters of the Blessed, O.S.B.S.: Founded 1935, in U.S.; motherhouse, St. Sylvester Convent, Marty, SD 57361. Care of American Indians.

Sacrament, Servants of the Blessed, S.S.S.: Founded 1858, in France, by St. Pierre Julien Eymard; in U.S., 1947. General motherhouse, Rome, Italy; American provincial house, 1818 Coal Pl. SE, Albuquerque, NM 87106. Contemplative.

Sacrament, Sisters of the Blessed, for Indians and Colored People, S.B.S.: Founded 1891, in U.S., by Bl. Katharine Drexel. General motherhouse, St. Elizabeth's Convent, Bensalem, PA 19020.

Sacrament, Sisters of the Most Holy, M.H.S.: Founded 1851, in France; in U.S., 1872. Generalate, 313 Corona Dr. (P.O. Box 30727), Lafayette, LA 70593.

Sacrament, Sisters Servants of the Blessed, S.J.S.: Founded 1904, in Mexico; in U.S., 1926. General motherhouse, Mexico; U.S. address, 215 Lomita St., El Segundo, CA 90245.

Sacramentine Nuns (Religious of the Order of the Blessed Sacrament and Our Lady), O.S.S.: Founded 1639, in France; in U.S., 1912. U.S. monasteries: 23 Park Ave., Yonkers, NY 10703; US 31, Conway, MI 49722. Perpetual adoration of the Holy Eucharist.

Sacred Heart, Daughters of Our Lady of the: Founded 1882, in France; in U.S., 1955. General motherhouse, Rome, Italy; U.S. address, 424 E. Browning Rd., Bellmawr, NJ 08031. Educational work.

Sacred Heart, Missionary Sisters of the (Cabrini Sisters), M.S.C.: Founded 1880, in Italy, by St. Frances Xavier Cabrini; in U.S., 1889. General motherhouse, Rome,

Italy; U.S. provinces: 222 E. 19th St., 5B, New York, NY 10003 (Eastern); 434 W. Deming Pl., Chicago, IL 60614 (Western). Educational, health, social and catechetical work.

Sacred Heart, Religious of the Apostolate of the, R.A.: General motherhouse, Madrid, Spain; U.S. address, 1310 W. 42nd Pl., Hialiah, FL 33012.

Sacred Heart, Society Devoted to the, S.D.S.H.: Founded 1940, in Hungary; in U.S., 1956. U.S. motherhouse, 9814 Sylvia Ave., Northridge, CA 91324. Educational work.

Sacred Heart, Society of the, R.S.C.J.: Founded 1800, in France; in U.S., 1818. Generalate, Rome, Italy. U.S. provincial house, 4389 W. Pine Blvd., St. Louis, MO 63108. Educational work.

Sacred Heart of Jesus, Apostles of, A.S.C.J.: Founded 1894, in Italy; in U.S., 1902. General motherhouse, Rome, Italy; U.S. motherhouse, 265 Benham St., Hamden, CT 06514. Educational, social work.

Sacred Heart of Jesus, Handmaids of the, A.C.J.: Founded 1877, in Spain. General motherhouse, Rome, Italy; U.S. province, 616 Coopertown Rd., Haverford, PA 19041. Educational, retreat work.

Sacred Heart of Jesus, Missionary Sisters of the Most (Hiltrup), M.S.C.: Founded 1899, in Germany; in U.S., 1908. General motherhouse, Rome, Italy; U.S. province, 51 Seminary Rd., Reading, PA 19605. Education, health care, pastoral ministry.

Sacred Heart of Jesus, Oblate Sisters of the, O.S.H.J.: Founded 1894; in U.S., 1949. General motherhouse, Rome, Italy; U.S. headquarters, 50 Warner Rd., Hubbard, OH 44425. Educational, social work.

Sacred Heart of Jesus, Servants of the Most, S.S.C.J.: Founded 1894, in Poland; in U.S., 1959. General motherhouse, Cracow, Poland; U.S. address, 231 Arch St., Cresson, PA 16630. Education, health care, social services.

Sacred Heart of Jesus, Sisters of the, S.S.C.J.: Founded 1816, in France; in U.S., 1903. General motherhouse, St. Jacut, Brittany, France; U.S. provincial house, 5922 Blanco Rd., San Antonio, TX 78216. Educational, hospital, domestic work.

Sacred Heart of Jesus and of the Poor, Servants of the (Mexican), S.S.H.J.P.: Founded 1885, in Mexico; in U.S., 1907. General motherhouse, Apartado 92, Puebla, Pue., Mexico; U.S. address, 3310 S. Zapata Hwy, Laredo, TX 78043.

Sacred Heart of Jesus and Our Lady of Guadalupe, Missionaries of the: U.S. address, 1212 E. Euclid Ave., Arlington Heights, IL 60660.

Sacred Heart of Jesus for Reparation, Congregation of the Handmaids of the, A.R.: Founded 1918, in Italy; in U.S., 1958. U.S. address, Sunshine Park, R.D. 3, Steubenville, OH 43952.

Sacred Heart of Mary, Religious of the, R.S.H.M.: Founded 1848, in France; in U.S., 1877. Generalate, Rome,

Italy. U.S. provinces: 50 Wilson Park Dr., Tarrytown, NY 10591; 441 N. Garfield Ave., Montebellow, CA 90640.

Sacred Hearts, Religious of the Holy Union of the, S.U.S.C.: Founded 1826, in France; in U.S., 1886. Generalate, Rome, Italy. U.S. provinces: 550 Rock St., Fall River, MA 02720; Box 993, Main St., Groton, MA 01450. Varied ministries.

Sacred Hearts and of Perpetual Adoration, Sisters of the, SS.CC.: Founded 1797, in France; in U.S., 1908. General motherhouse, Rome, Italy; U.S. provinces: 3253 Waialae Rd., Honolulu, HI 96816 (Pacific); 216 Lawrence St., Lawrence, MA 02720 (East Coast). Varied ministries.

Sacred Hearts of Jesus and Mary, Sisters of the, S.H.J.M.: Established 1953, in U.S. General motherhouse, Essex, England; U.S. address, 844 Don Carlo Dr., El Cerrito, CA 94530.

Savior, Company of the, C.S.: Founded 1952, in Spain; in U.S., 1962. General motherhouse, Madrid, Spain; U.S. foundation, 820 Clinton Ave., Bridgeport, CT 06604.

Savior, Sisters of the Divine, S.D.S.: Founded 1888, in Italy; in U.S., 1895. General motherhouse, Rome, Italy; U.S. province, 4311 N. 100th St., Milwaukee, WI 53222. Educational, hospital work.

Social Service, Sisters of, S.S.S.: Founded in Hungary, 1923, by Sr. Margaret Slachta. U.S. generalate, 296 Summit Ave., Buffalo, NY 14214. Social work.

Social Service, Sisters of, of Los Angeles, S.S.S.: Founded 1908, in Hungary; in U.S., 1926. General motherhouse, 1120 Westchester Pl., Los Angeles, CA 90019.

Teresa of Jesus, Society of St., S.T.J.: Founded 1876, in Spain; in U.S., 1910. General motherhouse, Rome, Italy; U.S. provincial house, 18080 St. Joseph's Way, Covington, LA 70433.

Thomas of Villanova, Congregation of Sisters of St., S.S.T.V.: Founded 1661, in France; in U.S., 1948. General motherhouse, Neuilly-sur-Seine, France; U.S. foundation, W. Rocks Rd., Norwalk, CT 06851.

Trinity, Missionary Servants of the Most Blessed, M.S.B.T.: Founded 1912, in U.S., by Very Rev. Thomas A. Judge. General motherhouse, 3501 Solly Ave., Philadelphia, PA 19136. Educational, social work; health services.

Trinity, Sisters Oblates to the Blessed, O.B.T.: Founded 1923, in Italy. U.S. novitiate, Beekman Rd., Hopewell Junction, NY 12533.

Trinity, Sisters of the Most Holy, O.Ss.T.: Founded 1198, in Rome; in U.S., 1920. General motherhouse, Rome, Italy; U.S. address, Immaculate Conception Province, 21281 Chardon Rd., Euclid, OH 44117. Educational work.

Trinity, Society of Our Lady of the Most Holy, S.O.L.T.: Motherhouse, P.O. Box 189, Skidmore, TX 78389.

Ursula of the Blessed Virgin, Society of the Sisters of St., S.U.: Founded 1606, in France; in U.S., 1902. General motherhouse, France; U.S. novitiate, 139 S. Mill Rd., Rhinebeck, NY 12572. Educational work.

Ursuline Nuns (Roman Union), O.S.U.: Founded 1535, in Italy; in U.S., 1727. Generalate, Rome, Italy. U.S. provinces: 323 E. 198th St., Bronx, NY 10458; 210 Glennon Heights Rd., Crystal City, MO 63019; 639 Angela Dr., Santa Rosa, CA 95401; 71 Lowder St., Dedham, MA 02026.

Ursuline Nuns of the Congregation of Paris, O.S.U.: Founded 1535, in Italy; in U.S., 1727, in New Orleans. U.S. motherhouses: 20860 St, Rte 251, St. Martin, OH 45118; 901 E. Miami St., Paola, KS 66071; 3115 Lexington Rd., Louisville, KY 40206; 2600 Lander Rd., Cleveland, OH 44124; Maple Mount, KY 42356; 4045 Indian Rd., Toledo, OH 43606; 4250 Shields Rd., Canfield, OH 44406; 1339 E. McMillan St., Cincinnati, OH 45206.

Ursuline Sisters of the Congregation of Tildonk, Belgium, O.S.U.: Founded 1535, in Italy; Tildonk congregation, 1832; in U.S., 1924. Generalate, Brussels, Belgium; U.S. address, 81-15 Utopia Parkway, Jamaica, NY 11432. Educational, foreign mission work.

Ursuline Sisters of Belleville, O.S.U.: Founded 1535, in Italy; in U.S., 1910; established as diocesan community, 1983. Central house, 1026 N. Douglas Ave., Belleville, IL 62221. Educational work.

Ursuline Sisters (Irish Ursuline Union), O.S.U.: Generalate, Dublin, Ireland; U.S. address, 1973 Torch Hill Rd., Columbus, GA 31903.

Venerini Sisters, Religious, M.P.V.: Founded 1685, in Italy; in U.S., 1909. General motherhouse, Rome, Italy; U.S. provincialate: 23 Edward St., Worcester, MA 01605.

Vincent de Paul, Sisters: See Charity of St. Vincent de Paul, Sisters of.

Visitation Nuns, V.H.M.: Founded 1610, in France; in U.S. (Georgetown, DC), 1799. Contemplative, educational work. Two federations in U.S.

First Federation of North America. Major pontifical enclosure. Pres., Mother Mary Jozefa Kowalewski, Monastery of the Visitation, Snellville, GA 30278. Addresses of monasteries belonging to the federation: 2300 Springhill Ave., Mobile, AL 36607; 370 North St., Pittsfield MA 01201; Rt. 1, Box 2055, Rockville, VA 23146; 5820 City Ave., Philadelphia, PA 19131; 1745 Parkside Blvd., Toledo, OH 43607; 2055 Ridgedale Dr., Snellville, GA 30278.

Second Federation of North America. Constitutional enclosure. Pres., Rev. Mother Mary Philomena Tisinger, Visitation Monastery of Georgetown, Washington, DC 20007. Addresses of monasteries belonging to the federation: 1500 35th St., Washington, DC 20007; 3020 N. Ballas Rd., St. Louis, MO 63131; 200 E. Second St., Frederick, MD 21701; Mt. St. Chantal Monastery of the Visitation, Wheeling, WV 26003; 8902 Ridge Blvd., Brooklyn, NY 11209; 2936 36th St., Rock Island, IL 61201; 2455 Visitation Dr., Mendota Heights, St. Paul, MN 55120.

Visitation of the Congregation of the Immaculate Heart of Mary, Sisters of the, S.V.M.: Founded 1952, in U.S. Motherhouse, 900 Alta Vista St., Dubuque, IA 52001. Educational work, parish ministry.

Vocationist Sisters (Sisters of the Divine Vocations): Founded 1921, in Italy; in U.S., 1967. General motherhouse, Naples, Italy; U.S. foundation, Perpetual Help Nursery, 172 Broad St., Newark, NJ 07104.

Wisdom, Daughters of, D.W.: Founded 1703, in France, by St. Louis Marie Grignon de Montfort; in U.S., 1904. General motherhouse, Vendée, France; U.S. province, 385 S. Ocean Ave., Islip, NY 11751. Education, health care, parish ministry, social services.

Xaverian Missionary Society of Mary, Inc., X.M.M.: Founded 1945, in Italy; in U.S., 1954. General motherhouse, Parma, Italy; U.S. address, 242 Salisbury St., Worcester, MA 01609.

WORKMAN, MARY JULIA (1871–1964)

Social reformer. Workman was the daughter of Los Angeles mayor William Henry Workman and Catholic leader Maria Boyle. Educated by the Sisters of the Holy Names in Oakland, California, and at the State Normal School, Los Angeles, Workman taught in the Los Angeles public schools for two decades. She founded the Brownson House Settlement Association in 1901 and led it for twenty years to serve inner-city residents. Workman associated with Catholic social justice leaders John A. Ryan of The Catholic University of America; Frederick Siedenburg, S.J., of Loyola University, Chicago; and Robert Lucey, later archbishop of San Antonio. In 1924 she founded the diocesan branch of the National Council of Catholic Women. She promoted world peace as an officer in the League of Nations Association and its successor, the United Nations Association, as well as in the Catholic Association for International Peace.

The first woman to join the Municipal League to monitor civic services, Workman was appointed to the Los Angeles Civil Service Commission in 1925, which she led, 1927–28. She campaigned by radio in 1938 for the recall of the corrupt mayor, Frank Shaw, and advised his successor, Fletcher Bowron, 1938–53. A lifelong Democrat, Workman served on the Southern California division of the California Democratic National Committee, and assisted Helen Gahagan Douglas in her congressional career, 1944–50. She championed the rights of Japanese Americans in World War II, denounced prejudice against African Americans, and supported the brief existence of the Catholic Interracial Council of Los Angeles, 1945–50. She aided in establishing both the League of Women Voters and the National Conference of Christians and Jews in Los Angeles. For her humanitarian work, Pope Pius XI awarded Workman the *Pro Ecclesia et Pontifice* Medal in 1926, the first awarded in the diocese.

Engh, M. E., S.J. "Mary Julia Workman, The Catholic Conscience of Los Angeles." *California History* 72 (Spring 1993) 2–19.

Workman, Mary J. "Brownson House: A Catholic Social Settlement." *Queens Work* 1 (November 1914) 299–303.

Year Book of the Brownson House Settlement Association (Los Angeles, 1915).

MICHAEL E. ENGH, S.J.

WORLD WAR I AND AMERICAN CATHOLICS

America's declaration of war in 1917 transformed both the country and the Catholic Church. Two and a half million men were mobilized, millions of women provided social and industrial war work, and the suddenly enlarged federal government imposed controls on labor, transportation, and industry. Crisis-driven adrenaline produced a feverish quality in public life as the whole country began to "join up."

Catholic leaders believed that the Church faced special challenges in responding to the crisis. The Catholic population of the United States included large numbers of immigrants whose origins tied them to countries now at war with the United States. The deep antagonism of Irish-Americans toward England also threatened Allied cooperation. Ecclesiastical authorities were anxious to demonstrate to the American public that foreign-born Catholics and their descendants would conform to wartime requirements and establish themselves as patriotic Americans.

The Knights of Columbus

The Irish-American Knights of Columbus immediately stepped up to provide moral and material support for the war effort. Founded in New Haven in 1882 as an insurance organization, the Knights announced their American Catholic aspirations in fraternal ritual, displaying the stars and stripes alongside the papal colors. In 1916 the Knights showed support for American military efforts when they supplied recreation and religious services to Catholic troops during the Mexican border engagement.

In 1917 they were eager to apply their experience to the vastly larger canvas of wartime mobilization. To support their efforts, the Knights launched an extensive fundraising campaign among hundreds of their local councils. With the returns from the drive, they recruited and deployed thousands of lay volunteers to stateside training camps and overseas operation. They also recruited Catholic chaplains to supplement those in the regular military. The Catholic troops appreciated the strenuous efforts of the Knights and the personable approach of their lay workers. The "Caseys" became a regular feature of camp life, and by the Armistice in November 1918, their extensive network of service "huts" reached even to Siberia.

In return for their patriotic activities, the Knights quickly won a new level of access in Washington. Along with other national service organizations like the Y.M.C.A., they enjoyed semiofficial governmental status and found the role very congenial. As their leaders communicated with War Department officials and eventually with General John J. Pershing himself, public officials began to turn to the Knights of Columbus for "the Catholic view" on questions of troop morale, recreation, and chaplain supply.

The Knights' venture into informal policy-making was soon overshadowed by the initiatives of a group of ecclesiastics and laymen calling themselves the Catholic Interests Committee of New York. Acutely aware of the mushrooming power of the federal government, these New Yorkers were convinced that the Church must develop some kind of official presence in Washington. Knights of Columbus, they believed, could not adequately represent the whole American Church. They planned to form a representative national body of American Catholics, with headquarters in the nation's capital. Theirs was not a novel idea. Mainline Protestant churches had established the New York headquarters of the Federal Council of Churches in 1908, and had subsequently opened an office in Washington, and the Y.M.C.A. had also demonstrated a powerful national presence. The influence of Protestant bodies on government policy spurred plans to develop a Catholic counterpart.

National Catholic War Council

Under the leadership of Paulist priest John J. Burke, the New Yorkers launched an initiative that resulted in the formation of the National Catholic War Council (NCWC). Gaining the participation of several of the more activist members of the American hierarchy, the NCWC claimed sweeping responsibility for the "national interests" of the American Church. Although strenuously resisting this new initiative, the Knights of Columbus eventually yielded to the NCWC, and Knights' war work became a component of the War Council.

Aiming to protect Catholic interests while they supported the American war effort, NCWC leaders cultivated contacts with federal officials in the War Department and in Congress, and established a working relationship between the Church and the national government. The council successfully lobbied for an increase in Catholic chaplain quotas, obtained permission to organize and staff visitors' centers in the U.S. training camps, and sent workers overseas to provide social services to U.S. troops and local populations in war regions.

Council chairman John Burke represented the War Council on the War Department's Commission on Training Camp Activities, an advisory committee concerned with "social hygiene" issues—prostitution, venereal disease, and the consumption of alcohol in the training camps. The CTCA was also interested in associated efforts to "protect" the women who worked in war-related industries or in war camp communities. Burke was eventually awarded the Distinguished Service Cross for his war work.

The success of the War Council in establishing a Washington presence became apparent in the course of planning and executing the United War Work campaign in the fall of 1918. NCWC leaders mobilized thousands of Catholic volunteers to work in the fund drive, after successfully resisting efforts to divide the campaign into separate appeals for the Protestant Y's and the American Red Cross, on the one hand, and Catholic and Jewish war organizations on the other. The obvious segregation and implied second-class citizenship of the original plan was unacceptable in the collaborative climate of wartime, and the vigorous protests of the NCWC quickly assured a united campaign.

On the day the Armistice was signed, the War Work Campaign kicked off a weeklong fund drive that netted pledges of one hundred and seventy million dollars, of which the NCWC received thirty million. When the council officially closed its books in 1930, it had expended thirty-two million dollars in public funds for camp work, rehabilitation schools, employment services, hospital social work, and medical dispensaries for servicemen and their families, the construction of visitors' houses in the camps, and the support of settlement houses in the cities. Twenty-three million of this total was spent by the Knights of Columbus, who also raised fourteen million more in their private campaigns. In the process of raising and spending these sums, the NCWC enhanced its reputation as the national voice of the Church.

The lessons gleaned from the wartime experience were quickly put to use by the council in the period of reconstruction. An intensive professional public relations effort brought national attention to the NCWC's Program of Social Reconstruction early in 1919. Authored by moral theologian John A. Ryan, and signed by the four bishops of the NCWC's Administrative Committee, the program became the hallmark of progressive Catholicism. NCWC supporters also turned their lobbying skills on the members of the American hierarchy themselves, in a successful campaign to create a permanent version of the NCWC.

National Catholic Welfare Council

In September 1919 the National Catholic Welfare Council (later, the National Catholic Welfare *Conference*) was approved by a majority of the bishops as the voluntary organization of the American hierarchy. A prototype for later national episcopal conferences, its annual meetings offered an occasion for the American bishops to meet and discuss common interests. Resolutions taken at those meetings, along with the interim leadership of bishops elected to the Administrative Committee, supplied effective, if

unofficial, authority for the NCWC staff as it worked to represent "Catholic welfare" in public life. Education, communications, and social welfare dominated the public agenda of the NCWC.

To support its claim to speak for American Catholics, staffers also set out to federate Catholic lay organizations under the umbrella of the NCWC, and to orchestrate the Catholic response on social issues of the day. Recalling their successful collaboration in war work, middle-class Catholic women responded to the call to share in the national work of the Church, joining the NCWC's lay affiliate, the National Council of Catholic Women. Widely known for its opposition to issues like birth control and a federal Department of Education, the NCCW also endorsed progressive measures for women and children. These included the federal Sheppard-Towner bill and state-sponsored "mother's pensions" programs. When the women's affiliate supported a child labor amendment in 1924, however, its leaders became the objects of a fiercely hostile reaction from opponents of the measure, including the dean of the Catholic hierarchy, Cardinal William O'Connell of Boston. After this point, the progressive energies of the NCCW receded from public view, while the parent organization continued to promote Catholic approaches to policy issues.

When World War I drew all eyes to Washington and created a national stage in public life, American Catholic leaders seized the opportunity to write the Catholic Church into the script. Armed with the conviction that they were supporting a just cause, they made a substantial contribution to the Allied victory. And as they provided a national focus for Catholics across the country, their efforts initiated a new era in the transformation of European Catholicism in the American context.

Kauffman, Christopher J. *Faith and Fraternalism: The History of the Knights of Columbus, 1882–1992.* New York: Harper & Row, 1982.

McKeown, Elizabeth. *War and Welfare: American Catholics and World War I.* New York: Garland Press, 1988.

McShane, Joseph M. *"Sufficiently Radical": Catholicism, Progressivism, and the Bishops' Program of 1919.* Washington, D.C.: The Catholic University of America Press, 1986.

Slawson, Douglas J. *The Foundation and First Decade of the National Catholic War Council.* Washington, D.C.: The Catholic University Press of America, 1992.

ELIZABETH McKEOWN

WORLD WAR II AND AMERICAN CATHOLICS

Catholic Americans played a substantial role in winning the Second World War. During these difficult years, American Catholics were confronted by a series of controversies involving their Church and various aspects of the global conflict. Yet, none of these crises undermined Catholic-American contributions on behalf of victory, whose attainment helped usher in an era of growth and greatness for the Church in the United States.

The prelude to World War II included several events that many Catholic Americans found awkward and embarrassing. In 1929 the Vatican formally recognized Italy's fascist regime in return for important territorial and legal concessions from the Italian government headed by Benito Mussolini. These Lateran Pacts of 1929 resulted in the recognition of the Vatican City State but also involved a concordat with the dictator destined to become Adolf Hitler's main ally during World War II.

During the Spanish Civil War of 1936–38, the Church wholly endorsed the right-wing, Hitler-supported forces led by General Francisco Franco in their rebellion against the Republican regime dominated by an anticlerical coalition of anarchists and Communists. While most outside observers viewed the Spanish conflict as a clear-cut Left versus Right ideological encounter, the Church subordinated political to religious and cultural considerations and hailed Franco as a heroic defender of faith and civilization against the demonic forces of atheism and Bolshevism, who were responsible for the deaths of some 8,000 clergy and religious. Ultimately victorious, Franco prudently chose not to bring Spain into World War II, a decision that undoubtedly made it easier for conservative Catholic Americans to back the war effort without reservation.

American Catholic Public Opinion

When World War II began in September 1939, most American Catholics preferred that their country maintain its traditional policy of isolationism. Given the strong anti-Communist stance of the Church, this isolationist sentiment intensified after Nazi Germany attacked its erstwhile Communist ally, the Soviet Union, in June 1941. When President Franklin Roosevelt decided to provide the beleaguered Soviets with Lend-Lease assistance, Catholic leaders bitterly opposed the move. Fr. James Gillis, C.S.P., editor of the conservative *Catholic World,* spoke for many of his coreligionists when he labeled the policy a "Covenant with Hell."

However, once America joined the fight in December 1941, an overwhelming majority of American Catholics gave their full support to the war effort. The U.S. Catholic bishops sent a letter to Roosevelt pledging their total cooperation in safeguarding "our God-given blessings of freedom." Bishop Fulton J. Sheen, a prominent radio orator who had been a staunch isolationist, now characterized the war as a "theological struggle" between good and evil. Francis Spellman, archbishop of New York and the Catholic Military Vicar, informed President Roosevelt:

"As an American and one of twenty-five million Catholic Americans I follow the identically glorious traditions of my country and my religion." Spellman, a friend of both Roosevelt and Pope Pius XII, would conduct a number of well-publicized, semidiplomatic foreign tours during the war on the President's behalf.

The Catholic contribution to America's military manpower was enormous. During the war, Catholics made up an estimated 25–35 percent of the country's total fighting strength. The most prominent Catholic men in uniform included Admiral William Leahy, an advisor to the President; General Walter Bedell Smith, chief of staff for General Dwight Eisenhower; and General William "Wild Bill" Donovan, director of the top-secret Office of Strategic Services. Perhaps the most poignant story of Catholic service and sacrifice concerned the five Sullivan brothers of Iowa, all of whom perished when the light cruiser U.S.S. *Juneau* was sunk during the Battle of the Solomon Islands.

A dedicated group of 3,270 commissioned chaplains, of whom 38 were killed and 90 wounded in action, tended to the ministerial needs of Catholic servicemen. Fr. Joseph O'Callaghan became the first chaplain in U.S. history to be awarded the Congressional Medal of Honor for his heroic action during a Japanese air attack upon the aircraft carrier U.S.S. *Franklin*. O'Callaghan was one of sixty-seven Catholics so honored during World War II.

Some slight opposition to the war did surface on the ideological fringes of U.S. Catholicism. Dorothy Day, leader of the pacifist, New York City-based Catholic Workers movement, declared that the male members of her organization would refuse induction into the armed forces, and that no one in the movement would work in munitions factories or purchase government bonds. On the far right, Fr. Charles Coughlin, the fanatically anti-Semitic "radio priest" from Detroit who only recently had been taken off the airwaves, praised the Nazis in his magazine *Social Justice* for supposedly bringing a "new Christian social order" to Europe. Under prodding from the government, the archbishop of Detroit silenced Coughlin in May 1942 and ordered that his seditious magazine cease publication.

The Holy See and the U.S.A.

More troubling was the Holy See's decision in March 1942 to establish diplomatic relations, for the first time, with Japan. Although this action consummated some twenty years of Vatican-Japanese negotiations, from an American standpoint the timing of the event—only a few months after the Pearl Harbor attack—could scarcely have been worse. In a private letter to Spellman, an angry and upset Roosevelt said he would "say nothing officially" about the event, yet his heart was "torn" by this "unnecessary move," this "great error of judgment" by the Holy See. However, the Japanese Mission at the Vatican had little or no measurable influence, and if anything the event inspired American Catholic leaders to support the war effort even more effusively.

More disturbing yet was the Pope's strict policy of public neutrality which he maintained throughout the war, even to the point of remaining silent about the Nazi atrocities against the Jews. Perhaps in an effort to insure that the Pope's stance was not misunderstood, the Catholic press always gave prominent coverage to any Nazi criticisms of His Holiness. Beyond that, Catholic-American clergymen castigated the Hitler regime at every opportunity throughout the war. This made it virtually impossible for non-Catholics to blame their Catholic countrymen for the Pope's refusal to choose sides.

When the fighting spread in 1943 to the Italian peninsula, Catholic American leaders expressed alarm that Rome would be devastated by Allied invaders. In a letter published in a major New York City newspaper, Archbishop Spellman pleaded for restraint by the U.S. military, as "millions of hearts would be saddened if history were obliged to record that Rome was destroyed by Americans." In May 1943 Pope Pius XII wrote to President Roosevelt, to ask that Rome's innocent civilians and "their many treasured shrines" be "spared as far as possible." Roosevelt sent reassurances that U.S. aviators had been instructed not to bomb within the Vatican City, but Rome was subjected to several Allied bombing raids, during which a number of churches and other historical and religious structures were damaged or destroyed.

The worst such destruction occurred in mid-February 1944 at the town of Cassino, along the ground route followed by the Allies in their advance toward Rome. Some 255 Flying Fortresses dropped 576 tons of explosives on the abbey of Monte Cassino, demolishing this historic shrine. General Mark Clark, the U.S. field commander on the scene, admitted after the war that the action had been "a tactical military mistake of the first magnitude." The shocked response of the American Catholic hierarchy was more immediate. During the annual patriotic memorial Mass at St. Patrick's Cathedral held on Washington's Birthday, 1944, Archbishop Spellman declared that he "must deplore the fact that the armed forces of our country have attacked the territory of a neutral state, thereby violating rights which are among those for which America is waging war." The archbishop called again for measures that would spare Rome, "the citadel of civilization," from further havoc. Fortunately, papal properties escaped much further damage in the fighting, and in early June the American Army marched into Rome and held it for the duration of the war.

On the home front, much of the American Catholic hierarchy opposed the establishment in 1942 of the Women's Auxiliary Army Corps, whose members became popu-

larly known as the WACs. Catholic leaders denounced the admission of women into the armed forces as a step toward the ruination of traditional family roles. Bishop John J. O'Hara, auxiliary to the Military Vicar and the most outspoken opponent of the measure, told one male audience he was certain that to preserve "the sanctity of the home" the men would "prefer to peel potatoes and darn [their] own socks rather than have women in the army." The *Boston Pilot* even denounced the WAAC idea as one of German, not American, origin. After Congress passed legislation establishing the WAAC, some Catholic clergymen urged that women refuse to enlist.

American Catholics and the Soviet Union

Although Catholic leaders recognized the necessity of the Soviet-American alliance of World War II, they continued to express hostility and suspicion toward the Communist regime. This ran counter to the prevailing national mood of friendship and admiration for the Soviets. But the diocesan newspapers, especially, routinely reminded readers that the USSR remained an atheist country, a dictatorship, and an enemy of the Church—facts that had not been altered by the desperate circumstances which had put America and the Soviet Union temporarily into the same military camp.

In the spring of 1944 the Soviet government made a rather comic attempt to recruit support in Catholic circles by secretly inviting Fr. Stanislaus Orlemanski, an obscure priest from Springfield, Massachusetts, to the Kremlin for a meeting with Joseph Stalin. When the Soviet press announced that the event had taken place, Catholic leaders throughout the United States condemned Stalin's "tricky manipulation." Orlemanski (who had written several complimentary articles about the USSR that had gone undetected in his diocese) was made to apologize, his priestly privileges were suspended, and he was sent to a monastery to do penance.

Concern for the postwar fate of Poland sharpened Catholic antipathy for Communism and the USSR all the more. All the diocesan newspapers and many individual clergy expressed anxiety about whether the Red Army, marching through Poland on its way to Berlin, would impose Soviet control over this land at war's end. Speaking for millions of Catholics, the Knights of Columbus passed a resolution branding as "unthinkable" any postwar settlement that denied democracy to Poland. Naturally, Catholic Americans sought the support of President Roosevelt. Unknown to them, the President, at the Teheran Conference with Stalin and Winston Churchill in November 1943, secretly had agreed to the Soviet leader's demand that the USSR's postwar borders be extended westward, at Poland's expense.

Roosevelt had to contend with the limitations of existing military realities, but he also knew that Catholic voters made up a big part of his "Grand Coalition." Fearing that Catholics would desert him in the presidential election of 1944 if they suspected that Poland was to be abandoned to Communism, FDR prevaricated on the issue. At one point he even had himself photographed in front of a large map of Poland with its prewar boundaries intact, then had this picture distributed widely in Polish-American and other heavily Catholic areas. Fortunately for Roosevelt's political fortunes, the potentially explosive Polish issue was substantially muted during the presidential campaign. FDR's opponent, Thomas Dewey, shied away from criticizing the Soviet ally, and he had no hard proof about the administration's postwar plans for Poland. Roosevelt, again enjoying massive Catholic support at the polls, swept to a fourth landslide victory.

The Yalta Conference in February 1945 cemented Poland's grim future as a Soviet satellite. Catholic Americans immediately reacted to the news with disgust and outrage. A headline over one diocesan press account—"President and Churchill Throw 9,000,000 Catholic Poles to Reds"—typified the reaction among Catholics to this fateful summit. Their dismay with the results of the Yalta Conference was one factor that led many Catholic Americans to support the subsequent Red-hunting excesses of Senator Joe McCarthy.

The American bishops issued no comment after the disclosure that atomic bombs had been dropped on the Japanese, bringing about their surrender and the end of the war. But immediate criticism did appear in the Catholic lay magazine *Commonweal* and the Jesuit-run *America,* two of the most liberal Catholic publications. *Commonweal* flatly asserted that "The name Hiroshima, the name Nagasaki are names for American guilt and shame." In contrast to the prevailing mood of euphoria, *America* looked pessimistically into the future of the new Atomic Age. Predicting that other nations eventually would acquire the technology to build atomic bombs, whose vast range of destruction "cannot be confined to anything that might be called an authentic military target," *America* could only hope "that the evil which will come from the atomic bomb may not outweigh the good which our war leaders, rightly or wrongly, hope to achieve by its use." Even earlier, in 1944, Jesuit moral theologian John C. Ford had criticized the American policy of obliteration bombing.

World War II affected the course of American Catholicism in several important ways. The horrors of war helped spur a religious revival in America, and attendance at Sunday Mass soared throughout the nation's parishes in the late 1940s and 1950s. World War II also contributed to the development of American Catholicism's first significant contemplative movement; most notably, novices entered the Trappist monasteries in unprecedented numbers during the postwar period. Finally, the unabashed patriotism displayed by the American Catholic population throughout World War II put an end to any serious manifestations of anti-Catholicism in respectable quarters. This full assimilation reached a pinnacle in 1960 with the election of the first Catholic president, John Fitzgerald Kennedy, whose heroics as the skipper of PT-109 in the Pacific Theater attracted the admiration of Catholic and non-Catholic Americans alike.

Dohen, Dorothy. *Nationalism and American Catholicism.* New York, 1967.

Flynn, George. *Roosevelt and Romanism: Catholics and American Diplomacy, 1937–1945.* Westport, Conn.: Greenwood Press, 1976.

Fogarty, Gerald P., S.J. *The Vatican and the American Hierarchy from 1870 to 1965.* Wilmington, 1985.

Ford, John C., S.J. "The Morality of Obliteration Bombing." *Theological Studies* 5 (1944) 261–309.

Hennesey, James, S.J. *American Catholics.* New York, 1981.

Sirgiovanni, George. *An Undercurrent of Suspicion: Anti-Communism in America during World War II.* New Brunswick, N.J.: Transaction Publishers, 1990.

GEORGE SIRGIOVANNI

WORSHIP (ORATE FRATRES)

The first issue of *Worship,* originally titled *Orate Fratres,* was published by the monks of St. John's Abbey in Collegeville, Minnesota, in 1926. The goal of the journal has been to develop a better understanding of the spiritual impact of the liturgy and to promote active participation in the worship of the Church.

Rooted in Benedictine tradition, the journal was edited by Dom Virgil Michel, along with other pioneers in the liturgical movement, including Donald Attwater of England, William Busch, Gerald Ellard, S.J., Martin Hellriegel, Justine Ward, and James O'Mahony, O.F.M. Cap., of Ireland.

Since Michel's death in 1938, the editorial policy has been under the direction of Godfrey Diekmann, Aelred Tegels, Michael Marx, and Kevin Seasoltz, all monks of St. John's Abbey. The journal's name was changed to *Worship* in 1951, a sign of the growing interest in the use of the vernacular in liturgical celebrations.

Since the Second Vatican Council, *Worship* has tried to help Christian communities internalize the meaning of the extensive liturgical changes that have taken place, to evaluate critically the effectiveness of those reforms, and to search for new rituals that enable worshipers to praise and serve God and to minister to God's people in the midst of rapidly changing cultural patterns in the world.

Although they have concentrated on a theoretical approach to liturgical issues, the editors have been convinced that the doctrinal study of liturgy is usually best situated at the level of concrete ritual structures and explicit pastoral problems. Before the council, pastoral issues were most challengingly addressed by H. A. Reinhold in his column, "Timely Tracts" (1938–54), and more recently by Robert Hovda in "The Amen Corner" (1983–92).

The journal has been firmly rooted in a Benedictine and a Roman Catholic tradition, but its editorial policy has never been narrowly confessional, as the membership of the editorial board, the list of authors, and the subjects addressed indicate. According to Seasoltz: "The Benedictine tradition has regularly provided a hospitable context in which the human search for God in liturgy, much more effectively than theology, tends to emphasize the truths which unite Christians; hence it is important for ecumenical encounters."

Since 1967 *Worship* has consciously sought to contribute to the ecumenical movement by the appointment of Protestant and Orthodox liturgical scholars to its editorial board. *Worship* has been distinguished for its covers and design as well as its content. The first cover was the work of Eric Gill. For more than forty years, Frank Kacmarcik has designed the layout and covers of the journal.

See also LITURGICAL MOVEMENT IN AMERICA, THE.

STEPHENIE OVERMAN

WOYWOD, STANISLAUS (1880–1941)

Franciscan friar, priest, educator, and canon lawyer. Stanislaus Woywod was born on August 10, 1880, in Guttstadt, Germany. During the *Kulturkampf*, he attended preparatory seminaries in Fulda and Obernberg, and then emigrated to the United States in 1897. On December 21, 1899, he entered the novitiate of the Holy Name province of the Order of Friars Minor, located in Paterson, New Jersey. He was ordained a priest at the Franciscan Friary Church in Paterson on June 4, 1906. For the next three years, he studied at the Franciscan international college in Rome, the Pontificium Atheneum Antonianum, from which he received degrees in both theology and canon law. Following the completion of his studies, he returned to Paterson, where he taught and served for six years as superior of the community.

Shortly after the promulgation of the 1917 Code of Canon Law, he published his first book, *The New Canon Law* (1918), an English paraphrase of and commentary on the Latin text of the Code. From 1920 to 1926, he served as professor of canon law at the seminary of St. Bonaventure University in Allegany, New York. In 1925 he published the first edition of what would become a standard canonical commentary, *A Practical Commentary on the Code of Canon Law*. (Subsequent editions were popularly known as "Woywod and Smith," to acknowledge the assistance of Fr. Callistus Smith, O.F.M., also a member of Holy Name province.) In 1930 Woywod was appointed the first rector and superior of Holy Name College, the new Franciscan house of formation, located in close proximity to The Catholic University of America in Washing-

ton, D.C. While fulfilling his spiritual and administrative responsibilities, he also served as the editor of *St. Anthony's Almanac* (now the *Catholic Almanac*), wrote numerous articles for the *American Ecclesiastical Review*, and provided canonical advice to bishops, priests, and religious. Additionally, his responses to pastoral questions in moral theology and canon law became a well-known feature of the *Homiletic and Pastoral Review*. Fr. Woywod died at St. Clare's Hospital in New York City on September 19, 1941.

See also FRANCISCAN FRIARS.

Donovan, J. P. "Code and the Homiletic These Thirty-One Years." *Homiletic and Pastoral Review* 50 (October 1949) 38–44.
Holy Name Province Provincial Annals 3 (October 1941) 177–79.
Necrology of Holy Name Province, 1994.

JOHN COUGHLIN, O.F.M.

WRIGHT, JOHN CARDINAL (1909–79)

Bishop, curial cardinal. Born in Dorchester, Massachusetts, on July 18, 1909, John Wright attended the Latin School, Boston College, St. John's Seminary, Brighton, and later the Pontifical North American College in Rome. He was ordained to the priesthood in 1935 in Rome, and returned after further studies to join the seminary faculty at St. John's Seminary in Brighton, where he taught theology from 1939 until 1943. He served as the secretary to both Cardinals O'Connell and Cushing, and was appointed auxiliary bishop to the archbishop of Boston in 1947, a post he held until his appointment as bishop of the newly erected see of Worcester in January, 1950.

John Cardinal Wright

His years in Worcester were dedicated to the establishment and organization of the new diocese and the overseeing of the various diocesan offices, parishes, and schools.

In 1959 Wright was translated to the Diocese of Pittsburgh, where he remained for ten years. Wright was an incessant preacher and teacher during his pastoral years, emphasizing themes of social justice, racial toleration, brotherly love, community solidarity, peace, justice, fair housing, proper education of the young, care of the elderly, the inspiration of youth, and the protection of the underprivileged, and he advocated the greater role of the laity in the mission of the Church. He was one of the cofounders of the International Commission for Religion and Peace long before the fashionable antiwar movements of the 1960s (*Osservatore Romano,* September 24, 1979).

Wright was a liberal Catholic in the line of Maritain, Newman, and Blondel, seeking links and dialogue between faith and culture. In 1961 he established a house for the Congregation of the Oratory in Pittsburgh. A devotee of Newman, "precisely because Newman combined deep love and loyalty to the faith with deep love and understanding of the world" (Clancy), Wright established the oratory in the midst of Pittsburgh's universities, "hoping that it would be a community where the love of the Church and love of liberal values—learning, freedom, civility and art—might come together" (Clancy).

Wright attended the Second Vatican Council, serving as a theological advisor during the preparatory work for the council itself.

In Rome

Wright was appointed prefect of the Sacred Congregation for the Clergy on April 22, 1969, and was created a cardinal by Pope Paul VI six days later. He was the first American to be named the head of a Roman congregation with worldwide responsibilities. He also served as a member of various other Roman congregations and commissions, including the Council for Public Affairs of the Church, the Sacred Congregation for the Doctrine of the Faith, as well as those for Bishops, Evangelization of Peoples, and Catholic Education (*Osservatore Romano,* August 20, 1979). He continued his work in Rome as prefect of the Congregation for the Clergy until his death in 1979.

Wright's one great love was the Church, to which he dedicated his prodigious intellectual gifts and personality. He sought dialogue between the modern culture and the Church's faith, teaching with verve, humor, and a wealth of knowledge, expressed in homily and writings, which strove to inspire love for God through fidelity to the Church's magisterium, in terms and manner both personable and clear. He died in Cambridge, Massachusetts, on August 10, 1979.

See also CARDINALS IN THE AMERICAN CHURCH; MASSACHUSETTS, CATHOLIC CHURCH IN; PENNSYLVANIA, CATHOLIC CHURCH IN; VATICAN COUNCIL II AND AMERICAN CATHOLICS.

Clancy, William. *Commonweal,* August 31, 1979.
Osservatore Romano, August 20, September 24, October 1, 1979.

STEPHEN M. DiGIOVANNI

Related Document

AMERICAN CATHOLICS AND THE INTELLECTUAL LIFE, 1956 [STATEMENT OF BISHOP JOHN J. WRIGHT]

One of the liveliest topics of discussion among educated Catholics during the 1950's centered around their failure to make a contribution to the cultural life of the nation in keeping with their numbers, wealth, and increasingly high percentage of college graduates. The Catholic Commission for Intellectual and Cultural Affairs took up the matter and devoted its annual meeting of 1955 in St. Louis largely to this subject. On May 14 at one of the sessions of the C.C.I.C.A., John Tracy Ellis, professor of church history in the Catholic University of America, read a paper entitled "American Catholics and the Intellectual Life" which, in turn, provoked a good deal of discussion. The paper was first published in *Thought* (Autumn, 1955) and appeared in book form the following summer with a preface by the Most Reverend John J. Wright.

(*Source:* Prefatory Note by John J. Wright to John Tracy Ellis, *American Catholics and the Intellectual Life* [Chicago: Heritage Foundation, Inc. 1956], pp. 5–10.)

. . . .

MONSIGNOR ELLIS' PAPER PROVOKED A REACTION THAT IS in itself irrefutable evidence of how well timed and accurate are his contentions. A great number of others were emboldened by his statements to lift their own voices on the urgency of a re-evaluation of Catholic intellectual life in the United States, and their witness frequently added proof both that the cause is critical and that it is far from hopeless. The passion with which the few dissenters from Monsignor Ellis' position set forth their indignant reservations proved that he had touched a tender nerve. In an article in *America,* Monsignor Ellis himself summarized some of the reactions to his original piece. He has received several hundred letters. All but four seem to be in agreement with his analysis. The article itself is an important contribution to the documentation on the "great debate," but there is no reason to believe that all the reactions are by any means yet registered. One awaits with mingled sentiments of dread and curiosity this season's commencement addresses, for example!

What we have called the "great debate" raging here in the United States at the moment is doubtless no more than a phase within our own land of an argument that has been going on in Europe for decades. Traditionally, the European intellectual has been acknowledged by his contemporaries, even those who might disagree with him, to have a 'vocation' beyond the limits of his own profession of writing or science or teaching. It is a vocation quite apart from that of the functionary or representative of Church or of State, and it has obvious and grave perils as well as elements of prestige. These perils are as real as ignominy, exile or prison, even death, the frequent destinies of the traditional intellectuals in Europe. And yet, the intellectual has usually enjoyed a veneration in Europe which scarcely has a parallel in the common American attitude toward those who take on the valiant role of questioner, critic, or intellectual trail blazer. The reader will note the "witty extravagance" which Monsignor Ellis recalls as differentiating the attitudes of Europeans and Americans toward intellectuals: in the old world an ordinary mortal on seeing a professor tipped his hat, while in America he taps his head.

Such a suspicious attitude toward the intellectual life is far from being an exclusive Catholic phenomenon in the United States. Indeed, this kink in the American character generally may be due, as an editorial in the Washington *Post and Times Herald* pointed out on December 19, 1955, to specifically non-Catholic sociological and even theological influences on the formation of our national character. For example, the thoroughly practical problems confronting the first settlers on New England's stern and rock-bound coast no doubt intensified the predisposition of their Calvinist theology to emphasize results rather than theories and to reverence achievement rather than abstract speculation. There is a characteristically American esteem for the word "industry," in all its senses, which has never been accorded to the word "intellectual" or any of its variations.

The anti-intellectual attitude, however, is more unbecoming and embarrassing in Catholics because it is so entirely inconsistent with any authentic Catholic position. So many of the heresies which have wounded the Church and despoiled her of whole nations have been voluntarist heresies, anti-intellectual in their roots and pretensions, that it is bitterly ironic when anti-intellectualism threatens to become characteristic of those who have remained faithful to her obedience.

One wonders whether Catholics themselves always appreciate the extent to which the battles of the Church against the modern heresies have been at one and the same time battles against the heresy of anti-intellectualism. Luther's "stat pro ratione voluntas," his voluntaristic *fides fiducialis* with its repudiation of the intellectual elements in the act of faith, and his violent but typical description of the intellect as the "devil's whore," are as much the evidence of his departure from Catholic traditions as any of his theses nailed to the chapel door. The blind fatalism of Calvin, the perverse austerities of Jansenism, the sentimentality and exaltation of instinct or religious emotion which, for all its show of scholarship, characterized Modernism, are all typical of the heresies which have divided the Christian flock in these last four centuries. In defending supernatural reve-

lation against these the Church was at the same time defending the validity of natural reason and the primacy of the intellect over the will, the emotions, the instincts or any of the other faculties to which voluntarism has always appealed, whether in Luther's dogma, the moral theories of Jansenius, the religious psychology of the moderns or the political philosophy of totalitarianism.

We usually think of the Council of Trent, the Vatican Council and the syllabus against Modernism in terms of the defense of revealed dogmas, and such, of course, they were. But he understands them poorly who fails to perceive that they were frequently Catholic affirmations of the validity of reason as well as of the reality of revelation, and that they bore witness to the essential part of rational elements even in the supernatural act of faith, and to the divine origin of the primacy and rights of the intellect in the natural order.

It is, therefore, a problem for the Church when any who might be taken as her representatives in any sense in the world of the campus, the press, or the forum reveal contempt for that "wild living intellect of man" of which Cardinal Newman spoke, or cynicism about the slow, sometimes faltering, but patient, persevering processes by which the intellectual seeks to wrest some measure of order from the chaos about us.

The problem is manifold Monsignor Ellis' paper and others which followed give good hope that its solution may be in process of realization. First of all, there is a problem of definitions. What precisely do we now mean when we use the word intellectual and when we speak of either the virtues of faults of "intellectualism"? It is this initial problem which has been highlighted by the editor of the Brooklyn *Tablet* in his evaluation of recent writings on the subject.

Then there is a problem which we can best call spiritual or apostolic. What is the vocation of the intellectual in the life of the Church? How can he best bear his specifically intellectual witness, a witness which may involve a living martyrdom, given the temper of the times and the suspicion with which even his own will all too often views his gifts and his works? How shall we persuade intellectuals to find in Christ, the *Logos,* the eternal Word made flesh to dwell among us, a divine prototype of their special vocation and unique dignity, as we have persuaded workers to find their model in the carpenter's Son, Christian youth to find a model in the youthful Christ's obedience to Joseph and Mary at Nazareth, and patriotic citizens to see the exemplar of their proper loyalty in the Christ who paid the coin of tribute and wept tears of predilection over the capital city of His nation? A spirituality of Christian humanism, centered about the concept of Christ the divine Intellectual, is a critical need of our generation if the evidence presented here proves as much as we have good reason to believe it does.

The problem of the apostolic role of the Catholic intellectual cannot be too often emphasized. Father Raymond L. Bruckberger, O.P., our friendly French critic, in an article in *Harper's Magazine* for February, 1956, on the patriotic responsibilities of the American intellectual, makes a point worthy of meditation by Catholic intellectuals who sincerely seek to understand their contemporary religious responsibilities. The American intellectual often tends to say that his country has failed him, that she will not give him the honor which is his due, and that he feels like a spiritual exile. Perhaps, the contrary is more nearly true, and the American intellectual is more deeply missed than is at first apparent. When the intellectual turns his back on his country and confines himself to berating her, his place remains empty, all the while that he complains that he has no place at all. A more valiant generation of European intellectuals accepted it as their destiny to be unappreciated and mocked for false prophets; in this they found a secret consolation and often their abiding glory.

Catholic intellectuals have a point for meditation here. Intellectually gifted Catholics suffer all too often from a "whining" tendency in their attitude toward the Church. They lament that they are not sufficiently appreciated or encouraged. They berate the indifference of their fellow Catholics to their vocation. In a curious paradox on the lips of Christians, particularly Christians with presumably keener powers of insight and understanding than the rest, they protest against being made martyrs. Where in the New Testament, the Church of the Fathers, or the history of the saints from Paul to Thomas More, were the genuinely thoughtful promised any other lot, whether at the hands of the world or at the hands of their uncomprehending brethren, than contradiction and constant testing?

Finally, and urgently, there is an intensely practical problem in this matter of American Catholic intellectual life. It is the problem of how we can increase the proportions of authentic scholars and trained, competent intellectuals among us.

Statistics have been offered recently which point up and analyze the dearth of Catholic lay scholars. These statistics have been challenged by those who resented certain of its implications, although their resentment did not inspire much in the way of effective refutation of the facts. The facts add up to a conclusion which is a primary justification for the republication of this present paper, by a man who dearly loves the Faith and is one of those who spare themselves nothing to contribute to the solution of whatever problems impede the freedom and well being of our Holy Mother the Church.

In the early days of the Church in America, humble Catholics struggled to retain the Faith in an anti-Catholic atmosphere. These early pioneers built schools and churches which are responsible for the survival of Catholic America today. These foundations for growth and expansion have been firmly rooted within the American tradition in our soil, but future progress and expansion will come only through a determined effort based upon the development of Catholic scholarship. It is to this problem that Monsignor Ellis addresses himself so effectively, and we recommend a reading and rereading of his provocative message at regular intervals. Both Catholicism and America have need of an intellectual apostolate of distinction.

(*Source*: John Tracy Ellis, ed. *Documents of American Catholic History*. Vol. 2:1866–1966. Wilmington, Del.: Michael Glazier, 1987, 641–46.)

WYNHOVEN, PETER M. H. (1884–1944)

Priest, social reformer. Foreign-born priests frequently recruited for the American Mission on visits to their native countries. In 1904 Dutch-born Fr. Arthur Drossaerts recruited twenty-year-old classical student Peter Wynhoven of Venray, Holland, for the Archdiocese of New Orleans. Peter completed his theological studies in New Orleans and St. Louis and was ordained in 1909. During his thirty-five years of ministry he was recognized "as one of the most talented, vigorous, and influential priests of the archdiocese."

He worked with three successive archbishops in three different areas of metropolitan New Orleans. Archbishop James Blenk (1905–17) used and sharpened young Fr. Wynhoven's organizational and communication skills as vice chancellor and manager of the *Morning Star* and at the same time encouraged his bent for social Catholic Action by allowing him to provide housing, nourishment, and jobs for downtrodden drifters in the French Quarter riverfront. Wynhoven called his boarding house St. Vincent Hotel and Free Labor Bureau.

During the administration of Archbishop John William Shaw (1918–34), Wynhoven was pastor of St. Joseph's, Gretna, directly across the Mississippi in the West Bank section of Jefferson parish. There he implemented his dream of special residences and skilled craft training for orphans: Hope Haven for boys dates from 1926, Madonna Manor for girls from 1932. To finance this innovative and expensive social action Wynhoven employed a gift for making friends with powerful people and a genius for public relations. Among the benefactors were affluent Protestant and Jewish leaders of the community. His vigor allowed him at the same time to serve his parish and supervise its physical and spiritual growth. A new church was built in Gretna and four parishes developed from missions. At the invitation of Archbishop Shaw he organized Associated Catholic Charities and founded the weekly *Catholic Action of the South,* whose editorials expressed the right of labor to organize and the necessity to muffle the attraction of Communism by removing the defects of laissez-faire capitalism. A similar-minded President Roosevelt appointed him chairman of a United States Regional Labor Board in October 1933.

When Joseph Francis Rummel was appointed Shaw's successor in 1935, Wynhoven was the organizer of the public reception. Rummel (1935–64), whose own genius was organization, was impressed. He appointed Wynhoven pastor of Our Lady of Lourdes on Napoleon Avenue, New Orleans, a thriving parish located a short distance from the archbishop's residence. Rummel appointed the now Msgr. Wynhoven general chairman of the Eighth National Eucharist Congress. In October 1938, thanks largely to Wynhoven's leadership, this three-day religious assembly inspired participants at all levels. As World War II was grinding to an end, Rummel also asked Wynhoven to head up the Youth Progess Program capital funds drive for secondary schools, a center for the Catholic Youth Organization, and a facility for emotionally disturbed youth. The drive achieved its goal, but Msgr. Wynhoven died on September 14, 1944, months prior to the liberation of his native Holland from Nazi occupation. He was interred on the grounds of Hope Haven at a spot he had selected. An administrator there, using Wynhoven's own journalistic style, commented: "He was a man of dedication. He would dream, make the dream a goal and he would achieve it."

Bezou, Henry C. *Lourdes on Napoleon Avenue.* New Orleans, 1980.

EARL F. NIEHAUS, S.M.

WYNNE, JOHN (1859–1948)

Jesuit priest, editor, author. Wynne was born on September 30, 1859, in New York City, and graduated with a B.A. degree from St. Francis Xavier's College in 1876. He then entered the Society of Jesus at West Park (New York) on July 30, 1876. After his early Jesuit training he studied philosophy (1879–82) and theology (1887–91) at Woodstock College (Maryland), and in the intervening years taught mathematics and classics at St. Francis Xavier (1882–86) and mathematics at Boston College (1886–87). He was ordained in 1890.

In 1891 Wynne joined the staff of the *Messenger of the Sacred Heart* and was its editor from 1892 until 1909. He was also national director (1892–1906) of the Apostleship of Prayer, whose number of centers, under his guidance, increased from 1,600 to 8,000. His *Messenger* articles demonstrating the contribution that the Augustinian, Franciscan, and Dominican friars made to the civilization of the Philippines, helped persuade President Theodore Roosevelt not to expel them from the islands at the time the United States occupied the archipelago. And for his defense of Belgian interests in the African Congo, he was made a Knight of the Order of Leopold.

John Joseph Wynne

Convinced of the need for a weekly to discuss world and national affairs from a Catholic viewpoint, he launched, in 1909, *America,* a magazine which continues to have influence on Catholic thinking in the United States. He was editor, however, for only a year. Since 1905 he had been assistant editor of the *Catholic Encyclopedia* (1907–14), and when editorial problems arose, he took over (1910) as editor and saw the project through to its conclusion. He later coedited *The New Catholic Dictionary* (1927). While fulfilling these positions he was also associate editor of the Universal Knowledge Foundation and lectured on religion (1918–24) at the College of the Sacred Heart in Manhattanville (New York).

In 1892 Wynne became director of the Shrine of Our Lady of Martyrs at Auriesville (New York), and thereafter he promoted the cause of the eight Jesuit missionaries who were martyred on North American soil. He became vice postulator of the cause in 1923 and his *Jesuit Martyrs of North America* (1925) is an account of their missionary exploits and heroic deaths. The eight were beatified in 1925 and canonized in 1930. He also collected and prepared the material for the cause of the Native American maiden Kateri Tekakwitha, who was beatified in 1980.

After a life of scholarly achievement and service to the American Catholic Church, he died at Fordham University (New York City) on November 30, 1948.

Ciani, John L., S.J. "A Man With Too Many Ideas." *America* 167 (1992) 494–98.

Loomie, Albert J., S.J. "Father John Joseph Wynne, 1859–1948." *Woodstock Letters* 80 (1951) 61–66.

Nevils, W. Coleman., S.J. "*America's* First Editor." *America* 80 (1948–49) 312.

JOSEPH N. TYLENDA, S.J.

WYOMING, CATHOLIC CHURCH IN

The Diocese of Cheyenne includes the whole of the state of Wyoming, encompassing nearly one hundred thousand square miles and a total population of about 450,000 people.

The Early Days: Three Vicariates Apostolic (1840–1887)

In 1840 Fr. Pierre Jean De Smet, S.J., said the first Mass in Wyoming Territory near what is now present-day Daniel, Wyoming. A group of Native Americans, who came upon him as he passed through the area on his way to minister to the Flathead tribes further north, asked the 'Black Robe' to make sacrifice to his God on their behalf as a gesture of friendship and a sign of good intent.

The territory grew as the Oregon Trail pioneers, the Union Pacific railroaders, the miners, the ranchers, and the farmers moved in: some to stay, some to move on farther west. Catholic missions and churches continued to expand under the jurisdiction of the vicariate apostolic of Oregon west of the Rocky Mountains and the vicariate apostolic of Indian Territory east of the Rockies through the mid-1800s. By the 1860s, the eastern portion had come under the vicariate apostolic of Nebraska Territory where it remained until 1887.

The Holy See created the Diocese of Cheyenne on August 2, 1887. One week later Maurice Francis Burke, a priest of the Archdiocese of Chicago, was appointed the first bishop. Bishop Burke was a native of Ireland as had been the two most recent vicars apostolic, James O'Gorman and James O'Connor, thus continuing a tradition of missionary zeal on the part of the Irish for the people of Wyoming that is still represented in the present-day clergy.

A New Diocese: Three Early Bishops (1887–1911)

This new bishop soon discovered that he faced an enormous task ministering to a multicultured people spread over a territory three times the size of his native homeland, assisted by only six priests, one lay brother, and twenty-one religious women. Altogether, they served approximately seventy-five hundred Catholics in eight churches, two schools, one hospital, and one Native American mission in an area of almost one hundred thousand square miles.

Fortunately, the building of the Union Pacific Railroad had made access possible to the major southern cities of Cheyenne, Laramie, Rawlins, Rock Springs, Green River, Kemmerer, and Evanston, and Bishop Burke became a determined railroad man. He added quite a bit of other travel by stagecoach and buckboard to the northern part of the territory. He spent a good deal of time in the north-central part of the state on the Wind River Reservation, home of the Shoshone and Arapahoe tribes near Riverton and Lander, where he presided over the laying of the cornerstone for St. Stephen's Indian Mission in June 1888.

Wyoming became a state July 10, 1890. Shortly thereafter in early 1893, Bishop Burke was reassigned to the Diocese of St. Joseph, and Fr. Hugh Commiskey, pastor of St. Laurence O'Toole in Laramie, was appointed administrator of the Diocese of Cheyenne until another bishop was selected. This turned out to be a period of almost four years. Finally, on November 30, 1896, another native of Ireland, Thomas Mathias Lenihan, was chosen for the see of Cheyenne. He traveled throughout the state overseeing building programs and administering the sacraments until his death on December 15, 1901. He was succeeded by James John Keane of Joliet, Illinois, who came to Wyoming at a time when the fortunes and optimism of the people were on a rebound from almost a decade of depression. That attitude and spirit was nowhere more evident than in the Catholic community that supported Bishop Keane as he incorporated the Diocese of Cheyenne according to Wyoming state law and required his pastors to do likewise in their parishes. He worked tirelessly to raise standards of accountability and records-keeping. Boards of trustees with both clergy and laity represented were formed. He spoke all over the country as a guest preacher and as a retreat master, always recruiting additional priests with a missionary spirit for the frontier. Wyoming benefited from the publicity both in more men committed to serve and in gifts of money pledged. One of his main priorities was the building of a cathedral. He purchased the present site at 2107 Capitol Avenue in view of the State Capitol and presided over the laying of the cornerstone on July 7, 1907. Both the cathedral under the patronage of St. Mary and the residence were completed and dedicated nineteen months later. Bishop Keane served the Diocese of Cheyenne for nine years until he was named an archbishop and transferred to the Archdiocese of Dubuque on August 11, 1911.

Bishop Patrick McGovern (1912–1951)

The fourth bishop of Cheyenne, Patrick Aloysius McGovern, a priest in Nebraska, was notified of his appointment on January 19, 1912, and was consecrated a short time later.

Bishop McGovern began his years of service in the Diocese of Cheyenne in April 1913 by calling a synod where he met with all the priests to formulate the statutes to provide for the orderly government of the clergy and the people. Later, near the end of his tenure, he would convene the Second Diocesan Synod in June 1948 at St. Stephen's Indian Mission, where he once again consulted with his priests in setting guidelines, legislation, and regulations "to promote ecclesiastical discipline and to strengthen the practice of religion within the limits of our jurisdiction."

When he died November 8, 1951, Bishop Patrick A. McGovern had accomplished, with the spirit-filled support of his priests, religious, and a vigorous frontier laity, most of the program of work that he had set for the Church in Wyoming.

Bishop Hubert M. Newell (1947–1978)

One of the most forward-thinking actions of Bishop McGovern had been to request that a coadjutor bishop be assigned to the Diocese of Cheyenne when he felt his health declining in the late 1940s. His petition to the Holy See was answered by the appointment of Hubert M. Newell, a priest and educator from the Archdiocese of Denver, as coadjutor bishop of Cheyenne on August 2, 1947. Bishop Newell was consecrated in Denver on September 24, 1947.

When Bishop McGovern died, Bishop Newell was ready for a smooth transition. One of his first actions was to set in place a diocesan newspaper modeled after the *Denver Catholic Register.*

The Diocese of Cheyenne had been detached from the province of Dubuque and had become part of the province of Denver when it was created November 15, 1941. The war years, coming so hard upon the depression era, combined with the financial pressures of a fast-growing Western Church, had left building repairs and remodeling projects waiting a long time. In some areas new missions and churches needed to be built. Bishop Newell saw a great need to call the laity into a new level of partnership in order to accomplish the tasks ahead.

Although altar and rosary societies had been active since the late 1880s, he called upon them to go a step further and organize a Council of Catholic Women in the diocese. He envisioned that they would be a strong lay force promoting the Christian life. Likewise, he encouraged the proven leaders from the Knights of Columbus to become even more involved and to expand their influence. Newell was quick to note the importance of the ministry of the Newman Aposolate to the young men and women attending the University of Wyoming, the only four-year institution of higher learning in the state and, therefore, the diocese. He lent his support to the group and they responded by initiating a large number of new members in the mid-1950s under the leadership of Fr. Frederick J. Kimmet and Fr. Charles F. Taylor.

Bishop Newell also encouraged the high-school students of the local parish CYO groups to become involved at the diocesan, regional, and national level. In 1959 the first diocesan-wide youth convention was held in Cheyenne with Fr. Charles Brady as diocesan youth director.

In 1955, at the close of the decade following World War II, *The Wyoming Catholic Register* was able to report that the Diocese of Cheyenne was alive and well: the total number of Catholics had risen to almost fifty thousand; many building programs for new churches and schools were at least in the planning stage; the number of sisters had increased dramatically from fifty-five in 1948 to one hundred eighteen in 1955. The prayerful, hardworking women of the Sisters of Charity of Leavenworth, the Sisters of Charity of the Blessed Virgin Mary, the Dominican Sisters of the Third Order of St. Dominic, the Sisters of the Third Order of St. Francis, the Sisters of Penance and Charity, and the Ursuline Sisters were of inestimable value in all that had been achieved so far.

In 1955 Bishop Newell announced a major program of remodeling and rebuilding as a job for the whole diocese, and not just in the local parishes and missions facing crisis situations. On Sunday, May 1, 1955, the pastors read his letter addressed to the people outlining the problem areas and setting a minimum of one million dollars as the amount necessary to do what was needed. Five weeks later almost two million dollars had been pledged.

Vatican Council II

When Vatican II convened October 11, 1962, Newell was in attendance. In February 1964, in keeping with the ecumenical movement which followed the 'opening of the window for a little fresh air' by Pope John XXIII and the continuation of the council by his successor, Pope Paul VI, Bishop Newell entertained the Ministerial Association of Cheyenne and other non-Catholic clergy of Laramie County at St. Joseph's Parish Hall in Cheyenne. A senate of priests was formed to give counsel and effective assistance to the bishop in his governance of the diocese; and the Diocesan Pastoral Council, one of only twenty yet in existence in the U.S.A., was elected at the deanery level and set in place to act in an advisory capacity to the bishop. About this same time, an elected Board of Catholic Education was given the mission of oversight of the schools and religious education programs in the parishes throughout the diocese. In 1974 Bishop Newell began commissioning men and women as lay ministers of the Eucharist, first at the cathedral and later in other parishes, to assist in the distribution of Communion. This was a great boon in a diocese where there were, and still are, more missions than parishes.

A short time later, the bishop began to think ahead to his planned retirement at age seventy-five, another innovation following Vatican II, and he petitioned the Holy See to appoint an auxiliary bishop for the Diocese of Cheyenne. On August 31, 1976, Bishop Joseph Hart, a native of Missouri and a priest for twenty years, was ordained at the Cathedral of St. Mary in Cheyenne.

In 1978 Bishop Hubert M. Newell retired after the Pontiff accepted his resignation. Since an auxiliary bishop does not automatically assume the office of ordinary, Wyoming Catholics were consulted by a questionnaire survey about the type of bishop they felt was needed. This was an innovation provided for in the norms issued by Pope Paul VI in 1972 for the selection of bishops. The results were tabulated by the Diocesan Pastoral Council and forwarded to Archbishop Jean Jadot, apostolic delegate to the U.S.A.

The main criteria cited in their choice for bishop was that he be a man of both openness in personal spirituality and filled with a deep concern for youth. A short time later, the apostolic delegate announced that Bishop Joseph Hart had been appointed to the see of Cheyenne.

Bishop Joseph Hart, 1976–Present

Bishop Joseph Hart was installed as ordinary of the Diocese of Cheyenne June 12, 1978, at St. Mary's Cathedral in Cheyenne by Archbishop Casey of Denver. The ceremonies included an Arapaho Cedar-Incense Prayer during which Ernest Sun Rhodes, a tribal elder and catechist at St. Stephen's Native American Mission, prayed for the bishop and the Church in Wyoming.

More and more, Bishop Hart has worked to involve the laity in the ministry of the Church in Wyoming through such avenues as frequent deanery meetings and an annual Diocesan Assembly where inspiration, education, and elections to the various advisory and governing boards and councils take place. Also, in the 1980s, the entire diocese participated in the three-year RENEW process whereby the laity and clergy collectively examined their personal spirituality, knowledge of and commitment to the faith, and partnership in evangelization.

During his episcopacy, Bishop Hart has been in the forefront of the discussion of moral issues that affect the lives of all people, and he has spoken out to educate everyone, not only Catholics, concerning the spiritual dangers of nuclear proliferation, capital punishment, and abortion.

In 1995 the state of Wyoming contained 47,008 Catholics in a total population of 467,000. There were 37 parishes and 42 missions, served by 37 diocesan priests and 11 religious order priests. There were also 37 sisters, one brother, and 3 permanent deacons.

Carlson, Gloria S. *A Brief History of the Diocese of Cheyenne.* Third Synod Documents. Cheyenne, May 1993.
McGovern, P. A. *History of the Diocese of Cheyenne.* Cheyenne, 1941.

GLORIA S. CARLSON

X

XAVIER UNIVERSITY

Xavier University in Cincinnati, Ohio, the fourth oldest Jesuit university and the sixth oldest Roman Catholic college in the United States, was founded in 1831 by Edward Dominic Fenwick, a Dominican priest who became the first bishop of Cincinnati in 1825. In 1829 Fenwick started a seminary and then, two years later, turned to establishing a college in Cincinnati. The Athenaeum, as the institution was known, opened its doors on October 17, 1831. It was, in the words of historian Lee J. Bennish, S.J., "the first Catholic institution of higher learning in the Northwest Territory."

There were sixty students in the first class. A six-year course of studies for the all-male school was planned because at that time there was no division between high-school and college education. Bishop John Baptist Purcell, Fenwick's successor, under pressure to use his few priests as frontier missionaries rather than educators, offered The Athenaeum to the Society of Jesus to continue the diocese's educational apostolate.

In the fall of 1840, eight Jesuits from the Jesuit college in St. Louis, led by Fr. John Elet, assumed control of the school, renamed St. Xavier College. A mercantile program of study was added to the classical program. In 1841 evening classes in German and bookkeeping were begun. Boarding students paid $130 per year for tuition, room and board, with an additional $25 for washing, mending, stationery, and doctor's fees. In 1919 St. Xavier's College of Arts and Sciences moved from downtown to its present location in the Avondale neighborhood. In 1930 the name of the college was changed to Xavier University. Xavier's undergraduate "day" colleges became coeducational in 1969, although women had been attending Xavier's evening colleges and graduate programs for many years.

Today (1995) Xavier University consists of the College of Arts and Sciences, the College of Business Administration, and the College of Social Sciences. Enrollment of undergraduate, graduate, full-time, and part-time students from 35 states and 17 countries approximates 6,200.

See also CATHOLIC UNIVERSITIES AND COLLEGES.

Xavier University, Cincinnati

Bennish, Lee J., S.J. *Continuity and Change: Xavier University 1831–1981.* Chicago: Loyola University Press, 1981.

CHARLES J. CAREY

XAVIER UNIVERSITY OF LOUISIANA

Xavier University of Louisiana, the only historically black, Catholic college in the Western Hemisphere, is located in New Orleans, Louisiana.

The college dates back to 1915 when Mother Katharine Drexel and the Sisters of the Blessed Sacrament founded the coeducational secondary school from which it evolved. Mother Katharine, supported by the interest of a substantial inheritance from her father, banker-financier Francis Drexel, founded and staffed many institutions throughout the United States in an effort to help educate Native Americans and blacks. She was beatified—the final step leading to sainthood—by Pope John Paul II in 1988.

Aware of the serious lack of Catholic-oriented education available to young blacks in the South, Mother Katharine came to New Orleans and established a high school on the site previously occupied by Southern University. A normal school, offering one of the few career fields (teaching) open to blacks at the time, was added two years later. In 1925 Xavier University became a reality when the College of Liberal Arts and Sciences was established. The first degrees were awarded three years later. In 1927 a College of Pharmacy was opened.

Recognizing the university's need for a separate identity and room to expand, Mother Katharine bought a tract of undeveloped land for a campus on the corner of Palmetto and Pine Streets in 1929. Construction of the U-shaped, Gothic administration building (now a city landmark) was completed in 1933.

The sisters remain a vital presence on campus, providing much-needed staffing and limited financial assistance, but today Xavier is governed by a biracial board of trustees. Its president, Dr. Norman Francis, is himself a Xavier graduate.

Xavier's special mission is to serve the black, Catholic community, but its doors have always been open to qualified students of any race or creed. In fact, in 1995 more than 50 percent of its students were of other religious affiliations, and close to 10 percent were of other races. The academic curriculum is liberal-arts oriented and offers training in some three dozen fields on the undergraduate, graduate, and professional degree level.

Xavier is recognized as a national leader in the field of minority science education. In both 1993 and 1994 the university placed more African Americans into medical schools than any other college in the nation, and it has educated nearly 25 percent of the 4,800 practicing black pharmacists in the U.S.A. More than 40 percent of Xavier's students continue their education by attending graduate or professional school.

See also CATHOLIC UNIVERSITIES AND COLLEGES.

RICHARD TUCKER

Y

YORKE, PETER (1864–1925)

Priest, social activist, editor. Peter Yorke was born in Galway, Ireland, on August 13, 1864, the son of Gregory Yorke, a sea captain, and Bridget Kelly. In 1882 Yorke began studies for the priesthood for the Diocese of Galway at St. Patrick's College in Maynooth. In 1886 he was adopted by the Archdiocese of San Francisco and sent to complete his studies at St. Mary's Seminary in Baltimore, Maryland, where he was ordained to the priesthood by Cardinal James Gibbons on December 17, 1887. After a brief stay in San Francisco, he was enrolled at The (new) Catholic University of America in Washington, D.C., as one of its first students. In 1891 he received a licentiate in theology.

He returned to San Francisco and was rapidly promoted. His first appointment was to St. Mary's Cathedral. In 1894 he was appointed chancellor for the archdiocese and secretary to Archbishop Patrick Riordan. The same year he was appointed editor of the archdiocesan newspaper, *The Monitor.* After a conflict with Riordan, he served briefly as an assistant at St. Peter's parish in San Francisco, before becoming pastor of St. Anthony's parish in Oakland from 1903 until 1913, and pastor at St. Peter's from 1913 until his death in 1925.

Yorke obtained legendary status among San Francisco Catholics for his prominent role in a number of conflicts and developments. First, as editor of *The Monitor* during the 1890s, he vanquished the anti-Catholic American Protective Association in San Francisco through public debate and exposés published in *The Monitor.* During this conflict Yorke developed his acerbic rhetorical style, castigating his opponents in most unflattering (and unpriestly) language. Second, he emerged as spiritual leader and chief publicist for the union during the great Teamsters Strike of 1901. Yorke placed the Church in San Francisco squarely on the side of labor, and enjoyed widespread respect and admiration from union leaders and rank and file as a labor priest. Third, he founded and edited a local Irish newspaper, *The Leader,* in 1902, which gave him a platform to discuss and publicize his views on various local issues, political and otherwise. Fourth, he published a series of *Textbooks of Religion* that adapted the Baltimore Catechism to appropriate grade levels. These texts were adopted and used throughout the archdiocese and elsewhere.

Yorke served as an unofficial superintendent of Catholic schools in the archdiocese, and was instrumental in the creation of the National Catholic Educational Association (NCEA) in 1904. Fifth, Yorke vigorously supported the fight for a free Irish state, particularly supporting the efforts of Eamon de Valera. Finally, as pastor at St. Peter's, Yorke introduced a variety of liturgical reforms including congregational singing, use of missals, and a Children's Mass, in which the children recited the appropriate responses in English.

Yorke died on Palm Sunday, April 5, 1925, and his death was commemorated yearly by a memorial Mass at St. Peter's Church, followed by a procession to his grave at Holy Cross Cemetery in Colma. It became a major Irish and labor celebration.

Brusher, Joseph, S.J. *Consecrated Thunderbolt: A Life of Father Peter C. Yorke of San Francisco.* Hawthorne, N.J.: Wagner, 1973.

Burns, Jeffrey M. "Que es esto? The Transformation of St. Peter's Parish in San Francisco." *American Congregations,* eds. James Wind and James Lewis. Chicago: University of Chicago Press, 1994.

JEFFREY M. BURNS

Z

ZAHM, JOHN AUGUSTINE (1851–1921)

Priest, scientist, theologian. Zahm was born on June 14, 1851, in New Lexington, Ohio, to Jacob Michael Zahm, a native of Alsace, and Mary Ellen Braddock of Loretto, Pennsylvania. He received his early education in New Lexington and in Huntington, Indiana, where his family settled in 1863. He eventually entered the University of Notre Dame where he earned bachelor's and master's degrees. He entered the Congregation of the Holy Cross on September 13, 1871, and was ordained a priest on June 11, 1875. From his ordination until 1892, Zahm taught physics at Notre Dame where he also held administrative posts and was instrumental in making Notre Dame the first American college to utilize electric lighting.

Beginning in 1892, Zahm gave up the study of the natural sciences in favor of writing and studying the relationship between the Catholic faith and the discoveries of the modern sciences. Zahm advocated a "via media" between literal creationism and new evolutionary theories that excluded God. Zahm put forth a theory of "theistic evolution" that tried to harmonize traditional Catholic theology with the findings of evolutionists. His important work, *Evolution and Dogma* (1896), argued that faith and science were compatible. Liberal Catholics of that era welcomed Zahm and his writings while conservatives regarded him and his beliefs with suspicion. Archbishop Michael A. Corrigan, a prominent conservative, forbade the use of Zahm's book at St. Joseph's Seminary, Dunwoodie. Yielding to conservative criticism, the Congregation of the Index asked Zahm to withdraw his book from publication, which he did.

After this rebuff, Zahm ceased writing about the relationship between faith and science. In 1898 he became the American provincial of the Congregation of the Holy Cross and worked to establish Holy Cross College, a house of studies adjacent to The Catholic University of America in Washington, D.C. When his term as provincial ended in 1906, Zahm began to travel widely, including a trip to South America with former President Theodore Roosevelt. He continued to write about his travels, including four volumes on South American history, but Zahm avoided any theological topics that had previously caused him so much grief. A man of both science and faith, Zahm became a victim in the struggle between a Rome growing fearful of the advances of modern science and those in the Church who were working to effect a rapprochement between scientific learning and the Christian faith.

See also HOLY CROSS, CONGREGATION OF (C.S.C.); MODERNISM IN AMERICA.

Weber, Ralph E. *Notre Dame's John Zahm: American Catholic Apologist and Educator.* Notre Dame, 1961.
Zahm, John A. *Evolution and Dogma.* Chicago, 1896.

ANTHONY D. ANDREASSI

ZLAMAL, OLDRICH (1879–1955)

Pioneer Czech priest. Oldrich Zlamal was born on April 4, 1879, in Kokory, Moravia, to Anton and Antoinette Zlamal. He began his priestly studies at the theology seminary at Olmütz, but his bishop released him for service to the

Czech and Slovak communities in Cleveland. Arriving in Cleveland, Zlamal was ordained to the priesthood on November 3, 1904.

His first assignment was as pastor of St. Wendelin parish in Cleveland where he built a school. At that time he also served the mission (later parish) of SS Cyril and Methodius in Lakewood, Ohio. In 1908 he was transferred to SS Cyril and Methodius parish in Youngstown, Ohio. In 1915 he succeeded the late Fr. Stephen Furdek as pastor of Our Lady of Lourdes parish in Cleveland. Zlamal, like many of his fellow Czech and Slovak immigrants, was vitally interested in the welfare of his homeland which was then part of the Austrian-Hungarian Empire. The Czech community in Cleveland was split along religious and political lines, but all desired independence for their nation.

The creation of the Czechoslovak republic after the First World War was applauded by many, but the rise of anti-Catholicism and apostasy in that country alarmed many American Czech Catholics. In 1919 the National Catholic Welfare Conference recruited prominent Czech priests in America to visit their native land. Zlamal was one who accepted the invitation to travel through Czechoslovakia speaking on democracy, self-government, and religious matters. Even though he was pastor of a growing parish, Zlamal found time for additional trips to Czechoslovakia. He organized a defense fund for the Czechs in 1938. After the Second World War, he organized a relief committee for Czechoslovakia.

Zlamal was honored by being named a domestic prelate in 1934. He died on March 24, 1955, in Cleveland.

Catholic Universe Bulletin, March 25, 1955.

Papers of Our Lady of Lourdes parish, Archives, Diocese of Cleveland, Ohio.

Stone, Norman and Eduard Strouhal, eds. *Czechoslovakia: Crossroads and Crises, 1918–88.* New York, 1989.

CHRISTINE L. KROSEL

Contributors

Mary Barbara Agnew, C.PP.S.
Mary Aimee, O.P.
John Allen
Patrick Allitt
Paracleta Amrich, SS.C.M.
Anthony D. Andreassi
R. Scott Appleby
Jack M. Arlotta
Regis J. Armstrong, O.F.M.Cap.
Mary Luke Arntz, S.N.D.
Robert Ashenoracher
Mary Christine Athans, B.V.M.
William A. Au
John J. Augenstein
Steven M. Avella
Joan Marie Aycock, O.S.U.
Barbara Baer, C.S.J.
Kenneth Baker, S.J.
Paul Bechtold, C.P.
Christopher Begg
Dianne Bergant, C.S.A.
Joan Bishop
Thomas E. Blantz, C.S.C.
William Bole
David Bovee
John W. Bowen, S.S.
Earl Boyea
Bruce Bradley
Patricia Brady
Ernest Brandewie
Patricia Brandt

Dominic Braud, O.S.B.
Bill Breault, S.J.
Margaret Brennan
Mary Virginia Brennan, V.H.M.
George Brown
Mary Elizabeth Brown
Cornelius Buckley, S.J.
Helen Marie Burns, R.S.M.
Jeffrey M. Burns
Don H. Buske
Patricia Byrne, C.S.J.
Una M. Cadegan
Margaret Cafferty, P.V.B.M.
Mary Consuela Callaghan, I.H.M.
Nelson J. Callahan
Anne Francis Campbell, O.L.M.
Owen Campion
Sister Campion, C.S.C.
Robert E. Carbonneau, C.P.
Charles J. Carey
Patrick W. Carey
Francis Maureen Carlin, O.P.
Gloria S. Carlson
Robert C. Carriker
Elisa A. Carrillo
Janet Carroll, M.M.
L. Franklin Carter
John W. Carven, C.M.
Juliana Casey, I.H.M.
Edward J. Cashin
Joseph J. Casino

Martinus Cawley, O.C.S.O.
Thomas H. Clancy, S.J.
M. Reparata Clarke, O.S.P.
Peter Clarke
Carol Dorr Clement
Keith Coffman
Patrick Cogan, S.A.
John J. Collins
Thomas E. Comber, C.S.P.
George L. Concordia, O.P.
Rory T. Conley
James T. Connelly, C.S.C.
Thomas Connolly, S.J.
Glenn R. Conrad
David R. Constosta
Kathleen Neils Conzen
Colman M. Cooke
Bridget Corey
Patricia J. Corkery, R.S.M.
John C. Cort
Mary Virginia Cotter, C.N.D.
John Coughlin, O.F.M.
Anne Courtney, S.C.
Paul E. Couture, S.S.E.
Colette Cowman
Clyde F. Crews
Donald F. Crosby, S.J.
Dominic L. Csorba, O.F.M.
Charles E. Curran
Robert Emmett Curran, S.J.
Judith Davies, O.S.F.
Cyprian Davis, O.S.B.
John Deedy
Anthony R. Dees
Patricia DeFerrari
Joseph A. Di Noia, O.P.
John A. Dick
Alberta Dieker, O.S.B.
Stephen M. DiGiovanni
William D. Dinges
Jim Dinn
Roy Domenico
Anna M. Donnelly
Charles F. Donovan, S.J.
Ann Dowart
Liselle Drake
Angelyn Dries, O.S.F.
Harry Dunkak, C.F.C.
Claudette Dwyer, R.S.M.
James B. Earley
Mary Pierre Ellebracht, C.PP.S.
Michael E. Engh, S.J.
Robert B. Eno, S.S.*
Edward J. Enright, O.S.A.

Jerome B. Ernst
Felipe J. Estevez
John Whitney Evans
Lucylle Evans
Elizabeth Farley, R.S.C.J.
Janice Farnham, R.J.M.
Angela Feeney, P.B.V.M.
Hugh Feiss, O.S.B.
James Terence Fisher
Constance Fitzgerald, O.C.D.
Robert Fitzgerald, S.J.
Gerald P. Fogarty, S.J.
Mary Eileen Foley, R.G.S.
Patrick Foley
Jim Forest
Tom Fox
Donald D. Fraser
Mariella Frye, M.H.S.H.
Virgil C. Funk
James P. Gaffey
Philip Gage, S.M.
Ann Miriam Gallagher, R.S.M.
Dennis J. Gallagher, O.S.A.
Alice Gallin, O.S.U.
Michael Gannon
John Garvey, S.J.
Michael Garvey
Mary Michael Gecewicz, C.S.F.N.
Virgina Geiger, S.S.N.D
Dawn M. Gibeau
Michael Glazier
Philip Gleason
Edward Gobetz
C. Walker Golar
William W. Goss
Virginia Meacham Gould
Joseph Grabenstein, F.S.C.
Dana Greene
Thomas R. Greene
Richard Gribble, C.S.C.
Leslie C. Griffin
Patrick Griffin
James Haley
James P. Hanigan
Sr. Mary Laurence Hanley, O.S.F.
Daniel J. Harrington, S.J.
Patrick Hart, O.C.S.O.
Robert W. Hayman
Robert Hecht
Barbara Hendricks, M.M.
James Hennesey, S.J.
Steven Henrich, O.S.C.
Florence Herman
Richard Hirsch

Peter E. Hogan, S.S.J.
Ephrem Hollerman, O.S.B.
Joseph G. Hubbert, C.M.
John Huels
M. Edmund Hussey
James Hynes
Nancy Hynes, O.S.B.
Alfred Isacsson, O.Carm.
Jean-Marie Jammes
Joseph Jensen, O.S.B.
Rosemary Jermann
Mary of Jesus, O.P.
Robert Johnson-Lally
William Jones
Janet Kalven
Josef Kalvoda
Paula M. Kane
Edward R. Kantowicz
Terrence G. Kardong, O.S.B.
Rosemarie Kasper, S.N.J.M.
Annemarie Kasteel
Christopher J. Kauffman
Aloysius Kelly, S.J.
David F. Kelly
Joseph F. Kelly
James J. Kenneally
Camilla Kennedy, M.M.
Karen M. Kennelly, C.S.J.
George Kilcourse
John J. Killoren, S.J.
Robert L. Kinast
J. Leo Klein, S.J.
Joseph A. Komonchak
Mueller Komp
Henry J. Koren, C.S.SP.
Patricia A. Kossman
Edward J. Kowrach
Carolyn Krebs, O.P.
Christine L. Krosel
Thomas A. Kuhlman
Bruce Kupelnick
Raymond J. Kupke
Edgar Kurt
Anthony J. Kuzniewski, S.J.
Gerald Laba, C.P.
Joseph H. Lackner, S.M.
Matthew LaFlamme
John Langlois, O.P.
Vincent A. Lapomarda, S.J.
Kathryn Lawlor, B.V.M.
Dolores R. Leckey
Albert H. Ledoux
Marie Lefevre, S.G.M.
Alfred E. Lemmon

Wasyl Lencyk
Bruce H. Lescher
Gerald Lewis
Joseph C. Linck, C.O.
Oscar H. Lipscomb
David Q. Liptak
Edward Lofton
Margaret Lorimer, C.S.A.
Thomas A. Lynch
Timothy MacDonald, S.A.
Benjamin Mackin, O. Praem.
Mary Roger Madden, S.P.
Paul Robert Magocsi
Mary Denis Maher, C.S.A.
Betty Ann Maheu, M.M.
George A. Maloney, S.J.
Charles M. Mangan
Mother Vincent Marie, O.C.D.
Berard L. Marthaler
Mary Lenore Martin, S.C.L.
Paul Maslach
Colleen J. Matan
Alphonse J. Matt, Jr.
Maria Mazzenga
Lawrence McAndrews
Lawrence J. McCaffrey
Dorothea McCarthy, R.C.D.
Jeremiah J. McCarthy
K. N. McCarthy
William D. McCarthy, M.M.
Gerald A. McCool, S.J.
Floyd McCoy
Grace McDonald, F.S.P.A.
Bernard McGarty, S.T.D.
Michael J. McGinniss, F.S.C.
James McGrath
Mary Nona McGreal, O.P.
Morris McGregor
Margaret McGuinness
Elizabeth McKeown
Joseph M. McLafferty
Marianna McLoughlin
James McLucas
Michael J. McNally
Patrick J. McNamara
Robert F. McNamara
Rosalie McQuaide, C.S.J.P.
Joseph M. McShane, S.J.
Julia McSherry
Thomas J. McSweeney
Regina A. Melican, O.P.
John Melingagio
Michael Mendl, S.D.B.
Roger Mercurio, C.P.

John Minogue, C.M.
Kathleen Maria Mitchell, F.S.P.
Sandra Yocum Mize
John T. Monaghan
Dominic V. Monti, O.F.M.
Bernice Maher Mooney
Terrence J. Moran, C.Ss.R.
Michael Morrison, S.J.
James Muldoon
Hermenia M. Muldrey, R.S.M.
Herman J. Muller, S.J.
Maureen Murphy
John Murray
Earl F. Niehaus, S.M.
Charles E. Nolan
Paschala Noonan, O.P.
Judith Noone, M.M.
C. Joseph Nuesse
Doyce B. Nunis, Jr.
M. Paulinus Oakes, R.S.M.
Mary J. Oates
Mary Kay Oosdyke
Louanna Orth, S.N.D.deN.
Paul J. Ostendorf, F.S.C.
Aurelia Ottersbach, S.L.
Stephenie Overman
David O'Brien
Peter F. O'Brien, S.J.
Maureen H. O'Connell
Thomas H. O'Connor
Joseph O'Hare, S.J.
Charles Edwards O'Neill
Kevin J. O'Reilly
James M. O'Toole
Wilfrid H. Paradis
Stanley Parmisano, O.P.
Philip J. Pascucci, S.D.B.
John T. Pawlikowski, O.S.M.
Steven Payne, O.C.D.
M. Basil Pennington, O.C.S.O.
Lillian A. Pereyra
Michael F. Perko, S.J.
Val J. Peter
Thomas J. Peterman
Loretta Petit, O.P.
Peter C. Phan
Michael Phayer
Margaret Phelan, R.S.C.J.
Stephanie Mary Pilachowski, S.S.N.D.
Martin Poluse
Charles Polzer, S.J.
Stafford Poole, C.M.
Raymond A. Prybis
James S. Pula

Tricia T. Pyne
William Quaintance, F.S.C.
Jarlath Quinn
Joseph Quinn
Margaret M. Quinn, C.S.J.
Stephanie Raha
Rachel Reeder
Margaret Mary Reher
Louis L. Renner, S.J.
Eileen F. Rice, O.P.
John T. Ridge
Randal Riede, C.F.X.
Joel Rippinger, O.S.B.
Michael J. Roach
Mary Jane Romero, O.S.B.
Theresa A. Ross-Jones
Joseph S. Rossi, S.J.
Silvan Rouse, C.P.
N. Daniel Rupp
Geroge E. Ryan
Stephen M. Ryan
Patrick Samway, S.J.
José M. Sánchez
Timothy J. Sarbaugh
Joseph A. Schiwek, Jr.
David E. Schlaver, C.S.C.
Wilfred P. Schoenberg, S.J.
Robert J. Schreiter, C.PP.S.
Thomas A. Shannon
Richard Shaw
Thomas J. Shelley
Richard J. Shmaruk
George Sirgiovanni
Leanne Sitter, C.S.A.
Edward Skillin
Douglas J. Slawson
Jeremiah Smith, O.F.M.Conv.
Karen Sue Smith
Richard G. Smith
Michael Socolow
Ancilla Sojka, C.S.F.N.
Paul J. Spaeth
Thomas W. Spalding
Alphonse P. Spilly, C.PP.S.
Thomas H. Stahel, S.J.
Carl F. Starkloff, S.J.
Thomas J. Steele, S.J.
Donald L. Stelluto
Michael F. Steltenkamp, S.J.
Robert L. Stern
George C. Stewart, Jr.
M. Mark Stolarik
Mary Ann Strain, C.P.
Bernard F. Stratman, S.M.

Carole Strawn, S.N.J.M.
Helen Streck, A.S.C.
Thomas Stritch
Mary Louise Sullivan
Dolores Super, O.S.B.
Edwina Sweeney, O.P.
Samuel Michael Taub
George H. Tavard
Christine Taylor
Vincent Tegeder, O.S.B.
Carm Ternes, O.S.B.
Thomas W. Tifft
M. Catherine Tilzey
Jennifer Tomshack
Linda Tonellato, O.P.
Martin G. Towey
Michael Tripka, T.O.R.
Robert Trisco
Robert R. Trotter
Richard Tucker
Joseph Tylenda, S.J.
R. Timothy Unsworth
Rodger Van Allen
Jaime R. Vidal
Jon L. Wakelyn

Timothy Walch
Nicholas E. Walsh*
Kees-Jan Waterman
Mary Adorata Watson, O.S.M.
Francis J. Weber
Beatrice Weisner, S.N.J.M.
Shawn Weldon
Joel Wells
Elaine Wheeler, D.C.
James D. White
Joseph M. White
Jean-Paul Wiest
William E. Wilkie
Elizabeth Willems, S.S.N.D.
Robert J. Wister
Patricia Wittberg, S.C.
William Wolkovich-Valkavičius
James M. Woods
David F. Wright, O.P.
Alexander Wyse, O.F.M.
Louis H. Yim
Gordon C. Zahn
Kenneth J. Zanca
Martin Zielinski
Mary Janice Ziolkowski, C.S.S.F.

* Deceased.

List of Illustrations

Index